THE McGRAW-HILL HANDBOOK OF FINANCIAL TABLES FOR REAL ESTATE

Dennis R. Kelley

Senior Vice President
Real Estate Advisory Division
LaSalle National Trust, N.A.

McGraw-Hill, Inc.

New York St. Louis San Francisco Auckland Bogotá
Caracas Lisbon London Madrid Mexico Milan
Montreal New Delhi Paris San Juan São Paulo
Singapore Sydney Tokyo Toronto

TO PATRICIA

Library of Congress Cataloging-in-Publication Data

Kelley, Dennis R.
    The McGraw-Hill handbook of financial tables for real estate /
Dennis R. Kelley.
       p.   cm.
    Includes index.
    ISBN 0-07-033781-0
    1. Business mathematics—Real estate business—Tables. 2. Real
estate business—Tables. 3. Real estate investment—Rates and
tables. I. Title.
HF5695.5.R3K45 1992
333.33'0212—dc20   92-7778
                                       CIP

1 2 3 4 5 6 7 8 9 0 HAL/HAL 9 8 7 6 5 4 3 2

ISBN 0-07-033781-0

The sponsoring editor for this book was Caroline Carney, the editing supervisor was Kimberly A. Goff, and the production supervisor was Pamela A. Pelton. This book was set in Baskerville. It was composed by McGraw-Hill's Professional Book Group composition unit.

Printed and bound by Halliday Litho.

CONTENTS

Yield on Mortgage Loans   43

4. Planning the Use of Proceeds

Establishing a Fund for Future Income or Expense   51

Withdrawals from a Fund   52

PREFACE

This book will make money for you two ways: First, by providing the financial math for your everyday real estate work load in a single source. All standard financial functions are included as well as dozens never before published. Solutions are presented at a wide variety of interest rates, in simple, easy-to-read format. There are no formulas or theories to keep in mind: The right answer is at your fingertips in seconds, and, when you find the first answer, similar cases surround it, letting you see the whole range of answers at once.

This book will make money for you also by building your toolbox of deal techniques. You will see how to dissect a deal and construct a financial solution point by point, even if you have no background in mathematics. With daily reference, you will soon find your transactions more informed, the range of options you offer clients broader, and your perception of deal making more acute. Without leaving your desk, you will advance in professional standing by demonstrating the financial path for bringing parties together.

The secret to this deal power lies in the book's construction, made up of financial tables and examples. The tables—89 of them—show you the answers to virtually every financial application that occurs in real estate. The examples tell you how to phrase the questions in real estate terms. With wider real estate coverage than ever before, 350 examples from actual real estate practice cover every point of the realty compass: sales, leasing, property management, home and commercial financing, appraising, investment analysis, and workouts.

Eight chapters divide the spectrum of real estate examples according to topics. Chapter 1, "Planning the Commercial Property Purchase," addresses the elements of the buying decision. Its analysis tools are the internal rate of return (IRR) and the net present value. Special emphasis is placed on the yield implied by a price and changing the price to achieve the desired yield.

Chapter 2 concentrates on home loans, presenting payments and mortgage terms and advanced planning for ordinary loans, reduced amortization schedules, growing-equity and rising-rate mortgages, and biweekly payment loans. Techniques to shorten the term of the loan and to cut interest by manageable prepayments are emphasized. Examples show refinancing and lock-in decisions in light of interest rate markets and how seller financing can cement the deal.

Income-producing property loans are the stars of Chapter 3, which focuses on loan techniques and strategies to better fit the financing to the deal and thorough coverage of constants, discounts, and yields. How to interpret the yield curve is shown, so you can let interest rate markets themselves make your rate predictions.

Few real estate books have addressed what to do with the money coming out of a real estate deal. Chapter 4 shows not only how to handle reserves and guarantees in the aftermath of a sale but also how to plan for retirement and estate use of the proceeds.

Chapter 5 is devoted to appraisal and market analysis. The emphasis here is less on the value of a deal or technique to any one investor and more on how the market in general— the typical buyer or seller—might respond. Standard appraisal techniques are given as well as new analysis tools never before published. Special attention is devoted to valuation of all sorts of long-term leases.

Chapter 6 turns to the topics that deal with decisions facing the teams that market the space, manage the property, and direct the corporate facilities. These topics include the leasing proposal, managing vacancy and below-market rents, choosing the lowest-cost alternatives for expenses, and replacing equipment.

Chapter 7 shows how to build the closing statement, to make prorations, to figure loan payoffs, and to adjust rent for tenants with CPI clauses. Interest and principal calculations of mortgages are presented.

Chapter 8 comprises elements from every preceding chapter from the point of view of deals gone sour. The explanations here show how to employ the book's techniques for controlling, replanning, and selling distressed property.

The hundreds of examples ensure that you will never need to search for a formula and then interpret it. The hundreds of thousands of precomputed solutions ensure that one book will have the answer you need for every deal you encounter. *The McGraw-Hill Handbook of Financial Tables for Real Estate* will add years of practical experience to your résumé, save you countless hours, and help you make deals.

ACKNOWLEDGMENTS

The deals of almost 30 years, the loans, the leases, sales and purchases, created my own need for this book and provided the examples that will pass that experience to you. The book has been shaped by hundreds of colleagues and adversaries, financiers, tenants, buyers and sellers, and to all of them my thanks.

In this space, I have the opportunity also to recompense with this small tribute those who shaped my responses to deals and gave me the know-how to make them. Laurence H. Cleland, MAI, taught, inspired and refreshed with humor and insight all who worked for him and a great many others throughout the industry. Lewis O. Kerwood, executive director, National Society for Real Estate Finance, has from the very first supported this book and strengthened it with his thorough reading and useful criticisms. Although its defects remain mine, the merits of this book find their sources in these two inestimable friends.

Ron Silverman, Cox Castle & Nicholson, broadened the viewpoint of the manuscript with helpful suggestions. Robert Langer, Ernst & Young, gave both technical expertise and encouragement. John Levy, NationsBanc Mortgage Corporation, provided insight from his unique position in the mortgage banking industry. The valuable critique of Maria Siccola of Cushman & Wakefield helped to define and structure the book. Robert Irwin's reading not only furnished tips but helped me avoid traps. Kelley Bergstrom, JMB Properties Company, responded instantly with strong, useful comments.

At McGraw-Hill Professional Book Group, the assistance and professionalism were awe-inspiring. Caroline Carney devoted amazing energy and talent to develop and structure the text. Kimberly Goff and Pamela Pelton managed a wide array of editorial and production needs while McGraw-Hill's Professional Book Group composition unit accomplished the daunting task of melding real estate mathematics with publishing technology.

To all of you, my earnest thanks and applause.

HOW TO USE THIS BOOK

This book is textbook, workbook, ideabook, and reference work. It works best as a daily companion, rather than as a book to be read cover to cover and set aside. The book's design will assist in deepening and broadening your knowledge not only of how real estate deals are constructed but of how the terms of deals are negotiated.

To take advantage of all its potential, familarize yourself with the contents of the book. Although you may work only in commercial real estate, take time to dig into the sections on home loans. As a property manager or leasing agent, you may doubt that the more exotic forms of real estate loans will have any impact on your day-to-day work. Nonetheless, read through the lending sections as well. In doing so, you will be cataloguing the types of problems that are solved for you in the book. That will make them much more likely to pop back from your memory when the need arises. And you will often find that approaches used in other areas of our industry apply to your business as well. Applying tested solutions to new situations gives birth to innovation in real estate.

Road Signs and Ground Rules   Ground rules apply to the use of financial tables. Reading these now will help you to remember that they are here, when the need arises for more detailed review.

Interest Rates   When talking about mortgage loans, people often use terms such as "9.50 percent loan." What is almost always meant in the United States is a monthly payment loan at a nominal annual rate of interest of 9.50 percent, payable monthly in arrears. And that will be the meaning in this book, unless stated otherwise. Loans that call for payments in advance or for other than monthly payments, will be indicated as they occur. If no other details are stated, the loan described has payments monthly in arrears.

Mortgage Constants   Mortgage constants appear in many of the tables. The mortgage constant is always the *annual* mortgage constant, which is the ratio of one year's worth of payments to the amount borrowed. Monthly payment loans have a constant that is twelve monthly payments divided by the loan amount. References in the real estate business to annual mortgage constants are so frequent that it is often called simply "the constant," or "the mortgage constant," without reference to the other key term, *annual*. In this book, constant, mortgage constant, constant annual percent, and annual mortgage constant all mean the same thing.

Taxes   This book offers many tax ideas but not tax advice. Use the ideas to build tax plans that fit your situation, but get tax advice to carry the ideas into practice. Income tax consequences can make what would otherwise be a fine strategem illogical or even illegal. The profitable path in real estate may conflict with tax laws, which have been changing rapidly, making a review with a tax advisor a critical portion of any realty plan.

Legal Aspects   Like taxes, legal questions influence every realty transaction. What may be common in one region may not be legal or ethical everywhere this book may be read. For example, offering to assume a tenant's lease at one location to induce the tenant to move to another may be unethical in some places. The *financial* aspects of a transaction would give no clue to that, however. Real estate professionals have no practical means to judge whether a financial technique comports with legal standards and community ethics. There is no substitute for competent legal advice in carrying out ordinary real estate transactions. Double this advice when carrying out unfamiliar transactions.

Accounting versus Economics   There are important differences between the economic value of a lease, of a loan or of a sale, and the accounting and tax treatment that is made of that value. Accounting seeks to present financial matters so as to make them comparable among companies, regardless whether that best presents economic reality for one company alone. Tax formulas are arbitrary and unrelated to real-world economics. The allowance for depreciation of a building, for example, is simply a tax fiction. But this book is about economic reality, so differences of economic treatment from accounting treatment occur. The aim is to bring you to the correct measure of real estate investment performance rather than to accounting or tax results.

Notes   Road signs in the form of comments, introduced by *Note:* appear in many places. Notes often do not bear directly on the financial points under discussion, but they give tips, detours to avoid, and, especially, points to discuss with legal counsel.

Decimals and Percentages   Often, entries in the tables are given in percentages. The examples include the step of converting the percentage to a decimal by moving the decimal point two places to the left, before proceeding with the math, even though it may be obvious how to deal with the number as a percentage. This prevents confusion with other cases, where the answers are *multiples* of something, and not percentages.

Defined Terms   Words that appear in bold type, such as **annual mortgage constant** are defined in the Glossary. Street talk of the real estate industry, such as as "neg am" or "25 percent of refi" has been avoided. But there is still an inescapable base of trade jargon in real estate. Looking up in the glossary the boldface words or expressions encountered in examples will aid your understanding of concepts and serve as a memory aide when you encounter these words in the field.

Multiple Titles   Some tables carry more than one title, for example, Table 38 carries the titles, "Annual Mortgage Constant, Payments in Advance" and "Annual Rent Constant." An example concerning such a table will refer only to the title that fits the example. Do not be concerned, if one of the titles does not apply to your case; the mathematics are the same for both applications.

New Applications   The tables illustrate the many different business functions that depend on a small group of mathematical concepts. The table titled "Deposit to Create a Sinking Fund" shows how to build a reserve to replace a physical asset, for example, a roof. The table also shows how to build a fund to "pay off" a nonprepayable loan. Identical mathematical logic supports the two examples, but the business logic differs. Suggesting alternative uses of the same mathematics may inspire applications beyond the examples given, and by all means develop these new uses. Reflect carefully, though, if a new application seems to deliver a riskless profit. The law of arbitrage assures us no profit occurs without risk or cost. A discovery that seems to guarantee a profit may signal an unidentified risk or an unaccounted cost.

Self-study Guides   The index is an excellent means to plan a self-study program. Select a topic and work through each of the examples given for it. As you work with a table, search for other examples from other topics that use the same table. This weaving of examples will soon build your comprehension of how the tables function in the cases that concern your business, and how to apply the tables in other cases.

Precision and Accuracy

The book presents completely accurate tables. The precision of the entries in the tables varies, however, from one table to the next. The values may be extended to six or seven decimal places in one spot and only to three or four in another. Numerous decimal places are likely to be given when the entry is intermediate; for example, a mortgage constant will usually be multiplied by a principal amount, whereas a yield on a loan is itself the answer. Mortgage constants receive nine or ten decimals, but yields receive five.

Becoming comfortable with financial calculations means extending the number of decimal places only to what is needed to express the business logic of the deal. Great precision can quickly place an answer within too narrow limits for the assumptions that created it.

For example, consider that if you bought a $200,000 mortgage loan as an investment that would pay you 120 monthly payments of $2,500 each, you would have a yield of

8.689 percent (following trade practice, we present the yield to five decimal places, .08689 or 8.689 percent). Changing the payments by just 10 cents increases the yield to 8.690 percent or lowers it to 8.688 percent, depending on whether the dime was added to or subtracted from the payment. In other words, it won't make a dime's worth of difference in your monthly income if the mortgage yield is 8.689 percent or 8.690 percent.

Effect of Precision on Monthly Payments

Inaccuracies will show up in every statement about financial matters, but these inaccuracies need not be misleading. Consider, for example, an apartment study where rents vary from

---

Assume a $1 million mortgage at 8.00 percent interest on a 30-year amortization schedule. The annual mortgage constant expressed to nine decimal places is 8.805174887 percent. Multiplying the loan amount by the constant with decreasing decimal places (and dividing by 12 to get the monthly payment) gives the following results:

Annual constant	Monthly payment
8.805174887%	$7,337.65
8.80517489%	7,337.65
8.8051749%	7,337.65
8.805175%	7,337.65
8.80518%	7,337.65
8.8052%	7,337.67
8.805%	$7,337.50

A large number of decimal places has little meaning in real world calculations. Five of the decimal places in this mortgage constant make a difference of only two cents on a $1 million base.

Figure 1. The effect of precision on monthly payments.

$236.00 to $241.50. Using, say, $238.00 per month as a typical rent would build in some inaccuracy already. Now suppose the next step is to multiply the typical rent by 96.116151. With enough decimal places, the following figures might appear on your caluclator:

$$\$238.00 \times 96.116151 = \$22,875.64394$$

This looks precise but is misleading. The answer is not nearly as accurate as it looks, especially since we know that the $238.00 figure was picked from a range of numbers for convenience.

Here are two ways to match the precision of answers to their accuracy:

1. Limit the precision of the answer to the *precision of the least precise element*. In the case above, $238.00 is less precise—two decimal places—than 96.116151 with six, so you would give the answer to two decimal places. In fact, since the values of the two decimals in $238.00 are zero, you could forget them also, and give the answer as $22,876. If you multiply $124.61 by 700, give the answer in hundreds, $87,200, not $87,227, since the less precise element is expressed in hundreds.

2. *Give the upper and lower limits*. In the example where rents could vary from $236.00 to $241.50, multiply both limits

$$\$236.00 \times 96.116151 = \$22,683$$

$$\$241.50 \times 96.116151 = \$23,212$$

Then report the answer as "$22,683 to $23,212." This would be especially useful, if $236.00 and $241.50 were known to be exactly the upper and lower limits.

Rounding

If answers obtained in these examples were intermediate values, then they might be accepted as is, for example, $22,683 or $23,212, and the work carried on. If the answers were final, though, appraisers and real estate analysts would study if their implied precision fit the circumstances. The degree of rounding can signal how reliable the figures may be.

Reading "$238.00 × 96.116151 = $22,876" gives the impression that this is accurate to 1 dollar more than $22,875 and less than $22,877. But in fact, we know from the assumptions that the answer lies between $22,683 and $23,212. A round off to $22,900, the nearest $100, would tell the reader that the actual figure is more than $22,800 and less than $23,000, fairly close to our intention. Going a step farther and rounding to $23,000 may give exactly the desired impression, more than $22,000 and less than $24,000, or may have gone too far. Ambiguity is preferable to a false sense of precision, however, and in any case can be reduced by showing the round-off process like this: "$238 × 96.116151 = $22,876, or, say, $23,000." If avoiding ambiguity is especially important, tell what the round off is: "270 × 92.521331 = $24,981 or, rounding to the nearest $1,000, $25,000."

In real estate accounting, such large round-offs would not be made. The round-off would be in most cases to the nearest penny or dollar. Note that mortgage payments are always rounded up to the next penny (and we recommend to the next multiple of $5.00) to ensure that the loan will be amortized within the stated period. Interest calculations, however, are always rounded down to the next lower penny to avoid charging any more interest than started in the note.

Examples in this book will often be left without rounding, to assist you in replicating the exact number printed. Any round-offs will be indicated. Remember that the best rule for rounding is the need concept: Extend the number of decimals only as far as needed to understand the deal. If a proposal describes an investment that "may produce between 8 percent and 9 percent per year," state simply that. Investment reports suggesting that an "internal rate of return of 8.689 percent could be realized" bear the burden of proving that the rate of return is neither 8.688 percent nor 8.690 percent. As we have seen, just $0.10 a month in income might be the difference between the rates.

Dennis R. Kelley

Chapter 1

PLANNING THE COMMERCIAL PROPERTY PURCHASE

The exploits of top real estate dealmakers seldom depend on sheer persuasiveness. Real estate is a business of numbers, and balancing numbers on all four sides of the real estate grid—income, expense, price and financing—creates success. Finding the balance widens agreement among buyer, seller, and financer and helps forecast how parties might react to successive counteroffers. Financial tables will help you find the balance and make the forecast quickly.

In this chapter, we will concentrate on the buying decision. The global questions that need to be asked before buying real estate are what can you pay, how much would you have to sell for, what would the yield be, and how long would it take to achieve that yield. The early examples deal with those questions. Following are methods to make the price more attractive, that is, to give each side more of what it really needs, and other means to tweak the purchase offer into purchase contract.

THE INTERNAL RATE OF RETURN

The **internal rate of return** (**IRR**) is the single, most widely used means to estimate real estate investment performance. The IRR gives a simple measure of performance despite the fact that hundreds or possibly thousands of factors go into the IRR's calculation.

The IRR is a yield and is stated as an annual percentage. For example, "the IRR is 11.50 percent for a 10-year holding period" means that all the cash income and capital gain or loss from the property over 10 years will exceed all cash costs, weighted for time, by 11.50 percent per year. Yield to maturity of corporate bonds and mortgage loans rests on the same math as the IRR, which may account for the popularity of the IRR with analysts.

Although IRRs see everyday use as performance measures, they are not without critics. The sheer number of factors that meld into a single number means that two properties with vastly different prospects could have the same IRR. Analysts have also shown that two different and mathematically valid IRRs can exist for a property. The many unknowns of real estate returns, critics say, should not be measured with the math used for bonds and mortgages, which are contracts with stated performance dates. These points have not overcome the convenience of a single number to measure realty investments, so the IRR has become part of commercial real estate's daily vocabulary.

Perhaps the greatest weakness of the IRR is its unique character; each IRR is custom-built. The measure is, after all, the return *internal* to a deal. Comparing the prospects for investment performance among competing opportunities with the IRR has been nearly impossible, because of the lack of standard terms. To render the IRR of one property comparable to that of other investments, Table 1 (p. 145) shows a set of standard, simplified IRRs. These follow from specified common circumstances; as tools for calibration, the IRRs allow the analyst to compare alternative prospective investments against a mathematical standard.

Example 1.   Finding the Internal Rate of Return of an Investment

Aaron Hasten has been offered an office building with a current **capitalization rate** of 9.00 percent per year. The property is priced far below reproduction cost, and Hasten wishes to know the IRR, if the property can be sold in 5 years for three times its cost, i.e., a 200 percent capital gain.

To find the IRR, enter Table 1, page 1 (p. 145), at the section for a 5-year holding period. Read across on the line for a 9.00 percent capitalization rate to the column headed 200 percent capital gain. The answer there, 27.824 percent, is the internal rate of return, if a 200 percent capital gain is realized in addition to a 9.00 percent cap rate over a 5-year holding period. Likely fluctuations in income and expenses suggest rounding off this estimate, at least to 27.8 percent and perhaps to 27 percent per year.

Example 2.   Comparing Calculated Internal Rate of Return to the Model Rate

Stacy Malloy has prepared a prospectus for Cinco Robles Apartments, including a 10-year income, expense, and future sale projection. The average **capitalization rate** of the property is 7.50 percent. Based on the increase in income over time, a sale is predicted at the end of the 10-year holding period at 200 percent of the investment required today, that is, a 100 percent capital gain. Based on these facts, the prospectus projects the IRR to be 13.17 percent per year.

To make the comparison, enter Table 1, page 2 (p. 146), at the section for a 10-year holding period. In the 10-year section, read across on the line for capitalization rate of 7.50 percent to the column headed 100 percent capital gain at end of period. The answer there, 12.551 percent, or, rounding, 12.5 percent, is the standard, simplified IRR for these circumstances. Since the IRR calculated by Malloy is over ½ percent higher—in IRR calcula-

tions, a significant difference—the assumptions underlying the calculated IRR should be retested. Stacy Malloy will reconsider such factors as income growth over the period, whether expenses are presumed to grow at a lesser rate than income, or whether she has miscalculated. A common source of conflicting IRRs is a spike in cash flow, perhaps from a projected partial sale or refinancing or because interest expense is paid from a reserve.

As with any financial table, the figure in Table 1 does not prove the calculated IRR correct. Neither figure can be called wrong. The table suggests only that the result of an analysis compares well (or poorly) with a known mathematical model. A deviation as great as 0.50 percent or 1.00 percent per year should be cause to review the assumptions to identify differences from the model.

PURCHASE PRICE FOR A GIVEN YIELD

We have seen the yield consequences for certain income and sale price information, but how would the price be altered to achieve a given yield? Income-producing property rarely offers current income exactly equal to the overall return sought by the investor. When a property's current income is greater than the investor's requirement, future capital growth will probably be less than that offered by other properties in the market. If the current income is less than that required by the investor, Table 2 (p. 151) shows the purchase price needed to match a yield objective to the predicted income and sale price.

Example 3.   Purchase Price for a Given Yield

Van Wyck is considering the purchase of a condominium as an investment. The property can be rented to provide a 5.00 percent annual **net operating income**, or **NOI**. Van Wyck is confident that the property will be sold after 5 years for $200,000 but would buy it only if a 12 percent to 13 percent per year overall return can be made.

To find the price that can be paid for the condominium today, turn to the section containing desired yields of 12.00 percent and 13.00 percent. First, read down the left column to the section for 12.00 percent and read across on the line for a 5-year holding period to the column headed 5.00 percent, the expected dividend rate. Read there the answer, 74.7666 percent, for a 12.00 percent yield. Below, in the section for a desired yield of 13.00 percent, read across on the 5-year holding period line to the 5.00 percent column, and find 71.8622 percent for a yield of 13.00 percent. Now multiply both factors times $200,000, the future selling price, to get

$$\$200,000 \times 0.718622 = \$143,724,$$

the price to yield 13 percent and

$$\$200,000 \times 0.747666 = \$149,533.20$$

the price to yield 12 percent per year. Rounding to the nearest $250, Van Wyck can afford to pay between $143,750 and $150,000 to receive the desired yield of 12 percent to 13 percent, if the property can be sold after five years for $200,000 and cash dividends of 5.00 percent will also be received.

Example 4. Purchase Price for a Given Yield When NOI Is Greater Than Required

Folansky Realtors have a target yield of 7.00 percent on their investments, using a presumed holding period of 10 years. The Pier Ridge Apartments have been offered to them with a pro forma that shows a 9.00 percent return on the asking price.

To find the purchase price that will give a 7.00 percent return under these conditions, enter Table 2 (p. 152) on the page for 9.0 percent capitalization rate. Read down the left column, desired yield, to the section for 7.00 percent, and in the section next to it, holding period, find the line for 10 years. Read across on that line to the column headed 9.00 percent and find 114.0472. Subtract 100.0000 percent to get 14.0472 percent, the percentage that can be paid in excess of the asking price and still obtain the 7.00 percent required return.

It is unlikely that Folansky will offer the extra 14 percent to the seller. More likely, Folansky will use it to establish a reserve for repairs or to cushion a fall in property value. It is not unheard of, though, for an investor to use this type of calculation to develop a preemptive bid on a top-quality property.

Example 5. Purchase Price for a Given Yield When NOI Is Lower Than Required

The Pyramid Company is offered a group of industrial warehouses leased to first-class tenants. The properties offer a 5.00 percent initial yield, which is expected to continue until the leases roll over in 5 years. Pyramid will not accept less than a 7.00 percent return.

To find the purchase price that meets Pyramid's standards, enter Table 2, page 1, the page that includes 5.00 percent capitalization rate from the property (p. 151). Under the left column, find the section with desired yield of 7.00 percent. Reading across on the line for 5 years to the column headed 5.00 percent, find the answer 91.7996 or not quite 91.8 percent. This is the maximum percentage of the offering price that could be paid to obtain the desired return, assuming the property value will rise to today's asking price in 5 years.

Example 6. Purchase Price for a Given Yield When NOI Will Rise

In the preceding example, if Pyramid Company estimated that, over 5 years, net operating income would rise from 5.00 percent per year to 7.00 percent, the average 6.00 percent could be used for the calculation. Enter Table 2 at 7.00 percent desired yield and find under 5 years and 6.00 percent capitalization rate the answer, 95.8998 percent, or almost 96 percent. A purchase at 96 percent of asking price would give them the desired yield, if cash return averages 6.00 percent.

Example 7. Maximum Price When an Option Exists

Spectron Investors would like to buy the industrial building that Mellaney Corporation occupies as a tenant. But the tenant has not only a lease with 10 years remaining at a fixed rental of $450,000 per year net but also an option to buy the building for $6 million.

Spectron uses a 10-year holding period in analyzing deals, so the 10-year lease is acceptable. But the risk is that the tenant might exercise its option, leaving Spectron with less than the 12.00 percent yield objective that it requires.

To find the maximum price Spectron can pay, first determine the dividend yield on the option price, to get

$$\frac{\text{Rent}}{\text{Option price}} = \frac{\$450,000}{\$6,000,000} = 7.5\% \text{ percent per year}$$

Now enter Table 2, page 3 (p. 153) and read down the left column to 12.00 percent and to the line in that section under holding period of 10 years. Read across on that line to the column headed 7.5 percent and find the factor 74.5740 percent, the percentage of price that may be paid. Now multiply this by the option price to get

$$\$6,000,000 \times 0.745740 = \$4,474,440$$

Rounding to the nearest \$25,000 gives you \$4,475,000. Spectron could afford to pay \$4,475,000 for the property with Mellaney's lease and still earn 12.00 percent overall on its investment, if the option is exercised.

NET PRESENT VALUE OF AN INVESTMENT

The IRR may be the most popular means to forecast real estate performance, but the **net present value** method, or **NPV,** is a close second. The present values of a great many standard cases are calculated for you in Table 3 (p. 155). Or the NPV can be found by discounting the income (see Example 184 in Chapter 5). In either case, the result is compared with today's cost or value, and the difference is the net present value of the property. Analysts favoring NPV appreciate that the result is expressed in terms of money, rather than percentages, which gives them the scale of profitability.

Example 8.   Finding the Net Present Value of a Proposed Investment

---

Stephana Verberle has been offered Cinema Park, a theme center offering a current capitalization rate of only 6.00 percent per year. But built-in rental increases and CPI protection suggest that the property can be sold in 5 years for 2½ times its purchase price, for a capital gain of 150 percent. At the same time, Cermin Apartments has been offered with a 10.00 percent cap rate. Since this property's income will rise slowly, the best sale price that can be expected in 5 years is a 33 percent capital gain. Either investment would require \$1.1 million. Verberle analyzes all offers on the basis of a 10.50 percent **discount rate.**

To begin the investment comparison, find the NPV of each investment. Find the 10.50 percent discount rate in Table 3. In the section for 5 years' holding period, first read across on the line for a cap rate of 6.50 percent. Under the column headed 150 percent capital gain, read the factor 173.428 percent, the

present value as a percentage of original cost of Cinema Park. Next, on the line for a cap rate of 10.00 percent, under the column headed 33 percent capital gain, find the factor 117.825 percent, the present value of Cermin Apartments. Subtract 100 percent from each of the factors, representing the original price, to get NPVs of 73.428 percent for Cinema Park and 17.825 percent for Cermin Apartments. Despite its lower cap rate, Cinema Park has a far higher NPV. However, the investment advantage of Cinema Park rests heavily on the expected capital gain; accordingly, Verberle will scrutinize the prospects for the gain carefully.

Example 9.   Constructing the Profitability Index

The preceding example gave no dollar figures for the investment, indicating only that the two investments would cost the same amount. More commonly, properties would carry different prices. To compare such cases, a **profitability index,** or **PI,** may be constructed. The PI is the ratio of the present value of the deal, calculated with the investor's required return as the discount rate, to its original cost. By custom, a PI is given as a decimal, not a percentage. A PI greater than 1.00 should be accepted, and those less than 1.00 should be rejected. Among acceptable projects, choosing that with the highest PI will maximize profit.

Table 3 is already constructed in the form of a profitability index, although as a percentage (therefore, divide the figure from Table 3 by 100). Using the present value figures from the preceding example computed at a discount rate of 10.50 percent, we would find a PI of 1.73428, or, rounding, 1.73, for Cinema Park and 1.17825, rounded to 1.18, for Cermin Apartments.

SALE PRICE FOR GIVEN OVERALL OR EQUITY YIELD

Real estate investment yield is not really known until after a sale. With sale proceeds in hand and the record of dividends received over the holding period, one can tote up the true yield. But real estate decisions need to be made before the true yield is known. To make these decisions, investors need to estimate how much of their required yield can be had from the income and how much must come from capital gain. Other investors are more concerned with capital loss and want to know how wrong they can be about a property before they will have missed their minimum acceptable yield.

Table 4 (pp. 169–181) shows the sale price, as a percentage of original investment, that would bring the overall yield up or down to a desired level. Section (a) of the table gives the increase where no leverage is used. Section (b) gives the same information for cases which involve leverage.

Example 10. Sale Price for a Given Overall Yield

The Pliny Partnership built an industrial building **on spec** at a cost of $1 million. They have just leased the building for $109,000 annual fixed rent for 10 years. The partners have an overall yield objective of 12 percent per year over a 10-year holding period. Knowing that they are getting 10.90 percent, or, rounding, 11.00 percent annual return ($109,000 divided by $1 million, rounded) from rentals during the lease term, they realize that a sale will have to bring a profit to achieve the target yield.

To find the required sale price, enter Table 4(a), page 3 (p. 171) where cap rates are 11.00 percent. Read down the left column to the section for cap rate of 11.00 percent and across on the line for holding period of 10 years. Find, under the column for desired yield 12.00 percent, the answer 117.549 percent. This is the percentage of original cost needed for the required 12.00 percent yield. Multiply this figure by the cost to get

$$\$1,000,000 \times 1.17549 = \$1,175,490$$

the sale price to raise 11.00 percent operating yield to 12.00 percent overall yield.

Stated differently, to get a 12 percent return, the property will have to be sold 10 years in the future for $1,175,000 in addition to the annual rentals of $109,000.

Example 11. Amount of Loss Acceptable before Return Is Jeopardized

AZAZ Pension Fund measures all investments against an 8.00 percent yield requirement and a 10-year holding period. To cover administrative costs and costs of benefits, AZAZ needs about 8.00 percent per year. Most properties offer better rates, but the Fund is more concerned with assured return than it

is with high return. Since real estate offers no guarantees of any particular rate of return, the Fund makes its analyses with sufficient room for error about future values. The Fund is considering the purchase of an older building with current income of 10.50 percent.

To find the required sale price, turn to the section of Table 4(a), page 3, where cap rates are 10.50 percent (p. 171). Within that section, find the line for a holding period of 10 years; on that line look under the column for desired yield 8.00 percent to find 63.784. This is the percentage of original purchase price that the property could be sold for to achieve an 8.00 percent return for the Fund. The Fund's analysis shows that real estate values are unlikely to fall 36.216 percent (that is, 100.000% − 63.784%), making the property a good candidate to give the necessary 8.00 percent yield.

Example 12. Payment Available to One Who Ensures Yield

Springboard Investaurants Ltd. proposes to syndicate a partnership that will own restaurants leased to fast-food chains. The partners are to receive a fixed rate of return during the expected 10-year holding period plus the opportunity for a capital gain when the restaurants are sold. The partners expect a total yield of 8.00 percent from the total of annual cash flow, plus a capital gain upon sale of the properties.

Numerous fast-food chains have offered long-term lease deals that offer a return of 9.50 percent. But these deals are notoriously risky, so Springboard's management proposes to pay a third party to ensure the 8.00 percent return to the partners. An insurance company is prepared to act as surety in return for 15 percent of the sale price of the properties after 10 years or, if lower, the amount which leaves Springboard an 8.00 percent annual return.

To find what the Springboard management should make of this offer, enter Table 4(a), page 3 (p. 171) at the section for 9.50 percent capitalization rate. On the line for a 10-year holding period, read across to the column for desired yield 8.00 percent. The answer there, 78.270 percent, is the percentage of the original cost needed to provide the desired return. The surety could receive as much as 21.730 percent of the original cost to ensure 8.00 percent, but since the surety will accept 15 percent, the transaction will give the investors at least 8.00 percent and leave room for capital gain as well.

Example 13. Shared Appreciation to Give a Lender a Specified Yield

Fillna Developers propose a joint venture with Perquisite Life Assurance. Perquisite would make a loan of 75 percent of appraised value. The loan would bear interest at 9.00 percent with an initial mortgage constant of 9.50 percent. Perquisite would also be entitled to 100 percent of cash flow and appreciation, until it had received 11.00 percent yield.

To find the sale price at the end of 10 years that would give the lender 11.00 percent yield, enter Table 4(a), page 3 (p. 171), the page for 9.50 percent cap rates. Read across on the line for a 10-year holding period to the 11.00 percent column. The factor there is 125.083 percent. Paying the lender an amount equal to 125 percent of the original loan will give the lender a yield of 11.00 percent if monthly payments at an annual constant of 9.50 percent have also been made.

Note That the monthly payments will have been applied to principal and interest does not enter into this calculation. The ordinary amortization schedule will only apply in the case where there is no capital gain.

SALE PRICE FOR A GIVEN EQUITY RETURN

Section (b) of Table 4 gives the information for a leveraged deal that section (a) gives for unleveraged property. The sensitivity of leveraged returns, called **cash-on-cash returns,** to changes in sales price is much greater than in the preceding section, since only the equity fraction of the investment gets the benefit of any gain (or detriment of loss). If both a mortgaged property and an unleveraged deal are offered, they should not be directly compared using these tables. First the cases should be modified by supposing a financing for the unleveraged deal similar to the mortgaged property. Then the leveraged case should be compared as if *free and clear* with the unleveraged property.

Example 14. Future Gain to Bring Equity Yield to Desired Level

Maria Gutfriend will bid on a sale-leaseback transaction, under which she will lease a freestanding ware-

house building on a 10-year term. She can obtain financing for 75 percent of the total cost at 10.50 percent interest, investing $260,000 equity. An annual return of 12 percent overall on her equity investment is her criterion. This would include return from cash flow after debt service and a capital gain from future profit on sale of the building. She proposes to bid a lease on the basis of 7.50 percent cash-on-cash return, hoping to get the remainder of her yield from future profit.

To find what the profit would have to be, begin by finding the total investment today. It is the equity divided by the equity-to-value ratio, or $260,000 ÷ 0.25 = $1,040,000. Now enter Table 4(b), page 3 (p. 175) with 7.50 percent equity rate and 12.00 percent desired yield. Read across in the section for 10.50 percent loan on the line for 10 years to the section for 12.00 percent desired yield. Find there in the column for 75 percent loan the factor 113.459 percent. Multiply the percentage by the total investment today to get

$$\$1,040,000 \times 1.13459 = \$1,179,974$$

or, rounding to the nearest $25,000, $1,175,000, the future sale price needed to bring overall yield from 7.50 percent cash-on-cash to 12.00 percent for the 10-year period.

USING FINANCING TO ALTER THE PRICE OR YIELD

Techniques up to this point have shown the yield or the price from a transaction. We now introduce financing as a means to alter the price or the yield, either to the owner or to a buyer.

Create Value by Paying Points

Table 5 (pp. 182–187) shows how lower mortgage payments on income-producing real estate mean an increase in value. Lower mortgage payments mean higher **net cash flow** after **debt service.** The increased cash flow means an increase in value, because most investors capitalize net cash flow after debt service at a lower yield than the lender requires. In a market where the lender demands a 10.00 percent return on investment, equity investors might look for only a 7.00 percent **cash-on-cash return.** Paying **points** to a lender to get a lower interest rate on the loan is a smart vehicle to get the increased value. The money paid for the points is outweighed in many cases by the increase in sale price. This program will generally be useful when interest rates are greater than cash-on-cash returns required in the market-place.

Example 15. Value Created by Paying Points

Ted Grilshire builds miniwarehouses for sale. Typically, investors who buy the projects use 75 percent mortgage financing and seek a 7.50 percent initial cash-on-cash return. Loans are available today for a 7-year term with amortization on a 30-year schedule at an interest rate of 11.00 percent. Ted would like to see the value of buying the loan down to 10.00 percent.

To get the number of points that could be paid, enter Table 5, page 2 (p. 183) (the page for equity rate of 7.50 percent) and find the section for 75 percent loan-to-value ratio. On the line for a cut in rate of 1.000 percent, read across to the column headed 11.00 percent and find 8.970 percent, the increase in value from buying down the loan from 11.00 percent to 10.00 percent.

By reference to Table 24 (pp. 282–288) and Examples 84 and 85 in Chapter 3, Ted will find that the buy-down would cost only 5.202 percent, adding a profit from the buy-down to the profit on the sale to the investor group.

Converting Interest to Principal or Principal to Interest

Interest and principal are equivalent; as shown in Table 10 (pp. 201–229) the two can be interchanged in fixed ratios. The table is fundamentally a loan price table, and examples in Chapter 3 will show the price of a loan to give a certain yield. But other uses that evolve from the principal-interest equivalence are illustrated in the following examples.

Example 16. Lower Interest Rate to Gain Higher Sale Price

Pierrot Corporate Finance proposes to sell its apartment complex with seller financing. Pierrot will provide a $2 million loan for 10 years on a 30-year schedule. It considers its offer of 10.25 percent interest equal to the market rate. A syndicator is willing to purchase, but the rate is too high to permit a current cash dividend to its investor-partners. Pierrot seeks a

rate in the 9.50 percent range to attract an offer from the syndicator.

To find the increase in purchase price necessary to justify this interest rate, enter Table 10, page 17, the page for 9.50 percent. Read down the left column to 10.25 percent desired yield. Read across on that line to the column for 10 years and find the factor 95.47434 percent, the percentage of the starting loan amount needed to bring the rate from 9.50 percent to 10.25 percent. Subtract this from 100 percent to get 4.52566 percent, and multiply by the $2 million loan amount:

$$\$2,000,000 \times 0.0452566 = \$90,513.20$$

This is the increase in purchase price that would justify accepting this below-market interest rate.

Example 17. Portion of Price Attributable to Below-Market Financing

To attract a buyer, a seller may offer to take back a **purchase money mortgage** at a lower interest rate than the current market. Swanee, Zeldig & Co. are offered a property at a price of $3.5 million consisting of $700,000 cash down payment with seller financing of $2.8 million at 6.00 percent interest for 5 years. Mortgage interest rates are generally 8.50 percent, so the treasurer of Swanee, Zeldig wants to separate the price of the property from the price of below-market financing.

Enter Table 10, page 3 (p. 203) at the section for an interest rate of 6.00 percent. Read down the desired yield column to 8.50 percent and across on that line to 5 years. The factor there, 90.15014 percent, is the percentage of face amount that would be paid for normal financing. Multiplying the loan by the factor will give

$$\$2,800,000 \times 0.9015014 = \$2,524,204$$

This gives the real financing; add the down payment of $700,000 for a comparable value of $3,224,204, or, rounding, $3,225,000. The real estate price is $3,225,000, and $275,000 is the price of the special financing.

Note Converting ordinary income into capital gain in this manner will be restricted for financial accounting or tax purposes, if the interest rate is clearly below market. Competent tax advice should always be obtained before putting into practice the methods described here.

ESTIMATING FUTURE RESULTS

Total Growth Converted to Compounded Annual Rate of Growth

Table 6 (pp. 188–190) shows the **compounded** annual rate of change for a given total amount of change. The simple annual rate is easily found: If the value of a property increased 125 percent over a 10-year holding period, the simple or straight-line rate of growth is easily found. Dividing 125 percent by 10 gives a 12.5 percent rate of increase. The compounded rate, found in Table 6, however, is only 8.447 percent, or roughly two-thirds of the straight-line rate.

Example 18. Total Return Converted to Compound Annual Return

Venett's prospectus for the financing of Eddison Venture shows a 65 percent total return over a projected 5-year life. This return is the total amount of cash, not discounted, that an investor would have in addition to the original investment if the projection results in fact occur.

To find the annual compounded return, enter Table 6 at 65 percent total growth—page 2 (p. 189). On the 5-year line, read under the column headed 65 percent the answer 10.534 percent, the equivalent annual rate of return, compounded, from 65 percent total return. This is not necessarily the same as the IRR for this deal: Table 6 assumes level annual cash flows, which may or may not have been the case in the Eddison Venture prospectus.

Example 19. Total Growth Converted to Annual Rate of Growth

Phyllis is deciding whether to buy an apartment complex. She has estimated that rents will increase a total of 75 percent over the next 8 years.

To find the annual rate of increase, enter Table 6, page 2 (p. 189). Read down the left column to 8 years and across to the column headed 75 percent to find 7.245 percent, the compounded annual rate of rent increase equal to 75 percent total increase over 8 years.

Example 20. Annual Rate of Price Growth from Total Rate

Macavery is nearing the end of a 5-year lease. The landlord is offering a renewal lease with an option to buy at the end of 5 years. Stating that the property is worth $750,000 today, the landlord is willing to grant an option at a price increase of 25 percent for 5 years from now.

To test whether the inflation expectation implied by the option price is reasonable, enter Table 6, page 1 (p. 188) at the section for 25 percent increase. Read down the years column to 5 and across to the 25 percent column. The answer there is 4.563 percent, or roughly 4.5 percent per year. The landlord's option price is a 4.5 percent compounded annual rate of price increase. Table C, the Consumer Price Index (p. 846), indicates that 5-year increases in the CPI of 25 percent or more occurred about half the time over the past 30 years.

Future Simple Rate of Return on Initial Investment

Real estate people work so much with compounded annual rates of return that we can lose sight of the acceleration inherent in our assumptions of growth. Table 7 (pp. 191–192) tells the annual rate of return on the *original* invested amount. For example, a deposit of $100 at 5.50 percent interest per year compounded monthly will increase $5.64 in the first year, $5.96 in the second, and $6.29 in the third. The compounded rate of interest remains 5.50 percent for each year, but the **future simple rates** are 5.64 percent, 5.96 percent, and 6.29 percent. Future simple rates illustrate the sensitivity of investments to compounding and how to isolate growth in a given year in the future.

Cross-Reference Although the **nominal annual rate** is only 5.50 percent, the **effective annual rate** is 5.64 percent. See Example 111 in Chapter 3 for a discussion of nominal and effective rates.

Example 21. Amount of Profit in a Future Year

Tim Brenner has leased a medical office complex on a net rental basis, with the rental increasing monthly at an annual rate of 7.0 percent per year. The property is worth $2.6 million today, and Brenner expects that its value will grow 7.0 percent each year with the rental increase. If he is correct in that assumption, which implies that capitalization rates remain the same, he wants to know the increase in property value in the tenth year of the lease.

Enter Table 7, page 1 (p. 191). Read down the elapsed years column to 10 and across on that line to the 7.00 percent column. The factor there, 13.55 percent, is the percentage increase for year 10. Multiply by today's value to get

$$\$2,600,000 \times 0.1355 = \$352,300$$

This is the value increase in the tenth year, if properties continue to be sold at today's cap rates.

Time When Compounded Profit Will Be Achieved

Table 68 (p. 772) tells the month in which an increase of compounded interest or profit will have been achieved, if interest or profit accumulates at a given compounded monthly rate. The entries are given in years and months. The answer is the month when the goal will be achieved. For example, an entry of 10Y 12m means that the desired increase in value will occur sometime in the twelfth month of the eleventh year.

Example 22. Time When Compounded Profit Should Have Occurred

Melisson has acquired 200 acres for future homesite development. Homesites are selling today for $21,000, and the plan is to hold the acreage until homesite prices reach $31,500, a 50 percent increase. In the past 3 years, as well as over the past 15 years, average annual price growth has been just over 7.25 percent per year.

To find when Melisson may expect to have achieved 50 percent value growth, enter Table 68 at the section for 50 percent increase. Read down the left column to 7.25 percent interest. On that line under the column headed 50 percent, read the answer 5Y 8m, meaning 5 years and 8 months. If the 7.25 percent nominal annual rate of increase continues, the value of homesites will have risen 50 percent in 5 years and 8 months after Melisson's purchase.

Time When Income on Deferred Tax Equals Tax

Many opportunities exist in real estate to defer taxation of a profit until a later date. Structuring tax-free exchanges according to the rules of Section 1031 of the *U.S. Internal Revenue Code,* or a variety of "near sales," by which shares in a corporation or interests in a partnership are created or exchanged, can push back payment of taxes. The methods to do this are complex, since the tax codes are written to speed, not defer, collection of taxes, and the process should be undertaken only with professional tax advice. However, it is useful to make quick calculations of the possible benefits of tax deferral before engaging the complete analysis that the advisor must make. Table 69 (p. 773) assists by showing the time to "re-earn" the taxes.

Consider a real estate seller faced with taxes from a desirable transaction. If closed in the ordinary way, the sale will mean a tax to pay. But if the tax can be deferred, the money *not* sent to the tax authorities can earn interest, taxable or not. After some years, the deferring transaction is closed out, and the tax must be paid. But interest earned on the deferred amount will at some point equal the deferred taxes plus tax on the extra earnings, so the wealth of the individual is nominally the same, as if the deal had been tax-free in the first place. Table 69 charts the time required to reach that stage, given the investor's tax bracket and the rate of return earned in the deferral period. The user may select interest that is taxable currently or deferred taxation.

Example 23. Time When Income on Deferred Tax Equals Tax

Deferred Taxation of Income

Fran Galatty has a buyer for The Elan Shop'n Park. With a price of $6.1 million cash for his equity, he would have to pay tax, federal and state, of $880,000, for net proceeds of $5,220,000. But a tax-free exchange of The Elan for a freestanding discount store leased for 25 years to a major retail chain could also be arranged. Based on a $6.1 million exchange value for this equity, the return from the exchange property would be 9.00 percent per year. Under current tax laws, Galatty expects to be in the 32 percent tax bracket for several years.

This section considers that depreciation and other charges would shelter all the income from tax until resale. To find the time for the deferred taxes to regenerate themselves through interest, enter Table 69 in the section for deferred taxation. On the line for 32 percent, read across to the column headed 9.00 percent. The answer, 10 years 2 months, means that, with 9.00 percent tax-deferred income, Galatty will have earned enough after 10 years and 2 months using the deferred taxes to pay the original deferred taxes plus the tax on the new earnings and still have left the full $6.1 million original price, as if the deal had been tax-free.

Current Taxation of Income

If Galatty's exchange property produces taxable income, the portion of Table 69 labeled "Current Taxation of Interest" is used. On the same facts of a 32 percent tax bracket and 9.00 percent interest rate, the factor is 11Y 5m, meaning 11 years and 5 months will be required before the income will have produced enough additional yield to offset the tax.

Note From these facts, it appears desirable always to defer tax and profit from use of the "government's" money. But as the law of arbitrage tells us, profit occurs only in an environment of risk or cost. Here the most important risk is having all the sales proceeds tied up in an exchange property in order to have the deferred tax portion regenerating itself. The entire amount is at risk in a property that might be unsuccessful. A lease to a major chain mitigates the investment risk in this example but does not eliminate it. Exchanging a sure $5,220,000, after tax, might produce something less. It is also possible that tax laws could change again and strip the deal of the intended tax benefits. The laws *have* changed almost annually in the past decade; further changes to tax codes are a risk that can neither be calculated nor avoided.

Consumer Price Index and Effects of Inflation

Example 24.   Change in CPI and Percent Difference

Tammy Salomon is analyzing the offering package for Chateau Griffon apartments. Using Table 6, she has found that gross rentals rose by a 1.6 percent compounded annual rate in the period from April 1980 to April 1990. To compare this with the national inflation rate, enter Table C, page 2, in the section for percentage change in CPI over 10 years earlier. Read down the left column to 90/80 and across to the column April. The answer there is 59.1 percent, the change in the national CPI from April 1980 through April 1990.

Using Table 6, Salomon will learn that this change is a 4.746 percent, or, rounding, 4.75 percent, compounded annual change, which seems to indicate that Chateau Griffon has not kept pace. Two comments may be made: Many communities have lower CPI indexes and rates of change than the national average. Second, growth in the CPI was softening rapidly in 1980. Real estate, which cannot be repriced as readily as groceries, tends not to achieve the inflationary peaks. All the same, Salomon has had a demonstration that the property responds slowly to inflation.

Example 25.   Rate of Inflation in a Future Year

Romy Barstow notes that the CPI has increased 5.50 percent in the past year. If the same rate of growth occurs in the CPI for the next 5 years, what will the inflation rate be in constant dollars, 5 years in the future?

Enter Table 7, page 1 (p. 191) at the section for 5.50 percent interest rate or rate of growth. On the line for 5 years elapsed, read across to the 5.50 percent column, and find there the factor 7.03 percent. With a 5.50 percent nominal annual rate of growth in the CPI, in 5 years' time the inflation rate that year will be 7.03 percent relative to today's purchasing power.

Example 26.   Total CPI Growth in a Period

Mr. Tanaka is investigating sale price inflation. Appraised values of small apartment buildings have been increasing at an annual rate of 7.0 percent over the past 5 years. If this inflation rate continues, what value would be indicated for a $900,000 property 10 years in the future?

First find the future value factor. It is under Table 46, page 7, the page for 7.00 percent interest (the rate of price increase will be substituted for interest here). On the line for 10 years under the annual payment section, read under the future value column the factor 1.9671514. Now multiply it by the current value to get

$$\$900{,}000 \times 1.9671514 = \$1{,}770{,}436$$

Rounding to the nearest $25,000, $1,775,000 is the value of a $900,000 property 10 years in the future if the present 7.0 percent annual rate of price growth continues.

Chapter 2

PLANNING THE SINGLE-FAMILY RESIDENTIAL MORTGAGE

This chapter is devoted to home loans, from the standpoint of both the borrower and the lender. Examples will show how to find mortgage payments and the yield, or APR, when points are paid. The chapter also supplies methods to lower the interest cost and to shorten the term of the loan as well as techniques for seller financing and buying down a loan. The chapter is divided into the following principal sections.

Mortgage payments and comparison of payment plans

Sorting out mortgage terms

Deciding to lock in or refinance a mortgage

Seller financing

Yields on home loan transactions

MORTGAGE PAYMENTS AND COMPARISONS OF PAYMENT PLANS

The most common home loan available in the United States today has a 30-year **amortization schedule.** But lenders have introduced an entire hothouse of hybrid mortgages, such as GEMs, rising-rate mortgages, and biweeklies to deal with every borrower's needs: Lowest interest cost, lowest initial payment, longest term, and largest amount borrowable. No one can put them all into a single package, since investment markets dictate mortgage terms. But with the variety of plans described here, the emphasis may be placed where it will best meet the borrower's particular needs.

Even though a loan may be for a 5-, 7- or 10-year term, the standard loan payment will be the amount that *if continued for 30 years* would fully amortize the loan. The **term** of the loan, then, may be for one period and the amortization schedule for another. The amortization schedule and interest rate determine how much the payments are; the term determines for how long the payments will be made.

Whenever the term of the loan is shorter than the amortization schedule, a lump sum called a **balloon** will be payable at the end of the term. A balloon payment will commonly be very much larger than the normal payment. It is necessary to understand not only the interest rate and the monthly payment but the amount of any balloon payment that will be required. (If the loan is *fully amortizing,* there will be no balloon payment.)

Loans may start out with one amortization schedule and end up with another. Biweekly loans begin with the standard 30-year amortization schedule. But since a half-payment is made every two weeks, the loan is fully amortized in fewer years than originally scheduled. The growing equity mortgage (GEM) uses monthly payments that begin at a normal rate and later increase, accelerating repayment.

Mortgage Payments

Example 27.   Payments on a 30-Year Home Loan

Carrollton's client is seeking a $75,000 mortgage loan at the current interest rate, which is 10.75 percent. The loan will have a 10-year term, but the payments will be based on a 30-year amortization schedule.

To find the monthly payment, turn to Table 18, page 4. Read down the left column to $75,000 and across on that line to the column headed 10.75 percent. The answer there is $700.11, the payment for a 10.75 percent loan on a 30-year schedule.

Example 28.   Monthly Payments on a Nonstandard Home Loan

The standard home loan tables cover 30- or 15-year amortization schedules or loans with biweekly or weekly payments. The commercial loan factors in Tables 35 through 38 (pp. 421–465) provide for a wide variety of other payment plans and interest rates. The commercial tables present figures for an **annual mortgage constant.** These constants are the percentage of the original loan amount that will be paid in one year and are used as follows:

The Mulder family is shopping for a $150,000 loan at 10.50 percent interest with an amortization schedule of 23 years, 7 months. There are two steps to finding the monthly payments:

1. Find the constant: Enter Table 35(b), page 11 (p. 442), the page for 10.50 percent interest. Read down the years column to 23 and across to the column headed 7 months to find 11.475010 percent, the annual constant.

2. Calculate the payments: Multiply the loan amount by the constant, and divide by 12 to get

$$\$150,000 \times 0.11475010 \div 12 = \$1,434.38$$

This is the monthly payment to amortize $150,000 at 10.50 percent in 23 years, 7 months.

Benefits of Accelerated Mortgage Payments

Home loan borrowers do well to pay their loans more rapidly than called for in their loan agreements. Tables 19 to 22 spotlight the means to save interest and reduce the loan balance more quickly. Finally, discussion further on in the chapter will show how making a "payments in advance" loan can also save interest, even though it does not shorten the life of the loan.

Time of Earlier Payoff, Time, and Interest Savings

This section describes Table 19 which illustrates just how much more quickly a loan will be paid and how much interest will be saved by even rather small extra monthly payments. Table 19 gives the comparisons with a standard 30-year loan amortization schedule.

Table 19 shows that the savings in interest will sometimes exceed 100 percent of the loan, which is true but which bears explanation. The total interest on a 30-year loan at, say, 10.00 percent interest is equal to 216 percent of the loan amount. Rapid payments might lower total interest, for example to 116 percent of the loan amount, saving an amount equal to 100 percent of the loan.

Example 29.   Time and Money Savings with Accelerated Mortgage Payments, New Mortgage

Sharon Zernill intends to apply for a $100,000 loan at 9.50 percent interest, to be amortized on a 30-year schedule. The payments on this loan will be $840.86 per month. She wishes to calculate what the savings would be if she consistently pays 10 percent more than the required payment, namely $924.95 per month.

Find Table 19, page 4 (p. 264). In the section for added payment of 10 percent, read across on the line for 30 years' time to original maturity to the section headed 9.50 percent interest. The first entry there, under new maturity, is 20Y 6m, meaning 20 years, 6 months. By paying 10 percent extra each month, she will reduce the term of her loan to 20 years, 6 months. As shown in the next column, this is a savings of 114 months, 9½ years' worth of payments. The third column shows that this is a savings in interest equal to 75.5 percent of the original loan amount. Since her loan will be for $100,000, the dollar savings to her will be

$$\$100,000 \times 0.755 = \$75,500$$

over the term of the loan. Note that the $84.09 paid each month costs only the inconvenience of making the extra payment. That is, all the $84.09 will be applied to principal each month, so the borrower gets the benefit of a lower balance at once and lower interest cost from then on.

Comparison of 15-year Amortization Schedules with 30-year Schedules

Paying a loan back faster than the customary 30-year amortization period, for example on a 15-year schedule, gives a homeowner a high return on a sound investment. If home loans are priced at 10.00 percent, it is unlikely that any better than about 8.75 percent would be available on savings accounts or bonds of reasonable quality. High-yielding bonds may offer a better rate but at far greater risk: The investment markets, by pricing some bonds at higher yields than home loans, are declaring those bonds to be riskier. Using available cash to invest in a fast amortization schedule, such as 15 years, gives the homeowner the same rate of return on the extra payment that the lender gets. Typically that return will be 1.5 percent to 2 percent better than the CD rate, especially when loans are above 10.00 percent interest.

Comparison of 15-Year with 30-Year Amortization

Table 20 (pp. 268–271) provides the comparisons that illustrate the benefits of 15-year amortization, as follows:

Monthly payment: Table 20 compares the monthly payment for a 30-year with a 15-year loan, and the percentage difference of the 15-year loan payment above the 30-year.

Mortgage balance: Tables 20 compares the year-end loan balances and the percentage difference of the 15-year balance below the 30-year.

Total interest paid: Table 20 compares the cumulative interest paid since the start of the loan and the difference of 30-year interest above the 15-year schedule.

Example 30.   Comparison of Interest Expense between 15-Year and 30-Year Loans

Pamela and Richard are shopping for a $100,000 mortgage loan. They have these quotes:

Interest of 10.00 percent for 30 years:

$ 877.57 per month

Interest of 10.00 percent for 15 years:

1,074.61 per month

The payment is $197.04 per month greater for the 15-year plan. By reviewing Table 20, their mortgage banker points out these aspects of the 15-year plan: The 15-year loan requires payments 22.5 percent higher than the 30-year schedule. This is its largest, perhaps its only, drawback. The 15-year term's advantages include

1. By definition, the 15-year loan will have been paid off in half the time of the 30-year schedule.

2. Even in the first year, the amount of interest paid on the loan will be noticeably lower with the 15-year plan. Refer to the section on total interest paid.

3. The principal balance reduces more rapidly with the 15-year schedule (refer to the section on mortgage balance) making more equity available to serve as a cushion against financial emergencies.

4. The interest paid over the life of the loan is immensely less. See total interest paid.

5. Finally, in 15 years Richard and Pamela could have a mortgage-burning party; at that time they would still owe 81.7 percent of the original balance if they had taken on a 30-year loan. By paying an extra $197 per month for the first 15 years, Pamela and Richard will avoid paying $878 per month later for 15 years.

Summarizing the 15-year plan: They will have made 180 payments that were $197.04 higher, a total of $35,467. But their household debt will be $81,665 less, and they will not have to make 180 payments (the second 15 years) of $877.57, a total of $158,000. This is a 10.00 percent compounded rate of return on the extra payments "invested."

The mortgage banker points out that many persons prefer a 30-year plan because it gives higher tax deductions. Paying more interest, however, is a poor way to save on taxes. In fact, if a person is in a 25 percent tax bracket, $3 out of every $4 in interest comes from the taxpayer's pocket, rather than from tax savings. From an economic standpoint, the smarter route is to pay $1 in taxes and avoid $3 in interest, which is what happens over time with rapid amortization.

Comparison of Biweekly or Weekly Payments with Monthly Payments

Loans with payments every 2 weeks have popular appeal: Many households receive paychecks 26 times per year, and the biweekly mortgage payment described in Table 21 (p. 272) meets their needs. The biweekly is profitable as well as convenient. Biweekly loans are made on the basis of a payment every 2 weeks equal to one-half the monthly payment on a normal mortgage with a 30-year amortization schedule. Because this adds up to 26 payments per year of one-half month each, the borrower prepays the loan by one full payment per year and speeds up the amortization. Since the payments made in the early loan years go primarily to interest, prepaying one full payment then is equal to prepaying many months of principal. For an 11.00 percent loan on biweekly payments, the borrower will have credit for 30 years of payments at the end of only 20 years. In exchange for paying every 2 weeks and prepaying 20 months' payments, the loan will have been paid off 120 months early, a substantial profit.

The savings effects are just as pronounced with weekly payments. Home loan borrowers who make the adjustment to weekly payments are often pleased with the convenience and delighted with the painless interest savings. Because the weekly payment loan has not caught on in the way the biweekly has, although data for weekly payments is also given in Table 21, the examples focus on biweekly payment loans.

Example 31.   Comparison of Biweekly with Monthly Payment Mortgages

---

Delphine and Norman are searching for a home loan. Friends suggest that they look into a biweekly mortgage. The interest rate being quoted is 10.25 percent. They are seeking a $150,000 loan. Reviewing Table 21 (p. 272), they develop the following information:

Monthly payment. To compare the payments, take the payment factors on the line for a 10.25 percent loan (they are for a $100,000 loan). Multi-

ply the desired loan by the factor and then divide by $100,000, as follows:

Monthly Payment:

$$\frac{\$150,000}{100,000} \times \$896.11 = \$1,344.17$$

Biweekly Payment:

$$\frac{\$150,000}{100,000} \times \$448.06 = \$672.09$$

The monthly payment will cost $1,344.17 per month or a total of $16,130 for 12 months. The biweekly will cost $672.09 every two weeks, or $17,474 per year, or 8.3 percent per year more.

Loan term. As shown in the third column in Table 21 (p. 272), Biweekly Payment, a 10.25 percent biweekly will be fully paid off in 20 years and 37 weeks, over 30 percent faster than with the conventional payments on a 30-year schedule. The extra payment per year has brought a return of almost three times its cost.

Interest savings. As shown in the next four columns of the biweekly section, interest savings begin in the very first year and compound regularly to a substantial sum over the life of the loan. The savings quoted in the total column are as of when the 30-year loan would have been paid off. The interest savings on a biweekly loan are not extraordinary, while making the biweekly payments. The real savings come when the biweekly is paid off but the 30-year borrower would still face years of additional payments. By the end of 30 years, the differences in interest between the two plans are astonishing.

Rising-Rate Mortgages

One of the best seller-financing plans developed in recent years is the rising-rate mortgage, or RRM. Although the abbreviation *RRM* has yet to take its place in industry jargon alongside ARMs, SAMs and GEMs, the technique behind the RRM fills a niche not provided by the others. Even Fannie Mae (the Federal National Mortgage Association) uses an RRM in selling property that it owns.

An RRM is a 30-year loan with an interest rate that begins low and rises by a specified increment each year. The increases might continue for 1 year or a number of years. The monthly payment rises with the rate, to keep pace with the original 30-year schedule. Designed to compete with the low "teaser" rates offered on some adjustable rate mortgage (ARM) plans, the RRM has the advantages that the exact interest and total payment are known in advance and negative amortization never occurs.

Table 22 (pp. 273–276) gives the information for rate increases of ¼ percent per year, or ½ percent, ¾ percent or 1 percent per year, for up to 10 years of increases. Each line of the table has an increase built into each year after the first. For three years of increases, starting at, say, 10.00 percent, the figures would all be selected from the line for 10.00 percent. If increases of ¼ percent per year are chosen, the payment for the first year is under year 1 at a 10.00 percent rate. For the second year, the payment is under year 2, and the rate is 10.25 percent. The third-year payment under year 3 includes interest at 10.50 percent, and for years 4 through 30 under year 4, the payments are for a rate of 10.75 percent. As long as the fourth-year figure continues to be used, the 10.75 percent rate will apply. The payment figure for any year, if continued for 30 years, will fully amortize the loan at that interest rate.

Cross-Reference Because of the rising-rate feature, payments in Table 22 are not correct for ordinary loans, which are discussed in Example 27 and shown in Table 18.

Example 32. Payments on a Rising-Rate Loan

Priscilla Chu has encouraged her client to offer purchase money mortgage financing to a prospective buyer, provided the buyer's credit checks out. The purchase money mortgage would render a good income to the client. And removing the hassle of finding financing may spur the buyer to make a buying decision or may lessen price negotiation.

The lenders in the market at the moment are offering a 9.50 percent loan, but ARMs with teaser rates of 9.00 percent are also available. Chu proposes a $200,000 rising-rate mortgage for 5 years with an interest rate of 9.00 percent in the first year, 9.25 percent in the second year, and 9.50 percent for years three, four, and five. There would be a balloon payment of the entire balance at the end of the fifth year. The buyer would get the benefit of the teaser rate but no uncertainty about future payments.

To find the monthly payments, enter Table 22, at the section for rate rises ¼ percent per year on page 1 (p. 273). On the line for an interest rate of 9.00 percent, read under payment for year 1, $804.63, the payment per $100,000 in the first year. Next to that under column 2, read $822.40; for years three, four, and five, read the figure under column 3, $840.00.

Multiply each of these by the loan amount and divide by $100,000 to get

$$\frac{\$200,000}{\$100,000} \times 804.63 = \$1,609.26 \text{ per month in year 1}$$

$$\frac{\$200,000}{\$100,000} \times 822.40 = 1,644.80 \text{ per month in year 2}$$

$$\frac{\$200,000}{\$100,000} \times 840.00$$
$$= 1,680.00 \text{ per month in years 3, 4, and 5}$$

The interest rates built into these payments are 9.00 percent for the first year, 9.25 percent for the second year, and 9.50 percent for years three, four, and five. If the payments continue at the rate of $1,680 per month, the loan will be fully amortized at the end of 30 years.

Note Most state laws and preprinted loan forms envision that a single interest rate will apply for the term of the loan. The chances for error in describing these multirate loans are considerable, so it is wise to have an attorney prepare the RRM interest rate and payment descriptions.

Example 33. Mortgage Balance on a Rising-Rate Loan

Three years ago, Mr. Boomsma received a rising-rate mortgage that had an initial interest rate of 9.25 percent and is at 9.75 percent now. To find the balance after 3 years on an RRM, enter Table 22, page 1 (p. 273), the page for rate rises of ¼ percent per year. On the line for an interest rate of 9.25 percent, read across to the 3-year column and find the answer, $97,963 the balance on an RRM rising ¼ percent per year after 3 years.

Growing Equity Mortgages (GEMs)

The next specialty mortgage technique, shown in Table 23 (pp. 277–281), is the growing equity mortgage, or GEM. Although advertisers for GEMs naturally choose themes inspired by the acronym, it is not simply puffery. The GEM loan produces concrete savings for the borrower while overcoming a major objection of most short amortization schedules. The GEM is a standard mortgage loan that starts out on a 30-year amortization schedule. Each year after the first, the payments increase by a previously agreed percentage, typically from 2.0 percent to 7.5 percent per year. All the increase in payment goes to principal and in effect begins to earn interest at the rate on the mortgage. This makes it especially attractive in high-rate periods. The increases may continue for as many years as desired—Table 23 shows up to 10 years of increases.

The GEM shares the advantages of the RRM in avoiding negative amortization and payment shock. But the modest, agreed-in-advance payment increases are powerful amortizers. If a loan with $900 monthly payments is selected to increase at 2.0 percent, the second-year payments will be $918.00, and the third and fourth years would be $936 and $950. But if the $950 rate is continued, just these small increases would cut the loan term to 24 years, 5 months. Over 5½ years of mortgage payments accomplished with mere 2.0 percent payment increases!

Table 23 has two sections, (a) the monthly payment section, and (b) the overall maturity of the GEM. The payment figures are given per $100,000 of loan, so divide the actual loan amount by $100,000 in figuring the payments, as shown in the examples.

Example 34. Monthly Payments on a Growing Equity Mortgage

Sal Calavito would like the benefits of a shorter amortization schedule. To qualify for the loan with present household income, he needs a 30-year amortization schedule, but he is confident he can handle 2.0 percent payment increases in coming years. His mortgage advisor points out that a growing equity mortgage would keep the benefit of the 30-year's lower payment at the start to help him qualify. Manageable payment increases later would cut overall mortgage interest. Based on her analysis of his income and prospects, she recommends a $180,000 GEM with 4 years of 2.0 percent increases. The loan will start at the standard payments for 30 years at 10.00 percent, the current rate in the market. By reference to Table 23 (b), she points out that increasing 2.0 percent per year for 4 years of increases will cut the overall amortization period from 30 years to 22 years, 6 months.

To find the monthly payments, enter Table 23, page 1 (p. 277), the page for 2.0 percent per year payment increases. Read down the left column to 10.00 percent, and take the figure from column 1 for the first-year payments. It is $877.58 (for a $100,000 loan). Take the figures under columns 2, 3, 4, and 5 for years 2, 3, 4, and 5 through 30, also. They are $895.13, $913.04, $931.31, and $949.94. Multiply

each of these by the ratio of the loan amount to $100,000 to get

$$\frac{\$180,000}{\$100,000} \times 877.58$$
$$= \$1,579.65 \text{ per month for the first year}$$

$$\frac{\$180,000}{\$100,000} \times 895.13$$
$$= \$1,611.24 \text{ per month for year two}$$

$$\frac{\$180,000}{\$100,000} \times 913.04$$
$$= \$1,643.48 \text{ per month in year three}$$

$$\frac{\$180,000}{\$100,000} \times 931.31$$
$$= \$1,676.36 \text{ per month in the fourth year}$$

$$\frac{\$180,000}{\$100,000} \times 949.94$$
$$= \$1,709.90 \text{ per month in the}$$
$$\text{fifth through thirtieth years}$$

The increases in payments will never exceed $130 per month over a standard 30-year loan, but the increases will wipe 90 months of payments from the mortgage bill.

SORTING OUT MORTGAGE TERMS

We turn now from concentration on mortgage payments to other terms of the mortgage.

Example 35. Total Interest Cost over Life of a Loan

Sandra Malin wants to know the total interest that will be paid over the life of a 25-year amortization schedule, if the interest rate is 7 percent, 8 percent, or 9 percent. She gets the annual mortgage constants on these loans by referring to Table 35 (a). The constants are 8.481350 percent, 9.261795 percent, and 10.070356 percent. Multiplying each of the constants by 25 to get the total payments on the loan, and subtracting 100.0000 percent (the amount of the loan), she gets

$$8.481350 \times 25 = 212.03375 - 100.0000$$
$$= 112.03375\%$$
$$9.261795 \times 25 = 231.54485 - 100.0000$$
$$= 131.544875\%$$
$$10.070356 \times 25 = 251.75890 - 100.0000$$
$$= 151.75890\%$$

These figures show the total interest to be paid over the life of the loan as a percentage of the original loan. Malin concludes that each 1.00 percent increase in the interest rate adds about 20 percent to the interest cost of the loan over a 25-year period.

Example 36.   Amount of Balloon Payment (Remaining Balance)

Carrollton's client took out a $75,000 loan at 10.75 percent interest. The loan is on a 30-year amortization schedule but will have a balloon payment at the end of 10 years. To find the amount of the balloon payment, find Table 42 (a), page 1 (p. 496). Read down the left column to 10.75 percent. On that line under 10 years, find 91.9479 percent, the percentage of the loan still unpaid. Multiply it by the original amount of the loan to get

$$\$75,000 \times 0.919479 = \$68,960.93$$

the mortgage balance and therefore the balloon payment due on the loan after 10 years.

Payments in Advance

It seems contradictory to borrow money and then make the loan payments in advance. But mortgage loans with payments in advance, the kind shown in Table 38 (pp. 458–465) are another means to shape financing for special needs. (Table 38 carries two titles; one refers to Annual Mortgage Constant, Payments in Advance, and the second reference is to Rent Constants for use with Chapter 6, Leasing, Property Management, and Maintenance.)

Example 37.   Interest Savings with Payments in Advance

Mr. and Mrs. Cree want the lowest interest cost over the life of the loan that they have applied for. They are seeking $100,000 at 10.75 percent on a 20-year schedule. Payments semiannually in advance appeal to them, but the first payment, at closing, would be $5,817.34 ($100,000 times the constant, 11.634676 percent, divided by 2 payments per year). An ordinary mortgage would require payments of $1,015.23 per month, starting 30 days after closing. They do not wish to reduce

their savings to make the necessary payment *in front*. They are earning 8.50 percent on their certificates of deposit.

Their mortgage counselor advises them that, over the first 6 months of the loan, the Crees would have paid $3,279 on average *earlier* than if they took the monthly plan. But they will have paid $274 *less* than the sum of six monthly payments on a regular loan. Early payment has saved them almost $300 in the first 6 months alone. The savings mount at the 10.75 percent **note rate** on the mortgage. Even though they will have paid $548 less the first year, their mortgage balance will be $48 lower at the end of it than with a normal loan and increasingly lower in later years. The Crees decide that, since 10.75 percent is better than the rates available on savings deposits, they will transfer part of their savings to a payments-in-advance mortgage program.

Time When Given Mortgage Balance Occurs

The balance declines slowly in the early stages of an amortizing mortgage loan, because the principal reduction is only a small part of the early payments. Ten years of monthly payments are needed to pay off the first tenth of a 9.50 percent, 30-year loan but only 13 months to pay off the last tenth of it. Table 67 tells when important mortgage balance benchmarks are achieved for different interest rates and amortization schedules. In using the table, small differences occur from the amortization schedules provided by lenders. Table 67 is precise, but round-offs of the mortgage payments can, over many years, add up to a month or so.

Example 38.   Time When Given Mortgage Balance Occurs

The Glouviers are considering loan alternatives for a new home. They plan to retire in 10 years' time and want to compare the mortgage balances at their retirement date. They would like to reduce their mortgage balance to 60 percent by that date. Present interest rates are 7.25 percent.

Turn to Table 67, page 2 (p. 767). Find 7.25 percent; under the column headed 60 percent, read the answers, finding 10Y 1m, or 10 years, 1 month on the 18-year line. An 18-year amortization plan will reach 60 percent unpaid balance at the end of 10 years and would meet the Glouviers' requirements.

Example 39. Mortgage Balance after Specified Time; Time When Tax Reserve May Be Dropped

Outrelle's mortgage loan commitment for a 10.50 percent, 25-year loan requires that a deposit for real estate taxes be maintained, interest-free, with the lender. Under the law in her state, the lender may no longer require such a deposit after the loan balance falls below 75 percent of the original amount.

To find when the loan is scheduled to reach 75 percent of original balance, turn to the portion of Table 67, page 5 (p. 770) for 10.50 percent loans. Read down the left column to 25 years' amortization and across to the column headed 75 percent. Read there the answer, 13Y 8m or 13 years, 8 months, the time when the loan will reach 75 percent of its original schedule.

Example 40.   Amount Owed to a Loan Guarantor

James and Penny have taken out a loan of $100,000 at 11.00 percent interest. The normal payments on this are more than they can afford. They feel their realistic payment for budget purposes is 8.50 percent. Their families are willing to help out by making the portion of the payment in excess of 8.50 percent. James and Penny want to know how much they would owe their families at the end of 5 years.

To find the amount of the accrual at the end of 5 years, enter Table 14, page 1 (p. 237) at the section for a pay rate of 8.50 percent, 30-year schedule. Read down the left column, year paid off, to 5 years, and across on that line to the column headed 11.00 percent. Find there the answer, 16.5663 percent, or, rounding, 16.6 percent, the accrual percentage. Multiply the loan amount by the accrual percentage to get

$$\$100{,}000 \times 0.165663 = \$16{,}566.30$$

the amount Penny and James would owe their families at the end of 5 years.

Example 41.   Number of Payments to Retire a Loan

Finn Kolson would like a mortgage payment program to retire a $60,000 loan at a 9.00 percent inter-

est rate using a 12.00 percent annual mortgage constant. To find the term of the loan, enter Table 59, page 2 (p. 723). Read down the annual constant column to 12.00 percent, and on that line under 9.00 percent, find the answer, 185.5, the term of the loan in months.

Note In practice, the loan would be written for 186 months with a final payment lower than normal.

Example 42.   Increase in Number of Payments as Payment Amount Decreases

One use of Table 59 is to illustrate the high cost over the long term of lower monthly payments. For example, as seen under the 9.75 percent column on page 2 (p. 723), about 207 months are needed to pay off a loan using payments of 1 percent of the original loan per month. This is 17 years, 3 months. Lowering the payment to 0.83 percent per month increases the loan term to 455.9 months or almost 38 years. A mere 17 percent decrease in the monthly payment costs a 120 percent increase in the loan term.

Example 43.   Amount of Mortgage Loan Available from a Given Payment

Mr. and Mrs. Killen are shopping for a mortgage loan on a 30-year **amortization schedule** at 9.50 percent interest. Their mortgage banking specialist has analyzed their financial situation and determined that the loan they qualify for should have payments of no more than $2200 per month.

To find the amount of mortgage they could take out, enter Table 58, page 1 (p. 716) at the section for a draw delay of 1 month (meaning that the first payment would be in 1 month) and 9.50 percent interest. This is the delay for the customary loan in the United States. Read down to 360 payments, and across on that line to the 9.50 percent column. The factor there, 118.92668, is the multiple of the loan payment that can be borrowed. Multiply it by the loan payment to get

$$\$2200 \times 118.92668 = \$261{,}638.70$$

which is the mortgage loan amount that will meet the Killens' requirements.

Example 44. Number of Monthly Deposits to Save for Down Payment

Sharon and Stephen estimate they will need $25,000 for a down payment on a home. They can set aside $740 per month in an account bearing interest at 8.00 percent. To find out how long it will take to build the fund, first find the monthly payment percentage:

$$\frac{\$740 \text{ monthly deposit}}{\$25,000 \text{ desired fund}} = 0.0296 = 2.96\%$$

Rounded, this would be 3.0 percent per month. Now enter Table 55, page 1 (p. 704) and read down the monthly deposit column to 3.00 percent and across on that line to the 8.00 percent interest column. The answer there is 30.0 months. Stephen and Sharon will reach their $25,000 goal in slightly over 2 years and 6 months, with $740 payments earning 8.00 percent per year interest. (It will require slightly more than the time in the table, because the deposit was rounded up slightly.)

Example 45. Additional Time to Complete a Partial Down Payment Fund

Therese has accumulated $30,000 of the $50,000 she estimates she will need for a down payment on a house. If she can set aside $500 per month and get 8.50 percent interest on the account, compounded monthly, how long will it take to accumulate the remaining 40 percent of the fund?

Begin by finding the monthly deposit percentage. It is $500 ÷ 50,000 = 0.010 = 1.00 percent per month. Now enter Table 56, page 4 (p. 709) at the section that starts from a partial fund of 60 percent. Read across on the line for monthly payment of 1.00 percent and under the 8.50 percent column find the answer, 25.7 months. It will take 26 months of such deposits added to a $30,000 beginning balance and interest at 8.50 percent to reach a $50,000 down payment.

Example 46. Deposit for Reserve for Home Loan Payment

The Nordstroms are planning to acquire a home in 3 years. Although they have the necessary down pay-

ment today, the payments on a loan would be more than they could comfortably handle from their current income. They would like to set aside a monthly reserve for 3 years that could be used to pay $300 per month during the first 2 years of the loan. Interest is likely to be 8.50 percent throughout the term of the reserve.

Enter Table 60, page 2 (p. 725) at the section for 3 years of deposit. Read across on the line for two years of withdrawal to the column headed 8.50 percent interest. The factor there, 53.8639 percent, is the needed rate of deposit. Multiply the dollar amount of withdrawal by the factor to get

$$\$300 \times 0.538639 = \$161.59$$

the monthly deposit needed for 36 months to permit withdrawals of $300 per month for 24 months, when interest is 8.50 percent per year.

Cost to Buy Down a Loan

Table 24 shows the cost of **mortgage buy-downs.** To buy a loan down is to pay the lender a fee in exchange for dropping the interest rate to a lower rate for a period of time. What makes it different from ordinary points paid on a loan is that the buy-down is usually paid by the seller. A buy-down is a useful sales technique, especially when loan rates are so high as to inhibit a prospective buyer. With adjustable rate mortgages (ARMs), the buy-down overcomes the fear that rates will come down in a year or two, leaving the buyer locked into a high-rate loan. The buy-down gives the benefit of a low rate today, while the adjustable feature will, the buyer hopes, keep the rate low in the future.

To effect a buy-down, the seller deposits the buy-down points with the lender at closing. Lenders will usually give some interest credit for the deposit. Most banks and Fannie Mae will give credit at 5.50 percent per year. Table 24 has four sections for each market interest rate. The first of these, on page 1 (p. xxx), gives buy-down points where 5.50 percent per year credit is given. The second section gives credit at the note rate. The third gives no credit at all; its figures are the sum of the difference between the payments at the market rate and the payments at the buy-down rate. The fourth section gives the credit for a rate of 1 percent per year less than the coupon rate. Especially in commercial deals, it is sometimes possible to negotiate a better rate than 5.50 percent, even though the lender will not credit the deposit at the full rate. Our suggestion for such a middle-ground rate is 1 percent under the note rate.

At the end of each section, there is a line labeled "3-2-1." This is a common buy-down, namely a 3-year program with an interest rate 3.00 percent below the market rate for the first year, 2.00 percent below market for the second year, and 1 percent below the market for the third year.

Example 47.   Cost to Buy Down a Home Loan, Standard Credit

Mr. and Mrs. Farragut have a buyer who has a loan quotation for a $135,000 loan at 11.00 percent interest, amortizing on a 30-year schedule, with the balance coming due at the end of 10 years. The buyer prefers a loan carrying an interest rate no higher than 9.25 percent and will sign a purchase offer if the Farraguts will buy the loan down to 9.25 percent for 3 years. The buyer's lender will give credit on the buy-down deposit at 5.50 percent.

To find the number of points to buy the 11.00 percent loan down to 9.25 percent, enter Table 24, page 5 (p. 286) in the section for market interest rate of 11.00 percent and buy-down credit rate of 5.50 percent. Read down the column for desired buy-down to 9.25 percent and across on that line to the column headed 3 years. Read there the answer, 4.294 percent, the percentage of original loan amount that will buy the 11.00 percent loan down to 9.25 percent for 3 years. Multiply the factor by the loan amount to get

$$\$135,000 \times 0.04294 = \$5,796.90$$

This is the dollar amount of the payment that the Farraguts would have to pay from their sale proceeds to buy the loan down.

Note   In calculating the annual percentage rate (APR), buy-down points paid by the seller are not included in the finance charge.

Example 48.   Cost to Buy Down a Home Loan, Mortgage Rate Credit

Per Tharnstrom has bought a house and arranged financing with a bank for a $100,000 loan on a 30-year schedule. The seller has agreed to provide financing at a current market rate, 12.00 percent, but will buy the purchase money mortgage interest rate down from 12.00 percent to 10.50 percent for 3 years. The seller will give credit at the note rate of 12.00 percent.

To find the buy-down amount, enter Table 24, page 7 (p. 288), the page for 12.00 percent interest,

and find the section for a buy-down credit rate of 12.00 percent. Read down the desired buy-down column to 10.50 percent and across to the 3-year column. The answer there, 3.428 percent, is the number of points that will buy the loan down from 12.00 percent to 10.50 percent for 3 years. Since the seller who is paying the buy-down points is also the lender receiving the points, no money need change hands. According to local law, the attorney may simply write the loan documents with the lower payments, or a buy-down deposit agreement may be created as if the lender were distinct from the seller.

DECIDING TO LOCK IN A MORTGAGE RATE OR TO REFINANCE AN EXISTING LOAN

Most of this section is written from the viewpoint of the home loan borrower, that is, a viewpoint directly opposite that of the lender. It is written to give you the forecasting tools that lenders use but in reverse. Although lenders are just as concerned with the rise and fall of interest rates as their borrowers, they have more room to recover from mistakes. A lender that makes a thousand loans hardly expects every one to be completely market smart. The home loan borrower on the other hand has one loan to be concerned with. For that reason, although the examples will demonstrate professional market analysis, many mortgage planners will counsel erring on the side of safety, that is, locking in rates for the longest time and allowing the least gamble in the future.

Example 49.   When to Lock in an ARM—The Pheldons

The Pheldon family has an **adjustable rate mortgage,** or **ARM.** The maximum interest rate permitted under the note is 11.25 percent. They have the opportunity in the next month to fix the rate at 10.00 percent for 3 years, provided they pay the lender a 2 percent fee.

To decide if it is worthwhile to lock in the rate now, we will label the 11.25 percent rate the market interest rate. The 10.00 percent rate that can be locked in is the desired buy-down. Now enter Table 24, page 5 (p. 286), the page for 11.25 percent market interest rate in the section for buy-down credit rate of 11.25 percent. Read down desired buy-down to 10.00 percent. Read across on that line to the column headed 3 years and find the factor 2.851 percent of the present balance of the loan. This is the economic difference between the two loan rates, given as a percentage of the loan balance. If the total cost to buy down the loan, including the 2 percent lender fee *and* any title or closing costs, is less than 2.851 percent of the loan, locking in the 10.00 percent rate would be economical.

Note Locking in the loan fixes the cost but may not be necessary. The Pheldons would look at the **yield curve** (see Using the Interest Rate Yield Curve later in this chapter) to estimate the chances that rates might rise. If rates appear to be falling, they may risk not locking in the loan to avoid the fee.

Example 50. When to Lock in an ARM—The Bellions

The Bellions' ARM loan is adjusted each January. The loan is now at 10.75 percent, but it could rise in each of the next three years by 1.00 percent to a maximum of 13.00 percent. The Bellions' alternative is to lock the rate in now at 10.00 percent by paying a fee of 2½ percent of the loan.

Begin by averaging the current rate and the maximum rate: (10.00 percent + 13.00 percent) ÷ 2 = 11.50 percent, the potential interest rate over the 3-year term. Now enter Table 24, page 6 (p. 287), the page for 11.50 percent, at the section for 11.50 percent buy-down credit rate. Read across on the line for a desired buy-down of 10.00 percent to the column headed 3 years, and find there the answer, 3.418 points, which is the economic charge to buy down on these terms. Since the lock-in can be obtained for only 2½ points, it would be economical to take it, if interest rates can reasonably be expected to actually rise over the next 3 years.

Example 51. Whether to Refinance a Mortgage Loan

Refinancing a loan with a different lender is similar to the preceding example. But with a refinancing, there are other fees that are not paid in the case of a simple lock-in with the same lender. In making the calculation, be certain to include all refinance costs.

William and Mary de Gloestin have an existing mortgage loan with 10.50 percent interest. A competing lender is advertising 5-year loans on 30-year amortization schedules with an interest rate of 9.00 percent and a 1½-point fee. When they call the lender and inquire about other charges, they learn

that there is a 1 percent broker's fee and title insurance charges. They will also have to pay their attorney's fees, about $800, or ½ of 1 percent. All of these add up to 4.0 percent or 4 points.

To find if this loan would be better than their existing loan, turn to the portion of Table 24, page 4 (p. 285) for a 10.50 percent market interest rate and the section for a buy-down credit rate of 10.50 percent. Read down the desired buy-down column to 9.00 percent and across on that line to 5 years of buy-down. The factor there, 5.123 percent, is the number of points to make the 9.00 percent offer equal to the 10.50 percent existing loan. Since the de Gloestins can refinance for only 4.0 points, it would save them money to do so.

Note The statement of the APR that most lenders are obliged to give is not suitable for making this comparison, because some costs of refinancing, such as title, closing, and attorney's fees, need not be included in the calculation of the APR.

Note In weighing these alternatives, it is unimportant what the points were, or what the APR was, at the time of the original loan. Those costs are paid and, at least by the lender, forgotten. The decision to refinance or lock in should be based only on the rate today versus the rate tomorrow and the cost to get it, as calculated in the example.

Using the Interest Rate Yield Curve

The **yield curve** is the simplest way to judge what professional investors think will happen to interest rates in the future. Some investment papers and magazines publish yield-curve graphs, but a chart of the curve may be easily constructed: Look in the *Wall Street Journal* or *Investor's Daily* for prices of government bonds of various maturities. If 3-year bonds are priced at noticeably higher rates than 1- or 2-year bonds, the market expects that interest rates will rise. If longer term bonds are only slightly higher than short rates, the market expects that rates will be about the same (it is normal that there is a small illiquidity premium on the rate of a longer-term bond). And if the rates on 3-year or 5-year bonds are the same or lower than on 1- or 2-year bonds, the market expects that interest rates will decline in the period after the coming year.

This forecasting tool gives an idea in what direction the market expects rates to move but not how much they will move. Table 34 (pp. 413–420) helps to put specific numbers to the amount of interest rate shift that is inherent in market interest rates. If, for example, you have the 4-year and the 5-year Treasury rates, Table 34 tells the rate the market forecasts for the fifth year.

To see how this can be so, assume that 4-year rates are 9.00 percent and 5-year rates are 9.125 percent. No rational investor would accept 9.00 percent, if 9.125 percent is offered. That investors do accept it means they think rates are going up in the fifth year. They insist on a premium now to get them to tie up their money for the extra year. In fact, from Table 34, we find the market expects 9.626 percent in the fifth year.

Interest rate study has many other complex points of theory. But the examples here and the use of Table 34 will assist the real estate investor to see if a decision is with, or against, the weight of what the market believes will happen.

Example 52. Whether to Lock in an ARM Loan: Interest Rate Forecast Using the Interest Rate Yield Curve

Thera Cross has the option to continue the present 10.00 percent rate on her ARM for another year or to lock it in at a rate of 10.50 percent. She learned from the newspaper that the yields on government bonds for 1-, 2-, and 3-year maturities are 8.25 percent, 8.27 percent, and 8.375 percent.

To begin the analysis, consider that the rates on 1-year and 2-year bonds are close enough to be considered the same. Now enter Table 34, page 2 (p. 414) at the page for the 2-year forward rate and the section that includes 8.375 percent 3-year rate. Read down the 2-year rate column to 8.25 percent, the rate closest to 8.27 percent, and across on that line to the 8.375 percent column. The rate there, 8.625 percent, is the rate predicted by market conditions to occur in the third year forward from now. Virtually no increase is expected next year, and only a 37-basis point increase 2 years from now; locking in would cost an immediate 50-basis point increase on her mortgage from 10.00 percent to 10.50 percent. Cross elects not to lock in this year and to review the matter again next year.

SELLER FINANCING

The examples that follow will help in the decision to provide seller financing. Thousands of home sellers have found that making a first or second mortgage loan to their buyer is an excellent means to get a sale

accomplished and to earn good income from a solid investment. The examples will generate the financial information you need to make the right decisions. But this information needs to be melded with input from tax and legal advisors as well.

Example 53. Higher Sale Price from Assumable Below-Market Mortgage Loan

Bill and Teresa Pfeiffer took out a 30-year loan 12 years ago at an interest rate of 7.50 percent per year. As they prepare to sell, the house has been appraised at $142,500. The original loan of $80,000 is now reduced to $66,200, or 46.5 percent of current value. Nonetheless, with interest rates now at 10.00 percent, the loan is valuable, since by its terms it may be assumed by a creditworthy buyer.

To find the value increment in the loan, enter Table 10, page 19 (p. 219). Read down the desired yield column to 7.50 percent and across on that line to the 7-year column. The factor there, 113.29638 percent, is the value of the loan today. Multiply the loan balance by the factor to get

$$\$66,200 \times 1.1329638 = \$75,002.20$$

Rounding, we get $75,000, the value of the loan. Since the borrower would only have to pay $66,200, the $8800 difference could be added to the price of the house, to make the offering price $151,300.

Few buyers would be prepared to put 56 percent down on the house, especially since, in our example, the value of the below-market financing would go to the Pfeiffers. If they are in a position to make an investment, the Pfeiffers might consider ways to build up a loan package equal to 80 percent of value, such as taking back a purchase money second mortgage, as shown in the next example, or making a **wraparound loan,** as described in Example 60 later in this chapter.

Example 54. Higher Sale Price through Below-Market Purchase Money Second Mortgage

Emily Ostlander has the opportunity to defer all taxes from the sale of her house by reinvesting in a new property. In addition she will provide the buyers a purchase money second mortgage for 20 percent of the $150,000 sales price. The buyers, who have a good credit history, can get open-market financing for a 10-year loan on a 30-year schedule at 10.50 percent. She intends to offer a below-market interest rate, for example 8.50 percent, in exchange for an increase in the sale price.

To find the sale price increase from the below-market second mortgage, enter Table 10, page 21 (p. 221), the page for 10.50 percent. Read down the desired yield column to 8.50 percent and across on that line to the 10-year column. The factor there is 113.05609 percent, indicating that the loan is worth 13 percent more than the amount borrowed.

Multiply the $30,000 loan amount ($150,000 × 20%) by the factor to get

$$\$30,000 \times 1.1305609 = \$33,916.83$$

Rounding, we get $33,900, the value of the loan. The premium value over the $30,000 face amount, $3900, could be added to the sale price to compensate for the below-market rate.

Monthly Payment to Retire a Given Portion of a Loan by a Certain Date

Few mortgage loans today have a term as long as the amortization schedule. As discussed earlier, when the loan comes due before it is fully amortized, the final payment is called a **balloon payment.** Many seller-financing plans are designed to achieve a specific loan balance by the balloon payment date. Table 36 (pp. 447–453) gives the figures to retire a given percentage of the loan within the desired term.

Example 55. Monthly Payment to Amortize Part of Purchase Money Loan by Certain Date

Perkiewicz is asked to take back an 8.25 percent purchase money mortgage loan in the amount of $100,000. He is willing to do so, provided the loan term will be 5 years, at the end of which 40 percent of the loan will have been paid off.

To find the monthly payment, enter Table 36, page 3 (450), at 8.25 percent interest and read down the years column to 5 years. Now read across to the column headed 40 percent, finding 14.73991 percent. This is the annual constant percent needed to repay 40 percent of the original principal during the first 5 years of the loan. Now multiply the loan amount by the annual mortgage constant and divide by 12 to get

$$\$100,000 \times 0.1473991 \div 12 = \$1,228.33$$

This is the monthly payment to amortize 40 percent of a $100,000, 8.25 percent mortgage loan in 5 years.

Note Under the entry 14.73991 percent is a figure in parentheses (9Y 12m). This means that it would take 9 years and almost 12 months of these payments to amortize the loan fully.

Example 56. Rapid Amortization of a Seller-Financed Loan

To make her property attractive at a price of $110,000, deFalco is willing to take back a $100,000 mortgage at 7.50 percent interest with a balloon at 10 years. Knowing that 91 percent is a risky loan-to-price ratio, she wants to be sure that the loan balance will have been paid down to $80,000 at the end of 5 years. In the second 5 years, she wants what would have been a 25-year schedule at the original loan date.

To find the payment for the first 5 years, enter Table 36, page 3 (p. 449), at 7.50 percent interest. Read down the years column to 5 years and across to the column headed 20 percent (percentage to be amortized), and read 10.80798 percent, the constant for the first 5 years.

Now enter Table 35 (a), page 3 (p. 423) at 7.50 percent and read down to 20 years, the number of years that will remain after the first segment. Read across to the column headed 7.50 percent and read 9.667118 percent, the constant for the second 5 years. Multiply the original balance by the first constant, and the reduced balance by the second constant to get the annual debt service. Divide each by 12 to get the monthly payments, rounding up in each case, as follows:

$$\$100,000 \times 0.1080798 = \$10,807.98 \div 12 = \$900.67$$

the monthly payment for the first 5 years that reduces the balance to 80 percent of original within that time, and

$$\$80,000 \times 0.09667118 = \$7733.69 \div 12 = \$644.48$$

the monthly payment for the remainder of the loan.

Example 57. More Secure Purchase Money Loan with Payments in Advance

The Levesques are considering taking back a **purchase money mortgage** on the home that they are selling. They are attracted by the advantage of the higher rate of return available from mortgage investments than those on certificates of deposit. But the lurking disadvantage, that the buyer might default, cutting their monthly income dangerously, looks like too great a risk to accept. They wish that there were a "security deposit" system for borrowers as there is for renters.

A solution might lie in offering the purchase money loan with payments in advance, as shown in Table 38. If they offer a program with payments semiannually in advance, they will have an average of 3 months' worth of payments (compared to the normal loan) to serve as security against default. And they can offer the borrower lower payments per year than the usual program at a bank or mortgage lender. (The buyer may object that this plan in effect requires a larger down payment, just when cash resources are strained, since half a year's payments must be made at closing. If the buyer is making a substantial down payment, such as 20 percent, it could be worthwhile to lend the borrower the additional cash to make the initial payment.)

Reverse Annuity Mortgages

For many households, a sale is not desired, but converting the equity locked up in the house into cash for current living costs is the goal. The reverse annuity mortgage is an excellent solution in such cases and is increasingly available.

Reverse annuity mortgages allow the lender to advance a payment to the borrower each month. The accumulated payments and the interest on them is paid off in a lump sum at the end of the mortgage. It is the reverse of a usual mortgage loan.

Example 58.   Payments from a Reverse Annuity Mortgage

Mr. Garofalo holds his house, appraised at $300,000, free and clear. Reverse annuity mortgages are available on the basis of 67 percent of value with interest at 9.25 percent per year. He is interested in a 10-year program.

To find the payments available from such a reverse annuity mortgage, enter Table 52, page 4 (p. 684) at 9.25 percent interest. Read down the monthly side column to 10 years and across to the 9.25 percent column, monthly payments. The factor there, 6.113927 percent, is the annual percentage available from the loan. To find the monthly payments, multiply by the loan amount ($300,000 × 0.67) and divide by 12, as follows:

$$\$200,000 \times 0.06113927 \div 12 = \$1018.99$$

per month, or, rounding, $1019 per month payment from a 10-year reverse annuity mortgage at 9.25 percent interest.

Note   Although reverse annuity mortgages are the reverse of normal cases, borrowers still prefer low interest rates to high. For the balance owing on a reverse annuity mortgage, see Example 146 in Chapter 4.

YIELDS ON HOME LOAN TRANSACTIONS

This section shows how to find the yields from the most common home loan transactions. Following trade practice, the yield is carried out to five decimal places, for example, 0.08691 or 8.691 percent. Recall, however, the discussion in the Introduction, warning that there may be little commercial significance to the last one or two decimal places of such yields. Chapter 3 has additional examples on this subject.

Annual Percentage Rate (APR)

The Truth-in-Lending Law (called "Regulation Z" by bankers) requires the mortgage lender in most home loan cases to give a written statement of the annual percentage rate (APR) of the loan. The APR takes into account the kinds of points, fees, and special charges that the lender may impose so as to give a single expression of loan cost. Although the rules for calculating the APR are complex, they apply to a great many lenders and they apply equally, so the APR quoted by one lender may be compared directly with that of another. As we will see in the examples further on, though, borrowing decisions based on the APR quotation are not always correct.

Example 59.   Annual Percentage Rate

Meeks Branley intends to apply for a 10-year loan on a 30-year schedule. Current market quotations are for 6.50 percent interest with 2.5 points to be paid at closing.

To find the APR, enter Table 25, page 5 (p. 293), the page for 6.50 percent interest, at the section for a 30-year schedule. Read down the left column, yield to end of year, to 10 years. Read across on that line to the column headed 2.5 points and find there the answer, 6.867 percent, the APR for a 6.50 percent loan maturing in 10 years on a 30-year schedule when 2.5 points are paid.

Note   Lenders quote certain charges such as application, origination, or inspection fees separately from points. In calculating the APR, lump all such charges together with the points and use the sum as the number of "points" for determining the APR. Do not include appraisal fees, seller-paid discount or buydown points, and closing fees such as title charges and attorney's fees in the APR calculation, as they are not part of the cost definition contained in the law.

Yield on Wraparound Mortgage Loan

Table 28 gives the Yield on Wraparound Mortgage Loans. A wraparound mortgage loan is one that in legal form is a second mortgage but in financial form is structured as a first mortgage. The wraparound lender determines a normal first mortgage, for example, a 75 percent loan to value, but disburses only the difference between it and the existing first mortgage. The difference is called the **new money.** The wraparound lender receives a mortgage payment based on the full mortgage, deducts a portion for the new money, and then makes the payment on the first mortgage (the old money). In most cases, wraparound financing gives a leverage effect to the yield on the new money.

Example 60. Yield on Seller-Financed Wraparound Mortgage Loan

Petrel Oskins has an 8.00 percent mortgage loan with 15 years remaining on the property she is selling. The balance is $240,000, and the loan can be assumed by a creditworthy buyer. Current mortgage loan rates are 10.50 percent, so Oskins has offered to take back a purchase money mortgage in the form of a wraparound. A buyer is interested if she will provide $320,000 wraparound financing on a 30-year schedule at an interest rate of 10.50 percent.

The new money here is $80,000, or 25 percent ($80,000 ÷ 320,000). Enter Table 28, page 7 (p. 345), the page for 10.50 percent overall interest rate, and the section for 25 percent new money, 75 percent old money. In the section for 30 years full term of the new loan, read across on the line for 15 years remaining term of the old loan to the column headed 8.00 percent. The yield there, 13.372, is the yield on the new money represented by Oskins's investment.

Note The wraparound loan document will make clear that the wraparound lender does not assume liability for the prior mortgage and that only if and

when the borrower puts in funds to make the prior loan payments will the lender faithfully remit them to the prior lender.

Example 61. Yield on Seller-Financed Shared Appreciation Mortgage (SAM)

Donald McBurnie is interested in buying a house, but present interest rates (12.50 percent) make the payments too expensive for him. To qualify for a loan, he would need an interest rate several percentage points lower. The owner of a property that he likes is willing to make a purchase money loan on a shared appreciation mortgage (SAM) basis. This type of loan is described in Table 29. The loan would have a 75 percent loan-to-value ratio and a fixed interest rate of 8.50 percent for 10 years on a 30-year schedule, but the seller-lender would also be entitled to 50 percent of any appreciation in price up to the end of the loan. If McBurnie did not want to sell at the end of 10 years, an appraisal would be obtained and the value reported would be used to determine the price appreciation, if any. In McBurnie's view, house prices are likely to continue the 5.0 percent annual rate of price increase that has been the recent experience in his community.

To measure if the SAM would be a cost-effective alternative for McBurnie, enter Table 29, page 17 (p. 371), the page for 5.0 percent growth rate, 75 percent loan-to-value ratio, and 8.50 percent interest. Read down to 10 years and across to 50 percent share of profit on sale. The answer there, 10.922 percent, means that the compounded annual yield to the lender from both the monthly interest and its share of the appreciation would equal 10.922 percent per year. This compares favorably with the 12.50 percent interest rate available in the open market.

Example 62. Selling a Purchase Money Mortgage at a Discount

Domiville will take back a $180,000 purchase money loan on a 30-year schedule at 8.00 percent interest. The loan will mature with a balloon payment in 5 years. A mortgage banker is willing to buy the loan. But current market rates are 9.00 percent, so Domiville will not be able to realize the full amount of the loan.

To find the price of the loan, enter Table 10, page 11 (p. 211), the section for 8.00 percent interest, the rate on the note Domiville is selling. Read down the column for desired yield to the line 9.00 percent and across on that line to the 5-years column. Read there the price 96.06900, the percentage of balance that the mortgage banker will pay. Multiply the loan amount by the percentage to get

$$\$180,000 \times 0.9606900 = \$172,924.20$$

the price of a $180,000 loan, 5-year term on a 30-year schedule, at 8.00 percent note rate priced to yield 9.00 percent. The discount, or points, in this example equals 3.931 percent (100.00 percent − 96.069 percent). If the loan is sold after it is made, Domiville will also be entitled to accrued interest. See Example 291 in Chapter 7 for a sample calculation.

Example 63.   Total Price after Number of Years of Increases

Persillion Homes have had an average price increase of 11.0 percent per year in the past 5 years. If this rate of price increase continues, Persillion would like to know the value of its homes 10 years from now.

To find the future prices, enter Table 46, page 23 (p. 567), the page for 11.00 percent interest, the interest rate here representing the rate of price growth. Under annual payments, find the factor on the line for 10 years under the column future value. It is 2.8394210. Convert this to a percentage by multiplying by 100 to get 283.94210. The average Persillion home would be worth 284 percent of its present price, if prices increase 11.0 percent compounded for the next 10 years.

Example 64.   Total Price Increase Converted to Annual Rate of Increase

Bette A. Hassad bought a house 7 years ago for $212,000. It has just been sold for $358,500. To find the compounded annual price increase, begin by finding the total percentage increase. It is

$$\frac{\text{Selling price}}{\text{Purchase price}} = \frac{\$358,500}{212,000} - 1.000 = 0.6910 = 69.1\%$$

Enter Table 6, page 2 (p. 189), at the section for 69 percent. Read down to 7 years and across to the column 69 percent. The answer there, 7.785 percent, is the compounded annual price increase over her 7-year holding period.

Example 65.   Time When Profit Objective Should Be Achieved

Stella Danuta has purchased a small apartment building in a fast-growing region. Prices have been rising at an annual rate of 6.0 percent per year. Danuta wishes to know, if this rate continues, how long it would be until the building would have increased in value by 50 percent.

Enter Table 68, page 1 (p. 772), at the section for 50 percent increase. Read down to 6.00 percent interest and across to the column headed 50 percent increase in value of original investment. The answer there, 6Y 10m, means that at this compounded rate of growth, the value should have grown 50 percent after 6 years and 10 months.

Chapter 3

PLANNING THE COMMERCIAL MORTGAGE LOAN

Commercial mortgage loans differ in important ways from the home loans described in the preceding chapter. Since commercial mortgages are seldom sold in the secondary market, the need for standard terms does not exist. Terms vary much more widely, especially as to numbers of points, lock-ins and prepayment premiums, and provisions for additional or later funding. Next, the income of the property financed outweighs the income of the owner. The commercial mortgage lender relies more on the property's ability to repay the debt comfortably than the owner's income or other assets. Finally, the rate of annual debt service outranks the interest rate as the figure of merit in commercial loans.

Chapter 3 is divided into four sections:

Annual Mortgage Constants Finding the percentage of the loan needed for payments on five types of mortgage loan

Loan Strategies Searching for the best fit of mortgage finance to property circumstances

Loan Underwriting Shaping the loan terms of long-term and construction financing

Yields on Loans Exploring the yield to lenders from eight varieties of financings

ANNUAL MORTGAGE CONSTANTS

Real estate finance people use the annual mortgage constant more than any other factor. The annual mortgage constant is the fundamental building block of most mortgage calculations. It expresses the *rate* of mortgage payment, rather than the *amount* of mortgage payment or mortgage interest. Financial people emphasize the rate of payment, because both principal and interest must come from cash flow. In real estate, debt service is the largest cash drain and draws the greatest attention.

An annual mortgage constant is the sum of 1 year's payments divided by the original amount of the loan. If a $100,000 loan requires monthly payments of $800, the annual mortgage constant is

$$\frac{\$800 \times 12}{\$100,000} = \frac{\$9,600}{\$100,000} = 0.096 = 9.600\% \text{ constant}$$

Note that the annual mortgage constant only deals with one typical year's payments. It does not matter if a loan will be fully amortized or will have a **balloon payment.** If we refer to a 25-year amortization schedule, the annual mortgage constant for the loan will be the same, whether the loan is made for the full 25 years or will require a balloon payment.

Now that we are better acquainted with the term, we will adopt industry usage and refer simply to "the constant." As easy as it was to find the constant when the payment was known, deriving the constant without knowing the payment requires some elaborate math. This book makes it unnecessary to understand the complex math that creates the constant. But you should be fairly comfortable with the use of constants before venturing too far into the forest of realty finance.

When people refer to the constant, they often mean the constant at the time the loan was made. The statement, "They took out a loan at a 9.600 percent constant" means the percentage relationship was true at the start of the loan. If payments of principal have been made since then, it is no longer true. The constant changes each time a principal payment is made. In our example above, we found the constant to be 9.600 percent. But after 1 year of amortization, the loan balance will have decreased. Let us assume it has declined to $98,340. The annual payments are still $9600. So the constant after 1 year will be 9.762 percent ($9,600 ÷ $98,340). The constant has to be higher, because amortizing the loan in a shorter time span takes a greater rate of payment. Balance of a loan, rate of payment, and constant are interconnected, so constants can be used to predict a loan balance, as will be seen in the examples.

Five sections of constants provide a broad range of financing plans, including full-year term with monthly payments—Table 35 (a); year and partial-year terms—Table 35 (b); using the annual mortgage constant to amortize part of a loan—Table 36; annual, semiannual, quarterly payments—Table 37; and payments in advance—Table 38.

Annual Mortgage Constant, Full-Year Term, Monthly Payments

The constants in Table 35 (a) are for the customary loan described at length in this book. This loan is often referred to as a *level payment annuity mortgage*. The payments are monthly, commencing 30 days after the closing of the loan, calculated to amortize the entire loan through level (equal) payments that are applied first to interest in arrears and then to principal repayment. The loan terms in section (a) of Table 35 are expressed in full 12-month years, giving all interest rates by tenths and by sixteenths from 5.00 percent through 15.00 percent, by ¼ percent through 19.00 percent, and by 1.00 percent through 24.00 percent per year. Section (b) of Table 35 gives constants for loans with a number of years plus some number of months, by ¼ percent, from 5.50 percent through 12.50 percent per year.

Example 66. Annual Mortgage Constant—Full-Year Term

Desmond Owens asks his mortgage banker to quote a loan at 8.75 percent interest to be amortized with monthly payments over 30 years. To find the constant, turn to Table 35 (a), page 4 (p. 425), the page for 8.75 percent interest. Read down the years column to 30 and across to the column headed by 8.75 percent; read 9.440405 percent, the annual constant for an 8.75 percent, 30-year loan.

Annual Mortgage Constant, Year and Partial-Year Term, Monthly Payments

Table 35 (b) gives the constants for mortgage loans with terms expressed in years and fractions of a year. The table ranges from 2 years to 40 years, 11 months.

Example 67. Annual Mortgage Constant—Year and Month Term

A loan at 7.50 percent interest is to have an amortization period of 27 years 6 months. To find the constant, enter Table 35 (b), page 5 (p. 436) at 7.50 percent. Read down the years column to 27 and across to the column headed 6, and read 8.600468 percent, the constant for a 27-year, 6-month loan.

Example 68. Annual Mortgage Constant, Interest Rate Changing during Loan

Flambeau Freres have agreed to buy the Catalana Cove Apartments. The seller will lend 80 percent of the $3 million purchase price on a 3-year loan, using a 30-year schedule. The interest rate is to be 10.00 percent in the first year and 9.00 percent in the second and third years.

Programming the mortgage payments here means setting up two loans:

1 year at 10.00 percent, 30-year schedule on the full amount of the loan

2 years at 9.00 percent, 29-year schedule on the balance at the end of the first year

Referring to Table 35 (a), page 6 (p. 426), the first constant is found in the column for 10.00 percent interest on the line for 30 years; it is 10.530859 percent. Using the same procedure, the second year constant is found at 9.00 percent on the 29-year line, 9.721891 percent.

Next, enter Table 42 (a) (p. 496) and find the balance at the end of 1 year on a 10.00 percent 30-year loan; it is 99.4441 percent. The program now can be laid out as follows:

First year:

$$\$2,400,000 \times 0.10530859 = \$252,740.62$$

Second and third years:

$$\$2,400,000 \times 0.994441 \times 0.09721891 = \$232,028.33$$

Dividing each of the annual debt services by 12 will give the monthly payments for each year.

Cross-Reference   For payments on a loan with a *rising* interest rate, see Example 32 in Chapter 2.

Annual Mortgage Constants to Amortize Part of a Loan by a Certain Date

Constructing real estate deals to achieve a specific loan balance by a certain date is simple with Table 36. The monthly payments developed from Table 36 will reduce the balance to the desired **balloon payment** at the desired date. Payments are monthly in arrears, as usual. Below each figure is an entry in parentheses giving the years and months needed to fully amortize the loan with this constant. So an entry of 7Y 12m means that the constant above it would amortize the loan fully during the twelfth month of the eighth year.

Example 69.   Constant to Amortize Part of a Loan by a Certain Date

To attract a buyer, Sean Steen is asked to take back an 8.25 percent purchase money mortgage loan. He will do so if the loan will come due at the end of 5 years with a balance then of 60 percent of the original loan amount.

To find the annual mortgage constant, enter Table 36 at 8.25 percent interest and read down to 5 years. Now read across to the column headed 40 percent, the amount to be amortized within 5 years, and read 14.73991 percent. This is the annual constant percent needed to repay 40 percent of the principal during the first 5 years of the loan.

The annual debt service and the monthly payments are obtained in the same manner as with other constants: multiply the loan amount by the annual

mortgage constant and divide by 12. Using an original loan amount of $100,000, the monthly payment is

$$\$100,000 \times 0.1473991 \div 12 = \$1,228.33$$

the monthly payment to amortize 40 percent of an 8.25 percent mortgage loan within 5 years.

Annual Mortgage Constants for Annual, Semiannual, and Quarterly Loans

Monthly payments are the most common in the United States, but the deal structure or the income capability of the property will sometimes dictate a different frequency. Table 37 gives the constants for quarterly, semiannual, and annual payment schedules. The payments are in arrears.

Example 70.   Payments on Annual Payment Loan

Eleanor Elsenau will purchase a parcel of land with the seller taking back a $35,000 purchase money mortgage at 9.25 percent, payable in seven equal annual installments to amortize the loan fully.

To find the payments on the loan, enter Table 37, page 2 (p. 455) at the section for 9.25 percent interest. Read down the left column to 7 years and across to the column headed 9.25 percent. Read there the factor 20.03603, the annual mortgage constant for the loan. Multiply the principal amount by the factor to get

$$\$35,000.00 \times 0.2003603 = \$7,012.62$$

the amount of each annual payment.

Note   Annual payment mortgages have the advantage for the lender that they earn more interest for a given loan amount and loan term than monthly payment loans. They have the disadvantages that they do not provide smooth cash flow, and financial difficulties of the borrower might not become apparent for as much as a year.

Mortgage Constants for Payments in Advance, Monthly, Quarterly, Semiannually

Table 38 is devoted to the constants on loans where the payments are made either monthly, quarterly, or semiannually in advance. When interest is paid in arrears, the annual constant is higher for quarterly payment loans than for monthly payments; the constant is higher still for annual payment loans. When the interest is paid in advance, the constant is lower for quarterly payments than for monthly, and lower still for semiannual payments in advance.

Example 71. Debt Service on a Loan with Payments in Advance

Constable wants a lower payment than that available from the customary mortgage on an 8.75 percent, 20-year fully amortizing loan in the amount of $675,000. She selects semiannual payments in advance.

To find the annual mortgage constant, enter Table 38, page 4 (p. 461) in the section for 8.75 percent interest. Read down the left column to 20 years and across on that line to the column for semiannual advance. The factor there, 10.227947 percent, is the annual mortgage constant for annual payment loans payable semiannually in advance. Multiply the loan amount by the constant to get

$$\$675,000 \times 0.10227947 = \$69,038.65$$

This is the annual debt service; divide by 2 (payments per year) to get

$$\$69,038.65 \div 2 = \$34,519.33$$

which is the dollar amount of the payment on a $675,000, 20-year loan with payments semiannually in advance.

Example 72. Mortgage Constant When Interest Rate Will Change at Specified Loan Balance

Val LLadding has agreed to sell the Parlous Arts Center, taking back a 12-year purchase money mortgage of $300,000, which represents a high loan-to-value ratio. The buyer has agreed to an initial interest rate of 11.00 percent. The interest rate is to drop to 8.50 percent when the loan balance reaches 80 percent, and the payments will be chosen to achieve the 80 percent mark at the end of 7.5 years. Thereafter, the interest rate will drop to 8.50 percent and follow a 22-year 6-month schedule (i.e., as if it had been on a 30-year schedule from the beginning).

To find the constants, enter Table 36 at 11.00 percent. Read down the column, years to balloon to 7.5 years. Across on that line under 20 percent to be amortized, read 12.72695 percent, the constant for the first 7.5 years. Now enter Table 35 (b), page 7 (p.

438), and read under 22 years 6 months the constant 9.984844 percent. Multiply the first constant by the original principal to get

$$\$300,000 \times 0.1272695 = \$38,180.85$$

the annual debt service in the first 7.5 years at 11.00 percent. Next multiply the second constant by the reduced principal to get

$$\$300,000 \times 0.80 \times 0.09984844 = \$23,963.63$$

This is the annual debt service in the last 4.5 years until the balloon at the twelfth year at 8.50 percent. Dividing each annual debt service by 12 will give the monthly payments, $3181.74 in the first 7.5 years and $1996.97 in the next 5 years.

Cross-Reference Examples 32 and 34 in Chapter 2 describe payments on rising rate mortgages and growing equity mortgages.

LOAN STRATEGIES

This section looks at the terms of the loan from the standpoint of the borrower. It presents ideas to bend, shape, or alter the financing plan in ways that better the borrower's position relative to the lender or to a possible buyer.

The Yield Curve Predicts Interest Rates

Investors create interest rate markets through millions of daily decisions. Banks, corporations, and governments lend to each other. Public and private persons across the earth buy some types of interest-bearing investments and sell others. The interest rates on mortgage loans are created in the process, as are the differences between short- and long-term rates. Depending on their views of the future, investors will tend to buy longer-term bonds and lower the long-term rates, or avoid longer-term bonds, causing long-term rates to rise to attract investors. Differences between long- and short-rates create the **yield curve.** This is a graph of all maturities of bonds of one issuer, usually the Treasury. When the curve shows that long-term bonds offer slightly more yield than short-term, the market is expecting interest rates to remain the same for a while, since long-term bonds normally pay a small illiquidity premium. If long-term bonds yield less than short-term rates, the market is expecting rates to fall sharply. Long-term rates that are noticeably higher than short rates indicate a coming rise in interest rates.

Although the direction of the trends created by professional investors is quite clear, it is not obvious how much investors expect rates to rise or fall. But this can be inferred by taking the measure of the market and utilizing Table 34. Consider a mid-term interest rate, say, for a 3-year bond: The rate is the sum of the rates for a 1-year bond, a 2-year bond, and a 3-year bond. By extracting from the 3-year interest the amount for the 2-year, we can see what is expected to happen in the third year. By extracting from the 2-year rate the rate for the 1-year bond, we can see what the market foretells for the second year. And the 1-year rate itself tells the market story for the coming year.

Establishing the market forecast inherent in rates will not guarantee interest rate success. Wars, political upheaval, and economic distress can all interfere with the expected outcome. But it is helpful for the real estate investor to know if actions planned are in line with what market makers expect.

Example 73. Using the Interest Rate Yield Curve to Forecast Rates

Phila Mondrian has the opportunity to place a 30-year fixed rate mortgage loan on Drummond Cliff Apartments at 11.15 percent per year. As an alternative, a 3-year interest-only **bullet loan** is available at the same rate. Consulting financial journals provides the information that Treasury rates for 4-year bonds are 10.500 percent, but 3-year bonds are yielding only 10.375 percent.

Turning to Table 34, page 7 (p. 419), enter the section for 10.50 percent at a 4-year rate. Read down the left column to a 3-year rate of 10.375 percent, and find under the 10.50 percent column the answer, 10.876 percent. Based on the interest rate markets, no unusual or large swing is expected going into the fourth year, the time when the 3-year loan would be coming due. Based on today's yield curve, there is no clear potential to improve the rate at the end of 3 years. Accordingly, Phila Mondrian decides to close a long-term fixed rate transaction.

Note Many times the yield curve will be so flat that the rates fall in between the ⅛ of 1 percent gradations of Table 34. This is normal and merely signals that the markets do not foresee important change. For those facing short-term rate swing decisions, detailed study of interest rate markets will be needed. For those making real estate decisions, the table should prove adequate to signal when the market expects major movements.

Create Value by Paying Points

Real estate buyers who use leverage often accept a lower rate of return on investment than mortgage lenders will accept for the mortgage rate. In shaping a loan program, the strategist first considers whether a mortgage buy-down could increase overall value. Table 5 shows a great many plans that will increase value. (See the discussion of buy-downs later in this chapter.) In many of these plans, the increase in value will be greater than the cost of the buy-down. The concept works best when interest rates are markedly higher than equity rates and the time to a sale is relatively short.

Example 74. Value Created by Paying Points

George Christopoulos builds 4- and 6-unit apartment buildings for sale. As part of the package, he arranges financing of 75 percent loan-to-value on a 30-year schedule. Currently, interest rates are 10.00 percent, and buyers will pay a price that will yield them 8.50 percent cash-on-cash return. He would like to buy the loan down to 8.50 percent, with a balloon payment at the end of 7 years.

To get the increase in value from a buy-down, enter Table 5, page 3 (p. 184), equity yield of 8.50 percent and the section for 75 percent loan-to-value ratio. On the line for a cut in rate of 1.50 percent, read across to the column headed 10.00 percent and find 11.505 percent, the increase in value from buying down the loan from 10.00 percent to 8.50 percent.

Referring to Table 24 and Examples 85 and 86, Christopoulos will find that the buy-down should be priced at only 7.561 points which will be paid on only 75 percent of value, or 5.67 percent as a percent of total property value, whereas the value increase is double that, making this a favorable exchange.

Example 75. Lower Constant versus Lower Interest Rate

Preparing financial projections for a new apartment project, Mr. Bredon has loan quotations from competing lenders. One lender offers a 10.60 percent loan for 22 years, fully amortized. The other offers an 11.00 percent interest rate but a longer amortization period, namely 30 years. To compare these, find the constants for each from Table 35 (a) following Example 66 above. This will give a constant for the first loan of 11.752975 percent and for the second loan of 11.427881 percent. Despite the higher interest rate on the second loan, its constant is lower. Since property is valued most often on its cash flow, the lower constant would be favored by many.

Lower Debt Service with Payments in Advance

At times, the entire business of real estate seems to revolve around lowering the annual mortgage constant on financing, and with good reason. The fundamental measure of value for investors who buy property with leverage is **cash-on-cash return.** A lower constant lowers the cash going to the lender and increases the cash-on-cash return, which makes the property more valuable.

One means to lower the annual constant is to make payments **in advance,** as set out in Table 38. It goes against the grain for real estate people to make payments early, but building the early payment into the financial structure can raise the value of the property. To see how that can be, consider that the normal mortgage payment is made monthly **in arrears,** the first payment being due 30 days after closing. The borrower has the money for 30 days before the lender gets its interest. When payments are monthly in advance, the first payment is deducted from the loan proceeds and the lender has the use of the payment for 30 days. The constant is lower to correct for that, and the lower constant creates higher cash-on-cash return.

On a 20-year loan at 10.75 percent interest, payments monthly in arrears, the annual mortgage constant is 12.18 percent. But with payments semiannually in advance, the constant is 11.63 percent, a full half-point less. That half-point represents an immediate increase in value of the property, magnified by the leverage ratio on the property. At the same time, the mortgage is safer, since the debt service coverage is greater.

The inconvenient part, obviously, is making the payments early. Payments semi-annually in advance will be made an average of more than 3 months earlier than normal. It costs interest to make the earlier payments, but the investment return on them equals the mortgage note rate, typically higher than that on short-term deposits.

Example 76.   Lower Constant with Payments in Advance

McGillifree had expected to refinance his apartments at a favorable rate. Various problems caused delays, and rates have now risen sharply. The current market quotation is 9.00 percent interest on a 30-year amortization schedule, with an annual mortgage constant of 9.655471 percent. Knowing that appraisers and buyers are sensitive to the constant on assumable financing, he is seeking a lower constant.

To find lower constants, enter Table 38, page 4 (p. 461), the page for 9.00 percent interest. On the line for 30-year amortization, the first column gives the monthly arrears figure which we have already seen. Next to that appear 9.583594 percent, for loans which pay monthly in advance, 9.456814 percent for loans which pay quarterly in advance, and 9.273542 percent for loans which pay semiannually in advance. The periodic payments are found by multiplying the principal by these factors. Dividing by the frequency of payment, 12, 4, or 2, will give the payment for each period.

Converting Interest to Principal or Principal to Interest

Table 10 demonstrates how paying points for a loan could be preferable to paying a high rate of interest. Buyers are more interested in property that has an assumable mortgage at a below-market rate. A seller who will carry back paper at a lower-than-market interest rate may facilitate a sale that full market rates would have inhibited. Then, too, the property's cash flow after debt service may permit a current cash dividend that might be unavailable otherwise, until income had grown considerably. Or, the lower mortgage payment may make it possible to meet a minimum debt-service coverage ratio required by the lender.

Paying a higher price for a property may also be preferable in some situations. An increase in purchase price means higher capital gain. In many countries, capital gains are taxed at a lower rate than interest income, and different rates are again being debated in the United States.

At the other end of the scale, it can be desirable to pay higher interest on the loan, in return for a lower purchase price or a larger or otherwise more favorable loan. When might this be desirable? Some foreign entities can receive interest free of U.S. tax under their home country's treaty with the United States. Or a seller facing recapture tax may exchange a lower purchase price for a higher rate on a purchase money mortgage, deferring some tax into future years.

Converting loan interest into loan principal or vice versa accomplishes all these tasks. Table 10 gives the necessary figures to translate one to the other. Current U.S. tax regulations and accounting practice restrict this to narrow limits. Competent tax advice should always be obtained before committing to such transactions. Later in this chapter, Table 10 also serves as a loan price table.

Example 77. Paying Higher Interest to Get a Lower Purchase Price

When a buyer prefers a lower purchase price but is willing to pay higher interest, the following case may be used, with or without down payment.

Using 100 Percent Financing

Excedent Partners is prepared to pay the $1 million asked for the office building that will become its U.S. headquarters. For internal allocation of costs, Excedent wants the lowest initial price but would be willing to pay a higher rate of interest. Buyer and seller agree that 9.50 percent is the market rate today for loans on such buildings. Both agree to structure a deal with 11.00 percent interest on a 10-year purchase money loan on a 30-year schedule, provided the buyer gets the benefit of a lower purchase price to compensate.

To find the conversion of principal to interest, enter Table 10, page 17 (p. 217), the page for 9.50 percent interest. Read down the column for desired yield to 11.00 percent and across on that line to the column headed 10 years. Read the amount 91.22043 percent, which means that if 100 percent financing is used, Excedent Partners should pay only $912,204.30 for the property.

Using a Down Payment

Let us assume Excedent's deal is acceptable to the seller, provided that the buyer puts 20 percent down. The seller will finance the rest at an 11.00 percent stated rate on a purchase money loan. The agreed price before conversion of principal to interest is $1 million. The financing amount would equal

Agreed price	$1,000,000
Less down payment	200,000
Subtotal	800,000
Times factor above	× 0.9122043
Financed amount	729,763
	+ 200,000
Total apparent purchase price	$929,763

The price that will be put in the contract will be $929,763. It looks as if Excedent Partners have "saved" over $70,000 on the cost of the building. But, of course, they will be paying higher interest over the life of the loan.

Note The seller will restrict prepayment to assure that the high-interest-rate loan, for which it has already given credit in the purchase price, will not be paid off before its scheduled maturity. If the loan is prepaid, the seller should receive a prepayment premium beginning at $70,237 ($800,000 less $729,763) and declining over the term. To find the correct amount of prepayment premium as of any date, use Table 42 as if a 10-year loan of $70,237 had been made at 11 percent interest.

Example 78. When to Forfeit a Commitment Deposit

Chausson has a mortgage loan **takeout commitment** for a 7-year loan on a 30-year schedule from Marvelous Life, issued when rates were 11.75 percent. The commitment permits him to cancel the transaction prior to closing, but if he does so, he will forfeit the 4-point standby fee (commitment deposit) that he has posted. Crucial Life has offered him a 7-year loan at 9.25 percent. It would cost one point to obtain the Crucial commitment.

To see if it is worthwhile to forfeit the commitment deposit, enter Table 10, page 26 (p. 226), for 11.75 percent loans. Read down the column for desired yield to 9.25 percent and across on that line to the column headed 7 years. The factor there, 112.65889 percent, states that it would be worth 12.7 points (112.65889 − 100.00) to obtain the lower-rate loan. Since Chausson can obtain it for only 5 points (losing the 4-point deposit plus one point paid to the new lender), it would be economic to drop the Marvelous Life commitment.

Note This example and these tables give only the financial consequences of forfeiting the deposit. Legal and ethical questions arise whenever nonperformance is at issue. Discuss these with counsel before proceeding.

Example 79. The Value of Below-Market Financing

Glengowan Savings is offering an office building for sale at $6 million. The savings bank will take back financing of 75 percent of the purchase price, at an interest rate of 8.00 percent, despite the fact that the market rate in the region is 10.00 percent. The financing would be for a 10-year term with 30-year amortization schedule.

To find how much of the purchase price is attributable to the bargain interest rate, first find the loan amount, which is 75 percent of $6 million or $4.5 million. Now enter Table 10, page 11 (p. 211), for an interest rate of 8.00 percent. Read down the desired rate column to 10.00 percent and across on that line to the column headed 10 years. The factor there, 87.93094 percent, is the percentage that the financing is worth in the open market. Multiplying the loan by the factor will give

$$\$4,500,000 \times 0.8793094 = \$3,956,892$$

the "real" financing. Adding the down payment of $1,500,000 gives the real estate value of $5,456,892. The real estate is being sold for about $5.45 million. The difference between the contract price and the real estate value is the premium paid for the under-market interest rate.

Cross-Reference   Example 294 in Chapter 7 describes how to account for the transaction.

Price of a Loan to Give a Specified Yield

The yield on a loan sold at a premium will be less than the mortgage rate. The yield will be more than the mortgage rate, however, in the case of a discount. Loans are often priced in percentages of the amount owed by the borrower. So a loan offered at a price of "108.50 plus accrued interest" means a price equal to 108.50 percent of the principal balance owed by the borrower at time of sale of the loan. Accrued interest owed by the borrower as of the sale date will automatically be added to the purchase price to find the total amount of the sale, unless agreement is otherwise made.

Example 80.   Price of a Loan Sold at a Discount

Samuels & Peron will receive a $700,000 purchase money mortgage loan as part payment for the sale of their Plaza Milano. The loan will bear interest at 9.50 percent and will run for 10 years on a 30-year schedule. In order to raise cash, they have asked their bank to buy the loan. The bank will do so, but only if it is priced to yield 11.00 percent.

To find the price of the loan, enter Table 10, page 17 (p. 217) for 9.50 percent interest. Read down the desired interest column to 11.00 percent and across on that line to the column headed 10 years. The factor there, 91.22043 percent, is the percentage of face value that will be paid for the loan. Multiply the face amount by the factor to get

$$\$700,000 \times 0.9122043 = \$638,543$$

the amount the bank will pay for the principal amount of the loan.

Since the sale to the bank will occur 3 days after the loan is closed with the borrower, there will be an interest proration in favor of Samuels & Peron for the 3 days' interest accrued on the loan as of the date of sale. To calculate this amount, see Example 291 in Chapter 7.

Example 81.   Price of a Loan Sold at a Premium

Clarrengle Peijovich made a forward commitment to buy a $500,000 loan on a 30-year fully amortizing schedule with 11.00 percent interest. The current market rate has dropped to 9.00 percent, and Peijovich will sell the loan as soon as it closes.

To find the price, enter Table 10, page 23 (p. 223), for 11.00 percent interest and full term. Read down the desired yield column to 9.00 percent and across on that line to the column headed full term. Read there the price of the loan, 118.35653 percent, the percentage of the loan to be paid for a 9.00 percent yield.

Multiply this percentage by the loan amount to get

$$\$500,000 \times 1.1835653 = \$591,782.65$$

the sale price of the loan as of the day the loan is made.

Interest on Constant Principal Repayment Loans

We are accustomed to working with real estate loans made on the level payment annuity method, where part of each payment goes to principal and part to interest. But many real estate deals call for a loan, such as those shown in Table 40, with constant principal repayment, where the same amount of principal is paid off with each payment. This makes it easy to determine what the loan balance will be from time to time. The principal part of each payment is the same, but the interest varies with each period, as does the annual debt service. Relative to level payment annuity loans, amortization is much more rapid in the early periods. Table 40 gives the interest as a percentage of the original loan.

Example 82. Interest on Constant Principal Repayment Loan, Monthly Payments

Creegan Fulsome will lend $100,000 to Absomol Partners, to be repaid over 100 months with 1.00 percent of the loan paid each month to principal, plus interest on the unpaid balance at 9.25 percent per year.

To find the interest paid in the first year, enter Table 40, page 3 (p. 476), at the section for 9.25 percent interest rate, monthly payments. Read across on the line, year 1, to the column headed 1.00 percent constant principal repayment, and find the factor, 8.7413 percent. This is the interest on the loan during the year. Multiply the original loan amount by the interest factor to get

$$\$100,000 \times 0.087413 = \$8,741.30$$

the interest accrued in year 1 of a constant principal repayment loan at 9.25 percent, repaying in 100 monthly periods.

Example 83. Principal Paid and Remaining Balance on Constant Principal Repayment Loan

Nguyen Dhu loaned $160,000 at 7.50 percent interest, to be repaid in 72 equal installments of principal plus interest on the unpaid balance. Nguyen Dhu wishes to know the amount paid off after 19 payments and the remaining principal balance at that time.

To find the amount paid off, multiply the original loan amount by the ratio of installments paid to total installments:

$$\$160,000 \times 19/72 = \$160,000 \times 0.263889$$
$$= \$42,222.22$$

the amount paid off after 19 payments. To find the remaining balance, subtract the amount paid off from the original loan:

$$\$160,000 - 42,222.22 = \$117,777.78$$

the remaining balance on a 72-payment loan after 19 payments.

Example 84. Debt Service on a Constant Principal Repayment Loan, Monthly Payments

Pegosian is forecasting the cash flow of Outlanden Apartments. The property is financed with a 10.50 percent loan requiring principal repayments each month equal to 1/120 of the original loan amount, which was $600,000. Pegosian wishes to know the annual debt service for the fifth year of this loan.

Enter Table 40, page 4 (p. 477). Read down the year column to 5 years and across on that line to the column headed 1/120. The factor there, 5.8187 percent, is the percentage of the loan paid as interest in the fifth year. Multiply it by the original balance to get

$$\$600,000 \times 0.058187 = \$34,912.20$$

interest in year 5. To get the principal repayment in that year, divide the number of payments in each year by the total number of payments in the loan, and multiply that by the original balance

$$12 \div 120 \times \$600,000 = \$60,000$$

the principal paid in the fifth (and each) year. The annual debt service for the fifth year is $94,912.20.

Cost to Buy Down a Loan

Table 24 shows the cost of **mortgage buy-downs.** Buying a loan down means paying a sum to induce a lender to lower the interest rate for a period. When a property does not have sufficient income to cover debt service on proposed financing, or simply owing to negotiation, a seller may find that paying for a buy-down creates more value than its cost and accomplishes a deal that could not go forward otherwise.

Table 24 gives the buy-downs for a wide variety of interest rates. For each rate, there are four sections of "buy-down credit," which is the discount given by the lender with whom the buy-down points are deposited. The four rates of credit are 5.50 percent per year, which is the standard used by Fannie Mae (FNMA) and many banks; 0 percent; the interest rate on the loan; and 1 percent under the interest rate on the loan.

Example 85. Cost to Buy Down a Loan, Deposit Credited

Hubert-Gredsiull & Co. have been offered a satisfactory price for their research facility, but the buyer, a developer, intends to convert the property to office use. In the rehabilitation period, the developer will have no income, and will therefore condition an offer on obtaining 7.00 percent financing for the first 3 years. Since the current interest rate is 9.50 percent, there is little chance of getting such financing unless Hubert-Gredsiull will buy down the loan. The lender will agree to credit the buy-down deposit at 5.50 percent interest.

To find the cost to buy this loan down, enter Table 24, page 2 (p. 283), the page for 9.50 percent interest at the section for a buy-down credit rate of 5.50 percent. Read down the desired buy-down column to 7.00 percent and across on that line to the 3-year column. The factor there, 5.814 percent, is the percentage of the loan to be paid to buy down the loan from 9.50 percent to 7.00 percent for 3 years.

Example 86. Cost to Buy Down a Loan, No Buy-Down Credit

Thelma Bigelow has a prospective purchaser who would make an acceptable offer, if the initial interest rate were 10.00 percent or less. Unfortunately, lenders are offering no better than 12.00 percent on 5-year loans, using 30-year schedules, and will give no credit for buy-down deposits. Bigelow is willing to make the buy-down, if it would cost less than 10 percent of the loan.

To find what a buy-down would cost, enter Table 24, page 7 (p. 288), the page for 12.00 percent, at the section for buy-down credit of zero percent. Read down the desired buy-down column to 10.00 percent. On that line, under the column headed 5 years, find the factor, 9.062 percent. It would cost 9.062 percent of the loan to make this buy-down.

Note In this case where the lender will give no buy-down credit, measure the difference between the buy-down at zero credit and at 5.50 percent credit. If the difference is more than a few hundred dollars, setting up an escrow at a bank or trust company may make sense. The escrowee trust company will be directed to deposit the funds at interest and pay the difference between the lender's required payment and the agreed rate, charging from a few hundred to a few thousand dollars for the service.

Example 87. Change in Interest Rate Needed to Offset a Difference in Rates

Albany & Troy have a floating rate construction loan available at 8.00 percent for a 12-month term, but the best fixed rate quotation is 10.50 percent. Rates are expected to rise sharply in the near future.

To find how much the rates could rise before offsetting the differential, enter Table 15, page 2 (p. 242), the page with 8.00 percent. Read down the 8.00 percent column to the figure closest to 10.50 percent, which happens to be 10.44 percent. On that line at the left read 4.00 percent. This means that the floating rate could rise a little over 4.00 percent and still give an interest cost less than a 10.50 percent fixed rate. If rates seem unlikely to rise 4.00 percent over the next year, the floating rate would be a logical choice.

Example 88. Maximum Price for an Interest Rate Swap

Roy Allco's construction lender will lend on a floating rate basis only. Its current quotation for the Royall Park loan is 1.25 percent over the prime rate, which currently is 9.00 percent. Allco expects the prime rate to rise as much as 3.00 percent over the 24 months that the loan will be outstanding. To protect against this rise, he would like his lender to buy an interest rate swap, by which the loan rate would be fixed at 10.25 percent.

To find out how much Allco can afford to pay for the swap, enter Table 15, page 5 (p. 245), for 10.25 percent interest. Read down the column for increase in rate of 3.00 percent, and across on the change in cost line to the 10.25 percent column. The factor there, 18.43 percent, means that the change in interest, if it happens, would cost 18 percent of the loan in additional interest. Allco could pay as much as 18 percent to obtain a fixed rate through an interest rate swap.

Note This is the maximum price that can be paid, since it would cost as much as the expected increase in interest. Allco should shop for quotations, as different banks will offer different prices based on *their* expectation of what will happen to interest rates. In any case, the fee should be substantially less, for example, half of the maximum.

LOAN UNDERWRITING

Loan underwriting is looked on as the province of the lender but deserves study by prospective borrowers as well. The well-prepared loan application will demonstrate that the applicant has considered the lender's preferences, needs, and yield requirements. Although some lenders will never change loan terms, a few will soften them, but only for the professionals who demonstrate their command of market terms and methods. This section relates only to underwriting, but appraisal methods are closely allied to this topic; they are discussed in Chapter 5.

Example 89. Measuring Value Locked in a Mortgage

Albamonte's shopping center has a 12.00 percent mortgage loan which has 10 years remaining before it becomes open for prepayment. He considers the loan to be about 67 percent of the current value of the center. Interest rates have declined since he took out the loan and now are at the level of 9.50 percent. Albamonte is considering selling the center and would like to know what value is tied up in the locked-in mortgage. The broker tells him that for sale purposes the market considers an 8.50 percent cash-on-cash return appropriate.

Enter Table 5, page 3 (p. 184), the page for an 8.50 percent equity rate, in the section for 67 percent loan-to-value ratio. In the 67 percent section, read across on the line for a cut in rate of 2.50 percent (12.00 percent − 9.50 percent) to the 12.00 percent interest column. The factor there is 17.671 percent, meaning that the value of the shopping center would be more than 1/6 higher, if the loan were at 9.50 percent rather than at 12.00 percent.

Debt Service Coverage

Debt service coverage is easily calculated: It is net operating income (NOI) before debt service divided by the amount of debt service to be paid in one year. It is a more important limit on loan amount than the loan-to-value ratio, because debt service coverage defines how well (or not) the project can make monthly payments on the loan. Table 12 shows how the interplay of debt service coverage and mortgage constant affect the lendable amount.

Example 90. Debt Service Coverage

A 75 percent loan has a mortgage constant of 9.00 percent. The equity yield is 7.50 percent. The debt service coverage is given in Table 12 (p. 234) at the section for 75 percent loan-to-value ratio. On the line for a 7.50 percent equity yield, under the 9.00 percent mortgage constant column, find the **debt ser-**

vice coverage ratio, 1.28 times, for these mortgage and equity terms.

Example 91. Improved Debt Service Coverage with Payments in Advance

The Pelton Partnership builds warehouses to sell. Its lender will make a 10.75 percent loan on a 20-year schedule, but only if debt service coverage is at least 1.25 times or better. Projected NOI of the company's next building is $150,000, giving the proposed $1 million loan only 1.23 times coverage.

To locate an improved constant, enter Table 38, page 6 (p. 463), the page for 10.75 percent interest. Reading across the line for a 20-year amortization schedule, find under quarterly advance the constant 11.894005 percent and under semiannual advance, 11.634676 percent. Either of these constants will be more than 1.25 times covered by the projected NOI of $150,000.

Feasible Loan Based on Debt Service Coverage

Table 11 gives the appropriate loan for given debt service and provides the formula for deferred payout situations.

Example 92. Feasible Amount of a Loan

Mike Friedman projects $100,000 annual net operating income from his apartment building. Interest rates are currently 9.25 percent. Conventional financing is available on a 30-year schedule. Friedman's mortgage banker informs him that lenders are requiring debt service coverage of 1.20 times (i.e., 1.20 times annual debt service) for apartments.

To find the amount that Friedman should be able to borrow, enter Table 11, page 2 (p. 231), the page that includes 9.25 percent. Read down the left column to 9.25 percent and the line in that section for 30-year amortization schedule. Read across to the column headed 1.20, and find 8.44. This is the lendable amount, that is, the multiple of NOI that may be borrowed. Multiply the NOI by the lendable amount to get

$$\$100,000 \times 8.44 = \$844,000$$

the amount that may be borrowed for a 9.25 percent loan on a 30-year schedule to give debt service coverage of 1.20 times.

Example 93. Loan Increases Based on Added Rental Income

Perriewit & Langley (P&L) will rehabilitate the Market Mall. Their rehab lender has agreed to a basic mortgage amount that includes a standard tenant improvement package. P&L believe that many tenants will take above-standard tenant improvement packages and will be willing to pay higher rent for them.

Because each package will be individually negotiated, it is difficult to say just what the extra rent will be. P&L seek a formula for the additional loan that the lender will advance, if leases are brought in at rents above pro forma. The lender wants 1.25 times debt service coverage. The discussion centers around a loan at 10.75 percent, 20-year schedule.

To find the loan "adder," enter Table 11, page 3 (p. 232), the page with 10.75 percent interest. Read down to 10.75 percent and the line for 20-year amortization schedule. Read across on that line to the column headed 1.25, and find 6.57, the lendable amount. For the loan formula, P&L will request that the lender advance $6.57 for each $1 of rental income above pro forma from approved leases.

Example 94. Rent Holdback Formulas in Mortgage Loan Commitment

Mortgage lenders use one debt service coverage for a **spec** (unleased) building, another for a building with some preleasing, and a third for fully leased property. Although a loan commitment may be made on the basis of fully-leased status, there will be a **leasing holdback** of part of the loan proceeds until that status becomes reality.

Palquo's lender analyzes applications for spec building loans using debt service coverage of 1.67 times. With 60 percent preleasing, it would use 1.25 times, while fully-leased buildings qualify for 1.15 times. Current loan quotes are for 8.00 percent interest on a 25-year schedule.

To develop the leasing holdback formula for Palquo's loan, enter Table 11, page 2 (p. 231), the page with 8.00 percent interest rate. From the 8.00 percent, 25-year schedule line, read the lendable amounts under these columns:

1.667 for 6.48 lendable amount

1.25 for 8.64 lendable amount

1.15 for 9.39 lendable amount

Dividing each lendable amount by the maximum lendable amount, the lender would advance 69 percent of the loan (6.48 ÷ 9.39) without regard to leasing, 92 percent of the loan (8.64 ÷ 9.39) when 60 percent leasing is achieved, and 100 percent of the loan when fully leased status is achieved.

In practice, lenders tend to be much more conservative than this schedule in setting rent holdback formulas. Most often this is the result of negotiation rather than of rational risk analysis. Table 11 may help demonstrate that one may appropriately permit more liberal holdbacks.

Equity Yield Implied by Financing Terms

Any given set of mortgage terms implies an equity yield. That is, if the loan is intended to have a certain loan-to-value ratio and the debt service coverage is estimated at a specified rate, then the equity yield can be inferred from those terms. The data in Table 13 serves as a useful check on how reasonable the mortgage terms are and whether the implied equity yield comports with estimates based on external data. It also shows where negative leverage leaves off and positive leverage begins.

Example 95. Equity Yield Implied by Mortgage Terms

Purvis St. John prepares proposals for the credit committee of the bank. The Bidgeon Builders' loan proposal is based on a 70 percent loan-to-value ratio, 11.00 percent mortgage constant, and debt service coverage of 1.175 times.

To find the implied equity yield, enter Table 13, page 2 (p. 236), the page for 11.00 percent mortgage constant. In the section for 70 percent loan-to-value ratio, read across on the line for 1.175 times debt service coverage to the 11.00 percent column and find the factor, 4.492 percent return on equity under these circumstances. This is consistent with the equity yield demanded in the marketplace, as indicated by the appraisal.

Example 96. Comparing Equity Yield Implied by Mortgage Terms to Loan Application

Mena Smithers has arranged a loan at 9.2 percent constant for her client. The proposal to the lender considers the deal to have a 75 percent loan-to-value ratio. Based on the estimated net operating income, the debt service coverage will be 1.2 times.

To find the equity yield implied by these terms, enter Table 13, page 1 (p. 235), the page which shows 9.2 percent annual mortgage constant. Read down the left column for loan-to-value ratio to the 75 percent section and find under the debt service coverage ratio the line for 1.200 times. Reading across on that line, find under the column headed 9.2 percent the answer 5.520 percent, the annual equity return associated with these mortgage terms.

If the loan proposal had indicated that the initial equity yield would be considerably more than 5.52 percent, she might be well advised to revisit the assumptions supporting that indication, as the "natural" yield does not support it.

Example 97.   Income Growth to Obtain Positive Leverage

Persifal Partners project that the financing available for their project will involve an 80 percent loan-to-value ratio and debt service coverage of 1.100 times. The loan will be at 9.80 percent constant.

To find the point of positive leverage, enter Table 13, page 2 (p. 236), the page with an annual mortgage constant of 9.80 percent. Locate the 80 percent loan-to-value section and within it the line for 1.100 times coverage. On that line under the column headed 9.80 percent constant, read 3.92 percent, the initial return on equity with these mortgage terms. Since the equity yield at about 4 percent is far below the constant of 9.80 percent, the property is very negatively leveraged. Down the column under 9.80 percent, the listing next to 1.250 times coverage shows an equity yield of 9.80 percent. The net operating income would have to be greater by 13.6 percent (1.25 ÷ 1.10) before the project would become positively leveraged. (Alternatively, the loan-to-value ratio could be lowered.)

Rapid Amortization of a Loan

Example 98.   Rapid Amortization of a Commercial Loan

Maartens has a lease with a major corporation for his entire building. The lease is for a term of 5 years. He has asked for a loan of $250,000 at 10.375 percent interest, based on the credit strength of the tenant, although $200,000 would be the maximum loan under ordinary conditions. The lender is willing to make the $250,000 loan, provided that the $50,000 "overboard" amount is fully amortized within the first 5 years. The other $200,000 would also be at 10.375 percent and would amortize on a 20-year schedule.

The total payment is the sum of the payment on the rapidly amortized portion plus the payment on the regular portion. First obtain the constants by entering Table 35 (a), page 6 (p. 426), at 10.375 percent interest. In the column at 5 years under 10.375 percent, read the first constant, 25.718436 percent, and, in the column under 20 years under 10.375 percent, read the second, 11.879969 percent. Now multiply the rapid amortization component by the first constant and the regular component by the second

$$\$50,000 \times 0.25718436 = \$12,859.22 \div 12 = \$1,071.61$$

$$200,000 \times 0.11879969 = \underline{23,759.94} \div 12 = \underline{1,980.00}$$
$$\$36,619.16 \div 12 = \$3,051.61$$

This is the total monthly debt service to amortize 20 percent of the loan in the first 5 years and the remainder over the following 15 years. The monthly payments to be inserted in the mortgage note are $3051.61 during the first 60 months and $1980.00 during the following 180 (240 − 60) months.

Cross-Reference   Another method of rapid amortization is shown in Example 56 in Chapter 2.

Amount Accrued on Bow-Tie Loans (Where Pay Rate Is Less Than Accrual Rate)

Table 14 gives the amount accrued on bow-tie loans. With a bow-tie loan, the interest rate paid in cash currently (called the **pay rate**) is less than the total interest rate accruing on the loan. The difference between the face rate on the loan and the pay rate is the accrual rate, and the interest not paid in cash is called the "accrual." The accrual is usually paid, at least in part, from a share of the cash flow of the mortgaged premises. Any accrual not paid from cash flow or other means must be paid at maturity.

This type of loan is useful but dangerous. Useful, because the loan makes possible financing for deals which could not otherwise support the accrual rate. Dangerous, because the accrual mounts rapidly to an unsupportable level. Table 14 assists selection of a bow-tie with manageable risk.

Example 99. Amount Accrued on Bow-Tie Loan

Mallkin Insurance considers making a real estate loan for an apartment complex to be built. Based on appraisals, the loan-to-value ratio will be 75 percent. But the project will not have adequate cash flow to pay the current interest rate of 10.50 percent in its first few years. A pay rate of 8.00 percent per year has been proposed by the prospective borrower. Mallkin will consider the bow-tie loan but would like the accrual to build up to no more than one-half of the 25 percent appraised equity in the deal.

To find when the accrual will exceed 12.5 percent of the property value, first consider that 12.5 percent of property value is one-sixth of the loan amount $(0.125 \div 0.75 = 0.16667)$ or 16.667 percent. So the question becomes how long will it be until the accrual reaches 16 percent of the loan?

Now enter Table 14, page 1 (p. 237), the page for pay rate of 8.00 percent. Reading down the column headed 10.50 percent, the accrual rate, note that the accrual reaches 16 percent—16.3477—at the end of the fifth year. Since Mallkin expects that the property will be flowing enough cash flow to service the accrual rate before the fifth year, the accrual should not reach the level of one-half of the equity in the deal.

Example 100. Minimum Interest Yield from a Lease

Devonre Bank has been asked to provide construction financing of $1.6 million on a warehouse. There is no takeout commitment for the 1-year loan. There is, however, a 15-year lease to Mapitra Console at a net rent of $178,000 per year. The bank officer would like to know what the yield to the bank would be if no takeout becomes available and the bank had to rely solely on the rentals to retire its loan. Begin by finding the rent constant. Do this by dividing the annual net rentals by the loan amount, to get

$$\$178,000 \div \$1,600,000 = 0.111250$$

or 11.125 percent annual rent constant. Now enter Table 35 (b) at its first page (p. 432). Read down the years column to 15 and across on that line searching for a constant close to 11.125 percent. Since none is found on this page, continue to the next page, staying on the 15-year line and the zero month column. The closest constant is on page 5 of the table, 11.124148 percent, the page for 7.50 percent.

Therefore, if no revenue but the rentals from Mapitra Console were received over the 15 years, the bank would have slightly more than 7.50 percent return on its money and its money back. The return is greater than 7.50 percent, because the rent constant is slightly greater than found in this example and because rent would come at the beginning of the month, whereas this is an end-of-month table.

Time When Given Mortgage Balance Occurs

The balance declines slowly in the early stages of a mortgage loan, because the interest takes most of the early payments, leaving only a small part as principal reduction. Ten years of monthly payments are needed to pay off the first tenth of a 9.50 percent, 30-year loan, but only 13 months are needed to pay off the last tenth. Table 67 tells when important mortgage balance benchmarks are achieved for different interest rates and amortization schedules.

Small differences will occur from the schedules provided by lenders. Table 67 is precise, but round-offs of mortgage payments can add up over many years to a month or so.

Example 101. Time When Given Mortgage Balance Occurs

Vogel will open Phase I of Phenomenon Business Park now. It is financed with an 11.00 percent mortgage on a 12-year schedule. He expects to start Phase II when the Phase I mortgage is paid down to 75 percent.

To find when the loan balance of Phase I will reach 75 percent, enter Table 67, page 5 (p. 770), at the section for 11.00 percent. Read across on the line for 12 years' amortization schedule to the 75 percent column. The answer 4Y 9m means that with the payment for the ninth month of the fifth year, the loan will be slightly under 75 percent of its original amount.

Number of Payments to Retire a Loan

Table 59 gives the number of monthly payments needed to fully amortize a mortgage loan. The table assumes that the first payment is made 30 days after closing the loan. In some places, the entry is "unl" for "unlimited," which means the payment is less than the interest accrued during a month and a loan would never be amortized.

Example 102. Difference in Number of Payments at Different Rates

Van der Griff is negotiating with Swenson regarding the purchase money mortgage to be taken back in connection with the sale of The Windows Apartments. There is no disagreement about the amount of the loan, $1 million, or that level monthly payments of $12,500 to principal and interest are to be made to amortize the loan fully. But they disagree on interest rate, the buyer holding out for a 7.50 percent rate and the seller insisting on 8.00 percent. Swenson wonders if the difference is important enough to be worth protracted negotiation.

To find the difference in the number of payments, first find the monthly constant. It is $12,500 ÷ $1,000,000 = 0.01250 = 1.25 percent. Now enter Table 59, page 1 (p. 722); read down the monthly payment column to 1.25 percent. Read across on that line and find under the column headed 7.50 percent the figure 111.2 months. To the right of it, under 8.00 percent, find 114.7 months. The higher interest rate will require 3.5, that is, 114.7 − 111.2, more months to amortize fully than the lower rate, or about 3.0 percent longer.

Amount of a Mortgage Amortized by a Given Payment

Table 58 is the reverse of a mortgage constant table and serves an important role in developing the financing plan. Rather than the amount of payment that will retire a given loan, the table gives the initial loan amount that may be paid off from specified payments and interest rate. The entries are given in multiples, not percentages, of the payment amount.

The payments begin after a "draw delay." The loan is made on day 1; then, after a delay of 1 month, 1 year, or more, the first payment is made. Interest compounded monthly accrues at the nominal annual rate chosen at all times.

Example 103. Amount of Loan Available from a Given Payment

Partners in Realty have negotiated a 20-year lease at a fixed rent from a major corporation. The lease will pay $7480 per month rent. Two lenders have given offers of financing. One will make the loan on the basis of 8.00 percent, fully amortized within the 20-year term of the lease. The other will charge 8.25 percent, but will accept a 5-year **hangout**. That is, the loan would run 25 years, leaving the last 5 years of payments to hang out in terms of credit risk against the **residual value** of the land. In either case, the debt service coverage requirement will be 1.10 times.

Begin by finding the amount available for debt service. It is $7480 ÷ 1.10 = $6800. To find the financing amounts of the two proposed loans, enter Table 58, page 1 (p. 716), at 8.00 percent. Read down the left column and get the first factor on the line for 240 months under 8.00 percent. It is 119.55429 times. Now on the line for 300 months, get the factor under the column for 8.25 percent interest, which is 126.83110 times. Multiply each factor by the monthly payment:

$$\$6,800 \times 119.55429 = \$812,969$$

the loan amount at 8.00 percent, 20 years, and

$$\$6,800 \times 126.83110 = \$862,451$$

the loan amount at 8.25 percent, 25 years, in either case based on debt service coverage of 1.10 times.

Construction Financing

Construction financing is the term applied in this book to all short- and medium-term loans up to 84 months used to build or rehabilitate property. From the financial point of view, the important characteristic of the construction loan is not construction per se but the process of drawing the loan funds down over time, usually with a floating rate. This lowers the average balance of the financing, heightens the sensitivity of yield to discounts, and makes interest rate swings in the late stages of the loan more costly.

Example 104. Effect of Change in Prime Rate

Mannesmann Builders is offered a 1-year construction loan package by its banker that includes interest at a rate of 2 percent over the **floating prime rate**. Since the prime is currently 8.75 percent, the present rate would be 10.75 percent but would go up or down as the prime rate fluctuates.

A finance company has offered Mannesmann a loan package that is equivalent except for a fixed interest rate of 11.50 percent. The bank loan is apparently a bargain, but Mannesmann is of the opinion that prime is likely to rise over the 2-year term of the construction loan. They feel that the probable rate rise is of the order of 2 percent over the term of the loan.

To find the effect of prime rate changes, enter Table 15, page 3 (p. 243), the page for a term of 12 months and 10.75 percent interest rate at start of loan. Read down the left column for an increase in rate of 2.00 percent and across to the column headed 10.75 percent. Find there the rate 11.97 percent, the equal level rate if interest goes up. This is the fixed rate that would produce equal interest cost, given that the loan balance is rising as the rate is rising. It is not the average interest *rate*; that would be 11.75 percent (10.75 + 12.75 divided by 2). The equal level rate is higher than the average rate because the highest balance on the loan coincides with the highest rate. The interest cost for the floating rate deal of 11.97 percent per year compares unfavorably with the rate quotation from the finance company of 11.50 percent fixed.

Example 105.   Whether to Lock in a Mortgage Loan

Promestica Corporate Builders has a construction loan at 11.25 percent, floating with the prime rate. The loan is expected to have a 50 percent average balance. They have the choice to stay with this loan for 3 more years or they can obtain a 9.00 percent fixed rate on a 3-year loan with 30-year schedule, by paying 2½ points.

Begin by finding the yield on the fixed rate loan. Enter Table 25, page 15 (p. 303), the page for 9.00 percent interest. In the 30-year section, read down the left column to 3 years and across to the column headed 2.50 points. The answer there, 9.977 percent, is the yield on the fixed rate loan. The yield on the fixed rate deal at 9.977 percent compares well with the current rate of 11.25 percent, which might float higher.

Promestica will consider also the cash flow implications. Since the annual constant of the fixed rate loan is 66 basis points higher than the interest rate, the cash flow cost of the fixed rate deal is almost 10.63 percent. Cash will also be needed for the 2½-point payment. This means that the actual cash outlays on the fixed rate deal will exceed 12.00 percent in the coming year. Although offset later by interest of only 9.00 percent, the short-term cash disadvantage might outweigh the yield advantage for many developments, where cash is critical in the early stages.

Average Balance on Construction Loans and Miniperms

The average balance on a **construction loan** or **minipermanent** (or **miniperm**) loan is shown in Table 16 (p. 253). The first half of the table covers construction loans, by which we mean loans of any short- or medium-term duration that are disbursed in monthly segments. The second half covers miniperms, which for our purposes are defined as construction loans followed by a period of several years after construction during which the loans remain outstanding.

Example 106.   Average Outstanding Balance on a Construction Loan

To find the average balance on a construction loan, enter the upper half of Table 16 (p. 253) and read down the column loan term to the correct line. Read across on that line to the appropriate initial draw: If the initial draw will be in proportion to the rest of the loan, for example one-twelfth of the loan on a 12-month loan, then the correct column will be that marked proportion. If the initial draw will be another ratio, use the column for the percentage closest to the actual case. Select the column headed by the number of months in the loan and read the answer, which is the percentage of the loan amount that will be outstanding on average throughout the loan.

Example 107.   Average Outstanding Balance on a Miniperm Loan

A miniperm loan is in effect a construction loan followed by a single-repayment loan of 1 to 5 years' duration. The loan balance builds up during the construction period to 100 percent and then remains outstanding until maturity. ASCII Programmers Group are calculating the interest cost of their new office building. They will receive a miniperm loan with 12 months' construction period, followed by a 5-year term loan.

To find the average balance, enter Table 16 (p. 253) and read down the left column, full funding, to 60 months, the time the full loan will be outstanding. Read across on that line to the 12-month column. The answer there, 92.36 percent, is the percentage of the loan that will be outstanding on average throughout the loan.

Amount of Construction Loan Interest Reserve

Construction lenders normally hold back a portion of the loan proceeds as a reserve, from which the interest payments are drawn over the life of the loan. Table 17 shows the interest reserve as a percentage of the full loan before consideration of the reserve. The reserve amount is usually added to give the total loan amount.

Except for the interest paid from the reserve, the loan is assumed to be drawn in equal proportionate **draws** each month to produce the average balance in question. Note that as loan interest is drawn from the interest reserve, there will be interest on the draws, in effect giving interest on interest. The table has allowed for such compounding.

Example 108. Amount of Construction Loan Interest Reserve

Hochton & Hoogkaamp are preparing the construction budget for Freelton Apartments. The cost before construction loan interest will be $1.56 million. The construction loan will be for 18 months at 9.50 percent interest. H&H believe that the average balance on the loan will be 55 percent. Enter Table 17, page 2 (p. 255), at the section for 18-month loans. Read across on the line for 55 percent average balance to the column headed 9.50 percent. The factor there, 8.39 percent, is the percentage of budget needed for the interest reserve. Multiply the factor by the loan amount to get

$$\$1,560,000 \times 0.0839 = \$130,884$$

or, rounding to the next thousand, $131,000, the needed interest reserve to service a 9.50 percent, 18-month loan with 55 percent average balance. The reserve will be added to the $1,560,000 base loan to give $1,691,000 total financing.

Example 109. Construction Loan Yield When Points Are Paid— Comparing Higher Interest with Points

Two lenders have given quotations for a construction loan. The first will make the loan at an interest rate of 3.5 percent over the **prime rate** with no points. Since the prime rate is 7.25 percent, this means a 10.75 percent interest rate. The second lender requires only 2.00 percent over prime but will charge a fee of 1.5 points. Either way, the loan would be for a term of 1 year and probably would have an outstanding balance of 60 percent of the loan amount. At the moment, it is expected that the prime rate will remain constant.

Enter Table 26, page 8 (p. 326), at the section for 9.25 percent (2.00 percent over a presumed 7.25 percent prime rate) and 1.5 points. Read across on the line for 12 months to the column headed 60 percent. Read there the yield on the loan, 11.914 percent. Since the quotation for 3.5 percent over prime rate gives a 10.75 percent cost, it is the better quotation, considering only probable interest cost.

Note The yield curve should be consulted to estimate if a constant prime-rate assumption is justified. See Example 73 earlier in this chapter.

Example 110. Amount of a Construction Loan Interest Reserve to Cover Rate Change

Kliquan is preparing the cost budget for a $1 million construction loan. The loan will bear interest at 1 percent over the prime rate, now 8 percent, and is expected to have an average balance of 55 percent. The loan will be for 2 years, and Kliquan wants to ensure that the interest reserve will be adequate to cover a rise of 1.50 percent in the interest rate.

To establish the amount of the reserve, first find the annual interest cost. Do this by entering Table 15, page 8 (p. 248), the page with 9.00 percent interest at the start of the loan and 24 months. Read down the column for increase in rate of 1.50 percent and across on the line for equal level rate to the column 9.00 percent. Find there the equal level rate of 9.96 percent. Multiply the loan amount by the equal level rate and the average loan balance to get

$$\$1,000,000 \times 0.55 \times 0.0996 \times 2 \text{ (years)} = \$109,560$$

the dollar amount of the interest reserve for the loan.

YIELD ON MORTGAGE LOANS

Nominal Rates versus Effective Rates

An interest rate equals its nominal rate only if the interest is paid at the end of the expressed interval. Reference to 8.00 percent per year should mean that interest is paid at the end of the year, but often monthly payments are actually made. Monthly payments give most of the interest before year-end, so the lender has use of it to earn additional interest. The higher rate is called the **effective annual rate.** Table 33 shows the effective rates for any nominal rate and the conversion of effective rates back to nominal rates.

Example 111.   Effective Interest Rate from Nominal Annual Rate

Selblanc has a commitment from Foreseeable Life at an interest rate stated to be "a nominal annual interest rate of 11.50 percent, payable monthly in arrears." To find the effective interest rate, enter Table 33 (a), page 4 (p. 408), and read down to a nominal rate of 11.50 percent. On that line under monthly, read 12.126 percent, the effective interest rate on the loan.

Yield on Loans When Points Are Paid

Charging points is one way to discount a loan. Real estate lenders prefer **points** to interest. A point is a payment to a lender equal to 1 percent of the amount of the loan. Points increase the yield to the lender, just as a higher rate of interest would do. But points have the advantage for the lender that, if the loan is prepaid, the lender retains the points, whereas the higher interest rate would cease.

Table 25 assumes that the points are paid **in front,** that is, at the beginning of the loan. If the points will be paid **in back,** that is, at time of payoff of the loan, see Example 118 or Table 27.

Example 112.   Yield on Mortgage Loan When Points Are Paid

Churchill Crenell offers mortgage financing at 8.00 percent on a 25-year amortization schedule. The loan will come due at the end of 10 years, and Crenell requires a payment at closing of 5 points (5 percent of the loan amount) for the loan.

To find the yield to the lender, enter Table 25, page 11 (p. 299), the page for 8.00 percent interest and 25-year schedule. Read down the column headed yield to end of year to 10 years. Read across on that line to the column headed 5.00 points and find the answer, 8.809 percent, the compounded annual yield to the lender.

If a truth-in-lending (TIL) disclosure is needed—for most commercial loans it is not—the **annual per-**centage rate, or APR, is also 8.809 percent, rounded for TIL purposes to 8.81 percent. This is also the yield to one who buys the loan at a discount of 5 points.

Example 113.   Yield on Balloon Loan When Points Are Paid and Yield on Loan Paid before Maturity

Five years ago, Lee Yapp borrowed at 10.00 percent on a 30-year loan schedule. Lee paid 4.00 points at that time. He now wishes to pay the loan in full, which his loan documents permit him to do without prepayment premium (but with no credit for the "unused" points). He wants to know what yield the lender will have had on the loan.

To find the yield to the lender, enter Table 25, page 19 (p. 307), the page for 10.00 percent interest. In the section for a 30-year schedule read down the left column to year 5 and across on that line to the column headed 4 points. Read there the answer, 11.070 percent, the yield to a lender who received 4 points at the start of the loan and is paid off at the end of the fifth year.

Yield on Construction Loan When Points Are Paid

Construction loan yield, when points are paid, is more difficult to calculate than ordinary loan yield. Added to the normal compound discount problem is the fact that the outstanding balance is changing each month, normally upward, as the construction progresses and **draws** on the loan are made. Points are more significant in the yield of a construction loan than in the usual case. Since this loan's average balance is much lower than that of a 20-year or 30-year loan, the points figure more prominently in the calculation. Table 26 gives the yield in these cases.

Example 114.   Yield on Construction Loan When Points Are Paid

A construction loan is available at an interest rate of 9.00 percent plus a fee of 2 points. The loan term is 18 months. The estimated average balance on the loan is 55 percent of the total commitment.

To find the yield to the lender, enter Table 26, page 8 (p. 326), the section for loans at 9.00 percent.

Read down the column, points paid, to 2.00 points. Now read across on the line for 18 months to the column headed 55 percent average balance. The yield there, 11.654 percent, is the annual yield to the lender on a loan with 55 percent average balance and a fee of 2 points.

Yield on Loan When Compensating Balances Are Kept

Compensating balances are bank deposits without interest that a commercial bank requires a borrower to keep. The lender gets additional yield from this arrangement, since it is lending back some of the borrower's own money (at least the part that is not needed for reserve requirements). The borrower benefits, because it would have some money on deposit in any case, for which nonbank lenders would give no credit at all.

Table 31 shows the yield to the lender when compensating balances are left. The balances to be reckoned with are "free balances," that is, those not needed to compensate the bank for other bank services, such as clearing checks.

Compensating balance arrangements may be based on the total amount of the bank's line of credit to the borrower. So compensating balances of 10 percent of the line means the borrower's deposits are to be 10 percent of the total available to be drawn. Other arrangements may call for a compensating balance equal to a part of the line plus a part of the loan itself; for example, 10 percent of the line plus 5 percent of the outstanding balance. This method of providing additional compensation compares fairly with payment of points, especially for borrowers with large cash flow through their accounts. (Note to bankers: The table gives the gross yield before deduction for reserve requirements.)

Example 115.   Yield on Loan When Compensating Balances Are Kept

CrediBank has offered a builder a line of credit for subdivision development at 9.25 percent plus compensating balances of 10 percent of the line and 10 percent of any amount borrowed. The builder expects that on average 50 percent of the line will be borrowed over the life of the loan. Since all the transaction elements are in proportion to time, the term of the loan is not necessary.

To find the yield to the lender, enter Table 31, page 1 (p. 401), in the section for 9.25 percent inter-

est. Read down to 10 percent of line plus 10 percent of loan and across on the line for 50 percent average balance to the column headed 9.25 percent. Read there the answer, 12.333 percent, the yield to the lender.

Example 116.   Yield on Loan When Some Deposits Already Maintained

Harell Property Managers are projecting the owner's cost for constructing an additional building in the Harell Office Park. A construction loan is available at 10.00 percent interest plus compensating balances of 10 percent of the commitment plus 10 percent of any borrowings. About 50 percent of the loan will be outstanding on average. Moreover the manager knows that deposits from the existing buildings are averaging about 10 percent of the construction commitment.

To find the yield to the lender, first consider that the "free" deposits from the existing buildings satisfy the requirement of "10 percent of commitment." Now enter Table 31, page 1 (p. 401), the page for 10.00 percent interest. Read across on the 5 percent of loan line to the column headed 10.00 percent and find there 10.526 percent, the cost of the borrowing to the owner in excess of the balances already maintained.

Example 117.   Yield on Loan When Buyer Deposits Maintained with the Lender

Parebrise-on-Sea Vacation Homes will be offered with a preconstruction sales program. Each purchaser will make an initial deposit of $500. Upon mortgage approval, they will bring this up to 10 percent of the purchase price. When the building foundation is complete, another 10 percent will be deposited; when the building is fully framed and under roof, a third 10 percent deposit will be posted. All deposits will be maintained in special escrow accounts at a commercial bank; interest will be paid in accordance with state law, which at present means 5.75 percent per year compounded monthly. Geoffrey Parebrise estimates the deposits will average 30 percent of the construction loan. The interest rate on the loan is expected to average 11.00 percent over the term of the loan. Since Parebrise has the power to direct at which bank the deposits will be lodged, he wants to point out to the construction lender the benefits it would have from these low-cost deposits.

First consider that, unlike other examples in this section, the bank is not getting these deposits "free," since it must pay interest on them. To find the effect of the "free" portion of the deposits, divide the free portion (11.00 percent − 5.75 percent = 5.25 percent) by the expected loan interest rate, to get

$$5.25\% \div 11.00\% = 0.4773 = 47.73\%$$

the effective portion of the deposits. Multiply this by the expected average deposits, 30 percent, to get

$$0.4773 \times 0.30 = 0.141319 = 14.3\%$$

or, rounding, 14 percent effective amount of deposits. Now enter Table 31 at the page for 11.00 percent interest. On the line for 15 percent, the closest deposit level, read under the 11.00 percent column the yield, 12.941 percent. The lender's effective yield would be slightly less than 12.941 percent from interest and use of low-cost deposits.

Yield on Loan When Prepayment Premium Is Paid and Yield from Points Paid at End of Loan

In a variety of cases, the loan agreement calls for one or more payments to the lender **in back,** that is, at the time of paying off a loan. Such payments raise the yield to the lender. The increase in yield is not as great as when points are paid **in front,** that is, at the start of the loan. Most often, the payment in back is a prepayment premium, but some deals are structured with loan points at the end of the loan term.

Example 118.   Yield on Loan When Prepayment Premium Is Paid

Connolly & Corklen made a loan on a 30-year schedule at 12.00 percent. Their borrower has the right to prepay with a 4-point premium (1 point equals 1 percent of the loan balance). Connolly & Corklen wish to know the yield on the loan, if it is prepaid at the end of the fifth loan year.

Start by entering Table 27, page 5 (p. 338), 12.00 percent interest. Read down the years to payoff column to 5 years and across on that line to the column headed 4 points. The answer there is 12.571 percent, the annual yield over the 5-year term to a lender who receives a 4-point prepayment premium on a 12.00 percent loan.

Cross-Reference   Table 43 gives the premium that would be needed to obtain a specified yield. Examples 302, 303, and 304 describe its use.

Yield on Wraparound Mortgage Loan

Table 28 gives the true yield to the lender on the **new money** loaned on a **wraparound mortgage loan.**

A property owner may consider refinancing loan on realty to tap the increased equity in the property without the expenses, capital gains taxes, and possible recapture attendant on a sale. At the same time, the owner does not want to give up the old interest rate if it is below the current market. The wraparound loan is designed to deal with this situation.

In a wraparound or **all-inclusive mortgage** loan, the lender writes a new loan, as if the old loan were being paid off and a new mortgage put on the property. But, in fact, the lender leaves the old mortgage in place and makes what is legally a second mortgage loan. The wraparound loan is written for the amount of the first plus the second mortgages, but the wraparound lender advances only the amount of the second, called the new money. The borrower makes one monthly payment to the wraparound lender (who in turn makes the first mortgage payment to the original lender).

Borrowers benefit, since interest rates on wraparound loans preserve at least some of the benefit of the old interest rate and give an overall rate lower than the market. For the wraparound lender, the yield on new money is usually better than can be had for a customary loan. The technique is particularly interesting for purchase money transactions, but the concept is valid for a wide range of mortgage deals.

Note   In purchase money transactions with noninstitutional lenders, the borrower will usually want to continue to make the payment to the old lender. The aim is to avoid a credit risk, namely that the wraparound lender fail to make the primary payment. At the same time, the wraparound lender will want to ensure that the old lender is paid on time, so it will want to receive the full payment, from which it will remit the payment to the old lender. Even though printed forms are available that seem proper for wraparound use, documentation of this impasse ought to be accomplished by legal counsel.

The wraparound lender should take care not to "assume" or otherwise imply that it guarantees payment to the first mortgagee. Its obligation should be limited to making the old mortgage payment when and if it receives the wraparound payments.

Example 119. Yield on New Money in a Wraparound Loan

Parallel Plaza is a 14-year-old shopping center which has a mortgage loan with $300,000 remaining at 6.50 percent interest. It has 10 years left until it will be fully amortized. Because of increased rents, the owner wants to refinance and take some equity out of the property. She hopes to obtain financing for $600,000, that is to say, $300,000 of new money. The current market quotation is 10.50 percent on a 25-year schedule, but her mortgage banker indicates that a wraparound loan is available for 9.5 percent for 25 years.

To find the yield to the lender, first obtain the ratio of new money to old money. The new money here is $300,000 in a $600,000 total, or 50 percent. So the new money/old money ratio is 50/50.

Now enter Table 28, page 4 (p. 342) (at the section for 50 percent new money). In the left column, find 25 years under new term. Within that section read across on the line under old term for 10 years to the column headed old rate for 6.50 percent. Find there 10.588 percent, the yield to the wraparound lender on the $300,000 new money in this transaction.

Yield on Shared Appreciation and Participating Mortgage Loans

Lenders recognize that inflation cuts the value of fixed rate mortgage loans. At the same time, it usually increases the value of the property whose construction or purchase was made possible by the lender. Seeing this as an imbalance, some lenders demand to receive a share of future profit, if any, by means of a shared appreciation mortgage, sometimes called a **SAM.**

In the customary shared appreciation loan, the lender receives a share of the profit at an agreed date. The profit is measured as the difference in the **net sale proceeds** or the **fair market value** of the property over its cost or appraised value at the time the loan is made. In Table 29, a growth rate is chosen to represent the value increase in the property. Thus, if a growth rate of 3 percent is selected, the results in the table will be based on the assumption that the value of the entire property will rise 3 percent each year, compounded.

A **participating** mortgage **loan** is, for the purposes of this book, a type of shared appreciation loan in which the lender receives not only a portion of the increase in value of the property over the term of the loan but also a portion of the increased cash flow during the term.

In Table 29, the lender is deemed to receive part of the appreciation, but no part of the annual cash flow. The companion table, Table 30, gives yields where the lender receives part of the annual increase in income of the property as well as part of the appreciation.

Note The terms *shared appreciation mortgage* and *participating mortgage* are not yet fixed by trade usage, so a lender is free to define them differently from what is presented here. The best course of action is to establish an express definition in the deal documentation. The financial calculations in Tables 29 and 30, however, follow the definition given here.

Example 120. Yield on Shared Appreciation Mortgage

Corvax has applied for a shared appreciation mortgage loan. The loan-to-value ratio will be 75 percent. The loan will have an amortization schedule of 30 years but will come due with a **balloon payment** at the end of 5 years. Market interest rates are 9.50 percent, but the lender will accept a coupon rate of 9.00 percent if it also receives 30 percent of the profit from sale of the property (or 30 percent of the increase in appraisal value, if Corvax decides not to sell). Corvax considers that a 3 percent annual rate of increase in property value is a reasonable expectation and would like to estimate the yield to the lender if that rate of growth occurs.

Enter Table 29, page 5 (p. 359), the page for a 75 percent loan-to-value ratio and a 3 percent growth rate of property value. Enter the section for 9.00 percent interest and read down the column for years to payoff to 5 years. Read across on the line to the column headed 30 percent (share of profit on sale) and find the yield, 10.004 percent, the yield on a 9.00 percent loan, 30-year schedule, 5-year term, if the lender receives 30 percent of the profit and the property value inflates 3 percent per year.

Example 121. When Yield Asked on Shared Appreciation Mortgage Greater than Available

Plenno Property is seeking a shared appreciation mortgage. The lender desires an 11.00 percent yield and will structure a 10-year deal based on 3 percent annual growth rate of property values. Plenno hopes to get a **face rate** of 9.00 percent, giving the lender a share of appreciation that will bring its total yield from 9.00 percent to 11.00 percent.

To find the share of profit needed to meet the lender's conditions, turn to Table 29, page 5 (p. 359), for property value increase of 3 percent per year and a 75 percent loan-to-value ratio. Enter the section for 9.00 percent, the rate that Plenno would like to achieve, and search on the 10-year line for an 11.00 percent rate. The lowest share that can meet the 11.00 percent requirement is the entry 11.091 under the 80 percent column, indicating that the lender would get four-fifths of the appreciation. Most likely this structure will not satisfy Plenno. Some alternatives would be (1) a lower loan-to-value ratio; (2) a higher fixed rate component, or (3) getting the lender to agree that a higher growth rate could be assumed.

Plenno might also consider a deal where the lender got 100 percent of the profit until it achieved an 11.00 percent yield, after which the profit would be split 50/50 or some other negotiated ratio.

Cross-Reference   Table 4 shows the future sale price that would yield 11.00 percent to the lender. Example 13 in Chapter 1 describes its use.

Yield on Participating Mortgage Loan

Example 122. Yield on Participating Mortgage Loan

Hasselly & Hafort have applied for a mortgage loan. The lender patterns its deals as follows: (1) a loan-to-value ratio of 75 percent, (2) initial debt service coverage ratio of 1.20 to 1.00, and (3) an interest rate consisting of a 10.00 percent fixed interest portion, plus a contingent interest of 50 percent of the increases in value and cash flow over the term of the loan. The loan will have a 10-year term and a 30-year amortization schedule. The CPI is expected to grow at an average of 3 percent annually over the 10-year term, and net rentals and real estate values should follow that same rate of increase.

To find the yield suggested by these deal terms and economic outlook, enter Table 30, page 12 (p. 384), the page for a 10.00 percent interest rate, 75 percent loan-to-value ratio, 3 percent growth rate, and 30-year schedule. Read down the debt coverage column to 1.200 and within that section read across

on the line for 10.0 years to payoff. Under the column for 50 percent share of increase in income and profit from sale, read the answer, 11.622 percent, the yield to the lender under this set of assumptions.

Example 123. Converting Participation Interest into Fixed Yield

Zlodny is seeking a participating mortgage loan from a foreign investor. The proposal to the lender is for a loan with an 80 percent loan-to-value ratio with 1.15 to 1 debt service coverage. Interest would consist of a 9.00 percent fixed rate plus a participation by the lender in 50 percent of the increases in cash flow and appreciation. The loan is to run for a 10-year term on a 30-year amortization schedule. The **financial pro forma** assumes 3 percent annual rate of growth of net rents. The investor points out that, under the tax treaty between its country and the United States, interest payments to it would be free of tax, whereas dividends from participation may be subject to withholding tax. The foreign lender therefore proposes that a fixed interest loan at a higher rate be used.

To find the fixed interest rate that would match Zlodny's proposal, find Table 30, page 11 (p. 383), the page for 9.00 percent interest, 75 percent loan-to-value ratio, 30-year amortization schedule, and 3 percent annual rate of growth. Now enter the section for 1.15 debt service coverage; on the line for 10 years, read across to the column headed 50 percent, where the answer, 10.660 percent, is given, the yield to the lender from these terms. Zlodny may suggest that in fairness the fixed rate should be made somewhat lower. About 18 percent of the overall yield, or $(10.66 - 9.00) \div 9.00$, of the participating loan requested by Zlodny would be contingent on future results. But under the lender's suggestion to fix the rate, it would become a firm obligation of the property, perhaps justifying a reduction in rate.

Simple Interest Yield from Add-on Interest

Add-on interest loans described in Table 32 are commonly used in financing cars, trucks, and various types of machinery. The payments are easily calculated. For example, assume a loan will run for 3 years at 4 percent interest add-on: 3 times 4 percent, or 12 percent, is added to the original amount of the loan, 100 percent. The total 112 percent is divided by 36 months to give a monthly payment of 3.1111 percent per month.

The yield from such a loan is more difficult to obtain. Table 32 gives the yield in actuarial terms, that is, true yield. The yields in Table 32 are also the annual percentage rate (APR), if the loan is a consumer loan governed by the truth-in-lending disclosure requirements.

Example 124.   Yield from Add-on Interest Loan

RCKT Scientific Corporate Services is buying a van to take service personnel to different portions of the RCKT Science Campus. The auto manufacturer offers financing at "6.90 percent APR" for 48 months. The local bank is prepared to handle the same loan at 4.00 percent add-on interest.

Since the manufacturer's loan is already quoted in APR terms, it is only necessary to look up the value of the bank quote. Find Table 32, page 1 (p. 403), the page for 4.00 percent add-on interest. Read down the months column to 48 and across to the column headed 4.00 percent, and read 7.474 percent, the annual interest yield from the add-on interest loan. From the standpoint of interest rate only, the loan from the manufacturer is about ½ percent per year better.

Example 125.   Yield on a Single-Payment Note

Norbert will take back a purchase money second mortgage as part of a sale. The mortgage is in lieu of $100,000 of sale proceeds. It is a "slow note," requiring no payments until the end of 5 years, when a single payment of $125,000 for both principal and interest will come due.

To find the yield, enter Table 6, page 1 (p. 188), and read down the left column to 5 years. Then read across to the column headed 25 percent, that is ($125,000 − 100,000) ÷ $100,000, and read the answer, 4.563 percent, the compounded annual yield from the slow note.

Chapter 4
PLANNING THE USE OF PROCEEDS

Planning what will be done with the money coming from real estate transactions may seem presumptuous, but it is sound on two levels. First, an axiom of real estate is that profits are made on the buy, not on the sell. The best deals are those where you anticipate the most probable outcome at the time of purchase. That way, the critical factors are negotiated keeping in mind your future buyer, the one who actually delivers the profit to you. Second, understanding the dynamics of reinvesting helps you to understand investing. Sketching tomorrow's potential highlights today's needs and makes concrete what is being given up in negotiations.

This chapter targets the uses of the financial tables as they apply to money problems other than just those of real estate, such as how to plan deposits that will pay inflation-adjusted dividends and how to balance gifts or bequests to heirs.

ESTABLISHING A FUND FOR FUTURE INCOME OR EXPENSE

The first group of examples shows how much must be placed on deposit at interest to give a certain number, amount, and type of payments.

Amount of Fund to Provide a Number of Withdrawals

Table 58 shows how much must be deposited to permit a given number of level withdrawals, that is, withdraw-als of the same monthly amount. The entries are given in multiples, not percentages, of the desired withdrawal. Payments are assumed to begin after a "draw delay." This may be 1 month or 1 year or more. After the selected draw delay, the first withdrawal is taken from the fund. Interest on the account balance is compounded monthly at the selected rate at all times.

Example 126. Deposit Needed to Build Education Fund

Ramon Ziegle will use proceeds of Mannick Manor to cover expenses of a delayed college education. A fund will be set aside now, and in 2 years, monthly payments of $5000 will be sent to Ziegle from the account which will be earning 8.50 percent interest.

To find the deposit needed to establish the fund, enter Table 58, page 2 (p. 717), at the section for a draw delay of 24 months and 8.50 percent interest. Read down the term column to 48 payments and across on that line to the column headed 8.50 percent. The factor there, 34.49122, is the investment as a multiple of the payments needed to provide the fund. Multiply it by the dollar amount of the payments to get

$$\$5000 \times 34.49122 = \$172,456$$

the amount that will fund 48 payments of $5000 per month with a 2-year delay after deposit, when the interest rate is 8.50 percent per year.

Example 127.   Amount Needed to Establish Trust Fund with Changing Distributions

Syrita and Jeffrey plan to establish a trust fund for their favorite charity's building program. They will make an original gift of $250,000, which will be deposited at interest, currently a rate of 10.00 percent. The fund and its interest earnings will be distributed in a 12-year program as follows: Monthly payments will be made to use up 60 percent of the fund in the first 5 years. Thereafter, monthly payments will be made at a rate to distribute the entire fund in 7 additional years.

To establish the first portion of the program, enter Table 36, page 5 (p. 451), the page for 10.00 percent interest. On the line for 5 years, read across to the 60 percent to the amortized column and find the factor, 19.29783 percent. Now enter Table 35 (a), page 6 (p. 426). Read across on the 7-year line to 10.00 percent; the factor there is 19.921421 percent. With the materials now to construct the payments, multiply the first factor by the full amount of the trust fund to get

$$\$250,000 \times 0.1929783 = \$48,244.58$$

or $4020.39 per month during the first 5 years of the program. Next, multiply the original fund by 40 percent, the amount remaining after 5 years, and by the second factor to get

$$\$250,000 \times 0.40 \times 0.19921421 = \$19,921.42$$

or $1660.12 per month during the remaining 7 years.

Fund to Provide Payments Changing at a Constant Rate

Table 47 illustrates the present value of payments that increase (section a) or decrease (section b) in each period. In either section, the assumption is that the payments change at a constant rate. So, an initial increase of 10 percent means that in subsequent years the increase will be 11.0 percent, 12.1 percent, and so on. Table 47 deals with a constant *rate* of change, such as 3 percent per period. Table 48 involves changes of a constant *amount* each period, such as $1000 per period. Both Tables 47 and 48 are constructed for payments at the end of each year.

WITHDRAWALS FROM A FUND
Fund to Permit Withdrawals Increasing at a Constant Rate

Example 128.   Fund to Permit Increasing Withdrawals

Martin Boland will place the proceeds of Rathskelly Cellars in an investment account. He wants to draw $60,000 per year from the account in the first year, with this amount increasing each year by 5.0 percent. The investment account carries a guaranteed minimum rate of 7.50 percent, although it might go higher. He wants the withdrawals to be available for 25 years minimum.

To find the necessary deposit to start this account, enter Table 47 (a), page 2 (p. 585) at the page for 5.0 percent annual rate of growth and 7.50 percent interest. Read down the left column to 25 years and under the 7.50 percent column find 17.78834, the multiple of the annual payment. Multiply this by the annual withdrawals to get

$$\$60,000 \times 17.78834 = \$1,067,300$$

the deposit to ensure 25 years of withdrawals, beginning at $60,000 in the first year, rising 5 percent per year thereafter, if interest is at least 7.50 percent per year.

Example 129.   Purchase Price of a Rising Annuity

Tilmon Farriday has asked his bank for an annuity that will pay out over a 10-year period. The payment at the end of the first year is to be $5000, then rising 10 percent each year thereafter. So the payments would be $5000, $5500, $6050, $6655, and so on. The bank's current interest rate on long-term deposits is 8.00 percent.

To find the amount the bank should charge, enter Table 47 (a), page 8 (p. 591), the section for 10 percent annual rate of growth. Read down to 10 years and across on that line to the 8.00 percent column. The factor there, 10.07023, is the multiple of the initial payment. Multiply the factor by the dollar amount of the initial payment to get

$$\$5000 \times 10.07023 = \$50,351.15$$

the price of an annuity to pay $5000 initially rising 10 percent each year when interest is 8.00 percent.

(Most banks compound interest more frequently than annually, so the price should be somewhat less.)

Fund to Permit Payments Changing by a Constant Amount

Table 48 provides for a series of payments which rise in constant amount each period, for example, a payment of $10,000, rising $500 per year. The amount of the first change (which occurs in the second year) is expressed as a percentage, but it is *not* compounded. So the $500 would be expressed as a 5 percent *initial* amount of growth.

Example 130. Fund to Permit Payments Rising in Constant Amount

---

Melinda Cassapolis will set aside part of the sale proceeds of Part-i-Mart to guarantee certain expenses that are now $40,000 but which have been rising at $2000 per year. The fund will earn interest at 6.50 percent per year.

To find the needed initial funding amount, first determine the amount of first-year growth. It is $2000 ÷ 100,000 = 0.05 or 5.0 percent. Enter Table 48 (a), page 2 (p. 612), at the section for 5.0 percent first-year growth. Read down the left column to 6 years and across to the 6.50 percent column. The factor there, 5.40179, is the multiple of the annual payment. Multiply it by the initial annual payment to get

$$\$40,000 \times 5.40179 = \$216,071.60$$

the funding that will be needed to ensure 6 years of payments starting at $40,000 and rising $2000 per year, with interest at 6.50 percent per year.

Payments Decreasing by a Constant Amount

Table 48 (b) gives the initial amount to provide a series of payments with stepped declines. The series begins at a certain level and after the first year declines by some amount, for example a $12,000 payment, declining $600 per year. The amount of the first change is expressed as a percentage but then remains constant in each succeeding year; for a $600 decrease, equal to 5 percent in the first year, the payments in succeeding years would be $12,000, $11,400, $10,800, and so on.

Negative numbers appear in the lower, later portions of the table, the result of the decline continuing at fixed amounts and becoming a larger portion of the total. It signifies that eventually there is no value to a stream of payments going below zero.

Example 131. Fund to Permit Payments Decreasing by Constant Amount

---

Perry Tan will establish a fund at 9.50 percent interest to assist his child with living expenses from age 21 to 30. Since the child will be entering the work force and presumably will receive increases in salary as time goes by, Tan will provide an initial amount of $12,000 per year which will decline by $1200, or 10 percent, each year.

To find the amount needed to establish this fund, enter Table 48 (b), page 8 (p. 630), at the section for 9.50 percent interest and 10.0 percent amount of first-year decline. On the 10-year line, under 9.50 percent, find the factor, 3.91705, and multiply it by the initial rate of payment to get

$$\$12,000 \times 3.91705 = \$47,005$$

or, rounding, $47,000, the amount needed to provide 10 years of payments beginning at $12,000 and declining $1200 per year.

Amount of Withdrawals Available from a Fund

Up to this point, we have considered only the initial amount necessary to create a fund from which certain payments could be drawn. We turn now to the amount of the payments that could be drawn from a fund.

Example 132. Amount of Monthly Withdrawals Available from a Deposit Account

---

Jennifer Marciak intends to deposit $100,000 in an account that will be invested to earn 10.50 percent per year, compounded monthly. She wants to draw a monthly check from the account, so that the fund and the interest earnings on it will be depleted at the end of 8 years, 7 months.

To find the amount of monthly withdrawals that will be available from this account, find Table 35 (b), page 11 (p. 442), the page for 10.50 percent. Read down the years column to 8 and across on that line to the 7 months column. The factor there, 17.726207 percent, is the percentage of the original deposit to be drawn each year. Multiply the deposit amount by the factor and divide by 12 to get

$$\$100,000 \times 0.17726207 \div 12 = \$1477.18$$

the monthly payment that may be drawn for 8 years and 7 months from an account earning interest at 10.50 percent per year, compounded monthly.

Example 133. Amount of Monthly Withdrawals from a Deposit Earning Taxable Income

For an account earning taxable interest, the size of the after-tax withdrawals will be considerably lower than the before-tax results. Ernst Beyer has sold Vienna Tor and will guarantee the performance of the property for 3 years. He will establish a $50,000 reserve account at a bank, from which cash flow may be drawn to supplement rentals, if that should be necessary. The account can earn 8.75 percent interest. If withdrawals must be available for 3 years minimum, what amount can be drawn monthly from the account, given that Beyer will remain in a 33 percent tax bracket in the coming years?

Begin by finding the after-tax income rate to Beyer. It is 100 minus the tax bracket, or 100 percent − 33 percent = 67 percent. The after-tax interest rate is 67 percent of the interest rate of the account, or

$$8.75 \times 0.67 = 5.8625$$

or, rounding to the nearest one-sixteenth of 1 percent, 5.875 percent. Now enter Table 35 (a), page 1 (p. 421), the page for 5.875 percent, and read down to 3 years. On that line under 5.875 percent, read the factor, 36.438398 percent. Multiply this by the deposit amount and divide by 12 to get

$$\$50,000 \times 0.36438398 \div 12 = \$1518.26$$

the minimum monthly after-tax draw available from the account.

Drawing Increasing Amounts from a Fund

Table 65 shows how to construct a series of payments that rise each year by a given percentage. The first withdrawal is assumed to be made on the day the ac-count is established. On each anniversary, the withdrawal increases by the annual rate of increase for that section. In addition to rising a certain percentage each year, the series of payments is also constructed so it has a present value equal to a series of payments of the amount shown as "level." The level amount is the time-weighted average payment from the series. A level withdrawal could be used in a series instead of the rising amounts.

The entries are given in percentages of the initial deposit and are annual figures; divide by 12 to get the monthly amount. Example 134 shows how to construct the rising series when the initial value of the fund is known. Example 135 shows how to proceed when the level or standard payment is known but the value or initial deposit is not known.

Example 134. Rising Withdrawals from a Fund

Madeleine MacPherson has sold Bahama Bay Apartments for cash. The equity proceeds after payment of the mortgage are $340,000. She wishes to establish a bank account that will pay this money to her monthly, so as to exhaust the account and the interest earned on it over a 10-year period. To offset the effects of the increased cost of living, she wants the payments to her to increase 3 percent each year. Her bank will give her a fixed 9.00 percent rate of interest on the account.

To find the initial payment, find Table 65, page 1 (p. 738). In the section for a 10-year plan, read across on the line for year 1 to the column headed 9.00 percent. The factor there, 13.31553 percent, is the first year total. Divide it by 12 and multiply by the dollar amount to get

$$\$340,000 \times 0.1331553 \div 12 = \$3772.73$$

the monthly check drawable in the first year. Each year after the first, the payments will rise by 3.0 percent. They can be calculated by the same procedure. For year 2, payments will be $3885.91 per month; the tenth-year payments will be $4922.56 per month.

Example 135. Rising Payment from an Obligation

Phelps Foley & Company will receive a purchase money mortgage as part of the payment for the parking lot adjoining their building. The note will provide $1000 per month for 60 months. The company would prefer to have the cash flow come in at an increasing rate, which would help to offset future office rental costs. A better plan for them would therefore be a payment that starts at less than $1000, but increases 5.0 percent each year. The borrower will pay the increasing payment if it is financially equivalent. The purchase money note is at 7.50 percent, so this would be an agreeable rate for the calculations.

To find a series of payments that rise 5.0 percent each year and equals the level payment of $1000 in present value, find Table 66, page 5 (p. 756). In the section for 5-year plans, take the payment for year 1 listed under the 7.50 percent column. It is 91.0594 percent. Multiply this by the normal amount, $1000, to get

$$\$1000 \times 0.910594 = \$910.59$$

the mortgage payment to be made in the first year instead of $1000. For year 2 the payment would again be the product of $1000 times the figure in the table, 95.6124 percent for year 2, and so on.

Note Unless Phelps Foley & Company are anxious to encourage prepayment, they would require that the loan be **closed** or that a prepayment premium be paid to offset the loss of yield.

Amount of Monthly Withdrawals from a Series of Deposits

The examples to this point have been based on a fund of known amount or payments of known amount. The next case is a hybrid, in which the fund will be created by a series of deposits. Table 61 gives the amount of monthly withdrawals that may be taken out of a fund for a given period, after a series of monthly deposits. The format assumes that monthly deposits of a known amount are made for a time, after which withdrawals are taken out, with interest at all times on the balance remaining in the account.

Example 136.   Amount of Monthly Withdrawals from a Series of Deposits

---

Belda Ganschau has leased an office building for 10 years to the General Services Administration (GSA), the branch of the U.S. federal government that arranges office leases. She can dependably set aside $1500 every month from the rentals as a kind of retirement pension. Based on interest rates of 7.50 percent on deposits over the 20 years, how much could

she draw out monthly over the 10 years following expiration of the lease?

Enter Table 61, page 1 (p. 726) at the section for 10 years of deposit. Read across on the line for 10 years of withdrawal to the column headed 7.50 percent interest. The answer there, 211.2065 percent, is the percentage of the deposits that she could withdraw. Multiply the dollar amount of the deposits by the factor to get

$$\$1500 \times 2.112065 = \$3168.10$$

the amount of monthly withdrawals that she could take for 10 years following 10 years of deposits, if interest is 7.50 percent per year throughout the term.

SEQUENTIAL PAYMENTS

Tables 62 through 64 are three simple tables that solve some most knotty problems, those to balance the payments when one party receives (or pays) a number of payments first then another party receives (or pays) for a succeeding period of time. In all cases, the interest rates are based on monthly compounding of interest, with payments assumed to be monthly on the last of the month.

Sequencing payments in the manner of tables such as these is not common. The reason is that interest rates fluctuate; over time, the values calculated from these tables could diverge widely from the correct balance of interests made at the outset. Sequential payment programs are most useful for those, such as relatives or business associates, who do not act **at arm's length.**

Succeeding Payment to Match Prior Payments

Table 62 describes the kind of plan where one party receives (or pays) a number of payments and a second party then receives (or pays) the *same number* of payments. The payments in the succeeding series are larger to compensate for the fact that they come later.

Example 137.   Payment in Second Series to Match Prior Series

---

Hokanson & Sawyer have received the bulk of the sale proceeds from their sale of real estate. There remains a purchase money mortgage that will pay $4800 per month for 72 months. The two partners are 50/50 owners of the mortgage. Hokanson needs to post a guarantee on another project with which Sawyer has no connection. Hokanson's bank will issue a letter of credit to secure the guarantee, if the parties will both pledge the first $3500 per month from the mortgage loan for 3 years. Sawyer's attorney wants to document how the payments from the mortgage loan will be distributed if the bank has to pay on the letter of credit and therefore starts to draw the $3500 per month. The interest rate on the purchase money note is 8.50 percent, so the parties agree to use that as the rate for this calculation.

Begin by finding the respective payments if the bank draws on the pledge. The monthly mortgage receipt is $4800, of which the bank would take $3500, Hokanson $650, and Sawyer $650.

Next enter Table 62 (p. 728) in the section for 8.50 percent. Find the factor on the line for 36 prior payments in the 8.50 percent column, 128.9302 percent. Multiply this by the portion that the bank may take to get

$$\$3500 \times 1.289302 = \$4,512.56$$

the payment that Sawyer will take in the second 36 months as his prior claim. Payments in the second 36 months would therefore be paid as follows: $4513 to Sawyer, then the remainder divided $143.50 to Hokanson and $143.50 to Sawyer.

Number of Succeeding Payments to Match Series of Prior Payments

In this variation, shown in Table 63, the second series of payments are the same *amount* as the prior series. The compensation to the receiver of the later payments is that more payments will be received. Entries in the table "Unl" for unlimited mean that the credit built up by the first series would never be exhausted by the succeeding series of payments.

Example 138. Number of Succeeding Payments to Match Series of Prior Payments— Llewellyn's Problem

Over time, Llewellyn would like to distribute the proceeds of the Phalanx House Apartments to his two children in equal shares. But his daughter is starting law school and has no income, and his son is well established in a good-paying job. Llewellyn will therefore arrange for the bank to pay out $3000 per month to his daughter for the next 36 months. After

that, his son will receive some greater number of payments, also at the rate of $3000 per month. The bank is paying 7.50 percent interest.

To find the number of succeeding payments, enter Table 63 (p. 729) at the line for 36 prior payments. Read across on that line to the 7.50 percent interest column and read there the answer, 46.48 months. In principle, the son would receive 46 payments of $3000 on the last day of each month and a final payment of $1440, or 0.48 × $3000. In practice, the final payment in a family setting like this might simply be rounded up to a whole payment, modestly overcompensating the party who had to wait.

Example 139. Number of Succeeding Payments to Match Series of Prior Payments— the Perreaults

Tambra Perreault has agreed to let her husband receive the first 42 payments from the purchase money mortgage the couple received on sale of Rancho Pano. The next group of payments would be received by her exclusively, and after that series the payments will be divided 50/50. The interest rate on the mortgage is 11.00 percent.

To find the number of payments that Tambra Perreault should receive, enter Table 63 (p. 729) at the section for 11.00 percent. Read down the column for number of prior payments to 42 and across to the column 11.00 percent, where the number 68.97 appears. Tambra Perreault will receive 69 payments after the first 36 payments. If precision is required, she would receive 68 full payments and 97 percent of the sixth-ninth payment. Thereafter, the payments would be divided 50/50.

Example 140. Dividing Responsibility for Mortgage Payments in Sequence

The payments shown in these tables may be payments received from a deposit or other income source, or they may be payments that the members of the sequence are responsible to pay. Pliny, Carella, and Germain have decided to buy a country house, using a mortgage loan that requires monthly payments of $1400. They have decided that Pliny will make the mortgage payments for the first 2 years. After that, Carella will make some number of payments, and, finally, Germain will make some number of payments. After this sequence, they will make a new decision on dividing the payment obligation. Current interest rates on multiyear deposits are 8.50 percent.

To find the terms of Carella's and Germain's payment segments, enter Table 63 (p. 729) and read down to 24 prior payments. Read across on that line to the column headed 8.50 percent interest, where the factor, 28.91, is found. So Carella, the second team member, will be responsible for 28.91 payments after the first 24 payments. Now read down the number of prior payments column to 27 and 30 months, the numbers closest above and below 28.91 payments. Read across first on the 27 month line to the 8.50 percent column and read the factor, 33.39, and, on the line for 30 months, read 38.11 payments. Interpolate for the correct answer by taking

$$\frac{(28.91 - 27.00) \times (38.11 - 33.39)}{30.00 - 27.00} = \frac{1.91 \times 4.72}{3.00}$$
$$= 0.63667 \times 4.72 = 3.005$$

or, rounding, 3 payments. Adding the 3 payments to 33.39 gives 36.39 payments for Germain's third position. The precision of these answers makes the payment process less convenient when the purpose was to make it more convenient. Simple rounding would make Carella's position 29 payments and Germain's 37 payments. The slight additional cost to the second two payers is compensated by the freedom to make the payments later.

Partition of a Payment Series into Segments of Equal Value

When a fixed deposit or a fixed number of payments are to be divided into segments, Table 64 gives the partitions that will result in equal present values of the segments. The answers are given in numbers of monthly payments received by (or paid by) each party serially. The present value of each series is the same as the others in its sequence.

Example 141. Partition of a Payment Series into Segments of Equal Value

---

Leandrah Lotomille owns a free-standing discount store leased to BingoMart for 20 more years at $6000 per month **triple net**. She wants her three children to have the income from the store in series, with the oldest receiving all the rental for a period, then the second child, and then the third. Banks are paying 8.00 percent interest on long-term deposits, so she

decides that this is the appropriate basis for making her calculations.

To find the periods for each segment, enter Table 64, page 3 (p. 732), the section for a three-party partition. Read down the column for total number of payments to 240. On the line for the first party, read under the 8.00 percent interest column the answer, 46.4724 payments. This is the number of months of rent that will go to the first child. Just below that answer, on the line for second party, is the answer 67.5901, the number of months that will go to the second child. On the next line, for third party, is the answer 125.9376, the number of payments the last child would receive. Many parents would simplify the payment sequence as 46, 67, and 127 payments.

If exact values are adhered to, the forty-seventh payment would be prorated 47.24 percent, or 46.4724 − 46.0000, to the oldest child, 52.76 percent to the middle child. Then the 115th payment (46.4724 + 67.5901 = 114.0625) would be divided 6.25 percent, or 114.0625 − 114.0000, to the middle child and 93.75 percent to the last.

Time When Compounded Profit Will Be Achieved

A number of tables provide that time when some financial event will have, or should have, occurred. Table 68 tells the month in which a specified account balance or profit level is or should be achieved. The table assumes that interest or profit accrues monthly at the end of each month on the accumulating balance.

Entries in Table 68 are given as the year and month when the increase will pass through the specified goal. For example, an entry of 10Y 12m means that the desired increase in value will have been achieved in the twelfth month of the eleventh year. At month end, the value will be slightly greater than specified. Investments such as certificates of deposit can only be "broken" on an interest date, making it necessary that the fund remain to the end of a certain period to ensure that the stated goal will actually have occurred. The parties should agree in advance who gets any residue of interest.

Example 142. Time When Compounded Profit Will Have Occurred

Bernice and her family will put the sale proceeds from their co-op shares in an account bearing interest at 7.75 percent per year, compounded monthly.

She has established as the goal to cash out the account when it reaches 150 percent of its opening value.

To find when the account will have achieved 50 percent growth (150 percent balance less 100 percent original amount), enter Table 68 (p. 772) at the section for 50 percent increase. Read down the left column to 7.75 percent interest. On that line under the column headed 50 percent read the answer 5Y 3m, meaning 5 years and 3 months. The value of the account will pass through 150 percent of the original balance at 5 years and 3 months from the starting date, if 7.75 percent interest is paid.

Example 143. Time When Withdrawals Will Reduce a Deposit to a Given Percentage

Theo Drontin has set up a deposit account from which he draws monthly payments. The deposit earns interest at 7.00 percent; withdrawals are calculated to reduce the account to 0 in 15 years. Drontin wishes to know when the account will have a balance of 50 percent of the starting figure.

Enter Table 67, page 2 (p. 767), in the 7.00 percent section and read across the line for 15 years to the 50 percent unpaid balance column. The entry there, 9Y 5m, means that the balance will pass through 50 percent during the fifth month of the tenth year and at the end of that month will be slightly less than 50 percent.

Example 144. Time When Compounded Deposit Growth Will Be Achieved

Selwyn Vraie will set aside $60,000 from the sale proceeds of his office to satisfy a requirement for $100,000 funding for his pension fund. If the deposit can earn at least 9.00 percent interest, how long will it take to build the needed fund?

Begin by finding the desired increase. Do this by dividing

$$\frac{\$100,000 \text{ desired fund} - \$60,000 \text{ initial fund}}{\$60,000 \text{ initial fund}}$$

$$= \frac{\$40,000}{\$60,000} = 0.6667 = 66.7\%$$

Now enter Table 68 (p. 772) in the section for a 66.7 percent increase and read down to 9.00 percent interest and across to the 66.7 percent column. The an-

swer, 5Y 9m, means the value of the deposit will pass through $100,000 in the ninth month of the sixth year, if 9.00 percent interest compounded monthly is earned.

Time When Income on Deferred Tax Equals Tax

A sale of real estate is a taxable event; unlike receiving mortgage loan proceeds, receipt of sale proceeds will require reporting any gain and paying tax on it. Through tax-free exchange of a property for "like-kind" property, the taxes may be deferred. The tax-free exchange, however, leaves the investor with a property rather than cash. The question becomes, "How long does it take to get enough yield from the exchange parcel to pay the tax (and any tax on the earnings)?"

Table 69 assists the decision whether to make the exchange or to go ahead with a sale and pay the tax. The table shows the length of time a sum of deferred taxes takes to regenerate itself. That is, the table charts the time until the additional earnings from reinvestment of a deferred tax equal the tax itself, given the investor's tax bracket and the rate of return that can be earned during the deferral period. The user may select taxable interest or deferred taxation.

Although Table 69 is based on investment of the portion of sales proceeds that would go for taxes, note that all the sales proceeds will be tied up in the exchange property.

Example 145. Time When Income on Deferred Tax Equals Tax

Letitia Gilroy has the opportunity to sell Brookbend at a satisfactory price in a fully taxable transaction. It is probable that a tax-free exchange could also be arranged, in which case no taxes would be paid currently. Good-quality properties that would be used in an exchange should earn 9.00 percent per year. Gilroy is in a 32 percent tax bracket.

To find the time until the tax would have been regenerated, enter Table 69 (p. 773) in the section for current taxation. On the line for 32 percent, read across to the column headed 9.00 percent interest rate. The answer, 11 years 5 months, means that, with 9.00 percent taxable income, Gilroy will have earned enough after 11 years and 5 months to pay the original tax plus the tax on the income and still have left the original price, as if the deal had been tax-free.

Note This example calculates the time needed for the amount that would have been sent as taxes to regenerate itself through earnings (net of the tax on those earnings). But to get to that situation, it will be necessary for Gilroy to tie up all the sale proceeds, not just the "tax portion," in an exchange property. Doing so is risky, and that is the point of Table 69, to help decide if just paying the taxes now might be safer.

Time When Given Balance of a Sinking Fund Occurs

Table 57 tells when a sinking fund will reach all or a part of its intended total, given a rate of deposit into the fund and the interest rate earned on the fund. Its logic parallels that of Table 67, which gives the same information for a series of payments *from* a fund. The entries are given in months from the date the first payment is made into the sinking fund.

Example 146. Time When Specified Percentage of a Sinking Fund Achieved

Galuggin will deposit $1000 monthly into a sinking fund at a bank which will pay 8.25 percent interest on the account. Galuggin's goal is to accumulate $100,000. At what points will the fund have reached 25 percent, 50 percent, 75 percent, and 100 percent of the intended total?

Begin by establishing the percentage represented by each monthly deposit. It is $1000 divided by $100,000, which equals 0.010 or 1.00 percent per month. Now enter Table 57, page 3 (p. 712), the page for 8.25 percent interest. Read down the monthly payment column to 1.00 percent and across on that line to the 25 percent column. The answer there is 23.00 months. Under 50 percent, the answer is 42.87 months. Under 75 percent, it is 60.35 months, and the fund will have been 100 percent achieved at 75.96 months. (Remember that for practical purposes, transactions should be assumed to occur at end of month.)

Number of Installments Available from a Deposit

Table 59 gives the number of equal monthly withdrawals that may be taken from a deposit that earns interest. The table assumes the first withdrawal is made 30 days after setting up the deposit. In some places, the entry is "unl" for "unlimited," meaning the draw is less than the interest accrued during a month. In such cases, the deposit would never be exhausted.

Example 147. Number of Installments Available from a Deposit

Monte Monteith has sold The DealCentre to a major corporation. He proposes that the sale price be paid to him in monthly installments of 1 percent of the price. Considering this arrangement to be in effect a loan, he feels that a fair rate of interest would be the current rate on business loans, which is 9.50 percent per year. Monteith wants to find the number of payments he would receive from the corporation, if they agree to this proposal.

Enter Table 59 on page 2 (p. 723) at the page for 9.50 percent interest. Read down the monthly payment section to 1.00 percent and across on that line to the 9.50 percent column. The answer there is 198.9, indicating that the account would last for 198 full payments and a final payment equal to nine-tenths of the others.

Example 148. Number of Payments to Retire an Obligation

Wilma Traut has agreed to pay her brother 2.00 percent per month of his half of the sale proceeds of Sparrowhill. Both agree that an interest rate of 6.00 percent per year should be imputed in the calculation.

To find the number of payments that she will make to her brother, enter Table 59 at the page with 6.00 percent interest. Read down the monthly payment column to 2.00 percent and across to the 6.00 percent column. The answer, 57.7, indicates that she will make 57 monthly payments of the same amount and a final payment equal to seven-tenths of the normal payment.

Example 149. Increase in Number of Withdrawals Available as Amount Decreases

Table 59 illustrates how rapidly the length of a distribution period expands, as the rate of distribution comes closer to the interest rate. A $100,000 fund established at 9.75 percent interest can pay out distributions of $1000 per month for 207 months—17 years 3 months. Lowering the payment to $830 per month increases the term to 455.9 months or almost 38 years. A mere 17 percent decrease in the monthly distribution creates a 120 percent increase in the term.

Example 150.   Difference in Number of Payments at Different Rates

Dr. Omnis plans to deposit $100,000 in a bank or savings institution and to draw that money out at the rate of $1250 per month. A bank with a good reputation offers 7.50 percent, compounded monthly, on such deposits. Another institution is advertising that it pays 8.00 percent. Dr. Omnis wonders if the interest rate makes much difference.

To find the difference in number of payments, first find the withdrawal percentage. It is 1.25 percent, that is, $1250 ÷ 100,000. Now enter Table 59, page 1 (p. 722) and read down the monthly payment column to 1.25 percent. Read across on that line and find under the column headed 7.50 percent the figure 111.2 months. To the right of it, under 8.00 percent, find 114.7 months. The account at higher interest will give 3.5 (or 114.7 − 111.2) more months of payments.

Number of Monthly Deposits to Build a Sinking Fund

Two of the tables describe the number of payments needed to ensure a certain sum will be on hand at a future date. Table 55 tells how long it will take to build a sinking fund by making monthly deposits at interest. Table 56 described in the next section will show the number of deposits to complete a fund already begun. The entries are expressed as the number of monthly deposits earning interest that are needed to build the fund.

Example 151.   Number of Monthly Deposits to Build a Sinking Fund

Mr. and Mrs. Mangano have leased their building to a major food store chain for 15 years at $6500 per month **triple net**. From this they must deduct a $4500 monthly mortgage payment. The remaining net cash flow will be paid automatically into a trust

for their daughter's education. Estimating that her college costs will be $120,000, they wish to know how long it will take for the trust to reach this level if interest of at least 7.50 percent per year can be achieved.

Begin by finding the monthly payment percentage. It is

$$\frac{\$2000 \text{ monthly deposit}}{\$120,000 \text{ desired fund}} = 0.01667$$
$$= 1.667\% \text{ payment per month}$$

Now enter Table 55 and read down the monthly payment column to 1.6667 percent. Across on that line under 7.50 percent, read the answer, 50.8 months. The desired fund level will have been reached in just under 4 years 3 months. (Although the tables are precise to one-tenth of a month, virtually all transactions will involve rounding off to the next whole month.)

Number of Deposits to Complete a Partial Sinking Fund

Often a sinking fund has been partially funded, or a lump-sum deposit will be made to start the fund. Table 56 gives the number of payments needed to fill out the remainder of the fund, while both new deposits and the existing funds earn interest at the given rate, compounded monthly. The entries are in numbers of months, but for all practical purposes the entry should be rounded to the next higher month. (Some of the entries in Table 56 are negative. This means that no deposit would be necessary to achieve the goal by the due date; the interest earnings on the initial balance alone would be enough to complete the fund. In fact, an amount equal to the negative percentage could be withdrawn each period.)

Example 152.   Number of Deposits to Complete a Partial Sinking Fund

Cindia Cillowin wants to establish a $100,000 endowment fund. The first $25,000 will come from a sale of land. The balance will come from monthly deposits of $1250 over a 90-month period. The initial deposit and the monthly additions will earn interest at 9.00 percent.

To begin, find the monthly payment percentage by dividing the payment by the desired fund. It is

$$\$1250 ÷ \$100,000 = 0.0125 = 1.25\%$$

per month. Now enter Table 56, page 3 (p. 708), at the section for starting from a partial fund of 25 percent. Read down the monthly payment column to 1.25 percent and across on that line to the 9.00 percent column, to get the answer, 44.2 months, the time to bring the $25,000 balance to $100,000 with monthly deposits of $1250 and interest at 9.00 percent per year.

VALUES IN THE FUTURE

The next examples come from the domain of the future worth tables found as part of Table 46 Present and Future Value. They give the results in the future of a deposit made today that accumulates interest. The interest may be compounded monthly or annually.

Example 153. Total Interest Earned from a Single Deposit or Investment

August Durgansin deposited $16,000 at 9.00 percent interest, compounded monthly, 12 years ago. What is the balance on the account and how much interest will have been earned in that period?

Enter Table 46, page 15 (p. 559), the section for 9.00 percent interest. Read down to 12 years and across to the monthly payment columns and the column for future value; read the factor, 2.9328368. Multiply the factor by the original deposit

$$\$16,000 \times 2.9328368 = \$46,925.39$$

the total balance on deposit. Now subtract 1.0000, representing the original deposit, from the factor and multiply again to get

$$\$16,000 \times 1.9328368 = \$30,925.39$$

the interest that will have been earned on the account over the 12 years, at 9.00 percent interest compounded monthly.

The future value of 1 per period, also found as part of Table 46, is the basis of life insurance cash values and pension plans. It gives the value in the future of a series of deposits made monthly or annually that accumulate interest. The values found in the future value of 1 section of the annuity tables are accumulated as a running total in the future value of 1 per period column.

Example 154. Terminal Value of a Series of Deposits—Future Value of 1 per Period

Larry French plans to put $1200 per month out of rents into a fund for replacements. He needs to know, if the money market account holding the deposits av-

erages 8.00 percent over the coming years, what the **terminal value** of the fund would be after 120 months.

Enter Table 46, page 11 (p. 555), the page for 8.00 percent interest; read down the right column to 120 months. On that line find under the column future value of 1 per period in the monthly payments section the factor, 182.9460352. Multiply this by the amount of the monthly deposit to get

$$\$1200 \times 182.9460352 = \$219,535.24$$

the future value of a series of 120 monthly deposits of $1200 with 8.00 percent interest.

Example 155. Total Interest Earned from a Series of Deposits

Cynthia Radiewicz intends to deposit $350 per month over a ten-year term. If she earns 8.00 percent interest throughout that time, compounded monthly, what will be the balance in the account? What will be the total interest earned?

Enter Table 46, page 11 (p. 555), at the section for monthly payments. Read down to 120 months and across to monthly payments, future value of 1 per period. The factor there is 182.9460352. Subtract 120 from this, representing the 120 monthly deposits she will have made, to get 62.9460352, the factor for the interest. Multiply the factors by the dollar amount of the deposits to get, first

$$\$350 \times 182.9460352 = \$64,031.11$$

the total balance in the account. Next, multiply the monthly deposit by the factor for the interest to get

$$\$350 \times 62.9460352 = \$22,031.11$$

the interest earned on the account over 10 years at 8.00 percent per year interest.

Example 156. Rate of Capital Growth Indicated by Total Growth

Hannigan & Blamely have sold their corporate office center for $6.5 million. They developed the property 10 years ago with an investment of $2.2 million. To find the annual rate of capital growth indicated by these terms, first find the percentage of overall growth. It is

$$\frac{\$6,600,000}{2,200,000} = 2.9545 = 295.45\%$$

or, rounding, 300 percent. Now enter Table 6, page 3 (p. 190), at the section for 200 percent growth. Read down the years column to 10 and across to the column headed 200 percent growth. The answer is 11.612 percent, the compounded annual rate of growth in value of the office building over the 10 years.

Future Simple Rate of Return on Initial Investment

Compounded annual rates of return mask the acceleration inherent in growth assumptions. Table 7 tells the annual rate of return on the *original* invested amount. A deposit of $100 at 5.50 percent interest per year compounded monthly will increase $5.64 in the first year, $5.96 in the second, and $6.29 in the third. The compounded rate of interest remains 5.50 percent for each year, but the **future simple** rates are 5.64 percent, 5.96 percent, and 6.29 percent.

Cross-Reference The deposit will grow $5.64 in the first year, even though the **nominal annual rate** is only 5.50 percent. The **effective annual rate** is thus 5.64 percent. See Example 111 in Chapter 3 for a discussion of nominal and effective rates.

Example 157. Future Simple Rate of Return on Initial Investment

Thielle Margine is projecting income from a 5-year cash deposit that will compound at 12.00 percent interest and accumulate. She wishes to know the annual rate of income in the fifth year of the deposit.

Enter Table 7 at 12.00 percent interest rate or rate of growth. Read down the elapsed years column to 5 and across on that line to the 12.00 percent column. The answer there is 20.45 percent. The annual rate of interest earned on the original deposit in its fifth year will be 20.4 percent on her initial investment.

Example 158. Bond Equivalent Yield

The Portsmans have sold their property and are considering alternative investments, such as mortgages, bonds, and Eurobonds. The mortgages pay interest monthly at the end of each month and can be obtained at a current interest rate of 7.125 percent.

Corporate bonds are paying 6.75 percent compounded semiannually, and Eurobonds are currently offering 7.00 percent.

To find the effective interest rates from each of these, first consider that since Eurobonds pay interest at the end of the year, their nominal and effective interest rates are the same, 7.00 percent. Now, enter Table 33 (a), page 2 (p. 406) at the line for 7.125 percent and find under monthly the effective rate, 7.362 percent per year, the effective rate for the mortgage loan investments. At 6.75 percent on page 1 (p. 405) under semiannual, find 6.864 percent, the effective yield on the corporate bonds.

Example 159. Growth Needed to Cover Carrying Costs

Palladia has $700,000 to invest from the sale of the House of Pertalina. Among the investment venues available are Treasury notes, currently yielding 5.00 percent, and a land partnership that invests in raw land sites believed to be in the path of growth in major cities. The land partnership uses 50 percent leverage and pays its lenders an average interest rate of 11.00 percent; its management fees and operating costs are 5.0 percent per year. The prospectus states that the partnership hopes to liquidate its holdings in 5 years.

To find the growth needed to cover these costs, begin by adding the opportunity cost of the sure yield of Treasury notes to the operating costs of the land partnership to get 10.50 percent. Now enter Table 9, page 3 (p. 200), the page for cost of carry 10.50 percent and the section for mortgage interest of 11.00 percent. On the line for 5 years' cumulative, read under the column in the 11.00 percent section headed 50 percent loan-to-value ratio, the factor 70.76 percent. The property value would have to increase by 71 percent in 5 years' time to cover the operating and mortgage costs in the land proposal.

Note Palladia is not asked to fund the mortgage payments and operating costs herself; rather they will be paid out of reserves established for the purpose. For financial analysis purposes, however, it is as if she herself were to make the payments, since the reserves are coming from the capital that she and the other partners would subscribe. (Since the reserves can themselves earn at least the Treasury rate, the example above modestly overstates the needed growth.)

Deposit to Create or Complete a Sinking Fund

A deposit to a **sinking fund** or deposit account is the inverse of a mortgage loan payment. Instead of paying back bit by bit a sum of money already received, its payments build up bit by bit to an amount needed to be paid in the future. Sinking funds are associated with future value, since it is at a date in the future that the fund will be needed. By contrast, mortgage loan payments are associated with present value, since they pay back an amount received at the present time. It was common in past times to depreciate properties using sinking funds, as well as to retire bond issues with them.

In Table 52 the entries show the deposit to start a fund from a zero balance. In Table 53 the entries show the deposit to complete a fund that already has some amount accumulated. The numbers in the monthly column are the totals for a year, the sum of 12 monthly deposits. To get the factor per month, the figure given must be divided by 12.

Example 160.   Deposit to Create a Fund for Replacement

In connection with the sale of Anders Place, Nils Anderson will need to make a payout 7 years from now for replacement of certain equipment. The amount needed would be $110,000 maximum. To build a reserve for this, he will set up an escrow with monthly deposits that can earn 7.00 percent interest.

To find the monthly deposit that he should set aside, enter Table 52, page 2 (p. 682), the page for 7.00 percent interest. On the line for 7 years, read under 7.00 percent the factor 11.555322 percent. Multiply this by the maximum needed fund to get

$$\$110,000 \times 0.11555322 = \$12,710.85 \text{ per year}$$

the deposit which will ensure a fund of at least $110,000 after 7 years at 7.00 percent interest.

Example 161.   Deposit to Complete a Partial Sinking Fund

June Kim has $25,000 on hand and wants to build a $100,000 fund in the next 90 months. She can obtain 9.00 percent interest compounded monthly from a money-market account at her bank.

To find the monthly deposit to complete this fund, enter Table 53, page 3 (p. 690) at the section for starting from a partial fund of 25 percent. On the line for 7.5 years, read the factor under the 9.00 percent column, 0.39899 percent. Multiply this by the total desired fund to get

$$\$100,000 \times 0.0039899 = \$398.99$$

or, rounding, $400.00 per month as the payment which, when added to a starting balance of $25,000 and interest of 9.00 percent, will produce a fund of $100,000 in 7.5 years.

Amount of Monthly Deposit to Obtain Withdrawals of Known Amount

Table 60 gives the number and amount of a series of monthly deposits to make possible a given number and amount of desired future withdrawals. The deposit series, to be made in an amount to be determined, will be followed by a series of withdrawals of stated amount. Interest accrues at all times at the selected rate.

Example 162.   Amount of Monthly Deposits to Obtain Withdrawals of Known Amount—$2500

Mike Robison wants to be able to draw $2500 per month in the 10-year period following his retirement 5 years from now. He can set aside part of current cash flow from management fees during the coming 5 years and earn an average 8.00 percent per year on the savings.

To find the deposit series to accomplish this withdrawal plan, enter Table 60, page 1 (p. 724), at the section for 5 years of deposits. On the line for 10 years of withdrawals, the factor is given under the 8.00 percent column, 112.1734 percent. Multiply it by the desired withdrawals to get

$$\$2500 \times 1.121734 = \$2804.34$$

the monthly deposit needed for 5 years at 8.00 percent to make possible 10 years of withdrawals of $2500 per month.

Example 163.   Amount of Monthly Deposits to Obtain Withdrawals of Known Amount—$2000

Sara Leonas intends to deposit part of the rentals from O'Corcoran Center in an account for her child's education. During the child's 4 years of high school, she will set aside an amount at interest of 9.00 percent. During the child's college years, she will draw out $2000 per month.

To find the needed deposits, enter Table 60, page 2 (p. 725), in the section for 9.00 percent interest and 4 years of deposits. On the line in that section for 4 years of withdrawals, read under the column 9.00 percent the factor 69.8614 percent. Multiply the desired withdrawal by the factor to get

$$\$2000 \times 0.698614 = \$1397.23$$

the necessary deposit over 4 years to ensure, with 9.00 percent interest, 48 monthly withdrawals of $2000 each.

Chapter 5

APPRAISING AND MARKET ANALYSIS

Chapter 5 emphasizes valuation techniques both at the macro level, as in comparing rates of inflation and population growth, and at the micro level, as when valuing leases at specific properties. The three sections of this chapter are

Capitalization. The fundamental technique of income-property appraising, estimating value from the income-generating capacity.

Valuation of leases. Appraisal of long-term leases, both to illustrate techniques used in all appraisals and those for the special characteristics that long-term leases present.

Appraisal techniques. Finding the IRR and the NPV of investments, making financial terms comparable, and preparing projections and analyses of income-property deals.

CAPITALIZATION

Capitalization is the heart of the income property appraisal. Starting with an estimate of income for one or several years, the appraiser estimates a rate of return on investment demanded by capital sources. If income produced at that rate gives value, then the income of the property under appraisal capitalized at (divided by) that rate ought to be worth a given amount. Increasing levels of sophisticated analysis are brought to bear on estimating the income pros-

pects of the property and on methods to compare the rates of return demanded by investors.

Direct Capitalization

Direct capitalization, as its name suggests, is the most straightforward and the most common means to value a property according to its income. The process consists of dividing present or average income by a **capitalization rate** to arrive at **capitalized value.** Even in this computer age, direct capitalization rates see everyday use. Prospectuses may lay out dozens of pages of analysis, but few investors would give even a second glance to a property that does not offer a "cap rate" close to the investor's minimum. The most widely used capitalization method is something called the "IRV model." IRV stands for

$$\frac{I}{R} = V \quad \text{or} \quad \frac{\text{Income}}{\text{Rate}} = \text{Value}$$

where R is the capitalization rate. The income is usually the current income of the property, or rather, a somewhat "smoothed" forecast of what the appraiser estimates income ought to be under normal conditions, neither giving credit to extraordinarily low expense ratios nor penalizing too heavily short-term vacancy or revenue problems. Although past income is an important guide to the earning capacity of the property, the appraiser keeps in mind that it is tomorrow's income that will pay the buyer the desired dividends.

Gross Rent Multiplier

The gross rent multiplier (GRM) is far less popular than it was in past decades. It is a useful method of finding value and serves also to check values derived by other, more sophisticated methods. The GRM model is

$$\text{Gross Rent} \times \text{GRM} = \text{Value}$$

where the gross rent is the sum of the rents taken in by a property during a year. Using the GRM method of property capitalization ignores the many differences of operating ratios and financing that occur. But its great advantage is that the gross rent of a property can usually be obtained from an owner, or even public sources, far more accurately than precise operating figures and financing details. The GRM works well for evaluating comparables in cases where there are a number of sales of quite similar properties.

Example 164. Using the Gross Rent Multiplier to Find Value

Leslie Pertins values Serenity Gate Townhomes at a gross rent multiple of 6.5. With an average of 1411 square feet, the townhomes rent for $12.25 per square foot per year, giving

$$1411 \text{ s.f.} \times \$12.25 \text{ per s.f.} \times 6.5 = \$112,351$$

per unit as their present value. Pertins believes rents can be raised at about one-half the rate of the Consumer Price Index (CPI) and wants to know, if this is so and the CPI rises 5.5 percent per year, the value increase 10 years in the future.

Begin by taking 50 percent of the 5.5 percent CPI growth to get 2.75 percent. Enter Table 77 (b), page 1 (p. 818), in the section for increases every year. On the line for 10 years, read across to the column headed 2.75 percent. The factor there is 35.11 cents per s.f. for every $10 per s.f. of base rent. Divide the base by $10 and multiply by the factor to get

$$\$12.25 \div \$10 \text{ per s.f.} \times 0.3511 \times 1411 \times 6.5 = \$3944.64$$

or, rounding, $4000 per unit value growth in the tenth year, if rents rise at one-half the CPI growth and it is 5.5 percent per year.

Mortgage-Equity Capitalization

Years ago, someone pointed out that most income-producing real estate is financed. The interest rate on the loan differs from the investor's expected *cash-on-cash* return in just about every case. This means that there really should be two Rs in the IRV model, the rate of payment on the mortgage and the rate of yield to the owner of the equity. Table 50 blends those two Rs into a single capitalization rate for a wide variety of equity and financing cases.

Example 165. Mortgage-Equity Capitalization Rate

Dewellous Koude has estimated that the **net operating income** of Koude Gardens apartments will be $350,000. Currently, mortgages on a 25-year amortization schedule are available with a 70 percent loan-to-value ratio at a 10.50 percent annual mortgage rate. Koude expects 8.50 percent cash-on-cash return on the indicated 30 percent equity position.

To find the blended capitalization rate, enter Table 50, page 9 (p. 658), at the section for 70 percent loan-to-value ratio and 10.25 percent mortgage constant. Read down the mortgage term column to 25 and across on that line to 70 percent loan-to-value ratio. Find there 10.48113 percent, the blended mortgage-equity capitalization rate.

Capitalization Rate to Account for Growth or Decline in Value

Capitalization rates, such as the IRV model or the mortgage-equity capitalization rates discussed above, do not account for the fact that the investor may expect to obtain a capital gain on the investment. That is, in ordinary models like IRV, the rates of return to the investor are **capitalized in perpetuity,** without assuming any increase or decrease in value. But in fact, the chance for capital appreciation is a major motive for acquiring real estate. The late L. W. Ellwood recognized the need for a capitalization rate that accounted for the investor's hope for capital gain, to conform the IRV model better to reality.

Table 51 has the same premise. It provides the capitalization rate that will account for an expected rise or fall in the value of the property. Moreover, the capital gain takes into account the degree of mortgage amortization that occurs during the assumed holding period.

Example 166. Capitalization Rate to Account for Increase or Decrease in Value

Zilligan is appraising Flanders Towers and considers that 7.50 percent per year is the appropriate return on equity investment. Mortgages with a 70 percent loan-to-value ratio are available at 10.00 percent interest on 30-year amortization schedules. By the time of a sale after a 15-year holding period, Zilligan estimates that the value of the property will have grown 25 percent.

To find the capitalization rate for this case, enter Table 51 at the page for equity yield 7.50 percent, mortgage ratio of 70 percent, and growth over term of 25 percent. Within this section, enter the section for 15-years time to sale and the line for 30-year amortization schedule. Read under the column headed 10.00 percent interest the answer, 8.1730 percent, the capitalization rate which accounts for 25 percent value growth with a 7.5 percent equity return and a 70 percent loan at 10.00 percent, 30 years.

Annuity Capitalization

The annual mortgage constant is equal to the sum of the interest rate plus the sinking fund factor. As such it provides a return *on* investment (the interest rate) and a return *of* investment (the sinking fund factor). Since this is exactly what is needed in capitalization, annual mortgage constants serve well as cap rates. The next example uses the constant that will amortize a given portion of a loan within a specified time, but any mortgage constant could be used in the cap rate model. The term, *annuity capitalization,* introduces a concept of capitalization based on the annuity tables.

Example 167. Capitalization Rate for a Diminishing Asset

Verlaine will lease a new building to a prominent research entity for 10 years, based on an 8.00 percent return on investment. The building is standard in most respects, but the tenant needs special-purpose improvements. These will cost 30 percent of the budget but be worthless (at least to Verlaine) at the end of 10 years. Verlaine seeks the rental to compensate for the fact that 30 percent of the initial cost must be recovered by the end of the tenth year.

The annual mortgage constant will be used as a capitalization rate. First, to find the factor, enter Ta-

ble 36, page 3 (p. 449), the page for 8.00 percent interest. Read down the years to balloon column to 10 years and across on that line to the column headed 30 percent. Read there the constant 9.96689 percent. This is the annual percentage of original cost which will return 8.00 percent per year to Verlaine *on* his investment and will have returned 30 percent *of* the investment over 10 years. This constant assumes payments at the end of the month; because rents are normally paid at the beginning, a slight bonus to the landlord is included.

Present and Future Values

Grouping the concepts of present and future value, as in Table 46, is more than a tradition in publishing formats. Seen side by side, the concepts of **compound discount** (present value) and **compound amount** (future value) are more easily grasped. Looking at the tables may be more instructive than reading definitions, so the first practical step in making these tables your own is to scan them. Watch the flow of the numbers from the top of each column to the bottom. Note the regression of present value, as the figures are painted into a corner that grows smaller and smaller. On the other hand, the progression of future worth presents greater challenge to the typesetter to fit the numbers into the column.

Placing the discussion of "annuity tables," as present and future value tables along with sinking funds and mortgage constants are known, in the section devoted to capitalization is not at all traditional. But the functions of present and future value tables are primarily to capitalize, that is to predicate value today on the future benefits a property could produce or to forecast the future sum arising from today's investment actions. We have had a brief look at the use of mortgage constants as capitalization rates and noted that the mortgage constant is the sum of the interest rate plus the sinking fund factor. We will introduce the other principal annuity functions as means to develop appraised values of property.

Present Value of 1

Given a choice of getting a sum of money today, let's say $100, or getting the same amount a year from now, everyone would choose $100 today. Not only is there some risk that the promised $100 will not arrive, but the cash today could be deposited and earn interest during the year. The **present value** of a payment in the future is less than the value of the same amount today. How much less depends on the interest rate that could be earned. Suppose that a deposit could earn 6.00 percent interest. It would be necessary to deposit about $94—$94.34 to be exact—to have $100.00 in 1 year from now. So the present value of $100 **discounted** for one year at 6.00 percent is $94.34. Some people would call this the **discounted amount**; it means the same as the present value. Discounting for more than 1 year might be referred to as present value or "compound discount."

How was the figure $94.34 derived? Either by referring to Table 46 or by dividing $100 by 1 plus the interest rate (1.06). If it remained this simple, Table 46 would be unnecessary. But the formula for the second year of discounting is $100 divided by 1.06 squared (1.06 × 1.06); for the third year 1.06 is cubed, and it gets progressively more complex. Reference to Table 46 is much faster.

Present value tables give the value today of one or more payments that will be received in the future. Since leases are exchanges of the use of real estate for one or more payments in the future, we will combine the treatment of present value with valuation of leases. Up to this point, we have capitalized income without close attention to its source, or to the lease, the specialized contract that produces the income. Now we will focus on the special cases of long-term leases, those with rising or falling income, and those with other characteristics.

VALUATION OF LEASES

Leases are estates in land and at the same time contracts. The effects of a lease on the ownership and rights to use real estate are in the province of lawyers, but the contractual elements of a lease are money transactions that may be valued, just as banking and finance deals are, by reference to financial tables giving the relation between time, interest rates, and value. The type of valuation described here is sometimes referred to as the **time value of money** approach. It means the same as present value approach or discounted value approach.

Here is an analogy of lease transactions to loans: In a loan, the lender turns over the use of a sum of money for a certain time, in exchange for the promise of the future return of the money and for a payment for its use. In a lease, the landlord, or lessor, turns over the use of real estate, in exchange for its future return and a payment for its use. The payment for the use of real estate is called "rent"; that for the use of money is called "interest." The return of money that is borrowed is called "repayment." The return of real estate that is leased is called "reversion."

In discussing how to value leases, we will always need to deal with **net rent,** that is, the money the landlord actually keeps after paying all property expenses such as real estate taxes, maintenance, and insurance. Often a lease will provide that all such costs are to be paid by the tenant, in which case the lease is called a **net lease.** The rent under a net lease is by definition the net rent. Because in times past, complex trade customs arose over who paid what, the terms "single net," "double net," and "triple net" came into leasing parlance. Only "triple net" remains, by which is meant a lease under which the tenant pays all property expenses. "Triple net" and "absolutely net" mean the same as "net," but it is still common in the industry to hear the other terms.

If rent under the lease is not net to the landlord, then the lease is a **gross lease.** The expenses that the landlord is obliged to pay must be estimated and deducted from the **gross rent,** before valuation may proceed. Since net rental in such cases will be only an estimate, a higher yield will be associated with a gross lease rather than with a net lease.

Example 168.   Present Value of a Future Sum, Annual Compounding

Cantwell & Sobraniec have rented 40 acres to Dunton for 1 year for $6000 net, payable at the end of the lease term. The appraiser estimates that today's fair rental rate for land is 8.25 percent per year of the land value.

To find the value of the rent today, enter Table 46, page 12 (p. 556), the page for 8.25 percent interest. Read on the line for 1 year across to the column for present value; find the factor 0.9237875. Multiply the factor by the rent payment to get

$$\$6000 \times 0.9237875 = \$5542.73$$

the present value of the rent at a discount rate of 8.25 percent per year.

Example 169.   Present Value of a Future Sum, Monthly Compounding

Pernod & Partners have sold Pernod Park for cash of $1 million plus a mortgage note of $3 million. The note comes due in 3 years and pays no interest or principal until then. Pernod's appraisers are valuing the transaction. They note that commercial lenders currently make 3-year mortgage loans of this type at an interest rate of 9.25 percent with monthly payments of interest.

To find the value of the sale, enter Table 46, page 16 (p. 560), the page for 9.25 percent interest. On the line for 36 months, find the factor in the column for monthly compounding present value, 0.7584822. Multiply this by the face amount of the note to get

$$\$3,000,000 \times 0.7584822 = \$2,275,447$$

the present value of the mortgage note. To this must be added the $1 million down payment. The present value of 1 received in the present is 1, so the down payment is worth $1 million, making the total value of the transaction $3,275,447, or, rounding to the nearest $25,000, $3,275,000, the value of the Pernod Park sale.

Example 170. Present Value of a Reversion

Li Chung owns 10 acres of land. He has leased the land to the local park district for 10 years for a rental of $1, despite the fact that the land would be worth $800,000 without the lease. At the end of the lease term, the land will revert back to Li Chung (the landlord's interest is therefore called the **reversion**). In the current market, an 11.00 percent per year discount rate would be normal for land leases.

To find the value of the reversion, enter Table 46, page 23 (p. 567), the page for 11.00 percent interest. Read down the left column to 10 years and find under the column for present value the factor 0.3521845, the present worth factor. Multiply the value of the land if the lease did not encumber it by the factor to get

$$\$800,000 \times 0.3521845 = \$281,747.60$$

the present value of the reversion. The value of the land as **encumbered** by the lease is only 35.2 percent of its **free and clear** value. Depending on tax laws, Li Chung may be entitled to a charitable deduction for the difference.

In this case, the value of the reversion represents the total present value of the property, since the income stream of $1 may be disregarded. In a more common case, there would be an income component in addition to the reversion. The two elements, income stream and reversion, make up the value of the **leased fee,** as shown later in this chapter.

Note that the capitalization process has moved from division by a capitalization rate to multiplication by an annuity factor. Except when using annual mortgage constants as cap rates, annuity capitaliza-

tion will be in the form of an income stream or a reversion multiplied by an annuity factor.

Present Value of 1 per Period

Present value calculations become more difficult if a series of payments will be received. If the payments will be in constant amount at predictable intervals, the portion of Table 46 for present worth of 1 per period can be used to solve the calculation.

We saw above that, at a 6.00 percent discount rate, the present value of $100 one year from now is $94.34, or $100 ÷ 1.06. It is also true that the present value of $100 two years from now is $89.00, or 94.34 ÷ 1.06; and for $100 three years from now, the present value is $83.96, or 89.00 ÷ 1.06. The present value of a series of three annual payments, $100 each, at 6.00 percent is $267.30, or $94.34 + 89.00 + 83.96. A series of payments such as this is often referred to as an **income stream** and also as an annuity. Either term signals that the present worth of 1 per period will be used. In Table 46, the sums in the column for present value of 1 per period are a running total of the figures in the column for present value of 1.

The present worth of 1 per period factors are often referred to as "Inwood coefficients," after William Inwood. Although Inwood was not the first to publish tables of these factors, his 1811 book was in English and in handy form, so his name became attached to the factors.

Example 171. Amount to Prepay a Lease for Its Term and Present Value of an Income Stream

Wielna owns a 40-acre farm which he intends to keep in the family. An apartment developer, however, would like to buy it. To avoid a sale and to ensure that eventually the land will revert to the family, Wielna is willing to lease the farm to the developer for 45 years at $100,000 net rent payable at the end of each year. Wielna is concerned about credit risk, so the developer has offered to prepay the rent. Both agree that 8.50 percent represents the fair market interest rate today.

To find the amount of rent to be prepaid, enter Table 46, page 13 (p. 557), the section for 8.50 percent and for present value. Read down the years column to 45 and across to the column present value of 1 per period and find the factor, 11.4653120, which is the present value of 45 annual payments of rent discounted at 8.50 percent. Multiply the annual rent by the factor to get

$$\$100,000 \times 11.4653120 = \$1,146,531.20$$

the amount of rent that will prepay $100,000 rent per year for 45 years at 8.50 percent; this also is the present value of that stream of rent payments.

Example 172.   Present Value of 1 per Period, Rent Payments at Beginning of Period

When payments of an annuity or income stream are to be made at the *beginning* of a period, use the factor in the table for one less period and add 1 to it, as follows: Suppose rent payments of $100,000 will be made to Wielna at the beginning of each year for 45 years. The appropriate rate of discount is 8.50 percent. To find the present value, proceed by entering Table 46, page 13 (p. 557), the page for 8.50 percent discount rate. Find the factor for 44 years (1 less than the number of payments). It is 11.4398636. Add 1.000000 to it to get 12.4398636. Thus, with payments at the beginning of the term, the value of the first payment is equal to 1, since it is received now. The remaining payments, 44 in this case, will follow 1 year apart. Multiply the factor by the rental amount to get

$$\$100,000 \times 12.4398636 = \$1,243,986.36$$

the present value of 45 payments of $100,000 per year at the beginning of the year, discounted at 8.50 percent per year.

We have introduced the term *discount* rate and have used it as a synonym for interest rate. In the industry today, they have the same meaning, but financial literature often distinguishes the rate used in discounting as the discount rate.

Example 173.   Value of a Leased Fee

In a lease contract, the real estate becomes the property of the tenant, with the landlord retaining the rights to receive the agreed rental and to receive back the property at the end of the lease term. The landlord's interest during the term of the lease, called the *leased fee*, consists of a rental component, called the *income stream* and a future interest called the *reversion*. In valuation of a leased fee, the two elements are valued separately and then totalled.

Malmo Tedlund & Co. have granted a lease of the Barragot Building land for 50 years at a net rent, payable at the end of the year, equal to 6.00 percent per year of its $2 million value. The first assumption in real estate appraising is that the land will be worth its value today of $2 million at the end of 50 years. To value the leased fee, first value the income stream. Begin by calculating the annual rent, as follows:

$$\$2,000,000 \times 0.0600 = \$120,000$$

per year annual land rent. Now enter Table 46, page 3 (p. 547), the page for 6.00 percent in the section for present value of 1 per period. Read down the time column to 50 years and across on that line to the column for present value of 1 per period. Read there the factor, 15.7618606. Multiply the annual rent by this factor to get

$$\$120,000 \times 15.7618606 = \$1,891,423$$

the present value of the rental income stream.

Now enter Table 46 again and find the present value of 1 also on the 50-year line with annual payments. The factor is 0.0542884. Multiply this by the presumed value of the future reversion, to get

$$\$2,000,000 \times 0.0542884 = 108,577$$

the present value of the reversion. The total of these two is $2 million. This was a time-consuming method to prove that a $2 million property is worth $2 million. But the method is precise and shows that the value of a leased fee is equal to the sum of the present value of the income stream plus the present value of the reversion. The same method will be used in more complex cases, where value is not known in advance or where the contract rental rate may diverge from the market rate.

Example 174.   Present Value of a Leasehold

Smithy Foods is the tenant under a lease for 12 more years. They have the right to sublease, and they have done so, to Perky Foods. While Smithy is paying $1240 per month net to its landlord, Perky is paying Smithy $2120 per month net for the same space for the same term. Smithy wants to sell its leasehold to an investor who requires a 9.75 percent yield.

To find the value of the leasehold, begin by taking the net income to the sublessor, Smithy, which is the difference between its rent income and its rent cost:

$$\$2120 - 1240 = \$880$$

per month net rental income. Now enter Table 46, page 18 (p. 562), on the page for 9.75 percent interest. Read down the right column to 120 months and across to the column for present worth of 1 per period under monthly payments. Read there the factor 76.4699968. Multiply this by Smithy's monthly income to get

$$\$880 \times 76.4699968 = \$67,294$$

the present value of Smithy's leasehold interest. When the rental under the lease, the **contract rental,** equals the market rental, also called the **economic rental,** the tenant's interest in the lease itself has no appraisal value. The tenant's furniture, fixtures, and equipment (FF&E), however, may have substantial value. The value of the leasehold is the value of the tenant's interest in the lease, plus the value of the FF&E. Whether the value of Smithy's leasehold arises from contract rental that is below market or from the value of the FF&E would require a market study of rentals.

Example 175. Present Value of a Stepped Sandwich Lease

A sandwich lease is a kind of leasehold, as in the previous example, where a tenant rents from a landlord and releases to another tenant, the subtenant. In major cities, the land under a building may be owned by one party and leased to another, who in turn leases to a building owner. The party in between is called the sandwich tenant.

Valorlaine Stores leased a land parcel during the 1930s for 110 years. The rent is $50,000 per year net. Their store is out-of-date, and they wish to demolish it. Happily, CrestCrown Developers would like to build a building there for the remaining 50 years on the lease. They have accepted Valorlaine's rent proposal for

Years 1 through 5: $200,000 per year

Years 6 through 50: 800,000 per year

All payments will be completely net and will be made at the beginning of each year. The appraiser wishes to value Valorlaine's sandwich lease, given the assessment that an 8.25 percent discount rate with annual compounding is appropriate to the transaction.

Set up the problem like this:

Years 1 to 5:

$200,000 − $50,000 = $150,000 net to Valorlaine

Years 6 to 50:

800,000 − 50,000 = 750,000 net to Valorlaine

Two factors of the present value of 1 per period will be needed: The first is found in the usual way. Enter Table 46, page 12 (p. 556), the page for 8.25 percent

discount rate. In the section for annual payments, find the factor for 4 years, that is one less than the first lease segment, under the column for present value of 1 per period, and add 1.00000 to get

$$3.2937791 + 1.000000 = 4.2937791$$

the present value factor for five annual payments at 8.25 percent interest, payments at beginning of year.

The second factor is found as follows: Enter Table 46, page 12 (p. 556), and get the present value of 1 per period for 49 years—11.8719945. Add 1.000000 to this to get 12.8719945. Then subtract from it the factor found in step 1:

$$12.8719945 - 4.2937791 = 8.5782154$$

the factor for 45 annual payments beginning 5 years in the future, payments at beginning of period.

Now multiply the annual rent by the factors obtained above and sum the results, as follows:

Years 1 to 5: $150,000 × 4.2937791 = $ 644,067

Years 6 to 50: 750,000 × 8.5782154 =   6,433,662

Total $7,077,729

the present value of Valorlaine's position for 50 years with a step-up in rent after 5 years, payments at beginning of period. Any number of step-ups or step-downs may be calculated in similar fashion, subtracting the factor for the period until the change from the factor for the total number of years.

Hoskold Present Value of 1 per Period

A mining engineer in the last century, Henry Davis Hoskold, found that ordinary Inwood tables did not adequately deal with the question of recapture of investment in mines. Some mines may be so large or difficult to work that they will pay out over a period of 10 or 20 years. Others may be so shallow or easy to work that they pay out in a few years. A mine that will be depleted in 3 years owes its high rate of return not to profitability, that is, return *on* investment, but to recapture, which is return *of* investment.

As capital is returned each year, there is an opportunity to reinvest to get a short-term rate of interest from bank deposits or quality bonds. A mine paying back its capital at 30 percent per year may be less valuable than one paying back 10 percent per year. If capital is returned in 3 years and the only alternative is, say, 3 percent interest, total wealth after 10 years may be less than if capital came back over a longer period. Hoskold solved this problem by using two rates, one internal to the property and the other determined by market rates.

A century after his work, Hoskold's principle has been brought to bear on real estate appraisal cases in the United States. The principle in Table 49 is that a primary rate is chosen for capitalization. This is the rate appropriate to speculative real estate deals, and is called the "speculative rate." A second rate, called the "safe rate," is the rate obtainable on money-good, readily available investments, such as governments or bank deposits. The Hoskold factors presented in Table 49 compound at only the safe rate, whereas the return on investment is received at the speculative rate. The Hoskold factor sets the stage for calculation of terminal wealth of an investor, a useful tool for investment comparisons.

Example 176. Hoskold Present Value of 1 per Period

Xenomon is appraising the leasehold of Capacity Containers' warehouse, which is leased to them by a consortium for a 25-year term. The property is a truck dock and will have no value at the end of the term. Capacity in turn leases the property to various shippers, who pay in the aggregate $125,000 more per year for the use of the property than Capacity is paying to the consortium. Capacity is thus a sandwich tenant. Since Capacity cannot for any practical purpose convert the property into something else, and since the present special purpose usage is somewhat speculative, Xenomon estimates that the correct rate for discounting the rentals is 12 percent. This will be the speculative rate in the Hoskold calculation. The current safe rate, that obtainable every day on high-quality bonds of as little as $1000, is 8.50 percent.

To find the Hoskold Present Value of 1 per Period, enter Table 49 on the page for 12.00 percent speculative rate and 8.50 percent safe rate. Read down the year column to 25 and across on that line to the column for 12.00 percent monthly. The factor there, 7.59721, is the Hoskold factor. Multiply it by the **sandwich rentals** to get

$$\$125,000 \times 7.59721 = \$949,651.25$$

or, rounding to the nearest $2500, $950,000, the value by Hoskold capitalization of $125,000 of annual sandwich rentals for 25 years.

Present Value of a Series of Rising or Falling Payments

Tables 47 and 48 present special cases of the present value of 1 per period (or Inwood) factors. Inwood factors assume that a constant payment is made each period, but in these tables it is assumed that the payments increase or decrease in each period. In Table 47, the assumption is that the payments change at a constant *rate*. So, an initial increase of 10 percent means that in subsequent years the increase will be 11.0 percent, 12.1 percent, and so on. In Table 48, the assumption is that the change is by a constant amount, that is, an increase of $3000 one year, $6000 the next, $9,000 the next, and so on.

Example 177. Present Value of a Series of Increasing Payments

James Pennoyer has leased to Burger Specials on the following terms: "Annual Rental shall be payable on the first day of each lease year and shall for the first year be $6000. Thereafter, rental each year shall be 3 percent greater than in the preceding year. The lease shall run for 15 years." Pennoyer considers 8.00 percent per annum to be the appropriate discount rate to value this income stream.

To find the present value of these rentals, enter Table 47 (a), page 5 (p. 588), the page for 3 percent annual rate of growth and 8.00 percent interest. Read down the left column to 14 years (1 less than the term) and across on that line to the column for 8.00 percent. Find the factor, 9.70044, and add 1.00000 to it (to account for the first year) to get the present value of 1 per period with increases of 3 percent per year. Multiply this by the initial rental to get

$$\$6000.00 \times 10.70044 = \$64,202.64$$

the present value of an annuity of $6000 per year, rising 3 percent per year. (The present value of $6000 per year flat for 15 years, i.e., not rising, would be $55,465.42.)

Example 178. Present Value of a Series of Decreasing Payments— Value of Rentals Expressed in Constant Dollars

Rastelnik holds a lease providing fixed rentals of $78,000 per year for 20 years. Although discount rates for such leases are 7.00 percent in the current market, Rastelnik feels that inflation will cut the purchasing power of the rentals by 2 percent every year.

To find the present value of the rentals in terms of constant purchasing power, enter Table 47 (b), page 1 (p. 596), the page for 7.00 percent interest and 2 percent annual decline. Read down the left column to 19 years (1 less than the lease term) and across on that line to the column for 7.00 percent. The factor there is 9.01815. Add 1.0000 to it, representing the first year. This gives the present value factor of 20 years of payments at 7.00 percent with payments declining 2 percent per year in real dollar terms. Multiply the factor by the rental to get

$$\$78,000 \times 10.01815 = \$781,415.70$$

the present value of the rentals in constant dollars, if inflation is 2 percent per year. (The present value in actual, rather than constant, dollars would be $884,176.)

Example 179.   Present Value of Rentals Growing with the CPI

Moira O'Shaughnessy has rented a freestanding store building to Goodie 2-Shoes on a 10-year lease for a rental of $55,000 per year net, adjusted each year by the change if any in the **Consumer Price Index** (CPI). She wishes to know the present value at 9.00 percent discount rate of the property, if (1) the CPI rises an average of 5 percent per year, and (2) the property can be sold at the end of 10 years for $550,000.

Begin by valuing the income stream, the annual rentals from the property. Enter Table 47 (a), page 6 (p. 589), the section for annual rate of growth of 5 percent. Read down to 10 years and across on that line to the column for 9.00 percent, and find the factor, 7.79843. Multiply this by the annual rental to get

$$\$55,000 \times 7.79843 = \$428,913.65$$

the present value of the rentals assuming 5 percent annual increases from the CPI and a 9.00 percent discount rate.

Now obtain from Table 46, page 15 (p. 599), the present value of of the reversion in the usual manner (for details, see Example 170): Enter there at 9.00 percent interest, read down to 10 years and under annual payments in the present value column find 0.4224108, the reversion factor. Multiply this by the estimated sale price to get

$$\$550,000 \times 0.4224108 = \$232,325.94$$

the present value of an expected $550,000 reversion discounted 10 years at 9.00 percent. Add the income stream value and the reversion to get

$$\$428,913.65 + 232,325.94 = \$661,239.59$$

the value of the property with rentals rising 5 percent per year and a $550,000 future sale price.

Note The example uses valuations based on annual payments, but real estate rentals most often are paid monthly. It is common appraisal practice to use annual figures when there are important elements of supposition in the valuation, as with the CPI and the future sale price in this example. The examples are illustrative only and do not preclude that an appraiser might select monthly figures in this case.

Example 180.   Value of Increasing Annuity at Different Discount Rates and Value of Increasing Percentage Rents

Herman Songin is valuing the rentals from the SpendMor Playtoys lease. SpendMor pays a minimum guarantee of $36,000 per year plus **percentage rent** of 3.5 percent of gross sales. In the past 5 years, the percentage rent has averaged $9000 and has been increasing 7 percent per year. Songin wants to value the rentals on the assumption that the percentage rents will continue to rise 7 percent per year. But, because of the uncertainty in the percentage rent forecast, he wants to apply a different, higher discount rate to them than that for the minimum guaranteed rentals.

Treat this case as if it were two different leases, one made up of the minimum guaranteed rent only and the other made up of the percentage rents only. The first lease is simply a stream of income at a fixed rate of $36,000 per year. It should be valued with the tables at Table 46 using the methods of Example 171. The discount rate will be that which is appropriate to rather secure income, such as reasonably rated corporate bonds. The second lease is one composed of percentage rentals only, that is, rent starts at $9000 per year, rising 7 percent per year. The discount rate would be that appropriate for more speculative transactions, perhaps 200 or 300 basis points above the rate for good bonds. The valuation is done following Example 177.

Payments Increasing by Constant Amount

Table 48 provides for a series of payments which rise in constant amount each period. The amount of the first change (which occurs in the second year) is expressed as a percentage, but it is *not* compounded. So $500 on a $10,000 base, expressed as a 5 percent initial amount of growth in the table, would mean payments of $10,000, $10,500, $11,000, and so on.

Example 181. Present Value of Rentals Rising in Constant Amount

Bildwill Developers has leased to Swearingen Medical for 10 years at an annual rental of $51,000 net, rising $3000 per year after the first year. At a discount rate of 9.00 percent, what is the present value of this lease?

Begin by finding the amount of 1st year growth. It is $3000 ÷ $51,000 = 0.0588 or 5.88 percent. Enter Table 48 (a), page 6 (p. 616), at 6.0 percent amount of 1st year growth, the closest rate available (the small difference will overstate the results slightly). Read down to 10 years and across on that line to the 9.00 percent column. The factor there, 7.88002, is the present value of 1 per period of a rising series. Multiply it by the annual rental to get

$$\$51,000 \times 7.88002 = \$401,881.02$$

the present value of a series of ten payments rising 6.0 percent per year after the first year, at a discount rate of 9.00 percent.

Payments Decreasing by a Constant Amount

Table 48 (b) illustrates the effect of stepped declines in the payments that are being valued. The series of payments begins at a certain level and after the first year declines by some amount, for example a $12,000 payment, declining $600 per year, giving $12,000, $11,400, $10,800, and so on. The amount of the first change is expressed as a percentage, but the amount remains constant in each succeeding year.

Some negative numbers appear in the lower, later portions of the table. These are the result of decline continuing at fixed amounts and becoming larger portions of the total. What this means is that eventually no value exists in a payment stream that becomes increasingly negative (for example, when rising expenses outstrip income).

Example 182. Present Value of Rents with CPI Clause Compared to Rents without

Emmanuel Seguin has the opportunity to lease an office to one of two major corporations. The possible deals are the following:

10-year lease $15 per square foot net, no CPI clause

10-year lease $12 per square foot net, full CPI protection

Seguin estimates his borrowing rate at 10.00 percent per year and believes that the Consumer Price Index, standing now at 150.3, will rise by 12 points each year.

To find which lease offers better value to Seguin, first measure the initial growth in the CPI. It is

$$12 \text{ points} \div 150.3 = 0.0798 = 7.98\%$$

or, rounding, 8.0 percent. Now consider that *growth* of the CPI is a *decline* in Seguin's purchasing power. Enter Table 48 (b), page 7 (p. 629), at the section for 8.0 percent amount of 1st year *decline*. Read down to 10 years and across on that line to the 10.00 percent interest column. The factor there is 4.31326, the present value of the declining series. Multiply it by the rental offered in the no-CPI lease to get

$$\$15.00 \times 4.31326 = 64.6989$$

the present value of the first lease with the inflation taken out.

Now enter Table 46, page 19 (p. 563), and obtain the factor for 10.00 percent interest, annual payments, 10 years. It is 6.1445671. Multiply it by the rental from the lease with CPI clause to get

$$\$12.00 \times 6.1445671 = 73.734805$$

the present value of the lease with the CPI clause. This says that $15 per square foot with no CPI clause will have about 12 percent less purchasing power over 10 years than a lease with $12 per square foot and full CPI protection, if the CPI rises 12 points per year from a 150 base and interest is 10.00 percent.

Note that the same calculations applied to the assumption that the CPI rises only 4.5 points per year (a 3 percent initial change) would produce a deflated present value of 81.86745 for the $15 lease, or about 11 percent *greater* purchasing power. One or two more "bracketing" steps would enable Seguin to establish how sensitive this problem is to a correct guess about inflation. He could then calculate the minimum inflation increase needed to make the first lease equivalent to the second.

Note No dollar signs were put before the answers above, although the answer could be expressed in dollars. That was to emphasize that the two values are indexes, created only to compare the relative merits. What counts is not the amount but which lease gives the higher value. For this reason, it is not critical that this example measures rentals, usually beginning of year payments, with end of year factors.

APPRAISAL TECHNIQUES

Up to this point, we have focused on capitalization, the process of finding value from estimated income, and specific kinds of capitalization, especially to find the value of long-term leases with income of varying characteristics. From the techniques to find the value, we proceed to techniques to analyze the quality of the income stream or to quantify the income or market factors and to separate what might affect one or few buyers from what affects the typical buyer.

The first two techniques in effect continue the capitalization discussion. The internal rate of return (IRR) of an investment and the net present value (NPV) of an investment are analyses often used in conjunction with capitalization. The tables we present will allow the IRR and NPV analysis to be tested and strengthened.

Internal Rate of Return of an Investment

The discount rate that discounts all expected future returns from a property back to the level of the property's original cost is the internal rate of return of the property. The IRR provides a single-number means to measure the performance of income-producing real estate. The mathematics of deriving IRRs is comparable to that for yield to maturity of corporate bonds and mortgage loan investments. But the potential for wide variances in the cash flows of operating real estate creates two problems in the use of IRRs: First, one IRR may not be fairly comparable with another, since the IRR tells nothing about the stability of the income stream. And an IRR for a property with wide swings in its cash inflows or outflows may not be unique; one property could have two or more IRRs, each mathematically valid.

To improve the comparability of IRRs, Table 1 presents the IRR for a variety of standard cases. Its entries serve as models to which calculated IRRs may be compared. Important differences may then be scrutinized for reasons as to the variance. The table assumes that monthly income is received at the capitalization rate chosen. At the end of a selected holding period, a capital gain or loss is deemed to be realized. The IRR is the annual rate of return which matches these assumptions to the initial cost.

Example 183.   The Internal Rate of Return of an Investment

Serge Krasnow is preparing an analysis of La Campina. The expected monthly cash flows will provide a return at a capitalization rate of 9.00 percent. Krasnow projects the eventual selling price after a 10-year holding period at 250 percent of today's value, and he wishes to know the IRR from this set of circumstances.

To find the IRR, enter Table 1, page 2 (p. 146), the page for capital gain and the section for a 10-year holding period. On the line for a cap rate of 9.00 percent, read across to the column for 150 percent capital gain. The rate there, 15.388 percent, is the IRR of a property whose monthly returns give a 9.00 percent capitalization rate and that is worth 250 percent of its initial value after 10 years.

Example 184.   IRR in a Capital Loss Situation

Peter Drobney is appraising The Inn at the Storehouse. Although well constructed, the location is secondary. Based on his analysis thus far, net operating income (NOI) appears to run at a rate of 11.50 percent per year. Drobney believes the largest capital loss in the next 5 years would be 30 percent of today's value.

To find the IRR in such an event, enter Table 1, page 5 (p. 149), the pages for capital loss cases and the section for 5 years. In that section, read across on the line for 11.50 percent cap rate to the column for 30 percent capital loss. The answer there, 6.391 percent, is the IRR in the event that 11.50 percent per year is received from the monthly income and the property can be sold after 5 years at only 70 percent of its present cost. The capital loss would cut about 5.00 percent per year from the return that the monthly cash flows produce.

Net Present Value of an Investment

If the income and eventual sales proceeds of a property are discounted to the present at a market discount rate and deducted from the original cost or proposed purchase price, the result is the net present value (NPV). Three outcomes can result from this process: The net present value is greater than zero, indicating the property furnishes more than the discount rate of return; the net present value may be zero, which means that the property furnishes exactly the discount rate as a rate of return; or the net present value is less than zero, meaning that less than the discount rate has been earned. The IRR is similarly more than, equal to, or less than the discount rate in these cases.

The NPV approach to investment analysis rests on the same logic as the IRR method, but NPV has the advantage that its results are expressed in money or percent of initial cost, so the scale of the project's profitability can be measured more easily. That is, a property which has an enormously high rate of return for 2 or 3 years, followed by a low rate for 10 or 15 years, may have a high IRR. When its overall profitability is compared with another property of lower IRR, it may be that at the end of 15 years, the investor with the lower IRR has greater actual wealth. The NPV approach copes with this.

More than one IRR may be valid for a given set of property circumstances. Two completely different IRRs may apply to a proposed investment, and mathematicians assure us it is not valid to exclude one because it seems unreasonable, such as 42 percent per year return. In the NPV approach, each value obtained is the only mathematically valid result for the circumstances.

Example 185. Calculating the Net Present Value

Cyrilla Saad is presented with a more complex appraisal assignment than generally described in Table 3 and wants to calculate the NPV for the case at hand. The Zeno Society Building currently operates at a cash flow deficit, owing principally to a below-market lease to The Zeno Society. The Zeno lease provides for a substantial rent increase 2 years from now. And other tenants in the building who have fixed-rate expense contributions will then begin paying their full proportionate share of operating expenses. As a result, the 5-year cash flow projection looks like the following:

The Zeno Society Building: Projected NOI Years 1 through 5 (thousands of dollars)

	Year				
	1	2	3	4	5
Net operating income	−126.00	−103.00	281.00	296.00	387.00

Cyrilla Saad estimates that capitalization rates appropriate for use in valuation of this property center around 8.00 percent, whereas overall discount rates are 11.25 percent. The cap rate would indicate a potential sale price 5 years in the future of $4,837,500, or $387,000 ÷ 0.0800, from which 5 percent should be subtracted for selling expenses. Given the $3 million proposed sale price of the building today, she will develop the NPV of the offering.

To begin the calculation, enter Table 46 at the page for 11.25 percent discount rate. In the annual payment section, take the factors in the future worth of 1 column for years 1 through 5, and divide the cash flow for each year by its corresponding factor from the table. The following is a simple way to lay this out:

The Zeno Society Building
Estimated NPV: Projected 5-Year Holding Period (thousands of dollars)

	Year				
	1	2	3	4	5
Operating income	−126.00	−103.00	281.00	296.00	387.00
Proceeds from sale*					4595.63
Total	−126.00	−103.00	281.00	296.00	4982.63
Discounted at 11.25%	÷ 1.1125000	÷ 1.2376563	÷ 1.3768926	÷ 1.5317930	÷ 1.7041197
Present value	−113.26	−83.22	204.08	193.24	2923.87

Sum of years 1 through 5, $3124.71, at 8.00 percent less 5 percent sale costs
*Fifth year NOI capitalized

The sum of the discounted values, $3,124,710, is the present value of the property. Deducting the $3,000,000 proposed selling price today gives $124,710, the net present value of the property at an 11.25 percent discount rate. Since the projection indicates the NPV is greater than zero, the proposed offering price is justified, based on market conditions found by Saad.

Note If the NPV had been exactly zero, the IRR in this proposal would have been equal to the discount rate.

Example 186. Net Present Value of an Investment

Dettle & Partners have been retained to form a feasibility study of Downtown Centre. The Centre is expected to deliver an initial capitalization rate of 7.50 percent per year. The appraisers believe that over a 10-year period, the value of the property will increase 200 percent. The current discount rate that they have derived from comparable market transactions is 11.50 percent per year.

To find the prospective NPV of the property, enter Table 3, page 9 (p. 163), the page for a discount rate of 11.50 percent. In the section for a 10-year holding period, read across on the line for a cap rate of 7.50 percent. Under the 200 percent capital gain column, read 139.966 percent, or nearly 140 percent. Subtracting the 100 percent that represents the original investment in the project, they find the NPV to be 40 percent. Many other factors will be included in the detailed cash flow projection and valuation. But this analysis from Table 3 will serve as an early warning device to signal if the value conclusion is within a reasonable range of this "model" figure.

Spreading Average Rents or Prices to Typical

Pricing real estate sale prices and rentals is a complex business. The pricing rationale of a housing subdivision or a high-rise apartment is often subjective. Appraisers, however, tend to put all of the units into an average that can be objectively compared to competition. Using the average means that individual units might be overlooked that would weigh the average differently; treating each unit individually risks that the ensemble of prices no longer reflects market reality.

Table 74 provides a simple price grid-maker. The analyst specifies the range of values that apply to a unit. For example, one-bedroom apartment rents may be set with a spread of 30 percent from the highest priced to the lowest, and one-bedroom units of type A may be said to be 25 percent better than those of type B. Using the percentage of each unit in the total, the analyst is given the weight of that unit's prices relative to the average. Multiplying each unit's weight by the average gives a well-spread chart of prices known to be equal or

very close to the average. Overall pricing will be fully comparable with average prices found at competition, and the logic of individual pricing decisions can be tested for reasonableness. When the actual prices of one-bedroom units are seen priced in dollars per month, for example, it may appear that 30 percent is too great a price range or not great enough.

Example 187. Spreading Average Rents to Unit Rents

Swinburne Apartments are under construction, and Byron Dylan is preparing a rent schedule for them. The 100-unit building will have 93,000 square feet of rentable space, and Dylan estimates market rent at 90 cents per square foot per month. The average apartment should therefore rent at $837 per month— 93,000 × 0.90 ÷ 100 (units). The apartment types are as follows:

One-bedroom: 30 rear view units, 30 front view units

Two-bedroom: 20 park view units, 20 lake view units

Based on average size and quality, Dylan feels that the two-bedroom units should have a 33 percent higher average rent than the one-bedroom average. So the section of Table 74, page 2 (p. 799), labeled "33% Premium A over B" will be selected, and for purposes of this analysis, "A" units shall be the two-bedrooms. Since 40 out of the 100 units are two-bedroom, the distribution selected will be 40 percent type A, 60 percent type B.

Turning to the apartments themselves, Dylan feels that the two-bedroom units are quite close to each other in quality, with the lake view being slightly superior. He awards only a 5 percent difference from high to low of the two-bedroom, the lake view being the high. Going to the 40 percent type A, 60 percent type B distribution, we take the high and low factors from the 40 percent type A portion to get 114.7 percent for the low (park view) and 120.6 for the high (lake view).

In the one-bedroom category, however, Dylan sees an important differential between the front and the rear views, which he places at a 25 percent spread high to low. The low and high figures are in the column for 25 percent spread from high to low in the B portion. The figures are 77.2 percent low and 99.3 percent for the high. We are ready to put the factors into the rent chart.

	Average	Factor	Unit Rent	Total Category
One bedroom				
30 rear view	$837.00	0.772	646.16	$19,384.80
30 front view	837.00	0.993	831.14	24,934.20
Subtotal: one bedroom			738.65 average	44,319.00
Two bedroom				
20 park view	837.00	1.147	960.04	19,200.80
20 lake view	837.00	1.206	1,009.42	20,188.40
Subtotal: Two bedroom			984.73 average	39,389.20
		Grand total = $837.08		$83,708.20

This program will meet the standards called for within close tolerances for round-offs. The average apartment is $837.08, within pennies of the desired target. The two-bedroom average is 33.3 percent greater than the one-bedroom, while the best two-bedroom is 5.1 percent higher than the low, and the best one-bedroom is 28.6 percent higher than the low one-bedroom. All differences from the specifications are due to rounding.

The rentals in this chart could simply be rounded off and used as is, if the intention is to sort the units into primary value categories regardless of the precise features in each unit. In today's property management world, however, this sort of mass estimation would serve only as a rough cut to establish the price ranges for comparison with competition. Further refinement would be made to value-price the apartments. In value pricing, special features and qualities of each apartment, as well as any demerits of size, location, or appointments are used to raise or lower its rent. Nonetheless, the rental spreads allow the appraiser to discern fundamental quality differences and to weight the pricing by value classes before proceeding to such refining.

Graduated Sales Prices

Table 66 shows how to build a graduated sales price chart in which the values are weighted for the time value of money and graduated upward over time. The table shows the percentage of "standard" or list price to be charged. By standard is meant the price that would be charged if a fixed sale plan were being quoted instead of a graduated plan. Each year after the first, the price rises by a percentage, from 3 percent to 10 percent according to the section selected, and remains at that level during that year. The present value of the prices in the graduated plan equals the present value of the standard prices for the same period. The assump-

tion is that sales occur uniformly each month over the term of the program.

Example 188. Graduated Sales Prices

The feasibility study of Stephen Leaworth concludes that Sinfonietta Townhouses will sell at an average price of $130,000. It is expected the developer will offer a discount at first and, once the sales pattern is established, increase prices 5 percent in the second and third years, so as to bring the value of sales, weighted for the time value of money, up to the $130,000 average. The study uses 11.00 percent as the cost of funds throughout.

To find the initial price, enter Table 66, page 5 (p. 756), the 3-year plan. Take the factors from the 11.00 percent column and multiply each by the desired average price, $130,000, to get

$130,000 × 0.954107 = $124,033.91 in year 1

$130,000 × 1.001812 = 130,235.56 in year 2

$130,000 × 1.051903 = 136,747.39 in year 3

These are the sales prices that will give 5 percent increases each year and that equal, in present value terms, an average of $130,000, if interest is 11.00 percent per year. Rounding these to give more logical prices of $124,000, $130,250, and $136,750 will not affect the valuation.

Spreading Tenant Alterations in Projections

Table 75 aids preparation of capital and expense projections by giving the progression of the cost for the next 15 years at any of twelve assumed inflation rates.

Example 189. Projecting Apartment Refitting and Make-Ready Cost

Soderstrom's analysis of Barefoot Bay Apartments will include a 5-year cash flow projection. The development has 200 apartments which cost an average of $240 to make ready for a tenant upon turnover. This would be $48,000, or 200 × $240, for the entire complex. Given an inflation estimate of 4 percent per year and 50 percent turnover of units, what will be the make-ready cost in 5 years?

Enter Table 75, page 1 (p. 803), the section for 4 percent inflation. Read down the year column to 5 and across to the column headed 50 percent turnover. Read there the factor 60.833 percent. Multiply this by the make-ready cost for the entire project to get

$$\$48,000 \times 0.60833 = \$29,199.84$$

or, rounding to the next $100, $29,200, the tenant make-ready cost 5 years from now, if inflation is 4 percent per year and turnover in the fifth year is 50 percent.

Total Growth or Decline Converted to Annual Rate of Growth

Table 6 gives the *compounded* annual rate of change for a given total amount of change. The simple annual rate is easily found: If the value of a property increased 125 percent over a 10-year holding period, the simple or straight-line rate of growth is easily found. Divide 125 percent by 10 to get a 12.5 percent rate of increase. The compounded rate, however, is only 8.45 percent, or roughly two-thirds of the straight-line rate.

Example 190. Total Growth Converted to Annual Rate of Growth

Candleson is deciding whether to buy the Clemency Ridge apartment complex. She has estimated that rents will increase a total of 75 percent over the next 8 years. To find the annual rate of increase, enter Table 6, page 2 (p. 189). Read down the left column to 8 years. Now read across to the column headed 75 percent and read 7.245 percent, the compounded annual rate of rent increase equal to a 75 percent total increase over 8 years.

Example 191. Annual Change in Revenue Growth from Total Change

Real estate tax revenues in the City of Boston rose 200 percent from 1983 through 1989. To find the rate of increase, enter Table 6, page 3 (p. 190), the page for a 200 percent increase. Read down to 6 years and across to 200 percent, to find 20.094 percent. The increase is say, 20 percent per year, compounded, over the 6-year period.

Rate of Change in CPI 1960 to 1990

The CPI is the most commonly used measure of changes in purchasing power and inflation in the United States. The index is published by the Bureau of Labor Statistics, U.S. Department of Labor. The principal series is known as CPI-U, All Urban Consumers, which covers about 80 percent of the U.S. population.

In addition to the index presented here, which is the U.S. City Average Index, regional indexes are published for each major metropolitan area. The current indexes use as their reference base the period 1982 to 1984.

Note Prior to the use of 1982–1984 as the reference base, the CPI for many years used a base of 1967 = 100. Many documents of course were prepared over the years requiring the use of the index with base 1967 = 100. Consult your attorney, but you should be able to use the figures in Table C, since it is the identical index recalculated by the government on the revised base.

Example 192. Percent Change in CPI over 1-, 3-, 5-, or 10-Year Term

Portions of Table C give the percentage change that has occurred between a given month and the same month 3, 5, or 10 years earlier, or between the average for the year and the third, fifth, or tenth year earlier. Each figure gives the percentage change in the index from the same time in the earlier period. The next example shows how to calculate the percentage difference for time differences other than 3, 5, or 10 years.

Example 193.   Calculating Percent Change in CPI

The CPI in January, 1989, stood at 121.1. Nine years earlier, the January CPI was 77.8. Begin by subtracting the earlier index from the later one, to get the index difference, as follows:

$$121.1 - 77.8 = 43.3$$

the index difference. Next, divide the index difference by the earlier index, to get

$$\frac{\text{Index difference}}{\text{January, 1980 index}} = \frac{43.3}{77.8} = 0.557 = 55.7\%$$

the percent change in index from January 1980 to January 1989.

Example 194.   Annual Rate of Inflation from Total Rate

In the property under appraisal, the landlord offers leases with a fixed annual increase of 2 percent per year. Anne Tomlen finds that the standard offering in the market is an annual increase equal to 35 percent of the change in the CPI. The CPI was 210.0 five years ago. Now after 5 years, it is 316.5.

To compare the landlord's terms with market conditions, begin by finding the percent change in the CPI. It is 318.5 divided by 210.0, which equals 1.5167. Subtract 1.00 to get 0.5167, or 51.67 percent interest. Rounding to 52 percent, enter Table 6 at the section for 52 percent increase. Read down the years column to 5 and across to the 52 percent column. The answer there is 8.734 percent. Multiply this by 35 percent to get

$$0.35 \times 0.08734 = 0.03057 = 3.057\%$$

or 3.0 percent actual annual increases under the CPI lease formulas. Based on the experience in the community over the past 5 years, the landlord's offer appears favorable to tenants.

Cross-Reference By looking through Table C, Tomlen will see that 5-year increases in the CPI of 52 percent or more were quite unusual between 1960 and 1991.

Example 195.   Rate of Inflation in a Future Year

Steinmetz is preparing a 5-year rent projection. Noting the CPI has increased 5.50 percent in the past year, Steinmetz needs to estimate what the inflation rate will be, relative to today's dollars, in the coming 5 years.

Enter Table 7 at the section for 5.50 percent interest rate. Under the 5.50 percent column, find the factors for years 1 through 5. They are

Year	Inflation Rate
1	5.64
2	5.96
3	6.30
4	6.65
5	7.03

If the present 5.50 percent nominal annual rate of growth occurs in the index over the coming 5 years, the inflation rate for year 1 of the study will be 5.64 percent; for year 2, it will be 5.96 percent relative to the prior year; for years 3, 4, and 5, the rates will be 6.30 percent, 6.65 percent, and 7.03 percent expressed in today's dollars. Stated differently, in year 5 it will take $107.03 of today's dollars to buy what $100 of today's dollars bought in the fourth year.

Example 196.   Periods in Which Growth Occurred

Okara's research shows that population growth in the region under study was 12.0 percent per year compounded during the period between the 1980 and 1990 censuses. If she assumes that the growth was "normal," that is, that it followed the compounded rate exactly, how long did it take for the first 25 percent of the growth to occur?

Enter Table 64, page 6 (p. 735), the section for four-party partitions and 120 months. On the line for fourth party, read across to the 12.00 percent column. The answer there, 45.6588 months, means that it required 46 months for the first 25 percent of population growth to occur under "normal" conditions. The remaining 25 percent segments can be found by continuing to read up in reverse order.

Example 197.   Calculating Rent Tied to the CPI

Rent on the Karel lease is $14.00 per square foot and is scheduled to change on July 1, 1990. The lease provides that the new rent will be the result of multiplying the base rent by a fraction, the numerator of which will be the CPI for May 1990 and the denominator of which will be the CPI for May 1985.

Enter Table C and read down the left column to 1985 and across on that line to the column headed May. The factor there, 107.3, is the denominator for the fraction. In that column on the line for 1990 is the factor, 129.2, the numerator of the fraction. The new rent will be

$$\$14.00 \text{ per square foot} \times \frac{129.2}{107.3} = \$14.00 \times 1.20503$$
$$= \$16.87$$

rent per square foot as of July 1, 1990.

Example 198.   Future Simple Rate of Increase in Rent

By future simple rate of increase is meant the increase, not compounded, that would occur in a future year relative to the initial year. Stan believes that rents in the region will rise 8.0 percent per year over the next 10 years. What would be the rent increase in the tenth year?

Here the rate of interest will be treated as the rate of rental growth. Enter Table 7, page 2 (p. 192), at 8.00 percent interest rate. Read down elapsed years to 10 and across on that line to the column headed 8.00 percent and find the factor, 17.01 percent. The increase in rent levels in the tenth year, as a percentage of first-year rent, will be 17 percent, if the expected 8.0 percent annual rate of growth is sustained. Note that this is not the cumulative rate of growth. It is the increase in the tenth year alone above the rent in the initial year.

Number of Installments Available from a Deposit

Table 59 gives the number of monthly payments that can be drawn from an interest-bearing deposit. Payments are assumed to be drawn from the deposit 30 days after setting it up. In some places, the entry is "unl" for "unlimited," which means the draw is less than the interest accrued in a month. The deposit in such case would never be exhausted.

Example 199.   Number of Installments Available from a Deposit

Lewis Cleborg is appraising Hereford House. The seller put $100,000 of the sale proceeds into an escrow fund for repairs and deferred maintenance. The bank holding the deposit will give 8.00 percent

interest and is to pay out $2500 per month. Cleborg wants to know for how long a period he can exclude capital repair costs from his projected cash flow.

To find the minimum number of draws available, begin by finding the percentage of the initial fund that each draw represents. It is

$$\$2,500 \div \$100,000 = 0.025 = 2.50\%$$

the monthly draw. Now enter Table 59, page 1 (p. 722), and read down the monthly payment column to 2.50 percent. Across on that line under 8.00 percent, find the answer 46.7, the number of monthly payments of $2500 that can be drawn from a $100,000 deposit earning 8.00 percent per year interest.

Example 200.   Time When Rentals Should Have Grown to a Certain Level

Birnbaum is projecting rentals of Le Palais Royal. He expects that rents should increase 9.0 percent per year in the coming years. At that rate, how long would be needed for rentals to have risen to 2.5 times their present level, that is, a 150 percent increase?

In this instance, the rate of increase will be represented by the interest rate. Enter Table 68, page 1 (p. 772), and read down the interest rate column to 9.00 percent. On that line under the column for a 150 percent increase, the answer, 10Y 3m, indicates that after 10 years and 3 months rents would be 250 percent of their present level, if a 9.0 percent growth rate is sustained.

Example 201.   Time When Population Growth Should Have Occurred

The City of Bella Vista Dunes has been growing rapidly. The population is expected to grow at 12.00 percent per year. If this growth occurs, when will the population have doubled?

Doubling means a 100 percent increase, so the answer will lie in Table 68 (p. 772), under the 100 percent increase column on the line for 12.00 percent "interest." The entry there is 5Y 10m or 5 years, 10 months from now. In principle, the population grows continuously, while this table assumes monthly increases in the number of residents. Any error arising from this inexactitude should be far outweighed by errors in polling formulas.

Time When Given Mortgage Balance Occurs

Table 67 tells when important mortgage balance benchmarks are achieved for different interest rates and amortization schedules. Small differences may occur from the schedules provided by lenders. Table 67 is precise, but lenders often round off mortgage payments, causing slight differences from the table.

Example 202.   Time When Given Mortgage Balance Occurs

For a feasibility study, Gallovas wants to include information about loan refinancing. He believes the property would make a good refinancing candidate when it has been reduced to 80 percent of its present balance. The loan bears interest at 9.50 percent and has 22 years remaining until full amortization.

Turn to the section of Table 67, page 4 (p. 769), the section for 9.50 percent. Read down the left column to 22 years' amortization of loan and across on that line to the column for 80 percent unpaid balance of loan. The time given there, 9Y 4m, indicates that the loan will pass through 80 percent balance in the ninth year and fourth month from now.

Note that it was not important what the original amortization schedule was, only the time remaining from now until full amortization. In other words, the amortization schedules of a 30-year loan that has been amortized for 7 years and that of a 23-year full amortization loan are identical.

Example 203.   Portion of Price Attributable to Below-Market Financing

---

To attract a buyer, a seller may offer to take back a **purchase money mortgage,** at a lower interest rate than the current market. McGorkle Bros. are preparing a comparable sales analysis for an appraisal. In one of the comparable sale cases, the seller sold the property at a price of $400,000, consisting of $100,000 cash down payment with seller financing at 6.00 percent interest for 5 years. At the time of the sale, mortgage interest rates were generally 8.50 percent, so it is clear that part of the sale was the price for the cheap loan, not for the real estate. The appraisers want to allocate the price between value of real estate and value of seller financing.

Enter Table 10, page 13 (p. 213), the section for a stated interest rate of 8.50 percent. Read down

the left column to 6.00 percent and across on that line to the column headed 5 years. The factor there, 110.56631 percent, is the percentage that should have been paid for the financing. Since only 100 percent was paid, dividing the loan by the factor will give

$$\$300,000 \div 1.1056631 = \$271,330$$

the "real" amount of the financing. To this must be added the down payment of $100,000 for a comparable value of $371,330. The difference between the comparable value and the contract price is the premium paid for the below-market financing. Appraisers will deem the sale price of this comparable to be $371,330.

Future Simple Rate of Return on Initial Investment

Table 7 provides the annual rate of return on the *original* invested amount. The table was used earlier in this chapter for a future rent increase. Here it will show the investment return in a future year. A deposit of $100 at 5.50 percent interest per year, compounded monthly, will increase $5.64 in the first year, $5.96 in the second, and $6.29 in the third. The compounded rate of interest remains 5.50 percent for each year, but the **future simple** rates are 5.64 percent, 5.96 percent, and 6.29 percent. Future simple rates shown by Table 7 illustrate the sensitivity of investments to compounding and how to isolate growth in a given year in the future.

Example 204.   Future Simple Rate of Return on Initial Investment

---

Firptin estimates that income on a 5-year appraisal projection will compound at 12.00 percent interest. She wishes to know the annual rate of income in the 5th year of the deposit.

Enter Table 7, page 2 (p. 192), the section for 12.00 percent interest rate or rate of growth. Read down the years elapsed column to 5 and across on that line to the 12.00 percent column. The answer there is 20.45 percent. The interest that she will earn on the original deposit in its 5th year will be 20.4 percent of her initial investment.

Deposit to Create a Sinking Fund

A deposit to a **sinking fund** builds up an amount needed to be paid in the future. Sinking funds are at the heart of the capitalization process as well as the annuity payment mortgage loan. The deposit to create a sinking fund is shown in Table 52; the deposit to complete a fund in which some money is already accumulated is given by Table 53. In the tables, the numbers in the monthly column are the totals for a year, the sum of 12 monthly deposits. To get the factor per month, divide the table entry by 12.

Example 205. Building a Reserve for Replacements

The Sentry & Sentinel newspaper chain has started to change over to electronic editing. In order to adapt their office quarters to the new system, they will need to build a fund of $800,000 over the next 60 months to be taken monthly from the company's current cash flow. They can obtain an average interest yield on the fund of 9.25 percent from a combination of bank deposits and commercial paper investments.

To find the amount to be deducted from the newspaper's earnings to build the fund, enter Table 52, page 4 (p. 684), the page for 9.25 percent interest. Read down the end-of-year column to year 5 and across on that line to the entry under 9.25 percent interest, monthly. The factor there, 15.805878, is the sum of 12 monthly deposits to the fund. Each year 15.805878 percent of the total fund must be set aside from monthly deposits. Multiply the factor by the desired future total and divide by 12 to get

$$\$800,000 \times 0.15805878 \div 12 = \$10,537.25$$

the monthly deposit needed to build an $800,000 sinking fund in 60 months when 9.25 percent interest is paid.

Chapter 6

LEASING, PROPERTY MANAGEMENT, AND MAINTENANCE

This chapter considers the operating life of income property from the time it is bought to the time it is sold. A broad topic, it is divided into sections according to the interests of the specialists who manage real estate assets: leasing agents, asset managers, property managers, and corporate facilities managers. The sections are:

Leasing

Rental income, concessions, vacancy, and impact of vacancy

Real estate operations, reserves, and replacements

Efficiency and money-saving matters

LEASING

Today's leasing specialist must be prepared to respond to a broad spectrum of financial inquiries: What is the yield, if this is the rent? What rent will bring this yield? What will these concessions do to the true rent? What will it cost to assume a tenant's present lease? All these and the financial consequences of lease terms, such as the CPI clause, are dealt with in this chapter. (Valuation of leases, however, is dealt with in Chapter 5.) As this chapter progresses, we move from income and yield questions through vacancy and expense analysis toward reserves and money-saving opportunities.

Annual Rent Constants

Annual rent constants serve the role in leasing that mortgage constants do in financing. They show the rent necessary to give a return on investment and the return of all or a part of the invested capital. Although rents in multitenant buildings are most often set by reference to competition, the rent constant is the building block most often used to construct the rent proposal in build-to-suit or single-tenant cases.

Example 206. Annual Rent Constants

Greenup Corporation has been asked to give its quotation for a **build-to-suit lease** of a new restaurant facility. Because the design is not yet fixed, costs may vary from \$1.3 million to \$1.75 million. Accordingly, bidders have been asked to submit quotations as a constant annual payment for rents which will be paid monthly in advance. Greenup will base its proposal on an 8.00 percent rent rate for 15 years.

To find the rent constant, enter Table 38, page 3 (p. 460), the page for 8.00 percent interest. Reading across on the 15-year line, find under monthly advance, 11.391879 percent, the annual rent constant. Since the rent constant is similar to a mortgage constant, this rental rate will give the landlord 8.00 percent annual return *on* its investment and the return *of* its investment over 15 years.

Example 207.   Rent Constant to Retire Investment Except Land

Seraphic Baking will put four of its Cookie Heaven drive-in cookie jars in the community. Its contractor will construct the company's standard building on a developer's prepared site for a guaranteed **turnkey** price of $750,000. Barneveld intends to bid for one of the locations. The proposal will be on a site that Seraphic has approved and has valued at $180,000. In addition, about $150,000 of fees, site preparation, and other costs will be involved for a total package of $1,080,000. Barneveld's offer will be based on an 11.00 percent return and the return of the investment except land over the 20-year term of the lease. Rents will be paid monthly in advance.

Enter Table 38, page 6 (p. 463), the section for 11.00 percent interest rate. Read down the year column to 20 and across to the section for monthly advance. The factor there, 12.273751 percent, is the rent constant for all but the land. Multiply the land by the desired return to get

$$\$180,000 \times 0.1100 = \$19,800$$

annual land rent. Now multiply the difference between the land value and the total cost by the rent constant to get

$$\$900,000 \times 0.12273751 = \$110,463.76$$

annual rent on the building. Adding the two rents and dividing by 12 gives $10,855.31 per month, the monthly rental that will retire all but $180,000 of the $1,080,000 investment in 20 years and give 11.00 percent per year return on the investment.

Example 208.   Minimum Rent for Kiosk

The Ninnish Corporation requires a 12.00 percent annual return on any investments. Fioley is proposing to management that they put a kiosk in Central Fairly Mall. The original cost is $65,000, including installa-

tion, electrical feeds, and so on. The kiosk will probably be obsolete in 7 years. (Since it will increase leasable area of the mall and decrease common area, the kiosk will be charged its share of CAM and real estate taxes as well as provide a return to the owners.) Fioley needs to figure the minimum rental needed to justify installing the kiosk.

Enter Table 38, page 7 (p. 464), the section for 12.00 percent. On the line for 7 years under monthly advance, find the factor, 20.973544 percent, the percentage of original cost that must be obtained **net.** Multiply the dollar cost by the factor to get

$$\$65,000 \times 0.20973544 = \$13,632.81$$

annual rent. Dividing by 12 gives $1,136.07, the minimum monthly rent payment (payable on the first of each month plus CAM and taxes) that must be obtained to justify the expenditure.

Note   In addition to expenses and the payment to justify its cost, most landlords would want a payment for use of the Mall's real estate and its business franchise. But, if other factors compensated, such as brightening a dull spot in the mall or adding a unique product line that could throw off percentage rents, the project might be approved on the prospect of returning only its tangible cost plus interest.

Example 209.   Number of Months to "Retire" a Lease

Kenda Jansik will respond to a request for proposal (RFP) for a build-to-suit lease. The RFP indicates a $600,000 cost. Jansik requires a 9.00 percent return on investment and believes a proposal using a 12.00 percent rent constant would be competitive.

To find the lease term that would give this return and retire the investment, enter Table 59, page 2 (p. 723), the section for 9.00 percent interest. Read down the annual constant column to 12.00 percent and on that line under 9.00 percent find the answer, 185.5, the number of months of the lease to retire the entire investment and give a 9.00 percent yield. Leases are most often written for numbers of full months, so in practice this would be a 15-year, 6-month lease.

Example 210.   Yield from Partially Amortizing Long-Term Lease

Kearney Propter owns a parcel of land valued at $200,000. Cars' Truck Company will give a lease for 15 years at $11,000 per month, triple net, if Propter will construct a terminal at a cost of $800,000 on the land. Propter considers that the land will hold its value during the lease and still be worth $200,000 at the end of the term. The truck terminal, however, will probably be worthless then.

To find the approximate yield in this lease proposal, first find the rent constant. To do this, divide the annual rent by the cost to get

$$\$132,000 \div \$1,000,000 = 13.20\%$$

annual rent constant. Now, considering that the rent must amortize 80 percent—$800,000 ÷ $1,000,000—of the total cost, enter Table 36, page 6 (p. 452). Search through the 80 percent columns on the line for 15 years for the factor closest to the rent constant of 13.20 percent. The closest factor is 13.11018 percent in the section for 11.00 percent interest. This means that the proposed rents would be sufficient to give a return of slightly more than 11.00 percent per year *on* the invested capital of $1 million and return of 80 percent *of* the investment over 15 years.

If Kearney Propter were willing to consider that the land would rise in value from $200,000 to, say, $300,000 over the term, the same calculation could be made based on amortizing 70 percent of the capital (full depreciation of the $800,000 truck terminal cost minus $100,000 gain in land value).

Example 211. Approximate Yield from Sale-Lease Transaction

Jaikoe Shipping has been offered a 15-year lease at $148,000 per year **triple net.** They will have the option at the end of the lease term to buy the facility for $1. Their estimate is that the facility would cost $1 million, if they tried to buy it today.

To find the apparent yield in this transaction, first find the rent constant by dividing the rent by the apparent cost to get

$$\$148,000 \div \$1,000,000 = 14.80\%$$

annual rent constant. Now enter Table 35 (a), page 8 (p. 428), and search on the line for 15 years for the constant closest to 14.80 percent. It is 14.790265 percent, which is found under 12.50 percent interest. The deal's apparent yield to the landlord is slightly greater than 12.50 percent per year.

Graduated Rent Plans

Landlords can make commercial rent proposals more attractive to tenants by graduating the rent. Lower rentals at the outset of a lease coincide with the ten-

ant's highest cash outlays as it moves into its space. Later, the rent is higher and, in the plans presented here, has an interest load built in to compensate for the delay in payment. Even with the interest, graduated rent plans will likely be attractive to tenants, because real estate deals are usually calculated with far lower interest rates than the cost of funds calculated by business enterprises.

Table 66 is used in cases where the "standard" rental is known. By standard is meant the rent that would be quoted if a fixed rent plan were being offered. Each year after the first, the rent rises by 3 percent to 10 percent, according to the section selected, and remains at that level for a year. The present value of all the rents in a graduated plan equals the present value of the "standard" rent for the same period.

In cases such as sale-leasebacks, where the standard rental is not known but the property cost or value is known, Table 65 shows how to construct the graduated rent deal. In these cases also, the rent rises on each anniversary by the annual rate of increase selected. The rising rent series is constructed so it has a present value equal to a series of payments at the "level" amount shown in each section. The level payment is the annual rent constant and could be substituted for the rising amounts. The entries in Table 65 are given in percentages of initial cost and are annual figures; divide by 12 to get the monthly amount.

Example 212. Rent Constants in a Rising Series and Graduated Rent When Market or Standard Level Is Unknown

Dental Diskettes must expand its distribution system. It has sent a request for proposal (RFP) to the business parks in the area, asking for a 10-year lease proposal for a new business center. The company's rapid growth mandates that it conserve cash to the utmost in the coming years. The RFP specifies that Dental Diskettes wishes to own the facility at the end of the 10-year lease term. To appeal to these dual needs, Halivy Developers plans a lease with graduated rents, allowing the lowest possible rent at the outset of the lease. The low payments early in the lease will be compensated by annual rent increases. Halivy has a mortgage quote based on 9.50 percent interest and would therefore consider that to be the cost of funds for this deal. Halivy's estimate of the cost to put the business center in place is $2.65 million.

To establish the rent plan, the figures in Table 65, page 13 (p. 750), will be used as rent constants. Choose the 10 percent annual rate of increase, as this will give the lowest initial rent and the steepest graduation. In the 10-year plan, take the payments from the 9.50 percent interest column. Convert each to a decimal and multiply it by the project development cost of $2,650,000. The rent for the first year will be

$$\$2,650,000 \times 0.1026779\% \div 12 = \$22,674.71$$

per month. For the second year, it will be

$$\$2,650,000 \times 0.1129457\% \div 12 = \$24,942.18$$

per month, and so on for each of the 10 years. The resulting series of rent payments will be the annual net rents for Dental Diskettes that will have the same present value as the level rent constant (15.40574 percent) to give 9.50 percent yield and pay back Halivy over 120 months.

Note A graduated lease for 15 years or more or one involving tax avoidance brings into play special U.S. tax rules that require straight-line treatment; that is, the rent for tax purposes would be the arithmetic average of the entire series of payments. The accounting treatment of these rents under generally accepted accounting principles will also require straight-line treatment in many situations.

Example 213.   Graduated Rent Plan

D'Amato Managers Corp. offers office space in the Dominion complex at $16.00 per square foot with a $4.00 expense stop (in effect, $12.00 net). Angela D'Amato would like to provide Harrensbrod Bakers a 5-year rent proposal with graduated rents. From discussions with Harrensbrod, she understands that a 6.0 percent rate of increase would be quite acceptable, as long as they get the lowest initial rent that they can. With bank loans currently priced at 9.00 percent, a deal using that rate would be competitive with the tenant's cost at its bank.

To find the rents for the proposal, enter Table 66, page 7 (p. 758), the page for 6.0 percent annual rate of increase and the 5-year lease section. Take each percentage in the 9.00 percent column and convert it to a decimal. Then multiply it by the net rent to get the rent for the year, as follows:

Year	Net Rent		Factor		This Year's Rent
1	$16.00	×	0.893795	=	$14.30
2	16.00	×	0.947423	=	15.16
3	16.00	×	1.004269	=	16.07
4	16.00	×	1.064525	=	17.03
5	16.00	×	1.128396	=	18.05

Each rental will be multiplied by the number of square feet and the results set out in the proposal. They are equal, at time value of money of 9.00 percent, to a proposal with a $16.00 flat rent, even though $16.00 rent is not reached until the third year.

Example 214.   Level Rent to Match Rising Rents

Devona McHugh has offered a 10-year lease to a prospective tenant. The rent would start at $12.00 per square foot triple net and call for 3.0 percent fixed annual rent increases. However, the prospective tenant insists on annual rent fixed for the 10-year period. McHugh would like to rework her quotation to give the tenant the benefit of a fixed rate but obtain the same economic benefit as a lease with 3.0 percent annual rent raises. Her mortgage interest rate is 10.00 percent, so she will use that as her cost of capital.

Enter Table 66, page 1 (p. 752), the page for annual rate of increase of 3.0 percent and the section for a 10-year lease. Under the column for 10.00 percent interest rate, take the factor for year 1 of the lease. It is 88.2120 percent. Divide the starting rent by this factor, as follows:

$$\$12.00 \div 0.882120 = \$13.60359$$

or $13.60, the fixed annual rental per square foot that on a 10-year lease will give the same economic benefit as a 10-year series starting at $12.00 and rising 3.0 percent per year, if interest rates are 10.00 percent per year.

Note This example would also be followed to substitute a graduated plan for a plan with a fixed rate plus CPI increases. The rate of increase in Table 66 would be selected according to the expected rise in the CPI or the rate of increase stated in the lease.

Create Value by Buying in Below-Market Leases

Landlords create value when they increase the **net operating income** of property. If a tenant has a long-term lease with below-market rentals, the net operating income is not at its full potential. The long-term lease blocks the landlord's chances at value creation. In effect, the tenant owns some of the market value of the property.

It makes sense for the landlord to unblock value increases by buying in the lease and writing a new one, using the figures from Table 73. That is, the landlord pays the tenant to rewrite its lease, in exchange for raising the rent to today's market rental. The plus for the tenant is that it receives cash now, the minus is higher rent in the future. But, in some cases, the landlord can pay the tenant a sum equal to all future rent increases and still make a profit. Even if that is not the case, the higher payments come in the future, whereas the tenant has the money to use now.

For the landlord, rewriting the lease not only creates value, it may induce a tenant with a few years left on its lease to extend the lease and to commit to do so now. New leases at market rates make property more saleable and mortgageable and easier to lease at higher rents to the next tenant.

The source of this win-win case lies in the higher returns that most U.S. companies expect compared to real estate investors. A company making 25 percent on its working capital may be happy to work a lease buy-in deal at 12.50 percent to 15.00 percent return, especially if the tenant has a tax-loss carryforward. Most landlords would be happy with 9.00 percent to 11.00 percent per year return on a "fresh" new lease from the tenant, so there is ample room to negotiate a mutually acceptable deal.

Note

1. Such transactions may be "fraudulent transfers" in case of bankruptcy and be set aside. If there is any practical risk that the tenant receiving the cash may not be around to pay it back through rental, this technique should be far from the landlord's mind.

2. Even more than in the normal case, the tenant receiving the cash should be restricted from assigning its position to a less creditworthy tenant. Since courts increasingly consider tenants to have the right to assign unless the landlord shows compelling reasons for restrictions, the attorney drafting the lease may wish to recite the special considerations supporting the negotiated restriction on assignment.

3. Some states require lease concessions to be stated on the face of the lease. In such cases, the payments to the tenant should be so declared.

Example 215.   Increased Value from Buying in a Lease

Nondiscounted Case

Hakin & Porter have a building in their office park occupied entirely by Gladwinkels Engineering. Glad-

winkels has 6 years remaining on their lease at $3.00 per square foot **triple net.** Gross rents in the area are $12.00 per square foot net or 4.0 times the Gladwinkels' rent. Hakin & Porter propose to offer Gladwinkels a new 6-year lease at $12.00 per square foot, together with a lump-sum payment of all the additional rent between $3.00 and $12.00 per square foot. Current capitalization rates are 8.50 percent per year.

To find the appropriate amounts, enter Table 73, page 2 (p. 793), the page for 8.50 percent capitalization rate and the section for ratio of target rent to old rent of 4.0 times ($12.00/$3.00). Read down the left column to 6 years and across on that line to the column in the 4.0 times section for non-discounted figures. Read there under the pay-to-tenant column 18.000 times. This means that the payment to Gladwinkels will be equal to 18 times the current rent of $3.00, or $54.00 per square foot. Next to this, under the column for value added, read 17.29412. This means that the landlord will still have improved the value of its property by 17.3 times the current annual rental, or $51.88 per square foot, even after deducting the payment to Gladwinkels.

Discounted Case

Hakin & Porter may be able to show Gladwinkels that the lump-sum payment should be discounted, since the rent payments will only come due over a period of 6 years. This calculation is made using the discounted columns. The other terms are as in the nondiscounted case above.

Enter Table 73, page 2 (p. 793), the section for ratio of target rent to old rent of 4.0 times on the 8.50 percent page. On the line for 6 years, read under the column in the discounted section for pay to tenant, the factor 14.06202. This means that the payment to Gladwinkels will be 14.06 times their current annual rent of $3.00, or $42.19. Next to this in the column for value added, read the factor 21.23210. This means that Hakin & Porter have, after deduction of the payment to Gladwinkels of $42.19, an increased value of their property of $63.70 per square foot.

Example 216.   Buying in a Lease Where Other Costs Arise

This type of lease buy-in will many times be acceptable only if the landlord includes some refurbishing of the premises. Let us assume that the tenant asks for a $5.00 per square foot painting and carpet allowance. The calculation is the same as in the previous cases. But, if market conditions are such that the landlord must offer an allowance of $5.00 per square foot to a new tenant, then the landlord will provide the carpet at its cost, and its value added will be lower by $5.00 per square foot. If a new tenant would not have received the carpet or its equivalent in an "open-market" case, then the tenant would pay for the carpet via a reduction in its payment from the landlord.

Increases in Rent from CPI Clauses or Fixed Rent Increases

Example 217. Actual Rent Increase from CPI Clause and Projecting Future Rents Adjusted by the CPI

The management of La Paloma have offered office space to Parachin Industries at $20.00 per square foot per year, increasing each year at the rate of 40 percent of the **Consumer Price Index.** They will include a renewal option after the 7-year term at a fixed price increase over the preceding year. To approximate what the rent increase would be at that time, they wish to know the increase in Parachin's rent in the seventh year of the lease, if the Consumer Price Index increases 6.0 percent per year.

Enter Table 77 (a), page 2 (p. 817), on the page for 6.0 percent annual growth in CPI and the section for 40 percent of CPI increases. On the line for year 7, read across to the column for 6.00 percent and find the increase factor, 40.16 cents per $10 of rent. Divide today's rent by $10 and multiply it by the increase factor to get

$$\$20 \div \$10 \times 40.16 = 80.32 \text{ cents}$$

the increase in rent in the seventh year of the lease under a 40 percent of CPI increase clause and 6.0 percent annual growth of the CPI.

Example 218. Future Simple Rate of Increase in Rent

Where the general rent level is desired, rather than the rent under a CPI clause as in the preceding example, Table 7 will give the answer as well. Esperaatin believes that rents in the region, which are $1.15 per square foot per month now, will rise 8.0 percent per year over the next 10 years. What would be the rent increase in the tenth year?

Enter Table 7, page 2 (p. 192), at 8.00 percent interest rate and use the interest rate as a rate of growth. Read down elapsed years to 10 and across on that line to the column headed 8.00 percent. The factor there, 17.01 percent, is the increase in rent levels in the tenth year. As a percentage of first year rents, rents will increase 17 percent in the tenth year in the future, if the expected 8.0 percent annual rate of growth is sustained.

Example 219. Rate of Inflation in a Future Year

Stenowick notes that the CPI has increased 5.25 percent in the past year. If the same rate of growth occurs for the next 5 years, Stenowick needs to estimate what the inflation rate will be, relative to today's dollars, 5 years in the future.

Enter Table 7, page 1 (p. 191), the section for 5.25 percent interest rate or rate of growth. On the line for 5 years elapsed, read across to the 5.25 percent column, and find there the factor, 6.63 percent. If the present 5.25 percent nominal annual rate of growth occurs in the index, in 5 years' time the inflation rate will be 6.63 percent, expressed in today's dollars. Stated differently, it will take $106.63 of today's dollars then to buy what $100 of today's dollars bought the year before.

Example 220. Rent Increase in Lease Period under CPI Clause

The Langley Corporation is a tenant in Bascom Hollow Haven. Its lease states that

if the CPI for any Lease Year (the "Current CPI") shall exceed the CPI for the Base Year (the "Base CPI"), then the Base Rent shall be increased, so that the Base Rent after the increase (the "Adjusted Base Rent") shall be the product of the Base Rent multiplied by the ratio of the Current CPI to the Base CPI, provided, however, that the accumulated increases above the Base Rent shall not exceed an average of 5 percent compounded per year.

The base CPI one year ago was 236.2; the current CPI today is 252.7, a 6.99 percent change. To find if this CPI exceeds the 5 percent compounded limit, enter Table 7, page 1 (p. 191), the section for an interest rate of 5.00 percent. Read down the years column to 5 and find under the 5.00 percent column, 6.25 percent, the permissible increase in the fifth year under the lease. The increase in year 5 will be limited to 6.25 percent rather than the 6.99 percent called for by the CPI.

Example 221. Actual Rent Increase under Fixed Rent Increase Clause

B. R. Carby Corporation is negotiating a lease in Granada Grande Business Park. Under the proposal, they would have a rent of $14.00 per square foot and a 2.75 percent fixed increase in rent every 2 years. They want to know what the increase would be in the tenth year of the 10-year lease.

To find the increase, enter Table 77 (b), page 1 (p. 818), the section for increases every 2 years. Read across on the line for 10 years to the column headed 2.75 percent increase. The factor there, 30.65 cents, is the increase then per $10 of initial rent. Multiply the initial rent by the factor to get

$$\$14.00 \div \$10 \times 30.65 = 42.91$$

or, rounding, 43 cents per square foot, the rent increase in the Carby lease in the tenth year after 2.75 percent fixed increases every 2 years.

Example 222. Present Value of Rents with CPI Clause Compared to Rents without

The tenant representative for Charlotta Style Enterprises has obtained two rental quotations in downtown office buildings. The first offers rental at $27 per square foot next, fixed for 10 years. The other offers $24 per square foot net with an adjustment each year at the rate of 50 percent of the CPI. Charlotta's facilities manager has told the broker to assume the CPI will rise 6 percent per year and that the firm's cost of funds is 11.00 percent per year.

To compare the leases, first enter Table 47 (a), page 9 (p. 592), at the section for a 3 percent annual rise (50 percent of 6 percent). On the line for 10 years, read across to the column headed 11.00 percent interest. The factor there is 6.58367.

Now enter Table 46, page 23 (p. 567), the page for 11.00 percent. On the line for 10 years, read under the column, present value of 1 per period, annual payments, the factor 5.8892320. Multiply the first factor by the rental from the lease *with* CPI clause to get

$$\$24.00 \times 6.58367 = 158.008$$

the present value of the lease with CPI clause. Multiply the second factor by the rent under the lease with a fixed rental to get

$$\$27.00 \times 5.8892320 = 159.009$$

the present value of the rent under the fixed rate proposal. Since the lease with CPI clause has a slightly lower cost index—lower is better from the point of view of the tenant—Charlotta Style Enterprises would be better off with the lease with a CPI clause, provided that the 6.00 percent inflation assumption is borne out. Since the cost indexes are very close, it would make sense for the tenant representative to try to negotiate a cap on the annual increase in the CPI clause.

Example 223. Comparing Lease Favorable to Tenant to "Standard" Lease and Premium to Buy a Leasehold with Favorable Tenant Lease

Boots at the Barn has been a phenomenally successful tenant at Madrid Mall Plus, so much so that a major chain is offering to buy the company's assets including its leasehold. The lease has 7 more years and is the last in the mall written on a gross basis. Boots at the Barn pays $12.00 per square foot and does not pay any portion of the real estate taxes or other expenses. All other tenants at the mall, in fact all over the region, pay a rental plus a share of taxes and expenses. The owners of Boots at the Barn want a credit in the sale price to reflect their favorable lease. Expenses have been rising in recent years at 60 cents per square foot per year. Buyer and seller are agreed that 10.00 percent is an appropriate discount rate for lease deals in this area.

Begin by finding the initial change as a percentage of current rental. It is $0.060 divided by $12 or 5.0 percent. Now consider that, because of the expense clause, rent to the landlord is *decreasing*, compared to the other tenants. Enter Table 47 (b), page 8 (p. 603), at the section for 5.0 percent amount of first-year decline. Read down to 7 years and across on that line to the column headed 10.00 percent interest. The factor there, 4.27762, gives a multiple of the current annual rental. Multiply the factor by $12 to get

$$\$12.00 \times 4.27762 = \$51.33$$

the value of a lease that decreases each year as compared to other tenants.

Now enter Table 46, page 19 (p. 563), the page for 10.00 percent discount rate and get the present value of 1 per period, monthly payments, on the line for 7 years. It is 60.2366674, or, dividing by 12 to give the annual rate, 5.0197228. Multiply it also by $12 to get

$$\$12.00 \times 5.0197228 = \$60.24$$

the value of a lease with fixed annual rental. Subtract the value obtained from the first step from $60.24 to get $8.91 per square foot, the premium value of a gross lease over a net lease, where the tenant pays $12 fixed rent per square foot and expenses have been rising at 60 cents per year.

Cost of Assuming a Tenant's Lease Obligation

Table 71 focuses on the cost of assuming a tenant's lease obligation. Commercial tenants resist relocating their quarters. Lower rent seldom induces a move, and when tenants do move, their motives will more likely be to gain operating or sales efficiency than better rental. However, the tenant's existing lease contract often inhibits such a move. The tenant may rebuff the lease offer, saying, "We've got years remaining on our existing lease." The landlord may counter, "I will assume your existing lease, if you sign a lease in my building."

Assuming the tenant's lease obligation may make good business sense for several economic reasons. In a brand-new building, the developer may reason that the space would be vacant anyway. Although it costs something to have a tenant occupying space in an otherwise empty building, demonstrating market acceptance and avoiding a "see-through" condition may more than justify the cost. And, in some markets, it may be possible to sublease the space taken over.

If it appears worthwhile to buy out the lease, the next step is to calculate the true rent the owner will receive net of the assumed lease. The average rent is often used, but averages ignore the fact that lease assumption payments go out early but new rent payments come in later. The present value of the net rent given in Table 71 is the more conservative calculation.

Example 224.   Cost of Assuming a Lease Where Old and New Areas Are the Same

San Ferrando has office space to let at $9.50 per square foot per year. He can get a 7-year lease from Jonesson, if he will assume Jonesson's existing lease, which has 2 years remaining at $6.00 per square foot. Current interest rates are 7.50 percent. San Ferrando's property manager is paid 3.50 percent on rents.

To get the true rent, enter Table 71, page 1 (p. 780), on the page for 7.50 percent interest and 3.50 percent management fee. Read down the left column, Old Rent, to $6.00. Now read across to the column headed by 7/2 and read $2.133, the true cost of the lease assumption.

Now subtract $2.133 from $9.50, the regular rent, to get $7.367, or, rounding $7.37, the true rent the landlord will be getting if he accepts the lease assumption proposal, and receives nothing from subleasing the assumed space.

Example 225.   Cost of Assuming a Lease Where New Area Different from Old

Example 224 assumes the same area is involved in the new and old leases. If this is not the case, take the ratio by dividing the old space by the new space. If the facts are the same as in Example 225, except that Jonesson's existing space is 43,000 square feet and the new space will be 75,000 feet, the old/new ratio is $43,000 \div 75,000 = 0.5733$ or 57.33 percent. Multiplying the cost of the assumption by the old/new ratio gives

$$\$2.133 \times 0.5733 = \$1.22$$

the cost of the sublease. Subtracting this from $9.50 gives

$$\$9.50 - 1.22 = \$8.28$$

the true rent to be received, where the existing space was 43,000 square feet and the new space is 75,000 square feet.

Example 226.   Amount of Rent to Ask for in a Lease Assumption Case

A leasing broker wishes to attract Quixotic Knits to the new shopping center in town. The prospect pays $5.00 per square foot per year now, and has 1 year remaining on her lease. She would be willing to take a 5-year lease, if the shopping center would assume her remaining lease obligation. The broker wants to calculate the rent to give the landlord $8.00 per square foot net of the cost of taking over the prospect's existing lease. Interest rates are 7.50 percent; the management fee is 3.5 percent of rents collected.

To measure what the broker should quote, enter Table 71, page 1 (p. 780), the page which contains $5.00 under old rent. Read down the old rent column to $5.00. Now read across to the column for new term of 5 years, old term of 1 year and read $1.204, the cost of the lease assumption per square foot.

If the same space is involved in the new lease as in the old, simply add this cost of the lease assumption to the asking rent, $8.00 + 1.204, to get $9.20, the rent the landlord must ask to receive $8.00 net of assumption costs.

If a different amount of space is involved, multiply the ratio of the old space to the new space times the factor. Using 2,000 square feet as Quixotic's existing space, and 3,000 square feet for its new space, the calculation would be

$$2,000 \div 3,000 \times \$1.204 = \$0.8027$$

or 80 cents, the additional rent. Adding this to landlord's $8.00 base rent gives $8.80, the rent to give landlord $8.00 net of the lease assumption, where the ratio of old space to new is 2 feet to 3 feet and 3.5 percent management fee is payable on rent.

Note The tenant's old lease most likely requires the tenant to pay base rent and additional charges, such as common area maintenance (CAM) and real estate taxes. The old rent to be used with Table 71 is the total of the base rent and all additional charges.

True Rent When Free Rent or Concessions Are Given

Landlords offer a range of price concessions today that may include free rent and other tenant inducements such as additional alterations or moving allowances. The package of rental concessions includes terms that often are not comparable. Table 76 puts all concessions into a single package and converts them to true rent. True rent is not truly a rent figure but an index that allows comparison of one lease concession package with another in a manner that takes into account interest cost on funds, cash equivalence of amounts, and time value of money. The free rent in the first column of the table gives a cost spread over the stated period, and the other concessions package is assumed to be a cash cost at the start of the lease.

Example 227. True Rent When Concessions Are Given

Jaglods Chain Co. has sought an offer from Commerce Tower for office space in the building. The landlord has responded that the 10-year deal would have a base rental of $15 per square foot per year and 4 months' free rent. Other concessions include a tenant alteration package that has an "above-

standard" value of $6.00 per square foot and a moving allowance of $1.50 per square foot. The current interest rate for Jaglods's borrowings is 10.00 percent per year.

To find the true rent, convert the concessions into the equivalent number of free months' rent. Do this by adding up the total concessions ($6.00 + 1.50) and dividing by the base rent. Then multiply by 12 to get

$$\$7.50 \div 15.00 \times 12$$
$$= 6 \text{ months' rent-equivalent of other concessions}$$

Now enter Table 76, page 6 (p. 811), at the section for 10.00 percent interest and 120-month lease term. Read down the left column to 4 months and across on that line to the column headed 6 months. The factor there, 90.094 percent, is the true rent factor. Multiply the nominal base rent by the factor to get

$$\$15.00 \times 0.90094 = \$13.51$$

the true rent when free rent of 4 months and other concessions equal to 6 months are given.

Cost of Providing Leasehold Improvements

Prospective tenants often demand special features or alterations not part of the normal rent package. The landlord is usually willing to install them and pass the cost on to the tenant in the form of additional rent over the life of the lease. In other cases, market forces may leave the landlord no choice but to include them without any additional rent. In either case, the common method to figure the additional rent is to straight-line the cost, that is, simply divide the cost by the number of years in the lease. That gives no credit for return on invested capital and nothing to compensate for management fees that will be charged when the additional rent is collected.

Table 70 spreads the cost of improvements over the life of a lease and adds in the selected rate of return on investment plus an allowance for management fees paid on the additional rent.

Example 228. Additional Rent to Pay for Leasehold Improvements

Soares, an office leasing broker, has been asked by a dentist for a 5-year lease at $18.00 per square foot per year. In addition the dentist wants alterations that will cost $26.00 per square foot. Soares needs to calculate the rent that should be quoted to give the owner a 10.50 percent return on investment and provide for a 3.5 percent management fee.

Turn to the portion of Table 70, page 3 (p. 776), for 10.50 percent equity yield and a management fee of 3.5 percent. Read down the column for improvements cost per square foot of rented area to $26.00. Then read across on that line to the column headed 5 years and read the answer, $6.889, which is the annual rent to be paid for improvements. Add this to the basic rent per square foot to be charged, $18.00, to get $24.89, the total rent quotation.

Example 229.   Additional Rent When Cost Applies Only to Usable Area

Office space is most often rented according to the formula for **net rentable area,** whereas tenant installations are priced according to the actual area the tenant occupies, called the **usable area.**

The ratio of the unusable area to the net rentable area is called the **loss factor.** If the tenant installation will be given only on the usable area, but the rent is quoted on the net rentable area, there is an added step to follow to get the additional rent. First, subtract the loss factor from 100 percent and multiply the result by the cost per square foot of usable area. Now enter the chart with this figure. Using the data from Example 227 for tenant alterations of $26.00 and the loss factor 8 percent, would give

$$\$26.00 \times 0.92 = \$23.92$$

or, rounding, $24.00, the alteration cost per square foot of rentable area. Now entering Table 70, page 3 (p. 776), the page for 10.50 percent equity yield, we would find at $24.00 per square foot and 5 years, the answer $6.359 or rounded $6.36. This is the additional rent to charge for a $26.00 alteration to be applied only to the usable area, where there is an 8 percent loss factor.

Example 230.   Additional Rent If Improvements Last Longer than Primary Lease Term

The tenant may sign a lease for only 5 years but have an option for 5 additional years or more. Tenant will want the cost of the tenant installation amortized over the lease term plus the option period(s). If the landlord agrees, simply find the correct factor as in the example above, but instead of the 5-year primary term, use a term of 5 years plus the 5-year option.

Enter Table 70 at the page for 10.50 percent and 3.5 percent management fee. On the line for $26.00, under the 10-year column find the answer, $4.325 per square foot.

The landlord gambles in this case, since the tenant may not stay after 5 years. The landlord risks having an unamortized portion of tenant improvements. Two solutions are available: One is set out in the example below. The other is to split the gamble in some defined fashion. In the case of the 5-year primary term and 5-year option, the landlord might elect to calculate the additional rent for a 7.5 year lease (using the average of the table's 7-year and 8-year figures). If the tenant takes the 5-year option, the landlord will have 2.5 years of profit from the extra rent. If tenant declines the 5-year option and moves out, the landlord is stuck with only 2.5 years of unamortized improvement cost.

Advantages of Free Rent over Leasehold Improvements

For a landlord, giving free rent may be preferable to giving a tenant-improvement allowance for a number of reasons: (1) Free rent does not require cash, no small matter in real estate, where cash is critical. (2) Often, interest cost can be covered out of an interest reserve held by the lender, whereas "hard" costs could not be drawn from the reserve. (3) There is an interest savings in free rent, since by definition the rent is given over time, whereas leasehold improvements must usually be paid for at the start of the lease. (4) It may be easier to negotiate exclusion of free rent from leasing commissions and management fees than the rent that compensates for tenant alteration. (5) And finally, having the tenant invest cash in its premises to be "reimbursed" later by free rent, provides a security deposit to ensure the tenant will stay.

Advantages of Leasehold Improvements over Free Rent

Advantages are not without counteradvantages. Here are some on the side of giving leasehold improvements: (1) Leasehold improvements are just that: improvements. They improve the image of the building, both in the eyes of tenants and their decision-makers, employees and customers, and in the eyes of other prospective tenants who visit the property. (2) At renewal time, it will be harder, or at least more costly, for a competing landlord to offer equivalent space, and the benefit of free rent will have been long forgotten. (3) The negotiating of leasehold improvements, involving as it does discussion of hard dollars, is more carefully done; giving away months of free rent feels painless, as the dollar cost is not actually being discussed. (4) Finally, if the tenant does move out, some portions of the improvements may be serviceable for the next tenant.

Example 231.   Unused Portion of Tenant Improvements

The simple solution in Example 229 involving a gamble may be adequate for smaller deals. But a major installation for a sophisticated tenant should not rest on a gamble for the landlord. Nor will the tenant want to risk paying more rent than is fair. In such case, the landlord should calculate what the unamortized rent amount will be at the end of 5 years and provide that tenant will pay this amount before moving out.

To find the unamortized portion of the tenant installation, treat the installation as a loan from the landlord and find the remaining loan balance. The interest rate is the landlord's cost of funds or a negotiated rate. The "loan term" is the amortization period for the improvements. To do this with the data from Example 229 above, enter Table 42 (b), page 21 (p. 517), for a 10.50 percent loan on a 10-year amortization schedule. The answer on the line for 5 years in the 10.50 percent interest column is 62.778274 percent. The lease would provide that, if tenant elects not to take the 5-year renewal, it will pay as additional rent the sum of $16.32, or $26.00 per square foot × 62.778274 percent remaining balance, for each square foot in the demised premises.

Note Leases often provide that tenant must pay the unamortized portion of tenant improvements within 10 days after lease expiration. Some courts have held that a payment is not rent if it is provided to be paid after the lease term, since there was no longer a lease in existence. Do not draft the clause yourself; give your attorney the calculations.

Example 232.   Amount of Rent to Exclude from Fees or Commissions

Martin Maskey is marketing retail space in the Harpal King Discount Center. A tenant will take a lease at $12.50 for 10 years, if a concession package worth $9.00 per square foot is given. Maskey will propose to the owner that, for purposes of calculating the commission, the concession package will be excluded from the $12.50 rent. An equity yield of 7.50 percent is appropriate.

To find the amount of the exclusion, enter Table 70, page 1 (p. 774), the page for 7.50 percent equity yield and 3.5 percent management fee. Read down the left column to $9.00 and then across on that line to the column for 10 years. The answer there is $1.32, the annual rent per square foot to be excluded from rent for purposes of calculating the commission on the lease.

Spreading Tenant Alterations in Projections

Table 76 aids preparation of capital and expense projections. If today's cost of a capital item—let's say tenant installations—and the tenant turnover ratio are known, the table gives the total tenant installation cost for any of the next 15 years at any of eight assumed inflation rates.

Example 233.   Projecting Apartment Refitting and Make-Ready Cost

Bellweather's apartment complex has 262 units. The average cost today is $188 to turn over a unit and make it ready for a new tenant. This would be $49,256, or 262 × $188, for the entire complex.

Given an estimate of 4 percent annual inflation and 33 percent turnover of units, what will be the make-ready cost in 5 years?

Enter Table 75, page 1 (p. 803), the section for 4 percent inflation. Read down the year column to 5 and across to the column headed 33 percent turnover. Read there the factor 40.555 percent. Multiply this by the make-ready cost for the entire project to get

$$\$49,256 \times 0.40555 = \$19,975.77$$

the make-ready cost 5 years from now, if inflation each year is 5 percent and 33 percent turnover occurs in the fifth year.

Example 234.   Future Office Alterations Costs

Meredith Hradup knows that tenant alterations today cost $22.50 per square foot. Her office building has 86,100 square feet. The cost today to do the entire building would be

$$86,100 \times \$22.50 = \$1,937,250$$

This is the total building alteration cost. Hradup is preparing a 5-year projected capital expenditure budget. Her assumptions are that inflation will be 3 percent per year and that tenant turnover is likely to be as follows:

Year	Tenant Turnover
1	0%
2	20
3	20
4	10
5	20

To find the tenant alterations costs, skip year 1 since it is zero. For year 2, enter Table 75, page 1 (p. 803), the page with 3 percent inflation rate. Read down the year column to year 2 and across on that line to the column headed 20 percent. The factor there is 21.218 percent. Multiply the total building alteration cost by this factor to get

$$\$1,937,250 \times 0.21218 = \$411,045.71$$

the cost for year 2.

Complete the other years in the same manner to get

Total Building Alteration Cost	Year	Turnover	Factor	Alteration Cost
$1,937,250	1	0%	0.000%	$ 0.00
	2	20	21.218	411,045.71
	3	20	21.855	423,385.99
	4	10	11.255	218,037.49
	5	20	23.185	449,151.41

These are the annual costs of alterations, adjusted for 3 percent annual inflation, based on the expected tenant turnover schedule.

Example 235.   Projecting Lease Commission Costs

The Falstritch Industrial Complex is fully rented for the next 5 years. Today's annual gross rent is $2,250,000. Rents are expected to grow 5 percent annually. Standard leasing commissions in the community are 3 percent of the total rent over first 5 years of the lease, which is equal to 15 percent of the first year's rent. What will the leasing commissions be 5 years in the future for a new lease of 50 percent of the complex?

First consider that the leasing commission today on a 5-year lease of 100 percent of the complex would be

$$\$2,250,000 \times 0.15 = \$337,500.00$$

Now enter Table 75, page 2 (p. 804), the section for 5.0 percent inflation rate. Read down the year column to year 5 and across on that line to the column for 50 percent turnover. Read there the factor, 63.814 percent, the percentage of total that applies. Multiply the total commission by the factor to get

$$\$337,500 \times 0.63814 = \$215,372.25$$

the commission 5 years from now on a 5-year lease or leases for 50 percent of the building, if rents rise 5 percent per year.

Spreading Average Rents or Prices to Typical Unit Values

Rental and sale pricing of real estate often rests on simple averages. But tenants and buyers discriminate among units with a park view ("too dull") or a highway view ("too busy") or front ("too noisy") or rear ("cheap"). Although renting plans would never be completed if hundreds of units had to be appraised separately, the use of averages can award too much value to some units while hiding the attractions of the best. Table 74 allows the rental or sales agent to prepare a price grid that weights the value differences between categories in such a way that the different prices equal the starting average.

Example 236.   Spreading Average Office Rents to Typical Rents

Graham & Simpson have built Standard Office Park. The park has two buildings, each containing 120,000 square feet. One building is a high-rise with ten floors of offices above two levels of parking, and the other is a mid-rise with five floors of offices. Graham

& Simpson want to price the space at an average of $14 per square foot. They also want to give effect to a 25 percent premium in the high-rise space over the mid-rise. Within the mid-rise, the space is all about the same, so a small price spread, 5 percent, exists from the best to the poorest. In the high-rise, however, the view and the image of the top floors make them superior. They feel that those floors should have a 20 percent spread from the low floors to the upper. One-half of floors 3 and 4, however, look out over the garage and should be discounted.

Enter Table 74, page 1 (p. 798), the section for 25 percent Premium A over B and the distribution of 50 percent Type A, 50 percent Type B. In that section, under Type B, in the column for 5 percent, read the factors 86.7 percent, 88.9 percent, and 91.1 percent for the low, mid, and high range. Graham & Simpson set up the following schedule:

Mid-Rise

Floors 1–2:	$14 × 0.867 = $12.14
Floor 3:	14 × 0.889 = 12.45
Floors 4–5:	14 × 0.911 = 12.75

For the high-rise building, they take the factors from the A section under 20 percent spread high to low, which are 100.00 percent, 111.1 percent, and 122.2 percent. They decide to treat the garage side of 3 and 4 as the lowest-priced "floor" and the better side as the floor above. Using the rules that there must be as many units (floors) at the high figure as at the low, they assign the rents as follows:

High-Rise

Floors 3–4 garage:	$14 × 1.000 = $14.00
Floors 3–4 parkside and 5 through 11:	14 × 1.111 = 15.55
Floor 12:	14 × 1.222 = 17.11

It is permissible to insert intermediate levels in the scheme, to give a broader range of values. So floors 5 and 6 could be priced $1.00 below the mid-range at $14.55, and floors 10 and 11 at $1.00 above mid-range at $16.55, without harming the symmetry or the average.

With this basic rent structure, Graham & Simpson are prepared to analyze the merits of the space in greater detail. They might, for example, decide that the mid-rise building and the first four levels of office in the high-rise should be priced equivalently. This would mean that the Type A space would become 30 percent of the total space (six floors of 12,000 square feet divided by 240,000 square feet total). A second round of pricing would be established.

Then the logic of the rents asked for the features offered would again be reviewed. The process can be used for greater and greater refinement and, most important, to test if the rentals arrived at by such approximations as "30 percent spread top to bottom" look sensible when they are laid out in actual numbers.

Cash Cost of Vacancy

Table 78 sets forth a tabular statement of vacancy cost expressed in terms of cash. It is common to express vacancy as a percentage of total existing units, but "16 percent vacant" or "84 percent occupied" do not convey how much real money is being missed from space that has no paying tenant. This table states vacancy in the same terms used for rentals, rent per square foot per month or year.

Example 237. Cash Cost of Vacancy

Mark is preparing a management survey for an apartment building, where the average rental is $0.88 per square foot per month or $10.56 per square foot per year. There are 261,000 rentable square feet in the property. He estimates they will experience 20 percent turnover during the coming year, or 52,200 square feet. Apartments turning over will be without a rent payer an average of 20 days.

First, enter Table 78, page 2 (p. 821), the section with $10.50, the nearest entry to $10.56. Read down the left column, time vacant to 20 days. Read across on that line to the column headed 10.50 and read the answer, 0.583, the annual cost in pennies of a square foot vacant for 20 days. Multiply this factor by the number of square feet expected to turn over to get

$$52,200 × 0.583 = \$30,432.60$$

or, rounding, $30,400, the annual cost of vacancy.

Example 238. Refurbishing Cost to Avoid Potential Vacancy

Xanfer Associates is landlord of the Xanfer Plaza Office Tower. A tenant is asking for a renewal lease at an annual rent of $13.75 per square foot. The tenant is also insisting that it receive refurbishing that is expected to cost $1.75 to $2.10 per square foot. The Tower manager expects that it would take 2 to 3 months of vacancy to obtain a replacement tenant.

To find out if the trade-off is worthwhile, enter Table 78, page 2 (p. 821), the page that includes $13.75. Read down the left column to 2 months. Read across on that line to the column headed 13.75 and read the answer, 2.292, the cost of a 2-month vacancy. Read just below it, 3.438, the cost of a 3-month vacancy.

Since a vacancy would cost from $2.29 to $3.44 per square foot, while refurbishing would be no more than $2.10 per square foot, Xanfer would be justified in refurbishing in order to retain the tenant.

Annual Reserve for Vacancy Converted to Spot Allowance

In projecting future returns for real estate, it is customary to estimate an annual reserve for vacancy of the property. This is done by deducting a constant portion, usually from 3 to 7 percent, of the gross revenue of the project at full-house, to reflect space which will be vacant from time to time. In reality, vacancy tends to occur in certain spots. For example, office building vacancy tends to be markedly greater at 5-year intervals, since most office leases are written for terms of 5 years or multiples of 5 years.

Table 79 converts an annual reserve allowance to a spot cost for vacancy. The annual reserve is presumed to be created from monthly deposits which grow at the interest rates obtainable on savings deposits. The result is given in months of vacancy that could be "paid" from the accumulated reserve.

Example 239.   Annual Reserve for Vacancy Converted to Spot Vacancy Allowance

Pim Pheldrin's appraisal of the Carrock Office Plaza income uses an annual reserve for vacancy of 5.0 percent. But the building is fully leased for 5 years, at which time about 33.3 percent of the tenants are expected to move out. Pim wishes to know how long that space could remain vacant without exceeding the accumulated reserve for vacancy in his appraisal. The current rate on savings deposits is 7.50 percent per year.

Enter Table 79, page 1 (p. 823), the section for 7.50 percent interest rate on savings. Read down the left column, annual reserve, to 5.0 percent, and read across on that line to the section for 33.3 percent turnover. Read under the column headed 5 years, the answer 11m 1, that is, 11 months and 1 day. This is the time that one-third of the building could be va-

cant 5 years from now without exceeding the accumulated reserve for vacancy.

Spot Vacancy Cost Converted to Annual Reserve

Table 80 is the reverse of Table 79. It assumes that the duration of vacancy that will occur is known and converts that into its equivalent annual reserve for vacancy.

Example 240.   Spot Vacancy Allowance Converted to Annual Vacancy Reserve

Taddikew is projecting the vacancy of Lyynedorn Office Park. The property is fully leased for 3 years into the future. At the end of 5 years, Taddikew expects that 60 percent of the tenants will turn over, that is, move out. Vacant spaces are expected to be without a rent payer for 9 months. The interest rate today on savings deposits is 8.50 percent.

To find the annual reserve to match the revenue loss of this turnover, enter Table 80 on the page for spot vacancy of 9 months. Within the section for interest rate on savings of 8.50 percent, read down the time span column to 36 months and across to the column headed 60 percent. The answer there, 2.2 percent, is the annual reserve that would cover a vacancy of 60 percent of the property for 6 months starting 3 years from now, if the reserve is built up using 8.50 percent interest.

Cash-on-Cash Return after Growth

Financial leverage can produce one of real estate's most desirable attributes: profit from the use of other people's money. It allows a buyer to acquire a larger property than could otherwise be had with the investor's own resources. For investors whose functional currency is not the U.S. dollar, buying with leverage hedges the currency risk in a U.S. investment and gives a springboard effect to yield: With mortgage financing at an 80 percent loan-to-value ratio, a mere 20 percent increase in property value doubles the investor's **cash-on-cash return,** also called "equity dividend." In principle, doubling cash-on-cash return doubles the value of the investor's equity.

Table 8 gives the effect of changes in net operating income on cash-on-cash return. The table illustrates how quickly the equity dividend can rise and how quickly the dividend evaporates under the stimulus of changing income and expenses. Change could come about by way of inflation or efficiency, so that a 1 percent growth rate means any combination of income and expense changes such that net operating income rises 1 percent each year.

Example 241. Effect of Income Increase on Cash-on-Cash Yield

Avril Apartments Associates operates Avril Terrace with an 80 percent loan-to-value mortgage that has an annual constant of 10.25 percent. The property currently delivers an 8.50 percent cash-on-cash return to the partnership. The projections indicate that the property's revenue will grow an average of 3 percent per year over the next 5 years.

To find what effect this growth would have on yield, enter Table 8, page 3 (p. 195), the page for a return of 8.50 percent cash-on-cash and 80 percent loan-to-value ratio. Read down the growth rate column to the section 3 percent, and across on the line for 5 years to the column headed 10.25 percent mortgage constant. The answer there is 16.384 percent; that is, after 5 years of growth in the net operating income of 3 percent per year, cash-on-cash return will have risen to over 16 percent per year.

Reciprocal Percentage Markups and Markdowns

Table F tells how much a number that has been marked down must be marked up to obtain the original figure. It also gives the necessary markup to provide a given margin, the figure with which to gross up expenses or to figure the gross revenue to produce an after-tax net revenue.

Example 242. Markup of Landlord's Charges

Stenzel's lease provides that landlord's bills for tenant alterations may include a fee, not to exceed 12 percent of the bill, for supervision by the managing agent. The cost of the work in Stenzel's space was $1450. For how much should Stenzel be billed?

Enter Table F, page 1 (p. 854), and read next to 12 percent markdown, 113.63636 markup. Multiply the dollar cost by the markup to get

$$\$1450 \times 1.1363636 = \$1647.73$$

the invoice to Stenzel marked up to cover the 12 percent supervision fee.

Example 243. Comparison of Operating Results to Inflation Rate

Spaniels Coast Apartments were financed 5 years ago with a 75 percent loan. The original constant was 9.75 percent. The original cash-on-cash return was 7.00 percent and is currently 12.00 percent per year. In the past five years, inflation has averaged 5.0 percent per year.

To find how the apartments have fared, enter Table 8 in the section for 75 percent loan-to-value and 7.00 percent cash-on-cash. In the portion for 5 percent growth rate, read across on the line for 5 years to the column headed 9.75 percent constant. The factor there, 17.015 percent, is what would have been expected if the rents and expenses kept pace with inflation. Since the current cash-on-cash is only 12.00 percent, the apartments are performing below the inflation rate. By searching this section for lower growth rates, it will be seen that a 12.00 percent return is consistent with roughly a 2.5 percent inflation rate.

Effect of Expense Change on Cash-on-Cash Return

Income-producing property operates with leverage of two kinds, financial and operating. Financial leverage is the use of debt or disparate classes of equity to increase the yield to the last party with a right to payment. Operating leverage comes about through reduced expenses, whether by massing purchasing power, using more efficient "machines," or passing costs to tenants that would otherwise have been paid by the landlord. Both types in their favorable aspect have the capacity to increase yield rapidly; both can be millstones when they become adverse. Their impact is geometric, if both are used and one or both becomes unfavorable.

Table 81 shows the cash-on-cash return when the expenses of a leveraged property increase or decrease. The table assumes that the investor begins with a certain equity return, debt service coverage ratio, and expense ratio. Then expenses are assumed to decrease or increase by some percentage, with the resulting cash-on-cash yield being the entry given by the table. The negative entries in the table indicate that the return to the landlord would be less than zero; the property would be in a cash deficit position.

Example 244.   Effect of Expense Change on Cash-on-Cash Return

Stennerud Stores operates a mall with 35 stores. The property is operating with an expense ratio (landlord's share) of 30 percent. The mortgage debt service ratio is 1.20 to 1 at present. With these circumstances, the owners receive a 7.00 percent cash-on-cash return. They anticipate a 20 percent increase in operating expenses in the coming year, about half of which can be passed on to tenants under the terms of the leases. They want to know the likely impact of this variance in expenses.

Begin with landlord's share of the expense increase, which is 50 percent of 20 percent, or 10 percent. Now enter Table 81, page 1 (p. 829), the section for a 7.00 percent cash-on-cash return. In the section for debt service coverage of 1.20 times, read across on the line for 30 percent expense ratio to the column for 10 percent (that is, +10 percent owing to the increase in the expenses). The answer there, 5.20 percent, is the cash-on-cash return that can be expected after a 10 percent increase in expenses borne by the landlord.

Asset-based Management Fee Converted to Income-Based Fee and Vice Versa

Asset management fees are often quoted in a percentage of the value of the property. The value may be that set by an annual appraisal, or it may be the value on the books of the owner. Property managers most often quote their fees in terms of the percentage of the actual income of the property that they collect. Table 83 provides the conversion of asset-based management fees to the income-based, and vice versa.

Example 245.   Asset-Based Fee Converted to Income-Based Fee

Rungeon and Company propose to take over asset management for Sarah's Corners Mini-Mall. Rungeon customarily offers a deal based on 0.75 percent of asset value, measured by the book value of the property each year. The owner has asked, however, that offers be expressed in terms of a percentage of rentals collected at the property. The analysis made by Rungeon indicates that the property will earn at a capitalization rate of 5.00 percent in the coming year, and at about 10.00 percent in the remaining 4 years of the 5-year contract. All rents at the Mini-Mall are net.

Enter Table 83, page 5 (p. 839), the section for net rentals at the upper half. Read down the column for asset-based fee to 0.75 percent and across on that line first to the column headed 6.00 percent capitalization rate. The factor there is 12.50 percent. Continue on that line to the column headed 10.00 percent and find the factor, 7.50 percent. The pricing portion of Rungeon's proposal will include a fee of 12.50 percent of rents collected during the first year and 7.50 percent of rents collected thereafter.

Note   The table allows for 7 percent vacancy and collection loss, which will cover most cases. If the vacancy will be substantially greater than this, say, above 20 percent, select a lower capitalization rate, as in the example above.

Example 246.   Income-Based Fee Converted to Asset-Based Fee

Spiratillo Property Management has quoted 6.25 percent of rents collected as its fee for the Brighton Arms Residences. The owners of Brighton Arms have also received a bid from First Town ThriftCo to handle the management for a fee of 0.90 percent of the property value, based on an appraisal to be performed annually. The Brighton Arms Residences today operates at a 25 percent expense ratio and earns at a capitalization rate of approximately 9.5 percent per year.

To find the better quotation, enter Table 83, page 1 (p. 835), the section for operating expense ratio of 25 percent in the lower half of the chart. Read down the column for income-based fee to 6.25 percent. Read across on that line to the column headed 9.5 percent interest. The percentage there, 0.792 percent, is the percentage of property value represented by the Spiratillo quote. The Spiratillo offer at an effective 0.792 percent of asset value is considerably lower than First Town ThriftCo's 0.90 percent price quotation.

Example 247.   Amortization of Building Equipment and Operating Expense Charge for Long-Lived Equipment

Leases in the Danau Office Tower provide for tenants to share operating expenses above certain levels.

Operating expenses include amortization of capital equipment, if the equipment serves to reduce operating expenses. The amortization is the straight-line life of the equipment plus the bank rate of interest on the unamortized portion.

Three years ago, a new energy management computer was installed at Danau at a cost of $48,000. The computer has an estimated life of 8 years. Bank interest averaged 9.00 percent last year. To find the capital equipment charge to be included in operating expenses for the fourth year, begin by taking the straight-line portion of the equipment's cost, which is

$$\$48,000 \div 8 \text{ years} = \$6000$$

the "principal" portion of the expense.

Now enter Table 40, page 9 (p. 482), the page for 9.00 percent interest, annual payments. Read down the years column to line 4 and across on that line to the column headed 8 years. The factor there, 5.6250 percent, is the interest factor for year 4. Multiply it by the original amount of the loan to get

$$\$48,000 \times 0.056250 = \$2700.00$$

the "interest cost" for the fourth year. Adding this to the principal gives $8700.00, the total cost to be included in operating expenses as amortization of the energy computer for year 4 of the computer's life.

Example 248. Amortization of Leasing Commissions or Tenant Alterations

Many real estate problems require the amount "not yet paid off" of something, whether the unearned part of a commission or the unamortized portion of tenant improvements. These problems can be treated as amortizing loans and the remaining balance found in Table 42 just as with amortizing loans.

Fanhall Links has rented a development office in a downtown office building. The landlord agrees to put in $26.00 per square foot of tenant improvements but wants Fanhall to pay for the unamortized portion if Fanhall does not renew at the end of 5 years. Current real estate loan rates are 10.50 percent. What is needed then is the "remaining loan balance" after 5 years for a 10.50 percent "loan" on a 10-year amortization schedule.

This can be found in Table 42 (b), page 21 (p. 517), the page for 10.50 percent loans, 10-year amortization schedule. Referring to the column for remaining balance at year end on the line for year 5, the answer is 62.778274 percent. The lease would provide that if Fanhall does not elect the 5-year re-

newal, it must pay as additional rent the sum of $16.32, or $26.00 per square foot × 62.778274 percent remaining balance, for each square foot in the demised premises.

Note For accounting purposes, the tenant improvements will most likely be written off straight-line, as part of the building. This example, and the following, give the *economic* results of the transaction; the accounting results follow accounting principles and may appear substantially different on financial statements from those shown here.

Example 249. Annuity Depreciation of Machinery

In many real estate applications, annuity depreciation corresponds better to the physical course of deterioration and obsolescence than standard accounting and tax methods. Most buildings and important components, such as air-conditioning compressors, depreciate little in the early periods, but degrade more and more rapidly in later years, following the same path as principal payments on a mortgage loan. Annuity depreciation treats the cost of property as if it were a loan to the company or profit center and depreciates the property at the rate of principal amortization of the loan. (There is no interest payment, but the cost of funds of the owner will be used as the interest rate to select the amortization schedule.)

Ventura Vallejo Gardens is selling land sites for future buildings. Among its equipment are trucks and several backhoes, all estimated to have a life of 5 remaining years. The firm borrows currently at 12.00 percent and uses that as its cost of funds. In preparing its 5-year financial forecasts, the company prefers to use annuity depreciation. To do so, it will project the machinery cost as if it were on a 5-year loan. Depreciation each year equals the principal repayment on a 5-year loan at 12.00 percent interest, as taken from Table 42. This planning assigns costs more tightly to the years in which physical deterioration is likely to occur. Since repairs on such equipment tend to rise markedly in the last periods of the equipment's life, trade-offs against the purchase of new equipment will be better analyzed.

Example 250. Yield from Add-on Interest Loan

Carranans Property Management is considering the purchase of a service van. The auto dealership offers financing at 4.90 percent add-on interest for 72 months. Their bank is prepared to handle the same loan at 8.50 percent interest.

To find the yield from the add-on loan, enter Table 32, page 1 (p. 403), the page for 4.90 percent interest. Read down the months column to 72 and across to the column headed 4.90 percent, and read 8.893, the annual interest yield from the add-on interest loan. From the standpoint of interest rate only, the bank loan appears more favorable.

Reserves for Repairs and Replacements

Example 251. Terminal Value of a Series of Deposits

Grilleton intends to deposit $1200 per month from the rentals it receives into a fund for replacements. Assuming that the interest rate on deposits will average 8.00 percent over the coming years, what will be the **terminal value** of the fund after 120 months?

Enter Table 46, page 11 (p. 555), the page for 8.00 percent interest; read down the right column to 120 months. On that line, find under the column for future value of 1 per period in the monthly payments section the factor, 182.9460352. Multiply this by the monthly deposit to get

$$\$1200 \times 182.9460352 = \$219{,}535.24$$

the future value of a series of 120 monthly deposits of $1200 with 8.00 percent interest.

Example 252. Building a Reserve for Replacements (One Time Payout)

Coriander Court Shopping Plaza has obtained a 15-year lease with Finer Stores, under which the landlord is required to install a high-tech electronic food court which must be replaced at the end of the fifth year of the lease. Replacement will cost $300,000. CCSP Associates, the owning partnership, wishes to establish a sinking fund to pay for the replacement. They will deposit monthly amounts deducted from the Finer rents into the fund. The interest rate on savings deposits is 7.00 percent, which they believe is a reasonable average to assume over the 60-month buildup of the fund.

To find the amount to be deducted from Finer's rent and deposited in the sinking fund, enter Table

52, page 2 (p. 682), the page for 7.00 percent interest. Read down the end-of-year column to year 5 and across on that line to the entry under 7.00 percent interest, monthly. The factor there, 16.761438, is the sum of 12 monthly deposits to the fund. That is, 16.761438 percent of the desired ending balance must be put aside each year with monthly deposits to obtain 100 percent at the end of 5 years. Now multiply the factor by the amount desired at the end of the sinking fund period to get

$$0.16761438 \div 12 \times \$300{,}000 = \$4190.36$$

the amount to be set aside each month to build a $300,000 sinking fund with 60 monthly deposits, when monthly deposits earn 7.00 percent per year interest.

Example 253. Building a Reserve for Replacement (Multipayout)

Czerwuht plans to repave the parking lot and paint the exterior of Winfalls Slip Yachting Mall. The work will take place over 3 years and cost an average of $8000 per month. Czerwuht would start the work 2 years from now, setting aside a monthly reserve in the meantime that would earn interest at an expected rate of 9.00 percent.

To find the monthly deposit needed, enter Table 60, page 2 (p. 725), the section for 2 years of deposit and 9.00 percent interest. On the line for 3 years of withdrawal, read across to the column headed 9.00 percent and read 120.0788 percent, the percentage of the future withdrawals needed. Multiply the dollar amount of withdrawals by the percentage to get

$$\$8000 \times 1.200788 = \$9606.30$$

the monthly deposits needed for 24 months, so that $8000 per month can then be withdrawn for 36 months, when interest is 9.00 percent per year.

Note The repairs are seasonal in nature, but the calculations here assume steady flows in and out. Deviations from a schedule would alter the amounts needed, but we submit that the assumptions here are broad enough to require this form of "smoothed" forecast.

Amount of Monthly Withdrawal Available from Deposits of 100

Table 61 gives the reverse of the Table 60 problem illustrated in the last example. Here the monthly deposit amount is known. The entries in the table tell how much the periodic withdrawals could be after the series of deposits.

Example 254. Expenses Payable from Monthly Deposits

In the year after the sale of The Deco Mall, the buyer will remit monthly the amount of delinquent rents due as of the closing date. The maximum amount that may be paid is $11,000 per month, but Congress Management believe only two-thirds will actually be paid. Rather than distribute the bad debt receipts to the owning partnership, Congress proposes to hold the funds in a money market account at 8.00 percent and to use it to cover repairs and decorating needed in the second and third years of ownership.

To find the amount available for repairs in the second and third years, begin by finding the dependable amount of the deposit. It is $7333 per month ($11,000 × ⅔). Enter Table 61, page 1 (p. 726), the page for 8.00 percent and the section for 1 year of deposit. On the line for 2 years of withdrawals, read across to the 8.00 percent column and read the factor, 56.3077 percent, the percentage of deposit. Multiply the monthly deposit by the factor to get

$$\$7333 \times 0.563077 = \$4129.04$$

the monthly withdrawal available for 24 months after 12 months of deposits of $7333 when interest is 8.00 percent.

Example 255. Single Deposit to Create Multipayout Repair Fund

Thom Fascinato estimates that, over the next 48 months, $9000 per month will be needed on average for the upgrade of Cannes Village Apartments. The pension fund owner will deposit the necessary sum at a bank, where the current rate for certificates of deposits with such monthly draws is 8.25 percent per year.

To find the deposit, enter Table 58, page 1 (p. 716), the section for draw delay of 1 month and 8.25 percent interest. Read down the number of payments column to 48 and across on that line to the column headed 8.25 percent. The factor there, 40.76567, is the needed investment as a multiple, not a percentage, of the payments. Multiply the average cost by the multiple to get

$$\$9000 \times 40.76567 = \$366,891$$

the deposit needed to provide $9000 per month over 48 months, when interest is 8.25 percent.

Deposit to Complete a Partial Sinking Fund

Part of the needed cash for a sinking fund may already be on hand. Perhaps the fund was started some time ago. Or, a seller may give a credit at closing to establish the fund. Having a partial balance in the fund lowers the deposit needed for completion compared to the ordinary sinking fund, since both the beginning balance and the periodic deposits will earn interest. Table 53 gives the reduced deposit. It assumes a partial fund is on hand the first day of the program, and that 1 month later, and each month after that, a deposit is made. Interest is compounded monthly on the entire balance in the fund. The entries are percentages of the total fund desired in the future.

Some entries are negative, meaning that the initial deposit and its interest alone will be enough to complete the sinking fund. The percentage amount of a negative entry could actually be withdrawn from the fund each month and still achieve the full balance by the specified time.

Example 256. Deposit to Complete a Partial Sinking Fund

Conduco Jarb Ltd. (CJL) has bought the Symnyms factory. CJL's engineer estimates that a new roof will be needed in 3 years at a probable cost of $90,000. By negotiation, CJL has obtained the seller's agreement to pay one-third of this, $30,000, as a kind of proration of the poor condition of the roof. Deposits earn interest currently at 9.00 percent per year.

To find the monthly deposit that CJL should make to complete the $90,000 fund, enter Table 53, page 3 (p. 690), the section for starting from a partial fund of 33.3 percent. Read across on the line for 3 years to the column headed 9.00 percent. The factor there, 1.36998 percent, is the percentage of the future fund to be deposited monthly. Multiply the future fund amount by the percentage to get

$$\$90,000 \times 0.0136998 = \$1232.98$$

the monthly deposit that, together with an initial deposit of $30,000 and interest on the total at 9.00 percent per year compounded monthly will build up to $90,000 by the end of 3 years.

Number of Deposits to Complete a Partial Sinking Fund

Table 56 gives the number of payments needed to fill out the remainder of a fund that already has some balance. Interest is assumed to be compounded monthly. The entries are in months and fractions of months but for all practical purposes should be rounded to the next higher month.

Example 257.   Number of Deposits to Complete a Partial Sinking Fund

Wigstan & Flagley, Attorneys, intend to remodel their offices. To cover the estimated $500,000 cost, they will set aside a reserve of $125,000 now and add $7500 per month to it. Deposits can earn 9.00 percent per year.

To find out how long it will take to meet their target, begin by finding the monthly deposit. It is 1.50 percent, or $7500 ÷ $500,000. Now enter Table 56, page 3 (p. 708), the section for starting from a partial fund of 25 percent and read down the monthly deposit column to 1.50 percent. Read across on that line to the 9.00 percent column. The answer, 38.5, appears there, meaning that it will take, rounded, 3 years and 3 months of such deposits, together with the initial reserve and interest of 9.00 percent to achieve a fund of $500,000.

Cumulative Balance on a Sinking Fund

Just as a sinking fund deposit is the inverse of a mortgage loan payment, the cumulative balance table for a sinking fund is the inverse of the remaining balance table for a mortgage loan. Table 54 gives the percentage of the desired fund that has been achieved at the end of any year. Although a remaining balance table always ends at zero, the cumulative balance table always ends at 100 percent.

Example 258.   Cumulative Balance on a Sinking Fund

Property workout specialists, Pellaskaus & Van Eckx, are tenants in the Banner Office Tower but plan to relocate their office at lease expiration 7 years from now and want to set up a reserve to cover the costs to be incurred in making the move. They will establish a sinking fund with 7-year funding. They wish to know

the balance that will be on hand 4 years from now. Interest rates on the fund will be 7.50 percent; deposits are to be made monthly.

To find the balance, enter Table 54, page 3 (p. 694), the page for 7.50 percent interest, 7-year funding. Read down the left column in the 7-year section to year 4. On that line under 7.50 percent monthly, read the answer, 50.691 percent, the balance accumulated on a 7-year sinking fund at 7.50 percent after 4 years.

Example 259.   Time When Compounded Deposit Growth Will Be Achieved

Speerwin Limited Company will set aside $60,000 from the sale proceeds of its parking lot to satisfy a required $100,000 funding for its pension fund. If the deposit can earn at least 9.00 percent interest, how long will it take to build the needed fund?

Begin by finding the desired percentage increase, which is found by dividing the increase needed in the fund by the initial balance, as follows:

$$\frac{\$100,000 \text{ fund} - \$60,000 \text{ initial fund}}{\$60,000 \text{ initial fund}} = \frac{\$40,000}{\$60,000}$$
$$= 0.6667$$
$$= 66.7\%$$

Now enter Table 68 (p. 772), in the section for a 66.7 percent increase and read down to 9.00 percent interest and across to the 66.7 percent column. The answer, 5Y 9m, means the value of the deposit will pass through $100,000 in the ninth month of the fifth year, if 9.00 percent interest compounded monthly is earned.

Establishing a Condo Building Reserve Fund

Example 260.   Partition of a Deposit Series into Segments of Equal Value

The Tour d'Argent residential park consists of two condominiums that share a common recreation area and wilderness preserve on a 50/50 basis. The highrise, La Tour, was constructed several years ago, but Les Maisons-Ville have only recently been completed. The two associations are agreed that a fund should be built up at the initial rate of $14,000 per month.

The fund will be used to construct additional common-area facilities. The condo board of La Tour would prefer to avoid funding additional projects at this time, but the board of Les Maisons-Ville is prepared to make the full deposit for 18 months, with La Tour to make some number of payments after that. The long-term deposits of the associations are currently earning 7.00 percent interest, so that seems to be a reasonable rate on which to base their agreement.

To find the number of payments of $14,000 that La Tour would make, enter Table 63 (p. 729), and read down the number of prior payments column to 18. Reading across on that line to the 7.00 percent interest column, find the answer 20.11 payments. Thus, after 18 payments are made by Les Maisons-Ville, 20 full payments of $14,000 should be made by La Tour d'Argent. Eleven percent (20.11 − 20.00) of the forty-first payment, $1540, or $14,000 × 0.11, should be paid by La Tour. The remaining $12,460 and all further payments will be divided equally between the two boards.

EFFICIENCY AND MONEY-SAVING OPERATIONS

Replacing a Capital Asset

We define a capital asset as one needed to make a larger asset work, or at least function smoothly, but which wears out only over a long time. Examples might be air conditioning compressors, elevators, even a roof. In the decision to replace one of these, the important questions are how long it will last, how much of it can be salvaged later, what operating costs are associated with it, and what interest could be earned on the money paid for it. Table 72 pulls all these questions into a single figure. The entries in the table are not costs but an index. The usefulness of the figures lies in comparing alternatives. The case with the lowest index is the best alternative.

In Table 72, a column is given for "maintenance." By maintenance is meant all costs associated with having this asset instead of another, whether or not precisely for maintenance. To take an extreme example, a passenger elevator that required an operator might be priced vastly below an automatic elevator, but the payroll of the operators would be added back as part of maintenance.

The index becomes lower as interest rates go up; this rewards assets with longer life. Generally the asset with a long life is desirable under high interest rates; that with low maintenance under low interest rates.

Example 261. Cost of Replacing a Capital Asset

Gridge-Mackrey Managers have slated two water pumps for replacement in the coming year. Among the possible replacements is a new model offered at $9500 which is guaranteed for 7 years. On the strength of the guarantee, they are willing to assign it a useful life of 7 years and a maintenance factor of zero percent. An alternative is a rebuilt unit that can be had for $5500 with a 1-year warranty. Based on experience reports from other users, they believe this unit would have a life of 5 years. After the 1-year warranty, they estimate the rebuilt machine would require annual maintenance at 10 percent of cost. They are disregarding salvage. All their capital budgeting is done with an assumed interest rate of 10.00 percent.

To compare these choices, first enter Table 72, page 2 (p. 789), the page for time to replacement of 5 years. In the section for zero percent salvage ratio, read across on the line for 10 percent maintenance to the 10.00 percent interest rate column. The index there, 3.5496, is the replacement index of the rebuilt pump.

Next, enter Table 72, page 3 (p. 790), the page for 7 years' time to replacement, again in the zero percent salvage ratio section. On the line for zero percent maintenance, read across to the column headed 10.00 percent interest rate. The index in this case is 1.9921 for the new, guaranteed pump.

Now multiply the original cost of each pump by its replacement index to get

$$\$9500 \times 1.9921 = \$18,925$$

comparison index cost for the new pump, and

$$\$5500 \times 3.5496 = \$19,523$$

comparison index for the rebuilt pump. On the basis of the comparison indexes, the new, guaranteed pump is the better choice, but only by a slender margin. Noting that the replacement index is heavily influenced by maintenance cost, the managers at Gridge-Mackrey will study the estimate of 10 percent maintenance for the rebuilt pump. If that estimate could be safely lowered to 5 percent, the comparison indexes will look entirely different.

Example 262. Maximum Capital Cost to Avoid Operating Expense Increase

Replacing burnt-out fluorescent lamps in the QuillnQuire Distributors warehouse costs over

$20,000 per year, labor and material included, and this is expected to increase 6 percent per year. A new type of lamp is guaranteed to burn for 7 years without replacement. QuillnQuire Facilities Management Department want to estimate how much they could pay for these lamps to avoid the annual replacement costs. Their main office requires a 10.00 percent cost of funds (interest rate) be figured on any capital expenditures.

Enter Table 47 (a), page 6 (p. 589), the section for an annual rate of growth of 6 percent. On the line for 7 years, read under the column headed 10.00 percent the factor, 5.71000, the multiple of savings that could be paid. Multiply this by the dollar amount to get

$$\$20,000 \times 5.71000 = \$114,200.00$$

the maximum price one could pay for the lamps installed, to avoid $20,000 annual expense growing at 6 percent annually, at 10.00 percent interest.

Example 263. Maximum Price for Money-Saving Equipment with Declining Benefits

Skilson Management are considering a new power sweeper for Skilson Value Mall. Although their existing machine works well, the new model could save at least $10,800 per year over its 10-year life. The savings would be reduced, however, by the need for increased maintenance and downtime as the machine ages and wears. This decline is estimated to reduce the savings at the rate of 5 percent per year. Interest rates for loans are at 10.00 percent, so this could be considered Skilson's cost of funds.

To find what could be paid for the machine, enter Table 47 (b), page 8 (p. 603), at annual rate of decline of 5 percent per year. On the line for 10 years, under the 10.00 percent column, find the factor, 5.12774. Multiplying it by the dollar amount of annual savings gives

$$\$10,800 \times 5.12774 = \$55,379.59$$

the maximum price for a machine that will save $10,800 per year, when the savings will decline 5 percent per year.

Note This example assumes that a new power sweeper is not needed currently but would be bought only to get the savings. If an ordinary model is needed anyway that would cost $22,300 but produce no savings, add $22,300 to the figure above to get the total that could be paid for the machine.

Example 264. Time to Payback of a Money-Saving Expenditure

Neal Chesterton is considering improvements to the HVAC system of Fillwint Club Offices. The work will cost $60,000, but savings of at least $12,000 per year can be expected. Given that Chesterton's cost of borrowing is 8.00 percent per year, how long will it take to recapture the improvements out of the savings?

Begin by finding the annual payback constant, as follows:

$$\frac{\$12,000 \text{ savings per year}}{\$60,000 \text{ cost of improvements}} = 0.200$$
$$= 20.0\% \text{ rate of payback}$$

Now enter Table 59, page 1 (p. 722), the page for 8.00 percent interest and read down the annual constant column to 20.00 percent. Read across on that line to the column headed 8.00 percent, and find the answer, 76.9 months. The HVAC improvements will have been paid for from savings in 77 months, if the $12,000 annual rate of savings is maintained.

Example 265. When All But Salvage Cost of Machine Is Recovered

Breugher intends to install new HVAC equipment that has an expected life of 10 years in Connaught Towers. The electric motors can always be salvaged for 20 percent of the equipment cost. If the property earns 8.50 percent yearly (that is, its cost of funds is 8.50 percent), how long will it be until the installation, net of salvage value, has been economically recovered?

Enter Table 67, page 3 (p. 768), the section for 8.50 percent interest. On the line for 10 years' amortization of loan, read across to the column headed 20 percent, and find the answer, 8 years 7 months, the time when the value of the equipment will have been economically depreciated down to its salvage value.

Note This example deals with the equipment on the basis of annuity depreciation, which differs substantially from accounting or tax depreciation. The intention with annuity depreciation is to estimate the probable economic impact on operations. See Example 249 for a discussion of annuity depreciation.

Chapter 7

CLOSING AND ACCOUNTING FOR SALES, LOANS, AND LEASES

This chapter will build your proficiency in the daily operations of real estate money matters. Its examples show how to develop the closing statement and make prorations of income, expenses, and interest payments and how to figure a loan payoff letter, prepayment premiums, loan principal and interest statements, and discounts on loans. The examples also demonstrate amortization of discounts and premiums on loans, rent adjustments under Consumer Price Index clauses, and transactions between partners.

CLOSING THE SALE

The real estate sale closing statement has been made complex by federal laws and federal forms. But at base the closing statement is merely a balance sheet of payments and credits a buyer and seller make to settle accounts. The simplest closing statement sets up three columns: item, seller's credit, and buyer's credit. The title of each element in the transaction is put in the first column, under *item*. The money appropriate to the item is placed under either the seller's credit or buyer's credit column. The seller's credit and buyer's credit columns are then totalled, and the difference between them is paid (usually) to the seller. A few of the closing items will be marked to be "paid outside the closing." Despite its simplicity, this form may be used to document even highly sophisticated transactions. Loan closings can equally well be accomplished with the same format, set up with columns for item, borrower's credit, and lender's credit.

Example 266. Preparing the Closing Statement

Spoerwagen & Cie have agreed to purchase Howth Industrial Estates for $7.25 million with a closing date of June 30. The contract provides that the day of closing will be a day of income and expense to the seller and that prorations of usual items are to be made on the basis of the number of days elapsed.

Rents under leases are all due on the first of the month, so there will be no rent proration. One tenant is 30 days delinquent, however, and Spoerwagen has accepted the risk of collecting the $2400 item. An annual insurance policy of $16,000 was taken out last September 1 and will be assigned to the buyer. Real estate taxes of $109,000 will be payable on the coming December 31. Monthly electric power that cost $7250 last period will be due on the 15th of July.

**Howth Industrial Estates
Closing Statement
Closing Date June 30**

Item	Seller's Credit	Buyer's Credit
Purchase price, per contract	$7,250,000.00	$
Brokerage commission (2.0%)		145,000.00
Mortgage loan assumption		
Principal (*see Ex. 278*)	$4,412,000.00	
Interest 30 days at 10.25%	37,685.83	
Total mortgage assumption		4,449,685.83
Assumption fee $44,120.00 to be paid by buyer outside closing.		
Prorations		
Rent (all rents due July 1, no proration)		
Delinquent rent credit	2,400.00	
Insurance (*see Ex. 269*)	2,717.81	
Electric power (*see Ex. 270*)		3,625.00
Real estate taxes (*see Ex. 269*)		54,052.05
(181 days)		
Title and recording charges of seller (buyer's transfer tax stamps of $7250 to be paid outside closing)		11,210.25
Total credits	$7,255,117.81	$4,663,573.13
Difference due seller to balance		2,591,544.68
Totals	$7,255,117.81	$7,255,117.81
Buyer's cash requirements		
Proceeds due seller		$2,591,544.68
Commission due broker		145,000.00
Title, transfer tax		18,460.25
Lender assumption fee		44,120.00
July 1 mortgage payment*		46,320.00
Buyer's cash to close		$2,845,444.93

*Not mentioned in the contract but required by the lender was that the July 1 payment be collected at closing.

Figure 7-1. Closing Statement

Title charges of $11,200 are the responsibility of the seller as is a recording fee of $10.25. Transfer tax stamps of $7250 are chargeable to the buyer.

Spoerwagen will take title **subject to** a mortgage loan that bears interest at 10.25 percent per year and is paid through May 31. After the June 1 payment, the balance was $4,412,000. The lender will charge a 1 percent assumption fee to permit Spoerwagen to take over the loan. The broker is entitled to a commission of 2.0 percent of the selling price. Each party will pay its attorney outside the closing.

The closing statement should look like Figure 7-1, except that references in italics are to examples in this chapter that show how the item was calculated.

Readers experienced in closings may protest that this closing statement is oversimplified, and that is partly true. The closing statement for a large apartment sale may include 50 or 100 items. This statement has been made small enough to comprehend and to serve as a

teaching device. But it is also true that many forms of closing statement are unnecessarily complex, so much so that they mask the business logic of what is being accomplished. If each element of Figure 7-1 is studied until its logic is thoroughly understood, the most complex forms for home or commercial closings may be attacked with confidence.

Prorations

Prorations, or *apportionments* as they are also called, are the means for buyer and seller to settle accounts that cannot be paid direct. For example, if an insurance policy is being transferred to the buyer but has already been paid by the seller, the seller will receive a proration credit for the unused portion of the policy. The most common proration is that for real estate taxes, which in many communities are paid only once or twice a year, usually after the period to which they apply.

In most cases, the buyer receives a credit for the taxes applicable to the seller's period of ownership but that the buyer will have to pay. Prorations are most likely made according to the number of days in the month, for expenses which are typically paid monthly, or the number of days in the year, for annual items such as real estate taxes. Accordingly, the first examples in this section deal with the number of days between two dates and the percentage of a year or month that has elapsed and the percentage remaining.

Days between Two Dates

Table A lets you quickly calculate the number of days between two dates. The number of days is important for sale and loan prorations and for determining the due date of, and interest on, a mortgage note.

Example 267.   Date When Given Number of Days Have Passed

Commercial Stamp Collecting's lease provides the option to cancel the lease if "such option is exercised within 200 days from the date hereof." The lease was signed on August 21 (the "date hereof"). To find the last day for exercising the cancellation option, enter the *upper* half of Table A, page 1 (p. 840), at August 21 and get its number, 233. Add 200 to it and enter the *lower* half of Table A to find 433. It is next to March 9. The exercise of option must be made on or before March 9 of the following year, unless it is leap year. If it is leap year, March 8 will be the final day.

Note If March 9 (or March 8 in leap year), the stated exercise date, falls on a weekend or holiday, it is *not* safe to assume that the exercise period is extended. Good business practice would be to serve the notice on or before the last business day, so that a dated receipt may be obtained.

Example 268.   Prorations Using Days between Dates

Merrick van Dyke is preparing a closing statement for the sale of an apartment. The prorations date is August 15. Annual sewer assessments of $6700 are already paid, however, through March 27 of the following year. The seller is therefore entitled to a proration credit at the closing.

To calculate the proration, begin by finding March 27 in the lower half of Table A (using leap year table if necessary). Its number is 451. Find August 15 in the upper part of the table; its number is 227. Subtracting the second from the first gives 451 − 227 = 224, the number of days between August 15 and March 27. Multiply the annual assessment by the ratio of 224 days to one year to get

$$\$6700 \times 224 \div 365 = \$6700 \times 0.6137 = \$4111.79$$

the proration credit due seller for the prepaid sewer assessment, assuming the proration date is a day of income and expense to the seller. If it is buyer's day, add 1 day to the 224 used above. The same result is achieved in Example 271 to show how to use percentage of year tables for prorations.

Percentage of Year or Month Elapsed, Percentage Remaining

Prorations may also be calculated by the percentage method given in Table B. In it, all calculations are considered to take place at the *end* of the day. So the figure for January 22 assumes the business day of January 22 has already passed. If the closing date is January 22 and the day of closing is a day of income and expense to the seller, then the figures for January 22 are used. If the day of closing is a day of income and expense to the buyer, the figures for January 21 are used. In leap year, use the separate portion of Table B marked leap year.

Example 269.   Proration of 1 Year's Real Estate Taxes

Brady Callanan's real estate taxes for the year are $16,300. The tax year is the calendar year. The property has been sold, and prorations are to be made as of April 1. The real estate taxes will be paid after the closing, so the buyer will be entitled to a proration credit. According to the contract, the day of closing is a day of income and expense to the seller.

Enter Table B, page 1 (p. 842), the section for percentage of year which has elapsed. Locate April 1 and find there the factor, 24.93 percent. Multiply the amount of the taxes by the percentage to get

$$\$16,300 \times 0.2493 = \$4063.59$$

the proration credit to buyer for real estate taxes on the sale.

Example 270.   Proration of 1 Month's Electricity

Constanza Germania is preparing a closing statement for the sale, as of August 15, of Goodhouse Apartments. Electricity is to be prorated on the basis of the prior month's bill, which was $26,855.00. The closing date is a day of income and expenses to the buyer.

Enter Table B in the section for percentage of month which has elapsed. Locate August *14* (the last day of seller's obligation) and find there the factor, 45.16 percent. Multiply the factor by the last bill to get

$$\$26,855.00 \times 0.4516 = \$12,127.72$$

the proration credit to buyer for electricity for 14 days of August.

Example 271.   Prorations across Different Years

Merrick van Dyke is preparing a closing statement for the sale of an apartment. The proration date is August 15. Annual sewer assessments of $6700 have already been paid, however, through March 27 of the following year.

To calculate the proration, enter the *lower* half of Table B, page 1 (p. 842), and find August 15. The percentage of the year remaining is 37.81 percent. Now find March 27 in the *upper* half of the table, where the answer is 23.56 percent. Add these two together to get 61.37 percent. Multiply the annual assessment by the percentage to get

$$\$6700 \times 0.6137 = \$4111.79$$

the proration credit due seller for the prepaid sewer assessment. The same result is achieved in Example 268 above.

Example 272.   Proration of Rentals for Closing

Eldonza's rent is $1600 per month, is payable on the first, and is current. The building has been sold, and the rents will be prorated between the buyer and the seller as of July 15, with the closing day being a day of income and expense to the seller.

Enter Table B at the section for Percentage of Month which remains. Read down the July column to the 15th, where the factor, 51.61 percent, appears. Multiply the dollar amount by the factor to get

$$\$1600 \times 0.5161 = \$825.76$$

the credit to seller for Eldonza's rent for July.

Example 273.   Number of Days between Two Dates and Maturity Date of a Note

Will Haas is taking a note from his buyer on November 20. The buyer agrees to pay the note on March 31 the next year. For how many days should the note be written?

Read the number for March 31 on the bottom half of Table A, page 1 (p. 840). It is 455. Now read the number for November 20 on the top half of the table. It is 324. Subtract the second number from the first to get

$$455 - 324 = 131 \text{ days}$$

the number of days that should be entered on the note. If the next year is leap year, the leap year table (Table A, page 2) would be used for March 31 or any date after February 28.

Note   Use Table D to determine if March 31 in that year will fall on a weekday, Monday through Friday. If not, the parties should agree to add or subtract days to bring the maturity to a business day. This avoids the problem of trying to deliver a payment when the banks are closed.

Balance on a Loan

Table 42 gives balances on loans at the end of any year. Additional columns give the interest and principal paid during each year and the total amount of interest and principal paid since the loan started. The first page of the table furnishes the most commonly needed remaining balances.

A special feature of Table 42 enables you to find the same information for any month within a year. Multiplication of one extra factor is needed to get the interim monthly data, an inconvenience which has the benefit of keeping the table to a reasonable size.

Two conventions are used in U.S. mortgage loans. First, unlike bond or bank loan payments, mortgage payments are customarily made on the first of the month including the interest for the preceding month. Second, interest for the payment date is not included in the payment. So a payment on June 1 includes the interest for May. If the loan is to be paid off on June 1, interest for that day will have to be added.

To prepare a loan payoff statement, it is necessary to know to which month the most recent payment applied. In our case, the most recent payment would have been May 1, which would have included the interest for April and the May 1 principal payment.

Example 274.   Balance of a Loan at End of Year

A $60,000 loan at 8.75 percent interest with a 30-year amortization schedule calls for a balloon payment (payment in full) at the end of five years. What will be the loan balance at that time?

To get the balance, turn to Table 42 (a) (p. 496), the portion of the table for the most commonly needed mortgage balances. Read down the left column to 8.75 percent and across to the column for balance at end of year 5 and read 95.6889 percent. This is the percentage of the loan remaining. Multiply the original loan amount by the percentage balance remaining to get

$$\$60,000 \times 0.956889 = \$57,413.34$$

the principal balance remaining on the loan at the end of 5 years. The total balloon payment will be this principal balance plus interest for the prior month, found by the method of the examples below.

Example 275.   Balance of a Loan during the Year and Amount of Principal Paid

What is the principal balance on a loan at 9.00 percent interest, 30-year amortization schedule after 5 years, 5 months? When the balance on the loan is desired for a month other than year end, there are two steps to finding it:

1. Get the balance at the end of year 5: Enter Table 42 (b), page 16 (p. 512), and in the section for 30 years, read down to year 5. The factor on that line under remaining balance year end is 95.880136 percent, the balance at the end of 5 years.

2. Get the balance 5 months later: In the same section, take the factor for curtail first month on the 6-year line; it is 0.084885 percent. At the bottom of the page, find the monthly factor for 5 months in the 9.00 percent year-to-date section. It is

5.113631. Multiply the curtail first month by the year-to-date factor to get

$$0.084885 \times 5.113631 = 0.434070 \text{ percent}$$

the percentage of principal repayment in the first 5 months of the sixth year. Subtract this from the balance at the end of year 5 to get

95.880136 percent − 0.434070 percent

= 95.446066 percent

the balance remaining on the loan after 5 years and 5 months.

Example 276.   Amount of Principal or Interest Paid for a Year

Table 42 also presents the division of payments into principal and interest for a year.

Principal Paid.   To get the principal paid for a given year, for example year 11, read the figure in the column for principal paid this year for year end 11. This is the percentage of the original loan amount that was repaid as principal during year 11. If the loan in question is a $500,000 loan at 7.50 percent interest on a 15-year amortization schedule, that figure is 7.923116 percent, found in Table 42 (b), page 9 (p. 505), for 7.50 percent interest in the 15-year schedule section, year end 11. To convert this to the dollar amount, multiply the original loan amount, $500,000, by the factor 0.07923116 to get $39,615.58, the amount of principal paid in the eleventh year.

Interest Paid.   To get the interest paid that year, read the percentage 3.201032 percent under the column for interest paid this year for line 11. Multiplying this by the original loan amount will give

$$\$500,000 \times 0.03201032 = \$16,005.16$$

the interest paid in the 12 payments of year 11.

The total principal and interest paid in a year will add up to the figure at the top of the schedule annual constant, *except* for the last year of a loan, when the final payment is often less than the normal payment.

Example 277.   Interest or Principal Paid Since Beginning of Loan

The total interest or principal paid since the beginning of the loan may be readily found from Table 42.

Assume a loan of $100,000 at 10.50 percent interest has been amortized for 7 years on a 10-year amortization schedule.

Interest Paid. The interest paid in the first 7 years of the loan is found in Table 42 (b), page 21 (p. 517), for 10.50 percent interest and the section for a 10-year schedule. Under the column for total interest paid, the factor at 7 years is 54.860737 percent. Multiply this by the original principal balance to get

$$\$100,000 \times 0.54860737 = \$54,860.74$$

the total interest paid on the loan in the first 7 years.

Principal Paid. The principal paid during the first 7 years is found by subtracting the principal balance at the end of the seventh year, 41.515339 percent in this case, from the original balance, 100 percent:

100.000000 percent − 41.515339 percent

= 58.484661 percent

the principal paid off during the first 7 years of a 10-year loan at 10.50 percent interest.

Example 278. Payoff Figures for a Mortgage Loan and Interest and Principal Balances at Any Given Date

Vermeuille is preparing a loan payoff statement for the Garinage loan. The principal balance after the April payment was $238,980. The loan bears interest at 10.75 percent. The May payment of $2800.00, due on May 1, has *not* been made. The loan is to be paid off on the eleventh day of May.

Begin by finding the principal balance. Since the May 1 payment has not been made, the principal balance remains $238,980. For the interest amount, calculate the April interest:

$$\$238,980 \times 0.1075 \div 12 = \$2140.86$$

Then calculate the May interest:

$$\$238,980 \times 0.1075 \times \frac{11}{365} = \$774.23$$

Total interest is therefore $2915.09. Add the principal balance of $238,980.00 and the total principal and interest due is $241,895.09, disregarding, for purposes of this illustration, any late payment fee or prepayment premium.

Example 279. Principal and Interest for Any Given Month in the Loan Term

Let us assume a loan of $100,000 at 9.00 percent interest on a 30-year amortization schedule. We need to know the principal and interest for the eighteenth month of the loan:

Principal Paid. To get a principal portion of the payment, enter Table 42 (b), page 16 (p. 512), the page for 9.00 percent, 30-year schedule. Since the needed payment occurs in the second year, read on the line for year 2 the section for curtail first month, 0.059302. Now enter the table at the bottom of the page under 9.00 percent, and take the monthly factor for this month for month 6. It is 1.045852. Multiply the two together to get

$$0.059302 \times 1.045852 = 0.062021 \text{ percent}$$

the percentage of principal paid off in the eighteenth month. To convert this to dollars, multiply the original loan amount by the principal percentage to get

$$\$100,000 \times 0.00062021 = \$62.02$$

the principal portion of the loan paid in the eighteenth month of a 30-year schedule.

Interest Paid. To get the interest for the eighteenth month, subtract the principal payment just above from the monthly payment. If the monthly payment is not known, obtain it by doing the following: Multiply the original balance of the loan by the factor 0.804623 percent. In the middle of page 16 of Table 42 (b) (p. 512), at the beginning of the 30-year schedule find the monthly payment to get

$$\$100,000 \times 0.00804623 = \$804.62$$

the monthly payment. Now subtract the principal portion from it to get

$804.62 monthly payment − $62.02 principal paid

= $742.60

interest for the eighteenth month of a 30-year schedule at 9.00 percent.

Remaining Balance on a Loan for Schedules Not Shown in Table 42

Remaining balance information is given in this book for most common amortization plans. But many loan plans which could not be included can be covered by use of the constant tables. The remaining balance is obtained by dividing the constant for the original loan by the constant for the loan at a desired date.

Example 280. Remaining Balance on a Loan from Annual Mortgage Constants

Herdron Corporation took out a 25-year loan at 9.00 percent interest 3 years and 2 months ago. In other words, the loan has 21 years, 10 months remaining to full amortization.

To get the balance today, enter Table 35 (b), page 8 (p. 439), the page for 9.00 percent. Read down the years column to 25 and under the column for 0 months read 10.070356 percent, the original term constant. Now find 21 years and across to the column for 10 months, and read 10.479584 percent, the remaining term constant. Divide the original term constant by the remaining term constant to get

$$\frac{\text{Original term of 25 years}}{\text{Remaining term of 21 years 10 months}}$$
$$= \frac{10.070356 \text{ percent}}{10.479584 \text{ percent}} = 96.095 \text{ percent}$$

The loan has a balance of 96.095 percent of the original amount. To get the balance in dollars, multiply the original amount by 0.96095. To get the amount paid off since the beginning of the loan, subtract the answer from 100 percent, as follows:

100.000 percent − 96.095 percent = 3.005 percent

paid off from the original balance.

This example could have been solved as well with Table 42, but it demonstrated that the answer produced by this method is the same as that in the "official" remaining balance table.

Example 281. Remaining Balance or Balloon Payment on Annual Pay Loan

MerryGold Industries holds a 10-year note at 6.50 percent interest, with annual payments to principal and interest. The borrower wishes to prepay the loan four months after the first payment has been made.

To get the payoff amount, begin by finding the principal balance after the first payment. To do this, enter Table 37, page 1 (p. 454), the page for 6.50 percent interest and locate the annual mortgage constant for a 10-year, 6.50 percent loan. This is

13.91047 percent. Now locate just above that the constant for a 9-year loan. This is 15.02380 percent. Divide the first figure by the second to get

13.91047 ÷ 15.02380 = 0.925896 or 92.5896 percent

the balance on the loan after 1 year. Multiplying this percentage by the original principal amount of the loan will give the principal balance in dollars. To get the interest owing on the loan, refer to Example 278 to find the interest for the 4 months since the last payment.

Example 282. Original Amount of a Loan When Payment and Constant Are Known

With the present balance of a loan, the interest rate, and the monthly payment, the original balance of the loan can be found.

Herdron Corporation's loan carries monthly payments of $1469. The loan bears interest at 9.00 percent and was originally for 25 years. Enter Table 35 (a), page 5 (p. 425), at 9.00 percent, 25 years, and find the original constant, 10.070356 percent. Multiply the monthly payment by 12 to get the annual debt service

$1,469.00 × 12 = $17,628.00

Divide the annual debt service by the constant to get

$$\frac{\text{annual debt service}}{\text{original mortgage constant}} = \frac{\$17,628}{0.10070356} = \$175,048$$

Most likely, the original amount of the loan was $175,000. Lenders often round off mortgage payments, which would make our example slightly erroneous. If a result is a few dollars away from an even thousand or hundred dollars, it is a fair guess that the round number was the original amount.

Example 283. Full Amortization Term of a Loan When Constant and Rate Are Known

Faris McNulty has acquired a shopping plaza subject to a mortgage with a balance of $661,780. It is a **full payout loan** that bears interest at 7.50 percent and requires a monthly payment of $8038.

To find the term to full amortization, begin by finding the annual constant. It is

$$\frac{\$8038 × 12}{\$661,780} = \frac{\$96,456.00}{\$661,780} = 0.145752$$
$$= 14.5752 \text{ percent}$$

Now enter Table 35 (b), page 5 (p. 436), and search in the 7.50 percent interest section for the constants closest to 14.5752 percent. At 9 years, 8 months, the constant is 14.574952 percent, and at 9 years, 7 months the constant is 14.661393 percent. The loan will be fully amortized in just under 9 years, 8 months. In practice, loans are not written for fractions of a month; most likely this loan will come due in 9 years, 8 months with the final payment being slightly lower than normal.

DISCOUNTED LOANS

Loan documents may specify an interest rate, or they may be **discounted,** meaning that one amount is shown on the face of the note, representing principal and interest, but a lesser amount, representing principal only, is all that is advanced to the borrower. The difference between the face amount and the lesser amount is the discount, which for most purposes is synonymous with interest. Table 41 has two parts. One provides interest for the actual number of days elapsed in a 365-day year. This is called "Actual/365" basis or "exact interest" or "exact time exact interest." This basis should be used in the United States, unless the parties have specifically agreed to use the other popular rate basis, "30/360," also called "ordinary interest" or "approximate time ordinary interest." By 30/360 is meant that each month is considered to have 30 days and the year to have 360 days. In 30/360 calculations, each day's interest will be 1/30 of a month's interest, a month's interest being 1/12 of a year's interest.

Table 41 is constructed with monthly compounding. That is, the lender's yield is calculated as a normal mortgage loan with monthly interest payments in arrears. For a loan of 2 months, the discount for 2 months will include interest on interest earned at the end of the first month. This yield is lower than that computed with bank discount. Under banker's discount formulas, the lender would receive interest on interest for 2 months.

Example 284. Discounted Value of Zero Interest Rate Note

Van Baarles will lend $100,000 to Kiley on a note with no interest rate stated, but for which they agree the correct rate would be 6.00 percent, based on market conditions. The note is to be payable in 6 months. The parties have agreed that 30/360 basis is to be used.

To find the actual cash to be loaned to Kiley, enter Table 41, page 6 (p. 491), the page for 6.00 percent interest, 30/360 basis. Read down the term column to 6 months and across on that line to the column headed 6.00 percent. Read there the answer, 97.05181 percent, the percentage discounted amount. Multiply the face amount by the percentage to get

$$\$100,000 \times 0.9705181 = \$97,051.81$$

the loan proceeds that will go to Kiley.

Note The use of 30/360 basis is generally accepted in the United States for real estate loans of at least 1 year. The reason is that 12/12 of a year's interest is no more nor less than the borrower agreed to, even though the payments might vary slightly from payments on an actual days basis. Even then, it is customary to prorate interest for the first and last months of the loan on an actual/365 basis. With a loan of less than one year, a noticeable difference would occur with 30/360 basis compared to actual/365, for example from February 1 to March 15. The lender's document should clearly state which basis is used, and the truth-in-lending disclosure to the borrower should take account of the basis being used.

Another basis is used by some lenders, called "actual/360," or "exact time ordinary interest," or "Banker's Rule," in which the lender charges 365 days' interest each 360 days. For example, Eurodollar bonds are priced this way. This method is not presented here, as it has become a source of much contention.

Example 285. Principal and Interest on a Discounted Loan

Hugh McMaster will close a real estate deal on July 1. He will give a note due 5 months later, that is, on November 30. The parties have agreed that 9.00 percent interest is a fair rate for the deal; their contract states that all amounts are to be based on the presumption of 30-day months in a year of 360 days.

To find the principal amount of the loan, enter Table 41, page 8 (p. 493), for 9.00 percent interest, 30/360 basis, and read down the term column to 5 months. Now read across to 9.00 percent and read there 96.33292, the percentage that is principal. Multiply the face amount by the principal percentage to get

$$\$100,000 \times 0.9633292 = \$96,332.92$$

the discounted amount or principal balance. Subtract that from $100,000 to get

$$\$100,000 - 96,332.92 = \$3667.08$$

the interest on the loan. So McMaster's note is equal to the principal of $96,332.92. That amount will be treated as part of the sale price (and therefore tax or recording fees should be paid on it), whereas the remaining $3667.08 will be reported by the seller as interest income and by the buyer as interest expense.

Note If a note is written for so many "days after date," the note comes due that number of days later, Saturdays, Sundays, and holidays included. If the due date is not a business day, the note is due the next business day, and interest continues to accrue until the loan is actually paid. Use the calendars in Table D to avoid having a note come due on a weekend.

If a note is written for a certain number of "months after date," the note comes due on the same date in the maturity month. If there is no such date in the maturity month, for example, the thirtieth for a note maturing in February, the note falls due on the last day of the maturity month.

Even though the contract stipulated 30/360 basis, that should be repeated in the note.

Example 286. Face Amount of Loan to Be Used on a Discounted Loan

Leah Cregstein has contracted to sell her warehouse. She is willing to accept $51,000 of the purchase price in the form of a purchase money note, due in one year, with a discount calculated to give her 11.00 percent interest. She needs to know the face amount of the note (in the preceding examples, the face amount was known).

To find the face amount, enter Table 41, page 10 (p. 495), the page for 11.00 percent interest. Read down the term column to 12 months and across to the column for 11.00 percent interest. The factor there is 89.62832 percent. *Divide* the discounted amount by this number to get

$$\$51,000 \div 0.8962832 = \$56,901.66$$

loan amount to be entered on the face of the note.

Example 287. Price of a Discounted Note after Original Loan Date and Amount to Prepay a Discounted Note

Fujikawa received a 6-month discounted note with a face amount of $100,000 in settlement of the purchase price of his house. The note was based on a discount rate of 8.00 percent per year, 30/360 basis.

The borrower wants to pay off the loan today after only 2 months, and Fujikawa is willing to accept the prepayment. To find the amount to pay off, treat the loan as if it were a 4-month note at 8.00 percent interest. Enter Table 41, page 8 (p. 493), the page for 8.00 percent, and read down the term column to 4 months. Read across on that line under the column 8.00 percent to find the factor 97.37719 percent. Multiply this by the face amount to get

$$\$100,000 \times 0.9737719 = \$97,377.19$$

the price of the note 4 months from maturity at 8.00 percent interest.

Note As a general principle, a lender need not accept prepayment, unless the note states it must do so.

Example 288. Price to Sell Note at Different Rate from Original

The price to sell a note is the same as the amount to pay it off, if interest rates are the same. The price to sell a note at a different rate can be found by recalculating the note. Katrinov holds a note in the face amount of $100,000, which matures in 6 months. He desires to sell the note today to his bank, whose current discount rate is 10.75 percent. They use 30/360 basis. The interest rate that was used in the original deal is not important, because the note buyer only needs to know that it will receive $100,000 in six months. Search Table 41, page 10 (p. 495), for the 10.75 percent interest factor at 6 months to find 94.78958 percent. Multiply the face amount by the factor to get

$$\$100,000 \times 0.9478958 = \$94,789.58$$

the value of the note today at 10.75 percent interest.

Example 289. Amount to Prepay a Discounted Note at Different Yield from Original

The original discount rate may be changed. Suppose that, to induce his borrower to prepay at the end of 2 months, that is, 4 months before maturity, Fujikawa is willing to accept a 6.00 percent discount rate rather than the 8.00 percent rate in the original deal.

Begin by finding the amount of value that was given for the loan at the time it was made. Do this by entering Table 41, page 8 (p. 493), the page for 8 percent. Read down the term of loan column to 6 months, and find under the column for 8.00 percent the original loan factor, 96.09170 percent. Now locate the factor for 6.00 percent for 2 months in Table 41, page 6 (p. 491). It is 99.00745 percent. Dividing the original loan factor by the 2-month factor gives

$$96.09170 \div 99.00745 = 97.05502 \text{ percent}$$

Multiply this answer by the $100,000 face amount to get

$$\$100,000 \times 0.9705502 = \$97,055.02$$

the amount to pay off the discounted note after 2 months to yield 6.00 percent to the lender instead of the original 8.00 percent.

Example 290.   Yield on a Discounted Note

Pils & Co. are estimating the value of the assets of a corporation they propose to buy. One asset is a purchase money note that the corporation received from the sale of its offices. The note matures in 29 days; its face amount is $1 million. The seller asks Pils to value the note at $994,000, or a price of 99.4000 percent of face.

To estimate the yield, enter Table 41, page 7 (p. 492), and read down to 29 days. Read across on that line, searching for 99.4000. Under the column for 7.50 percent, read 99.39959 which is the closest figure to 99.40000. The yield would be slightly greater than 7.50 percent per year.

Daily Interest on a Loan, 360- and 365-Day Year

Calculating interest on a loan for a short period is easy enough. But why bother when the figures are printed in Table 39, on either a 360-day or 365-day year? With a 365-day year, interest for 1 day is 1/365 of one year's interest, also known as "exact interest." This would be the normal basis for calculations, except when documents specify otherwise.

Before computers and tables as precise as these, the 360-day year was standard in the United States by which 1 day's interest is 1/360 of a year's interest. This is referred to as ordinary interest. It is commonly used in mortgage loan calculations, but the custom is to use a 365-day year for the first month of the loan and for the month of payoff.

In order to give a large number of decimal places in the answer, Table 39 gives interest on a loan of $100,000. Divide each answer by $100,000, as shown in the examples.

Example 291.   Daily Interest on a Loan—Actual/365 Basis and Interest Prorations for Closing

Grossinger wants to prorate interest on an actual/365 on a $53,865 loan for 11 days at 6.00 percent interest. Enter Table 39, page 5 (p. 470), the page for 6.00 percent. Read down number of days to 11 and find under 6.00 percent the figure $180.8219, the interest on $100,000 for 11 days. To get the interest for Grossinger's amount, divide the loan amount by $100,000 and multiply by the figure from the table, as follows:

$$\$53,865 \div \$100,000 \times \$180.8219$$

$$= 0.53865 \times \$180.8219$$

$$= \$97.40$$

the interest for 11 days at 6.00 percent, actual/365 basis, on $53,865.

Example 292.   Daily Interest on a Loan—30/360 Basis and Interest Prorations for Closing

Kat Robinson is preparing the closing statement for the sale of Getaway Apartments. The contract calls for all proration items, including interest, to be prorated on the basis of the number of days elapsed in months that are presumed to have 30 days each. Robinson wants the interest proration for 23 days for $2,625,000 at 11.25 percent interest.

To find the factor for 23 days, enter Table 39, page 3 (p. 468), the page for 11.25 percent interest, 30/360 basis. Read down the term column to 23 days and across to the column headed 11.25 percent. Read there the factor $718.7500, the interest for 23 days on $100,000. For the interest proration, divide the loan amount by $100,000 and multiply by the factor from the table to get

$$\$2,625,000 \div \$100,000 \times \$718.75 = 26.2500 \times 718.75$$

$$= \$18,867.19$$

the interest at 11.25 percent, 30/360 basis, on $2,625,000 for 23 days.

Example 293.   Amortizing a Loan with Variable Interest Rate

Bankers favor floating rate loans, even when making commercial mortgages. At the same time, bank examiners favor amortizing loans. How does one calculate the principal payments, when the interest rate, because it floats with prime or some other base rate, is not known? We take advantage of a property of the sinking fund, described by Hoskold in the last century, that a mortgage constant is equal to the effective interest rate on a loan plus the sinking fund payment to retire it.

Goodbank will lend only on a floating rate basis. Their loans are based on prime, which, let us say, is 8.00 percent at the moment. Himmin wants a 10-year loan with mortgage-type amortization.

To find the amount of the principal payments, begin by finding the monthly interest factor. It is equal to 1 plus 1/12 of the interest rate; thus, $1 + (0.08 \div 12)$ $= 1 + 0.00667 = 1.00667$, the monthly interest factor for the first month. Now enter Table 52, page 3 (p. 683), 8.00 percent, monthly payments. Read down the end of year column to 10, and across to the column headed 8.00 percent where the factor 6.559311 percent appears. Divide this by 12 and multiply this by the principal of the loan to get

$$\$100,000 \times 0.06559311 \div 12 = \$546.61$$

the payment to principal for the first month. For each succeeding month, multiply the first month's principal by the monthly interest factor, changing the interest factor when the floating rate changes

$$\text{Month 2: } \$546.61 \times 1.00667 = \$550.26$$

$$\text{Month 3: } 550.26 \times 1.00667 = 553.93$$

The principal from each preceding month is multiplied by this month's interest factor to get this month's principal. It is not necessary to start the calculation at the beginning of the loan. If a 30-year loan has been amortized for 7 years and the amortization is desired for the seventh year, start with the sinking fund factor for 23 years.

ACCOUNTING ADJUSTMENTS

Example 294. Accounting Adjustments to Price When Below-Market Debt Assumed

Table 10 applies to accounting for purchases when below-market debt is assumed. Fenian Capital Corporation has bought a warehouse for $600,000, with $500,000 of the purchase price represented by assumption of a 30-year loan on the property at 7.00 percent interest with 7 years remaining on the term. The land value is appraised at $150,000. Because the interest rate is well below the current market rate for such loans, namely 10.00 percent, the accountants state that Fenian will record the liability of the debt at a lower value than its face amount. The amount of this discount will equal the value by which the below-market debt exceeds the market value. The real estate asset will be carried with the same discount, lowering its value for depreciation purposes.

To find the value of the below-market debt, enter Table 10, page 7 (p. 207), for the section for a stated interest rate of 7.00 percent. Read down the column desired yield to 10.00 percent and across on that line to the column for 7 years and read the factor 85.46955 percent. This is the percentage of the loan that will be recorded as debt. Multiplying the factor by the face amount of the loan gives $427,348, the carrying value of the loan. The remaining 14.53045 percent, or $72,652, will be recorded as a discount from the total loan. On the asset side, the real estate will be reduced by the same amount, as follows:

Assets		Liabilities	
Real estate		Mortgage debt	$ 500,000
Land	$ 150,000		
Building	450,000		
less: discount for below-market debt	− 72,652	less: discount for below-market debt	− 72,652
Net building	377,348	Net indebtedness	$ 427,348
Total real estate	$ 527,348		

The real estate will be depreciated on the lower value, that is, $527,348 less $150,000 for land. The discount will be amortized over the remaining 7 years of the loan, as additional interest expense.

Example 295. Adjustments to Rentals for Financial Accounting Purposes

Under generally accepted accounting principles (GAAP) in the United States, free or reduced rentals conceded to a tenant are accounted for straight-line over the life of the lease: Harkis received a concession from the landlord of 6 months' free rent when he signed a lease for 60 months at a face rate of $1600 per month.

1. The rent expense on Harkis's books will show up as the straight-line value of 54/60 of the total rent each month, rather than as zero for the first 6 months and then $1600 for the following 54 months. To find the rent that Harkis will record as rent expense (and that the landlord will record as rent income), one may simply multiply the rent by the ratio of paying months to total months in the lease.

2. Technical Bulletin 85-3 of the Financial Accounting Standards Board, dated November 1985, permits only a straight-line case, which is equal to a zero interest rate. This is correct accounting but financially unrealistic. The tenant gets a bonus of interest rate savings in addition to the free rent. The landlord loses the amount of interest that would have been earned by the foregone rent. To find the economic rent, given that the landlord has an interest cost on the free rent it would otherwise have received, select an interest rate that best indicates the landlord's cost of funds. Let us say this is 8 percent. Enter Table 76, page 1 (p. 806), for 60-month lease term. On the line for 6 months free, read under no other concessions, 88.113 percent. Multiplying by the face rent gives

$$\$1600 \times 0.88113 = \$1410.13$$

the economic rent being paid.

Example 296.   Amortizing a Capital Lease

Barratry Bros. have acquired the assets of Snazzy's, a chain of retail stores. The flagship store in the chain is under lease to Snazzy's for 20 years. Because it is a **capital lease,** the leasehold interest will be set up on Snazzy's books as a fixed asset, a capital lease obligation. The corresponding liability will also be a capital lease obligation. A capital lease is treated as mortgage debt and written off according to the interest method. The value of both the fixed asset and the liability on the books will be the present value of the lease payments, discounted at the interest rate appropriate for a mortgage loan on this type of property. The "term" of the loan will be the lease period.

Each year as payments of rent are made, the amount shown in the remaining balance tables for that year as interest will be charged as interest expense. The portion shown as principal will be charged against the capital lease obligation liability, amortizing it over the lease term.

Example 297.   Amortization of Loan Premium or Discount

Amortization is the method of accounting for the premium or discount involved in a loan transaction. Presented here is the level yield method.

Amortization of Premium

The premium involved in a loan purchase is initially set up as an asset on the books of the lender. Part of the income taken in with each payment is used to lower the premium.

Assume a 30-year loan with 8.25 percent note rate was bought to yield 6.25 percent. To find the amount of the premium for year 1 of the loan, enter Table 10, page 12 (p. 212), the section for 8.25 percent interest. Read down the desired yield column to 6.25 percent and get the figure under the year 1 column, 101.92704 percent. Subtract the original principal, 100 percent, and get

101.92704 percent − 100.00000 percent

= 1.92704 percent

the percentage of the original loan to be charged against the premium account in the first year. In each succeeding year, subtract the prior year figure from the current year figure; in year 2, this will give

103.72263 percent − 101.92704 percent

= 1.79559 percent

amortization of the second year's premium.

Amortization of Discount

A loan discount is set up by the lender as a liability and then amortized. As the loan is paid, some of the discount is taken into income, raising the yield above that paid by the borrower. If an 8.25 percent loan is bought to yield 9.25 percent, find the first year's amortization of discount by entering Table 10, page 12 (p. 212), the page for an 8.25 percent loan. Read down the desired yield column to 9.25 percent and find next to it in the column for 1 year, 99.05171 percent. Subtract this from 100 percent to get

100.00000 percent − 99.05171 percent

= 0.94829 percent

the percentage of the original loan to be taken into income by a charge against the discount. For each later year, subtract the current year's figure from the preceding year's figure. So for year 2 of this example

99.05171 percent − 98.19406 percent

= 0.85765 percent

is the percentage of the original loan amount to be amortized as discount in year 2.

CONSUMER PRICE INDEX

The Consumer Price Index is the most commonly used measure of changes in purchasing power and inflation in the United States. Commonly called the CPI, the index is published by the Bureau of Labor Statistics, U.S. Department of Labor. The principal series is known as CPI-U, All Urban Consumers and covers about 80 percent of the U.S. population.

In addition to the index presented here, which is the United States City Average Index, there are regional indexes published for each major metropolitan area. The current indexes use as their reference base the period 1982 to 1984 = 100. Prior to this base, the index for many years used a base of 1967 = 100.

Example 298.   Calculating Rent Tied to the CPI

Rent on the Sormen lease is $14.00 per square foot and is scheduled to change on July 1, 1990. The lease provides that the new rent will be the result of multiplying the base rent by a fraction, the numerator of which will be the CPI for May 1990 and the denominator of which will be the CPI for May 1985.

Enter Table C, page 1 (p. 845), and read down the left column to 1985 and across on that line to the column for May. The factor there, 107.3, is the denominator for the fraction. In that column on the line for 1990 is the factor, 129.2, the numerator of the fraction. The new rent will be

$$\$14.00 \times \frac{129.2}{107.3} = \$14.00 \times 1.20410 = \$16.86$$

rental per square foot as of July 1, 1990.

Cross-Reference   For the value of rentals rising with the CPI, see Example 179. To find the value of rentals in constant dollars, see Example 178. Both are in Chapter 5.

Example 299.   Percent Change in CPI over 3-, 5-, or 10-Year Term

Portions of the CPI table, Table C, pages 1 and 2 (pp. 845–846) give the percentage change that has occurred between a given month and the same month 3, 5, or 10 years earlier, or between the average for the year and the third, fifth, or tenth year earlier. Each position in these charts gives the change in percent from the same time in the earlier period. The next example shows how to calculate the percentage difference for time differences other than 3, 5, or 10 years.

Example 300.   Calculating Percent Change in CPI

The CPI in January 1989, stood at 121.1. Nine years earlier, the January CPI was 77.8. Begin by subtracting the earlier index from the later one, to get the index difference, as follows:

$$121.1 - 77.8 = 43.3$$

the "index difference." Next, divide the index difference by the earlier index, to get

$$\frac{43.3}{77.8} = 0.557 = 55.7 \text{ percent}$$

the percent change in the index from January 1980 to January 1989.

Cross-Reference   The average rate of change in this period was 6.2 percent (55.7 ÷ 9) per year. To find the compounded annual rate of change, use Table 6 as explained in Example 194.

Conversion of U.S. Customary and International System (SI) Measures

Example 301.   Converting U.S. Customary to International System Measures

America Batista is analyzing the rent proposal for Place San Sebastian, where her U.S. headquarters will be located. The net rentable area is stated in the lease proposal to be 26,850 square feet. She wants the lease document to state this in SI units also.

To convert this to m², or square meters, enter Table E (p. 853). On the line for square feet, read across to m² and find 0.092903, the metric area of one square foot. Multiply the net rentable area by the conversion factor to get

$$26,850 \times 0.092903 = 2,494.44 \text{ m}^2$$

the SI equivalent of the net rentable area.

Note Although the tenant will undoubtedly use 2500 square meters as a useful approximation in working on the lease, the document itself should state the precise figure to record what the parties agreed to.

PREPAYMENTS

Borrowers tend to prepay loans when market interest rates fall below their borrowing rate. Prepayment in that situation reduces the lender's yield below its original expectations, because it can only reinvest the funds at a lower rate. Prepayments present the lender with the need to seek out new investments as well, a cost which is difficult to set out in a precise formula. Table 43 tells how large a **prepayment premium** is necessary to offset the loss of yield. The table assumes that at time of prepayment the lender can only reinvest in mortgages with a lower rate. The entries in Table 43 show what prepayment premium would equalize the yield on the replacement mortgage with that of the prepaid mortgage. The replacement mortgage is presumed to have the same original amortization schedule as the prepaid loan and a remaining term equal to the loan's remaining term.

Example 302. Prepayment Premium to Maintain Yield

Mykonos' mortgage loan bears interest at 12.00 percent on a 30-year schedule. Mykonos wants to prepay the loan, which has 8 years remaining on the original term. In the loan documents, the prepayment premium is specified as the amount which would maintain the lender's yield to maturity at 12.00 percent if reinvested at the current market rate for 30-year mortgages, which today is 9.50 percent per year.

To find the prepayment premium, enter Table 43, page 12 (p. 538), the page for 12.00 percent interest, 30-year schedule. Read down the left column to 8 years and across on that line to the column headed 9.50 percent. The answer there, 16.0934 percent, is the prepayment premium necessary to maintain the lender's yield at 12.00 percent in a 9.50 percent market for 8 years.

Note Loan documents often provide that replacement investments used to compare yields will not be the equivalent mortgage loans, but Treasuries or other high-quality bonds. This seems to produce a windfall for the lender, since such securities have lower rates than long-term mortgages. For this reason, courts sometimes refuse to apply the formula in the loan agreement. It may be wise to state in the documents that numerous internal costs attend the lender's making of a loan, whereas Treasury investments are (almost) expense-free. The yield difference is intended to compensate the lender's costs in making the mortgage being prepaid.

Example 303. Payment to Induce Prepayment

Table 43 may be used in reverse, to show what payment would compensate a borrower for giving up a below-market loan.

Kinsella Credit holds a $19,300 mortgage loan of the Bowman family, bearing interest at 8.00 percent, originally for 30 years with 7 years now remaining. The market interest rate is 10.50 percent, which, along with the proportionately higher cost to service small loan balances, causes Kinsella to want to induce them to pay it off.

To find the possible offer to the borrowers, enter Table 43, page 9 (p. 535), at 10.50 percent interest, 30-year schedule. Read down the year of prepayment to 23 years (30-year original loan less 7 years remaining). On that line, read under 8.00 percent the factor, 7.5588 percent, the percentage that Kinsella could afford to pay. Multiplying by the loan balance gives

$$\$19,300 \times 0.075588 = \$1458.85$$

the cash that Kinsella could offer to pay the Bowmans to induce them to prepay the loan, based only on opportunity cost of the low interest rate. If Kinsella's operating costs mean a loss on the servicing, they might add a further inducement to get rid of the loan.

Example 304. "Unused" Points at Time of Prepayment

If a lender has agreed to make a loan for a specified term and points are charged to increase its yield, the lender should be willing to credit the unused portion of the points if the loan is prepaid. Obviously a lender wants to keep the points, but, since lenders often require a prepayment premium calculated to compensate for the loss of yield, it seems fair to credit the unused points against the prepayment premium.

Gilquine Livery took out a loan on a 30-year schedule when rates were 12.00 percent. To reduce the coupon rate on the 7-year loan to 10.00 percent, they paid the lender 9.9 points. Five years have passed, and the loan is now **open for prepayment** at a premium of 3.0 percent of the loan balance. Gilquine wants the lender to give credit in the prepayment premium for the unused portion of the points.

To find the amount of such a credit, enter Table 10, page 27 (p. 227), the page for 12.00 percent. Read down the desired yield column to 10.00 percent. Read across on that line to the column headed 7 years and note the factor, 109.90091. Then read the factor under the column headed 5 years, 107.77062. Subtract the second factor from the first to get 109.90091 − 107.77062 = 2.13029 percent, the percentage of original loan which the lender does not need to maintain its 12.00 percent yield. In principle, this amount should be credited against the 3.0 percent prepayment premium provided for in the loan documents.

Note The lender is not obliged to give this credit, unless the loan documents or local law requires it. Such a credit must be negotiated before the loan is made, so it may be stated in the loan documents.

Interest Rebate by Rule of 78s

With add-on interest loans, the loan amount stated in the documents includes all the interest for the term of the loan. If the loan is prepaid, some interest will not have been earned by the lender, and the borrower is entitled to a rebate. Calculating the rebate has for years been done by the Rule of 78s, presented in Table 45. The entries are given as percentages of the original loan proceeds, that is, the amount of the loan before the interest is added on. The Rule of 78s considerably favors lenders, because it rebates less interest than if calculated on the actual balance outstanding. As a result, it is falling out of favor.

Example 305.   Interest Rebate by Rule of 78s

Selma Pathimin borrowed $5000 actual proceeds from DeSoto Finance. The loan was a 48-month loan at a rate of 4.50 percent per year add-on. Now after

36 payments have been made, she wishes to calculate the rebate she will receive if she prepays the loan.

Enter Table 45, page 1 (p. 543), the section for 48 months. On the line for 36 payments left, read across to the column headed 4.50 percent add-on interest rate. The factor there, 10.19388 percent, is the percentage of the original loan proceeds that will be rebated. Multiply the loan amount by the percentage to get

$$\$5000 \times 0.1019388 = \$509.69$$

the rebate from a 48-month loan at 4.50 percent add-on interest prepaid after 36 payments.

Example 306.   Sinking Fund to Pay Off a Nonprepayable Loan

Real estate loans which have no required amortization payment are called bullet loans. Freedom from amortization payments may be offset, however, by the lender's not permitting the loan to be prepaid. If rates on investments such as CDs or short-term bonds become better than the rate on the note, the borrower will find it profitable to establish a sinking fund with a trust company. Caricoordon Financial has 10 years remaining on a locked-in loan of $1 million at 9.00 percent. Double-AA rated bonds are currently paying over 10.00 percent, but the lender will not accept a prepayment. Caricoordon wants to build a sinking fund to retire the loan via amortization payments.

To find the payment to build such a retirement fund, enter Table 52, page 5 (p. 685), the page for 10.00 percent interest. Read down to year 10 and across to the column headed 10.00 percent monthly payments and note the factor there, 5.858088 percent. Divide the factor by 12 and multiply by the amount of the loan balance to get

$$0.05858088 \div 12 \times \$1,000,000 = \$4881.74$$

per month, the amount needed to amortize the loan using a sinking fund at 10.00 percent per year.

Conversion of Months' Interest Prepayment Premium to Percent Premium and Vice Versa

Just as early withdrawals from savings certificates are penalized a certain number of days' or months' interest, mortgage prepayments used to be penalized by a certain number of months' interest. This prepayment premium is less common today, but many existing documents still carry months' interest premiums. In

Table 44, they are converted to today's standard, which is a percentage of the outstanding balance being prepaid.

Example 307. Conversion of Months' Interest Premium to Percentage Premium

The Sales Closers have two mortgage quotations for their client, both at 10.50 percent interest and 15-year schedule. The prepayment premiums are different, however, in that the first quotation requires a prepayment premium of 4.00 percent of any amount prepaid, while the second calls for a premium of 6 months' interest on any prepayment.

To compare these quotations, enter Table 44 (p. 542), the section for 10.50 percent interest. Read down the percentage premium column to 4.00 percent. Across on that line under the 10.50 percent column is the factor, 4.57 months. A 4.00 percent prepayment premium equates to only a 4.57 month premium, making the percentage premium noticeably better. In fact in the 10.50 percent column a little below the 4.57 figure, the 6 months' interest figure is on the line for, and equates to, a 5.25 percent prepayment premium.

Example 308. Future Worth of 1 and Interest Accrued on a Security Deposit

Elementer's lease required a security deposit of $10,000. The lease provides that, if there is no default, Elementer will receive the security deposit back with 6.00 percent interest based on monthly compounding. Now after 60 months, the lease has ended with no default.

To find the amount of the deposit to be returned to Elementer, enter Table 46, page 4 (p. 548), the page for 6.25 percent interest. Read down the time column to 60 months and across on that line to the column in the monthly section headed future value. Read there the factor 1.3657299, the future value of 1. Multiply the original deposit by the factor to get

$$\$10,000.00 \times 1.3657299 = \$13,657.30$$

the amount of the deposit to be returned. (Elementer will report as interest income the $3657.30 difference between the deposit and the amount returned.)

Example 309. Total Interest Accrued on an Account

At its loan closing 12 years ago, Hieratic Properties deposited $16,000 with its lender in lieu of monthly real estate tax deposits. The agreement calls for the lender to return the deposit with interest at 9.00 percent interest, compounded monthly. The loan is about to be repaid, and Hieratic wishes to know the balance on the account and the interest earned.

Enter Table 46 at the section for 9.00 percent interest. Read down to 144 months and across to the columns for future value, monthly, and read the factor 2.9328368. Multiply the factor by the original deposit

$$\$16,000 \times 2.9328368 = \$46,925.39$$

the total balance on deposit. Now subtract 1.0000, representing the original deposit, from the factor and multiply again to get

$$\$16,000 \times 1.9328 = \$30,925.39$$

the interest that will have been earned on the account over the 12 years, at 9.00 percent interest compounded monthly.

Example 310. Interest on Delinquent Rent

Abbaney Management have noted that Torn's rent of $3100 is 26 days delinquent. Torn's lease calls for 8.00 percent interest on delinquent rent.

To find the interest on the delinquency, enter Table 39, page 6 (p. 471), the page for 8.00 percent interest, 365-day year. Read down the number-of-days column to 26 and take the factor in the 8.00 percent column, 569.8630. Multiply the amount of the late rent by the factor and divide by $100,000 to get

$$\$3100 \times 569.8630 \div \$100,000 = \$17.67$$

the interest on the delinquency.

Example 311. Real Estate Tax Deposit to Be Adjusted

Janilgan Business Park has just been completed, and the **permanent financing** is being closed. The lender's commitment calls for a monthly deposit to a tax reserve of 1/12 of the estimated annual real estate taxes. Ian Janilgan argues that, since the property will be taxed as vacant land for the next 2 years, only 1/12 of the current taxes, $1200 per month, should be deposited. The lender insists, however, that the full amount of the taxes, estimated in the appraisal to be $6100 per month, must be reserved. As a compromise, the lender is willing to allow any excess of deposits that is not needed in the first 2 years to be credited against the required deposits in the 3 years following (that is, years 3, 4, and 5). The lender will allow 6.00 percent interest on the deposits.

To find the monthly credit that Janilgan feels will be available, enter Table 61, page 1 (p. 726), the section for 6.00 percent interest and 2 years of deposit. Read across on the line for 3 years of withdrawal to the 6.00 percent column. The factor there, 77.3689 percent, is the percentage of the $4900 "excess" deposit ($6100 less $1200). Multiply the dollar amount of the excess payment by the percentage to get

$$\$4900 \times 0.773689 = \$3791.08$$

the monthly credit that Janilgan can expect in the third, fourth, and fifth years, if his assumption is correct about the taxes in the first 2 years.

DEPRECIATION AND COST RECOVERY OF ASSETS

Depreciation is an accounting charge against income to allow for the supposed decay of a property through age, wear, tear, and obsolescence. In the 1980s, the phrase "cost recovery system," was coined by the Internal Revenue Service to denote that depreciation, now to be called "cost recovery," would be fixed by tables rather than by formula.

Table 83 gives MACRS, Modified Accelerated Cost Recovery System, for a property life of 27½ years, which is used for rental housing after 1986 and for 31½ years, used for all other rental real estate after 1986. The alternative method, which in essence is 40-year straight-line depreciation, is also included. This table employs the mid-month convention, by which it is assumed that property is placed in service in the middle of its first operating month.

Since the eight tax laws of the 1980s have taken much of the excitement out of depreciation in the United States, use of the tables is straightforward. The annual percentage of depreciation or cost recovery is given in the upper portion of the table and the total recovery accumulated to date is given in the lower portion.

Example 312. Cost Recovery for a Given Year

Baarles Slaney acquired a 10-year-old office building. The closing took place during the seventh month of Slaney's fiscal year. An appraiser has estimated that 16 percent of the $1 million price of the property should be allocated to land, 84 percent to the building. There is no need to allocate anything to salvage value.

To determine the cost recovery deduction from U.S. income for the first year, enter Table 82, page 2 (p. 833), the page for 31½ years (since this is an office building). Read across under the section for month when property placed in service to 7 and read down the column under it. The first year's depreciation is 1.455 percent of the depreciable amount. Since 84 percent of the purchase price is the depreciable portion, multiply as follows:

$$0.84 \times \$1,000,000 \times 0.01455 = \$12,222$$

the cost recovery deductible against income for the first year. Calculate depreciation for the second year in the same way, but use the figure in column 7 for year 2 (it is 3.175 percent, and the recovery will be $26,670).

Baarles Slaney could have elected to use a 40-year life for the property. In that case, the factors would have been taken from the 40-year page of the table—Table 82, page 3 (p. 834). The first-year factor would be (for property placed in service in the seventh month) 1.146 percent, and the depreciation would be $9626.40.

Cross-Reference Example 249 in Chapter 6 discusses economic depreciation, distinguishing it from accounting and tax depreciation.

Example 313. Amortization of Leasing Commissions or Tenant Alterations

Ari Plochman has rented an office in the Place de Style and agrees to put in $26.00 per square foot of tenant improvements but wants the tenant to pay the unamortized portion of the improvements, if the tenant does not renew its lease at the end of 5 years. Current real estate loan rates are 10.50 percent.

Treat this as a 10.50 percent loan on a 10-year amortization schedule that will be paid off after 5 years. Enter Table 42 (b), page 21 (p. 768), the page for

10.50 percent loans, 10-year amortization schedule. In the column for remaining balance year-end on line 5 is the factor 62.778274 percent. If the tenant elects not to renew the lease, its rental for the last month of the lease shall be increased by $16.32 ($26.00 per square foot × 62.778274 percent) for each square foot in the lease.

Note For accounting purposes, the tenant improvements are written off straight-line as part of the building. This example gives the **economic** results of the transaction; the accounting results according to GAAP will appear substantially different from those shown here.

TRANSACTIONS BETWEEN PARTNERS

Joint venture and partnership agreements contain numerous deal points which are woven into a fabric that is virtually unique for every transaction. The examples that follow show how to use the tables to isolate specific deal points and solve them one by one. Doing so quantifies the give and take needed to balance the differing interests of the parties.

Example 314. When Balloon of Given Amount Will Occur

Haselow Finance will provide joint venture funding to Kienan Flyn's apartment property. The deal will be structured as an 8.75 percent participating mortgage with a 25-year amortization schedule. When the loan balance reaches 80 percent of the original amount, the deal will be converted to a simple partnership.

To find when the partnership conversion will occur, enter Table 67, page 3 (p. 768), the page for 8.75 percent. Read down the left column to 25 years' amortization. Read across on that line to the column headed 80 percent to find 10Y 10m, that is, 10 years and 10 months. The loan balance will pass through 80 percent at 10 years and 10 months from the start of the loan.

Example 315. Interest Reserve During Cash Flow Deficit Period

Cashon Life Company will enter a joint venture for Prospero Plaza. The 10-year income projections show that net operating income will be inadequate to cover the 10.0 percent preferred return that is a key element of the deal to Cashon Life. The shortfall will be 3.00 percent in the first year, declining to zero over the 4 years following. They wish to set up a budget item as a reserve for this operating deficit.

To find the amount to be reserved, consider that the average shortfall is about 1.50 percent. To give a margin for error, let us use 1.75 percent. Now enter Table 24, page 3 (p. 284), the page for market interest rate of 10.00 percent. In the section for buy-down credit of 10.00 percent, read down the desired buy-down column to 8.25 percent (10.00 − 1.75) and across on that line to the column headed 5 years. Read there the factor 5.945 percent, the percentage of the budget that should be set up as a reserve.

Example 316. Simultaneous Wraparound and Wraparound of Partner's Interest

Cargonom Corp. will buy the Cieleen factory, giving a down payment and a purchase money mortgage for $2.8 million and will convert the factory to multitenant use. The loan Cieleen Corporation will take back is at 8.50 percent interest for 10 years on a 30-year schedule, with the corporate guarantee of Cargonom. Cargonom in turn will bring in private investors. To compensate itself for its developer work and the value of its guarantee, Cargonom will make a simultaneous wraparound loan of $3.5 million at 10.00 percent for 10 years.

To find the yield on Cargonom's presumed $700,000 investment, enter Table 28, page 5 (p. 343), the page for 10.00 percent interest and 20 percent new money and 80 percent old money ($700,000 ÷ $3,500,000). In the 30-year new term section, read across on the line for 10 years' remaining term of old loan to the column headed 8.50 percent, and read the answer, 11.033 percent, the yield on the presumed $700,000 of new money in the wraparound.

Note Structured this way, the deal probably creates immediate taxable income to Cargonom. In a joint venture agreement, Cargonom would seek to create a preference return without receiving a mortgage loan interest. An arrangement that answers the tax difficulty requires sophisticated tax structuring, but the financial calculations would follow the example, even if the vehicle is not in true wraparound form.

Example 317. Conversion of Debt to Partner Equity

Affluent Life is analyzing a joint venture with developer Marlboro. Under the proposal, Affluent would hold a 9.50 percent mortgage on a 30-year schedule for the first 3 years of the venture, when it will convert the mortgage into equity. Based on its projections, Affluent would receive a 6.00 percent return on investment in the 5 years after conversion. Affluent believes it should receive credit for the loss of yield it would suffer.

To calculate the loss of yield, treat this proposal as an 8-year loan at 9.50 percent which will be repaid after 3 years when rates will be 6.00 percent. Enter Table 43 at the place for 9.50 percent interest rate and 30-year schedule. Read down the left column to 5 years and across on that line to the column for 6.00 percent market rate at time of prepayment. The answer there, 26.2557 percent, is the percentage of the loan to compensate the lender for loss of yield.

Example 318. Time When Partner's Capital Account Is Achieved

Djakarta Realty Company (DRC) will be the financial partner in the Struitt Lane Office Block. The deal with its partners is that the investment of DRC will be considered increased at 11.00 percent per year until its so-called capital account is double DRC's cash investment. (Thereafter, DRC will receive 8.00 percent preferred return on its capital account, with the remainder divided 50/50.)

Enter Table 68 in the section for 100 percent increase. The capital account will reach 200 percent of its original value, or a 100 percent increase, at the time indicated on the 11.00 percent interest line. The entry there, 6Y 4m indicates that the 100 percent increase will have been achieved after 6 years and 4 months from the original investment.

Example 319. Release Fees to Achieve a Given Yield

Paffrice is the general partner of Palladion Venture. The partners have made a mortgage loan to the partnership at 9.00 percent interest, 30-year schedule. Paffrice has the right to buy out the partners and pay off the loan, but, in such a case, she must make the yield during the time the loan was outstanding equal to 12.00 percent. Now after 5 years, Paffrice is prepared to do this.

To find the necessary points, enter Table 10, page 15 (p. 215), the page for 9.00 percent interest and 30-year amortization. Read down the left column to the yield of 12.00 percent and across on that line to the column headed 5 years. Read there the factor 88.94902 percent. Subtract this from 100 percent to get 11.05098, the number of points needed to raise the yield from 9.00 percent to 12.00 percent for a 5-year term.

Now enter Table 46, page 27 (p. 571), monthly payments, on the page for 12.00 percent. Read down the time column to 60 months and read under the future value the factor 1.8166967. Multiply this by the number of points to get

$$11.050980 \times 1.8166967 = 20.076279$$

the number of points to raise the yield to 12.00 percent from 9.00 percent when the points are paid 5 years after the start of the loan.

Note This case shows how to bring the yield up to a higher level from the start of the loan to date of prepayment. To compensate for a difference in yield from the time a loan is prepaid to the contract maturity, see Example 302 earlier in this chapter.

Example 320. Deposit Needed to Fund a Series of Purchase Payments

Aronson Cale is acquiring the Kingston Landworth property management portfolio. The purchase price includes a fixed payment portion, consisting of monthly payments of $3100 to both principal and interest, for 120 months. The draw period begins on the first anniversary of the closing, so the first payment will be made 12 months from the closing date. Cale will sign a note at 7.00 percent for this portion. There will also be an "earn-out," consisting of a participation in 25 percent of the profits for 120 months.

To find the required note amount for the fixed rate portion, enter Table 58, page 1 (p. 716), the section for draw delay of 12 months. Read down to 120 payments and across to 7.00 percent interest, and find the factor 80.78855. Multiply the monthly payment by the factor to get

$$\$3100 \times 80.78855 = \$250,444.51$$

the face amount of the note that will be retired by 120 monthly payments of $3100 at 7.00 percent interest.

Sequential Payments

Tables 62, 63, and 64 give the solutions to balance the payments when one party receives (or pays) a number of payments first, then another party receives (or pays) for a succeeding period of time.

Interest is based on monthly payments in arrears. Sequencing payments as shown here is not common. Substantial potential for fluctuation of interest rates means the actual values needed to balance the interests of the parties could differ from those calculated by use of the tables. For this reason, sequential payment programs are most useful for those acting at less than arm's-length, such as relatives or business associates.

Succeeding Payment to Match Prior Payments

In these plans, one party receives (or pays) a series of payments, and a second party receives (or pays) *the same number* of payments succeeding the first series. The payments in the succeeding series are larger, to compensate for the fact that they come later.

Example 321.   Succeeding Payment to Match Prior Payments and Balancing Partnership Distributions

Mondumain and Tippson are partners in Glinnsdale Park Business Center. Their first office building is coming on-line and will produce a dependable cash flow of $13,000 per month. Mondumain is under considerable cash pressure. It is agreed that, during the first 24 months, he will take $8000 per month from partnership cash flow first, and the remainder will be divided 50/50. To balance out their interests, Tippson will then draw some amount first during the second 24 months, and the balance will be split 50/50. The partners agree that interest on 2-year deposits today is 9.00 percent and that they will use this for the calculation.

To find the amount Tippson will take out during the second 24 months, enter Table 62 (p. 728), the line for 24 payments. Under the column headed 9.00 percent interest, read the factor 119.6414 percent, the percentage of the prior series that the succeeding

series must be. Multiply the dollar amount of the prior series payment by the percentage to get

$$\$8000 \times 1.196414 = \$9571.31$$

the amount of the 24 succeeding payments which will match the value of twenty-four prior payments of $8000 per month, when interest rates are 9.00 percent.

Note   It is not necessary to consider the 50/50 portion of the income split here. As long as the payment agreed to by the partners is actually earned by the partnership, their interests will be in balance. If a payment is not made for lack of earnings, the partners should have agreed in advance how the shortfall will be made up. They might agree it will be taken from the next month's income or to pay it later. Or they might decide to adjust the corresponding payment to the other partner; i.e., if the fifteenth payment to the first partner was 23 percent short, the fifteenth payment to the second partner would be shorted by 23 percent.

Example 322.   Prior Payment to Match Succeeding Payments

The Kilgallen heirs have agreed that one of them will draw an amount each year from the family partnership for managing its affairs. In the third year, the draw amount should be $4000 per month. Interest rates currently are 7.50 percent.

This case will be solved in reverse order, starting from the third year. To find the amount of the draws in the second and first years, enter Table 62 (p. 728), the line for 12 months and take the factor under 7.50 percent interest. It is 107.7633 percent. Divide $4000, the payment in the third year, by this to get

$$\$4000 \div 1.077633 = \$3711.73$$

the draw in the second year. From the line for 24 months, take the factor under 7.50 percent, 116.1292 percent, and again divide $4000 by it to get

$$\$4000 \div 1.161292 = \$3444.44$$

the draw in the first 12 months.

Example 323.   Alternating Partitions between Two Parties

Kronstad and Curcillo have established a partnership under which the partners will alternate taking a draw during the first 4 years. The draws will be taken from increases in partnership capital and will be non-cumulative. That is, if the increase in partnership capital is not sufficient to cover the draw, the shortfall will simply be missed; it will not be made up later.

It was decided by coin-toss that, in the first year, Kronstad would draw $3000 per month first, then Curcillo will draw. In the second year, it will be Curcillo's turn to draw first, Kronstad second. In the third and fourth years, they will again alternate positions. They will use 12.00 percent as their cost of capital.

To find the amount of the draws after the first year, enter Table 62 (p. 728). Take the factors under the 12.00 percent interest column for 12, 24, and 36 months. They are 112.6825 percent, 126.9735 percent, and 143.0769 percent. The first year's draws will be $3000 per month; the next year's draws will be $3000 times 1.126825; the third year's draws will be $3000 times 1.269735, and the fourth year's draws will be $3000 times 1.430769.

Example 324. Payments That May Be Drawn from a Deposit

Villogle is separating from his partner, who will retain the partnership's real estate. Villogle's share of the partnership's real estate value is $200,000. This amount will be deposited to a bank account and semi-annual checks paid to Villogle for 8 years.

To find the amount of each check, enter Table 37, page 2 (p. 455), the page for 7.75 percent interest. Read down the left column to 8 years and across on that line to the 7.75 percent semiannual column. The factor there, 17.00610, is the annual total as a percentage of the original value. Multiply Villogle's share by the percentage and divide by two to get

$200,000 × 17.00610 ÷ 2 (payments per year)

= $17,006.10

the amount of each semiannual payment to be made to Villogle. The example assumes the bank's fee for issuing the checks has been netted from the interest.

Chapter 8

LOAN AND PROPERTY WORKOUTS

This chapter draws on the examples of all previous chapters to focus on the special problems presented by distressed property or **real estate owned** (REO). What are problems to lenders or joint venturers disposing of distressed real estate are also opportunities for buyers who may be able to negotiate superior terms in difficult times. The needs of both are discussed in the examples. In many instances, one or more examples in earlier chapters will give additional insight on how to proceed. These can most often be identified in the Master Table Finder by the similarity of subject.

Interest Accrual, Reserves

Example 325. Interest Reserve During Cash Flow Deficit Period

Drummers Life Company has taken title to Canvas & Cornflowers Plaza and is reselling it with a **cash flow mortgage** that pays the lesser of 100 percent of the net operating income (NOI) or 10.00 percent per year. Under the cash flow mortgage, its projections show NOI will fall short of the 10.00 percent rate to the extent of 3.00 percent in the first year. The shortfall will continue but decline to zero over the four years following. Drummers is required to establish a reserve for this interest deficit.

To find the amount to be reserved, consider that the average shortfall is 1.50 percent per year. Now enter Table 24, page 3 (p. 284), the page for market interest rate of 10.00 percent and the section for buy-down credit of zero percent. Read down the desired buy-down column to 8.50 percent and across on that line to the column headed 5 years. Read there the factor, 6.519 percent, the percentage of the loan to be set up as a reserve.

Example 326. Interest Earned on Cash Flow Mortgage

Calamity Cross Mall was foreclosed by the construction lender, which is now ready to turn it over to a leasing and management team. CrossCal Rectifiers Ltd. will buy the Mall from the lender with $100,000 cash equity and a $2,800,000 **cash flow mortgage.** Under this loan, the lender will receive the lesser of 100 percent of net operating income (NOI) or 8.50 percent interest. CrossCal estimates that the leasing program will require 36 months before the NOI is sufficient to pay 8.50 percent interest, and during this period occupancy and income will be about 40 percent of potential. The lender needs to estimate its interest earnings in this period, and what they would have earned had the full 8.50 percent been paid.

Begin by estimating the annual interest earnings projected to be paid, which is

$$\$2,800,000 \times 0.085 \times 3 \text{ years} \times 0.40 = \$285,600$$

the amount that CrossCal estimates will actually be paid. Now enter Table 17 at the section for 36 months and 8.50 percent interest. Read across on the line for 100 percent average balance (in this case, meaning 100 percent of what the full interest would be) to the column headed 8.50 percent interest, and read 28.93 percent. Multiply the loan amount by the factor to get

$$\$2,800,000 \times 0.2893 = \$810,040$$

the interest earnings that the lender would have had if the full 8.50 percent interest had accrued throughout the 36-month period.

Example 327.   Interest Accrued on Loan Workout

Paul Blanquard Financiers S.A. holds a loan on The Monolith, a mixed-use project. The loan documents call for interest at 10.50 percent per year. But poor occupancy in the hotel and office portions prevents the owner from paying the full amount of the interest. Projections show the property could dependably pay only about 7.50 percent, so the borrower proposes to pay 7.50 percent currently and to accrue the difference for three years. After 3 years, both parties believe that market conditions will have improved sufficiently to permit resumption of normal payments. Blanquard wants to know what the accrual might be after 3 years, before he agrees to the plan.

To find the interest accrual, enter Table 14, page 1 (p. 237), the page for a pay rate of 7.50 percent, the rate the borrower can afford to make currently. Read down to 3 years and across to the 10.50 percent column. The answer there, 10.5252 percent, is the percentage of the current loan balance that will have accrued in the 3-year period. Paul Blanquard Financiers S.A. will now negotiate how this 10.5 percent accrual might be paid, for example, from increased revenue, from sale of the property, or from additional equity investment by the owners.

Example 328.   Mortgage Payment, Interest Rate Changing during Loan

---

Fredonia Design Park was foreclosed by a bank that is now preparing to list it for sale. To improve sale

prospects, their broker recommends that the bank offer $6.4 million purchase money financing on a rising rate mortgage. To fit the expected income pattern of the property, they recommend a 5-year loan on a 30-year schedule. Interest in the first year would be 5.50 percent, rising 1/4 percent in the second year to 5.75 percent, and another 1/4 percent to 6.00 percent during the third, fourth, and fifth years.

To find the payments, enter Table 22, page 1 (p. 273). In the section for rate rises of 1/4 percent per year, read across on the line for 5.50 percent interest rate and take the payment figures from the first three columns. They are $567.79, $583.22, and $598.47 per month per $100,000 of loan. Divide the loan amount by $100,000 and multiply by each of these factors to get

$$\frac{\$6,400,000}{\$100,000} \times 567.79 = \$36,338.56 \text{ per month in year 1}$$

$$\frac{\$6,400,000}{100,000} \times 583.22 = \$37,326.08 \text{ per month in year 2}$$

$$\frac{\$6,400,000}{100,000} \times 598.47 = \$38,302.08 \text{ per month}$$

in years 3, 4, and 5. If the bank made its presentations using constants, the payments from the table would have been multiplied by 12 and divided by 1000, giving the annual mortgage constant in percent.

Example 329.   Lower Interest Rate to Gain Higher Sale Price on Foreclosed Apartments

---

Fairstyle Bancorp proposes to sell an apartment complex with a $2 million loan for 10 years on a 30-year schedule. The property is believed to be priced right, but the market rate of 10.25 percent interest has been too high to attract an offer. A developer will make an offer, if the bank will take back a mortgage in the 9.50 percent range. The bank believes that, since there has been little price resistance, they may be able to add the below-market rate premium to the sales price.

To find the increase in purchase price necessary to justify this interest rate, enter Table 10, page 17 (p. 217), the page for 9.50 percent. Read down the left column to 10.25 percent desired yield. Read across on that line to the column headed 10 years and find the factor 95.47434 percent, the percentage of the starting loan amount needed to bring the rate from 9.50 percent to 10.25 percent. Subtract this from 100 percent to get 4.52566 percent. Multiply this by the $2 million loan amount to get

$$\$2,000,000 \times 0.0452566 = \$90,513$$

the increase in purchase price that would offset the below-market rate the bank is accepting.

Mortgage or Rent Forbearance Plans, Remarketing

Example 330.   Using Master Lease to Improve Price of REO

Bank Monnaie acquired Summertime, an Office Place, through foreclosure. In the months before and during litigation, the property was substantially leased on 3- to 5-year leases at rent levels that were drastically reduced by comparison with the original pro forma.

Bank Monnaie workout personnel feel that, although rents will never return to the level of the original pro forma, they should at least double in the coming 3 years. Unfortunately today's depressed rent levels—one-half Bank Monnaie's expectation—will not induce any purchase offer at a price the bank can live with. The bank is therefore considering selling the property with a master lease from the bank as master tenant for 93 percent of the property at what the bank views as the proper market rent. The actual tenants, the occupancy tenants, would continue to pay rent according to their leases, and, it is hoped, renew at higher rents when the leases expire. Today's initial investment yield demanded by buyers is 10.00 percent per year.

To find the potential price improvement for the bank, enter Table 73, page 3 (p. 294), the page for 10.00 percent interest and a ratio of target rent to old rent of 2.00 times. On the line for 3 years, read across in the discounted section the pay-to-tenant factor, 2.58260 times. This is the amount that will be paid over time to the buyer as master lease rent over what the occupancy tenants will be paying. Read under the columns for additional value gain, the factor 7.41740. This is the increase in purchase price that could be obtained, as a multiple of current rent, from a master lease at 2.00 times the current depressed annual rent. The bank should actually do somewhat better, since the bank's cost of funds is likely to be far less than real estate yields and since the bank would pay out the master lease cash over time.

Example 331.   Portion of Price of Real Estate Owned Attributable to Below-Market Financing

The auditors of The Credit House are reviewing a sale the company made, where, to attract a buyer. The Credit House took back a purchase money mortgage at a lower interest rate. The sale consisted of $1 million cash down payment and a $2 million loan at 6.00 percent interest for 5 years. At the time of the sale, mortgage interest rates were generally 8.50 percent. In effect the sale price consisted of a price for the real estate and a payment for the use of the cheap money. The auditors will now allocate the price between value of real estate and value of the loan.

Enter Table 10, page 13 (p. 213), the section for a stated interest rate of 8.50 percent. Read down the left column to 6.00 percent and across on that line to the column headed 5 years. The factor there, 110.56631 percent, is the percentage that should have been paid for the financing. Since only 100 percent was paid, dividing the loan by the factor will give

$$\frac{\$2,000,000}{1.1056631} = \$1,808,869 \text{ actual loan amount}$$

$$\frac{+1,000,000}{\$2,808,869} \text{ down payment}$$
$$\$2,808,869 \text{ actual real estate sale}$$

The difference between the actual real estate sale and the contract price is the premium paid for the below-market financing.

Example 332.   Whether Financing Takes Sale Value below First Refusal Threshhold

Swimbad Bank has taken back the Gorjus Office Plaza, developed by a party unrelated to Gorjus Corporation. Gorjus Corporation has a lease for 45 percent of the office space in the property and a right of first refusal on any sale. Gorjus has refused an offer at $21 million, so Swimbad is free to sell the property in the next year at any price above $21 million. Any price below $21 million must be resubmitted to Gorjus, who will have 90 days to match it. Nguyen Restructors has offered $23 million, provided that Swimbad take back a $17 million loan for 10 years on a 30-year schedule at 7.50 percent interest. The current market rate is 10.25 percent per year.

Swimbad would like to accept this offer without resubmitting it to Gorjus Corporation. The bank's legal department will feel better about not resubmitting if the economic value of the Nguyen package is greater than the $21 million threshhold established by Gorjus' earlier refusal.

To evaluate the package, enter Table 10, page 20 (p. 220), the page for 10.25 percent interest. Read down the desired yield column to 7.50 percent and across on that line to 10 years. The factor there is 118.71296 percent. Divide the amount of the financing by the factor to get

$$\frac{\$17,000,000}{1.1871296} = \$14,320,256 \text{ real loan value}$$

$$+\ 6,000,000 \text{ down payment}$$

$$\$20,320,256$$

This is the total value. Since the value of the sale, giving effect to market interest rates, is below $21 million, Swimbad's attorneys prefer that the offer be negotiated upward or else resubmitted to Gorjus to give it a further opportunity to exercise its refusal.

Example 333. Loan Increases on Distressed Sale from Added Rental Income

Sara Peabody will take over Roscoe Harbor Marina and rehabilitate it. Her rehab lender will advance the primary rehab moneys without regard to leasing. The economic rent needed to cover this loan is $9.00 per square foot per year net. Peabody will negotiate the individual tenant leases and the associated buildout of tenant improvements. For leases at rents above the $9.00 proforma, the lender will advance additional funds, using debt service coverage of 1.25 times. The loan is at 10.75 percent, 20-year schedule.

To find the additional loan proceeds formula, enter Table 11, page 3 (p. 232), the page with 10.75 percent interest. Read down to 10.75 percent and the line for 20-year amortization schedule. Read across on that line to the column headed 1.25 and find $6.57, the lendable amount. Peabody will request a draw from the lender of $6.57 for each $1 per square foot per year of net rental income above the $9.00 proforma that she obtains from approved tenants.

Example 334. Whether Foreclosing Lender Should Forfeit a Commitment Deposit

Stiegens Mortgage Bankers has provided construction financing for the Trail Riders Hotel, against a take-out commitment from The Creamery Council Trust for a 7-year loan on a 30-year schedule, with an interest rate of 11.75 percent. Stiegens has taken over the hotel from the developer and is now the assignee of the commitment. They have the right to cancel the commitment but in that event would forfeit the 4-point standby fee that the developer had posted. If the loan is delivered to The Council, however, the fee would be refunded. Under their mortgage banking lines of credit with Colossus Credit Company, Stiegens can obtain a seven-year loan at 9.25 percent. It would cost a 1-point fee to deliver the loan to Colossus.

To see if it is worthwhile to take the Colossus deal, enter Table 24, page 6 (p. 287), the page for 11.75 percent loans and the section for buy-down credit of 11.75 percent. Read down the column for desired buy-down to 9.25 percent and across on that line to the column in the 11.75 percent section headed 7 years. The factor there, 10.659 percent, is the value that could be paid to obtain the lower-rate loan. Stiegens can obtain it for only 5 points (forfeiture of the 4-point deposit plus the 1-point fee paid to the new lender), showing it to be economic to drop the commitment from The Creamery Council Trust.

Note Construction lender, permanent lender, and borrower often enter into a **tri-party or buy-sell agreement,** requiring the permanent lender to buy the loan from the construction lender and prohibiting the construction lender from delivering the loan to any other lender. This example assumes that Swimbad is free to deliver to The Creamery Council or not, as it sees fit.

Example 335. Amount to Complete a Loss Reserve on Repossessed Building

Salvo Buildcorp has repossessed Budget Town Bargain Box on which it held a second mortgage loan. The bank that holds the first mortgage wants Salvo to establish a $1 million reserve for renovation costs, beginning with an immediate deposit of $250,000. Salvo proposes to establish an escrow account at the bank which would earn 8.50 percent interest. Salvo will add monthly to the reserve out of rentals, so as to have $1 million total at the end of 3 years.

To find the deposits needed to complete the reserve, enter Table 53, page 3 (p. 690), the page and section for 8.50 percent interest and starting from partial fund of 25 percent. On the line for 3 years, read across to the 8.50 percent column and find the factor 1.65923 percent per month. Multiply this by the desired total fund to get

$$\$1,000,000 \times 0.0165923 = \$16,592$$

per month, the monthly reserve deposit which, with a starting balance of $250,000 and interest at 8.50 percent, will bring the account to $1 million at the end of 3 years.

Example 336. Amount Accrued on Bow-Tie Loan in Real Estate—Owned Account

Spritzer and Greis will acquire the Galaxy Garden Business Park from the lender who now holds it as real estate–owned. The loan for a 10-year period will have an 11.00 percent accrual rate but a pay rate of 8.50 percent per year or 100 percent of net operating income, whichever is higher, up to the accrual rate. The lender is confident that income will rise over the years but wishes to know the eventual accrual if only the pay rate is paid.

To find the accrual, enter Table 14 at the page and section for Pay Rate of 8.50 percent per year. Read down the year paid column to 10 and across to the accrual rate column of 11.00 percent. The factor there, 45.2079 percent, means that the accrued interest on the loan could be as much as 45 percent of the loan, if only the pay rate is actually paid.

Example 337. Time When Withdrawals Will Reduce Operating Reserve to Given Percentage

At the closing of Magnolia Court, LeCoeur Bank & Trust will deposit $650,000 in an escrow account bearing interest at the rate of 8.25 percent. The buyer may draw the amounts of operating deficits or extraordinary repairs from this account. The account is intended to last for 84 months; if the balance of the account goes below 60 percent before a certain date, LeCoeur will be obliged to restore the account with an additional sum. The question is when would the "natural" date for a 60 percent balance occur, i.e., if the account paid out uniformly for 84 months, when would it reach a 60 percent balance?

To find the 60 percent balance date, enter Table 67 in the section for 8.25 percent interest. Read down the left column to 7 years and across to the column Unpaid Balance of loan 60 percent. The answer

there, 3Y 4m, indicates that the balance would pass through the 60 percent level 3 years and 4 months after closing. The agreement will read that, if the account remains above 60 percent after 40 months, the "refreshment" of the account will not be required.

Example 338. Mortgage Forbearance Plan

Delaplage Apartments have experienced vacancy problems, and cash flow is currently insufficient to meet the mortgage payment. The mortgage lender is willing, for a period of 12 months, to accept payments that are $1800 per month lower than required in the loan documents. At the end of that time, however, the shortfall is to be made up by higher monthly payments in the 24 months following forbearance. The mortgage note is at 11.00 percent interest. In a forbearance plan such as this, the "deposit" will be the privilege to make reduced payments for 1 year, while the "withdrawal" will be the obligation to pay back for 2 years.

To find the monthly make-up payment, enter Table 61, page 2 (p. 727), the section for 1 year of deposit. On the line for 2 years of withdrawal, find under the column 11.00 percent, the factor, 58.8371 percent, the percentage of the monthly deposit which must be made up. Multiply the dollar amount of the monthly shortfall by the percentage to get

$$\$1800 \times 0.588371 = \$1059.07$$

the amount of the make-up payment in the latter 24 months to be added to the regular payment.

Note The procedure is the same, whether all or only part of the payment is deferred. If it is entirely deferred, the payment is zero during the forbearance period, the full amount of the monthly payment is used in the calculation in place of $1800, and the result will be the payment added to the regular payment during the make-up period.

Note The parties might choose an interest rate different from the note rate for the make-up payment, for example, the default rate under the mortgage. In such case, use the portion of the table for the interest rate of the forbearance plan, not that on the original note. Often a separate note is created for the total amount of the forbearance (number of months times the amount of monthly shortfall), especially if additional mortgagee's title insurance is required.

Example 339.   Deposit Needed to Secure Mortgage Forbearance

The Hope Brothers have asked their lender to forbear from monthly payments on the Kaligarry Korners Shop Stop for a period of 1 year. The purpose is to permit rehabilitation to be accomplished, during which no revenue will be coming in from tenants. To secure payment of the interest, they are prepared to deposit cash today into an interest-bearing account. The rehab work will begin in 1 year; when it is completed, the lender will reappraise the property. If the value increase permits the lender to rewrite the loan, it will do so, adding the accrued interest to the loan and returning the deposit to the Hope Brothers. If reappraisal does not support the loan rewrite, the deposit will cover the interest for the forbearance period. With the deposit pledged to it, the lender's collateral position will at all times meet the requirements of the authorities. The loan balance is $3 million, and the interest rate is 9.00 percent. The deposit will earn interest at 8.00 percent.

Begin by finding the monthly interest payment that would have been needed. It is

$$\$3,000,000 \times 0.09 \div 12 = \$22,500$$

per month interest. Now enter Table 58, page 1 (p. 716), at the section for a draw delay of 12 months. On the line for 12 payments, read across to the column headed 8.00 percent. The factor there, 10.68553, is the necessary multiple of the payments. Multiply the monthly interest payment by the factor to get

$$\$22,500 \times 10.68553 = \$240,424$$

the deposit needed today to secure the lender for 12 monthly payments of $22,500, beginning in 12 months.

Example 340.   Dividing Revenues from Defaulted Loan among Participating Lenders

The Sister Cities Bank is lead lender for Wolverton Mountain Office Refuge and has sold **participations** in 50 percent of the loan to two other banks. The loan is in default, and the participants feel that they should receive income first before the lead lender. The property is dependably producing about $41,000 per month, far below the amount needed to cover interest payments to the banks. The Sister Cities Bank will offer to let the participants receive all

$41,000 for 24 months, but Sister Cities would then receive all $41,000 for some number of months until they were again equal. This would give the participants current cash that they can report as income, with the hope that, after 2 years' delay, income may be restored to continue payments and cover Sister Cities' share as well. The Treasury Bill rate currently is 8.50 percent.

To find the number of payments that Sister Cities will be entitled to, enter Table 63 (p. 729), and read down the column for number of prior payments to 24 and on that line find under 8.50 percent 28.91 months. After 24 months of payments of $41,000 taken by the participants, Sister Cities Bank will be entitled to 28 full payments of $41,000, and plus 91 percent of the twenty-ninth payment. The other 9 percent of the twenty-ninth payment and further income will be divided 50/50 between Sister Cities and the participants. If the loan were to be paid off before Sister Cities received all its payments, it would be entitled to a preference from the payoff proceeds of the then present value at 8.50 percent of any payments it had not received.

Example 341.   Yield on Participating Mortgage Loan from Resold Property

The Fund for Realty Renewal has received a deed in lieu of foreclosure for GlasHaus, an office. A leasing team is prepared to buy it on the basis of no money down with a participating mortgage loan for 75 percent of the Fund's cost. The loan would run for 10 years and bear interest at 7.50 percent; the lender would also receive 80 percent of any increases in net operating income and in appraised value above today's levels. Based on the proforma, the debt service coverage ratio on this lease appears to be 1.20 times. The other 25 percent of the property value will be covered by a corporate loan to the leasing team, who will pledge their business assets to it and pay a market rate of interest for business loans. The parties agree that income and value should rise 3 percent per year over the loan term.

To find the potential yield to the lender, enter Table 30, page 3 (p. 375), the page and section for 3.0 percent annual rate of growth and 7.50 percent loans. Read down to 10 years and across to the column 80 percent share of income and value increases, and read there the answer, 10.209 percent, the yield on the participating mortgage loan, if the specified conditions come to pass.

Example 342. Cumulative Balance on Phantom Deposits

Artrichie Savings Bank foreclosed on the Harbor Hall Shopping Port and is reselling it to the workout team of Monigle & Zilligan. Under the deal with M&Z, the savings bank will set aside a portion of each monthly mortgage interest payment in a reserve for latent defects and major repairs. The amounts set aside will bear interest and be available to M&Z as needed. Of course, Artrichie, being a depositary itself, does not wish to set aside actual payments. The payments will be phantom payments, that is, they will simply be calculated and available for M&Z to draw, as if set up in an actual account. The agreed rate of interest is 6.00 percent, and the program is designed to build up to $1 million over 5 years. M&Z consider it highly probable that new air conditioning compressors will be needed in three years at a cost of $465,000. They want to verify that the "account" will have an adequate balance to cover this.

To find the balance on the account, proceed as if the payments were actually being set aside in cash. Enter Table 54, page 1, the page for 6.00 percent interest, 5-year funding. Reading across on the line for 3 years in the 5-year section, find under the heading 6.00 percent monthly, the factor 56.476 percent, the percentage of the future total that would be on hand. Multiply the eventual total by this factor to get

$$\$1,000,000 \times 0.56476 = \$564,760$$

the sum that the phantom deposits will amount to by the end of the third year of a 5-year schedule at 6.00 percent interest, substantially more than the predicted cost of the compressor replacements.

Note Many agreements call for a rate of interest to be calculated, as here, even though no account is actually set up. When an interest-bearing account is established, one party or another must pay taxes on the interest earned. Using the phantom account may avoid that problem, until the matter is fully resolved and the accounting can be made. In such cases, some attorneys prefer to avoid reference to "interest" payments and simply provide for increases in accordance with a certain schedule.

Example 343. Using a Graduated Rent Plan to Create Attractive Lease at Foreclosure

Standish & Co. have been awarded title to the Center of the Perimeter as part of a bankruptcy claim. Standish has $200 per rentable square foot invested in the Center. The building is vacant, but Wauhaukee Corporation is interested in leasing the entire property for 10 years. To make an attractive rent proposal, Standish decides to use 6.00 percent as the cost of funds in calculating the rent and to present a graduated lease plan, starting with low rents and rising 10 percent per year.

To find the initial rent for the proposal, begin by finding the standard rental. It is $200 × 0.06 = $12.00 per square foot per year net. Now enter Table 65, page 13 (p. 750), the page for 10 percent annual rise and 6.00 percent interest. In the section for 10-year plans, find on the line for year 1 under 6.00 percent the factor, 8.67925 percent. At the bottom of the 10-year section, find the level factor, 13.25618. Multiply the rent by the ratio of the first-year factor to the level factor to get

$$\$12.00 \text{ per s.f.} \times \frac{0.0867925}{0.1325618} = \$7.8568$$

or, $7.86 per square foot, the rental in the first year. Each year after the first the rental may be increased 10 percent by repeating the process above or simply increasing the prior year's rent by 10 percent. The result will be the rental which will give a 6.00 percent per year return on the investment of Standish, while rising 10 percent per year.

Example 344. Rent Increase to Compensate for Free Rent Period

Saltimbanque S.A. will lease a former Hand Bank branch for 12 years, if Hand Bank will give the first 2 years rent-free. Hand Bank was willing to accept $17,000 per month on a 10-year lease but has not yet disclosed this. They want to convert the rental into that which would compensate them, at 7.00 percent interest, for the free rent period.

To find the rent, enter Table 61, page 1 (p. 726), the page for 7.00 percent interest and the section for 2 years of deposit. On the line for 10 years of withdrawal, read under the 7.00 percent column, 29.8179 percent, the percentage of the deposit that will be needed. Multiply the foregone rent by the percentage to get

$$\$17,000 \times 0.298179 = \$5069$$

the additional rent that will compensate the free rent. Added to the base rent of $17,000, Hand Bank will quote a rental of $22,069 per month for the 10 years following a 2-year free rent period.

In this example, there is no way to know if $17,000 is a fair market rental. If it is, Hand Bank will probably not be able to negotiate the increase. Even if the resulting figures are only asking rents, subject to negotiation, knowing that the requested free rent has a value of $5000 per month deepens the landlord's appreciation for the value of the concession.

Example 345.   Real Price Underlying Offer with Below-Market Financing

Yeats and Barrell are offered a property at a price of $3 million consisting of $700,000 cash down payment with seller financing of $2.8 million at 6.00 percent interest for 5 years. Although mortgage interest rates are generally 8.50 percent per year, the company's internal cash generation makes it possible for them to allocate funds at 5.00 percent per year. Yeats and Barrell prefer to discuss the property without any premium in the price for a below-market loan.

Enter Table 10 at the section for a Stated Interest Rate of 8.50 percent. Read down the left column to 6.000 percent desired yield and across on that line to the column for 5 years. The factor there is 110.56631 percent. Dividing the loan by the factor will give

$$\$2,800,000 \div 1.1056631 = \$2,532,417$$

the market value of the loan to which must be added $700,000 for a total of $3,232,417, or, rounding, $3,232,500. The seller's offer has a real value of $3,232,500, which Yeats and Barrell will use as the starting point to value this property.

Yields from Transactions

Example 346.   Internal Rate of Return from Distressed Property

Stabilo Banking Corporation has ownership of The Couronna. Although the property is producing an 11.00 percent return on Stabilo's investment, the market is extremely soft, and no buyer has made an offer. Stabilo expects that they may have to hold the property for 5 years and even then will have to take a 50 percent loss to sell it.

To find the internal rate of return from this set of circumstances, enter Table 1, page 5 (p. 149), the page for capital loss situations and 5-year holding period. On the line for 11.00 percent capitalization rate, read the factor under 50 percent capital loss, 1.320 percent. The property would have an internal rate of return of 1.32 percent per year, if the income is sustained at 11.00 percent per year and a 50 percent loss of capital is experienced after 5 years of holding.

Example 347.   Amount of Loss Based on Depressed Rent

Stereo Covers Corporate Pension Trust has taken back three warehouses in Samantha's Corners that were collateral to mortgage loans it had made. The warehouses are fully leased but with depressed market conditions can produce only an 8.00 percent yield, far below the market requirement, which appears to demand at least a 10.50 percent current capitalization rate. The Trust anticipates that it will hold the properties for a period of 10 years, and wants to write the properties down to the value indicated by the market demand.

To find the required writedown, turn to Table 2, page 3 (p. 153), with capitalization rates of 10.50 percent. Read down the left column headed desired yield to 10.50 percent. In that section, on the line for a holding period of 10 years and find 84.9631. This is the percentage of their investment that the property would be sold for today to give a buyer 10.50 percent over 10 years. The Trust will therefore take a writedown of 15.0369 percent (100.000 percent − 84.9631 percent), at least until market conditions warrant further consideration.

Example 348.   Shared Appreciation to Give a Specified Yield on Workout

Cerberus Savings Bank has an offer for In the Styx Recording Hall. The price is satisfactory, but the buyer requires the seller to take back a 90-month purchase money mortgage at only 7.50 percent instead of the current market rate of 11.00 percent. The buyer is willing, however, to pass 100 percent of price appreciation at time of sale to the lender, until the lender has an 11.00 percent yield.

To find the sale price at the end of 7.5 years that would give 11.00 percent yield to the lender, enter Table 4 (a), page 2 (p. 170), on the page for 7.50 percent cap rates. In that section, read across on the line for holding period of 7.5 years to the column headed desired yield 11.00 percent. The factor there is 137.780 percent, the necessary percentage of the purchase money loan to bring its yield from 7.50 percent up to 11.00 percent.

Example 349. Future Gain to Bring Distressed Property Yield to Target

Ara Gail Hopeson will bid on a bank foreclosure. The bank offers 75 percent financing at 10.50 percent interest on a 30-year schedule for 10 years. She will only do the deal if a 12.00 percent equity return can be obtained on the needed investment of $260,000. Her analysis shows the property has a going-in equity rate of 7.50 percent.

Begin by finding the total property value. Divide the equity by the equity to value ratio to get $1.04 million, that is, $260,000 divided by 0.25. To find the profit that would produce the 12.00 percent equity target, enter Table 4 (b), page 3 (p. 175), the page for 7.50 percent equity rate and 12.00 percent desired yield. Read across in the section for 10.50 percent loan on the 10-year line to the section for 12.00 percent desired yield. Find there under 75 percent loan, the factor 113.459 percent. Multiply this percentage by the total property value to get

$$\$1,040,000 \times 1.13459 = \$1,179,974$$

or, rounding to the nearest $25,000, that is, $1,175,000, the future sale price to bring the overall yield from 7.50 percent cash-on-cash to 12.00 percent equity return for the 10-year period.

Example 350. Growth Needed to Cover REO Carrying Costs

Millie Foley Counselors are advising Altrue Bank concerning a second mortgage the bank has foreclosed and converted to real estate owned (REO). A first mortgage payable to another institution at 11.00 percent apparently has a 75 percent loan-to-value ratio, relative to Altrue's $250,000 position. The Millie Foley team estimate their client's cost to carry is 7.50 percent per year on the equity position. Given that no upturn is seen in the market for 4 years, they want to show the bank what value growth would be needed to justify holding the investment.

Enter Table 9, page 1 (p. 198), 7.50 percent cost of carry. In the section for 11.00 percent financing, read down to year 4. On the cumulative line, read under 75 percent financed, the factor 49.68 percent. The property value would have to grow 50 percent to cover these carrying costs. Since the value performance forecast does not at all support such a need, Millie Foley Counselors will recommend that Altrue Bank attempt to negotiate an interest reduction from the senior lender. If that fails, they will recommend writing off the REO and forfeiting it to the senior lender.

Glossary

abbreviations: esp. = especially; L. = Latin; opp = opposite of; q.v. = which see; syn = synonym

absolutely net: (syn = net and triple net) a lease under which the tenant pays all costs of operating the real estate but not such costs of ownership as inheritance or income taxes, leasing commissions, or costs of collecting rent from other tenants

accounting principles: the body of rules governing preparation of financial statements; in the United States, *generally accepted accounting principles,* q.v., is the common term

accrual: the earning of interest on a loan or accumulation of periodic expense; the amount of interest or expense owing

accrual rate: the rate at which interest is earned on a loan, whether or not paid currently; contrasted with pay rate, the rate at which interest must be paid currently

accrued interest: the interest earned on a loan since the last date paid in cash

accuracy: degree to which an answer or equation is correct (to be distinguished from precision; 2 + 2 = 3.9999 is precise, 2 + 2 = 4 is accurate)

actual/365 basis: syn = exact interest; interest calculated as 1/365 of one year's interest per day

add-on interest: interest calculated under an "add-on" formula by which interest is pre-computed for the loan term and added to principal

adjustable rate mortgage (ARM): any mortgage loan the interest rate of which is adjusted periodically, usually annually, according to an index. The rate is usually subject to a ceiling on upward adjustment in any year and over the term of the loan; also called variable rate mortgage

ad valorem tax: (L.: according to value) real estate taxes levied according to value; the ordinary real estate taxes in most regions; opp = according to income

advance: a disbursement of part of a loan; syn = draw

after-tax cash flow: cash flow remaining after deducting cash operating expenses, debt service, and income taxes; both principal and interest of mortgage payments are deducted, but depreciation is not

after-tax income: income after deducting operating expenses, interest, and income taxes; depreciation is deducted, but principal payments are not

all-inclusive mortgage: syn = wraparound, q.v.

amortization: reduction of a mortgage loan by periodic repayments of principal; the sum of the principal repayments in a given period; in accounting, the reduction of an intangible asset account by accounting charges, similar to depreciation for a tangible asset

amortization schedule: the time period over which a mortgage loan would be fully amortized by level annuity payments; a listing of the application of each mortgage payment to principal and interest

annual mortgage constant: quotient of 1 year's mortgage payments divided by the loan amount, expressed as a percentage (syn = constant, constant annual percent, and mortgage constant)

annual percentage rate (APR): the effective yield to a lender from interest, points, and certain fees calculated according to, and to comply with, the truth-in-lending law (T-I-L). Most lenders to consumers are obliged by law to disclose the APR in advertising and in loan commitments. The T-I-L is synonymous with the Federal Reserve Board's Regulation Z

annuity: any stream of periodic payments; an agreement by one to pay payments at certain dates to another, especially with the sense of certainty; leases and mortgages are, for investment analysis, forms of annuities

annuity payment mortgage: the customary mortgage loan, with level payments each applied part to interest and part to principal

appraisal: an estimate of the value of property as of a certain time. Real estate appraisals are most often made to estimate fair market value (which see). Insurance value appraisals are made to estimate replacement cost or the correct insurance coverage

appreciation: increase in the value of real estate

apportionment: syn = "proration," which see

assessment: in real estate taxation, the value of a project used to determine real estate taxes; in condominium or other property owners' associations, charge levied on owners or co-owners toward their shares of operating expenses

at a discount: a loan bought or sold for less than the amount owed by the borrower

at a premium: a loan bought or sold for more than the amount owed by the borrower

at arm's length: disinterested; unmarked by closeness or affection; to bargain at arm's length is to deal without conflict of interest, whether emotional or financial, toward the best ends of a transaction

at par: a loan bought or sold at the amount owed by the borrower

balance: the unpaid principal amount of a loan

balloon: a payment of all the balance of a loan required before normal amortization schedule

basis: for income tax purposes, the cost (after depreciation but excluding potential profit) of an investment in the hands of a taxpayer, the value of an asset from which profit or loss will be measured for tax purposes; for interest calculations, the number of days to be considered to fall in a month or year

basis point: 1/100 of 1 percent—the difference between interest rates of 7.50 percent and 7.75 percent is 25 basis points

bona fide purchaser for value (BFP): one who buys in a genuine transaction paying an actual price; opp = straw buyer; a BFP is protected from some irregularities in the transaction, esp. regarding fraud

bow-tie loan: a loan on which the rate of current cash payment, called the "pay rate," is less than the full interest rate, called the "accrual rate"; the difference, called the "accrual," accrues at a compounded rate

build-to-suit: a property constructed to order of its purchaser (versus built on speculation)

build-to-suit lease: a property constructed to order of a tenant who will occupy under a lease

bullet loan: a loan which neither requires nor permits amortization during its term, typically 3 to 10 years

buy-sell agreement: in construction lending, an agreement that the construction lender will deliver a loan to the permanent lender and the permanent lender will buy it; in partnerships, an agreement that, under certain conditions, one partner may force the other partner(s) to buy the offering partner's interest or to sell their interests to the offering partner

CAM: see common area maintenance

capitalization: the process of estimating value by reference to current and projected future income in which income is divided by one or more capitalization rates

capitalization rate or **cap rate:** the rate of return *on* an investment and *of* an investment demanded by investors in the market for certain types of property

capitalized in perpetuity: capitalization by which current net operating income is divided by a capitalization rate (capitalized) to give an estimate of value

capitalized value: the value estimated by capitalization, as opposed to that estimated by reference to cost or to market data

capital lease: a lease by which the tenant obtains most of the benefits and burdens of ownership; in accounting practice, only leases that meet certain technical standards are capital leases, but in investment analysis a broader spectrum of leases may be so called

cash flow mortgage: a loan on which current payments are declared equal to the cash flow from the property; used in workout cases where income is not sufficiently predictable to permit a fixed interest rate

cash-on-cash return: net cash flow available to the owner of a mortgaged property after payment of operating expenses and debt service

certificate of deposit (CD): an interest-bearing bank deposit made under a specific written agreement (the certificate)

closed: in regard to a loan or a sale, accomplished or no longer in commitment or "contract" stage; in regard to prepayment of a loan, noncallable, not permitted to be prepaid

common area maintenance (CAM): charges to maintain, repair, and insure the common areas of a property, esp. a shopping center, shared by tenants in proportion to their leased areas

compound amount: syn= future value

compound discount: discount for more than one interest period

compounded: accrued earnings added to principal

Consumer Price Index (CPI): measure of inflation and change in purchasing power of money, published by U.S. Department of Labor (see Table D)

construction loan: a loan disbursed periodically, usually monthly, according to the progress of construction; it may include a reserve from which the lender draws monthly interest

contract rent: rent fixed by lease or other contract, especially when distinguished from market rent

coupon rate: syn= face rate and note rate

customary unit also **U.S. customary unit:** the system of measures in use in the United States, using feet, yards, miles, square feet, square yards, and square miles

debt service: amounts, whether principal or interest, required to be paid periodically by the terms of a loan

debt service coverage: net operating income divided by annual debt service; the degree to which debt service can be paid from operating cash flow

discount: in lending, to deduct interest from the proceeds of a loan or the amount deducted; in investment analysis, to calculate the present value of a sum to be received in future

discounted amount: syn= present value or discounted value

discount rate: the interest rate inherent in a discounted loan or at which a present value is estimated

draw: to request a lender to disburse part of a loan, especially a construction loan

draws: the amounts periodically requested from a lender

economic rent: syn= market rent; rental found in the open-market; rent which would be established by economic (supply-demand) conditions, as opposed to contract rent; sometimes the rent net of concessions, as opposed to face rent

effective annual rate: the true rate of interest to a lender who receives payments more frequently than annually

encumbered: bound by one or more leases, mortgages, or judgment liens; opp= free and clear; in an office lease, a rentable area subject to an option or right of first refusal held by a tenant

encumbrance: most often a mortgage loan, but also a lease

exact interest: interest paid on the basis of a 365-day year

expense stop: a lease clause stating the maximum rate of expenses to be paid by the landlord; an expense stop of $4.00 per square foot means the landlord will pay the first $4.00 of expenses and tenant those in excess of $4.00. Real estate taxes are sometimes included in the expenses subject to the stop, sometimes subject to a separate stop called a "tax stop"

face rate: syn= coupon rate, note rate; the interest rate stated in a note

fair market value (FMV): the value in terms of money that a knowledgeable buyer willing and able to buy would pay a willing and knowledgeable seller for a property in the present, neither acting under undue pressures

Fannie Mae: the Federal National Mortgage Association, a private company originally created by the government, which is the leading purchaser of mortgages in the secondary markets

fee simple: the highest level of ownership; a holder in fee simple is free to take any action concerning the property; in English law, fee simple meant property unbound by inheritance rules, but in modern real estate practice it means free of encumbrances; sometimes used to indicate an appraisal made on the assumption that existing leases do not encumber the property

financial pro forma: an estimate of the outcome of property operations, usually made for several years

floating prime rate: an interest rate on a loan that adjusts when the bank's prime rate is adjusted

FNMA: see **Fannie Mae**

forbearance: agreement by a lender to moderate the time or amount of loan payments to ease a borrower's short-term problems

free and clear: not encumbered by a mortgage or leases

full payout lease: a lease that will provide a return on investment and return of invested capital within the lease term

full payout loan: a loan which will be fully amortized within its term

future simple rate: the simple interest rate which equates a compounded interest rate after compounding to the present; e.g., after two years of compounding at 5.50 percent, the future simple interest rate will be 5.8025 percent, while the compounded interest rate remains 5.50 percent.

future value: the sum of an investment or deposit and the interest earned on it

generally accepted accounting principles (GAAP): the body of accounting methods and standards used in audits of commercial companies

gross: inclusive of charges or taxes

gross lease: a lease that provides that the landlord pays some or all operating expenses and taxes

gross rent: rental under a gross lease or including operating expenses

ground rent: rent paid by the tenant of a lease of land for its use

hangout: amortization period of a loan beyond the term of the single or principal lease which supports the loan; a shopping center with a major store lease of 20 years and a 25-year loan has a 5-year hangout

in advance: interest that is paid on the first day of each compounding period

in arrears: interest paid at the end of each compounding period; in the U.S.A., interest on mortgage loans is paid in arrears (and usually on the day after the compounding period)

in back: at the end of the term of a loan

income stream: any series of payments made or dividends received from a lease or property; an annuity

in front: at the start of the term of a loan

installment: one of a series of payments to amortize a loan, consisting of interest and part of the principal of the loan; one of a series of payments of any type

internal rate of return (IRR): the annual discount rate, akin to yield to maturity of a bond or mortgage, that equates expected future returns on an investment to the present amount of the investment; more than one valid IRR may exist for a given set of circumstances

interest reserve: proceeds of a loan withheld for payment of interest over the life of the loan

kicker: any bonus interest paid a lender, especially measured in relation to income or to an increase in income of the property

leased fee: the interest of a landlord in property leased to a tenant, especially on a long-term lease

leasehold: the interest of a tenant under a lease, especially a long-term lease, in the leased property

leasing holdback: loan proceeds withheld until agreed leasing benchmarks are achieved

level payment annuity mortgage: loan with payments of both principal and interest

loan draws: partial disbursements of a construction loan made as construction progresses or other benchmarks are achieved

loan-to-value ratio: the maximum portion of sale price or appraised value, usually 75 percent to 85 percent, that a lender will advance on given collateral

loss factor: the percentage of rentable area not practically usable by tenants

master lease: a lease by a tenant that does not intend to occupy real estate but agrees to pay rent for it, thereby providing financial support to enhance a credit or sale proposal

minipermanent or **miniperm:** a medium-term, 3- to 7-year loan, amortizing on a long-term, 25- to 30-year schedule

money good: investments of unquestioned quality, e.g., Treasuries

mortgage buy-down: payment to a lender by a third party such as a seller or builder to induce the lender to lower its interest rate for a period

mortgage constant or **annual mortgage constant:** the quotient of one year's mortgage payments divided by the amount of the loan

negative amortization: the increase in loan indebtedness when loan payments are insufficient to pay accrued interest

net: after deduction of charges

net cash flow: operating result after deducting operating expenses and debt service payments from total income

net lease: syn= triple net lease; net, net lease, absolutely net lease: a lease under which the tenant pays all operating expenses, costs of maintenance and repairs, fire insurance premiums, and real estate taxes on the property

net operating income: operating result after deducting operating expenses from total income

net present value (NPV): the sum of future returns from a property, discounted for time, minus the present cost of the property

net rent: see **absolutely net**

net rentable area: area of an office, including both the portion available for use by the tenant and a pro rata share of the common restrooms, corridors, and building service rooms on the same floor; syn= rentable area, the term used by the Building Owners and Managers Association

new money: the loan proceeds from a wraparound mortgage loan in excess of the existing loan, or, generally, additional investment in a project, especially in a workout case

nominal annual rate: the stated annual rate of a loan; said to be the nominal rate because the yield to the lender is greater if payments are made more frequently than annually

note: written evidence of a debt; the debtor who signs the note is called the maker; the creditor named in the note is the payee; a creditor who holds (owns) the note, whether or not the original payee, is called the "holder"

note rate: the interest rate stated in a note; the yield to a lender from the interest rate in the note, as distinguished from the yield from fees, discount, or participation

on spec, on speculation: undertaken without advance leasing or sales contracts

open for prepayment: a loan that has reached the time when, by its terms, it may be prepaid

ordinary interest: interest calculated on the basis of a 360-day year

other real estate owned (OREO): syn= real estate owned, which see

par: the value of a note or other debt owed by the borrower

participating loan: a loan in which the lender receives part of any increase in operating income or in property value during the term of the loan

participation: a loan shared by more than one lender; the excess payments above fixed rate interest to a lender in a participating mortgage

payout: (syn= advance, draw) disbursement of all or part of a loan

pay rate: the rate at which interest must be paid in cash currently to the lender, implying that some of the interest is not paid currently but is accrued

percentage rent: a percentage of a tenant's sales or revenues paid as rent; often a guaranteed rental is also charged, e.g., $12,000 per year versus 3.5 percent of sales, in which case the greater amount is paid

permanent financing: any long- or medium-term financing arrangement, including equity financing, which serves to repay a construction loan

point: 1 percent of the amount of a loan, whether paid to a lender or seller of a loan to increase its yield or to pay the lender or a mortgage banker as compensation for arranging the loan premium

points: the excess paid for a loan above the amount owed by the borrower

prepayment premium: compensation to a lender required when payment made earlier than provided

present value: the value in money today of a payment or a lease reversion to be received in future

profitability index: the ratio of the present value of a property, measured by discounting its forecast future investment returns, to the present cost of the investment; see also **net present value**

prime rate: the general interest rate for short-term loans to highly qualified commercial borrowers; few lenders actually use the prime rate, calling it something else, such as their "base lending rate," but the prime rate is indicative of the level of commercial interest rates

pro forma: (L., for form's sake); used in real estate analysis, syn= financial projection, i.e., estimation of potential results from operations of an investment; used in accounting to describe a financial situation as if one or more conditions had been true instead of actual conditions

proration: division between buyer and seller of a property-related cost, usually at sale closing; syn= apportionment

purchase money mortgage: a loan made by the seller of a property to enable the purchaser to buy it; such loans have advantages over other debts in bankruptcy and other tests of lien priority

real estate owned (REO): (syn= other real estate owned, or OREO) term used by banks to designate real estate acquired from loan default

rentable area: syn= net rentable area; the term of the Building Owners and Managers Association (BOMA) for net rentable area; a precise definition of the area allocated to a tenant under an office lease (see "Standard Method for Measuring Floor Area in Office Buildings," American National Standards Institute, ANSI Z65.1-1980 reaffirmed 1989, available from BOMA)

rent holdback: loan proceeds withheld until agreed leasing benchmarks are achieved

request for proposal (RFP): solicitation, usually quite detailed, by a prospective purchaser or tenant that sellers or landlords submit offers to sell or to lease; an RFP usually does not signify any engagement by the solicitor to accept any given proposal

reversion: the return to the landlord of the use of leased property at the end of the lease term; the value of the property at the time of the reversion

SAM: see **shared appreciation mortgage**

sandwich: positioned between a fee titleholder and a subtenant

sandwich lease: a lease by a tenant as a sublandlord to a subtenant

sandwich rentals: the rent received by a tenant from a subtenant

sf, s.f.: square foot (0.092903 m²) (see Table E)

shared appreciation mortgage (SAM): a mortgage loan in which the lender receives a portion of any increase in value of the mortgaged property during the term of the loan; see also **participating loan**

sinking fund: an accumulation of deposits and interest thereon usually held to meet a future financial obligation, such as to retire bonds

spec: see **on spec**

straight line: the arithmetic average determined without regard to time value of money; e.g., the straight line depreciation of a building with a 40-year life is 2.5 percent per year

straw buyer: or straw man; one who acts as buyer, but for the account of another, especially a party with an interest in the property

subject to: encumbered by mortgage without assumption or agreement to pay; one taking title subject to a mortgage does not agree to be personally liable for payment

takeout commitment: a commitment for a mortgage loan which will retire an earlier financing, usually a construction loan; often synonymous with permanent financing

tax stop: the maximum portion of real estate taxes to be paid by a landlord under a lease; a real estate tax stop of $2.50 per square foot means that the landlord will pay that amount of taxes first and the tenant any in excess of that rate

term: in a loan, the time from the making of the loan until its required full repayment; in a lease, the time during which the tenant may occupy the leased premises

terminal value: the amount in a deposit account or sinking fund after a specified period; the value that would be achieved by an annuity compounding at a given rate

thirty/360 basis: syn= ordinary interest; interest at the rate of 30/360 of a year's interest per month, or 1/360 per day

time value of money: weighting money transactions according to the discount rate for investments

triparty agreement: most often an agreement among borrower, permanent lender, and construction lender, assuring the construction lender that, subject to conditions, the permanent lender will make a loan that will retire the construction lender's loan, and the permanent lender that the construction lender will not deliver the loan to any other party

triple net: see **absolutely net**

turnkey: completed, ready for immediate occupancy of the intended tenant

turnkey price: the price including work to suit tenant's specifications for its occupancy

unencumbered: with regard to financing syn= free and clear; property that is not bound by mortgages or leases; with regard to leasing, space in a building, especially offices, not subject to options in favor of tenants

usable area: the area of an office floor, net of common restrooms, corridors and building service rooms that a tenant may use; rentable area, q.v., reduced by a loss factor, q.v.

valued as if free and clear: an appraisal made on the assumption that a property is, or will be at time of sale, free of mortgage loans

wraparound loan: a mortgage loan by which the terms of an existing first mortgage are incorporated into a second mortgage loan; the borrower treats the wraparound as if it were the only loan on the property

yield curve: a graph of interest rates of various maturities of one security issuer, most often the government, used to indicate how investors predict interest will vary over time

Internal Rate of Return of an Investment

Holding Period	Capitalization Rate	Capital Gain on Sale of Property											
		20%	25%	33%	40%	50%	67%	75%	100%	150%	200%	250%	300%
	5.50	8.707	9.433	10.586	11.463	12.709	14.625	15.518	17.980	22.146	25.594	28.539	31.110
	5.75	8.938	9.660	10.807	11.679	12.918	14.826	15.715	18.165	22.315	25.752	28.688	31.251
	6.00	9.168	9.886	11.027	11.895	13.128	15.026	15.911	18.351	22.485	25.910	28.837	31.393
	6.25	9.399	10.113	11.248	12.111	13.338	15.227	16.108	18.537	22.655	26.068	28.986	31.535
	6.50	9.630	10.340	11.468	12.327	13.547	15.428	16.304	18.724	22.825	26.227	29.135	31.677
	6.75	9.861	10.567	11.689	12.543	13.758	15.628	16.501	18.910	22.996	26.386	29.285	31.820
5	7.00	10.092	10.794	11.910	12.759	13.968	15.830	16.699	19.097	23.166	26.545	29.435	31.962
years	7.25	10.323	11.021	12.131	12.976	14.178	16.031	16.896	19.283	23.337	26.704	29.585	32.105
	7.50	10.555	11.248	12.352	13.192	14.388	16.232	17.093	19.470	23.508	26.863	29.735	32.248
	7.75	10.786	11.476	12.574	13.409	14.599	16.434	17.291	19.658	23.680	27.023	29.886	32.392
	8.00	11.017	11.703	12.795	13.626	14.810	16.636	17.489	19.845	23.851	27.183	30.037	32.535
	8.25	11.249	11.931	13.016	13.843	15.021	16.838	17.687	20.033	24.023	27.343	30.188	32.679
	8.50	11.480	12.158	13.238	14.060	15.232	17.040	17.885	20.220	24.195	27.503	30.339	32.823
	8.75	11.712	12.386	13.460	14.278	15.443	17.242	18.083	20.408	24.367	27.663	30.490	32.967
	9.00	11.944	12.614	13.681	14.495	15.654	17.445	18.282	20.596	24.539	27.824	30.642	33.111
	9.25	12.175	12.842	13.903	14.712	15.866	17.647	18.480	20.785	24.712	27.985	30.794	33.256
	9.50	12.407	13.070	14.125	14.930	16.077	17.850	18.679	20.973	24.885	28.146	30.946	33.401
	9.75	12.639	13.298	14.348	15.148	16.289	18.053	18.878	21.162	25.058	28.308	31.099	33.546
	10.00	12.871	13.526	14.570	15.366	16.501	18.256	19.077	21.351	25.231	28.469	31.251	33.691
	10.25	13.103	13.754	14.792	15.584	16.713	18.460	19.277	21.540	25.404	28.631	31.404	33.837
	10.50	13.335	13.983	15.015	15.802	16.925	18.663	19.476	21.730	25.578	28.793	31.557	33.983
	10.75	13.568	14.211	15.237	16.020	17.138	18.867	19.676	21.919	25.752	28.955	31.710	34.129
	11.00	13.800	14.440	15.460	16.239	17.350	19.070	19.876	22.109	25.926	29.118	31.864	34.275
	11.25	14.032	14.668	15.683	16.457	17.563	19.274	20.076	22.299	26.100	29.281	32.018	34.421
	11.50	14.265	14.897	15.906	16.676	17.776	19.479	20.276	22.489	26.275	29.444	32.171	34.568
	11.75	14.498	15.126	16.129	16.895	17.989	19.683	20.477	22.679	26.449	29.607	32.326	34.715
	12.00	14.730	15.355	16.352	17.114	18.202	19.887	20.678	22.870	26.624	29.770	32.480	34.862
	12.25	14.963	15.584	16.575	17.333	18.415	20.092	20.878	23.060	26.799	29.934	32.635	35.009
	12.50	15.196	15.813	16.799	17.552	18.628	20.297	21.079	23.251	26.975	30.098	32.790	35.157
	15.00	17.528	18.109	19.039	19.751	20.770	22.354	23.099	25.171	28.741	31.749	34.351	36.646
	5.50	7.345	7.765	8.433	8.942	9.666	10.785	11.307	12.751	15.208	17.251	19.001	20.534
	5.75	7.577	7.992	8.654	9.159	9.878	10.987	11.506	12.939	15.380	17.411	19.153	20.678
	6.00	7.808	8.220	8.876	9.376	10.089	11.190	11.704	13.128	15.552	17.572	19.304	20.822
	6.25	8.040	8.448	9.098	9.594	10.301	11.392	11.903	13.316	15.725	17.733	19.456	20.967
	6.50	8.272	8.676	9.320	9.812	10.512	11.595	12.102	13.505	15.898	17.894	19.609	21.112
	6.75	8.504	8.905	9.543	10.030	10.724	11.799	12.302	13.694	16.071	18.056	19.761	21.257
8	7.00	8.737	9.133	9.766	10.248	10.937	12.002	12.501	13.883	16.245	18.218	19.914	21.403
years	7.25	8.969	9.362	9.988	10.467	11.149	12.206	12.701	14.073	16.419	18.381	20.068	21.549
	7.50	9.201	9.590	10.211	10.685	11.362	12.410	12.901	14.263	16.594	18.543	20.222	21.695
	7.75	9.434	9.819	10.434	10.904	11.575	12.615	13.102	14.454	16.768	18.707	20.376	21.842
	8.00	9.667	10.048	10.658	11.123	11.788	12.819	13.303	14.645	16.943	18.870	20.530	21.990
	8.25	9.900	10.278	10.881	11.343	12.002	13.024	13.504	14.836	17.119	19.034	20.685	22.137
	8.50	10.133	10.507	11.105	11.562	12.216	13.230	13.705	15.027	17.295	19.198	20.841	22.285
	8.75	10.366	10.736	11.329	11.782	12.430	13.435	13.907	15.219	17.471	19.363	20.996	22.434
	9.00	10.599	10.966	11.553	12.002	12.644	13.641	14.109	15.411	17.648	19.528	21.152	22.582
	9.25	10.832	11.196	11.777	12.222	12.858	13.847	14.311	15.603	17.824	19.694	21.309	22.731
	9.50	11.066	11.426	12.002	12.442	13.073	14.053	14.514	15.796	18.002	19.859	21.465	22.881
	9.75	11.300	11.656	12.226	12.663	13.288	14.260	14.717	15.989	18.179	20.026	21.623	23.031
	10.00	11.533	11.886	12.451	12.883	13.503	14.467	14.920	16.182	18.357	20.192	21.780	23.181
	10.25	11.767	12.116	12.676	13.104	13.718	14.674	15.123	16.375	18.536	20.359	21.938	23.331
	10.50	12.001	12.347	12.901	13.325	13.934	14.881	15.327	16.569	18.715	20.526	22.096	23.483
	10.75	12.235	12.578	13.126	13.547	14.150	15.089	15.531	16.764	18.894	20.694	22.255	23.634
	11.00	12.469	12.809	13.352	13.768	14.366	15.297	15.735	16.958	19.073	20.862	22.414	23.786
	11.25	12.704	13.039	13.577	13.990	14.582	15.505	15.940	17.153	19.253	21.031	22.574	23.938
	11.50	12.938	13.271	13.803	14.212	14.799	15.713	16.145	17.348	19.433	21.199	22.733	24.090
	11.75	13.173	13.502	14.029	14.434	15.015	15.922	16.350	17.544	19.613	21.368	22.894	24.243
	12.00	13.408	13.733	14.256	14.657	15.232	16.131	16.555	17.740	19.794	21.538	23.054	24.397
	12.25	13.643	13.965	14.482	14.879	15.450	16.341	16.761	17.936	19.976	21.708	23.215	24.550
	12.50	13.877	14.196	14.709	15.102	15.667	16.550	16.967	18.132	20.157	21.878	23.377	24.705
	15.00	16.234	16.521	16.984	17.341	17.854	18.661	19.043	20.115	21.994	23.603	25.012	26.267

Entry is the IRR in percent per year from monthly income and capital gain.

Internal Rate of Return of an Investment

Holding Period	Capitalization Rate	20%	25%	33%	Capital Gain on Sale of Property 40%	50%	67%	75%	100%	150%	200%	250%	300%
	5.50	6.895	7.214	7.721	8.108	8.661	9.516	9.915	11.023	12.914	14.493	15.850	17.040
	5.75	7.127	7.442	7.944	8.327	8.873	9.719	10.115	11.213	13.088	14.655	16.003	17.185
	6.00	7.360	7.671	8.167	8.545	9.086	9.923	10.315	11.403	13.262	14.818	16.156	17.332
	6.25	7.592	7.900	8.390	8.764	9.299	10.128	10.516	11.593	13.437	14.981	16.311	17.478
	6.50	7.825	8.129	8.613	8.983	9.512	10.332	10.717	11.784	13.612	15.145	16.465	17.625
	6.75	8.058	8.358	8.837	9.203	9.726	10.537	10.918	11.975	13.788	15.309	16.620	17.773
10 years	7.00	8.291	8.587	9.061	9.422	9.940	10.743	11.119	12.166	13.964	15.473	16.775	17.921
	7.25	8.524	8.817	9.285	9.642	10.154	10.948	11.321	12.358	14.140	15.638	16.931	18.070
	7.50	8.758	9.047	9.509	9.862	10.368	11.154	11.524	12.551	14.317	15.803	17.088	18.219
	7.75	8.991	9.277	9.733	10.083	10.583	11.361	11.726	12.743	14.495	15.969	17.245	18.368
	8.00	9.225	9.507	9.958	10.303	10.798	11.568	11.929	12.937	14.672	16.136	17.402	18.519
	8.25	9.459	9.737	10.183	10.524	11.013	11.775	12.133	13.130	14.851	16.303	17.560	18.669
	8.50	9.693	9.968	10.408	10.745	11.229	11.982	12.336	13.324	15.029	16.470	17.718	18.820
	8.75	9.927	10.198	10.633	10.967	11.445	12.190	12.540	13.518	15.208	16.638	17.877	18.971
	9.00	10.161	10.429	10.859	11.188	11.661	12.398	12.745	13.713	15.388	16.806	18.036	19.123
	9.25	10.396	10.660	11.085	11.410	11.878	12.606	12.950	13.908	15.568	16.974	18.196	19.276
	9.50	10.630	10.892	11.311	11.633	12.094	12.815	13.155	14.104	15.749	17.144	18.356	19.429
	9.75	10.865	11.123	11.537	11.855	12.311	13.024	13.360	14.300	15.930	17.313	18.517	19.582
	10.00	11.100	11.355	11.764	12.078	12.529	13.234	13.566	14.496	16.111	17.483	18.678	19.736
	10.25	11.335	11.587	11.990	12.301	12.746	13.443	13.772	14.693	16.293	17.654	18.839	19.890
	10.50	11.570	11.819	12.217	12.524	12.964	13.653	13.979	14.890	16.475	17.825	19.002	20.045
	10.75	11.806	12.051	12.444	12.747	13.183	13.864	14.186	15.088	16.658	17.997	19.164	20.201
	11.00	12.041	12.283	12.672	12.971	13.401	14.075	14.393	15.286	16.841	18.169	19.327	20.356
	11.25	12.277	12.516	12.899	13.195	13.620	14.286	14.601	15.484	17.025	18.341	19.491	20.513
	11.50	12.513	12.748	13.127	13.419	13.839	14.497	14.809	15.683	17.209	18.514	19.655	20.670
	11.75	12.749	12.981	13.355	13.643	14.058	14.709	15.017	15.882	17.394	18.688	19.820	20.827
	12.00	12.985	13.214	13.584	13.868	14.278	14.921	15.226	16.082	17.579	18.862	19.985	20.985
	12.25	13.221	13.448	13.812	14.093	14.498	15.134	15.435	16.282	17.765	19.036	20.151	21.143
	12.50	13.458	13.681	14.041	14.318	14.718	15.347	15.645	16.482	17.951	19.211	20.317	21.302
	15.00	15.829	16.024	16.339	16.583	16.936	17.493	17.759	18.509	19.837	20.989	22.007	22.920
	5.50	6.598	6.849	7.251	7.558	7.996	8.676	8.994	9.879	11.395	12.666	13.761	14.723
	5.75	6.831	7.079	7.474	7.777	8.210	8.881	9.196	10.070	11.571	12.830	13.916	14.871
	6.00	7.064	7.308	7.698	7.997	8.424	9.086	9.397	10.262	11.747	12.995	14.071	15.019
	6.25	7.297	7.538	7.923	8.217	8.638	9.292	9.599	10.454	11.924	13.160	14.228	15.168
	6.50	7.531	7.768	8.147	8.437	8.853	9.499	9.802	10.647	12.101	13.326	14.384	15.318
	6.75	7.765	7.998	8.372	8.658	9.068	9.705	10.005	10.840	12.279	13.492	14.542	15.468
12 years	7.00	7.999	8.228	8.597	8.879	9.283	9.913	10.209	11.034	12.457	13.659	14.700	15.618
	7.25	8.233	8.459	8.822	9.100	9.499	10.120	10.412	11.228	12.636	13.826	14.858	15.769
	7.50	8.467	8.690	9.048	9.322	9.715	10.328	10.617	11.422	12.816	13.994	15.017	15.921
	7.75	8.701	8.921	9.273	9.544	9.932	10.536	10.822	11.617	12.996	14.163	15.177	16.074
	8.00	8.936	9.152	9.499	9.766	10.148	10.745	11.027	11.813	13.176	14.332	15.337	16.226
	8.25	9.171	9.384	9.726	9.988	10.366	10.955	11.232	12.009	13.357	14.502	15.498	16.380
	8.50	9.406	9.616	9.952	10.211	10.583	11.164	11.438	12.206	13.539	14.672	15.659	16.534
	8.75	9.641	9.848	10.179	10.434	10.801	11.374	11.645	12.403	13.721	14.843	15.821	16.689
	9.00	9.876	10.080	10.406	10.658	11.019	11.585	11.852	12.600	13.904	15.015	15.984	16.844
	9.25	10.112	10.312	10.634	10.881	11.238	11.795	12.059	12.798	14.087	15.187	16.147	17.000
	9.50	10.348	10.545	10.862	11.105	11.457	12.007	12.267	12.997	14.271	15.360	16.311	17.157
	9.75	10.583	10.777	11.089	11.330	11.676	12.218	12.475	13.196	14.456	15.533	16.475	17.314
	10.00	10.820	11.010	11.318	11.554	11.895	12.430	12.684	13.395	14.641	15.707	16.640	17.471
	10.25	11.056	11.244	11.546	11.779	12.115	12.643	12.893	13.595	14.826	15.881	16.806	17.630
	10.50	11.292	11.477	11.775	12.004	12.336	12.856	13.102	13.796	15.012	16.056	16.972	17.789
	10.75	11.529	11.711	12.004	12.230	12.556	13.069	13.312	13.997	15.199	16.232	17.139	17.948
	11.00	11.766	11.945	12.233	12.456	12.777	13.283	13.523	14.198	15.386	16.408	17.307	18.108
	11.25	12.003	12.179	12.463	12.682	12.998	13.497	13.734	14.400	15.574	16.585	17.475	18.269
	11.50	12.240	12.413	12.692	12.908	13.220	13.711	13.945	14.603	15.762	16.763	17.643	18.431
	11.75	12.477	12.647	12.922	13.135	13.442	13.926	14.156	14.806	15.951	16.941	17.813	18.593
	12.00	12.714	12.882	13.153	13.362	13.664	14.141	14.368	15.009	16.141	17.119	17.983	18.755
	12.25	12.952	13.117	13.383	13.589	13.887	14.357	14.581	15.213	16.331	17.299	18.153	18.919
	12.50	13.190	13.352	13.614	13.817	14.110	14.573	14.794	15.417	16.521	17.478	18.324	19.083
	15.00	15.577	15.713	15.935	16.107	16.358	16.756	16.946	17.488	18.458	19.310	20.070	20.757

Entry is the IRR in percent per year from monthly income and capital gain.

Internal Rate of Return of an Investment

Holding Period	Capitalization Rate	20%	25%	33%	Capital Gain on Sale of Property 40%	50%	67%	75%	100%	150%	200%	250%	300%
15 years	5.50	6.305	6.490	6.786	7.013	7.338	7.845	8.083	8.745	9.888	10.852	11.687	12.423
	5.75	6.539	6.720	7.011	7.234	7.554	8.052	8.286	8.939	10.067	11.020	11.845	12.573
	6.00	6.773	6.951	7.237	7.456	7.770	8.260	8.490	9.134	10.246	11.187	12.004	12.725
	6.25	7.007	7.182	7.463	7.678	7.987	8.468	8.695	9.329	10.426	11.356	12.163	12.877
	6.50	7.242	7.413	7.689	7.900	8.203	8.677	8.900	9.525	10.607	11.525	12.324	13.030
	6.75	7.477	7.645	7.915	8.123	8.421	8.886	9.106	9.721	10.788	11.695	12.485	13.184
	7.00	7.712	7.877	8.142	8.346	8.639	9.096	9.313	9.918	10.970	11.866	12.647	13.339
	7.25	7.947	8.109	8.369	8.569	8.857	9.307	9.520	10.115	11.153	12.038	12.809	13.494
	7.50	8.183	8.342	8.597	8.793	9.075	9.518	9.727	10.313	11.337	12.210	12.972	13.650
	7.75	8.419	8.574	8.824	9.017	9.294	9.729	9.935	10.512	11.521	12.383	13.137	13.807
	8.00	8.655	8.807	9.053	9.242	9.514	9.941	10.144	10.712	11.706	12.557	13.301	13.964
	8.25	8.891	9.040	9.281	9.467	9.734	10.154	10.353	10.912	11.891	12.731	13.467	14.123
	8.50	9.128	9.274	9.510	9.692	9.954	10.367	10.562	11.112	12.077	12.906	13.633	14.282
	8.75	9.364	9.508	9.739	9.917	10.175	10.580	10.772	11.313	12.264	13.082	13.800	14.441
	9.00	9.601	9.742	9.968	10.143	10.396	10.794	10.983	11.515	12.452	13.259	13.968	14.602
	9.25	9.838	9.976	10.198	10.370	10.618	11.009	11.194	11.718	12.640	13.436	14.137	14.764
	9.50	10.076	10.210	10.428	10.597	10.840	11.224	11.406	11.921	12.829	13.614	14.306	14.926
	9.75	10.313	10.445	10.659	10.824	11.062	11.439	11.618	12.124	13.019	13.793	14.477	15.089
	10.00	10.551	10.680	10.889	11.051	11.285	11.655	11.831	12.329	13.209	13.973	14.648	15.252
	10.25	10.789	10.916	11.120	11.279	11.509	11.872	12.044	12.534	13.401	14.153	14.819	15.417
	10.50	11.027	11.151	11.352	11.507	11.732	12.089	12.258	12.739	13.592	14.335	14.992	15.582
	10.75	11.265	11.387	11.583	11.736	11.957	12.306	12.473	12.945	13.785	14.517	15.165	15.749
	11.00	11.504	11.623	11.815	11.965	12.181	12.524	12.688	13.152	13.978	14.699	15.339	15.916
	11.25	11.743	11.859	12.048	12.194	12.406	12.742	12.903	13.359	14.172	14.883	15.514	16.083
	11.50	11.982	12.096	12.280	12.423	12.631	12.961	13.119	13.567	14.367	15.067	15.690	16.252
	11.75	12.221	12.332	12.513	12.653	12.857	13.181	13.336	13.775	14.562	15.252	15.867	16.421
	12.00	12.460	12.569	12.746	12.884	13.083	13.401	13.553	13.985	14.758	15.438	16.044	16.592
	12.25	12.700	12.807	12.980	13.114	13.310	13.621	13.770	14.194	14.955	15.624	16.222	16.763
	12.50	12.940	13.044	13.213	13.345	13.537	13.842	13.988	14.404	15.153	15.812	16.401	16.934
	15.00	15.347	15.430	15.566	15.672	15.827	16.075	16.195	16.539	17.166	17.726	18.234	18.699
20 years	5.50	6.019	6.139	6.333	6.481	6.696	7.031	7.189	7.633	8.406	9.065	9.640	10.150
	5.75	6.254	6.372	6.560	6.705	6.914	7.242	7.397	7.831	8.589	9.237	9.803	10.306
	6.00	6.490	6.605	6.788	6.930	7.134	7.454	7.605	8.030	8.774	9.411	9.968	10.464
	6.25	6.727	6.838	7.017	7.155	7.354	7.666	7.814	8.230	8.960	9.585	10.133	10.622
	6.50	6.963	7.071	7.246	7.380	7.574	7.879	8.024	8.431	9.146	9.761	10.300	10.781
	6.75	7.200	7.305	7.475	7.606	7.795	8.093	8.235	8.633	9.334	9.937	10.468	10.942
	7.00	7.437	7.540	7.705	7.833	8.017	8.308	8.446	8.835	9.522	10.115	10.636	11.103
	7.25	7.675	7.774	7.935	8.059	8.239	8.523	8.658	9.039	9.711	10.293	10.806	11.266
	7.50	7.912	8.009	8.166	8.287	8.462	8.739	8.870	9.243	9.901	10.472	10.977	11.429
	7.75	8.150	8.245	8.397	8.515	8.685	8.955	9.084	9.448	10.093	10.653	11.149	11.594
	8.00	8.389	8.480	8.628	8.743	8.909	9.172	9.298	9.653	10.285	10.834	11.322	11.759
	8.25	8.627	8.716	8.860	8.972	9.134	9.390	9.513	9.860	10.478	11.017	11.496	11.926
	8.50	8.866	8.952	9.092	9.201	9.359	9.609	9.728	10.067	10.672	11.200	11.671	12.094
	8.75	9.105	9.189	9.325	9.431	9.584	9.828	9.944	10.275	10.867	11.385	11.847	12.263
	9.00	9.344	9.426	9.558	9.661	9.810	10.048	10.161	10.484	11.063	11.571	12.024	12.433
	9.25	9.584	9.663	9.792	9.892	10.037	10.268	10.379	10.694	11.260	11.757	12.202	12.604
	9.50	9.824	9.901	10.026	10.123	10.264	10.489	10.597	10.904	11.457	11.945	12.381	12.776
	9.75	10.064	10.139	10.260	10.354	10.492	10.711	10.816	11.116	11.656	12.133	12.561	12.950
	10.00	10.304	10.377	10.494	10.586	10.720	10.933	11.035	11.328	11.856	12.323	12.743	13.124
	10.25	10.545	10.615	10.729	10.818	10.948	11.156	11.256	11.541	12.056	12.514	12.925	13.299
	10.50	10.786	10.854	10.965	11.051	11.178	11.379	11.476	11.754	12.258	12.706	13.109	13.476
	10.75	11.027	11.093	11.200	11.285	11.407	11.603	11.698	11.969	12.460	12.898	13.293	13.654
	11.00	11.268	11.332	11.437	11.518	11.637	11.828	11.920	12.184	12.664	13.092	13.479	13.833
	11.25	11.510	11.572	11.673	11.752	11.868	12.053	12.143	12.400	12.868	13.287	13.666	14.013
	11.50	11.751	11.812	11.910	11.987	12.099	12.279	12.366	12.616	13.073	13.482	13.854	14.194
	11.75	11.993	12.052	12.147	12.221	12.331	12.506	12.590	12.834	13.279	13.679	14.043	14.376
	12.00	12.236	12.292	12.384	12.457	12.563	12.733	12.815	13.052	13.486	13.877	14.233	14.559
	12.25	12.478	12.533	12.622	12.692	12.795	12.960	13.040	13.271	13.694	14.076	14.424	14.744
	12.50	12.721	12.774	12.860	12.928	13.028	13.188	13.266	13.490	13.903	14.276	14.616	14.929
	15.00	15.157	15.195	15.258	15.307	15.380	15.498	15.556	15.724	16.038	16.327	16.596	16.846

Entry is the IRR in percent per year from monthly income and capital gain.

Internal Rate of Return of an Investment

Holding Period	Capitalization Rate	\multicolumn{12}{c}{Capital Gain on Sale of Property}										
		20%	25%	33%	40%	50%	67%	75%	100%	150%	200%	250%	300%
	5.50	5.855	5.938	6.071	6.175	6.324	6.559	6.671	6.985	7.540	8.017	8.438	8.813
	5.75	6.092	6.172	6.301	6.401	6.546	6.774	6.882	7.188	7.728	8.195	8.607	8.975
	6.00	6.330	6.407	6.532	6.629	6.769	6.990	7.095	7.392	7.919	8.375	8.777	9.139
	6.25	6.568	6.642	6.763	6.857	6.992	7.206	7.308	7.597	8.110	8.555	8.949	9.303
	6.50	6.806	6.878	6.995	7.085	7.216	7.424	7.523	7.803	8.302	8.737	9.123	9.469
	6.75	7.045	7.114	7.227	7.314	7.441	7.642	7.738	8.010	8.496	8.920	9.297	9.637
25 years	7.00	7.284	7.351	7.459	7.544	7.666	7.861	7.954	8.218	8.691	9.104	9.473	9.805
	7.25	7.523	7.588	7.693	7.774	7.893	8.081	8.171	8.427	8.887	9.290	9.650	9.975
	7.50	7.763	7.825	7.926	8.005	8.119	8.301	8.389	8.637	9.084	9.477	9.829	10.147
	7.75	8.003	8.063	8.160	8.236	8.347	8.523	8.607	8.848	9.282	9.665	10.008	10.320
	8.00	8.243	8.301	8.395	8.468	8.575	8.745	8.827	9.060	9.482	9.855	10.190	10.494
	8.25	8.484	8.539	8.630	8.701	8.803	8.968	9.047	9.273	9.682	10.045	10.372	10.669
	8.50	8.725	8.778	8.865	8.933	9.033	9.192	9.268	9.487	9.884	10.238	10.556	10.846
	8.75	8.966	9.017	9.101	9.167	9.263	9.416	9.490	9.702	10.087	10.431	10.741	11.025
	9.00	9.207	9.257	9.338	9.401	9.493	9.641	9.713	9.918	10.291	10.625	10.928	11.205
	9.25	9.449	9.497	9.575	9.635	9.724	9.867	9.936	10.134	10.497	10.821	11.116	11.386
	9.50	9.691	9.737	9.812	9.870	9.956	10.094	10.161	10.352	10.703	11.018	11.305	11.569
	9.75	9.933	9.977	10.049	10.106	10.188	10.321	10.386	10.571	10.911	11.217	11.496	11.753
	10.00	10.176	10.218	10.288	10.342	10.421	10.549	10.611	10.790	11.119	11.416	11.688	11.938
	10.25	10.419	10.460	10.526	10.578	10.655	10.778	10.838	11.011	11.329	11.617	11.881	12.125
	10.50	10.662	10.701	10.765	10.815	10.889	11.007	11.065	11.232	11.540	11.819	12.076	12.313
	10.75	10.905	10.943	11.004	11.052	11.123	11.238	11.293	11.454	11.752	12.023	12.272	12.503
	11.00	11.149	11.185	11.244	11.290	11.358	11.468	11.522	11.677	11.965	12.227	12.469	12.694
	11.25	11.393	11.427	11.484	11.528	11.594	11.700	11.751	11.901	12.179	12.433	12.668	12.886
	11.50	11.637	11.670	11.724	11.767	11.830	11.932	11.981	12.125	12.394	12.640	12.868	13.080
	11.75	11.881	11.913	11.965	12.006	12.066	12.164	12.212	12.351	12.610	12.848	13.069	13.275
	12.00	12.125	12.156	12.206	12.245	12.303	12.397	12.443	12.577	12.827	13.058	13.272	13.471
	12.25	12.370	12.399	12.447	12.485	12.541	12.631	12.675	12.804	13.045	13.268	13.475	13.669
	12.50	12.615	12.643	12.689	12.725	12.778	12.865	12.908	13.032	13.264	13.480	13.680	13.869
	15.00	15.073	15.091	15.121	15.145	15.179	15.237	15.265	15.347	15.505	15.655	15.797	15.932
	5.50	5.751	5.810	5.906	5.980	6.088	6.258	6.340	6.571	6.981	7.340	7.658	7.944
	5.75	5.990	6.047	6.138	6.210	6.313	6.477	6.555	6.778	7.176	7.523	7.833	8.112
	6.00	6.229	6.283	6.371	6.440	6.539	6.697	6.772	6.987	7.371	7.709	8.010	8.282
	6.25	6.469	6.521	6.605	6.670	6.766	6.917	6.990	7.197	7.568	7.896	8.188	8.453
	6.50	6.709	6.758	6.839	6.902	6.993	7.139	7.208	7.408	7.767	8.084	8.368	8.626
	6.75	6.949	6.997	7.074	7.134	7.221	7.361	7.428	7.620	7.967	8.274	8.550	8.800
30 years	7.00	7.190	7.235	7.309	7.366	7.450	7.584	7.649	7.833	8.168	8.465	8.733	8.977
	7.25	7.431	7.474	7.545	7.600	7.680	7.809	7.871	8.048	8.370	8.658	8.918	9.155
	7.50	7.673	7.714	7.781	7.834	7.911	8.034	8.093	8.264	8.574	8.852	9.104	9.334
	7.75	7.914	7.954	8.018	8.068	8.142	8.260	8.317	8.480	8.780	9.048	9.292	9.516
	8.00	8.156	8.194	8.255	8.303	8.374	8.487	8.541	8.698	8.987	9.246	9.482	9.699
	8.25	8.399	8.435	8.493	8.539	8.606	8.714	8.767	8.917	9.195	9.445	9.673	9.883
	8.50	8.642	8.676	8.732	8.775	8.839	8.943	8.993	9.138	9.404	9.645	9.866	10.070
	8.75	8.885	8.917	8.970	9.012	9.073	9.172	9.220	9.359	9.615	9.847	10.061	10.258
	9.00	9.128	9.159	9.210	9.249	9.308	9.402	9.448	9.581	9.827	10.051	10.257	10.448
	9.25	9.372	9.401	9.449	9.487	9.543	9.633	9.677	9.804	10.040	10.256	10.455	10.639
	9.50	9.616	9.644	9.690	9.726	9.779	9.865	9.907	10.028	10.255	10.462	10.654	10.832
	9.75	9.860	9.886	9.930	9.964	10.015	10.097	10.137	10.253	10.470	10.670	10.855	11.027
	10.00	10.104	10.130	10.171	10.204	10.252	10.330	10.368	10.480	10.687	10.879	11.057	11.223
	10.25	10.349	10.373	10.412	10.444	10.490	10.564	10.601	10.707	10.906	11.090	11.261	11.421
	10.50	10.594	10.617	10.654	10.684	10.728	10.799	10.833	10.935	11.125	11.302	11.466	11.621
	10.75	10.839	10.861	10.896	10.925	10.966	11.034	11.067	11.163	11.346	11.515	11.673	11.822
	11.00	11.085	11.105	11.139	11.166	11.205	11.269	11.301	11.393	11.567	11.730	11.882	12.025
	11.25	11.330	11.350	11.382	11.407	11.445	11.506	11.536	11.624	11.790	11.946	12.092	12.229
	11.50	11.576	11.594	11.625	11.649	11.685	11.743	11.771	11.855	12.014	12.163	12.303	12.435
	11.75	11.822	11.839	11.868	11.891	11.925	11.980	12.008	12.087	12.239	12.381	12.516	12.643
	12.00	12.068	12.085	12.112	12.134	12.166	12.219	12.244	12.320	12.465	12.601	12.730	12.852
	12.25	12.315	12.330	12.356	12.377	12.407	12.457	12.482	12.554	12.692	12.822	12.945	13.062
	12.50	12.561	12.576	12.601	12.620	12.649	12.696	12.720	12.788	12.920	13.044	13.162	13.274
	15.00	15.035	15.043	15.058	15.069	15.085	15.113	15.127	15.167	15.246	15.322	15.396	15.467

Entry is the IRR in percent per year from monthly income and capital gain.

Internal Rate of Return on an Investment

Holding Period	Capitalization Rate	10%	15%	16.67%	Capital Loss on Sale of Property 20%	25%	30%	33.33%	35%	40%	50%	60%	66.67%
	5.5	3.675	2.694	2.355	1.660	0.570	-0.587	-1.399	-1.818	-3.133	-6.069	-9.543	-12.275
	6.0	4.199	3.231	2.898	2.213	1.138	0.008	-0.799	-1.211	-2.503	-5.384	-8.785	-11.451
	6.5	4.722	3.769	3.440	2.765	1.706	0.585	-0.200	-0.604	-1.875	-4.702	-8.031	-10.633
	7.0	5.246	4.306	3.981	3.317	2.274	1.171	0.398	0.011	-1.249	-4.023	-7.281	-9.820
	7.5	5.769	4.842	4.523	3.867	2.840	1.754	0.995	0.602	-0.624	-3.346	-6.535	-9.01
	8.0	6.292	5.378	5.063	4.418	3.406	2.338	1.590	1.205	0.012	-2.672	-5.793	-8.213
5	8.5	6.815	5.914	5.604	4.968	3.971	2.919	2.184	1.806	0.621	-2.000	-5.056	-7.418
years	9.0	7.338	6.449	6.144	5.517	4.536	3.501	2.778	2.405	1.241	-1.331	-4.322	-6.628
	9.5	7.860	6.984	6.683	6.065	5.099	4.081	3.369	3.003	1.859	-0.665	-3.592	-5.844
	10.0	8.383	7.519	7.222	6.614	5.662	4.660	3.960	3.600	2.476	0.015	-2.866	-5.065
	10.5	8.905	8.053	7.761	7.161	6.224	5.238	4.550	4.196	3.092	0.661	-2.145	-4.291
	11.0	9.426	8.587	8.299	7.708	6.786	5.815	5.138	4.791	3.706	1.320	-1.426	-3.523
	11.5	9.948	9.121	8.836	8.255	7.347	6.391	5.726	5.384	4.318	1.977	-0.711	-2.759
	12.0	10.469	9.654	9.374	8.801	7.907	6.967	6.312	5.976	4.928	2.632	0.019	-2.000
	12.5	10.990	10.186	9.911	9.346	8.466	7.541	6.898	6.567	5.538	3.285	0.706	-1.247
	5.5	4.457	3.899	3.707	3.313	2.696	2.045	1.590	1.355	0.621	-1.002	-2.893	-4.354
	6.0	4.979	4.434	4.246	3.862	3.260	2.626	2.182	1.954	1.241	-0.332	-2.160	-3.567
	6.5	5.502	4.969	4.786	4.410	3.823	3.205	2.773	2.551	1.858	0.332	-1.434	-2.788
	7.0	6.024	5.503	5.324	4.958	4.385	3.782	3.362	3.146	2.473	0.992	-0.715	-2.017
	7.5	6.545	6.036	5.862	5.504	4.946	4.359	3.950	3.740	3.085	1.648	0.012	-1.254
	8.0	7.066	6.569	6.399	6.050	5.505	4.933	4.535	4.331	3.695	2.301	0.708	-0.499
8	8.5	7.587	7.102	6.935	6.595	6.064	5.507	5.119	4.920	4.302	2.951	1.411	0.248
years	9.0	8.107	7.633	7.471	7.139	6.621	6.078	5.701	5.508	4.907	3.596	2.108	0.989
	9.5	8.627	8.165	8.006	7.682	7.177	6.649	6.282	6.094	5.510	4.239	2.799	1.721
	10.0	9.147	8.695	8.540	8.224	7.732	7.218	6.861	6.678	6.110	4.877	3.486	2.447
	10.5	9.666	9.225	9.074	8.766	8.286	7.785	7.438	7.260	6.708	5.513	4.167	3.166
	11.0	10.185	9.755	9.607	9.307	8.839	8.351	8.013	7.840	7.304	6.145	4.844	3.879
	11.5	10.704	10.284	10.140	9.847	9.391	8.916	8.587	8.419	7.898	6.774	5.516	4.586
	12.0	11.222	10.812	10.672	10.386	9.942	9.479	9.160	8.996	8.490	7.399	6.183	5.287
	12.5	11.740	11.340	11.203	10.924	10.492	10.041	9.730	9.571	9.079	8.022	6.846	5.981
	5.5	4.715	4.296	4.152	3.857	3.397	2.911	2.573	2.399	1.856	0.662	-0.716	-1.769
	6.0	5.236	4.830	4.690	4.404	3.958	3.488	3.161	2.993	2.469	1.319	0.009	-1.005
	6.5	5.758	5.363	5.227	4.950	4.517	4.063	3.747	3.584	3.079	1.972	0.707	-0.251
	7.0	6.278	5.895	5.763	5.494	5.075	4.636	4.330	4.173	3.685	2.621	1.409	0.494
	7.5	6.798	6.426	6.299	6.038	5.632	5.207	4.911	4.760	4.289	3.265	2.103	1.231
	8.0	7.318	6.957	6.833	6.581	6.187	5.776	5.491	5.344	4.890	3.904	2.791	1.959
10	8.5	7.838	7.487	7.367	7.122	6.742	6.343	6.068	5.927	5.488	4.540	3.473	2.679
years	9.0	8.357	8.017	7.900	7.663	7.294	6.909	6.643	6.506	6.084	5.171	4.148	3.390
	9.5	8.875	8.545	8.432	8.202	7.846	7.473	7.216	7.084	6.677	5.798	4.817	4.093
	10.0	9.393	9.073	8.964	8.741	8.396	8.036	7.787	7.660	7.267	6.421	5.481	4.790
	10.5	9.911	9.601	9.495	9.279	8.944	8.596	8.356	8.234	7.854	7.041	6.139	5.478
	11.0	10.428	10.127	10.025	9.815	9.492	9.156	8.924	8.805	8.440	7.657	6.792	6.160
	11.5	10.945	10.653	10.554	10.351	10.038	9.713	9.489	9.375	9.022	8.269	7.439	6.836
	12.0	11.461	11.179	11.082	10.886	10.583	10.269	10.053	9.942	9.603	8.878	8.082	7.505
	12.5	11.977	11.703	11.610	11.420	11.127	10.823	10.615	10.508	10.180	9.483	8.720	8.167
	5.5	4.885	4.558	4.446	4.216	3.858	3.482	3.220	3.086	2.668	1.753	0.707	-0.085
	6.0	5.406	5.090	4.982	4.761	4.416	4.055	3.803	3.674	3.274	2.400	1.407	0.660
	6.5	5.926	5.621	5.517	5.304	4.972	4.625	4.384	4.260	3.876	3.042	2.099	1.392
	7.0	6.445	6.152	6.051	5.846	5.527	5.193	4.962	4.843	4.476	3.679	2.782	2.114
	7.5	6.964	6.681	6.584	6.387	6.079	5.759	5.537	5.423	5.071	4.311	3.459	2.827
	8.0	7.483	7.210	7.116	6.926	6.631	6.323	6.110	6.001	5.664	4.938	4.128	3.530
12	8.5	8.001	7.738	7.648	7.464	7.181	6.885	6.681	6.576	6.254	5.560	4.790	4.224
years	9.0	8.518	8.265	8.178	8.002	7.729	7.445	7.249	7.149	6.840	6.178	5.446	4.910
	9.5	9.035	8.791	8.708	8.538	8.276	8.003	7.815	7.719	7.424	6.792	6.095	5.588
	10.0	9.551	9.316	9.236	9.073	8.821	8.559	8.379	8.287	8.004	7.401	6.738	6.258
	10.5	10.067	9.841	9.764	9.607	9.365	9.114	8.941	8.853	8.582	8.006	7.376	6.920
	11.0	10.583	10.365	10.291	10.140	9.907	9.666	9.501	9.417	9.157	8.607	8.007	7.575
	11.5	11.098	10.888	10.817	10.672	10.448	10.217	10.059	9.978	9.730	9.204	8.634	8.224
	12.0	11.613	11.411	11.342	11.203	10.988	10.766	10.614	10.537	10.300	9.798	9.255	8.866
	12.5	12.127	11.933	11.867	11.733	11.526	11.314	11.168	11.094	10.867	10.388	9.871	9.502

Entry is the Internal Rate of Return in percent per year. Negative returns may not be unique.

Internal Rate of Return on an Investment

Holding Period	Capitalization Rate	10%	15%	16.67%	20%	25%	30%	33.33%	35%	40%	50%	60%	66.67%
						Capital Loss on Sale of Property							
15 years	5.5	5.053	4.816	4.735	4.569	4.311	4.042	3.855	3.759	3.462	2.817	2.091	1.548
	6.0	5.572	5.345	5.268	5.110	4.864	4.608	4.431	4.340	4.058	3.450	2.768	2.263
	6.5	6.090	5.874	5.800	5.649	5.416	5.172	5.003	4.917	4.651	4.077	3.437	2.965
	7.0	6.608	6.401	6.331	6.187	5.965	5.733	5.573	5.492	5.239	4.698	4.097	3.656
	7.5	7.125	6.928	6.861	6.724	6.512	6.292	6.141	6.063	5.824	5.313	4.749	4.338
	8.0	7.642	7.454	7.390	7.259	7.058	6.849	6.705	6.631	6.405	5.923	5.393	5.009
	8.5	8.158	7.978	7.917	7.793	7.602	7.403	7.267	7.197	6.983	6.528	6.030	5.671
	9.0	8.673	8.502	8.444	8.326	8.144	7.955	7.826	7.760	7.557	7.127	6.660	6.324
	9.5	9.188	9.025	8.970	8.857	8.684	8.505	8.382	8.320	8.128	7.723	7.283	6.969
	10.0	9.702	9.547	9.494	9.387	9.223	9.053	8.936	8.877	8.696	8.313	7.900	7.606
	10.5	10.216	10.068	10.018	9.916	9.760	9.598	9.488	9.432	9.261	8.900	8.511	8.236
	11.0	10.729	10.588	10.540	10.444	10.295	10.142	10.038	9.985	9.822	9.482	9.117	8.858
	11.5	11.241	11.108	11.062	10.970	10.829	10.684	10.585	10.535	10.381	10.060	9.717	9.474
	12.0	11.754	11.626	11.583	11.496	11.362	11.224	11.130	11.083	10.938	10.634	10.312	10.084
	12.5	12.265	12.144	12.103	12.020	11.893	11.763	11.674	11.629	11.491	11.205	10.901	10.688
20 years	5.5	5.215	5.065	5.014	4.909	4.748	4.581	4.465	4.406	4.223	3.833	3.401	3.086
	6.0	5.731	5.591	5.543	5.445	5.294	5.138	5.030	4.975	4.805	4.444	4.047	3.759
	6.5	6.247	6.115	6.070	5.979	5.838	5.692	5.591	5.540	5.382	5.048	4.683	4.419
	7.0	6.762	6.639	6.596	6.511	6.379	6.243	6.149	6.101	5.955	5.646	5.310	5.069
	7.5	7.277	7.161	7.121	7.041	6.918	6.791	6.704	6.659	6.524	6.237	5.928	5.707
	8.0	7.790	7.682	7.645	7.570	7.455	7.336	7.255	7.214	7.088	6.823	6.538	6.336
	8.5	8.303	8.201	8.167	8.097	7.990	7.879	7.804	7.765	7.648	7.403	7.141	6.956
	9.0	8.816	8.720	8.688	8.623	8.522	8.420	8.349	8.314	8.205	7.978	7.737	7.567
	9.5	9.327	9.238	9.208	9.147	9.053	8.958	8.892	8.859	8.759	8.548	8.326	8.170
	10.0	9.838	9.755	9.727	9.670	9.583	9.493	9.433	9.402	9.309	9.114	8.909	8.766
	10.5	10.348	10.271	10.244	10.191	10.110	10.027	9.971	9.942	9.855	9.676	9.486	9.355
	11.0	10.858	10.786	10.761	10.712	10.636	10.559	10.506	10.480	10.399	10.233	10.059	9.937
	11.5	11.367	11.300	11.277	11.231	11.160	11.088	11.040	11.015	10.941	10.787	10.626	10.514
	12.0	11.876	11.813	11.792	11.749	11.683	11.616	11.571	11.548	11.479	11.337	11.188	11.086
	12.5	12.384	12.325	12.306	12.265	12.205	12.143	12.101	12.079	12.015	11.883	11.746	11.652
25 years	5.5	5.307	5.206	5.172	5.103	4.995	4.885	4.808	4.770	4.651	4.398	4.124	3.927
	6.0	5.822	5.729	5.697	5.633	5.535	5.433	5.364	5.328	5.220	4.991	4.744	4.567
	6.5	6.335	6.250	6.221	6.162	6.071	5.978	5.915	5.882	5.784	5.576	5.353	5.195
	7.0	6.848	6.769	6.742	6.688	6.605	6.520	6.462	6.433	6.343	6.154	5.953	5.811
	7.5	7.360	7.287	7.263	7.213	7.137	7.059	7.006	6.979	6.897	6.726	6.545	6.417
	8.0	7.871	7.804	7.782	7.736	7.667	7.595	7.547	7.523	7.448	7.293	7.129	7.014
	8.5	8.381	8.320	8.299	8.258	8.194	8.129	8.085	8.062	7.994	7.853	7.706	7.603
	9.0	8.891	8.834	8.816	8.777	8.719	8.660	8.620	8.599	8.537	8.409	8.276	8.183
	9.5	9.399	9.348	9.331	9.296	9.243	9.188	9.152	9.133	9.077	8.961	8.840	8.757
	10.0	9.908	9.861	9.845	9.813	9.764	9.715	9.681	9.664	9.613	9.508	9.399	9.324
	10.5	10.415	10.372	10.358	10.329	10.284	10.239	10.209	10.193	10.147	10.051	9.953	9.885
	11.0	10.922	10.883	10.870	10.843	10.803	10.761	10.734	10.720	10.677	10.591	10.502	10.440
	11.5	11.429	11.393	11.381	11.356	11.319	11.282	11.257	11.244	11.206	11.127	11.046	10.991
	12.0	11.935	11.902	11.891	11.869	11.835	11.801	11.778	11.767	11.732	11.660	11.587	11.538
	12.5	12.440	12.410	12.400	12.380	12.349	12.318	12.298	12.287	12.255	12.191	12.125	12.080
30 years	5.5	5.365	5.295	5.271	5.223	5.149	5.073	5.021	4.994	4.914	4.744	4.562	4.433
	6.0	5.877	5.814	5.792	5.749	5.682	5.614	5.567	5.544	5.471	5.320	5.160	5.047
	6.5	6.389	6.331	6.312	6.273	6.213	6.151	6.110	6.088	6.024	5.890	5.747	5.648
	7.0	6.899	6.847	6.830	6.795	6.741	6.686	6.648	6.629	6.572	6.452	6.326	6.239
	7.5	7.409	7.362	7.346	7.315	7.266	7.217	7.183	7.166	7.115	7.009	6.897	6.820
	8.0	7.918	7.876	7.861	7.833	7.789	7.745	7.715	7.700	7.654	7.560	7.461	7.393
	8.5	8.426	8.388	8.375	8.350	8.311	8.271	8.244	8.231	8.190	8.105	8.018	7.958
	9.0	8.933	8.899	8.888	8.865	8.830	8.794	8.770	8.758	8.722	8.647	8.570	8.517
	9.5	9.440	9.409	9.399	9.378	9.347	9.315	9.294	9.283	9.251	9.184	9.116	9.069
	10.0	9.946	9.918	9.909	9.891	9.863	9.835	9.815	9.806	9.777	9.718	9.657	9.616
	10.5	10.451	10.427	10.419	10.402	10.377	10.352	10.335	10.326	10.300	10.248	10.194	10.157
	11.0	10.956	10.934	10.927	10.912	10.890	10.867	10.852	10.845	10.822	10.775	10.727	10.695
	11.5	11.461	11.441	11.435	11.421	11.402	11.381	11.368	11.361	11.341	11.299	11.257	11.228
	12.0	11.965	11.947	11.942	11.930	11.912	11.894	11.882	11.876	11.858	11.821	11.783	11.758
	12.5	12.469	12.453	12.448	12.437	12.421	12.405	12.395	12.389	12.373	12.340	12.307	12.285

Entry is the Internal Rate of Return in percent per year. Negative returns may not be unique.

Purchase Price for a Given Yield

Desired Yield	Holding Period	Capitalization Rate									
		0.00%	2.00%	3.00%	4.00%	5.00%	5.50%	6.00%	6.50%	7.50%	8.00%
5.50%	1.0	94.7867	96.6825	97.6303	98.5782	99.5261	100.0000	100.4739	100.9479	101.8957	102.3697
	2.0	89.8453	93.5379	95.3842	97.2305	99.0768	100.0000	100.9232	101.8463	103.6926	104.6158
	3.0	85.1614	90.5572	93.2552	95.9531	98.6510	100.0000	101.3490	102.6979	105.3959	106.7448
	4.0	80.7217	87.7320	91.2371	94.7423	98.2474	100.0000	101.7526	103.5051	107.0103	108.7629
	5.0	76.5135	85.0540	89.3243	93.5946	97.8649	100.0000	102.1351	104.2703	108.5406	110.6757
	7.5	66.9279	78.9541	84.9672	90.9803	96.9934	100.0000	103.0066	106.0131	112.0262	115.0328
	10.0	58.5431	73.6183	81.1560	88.6936	96.2312	100.0000	103.7688	107.5376	115.0752	118.8440
	12.5	51.2089	68.9511	77.8222	86.6933	95.5644	100.0000	104.4356	108.8711	117.7422	122.1778
	15.0	44.7934	64.8685	74.9061	84.9436	94.9812	100.0000	105.0188	110.0376	120.0751	125.0939
6.00%	1.0	94.3396	96.2264	97.1698	98.1132	99.0566	99.5283	100.0000	100.4717	101.4151	101.8868
	2.0	88.9997	92.6664	94.4998	96.3332	98.1666	99.0833	100.0000	100.9167	102.7501	103.6668
	3.0	83.9619	89.3080	91.9810	94.6540	97.3270	98.6635	100.0000	101.3365	104.0095	105.3460
	4.0	79.2094	86.1396	89.6047	93.0698	96.5349	98.2674	100.0000	101.7326	105.1977	106.9302
	5.0	74.7258	83.1506	87.3629	91.5753	95.7876	97.8938	100.0000	102.1062	106.3185	108.4247
	7.5	64.5961	76.3974	82.2981	88.1987	94.0994	97.0497	100.0000	102.9503	108.8510	111.8013
	10.0	55.8395	70.5597	77.9198	85.2798	92.6399	96.3200	100.0000	103.6800	111.0401	114.7202
	12.5	48.2700	65.5134	74.1350	82.7567	91.3783	95.6892	100.0000	104.3108	112.9325	117.2433
	15.0	41.7265	61.1510	70.8633	80.5755	90.2878	95.1439	100.0000	104.8561	114.5684	119.4245
6.50%	1.0	93.8967	95.7746	96.7136	97.6526	98.5915	99.0610	99.5305	100.0000	100.9390	101.4085
	2.0	88.1659	91.8072	93.6278	95.4484	97.2691	98.1794	99.0897	100.0000	101.8206	102.7309
	3.0	82.7849	88.0818	90.7303	93.3788	96.0273	97.3515	98.6758	100.0000	102.6485	103.9727
	4.0	77.7323	84.5839	88.0097	91.4355	94.8613	96.5742	98.2871	100.0000	103.4258	105.1387
	5.0	72.9881	81.2994	85.4551	89.6108	93.7665	95.8443	97.9222	100.0000	104.1557	106.2335
	7.5	62.3560	73.9387	79.7301	85.5215	91.3129	94.2086	97.1043	100.0000	105.7914	108.6871
	10.0	53.2726	67.6502	74.8391	82.0279	89.2167	92.8112	96.4056	100.0000	107.1888	110.7833
	12.5	45.5124	62.2778	70.6605	79.0432	87.4259	91.6173	95.8086	100.0000	108.3827	112.5741
	15.0	38.8826	57.6880	67.0906	76.4933	85.8960	90.5973	95.2987	100.0000	109.4027	114.1040
7.00%	1.0	93.4579	95.3271	96.2617	97.1963	98.1308	98.5981	99.0654	99.5327	100.4673	100.9346
	2.0	87.3439	90.9599	92.7679	94.5759	96.3840	97.2880	98.1920	99.0960	100.9040	101.8080
	3.0	81.6298	86.8784	89.5027	92.1270	94.7514	96.0635	97.3757	98.6878	101.3122	102.6243
	4.0	76.2895	83.0639	86.4511	89.8384	93.2256	94.9192	96.6128	98.3064	101.6936	103.3872
	5.0	71.2986	79.4990	83.5992	87.6994	91.7996	93.8497	95.8998	97.9499	102.0501	104.1002
	7.5	60.2035	71.5740	77.2592	82.9444	88.6296	91.4722	94.3148	97.1574	102.8426	105.6852
	10.0	50.8349	64.8821	71.9057	78.9292	85.9528	89.4646	92.9764	96.4882	103.5118	107.0236
	12.5	42.9243	59.2317	67.3853	75.5390	83.6927	87.7695	91.8463	95.9232	104.0768	108.1537
	15.0	36.2446	54.4604	63.5683	72.6762	81.7842	86.3381	90.8921	95.4460	104.5540	109.1079
7.50%	1.0	93.0233	94.8837	95.8140	96.7442	97.6744	98.1395	98.6047	99.0698	100.0000	100.4651
	2.0	86.5333	90.1244	91.9200	93.7155	95.5111	96.4089	97.3067	98.2044	100.0000	100.8978
	3.0	80.4960	85.6971	88.2976	90.8982	93.4987	94.7989	96.0992	97.3995	100.0000	101.3003
	4.0	74.8800	81.5787	84.9280	88.2774	91.6267	93.3013	94.9760	96.6507	100.0000	101.6747
	5.0	69.6558	77.7476	81.7935	85.8394	89.8853	91.9082	93.9312	95.9541	100.0000	102.0229
	7.5	58.1348	69.2989	74.8809	80.4629	86.0449	88.8360	91.6270	94.4180	100.0000	102.7910
	10.0	48.5194	62.2475	69.1116	75.9757	82.8398	86.2718	89.7039	93.1359	100.0000	103.4320
	12.5	40.4943	56.3625	64.2966	72.2307	80.1648	84.1318	88.0989	92.0659	100.0000	103.9670
	15.0	33.7966	51.4508	60.2779	69.1051	77.9322	82.3458	86.7593	91.1729	100.0000	104.4136
8.00%	1.0	92.5926	94.4444	95.3704	96.2963	97.2222	97.6852	98.1481	98.6111	99.5370	100.0000
	2.0	85.7339	89.3004	91.0837	92.8669	94.6502	95.5418	96.4335	97.3251	99.1084	100.0000
	3.0	79.3832	84.5374	87.1145	89.6916	92.2687	93.5573	94.8458	96.1344	98.7115	100.0000
	4.0	73.5030	80.1272	83.4394	86.7515	90.0636	91.7197	93.3757	95.0318	98.3439	100.0000
	5.0	68.0583	76.0437	80.0364	84.0292	88.0219	90.0182	92.0146	94.0109	98.0036	100.0000
	7.5	56.1464	67.1098	72.5915	78.0732	83.5549	86.2957	89.0366	91.7774	97.2591	100.0000
	10.0	46.3193	59.7395	66.4496	73.1597	79.8697	83.2248	86.5798	89.9349	96.6450	100.0000
	12.5	38.2123	53.6592	61.3827	69.1061	76.8296	80.6913	84.5531	88.4148	96.1383	100.0000
	15.0	31.5242	48.6431	57.2026	65.7621	74.3216	78.6013	82.8810	87.1608	95.7203	100.0000
8.50%	1.0	92.1659	94.0092	94.9309	95.8525	96.7742	97.2350	97.6959	98.1567	99.0783	99.5392
	2.0	84.9455	88.4878	90.2589	92.0300	93.8011	94.6867	95.5722	96.4578	98.2289	99.1144
	3.0	78.2908	83.3988	85.9529	88.5069	91.0609	92.3379	93.6149	94.8920	97.4460	98.7230
	4.0	72.1574	78.7086	81.9842	85.2598	88.5354	90.1732	91.8110	93.4488	96.7244	98.3622
	5.0	66.5045	74.3858	78.3265	82.2671	86.2077	88.1781	90.1484	92.1187	96.0594	98.0297
	7.5	54.2347	65.0030	70.3871	75.7713	81.1554	83.8475	86.5396	89.2317	94.6158	97.3079
	10.0	44.2285	57.3512	63.9126	70.4739	77.0353	80.3159	83.5966	86.8773	93.4386	96.7193
	12.5	36.0685	51.1112	58.6326	66.1539	73.6753	77.4359	81.1966	84.9573	92.4786	96.2393
	15.0	29.4140	46.0224	54.3267	62.6309	70.9352	75.0873	79.2394	83.3915	91.6958	95.8479
9.00%	1.0	91.7431	93.5780	94.4954	95.4128	96.3303	96.7890	97.2477	97.7064	98.6239	99.0826
	2.0	84.1680	87.6862	89.4453	91.2044	92.9636	93.8431	94.7227	95.6022	97.3613	98.2409
	3.0	77.2183	82.2809	84.8122	87.3435	89.8748	91.1405	92.4061	93.6718	96.2031	97.4687
	4.0	70.8425	77.3220	80.5617	83.8014	87.0411	88.6610	90.2808	91.9007	95.1404	96.7603
	5.0	64.9931	72.7724	76.6621	80.5517	84.4414	86.3862	88.3310	90.2759	94.1655	96.1103
	7.5	52.3964	62.9750	68.2643	73.5536	78.8428	81.4875	84.1321	86.7768	92.0661	94.7107
	10.0	42.2411	55.0764	61.4940	67.9117	74.3294	77.5382	80.7470	83.9559	90.3735	93.5823
	12.5	34.0541	48.7087	56.0360	63.3634	70.6907	74.3544	78.0180	81.6817	89.0090	92.6727
	15.0	27.4538	43.5752	51.6359	59.6965	67.7572	71.7876	75.8179	79.8483	87.9090	91.9393

Entry is the percentage of future sale price to give desired yield.

Purchase Price for a Given Yield

Desired Yield	Holding Period	8.50%	9.00%	9.50%	10.00%	10.50%	11.00%	11.50%	12.00%	12.50%	15.00%
					Capitalization Rate						
5.50%	1.0	102.8436	103.3175	103.7915	104.2654	104.7393	105.2133	105.6872	106.1611	106.6351	109.0047
	2.0	105.5390	106.4621	107.3853	108.3084	109.2316	110.1547	111.0779	112.0011	112.9242	117.5400
	3.0	108.0938	109.4428	110.7917	112.1407	113.4896	114.8386	116.1876	117.5365	118.8855	125.6303
	4.0	110.5154	112.2680	114.0206	115.7732	117.5257	119.2783	121.0309	122.7834	124.5360	133.2989
	5.0	112.8108	114.9460	117.0811	119.2163	121.3514	123.4865	125.6217	127.7568	129.8920	140.5677
	7.5	118.0393	121.0459	124.0525	127.0590	130.0656	133.0721	136.0787	139.0852	142.0918	157.1246
	10.0	122.6129	126.3817	130.1505	133.9193	137.6881	141.4569	145.2257	148.9945	152.7633	171.6074
	12.5	126.6134	131.0489	135.4845	139.9200	144.3556	148.7911	153.2267	157.6623	162.0978	184.2756
	15.0	130.1127	135.1315	140.1503	145.1691	150.1879	155.2066	160.2254	165.2442	170.2630	195.3569
6.00%	1.0	102.3585	102.8302	103.3019	103.7736	104.2453	104.7170	105.1887	105.6604	106.1321	108.4906
	2.0	104.5835	105.5002	106.4169	107.3336	108.2503	109.1670	110.0837	111.0003	111.9170	116.5005
	3.0	106.6825	108.0190	109.3555	110.6920	112.0285	113.3651	114.7016	116.0381	117.3746	124.0571
	4.0	108.6628	110.3953	112.1279	113.8604	115.5930	117.3255	119.0581	120.7906	122.5232	131.1859
	5.0	110.5309	112.6371	114.7433	116.8494	118.9556	121.0618	123.1680	125.2742	127.3803	137.9112
	7.5	114.7516	117.7019	120.6522	123.6026	126.5529	129.5032	132.4535	135.4039	138.3542	153.1058
	10.0	118.4002	122.0802	125.7603	129.4403	133.1204	136.8004	140.4805	144.1605	147.8405	166.2407
	12.5	121.5541	125.8650	130.1758	134.4866	138.7975	143.1083	147.4191	151.7300	156.0408	177.5949
	15.0	124.2806	129.1367	133.9929	138.8490	143.7051	148.5612	153.4173	158.2735	163.1296	187.4102
6.50%	1.0	101.8779	102.3474	102.8169	103.2864	103.7559	104.2254	104.6948	105.1643	105.6338	107.9812
	2.0	103.6413	104.5516	105.4619	106.3722	107.2825	108.1928	109.1031	110.0135	110.9238	115.4753
	3.0	105.2970	106.6212	107.9454	109.2697	110.5939	111.9182	113.2424	114.5666	115.8909	122.5121
	4.0	106.8516	108.5645	110.2774	111.9903	113.7032	115.4161	117.1290	118.8419	120.5548	129.1193
	5.0	108.3114	110.3892	112.4670	114.5449	116.6227	118.7006	120.7784	122.8563	124.9341	135.3233
	7.5	111.5828	114.4785	117.3742	120.2699	123.1656	126.0613	128.9570	131.8527	134.7484	149.2268
	10.0	114.3777	117.9721	121.5665	125.1609	128.7553	132.3498	135.9442	139.5386	143.1330	161.1051
	12.5	116.7654	120.9568	125.1481	129.3395	133.5308	137.7222	141.9135	146.1049	150.2962	171.2530
	15.0	118.8053	123.5067	128.2080	132.9094	137.6107	142.3120	147.0134	151.7147	156.4160	179.9227
7.00%	1.0	101.4019	101.8692	102.3365	102.8037	103.2710	103.7383	104.2056	104.6729	105.1402	107.4766
	2.0	102.7120	103.6160	104.5200	105.4241	106.3281	107.2321	108.1361	109.0401	109.9441	114.4642
	3.0	103.9365	105.2486	106.5608	107.8730	109.1851	110.4973	111.8094	113.1216	114.4337	120.9945
	4.0	105.0808	106.7744	108.4680	110.1616	111.8552	113.5489	115.2425	116.9361	118.6297	127.0977
	5.0	106.1503	108.2004	110.2505	112.3006	114.3507	116.4008	118.4509	120.5010	122.5511	132.8016
	7.5	108.5278	111.3704	114.2130	117.0556	119.8982	122.7408	125.5834	128.4260	131.2686	145.4817
	10.0	110.5354	114.0472	117.5590	121.0708	124.5825	128.0943	131.6061	135.1179	138.6297	156.1887
	12.5	112.2305	116.3073	120.3842	124.4610	128.5378	132.6147	136.6915	140.7683	144.8452	165.2294
	15.0	113.6619	118.2158	122.7698	127.3238	131.8777	136.4317	140.9856	145.5396	150.0935	172.8633
7.50%	1.0	100.9302	101.3953	101.8605	102.3256	102.7907	103.2558	103.7209	104.1860	104.6512	106.9767
	2.0	101.7956	102.6933	103.5911	104.4889	105.3867	106.2845	107.1823	108.0800	108.9778	113.4667
	3.0	102.6005	103.9008	105.2011	106.5013	107.8016	109.1018	110.4021	111.7024	113.0026	119.5040
	4.0	103.3493	105.0240	106.6987	108.3733	110.0480	111.7226	113.3973	115.0720	116.7466	125.1200
	5.0	104.0459	106.0688	108.0918	110.1147	112.1377	114.1606	116.1835	118.2065	120.2294	130.3442
	7.5	105.5820	108.3730	111.1640	113.9551	116.7461	119.5371	122.3281	125.1191	127.9101	141.8652
	10.0	106.8641	110.2961	113.7282	117.1602	120.5922	124.0243	127.4563	130.8884	134.3204	151.4806
	12.5	107.9341	111.9011	115.8682	119.8352	123.8023	127.7693	131.7364	135.7034	139.6705	159.5057
	15.0	108.8271	113.2407	117.6542	122.0678	126.4814	130.8949	135.3085	139.7221	144.1356	166.2034
8.00%	1.0	100.4630	100.9259	101.3889	101.8519	102.3148	102.7778	103.2407	103.7037	104.1667	106.4815
	2.0	100.8916	101.7833	102.6749	103.5665	104.4582	105.3498	106.2414	107.1331	108.0247	112.4829
	3.0	101.2885	102.5771	103.8656	105.1542	106.4427	107.7313	109.0198	110.3084	111.5969	118.0397
	4.0	101.6561	103.3121	104.9682	106.6243	108.2803	109.9364	111.5924	113.2485	114.9046	123.1849
	5.0	101.9964	103.9927	105.9891	107.9854	109.9818	111.9781	113.9745	115.9708	117.9672	127.9490
	7.5	102.7409	105.4817	108.2226	110.9634	113.7043	116.4451	119.1860	121.9268	124.6677	138.3719
	10.0	103.3550	106.7101	110.0651	113.4202	116.7752	120.1303	123.4853	126.8403	130.1954	146.9706
	12.5	103.8617	107.7235	111.5852	115.4469	119.3087	123.1704	127.0321	130.8939	134.7556	154.0642
	15.0	104.2797	108.5595	112.8392	117.1190	121.3987	125.6784	129.9582	134.2379	138.5177	159.9164
8.50%	1.0	100.0000	100.4608	100.9217	101.3825	101.8433	102.3041	102.7650	103.2258	103.6866	105.9908
	2.0	100.0000	100.8856	101.7711	102.6567	103.5422	104.4278	105.3133	106.1989	107.0845	111.5122
	3.0	100.0000	101.2770	102.5540	103.8310	105.1080	106.3851	107.6621	108.9391	110.2161	116.6012
	4.0	100.0000	101.6378	103.2756	104.9134	106.5512	108.1890	109.8268	111.4646	113.1024	121.2914
	5.0	100.0000	101.9703	103.9406	105.9110	107.8813	109.8516	111.8219	113.7923	115.7626	125.6142
	7.5	100.0000	102.6921	105.3842	108.0762	110.7683	113.4604	116.1525	118.8446	121.5366	134.9970
	10.0	100.0000	103.2807	106.5614	109.8420	113.1227	116.4034	119.6841	122.9647	126.2454	142.6488
	12.5	100.0000	103.7607	107.5214	111.2820	115.0427	118.8034	122.5641	126.3247	130.0854	148.8888
	15.0	100.0000	104.1521	108.3042	112.4564	116.6085	120.7606	124.9127	129.0648	133.2170	153.9776
9.00%	1.0	99.5413	100.0000	100.4587	100.9174	101.3761	101.8349	102.2936	102.7523	103.2110	105.5046
	2.0	99.1204	100.0000	100.8796	101.7591	102.6387	103.5182	104.3978	105.2773	106.1569	110.5547
	3.0	98.7344	100.0000	101.2656	102.5313	103.7969	105.0626	106.3282	107.5939	108.8595	115.1878
	4.0	98.3801	100.0000	101.6199	103.2397	104.8596	106.4794	108.0993	109.7192	111.3390	119.4383
	5.0	98.0552	100.0000	101.9448	103.8897	105.8345	107.7793	109.7241	111.6690	113.6138	123.3379
	7.5	97.3554	100.0000	102.6446	105.2893	107.9339	110.5786	113.2232	115.8679	118.5125	131.7357
	10.0	96.7912	100.0000	103.2088	106.4177	109.6265	112.8353	116.0441	119.2530	122.4618	138.5060
	12.5	96.3363	100.0000	103.6637	107.3273	110.9910	114.6547	118.3183	121.9820	125.6456	143.9640
	15.0	95.9697	100.0000	104.0303	108.0607	112.0910	116.1214	120.1517	124.1821	128.2124	148.3641

Entry is the percentage of future sale price to give desired yield.

Purchase Price for a Given Yield

Desired Yield	Holding Period	Capitalization Rate 0.00%	2.00%	3.00%	4.00%	5.00%	5.50%	6.00%	6.50%	7.50%	8.00%
9.50%	1.0	91.3242	93.1507	94.0639	94.9772	95.8904	96.3470	96.8037	97.2603	98.1735	98.6301
	2.0	83.4011	86.8956	88.6429	90.3901	92.1374	93.0110	93.8846	94.7582	96.5055	97.3791
	3.0	76.1654	81.1832	83.6921	86.2010	88.7099	89.9644	91.2188	92.4733	94.9822	96.2366
	4.0	69.5574	75.9664	79.1709	82.3754	85.5798	87.1821	88.7843	90.3866	93.5910	95.1933
	5.0	63.5228	71.2022	75.0419	78.8816	82.7213	84.6412	86.5610	88.4809	92.3206	94.2404
	7.5	50.6284	61.0224	66.2194	71.4164	76.6135	79.2120	81.8105	84.4090	89.6060	92.2045
	10.0	40.3514	52.9090	59.1878	65.4666	71.7454	74.8848	78.0242	81.1636	87.4424	90.5818
	12.5	32.1606	46.4425	53.5835	60.7245	67.8655	71.4360	75.0065	78.5770	85.7180	89.2885
	15.0	25.6323	41.2887	49.1169	56.9450	64.7732	68.6873	72.6014	76.5155	84.3436	88.2577
10.00%	1.0	90.9091	92.7273	93.6364	94.5455	95.4545	95.9091	96.3636	96.8182	97.7273	98.1818
	2.0	82.6446	86.1157	87.8512	89.5868	91.3223	92.1901	93.0579	93.9256	95.6612	96.5289
	3.0	75.1315	80.1052	82.5920	85.0789	87.5657	88.8092	90.0526	91.2960	93.7829	95.0263
	4.0	68.3013	74.6411	77.8109	80.9808	84.1507	85.7356	87.3205	88.9055	92.0753	93.6603
	5.0	62.0921	69.6737	73.4645	77.2553	81.0461	82.9415	84.8369	86.7322	90.5230	92.4184
	7.5	48.9277	59.1422	64.2494	69.3566	74.4639	77.0175	79.5711	82.1247	87.2319	89.7855
	10.0	38.5543	50.8435	56.9880	63.1326	69.2772	72.3494	75.4217	78.4940	84.6386	87.7109
	12.5	30.3803	44.3042	51.2662	58.2282	65.1901	68.6711	72.1521	75.6331	82.5951	86.0761
	15.0	23.9392	39.1514	46.7574	54.3635	61.9696	65.7726	69.5757	73.3787	80.9848	84.7878
10.50%	1.0	90.4977	92.3077	93.2127	94.1176	95.0226	95.4751	95.9276	96.3801	97.2851	97.7376
	2.0	81.8984	85.3463	87.0703	88.7943	90.5182	91.3802	92.2422	93.1042	94.8281	95.6901
	3.0	74.1162	79.0464	81.5116	83.9767	86.4418	87.6744	88.9069	90.1395	92.6046	93.8372
	4.0	67.0735	73.3452	76.4811	79.6169	82.7528	84.3207	85.8886	87.4566	90.5924	92.1604
	5.0	60.7000	68.1857	71.9286	75.6714	79.4143	81.2857	83.1571	85.0286	88.7714	90.6429
	7.5	47.2915	57.3312	62.3511	67.3709	72.3908	74.9007	77.4106	79.9206	84.9404	87.4504
	10.0	36.8449	48.8744	54.8892	60.9040	66.9187	69.9261	72.9335	75.9409	81.9557	84.9631
	12.5	28.7059	42.2857	49.0757	55.8656	62.6555	66.0504	69.4454	72.8404	79.6303	83.0252
	15.0	22.3648	37.1525	44.5463	51.9401	59.3340	63.0309	66.7278	70.4247	77.8185	81.5154
11.00%	1.0	90.0901	91.8919	92.7928	93.6937	94.5946	95.0450	95.4955	95.9459	96.8468	97.2973
	2.0	81.1622	84.5873	86.2998	88.0123	89.7249	90.5811	91.4374	92.2936	94.0062	94.8624
	3.0	73.1191	78.0066	80.4503	82.8940	85.3377	86.5596	87.7814	89.0033	91.4470	92.6689
	4.0	65.8731	72.0780	75.1804	78.2829	81.3853	82.9365	84.4878	86.0390	89.1414	90.6927
	5.0	59.3451	66.7369	70.4328	74.1287	77.8246	79.6726	81.5205	83.3685	87.0644	88.9123
	7.5	45.7170	55.5866	60.5215	65.4563	70.3911	72.8585	75.3259	77.7933	82.7281	85.1955
	10.0	35.2184	46.9969	52.8861	58.7754	64.6646	67.6092	70.5538	73.4985	79.3877	82.3323
	12.5	27.1308	40.3798	47.0042	53.6287	60.2532	63.5654	66.8776	70.1899	76.8144	80.1266
	15.0	20.9004	35.2822	42.4730	49.6639	56.8548	60.4502	64.0457	67.6411	74.8320	78.4274
11.50%	1.0	89.6861	91.4798	92.3767	93.2735	94.1704	94.6188	95.0673	95.5157	96.4126	96.8610
	2.0	80.4360	83.8384	85.5396	87.2408	88.9421	89.7927	90.6433	91.4939	93.1951	94.0457
	3.0	72.1399	76.9851	79.4077	81.8304	84.2530	85.4643	86.6756	87.8869	90.3095	91.5208
	4.0	64.6994	70.8387	73.9083	76.9779	80.0475	81.5823	83.1171	84.6519	87.7215	89.2564
	5.0	58.0264	65.3262	68.9760	72.6259	76.2758	78.1007	79.9257	81.7506	85.4005	87.2254
	7.5	44.2017	53.9057	58.7578	63.6098	68.4618	70.8878	73.3138	75.7399	80.5919	83.0179
	10.0	33.6706	45.2062	50.9740	56.7417	62.5095	65.3934	68.2773	71.1611	76.9289	79.8128
	12.5	25.6486	38.5793	45.0447	51.5100	57.9753	61.2080	64.4407	67.6733	74.1387	77.3713
	15.0	19.5379	33.5313	40.5280	47.5247	54.5214	58.0198	61.5181	65.0165	72.0132	75.5115
12.00%	1.0	89.2857	91.0714	91.9643	92.8571	93.7500	94.1964	94.6429	95.0893	95.9821	96.4286
	2.0	79.7194	83.0995	84.7895	86.4796	88.1696	89.0147	89.8597	90.7047	92.3948	93.2398
	3.0	71.1780	75.9817	78.3835	80.7854	83.1872	84.3881	85.5890	86.7899	89.1918	90.3927
	4.0	63.5518	69.6265	72.6639	75.7012	78.7386	80.2572	81.7759	83.2946	86.3319	87.8506
	5.0	56.7427	63.9522	67.5570	71.1618	74.7666	76.5690	78.3713	80.1737	83.7785	85.5809
	7.5	42.7430	52.2858	57.0573	61.8287	66.6001	68.9858	71.3715	73.7572	78.5286	80.9143
	10.0	32.1973	43.4978	49.1480	54.7982	60.4484	63.2736	66.0987	68.9238	74.5740	77.3991
	12.5	24.2535	36.8780	43.1902	49.5024	55.8146	58.9707	62.1268	65.2829	71.5951	74.7512
	15.0	18.2696	31.8914	38.7022	45.5131	52.3239	55.7294	59.1348	62.5402	69.3511	72.7565
12.50%	1.0	88.8889	90.6667	91.5556	92.4444	93.3333	93.7778	94.2222	94.6667	95.5556	96.0000
	2.0	79.0123	82.3704	84.0494	85.7284	87.4074	88.2469	89.0864	89.9259	91.6049	92.4444
	3.0	70.2332	74.9959	77.3772	79.7586	82.1399	83.3306	84.5213	85.7119	88.0933	89.2840
	4.0	62.4295	68.4408	71.4464	74.4521	77.4577	78.9605	80.4633	81.9662	84.9718	86.4746
	5.0	55.4929	62.6140	66.1746	69.7352	73.2957	75.0760	76.8563	78.6366	82.1972	83.9774
	7.5	41.3387	50.7245	55.4174	60.1103	64.8032	67.1497	69.4961	71.8426	76.5355	78.8819
	10.0	30.7946	41.8675	47.4039	52.9403	58.4768	61.2450	64.0132	66.7814	72.3178	75.0861
	12.5	22.9400	35.2696	41.4344	47.5992	53.7640	56.8464	59.9288	63.0112	69.1760	72.2584
	15.0	17.0888	30.3546	36.9875	43.6204	50.2533	53.5697	56.8862	60.2026	66.8355	70.1520
13.00%	1.0	88.4956	90.2655	91.1504	92.0354	92.9204	93.3628	93.8053	94.2478	95.1327	95.5752
	2.0	78.3147	81.6509	83.3190	84.9871	86.6552	87.4892	88.3233	89.1573	90.8254	91.6595
	3.0	69.3050	74.0273	76.3885	78.7496	81.1108	82.2914	83.4719	84.6525	87.0137	88.1942
	4.0	61.3319	67.2808	70.2553	73.2298	76.2042	77.6915	79.1787	80.6659	83.6404	85.1276
	5.0	54.2760	61.3105	64.8277	68.3449	71.8622	73.6208	75.3794	77.1380	80.6552	82.4138
	7.5	39.9864	49.2192	53.8357	58.4521	63.0685	65.3768	67.6850	69.9932	74.6096	76.9178
	10.0	29.4588	40.3113	45.7376	51.1638	56.5901	59.3032	62.0163	64.7294	70.1557	72.8688
	12.5	21.7030	33.7487	39.7715	45.7944	51.8172	54.8287	57.8401	60.8515	66.8744	69.8858
	15.0	15.9891	28.9138	35.3762	41.8386	48.3010	51.5322	54.7634	57.9945	64.4569	67.6881

Entry is the percentage of future sale price to give desired yield.

Purchase Price for a Given Yield

Desired Yield	Holding Period	Capitalization Rate									
		8.50%	9.00%	9.50%	10.00%	10.50%	11.00%	11.50%	12.00%	12.50%	15.00%
9.50%	1.0	99.0868	99.5434	100.0000	100.4566	100.9132	101.3699	101.8265	102.2831	102.7397	105.0228
	2.0	98.2527	99.1264	100.0000	100.8736	101.7473	102.6209	103.4945	104.3681	105.2418	109.6099
	3.0	97.4911	98.7455	100.0000	101.2545	102.5089	103.7634	105.0178	106.2723	107.5267	113.7990
	4.0	96.7955	98.3978	100.0000	101.6022	103.2045	104.8067	106.4090	108.0112	109.6134	117.6246
	5.0	96.1603	98.0801	100.0000	101.9199	103.8397	105.7596	107.6794	109.5993	111.5191	121.1184
	7.5	94.8030	97.4015	100.0000	102.5985	105.1970	107.7955	110.3940	112.9925	115.5910	128.5836
	10.0	93.7212	96.8606	100.0000	103.1394	106.2788	109.4182	112.5576	115.6970	118.8364	134.5334
	12.5	92.8590	96.4295	100.0000	103.5705	107.1410	110.7115	114.2820	117.8525	121.4230	139.2755
	15.0	92.1718	96.0859	100.0000	103.9141	107.8282	111.7423	115.6564	119.5704	123.4845	143.0550
10.00%	1.0	98.6364	99.0909	99.5455	100.0000	100.4545	100.9091	101.3636	101.8182	102.2727	104.5455
	2.0	97.3967	98.2645	99.1322	100.0000	100.8678	101.7355	102.6033	103.4711	104.3388	108.6777
	3.0	96.2697	97.5131	98.7566	100.0000	101.2434	102.4869	103.7303	104.9737	106.2171	112.4343
	4.0	95.2452	96.8301	98.4151	100.0000	101.5849	103.1699	104.7548	106.3397	107.9247	115.8493
	5.0	94.3138	96.2092	98.1046	100.0000	101.8954	103.7908	105.6862	107.5816	109.4770	118.9539
	7.5	92.3392	94.8928	97.4464	100.0000	102.5536	105.1072	107.6608	110.2145	112.7681	125.5361
	10.0	90.7831	93.8554	96.9277	100.0000	103.0723	106.1446	109.2169	112.2891	115.3614	130.7228
	12.5	89.5570	93.0380	96.5190	100.0000	103.4810	106.9620	110.4430	113.9239	117.4049	134.8099
	15.0	88.5909	92.3939	96.1970	100.0000	103.8030	107.6061	111.4091	115.2122	119.0152	138.0304
10.50%	1.0	98.1900	98.6425	99.0950	99.5475	100.0000	100.4525	100.9050	101.3575	101.8100	104.0724
	2.0	96.5521	97.4141	98.2760	99.1380	100.0000	100.8620	101.7240	102.5859	103.4479	107.7578
	3.0	95.0698	96.3023	97.5349	98.7674	100.0000	101.2326	102.4651	103.6977	104.9302	111.0931
	4.0	93.7283	95.2962	96.8641	98.4321	100.0000	101.5679	103.1359	104.7038	106.2717	114.1114
	5.0	92.5143	94.3857	96.2571	98.1286	100.0000	101.8714	103.7429	105.6143	107.4857	116.8429
	7.5	89.9603	92.4702	94.9801	97.4901	100.0000	102.5099	105.0199	107.5298	110.0397	122.5894
	10.0	87.9705	90.9778	93.9852	96.9926	100.0000	103.0074	106.0148	109.0222	112.0295	127.0665
	12.5	86.4202	89.8151	93.2101	96.6050	100.0000	103.3950	106.7899	110.1849	113.5798	130.5546
	15.0	85.2124	88.9093	92.6062	96.3031	100.0000	103.6969	107.3938	111.0907	114.7876	133.2722
11.00%	1.0	97.7477	98.1982	98.6486	99.0991	99.5495	100.0000	100.4505	100.9009	101.3514	103.6036
	2.0	95.7187	96.5750	97.4312	98.2875	99.1437	100.0000	100.8563	101.7125	102.5688	106.8501
	3.0	93.8907	95.1126	96.3344	97.5563	98.7781	100.0000	101.2219	102.4437	103.6656	109.7749
	4.0	92.2439	93.7951	95.3463	96.8976	98.4488	100.0000	101.5512	103.1024	104.6537	112.4098
	5.0	90.7603	92.6082	94.4562	96.3041	98.1521	100.0000	101.8479	103.6959	105.5438	114.7836
	7.5	87.6630	90.1304	92.5978	95.0652	97.5326	100.0000	102.4674	104.9348	107.4022	119.7393
	10.0	85.2769	88.2215	91.1662	94.1108	97.0554	100.0000	102.9446	105.8892	108.8338	123.5569
	12.5	83.4388	86.7511	90.0633	93.3755	96.6878	100.0000	103.3122	106.6245	109.9367	126.4979
	15.0	82.0228	85.6183	89.2137	92.8091	96.4046	100.0000	103.5954	107.1909	110.7863	128.7635
11.50%	1.0	97.3094	97.7578	98.2063	98.6547	99.1031	99.5516	100.0000	100.4484	100.8969	103.1390
	2.0	94.8963	95.7469	96.5976	97.4482	98.2988	99.1494	100.0000	100.8506	101.7012	105.9543
	3.0	92.7321	93.9435	95.1548	96.3661	97.5774	98.7887	100.0000	101.2113	102.4226	108.4792
	4.0	90.7912	92.3260	93.8608	95.3956	96.9304	98.4652	100.0000	101.5348	103.0696	110.7436
	5.0	89.0504	90.8753	92.7002	94.5252	96.3501	98.1751	100.0000	101.8249	103.6499	112.7746
	7.5	85.4439	87.8699	90.2959	92.7220	95.1480	97.5740	100.0000	102.4260	104.8520	116.9821
	10.0	82.6967	85.5806	88.4645	91.3483	94.2322	97.1161	100.0000	102.8839	105.7678	120.1872
	12.5	80.6040	83.8367	87.0693	90.3020	93.5347	96.7673	100.0000	103.2327	106.4653	122.6287
	15.0	79.0099	82.5082	86.0066	89.5049	93.0033	96.5016	100.0000	103.4984	106.9967	124.4885
12.00%	1.0	96.8750	97.3214	97.7679	98.2143	98.6607	99.1071	99.5536	100.0000	100.4464	102.6786
	2.0	94.0848	94.9298	95.7749	96.6199	97.4649	98.3099	99.1550	100.0000	100.8450	105.0702
	3.0	91.5936	92.7945	93.9954	95.1963	96.3973	97.5982	98.7991	100.0000	101.2009	107.2055
	4.0	89.3693	90.8880	92.4066	93.9253	95.4440	96.9627	98.4813	100.0000	101.5187	109.1120
	5.0	87.3833	89.1857	90.9881	92.7904	94.5928	96.3952	98.1976	100.0000	101.8024	110.8143
	7.5	83.3000	85.6858	88.0715	90.4572	92.8429	95.2286	97.6143	100.0000	102.3857	114.3142
	10.0	80.2242	83.0493	85.8744	88.6996	91.5247	94.3498	97.1749	100.0000	102.8251	116.9507
	12.5	77.9073	81.0634	84.2195	87.3756	90.5317	93.6878	96.8439	100.0000	103.1561	118.9366
	15.0	76.1620	79.5674	82.9728	86.3783	89.7837	93.1891	96.5946	100.0000	103.4054	120.4326
12.50%	1.0	96.4444	96.8889	97.3333	97.7778	98.2222	98.6667	99.1111	99.5556	100.0000	102.2222
	2.0	93.2840	94.1235	94.9630	95.8025	96.6420	97.4815	98.3210	99.1605	100.0000	104.1975
	3.0	90.4746	91.6653	92.8560	94.0466	95.2373	96.4280	97.6187	98.8093	100.0000	105.9534
	4.0	87.9774	89.4803	90.9831	92.4859	93.9887	95.4915	96.9944	98.4972	100.0000	107.5141
	5.0	85.7577	87.5380	89.3183	91.0986	92.8789	94.6591	96.4394	98.2197	100.0000	108.9014
	7.5	81.2284	83.5748	85.9213	88.2677	90.6142	92.9606	95.3071	97.6535	100.0000	111.7323
	10.0	77.8543	80.6225	83.3907	86.1589	88.9271	91.6954	94.4636	97.2318	100.0000	113.8411
	12.5	75.3408	78.4232	81.5056	84.5880	87.6704	90.7528	93.8352	96.9176	100.0000	115.4120
	15.0	73.4684	76.7849	80.1013	83.4178	86.7342	90.0507	93.3671	96.6836	100.0000	116.5822
13.00%	1.0	96.0177	96.4602	96.9027	97.3451	97.7876	98.2301	98.6726	99.1150	99.5575	101.7699
	2.0	92.4935	93.3276	94.1616	94.9957	95.8297	96.6638	97.4978	98.3319	99.1659	103.3362
	3.0	89.3748	90.5554	91.7360	92.9165	94.0971	95.2777	96.4583	97.6388	98.8194	104.7223
	4.0	86.6149	88.1021	89.5894	91.0766	92.5638	94.0511	95.5383	97.0255	98.5128	105.9489
	5.0	84.1725	85.9311	87.6897	89.4483	91.2069	92.9655	94.7242	96.4828	98.2414	107.0345
	7.5	79.2261	81.5343	83.8425	86.1507	88.4589	90.7671	93.0754	95.3836	97.6918	109.2329
	10.0	75.5819	78.2950	81.0082	83.7213	86.4344	89.1475	91.8606	94.5738	97.2869	110.8525
	12.5	72.8972	75.9086	78.9200	81.9315	84.9429	87.9543	90.9657	93.9772	96.9886	112.0457
	15.0	70.9193	74.1505	77.3817	80.6129	83.8441	87.0752	90.3064	93.5376	96.7688	112.9248

Entry is the percentage of future sale price to give desired yield.

Net Present Value of an Investment

Discount Rate 9.50%

Holding Period	Capitalization Rate	Capital Gain on Sale of Property 25%	33%	40%	50%	67%	75%	100%	150%	200%	300%
	5.5	99.705	104.897	109.050	115.281	125.665	130.857	146.433	177.585	208.738	271.043
	6.0	101.688	106.881	111.034	117.265	127.649	132.841	148.417	179.569	210.722	273.027
	6.5	103.672	108.864	113.018	119.249	129.633	134.825	150.401	181.553	212.706	275.011
	7.0	105.656	110.848	115.002	121.233	131.617	136.809	152.385	183.537	214.690	276.995
	7.5	107.640	112.832	116.986	123.217	133.601	138.793	154.369	185.521	216.674	278.978
5 years	8.0	109.624	114.816	118.970	125.201	135.585	140.777	156.353	187.505	218.658	280.962
	8.5	111.608	116.800	120.954	127.184	137.569	142.761	158.337	189.489	220.642	282.946
	9.0	113.592	118.784	122.938	129.168	139.553	144.745	160.321	191.473	222.626	284.930
	9.5	115.576	120.768	124.922	131.152	141.537	146.729	162.305	193.457	224.610	286.914
	10.0	117.560	122.752	126.906	133.136	143.520	148.713	164.289	195.441	226.593	288.898
	10.5	119.544	124.736	128.890	135.120	145.504	150.696	166.273	197.425	228.577	290.882
	11.0	121.528	126.720	130.874	137.104	147.488	152.680	168.257	199.409	230.561	292.866
	11.5	123.512	128.704	132.858	139.088	149.472	154.664	170.241	201.393	232.545	294.850
	12.0	125.496	130.688	134.842	141.072	151.456	156.648	172.225	203.377	234.529	296.834
	12.5	127.480	132.672	136.826	143.056	153.440	158.632	174.209	205.361	236.513	298.818
	5.5	89.372	93.280	96.408	101.098	108.916	112.825	124.551	148.005	171.458	218.365
	6.0	92.166	96.075	99.202	103.893	111.710	115.619	127.346	150.799	174.252	221.159
	6.5	94.960	98.869	101.996	106.687	114.505	118.414	130.140	153.594	177.047	223.953
	7.0	97.755	101.664	104.791	109.481	117.299	121.208	132.935	156.388	179.841	226.748
	7.5	100.549	104.458	107.585	112.276	120.094	124.002	135.729	159.182	182.636	229.542
8 years	8.0	103.343	107.252	110.379	115.070	122.888	126.797	138.523	161.977	185.430	232.337
	8.5	106.138	110.047	113.174	117.865	125.682	129.591	141.318	164.771	188.224	235.131
	9.0	108.932	112.841	115.968	120.659	128.477	132.386	144.112	167.566	191.019	237.925
	9.5	111.727	115.636	118.763	123.453	131.271	135.180	146.907	170.360	193.813	240.720
	10.0	114.521	118.430	121.557	126.248	134.065	137.974	149.701	173.154	196.608	243.514
	10.5	117.315	121.224	124.351	129.042	136.860	140.769	152.495	175.949	199.402	246.309
	11.0	120.110	124.019	127.146	131.836	139.654	143.563	155.290	178.743	202.196	249.103
	11.5	122.904	126.813	129.940	134.631	142.449	146.358	158.084	181.537	204.991	251.897
	12.0	125.699	129.607	132.735	137.425	145.243	149.152	160.879	184.332	207.785	254.692
	12.5	128.493	132.402	135.529	140.220	148.037	151.946	163.673	187.126	210.580	257.486
	5.5	83.944	87.179	89.767	93.649	100.119	103.354	113.058	132.468	151.877	190.696
	6.0	87.164	90.399	92.987	96.869	103.339	106.574	116.278	135.688	155.097	193.916
	6.5	90.384	93.619	96.207	100.089	106.559	109.794	119.498	138.908	158.317	197.136
	7.0	93.604	96.839	99.427	103.309	109.779	113.014	122.719	142.128	161.537	200.356
	7.5	96.824	100.059	102.647	106.529	112.999	116.234	125.939	145.348	164.757	203.576
10 years	8.0	100.045	103.279	105.867	109.749	116.219	119.454	129.159	148.568	167.977	206.796
	8.5	103.265	106.499	109.087	112.969	119.439	122.674	132.379	151.788	171.198	210.016
	9.0	106.485	109.720	112.307	116.189	122.659	125.894	135.599	155.008	174.418	213.236
	9.5	109.705	112.940	115.528	119.409	125.879	129.114	138.819	158.228	177.638	216.457
	10.0	112.925	116.160	118.748	122.629	129.099	132.334	142.039	161.448	180.858	219.677
	10.5	116.145	119.380	121.968	125.850	132.319	135.554	145.259	164.668	184.078	222.897
	11.0	119.365	122.600	125.188	129.070	135.539	138.774	148.479	167.888	187.298	226.117
	11.5	122.585	125.820	128.408	132.290	138.759	141.994	151.699	171.108	190.518	229.337
	12.0	125.805	129.040	131.628	135.510	141.980	145.214	154.919	174.329	193.738	232.557
	12.5	129.025	132.260	134.848	138.730	145.200	148.434	158.139	177.549	196.958	235.777
	5.5	79.453	82.130	84.272	87.484	92.838	95.515	103.547	119.610	135.672	167.798
	6.0	83.025	85.702	87.844	91.056	96.411	99.088	107.119	123.182	139.245	171.370
	6.5	86.597	89.274	91.416	94.629	99.983	102.660	110.692	126.754	142.817	174.943
	7.0	90.170	92.847	94.989	98.201	103.555	106.232	114.264	130.327	146.389	178.515
	7.5	93.742	96.419	98.561	101.773	107.128	109.805	117.836	133.899	149.962	182.087
12 years	8.0	97.314	99.992	102.133	105.346	110.700	113.377	121.409	137.471	153.534	185.660
	8.5	100.887	103.564	105.706	108.918	114.272	116.950	124.981	141.044	157.106	189.232
	9.0	104.459	107.136	109.278	112.490	117.845	120.522	128.553	144.616	160.679	192.804
	9.5	108.031	110.709	112.850	116.063	121.417	124.094	132.126	148.188	164.251	196.377
	10.0	111.604	114.281	116.423	119.635	124.989	127.667	135.698	151.761	167.824	199.949
	10.5	115.176	117.853	119.995	123.207	128.562	131.239	139.270	155.333	171.396	203.521
	11.0	118.748	121.426	123.567	126.780	132.134	134.811	142.843	158.905	174.968	207.094
	11.5	122.321	124.998	127.140	130.352	135.706	138.384	146.415	162.478	178.541	210.666
	12.0	125.893	128.570	130.712	133.924	139.279	141.956	149.987	166.050	182.113	214.238
	12.5	129.465	132.143	134.284	137.497	142.851	145.528	153.560	169.622	185.685	217.811

Entry is the value of monthly income and capital gain as a percentage of initial investment.

Net Present Value of an Investment

Discount Rate 9.50%

Holding Period	Capitalization Rate	Capital Gain on Sale of Property									
		25%	33%	40%	50%	67%	75%	100%	150%	200%	300%
	5.5	74.125	76.140	77.753	80.171	84.202	86.218	92.264	104.357	116.450	140.636
	6.0	78.115	80.131	81.743	84.162	88.193	90.208	96.255	108.347	120.440	144.626
	6.5	82.105	84.121	85.733	88.152	92.183	94.198	100.245	112.338	124.431	148.617
	7.0	86.095	88.111	89.723	92.142	96.173	98.188	104.235	116.328	128.421	152.607
	7.5	90.086	92.101	93.714	96.132	100.163	102.179	108.225	120.318	132.411	156.597
15 years	8.0	94.076	96.091	97.704	100.122	104.153	106.169	112.215	124.308	136.401	160.587
	8.5	98.066	100.082	101.694	104.113	108.144	110.159	116.206	128.299	140.392	164.578
	9.0	102.056	104.072	105.684	108.103	112.134	114.149	120.196	132.289	144.382	168.568
	9.5	106.046	108.062	109.674	112.093	116.124	118.139	124.186	136.279	148.372	172.558
	10.0	110.037	112.052	113.665	116.083	120.114	122.130	128.176	140.269	152.362	176.548
	10.5	114.027	116.042	117.655	120.073	124.104	126.120	132.166	144.259	156.352	180.538
	11.0	118.017	120.033	121.645	124.064	128.095	130.110	136.157	148.250	160.343	184.529
	11.5	122.007	124.023	125.635	128.054	132.085	134.100	140.147	152.240	164.333	188.519
	12.0	125.998	128.013	129.625	132.044	136.075	138.091	144.137	156.230	168.323	192.509
	12.5	129.988	132.003	133.616	136.034	140.065	142.081	148.127	160.220	172.313	196.499
	5.5	68.007	69.263	70.267	71.774	74.286	75.541	79.309	86.843	94.378	109.447
	6.0	72.477	73.733	74.737	76.244	78.756	80.011	83.779	91.313	98.848	113.917
	6.5	76.947	78.203	79.207	80.714	83.226	84.481	88.249	95.783	103.318	118.387
	7.0	81.417	82.673	83.677	85.184	87.696	88.952	92.719	100.253	107.788	122.857
	7.5	85.887	87.143	88.147	89.654	92.166	93.422	97.189	104.723	112.258	127.327
20 years	8.0	90.357	91.613	92.617	94.124	96.636	97.892	101.659	109.193	116.728	131.797
	8.5	94.827	96.083	97.088	98.594	101.106	102.362	106.129	113.663	121.198	136.267
	9.0	99.297	100.553	101.558	103.064	105.576	106.832	110.599	118.133	125.668	140.737
	9.5	103.767	105.023	106.028	107.535	110.046	111.302	115.069	122.604	130.138	145.207
	10.0	108.237	109.493	110.498	112.005	114.516	115.772	119.539	127.074	134.608	149.677
	10.5	112.707	113.963	114.968	116.475	118.986	120.242	124.009	131.544	139.078	154.147
	11.0	117.177	118.433	119.438	120.945	123.456	124.712	128.479	136.014	143.548	158.617
	11.5	121.647	122.903	123.908	125.415	127.926	129.182	132.949	140.484	148.018	163.087
	12.0	126.118	127.373	128.378	129.885	132.396	133.652	137.419	144.954	152.488	167.557
	12.5	130.588	131.843	132.848	134.355	136.866	138.122	141.889	149.424	156.958	172.027
	5.5	64.195	64.977	65.603	66.542	68.107	68.889	71.237	75.931	80.625	90.014
	6.0	68.964	69.746	70.372	71.311	72.876	73.658	76.006	80.700	85.394	94.783
	6.5	73.733	74.515	75.141	76.080	77.645	78.427	80.775	85.469	90.163	99.552
	7.0	78.502	79.284	79.910	80.849	82.414	83.196	85.544	90.238	94.932	104.321
	7.5	83.271	84.054	84.679	85.618	87.183	87.965	90.313	95.007	99.701	109.090
25 years	8.0	88.040	88.823	89.448	90.387	91.952	92.734	95.082	99.776	104.470	113.859
	8.5	92.809	93.592	94.217	95.156	96.721	97.504	99.851	104.545	109.239	118.628
	9.0	97.578	98.361	98.986	99.925	101.490	102.273	104.620	109.314	114.008	123.397
	9.5	102.347	103.130	103.755	104.694	106.259	107.042	109.389	114.083	118.777	128.166
	10.0	107.116	107.899	108.525	109.463	111.028	111.811	114.158	118.852	123.546	132.935
	10.5	111.885	112.668	113.294	114.232	115.797	116.580	118.927	123.621	128.315	137.704
	11.0	116.654	117.437	118.063	119.001	120.566	121.349	123.696	128.390	133.084	142.473
	11.5	121.423	122.206	122.832	123.770	125.335	126.118	128.465	133.159	137.853	147.242
	12.0	126.192	126.975	127.601	128.539	130.104	130.887	133.234	137.928	142.623	152.011
	12.5	130.961	131.744	132.370	133.308	134.873	135.656	138.003	142.697	147.392	156.780
	5.5	61.820	62.308	62.698	63.283	64.257	64.745	66.207	69.132	72.057	77.907
	6.0	66.775	67.263	67.653	68.238	69.213	69.700	71.163	74.087	77.012	82.862
	6.5	71.731	72.218	72.608	73.193	74.168	74.656	76.118	79.043	81.968	87.817
	7.0	76.686	77.173	77.563	78.148	79.123	79.611	81.073	83.998	86.923	92.772
	7.5	81.641	82.129	82.519	83.104	84.079	84.566	86.028	88.953	91.878	97.728
30 years	8.0	86.597	87.084	87.474	88.059	89.034	89.521	90.984	93.909	96.833	102.683
	8.5	91.552	92.039	92.429	93.014	93.989	94.477	95.939	98.864	101.789	107.638
	9.0	96.507	96.995	97.385	97.970	98.944	99.432	100.894	103.819	106.744	112.594
	9.5	101.462	101.950	102.340	102.925	103.900	104.387	105.850	108.774	111.699	117.549
	10.0	106.418	106.905	107.295	107.880	108.855	109.342	110.805	113.730	116.655	122.504
	10.5	111.373	111.860	112.250	112.835	113.810	114.298	115.760	118.685	121.610	127.459
	11.0	116.328	116.816	117.206	117.791	118.766	119.253	120.715	123.640	126.565	132.415
	11.5	121.284	121.771	122.161	122.746	123.721	124.208	125.671	128.596	131.520	137.370
	12.0	126.239	126.726	127.116	127.701	128.676	129.164	130.626	133.551	136.476	142.325
	12.5	131.194	131.682	132.072	132.657	133.631	134.119	135.581	138.506	141.431	147.281

Entry is the value of monthly income and capital gain as a percentage of initial investment.

Net Present Value of an Investment

Discount Rate 10.00%

Holding Period	Capitalization Rate	25%	33%	40%	Capital Gain on Sale of Property 50%	67%	75%	100%	150%	200%	300%
	5.5	97.545	102.610	106.662	112.740	122.870	127.935	143.130	173.519	203.909	264.688
	6.0	99.506	104.571	108.623	114.701	124.831	129.896	145.091	175.480	205.870	266.649
	6.5	101.467	106.532	110.584	116.662	126.792	131.857	147.052	177.441	207.831	268.610
	7.0	103.428	108.493	112.545	118.623	128.753	133.818	149.013	179.402	209.792	270.571
	7.5	105.389	110.454	114.506	120.584	130.714	135.779	150.974	181.363	211.753	272.532
5 years	8.0	107.351	112.415	116.467	122.545	132.675	137.740	152.935	183.324	213.714	274.493
	8.5	109.312	114.377	118.428	124.506	134.636	139.701	154.896	185.285	215.675	276.454
	9.0	111.273	116.338	120.389	126.467	136.597	141.662	156.857	187.246	217.636	278.415
	9.5	113.234	118.299	122.351	128.428	138.558	143.623	158.818	189.207	219.597	280.376
	10.0	115.195	120.260	124.312	130.389	140.519	145.584	160.779	191.168	221.558	282.337
	10.5	117.156	122.221	126.273	132.351	142.480	147.545	162.740	193.130	223.519	284.298
	11.0	119.117	124.182	128.234	134.312	144.441	149.506	164.701	195.091	225.480	286.259
	11.5	121.078	126.143	130.195	136.273	146.402	151.467	166.662	197.052	227.441	288.220
	12.0	123.039	128.104	132.156	138.234	148.364	153.428	168.623	199.013	229.402	290.181
	12.5	125.000	130.065	134.117	140.195	150.325	155.389	170.584	200.974	231.363	292.142
	5.5	86.558	90.314	93.320	97.828	105.342	109.099	120.369	142.910	165.452	210.534
	6.0	89.303	93.060	96.066	100.574	108.088	111.845	123.115	145.656	168.197	213.280
	6.5	92.049	95.806	98.812	103.320	110.834	114.590	125.861	148.402	170.943	216.026
	7.0	94.795	98.552	101.558	106.066	113.580	117.336	128.607	151.148	173.689	218.771
	7.5	97.541	101.298	104.303	108.812	116.325	120.082	131.353	153.894	176.435	221.517
8 years	8.0	100.287	104.044	107.049	111.558	119.071	122.828	134.099	156.640	179.181	224.263
	8.5	103.033	106.790	109.795	114.303	121.817	125.574	136.845	159.386	181.927	227.009
	9.0	105.779	109.536	112.541	117.049	124.563	128.320	139.590	162.132	184.673	229.755
	9.5	108.525	112.282	115.287	119.795	127.309	131.066	142.336	164.877	187.419	232.501
	10.0	111.271	115.027	118.033	122.541	130.055	133.812	145.082	167.623	190.165	235.247
	10.5	114.016	117.773	120.779	125.287	132.801	136.558	147.828	170.369	192.910	237.993
	11.0	116.762	120.519	123.525	128.033	135.547	139.303	150.574	173.115	195.656	240.739
	11.5	119.508	123.265	126.271	130.779	138.292	142.049	153.320	175.861	198.402	243.484
	12.0	122.254	126.011	129.016	133.525	141.038	144.795	156.066	178.607	201.148	246.230
	12.5	125.000	128.757	131.762	136.271	143.784	147.541	158.812	181.353	203.894	248.976
	5.5	80.859	83.937	86.400	90.094	96.251	99.329	108.564	127.035	145.505	182.446
	6.0	84.012	87.090	89.553	93.247	99.404	102.482	111.717	130.188	148.658	185.599
	6.5	87.165	90.243	92.706	96.400	102.557	105.635	114.870	133.341	151.811	188.752
	7.0	90.317	93.396	95.859	99.553	105.710	108.788	118.023	136.494	154.964	191.905
	7.5	93.470	96.549	99.012	102.706	108.862	111.941	121.176	139.647	158.117	195.058
10 years	8.0	96.623	99.702	102.165	105.859	112.015	115.094	124.329	142.799	161.270	198.211
	8.5	99.776	102.855	105.317	109.012	115.168	118.247	127.482	145.952	164.423	201.364
	9.0	102.929	106.008	108.470	112.165	118.321	121.400	130.635	149.105	167.576	204.517
	9.5	106.082	109.161	111.623	115.317	121.474	124.553	133.788	152.258	170.729	207.670
	10.0	109.235	112.314	114.776	118.470	124.627	127.706	136.941	155.411	173.882	210.823
	10.5	112.388	115.467	117.929	121.623	127.780	130.859	140.094	158.564	177.035	213.976
	11.0	115.541	118.620	121.082	124.776	130.933	134.012	143.247	161.717	180.188	217.129
	11.5	118.694	121.772	124.235	127.929	134.086	137.165	146.400	164.870	183.341	220.281
	12.0	121.847	124.925	127.388	131.082	137.239	140.317	149.553	168.023	186.494	223.434
	12.5	125.000	128.078	130.541	134.235	140.392	143.470	152.706	171.176	189.647	226.587
	5.5	76.189	78.711	80.729	83.756	88.801	91.324	98.891	114.026	129.161	159.431
	6.0	79.675	82.198	84.216	87.243	92.288	94.810	102.378	117.512	132.647	162.917
	6.5	83.162	85.684	87.702	90.729	95.774	98.297	105.864	120.999	136.134	166.404
	7.0	86.648	89.171	91.189	94.216	99.261	101.783	109.351	124.485	139.620	169.890
	7.5	90.135	92.657	94.675	97.702	102.747	105.270	112.837	127.972	143.107	173.377
12 years	8.0	93.621	96.144	98.162	101.189	106.234	108.756	116.324	131.459	146.593	176.863
	8.5	97.108	99.630	101.648	104.675	109.720	112.243	119.810	134.945	150.080	180.350
	9.0	100.594	103.117	105.135	108.162	113.207	115.729	123.297	138.432	153.566	183.836
	9.5	104.081	106.603	108.621	111.648	116.693	119.216	126.783	141.918	157.053	187.323
	10.0	107.567	110.090	112.108	115.135	120.180	122.702	130.270	145.405	160.539	190.809
	10.5	111.054	113.576	115.594	118.621	123.666	126.189	133.756	148.891	164.026	194.296
	11.0	114.540	117.063	119.081	122.108	127.153	129.675	137.243	152.378	167.512	197.782
	11.5	118.027	120.549	122.567	125.594	130.639	133.162	140.729	155.864	170.999	201.269
	12.0	121.513	124.036	126.054	129.081	134.126	136.648	144.216	159.351	174.485	204.755
	12.5	125.000	127.522	129.540	132.567	137.612	140.135	147.702	162.837	177.972	208.242

Entry is the value of monthly income and capital gain as a percentage of initial investment.

Net Present Value of an Investment

Discount Rate 10.00%

Holding Period	Capitalization Rate	25%	33%	40%	Capital Gain on Sale of Property 50%	67%	75%	100%	150%	200%	300%
	5.5	70.717	72.588	74.084	76.330	80.072	81.943	87.556	98.782	110.008	132.460
	6.0	74.594	76.465	77.962	80.207	83.949	85.820	91.433	102.659	113.885	136.338
	6.5	78.471	80.342	81.839	84.084	87.826	89.698	95.311	106.537	117.763	140.215
	7.0	82.349	84.220	85.717	87.962	91.704	93.575	99.188	110.414	121.640	144.093
	7.5	86.226	88.097	89.594	91.839	95.581	97.452	103.065	114.291	125.518	147.970
15 years	8.0	90.104	91.975	93.471	95.717	99.459	101.330	106.943	118.169	129.395	151.847
	8.5	93.981	95.852	97.349	99.594	103.336	105.207	110.820	122.046	133.272	155.725
	9.0	97.858	99.729	101.226	103.471	107.213	109.084	114.698	125.924	137.150	159.602
	9.5	101.736	103.607	105.104	107.349	111.091	112.962	118.575	129.801	141.027	163.479
	10.0	105.613	107.484	108.981	111.226	114.968	116.839	122.452	133.678	144.905	167.357
	10.5	109.490	111.361	112.858	115.104	118.846	120.717	126.330	137.556	148.782	171.234
	11.0	113.368	115.239	116.736	118.981	122.723	124.594	130.207	141.433	152.659	175.112
	11.5	117.245	119.116	120.613	122.858	126.600	128.471	134.084	145.311	156.537	178.989
	12.0	121.123	122.994	124.490	126.736	130.478	132.349	137.962	149.188	160.414	182.866
	12.5	125.000	126.871	128.368	130.613	134.355	136.226	141.839	153.065	164.291	186.744
	5.5	64.552	65.690	66.599	67.964	70.238	71.376	74.787	81.610	88.433	102.080
	6.0	68.870	70.007	70.917	72.282	74.556	75.693	79.105	85.928	92.751	106.397
	6.5	73.188	74.325	75.235	76.599	78.874	80.011	83.422	90.246	97.069	110.715
	7.0	77.505	78.643	79.552	80.917	83.191	84.329	87.740	94.563	101.386	115.033
	7.5	81.823	82.960	83.870	85.235	87.509	88.646	92.058	98.881	105.704	119.350
20 years	8.0	86.141	87.278	88.188	89.552	91.827	92.964	96.376	103.199	110.022	123.668
	8.5	90.459	91.596	92.505	93.870	96.144	97.282	100.693	107.516	114.339	127.986
	9.0	94.776	95.913	96.823	98.188	100.462	101.599	105.011	111.834	118.657	132.303
	9.5	99.094	100.231	101.141	102.505	104.780	105.917	109.329	116.152	122.975	136.621
	10.0	103.412	104.549	105.459	106.823	109.098	110.235	113.646	120.469	127.293	140.939
	10.5	107.729	108.866	109.776	111.141	113.415	114.552	117.964	124.787	131.610	145.256
	11.0	112.047	113.184	114.094	115.459	117.733	118.870	122.282	129.105	135.928	149.574
	11.5	116.365	117.502	118.412	119.776	122.051	123.188	126.599	133.422	140.246	153.892
	12.0	120.682	121.820	122.729	124.094	126.368	127.505	130.917	137.740	144.563	158.210
	12.5	125.000	126.137	127.047	128.412	130.686	131.823	135.235	142.058	148.881	162.527
	5.5	60.806	61.497	62.050	62.879	64.262	64.953	67.026	71.173	75.320	83.615
	6.0	65.391	66.082	66.635	67.465	68.847	69.538	71.612	75.759	79.906	88.200
	6.5	69.976	70.668	71.221	72.050	73.432	74.123	76.197	80.344	84.491	92.785
	7.0	74.562	75.253	75.806	76.635	78.018	78.709	80.782	84.929	89.076	97.370
	7.5	79.147	79.838	80.391	81.221	82.603	83.294	85.368	89.515	93.662	101.956
25 years	8.0	83.732	84.424	84.976	85.806	87.188	87.879	89.953	94.100	98.247	106.541
	8.5	88.318	89.009	89.562	90.391	91.773	92.465	94.538	98.685	102.832	111.126
	9.0	92.903	93.594	94.147	94.976	96.359	97.050	99.123	103.271	107.418	115.712
	9.5	97.488	98.179	98.732	99.562	100.944	101.635	103.709	107.856	112.003	120.297
	10.0	102.074	102.765	103.318	104.147	105.529	106.221	108.294	112.441	116.588	124.882
	10.5	106.659	107.350	107.903	108.732	110.115	110.806	112.879	117.026	121.173	129.467
	11.0	111.244	111.935	112.488	113.318	114.700	115.391	117.465	121.612	125.759	134.053
	11.5	115.829	116.521	117.074	117.903	119.285	119.976	122.050	126.197	130.344	138.638
	12.0	120.415	121.106	121.659	122.488	123.871	124.562	126.635	130.782	134.929	143.223
	12.5	125.000	125.691	126.244	127.074	128.456	129.147	131.221	135.368	139.515	147.809
	5.5	58.529	58.949	59.285	59.789	60.629	61.049	62.310	64.830	67.351	72.392
	6.0	63.277	63.697	64.033	64.537	65.377	65.797	67.057	69.578	72.099	77.140
	6.5	68.025	68.445	68.781	69.285	70.125	70.545	71.806	74.326	76.846	81.888
	7.0	72.773	73.193	73.529	74.033	74.873	75.293	76.553	79.074	81.594	86.635
	7.5	77.521	77.941	78.277	78.781	79.621	80.041	81.301	83.822	86.342	91.383
30 years	8.0	82.268	82.689	83.025	83.529	84.369	84.789	86.049	88.570	91.090	96.131
	8.5	87.016	87.437	87.773	88.277	89.117	89.537	90.797	93.318	95.838	100.879
	9.0	91.764	92.184	92.521	93.025	93.865	94.285	95.545	98.066	100.586	105.627
	9.5	96.512	96.932	97.268	97.773	98.613	99.033	100.293	102.814	105.334	110.375
	10.0	101.260	101.680	102.016	102.521	103.361	103.781	105.041	107.562	110.082	115.123
	10.5	106.008	106.428	106.764	107.268	108.109	108.529	109.789	112.310	114.830	119.871
	11.0	110.756	111.176	111.512	112.016	112.857	113.277	114.537	117.057	119.578	124.619
	11.5	115.504	115.924	116.260	116.764	117.605	118.025	119.285	121.805	124.326	129.367
	12.0	120.252	120.672	121.008	121.512	122.352	122.773	124.033	126.553	129.074	134.115
	12.5	125.000	125.420	125.756	126.260	127.100	127.521	128.781	131.301	133.822	138.863

Entry is the value of monthly income and capital gain as a percentage of initial investment.

Net Present Value of an Investment

Discount Rate 10.50%

Holding Period	Capitalization Rate	Capital Gain on Sale of Property									
		25%	33%	40%	50%	67%	75%	100%	150%	200%	300%
	5.5	95.437	100.378	104.331	110.260	120.142	125.083	139.906	169.551	199.197	258.487
	6.0	97.376	102.317	106.270	112.199	122.081	127.021	141.844	171.490	201.135	260.426
	6.5	99.315	104.255	108.208	114.137	124.019	128.960	143.783	173.428	203.074	262.365
	7.0	101.253	106.194	110.147	116.076	125.958	130.898	145.721	175.367	205.012	264.303
	7.5	103.192	108.132	112.085	118.014	127.896	132.837	147.660	177.305	206.951	266.242
5 years	8.0	105.130	110.071	114.024	119.953	129.835	134.776	149.598	179.244	208.889	268.180
	8.5	107.069	112.010	115.962	121.891	131.773	136.714	151.537	181.182	210.828	270.119
	9.0	109.007	113.948	117.901	123.830	133.712	138.653	153.475	183.121	212.766	272.057
	9.5	110.946	115.887	119.839	125.768	135.650	140.591	155.414	185.059	214.705	273.996
	10.0	112.884	117.825	121.778	127.707	137.589	142.530	157.352	186.998	216.643	275.934
	10.5	114.823	119.764	123.716	129.645	139.527	144.468	159.291	188.936	218.582	277.873
	11.0	116.761	121.702	125.655	131.584	141.466	146.407	161.229	190.875	220.520	279.811
	11.5	118.700	123.641	127.593	133.523	143.404	148.345	163.168	192.813	222.459	281.750
	12.0	120.638	125.579	129.532	135.461	145.343	150.284	165.106	194.752	224.397	283.688
	12.5	122.577	127.518	131.470	137.400	147.281	152.222	167.045	196.690	226.336	285.627
	5.5	83.846	87.457	90.346	94.679	101.900	105.511	116.343	138.008	159.672	203.002
	6.0	86.545	90.156	93.044	97.377	104.599	108.209	119.042	140.706	162.371	205.700
	6.5	89.243	92.854	95.743	100.076	107.297	110.908	121.740	143.405	165.070	208.399
	7.0	91.942	95.553	98.441	102.774	109.996	113.607	124.439	146.104	167.768	211.097
	7.5	94.641	98.251	101.140	105.473	112.695	116.305	127.138	148.802	170.467	213.796
8 years	8.0	97.339	100.950	103.839	108.172	115.393	119.004	129.836	151.501	173.165	216.495
	8.5	100.038	103.649	106.537	110.870	118.092	121.702	132.535	154.199	175.864	219.193
	9.0	102.736	106.347	109.236	113.569	120.790	124.401	135.233	156.898	178.563	221.892
	9.5	105.435	109.046	111.934	116.267	123.489	127.100	137.932	159.597	181.261	224.590
	10.0	108.134	111.744	114.633	118.966	126.188	129.798	140.631	162.295	183.960	227.289
	10.5	110.832	114.443	117.332	121.665	128.886	132.497	143.329	164.994	186.658	229.988
	11.0	113.531	117.142	120.030	124.363	131.585	135.196	146.028	167.692	189.357	232.686
	11.5	116.230	119.840	122.729	127.062	134.283	137.894	148.726	170.391	192.056	235.385
	12.0	118.928	122.539	125.428	129.760	136.982	140.593	151.425	173.090	194.754	238.084
	12.5	121.627	125.238	128.126	132.459	139.681	143.291	154.124	175.788	197.453	240.782
	5.5	77.910	80.839	83.183	86.698	92.557	95.487	104.275	121.852	139.429	174.583
	6.0	80.997	83.927	86.271	89.786	95.645	98.575	107.363	124.940	142.517	177.671
	6.5	84.085	87.015	89.358	92.874	98.733	101.662	110.451	128.028	145.605	180.759
	7.0	87.173	90.103	92.446	95.962	101.821	104.750	113.539	131.116	148.693	183.847
	7.5	90.261	93.191	95.534	99.050	104.909	107.838	116.627	134.204	151.781	186.935
10 years	8.0	93.349	96.279	98.622	102.138	107.997	110.926	119.715	137.292	154.869	190.023
	8.5	96.437	99.366	101.710	105.225	111.084	114.014	122.803	140.380	157.957	193.111
	9.0	99.525	102.454	104.798	108.313	114.172	117.102	125.890	143.467	161.045	196.199
	9.5	102.613	105.542	107.886	111.401	117.260	120.190	128.978	146.555	164.132	199.287
	10.0	105.701	108.630	110.974	114.489	120.348	123.278	132.066	149.643	167.220	202.374
	10.5	108.789	111.718	114.062	117.577	123.436	126.366	135.154	152.731	170.308	205.462
	11.0	111.876	114.806	117.150	120.665	126.524	129.453	138.242	155.819	173.396	208.550
	11.5	114.964	117.894	120.237	123.753	129.612	132.541	141.330	158.907	176.484	211.638
	12.0	118.052	120.982	123.325	126.841	132.700	135.629	144.418	161.995	179.572	214.726
	12.5	121.140	124.070	126.413	129.929	135.788	138.717	147.506	165.083	182.660	217.814
	5.5	73.093	75.470	77.371	80.223	84.977	87.354	94.484	108.745	123.005	151.527
	6.0	76.497	78.873	80.775	83.627	88.381	90.757	97.888	112.149	126.409	154.931
	6.5	79.900	82.277	84.179	87.031	91.784	94.161	101.292	115.552	129.813	158.334
	7.0	83.304	85.681	87.582	90.435	95.188	97.565	104.695	118.956	133.217	161.738
	7.5	86.708	89.085	90.986	93.838	98.592	100.969	108.099	122.360	136.620	165.142
12 years	8.0	90.112	92.488	94.390	97.242	101.996	104.372	111.503	125.763	140.024	168.546
	8.5	93.515	95.892	97.794	100.646	105.399	107.776	114.906	129.167	143.428	171.949
	9.0	96.919	99.296	101.197	104.050	108.803	111.180	118.310	132.571	146.832	175.353
	9.5	100.323	102.700	104.601	107.453	112.207	114.584	121.714	135.975	150.235	178.757
	10.0	103.727	106.103	108.005	110.857	115.611	117.987	125.118	139.378	153.639	182.161
	10.5	107.130	109.507	111.409	114.261	119.014	121.391	128.521	142.782	157.043	185.564
	11.0	110.534	112.911	114.812	117.664	122.418	124.795	131.925	146.186	160.447	188.968
	11.5	113.938	116.315	118.216	121.068	125.822	128.199	135.329	149.590	163.850	192.372
	12.0	117.342	119.718	121.620	124.472	129.226	131.602	138.733	152.993	167.254	195.776
	12.5	120.745	123.122	125.024	127.876	132.629	135.006	142.136	156.397	170.658	199.179

Entry is the value of monthly income and capital gain as a percentage of initial investment.

Net Present Value of an Investment

Discount Rate 10.50%

Holding Period	Capitalization Rate	25%	33%	40%	Capital Gain on Sale of Property 50%	67%	75%	100%	150%	200%	300%
	5.5	67.517	69.254	70.644	72.728	76.202	77.939	83.149	93.571	103.993	124.836
	6.0	71.286	73.023	74.413	76.497	79.971	81.708	86.919	97.340	107.762	128.605
	6.5	75.056	76.793	78.182	80.267	83.740	85.477	90.688	101.110	111.531	132.375
	7.0	78.825	80.562	81.952	84.036	87.510	89.247	94.458	104.879	115.301	136.144
	7.5	82.595	84.332	85.721	87.805	91.279	93.016	98.227	108.649	119.070	139.913
15 years	8.0	86.364	88.101	89.490	91.575	95.049	96.786	101.996	112.418	122.840	143.683
	8.5	90.133	91.870	93.260	95.344	98.818	100.555	105.766	116.187	126.609	147.452
	9.0	93.903	95.640	97.029	99.113	102.587	104.324	109.535	119.957	130.378	151.221
	9.5	97.672	99.409	100.799	102.883	106.357	108.094	113.304	123.726	134.148	154.991
	10.0	101.441	103.178	104.568	106.652	110.126	111.863	117.074	127.495	137.917	158.760
	10.5	105.211	106.948	108.337	110.422	113.895	115.632	120.843	131.265	141.686	162.530
	11.0	108.980	110.717	112.107	114.191	117.665	119.402	124.613	135.034	145.456	166.299
	11.5	112.750	114.486	115.876	117.960	121.434	123.171	128.382	138.804	149.225	170.068
	12.0	116.519	118.256	119.645	121.730	125.204	126.941	132.151	142.573	152.995	173.838
	12.5	120.288	122.025	123.415	125.499	128.973	130.710	135.921	146.342	156.764	177.607
	5.5	61.355	62.385	63.209	64.445	66.505	67.534	70.624	76.803	82.982	95.340
	6.0	65.529	66.559	67.382	68.618	70.678	71.708	74.797	80.976	87.155	99.514
	6.5	69.702	70.732	71.556	72.792	74.851	75.881	78.971	85.150	91.329	103.687
	7.0	73.876	74.905	75.729	76.965	79.025	80.055	83.144	89.323	95.502	107.860
	7.5	78.049	79.079	79.903	81.139	83.198	84.228	87.318	93.497	99.676	112.034
20 years	8.0	82.222	83.252	84.076	85.312	87.372	88.401	91.491	97.670	103.849	116.207
	8.5	86.396	87.426	88.250	89.485	91.545	92.575	95.664	101.843	108.023	120.381
	9.0	90.569	91.599	92.423	93.659	95.718	96.748	99.838	106.017	112.196	124.554
	9.5	94.743	95.773	96.596	97.832	99.892	100.922	104.011	110.190	116.369	128.728
	10.0	98.916	99.946	100.770	102.006	104.065	105.095	108.185	114.364	120.543	132.901
	10.5	103.090	104.119	104.943	106.179	108.239	109.269	112.358	118.537	124.716	137.074
	11.0	107.263	108.293	109.117	110.352	112.412	113.442	116.532	122.711	128.890	141.248
	11.5	111.436	112.466	113.290	114.526	116.586	117.615	120.705	126.884	133.063	145.421
	12.0	115.610	116.640	117.464	118.699	120.759	121.789	124.878	131.057	137.237	149.595
	12.5	119.783	120.813	121.637	122.873	124.932	125.962	129.052	135.231	141.410	153.768
	5.5	57.702	58.313	58.801	59.534	60.755	61.366	63.197	66.861	70.525	77.852
	6.0	62.115	62.726	63.214	63.947	65.168	65.779	67.610	71.274	74.938	82.265
	6.5	66.528	67.139	67.627	68.360	69.581	70.192	72.023	75.687	79.351	86.678
	7.0	70.941	71.551	72.040	72.773	73.994	74.605	76.436	80.100	83.764	91.091
	7.5	75.354	75.964	76.453	77.186	78.407	79.018	80.849	84.513	88.177	95.504
25 years	8.0	79.767	80.377	80.866	81.599	82.820	83.430	85.262	88.926	92.590	99.917
	8.5	84.180	84.790	85.279	86.012	87.233	87.843	89.675	93.339	97.003	104.330
	9.0	88.593	89.203	89.692	90.425	91.646	92.256	94.088	97.752	101.416	108.743
	9.5	93.006	93.616	94.105	94.838	96.059	96.669	98.501	102.165	105.829	113.156
	10.0	97.419	98.029	98.518	99.251	100.472	101.082	102.914	106.578	110.242	117.569
	10.5	101.832	102.442	102.931	103.664	104.885	105.495	107.327	110.991	114.654	121.982
	11.0	106.245	106.855	107.344	108.077	109.298	109.908	111.740	115.404	119.067	126.395
	11.5	110.658	111.268	111.757	112.490	113.711	114.321	116.153	119.817	123.480	130.808
	12.0	115.071	115.681	116.170	116.903	118.124	118.734	120.566	124.230	127.893	135.221
	12.5	119.484	120.094	120.583	121.316	122.537	123.147	124.979	128.643	132.306	139.634
	5.5	55.536	55.898	56.187	56.622	57.346	57.708	58.794	60.966	63.138	67.483
	6.0	60.091	60.453	60.742	61.177	61.901	62.263	63.349	65.521	67.694	72.038
	6.5	64.646	65.008	65.298	65.732	66.456	66.818	67.904	70.076	72.249	76.593
	7.0	69.201	69.563	69.853	70.287	71.011	71.373	72.459	74.631	76.804	81.148
	7.5	73.756	74.118	74.408	74.842	75.566	75.928	77.014	79.186	81.359	85.703
30 years	8.0	78.311	78.673	78.963	79.397	80.121	80.483	81.569	83.741	85.914	90.258
	8.5	82.866	83.228	83.518	83.952	84.676	85.038	86.124	88.296	90.469	94.813
	9.0	87.421	87.783	88.073	88.507	89.231	89.593	90.679	92.852	95.024	99.368
	9.5	91.976	92.338	92.628	93.062	93.786	94.148	95.234	97.407	99.579	103.923
	10.0	96.531	96.893	97.183	97.617	98.341	98.703	99.789	101.962	104.134	108.478
	10.5	101.086	101.448	101.738	102.172	102.896	103.258	104.344	106.517	108.689	113.033
	11.0	105.641	106.003	106.293	106.727	107.451	107.813	108.899	111.072	113.244	117.588
	11.5	110.196	110.558	110.848	111.282	112.006	112.368	113.454	115.627	117.799	122.143
	12.0	114.751	115.113	115.403	115.837	116.561	116.923	118.009	120.182	122.354	126.698
	12.5	119.306	119.668	119.958	120.392	121.116	121.478	122.565	124.737	126.909	131.253

Entry is the value of monthly income and capital gain as a percentage of initial investment.

Net Present Value of an Investment

Discount Rate 11.00%
- -

Holding Period	Capitalization Rate	25%	33%	40%	Capital Gain on Sale of Property 50%	67%	75%	100%	150%	200%	300%
	5.5	93.380	98.200	102.056	107.840	117.480	122.299	136.759	165.679	194.599	252.439
	6.0	95.296	100.116	103.972	109.756	119.396	124.216	138.676	167.596	196.515	254.355
	6.5	97.212	102.032	105.888	111.672	121.312	126.132	140.592	169.512	198.432	256.271
	7.0	99.129	103.949	107.805	113.589	123.229	128.049	142.509	171.428	200.348	258.188
	7.5	101.045	105.865	109.721	115.505	125.145	129.965	144.425	173.345	202.265	260.104
5 years	8.0	102.962	107.782	111.638	117.422	127.061	131.881	146.341	175.261	204.181	262.020
	8.5	104.878	109.698	113.554	119.338	128.978	133.798	148.258	177.177	206.097	263.937
	9.0	106.794	111.614	115.470	121.254	130.894	135.714	150.174	179.094	208.014	265.853
	9.5	108.711	113.531	117.387	123.171	132.811	137.631	152.090	181.010	209.930	267.770
	10.0	110.627	115.447	119.303	125.087	134.727	139.547	154.007	182.927	211.846	269.686
	10.5	112.544	117.363	121.219	127.003	136.643	141.463	155.923	184.843	213.763	271.602
	11.0	114.460	119.280	123.136	128.920	138.560	143.380	157.840	186.759	215.679	273.519
	11.5	116.376	121.196	125.052	130.836	140.476	145.296	159.756	188.676	217.596	275.435
	12.0	118.293	123.113	126.969	132.753	142.392	147.212	161.672	190.592	219.512	277.352
	12.5	120.209	125.029	128.885	134.669	144.309	149.129	163.589	192.509	221.428	279.268
	5.5	81.234	84.704	87.480	91.645	98.586	102.056	112.467	133.290	154.112	195.757
	6.0	83.886	87.356	90.133	94.297	101.238	104.708	115.120	135.942	156.764	198.409
	6.5	86.539	90.009	92.785	96.950	103.891	107.361	117.772	138.595	159.417	201.062
	7.0	89.191	92.661	95.438	99.602	10C.543	110.013	120.425	141.247	162.069	203.714
	7.5	91.844	95.314	98.090	102.255	109.196	112.666	123.077	143.900	164.722	206.367
8 years	8.0	94.496	97.967	100.743	104.907	111.848	115.318	125.730	146.552	167.374	209.019
	8.5	97.149	100.619	103.395	107.560	114.501	117.971	128.382	149.205	170.027	211.672
	9.0	99.801	103.272	106.048	110.212	117.153	120.624	131.035	151.857	172.679	214.324
	9.5	102.454	105.924	108.700	112.865	119.806	123.276	133.687	154.510	175.332	216.977
	10.0	105.106	108.577	111.353	115.517	122.458	125.929	136.340	157.162	177.984	219.629
	10.5	107.759	111.229	114.005	118.170	125.111	128.581	138.992	159.815	180.637	222.282
	11.0	110.411	113.882	116.658	120.822	127.763	131.234	141.645	162.467	183.290	224.934
	11.5	113.064	116.534	119.310	123.475	130.416	133.886	144.297	165.120	185.942	227.587
	12.0	115.716	119.187	121.963	126.127	133.068	136.539	146.950	167.772	188.595	230.239
	12.5	118.369	121.839	124.615	128.780	135.721	139.191	149.602	170.425	191.247	232.892
	5.5	75.091	77.878	80.109	83.454	89.030	91.818	100.181	116.908	133.635	167.090
	6.0	78.115	80.903	83.134	86.479	92.055	94.843	103.206	119.933	136.660	170.114
	6.5	81.140	83.928	86.158	89.504	95.079	97.867	106.231	122.958	139.685	173.139
	7.0	84.165	86.953	89.183	92.529	98.104	100.892	109.256	125.983	142.710	176.164
	7.5	87.190	89.978	92.208	95.553	101.129	103.917	112.281	129.008	145.735	179.189
10 years	8.0	90.215	93.003	95.233	98.578	104.154	106.942	115.305	132.032	148.759	182.214
	8.5	93.239	96.027	98.258	101.603	107.179	109.967	118.330	135.057	151.784	185.238
	9.0	96.264	99.052	101.282	104.628	110.204	112.991	121.355	138.082	154.809	188.263
	9.5	99.289	102.077	104.307	107.653	113.228	116.016	124.380	141.107	157.834	191.288
	10.0	102.314	105.102	107.332	110.677	116.253	119.041	127.405	144.132	160.859	194.313
	10.5	105.339	108.127	110.357	113.702	119.278	122.066	130.429	147.156	163.884	197.338
	11.0	108.364	111.151	113.382	116.727	122.303	125.091	133.454	150.181	166.908	200.363
	11.5	111.388	114.176	116.406	119.752	125.328	128.115	136.479	153.206	169.933	203.387
	12.0	114.413	117.201	119.431	122.777	128.352	131.140	139.504	156.231	172.958	206.412
	12.5	117.438	120.226	122.456	125.802	131.377	134.165	142.529	159.256	175.983	209.437
	5.5	70.156	72.395	74.187	76.875	81.354	83.593	90.312	103.749	117.186	144.061
	6.0	73.480	75.719	77.511	80.198	84.677	86.917	93.636	107.073	120.510	147.385
	6.5	76.804	79.043	80.835	83.522	88.001	90.241	96.960	110.397	123.834	150.709
	7.0	80.128	82.367	84.159	86.846	91.325	93.565	100.283	113.721	127.158	154.032
	7.5	83.451	85.691	87.483	90.170	94.649	96.889	103.607	117.045	130.482	157.356
12 years	8.0	86.775	89.015	90.806	93.494	97.973	100.213	106.931	120.368	133.806	160.680
	8.5	90.099	92.339	94.130	96.818	101.297	103.536	110.255	123.692	137.130	164.004
	9.0	93.423	95.663	97.454	100.142	104.621	106.860	113.579	127.016	140.453	167.328
	9.5	96.747	98.987	100.778	103.466	107.945	110.184	116.903	130.340	143.777	170.652
	10.0	100.071	102.310	104.102	106.789	111.269	113.508	120.227	133.664	147.101	173.976
	10.5	103.395	105.634	107.426	110.113	114.592	116.832	123.551	136.988	150.425	177.300
	11.0	106.719	108.958	110.750	113.437	117.916	120.156	126.875	140.312	153.749	180.624
	11.5	110.043	112.282	114.074	116.761	121.240	123.480	130.198	143.636	157.073	183.947
	12.0	113.366	115.606	117.398	120.085	124.564	126.804	133.522	146.960	160.397	187.271
	12.5	116.690	118.930	120.721	123.409	127.888	130.128	136.846	150.283	163.721	190.595

- -
Entry is the value of monthly income and capital gain as a percentage of initial investment.

Net Present Value of an Investment

Discount Rate 11.00%

Holding Period	Capitalization Rate	25%	33%	40%	Capital Gain on Sale of Property 50%	67%	75%	100%	150%	200%	300%
	5.5	64.512	66.125	67.415	69.350	72.575	74.187	79.025	88.700	98.374	117.724
	6.0	68.178	69.791	71.081	73.016	76.241	77.853	82.691	92.365	102.040	121.390
	6.5	71.844	73.457	74.747	76.682	79.907	81.519	86.356	96.031	105.706	125.056
	7.0	75.510	77.123	78.413	80.348	83.572	85.185	90.022	99.697	109.372	128.722
	7.5	79.176	80.788	82.078	84.013	87.238	88.851	93.688	103.363	113.038	132.388
15 years	8.0	82.842	84.454	85.744	87.679	90.904	92.517	97.354	107.029	116.704	136.054
	8.5	86.508	88.120	89.410	91.345	94.570	96.183	101.020	110.695	120.370	139.720
	9.0	90.174	91.786	93.076	95.011	98.236	99.849	104.686	114.361	124.036	143.386
	9.5	93.840	95.452	96.742	98.677	101.902	103.515	108.352	118.027	127.702	147.051
	10.0	97.506	99.118	100.408	102.343	105.568	107.180	112.018	121.693	131.368	150.717
	10.5	101.172	102.784	104.074	106.009	109.234	110.846	115.684	125.359	135.034	154.383
	11.0	104.837	106.450	107.740	109.675	112.900	114.512	119.350	129.025	138.700	158.049
	11.5	108.503	110.116	111.406	113.341	116.566	118.178	123.016	132.691	142.365	161.715
	12.0	112.169	113.782	115.072	117.007	120.232	121.844	126.682	136.356	146.031	165.381
	12.5	115.835	117.448	118.738	120.673	123.898	125.510	130.348	140.022	149.697	169.047
	5.5	58.394	59.327	60.073	61.192	63.057	63.990	66.788	72.384	77.980	89.171
	6.0	62.431	63.363	64.109	65.229	67.094	68.027	70.824	76.420	82.016	93.208
	6.5	66.467	67.400	68.146	69.265	71.131	72.063	74.861	80.457	86.053	97.245
	7.0	70.504	71.437	72.183	73.302	75.167	76.100	78.898	84.494	90.090	101.282
	7.5	74.541	75.473	76.220	77.339	79.204	80.137	82.935	88.531	94.126	105.318
20 years	8.0	78.578	79.510	80.256	81.375	83.241	84.173	86.971	92.567	98.163	109.355
	8.5	82.614	83.547	84.293	85.412	87.278	88.210	91.008	96.604	102.200	113.392
	9.0	86.651	87.584	88.330	89.449	91.314	92.247	95.045	100.641	106.237	117.429
	9.5	90.688	91.620	92.367	93.486	95.351	96.284	99.082	104.678	110.273	121.465
	10.0	94.724	95.657	96.403	97.522	99.388	100.320	103.118	108.714	114.310	125.502
	10.5	98.761	99.694	100.440	101.559	103.424	104.357	107.155	112.751	118.347	129.539
	11.0	102.798	103.731	104.477	105.596	107.461	108.394	111.192	116.788	122.384	133.575
	11.5	106.835	107.767	108.513	109.633	111.498	112.431	115.229	120.824	126.420	137.612
	12.0	110.871	111.804	112.550	113.669	115.535	116.467	119.265	124.861	130.457	141.649
	12.5	114.908	115.841	116.587	117.706	119.571	120.504	123.302	128.898	134.494	145.686
	5.5	54.855	55.394	55.826	56.473	57.552	58.092	59.710	62.947	66.183	72.657
	6.0	59.106	59.646	60.077	60.725	61.803	62.343	63.961	67.198	70.434	76.908
	6.5	63.357	63.897	64.328	64.976	66.055	66.594	68.212	71.449	74.686	81.159
	7.0	67.609	68.148	68.580	69.227	70.306	70.845	72.464	75.700	78.937	85.410
	7.5	71.860	72.399	72.831	73.478	74.557	75.096	76.715	79.951	83.188	89.661
25 years	8.0	76.111	76.650	77.082	77.729	78.808	79.348	80.966	84.203	87.439	93.913
	8.5	80.362	80.902	81.333	81.981	83.059	83.599	85.217	88.454	91.691	98.164
	9.0	84.613	85.153	85.584	86.232	87.311	87.850	89.468	92.705	95.942	102.415
	9.5	88.865	89.404	89.836	90.483	91.562	92.101	93.720	96.956	100.193	106.666
	10.0	93.116	93.655	94.087	94.734	95.813	96.353	97.971	101.208	104.444	110.917
	10.5	97.367	97.907	98.338	98.985	100.064	100.604	102.222	105.459	108.695	115.169
	11.0	101.618	102.158	102.589	103.237	104.316	104.855	106.473	109.710	112.947	119.420
	11.5	105.870	106.409	106.841	107.488	108.567	109.106	110.725	113.961	117.198	123.671
	12.0	110.121	110.660	111.092	111.739	112.818	113.357	114.976	118.212	121.449	127.922
	12.5	114.372	114.911	115.343	115.990	117.069	117.609	119.227	122.464	125.700	132.174
	5.5	52.808	53.120	53.370	53.744	54.368	54.680	55.616	57.488	59.360	63.104
	6.0	57.183	57.495	57.745	58.119	58.743	59.055	59.991	61.864	63.736	67.480
	6.5	61.559	61.871	62.120	62.495	63.119	63.431	64.367	66.239	68.111	71.855
	7.0	65.934	66.246	66.496	66.870	67.494	67.806	68.742	70.614	72.486	76.230
	7.5	70.309	70.621	70.871	71.245	71.869	72.181	73.117	74.989	76.861	80.606
30 years	8.0	74.684	74.996	75.246	75.620	76.244	76.556	77.493	79.365	81.237	84.981
	8.5	79.060	79.372	79.621	79.996	80.620	80.932	81.868	83.740	85.612	89.356
	9.0	83.435	83.747	83.997	84.371	84.995	85.307	86.243	88.115	89.987	93.731
	9.5	87.810	88.122	88.372	88.746	89.370	89.682	90.618	92.490	94.362	98.107
	10.0	92.185	92.498	92.747	93.122	93.746	94.058	94.994	96.866	98.738	102.482
	10.5	96.561	96.873	97.122	97.497	98.121	98.433	99.369	101.241	103.113	106.857
	11.0	100.936	101.248	101.498	101.872	102.496	102.808	103.744	105.616	107.488	111.232
	11.5	105.311	105.623	105.873	106.247	106.871	107.183	108.119	109.991	111.864	115.608
	12.0	109.687	109.999	110.248	110.623	111.247	111.559	112.495	114.367	116.239	119.983
	12.5	114.062	114.374	114.623	114.998	115.622	115.934	116.870	118.742	120.614	124.358

Entry is the value of monthly income and capital gain as a percentage of initial investment.

Net Present Value of an Investment

Discount Rate 11.50%

Holding Period	Capitalization Rate	25%	33%	40%	Capital Gain on Sale of Property 50%	67%	75%	100%	150%	200%	300%
	5.5	91.371	96.073	99.835	105.477	114.882	119.584	133.690	161.902	190.115	246.539
	6.0	93.266	97.968	101.730	107.372	116.776	121.478	135.584	163.797	192.009	248.434
	6.5	95.160	99.863	103.624	109.267	118.671	123.373	137.479	165.691	193.904	250.329
	7.0	97.055	101.757	105.519	111.161	120.565	125.267	139.374	167.586	195.798	252.223
	7.5	98.950	103.652	107.413	113.056	122.460	127.162	141.268	169.481	197.693	254.118
5 years	8.0	100.844	105.546	109.308	114.950	124.354	129.057	143.163	171.375	199.588	256.012
	8.5	102.739	107.441	111.202	116.845	126.249	130.951	145.057	173.270	201.482	257.907
	9.0	104.633	109.335	113.097	118.740	128.144	132.846	146.952	175.164	203.377	259.801
	9.5	106.528	111.230	114.992	120.634	130.038	134.740	148.846	177.059	205.271	261.696
	10.0	108.422	113.125	116.886	122.529	131.933	136.635	150.741	178.953	207.166	263.591
	10.5	110.317	115.019	118.781	124.423	133.827	138.529	152.636	180.848	209.060	265.485
	11.0	112.212	116.914	120.675	126.318	135.722	140.424	154.530	182.743	210.955	267.380
	11.5	114.106	118.808	122.570	128.212	137.617	142.319	156.425	184.637	212.850	269.274
	12.0	116.001	120.703	124.464	130.107	139.511	144.213	158.319	186.532	214.744	271.169
	12.5	117.895	122.597	126.359	132.002	141.406	146.108	160.214	188.426	216.639	273.063
	5.5	78.716	82.052	84.720	88.723	95.394	98.730	108.737	128.750	148.763	188.790
	6.0	81.324	84.659	87.328	91.331	98.002	101.337	111.344	131.358	151.371	191.398
	6.5	83.931	87.267	89.935	93.938	100.609	103.945	113.952	133.965	153.978	194.005
	7.0	86.539	89.875	92.543	96.546	103.217	106.552	116.559	136.573	156.586	196.613
	7.5	89.146	92.482	95.151	99.153	105.824	109.160	119.167	139.180	159.194	199.220
8 years	8.0	91.754	95.090	97.758	101.761	108.432	111.767	121.774	141.788	161.801	201.828
	8.5	94.362	97.697	100.366	104.368	111.039	114.375	124.382	144.395	164.409	204.435
	9.0	96.969	100.305	102.973	106.976	113.647	116.983	126.989	147.003	167.016	207.043
	9.5	99.577	102.912	105.581	109.583	116.254	119.590	129.597	149.610	169.624	209.651
	10.0	102.184	105.520	108.188	112.191	118.862	122.198	132.204	152.218	172.231	212.258
	10.5	104.792	108.127	110.796	114.798	121.470	124.805	134.812	154.825	174.839	214.866
	11.0	107.399	110.735	113.403	117.406	124.077	127.413	137.419	157.433	177.446	217.473
	11.5	110.007	113.342	116.011	120.013	126.685	130.020	140.027	160.040	180.054	220.081
	12.0	112.614	115.950	118.618	122.621	129.292	132.628	142.634	162.648	182.661	222.688
	12.5	115.222	118.557	121.226	125.228	131.900	135.235	145.242	165.255	185.269	225.296
	5.5	72.396	75.049	77.172	80.356	85.662	88.315	96.275	112.193	128.112	159.950
	6.0	75.360	78.013	80.136	83.319	88.626	91.279	99.238	115.157	131.076	162.913
	6.5	78.324	80.977	83.099	86.283	91.589	94.242	102.202	118.120	134.039	165.877
	7.0	81.287	83.940	86.063	89.247	94.553	97.206	105.165	121.084	137.003	168.840
	7.5	84.251	86.904	89.026	92.210	97.516	100.169	108.129	124.048	139.966	171.804
10 years	8.0	87.214	89.867	91.990	95.174	100.480	103.133	111.092	127.011	142.930	174.768
	8.5	90.178	92.831	94.954	98.137	103.444	106.097	114.056	129.975	145.894	177.731
	9.0	93.141	95.795	97.917	101.101	106.407	109.060	117.020	132.938	148.857	180.695
	9.5	96.105	98.758	100.881	104.064	109.371	112.024	119.983	135.902	151.821	183.658
	10.0	99.069	101.722	103.844	107.028	112.334	114.987	122.947	138.866	154.784	186.622
	10.5	102.032	104.685	106.808	109.992	115.298	117.951	125.910	141.829	157.748	189.585
	11.0	104.996	107.649	109.771	112.955	118.261	120.915	128.874	144.793	160.712	192.549
	11.5	107.959	110.613	112.735	115.919	121.225	123.878	131.838	147.756	163.675	195.513
	12.0	110.923	113.576	115.699	118.882	124.189	126.842	134.801	150.720	166.639	198.476
	12.5	113.887	116.540	118.662	121.846	127.152	129.805	137.765	153.683	169.602	201.440
	5.5	67.369	69.480	71.168	73.700	77.921	80.031	86.362	99.024	111.686	137.010
	6.0	70.616	72.726	74.415	76.947	81.168	83.278	89.609	102.271	114.933	140.256
	6.5	73.863	75.973	77.662	80.194	84.415	86.525	92.856	105.518	118.179	143.503
	7.0	77.110	79.220	80.908	83.441	87.661	89.772	96.103	108.764	121.426	146.750
	7.5	80.357	82.467	84.155	86.688	90.908	93.018	99.349	112.011	124.673	149.997
12 years	8.0	83.603	85.714	87.402	89.934	94.155	96.265	102.596	115.258	127.920	153.244
	8.5	86.850	88.960	90.649	93.181	97.402	99.512	105.843	118.505	131.167	156.490
	9.0	90.097	92.207	93.896	96.428	100.649	102.759	109.090	121.752	134.413	159.737
	9.5	93.344	95.454	97.142	99.675	103.895	106.006	112.337	124.998	137.660	162.984
	10.0	96.591	98.701	100.389	102.921	107.142	109.252	115.583	128.245	140.907	166.231
	10.5	99.837	101.948	103.636	106.168	110.389	112.499	118.830	131.492	144.154	169.478
	11.0	103.084	105.194	106.883	109.415	113.636	115.746	122.077	134.739	147.401	172.724
	11.5	106.331	108.441	110.129	112.662	116.882	118.993	125.324	137.986	150.647	175.971
	12.0	109.578	111.688	113.376	115.909	120.129	122.240	128.571	141.232	153.894	179.218
	12.5	112.825	114.935	116.623	119.155	123.376	125.486	131.817	144.479	157.141	182.465

Entry is the value of monthly income and capital gain as a percentage of initial investment.

Net Present Value of an Investment

Discount Rate 11.50%

Holding Period	Capitalization Rate	25%	33%	40%	Capital Gain on Sale of Property 50%	67%	75%	100%	150%	200%	300%
	5.5	61.690	63.187	64.384	66.181	69.175	70.672	75.163	84.145	93.127	111.092
	6.0	65.257	66.754	67.951	69.748	72.742	74.239	78.730	87.712	96.694	114.658
	6.5	68.823	70.320	71.518	73.314	76.308	77.805	82.297	91.279	100.261	118.225
	7.0	72.390	73.887	75.085	76.881	79.875	81.372	85.863	94.845	103.828	121.792
	7.5	75.957	77.454	78.652	80.448	83.442	84.939	89.430	98.412	107.394	125.359
15 years	8.0	79.524	81.021	82.218	84.015	87.009	88.506	92.997	101.979	110.961	128.925
	8.5	83.090	84.587	85.785	87.582	90.576	92.073	96.564	105.546	114.528	132.492
	9.0	86.657	88.154	89.352	91.148	94.142	95.639	100.130	109.113	118.095	136.059
	9.5	90.224	91.721	92.919	94.715	97.709	99.206	103.697	112.679	121.661	139.626
	10.0	93.791	95.288	96.485	98.282	101.276	102.773	107.264	116.246	125.228	143.192
	10.5	97.358	98.855	100.052	101.849	104.843	106.340	110.831	119.813	128.795	146.759
	11.0	100.924	102.421	103.619	105.415	108.409	109.906	114.397	123.380	132.362	150.326
	11.5	104.491	105.988	107.186	108.982	111.976	113.473	117.964	126.946	135.929	153.893
	12.0	108.058	109.555	110.752	112.549	115.543	117.040	121.531	130.513	139.495	157.460
	12.5	111.625	113.122	114.319	116.116	119.110	120.607	125.098	134.080	143.062	161.026
	5.5	55.649	56.493	57.169	58.183	59.872	60.717	63.251	68.319	73.387	83.523
	6.0	59.556	60.400	61.076	62.090	63.779	64.624	67.158	72.226	77.294	87.431
	6.5	63.463	64.308	64.983	65.997	67.686	68.531	71.065	76.133	81.201	91.338
	7.0	67.370	68.215	68.890	69.904	71.593	72.438	74.972	80.040	85.109	95.245
	7.5	71.277	72.122	72.798	73.811	75.501	76.345	78.879	83.947	89.016	99.152
20 years	8.0	75.184	76.029	76.705	77.718	79.408	80.252	82.786	87.855	92.923	103.059
	8.5	79.091	79.936	80.612	81.625	83.315	84.160	86.694	91.762	96.830	106.966
	9.0	82.998	83.843	84.519	85.533	87.222	88.067	90.601	95.669	100.737	110.873
	9.5	86.906	87.750	88.426	89.440	91.129	91.974	94.508	99.576	104.644	114.780
	10.0	90.813	91.657	92.333	93.347	95.036	95.881	98.415	103.483	108.551	118.688
	10.5	94.720	95.565	96.240	97.254	98.943	99.788	102.322	107.390	112.458	122.595
	11.0	98.627	99.472	100.147	101.161	102.850	103.695	106.229	111.297	116.365	126.502
	11.5	102.534	103.379	104.055	105.068	106.758	107.602	110.136	115.204	120.273	130.409
	12.0	106.441	107.286	107.962	108.975	110.665	111.509	114.043	119.112	124.180	134.316
	12.5	110.348	111.193	111.869	112.882	114.572	115.416	117.951	123.019	128.087	138.223
	5.5	52.240	52.717	53.098	53.670	54.623	55.100	56.529	59.389	62.249	67.968
	6.0	56.339	56.816	57.197	57.769	58.722	59.199	60.629	63.488	66.348	72.067
	6.5	60.438	60.915	61.296	61.868	62.821	63.298	64.728	67.587	70.447	76.167
	7.0	64.537	65.014	65.395	65.967	66.921	67.397	68.827	71.687	74.546	80.266
	7.5	68.637	69.113	69.494	70.066	71.020	71.496	72.926	75.786	78.646	84.365
25 years	8.0	72.736	73.212	73.594	74.166	75.119	75.595	77.025	79.885	82.745	88.464
	8.5	76.835	77.312	77.693	78.265	79.218	79.695	81.124	83.984	86.844	92.563
	9.0	80.934	81.411	81.792	82.364	83.317	83.794	85.224	88.083	90.943	96.662
	9.5	85.033	85.510	85.891	86.463	87.416	87.893	89.323	92.182	95.042	100.762
	10.0	89.132	89.609	89.990	90.562	91.515	91.992	93.422	96.282	99.141	104.861
	10.5	93.232	93.708	94.089	94.661	95.615	96.091	97.521	100.381	103.240	108.960
	11.0	97.331	97.807	98.189	98.761	99.714	100.190	101.620	104.480	107.340	113.059
	11.5	101.430	101.906	102.288	102.860	103.813	104.290	105.719	108.579	111.439	117.158
	12.0	105.529	106.006	106.387	106.959	107.912	108.389	109.819	112.678	115.538	121.257
	12.5	109.628	110.105	110.486	111.058	112.011	112.488	113.918	116.777	119.637	125.356
	5.5	50.317	50.586	50.801	51.123	51.661	51.930	52.737	54.351	55.964	59.191
	6.0	54.524	54.793	55.008	55.331	55.869	56.138	56.944	58.558	60.172	63.399
	6.5	58.732	59.001	59.216	59.538	60.076	60.345	61.152	62.766	64.379	67.606
	7.0	62.939	63.208	63.423	63.746	64.284	64.553	65.360	66.973	68.587	71.814
	7.5	67.147	67.416	67.631	67.953	68.491	68.760	69.567	71.181	72.794	76.021
30 years	8.0	71.354	71.623	71.838	72.161	72.699	72.968	73.775	75.388	77.002	80.229
	8.5	75.562	75.831	76.046	76.368	76.906	77.175	77.982	79.596	81.209	84.436
	9.0	79.769	80.038	80.253	80.576	81.114	81.383	82.190	83.803	85.417	88.644
	9.5	83.977	84.246	84.461	84.784	85.321	85.590	86.397	88.011	89.624	92.851
	10.0	88.184	88.453	88.668	88.991	89.529	89.798	90.605	92.218	93.832	97.059
	10.5	92.392	92.661	92.876	93.199	93.736	94.005	94.812	96.426	98.039	101.266
	11.0	96.599	96.868	97.083	97.406	97.944	98.213	99.020	100.633	102.247	105.474
	11.5	100.807	101.076	101.291	101.614	102.151	102.420	103.227	104.841	106.454	109.681
	12.0	105.014	105.283	105.498	105.821	106.359	106.628	107.435	109.048	110.662	113.889
	12.5	109.222	109.491	109.706	110.029	110.566	110.835	111.642	113.256	114.869	118.096

Entry is the value of monthly income and capital gain as a percentage of initial investment.

Net Present Value of an Investment

Discount Rate 12.00%

Holding Period	Capitalization Rate	25%	33%	40%	Capital Gain on Sale of Property 50%	67%	75%	100%	150%	200%	300%
	5.5	89.411	93.998	97.667	103.172	112.346	116.933	130.694	158.217	185.739	240.784
	6.0	91.284	95.871	99.540	105.045	114.219	118.806	132.567	160.090	187.612	242.657
	6.5	93.157	97.744	101.414	106.918	116.092	120.679	134.441	161.963	189.486	244.531
	7.0	95.030	99.617	103.287	108.791	117.965	122.552	136.314	163.836	191.359	246.404
	7.5	96.903	101.490	105.160	110.664	119.839	124.426	138.187	165.709	193.232	248.277
5 years	8.0	98.776	103.363	107.033	112.537	121.712	126.299	140.060	167.582	195.105	250.150
	8.5	100.649	105.236	108.906	114.411	123.585	128.172	141.933	169.456	196.978	252.023
	9.0	102.522	107.110	110.779	116.284	125.458	130.045	143.806	171.329	198.851	253.896
	9.5	104.396	108.983	112.652	118.157	127.331	131.918	145.679	173.202	200.724	255.769
	10.0	106.269	110.856	114.525	120.030	129.204	133.791	147.552	175.075	202.597	257.642
	10.5	108.142	112.729	116.399	121.903	131.077	135.664	149.426	176.948	204.471	259.516
	11.0	110.015	114.602	118.272	123.776	132.950	137.537	151.299	178.821	206.344	261.389
	11.5	111.888	116.475	120.145	125.649	134.824	139.411	153.172	180.694	208.217	263.262
	12.0	113.761	118.348	122.018	127.522	136.697	141.284	155.045	182.567	210.090	265.135
	12.5	115.634	120.221	123.891	129.396	138.570	143.157	156.918	184.441	211.963	267.008
	5.5	76.291	79.497	82.061	85.909	92.321	95.527	105.145	124.381	143.617	182.089
	6.0	78.854	82.060	84.625	88.472	94.884	98.090	107.708	126.945	146.181	184.653
	6.5	81.418	84.624	87.189	91.036	97.448	100.654	110.272	129.508	148.744	187.217
	7.0	83.982	87.188	89.752	93.600	100.012	103.218	112.836	132.072	151.308	189.780
	7.5	86.545	89.751	92.316	96.163	102.575	105.781	115.399	134.636	153.872	192.344
8 years	8.0	89.109	92.315	94.880	98.727	105.139	108.345	117.963	137.199	156.435	194.908
	8.5	91.673	94.879	97.443	101.291	107.703	110.909	120.527	139.763	158.999	197.471
	9.0	94.236	97.442	100.007	103.854	110.266	113.472	123.090	142.327	161.563	200.035
	9.5	96.800	100.006	102.571	106.418	112.830	116.036	125.654	144.890	164.126	202.599
	10.0	99.363	102.569	105.134	108.982	115.394	118.600	128.218	147.454	166.690	205.162
	10.5	101.927	105.133	107.698	111.545	117.957	121.163	130.781	150.018	169.254	207.726
	11.0	104.491	107.697	110.262	114.109	120.521	123.727	133.345	152.581	171.817	210.290
	11.5	107.054	110.260	112.825	116.673	123.085	126.291	135.909	155.145	174.381	212.853
	12.0	109.618	112.824	115.389	119.236	125.648	128.854	138.472	157.708	176.945	215.417
	12.5	112.182	115.388	117.953	121.800	128.212	131.418	141.036	160.272	179.508	217.981
	5.5	69.820	72.345	74.365	77.395	82.445	84.970	92.545	107.695	122.845	153.144
	6.0	72.725	75.250	77.270	80.299	85.349	87.874	95.449	110.599	125.749	156.048
	6.5	75.629	78.154	80.174	83.204	88.254	90.779	98.353	113.503	128.653	158.952
	7.0	78.533	81.058	83.078	86.108	91.158	93.683	101.258	116.407	131.557	161.857
	7.5	81.437	83.962	85.982	89.012	94.062	96.587	104.162	119.312	134.461	164.761
10 years	8.0	84.341	86.866	88.886	91.916	96.966	99.491	107.066	122.216	137.365	167.665
	8.5	87.246	89.771	91.790	94.820	99.870	102.395	109.970	125.120	140.270	170.569
	9.0	90.150	92.675	94.695	97.725	102.775	105.299	112.874	128.024	143.174	173.473
	9.5	93.054	95.579	97.599	100.629	105.679	108.204	115.779	130.928	146.078	176.378
	10.0	95.958	98.483	100.503	103.533	108.583	111.108	118.683	133.832	148.982	179.282
	10.5	98.862	101.387	103.407	106.437	111.487	114.012	121.587	136.737	151.886	182.186
	11.0	101.766	104.291	106.311	109.341	114.391	116.916	124.491	139.641	154.791	185.090
	11.5	104.671	107.196	109.216	112.246	117.295	119.820	127.395	142.545	157.695	187.994
	12.0	107.575	110.100	112.120	115.150	120.200	122.725	130.299	145.449	160.599	190.898
	12.5	110.479	113.004	115.024	118.054	123.104	125.629	133.204	148.353	163.503	193.803
	5.5	64.725	66.713	68.304	70.690	74.668	76.656	82.622	94.553	106.485	130.348
	6.0	67.897	69.886	71.477	73.863	77.840	79.829	85.794	97.726	109.657	133.520
	6.5	71.070	73.058	74.649	77.035	81.012	83.001	88.967	100.898	112.830	136.692
	7.0	74.242	76.230	77.821	80.208	84.185	86.173	92.139	104.070	116.002	139.865
	7.5	77.414	79.403	80.994	83.380	87.357	89.346	95.311	107.243	119.174	143.037
12 years	8.0	80.587	82.575	84.166	86.552	90.530	92.518	98.484	110.415	122.347	146.210
	8.5	83.759	85.748	87.338	89.725	93.702	95.690	101.656	113.588	125.519	149.382
	9.0	86.931	88.920	90.511	92.897	96.874	98.863	104.829	116.760	128.691	152.554
	9.5	90.104	92.092	93.683	96.070	100.047	102.035	108.001	119.932	131.864	155.727
	10.0	93.276	95.265	96.856	99.242	103.219	105.208	111.173	123.105	135.036	158.899
	10.5	96.449	98.437	100.028	102.414	106.391	108.380	114.346	126.277	138.209	162.071
	11.0	99.621	101.610	103.200	105.587	109.564	111.552	117.518	129.450	141.381	165.244
	11.5	102.793	104.782	106.373	108.759	112.736	114.725	120.690	132.622	144.553	168.416
	12.0	105.966	107.954	109.545	111.931	115.909	117.897	123.863	135.794	147.726	171.589
	12.5	109.138	111.127	112.718	115.104	119.081	121.070	127.035	138.967	150.898	174.761

Entry is the value of monthly income and capital gain as a percentage of initial investment.

Net Present Value of an Investment

Discount Rate 12.00%

Holding Period	Capitalization Rate	25%	33%	40%	Capital Gain on Sale of Property 50%	67%	75%	100%	150%	200%	300%
	5.5	59.037	60.427	61.539	63.207	65.986	67.376	71.546	79.885	88.224	104.902
	6.0	62.509	63.899	65.011	66.678	69.458	70.848	75.018	83.357	91.696	108.374
	6.5	65.980	67.370	68.482	70.150	72.930	74.320	78.489	86.828	95.168	111.846
	7.0	69.452	70.842	71.954	73.622	76.402	77.791	81.961	90.300	98.639	115.318
	7.5	72.924	74.314	75.426	77.094	79.873	81.263	85.433	93.772	102.111	118.789
15 years	8.0	76.396	77.786	78.897	80.565	83.345	84.735	88.904	97.244	105.583	122.261
	8.5	79.867	81.257	82.369	84.037	86.817	88.207	92.376	100.715	109.055	125.733
	9.0	83.339	84.729	85.841	87.509	90.288	91.678	95.848	104.187	112.526	129.205
	9.5	86.811	88.201	89.313	90.980	93.760	95.150	99.320	107.659	115.998	132.676
	10.0	90.283	91.673	92.784	94.452	97.232	98.622	102.791	111.131	119.470	136.148
	10.5	93.754	95.144	96.256	97.924	100.704	102.094	106.263	114.602	122.941	139.620
	11.0	97.226	98.616	99.728	101.396	104.175	105.565	109.735	118.074	126.413	143.092
	11.5	100.698	102.088	103.200	104.867	107.647	109.037	113.207	121.546	129.885	146.563
	12.0	104.170	105.559	106.671	108.339	111.119	112.509	116.678	125.018	133.357	150.035
	12.5	107.641	109.031	110.143	111.811	114.591	115.980	120.150	128.489	136.828	153.507
	5.5	53.101	53.866	54.478	55.396	56.927	57.692	59.987	64.577	69.167	78.348
	6.0	56.885	57.650	58.263	59.181	60.711	61.476	63.771	68.361	72.951	82.132
	6.5	60.670	61.435	62.047	62.965	64.495	65.260	67.555	72.145	76.736	85.916
	7.0	64.454	65.219	65.831	66.749	68.279	69.044	71.339	75.929	80.520	89.700
	7.5	68.238	69.003	69.615	70.533	72.063	72.828	75.123	79.714	84.304	93.484
20 years	8.0	72.022	72.787	73.399	74.317	75.847	76.612	78.907	83.498	88.088	97.269
	8.5	75.806	76.571	77.183	78.101	79.631	80.396	82.692	87.282	91.872	101.053
	9.0	79.590	80.355	80.967	81.885	83.416	84.181	86.476	91.066	95.656	104.837
	9.5	83.374	84.139	84.752	85.670	87.200	87.965	90.260	94.850	99.440	108.621
	10.0	87.159	87.924	88.536	89.454	90.984	91.749	94.044	98.634	103.225	112.405
	10.5	90.943	91.708	92.320	93.238	94.768	95.533	97.828	102.418	107.009	116.189
	11.0	94.727	95.492	96.104	97.022	98.552	99.317	101.612	106.203	110.793	119.973
	11.5	98.511	99.276	99.888	100.806	102.336	103.101	105.396	109.987	114.577	123.758
	12.0	102.295	103.060	103.672	104.590	106.120	106.885	109.181	113.771	118.361	127.542
	12.5	106.079	106.844	107.456	108.374	109.905	110.670	112.965	117.555	122.145	131.326
	5.5	49.834	50.255	50.592	51.097	51.940	52.361	53.624	56.151	58.678	63.731
	6.0	53.790	54.211	54.548	55.053	55.896	56.317	57.580	60.107	62.634	67.687
	6.5	57.746	58.167	58.504	59.010	59.852	60.273	61.536	64.063	66.590	71.643
	7.0	61.702	62.123	62.460	62.966	63.808	64.229	65.492	68.019	70.546	75.599
	7.5	65.658	66.080	66.416	66.922	67.764	68.185	69.449	71.975	74.502	79.555
25 years	8.0	69.615	70.036	70.373	70.878	71.720	72.141	73.405	75.931	78.458	83.512
	8.5	73.571	73.992	74.329	74.834	75.676	76.097	77.361	79.887	82.414	87.468
	9.0	77.527	77.948	78.285	78.790	79.632	80.053	81.317	83.844	86.370	91.424
	9.5	81.483	81.904	82.241	82.746	83.588	84.010	85.273	87.800	90.326	95.380
	10.0	85.439	85.860	86.197	86.702	87.545	87.966	89.229	91.756	94.282	99.336
	10.5	89.395	89.816	90.153	90.658	91.501	91.922	93.185	95.712	98.239	103.292
	11.0	93.351	93.772	94.109	94.615	95.457	95.878	97.141	99.668	102.195	107.248
	11.5	97.307	97.728	98.065	98.571	99.413	99.834	101.097	103.624	106.151	111.204
	12.0	101.263	101.684	102.021	102.527	103.369	103.790	105.053	107.580	110.107	115.160
	12.5	105.219	105.641	105.977	106.483	107.325	107.746	109.010	111.536	114.063	119.116
	5.5	48.035	48.267	48.453	48.731	49.195	49.426	50.122	51.513	52.903	55.685
	6.0	52.086	52.318	52.504	52.782	53.245	53.477	54.173	55.563	56.954	59.736
	6.5	56.137	56.369	56.554	56.832	57.296	57.528	58.223	59.614	61.005	63.787
	7.0	60.188	60.420	60.605	60.883	61.347	61.579	62.274	63.665	65.056	67.837
	7.5	64.239	64.470	64.656	64.934	65.398	65.629	66.325	67.716	69.106	71.888
30 years	8.0	68.289	68.521	68.707	68.985	69.448	69.680	70.376	71.766	73.157	75.939
	8.5	72.340	72.572	72.757	73.035	73.499	73.731	74.426	75.817	77.208	79.990
	9.0	76.391	76.623	76.808	77.086	77.550	77.782	78.477	79.868	81.259	84.040
	9.5	80.442	80.673	80.859	81.137	81.601	81.832	82.528	83.919	85.310	88.091
	10.0	84.492	84.724	84.910	85.188	85.651	85.883	86.579	87.969	89.360	92.142
	10.5	88.543	88.775	88.960	89.239	89.702	89.934	90.629	92.020	93.411	96.193
	11.0	92.594	92.826	93.011	93.289	93.753	93.985	94.680	96.071	97.462	100.243
	11.5	96.645	96.876	97.062	97.340	97.804	98.035	98.731	100.122	101.513	104.294
	12.0	100.695	100.927	101.113	101.391	101.854	102.086	102.782	104.173	105.563	108.345
	12.5	104.746	104.978	105.163	105.442	105.905	106.137	106.832	108.223	109.614	112.396

Entry is the value of monthly income and capital gain as a percentage of initial investment.

Net Present Value of an Investment

Discount Rate 15.00%

Holding Period	Capitalization Rate	25%	33%	40%	Capital Gain on Sale of Property						
					50%	67%	75%	100%	150%	200%	300%
	5.5	78.587	82.541	85.705	90.451	98.360	102.315	114.179	137.907	161.636	209.092
	6.0	80.338	84.293	87.457	92.202	100.112	104.066	115.931	139.659	163.387	210.844
	6.5	82.090	86.044	89.208	93.954	101.863	105.818	117.682	141.410	165.139	212.595
	7.0	83.841	87.796	90.959	95.705	103.615	107.569	119.433	143.162	166.890	214.347
	7.5	85.592	89.547	92.711	97.457	105.366	109.321	121.185	144.913	168.641	216.098
5 years	8.0	87.344	91.299	94.462	99.208	107.117	111.072	122.936	146.665	170.393	217.849
	8.5	89.095	93.050	96.214	100.959	108.869	112.824	124.688	148.416	172.144	219.601
	9.0	90.847	94.801	97.965	102.711	110.620	114.575	126.439	150.167	173.896	221.352
	9.5	92.598	96.553	99.717	104.462	112.372	116.327	128.191	151.919	175.647	223.104
	10.0	94.350	98.304	101.468	106.214	114.123	118.078	129.942	153.670	177.399	224.855
	10.5	96.101	100.056	103.220	107.965	115.875	119.829	131.694	155.422	179.150	226.607
	11.0	97.853	101.807	104.971	109.717	117.626	121.581	133.445	157.173	180.902	228.358
	11.5	99.604	103.559	106.722	111.468	119.378	123.332	135.196	158.925	182.653	230.110
	12.0	101.355	105.310	108.474	113.220	121.129	125.084	136.948	160.676	184.404	231.861
	12.5	103.107	107.062	110.225	114.971	122.880	126.835	138.699	162.428	186.156	233.612
	5.5	63.471	65.999	68.022	71.057	76.114	78.643	86.229	101.401	116.573	146.917
	6.0	65.792	68.321	70.344	73.379	78.436	80.965	88.551	103.723	118.895	149.239
	6.5	68.114	70.643	72.666	75.700	80.758	83.286	90.872	106.044	121.217	151.561
	7.0	70.436	72.965	74.988	78.022	83.080	85.608	93.194	108.366	123.538	153.882
	7.5	72.758	75.287	77.310	80.344	85.401	87.930	95.516	110.688	125.860	156.204
8 years	8.0	75.080	77.609	79.632	82.666	87.723	90.252	97.838	113.010	128.182	158.526
	8.5	77.402	79.930	81.953	84.988	90.045	92.574	100.160	115.332	130.504	160.848
	9.0	79.724	82.252	84.275	87.310	92.367	94.896	102.482	117.654	132.826	163.170
	9.5	82.046	84.574	86.597	89.632	94.689	97.218	104.804	119.976	135.148	165.492
	10.0	84.367	86.896	88.919	91.953	97.011	99.539	107.125	122.298	137.470	167.814
	10.5	86.689	89.218	91.241	94.275	99.333	101.861	109.447	124.619	139.791	170.136
	11.0	89.011	91.540	93.563	96.597	101.654	104.183	111.769	126.941	142.113	172.457
	11.5	91.333	93.862	95.885	98.919	103.976	106.505	114.091	129.263	144.435	174.779
	12.0	93.655	96.184	98.206	101.241	106.298	108.827	116.413	131.585	146.757	177.101
	12.5	95.977	98.505	100.528	103.563	108.620	111.149	118.735	133.907	149.079	179.423
	5.5	56.560	58.437	59.939	62.191	65.944	67.821	73.451	84.712	95.973	118.494
	6.0	59.143	61.020	62.521	64.773	68.527	70.404	76.034	87.295	98.555	121.077
	6.5	61.726	63.602	65.104	67.356	71.110	72.986	78.617	89.877	101.138	123.659
	7.0	64.308	66.185	67.687	69.939	73.692	75.569	81.199	92.460	103.721	126.242
	7.5	66.891	68.768	70.269	72.521	76.275	78.152	83.782	95.043	106.303	128.824
10 years	8.0	69.474	71.350	72.852	75.104	78.857	80.734	86.365	97.625	108.886	131.407
	8.5	72.056	73.933	75.434	77.687	81.440	83.317	88.947	100.208	111.468	133.990
	9.0	74.639	76.516	78.017	80.269	84.023	85.899	91.530	102.790	114.051	136.572
	9.5	77.221	79.098	80.600	82.852	86.605	88.482	94.112	105.373	116.634	139.155
	10.0	79.804	81.681	83.182	85.434	89.188	91.065	96.695	107.956	119.216	141.738
	10.5	82.387	84.263	85.765	88.017	91.771	93.647	99.278	110.538	121.799	144.320
	11.0	84.969	86.846	88.348	90.600	94.353	96.230	101.860	113.121	124.382	146.903
	11.5	87.552	89.429	90.930	93.182	96.936	98.813	104.443	115.704	126.964	149.485
	12.0	90.135	92.011	93.513	95.765	99.518	101.395	107.026	118.286	129.547	152.068
	12.5	92.717	94.594	96.095	98.348	102.101	103.978	109.608	120.869	132.129	154.651
	5.5	51.432	52.825	53.939	55.611	58.396	59.789	63.968	72.326	80.683	97.399
	6.0	54.208	55.601	56.715	58.387	61.173	62.565	66.744	75.102	83.459	100.175
	6.5	56.984	58.377	59.491	61.163	63.949	65.342	69.520	77.878	86.236	102.951
	7.0	59.760	61.153	62.268	63.939	66.725	68.118	72.297	80.654	89.012	105.727
	7.5	62.536	63.929	65.044	66.715	69.501	70.894	75.073	83.430	91.788	108.503
12 years	8.0	65.313	66.705	67.820	69.491	72.277	73.670	77.849	86.207	94.564	111.279
	8.5	68.089	69.482	70.596	72.268	75.053	76.446	80.625	88.983	97.340	114.055
	9.0	70.865	72.258	73.372	75.044	77.830	79.222	83.401	91.759	100.116	116.832
	9.5	73.641	75.034	76.148	77.820	80.606	81.999	86.177	94.535	102.893	119.608
	10.0	76.417	77.810	78.924	80.596	83.382	84.775	88.954	97.311	105.669	122.384
	10.5	79.193	80.586	81.701	83.372	86.158	87.551	91.730	100.087	108.445	125.160
	11.0	81.970	83.362	84.477	86.148	88.934	90.327	94.506	102.863	111.221	127.936
	11.5	84.746	86.139	87.253	88.924	91.710	93.103	97.282	105.640	113.997	130.712
	12.0	87.522	88.915	90.029	91.701	94.486	95.879	100.058	108.416	116.773	133.489
	12.5	90.298	91.691	92.805	94.477	97.263	98.656	102.834	111.192	119.550	136.265

Entry is the value of monthly income and capital gain as a percentage of initial investment.

Net Present Value of an Investment

Discount Rate 15.00%

Holding Period	Capitalization Rate	25%	33%	40%	Capital Gain on Sale of Property 50%	67%	75%	100%	150%	200%	300%
	5.5	46.108	46.998	47.711	48.780	50.561	51.451	54.123	59.467	64.811	75.499
	6.0	49.085	49.975	50.688	51.757	53.538	54.429	57.101	62.444	67.788	78.476
	6.5	52.062	52.952	53.665	54.734	56.515	57.406	60.078	65.421	70.765	81.453
	7.0	55.039	55.929	56.642	57.711	59.492	60.383	63.055	68.399	73.742	84.430
	7.5	58.016	58.907	59.619	60.688	62.469	63.360	66.032	71.376	76.720	87.407
15 years	8.0	60.993	61.884	62.596	63.665	65.446	66.337	69.009	74.353	79.697	90.384
	8.5	63.970	64.861	65.573	66.642	68.423	69.314	71.986	77.330	82.674	93.362
	9.0	66.947	67.838	68.550	69.619	71.400	72.291	74.963	80.307	85.651	96.339
	9.5	69.924	70.815	71.527	72.596	74.377	75.268	77.940	83.284	88.628	99.316
	10.0	72.901	73.792	74.504	75.573	77.354	78.245	80.917	86.261	91.605	102.293
	10.5	75.878	76.769	77.481	78.550	80.332	81.222	83.894	89.238	94.582	105.270
	11.0	78.855	79.746	80.459	81.527	83.309	84.199	86.871	92.215	97.559	108.247
	11.5	81.832	82.723	83.436	84.504	86.286	87.176	89.848	95.192	100.536	111.224
	12.0	84.810	85.700	86.413	87.481	89.263	90.153	92.825	98.169	103.513	114.201
	12.5	87.787	88.677	89.390	90.459	92.240	93.131	95.802	101.146	106.490	117.178
	5.5	41.147	41.570	41.908	42.415	43.260	43.683	44.951	47.487	50.023	55.095
	6.0	44.311	44.734	45.072	45.579	46.425	46.847	48.115	50.651	53.187	58.259
	6.5	47.476	47.898	48.236	48.744	49.589	50.012	51.280	53.816	56.352	61.424
	7.0	50.640	51.062	51.401	51.908	52.753	53.176	54.444	56.980	59.516	64.588
	7.5	53.804	54.227	54.565	55.072	55.917	56.340	57.608	60.144	62.680	67.752
20 years	8.0	56.968	57.391	57.729	58.236	59.082	59.504	60.772	63.308	65.844	70.917
	8.5	60.133	60.555	60.893	61.401	62.246	62.669	63.937	66.473	69.009	74.081
	9.0	63.297	63.720	64.058	64.565	65.410	65.833	67.101	69.637	72.173	77.245
	9.5	66.461	66.884	67.222	67.729	68.574	68.997	70.265	72.801	75.337	80.409
	10.0	69.625	70.048	70.386	70.893	71.739	72.161	73.429	75.965	78.502	83.574
	10.5	72.790	73.212	73.550	74.058	74.903	75.326	76.594	79.130	81.666	86.738
	11.0	75.954	76.377	76.715	77.222	78.067	78.490	79.758	82.294	84.830	89.902
	11.5	79.118	79.541	79.879	80.386	81.232	81.654	82.922	85.458	87.994	93.066
	12.0	82.282	82.705	83.043	83.550	84.396	84.818	86.086	88.623	91.159	96.231
	12.5	85.447	85.869	86.208	86.715	87.560	87.983	89.251	91.787	94.323	99.395
	5.5	38.793	38.993	39.154	39.395	39.796	39.996	40.598	41.802	43.005	45.412
	6.0	42.046	42.247	42.407	42.648	43.049	43.249	43.851	45.055	46.258	48.665
	6.5	45.299	45.500	45.660	45.901	46.302	46.503	47.104	48.308	49.511	51.918
	7.0	48.552	48.753	48.913	49.154	49.555	49.756	50.357	51.561	52.764	55.172
	7.5	51.805	52.006	52.166	52.407	52.808	53.009	53.611	54.814	56.018	58.425
25 years	8.0	55.058	55.259	55.419	55.660	56.061	56.262	56.864	58.067	59.271	61.678
	8.5	58.311	58.512	58.673	58.913	59.314	59.515	60.117	61.320	62.524	64.931
	9.0	61.565	61.765	61.926	62.166	62.567	62.768	63.370	64.573	65.777	68.184
	9.5	64.818	65.018	65.179	65.419	65.821	66.021	66.623	67.826	69.030	71.437
	10.0	68.071	68.271	68.432	68.673	69.074	69.274	69.876	71.080	72.283	74.690
	10.5	71.324	71.524	71.685	71.926	72.327	72.527	73.129	74.333	75.536	77.943
	11.0	74.577	74.778	74.938	75.179	75.580	75.780	76.382	77.586	78.789	81.196
	11.5	77.830	78.031	78.191	78.432	78.833	79.034	79.635	80.839	82.042	84.449
	12.0	81.083	81.284	81.444	81.685	82.086	82.287	82.888	84.092	85.295	87.703
	12.5	84.336	84.537	84.697	84.938	85.339	85.540	86.142	87.345	88.549	90.956
	5.5	37.676	37.771	37.847	37.961	38.152	38.247	38.532	39.104	39.675	40.817
	6.0	40.971	41.066	41.142	41.257	41.447	41.542	41.828	42.399	42.970	44.112
	6.5	44.266	44.361	44.438	44.552	44.742	44.837	45.123	45.694	46.265	47.408
	7.0	47.561	47.657	47.733	47.847	48.037	48.133	48.418	48.989	49.560	50.703
	7.5	50.857	50.952	51.028	51.142	51.333	51.428	51.713	52.285	52.856	53.998
30 years	8.0	54.152	54.247	54.323	54.438	54.628	54.723	55.009	55.580	56.151	57.293
	8.5	57.447	57.542	57.619	57.733	57.923	58.018	58.304	58.875	59.446	60.589
	9.0	60.742	60.838	60.914	61.028	61.218	61.314	61.599	62.170	62.742	63.884
	9.5	64.038	64.133	64.209	64.323	64.514	64.609	64.894	65.466	66.037	67.179
	10.0	67.333	67.428	67.504	67.619	67.809	67.904	68.190	68.761	69.332	70.474
	10.5	70.628	70.723	70.800	70.914	71.104	71.199	71.485	72.056	72.627	73.770
	11.0	73.924	74.019	74.095	74.209	74.399	74.495	74.780	75.351	75.923	77.065
	11.5	77.219	77.314	77.390	77.504	77.695	77.790	78.075	78.647	79.218	80.360
	12.0	80.514	80.609	80.685	80.800	80.990	81.085	81.371	81.942	82.513	83.655
	12.5	83.809	83.904	83.981	84.095	84.285	84.380	84.666	85.237	85.808	86.951

Entry is the value of monthly income and capital gain as a percentage of initial investment.

Sale Price to Achieve A Given Overall Yield

	Holding Period	5.50%	6.00%	6.50%	7.00%	7.25%	Desired Yield 7.50%	7.75%	8.00%	8.25%	8.50%	8.75%	9.00%
	2.5	100.000	101.307	102.623	103.949	104.616	105.285	105.956	106.630	107.306	107.985	108.666	109.349
	5	100.000	102.819	105.694	108.626	110.114	111.617	113.134	114.667	116.214	117.776	119.354	120.947
Cap	7.5	100.000	104.567	109.288	114.165	116.664	119.204	121.785	124.408	127.074	129.783	132.535	135.332
Rate	10	100.000	106.590	113.494	120.725	124.466	128.294	132.210	136.216	140.314	144.505	148.792	153.175
5.50%	12.5	100.000	108.931	118.419	128.493	133.760	139.186	144.775	150.530	156.456	162.559	168.841	175.309
	15	100.000	111.638	124.182	137.694	144.832	152.237	159.917	167.880	176.137	184.697	193.569	202.763
	17.5	100.000	114.770	130.929	148.589	158.020	167.874	178.165	188.912	200.131	211.843	224.065	236.818
	20.0	100.000	118.393	138.825	161.493	173.731	186.609	200.157	214.405	229.385	245.131	261.677	279.061
	2.5	98.698	100.000	101.312	102.633	103.297	103.964	104.633	105.304	105.978	106.654	107.333	108.014
	5	97.209	100.000	102.847	105.751	107.224	108.713	110.215	111.733	113.266	114.813	116.376	117.954
Cap	7.5	95.508	100.000	104.644	109.443	111.903	114.403	116.944	119.526	122.151	124.819	127.530	130.284
Rate	10	93.562	100.000	106.747	113.816	117.476	121.221	125.052	128.973	132.984	137.088	141.285	145.579
6.00%	12.5	91.338	100.000	109.209	118.995	124.115	129.390	134.825	140.424	146.192	152.132	158.250	164.550
	15	88.796	100.000	112.091	125.129	132.023	139.178	146.602	154.304	162.294	170.581	179.174	188.083
	17.5	85.889	100.000	115.464	132.393	141.443	150.905	160.795	171.129	181.926	193.203	204.978	217.273
	20.0	82.566	100.000	119.413	140.996	152.662	164.957	177.900	191.524	205.861	220.943	236.804	253.481
	2.5	97.396	98.693	100.000	101.316	101.978	102.642	103.309	103.978	104.649	105.323	105.999	106.678
	5	94.419	97.181	100.000	102.875	104.335	105.808	107.297	108.800	110.318	111.851	113.399	114.962
Cap	7.5	91.016	95.433	100.000	104.722	107.142	109.602	112.103	114.645	117.229	119.855	122.524	125.237
Rate	10	87.125	93.410	100.000	106.908	110.486	114.147	117.895	121.730	125.654	129.670	133.779	137.982
6.50%	12.5	82.677	91.069	100.000	109.498	114.469	119.593	124.875	130.318	135.927	141.706	147.659	153.792
	15	77.591	88.362	100.000	112.565	119.214	126.118	133.287	140.728	148.451	156.465	164.778	173.402
	17.5	71.778	85.230	100.000	116.196	124.866	133.937	143.425	153.347	163.720	174.562	185.891	197.727
	20.0	65.132	81.607	100.000	120.498	131.599	143.305	155.643	168.643	182.336	196.754	211.930	227.900
	2.5	96.094	97.386	98.688	100.000	100.659	101.321	101.985	102.652	103.321	103.992	104.666	105.343
	5	91.628	94.363	97.153	100.000	101.445	102.904	104.378	105.867	107.370	108.888	110.421	111.969
Cap	7.5	86.523	90.865	95.356	100.000	102.381	104.801	107.262	109.763	112.306	114.891	117.519	120.190
Rate	10	80.687	86.819	93.253	100.000	103.495	107.074	110.737	114.487	118.325	122.253	126.272	130.386
7.00%	12.5	74.015	82.139	90.791	100.000	104.823	109.797	114.925	120.212	125.662	131.279	137.068	143.033
	15	66.387	76.724	87.909	100.000	106.405	113.059	119.972	127.152	134.608	142.348	150.383	158.722
	17.5	57.667	70.460	84.536	100.000	108.289	116.968	126.055	135.565	145.514	155.922	166.804	178.182
	20.0	47.698	63.214	80.587	100.000	110.533	121.652	133.386	145.762	158.811	172.566	187.057	202.320

	Holding Period	9.25%	9.50%	9.75%	10.00%	10.25%	Desired Yield 10.50%	10.75%	11.00%	11.50%	12.00%	12.50%	15.00%
	2.5	110.035	110.724	111.414	112.108	112.803	113.501	114.202	114.905	116.318	117.741	119.174	126.487
	5	122.555	124.178	125.818	127.473	129.144	130.831	132.534	134.253	137.740	141.294	144.914	164.053
Cap	7.5	138.173	141.060	143.993	146.972	149.999	153.074	156.196	159.368	165.862	172.560	179.466	217.328
Rate	10	157.658	162.241	166.927	171.718	176.616	181.623	186.740	191.971	202.780	214.067	225.850	292.885
5.50%	12.5	181.965	188.817	195.867	203.122	210.587	218.267	226.166	234.292	251.244	269.168	288.115	400.041
	15	212.290	222.161	232.386	242.976	253.944	265.300	277.058	289.229	314.866	342.318	371.700	552.014
	17.5	250.121	263.997	278.466	293.553	309.278	325.669	342.748	360.543	398.387	439.426	483.902	767.542
	20.0	297.318	316.489	336.614	357.738	379.902	403.154	427.542	453.116	508.030	568.341	634.525	1073.21
	2.5	108.697	109.383	110.072	110.762	111.456	112.151	112.849	113.550	114.958	116.377	117.805	125.093
	5	119.547	121.156	122.780	124.420	126.076	127.748	129.435	131.139	134.595	138.117	141.706	160.681
Cap	7.5	133.083	135.928	138.817	141.753	144.736	147.766	150.844	153.971	160.374	166.978	173.790	211.153
Rate	10	149.970	154.461	159.054	163.750	168.551	173.461	178.479	183.610	194.215	205.292	216.861	282.733
6.00%	12.5	171.037	177.715	184.589	191.664	198.946	206.440	214.151	222.084	238.640	256.155	274.678	384.250
	15	197.318	206.891	216.811	227.090	237.739	248.770	260.195	272.027	296.961	323.678	352.292	528.224
	17.5	230.105	243.498	257.470	272.047	287.249	303.102	319.629	336.857	373.521	413.316	456.481	732.409
	20.0	271.009	289.428	308.777	329.100	350.438	372.839	396.347	421.014	474.028	532.315	596.345	1021.99
	2.5	107.359	108.043	108.729	109.417	110.108	110.801	111.497	112.195	113.598	115.012	116.435	123.699
	5	116.540	118.134	119.743	121.368	123.008	124.665	126.337	128.025	131.450	134.941	138.498	157.310
Cap	7.5	127.994	130.795	133.642	136.534	139.473	142.459	145.492	148.574	154.885	161.397	168.114	204.978
Rate	10	142.282	146.681	151.180	155.781	160.486	165.298	170.218	175.249	185.650	196.518	207.871	272.582
6.50%	12.5	160.108	166.613	173.310	180.206	187.306	194.613	202.135	209.875	226.037	243.142	261.241	368.458
	15	182.346	191.621	201.236	211.204	221.534	232.240	243.333	254.824	279.055	305.038	332.885	504.434
	17.5	210.089	222.998	236.474	250.541	265.220	280.535	296.510	313.171	348.656	387.206	429.059	697.275
	20.0	244.700	262.367	280.940	300.463	320.975	342.523	365.153	388.913	440.025	496.288	558.164	970.771
	2.5	106.021	106.702	107.386	108.072	108.760	109.451	110.144	110.840	112.239	113.647	115.065	122.305
	5	113.533	115.112	116.706	118.315	119.941	121.582	123.238	124.911	128.305	131.764	135.289	153.939
Cap	7.5	122.904	125.663	128.466	131.315	134.210	137.152	140.140	143.177	149.397	155.815	162.438	198.803
Rate	10	134.595	138.901	143.306	147.812	152.422	157.136	161.957	166.888	177.085	187.744	198.882	262.430
7.00%	12.5	149.179	155.510	162.032	168.748	175.665	182.787	190.119	197.667	213.433	230.129	247.804	352.666
	15	167.374	176.351	185.661	195.317	205.330	215.710	226.470	237.621	261.150	286.399	313.478	480.643
	17.5	190.073	202.498	215.478	229.035	243.190	257.968	273.391	289.486	323.790	361.097	401.638	662.141
	20.0	218.391	235.306	253.103	271.825	291.512	312.208	333.958	356.811	406.023	460.262	519.984	919.549

Entry is percentage of original cost needed at sale to achieve desired yield.

Sale Price to Achieve A Given Overall Yield

	Holding Period						Desired Yield						
		5.50%	6.00%	6.50%	7.00%	7.25%	7.50%	7.75%	8.00%	8.25%	8.50%	8.75%	9.00%
	2.5	94.792	96.080	97.377	98.684	99.341	100.000	100.662	101.326	101.993	102.662	103.333	104.007
	5	88.838	91.544	94.306	97.125	98.555	100.000	101.459	102.933	104.422	105.925	107.444	108.977
Cap	7.5	82.031	86.298	90.712	95.278	97.619	100.000	102.421	104.882	107.384	109.928	112.513	115.142
Rate	10	74.249	80.229	86.506	93.092	96.505	100.000	103.579	107.243	110.995	114.835	118.766	122.789
7.50%	12.5	65.353	73.208	81.581	90.502	95.177	100.000	104.975	110.106	115.397	120.853	126.477	132.275
	15	55.183	65.086	75.818	87.435	93.595	100.000	106.657	113.576	120.765	128.232	135.988	144.041
	17.5	43.556	55.691	69.071	83.804	91.711	100.000	108.685	117.782	127.309	137.281	147.717	158.636
	20.0	30.264	44.822	61.175	79.502	89.467	100.000	111.129	122.881	135.287	148.377	162.184	176.740
	2.5	93.490	94.773	96.065	97.367	98.022	98.679	99.338	100.000	100.664	101.331	102.000	102.671
	5	86.047	88.726	91.460	94.249	95.665	97.096	98.541	100.000	101.474	102.963	104.466	105.985
Cap	7.5	77.539	81.731	86.069	90.557	92.858	95.199	97.579	100.000	102.461	104.964	107.508	110.095
Rate	10	67.812	73.638	79.758	86.184	89.514	92.926	96.421	100.000	103.665	107.418	111.260	115.193
8.00%	12.5	56.691	64.277	72.372	81.005	85.531	90.203	95.025	100.000	105.132	110.426	115.886	121.517
	15	43.978	53.448	63.727	74.871	80.786	86.941	93.343	100.000	106.922	114.116	121.593	129.361
	17.5	29.445	40.921	53.607	67.607	75.134	83.032	91.315	100.000	109.103	118.641	128.630	139.091
	20.0	12.829	26.429	41.762	59.004	68.401	78.348	88.871	100.000	111.762	124.189	137.310	151.160
	2.5	92.188	93.466	94.754	96.051	96.703	97.358	98.015	98.674	99.336	100.000	100.667	101.336
	5	83.257	85.907	88.613	91.374	92.776	94.192	95.622	97.067	98.526	100.000	101.489	102.992
Cap	7.5	73.047	77.163	81.425	85.835	88.097	90.398	92.738	95.118	97.539	100.000	102.503	105.047
Rate	10	61.374	67.048	73.011	79.275	82.524	85.853	89.263	92.757	96.335	100.000	103.753	107.596
8.50%	12.5	48.030	55.347	63.163	71.507	75.885	80.407	85.075	89.894	94.868	100.000	105.295	110.758
	15	32.774	41.810	51.636	62.306	67.977	73.882	80.028	86.424	93.078	100.000	107.198	114.680
	17.5	15.334	26.151	38.143	51.411	58.557	66.063	73.945	82.218	90.897	100.000	109.543	119.545
	20.0	---	8.036	22.349	38.507	47.335	56.695	66.614	77.119	88.238	100.000	112.437	125.580
	2.5	90.886	92.159	93.442	94.734	95.384	96.036	96.691	97.348	98.007	98.669	99.333	100.000
	5	80.466	83.089	85.766	88.499	89.886	91.287	92.703	94.133	95.578	97.037	98.511	100.000
Cap	7.5	68.554	72.596	76.781	81.113	83.336	85.597	87.897	90.237	92.616	95.036	97.497	100.000
Rate	10	54.936	60.458	66.264	72.367	75.534	78.779	82.105	85.513	89.005	92.582	96.247	100.000
9.00%	12.5	39.368	46.416	53.954	62.009	66.240	70.610	75.125	79.788	84.603	89.574	94.705	100.000
	15	21.570	30.172	39.545	49.742	55.168	60.822	66.713	72.848	79.235	85.884	92.802	100.000
	17.5	1.223	11.381	22.679	35.214	41.980	49.095	56.575	64.435	72.691	81.359	90.457	100.000
	20.0	---	---	2.937	18.009	26.269	35.043	44.357	54.238	64.713	75.811	87.563	100.000

	Holding Period						Desired Yield						
		9.25%	9.50%	9.75%	10.00%	10.25%	10.50%	10.75%	11.00%	11.50%	12.00%	12.50%	15.00%
	2.5	104.683	105.362	106.043	106.726	107.412	108.101	108.792	109.485	110.879	112.282	113.696	120.911
	5	110.526	112.089	113.668	115.263	116.873	118.498	120.140	121.797	125.160	128.588	132.081	150.568
Cap	7.5	117.814	120.530	123.290	126.096	128.947	131.844	134.788	137.780	143.908	150.234	156.762	192.628
Rate	10	126.907	131.121	135.432	139.844	144.357	148.974	153.696	158.527	168.520	178.969	189.893	252.278
7.50%	12.5	138.251	144.408	150.753	157.290	164.024	170.960	178.103	185.459	200.829	217.117	234.368	336.875
	15	152.402	161.080	170.087	179.431	189.125	199.180	209.607	220.419	243.244	267.759	294.071	456.853
	17.5	170.057	181.999	194.482	207.529	221.161	235.401	250.273	265.800	298.925	334.987	374.216	627.007
	20.0	192.082	208.245	225.266	243.188	262.048	281.892	302.764	324.710	372.020	424.236	481.804	868.327
	2.5	103.345	104.021	104.700	105.381	106.065	106.751	107.439	108.130	109.519	110.918	112.326	119.517
	5	107.518	109.067	110.631	112.210	113.805	115.415	117.041	118.683	122.015	125.411	128.873	147.197
Cap	7.5	112.724	115.398	118.115	120.877	123.684	126.537	129.436	132.383	138.420	144.652	151.086	186.452
Rate	10	119.219	123.340	127.558	131.875	136.292	140.811	145.435	150.166	159.955	170.195	180.904	242.126
8.00%	12.5	127.322	133.306	139.475	145.832	152.383	159.133	166.087	173.250	188.226	204.104	220.931	321.083
	15	137.430	145.810	154.512	163.545	172.921	182.650	192.745	203.216	225.339	249.119	274.664	433.063
	17.5	150.040	161.499	173.486	186.023	199.132	212.834	227.154	242.114	274.059	308.877	346.794	591.873
	20.0	165.773	181.183	197.429	214.550	232.585	251.577	271.569	292.609	338.018	388.210	443.623	817.105
	2.5	102.007	102.681	103.357	104.036	104.717	105.401	106.087	106.775	108.159	109.553	110.957	118.123
	5	104.511	106.045	107.593	109.158	110.737	112.332	113.943	115.570	118.870	122.235	125.665	143.825
Cap	7.5	107.635	110.265	112.939	115.657	118.421	121.229	124.084	126.986	132.931	139.071	145.409	180.277
Rate	10	111.532	115.560	119.685	123.906	128.227	132.649	137.174	141.805	151.390	161.421	171.914	231.974
8.50%	12.5	116.393	122.204	128.196	134.374	140.743	147.307	154.071	161.042	175.622	191.091	207.494	305.291
	15	122.458	130.540	138.937	147.659	156.716	166.120	175.882	186.013	207.433	230.479	255.257	409.273
	17.5	130.024	140.999	152.490	164.518	177.103	190.268	204.035	218.429	249.193	282.768	319.373	556.740
	20.0	139.464	154.122	169.592	185.913	203.122	221.262	240.375	260.507	304.015	352.184	405.443	765.883
	2.5	100.669	101.340	102.014	102.691	103.369	104.050	104.734	105.420	106.799	108.188	109.587	116.729
	5	101.504	103.022	104.556	106.105	107.669	109.249	110.845	112.456	115.725	119.059	122.457	140.454
Cap	7.5	102.545	105.133	107.763	110.438	113.158	115.922	118.732	121.589	127.443	133.489	139.733	174.102
Rate	10	103.844	107.780	111.811	115.937	120.162	124.487	128.913	133.444	142.825	152.646	162.925	221.822
9.00%	12.5	105.464	111.102	116.918	122.916	129.102	135.480	142.055	148.834	163.018	178.078	194.057	289.500
	15	107.486	115.270	123.362	131.772	140.511	149.590	159.019	168.811	189.528	211.839	235.850	385.482
	17.5	110.008	120.500	131.494	143.012	155.073	167.701	180.916	194.743	224.328	256.658	291.951	521.606
	20.0	113.155	127.061	141.755	157.275	173.658	190.946	209.181	228.406	270.013	316.157	367.263	714.662

Entry is percentage of original cost needed at sale to achieve desired yield.

Sale Price to Achieve A Given Overall Yield

	Holding Period	Desired Yield											
		5.50%	6.00%	6.50%	7.00%	7.25%	7.50%	7.75%	8.00%	8.25%	8.50%	8.75%	9.00%
	2.5	89.584	90.852	92.130	93.418	94.065	94.715	95.367	96.022	96.679	97.338	98.000	98.664
	5	77.676	80.270	82.919	85.623	86.996	88.383	89.785	91.200	92.630	94.075	95.534	97.008
Cap	7.5	64.062	68.029	72.137	76.392	78.575	80.796	83.056	85.355	87.694	90.072	92.492	94.953
Rate	10	48.499	53.867	59.517	65.459	68.543	71.706	74.948	78.270	81.675	85.165	88.740	92.404
9.50%	12.5	30.706	37.485	44.744	52.511	56.594	60.814	65.175	69.682	74.338	79.147	84.114	89.242
	15	10.366	18.534	27.453	37.177	42.359	47.763	53.398	59.272	65.392	71.768	78.407	85.320
	17.5	---	---	7.214	19.018	25.402	32.126	39.205	46.653	54.486	62.719	71.370	80.455
	20.0	---	---	---	---	5.203	13.391	22.100	31.357	41.189	51.623	62.690	74.420
	2.5	88.282	89.546	90.819	92.102	92.747	93.394	94.044	94.696	95.351	96.008	96.667	97.329
	5	74.885	77.452	80.072	82.748	84.106	85.479	86.866	88.267	89.682	91.112	92.556	94.015
Cap	7.5	59.570	63.461	67.493	71.670	73.814	75.995	78.215	80.474	82.771	85.109	87.487	89.905
Rate	10	42.061	47.277	52.769	58.551	61.553	64.632	67.790	71.027	74.346	77.747	81.234	84.807
10.00%	12.5	22.045	28.555	35.535	43.014	46.948	51.017	55.225	59.576	64.073	68.721	73.523	78.483
	15	---	6.896	15.362	24.613	29.550	34.704	40.083	45.696	51.549	57.652	64.012	70.639
	17.5	---	---	---	2.822	8.825	15.158	21.835	28.871	36.280	44.078	52.283	60.909
	20.0	---	---	---	---	---	---	---	8.476	17.664	27.434	37.816	48.840
	2.5	86.980	88.239	89.507	90.785	91.428	92.073	92.720	93.370	94.022	94.677	95.334	95.993
	5	72.095	74.633	77.225	79.872	81.217	82.575	83.947	85.333	86.734	88.149	89.579	91.023
Cap	7.5	55.078	58.894	62.849	66.948	69.053	71.194	73.374	75.592	77.849	80.145	82.481	84.858
Rate	10	35.623	40.686	46.022	51.642	54.563	57.559	60.632	63.784	67.016	70.330	73.728	77.211
10.50%	12.5	13.383	19.624	26.326	33.516	37.302	41.221	45.276	49.470	53.808	58.294	62.932	67.725
	15	---	---	3.271	12.048	16.741	21.645	26.769	32.120	37.706	43.535	49.617	55.959
	17.5	---	---	---	---	---	---	4.465	11.088	18.074	25.438	33.196	41.364
	20.0	---	---	---	---	---	---	---	---	---	3.246	12.943	23.260
	2.5	85.678	86.932	88.196	89.469	90.109	90.752	91.397	92.044	92.694	93.346	94.001	94.657
	5	69.304	71.815	74.379	76.997	78.327	79.671	81.028	82.400	83.786	85.187	86.601	88.031
Cap	7.5	50.585	54.327	58.206	62.227	64.292	66.394	68.533	70.710	72.926	75.181	77.476	79.810
Rate	10	29.186	34.096	39.275	44.734	47.572	50.485	53.474	56.540	59.686	62.912	66.221	69.614
11.00%	12.5	4.721	10.693	17.117	24.018	27.656	31.424	35.326	39.364	43.544	47.868	52.341	56.967
	15	---	---	---	---	3.932	8.586	13.454	18.544	23.863	29.419	35.222	41.278
	17.5	---	---	---	---	---	---	---	---	---	6.797	14.109	21.818
	20.0	---	---	---	---	---	---	---	---	---	---	---	---

	Holding Period	Desired Yield											
		9.25%	9.50%	9.75%	10.00%	10.25%	10.50%	10.75%	11.00%	11.50%	12.00%	12.50%	15.00%
	2.5	99.331	100.000	100.671	101.345	102.022	102.700	103.381	104.065	105.439	106.824	108.218	115.335
	5	98.496	100.000	101.519	103.053	104.602	106.166	107.746	109.342	112.580	115.882	119.249	137.083
Cap	7.5	97.455	100.000	102.588	105.219	107.895	110.615	113.380	116.191	121.954	127.908	134.057	167.927
Rate	10	96.156	100.000	103.937	107.969	112.097	116.325	120.652	125.083	134.260	143.872	153.936	211.670
9.50%	12.5	94.536	100.000	105.639	111.458	117.461	123.653	130.040	136.625	150.415	165.065	180.621	273.708
	15	92.514	100.000	107.787	115.886	124.307	133.060	142.157	151.608	171.622	193.199	216.443	361.692
	17.5	89.992	100.000	110.498	121.506	133.044	145.134	157.797	171.057	199.462	230.548	264.530	486.472
	20.0	86.845	100.000	113.918	128.638	144.195	160.631	177.986	196.304	236.010	280.131	329.082	663.440
	2.5	97.993	98.660	99.329	100.000	100.674	101.350	102.029	102.710	104.080	105.459	106.848	113.941
	5	95.489	96.978	98.481	100.000	101.534	103.083	104.648	106.228	109.435	112.706	116.041	133.712
Cap	7.5	92.365	94.867	97.412	100.000	102.632	105.307	108.028	110.794	116.466	122.326	128.381	161.752
Rate	10	88.468	92.220	96.063	100.000	104.032	108.162	112.391	116.722	125.695	135.097	144.946	201.519
10.00%	12.5	83.607	88.898	94.361	100.000	105.820	111.827	118.024	124.417	137.811	152.052	167.184	257.916
	15	77.542	84.730	92.213	100.000	108.102	116.530	125.294	134.405	153.717	174.559	197.036	337.902
	17.5	69.976	79.500	89.502	100.000	111.015	122.567	134.678	147.371	174.597	204.439	237.108	451.338
	20.0	60.536	72.939	86.082	100.000	114.732	130.315	146.792	164.203	202.008	244.105	290.902	612.218
	2.5	96.655	97.319	97.986	98.655	99.326	100.000	100.676	101.355	102.720	104.094	105.478	112.547
	5	92.482	93.955	95.444	96.947	98.466	100.000	101.549	103.114	106.290	109.529	112.833	130.341
Cap	7.5	87.276	89.735	92.237	94.781	97.368	100.000	102.676	105.397	110.977	116.745	122.705	155.577
Rate	10	80.781	84.440	88.189	92.031	95.968	100.000	104.130	108.361	117.130	126.323	135.957	191.367
10.50%	12.5	72.678	77.796	83.082	88.542	94.180	100.000	106.008	112.208	125.207	139.039	153.747	242.125
	15	62.570	69.460	76.638	84.114	91.898	100.000	108.431	117.203	135.811	155.920	177.628	314.112
	17.5	49.960	59.001	68.506	78.494	88.985	100.000	111.559	123.686	149.731	178.329	209.686	416.204
	20.0	34.227	45.878	58.245	71.362	85.268	100.000	115.597	132.101	168.005	208.079	252.721	560.996
	2.5	95.317	95.979	96.643	97.309	97.978	98.650	99.324	100.000	101.360	102.729	104.109	111.153
	5	89.474	90.933	92.407	93.895	95.398	96.917	98.451	100.000	103.145	106.353	109.624	126.970
Cap	7.5	82.186	84.602	87.061	89.562	92.105	94.693	97.324	100.000	105.489	111.163	117.029	149.401
Rate	10	73.093	76.660	80.315	84.063	87.903	91.838	95.870	100.000	108.565	117.549	126.968	181.215
11.00%	12.5	61.749	66.694	71.804	77.084	82.539	88.173	93.992	100.000	112.604	126.026	140.310	226.333
	15	47.598	54.190	61.063	68.228	75.693	83.470	91.569	100.000	117.906	137.280	158.221	290.322
	17.5	29.943	38.501	47.510	56.988	66.956	77.433	88.441	100.000	124.866	152.219	182.265	381.071
	20.0	7.918	18.817	30.408	42.725	55.805	69.685	84.403	100.000	134.003	172.052	214.541	509.774

Entry is percentage of original cost needed at sale to achieve desired yield.

Sale Price to Achieve A Given Overall Yield

	Holding Period	\multicolumn{12}{c}{Desired Yield}
		5.50%	6.00%	6.50%	7.00%	7.25%	7.50%	7.75%	8.00%	8.25%	8.50%	8.75%	9.00%
	2.5	84.376	85.625	86.884	88.153	88.790	89.431	90.073	90.718	91.365	92.015	92.667	93.322
	5	66.514	68.996	71.532	74.122	75.437	76.766	78.110	79.467	80.838	82.224	83.624	85.038
Cap	7.5	46.093	49.759	53.562	57.505	59.531	61.593	63.692	65.829	68.004	70.217	72.470	74.763
Rate	10	22.748	27.506	32.528	37.826	40.582	43.412	46.316	49.297	52.356	55.495	58.715	62.018
11.50%	12.5	---	1.763	7.907	14.520	18.011	21.628	25.376	29.258	33.279	37.441	41.750	46.208
	15	---	---	---	---	---	---	0.139	4.968	10.020	15.303	20.826	26.598
	17.5	---	---	---	---	---	---	---	---	---	---	---	2.273
	20.0	---	---	---	---	---	---	---	---	---	---	---	---
	2.5	83.074	84.318	85.572	86.836	87.472	88.109	88.750	89.392	90.037	90.684	91.334	91.986
	5	63.723	66.177	68.685	71.246	72.547	73.862	75.191	76.534	77.890	79.261	80.646	82.046
Cap	7.5	41.601	45.192	48.918	52.783	54.769	56.792	58.851	60.947	63.081	65.254	67.465	69.716
Rate	10	16.310	20.915	25.781	30.918	33.592	36.338	39.158	42.054	45.026	48.077	51.208	54.421
12.00%	12.5	---	---	---	5.023	8.365	11.831	15.426	19.152	23.014	27.015	31.159	35.450
	15	---	---	---	---	---	---	---	---	---	---	1.187	6.431
	17.5	---	---	---	---	---	---	---	---	---	---	---	---
	20.0	---	---	---	---	---	---	---	---	---	---	---	---
	2.5	81.772	83.012	84.261	85.520	86.153	86.788	87.426	88.066	88.709	89.354	90.001	90.651
	5	60.932	63.359	65.838	68.371	69.658	70.958	72.272	73.600	74.942	76.298	77.669	79.053
Cap	7.5	37.109	40.625	44.274	48.062	50.008	51.991	54.010	56.065	58.159	60.290	62.460	64.668
Rate	10	9.873	14.325	19.033	24.009	26.601	29.265	32.000	34.810	37.696	40.660	43.702	46.825
12.50%	12.5	---	---	---	---	---	2.035	5.476	9.046	12.749	16.588	20.568	24.691
	15	---	---	---	---	---	---	---	---	---	---	---	---
	17.5	---	---	---	---	---	---	---.	---	---	---	---	---
	20.0	---	---	---	---	---	---	---	---	---	---	---	---
	2.5	80.470	81.705	82.949	84.203	84.834	85.467	86.102	86.740	87.380	88.023	88.668	89.315
	5	58.142	60.540	62.991	65.496	66.768	68.054	69.354	70.667	71.994	73.336	74.691	76.061
Cap	7.5	32.616	36.057	39.630	43.340	45.247	47.190	49.169	51.184	53.236	55.326	57.454	59.621
Rate	10	3.435	7.735	12.286	17.101	19.611	22.191	24.843	27.567	30.367	33.242	36.195	39.228
13.00%	12.5	---	---	---	---	---	---	---	---	2.484	6.162	9.977	13.933
	15	---	---	---	---	---	---	---	---	---	---	---	---
	17.5	---	---	---	---	---	---	---	---	---	---	---	---
	20.0	---	---	---	---	---	---	---	---	---	---	---	---

	Holding Period	\multicolumn{12}{c}{Desired Yield}
		9.25%	9.50%	9.75%	10.00%	10.25%	10.50%	10.75%	11.00%	11.50%	12.00%	12.50%	15.00%
	2.5	93.979	94.638	95.300	95.964	96.631	97.300	97.971	98.645	100.000	101.365	102.739	109.759
	5	86.467	87.911	89.369	90.842	92.331	93.834	95.352	96.886	100.000	103.176	106.416	123.598
Cap	7.5	77.096	79.470	81.885	84.343	86.842	89.385	91.972	94.603	100.000	105.582	111.352	143.226
Rate	10	65.405	68.879	72.442	76.094	79.838	83.675	87.609	91.639	100.000	108.774	117.979	171.063
11.50%	12.5	50.821	55.592	60.525	65.626	70.898	76.347	81.976	87.792	100.000	113.013	126.874	210.542
	15	32.626	38.920	45.488	52.341	59.489	66.940	74.706	82.797	100.000	118.640	138.814	266.531
	17.5	9.927	18.001	26.514	35.482	44.927	54.866	65.322	76.314	100.000	126.110	154.843	345.937
	20.0	---	---	2.571	14.087	26.342	39.369	53.208	67.899	100.000	136.026	176.361	458.553
	2.5	92.641	93.298	93.957	94.619	95.283	95.950	96.619	97.290	98.640	100.000	101.370	108.364
	5	83.460	84.888	86.332	87.790	89.263	90.751	92.254	93.772	96.855	100.000	103.208	120.227
Cap	7.5	72.006	74.337	76.710	79.123	81.579	84.078	86.620	89.206	94.511	100.000	105.676	137.051
Rate	10	57.718	61.099	64.568	68.125	71.773	75.513	79.348	83.278	91.435	100.000	108.989	160.911
12.00%	12.5	39.892	44.490	49.247	54.168	59.257	64.520	69.960	75.583	87.396	100.000	113.437	194.750
	15	17.654	23.649	29.913	36.455	43.284	50.410	57.843	65.595	82.094	100.000	119.407	242.741
	17.5	---	---	5.518	13.977	22.897	32.299	42.203	52.629	75.134	100.000	127.422	310.803
	20.0	---	---	---	---	---	9.054	22.014	35.797	65.997	100.000	138.180	407.331
	2.5	91.303	91.957	92.614	93.274	93.935	94.599	95.266	95.935	97.280	98.635	100.000	106.970
	5	80.453	81.866	83.294	84.737	86.195	87.668	89.155	90.658	93.710	96.824	100.000	116.856
Cap	7.5	66.917	69.205	71.534	73.904	76.316	78.771	81.268	83.809	89.023	94.418	100.000	130.876
Rate	10	50.030	53.319	56.694	60.156	63.708	67.351	71.087	74.917	82.870	91.226	100.000	150.759
12.50%	12.5	28.963	33.387	37.968	42.710	47.617	52.693	57.945	63.375	74.793	86.987	100.000	178.958
	15	2.682	8.379	14.339	20.569	27.079	33.880	40.981	48.392	64.189	81.360	100.000	218.951
	17.5	---	---	---	---	0.868	9.732	19.084	28.943	50.269	73.890	100.000	275.669
	20.0	---	---	---	---	---	---	---	3.696	31.995	63.974	100.000	356.109
	2.5	89.965	90.617	91.271	91.928	92.588	93.249	93.913	94.580	95.920	97.271	98.630	105.576
	5	77.445	78.844	80.257	81.685	83.127	84.585	86.057	87.547	90.565	93.647	96.792	113.485
Cap	7.5	61.827	64.072	66.358	68.685	71.053	73.463	75.916	78.411	83.534	88.837	94.324	124.701
Rate	10	42.342	45.539	48.820	52.188	55.643	59.189	62.826	66.556	74.305	82.451	91.011	140.607
13.00%	12.5	18.035	22.285	26.690	31.252	35.976	40.867	45.929	51.166	62.189	73.974	86.563	163.167
	15	---	---	---	4.683	10.875	17.350	24.118	31.189	46.283	62.720	80.593	195.161
	17.5	---	---	---	---	---	---	---	5.257	25.403	47.781	72.578	240.535
	20.0	---	---	---	---	---	---	---	---	---	27.948	61.820	304.887

Entry is percentage of original cost needed at sale to achieve desired yield.

Sale Price for a Given Return on Equity

7.50% Equity Rate

Mortgage	Holding Period Years	5.00% 60% Loan	75% Loan	90% Loan	Desired Yield 6.00% 60% Loan	75% Loan	90% Loan	6.50% 60% Loan	75% Loan	90% Loan	7.00% 60% Loan	75% Loan	90% Loan
6.00%	5 Years	90.307	91.337	92.368	92.450	92.677	92.903	93.555	93.367	93.180	94.682	94.072	93.461
	7.5 "	84.395	86.017	87.639	87.751	88.114	88.478	89.517	89.218	88.919	91.343	90.359	89.376
	10 "	77.634	79.903	82.173	82.303	82.822	83.340	84.814	84.391	83.968	87.448	86.037	84.626
30 Yrs	12.5 "	69.899	72.877	75.854	75.987	76.681	77.376	79.336	78.775	78.213	82.904	81.005	79.105
	15 "	61.051	64.800	68.549	68.664	69.558	70.453	72.956	72.241	71.526	77.604	75.146	72.688
6.50%	5 Years	90.641	91.755	92.868	92.784	93.094	93.404	93.889	93.785	93.680	95.016	94.489	93.962
	7.5 "	84.893	86.640	88.386	88.250	88.737	89.225	90.015	89.841	89.667	91.842	90.983	90.123
	10 "	78.288	80.721	83.154	82.957	83.639	84.321	85.468	85.208	84.949	88.102	86.855	85.608
30 Yrs	12.5 "	70.693	73.869	77.044	76.780	77.673	78.566	80.129	79.766	79.403	83.698	81.997	80.295
	15 "	61.957	65.933	69.908	69.570	70.691	71.812	73.863	73.374	72.885	78.510	76.278	74.047
7.00%	5 Years	90.953	92.145	93.337	93.097	93.485	93.873	94.202	94.175	94.149	95.329	94.880	94.431
	7.5 "	85.363	87.227	89.091	88.720	89.325	89.930	90.485	90.429	90.372	92.312	91.570	90.828
	10 "	78.910	81.498	84.087	83.579	84.417	85.254	86.090	85.986	85.882	88.724	87.632	86.540
30 Yrs	12.5 "	71.453	74.819	78.185	77.541	78.624	79.707	80.890	80.717	80.544	84.458	82.947	81.436
	15 "	62.833	67.028	71.222	70.446	71.786	73.126	74.738	74.469	74.199	79.386	77.373	75.361
7.50%	5 Years	91.245	92.510	93.774	93.388	93.849	94.310	94.493	94.540	94.586	95.620	95.244	94.868
	7.5 "	85.806	87.780	89.754	89.162	89.878	90.593	90.927	90.981	91.035	92.754	92.123	91.492
	10 "	79.499	82.235	84.971	84.169	85.154	86.138	86.679	86.723	86.766	89.314	88.369	87.425
30 Yrs	12.5 "	72.180	75.728	79.276	78.268	79.532	80.797	81.617	81.626	81.635	85.185	83.856	82.527
	15 "	63.678	68.084	72.489	71.291	72.842	74.393	75.583	75.525	75.466	80.230	78.429	76.628
8.00%	5 Years	91.516	92.849	94.181	93.660	94.188	94.717	94.764	94.879	94.994	95.892	95.584	95.275
	7.5 "	86.220	88.298	90.377	89.576	90.396	91.216	91.342	91.500	91.657	93.169	92.641	92.114
	10 "	80.057	82.932	85.808	84.726	85.851	86.975	87.237	87.420	87.603	89.872	89.066	88.261
30 Yrs	12.5 "	72.874	76.595	80.316	78.961	80.400	81.838	82.311	82.493	82.675	85.879	84.723	83.567
	15 "	64.490	69.100	73.709	72.103	73.858	75.612	76.396	76.541	76.685	81.043	79.445	77.847
8.50%	5 Years	91.769	93.164	94.560	93.912	94.504	95.096	95.017	95.194	95.372	96.144	95.899	95.654
	7.5 "	86.609	88.784	90.959	89.965	90.882	91.798	91.731	91.985	92.240	93.557	93.127	92.696
	10 "	80.584	83.591	86.598	85.253	86.509	87.765	87.764	88.078	88.393	90.398	89.725	89.051
30 Yrs	12.5 "	73.534	77.421	81.307	79.622	81.225	82.829	82.971	83.318	83.666	86.539	85.549	84.558
	15 "	65.271	70.076	74.880	72.884	74.834	76.783	77.177	77.517	77.856	81.824	80.421	79.018
9.00%	5 Years	92.002	93.457	94.911	94.146	94.796	95.447	95.251	95.487	95.723	96.378	96.191	96.005
	7.5 "	86.972	89.238	91.504	90.328	91.336	92.343	92.094	92.439	92.785	93.920	93.581	93.241
	10 "	81.080	84.211	87.342	85.749	87.130	88.510	88.260	88.699	89.137	90.895	90.345	89.796
30 Yrs	12.5 "	74.162	78.205	82.248	80.250	82.010	83.770	83.599	84.103	84.608	87.167	86.333	85.500
	15 "	66.020	71.011	76.003	73.633	75.770	77.906	77.926	78.452	78.979	82.573	81.357	80.141
9.50%	5 Years	92.219	93.727	95.236	94.362	95.067	95.771	95.467	95.757	96.048	96.594	96.462	96.329
	7.5 "	87.311	89.662	92.012	90.667	91.759	92.851	92.433	92.863	93.293	94.259	94.004	93.749
	10 "	81.547	84.795	88.043	86.216	87.713	89.210	88.727	89.282	89.838	91.361	90.929	90.496
30 Yrs	12.5 "	74.758	78.950	83.141	80.845	82.754	84.663	84.194	84.847	85.501	87.763	87.078	86.393
	15 "	66.736	71.907	77.077	74.349	76.665	78.981	78.642	79.348	80.054	83.289	82.252	81.215
10.00%	5 Years	92.419	93.977	95.535	94.562	95.317	96.071	95.667	96.007	96.347	96.794	96.712	96.629
	7.5 "	87.626	90.056	92.485	90.982	92.153	93.324	92.748	93.257	93.766	94.574	94.398	94.222
	10 "	81.985	85.342	88.700	86.654	88.261	89.867	89.165	89.830	90.495	91.799	91.476	91.153
30 Yrs	12.5 "	75.321	79.654	83.987	81.408	83.459	85.509	84.758	85.552	86.346	88.326	87.782	87.238
	15 "	67.420	72.762	78.103	75.033	77.520	80.007	79.326	80.203	81.080	83.973	83.107	82.242
10.50%	5 Years	92.603	94.208	95.812	94.747	95.547	96.348	95.852	96.238	96.624	96.979	96.942	96.906
	7.5 "	87.919	90.422	92.925	91.275	92.520	93.764	93.041	93.623	94.206	94.868	94.765	94.662
	10 "	82.396	85.856	89.316	87.065	88.774	90.483	89.576	90.343	91.111	92.210	91.990	91.769
30 Yrs	12.5 "	75.854	80.320	84.786	81.941	84.125	86.308	85.291	86.218	87.145	88.859	88.448	88.037
	15 "	68.073	73.577	79.082	75.686	78.335	80.985	79.978	81.018	82.058	84.625	83.923	83.220
11.00%	5 Years	92.773	94.420	96.067	94.917	95.760	96.603	96.021	96.450	96.879	97.149	97.155	97.161
	7.5 "	88.191	90.762	93.333	91.547	92.860	94.172	93.313	93.963	94.614	95.140	95.105	95.070
	10 "	82.780	86.336	89.892	87.449	89.254	91.059	89.960	90.823	91.687	92.594	92.470	92.346
30 Yrs	12.5 "	76.357	80.949	85.540	82.444	84.753	87.062	85.793	86.846	87.899	89.362	89.077	88.791
	15 "	68.694	74.354	80.014	76.307	79.112	81.917	80.600	81.795	82.990	85.247	84.699	84.152
11.50%	5 Years	92.929	94.615	96.301	95.073	95.955	96.837	96.177	96.645	97.113	97.305	97.350	97.395
	7.5 "	88.443	91.077	93.711	91.799	93.175	94.550	93.565	94.278	94.991	95.391	95.420	95.448
	10 "	83.138	86.784	90.430	87.808	89.703	91.597	90.318	91.272	92.225	92.953	92.918	92.884
30 Yrs	12.5 "	76.830	81.540	86.251	82.918	85.345	87.772	86.267	87.438	88.610	89.835	89.669	89.502
	15 "	69.284	75.092	80.900	76.897	79.850	82.803	81.190	82.533	83.876	85.837	85.437	85.038

Entry is percentage of original cost needed at sale to achieve desired yield.

Sale Price for a Given Return on Equity

7.50% Equity Rate

Entry is percentage of original cost needed at sale to achieve desired yield.

Mortgage	Holding Period Years	Desired Yield 7.50% 60% Loan	7.50% 75% Loan	7.50% 90% Loan	8.00% 60% Loan	8.00% 75% Loan	8.00% 90% Loan	8.50% 60% Loan	8.50% 75% Loan	8.50% 90% Loan	9.00% 60% Loan	9.00% 75% Loan	9.00% 90% Loan
6.00% 30 Yrs	5 Years	95.833	94.791	93.749	97.006	95.524	94.042	98.203	96.272	94.341	99.423	97.035	94.647
	7.5	93.232	91.540	89.848	95.185	92.760	90.336	97.203	94.022	90.841	99.289	95.325	91.362
	10	90.211	87.764	85.317	93.109	89.575	86.041	96.145	91.473	86.801	99.327	93.462	87.596
	12.5	86.703	83.379	80.055	90.746	85.906	81.066	95.045	88.593	82.141	99.614	91.448	83.283
	15	82.629	78.287	73.944	88.060	81.681	75.302	93.922	85.345	76.767	100.246	89.297	78.348
6.50% 30 Yrs	5 Years	96.167	95.208	94.250	97.340	95.942	94.543	98.537	96.690	94.842	99.757	97.452	95.148
	7.5	93.730	92.163	90.596	95.683	93.383	91.084	97.701	94.645	91.588	99.787	95.949	92.110
	10	90.866	88.582	86.298	93.763	90.393	87.023	96.800	92.291	87.782	99.981	94.279	88.577
	12.5	87.497	84.371	81.245	91.539	86.898	82.256	95.838	89.584	83.331	100.407	92.440	84.473
	15	83.535	79.419	75.303	88.966	82.813	76.661	94.828	86.477	78.126	101.152	90.430	79.707
7.00% 30 Yrs	5 Years	96.479	95.599	94.718	97.652	96.332	95.012	98.849	97.080	95.311	100.070	97.843	95.616
	7.5	94.200	92.751	91.301	96.153	93.971	91.789	98.171	95.232	92.293	100.257	96.536	92.815
	10	91.487	89.359	87.231	94.385	91.170	87.956	97.422	93.068	88.715	100.603	95.057	89.510
	12.5	88.257	85.322	82.386	92.300	87.848	83.397	96.598	90.535	84.471	101.167	93.390	85.613
	15	84.411	80.514	76.617	89.842	83.908	77.975	95.704	87.572	79.440	102.028	91.525	81.021
7.50% 30 Yrs	5 Years	96.770	95.963	95.156	97.944	96.696	95.449	99.141	97.444	95.748	100.361	98.207	96.053
	7.5	94.642	93.303	91.964	96.595	94.523	92.452	98.613	95.785	92.956	100.699	97.089	93.478
	10	92.077	90.096	88.116	94.974	91.907	88.840	98.011	93.805	89.599	101.193	95.794	90.395
	12.5	88.984	86.230	83.477	93.027	88.757	84.487	97.326	91.444	85.562	101.894	94.299	86.704
	15	85.256	81.570	77.884	90.687	84.964	79.242	96.549	88.628	80.707	102.873	92.580	82.288
8.00% 30 Yrs	5 Years	97.042	96.302	95.563	98.215	97.036	95.856	99.412	97.784	96.155	100.633	98.547	96.461
	7.5	95.057	93.822	92.586	97.010	95.042	93.074	99.028	96.303	93.579	101.114	97.607	94.100
	10	92.635	90.794	88.952	95.532	92.604	89.677	98.569	94.502	90.436	101.751	96.491	91.231
	12.5	89.678	87.098	84.517	93.720	89.624	85.528	98.019	92.311	86.602	102.588	95.166	87.745
	15	86.069	82.586	79.103	91.499	85.980	80.461	97.362	89.644	81.927	103.686	93.597	83.508
8.50% 30 Yrs	5 Years	97.294	96.618	95.941	98.467	97.351	96.235	99.664	98.099	96.534	100.885	98.862	96.839
	7.5	95.446	94.307	93.169	97.398	95.528	93.657	99.417	96.789	94.161	101.503	98.093	94.683
	10	93.161	91.452	89.742	96.059	93.263	90.467	99.096	95.161	91.226	102.277	97.149	92.021
	12.5	90.338	87.923	85.508	94.381	90.450	86.518	98.680	93.136	87.593	103.249	95.992	88.735
	15	86.850	83.562	80.275	92.280	86.956	81.632	98.143	90.620	83.098	104.466	94.572	84.679
9.00% 30 Yrs	5 Years	97.528	96.910	96.292	98.701	97.643	96.586	99.898	98.391	96.885	101.119	99.154	97.190
	7.5	95.809	94.761	93.714	97.762	95.982	94.202	99.780	97.243	94.706	101.866	98.547	95.228
	10	93.658	92.072	90.487	96.555	93.883	91.211	99.592	95.781	91.970	102.774	97.770	92.766
	12.5	90.966	88.708	86.450	95.009	91.234	87.460	99.308	93.921	88.535	103.876	96.777	89.677
	15	87.598	84.498	81.398	93.029	87.892	82.755	98.891	91.556	84.221	105.215	95.508	85.802
9.50% 30 Yrs	5 Years	97.745	97.181	96.617	98.918	97.914	96.910	100.115	98.662	97.209	101.335	99.425	97.515
	7.5	96.148	95.185	94.222	98.100	96.405	94.710	100.119	97.667	95.214	102.205	98.970	95.736
	10	94.125	92.656	91.187	97.022	94.467	91.911	100.059	96.365	92.671	103.240	98.353	93.466
	12.5	91.562	89.452	87.343	95.604	91.979	88.353	99.903	94.665	89.428	104.472	97.521	90.570
	15	88.315	85.393	82.472	93.745	88.787	83.830	99.608	92.451	85.295	105.931	96.404	86.876
10.00% 30 Yrs	5 Years	97.945	97.431	96.917	99.118	98.164	97.210	100.315	98.912	97.509	101.535	99.675	97.815
	7.5	96.463	95.579	94.695	98.416	96.799	95.183	100.434	98.061	95.687	102.520	99.364	96.209
	10	94.563	93.203	91.844	97.460	95.014	92.568	100.497	96.912	93.328	103.679	98.901	94.123
	12.5	92.125	90.157	88.188	96.168	92.683	89.198	100.466	95.370	90.273	105.035	98.225	91.415
	15	88.999	86.248	83.498	94.429	89.642	84.856	100.292	93.306	86.321	106.615	97.259	87.902
10.50% 30 Yrs	5 Years	98.129	97.661	97.194	99.302	98.395	97.487	100.499	99.143	97.786	101.720	99.906	98.091
	7.5	96.756	95.945	95.134	98.709	97.166	95.622	100.727	98.427	96.127	102.813	99.731	96.649
	10	94.973	93.717	92.460	97.871	95.528	93.184	100.907	97.426	93.944	104.089	99.414	94.739
	12.5	92.658	90.823	88.987	96.700	93.349	89.998	100.999	96.036	91.072	105.568	98.891	92.215
	15	89.651	87.064	84.477	95.082	90.458	85.834	100.944	94.122	87.300	107.268	98.074	88.881
11.00% 30 Yrs	5 Years	98.299	97.874	97.448	99.472	98.607	97.742	100.669	99.355	98.041	101.890	100.118	98.346
	7.5	97.028	96.285	95.542	98.981	97.506	96.031	100.999	98.767	96.535	103.085	100.071	97.057
	10	95.358	94.197	93.036	98.255	96.008	93.761	101.292	97.906	94.520	104.473	99.894	95.315
	12.5	93.161	91.451	89.741	97.203	93.978	90.752	101.502	96.664	91.827	106.071	99.520	92.969
	15	90.272	87.841	85.409	95.703	91.235	86.766	101.565	94.899	88.232	107.889	98.851	89.813
11.50% 30 Yrs	5 Years	98.455	98.068	97.682	99.628	98.802	97.976	100.825	99.550	98.275	102.046	100.313	98.580
	7.5	97.280	96.600	95.920	99.233	97.821	96.408	101.251	99.082	96.913	103.337	100.386	97.434
	10	95.716	94.645	93.574	98.614	96.456	94.299	101.650	98.354	95.058	104.832	100.343	95.853
	12.5	93.634	92.043	90.452	97.677	94.569	91.462	101.976	97.256	92.537	106.544	100.112	93.679
	15	90.863	88.579	86.294	96.293	91.973	87.652	102.156	95.637	89.118	108.479	99.589	90.698

Sale Price for a Given Return on Equity

7.50% Equity Rate

Mortgage	Holding Period Years	Desired Yield 9.50% 60% Loan	75% Loan	90% Loan	10.00% 60% Loan	75% Loan	90% Loan	11.00% 60% Loan	75% Loan	90% Loan	12.00% 60% Loan	75% Loan	90% Loan
6.00% 30 Yrs	5 Years 7.5 " 10 " 12.5 " 15 "	100.668 101.444 102.660 104.467 107.062	97.813 96.672 95.544 94.481 93.557	94.958 91.901 88.429 84.496 80.052	101.938 103.670 106.149 109.620 114.402	98.606 98.064 97.725 97.702 98.144	95.275 92.457 89.302 85.784 81.887	104.552 108.344 113.622 120.887 130.797	100.240 100.985 102.396 104.744 108.391	95.929 93.626 91.170 88.601 85.986	107.268 113.325 121.799 133.550 149.733	101.938 104.098 107.507 112.658 120.226	96.608 94.871 93.214 91.767 90.720
6.50% 30 Yrs	5 Years 7.5 " 10 " 12.5 " 15 "	101.002 101.942 103.314 105.260 107.968	98.231 97.295 96.362 95.473 94.689	95.459 92.649 89.410 85.686 81.411	102.272 104.169 106.803 110.413 115.308	99.024 98.687 98.543 98.694 99.277	95.776 93.205 90.283 86.974 83.246	104.885 108.842 114.276 121.680 131.703	100.658 101.608 103.214 105.736 109.524	96.430 94.374 92.151 89.791 87.345	107.602 113.824 122.453 134.343 150.639	102.355 104.721 108.324 113.650 121.359	97.109 95.619 94.195 92.957 92.079
7.00% 30 Yrs	5 Years 7.5 " 10 " 12.5 " 15 "	101.315 102.412 103.936 106.021 108.844	98.621 97.883 97.139 96.424 95.784	95.927 93.354 90.343 86.827 82.725	102.584 104.639 107.425 111.173 116.184	99.414 99.274 99.320 99.644 100.372	96.245 93.910 91.216 88.115 84.560	105.198 109.312 114.898 122.441 132.579	101.048 102.195 103.991 106.686 110.619	96.898 95.079 93.084 90.932 88.659	107.914 114.294 123.075 135.104 151.515	102.746 105.309 109.102 114.601 122.454	97.577 96.324 95.128 94.098 93.393
7.50% 30 Yrs	5 Years 7.5 " 10 " 12.5 " 15 "	101.606 102.854 104.525 106.748 109.688	98.985 98.436 97.876 97.333 96.840	96.365 94.017 91.228 87.917 83.992	102.876 105.081 108.014 111.900 117.029	99.779 99.827 100.057 100.553 101.428	96.682 94.573 92.100 89.206 85.827	105.489 109.754 115.488 123.168 133.424	101.412 102.747 104.728 107.595 111.675	97.335 95.742 93.968 92.022 89.926	108.206 114.736 123.665 135.831 152.360	103.110 105.861 109.839 115.510 123.510	98.015 96.987 96.013 95.188 94.660
8.00% 30 Yrs	5 Years 7.5 " 10 " 12.5 " 15 "	101.878 103.269 105.083 107.441 110.501	99.325 98.954 98.574 98.200 97.856	96.772 94.639 92.064 88.958 85.211	103.147 105.496 108.572 112.594 117.841	100.118 100.346 100.754 101.420 102.444	97.089 95.195 92.937 90.246 87.047	105.761 110.169 116.046 123.861 134.236	101.752 103.267 105.425 108.462 112.691	97.743 96.364 94.805 93.063 91.145	108.477 115.151 124.223 136.525 153.172	103.449 106.380 110.536 116.377 124.526	98.422 97.609 96.849 96.229 95.879
8.50% 30 Yrs	5 Years 7.5 " 10 " 12.5 " 15 "	102.130 103.658 105.610 108.102 111.282	99.640 99.440 99.232 99.025 98.832	97.150 95.222 92.854 89.949 86.383	103.399 105.884 109.099 113.255 118.622	100.433 100.831 101.413 102.246 103.420	97.467 95.778 93.727 91.237 88.218	106.013 110.558 116.572 124.522 135.017	102.067 103.752 106.084 109.288 113.667	98.121 96.947 95.595 94.054 92.316	108.729 115.539 124.749 137.185 153.953	103.765 106.866 111.194 117.202 125.502	98.800 98.192 97.639 97.219 97.050
9.00% 30 Yrs	5 Years 7.5 " 10 " 12.5 " 15 "	102.364 104.021 106.106 108.730 112.031	99.932 99.894 99.853 99.810 99.768	97.501 95.767 93.599 90.890 87.506	103.633 106.247 109.595 113.882 119.371	100.726 101.285 102.033 103.030 104.356	97.818 96.323 94.471 92.179 89.341	106.247 110.921 117.069 125.150 135.766	102.359 104.206 106.704 110.073 114.603	98.472 97.492 96.340 94.995 93.440	108.963 115.902 125.246 137.813 154.702	104.057 107.320 111.815 117.987 126.438	99.151 98.737 98.384 98.161 98.173
9.50% 30 Yrs	5 Years 7.5 " 10 " 12.5 " 15 "	102.580 104.360 106.573 109.325 112.747	100.203 100.317 100.436 100.554 100.663	97.826 96.275 94.299 91.783 88.580	103.850 106.586 110.062 114.478 120.087	100.996 101.709 102.617 103.775 105.251	98.143 96.831 95.171 93.072 90.415	106.464 111.260 117.535 125.745 136.482	102.630 104.630 107.288 110.817 115.498	98.797 98.000 97.040 95.888 94.514	109.180 116.241 125.712 138.408 155.418	104.328 107.743 112.398 118.731 127.333	99.476 99.245 99.084 99.054 99.248
10.00% 30 Yrs	5 Years 7.5 " 10 " 12.5 " 15 "	102.780 104.675 107.011 109.889 113.431	100.453 100.711 100.984 101.259 101.518	98.126 96.748 94.956 92.629 89.606	104.050 106.901 110.500 115.041 120.771	101.246 102.103 103.164 104.479 106.106	98.443 97.304 95.829 93.917 91.441	106.663 111.575 117.974 126.309 137.166	102.880 105.024 107.835 111.521 116.353	99.097 98.473 97.697 96.734 95.540	109.380 116.557 126.150 138.972 156.102	104.578 108.137 112.946 119.436 128.188	99.776 99.718 99.741 99.900 100.274
10.50% 30 Yrs	5 Years 7.5 " 10 " 12.5 " 15 "	102.965 104.968 107.422 110.421 114.083	100.684 101.078 101.497 101.925 102.334	98.402 97.187 95.572 93.428 90.585	104.234 107.195 110.911 115.574 121.424	101.477 102.469 103.678 105.145 106.922	98.720 97.744 96.444 94.716 92.420	106.848 111.868 118.384 126.842 137.819	103.111 105.390 108.348 112.187 117.169	99.373 98.912 98.313 97.533 96.519	109.564 116.850 126.561 139.505 156.755	104.808 108.504 113.459 120.102 129.004	100.052 100.158 100.357 100.699 101.253
11.00% 30 Yrs	5 Years 7.5 " 10 " 12.5 " 15 "	103.134 105.240 107.806 110.924 114.705	100.896 101.418 101.977 102.553 103.111	98.657 97.595 96.148 94.182 91.517	104.404 107.467 111.295 116.077 122.045	101.689 102.809 104.158 105.774 107.698	98.974 98.152 97.021 95.470 93.352	107.018 112.140 118.768 127.344 138.440	103.323 105.730 108.829 112.816 117.945	99.628 99.320 98.889 98.287 97.450	109.734 117.122 126.945 140.007 157.376	105.020 108.844 113.939 120.730 129.780	100.307 100.566 100.933 101.453 102.184
11.50% 30 Yrs	5 Years 7.5 " 10 " 12.5 " 15 "	103.290 105.492 108.165 111.398 115.295	101.091 101.733 102.425 103.145 103.849	98.891 97.973 96.686 94.892 92.402	104.560 107.718 111.654 116.550 122.635	101.884 103.124 104.606 106.366 108.436	99.208 98.530 97.559 96.181 94.237	107.174 112.392 119.127 127.818 139.030	103.518 106.045 109.277 113.408 118.683	99.862 99.698 99.427 98.997 98.336	109.890 117.374 127.304 140.481 157.966	105.215 109.159 114.388 121.322 130.518	100.541 100.944 101.471 102.163 103.070

Entry is percentage of original cost needed at sale to achieve desired yield.

Sale Price for a Given Return on Equity

9.00% Equity Rate

Mortgage	Holding Period Years	5.00% 60% Loan	5.00% 75% Loan	5.00% 90% Loan	Desired Yield 6.00% 60% Loan	6.00% 75% Loan	6.00% 90% Loan	6.50% 60% Loan	6.50% 75% Loan	6.50% 90% Loan	7.00% 60% Loan	7.00% 75% Loan	7.00% 90% Loan
6.00%	5 Years	86.992	89.265	91.539	89.068	90.563	92.058	90.139	91.232	92.326	91.232	91.915	92.599
	7.5 "	79.093	82.703	86.313	82.270	84.689	87.107	83.944	85.735	87.526	85.677	86.818	87.959
	10 "	70.087	75.186	80.286	74.394	77.879	81.363	76.717	79.330	81.944	79.158	80.856	82.554
30 Yrs	12.5 "	59.817	66.575	73.334	65.270	69.983	74.697	68.285	71.868	75.451	71.507	73.882	76.256
	15 "	48.104	56.708	65.313	54.698	60.830	66.961	58.447	63.173	67.898	62.526	65.722	68.918
6.50%	5 Years	87.326	89.683	92.040	89.402	90.980	92.559	90.473	91.650	92.826	91.566	92.333	93.100
	7.5 "	79.591	83.326	87.061	82.769	85.312	87.855	84.443	86.358	88.274	86.176	87.441	88.707
	10 "	70.741	76.004	81.267	75.049	78.696	82.344	77.371	80.148	82.925	79.813	81.674	83.535
30 Yrs	12.5 "	60.610	67.567	74.524	66.063	70.975	75.887	69.078	72.860	76.641	72.301	74.873	77.446
	15 "	49.010	57.841	66.672	55.604	61.962	68.320	59.353	64.306	69.258	63.432	66.855	70.277
7.00%	5 Years	87.638	90.073	92.508	89.714	91.371	93.027	90.785	92.040	93.295	91.878	92.723	93.568
	7.5 "	80.061	83.914	87.766	83.239	85.899	88.560	84.913	86.946	88.979	86.646	88.029	89.412
	10 "	71.363	76.781	82.200	75.670	79.474	83.277	77.993	80.925	83.858	80.434	82.451	84.468
30 Yrs	12.5 "	61.371	68.517	75.664	66.824	71.926	77.027	69.839	73.810	77.781	73.061	75.824	78.587
	15 "	49.886	58.936	67.986	56.480	63.057	69.634	60.229	65.400	70.571	64.308	67.950	71.591
7.50%	5 Years	87.929	90.437	92.945	90.006	91.735	93.465	91.077	92.405	93.732	92.170	93.088	94.006
	7.5 "	80.503	84.466	88.429	83.681	86.452	89.223	85.355	87.498	89.642	87.088	88.581	90.075
	10 "	71.952	77.518	83.084	76.260	80.211	84.161	78.583	81.662	84.742	81.024	83.188	85.352
30 Yrs	12.5 "	62.098	69.426	76.755	67.551	72.834	78.118	70.566	74.719	78.872	73.788	76.733	79.677
	15 "	50.730	59.991	69.253	57.325	64.113	70.901	61.074	66.456	71.838	65.153	69.005	72.858
8.00%	5 Years	88.201	90.777	93.353	90.277	92.075	93.872	91.348	92.744	94.139	92.441	93.427	94.413
	7.5 "	80.918	84.985	89.051	84.096	86.971	89.845	85.770	88.017	90.264	87.503	89.100	90.697
	10 "	72.510	78.216	83.921	76.818	80.908	84.998	79.140	82.360	85.579	81.582	83.885	86.189
30 Yrs	12.5 "	62.791	70.293	77.795	68.244	73.701	79.159	71.260	75.586	79.912	74.482	77.600	80.718
	15 "	51.543	61.008	70.472	58.138	65.129	72.121	61.887	67.472	73.058	65.966	70.022	74.078
8.50%	5 Years	88.453	91.092	93.731	90.530	92.390	94.250	91.601	93.059	94.518	92.694	93.742	94.791
	7.5 "	81.307	85.470	89.634	84.484	87.456	90.428	86.158	88.502	90.847	87.891	89.586	91.280
	10 "	73.037	78.874	84.711	77.345	81.566	85.788	79.667	83.018	86.369	82.108	84.544	86.979
30 Yrs	12.5 "	63.452	71.119	78.786	68.905	74.527	80.149	71.920	76.412	80.903	75.142	78.425	81.709
	15 "	52.324	61.984	71.643	58.919	66.105	73.292	62.668	68.448	74.229	66.747	70.998	75.249
9.00%	5 Years	88.687	91.384	94.082	90.764	92.682	94.601	91.834	93.352	94.869	92.927	94.035	95.142
	7.5 "	81.670	85.924	90.179	84.847	87.910	90.973	86.521	88.956	91.392	88.254	90.040	91.825
	10 "	73.533	79.494	85.456	77.841	82.187	86.533	80.163	83.638	87.113	82.605	85.164	87.723
30 Yrs	12.5 "	64.080	71.904	79.728	69.533	75.312	81.091	72.548	77.196	81.845	75.770	79.210	82.650
	15 "	53.073	62.919	72.766	59.667	67.041	74.415	63.416	69.384	75.352	67.495	71.933	76.372
9.50%	5 Years	88.904	91.655	94.407	90.980	92.953	94.926	92.051	93.622	95.193	93.144	94.305	95.467
	7.5 "	82.009	86.348	90.687	85.186	88.334	91.481	86.860	89.380	91.900	88.593	90.463	92.333
	10 "	74.000	80.078	86.156	78.308	82.770	87.233	80.630	84.222	87.813	83.071	85.748	88.424
30 Yrs	12.5 "	64.675	72.648	80.621	70.128	76.056	81.984	73.143	77.940	82.738	76.365	79.954	83.543
	15 "	53.789	63.815	73.840	60.383	67.936	75.489	64.132	70.279	76.426	68.211	72.829	77.446
10.00%	5 Years	89.104	91.905	94.707	91.180	93.203	95.226	92.251	93.872	95.493	93.344	94.555	95.767
	7.5 "	82.324	86.742	91.160	85.501	88.728	91.954	87.175	89.774	92.373	88.908	90.857	92.806
	10 "	74.438	80.626	86.813	78.746	83.318	87.890	81.068	84.770	88.471	83.510	86.295	89.081
30 Yrs	12.5 "	65.239	73.353	81.466	70.692	76.761	82.830	73.707	78.645	83.583	76.929	80.659	84.389
	15 "	54.473	64.670	74.867	61.068	68.791	76.515	64.817	71.135	77.453	68.896	73.684	78.472
10.50%	5 Years	89.288	92.136	94.983	91.365	93.433	95.502	92.435	94.103	95.770	93.528	94.786	96.043
	7.5 "	82.617	87.108	91.600	85.795	89.094	92.394	87.469	90.141	92.812	89.202	91.224	93.246
	10 "	74.849	81.139	87.429	79.156	83.831	88.506	81.479	85.283	89.087	83.920	86.809	89.697
30 Yrs	12.5 "	65.772	74.019	82.265	71.224	77.427	83.629	74.240	79.311	84.383	77.462	81.325	85.188
	15 "	55.125	65.485	75.845	61.720	69.607	77.494	65.469	71.950	78.431	69.548	74.499	79.451
11.00%	5 Years	89.458	92.348	95.238	91.534	93.646	95.757	92.605	94.315	96.025	93.698	94.998	96.298
	7.5 "	82.889	87.448	92.008	86.067	89.434	92.802	87.741	90.480	93.220	89.474	91.564	93.654
	10 "	75.233	81.619	88.005	79.541	84.311	89.082	81.863	85.763	89.663	84.304	87.289	90.273
30 Yrs	12.5 "	66.274	74.647	83.020	71.727	78.055	84.383	74.742	79.939	85.137	77.964	81.953	85.942
	15 "	55.747	66.262	76.777	62.341	70.383	78.426	66.090	72.727	79.363	70.169	75.276	80.383
11.50%	5 Years	89.614	92.543	95.472	91.690	93.841	95.991	92.761	94.510	96.259	93.854	95.193	96.532
	7.5 "	83.141	87.763	92.385	86.318	89.749	93.180	87.992	90.795	93.598	89.725	91.878	94.031
	10 "	75.592	82.067	88.543	79.899	84.760	89.620	82.222	86.211	90.201	84.663	87.737	90.811
30 Yrs	12.5 "	66.748	75.239	83.730	72.201	78.647	85.093	75.216	80.531	85.847	78.438	82.545	86.652
	15 "	56.337	67.000	77.663	62.932	71.122	79.312	66.681	73.465	80.249	70.760	76.014	81.268

Sale Price for a Given Return on Equity

9.00% Equity Rate

Mortgage	Holding Period Years	Desired Yield 7.50% 60% Loan	75% Loan	90% Loan	8.00% 60% Loan	75% Loan	90% Loan	8.50% 60% Loan	75% Loan	90% Loan	9.00% 60% Loan	75% Loan	90% Loan
6.00%	5 Years	92.348	92.613	92.878	93.486	93.324	93.162	94.648	94.050	93.453	95.833	94.791	93.749
	7.5 "	87.471	87.939	88.408	89.327	89.099	88.872	91.246	90.299	89.351	93.232	91.540	89.848
	10 "	81.723	82.459	83.195	84.417	84.143	83.869	87.244	85.910	84.575	90.211	87.764	85.317
30 Yrs	12.5 "	74.948	76.032	77.116	78.619	78.326	78.034	82.533	80.773	79.013	86.703	83.379	80.055
	15 "	66.958	68.492	70.026	71.768	71.499	71.229	76.983	74.758	72.532	82.629	78.287	73.944
6.50%	5 Years	92.682	93.030	93.379	93.820	93.742	93.663	94.981	94.468	93.954	96.167	95.208	94.250
	7.5 "	87.969	88.562	89.155	89.825	89.722	89.619	91.745	90.922	90.099	93.730	92.163	90.596
	10 "	82.377	83.277	84.176	85.071	84.960	84.850	87.899	86.728	85.557	90.866	88.582	86.298
30 Yrs	12.5 "	75.741	77.024	78.306	79.412	79.318	79.224	83.326	81.764	80.203	87.497	84.371	81.245
	15 "	67.864	69.625	71.385	72.675	72.631	72.588	77.889	75.890	73.891	83.535	79.419	75.303
7.00%	5 Years	92.994	93.421	93.847	94.132	94.132	94.132	95.294	94.858	94.422	96.479	95.599	94.718
	7.5 "	88.439	89.150	89.860	90.295	90.310	90.324	92.215	91.510	90.804	94.200	92.751	91.301
	10 "	82.999	84.054	85.109	85.693	85.738	85.783	88.520	87.505	86.489	91.487	89.359	87.231
30 Yrs	12.5 "	76.501	77.974	79.447	80.173	80.269	80.365	84.087	82.715	81.343	88.257	85.322	82.386
	15 "	68.740	70.720	72.699	73.551	73.726	73.902	78.765	76.985	75.205	84.411	80.514	76.617
7.50%	5 Years	93.285	93.785	94.284	94.424	94.496	94.569	95.585	95.222	94.859	96.770	95.963	95.156
	7.5 "	88.881	89.702	90.523	90.737	90.862	90.987	92.657	92.062	91.467	94.642	93.303	91.964
	10 "	83.589	84.791	85.994	86.282	86.475	86.667	89.110	88.242	87.374	92.077	90.096	88.116
30 Yrs	12.5 "	77.229	78.883	80.538	80.900	81.177	81.455	84.814	83.624	82.434	88.984	86.230	83.477
	15 "	69.585	71.776	73.966	74.395	74.782	75.169	79.610	78.041	76.473	85.256	81.570	77.884
8.00%	5 Years	93.557	94.124	94.692	94.695	94.836	94.976	95.857	95.562	95.267	97.042	96.302	95.563
	7.5 "	89.296	90.221	91.146	91.152	91.381	91.610	93.072	92.581	92.090	95.057	93.822	92.586
	10 "	84.147	85.488	86.830	86.840	87.172	87.504	89.668	88.939	88.210	92.635	90.794	88.952
30 Yrs	12.5 "	77.922	79.750	81.578	81.593	82.045	82.496	85.507	84.491	83.474	89.678	87.098	84.517
	15 "	70.398	72.792	75.186	75.208	75.798	76.388	80.422	79.057	77.692	86.069	82.586	79.103
8.50%	5 Years	93.809	94.440	95.070	94.947	95.151	95.355	96.109	95.877	95.645	97.294	96.618	95.941
	7.5 "	89.685	90.707	91.728	91.540	91.866	92.192	93.460	93.066	92.672	95.446	94.307	93.169
	10 "	84.673	86.147	87.620	87.367	87.830	88.294	90.194	89.597	89.000	93.161	91.452	89.742
30 Yrs	12.5 "	78.583	80.576	82.569	82.254	82.870	83.487	86.168	85.316	84.465	90.338	87.923	85.508
	15 "	71.179	73.768	76.357	75.989	76.774	77.559	81.203	80.033	78.863	86.850	83.562	80.275
9.00%	5 Years	94.043	94.732	95.421	95.181	95.444	95.706	96.343	96.169	95.996	97.528	96.910	96.292
	7.5 "	90.048	91.161	92.273	91.904	92.320	92.737	93.824	93.520	93.217	95.809	94.761	93.714
	10 "	85.170	86.767	88.365	87.863	88.451	89.038	90.691	90.218	89.745	93.658	92.072	90.487
30 Yrs	12.5 "	79.210	81.361	83.511	82.882	83.655	84.428	86.796	86.101	85.407	90.966	88.708	86.450
	15 "	71.927	74.704	77.480	76.738	77.710	78.682	81.952	80.969	79.986	87.598	84.498	81.398
9.50%	5 Years	94.260	95.003	95.746	95.398	95.714	96.030	96.560	96.440	96.321	97.745	97.181	96.617
	7.5 "	90.387	91.584	92.781	92.242	92.744	93.245	94.162	93.944	93.725	96.148	95.185	94.222
	10 "	85.636	87.351	89.065	88.330	89.034	89.738	91.158	90.801	90.445	94.125	92.656	91.187
30 Yrs	12.5 "	79.806	82.105	84.404	83.477	84.399	85.321	87.391	86.845	86.300	91.562	89.452	87.343
	15 "	72.644	75.599	78.554	77.454	78.605	79.757	82.668	81.864	81.060	88.315	85.393	82.472
10.00%	5 Years	94.460	95.253	96.046	95.598	95.964	96.330	96.759	96.690	96.621	97.945	97.431	96.917
	7.5 "	90.702	91.978	93.254	92.558	93.138	93.718	94.478	94.338	94.198	96.463	95.579	94.695
	10 "	86.075	87.898	89.722	88.768	89.582	90.396	91.596	91.349	91.102	94.563	93.203	91.844
30 Yrs	12.5 "	80.369	82.809	85.249	84.040	85.104	86.167	87.955	87.550	87.145	92.125	90.157	88.188
	15 "	73.328	76.454	79.580	78.138	79.460	80.783	83.352	82.719	82.086	88.999	86.248	83.498
10.50%	5 Years	94.644	95.483	96.322	95.782	96.195	96.607	96.944	96.921	96.897	98.129	97.661	97.194
	7.5 "	90.995	92.345	93.694	92.851	93.504	94.158	94.771	94.704	94.638	96.756	95.945	95.134
	10 "	86.485	88.412	90.338	89.179	90.095	91.011	92.006	91.862	91.718	94.973	93.717	92.460
30 Yrs	12.5 "	80.902	83.475	86.048	84.573	85.770	86.966	88.487	88.216	87.944	92.658	90.823	88.987
	15 "	73.980	77.269	80.559	78.790	80.276	81.761	84.005	83.535	83.065	89.651	87.064	84.477
11.00%	5 Years	94.814	95.695	96.577	95.952	96.407	96.862	97.114	97.133	97.152	98.299	97.874	97.448
	7.5 "	91.267	92.685	94.102	93.123	93.844	94.566	95.043	95.044	95.046	97.028	96.285	95.542
	10 "	86.869	88.892	90.914	89.563	90.575	91.588	92.391	92.343	92.295	95.358	94.197	93.036
30 Yrs	12.5 "	81.405	84.104	86.802	85.076	86.398	87.720	88.990	88.844	88.699	93.161	91.451	89.741
	15 "	74.601	78.046	81.491	79.412	81.052	82.693	84.626	84.311	83.997	90.272	87.841	85.409
11.50%	5 Years	94.970	95.890	96.811	96.108	96.602	97.096	97.270	97.328	97.386	98.455	98.068	97.682
	7.5 "	91.519	92.999	94.480	93.375	94.159	94.944	95.295	95.359	95.424	97.280	96.600	95.920
	10 "	87.228	89.340	91.452	89.922	91.024	92.126	92.749	92.791	92.833	95.716	94.645	93.574
30 Yrs	12.5 "	81.879	84.696	87.513	85.550	86.990	88.430	89.464	89.436	89.409	93.634	92.043	90.452
	15 "	75.192	78.784	82.377	80.002	81.791	83.579	85.216	85.050	84.883	90.863	88.579	86.294

Entry is percentage of original cost needed at sale to achieve desired yield.

Sale Price for a Given Return on Equity

9.00% Equity Rate

Mortgage	Holding Period Years	9.50% 60% Loan	75% Loan	90% Loan	10.00% 60% Loan	75% Loan	90% Loan	11.00% 60% Loan	75% Loan	90% Loan	12.00% 60% Loan	75% Loan	90% Loan
6.00% 30 Yrs	5 Years	97.042	95.546	94.051	98.275	96.317	94.359	100.815	97.905	94.994	103.456	99.555	95.655
	7.5 "	95.285	92.823	90.361	97.407	94.149	90.892	101.867	96.937	92.007	106.628	99.912	93.197
	10 "	93.323	89.709	86.095	96.586	91.749	86.911	103.589	96.125	88.662	111.270	100.926	90.582
	12.5 "	91.144	86.155	81.165	95.870	89.108	82.347	106.237	95.588	84.939	117.935	102.899	87.863
	15 "	88.737	82.104	75.471	95.338	86.230	77.121	110.154	95.489	80.825	127.365	106.246	85.128
6.50% 30 Yrs	5 Years	97.375	95.964	94.552	98.609	96.734	94.860	101.149	98.322	95.495	103.790	99.973	96.156
	7.5 "	95.783	93.446	91.109	97.906	94.773	91.639	102.366	97.560	92.754	107.126	100.535	93.944
	10 "	93.978	90.527	87.076	97.241	92.566	87.892	104.243	96.943	89.643	111.924	101.744	91.563
	12.5 "	91.938	87.147	82.355	96.663	90.100	83.537	107.030	96.579	86.129	118.728	103.890	89.053
	15 "	89.643	83.237	76.830	96.244	87.362	78.480	111.060	96.622	82.184	128.271	107.379	86.487
7.00% 30 Yrs	5 Years	97.688	96.354	95.021	98.921	97.125	95.329	101.461	98.713	95.964	104.102	100.363	96.624
	7.5 "	96.253	94.034	91.814	98.376	95.360	92.344	102.836	98.148	93.459	107.596	101.123	94.650
	10 "	94.600	91.304	88.009	97.862	93.344	88.825	104.865	97.720	90.576	112.546	102.521	92.496
	12.5 "	92.698	88.097	83.496	97.424	91.051	84.678	107.791	97.530	87.269	119.488	104.841	90.194
	15 "	90.519	84.332	78.144	97.120	88.457	79.794	111.936	97.717	83.498	129.147	108.474	87.801
7.50% 30 Yrs	5 Years	97.979	96.719	95.458	99.213	97.489	95.766	101.753	99.077	96.401	104.394	100.728	97.062
	7.5 "	96.695	94.586	92.477	98.818	95.913	93.008	103.278	98.700	94.123	108.038	101.675	95.313
	10 "	95.189	92.041	88.894	98.452	94.081	89.709	105.455	98.457	91.460	113.136	103.258	93.380
	12.5 "	93.425	89.006	84.587	98.151	91.959	85.768	108.518	98.439	88.360	120.215	105.750	91.284
	15 "	91.364	85.388	79.411	97.965	89.513	81.061	112.780	98.773	84.765	129.992	109.530	89.068
8.00% 30 Yrs	5 Years	98.251	97.058	95.865	99.484	97.829	96.173	102.024	99.416	96.808	104.665	101.067	97.469
	7.5 "	97.110	95.105	93.099	99.233	96.431	93.630	103.693	99.219	94.745	108.453	102.194	95.935
	10 "	95.747	92.739	89.730	99.010	94.778	90.546	106.012	99.155	92.297	113.693	103.955	94.217
	12.5 "	94.119	89.873	85.627	98.844	92.827	86.809	109.211	99.306	89.400	120.909	106.617	92.325
	15 "	92.177	86.404	80.630	98.778	90.529	82.281	113.593	99.789	85.984	130.805	110.546	90.287
8.50% 30 Yrs	5 Years	98.503	97.373	96.243	99.736	98.144	96.552	102.276	99.732	97.187	104.918	101.382	97.847
	7.5 "	97.499	95.590	93.682	99.621	96.917	94.212	104.081	99.704	95.328	108.841	102.679	96.518
	10 "	96.274	93.397	90.520	99.536	95.436	91.336	106.539	99.813	93.087	114.220	104.613	95.007
	12.5 "	94.779	90.699	86.618	99.505	93.652	87.799	109.872	100.131	90.391	121.570	107.443	93.315
	15 "	92.958	87.380	81.802	99.559	91.505	83.452	114.374	100.765	87.156	131.585	111.522	91.458
9.00% 30 Yrs	5 Years	98.737	97.666	96.594	99.970	98.436	96.903	102.510	100.024	97.538	105.152	101.675	98.198
	7.5 "	97.862	96.044	94.227	99.984	97.371	94.757	104.444	100.158	95.872	109.205	103.134	97.062
	10 "	96.770	94.017	91.265	100.033	96.057	92.081	107.036	100.433	93.831	114.716	105.234	95.752
	12.5 "	95.407	91.483	87.560	100.133	94.437	88.741	110.500	100.916	91.333	122.197	108.227	94.257
	15 "	93.706	88.316	82.925	100.307	92.441	84.575	115.123	101.701	88.279	132.334	112.458	92.582
9.50% 30 Yrs	5 Years	98.954	97.936	96.919	100.187	98.707	97.227	102.727	100.295	97.862	105.368	101.945	98.523
	7.5 "	98.201	96.468	94.735	100.323	97.794	95.265	104.783	100.582	96.380	109.543	103.557	97.571
	10 "	97.237	94.601	91.965	100.500	96.640	92.781	107.502	101.017	94.531	115.183	105.817	96.452
	12.5 "	96.003	92.228	88.453	100.728	95.181	89.634	111.095	101.660	92.226	122.793	108.972	95.150
	15 "	94.423	89.211	83.999	101.024	93.336	85.649	115.839	102.596	89.353	133.050	113.353	93.656
10.00% 30 Yrs	5 Years	99.153	98.186	97.219	100.387	98.957	97.527	102.927	100.545	98.162	105.568	102.195	98.823
	7.5 "	98.516	96.862	95.208	100.638	98.188	95.738	105.098	100.976	96.853	109.859	103.951	98.044
	10 "	97.675	95.149	92.622	100.938	97.188	93.438	107.940	101.564	95.189	115.621	106.365	97.109
	12.5 "	96.566	92.932	89.298	101.292	95.886	90.480	111.659	102.365	93.071	123.356	109.676	95.996
	15 "	95.107	90.066	85.025	101.708	94.191	86.675	116.523	103.451	90.379	133.734	114.208	94.682
10.50% 30 Yrs	5 Years	99.338	98.417	97.496	100.571	99.188	97.804	103.111	100.775	98.439	105.752	102.426	99.099
	7.5 "	98.809	97.228	95.648	100.932	98.555	96.178	105.392	101.342	97.293	110.152	104.318	98.483
	10 "	98.085	95.662	93.238	101.348	97.701	94.054	108.351	102.078	95.804	116.032	106.878	97.725
	12.5 "	97.099	93.598	90.097	101.824	96.552	91.279	112.191	103.031	93.870	123.889	110.342	96.795
	15 "	95.759	90.881	86.004	102.360	95.007	87.654	117.175	104.267	91.358	134.387	115.024	95.661
11.00% 30 Yrs	5 Years	99.508	98.629	97.750	100.741	99.400	98.059	103.281	100.987	98.694	105.922	102.638	99.354
	7.5 "	99.081	97.568	96.056	101.204	98.895	96.586	105.664	101.682	97.701	110.424	104.658	98.891
	10 "	98.470	96.142	93.814	101.733	98.181	94.630	108.735	102.558	96.381	116.416	107.359	98.301
	12.5 "	97.602	94.227	90.851	102.327	97.180	92.033	112.694	103.659	94.625	124.392	110.970	97.549
	15 "	96.380	91.658	86.936	102.981	95.784	88.586	117.797	105.043	92.290	135.008	115.800	96.593
11.50% 30 Yrs	5 Years	99.664	98.824	97.984	100.897	99.595	98.293	103.437	101.182	98.928	106.078	102.833	99.588
	7.5 "	99.333	97.883	96.433	101.455	99.210	96.964	105.916	101.997	98.079	110.676	104.972	99.269
	10 "	98.828	96.590	94.352	102.091	98.630	95.168	109.094	103.006	96.919	116.775	107.807	98.839
	12.5 "	98.075	94.819	91.562	102.801	97.772	92.743	113.168	104.251	95.335	124.865	111.562	98.259
	15 "	96.971	92.396	87.821	103.572	96.522	89.472	118.387	105.781	93.175	135.599	116.538	97.478

Entry is percentage of original cost needed at sale to achieve desired yield.

Sale Price for a Given Return on Equity

10.50% Equity Rate

		Desired Yield											
		5.00%			6.00%			6.50%			7.00%		
	Holding Period	60%	75%	90%	60%	75%	90%	60%	75%	90%	60%	75%	90%
Mortgage	Years	Loan	Loan	Loan	Loan	Loan	Loan	Loan	Loan	Loan	Loan	Loan	Loan
6.00%	5 Years	83.676	87.193	90.710	85.686	88.449	91.212	86.723	89.097	91.471	87.782	89.759	91.736
	7.5 "	73.791	79.389	84.988	76.789	81.263	85.737	78.372	82.252	86.133	80.011	83.277	86.543
	10 "	62.540	70.470	78.399	66.486	72.936	79.386	68.620	74.270	79.919	70.868	75.675	80.481
30 Yrs	12.5 "	49.734	60.274	70.813	54.553	63.285	72.018	57.234	64.961	72.688	60.110	66.758	73.407
	15 "	35.156	48.616	62.076	40.733	52.101	63.470	43.938	54.104	64.271	47.449	56.299	65.149
6.50%	5 Years	84.010	87.610	91.211	86.020	88.867	91.713	87.057	89.515	91.972	88.116	90.176	92.237
	7.5 "	74.289	80.012	85.735	77.288	81.886	86.485	78.870	82.875	86.881	80.510	83.900	87.290
	10 "	63.194	71.287	79.381	67.140	73.754	80.367	69.275	75.088	80.901	71.523	76.493	81.463
30 Yrs	12.5 "	50.528	61.266	72.003	55.346	64.277	73.208	58.027	65.953	73.878	60.903	67.750	74.597
	15 "	36.063	49.749	63.435	41.639	53.234	64.829	44.844	55.237	65.630	48.355	57.431	66.508
7.00%	5 Years	84.323	88.001	91.679	86.332	89.257	92.182	87.369	89.905	92.441	88.428	90.567	92.706
	7.5 "	74.759	80.600	86.440	77.758	82.474	87.190	79.340	83.463	87.586	80.980	84.488	87.995
	10 "	63.816	72.065	80.313	67.762	74.531	81.300	69.896	75.865	81.833	72.144	77.270	82.395
30 Yrs	12.5 "	51.288	62.216	73.144	56.107	65.228	74.348	58.788	66.903	75.019	61.664	68.701	75.737
	15 "	36.938	50.844	64.749	42.515	54.329	66.143	45.720	56.332	66.944	49.231	58.526	67.822
7.50%	5 Years	84.614	88.365	92.117	86.624	89.621	92.619	87.661	90.269	92.878	88.719	90.931	93.143
	7.5 "	75.201	81.152	87.103	78.200	83.026	87.853	79.782	84.015	88.249	81.422	85.040	88.658
	10 "	64.406	72.802	81.198	68.352	75.268	82.184	70.486	76.602	82.718	72.734	78.007	83.280
30 Yrs	12.5 "	52.015	63.125	74.234	56.834	66.136	75.439	59.515	67.812	76.109	62.391	69.609	76.828
	15 "	37.783	51.899	66.016	43.359	55.385	67.410	46.565	57.388	68.211	50.075	59.582	69.089
8.00%	5 Years	84.886	88.705	92.524	86.895	89.961	93.026	87.932	90.609	93.285	88.991	91.270	93.550
	7.5 "	75.616	81.671	87.726	78.615	83.545	88.475	80.197	84.534	88.871	81.837	85.559	89.281
	10 "	64.963	73.499	82.034	68.909	75.965	83.021	71.044	77.299	83.554	73.292	78.704	84.116
30 Yrs	12.5 "	52.709	63.992	75.275	57.528	67.003	76.479	60.208	68.679	77.150	63.084	70.476	77.869
	15 "	38.596	52.916	67.235	44.172	56.401	68.629	47.377	58.404	69.431	50.888	60.598	70.308
8.50%	5 Years	85.138	89.020	92.902	87.147	90.276	93.405	88.184	90.924	93.664	89.243	91.586	93.928
	7.5 "	76.004	82.156	88.308	79.003	84.031	89.058	80.586	85.020	89.454	82.225	86.044	89.864
	10 "	65.490	74.157	82.824	69.436	76.624	83.811	71.570	77.957	84.345	73.819	79.363	84.907
30 Yrs	12.5 "	53.370	64.818	76.266	58.188	67.829	77.470	60.869	69.505	78.140	63.745	71.302	78.859
	15 "	39.377	53.892	68.406	44.953	57.377	69.800	48.158	59.380	70.602	51.669	61.574	71.479
9.00%	5 Years	85.372	89.312	93.253	87.381	90.568	93.755	88.418	91.216	94.015	89.477	91.878	94.279
	7.5 "	76.368	82.610	88.853	79.366	84.485	89.603	80.949	85.474	89.998	82.588	86.498	90.408
	10 "	65.986	74.778	83.569	69.932	77.244	84.555	72.067	78.578	85.089	74.315	79.983	85.651
30 Yrs	12.5 "	53.997	65.602	77.207	58.816	68.614	78.412	61.497	70.289	79.082	64.373	72.087	79.801
	15 "	40.125	54.827	69.529	45.702	58.312	70.923	48.907	60.316	71.725	52.418	62.510	72.602
9.50%	5 Years	85.588	89.583	93.578	87.598	90.839	94.080	88.635	91.487	94.339	89.694	92.149	94.604
	7.5 "	76.706	83.034	89.361	79.705	84.908	90.111	81.287	85.897	90.507	82.927	86.922	90.916
	10 "	66.453	75.361	84.269	70.399	77.827	85.256	72.534	79.161	85.789	74.782	80.566	86.351
30 Yrs	12.5 "	54.593	66.346	78.100	59.411	69.358	79.305	62.092	71.034	79.975	64.968	72.831	80.694
	15 "	40.842	55.723	70.604	46.418	59.208	71.998	49.623	61.211	72.799	53.134	63.405	73.677
10.00%	5 Years	85.788	89.833	93.878	87.798	91.089	94.380	88.835	91.737	94.639	89.894	92.399	94.904
	7.5 "	77.022	83.428	89.834	80.021	85.302	90.584	81.603	86.291	90.980	83.242	87.316	91.389
	10 "	66.891	75.909	84.926	70.837	78.375	85.913	72.972	79.709	86.446	75.220	81.114	87.008
30 Yrs	12.5 "	55.156	67.051	78.946	59.975	70.063	80.150	62.656	71.738	80.821	65.532	73.536	81.540
	15 "	41.526	56.578	71.630	47.102	60.063	73.024	50.307	62.066	73.825	53.818	64.261	74.703
10.50%	5 Years	85.973	90.064	94.154	87.982	91.320	94.657	89.019	91.968	94.916	90.078	92.629	95.181
	7.5 "	77.315	83.794	90.274	80.314	85.669	91.024	81.896	86.658	91.419	83.536	87.682	91.829
	10 "	67.302	76.422	85.542	71.248	78.888	86.529	73.382	80.222	87.062	75.630	81.627	87.624
30 Yrs	12.5 "	55.689	67.717	79.745	60.508	70.729	80.950	63.188	72.404	81.620	66.064	74.202	82.339
	15 "	42.178	57.393	72.609	47.754	60.879	74.003	50.960	62.882	74.804	54.471	65.076	75.682
11.00%	5 Years	86.142	90.276	94.409	88.152	91.532	94.911	89.189	92.180	95.171	90.248	92.842	95.435
	7.5 "	77.587	84.134	90.682	80.586	86.009	91.432	82.168	86.998	91.827	83.808	88.022	92.237
	10 "	67.686	76.902	86.118	71.632	79.369	87.105	73.766	80.702	87.639	76.015	82.108	88.201
30 Yrs	12.5 "	56.192	68.345	80.499	61.010	71.357	81.704	63.691	73.032	82.374	66.567	74.830	83.093
	15 "	42.800	58.170	73.540	48.376	61.655	74.934	51.581	63.658	75.736	55.092	65.853	76.613
11.50%	5 Years	86.298	90.471	94.643	88.308	91.727	95.146	89.345	92.375	95.405	90.404	93.037	95.669
	7.5 "	77.839	84.449	91.060	80.838	86.324	91.810	82.420	87.312	92.205	84.059	88.337	92.615
	10 "	68.045	77.351	86.657	71.991	79.817	87.643	74.125	81.151	88.177	76.373	82.556	88.739
30 Yrs	12.5 "	56.665	68.937	81.209	61.484	71.949	82.414	64.165	73.624	83.084	67.041	75.422	83.803
	15 "	43.390	58.908	74.426	48.966	62.393	75.820	52.171	64.396	76.621	55.682	66.591	77.499

Sale Price for a Given Return on Equity

10.50% Equity Rate

Mortgage	Holding Period Years	7.50% 60% Loan	75% Loan	90% Loan	Desired Yield 8.00% 60% Loan	75% Loan	90% Loan	8.50% 60% Loan	75% Loan	90% Loan	9.00% 60% Loan	75% Loan	90% Loan
6.00%	5 Years	88.863	90.434	92.006	89.966	91.124	92.282	91.092	91.828	92.564	92.242	92.547	92.851
	7.5 "	81.710	84.338	86.967	83.469	85.438	87.407	85.290	86.576	87.862	87.175	87.754	88.334
	10 "	73.235	77.154	81.073	75.725	78.710	81.696	78.343	80.347	82.350	81.096	82.067	83.038
30 Yrs	12.5 "	63.192	68.685	74.177	66.491	70.747	75.002	70.021	72.953	75.885	73.793	75.311	76.828
	15 "	51.287	58.698	66.108	55.477	61.317	67.156	60.043	64.170	68.298	65.013	67.276	69.540
6.50%	5 Years	89.196	90.852	92.507	90.300	91.542	92.783	91.426	92.246	93.065	92.576	92.964	93.352
	7.5 "	82.208	84.962	87.715	83.967	86.061	88.155	85.788	87.199	88.610	87.674	88.377	89.081
	10 "	73.889	77.972	82.054	76.379	79.528	82.677	78.998	81.164	83.331	81.750	82.885	84.019
30 Yrs	12.5 "	63.985	69.676	75.367	67.285	71.739	76.192	70.814	73.945	77.075	74.587	76.302	78.018
	15 "	52.193	59.830	67.468	56.383	62.449	68.515	60.950	65.303	69.657	65.919	68.409	70.899
7.00%	5 Years	89.509	91.242	92.976	90.612	91.932	93.252	91.739	92.636	93.533	92.888	93.354	93.821
	7.5 "	82.678	85.549	88.420	84.437	86.648	88.860	86.258	87.787	89.315	88.144	88.965	89.786
	10 "	74.511	78.749	82.987	77.001	80.305	83.610	79.619	81.942	84.264	82.372	83.662	84.952
30 Yrs	12.5 "	64.746	70.627	76.508	68.045	72.689	77.333	71.575	74.895	78.215	75.347	77.253	79.158
	15 "	53.069	60.925	68.782	57.259	63.544	69.829	61.826	66.398	70.971	66.795	69.504	72.213
7.50%	5 Years	89.800	91.607	93.413	90.904	92.296	93.689	92.030	93.000	93.971	93.180	93.719	94.258
	7.5 "	83.120	86.102	89.083	84.879	87.201	89.523	86.700	88.339	89.978	88.586	89.518	90.449
	10 "	75.101	79.486	83.871	77.590	81.042	84.494	80.209	82.679	85.149	82.961	84.399	85.837
30 Yrs	12.5 "	65.473	71.536	77.599	68.772	73.598	78.424	72.302	75.804	79.306	76.074	78.162	80.249
	15 "	53.914	61.981	70.049	58.104	64.600	71.096	62.670	67.454	72.238	67.640	70.560	73.480
8.00%	5 Years	90.072	91.946	93.820	91.175	92.636	94.096	92.302	93.340	94.378	93.451	94.058	94.665
	7.5 "	83.535	86.620	89.705	85.294	87.720	90.145	87.115	88.858	90.600	89.000	90.036	91.072
	10 "	75.658	80.183	84.708	78.148	81.739	85.331	80.767	83.376	85.985	83.519	85.096	86.673
30 Yrs	12.5 "	66.166	72.403	78.639	69.466	74.465	79.464	72.996	76.671	80.346	76.768	79.029	81.290
	15 "	54.727	62.997	71.268	58.917	65.616	72.315	63.483	68.470	73.457	68.452	71.576	74.699
8.50%	5 Years	90.324	92.261	94.199	91.428	92.951	94.475	92.554	93.655	94.756	93.703	94.373	95.043
	7.5 "	83.924	87.106	90.288	85.683	88.205	90.728	87.504	89.343	91.183	89.389	90.522	91.654
	10 "	76.185	80.842	85.498	78.675	82.398	86.121	81.293	84.034	86.775	84.046	85.754	87.463
30 Yrs	12.5 "	66.827	73.228	79.630	70.126	75.291	80.455	73.656	77.497	81.337	77.428	79.854	82.280
	15 "	55.508	63.973	72.439	59.698	66.592	73.486	64.264	69.446	74.628	69.233	72.552	75.870
9.00%	5 Years	90.558	92.554	94.550	91.662	93.244	94.826	92.788	93.947	95.107	93.937	94.666	95.394
	7.5 "	84.287	87.560	90.833	86.046	88.659	91.273	87.867	89.798	91.728	89.752	90.976	92.199
	10 "	76.681	81.462	86.243	79.171	83.018	86.865	81.790	84.655	87.520	84.542	86.375	88.208
30 Yrs	12.5 "	67.455	74.013	80.572	70.754	76.075	81.397	74.284	78.281	82.279	78.056	80.639	83.222
	15 "	56.256	64.909	73.562	60.446	67.528	74.610	65.013	70.382	75.751	69.982	73.488	76.993
9.50%	5 Years	90.775	92.824	94.874	91.878	93.514	95.150	93.004	94.218	95.432	94.154	94.936	95.719
	7.5 "	84.626	87.983	91.341	86.385	89.083	91.781	88.206	90.221	92.236	90.091	91.399	92.707
	10 "	77.148	82.046	86.943	79.638	83.602	87.565	82.257	85.238	88.220	85.009	86.958	88.908
30 Yrs	12.5 "	68.050	74.757	81.465	71.350	76.820	82.290	74.879	79.026	83.172	78.652	81.383	84.115
	15 "	56.973	65.804	74.636	61.162	68.423	75.684	65.729	71.277	76.825	70.698	74.383	78.068
10.00%	5 Years	90.975	93.074	95.174	92.078	93.764	95.450	93.204	94.468	95.732	94.354	95.186	96.019
	7.5 "	84.941	88.377	91.814	86.700	89.477	92.254	88.521	90.615	92.709	90.406	91.793	93.180
	10 "	77.586	82.593	87.600	80.076	84.149	88.223	82.695	85.786	88.877	85.447	87.506	89.565
30 Yrs	12.5 "	68.614	75.462	82.310	71.913	77.524	83.135	75.443	79.730	84.017	79.215	82.088	84.960
	15 "	57.657	66.660	75.663	61.847	69.278	76.710	66.413	72.132	77.852	71.382	75.238	79.094
10.50%	5 Years	91.159	93.305	95.451	92.262	93.995	95.727	93.389	94.699	96.008	94.538	95.417	96.296
	7.5 "	85.234	88.744	92.254	86.993	89.843	92.694	88.814	90.982	93.149	90.699	92.160	93.620
	10 "	77.997	83.106	88.216	80.487	84.663	88.838	83.105	86.299	89.493	85.858	88.019	90.181
30 Yrs	12.5 "	69.146	76.128	83.109	72.446	78.190	83.934	75.976	80.396	84.816	79.748	82.754	85.760
	15 "	58.309	67.475	76.641	62.499	70.094	77.689	67.065	72.948	78.830	72.035	76.054	80.073
11.00%	5 Years	91.329	93.517	95.706	92.432	94.207	95.982	93.559	94.911	96.263	94.708	95.629	96.550
	7.5 "	85.506	89.084	92.662	87.265	90.183	93.102	89.086	91.322	93.557	90.971	92.500	94.028
	10 "	78.381	83.587	88.792	80.871	85.143	89.415	83.489	86.779	90.069	86.242	88.500	90.757
30 Yrs	12.5 "	69.649	76.756	83.863	72.949	78.819	84.688	76.478	81.025	85.571	80.251	83.382	86.514
	15 "	58.930	68.252	77.573	63.120	70.870	78.621	67.687	73.724	79.762	72.656	76.830	81.004
11.50%	5 Years	91.485	93.712	95.940	92.588	94.402	96.216	93.714	95.106	96.497	94.864	95.824	96.784
	7.5 "	85.758	89.399	93.040	87.517	90.498	93.479	89.338	91.636	93.935	91.223	92.815	94.406
	10 "	78.740	84.035	89.330	81.230	85.591	89.953	83.848	87.228	90.607	86.601	88.948	91.295
30 Yrs	12.5 "	70.123	77.348	84.574	73.422	79.411	85.399	76.952	81.617	86.281	80.724	83.974	87.224
	15 "	59.521	68.990	78.459	63.711	71.608	79.506	68.277	74.462	80.648	73.246	77.568	81.890

Entry is percentage of original cost needed at sale to achieve desired yield.

Sale Price for a Given Return on Equity

10.50% Equity Rate

Mortgage	Holding Period Years	9.50% 60% Loan	9.50% 75% Loan	9.50% 90% Loan	Desired Yield 10.00% 60% Loan	10.00% 75% Loan	10.00% 90% Loan	11.00% 60% Loan	11.00% 75% Loan	11.00% 90% Loan	12.00% 60% Loan	12.00% 75% Loan	12.00% 90% Loan
6.00%	5 Years	93.415	93.280	93.144	94.612	94.028	93.444	97.078	95.569	94.060	99.644	97.173	94.702
	7.5 "	89.126	88.974	88.821	91.144	90.235	89.326	95.391	92.889	90.388	99.930	95.726	91.522
30 Yrs	10 "	83.987	83.874	83.761	87.024	85.772	84.520	93.556	89.855	86.153	100.741	94.345	87.949
	12.5 "	77.822	77.828	77.835	82.120	80.515	78.909	91.587	86.431	81.276	102.319	93.139	83.959
	15 "	70.413	70.652	70.890	76.275	74.315	72.355	89.510	82.587	75.664	104.997	92.267	79.536
6.50%	5 Years	93.749	93.697	93.645	94.946	94.445	93.945	97.412	95.987	94.561	99.978	97.591	95.203
	7.5 "	89.624	89.597	89.569	91.643	90.858	90.074	95.889	93.512	91.135	100.428	96.349	92.270
30 Yrs	10 "	84.641	84.692	84.742	87.678	86.590	85.502	94.210	90.672	87.135	101.395	95.163	88.931
	12.5 "	78.615	78.820	79.025	82.914	81.507	80.099	92.380	87.423	82.466	103.112	94.131	85.149
	15 "	71.319	71.784	72.249	77.181	75.448	73.714	90.416	83.720	77.023	105.903	93.399	80.895
7.00%	5 Years	94.061	94.088	94.114	95.258	94.836	94.413	97.725	96.377	95.030	100.291	97.981	95.671
	7.5 "	90.094	90.184	90.274	92.113	91.446	90.779	96.359	94.100	91.840	100.898	96.937	92.975
30 Yrs	10 "	85.263	85.469	85.675	88.300	87.367	86.434	94.832	91.450	88.067	102.017	95.940	89.863
	12.5 "	79.376	79.771	80.166	83.674	82.457	81.240	93.141	88.374	83.607	103.873	95.081	86.290
	15 "	72.195	72.879	73.563	78.057	76.543	75.028	91.292	84.815	78.337	106.779	94.494	82.209
7.50%	5 Years	94.353	94.452	94.551	95.549	95.200	94.850	98.016	96.742	95.467	100.582	98.345	96.109
	7.5 "	90.536	90.737	90.937	92.555	91.998	91.442	96.801	94.652	92.503	101.340	97.489	93.638
30 Yrs	10 "	85.853	86.206	86.560	88.890	88.104	87.319	95.421	92.187	88.952	102.606	96.677	90.748
	12.5 "	80.103	80.679	81.256	84.401	83.366	82.331	93.868	89.283	84.697	104.600	95.990	87.380
	15 "	73.040	73.935	74.830	78.902	77.599	76.295	92.137	85.871	79.604	107.624	95.550	83.476
8.00%	5 Years	94.624	94.791	94.958	95.821	95.539	95.258	98.287	97.081	95.874	100.854	98.685	96.516
	7.5 "	90.951	91.255	91.559	92.970	92.517	92.064	97.216	95.171	93.126	101.755	98.008	94.260
30 Yrs	10 "	86.411	86.903	87.396	89.447	88.801	88.155	95.979	92.884	89.788	103.164	97.374	91.585
	12.5 "	80.796	81.546	82.297	85.095	84.233	83.371	94.561	90.150	85.738	105.294	96.857	88.421
	15 "	73.853	74.951	76.049	79.714	78.615	77.515	92.950	86.887	80.824	108.437	96.566	84.695
8.50%	5 Years	94.876	95.107	95.337	96.073	95.855	95.636	98.540	97.396	96.253	101.106	99.000	96.894
	7.5 "	91.340	91.741	92.142	93.358	93.002	92.647	97.605	95.656	93.708	102.144	98.493	94.843
30 Yrs	10 "	86.937	87.562	88.186	89.974	89.460	88.945	96.506	93.542	90.578	103.691	98.033	92.375
	12.5 "	81.457	82.372	83.287	85.755	85.059	84.362	95.222	90.975	86.729	105.954	97.683	89.412
	15 "	74.634	75.927	77.220	80.495	79.591	78.686	93.731	87.863	81.995	109.218	97.542	85.866
9.00%	5 Years	95.110	95.399	95.688	96.307	96.147	95.987	98.774	97.689	96.604	101.340	99.292	97.245
	7.5 "	91.703	92.195	92.687	93.721	93.456	93.192	97.968	96.111	94.253	102.507	98.947	95.388
30 Yrs	10 "	87.434	88.182	88.931	90.470	90.080	89.690	97.002	94.163	91.323	104.187	98.653	93.119
	12.5 "	82.085	83.157	84.229	86.383	85.843	85.304	95.850	91.760	87.670	106.582	98.468	90.353
	15 "	75.382	76.863	78.344	81.244	80.526	79.809	94.479	88.799	83.118	109.966	98.478	86.990
9.50%	5 Years	95.327	95.670	96.012	96.524	96.418	96.312	98.990	97.959	96.928	101.556	99.563	97.570
	7.5 "	92.042	92.618	93.195	94.060	93.880	93.700	98.307	96.534	94.761	102.846	99.371	95.896
30 Yrs	10 "	87.901	88.766	89.631	90.937	90.664	90.390	97.469	94.746	92.023	104.654	99.237	93.819
	12.5 "	82.680	83.901	85.122	86.978	86.588	86.197	96.445	92.504	88.563	107.177	99.212	91.246
	15 "	76.099	77.758	79.418	81.960	81.422	80.883	95.196	89.694	84.192	110.682	99.373	88.064
10.00%	5 Years	95.527	95.920	96.312	96.724	96.668	96.612	99.190	98.209	97.228	101.756	99.813	97.870
	7.5 "	92.357	93.013	93.668	94.375	94.274	94.173	98.622	96.928	95.234	103.161	99.765	96.369
30 Yrs	10 "	88.339	89.313	90.288	91.375	91.211	91.047	97.907	95.294	92.680	105.092	99.784	94.476
	12.5 "	83.244	84.606	85.967	87.542	87.292	87.042	97.009	93.209	89.409	107.741	99.916	92.092
	15 "	76.783	78.613	80.444	82.644	82.277	81.909	95.880	90.549	85.218	111.367	100.228	89.090
10.50%	5 Years	95.711	96.150	96.589	96.908	96.898	96.888	99.375	98.440	97.505	101.941	100.044	98.146
	7.5 "	92.650	93.379	94.108	94.669	94.640	94.612	98.915	97.295	95.674	103.454	100.131	96.809
30 Yrs	10 "	88.749	89.827	90.904	91.786	91.725	91.663	98.318	95.807	93.296	105.503	100.298	95.092
	12.5 "	83.776	85.271	86.767	88.075	87.958	87.841	97.541	93.875	90.208	108.274	100.582	92.891
	15 "	77.435	79.429	81.423	83.297	83.092	82.888	96.532	91.365	86.197	112.019	101.044	90.069
11.00%	5 Years	95.881	96.362	96.844	97.078	97.110	97.143	99.544	98.652	97.760	102.111	100.256	98.401
	7.5 "	92.922	93.719	94.516	94.941	94.980	95.020	99.187	97.635	96.082	103.726	100.471	97.217
30 Yrs	10 "	89.133	90.307	91.480	92.170	92.205	92.239	98.702	96.287	93.872	105.887	100.778	95.669
	12.5 "	84.279	85.900	87.521	88.578	88.587	88.595	98.044	94.503	90.962	108.776	101.211	93.645
	15 "	78.056	80.205	82.355	83.918	83.869	83.820	97.153	92.141	87.129	112.640	101.820	91.001
11.50%	5 Years	96.037	96.557	97.078	97.234	97.305	97.377	99.700	98.847	97.994	102.267	100.451	98.635
	7.5 "	93.174	94.034	94.894	95.192	95.295	95.398	99.439	97.949	96.460	103.978	100.786	97.595
30 Yrs	10 "	89.492	90.755	92.018	92.529	92.653	92.778	99.061	96.736	94.411	106.246	101.226	96.207
	12.5 "	84.753	86.492	88.231	89.051	89.178	89.306	98.518	95.095	91.672	109.250	101.803	94.355
	15 "	78.647	80.944	83.240	84.508	84.607	84.706	97.744	92.879	88.015	113.231	102.558	91.886

Entry is percentage of original cost needed at sale to achieve desired yield.

Create Value by Paying Points

Equity Rate 6.50%

Loan to Value	Cut in Rate	8.00%	8.25%	8.50%	8.75%	9.00%	9.25%	9.50%	9.75%	11.00%	11.50%	12.00%	12.50%
						Initial Interest Rate							
67% Loan to Value	0.25	2.136	2.154	2.172	2.189	2.206	2.222	2.237	2.252	2.319	2.342	2.363	2.383
	0.50	4.252	4.290	4.326	4.361	4.395	4.428	4.459	4.490	4.626	4.673	4.716	4.756
	0.75	6.349	6.406	6.462	6.515	6.567	6.617	6.665	6.712	6.920	6.992	7.059	7.120
	1.00	8.426	8.503	8.578	8.651	8.721	8.789	8.854	8.917	9.200	9.299	9.389	9.473
	1.50	12.516	12.636	12.752	12.865	12.973	13.079	13.180	13.278	13.719	13.873	14.015	14.146
	2.00	16.519	16.683	16.843	16.997	17.147	17.292	17.433	17.568	18.179	18.392	18.590	18.772
	2.50	20.428	20.639	20.845	21.044	21.237	21.425	21.606	21.782	22.574	22.852	23.109	23.346
	3.00	24.239	24.500	24.754	25.000	25.240	25.472	25.697	25.915	26.900	27.247	27.568	27.865
75% Loan to Value	0.25	2.403	2.423	2.443	2.463	2.482	2.500	2.517	2.534	2.609	2.635	2.659	2.681
	0.50	4.784	4.826	4.867	4.906	4.944	4.981	5.017	5.051	5.204	5.257	5.306	5.351
	0.75	7.143	7.207	7.269	7.330	7.388	7.444	7.498	7.551	7.785	7.866	7.941	8.010
	1.00	9.479	9.566	9.651	9.732	9.811	9.887	9.961	10.032	10.350	10.461	10.563	10.657
	1.50	14.081	14.216	14.346	14.473	14.595	14.713	14.828	14.938	15.434	15.607	15.767	15.914
	2.00	18.583	18.768	18.948	19.122	19.290	19.454	19.612	19.764	20.451	20.691	20.913	21.118
	2.50	22.981	23.219	23.450	23.675	23.892	24.103	24.307	24.505	25.395	25.708	25.997	26.264
	3.00	27.269	27.563	27.848	28.125	28.395	28.656	28.909	29.154	30.262	30.652	31.014	31.348
80% Loan to Value	0.25	2.563	2.585	2.606	2.627	2.647	2.666	2.685	2.703	2.783	2.811	2.836	2.860
	0.50	5.103	5.148	5.191	5.233	5.274	5.313	5.351	5.388	5.551	5.608	5.660	5.708
	0.75	7.619	7.688	7.754	7.818	7.880	7.940	7.998	8.054	8.304	8.390	8.470	8.544
	1.00	10.111	10.204	10.294	10.381	10.465	10.547	10.625	10.701	11.040	11.158	11.267	11.367
	1.50	15.020	15.163	15.303	15.437	15.568	15.694	15.816	15.934	16.463	16.648	16.818	16.975
	2.00	19.822	20.020	20.211	20.397	20.577	20.751	20.919	21.082	21.814	22.071	22.308	22.526
	2.50	24.513	24.767	25.014	25.253	25.485	25.710	25.928	26.138	27.088	27.422	27.730	28.015
	3.00	29.087	29.400	29.705	30.000	30.288	30.566	30.836	31.098	32.279	32.636	33.082	33.438
85% Loan to Value	0.25	2.723	2.746	2.769	2.791	2.812	2.833	2.853	2.872	2.957	2.986	3.013	3.038
	0.50	5.422	5.469	5.516	5.560	5.604	5.645	5.686	5.724	5.898	5.958	6.013	6.064
	0.75	8.095	8.168	8.239	8.307	8.373	8.436	8.498	8.557	8.823	8.915	9.000	9.078
	1.00	10.743	10.842	10.937	11.030	11.119	11.206	11.289	11.370	11.730	11.856	11.972	12.078
	1.50	15.959	16.111	16.259	16.402	16.541	16.675	16.805	16.930	17.492	17.688	17.869	18.036
	2.00	21.061	21.271	21.474	21.671	21.863	22.048	22.227	22.400	23.178	23.450	23.702	23.934
	2.50	26.045	26.315	26.577	26.831	27.078	27.317	27.548	27.772	28.781	29.136	29.464	29.766
	3.00	30.905	31.238	31.561	31.875	32.181	32.477	32.763	33.041	34.297	34.739	35.149	35.528

Equity Rate 7.00%

Loan to Value	Cut in Rate	8.00%	8.25%	8.50%	8.75%	9.00%	9.25%	9.50%	9.75%	11.00%	11.50%	12.00%	12.50%
67% Loan to Value	0.25	1.983	2.000	2.017	2.033	2.048	2.063	2.078	2.091	2.153	2.175	2.195	2.213
	0.50	3.949	3.983	4.017	4.050	4.081	4.111	4.141	4.169	4.295	4.339	4.380	4.417
	0.75	5.896	5.949	6.000	6.050	6.098	6.144	6.189	6.232	6.425	6.493	6.554	6.611
	1.00	7.824	7.896	7.966	8.033	8.098	8.161	8.222	8.280	8.543	8.635	8.719	8.796
	1.50	11.622	11.734	11.841	11.946	12.047	12.144	12.239	12.330	12.739	12.882	13.014	13.135
	2.00	15.339	15.491	15.639	15.783	15.922	16.057	16.187	16.313	16.880	17.079	17.262	17.431
	2.50	18.969	19.165	19.356	19.541	19.721	19.895	20.063	20.226	20.961	21.219	21.458	21.678
	3.00	22.508	22.750	22.986	23.215	23.437	23.652	23.861	24.064	24.978	25.300	25.599	25.875
75% Loan to Value	0.25	2.231	2.250	2.269	2.287	2.304	2.321	2.337	2.353	2.423	2.447	2.469	2.489
	0.50	4.442	4.481	4.519	4.556	4.591	4.625	4.658	4.690	4.832	4.882	4.927	4.969
	0.75	6.633	6.692	6.750	6.806	6.860	6.912	6.963	7.011	7.229	7.304	7.374	7.438
	1.00	8.802	8.883	8.961	9.037	9.110	9.181	9.250	9.316	9.611	9.714	9.809	9.896
	1.50	13.075	13.200	13.321	13.439	13.552	13.662	13.769	13.871	14.332	14.493	14.641	14.777
	2.00	17.256	17.428	17.594	17.756	17.913	18.064	18.211	18.353	18.990	19.213	19.420	19.610
	2.50	21.340	21.561	21.775	21.984	22.186	22.381	22.571	22.754	23.581	23.872	24.140	24.388
	3.00	25.321	25.594	25.859	26.116	26.366	26.609	26.844	27.072	28.100	28.463	28.799	29.109
80% Loan to Value	0.25	2.380	2.400	2.420	2.439	2.458	2.476	2.493	2.510	2.584	2.610	2.634	2.655
	0.50	4.738	4.780	4.820	4.859	4.897	4.934	4.969	5.003	5.154	5.207	5.255	5.300
	0.75	7.075	7.139	7.200	7.260	7.317	7.373	7.427	7.479	7.710	7.791	7.865	7.933
	1.00	9.389	9.475	9.559	9.640	9.718	9.793	9.866	9.937	10.252	10.361	10.463	10.555
	1.50	13.947	14.080	14.210	14.335	14.456	14.573	14.687	14.796	15.287	15.459	15.617	15.762
	2.00	18.406	18.590	18.767	18.940	19.107	19.268	19.425	19.576	20.256	20.494	20.714	20.917
	2.50	22.762	22.998	23.227	23.449	23.665	23.873	24.076	24.271	25.153	25.463	25.750	26.014
	3.00	27.009	27.300	27.583	27.857	28.124	28.383	28.634	28.876	29.974	30.360	30.719	31.050
85% Loan to Value	0.25	2.528	2.550	2.571	2.592	2.612	2.631	2.649	2.667	2.746	2.773	2.798	2.821
	0.50	5.034	5.079	5.122	5.163	5.203	5.242	5.279	5.316	5.477	5.532	5.584	5.631
	0.75	7.517	7.585	7.650	7.714	7.775	7.834	7.891	7.946	8.192	8.278	8.357	8.429
	1.00	9.976	10.067	10.156	10.242	10.325	10.405	10.483	10.558	10.892	11.009	11.116	11.215
	1.50	14.819	14.960	15.098	15.231	15.359	15.484	15.604	15.721	16.243	16.425	16.593	16.748
	2.00	19.557	19.751	19.940	20.123	20.301	20.473	20.639	20.800	21.522	21.775	22.009	22.224
	2.50	24.185	24.435	24.679	24.915	25.144	25.366	25.580	25.788	26.725	27.055	27.359	27.640
	3.00	28.697	29.006	29.307	29.599	29.882	30.157	30.423	30.681	31.847	32.258	32.639	32.990

Entry is capitalized value of reduced constant as percent of total property value.

Create Value by Paying Points

Equity Rate 7.50%

Loan to Value	Cut in Rate	Initial Interest Rate											
		8.00%	8.25%	8.50%	8.75%	9.00%	9.25%	9.50%	9.75%	11.00%	11.50%	12.00%	12.50%
67% Loan to Value	0.25	1.851	1.867	1.882	1.897	1.912	1.926	1.939	1.952	2.010	2.030	2.048	2.065
	0.50	3.685	3.718	3.749	3.780	3.809	3.837	3.865	3.891	4.009	4.050	4.088	4.122
	0.75	5.503	5.552	5.600	5.646	5.691	5.735	5.776	5.817	5.997	6.060	6.117	6.170
	1.00	7.303	7.370	7.435	7.497	7.558	7.617	7.674	7.728	7.974	8.059	8.138	8.210
	1.50	10.848	10.951	11.052	11.149	11.244	11.335	11.423	11.508	11.890	12.023	12.146	12.260
	2.00	14.316	14.459	14.597	14.731	14.861	14.987	15.108	15.226	15.755	15.940	16.111	16.269
	2.50	17.704	17.887	18.065	18.238	18.406	18.568	18.726	18.878	19.564	19.805	20.028	20.233
	3.00	21.007	21.233	21.453	21.667	21.874	22.076	22.271	22.459	23.313	23.614	23.892	24.150
75% Loan to Value	0.25	2.082	2.100	2.118	2.134	2.151	2.166	2.181	2.196	2.261	2.284	2.304	2.323
	0.50	4.146	4.183	4.218	4.252	4.285	4.317	4.348	4.377	4.510	4.556	4.599	4.637
	0.75	6.191	6.246	6.300	6.352	6.403	6.451	6.498	6.544	6.747	6.817	6.882	6.942
	1.00	8.215	8.291	8.364	8.435	8.503	8.569	8.633	8.694	8.970	9.066	9.155	9.236
	1.50	12.204	12.320	12.433	12.543	12.649	12.752	12.851	12.947	13.376	13.526	13.665	13.792
	2.00	16.106	16.266	16.421	16.572	16.718	16.860	16.997	17.129	17.724	17.932	18.125	18.302
	2.50	19.917	20.123	20.324	20.518	20.707	20.889	21.066	21.237	22.009	22.280	22.531	22.762
	3.00	23.633	23.888	24.135	24.375	24.609	24.835	25.054	25.267	26.227	26.565	26.879	27.168
80% Loan to Value	0.25	2.221	2.240	2.259	2.277	2.294	2.311	2.327	2.342	2.412	2.436	2.458	2.478
	0.50	4.422	4.461	4.499	4.536	4.571	4.605	4.638	4.669	4.811	4.860	4.905	4.947
	0.75	6.603	6.663	6.720	6.776	6.830	6.882	6.932	6.980	7.196	7.272	7.341	7.405
	1.00	8.763	8.844	8.921	8.997	9.070	9.140	9.208	9.274	9.568	9.671	9.765	9.852
	1.50	13.017	13.142	13.262	13.379	13.492	13.602	13.707	13.810	14.268	14.428	14.576	14.712
	2.00	17.179	17.350	17.516	17.677	17.833	17.984	18.130	18.271	18.906	19.128	19.333	19.522
	2.50	21.245	21.465	21.678	21.886	22.087	22.282	22.471	22.653	23.476	23.766	24.033	24.280
	3.00	25.209	25.480	25.744	26.000	26.249	26.491	26.725	26.951	27.976	28.336	28.671	28.980
85% Loan to Value	0.25	2.360	2.380	2.400	2.419	2.437	2.455	2.472	2.489	2.563	2.588	2.612	2.633
	0.50	4.699	4.740	4.780	4.819	4.856	4.893	4.927	4.961	5.111	5.164	5.212	5.256
	0.75	7.016	7.079	7.140	7.199	7.256	7.312	7.365	7.416	7.646	7.726	7.800	7.867
	1.00	9.311	9.396	9.479	9.559	9.637	9.712	9.784	9.854	10.166	10.275	10.375	10.467
	1.50	13.831	13.963	14.091	14.215	14.336	14.452	14.564	14.673	15.160	15.330	15.487	15.631
	2.00	18.253	18.435	18.611	18.782	18.948	19.108	19.263	19.413	20.087	20.323	20.542	20.743
	2.50	22.573	22.806	23.033	23.254	23.467	23.675	23.875	24.069	24.944	25.251	25.535	25.797
	3.00	26.784	27.073	27.353	27.625	27.890	28.146	28.395	28.636	29.724	30.107	30.463	30.791

Equity Rate 8.00%

Loan to Value	Cut in Rate	Initial Interest Rate											
		8.00%	8.25%	8.50%	8.75%	9.00%	9.25%	9.50%	9.75%	11.00%	11.50%	12.00%	12.50%
67% Loan to Value	0.25	1.735	1.750	1.765	1.779	1.792	1.805	1.818	1.830	1.884	1.903	1.920	1.936
	0.50	3.455	3.485	3.515	3.543	3.571	3.598	3.623	3.648	3.758	3.797	3.832	3.865
	0.75	5.159	5.205	5.250	5.294	5.336	5.376	5.415	5.453	5.622	5.681	5.735	5.785
	1.00	6.846	6.909	6.970	7.029	7.086	7.141	7.194	7.245	7.475	7.555	7.629	7.697
	1.50	10.170	10.267	10.361	10.452	10.541	10.626	10.709	10.789	11.147	11.272	11.387	11.493
	2.00	13.421	13.555	13.685	13.810	13.932	14.050	14.164	14.274	14.770	14.944	15.104	15.252
	2.50	16.598	16.769	16.936	17.098	17.255	17.408	17.555	17.698	18.341	18.567	18.776	18.969
	3.00	19.694	19.906	20.112	20.313	20.507	20.696	20.879	21.056	21.856	22.138	22.399	22.640
75% Loan to Value	0.25	1.952	1.969	1.985	2.001	2.016	2.031	2.045	2.059	2.120	2.141	2.160	2.178
	0.50	3.887	3.921	3.954	3.986	4.017	4.047	4.076	4.104	4.228	4.271	4.311	4.348
	0.75	5.804	5.856	5.906	5.955	6.003	6.048	6.092	6.135	6.325	6.391	6.452	6.508
	1.00	7.702	7.773	7.841	7.907	7.972	8.033	8.093	8.151	8.410	8.500	8.583	8.659
	1.50	11.441	11.550	11.656	11.759	11.858	11.955	12.048	12.137	12.540	12.681	12.811	12.930
	2.00	15.099	15.249	15.395	15.537	15.674	15.806	15.934	16.058	16.616	16.812	16.992	17.158
	2.50	18.672	18.866	19.053	19.236	19.412	19.584	19.750	19.910	20.634	20.888	21.123	21.340
	3.00	22.156	22.395	22.627	22.852	23.071	23.283	23.488	23.688	24.588	24.905	25.199	25.470
80% Loan to Value	0.25	2.082	2.100	2.118	2.134	2.151	2.166	2.181	2.196	2.261	2.284	2.304	2.323
	0.50	4.146	4.183	4.218	4.252	4.285	4.317	4.348	4.377	4.510	4.556	4.599	4.637
	0.75	6.191	6.246	6.300	6.352	6.403	6.451	6.498	6.544	6.747	6.817	6.882	6.942
	1.00	8.215	8.291	8.364	8.435	8.503	8.569	8.633	8.694	8.970	9.066	9.155	9.236
	1.50	12.204	12.320	12.433	12.543	12.649	12.752	12.851	12.947	13.376	13.526	13.665	13.792
	2.00	16.106	16.266	16.421	16.572	16.718	16.860	16.997	17.129	17.724	17.932	18.125	18.302
	2.50	19.917	20.123	20.324	20.518	20.707	20.889	21.066	21.237	22.009	22.280	22.531	22.762
	3.00	23.633	23.888	24.135	24.375	24.609	24.835	25.054	25.267	26.227	26.565	26.879	27.168
85% Loan to Value	0.25	2.212	2.232	2.250	2.268	2.285	2.302	2.318	2.333	2.402	2.426	2.448	2.469
	0.50	4.405	4.444	4.481	4.518	4.553	4.587	4.620	4.651	4.792	4.841	4.886	4.927
	0.75	6.578	6.637	6.694	6.749	6.803	6.855	6.905	6.953	7.168	7.243	7.312	7.376
	1.00	8.729	8.809	8.887	8.962	9.034	9.105	9.172	9.238	9.531	9.633	9.727	9.813
	1.50	12.966	13.090	13.210	13.327	13.440	13.549	13.654	13.756	14.212	14.372	14.519	14.654
	2.00	17.112	17.283	17.448	17.608	17.763	17.914	18.059	18.200	18.832	19.053	19.258	19.446
	2.50	21.162	21.381	21.594	21.800	22.001	22.195	22.383	22.565	23.385	23.673	23.939	24.185
	3.00	25.110	25.381	25.643	25.899	26.147	26.387	26.620	26.846	27.866	28.226	28.559	28.866

Entry is capitalized value of reduced constant as percent of total property value.

Create Value by Paying Points

Equity Rate 8.50%

Loan to Value	Cut in Rate	Initial Interest Rate											
		8.00%	8.25%	8.50%	8.75%	9.00%	9.25%	9.50%	9.75%	11.00%	11.50%	12.00%	12.50%
67% Loan to Value	0.25	1.633	1.647	1.661	1.674	1.687	1.699	1.711	1.722	1.773	1.791	1.807	1.822
	0.50	3.252	3.280	3.308	3.335	3.361	3.386	3.410	3.433	3.537	3.573	3.607	3.637
	0.75	4.855	4.899	4.941	4.982	5.022	5.060	5.097	5.132	5.291	5.347	5.398	5.445
	1.00	6.443	6.503	6.560	6.615	6.669	6.721	6.771	6.819	7.035	7.111	7.180	7.244
	1.50	9.571	9.663	9.752	9.838	9.921	10.001	10.079	10.154	10.491	10.609	10.717	10.817
	2.00	12.632	12.758	12.880	12.998	13.112	13.223	13.331	13.435	13.901	14.065	14.216	14.355
	2.50	15.621	15.783	15.940	16.093	16.240	16.384	16.523	16.657	17.262	17.475	17.671	17.853
	3.00	18.536	18.735	18.929	19.118	19.301	19.478	19.650	19.817	20.570	20.836	21.081	21.309
75% Loan to Value	0.25	1.837	1.853	1.868	1.883	1.898	1.911	1.925	1.938	1.995	2.015	2.033	2.050
	0.50	3.658	3.690	3.722	3.752	3.781	3.809	3.836	3.862	3.979	4.020	4.058	4.092
	0.75	5.462	5.511	5.559	5.605	5.649	5.692	5.734	5.774	5.953	6.015	6.072	6.125
	1.00	7.249	7.315	7.380	7.442	7.503	7.561	7.617	7.672	7.915	8.000	8.078	8.149
	1.50	10.768	10.871	10.971	11.067	11.161	11.251	11.339	11.423	11.803	11.935	12.057	12.170
	2.00	14.211	14.352	14.490	14.623	14.752	14.876	14.997	15.114	15.639	15.823	15.993	16.149
	2.50	17.574	17.756	17.933	18.104	18.270	18.432	18.588	18.739	19.420	19.659	19.880	20.084
	3.00	20.853	21.077	21.296	21.508	21.714	21.913	22.107	22.294	23.142	23.440	23.717	23.972
80% Loan to Value	0.25	1.960	1.977	1.993	2.009	2.024	2.039	2.053	2.067	2.128	2.149	2.169	2.187
	0.50	3.902	3.936	3.970	4.002	4.033	4.063	4.092	4.120	4.245	4.288	4.328	4.365
	0.75	5.826	5.879	5.930	5.979	6.026	6.072	6.116	6.159	6.350	6.416	6.477	6.533
	1.00	7.732	7.803	7.872	7.938	8.003	8.065	8.125	8.183	8.443	8.533	8.616	8.693
	1.50	11.486	11.596	11.702	11.805	11.905	12.001	12.095	12.185	12.589	12.731	12.861	12.981
	2.00	15.158	15.309	15.455	15.597	15.735	15.868	15.997	16.121	16.681	16.878	17.059	17.226
	2.50	18.745	18.940	19.128	19.311	19.489	19.660	19.827	19.988	20.715	20.970	21.206	21.423
	3.00	22.243	22.482	22.715	22.941	23.161	23.374	23.581	23.780	24.684	25.003	25.298	25.570
85% Loan to Value	0.25	2.082	2.100	2.118	2.134	2.151	2.166	2.181	2.196	2.261	2.284	2.304	2.323
	0.50	4.146	4.183	4.218	4.252	4.285	4.317	4.348	4.377	4.510	4.556	4.599	4.637
	0.75	6.191	6.246	6.300	6.352	6.403	6.451	6.498	6.544	6.747	6.817	6.882	6.942
	1.00	8.215	8.291	8.364	8.435	8.503	8.569	8.633	8.694	8.970	9.066	9.155	9.236
	1.50	12.204	12.320	12.433	12.543	12.649	12.752	12.851	12.947	13.376	13.526	13.665	13.792
	2.00	16.106	16.266	16.421	16.572	16.718	16.860	16.997	17.129	17.724	17.932	18.125	18.302
	2.50	19.917	20.123	20.324	20.518	20.707	20.889	21.066	21.237	22.009	22.280	22.531	22.762
	3.00	23.633	23.888	24.135	24.375	24.609	24.835	25.054	25.267	26.227	26.565	26.879	27.168

Equity Rate 9.00%

Loan to Value	Cut in Rate	Initial Interest Rate											
		8.00%	8.25%	8.50%	8.75%	9.00%	9.25%	9.50%	9.75%	11.00%	11.50%	12.00%	12.50%
67% Loan to Value	0.25	1.542	1.556	1.569	1.581	1.593	1.605	1.616	1.627	1.675	1.692	1.707	1.721
	0.50	3.071	3.098	3.124	3.150	3.174	3.198	3.221	3.243	3.341	3.375	3.406	3.435
	0.75	4.586	4.627	4.667	4.705	4.743	4.779	4.814	4.847	4.998	5.050	5.098	5.142
	1.00	6.086	6.141	6.195	6.248	6.298	6.347	6.395	6.440	6.645	6.716	6.781	6.841
	1.50	9.040	9.126	9.210	9.291	9.370	9.446	9.519	9.590	9.908	10.020	10.122	10.216
	2.00	11.930	12.049	12.164	12.276	12.384	12.489	12.590	12.688	13.129	13.283	13.426	13.557
	2.50	14.753	14.906	15.054	15.199	15.338	15.474	15.605	15.731	16.303	16.504	16.690	16.861
	3.00	17.506	17.694	17.878	18.056	18.229	18.396	18.559	18.716	19.427	19.678	19.910	20.125
75% Loan to Value	0.25	1.735	1.750	1.765	1.779	1.792	1.805	1.818	1.830	1.884	1.903	1.920	1.936
	0.50	3.455	3.485	3.515	3.543	3.571	3.598	3.623	3.648	3.758	3.797	3.832	3.865
	0.75	5.159	5.205	5.250	5.294	5.336	5.376	5.415	5.453	5.622	5.681	5.735	5.785
	1.00	6.846	6.909	6.970	7.029	7.086	7.141	7.194	7.245	7.475	7.555	7.629	7.697
	1.50	10.170	10.267	10.361	10.452	10.541	10.626	10.709	10.789	11.147	11.272	11.387	11.493
	2.00	13.421	13.555	13.685	13.810	13.932	14.050	14.164	14.274	14.770	14.944	15.104	15.252
	2.50	16.598	16.769	16.936	17.098	17.255	17.408	17.555	17.698	18.341	18.567	18.776	18.969
	3.00	19.694	19.906	20.112	20.313	20.507	20.696	20.879	21.056	21.856	22.138	22.399	22.640
80% Loan to Value	0.25	1.851	1.867	1.882	1.897	1.912	1.926	1.939	1.952	2.010	2.030	2.048	2.065
	0.50	3.685	3.718	3.749	3.780	3.809	3.837	3.865	3.891	4.009	4.050	4.088	4.122
	0.75	5.503	5.552	5.600	5.646	5.691	5.735	5.776	5.817	5.997	6.060	6.117	6.170
	1.00	7.303	7.370	7.435	7.497	7.558	7.617	7.674	7.728	7.974	8.059	8.138	8.210
	1.50	10.848	10.951	11.052	11.149	11.244	11.335	11.423	11.508	11.890	12.023	12.146	12.260
	2.00	14.316	14.459	14.597	14.731	14.861	14.987	15.108	15.226	15.755	15.940	16.111	16.269
	2.50	17.704	17.887	18.065	18.238	18.406	18.568	18.726	18.878	19.564	19.805	20.028	20.233
	3.00	21.007	21.233	21.453	21.667	21.874	22.076	22.271	22.459	23.313	23.614	23.892	24.150
85% Loan to Value	0.25	1.967	1.984	2.000	2.016	2.031	2.046	2.060	2.074	2.135	2.157	2.176	2.194
	0.50	3.916	3.950	3.984	4.016	4.047	4.077	4.106	4.134	4.260	4.303	4.343	4.380
	0.75	5.847	5.899	5.950	5.999	6.047	6.093	6.137	6.180	6.372	6.438	6.500	6.556
	1.00	7.759	7.830	7.899	7.966	8.031	8.093	8.153	8.211	8.472	8.563	8.646	8.723
	1.50	11.526	11.636	11.743	11.846	11.946	12.043	12.137	12.227	12.633	12.775	12.906	13.026
	2.00	15.211	15.362	15.509	15.652	15.790	15.923	16.052	16.177	16.739	16.936	17.118	17.285
	2.50	18.811	19.005	19.194	19.378	19.556	19.729	19.896	20.058	20.786	21.042	21.279	21.498
	3.00	22.320	22.560	22.794	23.021	23.242	23.455	23.662	23.863	24.770	25.090	25.386	25.659

Entry is capitalized value of reduced constant as percent of total property value.

Create Value by Paying Points

Equity Rate 9.50%

Loan to Value	Cut in Rate	8.00%	8.25%	8.50%	8.75%	9.00%	9.25%	9.50%	9.75%	11.00%	11.50%	12.00%	12.50%
						Initial Interest Rate							
67% Loan to Value	0.25	1.461	1.474	1.486	1.498	1.509	1.520	1.531	1.541	1.587	1.603	1.617	1.630
	0.50	2.909	2.935	2.960	2.984	3.007	3.029	3.051	3.072	3.165	3.197	3.227	3.254
	0.75	4.344	4.383	4.421	4.458	4.493	4.527	4.560	4.592	4.734	4.784	4.830	4.871
	1.00	5.765	5.818	5.869	5.919	5.967	6.013	6.058	6.101	6.295	6.362	6.424	6.481
	1.50	8.564	8.646	8.725	8.802	8.876	8.948	9.018	9.085	9.387	9.492	9.589	9.679
	2.00	11.302	11.415	11.524	11.630	11.732	11.832	11.928	12.020	12.438	12.584	12.719	12.844
	2.50	13.977	14.122	14.262	14.399	14.531	14.659	14.783	14.903	15.445	15.635	15.811	15.974
	3.00	16.585	16.763	16.937	17.105	17.269	17.428	17.582	17.731	18.405	18.642	18.862	19.066
75% Loan to Value	0.25	1.644	1.658	1.672	1.685	1.698	1.710	1.722	1.734	1.785	1.803	1.819	1.834
	0.50	3.273	3.302	3.330	3.357	3.383	3.408	3.432	3.456	3.561	3.597	3.630	3.661
	0.75	4.887	4.931	4.974	5.015	5.055	5.093	5.130	5.166	5.326	5.382	5.433	5.480
	1.00	6.486	6.545	6.603	6.659	6.713	6.765	6.815	6.864	7.082	7.158	7.227	7.292
	1.50	9.634	9.726	9.816	9.902	9.986	10.067	10.145	10.221	10.560	10.679	10.788	10.889
	2.00	12.715	12.842	12.964	13.083	13.199	13.310	13.418	13.523	13.993	14.157	14.309	14.449
	2.50	15.724	15.887	16.045	16.198	16.347	16.492	16.631	16.766	17.376	17.590	17.788	17.970
	3.00	18.658	18.859	19.054	19.244	19.428	19.607	19.780	19.947	20.706	20.973	21.220	21.449
80% Loan to Value	0.25	1.753	1.769	1.783	1.797	1.811	1.824	1.837	1.849	1.904	1.923	1.940	1.957
	0.50	3.491	3.522	3.552	3.581	3.609	3.635	3.661	3.686	3.798	3.837	3.872	3.905
	0.75	5.213	5.260	5.305	5.349	5.392	5.433	5.472	5.511	5.681	5.741	5.795	5.846
	1.00	6.918	6.982	7.043	7.103	7.160	7.216	7.270	7.322	7.554	7.635	7.709	7.778
	1.50	10.277	10.375	10.470	10.562	10.652	10.738	10.822	10.902	11.264	11.391	11.507	11.614
	2.00	13.563	13.698	13.829	13.956	14.079	14.198	14.313	14.424	14.926	15.101	15.263	15.412
	2.50	16.772	16.946	17.115	17.278	17.437	17.591	17.740	17.884	18.534	18.762	18.973	19.168
	3.00	19.902	20.116	20.324	20.527	20.723	20.914	21.098	21.277	22.086	22.371	22.635	22.879
85% Loan to Value	0.25	1.863	1.879	1.895	1.910	1.924	1.938	1.952	1.965	2.023	2.043	2.062	2.079
	0.50	3.710	3.742	3.774	3.804	3.834	3.863	3.890	3.917	4.035	4.077	4.114	4.149
	0.75	5.539	5.589	5.637	5.684	5.729	5.772	5.814	5.855	6.036	6.100	6.158	6.211
	1.00	7.351	7.418	7.483	7.547	7.608	7.667	7.724	7.779	8.026	8.112	8.191	8.264
	1.50	10.919	11.023	11.125	11.223	11.318	11.409	11.498	11.584	11.968	12.103	12.226	12.340
	2.00	14.410	14.554	14.693	14.828	14.959	15.085	15.208	15.326	15.858	16.045	16.217	16.376
	2.50	17.821	18.005	18.184	18.358	18.527	18.690	18.849	19.002	19.692	19.935	20.159	20.366
	3.00	21.145	21.373	21.594	21.809	22.018	22.221	22.417	22.607	23.466	23.769	24.049	24.309

Equity Rate 10.00%

Loan to Value	Cut in Rate	8.00%	8.25%	8.50%	8.75%	9.00%	9.25%	9.50%	9.75%	11.00%	11.50%	12.00%	12.50%
67% Loan to Value	0.25	1.388	1.400	1.412	1.423	1.434	1.444	1.454	1.464	1.507	1.522	1.536	1.549
	0.50	2.764	2.788	2.812	2.835	2.857	2.878	2.899	2.918	3.007	3.037	3.066	3.092
	0.75	4.127	4.164	4.200	4.235	4.268	4.301	4.332	4.363	4.498	4.545	4.588	4.628
	1.00	5.477	5.527	5.576	5.623	5.669	5.713	5.755	5.796	5.980	6.044	6.103	6.157
	1.50	8.136	8.213	8.289	8.362	8.433	8.501	8.567	8.631	8.918	9.018	9.110	9.195
	2.00	10.737	10.844	10.948	11.048	11.146	11.240	11.331	11.419	11.816	11.955	12.083	12.201
	2.50	13.278	13.415	13.549	13.679	13.804	13.926	14.044	14.158	14.673	14.854	15.021	15.175
	3.00	15.755	15.925	16.090	16.250	16.406	16.557	16.703	16.845	17.485	17.710	17.919	18.112
75% Loan to Value	0.25	1.562	1.575	1.588	1.601	1.613	1.625	1.636	1.647	1.696	1.713	1.728	1.743
	0.50	3.110	3.137	3.163	3.189	3.214	3.238	3.261	3.283	3.383	3.417	3.449	3.478
	0.75	4.643	4.685	4.725	4.764	4.802	4.839	4.874	4.908	5.060	5.113	5.162	5.206
	1.00	6.162	6.218	6.273	6.326	6.377	6.427	6.475	6.521	6.728	6.800	6.866	6.927
	1.50	9.153	9.240	9.325	9.407	9.487	9.564	9.638	9.710	10.032	10.145	10.249	10.344
	2.00	12.079	12.199	12.316	12.429	12.539	12.645	12.748	12.847	13.293	13.449	13.594	13.727
	2.50	14.938	15.092	15.243	15.388	15.530	15.667	15.800	15.928	16.507	16.710	16.898	17.072
	3.00	17.725	17.916	18.101	18.281	18.456	18.626	18.791	18.950	19.670	19.924	20.159	20.376
80% Loan to Value	0.25	1.666	1.680	1.694	1.708	1.721	1.733	1.745	1.757	1.809	1.827	1.843	1.859
	0.50	3.317	3.346	3.374	3.402	3.428	3.454	3.478	3.502	3.608	3.645	3.679	3.710
	0.75	4.952	4.997	5.040	5.082	5.122	5.161	5.199	5.235	5.397	5.454	5.506	5.553
	1.00	6.572	6.633	6.691	6.748	6.802	6.855	6.906	6.956	7.176	7.253	7.324	7.389
	1.50	9.763	9.856	9.947	10.034	10.119	10.201	10.281	10.357	10.701	10.821	10.932	11.034
	2.00	12.885	13.013	13.137	13.258	13.375	13.488	13.597	13.703	14.179	14.346	14.500	14.642
	2.50	15.934	16.099	16.259	16.414	16.565	16.711	16.853	16.990	17.607	17.824	18.025	18.210
	3.00	18.907	19.110	19.308	19.500	19.687	19.868	20.043	20.213	20.982	21.252	21.503	21.735
85% Loan to Value	0.25	1.770	1.785	1.800	1.814	1.828	1.841	1.854	1.867	1.922	1.941	1.959	1.975
	0.50	3.524	3.555	3.585	3.614	3.642	3.669	3.696	3.721	3.834	3.873	3.909	3.942
	0.75	5.262	5.309	5.355	5.399	5.442	5.484	5.524	5.562	5.735	5.795	5.850	5.900
	1.00	6.983	7.047	7.109	7.169	7.228	7.284	7.338	7.390	7.625	7.706	7.781	7.851
	1.50	10.373	10.472	10.568	10.661	10.752	10.839	10.923	11.005	11.370	11.497	11.615	11.723
	2.00	13.690	13.826	13.958	14.086	14.211	14.331	14.447	14.560	15.065	15.243	15.406	15.557
	2.50	16.930	17.105	17.275	17.440	17.601	17.756	17.906	18.052	18.708	18.938	19.151	19.348
	3.00	20.088	20.304	20.515	20.719	20.917	21.110	21.296	21.477	22.293	22.581	22.847	23.093

Entry is capitalized value of reduced constant as percent of total property value.

Create Value by Paying Points

Equity Rate 10.50%

Loan to Value	Cut in Rate	Initial Interest Rate											
		8.00%	8.25%	8.50%	8.75%	9.00%	9.25%	9.50%	9.75%	11.00%	11.50%	12.00%	12.50%
67% Loan to Value	0.25	1.322	1.333	1.345	1.355	1.366	1.375	1.385	1.394	1.436	1.450	1.463	1.475
	0.50	2.632	2.656	2.678	2.700	2.721	2.741	2.761	2.779	2.864	2.893	2.920	2.944
	0.75	3.931	3.966	4.000	4.033	4.065	4.096	4.126	4.155	4.284	4.328	4.370	4.407
	1.00	5.216	5.264	5.310	5.355	5.399	5.441	5.481	5.520	5.695	5.756	5.813	5.864
	1.50	7.748	7.822	7.894	7.964	8.031	8.096	8.159	8.220	8.493	8.588	8.676	8.757
	2.00	10.226	10.328	10.426	10.522	10.615	10.705	10.792	10.876	11.253	11.386	11.508	11.620
	2.50	12.646	12.777	12.904	13.027	13.147	13.263	13.375	13.484	13.974	14.146	14.305	14.452
	3.00	15.005	15.167	15.324	15.476	15.625	15.768	15.908	16.042	16.652	16.867	17.066	17.250
75% Loan to Value	0.25	1.487	1.500	1.513	1.525	1.536	1.547	1.558	1.569	1.615	1.631	1.646	1.660
	0.50	2.961	2.988	3.013	3.037	3.061	3.084	3.106	3.127	3.221	3.254	3.285	3.312
	0.75	4.422	4.462	4.500	4.537	4.573	4.608	4.642	4.674	4.819	4.869	4.916	4.958
	1.00	5.868	5.922	5.974	6.025	6.074	6.121	6.166	6.210	6.407	6.476	6.539	6.597
	1.50	8.717	8.800	8.881	8.959	9.035	9.108	9.179	9.248	9.555	9.662	9.761	9.852
	2.00	11.504	11.619	11.730	11.837	11.942	12.043	12.141	12.235	12.660	12.809	12.946	13.073
	2.50	14.226	14.374	14.517	14.656	14.790	14.921	15.047	15.170	15.721	15.914	16.094	16.259
	3.00	16.881	17.063	17.239	17.411	17.578	17.739	17.896	18.048	18.734	18.975	19.199	19.406
80% Loan to Value	0.25	1.586	1.600	1.613	1.626	1.639	1.651	1.662	1.673	1.723	1.740	1.756	1.770
	0.50	3.159	3.187	3.214	3.240	3.265	3.289	3.313	3.335	3.436	3.471	3.504	3.533
	0.75	4.717	4.759	4.800	4.840	4.878	4.915	4.951	4.986	5.140	5.194	5.244	5.289
	1.00	6.259	6.317	6.372	6.426	6.478	6.529	6.577	6.624	6.834	6.908	6.975	7.037
	1.50	9.298	9.387	9.473	9.556	9.637	9.715	9.791	9.864	10.191	10.306	10.411	10.508
	2.00	12.271	12.393	12.512	12.626	12.738	12.846	12.950	13.051	13.504	13.663	13.809	13.945
	2.50	15.175	15.332	15.485	15.633	15.776	15.916	16.050	16.181	16.769	16.975	17.166	17.343
	3.00	18.006	18.200	18.389	18.572	18.749	18.922	19.089	19.251	19.983	20.240	20.479	20.700
85% Loan to Value	0.25	1.686	1.700	1.714	1.728	1.741	1.754	1.766	1.778	1.830	1.849	1.865	1.881
	0.50	3.356	3.386	3.414	3.442	3.469	3.495	3.520	3.544	3.651	3.688	3.723	3.754
	0.75	5.011	5.056	5.100	5.142	5.183	5.223	5.261	5.297	5.462	5.519	5.571	5.620
	1.00	6.651	6.712	6.771	6.828	6.883	6.937	6.989	7.038	7.262	7.339	7.411	7.477
	1.50	9.879	9.974	10.065	10.154	10.240	10.323	10.403	10.481	10.828	10.950	11.062	11.165
	2.00	13.038	13.168	13.294	13.416	13.534	13.648	13.759	13.866	14.348	14.517	14.673	14.816
	2.50	16.123	16.290	16.452	16.610	16.762	16.910	17.054	17.192	17.817	18.036	18.239	18.427
	3.00	19.132	19.338	19.538	19.732	19.921	20.105	20.282	20.454	21.231	21.505	21.759	21.993

Equity Rate 11.00%

Loan to Value	Cut in Rate	8.00%	8.25%	8.50%	8.75%	9.00%	9.25%	9.50%	9.75%	11.00%	11.50%	12.00%	12.50%
67% Loan to Value	0.25	1.262	1.273	1.283	1.294	1.303	1.313	1.322	1.331	1.370	1.384	1.397	1.408
	0.50	2.513	2.535	2.556	2.577	2.597	2.616	2.635	2.653	2.733	2.761	2.787	2.811
	0.75	3.752	3.786	3.818	3.850	3.880	3.910	3.938	3.966	4.089	4.132	4.171	4.207
	1.00	4.979	5.025	5.069	5.112	5.153	5.193	5.232	5.269	5.436	5.495	5.548	5.598
	1.50	7.396	7.467	7.535	7.602	7.666	7.728	7.788	7.846	8.107	8.198	8.282	8.359
	2.00	9.761	9.858	9.952	10.044	10.132	10.218	10.301	10.381	10.742	10.868	10.985	11.092
	2.50	12.071	12.196	12.317	12.435	12.549	12.660	12.767	12.871	13.339	13.503	13.655	13.795
	3.00	14.323	14.477	14.627	14.773	14.914	15.052	15.184	15.313	15.895	16.100	16.290	16.466
75% Loan to Value	0.25	1.420	1.432	1.444	1.455	1.466	1.477	1.487	1.497	1.542	1.557	1.571	1.584
	0.50	2.827	2.852	2.876	2.899	2.922	2.943	2.964	2.985	3.075	3.106	3.135	3.162
	0.75	4.221	4.259	4.296	4.331	4.365	4.399	4.431	4.462	4.600	4.648	4.692	4.733
	1.00	5.601	5.653	5.703	5.751	5.797	5.843	5.886	5.928	6.116	6.182	6.242	6.297
	1.50	8.321	8.400	8.477	8.552	8.624	8.694	8.762	8.827	9.120	9.223	9.317	9.404
	2.00	10.981	11.090	11.196	11.299	11.399	11.495	11.589	11.679	12.085	12.227	12.358	12.479
	2.50	13.580	13.720	13.857	13.990	14.118	14.243	14.363	14.480	15.006	15.191	15.362	15.520
	3.00	16.114	16.287	16.456	16.620	16.779	16.933	17.083	17.227	17.882	18.113	18.326	18.524
80% Loan to Value	0.25	1.514	1.527	1.540	1.552	1.564	1.576	1.587	1.597	1.644	1.661	1.676	1.690
	0.50	3.015	3.042	3.068	3.092	3.116	3.140	3.162	3.184	3.280	3.314	3.344	3.373
	0.75	4.502	4.543	4.582	4.620	4.657	4.692	4.726	4.759	4.907	4.958	5.005	5.049
	1.00	5.975	6.030	6.083	6.134	6.184	6.232	6.278	6.323	6.524	6.594	6.658	6.717
	1.50	8.875	8.960	9.042	9.122	9.199	9.274	9.346	9.416	9.728	9.837	9.938	10.031
	2.00	11.713	11.830	11.943	12.053	12.159	12.262	12.361	12.457	12.890	13.042	13.182	13.311
	2.50	14.485	14.635	14.781	14.922	15.059	15.192	15.321	15.445	16.007	16.204	16.386	16.554
	3.00	17.188	17.373	17.553	17.727	17.897	18.062	18.221	18.376	19.074	19.320	19.548	19.759
85% Loan to Value	0.25	1.609	1.623	1.636	1.649	1.662	1.674	1.686	1.697	1.747	1.765	1.781	1.795
	0.50	3.204	3.232	3.259	3.286	3.311	3.336	3.360	3.383	3.485	3.521	3.553	3.583
	0.75	4.784	4.827	4.868	4.909	4.948	4.985	5.022	5.057	5.213	5.268	5.318	5.364
	1.00	6.348	6.407	6.463	6.518	6.570	6.622	6.671	6.718	6.932	7.006	7.074	7.137
	1.50	9.430	9.520	9.608	9.692	9.774	9.853	9.930	10.004	10.336	10.452	10.559	10.658
	2.00	12.445	12.569	12.689	12.806	12.919	13.028	13.134	13.236	13.696	13.857	14.006	14.143
	2.50	15.390	15.550	15.705	15.855	16.001	16.142	16.278	16.411	17.007	17.217	17.410	17.589
	3.00	18.262	18.459	18.650	18.835	19.016	19.191	19.360	19.524	20.266	20.528	20.770	20.994

Entry is capitalized value of reduced constant as percent of total property value.

Create Value by Paying Points

Equity Rate 11.50%

Loan to Value	Cut in Rate	8.00%	8.25%	8.50%	8.75%	9.00%	9.25%	9.50%	9.75%	11.00%	11.50%	12.00%	12.50%
							Initial Interest Rate						
	0.25	1.207	1.218	1.228	1.237	1.247	1.256	1.265	1.273	1.311	1.324	1.336	1.347
	0.50	2.403	2.425	2.445	2.465	2.484	2.503	2.520	2.538	2.615	2.641	2.666	2.688
67%	0.75	3.589	3.621	3.652	3.682	3.712	3.740	3.767	3.794	3.911	3.952	3.990	4.024
Loan	1.00	4.763	4.806	4.849	4.890	4.929	4.968	5.005	5.040	5.200	5.256	5.307	5.354
to	1.50	7.075	7.142	7.208	7.271	7.333	7.392	7.450	7.505	7.754	7.841	7.922	7.995
Value	2.00	9.337	9.430	9.520	9.607	9.692	9.774	9.853	9.930	10.275	10.396	10.507	10.610
	2.50	11.546	11.666	11.782	11.894	12.004	12.110	12.212	12.312	12.759	12.916	13.061	13.196
	3.00	13.700	13.848	13.991	14.131	14.266	14.397	14.524	14.647	15.204	15.400	15.582	15.750
	0.25	1.358	1.370	1.381	1.392	1.403	1.413	1.423	1.432	1.475	1.489	1.503	1.515
	0.50	2.704	2.728	2.751	2.773	2.795	2.815	2.836	2.855	2.941	2.971	2.999	3.024
75%	0.75	4.037	4.074	4.109	4.143	4.176	4.207	4.238	4.268	4.400	4.446	4.488	4.527
Loan	1.00	5.358	5.407	5.455	5.501	5.545	5.589	5.630	5.670	5.850	5.913	5.970	6.023
to	1.50	7.959	8.035	8.109	8.180	8.249	8.316	8.381	8.443	8.724	8.822	8.912	8.995
Value	2.00	10.504	10.608	10.710	10.808	10.903	10.996	11.085	11.171	11.559	11.695	11.821	11.936
	2.50	12.989	13.124	13.254	13.381	13.504	13.623	13.739	13.850	14.354	14.531	14.694	14.845
	3.00	15.413	15.579	15.740	15.897	16.049	16.197	16.340	16.478	17.105	17.325	17.530	17.719
	0.25	1.449	1.461	1.473	1.485	1.496	1.507	1.518	1.528	1.573	1.589	1.603	1.616
	0.50	2.884	2.910	2.934	2.958	2.981	3.003	3.025	3.045	3.137	3.170	3.199	3.226
80%	0.75	4.307	4.345	4.383	4.419	4.454	4.488	4.521	4.552	4.693	4.742	4.788	4.829
Loan	1.00	5.715	5.768	5.818	5.868	5.915	5.961	6.005	6.048	6.240	6.307	6.368	6.425
to	1.50	8.489	8.571	8.649	8.725	8.799	8.871	8.940	9.006	9.305	9.410	9.506	9.595
Value	2.00	11.204	11.315	11.424	11.529	11.630	11.729	11.824	11.916	12.330	12.475	12.609	12.732
	2.50	13.855	13.999	14.138	14.273	14.405	14.532	14.655	14.774	15.311	15.499	15.674	15.835
	3.00	16.440	16.617	16.790	16.957	17.119	17.277	17.429	17.577	18.245	18.480	18.698	18.900
	0.25	1.539	1.552	1.565	1.578	1.590	1.601	1.612	1.623	1.671	1.688	1.703	1.717
	0.50	3.064	3.091	3.118	3.143	3.167	3.191	3.214	3.236	3.334	3.368	3.399	3.428
85%	0.75	4.576	4.617	4.657	4.695	4.732	4.768	4.803	4.837	4.987	5.039	5.087	5.131
Loan	1.00	6.072	6.128	6.182	6.234	6.285	6.334	6.381	6.426	6.630	6.701	6.767	6.827
to	1.50	9.020	9.106	9.190	9.271	9.349	9.425	9.498	9.569	9.887	9.998	10.100	10.194
Value	2.00	11.904	12.023	12.138	12.249	12.357	12.462	12.563	12.661	13.100	13.254	13.397	13.528
	2.50	14.721	14.874	15.022	15.165	15.305	15.440	15.571	15.697	16.268	16.468	16.653	16.824
	3.00	17.468	17.656	17.839	18.017	18.189	18.356	18.518	18.675	19.385	19.635	19.867	20.081

Equity Rate 12.00%

Loan to Value	Cut in Rate	8.00%	8.25%	8.50%	8.75%	9.00%	9.25%	9.50%	9.75%	11.00%	11.50%	12.00%	12.50%
	0.25	1.157	1.167	1.176	1.186	1.195	1.204	1.212	1.220	1.256	1.269	1.280	1.291
	0.50	2.303	2.324	2.343	2.362	2.381	2.398	2.415	2.432	2.506	2.531	2.555	2.576
67%	0.75	3.439	3.470	3.500	3.529	3.557	3.584	3.610	3.635	3.748	3.787	3.823	3.857
Loan	1.00	4.564	4.606	4.647	4.686	4.724	4.761	4.796	4.830	4.983	5.037	5.086	5.131
to	1.50	6.780	6.845	6.907	6.968	7.027	7.084	7.139	7.193	7.431	7.515	7.592	7.662
Value	2.00	8.948	9.037	9.123	9.207	9.288	9.367	9.443	9.516	9.847	9.962	10.069	10.168
	2.50	11.065	11.180	11.291	11.399	11.504	11.605	11.703	11.799	12.227	12.378	12.517	12.646
	3.00	13.130	13.271	13.408	13.542	13.671	13.797	13.919	14.037	14.571	14.759	14.933	15.094
	0.25	1.301	1.313	1.324	1.334	1.344	1.354	1.363	1.373	1.413	1.427	1.440	1.452
	0.50	2.591	2.614	2.636	2.658	2.678	2.698	2.717	2.736	2.819	2.848	2.874	2.898
75%	0.75	3.869	3.904	3.938	3.970	4.002	4.032	4.062	4.090	4.217	4.261	4.301	4.339
Loan	1.00	5.135	5.182	5.227	5.272	5.314	5.356	5.396	5.434	5.606	5.666	5.722	5.772
to	1.50	7.627	7.700	7.771	7.839	7.906	7.970	8.032	8.092	8.360	8.454	8.540	8.620
Value	2.00	10.066	10.166	10.263	10.358	10.449	10.537	10.623	10.706	11.078	11.208	11.328	11.439
	2.50	12.448	12.577	12.702	12.824	12.942	13.056	13.166	13.273	13.756	13.925	14.082	14.226
	3.00	14.771	14.930	15.084	15.235	15.380	15.522	15.659	15.792	16.392	16.603	16.799	16.980
	0.25	1.388	1.400	1.412	1.423	1.434	1.444	1.454	1.464	1.507	1.522	1.536	1.549
	0.50	2.764	2.788	2.812	2.835	2.857	2.878	2.899	2.918	3.007	3.037	3.066	3.092
80%	0.75	4.127	4.164	4.200	4.235	4.268	4.301	4.332	4.363	4.498	4.545	4.588	4.628
Loan	1.00	5.477	5.527	5.576	5.623	5.669	5.713	5.755	5.796	5.980	6.044	6.103	6.157
to	1.50	8.136	8.213	8.289	8.362	8.433	8.501	8.567	8.631	8.918	9.018	9.110	9.195
Value	2.00	10.737	10.844	10.948	11.048	11.146	11.240	11.331	11.419	11.816	11.955	12.083	12.201
	2.50	13.278	13.415	13.549	13.679	13.804	13.926	14.044	14.158	14.673	14.854	15.021	15.175
	3.00	15.755	15.925	16.090	16.250	16.406	16.557	16.703	16.845	17.485	17.710	17.919	18.112
	0.25	1.475	1.488	1.500	1.512	1.523	1.534	1.545	1.556	1.602	1.618	1.632	1.646
	0.50	2.937	2.963	2.988	3.012	3.035	3.058	3.080	3.101	3.195	3.227	3.257	3.285
85%	0.75	4.385	4.424	4.463	4.500	4.535	4.570	4.603	4.635	4.779	4.829	4.875	4.917
Loan	1.00	5.819	5.873	5.924	5.974	6.023	6.070	6.115	6.159	6.354	6.422	6.485	6.542
to	1.50	8.644	8.727	8.807	8.885	8.960	9.032	9.103	9.170	9.475	9.581	9.679	9.769
Value	2.00	11.408	11.522	11.632	11.739	11.842	11.942	12.039	12.133	12.555	12.702	12.838	12.964
	2.50	14.108	14.254	14.396	14.534	14.667	14.797	14.922	15.043	15.590	15.782	15.959	16.123
	3.00	16.740	16.920	17.096	17.266	17.431	17.591	17.747	17.897	18.577	18.817	19.039	19.244

Entry is capitalized value of reduced constant as percent of total property value.

Total Growth Converted to Annual Rate

Total Growth During Time Span

Time Span	10%	11%	12%	13%	14%	15%	16%	17%	18%	19%	20%	21%	22%	23%	24%	25%
2	4.880	5.356	5.830	6.301	6.770	7.238	7.703	8.166	8.627	9.087	9.544	10.000	10.453	10.905	11.355	11.803
3	3.228	3.540	3.849	4.158	4.464	4.768	5.072	5.373	5.672	5.970	6.266	6.560	6.853	7.144	7.433	7.722
4	2.411	2.643	2.873	3.102	3.329	3.555	3.780	4.003	4.224	4.444	4.663	4.880	5.096	5.311	5.525	5.737
5	1.924	2.109	2.292	2.474	2.655	2.834	3.012	3.189	3.365	3.540	3.713	3.886	4.057	4.227	4.396	4.563
6	1.601	1.755	1.906	2.058	2.208	2.356	2.504	2.651	2.796	2.941	3.085	3.228	3.370	3.511	3.650	3.789
7	1.371	1.502	1.632	1.762	1.889	2.016	2.143	2.268	2.393	2.516	2.639	2.760	2.881	3.001	3.121	3.239
8	1.198	1.313	1.426	1.539	1.651	1.762	1.872	1.981	2.090	2.198	2.305	2.411	2.516	2.621	2.725	2.828
9	1.065	1.167	1.267	1.367	1.466	1.565	1.663	1.759	1.856	1.952	2.047	2.141	2.234	2.327	2.419	2.510
10	0.957	1.049	1.139	1.229	1.318	1.407	1.495	1.582	1.668	1.754	1.839	1.924	2.008	2.091	2.174	2.256
11	0.871	0.953	1.035	1.117	1.198	1.279	1.358	1.438	1.516	1.594	1.672	1.748	1.824	1.899	1.974	2.049
12	0.798	0.873	0.948	1.024	1.098	1.171	1.245	1.317	1.388	1.460	1.531	1.601	1.671	1.740	1.808	1.877
13	0.736	0.806	0.876	0.944	1.013	1.081	1.148	1.215	1.281	1.347	1.412	1.477	1.542	1.605	1.669	1.732
14	0.683	0.748	0.813	0.877	0.940	1.003	1.065	1.128	1.189	1.251	1.311	1.370	1.431	1.489	1.549	1.606
15	0.637	0.698	0.758	0.818	0.878	0.936	0.994	1.052	1.109	1.166	1.223	1.278	1.334	1.390	1.444	1.499
16	0.597	0.654	0.710	0.767	0.822	0.877	0.931	0.986	1.039	1.093	1.146	1.199	1.250	1.302	1.353	1.404
17	0.562	0.616	0.668	0.721	0.774	0.826	0.877	0.927	0.978	1.028	1.078	1.128	1.177	1.225	1.273	1.321
18	0.531	0.582	0.631	0.682	0.730	0.780	0.828	0.876	0.923	0.971	1.018	1.064	1.111	1.156	1.202	1.247
19	0.503	0.550	0.598	0.646	0.692	0.738	0.785	0.830	0.875	0.919	0.964	1.009	1.052	1.095	1.139	1.181
20	0.477	0.523	0.568	0.612	0.657	0.701	0.744	0.788	0.831	0.873	0.915	0.957	0.999	1.040	1.081	1.121
21	0.455	0.498	0.541	0.584	0.626	0.668	0.709	0.750	0.792	0.832	0.872	0.911	0.951	0.991	1.029	1.068
22	0.434	0.475	0.517	0.557	0.597	0.637	0.677	0.716	0.755	0.794	0.833	0.870	0.907	0.945	0.982	1.020
23	0.415	0.455	0.494	0.533	0.571	0.610	0.647	0.685	0.722	0.760	0.796	0.833	0.868	0.904	0.940	0.974
24	0.398	0.436	0.473	0.510	0.548	0.584	0.620	0.656	0.692	0.727	0.763	0.797	0.832	0.866	0.900	0.934
25	0.381	0.418	0.454	0.490	0.525	0.560	0.595	0.629	0.664	0.698	0.731	0.765	0.798	0.831	0.864	0.896

Span	26%	27%	28%	29%	30%	31%	32%	33%	34%	35%	36%	37%	38%	39%	40%	41%
2	12.249	12.694	13.137	13.578	14.017	14.455	14.891	15.325	15.758	16.189	16.619	17.046	17.473	17.898	18.321	18.743
3	8.008	8.293	8.577	8.859	9.139	9.419	9.696	9.972	10.248	10.521	10.793	11.064	11.333	11.601	11.869	12.134
4	5.947	6.157	6.365	6.573	6.778	6.983	7.187	7.389	7.591	7.791	7.990	8.188	8.385	8.580	8.775	8.969
5	4.730	4.896	5.061	5.224	5.387	5.549	5.709	5.869	6.028	6.185	6.342	6.498	6.653	6.807	6.961	7.113
6	3.927	4.064	4.200	4.336	4.469	4.603	4.736	4.867	4.999	5.129	5.258	5.387	5.515	5.641	5.768	5.894
7	3.357	3.474	3.589	3.704	3.819	3.933	4.046	4.158	4.270	4.380	4.490	4.600	4.709	4.817	4.924	5.031
8	2.931	3.032	3.133	3.234	3.333	3.432	3.531	3.629	3.726	3.822	3.918	4.013	4.108	4.202	4.295	4.388
9	2.601	2.691	2.781	2.870	2.958	3.046	3.133	3.219	3.305	3.390	3.475	3.560	3.644	3.727	3.809	3.891
10	2.338	2.418	2.499	2.579	2.658	2.737	2.815	2.892	2.969	3.046	3.122	3.198	3.273	3.347	3.421	3.495
11	2.123	2.197	2.270	2.342	2.414	2.485	2.556	2.626	2.696	2.765	2.835	2.903	2.971	3.039	3.106	3.173
12	1.944	2.011	2.079	2.145	2.210	2.276	2.340	2.404	2.469	2.532	2.595	2.658	2.720	2.782	2.844	2.904
13	1.793	1.855	1.917	1.978	2.038	2.099	2.159	2.218	2.277	2.336	2.394	2.452	2.509	2.565	2.622	2.678
14	1.665	1.722	1.778	1.836	1.891	1.948	2.003	2.058	2.112	2.166	2.221	2.274	2.327	2.380	2.433	2.485
15	1.553	1.606	1.659	1.712	1.764	1.816	1.868	1.919	1.970	2.021	2.071	2.121	2.171	2.219	2.268	2.317
16	1.454	1.505	1.554	1.604	1.653	1.702	1.750	1.798	1.846	1.893	1.940	1.987	2.033	2.079	2.125	2.171
17	1.369	1.416	1.463	1.509	1.555	1.601	1.647	1.692	1.736	1.781	1.825	1.869	1.913	1.956	1.999	2.041
18	1.292	1.336	1.381	1.425	1.468	1.512	1.554	1.597	1.639	1.681	1.722	1.764	1.806	1.846	1.887	1.927
19	1.224	1.266	1.308	1.349	1.390	1.431	1.472	1.512	1.552	1.592	1.631	1.671	1.709	1.748	1.787	1.824
20	1.162	1.202	1.241	1.281	1.320	1.359	1.397	1.436	1.474	1.511	1.549	1.586	1.623	1.660	1.696	1.732
21	1.107	1.144	1.183	1.220	1.257	1.294	1.331	1.367	1.404	1.439	1.475	1.510	1.546	1.581	1.615	1.650
22	1.056	1.093	1.128	1.165	1.200	1.235	1.270	1.304	1.339	1.373	1.408	1.441	1.475	1.508	1.541	1.574
23	1.010	1.044	1.079	1.113	1.147	1.181	1.215	1.247	1.281	1.313	1.346	1.378	1.411	1.442	1.474	1.505
24	0.968	1.000	1.034	1.067	1.099	1.131	1.164	1.195	1.227	1.258	1.289	1.320	1.351	1.381	1.412	1.442
25	0.928	0.960	0.992	1.023	1.054	1.085	1.116	1.147	1.177	1.207	1.237	1.267	1.296	1.325	1.354	1.383

Span	42%	43%	44%	45%	46%	47%	48%	49%	50%	51%	52%	53%	54%	55%	56%	57%
2	19.163	19.582	20.000	20.415	20.830	21.243	21.655	22.065	22.474	22.882	23.288	23.693	24.096	24.498	24.899	25.299
3	12.399	12.662	12.924	13.185	13.445	13.703	13.960	14.217	14.471	14.725	14.978	15.229	15.480	15.730	15.978	16.225
4	9.162	9.353	9.544	9.734	9.922	10.110	10.297	10.483	10.668	10.852	11.035	11.217	11.398	11.579	11.758	11.937
5	7.264	7.415	7.565	7.714	7.862	8.009	8.156	8.302	8.447	8.591	8.734	8.877	9.019	9.160	9.301	9.440
6	6.018	6.142	6.266	6.388	6.510	6.632	6.752	6.872	6.991	7.109	7.228	7.345	7.461	7.577	7.693	7.807
7	5.136	5.242	5.347	5.451	5.555	5.658	5.761	5.862	5.963	6.064	6.164	6.264	6.363	6.461	6.558	6.656
8	4.480	4.572	4.663	4.754	4.844	4.933	5.022	5.111	5.198	5.286	5.373	5.459	5.545	5.631	5.715	5.800
9	3.973	4.054	4.134	4.214	4.295	4.374	4.452	4.531	4.608	4.685	4.762	4.838	4.914	4.990	5.065	5.140
10	3.568	3.641	3.713	3.785	3.856	3.927	3.998	4.068	4.137	4.207	4.275	4.344	4.412	4.480	4.547	4.614
11	3.239	3.305	3.370	3.435	3.500	3.564	3.628	3.692	3.755	3.818	3.880	3.942	4.004	4.064	4.125	4.186
12	2.965	3.026	3.085	3.144	3.204	3.262	3.320	3.379	3.436	3.493	3.551	3.607	3.663	3.720	3.775	3.830
13	2.734	2.789	2.845	2.899	2.954	3.008	3.062	3.115	3.168	3.221	3.273	3.325	3.377	3.428	3.480	3.531
14	2.536	2.588	2.638	2.690	2.740	2.790	2.840	2.889	2.939	2.987	3.036	3.084	3.133	3.180	3.227	3.275
15	2.365	2.413	2.461	2.508	2.555	2.602	2.648	2.694	2.740	2.785	2.831	2.876	2.920	2.965	3.009	3.052
16	2.215	2.261	2.305	2.349	2.393	2.437	2.480	2.524	2.566	2.609	2.651	2.694	2.735	2.777	2.818	2.859
17	2.084	2.126	2.168	2.210	2.251	2.292	2.333	2.374	2.414	2.453	2.493	2.533	2.572	2.612	2.651	2.688
18	1.967	2.007	2.047	2.085	2.125	2.164	2.202	2.240	2.278	2.316	2.353	2.391	2.427	2.465	2.502	2.537
19	1.863	1.901	1.937	1.975	2.012	2.048	2.085	2.121	2.157	2.193	2.228	2.264	2.299	2.333	2.368	2.402
20	1.768	1.804	1.839	1.875	1.910	1.944	1.979	2.013	2.048	2.081	2.115	2.149	2.182	2.215	2.248	2.281
21	1.683	1.718	1.752	1.785	1.818	1.852	1.884	1.917	1.949	1.982	2.014	2.045	2.077	2.109	2.140	2.171
22	1.607	1.639	1.671	1.703	1.735	1.767	1.798	1.829	1.860	1.891	1.921	1.952	1.982	2.012	2.042	2.071
23	1.537	1.567	1.598	1.629	1.658	1.689	1.719	1.749	1.778	1.808	1.837	1.866	1.895	1.924	1.952	1.981
24	1.471	1.501	1.531	1.560	1.589	1.618	1.646	1.675	1.704	1.731	1.760	1.788	1.815	1.843	1.870	1.897
25	1.412	1.440	1.469	1.497	1.525	1.552	1.580	1.607	1.635	1.662	1.688	1.715	1.742	1.768	1.794	1.820

Entry is the annual percentage rate of the total growth.

Total Growth Converted to Annual Rate

Time Span	58%	59%	60%	61%	62%	Total Growth During Time Span 63%	64%	65%	66%	67%	68%	69%	70%	71%	72%	73%
2	25.698	26.095	26.491	26.885	27.279	27.671	28.062	28.452	28.840	29.228	29.614	30.000	30.384	30.766	31.148	31.529
3	16.471	16.716	16.960	17.204	17.446	17.687	17.928	18.166	18.404	18.642	18.878	19.113	19.348	19.582	19.814	20.046
4	12.115	12.292	12.468	12.643	12.818	12.991	13.164	13.336	13.508	13.678	13.848	14.017	14.185	14.353	14.520	14.686
5	9.580	9.718	9.856	9.993	10.129	10.264	10.399	10.534	10.667	10.800	10.933	11.065	11.196	11.326	11.456	11.585
6	7.922	8.036	8.148	8.261	8.373	8.483	8.594	8.705	8.813	8.923	9.032	9.139	9.246	9.354	9.459	9.565
7	6.753	6.849	6.945	7.040	7.135	7.229	7.322	7.416	7.509	7.601	7.693	7.785	7.875	7.965	8.055	8.145
8	5.884	5.967	6.051	6.133	6.215	6.297	6.378	6.459	6.540	6.620	6.699	6.778	6.857	6.936	7.014	7.091
9	5.214	5.288	5.361	5.434	5.506	5.578	5.651	5.722	5.793	5.864	5.934	6.003	6.073	6.142	6.211	6.280
10	4.680	4.746	4.812	4.877	4.942	5.007	5.071	5.135	5.198	5.262	5.324	5.387	5.449	5.511	5.572	5.634
11	4.246	4.306	4.365	4.425	4.483	4.542	4.600	4.658	4.715	4.772	4.829	4.886	4.942	4.998	5.054	5.109
12	3.886	3.940	3.994	4.049	4.102	4.155	4.209	4.261	4.313	4.366	4.418	4.469	4.521	4.572	4.623	4.674
13	3.581	3.632	3.682	3.731	3.781	3.830	3.879	3.927	3.975	4.023	4.071	4.119	4.166	4.213	4.260	4.307
14	3.321	3.368	3.414	3.461	3.506	3.551	3.597	3.641	3.687	3.731	3.776	3.819	3.862	3.907	3.949	3.993
15	3.096	3.140	3.182	3.226	3.269	3.310	3.353	3.395	3.436	3.478	3.519	3.560	3.601	3.642	3.681	3.722
16	2.900	2.941	2.981	3.021	3.061	3.101	3.140	3.179	3.218	3.257	3.295	3.334	3.372	3.410	3.447	3.485
17	2.727	2.765	2.803	2.841	2.879	2.915	2.953	2.990	3.026	3.063	3.098	3.134	3.170	3.206	3.242	3.277
18	2.574	2.609	2.646	2.681	2.716	2.751	2.786	2.822	2.856	2.890	2.924	2.958	2.991	3.025	3.058	3.092
19	2.437	2.471	2.504	2.538	2.572	2.605	2.638	2.671	2.703	2.736	2.768	2.800	2.832	2.864	2.895	2.927
20	2.313	2.345	2.377	2.409	2.441	2.472	2.504	2.535	2.566	2.597	2.627	2.658	2.688	2.718	2.748	2.778
21	2.202	2.233	2.264	2.293	2.324	2.353	2.384	2.414	2.442	2.472	2.502	2.530	2.559	2.587	2.616	2.645
22	2.101	2.130	2.160	2.188	2.217	2.246	2.275	2.302	2.330	2.358	2.386	2.414	2.441	2.469	2.496	2.523
23	2.008	2.037	2.064	2.092	2.120	2.147	2.174	2.202	2.228	2.255	2.281	2.307	2.334	2.360	2.386	2.411
24	1.924	1.951	1.977	2.004	2.031	2.056	2.082	2.109	2.134	2.160	2.185	2.210	2.235	2.261	2.285	2.310
25	1.846	1.872	1.897	1.923	1.948	1.973	1.998	2.023	2.047	2.072	2.096	2.121	2.145	2.169	2.192	2.216

Span	74%	75%	76%	77%	78%	79%	80%	81%	82%	83%	84%	85%	86%	87%	88%	90%
2	31.909	32.287	32.664	33.041	33.416	33.790	34.164	34.536	34.907	35.277	35.646	36.014	36.381	36.747	37.113	37.840
3	20.277	20.507	20.736	20.964	21.191	21.419	21.644	21.868	22.093	22.316	22.538	22.760	22.981	23.200	23.420	23.856
4	14.851	15.016	15.180	15.343	15.506	15.668	15.829	15.989	16.149	16.308	16.467	16.625	16.782	16.939	17.095	17.405
5	11.714	11.842	11.970	12.097	12.223	12.349	12.474	12.599	12.723	12.847	12.970	13.092	13.214	13.336	13.457	13.697
6	9.671	9.775	9.880	9.984	10.087	10.190	10.293	10.394	10.495	10.597	10.697	10.797	10.897	10.995	11.094	11.290
7	8.234	8.323	8.411	8.498	8.586	8.673	8.760	8.846	8.932	9.017	9.101	9.186	9.270	9.354	9.437	9.603
8	7.168	7.245	7.322	7.398	7.473	7.549	7.623	7.698	7.772	7.846	7.920	7.993	8.066	8.138	8.210	8.353
9	6.348	6.416	6.483	6.550	6.616	6.683	6.749	6.814	6.880	6.945	7.010	7.074	7.139	7.202	7.266	7.392
10	5.695	5.755	5.815	5.875	5.935	5.994	6.054	6.112	6.171	6.229	6.287	6.345	6.402	6.459	6.516	6.629
11	5.164	5.219	5.274	5.327	5.381	5.435	5.489	5.542	5.595	5.648	5.700	5.752	5.804	5.856	5.906	6.008
12	4.724	4.773	4.824	4.873	4.922	4.972	5.020	5.068	5.117	5.165	5.212	5.260	5.307	5.354	5.402	5.494
13	4.353	4.399	4.445	4.490	4.535	4.580	4.625	4.670	4.714	4.758	4.802	4.846	4.890	4.933	4.976	5.062
14	4.035	4.079	4.121	4.162	4.205	4.246	4.288	4.329	4.371	4.411	4.451	4.492	4.532	4.573	4.612	4.691
15	3.762	3.801	3.841	3.880	3.918	3.958	3.997	4.034	4.073	4.111	4.148	4.186	4.224	4.261	4.298	4.371
16	3.522	3.559	3.596	3.633	3.669	3.706	3.741	3.778	3.813	3.849	3.884	3.920	3.954	3.990	4.024	4.093
17	3.311	3.346	3.381	3.416	3.450	3.485	3.518	3.552	3.585	3.619	3.652	3.685	3.718	3.750	3.783	3.848
18	3.125	3.158	3.191	3.223	3.255	3.287	3.319	3.351	3.383	3.415	3.445	3.477	3.507	3.539	3.569	3.630
19	2.958	2.989	3.020	3.051	3.082	3.111	3.142	3.172	3.202	3.232	3.262	3.291	3.320	3.349	3.378	3.436
20	2.808	2.837	2.866	2.896	2.925	2.953	2.982	3.011	3.039	3.067	3.095	3.123	3.151	3.179	3.206	3.261
21	2.672	2.701	2.729	2.756	2.784	2.811	2.839	2.866	2.892	2.920	2.946	2.973	2.999	3.025	3.052	3.103
22	2.549	2.577	2.603	2.629	2.656	2.681	2.708	2.733	2.760	2.785	2.811	2.836	2.861	2.886	2.910	2.960
23	2.438	2.463	2.488	2.513	2.539	2.563	2.589	2.613	2.638	2.662	2.687	2.711	2.735	2.759	2.783	2.830
24	2.335	2.359	2.383	2.408	2.431	2.455	2.480	2.503	2.526	2.550	2.573	2.596	2.620	2.642	2.665	2.710
25	2.240	2.263	2.287	2.310	2.333	2.356	2.379	2.401	2.424	2.446	2.469	2.491	2.513	2.535	2.557	2.600

Span	91%	92%	93%	94%	95%	96%	97%	98%	99%	100%	105%	110%	115%	120%	125%	130%
2	38.202	38.564	38.924	39.283	39.642	40.000	40.356	40.712	41.067	41.421	43.178	44.913	46.628	48.323	50.000	51.657
3	24.073	24.289	24.504	24.720	24.933	25.146	25.359	25.571	25.781	25.992	27.033	28.058	29.066	30.059	31.037	32.001
4	17.559	17.713	17.866	18.018	18.170	18.321	18.472	18.622	18.771	18.920	19.657	20.380	21.090	21.788	22.474	23.149
5	13.816	13.935	14.054	14.172	14.289	14.406	14.523	14.639	14.754	14.869	15.438	15.996	16.543	17.080	17.607	18.126
6	11.388	11.485	11.581	11.678	11.774	11.868	11.964	12.059	12.152	12.246	12.709	13.163	13.607	14.043	14.472	14.891
7	9.685	9.767	9.848	9.929	10.010	10.091	10.171	10.250	10.330	10.409	10.799	11.181	11.555	11.922	12.283	12.636
8	8.424	8.495	8.566	8.636	8.706	8.775	8.844	8.913	8.982	9.050	9.387	9.717	10.041	10.357	10.668	10.972
9	7.455	7.517	7.579	7.641	7.703	7.764	7.824	7.885	7.945	8.006	8.303	8.593	8.877	9.156	9.428	9.696
10	6.684	6.740	6.796	6.851	6.906	6.961	7.015	7.069	7.123	7.177	7.442	7.701	7.955	8.203	8.447	8.685
11	6.059	6.109	6.160	6.210	6.259	6.309	6.358	6.407	6.455	6.504	6.744	6.977	7.207	7.431	7.650	7.866
12	5.541	5.586	5.632	5.678	5.723	5.768	5.813	5.857	5.902	5.946	6.164	6.378	6.587	6.791	6.991	7.188
13	5.103	5.145	5.188	5.229	5.271	5.313	5.354	5.395	5.436	5.477	5.677	5.873	6.065	6.252	6.437	6.616
14	4.730	4.770	4.808	4.848	4.886	4.925	4.962	5.000	5.038	5.075	5.261	5.443	5.620	5.794	5.963	6.130
15	4.408	4.445	4.480	4.517	4.553	4.588	4.624	4.659	4.694	4.729	4.901	5.071	5.235	5.396	5.555	5.710
16	4.127	4.161	4.195	4.228	4.262	4.295	4.329	4.361	4.395	4.427	4.589	4.746	4.900	5.051	5.199	5.343
17	3.879	3.912	3.943	3.975	4.007	4.038	4.069	4.100	4.131	4.162	4.313	4.461	4.605	4.747	4.885	5.022
18	3.660	3.691	3.720	3.750	3.780	3.810	3.838	3.868	3.896	3.926	4.069	4.208	4.344	4.478	4.608	4.736
19	3.464	3.493	3.521	3.550	3.577	3.605	3.633	3.660	3.688	3.716	3.851	3.982	4.111	4.237	4.360	4.482
20	3.288	3.315	3.342	3.368	3.395	3.421	3.448	3.474	3.500	3.526	3.654	3.779	3.901	4.021	4.137	4.252
21	3.130	3.155	3.181	3.206	3.231	3.256	3.282	3.306	3.331	3.355	3.477	3.597	3.713	3.826	3.937	4.046
22	2.985	3.009	3.034	3.058	3.082	3.106	3.130	3.154	3.177	3.201	3.316	3.429	3.541	3.649	3.755	3.859
23	2.853	2.876	2.900	2.923	2.946	2.969	2.992	3.014	3.037	3.059	3.171	3.278	3.384	3.488	3.588	3.688
24	2.733	2.755	2.777	2.800	2.822	2.843	2.865	2.887	2.908	2.930	3.036	3.140	3.241	3.339	3.437	3.531
25	2.622	2.643	2.664	2.686	2.707	2.728	2.749	2.770	2.790	2.811	2.912	3.012	3.109	3.204	3.296	3.387

Entry is the annual percentage rate of the total growth.

Total Growth Converted to Annual Rate

Total Growth During Time Span

Time Span	135%	140%	145%	150%	155%	160%	165%	170%	175%	180%	185%	190%	195%	200%	210%	220%
2	53.297	54.919	56.524	58.113	59.687	61.245	62.788	64.316	65.831	67.332	68.819	70.293	71.755	73.205	76.068	78.885
3	32.950	33.886	34.810	35.720	36.620	37.507	38.382	39.247	40.102	40.945	41.780	42.604	43.419	44.225	45.809	47.361
4	23.813	24.466	25.109	25.743	26.367	26.982	27.588	28.186	28.775	29.356	29.930	30.496	31.055	31.607	32.690	33.748
5	18.635	19.135	19.628	20.112	20.589	21.058	21.520	21.975	22.423	22.865	23.301	23.731	24.155	24.573	25.392	26.191
6	15.304	15.710	16.108	16.499	16.885	17.263	17.636	18.003	18.365	18.720	19.072	19.417	19.757	20.094	20.751	21.392
7	12.982	13.322	13.657	13.985	14.308	14.626	14.938	15.245	15.547	15.846	16.139	16.427	16.713	16.993	17.542	18.077
8	11.271	11.564	11.852	12.135	12.413	12.686	12.955	13.219	13.479	13.735	13.987	14.235	14.479	14.720	15.191	15.649
9	9.958	10.216	10.469	10.717	10.961	11.201	11.437	11.668	11.896	12.120	12.341	12.559	12.772	12.983	13.396	13.796
10	8.919	9.149	9.374	9.595	9.813	10.026	10.236	10.442	10.645	10.844	11.041	11.234	11.424	11.612	11.978	12.334
11	8.077	8.284	8.487	8.687	8.882	9.075	9.263	9.450	9.633	9.812	9.989	10.163	10.335	10.503	10.833	11.153
12	7.379	7.568	7.753	7.934	8.113	8.288	8.460	8.629	8.796	8.959	9.120	9.278	9.433	9.587	9.887	10.178
13	6.793	6.967	7.136	7.303	7.467	7.627	7.785	7.939	8.092	8.243	8.389	8.535	8.677	8.818	9.093	9.360
14	6.293	6.453	6.610	6.764	6.915	7.063	7.209	7.352	7.493	7.632	7.768	7.902	8.033	8.163	8.416	8.663
15	5.861	6.010	6.156	6.299	6.440	6.577	6.712	6.846	6.976	7.105	7.232	7.356	7.478	7.599	7.834	8.063
16	5.485	5.624	5.760	5.893	6.025	6.153	6.280	6.404	6.527	6.646	6.765	6.880	6.995	7.107	7.327	7.540
17	5.155	5.285	5.413	5.538	5.661	5.781	5.900	6.016	6.132	6.244	6.355	6.463	6.570	6.676	6.881	7.082
18	4.861	4.984	5.104	5.222	5.339	5.451	5.563	5.673	5.781	5.886	5.991	6.093	6.194	6.294	6.487	6.676
19	4.600	4.716	4.829	4.941	5.050	5.158	5.263	5.367	5.468	5.568	5.667	5.763	5.859	5.953	6.135	6.313
20	4.364	4.474	4.582	4.688	4.791	4.893	4.993	5.091	5.188	5.282	5.376	5.467	5.557	5.646	5.820	5.988
21	4.152	4.257	4.359	4.460	4.558	4.656	4.750	4.844	4.935	5.025	5.114	5.201	5.286	5.370	5.535	5.695
22	3.960	4.060	4.157	4.253	4.347	4.439	4.529	4.618	4.705	4.791	4.876	4.959	5.040	5.120	5.277	5.429
23	3.785	3.879	3.973	4.064	4.154	4.242	4.328	4.413	4.496	4.579	4.659	4.738	4.816	4.892	5.042	5.188
24	3.624	3.715	3.804	3.891	3.978	4.061	4.144	4.226	4.305	4.383	4.461	4.536	4.610	4.684	4.827	4.966
25	3.476	3.563	3.649	3.733	3.815	3.896	3.975	4.052	4.129	4.204	4.278	4.350	4.422	4.492	4.629	4.762

Span	230%	240%	250%	260%	270%	280%	290%	300%	310%	320%	330%	340%	350%	360%	370%	380%
2	81.659	84.390	87.082	89.736	92.353	94.935	97.484	100.00	102.48	104.94	107.36	109.76	112.13	114.48	116.79	119.09
3	48.880	50.369	51.830	53.262	54.668	56.049	57.406	58.740	60.052	61.343	62.613	63.864	65.096	66.310	67.507	68.686
4	34.780	35.790	36.778	37.744	38.691	39.619	40.529	41.421	42.297	43.156	44.001	44.831	45.647	46.450	47.239	48.016
5	26.970	27.730	28.473	29.199	29.909	30.604	31.284	31.950	32.604	33.244	33.873	34.490	35.096	35.691	36.276	36.851
6	22.017	22.625	23.219	23.799	24.365	24.919	25.462	25.992	26.512	27.021	27.519	28.009	28.490	28.961	29.424	29.880
7	18.597	19.104	19.598	20.080	20.551	21.011	21.461	21.902	22.332	22.754	23.167	23.573	23.969	24.360	24.743	25.118
8	16.095	16.529	16.952	17.364	17.767	18.160	18.544	18.920	19.288	19.648	20.000	20.345	20.684	21.016	21.342	21.662
9	14.186	14.565	14.935	15.295	15.646	15.990	16.325	16.653	16.973	17.287	17.594	17.895	18.189	18.478	18.762	19.040
10	12.681	13.018	13.346	13.665	13.977	14.282	14.579	14.869	15.153	15.431	15.703	15.969	16.230	16.486	16.737	16.983
11	11.465	11.768	12.063	12.350	12.630	12.904	13.170	13.431	13.686	13.935	14.179	14.419	14.653	14.882	15.107	15.327
12	10.461	10.736	11.004	11.265	11.519	11.768	12.009	12.246	12.478	12.703	12.924	13.141	13.353	13.561	13.765	13.964
13	9.619	9.871	10.116	10.355	10.588	10.815	11.036	11.253	11.465	11.672	11.874	12.071	12.266	12.456	12.642	12.824
14	8.902	9.134	9.361	9.581	9.796	10.005	10.210	10.409	10.604	10.795	10.981	11.163	11.341	11.517	11.688	11.856
15	8.285	8.500	8.710	8.915	9.113	9.308	9.498	9.682	9.863	10.040	10.212	10.381	10.547	10.709	10.868	11.024
16	7.747	7.948	8.144	8.335	8.520	8.701	8.878	9.050	9.219	9.383	9.544	9.702	9.856	10.007	10.155	10.300
17	7.276	7.464	7.647	7.826	8.000	8.169	8.335	8.497	8.654	8.808	8.959	9.106	9.251	9.392	9.530	9.666
18	6.858	7.035	7.207	7.376	7.539	7.699	7.855	8.006	8.155	8.299	8.441	8.579	8.715	8.847	8.978	9.106
19	6.486	6.653	6.815	6.974	7.129	7.279	7.426	7.569	7.709	7.846	7.979	8.110	8.238	8.363	8.486	8.606
20	6.151	6.309	6.464	6.614	6.760	6.902	7.041	7.177	7.309	7.439	7.565	7.689	7.810	7.928	8.045	8.158
21	5.850	6.001	6.147	6.289	6.429	6.564	6.695	6.824	6.949	7.073	7.193	7.310	7.425	7.537	7.648	7.756
22	5.577	5.721	5.859	5.996	6.127	6.256	6.381	6.504	6.623	6.741	6.854	6.966	7.076	7.183	7.288	7.390
23	5.328	5.465	5.598	5.727	5.854	5.976	6.096	6.213	6.327	6.439	6.547	6.654	6.758	6.860	6.960	7.058
24	5.101	5.231	5.358	5.482	5.602	5.720	5.835	5.946	6.055	6.162	6.266	6.368	6.468	6.565	6.660	6.754
25	4.891	5.016	5.138	5.257	5.372	5.485	5.594	5.701	5.806	5.908	6.008	6.105	6.200	6.294	6.385	6.475

Span	390%	400%	410%	420%	430%	440%	450%	460%	470%	480%	490%	500%	600%	700%	750%	800%
2	121.36	123.61	125.83	128.04	130.22	132.38	134.52	136.64	138.75	140.83	142.90	144.95	164.58	182.84	191.55	200.00
3	69.849	70.998	72.130	73.247	74.352	75.441	76.517	77.581	78.631	79.670	80.697	81.712	91.293	100.00	104.08	108.01
4	48.781	49.534	50.277	51.008	51.729	52.439	53.140	53.832	54.514	55.187	55.852	56.508	62.657	68.179	70.747	73.205
5	37.416	37.972	38.520	39.059	39.590	40.113	40.628	41.135	41.636	42.129	42.616	43.096	47.577	51.571	53.420	55.184
6	30.326	30.766	31.199	31.623	32.042	32.454	32.859	33.259	33.653	34.041	34.423	34.801	38.308	41.421	42.857	44.225
7	25.487	25.850	26.206	26.557	26.902	27.242	27.575	27.904	28.227	28.547	28.861	29.171	32.047	34.590	35.760	36.874
8	21.976	22.284	22.587	22.885	23.178	23.466	23.750	24.029	24.303	24.574	24.840	25.103	27.537	29.683	30.670	31.607
9	19.313	19.581	19.845	20.103	20.358	20.608	20.854	21.097	21.335	21.570	21.801	22.028	24.136	25.992	26.844	27.651
10	17.224	17.461	17.694	17.923	18.148	18.369	18.586	18.800	19.011	19.218	19.422	19.623	21.481	23.114	23.863	24.573
11	15.543	15.756	15.964	16.169	16.370	16.568	16.764	16.955	17.143	17.328	17.511	17.690	19.351	20.809	21.476	22.110
12	14.160	14.353	14.542	14.727	14.910	15.089	15.264	15.438	15.608	15.776	15.941	16.104	17.604	18.921	19.523	20.094
13	13.003	13.180	13.352	13.521	13.687	13.852	14.012	14.170	14.325	14.479	14.630	14.778	16.147	17.346	17.895	18.414
14	12.021	12.183	12.341	12.497	12.651	12.801	12.949	13.095	13.238	13.378	13.516	13.654	14.912	16.012	16.516	16.993
15	11.176	11.326	11.474	11.617	11.759	11.899	12.035	12.170	12.303	12.433	12.561	12.688	13.851	14.870	15.335	15.776
16	10.442	10.582	10.719	10.853	10.985	11.115	11.242	11.368	11.491	11.612	11.732	11.849	12.932	13.878	14.311	14.720
17	9.800	9.930	10.058	10.183	10.308	10.429	10.548	10.665	10.781	10.894	11.005	11.115	12.128	13.012	13.415	13.797
18	9.230	9.354	9.473	9.592	9.707	9.822	9.933	10.044	10.153	10.258	10.364	10.466	11.417	12.246	12.625	12.983
19	8.724	8.840	8.953	9.065	9.174	9.281	9.387	9.491	9.593	9.694	9.792	9.889	10.784	11.566	11.922	12.260
20	8.270	8.379	8.487	8.592	8.696	8.797	8.897	8.995	9.092	9.187	9.280	9.372	10.218	10.956	11.293	11.612
21	7.862	7.965	8.067	8.167	8.266	8.362	8.456	8.549	8.641	8.731	8.820	8.907	9.709	10.409	10.728	11.030
22	7.491	7.590	7.687	7.781	7.875	7.966	8.057	8.146	8.232	8.318	8.402	8.485	9.248	9.913	10.216	10.503
23	7.154	7.248	7.341	7.431	7.520	7.608	7.694	7.777	7.861	7.942	8.023	8.102	8.828	9.462	9.751	10.024
24	6.845	6.936	7.024	7.110	7.196	7.280	7.361	7.442	7.522	7.599	7.676	7.752	8.445	9.051	9.326	9.587
25	6.563	6.649	6.734	6.816	6.898	6.978	7.056	7.134	7.209	7.284	7.357	7.430	8.094	8.673	8.937	9.186

Entry is the annual percentage rate of the total growth.

Future Simple Rate of Return on Initial Investment

| Elapsed Years | \multicolumn{11}{c}{Interest Rate (compounded monthly)} |
	2.00%	2.25%	2.50%	2.75%	3.00%	3.25%	3.50%	3.75%	4.00%	4.25%	4.50%
1	2.02	2.27	2.53	2.78	3.04	3.30	3.56	3.82	4.07	4.33	4.59
2	2.06	2.33	2.59	2.86	3.13	3.41	3.68	3.96	4.24	4.52	4.81
3	2.10	2.38	2.66	2.94	3.23	3.52	3.81	4.11	4.41	4.72	5.03
4	2.14	2.43	2.73	3.02	3.33	3.64	3.95	4.27	4.59	4.92	5.26
5	2.19	2.49	2.79	3.11	3.43	3.76	4.09	4.43	4.78	5.14	5.50
6	2.23	2.54	2.87	3.19	3.53	3.88	4.24	4.60	4.97	5.36	5.75
7	2.28	2.60	2.94	3.28	3.64	4.01	4.39	4.78	5.18	5.59	6.01
8	2.32	2.66	3.01	3.38	3.75	4.14	4.54	4.96	5.39	5.83	6.29
9	2.37	2.72	3.09	3.47	3.87	4.28	4.70	5.15	5.61	6.09	6.58
10	2.42	2.78	3.17	3.57	3.98	4.42	4.87	5.34	5.84	6.35	6.88
11	2.46	2.85	3.25	3.67	4.10	4.56	5.04	5.55	6.07	6.62	7.20
12	2.51	2.91	3.33	3.77	4.23	4.71	5.22	5.76	6.32	6.91	7.53
13	2.57	2.98	3.41	3.87	4.36	4.87	5.41	5.98	6.58	7.21	7.88
14	2.62	3.04	3.50	3.98	4.49	5.03	5.60	6.21	6.85	7.52	8.24
15	2.67	3.11	3.59	4.09	4.63	5.20	5.80	6.44	7.13	7.85	8.62
16	2.72	3.18	3.68	4.20	4.77	5.37	6.01	6.69	7.42	8.19	9.01
17	2.78	3.26	3.77	4.32	4.91	5.54	6.22	6.95	7.72	8.54	9.43
18	2.83	3.33	3.87	4.44	5.06	5.73	6.44	7.21	8.03	8.91	9.86
19	2.89	3.41	3.96	4.57	5.22	5.92	6.67	7.49	8.36	9.30	10.31
20	2.95	3.48	4.06	4.69	5.37	6.11	6.91	7.77	8.70	9.70	10.78
21	3.01	3.56	4.17	4.82	5.54	6.31	7.16	8.07	9.06	10.12	11.28
22	3.07	3.64	4.27	4.96	5.71	6.52	7.41	8.37	9.42	10.56	11.80
23	3.13	3.73	4.38	5.10	5.88	6.74	7.67	8.69	9.81	11.02	12.34
24	3.20	3.81	4.49	5.24	6.06	6.96	7.95	9.03	10.21	11.50	12.91
25	3.26	3.90	4.60	5.38	6.24	7.19	8.23	9.37	10.62	12.00	13.50
26	3.33	3.99	4.72	5.53	6.43	7.43	8.52	9.73	11.06	12.52	14.12
27	3.39	4.08	4.84	5.69	6.63	7.67	8.82	10.10	11.51	13.06	14.77
28	3.46	4.17	4.96	5.85	6.83	7.92	9.14	10.48	11.98	13.63	15.45
29	3.53	4.27	5.09	6.01	7.04	8.19	9.46	10.88	12.46	14.22	16.16
30	3.60	4.36	5.22	6.18	7.25	8.46	9.80	11.30	12.97	14.83	16.90

| Elapsed Years | \multicolumn{11}{c}{Interest Rate (compounded monthly)} |
	4.75%	5.00%	5.25%	5.50%	5.75%	6.00%	6.25%	6.50%	6.75%	7.00%	7.25%
1	4.85	5.12	5.38	5.64	5.90	6.17	6.43	6.70	6.96	7.23	7.50
2	5.09	5.38	5.67	5.96	6.25	6.55	6.85	7.15	7.45	7.75	8.06
3	5.34	5.65	5.97	6.30	6.62	6.95	7.29	7.62	7.97	8.31	8.66
4	5.60	5.94	6.29	6.65	7.01	7.38	7.75	8.13	8.52	8.91	9.31
5	5.87	6.25	6.63	7.03	7.43	7.84	8.25	8.68	9.11	9.56	10.01
6	6.15	6.57	6.99	7.42	7.87	8.32	8.78	9.26	9.75	10.25	10.76
7	6.45	6.90	7.36	7.84	8.33	8.83	9.35	9.88	10.43	10.99	11.57
8	6.77	7.25	7.76	8.28	8.82	9.38	9.95	10.54	11.15	11.78	12.43
9	7.09	7.63	8.18	8.75	9.34	9.96	10.59	11.25	11.93	12.64	13.36
10	7.44	8.02	8.62	9.24	9.89	10.57	11.27	12.00	12.76	13.55	14.37
11	7.80	8.43	9.08	9.76	10.48	11.22	12.00	12.81	13.65	14.53	15.44
12	8.18	8.86	9.57	10.32	11.10	11.91	12.77	13.66	14.60	15.58	16.60
13	8.57	9.31	10.08	10.90	11.75	12.65	13.59	14.58	15.62	16.70	17.85
14	8.99	9.79	10.63	11.51	12.45	13.43	14.46	15.56	16.70	17.91	19.18
15	9.43	10.29	11.20	12.16	13.18	14.26	15.40	16.60	17.87	19.21	20.62
16	9.89	10.81	11.80	12.85	13.96	15.14	16.39	17.71	19.11	20.60	22.17
17	10.37	11.37	12.44	13.57	14.78	16.07	17.44	18.89	20.44	22.08	23.83
18	10.87	11.95	13.10	14.34	15.66	17.06	18.56	20.16	21.86	23.68	25.61
19	11.40	12.56	13.81	15.15	16.58	18.11	19.75	21.51	23.39	25.39	27.53
20	11.95	13.20	14.55	16.00	17.56	19.23	21.03	22.95	25.02	27.23	29.60
21	12.53	13.88	15.33	16.90	18.59	20.42	22.38	24.49	26.76	29.20	31.82
22	13.14	14.59	16.16	17.86	19.69	21.68	23.82	26.13	28.62	31.31	34.20
23	13.78	15.33	17.03	18.86	20.86	23.01	25.35	27.88	30.61	33.57	36.77
24	14.44	16.12	17.94	19.93	22.09	24.43	26.98	29.74	32.74	36.00	39.52
25	15.15	16.94	18.91	21.05	23.39	25.94	28.72	31.74	35.02	38.60	42.48
26	15.88	17.81	19.93	22.24	24.77	27.54	30.56	33.86	37.46	41.39	45.67
27	16.65	18.72	21.00	23.49	26.23	29.24	32.53	36.13	40.07	44.38	49.09
28	17.46	19.68	22.13	24.82	27.78	31.04	34.62	38.55	42.86	47.59	52.77
29	18.31	20.69	23.32	26.22	29.42	32.96	36.85	41.13	45.85	51.03	56.73
30	19.20	21.75	24.57	27.70	31.16	34.99	39.22	43.89	49.04	54.72	60.98

Entry is the percentage return then on the amount invested now.

Future Simple Rate of Return on Initial Investment

Elapsed Years	\	Interest Rate (compounded monthly)									
	7.50%	7.75%	8.00%	8.25%	8.50%	8.75%	9.00%	9.25%	9.50%	9.75%	10.00%
1	7.76	8.03	8.30	8.57	8.84	9.11	9.38	9.65	9.92	10.20	10.47
2	8.37	8.68	8.99	9.30	9.62	9.94	10.26	10.58	10.91	11.24	11.57
3	9.02	9.37	9.73	10.10	10.47	10.84	11.22	11.61	11.99	12.38	12.78
4	9.72	10.13	10.54	10.97	11.40	11.83	12.28	12.73	13.18	13.65	14.12
5	10.47	10.94	11.42	11.91	12.40	12.91	13.43	13.95	14.49	15.04	15.60
6	11.28	11.82	12.37	12.93	13.50	14.09	14.69	15.30	15.93	16.57	17.23
7	12.16	12.77	13.39	14.03	14.69	15.37	16.06	16.78	17.51	18.26	19.03
8	13.10	13.79	14.50	15.24	15.99	16.77	17.57	18.40	19.25	20.12	21.03
9	14.12	14.90	15.71	16.54	17.41	18.30	19.22	20.17	21.16	22.18	23.23
10	15.22	16.10	17.01	17.96	18.94	19.96	21.02	22.12	23.26	24.44	25.66
11	16.40	17.39	18.42	19.50	20.62	21.78	23.00	24.26	25.57	26.93	28.35
12	17.67	18.79	19.95	21.17	22.44	23.77	25.15	26.60	28.10	29.68	31.31
13	19.04	20.29	21.61	22.98	24.42	25.93	27.51	29.16	30.89	32.70	34.59
14	20.52	21.92	23.40	24.95	26.58	28.30	30.09	31.98	33.96	36.04	38.22
15	22.11	23.69	25.34	27.09	28.93	30.87	32.92	35.07	37.33	39.71	42.22
16	23.83	25.59	27.45	29.41	31.49	33.69	36.00	38.45	41.03	43.76	46.64
17	25.68	27.64	29.73	31.93	34.27	36.75	39.38	42.16	45.11	48.22	51.52
18	27.67	29.86	32.19	34.67	37.30	40.10	43.08	46.23	49.58	53.14	56.92
19	29.82	32.26	34.86	37.64	40.60	43.76	47.12	50.69	54.51	58.56	62.88
20	32.14	34.85	37.76	40.87	44.19	47.74	51.54	55.59	59.91	64.53	69.46
21	34.63	37.65	40.89	44.37	48.10	52.09	56.37	60.95	65.86	71.11	76.73
22	37.32	40.67	44.29	48.17	52.35	56.84	61.66	66.84	72.40	78.37	84.77
23	40.22	43.94	47.96	52.30	56.97	62.01	67.44	73.29	79.58	86.36	93.65
24	43.34	47.47	51.94	56.78	62.01	67.66	73.77	80.36	87.48	95.16	103.45
25	46.70	51.28	56.25	61.65	67.49	73.83	80.69	88.12	96.16	104.87	114.28
26	50.33	55.40	60.92	66.93	73.46	80.55	88.26	96.63	105.71	115.56	126.25
27	54.24	59.85	65.98	72.66	79.95	87.89	96.54	105.95	116.20	127.35	139.47
28	58.45	64.66	71.46	78.89	87.02	95.90	105.59	116.18	127.73	140.33	154.08
29	62.98	69.85	77.39	85.65	94.71	104.63	115.50	127.39	140.41	154.65	170.21
30	67.87	75.46	83.81	92.99	103.08	114.16	126.33	139.69	154.34	170.42	188.03

Elapsed Years	\	Interest Rate (compounded monthly)									
	10.25%	10.50%	10.75%	11.00%	11.25%	11.50%	11.75%	12.00%	12.25%	12.50%	12.75%
1	10.75	11.02	11.30	11.57	11.85	12.13	12.40	12.68	12.96	13.24	13.52
2	11.90	12.23	12.57	12.91	13.25	13.60	13.94	14.29	14.64	15.00	15.35
3	13.18	13.58	13.99	14.41	14.82	15.24	15.67	16.10	16.54	16.98	17.43
4	14.60	15.08	15.57	16.07	16.58	17.09	17.62	18.15	18.68	19.23	19.78
5	16.16	16.74	17.33	17.93	18.54	19.17	19.80	20.45	21.11	21.78	22.46
6	17.90	18.59	19.29	20.01	20.74	21.49	22.26	23.04	23.84	24.66	25.49
7	19.82	20.64	21.47	22.32	23.20	24.10	25.02	25.96	26.93	27.92	28.94
8	21.95	22.91	23.89	24.91	25.95	27.02	28.12	29.26	30.42	31.62	32.86
9	24.31	25.43	26.59	27.79	29.02	30.29	31.61	32.97	34.36	35.81	37.30
10	26.93	28.24	29.60	31.00	32.46	33.97	35.53	37.15	38.82	40.55	42.34
11	29.82	31.35	32.94	34.59	36.31	38.09	39.94	41.86	43.85	45.92	48.07
12	33.02	34.80	36.66	38.59	40.61	42.71	44.89	47.17	49.53	52.00	54.57
13	36.57	38.64	40.80	43.06	45.42	47.88	50.46	53.15	55.96	58.89	61.95
14	40.50	42.90	45.41	48.04	50.80	53.69	56.72	59.89	63.21	66.68	70.32
15	44.85	47.62	50.54	53.60	56.82	60.20	63.75	67.48	71.40	75.51	79.83
16	49.67	52.87	56.25	59.80	63.55	67.50	71.66	76.04	80.66	85.51	90.63
17	55.01	58.70	62.60	66.72	71.08	75.69	80.55	85.69	91.11	96.84	102.88
18	60.92	65.17	69.67	74.44	79.50	84.86	90.54	96.55	102.92	109.66	116.79
19	67.47	72.35	77.54	83.06	88.92	95.15	101.77	108.80	116.26	124.18	132.58
20	74.72	80.32	86.30	92.67	99.46	106.69	114.39	122.60	131.33	140.62	150.51
21	82.75	89.18	96.05	103.39	111.24	119.63	128.58	138.14	148.35	159.24	170.87
22	91.64	99.00	106.90	115.36	124.43	134.14	144.53	155.67	167.58	180.33	193.97
23	101.49	109.91	118.97	128.71	139.17	150.40	162.46	175.41	189.30	204.21	220.20
24	112.39	122.03	132.41	143.60	155.66	168.64	182.61	197.65	213.84	231.25	249.97
25	124.47	135.47	147.37	160.22	174.10	189.09	205.26	222.72	241.55	261.87	283.78
26	137.84	150.40	164.02	178.76	194.73	212.02	230.72	250.97	272.86	296.55	322.15
27	152.65	166.98	182.54	199.45	217.80	237.72	259.34	282.80	308.23	335.81	365.71
28	169.06	185.38	203.16	222.53	243.61	266.55	291.51	318.66	348.18	380.28	415.16
29	187.22	205.81	226.11	248.28	272.47	298.87	327.67	359.08	393.32	430.63	471.30
30	207.34	228.49	251.65	277.01	304.76	335.11	368.31	404.62	444.30	487.66	535.03

Entry is the percentage return then on the amount invested now.

Cash on Cash Return After Growth

5.50% Cash on Cash   67% Loan to Value Ratio

Growth Rate	Time Period	5.50%	5.75%	6.00%	6.25%	6.50%	6.75%	7.00%	7.25%	7.50%	7.75%	8.00%	8.25%
						Annual Mortgage Constant							
2%	3	6.520	6.551	6.582	6.613	6.644	6.675	6.707	6.738	6.769	6.800	6.831	6.862
	5	7.235	7.288	7.340	7.393	7.446	7.499	7.552	7.604	7.657	7.710	7.763	7.816
	7.5	7.978	8.054	8.129	8.205	8.280	8.355	8.431	8.506	8.582	8.657	8.733	8.808
	10	9.150	9.261	9.372	9.483	9.595	9.706	9.817	9.928	10.039	10.150	10.261	10.373
3%	3	7.045	7.093	7.140	7.187	7.234	7.281	7.328	7.375	7.422	7.469	7.516	7.563
	5	8.155	8.235	8.316	8.397	8.478	8.559	8.640	8.720	8.801	8.882	8.963	9.044
	7.5	9.331	9.448	9.565	9.681	9.798	9.915	10.031	10.148	10.265	10.381	10.498	10.615
	10	11.232	11.407	11.581	11.756	11.930	12.105	12.279	12.454	12.628	12.803	12.978	13.152
4%	3	7.581	7.644	7.708	7.771	7.835	7.898	7.961	8.025	8.088	8.151	8.215	8.278
	5	9.111	9.221	9.331	9.441	9.551	9.661	9.771	9.881	9.991	10.101	10.211	10.321
	7.5	10.766	10.926	11.086	11.247	11.407	11.567	11.728	11.888	12.048	12.209	12.369	12.529
	10	13.504	13.748	13.992	14.235	14.479	14.723	14.967	15.210	15.454	15.698	15.942	16.185
5%	3	8.127	8.207	8.287	8.367	8.447	8.527	8.607	8.687	8.767	8.847	8.927	9.007
	5	10.105	10.245	10.385	10.525	10.666	10.806	10.946	11.086	11.227	11.367	11.507	11.647
	7.5	12.285	12.492	12.698	12.905	13.112	13.318	13.525	13.731	13.938	14.145	14.351	14.558
	10	15.982	16.301	16.620	16.939	17.258	17.578	17.897	18.216	18.535	18.854	19.174	19.493
6%	3	8.684	8.781	8.878	8.974	9.071	9.168	9.265	9.362	9.459	9.556	9.653	9.750
	5	11.137	11.309	11.480	11.652	11.824	11.995	12.167	12.339	12.510	12.682	12.854	13.026
	7.5	13.894	14.149	14.405	14.661	14.916	15.172	15.428	15.683	15.939	16.195	16.450	16.706
	10	18.681	19.082	19.484	19.885	20.286	20.688	21.089	21.491	21.892	22.294	22.695	23.096

5.50% Cash on Cash   75% Loan to Value Ratio

Growth Rate	Time Period	5.50%	5.75%	6.00%	6.25%	6.50%	6.75%	7.00%	7.25%	7.50%	7.75%	8.00%	8.25%
2%	3	6.847	6.892	6.938	6.984	7.030	7.076	7.122	7.168	7.214	7.260	7.306	7.352
	5	7.790	7.868	7.946	8.024	8.102	8.180	8.258	8.336	8.414	8.492	8.570	8.648
	7.5	8.771	8.883	8.994	9.106	9.217	9.329	9.440	9.552	9.663	9.775	9.886	9.998
	10	10.318	10.482	10.646	10.811	10.975	11.139	11.303	11.468	11.632	11.796	11.960	12.125
3%	3	7.540	7.610	7.679	7.749	7.818	7.888	7.957	8.027	8.096	8.166	8.235	8.305
	5	9.004	9.123	9.243	9.362	9.482	9.601	9.721	9.840	9.960	10.079	10.199	10.318
	7.5	10.557	10.730	10.902	11.074	11.247	11.419	11.592	11.764	11.936	12.109	12.281	12.454
	10	13.066	13.324	13.582	13.840	14.098	14.356	14.614	14.872	15.130	15.388	15.646	15.903
4%	3	8.247	8.341	8.434	8.528	8.622	8.715	8.809	8.903	8.996	9.090	9.183	9.277
	5	10.266	10.429	10.591	10.754	10.916	11.079	11.241	11.404	11.566	11.729	11.891	12.054
	7.5	12.450	12.687	12.924	13.161	13.398	13.635	13.872	14.109	14.346	14.583	14.820	15.057
	10	16.065	16.426	16.786	17.146	17.506	17.866	18.226	18.587	18.947	19.307	19.667	20.027
5%	3	8.968	9.086	9.204	9.322	9.441	9.559	9.677	9.795	9.913	10.032	10.150	10.268
	5	11.578	11.785	11.993	12.200	12.407	12.614	12.821	13.029	13.236	13.443	13.650	13.858
	7.5	14.456	14.762	15.067	15.372	15.678	15.983	16.288	16.593	16.899	17.204	17.509	17.815
	10	19.336	19.807	20.279	20.751	21.222	21.694	22.166	22.637	23.109	23.581	24.052	24.524
6%	3	9.702	9.846	9.989	10.132	10.275	10.419	10.562	10.705	10.848	10.992	11.135	11.278
	5	12.941	13.195	13.448	13.702	13.956	14.209	14.463	14.717	14.970	15.224	15.478	15.731
	7.5	16.580	16.958	17.335	17.713	18.091	18.468	18.846	19.224	19.602	19.979	20.357	20.735
	10	22.899	23.492	24.085	24.678	25.271	25.864	26.457	27.051	27.644	28.237	28.830	29.423

5.50% Cash on Cash   80% Loan to Value Ratio

Growth Rate	Time Period	5.50%	5.75%	6.00%	6.25%	6.50%	6.75%	7.00%	7.25%	7.50%	7.75%	8.00%	8.25%
2%	3	7.183	7.244	7.306	7.367	7.428	7.489	7.550	7.612	7.673	7.734	7.795	7.857
	5	8.362	8.466	8.570	8.674	8.779	8.883	8.987	9.091	9.195	9.299	9.403	9.507
	7.5	9.589	9.738	9.886	10.035	10.184	10.332	10.481	10.630	10.778	10.927	11.076	11.224
	10	11.522	11.741	11.960	12.179	12.398	12.617	12.836	13.055	13.274	13.493	13.712	13.931
3%	3	8.050	8.143	8.235	8.328	8.421	8.514	8.606	8.699	8.792	8.885	8.977	9.070
	5	9.880	10.039	10.199	10.358	10.517	10.676	10.836	10.995	11.154	11.314	11.473	11.632
	7.5	11.822	12.051	12.281	12.511	12.741	12.971	13.201	13.431	13.661	13.890	14.120	14.350
	10	14.958	15.302	15.646	15.989	16.333	16.677	17.021	17.365	17.709	18.053	18.397	18.741
4%	3	8.934	9.059	9.183	9.308	9.433	9.558	9.683	9.808	9.933	10.058	10.182	10.307
	5	11.458	11.675	11.891	12.108	12.325	12.541	12.758	12.975	13.191	13.408	13.624	13.841
	7.5	14.188	14.504	14.820	15.136	15.452	15.768	16.084	16.400	16.716	17.032	17.347	17.663
	10	18.707	19.187	19.667	20.147	20.628	21.108	21.588	22.068	22.549	23.029	23.509	23.989
5%	3	9.835	9.992	10.150	10.308	10.465	10.623	10.780	10.938	11.096	11.253	11.411	11.569
	5	13.098	13.374	13.650	13.927	14.203	14.479	14.755	15.032	15.308	15.584	15.861	16.137
	7.5	16.695	17.102	17.509	17.917	18.324	18.731	19.138	19.545	19.952	20.359	20.766	21.173
	10	22.795	23.423	24.052	24.681	25.310	25.939	26.568	27.197	27.826	28.455	29.084	29.712
6%	3	10.753	10.944	11.135	11.326	11.517	11.708	11.899	12.090	12.281	12.472	12.663	12.854
	5	14.801	15.139	15.478	15.816	16.154	16.492	16.831	17.169	17.507	17.845	18.183	18.522
	7.5	19.350	19.853	20.357	20.861	21.364	21.868	22.372	22.875	23.379	23.883	24.386	24.890
	10	27.248	28.039	28.830	29.621	30.412	31.203	31.993	32.784	33.575	34.366	35.157	35.948

Entry is the percentage return on equity after the time period, if the growth rate is sustained.

Cash on Cash Return After Growth

7.00% Cash on Cash   67% Loan to Value Ratio

Growth Rate	Time Period	7.00%	7.25%	7.50%	7.75%	8.00%	8.25%	8.50%	8.75%	9.00%	9.25%	9.50%	9.75%
						Annual Mortgage Constant							
2%	3	8.298	8.329	8.360	8.392	8.423	8.454	8.485	8.516	8.547	8.578	8.609	8.640
	5	9.208	9.261	9.313	9.366	9.419	9.472	9.525	9.578	9.630	9.683	9.736	9.789
	7.5	10.154	10.229	10.305	10.380	10.456	10.531	10.607	10.682	10.758	10.833	10.909	10.984
	10	11.645	11.756	11.868	11.979	12.090	12.201	12.312	12.423	12.535	12.646	12.757	12.868
3%	3	8.967	9.014	9.061	9.108	9.155	9.202	9.249	9.296	9.343	9.391	9.438	9.485
	5	10.379	10.459	10.540	10.621	10.702	10.783	10.864	10.944	11.025	11.106	11.187	11.268
	7.5	11.876	11.993	12.109	12.226	12.343	12.460	12.576	12.693	12.810	12.926	13.043	13.160
	10	14.295	14.470	14.644	14.819	14.993	15.168	15.343	15.517	15.692	15.866	16.041	16.215
4%	3	9.649	9.712	9.775	9.839	9.902	9.966	10.029	10.092	10.156	10.219	10.282	10.346
	5	11.596	11.706	11.816	11.926	12.036	12.146	12.255	12.365	12.475	12.585	12.695	12.805
	7.5	13.702	13.862	14.022	14.183	14.343	14.503	14.664	14.824	14.984	15.145	15.305	15.466
	10	17.187	17.431	17.675	17.918	18.162	18.406	18.650	18.893	19.137	19.381	19.625	19.868
5%	3	10.344	10.424	10.504	10.584	10.664	10.744	10.824	10.904	10.984	11.064	11.144	11.224
	5	12.861	13.001	13.141	13.281	13.421	13.562	13.702	13.842	13.982	14.123	14.263	14.403
	7.5	15.635	15.842	16.049	16.255	16.462	16.669	16.875	17.082	17.289	17.495	17.702	17.908
	10	20.340	20.659	20.979	21.298	21.617	21.936	22.255	22.575	22.894	23.213	23.532	23.852
6%	3	11.052	11.149	11.246	11.343	11.440	11.537	11.634	11.731	11.827	11.924	12.021	12.118
	5	14.174	14.346	14.518	14.690	14.861	15.033	15.205	15.376	15.548	15.720	15.891	16.063
	7.5	17.683	17.939	18.194	18.450	18.706	18.961	19.217	19.472	19.728	19.984	20.239	20.495
	10	23.776	24.177	24.578	24.980	25.381	25.783	26.184	26.585	26.987	27.388	27.790	28.191

7.00% Cash on Cash   75% Loan to Value Ratio

Growth Rate	Time Period	7.00%	7.25%	7.50%	7.75%	8.00%	8.25%	8.50%	8.75%	9.00%	9.25%	9.50%	9.75%
2%	3	8.714	8.760	8.806	8.852	8.897	8.943	8.989	9.035	9.081	9.127	9.173	9.219
	5	9.914	9.992	10.070	10.148	10.227	10.305	10.383	10.461	10.539	10.617	10.695	10.773
	7.5	11.163	11.275	11.386	11.498	11.609	11.721	11.832	11.944	12.055	12.167	12.278	12.390
	10	13.132	13.296	13.460	13.625	13.789	13.953	14.117	14.282	14.446	14.610	14.774	14.939
3%	3	9.596	9.666	9.735	9.805	9.875	9.944	10.014	10.083	10.153	10.222	10.292	10.361
	5	11.460	11.579	11.699	11.818	11.937	12.057	12.176	12.296	12.415	12.535	12.654	12.774
	7.5	13.436	13.609	13.781	13.954	14.126	14.298	14.471	14.643	14.816	14.988	15.161	15.333
	10	16.630	16.888	17.146	17.403	17.661	17.919	18.177	18.435	18.693	18.951	19.209	19.467
4%	3	10.496	10.590	10.683	10.777	10.871	10.964	11.058	11.152	11.245	11.339	11.433	11.526
	5	13.066	13.229	13.391	13.554	13.716	13.879	14.041	14.204	14.366	14.529	14.691	14.854
	7.5	15.846	16.083	16.320	16.557	16.794	17.031	17.268	17.505	17.742	17.979	18.216	18.453
	10	20.447	20.807	21.167	21.527	21.888	22.248	22.608	22.968	23.328	23.688	24.049	24.409
5%	3	11.413	11.532	11.650	11.768	11.886	12.005	12.123	12.241	12.359	12.477	12.596	12.714
	5	14.736	14.943	15.150	15.358	15.565	15.772	15.979	16.186	16.394	16.601	16.808	17.015
	7.5	18.399	18.704	19.009	19.315	19.620	19.925	20.231	20.536	20.841	21.147	21.452	21.757
	10	24.609	25.081	25.552	26.024	26.496	26.967	27.439	27.911	28.382	28.854	29.326	29.797
6%	3	12.348	12.492	12.635	12.778	12.921	13.065	13.208	13.351	13.495	13.638	13.781	13.924
	5	16.470	16.724	16.978	17.231	17.485	17.739	17.992	18.246	18.500	18.753	19.007	19.261
	7.5	21.102	21.479	21.857	22.235	22.613	22.990	23.368	23.746	24.123	24.501	24.879	25.257
	10	29.144	29.737	30.330	30.923	31.516	32.109	32.703	33.296	33.889	34.482	35.075	35.668

7.00% Cash on Cash   80% Loan to Value Ratio

Growth Rate	Time Period	7.00%	7.25%	7.50%	7.75%	8.00%	8.25%	8.50%	8.75%	9.00%	9.25%	9.50%	9.75%
2%	3	9.142	9.203	9.265	9.326	9.387	9.448	9.510	9.571	9.632	9.693	9.754	9.816
	5	10.643	10.747	10.851	10.955	11.059	11.163	11.267	11.371	11.475	11.580	11.684	11.788
	7.5	12.204	12.353	12.501	12.650	12.799	12.947	13.096	13.245	13.393	13.542	13.691	13.840
	10	14.665	14.884	15.103	15.322	15.541	15.760	15.979	16.198	16.417	16.636	16.855	17.074
3%	3	10.245	10.338	10.431	10.524	10.616	10.709	10.802	10.895	10.987	11.080	11.173	11.265
	5	12.575	12.734	12.893	13.052	13.212	13.371	13.530	13.690	13.849	14.008	14.167	14.327
	7.5	15.046	15.275	15.505	15.735	15.965	16.195	16.425	16.655	16.885	17.114	17.344	17.574
	10	19.037	19.381	19.725	20.069	20.413	20.757	21.101	21.444	21.788	22.132	22.476	22.820
4%	3	11.370	11.495	11.620	11.745	11.870	11.995	12.119	12.244	12.369	12.494	12.619	12.744
	5	14.583	14.800	15.016	15.233	15.449	15.666	15.883	16.099	16.316	16.533	16.749	16.966
	7.5	18.058	18.374	18.689	19.005	19.321	19.637	19.953	20.269	20.585	20.901	21.217	21.533
	10	23.809	24.289	24.769	25.249	25.730	26.210	26.690	27.170	27.651	28.131	28.611	29.091
5%	3	12.517	12.674	12.832	12.990	13.147	13.305	13.463	13.620	13.778	13.935	14.093	14.251
	5	16.670	16.946	17.222	17.499	17.775	18.051	18.328	18.604	18.880	19.156	19.433	19.709
	7.5	21.249	21.656	22.063	22.470	22.877	23.284	23.691	24.098	24.505	24.912	25.320	25.727
	10	29.011	29.640	30.269	30.898	31.527	32.156	32.785	33.414	34.042	34.671	35.300	35.929
6%	3	13.686	13.877	14.068	14.259	14.450	14.641	14.832	15.023	15.214	15.405	15.596	15.787
	5	18.838	19.176	19.514	19.853	20.191	20.529	20.867	21.205	21.544	21.882	22.220	22.558
	7.5	24.627	25.131	25.634	26.138	26.642	27.145	27.649	28.152	28.656	29.160	29.663	30.167
	10	34.680	35.471	36.261	37.052	37.843	38.634	39.425	40.216	41.006	41.797	42.588	43.379

Entry is the percentage return on equity after the time period, if the growth rate is sustained.

Cash on Cash Return After Growth

8.50% Cash on Cash   67% Loan to Value Ratio

Growth Rate	Time Period	8.50%	8.75%	9.00%	9.25%	9.50%	9.75%	10.00%	10.25%	10.50%	10.75%	11.00%	11.25%
					Annual Mortgage Constant								
2%	3	10.077	10.108	10.139	10.170	10.201	10.232	10.263	10.294	10.325	10.356	10.387	10.418
	5	11.181	11.234	11.287	11.339	11.392	11.445	11.498	11.551	11.604	11.656	11.709	11.762
	7.5	12.330	12.405	12.481	12.556	12.632	12.707	12.783	12.858	12.934	13.009	13.084	13.160
	10	14.141	14.252	14.363	14.474	14.585	14.697	14.808	14.919	15.030	15.141	15.252	15.363
3%	3	10.888	10.935	10.983	11.030	11.077	11.124	11.171	11.218	11.265	11.312	11.359	11.406
	5	12.603	12.683	12.764	12.845	12.926	13.007	13.088	13.168	13.249	13.330	13.411	13.492
	7.5	14.421	14.538	14.654	14.771	14.888	15.004	15.121	15.238	15.354	15.471	15.588	15.704
	10	17.358	17.533	17.708	17.882	18.057	18.231	18.406	18.580	18.755	18.930	19.104	19.279
4%	3	11.716	11.780	11.843	11.906	11.970	12.033	12.096	12.160	12.223	12.287	12.350	12.413
	5	14.080	14.190	14.300	14.410	14.520	14.630	14.740	14.850	14.960	15.070	15.180	15.290
	7.5	16.638	16.798	16.958	17.119	17.279	17.439	17.600	17.760	17.921	18.081	18.241	18.402
	10	20.870	21.114	21.357	21.601	21.845	22.089	22.332	22.576	22.820	23.064	23.308	23.551
5%	3	12.560	12.640	12.720	12.800	12.880	12.960	13.040	13.120	13.200	13.280	13.360	13.440
	5	15.616	15.757	15.897	16.037	16.177	16.318	16.458	16.598	16.738	16.878	17.019	17.159
	7.5	18.986	19.193	19.399	19.606	19.812	20.019	20.226	20.432	20.639	20.846	21.052	21.259
	10	24.699	25.018	25.337	25.656	25.976	26.295	26.614	26.933	27.252	27.572	27.891	28.210
6%	3	13.420	13.517	13.614	13.711	13.808	13.905	14.002	14.099	14.196	14.293	14.390	14.487
	5	17.212	17.384	17.555	17.727	17.899	18.070	18.242	18.414	18.585	18.757	18.929	19.100
	7.5	21.472	21.728	21.984	22.239	22.495	22.750	23.006	23.262	23.517	23.773	24.029	24.284
	10	28.870	29.272	29.673	30.075	30.476	30.877	31.279	31.680	32.082	32.483	32.884	33.286

8.50% Cash on Cash   75% Loan to Value Ratio

Growth Rate	Time Period	8.50%	8.75%	9.00%	9.25%	9.50%	9.75%	10.00%	10.25%	10.50%	10.75%	11.00%	11.25%
2%	3	10.581	10.627	10.673	10.719	10.765	10.811	10.857	10.902	10.948	10.994	11.040	11.086
	5	12.039	12.117	12.195	12.273	12.351	12.429	12.507	12.585	12.663	12.741	12.819	12.897
	7.5	13.555	13.667	13.778	13.890	14.001	14.113	14.224	14.336	14.447	14.559	14.670	14.782
	10	15.946	16.110	16.274	16.439	16.603	16.767	16.931	17.096	17.260	17.424	17.588	17.753
3%	3	11.653	11.722	11.792	11.861	11.931	12.000	12.070	12.140	12.209	12.279	12.348	12.418
	5	13.915	14.035	14.154	14.274	14.393	14.513	14.632	14.752	14.871	14.990	15.110	15.229
	7.5	16.316	16.488	16.661	16.833	17.005	17.178	17.350	17.523	17.695	17.867	18.040	18.212
	10	20.193	20.451	20.709	20.967	21.225	21.483	21.741	21.999	22.257	22.515	22.773	23.030
4%	3	12.745	12.839	12.933	13.026	13.120	13.214	13.307	13.401	13.495	13.588	13.682	13.776
	5	15.866	16.029	16.191	16.354	16.516	16.679	16.841	17.004	17.166	17.329	17.491	17.654
	7.5	19.242	19.479	19.716	19.953	20.189	20.426	20.663	20.900	21.137	21.374	21.611	21.848
	10	24.828	25.188	25.549	25.909	26.269	26.629	26.989	27.350	27.710	28.070	28.430	28.790
5%	3	13.859	13.977	14.096	14.214	14.332	14.450	14.569	14.687	14.805	14.923	15.041	15.160
	5	17.894	18.101	18.308	18.515	18.722	18.930	19.137	19.344	19.551	19.758	19.966	20.173
	7.5	22.341	22.647	22.952	23.257	23.563	23.868	24.173	24.479	24.784	25.089	25.395	25.700
	10	29.882	30.354	30.826	31.297	31.769	32.241	32.712	33.184	33.656	34.127	34.599	35.071
6%	3	14.995	15.138	15.281	15.424	15.568	15.711	15.854	15.997	16.141	16.284	16.427	16.570
	5	20.000	20.253	20.507	20.761	21.014	21.268	21.522	21.775	22.029	22.283	22.536	22.790
	7.5	25.623	26.001	26.379	26.757	27.134	27.512	27.890	28.267	28.645	29.023	29.401	29.778
	10	35.389	35.982	36.575	37.168	37.761	38.355	38.948	39.541	40.134	40.727	41.320	41.913

8.50% Cash on Cash   80% Loan to Value Ratio

Growth Rate	Time Period	8.50%	8.75%	9.00%	9.25%	9.50%	9.75%	10.00%	10.25%	10.50%	10.75%	11.00%	11.25%
2%	3	11.101	11.163	11.224	11.285	11.346	11.407	11.469	11.530	11.591	11.652	11.713	11.775
	5	12.923	13.028	13.132	13.236	13.340	13.444	13.548	13.652	13.756	13.860	13.964	14.068
	7.5	14.819	14.968	15.117	15.265	15.414	15.563	15.711	15.860	16.009	16.157	16.306	16.455
	10	17.807	18.026	18.245	18.464	18.683	18.902	19.121	19.340	19.559	19.778	19.997	20.216
3%	3	12.441	12.534	12.626	12.719	12.812	12.905	12.997	13.090	13.183	13.275	13.368	13.461
	5	15.269	15.428	15.588	15.747	15.906	16.066	16.225	16.384	16.543	16.703	16.862	17.021
	7.5	18.270	18.500	18.729	18.959	19.189	19.419	19.649	19.879	20.109	20.339	20.568	20.798
	10	23.116	23.460	23.804	24.148	24.492	24.836	25.180	25.524	25.868	26.212	26.556	26.900
4%	3	13.807	13.932	14.056	14.181	14.306	14.431	14.556	14.681	14.806	14.930	15.055	15.180
	5	17.708	17.924	18.141	18.358	18.574	18.791	19.008	19.224	19.441	19.658	19.874	20.091
	7.5	21.927	22.243	22.559	22.875	23.191	23.507	23.823	24.139	24.455	24.770	25.086	25.402
	10	28.910	29.391	29.871	30.351	30.831	31.312	31.792	32.272	32.752	33.233	33.713	34.193
5%	3	15.199	15.357	15.514	15.672	15.830	15.987	16.145	16.302	16.460	16.618	16.775	16.933
	5	20.242	20.518	20.795	21.071	21.347	21.623	21.900	22.176	22.452	22.729	23.005	23.281
	7.5	25.802	26.209	26.616	27.023	27.430	27.837	28.244	28.651	29.059	29.466	29.873	30.280
	10	35.228	35.857	36.486	37.115	37.744	38.372	39.001	39.630	40.259	40.888	41.517	42.146
6%	3	16.618	16.809	17.000	17.191	17.382	17.573	17.764	17.955	18.146	18.337	18.528	18.719
	5	22.875	23.213	23.551	23.889	24.227	24.566	24.904	25.242	25.580	25.919	26.257	26.595
	7.5	29.904	30.408	30.912	31.415	31.919	32.422	32.926	33.430	33.933	34.437	34.941	35.444
	10	42.111	42.902	43.693	44.484	45.274	46.065	46.856	47.647	48.438	49.229	50.020	50.810

Entry is the percentage return on equity after the time period, if the growth rate is sustained.

Cash on Cash Return After Growth

10.00% Cash on Cash   67% Loan to Value Ratio

Growth Rate	Time Period	Annual Mortgage Constant											
		10.00%	10.25%	10.50%	10.75%	11.00%	11.25%	11.50%	11.75%	12.00%	12.25%	12.50%	12.75%
2%	3	11.855	11.886	11.917	11.948	11.979	12.010	12.041	12.072	12.103	12.134	12.165	12.197
	5	13.154	13.207	13.260	13.312	13.365	13.418	13.471	13.524	13.577	13.629	13.682	13.735
	7.5	14.506	14.581	14.657	14.732	14.808	14.883	14.958	15.034	15.109	15.185	15.260	15.336
	10	16.636	16.747	16.859	16.970	17.081	17.192	17.303	17.414	17.525	17.637	17.748	17.859
3%	3	12.810	12.857	12.904	12.951	12.998	13.045	13.092	13.139	13.186	13.234	13.281	13.328
	5	14.826	14.907	14.988	15.069	15.150	15.231	15.312	15.392	15.473	15.554	15.635	15.716
	7.5	16.966	17.083	17.199	17.316	17.433	17.549	17.666	17.783	17.899	18.016	18.133	18.249
	10	20.422	20.596	20.771	20.945	21.120	21.295	21.469	21.644	21.818	21.993	22.167	22.342
4%	3	13.784	13.847	13.911	13.974	14.037	14.101	14.164	14.227	14.291	14.354	14.418	14.481
	5	16.565	16.675	16.785	16.895	17.005	17.115	17.225	17.335	17.445	17.555	17.665	17.775
	7.5	19.574	19.734	19.894	20.055	20.215	20.375	20.536	20.696	20.857	21.017	21.177	21.338
	10	24.553	24.797	25.040	25.284	25.528	25.772	26.015	26.259	26.503	26.747	26.990	27.234
5%	3	14.777	14.857	14.937	15.017	15.097	15.177	15.257	15.337	15.417	15.497	15.577	15.657
	5	18.372	18.512	18.653	18.793	18.933	19.073	19.214	19.354	19.494	19.634	19.775	19.915
	7.5	22.336	22.543	22.750	22.956	23.163	23.370	23.576	23.783	23.989	24.196	24.403	24.609
	10	29.057	29.377	29.696	30.015	30.334	30.653	30.973	31.292	31.611	31.930	32.250	32.569
6%	3	15.788	15.885	15.982	16.079	16.176	16.273	16.370	16.467	16.564	16.661	16.758	16.855
	5	20.249	20.421	20.593	20.764	20.936	21.108	21.279	21.451	21.623	21.794	21.966	22.138
	7.5	25.262	25.517	25.773	26.028	26.284	26.540	26.795	27.051	27.307	27.562	27.818	28.073
	10	33.965	34.366	34.768	35.169	35.571	35.972	36.374	36.775	37.176	37.578	37.979	38.381

10.00% Cash on Cash   75% Loan to Value Ratio

Growth Rate	Time Period	10.00%	10.25%	10.50%	10.75%	11.00%	11.25%	11.50%	11.75%	12.00%	12.25%	12.50%	12.75%
2%	3	12.448	12.494	12.540	12.586	12.632	12.678	12.724	12.770	12.816	12.861	12.907	12.953
	5	14.163	14.241	14.319	14.397	14.475	14.554	14.632	14.710	14.788	14.866	14.944	15.022
	7.5	15.947	16.059	16.170	16.282	16.393	16.505	16.617	16.728	16.840	16.951	17.063	17.174
	10	18.760	18.924	19.088	19.253	19.417	19.581	19.745	19.909	20.074	20.238	20.402	20.566
3%	3	13.709	13.779	13.848	13.918	13.987	14.057	14.126	14.196	14.265	14.335	14.405	14.474
	5	16.371	16.490	16.610	16.729	16.849	16.968	17.088	17.207	17.327	17.446	17.566	17.685
	7.5	19.195	19.367	19.540	19.712	19.885	20.057	20.229	20.402	20.574	20.747	20.919	21.091
	10	23.757	24.015	24.273	24.530	24.788	25.046	25.304	25.562	25.820	26.078	26.336	26.594
4%	3	14.995	15.088	15.182	15.276	15.369	15.463	15.556	15.650	15.744	15.837	15.931	16.025
	5	18.666	18.829	18.991	19.154	19.316	19.479	19.641	19.804	19.966	20.129	20.291	20.454
	7.5	22.637	22.874	23.111	23.348	23.585	23.822	24.059	24.296	24.533	24.770	25.007	25.244
	10	29.210	29.570	29.930	30.290	30.651	31.011	31.371	31.731	32.091	32.451	32.812	33.172
5%	3	16.305	16.423	16.541	16.660	16.778	16.896	17.014	17.133	17.251	17.369	17.487	17.605
	5	21.051	21.258	21.466	21.673	21.880	22.087	22.295	22.502	22.709	22.916	23.123	23.331
	7.5	26.284	26.589	26.895	27.200	27.505	27.811	28.116	28.421	28.727	29.032	29.337	29.643
	10	35.156	35.627	36.099	36.571	37.042	37.514	37.986	38.457	38.929	39.401	39.872	40.344
6%	3	17.641	17.784	17.927	18.070	18.214	18.357	18.500	18.643	18.787	18.930	19.073	19.217
	5	23.529	23.783	24.036	24.290	24.544	24.797	25.051	25.305	25.558	25.812	26.066	26.319
	7.5	30.145	30.523	30.901	31.278	31.656	32.034	32.412	32.789	33.167	33.545	33.922	34.300
	10	41.634	42.227	42.820	43.413	44.006	44.600	45.193	45.786	46.379	46.972	47.565	48.158

10.00% Cash on Cash   80% Loan to Value Ratio

Growth Rate	Time Period	10.00%	10.25%	10.50%	10.75%	11.00%	11.25%	11.50%	11.75%	12.00%	12.25%	12.50%	12.75%
2%	3	13.060	13.122	13.183	13.244	13.305	13.366	13.428	13.489	13.550	13.611	13.672	13.734
	5	15.204	15.308	15.412	15.516	15.620	15.724	15.829	15.933	16.037	16.141	16.245	16.349
	7.5	17.434	17.583	17.732	17.880	18.029	18.178	18.326	18.475	18.624	18.772	18.921	19.070
	10	20.950	21.169	21.388	21.607	21.826	22.045	22.264	22.483	22.702	22.921	23.140	23.359
3%	3	14.636	14.729	14.822	14.915	15.007	15.100	15.193	15.285	15.378	15.471	15.564	15.656
	5	17.964	18.123	18.282	18.442	18.601	18.760	18.919	19.079	19.238	19.397	19.556	19.716
	7.5	21.494	21.724	21.953	22.183	22.413	22.643	22.873	23.103	23.333	23.563	23.792	24.022
	10	27.196	27.540	27.884	28.228	28.571	28.915	29.259	29.603	29.947	30.291	30.635	30.979
4%	3	16.243	16.368	16.493	16.618	16.743	16.868	16.992	17.117	17.242	17.367	17.492	17.617
	5	20.833	21.049	21.266	21.483	21.699	21.916	22.133	22.349	22.566	22.783	22.999	23.216
	7.5	25.797	26.113	26.428	26.744	27.060	27.376	27.692	28.008	28.324	28.640	28.956	29.272
	10	34.012	34.492	34.973	35.453	35.933	36.413	36.894	37.374	37.854	38.334	38.815	39.295
5%	3	17.881	18.039	18.196	18.354	18.512	18.669	18.827	18.985	19.142	19.300	19.457	19.615
	5	23.814	24.090	24.367	24.643	24.919	25.195	25.472	25.748	26.024	26.301	26.577	26.853
	7.5	30.355	30.762	31.169	31.576	31.983	32.391	32.798	33.205	33.612	34.019	34.426	34.833
	10	41.445	42.074	42.703	43.331	43.960	44.589	45.218	45.847	46.476	47.105	47.734	48.363
6%	3	19.551	19.742	19.933	20.124	20.315	20.506	20.697	20.888	21.079	21.270	21.461	21.652
	5	26.911	27.250	27.588	27.926	28.264	28.602	28.941	29.279	29.617	29.955	30.294	30.632
	7.5	35.182	35.685	36.189	36.692	37.196	37.700	38.203	38.707	39.211	39.714	40.218	40.721
	10	49.542	50.333	51.124	51.915	52.706	53.497	54.287	55.078	55.869	56.660	57.451	58.242

Entry is the percentage return on equity after the time period, if the growth rate is sustained.

Cash on Cash Return After Growth

11.50% Cash on Cash   67% Loan to Value Ratio

Growth Rate	Time Period	Annual Mortgage Constant											
		8.50%	9.00%	9.50%	10.00%	10.50%	11.00%	11.50%	12.00%	12.50%	13.00%	13.50%	14.00%
2%	3	13.260	13.322	13.384	13.447	13.509	13.571	13.633	13.695	13.757	13.819	13.882	13.944
	5	14.493	14.599	14.704	14.810	14.916	15.021	15.127	15.233	15.338	15.444	15.550	15.655
	7.5	15.776	15.927	16.078	16.229	16.380	16.531	16.681	16.832	16.983	17.134	17.285	17.436
	10	17.798	18.020	18.242	18.465	18.687	18.909	19.132	19.354	19.576	19.799	20.021	20.243
3%	3	14.167	14.261	14.355	14.449	14.543	14.637	14.731	14.826	14.920	15.014	15.108	15.202
	5	16.080	16.242	16.404	16.565	16.727	16.889	17.050	17.212	17.374	17.536	17.697	17.859
	7.5	18.111	18.344	18.577	18.811	19.044	19.277	19.511	19.744	19.977	20.211	20.444	20.678
	10	21.390	21.739	22.088	22.438	22.787	23.136	23.485	23.834	24.183	24.532	24.881	25.231
4%	3	15.091	15.218	15.344	15.471	15.598	15.725	15.851	15.978	16.105	16.232	16.358	16.485
	5	17.730	17.950	18.170	18.390	18.610	18.830	19.050	19.270	19.490	19.710	19.930	20.150
	7.5	20.585	20.906	21.227	21.548	21.868	22.189	22.510	22.830	23.151	23.472	23.793	24.113
	10	25.311	25.798	26.286	26.773	27.261	27.748	28.236	28.723	29.211	29.698	30.186	30.673
5%	3	16.033	16.193	16.353	16.513	16.673	16.833	16.993	17.153	17.313	17.473	17.633	17.793
	5	19.445	19.726	20.006	20.287	20.567	20.848	21.128	21.408	21.689	21.969	22.250	22.530
	7.5	23.207	23.620	24.034	24.447	24.860	25.274	25.687	26.100	26.513	26.927	27.340	27.753
	10	29.585	30.224	30.862	31.501	32.139	32.778	33.416	34.054	34.693	35.331	35.970	36.608
6%	3	16.993	17.187	17.381	17.575	17.769	17.963	18.157	18.351	18.544	18.738	18.932	19.126
	5	21.227	21.570	21.913	22.257	22.600	22.943	23.287	23.630	23.973	24.317	24.660	25.003
	7.5	25.983	26.494	27.006	27.517	28.028	28.539	29.051	29.562	30.073	30.585	31.096	31.607
	10	34.243	35.046	35.849	36.651	37.454	38.257	39.060	39.863	40.666	41.468	42.271	43.074

11.50% Cash on Cash   75% Loan to Value Ratio

Growth Rate	Time Period	8.50%	9.00%	9.50%	10.00%	10.50%	11.00%	11.50%	12.00%	12.50%	13.00%	13.50%	14.00%
2%	3	13.765	13.857	13.948	14.040	14.132	14.224	14.316	14.407	14.499	14.591	14.683	14.775
	5	15.351	15.507	15.663	15.819	15.975	16.132	16.288	16.444	16.600	16.756	16.912	17.068
	7.5	17.001	17.224	17.447	17.670	17.893	18.117	18.340	18.563	18.786	19.009	19.232	19.455
	10	19.603	19.931	20.260	20.588	20.917	21.245	21.574	21.902	22.231	22.559	22.888	23.216
3%	3	14.931	15.070	15.209	15.348	15.487	15.626	15.765	15.905	16.044	16.183	16.322	16.461
	5	17.393	17.632	17.871	18.110	18.349	18.588	18.827	19.066	19.304	19.543	19.782	20.021
	7.5	20.005	20.350	20.695	21.040	21.385	21.729	22.074	22.419	22.764	23.109	23.453	23.798
	10	24.225	24.741	25.257	25.773	26.288	26.804	27.320	27.836	28.352	28.868	29.384	29.900
4%	3	16.120	16.307	16.495	16.682	16.869	17.056	17.244	17.431	17.618	17.806	17.993	18.180
	5	19.516	19.841	20.166	20.491	20.816	21.141	21.466	21.791	22.116	22.441	22.766	23.091
	7.5	23.189	23.663	24.137	24.611	25.085	25.559	26.033	26.507	26.981	27.455	27.928	28.402
	10	29.269	29.989	30.710	31.430	32.151	32.871	33.591	34.312	35.032	35.752	36.473	37.193
5%	3	17.332	17.569	17.805	18.041	18.278	18.514	18.751	18.987	19.224	19.460	19.696	19.933
	5	21.722	22.137	22.551	22.966	23.380	23.795	24.209	24.623	25.038	25.452	25.867	26.281
	7.5	26.563	27.173	27.784	28.395	29.005	29.616	30.227	30.837	31.448	32.059	32.669	33.280
	10	34.769	35.712	36.656	37.599	38.542	39.486	40.429	41.372	42.316	43.259	44.203	45.146
6%	3	18.568	18.854	19.141	19.427	19.714	20.000	20.287	20.573	20.860	21.146	21.433	21.719
	5	24.014	24.522	25.029	25.536	26.044	26.551	27.058	27.566	28.073	28.580	29.088	29.595
	7.5	30.134	30.890	31.645	32.401	33.156	33.912	34.667	35.422	36.178	36.933	37.689	38.444
	10	40.761	41.948	43.134	44.320	45.506	46.693	47.879	49.065	50.252	51.438	52.624	53.810

11.50% Cash on Cash   80% Loan to Value Ratio

Growth Rate	Time Period	8.50%	9.00%	9.50%	10.00%	10.50%	11.00%	11.50%	12.00%	12.50%	13.00%	13.50%	14.00%
2%	3	14.285	14.407	14.530	14.652	14.775	14.897	15.019	15.142	15.264	15.387	15.509	15.632
	5	16.236	16.444	16.652	16.860	17.068	17.276	17.485	17.693	17.901	18.109	18.317	18.525
	7.5	18.265	18.563	18.860	19.157	19.455	19.752	20.049	20.347	20.644	20.942	21.239	21.536
	10	21.464	21.902	22.340	22.778	23.216	23.654	24.092	24.530	24.968	25.406	25.844	26.282
3%	3	15.719	15.905	16.090	16.275	16.461	16.646	16.832	17.017	17.203	17.388	17.574	17.759
	5	18.747	19.066	19.384	19.703	20.021	20.340	20.658	20.977	21.295	21.614	21.932	22.251
	7.5	21.959	22.419	22.879	23.339	23.798	24.258	24.718	25.177	25.637	26.097	26.557	27.016
	10	27.148	27.836	28.524	29.212	29.900	30.587	31.275	31.963	32.651	33.339	34.027	34.714
4%	3	17.181	17.431	17.681	17.930	18.180	18.430	18.680	18.929	19.179	19.429	19.679	19.928
	5	21.358	21.791	22.224	22.658	23.091	23.524	23.958	24.391	24.824	25.257	25.691	26.124
	7.5	25.875	26.507	27.139	27.770	28.402	29.034	29.666	30.298	30.930	31.562	32.194	32.825
	10	33.351	34.312	35.272	36.233	37.193	38.154	39.114	40.075	41.035	41.996	42.956	43.916
5%	3	18.672	18.987	19.302	19.618	19.933	20.248	20.563	20.879	21.194	21.509	21.824	22.140
	5	24.071	24.623	25.176	25.729	26.281	26.834	27.386	27.939	28.491	29.044	29.596	30.149
	7.5	30.023	30.837	31.651	32.466	33.280	34.094	34.908	35.722	36.537	37.351	38.165	38.979
	10	40.115	41.372	42.630	43.888	45.146	46.404	47.661	48.919	50.177	51.435	52.693	53.950
6%	3	20.191	20.573	20.955	21.337	21.719	22.101	22.483	22.865	23.247	23.630	24.012	24.394
	5	26.889	27.566	28.242	28.919	29.595	30.272	30.948	31.624	32.301	32.977	33.654	34.330
	7.5	34.415	35.422	36.430	37.437	38.444	39.451	40.459	41.466	42.473	43.481	44.488	45.495
	10	47.484	49.065	50.647	52.229	53.810	55.392	56.974	58.555	60.137	61.719	63.301	64.882

Entry is the percentage return on equity after the time period, if the growth rate is sustained.

Growth Needed to Cover Carrying Costs

Cost of carry 7.50%

Elapsed Time		Mortgage Rate 6.00% Percent Financed:				Mortgage Rate 7.00% Percent Financed:				Mortgage Rate 8.00% Percent Financed:			
		0%	50%	75%	100%	0%	50%	75%	100%	0%	50%	75%	100%
1	Annual Amount	7.76	6.96	6.56	6.17	7.76	7.50	7.36	7.23	7.76	8.03	8.17	8.30
	Cumulative	7.76	6.96	6.56	6.17	7.76	7.50	7.36	7.23	7.76	8.03	8.17	8.30
2	Annual Amount	8.37	7.45	7.00	6.55	8.37	8.06	7.90	7.75	8.37	8.68	8.83	8.99
	Cumulative	16.13	14.41	13.56	12.72	16.13	15.55	15.27	14.98	16.13	16.71	17.00	17.29
3	Annual Amount	9.02	7.97	7.45	6.95	9.02	8.66	8.49	8.31	9.02	9.37	9.55	9.73
	Cumulative	25.14	22.38	21.01	19.67	25.14	24.22	23.75	23.29	25.14	26.08	26.55	27.02
4	Annual Amount	9.72	8.52	7.94	7.38	9.72	9.31	9.11	8.91	9.72	10.13	10.33	10.54
	Cumulative	34.86	30.90	28.96	27.05	34.86	33.53	32.86	32.21	34.86	36.21	36.88	37.57
5	Annual Amount	10.47	9.11	8.47	7.84	10.47	10.01	9.78	9.56	10.47	10.94	11.18	11.42
	Cumulative	45.33	40.01	37.42	34.89	45.33	43.54	42.65	41.76	45.33	47.15	48.06	48.98
6	Annual Amount	11.28	9.75	9.02	8.32	11.28	10.76	10.50	10.25	11.28	11.82	12.09	12.37
	Cumulative	56.61	49.76	46.45	43.20	56.61	54.29	53.15	52.01	56.61	58.96	60.15	61.35
7	Annual Amount	12.16	10.43	9.61	8.83	12.16	11.57	11.28	10.99	12.16	12.77	13.08	13.39
	Cumulative	68.77	60.19	56.06	52.04	68.77	65.86	64.42	63.00	68.77	71.73	73.23	74.74
8	Annual Amount	13.10	11.15	10.24	9.38	13.10	12.43	12.11	11.78	13.10	13.79	14.15	14.50
	Cumulative	81.87	71.34	66.30	61.41	81.87	78.29	76.53	74.78	81.87	85.52	87.38	89.25
9	Annual Amount	14.12	11.93	10.92	9.96	14.12	13.36	13.00	12.64	14.12	14.90	15.30	15.71
	Cumulative	95.99	83.27	77.22	71.37	95.99	91.66	89.53	87.42	95.99	100.42	102.68	104.95
10	Annual Amount	15.22	12.76	11.63	10.57	15.22	14.37	13.95	13.55	15.22	16.10	16.55	17.01
	Cumulative	111.21	96.03	88.86	81.94	111.21	106.02	103.48	100.97	111.21	116.52	119.22	121.96
12	Annual Amount	34.07	28.25	25.61	23.14	34.07	32.04	31.06	30.11	34.07	36.18	37.26	38.37
	Cumulative	145.27	124.28	114.46	105.08	145.27	138.07	134.54	131.07	145.27	152.69	156.49	160.34
15	Annual Amount	61.67	50.19	45.07	40.33	61.67	57.65	55.71	53.82	61.67	65.90	68.10	70.35
	Cumulative	206.95	174.47	159.53	145.41	206.95	195.72	190.26	184.89	206.95	218.60	224.59	230.69

Time		Mortgage Rate 9.00% Percent Financed:				Mortgage Rate 10.00% Percent Financed:				Mortgage Rate 11.00% Percent Financed:			
		0%	50%	75%	100%	0%	50%	75%	100%	0%	50%	75%	100%
1	Annual Amount	7.76	8.57	8.97	9.38	7.76	9.11	9.79	10.47	7.76	9.65	10.61	11.57
	Cumulative	7.76	8.57	8.97	9.38	7.76	9.11	9.79	10.47	7.76	9.65	10.61	11.57
2	Annual Amount	8.37	9.30	9.78	10.26	8.37	9.94	10.75	11.57	8.37	10.58	11.73	12.91
	Cumulative	16.13	17.87	18.75	19.64	16.13	19.05	20.54	22.04	16.13	20.24	22.34	24.48
3	Annual Amount	9.02	10.10	10.66	11.22	9.02	10.84	11.80	12.78	9.02	11.61	12.98	14.41
	Cumulative	25.14	27.97	29.41	30.86	25.14	29.89	32.33	34.82	25.14	31.84	35.32	38.89
4	Annual Amount	9.72	10.97	11.61	12.28	9.72	11.83	12.95	14.12	9.72	12.73	14.36	16.07
	Cumulative	34.86	38.94	41.02	43.14	34.86	41.73	45.29	48.94	34.86	44.57	49.68	54.96
5	Annual Amount	10.47	11.91	12.66	13.43	10.47	12.91	14.22	15.60	10.47	13.95	15.88	17.93
	Cumulative	45.33	50.85	53.68	56.57	45.33	54.64	59.51	64.53	45.33	58.52	65.55	72.89
6	Annual Amount	11.28	12.93	13.79	14.69	11.28	14.09	15.61	17.23	11.28	15.30	17.56	20.01
	Cumulative	56.61	63.77	67.47	71.26	56.61	68.72	75.12	81.76	56.61	73.82	83.12	92.90
7	Annual Amount	12.16	14.03	15.03	16.06	12.16	15.37	17.14	19.03	12.16	16.78	19.43	22.32
	Cumulative	68.77	77.81	82.50	87.32	68.77	84.09	92.26	100.79	68.77	90.60	102.54	115.22
8	Annual Amount	13.10	15.24	16.38	17.57	13.10	16.77	18.82	21.03	13.10	18.40	21.49	24.91
	Cumulative	81.87	93.04	98.88	104.89	81.87	100.86	111.08	121.82	81.87	109.00	124.03	140.13
9	Annual Amount	14.12	16.54	17.85	19.22	14.12	18.30	20.66	23.23	14.12	20.17	23.77	27.79
	Cumulative	95.99	109.59	116.73	124.11	95.99	119.16	131.75	145.04	95.99	129.17	147.79	167.91
10	Annual Amount	15.22	17.96	19.45	21.02	15.22	19.96	22.68	25.66	15.22	22.12	26.29	31.00
	Cumulative	111.21	127.54	136.18	145.14	111.21	139.13	154.43	170.70	111.21	151.29	174.08	198.91
12	Annual Amount	34.07	40.67	44.29	48.15	34.07	45.55	52.25	59.66	34.07	50.85	61.24	73.18
	Cumulative	145.27	168.21	180.47	193.28	145.27	184.68	206.68	230.36	145.27	202.15	235.32	272.10
15	Annual Amount	61.67	75.03	82.49	90.52	61.67	85.10	99.16	115.03	61.67	96.21	118.44	144.70
	Cumulative	206.95	243.24	262.96	283.80	206.95	269.78	305.84	345.39	206.95	298.36	353.75	416.80

Growth Needed to Cover Carrying Costs

Cost of carry 9.00%

Elapsed Time		Mortgage Rate 7.00% Percent Financed:				Mortgage Rate 8.00% Percent Financed:				Mortgage Rate 9.00% Percent Financed:			
		0%	50%	75%	100%	0%	50%	75%	100%	0%	50%	75%	100%
1	Annual Amount	9.38	8.30	7.76	7.23	9.38	8.84	8.57	8.30	9.38	9.38	9.38	9.38
	Cumulative	9.38	8.30	7.76	7.23	9.38	8.84	8.57	8.30	9.38	9.38	9.38	9.38
2	Annual Amount	10.26	8.99	8.37	7.75	10.26	9.62	9.30	8.99	10.26	10.26	10.26	10.26
	Cumulative	19.64	17.29	16.13	14.98	19.64	18.46	17.87	17.29	19.64	19.64	19.64	19.64
3	Annual Amount	11.22	9.73	9.02	8.31	11.22	10.47	10.10	9.73	11.22	11.22	11.22	11.22
	Cumulative	30.86	27.02	25.14	23.29	30.86	28.93	27.97	27.02	30.86	30.86	30.86	30.86
4	Annual Amount	12.28	10.54	9.72	8.91	12.28	11.40	10.97	10.54	12.28	12.28	12.28	12.28
	Cumulative	43.14	37.57	34.86	32.21	43.14	40.33	38.94	37.57	43.14	43.14	43.14	43.14
5	Annual Amount	13.43	11.42	10.47	9.56	13.43	12.40	11.91	11.42	13.43	13.43	13.43	13.43
	Cumulative	56.57	48.98	45.33	41.76	56.57	52.73	50.85	48.98	56.57	56.57	56.57	56.57
6	Annual Amount	14.69	12.37	11.28	10.25	14.69	13.50	12.93	12.37	14.69	14.69	14.69	14.69
	Cumulative	71.26	61.35	56.61	52.01	71.26	66.23	63.77	61.35	71.26	71.26	71.26	71.26
7	Annual Amount	16.06	13.39	12.16	10.99	16.06	14.69	14.03	13.39	16.06	16.06	16.06	16.06
	Cumulative	87.32	74.74	68.77	63.00	87.32	80.92	77.81	74.74	87.32	87.32	87.32	87.32
8	Annual Amount	17.57	14.50	13.10	11.78	17.57	15.99	15.24	14.50	17.57	17.57	17.57	17.57
	Cumulative	104.89	89.25	81.87	74.78	104.89	96.92	93.04	89.25	104.89	104.89	104.89	104.89
9	Annual Amount	19.22	15.71	14.12	12.64	19.22	17.41	16.54	15.71	19.22	19.22	19.22	19.22
	Cumulative	124.11	104.95	95.99	87.42	124.11	114.32	109.59	104.95	124.11	124.11	124.11	124.11
10	Annual Amount	21.02	17.01	15.22	13.55	21.02	18.94	17.96	17.01	21.02	21.02	21.02	21.02
	Cumulative	145.14	121.96	111.21	100.97	145.14	133.26	127.54	121.96	145.14	145.14	145.14	145.14
12	Annual Amount	48.15	38.37	34.07	30.11	48.15	43.06	40.67	38.37	48.15	48.15	48.15	48.15
	Cumulative	193.28	160.34	145.27	131.07	193.28	176.32	168.21	160.34	193.28	193.28	193.28	193.28
15	Annual Amount	90.52	70.35	61.67	53.82	90.52	79.94	75.03	70.35	90.52	90.52	90.52	90.52
	Cumulative	283.80	230.69	206.95	184.89	283.80	256.27	243.24	230.69	283.80	283.80	283.80	283.80

Time		Mortgage Rate 10.00% Percent Financed:				Mortgage Rate 11.00% Percent Financed:				Mortgage Rate 12.00% Percent Financed:			
		0%	50%	75%	100%	0%	50%	75%	100%	0%	50%	75%	100%
1	Annual Amount	9.38	9.92	10.20	10.47	9.38	10.47	11.02	11.57	9.38	11.02	11.85	12.68
	Cumulative	9.38	9.92	10.20	10.47	9.38	10.47	11.02	11.57	9.38	11.02	11.85	12.68
2	Annual Amount	10.26	10.91	11.24	11.57	10.26	11.57	12.23	12.91	10.26	12.23	13.25	14.29
	Cumulative	19.64	20.83	21.44	22.04	19.64	22.04	23.26	24.48	19.64	23.26	25.10	26.97
3	Annual Amount	11.22	11.99	12.38	12.78	11.22	12.78	13.58	14.41	11.22	13.58	14.82	16.10
	Cumulative	30.86	32.83	33.82	34.82	30.86	34.82	36.84	38.89	30.86	36.84	39.92	43.08
4	Annual Amount	12.28	13.18	13.65	14.12	12.28	14.12	15.08	16.07	12.28	15.08	16.58	18.15
	Cumulative	43.14	46.01	47.47	48.94	43.14	48.94	51.92	54.96	43.14	51.92	56.50	61.22
5	Annual Amount	13.43	14.49	15.04	15.60	13.43	15.60	16.74	17.93	13.43	16.74	18.54	20.45
	Cumulative	56.57	60.50	62.50	64.53	56.57	64.53	68.66	72.89	56.57	68.66	75.05	81.67
6	Annual Amount	14.69	15.93	16.57	17.23	14.69	17.23	18.59	20.01	14.69	18.59	20.74	23.04
	Cumulative	71.26	76.43	79.08	81.76	71.26	81.76	87.25	92.90	71.26	87.25	95.79	104.71
7	Annual Amount	16.06	17.51	18.26	19.03	16.06	19.03	20.64	22.32	16.06	20.64	23.20	25.96
	Cumulative	87.32	93.94	97.34	100.79	87.32	100.79	107.88	115.22	87.32	107.88	118.98	130.67
8	Annual Amount	17.57	19.25	20.12	21.03	17.57	21.03	22.91	24.91	17.57	22.91	25.95	29.26
	Cumulative	104.89	113.19	117.46	121.82	104.89	121.82	130.79	140.13	104.89	130.79	144.93	159.93
9	Annual Amount	19.22	21.16	22.18	23.23	19.22	23.23	25.43	27.79	19.22	25.43	29.02	32.97
	Cumulative	124.11	134.35	139.64	145.04	124.11	145.04	156.23	167.91	124.11	156.23	173.95	192.89
10	Annual Amount	21.02	23.26	24.44	25.66	21.02	25.66	28.24	31.00	21.02	28.24	32.46	37.15
	Cumulative	145.14	157.61	164.07	170.70	145.14	170.70	184.46	198.91	145.14	184.46	206.41	230.04
12	Annual Amount	48.15	53.67	56.61	59.66	48.15	59.66	66.15	73.18	48.15	66.15	76.91	89.02
	Cumulative	193.28	211.28	220.68	230.36	193.28	230.36	250.62	272.10	193.28	250.62	283.32	319.06
15	Annual Amount	90.52	102.18	108.45	115.03	90.52	115.03	129.16	144.70	90.52	129.16	153.04	180.52
	Cumulative	283.80	313.46	329.13	345.39	283.80	345.39	379.78	416.80	283.80	379.78	436.36	499.58

Growth Needed to Cover Carrying Costs

Cost of carry 10.50%

Elapsed Time		Mortgage Rate 8.00% Percent Financed:				Mortgage Rate 9.00% Percent Financed:				Mortgage Rate 10.00% Percent Financed:			
		0%	50%	75%	100%	0%	50%	75%	100%	0%	50%	75%	100%
1	Annual Amount	11.02	9.65	8.97	8.30	11.02	10.20	9.79	9.38	11.02	10.75	10.61	10.47
	Cumulative	11.02	9.65	8.97	8.30	11.02	10.20	9.79	9.38	11.02	10.75	10.61	10.47
2	Annual Amount	12.23	10.58	9.78	8.99	12.23	11.24	10.75	10.26	12.23	11.90	11.73	11.57
	Cumulative	23.26	20.24	18.75	17.29	23.26	21.44	20.54	19.64	23.26	22.65	22.34	22.04
3	Annual Amount	13.58	11.61	10.66	9.73	13.58	12.38	11.80	11.22	13.58	13.18	12.98	12.78
	Cumulative	36.84	31.84	29.41	27.02	36.84	33.82	32.33	30.86	36.84	35.82	35.32	34.82
4	Annual Amount	15.08	12.73	11.61	10.54	15.08	13.65	12.95	12.28	15.08	14.60	14.36	14.12
	Cumulative	51.92	44.57	41.02	37.57	51.92	47.47	45.29	43.14	51.92	50.42	49.68	48.94
5	Annual Amount	16.74	13.95	12.66	11.42	16.74	15.04	14.22	13.43	16.74	16.16	15.88	15.60
	Cumulative	68.66	58.52	53.68	48.98	68.66	62.50	59.51	56.57	68.66	66.58	65.55	64.53
6	Annual Amount	18.59	15.30	13.79	12.37	18.59	16.57	15.61	14.69	18.59	17.90	17.56	17.23
	Cumulative	87.25	73.82	67.47	61.35	87.25	79.08	75.12	71.26	87.25	84.48	83.12	81.76
7	Annual Amount	20.64	16.78	15.03	13.39	20.64	18.26	17.14	16.06	20.64	19.82	19.43	19.03
	Cumulative	107.88	90.60	82.50	74.74	107.88	97.34	92.26	87.32	107.88	104.31	102.54	100.79
8	Annual Amount	22.91	18.40	16.38	14.50	22.91	20.12	18.82	17.57	22.91	21.95	21.49	21.03
	Cumulative	130.79	109.00	98.88	89.25	130.79	117.46	111.08	104.89	130.79	126.26	124.03	121.82
9	Annual Amount	25.43	20.17	17.85	15.71	25.43	22.18	20.66	19.22	25.43	24.31	23.77	23.23
	Cumulative	156.23	129.17	116.73	104.95	156.23	139.64	131.75	124.11	156.23	150.57	147.79	145.04
10	Annual Amount	28.24	22.12	19.45	17.01	28.24	24.44	22.68	21.02	28.24	26.93	26.29	25.66
	Cumulative	184.46	151.29	136.18	121.96	184.46	164.07	154.43	145.14	184.46	177.50	174.08	170.70
12	Annual Amount	66.15	50.85	44.29	38.37	66.15	56.61	52.25	48.15	66.15	62.84	61.24	59.66
	Cumulative	250.62	202.15	180.47	160.34	250.62	220.68	206.68	193.28	250.62	240.34	235.32	230.36
15	Annual Amount	129.16	96.21	82.49	70.35	129.16	108.45	99.16	90.52	129.16	121.93	118.44	115.03
	Cumulative	379.78	298.36	262.96	230.69	379.78	329.13	305.84	283.80	379.78	362.27	353.75	345.39

Time		Mortgage Rate 11.00% Percent Financed:				Mortgage Rate 12.00% Percent Financed:				Mortgage Rate 13.00% Percent Financed:			
		0%	50%	75%	100%	0%	50%	75%	100%	0%	50%	75%	100%
1	Annual Amount	11.02	11.30	11.43	11.57	11.02	11.85	12.26	12.68	11.02	12.40	13.10	13.80
	Cumulative	11.02	11.30	11.43	11.57	11.02	11.85	12.26	12.68	11.02	12.40	13.10	13.80
2	Annual Amount	12.23	12.57	12.74	12.91	12.23	13.25	13.77	14.29	12.23	13.94	14.82	15.71
	Cumulative	23.26	23.87	24.17	24.48	23.26	25.10	26.03	26.97	23.26	26.35	27.92	29.51
3	Annual Amount	13.58	13.99	14.20	14.41	13.58	14.82	15.46	16.10	13.58	15.67	16.76	17.88
	Cumulative	36.84	37.86	38.37	38.89	36.84	39.92	41.49	43.08	36.84	42.02	44.68	47.39
4	Annual Amount	15.08	15.57	15.82	16.07	15.08	16.58	17.35	18.15	15.08	17.62	18.96	20.34
	Cumulative	51.92	53.43	54.19	54.96	51.92	56.50	58.85	61.22	51.92	59.63	63.63	67.73
5	Annual Amount	16.74	17.33	17.63	17.93	16.74	18.54	19.48	20.45	16.74	19.80	21.44	23.15
	Cumulative	68.66	70.76	71.82	72.89	68.66	75.05	78.33	81.67	68.66	79.43	85.07	90.89
6	Annual Amount	18.59	19.29	19.65	20.01	18.59	20.74	21.87	23.04	18.59	22.26	24.25	26.35
	Cumulative	87.25	90.05	91.47	92.90	87.25	95.79	100.20	104.71	87.25	101.69	109.32	117.23
7	Annual Amount	20.64	21.47	21.89	22.32	20.64	23.20	24.55	25.96	20.64	25.02	27.42	29.99
	Cumulative	107.88	111.52	113.36	115.22	107.88	118.98	124.75	130.67	107.88	126.71	136.75	147.22
8	Annual Amount	22.91	23.89	24.40	24.91	22.91	25.95	27.57	29.26	22.91	28.12	31.02	34.12
	Cumulative	130.79	135.41	137.76	140.13	130.79	144.93	152.32	159.93	130.79	154.83	167.76	181.34
9	Annual Amount	25.43	26.59	27.18	27.79	25.43	29.02	30.95	32.97	25.43	31.61	35.08	38.83
	Cumulative	156.23	162.00	164.94	167.91	156.23	173.95	183.27	192.89	156.23	186.44	202.84	220.18
10	Annual Amount	28.24	29.60	30.29	31.00	28.24	32.46	34.74	37.15	28.24	35.53	39.68	44.19
	Cumulative	184.46	191.60	195.24	198.91	184.46	206.41	218.01	230.04	184.46	221.97	242.52	264.37
12	Annual Amount	66.15	69.60	71.37	73.18	66.15	76.91	82.79	89.02	66.15	84.83	95.63	107.53
	Cumulative	250.62	261.20	266.61	272.10	250.62	283.32	300.80	319.06	250.62	306.80	338.15	371.91
15	Annual Amount	129.16	136.75	140.68	144.70	129.16	153.04	166.30	180.52	129.16	170.93	195.76	223.63
	Cumulative	379.78	397.95	407.28	416.80	379.78	436.36	467.10	499.58	379.78	477.72	533.91	595.54

Price of a Mortgage to Give a Specified Yield
Conversion of Interest to Principal or Principal to Interest
5.50% Interest Rate 30 Years Amortization Schedule

Desired Yield	1 Year	2 Years	3 Years	4 Years	5 Years	6 Years	7 Years	8 Years	9 Years	10 Years	11 Years	12 Years
					Prepaid or Ballooned at							
2.500	102.94176	105.77108	108.48952	111.09859	113.59967	115.99413	118.28322	120.46813	122.55000	124.52985	126.40869	128.18740
2.75	102.69299	105.27660	107.75278	110.12341	112.39027	114.55507	116.61946	118.58499	120.45315	122.22535	123.90293	125.48717
3.00	102.44489	104.78463	107.02150	109.15768	111.19527	113.13628	114.98265	116.73622	118.39877	119.97199	121.45751	122.85688
3.25	102.19745	104.29516	106.29565	108.20132	110.01452	111.73748	113.37234	114.92116	116.38594	117.76857	119.07087	120.29458
3.500	101.95067	103.80817	105.57516	107.25423	108.84783	110.35835	111.78807	113.13918	114.41378	115.61391	116.74150	117.79841
3.625	101.82753	103.56560	105.21693	106.78412	108.26970	109.67608	111.00556	112.26038	113.44268	114.55451	115.59783	116.57454
3.750	101.70455	103.32365	104.86002	106.31630	107.69503	108.99861	110.22940	111.38962	112.48142	113.50687	114.46793	115.36652
3.875	101.58174	103.08231	104.50444	105.85075	107.12378	108.32593	109.45953	110.52681	111.52990	112.47085	113.35163	114.17412
4.000	101.45909	102.84158	104.15017	105.38746	106.55594	107.65799	108.69590	109.67187	110.58800	111.44632	112.24874	112.99713
4.125	101.33660	102.60146	103.79722	104.92641	105.99148	106.99475	107.93845	108.82473	109.65564	110.43313	111.15910	111.83533
4.250	101.21428	102.36195	103.44557	104.46760	105.43039	106.33618	107.18714	107.98532	108.73270	109.43117	110.08253	110.68852
4.375	101.09212	102.12305	103.09523	104.01102	104.87264	105.68225	106.44191	107.15356	107.81908	108.44028	109.01887	109.55647
4.50	100.97013	101.88476	102.74619	103.55664	104.31822	105.03293	105.70270	106.32937	106.91469	107.46035	107.96794	108.43900
4.625	100.84829	101.64706	102.39844	103.10447	103.76710	104.38817	104.96947	105.51268	106.01943	106.49124	106.92960	107.33590
4.75	100.72662	101.40997	102.05198	102.65449	103.21926	103.74795	104.24217	104.70343	105.13319	105.53283	105.90367	106.24695
4.875	100.60512	101.17349	101.70681	102.20669	102.67468	103.11223	103.52074	103.90154	104.25588	104.58499	104.88999	105.17198
5.000	100.48377	100.93760	101.36291	101.76106	102.13334	102.48098	102.80514	103.10693	103.38741	103.64759	103.88841	104.11079
5.125	100.36258	100.70231	101.02028	101.31759	101.59522	101.85416	102.09531	102.31954	102.52768	102.72051	102.89877	103.06318
5.25	100.24156	100.46761	100.67893	100.87626	101.06031	101.23175	101.39121	101.53930	101.67660	101.80363	101.92093	102.02897
5.50	100.00000	100.00000	100.00000	100.00000	100.00000	100.00000	100.00000	100.00000	100.00000	100.00000	100.00000	100.00000
5.750	99.75908	99.53476	99.32609	99.13220	98.95226	98.78548	98.63112	98.48848	98.35689	98.23574	98.12444	98.02243
5.875	99.63886	99.30302	98.99100	98.70144	98.43305	98.18460	97.95493	97.74296	97.54767	97.36810	97.20331	97.05247
6.00	99.51881	99.07186	98.65715	98.27277	97.91693	97.58793	97.28418	97.00420	96.74656	96.50995	96.29310	96.09484
6.125	99.39891	98.84130	98.32454	97.84617	97.40386	96.99544	96.61883	96.27212	95.95347	95.66119	95.39366	95.14936
6.25	99.27917	98.61131	97.99316	97.42163	96.89385	96.40710	95.95883	95.54665	95.16831	94.82171	94.50485	94.21587
6.375	99.15959	98.38191	97.66300	96.99914	96.38686	95.82288	95.30413	94.82774	94.39101	93.99140	93.62654	93.29420
6.50	99.04017	98.15309	97.33406	96.57870	95.88288	95.24275	94.65469	94.11532	93.62146	93.17015	92.75860	92.38419
6.625	98.92091	97.92484	97.00634	96.16028	95.38188	94.66668	94.01046	93.40933	92.85961	92.35786	91.90088	91.48567
6.750	98.80181	97.69718	96.67983	95.74388	94.88386	94.09463	93.37141	92.70971	92.10535	91.55442	91.05328	90.59850
6.875	98.68286	97.47009	96.35452	95.32950	94.38879	93.52659	92.73748	92.01639	91.35861	90.75973	90.21564	89.72250
7.00	98.56408	97.24357	96.03042	94.91711	93.89665	92.96252	92.10863	91.32932	90.61931	89.97369	89.38785	88.85754
7.125	98.44545	97.01763	95.70751	94.50671	93.40743	92.40239	91.48482	90.64844	89.88738	89.19618	88.56978	88.00346
7.25	98.32698	96.79225	95.38580	94.09830	92.92110	91.84617	90.86601	89.97368	89.16272	88.42713	87.76131	87.16010
7.375	98.20867	96.56745	95.06527	93.69185	92.43766	91.29383	90.25215	89.30500	88.44527	87.66641	86.96232	86.32733
7.500	98.09052	96.34322	94.74593	93.28736	91.95707	90.74535	89.64321	88.64232	87.73495	86.91395	86.17268	85.50499
7.750	97.85468	95.89645	94.11077	92.48423	91.00441	89.65984	88.43989	87.33477	86.33359	85.43338	84.62099	83.89105
8.00	97.61947	95.45193	93.48029	91.68882	90.06299	88.58941	87.25573	86.05058	84.96345	83.98466	83.10531	82.31717
8.25	97.38489	95.00965	92.85446	90.90105	89.13266	87.53384	86.09040	84.78930	83.61853	82.56706	81.62474	80.78226
8.50	97.15093	94.56961	92.23323	90.12085	88.21328	86.49291	84.94349	83.55051	82.30007	81.17984	80.17839	79.28526
9.00	96.68487	93.69617	91.00444	88.58285	86.40687	84.45415	82.70428	81.13866	79.74031	78.49377	77.38493	76.40092

Yield	13 Years	14 Years	15 Years	16 Years	17 Years	18 Years	19 Years	20 Years	22 Years	25 Years	27 Years	Full Term
2.500	129.86684	131.44776	132.93087	134.31679	135.60608	136.79922	137.89664	138.89868	140.61768	142.48557	143.25707	143.70007
2.75	126.97925	128.38031	129.69141	130.91355	132.04764	133.09454	134.05506	134.92991	136.42522	138.04026	138.70312	139.08176
3.00	124.17156	125.40297	126.55244	127.62125	128.61059	129.52159	130.35535	131.11285	132.40285	133.78775	134.35257	134.67352
3.25	121.44139	122.51287	123.51057	124.43595	125.29009	126.07522	126.79171	127.44105	128.54281	129.71851	130.19499	130.46433
3.500	118.78642	119.70725	120.56254	121.35384	122.08267	122.75046	123.35858	123.90834	124.83773	125.82352	126.22052	126.44376
3.625	117.48644	118.33528	119.12271	119.85034	120.51968	121.13220	121.68930	122.19230	123.04109	123.93869	124.29902	124.50112
3.750	116.20443	116.98343	117.70518	118.37127	118.98325	119.54258	120.05087	120.50885	121.28059	122.09425	122.41986	122.60201
3.875	114.94013	115.65138	116.30955	116.91621	117.47288	117.98104	118.44206	118.85728	119.55539	120.28920	120.58193	120.74526
4.000	113.69325	114.33882	114.93545	115.48471	115.98809	116.44702	116.86287	117.23693	117.86470	118.52259	118.78420	118.92979
4.125	112.46356	113.04543	113.58253	114.07637	114.52839	114.93999	115.31248	115.64713	116.20773	116.79345	117.02563	117.15451
4.250	111.25078	111.77092	112.25043	112.69077	113.09332	113.45941	113.79031	114.08723	114.58370	115.10087	115.30524	115.41837
4.375	110.05468	110.51497	110.93879	111.32750	111.68241	112.00478	112.29579	112.55660	112.99189	113.44396	113.62204	113.72036
4.50	108.87499	109.27730	109.64727	109.98617	110.29522	110.57558	110.82835	111.05461	111.43155	111.82184	111.97510	112.05950
4.625	107.71147	108.05761	108.37553	108.66639	108.93129	109.17131	109.38744	109.58066	109.90197	110.23366	110.36350	110.43481
4.75	106.56389	106.85563	107.12324	107.36777	107.59021	107.79149	107.97252	108.13416	108.40246	108.67860	108.78635	108.84538
4.875	105.43201	105.67106	105.89007	106.08994	106.27153	106.43565	106.58306	106.71452	106.93234	107.15585	107.24278	107.29028
5.000	104.31559	104.50363	104.67570	104.83254	104.97485	105.10331	105.21855	105.32119	105.49095	105.66462	105.73195	105.76865
5.125	103.21440	103.35308	103.47982	103.59519	103.69975	103.79401	103.87848	103.95361	104.07764	104.20415	104.25305	104.27963
5.25	102.12822	102.21913	102.30211	102.37755	102.44584	102.50732	102.56235	102.61123	102.69179	102.77371	102.80527	102.82238
5.50	100.00000	100.00000	100.00000	100.00000	100.00000	100.00000	100.00000	100.00000	100.00000	100.00000	100.00000	100.00000
5.750	97.92918	97.84419	97.76700	97.69717	97.63428	97.57793	97.52776	97.48430	97.41084	97.33019	97.31019	97.29531
5.875	96.91476	96.78941	96.67571	96.57296	96.48055	96.39785	96.32430	96.25936	96.15332	96.04709	96.00681	95.98525
6.00	95.91406	95.74972	95.60083	95.46647	95.34575	95.23786	95.14203	95.05753	94.91979	94.78221	94.73020	94.70244
6.125	94.92689	94.72489	94.54211	94.37737	94.22954	94.09759	93.98053	93.87744	93.70970	93.54266	93.47972	93.44621
6.25	93.95303	93.71468	93.49927	93.30536	93.13158	92.97666	92.83939	92.71864	92.52254	92.32785	92.25471	92.21587
6.375	92.99229	92.71886	92.47205	92.25015	92.05153	91.87468	91.71818	91.58069	91.35780	91.13717	91.05456	91.01080
6.50	92.04449	91.73720	91.46019	91.21143	90.98906	90.79131	90.61652	90.46316	90.21500	89.97008	89.87866	89.83036
6.625	91.10942	90.76949	90.46343	90.18893	89.94385	89.72618	89.53402	89.36563	89.09363	88.82600	88.72642	88.67395
6.750	90.18690	89.81550	89.48236	89.18236	88.91559	88.67894	88.47030	88.28768	87.99325	87.70440	87.59726	87.54096
6.875	89.27674	88.87502	88.51422	88.19143	87.90395	87.64925	87.42497	87.22891	86.91337	86.60475	86.49064	86.43083
7.00	88.37877	87.94784	87.56128	87.21588	86.90865	86.63678	86.39768	86.18892	85.85357	85.52653	85.40600	85.34298
7.125	87.49281	87.03374	86.62247	86.25544	85.92937	85.64119	85.38806	85.16733	84.81339	84.46925	84.34282	84.27689
7.25	86.61867	86.13254	85.69755	85.30985	84.96583	84.66218	84.39578	84.16377	83.79241	83.43242	83.30058	83.23201
7.375	85.75618	85.24401	84.78630	84.37884	84.01774	83.69941	83.42048	83.17785	82.79021	82.41555	82.27878	82.20782
7.500	84.90518	84.36797	83.88848	83.46216	83.08482	82.75258	82.46183	82.20923	81.80638	81.41820	81.27663	81.20384
7.750	83.23695	82.65257	82.13227	81.67081	81.26339	80.90554	80.59316	80.32245	79.89227	79.48021	79.33121	79.25451
8.00	81.61267	80.98482	80.42719	79.93387	79.49939	79.11872	78.78724	78.50069	78.04699	77.61499	77.45976	77.38027
8.25	80.03105	79.36324	78.77159	78.24946	77.79075	77.38986	77.04163	76.74135	76.26762	75.81923	75.65912	75.57756
8.50	78.49086	77.78641	77.16385	76.61580	76.13551	75.71679	75.35399	75.04191	74.55135	74.08979	73.92602	73.84303
9.00	75.53001	74.76154	74.08576	73.49381	72.97761	72.52982	72.14374	71.81329	71.29759	70.81810	70.65013	70.56588

Entry is the percentage of loan balance to give the desired yield to the selected time.

Price of a Mortgage to Give a Specified Yield
Conversion of Interest to Principal or Principal to Interest
5.75% Interest Rate   30 Years Amortization Schedule

Desired Yield	1 Year	2 Years	3 Years	4 Years	Prepaid or Ballooned at 5 Years	6 Years	7 Years	8 Years	9 Years	10 Years	11 Years	12 Years
2.750	102.93863	105.75965	108.46511	111.05694	113.53701	115.90708	118.16882	120.32385	122.37367	124.31970	126.16331	127.90575
3.00	102.69013	105.26616	107.73052	110.08550	112.33331	114.47607	116.51581	118.45446	120.29387	122.03581	123.68194	125.23388
3.25	102.44229	104.77518	107.00137	109.12346	111.14393	113.06518	114.88951	116.61910	118.25608	119.80244	121.26012	122.63097
3.500	102.19512	104.28668	106.27762	108.17073	109.96870	111.67412	113.28947	114.81713	116.25938	117.61841	118.89632	120.09510
3.750	101.94860	103.80066	105.55922	107.22722	108.80744	110.30259	111.71526	113.04791	114.30292	115.48257	116.58904	117.62442
3.875	101.82559	103.55857	105.20202	106.75889	108.23200	109.62407	110.93769	112.17537	113.33950	114.43236	115.45614	116.41296
4.00	101.70274	103.31710	104.84615	106.29283	107.65998	108.95031	110.16642	111.31079	112.38582	113.39377	114.33684	115.21713
4.125	101.58006	103.07624	104.49159	105.82903	107.09137	108.28130	109.40139	110.45409	111.44176	112.36667	113.23096	114.03670
4.25	101.45754	102.83599	104.13834	105.36748	106.52615	107.61700	108.64254	109.60518	110.50724	111.35091	112.13832	112.87147
4.375	101.33519	102.59635	103.78640	104.90816	105.96429	106.95736	107.88982	108.76400	109.58214	110.34638	111.05876	111.72122
4.50	101.21300	102.35731	103.43577	104.45106	105.40577	106.30236	107.14318	107.93046	108.66636	109.35292	109.99210	110.58575
4.625	101.09097	102.11888	103.08643	103.99618	104.85058	105.65197	106.40257	107.10450	107.75981	108.37042	108.93818	109.46485
4.75	100.96910	101.88106	102.73839	103.54350	104.29869	105.00614	105.66793	106.28605	106.86239	107.39874	107.89684	108.35832
4.875	100.84740	101.64383	102.39163	103.09301	103.75008	104.36485	104.93922	105.47502	105.97399	106.43776	106.86792	107.26595
5.000	100.72586	101.40721	102.04616	102.64470	103.20473	103.72806	104.21639	104.67136	105.09452	105.48735	105.85125	106.18756
5.125	100.60448	101.17119	101.70197	102.19856	102.66263	103.09573	103.49938	103.87498	104.22389	104.54739	104.84669	105.12295
5.25	100.48326	100.93576	101.35905	101.75458	102.12374	102.46785	102.78815	103.08582	103.36200	103.61775	103.85407	104.07193
5.375	100.36220	100.70093	101.01739	101.31274	101.58805	101.84436	102.08264	102.30382	102.50876	102.69831	102.87324	103.03430
5.50	100.24131	100.46669	100.67701	100.87304	101.05555	101.22525	101.38281	101.52889	101.66407	101.78895	101.90405	102.00990
5.75	100.00000	100.00000	100.00000	100.00000	100.00000	100.00000	100.00000	100.00000	100.00000	100.00000	100.00000	100.00000
6.00	99.75934	99.53566	99.32799	99.13538	98.95694	98.79185	98.63933	98.49863	98.36906	98.24998	98.14075	98.04081
6.125	99.63924	99.30438	98.99385	98.70619	98.44004	98.19411	97.96717	97.75810	97.56580	97.38928	97.22757	97.07980
6.25	99.51931	99.07367	98.66094	98.27908	97.92621	97.60055	97.30042	97.02425	96.77056	96.53797	96.32517	96.13094
6.375	99.39954	98.84355	98.32926	97.85403	97.41542	97.01114	96.63901	96.29702	95.98326	95.69594	95.43341	95.19407
6.500	99.27993	98.61402	97.99880	97.43103	96.90766	96.42585	95.98291	95.57634	95.20380	94.86309	94.55214	94.26904
6.625	99.16048	98.38506	97.66957	97.01007	96.40291	95.84464	95.33206	94.86216	94.43212	94.03930	93.68125	93.35566
6.750	99.04118	98.15668	97.34155	96.59114	95.90114	95.26750	94.68643	94.15441	93.66812	93.22447	92.82060	92.45379
6.875	98.92205	97.92888	97.01474	96.17424	95.40235	94.69439	94.04597	93.45302	92.91172	92.41850	91.97005	91.56326
7.00	98.80307	97.70166	96.68914	95.75934	94.90651	94.12527	93.41064	92.75795	92.16284	91.62128	91.12948	90.68393
7.125	98.68425	97.47500	96.36474	95.34644	94.41360	93.56013	92.78039	92.06912	91.42141	90.83270	90.29876	89.81563
7.25	98.56559	97.24892	96.04153	94.93553	93.92360	92.99893	92.15518	91.38648	90.68734	90.05268	89.47777	88.95822
7.375	98.44709	97.02342	95.71952	94.52660	93.43650	92.44164	91.53497	90.70997	89.96055	89.28110	88.66638	88.11154
7.500	98.32874	96.79848	95.39870	94.11965	92.95229	91.88823	90.91972	90.03952	89.24097	88.51787	87.86447	87.27545
7.625	98.21056	96.57411	95.07906	93.71465	92.47093	91.33868	90.30307	89.37509	88.52853	87.76289	87.07192	86.44980
7.75	98.09253	96.35031	94.76059	93.31160	91.99241	90.79296	89.70390	88.71662	87.82313	87.01607	86.28862	85.63446
8.00	97.85694	95.90439	94.12719	92.51131	91.04385	89.71288	88.50741	87.41731	86.43322	85.54652	84.74926	84.03411
8.250	97.62197	95.46073	93.49844	91.71871	90.10645	88.64777	87.32992	86.14114	85.07063	84.10845	83.24548	82.47331
8.50	97.38763	95.01930	92.87431	90.93371	89.18007	87.59742	86.17110	84.88767	83.73480	82.70116	81.77639	80.95097
8.75	97.15392	94.58009	92.25478	90.15624	88.26458	86.56161	85.03065	83.65648	82.42515	81.32392	80.34111	79.46607
9.25	96.68834	93.70831	91.02933	88.62359	86.46575	84.53275	82.80362	81.25924	79.88225	78.65684	77.56862	76.60452

Yield	13 Years	14 Years	15 Years	16 Years	17 Years	18 Years	19 Years	20 Years	22 Years	25 Years	27 Years	Full Term
2.750	129.54821	131.09180	132.53755	133.88641	135.13926	136.29689	137.36001	138.32929	139.98847	141.78512	142.52461	142.94806
3.00	126.69312	128.06111	129.33920	130.52866	131.63071	132.64646	133.57697	134.42322	135.86652	137.41999	138.05535	138.41728
3.25	123.91672	125.11907	126.23961	127.27986	128.24125	129.12515	129.93287	130.66562	131.91076	133.24288	133.78428	134.09108
3.500	121.21667	122.26288	123.23548	124.13613	124.96644	125.72793	126.42205	127.05018	128.11364	129.24455	129.70128	129.95875
3.750	118.59071	119.48982	120.32359	121.09376	121.80202	122.44995	123.03909	123.57090	124.46799	125.41624	125.79679	126.01019
3.875	117.30482	118.13364	118.90126	119.60946	120.25991	120.85422	121.39393	121.88051	122.69981	123.56323	123.90864	124.10184
4.00	116.03663	116.79726	117.50085	118.14916	118.74387	119.28658	119.77881	120.22203	120.96696	121.74965	122.06177	122.23589
4.125	114.78587	115.48036	116.12198	116.71244	117.25341	117.74647	118.19311	118.59478	119.26864	119.97452	120.25513	120.41126
4.25	113.55230	114.18265	114.76428	115.29888	115.78806	116.23335	116.63623	116.99809	117.60405	118.23690	118.48769	118.62686
4.375	112.33565	112.90381	113.42741	113.90807	114.34734	114.74671	115.10758	115.43131	115.97244	116.53588	116.75846	116.88165
4.50	111.13567	111.64354	112.11100	112.53960	112.93080	113.28601	113.60660	113.89383	114.37306	114.87056	115.06646	115.17462
4.625	109.95211	110.40156	110.81473	111.19307	111.53797	111.85077	112.13271	112.38500	112.80518	113.24006	113.41077	113.50477
4.75	108.78473	109.17756	109.53824	109.86810	110.16843	110.44047	110.68536	110.90424	111.26809	111.64355	111.79046	111.87115
4.875	107.63328	107.97127	108.28120	108.56430	108.82114	109.05463	109.26403	109.45094	109.76110	110.08019	110.20465	110.27282
5.000	106.49754	106.78240	107.04329	107.28131	107.49747	107.69278	107.86817	108.02454	108.28353	108.54917	108.65246	108.70890
5.125	105.37727	105.61069	105.82420	106.01874	106.19521	106.35446	106.49728	106.62445	106.83471	107.04973	107.13307	107.17848
5.25	104.27223	104.45585	104.62359	104.77625	104.91455	105.03919	105.15085	105.25014	105.41401	105.58108	105.64564	105.68072
5.375	103.18221	103.31762	103.44117	103.55347	103.65508	103.74655	103.82838	103.90107	104.02080	104.14250	104.18938	104.21479
5.50	102.10697	102.19574	102.27663	102.35007	102.41643	102.47609	102.52940	102.57669	102.65445	102.73326	102.76352	102.77988
5.75	100.00000	100.00000	100.00000	100.00000	100.00000	100.00000	100.00000	100.00000	100.00000	100.00000	100.00000	100.00000
6.00	97.94960	97.86662	97.79137	97.72340	97.66228	97.60760	97.55898	97.51607	97.44602	97.37588	97.34929	97.33506
6.125	96.94510	96.82270	96.71185	96.61184	96.52203	96.44178	96.37052	96.30770	96.20533	96.10313	96.06451	96.04390
6.25	95.95412	95.79365	95.64849	95.51770	95.40038	95.29569	95.20285	95.12109	94.98812	94.85577	94.80591	94.77937
6.375	94.97647	94.77922	94.60103	94.44067	94.29701	94.16897	94.05555	93.95581	93.79388	93.63318	93.57283	93.54079
6.500	94.01195	93.77920	93.56920	93.38045	93.21156	93.06122	92.92822	92.81141	92.62210	92.43479	92.36467	92.32754
6.625	93.06037	92.79336	92.55274	92.33674	92.14371	91.97210	91.82047	91.68745	91.47228	91.26002	91.18081	91.13898
6.750	92.12153	91.82147	91.55139	91.30926	91.09314	90.90125	90.73190	90.58352	90.34395	90.10832	90.02067	89.97449
6.875	91.19525	90.86331	90.56492	90.29773	90.05954	89.84831	89.66213	89.49921	89.23663	88.97914	88.88367	88.83350
7.00	90.28134	89.91867	89.59306	89.30186	89.04259	88.81295	88.61079	88.43411	88.14987	87.87197	87.76925	87.71544
7.125	89.37963	88.98734	88.63558	88.32138	88.04198	87.79482	87.57751	87.38782	87.08321	86.78628	86.67687	86.61968
7.25	88.48993	88.06912	87.69224	87.35603	87.05743	86.79361	86.56194	86.35997	86.03621	85.72157	85.60601	85.54576
7.375	87.61207	87.16378	86.76281	86.40554	86.08864	85.80899	85.56372	85.35017	85.00846	84.67736	84.55614	84.49310
7.500	86.74587	86.27115	85.84706	85.46966	85.13531	84.84064	84.58252	84.35805	83.99953	83.65317	83.52677	83.46121
7.625	85.89116	85.39101	84.94476	84.54813	84.19718	83.88826	83.61800	83.38326	83.00902	82.64855	82.51741	82.44956
7.75	85.04778	84.52318	84.05569	83.64070	83.27396	82.95155	82.66982	82.42544	82.03652	81.66303	81.52758	81.45769
8.00	83.39432	82.82366	82.31637	81.86718	81.47119	81.12393	80.82125	80.55933	80.14402	79.74756	79.60469	79.53135
8.250	81.78421	81.17109	80.62742	80.14719	79.72491	79.35550	79.03431	78.75707	78.31904	77.90338	77.75454	77.67853
8.50	80.21619	79.56403	78.98718	78.47892	78.03309	77.64404	77.30662	77.01608	76.55871	76.12728	75.97376	75.89578
8.75	78.68903	78.00109	77.39409	76.86059	76.39378	75.98744	75.63589	75.33394	74.86031	74.41619	74.25917	74.17981
9.25	75.75264	75.00217	74.34328	73.76703	73.26531	72.83074	72.45663	72.13690	71.63898	71.17761	71.01654	70.93598

Entry is the percentage of loan balance to give the desired yield to the selected time.

Price of a Mortgage to Give a Specified Yield
Conversion of Interest to Principal or Principal to Interest
6.00% Interest Rate 30 Years Amortization Schedule

Desired Yield	1 Year	2 Years	3 Years	4 Years	5 Years	6 Years	7 Years	8 Years	9 Years	10 Years	11 Years	12 Years
					Prepaid or Ballooned at							
3.000	102.93547	105.74813	108.44051	111.01504	113.47402	115.81967	118.05409	120.17930	122.19721	124.10963	125.91828	127.62479
3.250	102.68724	105.25564	107.70809	110.04735	112.27605	114.39674	116.41185	118.32369	120.13447	121.84633	123.46126	124.98121
3.500	102.43967	104.76565	106.98109	109.08901	111.09232	112.99379	114.79609	116.50177	118.11327	119.63294	121.06300	122.40559
3.750	102.19276	104.27814	106.25946	108.13994	109.92264	111.61051	113.20636	114.71290	116.13273	117.46830	118.72199	119.89608
4.00	101.94651	103.79309	105.54317	107.20003	108.76684	110.24661	111.64223	112.95646	114.19196	115.35126	116.43677	117.45083
4.125	101.82364	103.55149	105.18701	106.73349	108.19410	109.57184	110.86962	112.09020	113.23623	114.31023	115.31464	116.25175
4.25	101.70092	103.31050	104.83217	106.26921	107.62476	108.90181	110.10325	111.23182	112.29013	113.28070	114.20592	115.06808
4.375	101.57837	103.07012	104.47864	105.80717	107.05880	108.23649	109.34307	110.38123	111.35355	112.26251	113.11044	113.89959
4.50	101.45598	102.83035	104.12642	105.34737	106.49621	107.57584	108.58901	109.53836	110.42640	111.25553	112.02803	112.74609
4.625	101.33376	102.59119	103.77551	104.88979	105.93696	106.91982	107.84103	108.70314	109.50857	110.25963	110.95853	111.60737
4.750	101.21170	102.35263	103.42589	104.43442	105.38103	106.26840	107.09908	107.87550	108.59997	109.27469	109.90177	110.48321
4.875	101.08980	102.11468	103.07756	103.98125	104.82841	105.62155	106.36311	107.05536	107.70048	108.30057	108.85759	109.37342
5.000	100.96806	101.87732	102.73053	103.53028	104.27906	104.97924	105.63306	106.24264	106.81003	107.33714	107.82582	108.27780
5.125	100.84649	101.64057	102.38477	103.08148	103.73298	104.34143	104.90888	105.43729	105.92851	106.38429	106.80631	107.19616
5.25	100.72508	101.40442	102.04029	102.63485	103.19013	103.70808	104.19053	104.63922	105.05582	105.44188	105.79890	106.12829
5.375	100.60383	101.16887	101.69709	102.19038	102.65051	103.07917	103.47795	103.84837	104.19187	104.50979	104.80343	105.07401
5.50	100.48274	100.93391	101.35516	101.74805	102.11409	102.45466	102.77110	103.06467	103.33657	103.58791	103.81976	104.03314
5.625	100.36181	100.69954	101.01448	101.30786	101.58084	101.83452	102.06993	102.28805	102.48982	102.67610	102.84773	103.00548
5.750	100.24105	100.46577	100.67507	100.86980	101.05076	101.21872	101.37439	101.51845	101.65154	101.77426	101.88719	101.99086
6.00	100.00000	100.00000	100.00000	100.00000	100.00000	100.00000	100.00000	100.00000	100.00000	100.00000	100.00000	100.00000
6.25	99.75959	99.53658	99.32990	99.13857	98.96165	98.79825	98.64756	98.50880	98.38125	98.26421	98.15705	98.05916
6.375	99.63963	99.30575	98.99671	98.71097	98.44707	98.20366	97.97946	97.77326	97.58395	97.41046	97.25181	97.10707
6.500	99.51982	99.07550	98.66475	98.28543	97.93555	97.61322	97.31670	97.04444	96.79458	96.56599	96.35721	96.16697
6.625	99.40018	98.84583	98.33401	97.86194	97.42705	97.02691	96.65925	96.32197	96.01307	95.73070	95.47312	95.23870
6.750	99.28069	98.61675	98.00449	97.44049	96.92155	96.44468	96.00706	95.60610	95.23933	94.90448	94.59940	94.32210
6.875	99.16137	98.38824	97.67618	97.02107	96.41905	95.86650	95.36009	94.89665	94.47327	94.08721	93.73592	93.41701
7.000	99.04220	98.16031	97.34909	96.60367	95.91951	95.29236	94.71828	94.19358	93.71482	93.27881	92.88255	92.52327
7.125	98.92319	97.93295	97.02320	96.18828	95.42292	94.72222	94.08160	93.49681	92.96389	92.47915	92.03916	91.64072
7.250	98.80434	97.70617	96.69852	95.77489	94.92927	94.15605	93.45000	92.80629	92.22040	91.68815	91.20563	90.76922
7.375	98.68565	97.47996	96.37503	95.36349	94.43854	93.59382	92.82345	92.12196	91.48428	90.90569	90.38182	89.90860
7.500	98.56711	97.25432	96.05273	94.95407	93.95070	93.03550	92.20189	91.44376	90.75544	90.13169	89.56762	89.05872
7.625	98.44874	97.02926	95.73162	94.54662	93.46574	92.48106	91.58529	90.77163	90.03382	89.36604	88.76291	88.21944
7.75	98.33052	96.80476	95.41169	94.14113	92.98364	91.93048	90.97360	90.10551	89.31932	88.60864	87.96756	87.39061
7.875	98.21245	96.58082	95.09294	93.73759	92.50438	91.38373	90.36678	89.44535	88.61188	87.85940	87.18145	86.57209
8.00	98.09455	96.35745	94.77537	93.33599	92.02795	90.84077	89.76479	88.79109	87.91143	87.11822	86.40448	85.76373
8.25	97.85921	95.91240	94.14372	92.53857	91.08350	89.76615	88.57515	87.50003	86.53116	85.65969	84.87745	84.17696
8.50	97.62449	95.46960	93.51672	91.74789	90.15014	88.70328	87.40435	86.23191	85.17795	84.23229	83.38557	82.62922
8.75	97.39040	95.02902	92.89432	90.96658	89.22774	87.66128	86.25207	84.98627	83.85122	82.83532	81.92796	81.11945
9.00	97.15693	94.59066	92.27649	90.19186	88.31616	86.63060	85.11800	83.76271	82.55041	81.46806	80.50375	79.64662
9.50	96.69184	93.72055	91.05440	88.66459	86.52495	84.61170	82.90329	81.38012	80.02440	78.81999	77.75224	76.80787

Yield	13 Years	14 Years	15 Years	16 Years	17 Years	18 Years	19 Years	20 Years	22 Years	25 Years	27 Years	Full Term
3.000	129.23069	130.73744	132.14639	133.45880	134.67586	135.79867	136.82824	137.76550	139.36638	141.09388	141.80242	142.20702
3.250	126.40798	127.74333	128.98889	130.14622	131.21680	132.20201	133.10315	133.92146	135.31406	136.80776	137.41654	137.76237
3.500	123.66275	124.83642	125.92845	126.94060	127.87455	128.73189	129.51412	130.22268	131.42410	132.70498	133.22374	133.51690
3.750	120.99271	122.01397	122.96183	123.83817	124.64479	125.38340	126.05562	126.66302	127.68915	128.77658	129.21421	129.46023
4.00	118.39564	119.27331	120.08588	120.83527	121.52332	122.15179	122.72236	123.23662	124.10223	125.01403	125.37868	125.58260
4.125	117.12378	117.93285	118.68096	119.37004	120.00194	120.57840	121.10110	121.57163	122.36218	123.19242	123.52340	123.70801
4.25	115.86936	116.61186	117.29757	117.92839	118.50614	119.03255	119.50927	119.93787	120.65667	121.40928	121.70837	121.87475
4.375	114.63212	115.31006	115.93537	116.50990	117.03545	117.51370	117.94620	118.33459	118.98491	119.66368	119.93256	120.08176
4.50	113.41180	114.02713	114.59398	115.11416	115.58939	116.02132	116.41150	116.76143	117.34614	117.95469	118.19499	118.32799
4.625	112.20814	112.76277	113.27306	113.74076	114.16751	114.55489	114.90440	115.21746	115.73961	116.28142	116.49469	116.61242
4.750	111.02091	111.51669	111.97228	112.38931	112.76936	113.11392	113.42440	113.70217	114.16460	114.64300	114.83072	114.93407
4.875	109.84986	110.28861	110.69128	111.05942	111.39450	111.69790	111.97092	112.21495	112.62040	113.03859	113.20217	113.29199
5.000	108.69475	109.07823	109.42974	109.75071	110.04249	110.30636	110.54355	110.75521	111.10631	111.46736	111.60814	111.68524
5.125	107.55533	107.88527	108.18733	108.46280	108.71291	108.93881	109.14162	109.32237	109.62166	109.92851	110.04777	110.11292
5.25	106.43139	106.70947	106.96314	107.19533	107.40534	107.59480	107.76467	107.91588	108.16580	108.42125	108.52023	108.57416
5.375	105.32269	105.55055	105.75864	105.94794	106.11939	106.27386	106.41219	106.53517	106.73806	106.94483	107.02469	107.06809
5.50	104.22900	104.40825	104.57173	104.72028	104.85464	104.97555	105.08369	105.17971	105.33784	105.49851	105.56037	105.59390
5.625	103.15010	103.28229	103.40271	103.51199	103.61071	103.69943	103.77869	103.84898	103.96452	104.08156	104.12648	104.15076
5.750	102.08578	102.17244	102.25128	102.32273	102.38721	102.44508	102.49671	102.54245	102.61749	102.69327	102.72227	102.73790
6.00	100.00000	100.00000	100.00000	100.00000	100.00000	100.00000	100.00000	100.00000	100.00000	100.00000	100.00000	100.00000
6.25	97.96998	97.88896	97.81562	97.74948	97.69010	97.63706	97.58997	97.54847	97.48087	97.41342	97.38792	97.37433
6.375	96.97536	96.85587	96.74783	96.65051	96.56325	96.48541	96.41639	96.35563	96.25685	96.15856	96.12155	96.10185
6.500	95.99407	95.83741	95.69593	95.56866	95.45468	95.35313	95.26320	95.18413	95.05582	94.92853	94.88075	94.85538
6.625	95.02592	94.83336	94.65968	94.50364	94.36406	94.23986	94.13000	94.03354	93.87728	93.72273	93.66490	93.63427
6.750	94.07072	93.84350	93.63881	93.45514	93.29105	93.14522	93.01640	92.90342	92.72073	92.54059	92.47340	92.43791
6.875	93.12826	92.86759	92.63307	92.42288	92.23534	92.06887	91.92200	91.79336	91.58571	91.38157	91.30566	91.26568
7.000	92.19837	91.90543	91.64220	91.40658	91.19661	91.01046	90.84642	90.70293	90.47173	90.24511	90.16111	90.11698
7.125	91.28086	90.95680	90.66597	90.40596	90.17454	89.96963	89.78930	89.63174	89.37833	89.13070	89.03919	88.99125
7.250	90.37555	90.02148	89.70142	89.42075	89.16884	88.94607	88.75029	88.57939	88.30508	88.03781	87.93937	87.88792
7.375	89.48225	89.09928	88.75643	88.45067	88.17921	87.93944	87.72896	87.54550	87.25153	86.96595	86.86110	86.80644
7.500	88.60080	88.18998	87.82265	87.49547	87.20536	86.94943	86.72503	86.52969	86.21726	85.91463	85.80388	85.74629
7.625	87.73103	87.29339	86.90256	86.55489	86.24699	85.97571	85.73814	85.53160	85.20183	84.88338	84.76720	84.70695
7.75	86.87275	86.40930	85.99594	85.62868	85.30383	85.01797	84.76795	84.55085	84.20485	83.87174	83.75059	83.68792
7.875	86.02580	85.53753	85.10256	84.71659	84.37561	84.07593	83.81414	83.58711	83.22593	82.87924	82.75355	82.68871
8.00	85.19003	84.67787	84.22221	83.81837	83.46205	83.14927	82.87639	82.64002	82.26468	81.90546	81.77564	81.70884
8.25	83.55132	82.99419	82.49974	82.06260	81.67786	81.34098	81.04779	80.79446	80.39364	80.01232	79.87539	79.80529
8.50	81.95536	81.35677	80.82685	80.35952	79.94921	79.59084	79.27972	79.01157	78.58883	78.18904	78.04638	77.97373
8.75	80.40090	79.76421	79.20194	78.70732	78.27413	77.89670	77.56986	77.28885	76.84743	76.43246	76.28533	76.21078
9.00	78.88676	78.21512	77.62347	77.10428	76.65070	76.25649	75.91595	75.62391	75.16679	74.73962	74.58912	74.51326
9.50	75.97480	75.24210	74.59985	74.03905	73.55155	73.12995	72.76756	72.45830	71.97773	71.53395	71.37957	71.30255

Entry is the percentage of loan balance to give the desired yield to the selected time.

Price of a Mortgage to Give a Specified Yield
Conversion of Interest to Principal or Principal to Interest
6.25% Interest Rate   30 Years Amortization Schedule

Prepaid or Ballooned at

Desired Yield	1 Year	2 Years	3 Years	4 Years	5 Years	6 Years	7 Years	8 Years	9 Years	10 Years	11 Years	12 Years
3.250	102.93229	105.73652	108.41575	110.97289	113.41074	115.73195	117.93908	120.03456	122.02071	123.89973	125.67372	127.34466
3.500	102.68433	105.24504	107.68551	110.00898	112.21853	114.31714	116.30763	118.19274	119.97503	121.65700	123.24100	124.72927
3.750	102.43703	104.75605	106.96067	109.05437	111.04046	112.92214	114.70244	116.38427	117.97043	119.46357	120.86625	122.18087
4.000	102.19039	104.26952	106.24118	108.10897	109.87636	111.54666	113.12304	114.60853	116.00603	117.31830	118.54799	119.69762
4.25	101.94441	103.78546	105.52700	107.17270	108.72605	110.19042	111.56901	112.86489	114.08096	115.22004	116.28478	117.27772
4.375	101.82166	103.54435	105.17189	106.70795	108.15601	109.51943	110.80138	112.00491	113.13292	114.18820	115.17338	116.09098
4.50	101.69908	103.30385	104.81810	106.24545	107.58936	108.85314	110.03992	111.15272	112.19440	113.16770	114.07521	114.91943
4.625	101.57667	103.06396	104.46561	105.78518	107.02607	108.19151	109.28460	110.30826	111.26531	112.15841	112.99012	113.76286
4.750	101.45441	102.82467	104.11442	105.32714	106.46612	107.53453	108.53535	109.47144	110.34553	111.16020	111.91793	112.62105
4.875	101.33232	102.58599	103.76454	104.87131	105.90950	106.88214	107.79212	108.64220	109.43497	110.17295	110.85848	111.49381
5.000	101.21039	102.34791	103.41594	104.41768	105.35617	106.23432	107.05487	107.82045	108.53354	109.19651	109.81160	110.38094
5.125	101.08862	102.11044	103.06863	103.96624	104.80613	105.59103	106.32354	107.00613	107.64113	108.23076	108.77713	109.28223
5.25	100.96702	101.87357	102.72261	103.51697	104.25934	104.95224	105.59809	106.19917	106.75765	107.27558	107.75491	108.19750
5.375	100.84558	101.63729	102.37786	103.06988	103.71579	104.31792	104.87846	105.39950	105.88300	106.33085	106.74480	107.12654
5.500	100.72430	101.40161	102.03439	102.62494	103.17547	103.68803	104.16460	104.60704	105.01709	105.39643	105.74663	106.06917
5.625	100.60318	101.16653	101.69218	102.18125	102.63834	103.06254	103.45647	103.82173	104.15983	104.47221	104.76024	105.02520
5.750	100.48222	100.93204	101.35124	101.74149	102.10439	102.44143	102.75401	103.04349	103.31112	103.55808	103.78550	103.99445
5.875	100.36143	100.69815	101.01155	101.30296	101.57360	101.82464	102.05719	102.27227	102.47087	102.65391	102.82225	102.97673
6.00	100.24079	100.46484	100.67312	100.86654	101.04595	101.21217	101.36594	101.50799	101.63899	101.75958	101.87035	101.97187
6.250	100.00000	100.00000	100.00000	100.00000	100.00000	100.00000	100.00000	100.00000	100.00000	100.00000	100.00000	100.00000
6.500	99.75985	99.53750	99.33183	99.14179	98.96638	98.80468	98.65582	98.51900	98.39344	98.27844	98.17332	98.07747
6.625	99.64002	99.30713	98.99960	98.71578	98.45414	98.21325	97.99178	97.78845	97.60211	97.43164	97.27601	97.13428
6.750	99.52034	99.07734	98.66858	98.29182	97.94493	97.62595	97.33303	97.06446	96.81862	96.59401	96.38921	96.20292
6.875	99.40082	98.84813	98.33879	97.86990	97.43872	97.04273	96.67955	96.34697	96.04291	95.76545	95.51278	95.28323
7.000	99.28147	98.61950	98.01021	97.45001	96.93551	96.46358	96.03128	95.63590	95.27488	94.94585	94.64659	94.37505
7.125	99.16227	98.39144	97.68285	97.03213	96.43526	95.88845	95.38818	94.93120	94.51446	94.13511	93.79052	93.47822
7.250	99.04323	98.16396	97.35668	96.61627	95.93796	95.31732	94.75021	94.23281	93.76155	93.33312	92.94442	92.59259
7.375	98.92435	97.93705	97.03172	96.20241	95.44360	94.75016	94.11732	93.54067	93.01610	92.53978	92.10818	91.71801
7.500	98.80562	97.71072	96.70796	95.79054	94.95215	94.18694	93.48947	92.85472	92.27800	91.75500	91.28168	90.85432
7.625	98.68706	97.48496	96.38539	95.38065	94.46360	93.62763	92.86662	92.17489	91.54720	90.97866	90.46478	90.00137
7.750	98.56865	97.25976	96.06400	94.97272	93.97792	93.07220	92.24872	91.50114	90.82360	90.21068	89.65737	89.15902
7.875	98.45040	97.03514	95.74380	94.56676	93.49511	92.52064	91.63574	90.83340	90.10714	89.45096	88.85932	88.32712
8.000	98.33231	96.81108	95.42478	94.16274	93.01514	91.97289	91.02763	90.17162	89.39773	88.69939	88.07052	87.50554
8.125	98.21437	96.58759	95.10693	93.76067	92.53799	91.42895	90.42435	89.51573	88.69531	87.95589	87.29086	86.69412
8.250	98.09659	96.36466	94.79025	93.36052	92.06366	90.88877	89.82586	88.86569	87.99979	87.22036	86.52021	85.89274
8.50	97.86150	95.92048	94.16038	92.56598	91.12334	89.81963	88.64308	87.58291	86.62919	85.77284	85.00550	84.31952
8.750	97.62703	95.47864	93.53513	91.77905	90.19405	88.76524	87.47899	86.32284	85.28537	84.35611	83.52552	82.78482
9.000	97.39319	95.03882	92.91446	90.99964	89.27564	87.72539	86.33327	85.08506	83.96775	82.96946	82.07938	81.28760
9.25	97.15996	94.60131	92.29835	90.22769	88.36799	86.69986	85.20561	83.86913	82.67578	81.61220	80.66624	79.82685
9.75	96.69537	93.73289	91.07965	88.70584	86.58444	84.69097	83.00326	81.50122	80.16667	78.98314	77.93570	77.01085

Yield	13 Years	14 Years	15 Years	16 Years	17 Years	18 Years	19 Years	20 Years	22 Years	25 Years	27 Years	Full Term
3.250	128.91444	130.38485	131.75755	133.03413	134.21608	135.30478	136.30153	137.20753	138.75162	140.41201	141.09064	141.47708
3.500	126.12396	127.42710	128.64063	129.76638	130.80608	131.76137	132.63380	133.42482	134.76804	136.20373	136.78682	137.11713
3.750	123.40977	124.55514	125.61910	126.60363	127.51065	128.34196	129.09927	129.78422	130.94304	132.17420	132.67108	132.95108
4.000	120.76961	121.76626	122.68976	123.54219	124.32556	125.04175	125.69257	126.27972	127.26949	128.31472	128.73390	128.96889
4.25	118.20130	119.05783	119.84952	120.57848	121.24670	121.85610	122.40850	122.90563	123.74058	124.61701	124.96628	125.16106
4.375	116.94343	117.73300	118.46189	119.13219	119.74588	120.30486	120.81091	121.26577	122.02832	122.82636	123.14339	123.31972
4.50	115.70272	116.42734	117.09543	117.70906	118.27016	118.78060	119.24215	119.65648	120.34982	121.07325	121.35973	121.51866
4.625	114.47893	115.14054	115.74979	116.30867	116.81908	117.28282	117.70162	118.07711	118.70431	119.35676	119.61432	119.75683
4.750	113.27181	113.87232	114.42462	114.93062	115.39217	115.81099	116.18876	116.52704	117.09105	117.67601	117.90619	118.03323
4.875	112.08110	112.62238	113.11957	113.57452	113.98898	114.36462	114.70300	115.00564	115.50931	116.03012	116.23441	116.34687
5.000	110.90657	111.39042	111.83431	112.23998	112.60909	112.94320	113.24381	113.51233	113.95839	114.41826	114.59807	114.69680
5.125	109.74798	110.17616	110.56850	110.92662	111.25205	111.54626	111.81063	112.04649	112.43760	112.83959	112.99628	113.08208
5.25	108.60508	108.97934	109.32183	109.63406	109.91744	110.17331	110.40296	110.60757	110.94626	111.29332	111.42817	111.50182
5.375	107.47766	107.79966	108.09397	108.36194	108.60484	108.82390	109.02026	109.19500	109.48373	109.77867	109.89291	109.95515
5.500	106.36547	106.63686	106.88461	107.10990	107.31386	107.49758	107.66204	107.80823	108.04930	108.29487	108.38968	108.44120
5.625	105.26830	105.49068	105.69343	105.87758	106.04409	106.19388	106.32782	106.44671	106.64243	106.84119	106.91769	106.95915
5.750	104.18592	104.36085	104.52015	104.66465	104.79514	104.91239	105.01710	105.10993	105.26246	105.41691	105.47617	105.50820
5.875	103.11811	103.24712	103.36445	103.47075	103.56663	103.65267	103.72941	103.79736	103.90882	104.02133	104.06436	104.08756
6.00	102.06466	102.14923	102.22605	102.29556	102.35818	102.41430	102.46430	102.50851	102.58090	102.65375	102.68153	102.69647
6.250	100.00000	100.00000	100.00000	100.00000	100.00000	100.00000	100.00000	100.00000	100.00000	100.00000	100.00000	100.00000
6.500	97.99028	97.91121	97.83975	97.77541	97.71773	97.66630	97.62071	97.58059	97.51538	97.45053	97.42611	97.41312
6.625	97.00552	96.88890	96.78362	96.68896	96.60420	96.52871	96.46188	96.40315	96.30785	96.21337	96.17791	96.15909
6.750	96.03389	95.88099	95.74314	95.61933	95.50863	95.41014	95.32307	95.24663	95.12284	95.00047	94.95470	94.93047
6.875	95.07522	94.88728	94.71805	94.56625	94.43068	94.31023	94.20386	94.11060	93.95986	93.81128	93.75588	93.72662
7.000	94.12929	93.90763	93.70809	93.52941	93.37003	93.22861	93.10388	92.99465	92.81841	92.64523	92.58086	92.54695
7.125	93.19594	92.94153	92.71301	92.50854	92.32638	92.16494	92.02273	91.89836	91.69804	91.50178	91.42907	91.39087
7.250	92.27497	91.98906	91.73257	91.50335	91.29941	91.11888	90.96006	90.82132	90.59828	90.38042	90.29995	90.25779
7.375	91.36620	91.04992	90.76653	90.51359	90.28882	90.09010	89.91549	89.76315	89.51869	89.28061	89.19296	89.14715
7.500	90.46946	90.12389	89.81465	89.53897	89.29430	89.07827	88.88867	88.72346	88.45883	88.20188	88.10757	88.05841
7.625	89.58456	89.21078	88.87670	88.57925	88.31558	88.08306	87.87924	87.70188	87.41827	87.14372	87.04327	86.99105
7.750	88.71134	88.31038	87.95244	87.63415	87.35236	87.10416	86.88688	86.69803	86.39660	86.10566	85.99956	85.94454
7.875	87.84963	87.42249	87.04166	86.70344	86.40436	86.14128	85.91124	85.71155	85.39341	85.08725	84.97595	84.91838
8.000	86.99926	86.54692	86.14414	85.78685	85.47132	85.19409	84.95200	84.74210	84.40830	84.08803	83.97196	83.91209
8.125	86.16005	85.68349	85.25965	84.88415	84.55295	84.26232	84.00883	83.78933	83.44088	83.10756	82.98714	82.92519
8.250	85.33186	84.83199	84.38798	83.99510	83.64899	83.34566	83.08142	82.85290	82.49078	82.14541	82.02104	81.95722
8.50	83.70787	83.16409	82.68228	82.25700	81.88329	81.55658	81.27268	81.02775	80.64105	80.27443	80.14324	80.07627
8.750	82.12602	81.54178	81.02540	80.57074	80.17220	79.82464	79.52338	79.26411	78.85625	78.47187	78.33519	78.26578
9.000	80.58511	79.96367	79.41577	78.93456	78.51378	78.14774	77.83124	77.55954	77.13366	76.73468	76.59371	76.52248
9.25	79.08395	78.42840	77.85186	77.34674	76.90616	76.52384	76.19408	75.91170	75.47068	75.05995	74.91575	74.84327
9.75	76.19638	75.48122	74.85537	74.30976	73.83621	73.42732	73.07639	72.77737	72.31370	71.88700	71.73908	71.66549

Entry is the percentage of loan balance to give the desired yield to the selected time.

Price of a Mortgage to Give a Specified Yield
Conversion of Interest to Principal or Principal to Interest
6.50% Interest Rate   30 Years Amortization Schedule

Desired Yield	Prepaid or Ballooned at											
	1 Year	2 Years	3 Years	4 Years	5 Years	6 Years	7 Years	8 Years	9 Years	10 Years	11 Years	12 Years
3.500	102.92908	105.72483	108.39083	110.93052	113.34718	115.64396	117.82384	119.88970	121.84425	123.69011	125.42974	127.06550
3.750	102.68139	105.23436	107.66279	109.97040	112.16076	114.23728	116.20321	118.06167	119.81563	121.46792	123.02125	124.47819
4.000	102.43437	104.74637	106.94012	109.01954	110.98839	112.85026	114.60859	116.26667	117.82761	119.29442	120.66994	121.95690
4.250	102.18800	104.26085	106.22278	108.07784	109.82988	111.48261	113.03955	114.50406	115.87935	117.16848	118.37437	119.49982
4.500	101.94229	103.77778	105.51073	107.14521	108.68508	110.13406	111.49565	112.77322	113.96998	115.08898	116.13312	117.10518
4.625	101.81968	103.53716	105.15668	106.68227	108.11777	109.46685	110.73299	111.91953	113.02963	114.06630	115.03243	115.93073
4.750	101.69723	103.29715	104.80394	106.22156	107.55381	108.80430	109.97646	111.07355	112.09869	113.05483	113.94480	114.77126
4.875	101.57495	103.05775	104.45249	105.76308	106.99320	108.14639	109.22600	110.23522	111.17707	112.05444	112.87006	113.62655
5.000	101.45283	102.81895	104.10235	105.30680	106.43591	107.49308	108.48157	109.40445	110.26467	111.06499	111.80806	112.49641
5.125	101.33087	102.58076	103.75350	104.85273	105.88192	106.84434	107.74311	108.58119	109.36138	110.08635	110.75863	111.38062
5.25	101.20907	102.34316	103.40593	104.40085	105.33120	106.20012	107.01057	107.76535	108.46712	109.11841	109.72161	110.27899
5.375	101.08744	102.10617	103.05965	103.95114	104.78375	105.56041	106.28390	106.95686	107.58178	108.16102	108.69683	109.19133
5.500	100.96597	101.86978	102.71464	103.50360	104.23953	104.92515	105.56305	106.15565	106.70527	107.21408	107.68415	108.11744
5.625	100.84466	101.63398	102.37091	103.05822	103.69653	104.29434	104.84797	105.36166	105.83750	106.27746	106.68341	107.05714
5.750	100.72351	101.39878	102.02844	102.61498	103.16073	103.66792	104.13862	104.57482	104.97837	105.35103	105.69446	106.01023
5.875	100.60252	101.16418	101.68724	102.17388	102.62611	103.04586	103.43494	103.79505	104.12779	104.43468	104.71714	104.97654
6.00	100.48170	100.93016	101.34730	101.73490	102.09465	102.42815	102.73689	103.02229	103.28567	103.52828	103.75132	103.95587
6.125	100.36103	100.69674	101.00860	101.29803	101.56633	101.81473	102.04442	102.25647	102.45192	102.63173	102.79683	102.94806
6.250	100.24053	100.46391	100.67116	100.86326	101.04112	101.20559	101.35747	101.49752	101.62645	101.74491	101.85354	101.95293
6.500	100.00000	100.00000	100.00000	100.00000	100.00000	100.00000	100.00000	100.00000	100.00000	100.00000	100.00000	100.00000
6.750	99.76011	99.53843	99.33377	99.14502	98.97113	98.81112	98.66410	98.52920	98.40563	98.29265	98.18956	98.09572
6.875	99.64041	99.30852	99.00250	98.72061	98.46124	98.22288	98.00412	97.80366	97.62027	97.45279	97.30017	97.16141
7.000	99.52086	99.07919	98.67244	98.29824	97.95435	97.63872	97.34940	97.08461	96.84267	96.62200	96.42115	96.23876
7.125	99.40147	98.85044	98.34360	97.87790	97.45045	97.05861	96.69990	96.37199	96.07275	95.80017	95.55237	95.32763
7.250	99.28225	98.62227	98.01598	97.45957	96.94952	96.48254	96.05556	95.66574	95.31044	94.98719	94.69370	94.42785
7.375	99.16318	98.39467	97.68955	97.04326	96.45154	95.91046	95.41635	94.96580	94.55565	94.18296	93.84502	93.53927
7.500	99.04426	98.16764	97.36433	96.62894	95.95650	95.34235	94.78222	94.27210	93.80830	93.38739	93.00619	92.66173
7.625	98.92551	97.94119	97.04030	96.21662	95.46436	94.77819	94.15313	93.58459	93.06832	92.60037	92.17709	91.79509
7.750	98.80692	97.71530	96.71747	95.80627	94.97513	94.21793	93.52903	92.90321	92.33562	91.82180	91.35760	90.93919
7.875	98.68848	97.48999	96.39582	95.39789	94.48877	93.66156	92.90989	92.22790	91.61013	91.05158	90.54760	90.09389
8.000	98.57020	97.26525	96.07535	94.99147	94.00527	93.10904	92.29567	91.55860	90.89178	90.28962	89.74696	89.25905
8.125	98.45207	97.04107	95.75606	94.58701	93.52461	92.56034	91.68631	90.89525	90.18048	89.53581	88.95558	88.43452
8.250	98.33411	96.81745	95.43795	94.18447	93.04678	92.01545	91.08178	90.23781	89.47616	88.79008	88.17332	87.62017
8.375	98.21630	96.59440	95.12100	93.78387	92.57176	91.47432	90.48205	89.58621	88.77875	88.05231	87.40009	86.81584
8.500	98.09864	96.37191	94.80522	93.38519	92.09953	90.93694	89.88706	88.94039	88.08818	87.32243	86.63576	86.02142
8.75	97.86381	95.92861	94.17714	92.59355	91.16336	89.87329	88.71118	87.66590	86.72726	85.88593	85.13336	84.46173
9.000	97.62959	95.48754	93.55366	91.80948	90.23815	88.82429	87.55382	86.41391	85.39282	84.47986	83.66525	82.94005
9.25	97.39600	95.04869	92.93474	91.03289	89.23376	87.78971	86.41467	85.18398	84.08432	83.10354	82.23057	81.45536
9.50	97.16302	94.61204	92.32036	90.26372	88.42006	86.76937	85.29343	83.97571	82.80120	81.75626	80.82850	80.00665
10.000	96.69893	93.74532	91.10507	88.74732	86.64420	84.77051	83.10347	81.62251	80.30902	79.14621	78.11891	77.21339

Yield	13 Years	14 Years	15 Years	16 Years	17 Years	18 Years	19 Years	20 Years	22 Years	25 Years	27 Years	Full Term
3.500	128.59960	130.03417	131.37121	132.61259	133.76010	134.81540	135.78006	136.65555	138.14436	139.73969	140.38942	140.75838
3.750	125.84119	127.11259	128.29459	129.38931	130.39872	131.32471	132.93346	132.93346	134.22860	135.60805	136.16632	136.48170
4.000	123.15788	124.27536	125.31169	126.26909	127.14970	127.95552	128.68847	129.35036	130.46772	131.65067	132.12641	132.39375
4.250	120.54747	121.51985	122.41937	123.24832	124.00888	124.70312	125.33301	125.90041	126.85478	127.85909	128.26044	128.48481
4.500	118.00779	118.84348	119.61462	120.32350	120.97227	121.56300	122.09764	122.57805	123.38314	124.22528	124.55970	124.74568
4.625	116.76383	117.53419	118.24417	118.89601	119.49184	120.03369	120.52348	120.96304	121.69833	122.46514	122.76869	122.93706
4.750	115.53678	116.24376	116.89452	117.49125	118.03603	118.53084	118.97755	119.37795	120.04650	120.74163	121.01593	121.16769
4.875	114.32638	114.97160	115.56534	116.10883	116.60439	117.05393	117.45927	117.82214	118.42692	119.05386	119.30047	119.43655
5.000	113.13240	113.71830	114.25627	114.74835	115.19647	115.60247	115.96810	116.29501	116.83887	117.40095	117.62135	117.74265
5.125	111.95458	112.48269	112.96699	113.40942	113.81183	114.17596	114.50348	114.79595	115.28162	115.78207	115.97768	116.08506
5.25	110.79270	111.26478	111.69716	112.09167	112.45004	112.77393	113.06488	113.32437	113.75451	114.19639	114.36857	114.46284
5.375	109.64651	110.06428	110.44465	110.79471	111.11068	111.39588	111.65177	111.87971	112.25684	112.64312	112.79316	112.87509
5.500	108.51578	108.88094	109.21455	109.51819	109.79333	110.04138	110.26365	110.46139	110.78798	111.12148	111.25060	111.32093
5.625	107.40029	107.71447	108.00115	108.26175	108.49759	108.70995	108.90000	109.06887	109.34727	109.63071	109.74010	109.79953
5.750	106.29981	106.56461	106.80593	107.02503	107.22307	107.40116	107.56035	107.70162	107.93409	108.17006	108.26085	108.31005
5.875	105.21412	105.43110	105.62860	105.80769	105.96936	106.11457	106.24420	106.35910	106.54784	106.73884	106.81209	106.85168
6.00	104.14300	104.31369	104.46886	104.60938	104.73609	104.84975	104.95109	105.04081	105.18790	105.33632	105.39306	105.42365
6.125	103.08624	103.21212	103.32641	103.42979	103.52288	103.60629	103.68057	103.74624	103.85372	103.96183	104.00304	104.02519
6.250	102.04362	102.12614	102.20097	102.26857	102.32937	102.38378	102.43217	102.47490	102.54470	102.61471	102.64131	102.65557
6.500	100.00000	100.00000	100.00000	100.00000	100.00000	100.00000	100.00000	100.00000	100.00000	100.00000	100.00000	100.00000
6.750	98.01051	97.93336	97.86375	97.80117	97.74517	97.69531	97.65118	97.61240	97.54952	97.48720	97.46382	97.45142
6.875	97.03556	96.92177	96.81923	96.72716	96.64486	96.57168	96.50696	96.45023	96.35833	96.26753	96.23358	96.21560
7.000	96.07357	95.92438	95.79009	95.66968	95.56219	95.46672	95.38243	95.30856	95.18918	95.07158	95.02775	95.00461
7.125	95.12433	94.94095	94.77610	94.62846	94.49683	94.38006	94.27710	94.18697	94.04159	93.89881	93.84576	93.81782
7.250	94.18766	93.97127	93.77699	93.60322	93.44847	93.31136	93.19062	93.08506	92.91510	92.74867	92.68702	92.65465
7.375	93.26337	93.01513	92.79253	92.59366	92.41679	92.26028	92.12263	92.00042	91.80924	91.62063	91.55100	91.51452
7.500	92.35129	92.07232	91.82246	91.59954	91.40151	91.22649	91.07275	90.93867	90.72357	90.51420	90.43713	90.39687
7.625	91.45124	91.14263	90.86657	90.62057	90.40231	90.20966	90.04064	89.89341	89.65765	89.42885	89.34491	89.30116
7.750	90.56304	90.22585	89.92461	89.65649	89.41891	89.20947	89.02594	88.86628	88.61106	88.36412	88.27380	88.22686
7.875	89.68651	89.32179	88.99635	88.70706	88.45103	88.22561	88.02832	87.85689	87.58338	87.31952	87.22332	87.17345
8.000	88.82150	88.43025	88.08157	87.77201	87.49838	87.25776	87.04743	86.86490	86.57421	86.29460	86.19298	86.14044
8.125	87.96783	87.55104	87.18005	86.85110	86.56070	86.30563	86.08296	85.88996	85.58314	85.28890	85.18231	85.12733
8.250	87.12533	86.68396	86.29158	85.94409	85.63770	85.36893	85.13458	84.93171	84.60979	84.30199	84.19083	84.13365
8.375	86.29385	85.82882	85.41594	85.05073	84.72913	84.44736	84.20199	83.98983	83.65378	83.33343	83.21811	83.15894
8.500	85.47322	84.98546	84.55292	84.17080	83.83472	83.54064	83.28486	83.06398	82.71474	82.38281	82.26370	82.20275
8.75	83.86389	83.33329	82.86392	82.45030	82.08741	81.77065	81.49583	81.25910	80.88615	80.53379	80.40815	80.34418
9.000	82.29613	81.72603	81.22298	80.78078	80.39378	80.05681	79.76518	79.51459	79.12123	78.75179	78.62089	78.55459
9.25	80.76872	80.16233	79.62857	79.16053	78.75193	78.39705	78.09067	77.82805	77.41731	77.03383	76.89882	76.83079
9.50	79.28053	78.64084	78.07917	77.58788	77.16005	76.78937	76.47015	76.19721	75.77186	75.37709	75.23898	75.16975
10.000	76.41729	75.71942	75.10971	74.57903	74.11918	73.72273	73.38301	73.09398	72.64677	72.23663	72.09496	72.02467

Entry is the percentage of loan balance to give the desired yield to the selected time.

Price of a Mortgage to Give a Specified Yield
Conversion of Interest to Principal or Principal to Interest
6.75% Interest Rate 30 Years Amortization Schedule

Desired Yield	1 Year	2 Years	3 Years	4 Years	Prepaid or Ballooned at 5 Years	6 Years	7 Years	8 Years	9 Years	10 Years	11 Years	12 Years
3.750	102.92585	105.71305	108.36576	110.88794	113.28338	115.55572	117.70842	119.74477	121.66792	123.48086	125.18646	126.78742
4.000	102.67844	105.22361	107.63993	109.93163	112.10277	114.15720	116.09862	117.93054	119.65632	121.27916	122.80211	124.22807
4.250	102.43169	104.73663	106.91944	108.98453	110.93611	112.77819	114.51460	116.14901	117.68488	119.12555	120.47418	121.73378
4.500	102.18559	104.25211	106.20427	108.04655	109.78323	111.41839	112.95593	114.39953	115.75274	117.01891	118.20123	119.30276
4.750	101.94015	103.77004	105.49436	107.11758	108.64396	110.07753	111.42216	112.68151	113.85906	114.95813	115.98187	116.93327
4.875	101.81768	103.52992	105.14137	106.65646	108.07937	109.41412	110.66449	111.83411	112.92639	113.94460	114.89185	115.77108
5.000	101.69537	103.29041	104.78969	106.19755	107.51813	108.75534	109.91289	110.99434	112.00303	112.94215	113.81473	114.62364
5.125	101.57322	103.05149	104.43930	105.74086	106.96020	108.10115	109.16731	110.16214	111.08888	111.95063	112.75032	113.49075
5.25	101.45123	102.81319	104.09020	105.28636	106.40558	107.45153	108.42770	109.33743	110.18384	110.96992	111.69848	112.37221
5.375	101.32941	102.57548	103.74239	104.83406	105.85423	106.80643	107.69401	108.52014	109.28782	109.99990	110.65905	111.26782
5.500	101.20775	102.33838	103.39586	104.38393	105.30614	106.16583	106.96619	107.71021	108.40073	109.04043	109.63185	110.11740
5.625	101.08625	102.10187	103.05061	103.93597	104.76128	105.52970	106.24418	106.90755	107.52245	108.09140	108.61675	109.10074
5.750	100.96491	101.86596	102.70663	103.49016	104.21964	104.89799	105.52795	106.11211	106.65291	107.15268	107.61357	108.03766
5.875	100.84373	101.63065	102.36391	103.04650	103.68120	104.27069	104.81743	105.32380	105.79201	106.22415	106.62218	106.98797
6.00	100.72272	101.39593	102.02246	102.60497	103.14594	103.64774	104.11259	104.54257	104.93966	105.30569	105.64242	105.95149
6.125	100.60186	101.16180	101.68227	102.16556	102.61384	103.02914	103.41337	103.76835	104.09576	104.39719	104.67415	104.92804
6.25	100.48117	100.92827	101.34333	101.72827	102.08487	102.41483	102.71973	103.00107	103.26023	103.49853	103.71721	103.91743
6.375	100.36064	100.69532	101.00564	101.29307	101.55902	101.80480	102.03162	102.24065	102.43297	102.60959	102.77147	102.91950
6.50	100.24026	100.46296	100.66919	100.85997	101.03627	101.19900	101.34899	101.48705	101.61391	101.73027	101.83678	101.93406
6.750	100.00000	100.00000	100.00000	100.00000	100.00000	100.00000	100.00000	100.00000	100.00000	100.00000	100.00000	100.00000
7.000	99.76037	99.53937	99.33573	99.14827	98.97590	98.81759	98.67239	98.53941	98.41782	98.30685	98.20577	98.11391
7.125	99.64080	99.30993	99.00542	98.72546	98.46836	98.23252	98.01649	97.81888	97.63842	97.47392	97.32428	97.18845
7.250	99.52138	99.08106	98.67633	98.30469	97.96381	97.65152	97.36580	97.10478	96.86670	96.64995	96.45302	96.27450
7.375	99.40213	98.85277	98.34845	97.88594	97.46223	97.07454	96.72028	96.39704	96.10258	95.83484	95.59187	95.37189
7.500	99.28303	98.62506	98.02177	97.46919	96.96360	96.50156	96.07988	95.69561	95.34599	95.02847	94.74071	94.48049
7.625	99.16409	98.39791	97.69630	97.05444	96.46790	95.93254	95.44456	95.00042	94.59683	94.23076	93.89939	93.60012
7.750	99.04531	98.17135	97.37202	96.64168	95.97511	95.36747	94.81428	94.31142	93.85504	93.44160	93.06781	92.73065
7.875	98.92668	97.94535	97.04893	96.23090	95.48521	94.80630	94.18900	93.62854	93.12053	92.66088	92.24584	91.87193
8.000	98.80822	97.71992	96.72703	95.82208	94.99820	94.24902	93.56867	92.95174	92.39322	91.88852	91.43335	91.02381
8.125	98.68991	97.49506	96.40631	95.41523	94.51404	93.69558	92.95325	92.28094	91.67305	91.12441	90.63023	90.18614
8.250	98.57176	97.27077	96.08677	95.01032	94.03273	93.14598	92.34270	91.61610	90.95994	90.36846	89.83636	89.35878
8.375	98.45376	97.04704	95.76840	94.60736	93.55424	92.60017	91.73698	90.95716	90.25381	89.62057	89.05163	88.54160
8.50	98.33592	96.82387	95.45120	94.20632	93.07856	92.05813	91.13605	90.30406	89.55458	88.88066	88.27591	87.73445
8.625	98.21824	96.60126	95.13517	93.80720	92.60566	91.51983	90.53986	89.65674	88.86219	88.14863	87.50909	86.93766
8.75	98.10071	96.37922	94.82029	93.40999	92.13554	90.98524	89.94839	89.01516	88.17656	87.42438	86.75107	86.14972
9.00	97.86613	95.93680	94.19400	92.62126	91.20355	89.92711	88.77941	87.74897	86.82532	85.99889	85.26096	84.60353
9.25	97.63217	95.49661	93.57230	91.84006	90.28244	88.88351	87.62879	86.50505	85.50027	84.60349	83.80471	83.09484
9.50	97.39883	95.05863	92.95514	91.06631	89.37208	87.85424	86.49623	85.28300	84.20089	83.23748	82.38148	81.62264
9.75	97.16610	94.62285	92.34251	90.29993	88.47234	86.83908	85.38142	84.08239	82.92663	81.90019	80.99044	80.18596
10.25	96.70251	93.75784	91.13064	88.78901	86.70421	84.85029	83.20389	81.74392	80.45138	79.30915	78.30178	77.41539

Yield	13 Years	14 Years	15 Years	16 Years	17 Years	18 Years	19 Years	20 Years	22 Years	25 Years	27 Years	Full Term
3.750	128.28631	129.68557	130.98752	132.19434	133.30808	134.33070	135.26403	136.10976	137.54478	139.07704	139.69888	140.05102
4.000	125.55979	126.79991	127.95091	129.01515	129.99487	130.89219	131.70912	132.44755	133.69591	135.02085	135.55516	135.85616
4.250	122.90721	123.99720	125.00635	125.93711	126.79182	127.57270	128.28185	128.92126	129.99828	131.13450	131.58983	131.84499
4.500	120.32638	121.27485	122.15079	122.95667	123.69488	124.36764	124.97708	125.52522	126.44513	127.40979	127.79392	128.00807
4.750	117.81519	118.63033	119.38126	120.07042	120.70013	121.27259	121.78988	122.25398	123.03002	123.83892	124.15900	124.33651
4.875	116.58507	117.33650	118.02787	118.66158	119.23991	119.76500	120.23890	120.66354	121.37230	122.10885	122.39939	122.56009
5.000	115.37160	116.06121	116.69492	117.27506	117.80384	118.28334	118.71556	119.10237	119.74681	120.41453	120.67706	120.82190
5.125	114.17453	114.80419	115.38208	115.91047	116.39147	116.82711	117.21930	117.56986	118.15283	118.75503	118.99107	119.12096
5.25	112.99363	113.56514	114.08902	114.56742	115.00237	115.39582	115.74959	116.06541	116.58966	117.12957	117.34053	117.45631
5.375	111.82864	112.34378	112.81539	113.24553	113.63612	113.98900	114.30589	114.58844	115.05660	115.53731	115.72454	115.82704
5.500	110.67934	111.13983	111.56088	111.94443	112.29228	112.60616	112.88767	113.13837	113.55300	113.97746	114.14226	114.23224
5.625	109.54550	109.95301	110.32517	110.66376	110.97045	111.24684	111.49443	111.71464	112.07818	112.44923	112.59284	112.67105
5.750	108.42688	108.78307	109.10795	109.40315	109.67022	109.91060	110.12567	110.31671	110.63153	110.95188	111.07548	111.14261
5.875	107.32327	107.62973	107.90891	108.16227	108.39120	108.59699	108.78008	108.94403	109.21240	109.48466	109.58938	109.64610
6.00	106.23445	106.49274	106.72775	106.94076	107.13299	107.30558	107.45961	107.59609	107.82019	108.04687	108.13377	108.18072
6.125	105.16019	105.37184	105.56417	105.73828	105.89521	106.03594	106.16137	106.27238	106.45431	106.63779	106.70791	106.74570
6.25	104.10028	104.26677	104.41788	104.55451	104.67750	104.78765	104.88571	104.97238	105.11418	105.25675	105.31106	105.34026
6.375	103.05451	103.17730	103.28860	103.38911	103.47947	103.56031	103.63218	103.69562	103.79923	103.90309	103.94253	103.96368
6.50	102.02268	102.10317	102.17604	102.24177	102.30078	102.35351	102.40033	102.44162	102.50891	102.57616	102.60162	102.61524
6.750	100.00000	100.00000	100.00000	100.00000	100.00000	100.00000	100.00000	100.00000	100.00000	100.00000	100.00000	100.00000
7.000	98.03065	97.95539	97.88760	97.82676	97.77240	97.72408	97.68138	97.64391	97.58329	97.52342	97.50105	97.48920
7.125	97.06549	96.95448	96.85462	96.76510	96.68522	96.61429	96.55170	96.49685	96.40826	96.32103	96.28853	96.27138
7.250	96.11308	95.96754	95.83677	95.71970	95.61535	95.52282	95.44127	95.36989	95.25481	95.14126	95.09988	95.07778
7.375	95.17324	94.99435	94.83381	94.69027	94.56249	94.44932	94.34969	94.26261	94.12246	93.98529	93.93451	93.90784
7.500	94.24578	94.03470	93.84549	93.67653	93.52632	93.39344	93.27661	93.17462	93.01077	92.85088	92.79187	92.76096
7.625	93.33053	93.08837	92.87158	92.67823	92.50654	92.35488	92.22165	92.10552	91.91928	91.73808	91.67142	91.63660
7.750	92.42731	92.15517	91.91184	91.69509	91.50286	91.33324	91.18447	91.05492	90.84756	90.64641	90.57264	90.53420
7.875	91.53593	91.23488	90.96603	90.72685	90.51498	90.32827	90.16471	90.02246	89.79518	89.57537	89.49501	89.45324
8.000	90.65624	90.32731	90.03393	89.77325	89.54263	89.33946	89.16204	89.00777	88.76173	88.52449	88.43803	88.39321
8.125	89.78806	89.43227	89.11532	88.83404	88.58551	88.36703	88.17612	88.01049	87.74681	87.49331	87.40122	87.35361
8.250	88.93122	88.54955	88.20997	87.90898	87.64337	87.41016	87.20663	87.03027	86.75001	86.48139	86.38411	86.33394
8.375	88.08556	87.67897	87.31767	86.99783	86.71592	86.46829	86.25324	86.06678	85.77096	85.48827	85.38623	85.33374
8.50	87.25091	86.82034	86.43820	86.10034	85.80291	85.54242	85.31564	85.11963	84.80926	84.51355	84.40713	84.35255
8.625	86.42712	85.97348	85.57137	85.21627	84.90408	84.63099	84.39354	84.18855	83.86457	83.55679	83.44639	83.38990
8.75	85.61403	85.13821	84.71695	84.34542	84.01917	83.73414	83.48662	83.27320	82.93650	82.61760	82.50357	82.44537
9.00	84.01933	83.50170	83.04458	82.64240	82.29013	81.98312	81.71717	81.48844	81.12887	80.79034	80.67005	80.60898
9.25	82.46560	81.90945	81.41952	80.98955	80.61386	80.28726	80.00504	79.76291	79.38366	79.02871	78.90339	78.84010
9.50	80.95167	80.36009	79.84025	79.38516	78.98850	78.64453	78.34803	78.09429	77.69827	77.32983	77.20057	77.13562
9.75	79.47639	78.85233	78.30530	77.82760	77.41226	77.05299	76.74406	76.48034	76.07023	75.69094	75.55871	75.49261
10.25	76.63742	75.95660	75.36277	74.84675	74.40033	74.01607	73.68730	73.40801	72.97683	72.58275	72.44711	72.38000

Entry is the percentage of loan balance to give the desired yield to the selected time.

Price of a Mortgage to Give a Specified Yield
Conversion of Interest to Principal or Principal to Interest
7.00% Interest Rate 30 Years Amortization Schedule

Desired Yield	1 Year	2 Years	3 Years	4 Years	5 Years	6 Years	7 Years	8 Years	9 Years	10 Years	11 Years	12 Years
4.00	102.92260	105.70120	108.34055	110.84516	113.21937	115.46729	117.59287	119.59984	121.49178	123.27208	124.94398	126.51055
4.250	102.67547	105.21278	107.61693	109.89269	112.04458	114.07695	115.99391	117.79941	119.49720	121.09082	122.58369	123.97902
4.500	102.42899	104.72682	106.89865	108.94937	110.88365	112.70595	114.42050	116.03134	117.54231	118.95705	120.27905	121.51160
4.75	102.18317	104.24332	106.18565	108.01511	109.73641	111.35402	112.87220	114.29500	115.62627	116.86965	118.02864	119.10652
5.000	101.93800	103.76225	105.47790	107.08983	108.60269	110.02088	111.34859	112.58979	113.74825	114.82755	115.83109	116.76208
5.125	101.81566	103.52263	105.12598	106.63053	108.04085	109.36127	110.59591	111.74867	112.82325	113.82316	114.75172	115.61208
5.25	101.69349	103.28361	104.77536	106.17344	107.48232	108.70625	109.84925	110.91512	111.90746	112.82969	113.68506	114.47662
5.375	101.57148	103.04520	104.42603	105.71854	106.92709	108.05580	109.10855	110.08905	111.00077	111.84703	112.63095	113.35549
5.50	101.44962	102.80739	104.07798	105.26583	106.37514	107.40987	108.37377	109.27040	110.10310	110.87505	111.58924	112.24852
5.625	101.32794	102.57018	103.73122	104.81530	105.82644	106.76844	107.64486	108.45909	109.21434	109.91361	110.55976	111.15549
5.750	101.20641	102.33356	103.38573	104.36693	105.28098	106.13146	106.92176	107.65506	108.33440	108.96260	109.54237	110.07622
5.875	101.08505	102.09755	103.04151	103.92072	104.73874	105.49892	106.20442	106.85824	107.46318	108.02190	108.53690	109.01052
6.00	100.96384	101.86213	102.69866	103.47665	104.19969	104.87077	105.49280	106.06856	106.60060	107.09139	107.54320	107.95820
6.125	100.84280	101.62730	102.35688	103.03472	103.66382	104.24698	104.78686	105.25894	105.74657	106.17094	106.56113	106.91908
6.25	100.72192	101.39306	102.01645	102.59491	103.13110	103.62752	104.08653	104.51033	104.90098	105.26044	105.59054	105.89299
6.375	100.60120	101.15942	101.67727	102.15720	102.60152	103.01237	103.39178	103.74165	104.06376	104.35978	104.63128	104.87973
6.50	100.48064	100.92636	101.33934	101.72160	102.07506	102.40148	102.70256	102.97984	103.23481	103.46883	103.68321	103.87914
6.625	100.36024	100.69389	101.00265	101.28809	101.55169	101.79483	102.01881	102.22484	102.41404	102.58749	102.74618	102.89104
6.750	100.24000	100.46201	100.66720	100.85666	101.03141	101.19239	101.34050	101.47657	101.60138	101.71565	101.82006	101.91526
7.00	100.00000	100.00000	100.00000	100.00000	100.00000	100.00000	100.00000	100.00000	100.00000	100.00000	100.00000	100.00000
7.250	99.76064	99.54031	99.33769	99.15153	98.98068	98.82407	98.68069	98.54962	98.43000	98.32102	98.22193	98.13204
7.375	99.64120	99.31134	99.00836	98.73034	98.47551	98.24220	98.02887	97.83410	97.65656	97.49501	97.34831	97.21539
7.500	99.52191	99.08294	98.68024	98.31117	97.97330	97.66435	97.38222	97.12495	96.89072	96.67786	96.48480	96.31010
7.625	99.40279	98.85511	98.35332	97.89401	97.47405	97.09050	96.74069	96.42209	96.13239	95.86945	95.63126	95.41599
7.75	99.28382	98.62786	98.02760	97.47885	96.97772	96.52062	96.10423	95.72548	95.38151	95.06969	94.78758	94.53293
7.875	99.16501	98.40118	97.70308	97.06567	96.48430	95.95468	95.47282	95.03505	94.63798	94.27848	93.95363	93.66076
8.00	99.04636	98.17508	97.37975	96.65447	95.99378	95.39264	94.84639	94.35075	93.90174	93.49571	93.12928	92.79933
8.125	98.92786	97.94954	97.05761	96.24524	95.50614	94.83448	94.22492	93.67251	93.17270	92.72129	92.31441	91.94850
8.250	98.80953	97.72457	96.73665	95.83797	95.02135	94.28018	93.60836	93.00028	92.45079	91.95513	91.50891	91.10812
8.375	98.69135	97.50016	96.41686	95.43265	94.53941	93.72970	92.99666	92.33401	91.73594	91.19712	90.71266	90.27805
8.50	98.57333	97.27632	96.09825	95.02926	94.06028	93.18301	92.38980	91.67363	91.02806	90.44717	89.92554	89.45816
8.625	98.45546	97.05304	95.78081	94.62780	93.58397	92.64009	91.78772	91.01909	90.32709	89.70520	89.14743	88.64830
8.75	98.33775	96.83033	95.46453	94.22826	93.11044	92.10092	91.19039	90.37033	89.63295	88.97110	88.37823	87.84834
8.875	98.22020	96.60817	95.14941	93.83063	92.63699	91.56545	90.59776	89.72731	88.94558	88.24479	87.61782	87.05815
9.000	98.10280	96.38657	94.83545	93.43490	92.17168	91.03367	90.00980	89.08996	88.26490	87.52618	86.86609	86.27759
9.25	97.86847	95.94505	94.21096	92.64910	91.24388	89.98107	88.84773	87.83207	86.92332	86.11168	85.38824	84.74485
9.50	97.63476	95.50574	93.59105	91.87079	90.32688	88.94289	87.70387	86.59662	85.60767	84.72693	83.94383	83.24911
9.75	97.40168	95.06864	92.97566	91.09989	89.42057	87.91893	86.57791	85.38207	84.31740	83.37122	82.53202	81.78938
10.00	97.16921	94.63373	92.36478	90.33632	88.52481	86.90897	85.46955	84.18913	83.05199	82.04391	81.15201	80.36470
10.50	96.70611	93.77044	91.15635	88.83090	86.76443	84.93029	83.30447	81.86540	80.59368	79.47186	78.48425	77.61675

Yield	13 Years	14 Years	15 Years	16 Years	17 Years	18 Years	19 Years	20 Years	22 Years	25 Years	27 Years	Full Term
4.00	127.97469	129.33919	130.60664	131.77954	132.86021	133.85086	134.75358	135.57031	136.95303	138.42420	139.01913	139.35509
4.250	125.27989	126.48920	127.60971	128.64404	129.59468	130.46397	131.25412	131.96723	133.17010	134.44224	134.95344	135.24061
4.500	122.65785	123.72077	124.70320	125.60781	126.43716	127.19364	127.87956	128.49705	129.53484	130.62579	131.06142	131.30487
4.75	120.10644	121.03136	121.88411	122.66737	123.38367	124.03541	124.62489	125.15425	126.04067	126.96690	127.33443	127.53875
5.000	117.62358	118.41849	119.14556	119.81936	120.43039	120.98498	121.48532	121.93353	122.68132	123.45801	123.76426	123.93362
5.125	116.40723	117.14001	117.81309	118.42901	118.99018	119.49888	119.95726	120.36736	121.05032	121.75756	122.03554	122.18887
5.25	115.20727	115.87977	116.49671	117.06057	117.57366	118.03820	118.45626	118.82983	119.45082	120.09195	120.34315	120.48135
5.375	114.02346	114.63749	115.20010	115.71365	116.18039	116.60244	116.98179	117.32035	117.88211	118.46035	118.68619	118.81012
5.50	112.85555	113.41289	113.92291	114.38789	114.80995	115.19112	115.53331	115.83832	116.34350	116.86193	117.06378	117.17425
5.625	111.70333	112.20569	112.66483	113.08290	113.46191	113.80378	114.11031	114.38318	114.83432	115.29591	115.47505	115.57285
5.750	110.56655	111.01561	111.42554	111.79832	112.13587	112.43995	112.71226	112.95437	113.35392	113.76150	113.91919	114.00504
5.875	109.44499	109.84240	110.20472	110.53381	110.83141	111.09918	111.33867	111.55135	111.90167	112.25797	112.39538	112.47000
6.00	108.33842	108.68578	109.00207	109.28900	109.54815	109.78103	109.98906	110.17357	110.47694	110.78456	110.90282	110.96688
6.125	107.24663	107.54549	107.81729	108.06355	108.28569	108.48507	108.66295	108.82052	109.07913	109.34057	109.44076	109.49489
6.25	106.16940	106.42129	106.65009	106.85713	107.04366	107.21087	107.35987	107.49168	107.70763	107.92530	108.00845	108.05326
6.375	105.10651	105.31292	105.50015	105.66940	105.82168	105.95802	106.07935	106.18656	106.36189	106.53807	106.60517	106.64122
6.50	104.05776	104.22013	104.36725	104.50004	104.61939	104.72611	104.82096	104.90467	105.04132	105.17822	105.23019	105.25805
6.625	103.02293	103.14268	103.25104	103.34873	103.43642	103.51473	103.58426	103.64553	103.74538	103.84511	103.88285	103.90303
6.750	102.00183	102.08033	102.15128	102.21516	102.27243	102.32351	102.36881	102.40868	102.47353	102.53811	102.56247	102.57546
7.00	100.00000	100.00000	100.00000	100.00000	100.00000	100.00000	100.00000	100.00000	100.00000	100.00000	100.00000	100.00000
7.250	98.05070	97.97731	97.91130	97.85217	97.79941	97.75259	97.71129	97.67511	97.61668	97.55919	97.53778	97.52648
7.375	97.09527	96.98701	96.88978	96.80277	96.72525	96.65654	96.59599	96.54302	96.45764	96.37387	96.34277	96.32640
7.500	96.15240	96.01047	95.88315	95.76935	95.66809	95.57845	95.49955	95.43061	95.31971	95.21122	95.17107	95.14998
7.625	95.22192	95.04746	94.89115	94.75163	94.62763	94.51799	94.42161	94.33750	94.20244	94.07071	94.02211	93.99666
7.75	94.30364	94.09778	93.91357	93.74934	93.60356	93.47482	93.36180	93.26329	93.10539	92.95184	92.89537	92.86587
7.875	93.39738	93.16122	92.95014	92.76220	92.59559	92.44863	92.31977	92.20760	92.02811	91.85411	91.79031	91.75708
8.00	92.50298	92.23757	92.00066	91.78997	91.60342	91.43908	91.29517	91.17005	90.97020	90.77702	90.70643	90.66975
8.125	91.62025	91.32665	91.06488	90.83239	90.62679	90.44588	90.28766	90.15027	89.93122	89.72013	89.64322	89.60337
8.250	90.74903	90.42824	90.14259	89.88920	89.66539	89.46872	89.29692	89.14791	88.91079	88.68295	88.60021	88.55744
8.375	89.88916	89.54216	89.23357	88.96016	88.71897	88.50729	88.32260	88.16262	87.90850	87.66505	87.57692	87.53148
8.50	89.04046	88.66822	88.33760	88.04502	87.78725	87.56130	87.36441	87.19406	86.92396	86.66598	86.57288	86.52501
8.625	88.20278	87.80624	87.45446	87.14356	86.86998	86.63046	86.42201	86.24189	85.95681	85.68532	85.58766	85.53758
8.75	87.37595	86.95602	86.58395	86.25553	85.96689	85.71449	85.49511	85.30578	85.00666	84.72266	84.62082	84.56872
8.875	86.55982	86.11739	85.72587	85.38071	85.07773	84.81312	84.58342	84.38542	84.07317	83.77758	83.67193	83.61802
9.000	85.75424	85.29017	84.88001	84.51886	84.20225	83.92608	83.68662	83.48048	83.15598	82.84970	82.74057	82.68504
9.25	84.17411	83.66927	83.22418	82.83325	82.49136	82.19390	81.93662	81.71568	81.36913	81.04399	80.92888	80.87059
9.50	82.63437	82.09195	81.61491	81.19696	80.83235	80.51590	80.24287	80.00899	79.64347	79.30256	79.18263	79.12222
9.75	81.13386	80.55689	80.05072	79.60834	79.22338	78.89009	78.60325	78.35815	77.97647	77.62259	77.49888	77.43689
10.00	79.67146	79.06280	78.53016	78.06579	77.66271	77.31458	77.01572	76.76097	76.36570	76.00140	75.87485	75.81176
10.50	76.85669	76.19266	75.61444	75.11282	74.67955	74.30721	73.98914	73.71936	73.30377	72.92526	72.79543	72.73138

Entry is the percentage of loan balance to give the desired yield to the selected time.

Price of a Mortgage to Give a Specified Yield
Conversion of Interest to Principal or Principal to Interest
7.25% Interest Rate   30 Years Amortization Schedule

Desired Yield	1 Year	2 Years	3 Years	4 Years	Prepaid or Ballooned at 5 Years	6 Years	7 Years	8 Years	9 Years	10 Years	11 Years	12 Years
4.25	102.91933	105.68928	108.31520	110.80221	113.15516	115.37870	117.47724	119.45497	121.31591	123.06385	124.70240	126.23500
4.500	102.67247	105.20189	107.59382	109.85358	111.98622	113.99654	115.88913	117.66834	119.33831	120.90298	122.36607	123.73116
4.75	102.42627	104.71696	106.87775	108.91406	110.83104	112.63358	114.32633	115.91372	117.39994	118.78898	120.08463	121.29047
5.00	102.18073	104.23447	106.16694	107.98355	109.68945	111.28953	112.78842	114.19051	115.49998	116.72078	117.85667	118.91120
5.25	101.93584	103.75442	105.46135	107.06197	108.56130	109.96412	111.27496	112.49810	113.63761	114.69731	115.68085	116.59167
5.375	101.81364	103.51530	105.11051	106.60449	108.00220	109.30832	110.52728	111.66327	112.72027	113.70202	114.61208	115.45380
5.50	101.69160	103.27678	104.76095	106.14922	107.44641	108.65708	109.78556	110.83592	111.81203	112.71752	113.55585	114.33026
5.625	101.56972	103.03887	104.41268	105.69613	106.89388	108.01036	109.04975	110.01598	110.91279	111.74369	112.51200	113.22085
5.750	101.44801	102.80155	104.06570	105.24521	106.34461	107.36813	108.31980	109.20338	110.02246	110.78040	111.48038	112.12538
5.875	101.32645	102.56484	103.71999	104.79647	105.79857	106.73037	107.59566	108.39806	109.14095	109.82754	110.46082	111.04365
6.00	101.20506	102.32872	103.37555	104.34987	105.25575	106.09702	106.87729	107.59993	108.26816	108.88497	109.45319	109.97549
6.125	101.08384	102.09319	103.03237	103.90542	104.71612	105.46807	106.16463	106.80894	107.40399	107.95258	108.45732	108.92069
6.25	100.96277	101.85826	102.69046	103.46309	104.17967	104.84349	105.45763	106.02501	106.54837	107.03025	107.47307	107.87909
6.375	100.84186	101.62392	102.34981	103.02289	103.64637	104.22323	104.75625	105.24809	105.70118	106.11786	106.50029	106.85050
6.50	100.72111	101.39018	102.01040	102.58480	103.11621	103.60726	104.06045	104.47809	104.86236	105.21530	105.53883	105.83473
6.625	100.60053	101.15702	101.67224	102.14882	102.58916	102.99557	103.37017	103.71495	104.03180	104.32245	104.58855	104.83163
6.750	100.48010	100.92445	101.33533	101.71491	102.06521	102.38811	102.68536	102.95862	103.20942	103.43921	103.64931	103.84101
6.875	100.35984	100.69246	100.99965	101.28309	101.54434	101.78485	102.00599	102.20902	102.39514	102.56545	102.72098	102.86270
7.000	100.23973	100.46106	100.66521	100.85334	101.02653	101.18577	101.33200	101.46609	101.58886	101.70106	101.80340	101.89654
7.25	100.00000	100.00000	100.00000	100.00000	100.00000	100.00000	100.00000	100.00000	100.00000	100.00000	100.00000	100.00000
7.500	99.76090	99.54126	99.33966	99.15481	98.98548	98.83056	98.68900	98.55984	98.44217	98.33516	98.23804	98.15009
7.625	99.64159	99.31276	99.01131	98.73524	98.48268	98.25189	98.04127	97.84932	97.67468	97.51606	97.37227	97.24222
7.75	99.52244	99.08483	98.68417	98.31769	97.98283	97.67721	97.39865	97.14511	96.91471	96.70570	96.51648	96.34555
7.875	99.40345	98.85747	98.35822	97.90213	97.48590	97.10650	96.76112	96.44714	96.16217	95.90399	95.67053	95.45991
8.00	99.28461	98.63069	98.03347	97.48855	96.99189	96.53973	96.12861	95.75535	95.41699	95.11082	94.83431	94.58516
8.125	99.16594	98.40448	97.70990	97.07695	96.50076	95.97686	95.50110	95.06968	94.67909	94.32609	94.00769	93.72214
8.250	99.04742	98.17883	97.38753	96.66732	96.01252	95.41787	94.87853	94.39007	93.94839	93.54971	93.19055	92.86772
8.375	98.92905	97.95375	97.06634	96.25965	95.52713	94.86072	94.26088	93.71648	93.22482	92.78158	92.38277	92.02476
8.50	98.81085	97.72924	96.74632	95.85393	95.04458	94.31140	93.64809	93.04883	92.50830	92.02160	91.58424	91.19210
8.625	98.69280	97.50530	96.42747	95.45014	94.56485	93.76388	93.04012	92.38707	91.79875	91.26968	90.79484	90.36961
8.75	98.57491	97.28191	96.10980	95.04828	94.08793	93.22012	92.43694	91.73115	91.09611	90.52573	90.01444	89.55715
8.875	98.45717	97.05909	95.79328	94.64833	93.61379	92.68010	91.83851	91.08102	90.40030	89.78965	89.24295	88.75459
9.00	98.33959	96.83683	95.47793	94.25030	93.14243	92.14379	91.24478	90.43661	89.71125	89.06136	88.48025	87.96179
9.125	98.22217	96.61512	95.16373	93.85417	92.67382	91.61117	90.65572	89.79787	89.02888	88.34076	87.72623	87.17863
9.25	98.10490	96.39398	94.85068	93.45992	92.20794	91.08221	90.07128	89.16476	88.35314	87.62777	86.98078	86.40497
9.50	97.87083	95.95335	94.22802	92.67706	91.28434	90.03514	88.91614	87.91518	87.02123	86.22426	85.51516	84.88564
9.75	97.63738	95.51493	93.60990	91.90165	90.37147	89.00240	87.77904	86.68744	85.71496	84.85013	84.08256	83.40281
10.00	97.40455	95.07871	92.99629	91.13361	89.46922	87.98376	86.65968	85.48114	84.43381	83.50472	82.68215	81.95551
10.25	97.17233	94.64467	92.38716	90.37286	88.57746	86.97902	85.55778	84.29588	83.17725	82.18736	81.31314	80.54278
10.75	96.70975	93.78312	91.18221	88.87297	86.82486	85.01046	83.40516	81.98690	80.73586	79.63428	78.66623	77.81740

Yield	13 Years	14 Years	15 Years	16 Years	17 Years	18 Years	19 Years	20 Years	22 Years	25 Years	27 Years	Full Term
4.25	127.66489	128.99515	130.22871	131.36833	132.41662	133.37603	134.24888	135.03736	136.36924	137.78128	138.35025	138.67066
4.500	125.00159	126.18058	127.27113	128.27613	129.19829	130.04016	130.80418	131.49263	132.65129	133.87231	134.36122	134.63510
4.75	122.40991	123.44619	124.40236	125.28132	126.08583	126.81847	127.48170	128.07785	129.07750	130.12464	130.54128	130.77346
5.00	119.88774	120.78948	121.61945	122.38050	123.07535	123.70656	124.27655	124.78762	125.64148	126.53052	126.88203	127.07690
5.25	117.43304	118.20803	118.91956	119.57040	120.16314	120.70025	121.18406	121.61678	122.33711	123.08263	123.37554	123.53707
5.375	116.23038	116.94479	117.59990	118.19837	118.74275	119.23542	119.67866	120.07459	120.73248	121.41133	121.67720	121.82345
5.50	115.04385	115.69950	116.29997	116.84785	117.34559	117.79550	118.19975	118.56041	119.15861	119.77401	120.01428	120.14609
5.625	113.87321	114.47187	115.01945	115.51846	115.97124	116.37999	116.74682	117.07368	117.61402	118.16986	118.38587	118.50407
5.750	112.71824	113.26162	113.75803	114.20983	114.61927	114.98844	115.31933	115.61380	116.10044	116.59808	116.79114	116.89651
5.875	111.57870	112.06848	112.51537	112.92160	113.28928	113.62038	113.91678	114.18024	114.61482	115.05790	115.22925	115.32252
6.00	110.45437	110.89219	111.29117	111.65341	111.98086	112.27537	112.53868	112.77244	113.15733	113.54857	113.69939	113.78128
6.125	109.34502	109.73248	110.08514	110.40491	110.69361	110.95296	111.18454	111.38987	111.72735	112.06936	112.20079	112.27196
6.25	108.25043	108.58910	108.89695	109.17576	109.42716	109.65272	109.85388	110.03202	110.32426	110.61955	110.73267	110.79377
6.375	107.17040	107.46178	107.72633	107.96562	108.18112	108.37423	108.54623	108.69836	108.94749	109.19846	109.29429	109.34592
6.50	106.10470	106.35029	106.57298	106.77416	106.95512	107.11707	107.26115	107.38842	107.59645	107.80540	107.88493	107.92767
6.625	105.05312	105.25436	105.43662	105.60106	105.74879	105.88084	105.99817	106.10169	106.27058	106.43971	106.50389	106.53828
6.750	104.01546	104.17377	104.31697	104.44600	104.56179	104.66515	104.75687	104.83770	104.96933	105.10076	105.15047	105.17704
6.875	102.99152	103.10827	103.21374	103.30867	103.39374	103.46959	103.53682	103.59598	103.69217	103.78791	103.82401	103.84326
7.000	101.98109	102.05763	102.12669	102.18876	102.24432	102.29380	102.33760	102.37609	102.43856	102.50056	102.52387	102.53626
7.25	100.00000	100.00000	100.00000	100.00000	100.00000	100.00000	100.00000	100.00000	100.00000	100.00000	100.00000	100.00000
7.500	98.07064	97.99909	97.93484	97.87738	97.82620	97.78085	97.74091	97.70597	97.64969	97.59450	97.57401	97.56323
7.625	97.12490	97.01093	96.92471	96.84016	96.76495	96.69804	96.63984	96.58869	96.50464	96.42603	96.39628	96.38066
7.75	96.19153	96.05315	95.92921	95.81863	95.72040	95.63357	95.55727	95.49071	95.38386	95.27971	95.24130	95.22119
7.875	95.27036	95.10026	94.94812	94.81253	94.69223	94.58603	94.49283	94.41162	94.28150	94.15504	94.10855	94.08427
8.00	94.36121	94.16049	93.98118	93.82159	93.68017	93.55547	93.44617	93.35106	93.19893	93.05152	92.99750	92.96937
8.125	93.46391	93.23364	93.02818	92.84555	92.68397	92.54156	92.41695	92.30804	92.13572	91.96867	91.90764	91.87594
8.250	92.57828	92.31950	92.08889	91.88416	91.70317	91.54399	91.40482	91.28400	91.09146	90.90601	90.83848	90.80349
8.375	91.70416	91.41788	91.16309	90.93715	90.73768	90.56246	90.40945	90.27679	90.06575	89.86309	89.78952	89.75151
8.50	90.84137	90.52859	90.25054	90.00430	89.78717	89.59667	89.43032	89.28665	89.05820	88.83946	88.76031	88.71591
8.625	89.98976	89.65143	89.35105	89.08536	88.85136	88.64632	88.46771	88.31324	88.06841	87.83468	87.75037	87.70703
8.75	89.14917	88.78623	88.46439	88.18008	87.92999	87.71113	87.52072	87.35623	87.09601	86.84833	86.75927	86.71360
8.875	88.31943	87.93279	87.59037	87.28824	87.02282	86.79081	86.58922	86.41530	86.14063	85.87999	85.78657	85.73879
9.00	87.50039	87.09094	86.72877	86.40961	86.12957	85.88510	85.67293	85.49012	85.20193	84.92926	84.83184	84.78214
9.125	86.69190	86.26050	85.87939	85.54396	85.25001	84.99371	84.77156	84.58037	84.27953	83.99575	83.89467	83.84324
9.25	85.89380	85.44130	85.04205	84.69108	84.38390	84.11639	83.88481	83.68576	83.37311	83.07906	82.97466	82.92168
9.50	84.32818	83.83592	83.40266	83.02275	82.69105	82.40291	82.15409	81.94075	81.60686	81.29469	81.18456	81.12896
9.75	82.80236	82.27346	81.80910	81.40293	81.04918	80.74264	80.47859	80.25275	79.90058	79.57327	79.45853	79.40089
10.00	81.31522	80.75263	80.25991	79.82999	79.45650	79.13365	78.85624	78.61956	78.25180	77.91204	77.79369	77.73455
10.25	79.86565	79.27216	78.75366	78.30238	77.91129	77.57407	77.28502	77.03903	76.65818	76.30840	76.18733	76.12714
10.75	77.07499	76.42750	75.86462	75.37713	74.95675	74.59607	74.28844	74.02792	73.62748	73.26405	73.13984	73.07873

Entry is the percentage of loan balance to give the desired yield to the selected time.

Price of a Mortgage to Give a Specified Yield
Conversion of Interest to Principal or Principal to Interest
7.50% Interest Rate 30 Years Amortization Schedule

Desired Yield	1 Year	2 Years	3 Years	4 Years	5 Years	6 Years	7 Years	8 Years	9 Years	10 Years	11 Years	12 Years
4.500	102.91603	105.67728	108.28974	110.75910	113.09079	115.28998	117.36157	119.31023	121.14039	122.85626	124.46183	125.96088
4.75	102.66946	105.19093	107.57060	109.81433	111.92770	113.91602	115.78432	117.53738	119.17974	120.71570	122.14935	123.48457
5.00	102.42354	104.70703	106.85675	108.87862	110.77829	112.56110	114.23214	115.79620	117.25786	118.62142	119.89100	121.07046
5.250	102.17827	104.22557	106.14813	107.95187	109.64237	111.22495	112.70460	114.08610	115.37393	116.57235	117.68540	118.71686
5.50	101.93366	103.74653	105.44473	107.03400	108.51980	109.90728	111.20131	112.40649	113.52716	114.56745	115.53121	116.42212
5.625	101.81159	103.50792	105.09496	106.57836	107.96346	109.25529	110.45862	111.57793	112.61747	113.58123	114.47299	115.29632
5.750	101.68969	103.26991	104.74648	106.12491	107.41039	108.60783	109.72184	110.75678	111.71677	112.60567	113.42715	114.18464
5.875	101.56796	103.03250	104.39928	105.67363	106.86058	107.96486	108.99092	109.94297	110.82497	111.64065	112.39351	113.08688
6.000	101.44638	102.79568	104.05335	105.22452	106.31400	107.32634	108.26580	109.13642	109.94198	110.68603	111.37194	112.00285
6.125	101.32496	102.55947	103.70870	104.77756	105.77063	106.69224	107.54645	108.33707	109.06770	109.74171	110.36227	110.93237
6.250	101.20371	102.32384	103.36531	104.33274	105.23045	106.06253	106.83280	107.54484	108.20204	108.80755	109.36436	109.87525
6.375	101.08262	102.08881	103.02319	103.89005	104.69345	105.43718	106.12481	106.75968	107.34491	107.88345	108.37805	108.83130
6.50	100.96169	101.85438	102.68232	103.44948	104.15960	104.81616	105.42244	105.98150	106.49622	106.96928	107.40320	107.80036
6.625	100.84092	101.62053	102.34270	103.01102	103.62888	104.19944	104.72564	105.21026	105.65588	106.04923	106.43967	106.78224
6.750	100.72031	101.38727	102.00433	102.57466	103.10128	103.58697	104.03435	104.44587	104.82380	105.17028	105.48731	105.77676
6.875	100.59986	101.15460	101.66719	102.14039	102.57677	102.97874	103.34854	103.68828	103.99990	104.28523	104.54599	104.78376
7.000	100.47957	100.92252	101.33130	101.70820	102.05534	102.37471	102.66816	102.93741	103.18408	103.40966	103.61555	103.80306
7.125	100.35943	100.69102	100.99664	101.27807	101.53697	101.77485	101.99316	102.19322	102.37627	102.54346	102.69587	102.83450
7.25	100.23946	100.46010	100.66320	100.85001	101.02163	101.17914	101.32350	101.45563	101.57637	101.68652	101.78680	101.87791
7.500	100.00000	100.00000	100.00000	100.00000	100.00000	100.00000	100.00000	100.00000	100.00000	100.00000	100.00000	100.00000
7.75	99.76117	99.54222	99.34165	99.15810	98.99030	98.83707	98.69732	98.57004	98.45431	98.34926	98.25409	98.16806
7.875	99.64199	99.31419	99.01428	98.74016	98.48987	98.26160	98.05367	97.86454	97.69277	97.53705	97.39615	97.26893
8.00	99.52298	99.08673	98.68811	98.32422	97.99238	97.69010	97.41510	97.16527	96.93866	96.73347	96.54804	96.38084
8.125	99.40412	98.85985	98.36314	97.91027	97.49779	97.12253	96.78156	96.47218	96.19190	95.93844	95.70966	95.50363
8.25	99.28541	98.63353	98.03936	97.49829	97.00609	96.55886	96.15300	95.78520	95.45242	95.15184	94.88088	94.63715
8.375	99.16687	98.40779	97.71676	97.08828	96.51727	95.99907	95.52940	95.10429	94.72013	94.37358	94.06157	93.78126
8.50	99.04848	98.18261	97.39534	96.68022	96.03130	95.44313	94.91069	94.42938	93.99497	93.60357	93.25161	92.93582
8.625	98.93025	97.95799	97.07510	96.27411	95.54818	94.89101	94.29686	93.76042	93.27685	92.84171	92.45090	92.10068
8.75	98.81217	97.73395	96.75604	95.86994	95.06787	94.34268	93.68784	93.09735	92.56571	92.08790	91.65931	91.27571
8.875	98.69426	97.51046	96.43814	95.46770	94.59037	93.79812	93.08361	92.44011	91.86147	91.34206	90.87673	90.46076
9.00	98.57650	97.28754	96.12140	95.06737	94.11565	93.25729	92.48412	91.78865	91.14556	90.60409	90.10305	89.65571
9.125	98.45889	97.06517	95.80582	94.66895	93.64370	92.72018	91.88933	91.14292	90.47340	89.87390	89.33815	88.86042
9.25	98.34144	96.84337	95.49140	94.27243	93.17451	92.18675	91.29921	90.50286	89.78943	89.15140	88.58193	88.07476
9.375	98.22415	96.62212	95.17812	93.87779	92.70805	91.65697	90.71371	89.86841	89.11207	88.43651	87.83427	87.29859
9.50	98.10701	96.40142	94.86599	93.48504	92.24430	91.13082	90.13280	89.23953	88.44126	87.72913	87.09508	86.53180
9.750	97.87320	95.96169	94.24515	92.70513	91.32491	90.08931	88.98458	87.99825	87.11900	86.33657	85.64166	85.02584
10.00	97.64001	95.52417	93.62884	91.93263	90.41619	89.06201	87.85425	86.77861	85.82211	84.97305	84.22083	83.55587
10.25	97.40743	95.08884	93.01702	91.16746	89.51801	88.04870	86.74151	85.58019	84.55006	83.63791	82.83179	82.12095
10.500	97.17548	94.65569	92.40967	90.40955	88.63025	87.04919	85.64607	84.40260	83.30234	82.33049	81.47375	80.72014
11.00	96.71340	93.79588	91.20819	88.91521	86.88546	85.09077	83.50593	82.10836	80.87787	79.79635	78.84764	78.01726

Yield	13 Years	14 Years	15 Years	16 Years	17 Years	18 Years	19 Years	20 Years	22 Years	25 Years	27 Years	Full Term
4.500	127.35700	128.65360	129.85388	130.96088	131.97747	132.90635	133.75008	134.51104	135.79354	137.14836	137.69233	137.99779
4.75	124.72501	125.87416	126.93530	127.91154	128.80583	129.62092	130.35945	131.02388	132.13960	133.31116	133.77859	134.03970
5.00	122.16349	123.17355	124.10393	124.95775	125.73795	126.44729	127.08840	127.66376	128.62638	129.63111	130.02945	130.25081
5.250	119.67036	120.54930	121.35689	122.09618	122.77004	123.38118	123.93217	124.42541	125.24765	126.10070	126.43678	126.62257
5.50	117.24364	117.99904	118.69140	119.32362	119.89846	120.41850	120.88619	121.30382	121.99748	122.71283	122.99288	123.14689
5.625	116.05458	116.75094	117.38839	117.96955	118.49769	118.97471	119.40317	119.78530	120.41884	121.07023	121.32443	121.46386
5.750	114.88139	115.52048	116.10477	116.63699	117.11970	117.55531	117.94610	118.29419	118.87024	119.46075	119.69047	119.81615
5.875	113.72385	114.30738	114.84022	115.32496	115.76407	116.15984	116.51444	116.82991	117.35103	117.88362	118.09015	118.20285
6.000	112.58173	113.11138	113.59442	114.03331	114.43039	114.78784	115.10770	115.39192	115.86055	116.33807	116.52265	116.62312
6.125	111.45480	111.93221	112.36706	112.76169	113.11827	113.43886	113.72559	113.97966	114.39817	114.82716	114.98776	115.07610
6.250	110.34284	110.76960	111.15784	111.50973	111.82730	112.11246	112.36700	112.59262	112.96327	113.33870	113.48290	113.56098
6.375	109.24563	109.62331	109.96647	110.27710	110.55710	110.80821	111.03208	111.23026	111.55526	111.88345	112.00911	112.07697
6.50	108.16296	108.49307	108.79263	109.06347	109.30730	109.52569	109.72016	109.89209	110.17353	110.45689	110.56504	110.62330
6.625	107.09460	107.37863	107.63606	107.86851	108.07751	108.26449	108.43077	108.57761	108.81752	109.05835	109.14998	109.19921
6.750	106.04036	106.27975	106.49646	106.69189	106.86739	107.02420	107.16348	107.28632	107.48667	107.68717	107.76322	107.80397
6.875	105.00003	105.19620	105.37355	105.53330	105.67657	105.80443	105.91786	106.01777	106.18042	106.34272	106.40408	106.43688
7.000	103.97340	104.12772	104.26706	104.39242	104.50471	104.60479	104.69346	104.77147	104.89825	105.02436	105.07189	105.09723
7.125	102.96028	103.07409	103.17672	103.26894	103.35145	103.42489	103.48988	103.54699	103.63962	103.73150	103.76602	103.78437
7.25	101.96047	102.03508	102.10227	102.16258	102.21646	102.26437	102.30671	102.34387	102.40404	102.46353	102.48581	102.49763
7.500	100.00000	100.00000	100.00000	100.00000	100.00000	100.00000	100.00000	100.00000	100.00000	100.00000	100.00000	100.00000
7.75	98.09048	98.02073	97.95821	97.90238	97.85275	97.80884	97.77022	97.73650	97.68230	97.62933	97.60974	97.59946
7.875	97.15437	97.05148	96.95938	96.87724	96.80430	96.73986	96.68325	96.63388	96.55466	96.47749	96.44904	96.43415
8.00	96.23044	96.09555	95.97459	95.86752	95.77224	95.68816	95.61440	95.55015	95.44725	95.34730	95.31017	95.29140
8.125	95.31854	95.15273	95.00467	94.87295	94.75627	94.65344	94.56334	94.48495	94.35963	94.23827	94.19381	94.17066
8.25	94.41847	94.22281	94.04832	93.89328	93.75611	93.63536	93.52970	93.43789	93.29137	93.14991	93.09825	93.07142
8.375	93.53007	93.30561	93.10567	92.92824	92.77147	92.63363	92.51316	92.40861	92.24207	92.08175	92.02340	91.99316
8.50	92.65318	92.40092	92.17650	91.97760	91.80207	91.64793	91.51338	91.39675	91.21132	91.03334	90.96768	90.93539
8.625	91.78761	91.50855	91.26060	91.04110	90.84764	90.67796	90.53003	90.40198	90.19873	90.00423	89.93388	89.89763
8.75	90.93322	90.62832	90.35774	90.11851	89.90791	89.72344	89.56282	89.42394	89.20391	88.99398	88.91830	88.87939
8.875	90.08984	89.76003	89.46771	89.20959	88.98263	88.78408	88.61141	88.46230	88.22649	88.00218	87.92156	87.88022
9.00	89.25731	88.90351	88.59032	88.31410	88.07154	87.85960	87.67551	87.51674	87.26610	87.02840	86.94323	86.89968
9.125	88.43548	88.05858	87.72534	87.43182	87.17438	86.94972	86.75482	86.58693	86.32239	86.07224	85.98290	85.93734
9.25	87.62419	87.22505	86.87260	86.56252	86.29091	86.05417	85.84905	85.67258	85.39500	85.13331	85.04015	84.99275
9.375	86.82329	86.40276	86.03187	85.70599	85.42088	85.17269	84.95791	84.77336	84.48360	84.21123	84.11458	84.06553
9.50	86.03263	85.59153	85.20298	84.86201	84.56406	84.30502	84.08112	83.88898	83.58785	83.30563	83.20579	83.15526
9.750	84.48146	84.00159	83.57995	83.21085	82.88912	82.61009	82.36953	82.16358	81.84199	81.54238	81.43706	81.38403
10.00	82.96951	82.45392	82.00201	81.60739	81.26427	80.96742	80.71213	80.49412	80.15491	79.84076	79.73103	79.67607
10.25	81.49568	80.94724	80.46772	80.05004	79.68776	79.37512	79.10690	78.87843	78.52421	78.19810	78.08492	78.02851
10.500	80.05889	79.48032	78.97572	78.53726	78.15792	77.83135	77.55189	77.31442	76.94758	76.61186	76.49607	76.43867
11.00	77.29225	76.66102	76.11322	75.63958	75.23182	74.88253	74.58509	74.33360	73.94788	73.59904	73.48025	73.42196

Entry is the percentage of loan balance to give the desired yield to the selected time.

Price of a Mortgage to Give a Specified Yield
Conversion of Interest to Principal or Principal to Interest
7.75% Interest Rate   30 Years Amortization Schedule

Desired Yield	1 Year	2 Years	3 Years	4 Years	Prepaid or Ballooned at 5 Years	6 Years	7 Years	8 Years	9 Years	10 Years	11 Years	12 Years
4.750	102.91272	105.66522	108.26415	110.71584	113.02628	115.20117	117.24593	119.16568	120.96530	122.64940	124.22235	125.68830
5.00	102.66642	105.17991	107.54727	109.77495	111.86906	113.83542	115.67952	117.40658	119.02154	120.52907	121.93361	123.23935
5.250	102.42079	104.69705	106.83565	108.84306	110.72542	112.48855	114.13795	115.67882	117.11610	118.45444	119.69824	120.85167
5.500	102.17580	104.21662	106.12924	107.92008	109.59519	111.16029	112.62080	113.98182	115.24818	116.42443	117.51488	118.52359
5.750	101.93147	103.73861	105.42802	107.00593	108.47820	109.85037	111.12766	112.31498	113.41698	114.43802	115.38223	116.25349
5.875	101.80954	103.50005	105.07934	106.55214	107.92463	109.20221	110.38997	111.49270	112.51490	113.46085	114.33452	115.13969
6.000	101.68778	103.26300	104.73194	106.10052	107.37430	108.55853	109.65813	110.67774	111.62173	112.49419	113.29901	114.03979
6.125	101.56618	103.02609	104.38581	105.65106	106.82720	107.91930	108.93209	109.87004	110.73734	111.53794	112.27554	112.95362
6.250	101.44474	102.78978	104.04096	105.20375	106.28332	107.28449	108.21181	109.06953	109.86167	110.59197	111.26397	111.88097
6.375	101.32346	102.55406	103.69737	104.75859	105.74262	106.65407	107.49723	108.27615	108.99460	109.65616	110.26414	110.82167
6.50	101.20235	102.31894	103.35504	104.31555	105.20510	106.02800	106.78831	107.48981	108.13606	108.73039	109.27591	109.77554
6.625	101.08139	102.08441	103.01396	103.87463	104.67073	105.40626	106.08500	106.71047	107.28595	107.81454	108.29912	108.74239
6.750	100.96060	101.85047	102.67414	103.43582	104.13948	104.78881	105.38725	105.93804	106.44418	106.90851	107.33364	107.72204
6.875	100.83997	101.61712	102.33556	102.99911	103.61135	104.17562	104.69502	105.17247	105.61067	106.01217	106.37932	106.71433
7.000	100.71949	101.38435	101.99822	102.56449	103.08632	103.56666	104.00826	104.41368	104.78532	105.12541	105.43602	105.71909
7.125	100.59918	101.15217	101.66212	102.13194	102.56436	102.96190	103.32692	103.66163	103.96806	104.24813	104.50360	104.73613
7.250	100.47902	100.92058	101.32725	101.70146	102.04545	102.36130	102.65096	102.91623	103.15879	103.38020	103.58193	103.76531
7.375	100.35903	100.68956	100.99361	101.27304	101.52958	101.76485	101.98033	102.17743	102.35743	102.52154	102.67086	102.80644
7.500	100.23919	100.45913	100.66119	100.84666	101.01673	101.17250	101.31499	101.44517	101.56390	101.67202	101.77027	101.85937
7.750	100.00000	100.00000	100.00000	100.00000	100.00000	100.00000	100.00000	100.00000	100.00000	100.00000	100.00000	100.00000
8.00	99.76144	99.54317	99.34364	99.16140	98.99512	98.84358	98.70563	98.58024	98.46643	98.36332	98.27007	98.18593
8.125	99.64240	99.31562	99.01726	98.74510	98.49708	98.27132	98.06607	97.87974	97.71083	97.55797	97.41992	97.29551
8.25	99.52351	99.08864	98.69208	98.33078	98.00195	97.70299	97.43154	97.18541	96.96256	96.76116	96.57948	96.41596
8.375	99.40479	98.86223	98.36808	97.91844	97.50970	97.13857	96.80200	96.49719	96.22157	95.97278	95.74864	95.54713
8.50	99.28622	98.63639	98.04527	97.50806	97.02033	96.57802	96.17740	95.81503	95.48778	95.19274	94.92726	94.68889
8.625	99.16781	98.41111	97.72365	97.09964	96.53382	96.02132	95.55770	95.13887	94.76110	94.42093	94.11523	93.84109
8.75	99.04955	98.18640	97.40319	96.69317	96.05014	95.46843	94.94286	94.46866	94.04146	93.65727	93.31243	93.00358
8.875	98.93145	97.96226	97.08391	96.28863	95.56927	94.91934	94.33284	93.80433	93.32879	92.90166	92.51876	92.17623
9.00	98.81351	97.73868	96.76580	95.88601	95.09122	94.37400	93.72760	93.14583	92.62302	92.15401	91.73408	91.35891
9.125	98.69573	97.51565	96.44885	95.48532	94.61594	93.83240	93.12710	92.49370	91.92407	91.41423	90.95830	90.55148
9.25	98.57810	97.29319	96.13305	95.08653	94.14344	93.29452	92.53131	91.84610	91.23188	90.68223	90.19131	89.75380
9.375	98.46062	97.07129	95.81841	94.68963	93.67368	92.76031	91.94017	91.20477	90.54636	89.95791	89.43298	88.96574
9.50	98.34330	96.84994	95.50492	94.29463	93.20666	92.22975	91.35365	90.56905	89.86746	89.24119	88.68322	88.18718
9.625	98.22614	96.62915	95.19258	93.90150	92.74236	91.70283	90.77172	89.93889	89.19510	88.53198	87.94191	87.41799
9.750	98.10914	96.40891	94.88137	93.51024	92.28075	91.17950	90.19434	89.31424	88.52921	87.83019	87.20896	86.65805
10.000	97.87559	95.97009	94.26237	92.73330	91.36558	90.14355	89.05305	88.08126	87.21659	86.44856	85.76769	85.16538
10.25	97.64265	95.53346	93.64787	91.96372	90.46101	89.12170	87.92949	86.86970	85.92907	85.09563	84.35859	83.70823
10.500	97.41034	95.09902	93.03785	91.20143	89.56692	88.11373	86.82337	85.67916	84.66611	83.77073	82.98089	82.28564
10.750	97.17864	94.66676	92.43227	90.44636	88.68317	87.11946	85.73439	84.50924	83.42722	82.47324	81.63379	80.89670
11.25	96.71707	93.80870	91.23430	88.95759	86.94620	85.17120	83.60673	82.22975	81.01963	79.95800	79.02842	78.21624

Yield	13 Years	14 Years	15 Years	16 Years	17 Years	18 Years	19 Years	20 Years	22 Years	25 Years	27 Years	Full Term
4.750	127.05116	128.31465	129.48226	130.55729	131.54288	132.44196	133.25729	133.99147	135.22604	136.52552	137.04540	137.33651
5.00	124.45025	125.57007	126.60233	127.55039	128.41741	129.20636	129.92004	130.56109	131.63513	132.75885	133.20558	133.45443
5.250	121.91867	122.90295	123.80803	124.63721	125.39362	126.08022	126.69976	127.25489	128.18155	129.14527	129.52598	129.73695
5.500	119.45439	120.31090	121.09653	121.81449	122.46782	123.05937	123.59183	124.06773	124.85926	125.67751	125.99872	126.17579
5.750	117.05546	117.79159	118.46512	119.07911	119.63644	120.13981	120.59178	120.99474	121.66250	122.34868	122.61633	122.76312
5.875	115.87990	116.55850	117.17862	117.74322	118.25508	118.71681	119.13088	119.49958	120.10947	120.73429	120.97725	121.11015
6.000	114.71997	115.34276	115.91117	116.42805	116.89606	117.31771	117.69536	118.03122	118.58578	119.15221	119.37177	119.49156
6.125	113.57544	114.14409	114.66245	115.13322	115.55896	115.94204	116.28473	116.58912	117.09079	117.60167	117.79907	117.90649
6.250	112.44609	112.96223	113.43214	113.85839	114.24338	114.58937	114.89849	115.17272	115.62387	116.08192	116.25835	116.35411
6.375	111.33168	111.79692	112.21996	112.60321	112.94893	113.25926	113.53616	113.78151	114.18440	114.59224	114.74883	114.83360
6.50	110.23201	110.64790	111.02559	111.36734	111.67524	111.95127	112.19726	112.41495	112.77179	113.13191	113.26975	113.34417
6.625	109.14686	109.51492	109.84875	110.15044	110.42191	110.66498	110.88134	111.07256	111.38543	111.70025	111.82037	111.88505
6.750	108.07602	108.39772	108.68915	108.95219	109.18859	109.39999	109.58793	109.75383	110.02478	110.29659	110.39997	110.45550
6.875	107.01928	107.29607	107.54651	107.77226	107.97491	108.15590	108.31660	108.45828	108.68925	108.92027	109.00785	109.05478
7.000	105.97643	106.20972	106.42054	106.61035	106.78051	106.93230	107.06690	107.18543	107.37831	107.57065	107.64334	107.68218
7.125	104.94727	105.13844	105.31098	105.46612	105.60504	105.72881	105.83843	105.93483	106.09142	106.24711	106.30577	106.33703
7.250	103.93160	104.08199	104.21755	104.33930	104.44817	104.54505	104.63075	104.70602	104.82807	104.94905	104.99449	105.01864
7.375	102.92924	103.04014	103.14000	103.22956	103.30956	103.38065	103.44346	103.49856	103.58774	103.67588	103.70887	103.72637
7.500	101.93997	102.01268	102.07805	102.13662	102.18887	102.23525	102.27617	102.31202	102.36994	102.42702	102.44832	102.45958
7.750	100.00000	100.00000	100.00000	100.00000	100.00000	100.00000	100.00000	100.00000	100.00000	100.00000	100.00000	100.00000
8.00	98.11020	98.04222	97.98140	97.92718	97.87905	97.83655	97.79922	97.76668	97.71450	97.66369	97.64496	97.63516
8.125	97.18366	97.08339	96.99379	96.91402	96.84329	96.78090	96.72619	96.67856	96.60229	96.52825	96.50106	96.48686
8.25	96.26913	96.13767	96.02033	95.91600	95.82361	95.74222	95.67093	95.60894	95.50986	95.41398	95.37887	95.36059
8.375	95.36643	95.20484	95.06080	94.93287	94.81973	94.72018	94.63310	94.55746	94.43680	94.32037	94.27788	94.25581
8.50	94.47540	94.28471	94.11495	93.96437	93.83136	93.71448	93.61235	93.52376	93.38269	93.24698	93.19760	93.17202
8.625	93.59585	93.37710	93.18258	93.01025	92.85823	92.72480	92.60837	92.50748	92.34714	92.19333	92.13755	92.10873
8.75	92.72764	92.48180	92.26346	92.07028	91.90007	91.75086	91.62081	91.50828	91.32974	91.15899	91.09726	91.06565
8.875	91.87059	91.59862	91.35739	91.14420	90.95661	90.79235	90.64938	90.52581	90.33012	90.14352	90.07627	90.04171
9.00	91.02455	90.72739	90.46414	90.23179	90.02758	89.84901	89.69376	89.55974	89.34790	89.14649	89.07414	89.03705
9.125	90.18935	89.86792	89.58352	89.33281	89.11274	88.92053	88.75364	88.60975	88.38290	88.16750	88.09044	88.05103
9.25	89.36485	89.02003	88.71532	88.44704	88.21184	88.00666	87.82874	87.67553	87.43421	87.20615	87.12474	87.08322
9.375	88.55088	88.18355	87.85934	87.57425	87.32462	87.10713	86.91875	86.75674	86.50203	86.26203	86.17663	86.13319
9.50	87.74730	87.35829	87.01538	86.71422	86.45084	86.22166	86.02340	85.85311	85.58585	85.33478	85.24571	85.20053
9.625	86.95395	86.54410	86.18326	85.86673	85.59027	85.35000	85.14241	84.96431	84.68532	84.42400	84.33160	84.28484
9.750	86.17070	85.74080	85.36277	85.03159	84.74267	84.49189	84.27549	84.09007	83.80012	83.52935	83.43391	83.38574
10.000	84.63390	84.16621	83.75598	83.39747	83.08550	82.81537	82.58285	82.38412	82.07446	81.78700	81.68632	81.63576
10.25	83.13575	82.63324	82.19356	81.81026	81.47754	81.19017	80.94341	80.73303	80.40641	80.10499	80.00009	79.94769
10.500	81.67517	81.14064	80.67410	80.26839	79.91710	79.61442	79.35517	79.13468	78.79361	78.48072	78.37251	78.31874
10.750	80.25110	79.68720	79.19625	78.77037	78.40251	78.08636	77.81624	77.58706	77.23384	76.91171	76.80101	76.74628
11.25	77.50837	76.89315	76.36016	75.90009	75.50467	75.16651	74.87901	74.63630	74.26488	73.93016	73.81659	73.76101

Entry is the percentage of loan balance to give the desired yield to the selected time.

Price of a Mortgage to Give a Specified Yield
Conversion of Interest to Principal or Principal to Interest

8.00% Interest Rate   30 Years Amortization Schedule

Desired Yield	1 Year	2 Years	3 Years	4 Years	Prepaid or Ballooned at 5 Years	6 Years	7 Years	8 Years	9 Years	10 Years	11 Years	12 Years
5.000	102.90939	105.65310	108.23847	110.67245	112.96165	115.11230	117.13034	119.02136	120.79069	122.44334	123.98406	125.41736
5.250	102.66338	105.16884	107.52385	109.73544	111.81031	113.75476	115.57477	117.27599	118.86377	120.34316	121.71894	122.99560
5.500	102.41802	104.68702	106.81446	108.80739	110.67245	112.41595	114.04380	115.56163	116.97473	118.28809	119.50642	120.63418
5.750	102.17332	104.20763	106.11028	107.88820	109.54792	111.09559	112.53703	113.87770	115.12276	116.27706	117.34519	118.33146
6.000	101.92926	103.73064	105.41125	106.97778	108.43653	109.79343	111.05404	112.22362	113.30708	114.30908	115.23396	116.08584
6.125	101.80748	103.49305	105.06366	106.52584	107.88572	109.14908	110.32134	111.40759	112.41261	113.34091	114.19671	114.98397
6.250	101.68585	103.25605	104.71734	106.07605	107.33814	108.50919	109.59444	110.59882	111.52693	112.38313	113.17148	113.89579
6.375	101.56439	103.01965	104.37229	105.62842	106.79377	107.87371	108.87329	109.79722	110.64995	111.43562	112.15813	112.82113
6.500	101.44309	102.78385	104.02851	105.18292	106.25258	107.24262	108.15783	109.00275	109.78157	110.49826	111.15651	111.75979
6.625	101.32196	102.54864	103.68598	104.73956	105.71456	106.61587	107.44803	108.21532	108.92170	109.57092	110.16647	110.71161
6.750	101.20098	102.31402	103.34471	104.29831	105.17970	105.99345	106.74384	107.43487	108.07026	108.65351	109.18787	109.67639
6.875	101.08016	102.07999	103.00470	103.85917	104.64796	105.37531	106.04520	106.66133	107.22715	107.74589	108.22056	108.65397
7.000	100.95951	101.84654	102.66592	103.42212	104.11933	104.76144	105.35208	105.89464	106.39228	106.84795	107.26439	107.64417
7.125	100.83901	101.61369	102.32839	102.98717	103.59379	104.15178	104.66441	105.13473	105.56558	105.95959	106.31924	106.64681
7.250	100.71867	101.38142	101.99209	102.55428	103.07133	103.54633	103.98217	104.38155	104.74695	105.08070	105.38496	105.66174
7.375	100.59850	101.14973	101.65703	102.12347	102.55192	102.94504	103.30530	103.63501	103.93630	104.21115	104.46141	104.68878
7.500	100.47848	100.91863	101.32319	101.69470	102.03554	102.34788	102.63376	102.89507	103.13356	103.35085	103.54845	103.72776
7.625	100.35862	100.68810	100.99057	101.26790	101.52218	101.75483	101.96751	102.16187	102.33865	102.49970	102.64597	102.77854
7.750	100.23892	100.45816	100.65917	100.84330	101.01181	101.16585	101.30649	101.43472	101.55147	101.65757	101.75382	101.84094
8.000	100.00000	100.00000	100.00000	100.00000	100.00000	100.00000	100.00000	100.00000	100.00000	100.00000	100.00000	100.00000
8.25	99.76171	99.54414	99.34564	99.16471	98.99996	98.85009	98.71395	98.59042	98.47852	98.37733	98.28599	98.20371
8.375	99.64280	99.31707	99.02026	98.75005	98.50430	98.28105	98.07847	97.89491	97.72884	97.57883	97.44359	97.32194
8.50	99.52405	99.09056	98.69606	98.33736	98.01154	97.71590	97.44799	97.20552	96.98641	96.78875	96.61079	96.45089
8.625	99.40546	98.86463	98.37305	97.92664	97.52164	97.15463	96.82244	96.52217	96.25117	96.00701	95.78744	95.59041
8.750	99.28703	98.63926	98.05122	97.51787	97.03460	96.59720	96.20179	95.84482	95.52305	95.23350	94.97343	94.74035
8.875	99.16875	98.41446	97.73056	97.11104	96.55039	96.04358	95.58599	95.17341	94.80196	94.46812	94.16866	93.90059
9.000	99.05063	98.19022	97.41108	96.70615	96.06900	95.49375	94.97502	94.50788	94.08784	93.71080	93.37299	93.07099
9.125	98.93266	97.96655	97.09276	96.30318	95.59041	94.94768	94.36882	93.84817	93.38061	92.96142	92.58632	92.25139
9.25	98.81485	97.74343	96.77560	95.90213	95.11461	94.40535	93.76735	93.19424	92.68020	92.21991	91.80854	91.44168
9.375	98.69720	97.52087	96.45960	95.50299	94.64157	93.86672	93.17059	92.54603	91.98653	91.48616	91.03953	90.64172
9.50	98.57971	97.29888	96.14476	95.10574	94.17128	93.33177	92.57848	91.90348	91.29954	90.76010	90.27919	89.85138
9.625	98.46236	97.07744	95.83106	94.71038	93.70372	92.80047	91.99099	91.26654	90.61916	90.04164	89.52741	89.07053
9.750	98.34518	96.85655	95.51851	94.31690	93.23888	92.27280	91.40809	90.63516	89.94532	89.33068	88.78408	88.29904
9.875	98.22815	96.63622	95.20710	93.92528	92.77674	91.74872	90.82972	90.00928	89.27795	88.62714	88.04910	87.53679
10.00	98.11127	96.41644	94.89682	93.53553	92.31727	91.22822	90.25586	89.38886	88.61698	87.93094	87.32236	86.78365
10.250	97.87799	95.97852	94.27966	92.76156	91.40633	90.19784	89.12150	88.16417	87.31398	86.56020	85.89320	85.30423
10.500	97.64532	95.54280	93.66698	91.99491	90.50593	89.18144	88.00472	86.96069	86.03579	85.21782	84.49580	83.85983
10.750	97.41326	95.10926	93.05877	91.23551	89.61592	88.17883	86.90521	85.77802	84.78191	83.90315	83.12938	82.44952
11.000	97.18182	94.67789	92.45497	90.48330	88.73620	87.18979	85.82270	84.61576	83.55183	82.61555	81.79318	81.07241
11.500	96.72077	93.82160	91.26051	89.00012	87.00708	85.25170	83.70753	82.35100	81.16111	80.11916	79.20849	78.41427

Yield	13 Years	14 Years	15 Years	16 Years	17 Years	18 Years	19 Years	20 Years	22 Years	25 Years	27 Years	Full Term
5.000	126.74748	127.97842	129.11398	130.15771	131.11299	131.98297	132.77063	133.47878	134.66683	135.91283	136.40951	136.68685
5.250	124.17741	125.26839	126.27233	127.19279	128.03515	128.79657	129.48605	130.10437	131.13795	132.21544	132.64225	132.87933
5.500	121.67555	122.63450	123.51474	124.31979	125.05296	125.71734	126.31588	126.85132	127.74309	128.66718	129.03091	129.23191
5.750	119.23991	120.07438	120.83846	121.53553	122.16878	122.74121	123.25561	123.71465	124.47638	125.26100	125.56788	125.73658
6.000	116.86856	117.58576	118.24082	118.83695	119.37716	119.86426	120.30091	120.68958	121.33222	121.99020	122.24593	122.38578
6.125	115.70642	116.36756	116.97068	117.51886	118.01500	118.46181	118.86183	119.21748	119.80442	120.40357	120.63570	120.76232
6.250	114.55965	115.16642	115.71924	116.22109	116.67473	117.08276	117.44761	117.77158	118.30527	118.84843	119.05821	119.17234
6.375	113.42803	113.98206	114.48621	114.94329	115.35595	115.72667	116.05774	116.35135	116.83415	117.32405	117.51266	117.61500
6.500	112.31135	112.81423	113.27126	113.68511	114.05828	114.39310	114.69175	114.95627	115.39045	115.82969	115.99826	116.08949
6.625	111.20939	111.66266	112.07411	112.44622	112.78133	113.08163	113.34916	113.58582	113.97356	114.36465	114.51427	114.59504
6.750	110.12192	110.52712	110.89446	111.22628	111.52473	111.79184	112.02951	112.23949	112.58291	112.92825	113.05995	113.13086
6.875	109.04875	109.40734	109.73203	110.02495	110.28810	110.52352	110.73235	110.91680	111.21791	111.51981	111.63458	111.69621
7.000	107.98966	108.30309	108.58654	108.84194	109.07108	109.27566	109.45723	109.61726	109.87802	110.13868	110.23746	110.29037
7.125	106.94444	107.21412	107.45770	107.67690	107.87333	108.04848	108.20374	108.34040	108.56270	108.78424	108.86792	108.91263
7.250	105.91291	106.14021	106.34525	106.52955	106.69449	106.84138	106.97143	107.08577	107.27140	107.45585	107.52530	107.56231
7.375	104.89485	105.08111	105.24892	105.39957	105.53422	105.65400	105.75990	105.85290	106.00361	106.15291	106.20896	106.23874
7.500	103.89008	104.03660	104.16845	104.28666	104.39219	104.48595	104.56875	104.64136	104.75882	104.87484	104.91826	104.94127
7.625	102.89839	103.00645	103.10357	103.19053	103.26808	103.33688	103.39756	103.45072	103.53655	103.62107	103.65260	103.66926
7.750	101.91961	101.99045	102.05403	102.11090	102.16155	102.20643	102.24596	102.28055	102.33630	102.39103	102.41138	102.42211
8.000	100.00000	100.00000	100.00000	100.00000	100.00000	100.00000	100.00000	100.00000	100.00000	100.00000	100.00000	100.00000
8.25	98.12979	98.06356	98.00440	97.95175	97.90510	97.86397	97.82791	97.79652	97.74629	97.69756	97.67967	97.67033
8.375	97.21277	97.11508	97.02793	96.95046	96.88191	96.82153	96.76867	96.72271	96.64941	96.57831	96.55232	96.53879
8.50	96.30757	96.17948	96.06536	95.96405	95.87450	95.79573	95.72685	95.66704	95.57169	95.47972	95.44617	95.42876
8.625	95.41403	95.25658	95.11648	94.99226	94.88259	94.78625	94.70211	94.62914	94.51301	94.40135	94.36074	94.33971
8.750	94.53197	94.34618	94.18106	94.03484	93.90591	93.79279	93.69412	93.60865	93.47288	93.34271	93.29553	93.27116
8.875	93.66123	93.44808	93.25888	93.09155	92.94419	92.81505	92.70255	92.60523	92.45090	92.30339	92.25008	92.22262
9.000	92.80165	92.56211	92.35013	92.16216	91.99790	91.85275	91.72710	91.61726	91.44670	91.28293	91.22394	91.19363
9.125	91.95306	91.68807	91.45342	91.24642	91.06457	90.90560	90.76746	90.64825	90.45989	90.28093	90.21667	90.18373
9.25	91.11532	90.82578	90.56972	90.34411	90.14615	89.97332	89.82332	89.69403	89.49012	89.29696	89.22782	89.19248
9.375	90.28826	89.97507	89.69844	89.45499	89.24166	89.05564	88.89438	88.75557	88.53704	88.33063	88.25698	88.21943
9.50	89.47173	89.13575	88.83936	88.57885	88.35085	88.15228	87.98036	87.83256	87.60028	87.38155	87.30375	87.26419
9.625	88.66558	88.30766	87.99231	87.71547	87.47348	87.26299	87.08098	86.92469	86.67952	86.44933	86.36772	86.32632
9.750	87.86967	87.49063	87.15708	86.86464	86.60932	86.38751	86.19595	86.03166	85.77441	85.53361	85.44850	85.40544
9.875	87.08384	86.68448	86.33349	86.02613	85.75813	85.52559	85.32500	85.15319	84.88465	84.63401	84.54571	84.50115
10.00	86.30795	85.88906	85.52135	85.19976	84.91968	84.67697	84.46787	84.28899	84.00990	83.75019	83.65898	83.61307
10.250	84.78544	84.32973	83.93070	83.58257	83.28013	83.01869	82.79402	82.60229	82.30423	82.02851	81.93229	81.88411
10.500	83.30103	82.81138	82.38369	82.01149	81.68894	81.41080	81.17237	80.96940	80.65501	80.36590	80.26565	80.21570
10.750	81.85363	81.33278	80.87896	80.48500	80.14443	79.85149	79.60098	79.38826	79.05995	78.75983	78.65641	78.60517
11.000	80.44221	79.89274	79.41518	79.00162	78.64500	78.33900	78.07798	77.85689	77.51687	77.20789	77.10210	77.04994
11.500	77.72329	77.12380	76.60533	76.15856	75.77522	75.44792	75.17010	74.93593	74.57840	74.25734	74.14879	74.09582

Entry is the percentage of loan balance to give the desired yield to the selected time.

Price of a Mortgage to Give a Specified Yield
Conversion of Interest to Principal or Principal to Interest
8.25% Interest Rate   30 Years Amortization Schedule

Desired Yield	1 Year	2 Years	3 Years	4 Years	5 Years	6 Years	7 Years	8 Years	9 Years	10 Years	11 Years	12 Years
						Prepaid or Ballooned at						
5.250	102.90603	105.64091	108.21268	110.62895	112.89692	115.02341	117.01485	118.87734	120.61663	122.23816	123.74705	125.14816
5.500	102.66031	105.15771	107.50033	109.69584	111.75147	113.67408	115.47011	117.14567	118.70651	120.15804	121.50540	122.75340
5.750	102.41524	104.67694	106.79320	108.77163	110.61941	112.34332	113.94974	115.44468	116.83380	118.12244	119.31561	120.41806
6.000	102.17082	104.19859	106.09124	107.85623	109.50057	111.03087	112.45333	113.77379	114.99773	116.13032	117.17639	118.14052
6.250	101.92704	103.72263	105.39441	106.94956	108.39480	109.73646	110.98049	112.13243	113.19753	114.18067	115.08647	115.91924
6.375	101.80540	103.48555	105.04791	106.49946	107.84676	109.09594	110.25277	111.32265	112.31064	113.22147	114.05961	114.82921
6.500	101.68392	103.24907	104.70268	106.05152	107.30193	108.45983	109.53081	110.52005	111.43243	112.27253	113.04461	113.75267
6.625	101.56260	103.01318	104.35872	105.60572	106.76028	107.82811	108.81453	109.72455	110.56282	111.33372	112.04132	112.68945
6.750	101.44144	102.77789	104.01601	105.16204	106.22180	107.20072	108.10391	108.93609	109.70171	110.40493	111.04960	111.63936
6.875	101.32044	102.54318	103.67456	104.72048	105.68646	106.57766	107.39888	108.15460	108.84902	109.48604	110.06930	110.60222
7.000	101.19960	102.30907	103.33435	104.28120	105.15425	105.95888	106.69940	107.38002	108.00465	108.57694	109.10028	109.57785
7.125	101.07892	102.07554	102.99539	103.84366	104.62516	105.34435	106.00544	106.61228	107.16852	107.67751	108.14239	108.56609
7.250	100.95841	101.84260	102.65768	103.40839	104.09914	104.73405	105.31693	105.85132	106.34054	106.78764	107.19550	107.56676
7.375	100.83805	101.61024	102.32119	102.97519	103.57620	104.12794	104.63383	105.09707	105.52062	105.90723	106.25946	106.57970
7.500	100.71785	101.37847	101.98594	102.54405	103.05631	103.52599	103.95611	104.34947	104.70868	105.03616	105.33415	105.60473
7.625	100.59781	101.14726	101.65191	102.11497	102.53946	102.92817	103.28370	103.60845	103.90464	104.17433	104.41942	104.64170
7.750	100.47793	100.91667	101.31910	101.68793	102.02561	102.33445	102.61658	102.87396	103.10841	103.32162	103.51515	103.69044
7.875	100.35821	100.68664	100.98752	101.26292	101.51476	101.74481	101.95469	102.14593	102.31991	102.47794	102.62120	102.75080
8.000	100.23865	100.45718	100.65714	100.83994	101.00689	101.15920	101.29799	101.42430	101.53907	101.64318	101.73744	101.82261
8.250	100.00000	100.00000	100.00000	100.00000	100.00000	100.00000	100.00000	100.00000	100.00000	100.00000	100.00000	100.00000
8.50	99.76198	99.54511	99.34765	99.16803	99.00480	98.85661	98.72225	98.60059	98.49058	98.39128	98.30182	98.22139
8.625	99.64321	99.31852	99.02326	98.75501	98.51154	98.29078	98.09087	97.91007	97.74680	97.59960	97.46715	97.34822
8.750	99.52460	99.09250	98.70006	98.34396	98.02114	97.72882	97.46442	97.22559	97.01019	96.81624	96.64194	96.48562
8.875	99.40614	98.86704	98.37803	97.93486	97.53360	97.17069	96.84286	96.54711	96.28069	96.04111	95.82605	95.63343
9.000	99.28784	98.64215	98.05718	97.52770	97.04889	96.61638	96.22616	95.87456	95.55823	95.27410	95.01939	94.79153
9.125	99.16970	98.41782	97.73750	97.12247	96.56700	96.06585	95.61427	95.20788	94.84272	94.51514	94.22183	93.95976
9.25	99.05171	98.19406	97.41899	96.71917	96.08790	95.51909	95.00715	94.54703	94.13409	93.76412	93.43326	93.13801
9.375	98.93388	97.97085	97.10164	96.31778	95.61159	94.97605	94.40477	93.89195	93.43229	93.02096	92.65357	92.32613
9.50	98.81621	97.74821	96.78544	95.91830	95.13804	94.43671	93.80708	93.24258	92.73722	92.28556	91.88265	91.52399
9.625	98.69869	97.52612	96.47040	95.52071	94.66724	93.90105	93.21405	92.59887	92.04882	91.55783	91.12038	90.73147
9.750	98.58132	97.30459	96.15651	95.12501	94.19917	93.36904	92.62563	91.96076	91.36703	90.83770	90.36667	89.94842
9.875	98.46412	97.08361	95.84376	94.73119	93.73381	92.84066	92.04179	91.32821	90.69177	90.12506	89.62141	89.17473
10.000	98.34706	96.86319	95.53215	94.33923	93.27115	92.31587	91.46249	90.70116	90.02297	89.41984	88.88448	88.41028
10.125	98.23016	96.64332	95.22167	93.94913	92.81117	91.79465	90.88769	90.07956	89.36057	88.72196	88.15579	87.65493
10.250	98.11342	96.42400	94.91233	93.56088	92.35386	91.27698	90.31735	89.46336	88.70451	88.03132	87.43524	86.90787
10.500	97.88040	95.98700	94.29701	92.78989	91.44716	90.25216	89.18992	88.24695	87.41111	86.67145	86.01814	85.44233
10.750	97.64799	95.55219	93.68617	92.02618	90.55092	89.24122	88.07991	87.05154	86.14225	85.33959	84.63239	84.01062
11.000	97.41620	95.11955	93.07976	91.26969	89.66501	88.24396	86.98702	85.87672	84.89742	84.03510	83.27722	82.61253
11.250	97.18502	94.68907	92.47776	90.52033	88.78932	87.26017	85.91097	84.72212	83.67613	82.75737	81.95188	81.24718
11.750	96.72449	93.83456	91.28683	89.04276	87.06805	85.33226	83.80829	82.47208	81.30224	80.27977	79.38778	78.61127

Yield	13 Years	14 Years	15 Years	16 Years	17 Years	18 Years	19 Years	20 Years	22 Years	25 Years	27 Years	Full Term
5.250	126.44605	127.64502	128.74915	129.76224	130.68790	131.52950	132.29022	132.97305	134.11599	135.31033	135.78469	136.04882
5.500	123.90658	124.96924	125.94539	126.83884	127.65315	128.39168	129.05758	129.65380	130.64814	131.68098	132.08861	132.31440
5.750	121.43421	122.36827	123.22416	124.00559	124.71603	125.35876	125.93684	126.45314	127.31107	128.19688	128.54427	128.73570
6.000	119.02699	119.83980	120.58275	121.25937	121.87301	122.42677	122.92360	123.36624	124.09907	124.85119	125.14430	125.30497
6.250	116.68301	117.38160	118.01855	118.59720	119.12068	119.59191	120.01364	120.38843	121.00670	121.63743	121.88168	122.01488
6.375	115.53418	116.17817	116.76462	117.29672	117.77750	118.20975	118.59611	118.93905	119.50374	120.07809	120.29980	120.42040
6.500	114.40047	114.99150	115.52905	116.01618	116.45577	116.85051	117.20290	117.51530	118.02876	118.54944	118.74981	118.85851
6.625	113.28167	113.82133	114.31155	114.75523	115.15512	115.51376	115.83353	116.11665	116.58116	117.05078	117.23092	117.32840
6.750	112.17757	112.66741	113.11181	113.51354	113.87516	114.19907	114.48752	114.74260	115.16032	115.58139	115.74240	115.82930
6.875	111.08796	111.52948	111.92956	112.29076	112.61551	112.90603	113.16442	113.39263	113.76568	114.14059	114.28350	114.36043
7.000	110.01261	110.40730	110.76450	111.08659	111.37580	111.63422	111.86377	112.06626	112.39667	112.72773	112.85352	112.92106
7.125	108.95132	109.30062	109.61634	109.90069	110.15569	110.38325	110.58514	110.76302	111.05272	111.34213	111.45176	111.51046
7.250	107.90390	108.20921	108.48483	108.73275	108.95480	109.15272	109.32810	109.48242	109.73342	109.98319	110.07754	110.12793
7.375	106.87013	107.13283	107.36968	107.58246	107.77281	107.94226	108.09222	108.22401	108.43788	108.65027	108.73020	108.77279
7.500	105.84983	106.07124	106.27063	106.44952	106.60936	106.75148	106.87709	106.98735	107.16595	107.34277	107.40912	107.44437
7.625	104.84279	105.02423	105.18741	105.33364	105.46413	105.58001	105.68231	105.77198	105.91699	106.06012	106.11365	106.14202
7.750	103.84883	103.99156	104.11977	104.23452	104.33679	104.42750	104.50747	104.57749	104.69051	104.80174	104.84321	104.86513
7.875	102.86776	102.97302	103.06746	103.15187	103.22702	103.29358	103.35220	103.40346	103.48604	103.56707	103.59719	103.61306
8.000	101.89938	101.96839	102.03022	102.08542	102.13450	102.17792	102.21611	102.24946	102.30310	102.35558	102.37502	102.38524
8.250	100.00000	100.00000	100.00000	100.00000	100.00000	100.00000	100.00000	100.00000	100.00000	100.00000	100.00000	100.00000
8.50	98.14926	98.08474	98.02721	97.97610	97.93089	97.89109	97.85626	97.82599	97.77766	97.73094	97.71385	97.70496
8.625	97.24169	97.14652	97.06177	96.98658	96.92014	96.86172	96.81066	96.76634	96.69572	96.62764	96.60282	96.58994
8.750	96.34576	96.22098	96.11001	96.01166	95.92487	95.84866	95.78213	95.72445	95.63270	95.54454	95.51249	95.49590
8.875	95.46131	95.30794	95.17169	95.05110	94.94482	94.85161	94.77034	94.69997	94.58823	94.48117	94.44238	94.42235
9.000	94.58817	94.40718	94.24661	94.10467	93.97972	93.87027	93.77496	93.69254	93.56190	93.43711	93.39203	93.36882
9.125	93.72618	93.51854	93.33456	93.17212	93.02930	92.90436	92.79569	92.70183	92.55333	92.41191	92.36099	92.33483
9.25	92.87517	92.64182	92.43531	92.25321	92.09330	91.95319	91.83222	91.72752	91.56527	91.40516	91.34880	91.31993
9.375	92.03500	91.77685	91.54867	91.34772	91.17148	91.01767	90.88423	90.76927	90.58803	90.41644	90.35505	90.32368
9.50	91.20550	90.92344	90.67444	90.45542	90.26357	90.09635	89.95145	89.82677	89.63056	89.44537	89.37931	89.34564
9.625	90.38653	90.08143	89.81242	89.57608	89.36933	89.18935	89.03358	88.89917	88.68843	88.49154	88.42118	88.38541
9.750	89.57792	89.25063	88.96240	88.70950	88.48853	88.29641	88.13034	87.98780	87.76429	87.55457	87.48025	87.44256
9.875	88.77955	88.43088	88.12421	87.85546	87.62093	87.41727	87.24145	87.09072	86.85481	86.63411	86.55614	86.51670
10.000	87.99125	87.62201	87.29765	87.01374	86.76630	86.55169	86.36664	86.20820	85.96066	85.72978	85.64847	85.60745
10.125	87.21290	86.82385	86.48253	86.18415	85.92440	85.69941	85.50564	85.33994	85.08154	84.84123	84.75686	84.71441
10.250	86.44433	86.03626	85.67867	85.36647	85.09503	84.86019	84.65820	84.48568	84.21712	83.96811	83.88098	83.83724
10.500	84.93603	84.49209	84.10404	83.76607	83.47296	83.22000	83.00296	82.81805	82.53123	82.26687	82.17494	82.12904
10.750	83.46527	82.98827	82.57235	82.21100	81.89839	81.62927	81.39895	81.20319	80.90065	80.62345	80.52766	80.48009
11.000	82.03099	81.52358	81.08225	80.69977	80.36970	80.08625	79.84425	79.63909	79.32316	79.03539	78.93659	78.88776
11.250	80.63216	80.09687	79.63243	79.23093	78.88530	78.58922	78.33707	78.12382	77.79662	77.50035	77.39927	77.34958
11.750	77.93692	77.35289	76.84866	76.41492	76.04338	75.72667	75.45829	75.23244	74.88837	74.58050	74.47679	74.42633

Entry is the percentage of loan balance to give the desired yield to the selected time.

Price of a Mortgage to Give a Specified Yield
Conversion of Interest to Principal or Principal to Interest
8.50% Interest Rate   30 Years Amortization Schedule

Desired Yield	1 Year	2 Years	3 Years	4 Years	Prepaid or Ballooned at 5 Years	6 Years	7 Years	8 Years	9 Years	10 Years	11 Years	12 Years
5.500	102.90267	105.62868	108.18681	110.58535	112.83213	114.93453	116.89952	118.73368	120.44320	122.03394	123.51141	124.88079
5.750	102.65723	105.14654	107.47674	109.65614	111.69257	113.59340	115.36559	117.01566	118.54980	119.97378	121.29308	122.51283
6.000	102.41244	104.66682	106.77186	108.73578	110.56631	112.27070	113.85579	115.32800	116.69337	117.95755	119.12589	120.20338
6.250	102.16831	104.18951	106.07213	107.82419	109.45318	110.96616	112.36974	113.67012	114.87314	115.98424	117.00855	117.95086
6.500	101.92482	103.71459	105.37752	106.92127	108.35302	109.67950	110.90702	112.04146	113.08835	114.05285	114.93980	115.75373
6.625	101.80331	103.47803	105.03212	106.47303	107.80775	109.04280	110.18429	111.23791	112.20901	113.10257	113.92327	114.67547
6.750	101.68197	103.24206	104.68798	106.02694	107.26567	108.41048	109.46725	110.44146	111.33825	112.16242	112.91844	113.61050
6.875	101.56079	103.00668	104.34510	105.58296	106.72675	107.78250	108.75585	109.65204	110.47599	111.23227	111.92516	112.55863
7.000	101.43977	102.77190	104.00347	105.14111	106.19098	107.15884	108.05004	108.86958	109.62213	110.31201	110.94328	111.51970
7.125	101.31892	102.53770	103.66309	104.70135	105.65833	106.53945	107.34978	108.09403	108.77658	109.40153	109.97266	110.49353
7.250	101.19822	102.30409	103.32396	104.26370	105.12878	105.92431	106.65502	107.32530	107.93926	108.50070	109.01317	109.47995
7.375	101.07768	102.07107	102.98606	103.82812	104.60233	105.31340	105.96571	106.56335	107.11008	107.60943	108.06465	108.47878
7.500	100.95730	101.83863	102.64940	103.39462	104.07894	104.70667	105.28182	105.80810	106.28896	106.72760	107.12698	107.48985
7.625	100.83708	101.60678	102.31397	102.96318	103.55589	104.10410	104.60328	105.05949	105.47581	105.85510	106.20001	106.51301
7.750	100.71702	101.37551	101.97977	102.53379	103.04128	103.50565	103.93007	104.31746	104.67054	104.99182	105.28362	105.54809
7.875	100.59712	101.14481	101.64678	102.10645	102.52698	102.91130	103.26213	103.58195	103.87308	104.13766	104.37767	104.59492
8.000	100.47738	100.91470	101.31501	101.68114	102.01567	102.32103	102.59942	102.85289	103.08334	103.29251	103.48202	103.65336
8.125	100.35780	100.68516	100.98445	101.25784	101.50734	101.73479	101.94189	102.13023	102.30124	102.45628	102.59656	102.72323
8.250	100.23837	100.45620	100.65510	100.83656	101.00196	101.15255	101.28951	101.41390	101.52671	101.62885	101.72115	101.80440
8.500	100.00000	100.00000	100.00000	100.00000	100.00000	100.00000	100.00000	100.00000	100.00000	100.00000	100.00000	100.00000
8.750	99.76226	99.54608	99.34967	99.17136	99.00965	98.86314	98.73055	98.61073	98.50260	98.40518	98.31758	98.23896
8.875	99.64362	99.31998	99.02628	98.75999	98.51878	98.30052	98.10325	97.92519	97.76470	97.62029	97.49059	97.37434
9.000	99.52514	99.09444	98.70407	98.35057	98.03076	97.74173	97.48083	97.24563	97.03390	96.84362	96.67293	96.52013
9.125	99.40682	98.86946	98.38303	97.94309	97.54557	97.18676	96.86326	96.57199	96.31012	96.07506	95.86447	95.67619
9.250	99.28866	98.64505	98.06317	97.53755	97.06320	96.63557	96.25051	95.90423	95.59329	95.31454	95.06511	94.84239
9.375	99.17065	98.42120	97.74447	97.13393	96.58362	96.08813	95.64252	95.24229	94.88335	94.56196	94.27474	94.01858
9.500	99.05280	98.19791	97.42693	96.73222	96.10682	95.54442	95.03926	94.58611	94.18021	93.81722	93.49323	93.20463
9.625	98.93510	97.97518	97.11055	96.33242	95.63279	95.00041	94.44069	93.93564	93.48380	93.08025	92.72048	92.40002
9.750	98.81756	97.75301	96.79532	95.93450	95.16150	94.46808	93.84677	93.29082	92.79406	92.35094	91.95638	91.60581
9.875	98.70018	97.53139	96.48124	95.53848	94.69294	93.93539	93.25747	92.65160	92.11092	91.62921	91.20083	90.82068
10.000	98.58295	97.31033	96.16830	95.14433	94.22709	93.40632	92.67274	92.01793	91.43431	90.91498	90.45372	90.04489
10.125	98.46588	97.08982	95.85650	94.75205	93.76394	92.88085	92.09254	91.38976	90.76415	90.20815	89.71493	89.27832
10.250	98.34896	96.86986	95.54583	94.36162	93.30346	92.35894	91.51684	90.76704	90.10039	89.50865	88.98438	88.52086
10.375	98.23219	96.65045	95.23630	93.97304	92.84565	91.84058	90.94560	90.14970	89.44295	88.81640	88.26196	87.77238
10.500	98.11558	96.43160	94.92789	93.58630	92.39049	91.32573	90.37879	89.53772	88.79178	88.13130	87.54757	87.03276
10.750	97.88282	95.99552	94.31443	92.81829	91.48803	90.30649	89.25828	88.32957	87.50795	86.78225	86.14247	85.57962
11.000	97.65068	95.56162	93.70542	92.05753	90.59597	89.30102	88.15503	87.14221	86.24839	85.46088	84.76832	84.16054
11.250	97.41915	95.12989	93.10083	91.30395	89.71417	88.30310	87.06876	85.97524	85.01259	84.16654	83.42435	82.77462
11.500	97.18823	94.70031	92.50063	90.55746	88.84251	87.33057	85.99917	84.82829	83.80008	82.89865	82.10982	81.42098
12.000	96.72823	93.84757	91.31324	89.08550	87.12912	85.41284	83.90897	82.59294	81.44298	80.43978	79.56624	78.80719

Yield	13 Years	14 Years	15 Years	16 Years	17 Years	18 Years	19 Years	20 Years	22 Years	25 Years	27 Years	Full Term
5.500	126.14697	127.31456	128.38787	129.37099	130.26772	131.08165	131.81615	132.47437	133.57358	134.71804	135.17094	135.42240
5.750	123.63786	124.67270	125.62162	126.48864	127.27751	127.99176	128.63471	129.20946	130.16577	131.15548	131.54467	131.75964
6.000	121.19473	122.10435	122.93637	123.69469	124.38294	125.00455	125.56271	126.06043	126.88555	127.73438	128.06607	128.24832
6.250	118.81569	119.60724	120.32948	120.98610	121.58057	122.11614	122.59586	123.02256	123.72738	124.44812	124.72797	124.88095
6.500	116.49887	117.17919	117.79839	118.35993	118.86707	119.32282	119.73003	120.09134	120.68598	121.29040	121.52561	121.65043
6.625	115.36324	115.99039	116.56050	117.07688	117.54264	117.96070	118.33376	118.66436	119.20748	119.75787	119.96957	120.08439
6.750	114.24249	114.81807	115.34064	115.81338	116.23925	116.62103	116.96129	117.26245	117.75629	118.25526	118.44657	118.55007
6.875	113.13641	113.66197	114.13852	114.56910	114.95651	115.30337	115.61214	115.88508	116.33184	116.78188	116.95389	117.04670
7.000	112.04480	112.52183	112.95385	113.34371	113.69405	114.00733	114.28585	114.53175	114.93353	115.33704	115.49078	115.57352
7.125	110.96743	111.39742	111.78635	112.13689	112.45150	112.73428	112.98198	113.20199	113.56080	113.92008	114.05654	114.12978
7.250	109.90410	110.28848	110.63573	110.94831	111.22850	111.47844	111.70010	111.89531	112.21310	112.53036	112.65047	112.71478
7.375	108.85462	109.19479	109.50172	109.77767	110.02471	110.24481	110.43976	110.61124	110.88989	111.16724	111.27191	111.32781
7.500	107.81877	108.11611	108.38405	108.62465	108.83898	109.03121	109.20055	109.34932	109.59064	109.83011	109.92020	109.96818
7.625	106.79637	107.05220	107.28246	107.48896	107.67337	107.83726	107.98207	108.10912	108.31483	108.51837	108.59470	108.63525
7.750	105.78721	106.00284	106.19668	106.37029	106.52515	106.66260	106.78390	106.89019	107.06198	107.23144	107.29479	107.32836
7.875	104.79112	104.96781	105.12645	105.26837	105.39479	105.50687	105.60565	105.69210	105.83158	105.96875	106.01987	106.04688
8.000	103.80789	103.94689	104.07153	104.18290	104.28198	104.36971	104.44694	104.51444	104.62315	104.72975	104.76934	104.79022
8.125	102.83734	102.93986	103.03167	103.11360	103.18640	103.25078	103.30738	103.35680	103.43623	103.51389	103.54265	103.55776
8.250	101.87930	101.94650	102.00662	102.06019	102.10774	102.14974	102.18661	102.21877	102.27036	102.32065	102.33922	102.34895
8.500	100.00000	100.00000	100.00000	100.00000	100.00000	100.00000	100.00000	100.00000	100.00000	100.00000	100.00000	100.00000
8.750	98.16858	98.10574	98.04982	98.00022	97.95641	97.91792	97.88428	97.85510	97.80861	97.76384	97.74752	97.73905
8.875	97.27040	97.17771	97.09532	97.02234	96.95797	96.90147	96.85217	96.80944	96.74150	96.67626	96.65255	96.64028
9.000	96.38368	96.26216	96.15426	96.05882	95.97473	95.90102	95.83677	95.78116	95.69291	95.60841	95.57780	95.56200
9.125	95.50826	95.35888	95.22643	95.10939	95.00642	94.91626	94.83778	94.76993	94.66245	94.55984	94.52280	94.50373
9.250	94.64398	94.46771	94.31160	94.17384	94.05278	93.94692	93.85488	93.77541	93.64975	93.53014	93.48710	93.46499
9.375	93.79067	93.58845	93.40957	93.25192	93.11355	92.99270	92.88776	92.79727	92.65443	92.51888	92.47025	92.44534
9.500	92.94818	92.72092	92.52014	92.34341	92.18803	92.05333	91.93613	91.83518	91.67613	91.52564	91.47183	91.44433
9.625	92.11637	91.86495	91.64311	91.44807	91.27731	91.12854	90.99968	90.88884	90.71450	90.55004	90.49141	90.46154
9.750	91.29506	91.02035	90.77827	90.56569	90.37981	90.21807	90.07814	89.95793	89.76919	89.59168	89.52861	89.49654
9.875	90.48412	90.18697	89.92543	89.69606	89.49324	89.32164	89.17122	89.04215	88.83987	88.65019	88.58300	88.54894
10.000	89.68340	89.36463	89.08440	88.83895	88.62485	88.43901	88.27864	88.14121	87.92620	87.72519	87.65422	87.61832
10.125	88.89274	88.55315	88.25500	87.99416	87.76693	87.56993	87.40014	87.25481	87.02787	86.81633	86.74187	86.70431
10.250	88.11202	87.75239	87.43703	87.16149	86.92173	86.71414	86.53544	86.38268	86.14456	85.92325	85.84560	85.80654
10.375	87.34109	86.96218	86.63032	86.34072	86.08905	85.87141	85.68430	85.52453	85.27595	85.04561	84.96505	84.92462
10.500	86.57980	86.18235	85.83469	85.53167	85.26866	85.04151	84.84644	84.68010	84.42176	84.18308	84.09986	84.05821
10.750	85.08563	84.65324	84.27595	83.94793	83.66392	83.41923	83.20964	83.03134	82.75543	82.50203	82.41424	82.37052
11.000	83.62844	83.16384	82.75946	82.40874	82.10584	81.84552	81.62308	81.43434	81.14330	80.87758	80.78611	80.74080
11.250	82.20719	81.71298	81.28388	80.91265	80.59283	80.31864	80.08494	79.88712	79.58319	79.30735	79.21299	79.16648
11.500	80.82088	80.29951	79.84795	79.45825	79.12334	78.83694	78.59342	78.38781	78.07303	77.78904	77.69250	77.64517
12.000	78.14919	77.58034	77.09008	76.66909	76.30907	76.00270	75.74351	75.52573	75.19473	74.89960	74.80055	74.75249

Entry is the percentage of loan balance to give the desired yield to the selected time.

Price of a Mortgage to Give a Specified Yield
Conversion of Interest to Principal or Principal to Interest
8.75% Interest Rate 30 Years Amortization Schedule

Desired Yield	1 Year	2 Years	3 Years	4 Years	Prepaid or Ballooned at 5 Years	6 Years	7 Years	8 Years	9 Years	10 Years	11 Years	12 Years
5.750	102.89928	105.61639	108.16086	110.54167	112.76729	114.84569	116.78437	118.59041	120.27045	121.83075	123.27720	124.61533
6.000	102.65413	105.13531	107.45307	109.61637	111.63363	113.51277	115.26123	116.88602	118.39370	119.79044	121.08205	122.27397
6.250	102.40963	104.65665	106.75046	108.69987	110.51317	112.19812	113.76200	115.21165	116.55348	117.79348	118.93731	119.99023
6.500	102.16578	104.18039	106.05297	107.79208	109.40575	110.90147	112.28627	113.56674	114.74902	115.83888	116.84170	117.76253
6.750	101.92258	103.70652	105.36057	106.89292	108.31121	109.62257	110.83366	111.95073	112.97958	113.92565	114.79400	115.58938
6.875	101.80122	103.47047	105.01627	106.44655	107.76872	108.98969	110.11591	111.15340	112.10777	112.98425	113.78775	114.52280
7.000	101.68002	103.23502	104.67323	106.00230	107.22939	108.36115	109.40378	110.36308	111.24443	112.05285	112.79302	113.46930
7.125	101.55898	103.00016	104.33143	105.56016	106.69320	107.73692	108.69725	109.57972	110.38948	111.13132	111.80968	112.42872
7.250	101.43810	102.76588	103.99089	105.12013	106.16013	107.11696	107.99625	108.80325	109.54284	110.21955	110.83758	111.40087
7.375	101.31738	102.53220	103.65159	104.68219	105.63017	106.50125	107.30075	108.03361	108.70441	109.31742	109.87659	110.38559
7.500	101.19683	102.29910	103.31353	104.24633	105.10329	105.88976	106.61070	107.27073	107.87412	108.42484	108.92656	109.38271
7.625	101.07643	102.06658	102.97670	103.81255	104.57948	105.28245	105.92605	106.51454	107.05187	107.54168	107.98736	108.39206
7.750	100.95619	101.83465	102.64110	103.38082	104.05871	104.67929	105.24676	105.76499	106.23758	106.66784	107.05885	107.41346
7.875	100.83611	101.60330	102.30673	102.95115	103.54097	104.08026	104.57278	105.02201	105.43116	105.80321	106.14090	106.44677
8.000	100.71619	101.37253	101.97357	102.52352	103.02624	103.48532	103.90407	104.28554	104.63254	104.94769	105.23338	105.49182
8.125	100.59643	101.14234	101.64163	102.09791	102.51450	102.89444	103.24058	103.55501	103.84164	104.10117	104.33615	104.54846
8.250	100.47683	100.91272	101.31090	101.67433	102.00573	102.30760	102.58228	102.83187	103.05836	103.26354	103.44908	103.61652
8.375	100.35738	100.68368	100.98138	101.25276	101.49991	101.72477	101.92911	102.11456	102.28264	102.43471	102.57206	102.69585
8.500	100.23810	100.45522	100.65306	100.83318	100.99703	101.14591	101.28103	101.40352	101.51439	101.61458	101.70496	101.78631
8.750	100.00000	100.00000	100.00000	100.00000	100.00000	100.00000	100.00000	100.00000	100.00000	100.00000	100.00000	100.00000
9.000	99.76253	99.54706	99.35169	99.17470	99.01450	98.86965	98.73884	98.62085	98.51458	98.41902	98.33324	98.25642
9.125	99.64403	99.32144	99.02931	98.76498	98.52603	98.31025	98.11561	97.94027	97.78254	97.64088	97.51389	97.40029
9.250	99.52569	99.09658	98.70809	98.35720	98.04039	97.75464	97.49472	97.26561	97.05752	96.87086	96.70374	96.55442
9.375	99.40751	98.87189	98.38805	97.95135	97.55756	97.20282	96.88364	96.59682	96.33944	96.10887	95.90268	95.71868
9.500	99.28948	98.64796	98.06917	97.54742	97.07752	96.65475	96.27482	95.93384	95.62824	95.35480	95.11058	94.89292
9.625	99.17161	98.42459	97.75146	97.14541	96.60026	96.11040	95.67073	95.27661	94.92383	94.60857	94.32735	94.07701
9.750	99.05389	98.20178	97.43490	96.74530	96.12589	95.56975	95.07132	94.62509	94.22616	93.87009	93.55287	93.27083
9.875	98.93633	97.97952	97.11949	96.34708	95.65401	95.03277	94.47656	93.97922	93.53514	93.13927	92.78702	92.47424
10.000	98.81893	97.75783	96.80523	95.95074	95.18498	94.49944	93.88641	93.33894	92.85071	92.41603	92.02972	91.68711
10.125	98.70168	97.53668	96.49211	95.55628	94.71866	93.96692	93.30083	92.70421	92.17281	91.70027	91.28084	90.90932
10.250	98.58458	97.31609	96.18012	95.16369	94.25504	93.44359	92.71978	92.07497	91.50136	90.99191	90.54029	90.14075
10.375	98.46764	97.09605	95.86928	94.77295	93.79409	92.92103	92.14322	91.45116	90.83629	90.29088	89.80796	89.38126
10.500	98.35086	96.87656	95.55956	94.38405	93.33581	92.40201	91.57112	90.83275	90.17755	89.59707	89.08375	88.63075
10.625	98.23423	96.65762	95.25097	93.99699	92.88016	91.88660	91.00344	90.21968	89.52506	88.91042	88.36757	87.88910
10.750	98.11775	96.43923	94.94350	93.61177	92.42715	91.37448	90.44015	89.61190	88.87875	88.23084	87.65930	87.15618
11.000	97.88526	96.00407	94.33190	92.84676	91.52894	90.36081	89.32656	88.41200	87.60447	86.89258	86.26615	85.71608
11.250	97.65338	95.57109	93.72474	92.08895	90.64106	89.36080	88.23007	87.23268	86.35418	85.58164	84.90354	84.30955
11.500	97.42212	95.14027	93.12197	91.33827	89.76337	88.37424	87.15039	86.07354	85.12739	84.29743	83.57071	82.93572
11.750	97.19146	94.71159	92.52357	90.59466	88.89575	87.40095	86.08726	84.93421	83.92362	83.03932	82.26695	81.59373
12.250	96.73198	93.86065	91.33974	89.12834	87.19024	85.49341	84.00953	82.71353	81.58326	80.59913	79.74379	79.00194

Yield	13 Years	14 Years	15 Years	16 Years	17 Years	18 Years	19 Years	20 Years	22 Years	25 Years	27 Years	Full Term
5.750	125.85034	126.98712	128.03026	128.98405	129.85254	130.63951	131.34850	131.98282	133.03967	134.13599	134.56825	134.80757
6.000	123.37131	124.37886	125.30111	126.14227	126.90631	127.59690	128.21753	128.77141	129.69088	130.63897	131.01043	131.21503
6.250	120.95718	121.84281	122.65145	123.38717	124.05376	124.65479	125.19357	125.67322	126.46657	127.27972	127.59630	127.76976
6.500	118.60608	119.37677	120.07871	120.71577	121.29153	121.80938	122.27244	122.68367	123.36135	124.05180	124.31892	124.46452
6.750	116.31620	116.97858	117.58039	118.12521	118.61639	119.05706	119.45014	119.79834	120.37009	120.94913	121.17173	121.29243
6.875	115.19365	115.80428	116.35838	116.85937	117.31049	117.71472	118.07484	118.39345	118.91566	119.44294	119.64500	119.75429
7.000	114.08576	114.64617	115.15407	115.61273	116.02521	116.39435	116.72281	117.01305	117.48789	117.96591	118.14852	118.24702
7.125	112.99230	113.50400	113.96718	114.38493	114.76016	115.09555	115.39361	115.65665	116.08622	116.51737	116.68156	116.76989
7.250	111.91306	112.37753	112.79742	113.17567	113.51499	113.81791	114.08678	114.32377	114.71009	115.09666	115.24341	115.32216
7.375	110.84784	111.26651	111.64452	111.98463	112.28935	112.56104	112.80189	113.01392	113.35893	113.70313	113.83338	113.90310
7.500	109.79645	110.17070	110.50821	110.81148	111.08287	111.32454	111.53851	111.72665	112.03222	112.33616	112.45082	112.51203
7.625	108.75866	109.08988	109.38820	109.65593	109.89521	110.10803	110.29623	110.46149	110.72942	110.99505	111.09505	111.14826
7.750	107.73430	108.02381	108.28424	108.51768	108.72605	108.91115	109.07462	109.21801	109.45004	109.67947	109.76546	109.81113
7.875	106.72317	106.97227	107.19607	107.39642	107.57504	107.73352	107.87330	107.99576	108.19356	108.38856	108.46142	108.50002
8.000	105.72508	105.93503	106.12343	106.29188	106.44187	106.57478	106.69187	106.79432	106.95950	107.12186	107.18233	107.21428
8.125	104.73984	104.91188	105.06607	105.20377	105.32622	105.43459	105.52995	105.61328	105.74739	105.87881	105.92760	105.95332
8.250	103.76726	103.90260	104.02375	104.13180	104.22777	104.31260	104.38715	104.45222	104.55675	104.65888	104.69667	104.71654
8.375	102.80716	102.90698	102.99621	103.07571	103.14622	103.20848	103.26312	103.31075	103.38713	103.46153	103.48898	103.50337
8.500	101.85937	101.92481	101.98323	102.03522	102.08127	102.12188	102.15748	102.18847	102.23809	102.28627	102.30399	102.31325
8.750	100.00000	100.00000	100.00000	100.00000	100.00000	100.00000	100.00000	100.00000	100.00000	100.00000	100.00000	100.00000
9.000	98.18776	98.12658	98.07222	98.02409	97.98166	97.94444	97.91197	97.88384	97.83914	97.79624	97.78066	97.77259
9.125	97.29890	97.20865	97.12857	97.05775	96.99544	96.94077	96.89317	96.85199	96.78666	96.72415	96.70152	96.68984
9.250	96.42132	96.30299	96.19812	96.10551	96.02406	95.95278	95.89076	95.83716	95.75229	95.67133	95.64211	95.62707
9.375	95.55486	95.40941	95.28067	95.16711	95.06737	94.98018	94.90442	94.83902	94.73566	94.63735	94.60199	94.58383
9.500	94.69937	94.52774	94.37600	94.24233	94.12507	94.02270	93.93384	93.85725	93.73641	93.62181	93.58071	93.55967
9.625	93.85469	93.65778	93.48392	93.33095	93.19692	93.08005	92.97874	92.89152	92.75416	92.62428	92.57786	92.55414
9.750	93.02067	92.79937	92.60422	92.43273	92.28266	92.15197	92.03882	91.94152	91.78857	91.64438	91.59300	91.56682
9.875	92.19714	91.95233	91.73670	91.54745	91.38205	91.23819	91.11378	91.00694	90.83929	90.68171	90.62574	90.59730
10.000	91.38397	91.11648	90.88117	90.67491	90.49485	90.33844	90.20335	90.08748	89.90598	89.73590	89.67568	89.64516
10.125	90.58101	90.29166	90.03744	89.81488	89.62084	89.45248	89.30726	89.18285	88.98833	88.80658	88.74244	88.71001
10.250	89.78811	89.47771	89.20533	88.96716	88.75977	88.58006	88.42523	88.29276	88.08600	87.89339	87.82563	87.79146
10.375	89.00513	88.67445	88.38464	88.13154	87.91143	87.72092	87.55700	87.41692	87.19868	86.99598	86.92490	86.88914
10.500	88.23193	87.88174	87.57520	87.30783	87.07559	86.87484	86.70231	86.55507	86.32607	86.11402	86.03988	86.00269
10.625	87.46837	87.09940	86.77683	86.49582	86.25203	86.04157	85.86091	85.70692	85.46786	85.24715	85.17023	85.13175
10.750	86.71431	86.32729	85.98935	85.69532	85.44055	85.22088	85.03255	84.87222	84.62377	84.39506	84.31562	84.27596
11.000	85.23417	84.81313	84.44639	84.12809	83.85298	83.61635	83.41399	83.24213	82.97679	82.73397	82.65015	82.60854
11.250	83.79047	83.33806	82.94498	82.60466	82.31124	82.05949	81.84473	81.66280	81.38290	81.12828	81.04095	80.99781
11.500	82.38217	81.90092	81.48382	81.12359	80.81378	80.54862	80.32298	80.13230	79.84000	79.57567	79.48558	79.44130
11.750	81.00831	80.50060	80.06166	79.68350	79.35908	79.08210	78.84698	78.64698	78.64879	78.34605	78.07391	77.98174	77.93668
12.250	78.36003	77.80608	77.32952	76.92099	76.57223	76.27594	76.02568	75.81576	75.49741	75.21459	75.12001	75.07425

Entry is the percentage of loan balance to give the desired yield to the selected time.

Price of a Mortgage to Give a Specified Yield
Conversion of Interest to Principal or Principal to Interest
9.00% Interest Rate   30 Years Amortization Schedule

Desired Yield	Prepaid or Ballooned at											
	1 Year	2 Years	3 Years	4 Years	5 Years	6 Years	7 Years	8 Years	9 Years	10 Years	11 Years	12 Years
6.000	102.89588	105.60406	108.13483	110.49792	112.70242	114.75692	116.66945	118.44759	120.09843	121.62865	123.04451	124.35187
6.250	102.65102	105.12405	107.42934	109.57653	111.57466	113.43219	115.15708	116.75677	118.23826	119.60808	120.87238	122.03690
6.500	102.40681	104.64645	106.72899	108.66390	110.46001	112.12559	113.66839	115.09566	116.41418	117.63029	118.74993	119.77865
6.750	102.16325	104.17124	106.03375	107.75993	109.35830	110.83683	112.20297	113.46368	114.62543	115.69429	116.67592	117.57559
7.000	101.92033	103.69841	105.34358	106.86453	108.26938	109.56567	110.76045	111.86028	112.87127	113.79912	114.64912	115.42623
7.125	101.79911	103.46289	105.00038	106.42002	107.72966	108.93661	110.04766	111.06914	112.00694	112.86655	113.65307	114.37124
7.250	101.67805	103.22795	104.65843	105.97763	107.19309	108.31185	109.34044	110.28494	111.15099	111.94385	112.66838	113.32914
7.375	101.55716	102.99361	104.31773	105.53733	106.65963	107.69136	108.63876	109.50763	110.30333	111.03089	111.69492	112.29975
7.500	101.43642	102.75985	103.97828	105.09912	106.12928	107.07512	107.94257	108.73713	109.46388	110.12756	110.73254	111.28290
7.625	101.31584	102.52667	103.64006	104.66300	105.60200	106.46308	107.25182	107.97338	108.63254	109.23375	109.78111	110.27843
7.750	101.19543	102.29409	103.30307	104.22895	105.07779	105.85523	106.56647	107.21632	107.80924	108.34936	108.84049	109.28617
7.875	101.07517	102.06208	102.96731	103.79695	104.55662	105.25152	105.88646	106.46588	106.99389	107.47427	107.91055	108.30596
8.000	100.95507	101.83066	102.63278	103.36700	104.03848	104.65194	105.21177	105.72201	106.18640	106.60839	106.99115	107.33762
8.125	100.83514	101.59981	102.29946	102.93910	103.52334	104.05644	104.54233	104.98464	105.38670	105.75159	106.08215	106.38101
8.250	100.71536	101.36955	101.96736	102.51322	103.01119	103.46500	103.87812	104.25371	104.59470	104.90378	105.18344	105.43596
8.375	100.59573	101.13986	101.63647	102.08936	102.50200	102.87759	103.21908	103.52915	103.81032	104.06486	104.29488	104.50232
8.500	100.47627	100.91074	101.30679	101.66751	101.99577	102.29419	102.56517	102.81092	103.03348	103.23472	103.41635	103.57994
8.625	100.35697	100.68220	100.97830	101.24766	101.49248	101.71475	101.91635	102.09895	102.26411	102.41326	102.54771	102.66867
8.750	100.23782	100.45423	100.65101	100.82980	100.99209	101.13926	101.27257	101.39317	101.50212	101.60039	101.68886	101.76835
9.000	100.00000	100.00000	100.00000	100.00000	100.00000	100.00000	100.00000	100.00000	100.00000	100.00000	100.00000	100.00000
9.250	99.76281	99.54804	99.35372	99.17804	99.01935	98.87617	98.74711	98.63094	98.52651	98.43278	98.34882	98.27375
9.375	99.64445	99.32291	99.03234	98.76997	98.53328	98.31997	98.12795	97.95531	97.80031	97.66137	97.53706	97.42606
9.500	99.52624	99.09834	98.71213	98.36383	98.05002	97.76755	97.51358	97.28554	97.08105	96.89798	96.73438	96.58848
9.625	99.40820	98.87433	98.39308	97.95962	97.56955	97.21887	96.90398	96.62157	96.36865	96.14250	95.94066	95.76087
9.750	99.29031	98.65088	98.07520	97.55731	97.09185	96.67392	96.29910	95.96335	95.66305	95.39486	95.15579	94.94311
9.875	99.17257	98.42800	97.75847	97.15691	96.61691	96.13266	95.69889	95.31084	94.96416	94.65495	94.37966	94.13505
10.000	99.05499	98.20566	97.44289	96.75840	96.14471	95.59507	95.10333	94.66396	94.27193	93.92270	93.61216	93.33658
10.125	98.93757	97.98389	97.12845	96.36177	95.67524	95.06112	94.51238	94.02268	93.58628	93.19801	92.85318	92.54756
10.250	98.82030	97.76266	96.81516	95.96701	95.20848	94.53078	93.92598	93.38693	92.90715	92.48080	92.10263	91.76786
10.375	98.70318	97.54199	96.50301	95.57411	94.74440	94.00403	93.34412	92.75667	92.23446	91.77099	91.36039	90.99737
10.500	98.58623	97.32188	96.19199	95.18308	94.28301	93.48084	92.76674	92.13184	91.56815	91.06849	90.62637	90.23597
10.625	98.46942	97.10231	95.88209	94.79388	93.82427	92.96119	92.19382	91.51240	90.90816	90.37321	89.90046	89.48352
10.750	98.35277	96.88329	95.57333	94.40652	93.36817	92.44505	91.62532	90.89829	90.25441	89.68508	89.18256	88.73992
10.875	98.23627	96.66481	95.26568	94.02099	92.91470	91.93240	91.06119	90.28947	89.60685	89.00401	88.47257	88.00505
11.000	98.11993	96.44689	94.95915	93.63728	92.46384	91.42321	90.50140	89.68588	88.96541	88.32992	87.77041	87.27879
11.250	97.88771	96.01266	94.34942	92.87527	91.56988	90.41511	89.39472	88.49421	87.70063	87.00239	86.38914	85.85164
11.500	97.65610	95.58060	93.74411	92.12042	90.68618	89.42055	88.30498	87.32290	86.45958	85.70185	85.03801	84.45760
11.750	97.42510	95.15069	93.14317	91.37267	89.81260	88.43305	87.23190	86.17158	85.24177	84.42771	83.71627	83.09579
12.000	97.19471	94.72292	92.54658	90.63193	88.94902	87.47130	86.17521	85.03986	84.04672	83.17936	82.42322	81.76538
12.500	96.73575	93.87377	91.36631	89.17125	87.25140	85.57394	84.10993	82.83381	81.72305	80.75776	79.92039	79.19548

Yield	13 Years	14 Years	15 Years	16 Years	17 Years	18 Years	19 Years	20 Years	22 Years	25 Years	27 Years	Full Term
6.000	125.55625	126.66281	127.67639	128.60152	129.44246	130.20316	130.88734	131.49847	132.51429	133.56417	133.97661	134.20431
6.250	123.10703	124.08779	124.98392	125.79982	126.53962	127.20718	127.80609	128.33973	129.22351	130.13146	130.48589	130.68055
6.500	120.72164	121.58373	122.36948	123.08310	123.72855	124.30953	124.82947	125.29160	126.05416	126.83289	127.13496	127.30000
6.750	118.39823	119.14845	119.83052	120.44845	121.00596	121.50654	121.95341	122.34961	123.00102	123.66225	123.91712	124.05565
7.000	116.13504	116.77984	117.36461	117.89307	118.36869	118.79467	119.17401	119.50950	120.05908	120.61362	120.82602	120.94087
7.125	115.02548	115.61989	116.15830	116.64427	117.08109	117.47184	117.81938	118.12635	118.62832	119.13329	119.32610	119.43009
7.250	113.93032	114.47586	114.96938	115.41428	115.81369	116.17053	116.48751	116.76716	117.22359	117.68140	117.85564	117.94937
7.375	112.84937	113.34749	113.79756	114.20278	114.56612	114.89034	115.17798	115.43142	115.84434	116.25726	116.41393	116.49798
7.500	111.78241	112.23455	112.64256	113.00947	113.33804	113.63087	113.89034	114.11868	114.49002	114.86026	115.00029	115.07522
7.625	110.72924	111.13679	111.50412	111.83402	112.12909	112.39173	112.62416	112.82846	113.16010	113.48976	113.61404	113.68038
7.750	109.68966	110.05399	110.38195	110.67613	110.93892	111.17254	111.37904	111.56031	111.85404	112.14515	112.25455	112.31280
7.875	108.66349	108.98592	109.27580	109.53550	109.76721	109.97294	110.15456	110.31380	110.57135	110.82584	110.92118	110.97181
8.000	107.65052	107.93235	108.18541	108.41185	108.61363	108.79256	108.95033	109.08848	109.31153	109.53126	109.61332	109.65678
8.125	106.65057	106.89306	107.11053	107.30488	107.47785	107.63104	107.76595	107.88393	108.07408	108.26084	108.33037	108.36709
8.250	105.66344	105.86783	106.05090	106.21430	106.35955	106.48803	106.60104	106.69974	106.85853	107.01403	107.07174	107.10214
8.375	104.68896	104.85645	105.00628	105.13985	105.25843	105.36319	105.45542	105.53551	105.66443	105.79030	105.83687	105.86133
8.500	103.72695	103.85870	103.97643	104.08124	104.17418	104.25619	104.32814	104.39083	104.49131	104.58913	104.62520	104.64410
8.625	102.77722	102.87439	102.96111	103.03822	103.10650	103.16668	103.21942	103.26531	103.33874	103.41000	103.43619	103.44989
8.750	101.83960	101.90330	101.96008	102.01050	102.05510	102.09436	102.12872	102.15858	102.20627	102.25242	102.26933	102.27815
9.000	100.00000	100.00000	100.00000	100.00000	100.00000	100.00000	100.00000	100.00000	100.00000	100.00000	100.00000	100.00000
9.250	98.20679	98.14723	98.09440	98.04772	98.00663	97.97064	97.93931	97.91220	97.86923	97.82814	97.81327	97.80560
9.375	97.32718	97.23932	97.16149	97.09280	97.03242	96.97960	96.93366	96.89398	96.83118	96.77130	96.74971	96.73859
9.500	96.45867	96.34347	96.24156	96.15172	96.07285	96.00430	95.94407	95.89243	95.81084	95.73329	95.70541	95.69110
9.625	95.60111	95.45951	95.33440	95.22424	95.12765	95.04336	94.97023	94.90722	94.80786	94.71369	94.67994	94.66266
9.750	94.75435	94.58725	94.43980	94.31013	94.19657	94.09761	94.01185	93.93804	93.82187	93.71210	93.67288	93.65285
9.875	93.91822	93.72653	93.55757	93.40917	93.27938	93.16640	93.06862	92.98457	92.85252	92.72811	92.68381	92.66124
10.000	93.09259	92.87716	92.68751	92.52115	92.37582	92.24947	92.14026	92.04651	91.89946	91.76135	91.71232	91.68741
10.125	92.27731	92.03897	91.82942	91.64584	91.48566	91.34658	91.22650	91.12355	90.96238	90.81144	90.75802	90.73095
10.250	91.47221	91.21180	90.98313	90.78303	90.60866	90.45745	90.32706	90.21541	90.04092	89.87800	89.82053	89.79148
10.375	90.67717	90.39548	90.14843	89.93252	89.74460	89.58184	89.44168	89.32180	89.13478	88.96069	88.89947	88.86861
10.500	89.89204	89.58985	89.32515	89.09410	88.89326	88.71952	88.57008	88.44243	88.24365	88.05915	87.99448	87.96196
10.625	89.11667	88.79474	88.51310	88.26757	88.05440	87.87023	87.71201	87.57703	87.36721	87.17305	87.10520	87.07117
10.750	88.35094	88.01001	87.71211	87.45274	87.22782	87.03374	86.86722	86.72533	86.50517	86.30204	86.23129	86.19590
10.875	87.59470	87.23549	86.92201	86.64940	86.41331	86.20983	86.03546	85.88707	85.65724	85.44581	85.37241	85.33578
11.000	86.84782	86.47103	86.14262	85.85738	85.61065	85.39827	85.21650	85.06199	84.82313	84.60405	84.52822	84.49048
11.250	85.38162	84.97171	84.61530	84.30652	84.04008	83.81130	83.61599	83.45038	83.19527	82.96266	82.88267	82.84306
11.500	83.95131	83.51086	83.12885	82.79870	82.51454	82.27114	82.06385	81.88853	81.61942	81.37551	81.29215	81.25109
11.750	82.55589	82.08736	81.68199	81.33252	81.03248	80.77611	80.55832	80.37457	80.09354	79.84032	79.75433	79.71219
12.000	81.19438	80.70009	80.27350	79.90664	79.59244	79.32464	79.09770	78.90670	78.61564	78.35493	78.26696	78.22407
12.500	78.56938	78.03005	77.56690	77.17056	76.83278	76.54632	76.30475	76.10245	75.79636	75.52542	75.43515	75.39159

Entry is the percentage of loan balance to give the desired yield to the selected time.

Price of a Mortgage to Give a Specified Yield
Conversion of Interest to Principal or Principal to Interest
9.25% Interest Rate   30 Years Amortization Schedule

Desired Yield	1 Year	2 Years	3 Years	4 Years	5 Years	6 Years	7 Years	8 Years	9 Years	10 Years	11 Years	12 Years
6.250	102.89247	105.59168	108.10875	110.45411	112.63755	114.66825	116.55480	118.30527	119.92722	121.42772	122.81340	124.09048
6.500	102.64790	105.11274	107.40555	109.53665	111.51569	113.35171	115.05317	116.62798	118.08354	119.42677	120.66413	121.80169
6.750	102.40398	104.63620	106.70748	108.62788	110.40684	112.05314	113.57499	114.98006	116.27551	117.46802	118.56382	119.56872
7.000	102.16070	104.16205	106.01449	107.72773	109.31084	110.77226	112.11986	113.36096	114.50239	115.55051	116.51124	117.39009
7.250	101.91807	103.69027	105.32654	106.83610	108.22754	109.50884	110.68741	111.77014	112.76345	113.67330	114.50ᶜ21	115.26434
7.375	101.79700	103.45527	104.98445	106.39346	107.69061	108.88359	109.97956	110.98517	111.90658	112.74951	113.51929	114.22084
7.500	101.67608	103.22086	104.64360	105.95292	107.15679	108.26261	109.27724	110.20707	111.05798	111.83545	112.54457	113.19004
7.625	101.55533	102.98703	104.30400	105.51446	106.62606	107.64586	108.58041	109.43577	110.21757	110.93101	111.58092	112.17176
7.750	101.43473	102.75379	103.96563	105.07809	106.09842	107.03332	107.88901	108.67122	109.38527	110.03608	110.62820	111.16583
7.875	101.31430	102.52113	103.62849	104.64378	105.57383	106.42495	107.20299	107.91334	108.56099	109.15055	109.68626	110.17208
8.000	101.19402	102.28906	103.29259	104.21153	105.05228	105.82073	106.52233	107.16209	107.74465	108.27430	108.75499	109.19036
8.125	101.07391	102.05756	102.95790	103.78133	104.53376	105.22063	105.84696	106.41738	106.93616	107.40724	107.83424	108.22050
8.250	100.95395	101.82665	102.62443	103.35317	104.01824	104.62461	105.17685	105.67917	106.13545	106.54926	106.92388	107.26235
8.375	100.83416	101.59631	102.29218	102.92703	103.50570	104.03264	104.51195	104.94739	105.34243	105.70025	106.02378	106.31573
8.500	100.71452	101.36655	101.96114	102.50291	102.99613	103.44470	103.85222	104.22198	104.55702	104.86011	105.13383	105.38051
8.625	100.59504	101.13736	101.63130	102.08080	102.48951	102.86076	103.19762	103.50288	103.77914	104.02875	104.25388	104.45653
8.750	100.47571	100.90875	101.30266	101.66069	101.98582	102.28079	102.54810	102.79004	103.00871	103.20605	103.38382	103.54363
8.875	100.35655	100.68071	100.97521	101.24256	101.48504	101.70475	101.90361	102.08338	102.24566	102.39192	102.52352	102.64168
9.000	100.23754	100.45324	100.64896	100.82641	100.98716	101.13263	101.26413	101.38286	101.48991	101.58627	101.67286	101.75052
9.250	100.00000	100.00000	100.00000	100.00000	100.00000	100.00000	100.00000	100.00000	100.00000	100.00000	100.00000	100.00000
9.500	99.76309	99.54903	99.35575	99.18138	99.02421	98.88268	98.75537	98.64099	98.53838	98.44647	98.36429	98.29096
9.625	99.64486	99.32438	99.03538	98.77497	98.54054	98.32969	98.14026	97.97030	97.81800	97.68176	97.56009	97.45165
9.750	99.52680	99.10030	98.71618	98.37048	98.05965	97.78044	97.52991	97.30540	97.10448	96.92495	96.76483	96.62229
9.875	99.40889	98.87678	98.39813	97.96790	97.58154	97.23491	96.92428	96.64625	96.39774	96.17597	95.97841	95.80277
10.000	99.29114	98.65382	98.08123	97.56722	97.10618	96.69307	96.32332	95.99278	95.69771	95.43471	95.20071	94.99294
10.125	99.17354	98.43141	97.76549	97.16842	96.63356	96.15490	95.72700	95.34495	95.00432	94.70110	94.43164	94.19268
10.250	99.05609	98.20956	97.45089	96.77151	96.16367	95.62036	95.13528	94.70271	94.31751	93.97504	93.67108	93.40186
10.375	98.93881	97.98826	97.13744	96.37547	95.69648	95.08943	94.54811	94.06600	93.63721	93.25645	92.91893	92.62036
10.500	98.82167	97.76752	96.82512	95.98330	95.23198	94.56209	93.96548	93.43477	92.96335	92.54525	92.17509	91.84805
10.625	98.70470	97.54733	96.51394	95.59197	94.77015	94.03831	93.38732	92.80897	92.29586	91.84135	91.43946	91.08481
10.750	98.58787	97.32768	96.20388	95.20204	94.31098	93.51806	92.81362	92.18854	91.63467	91.14466	90.71192	90.33052
10.875	98.47121	97.10859	95.89494	94.81485	93.85445	93.00132	92.24432	91.57345	90.97973	90.45512	89.99239	89.58507
11.000	98.35469	96.89004	95.58713	94.42903	93.40054	92.48806	91.67940	90.96363	90.33097	89.77263	89.28077	88.84833
11.125	98.23833	96.67203	95.28043	94.04502	92.94924	91.97826	91.11882	90.35905	89.68831	89.09712	88.57695	88.12020
11.250	98.12212	96.45457	94.97485	93.66283	92.50053	91.47189	90.56254	89.75964	89.05171	88.42850	87.88084	87.40055
11.500	97.89017	96.02128	94.36699	92.90382	91.61083	90.46936	89.46275	88.57618	87.79641	87.11165	86.51140	85.98628
11.750	97.65883	95.59014	93.76353	92.15194	90.73131	89.48026	88.37975	87.41286	86.56456	85.82147	85.17168	84.60464
12.000	97.42809	95.16115	93.16443	91.40710	89.86185	88.50440	87.31325	86.26933	85.35569	84.55735	83.86908	83.25478
12.250	97.19797	94.73429	92.56965	90.66925	89.00232	87.54160	86.26300	85.14520	84.16933	83.31871	82.57858	81.93588
12.750	96.73954	93.88694	91.39296	89.21423	87.31258	85.65442	84.21015	82.95375	81.86230	80.91562	80.09597	79.38774

Yield	13 Years	14 Years	15 Years	16 Years	17 Years	18 Years	19 Years	20 Years	22 Years	25 Years	27 Years	Full Term
6.250	125.26476	126.34169	127.32634	128.22348	129.03754	129.77267	130.43274	131.02136	131.99748	133.00258	133.39598	133.61255
6.500	122.84508	123.79959	124.67015	125.46136	126.17752	126.82264	127.40045	127.91444	128.76369	129.63293	129.97101	130.15615
6.750	120.48816	121.32718	122.09051	122.78254	123.40738	123.96884	124.47047	124.91558	125.64836	126.39390	126.68203	126.83901
7.000	118.19220	118.92234	119.58496	120.18420	120.72391	121.20767	121.63881	122.02043	122.64639	123.27945	123.52257	123.65434
7.250	115.95545	116.58300	117.15110	117.66359	118.12402	118.53570	118.90168	119.22483	119.75295	120.28387	120.48648	120.59572
7.375	114.85875	115.43727	115.96033	116.43161	116.85448	117.23212	117.56742	117.86310	118.34547	118.82895	119.01287	119.11177
7.500	113.77622	114.30717	114.78663	115.21808	115.60474	115.94960	116.25543	116.52479	116.96341	117.40172	117.56793	117.65709
7.625	112.70766	113.19247	113.62971	114.02269	114.37443	114.68776	114.96528	115.20941	115.60621	116.00156	116.15100	116.23095
7.750	111.65287	112.09292	112.48931	112.84513	113.16322	113.44621	113.69656	113.91650	114.27336	114.62784	114.76141	114.83269
7.875	110.61164	111.00830	111.36516	111.68509	111.97075	112.22458	112.44884	112.64562	112.96432	113.27995	113.39851	113.46161
8.000	109.58379	109.93838	110.25700	110.54229	110.79670	111.02248	111.22172	111.39632	111.67860	111.95732	112.06168	112.11708
8.125	108.56912	108.88293	109.16456	109.41642	109.64073	109.83956	110.01480	110.16818	110.41569	110.65935	110.75030	110.79846
8.250	107.56744	107.84174	108.08760	108.30720	108.50254	108.67547	108.82769	108.96076	109.17511	109.38550	109.46378	109.50512
8.375	106.57857	106.81458	107.02586	107.21434	107.38179	107.52985	107.66002	107.77367	107.95640	108.13522	108.20154	108.23648
8.500	105.60232	105.80125	105.97911	106.13758	106.27819	106.40237	106.51140	106.60648	106.75908	106.90797	106.96302	106.99194
8.625	104.63852	104.80153	104.94710	105.07663	105.19143	105.29268	105.38148	105.45881	105.58271	105.70323	105.74765	105.77093
8.750	103.68698	103.81521	103.92959	104.03124	104.12121	104.20047	104.26989	104.33028	104.42685	104.52051	104.55492	104.57290
8.875	102.74753	102.84210	102.92635	103.00113	103.06724	103.12541	103.17629	103.22050	103.29106	103.35929	103.38428	103.39731
9.000	101.81999	101.88199	101.93715	101.98606	102.02924	102.06718	102.10033	102.12909	102.17493	102.21912	102.23525	102.24364
9.250	100.00000	100.00000	100.00000	100.00000	100.00000	100.00000	100.00000	100.00000	100.00000	100.00000	100.00000	100.00000
9.500	98.22567	98.16769	98.11637	98.07109	98.03132	97.99653	97.96630	97.94019	97.89889	97.85954	97.84536	97.83806
9.625	97.35522	97.26971	97.19410	97.12748	97.06902	97.01797	96.97364	96.93542	96.87506	96.81773	96.79712	96.78655
9.750	96.49571	96.38359	96.28457	96.19744	96.12108	96.05448	95.99672	95.94697	95.86865	95.79430	95.76770	95.75408
9.875	95.64698	95.50916	95.38760	95.28076	95.18725	95.10578	95.03522	94.97453	94.87903	94.78886	94.75666	94.74022
10.000	94.80887	94.64624	94.50298	94.37722	94.26727	94.17162	94.08887	94.01777	93.90612	93.80101	93.76359	93.74454
10.125	93.98125	93.79466	93.63050	93.48658	93.36092	93.25172	93.15737	93.07641	92.94949	92.83036	92.78810	92.76662
10.250	93.16395	92.95425	92.76999	92.60865	92.46794	92.34583	92.24045	92.15014	92.00881	91.87655	91.82973	91.80607
10.375	92.35683	92.12485	91.92126	91.74320	91.58812	91.45369	91.33783	91.23866	91.08375	90.93921	90.88825	90.86250
10.500	91.55975	91.30628	91.08410	90.89004	90.72122	90.57506	90.44925	90.34169	90.17399	90.01798	89.96314	89.93551
10.625	90.77257	90.49839	90.25835	90.04895	89.86701	89.70970	89.57444	89.45896	89.27822	89.11251	89.05410	89.02474
10.750	89.99514	89.70101	89.44383	89.21974	89.02528	88.85735	88.71316	88.59018	88.39913	88.22246	88.16076	88.12982
10.875	89.22734	88.91399	88.64034	88.40221	88.19582	88.01780	87.86513	87.73510	87.53344	87.34751	87.28278	87.25040
11.000	88.46902	88.13717	87.84774	87.59617	87.37841	87.19082	87.03013	86.89344	86.68184	86.48732	86.41982	86.38614
11.125	87.72005	87.37041	87.06583	86.80143	86.57284	86.37617	86.20791	86.06496	85.84406	85.64159	85.57155	85.53670
11.250	86.98030	86.61355	86.29445	86.01780	85.77891	85.57363	85.39823	85.24939	85.01981	84.81001	84.73766	84.70175
11.500	85.52794	85.12894	84.78265	84.48315	84.22519	84.00406	83.81558	83.65604	83.41084	83.18809	83.11176	83.07407
11.750	84.11093	83.68221	83.31103	82.99081	82.71568	82.48041	82.28039	82.11148	81.85283	81.61924	81.53971	81.50064
12.000	82.72829	82.27223	81.87836	81.53940	81.24889	81.00109	80.79092	80.61389	80.34377	80.10127	80.01923	79.97913
12.250	81.37906	80.89792	80.48343	80.12760	79.82337	79.56452	79.34553	79.16152	78.88175	78.63207	78.54813	78.50732
12.750	78.77717	78.25219	77.80216	77.41773	77.09068	76.81378	76.58066	76.38576	76.09155	75.83206	75.74592	75.70448

Entry is the percentage of loan balance to give the desired yield to the selected time.

Price of a Mortgage to Give a Specified Yield
Conversion of Interest to Principal or Principal to Interest
9.50% Interest Rate   30 Years Amortization Schedule

Desired Yield	1 Year	2 Years	3 Years	4 Years	5 Years	6 Years	7 Years	8 Years	9 Years	10 Years	11 Years	12 Years
6.500	102.88904	105.57926	108.08260	110.41026	112.57270	114.57971	116.44045	118.16350	119.75685	121.22800	122.58395	123.83124
6.750	102.64476	105.10140	107.38171	109.49672	111.45673	113.27135	114.94954	116.49968	117.92958	119.24654	120.45736	121.56839
7.00	102.40113	104.62593	106.68592	108.59183	110.35368	111.98079	113.48184	114.86491	116.13753	117.30673	118.37902	119.36050
7.250	102.15814	104.15284	105.99518	107.69550	109.26340	110.70779	112.03697	113.25864	114.37996	115.40760	116.34773	117.20609
7.500	101.91580	103.68211	105.30947	106.80765	108.18572	109.45208	110.61455	111.68034	112.65616	113.54822	114.36230	115.10374
7.625	101.79487	103.44763	104.96848	106.36687	107.65156	108.83064	109.91164	110.90151	111.80669	112.63316	113.38644	114.07165
7.75	101.67410	103.21374	104.62874	105.92819	107.12049	108.21343	109.21421	110.12948	110.96541	111.72770	112.42162	113.05205
7.875	101.55349	102.98043	104.29023	105.49158	106.59250	107.60042	108.52220	109.36418	110.13222	110.83173	111.46771	112.04478
8.00	101.43304	102.74771	103.95296	105.05703	106.06756	106.99158	107.83558	108.60555	109.30704	109.94514	110.52457	111.04968
8.125	101.31275	102.51557	103.61691	104.62454	105.54566	106.38688	107.15429	107.85353	108.48978	109.06782	109.59207	110.06657
8.250	101.19262	102.28401	103.28208	104.19410	105.02678	105.78629	106.47830	107.10805	107.68037	108.19968	108.67007	109.09531
8.375	101.07264	102.05303	102.94847	103.76570	104.51090	105.18978	105.80756	106.36906	106.87871	107.34059	107.75845	108.13572
8.50	100.95283	101.82262	102.61607	103.33932	103.99800	104.59732	105.14202	105.63649	106.08474	106.49047	106.85707	107.18766
8.625	100.83317	101.59279	102.28488	102.91495	103.48807	104.00888	104.48164	104.91028	105.29837	105.64920	105.96581	106.25097
8.75	100.71367	101.36354	101.95490	102.49259	102.98108	103.42443	103.82639	104.19037	104.51951	104.81669	105.08455	105.32549
8.875	100.59433	101.13486	101.62611	102.07223	102.47702	102.84395	103.17621	103.47670	103.74810	103.99284	104.21316	104.41109
9.00	100.47515	100.90675	101.29852	101.65385	101.97587	102.26740	102.53107	102.76922	102.98406	103.17754	103.35151	103.50760
9.125	100.35613	100.67921	100.97211	101.23745	101.47761	101.69476	101.89091	102.06787	102.22730	102.37071	102.49949	102.61490
9.25	100.23726	100.45224	100.64690	100.82301	100.98222	101.12600	101.25571	101.37259	101.47775	101.57224	101.65697	101.73282
9.50	100.00000	100.00000	100.00000	100.00000	100.00000	100.00000	100.00000	100.00000	100.00000	100.00000	100.00000	100.00000
9.750	99.76336	99.55001	99.35779	99.18473	99.02907	98.88918	98.76360	98.65102	98.55021	98.46009	98.37967	98.30804
9.875	99.64528	99.32586	99.03843	98.77998	98.54779	98.33939	98.15255	97.98524	97.83562	97.70203	97.58296	97.47704
10.000	99.52735	99.10227	98.72023	98.37713	98.06928	97.79332	97.54620	97.32519	97.12780	96.95177	96.79507	96.65585
10.125	99.40958	98.87924	98.40318	97.97619	97.59353	97.25093	96.94453	96.67084	96.42669	96.20924	96.01590	95.84435
10.25	99.29197	98.65676	98.08729	97.57713	97.12051	96.71220	96.34749	96.02211	95.73221	95.47434	95.24534	95.04240
10.375	99.17451	98.43484	97.77253	97.17995	96.65021	96.17711	95.75504	95.37895	95.04430	94.74698	94.48329	94.24988
10.500	99.05720	98.21347	97.45892	96.78464	96.18262	95.64562	95.16714	94.74133	94.36289	94.02709	93.72963	93.46666
10.625	98.94005	97.99266	97.14645	96.39120	95.71771	95.11772	94.58377	94.10918	93.68791	93.31457	92.98426	92.69262
10.750	98.82306	97.77239	96.83510	95.99960	95.25547	94.59337	94.00487	93.48245	93.01930	92.60934	92.24709	91.92764
10.875	98.70622	97.55268	96.52489	95.60985	94.79589	94.07255	93.43042	92.86109	92.35698	91.91132	91.51801	91.17160
11.000	98.58953	97.33351	96.21580	95.22193	94.33895	93.55523	92.86038	92.24505	91.70090	91.22043	90.79693	90.42438
11.125	98.47300	97.11489	95.90782	94.83583	93.88462	93.04140	92.29470	91.63429	91.05099	90.53659	90.08374	89.68587
11.25	98.35662	96.89681	95.60096	94.45155	93.43291	92.53102	91.73336	91.02875	90.40718	89.85971	89.37835	88.95595
11.375	98.24039	96.67928	95.29522	94.06908	92.98378	92.02406	91.17632	90.42839	89.76942	89.18972	88.68066	88.23451
11.50	98.12432	96.46229	94.99058	93.68840	92.53723	91.52052	90.62354	89.83315	89.13763	88.52655	87.99058	87.52143
11.75	97.89264	96.02992	94.38460	92.93240	91.65578	90.52354	89.53063	88.65787	87.89177	87.22003	86.63288	86.11995
12.00	97.66156	95.59971	93.78299	92.18349	90.77644	89.53989	88.45435	87.50252	86.66909	85.94044	85.30452	84.75063
12.25	97.43110	95.17164	93.18573	91.44158	89.91109	88.56938	87.39443	86.36675	85.46913	84.68630	84.00479	83.41264
12.50	97.20124	94.74570	92.59277	90.70662	89.05561	87.61182	86.35059	85.25020	84.29142	83.45733	82.73298	82.10518
13.000	96.74334	93.90016	91.41966	89.25725	87.37376	85.73480	84.31015	83.07330	82.00096	81.07267	80.27049	79.57866

Yield	13 Years	14 Years	15 Years	16 Years	17 Years	18 Years	19 Years	20 Years	22 Years	25 Years	27 Years	Full Term
6.500	124.97597	126.02385	126.98020	127.84999	128.63785	129.34810	129.98474	130.55154	131.48924	132.45120	132.82631	133.03223
6.750	122.58553	123.51430	124.35985	125.12695	125.82007	126.44335	127.00067	127.49560	128.31144	129.14338	129.46575	129.64179
7.00	120.25680	121.07321	121.81461	122.48556	123.09030	123.63276	124.11660	124.54522	125.24917	125.96273	126.23749	126.38675
7.250	117.98803	118.69849	119.34208	119.92307	120.44542	120.91282	121.32868	121.69615	122.29750	122.90342	123.13525	123.26055
7.500	115.77748	116.38812	116.93991	117.43679	117.88242	118.28018	118.63319	118.94436	119.45173	119.95989	120.15310	120.25697
7.625	114.69352	115.25645	115.76450	116.22143	116.63071	116.99558	117.31899	117.60373	118.06714	118.52989	118.70528	118.79933
7.75	113.62350	114.14015	114.60585	115.02416	115.39840	115.73160	116.02659	116.28597	116.70735	117.12688	117.28538	117.37016
7.875	112.56722	113.03897	113.46367	113.84468	114.18512	114.48786	114.75555	114.99063	115.37185	115.75025	115.89276	115.96879
8.00	111.52448	111.95268	112.33770	112.68269	112.99056	113.26399	113.50546	113.71726	114.06010	114.39939	114.52677	114.59455
8.125	110.49509	110.88107	111.22769	111.53789	111.81436	112.05961	112.27593	112.46543	112.77161	113.07372	113.18678	113.24679
8.250	109.47885	109.82389	110.13337	110.40998	110.65622	110.87437	111.06655	111.23470	111.50588	111.77267	111.87219	111.92487
8.375	108.47558	108.78095	109.05449	109.29869	109.51580	109.70792	109.87694	110.02465	110.26244	110.49567	110.58240	110.62820
8.50	107.48509	107.75201	107.99082	108.20373	108.39280	108.55989	108.70672	108.83487	109.04081	109.24219	109.31684	109.35615
8.625	106.50721	106.73687	106.94209	107.12483	107.28691	107.42997	107.55552	107.66497	107.84052	108.01169	108.07494	108.10816
8.75	105.54174	105.73531	105.90807	106.06172	106.19782	106.31780	106.42297	106.51454	106.66115	106.80366	106.85616	106.88366
8.875	104.58851	104.74714	104.88853	105.01413	105.12524	105.22307	105.30873	105.38320	105.50223	105.61760	105.65996	105.68210
9.00	103.64735	103.77214	103.88323	103.98179	104.06888	104.14546	104.21243	104.27058	104.36336	104.45301	104.48583	104.50293
9.125	102.71809	102.81012	102.89195	102.96446	103.02845	103.08465	103.13373	103.17631	103.24410	103.30942	103.33325	103.34564
9.25	101.80055	101.86089	101.91447	101.96189	102.00368	102.04034	102.07232	102.10002	102.14405	102.18635	102.20174	102.20971
9.50	100.00000	100.00000	100.00000	100.00000	100.00000	100.00000	100.00000	100.00000	100.00000	100.00000	100.00000	100.00000
9.750	98.24438	98.18797	98.13811	98.09405	98.05571	98.02210	97.99293	97.96779	97.92811	97.89044	97.87692	97.86997
9.875	97.38303	97.29981	97.22637	97.16177	97.10519	97.05586	97.01310	96.97629	96.91830	96.86341	96.84377	96.83371
10.000	96.53244	96.42333	96.32715	96.24267	96.16876	96.10440	96.04868	96.00077	95.92543	95.85435	95.82898	95.81603
10.125	95.69246	95.55835	95.44027	95.33668	95.24616	95.16744	95.09938	95.04092	94.94916	94.86285	94.83214	94.81650
10.25	94.86295	94.70468	94.56552	94.44358	94.33716	94.24473	94.16490	94.09643	93.98915	93.88853	93.85285	93.83473
10.375	94.04374	93.86217	93.70271	93.56316	93.44152	93.33600	93.24499	93.16702	93.04507	92.93103	92.89072	92.87030
10.500	93.23471	93.03065	92.85166	92.69521	92.55901	92.44102	92.33936	92.25238	92.11659	91.98998	91.94537	91.92283
10.625	92.43569	92.20994	92.01218	91.83953	91.68841	91.55952	91.44775	91.35224	91.20339	91.06503	91.01642	90.99193
10.750	91.64657	91.39992	91.18408	90.99590	90.83249	90.69126	90.56990	90.46631	90.30517	90.15582	90.10352	90.07724
10.875	90.86718	90.60036	90.36719	90.16414	89.98803	89.83602	89.70554	89.59432	89.42162	89.26202	89.20631	89.17839
11.000	90.09740	89.81117	89.56134	89.34405	89.15582	88.99355	88.85445	88.73601	88.55244	88.38330	88.32445	88.29503
11.125	89.33710	89.03216	88.76634	88.53543	88.33565	88.16363	88.01635	87.89111	87.69735	87.51935	87.45761	87.42682
11.25	88.58614	88.26320	87.98204	87.73810	87.52731	87.34604	87.19103	87.05938	86.85606	86.66984	86.60545	86.57342
11.375	87.84438	87.50412	87.20825	86.95187	86.73060	86.54055	86.37823	86.24055	86.02830	85.83446	85.76766	85.73451
11.50	87.11170	86.75479	86.44482	86.17655	85.94532	85.74695	85.57774	85.43438	85.21379	85.01293	84.94392	84.90977
11.75	85.67308	85.28478	84.94839	84.65797	84.40826	84.19458	84.01275	83.85909	83.62348	83.41022	83.33742	83.30158
12.00	84.26927	83.85204	83.49148	83.18096	82.91463	82.68728	82.49431	82.33164	82.08310	81.85946	81.78360	81.74644
12.25	82.89932	82.45548	82.07287	81.74418	81.46296	81.22349	81.02074	80.85024	80.59068	80.35851	80.28025	80.24211
12.50	81.56229	81.09404	80.69138	80.34633	80.05184	79.80169	79.59042	79.41319	79.14435	78.90531	78.82524	78.78642
13.000	78.98336	78.47244	78.03525	77.66246	77.34586	77.07827	76.85337	76.66564	76.38292	76.13448	76.05231	76.01289

Entry is the percentage of loan balance to give the desired yield to the selected time.

Price of a Mortgage to Give a Specified Yield
Conversion of Interest to Principal or Principal to Interest
9.75% Interest Rate   30 Years Amortization Schedule

Desired Yield	1 Year	2 Years	3 Years	4 Years	Prepaid or Ballooned at 5 Years	6 Years	7 Years	8 Years	9 Years	10 Years	11 Years	12 Years
6.750	102.88560	105.56680	108.05641	110.36638	112.50788	114.49133	116.32645	118.02231	119.58738	121.02956	122.35621	123.57420
7.00	102.64161	105.09002	107.35782	109.45677	111.39781	113.19112	114.84621	116.37190	117.77644	119.06747	120.25214	121.33707
7.250	102.39827	104.61562	106.66431	108.55576	110.30056	111.90857	113.38896	114.75022	116.00027	117.14645	118.19559	119.15403
7.500	102.15558	104.14359	105.97584	107.66325	109.21598	110.64343	111.95431	113.15673	114.25817	115.26558	116.18541	117.02363
7.75	101.91352	103.67392	105.29236	106.77917	108.14392	109.39543	110.54190	111.59089	112.54941	113.42393	114.22044	114.94448
7.875	101.79274	103.43997	104.95249	106.34027	107.61253	108.77779	109.84392	110.81819	111.70733	112.51754	113.25456	113.92369
8.00	101.67211	103.20660	104.61385	105.90344	107.08421	108.16434	109.15135	110.05221	110.87332	111.62062	112.29956	112.91521
8.125	101.55165	102.97382	104.27644	105.46867	106.55895	107.55506	108.46416	109.29288	110.04731	110.73306	111.35532	111.91886
8.25	101.43134	102.74161	103.94026	105.03596	106.03672	106.94991	107.78230	108.54015	109.22921	109.85476	110.42169	110.93449
8.375	101.31119	102.50999	103.60530	104.60529	105.51751	106.34887	107.10573	107.79396	108.41894	108.98561	109.49855	109.96193
8.50	101.19120	102.27895	103.27155	104.17666	105.00129	105.75190	106.43440	107.05424	107.61641	108.12551	108.58576	109.00103
8.625	101.07137	102.04848	102.93902	103.75005	104.48806	105.15898	105.76827	106.32093	106.82156	107.27436	107.68320	108.05163
8.75	100.95170	101.81859	102.60769	103.32546	103.97778	104.57007	105.10729	105.59397	106.03429	106.43205	106.79074	107.11358
8.875	100.83218	101.58927	102.27757	102.90287	103.47045	103.98516	104.45143	104.87331	105.25453	105.59847	105.90826	106.18673
9.00	100.71283	101.36052	101.94864	102.48227	102.96604	103.40420	103.80063	104.15888	104.48220	104.77354	105.03562	105.27092
9.125	100.59363	101.13235	101.62091	102.06365	102.46453	102.82717	103.15486	103.45063	103.71722	103.95715	104.17272	104.36602
9.25	100.47459	100.90475	101.29437	101.64701	101.96592	102.25404	102.51408	102.74850	102.95952	103.14921	103.31943	103.47187
9.375	100.35571	100.67771	100.96901	101.23234	101.47018	101.68479	101.87825	102.05242	102.20903	102.34962	102.47562	102.58833
9.50	100.23698	100.45124	100.64483	100.81962	100.97729	101.11939	101.24732	101.36235	101.46566	101.55828	101.64120	101.71527
9.75	100.00000	100.00000	100.00000	100.00000	100.00000	100.00000	100.00000	100.00000	100.00000	100.00000	100.00000	100.00000
10.000	99.76364	99.55101	99.35983	99.18808	99.03392	98.89567	98.77182	98.66100	98.56197	98.47362	98.39493	98.32498
10.125	99.64570	99.32325	99.04149	98.78499	98.55504	98.34908	98.16480	98.00012	97.85315	97.72218	97.60567	97.50223
10.25	99.52791	99.10425	98.72429	98.38379	98.07891	97.80617	97.56245	97.34491	97.15101	96.97844	96.82511	96.68915
10.375	99.41028	98.88170	98.40825	97.98448	97.60551	97.26692	96.96472	96.69533	96.45550	96.24232	96.05314	95.88560
10.50	99.29280	98.65972	98.09335	97.58705	97.13484	96.73130	96.37159	96.05132	95.76655	95.51373	95.28967	95.09147
10.625	99.17548	98.43828	97.77959	97.19149	96.66686	96.19928	95.78300	95.41283	95.08409	94.79260	94.53458	94.30663
10.75	99.05832	98.21740	97.46696	96.79779	96.20156	95.67084	95.19893	94.77980	94.40805	94.07883	93.78777	93.53095
10.875	98.94130	97.99706	97.15547	96.40593	95.73894	95.14596	94.61933	94.15219	93.73837	93.37234	93.04914	92.76432
11.000	98.82444	97.77728	96.84511	96.01592	95.27896	94.62459	94.04417	93.52994	93.07498	92.67306	92.31860	92.00632
11.125	98.70774	97.55804	96.53586	95.62774	94.82163	94.10673	93.47341	92.91301	92.41781	91.98089	91.59604	91.25773
11.25	98.59119	97.33935	96.22774	95.24138	94.36691	93.59235	92.90701	92.30135	91.76681	91.29576	90.88136	90.51753
11.375	98.47480	97.12121	95.92073	94.85684	93.91479	93.08141	92.34495	91.69490	91.12190	90.61758	90.17447	89.78591
11.50	98.35855	96.90360	95.61483	94.47410	93.46526	92.57391	91.78718	91.09363	90.48303	89.94629	89.47528	89.06275
11.625	98.24246	96.68654	95.31003	94.09316	93.01831	92.06980	91.23367	90.49747	89.85014	89.28180	88.77846	88.34795
11.750	98.12653	96.47002	95.00634	93.71400	92.57391	91.56907	90.68438	89.90639	89.22315	88.62404	88.09959	87.64140
12.00	97.89512	96.03860	94.40224	92.96101	91.69271	90.57764	89.59833	88.73926	87.98668	87.32839	86.75357	86.25261
12.25	97.66431	95.60932	93.80249	92.21506	90.82156	89.59944	88.52875	87.59186	86.77313	86.05875	85.43649	84.89553
12.50	97.43412	95.18217	93.20707	91.47609	89.96032	88.63426	87.47539	86.46383	85.58204	84.81454	84.14765	83.56934
12.750	97.20453	94.75714	92.61594	90.74402	89.10888	87.68193	86.43797	85.35461	84.41295	83.59518	82.88638	82.27323
13.25	96.74716	93.91341	91.44641	89.30031	87.43493	85.81507	84.40991	83.19243	82.13899	81.22885	80.44389	79.76820

Yield	13 Years	14 Years	15 Years	16 Years	17 Years	18 Years	19 Years	20 Years	22 Years	25 Years	27 Years	Full Term
6.750	124.68993	125.70936	126.63803	127.48113	128.24346	128.92949	129.54339	130.08903	130.98958	131.90999	132.26756	132.46330
7.00	122.32844	123.23200	124.05308	124.79665	125.46731	126.06958	126.60677	127.08323	127.86676	128.66277	128.97007	129.13741
7.250	120.02763	120.82188	121.54184	122.19221	122.77736	123.30134	123.76790	124.18053	124.85661	125.53936	125.80128	125.94317
7.500	117.78577	118.47695	119.10193	119.66511	120.17055	120.62203	121.02304	121.37681	121.95436	122.53412	122.75512	122.87423
7.75	115.60117	116.19524	116.73108	117.21273	117.64393	118.02815	118.36856	118.66813	119.15542	119.64165	119.82584	119.92458
7.875	114.52983	115.07749	115.57085	116.01378	116.40981	116.76225	117.07413	117.34825	117.79332	118.23611	118.40331	118.49272
8.00	113.47220	113.97483	114.42707	114.83256	115.19469	115.51655	115.80101	116.05072	116.45544	116.85687	117.00798	117.08857
8.125	112.42808	112.88703	113.29946	113.66880	113.99822	114.29066	114.54879	114.77511	115.14125	115.50334	115.63920	115.71147
8.25	111.39728	111.81387	112.18776	112.52218	112.82009	113.08421	113.31708	113.52098	113.85026	114.17492	114.29636	114.36079
8.375	110.37961	110.75512	111.09173	111.39242	111.65996	111.89686	112.10546	112.28790	112.58197	112.87106	112.97885	113.03589
8.50	109.37487	109.71056	110.01110	110.27924	110.51751	110.72824	110.91357	111.07545	111.33591	111.59120	111.68608	111.73616
8.625	108.38290	108.67999	108.94563	109.18235	109.39244	109.57802	109.74102	109.88322	110.11161	110.33479	110.41748	110.46101
8.75	107.40349	107.66318	107.89509	108.10148	108.28444	108.44585	108.58744	108.71082	108.90861	109.10132	109.17249	109.20986
8.875	106.43649	106.65992	106.85922	107.03637	107.19321	107.33140	107.45248	107.55785	107.72647	107.89026	107.95056	107.98214
9.00	105.48170	105.67003	105.83780	105.98674	106.11845	106.23435	106.33577	106.42392	106.56474	106.70112	106.75117	106.77731
9.125	104.53895	104.69328	104.83059	104.95235	105.05987	105.15438	105.23697	105.30868	105.42301	105.53340	105.57379	105.59484
9.25	103.60808	103.72949	103.83738	103.93292	104.01719	104.09117	104.15575	104.21174	104.30085	104.38664	104.41793	104.43419
9.375	102.68892	102.77846	102.85793	102.92822	102.99014	103.04443	103.09176	103.13275	103.19787	103.26037	103.28309	103.29487
9.50	101.78129	101.83999	101.89202	101.93799	101.97843	102.01385	102.04469	102.07136	102.11365	102.15413	102.16880	102.17638
9.75	100.00000	100.00000	100.00000	100.00000	100.00000	100.00000	100.00000	100.00000	100.00000	100.00000	100.00000	100.00000
10.000	98.26293	98.20304	98.15963	98.11707	98.07983	98.04735	98.01921	97.99501	97.95689	97.92085	97.90795	97.90135
10.125	97.41060	97.32963	97.25830	97.19568	97.14093	97.09328	97.05204	97.01659	96.96089	96.90837	96.88963	96.88007
10.25	96.56885	96.46269	96.36929	96.28739	96.21586	96.15369	96.09995	96.05383	95.98146	95.91343	95.88924	95.87693
10.375	95.73755	95.60706	95.49239	95.39196	95.30437	95.22832	95.16268	95.10640	95.01826	94.93565	94.90638	94.89151
10.50	94.91655	94.76256	94.62741	94.50920	94.40621	94.31692	94.23994	94.17401	94.07097	93.97467	93.94065	93.92342
10.625	94.10570	93.92903	93.77417	93.63888	93.52171	93.41924	93.33146	93.25639	93.13925	93.03011	92.99168	92.97226
10.75	93.30485	93.10631	92.93248	92.78082	92.64901	92.53502	92.43698	92.35323	92.22280	92.10163	92.05909	92.03766
10.875	92.51388	92.29293	92.10216	91.93479	91.78952	91.66403	91.55624	91.46428	91.32130	91.18888	91.14254	91.11925
11.000	91.73264	91.49264	91.28304	91.10061	90.94247	90.80603	90.68898	90.58924	90.43446	90.29152	90.24166	90.21667
11.125	90.96099	90.70138	90.47493	90.27808	90.10765	89.96079	89.83496	89.72787	89.56197	89.40923	89.35611	89.32956
11.25	90.19879	89.92029	89.67766	89.46701	89.28485	89.12808	88.99392	88.87989	88.70355	88.54168	88.48557	88.45759
11.375	89.44593	89.14923	88.89107	88.66721	88.47387	88.30769	88.16564	88.04506	87.85893	87.68857	87.62970	87.60042
11.50	88.70226	88.38805	88.11498	87.87849	87.67450	87.49938	87.34988	87.22312	87.02781	86.84958	86.78819	86.75773
11.625	87.96766	87.63660	87.34924	87.10069	86.88655	86.70294	86.54640	86.41383	86.20994	86.02442	85.96072	85.92921
11.750	87.24200	86.89473	86.59368	86.33361	86.10982	85.91818	85.75498	85.61695	85.40504	85.21281	85.14701	85.11454
12.00	85.81701	85.43920	85.11248	84.83093	84.58927	84.38282	84.20746	84.05950	83.83317	83.62698	83.55964	83.52556
12.25	84.42630	84.02034	83.67015	83.36910	83.11135	82.89171	82.70559	82.54895	82.31020	82.09616	82.02382	81.98849
12.50	83.06894	82.63209	82.26548	81.94682	81.67465	81.44300	81.24775	81.08357	80.83422	80.61200	80.53738	80.50112
12.750	81.74401	81.28840	80.89732	80.56279	80.27778	80.03611	79.83233	79.66168	79.40342	79.17462	79.09827	79.06136
13.25	79.18788	78.69074	78.26612	77.90469	77.59828	77.33974	77.12283	76.94206	76.67045	76.43265	76.35430	76.31681

Entry is the percentage of loan balance to give the desired yield to the selected time.

Price of a Mortgage to Give a Specified Yield
Conversion of Interest to Principal or Principal to Interest
10.00% Interest Rate 30 Years Amortization Schedule

Desired Yield	Prepaid or Ballooned at 1 Year	2 Years	3 Years	4 Years	5 Years	6 Years	7 Years	8 Years	9 Years	10 Years	11 Years	12 Years
7.00	102.88214	105.55431	108.03018	110.32249	112.44313	114.40314	116.21282	117.88175	119.41887	120.83246	122.13026	123.31945
7.250	102.63845	105.07861	107.33390	109.41681	111.33894	113.11107	114.74322	116.24469	117.62414	118.88959	120.04850	121.10779
7.500	102.39541	104.60528	106.64267	108.51967	110.24748	111.83650	113.29638	114.63604	115.86377	116.98725	118.01358	118.94936
7.75	102.15300	104.13432	105.95646	107.63099	109.16860	110.57919	111.87193	113.05527	114.13704	115.12450	116.02435	116.84276
8.00	101.91124	103.66571	105.27523	106.75069	108.10215	109.33889	110.46949	111.50184	112.44326	113.30046	114.07966	114.78660
8.125	101.79060	103.43229	104.93647	106.31365	107.57353	108.72504	109.77641	110.73523	111.60850	112.40267	113.12369	113.77701
8.25	101.67012	103.19944	104.59894	105.87868	107.04797	108.11535	109.08870	109.97527	110.78173	111.51424	112.17844	112.77954
8.375	101.54979	102.96718	104.26263	105.44576	106.52543	107.50978	108.40631	109.22189	109.96286	110.63504	111.24378	111.79402
8.50	101.42963	102.73550	103.92754	105.01488	106.00591	106.90832	107.72920	108.47503	109.15180	109.76497	110.31959	110.82028
8.625	101.30963	102.50440	103.59367	104.58604	105.48938	106.31093	107.05732	107.73464	108.34847	108.90394	109.40574	109.85818
8.75	101.18978	102.27387	103.26101	104.15921	104.97583	105.71758	106.39064	107.00065	107.55280	108.05183	108.50209	108.90755
8.875	101.07009	102.04392	102.92955	103.73440	104.46523	105.12824	105.72910	106.27301	106.76471	107.20855	107.60852	107.96825
9.00	100.95056	101.81454	102.59930	103.31159	103.95757	104.54288	105.07267	105.55164	105.98411	106.37400	106.72491	107.04013
9.125	100.83119	101.58573	102.27025	102.89077	103.45284	103.96148	104.42130	104.83650	105.21092	105.54807	105.85113	106.12303
9.25	100.71198	101.35750	101.94238	102.47194	102.95100	103.38400	103.77495	104.12753	104.44508	104.73067	104.98706	105.21681
9.375	100.59292	101.12984	101.61571	102.05507	102.45206	102.81042	103.13358	103.42467	103.68651	103.92170	104.13258	104.32132
9.50	100.47403	100.90274	101.29022	101.64017	101.95598	102.24071	102.49715	102.72785	102.93512	103.12106	103.28758	103.43643
9.625	100.35528	100.67621	100.96591	101.22722	101.46275	101.67484	101.86562	102.03704	102.19085	102.32867	102.45194	102.56199
9.750	100.23670	100.45024	100.64277	100.81622	100.97236	101.11278	101.23894	101.35216	101.45362	101.54442	101.62553	101.69786
10.00	100.00000	100.00000	100.00000	100.00000	100.00000	100.00000	100.00000	100.00000	100.00000	100.00000	100.00000	100.00000
10.25	99.76393	99.55200	99.36188	99.19144	99.03877	98.90214	98.78000	98.67094	98.57368	98.48707	98.41009	98.34178
10.375	99.64612	99.32884	99.04454	98.79000	98.56228	98.35875	98.17701	98.01494	97.87058	97.74220	97.62822	97.52721
10.50	99.52847	99.10623	98.72836	98.39045	98.08853	97.81900	97.57865	97.36455	97.17410	97.00493	96.85493	96.72217
10.625	99.41098	98.88418	98.41332	97.99278	97.61749	97.28288	96.98486	96.71973	96.48417	96.27519	96.09011	95.92652
10.75	99.29364	98.66268	98.09942	97.59698	97.14915	96.75036	96.39562	96.08041	95.80071	95.55289	95.33367	95.14014
10.875	99.17646	98.44173	97.78666	97.20303	96.68349	96.22142	95.81088	95.44656	95.12367	94.83794	94.58550	94.36292
11.000	99.05943	98.22133	97.47502	96.81093	96.22049	95.69602	95.23061	94.81811	94.45298	94.13026	93.84550	93.59473
11.125	98.94256	98.00148	97.16451	96.42067	95.76015	95.17414	94.65478	94.19503	93.78857	93.42977	93.11357	92.83545
11.25	98.82584	97.78218	96.85512	96.03225	95.30244	94.65576	94.08334	93.57725	93.13037	92.73638	92.38960	92.08497
11.375	98.70927	97.56342	96.54686	95.64564	94.84734	94.14085	93.51627	92.96473	92.47833	92.05003	91.67351	91.34316
11.50	98.59286	97.34521	96.23970	95.26084	94.39485	93.62939	92.95351	92.35742	91.83238	91.37062	90.96520	90.60993
11.625	98.47660	97.12754	95.93365	94.87785	93.94494	93.12136	92.39505	91.75528	91.19246	90.69809	90.26457	89.88515
11.75	98.36050	96.91042	95.62871	94.49666	93.49760	92.61672	91.84084	91.15824	90.55850	90.03235	89.57153	89.16871
11.875	98.24454	96.69383	95.32487	94.11724	93.05281	92.11545	91.29085	90.56628	89.93045	89.37332	88.88598	88.46051
12.00	98.12874	96.47778	95.02212	93.73961	92.61056	91.61753	90.74504	89.97934	89.30822	88.72094	88.20784	87.76043
12.250	97.89760	96.04729	94.41991	92.98963	91.73362	90.63165	89.66583	88.82032	88.08112	87.43580	86.87342	86.38424
12.50	97.66707	95.61895	93.82203	92.24666	90.86664	89.65888	88.60295	87.68084	86.87665	86.17635	85.56755	85.03931
12.750	97.43715	95.19272	93.22845	91.51061	90.00952	88.69903	87.55612	86.56052	85.69439	84.94201	84.28955	83.72482
13.00	97.20783	94.76862	92.63915	90.78143	89.16212	87.75192	86.52509	85.45902	84.53388	83.73222	83.03874	82.44000
13.500	96.75100	93.92671	91.47322	89.34339	87.49605	85.89520	84.50938	83.31110	82.27635	81.38413	80.61612	79.95630

Yield	13 Years	14 Years	15 Years	16 Years	17 Years	18 Years	19 Years	20 Years	22 Years	25 Years	27 Years	Full Term
7.00	124.40671	125.39827	126.29989	127.11694	127.85440	128.51690	129.10873	129.63386	130.49850	131.37889	131.71966	131.90565
7.250	122.07388	122.95274	123.74991	124.47051	125.11930	125.70070	126.21879	126.67735	127.42964	128.19106	128.48392	128.64293
7.500	119.80070	120.57325	121.27224	121.90253	122.46860	122.97461	123.42441	123.82153	124.47068	125.12377	125.37337	125.50820
7.75	117.58547	118.25778	118.86457	119.41035	119.89932	120.33532	120.72192	121.06241	121.61695	122.17153	122.38215	122.49533
8.00	115.42655	116.00441	116.52465	116.99144	117.40859	117.77963	118.10782	118.39614	118.86402	119.32915	119.50468	119.59852
8.125	114.36771	114.90042	115.37942	115.80868	116.19181	116.53217	116.83285	117.09668	117.52403	117.94760	118.10694	118.19191
8.25	113.32234	113.81125	114.25033	114.64332	114.99364	115.30448	115.57872	115.81906	116.20767	116.59168	116.73568	116.81227
8.375	112.29026	112.73669	113.13712	113.49506	113.81376	114.09617	114.34504	114.56287	114.91443	115.26080	115.39029	115.45897
8.50	111.27129	111.67651	112.03952	112.36362	112.65183	112.90691	113.13141	113.32767	113.64384	113.95442	114.07015	114.13138
8.625	110.26522	110.63408	110.95730	111.24872	111.50754	111.73634	111.93745	112.11304	112.39541	112.67196	112.77469	112.82890
8.75	109.27188	109.59841	109.89020	110.15008	110.38059	110.58411	110.76278	110.91859	111.16869	111.41290	111.50333	111.55092
8.875	108.29109	108.58007	108.83799	109.06741	109.27066	109.44989	109.60704	109.74390	109.96321	110.17671	110.25552	110.29689
9.00	107.32266	107.57526	107.80043	108.00046	108.17746	108.33334	108.46986	108.58861	108.77853	108.96288	109.03071	109.06623
9.125	106.36643	106.58377	106.77728	106.94897	107.10070	107.23416	107.35089	107.45231	107.61423	107.77092	107.82839	107.85841
9.25	105.42222	105.60541	105.76831	105.91266	106.04008	106.15201	106.24980	106.33465	106.46986	106.60033	106.64803	106.67288
9.375	104.48986	104.63998	104.77330	104.89130	104.99532	105.08660	105.16623	105.23525	105.34503	105.45065	105.48914	105.50914
9.50	103.56918	103.68728	103.79203	103.88463	103.96616	104.03760	104.09987	104.15376	104.23933	104.32140	104.35122	104.36667
9.625	102.66001	102.74711	102.82427	102.89240	102.95231	103.00474	103.05037	103.08982	103.15235	103.21215	103.23381	103.24500
9.750	101.76220	101.81930	101.86982	101.91437	101.95350	101.98771	102.01744	102.04311	102.08373	102.12245	102.13643	102.14364
10.00	100.00000	100.00000	100.00000	100.00000	100.00000	100.00000	100.00000	100.00000	100.00000	100.00000	100.00000	100.00000
10.25	98.28132	98.22792	98.18091	98.13966	98.10362	98.07226	98.04514	98.02183	97.98523	97.95075	97.93846	97.93218
10.375	97.43791	97.35915	97.28990	97.22920	97.17623	97.13020	97.09044	97.05633	97.00283	96.95258	96.93473	96.92564
10.50	96.60493	96.50167	96.41097	96.33159	96.26239	96.20234	96.15053	96.10613	96.03664	95.97155	95.94850	95.93680
10.625	95.78223	95.65530	95.54395	95.44662	95.36187	95.28842	95.22513	95.17095	95.08632	95.00729	94.97938	94.96525
10.75	94.96967	94.81987	94.68865	94.57407	94.47443	94.38819	94.31397	94.25051	94.15155	94.05942	94.02699	94.01061
10.875	94.16709	93.99524	93.84487	93.71375	93.59986	93.50141	93.41678	93.34451	93.23202	93.12761	93.09097	93.07252
11.000	93.37437	93.18124	93.01245	92.86545	92.73793	92.62783	92.53330	92.45269	92.32743	92.21150	92.17095	92.15058
11.125	92.59137	92.37770	92.19120	92.02898	91.88842	91.76722	91.66329	91.57477	91.43747	91.31077	91.26660	91.24446
11.25	91.81794	91.58448	91.38095	91.20413	91.05113	90.91935	90.80649	90.71049	90.56184	90.42509	90.37755	90.35380
11.375	91.05396	90.80141	90.58153	90.39074	90.22584	90.08400	89.96267	89.85958	89.70027	89.55413	89.50350	89.47826
11.50	90.29929	90.02836	89.79277	89.58859	89.41235	89.26093	89.13158	89.02181	88.85247	88.69759	88.64410	88.61751
11.625	89.55380	89.26517	89.01449	88.79752	88.61046	88.44994	88.31299	88.19691	88.01816	87.85516	87.79905	87.77122
11.75	88.81737	88.51170	88.24655	88.01733	87.81996	87.65081	87.50666	87.38464	87.19708	87.02655	86.96803	86.93908
11.875	88.08986	87.76780	87.48878	87.24786	87.04068	86.86334	86.71239	86.58478	86.38897	86.21147	86.15075	86.12079
12.00	87.37116	87.03334	86.74101	86.48893	86.27241	86.08730	85.92995	85.79708	85.59357	85.40963	85.34691	85.31604
12.250	85.95968	85.59215	85.27490	85.00200	84.76817	84.56877	84.39968	84.25725	84.03989	83.84459	83.77842	83.74602
12.50	84.58198	84.18705	83.84700	83.55521	83.30581	83.09366	82.91420	82.76341	82.53412	82.32931	82.26035	82.22677
12.750	83.23712	82.81699	82.45615	82.14727	81.88393	81.66047	81.47190	81.31386	81.07439	80.86176	80.79062	80.75615
13.00	81.92419	81.48096	81.10120	80.77694	80.50117	80.26774	80.07124	79.90696	79.65893	79.44000	79.36721	79.33212
13.500	79.39068	78.90704	78.49471	78.14437	77.84789	77.59816	77.38899	77.21497	76.95411	76.72656	76.65186	76.61622

Entry is the percentage of loan balance to give the desired yield to the selected time.

Price of a Mortgage to Give a Specified Yield
Conversion of Interest to Principal or Principal to Interest
10.25% Interest Rate 30 Years Amortization Schedule

Desired Yield	1 Year	2 Years	3 Years	4 Years	5 Years	6 Years	7 Years	8 Years	9 Years	10 Years	11 Years	12 Years
					Prepaid or Ballooned at							
7.250	102.87868	105.54179	108.00391	110.27859	112.37844	114.31515	116.09959	117.74187	119.25135	120.63674	121.90613	123.06702
7.500	102.63528	105.06717	107.30994	109.37684	111.28013	113.03120	114.64059	116.11809	117.47274	118.71296	119.84650	120.88059
7.75	102.39253	104.59492	106.62101	108.48358	110.19446	111.76461	113.20413	114.52240	115.72807	116.82915	117.83303	118.74655
8.000	102.15042	104.12503	105.93707	107.59873	109.12128	110.51511	111.78983	112.95428	114.01663	114.98440	115.86456	116.66352
8.25	101.90895	103.65748	105.25808	106.72220	108.06043	109.28248	110.39733	111.41321	112.33772	113.17784	113.94000	114.63013
8.375	101.78845	103.42459	104.92043	106.28703	107.53458	108.67241	109.70914	110.65266	111.51025	112.28860	112.99385	113.63165
8.50	101.66811	103.19227	104.58400	105.85392	107.01176	108.06647	109.02626	109.89869	110.69067	111.40858	112.05826	112.64508
8.625	101.54794	102.96053	104.24880	105.42284	106.49195	107.46462	108.34866	109.15122	109.87889	110.53768	111.13312	111.67028
8.750	101.42792	102.72937	103.91480	104.99380	105.97513	106.86683	107.67628	108.41022	109.07483	109.67579	110.21829	110.70709
8.875	101.30806	102.49879	103.58202	104.56677	105.46128	106.27308	107.00908	107.67560	108.27841	108.82282	109.31365	109.75534
9.000	101.18836	102.26878	103.25045	104.14176	104.95039	105.68334	106.34703	106.94731	107.48956	107.97865	108.41907	108.81490
9.125	101.06881	102.03934	102.92007	103.71875	104.44243	105.09757	105.69007	106.22530	106.70818	107.14319	107.53442	107.88561
9.25	100.94943	101.81048	102.59090	103.29772	103.93739	104.51575	105.03817	105.50950	105.93421	106.31634	106.65958	106.96732
9.375	100.83020	101.58219	102.26291	102.87868	103.43525	103.93786	104.39128	104.79986	105.16757	105.49800	105.79444	106.05989
9.50	100.71113	101.35447	101.93611	102.46161	102.93599	103.36385	103.74936	104.09632	104.40818	104.68808	104.93887	105.16316
9.625	100.59222	101.12731	101.61050	102.04649	102.43960	102.79371	103.11238	103.39882	103.65597	103.88647	104.09276	104.27701
9.750	100.47346	100.90072	101.28606	101.63333	101.94605	102.22740	102.48028	102.70731	102.91086	103.09310	103.25598	103.40130
9.875	100.35486	100.67470	100.96279	101.22211	101.45534	101.66491	101.85304	102.02172	102.17278	102.30785	102.42843	102.53587
10.00	100.23642	100.44924	100.64070	100.81282	100.96743	101.10619	101.23060	101.34201	101.44166	101.53065	101.60999	101.68060
10.25	100.00000	100.00000	100.00000	100.00000	100.00000	100.00000	100.00000	100.00000	100.00000	100.00000	100.00000	100.00000
10.50	99.76421	99.55300	99.36392	99.19479	99.04361	98.90861	98.78817	98.68084	98.58532	98.50044	98.42513	98.35844
10.625	99.64654	99.33033	99.04761	98.79502	98.56952	98.36840	98.18919	98.02969	97.88792	97.76209	97.65059	97.55199
10.75	99.52904	99.10821	98.73244	98.39712	98.09814	97.83181	97.59479	97.38410	97.19706	97.03126	96.88452	96.75491
10.875	99.41168	98.88665	98.41840	98.00108	97.62946	97.29881	97.00493	96.74401	96.51267	96.30785	96.12681	95.96709
11.00	99.29448	98.66564	98.10550	97.60691	97.16345	96.76938	96.41956	96.10938	95.83469	95.59178	95.37735	95.18841
11.125	99.17744	98.44519	97.79373	97.21458	96.70010	96.24350	95.83867	95.48014	95.16304	94.88298	94.63605	94.41874
11.25	99.06055	98.22527	97.48309	96.82408	96.23941	95.72114	95.26220	94.85626	94.49766	94.18135	93.90280	93.65797
11.375	98.94382	98.00591	97.17356	96.43542	95.78134	95.20227	94.69012	94.23768	93.83849	93.48682	93.17751	92.90598
11.50	98.82724	97.78709	96.86516	96.04858	95.32589	94.68686	94.12239	93.62435	93.18547	92.79930	92.46008	92.16266
11.625	98.71081	97.56882	96.55786	95.66354	94.87303	94.17490	93.55899	93.01622	92.53853	92.11873	91.75042	91.42789
11.75	98.59453	97.35109	96.25168	95.28031	94.42276	93.66636	92.99986	92.41325	91.89761	91.44501	91.04842	90.70156
11.875	98.47841	97.13390	95.94660	94.89887	93.97505	93.16121	92.44499	91.81538	91.26264	90.77808	90.35401	89.98357
12.00	98.36244	96.91725	95.64261	94.51922	93.52990	92.65944	91.89433	91.22258	90.63357	90.11786	89.66707	89.27379
12.125	98.24663	96.70113	95.33973	94.14134	93.08728	92.16100	91.34784	90.63479	90.01034	89.46427	88.98754	88.57213
12.25	98.13097	96.48556	95.03793	93.76522	92.64718	91.66589	90.80550	90.05197	89.39288	88.81723	88.31530	87.87849
12.50	97.90010	96.05601	94.43760	93.01826	91.77449	90.68554	89.73312	88.90104	88.17505	87.54254	86.99240	86.51480
12.750	97.66984	95.62860	93.84159	92.27826	90.91169	89.71819	88.67690	87.76944	86.97963	86.29322	85.69767	85.18192
13.00	97.44019	95.20331	93.24986	91.54515	90.05867	88.76366	87.63660	86.65681	85.80615	85.06869	84.43043	83.87906
13.25	97.21114	94.78012	92.66238	90.81886	89.21532	87.82177	86.61194	85.56280	84.65418	83.86841	83.19002	82.60544
13.75	96.75484	93.94004	91.50006	89.38649	87.55712	85.97517	84.60854	83.42928	82.41300	81.53846	80.78715	80.14293

Yield	13 Years	14 Years	15 Years	16 Years	17 Years	18 Years	19 Years	20 Years	22 Years	25 Years	27 Years	Full Term
7.250	124.12638	125.09065	125.96584	126.75748	127.47073	128.11035	128.68076	129.18603	130.01598	130.85787	131.18251	131.35920
7.500	121.82189	122.67658	123.45038	124.14858	124.77608	125.33740	125.83674	126.27797	127.00009	127.72822	128.00722	128.15828
7.75	119.57605	120.32735	121.00586	121.61656	122.16406	122.65261	123.08613	123.46824	124.09136	124.71590	124.95371	125.08179
8.000	117.38718	118.04100	118.63001	119.15884	119.63177	120.05273	120.42535	120.75297	121.28528	121.81563	122.01629	122.12382
8.25	115.25368	115.81565	116.32065	116.77294	117.17641	117.53465	117.85098	118.12841	118.57754	119.02235	119.18959	119.27873
8.375	114.20719	114.72526	115.19024	115.60616	115.97673	116.30536	116.59516	116.84903	117.25926	117.66433	117.81614	117.89686
8.50	113.17397	113.64944	114.07567	114.45645	114.79529	115.09540	115.35974	115.59100	115.96403	116.33128	116.46848	116.54124
8.625	112.15381	112.58797	112.97667	113.32350	113.63175	113.90443	114.14430	114.35390	114.69138	115.02263	115.14600	115.21125
8.750	111.14653	111.54062	111.89301	112.20705	112.48581	112.73209	112.94848	113.13733	113.44084	113.73786	113.84812	113.90630
8.875	110.15195	110.50718	110.82444	111.10681	111.35715	111.57805	111.77190	111.94086	112.21193	112.47641	112.57428	112.62578
9.000	109.16989	109.48745	109.77071	110.02251	110.24547	110.44198	110.61419	110.76412	111.00421	111.23776	111.32392	111.36914
9.125	108.20017	108.48122	108.73159	108.95389	109.15048	109.32353	109.47500	109.60671	109.81723	110.02142	110.09651	110.13581
9.25	107.24262	107.48828	107.70686	107.90069	108.07189	108.22240	108.35398	108.46825	108.65057	108.82688	108.89151	108.92525
9.375	106.29706	106.50843	106.69627	106.86264	107.00940	107.13826	107.25078	107.34837	107.50380	107.65366	107.70842	107.73694
9.50	105.36332	105.54148	105.69961	105.83949	105.96273	106.07081	106.16506	106.24671	106.37652	106.50129	106.54674	106.57035
9.625	104.44124	104.58724	104.71666	104.83100	104.93162	105.01974	105.09651	105.16292	105.26831	105.36932	105.40599	105.42499
9.750	103.53065	103.64550	103.74719	103.83692	103.91578	103.98477	104.04478	104.09664	104.17879	104.25728	104.28570	104.30038
9.875	102.63139	102.71610	102.79100	102.85701	102.91496	102.96559	103.00957	103.04754	103.10757	103.16476	103.18539	103.19603
10.00	101.74330	101.79883	101.84788	101.89104	101.92889	101.96192	101.99058	102.01528	102.05427	102.09131	102.10463	102.11148
10.25	100.00000	100.00000	100.00000	100.00000	100.00000	100.00000	100.00000	100.00000	100.00000	100.00000	100.00000	100.00000
10.50	98.29952	98.24759	98.20196	98.16199	98.12712	98.09684	98.07070	98.04827	98.01314	97.98015	97.96844	97.96248
10.625	97.46497	97.38837	97.32114	97.26232	97.21108	97.16664	97.12832	97.09548	97.04413	96.99607	96.97905	96.97042
10.75	96.64067	96.54024	96.45219	96.37527	96.30833	96.25035	96.20041	96.15768	96.09097	96.02872	96.00675	95.99563
10.875	95.82649	95.70304	95.59495	95.50063	95.41865	95.34773	95.28672	95.23459	95.15333	95.07774	95.05115	95.03772
11.00	95.02229	94.87660	94.74921	94.63818	94.54180	94.45853	94.38698	94.32591	94.23091	94.14278	94.11188	94.09632
11.125	94.22792	94.06078	93.91480	93.78774	93.67757	93.58251	93.50092	93.43138	93.32339	93.22351	93.18860	93.17107
11.25	93.44325	93.25540	93.09155	92.94910	92.82575	92.71943	92.62831	92.55073	92.43048	92.31959	92.28096	92.26160
11.375	92.66814	92.46033	92.27927	92.12207	91.98611	91.86908	91.76889	91.68370	91.55188	91.43070	91.38860	91.36757
11.50	91.90246	91.67539	91.47781	91.30646	91.15846	91.03121	90.92242	90.83003	90.68732	90.55551	90.51122	90.48864
11.625	91.14608	90.90045	90.68698	90.50210	90.34259	90.20562	90.08866	89.98946	89.83650	89.69672	89.64847	89.62449
11.75	90.39886	90.13536	89.90664	89.70878	89.53830	89.39209	89.26739	89.16175	88.99917	88.85102	88.80005	88.77478
11.875	89.66069	89.37996	89.13660	88.92634	88.74539	88.59039	88.45837	88.34666	88.17504	88.01913	87.96566	87.93921
12.00	88.93143	88.63431	88.37672	88.15459	87.96367	87.80033	87.66137	87.54394	87.36386	87.20075	87.14498	87.11747
12.125	88.21096	87.89771	87.62683	87.39337	87.19295	87.02170	86.87619	86.75338	86.56538	86.39560	86.33773	86.30927
12.25	87.49916	87.17058	86.88678	86.64250	86.43304	86.25430	86.10261	85.97474	85.77934	85.60340	85.54363	85.51430
12.50	86.10108	85.74360	85.43561	85.17115	84.94496	84.75240	84.58940	84.45233	84.24363	84.05682	83.99376	83.96297
12.750	84.73627	84.35214	84.02201	83.73924	83.49798	83.29312	83.12011	82.97499	82.75484	82.55893	82.49321	82.46130
13.00	83.40380	82.99517	82.64484	82.34551	82.09076	81.87497	81.69319	81.54108	81.31116	81.10776	81.03996	81.00720
13.25	82.10279	81.67167	81.30298	80.98874	80.72197	80.49654	80.30712	80.14901	79.91086	79.70143	79.63206	79.59872
13.75	79.59173	79.12131	78.72098	78.38146	78.09465	77.85349	77.65183	77.48435	77.23388	77.01620	76.94501	76.91114

Entry is the percentage of loan balance to give the desired yield to the selected time.

Price of a Mortgage to Give a Specified Yield
Conversion of Interest to Principal or Principal to Interest
10.50% Interest Rate   30 Years Amortization Schedule

Desired Yield	1 Year	2 Years	3 Years	4 Years	5 Years	6 Years	7 Years	8 Years	9 Years	10 Years	11 Years	12 Years
					Prepaid or Ballooned at							
7.500	102.87520	105.52924	107.97761	110.23471	112.31385	114.22740	115.98681	117.60269	119.08486	120.44245	121.68389	122.81698
7.75	102.63210	105.05571	107.28596	109.33688	111.22141	112.95155	114.53837	115.99212	117.32228	118.53761	119.64620	120.65553
8.000	102.38964	104.58454	106.59932	108.44749	110.14152	111.69290	113.11224	114.40933	115.59321	116.67219	117.65398	118.54564
8.25	102.14783	104.11572	105.91765	107.56647	109.07402	110.45120	111.70805	112.85380	113.89694	114.84531	115.70610	116.48594
8.50	101.90665	103.64924	105.24090	106.69372	108.01876	109.22622	110.32544	111.32501	112.23282	113.05609	113.80149	114.47512
8.625	101.78630	103.41687	104.90437	106.26042	107.49568	108.61993	109.64212	110.57050	111.41260	112.17534	112.86507	113.48762
8.750	101.66611	103.18508	104.56905	105.82916	106.97560	108.01776	108.96406	109.82248	110.60016	111.30368	111.93907	112.51186
8.875	101.54607	102.95386	104.23495	105.39993	106.45851	107.41957	108.29122	109.08091	109.79543	110.44102	111.02337	111.54768
9.000	101.42620	102.72323	103.90206	104.97272	105.94439	106.82545	107.62356	108.34572	108.99833	109.58725	110.11782	110.59493
9.125	101.30648	102.49317	103.57037	104.54752	105.43322	106.23533	106.96102	107.61685	108.20878	108.74227	109.22231	109.65345
9.25	101.18693	102.26368	103.23988	104.12431	104.92498	105.64918	106.30358	106.89424	107.42669	107.90598	108.33672	108.72309
9.375	101.06753	102.03476	102.91059	103.70309	104.41966	105.06698	105.65118	106.17783	106.65199	107.07829	107.46092	107.80372
9.50	100.94829	101.80642	102.58248	103.28386	103.91723	104.48869	105.00379	105.46757	105.88461	106.25909	106.59479	106.89517
9.625	100.82920	101.57864	102.25557	102.86659	103.41768	103.91429	104.36137	104.76340	105.12447	105.44828	105.73821	105.99731
9.750	100.71027	101.35143	101.92984	102.45127	102.92099	103.34375	103.72387	104.06526	104.37149	104.64579	104.89107	105.11001
9.875	100.59150	101.12479	101.60528	102.03791	102.42715	102.77704	103.09125	103.37310	103.62561	103.85150	104.05325	104.23311
10.000	100.47289	100.89871	101.28190	101.62649	101.93613	102.21413	102.46347	102.68686	102.88674	103.06533	103.22464	103.36648
10.125	100.35443	100.67319	100.95968	101.21700	101.44793	101.65500	101.84050	102.00648	102.15481	102.28718	102.40511	102.50999
10.250	100.23613	100.44823	100.63863	100.80942	100.96252	101.09962	101.22229	101.33191	101.42976	101.51697	101.59457	101.66350
10.500	100.00000	100.00000	100.00000	100.00000	100.00000	100.00000	100.00000	100.00000	100.00000	100.00000	100.00000	100.00000
10.75	99.76449	99.55399	99.36597	99.19814	99.04845	98.91505	98.79630	98.69069	98.59689	98.51371	98.44005	98.37496
10.875	99.64697	99.33182	99.05068	98.80003	98.57675	98.37802	98.20132	98.04438	97.90516	97.78185	97.67280	97.57654
11.00	99.52960	99.11021	98.73652	98.40378	98.10774	97.84458	97.61087	97.40356	97.21989	97.05740	96.91389	96.78737
11.125	99.41239	98.88914	98.42349	98.00938	97.64140	97.31470	97.02492	96.76819	96.54101	96.34029	96.16322	96.00731
11.25	99.29533	98.66862	98.11159	97.61683	97.17773	96.78836	96.44343	96.13821	95.86846	95.63042	95.42069	95.23625
11.375	99.17842	98.44865	97.80082	97.22612	96.71700	96.26553	95.86635	95.51357	95.20218	94.92771	94.68620	94.47408
11.50	99.06168	98.22923	97.49116	96.83723	96.25829	95.74620	95.29367	94.89422	94.54209	94.23210	93.95966	93.72067
11.625	98.94508	98.01035	97.18263	96.45016	95.80250	95.23032	94.72533	94.28013	93.88813	93.54349	93.24096	92.97591
11.75	98.82864	97.79202	96.87520	96.06490	95.34930	94.71789	94.16130	93.67122	93.24025	92.86180	92.53002	92.23969
11.875	98.71235	97.57424	96.56888	95.68144	94.89869	94.20887	93.60155	93.06747	92.59838	92.18697	91.82673	91.51189
12.00	98.59621	97.35697	96.26367	95.29978	94.45064	93.70324	93.04605	92.46882	91.96246	91.51891	91.13101	90.79242
12.125	98.48023	97.14026	95.95955	94.91989	94.00513	93.20098	92.49475	91.87522	91.33242	90.85754	90.44276	90.08115
12.250	98.36440	96.92409	95.65653	94.54178	93.56216	92.70205	91.94762	91.28662	90.70821	90.20280	89.76189	89.37798
12.375	98.24872	96.70845	95.35460	94.16543	93.12171	92.20645	91.40464	90.70299	90.08977	89.55460	89.08832	88.68282
12.500	98.13320	96.49335	95.05376	93.79084	92.68376	91.71414	90.86575	90.12427	89.47704	88.91289	88.42195	87.99554
12.750	97.90260	96.06475	94.45532	93.04688	91.81530	90.73931	89.80017	88.98140	88.26846	87.64858	87.11049	86.64426
13.00	97.67262	95.63828	93.86118	92.30985	90.95668	89.77737	88.75060	87.85764	87.08204	86.40932	85.82681	85.32335
13.25	97.44323	95.21391	93.27130	91.57968	90.10777	88.82615	87.71680	86.75266	85.91730	85.19455	84.57026	84.03201
13.500	97.21446	94.79165	92.68565	90.85628	89.26845	87.89145	86.69849	85.66610	84.77382	84.00372	83.34018	82.76951
14.00	96.75870	93.95339	91.52693	89.42958	87.61812	86.05495	84.70737	83.54693	82.54891	81.69180	80.95693	80.32803

Yield	13 Years	14 Years	15 Years	16 Years	17 Years	18 Years	19 Years	20 Years	22 Years	25 Years	27 Years	Full Term
7.500	123.84897	124.78655	125.63591	126.40279	127.09248	127.70988	128.25951	128.74555	129.54200	130.34686	130.65605	130.82384
7.75	121.57252	122.40355	123.15453	123.83089	124.43766	124.97949	125.46065	125.88509	126.57807	127.27418	127.53991	127.68337
8.000	119.35372	120.08423	120.74273	121.33433	121.86375	122.33534	122.75308	123.12066	123.71864	124.31573	124.54222	124.66387
8.25	117.19093	117.82666	118.39830	118.91060	119.36792	119.77426	120.13332	120.44849	120.95933	121.46637	121.65749	121.75961
8.50	115.08257	115.62899	116.11912	116.55727	116.94742	117.29323	117.59805	117.86493	118.29595	118.72122	118.88051	118.96518
8.625	114.04832	114.55206	115.00334	115.40626	115.76640	116.08182	116.36109	116.60530	116.99899	117.38627	117.53087	117.60753
8.750	113.02710	113.48943	113.90309	114.27198	114.59964	114.88934	115.14406	115.36653	115.72453	116.07564	116.20633	116.27543
8.875	112.01874	112.44089	112.81814	113.15414	113.45222	113.71544	113.94659	114.14822	114.47210	114.78881	114.90631	114.96829
9.000	111.02304	111.40623	111.74824	112.05247	112.32204	112.55978	112.76830	112.94997	113.24125	113.52523	113.63026	113.68551
9.125	110.03983	110.38524	110.69315	110.96670	111.20879	111.42203	111.60883	111.77137	112.03152	112.28438	112.37761	112.42653
9.25	109.06893	109.37771	109.65263	109.89657	110.11218	110.30186	110.46782	110.61205	110.84247	111.06577	111.14784	111.19079
9.375	108.11017	108.38345	108.62645	108.84181	109.03192	109.19896	109.34493	109.47163	109.67368	109.86890	109.94043	109.97776
9.50	107.16337	107.40224	107.61439	107.80217	107.96762	108.11301	108.23981	108.34974	108.52472	108.69300	108.75486	108.78691
9.625	106.22837	106.43391	106.61622	106.77739	106.91931	107.04371	107.15214	107.24602	107.39520	107.53848	107.59064	107.61773
9.750	105.30500	105.47824	105.63172	105.76723	105.88641	105.99074	106.08157	106.16012	106.28470	106.40400	106.44730	106.46972
9.875	104.39310	104.53506	104.66068	104.77145	104.86875	104.95382	105.02780	105.09169	105.19284	105.28941	105.32435	105.34240
10.000	103.49250	103.60418	103.70288	103.78981	103.86607	103.93266	103.99050	104.04039	104.11923	104.19428	104.22135	104.23529
10.125	102.60304	102.68541	102.75811	102.82207	102.87810	102.92698	102.96937	103.00589	103.06350	103.11818	103.13784	103.14794
10.250	101.72458	101.77858	101.82618	101.86800	101.90460	101.93648	101.96410	101.98787	102.02529	102.06070	102.07339	102.07990
10.500	100.00000	100.00000	100.00000	100.00000	100.00000	100.00000	100.00000	100.00000	100.00000	100.00000	100.00000	100.00000
10.75	98.31755	98.26706	98.22276	98.18404	98.15032	98.12109	98.09590	98.07432	98.04060	98.00906	97.99790	97.99224
10.875	97.49176	97.41728	97.35202	97.29504	97.24549	97.20259	97.16565	97.13406	97.08477	97.03882	97.02261	97.01441
11.00	96.67607	96.57841	96.49295	96.41843	96.35369	96.29772	96.24959	96.20848	96.14445	96.08492	96.06399	96.05343
11.125	95.87043	95.75028	95.64536	95.55399	95.47471	95.40624	95.34745	95.29729	95.21930	95.14702	95.12168	95.10893
11.25	95.07441	94.93274	94.80909	94.70152	94.60831	94.52792	94.45897	94.40022	94.30903	94.22477	94.19533	94.18055
11.375	94.28817	94.12563	93.98394	93.86084	93.75430	93.66252	93.58390	93.51700	93.41334	93.31784	93.28458	93.26792
11.50	93.51147	93.32880	93.16976	93.03175	92.91246	92.80982	92.72200	92.64737	92.53194	92.42591	92.38910	92.37072
11.625	92.74418	92.54210	92.36636	92.21406	92.08257	91.96969	91.87303	91.79107	91.66455	91.54867	91.50857	91.48859
11.75	91.98618	91.76537	91.57359	91.40758	91.26445	91.14160	91.03675	90.94786	90.81088	90.68580	90.64265	90.62121
11.875	91.23733	90.99847	90.79127	90.61214	90.45788	90.32565	90.21293	90.11749	89.97067	89.83701	89.79104	89.76826
12.00	90.49750	90.24125	90.01925	89.82756	89.66628	89.52152	89.40135	89.29971	89.14365	89.00199	88.95343	88.92943
12.125	89.76657	89.49358	89.25736	89.05365	88.87865	88.72901	88.60177	88.49429	88.32957	88.18047	88.12953	88.10441
12.250	89.04442	88.75531	88.50546	88.29025	88.10560	87.94791	87.81399	87.70100	87.52815	87.37217	87.31904	87.29291
12.375	88.33092	88.02631	87.76338	87.53718	87.34335	87.17802	87.03778	86.91962	86.73917	86.57681	86.52168	86.49464
12.500	87.62596	87.30643	87.03097	86.79428	86.59172	86.41915	86.27295	86.14992	85.96237	85.79412	85.73718	85.70931
12.750	86.24118	85.89354	85.59458	85.33835	85.11959	84.93369	84.77659	84.64471	84.44438	84.26574	84.20565	84.17641
13.00	84.88914	84.51559	84.19514	83.92116	83.68784	83.49005	83.32331	83.18368	82.97235	82.78500	82.72239	82.69207
13.25	83.56896	83.17157	82.83152	82.54150	82.29512	82.08678	81.91158	81.76523	81.54452	81.35000	81.28541	81.25429
13.500	82.27976	81.86051	81.50263	81.19816	80.94015	80.72251	80.53994	80.38780	80.15920	79.95891	79.89282	79.86115
14.00	79.79097	79.33349	78.94490	78.61593	78.33852	78.10568	77.91133	77.75017	77.50974	77.30155	77.23372	77.20154

Entry is the percentage of loan balance to give the desired yield to the selected time.

Price of a Mortgage to Give a Specified Yield
Conversion of Interest to Principal or Principal to Interest

10.75% Interest Rate   30 Years Amortization Schedule

Desired Yield	1 Year	2 Years	3 Years	4 Years	Prepaid or Ballooned at 5 Years	6 Years	7 Years	8 Years	9 Years	10 Years	11 Years	12 Years
7.750	102.87171	105.51666	107.95130	110.19084	112.24937	114.13991	115.87450	117.46425	118.91946	120.24964	121.46357	122.56938
8.000	102.62891	105.04422	107.26196	109.29694	111.16279	112.87213	114.43656	115.86682	117.17279	118.36359	119.44762	120.43265
8.25	102.38675	104.57413	106.57761	108.41142	110.08867	111.62140	113.02072	114.29686	115.45921	116.51642	117.47647	118.34666
8.500	102.14523	104.10639	105.89821	107.53422	109.02684	110.38748	111.62661	112.75384	113.77803	114.70727	115.54900	116.31007
8.750	101.90434	103.64097	105.22372	106.66525	107.97717	109.17013	110.25385	111.23728	112.12859	112.93526	113.66416	114.32157
8.875	101.78414	103.40913	104.88830	106.23382	107.45685	108.56759	109.57538	110.48877	111.31556	112.06292	112.73740	113.34486
9.000	101.66409	103.17787	104.55409	105.80442	106.93951	107.96911	108.90212	109.74668	110.51023	111.19956	111.82090	112.37990
9.125	101.54420	102.94718	104.22109	105.37703	106.42513	107.37465	108.23402	109.01096	109.71250	110.34508	110.91454	111.42624
9.250	101.42448	102.71707	103.88930	104.95165	105.91370	106.78418	107.57105	108.28155	108.92231	109.49936	110.01819	110.48383
9.375	101.30491	102.48753	103.55870	104.52827	105.40520	106.19769	106.91316	107.55840	108.13958	108.66232	109.13174	109.55251
9.500	101.18549	102.25857	103.22930	104.10687	104.89962	105.61513	106.26031	106.84143	107.36422	107.83385	108.25506	108.63215
9.625	101.06624	102.03017	102.90109	103.68745	104.39692	105.03648	105.61245	106.13060	106.59616	107.01386	107.38803	107.72259
9.750	100.94714	101.80234	102.57407	103.27000	103.89710	104.46171	104.96956	105.42585	105.83532	106.22025	106.53053	106.82369
9.875	100.82820	101.57508	102.24822	102.85450	103.40014	103.89080	104.33158	104.72713	105.08164	105.39893	105.68245	105.93532
10.000	100.70942	101.34838	101.92355	102.44095	102.90602	103.32371	103.69847	104.03436	104.33503	104.60380	104.84367	105.05734
10.125	100.59079	101.12225	101.60006	102.02934	102.41473	102.76042	103.07020	103.34751	103.59543	103.81678	104.01407	104.18960
10.250	100.47232	100.89668	101.27773	101.61965	101.92624	102.20090	102.44673	102.66651	102.86277	103.03776	103.19355	103.33198
10.375	100.35401	100.67167	100.95656	101.21188	101.44053	101.64512	101.82801	101.99132	102.13696	102.26666	102.38199	102.48434
10.500	100.23585	100.44723	100.63656	100.80603	100.95761	101.09307	101.21401	101.32187	101.41794	101.50340	101.57928	101.64655
10.750	100.00000	100.00000	100.00000	100.00000	100.00000	100.00000	100.00000	100.00000	100.00000	100.00000	100.00000	100.00000
11.00	99.76477	99.55500	99.36803	99.20150	99.05328	98.92148	98.80440	98.70049	98.60839	98.52688	98.45485	98.39132
11.125	99.64739	99.33332	99.05375	98.80504	98.58397	98.38762	98.21340	98.05899	97.92229	97.80146	97.69482	97.60088
11.25	99.53017	99.11220	98.74060	98.41044	98.11732	97.85731	97.62689	97.42292	97.24258	97.08336	96.94301	96.81953
11.375	99.41309	98.89163	98.42858	98.01702	97.65333	97.33054	97.04484	96.79224	96.56918	96.37329	96.19933	96.04717
11.500	99.29618	98.67160	98.11768	97.62676	97.19199	96.80728	96.46720	96.16689	95.90204	95.66878	95.46368	95.28367
11.625	99.17941	98.45212	97.80791	97.23766	96.73327	96.28750	95.89393	95.54683	95.24108	94.97214	94.73595	94.52892
11.750	99.06280	98.23319	97.49925	96.85038	96.27715	95.77119	95.32502	94.93200	94.58625	94.28249	94.01606	93.78280
11.875	98.94635	98.01480	97.19170	96.46490	95.82363	95.25830	94.76040	94.32237	93.93747	93.59976	93.30390	93.04521
12.00	98.83004	97.79695	96.88525	96.08123	95.37269	94.74883	94.20006	93.71787	93.29470	92.92386	92.59940	92.31603
12.125	98.71389	97.57964	96.57991	95.69934	94.92431	94.24274	93.64396	93.11847	92.65787	92.25473	91.90244	91.59515
12.250	98.59790	97.36287	96.27567	95.31923	94.47847	93.74002	93.09206	92.52411	92.02692	91.59228	91.21294	90.88247
12.375	98.48205	97.14664	95.97252	94.94090	94.03516	93.24063	92.54432	91.93475	91.40179	90.93645	90.53081	90.17787
12.500	98.36636	96.93095	95.67046	94.56433	93.59437	92.74456	92.00072	91.35035	90.78241	90.28715	89.85597	89.48126
12.625	98.25082	96.71579	95.36949	94.18951	93.15608	92.25177	91.46122	90.77085	90.16873	89.64432	89.18831	88.79253
12.750	98.13543	96.50117	95.06960	93.81644	92.72028	91.76226	90.92578	90.19622	89.56070	89.00788	88.52777	88.11157
13.00	97.90512	96.07351	94.47305	93.07550	91.85606	90.79293	89.86697	89.06136	88.36133	87.75389	87.22766	86.77260
13.250	97.67540	95.64797	93.88078	92.34144	91.00160	89.83639	88.82403	87.94542	87.18384	86.52463	85.95495	85.46355
13.500	97.44629	95.22444	93.29275	91.61420	90.15769	88.89246	87.79669	86.84805	86.02780	85.31956	84.70001	84.18366
13.75	97.21778	94.80321	92.70894	90.89369	89.32150	87.96096	86.78472	85.76892	84.89276	84.13812	83.48919	82.93218
14.250	96.76257	93.96678	91.55382	89.47266	87.67904	86.13453	84.80583	83.66402	82.68403	81.84412	81.12542	80.51156

Yield	13 Years	14 Years	15 Years	16 Years	17 Years	18 Years	19 Years	20 Years	22 Years	25 Years	27 Years	Full Term
7.750	123.57455	124.48601	125.31016	126.05290	126.71967	127.31548	127.84498	128.31242	129.07653	129.84576	130.14016	130.29947
8.000	121.32582	122.13371	122.86240	123.51747	124.10409	124.62698	125.09052	125.49871	126.16356	126.82887	127.08190	127.21810
8.25	119.13375	119.84393	120.48289	121.05588	121.56772	122.02282	122.42527	122.77879	123.35250	123.92318	124.13884	124.25434
8.500	116.99675	117.61479	118.16948	118.66566	119.10779	119.49994	119.84586	120.14897	120.63908	121.12371	121.30570	121.40265
8.750	114.91326	115.44448	115.92007	116.34444	116.72164	117.05538	117.34904	117.60572	118.01926	118.42573	118.57741	118.65780
8.875	113.89111	114.38084	114.81873	115.20989	115.55543	115.86158	116.13062	116.36550	116.74322	117.11339	117.25108	117.32387
9.000	112.88177	113.33124	113.73264	114.08993	114.40671	114.68630	114.93170	115.14567	115.48915	115.82475	115.94919	116.01481
9.125	111.88507	112.29549	112.66156	112.98699	113.27518	113.52921	113.75190	113.94583	114.25658	114.55929	114.67119	114.73003
9.250	110.90083	111.27337	111.60524	111.89991	112.16053	112.38997	112.59086	112.76559	113.04506	113.31650	113.41651	113.46897
9.375	109.92887	110.26468	110.56346	110.82842	111.06247	111.26827	111.44824	111.60417	111.85417	112.09587	112.18464	112.23109
9.500	108.96901	109.26921	109.53598	109.77226	109.98071	110.16378	110.32367	110.46239	110.68347	110.89691	110.97506	111.01584
9.625	108.02109	108.28678	108.52258	108.73117	108.91497	109.07619	109.21682	109.33868	109.53254	109.71915	109.78726	109.82270
9.750	107.08494	107.31717	107.52303	107.70491	107.86498	108.00520	108.12737	108.23310	108.40099	108.56212	108.62074	108.65117
9.875	106.16039	106.36021	106.53713	106.69323	106.83045	106.95051	107.05497	107.14527	107.28841	107.42536	107.47504	107.50076
10.000	105.24728	105.41571	105.56464	105.69589	105.81112	105.91182	105.99933	106.07487	106.19441	106.30845	106.34967	106.37097
10.125	104.34545	104.48347	104.60536	104.71266	104.80673	104.88884	104.96011	105.02156	105.11861	105.21093	105.24420	105.26134
10.250	103.45473	103.56332	103.65909	103.74329	103.81702	103.88130	103.93702	103.98500	104.06065	104.13240	104.15817	104.17141
10.375	102.57499	102.65507	102.72562	102.78756	102.84174	102.88891	102.92975	102.96488	103.02016	103.07243	103.09115	103.10074
10.500	101.70605	101.75855	101.80474	101.84525	101.88064	101.91141	101.93802	101.96088	101.99679	102.03064	102.04272	102.04890
10.750	100.00000	100.00000	100.00000	100.00000	100.00000	100.00000	100.00000	100.00000	100.00000	100.00000	100.00000	100.00000
11.00	98.33541	98.28631	98.24333	98.20582	98.17321	98.14500	98.12073	98.09998	98.06762	98.03747	98.02684	98.02150
11.125	97.51829	97.44587	97.38255	97.32736	97.27944	97.23804	97.20245	97.17207	97.12477	97.08084	97.06540	97.05762
11.25	96.71111	96.61616	96.53323	96.46105	96.39845	96.34443	96.29806	96.25852	96.19707	96.14017	96.12024	96.11021
11.375	95.91373	95.79701	95.69520	95.60669	95.53003	95.46395	95.40730	95.35906	95.28422	95.21512	95.19100	95.17889
11.500	95.12601	94.98828	94.86828	94.76409	94.67396	94.59637	94.52993	94.47342	94.38592	94.30537	94.27733	94.26330
11.625	94.34782	94.18979	94.05230	93.93305	93.83004	93.74146	93.66570	93.60135	93.50188	93.41059	93.37891	93.36309
11.750	93.57902	93.40142	93.24708	93.11339	92.99805	92.89899	92.81437	92.74258	92.63182	92.53046	92.49540	92.47794
11.875	92.81948	92.62300	92.45246	92.30493	92.17780	92.06874	91.97571	91.89687	91.77546	91.66468	91.62649	91.60752
12.00	92.06908	91.85439	91.66828	91.50748	91.36908	91.25051	91.14948	91.06398	90.93254	90.81296	90.77186	90.75150
12.125	91.32769	91.09545	90.89438	90.72086	90.57170	90.44408	90.33547	90.24366	90.10278	89.97499	89.93122	89.90958
12.250	90.59518	90.34604	90.13059	89.94490	89.78548	89.64924	89.53344	89.43568	89.28593	89.15050	89.10425	89.08145
12.375	89.87143	89.60601	89.37677	89.17943	89.01022	88.86579	88.74319	88.63981	88.48173	88.33920	88.29068	88.26682
12.500	89.15632	88.87523	88.63275	88.42428	88.24574	88.09354	87.96450	87.85582	87.68995	87.54083	87.49023	87.46541
12.625	88.44973	88.15356	87.89839	87.67928	87.49186	87.33229	87.19716	87.08350	86.91033	86.75511	86.70261	86.67692
12.750	87.75155	87.44087	87.17354	86.94427	86.74840	86.58184	86.44097	86.32262	86.14265	85.98179	85.92756	85.90109
13.00	86.37993	86.04193	85.75180	85.50358	85.29206	85.11262	84.96124	84.83438	84.64214	84.47135	84.41412	84.38635
13.250	85.04056	84.67736	84.36637	84.10097	83.87535	83.68444	83.52377	83.38946	83.18666	83.00754	82.94791	82.91911
13.500	83.73256	83.34618	83.01616	82.73522	82.49698	82.29588	82.12706	81.98627	81.77447	81.58850	81.52698	81.49742
13.75	82.45508	82.04743	81.70011	81.40517	81.15568	80.94560	80.76967	80.62333	80.40394	80.21245	80.14950	80.11942
14.250	79.98837	79.54355	79.16641	78.84773	78.57949	78.35473	78.16745	78.01242	77.78167	77.58262	77.51802	77.48745

Entry is the percentage of loan balance to give the desired yield to the selected time.

Price of a Mortgage to Give a Specified Yield
Conversion of Interest to Principal or Principal to Interest
11.00% Interest Rate   30 Years Amortization Schedule

Desired Yield	1 Year	2 Years	3 Years	4 Years	5 Years	6 Years	7 Years	8 Years	9 Years	10 Years	11 Years	12 Years
					Prepaid or Ballooned at							
8.000	102.86822	105.50406	107.92497	110.14701	112.18502	114.05270	115.76268	117.32659	118.75518	120.05835	121.24524	122.32425
8.25	102.62571	105.03271	107.23795	109.25702	111.10429	112.79296	114.33521	115.74222	117.02431	118.19093	119.25082	120.21199
8.500	102.38385	104.56371	106.55590	108.37538	110.03592	111.55013	112.92961	114.18501	115.32611	116.36187	117.30053	118.14966
8.750	102.14262	104.09704	105.87877	107.50200	108.97976	110.32395	111.54552	112.65445	113.65991	114.57029	115.39329	116.13593
9.000	101.90203	103.63269	105.20652	106.63680	107.93566	109.11421	110.18258	111.15003	112.02505	112.81536	113.52804	114.16954
9.125	101.78197	103.40138	104.87222	106.20724	107.41809	108.51542	109.50893	110.40748	111.21917	111.95138	112.61084	113.20370
9.250	101.66207	103.17065	104.53912	105.77969	106.90348	107.92065	108.84044	109.67129	110.42089	111.09625	111.70375	112.24923
9.375	101.54233	102.94049	104.20723	105.35415	106.39182	107.32987	108.17707	108.94140	109.63012	110.24987	110.80666	111.30599
9.500	101.42275	102.71091	103.87653	104.93060	105.88308	106.74305	107.51877	108.21774	108.84680	109.41215	109.91944	110.37381
9.625	101.30332	102.48189	103.54703	104.50903	105.37724	106.16016	106.86550	107.50027	108.07083	108.58298	109.04196	109.45255
9.750	101.18406	102.25345	103.21872	104.08944	104.87430	105.58118	106.21722	106.78892	107.30215	107.76227	108.17411	108.54208
9.875	101.06495	102.02557	102.89159	103.67182	104.37423	105.00607	105.57389	106.08363	106.54069	106.94993	107.31577	107.64224
10.000	100.94599	101.79826	102.56564	103.25614	103.87702	104.43481	104.93547	105.38436	105.78636	106.14585	106.46683	106.75291
10.125	100.82720	101.57151	102.24087	102.84242	103.38264	103.86737	104.30191	104.69105	105.03909	105.34995	105.62717	105.87393
10.250	100.70856	101.34533	101.91727	102.43063	102.89108	103.30373	103.67319	104.00363	104.29881	104.56214	104.79667	105.00518
10.375	100.59008	101.11971	101.59483	102.02076	102.40232	102.74385	103.04925	103.32206	103.56546	103.78232	103.97523	104.14652
10.500	100.47175	100.89466	101.27356	101.61282	101.91635	102.18771	102.43006	102.64628	102.83895	103.01040	103.16273	103.29781
10.625	100.35358	100.67016	100.95344	101.20678	101.43315	101.63528	101.81558	101.97623	102.11922	102.24630	102.35906	102.45894
10.750	100.23556	100.44622	100.63448	100.80263	100.95271	101.08653	101.20576	101.31188	101.40620	101.48992	101.56412	101.62976
11.000	100.00000	100.00000	100.00000	100.00000	100.00000	100.00000	100.00000	100.00000	100.00000	100.00000	100.00000	100.00000
11.25	99.76506	99.55600	99.37008	99.20485	99.05810	98.92789	98.81246	98.71024	98.61982	98.53996	98.46953	98.40753
11.375	99.64782	99.33482	99.05682	98.81005	98.59117	98.39719	98.22543	98.07352	97.93932	97.82093	97.71666	97.62498
11.500	99.53073	99.11420	98.74468	98.41709	98.12689	97.87001	97.64285	97.44218	97.26512	97.10913	96.97190	96.85139
11.625	99.41380	98.89412	98.43367	98.02597	97.66524	97.34634	97.06467	96.81616	96.59717	96.40446	96.23514	96.08665
11.750	99.29702	98.67459	98.12378	97.63667	97.20622	96.82615	96.49087	96.19542	95.93540	95.70686	95.50631	95.33064
11.875	99.18040	98.45560	97.81500	97.24919	96.74980	96.30941	95.92140	95.57991	95.27372	95.01623	94.78529	94.58325
12.00	99.06393	98.23716	97.50733	96.86351	96.29598	95.79610	95.35623	94.96958	94.63013	94.33251	94.07199	93.84436
12.125	98.94762	98.01925	97.20077	96.47963	95.84472	95.28620	94.79533	94.36439	93.98651	93.65562	93.36633	93.11387
12.250	98.83145	97.80189	96.89531	96.09754	95.39603	94.77968	94.23866	93.76428	93.34882	92.98547	92.66820	92.39167
12.375	98.71544	97.58507	96.59095	95.71722	94.94988	94.27652	93.68619	93.16920	92.71700	92.32200	91.97752	91.67765
12.500	98.59959	97.36878	96.28768	95.33868	94.50625	93.77669	93.13787	92.57912	92.09098	91.66513	91.29420	90.97170
12.625	98.48388	97.15304	95.98550	94.96190	94.06514	93.28017	92.59369	91.99398	91.47072	91.01479	90.61815	90.27371
12.750	98.36833	96.93782	95.68440	94.58687	93.62653	92.78694	92.05360	91.41375	90.85615	90.37090	89.94927	89.58360
12.875	98.25293	96.72314	95.38439	94.21358	93.19040	92.29696	91.51756	90.83837	90.24721	89.73339	89.28749	88.90125
13.000	98.13768	96.50899	95.08545	93.84203	92.75673	91.81023	90.98556	90.26780	89.64385	89.10219	88.63272	88.22656
13.25	97.90763	96.08228	94.49079	93.10410	91.89674	90.84640	89.93350	89.14092	88.45362	87.85845	87.34308	86.89979
13.500	97.67819	95.65769	93.90039	92.37301	91.04644	89.89524	88.89716	88.03275	87.28503	86.63913	86.08207	85.60250
13.75	97.44936	95.23519	93.31422	91.64870	90.20257	88.95659	87.87627	86.94296	86.13763	85.44368	84.84666	84.33306
14.00	97.22112	94.81478	92.73224	90.93109	89.37445	88.03026	86.87060	85.87121	85.01099	84.27158	83.63701	83.09341
14.500	96.76645	93.98019	91.58073	89.51572	87.73984	86.21388	84.90390	83.78053	82.81835	81.99538	81.29259	80.69351

Yield	13 Years	14 Years	15 Years	16 Years	17 Years	18 Years	19 Years	20 Years	22 Years	25 Years	27 Years	Full Term
8.000	123.30315	124.18908	124.98862	125.70784	126.35232	126.92718	127.43717	127.88661	128.61951	129.35452	129.63475	129.78596
8.25	121.08181	121.86708	122.57402	123.20836	123.77536	124.27988	124.72634	125.11882	125.75652	126.39224	126.63309	126.76238
8.500	118.91618	119.60647	120.22637	120.78122	121.27566	121.71507	122.10269	122.44261	122.99290	123.53821	123.74350	123.85313
8.750	116.80467	117.40541	117.94355	118.42404	118.85140	119.22977	119.56295	119.85440	120.32451	120.78760	120.96084	121.05287
9.000	114.74577	115.26213	115.72353	116.13448	116.49909	116.82110	117.10395	117.35076	117.74743	118.13583	118.28022	118.35653
9.125	113.73559	114.21161	114.63645	115.01436	115.34924	115.64463	115.90377	116.12962	116.49194	116.84565	116.97673	117.04582
9.250	112.73800	113.17490	113.56433	113.91031	114.21652	114.48629	114.72266	114.92840	115.25787	115.57857	115.69703	115.75931
9.375	111.75284	112.15177	112.50693	112.82207	113.10064	113.34575	113.56025	113.74672	114.04480	114.33407	114.44058	114.49644
9.500	110.77993	111.14204	111.46402	111.74937	112.00129	112.22268	112.41618	112.58419	112.85227	113.11165	113.20686	113.25666
9.625	109.81909	110.14550	110.43538	110.69196	110.91820	111.11678	111.29013	111.44045	111.67987	111.91084	111.99535	112.03944
9.750	108.87015	109.16196	109.42078	109.64958	109.85108	110.02773	110.18173	110.31512	110.52719	110.73116	110.80555	110.84427
9.875	107.93296	108.19121	108.41999	108.62199	108.79966	108.95522	109.09068	109.20786	109.39381	109.57214	109.63698	109.67063
10.000	107.00734	107.23308	107.43280	107.60893	107.76366	107.89896	108.01664	108.11830	108.27935	108.43333	108.48914	108.51803
10.125	106.09312	106.28736	106.45900	106.61018	106.74282	106.85866	106.95929	107.04612	107.18342	107.31430	107.36159	107.38600
10.250	105.19016	105.35388	105.49838	105.62549	105.73687	105.83403	105.91833	105.99097	106.10564	106.21462	106.25387	106.27408
10.375	104.29830	104.43246	104.55072	104.65463	104.74557	104.82480	104.89344	104.95254	105.04564	105.13386	105.16553	105.18180
10.500	103.41737	103.52291	103.61584	103.69738	103.76865	103.83067	103.88434	103.93049	104.00305	104.07162	104.09615	104.10872
10.625	102.54722	102.62507	102.69351	102.75350	102.80588	102.85139	102.89073	102.92451	102.97754	103.02749	103.04531	103.05442
10.750	101.68771	101.73874	101.78356	101.82279	101.85700	101.88669	101.91232	101.93430	101.96875	102.00110	102.01261	102.01847
11.000	100.00000	100.00000	100.00000	100.00000	100.00000	100.00000	100.00000	100.00000	100.00000	100.00000	100.00000	100.00000
11.25	98.35307	98.30535	98.26364	98.22732	98.19580	98.16858	98.14520	98.12524	98.09420	98.06539	98.05527	98.05017
11.375	97.54455	97.47415	97.41271	97.35926	97.31294	97.27299	97.23871	97.20949	97.16412	97.12213	97.10744	97.10005
11.500	96.74580	96.65350	96.57304	96.50313	96.44262	96.39039	96.34582	96.30780	96.24885	96.19447	96.17550	96.16597
11.625	95.95669	95.84323	95.74445	95.65873	95.58463	95.52086	95.46629	95.41989	95.34810	95.28207	95.25910	95.24760
11.750	95.17709	95.04320	94.92677	94.82587	94.73874	94.66387	94.59987	94.54553	94.46159	94.38460	94.35791	94.34458
11.875	94.40687	94.25325	94.11984	94.00436	93.90478	93.81930	93.74632	93.68444	93.58902	93.50176	93.47160	93.45659
12.00	93.64589	93.47324	93.32349	93.19402	93.08252	92.98692	92.90542	92.83638	92.73012	92.63324	92.59987	92.58329
12.125	92.89402	92.70302	92.53575	92.39347	92.27177	92.16654	92.07692	92.00110	91.88463	91.77875	91.74239	91.72438
12.250	92.15115	91.94245	91.76187	91.60614	91.47235	91.35793	91.26061	91.17838	91.05228	90.93799	90.89887	90.87953
12.375	91.41714	91.19138	90.99629	90.82824	90.68405	90.56089	90.45626	90.36797	90.23282	90.11069	90.06901	90.04846
12.500	90.69188	90.44969	90.24065	90.06081	89.90669	89.77522	89.66367	89.56965	89.42599	89.29655	89.25252	89.23087
12.625	89.97524	89.71722	89.49480	89.30368	89.14010	89.00072	88.88262	88.78320	88.63155	88.49532	88.44912	88.42647
12.750	89.26711	88.99386	88.75859	88.55668	88.38408	88.23721	88.11290	88.00838	87.84925	87.70672	87.65854	87.63498
12.875	88.56737	88.27945	88.03187	87.81966	87.63847	87.48448	87.35431	87.24500	87.07887	86.93051	86.88052	86.85613
13.000	87.87590	87.57388	87.31450	87.09245	86.90309	86.74235	86.60665	86.49283	86.32017	86.16643	86.11478	86.08966
13.25	86.51733	86.18874	85.90723	85.66683	85.46234	85.28918	85.14335	85.02134	84.83691	84.67367	84.61918	84.59280
13.500	85.19051	84.83742	84.53567	84.27862	84.06051	83.87627	83.72149	83.59232	83.39775	83.22654	83.16976	83.14242
13.75	83.89458	83.51896	83.19874	82.92664	82.69632	82.50224	82.20422	82.00100	81.82325	81.76467	81.73660	
14.00	82.62871	82.23242	81.89540	81.60974	81.36854	81.16580	80.99632	80.85557	80.64509	80.46205	80.40211	80.37354
14.500	80.18390	79.75145	79.38551	79.07685	78.81751	78.60060	78.42017	78.27108	78.04968	77.85942	77.79790	77.76888

Entry is the percentage of loan balance to give the desired yield to the selected time.

Price of a Mortgage to Give a Specified Yield
Conversion of Interest to Principal or Principal to Interest
11.25% Interest Rate   30 Years Amortization Schedule

Desired Yield	1 Year	2 Years	3 Years	4 Years	5 Years	6 Years	7 Years	8 Years	9 Years	10 Years	11 Years	12 Years
8.250	102.86471	105.49145	107.89863	110.10321	112.12082	113.96580	115.65138	117.18974	118.59205	119.86862	121.02891	122.08164
8.500	102.62251	105.02119	107.21393	109.21715	111.04591	112.71407	114.23433	115.61835	116.87686	118.01967	119.05582	119.99358
8.750	102.38094	104.55327	106.53417	108.33937	109.96328	111.47910	112.83892	114.07382	115.19393	116.20856	117.12620	117.95465
9.000	102.14001	104.08768	105.85931	107.46981	108.93277	110.26065	111.46480	112.55562	113.54260	114.43442	115.23899	115.96356
9.250	101.89971	103.62440	105.18932	106.60837	107.89424	109.05848	110.11163	111.06329	111.92223	112.69642	113.39315	114.01904
9.375	101.77980	103.39362	104.85613	106.18068	107.37942	108.46343	109.44278	110.32667	111.12344	111.84072	112.48542	113.06386
9.500	101.66005	103.16342	104.52415	105.75498	106.86753	107.87236	108.77905	109.59634	110.33216	110.99375	111.58766	112.11987
9.625	101.54045	102.93379	104.19336	105.33128	106.35857	107.28524	108.12037	108.87223	109.54831	110.15542	110.69975	111.18693
9.750	101.42102	102.70473	103.86376	104.90956	105.85252	106.70205	107.46673	108.15429	108.77180	109.32562	109.82156	110.26488
9.875	101.30174	102.47624	103.53535	104.48981	105.34934	106.12276	106.81806	107.44247	108.00256	108.50426	108.95298	109.35359
10.000	101.18262	102.24832	103.20813	104.07203	104.84904	105.54734	106.17433	106.73670	107.24051	107.69125	108.09389	108.45290
10.125	101.06365	102.02096	102.88209	103.65620	104.35159	104.97576	105.53550	106.03693	106.48559	106.88649	107.24416	107.56269
10.250	100.94484	101.79417	102.55722	103.24231	103.85697	104.40800	104.90153	105.34311	105.73772	106.08989	106.40370	106.68282
10.375	100.82619	101.56794	102.23351	102.83035	103.36517	103.84403	104.27239	104.65517	104.99683	105.30136	105.57238	105.81314
10.500	100.70770	101.34228	101.91098	102.42032	102.87617	103.28381	103.64802	103.97307	104.26284	104.52080	104.75009	104.95353
10.625	100.58936	101.11717	101.58961	102.01220	102.38995	102.72733	103.02839	103.29675	103.53568	103.74813	103.93672	104.10385
10.750	100.47118	100.89263	101.26939	101.60599	101.90649	102.17456	102.41346	102.62616	102.81529	102.98325	103.13217	103.26398
10.875	100.35315	100.66864	100.95032	101.20167	101.42579	101.62546	101.80320	101.96124	102.10160	102.22609	102.33633	102.43378
11.000	100.23528	100.44520	100.63241	100.79924	100.94782	101.08002	101.19756	101.30194	101.39453	101.47655	101.54909	101.61314
11.250	100.00000	100.00000	100.00000	100.00000	100.00000	100.00000	100.00000	100.00000	100.00000	100.00000	100.00000	100.00000
11.500	99.76534	99.55700	99.37213	99.20819	99.06292	98.93428	98.82004	98.71993	98.63117	98.55293	98.48408	98.42359
11.625	99.64824	99.33633	99.05989	98.81505	98.59836	98.40672	98.23741	98.08797	97.95623	97.84025	97.73831	97.64886
11.750	99.53130	99.11620	98.74877	98.42374	98.13643	97.88267	97.65873	97.46133	97.28752	97.13470	97.00053	96.88295
11.875	99.41451	98.89662	98.43877	98.03426	97.67713	97.36208	97.08442	96.83995	96.62498	96.43619	96.27065	96.12576
12.000	99.29788	98.67758	98.12988	97.64658	97.22042	96.84495	96.51443	96.22380	95.96854	95.74464	95.54857	95.37717
12.125	99.18139	98.45908	97.82210	97.26071	96.76631	96.33124	95.94875	95.61282	95.31814	95.05999	94.83420	94.63707
12.250	99.06507	98.24113	97.51542	96.87664	96.31476	95.82094	95.38732	95.00696	94.67372	94.38215	94.12745	93.90534
12.375	98.94889	98.02372	97.20985	96.49435	95.86577	95.31401	94.83011	94.40618	94.03522	93.71105	93.42822	93.18189
12.500	98.83287	97.80684	96.90537	96.11384	95.41932	94.81043	94.27709	93.81043	93.40258	93.04662	92.73642	92.46660
12.625	98.71700	97.59051	96.60199	95.73509	94.97540	94.31018	93.72823	93.21966	92.77573	92.38877	92.05197	91.75937
12.750	98.60128	97.37470	96.29969	95.35811	94.53398	93.81324	93.18349	92.63383	92.15463	91.73743	91.37477	91.06009
12.875	98.48571	97.15944	95.99848	94.98288	94.09506	93.31958	92.64284	92.05289	91.53921	91.09254	90.70474	90.36866
13.000	98.37030	96.94470	95.69835	94.60939	93.65862	92.82918	92.10625	91.47680	90.92941	90.45402	90.04179	89.68496
13.125	98.25504	96.73050	95.39929	94.23763	93.22464	92.34201	91.57367	90.90552	90.32518	89.82180	89.38584	89.00896
13.250	98.13993	96.51683	95.10131	93.86760	92.79311	91.85806	91.04508	90.33899	89.72646	89.19580	88.73680	88.34048
13.500	97.91016	96.09107	94.50854	93.13268	91.93734	90.89969	89.99974	89.22004	88.54532	87.96224	87.45913	87.02580
13.750	97.68099	95.66742	93.92001	92.40456	91.09120	89.95390	88.96997	88.11961	87.38556	86.75278	86.20813	85.74018
14.000	97.45243	95.24585	93.33569	91.68317	90.25456	89.02051	87.95551	87.03736	86.24675	85.56689	84.98317	84.48288
14.250	97.22447	94.82638	92.75555	90.96845	89.42731	88.00934	86.95612	85.97297	85.12847	84.40406	83.78362	83.25319
14.750	96.77034	93.99362	91.60766	89.55874	87.80053	86.29299	85.00156	83.89643	82.95183	82.14555	81.45840	80.87381

Yield	13 Years	14 Years	15 Years	16 Years	17 Years	18 Years	19 Years	20 Years	22 Years	25 Years	27 Years	Full Term
8.250	123.03481	123.89578	124.67131	125.36763	125.99044	126.54498	127.03606	127.46810	128.17090	128.87302	129.13971	129.28318
8.500	120.84055	121.60370	122.28941	122.90356	123.45151	123.93819	124.36811	124.74540	125.35692	125.96420	126.19341	126.31608
8.750	118.70104	119.37189	119.97318	120.51038	120.98849	121.41209	121.78535	122.11211	122.63982	123.16074	123.35611	123.46014
9.000	116.61473	117.19856	117.72055	118.18575	118.59875	118.96376	119.28460	119.56477	120.01560	120.45798	120.62285	120.71018
9.250	114.58014	115.08196	115.52953	115.92740	116.27976	116.59040	116.86278	117.10004	117.48043	117.85149	117.98890	118.06131
9.375	113.58178	114.04441	114.45650	114.82240	115.14603	115.43099	115.68054	115.89765	116.24510	116.58302	116.70776	116.77333
9.500	112.59581	113.02041	113.39816	113.73315	114.02907	114.28932	114.51694	114.71472	115.03068	115.33705	115.44979	115.50889
9.625	111.62206	112.00977	112.35427	112.65939	112.92861	113.16506	113.37162	113.55089	113.83674	114.11309	114.21446	114.26747
9.750	110.66034	111.01227	111.32460	111.60088	111.84434	112.05791	112.24426	112.40577	112.66286	112.91065	113.00127	113.04852
9.875	109.71050	110.02774	110.30893	110.55735	110.77600	110.96765	111.13450	111.27901	111.50862	111.72927	111.80971	111.85155
10.000	108.77237	109.05597	109.30703	109.52856	109.72330	109.89371	110.04202	110.17025	110.37363	110.56849	110.63930	110.67603
10.125	107.84578	108.09677	108.31869	108.51427	108.68598	108.83605	108.96650	109.07915	109.25749	109.42785	109.48956	109.52149
10.250	106.93057	107.14997	107.34371	107.51424	107.66378	107.79430	107.90763	108.00536	108.15982	108.30692	108.36004	108.38745
10.375	106.02658	106.21536	106.38186	106.52823	106.65642	106.76818	106.86508	106.94856	107.08024	107.20528	107.25028	107.27345
10.500	105.13366	105.29278	105.43295	105.55602	105.66367	105.75740	105.83858	105.90842	106.01838	106.12250	106.15986	106.17904
10.625	104.25165	104.38205	104.49677	104.59737	104.68526	104.76169	104.82780	104.88461	104.97390	105.05818	105.08833	105.10377
10.750	103.38040	103.48298	103.57312	103.65207	103.72095	103.78079	103.83247	103.87683	103.94643	104.01193	104.03529	104.04722
10.875	102.51975	102.59541	102.66181	102.71989	102.77051	102.81442	102.85231	102.88478	102.93564	102.98336	103.00032	103.00897
11.000	101.66957	101.71917	101.76264	101.80063	101.83369	101.86233	101.88702	101.90815	101.94119	101.97209	101.98304	101.98861
11.250	100.00000	100.00000	100.00000	100.00000	100.00000	100.00000	100.00000	100.00000	100.00000	100.00000	100.00000	100.00000
11.500	98.37055	98.32417	98.28371	98.24854	98.21808	98.19182	98.16930	98.15011	98.12034	99.09281	98.08318	98.07834
11.625	97.57053	97.50211	97.44251	97.39075	97.34599	97.30744	97.27443	97.24634	97.20282	97.16271	97.14872	97.14170
11.750	96.78013	96.69041	96.61236	96.54467	96.48619	96.43590	96.39238	96.35632	96.29979	96.24783	96.22976	96.22073
11.875	95.99921	95.88893	95.79310	95.71010	95.63848	95.57696	95.52441	95.47980	95.41095	95.34785	95.32599	95.31507
12.000	95.22764	95.09751	94.98456	94.88686	94.80265	94.73042	94.66878	94.61653	94.53602	94.46247	94.43706	94.42441
12.125	94.46530	94.31600	94.18658	94.07476	93.97851	93.89604	93.82576	93.76626	93.67474	93.59137	93.56267	93.54842
12.250	93.71206	93.54426	93.39899	93.27363	93.16585	93.07363	92.99513	92.92875	92.82684	92.73428	92.70251	92.68677
12.375	92.96779	92.78215	92.62163	92.48328	92.36449	92.26290	92.17665	92.10376	91.99205	91.89089	91.85627	91.83918
12.500	92.23237	92.02953	91.85435	91.70355	91.57424	91.46385	91.37012	91.29106	91.17012	91.06092	91.02367	91.00532
12.625	91.50568	91.28266	91.09699	90.93427	90.79491	90.67608	90.57532	90.49043	90.36080	90.24410	90.20442	90.18493
12.750	90.78760	90.55220	90.34940	90.17527	90.02631	89.89946	89.79203	89.70163	89.56384	89.44016	89.39824	89.37770
12.875	90.07800	89.82721	89.61144	89.42638	89.26827	89.13380	89.02005	88.92446	88.77900	88.64884	88.60486	88.58336
13.000	89.37678	89.11118	88.88294	88.68744	88.52061	88.37891	88.25918	88.15869	88.00606	87.86987	87.82401	87.80165
13.125	88.68381	88.40397	88.16378	87.95829	87.78317	87.63459	87.50922	87.40413	87.24478	87.10302	87.05543	87.03229
13.250	87.99899	87.70544	87.45380	87.23879	87.05577	86.90068	86.76998	86.66055	86.49494	86.34803	86.29887	86.27502
13.500	86.65334	86.33396	86.06086	85.82808	85.63042	85.46335	85.32290	85.20559	85.02869	84.87270	84.82083	84.79580
13.750	85.33896	84.99577	84.70302	84.45411	84.24329	84.06553	83.91645	83.79225	83.60563	83.44203	83.38798	83.36202
14.000	84.05500	83.68989	83.37923	83.11574	82.89312	82.70587	82.54923	82.41904	82.22413	82.05427	81.97850	81.97186
14.250	82.80063	82.41543	82.08847	81.81185	81.57871	81.38309	81.21986	81.08453	80.88263	80.70772	80.65066	80.62354
14.750	80.37752	79.95717	79.60214	79.30325	79.05257	78.84328	78.66950	78.52613	78.31377	78.13195	78.07338	78.04583

Entry is the percentage of loan balance to give the desired yield to the selected time.

Price of a Mortgage to Give a Specified Yield
Conversion of Interest to Principal or Principal to Interest
11.50% Interest Rate   30 Years Amortization Schedule

Desired Yield	1 Year	2 Years	3 Years	4 Years	Prepaid or Ballooned at 5 Years	6 Years	7 Years	8 Years	9 Years	10 Years	11 Years	12 Years
8.50	102.86120	105.47882	107.87229	110.05948	112.05677	113.87922	115.54064	117.05372	118.43011	119.68048	120.81464	121.84158
8.750	102.61929	105.00965	107.18991	109.17732	110.98768	112.63547	114.13394	115.49524	116.73048	117.84985	118.86267	119.77746
9.00	102.37802	104.54282	106.51245	108.30341	109.93078	111.40834	112.74868	113.96330	115.06271	116.05653	116.95351	117.76168
9.25	102.13739	104.07830	105.83986	107.43766	108.88591	110.19758	111.38448	112.45740	113.42614	114.29967	115.08613	115.79297
9.50	101.89739	103.61610	105.17212	106.57998	107.85292	109.00295	110.04102	110.97707	111.82014	112.57846	113.25951	113.87009
9.625	101.77762	103.38585	104.84004	106.15415	107.34084	108.41162	109.37696	110.24634	111.02840	111.73097	112.36117	112.92546
9.75	101.65802	103.15618	104.50917	105.73031	106.83167	107.82424	108.71795	109.52183	110.24407	110.89210	111.47265	111.99184
9.875	101.53857	102.92708	104.17949	105.30844	106.32541	107.24078	108.06396	108.80348	109.46707	110.06174	110.59383	111.06909
10.00	101.41928	102.69855	103.85099	104.88855	105.82203	106.66121	107.41494	108.09123	108.69733	109.23981	109.72459	110.15707
10.125	101.30015	102.47058	103.52368	104.47062	105.32151	106.08550	106.77085	107.38502	107.93477	108.42619	108.86482	109.25563
10.25	101.18117	102.24318	103.19754	104.05464	104.82384	105.51363	106.13165	106.68480	107.17931	107.62082	108.01440	108.36463
10.375	101.06235	102.01635	102.87258	103.64059	104.32900	104.94557	105.49730	105.99051	106.43089	106.82358	107.17321	107.48395
10.500	100.94369	101.79008	102.54879	103.22848	103.83697	104.38129	104.86776	105.30210	105.68943	106.03439	106.34114	106.61343
10.625	100.82518	101.56437	102.22616	102.81830	103.34774	103.82077	104.24300	104.61951	104.95486	105.25316	105.51808	105.75296
10.75	100.70683	101.33922	101.90469	102.41002	102.86129	103.26397	103.62297	103.94269	104.22711	104.47979	104.70393	104.90240
10.875	100.58864	101.11463	101.58438	102.00365	102.37760	102.71087	103.00763	103.27159	103.50612	103.71421	103.89857	104.06162
11.000	100.47060	100.89059	101.26522	101.59917	101.89666	102.16145	102.39694	102.60615	102.79180	102.95632	103.10190	103.23049
11.125	100.35272	100.66712	100.94720	101.19657	101.41844	101.61568	101.79088	101.94633	102.08410	102.20604	102.31381	102.40888
11.25	100.23499	100.44419	100.63033	100.79585	100.94294	101.07353	101.18939	101.29206	101.38294	101.46328	101.53420	101.59668
11.50	100.00000	100.00000	100.00000	100.00000	100.00000	100.00000	100.00000	100.00000	100.00000	100.00000	100.00000	100.00000
11.750	99.76563	99.55801	99.37419	99.21154	99.06772	98.94065	98.82848	98.72927	98.64245	98.56581	98.49850	98.43948
11.875	99.64867	99.33783	99.06296	98.82005	98.60553	98.41623	98.24933	98.10234	97.97303	97.85942	97.75976	97.67250
12.00	99.53187	99.11820	98.75286	98.43039	98.14596	97.89528	97.67454	97.48037	97.30976	97.16006	97.02891	96.91420
12.125	99.41522	98.89912	98.44386	98.04253	97.68898	97.37777	97.10407	96.86361	96.65259	96.46766	96.30584	96.16449
12.25	99.29873	98.68057	98.13598	97.65648	97.23459	96.86369	96.53789	96.25201	96.00145	95.78214	95.59046	95.42324
12.375	99.18239	98.46257	97.82920	97.27222	96.78277	96.35300	95.97596	95.64553	95.35268	95.10341	94.88269	94.69036
12.500	99.06620	98.24511	97.52352	96.88975	96.33350	95.84568	95.41825	95.04412	94.71701	94.43141	94.18242	93.96573
12.625	98.95017	98.02819	97.21893	96.50905	95.88677	95.34172	94.86473	94.44773	94.08360	93.76606	93.48957	93.24925
12.750	98.83428	97.81180	96.91544	96.13012	95.44256	94.84107	94.31535	93.85631	93.45597	93.10728	92.80405	92.54081
12.875	98.71855	97.59595	96.61303	95.75294	95.00086	94.34373	93.77008	93.26983	92.83407	92.45501	92.12577	91.84030
13.00	98.60297	97.38063	96.31171	95.37752	94.56165	93.84967	93.22600	92.68823	92.21785	91.80917	91.45464	91.14763
13.125	98.48755	97.16585	96.01146	95.00383	94.12491	93.35885	92.69177	92.11146	91.60723	91.16969	90.79059	90.46270
13.25	98.37227	96.95160	95.71230	94.63188	93.69063	92.87127	92.15865	91.53950	91.00218	90.53649	90.13351	89.78540
13.375	98.25715	96.73787	95.41420	94.26165	93.25881	92.38690	91.62952	90.97229	90.40262	89.90952	89.48334	89.11564
13.500	98.14218	96.52468	95.11717	93.89314	92.82941	91.90571	91.10433	90.40978	89.80852	89.28870	88.83998	88.45332
13.750	97.91269	96.09987	94.52629	93.16122	91.97785	90.95280	90.06569	89.29872	88.63641	88.06523	87.57340	87.15063
14.00	97.68380	95.67716	93.93964	92.43607	91.13585	90.01236	89.04246	88.20599	87.48544	86.86556	86.33312	85.87657
14.250	97.45551	95.25653	93.35717	91.71761	90.30328	89.08422	88.03440	87.13124	86.35516	85.68691	85.11852	84.63042
14.500	97.22783	94.83799	92.77886	91.00577	89.48004	88.16820	87.04126	86.07415	85.24518	84.53554	83.92900	83.41147
15.000	96.77424	94.00707	91.63458	89.60172	87.86108	86.37183	85.09879	84.01169	83.08444	82.29460	81.62282	81.05246

Yield	13 Years	14 Years	15 Years	16 Years	17 Years	18 Years	19 Years	20 Years	22 Years	25 Years	27 Years	Full Term
8.50	122.76956	123.60614	124.35826	125.03229	125.63404	126.16886	126.64164	127.05686	127.73065	128.40118	128.65490	128.79101
8.750	120.60206	121.34359	122.00861	122.60310	123.13253	123.60190	124.01581	124.37841	124.96469	125.54466	125.76273	125.87911
9.00	118.48835	119.14021	119.72336	120.24337	120.70532	121.11386	121.47323	121.78727	122.29320	122.79070	122.97658	123.07527
9.25	116.42695	116.99425	117.50050	117.95081	118.34986	118.70190	119.01079	119.28006	119.71229	120.13479	120.29165	120.37450
9.50	114.41638	114.90400	115.33806	115.72321	116.06367	116.36328	116.62551	116.85355	117.21825	117.57264	117.70338	117.77207
9.625	113.42971	113.87925	114.27891	114.63310	114.94581	115.22065	115.46091	115.66957	116.00270	116.32544	116.44412	116.50633
9.75	112.45522	112.86781	113.23417	113.55844	113.84438	114.09538	114.31452	114.50462	114.80755	115.10016	115.20743	115.26350
9.875	111.49274	111.86948	112.20360	112.49897	112.75909	112.98715	113.18602	113.35832	113.63239	113.89633	113.99278	114.04307
10.00	110.54210	110.88407	111.18698	111.45443	111.68968	111.89567	112.07507	112.23031	112.47680	112.71347	112.79969	112.84452
10.125	109.60313	109.91139	110.18411	110.42459	110.63586	110.82062	110.98135	111.12024	111.34039	111.55114	111.62767	111.66736
10.25	108.67567	108.95125	109.19475	109.40920	109.59737	109.76173	109.90452	110.02777	110.22276	110.40888	110.47625	110.51110
10.375	107.75957	108.00347	108.21870	108.40803	108.57394	108.71869	108.84428	108.95256	109.12355	109.28626	109.34498	109.37528
10.500	106.85466	107.06785	107.25555	107.42084	107.56533	107.69122	107.80033	107.89427	108.04236	108.18287	108.23341	108.25942
10.625	105.96078	106.14422	106.30570	106.44740	106.57126	106.67906	106.77236	106.85259	106.97884	107.09827	107.14110	107.16308
10.75	105.07778	105.23241	105.36835	105.48749	105.59151	105.68191	105.76007	105.82720	105.93264	106.03208	106.06763	106.08583
10.875	104.20552	104.33223	104.44349	104.54088	104.62581	104.69953	104.76318	104.81779	104.90340	104.98390	105.01259	105.02723
11.000	103.34383	103.44352	103.53094	103.60737	103.67393	103.73164	103.78141	103.82405	103.89078	103.95334	103.97557	103.98688
11.125	102.49258	102.56610	102.63050	102.68673	102.73564	102.77800	102.81447	102.84569	102.89445	102.94004	102.95618	102.96438
11.25	101.65162	101.69982	101.74199	101.77876	101.81071	101.83834	101.86210	101.88242	101.91409	101.94361	101.95403	101.95931
11.50	100.00000	100.00000	100.00000	100.00000	100.00000	100.00000	100.00000	100.00000	100.00000	100.00000	100.00000	100.00000
11.750	98.38785	98.34277	98.30353	98.26948	98.24005	98.21472	98.19303	98.17459	98.14605	98.11975	98.11059	98.10599
11.875	97.59623	97.52974	97.47193	97.42183	97.37857	97.34139	97.30960	97.28261	97.24088	97.20256	97.18925	97.18259
12.00	96.81408	96.72690	96.65510	96.58567	96.52916	96.48064	96.43922	96.40408	96.34987	96.30024	96.28306	96.27448
12.125	96.04126	95.93410	95.84115	95.76080	95.69159	95.63225	95.58165	95.53877	95.47275	95.41248	95.39168	95.38132
12.25	95.27765	95.15119	95.04164	94.94705	94.86568	94.79601	94.73666	94.68644	94.60924	94.53897	94.51480	94.50280
12.375	94.52312	94.37803	94.25250	94.14424	94.05124	93.97169	93.90402	93.84682	93.75907	93.67943	93.65212	93.63859
12.500	93.77754	93.61447	93.47357	93.35220	93.24806	93.15910	93.08351	93.01977	92.92198	92.83356	92.80333	92.78840
12.625	93.04078	92.86038	92.70469	92.57075	92.45596	92.35802	92.27492	92.20485	92.09773	92.00109	91.96815	91.95193
12.750	92.31274	92.11562	91.94571	91.79972	91.67476	91.56827	91.47802	91.40203	91.28606	91.18174	91.14630	91.12899
12.875	91.59329	91.38005	91.19648	91.03894	90.90427	90.78965	90.69262	90.61103	90.48672	90.37524	90.33749	90.31899
13.00	90.88231	90.65355	90.45685	90.28826	90.14432	90.02196	89.91851	89.83162	89.69948	89.58134	89.54145	89.52195
13.125	90.17968	89.93597	89.72667	89.54751	89.39473	89.26501	89.15548	89.06360	88.92412	88.79977	88.75792	88.73752
13.25	89.48530	89.22719	89.00581	88.81654	88.65532	88.51863	88.40335	88.30675	88.16039	88.03029	87.98664	87.96542
13.375	88.79904	88.52709	88.29412	88.09518	87.92595	87.78263	87.66190	87.56088	87.40808	87.27265	87.22737	87.20540
13.500	88.12081	87.83553	87.59145	87.38329	87.20642	87.05683	86.93097	86.82578	86.66696	86.52662	86.47984	86.45721
13.750	86.78796	86.47758	86.21267	85.98731	85.79630	85.63514	85.49989	85.38713	85.21748	85.06846	85.01910	84.99535
14.00	85.48589	85.15236	84.86840	84.62742	84.42369	84.25221	84.10866	83.98927	83.81030	83.65401	83.60257	83.57794
14.250	84.21377	83.85895	83.55761	83.30251	83.08737	82.90674	82.75590	82.63076	82.44384	82.28156	82.22849	82.20321
14.500	82.97080	82.59645	82.27931	82.01149	81.78618	81.59748	81.44028	81.31019	81.11657	80.94947	80.89517	80.86943
15.000	80.56919	80.16068	79.81630	79.52691	79.28465	79.08276	78.91540	78.77758	78.57392	78.40022	78.34447	78.31833

Entry is the percentage of loan balance to give the desired yield to the selected time.

Price of a Mortgage to Give a Specified Yield
Conversion of Interest to Principal or Principal to Interest
11.75% Interest Rate 30 Years Amortization Schedule

Desired Yield	Prepaid or Ballooned at 1 Year	2 Years	3 Years	4 Years	5 Years	6 Years	7 Years	8 Years	9 Years	10 Years	11 Years	12 Years
8.750	102.85768	105.46617	107.84596	110.01580	111.99289	113.79298	115.43047	116.91858	118.26938	119.49396	120.60245	121.60411
9.00	102.61607	104.99810	107.16590	109.13755	110.92961	112.55718	114.03408	115.37291	116.58520	117.68149	118.67138	119.56366
9.25	102.37510	104.53236	106.49073	108.26750	109.87842	111.33785	112.65889	113.85348	114.93247	115.90580	116.78249	117.57077
9.500	102.13476	104.06892	105.82041	107.40555	108.83917	110.13475	111.30458	112.35979	113.31055	114.16607	114.93474	115.62419
9.75	101.89506	103.60778	105.15491	106.55163	107.81171	108.94765	109.97078	110.89139	111.71881	112.46150	113.12715	113.72271
9.875	101.77544	103.37807	104.82396	106.12766	107.30236	108.36002	109.31147	110.16652	110.93406	111.62216	112.23811	112.78852
10.00	101.65598	103.14893	104.49420	105.70566	106.79591	107.77631	108.65717	109.44779	110.15663	110.79131	111.35873	111.86516
10.125	101.53668	102.92036	104.16562	105.28564	106.29234	107.19649	108.00782	108.73516	109.38644	109.96886	110.48892	110.95250
10.25	101.41754	102.69236	103.83822	104.86757	105.79162	106.62052	107.36341	108.02855	108.62341	109.15471	109.62854	110.05039
10.375	101.29855	102.46492	103.51200	104.45145	105.29375	106.04838	106.72387	107.32792	107.86747	108.34878	108.77749	109.15870
10.500	101.17972	102.23804	103.18696	104.03727	104.79871	105.48005	106.08918	106.63321	107.11855	107.55097	107.93565	108.27729
10.625	101.06105	102.01173	102.86308	103.62501	104.30647	104.91549	105.45929	105.94437	106.37658	106.76119	107.10292	107.40602
10.75	100.94253	101.78598	102.54036	103.21468	103.81703	104.35468	104.83416	105.26314	105.64149	105.97935	106.27917	106.54477
10.875	100.82417	101.56079	102.21881	102.80626	103.33036	103.79759	104.21376	104.58407	104.91320	105.20536	105.46430	105.69341
11.000	100.70597	101.33616	101.89840	102.39974	102.84646	103.24420	103.59804	103.91250	104.19165	104.43913	104.65820	104.85180
11.125	100.58792	101.11208	101.57915	101.99511	102.36529	102.69448	102.98697	103.24659	103.47677	103.68058	103.86077	104.01981
11.25	100.47003	100.88856	101.26105	101.59236	101.88685	102.14840	102.38051	102.58627	102.76848	102.92962	103.07191	103.19733
11.375	100.35229	100.66559	100.94408	101.19148	101.41111	101.60594	101.77862	101.93151	102.06673	102.18616	102.29150	102.38423
11.50	100.23470	100.44318	100.62826	100.79247	100.93807	101.06707	101.18126	101.28224	101.37144	101.45013	101.51944	101.58039
11.75	100.00000	100.00000	100.00000	100.00000	100.00000	100.00000	100.00000	100.00000	100.00000	100.00000	100.00000	100.00000
12.00	99.76591	99.55901	99.37624	99.21487	99.07250	98.94699	98.83643	98.73915	98.65364	98.57858	98.51279	98.45522
12.125	99.64910	99.33934	99.06604	98.82504	98.61268	98.42569	98.26119	98.11662	97.98970	97.87843	97.78102	97.69590
12.25	99.53244	99.12021	98.75694	98.43702	98.15545	97.90784	97.69027	97.49929	97.33185	97.18522	97.05703	96.94513
12.375	99.41594	98.90162	98.44896	98.05080	97.70081	97.39340	97.12363	96.88712	96.68001	96.49888	96.34071	96.20282
12.50	99.29958	98.68357	98.14208	97.66637	97.24873	96.88235	96.56123	96.28006	96.03413	95.81932	95.63197	95.46886
12.625	99.18339	98.46606	97.83629	97.28372	96.79920	96.37467	96.00305	95.67805	95.39415	95.14648	94.93073	94.74312
12.750	99.06734	98.24909	97.53161	96.90284	96.35220	95.87034	95.44904	95.08106	94.76001	94.48027	94.23689	94.02552
12.875	98.95144	98.03266	97.22801	96.52373	95.90772	95.36932	94.89917	94.48903	94.13164	93.82062	93.55037	93.31594
13.00	98.83570	97.81676	96.92550	96.14638	95.46574	94.87160	94.35342	93.90192	93.50899	93.16746	92.87107	92.61428
13.125	98.72011	97.60140	96.62407	95.77077	95.02625	94.37715	93.81173	93.31970	92.89200	92.52073	92.19891	91.92044
13.25	98.60468	97.38657	96.32372	95.39690	94.58924	93.88565	93.27409	92.74230	92.28062	91.88034	91.53380	91.23431
13.375	98.48939	97.17227	96.02445	95.02476	94.15468	93.39798	92.74046	92.16969	91.67479	91.24622	90.87566	90.55581
13.500	98.37425	96.95849	95.72624	94.65435	93.72257	92.91321	92.21081	91.60183	91.07444	90.61832	90.22441	89.88483
13.625	98.25927	96.74525	95.42910	94.28565	93.29289	92.43163	91.68510	91.03866	90.47953	89.99655	89.57997	89.22128
13.75	98.14444	96.53254	95.13303	93.91865	92.86562	91.95320	91.16330	90.48015	89.89000	89.38086	88.94225	88.56506
14.00	97.91522	96.10868	94.54404	93.18973	92.01826	91.00572	90.13131	89.37694	88.72687	88.16741	87.68665	87.27424
14.250	97.68661	95.68691	93.95926	92.46754	91.18039	90.07061	89.11460	88.29186	87.58462	86.97746	86.45701	86.01163
14.50	97.45860	95.26722	93.37865	91.75200	90.35189	89.14770	88.11290	87.22457	86.46283	85.81049	85.25269	84.77653
14.75	97.23119	94.84961	92.80217	91.04305	89.53265	88.23680	87.12599	86.17475	85.36109	84.66600	84.07311	83.56825
15.25	96.77815	94.02054	91.66151	89.64465	87.92149	86.45038	85.19556	84.12628	83.21615	82.44249	81.78583	81.22942

Yield	13 Years	14 Years	15 Years	16 Years	17 Years	18 Years	19 Years	20 Years	22 Years	25 Years	27 Years	Full Term
8.750	122.50743	123.32019	124.04949	124.70181	125.28312	125.79882	126.25389	126.65286	127.29867	127.93889	128.18021	128.30929
9.00	120.36635	121.08678	121.73162	122.30697	122.81841	123.27102	123.66942	124.01783	124.57978	125.13354	125.34095	125.45133
9.25	118.27815	118.91145	119.47691	119.98019	120.42645	120.82040	121.16630	121.46806	121.95300	122.42802	122.60649	122.69842
9.500	116.24134	116.79250	117.28340	117.71923	118.10472	118.44419	118.74152	119.00026	119.41455	119.81797	119.96717	120.04575
9.75	114.25450	114.72825	115.14916	115.52192	115.85082	116.13973	116.39215	116.61127	116.96085	117.29923	117.42359	117.48874
9.875	113.27939	113.71614	114.10369	114.44649	114.74858	115.01360	115.24487	115.44538	115.76470	116.07286	116.18576	116.24475
10.00	112.31624	112.71709	113.07235	113.38620	113.66243	113.90447	114.11542	114.29808	114.58845	114.86785	114.96989	115.02307
10.125	111.36490	111.73093	112.05492	112.34079	112.59209	112.81201	113.00344	113.16900	113.43171	113.68374	113.77549	113.82318
10.25	110.42520	110.75745	111.05119	111.31004	111.53730	111.73594	111.90863	112.05780	112.29408	112.52007	112.60208	112.64460
10.375	109.49698	109.79648	110.06093	110.29369	110.49778	110.67596	110.83067	110.96414	111.17516	111.37640	111.44920	111.48685
10.500	108.58008	108.84782	109.08394	109.29150	109.47329	109.63178	109.76923	109.88767	110.07458	110.25230	110.31639	110.34944
10.625	107.67434	107.91130	108.12001	108.30326	108.46355	108.60313	108.72403	108.82807	108.99198	109.14735	109.20321	109.23194
10.75	106.77960	106.98673	107.16895	107.32873	107.46832	107.58972	107.69475	107.78502	107.92697	108.06114	108.10922	108.13389
10.875	105.89572	106.07394	106.23054	106.36768	106.48735	106.59129	106.68111	106.75821	106.87923	106.99327	107.03401	107.05486
11.000	105.02253	105.17276	105.30459	105.41990	105.52039	105.60758	105.68281	105.74732	105.84839	105.94335	105.97717	105.99443
11.125	104.15990	104.28301	104.39091	104.48517	104.56722	104.63831	104.69958	104.75206	104.83412	104.91100	104.93828	104.95218
11.25	103.30768	103.40453	103.48931	103.56328	103.62759	103.68324	103.73115	103.77212	103.83609	103.89584	103.91698	103.92771
11.375	102.46572	102.53715	102.59960	102.65402	102.70128	102.74212	102.77723	102.80723	102.85398	102.89751	102.91286	102.92064
11.50	101.63388	101.68071	101.72160	101.75719	101.78805	101.81470	101.83758	101.85710	101.88746	101.91565	101.92557	101.93057
11.75	100.00000	100.00000	100.00000	100.00000	100.00000	100.00000	100.00000	100.00000	100.00000	100.00000	100.00000	100.00000
12.00	98.40495	98.36116	98.32310	98.29015	98.26171	98.23728	98.21641	98.19868	98.17132	98.14621	98.13749	98.13313
12.125	97.62165	97.55709	97.50099	97.45250	97.41070	97.37485	97.34424	97.31830	97.27830	97.24171	97.22904	97.22273
12.25	96.84767	96.76296	96.68955	96.62612	96.57152	96.52474	96.48486	96.45109	96.39912	96.35173	96.33538	96.32724
12.375	96.08286	95.97874	95.88860	95.81083	95.74396	95.68674	95.63802	95.59682	95.53353	95.47597	95.45618	95.44635
12.50	95.32712	95.20424	95.09801	95.00645	94.92784	94.86064	94.80351	94.75524	94.68124	94.61414	94.59114	94.57975
12.625	94.58030	94.43933	94.31760	94.21281	94.12295	94.04624	93.98109	93.92613	93.84200	93.76595	93.73996	93.72713
12.750	93.84230	93.68386	93.54721	93.42974	93.32912	93.24333	93.17056	93.10925	93.01556	92.93112	92.90236	92.88820
12.875	93.11299	92.93770	92.78671	92.65707	92.54616	92.45171	92.37171	92.30437	92.20168	92.10939	92.07805	92.06266
13.00	92.39224	92.20071	92.03593	91.89462	91.77389	91.67120	91.58432	91.51128	91.40010	91.30048	91.26676	91.25024
13.125	91.67996	91.47276	91.29474	91.14225	91.01213	90.90159	90.80819	90.72977	90.61060	90.50413	90.46821	90.45066
13.25	90.97600	90.75373	90.56297	90.39979	90.26071	90.14271	90.04312	89.95961	89.83294	89.72010	89.68215	89.66366
13.375	90.28028	90.04347	89.84050	89.66708	89.51946	89.39436	89.28892	89.20061	89.06689	88.94813	88.90832	88.88897
13.500	89.59266	89.34187	89.12718	88.94397	88.78821	88.65638	88.54539	88.45256	88.31224	88.18799	88.14646	88.12633
13.625	88.91305	88.64880	88.42287	88.23030	88.06679	87.92857	87.81235	87.71526	87.56876	87.43947	87.39634	87.37550
13.75	88.24133	87.96414	87.72743	87.52593	87.35505	87.21077	87.08961	86.98852	86.83625	86.70222	86.65771	86.63624
14.00	86.92115	86.61956	86.36266	86.14451	85.95996	85.80453	85.67432	85.56594	85.40330	85.26098	85.21401	85.19148
14.250	85.63128	85.30719	85.03181	84.79854	84.60169	84.43631	84.29811	84.18337	84.01178	83.86251	83.81357	83.79020
14.50	84.37089	84.02612	83.73388	83.48694	83.27907	83.10486	82.95963	82.83936	82.66015	82.50516	82.45466	82.43068
14.75	83.13921	82.77546	82.46788	82.20863	81.99093	81.80894	81.65760	81.53257	81.34693	81.18733	81.13566	81.11124
15.25	80.75891	80.36195	80.02795	79.74782	79.51374	79.31902	79.15789	79.02543	78.83016	78.66425	78.61121	78.58640

Entry is the percentage of loan balance to give the desired yield to the selected time.

Price of a Mortgage to Give a Specified Yield
Conversion of Interest to Principal or Principal to Interest

12.00% Interest Rate   30 Years Amortization Schedule

Desired Prepaid or Ballooned at

Yield	1 Year	2 Years	3 Years	4 Years	5 Years	6 Years	7 Years	8 Years	9 Years	10 Years	11 Years	12 Years
9.00	102.85415	105.45351	107.81963	109.97220	111.92921	113.70710	115.32090	116.78432	118.10991	119.30910	120.39237	121.36925
9.25	102.61284	104.98654	107.14189	109.09785	110.87171	112.47922	113.93475	115.25138	116.44104	117.51461	118.48199	119.35220
9.50	102.37217	104.52188	106.46901	108.23164	109.82621	111.26766	112.56960	113.74438	114.80324	115.75640	116.61315	117.38194
9.75	102.13213	104.05953	105.80097	107.37350	108.79256	110.07219	111.22510	112.26283	113.19585	114.03365	114.78484	115.45724
10.00	101.89272	103.59946	105.13772	106.52333	107.77062	108.89257	109.90091	110.80627	111.61825	112.34557	112.99609	113.57693
10.125	101.77326	103.37029	104.80788	106.10121	107.26400	108.30863	109.24633	110.08721	110.84044	111.51429	112.11624	112.65305
10.25	101.65395	103.14168	104.47923	105.68106	106.76025	107.72858	108.59670	109.37424	110.06985	110.69139	111.24593	111.73984
10.375	101.53479	102.91364	104.15176	105.26287	106.25936	107.15238	107.95199	108.66728	109.30641	109.87678	110.38502	110.83715
10.500	101.41580	102.68616	103.82546	104.84662	105.76130	106.58000	107.31215	107.96628	108.55005	109.07036	109.53342	109.94485
10.625	101.29696	102.45925	103.50033	104.43231	105.26607	106.01142	106.67715	107.27120	107.80069	108.27204	108.69101	109.06280
10.75	101.17827	102.23290	103.17637	104.01993	104.77365	105.44660	106.04694	106.58196	107.05826	107.48173	107.85767	108.19087
10.875	101.05975	102.00711	102.85358	103.60946	104.28401	104.88553	105.42148	105.89853	106.32269	106.69934	107.03330	107.32893
11.000	100.94138	101.78188	102.53194	103.20090	103.79715	104.32818	104.80074	105.22085	105.59391	105.92478	106.21779	106.47684
11.125	100.82316	101.55721	102.21145	102.79424	103.31303	103.77452	104.18467	104.54885	104.87186	105.15797	105.41103	105.63448
11.25	100.70510	101.33309	101.89212	102.38947	102.83166	103.22452	103.57325	103.88250	104.15645	104.39881	104.61291	104.80173
11.375	100.58720	101.10953	101.57393	101.98658	102.35301	102.67815	102.96642	103.22174	103.44763	103.64723	103.82334	103.97845
11.50	100.46945	100.88652	101.25688	101.58556	101.87706	102.13540	102.36416	102.56652	102.74534	102.90314	103.04220	103.16453
11.625	100.35186	100.66407	100.94096	101.18640	101.40380	101.59624	101.76642	101.91679	102.04949	102.16665	102.26940	102.35984
11.750	100.23442	100.44216	100.62618	100.78909	100.93322	101.06063	101.17318	101.27249	101.36003	101.43709	101.50483	101.56427
12.00	100.00000	100.00000	100.00000	100.00000	100.00000	100.00000	100.00000	100.00000	100.00000	100.00000	100.00000	100.00000
12.25	99.76620	99.56002	99.37829	99.21321	99.07728	98.95331	98.84434	98.74867	98.66475	98.59124	98.52694	98.47079
12.375	99.64953	99.34085	99.06911	98.83003	98.61981	98.43512	98.27300	98.13081	98.00626	97.89728	97.80208	97.71906
12.50	99.53301	99.12222	98.76103	98.44364	98.16493	97.92035	97.70592	97.51810	97.35377	97.21018	97.08488	96.97575
12.625	99.41665	98.90413	98.45405	98.05905	97.71260	97.40897	97.14309	96.91049	96.70723	96.52984	96.37525	96.24077
12.750	99.30044	98.68657	98.14817	97.67623	97.26282	96.90095	96.58446	96.30792	96.06657	95.85620	95.67310	95.51400
12.875	99.18438	98.46956	97.84339	97.29519	96.81557	96.39626	96.02999	95.71036	95.43175	95.18919	94.97833	94.79534
13.00	99.06848	98.25308	97.53970	96.91591	96.37084	95.89490	95.47967	95.11776	94.80268	94.52872	94.29086	94.08469
13.125	98.95273	98.03714	97.23709	96.53839	95.92861	95.39682	94.93344	94.53007	94.17933	93.87473	93.61060	93.38195
13.250	98.83713	97.82173	96.93556	96.16261	95.48886	94.90201	94.39129	93.94725	93.56162	93.22715	92.93746	92.68700
13.375	98.72168	97.60685	96.63511	95.78857	95.05158	94.41044	93.85317	93.36926	92.94951	92.58590	92.27137	91.99976
13.500	98.60638	97.39251	96.33573	95.41625	94.61676	93.92210	93.31905	92.79604	92.34294	91.95092	91.61223	91.32012
13.625	98.49123	97.17869	96.03743	95.04566	94.18437	93.43696	92.78891	92.22756	91.74185	91.32213	90.95996	90.64799
13.75	98.37624	96.96540	95.74018	94.67678	93.75442	92.95499	92.26270	91.66377	91.14618	90.69947	90.31448	89.98327
13.875	98.26139	96.75264	95.44400	94.30960	93.32687	92.47618	91.74040	91.10463	90.55589	90.08287	89.67572	89.32586
14.000	98.14670	96.54040	95.14888	93.94412	92.90073	92.00049	91.22197	90.55010	89.97091	89.47226	89.04358	88.67568
14.250	97.91777	96.11749	94.56179	93.21820	92.05856	91.05843	90.19661	89.45469	88.81669	88.26876	87.79889	87.39662
14.50	97.68943	95.69667	93.97888	92.49896	91.22481	90.12864	89.18638	88.37721	87.68310	87.08846	86.57978	86.14536
14.75	97.46170	95.27793	93.40012	91.78634	90.40037	89.21093	88.19102	87.31733	86.56973	85.93084	85.38565	84.92121
15.000	97.23456	94.86124	92.82548	91.08027	89.58511	88.30514	87.21031	86.27475	85.47618	84.79542	84.21593	83.72349
15.50	96.78206	94.03401	91.68843	89.68751	87.98173	86.52864	85.29185	84.24019	83.34695	82.58922	81.94739	81.40466

Yield	13 Years	14 Years	15 Years	16 Years	17 Years	18 Years	19 Years	20 Years	22 Years	25 Years	27 Years	Full Term
9.00	122.24845	123.03795	123.74500	124.37622	124.93766	125.43484	125.87277	126.25604	126.87491	127.48604	127.71551	127.83789
9.25	120.13347	120.83328	121.45845	122.01519	122.50917	122.94551	123.32891	123.66362	124.20213	124.73073	124.92797	125.03261
9.50	118.07044	118.68563	119.23385	119.72085	120.15187	120.53167	120.86455	121.15445	121.61916	122.07261	122.24074	122.32948
9.75	116.05793	116.59333	117.06926	117.49100	117.86334	118.19061	118.47675	118.72532	119.12234	119.50745	119.64933	119.72383
10.00	114.09454	114.55474	114.96282	115.32353	115.64121	115.91974	116.16267	116.37317	116.70819	117.03121	117.14947	117.21125
10.125	113.13083	113.55509	113.93083	114.26256	114.55434	114.80985	115.03242	115.22505	115.53106	115.82524	115.93260	115.98854
10.25	112.17889	112.56828	112.91271	113.21642	113.48323	113.71658	113.91959	114.09508	114.37336	114.64008	114.73711	114.78754
10.375	111.23856	111.59412	111.90824	112.18488	112.42760	112.63963	112.82387	112.98292	113.23469	113.47528	113.56253	113.60776
10.500	110.30967	110.63243	110.91721	111.16770	111.38721	111.57872	111.74492	111.88823	112.11466	112.33040	112.40839	112.44872
10.625	109.39206	109.68301	109.93940	110.16464	110.36178	110.53356	110.68245	110.81068	111.01291	111.20503	111.27425	111.30995
10.75	108.48559	108.74569	108.97461	109.17547	109.35105	109.50386	109.63615	109.74993	109.92906	110.09872	110.15967	110.19102
10.875	107.59009	107.82028	108.02264	108.19997	108.35479	108.48937	108.60572	108.70568	108.86276	109.01109	109.06421	109.09146
11.000	106.70541	106.90663	107.08329	107.23791	107.37274	107.48979	107.59087	107.67760	107.81365	107.94173	107.98746	108.01085
11.125	105.83148	106.00454	106.15636	106.28908	106.40467	106.50489	106.59133	106.66540	106.78138	106.89026	106.92900	106.94877
11.25	104.96792	105.11385	105.24167	105.35326	105.45032	105.53438	105.60679	105.66877	105.76563	105.85629	105.88845	105.90482
11.375	104.11481	104.23440	104.33902	104.43024	104.50949	104.57803	104.63700	104.68741	104.76606	104.83946	104.86541	104.87858
11.50	103.27194	103.36602	103.44822	103.51981	103.58192	103.63558	103.68169	103.72105	103.78236	103.83940	103.85950	103.86969
11.625	102.43916	102.50855	102.56910	102.62177	102.66741	102.70679	102.74059	102.76941	102.81421	102.85577	102.87037	102.87774
11.750	101.61633	101.66183	101.70147	101.73592	101.76573	101.79142	101.81344	101.83219	101.86129	101.88821	101.89764	101.90239
12.00	100.00000	100.00000	100.00000	100.00000	100.00000	100.00000	100.00000	100.00000	100.00000	100.00000	100.00000	100.00000
12.25	98.42186	98.37932	98.34242	98.31053	98.28306	98.25950	98.23941	98.22239	98.19616	98.17218	98.16389	98.15976
12.375	97.64679	97.58403	97.52967	97.48274	97.44237	97.40780	97.37835	97.35342	97.31508	97.28014	97.26810	97.26211
12.50	96.88088	96.79859	96.72740	96.66602	96.61328	96.56817	96.52979	96.49735	96.44829	96.40229	96.38674	96.37902
12.625	96.12400	96.02284	95.93545	95.86018	95.79559	95.74041	95.69353	95.65394	95.59328	95.53832	95.51950	95.51018
12.750	95.37603	95.25666	95.15366	95.06505	94.98911	94.92432	94.86933	94.82296	94.75203	94.68796	94.66608	94.65529
12.875	94.63686	94.49990	94.38187	94.28046	94.19366	94.11969	94.05699	94.00418	93.92355	93.85093	93.82621	93.81405
13.00	93.90635	93.75243	93.61999	93.50564	93.40905	93.32633	93.25629	93.19738	93.10758	93.02696	92.99902	92.98617
13.125	93.18439	93.01410	92.86770	92.74223	92.63510	92.54403	92.46703	92.40233	92.30390	92.21578	92.18598	92.17138
13.250	92.47087	92.28480	92.12503	91.98827	91.87164	91.77263	91.68900	91.61883	91.51226	91.41714	91.38507	91.36941
13.375	91.76567	91.56438	91.39176	91.24419	91.11805	91.01191	90.92201	90.84666	90.73244	90.63079	90.59662	90.57998
13.500	91.06868	90.85273	90.66777	90.50984	90.37550	90.26171	90.16586	90.08562	89.96421	89.85647	89.82037	89.80283
13.625	90.37978	90.14972	89.95291	89.78507	89.64247	89.52185	89.42036	89.33551	89.20734	89.09395	89.05608	89.03772
13.75	89.69886	89.45521	89.24704	89.06973	88.91926	88.79215	88.68532	88.59612	88.46163	88.34299	88.30349	88.28440
13.875	89.02582	88.76910	88.55002	88.36366	88.20571	88.07243	87.96056	87.86727	87.72686	87.60336	87.56238	87.54262
14.000	88.36056	88.09126	87.86173	87.66672	87.50165	87.36253	87.24590	87.14877	87.00282	86.87484	86.83251	86.81215
14.250	87.05291	86.75991	86.51080	86.29967	86.12139	85.97152	85.84619	85.74205	85.58616	85.45026	85.40559	85.38421
14.50	85.77511	85.46025	85.19322	84.96746	84.77730	84.61783	84.48480	84.37455	84.21008	84.06754	84.02099	83.99883
14.75	84.52634	84.19138	83.90800	83.66901	83.46820	83.30021	83.16042	83.04485	82.87307	82.72507	82.67704	82.65429
15.000	83.30584	82.95243	82.65418	82.40327	82.19297	82.01747	81.87180	81.75166	81.57371	81.42131	81.37216	81.34900
15.50	80.94663	80.56096	80.23709	79.96596	79.73983	79.55206	79.39696	79.26968	79.08250	78.92406	78.87361	78.85008

Entry is the percentage of loan balance to give the desired yield to the selected time.

Price of a Mortgage to Give a Specified Yield
Conversion of Interest to Principal or Principal to Interest
12.25% Interest Rate   30 Years Amortization Schedule

Desired Yield	Prepaid or Ballooned at 1 Year	2 Years	3 Years	4 Years	5 Years	6 Years	7 Years	8 Years	9 Years	10 Years	11 Years	12 Years
9.25	102.85062	105.44085	107.79332	109.92868	111.86572	113.62160	115.21194	116.65098	117.95171	119.12593	120.18443	121.13702
9.50	102.60961	104.97497	107.11790	109.05822	110.81399	112.40160	113.83598	115.13068	116.29804	117.34925	118.29452	119.14310
9.75	102.36924	104.51140	106.44731	108.19586	109.77416	111.19778	112.48080	113.63602	114.67502	115.60835	116.44552	117.19521
10.000	102.12950	104.05013	105.78154	107.34150	108.74610	110.00990	111.14606	112.16651	113.08205	113.90241	114.63645	115.29215
10.25	101.89039	103.59114	105.12054	106.49508	107.72966	108.83773	109.83143	110.72172	111.51849	112.23068	112.86634	113.43275
10.375	101.77107	103.36250	104.79181	106.07482	107.22575	108.25747	109.18155	110.00844	110.74756	111.40739	111.99560	112.51907
10.500	101.65190	103.13442	104.46427	105.65651	106.72470	107.68106	108.53658	109.30117	109.98376	110.59237	111.13424	111.61589
10.625	101.53290	102.90691	104.13790	105.24014	106.22648	107.10846	107.89647	108.59985	109.22702	109.78552	110.28216	110.72306
10.75	101.41405	102.67996	103.81270	104.82571	105.73108	106.53965	107.26118	107.90443	108.47726	108.98675	109.43925	109.84046
10.875	101.29536	102.45358	103.48867	104.41321	105.23848	105.97461	106.63068	107.21485	107.73442	108.19597	108.60539	108.96794
11.000	101.17682	102.22775	103.16580	104.00262	104.74866	105.41330	106.00493	106.53105	106.99843	107.41310	107.78047	108.10539
11.125	101.05844	102.00248	102.84408	103.59393	104.26162	104.85571	105.38388	105.85300	106.26921	106.63803	106.96438	107.25266
11.25	100.94022	101.77778	102.52352	103.18714	103.77732	104.30179	104.76750	105.18062	105.54670	105.87069	106.15702	106.40964
11.375	100.82215	101.55362	102.20411	102.78224	103.29576	103.75154	104.15575	104.51387	104.83083	105.11100	105.35829	105.57619
11.500	100.70423	101.33002	101.88584	102.37922	102.81691	103.20492	103.54859	103.85270	104.12153	104.35885	104.56807	104.75220
11.625	100.58648	101.10698	101.56871	101.97807	102.34077	102.66190	102.94598	103.19706	103.41873	103.61418	103.78627	103.93754
11.750	100.46887	100.88449	101.25271	101.57877	101.86731	102.12246	102.34790	102.54690	102.72237	102.87689	103.01278	103.13208
11.875	100.35142	100.66254	100.93785	101.18133	101.39652	101.58658	101.75429	101.90216	102.03238	102.14691	102.24751	102.33572
12.00	100.23413	100.44115	100.62411	100.78572	100.92838	101.05422	101.16513	101.26280	101.34870	101.42416	101.49035	101.54832
12.250	100.00000	100.00000	100.00000	100.00000	100.00000	100.00000	100.00000	100.00000	100.00000	100.00000	100.00000	100.00000
12.50	99.76649	99.56103	99.38034	99.22153	99.08204	98.95960	98.85221	98.75812	98.67577	98.60379	98.54096	98.48620
12.625	99.64996	99.34236	99.07218	98.83500	98.62693	98.44451	98.28473	98.14491	98.02268	97.91597	97.82294	97.74197
12.750	99.53359	99.12423	98.76511	98.45025	98.17437	97.93281	97.72149	97.53679	97.37553	97.23491	97.11248	97.00604
12.875	99.41737	98.90663	98.45914	98.06728	97.72436	97.42447	97.16244	96.93370	96.73424	96.56053	96.40947	96.27831
13.00	99.30130	98.68958	98.15427	97.68609	97.27687	96.91946	96.60755	96.33561	96.09877	95.89276	95.71383	95.55867
13.125	99.18538	98.47306	97.85048	97.30665	96.83190	96.41776	96.05680	95.74247	95.46906	95.23153	95.02548	94.84702
13.250	99.06962	98.25707	97.54778	96.92896	96.38943	95.91935	95.51013	95.15423	94.84504	94.57676	94.34431	94.14325
13.375	98.95401	98.04162	97.24616	96.55302	95.94943	95.42420	94.96753	94.57085	94.22666	93.92838	93.67026	93.44727
13.500	98.83855	97.82670	96.94561	96.17882	95.51190	94.93229	94.42896	93.99229	93.61387	93.28632	93.00324	92.75897
13.625	98.72324	97.61231	96.64614	95.80634	95.07683	94.44360	93.89349	93.41850	93.00660	92.65052	92.34315	92.07826
13.750	98.60809	97.39845	96.34774	95.43557	94.64419	93.95810	93.36377	92.84943	92.40080	92.02090	91.68992	91.40504
13.875	98.49308	97.18512	96.05040	95.06652	94.21398	93.47577	92.83709	92.28505	91.80841	91.39739	91.04347	90.73921
14.000	98.37823	96.97231	95.75412	94.69917	93.78617	92.99659	92.31431	91.72531	91.21739	90.77994	90.40371	90.08069
14.125	98.26352	96.76003	95.45890	94.33351	93.36076	92.52054	91.79540	91.17018	90.63168	90.16846	89.77057	89.42937
14.250	98.14897	96.54827	95.16473	93.96954	92.93773	92.04760	91.28033	90.61959	90.05122	89.56290	89.14397	88.78517
14.50	97.92031	96.12632	94.57953	93.24662	92.09874	91.11093	90.26157	89.53194	88.90584	88.36927	87.91008	87.51776
14.750	97.69225	95.70644	93.99849	92.53033	91.26910	90.18642	89.25778	88.46202	87.78086	87.19853	86.70141	86.27774
15.000	97.46479	95.28863	93.42158	91.82062	90.44870	89.27390	88.26873	87.40951	86.67586	86.05019	85.51740	85.06444
15.25	97.23793	94.87288	92.84878	91.11742	89.63742	88.37320	87.29418	86.37412	85.59044	84.92377	84.35745	83.87717
15.75	96.78598	94.04750	91.71534	89.73030	88.04180	86.60658	85.38765	84.35340	83.47679	82.73474	82.10750	81.57817

Yield	13 Years	14 Years	15 Years	16 Years	17 Years	18 Years	19 Years	20 Years	22 Years	25 Years	27 Years	Full Term
9.25	121.99264	122.75943	123.44480	124.05550	124.59767	125.07689	125.49824	125.86636	126.45927	127.04250	127.26065	127.37665
9.50	119.90341	120.58310	121.18911	121.72776	122.20478	122.62537	122.99426	123.31574	123.83167	124.33614	124.52365	124.62284
9.75	117.86525	118.46275	118.99417	119.46535	119.88158	120.24767	120.56796	120.84640	121.29163	121.72439	121.88423	121.96835
10.000	115.87673	116.39674	116.85809	117.26613	117.62569	117.94115	118.21647	118.45522	118.83561	119.20314	119.33803	119.40866
10.25	113.93649	114.38347	114.77904	115.12804	115.43482	115.70331	115.93705	116.13924	116.46022	116.76851	116.88094	116.93951
10.375	112.98405	113.39612	113.76036	114.08131	114.36308	114.60938	114.82353	115.00855	115.30175	115.58251	115.68458	115.73761
10.500	112.04318	112.42138	112.75527	113.04911	113.30677	113.53171	113.72705	113.89560	114.16223	114.41679	114.50904	114.55684
10.625	111.11372	111.45907	111.76357	112.03123	112.26563	112.47001	112.64728	112.80006	113.04128	113.27090	113.35386	113.39673
10.75	110.19551	110.50899	110.78506	111.02742	111.23940	111.42401	111.58393	111.72158	111.93853	112.14444	112.21859	112.25681
10.875	109.28839	109.57098	109.81952	110.03745	110.22783	110.39342	110.53669	110.65985	110.85362	111.03698	111.10280	111.13664
11.000	108.39222	108.64485	108.86677	109.06111	109.23067	109.37797	109.50526	109.61455	109.78618	109.94811	110.00606	110.03578
11.125	107.50683	107.73042	107.92659	108.09816	108.24768	108.37740	108.48936	108.58537	108.73588	108.87745	108.92795	108.95379
11.25	106.63209	106.82753	106.99879	107.14840	107.27861	107.39144	107.48870	107.57201	107.70236	107.82461	107.86808	107.89026
11.375	105.76784	105.93601	106.08319	106.21160	106.32322	106.41983	106.50301	106.57416	106.68529	106.78921	106.82604	106.84479
11.500	104.91394	105.05569	105.17959	105.28756	105.38130	105.46223	105.53201	105.59154	105.68435	105.77088	105.80146	105.81697
11.625	104.07024	104.18641	104.28782	104.37608	104.45261	104.51869	104.57544	104.62386	104.69922	104.76927	104.79394	104.80643
11.750	103.23661	103.32800	103.40768	103.47695	103.53693	103.58866	103.63303	103.67084	103.72958	103.78403	103.80314	103.81279
11.875	102.41291	102.48031	102.53901	102.58997	102.63405	102.67201	102.70453	102.73221	102.77514	102.81481	102.82869	102.83568
12.00	101.59899	101.64318	101.68162	101.71494	101.74373	101.76850	101.78969	101.80770	101.83559	101.86128	101.87024	101.87474
12.250	100.00000	100.00000	100.00000	100.00000	100.00000	100.00000	100.00000	100.00000	100.00000	100.00000	100.00000	100.00000
12.50	98.43858	98.39725	98.36148	98.33062	98.30409	98.28139	98.26206	98.24570	98.22057	98.19768	98.18980	98.18588
12.625	97.67164	97.61068	97.55798	97.51257	97.47358	97.44025	97.41191	97.38796	97.35123	97.31788	97.30643	97.30075
12.750	96.91371	96.83378	96.76477	96.70537	96.65444	96.61095	96.57402	96.54285	96.49513	96.45193	96.43715	96.42983
12.875	96.16467	96.06641	95.98168	95.90885	95.84648	95.79328	95.74816	95.71014	95.65201	95.59955	95.58165	95.57282
13.00	95.42439	95.30844	95.20858	95.12285	95.04951	94.98705	94.93413	94.88959	94.82162	94.76046	94.73966	94.72942
13.125	94.69277	94.55974	94.44531	94.34719	94.26336	94.19205	94.13171	94.08098	94.00371	93.93440	93.91090	93.89936
13.250	93.96968	93.82016	93.69171	93.58171	93.48784	93.40809	93.34069	93.28410	93.19806	93.12110	93.09508	93.08235
13.375	93.25500	93.08958	92.94765	92.82625	92.72278	92.63499	92.56088	92.49873	92.40441	92.32030	92.29196	92.27812
13.500	92.54862	92.36787	92.21298	92.08065	91.96801	91.87255	91.79208	91.72467	91.62255	91.53175	91.50126	91.48641
13.625	91.85043	91.65491	91.48755	91.34476	91.22336	91.12061	91.03409	90.96171	90.85226	90.75522	90.72273	90.70695
13.750	91.16031	90.95055	90.77124	90.61842	90.48867	90.37897	90.28673	90.20965	90.09330	89.99046	89.95613	89.93950
13.875	90.47817	90.25469	90.06389	89.90149	89.76376	89.64748	89.54981	89.46830	89.34547	89.23723	89.20122	89.18382
14.000	89.80388	89.56721	89.36538	89.19381	89.04894	88.92594	88.82314	88.73745	88.60856	88.49531	88.45776	88.43965
14.125	89.13735	88.88797	88.67558	88.49524	88.34269	88.21420	88.10655	88.01693	87.88237	87.76448	87.72551	87.70677
14.250	88.47846	88.21687	87.99435	87.80564	87.64621	87.51209	87.39986	87.30654	87.16668	87.04451	87.00425	86.98495
14.50	87.18322	86.89861	86.65709	86.45279	86.28061	86.13611	86.01550	85.91547	85.76607	85.63634	85.59386	85.57359
14.750	85.91737	85.61152	85.35263	85.13417	84.95050	84.79676	84.66874	84.56282	84.40520	84.26913	84.22486	84.20385
15.000	84.68010	84.35472	84.07998	83.84871	83.65475	83.49280	83.35827	83.24725	83.08262	82.94134	82.89566	82.87409
15.25	83.47066	83.12736	82.83820	82.59540	82.39227	82.22308	82.08288	81.96746	81.79694	81.65144	81.60470	81.58274
15.75	81.13235	80.75770	80.44370	80.18133	79.96291	79.78187	79.63261	79.51033	79.33094	79.17968	79.13170	79.10938

Entry is the percentage of loan balance to give the desired yield to the selected time.

Price of a Mortgage to Give a Specified Yield
Conversion of Interest to Principal or Principal to Interest
12.50% Interest Rate   30 Years Amortization Schedule

Desired Yield	Prepaid or Ballooned at											
	1 Year	2 Years	3 Years	4 Years	5 Years	6 Years	7 Years	8 Years	9 Years	10 Years	11 Years	12 Years
9.500	102.84708	105.42818	107.76703	109.88525	111.80245	113.53650	115.10363	116.51859	117.79480	118.94446	119.97866	120.90746
9.75	102.60637	104.96340	107.09392	109.01868	110.75646	112.32434	113.73779	115.01083	116.15619	117.18543	118.10899	118.93639
10.000	102.36630	104.50092	106.42563	108.16014	109.72229	111.12822	112.39252	113.52841	114.54786	115.46167	116.27963	117.01060
10.250	102.12686	104.04073	105.76212	107.30957	108.69980	109.94789	111.06748	112.07088	112.96917	113.77239	114.48958	115.12891
10.500	101.88804	103.58281	105.10337	106.46689	107.68884	108.78314	109.76235	110.63776	111.41953	112.11684	112.73791	113.29020
10.625	101.76887	103.35470	104.77576	106.04847	107.18764	108.20654	109.11715	109.93022	110.65542	111.30147	111.87618	112.38660
10.75	101.64986	103.12716	104.44932	105.63200	106.68927	107.63375	108.47680	109.22861	109.89835	110.49425	111.02370	111.49333
10.875	101.53100	102.90018	104.12405	105.21746	106.19371	107.06474	107.84126	108.53289	109.14826	109.69509	110.18035	110.61025
11.000	101.41230	102.67376	103.79995	104.80485	105.70095	106.49949	107.21050	107.84300	108.40506	108.90391	109.34603	109.73723
11.125	101.29376	102.44790	103.47701	104.39414	105.21098	105.93797	106.58448	107.15889	107.66869	108.12060	108.52063	108.87415
11.25	101.17537	102.22260	103.15523	103.98534	104.72376	105.38015	105.96316	106.48050	106.93908	107.34509	107.70404	108.02086
11.375	101.05713	101.99786	102.83459	103.57844	104.23930	104.82601	105.34649	105.80777	106.21616	106.57728	106.89615	107.17725
11.50	100.93906	101.77367	102.51511	103.17342	103.75756	104.27553	104.73444	105.14067	105.49987	105.81710	106.09686	106.34318
11.625	100.82113	101.55004	102.19676	102.77027	103.27854	103.72867	104.12698	104.47913	104.79013	105.06445	105.30607	105.51855
11.750	100.70336	101.32696	101.87956	102.36899	102.80221	103.18540	103.52407	103.82311	104.08688	104.31925	104.52367	104.70321
11.875	100.58575	101.10443	101.56349	101.96957	102.32857	102.64571	102.92566	103.17255	103.39005	103.58142	103.74957	103.89707
12.00	100.46829	100.88245	101.24855	101.57200	101.85759	102.10957	102.33173	102.52741	102.69958	102.85088	102.98366	103.09998
12.125	100.35099	100.66102	100.93473	101.17626	101.38926	101.57696	101.74223	101.88763	102.01540	102.12755	102.22584	102.31185
12.25	100.23384	100.44013	100.62204	100.78236	100.92356	101.04784	101.15714	101.25317	101.33746	101.41134	101.47602	101.53255
12.50	100.00000	100.00000	100.00000	100.00000	100.00000	100.00000	100.00000	100.00000	100.00000	100.00000	100.00000	100.00000
12.750	99.76678	99.56204	99.38240	99.22485	99.08678	98.96586	98.86004	98.76752	98.68671	98.61623	98.55483	98.50144
12.875	99.65039	99.34387	99.07525	98.83996	98.63401	98.45386	98.29641	98.15892	98.03898	97.93450	97.84359	97.76464
13.00	99.53416	99.12624	98.76919	98.45585	98.18379	97.94522	97.73697	97.55534	97.39711	97.25943	97.13979	97.03601
13.125	99.41808	98.90914	98.46423	98.07550	97.73608	97.43991	97.18168	96.95676	96.76104	96.59096	96.44335	96.31546
13.25	99.30216	98.69258	98.16036	97.69592	97.29088	96.93790	96.63052	96.36311	96.13072	95.92900	95.75417	95.60287
13.375	99.18639	98.47656	97.85757	97.31808	96.84818	96.43917	96.08345	95.77436	95.50608	95.27350	95.07216	94.89815
13.500	99.07077	98.26107	97.55586	96.94199	96.40795	95.94370	95.54043	95.19046	94.88707	94.62438	94.39725	94.20119
13.625	98.95530	98.04611	97.25522	96.56763	95.97019	95.45146	95.00143	94.61136	94.27363	93.98156	93.72935	93.51190
13.75	98.83998	97.83167	96.95566	96.19499	95.53488	94.96244	94.46642	94.03703	93.66570	93.34499	93.06837	92.83018
13.875	98.72481	97.61777	96.65717	95.82407	95.10200	94.47660	93.93537	93.46742	93.06324	92.71458	92.41424	92.15594
14.00	98.60980	97.40440	96.35973	95.45486	94.67154	93.99394	93.40825	92.90248	92.46618	92.09028	91.76686	91.48907
14.125	98.49493	97.19155	96.06336	95.08734	94.24349	93.51441	92.88502	92.34217	91.87447	91.47201	91.12617	90.82948
14.250	98.38022	96.97923	95.76804	94.72152	93.81783	93.03801	92.36565	91.78646	91.28806	90.85971	90.49208	90.17709
14.375	98.26565	96.76742	95.47378	94.35738	93.39454	92.56471	91.85011	91.23529	90.70689	90.25332	89.86452	89.53180
14.50	98.15124	96.55614	95.18056	93.99492	92.97361	92.09449	91.33837	90.68863	90.13091	89.65276	89.24340	88.89352
14.75	97.92286	96.13515	94.59725	93.27498	92.13879	91.16320	90.32617	89.60868	88.99432	88.46891	88.02021	87.63764
15.000	97.69508	95.71622	94.01808	92.56164	91.31325	90.24396	89.32879	88.54627	87.87788	87.30767	86.82190	86.40876
15.25	97.46790	95.29935	93.44303	91.85484	90.49688	89.33660	88.34602	87.50110	86.78118	86.16853	85.64790	85.20619
15.50	97.24131	94.88453	92.87205	91.15451	89.68957	88.44096	87.37760	86.47284	85.70384	85.05103	84.49764	84.02929
16.00	96.78991	94.06100	91.74222	89.77301	88.10168	86.68418	85.48293	84.46587	83.60568	82.87905	82.26612	81.74993

Yield	13 Years	14 Years	15 Years	16 Years	17 Years	18 Years	19 Years	20 Years	22 Years	25 Years	27 Years	Full Term
9.500	121.74001	122.48464	123.14890	123.73964	124.26311	124.72494	125.13027	125.48376	126.05169	126.60815	126.81549	126.92542
9.75	119.67621	120.33626	120.92361	121.44466	121.90522	122.31056	122.66542	122.97413	123.46833	123.94966	124.12787	124.22188
10.000	117.66258	118.24283	118.75788	119.21367	119.61555	119.96836	120.27648	120.54386	120.97034	121.38326	121.53518	121.61490
10.250	115.69775	116.20274	116.64989	117.04461	117.39178	117.69580	117.96066	118.18992	118.55430	118.90498	119.03319	119.10012
10.500	113.78036	114.21444	114.59785	114.93455	115.23166	115.49041	115.71527	115.90944	116.21691	116.51107	116.61793	116.67344
10.625	112.83905	113.23923	113.59226	113.90274	114.17480	114.41217	114.61819	114.79586	115.07672	115.34462	115.44163	115.49189
10.75	111.90911	112.27640	112.60002	112.88427	113.13305	113.34983	113.53776	113.69962	113.95503	114.19792	114.28561	114.33091
10.875	110.99039	111.32578	111.62091	111.87983	112.10616	112.30313	112.47367	112.62038	112.85416	113.07056	113.14941	113.19004
11.000	110.08272	110.38717	110.65474	110.88919	111.09387	111.27179	111.42564	111.55783	111.76565	111.96213	112.03261	112.06884
11.125	109.18597	109.46040	109.70130	109.91212	110.09594	110.25553	110.39336	110.51164	110.69726	110.87222	110.93478	110.96686
11.25	108.29997	108.54531	108.76040	108.94841	109.11213	109.25410	109.37655	109.48151	109.64592	109.80044	109.85552	109.88368
11.375	107.42458	107.64171	107.83185	107.99783	108.14219	108.26722	108.37493	108.46713	108.61131	108.74641	108.79441	108.81889
11.50	106.55965	106.74945	106.91545	107.06017	107.18590	107.29465	107.38822	107.46822	107.59309	107.70975	107.75107	107.77209
11.625	105.70504	105.86836	106.01101	106.13524	106.24302	106.33613	106.41615	106.48448	106.59094	106.69010	106.72511	106.74288
11.750	104.86060	104.99827	105.11836	105.22281	105.31333	105.39142	105.45845	105.51562	105.60453	105.68711	105.71617	105.73088
11.875	104.02620	104.13902	104.23732	104.32270	104.39660	104.46028	104.51488	104.56138	104.63357	104.70042	104.72387	104.73571
12.00	103.20170	103.29046	103.36769	103.43470	103.49262	103.54248	103.58516	103.62147	103.67775	103.72970	103.74787	103.75702
12.125	102.38697	102.45243	102.50932	102.55862	102.60118	102.63777	102.66906	102.69564	102.73677	102.77462	102.78782	102.79444
12.25	101.58186	101.62477	101.66203	101.69427	101.72207	101.74594	101.76632	101.78362	101.81033	101.83485	101.84337	101.84764
12.50	100.00000	100.00000	100.00000	100.00000	100.00000	100.00000	100.00000	100.00000	100.00000	100.00000	100.00000	100.00000
12.750	98.45510	98.41496	98.38030	98.35044	98.32482	98.30294	98.28434	98.26863	98.24455	98.22271	98.21522	98.21151
12.875	97.69619	97.63699	97.58591	97.54198	97.50433	97.47221	97.44494	97.42194	97.38855	97.35493	97.34400	97.33866
13.00	96.94616	96.86853	96.80164	96.74417	96.69499	96.65308	96.61755	96.58761	96.54189	96.50067	96.48661	96.47968
13.125	96.20486	96.10944	96.02731	95.95685	95.89662	95.84535	95.80194	95.76542	95.70973	95.65967	95.64265	95.63428
13.25	95.47220	95.35958	95.26279	95.17984	95.10902	95.04882	94.99791	94.95513	94.89001	94.83165	94.81188	94.80217
13.375	94.74804	94.61884	94.50792	94.41299	94.33204	94.26331	94.20526	94.15653	94.08251	94.01636	93.99402	93.98308
13.500	94.03227	93.88706	93.76256	93.65613	93.56549	93.48862	93.42378	93.36942	93.28699	93.21354	93.18881	93.17674
13.625	93.32479	93.16414	93.02656	92.90911	92.80919	92.72457	92.65328	92.59359	92.50322	92.42295	92.39601	92.38289
13.75	92.62547	92.44993	92.29979	92.17176	92.06300	91.97099	91.89356	91.82882	91.73099	91.64433	91.61534	91.60126
13.875	91.93422	91.74432	91.58210	91.44395	91.32673	91.22769	91.14445	91.07493	90.97006	90.87746	90.84657	90.83161
14.00	91.25091	91.04718	90.87337	90.72552	90.60022	90.49449	90.40574	90.33171	90.22024	90.12209	90.08946	90.07369
14.125	90.57544	90.35840	90.17344	90.01632	89.88333	89.77124	89.67727	89.59898	89.48131	89.37801	89.34377	89.32727
14.250	89.90771	89.67784	89.48221	89.31621	89.17588	89.05776	88.95885	88.87655	88.75307	88.64498	88.60928	88.59211
14.375	89.24761	89.00541	88.79952	88.62505	88.47774	88.35389	88.25031	88.16423	88.03531	87.92280	87.88575	87.86799
14.50	88.59504	88.34097	88.12527	87.94270	87.78874	87.65946	87.55148	87.46185	87.32785	87.21125	87.17298	87.15468
14.75	87.31208	87.03564	86.80153	86.60387	86.43759	86.29832	86.18227	86.08619	85.94305	85.81923	85.77884	85.75963
15.000	86.05804	85.76098	85.51003	85.29866	85.12130	84.97310	84.84993	84.74819	84.59718	84.46731	84.42522	84.40530
15.25	84.83216	84.51612	84.24980	84.02604	83.83874	83.68263	83.55319	83.44655	83.28882	83.15397	83.11054	83.09009
15.50	83.63367	83.30024	83.01993	82.78501	82.58885	82.42526	82.29087	82.18001	82.01662	81.87775	81.83331	81.81249
16.00	81.31605	80.95216	80.64776	80.39391	80.18298	80.00847	79.86434	79.74739	79.57551	79.43113	79.38551	79.36436

Entry is the percentage of loan balance to give the desired yield to the selected time.

Feasible Loan Based on Debt Service Coverage

Interest Rate	Amortization Schedule	Debt Service Coverage											
		1.00	1.10	1.125	1.15	1.175	1.20	1.25	1.30	1.33	1.40	1.50	1.667
5.50%	10	7.68	6.98	6.83	6.68	6.54	6.40	6.14	5.91	5.77	5.48	5.12	4.61
	15	10.20	9.27	9.07	8.87	8.68	8.50	8.16	7.85	7.67	7.28	6.80	6.12
	20	12.11	11.01	10.77	10.53	10.31	10.10	9.69	9.32	9.11	8.65	8.08	7.27
	22.5	12.89	11.72	11.46	11.21	10.97	10.74	10.31	9.92	9.69	9.21	8.59	7.74
	25	13.57	12.34	12.06	11.80	11.55	11.31	10.86	10.44	10.20	9.69	9.05	8.14
	27.5	14.16	12.87	12.59	12.31	12.05	11.80	11.33	10.89	10.65	10.12	9.44	8.50
	30	14.68	13.34	13.05	12.76	12.49	12.23	11.74	11.29	11.04	10.48	9.78	8.81
	35	15.52	14.11	13.79	13.49	13.21	12.93	12.41	11.94	11.67	11.08	10.35	9.31
5.75%	10	7.59	6.90	6.75	6.60	6.46	6.33	6.07	5.84	5.71	5.42	5.06	4.56
	15	10.04	9.12	8.92	8.73	8.54	8.36	8.03	7.72	7.55	7.17	6.69	6.02
	20	11.87	10.79	10.55	10.32	10.10	9.89	9.50	9.13	8.92	8.48	7.91	7.12
	22.5	12.61	11.46	11.21	10.96	10.73	10.51	10.09	9.70	9.48	9.01	8.40	7.56
	25	13.25	12.04	11.77	11.52	11.27	11.04	10.60	10.19	9.96	9.46	8.83	7.95
	27.5	13.80	12.55	12.27	12.00	11.74	11.50	11.04	10.62	10.38	9.86	9.20	8.28
	30	14.28	12.98	12.69	12.42	12.15	11.90	11.42	10.98	10.74	10.20	9.52	8.57
	35	15.06	13.69	13.38	13.09	12.81	12.55	12.04	11.58	11.32	10.75	10.04	9.03
6.00%	10	7.51	6.82	6.67	6.53	6.39	6.26	6.00	5.77	5.64	5.36	5.00	4.50
	15	9.88	8.98	8.78	8.59	8.40	8.23	7.90	7.60	7.43	7.05	6.58	5.93
	20	11.63	10.57	10.34	10.11	9.90	9.69	9.31	8.95	8.75	8.31	7.75	6.98
	22.5	12.33	11.21	10.96	10.72	10.49	10.28	9.87	9.49	9.27	8.81	8.22	7.40
	25	12.93	11.76	11.50	11.25	11.01	10.78	10.35	9.95	9.72	9.24	8.62	7.76
	27.5	13.45	12.23	11.96	11.70	11.45	11.21	10.76	10.35	10.11	9.61	8.97	8.07
	30	13.90	12.64	12.35	12.09	11.83	11.58	11.12	10.69	10.45	9.93	9.27	8.34
	35	14.62	13.29	12.99	12.71	12.44	12.18	11.69	11.24	10.99	10.44	9.74	8.77
6.25%	10	7.42	6.75	6.60	6.45	6.32	6.18	5.94	5.71	5.58	5.30	4.95	4.45
	15	9.72	8.84	8.64	8.45	8.27	8.10	7.78	7.48	7.31	6.94	6.48	5.83
	20	11.40	10.36	10.13	9.91	9.70	9.50	9.12	8.77	8.57	8.14	7.60	6.84
	22.5	12.06	10.97	10.72	10.49	10.27	10.05	9.65	9.28	9.07	8.62	8.04	7.24
	25	12.63	11.48	11.23	10.98	10.75	10.53	10.11	9.72	9.50	9.02	8.42	7.58
	27.5	13.12	11.93	11.66	11.41	11.16	10.93	10.49	10.09	9.86	9.37	8.75	7.87
	30	13.53	12.30	12.03	11.77	11.52	11.28	10.83	10.41	10.18	9.67	9.02	8.12
	35	14.19	12.90	12.62	12.34	12.08	11.83	11.36	10.92	10.67	10.14	9.46	8.52
6.50%	10	7.34	6.67	6.52	6.38	6.25	6.12	5.87	5.65	5.52	5.24	4.89	4.40
	15	9.57	8.70	8.50	8.32	8.14	7.97	7.65	7.36	7.19	6.83	6.38	5.74
	20	11.18	10.16	9.94	9.72	9.51	9.31	8.94	8.60	8.40	7.98	7.45	6.71
	22.5	11.81	10.73	10.49	10.27	10.05	9.84	9.45	9.08	8.88	8.43	7.87	7.08
	25	12.34	11.22	10.97	10.73	10.50	10.28	9.87	9.49	9.28	8.82	8.23	7.41
	27.5	12.80	11.63	11.38	11.13	10.89	10.66	10.24	9.84	9.62	9.14	8.53	7.68
	30	13.18	11.99	11.72	11.46	11.22	10.99	10.55	10.14	9.91	9.42	8.79	7.91
	35	13.79	12.54	12.26	11.99	11.74	11.49	11.03	10.61	10.37	9.85	9.20	8.28
6.75%	10	7.26	6.60	6.45	6.31	6.18	6.05	5.81	5.58	5.46	5.18	4.84	4.35
	15	9.42	8.56	8.37	8.19	8.01	7.85	7.53	7.24	7.08	6.73	6.28	5.65
	20	10.96	9.96	9.74	9.53	9.33	9.13	8.77	8.43	8.24	7.83	7.31	6.58
	22.5	11.56	10.51	10.27	10.05	9.84	9.63	9.25	8.89	8.69	8.25	7.70	6.93
	25	12.06	10.96	10.72	10.49	10.26	10.05	9.65	9.28	9.07	8.62	8.04	7.24
	27.5	12.49	11.35	11.10	10.86	10.63	10.41	9.99	9.61	9.39	8.92	8.33	7.49
	30	12.85	11.68	11.42	11.17	10.93	10.71	10.28	9.88	9.66	9.18	8.57	7.71
	35	13.41	12.19	11.92	11.66	11.41	11.18	10.73	10.32	10.08	9.58	8.94	8.05
7.00%	10	7.18	6.52	6.38	6.24	6.11	5.98	5.74	5.52	5.40	5.13	4.78	4.31
	15	9.27	8.43	8.24	8.06	7.89	7.73	7.42	7.13	6.97	6.62	6.18	5.56
	20	10.75	9.77	9.55	9.35	9.15	8.96	8.60	8.27	8.08	7.68	7.17	6.45
	22.5	11.31	10.29	10.06	9.84	9.63	9.43	9.05	8.70	8.51	8.08	7.54	6.79
	25	11.79	10.72	10.48	10.25	10.03	9.83	9.43	9.07	8.87	8.42	7.86	7.07
	27.5	12.19	11.08	10.84	10.60	10.37	10.16	9.75	9.38	9.17	8.71	8.13	7.31
	30	12.53	11.39	11.13	10.89	10.66	10.44	10.02	9.64	9.42	8.95	8.35	7.52
	35	13.04	11.86	11.59	11.34	11.10	10.87	10.44	10.03	9.81	9.32	8.70	7.83
7.25%	10	7.10	6.45	6.31	6.17	6.04	5.92	5.68	5.46	5.34	5.07	4.73	4.26
	15	9.13	8.30	8.11	7.94	7.77	7.61	7.30	7.02	6.86	6.52	6.09	5.48
	20	10.54	9.59	9.37	9.17	8.97	8.79	8.43	8.11	7.93	7.53	7.03	6.33
	22.5	11.08	10.07	9.85	9.64	9.43	9.23	8.86	8.52	8.33	7.91	7.39	6.65
	25	11.53	10.48	10.25	10.03	9.81	9.61	9.22	8.87	8.67	8.24	7.69	6.92
	27.5	11.90	10.82	10.58	10.35	10.13	9.92	9.52	9.16	8.95	8.50	7.94	7.14
	30	12.22	11.11	10.86	10.62	10.40	10.18	9.77	9.40	9.18	8.73	8.14	7.33
	35	12.69	11.54	11.28	11.04	10.80	10.58	10.16	9.76	9.54	9.07	8.46	7.62

Entry is the feasible loan as a multiple of net operating income.

Feasible Loan Based on Debt Service Coverage

Interest Rate	Amortization Schedule	Debt Service Coverage											
		1.00	1.10	1.125	1.15	1.175	1.20	1.25	1.30	1.33	1.40	1.50	1.667
7.50%	10	7.02	6.38	6.24	6.10	5.97	5.85	5.62	5.40	5.28	5.01	4.68	4.21
	15	8.99	8.17	7.99	7.82	7.65	7.49	7.19	6.91	6.76	6.42	5.99	5.39
	20	10.34	9.40	9.19	9.00	8.80	8.62	8.28	7.96	7.78	7.39	6.90	6.21
	22.5	10.85	9.87	9.65	9.44	9.24	9.04	8.68	8.35	8.16	7.75	7.24	6.51
	25	11.28	10.25	10.02	9.81	9.60	9.40	9.02	8.67	8.48	8.05	7.52	6.77
	27.5	11.63	10.57	10.34	10.11	9.90	9.69	9.30	8.94	8.74	8.31	7.75	6.98
	30	11.92	10.83	10.59	10.36	10.14	9.93	9.53	9.17	8.96	8.51	7.95	7.15
	35	12.36	11.24	10.99	10.75	10.52	10.30	9.89	9.51	9.29	8.83	8.24	7.42
7.75%	10	6.94	6.31	6.17	6.04	5.91	5.79	5.56	5.34	5.22	4.96	4.63	4.17
	15	8.85	8.05	7.87	7.70	7.53	7.38	7.08	6.81	6.66	6.32	5.90	5.31
	20	10.15	9.23	9.02	8.83	8.64	8.46	8.12	7.81	7.63	7.25	6.77	6.09
	22.5	10.63	9.67	9.45	9.25	9.05	8.86	8.51	8.18	8.00	7.60	7.09	6.38
	25	11.03	10.03	9.81	9.59	9.39	9.19	8.83	8.49	8.30	7.88	7.36	6.62
	27.5	11.36	10.33	10.10	9.88	9.67	9.47	9.09	8.74	8.54	8.12	7.57	6.82
	30	11.63	10.57	10.34	10.11	9.90	9.69	9.31	8.95	8.75	8.31	7.75	6.98
	35	12.04	10.94	10.70	10.47	10.25	10.03	9.63	9.26	9.05	8.60	8.03	7.22
8.00%	10	6.87	6.24	6.11	5.97	5.85	5.72	5.49	5.28	5.16	4.91	4.58	4.12
	15	8.72	7.93	7.75	7.58	7.42	7.27	6.98	6.71	6.56	6.23	5.81	5.23
	20	9.96	9.06	8.86	8.66	8.48	8.30	7.97	7.66	7.49	7.12	6.64	5.98
	22.5	10.42	9.47	9.26	9.06	8.87	8.68	8.34	8.02	7.84	7.44	6.95	6.25
	25	10.80	9.82	9.60	9.39	9.19	9.00	8.64	8.31	8.12	7.71	7.20	6.48
	27.5	11.10	10.10	9.87	9.66	9.45	9.25	8.88	8.54	8.35	7.93	7.40	6.66
	30	11.36	10.32	10.10	9.88	9.67	9.46	9.09	8.74	8.54	8.11	7.57	6.81
	35	11.73	10.67	10.43	10.20	9.99	9.78	9.39	9.03	8.82	8.38	7.82	7.04
8.25%	10	6.79	6.18	6.04	5.91	5.78	5.66	5.44	5.23	5.11	4.85	4.53	4.08
	15	8.59	7.81	7.64	7.47	7.31	7.16	6.87	6.61	6.46	6.14	5.73	5.15
	20	9.78	8.89	8.69	8.50	8.32	8.15	7.82	7.52	7.35	6.99	6.52	5.87
	22.5	10.22	9.29	9.08	8.88	8.69	8.51	8.17	7.86	7.68	7.30	6.81	6.13
	25	10.57	9.61	9.39	9.19	9.00	8.81	8.46	8.13	7.95	7.55	7.05	6.34
	27.5	10.86	9.87	9.65	9.44	9.24	9.05	8.69	8.35	8.16	7.76	7.24	6.51
	30	11.09	10.08	9.86	9.65	9.44	9.24	8.87	8.53	8.34	7.92	7.39	6.66
	35	11.44	10.40	10.17	9.95	9.74	9.53	9.15	8.80	8.60	8.17	7.63	6.86
8.50%	10	6.72	6.11	5.97	5.84	5.72	5.60	5.38	5.17	5.05	4.80	4.48	4.03
	15	8.46	7.69	7.52	7.36	7.20	7.05	6.77	6.51	6.36	6.04	5.64	5.08
	20	9.60	8.73	8.54	8.35	8.17	8.00	7.68	7.39	7.22	6.86	6.40	5.76
	22.5	10.02	9.10	8.90	8.71	8.52	8.35	8.01	7.70	7.53	7.15	6.68	6.01
	25	10.35	9.41	9.20	9.00	8.81	8.62	8.28	7.96	7.78	7.39	6.90	6.21
	27.5	10.62	9.65	9.44	9.23	9.04	8.85	8.50	8.17	7.98	7.59	7.08	6.37
	30	10.84	9.85	9.63	9.42	9.22	9.03	8.67	8.34	8.15	7.74	7.23	6.50
	35	11.16	10.14	9.92	9.70	9.50	9.30	8.93	8.58	8.39	7.97	7.44	6.69
8.75%	10	6.65	6.04	5.91	5.78	5.66	5.54	5.32	5.11	5.00	4.75	4.43	3.99
	15	8.34	7.58	7.41	7.25	7.10	6.95	6.67	6.41	6.27	5.96	5.56	5.00
	20	9.43	8.57	8.38	8.20	8.03	7.86	7.54	7.25	7.09	6.74	6.29	5.66
	22.5	9.82	8.93	8.73	8.54	8.36	8.18	7.86	7.55	7.38	7.02	6.55	5.89
	25	10.14	9.21	9.01	8.81	8.63	8.45	8.11	7.80	7.62	7.24	6.76	6.08
	27.5	10.39	9.44	9.23	9.03	8.84	8.66	8.31	7.99	7.81	7.42	6.93	6.23
	30	10.59	9.63	9.42	9.21	9.02	8.83	8.47	8.15	7.96	7.57	7.06	6.36
	35	10.89	9.90	9.68	9.47	9.27	9.07	8.71	8.38	8.19	7.78	7.26	6.53
9.00%	10	6.58	5.98	5.85	5.72	5.60	5.48	5.26	5.06	4.95	4.70	4.39	3.95
	15	8.22	7.47	7.30	7.14	6.99	6.85	6.57	6.32	6.18	5.87	5.48	4.93
	20	9.26	8.42	8.23	8.05	7.88	7.72	7.41	7.12	6.96	6.62	6.17	5.56
	22.5	9.63	8.76	8.56	8.38	8.20	8.03	7.71	7.41	7.24	6.88	6.42	5.78
	25	9.93	9.03	8.83	8.63	8.45	8.28	7.94	7.64	7.47	7.09	6.62	5.96
	27.5	10.17	9.24	9.04	8.84	8.65	8.47	8.13	7.82	7.64	7.26	6.78	6.10
	30	10.36	9.42	9.21	9.01	8.81	8.63	8.29	7.97	7.79	7.40	6.90	6.21
	35	10.63	9.66	9.45	9.24	9.05	8.86	8.50	8.18	7.99	7.59	7.09	6.38
9.25%	10	6.51	5.92	5.79	5.66	5.54	5.42	5.21	5.01	4.89	4.65	4.34	3.91
	15	8.10	7.36	7.20	7.04	6.89	6.75	6.48	6.23	6.09	5.78	5.40	4.86
	20	9.10	8.27	8.09	7.91	7.74	7.58	7.28	7.00	6.84	6.50	6.07	5.46
	22.5	9.45	8.59	8.40	8.22	8.04	7.88	7.56	7.27	7.11	6.75	6.30	5.67
	25	9.73	8.85	8.65	8.46	8.28	8.11	7.78	7.49	7.32	6.95	6.49	5.84
	27.5	9.95	9.05	8.85	8.65	8.47	8.29	7.96	7.66	7.48	7.11	6.64	5.97
	30	10.13	9.21	9.00	8.81	8.62	8.44	8.10	7.79	7.62	7.24	6.75	6.08
	35	10.38	9.44	9.23	9.03	8.83	8.65	8.30	7.99	7.81	7.42	6.92	6.23

Entry is the feasible loan as a multiple of net operating income.

Feasible Loan Based on Debt Service Coverage

Interest Rate	Amortization Schedule	1.00	1.10	1.125	1.15	1.175	1.20	1.25	1.30	1.33	1.40	1.50	1.667
						Debt Service Coverage							
9.50%	10	6.44	5.85	5.72	5.60	5.48	5.37	5.15	4.95	4.84	4.60	4.29	3.86
	15	7.98	7.25	7.09	6.94	6.79	6.65	6.38	6.14	6.00	5.70	5.32	4.79
	20	8.94	8.13	7.95	7.77	7.61	7.45	7.15	6.88	6.72	6.39	5.96	5.36
	22.5	9.27	8.43	8.24	8.06	7.89	7.73	7.42	7.13	6.97	6.62	6.18	5.56
	25	9.54	8.67	8.48	8.29	8.12	7.95	7.63	7.34	7.17	6.81	6.36	5.72
	27.5	9.75	8.86	8.66	8.47	8.29	8.12	7.80	7.50	7.33	6.96	6.50	5.85
	30	9.91	9.01	8.81	8.62	8.43	8.26	7.93	7.62	7.45	7.08	6.61	5.95
	35	10.14	9.22	9.02	8.82	8.63	8.45	8.11	7.80	7.63	7.24	6.76	6.09
9.75%	10	6.37	5.79	5.66	5.54	5.42	5.31	5.10	4.90	4.79	4.55	4.25	3.82
	15	7.87	7.15	6.99	6.84	6.69	6.56	6.29	6.05	5.91	5.62	5.24	4.72
	20	8.79	7.99	7.81	7.64	7.48	7.32	7.03	6.76	6.61	6.28	5.86	5.27
	22.5	9.10	8.28	8.09	7.92	7.75	7.59	7.28	7.00	6.84	6.50	6.07	5.46
	25	9.35	8.50	8.31	8.13	7.96	7.79	7.48	7.19	7.03	6.68	6.23	5.61
	27.5	9.55	8.68	8.49	8.30	8.12	7.96	7.64	7.34	7.18	6.82	6.36	5.73
	30	9.70	8.82	8.62	8.43	8.25	8.08	7.76	7.46	7.29	6.93	6.47	5.82
	35	9.91	9.01	8.81	8.62	8.44	8.26	7.93	7.63	7.45	7.08	6.61	5.95
10.00%	10	6.31	5.73	5.61	5.48	5.37	5.25	5.04	4.85	4.74	4.50	4.20	3.78
	15	7.75	7.05	6.89	6.74	6.60	6.46	6.20	5.97	5.83	5.54	5.17	4.65
	20	8.64	7.85	7.68	7.51	7.35	7.20	6.91	6.64	6.49	6.17	5.76	5.18
	22.5	8.94	8.12	7.94	7.77	7.61	7.45	7.15	6.87	6.72	6.38	5.96	5.36
	25	9.17	8.34	8.15	7.97	7.80	7.64	7.34	7.05	6.90	6.55	6.11	5.50
	27.5	9.35	8.50	8.31	8.13	7.96	7.79	7.48	7.19	7.03	6.68	6.24	5.61
	30	9.50	8.63	8.44	8.26	8.08	7.91	7.60	7.30	7.14	6.78	6.33	5.70
	35	9.69	8.81	8.62	8.43	8.25	8.08	7.75	7.46	7.29	6.92	6.46	5.82
10.25%	10	6.24	5.67	5.55	5.43	5.31	5.20	4.99	4.80	4.69	4.46	4.16	3.74
	15	7.65	6.95	6.80	6.65	6.51	6.37	6.12	5.88	5.75	5.46	5.10	4.59
	20	8.49	7.72	7.55	7.38	7.22	7.07	6.79	6.53	6.38	6.06	5.66	5.09
	22.5	8.77	7.98	7.80	7.63	7.47	7.31	7.02	6.75	6.60	6.27	5.85	5.26
	25	9.00	8.18	8.00	7.82	7.66	7.50	7.20	6.92	6.76	6.43	6.00	5.40
	27.5	9.17	8.33	8.15	7.97	7.80	7.64	7.33	7.05	6.89	6.55	6.11	5.50
	30	9.30	8.45	8.27	8.09	7.91	7.75	7.44	7.15	6.99	6.64	6.20	5.58
	35	9.48	8.62	8.43	8.25	8.07	7.90	7.59	7.29	7.13	6.77	6.32	5.69
10.50%	10	6.18	5.61	5.49	5.37	5.26	5.15	4.94	4.75	4.64	4.41	4.12	3.71
	15	7.54	6.85	6.70	6.56	6.42	6.28	6.03	5.80	5.67	5.38	5.03	4.52
	20	8.35	7.59	7.42	7.26	7.10	6.96	6.68	6.42	6.28	5.96	5.56	5.01
	22.5	8.62	7.83	7.66	7.49	7.33	7.18	6.89	6.63	6.48	6.16	5.75	5.17
	25	8.83	8.02	7.85	7.67	7.51	7.35	7.06	6.79	6.64	6.30	5.88	5.30
	27.5	8.99	8.17	7.99	7.81	7.65	7.49	7.19	6.91	6.76	6.42	5.99	5.39
	30	9.11	8.28	8.10	7.92	7.75	7.59	7.29	7.01	6.85	6.51	6.07	5.47
	35	9.28	8.43	8.25	8.07	7.90	7.73	7.42	7.14	6.98	6.63	6.19	5.57
10.75%	10	6.11	5.56	5.43	5.31	5.20	5.09	4.89	4.70	4.60	4.37	4.07	3.67
	15	7.43	6.76	6.61	6.46	6.33	6.20	5.95	5.72	5.59	5.31	4.96	4.46
	20	8.21	7.46	7.30	7.14	6.99	6.84	6.57	6.31	6.17	5.86	5.47	4.92
	22.5	8.47	7.70	7.52	7.36	7.20	7.05	6.77	6.51	6.36	6.05	5.64	5.08
	25	8.66	7.87	7.70	7.53	7.37	7.22	6.93	6.66	6.51	6.19	5.77	5.20
	27.5	8.81	8.01	7.83	7.66	7.50	7.34	7.05	6.78	6.63	6.29	5.87	5.29
	30	8.93	8.12	7.94	7.76	7.60	7.44	7.14	6.87	6.71	6.38	5.95	5.36
	35	9.08	8.26	8.07	7.90	7.73	7.57	7.27	6.99	6.83	6.49	6.06	5.45
11.00%	10	6.05	5.50	5.38	5.26	5.15	5.04	4.84	4.65	4.55	4.32	4.03	3.63
	15	7.33	6.67	6.52	6.38	6.24	6.11	5.87	5.64	5.51	5.24	4.89	4.40
	20	8.07	7.34	7.18	7.02	6.87	6.73	6.46	6.21	6.07	5.77	5.38	4.84
	22.5	8.32	7.56	7.39	7.23	7.08	6.93	6.65	6.40	6.25	5.94	5.54	4.99
	25	8.50	7.73	7.56	7.39	7.24	7.09	6.80	6.54	6.39	6.07	5.67	5.10
	27.5	8.64	7.86	7.68	7.52	7.36	7.20	6.91	6.65	6.50	6.17	5.76	5.19
	30	8.75	7.96	7.78	7.61	7.45	7.29	7.00	6.73	6.58	6.25	5.83	5.25
	35	8.89	8.09	7.91	7.73	7.57	7.41	7.12	6.84	6.69	6.35	5.93	5.34
11.25%	10	5.99	5.44	5.32	5.21	5.10	4.99	4.79	4.61	4.50	4.28	3.99	3.59
	15	7.23	6.57	6.43	6.29	6.15	6.03	5.79	5.56	5.44	5.17	4.82	4.34
	20	7.94	7.22	7.06	6.91	6.76	6.62	6.35	6.11	5.97	5.67	5.29	4.77
	22.5	8.17	7.43	7.27	7.11	6.96	6.81	6.54	6.29	6.15	5.84	5.45	4.90
	25	8.35	7.59	7.42	7.26	7.10	6.96	6.68	6.42	6.28	5.96	5.57	5.01
	27.5	8.48	7.71	7.54	7.37	7.22	7.07	6.78	6.52	6.38	6.06	5.65	5.09
	30	8.58	7.80	7.63	7.46	7.30	7.15	6.86	6.60	6.45	6.13	5.72	5.15
	35	8.71	7.92	7.74	7.58	7.41	7.26	6.97	6.70	6.55	6.22	5.81	5.23

Entry is the feasible loan as a multiple of net operating income.

Feasible Loan Based on Debt Service Coverage

Interest Rate	Amortization Schedule	1.00	1.10	1.125	1.15	1.175	1.20	1.25	1.30	1.33	1.40	1.50	1.667
						Debt Service Coverage							
11.50%	10	5.93	5.39	5.27	5.15	5.04	4.94	4.74	4.56	4.46	4.23	3.95	3.56
	15	7.13	6.49	6.34	6.20	6.07	5.94	5.71	5.49	5.36	5.10	4.76	4.28
	20	7.81	7.10	6.95	6.79	6.65	6.51	6.25	6.01	5.88	5.58	5.21	4.69
	22.5	8.03	7.30	7.14	6.99	6.84	6.69	6.43	6.18	6.04	5.74	5.36	4.82
	25	8.20	7.45	7.29	7.13	6.98	6.83	6.56	6.31	6.16	5.86	5.47	4.92
	27.5	8.32	7.57	7.40	7.24	7.08	6.94	6.66	6.40	6.26	5.94	5.55	4.99
	30	8.42	7.65	7.48	7.32	7.16	7.01	6.73	6.47	6.33	6.01	5.61	5.05
	35	8.54	7.76	7.59	7.42	7.27	7.11	6.83	6.57	6.42	6.10	5.69	5.12
11.75%	10	5.87	5.33	5.22	5.10	4.99	4.89	4.69	4.51	4.41	4.19	3.91	3.52
	15	7.04	6.40	6.26	6.12	5.99	5.86	5.63	5.41	5.29	5.03	4.69	4.22
	20	7.69	6.99	6.84	6.69	6.54	6.41	6.15	5.92	5.78	5.49	5.13	4.61
	22.5	7.90	7.18	7.02	6.87	6.72	6.58	6.32	6.08	5.94	5.64	5.27	4.74
	25	8.05	7.32	7.16	7.00	6.85	6.71	6.44	6.19	6.05	5.75	5.37	4.83
	27.5	8.17	7.43	7.26	7.10	6.95	6.81	6.54	6.28	6.14	5.84	5.45	4.90
	30	8.26	7.51	7.34	7.18	7.03	6.88	6.60	6.35	6.21	5.90	5.50	4.95
	35	8.37	7.61	7.44	7.28	7.12	6.97	6.69	6.44	6.29	5.98	5.58	5.02
12.00%	10	5.81	5.28	5.16	5.05	4.94	4.84	4.65	4.47	4.37	4.15	3.87	3.49
	15	6.94	6.31	6.17	6.04	5.91	5.79	5.55	5.34	5.22	4.96	4.63	4.17
	20	7.57	6.88	6.73	6.58	6.44	6.31	6.05	5.82	5.69	5.41	5.05	4.54
	22.5	7.77	7.06	6.90	6.75	6.61	6.47	6.21	5.97	5.84	5.55	5.18	4.66
	25	7.91	7.19	7.03	6.88	6.73	6.59	6.33	6.09	5.95	5.65	5.27	4.75
	27.5	8.02	7.29	7.13	6.97	6.83	6.68	6.42	6.17	6.03	5.73	5.35	4.81
	30	8.10	7.37	7.20	7.04	6.89	6.75	6.48	6.23	6.09	5.79	5.40	4.86
	35	8.21	7.46	7.29	7.14	6.98	6.84	6.56	6.31	6.17	5.86	5.47	4.92
12.25%	10	5.75	5.23	5.11	5.00	4.89	4.79	4.60	4.42	4.32	4.11	3.83	3.45
	15	6.85	6.23	6.09	5.96	5.83	5.71	5.48	5.27	5.15	4.89	4.57	4.11
	20	7.45	6.77	6.62	6.48	6.34	6.21	5.96	5.73	5.60	5.32	4.97	4.47
	22.5	7.64	6.94	6.79	6.64	6.50	6.36	6.11	5.87	5.74	5.46	5.09	4.58
	25	7.78	7.07	6.91	6.76	6.62	6.48	6.22	5.98	5.85	5.55	5.18	4.67
	27.5	7.88	7.16	7.00	6.85	6.70	6.56	6.30	6.06	5.92	5.63	5.25	4.73
	30	7.95	7.23	7.07	6.92	6.77	6.63	6.36	6.12	5.98	5.68	5.30	4.77
	35	8.05	7.32	7.15	7.00	6.85	6.71	6.44	6.19	6.05	5.75	5.37	4.83
12.50%	10	5.69	5.18	5.06	4.95	4.85	4.74	4.55	4.38	4.28	4.07	3.80	3.42
	15	6.76	6.15	6.01	5.88	5.75	5.63	5.41	5.20	5.08	4.83	4.51	4.06
	20	7.33	6.67	6.52	6.38	6.24	6.11	5.87	5.64	5.51	5.24	4.89	4.40
	22.5	7.51	6.83	6.68	6.53	6.39	6.26	6.01	5.78	5.65	5.37	5.01	4.51
	25	7.64	6.95	6.79	6.65	6.50	6.37	6.11	5.88	5.75	5.46	5.10	4.59
	27.5	7.74	7.03	6.88	6.73	6.59	6.45	6.19	5.95	5.82	5.53	5.16	4.64
	30	7.81	7.10	6.94	6.79	6.65	6.51	6.25	6.01	5.87	5.58	5.21	4.68
	35	7.90	7.18	7.02	6.87	6.72	6.58	6.32	6.07	5.94	5.64	5.26	4.74
12.75%	10	5.64	5.12	5.01	4.90	4.80	4.70	4.51	4.34	4.24	4.03	3.76	3.38
	15	6.67	6.07	5.93	5.80	5.68	5.56	5.34	5.13	5.02	4.77	4.45	4.00
	20	7.22	6.57	6.42	6.28	6.15	6.02	5.78	5.56	5.43	5.16	4.81	4.33
	22.5	7.39	6.72	6.57	6.43	6.29	6.16	5.91	5.69	5.56	5.28	4.93	4.43
	25	7.51	6.83	6.68	6.53	6.39	6.26	6.01	5.78	5.65	5.37	5.01	4.51
	27.5	7.60	6.91	6.76	6.61	6.47	6.34	6.08	5.85	5.72	5.43	5.07	4.56
	30	7.67	6.97	6.82	6.67	6.53	6.39	6.13	5.90	5.77	5.48	5.11	4.60
	35	7.75	7.05	6.89	6.74	6.60	6.46	6.20	5.96	5.83	5.54	5.17	4.65
13.00%	10	5.58	5.07	4.96	4.85	4.75	4.65	4.46	4.29	4.20	3.99	3.72	3.35
	15	6.59	5.99	5.85	5.73	5.61	5.49	5.27	5.07	4.95	4.70	4.39	3.95
	20	7.11	6.47	6.32	6.19	6.05	5.93	5.69	5.47	5.35	5.08	4.74	4.27
	22.5	7.27	6.61	6.46	6.32	6.19	6.06	5.82	5.59	5.47	5.19	4.85	4.36
	25	7.39	6.72	6.57	6.43	6.29	6.16	5.91	5.68	5.56	5.28	4.93	4.43
	27.5	7.47	6.79	6.64	6.50	6.36	6.23	5.98	5.75	5.62	5.34	4.98	4.48
	30	7.53	6.85	6.70	6.55	6.41	6.28	6.03	5.79	5.66	5.38	5.02	4.52
	35	7.61	6.92	6.76	6.62	6.48	6.34	6.09	5.85	5.72	5.44	5.07	4.57
13.25%	10	5.53	5.02	4.91	4.81	4.70	4.61	4.42	4.25	4.16	3.95	3.68	3.32
	15	6.50	5.91	5.78	5.65	5.53	5.42	5.20	5.00	4.89	4.64	4.33	3.90
	20	7.01	6.37	6.23	6.09	5.96	5.84	5.60	5.39	5.27	5.00	4.67	4.20
	22.5	7.16	6.51	6.36	6.22	6.09	5.96	5.73	5.51	5.38	5.11	4.77	4.29
	25	7.27	6.61	6.46	6.32	6.18	6.06	5.81	5.59	5.46	5.19	4.84	4.36
	27.5	7.35	6.68	6.53	6.39	6.25	6.12	5.88	5.65	5.52	5.25	4.90	4.41
	30	7.40	6.73	6.58	6.44	6.30	6.17	5.92	5.69	5.57	5.29	4.93	4.44
	35	7.47	6.79	6.64	6.50	6.36	6.23	5.98	5.75	5.62	5.34	4.98	4.48

Entry is the feasible loan as a multiple of net operating income.

Debt Service Coverage

Loan to Value	Equity Yield	7.50%	8.00%	8.25%	8.50%	Annual Mortgage Constant 8.75%	9.00%	9.25%	9.50%	9.75%	10.00%	10.25%	10.50%	11.00%	12.00%
	6.00%	1.53	1.50	1.48	1.47	1.46	1.44	1.43	1.42	1.41	1.40	1.39	1.38	1.36	1.33
	6.50	1.58	1.54	1.53	1.51	1.50	1.48	1.47	1.46	1.44	1.43	1.42	1.41	1.39	1.36
	7.00	1.62	1.58	1.57	1.55	1.53	1.52	1.50	1.49	1.48	1.47	1.46	1.44	1.42	1.39
	7.50	1.67	1.63	1.61	1.59	1.57	1.56	1.54	1.53	1.51	1.50	1.49	1.48	1.45	1.42
	8.00	1.71	1.67	1.65	1.63	1.61	1.59	1.58	1.56	1.55	1.53	1.52	1.51	1.48	1.44
60%	8.50	1.76	1.71	1.69	1.67	1.65	1.63	1.61	1.60	1.58	1.57	1.55	1.54	1.52	1.47
	9.00	1.80	1.75	1.73	1.71	1.69	1.67	1.65	1.63	1.62	1.60	1.59	1.57	1.55	1.50
	9.50	1.84	1.79	1.77	1.75	1.72	1.70	1.68	1.67	1.65	1.63	1.62	1.60	1.58	1.53
	10.00	1.89	1.83	1.81	1.78	1.76	1.74	1.72	1.70	1.68	1.67	1.65	1.63	1.61	1.56
	11.00	1.98	1.92	1.89	1.86	1.84	1.81	1.79	1.77	1.75	1.73	1.72	1.70	1.67	1.61
	12.00	2.07	2.00	1.97	1.94	1.91	1.89	1.86	1.84	1.82	1.80	1.78	1.76	1.73	1.67
	6.00%	1.39	1.37	1.36	1.35	1.34	1.33	1.32	1.31	1.30	1.30	1.29	1.28	1.27	1.25
	6.50	1.43	1.40	1.39	1.38	1.37	1.36	1.35	1.34	1.33	1.32	1.31	1.30	1.29	1.27
	7.00	1.46	1.43	1.42	1.41	1.39	1.38	1.37	1.36	1.35	1.34	1.34	1.33	1.31	1.29
	7.50	1.49	1.46	1.45	1.43	1.42	1.41	1.40	1.39	1.38	1.37	1.36	1.35	1.34	1.31
	8.00	1.53	1.49	1.48	1.46	1.45	1.44	1.43	1.41	1.40	1.39	1.38	1.38	1.36	1.33
67%	8.50	1.56	1.52	1.51	1.49	1.48	1.47	1.45	1.44	1.43	1.42	1.41	1.40	1.38	1.35
	9.00	1.59	1.55	1.54	1.52	1.51	1.49	1.48	1.47	1.45	1.44	1.43	1.42	1.40	1.37
	9.50	1.62	1.58	1.57	1.55	1.53	1.52	1.51	1.49	1.48	1.47	1.46	1.45	1.43	1.39
	10.00	1.66	1.62	1.60	1.58	1.56	1.55	1.53	1.52	1.51	1.49	1.48	1.47	1.45	1.41
	11.00	1.72	1.68	1.66	1.64	1.62	1.60	1.59	1.57	1.56	1.54	1.53	1.52	1.49	1.45
	12.00	1.79	1.74	1.72	1.70	1.68	1.66	1.64	1.62	1.61	1.59	1.58	1.56	1.54	1.49
	6.00%	1.34	1.32	1.31	1.30	1.29	1.29	1.28	1.27	1.26	1.26	1.25	1.24	1.23	1.21
	6.50	1.37	1.35	1.34	1.33	1.32	1.31	1.30	1.29	1.29	1.28	1.27	1.27	1.25	1.23
	7.00	1.40	1.38	1.36	1.35	1.34	1.33	1.32	1.32	1.31	1.30	1.29	1.29	1.27	1.25
	7.50	1.43	1.40	1.39	1.38	1.37	1.36	1.35	1.34	1.33	1.32	1.31	1.31	1.29	1.27
	8.00	1.46	1.43	1.42	1.40	1.39	1.38	1.37	1.36	1.35	1.34	1.33	1.33	1.31	1.29
70%	8.50	1.49	1.46	1.44	1.43	1.42	1.40	1.39	1.38	1.37	1.36	1.36	1.35	1.33	1.30
	9.00	1.51	1.48	1.47	1.45	1.44	1.43	1.42	1.41	1.40	1.39	1.38	1.37	1.35	1.32
	9.50	1.54	1.51	1.49	1.48	1.47	1.45	1.44	1.43	1.42	1.41	1.40	1.39	1.37	1.34
	10.00	1.57	1.54	1.52	1.50	1.49	1.48	1.46	1.45	1.44	1.43	1.42	1.41	1.39	1.36
	11.00	1.63	1.59	1.57	1.55	1.54	1.52	1.51	1.50	1.48	1.47	1.46	1.45	1.43	1.39
	12.00	1.69	1.64	1.62	1.61	1.59	1.57	1.56	1.54	1.53	1.51	1.50	1.49	1.47	1.43
	6.00%	1.27	1.25	1.24	1.24	1.23	1.22	1.22	1.21	1.21	1.20	1.20	1.19	1.18	1.17
	6.50	1.29	1.27	1.26	1.25	1.25	1.24	1.23	1.23	1.22	1.22	1.21	1.21	1.20	1.18
	7.00	1.31	1.29	1.28	1.27	1.27	1.26	1.25	1.25	1.24	1.23	1.23	1.22	1.21	1.19
	7.50	1.33	1.31	1.30	1.29	1.29	1.28	1.27	1.26	1.26	1.25	1.24	1.24	1.23	1.21
	8.00	1.36	1.33	1.32	1.31	1.30	1.30	1.29	1.28	1.27	1.27	1.26	1.25	1.24	1.22
75%	8.50	1.38	1.35	1.34	1.33	1.32	1.31	1.31	1.30	1.29	1.28	1.28	1.27	1.26	1.24
	9.00	1.40	1.38	1.36	1.35	1.34	1.33	1.32	1.32	1.31	1.30	1.29	1.29	1.27	1.25
	9.50	1.42	1.40	1.38	1.37	1.36	1.35	1.34	1.33	1.32	1.32	1.31	1.30	1.29	1.26
	10.00	1.44	1.42	1.40	1.39	1.38	1.37	1.36	1.35	1.34	1.33	1.33	1.32	1.30	1.28
	11.00	1.49	1.46	1.44	1.43	1.42	1.41	1.40	1.39	1.38	1.37	1.36	1.35	1.33	1.31
	12.00	1.53	1.50	1.48	1.47	1.46	1.44	1.43	1.42	1.41	1.40	1.39	1.38	1.36	1.33
	6.00%	1.20	1.19	1.18	1.18	1.17	1.17	1.16	1.16	1.15	1.15	1.15	1.14	1.14	1.13
	6.50	1.22	1.20	1.20	1.19	1.19	1.18	1.18	1.17	1.17	1.16	1.16	1.15	1.15	1.14
	7.00	1.23	1.22	1.21	1.21	1.20	1.19	1.19	1.18	1.18	1.18	1.17	1.17	1.16	1.15
	7.50	1.25	1.23	1.23	1.22	1.21	1.21	1.20	1.20	1.19	1.19	1.18	1.18	1.17	1.16
	8.00	1.27	1.25	1.24	1.24	1.23	1.22	1.22	1.21	1.21	1.20	1.20	1.19	1.18	1.17
80%	8.50	1.28	1.27	1.26	1.25	1.24	1.24	1.23	1.22	1.22	1.21	1.21	1.20	1.19	1.18
	9.00	1.30	1.28	1.27	1.26	1.26	1.25	1.24	1.24	1.23	1.23	1.22	1.21	1.20	1.19
	9.50	1.32	1.30	1.29	1.28	1.27	1.26	1.26	1.25	1.24	1.24	1.23	1.23	1.22	1.20
	10.00	1.33	1.31	1.30	1.29	1.29	1.28	1.27	1.26	1.26	1.25	1.24	1.24	1.23	1.21
	11.00	1.37	1.34	1.33	1.32	1.31	1.31	1.30	1.29	1.28	1.28	1.27	1.26	1.25	1.23
	12.00	1.40	1.37	1.36	1.35	1.34	1.33	1.32	1.32	1.31	1.30	1.29	1.29	1.27	1.25
	6.00%	1.14	1.13	1.13	1.12	1.12	1.12	1.11	1.11	1.11	1.11	1.10	1.10	1.10	1.09
	6.50	1.15	1.14	1.14	1.13	1.13	1.13	1.12	1.12	1.12	1.11	1.11	1.11	1.10	1.10
	7.00	1.16	1.15	1.15	1.15	1.14	1.14	1.13	1.13	1.13	1.12	1.12	1.12	1.11	1.10
	7.50	1.18	1.17	1.16	1.16	1.15	1.15	1.14	1.14	1.14	1.13	1.13	1.13	1.12	1.11
	8.00	1.19	1.18	1.17	1.17	1.16	1.16	1.15	1.15	1.14	1.14	1.14	1.13	1.13	1.12
85%	8.50	1.20	1.19	1.18	1.18	1.17	1.17	1.16	1.16	1.15	1.15	1.15	1.14	1.14	1.13
	9.00	1.21	1.20	1.19	1.19	1.18	1.18	1.17	1.17	1.16	1.16	1.15	1.15	1.14	1.13
	9.50	1.22	1.21	1.20	1.20	1.19	1.19	1.18	1.18	1.17	1.17	1.16	1.16	1.15	1.14
	10.00	1.24	1.22	1.21	1.21	1.20	1.20	1.19	1.19	1.18	1.18	1.17	1.17	1.16	1.15
	11.00	1.26	1.24	1.24	1.23	1.22	1.22	1.21	1.20	1.20	1.19	1.19	1.18	1.18	1.16
	12.00	1.28	1.26	1.26	1.25	1.24	1.24	1.23	1.22	1.22	1.21	1.21	1.20	1.19	1.18

Equity Yield Implied by Mortgage Terms

Loan to Value Ratio	Debt Service Coverage Ratio	Annual Mortgage Constant											
		7.20%	7.40%	7.60%	7.80%	8.00%	8.20%	8.40%	8.60%	8.80%	9.00%	9.20%	9.40%
50%	1.100	0.720	0.740	0.760	0.780	0.800	0.820	0.840	0.860	0.880	0.900	0.920	0.940
	1.125	0.900	0.925	0.950	0.975	1.000	1.025	1.050	1.075	1.100	1.125	1.150	1.175
	1.150	1.080	1.110	1.140	1.170	1.200	1.230	1.260	1.290	1.320	1.350	1.380	1.410
	1.175	1.260	1.295	1.330	1.365	1.400	1.435	1.470	1.505	1.540	1.575	1.610	1.645
	1.200	1.440	1.480	1.520	1.560	1.600	1.640	1.680	1.720	1.760	1.800	1.840	1.880
	1.250	1.800	1.850	1.900	1.950	2.000	2.050	2.100	2.150	2.200	2.250	2.300	2.350
	1.300	2.160	2.220	2.280	2.340	2.400	2.460	2.520	2.580	2.640	2.700	2.760	2.820
	1.400	2.880	2.960	3.040	3.120	3.200	3.280	3.360	3.440	3.520	3.600	3.680	3.760
	1.500	3.600	3.700	3.800	3.900	4.000	4.100	4.200	4.300	4.400	4.500	4.600	4.700
67%	1.100	1.440	1.480	1.520	1.560	1.600	1.640	1.680	1.720	1.760	1.800	1.840	1.880
	1.125	1.800	1.850	1.900	1.950	2.000	2.050	2.100	2.150	2.200	2.250	2.300	2.350
	1.150	2.160	2.220	2.280	2.340	2.400	2.460	2.520	2.580	2.640	2.700	2.760	2.820
	1.175	2.520	2.590	2.660	2.730	2.800	2.870	2.940	3.010	3.080	3.150	3.220	3.290
	1.200	2.880	2.960	3.040	3.120	3.200	3.280	3.360	3.440	3.520	3.600	3.680	3.760
	1.250	3.600	3.700	3.800	3.900	4.000	4.100	4.200	4.300	4.400	4.500	4.600	4.700
	1.300	4.320	4.440	4.560	4.680	4.800	4.920	5.040	5.160	5.280	5.400	5.520	5.640
	1.400	5.760	5.920	6.080	6.240	6.400	6.560	6.720	6.880	7.040	7.200	7.360	7.520
	1.500	7.200	7.400	7.600	7.800	8.000	8.200	8.400	8.600	8.800	9.000	9.200	9.400
70%	1.100	1.680	1.727	1.773	1.820	1.867	1.913	1.960	2.007	2.053	2.100	2.147	2.193
	1.125	2.100	2.158	2.217	2.275	2.333	2.392	2.450	2.508	2.567	2.625	2.683	2.742
	1.150	2.520	2.590	2.660	2.730	2.800	2.870	2.940	3.010	3.080	3.150	3.220	3.290
	1.175	2.940	3.022	3.103	3.185	3.267	3.348	3.430	3.512	3.593	3.675	3.757	3.838
	1.200	3.360	3.453	3.547	3.640	3.733	3.827	3.920	4.013	4.107	4.200	4.293	4.387
	1.250	4.200	4.317	4.433	4.550	4.667	4.783	4.900	5.017	5.133	5.250	5.367	5.483
	1.300	5.040	5.180	5.320	5.460	5.600	5.740	5.880	6.020	6.160	6.300	6.440	6.580
	1.400	6.720	6.907	7.093	7.280	7.467	7.653	7.840	8.027	8.213	8.400	8.587	8.773
	1.500	8.400	8.633	8.867	9.100	9.333	9.567	9.800	10.033	10.267	10.500	10.733	10.967
75%	1.100	2.160	2.220	2.280	2.340	2.400	2.460	2.520	2.580	2.640	2.700	2.760	2.820
	1.125	2.700	2.775	2.850	2.925	3.000	3.075	3.150	3.225	3.300	3.375	3.450	3.525
	1.150	3.240	3.330	3.420	3.510	3.600	3.690	3.780	3.870	3.960	4.050	4.140	4.230
	1.175	3.780	3.885	3.990	4.095	4.200	4.305	4.410	4.515	4.620	4.725	4.830	4.935
	1.200	4.320	4.440	4.560	4.680	4.800	4.920	5.040	5.160	5.280	5.400	5.520	5.640
	1.250	5.400	5.550	5.700	5.850	6.000	6.150	6.300	6.450	6.600	6.750	6.900	7.050
	1.300	6.480	6.660	6.840	7.020	7.200	7.380	7.560	7.740	7.920	8.100	8.280	8.460
	1.400	8.640	8.880	9.120	9.360	9.600	9.840	10.080	10.320	10.560	10.800	11.040	11.280
	1.500	10.800	11.100	11.400	11.700	12.000	12.300	12.600	12.900	13.200	13.500	13.800	14.100
80%	1.100	2.880	2.960	3.040	3.120	3.200	3.280	3.360	3.440	3.520	3.600	3.680	3.760
	1.125	3.600	3.700	3.800	3.900	4.000	4.100	4.200	4.300	4.400	4.500	4.600	4.700
	1.150	4.320	4.440	4.560	4.680	4.800	4.920	5.040	5.160	5.280	5.400	5.520	5.640
	1.175	5.040	5.180	5.320	5.460	5.600	5.740	5.880	6.020	6.160	6.300	6.440	6.580
	1.200	5.760	5.920	6.080	6.240	6.400	6.560	6.720	6.880	7.040	7.200	7.360	7.520
	1.250	7.200	7.400	7.600	7.800	8.000	8.200	8.400	8.600	8.800	9.000	9.200	9.400
	1.300	8.640	8.880	9.120	9.360	9.600	9.840	10.080	10.320	10.560	10.800	11.040	11.280
	1.400	11.520	11.840	12.160	12.480	12.800	13.120	13.440	13.760	14.080	14.400	14.720	15.040
	1.500	14.400	14.800	15.200	15.600	16.000	16.400	16.800	17.200	17.600	18.000	18.400	18.800
85%	1.100	4.080	4.193	4.307	4.420	4.533	4.647	4.760	4.873	4.987	5.100	5.213	5.327
	1.125	5.100	5.242	5.383	5.525	5.667	5.808	5.950	6.092	6.233	6.375	6.517	6.658
	1.150	6.120	6.290	6.460	6.630	6.800	6.970	7.140	7.310	7.480	7.650	7.820	7.990
	1.175	7.140	7.338	7.537	7.735	7.933	8.132	8.330	8.528	8.727	8.925	9.123	9.322
	1.200	8.160	8.387	8.613	8.840	9.067	9.293	9.520	9.747	9.973	10.200	10.427	10.653
	1.250	10.200	10.483	10.767	11.050	11.333	11.617	11.900	12.183	12.467	12.750	13.033	13.317
	1.300	12.240	12.580	12.920	13.260	13.600	13.940	14.280	14.620	14.960	15.300	15.640	15.980
	1.400	16.320	16.773	17.227	17.680	18.133	18.587	19.040	19.493	19.947	20.400	20.853	21.307
	1.500	20.400	20.967	21.533	22.100	22.667	23.233	23.800	24.367	24.933	25.500	26.067	26.633
90%	1.100	6.480	6.660	6.840	7.020	7.200	7.380	7.560	7.740	7.920	8.100	8.280	8.460
	1.125	8.100	8.325	8.550	8.775	9.000	9.225	9.450	9.675	9.900	10.125	10.350	10.575
	1.150	9.720	9.990	10.260	10.530	10.800	11.070	11.340	11.610	11.880	12.150	12.420	12.690
	1.175	11.340	11.655	11.970	12.285	12.600	12.915	13.230	13.545	13.860	14.175	14.490	14.805
	1.200	12.960	13.320	13.680	14.040	14.400	14.760	15.120	15.480	15.840	16.200	16.560	16.920
	1.250	16.200	16.650	17.100	17.550	18.000	18.450	18.900	19.350	19.800	20.250	20.700	21.150
	1.300	19.440	19.980	20.520	21.060	21.600	22.140	22.680	23.220	23.760	24.300	24.840	25.380
	1.400	25.920	26.640	27.360	28.080	28.800	29.520	30.240	30.960	31.680	32.400	33.120	33.840
	1.500	32.400	33.300	34.200	35.100	36.000	36.900	37.800	38.700	39.600	40.500	41.400	42.300

Entry is the percentage return on equity consistent with these mortgage terms.

Equity Yield Implied by Mortgage Terms

Loan to Value Ratio	Debt Service Coverage Ratio	Annual Mortgage Constant											
		9.60%	9.80%	10.00%	10.20%	10.40%	10.60%	10.80%	11.00%	11.20%	11.40%	11.60%	11.80%
50%	1.100	0.960	0.980	1.000	1.020	1.040	1.060	1.080	1.100	1.120	1.140	1.160	1.180
	1.125	1.200	1.225	1.250	1.275	1.300	1.325	1.350	1.375	1.400	1.425	1.450	1.475
	1.150	1.440	1.470	1.500	1.530	1.560	1.590	1.620	1.650	1.680	1.710	1.740	1.770
	1.175	1.680	1.715	1.750	1.785	1.820	1.855	1.890	1.925	1.960	1.995	2.030	2.065
	1.200	1.920	1.960	2.000	2.040	2.080	2.120	2.160	2.200	2.240	2.280	2.320	2.360
	1.250	2.400	2.450	2.500	2.550	2.600	2.650	2.700	2.750	2.800	2.850	2.900	2.950
	1.300	2.880	2.940	3.000	3.060	3.120	3.180	3.240	3.300	3.360	3.420	3.480	3.540
	1.400	3.840	3.920	4.000	4.080	4.160	4.240	4.320	4.400	4.480	4.560	4.640	4.720
	1.500	4.800	4.900	5.000	5.100	5.200	5.300	5.400	5.500	5.600	5.700	5.800	5.900
67%	1.100	1.920	1.960	2.000	2.040	2.080	2.120	2.160	2.200	2.240	2.280	2.320	2.360
	1.125	2.400	2.450	2.500	2.550	2.600	2.650	2.700	2.750	2.800	2.850	2.900	2.950
	1.150	2.880	2.940	3.000	3.060	3.120	3.180	3.240	3.300	3.360	3.420	3.480	3.540
	1.175	3.360	3.430	3.500	3.570	3.640	3.710	3.780	3.850	3.920	3.990	4.060	4.130
	1.200	3.840	3.920	4.000	4.080	4.160	4.240	4.320	4.400	4.480	4.560	4.640	4.720
	1.250	4.800	4.900	5.000	5.100	5.200	5.300	5.400	5.500	5.600	5.700	5.800	5.900
	1.300	5.760	5.880	6.000	6.120	6.240	6.360	6.480	6.600	6.720	6.840	6.960	7.080
	1.400	7.680	7.840	8.000	8.160	8.320	8.480	8.640	8.800	8.960	9.120	9.280	9.440
	1.500	9.600	9.800	10.000	10.200	10.400	10.600	10.800	11.000	11.200	11.400	11.600	11.800
70%	1.100	2.240	2.287	2.333	2.380	2.427	2.473	2.520	2.567	2.613	2.660	2.707	2.753
	1.125	2.800	2.858	2.917	2.975	3.033	3.092	3.150	3.208	3.267	3.325	3.383	3.442
	1.150	3.360	3.430	3.500	3.570	3.640	3.710	3.780	3.850	3.920	3.990	4.060	4.130
	1.175	3.920	4.002	4.083	4.165	4.247	4.328	4.410	4.492	4.573	4.655	4.737	4.818
	1.200	4.480	4.573	4.667	4.760	4.853	4.947	5.040	5.133	5.227	5.320	5.413	5.507
	1.250	5.600	5.717	5.833	5.950	6.067	6.183	6.300	6.417	6.533	6.650	6.767	6.883
	1.300	6.720	6.860	7.000	7.140	7.280	7.420	7.560	7.700	7.840	7.980	8.120	8.260
	1.400	8.960	9.147	9.333	9.520	9.707	9.893	10.080	10.267	10.453	10.640	10.827	11.013
	1.500	11.200	11.433	11.667	11.900	12.133	12.367	12.600	12.833	13.067	13.300	13.533	13.767
75%	1.100	2.880	2.940	3.000	3.060	3.120	3.180	3.240	3.300	3.360	3.420	3.480	3.540
	1.125	3.600	3.675	3.750	3.825	3.900	3.975	4.050	4.125	4.200	4.275	4.350	4.425
	1.150	4.320	4.410	4.500	4.590	4.680	4.770	4.860	4.950	5.040	5.130	5.220	5.310
	1.175	5.040	5.145	5.250	5.355	5.460	5.565	5.670	5.775	5.880	5.985	6.090	6.195
	1.200	5.760	5.880	6.000	6.120	6.240	6.360	6.480	6.600	6.720	6.840	6.960	7.080
	1.250	7.200	7.350	7.500	7.650	7.800	7.950	8.100	8.250	8.400	8.550	8.700	8.850
	1.300	8.640	8.820	9.000	9.180	9.360	9.540	9.720	9.900	10.080	10.260	10.440	10.620
	1.400	11.520	11.760	12.000	12.240	12.480	12.720	12.960	13.200	13.440	13.680	13.920	14.160
	1.500	14.400	14.700	15.000	15.300	15.600	15.900	16.200	16.500	16.800	17.100	17.400	17.700
80%	1.100	3.840	3.920	4.000	4.080	4.160	4.240	4.320	4.400	4.480	4.560	4.640	4.720
	1.125	4.800	4.900	5.000	5.100	5.200	5.300	5.400	5.500	5.600	5.700	5.800	5.900
	1.150	5.760	5.880	6.000	6.120	6.240	6.360	6.480	6.600	6.720	6.840	6.960	7.080
	1.175	6.720	6.860	7.000	7.140	7.280	7.420	7.560	7.700	7.840	7.980	8.120	8.260
	1.200	7.680	7.840	8.000	8.160	8.320	8.480	8.640	8.800	8.960	9.120	9.280	9.440
	1.250	9.600	9.800	10.000	10.200	10.400	10.600	10.800	11.000	11.200	11.400	11.600	11.800
	1.300	11.520	11.760	12.000	12.240	12.480	12.720	12.960	13.200	13.440	13.680	13.920	14.160
	1.400	15.360	15.680	16.000	16.320	16.640	16.960	17.280	17.600	17.920	18.240	18.560	18.880
	1.500	19.200	19.600	20.000	20.400	20.800	21.200	21.600	22.000	22.400	22.800	23.200	23.600
85%	1.100	5.440	5.553	5.667	5.780	5.893	6.007	6.120	6.233	6.347	6.460	6.573	6.687
	1.125	6.800	6.942	7.083	7.225	7.367	7.508	7.650	7.792	7.933	8.075	8.217	8.358
	1.150	8.160	8.330	8.500	8.670	8.840	9.010	9.180	9.350	9.520	9.690	9.860	10.030
	1.175	9.520	9.718	9.917	10.115	10.313	10.512	10.710	10.908	11.107	11.305	11.503	11.702
	1.200	10.880	11.107	11.333	11.560	11.787	12.013	12.240	12.467	12.693	12.920	13.147	13.373
	1.250	13.600	13.883	14.167	14.450	14.733	15.017	15.300	15.583	15.867	16.150	16.433	16.717
	1.300	16.320	16.660	17.000	17.340	17.680	18.020	18.360	18.700	19.040	19.380	19.720	20.060
	1.400	21.760	22.213	22.667	23.120	23.573	24.027	24.480	24.933	25.387	25.840	26.293	26.747
	1.500	27.200	27.767	28.333	28.900	29.467	30.033	30.600	31.167	31.733	32.300	32.867	33.433
90%	1.100	8.640	8.820	9.000	9.180	9.360	9.540	9.720	9.900	10.080	10.260	10.440	10.620
	1.125	10.800	11.025	11.250	11.475	11.700	11.925	12.150	12.375	12.600	12.825	13.050	13.275
	1.150	12.960	13.230	13.500	13.770	14.040	14.310	14.580	14.850	15.120	15.390	15.660	15.930
	1.175	15.120	15.435	15.750	16.065	16.380	16.695	17.010	17.325	17.640	17.955	18.270	18.585
	1.200	17.280	17.640	18.000	18.360	18.720	19.080	19.440	19.800	20.160	20.520	20.880	21.240
	1.250	21.600	22.050	22.500	22.950	23.400	23.850	24.300	24.750	25.200	25.650	26.100	26.550
	1.300	25.920	26.460	27.000	27.540	28.080	28.620	29.160	29.700	30.240	30.780	31.320	31.860
	1.400	34.560	35.280	36.000	36.720	37.440	38.160	38.880	39.600	40.320	41.040	41.760	42.480
	1.500	43.200	44.100	45.000	45.900	46.800	47.700	48.600	49.500	50.400	51.300	52.200	53.100

Entry is the percentage return on equity consistent with these mortgage terms.

Amount Accrued on Bow-Tie Loans
(Pay Rate Less Than Accrual Rate)

Pay Rate   7.50%   30 Year Schedule

Year Paid	8.00%	8.25%	8.50%	8.75%	9.00%	9.25%	9.50%	9.75%	10.00%	10.25%	10.50%	10.75%
						Accrual Rate						
1	0.5187	0.7790	1.0399	1.3014	1.5634	1.8261	2.0894	2.3533	2.6178	2.8829	3.1487	3.4150
2	1.0805	1.6248	2.1717	2.7213	3.2736	3.8285	4.3862	4.9466	5.5098	6.0757	6.6443	7.2158
3	1.6890	2.5430	3.4036	4.2706	5.1441	6.0242	6.9110	7.8044	8.7045	9.6115	10.5252	11.4459
4	2.3479	3.5400	4.7443	5.9610	7.1901	8.4318	9.6863	10.9536	12.2339	13.5272	14.8338	16.1538
5	3.0615	4.6224	6.2035	7.8053	9.4280	11.0718	12.7370	14.4239	16.1327	17.8637	19.6172	21.3935
6	3.8344	5.7975	7.7918	9.8177	11.8759	13.9667	16.0906	18.2481	20.4399	22.6662	24.9278	27.2251
7	4.6714	7.0733	9.5204	12.0135	14.5534	17.1409	19.7770	22.4624	25.1980	27.9848	30.8236	33.7154
8	5.5779	8.4584	11.4018	14.4092	17.4820	20.6216	23.8292	27.1063	30.4544	33.8748	37.3691	40.9388
9	6.5596	9.9623	13.4495	17.0232	20.6854	24.4382	28.2836	32.2239	36.2612	40.3978	44.6360	48.9782
10	7.6228	11.5950	15.6782	19.8753	24.1893	28.6232	33.1801	37.8633	42.6760	47.6217	52.7037	57.9256
11	8.7742	13.3676	18.1039	22.9872	28.0219	33.2121	38.5626	44.0778	49.7626	55.6218	61.6605	67.8838
12	10.0212	15.2921	20.7440	26.3826	32.2139	38.2440	44.4792	50.9261	57.5912	64.4816	71.6044	78.9668
13	11.3717	17.3816	23.6175	30.0874	36.7993	43.7616	50.9831	58.4727	66.2396	74.2934	82.6441	91.3018
14	12.8343	19.6500	26.7450	34.1296	41.8148	49.8118	58.1325	66.7889	75.7936	85.1596	94.9004	105.0301
15	14.4183	22.1129	30.1489	38.5400	47.3007	56.4460	65.9914	75.9532	86.3480	97.1934	108.5075	120.3091
16	16.1337	24.7868	33.8536	43.3522	53.3013	63.7206	74.6304	86.0520	98.0076	110.5202	123.6140	137.3139
17	17.9916	27.6899	37.8859	48.6028	59.8648	71.6973	84.1267	97.1806	110.8881	125.2792	140.3854	156.2397
18	20.0036	30.8417	42.2745	54.3316	67.0440	80.4439	94.5654	109.4442	125.1173	141.6240	159.0050	177.3032
19	22.1826	34.2636	47.0511	60.5824	74.8966	90.0348	106.0403	122.9583	140.8366	159.7252	179.6766	200.7460
20	24.5425	37.9788	52.2499	67.4026	83.4859	100.5515	118.6539	137.8506	158.2018	179.7714	202.6262	226.8369
21	27.0983	42.0123	57.9082	74.8440	92.8809	112.0833	132.5195	154.2615	177.3855	201.9717	228.1050	255.8750
22	29.8662	46.3914	64.0667	82.9634	103.1572	124.7281	147.7611	172.3460	198.5779	226.5575	256.3916	288.1931
23	32.8638	51.1458	70.7695	91.8224	114.3975	138.5935	164.5155	192.2747	221.9894	253.7852	287.7955	324.1618
24	36.1102	56.3076	78.0648	101.4884	126.6922	153.7973	182.9327	214.2356	247.8524	283.9387	322.6603	364.1935
25	39.6261	61.9118	86.0049	112.0349	140.1402	170.4686	203.1777	238.4361	276.4236	317.3323	361.3672	408.7471

Pay Rate   8.00%   30 Year Schedule

Year Paid	8.50%	8.75%	9.00%	9.25%	9.50%	9.75%	10.00%	10.25%	10.50%	10.75%	11.00%	11.25%
						Accrual Rate						
1	0.5199	0.7808	1.0423	1.3044	1.5671	1.8304	2.0943	2.3588	2.6239	2.8896	3.1560	3.4229
2	1.0859	1.6328	2.1824	2.7347	3.2897	3.8474	4.4078	4.9710	5.5369	6.1057	6.6771	7.2514
3	1.7018	2.5623	3.4294	4.3030	5.1832	6.0701	6.9636	7.8639	8.7710	9.6850	10.6058	11.5335
4	2.3721	3.5766	4.7934	6.0227	7.2647	8.5195	9.7871	11.0677	12.3615	13.6686	14.9890	16.3230
5	3.1018	4.6832	6.2853	7.9085	9.5528	11.2186	12.9062	14.6158	16.3477	18.1022	19.8795	21.6800
6	3.8959	5.8906	7.9173	9.9762	12.0679	14.1930	16.3519	18.5451	20.7732	23.0366	25.3359	27.6717
7	4.7602	7.2081	9.7022	12.2435	14.8327	17.4707	20.1584	22.8966	25.6863	28.5284	31.4237	34.3733
8	5.7009	8.6455	11.6547	14.7297	17.8719	21.0827	24.3635	27.7158	31.1409	34.6405	38.2160	41.8690
9	6.7247	10.2139	13.7903	17.4558	21.2127	25.0630	29.0090	33.0527	37.1967	41.4431	45.7943	50.2529
10	7.8391	11.9252	16.1262	20.4451	24.8851	29.4492	34.1408	38.9632	43.9198	49.0140	54.2495	59.6300
11	9.0520	13.7923	18.6812	23.7230	28.9219	34.2827	39.8101	45.5088	51.3838	57.4401	63.6832	70.1183
12	10.3720	15.8296	21.4760	27.3172	33.3594	39.6092	46.0730	52.7577	59.6703	66.8181	74.2085	81.8492
13	11.8087	18.0524	24.5329	31.2583	38.2373	45.4788	52.9917	60.7855	68.8701	77.2554	85.9518	94.9701
14	13.3725	20.4777	27.8765	35.5799	43.5994	51.9469	60.6349	69.6760	79.0837	88.8716	99.0540	109.6457
15	15.0744	23.1240	31.5338	40.3186	49.4936	59.0747	69.0784	79.5219	90.4229	101.8000	113.6724	126.0601
16	16.9268	26.0113	35.5342	45.5147	55.9728	66.9293	78.4061	90.4257	103.0117	116.1887	129.9824	144.4194
17	18.9429	29.1617	39.9099	51.2123	63.0950	75.5849	88.7105	102.5011	116.9878	132.2028	148.1798	164.9540
18	21.1373	32.5990	44.6960	57.4599	70.9241	85.1232	100.0939	115.8742	132.5042	150.0258	168.4829	187.9216
19	23.5256	36.3494	49.9311	64.3106	79.5302	95.6342	112.6693	130.6842	149.7305	169.8620	191.1356	213.6106
20	26.1250	40.4415	55.6572	71.8225	88.9904	107.2171	126.5615	147.0857	168.8552	191.9389	216.4095	242.3434
21	28.9541	44.9064	61.9206	80.0595	99.3896	119.9812	141.9084	165.2496	190.0875	216.5096	244.6081	274.4806
22	32.0333	49.7780	68.7714	89.0915	110.8208	134.0469	158.8623	185.3652	213.6597	243.8557	276.0699	310.4256
23	35.3847	55.0934	76.2650	98.9954	123.3866	149.5470	177.5915	207.6425	239.8296	274.2908	311.1723	350.6296
24	39.0324	60.8930	84.4615	109.8552	137.1995	166.6277	198.2819	232.3135	268.8836	308.1637	350.3368	395.5973
25	43.0024	67.2209	93.4268	121.7633	152.3833	185.4503	221.1389	259.6355	301.1393	345.8629	394.0333	445.8929

Entry is accrued compound interest as percentage of original loan amount.

Amount Accrued on Bow-Tie Loans
(Pay Rate Less Than Accrual Rate)

Pay Rate   8.50%   30 Year Schedule

Year Paid	9.00%	9.25%	9.50%	9.75%	Accrual Rate 10.00%	10.25%	10.50%	10.75%	11.00%	11.25%	11.50%	11.75%
1	0.5211	0.7826	1.0447	1.3074	1.5707	1.8346	2.0991	2.3642	2.6300	2.8963	3.1633	3.4309
2	1.0912	1.6408	2.1931	2.7481	3.3059	3.8663	4.4296	4.9955	5.5643	6.1358	6.7102	7.2873
3	1.7147	2.5818	3.4555	4.3358	5.2227	6.1164	7.0168	7.9241	8.8382	9.7592	10.6871	11.6221
4	2.3967	3.6136	4.8431	6.0853	7.3403	8.6082	9.8892	11.1834	12.4909	13.8118	15.1463	16.4945
5	3.1427	4.7451	6.3685	8.0133	9.6796	11.3678	13.0782	14.8109	16.5663	18.3446	20.1462	21.9714
6	3.9586	5.9857	8.0453	10.1379	12.2639	14.4240	16.6185	18.8481	21.1133	23.4145	25.7524	28.1275
7	4.8511	7.3461	9.8885	12.4791	15.1188	17.8085	20.5491	23.3414	26.1864	29.0851	32.0384	35.0473
8	5.8273	8.8378	11.9146	15.0591	18.2726	21.5567	24.9127	28.3422	31.8467	35.4276	39.0867	42.8254
9	6.8951	10.4735	14.1418	17.9022	21.7567	25.7077	29.7573	33.9080	38.1619	42.5216	46.9896	51.5683
10	8.0631	12.2671	16.5901	21.0352	25.6056	30.3047	35.1358	40.1024	45.2079	50.4562	55.8508	61.3956
11	9.3406	14.2338	19.2813	24.4877	29.8576	35.3957	41.1070	46.9965	53.0693	59.3309	65.7865	72.4420
12	10.7380	16.3903	22.2396	28.2923	34.5547	41.0338	47.7362	54.6694	61.8404	69.2570	76.9270	84.8585
13	12.2664	18.7550	25.4916	32.4848	39.7438	47.2776	55.0961	63.2089	71.6265	80.3594	89.4184	98.8151
14	13.9383	21.3479	29.0663	37.1049	45.4762	54.1925	63.2670	72.7131	82.5450	92.7771	103.4246	114.5029
15	15.7669	24.1911	32.9957	42.1962	51.8088	61.8503	72.3383	83.2909	94.7270	106.6662	119.1290	132.1366
16	17.7671	27.3088	37.3152	47.8067	58.8045	70.3311	82.4093	95.0635	108.3187	122.2010	136.7378	151.9575
17	19.9549	30.7274	42.0633	53.9892	66.5328	79.7231	93.5903	108.1659	123.4831	139.5764	156.4819	174.2371
18	22.3480	34.4760	47.2827	60.8023	75.0704	90.1244	106.0033	122.7484	140.4024	159.0106	178.6200	199.2801
19	24.9655	38.5863	53.0201	68.3102	84.5020	101.6433	119.7844	138.9780	159.2796	180.7475	203.4427	227.4295
20	27.8286	43.0935	59.3270	76.5836	94.9211	114.4000	135.0841	157.0409	180.3413	205.0598	231.2753	259.0705
21	30.9603	48.0357	66.2597	85.7008	106.4313	128.5274	152.0700	177.1442	203.8401	232.2528	262.4828	294.6362
22	34.3857	53.4549	73.8806	95.7478	119.1467	144.1730	170.9278	199.5183	230.0582	262.6679	297.4746	334.6135
23	38.1325	59.3972	82.2577	106.8193	133.1596	161.4997	191.8637	224.4197	259.3103	296.6866	336.7095	379.5495
24	42.2307	65.9131	91.4663	119.0198	148.7114	180.6683	215.1068	252.1340	291.9473	334.7361	380.7019	430.0593
25	46.7134	73.0580	101.5889	132.4645	165.8542	201.9388	240.9115	282.9788	328.3611	377.2940	430.0289	486.8343

Pay Rate   9.00%   30 Year Schedule

Year Paid	9.50%	9.75%	10.00%	10.25%	Accrual Rate 10.50%	10.75%	11.00%	11.25%	11.50%	11.75%	12.00%	12.25%
1	0.5224	0.7844	1.0471	1.3104	1.5743	1.8389	2.1040	2.3697	2.6361	2.9030	3.1706	3.4388
2	1.0966	1.6489	2.2039	2.7617	3.3222	3.8854	4.4514	5.0202	5.5918	6.1662	6.7434	7.3234
3	1.7277	2.6015	3.4818	4.3689	5.2626	6.1632	7.0705	7.9848	8.9059	9.8341	10.7692	11.7115
4	2.4216	3.6512	4.8935	6.1487	7.4169	8.6982	9.9927	11.3006	12.6219	13.9569	15.3057	16.6683
5	3.1843	4.8080	6.4531	8.1199	9.8086	11.5196	13.2530	15.0092	16.7885	18.5911	20.4174	22.2676
6	4.0226	6.0827	8.1759	10.3028	12.4639	14.6596	16.8906	19.1573	21.4604	23.8002	26.1775	28.5927
7	4.9442	7.4875	10.0792	12.7204	15.4118	18.1544	20.9492	23.7969	26.6997	29.6554	32.6681	35.7377
8	5.9573	9.0354	12.1818	15.3976	18.6846	22.0440	25.4773	28.9863	32.5722	36.2369	39.9818	43.8087
9	7.0709	10.7413	14.5045	18.3626	22.3180	26.3729	30.5295	34.7904	39.1580	43.6347	48.2231	52.9259
10	8.2950	12.6211	17.0704	21.6462	26.3519	31.1907	36.1664	41.2823	46.5423	51.9502	57.5097	63.2248
11	9.6406	14.6926	19.9050	25.2826	30.8303	36.5528	42.4555	48.5434	54.8221	61.2970	67.9740	74.8587
12	11.1198	16.9754	23.0365	29.3098	35.8022	42.5206	49.4723	56.6649	64.1059	71.8033	79.7654	88.0005
13	12.7458	19.4909	26.4958	33.7697	41.3220	49.1625	57.3012	65.7486	74.5154	83.6128	93.0523	102.8458
14	14.5331	22.2630	30.3174	38.7089	47.4502	56.5547	66.0360	75.9086	86.1871	96.8871	108.0242	119.6152
15	16.4979	25.3177	34.5392	44.1788	54.2537	64.7818	75.7816	87.2724	99.2742	111.8079	124.8950	138.5582
16	18.6576	28.6840	39.2030	50.2365	61.8070	73.9383	86.6549	99.9826	113.9482	128.5795	143.9055	159.9566
17	21.0317	32.3935	44.3552	56.9451	70.1927	84.1291	98.7865	114.1989	130.4015	147.4314	165.3269	184.1286
18	23.6414	36.4814	50.0469	64.3745	79.5025	95.4710	112.3220	130.0996	148.8500	168.6216	189.4652	211.4337
19	26.5101	40.9861	56.3346	72.6023	89.8383	108.0940	127.4237	147.8843	169.5355	192.4404	216.6647	242.2780
20	29.6635	45.9502	63.2807	81.7143	101.3131	122.1430	144.2730	167.7762	192.7294	219.2135	247.3138	277.1202
21	33.1299	51.4205	70.9542	91.8053	114.0525	137.7788	163.0721	190.0250	218.7357	249.3076	281.8501	316.4787
22	36.9403	57.4487	79.4311	102.9807	128.1958	155.1809	184.0466	214.9101	247.8955	283.1345	320.7663	360.9386
23	41.1289	64.0916	88.7958	115.3569	143.8978	174.5487	207.4482	242.7436	280.5912	321.1572	364.6181	411.1614
24	45.7332	71.4119	99.1410	129.0631	161.3301	196.1042	233.5579	273.8750	317.2516	363.8963	414.0315	467.8938
25	50.7944	79.4787	110.5695	144.2420	180.6836	220.0946	262.6889	308.6951	358.3574	411.9367	469.7117	531.9798

Entry is accrued compound interest as percentage of original loan amount.

Amount Accrued on Bow-Tie Loans
(Pay Rate Less Than Accrual Rate)

Pay Rate   9.50%   30 Year Schedule

Year Paid	10.00%	10.25%	10.50%	10.75%	Accrual Rate 11.00%	11.25%	11.50%	11.75%	12.00%	12.25%	12.50%	12.75%
1	0.5236	0.7863	1.0496	1.3135	1.5780	1.8431	2.1089	2.3752	2.6422	2.9098	3.1780	3.4468
2	1.1020	1.6570	2.2148	2.7753	3.3386	3.9046	4.4734	5.0450	5.6195	6.1967	6.7768	7.3597
3	1.7409	2.6213	3.5084	4.4023	5.3029	6.2104	7.1247	8.0460	8.9743	9.9097	10.8521	11.8017
4	2.4468	3.6892	4.9446	6.2130	7.4945	8.7893	10.0975	11.4193	12.7547	14.1039	15.4671	16.8444
5	3.2265	4.8719	6.5391	8.2283	9.9398	11.6739	13.4308	15.2109	17.0145	18.8418	20.6932	22.5689
6	4.0880	6.1817	8.3093	10.4712	12.6680	14.9002	17.1683	19.4729	21.8146	24.1938	26.6113	29.0675
7	5.0396	7.6322	10.2745	12.9674	15.7119	18.5087	21.3590	24.2635	27.2234	30.2396	33.3130	36.4448
8	6.0909	9.2386	12.4564	15.7457	19.1080	22.5449	26.0578	29.6484	33.3182	37.0689	40.9022	44.8197
9	7.2522	11.0176	14.8787	18.8378	22.8972	27.0592	31.3264	35.7011	40.1860	44.7835	49.4963	54.3271
10	8.5352	12.9877	17.5679	22.2791	27.1248	32.1085	37.2339	42.5047	47.9247	53.4979	59.2284	65.1201
11	9.9525	15.1696	20.5535	26.1092	31.8416	37.7560	43.8577	50.1521	56.6450	63.3420	70.2491	77.3725
12	11.5182	17.5859	23.8681	30.3719	37.1043	44.0727	51.2847	58.7482	66.4712	74.4620	82.7292	91.2818
13	13.2479	20.2618	27.5480	35.1161	42.9759	51.1378	59.6123	68.4104	77.5436	87.0233	96.8619	107.0718
14	15.1587	23.2253	31.6335	40.3962	49.5270	59.0400	68.9497	79.2712	90.0202	101.2128	112.8660	124.9970
15	17.2696	26.5073	36.1692	46.2727	56.8362	67.8785	79.4194	91.4792	104.0792	117.2416	130.9892	145.3460
16	19.6015	30.1419	41.2047	52.8131	64.9912	77.7643	91.1586	105.2014	119.9212	135.3479	151.5123	168.4466
17	22.1776	34.1670	46.7951	60.0922	74.0899	88.8214	104.3212	120.6257	137.7724	155.8011	174.7529	194.6710
18	25.0235	38.6247	53.0017	68.1935	84.2415	101.1886	119.0800	137.9632	157.8876	178.9054	201.0710	224.4414
19	28.1673	43.5614	59.8922	77.2100	95.5678	115.0211	135.6284	157.4512	180.5539	205.0044	230.8740	258.2375
20	31.6404	49.0286	67.5421	87.2450	108.2048	130.4926	154.1835	179.3565	206.0949	234.4863	264.6234	296.6034
21	35.4771	55.0832	76.0350	98.4134	122.3041	147.7973	174.9886	203.9789	234.8750	267.7896	302.8418	340.1573
22	39.7156	61.7884	85.4639	110.8435	138.0349	167.1523	198.3164	231.6555	267.3053	305.4096	346.1209	389.6005
23	44.3979	69.2142	95.9318	124.6776	155.5862	188.8006	224.4730	262.7650	303.8485	347.9058	395.1308	445.7295
24	49.5705	77.4378	107.5534	140.0744	175.1684	213.0139	253.8013	297.7334	345.0262	395.9102	450.6304	509.4484
25	55.2847	86.5452	120.4557	157.2104	197.0167	240.0962	286.6859	337.0391	391.4264	450.1368	513.4791	581.7833

Pay Rate 10.00%   30 Year Schedule

Year Paid	10.50%	10.75%	11.00%	11.25%	Accrual Rate 11.50%	11.75%	12.00%	12.25%	12.50%	12.75%	13.00%	13.25%
1	0.5248	0.7881	1.0520	1.3165	1.5816	1.8474	2.1138	2.3807	2.6483	2.9165	3.1854	3.4548
2	1.1074	1.6652	2.2257	2.7890	3.3551	3.9239	4.4956	5.0700	5.6473	6.2274	6.8104	7.3962
3	1.7542	2.6414	3.5353	4.4360	5.3436	6.2580	7.1795	8.1079	9.0434	9.9861	10.9358	11.8928
4	2.4723	3.7278	4.9963	6.2781	7.5732	8.8817	10.2038	11.5396	12.8893	14.2529	15.6307	17.0228
5	3.2695	4.9370	6.6265	8.3385	10.0731	11.8307	13.6116	15.4160	17.2443	19.0967	20.9736	22.8752
6	4.1546	6.2827	8.4453	10.6430	12.8762	15.1456	17.4517	19.7950	22.1761	24.5956	27.0540	29.5520
7	5.1373	7.7805	10.4746	13.2205	16.0192	18.8716	21.7787	24.7415	27.7609	30.8379	33.9737	37.1693
8	6.2282	9.4474	12.7387	16.1035	19.5433	23.0598	26.6545	30.3291	34.0852	37.9244	41.8486	45.8594
9	7.4393	11.3027	15.2648	19.3280	23.4948	27.7675	32.1488	36.6410	41.2469	45.9691	50.8104	55.7735
10	8.7840	13.3675	18.0832	22.9346	27.9254	33.0592	38.3398	43.7710	49.3570	55.1016	61.0092	67.0840
11	10.2768	15.6655	21.2277	26.9686	32.8933	39.0072	45.3160	51.8253	58.5410	65.4691	72.6158	79.9877
12	11.9341	18.2231	24.7362	31.4805	38.4635	45.6930	53.1769	60.9234	68.9410	77.2384	85.8246	94.7088
13	13.7740	21.0696	28.6506	36.5270	44.7092	53.2081	62.0348	71.2009	80.7183	90.5992	100.8565	111.5033
14	15.8167	24.2377	33.0180	42.1714	51.7123	61.6554	72.0162	82.8105	94.0550	105.7667	117.9633	130.6634
15	18.0846	27.7636	37.8908	48.4847	59.5645	71.1505	83.2634	95.9249	109.1577	122.9851	137.4315	152.5222
16	20.6023	31.6878	43.3275	55.5459	68.3689	81.8233	95.9370	110.7392	126.2602	142.5318	159.5869	177.4598
17	23.3976	36.0553	49.3933	63.4438	78.2409	93.8200	110.2180	127.4736	145.6274	164.7216	184.8004	205.9099
18	26.5008	40.9161	56.1610	72.2775	89.3100	107.3047	126.3101	146.3772	167.5592	189.9120	213.4942	238.3672
19	29.9461	46.3260	63.7119	82.1579	101.7213	122.4620	144.4431	167.7309	192.3950	218.5086	246.1487	275.3961
20	33.7710	52.3470	72.1365	93.2090	115.6376	139.4995	164.8759	191.8525	220.5195	250.9721	283.3106	317.6405
21	38.0175	59.0481	81.5360	105.5695	131.2414	158.6503	187.9000	219.1006	252.3681	287.8254	325.6020	365.8351
22	42.7319	66.5061	92.0233	119.3945	148.7373	180.1765	213.8442	249.8806	288.4341	329.6620	373.7310	420.8179
23	47.9659	74.8066	103.7241	134.8576	168.3547	204.3728	243.0788	284.6502	329.2757	377.1558	428.5034	483.5450
24	53.7767	84.0447	116.7789	152.1528	190.3510	231.5704	276.0210	323.9265	375.5254	431.0717	490.8362	555.1073
25	60.2279	94.3263	131.3444	171.4973	215.0144	262.1415	313.1411	368.2937	427.8993	492.2782	561.7729	636.7491

Entry is accrued compound interest as percentage of original loan amount.

Amount Accrued on Bow-Tie Loans
(Pay Rate Less Than Accrual Rate)

Pay Rate 10.50%   30 Year Schedule

Year Paid	11.00%	11.25%	11.50%	11.75%	12.00%	12.25%	12.50%	12.75%	13.00%	13.25%	13.50%	13.75%
					Accrual Rate							
1	0.5260	0.7899	1.0544	1.3196	1.5853	1.8517	2.1187	2.3863	2.6545	2.9233	3.1928	3.4628
2	1.1129	1.6734	2.2367	2.8028	3.3717	3.9434	4.5179	5.0952	5.6753	6.2584	6.8442	7.4330
3	1.7676	2.6616	3.5624	4.4700	5.3846	6.3062	7.2348	8.1704	9.1132	10.0632	11.0204	11.9848
4	2.4982	3.7669	5.0488	6.3440	7.6528	8.9752	10.3114	11.6615	13.0256	14.4039	15.7965	17.2035
5	3.3133	5.0031	6.7154	8.4505	10.2087	11.9903	13.7955	15.6246	17.4780	19.3560	21.2588	23.1868
6	4.2227	6.3858	8.5841	10.8183	13.0887	15.3961	17.7409	20.1236	22.5450	25.0056	27.5059	30.0466
7	5.2373	7.9323	10.6795	13.4797	16.3340	19.2434	22.2087	25.2310	28.3114	31.4509	34.6505	37.9114
8	6.3693	9.6621	13.0289	16.4713	19.9909	23.5893	27.2681	31.0291	34.8738	38.8041	42.8217	46.9285
9	7.6324	11.5968	15.6632	19.8340	24.1116	28.4986	32.9975	37.6111	42.3420	47.1930	52.1669	57.2666
10	9.0416	13.7608	18.6169	23.6137	28.7548	34.0441	39.4856	45.0832	50.8410	56.7634	62.8547	69.1193
11	10.6139	16.1811	21.9288	27.8623	33.9870	40.3085	46.8328	53.5656	60.5132	67.6819	75.0781	82.7084
12	12.3681	18.8883	25.6423	32.6379	39.8827	47.3849	55.1528	63.1951	71.5205	80.1382	89.0576	98.2885
13	14.3253	21.9162	29.8061	38.0058	46.5261	55.3785	64.5746	74.1266	84.0471	94.3490	105.0457	116.1511
14	16.5090	25.3029	34.4749	44.0396	54.0121	64.4082	75.2440	86.5364	98.3028	110.5614	123.3308	136.6306
15	18.9454	29.0908	39.7097	50.8218	62.4475	74.6083	87.3261	100.6242	114.5262	129.0573	144.2431	160.1106
16	21.6637	33.3275	45.5793	58.4452	71.9527	86.1305	101.0082	116.6169	132.9890	150.1583	168.1599	187.0304
17	24.6966	38.0663	52.1606	67.0143	82.6635	99.1462	116.5019	134.7722	154.0003	174.2315	195.5129	217.8942
18	28.0805	43.3665	59.5400	76.6462	94.7326	113.8489	134.0473	155.3825	177.9118	201.6953	226.7959	253.2796
19	31.8559	49.2948	67.8142	87.4729	108.3324	130.4574	153.9160	178.7798	205.1239	233.0275	262.5734	293.8492
20	36.0683	55.9254	77.0918	99.6425	123.6569	149.2186	176.4156	205.3408	236.0922	268.7727	303.4913	340.3624
21	40.7680	63.3417	87.4943	113.3216	140.9250	170.4116	201.8945	235.4935	271.3350	309.5528	350.2880	393.6901
22	46.0116	71.6367	99.1582	128.6975	160.3832	194.3516	230.7472	269.7234	311.4425	356.0767	403.8082	454.8305
23	51.8621	80.9145	112.2365	145.9806	182.3091	221.3946	263.4205	308.5820	357.0862	409.1535	465.0179	524.9283
24	58.3895	91.2917	126.9006	165.4074	207.0157	251.9428	300.4203	352.6950	409.0301	469.7061	535.0218	605.2957
25	65.6722	102.8984	143.3430	187.2440	234.8558	286.4507	342.3194	402.7731	468.1441	538.7877	615.0836	697.4374

Pay Rate 11.00%   30 Year Schedule

Year Paid	11.50%	11.75%	12.00%	12.25%	12.50%	12.75%	13.00%	13.25%	13.50%	13.75%	14.00%	14.25%
					Accrual Rate							
1	0.5272	0.7917	1.0569	1.3226	1.5890	1.8560	2.1236	2.3918	2.6606	2.9301	3.2002	3.4709
2	1.1184	1.6817	2.2478	2.8167	3.3884	3.9629	4.5403	5.1205	5.7035	6.2895	6.8783	7.4700
3	1.7812	2.6820	3.5897	4.5044	5.4261	6.3548	7.2906	8.2335	9.1836	10.1410	11.1057	12.0777
4	2.5244	3.8064	5.1019	6.4109	7.7336	9.0700	10.4205	11.7850	13.1637	14.5568	15.9644	17.3867
5	3.3577	5.0703	6.8058	8.5645	10.3466	12.1525	13.9824	15.8367	17.7157	19.6196	21.5488	23.5036
6	4.2921	6.4910	8.7258	10.9972	13.3056	15.6517	18.0360	20.4591	22.9216	25.4240	27.9671	30.5514
7	5.3397	8.0878	10.8894	13.7453	16.6565	19.6241	22.6491	25.7326	28.8755	32.0789	35.3440	38.6718
8	6.5144	9.8828	13.3273	16.8495	20.4511	24.1337	27.8990	31.7488	35.6848	39.7087	43.8225	48.0279
9	7.8316	11.9004	16.0744	20.3561	24.7481	29.2531	33.8736	38.6124	43.4724	48.4563	53.5672	58.8080
10	9.3085	14.1682	19.1699	24.3172	29.6142	35.0647	40.6728	46.4428	52.3789	58.4855	64.7672	71.2286
11	10.9644	16.7174	22.6580	28.7918	35.1246	41.6621	48.4106	55.3761	62.5650	69.9841	77.6399	85.5395
12	12.8212	19.5827	26.5885	33.8464	41.3646	49.1517	57.2164	65.5676	74.2147	83.1672	92.4350	102.0282
13	14.9031	22.8035	31.0174	39.5561	48.4310	57.6540	67.2377	77.1946	87.5381	98.2817	109.4386	121.0263
14	17.2374	26.4237	36.0081	46.0058	56.4330	67.3061	78.6422	90.4593	102.7757	115.6105	128.9837	142.9157
15	19.8548	30.4931	41.6317	53.2916	65.4946	78.2632	91.6210	105.5923	120.2026	135.4782	151.4466	168.1363
16	22.7896	35.0671	47.9685	61.5218	75.7561	90.7020	106.3912	122.8568	140.1332	158.2565	177.2641	197.1951
17	26.0803	40.2086	55.1090	70.8187	87.3765	104.8228	123.2003	142.5530	162.9274	184.3720	206.9373	230.6762
18	29.7700	45.9877	63.1551	81.3206	100.5355	120.8531	142.3295	165.0234	188.9966	214.3135	241.0419	269.2526
19	33.9071	52.4837	72.2216	93.1838	115.4370	139.0509	164.0991	190.6588	218.8112	248.6416	280.2397	313.6999
20	38.5459	59.7855	82.4379	106.5847	132.3117	159.7095	188.8737	219.9050	252.9094	287.9990	325.2915	364.9113
21	43.7471	67.9930	93.9500	121.7226	151.4209	183.1616	217.0680	253.2704	291.9067	333.1224	377.0714	423.9164
22	49.5791	77.2185	106.9221	138.8225	173.0604	209.7849	249.1540	291.3354	336.5068	384.8565	436.5842	491.9013
23	56.1182	87.5883	121.5394	158.1390	197.5654	240.0082	285.6689	334.7619	387.5149	444.1701	504.9847	570.2324
24	63.4503	99.2445	138.0105	179.9592	225.3152	274.3183	327.2241	384.3050	445.8515	512.1733	583.6004	660.4843
25	71.6715	112.3464	156.5706	204.6076	256.7396	313.2679	374.5153	440.8263	512.5696	590.1394	673.9566	764.4714

Effect of Rate Changes on Construction Financing Cost

Term of 12 Months

Increase in rate of		Interest Rate at Start of Loan									
		5.50%	5.75%	6.00%	6.25%	6.50%	6.75%	7.00%	7.25%	7.50%	7.75%
0.50%	Equal level rate	5.81%	6.06%	6.31%	6.56%	6.81%	7.06%	7.31%	7.56%	7.81%	8.06%
	Change in cost	5.56%	5.31%	5.09%	4.89%	4.70%	4.53%	4.37%	4.21%	4.07%	3.94%
1.00%	Equal level rate	6.11%	6.36%	6.61%	6.86%	7.11%	7.36%	7.61%	7.86%	8.11%	8.36%
	Change in cost	11.11%	10.63%	10.19%	9.78%	9.40%	9.05%	8.73%	8.43%	8.15%	7.89%
1.25%	Equal level rate	6.26%	6.51%	6.76%	7.01%	7.26%	7.51%	7.76%	8.01%	8.26%	8.51%
	Change in cost	13.89%	13.29%	12.73%	12.22%	11.75%	11.32%	10.91%	10.54%	10.19%	9.86%
1.50%	Equal level rate	6.42%	6.67%	6.92%	7.17%	7.42%	7.67%	7.92%	8.17%	8.42%	8.67%
	Change in cost	16.67%	15.94%	15.28%	14.67%	14.10%	13.58%	13.10%	12.64%	12.22%	11.83%
1.75%	Equal level rate	6.57%	6.82%	7.07%	7.32%	7.57%	7.82%	8.07%	8.32%	8.57%	8.82%
	Change in cost	19.44%	18.60%	17.82%	17.11%	16.45%	15.84%	15.28%	14.75%	14.26%	13.80%
2.00%	Equal level rate	6.72%	6.97%	7.22%	7.47%	7.72%	7.97%	8.22%	8.47%	8.72%	8.97%
	Change in cost	22.22%	21.26%	20.37%	19.56%	18.80%	18.11%	17.46%	16.86%	16.30%	15.77%
2.50%	Equal level rate	7.03%	7.28%	7.53%	7.78%	8.03%	8.28%	8.53%	8.78%	9.03%	9.28%
	Change in cost	27.78%	26.57%	25.46%	24.44%	23.50%	22.63%	21.83%	21.07%	20.37%	19.71%
3.00%	Equal level rate	7.33%	7.58%	7.83%	8.08%	8.33%	8.58%	8.83%	9.08%	9.33%	9.58%
	Change in cost	33.33%	31.88%	30.56%	29.33%	28.21%	27.16%	26.19%	25.29%	24.44%	23.66%
3.50%	Equal level rate	7.64%	7.89%	8.14%	8.39%	8.64%	8.89%	9.14%	9.39%	9.64%	9.89%
	Change in cost	38.89%	37.20%	35.65%	34.22%	32.91%	31.69%	30.56%	29.50%	28.52%	27.60%
4.00%	Equal level rate	7.94%	8.19%	8.44%	8.69%	8.94%	9.19%	9.44%	9.69%	9.94%	10.19%
	Change in cost	44.44%	42.51%	40.74%	39.11%	37.61%	36.21%	34.92%	33.72%	32.59%	31.54%
4.50%	Equal level rate	8.25%	8.50%	8.75%	9.00%	9.25%	9.50%	9.75%	10.00%	10.25%	10.50%
	Change in cost	50.00%	47.83%	45.83%	44.00%	42.31%	40.74%	39.29%	37.93%	36.67%	35.48%
5.00%	Equal level rate	8.56%	8.81%	9.06%	9.31%	9.56%	9.81%	10.06%	10.31%	10.56%	10.81%
	Change in cost	55.56%	53.14%	50.93%	48.89%	47.01%	45.27%	43.65%	42.15%	40.74%	39.43%

Decrease in rate of		Interest Rate at Start of Loan									
		5.50%	5.75%	6.00%	6.25%	6.50%	6.75%	7.00%	7.25%	7.50%	7.75%
0.50%	Equal level rate	5.19%	5.44%	5.69%	5.94%	6.19%	6.44%	6.69%	6.94%	7.19%	7.44%
	Change in cost	-5.56%	-5.31%	-5.09%	-4.89%	-4.70%	-4.53%	-4.37%	-4.21%	-4.07%	-3.94%
1.00%	Equal level rate	4.89%	5.14%	5.39%	5.64%	5.89%	6.14%	6.39%	6.64%	6.89%	7.14%
	Change in cost	-11.11%	-10.63%	-10.19%	-9.78%	-9.40%	-9.05%	-8.73%	-8.43%	-8.15%	-7.89%
1.25%	Equal level rate	4.74%	4.99%	5.24%	5.49%	5.74%	5.99%	6.24%	6.49%	6.74%	6.99%
	Change in cost	-13.89%	-13.29%	-12.73%	-12.22%	-11.75%	-11.32%	-10.91%	-10.54%	-10.19%	-9.86%
1.50%	Equal level rate	4.58%	4.83%	5.08%	5.33%	5.58%	5.83%	6.08%	6.33%	6.58%	6.83%
	Change in cost	-16.67%	-15.94%	-15.28%	-14.67%	-14.10%	-13.58%	-13.10%	-12.64%	-12.22%	-11.83%
1.75%	Equal level rate	4.43%	4.68%	4.93%	5.18%	5.43%	5.68%	5.93%	6.18%	6.43%	6.68%
	Change in cost	-19.44%	-18.60%	-17.82%	-17.11%	-16.45%	-15.84%	-15.28%	-14.75%	-14.26%	-13.80%
2.00%	Equal level rate	4.28%	4.53%	4.78%	5.03%	5.28%	5.53%	5.78%	6.03%	6.28%	6.53%
	Change in cost	-22.22%	-21.26%	-20.37%	-19.56%	-18.80%	-18.11%	-17.46%	-16.86%	-16.30%	-15.77%
2.50%	Equal level rate	3.97%	4.22%	4.47%	4.72%	4.97%	5.22%	5.47%	5.72%	5.97%	6.22%
	Change in cost	-27.78%	-26.57%	-25.46%	-24.44%	-23.50%	-22.63%	-21.83%	-21.07%	-20.37%	-19.71%
3.00%	Equal level rate	3.67%	3.92%	4.17%	4.42%	4.67%	4.92%	5.17%	5.42%	5.67%	5.92%
	Change in cost	-33.33%	-31.88%	-30.56%	-29.33%	-28.21%	-27.16%	-26.19%	-25.29%	-24.44%	-23.66%
3.50%	Equal level rate	3.36%	3.61%	3.86%	4.11%	4.36%	4.61%	4.86%	5.11%	5.36%	5.61%
	Change in cost	-38.89%	-37.20%	-35.65%	-34.22%	-32.91%	-31.69%	-30.56%	-29.50%	-28.52%	-27.60%
4.00%	Equal level rate	3.06%	3.31%	3.56%	3.81%	4.06%	4.31%	4.56%	4.81%	5.06%	5.31%
	Change in cost	-44.44%	-42.51%	-40.74%	-39.11%	-37.61%	-36.21%	-34.92%	-33.72%	-32.59%	-31.54%
4.50%	Equal level rate	2.75%	3.00%	3.25%	3.50%	3.75%	4.00%	4.25%	4.50%	4.75%	5.00%
	Change in cost	-50.00%	-47.83%	-45.83%	-44.00%	-42.31%	-40.74%	-39.29%	-37.93%	-36.67%	-35.48%
5.00%	Equal level rate	2.44%	2.69%	2.94%	3.19%	3.44%	3.69%	3.94%	4.19%	4.44%	4.69%
	Change in cost	-55.56%	-53.14%	-50.93%	-48.89%	-47.01%	-45.27%	-43.65%	-42.15%	-40.74%	-39.43%

Equal level rate is the single rate that would produce equal interest cost.
Change in cost is percent change from interest if original rate remained in effect.

Effect of Rate Changes on Construction Financing Cost

Term of 12 Months

Increase in rate of		Interest Rate at Start of Loan									
		8.00%	8.25%	8.50%	8.75%	9.00%	9.25%	9.50%	9.75%	10.00%	10.25%
0.50%	Equal level rate	8.31%	8.56%	8.81%	9.06%	9.31%	9.56%	9.81%	10.06%	10.31%	10.56%
	Change in cost	3.82%	3.70%	3.59%	3.49%	3.40%	3.30%	3.22%	3.13%	3.06%	2.98%
1.00%	Equal level rate	8.61%	8.86%	9.11%	9.36%	9.61%	9.86%	10.11%	10.36%	10.61%	10.86%
	Change in cost	7.64%	7.41%	7.19%	6.98%	6.79%	6.61%	6.43%	6.27%	6.11%	5.96%
1.25%	Equal level rate	8.76%	9.01%	9.26%	9.51%	9.76%	10.01%	10.26%	10.51%	10.76%	11.01%
	Change in cost	9.55%	9.26%	8.99%	8.73%	8.49%	8.26%	8.04%	7.83%	7.64%	7.45%
1.50%	Equal level rate	8.92%	9.17%	9.42%	9.67%	9.92%	10.17%	10.42%	10.67%	10.92%	11.17%
	Change in cost	11.46%	11.11%	10.78%	10.48%	10.19%	9.91%	9.65%	9.40%	9.17%	8.94%
1.75%	Equal level rate	9.07%	9.32%	9.57%	9.82%	10.07%	10.32%	10.57%	10.82%	11.07%	11.32%
	Change in cost	13.37%	12.96%	12.58%	12.22%	11.88%	11.56%	11.26%	10.97%	10.69%	10.43%
2.00%	Equal level rate	9.22%	9.47%	9.72%	9.97%	10.22%	10.47%	10.72%	10.97%	11.22%	11.47%
	Change in cost	15.28%	14.81%	14.38%	13.97%	13.58%	13.21%	12.87%	12.54%	12.22%	11.92%
2.50%	Equal level rate	9.53%	9.78%	10.03%	10.28%	10.53%	10.78%	11.03%	11.28%	11.53%	11.78%
	Change in cost	19.10%	18.52%	17.97%	17.46%	16.98%	16.52%	16.08%	15.67%	15.28%	14.91%
3.00%	Equal level rate	9.83%	10.08%	10.33%	10.58%	10.83%	11.08%	11.33%	11.58%	11.83%	12.08%
	Change in cost	22.92%	22.22%	21.57%	20.95%	20.37%	19.82%	19.30%	18.80%	18.33%	17.89%
3.50%	Equal level rate	10.14%	10.39%	10.64%	10.89%	11.14%	11.39%	11.64%	11.89%	12.14%	12.39%
	Change in cost	26.74%	25.93%	25.16%	24.44%	23.77%	23.12%	22.51%	21.94%	21.39%	20.87%
4.00%	Equal level rate	10.44%	10.69%	10.94%	11.19%	11.44%	11.69%	11.94%	12.19%	12.44%	12.69%
	Change in cost	30.56%	29.63%	28.76%	27.94%	27.16%	26.43%	25.73%	25.07%	24.44%	23.85%
4.50%	Equal level rate	10.75%	11.00%	11.25%	11.50%	11.75%	12.00%	12.25%	12.50%	12.75%	13.00%
	Change in cost	34.37%	33.33%	32.35%	31.43%	30.56%	29.73%	28.95%	28.21%	27.50%	26.83%
5.00%	Equal level rate	11.06%	11.31%	11.56%	11.81%	12.06%	12.31%	12.56%	12.81%	13.06%	13.31%
	Change in cost	38.19%	37.04%	35.95%	34.92%	33.95%	33.03%	32.16%	31.34%	30.56%	29.81%

Decrease in rate of		Interest Rate at Start of Loan									
		8.00%	8.25%	8.50%	8.75%	9.00%	9.25%	9.50%	9.75%	10.00%	10.25%
0.50%	Equal level rate	7.69%	7.94%	8.19%	8.44%	8.69%	8.94%	9.19%	9.44%	9.69%	9.94%
	Change in cost	-3.82%	-3.70%	-3.59%	-3.49%	-3.40%	-3.30%	-3.22%	-3.13%	-3.06%	-2.98%
1.00%	Equal level rate	7.39%	7.64%	7.89%	8.14%	8.39%	8.64%	8.89%	9.14%	9.39%	9.64%
	Change in cost	-7.64%	-7.41%	-7.19%	-6.98%	-6.79%	-6.61%	-6.43%	-6.27%	-6.11%	-5.96%
1.25%	Equal level rate	7.24%	7.49%	7.74%	7.99%	8.24%	8.49%	8.74%	8.99%	9.24%	9.49%
	Change in cost	-9.55%	-9.26%	-8.99%	-8.73%	-8.49%	-8.26%	-8.04%	-7.83%	-7.64%	-7.45%
1.50%	Equal level rate	7.08%	7.33%	7.58%	7.83%	8.08%	8.33%	8.58%	8.83%	9.08%	9.33%
	Change in cost	-11.46%	-11.11%	-10.78%	-10.48%	-10.19%	-9.91%	-9.65%	-9.40%	-9.17%	-8.94%
1.75%	Equal level rate	6.93%	7.18%	7.43%	7.68%	7.93%	8.18%	8.43%	8.68%	8.93%	9.18%
	Change in cost	-13.37%	-12.96%	-12.58%	-12.22%	-11.88%	-11.56%	-11.26%	-10.97%	-10.69%	-10.43%
2.00%	Equal level rate	6.78%	7.03%	7.28%	7.53%	7.78%	8.03%	8.28%	8.53%	8.78%	9.03%
	Change in cost	-15.28%	-14.81%	-14.38%	-13.97%	-13.58%	-13.21%	-12.87%	-12.54%	-12.22%	-11.92%
2.50%	Equal level rate	6.47%	6.72%	6.97%	7.22%	7.47%	7.72%	7.97%	8.22%	8.47%	8.72%
	Change in cost	-19.10%	-18.52%	-17.97%	-17.46%	-16.98%	-16.52%	-16.08%	-15.67%	-15.28%	-14.91%
3.00%	Equal level rate	6.17%	6.42%	6.67%	6.92%	7.17%	7.42%	7.67%	7.92%	8.17%	8.42%
	Change in cost	-22.92%	-22.22%	-21.57%	-20.95%	-20.37%	-19.82%	-19.30%	-18.80%	-18.33%	-17.89%
3.50%	Equal level rate	5.86%	6.11%	6.36%	6.61%	6.86%	7.11%	7.36%	7.61%	7.86%	8.11%
	Change in cost	-26.74%	-25.93%	-25.16%	-24.44%	-23.77%	-23.12%	-22.51%	-21.94%	-21.39%	-20.87%
4.00%	Equal level rate	5.56%	5.81%	6.06%	6.31%	6.56%	6.81%	7.06%	7.31%	7.56%	7.81%
	Change in cost	-30.56%	-29.63%	-28.76%	-27.94%	-27.16%	-26.43%	-25.73%	-25.07%	-24.44%	-23.85%
4.50%	Equal level rate	5.25%	5.50%	5.75%	6.00%	6.25%	6.50%	6.75%	7.00%	7.25%	7.50%
	Change in cost	-34.38%	-33.33%	-32.35%	-31.43%	-30.56%	-29.73%	-28.95%	-28.21%	-27.50%	-26.83%
5.00%	Equal level rate	4.94%	5.19%	5.44%	5.69%	5.94%	6.19%	6.44%	6.69%	6.94%	7.19%
	Change in cost	-38.19%	-37.04%	-35.95%	-34.92%	-33.95%	-33.03%	-32.16%	-31.34%	-30.56%	-29.81%

Equal level rate is the single rate that would produce equal interest cost.
Change in cost is percent change from interest if original rate remained in effect.

Effect of Rate Changes on Construction Financing Cost

Term of 12 Months

Increase in rate of		\multicolumn{10}{c}{Interest Rate at Start of Loan}									
		10.50%	10.75%	11.00%	11.25%	11.50%	11.75%	12.00%	12.25%	12.50%	12.75%
0.50%	Equal level rate	10.81%	11.06%	11.31%	11.56%	11.81%	12.06%	12.31%	12.56%	12.81%	13.06%
	Change in cost	2.91%	2.84%	2.78%	2.72%	2.66%	2.60%	2.55%	2.49%	2.44%	2.40%
1.00%	Equal level rate	11.11%	11.36%	11.61%	11.86%	12.11%	12.36%	12.61%	12.86%	13.11%	13.36%
	Change in cost	5.82%	5.68%	5.56%	5.43%	5.31%	5.20%	5.09%	4.99%	4.89%	4.79%
1.25%	Equal level rate	11.26%	11.51%	11.76%	12.01%	12.26%	12.51%	12.76%	13.01%	13.26%	13.51%
	Change in cost	7.28%	7.11%	6.94%	6.79%	6.64%	6.50%	6.37%	6.24%	6.11%	5.99%
1.50%	Equal level rate	11.42%	11.67%	11.92%	12.17%	12.42%	12.67%	12.92%	13.17%	13.42%	13.67%
	Change in cost	8.73%	8.53%	8.33%	8.15%	7.97%	7.80%	7.64%	7.48%	7.33%	7.19%
1.75%	Equal level rate	11.57%	11.82%	12.07%	12.32%	12.57%	12.82%	13.07%	13.32%	13.57%	13.82%
	Change in cost	10.19%	9.95%	9.72%	9.51%	9.30%	9.10%	8.91%	8.73%	8.56%	8.39%
2.00%	Equal level rate	11.72%	11.97%	12.22%	12.47%	12.72%	12.97%	13.22%	13.47%	13.72%	13.97%
	Change in cost	11.64%	11.37%	11.11%	10.86%	10.63%	10.40%	10.19%	9.98%	9.78%	9.59%
2.50%	Equal level rate	12.03%	12.28%	12.53%	12.78%	13.03%	13.28%	13.53%	13.78%	14.03%	14.28%
	Change in cost	14.55%	14.21%	13.89%	13.58%	13.29%	13.00%	12.73%	12.47%	12.22%	11.98%
3.00%	Equal level rate	12.33%	12.58%	12.83%	13.08%	13.33%	13.58%	13.83%	14.08%	14.33%	14.58%
	Change in cost	17.46%	17.05%	16.67%	16.30%	15.94%	15.60%	15.28%	14.97%	14.67%	14.38%
3.50%	Equal level rate	12.64%	12.89%	13.14%	13.39%	13.64%	13.89%	14.14%	14.39%	14.64%	14.89%
	Change in cost	20.37%	19.90%	19.44%	19.01%	18.60%	18.20%	17.82%	17.46%	17.11%	16.78%
4.00%	Equal level rate	12.94%	13.19%	13.44%	13.69%	13.94%	14.19%	14.44%	14.69%	14.94%	15.19%
	Change in cost	23.28%	22.74%	22.22%	21.73%	21.26%	20.80%	20.37%	19.95%	19.56%	19.17%
4.50%	Equal level rate	13.25%	13.50%	13.75%	14.00%	14.25%	14.50%	14.75%	15.00%	15.25%	15.50%
	Change in cost	26.19%	25.58%	25.00%	24.44%	23.91%	23.40%	22.92%	22.45%	22.00%	21.57%
5.00%	Equal level rate	13.56%	13.81%	14.06%	14.31%	14.56%	14.81%	15.06%	15.31%	15.56%	15.81%
	Change in cost	29.10%	28.42%	27.78%	27.16%	26.57%	26.00%	25.46%	24.94%	24.44%	23.97%

Decrease in rate of		\multicolumn{10}{c}{Interest Rate at Start of Loan}									
		10.50%	10.75%	11.00%	11.25%	11.50%	11.75%	12.00%	12.25%	12.50%	12.75%
0.50%	Equal level rate	10.19%	10.44%	10.69%	10.94%	11.19%	11.44%	11.69%	11.94%	12.19%	12.44%
	Change in cost	-2.91%	-2.84%	-2.78%	-2.72%	-2.66%	-2.60%	-2.55%	-2.49%	-2.44%	-2.40%
1.00%	Equal level rate	9.89%	10.14%	10.39%	10.64%	10.89%	11.14%	11.39%	11.64%	11.89%	12.14%
	Change in cost	-5.82%	-5.68%	-5.56%	-5.43%	-5.31%	-5.20%	-5.09%	-4.99%	-4.89%	-4.79%
1.25%	Equal level rate	9.74%	9.99%	10.24%	10.49%	10.74%	10.99%	11.24%	11.49%	11.74%	11.99%
	Change in cost	-7.28%	-7.11%	-6.94%	-6.79%	-6.64%	-6.50%	-6.37%	-6.24%	-6.11%	-5.99%
1.50%	Equal level rate	9.58%	9.83%	10.08%	10.33%	10.58%	10.83%	11.08%	11.33%	11.58%	11.83%
	Change in cost	-8.73%	-8.53%	-8.33%	-8.15%	-7.97%	-7.80%	-7.64%	-7.48%	-7.33%	-7.19%
1.75%	Equal level rate	9.43%	9.68%	9.93%	10.18%	10.43%	10.68%	10.93%	11.18%	11.43%	11.68%
	Change in cost	-10.19%	-9.95%	-9.72%	-9.51%	-9.30%	-9.10%	-8.91%	-8.73%	-8.56%	-8.39%
2.00%	Equal level rate	9.28%	9.53%	9.78%	10.03%	10.28%	10.53%	10.78%	11.03%	11.28%	11.53%
	Change in cost	-11.64%	-11.37%	-11.11%	-10.86%	-10.63%	-10.40%	-10.19%	-9.98%	-9.78%	-9.59%
2.50%	Equal level rate	8.97%	9.22%	9.47%	9.72%	9.97%	10.22%	10.47%	10.72%	10.97%	11.22%
	Change in cost	-14.55%	-14.21%	-13.89%	-13.58%	-13.29%	-13.00%	-12.73%	-12.47%	-12.22%	-11.98%
3.00%	Equal level rate	8.67%	8.92%	9.17%	9.42%	9.67%	9.92%	10.17%	10.42%	10.67%	10.92%
	Change in cost	-17.46%	-17.05%	-16.67%	-16.30%	-15.94%	-15.60%	-15.28%	-14.97%	-14.67%	-14.38%
3.50%	Equal level rate	8.36%	8.61%	8.86%	9.11%	9.36%	9.61%	9.86%	10.11%	10.36%	10.61%
	Change in cost	-20.37%	-19.90%	-19.44%	-19.01%	-18.60%	-18.20%	-17.82%	-17.46%	-17.11%	-16.78%
4.00%	Equal level rate	8.06%	8.31%	8.56%	8.81%	9.06%	9.31%	9.56%	9.81%	10.06%	10.31%
	Change in cost	-23.28%	-22.74%	-22.22%	-21.73%	-21.26%	-20.80%	-20.37%	-19.95%	-19.56%	-19.17%
4.50%	Equal level rate	7.75%	8.00%	8.25%	8.50%	8.75%	9.00%	9.25%	9.50%	9.75%	10.00%
	Change in cost	-26.19%	-25.58%	-25.00%	-24.44%	-23.91%	-23.40%	-22.92%	-22.45%	-22.00%	-21.57%
5.00%	Equal level rate	7.44%	7.69%	7.94%	8.19%	8.44%	8.69%	8.94%	9.19%	9.44%	9.69%
	Change in cost	-29.10%	-28.42%	-27.78%	-27.16%	-26.57%	-26.00%	-25.46%	-24.94%	-24.44%	-23.97%

Equal level rate is the single rate that would produce equal interest cost.
Change in cost is percent change from interest if original rate remained in effect.

Effect of Rate Changes on Construction Financing Cost

Term of 18 Months

Increase in rate of		Interest Rate at Start of Loan									
		5.50%	5.75%	6.00%	6.25%	6.50%	6.75%	7.00%	7.25%	7.50%	7.75%
0.50%	Equal level rate	5.81%	6.06%	6.31%	6.56%	6.81%	7.06%	7.31%	7.56%	7.81%	8.06%
	Change in cost	5.72%	5.48%	5.25%	5.04%	4.84%	4.66%	4.50%	4.34%	4.20%	4.06%
1.00%	Equal level rate	6.13%	6.38%	6.63%	6.88%	7.13%	7.38%	7.63%	7.88%	8.13%	8.38%
	Change in cost	11.45%	10.95%	10.49%	10.07%	9.69%	9.33%	8.99%	8.68%	8.40%	8.12%
1.25%	Equal level rate	6.29%	6.54%	6.79%	7.04%	7.29%	7.54%	7.79%	8.04%	8.29%	8.54%
	Change in cost	14.31%	13.69%	13.12%	12.59%	12.11%	11.66%	11.24%	10.86%	10.49%	10.16%
1.50%	Equal level rate	6.44%	6.69%	6.94%	7.19%	7.44%	7.69%	7.94%	8.19%	8.44%	8.69%
	Change in cost	17.17%	16.43%	15.74%	15.11%	14.53%	13.99%	13.49%	13.03%	12.59%	12.19%
1.75%	Equal level rate	6.60%	6.85%	7.10%	7.35%	7.60%	7.85%	8.10%	8.35%	8.60%	8.85%
	Change in cost	20.03%	19.16%	18.36%	17.63%	16.95%	16.32%	15.74%	15.20%	14.69%	14.22%
2.00%	Equal level rate	6.76%	7.01%	7.26%	7.51%	7.76%	8.01%	8.26%	8.51%	8.76%	9.01%
	Change in cost	22.90%	21.90%	20.99%	20.15%	19.37%	18.66%	17.99%	17.37%	16.79%	16.25%
2.50%	Equal level rate	7.07%	7.32%	7.57%	7.82%	8.07%	8.32%	8.57%	8.82%	9.07%	9.32%
	Change in cost	28.62%	27.38%	26.23%	25.19%	24.22%	23.32%	22.49%	21.71%	20.99%	20.31%
3.00%	Equal level rate	7.39%	7.64%	7.89%	8.14%	8.39%	8.64%	8.89%	9.14%	9.39%	9.64%
	Change in cost	34.34%	32.85%	31.48%	30.22%	29.06%	27.98%	26.98%	26.05%	25.19%	24.37%
3.50%	Equal level rate	7.70%	7.95%	8.20%	8.45%	8.70%	8.95%	9.20%	9.45%	9.70%	9.95%
	Change in cost	40.07%	38.33%	36.73%	35.26%	33.90%	32.65%	31.48%	30.40%	29.38%	28.43%
4.00%	Equal level rate	8.02%	8.27%	8.52%	8.77%	9.02%	9.27%	9.52%	9.77%	10.02%	10.27%
	Change in cost	45.79%	43.80%	41.98%	40.30%	38.75%	37.31%	35.98%	34.74%	33.58%	32.50%
4.50%	Equal level rate	8.33%	8.58%	8.83%	9.08%	9.33%	9.58%	9.83%	10.08%	10.33%	10.58%
	Change in cost	51.52%	49.28%	47.22%	45.33%	43.59%	41.98%	40.48%	39.08%	37.78%	36.56%
5.00%	Equal level rate	8.65%	8.90%	9.15%	9.40%	9.65%	9.90%	10.15%	10.40%	10.65%	10.90%
	Change in cost	57.24%	54.75%	52.47%	50.37%	48.43%	46.64%	44.97%	43.42%	41.98%	40.62%

Decrease in rate of		Interest Rate at Start of Loan									
		5.50%	5.75%	6.00%	6.25%	6.50%	6.75%	7.00%	7.25%	7.50%	7.75%
0.50%	Equal level rate	5.19%	5.44%	5.69%	5.94%	6.19%	6.44%	6.69%	6.94%	7.19%	7.44%
	Change in cost	-5.72%	-5.48%	-5.25%	-5.04%	-4.84%	-4.66%	-4.50%	-4.34%	-4.20%	-4.06%
1.00%	Equal level rate	4.87%	5.12%	5.37%	5.62%	5.87%	6.12%	6.37%	6.62%	6.87%	7.12%
	Change in cost	-11.45%	-10.95%	-10.49%	-10.07%	-9.69%	-9.33%	-8.99%	-8.68%	-8.40%	-8.12%
1.25%	Equal level rate	4.71%	4.96%	5.21%	5.46%	5.71%	5.96%	6.21%	6.46%	6.71%	6.96%
	Change in cost	-14.31%	-13.69%	-13.12%	-12.59%	-12.11%	-11.66%	-11.24%	-10.86%	-10.49%	-10.16%
1.50%	Equal level rate	4.56%	4.81%	5.06%	5.31%	5.56%	5.81%	6.06%	6.31%	6.56%	6.81%
	Change in cost	-17.17%	-16.43%	-15.74%	-15.11%	-14.53%	-13.99%	-13.49%	-13.03%	-12.59%	-12.19%
1.75%	Equal level rate	4.40%	4.65%	4.90%	5.15%	5.40%	5.65%	5.90%	6.15%	6.40%	6.65%
	Change in cost	-20.03%	-19.16%	-18.36%	-17.63%	-16.95%	-16.32%	-15.74%	-15.20%	-14.69%	-14.22%
2.00%	Equal level rate	4.24%	4.49%	4.74%	4.99%	5.24%	5.49%	5.74%	5.99%	6.24%	6.49%
	Change in cost	-22.90%	-21.90%	-20.99%	-20.15%	-19.37%	-18.66%	-17.99%	-17.37%	-16.79%	-16.25%
2.50%	Equal level rate	3.93%	4.18%	4.43%	4.68%	4.93%	5.18%	5.43%	5.68%	5.93%	6.18%
	Change in cost	-28.62%	-27.38%	-26.23%	-25.19%	-24.22%	-23.32%	-22.49%	-21.71%	-20.99%	-20.31%
3.00%	Equal level rate	3.61%	3.86%	4.11%	4.36%	4.61%	4.86%	5.11%	5.36%	5.61%	5.86%
	Change in cost	-34.34%	-32.85%	-31.48%	-30.22%	-29.06%	-27.98%	-26.98%	-26.05%	-25.19%	-24.37%
3.50%	Equal level rate	3.30%	3.55%	3.80%	4.05%	4.30%	4.55%	4.80%	5.05%	5.30%	5.55%
	Change in cost	-40.07%	-38.33%	-36.73%	-35.26%	-33.90%	-32.65%	-31.48%	-30.40%	-29.38%	-28.43%
4.00%	Equal level rate	2.98%	3.23%	3.48%	3.73%	3.98%	4.23%	4.48%	4.73%	4.98%	5.23%
	Change in cost	-45.79%	-43.80%	-41.98%	-40.30%	-38.75%	-37.31%	-35.98%	-34.74%	-33.58%	-32.50%
4.50%	Equal level rate	2.67%	2.92%	3.17%	3.42%	3.67%	3.92%	4.17%	4.42%	4.67%	4.92%
	Change in cost	-51.52%	-49.28%	-47.22%	-45.33%	-43.59%	-41.98%	-40.48%	-39.08%	-37.78%	-36.56%
5.00%	Equal level rate	2.35%	2.60%	2.85%	3.10%	3.35%	3.60%	3.85%	4.10%	4.35%	4.60%
	Change in cost	-57.24%	-54.75%	-52.47%	-50.37%	-48.43%	-46.64%	-44.97%	-43.42%	-41.98%	-40.62%

Equal level rate is the single rate that would produce equal interest cost.
Change in cost is percent change from interest if original rate remained in effect.

Effect of Rate Changes on Construction Financing Cost

Term of 18 Months

Increase in rate of		Interest Rate at Start of Loan									
		8.00%	8.25%	8.50%	8.75%	9.00%	9.25%	9.50%	9.75%	10.00%	10.25%
0.50%	Equal level rate	8.31%	8.56%	8.81%	9.06%	9.31%	9.56%	9.81%	10.06%	10.31%	10.56%
	Change in cost	3.94%	3.82%	3.70%	3.60%	3.50%	3.40%	3.31%	3.23%	3.15%	3.07%
1.00%	Equal level rate	8.63%	8.88%	9.13%	9.38%	9.63%	9.88%	10.13%	10.38%	10.63%	10.88%
	Change in cost	7.87%	7.63%	7.41%	7.20%	7.00%	6.81%	6.63%	6.46%	6.30%	6.14%
1.25%	Equal level rate	8.79%	9.04%	9.29%	9.54%	9.79%	10.04%	10.29%	10.54%	10.79%	11.04%
	Change in cost	9.84%	9.54%	9.26%	8.99%	8.74%	8.51%	8.28%	8.07%	7.87%	7.68%
1.50%	Equal level rate	8.94%	9.19%	9.44%	9.69%	9.94%	10.19%	10.44%	10.69%	10.94%	11.19%
	Change in cost	11.81%	11.45%	11.11%	10.79%	10.49%	10.21%	9.94%	9.69%	9.44%	9.21%
1.75%	Equal level rate	9.10%	9.35%	9.60%	9.85%	10.10%	10.35%	10.60%	10.85%	11.10%	11.35%
	Change in cost	13.77%	13.36%	12.96%	12.59%	12.24%	11.91%	11.60%	11.30%	11.02%	10.75%
2.00%	Equal level rate	9.26%	9.51%	9.76%	10.01%	10.26%	10.51%	10.76%	11.01%	11.26%	11.51%
	Change in cost	15.74%	15.26%	14.81%	14.39%	13.99%	13.61%	13.26%	12.92%	12.59%	12.29%
2.50%	Equal level rate	9.57%	9.82%	10.07%	10.32%	10.57%	10.82%	11.07%	11.32%	11.57%	11.82%
	Change in cost	19.68%	19.08%	18.52%	17.99%	17.49%	17.02%	16.57%	16.14%	15.74%	15.36%
3.00%	Equal level rate	9.89%	10.14%	10.39%	10.64%	10.89%	11.14%	11.39%	11.64%	11.89%	12.14%
	Change in cost	23.61%	22.90%	22.22%	21.59%	20.99%	20.42%	19.88%	19.37%	18.89%	18.43%
3.50%	Equal level rate	10.20%	10.45%	10.70%	10.95%	11.20%	11.45%	11.70%	11.95%	12.20%	12.45%
	Change in cost	27.55%	26.71%	25.93%	25.19%	24.49%	23.82%	23.20%	22.60%	22.04%	21.50%
4.00%	Equal level rate	10.52%	10.77%	11.02%	11.27%	11.52%	11.77%	12.02%	12.27%	12.52%	12.77%
	Change in cost	31.48%	30.53%	29.63%	28.78%	27.98%	27.23%	26.51%	25.83%	25.19%	24.57%
4.50%	Equal level rate	10.83%	11.08%	11.33%	11.58%	11.83%	12.08%	12.33%	12.58%	12.83%	13.08%
	Change in cost	35.42%	34.34%	33.33%	32.38%	31.48%	30.63%	29.82%	29.06%	28.33%	27.64%
5.00%	Equal level rate	11.15%	11.40%	11.65%	11.90%	12.15%	12.40%	12.65%	12.90%	13.15%	13.40%
	Change in cost	39.35%	38.16%	37.04%	35.98%	34.98%	34.03%	33.14%	32.29%	31.48%	30.71%

Decrease in rate of		Interest Rate at Start of Loan									
		8.00%	8.25%	8.50%	8.75%	9.00%	9.25%	9.50%	9.75%	10.00%	10.25%
0.50%	Equal level rate	7.69%	7.94%	8.19%	8.44%	8.69%	8.94%	9.19%	9.44%	9.69%	9.94%
	Change in cost	-3.94%	-3.82%	-3.70%	-3.60%	-3.50%	-3.40%	-3.31%	-3.23%	-3.15%	-3.07%
1.00%	Equal level rate	7.37%	7.62%	7.87%	8.12%	8.37%	8.62%	8.87%	9.12%	9.37%	9.62%
	Change in cost	-7.87%	-7.63%	-7.41%	-7.20%	-7.00%	-6.81%	-6.63%	-6.46%	-6.30%	-6.14%
1.25%	Equal level rate	7.21%	7.46%	7.71%	7.96%	8.21%	8.46%	8.71%	8.96%	9.21%	9.46%
	Change in cost	-9.84%	-9.54%	-9.26%	-8.99%	-8.74%	-8.51%	-8.28%	-8.07%	-7.87%	-7.68%
1.50%	Equal level rate	7.06%	7.31%	7.56%	7.81%	8.06%	8.31%	8.56%	8.81%	9.06%	9.31%
	Change in cost	-11.81%	-11.45%	-11.11%	-10.79%	-10.49%	-10.21%	-9.94%	-9.69%	-9.44%	-9.21%
1.75%	Equal level rate	6.90%	7.15%	7.40%	7.65%	7.90%	8.15%	8.40%	8.65%	8.90%	9.15%
	Change in cost	-13.77%	-13.36%	-12.96%	-12.59%	-12.24%	-11.91%	-11.60%	-11.30%	-11.02%	-10.75%
2.00%	Equal level rate	6.74%	6.99%	7.24%	7.49%	7.74%	7.99%	8.24%	8.49%	8.74%	8.99%
	Change in cost	-15.74%	-15.26%	-14.81%	-14.39%	-13.99%	-13.61%	-13.26%	-12.92%	-12.59%	-12.29%
2.50%	Equal level rate	6.43%	6.68%	6.93%	7.18%	7.43%	7.68%	7.93%	8.18%	8.43%	8.68%
	Change in cost	-19.68%	-19.08%	-18.52%	-17.99%	-17.49%	-17.02%	-16.57%	-16.14%	-15.74%	-15.36%
3.00%	Equal level rate	6.11%	6.36%	6.61%	6.86%	7.11%	7.36%	7.61%	7.86%	8.11%	8.36%
	Change in cost	-23.61%	-22.90%	-22.22%	-21.59%	-20.99%	-20.42%	-19.88%	-19.37%	-18.89%	-18.43%
3.50%	Equal level rate	5.80%	6.05%	6.30%	6.55%	6.80%	7.05%	7.30%	7.55%	7.80%	8.05%
	Change in cost	-27.55%	-26.71%	-25.93%	-25.19%	-24.49%	-23.82%	-23.20%	-22.60%	-22.04%	-21.50%
4.00%	Equal level rate	5.48%	5.73%	5.98%	6.23%	6.48%	6.73%	6.98%	7.23%	7.48%	7.73%
	Change in cost	-31.48%	-30.53%	-29.63%	-28.78%	-27.98%	-27.23%	-26.51%	-25.83%	-25.19%	-24.57%
4.50%	Equal level rate	5.17%	5.42%	5.67%	5.92%	6.17%	6.42%	6.67%	6.92%	7.17%	7.42%
	Change in cost	-35.42%	-34.34%	-33.33%	-32.38%	-31.48%	-30.63%	-29.82%	-29.06%	-28.33%	-27.64%
5.00%	Equal level rate	4.85%	5.10%	5.35%	5.60%	5.85%	6.10%	6.35%	6.60%	6.85%	7.10%
	Change in cost	-39.35%	-38.16%	-37.04%	-35.98%	-34.98%	-34.03%	-33.14%	-32.29%	-31.48%	-30.71%

Equal level rate is the single rate that would produce equal interest cost.
Change in cost is percent change from interest if original rate remained in effect.

Effect of Rate Changes on Construction Financing Cost

Term of 18 Months

Increase in rate of		Interest Rate at Start of Loan									
		10.50%	10.75%	11.00%	11.25%	11.50%	11.75%	12.00%	12.25%	12.50%	12.75%
0.50%	Equal level rate	10.81%	11.06%	11.31%	11.56%	11.81%	12.06%	12.31%	12.56%	12.81%	13.06%
	Change in cost	3.00%	2.93%	2.86%	2.80%	2.74%	2.68%	2.62%	2.57%	2.52%	2.47%
1.00%	Equal level rate	11.13%	11.38%	11.63%	11.88%	12.13%	12.38%	12.63%	12.88%	13.13%	13.38%
	Change in cost	6.00%	5.86%	5.72%	5.60%	5.48%	5.36%	5.25%	5.14%	5.04%	4.94%
1.25%	Equal level rate	11.29%	11.54%	11.79%	12.04%	12.29%	12.54%	12.79%	13.04%	13.29%	13.54%
	Change in cost	7.50%	7.32%	7.15%	7.00%	6.84%	6.70%	6.56%	6.42%	6.30%	6.17%
1.50%	Equal level rate	11.44%	11.69%	11.94%	12.19%	12.44%	12.69%	12.94%	13.19%	13.44%	13.69%
	Change in cost	8.99%	8.79%	8.59%	8.40%	8.21%	8.04%	7.87%	7.71%	7.56%	7.41%
1.75%	Equal level rate	11.60%	11.85%	12.10%	12.35%	12.60%	12.85%	13.10%	13.35%	13.60%	13.85%
	Change in cost	10.49%	10.25%	10.02%	9.79%	9.58%	9.38%	9.18%	8.99%	8.81%	8.64%
2.00%	Equal level rate	11.76%	12.01%	12.26%	12.51%	12.76%	13.01%	13.26%	13.51%	13.76%	14.01%
	Change in cost	11.99%	11.71%	11.45%	11.19%	10.95%	10.72%	10.49%	10.28%	10.07%	9.88%
2.50%	Equal level rate	12.07%	12.32%	12.57%	12.82%	13.07%	13.32%	13.57%	13.82%	14.07%	14.32%
	Change in cost	14.99%	14.64%	14.31%	13.99%	13.69%	13.40%	13.12%	12.85%	12.59%	12.35%
3.00%	Equal level rate	12.39%	12.64%	12.89%	13.14%	13.39%	13.64%	13.89%	14.14%	14.39%	14.64%
	Change in cost	17.99%	17.57%	17.17%	16.79%	16.43%	16.08%	15.74%	15.42%	15.11%	14.81%
3.50%	Equal level rate	12.70%	12.95%	13.20%	13.45%	13.70%	13.95%	14.20%	14.45%	14.70%	14.95%
	Change in cost	20.99%	20.50%	20.03%	19.59%	19.16%	18.75%	18.36%	17.99%	17.63%	17.28%
4.00%	Equal level rate	13.02%	13.27%	13.52%	13.77%	14.02%	14.27%	14.52%	14.77%	15.02%	15.27%
	Change in cost	23.99%	23.43%	22.90%	22.39%	21.90%	21.43%	20.99%	20.56%	20.15%	19.75%
4.50%	Equal level rate	13.33%	13.58%	13.83%	14.08%	14.33%	14.58%	14.83%	15.08%	15.33%	15.58%
	Change in cost	26.98%	26.36%	25.76%	25.19%	24.64%	24.11%	23.61%	23.13%	22.67%	22.22%
5.00%	Equal level rate	13.65%	13.90%	14.15%	14.40%	14.65%	14.90%	15.15%	15.40%	15.65%	15.90%
	Change in cost	29.98%	29.29%	28.62%	27.98%	27.38%	26.79%	26.23%	25.70%	25.19%	24.69%

Decrease in rate of		Interest Rate at Start of Loan									
		10.50%	10.75%	11.00%	11.25%	11.50%	11.75%	12.00%	12.25%	12.50%	12.75%
0.50%	Equal level rate	10.19%	10.44%	10.69%	10.94%	11.19%	11.44%	11.69%	11.94%	12.19%	12.44%
	Change in cost	-3.00%	-2.93%	-2.86%	-2.80%	-2.74%	-2.68%	-2.62%	-2.57%	-2.52%	-2.47%
1.00%	Equal level rate	9.87%	10.12%	10.37%	10.62%	10.87%	11.12%	11.37%	11.62%	11.87%	12.12%
	Change in cost	-6.00%	-5.86%	-5.72%	-5.60%	-5.48%	-5.36%	-5.25%	-5.14%	-5.04%	-4.94%
1.25%	Equal level rate	9.71%	9.96%	10.21%	10.46%	10.71%	10.96%	11.21%	11.46%	11.71%	11.96%
	Change in cost	-7.50%	-7.32%	-7.15%	-7.00%	-6.84%	-6.70%	-6.56%	-6.42%	-6.30%	-6.17%
1.50%	Equal level rate	9.56%	9.81%	10.06%	10.31%	10.56%	10.81%	11.06%	11.31%	11.56%	11.81%
	Change in cost	-8.99%	-8.79%	-8.59%	-8.40%	-8.21%	-8.04%	-7.87%	-7.71%	-7.56%	-7.41%
1.75%	Equal level rate	9.40%	9.65%	9.90%	10.15%	10.40%	10.65%	10.90%	11.15%	11.40%	11.65%
	Change in cost	-10.49%	-10.25%	-10.02%	-9.79%	-9.58%	-9.38%	-9.18%	-8.99%	-8.81%	-8.64%
2.00%	Equal level rate	9.24%	9.49%	9.74%	9.99%	10.24%	10.49%	10.74%	10.99%	11.24%	11.49%
	Change in cost	-11.99%	-11.71%	-11.45%	-11.19%	-10.95%	-10.72%	-10.49%	-10.28%	-10.07%	-9.88%
2.50%	Equal level rate	8.93%	9.18%	9.43%	9.68%	9.93%	10.18%	10.43%	10.68%	10.93%	11.18%
	Change in cost	-14.99%	-14.64%	-14.31%	-13.99%	-13.69%	-13.40%	-13.12%	-12.85%	-12.59%	-12.35%
3.00%	Equal level rate	8.61%	8.86%	9.11%	9.36%	9.61%	9.86%	10.11%	10.36%	10.61%	10.86%
	Change in cost	-17.99%	-17.57%	-17.17%	-16.79%	-16.43%	-16.08%	-15.74%	-15.42%	-15.11%	-14.81%
3.50%	Equal level rate	8.30%	8.55%	8.80%	9.05%	9.30%	9.55%	9.80%	10.05%	10.30%	10.55%
	Change in cost	-20.99%	-20.50%	-20.03%	-19.59%	-19.16%	-18.75%	-18.36%	-17.99%	-17.63%	-17.28%
4.00%	Equal level rate	7.98%	8.23%	8.48%	8.73%	8.98%	9.23%	9.48%	9.73%	9.98%	10.23%
	Change in cost	-23.99%	-23.43%	-22.90%	-22.39%	-21.90%	-21.43%	-20.99%	-20.56%	-20.15%	-19.75%
4.50%	Equal level rate	7.67%	7.92%	8.17%	8.42%	8.67%	8.92%	9.17%	9.42%	9.67%	9.92%
	Change in cost	-26.98%	-26.36%	-25.76%	-25.19%	-24.64%	-24.11%	-23.61%	-23.13%	-22.67%	-22.22%
5.00%	Equal level rate	7.35%	7.60%	7.85%	8.10%	8.35%	8.60%	8.85%	9.10%	9.35%	9.60%
	Change in cost	-29.98%	-29.29%	-28.62%	-27.98%	-27.38%	-26.79%	-26.23%	-25.70%	-25.19%	-24.69%

Equal level rate is the single rate that would produce equal interest cost.
Change in cost is percent change from interest if original rate remained in effect.

Effect of Rate Changes on Construction Financing Cost

Term of 24 Months

Increase in rate of		Interest Rate at Start of Loan									
		5.50%	5.75%	6.00%	6.25%	6.50%	6.75%	7.00%	7.25%	7.50%	7.75%
0.50%	Equal level rate	5.82%	6.07%	6.32%	6.57%	6.82%	7.07%	7.32%	7.57%	7.82%	8.07%
	Change in cost	5.81%	5.56%	5.32%	5.11%	4.91%	4.73%	4.56%	4.41%	4.26%	4.12%
1.00%	Equal level rate	6.14%	6.39%	6.64%	6.89%	7.14%	7.39%	7.64%	7.89%	8.14%	8.39%
	Change in cost	11.62%	11.11%	10.65%	10.22%	9.83%	9.47%	9.13%	8.81%	8.52%	8.24%
1.25%	Equal level rate	6.30%	6.55%	6.80%	7.05%	7.30%	7.55%	7.80%	8.05%	8.30%	8.55%
	Change in cost	14.52%	13.89%	13.31%	12.78%	12.29%	11.83%	11.41%	11.02%	10.65%	10.30%
1.50%	Equal level rate	6.46%	6.71%	6.96%	7.21%	7.46%	7.71%	7.96%	8.21%	8.46%	8.71%
	Change in cost	17.42%	16.67%	15.97%	15.33%	14.74%	14.20%	13.69%	13.22%	12.78%	12.37%
1.75%	Equal level rate	6.62%	6.87%	7.12%	7.37%	7.62%	7.87%	8.12%	8.37%	8.62%	8.87%
	Change in cost	20.33%	19.44%	18.63%	17.89%	17.20%	16.56%	15.97%	15.42%	14.91%	14.43%
2.00%	Equal level rate	6.78%	7.03%	7.28%	7.53%	7.78%	8.03%	8.28%	8.53%	8.78%	9.03%
	Change in cost	23.23%	22.22%	21.30%	20.44%	19.66%	18.93%	18.25%	17.62%	17.04%	16.49%
2.50%	Equal level rate	7.10%	7.35%	7.60%	7.85%	8.10%	8.35%	8.60%	8.85%	9.10%	9.35%
	Change in cost	29.04%	27.78%	26.62%	25.56%	24.57%	23.66%	22.82%	22.03%	21.30%	20.61%
3.00%	Equal level rate	7.42%	7.67%	7.92%	8.17%	8.42%	8.67%	8.92%	9.17%	9.42%	9.67%
	Change in cost	34.85%	33.33%	31.94%	30.67%	29.49%	28.40%	27.38%	26.44%	25.56%	24.73%
3.50%	Equal level rate	7.74%	7.99%	8.24%	8.49%	8.74%	8.99%	9.24%	9.49%	9.74%	9.99%
	Change in cost	40.66%	38.89%	37.27%	35.78%	34.40%	33.13%	31.94%	30.84%	29.81%	28.85%
4.00%	Equal level rate	8.06%	8.31%	8.56%	8.81%	9.06%	9.31%	9.56%	9.81%	10.06%	10.31%
	Change in cost	46.46%	44.44%	42.59%	40.89%	39.32%	37.86%	36.51%	35.25%	34.07%	32.97%
4.50%	Equal level rate	8.37%	8.63%	8.88%	9.13%	9.38%	9.62%	9.88%	10.13%	10.38%	10.63%
	Change in cost	52.27%	50.00%	47.92%	46.00%	44.23%	42.59%	41.07%	39.66%	38.33%	37.10%
5.00%	Equal level rate	8.69%	8.94%	9.19%	9.44%	9.69%	9.94%	10.19%	10.44%	10.69%	10.94%
	Change in cost	58.08%	55.56%	53.24%	51.11%	49.15%	47.33%	45.63%	44.06%	42.59%	41.22%

Decrease in rate of		Interest Rate at Start of Loan									
		5.50%	5.75%	6.00%	6.25%	6.50%	6.75%	7.00%	7.25%	7.50%	7.75%
0.50%	Equal level rate	5.18%	5.43%	5.68%	5.93%	6.18%	6.43%	6.68%	6.93%	7.18%	7.43%
	Change in cost	-5.81%	-5.56%	-5.32%	-5.11%	-4.91%	-4.73%	-4.56%	-4.41%	-4.26%	-4.12%
1.00%	Equal level rate	4.86%	5.11%	5.36%	5.61%	5.86%	6.11%	6.36%	6.61%	6.86%	7.11%
	Change in cost	-11.62%	-11.11%	-10.65%	-10.22%	-9.83%	-9.47%	-9.13%	-8.81%	-8.52%	-8.24%
1.25%	Equal level rate	4.70%	4.95%	5.20%	5.45%	5.70%	5.95%	6.20%	6.45%	6.70%	6.95%
	Change in cost	-14.52%	-13.89%	-13.31%	-12.78%	-12.29%	-11.83%	-11.41%	-11.02%	-10.65%	-10.30%
1.50%	Equal level rate	4.54%	4.79%	5.04%	5.29%	5.54%	5.79%	6.04%	6.29%	6.54%	6.79%
	Change in cost	-17.42%	-16.67%	-15.97%	-15.33%	-14.74%	-14.20%	-13.69%	-13.22%	-12.78%	-12.37%
1.75%	Equal level rate	4.38%	4.63%	4.88%	5.13%	5.38%	5.63%	5.88%	6.13%	6.38%	6.63%
	Change in cost	-20.33%	-19.44%	-18.63%	-17.89%	-17.20%	-16.56%	-15.97%	-15.42%	-14.91%	-14.43%
2.00%	Equal level rate	4.22%	4.47%	4.72%	4.97%	5.22%	5.47%	5.72%	5.97%	6.22%	6.47%
	Change in cost	-23.23%	-22.22%	-21.30%	-20.44%	-19.66%	-18.93%	-18.25%	-17.62%	-17.04%	-16.49%
2.50%	Equal level rate	3.90%	4.15%	4.40%	4.65%	4.90%	5.15%	5.40%	5.65%	5.90%	6.15%
	Change in cost	-29.04%	-27.78%	-26.62%	-25.56%	-24.57%	-23.66%	-22.82%	-22.03%	-21.30%	-20.61%
3.00%	Equal level rate	3.58%	3.83%	4.08%	4.33%	4.58%	4.83%	5.08%	5.33%	5.58%	5.83%
	Change in cost	-34.85%	-33.33%	-31.94%	-30.67%	-29.49%	-28.40%	-27.38%	-26.44%	-25.56%	-24.73%
3.50%	Equal level rate	3.26%	3.51%	3.76%	4.01%	4.26%	4.51%	4.76%	5.01%	5.26%	5.51%
	Change in cost	-40.66%	-38.89%	-37.27%	-35.78%	-34.40%	-33.13%	-31.94%	-30.84%	-29.81%	-28.85%
4.00%	Equal level rate	2.94%	3.19%	3.44%	3.69%	3.94%	4.19%	4.44%	4.69%	4.94%	5.19%
	Change in cost	-46.46%	-44.44%	-42.59%	-40.89%	-39.32%	-37.86%	-36.51%	-35.25%	-34.07%	-32.97%
4.50%	Equal level rate	2.62%	2.87%	3.12%	3.37%	3.63%	3.87%	4.13%	4.38%	4.63%	4.87%
	Change in cost	-52.27%	-50.00%	-47.92%	-46.00%	-44.23%	-42.59%	-41.07%	-39.66%	-38.33%	-37.10%
5.00%	Equal level rate	2.31%	2.56%	2.81%	3.06%	3.31%	3.56%	3.81%	4.06%	4.31%	4.56%
	Change in cost	-58.08%	-55.56%	-53.24%	-51.11%	-49.15%	-47.33%	-45.63%	-44.06%	-42.59%	-41.22%

Equal level rate is the single rate that would produce equal interest cost.
Change in cost is percent change from interest if original rate remained in effect.

Effect of Rate Changes on Construction Financing Cost

Term of 24 Months

Increase in rate of		Interest Rate at Start of Loan									
		8.00%	8.25%	8.50%	8.75%	9.00%	9.25%	9.50%	9.75%	10.00%	10.25%
0.50%	Equal level rate	8.32%	8.57%	8.82%	9.07%	9.32%	9.57%	9.82%	10.07%	10.32%	10.57%
	Change in cost	3.99%	3.87%	3.76%	3.65%	3.55%	3.45%	3.36%	3.28%	3.19%	3.12%
1.00%	Equal level rate	8.64%	8.89%	9.14%	9.39%	9.64%	9.89%	10.14%	10.39%	10.64%	10.89%
	Change in cost	7.99%	7.74%	7.52%	7.30%	7.10%	6.91%	6.73%	6.55%	6.39%	6.23%
1.25%	Equal level rate	8.80%	9.05%	9.30%	9.55%	9.80%	10.05%	10.30%	10.55%	10.80%	11.05%
	Change in cost	9.98%	9.68%	9.40%	9.13%	8.87%	8.63%	8.41%	8.19%	7.99%	7.79%
1.50%	Equal level rate	8.96%	9.21%	9.46%	9.71%	9.96%	10.21%	10.46%	10.71%	10.96%	11.21%
	Change in cost	11.98%	11.62%	11.27%	10.95%	10.65%	10.36%	10.09%	9.83%	9.58%	9.35%
1.75%	Equal level rate	9.12%	9.37%	9.62%	9.87%	10.12%	10.37%	10.62%	10.87%	11.12%	11.37%
	Change in cost	13.98%	13.55%	13.15%	12.78%	12.42%	12.09%	11.77%	11.47%	11.18%	10.91%
2.00%	Equal level rate	9.28%	9.53%	9.78%	10.03%	10.28%	10.53%	10.78%	11.03%	11.28%	11.53%
	Change in cost	15.97%	15.49%	15.03%	14.60%	14.20%	13.81%	13.45%	13.11%	12.78%	12.47%
2.50%	Equal level rate	9.60%	9.85%	10.10%	10.35%	10.60%	10.85%	11.10%	11.35%	11.60%	11.85%
	Change in cost	19.97%	19.36%	18.79%	18.25%	17.75%	17.27%	16.81%	16.38%	15.97%	15.58%
3.00%	Equal level rate	9.92%	10.17%	10.42%	10.67%	10.92%	11.17%	11.42%	11.67%	11.92%	12.17%
	Change in cost	23.96%	23.23%	22.55%	21.90%	21.30%	20.72%	20.18%	19.66%	19.17%	18.70%
3.50%	Equal level rate	10.24%	10.49%	10.74%	10.99%	11.24%	11.49%	11.74%	11.99%	12.24%	12.49%
	Change in cost	27.95%	27.10%	26.31%	25.56%	24.85%	24.17%	23.54%	22.93%	22.36%	21.82%
4.00%	Equal level rate	10.56%	10.81%	11.06%	11.31%	11.56%	11.81%	12.06%	12.31%	12.56%	12.81%
	Change in cost	31.94%	30.98%	30.07%	29.21%	28.40%	27.63%	26.90%	26.21%	25.56%	24.93%
4.50%	Equal level rate	10.87%	11.13%	11.37%	11.63%	11.88%	12.13%	12.37%	12.62%	12.88%	13.12%
	Change in cost	35.94%	34.85%	33.82%	32.86%	31.94%	31.08%	30.26%	29.49%	28.75%	28.05%
5.00%	Equal level rate	11.19%	11.44%	11.69%	11.94%	12.19%	12.44%	12.69%	12.94%	13.19%	13.44%
	Change in cost	39.93%	38.72%	37.58%	36.51%	35.49%	34.53%	33.63%	32.76%	31.94%	31.17%

Decrease in rate of		Interest Rate at Start of Loan									
		8.00%	8.25%	8.50%	8.75%	9.00%	9.25%	9.50%	9.75%	10.00%	10.25%
0.50%	Equal level rate	7.68%	7.93%	8.18%	8.43%	8.68%	8.93%	9.18%	9.43%	9.68%	9.93%
	Change in cost	-3.99%	-3.87%	-3.76%	-3.65%	-3.55%	-3.45%	-3.36%	-3.28%	-3.19%	-3.12%
1.00%	Equal level rate	7.36%	7.61%	7.86%	8.11%	8.36%	8.61%	8.86%	9.11%	9.36%	9.61%
	Change in cost	-7.99%	-7.74%	-7.52%	-7.30%	-7.10%	-6.91%	-6.73%	-6.55%	-6.39%	-6.23%
1.25%	Equal level rate	7.20%	7.45%	7.70%	7.95%	8.20%	8.45%	8.70%	8.95%	9.20%	9.45%
	Change in cost	-9.98%	-9.68%	-9.40%	-9.13%	-8.87%	-8.63%	-8.41%	-8.19%	-7.99%	-7.79%
1.50%	Equal level rate	7.04%	7.29%	7.54%	7.79%	8.04%	8.29%	8.54%	8.79%	9.04%	9.29%
	Change in cost	-11.98%	-11.62%	-11.27%	-10.95%	-10.65%	-10.36%	-10.09%	-9.83%	-9.58%	-9.35%
1.75%	Equal level rate	6.88%	7.13%	7.38%	7.63%	7.88%	8.13%	8.38%	8.63%	8.88%	9.13%
	Change in cost	-13.98%	-13.55%	-13.15%	-12.78%	-12.42%	-12.09%	-11.77%	-11.47%	-11.18%	-10.91%
2.00%	Equal level rate	6.72%	6.97%	7.22%	7.47%	7.72%	7.97%	8.22%	8.47%	8.72%	8.97%
	Change in cost	-15.97%	-15.49%	-15.03%	-14.60%	-14.20%	-13.81%	-13.45%	-13.11%	-12.78%	-12.47%
2.50%	Equal level rate	6.40%	6.65%	6.90%	7.15%	7.40%	7.65%	7.90%	8.15%	8.40%	8.65%
	Change in cost	-19.97%	-19.36%	-18.79%	-18.25%	-17.75%	-17.27%	-16.81%	-16.38%	-15.97%	-15.58%
3.00%	Equal level rate	6.08%	6.33%	6.58%	6.83%	7.08%	7.33%	7.58%	7.83%	8.08%	8.33%
	Change in cost	-23.96%	-23.23%	-22.55%	-21.90%	-21.30%	-20.72%	-20.18%	-19.66%	-19.17%	-18.70%
3.50%	Equal level rate	5.76%	6.01%	6.26%	6.51%	6.76%	7.01%	7.26%	7.51%	7.76%	8.01%
	Change in cost	-27.95%	-27.10%	-26.31%	-25.56%	-24.85%	-24.17%	-23.54%	-22.93%	-22.36%	-21.82%
4.00%	Equal level rate	5.44%	5.69%	5.94%	6.19%	6.44%	6.69%	6.94%	7.19%	7.44%	7.69%
	Change in cost	-31.94%	-30.98%	-30.07%	-29.21%	-28.40%	-27.63%	-26.90%	-26.21%	-25.56%	-24.93%
4.50%	Equal level rate	5.13%	5.38%	5.62%	5.88%	6.13%	6.37%	6.62%	6.88%	7.12%	7.38%
	Change in cost	-35.94%	-34.85%	-33.82%	-32.86%	-31.94%	-31.08%	-30.26%	-29.49%	-28.75%	-28.05%
5.00%	Equal level rate	4.81%	5.06%	5.31%	5.56%	5.81%	6.06%	6.31%	6.56%	6.81%	7.06%
	Change in cost	-39.93%	-38.72%	-37.58%	-36.51%	-35.49%	-34.53%	-33.63%	-32.76%	-31.94%	-31.17%

Equal level rate is the single rate that would produce equal interest cost.
Change in cost is percent change from interest if original rate remained in effect.

Effect of Rate Changes on Construction Financing Cost

Term of 24 Months

Increase

Increase in rate of		Interest Rate at Start of Loan									
		10.50%	10.75%	11.00%	11.25%	11.50%	11.75%	12.00%	12.25%	12.50%	12.75%
0.50%	Equal level rate	10.82%	11.07%	11.32%	11.57%	11.82%	12.07%	12.32%	12.57%	12.82%	13.07%
	Change in cost	3.04%	2.97%	2.90%	2.84%	2.78%	2.72%	2.66%	2.61%	2.56%	2.51%
1.00%	Equal level rate	11.14%	11.39%	11.64%	11.89%	12.14%	12.39%	12.64%	12.89%	13.14%	13.39%
	Change in cost	6.08%	5.94%	5.81%	5.68%	5.56%	5.44%	5.32%	5.22%	5.11%	5.01%
1.25%	Equal level rate	11.30%	11.55%	11.80%	12.05%	12.30%	12.55%	12.80%	13.05%	13.30%	13.55%
	Change in cost	7.61%	7.43%	7.26%	7.10%	6.94%	6.80%	6.66%	6.52%	6.39%	6.26%
1.50%	Equal level rate	11.46%	11.71%	11.96%	12.21%	12.46%	12.71%	12.96%	13.21%	13.46%	13.71%
	Change in cost	9.13%	8.91%	8.71%	8.52%	8.33%	8.16%	7.99%	7.82%	7.67%	7.52%
1.75%	Equal level rate	11.62%	11.87%	12.12%	12.37%	12.62%	12.87%	13.12%	13.37%	13.62%	13.87%
	Change in cost	10.65%	10.40%	10.16%	9.94%	9.72%	9.52%	9.32%	9.13%	8.94%	8.77%
2.00%	Equal level rate	11.78%	12.03%	12.28%	12.53%	12.78%	13.03%	13.28%	13.53%	13.78%	14.03%
	Change in cost	12.17%	11.89%	11.62%	11.36%	11.11%	10.87%	10.65%	10.43%	10.22%	10.02%
2.50%	Equal level rate	12.10%	12.35%	12.60%	12.85%	13.10%	13.35%	13.60%	13.85%	14.10%	14.35%
	Change in cost	15.21%	14.86%	14.52%	14.20%	13.89%	13.59%	13.31%	13.04%	12.78%	12.53%
3.00%	Equal level rate	12.42%	12.67%	12.92%	13.17%	13.42%	13.67%	13.92%	14.17%	14.42%	14.67%
	Change in cost	18.25%	17.83%	17.42%	17.04%	16.67%	16.31%	15.97%	15.65%	15.33%	15.03%
3.50%	Equal level rate	12.74%	12.99%	13.24%	13.49%	13.74%	13.99%	14.24%	14.49%	14.74%	14.99%
	Change in cost	21.30%	20.80%	20.33%	19.88%	19.44%	19.03%	18.63%	18.25%	17.89%	17.54%
4.00%	Equal level rate	13.06%	13.31%	13.56%	13.81%	14.06%	14.31%	14.56%	14.81%	15.06%	15.31%
	Change in cost	24.34%	23.77%	23.23%	22.72%	22.22%	21.75%	21.30%	20.86%	20.44%	20.04%
4.50%	Equal level rate	13.38%	13.63%	13.88%	14.13%	14.38%	14.63%	14.88%	15.13%	15.37%	15.63%
	Change in cost	27.38%	26.74%	26.14%	25.56%	25.00%	24.47%	23.96%	23.47%	23.00%	22.55%
5.00%	Equal level rate	13.69%	13.94%	14.19%	14.44%	14.69%	14.94%	15.19%	15.44%	15.69%	15.94%
	Change in cost	30.42%	29.72%	29.04%	28.40%	27.78%	27.19%	26.62%	26.08%	25.56%	25.05%

Decrease

Decrease in rate of		Interest Rate at Start of Loan									
		10.50%	10.75%	11.00%	11.25%	11.50%	11.75%	12.00%	12.25%	12.50%	12.75%
0.50%	Equal level rate	10.18%	10.43%	10.68%	10.93%	11.18%	11.43%	11.68%	11.93%	12.18%	12.43%
	Change in cost	-3.04%	-2.97%	-2.90%	-2.84%	-2.78%	-2.72%	-2.66%	-2.61%	-2.56%	-2.51%
1.00%	Equal level rate	9.86%	10.11%	10.36%	10.61%	10.86%	11.11%	11.36%	11.61%	11.86%	12.11%
	Change in cost	-6.08%	-5.94%	-5.81%	-5.68%	-5.56%	-5.44%	-5.32%	-5.22%	-5.11%	-5.01%
1.25%	Equal level rate	9.70%	9.95%	10.20%	10.45%	10.70%	10.95%	11.20%	11.45%	11.70%	11.95%
	Change in cost	-7.61%	-7.43%	-7.26%	-7.10%	-6.94%	-6.80%	-6.66%	-6.52%	-6.39%	-6.26%
1.50%	Equal level rate	9.54%	9.79%	10.04%	10.29%	10.54%	10.79%	11.04%	11.29%	11.54%	11.79%
	Change in cost	-9.13%	-8.91%	-8.71%	-8.52%	-8.33%	-8.16%	-7.99%	-7.82%	-7.67%	-7.52%
1.75%	Equal level rate	9.38%	9.63%	9.88%	10.13%	10.38%	10.63%	10.88%	11.13%	11.38%	11.63%
	Change in cost	-10.65%	-10.40%	-10.16%	-9.94%	-9.72%	-9.52%	-9.32%	-9.13%	-8.94%	-8.77%
2.00%	Equal level rate	9.22%	9.47%	9.72%	9.97%	10.22%	10.47%	10.72%	10.97%	11.22%	11.47%
	Change in cost	-12.17%	-11.89%	-11.62%	-11.36%	-11.11%	-10.87%	-10.65%	-10.43%	-10.22%	-10.02%
2.50%	Equal level rate	8.90%	9.15%	9.40%	9.65%	9.90%	10.15%	10.40%	10.65%	10.90%	11.15%
	Change in cost	-15.21%	-14.86%	-14.52%	-14.20%	-13.89%	-13.59%	-13.31%	-13.04%	-12.78%	-12.53%
3.00%	Equal level rate	8.58%	8.83%	9.08%	9.33%	9.58%	9.83%	10.08%	10.33%	10.58%	10.83%
	Change in cost	-18.25%	-17.83%	-17.42%	-17.04%	-16.67%	-16.31%	-15.97%	-15.65%	-15.33%	-15.03%
3.50%	Equal level rate	8.26%	8.51%	8.76%	9.01%	9.26%	9.51%	9.76%	10.01%	10.26%	10.51%
	Change in cost	-21.30%	-20.80%	-20.33%	-19.88%	-19.44%	-19.03%	-18.63%	-18.25%	-17.89%	-17.54%
4.00%	Equal level rate	7.94%	8.19%	8.44%	8.69%	8.94%	9.19%	9.44%	9.69%	9.94%	10.19%
	Change in cost	-24.34%	-23.77%	-23.23%	-22.72%	-22.22%	-21.75%	-21.30%	-20.86%	-20.44%	-20.04%
4.50%	Equal level rate	7.63%	7.87%	8.13%	8.38%	8.63%	8.88%	9.13%	9.37%	9.63%	9.87%
	Change in cost	-27.38%	-26.74%	-26.14%	-25.56%	-25.00%	-24.47%	-23.96%	-23.47%	-23.00%	-22.55%
5.00%	Equal level rate	7.31%	7.56%	7.81%	8.06%	8.31%	8.56%	8.81%	9.06%	9.31%	9.56%
	Change in cost	-30.42%	-29.72%	-29.04%	-28.40%	-27.78%	-27.19%	-26.62%	-26.08%	-25.56%	-25.05%

Equal level rate is the single rate that would produce equal interest cost.
Change in cost is percent change from interest if original rate remained in effect.

Effect of Rate Changes on Construction Financing Cost

Term of 36 Months

Increase in rate of		5.50%	5.75%	6.00%	6.25%	6.50%	6.75%	7.00%	7.25%	7.50%	7.75%
					Interest Rate at Start of Loan						
0.50%	Equal level rate	5.82%	6.07%	6.32%	6.57%	6.82%	7.07%	7.32%	7.57%	7.82%	8.07%
	Change in cost	5.89%	5.64%	5.40%	5.19%	4.99%	4.80%	4.63%	4.47%	4.32%	4.18%
1.00%	Equal level rate	6.15%	6.40%	6.65%	6.90%	7.15%	7.40%	7.65%	7.90%	8.15%	8.40%
	Change in cost	11.78%	11.27%	10.80%	10.37%	9.97%	9.60%	9.26%	8.94%	8.64%	8.36%
1.25%	Equal level rate	6.31%	6.56%	6.81%	7.06%	7.31%	7.56%	7.81%	8.06%	8.31%	8.56%
	Change in cost	14.73%	14.09%	13.50%	12.96%	12.46%	12.00%	11.57%	11.17%	10.80%	10.45%
1.50%	Equal level rate	6.47%	6.72%	6.97%	7.22%	7.47%	7.72%	7.97%	8.22%	8.47%	8.72%
	Change in cost	17.68%	16.91%	16.20%	15.56%	14.96%	14.40%	13.89%	13.41%	12.96%	12.54%
1.75%	Equal level rate	6.63%	6.88%	7.13%	7.38%	7.63%	7.88%	8.13%	8.38%	8.63%	8.88%
	Change in cost	20.62%	19.73%	18.90%	18.15%	17.45%	16.80%	16.20%	15.64%	15.12%	14.64%
2.00%	Equal level rate	6.80%	7.05%	7.30%	7.55%	7.80%	8.05%	8.30%	8.55%	8.80%	9.05%
	Change in cost	23.57%	22.54%	21.60%	20.74%	19.94%	19.20%	18.52%	17.88%	17.28%	16.73%
2.50%	Equal level rate	7.12%	7.37%	7.62%	7.87%	8.12%	8.37%	8.62%	8.87%	9.12%	9.37%
	Change in cost	29.46%	28.18%	27.01%	25.93%	24.93%	24.01%	23.15%	22.35%	21.60%	20.91%
3.00%	Equal level rate	7.44%	7.69%	7.94%	8.19%	8.44%	8.69%	8.94%	9.19%	9.44%	9.69%
	Change in cost	35.35%	33.82%	32.41%	31.11%	29.91%	28.81%	27.78%	26.82%	25.93%	25.09%
3.50%	Equal level rate	7.77%	8.02%	8.27%	8.52%	8.77%	9.02%	9.27%	9.52%	9.77%	10.02%
	Change in cost	41.25%	39.45%	37.81%	36.30%	34.90%	33.61%	32.41%	31.29%	30.25%	29.27%
4.00%	Equal level rate	8.09%	8.34%	8.59%	8.84%	9.09%	9.34%	9.59%	9.84%	10.09%	10.34%
	Change in cost	47.14%	45.09%	43.21%	41.48%	39.89%	38.41%	37.04%	35.76%	34.57%	33.45%
4.50%	Equal level rate	8.42%	8.67%	8.92%	9.17%	9.42%	9.67%	9.92%	10.17%	10.42%	10.67%
	Change in cost	53.03%	50.72%	48.61%	46.67%	44.87%	43.21%	41.67%	40.23%	38.89%	37.63%
5.00%	Equal level rate	8.74%	8.99%	9.24%	9.49%	9.74%	9.99%	10.24%	10.49%	10.74%	10.99%
	Change in cost	58.92%	56.36%	54.01%	51.85%	49.86%	48.01%	46.30%	44.70%	43.21%	41.82%

Decrease in rate of		5.50%	5.75%	6.00%	6.25%	6.50%	6.75%	7.00%	7.25%	7.50%	7.75%
					Interest Rate at Start of Loan						
0.50%	Equal level rate	5.18%	5.43%	5.68%	5.93%	6.18%	6.43%	6.68%	6.93%	7.18%	7.43%
	Change in cost	-5.89%	-5.64%	-5.40%	-5.19%	-4.99%	-4.80%	-4.63%	-4.47%	-4.32%	-4.18%
1.00%	Equal level rate	4.85%	5.10%	5.35%	5.60%	5.85%	6.10%	6.35%	6.60%	6.85%	7.10%
	Change in cost	-11.78%	-11.27%	-10.80%	-10.37%	-9.97%	-9.60%	-9.26%	-8.94%	-8.64%	-8.36%
1.25%	Equal level rate	4.69%	4.94%	5.19%	5.44%	5.69%	5.94%	6.19%	6.44%	6.69%	6.94%
	Change in cost	-14.73%	-14.09%	-13.50%	-12.96%	-12.46%	-12.00%	-11.57%	-11.17%	-10.80%	-10.45%
1.50%	Equal level rate	4.53%	4.78%	5.03%	5.28%	5.53%	5.78%	6.03%	6.28%	6.53%	6.78%
	Change in cost	-17.68%	-16.91%	-16.20%	-15.56%	-14.96%	-14.40%	-13.89%	-13.41%	-12.96%	-12.54%
1.75%	Equal level rate	4.37%	4.62%	4.87%	5.12%	5.37%	5.62%	5.87%	6.12%	6.37%	6.62%
	Change in cost	-20.62%	-19.73%	-18.90%	-18.15%	-17.45%	-16.80%	-16.20%	-15.64%	-15.12%	-14.64%
2.00%	Equal level rate	4.20%	4.45%	4.70%	4.95%	5.20%	5.45%	5.70%	5.95%	6.20%	6.45%
	Change in cost	-23.57%	-22.54%	-21.60%	-20.74%	-19.94%	-19.20%	-18.52%	-17.88%	-17.28%	-16.73%
2.50%	Equal level rate	3.88%	4.13%	4.38%	4.63%	4.88%	5.13%	5.38%	5.63%	5.88%	6.13%
	Change in cost	-29.46%	-28.18%	-27.01%	-25.93%	-24.93%	-24.01%	-23.15%	-22.35%	-21.60%	-20.91%
3.00%	Equal level rate	3.56%	3.81%	4.06%	4.31%	4.56%	4.81%	5.06%	5.31%	5.56%	5.81%
	Change in cost	-35.35%	-33.82%	-32.41%	-31.11%	-29.91%	-28.81%	-27.78%	-26.82%	-25.93%	-25.09%
3.50%	Equal level rate	3.23%	3.48%	3.73%	3.98%	4.23%	4.48%	4.73%	4.98%	5.23%	5.48%
	Change in cost	-41.25%	-39.45%	-37.81%	-36.30%	-34.90%	-33.61%	-32.41%	-31.29%	-30.25%	-29.27%
4.00%	Equal level rate	2.91%	3.16%	3.41%	3.66%	3.91%	4.16%	4.41%	4.66%	4.91%	5.16%
	Change in cost	-47.14%	-45.09%	-43.21%	-41.48%	-39.89%	-38.41%	-37.04%	-35.76%	-34.57%	-33.45%
4.50%	Equal level rate	2.58%	2.83%	3.08%	3.33%	3.58%	3.83%	4.08%	4.33%	4.58%	4.83%
	Change in cost	-53.03%	-50.72%	-48.61%	-46.67%	-44.87%	-43.21%	-41.67%	-40.23%	-38.89%	-37.63%
5.00%	Equal level rate	2.26%	2.51%	2.76%	3.01%	3.26%	3.51%	3.76%	4.01%	4.26%	4.51%
	Change in cost	-58.92%	-56.36%	-54.01%	-51.85%	-49.86%	-48.01%	-46.30%	-44.70%	-43.21%	-41.82%

Equal level rate is the single rate that would produce equal interest cost.
Change in cost is percent change from interest if original rate remained in effect.

Effect of Rate Changes on Construction Financing Cost

Term of 36 Months

Increase in rate of		Interest Rate at Start of Loan									
		8.00%	8.25%	8.50%	8.75%	9.00%	9.25%	9.50%	9.75%	10.00%	10.25%
0.50%	Equal level rate	8.32%	8.57%	8.82%	9.07%	9.32%	9.57%	9.82%	10.07%	10.32%	10.57%
	Change in cost	4.05%	3.93%	3.81%	3.70%	3.60%	3.50%	3.41%	3.32%	3.24%	3.16%
1.00%	Equal level rate	8.65%	8.90%	9.15%	9.40%	9.65%	9.90%	10.15%	10.40%	10.65%	10.90%
	Change in cost	8.10%	7.86%	7.63%	7.41%	7.20%	7.01%	6.82%	6.65%	6.48%	6.32%
1.25%	Equal level rate	8.81%	9.06%	9.31%	9.56%	9.81%	10.06%	10.31%	10.56%	10.81%	11.06%
	Change in cost	10.13%	9.82%	9.53%	9.26%	9.00%	8.76%	8.53%	8.31%	8.10%	7.90%
1.50%	Equal level rate	8.97%	9.22%	9.47%	9.72%	9.97%	10.22%	10.47%	10.72%	10.97%	11.22%
	Change in cost	12.15%	11.78%	11.44%	11.11%	10.80%	10.51%	10.23%	9.97%	9.72%	9.49%
1.75%	Equal level rate	9.13%	9.38%	9.63%	9.88%	10.13%	10.38%	10.63%	10.88%	11.13%	11.38%
	Change in cost	14.18%	13.75%	13.34%	12.96%	12.60%	12.26%	11.94%	11.63%	11.34%	11.07%
2.00%	Equal level rate	9.30%	9.55%	9.80%	10.05%	10.30%	10.55%	10.80%	11.05%	11.30%	11.55%
	Change in cost	16.20%	15.71%	15.25%	14.81%	14.40%	14.01%	13.65%	13.30%	12.96%	12.65%
2.50%	Equal level rate	9.62%	9.87%	10.12%	10.37%	10.62%	10.87%	11.12%	11.37%	11.62%	11.87%
	Change in cost	20.25%	19.64%	19.06%	18.52%	18.00%	17.52%	17.06%	16.62%	16.20%	15.81%
3.00%	Equal level rate	9.94%	10.19%	10.44%	10.69%	10.94%	11.19%	11.44%	11.69%	11.94%	12.19%
	Change in cost	24.31%	23.57%	22.88%	22.22%	21.60%	21.02%	20.47%	19.94%	19.44%	18.97%
3.50%	Equal level rate	10.27%	10.52%	10.77%	11.02%	11.27%	11.52%	11.77%	12.02%	12.27%	12.52%
	Change in cost	28.36%	27.50%	26.69%	25.93%	25.21%	24.52%	23.88%	23.27%	22.69%	22.13%
4.00%	Equal level rate	10.59%	10.84%	11.09%	11.34%	11.59%	11.84%	12.09%	12.34%	12.59%	12.84%
	Change in cost	32.41%	31.43%	30.50%	29.63%	28.81%	28.03%	27.29%	26.59%	25.93%	25.29%
4.50%	Equal level rate	10.92%	11.17%	11.42%	11.67%	11.92%	12.17%	12.42%	12.67%	12.92%	13.17%
	Change in cost	36.46%	35.35%	34.31%	33.33%	32.41%	31.53%	30.70%	29.91%	29.17%	28.46%
5.00%	Equal level rate	11.24%	11.49%	11.74%	11.99%	12.24%	12.49%	12.74%	12.99%	13.24%	13.49%
	Change in cost	40.51%	39.28%	38.13%	37.04%	36.01%	35.04%	34.11%	33.24%	32.41%	31.62%

Decrease in rate of		Interest Rate at Start of Loan									
		8.00%	8.25%	8.50%	8.75%	9.00%	9.25%	9.50%	9.75%	10.00%	10.25%
0.50%	Equal level rate	7.68%	7.93%	8.18%	8.43%	8.68%	8.93%	9.18%	9.43%	9.68%	9.93%
	Change in cost	-4.05%	-3.93%	-3.81%	-3.70%	-3.60%	-3.50%	-3.41%	-3.32%	-3.24%	-3.16%
1.00%	Equal level rate	7.35%	7.60%	7.85%	8.10%	8.35%	8.60%	8.85%	9.10%	9.35%	9.60%
	Change in cost	-8.10%	-7.86%	-7.63%	-7.41%	-7.20%	-7.01%	-6.82%	-6.65%	-6.48%	-6.32%
1.25%	Equal level rate	7.19%	7.44%	7.69%	7.94%	8.19%	8.44%	8.69%	8.94%	9.19%	9.44%
	Change in cost	-10.13%	-9.82%	-9.53%	-9.26%	-9.00%	-8.76%	-8.53%	-8.31%	-8.10%	-7.90%
1.50%	Equal level rate	7.03%	7.28%	7.53%	7.78%	8.03%	8.28%	8.53%	8.78%	9.03%	9.28%
	Change in cost	-12.15%	-11.78%	-11.44%	-11.11%	-10.80%	-10.51%	-10.23%	-9.97%	-9.72%	-9.49%
1.75%	Equal level rate	6.87%	7.12%	7.37%	7.62%	7.87%	8.12%	8.37%	8.62%	8.87%	9.12%
	Change in cost	-14.18%	-13.75%	-13.34%	-12.96%	-12.60%	-12.26%	-11.94%	-11.63%	-11.34%	-11.07%
2.00%	Equal level rate	6.70%	6.95%	7.20%	7.45%	7.70%	7.95%	8.20%	8.45%	8.70%	8.95%
	Change in cost	-16.20%	-15.71%	-15.25%	-14.81%	-14.40%	-14.01%	-13.65%	-13.30%	-12.96%	-12.65%
2.50%	Equal level rate	6.38%	6.63%	6.88%	7.13%	7.38%	7.63%	7.88%	8.13%	8.38%	8.63%
	Change in cost	-20.25%	-19.64%	-19.06%	-18.52%	-18.00%	-17.52%	-17.06%	-16.62%	-16.20%	-15.81%
3.00%	Equal level rate	6.06%	6.31%	6.56%	6.81%	7.06%	7.31%	7.56%	7.81%	8.06%	8.31%
	Change in cost	-24.31%	-23.57%	-22.88%	-22.22%	-21.60%	-21.02%	-20.47%	-19.94%	-19.44%	-18.97%
3.50%	Equal level rate	5.73%	5.98%	6.23%	6.48%	6.73%	6.98%	7.23%	7.48%	7.73%	7.98%
	Change in cost	-28.36%	-27.50%	-26.69%	-25.93%	-25.21%	-24.52%	-23.88%	-23.27%	-22.69%	-22.13%
4.00%	Equal level rate	5.41%	5.66%	5.91%	6.16%	6.41%	6.66%	6.91%	7.16%	7.41%	7.66%
	Change in cost	-32.41%	-31.43%	-30.50%	-29.63%	-28.81%	-28.03%	-27.29%	-26.59%	-25.93%	-25.29%
4.50%	Equal level rate	5.08%	5.33%	5.58%	5.83%	6.08%	6.33%	6.58%	6.83%	7.08%	7.33%
	Change in cost	-36.46%	-35.35%	-34.31%	-33.33%	-32.41%	-31.53%	-30.70%	-29.91%	-29.17%	-28.46%
5.00%	Equal level rate	4.76%	5.01%	5.26%	5.51%	5.76%	6.01%	6.26%	6.51%	6.76%	7.01%
	Change in cost	-40.51%	-39.28%	-38.13%	-37.04%	-36.01%	-35.04%	-34.11%	-33.24%	-32.41%	-31.62%

Equal level rate is the single rate that would produce equal interest cost.
Change in cost is percent change from interest if original rate remained in effect.

Effect of Rate Changes on Construction Financing Cost

Term of 36 Months

Increase in rate of		Interest Rate at Start of Loan									
		10.50%	10.75%	11.00%	11.25%	11.50%	11.75%	12.00%	12.25%	12.50%	12.75%
0.50%	Equal level rate	10.82%	11.07%	11.32%	11.57%	11.82%	12.07%	12.32%	12.57%	12.82%	13.07%
	Change in cost	3.09%	3.01%	2.95%	2.88%	2.82%	2.76%	2.70%	2.65%	2.59%	2.54%
1.00%	Equal level rate	11.15%	11.40%	11.65%	11.90%	12.15%	12.40%	12.65%	12.90%	13.15%	13.40%
	Change in cost	6.17%	6.03%	5.89%	5.76%	5.64%	5.52%	5.40%	5.29%	5.19%	5.08%
1.25%	Equal level rate	11.31%	11.56%	11.81%	12.06%	12.31%	12.56%	12.81%	13.06%	13.31%	13.56%
	Change in cost	7.72%	7.54%	7.37%	7.20%	7.05%	6.90%	6.75%	6.61%	6.48%	6.35%
1.50%	Equal level rate	11.47%	11.72%	11.97%	12.22%	12.47%	12.72%	12.97%	13.22%	13.47%	13.72%
	Change in cost	9.26%	9.04%	8.84%	8.64%	8.45%	8.27%	8.10%	7.94%	7.78%	7.63%
1.75%	Equal level rate	11.63%	11.88%	12.13%	12.38%	12.63%	12.88%	13.13%	13.38%	13.63%	13.88%
	Change in cost	10.80%	10.55%	10.31%	10.08%	9.86%	9.65%	9.45%	9.26%	9.07%	8.90%
2.00%	Equal level rate	11.80%	12.05%	12.30%	12.55%	12.80%	13.05%	13.30%	13.55%	13.80%	14.05%
	Change in cost	12.35%	12.06%	11.78%	11.52%	11.27%	11.03%	10.80%	10.58%	10.37%	10.17%
2.50%	Equal level rate	12.12%	12.37%	12.62%	12.87%	13.12%	13.37%	13.62%	13.87%	14.12%	14.37%
	Change in cost	15.43%	15.07%	14.73%	14.40%	14.09%	13.79%	13.50%	13.23%	12.96%	12.71%
3.00%	Equal level rate	12.44%	12.69%	12.94%	13.19%	13.44%	13.69%	13.94%	14.19%	14.44%	14.69%
	Change in cost	18.52%	18.09%	17.68%	17.28%	16.91%	16.55%	16.20%	15.87%	15.56%	15.25%
3.50%	Equal level rate	12.77%	13.02%	13.27%	13.52%	13.77%	14.02%	14.27%	14.52%	14.77%	15.02%
	Change in cost	21.60%	21.10%	20.62%	20.16%	19.73%	19.31%	18.90%	18.52%	18.15%	17.79%
4.00%	Equal level rate	13.09%	13.34%	13.59%	13.84%	14.09%	14.34%	14.59%	14.84%	15.09%	15.34%
	Change in cost	24.69%	24.12%	23.57%	23.05%	22.54%	22.06%	21.60%	21.16%	20.74%	20.33%
4.50%	Equal level rate	13.42%	13.67%	13.92%	14.17%	14.42%	14.67%	14.92%	15.17%	15.42%	15.67%
	Change in cost	27.78%	27.13%	26.52%	25.93%	25.36%	24.82%	24.31%	23.81%	23.33%	22.88%
5.00%	Equal level rate	13.74%	13.99%	14.24%	14.49%	14.74%	14.99%	15.24%	15.49%	15.74%	15.99%
	Change in cost	30.86%	30.15%	29.46%	28.81%	28.18%	27.58%	27.01%	26.46%	25.93%	25.42%

Decrease in rate of		Interest Rate at Start of Loan									
		10.50%	10.75%	11.00%	11.25%	11.50%	11.75%	12.00%	12.25%	12.50%	12.75%
0.50%	Equal level rate	10.18%	10.43%	10.68%	10.93%	11.18%	11.43%	11.68%	11.93%	12.18%	12.43%
	Change in cost	-3.09%	-3.01%	-2.95%	-2.88%	-2.82%	-2.76%	-2.70%	-2.65%	-2.59%	-2.54%
1.00%	Equal level rate	9.85%	10.10%	10.35%	10.60%	10.85%	11.10%	11.35%	11.60%	11.85%	12.10%
	Change in cost	-6.17%	-6.03%	-5.89%	-5.76%	-5.64%	-5.52%	-5.40%	-5.29%	-5.19%	-5.08%
1.25%	Equal level rate	9.69%	9.94%	10.19%	10.44%	10.69%	10.94%	11.19%	11.44%	11.69%	11.94%
	Change in cost	-7.72%	-7.54%	-7.37%	-7.20%	-7.05%	-6.90%	-6.75%	-6.61%	-6.48%	-6.35%
1.50%	Equal level rate	9.53%	9.78%	10.03%	10.28%	10.53%	10.78%	11.03%	11.28%	11.53%	11.78%
	Change in cost	-9.26%	-9.04%	-8.84%	-8.64%	-8.45%	-8.27%	-8.10%	-7.94%	-7.78%	-7.63%
1.75%	Equal level rate	9.37%	9.62%	9.87%	10.12%	10.37%	10.62%	10.87%	11.12%	11.37%	11.62%
	Change in cost	-10.80%	-10.55%	-10.31%	-10.08%	-9.86%	-9.65%	-9.45%	-9.26%	-9.07%	-8.90%
2.00%	Equal level rate	9.20%	9.45%	9.70%	9.95%	10.20%	10.45%	10.70%	10.95%	11.20%	11.45%
	Change in cost	-12.35%	-12.06%	-11.78%	-11.52%	-11.27%	-11.03%	-10.80%	-10.58%	-10.37%	-10.17%
2.50%	Equal level rate	8.88%	9.13%	9.38%	9.63%	9.88%	10.13%	10.38%	10.63%	10.88%	11.13%
	Change in cost	-15.43%	-15.07%	-14.73%	-14.40%	-14.09%	-13.79%	-13.50%	-13.23%	-12.96%	-12.71%
3.00%	Equal level rate	8.56%	8.81%	9.06%	9.31%	9.56%	9.81%	10.06%	10.31%	10.56%	10.81%
	Change in cost	-18.52%	-18.09%	-17.68%	-17.28%	-16.91%	-16.55%	-16.20%	-15.87%	-15.56%	-15.25%
3.50%	Equal level rate	8.23%	8.48%	8.73%	8.98%	9.23%	9.48%	9.73%	9.98%	10.23%	10.48%
	Change in cost	-21.60%	-21.10%	-20.62%	-20.16%	-19.73%	-19.31%	-18.90%	-18.52%	-18.15%	-17.79%
4.00%	Equal level rate	7.91%	8.16%	8.41%	8.66%	8.91%	9.16%	9.41%	9.66%	9.91%	10.16%
	Change in cost	-24.69%	-24.12%	-23.57%	-23.05%	-22.54%	-22.06%	-21.60%	-21.16%	-20.74%	-20.33%
4.50%	Equal level rate	7.58%	7.83%	8.08%	8.33%	8.58%	8.83%	9.08%	9.33%	9.58%	9.83%
	Change in cost	-27.78%	-27.13%	-26.52%	-25.93%	-25.36%	-24.82%	-24.31%	-23.81%	-23.33%	-22.88%
5.00%	Equal level rate	7.26%	7.51%	7.76%	8.01%	8.26%	8.51%	8.76%	9.01%	9.26%	9.51%
	Change in cost	-30.86%	-30.15%	-29.46%	-28.81%	-28.18%	-27.58%	-27.01%	-26.46%	-25.93%	-25.42%

Equal level rate is the single rate that would produce equal interest cost.
Change in cost is percent change from interest if original rate remained in effect.

Average Balance on Construction & Mini-Perm Loans

Average Balance on Construction Loans

Loan Term	Proportion	2.5%	5.0%	7.5%	10.0%	Initial Draw 12.5%	15.0%	20.0%	25.0%	33.3%	40.0%	50.0%
6	58.33	59.79	61.25	62.71	64.17	65.63	67.08	70.00	72.92	77.78	81.67	87.50
9	55.56	56.94	58.33	59.72	61.11	62.50	63.89	66.67	69.44	74.07	77.78	83.33
12	54.17	55.52	56.88	58.23	59.58	60.94	62.29	65.00	67.71	72.22	75.83	81.25
15	53.33	54.67	56.00	57.33	58.67	60.00	61.33	64.00	66.67	71.11	74.67	80.00
18	52.78	54.10	55.42	56.74	58.06	59.38	60.69	63.33	65.97	70.37	73.89	79.17
21	52.38	53.69	55.00	56.31	57.62	58.93	60.24	62.86	65.48	69.84	73.33	78.57
24	52.08	53.39	54.69	55.99	57.29	58.59	59.90	62.50	65.10	69.44	72.92	78.13
27	51.85	53.15	54.44	55.74	57.04	58.33	59.63	62.22	64.81	69.14	72.59	77.78
30	51.67	52.96	54.25	55.54	56.83	58.13	59.42	62.00	64.58	68.89	72.33	77.50
33	51.52	52.80	54.09	55.38	56.67	57.95	59.24	61.82	64.39	68.69	72.12	77.27
36	51.39	52.67	53.96	55.24	56.53	57.81	59.10	61.67	64.24	68.52	71.94	77.08
39	51.28	52.56	53.85	55.13	56.41	57.69	58.97	61.54	64.10	68.38	71.79	76.92
42	51.19	52.47	53.75	55.03	56.31	57.59	58.87	61.43	63.99	68.25	71.67	76.79
45	51.11	52.39	53.67	54.94	56.22	57.50	58.78	61.33	63.89	68.15	71.56	76.67
48	51.04	52.32	53.59	54.87	56.15	57.42	58.70	61.25	63.80	68.06	71.46	76.56
51	50.98	52.25	53.53	54.80	56.08	57.35	58.63	61.18	63.73	67.97	71.37	76.47
54	50.93	52.20	53.47	54.75	56.02	57.29	58.56	61.11	63.66	67.90	71.30	76.39
57	50.88	52.15	53.42	54.69	55.96	57.24	58.51	61.05	63.60	67.84	71.23	76.32
60	50.83	52.10	53.38	54.65	55.92	57.19	58.46	61.00	63.54	67.78	71.17	76.25
66	50.76	52.03	53.30	54.56	55.83	57.10	58.37	60.91	63.45	67.68	71.06	76.14
72	50.69	51.96	53.23	54.50	55.76	57.03	58.30	60.83	63.37	67.59	70.97	76.04
78	50.64	51.91	53.17	54.44	55.71	56.97	58.24	60.77	63.30	67.52	70.90	75.96
84	50.60	51.86	53.13	54.39	55.65	56.92	58.18	60.71	63.24	67.46	70.83	75.89

Entries are percentages of full loan amount.

Average Balance on Mini-Permanent Loans

Full Funding	6	9	12	15	Construction Period (Proportionate Funding) 18	21	24	27	30	33	36
6	79.2%	73.3%	69.4%	66.7%	64.6%	63.0%	61.7%	60.6%	59.7%	59.0%	58.3%
9	83.33	77.78	73.81	70.83	68.52	66.67	65.15	63.89	62.82	61.90	61.11
12	86.11	80.95	77.08	74.07	71.67	69.70	68.06	66.67	65.48	64.44	63.54
15	88.10	83.33	79.63	76.67	74.24	72.22	70.51	69.05	67.78	66.67	65.69
18	89.58	85.19	81.67	78.79	76.39	74.36	72.62	71.11	69.79	68.63	67.59
21	90.74	86.67	83.33	80.56	78.21	76.19	74.44	72.92	71.57	70.37	69.30
24	91.67	87.88	84.72	82.05	79.76	77.78	76.04	74.51	73.15	71.93	70.83
27	92.42	88.89	85.90	83.33	81.11	79.17	77.45	75.93	74.56	73.33	72.22
30	93.06	89.74	86.90	84.44	82.29	80.39	78.70	77.19	75.83	74.60	73.48
33	93.59	90.48	87.78	85.42	83.33	81.48	79.82	78.33	76.98	75.76	74.64
36	94.05	91.11	88.54	86.27	84.26	82.46	80.83	79.37	78.03	76.81	75.69
39	94.44	91.67	89.22	87.04	85.09	83.33	81.75	80.30	78.99	77.78	76.67
42	94.79	92.16	89.81	87.72	85.83	84.13	82.58	81.16	79.86	78.67	77.56
45	95.10	92.59	90.35	88.33	86.51	84.85	83.33	81.94	80.67	79.49	78.40
48	95.37	92.98	90.83	88.89	87.12	85.51	84.03	82.67	81.41	80.25	79.17
51	95.61	93.33	91.27	89.39	87.68	86.11	84.67	83.33	82.10	80.95	79.89
54	95.83	93.65	91.67	89.86	88.19	86.67	85.26	83.95	82.74	81.61	80.56
57	96.03	93.94	92.03	90.28	88.67	87.18	85.80	84.52	83.33	82.22	81.18
60	96.21	94.20	92.36	90.67	89.10	87.65	86.31	85.06	83.89	82.80	81.77
66	96.53	94.67	92.95	91.36	89.88	88.51	87.22	86.02	84.90	83.84	82.84
72	96.79	95.06	93.45	91.95	90.56	89.25	88.02	86.87	85.78	84.76	83.80
78	97.02	95.40	93.89	92.47	91.15	89.90	88.73	87.62	86.57	85.59	84.65
84	97.22	95.70	94.27	92.93	91.67	90.48	89.35	88.29	87.28	86.32	85.42

Entries are percentages of full loan amount.

Interest Reserve on Construction Loans

Loan Term	Average Balance	5.50%	5.75%	6.00%	6.25%	6.50%	6.75%	7.00%	7.25%	7.50%	7.75%	8.00%	8.25%	8.50%
								Interest Rate						
6	40	1.11%	1.16%	1.22%	1.27%	1.32%	1.37%	1.42%	1.47%	1.52%	1.58%	1.63%	1.68%	1.73%
	50	1.39	1.45	1.52	1.58	1.65	1.71	1.78	1.84	1.90	1.97	2.03	2.10	2.16
	55	1.53	1.60	1.67	1.74	1.81	1.88	1.95	2.02	2.09	2.17	2.24	2.31	2.38
	60	1.67	1.75	1.82	1.90	1.98	2.05	2.13	2.21	2.29	2.36	2.44	2.52	2.60
	67	1.85	1.94	2.03	2.11	2.20	2.28	2.37	2.45	2.54	2.63	2.71	2.80	2.88
	75	2.09	2.18	2.28	2.37	2.47	2.57	2.66	2.76	2.86	2.95	3.05	3.15	3.24
	80	2.23	2.33	2.43	2.53	2.64	2.74	2.84	2.94	3.05	3.15	3.25	3.36	3.46
	85	2.36	2.47	2.58	2.69	2.80	2.91	3.02	3.13	3.24	3.35	3.46	3.57	3.68
	90	2.50	2.62	2.73	2.85	2.96	3.08	3.20	3.31	3.43	3.54	3.66	3.78	3.89
	100	2.78	2.91	3.04	3.17	3.29	3.42	3.55	3.68	3.81	3.94	4.07	4.20	4.33
12	40	2.26%	2.36%	2.47%	2.57%	2.68%	2.79%	2.89%	3.00%	3.11%	3.21%	3.32%	3.43%	3.54%
	50	2.82	2.95	3.08	3.22	3.35	3.48	3.61	3.75	3.88	4.02	4.15	4.28	4.42
	55	3.10	3.25	3.39	3.54	3.68	3.83	3.98	4.12	4.27	4.42	4.56	4.71	4.86
	60	3.38	3.54	3.70	3.86	4.02	4.18	4.34	4.50	4.66	4.82	4.98	5.14	5.30
	67	3.76	3.94	4.11	4.29	4.46	4.64	4.82	5.00	5.18	5.35	5.53	5.71	5.89
	75	4.23	4.43	4.63	4.82	5.02	5.22	5.42	5.62	5.82	6.02	6.22	6.43	6.63
	80	4.51	4.72	4.93	5.15	5.36	5.57	5.78	6.00	6.21	6.43	6.64	6.86	7.07
	85	4.79	5.02	5.24	5.47	5.69	5.92	6.14	6.37	6.60	6.83	7.05	7.28	7.51
	90	5.08	5.31	5.55	5.79	6.03	6.27	6.51	6.75	6.99	7.23	7.47	7.71	7.96
	100	5.64	5.90	6.17	6.43	6.70	6.96	7.23	7.50	7.76	8.03	8.30	8.57	8.84
18	40	3.43%	3.59%	3.76%	3.92%	4.08%	4.25%	4.41%	4.58%	4.75%	4.91%	5.08%	5.25%	5.42%
	50	4.29	4.49	4.70	4.90	5.11	5.31	5.52	5.73	5.93	6.14	6.35	6.56	6.77
	55	4.72	4.94	5.17	5.39	5.62	5.84	6.07	6.30	6.53	6.76	6.99	7.22	7.45
	60	5.15	5.39	5.64	5.88	6.13	6.37	6.62	6.87	7.12	7.37	7.62	7.88	8.13
	67	5.72	5.99	6.26	6.53	6.81	7.08	7.36	7.63	7.91	8.19	8.47	8.75	9.03
	75	6.43	6.74	7.04	7.35	7.66	7.97	8.28	8.59	8.90	9.21	9.53	9.84	10.16
	80	6.86	7.19	7.51	7.84	8.17	8.50	8.83	9.16	9.49	9.83	10.16	10.50	10.84
	85	7.29	7.64	7.98	8.33	8.68	9.03	9.38	9.73	10.09	10.44	10.80	11.16	11.52
	90	7.72	8.09	8.45	8.82	9.19	9.56	9.93	10.31	10.68	11.06	11.43	11.81	12.19
	100	8.58	8.99	9.39	9.80	10.21	10.62	11.04	11.45	11.87	12.29	12.70	13.13	13.55
24	40	4.64%	4.86%	5.09%	5.31%	5.54%	5.76%	5.99%	6.22%	6.45%	6.68%	6.92%	7.15%	7.38%
	50	5.80	6.08	6.36	6.64	6.92	7.21	7.49	7.78	8.06	8.35	8.64	8.94	9.23
	55	6.38	6.69	6.99	7.30	7.61	7.93	8.24	8.55	8.87	9.19	9.51	9.83	10.15
	60	6.96	7.29	7.63	7.97	8.31	8.65	8.99	9.33	9.68	10.02	10.37	10.72	11.08
	67	7.73	8.10	8.48	8.85	9.23	9.61	9.99	10.37	10.75	11.14	11.53	11.92	12.31
	75	8.70	9.12	9.54	9.96	10.38	10.81	11.24	11.67	12.10	12.53	12.97	13.40	13.84
	80	9.28	9.73	10.17	10.62	11.07	11.53	11.98	12.44	12.90	13.37	13.83	14.30	14.77
	85	9.86	10.33	10.81	11.29	11.77	12.25	12.73	13.22	13.71	14.20	14.70	15.19	15.69
	90	10.44	10.94	11.44	11.95	12.46	12.97	13.48	14.00	14.52	15.04	15.56	16.09	16.61
	100	11.60	12.16	12.72	13.28	13.84	14.41	14.98	15.55	16.13	16.71	17.29	17.87	18.46
30	40	5.88%	6.17%	6.46%	6.75%	7.04%	7.33%	7.63%	7.92%	8.22%	8.52%	8.82%	9.13%	9.43%
	50	7.35	7.71	8.07	8.43	8.80	9.16	9.53	9.90	10.28	10.65	11.03	11.41	11.79
	55	8.09	8.48	8.88	9.28	9.68	10.08	10.49	10.89	11.30	11.72	12.13	12.55	12.97
	60	8.82	9.25	9.68	10.12	10.56	11.00	11.44	11.88	12.33	12.78	13.24	13.69	14.15
	67	9.80	10.28	10.76	11.24	11.73	12.22	12.71	13.20	13.70	14.20	14.71	15.21	15.72
	75	11.03	11.56	12.11	12.65	13.19	13.74	14.30	14.85	15.41	15.98	16.54	17.11	17.69
	80	11.76	12.34	12.91	13.49	14.07	14.66	15.25	15.84	16.44	17.04	17.65	18.26	18.87
	85	12.50	13.11	13.72	14.33	14.95	15.58	16.20	16.84	17.47	18.11	18.75	19.40	20.05
	90	13.23	13.88	14.53	15.18	15.83	16.49	17.16	17.83	18.50	19.17	19.85	20.54	21.23
	100	14.70	15.42	16.14	16.86	17.59	18.33	19.06	19.81	20.55	21.30	22.06	22.82	23.58
36	40	7.16%	7.51%	7.87%	8.23%	8.59%	8.95%	9.32%	9.69%	10.06%	10.43%	10.81%	11.19%	11.57%
	50	8.95	9.39	9.83	10.28	10.73	11.19	11.65	12.11	12.57	13.04	13.51	13.99	14.47
	55	9.84	10.33	10.82	11.31	11.81	12.31	12.81	13.32	13.83	14.34	14.86	15.39	15.91
	60	10.74	11.27	11.80	12.34	12.88	13.43	13.98	14.53	15.09	15.65	16.21	16.78	17.36
	67	11.93	12.52	13.11	13.71	14.31	14.92	15.53	16.14	16.76	17.39	18.02	18.65	19.29
	75	13.42	14.08	14.75	15.42	16.10	16.78	17.47	18.16	18.86	19.56	20.27	20.98	21.70
	80	14.32	15.02	15.73	16.45	17.17	17.90	18.63	19.37	20.12	20.86	21.62	22.38	23.14
	85	15.21	15.96	16.72	17.48	18.25	19.02	19.80	20.58	21.37	22.17	22.97	23.78	24.59
	90	16.11	16.90	17.70	18.51	19.32	20.14	20.96	21.79	22.63	23.47	24.32	25.18	26.04
	100	17.89	18.78	19.67	20.56	21.47	22.38	23.29	24.22	25.14	26.08	27.02	27.97	28.93
48	40	9.82%	10.32%	10.82%	11.33%	11.84%	12.36%	12.88%	13.41%	13.94%	14.48%	15.03%	15.58%	16.13%
	50	12.27	12.90	13.52	14.16	14.80	15.45	16.10	16.76	17.43	18.10	18.78	19.47	20.16
	55	13.50	14.18	14.88	15.58	16.28	16.99	17.71	18.44	19.17	19.91	20.66	21.42	22.18
	60	14.73	15.47	16.23	16.99	17.76	18.54	19.32	20.12	20.92	21.72	22.54	23.36	24.20
	67	16.36	17.19	18.03	18.88	19.73	20.60	21.47	22.35	23.24	24.14	25.04	25.96	26.88
	75	18.41	19.34	20.29	21.24	22.20	23.17	24.15	25.14	26.14	27.16	28.17	29.20	30.24
	80	19.64	20.63	21.64	22.66	23.68	24.72	25.76	26.82	27.89	28.97	30.05	31.15	32.26
	85	20.86	21.92	22.99	24.07	25.16	26.26	27.37	28.50	29.63	30.78	31.93	33.10	34.28
	90	22.09	23.21	24.34	25.49	26.64	27.81	28.98	30.17	31.37	32.59	33.81	35.05	36.29
	100	24.55	25.79	27.05	28.32	29.60	30.90	32.21	33.53	34.86	36.21	37.57	38.94	40.33

Entry is percentage of loan amount exclusive of reserve.

Interest Reserve on Construction Loans

Loan Term	Average Balance	Interest Rate												
		8.75%	9.00%	9.25%	9.50%	9.75%	10.00%	10.25%	10.50%	10.75%	11.00%	11.50%	12.00%	12.50%
6	40	1.78%	1.83%	1.89%	1.94%	1.99%	2.04%	2.09%	2.15%	2.20%	2.25%	2.36%	2.46%	2.57%
	50	2.23	2.29	2.36	2.42	2.49	2.55	2.62	2.68	2.75	2.81	2.94	3.08	3.21
	55	2.45	2.52	2.59	2.66	2.74	2.81	2.88	2.95	3.02	3.10	3.24	3.38	3.53
	60	2.67	2.75	2.83	2.91	2.99	3.06	3.14	3.22	3.30	3.38	3.53	3.69	3.85
	67	2.97	3.06	3.14	3.23	3.32	3.40	3.49	3.58	3.66	3.75	3.93	4.10	4.28
	75	3.34	3.44	3.54	3.63	3.73	3.83	3.93	4.02	4.12	4.22	4.42	4.61	4.81
	80	3.56	3.67	3.77	3.88	3.98	4.08	4.19	4.29	4.40	4.50	4.71	4.92	5.13
	85	3.79	3.90	4.01	4.12	4.23	4.34	4.45	4.56	4.67	4.78	5.01	5.23	5.45
	90	4.01	4.13	4.24	4.36	4.48	4.59	4.71	4.83	4.95	5.06	5.30	5.54	5.77
	100	4.46	4.59	4.72	4.85	4.98	5.11	5.24	5.37	5.50	5.63	5.89	6.15	6.42
12	40	3.64%	3.75%	3.86%	3.97%	4.08%	4.19%	4.30%	4.41%	4.52%	4.63%	4.85%	5.07%	5.30%
	50	4.55	4.69	4.83	4.96	5.10	5.24	5.37	5.51	5.65	5.79	6.06	6.34	6.62
	55	5.01	5.16	5.31	5.46	5.61	5.76	5.91	6.06	6.21	6.36	6.67	6.98	7.28
	60	5.47	5.63	5.79	5.95	6.12	6.28	6.45	6.61	6.78	6.94	7.28	7.61	7.94
	67	6.07	6.25	6.43	6.62	6.80	6.98	7.16	7.35	7.53	7.71	8.08	8.46	8.83
	75	6.83	7.04	7.24	7.44	7.65	7.85	8.06	8.27	8.47	8.68	9.09	9.51	9.93
	80	7.29	7.50	7.72	7.94	8.16	8.38	8.60	8.82	9.04	9.26	9.70	10.15	10.59
	85	7.74	7.97	8.20	8.44	8.67	8.90	9.13	9.37	9.60	9.84	10.31	10.78	11.26
	90	8.20	8.44	8.69	8.93	9.18	9.42	9.67	9.92	10.17	10.41	10.91	11.41	11.92
	100	9.11	9.38	9.65	9.92	10.20	10.47	10.75	11.02	11.30	11.57	12.13	12.68	13.24
18	40	5.59%	5.76%	5.93%	6.10%	6.27%	6.44%	6.62%	6.79%	6.97%	7.14%	7.49%	7.85%	8.20%
	50	6.99	7.20	7.41	7.63	7.84	8.06	8.27	8.49	8.71	8.93	9.36	9.81	10.25
	55	7.68	7.92	8.15	8.39	8.62	8.86	9.10	9.34	9.58	9.82	10.30	10.79	11.28
	60	8.38	8.64	8.89	9.15	9.41	9.67	9.93	10.19	10.45	10.71	11.24	11.77	12.30
	67	9.31	9.60	9.88	10.17	10.45	10.74	11.03	11.32	11.61	11.90	12.49	13.08	13.67
	75	10.48	10.80	11.12	11.44	11.76	12.08	12.41	12.73	13.06	13.39	14.05	14.71	15.38
	80	11.18	11.52	11.86	12.20	12.54	12.89	13.24	13.58	13.93	14.28	14.98	15.69	16.40
	85	11.88	12.24	12.60	12.96	13.33	13.69	14.06	14.43	14.80	15.17	15.92	16.67	17.43
	90	12.57	12.96	13.34	13.73	14.11	14.50	14.89	15.28	15.67	16.07	16.86	17.65	18.46
	100	13.97	14.40	14.82	15.25	15.68	16.11	16.54	16.98	17.41	17.85	18.73	19.61	20.51
24	40	7.62%	7.86%	8.09%	8.33%	8.57%	8.82%	9.06%	9.30%	9.55%	9.79%	10.29%	10.79%	11.29%
	50	9.52	9.82	10.12	10.42	10.72	11.02	11.32	11.63	11.93	12.24	12.86	13.49	14.12
	55	10.48	10.80	11.13	11.46	11.79	12.12	12.46	12.79	13.13	13.47	14.15	14.84	15.53
	60	11.43	11.78	12.14	12.50	12.86	13.22	13.59	13.95	14.32	14.69	15.43	16.18	16.94
	67	12.70	13.09	13.49	13.89	14.29	14.69	15.10	15.50	15.91	16.32	17.15	17.98	18.82
	75	14.29	14.73	15.18	15.63	16.08	16.53	16.98	17.44	17.90	18.36	19.29	20.23	21.18
	80	15.24	15.71	16.19	16.67	17.15	17.63	18.12	18.60	19.09	19.59	20.58	21.58	22.59
	85	16.19	16.70	17.20	17.71	18.22	18.73	19.25	19.77	20.29	20.81	21.86	22.93	24.00
	90	17.14	17.68	18.21	18.75	19.29	19.84	20.38	20.93	21.48	22.03	23.15	24.28	25.41
	100	19.05	19.64	20.24	20.83	21.44	22.04	22.65	23.26	23.87	24.48	25.72	26.97	28.24
30	40	9.74%	10.05%	10.36%	10.68%	10.99%	11.31%	11.63%	11.95%	12.27%	12.60%	13.25%	13.91%	14.59%
	50	12.18	12.56	12.95	13.34	13.74	14.13	14.53	14.93	15.34	15.74	16.56	17.39	18.23
	55	13.39	13.82	14.25	14.68	15.11	15.55	15.99	16.43	16.87	17.32	18.22	19.13	20.05
	60	14.61	15.08	15.54	16.01	16.49	16.96	17.44	17.92	18.41	18.89	19.88	20.87	21.88
	67	16.24	16.75	17.27	17.79	18.32	18.85	19.38	19.91	20.45	20.99	22.08	23.19	24.31
	75	18.26	18.85	19.43	20.02	20.61	21.20	21.80	22.40	23.01	23.62	24.85	26.09	27.35
	80	19.48	20.10	20.72	21.35	21.98	22.62	23.25	23.90	24.54	25.19	26.50	27.83	29.17
	85	20.70	21.36	22.02	22.69	23.36	24.03	24.71	25.39	26.07	26.77	28.16	29.57	30.99
	90	21.92	22.61	23.32	24.02	24.73	25.44	26.16	26.88	27.61	28.34	29.81	31.31	32.82
	100	24.35	25.13	25.91	26.69	27.48	28.27	29.07	29.87	30.68	31.49	33.13	34.78	36.46
36	40	11.96%	12.35%	12.74%	13.13%	13.53%	13.93%	14.33%	14.74%	15.14%	15.56%	16.39%	17.23%	18.09%
	50	14.95	15.43	15.92	16.41	16.91	17.41	17.91	18.42	18.93	19.44	20.48	21.54	22.61
	55	16.44	16.98	17.51	18.05	18.60	19.15	19.70	20.26	20.82	21.39	22.53	23.69	24.87
	60	17.94	18.52	19.11	19.70	20.29	20.89	21.49	22.10	22.72	23.33	24.58	25.85	27.13
	67	19.93	20.58	21.23	21.88	22.55	23.21	23.88	24.56	25.24	25.93	27.31	28.72	30.14
	75	22.42	23.15	23.88	24.62	25.36	26.11	26.87	27.63	28.39	29.17	30.73	32.31	33.91
	80	23.92	24.69	25.47	26.26	27.06	27.85	28.66	29.47	30.29	31.11	32.77	34.46	36.17
	85	25.41	26.23	27.07	27.90	28.75	29.60	30.45	31.31	32.18	33.05	34.82	36.62	38.43
	90	26.90	27.78	28.66	29.54	30.44	31.34	32.24	33.15	34.07	35.00	36.87	38.77	40.70
	100	29.89	30.86	31.84	32.83	33.82	34.82	35.82	36.84	37.86	38.89	40.97	43.08	45.22
48	40	16.69%	17.26%	17.83%	18.40%	18.99%	19.57%	20.17%	20.77%	21.37%	21.98%	23.22%	24.49%	25.78%
	50	20.86	21.57	22.28	23.00	23.73	24.47	25.21	25.96	26.72	27.48	29.03	30.61	32.22
	55	22.95	23.73	24.51	25.31	26.11	26.91	27.73	28.56	29.39	30.23	31.93	33.67	35.45
	60	25.04	25.88	26.74	27.61	28.48	29.36	30.25	31.15	32.06	32.98	34.84	36.73	38.67
	67	27.82	28.76	29.71	30.67	31.64	32.62	33.61	34.61	35.62	36.64	38.71	40.82	42.96
	75	31.30	32.36	33.43	34.51	35.60	36.70	37.81	38.94	40.07	41.22	43.55	45.92	48.33
	80	33.38	34.51	35.65	36.81	37.97	39.15	40.34	41.53	42.75	43.97	46.45	48.98	51.56
	85	35.47	36.67	37.88	39.11	40.35	41.60	42.86	44.13	45.42	46.72	49.35	52.04	54.78
	90	37.55	38.83	40.11	41.41	42.72	44.04	45.38	46.73	48.09	49.46	52.25	55.10	58.00
	100	41.73	43.14	44.57	46.01	47.47	48.94	50.42	51.92	53.43	54.96	58.06	61.22	64.45

Payments on Monthly & Biweekly Home Loans

30 Year Schedule

Amount of Loan	5.50% Monthly	Biweekly	5.75% Monthly	Biweekly	6.00% Monthly	Biweekly	6.25% Monthly	Biweekly	6.50% Monthly	Biweekly	6.75% Monthly	Biweekly
$50,000	283.90	141.95	291.79	145.90	299.78	149.89	307.86	153.93	316.04	158.02	324.30	162.15
51,000	289.58	144.79	297.63	148.82	305.78	152.89	314.02	157.01	322.36	161.18	330.79	165.40
52,000	295.26	147.63	303.46	151.73	311.77	155.89	320.18	160.09	328.68	164.34	337.28	168.64
53,000	300.93	150.47	309.30	154.65	317.77	158.89	326.34	163.17	335.00	167.50	343.76	171.88
54,000	306.61	153.31	315.13	157.57	323.76	161.88	332.49	166.25	341.32	170.66	350.25	175.13
55,000	312.29	156.15	320.97	160.49	329.76	164.88	338.65	169.33	347.64	173.82	356.73	178.37
56,000	317.97	158.99	326.81	163.41	335.75	167.88	344.81	172.41	353.96	176.98	363.22	181.61
57,000	323.64	161.82	332.64	166.32	341.75	170.88	350.96	175.48	360.28	180.14	369.71	184.86
58,000	329.32	164.66	338.48	169.24	347.74	173.87	357.12	178.56	366.60	183.30	376.19	188.10
59,000	335.00	167.50	344.31	172.16	353.74	176.87	363.28	181.64	372.93	186.47	382.68	191.34
60,000	340.68	170.34	350.15	175.08	359.74	179.87	369.44	184.72	379.25	189.63	389.16	194.58
61,000	346.36	173.18	355.98	177.99	365.73	182.87	375.59	187.80	385.57	192.79	395.65	197.83
62,000	352.03	176.02	361.82	180.91	371.73	185.87	381.75	190.88	391.89	195.95	402.14	201.07
63,000	357.71	178.86	367.66	183.83	377.72	188.86	387.91	193.96	398.21	199.11	408.62	204.31
64,000	363.39	181.70	373.49	186.75	383.72	191.86	394.06	197.03	404.53	202.27	415.11	207.56
65,000	369.07	184.54	379.33	189.67	389.71	194.86	400.22	200.11	410.85	205.43	421.59	210.80
66,000	374.75	187.38	385.16	192.58	395.71	197.86	406.38	203.19	417.17	208.59	428.08	214.04
67,000	380.42	190.21	391.00	195.50	401.70	200.85	412.54	206.27	423.49	211.75	434.57	217.29
68,000	386.10	193.05	396.83	198.42	407.70	203.85	418.69	209.35	429.81	214.91	441.05	220.53
69,000	391.78	195.89	402.67	201.34	413.69	206.85	424.85	212.43	436.13	218.07	447.54	223.77
70,000	397.46	198.73	408.51	204.26	419.69	209.85	431.01	215.51	442.45	221.23	454.02	227.01
71,000	403.14	201.57	414.34	207.17	425.69	212.85	437.16	218.58	448.77	224.39	460.51	230.26
72,000	408.81	204.41	420.18	210.09	431.68	215.84	443.32	221.66	455.09	227.55	467.00	233.50
73,000	414.49	207.25	426.01	213.01	437.68	218.84	449.48	224.74	461.41	230.71	473.48	236.74
74,000	420.17	210.09	431.85	215.93	443.67	221.84	455.64	227.82	467.74	233.87	479.97	239.99
75,000	425.85	212.93	437.68	218.84	449.67	224.84	461.79	230.90	474.06	237.03	486.45	243.23
76,000	431.52	215.76	443.52	221.76	455.66	227.83	467.95	233.98	480.38	240.19	492.94	246.47
77,000	437.20	218.60	449.36	224.68	461.66	230.83	474.11	237.06	486.70	243.35	499.43	249.72
78,000	442.88	221.44	455.19	227.60	467.65	233.83	480.26	240.13	493.02	246.51	505.91	252.96
79,000	448.56	224.28	461.03	230.52	473.65	236.83	486.42	243.21	499.34	249.67	512.40	256.20
80,000	454.24	227.12	466.86	233.43	479.65	239.83	492.58	246.29	505.66	252.83	518.88	259.44
81,000	459.91	229.96	472.70	236.35	485.64	242.82	498.74	249.37	511.98	255.99	525.37	262.69
82,000	465.59	232.80	478.53	239.27	491.64	245.82	504.89	252.45	518.30	259.15	531.86	265.93
83,000	471.27	235.64	484.37	242.19	497.63	248.82	511.05	255.53	524.62	262.31	538.34	269.17
84,000	476.95	238.48	490.21	245.11	503.63	251.82	517.21	258.61	530.94	265.47	544.83	272.42
85,000	482.63	241.32	496.04	248.02	509.62	254.81	523.36	261.68	537.26	268.63	551.31	275.66
86,000	488.30	244.15	501.88	250.94	515.62	257.81	529.52	264.76	543.58	271.79	557.80	278.90
87,000	493.98	246.99	507.71	253.86	521.61	260.81	535.68	267.84	549.90	274.95	564.29	282.15
88,000	499.66	249.83	513.55	256.78	527.61	263.81	541.84	270.92	556.22	278.11	570.77	285.39
89,000	505.34	252.67	519.38	259.69	533.60	266.80	547.99	274.00	562.55	281.28	577.26	288.63
90,000	511.02	255.51	525.22	262.61	539.60	269.80	554.15	277.08	568.87	284.44	583.74	291.87
91,000	516.69	258.35	531.06	265.53	545.60	272.80	560.31	280.16	575.19	287.60	590.23	295.12
92,000	522.37	261.19	536.89	268.45	551.59	275.80	566.46	283.23	581.51	290.76	596.72	298.36
93,000	528.05	264.03	542.73	271.37	557.59	278.80	572.62	286.31	587.83	293.92	603.20	301.60
94,000	533.73	266.87	548.56	274.28	563.58	281.79	578.78	289.39	594.15	297.08	609.69	304.85
95,000	539.40	269.70	554.40	277.20	569.58	284.79	584.94	292.47	600.47	300.24	616.17	308.09
96,000	545.08	272.54	560.23	280.12	575.57	287.79	591.09	295.55	606.79	303.40	622.66	311.33
97,000	550.76	275.38	566.07	283.04	581.57	290.79	597.25	298.63	613.11	306.56	629.15	314.58
98,000	556.44	278.22	571.91	285.96	587.56	293.78	603.41	301.71	619.43	309.72	635.63	317.82
99,000	562.12	281.06	577.74	288.87	593.56	296.78	609.56	304.78	625.75	312.88	642.12	321.06
100,000	567.79	283.90	583.58	291.79	599.56	299.78	615.72	307.86	632.07	316.04	648.60	324.30
110,000	624.57	312.29	641.94	320.97	659.51	329.76	677.29	338.65	695.28	347.64	713.46	356.73
120,000	681.35	340.68	700.29	350.15	719.47	359.74	738.87	369.44	758.49	379.25	778.32	389.16
130,000	738.13	369.07	758.65	379.33	779.42	389.71	800.44	400.22	821.69	410.85	843.18	421.59
140,000	794.91	397.46	817.01	408.51	839.38	419.69	862.01	431.01	884.90	442.45	908.04	454.02
150,000	851.69	425.85	875.36	437.68	899.33	449.67	923.58	461.79	948.11	474.06	972.90	486.45
160,000	908.47	454.24	933.72	466.86	959.29	479.65	985.15	492.58	1011.31	505.66	1037.76	518.88
170,000	965.25	482.63	992.08	496.04	1019.24	509.62	1046.72	523.36	1074.52	537.26	1102.62	551.31
180,000	1022.03	511.02	1050.44	525.22	1079.20	539.60	1108.30	554.15	1137.73	568.87	1167.48	583.74
190,000	1078.80	539.40	1108.79	554.40	1139.15	569.58	1169.87	584.94	1200.93	600.47	1232.34	616.17
200,000	1135.58	567.79	1167.15	583.58	1199.11	599.56	1231.44	615.72	1264.14	632.07	1297.20	648.60
210,000	1192.36	596.18	1225.51	612.76	1259.06	629.53	1293.01	646.51	1327.35	663.68	1362.06	681.03
220,000	1249.14	624.57	1283.87	641.94	1319.02	659.51	1354.58	677.29	1390.55	695.28	1426.92	713.46
230,000	1305.92	652.96	1342.22	671.11	1378.97	689.49	1416.15	708.08	1453.76	726.88	1491.78	745.89
240,000	1362.70	681.35	1400.58	700.29	1438.93	719.47	1477.73	738.87	1516.97	758.49	1556.64	778.32
250,000	1419.48	709.74	1458.94	729.47	1498.88	749.44	1539.30	769.65	1580.18	790.09	1621.50	810.75
260,000	1476.26	738.13	1517.29	758.65	1558.84	779.42	1600.87	800.44	1643.38	821.69	1686.36	843.18
270,000	1533.04	766.52	1575.65	787.83	1618.79	809.40	1662.44	831.22	1706.59	853.30	1751.22	875.61
280,000	1589.81	794.91	1634.01	817.01	1678.75	839.38	1724.01	862.01	1769.80	884.90	1816.08	908.04
290,000	1646.59	823.30	1692.37	846.19	1738.70	869.35	1785.58	892.79	1833.00	916.50	1880.94	940.47
300,000	1703.37	851.69	1750.72	875.36	1798.66	899.33	1847.16	923.58	1896.21	948.11	1945.80	972.90
310,000	1760.15	880.08	1809.08	904.54	1858.61	929.31	1908.73	954.37	1959.42	979.71	2010.66	1005.33
320,000	1816.93	908.47	1867.44	933.72	1918.57	959.29	1970.30	985.15	2022.62	1011.31	2075.52	1037.76
330,000	1873.71	936.86	1925.80	962.90	1978.52	989.26	2031.87	1015.94	2085.83	1042.92	2140.38	1070.19
340,000	1930.49	965.25	1984.15	992.08	2038.48	1019.24	2093.44	1046.72	2149.04	1074.52	2205.24	1102.62
350,000	1987.27	993.64	2042.51	1021.26	2098.43	1049.22	2155.01	1077.51	2212.24	1106.12	2270.10	1135.05
Adder per $1,000	$5.68	$2.84	$5.84	$2.92	$6.00	$3.00	$6.16	$3.08	$6.33	$3.17	$6.49	$3.25

Payments on Monthly & Biweekly Home Loans

30 Year Schedule

Amount of Loan	7.00% Monthly	Biweekly	7.25% Monthly	Biweekly	7.50% Monthly	Biweekly	7.75% Monthly	Biweekly	8.00% Monthly	Biweekly	8.25% Monthly	Biweekly
$50,000	332.66	166.33	341.09	170.55	349.61	174.81	358.21	179.11	366.89	183.45	375.64	187.82
51,000	339.31	169.66	347.91	173.96	356.60	178.30	365.38	182.69	374.22	187.11	383.15	191.58
52,000	345.96	172.98	354.74	177.37	363.60	181.80	372.54	186.27	381.56	190.78	390.66	195.33
53,000	352.62	176.31	361.56	180.78	370.59	185.30	379.70	189.85	388.90	194.45	398.18	199.09
54,000	359.27	179.64	368.38	184.19	377.58	188.79	386.87	193.44	396.24	198.12	405.69	202.85
55,000	365.92	182.96	375.20	187.60	384.57	192.29	394.03	197.02	403.58	201.79	413.20	206.60
56,000	372.57	186.29	382.02	191.01	391.57	195.79	401.20	200.60	410.91	205.46	420.71	210.36
57,000	379.23	189.62	388.85	194.43	398.56	199.28	408.36	204.18	418.25	209.13	428.23	214.12
58,000	385.88	192.94	395.67	197.84	405.55	202.78	415.52	207.76	425.59	212.80	435.74	217.87
59,000	392.53	196.27	402.49	201.25	412.54	206.27	422.69	211.35	432.93	216.47	443.25	221.63
60,000	399.19	199.60	409.31	204.66	419.53	209.77	429.85	214.93	440.26	220.13	450.77	225.39
61,000	405.84	202.92	416.13	208.07	426.53	213.27	437.02	218.51	447.60	223.80	458.28	229.14
62,000	412.49	206.25	422.95	211.48	433.52	216.76	444.18	222.09	454.94	227.47	465.79	232.90
63,000	419.15	209.58	429.78	214.89	440.51	220.26	451.34	225.67	462.28	231.14	473.30	236.65
64,000	425.80	212.90	436.60	218.30	447.50	223.75	458.51	229.26	469.61	234.81	480.82	240.41
65,000	432.45	216.23	443.42	221.71	454.49	227.25	465.67	232.84	476.95	238.48	488.33	244.17
66,000	439.10	219.55	450.24	225.12	461.49	230.75	472.84	236.42	484.29	242.15	495.84	247.92
67,000	445.76	222.88	457.06	228.53	468.48	234.24	480.00	240.00	491.63	245.82	503.35	251.68
68,000	452.41	226.21	463.88	231.94	475.47	237.74	487.17	243.59	498.96	249.48	510.87	255.44
69,000	459.06	229.53	470.71	235.36	482.46	241.23	494.33	247.17	506.30	253.15	518.38	259.19
70,000	465.72	232.86	477.53	238.77	489.46	244.73	501.49	250.75	513.64	256.82	525.89	262.95
71,000	472.37	236.19	484.35	242.18	496.45	248.23	508.66	254.33	520.98	260.49	533.40	266.70
72,000	479.02	239.51	491.17	245.59	503.44	251.72	515.82	257.91	528.32	264.16	540.92	270.46
73,000	485.68	242.84	497.99	249.00	510.43	255.22	522.99	261.50	535.65	267.83	548.43	274.22
74,000	492.33	246.17	504.82	252.41	517.42	258.71	530.15	265.08	542.99	271.50	555.94	277.97
75,000	498.98	249.49	511.64	255.82	524.42	262.21	537.31	268.66	550.33	275.17	563.46	281.73
76,000	505.63	252.82	518.46	259.23	531.41	265.71	544.48	272.24	557.67	278.84	570.97	285.49
77,000	512.29	256.15	525.28	262.64	538.40	269.20	551.64	275.82	565.00	282.50	578.48	289.24
78,000	518.94	259.47	532.10	266.05	545.39	272.70	558.81	279.41	572.34	286.17	585.99	293.00
79,000	525.59	262.80	538.92	269.46	552.38	276.19	565.97	282.99	579.68	289.84	593.51	296.76
80,000	532.25	266.13	545.75	272.88	559.38	279.69	573.13	286.57	587.02	293.51	601.02	300.51
81,000	538.90	269.45	552.57	276.29	566.37	283.19	580.30	290.15	594.35	297.18	608.53	304.27
82,000	545.55	272.78	559.39	279.70	573.36	286.68	587.46	293.73	601.69	300.85	616.04	308.02
83,000	552.21	276.11	566.21	283.11	580.35	290.18	594.63	297.32	609.03	304.52	623.56	311.78
84,000	558.86	279.43	573.03	286.52	587.35	293.68	601.79	300.90	616.37	308.19	631.07	315.54
85,000	565.51	282.76	579.85	289.93	594.34	297.17	608.96	304.48	623.70	311.85	638.58	319.29
86,000	572.17	286.09	586.68	293.34	601.33	300.67	616.12	308.06	631.04	315.52	646.09	323.05
87,000	578.82	289.41	593.50	296.75	608.32	304.16	623.28	311.64	638.38	319.19	653.61	326.81
88,000	585.47	292.74	600.32	300.16	615.31	307.66	630.45	315.23	645.72	322.86	661.12	330.56
89,000	592.12	296.06	607.14	303.57	622.31	311.16	637.61	318.81	653.06	326.53	668.63	334.32
90,000	598.78	299.39	613.96	306.98	629.30	314.65	644.78	322.39	660.39	330.20	676.15	338.08
91,000	605.43	302.72	620.79	310.40	636.29	318.15	651.94	325.97	667.73	333.87	683.66	341.83
92,000	612.08	306.04	627.61	313.81	643.28	321.64	659.10	329.55	675.07	337.54	691.17	345.59
93,000	618.74	309.37	634.43	317.22	650.27	325.14	666.27	333.14	682.41	341.21	698.68	349.34
94,000	625.39	312.70	641.25	320.63	657.27	328.64	673.43	336.72	689.74	344.87	706.20	353.10
95,000	632.04	316.02	648.07	324.04	664.26	332.13	680.60	340.30	697.08	348.54	713.71	356.86
96,000	638.70	319.35	654.89	327.45	671.25	335.63	687.76	343.88	704.42	352.21	721.22	360.61
97,000	645.35	322.68	661.72	330.86	678.24	339.12	694.92	347.46	711.76	355.88	728.73	364.37
98,000	652.00	326.00	668.54	334.27	685.24	342.62	702.09	351.05	719.09	359.55	736.25	368.13
99,000	658.65	329.33	675.36	337.68	692.23	346.12	709.25	354.63	726.43	363.22	743.76	371.88
100,000	665.31	332.66	682.18	341.09	699.22	349.61	716.42	358.21	733.77	366.89	751.27	375.64
110,000	731.84	365.92	750.40	375.20	769.14	384.57	788.06	394.03	807.15	403.58	826.40	413.20
120,000	798.37	399.19	818.62	409.31	839.06	419.53	859.70	429.85	880.52	440.26	901.53	450.77
130,000	864.90	432.45	886.83	443.42	908.98	454.49	931.34	465.67	953.90	476.95	976.65	488.33
140,000	931.43	465.72	955.05	477.53	978.91	489.46	1002.98	501.49	1027.28	513.64	1051.78	525.89
150,000	997.96	498.98	1023.27	511.64	1048.83	524.42	1074.62	537.31	1100.65	550.33	1126.91	563.46
160,000	1064.49	532.25	1091.49	545.75	1118.75	559.38	1146.26	573.13	1174.03	587.02	1202.03	601.02
170,000	1131.02	565.51	1159.70	579.85	1188.67	594.34	1217.91	608.96	1247.40	623.70	1277.16	638.58
180,000	1197.55	598.78	1227.92	613.96	1258.59	629.30	1289.55	644.78	1320.78	660.39	1352.29	676.15
190,000	1264.08	632.04	1296.14	648.07	1328.51	664.26	1361.19	680.60	1394.16	697.08	1427.41	713.71
200,000	1330.61	665.31	1364.36	682.18	1398.43	699.22	1432.83	716.42	1467.53	733.77	1502.54	751.27
210,000	1397.14	698.57	1432.58	716.29	1468.36	734.18	1504.47	752.24	1540.91	770.46	1577.67	788.84
220,000	1463.67	731.84	1500.79	750.40	1538.28	769.14	1576.11	788.06	1614.29	807.15	1652.79	826.40
230,000	1530.20	765.10	1569.01	784.51	1608.20	804.10	1647.75	823.88	1687.66	843.83	1727.92	863.96
240,000	1596.73	798.37	1637.23	818.62	1678.12	839.06	1719.39	859.70	1761.04	880.52	1803.05	901.53
250,000	1663.26	831.63	1705.45	852.73	1748.04	874.02	1791.04	895.52	1834.42	917.21	1878.17	939.09
260,000	1729.79	864.90	1773.66	886.83	1817.96	908.98	1862.68	931.34	1907.79	953.90	1953.30	976.65
270,000	1796.32	898.16	1841.88	920.94	1887.88	943.94	1934.32	967.16	1981.17	990.59	2028.43	1014.22
280,000	1862.85	931.43	1910.10	955.05	1957.81	978.91	2005.96	1002.98	2054.55	1027.28	2103.55	1051.78
290,000	1929.38	964.69	1978.32	989.16	2027.73	1013.87	2077.60	1038.80	2127.92	1063.96	2178.68	1089.34
300,000	1995.91	997.96	2046.53	1023.27	2097.65	1048.83	2149.24	1074.62	2201.30	1100.65	2253.81	1126.91
310,000	2062.44	1031.22	2114.75	1057.38	2167.57	1083.79	2220.88	1110.44	2274.68	1137.34	2328.93	1164.47
320,000	2128.97	1064.49	2182.97	1091.49	2237.49	1118.75	2292.52	1146.26	2348.05	1174.03	2404.06	1202.03
330,000	2195.50	1097.75	2251.19	1125.60	2307.41	1153.71	2364.17	1182.09	2421.43	1210.72	2479.19	1239.60
340,000	2262.03	1131.02	2319.40	1159.70	2377.33	1188.67	2435.81	1217.91	2494.80	1247.40	2554.31	1277.16
350,000	2328.56	1164.28	2387.62	1193.81	2447.26	1223.63	2507.45	1253.73	2568.18	1284.09	2629.44	1314.72
Adder per $1,000	$6.66	$3.33	$6.83	$3.42	$7.00	$3.50	$7.17	$3.59	$7.34	$3.67	$7.52	$3.76

Payments on Monthly & Biweekly Home Loans

30 Year Schedule

Amount of Loan	8.50% Monthly	Biweekly	8.75% Monthly	Biweekly	9.00% Monthly	Biweekly	9.25% Monthly	Biweekly	9.50% Monthly	Biweekly	9.75% Monthly	Biweekly
$50,000	384.46	192.23	393.36	196.68	402.32	201.16	411.34	205.67	420.43	210.22	429.58	214.79
51,000	392.15	196.08	401.22	200.61	410.36	205.18	419.57	209.79	428.84	214.42	438.17	219.09
52,000	399.84	199.92	409.09	204.55	418.41	209.21	427.80	213.90	437.25	218.63	446.77	223.39
53,000	407.53	203.77	416.96	208.48	426.46	213.23	436.02	218.01	445.66	222.83	455.36	227.68
54,000	415.22	207.61	424.82	212.41	434.50	217.25	444.25	222.13	454.07	227.04	463.95	231.98
55,000	422.91	211.46	432.69	216.35	442.55	221.28	452.48	226.24	462.47	231.24	472.54	236.27
56,000	430.60	215.30	440.56	220.28	450.59	225.30	460.70	230.35	470.88	235.44	481.13	240.57
57,000	438.29	219.15	448.42	224.21	458.64	229.32	468.93	234.47	479.29	239.65	489.72	244.86
58,000	445.97	222.99	456.29	228.15	466.69	233.35	477.16	238.58	487.70	243.85	498.31	249.16
59,000	453.66	226.83	464.16	232.08	474.73	237.37	485.38	242.69	496.11	248.06	506.91	253.46
60,000	461.35	230.68	472.03	236.02	482.78	241.39	493.61	246.81	504.52	252.26	515.50	257.75
61,000	469.04	234.52	479.89	239.95	490.82	245.41	501.84	250.92	512.93	256.47	524.09	262.05
62,000	476.73	238.37	487.76	243.88	498.87	249.44	510.06	255.03	521.33	260.67	532.68	266.34
63,000	484.42	242.21	495.63	247.82	506.92	253.46	518.29	259.15	529.74	264.87	541.27	270.64
64,000	492.11	246.06	503.49	251.75	514.96	257.48	526.52	263.26	538.15	269.08	549.86	274.93
65,000	499.80	249.90	511.36	255.68	523.01	261.51	534.74	267.37	546.56	273.28	558.46	279.23
66,000	507.49	253.75	519.23	259.62	531.06	265.53	542.97	271.49	554.97	277.49	567.05	283.53
67,000	515.18	257.59	527.09	263.55	539.10	269.55	551.20	275.60	563.38	281.69	575.64	287.82
68,000	522.87	261.44	534.96	267.48	547.15	273.58	559.42	279.71	571.79	285.90	584.23	292.12
69,000	530.56	265.28	542.83	271.42	555.19	277.60	567.65	283.83	580.19	290.10	592.82	296.41
70,000	538.24	269.12	550.70	275.35	563.24	281.62	575.88	287.94	588.60	294.30	601.41	300.71
71,000	545.93	272.97	558.56	279.28	571.29	285.65	584.10	292.05	597.01	298.51	610.00	305.00
72,000	553.62	276.81	566.43	283.22	579.33	289.67	592.33	296.17	605.42	302.71	618.60	309.30
73,000	561.31	280.66	574.30	287.15	587.38	293.69	600.56	300.28	613.83	306.92	627.19	313.60
74,000	569.00	284.50	582.16	291.08	595.43	297.72	608.78	304.39	622.24	311.12	635.78	317.89
75,000	576.69	288.35	590.03	295.02	603.47	301.74	617.01	308.51	630.65	315.33	644.37	322.19
76,000	584.38	292.19	597.90	298.95	611.52	305.76	625.24	312.62	639.05	319.53	652.96	326.48
77,000	592.07	296.04	605.76	302.88	619.56	309.78	633.47	316.74	647.46	323.73	661.55	330.78
78,000	599.76	299.88	613.63	306.82	627.61	313.81	641.69	320.85	655.87	327.94	670.15	335.08
79,000	607.45	303.73	621.50	310.75	635.66	317.83	649.92	324.96	664.28	332.14	678.74	339.37
80,000	615.14	307.57	629.37	314.69	643.70	321.85	658.15	329.08	672.69	336.35	687.33	343.67
81,000	622.82	311.41	637.23	318.62	651.75	325.88	666.37	333.19	681.10	340.55	695.92	347.96
82,000	630.51	315.26	645.10	322.55	659.80	329.90	674.60	337.30	689.51	344.76	704.51	352.26
83,000	638.20	319.10	652.97	326.49	667.84	333.92	682.83	341.42	697.91	348.96	713.10	356.55
84,000	645.89	322.95	660.83	330.42	675.89	337.95	691.05	345.53	706.32	353.16	721.69	360.85
85,000	653.58	326.79	668.70	334.35	683.93	341.97	699.28	349.64	714.73	357.37	730.29	365.15
86,000	661.27	330.64	676.57	338.29	691.98	345.99	707.51	353.76	723.14	361.57	738.88	369.44
87,000	668.96	334.48	684.43	342.22	700.03	350.02	715.73	357.87	731.55	365.78	747.47	373.74
88,000	676.65	338.33	692.30	346.15	708.07	354.04	723.96	361.98	739.96	369.98	756.06	378.03
89,000	684.34	342.17	700.17	350.09	716.12	358.06	732.19	366.10	748.37	374.19	764.65	382.33
90,000	692.03	346.02	708.04	354.02	724.17	362.09	740.41	370.21	756.77	378.39	773.24	386.62
91,000	699.72	349.86	715.90	357.95	732.21	366.11	748.64	374.32	765.18	382.59	781.84	390.92
92,000	707.41	353.71	723.77	361.89	740.26	370.13	756.87	378.44	773.59	386.80	790.43	395.22
93,000	715.09	357.55	731.64	365.82	748.30	374.15	765.09	382.55	782.00	391.00	799.02	399.51
94,000	722.78	361.39	739.50	369.75	756.35	378.18	773.32	386.66	790.41	395.21	807.61	403.81
95,000	730.47	365.24	747.37	373.69	764.40	382.20	781.55	390.78	798.82	399.41	816.20	408.10
96,000	738.16	369.08	755.24	377.62	772.44	386.22	789.77	394.89	807.23	403.62	824.79	412.40
97,000	745.85	372.93	763.10	381.55	780.49	390.25	798.00	399.00	815.63	407.82	833.38	416.69
98,000	753.54	376.77	770.97	385.49	788.54	394.27	806.23	403.12	824.04	412.02	841.98	420.99
99,000	761.23	380.62	778.84	389.42	796.58	398.29	814.45	407.23	832.45	416.23	850.57	425.29
100,000	768.92	384.46	786.71	393.36	804.63	402.32	822.68	411.34	840.86	420.43	859.16	429.58
110,000	845.81	422.91	865.38	432.69	885.09	442.55	904.95	452.48	924.94	462.47	945.07	472.54
120,000	922.70	461.35	944.05	472.03	965.55	482.78	987.22	493.61	1009.03	504.52	1030.99	515.50
130,000	999.59	499.80	1022.72	511.36	1046.01	523.01	1069.48	534.74	1093.12	546.56	1116.91	558.46
140,000	1076.48	538.24	1101.39	550.70	1126.48	563.24	1151.75	575.88	1177.20	588.60	1202.82	601.41
150,000	1153.38	576.69	1180.06	590.03	1206.94	603.47	1234.02	617.01	1261.29	630.65	1288.74	644.37
160,000	1230.27	615.14	1258.73	629.37	1287.40	643.70	1316.29	658.15	1345.37	672.69	1374.65	687.33
170,000	1307.16	653.58	1337.40	668.70	1367.86	683.93	1398.55	699.28	1429.46	714.73	1460.57	730.29
180,000	1384.05	692.03	1416.07	708.04	1448.33	724.17	1480.82	740.41	1513.54	756.77	1546.48	773.24
190,000	1460.94	730.47	1494.74	747.37	1528.79	764.40	1563.09	781.55	1597.63	798.82	1632.40	816.20
200,000	1537.83	768.92	1573.41	786.71	1609.25	804.63	1645.36	822.68	1681.71	840.86	1718.31	859.16
210,000	1614.72	807.36	1652.08	826.04	1689.71	844.86	1727.62	863.81	1765.80	882.90	1804.23	902.12
220,000	1691.61	845.81	1730.75	865.38	1770.17	885.09	1809.89	904.95	1849.88	924.94	1890.14	945.07
230,000	1768.51	884.26	1809.42	904.71	1850.64	925.32	1892.16	946.08	1933.97	966.99	1976.06	988.03
240,000	1845.40	922.70	1888.09	944.05	1931.10	965.55	1974.43	987.22	2018.06	1009.03	2061.98	1030.99
250,000	1922.29	961.15	1966.76	983.38	2011.56	1005.78	2056.69	1028.35	2102.14	1051.07	2147.89	1073.95
260,000	1999.18	999.59	2045.43	1022.72	2092.02	1046.01	2138.96	1069.48	2186.23	1093.12	2233.81	1116.91
270,000	2076.07	1038.04	2124.10	1062.05	2172.49	1086.25	2221.23	1110.62	2270.31	1135.16	2319.72	1159.86
280,000	2152.96	1076.48	2202.77	1101.39	2252.95	1126.48	2303.50	1151.75	2354.40	1177.20	2405.64	1202.82
290,000	2229.85	1114.93	2281.44	1140.72	2333.41	1166.71	2385.76	1192.88	2438.48	1219.24	2491.55	1245.78
300,000	2306.75	1153.38	2360.11	1180.06	2413.87	1206.94	2468.03	1234.02	2522.57	1261.29	2577.47	1288.74
310,000	2383.64	1191.82	2438.78	1219.39	2494.34	1247.17	2550.30	1275.15	2606.65	1303.33	2663.38	1331.69
320,000	2460.53	1230.27	2517.45	1258.73	2574.80	1287.40	2632.57	1316.29	2690.74	1345.37	2749.30	1374.65
330,000	2537.42	1268.71	2596.12	1298.06	2655.26	1327.63	2714.83	1357.42	2774.82	1387.41	2835.21	1417.61
340,000	2614.31	1307.16	2674.79	1337.40	2735.72	1367.86	2797.10	1398.55	2858.91	1429.46	2921.13	1460.57
350,000	2691.20	1345.60	2753.46	1376.73	2816.18	1408.09	2879.37	1439.69	2942.99	1471.50	3007.05	1503.53
Adder per $1,000	$7.69	$3.85	$7.87	$3.94	$8.05	$4.03	$8.23	$4.12	$8.41	$4.21	$8.60	$4.30

Payments on Monthly & Biweekly Home Loans

30 Year Schedule

Amount of Loan	10.00% Monthly	Biweekly	10.25% Monthly	Biweekly	10.50% Monthly	Biweekly	10.75% Monthly	Biweekly	11.00% Monthly	Biweekly	11.25% Monthly	Biweekly
$50,000	438.79	219.40	448.06	224.03	457.37	228.69	466.75	233.38	476.17	238.09	485.64	242.82
51,000	447.57	223.79	457.02	228.51	466.52	233.26	476.08	238.04	485.69	242.85	495.35	247.68
52,000	456.34	228.17	465.98	232.99	475.67	237.84	485.42	242.71	495.21	247.61	505.06	252.53
53,000	465.12	232.56	474.94	237.47	484.82	242.41	494.75	247.38	504.74	252.37	514.77	257.39
54,000	473.89	236.95	483.90	241.95	493.96	246.98	504.08	252.04	514.26	257.13	524.49	262.25
55,000	482.67	241.34	492.86	246.43	503.11	251.56	513.42	256.71	523.78	261.89	534.20	267.10
56,000	491.45	245.73	501.82	250.91	512.26	256.13	522.75	261.38	533.31	266.66	543.91	271.96
57,000	500.22	250.11	510.78	255.39	521.41	260.71	532.09	266.05	542.83	271.42	553.62	276.81
58,000	509.00	254.50	519.74	259.87	530.55	265.28	541.42	270.71	552.35	276.18	563.34	281.67
59,000	517.77	258.89	528.70	264.35	539.70	269.85	550.76	275.38	561.88	280.94	573.05	286.53
60,000	526.55	263.28	537.67	268.84	548.85	274.43	560.09	280.05	571.40	285.70	582.76	291.38
61,000	535.32	267.66	546.63	273.32	558.00	279.00	569.43	284.72	580.92	290.46	592.47	296.24
62,000	544.10	272.05	555.59	277.80	567.14	283.57	578.76	289.38	590.45	295.23	602.19	301.10
63,000	552.88	276.44	564.55	282.28	576.29	288.15	588.10	294.05	599.97	299.99	611.90	305.95
64,000	561.65	280.83	573.51	286.76	585.44	292.72	597.43	298.72	609.49	304.75	621.61	310.81
65,000	570.43	285.22	582.47	291.24	594.59	297.30	606.77	303.39	619.02	309.51	631.32	315.66
66,000	579.20	289.60	591.43	295.72	603.73	301.87	616.10	308.05	628.54	314.27	641.04	320.52
67,000	587.98	293.99	600.39	300.20	612.88	306.44	625.44	312.72	638.06	319.03	650.75	325.38
68,000	596.75	298.38	609.35	304.68	622.03	311.02	634.77	317.39	647.58	323.79	660.46	330.23
69,000	605.53	302.77	618.31	309.16	631.18	315.59	644.11	322.06	657.11	328.56	670.18	335.09
70,000	614.31	307.16	627.28	313.64	640.32	320.16	653.44	326.72	666.63	333.32	679.89	339.95
71,000	623.08	311.54	636.24	318.12	649.47	324.74	662.78	331.39	676.15	338.08	689.60	344.80
72,000	631.86	315.93	645.20	322.60	658.62	329.31	672.11	336.06	685.68	342.84	699.31	349.66
73,000	640.63	320.32	654.16	327.08	667.76	333.88	681.45	340.73	695.20	347.60	709.03	354.52
74,000	649.41	324.71	663.12	331.56	676.91	338.46	690.78	345.39	704.72	352.36	718.74	359.37
75,000	658.18	329.09	672.08	336.04	686.06	343.03	700.12	350.06	714.25	357.13	728.45	364.23
76,000	666.96	333.48	681.04	340.52	695.21	347.61	709.45	-354.73	723.77	361.89	738.16	369.08
77,000	675.74	337.87	690.00	345.00	704.35	352.18	718.79	359.40	733.29	366.65	747.88	373.94
78,000	684.51	342.26	698.96	349.48	713.50	356.75	728.12	364.06	742.82	371.41	757.59	378.80
79,000	693.29	346.65	707.92	353.96	722.65	361.33	737.46	368.73	752.34	376.17	767.30	383.65
80,000	702.06	351.03	716.89	358.45	731.80	365.90	746.79	373.40	761.86	380.93	777.01	388.51
81,000	710.84	355.42	725.85	362.93	740.94	370.47	756.12	378.06	771.39	385.70	786.73	393.37
82,000	719.61	359.81	734.81	367.41	750.09	375.05	765.46	382.73	780.91	390.46	796.44	398.22
83,000	728.39	364.20	743.77	371.89	759.24	379.62	774.79	387.40	790.43	395.22	806.15	403.08
84,000	737.17	368.59	752.73	376.37	768.39	384.20	784.13	392.07	799.96	399.98	815.86	407.93
85,000	745.94	372.97	761.69	380.85	777.53	388.77	793.46	396.73	809.48	404.74	825.58	412.79
86,000	754.72	377.36	770.65	385.33	786.68	393.34	802.80	401.40	819.00	409.50	835.29	417.65
87,000	763.49	381.75	779.61	389.81	795.83	397.92	812.13	406.07	828.53	414.27	845.00	422.50
88,000	772.27	386.14	788.57	394.29	804.98	402.49	821.47	410.74	838.05	419.03	854.71	427.36
89,000	781.04	390.52	797.54	398.77	814.12	407.06	830.80	415.40	847.57	423.79	864.43	432.22
90,000	789.82	394.91	806.50	403.25	823.27	411.64	840.14	420.07	857.10	428.55	874.14	437.07
91,000	798.60	399.30	815.46	407.73	832.42	416.21	849.47	424.74	866.62	433.31	883.85	441.93
92,000	807.37	403.69	824.42	412.21	841.57	420.79	858.81	429.41	876.14	438.07	893.57	446.79
93,000	816.15	408.08	833.38	416.69	850.71	425.36	868.14	434.07	885.67	442.84	903.28	451.64
94,000	824.92	412.46	842.34	421.17	859.86	429.93	877.48	438.74	895.19	447.60	912.99	456.50
95,000	833.70	416.85	851.30	425.65	869.01	434.51	886.81	443.41	904.71	452.36	922.70	461.35
96,000	842.47	421.24	860.26	430.13	878.15	439.08	896.15	448.08	914.24	457.12	932.42	466.21
97,000	851.25	425.63	869.22	434.61	887.30	443.65	905.48	452.74	923.76	461.88	942.13	471.07
98,000	860.03	430.02	878.18	439.09	896.45	448.23	914.82	457.41	-933.28	466.64	951.84	475.92
99,000	868.80	434.40	887.15	443.58	905.60	452.80	924.15	462.08	942.81	471.41	961.55	480.78
100,000	877.58	438.79	896.11	448.06	914.74	457.37	933.49	466.75	952.33	476.17	971.27	485.64
110,000	965.33	482.67	985.72	492.86	1006.22	503.11	1026.83	513.42	1047.56	523.78	1068.39	534.20
120,000	1053.09	526.55	1075.33	537.67	1097.69	548.85	1120.18	560.09	1142.79	571.40	1165.52	582.76
130,000	1140.85	570.43	1164.94	582.47	1189.17	594.59	1213.53	606.77	1238.03	619.02	1262.64	631.32
140,000	1228.61	614.31	1254.55	627.28	1280.64	640.32	1306.88	653.44	1333.26	666.63	1359.77	679.89
150,000	1316.36	658.18	1344.16	672.08	1372.11	686.06	1400.23	700.12	1428.49	714.25	1456.90	728.45
160,000	1404.12	702.06	1433.77	716.89	1463.59	731.80	1493.58	746.79	1523.72	761.86	1554.02	777.01
170,000	1491.88	745.94	1523.38	761.69	1555.06	777.53	1586.92	793.46	1618.95	809.48	1651.15	825.58
180,000	1579.63	789.82	1612.99	806.50	1646.54	823.27	1680.27	840.14	1714.19	857.10	1748.28	874.14
190,000	1667.39	833.70	1702.60	851.30	1738.01	869.01	1773.62	886.81	1809.42	904.71	1845.40	922.70
200,000	1755.15	877.58	1792.21	896.11	1829.48	914.74	1866.97	933.49	1904.65	952.33	1942.53	971.27
210,000	1842.91	921.46	1881.82	940.91	1920.96	960.48	1960.32	980.16	1999.88	999.94	2039.65	1019.83
220,000	1930.66	965.33	1971.43	985.72	2012.43	1006.22	2053.66	1026.83	2095.12	1047.56	2136.78	1068.39
230,000	2018.42	1009.21	2061.04	1030.52	2103.91	1051.96	2147.01	1073.51	2190.35	1095.18	2233.91	1116.96
240,000	2106.18	1053.09	2150.65	1075.33	2195.38	1097.69	2240.36	1120.18	2285.58	1142.79	2331.03	1165.52
250,000	2193.93	1096.97	2240.26	1120.13	2286.85	1143.43	2333.71	1166.86	2380.81	1190.41	2428.16	1214.08
260,000	2281.69	1140.85	2329.87	1164.94	2378.33	1189.17	2427.06	1213.53	2476.05	1238.03	2525.28	1262.64
270,000	2369.45	1184.73	2419.48	1209.74	2469.80	1234.90	2520.40	1260.20	2571.28	1285.64	2622.41	1311.21
280,000	2457.21	1228.61	2509.09	1254.55	2561.27	1280.64	2613.75	1306.88	2666.51	1333.26	2719.54	1359.77
290,000	2544.96	1272.48	2598.70	1299.35	2652.75	1326.38	2707.10	1353.55	2761.74	1380.87	2816.66	1408.33
300,000	2632.72	1316.36	2688.31	1344.16	2744.22	1372.11	2800.45	1400.23	2856.98	1428.49	2913.79	1456.90
310,000	2720.48	1360.24	2777.92	1388.96	2835.70	1417.85	2893.80	1446.90	2952.21	1476.11	3010.92	1505.46
320,000	2808.23	1404.12	2867.53	1433.77	2927.17	1463.59	2987.15	1493.58	3047.44	1523.72	3108.04	1554.02
330,000	2895.99	1448.00	2957.14	1478.57	3018.64	1509.32	3080.49	1540.25	3142.67	1571.34	3205.17	1602.59
340,000	2983.75	1491.88	3046.75	1523.38	3110.12	1555.06	3173.84	1586.92	3237.90	1618.95	3302.29	1651.15
350,000	3071.51	1535.76	3136.36	1568.18	3201.59	1600.80	3267.19	1633.60	3333.14	1666.57	3399.42	1699.71
Adder per $1,000	$8.78	$4.39	$8.97	$4.49	$9.15	$4.58	$9.34	$4.67	$9.53	$4.77	$9.72	$4.86

Payments on Monthly & Biweekly Home Loans

30 Year Schedule

Amount of Loan	11.50% Monthly	Biweekly	11.75% Monthly	Biweekly	12.00% Monthly	Biweekly	12.25% Monthly	Biweekly	12.50% Monthly	Biweekly	12.75% Monthly	Biweekly
$50,000	495.15	247.58	504.71	252.36	514.31	257.16	523.95	261.98	533.63	266.82	543.35	271.68
51,000	505.05	252.53	514.80	257.40	524.60	262.30	534.43	267.22	544.31	272.16	554.22	277.11
52,000	514.96	257.48	524.90	262.45	534.88	267.44	544.91	272.46	554.98	277.49	565.09	282.55
53,000	524.86	262.43	534.99	267.50	545.17	272.59	555.39	277.70	565.65	282.83	575.95	287.98
54,000	534.76	267.38	545.09	272.55	555.46	277.73	565.87	282.94	576.32	288.16	586.82	293.41
55,000	544.67	272.34	555.18	277.59	565.74	282.87	576.35	288.18	587.00	293.50	597.69	298.85
56,000	554.57	277.29	565.27	282.64	576.03	288.02	586.83	293.42	597.67	298.84	608.55	304.28
57,000	564.47	282.24	575.37	287.69	586.31	293.16	597.31	298.66	608.34	304.17	619.42	309.71
58,000	574.37	287.19	585.46	292.73	596.60	298.30	607.78	303.89	619.01	309.51	630.29	315.15
59,000	584.28	292.14	595.56	297.78	606.89	303.45	618.26	309.13	629.69	314.85	641.15	320.58
60,000	594.18	297.09	605.65	302.83	617.17	308.59	628.74	314.37	640.36	320.18	652.02	326.01
61,000	604.08	302.04	615.74	307.87	627.46	313.73	639.22	319.61	651.03	325.52	662.89	331.45
62,000	613.99	307.00	625.84	312.92	637.74	318.87	649.70	324.85	661.70	330.85	673.75	336.88
63,000	623.89	311.95	635.93	317.97	648.03	324.02	660.18	330.09	672.38	336.19	684.62	342.31
64,000	633.79	316.90	646.03	323.02	658.32	329.16	670.66	335.33	683.05	341.53	695.49	347.75
65,000	643.69	321.85	656.12	328.06	668.60	334.30	681.14	340.57	693.72	346.86	706.36	353.18
66,000	653.60	326.80	666.22	333.11	678.89	339.45	691.62	345.81	704.40	352.20	717.22	358.61
67,000	663.50	331.75	676.31	338.16	689.18	344.59	702.10	351.05	715.07	357.54	728.09	364.05
68,000	673.40	336.70	686.40	343.20	699.46	349.73	712.57	356.29	725.74	362.87	738.96	369.48
69,000	683.31	341.66	696.50	348.25	709.75	354.88	723.05	361.53	736.41	368.21	749.82	374.91
70,000	693.21	346.61	706.59	353.30	720.03	360.02	733.53	366.77	747.09	373.55	760.69	380.35
71,000	703.11	351.56	716.69	358.35	730.32	365.16	744.01	372.01	757.76	378.88	771.56	385.78
72,000	713.01	356.51	726.78	363.39	740.61	370.31	754.49	377.25	768.43	384.22	782.42	391.21
73,000	722.92	361.46	736.87	368.44	750.89	375.45	764.97	382.49	779.10	389.55	793.29	396.65
74,000	732.82	366.41	746.97	373.49	761.18	380.59	775.45	387.73	789.78	394.89	804.16	402.08
75,000	742.72	371.36	757.06	378.53	771.46	385.73	785.93	392.97	800.45	400.23	815.02	407.51
76,000	752.63	376.32	767.16	383.58	781.75	390.88	796.41	398.21	811.12	405.56	825.89	412.95
77,000	762.53	381.27	777.25	388.63	792.04	396.02	806.89	403.45	821.79	410.90	836.76	418.38
78,000	772.43	386.22	787.34	393.67	802.32	401.16	817.36	408.68	832.47	416.24	847.63	423.82
79,000	782.34	391.17	797.44	398.72	812.61	406.31	827.84	413.92	843.14	421.57	858.49	429.25
80,000	792.24	396.12	807.53	403.77	822.90	411.45	838.32	419.16	853.81	426.91	869.36	434.68
81,000	802.14	401.07	817.63	408.82	833.18	416.59	848.80	424.40	864.48	432.24	880.23	440.12
82,000	812.04	406.02	827.72	413.86	843.47	421.74	859.28	429.64	875.16	437.58	891.09	445.55
83,000	821.95	410.98	837.82	418.91	853.75	426.88	869.76	434.88	885.83	442.92	901.96	450.98
84,000	831.85	415.93	847.91	423.96	864.04	432.02	880.24	440.12	896.50	448.25	912.83	456.42
85,000	841.75	420.88	858.00	429.00	874.33	437.17	890.72	445.36	907.17	453.59	923.69	461.85
86,000	851.66	425.83	868.10	434.05	884.61	442.31	901.20	450.60	917.85	458.93	934.56	467.28
87,000	861.56	430.78	878.19	439.10	894.90	447.45	911.67	455.84	928.52	464.26	945.43	472.72
88,000	871.46	435.73	888.29	444.15	905.18	452.59	922.15	461.08	939.19	469.60	956.30	478.15
89,000	881.36	440.68	898.38	449.19	915.47	457.74	932.63	466.32	949.86	474.93	967.16	483.58
90,000	891.27	445.64	908.47	454.24	925.76	462.88	943.11	471.56	960.54	480.27	978.03	489.02
91,000	901.17	450.59	918.57	459.29	936.04	468.02	953.59	476.80	971.21	485.61	988.90	494.45
92,000	911.07	455.54	928.66	464.33	946.33	473.17	964.07	482.04	981.88	490.94	999.76	499.88
93,000	920.98	460.49	938.76	469.38	956.61	478.31	974.55	487.28	992.55	496.28	1010.63	505.32
94,000	930.88	465.44	948.85	474.43	966.90	483.45	985.03	492.52	1003.23	501.62	1021.50	510.75
95,000	940.78	470.39	958.94	479.47	977.19	488.60	995.51	497.76	1013.90	506.95	1032.36	516.18
96,000	950.68	475.34	969.04	484.52	987.47	493.74	1005.99	503.00	1024.57	512.29	1043.23	521.62
97,000	960.59	480.30	979.13	489.57	997.76	498.88	1016.46	508.23	1035.25	517.63	1054.10	527.05
98,000	970.49	485.25	989.23	494.62	1008.05	504.03	1026.94	513.47	1045.92	522.96	1064.96	532.48
99,000	980.39	490.20	999.32	499.66	1018.33	509.17	1037.42	518.71	1056.59	528.30	1075.83	537.92
100,000	990.30	495.15	1009.41	504.71	1028.62	514.31	1047.90	523.95	1067.26	533.63	1086.70	543.35
110,000	1089.33	544.67	1110.36	555.18	1131.48	565.74	1152.69	576.35	1173.99	587.00	1195.37	597.69
120,000	1188.35	594.18	1211.30	605.65	1234.34	617.17	1257.48	628.74	1280.71	640.36	1304.04	652.02
130,000	1287.38	643.69	1312.24	656.12	1337.20	668.60	1362.27	681.14	1387.44	693.72	1412.71	706.36
140,000	1386.41	693.21	1413.18	706.59	1440.06	720.03	1467.06	733.53	1494.17	747.09	1521.38	760.69
150,000	1485.44	742.72	1514.12	757.06	1542.92	771.46	1571.85	785.93	1600.89	800.45	1630.04	815.02
160,000	1584.47	792.24	1615.06	807.53	1645.79	822.90	1676.64	838.32	1707.62	853.81	1738.71	869.36
170,000	1683.50	841.75	1716.00	858.00	1748.65	874.33	1781.43	890.72	1814.34	907.17	1847.38	923.69
180,000	1782.53	891.27	1816.94	908.47	1851.51	925.76	1886.22	943.11	1921.07	960.54	1956.05	978.03
190,000	1881.56	940.78	1917.88	958.94	1954.37	977.19	1991.01	995.51	2027.79	1013.90	2064.72	1032.36
200,000	1980.59	990.30	2018.82	1009.41	2057.23	1028.62	2095.80	1047.90	2134.52	1067.26	2173.39	1086.70
210,000	2079.62	1039.81	2119.77	1059.89	2160.09	1080.05	2200.59	1100.30	2241.25	1120.63	2282.06	1141.03
220,000	2178.65	1089.33	2220.71	1110.36	2262.95	1131.48	2305.38	1152.69	2347.97	1173.99	2390.73	1195.37
230,000	2277.68	1138.84	2321.65	1160.83	2365.81	1182.91	2410.17	1205.09	2454.70	1227.35	2499.40	1249.70
240,000	2376.70	1188.35	2422.59	1211.30	2468.68	1234.34	2514.96	1257.48	2561.42	1280.71	2608.07	1304.04
250,000	2475.73	1237.87	2523.53	1261.77	2571.54	1285.77	2619.75	1309.88	2668.15	1334.08	2716.74	1358.37
260,000	2574.76	1287.38	2624.47	1312.24	2674.40	1337.20	2724.54	1362.27	2774.88	1387.44	2825.41	1412.71
270,000	2673.79	1336.90	2725.41	1362.71	2777.26	1388.63	2829.33	1414.67	2881.60	1440.80	2934.08	1467.04
280,000	2772.82	1386.41	2826.35	1413.18	2880.12	1440.06	2934.11	1467.06	2988.33	1494.17	3042.75	1521.38
290,000	2871.85	1435.93	2927.29	1463.65	2982.98	1491.49	3038.90	1519.45	3095.05	1547.53	3151.42	1575.71
300,000	2970.88	1485.44	3028.23	1514.12	3085.84	1542.92	3143.69	1571.85	3201.78	1600.89	3260.08	1630.04
310,000	3069.91	1534.96	3129.18	1564.59	3188.70	1594.35	3248.48	1624.24	3308.50	1654.25	3368.75	1684.38
320,000	3168.94	1584.47	3230.12	1615.06	3291.57	1645.79	3353.27	1676.64	3415.23	1707.62	3477.42	1738.71
330,000	3267.97	1633.99	3331.06	1665.53	3394.43	1697.22	3458.06	1729.03	3521.96	1760.98	3586.09	1793.05
340,000	3367.00	1683.50	3432.00	1716.00	3497.29	1748.65	3562.85	1781.43	3628.68	1814.34	3694.76	1847.38
350,000	3466.02	1733.01	3532.94	1766.47	3600.15	1800.08	3667.64	1833.82	3735.41	1867.71	3803.43	1901.72
Adder per $1,000	$9.91	$4.96	$10.10	$5.05	$10.29	$5.15	$10.48	$5.24	$10.68	$5.34	$10.87	$5.44

Benefits of Accelerated Mortgage Repayment
Time of Earlier Payoff and Interest Savings

Original schedule 30 years

Added Payment	Normal Payoff	New Payoff (6.00%)	Time Saved	Money Saved	New Payoff (6.25%)	Time Saved	Money Saved	New Payoff (6.50%)	Time Saved	Money Saved	New Payoff (6.75%)	Time Saved	Money Saved
2.5%	5.0	4Y 10m	2	0.5%	4Y 10m	2	0.5%	4Y 10m	2	0.5%	4Y 10m	2	0.5%
	10.0	9Y 8m	4	1.2%	9Y 8m	4	1.3%	9Y 8m	4	1.3%	9Y 8m	4	1.4%
	12.5	12Y 1m	5	1.7%	12Y 1m	5	1.8%	12Y 0m	6	1.9%	12Y 0m	6	2.0%
	15.0	14Y 5m	7	2.2%	14Y 5m	7	2.4%	14Y 5m	7	2.6%	14Y 5m	7	2.8%
	20.0	19Y 1m	11	3.8%	19Y 1m	11	4.1%	19Y 0m	12	4.4%	19Y 0m	12	4.7%
	25.0	23Y 8m	16	5.9%	23Y 7m	17	6.4%	23Y 7m	17	7.0%	23Y 6m	18	7.6%
	27.5	25Y 11m	19	7.3%	25Y 10m	20	8.0%	25Y 9m	21	8.7%	25Y 8m	22	9.5%
	30.0	28Y 1m	23	8.8%	27Y 12m	24	9.7%	27Y 11m	25	10.7%	27Y 10m	26	11.7%
5%	5.0	4Y 9m	3	0.9%	4Y 9m	3	1.0%	4Y 9m	3	1.0%	4Y 9m	3	1.0%
	10.0	9Y 4m	8	2.3%	9Y 4m	8	2.4%	9Y 4m	8	2.6%	9Y 4m	8	2.7%
	12.5	11Y 8m	10	3.2%	11Y 7m	11	3.4%	11Y 7m	11	3.6%	11Y 7m	11	3.9%
	15.0	13Y 11m	13	4.3%	13Y 10m	14	4.6%	13Y 10m	14	4.9%	13Y 10m	14	5.3%
	20.0	18Y 3m	21	7.1%	18Y 3m	21	7.7%	18Y 2m	22	8.3%	18Y 1m	23	8.9%
	25.0	22Y 5m	31	11.1%	22Y 4m	32	12.0%	22Y 3m	33	13.0%	22Y 2m	34	14.1%
	27.5	24Y 6m	36	13.5%	24Y 4m	38	14.7%	24Y 3m	39	16.0%	24Y 1m	41	17.4%
	30.0	26Y 5m	43	16.3%	26Y 3m	45	17.8%	26Y 2m	46	19.5%	25Y 12m	48	21.2%
8%	5.0	4Y 7m	5	1.3%	4Y 7m	5	1.4%	4Y 7m	5	1.5%	4Y 7m	5	1.5%
	10.0	9Y 1m	11	3.3%	9Y 1m	11	3.5%	9Y 1m	11	3.7%	9Y 0m	12	3.9%
	12.5	11Y 3m	15	4.6%	11Y 3m	15	4.9%	11Y 3m	15	5.2%	11Y 2m	16	5.6%
	15.0	13Y 5m	19	6.2%	13Y 4m	20	6.6%	13Y 4m	20	7.1%	13Y 4m	20	7.5%
	20.0	17Y 6m	30	10.2%	17Y 5m	31	11.0%	17Y 5m	31	11.8%	17Y 4m	32	12.7%
	25.0	21Y 5m	43	15.6%	21Y 3m	45	16.9%	21Y 2m	46	18.3%	21Y 0m	48	19.8%
	27.5	23Y 3m	51	18.9%	23Y 1m	53	20.5%	22Y 11m	55	22.3%	22Y 9m	57	24.2%
	30.0	24Y 12m	60	22.6%	24Y 10m	62	24.7%	24Y 7m	65	26.9%	24Y 5m	67	29.2%
10%	5.0	4Y 6m	6	1.7%	4Y 6m	6	1.8%	4Y 6m	6	1.9%	4Y 6m	6	2.0%
	10.0	8Y 10m	14	4.3%	8Y 9m	15	4.5%	8Y 9m	15	4.8%	8Y 9m	15	5.1%
	12.5	10Y 11m	19	5.9%	10Y 10m	20	6.3%	10Y 10m	20	6.7%	10Y 10m	20	7.1%
	15.0	12Y 11m	25	7.9%	12Y 11m	25	8.5%	12Y 10m	26	9.0%	12Y 10m	26	9.6%
	20.0	16Y 10m	38	12.9%	16Y 9m	39	13.9%	16Y 8m	40	14.9%	16Y 7m	41	16.0%
	25.0	20Y 5m	55	19.6%	20Y 4m	56	21.2%	20Y 2m	58	22.9%	20Y 0m	60	24.7%
	27.5	22Y 1m	65	23.6%	21Y 11m	67	25.6%	21Y 9m	69	27.7%	21Y 7m	71	30.0%
	30.0	23Y 9m	75	28.1%	23Y 6m	78	30.6%	23Y 4m	80	33.2%	23Y 1m	83	35.9%
15%	5.0	4Y 3m	9	2.4%	4Y 3m	9	2.6%	4Y 3m	9	2.7%	4Y 3m	9	2.8%
	10.0	8Y 4m	20	6.0%	8Y 3m	21	6.4%	8Y 3m	21	6.7%	8Y 3m	21	7.1%
	12.5	10Y 3m	27	8.3%	10Y 2m	28	8.8%	10Y 2m	28	9.4%	10Y 2m	28	9.9%
	15.0	12Y 1m	35	11.0%	12Y 1m	35	11.7%	12Y 0m	36	12.5%	11Y 11m	37	13.3%
	20.0	15Y 7m	53	17.7%	15Y 6m	54	19.0%	15Y 5m	55	20.4%	15Y 4m	56	21.8%
	25.0	18Y 9m	75	26.4%	18Y 7m	77	28.5%	18Y 5m	79	30.7%	18Y 3m	81	32.9%
	27.5	20Y 3m	87	31.6%	20Y 0m	90	34.1%	19Y 10m	92	36.8%	19Y 7m	95	39.6%
	30.0	21Y 7m	101	37.3%	21Y 4m	104	40.4%	21Y 1m	107	43.6%	20Y 10m	110	46.9%
25%	5.0	3Y 10m	14	3.7%	3Y 10m	14	3.9%	3Y 10m	14	4.1%	3Y 10m	14	4.2%
	10.0	7Y 6m	30	8.9%	7Y 5m	31	9.4%	7Y 5m	31	10.0%	7Y 5m	31	10.5%
	12.5	9Y 2m	40	12.2%	9Y 1m	41	13.0%	9Y 1m	41	13.7%	9Y 0m	42	14.5%
	15.0	10Y 9m	51	16.0%	10Y 8m	52	17.0%	10Y 7m	53	18.1%	10Y 7m	53	19.2%
	20.0	13Y 8m	76	25.2%	13Y 6m	78	27.0%	13Y 5m	79	28.8%	13Y 4m	80	30.7%
	25.0	16Y 2m	106	36.7%	16Y 0m	108	39.4%	15Y 10m	110	42.2%	15Y 8m	112	45.1%
	27.5	17Y 4m	122	43.3%	17Y 1m	125	46.5%	16Y 11m	127	49.9%	16Y 8m	130	53.4%
	30.0	18Y 5m	139	50.5%	18Y 1m	143	54.4%	17Y 10m	146	58.3%	17Y 7m	149	62.4%
33%	5.0	3Y 7m	17	4.5%	3Y 7m	17	4.7%	3Y 7m	17	5.0%	3Y 7m	17	5.2%
	10.0	6Y 11m	37	10.8%	6Y 11m	37	11.4%	6Y 10m	38	12.1%	6Y 10m	38	12.7%
	12.5	8Y 5m	49	14.7%	8Y 5m	49	15.6%	8Y 4m	50	16.5%	8Y 4m	50	17.5%
	15.0	9Y 10m	62	19.2%	9Y 9m	63	20.4%	9Y 9m	63	21.6%	9Y 8m	64	22.9%
	20.0	12Y 5m	91	29.8%	12Y 4m	92	31.8%	12Y 2m	94	33.9%	12Y 1m	95	36.0%
	25.0	14Y 8m	124	42.8%	14Y 5m	127	45.8%	14Y 3m	129	48.9%	14Y 1m	131	52.1%
	27.5	15Y 7m	143	50.2%	15Y 4m	146	53.8%	15Y 2m	148	57.5%	14Y 11m	151	61.3%
	30.0	16Y 6m	162	58.2%	16Y 3m	165	62.3%	15Y 11m	169	66.7%	15Y 8m	172	71.1%
50%	5.0	3Y 2m	22	6.0%	3Y 2m	22	6.3%	3Y 2m	22	6.5%	3Y 2m	22	6.8%
	10.0	5Y 12m	48	14.0%	5Y 11m	49	14.8%	5Y 11m	49	15.6%	5Y 10m	50	16.4%
	12.5	7Y 3m	63	18.9%	7Y 2m	64	20.0%	7Y 2m	64	21.1%	7Y 1m	65	22.2%
	15.0	8Y 5m	79	24.4%	8Y 4m	80	25.8%	8Y 3m	81	27.3%	8Y 2m	82	28.8%
	20.0	10Y 6m	114	37.1%	10Y 4m	116	39.4%	10Y 3m	117	41.8%	10Y 1m	119	44.3%
	25.0	12Y 2m	154	52.1%	11Y 12m	156	55.6%	11Y 10m	158	59.1%	11Y 8m	160	62.7%
	27.5	12Y 11m	175	60.5%	12Y 8m	178	64.5%	12Y 6m	180	68.7%	12Y 3m	183	72.9%
	30.0	13Y 7m	197	69.4%	13Y 4m	200	74.1%	13Y 1m	203	78.9%	12Y 10m	206	83.8%

Benefits of Accelerated Mortgage Repayment
Time of Earlier Payoff and Interest Savings

Original schedule 30 years

Added Payment	Time to Normal Payoff	New Payoff	Time Saved	7.00% Money Saved	New Payoff	Time Saved	7.25% Money Saved	New Payoff	Time Saved	7.50% Money Saved	New Payoff	Time Saved	7.75% Money Saved
2.5%	5.0	4Y 10m	2	0.6%	4Y 10m	2	0.6%	4Y 10m	2	0.6%	4Y 10m	2	0.6%
	10.0	9Y 8m	4	1.5%	9Y 8m	4	1.6%	9Y 8m	4	1.7%	9Y 8m	4	1.8%
	12.5	12Y 0m	6	2.1%	12Y 0m	6	2.3%	12Y 0m	6	2.4%	11Y 12m	6	2.5%
	15.0	14Y 4m	8	2.9%	14Y 4m	8	3.1%	14Y 4m	8	3.3%	14Y 4m	8	3.5%
	20.0	18Y 12m	12	5.1%	18Y 11m	13	5.5%	18Y 11m	13	5.9%	18Y 11m	13	6.3%
	25.0	23Y 5m	19	8.3%	23Y 5m	19	9.0%	23Y 4m	20	9.7%	23Y 3m	21	10.5%
	27.5	25Y 7m	23	10.3%	25Y 6m	24	11.2%	25Y 5m	25	12.2%	25Y 4m	26	13.2%
	30.0	27Y 8m	28	12.8%	27Y 7m	29	13.9%	27Y 6m	30	15.2%	27Y 5m	31	16.5%
5%	5.0	4Y 9m	3	1.1%	4Y 9m	3	1.1%	4Y 9m	3	1.2%	4Y 9m	3	1.3%
	10.0	9Y 4m	8	2.9%	9Y 4m	8	3.0%	9Y 4m	8	3.2%	9Y 4m	8	3.4%
	12.5	11Y 7m	11	4.1%	11Y 7m	11	4.3%	11Y 7m	11	4.6%	11Y 6m	12	4.9%
	15.0	13Y 9m	15	5.6%	13Y 9m	15	6.0%	13Y 9m	15	6.3%	13Y 9m	15	6.7%
	20.0	18Y 1m	23	9.6%	18Y 0m	24	10.3%	17Y 12m	24	11.0%	17Y 11m	25	11.8%
	25.0	22Y 1m	35	15.3%	21Y 12m	36	16.5%	21Y 11m	37	17.8%	21Y 10m	38	19.2%
	27.5	23Y 12m	42	18.9%	23Y 10m	44	20.5%	23Y 9m	45	22.1%	23Y 7m	47	23.9%
	30.0	25Y 10m	50	23.1%	25Y 8m	52	25.0%	25Y 6m	54	27.1%	25Y 4m	56	29.4%
8%	5.0	4Y 7m	5	1.6%	4Y 7m	5	1.7%	4Y 7m	5	1.7%	4Y 7m	5	1.8%
	10.0	9Y 0m	12	4.2%	9Y 0m	12	4.4%	9Y 0m	12	4.6%	8Y 12m	12	4.9%
	12.5	11Y 2m	16	5.9%	11Y 2m	16	6.2%	11Y 2m	16	6.6%	11Y 1m	17	7.0%
	15.0	13Y 3m	21	8.0%	13Y 3m	21	8.5%	13Y 2m	22	9.1%	13Y 2m	22	9.6%
	20.0	17Y 3m	33	13.6%	17Y 2m	34	14.6%	17Y 1m	35	15.6%	17Y 0m	36	16.6%
	25.0	20Y 11m	49	21.3%	20Y 10m	50	23.0%	20Y 8m	52	24.7%	20Y 6m	54	26.5%
	27.5	22Y 7m	59	26.1%	22Y 6m	60	28.2%	22Y 4m	62	30.4%	22Y 2m	64	32.6%
	30.0	24Y 3m	69	31.6%	24Y 0m	72	34.2%	23Y 10m	74	36.9%	23Y 7m	77	39.7%
10%	5.0	4Y 6m	6	2.1%	4Y 6m	6	2.2%	4Y 6m	6	2.3%	4Y 5m	7	2.4%
	10.0	8Y 9m	15	5.4%	8Y 9m	15	5.6%	8Y 9m	15	5.9%	8Y 8m	16	6.2%
	12.5	10Y 10m	20	7.6%	10Y 9m	21	8.0%	10Y 9m	21	8.5%	10Y 9m	21	8.9%
	15.0	12Y 9m	27	10.2%	12Y 9m	27	10.9%	12Y 8m	28	11.5%	12Y 8m	28	12.2%
	20.0	16Y 6m	42	17.2%	16Y 5m	43	18.3%	16Y 4m	44	19.6%	16Y 3m	45	20.9%
	25.0	19Y 11m	61	26.6%	19Y 9m	63	28.5%	19Y 7m	65	30.6%	19Y 5m	67	32.7%
	27.5	21Y 11m	73	32.3%	21Y 9m	75	34.8%	21Y 7m	77	37.4%	20Y 10m	80	40.1%
	30.0	22Y 10m	86	38.8%	22Y 8m	88	41.8%	22Y 5m	91	45.0%	22Y 2m	94	48.3%
15%	5.0	4Y 3m	9	2.9%	4Y 3m	9	3.1%	4Y 3m	9	3.2%	4Y 3m	9	3.3%
	10.0	8Y 3m	21	7.5%	8Y 2m	22	7.9%	8Y 2m	22	8.3%	8Y 2m	22	8.7%
	12.5	10Y 1m	29	10.5%	10Y 1m	29	11.1%	10Y 1m	29	11.7%	10Y 0m	30	12.4%
	15.0	11Y 11m	37	14.1%	11Y 10m	38	15.0%	11Y 10m	38	15.9%	11Y 9m	39	16.8%
	20.0	15Y 3m	57	23.3%	15Y 1m	59	24.8%	15Y 0m	60	26.4%	14Y 11m	61	28.0%
	25.0	18Y 1m	83	35.3%	17Y 11m	85	37.8%	17Y 9m	87	40.3%	17Y 7m	89	43.0%
	27.5	19Y 5m	97	42.5%	19Y 2m	100	45.5%	18Y 12m	102	48.7%	18Y 9m	105	51.9%
	30.0	20Y 7m	113	50.4%	20Y 4m	116	54.1%	20Y 1m	119	57.9%	19Y 10m	122	61.8%
25%	5.0	3Y 10m	14	4.4%	3Y 10m	14	4.6%	3Y 10m	14	4.8%	3Y 10m	14	5.0%
	10.0	7Y 4m	32	11.1%	7Y 4m	32	11.6%	7Y 4m	32	12.2%	7Y 3m	33	12.8%
	12.5	8Y 12m	42	15.3%	8Y 11m	43	16.2%	8Y 11m	43	17.0%	8Y 10m	44	17.9%
	15.0	10Y 6m	54	20.3%	10Y 5m	55	21.5%	10Y 4m	56	22.7%	10Y 4m	56	23.9%
	20.0	13Y 2m	82	32.6%	13Y 1m	83	34.6%	12Y 12m	84	36.7%	12Y 10m	86	38.8%
	25.0	15Y 6m	114	48.0%	15Y 3m	117	51.1%	15Y 1m	119	54.3%	14Y 11m	121	57.6%
	27.5	16Y 5m	133	57.0%	16Y 3m	135	60.7%	15Y 12m	138	64.5%	15Y 9m	141	68.5%
	30.0	17Y 4m	152	66.7%	17Y 1m	155	71.1%	16Y 10m	158	75.6%	16Y 6m	162	80.2%
33%	5.0	3Y 7m	17	5.4%	3Y 7m	17	5.7%	3Y 7m	17	5.9%	3Y 7m	17	6.2%
	10.0	6Y 10m	38	13.4%	6Y 9m	39	14.0%	6Y 9m	39	14.7%	6Y 9m	39	15.4%
	12.5	8Y 3m	51	18.4%	8Y 2m	52	19.4%	8Y 2m	52	20.4%	8Y 1m	53	21.4%
	15.0	9Y 7m	65	24.2%	9Y 6m	66	25.6%	9Y 5m	67	26.9%	9Y 5m	67	28.4%
	20.0	11Y 11m	97	38.2%	11Y 10m	98	40.5%	11Y 9m	99	42.8%	11Y 7m	101	45.2%
	25.0	13Y 11m	133	55.4%	13Y 8m	136	58.8%	13Y 6m	138	62.3%	13Y 4m	140	65.9%
	27.5	14Y 8m	154	65.2%	14Y 6m	156	69.2%	14Y 3m	159	73.4%	14Y 1m	161	77.7%
	30.0	15Y 5m	175	75.7%	15Y 2m	178	80.4%	14Y 11m	181	85.3%	14Y 8m	184	90.3%
50%	5.0	3Y 2m	22	7.2%	3Y 2m	22	7.5%	3Y 1m	23	7.8%	3Y 1m	23	8.1%
	10.0	5Y 10m	50	17.2%	5Y 10m	50	18.0%	5Y 9m	51	18.9%	5Y 9m	51	19.8%
	12.5	7Y 0m	66	23.4%	6Y 12m	66	24.6%	6Y 11m	67	25.8%	6Y 11m	67	27.0%
	15.0	8Y 1m	83	30.4%	8Y 1m	83	32.0%	7Y 12m	84	33.7%	7Y 11m	85	35.3%
	20.0	9Y 12m	120	46.8%	9Y 10m	122	49.4%	9Y 9m	123	52.1%	9Y 7m	125	54.8%
	25.0	11Y 5m	163	66.4%	11Y 3m	165	70.2%	11Y 1m	167	74.1%	10Y 11m	169	78.1%
	27.5	12Y 1m	185	77.3%	11Y 10m	188	81.7%	11Y 8m	190	86.3%	11Y 5m	193	90.9%
	30.0	12Y 7m	209	88.8%	12Y 4m	212	93.9%	12Y 1m	215	99.2%	11Y 11m	217	104.5%

Benefits of Accelerated Mortgage Repayment
Time of Earlier Payoff and Interest Savings

Original schedule 30 years

Added Payment	Time to Normal Payoff	8.00% New Payoff	Time Saved	Money Saved	8.25% New Payoff	Time Saved	Money Saved	8.50% New Payoff	Time Saved	Money Saved	8.75% New Payoff	Time Saved	Money Saved
2.5%	5.0	4Y 10m	2	0.7%	4Y 10m	2	0.7%	4Y 10m	2	0.7%	4Y 10m	2	0.8%
	10.0	9Y 8m	4	1.8%	9Y 8m	4	1.9%	9Y 7m	5	2.0%	9Y 7m	5	2.1%
	12.5	11Y 12m	6	2.7%	11Y 12m	6	2.8%	11Y 12m	6	3.0%	11Y 12m	6	3.2%
	15.0	14Y 4m	8	3.8%	14Y 4m	8	4.0%	14Y 3m	9	4.2%	14Y 3m	9	4.5%
	20.0	18Y 10m	14	6.8%	18Y 10m	14	7.3%	18Y 9m	15	7.8%	18Y 9m	15	8.3%
	25.0	23Y 2m	22	11.3%	23Y 2m	22	12.2%	23Y 1m	23	13.1%	22Y 12m	24	14.1%
	27.5	25Y 3m	27	14.3%	25Y 2m	28	15.5%	25Y 1m	29	16.8%	24Y 12m	30	18.1%
	30.0	27Y 3m	33	18.0%	27Y 2m	34	19.5%	27Y 0m	36	21.1%	26Y 11m	37	22.8%
5%	5.0	4Y 9m	3	1.3%	4Y 9m	3	1.4%	4Y 8m	4	1.4%	4Y 8m	4	1.5%
	10.0	9Y 4m	8	3.5%	9Y 3m	9	3.7%	9Y 3m	9	3.9%	9Y 3m	9	4.1%
	12.5	11Y 6m	12	5.1%	11Y 6m	12	5.4%	11Y 6m	12	5.7%	11Y 6m	12	6.0%
	15.0	13Y 8m	16	7.1%	13Y 8m	16	7.6%	13Y 8m	16	8.0%	13Y 7m	17	8.5%
	20.0	17Y 10m	26	12.6%	17Y 10m	26	13.5%	17Y 9m	27	14.3%	17Y 8m	28	15.3%
	25.0	21Y 8m	40	20.6%	21Y 7m	41	22.1%	21Y 6m	42	23.7%	21Y 4m	44	25.4%
	27.5	23Y 6m	48	25.7%	23Y 4m	50	27.7%	23Y 2m	52	29.7%	23Y 0m	54	31.9%
	30.0	25Y 2m	58	31.7%	24Y 12m	60	34.2%	24Y 9m	63	36.8%	24Y 7m	65	39.5%
8%	5.0	4Y 7m	5	1.9%	4Y 7m	5	2.0%	4Y 7m	5	2.1%	4Y 7m	5	2.1%
	10.0	8Y 12m	12	5.1%	8Y 12m	12	5.4%	8Y 11m	13	5.6%	8Y 11m	13	5.9%
	12.5	11Y 1m	17	7.4%	11Y 1m	17	7.8%	11Y 1m	17	8.2%	11Y 0m	18	8.6%
	15.0	13Y 2m	22	10.2%	13Y 1m	23	10.8%	13Y 1m	23	11.4%	13Y 0m	24	12.0%
	20.0	16Y 12m	36	17.7%	16Y 11m	37	18.9%	16Y 10m	38	20.1%	16Y 9m	39	21.3%
	25.0	20Y 5m	55	28.4%	20Y 3m	57	30.4%	20Y 2m	58	32.4%	19Y 12m	60	34.6%
	27.5	21Y 12m	66	35.0%	21Y 9m	69	37.6%	21Y 7m	71	40.2%	21Y 5m	73	42.9%
	30.0	23Y 5m	79	42.7%	23Y 2m	82	45.8%	22Y 11m	85	49.1%	22Y 9m	87	52.5%
10%	5.0	4Y 5m	7	2.5%	4Y 5m	7	2.6%	4Y 5m	7	2.7%	4Y 5m	7	2.8%
	10.0	8Y 8m	16	6.6%	8Y 8m	16	6.9%	8Y 8m	16	7.2%	8Y 8m	16	7.6%
	12.5	10Y 8m	22	9.4%	10Y 8m	22	9.9%	10Y 8m	22	10.4%	10Y 7m	23	11.0%
	15.0	12Y 7m	29	12.9%	12Y 7m	29	13.7%	12Y 6m	30	14.4%	12Y 6m	30	15.2%
	20.0	16Y 2m	46	22.2%	16Y 1m	47	23.6%	15Y 12m	48	25.0%	15Y 11m	49	26.5%
	25.0	19Y 4m	68	35.0%	19Y 2m	70	37.3%	18Y 12m	72	39.8%	18Y 10m	74	42.3%
	27.5	20Y 8m	82	42.9%	20Y 6m	84	45.8%	20Y 3m	87	48.9%	20Y 1m	89	52.0%
	30.0	21Y 11m	97	51.8%	21Y 8m	100	55.4%	21Y 5m	103	59.1%	21Y 3m	105	63.0%
15%	5.0	4Y 3m	9	3.5%	4Y 3m	9	3.6%	4Y 3m	9	3.8%	4Y 3m	9	3.9%
	10.0	8Y 2m	22	9.2%	8Y 2m	22	9.6%	8Y 1m	23	10.1%	8Y 1m	23	10.5%
	12.5	9Y 12m	30	13.0%	9Y 11m	31	13.7%	9Y 11m	31	14.4%	9Y 10m	32	15.1%
	15.0	11Y 8m	40	17.7%	11Y 8m	40	18.7%	11Y 7m	41	19.7%	11Y 6m	42	20.7%
	20.0	14Y 10m	62	29.8%	14Y 9m	63	31.5%	14Y 7m	65	33.4%	14Y 6m	66	35.3%
	25.0	17Y 5m	91	45.8%	17Y 3m	93	48.6%	17Y 1m	95	51.6%	16Y 11m	97	54.7%
	27.5	18Y 7m	107	55.3%	18Y 4m	110	58.9%	18Y 2m	112	62.5%	17Y 11m	115	66.3%
	30.0	19Y 7m	125	65.9%	19Y 4m	128	70.2%	19Y 1m	131	74.5%	18Y 10m	134	79.0%
25%	5.0	3Y 10m	14	5.2%	3Y 10m	14	5.4%	3Y 10m	14	5.7%	3Y 10m	14	5.9%
	10.0	7Y 3m	33	13.4%	7Y 3m	33	14.0%	7Y 3m	33	14.7%	7Y 2m	34	15.3%
	12.5	8Y 10m	44	18.8%	8Y 9m	45	19.8%	8Y 9m	45	20.7%	8Y 8m	46	21.7%
	15.0	10Y 3m	57	25.2%	10Y 2m	58	26.5%	10Y 1m	59	27.8%	10Y 1m	59	29.2%
	20.0	12Y 9m	87	41.0%	12Y 7m	89	43.3%	12Y 6m	90	45.6%	12Y 5m	91	48.0%
	25.0	14Y 9m	123	61.0%	14Y 7m	125	64.5%	14Y 4m	128	68.1%	14Y 2m	130	71.8%
	27.5	15Y 7m	143	72.5%	15Y 4m	146	76.7%	15Y 1m	149	81.0%	14Y 11m	151	85.4%
	30.0	16Y 3m	165	85.0%	16Y 0m	168	89.9%	15Y 9m	171	95.0%	15Y 6m	174	100.1%
33%	5.0	3Y 7m	17	6.4%	3Y 7m	17	6.7%	3Y 7m	17	6.9%	3Y 7m	17	7.2%
	10.0	6Y 8m	40	16.2%	6Y 8m	40	16.9%	6Y 8m	40	17.6%	6Y 7m	41	18.4%
	12.5	8Y 1m	53	22.5%	8Y 0m	54	23.6%	7Y 12m	54	24.6%	7Y 11m	55	25.8%
	15.0	9Y 4m	68	29.8%	9Y 3m	69	31.3%	9Y 2m	70	32.8%	9Y 1m	71	34.4%
	20.0	11Y 6m	102	47.6%	11Y 4m	104	50.2%	11Y 3m	105	52.7%	11Y 1m	107	55.4%
	25.0	13Y 2m	142	69.6%	12Y 12m	144	73.4%	12Y 9m	147	77.3%	12Y 7m	149	81.2%
	27.5	13Y 10m	164	82.0%	13Y 7m	167	86.5%	13Y 5m	169	91.1%	13Y 2m	172	95.8%
	30.0	14Y 5m	187	95.4%	14Y 2m	190	100.6%	13Y 11m	193	105.9%	13Y 8m	196	111.3%
50%	5.0	3Y 1m	23	8.4%	3Y 1m	23	8.7%	3Y 1m	23	9.0%	3Y 1m	23	9.4%
	10.0	5Y 9m	51	20.6%	5Y 8m	52	21.5%	5Y 8m	52	22.5%	5Y 8m	52	23.4%
	12.5	6Y 10m	68	28.3%	6Y 10m	68	29.6%	6Y 9m	69	30.9%	6Y 8m	70	32.3%
	15.0	7Y 10m	86	37.0%	7Y 9m	87	38.8%	7Y 9m	87	40.6%	7Y 8m	88	42.4%
	20.0	9Y 6m	126	57.6%	9Y 5m	127	60.5%	9Y 3m	129	63.4%	9Y 2m	130	66.4%
	25.0	10Y 9m	171	82.1%	10Y 7m	173	86.3%	10Y 5m	175	90.5%	10Y 3m	177	94.8%
	27.5	11Y 3m	195	95.7%	11Y 1m	197	100.5%	10Y 10m	200	105.4%	10Y 8m	202	110.4%
	30.0	11Y 8m	220	110.0%	11Y 5m	223	115.6%	11Y 3m	225	121.2%	11Y 0m	228	126.9%

Benefits of Accelerated Mortgage Repayment
Time of Earlier Payoff and Interest Savings

Original schedule 30 years

Added Payment	Time to Normal Payoff	New Payoff	9.00% Time Saved	Money Saved	New Payoff	9.25% Time Saved	Money Saved	New Payoff	9.50% Time Saved	Money Saved	New Payoff	9.75% Time Saved	Money Saved
2.5%	5.0	4Y 10m	2	0.8%	4Y 10m	2	0.8%	4Y 10m	2	0.8%	4Y 10m	2	0.9%
	10.0	9Y 7m	5	2.2%	9Y 7m	5	2.4%	9Y 7m	5	2.5%	9Y 7m	5	2.6%
	12.5	11Y 11m	7	3.3%	11Y 11m	7	3.5%	11Y 11m	7	3.7%	11Y 11m	7	3.9%
	15.0	14Y 3m	9	4.7%	14Y 3m	9	5.0%	14Y 3m	9	5.3%	14Y 2m	10	5.6%
	20.0	18Y 9m	15	8.8%	18Y 8m	16	9.4%	18Y 8m	16	10.0%	18Y 7m	17	10.6%
	25.0	22Y 11m	25	15.2%	22Y 10m	26	16.3%	22Y 9m	27	17.5%	22Y 8m	28	18.7%
	27.5	24Y 11m	31	19.5%	24Y 10m	32	20.9%	24Y 8m	34	22.5%	24Y 7m	35	24.2%
	30.0	26Y 9m	39	24.6%	26Y 8m	40	26.6%	26Y 6m	42	28.6%	26Y 4m	44	30.8%
5%	5.0	4Y 8m	4	1.5%	4Y 8m	4	1.6%	4Y 8m	4	1.6%	4Y 8m	4	1.7%
	10.0	9Y 3m	9	4.3%	9Y 3m	9	4.5%	9Y 3m	9	4.7%	9Y 3m	9	4.9%
	12.5	11Y 5m	13	6.3%	11Y 5m	13	6.7%	11Y 5m	13	7.0%	11Y 5m	13	7.3%
	15.0	13Y 7m	17	8.9%	13Y 7m	17	9.4%	13Y 6m	18	9.9%	13Y 6m	18	10.5%
	20.0	17Y 7m	29	16.3%	17Y 7m	29	17.3%	17Y 6m	30	18.3%	17Y 5m	31	19.4%
	25.0	21Y 3m	45	27.1%	21Y 2m	46	29.0%	21Y 0m	48	30.9%	20Y 11m	49	32.9%
	27.5	22Y 11m	55	34.2%	22Y 9m	57	36.5%	22Y 7m	59	39.0%	22Y 5m	61	41.6%
	30.0	24Y 5m	67	42.4%	24Y 2m	70	45.4%	23Y 12m	72	48.6%	23Y 9m	75	51.9%
8%	5.0	4Y 7m	5	2.2%	4Y 7m	5	2.3%	4Y 7m	5	2.4%	4Y 7m	5	2.5%
	10.0	8Y 11m	13	6.2%	8Y 11m	13	6.5%	8Y 11m	13	6.8%	8Y 11m	13	7.1%
	12.5	10Y 12m	18	9.1%	10Y 12m	18	9.5%	10Y 11m	19	10.0%	10Y 11m	19	10.5%
	15.0	12Y 12m	24	12.7%	12Y 11m	25	13.4%	12Y 11m	25	14.1%	12Y 10m	26	14.8%
	20.0	16Y 8m	40	22.6%	16Y 7m	41	24.0%	16Y 6m	42	25.4%	16Y 5m	43	26.8%
	25.0	19Y 10m	62	36.9%	19Y 8m	64	39.2%	19Y 7m	65	41.7%	19Y 5m	67	44.2%
	27.5	21Y 3m	75	45.8%	21Y 1m	77	48.8%	20Y 11m	79	51.9%	20Y 8m	82	55.1%
	30.0	22Y 6m	90	56.1%	22Y 3m	93	59.8%	22Y 1m	95	63.6%	21Y 10m	98	67.6%
10%	5.0	4Y 5m	7	2.9%	4Y 5m	7	3.0%	4Y 5m	7	3.1%	4Y 5m	7	3.2%
	10.0	8Y 7m	17	7.9%	8Y 7m	17	8.3%	8Y 7m	17	8.6%	8Y 7m	17	9.0%
	12.5	10Y 7m	23	11.5%	10Y 7m	23	12.1%	10Y 6m	24	12.7%	10Y 6m	24	13.3%
	15.0	12Y 5m	31	16.0%	12Y 5m	31	16.9%	12Y 4m	32	17.7%	12Y 4m	32	18.6%
	20.0	15Y 10m	50	28.1%	15Y 9m	51	29.7%	15Y 8m	52	31.4%	15Y 6m	54	33.2%
	25.0	18Y 8m	76	45.0%	18Y 6m	78	47.7%	18Y 4m	80	50.6%	18Y 2m	82	53.5%
	27.5	19Y 11m	91	55.3%	19Y 8m	94	58.8%	19Y 6m	96	62.3%	19Y 3m	99	66.0%
	30.0	20Y 12m	108	67.0%	20Y 9m	111	71.2%	20Y 6m	114	75.5%	20Y 3m	117	79.9%
15%	5.0	4Y 2m	10	4.1%	4Y 2m	10	4.2%	4Y 2m	10	4.4%	4Y 2m	10	4.5%
	10.0	8Y 1m	23	11.0%	8Y 1m	23	11.5%	8Y 0m	24	12.0%	8Y 0m	24	12.5%
	12.5	9Y 10m	32	15.9%	9Y 10m	32	16.6%	9Y 9m	33	17.4%	9Y 9m	33	18.2%
	15.0	11Y 6m	42	21.8%	11Y 5m	43	22.9%	11Y 5m	43	24.0%	11Y 4m	44	25.2%
	20.0	14Y 5m	67	37.2%	14Y 3m	69	39.3%	14Y 2m	70	41.4%	14Y 1m	71	43.5%
	25.0	16Y 9m	99	57.9%	16Y 7m	101	61.1%	16Y 5m	103	64.5%	16Y 3m	105	68.0%
	27.5	17Y 9m	117	70.1%	17Y 6m	120	74.1%	17Y 3m	123	78.2%	17Y 1m	125	82.5%
	30.0	18Y 7m	137	83.7%	18Y 4m	140	88.4%	18Y 1m	143	93.3%	17Y 10m	146	98.3%
25%	5.0	3Y 10m	14	6.1%	3Y 10m	14	6.3%	3Y 10m	14	6.5%	3Y 9m	15	6.7%
	10.0	7Y 2m	34	16.0%	7Y 2m	34	16.7%	7Y 1m	35	17.4%	7Y 1m	35	18.1%
	12.5	8Y 8m	46	22.7%	8Y 7m	47	23.7%	8Y 7m	47	24.8%	8Y 6m	48	25.8%
	15.0	9Y 12m	60	30.6%	9Y 11m	61	32.1%	9Y 10m	62	33.6%	9Y 9m	63	35.1%
	20.0	12Y 3m	93	50.5%	12Y 2m	94	53.0%	12Y 0m	96	55.6%	11Y 11m	97	58.3%
	25.0	13Y 12m	132	75.5%	13Y 10m	134	79.4%	13Y 8m	136	83.4%	13Y 6m	138	87.4%
	27.5	14Y 8m	154	89.9%	14Y 6m	156	94.5%	14Y 3m	159	99.2%	14Y 1m	161	104.0%
	30.0	15Y 3m	177	105.4%	15Y 0m	180	110.7%	14Y 9m	183	116.2%	14Y 7m	185	121.8%
33%	5.0	3Y 6m	18	7.4%	3Y 6m	18	7.7%	3Y 6m	18	8.0%	3Y 6m	18	8.2%
	10.0	6Y 6m	41	19.2%	6Y 6m	42	20.0%	6Y 6m	42	20.8%	6Y 6m	42	21.6%
	12.5	7Y 11m	55	26.9%	7Y 10m	56	28.1%	7Y 9m	57	29.3%	7Y 9m	57	30.5%
	15.0	9Y 1m	71	36.0%	8Y 12m	72	37.6%	8Y 11m	73	39.3%	8Y 10m	74	41.0%
	20.0	10Y 12m	108	58.1%	10Y 10m	110	60.9%	10Y 9m	111	63.7%	10Y 8m	112	66.6%
	25.0	12Y 5m	151	85.3%	12Y 3m	153	89.4%	12Y 1m	155	93.6%	11Y 11m	157	97.9%
	27.5	12Y 12m	174	100.5%	12Y 9m	177	105.4%	12Y 7m	179	110.4%	12Y 5m	181	115.4%
	30.0	13Y 6m	198	116.8%	13Y 3m	201	122.5%	13Y 0m	204	128.2%	12Y 9m	207	134.0%
50%	5.0	3Y 1m	23	9.7%	3Y 1m	23	10.0%	3Y 1m	23	10.4%	3Y 1m	23	10.7%
	10.0	5Y 7m	53	24.3%	5Y 7m	53	25.3%	5Y 6m	54	26.3%	5Y 6m	54	27.3%
	12.5	6Y 8m	70	33.6%	6Y 7m	71	35.0%	6Y 7m	71	36.5%	6Y 6m	72	37.9%
	15.0	7Y 7m	89	44.3%	7Y 6m	90	46.2%	7Y 5m	91	48.1%	7Y 4m	92	50.1%
	20.0	9Y 1m	131	69.4%	8Y 11m	133	72.5%	8Y 10m	134	75.6%	8Y 9m	135	78.8%
	25.0	10Y 1m	179	99.1%	9Y 11m	181	103.6%	9Y 9m	183	108.1%	9Y 8m	184	112.7%
	27.5	10Y 6m	204	115.5%	10Y 4m	206	120.7%	10Y 2m	208	126.0%	9Y 12m	210	131.3%
	30.0	10Y 10m	230	132.8%	10Y 8m	232	138.7%	10Y 5m	235	144.7%	10Y 3m	237	150.8%

Benefits of Accelerated Mortgage Repayment
Time of Earlier Payoff and Interest Savings

Original schedule 30 years

Added Payment	Time to Normal Payoff	New Payoff	10.00% Time Saved	10.00% Money Saved	New Payoff	10.25% Time Saved	10.25% Money Saved	New Payoff	10.50% Time Saved	10.50% Money Saved	New Payoff	10.75% Time Saved	10.75% Money Saved
2.5%	5.0	4Y 10m	2	0.9%	4Y 10m	2	0.9%	4Y 10m	2	1.0%	4Y 10m	2	1.0%
	10.0	9Y 7m	5	2.7%	9Y 7m	5	2.8%	9Y 7m	5	2.9%	9Y 7m	5	3.1%
	12.5	11Y 11m	7	4.1%	11Y 11m	7	4.3%	11Y 11m	7	4.5%	11Y 11m	7	4.7%
	15.0	14Y 2m	10	5.9%	14Y 2m	10	6.2%	14Y 2m	10	6.5%	14Y 2m	10	6.9%
	20.0	18Y 7m	17	11.3%	18Y 6m	18	12.0%	18Y 6m	18	12.7%	18Y 5m	19	13.5%
	25.0	22Y 7m	29	20.0%	22Y 6m	30	21.3%	22Y 5m	31	22.8%	22Y 4m	32	24.3%
	27.5	24Y 6m	36	25.9%	24Y 4m	38	27.7%	24Y 3m	39	29.7%	24Y 1m	41	31.7%
	30.0	26Y 2m	46	33.1%	26Y 1m	47	35.5%	25Y 11m	49	38.0%	25Y 9m	51	40.7%
5%	5.0	4Y 8m	4	1.8%	4Y 8m	4	1.8%	4Y 8m	4	1.9%	4Y 8m	4	1.9%
	10.0	9Y 3m	9	5.1%	9Y 2m	10	5.4%	9Y 2m	10	5.6%	9Y 2m	10	5.8%
	12.5	11Y 5m	13	7.7%	11Y 4m	14	8.1%	11Y 4m	14	8.5%	11Y 4m	14	8.9%
	15.0	13Y 6m	18	11.0%	13Y 5m	19	11.6%	13Y 5m	19	12.2%	13Y 5m	19	12.8%
	20.0	17Y 4m	32	20.6%	17Y 3m	33	21.8%	17Y 3m	33	23.0%	17Y 2m	34	24.3%
	25.0	20Y 9m	51	35.0%	20Y 7m	53	37.2%	20Y 6m	54	39.5%	20Y 4m	56	41.9%
	27.5	22Y 3m	63	44.4%	22Y 1m	65	47.2%	21Y 11m	67	50.2%	21Y 9m	69	53.2%
	30.0	23Y 7m	77	55.3%	23Y 4m	80	58.9%	23Y 2m	82	62.6%	22Y 11m	85	66.5%
8%	5.0	4Y 7m	5	2.6%	4Y 7m	5	2.6%	4Y 7m	5	2.7%	4Y 7m	5	2.8%
	10.0	8Y 10m	14	7.4%	8Y 10m	14	7.7%	8Y 10m	14	8.0%	8Y 10m	14	8.3%
	12.5	10Y 11m	19	11.0%	10Y 11m	19	11.5%	10Y 10m	20	12.0%	10Y 10m	20	12.5%
	15.0	12Y 10m	26	15.5%	12Y 10m	26	16.3%	12Y 9m	27	17.1%	12Y 9m	27	18.0%
	20.0	16Y 4m	44	28.3%	16Y 3m	45	29.9%	16Y 2m	46	31.5%	16Y 1m	47	33.2%
	25.0	19Y 3m	69	46.9%	19Y 1m	71	49.6%	18Y 11m	73	52.5%	18Y 10m	74	55.4%
	27.5	20Y 6m	84	58.5%	20Y 4m	86	61.9%	20Y 1m	89	65.5%	19Y 11m	91	69.2%
	30.0	21Y 7m	101	71.7%	21Y 4m	104	75.9%	21Y 1m	107	80.3%	20Y 10m	110	84.9%
10%	5.0	4Y 5m	7	3.3%	4Y 5m	7	3.4%	4Y 5m	7	3.5%	4Y 5m	7	3.7%
	10.0	8Y 7m	17	9.4%	8Y 6m	18	9.8%	8Y 6m	18	10.2%	8Y 6m	18	10.6%
	12.5	10Y 6m	24	13.9%	10Y 5m	25	14.5%	10Y 5m	25	15.2%	10Y 4m	26	15.9%
	15.0	12Y 3m	33	19.6%	12Y 3m	33	20.5%	12Y 2m	34	21.5%	12Y 1m	35	22.5%
	20.0	15Y 5m	55	35.0%	15Y 4m	56	36.8%	15Y 3m	57	38.8%	15Y 2m	58	40.8%
	25.0	18Y 0m	84	56.5%	17Y 10m	86	59.7%	17Y 8m	88	62.9%	17Y 6m	90	66.3%
	27.5	19Y 1m	101	69.7%	18Y 10m	104	73.6%	18Y 8m	106	77.6%	18Y 5m	109	81.8%
	30.0	19Y 12m	120	84.5%	19Y 9m	123	89.2%	19Y 6m	126	94.0%	19Y 3m	129	99.0%
15%	5.0	4Y 2m	10	4.7%	4Y 2m	10	4.8%	4Y 2m	10	5.0%	4Y 2m	10	5.2%
	10.0	7Y 12m	24	13.0%	7Y 12m	24	13.6%	7Y 11m	25	14.1%	7Y 11m	25	14.7%
	12.5	9Y 8m	34	19.0%	9Y 8m	34	19.8%	9Y 7m	35	20.7%	9Y 7m	35	21.6%
	15.0	11Y 3m	45	26.4%	11Y 3m	45	27.6%	11Y 2m	46	28.9%	11Y 1m	47	30.2%
	20.0	13Y 11m	73	45.7%	13Y 10m	74	48.0%	13Y 9m	75	50.4%	13Y 7m	77	52.8%
	25.0	16Y 0m	108	71.5%	15Y 10m	110	75.2%	15Y 8m	112	79.0%	15Y 6m	114	82.8%
	27.5	16Y 10m	128	86.8%	16Y 8m	130	91.2%	16Y 5m	133	95.8%	16Y 3m	135	100.4%
	30.0	17Y 7m	149	103.5%	17Y 4m	152	108.7%	17Y 1m	155	114.1%	16Y 10m	158	119.5%
25%	5.0	3Y 9m	15	7.0%	3Y 9m	15	7.2%	3Y 9m	15	7.4%	3Y 9m	15	7.7%
	10.0	7Y 1m	35	18.8%	7Y 0m	36	19.6%	6Y 12m	36	20.3%	6Y 12m	36	21.1%
	12.5	8Y 6m	48	26.9%	8Y 5m	49	28.1%	8Y 5m	49	29.2%	8Y 4m	50	30.4%
	15.0	9Y 9m	63	36.6%	9Y 8m	64	38.2%	9Y 7m	65	39.9%	9Y 6m	66	41.5%
	20.0	11Y 9m	99	61.0%	11Y 8m	100	63.8%	11Y 7m	101	66.6%	11Y 5m	103	69.5%
	25.0	13Y 3m	141	91.5%	13Y 1m	143	95.7%	12Y 11m	145	100.0%	12Y 9m	147	104.4%
	27.5	13Y 10m	164	108.9%	13Y 8m	166	113.9%	13Y 5m	169	118.9%	13Y 3m	171	124.1%
	30.0	14Y 4m	188	127.5%	14Y 1m	191	133.2%	13Y 10m	194	139.1%	13Y 8m	196	145.0%
33%	5.0	3Y 6m	18	8.5%	3Y 6m	18	8.8%	3Y 6m	18	9.1%	3Y 6m	18	9.3%
	10.0	6Y 5m	43	22.5%	6Y 5m	43	23.3%	6Y 5m	43	24.2%	6Y 4m	44	25.1%
	12.5	7Y 8m	58	31.8%	7Y 8m	58	33.1%	7Y 7m	59	34.4%	7Y 7m	59	35.7%
	15.0	8Y 9m	75	42.8%	8Y 9m	75	44.5%	8Y 8m	76	46.4%	8Y 7m	77	48.2%
	20.0	10Y 6m	114	69.6%	10Y 5m	115	72.6%	10Y 3m	117	75.6%	10Y 2m	118	78.8%
	25.0	11Y 9m	159	102.3%	11Y 7m	161	106.7%	11Y 5m	163	111.2%	11Y 3m	165	115.8%
	27.5	12Y 2m	184	120.5%	12Y 0m	186	125.7%	11Y 10m	188	131.0%	11Y 8m	190	136.4%
	30.0	12Y 7m	209	139.9%	12Y 4m	212	145.9%	12Y 2m	214	151.9%	11Y 11m	217	158.1%
50%	5.0	3Y 1m	23	11.1%	3Y 0m	24	11.4%	3Y 0m	24	11.8%	3Y 0m	24	12.1%
	10.0	5Y 6m	54	28.3%	5Y 5m	55	29.3%	5Y 5m	55	30.4%	5Y 5m	55	31.4%
	12.5	6Y 6m	72	39.4%	6Y 5m	73	40.9%	6Y 4m	74	42.4%	6Y 4m	74	43.9%
	15.0	7Y 4m	92	52.1%	7Y 3m	93	54.1%	7Y 2m	94	56.2%	7Y 1m	95	58.3%
	20.0	8Y 7m	137	82.1%	8Y 6m	138	85.4%	8Y 5m	139	88.7%	8Y 3m	141	92.1%
	25.0	9Y 6m	186	117.4%	9Y 4m	188	122.1%	9Y 2m	190	126.9%	9Y 1m	191	131.7%
	27.5	9Y 10m	212	136.7%	9Y 8m	214	142.1%	9Y 6m	216	147.7%	9Y 4m	218	153.3%
	30.0	10Y 1m	239	156.9%	9Y 11m	241	163.1%	9Y 9m	243	169.4%	9Y 6m	246	175.7%

Benefits of Accelerated Mortgage Repayment
Time of Earlier Payoff and Interest Savings

Original schedule 30 years

Added Payment	Time to Normal Payoff	11.00% New Payoff	Time Saved	Money Saved	11.25% New Payoff	Time Saved	Money Saved	11.50% New Payoff	Time Saved	Money Saved	11.75% New Payoff	Time Saved	Money Saved
2.5%	5.0	4Y 10m	2	1.0%	4Y 10m	2	1.1%	4Y 10m	2	1.1%	4Y 10m	2	1.1%
	10.0	9Y 7m	5	3.2%	9Y 7m	5	3.3%	9Y 7m	5	3.5%	9Y 7m	5	3.6%
	12.5	11Y 10m	8	4.9%	11Y 10m	8	5.2%	11Y 10m	8	5.4%	11Y 10m	8	5.6%
	15.0	14Y 1m	11	7.2%	14Y 1m	11	7.6%	14Y 1m	11	8.0%	14Y 1m	11	8.4%
	20.0	18Y 5m	19	14.3%	18Y 4m	20	15.2%	18Y 3m	21	16.0%	18Y 3m	21	16.9%
	25.0	22Y 3m	33	25.9%	22Y 2m	34	27.5%	22Y 1m	35	29.3%	21Y 11m	37	31.1%
	27.5	23Y 12m	42	33.8%	23Y 10m	44	36.1%	23Y 9m	45	38.4%	23Y 7m	47	40.9%
	30.0	25Y 7m	53	43.5%	25Y 5m	55	46.4%	25Y 2m	58	49.5%	25Y 0m	60	52.7%
5%	5.0	4Y 8m	4	2.0%	4Y 8m	4	2.1%	4Y 8m	4	2.1%	4Y 8m	4	2.2%
	10.0	9Y 2m	10	6.1%	9Y 2m	10	6.3%	9Y 2m	10	6.6%	9Y 2m	10	6.9%
	12.5	11Y 4m	14	9.3%	11Y 3m	15	9.7%	11Y 3m	15	10.1%	11Y 3m	15	10.6%
	15.0	13Y 4m	20	13.4%	13Y 4m	20	14.1%	13Y 3m	21	14.8%	13Y 3m	21	15.5%
	20.0	17Y 1m	35	25.7%	16Y 12m	36	27.1%	16Y 11m	37	28.5%	16Y 10m	38	30.1%
	25.0	20Y 3m	57	44.3%	20Y 1m	59	46.9%	19Y 11m	61	49.6%	19Y 10m	62	52.4%
	27.5	21Y 7m	71	56.4%	21Y 4m	74	59.8%	21Y 2m	76	63.2%	20Y 12m	78	66.7%
	30.0	22Y 8m	88	70.5%	22Y 6m	90	74.6%	22Y 3m	93	78.9%	22Y 0m	96	83.3%
8%	5.0	4Y 7m	5	2.9%	4Y 7m	5	3.0%	4Y 6m	6	3.1%	4Y 6m	6	3.2%
	10.0	8Y 10m	14	8.7%	8Y 10m	14	9.0%	8Y 9m	15	9.4%	8Y 9m	15	9.8%
	12.5	10Y 10m	20	13.1%	10Y 9m	21	13.7%	10Y 9m	21	14.3%	10Y 9m	21	14.9%
	15.0	12Y 8m	28	18.8%	12Y 8m	28	19.7%	12Y 7m	29	20.6%	12Y 6m	30	21.6%
	20.0	15Y 12m	48	35.0%	15Y 11m	49	36.8%	15Y 10m	50	38.7%	15Y 8m	52	40.6%
	25.0	18Y 8m	76	58.4%	18Y 6m	78	61.6%	18Y 4m	80	64.8%	18Y 2m	82	68.2%
	27.5	19Y 8m	94	73.1%	19Y 6m	96	77.0%	19Y 4m	98	81.1%	19Y 1m	101	85.2%
	30.0	20Y 7m	113	89.5%	20Y 5m	115	94.3%	20Y 2m	118	99.3%	19Y 11m	121	104.3%
10%	5.0	4Y 5m	7	3.8%	4Y 5m	7	3.9%	4Y 5m	7	4.0%	4Y 5m	7	4.1%
	10.0	8Y 6m	18	11.1%	8Y 6m	18	11.5%	8Y 5m	19	12.0%	8Y 5m	19	12.4%
	12.5	10Y 4m	26	16.6%	10Y 4m	26	17.3%	10Y 3m	27	18.0%	10Y 3m	27	18.8%
	15.0	12Y 1m	35	23.6%	12Y 0m	36	24.6%	11Y 12m	36	25.8%	11Y 11m	37	26.9%
	20.0	15Y 0m	60	42.8%	14Y 11m	61	44.9%	14Y 10m	62	47.1%	14Y 9m	63	49.3%
	25.0	17Y 4m	92	69.7%	17Y 2m	94	73.2%	16Y 12m	96	76.9%	16Y 10m	98	80.6%
	27.5	18Y 3m	111	86.0%	18Y 0m	114	90.3%	17Y 10m	116	94.8%	17Y 7m	119	99.3%
	30.0	18Y 12m	132	104.1%	18Y 9m	135	109.3%	18Y 6m	138	114.6%	18Y 3m	141	120.0%
15%	5.0	4Y 2m	10	5.3%	4Y 2m	10	5.5%	4Y 2m	10	5.7%	4Y 2m	10	5.8%
	10.0	7Y 11m	25	15.3%	7Y 10m	26	15.8%	7Y 10m	26	16.4%	7Y 10m	26	17.1%
	12.5	9Y 7m	35	22.5%	9Y 6m	36	23.4%	9Y 6m	36	24.4%	9Y 5m	37	25.3%
	15.0	11Y 0m	48	31.5%	10Y 12m	48	32.9%	10Y 11m	49	34.3%	10Y 10m	50	35.7%
	20.0	13Y 6m	78	55.3%	13Y 5m	79	57.8%	13Y 3m	81	60.4%	13Y 2m	82	63.1%
	25.0	15Y 4m	116	86.7%	15Y 2m	118	90.8%	14Y 12m	120	94.9%	14Y 10m	122	99.1%
	27.5	16Y 0m	138	105.2%	15Y 10m	140	110.0%	15Y 7m	143	114.9%	15Y 5m	145	119.9%
	30.0	16Y 7m	161	125.1%	16Y 4m	164	130.8%	16Y 1m	167	136.6%	15Y 10m	170	142.4%
25%	5.0	3Y 9m	15	7.9%	3Y 9m	15	8.2%	3Y 9m	15	8.4%	3Y 9m	15	8.7%
	10.0	6Y 11m	37	21.9%	6Y 11m	37	22.7%	6Y 11m	37	23.5%	6Y 10m	38	24.3%
	12.5	8Y 3m	51	31.6%	8Y 3m	51	32.8%	8Y 2m	52	34.1%	8Y 2m	52	35.3%
	15.0	9Y 6m	66	43.3%	9Y 5m	67	45.0%	9Y 4m	68	46.8%	9Y 3m	69	48.6%
	20.0	11Y 4m	104	72.5%	11Y 2m	106	75.5%	11Y 1m	107	78.6%	10Y 12m	108	81.7%
	25.0	12Y 7m	149	108.9%	12Y 5m	151	113.4%	12Y 3m	153	118.0%	12Y 1m	155	122.6%
	27.5	13Y 1m	173	129.3%	12Y 10m	176	134.7%	12Y 8m	178	140.0%	12Y 6m	180	145.5%
	30.0	13Y 5m	199	151.1%	13Y 3m	201	157.2%	13Y 0m	204	163.4%	12Y 10m	206	169.6%
33%	5.0	3Y 6m	18	9.6%	3Y 6m	18	9.9%	3Y 6m	18	10.2%	3Y 6m	18	10.5%
	10.0	6Y 4m	44	26.0%	6Y 4m	44	26.9%	6Y 3m	45	27.9%	6Y 3m	45	28.8%
	12.5	7Y 6m	60	37.1%	7Y 6m	60	38.4%	7Y 5m	61	39.9%	7Y 4m	62	41.3%
	15.0	8Y 6m	78	50.1%	8Y 5m	79	52.1%	8Y 5m	79	54.0%	8Y 4m	80	56.0%
	20.0	10Y 1m	119	82.0%	9Y 11m	121	85.2%	9Y 10m	122	88.5%	9Y 9m	123	91.8%
	25.0	11Y 1m	167	120.5%	10Y 11m	169	125.2%	10Y 9m	171	130.0%	10Y 8m	172	134.9%
	27.5	11Y 6m	192	141.8%	11Y 3m	195	147.3%	11Y 1m	197	152.9%	10Y 11m	199	158.5%
	30.0	11Y 9m	219	164.3%	11Y 7m	221	170.6%	11Y 4m	224	176.9%	11Y 2m	226	183.3%
50%	5.0	3Y 0m	24	12.5%	3Y 0m	24	12.9%	2Y 12m	24	13.3%	2Y 12m	24	13.6%
	10.0	5Y 4m	56	32.5%	5Y 4m	56	33.6%	5Y 4m	56	34.7%	5Y 3m	57	35.9%
	12.5	6Y 3m	75	45.5%	6Y 3m	75	47.1%	6Y 2m	76	48.7%	6Y 2m	76	50.4%
	15.0	7Y 1m	95	60.4%	6Y 12m	96	62.6%	6Y 11m	97	64.8%	6Y 10m	98	67.1%
	20.0	8Y 2m	142	95.6%	8Y 1m	143	99.1%	7Y 12m	144	102.6%	7Y 11m	145	106.2%
	25.0	8Y 11m	193	136.6%	8Y 9m	195	141.6%	8Y 8m	196	146.6%	8Y 6m	198	151.7%
	27.5	9Y 2m	220	158.9%	9Y 0m	222	164.6%	8Y 11m	223	170.4%	8Y 9m	225	176.2%
	30.0	9Y 4m	248	182.2%	9Y 3m	249	188.6%	9Y 1m	251	195.1%	8Y 11m	253	201.7%

Benefits of Accelerated Mortgage Repayment
Time of Earlier Payoff and Interest Savings
Original schedule 30 years

Added Payment	Time to Normal Payoff	New Payoff	12.00% Time Saved	Money Saved	New Payoff	12.25% Time Saved	Money Saved	New Payoff	12.50% Time Saved	Money Saved	New Payoff	12.75% Time Saved	Money Saved
2.5%	5.0	4Y 10m	2	1.2%	4Y 10m	2	1.2%	4Y 10m	2	1.3%	4Y 10m	2	1.3%
	10.0	9Y 7m	5	3.8%	9Y 6m	6	3.9%	9Y 6m	6	4.1%	9Y 6m	6	4.2%
	12.5	11Y 10m	8	5.9%	11Y 10m	8	6.2%	11Y 10m	8	6.4%	11Y 9m	9	6.7%
	15.0	14Y 0m	12	8.8%	14Y 0m	12	9.2%	13Y 12m	12	9.7%	13Y 12m	12	10.1%
	20.0	18Y 2m	22	17.9%	18Y 2m	22	18.9%	18Y 1m	23	19.9%	18Y 0m	24	21.0%
	25.0	21Y 10m	38	33.0%	21Y 9m	39	35.0%	21Y 7m	41	37.1%	21Y 6m	42	39.3%
	27.5	23Y 5m	49	43.5%	23Y 3m	51	46.1%	23Y 2m	52	48.9%	22Y 12m	54	51.9%
	30.0	24Y 10m	62	56.1%	24Y 8m	64	59.6%	24Y 5m	67	63.2%	24Y 3m	69	66.9%
5%	5.0	4Y 8m	4	2.3%	4Y 8m	4	2.4%	4Y 8m	4	2.4%	4Y 8m	4	2.5%
	10.0	9Y 2m	10	7.1%	9Y 1m	11	7.4%	9Y 1m	11	7.7%	9Y 1m	11	8.0%
	12.5	11Y 3m	15	11.0%	11Y 2m	16	11.5%	11Y 2m	16	12.0%	11Y 2m	16	12.5%
	15.0	13Y 3m	21	16.2%	13Y 2m	22	17.0%	13Y 2m	22	17.8%	13Y 1m	23	18.6%
	20.0	16Y 9m	39	31.6%	16Y 8m	40	33.3%	16Y 7m	41	34.9%	16Y 6m	42	36.7%
	25.0	19Y 8m	64	55.2%	19Y 6m	66	58.2%	19Y 4m	68	61.3%	19Y 2m	70	64.4%
	27.5	20Y 10m	80	70.4%	20Y 7m	83	74.2%	20Y 5m	85	78.1%	20Y 3m	87	82.1%
	30.0	21Y 10m	98	87.8%	21Y 7m	101	92.5%	21Y 4m	104	97.3%	21Y 1m	107	102.3%
8%	5.0	4Y 6m	6	3.3%	4Y 6m	6	3.4%	4Y 6m	6	3.5%	4Y 6m	6	3.6%
	10.0	8Y 9m	15	10.2%	8Y 9m	15	10.5%	8Y 9m	15	10.9%	8Y 8m	16	11.4%
	12.5	10Y 8m	22	15.5%	10Y 8m	22	16.2%	10Y 8m	22	16.8%	10Y 7m	23	17.5%
	15.0	12Y 6m	30	22.6%	12Y 5m	31	23.6%	12Y 5m	31	24.6%	12Y 4m	32	25.7%
	20.0	15Y 7m	53	42.6%	15Y 6m	54	44.7%	15Y 5m	55	46.8%	15Y 4m	56	49.0%
	25.0	17Y 12m	84	71.6%	17Y 10m	86	75.1%	17Y 8m	88	78.8%	17Y 6m	90	82.5%
	27.5	18Y 11m	103	89.5%	18Y 8m	106	93.9%	18Y 6m	108	98.4%	18Y 4m	110	103.0%
	30.0	19Y 8m	124	109.5%	19Y 5m	127	114.7%	19Y 2m	130	120.1%	18Y 11m	133	125.6%
10%	5.0	4Y 5m	7	4.3%	4Y 5m	7	4.4%	4Y 5m	7	4.5%	4Y 5m	7	4.7%
	10.0	8Y 5m	19	12.9%	8Y 5m	19	13.4%	8Y 4m	20	13.9%	8Y 4m	20	14.4%
	12.5	10Y 3m	27	19.5%	10Y 2m	28	20.3%	10Y 2m	28	21.1%	10Y 1m	29	22.0%
	15.0	11Y 10m	38	28.1%	11Y 10m	38	29.3%	11Y 9m	39	30.5%	11Y 8m	40	31.8%
	20.0	14Y 8m	64	51.7%	14Y 6m	66	54.0%	14Y 5m	67	56.5%	14Y 4m	68	59.0%
	25.0	16Y 8m	100	84.4%	16Y 6m	102	88.3%	16Y 4m	104	92.3%	16Y 2m	106	96.4%
	27.5	17Y 5m	121	104.0%	17Y 3m	123	108.8%	17Y 0m	126	113.6%	16Y 10m	128	118.6%
	30.0	18Y 0m	144	125.5%	17Y 9m	147	131.2%	17Y 7m	149	136.9%	17Y 4m	152	142.7%
15%	5.0	4Y 2m	10	6.0%	4Y 2m	10	6.2%	4Y 2m	10	6.4%	4Y 2m	10	6.5%
	10.0	7Y 10m	26	17.7%	7Y 9m	27	18.3%	7Y 9m	27	19.0%	7Y 9m	27	19.7%
	12.5	9Y 5m	37	26.3%	9Y 4m	38	27.4%	9Y 4m	38	28.4%	9Y 3m	39	29.5%
	15.0	10Y 10m	50	37.2%	10Y 9m	51	38.7%	10Y 8m	52	40.3%	10Y 7m	53	41.8%
	20.0	13Y 1m	83	65.8%	12Y 11m	85	68.6%	12Y 10m	86	71.5%	12Y 9m	87	74.4%
	25.0	14Y 8m	124	103.4%	14Y 5m	127	107.7%	14Y 3m	129	112.2%	14Y 1m	131	116.7%
	27.5	15Y 2m	148	125.1%	14Y 12m	150	130.3%	14Y 10m	152	135.5%	14Y 7m	155	140.9%
	30.0	15Y 8m	172	148.4%	15Y 5m	175	154.4%	15Y 2m	178	160.5%	14Y 12m	180	166.7%
25%	5.0	3Y 9m	15	8.9%	3Y 9m	15	9.2%	3Y 9m	15	9.4%	3Y 9m	15	9.7%
	10.0	6Y 10m	38	25.2%	6Y 10m	38	26.0%	6Y 9m	39	26.9%	6Y 9m	39	27.8%
	12.5	8Y 1m	53	36.6%	8Y 1m	53	38.0%	8Y 0m	54	39.3%	7Y 12m	54	40.7%
	15.0	9Y 2m	70	50.4%	9Y 2m	70	52.3%	9Y 1m	71	54.2%	8Y 12m	72	56.2%
	20.0	10Y 10m	110	84.9%	10Y 9m	111	88.2%	10Y 8m	112	91.5%	10Y 6m	114	94.8%
	25.0	11Y 11m	157	127.4%	11Y 9m	159	132.2%	11Y 7m	161	137.0%	11Y 6m	162	142.0%
	27.5	12Y 4m	182	151.0%	12Y 2m	184	156.6%	11Y 11m	187	162.3%	11Y 9m	189	168.0%
	30.0	12Y 7m	209	176.0%	12Y 5m	211	182.4%	12Y 2m	214	188.8%	12Y 0m	216	195.3%
33%	5.0	3Y 5m	19	10.8%	3Y 5m	19	11.1%	3Y 5m	19	11.4%	3Y 5m	19	11.7%
	10.0	6Y 3m	45	29.8%	6Y 2m	46	30.8%	6Y 2m	46	31.8%	6Y 2m	46	32.8%
	12.5	7Y 4m	62	42.7%	7Y 3m	63	44.2%	7Y 3m	63	45.7%	7Y 2m	64	47.3%
	15.0	8Y 3m	81	58.1%	8Y 2m	82	60.1%	8Y 1m	83	62.2%	8Y 1m	83	64.4%
	20.0	9Y 7m	125	95.2%	9Y 6m	126	98.7%	9Y 5m	127	102.2%	9Y 4m	128	105.7%
	25.0	10Y 6m	174	139.8%	10Y 4m	176	144.8%	10Y 2m	178	149.8%	10Y 1m	179	154.9%
	27.5	10Y 9m	201	164.2%	10Y 7m	203	170.0%	10Y 5m	205	175.8%	10Y 4m	206	181.7%
	30.0	10Y 12m	228	189.8%	10Y 10m	230	196.3%	10Y 8m	232	202.9%	10Y 6m	234	209.5%
50%	5.0	2Y 12m	24	14.0%	2Y 12m	24	14.4%	2Y 12m	24	14.8%	2Y 12m	24	15.2%
	10.0	5Y 3m	57	37.0%	5Y 2m	58	38.2%	5Y 2m	58	39.4%	5Y 2m	58	40.6%
	12.5	6Y 1m	77	52.1%	6Y 1m	77	53.8%	5Y 12m	78	55.5%	5Y 11m	79	57.2%
	15.0	6Y 9m	99	69.3%	6Y 9m	99	71.7%	6Y 8m	100	74.0%	6Y 7m	101	76.4%
	20.0	7Y 9m	147	109.9%	7Y 8m	148	113.6%	7Y 7m	149	117.3%	7Y 6m	150	121.1%
	25.0	8Y 5m	199	156.8%	8Y 3m	201	162.0%	8Y 2m	202	167.2%	8Y 0m	204	172.5%
	27.5	8Y 7m	227	182.1%	8Y 6m	228	188.0%	8Y 4m	230	194.0%	8Y 2m	232	200.0%
	30.0	8Y 9m	255	208.3%	8Y 7m	257	215.0%	8Y 5m	259	221.7%	8Y 4m	260	228.5%

Comparison of 15-Year vs 30-Year Amortization

Monthly Payment

	5.50%			5.75%			6.00%			6.25%		
	30 Year	15 Year	Percent	30 Year	15 Year	Percent	30 Year	15 Year	Percent	30 Year	15 Year	Percent
	Year	Year	Variance	Year	Year	Variance	Year	Year	Variance	Year	Year	Variance
	0.5678	0.8171	43.9	0.5836	0.8304	42.3	0.5996	0.8439	40.7	0.6157	0.8574	39.3

Mortgage Balance

Year	30 Yr	15 Yr	% Var	30 Yr	15 Yr	% Var	30 Yr	15 Yr	% Var	30 Yr	15 Yr	% Var
1	98.653	95.585	3.2	98.714	95.672	3.2	98.772	95.758	3.1	98.828	95.843	3.1
2	97.230	90.921	6.9	97.351	91.089	6.9	97.468	91.255	6.8	97.581	91.419	6.7
3	95.726	85.993	11.3	95.908	86.235	11.2	96.084	86.474	11.1	96.254	86.710	11.0
4	94.138	80.788	16.5	94.380	81.095	16.4	94.615	81.398	16.2	94.841	81.699	16.1
5	92.461	75.289	22.8	92.762	75.651	22.6	93.054	76.009	22.4	93.337	76.365	22.2
6	90.688	69.480	30.5	91.048	69.885	30.3	91.398	70.288	30.0	91.737	70.688	29.8
7	88.816	63.343	40.2	89.234	63.779	39.9	89.639	64.213	39.6	90.034	64.645	39.3
8	86.838	56.860	52.7	87.311	57.313	52.3	87.772	57.765	51.9	88.221	58.214	51.5
9	84.748	50.012	69.5	85.276	50.465	69.0	85.790	50.918	68.5	86.291	51.370	68.0
10	82.541	42.777	93.0	83.120	43.213	92.4	83.686	43.649	91.7	84.238	44.085	91.1
11	80.209	35.134	128.3	80.837	35.532	127.5	81.451	35.932	126.7	82.052	36.332	125.8
12	77.746	27.059	187.3	78.419	27.398	186.2	79.079	27.738	185.1	79.726	28.080	183.9
13	75.143	18.530	305.5	75.859	18.784	303.8	76.561	19.040	302.1	77.250	19.297	300.3
14	72.394	9.519	660.5	73.147	9.661	657.1	73.887	9.805	653.6	74.615	9.949	650.0
15	69.490	---	---	70.275	---	---	71.049	---	---	71.810	---	---

Total Interest Paid

Year	30 Yr	15 Yr	% Var	30 Yr	15 Yr	% Var	30 Yr	15 Yr	% Var	30 Yr	15 Yr	% Var
1	5.466	5.390	1.4	5.716	5.637	1.4	5.967	5.885	1.4	6.217	6.132	1.4
2	10.857	10.531	3.1	11.357	11.019	3.1	11.857	11.508	3.0	12.358	11.997	3.0
3	16.167	15.408	4.9	16.917	16.130	4.9	17.668	16.853	4.8	18.419	17.577	4.8
4	21.392	20.008	6.9	22.392	20.954	6.9	23.393	21.903	6.8	24.395	22.855	6.7
5	26.528	24.314	9.1	27.777	25.475	9.0	29.027	26.641	9.0	30.280	27.810	8.9
6	31.569	28.310	11.5	33.066	29.675	11.4	34.566	31.045	11.3	36.069	32.422	11.2
7	36.510	31.978	14.2	38.254	33.534	14.1	40.002	35.097	14.0	41.754	36.669	13.9
8	41.346	35.300	17.1	43.334	37.033	17.0	45.329	38.775	16.9	47.330	40.527	16.8
9	46.070	38.257	20.4	48.302	40.149	20.3	50.542	42.054	20.2	52.789	43.972	20.1
10	50.676	40.827	24.1	53.149	42.862	24.0	55.632	44.912	23.9	58.124	46.976	23.7
11	55.157	42.989	28.3	57.869	45.146	28.2	60.592	47.321	28.0	63.327	49.512	27.9
12	59.507	44.719	33.1	62.454	46.977	32.9	65.415	49.254	32.8	68.389	51.549	32.7
13	63.718	45.995	38.5	66.896	48.328	38.4	70.091	50.681	38.3	73.302	53.055	38.2
14	67.783	46.789	44.9	71.187	49.170	44.8	74.612	51.573	44.7	78.055	53.996	44.6
15	71.692	47.075	52.3	75.318	49.474	52.2	78.968	51.894	52.2	82.639	54.336	52.1

Monthly Payment

	6.50%			6.75%			7.00%			7.25%		
	30 Year	15 Year	Percent	30 Year	15 Year	Percent	30 Year	15 Year	Percent	30 Year	15 Year	Percent
	Year	Year	Variance	Year	Year	Variance	Year	Year	Variance	Year	Year	Variance
	0.6321	0.8711	37.8	0.6486	0.8849	36.4	0.6653	0.8988	35.1	0.6822	0.9129	33.8

Mortgage Balance

Year	30 Yr	15 Yr	% Var	30 Yr	15 Yr	% Var	30 Yr	15 Yr	% Var	30 Yr	15 Yr	% Var
1	98.882	95.927	3.1	98.934	96.009	3.0	98.984	96.090	3.0	99.032	96.170	3.0
2	97.690	91.581	6.7	97.794	91.740	6.6	97.895	91.898	6.5	97.992	92.053	6.5
3	96.417	86.944	10.9	96.575	87.174	10.8	96.727	87.402	10.7	96.873	87.627	10.6
4	95.060	81.996	15.9	95.271	82.290	15.8	95.475	82.582	15.6	95.671	82.870	15.4
5	93.611	76.717	22.0	93.876	77.067	21.8	94.132	77.413	21.6	94.379	77.756	21.4
6	92.065	71.085	29.5	92.384	71.479	29.2	92.692	71.870	29.0	92.990	72.259	28.7
7	90.416	65.075	38.9	90.787	65.502	38.6	91.147	65.927	38.3	91.496	66.349	37.9
8	88.657	58.663	51.1	89.080	59.109	50.7	89.492	59.554	50.3	89.891	59.997	49.8
9	86.779	51.821	67.5	87.254	52.271	66.9	87.716	52.720	66.4	88.165	53.168	65.8
10	84.776	44.521	90.4	85.301	44.957	89.7	85.812	45.393	89.0	86.310	45.828	88.3
11	82.639	36.732	125.0	83.212	37.134	124.1	83.771	37.535	123.2	84.316	37.937	122.3
12	80.358	28.422	182.7	80.977	28.765	181.5	81.582	29.110	180.3	82.173	29.455	179.0
13	77.925	19.555	298.5	78.587	19.815	296.6	79.235	20.075	294.7	79.869	20.337	292.7
14	75.329	10.094	646.2	76.030	10.241	642.4	76.718	10.388	638.5	77.392	10.536	634.5
15	72.559	---	---	73.295	---	---	74.019	---	---	74.729	---	---

Total Interest Paid

Year	30 Yr	15 Yr	% Var	30 Yr	15 Yr	% Var	30 Yr	15 Yr	% Var	30 Yr	15 Yr	% Var
1	6.467	6.380	1.4	6.717	6.628	1.3	6.968	6.876	1.3	7.218	7.124	1.3
2	12.859	12.487	3.0	13.361	12.978	2.9	13.862	13.470	2.9	14.364	13.962	2.9
3	19.172	18.304	4.7	19.925	19.031	4.7	20.678	19.760	4.6	21.432	20.490	4.6
4	25.399	23.809	6.7	26.403	24.766	6.6	27.409	25.726	6.5	28.416	26.687	6.5
5	31.535	28.984	8.8	32.792	30.161	8.7	34.050	31.342	8.6	35.309	32.528	8.6
6	37.574	33.804	11.2	39.083	35.192	11.1	40.593	36.586	11.0	42.106	37.985	10.9
7	43.510	38.248	13.8	45.270	39.834	13.6	47.033	41.428	13.5	48.799	43.030	13.4
8	49.335	42.289	16.7	51.346	44.060	16.5	53.361	45.841	16.4	55.380	47.632	16.3
9	55.043	45.901	19.9	57.303	47.841	19.8	59.569	49.794	19.6	61.840	51.757	19.5
10	60.624	49.054	23.6	63.133	51.146	23.4	65.649	53.252	23.3	68.172	55.371	23.1
11	66.072	51.719	27.8	68.827	53.942	27.6	71.591	56.181	27.4	74.364	58.435	27.3
12	71.376	53.862	32.5	74.375	56.192	32.4	77.385	58.541	32.2	80.406	60.907	32.0
13	76.528	55.448	38.0	79.768	57.861	37.9	83.022	60.293	37.7	86.288	62.744	37.5
14	81.517	56.440	44.4	84.995	58.905	44.3	88.489	61.391	44.1	91.997	63.897	44.0
15	86.331	56.799	52.0	90.043	59.284	51.9	93.773	61.789	51.8	97.521	64.315	51.6

Entries are percentages of original loan amount.

Comparison of 15-Year vs 30-Year Amortization

Monthly Payment

	7.50%			7.75%			8.00%			8.25%		
	30 Year	15 Year	Percent Variance	30 Year	15 Year	Percent Variance	30 Year	15 Year	Percent Variance	30 Year	15 Year	Percent Variance
	0.6992	0.9270	32.6	0.7164	0.9413	31.4	0.7338	0.9557	30.2	0.7513	0.9701	29.1

Mortgage Balance

	30	15	PV	30	15	PV	30	15	PV	30	15	PV
1	99.078	96.249	2.9	99.122	96.326	2.9	99.165	96.402	2.9	99.205	96.477	2.8
2	98.085	92.206	6.4	98.174	92.357	6.3	98.260	92.506	6.2	98.342	92.652	6.1
3	97.014	87.850	10.4	97.150	88.069	10.3	97.280	88.286	10.2	97.405	88.500	10.1
4	95.861	83.155	15.3	96.043	83.437	15.1	96.219	83.716	14.9	96.388	83.991	14.8
5	94.617	78.096	21.2	94.848	78.433	20.9	95.070	78.766	20.7	95.284	79.097	20.5
6	93.278	72.644	28.4	93.556	73.027	28.1	93.825	73.406	27.8	94.085	73.782	27.5
7	91.834	66.769	37.5	92.161	67.186	37.2	92.477	67.601	36.8	92.783	68.013	36.4
8	90.278	60.438	49.4	90.654	60.877	48.9	91.018	61.314	48.4	91.370	61.749	48.0
9	88.602	53.615	65.3	89.025	54.061	64.7	89.437	54.505	64.1	89.836	54.948	63.5
10	86.795	46.263	87.6	87.266	46.697	86.9	87.725	47.131	86.1	88.170	47.565	85.4
11	84.848	38.340	121.3	85.366	38.742	120.3	85.870	39.145	119.4	86.361	39.548	118.4
12	82.750	29.802	177.7	83.313	30.149	176.3	83.862	30.497	175.0	84.398	30.845	173.6
13	80.489	20.600	290.7	81.095	20.865	288.7	81.688	21.130	286.6	82.266	21.396	284.5
14	78.052	10.685	630.5	78.699	10.835	626.3	79.332	10.986	622.1	79.952	11.138	617.8
15	75.427	---	---	76.111	---	---	76.782	---	---	77.439	---	---

Total Interest Paid

Year	30	15	PV	30	15	PV	30	15	PV	30	15	PV
1	7.469	7.373	1.3	7.719	7.621	1.3	7.970	7.870	1.3	8.220	8.119	1.3
2	14.866	14.454	2.8	15.368	14.948	2.8	15.870	15.441	2.8	16.373	15.936	2.7
3	22.186	21.222	4.5	22.941	21.955	4.5	23.696	22.689	4.4	24.451	23.425	4.4
4	29.423	27.652	6.4	30.431	28.618	6.3	31.440	29.587	6.3	32.449	30.558	6.2
5	36.570	33.717	8.5	37.832	34.909	8.4	39.096	36.105	8.3	40.360	37.305	8.2
6	43.621	39.389	10.7	45.138	40.798	10.6	46.656	42.213	10.5	48.176	43.633	10.4
7	50.568	44.638	13.3	52.340	46.253	13.2	54.114	47.876	13.0	55.890	49.505	12.9
8	57.403	49.431	16.1	59.429	51.239	16.0	61.459	53.057	15.8	63.492	54.882	15.7
9	64.117	53.733	19.3	66.398	55.719	19.2	68.683	57.716	19.0	70.973	59.723	18.8
10	70.701	57.504	22.9	73.236	59.650	22.8	75.776	61.810	22.6	78.322	63.981	22.4
11	77.144	60.705	27.1	79.932	62.991	26.9	82.727	65.291	26.7	85.529	67.607	26.5
12	83.437	63.291	31.8	86.476	65.692	31.6	89.524	68.110	31.4	92.580	70.545	31.2
13	89.566	65.214	37.3	92.855	67.704	37.1	96.155	70.212	36.9	99.464	72.738	36.7
14	95.520	66.423	43.8	99.056	68.969	43.6	102.605	71.536	43.4	106.165	74.121	43.2
15	101.285	66.862	51.5	105.065	69.430	51.3	108.859	72.017	51.2	112.667	74.625	51.0

Monthly Payment

	8.50%			8.75%			9.00%			9.25%		
	30 Year	15 Year	Percent Variance	30 Year	15 Year	Percent Variance	30 Year	15 Year	Percent Variance	30 Year	15 Year	Percent Variance
	0.7689	0.9847	28.1	0.7867	0.9994	27.0	0.8046	1.0143	26.1	0.8227	1.0292	25.1

Mortgage Balance

	30	15	PV	30	15	PV	30	15	PV	30	15	PV
1	99.244	96.551	2.8	99.281	96.623	2.8	99.317	96.695	2.7	99.351	96.765	2.7
2	98.421	92.797	6.1	98.497	92.939	6.0	98.570	93.079	5.9	98.639	93.217	5.8
3	97.526	88.711	9.9	97.641	88.919	9.8	97.752	89.125	9.7	97.858	89.327	9.6
4	96.551	84.264	14.6	96.708	84.533	14.4	96.858	84.799	14.2	97.003	85.062	14.0
5	95.490	79.424	20.2	95.689	79.747	20.0	95.880	80.068	19.7	96.064	80.385	19.5
6	94.336	74.156	27.2	94.577	74.526	26.9	94.810	74.893	26.6	95.035	75.257	26.3
7	93.079	68.422	36.0	93.365	68.829	35.6	93.640	69.232	35.3	93.907	69.633	34.9
8	91.711	62.182	47.5	92.041	62.612	47.0	92.361	63.041	46.5	92.669	63.467	46.0
9	90.223	55.390	62.9	90.598	55.830	62.3	90.961	56.268	61.7	91.313	56.705	61.0
10	88.603	47.997	84.6	89.022	48.429	83.8	89.430	48.861	83.0	89.825	49.291	82.2
11	86.839	39.952	117.4	87.304	40.355	116.3	87.755	40.758	115.3	88.193	41.161	114.3
12	84.920	31.195	172.2	85.428	31.545	170.8	85.923	31.895	169.4	86.405	32.247	167.9
13	82.831	21.664	282.3	83.382	21.932	280.2	83.919	22.201	278.0	84.443	22.472	275.8
14	80.557	11.290	613.5	81.149	11.444	609.1	81.728	11.598	604.7	82.292	11.753	600.2
15	78.083	---	---	78.713	---	---	79.330	---	---	79.934	---	---

Total Interest Paid

Year	30	15	PV	30	15	PV	30	15	PV	30	15	PV
1	8.471	8.368	1.2	8.722	8.617	1.2	8.972	8.866	1.2	9.223	9.115	1.2
2	16.875	16.430	2.7	17.378	16.926	2.7	17.880	17.422	2.6	18.383	17.918	2.6
3	25.207	24.161	4.3	25.962	24.899	4.3	26.719	25.638	4.2	27.475	26.378	4.2
4	33.459	31.531	6.1	34.469	32.507	6.0	35.480	33.484	6.0	36.491	34.463	5.9
5	41.625	38.508	8.1	42.891	39.714	8.0	44.157	40.924	7.9	45.425	42.137	7.8
6	49.697	45.057	10.3	51.220	46.486	10.2	52.743	47.920	10.1	54.268	49.358	9.9
7	57.668	51.140	12.8	59.448	52.782	12.6	61.229	54.431	12.5	63.011	56.085	12.3
8	65.527	56.717	15.5	67.565	58.559	15.4	69.604	60.410	15.2	71.646	62.269	15.1
9	73.265	61.742	18.7	75.561	63.770	18.5	77.860	65.809	18.3	80.161	67.858	18.1
10	80.872	66.166	22.2	83.426	68.363	22.0	85.984	70.573	21.8	88.546	72.794	21.6
11	88.336	69.937	26.3	91.148	72.282	26.1	93.965	74.641	25.9	96.787	77.015	25.7
12	95.643	72.997	31.0	98.713	75.465	30.8	101.789	77.950	30.6	104.870	80.450	30.4
13	102.781	75.283	36.5	106.107	77.846	36.3	109.441	80.427	36.1	112.781	83.026	35.8
14	109.735	76.727	43.0	113.315	79.351	42.8	116.904	81.995	42.6	120.502	84.657	42.3
15	116.487	77.253	50.8	120.320	79.901	50.6	124.163	82.568	50.4	128.016	85.255	50.2

Entries are percentages of original loan amount.

Comparison of 15-Year vs 30-Year Amortization

Monthly Payment

	9.50%			9.75%			10.00%			10.25%		
	30 Year 0.8409	15 Year 1.0442	Percent Variance 24.2	30 Year 0.8592	15 Year 1.0594	Percent Variance 23.3	30 Year 0.8776	15 Year 1.0746	Percent Variance 22.5	30 Year 0.8961	15 Year 1.0900	Percent Variance 21.6

Mortgage Balance

	30	15	Var	30	15	Var	30	15	Var	30	15	Var
1	99.383	96.834	2.6	99.414	96.902	2.6	99.444	96.968	2.6	99.472	97.034	2.5
2	98.706	93.353	5.7	98.769	93.487	5.6	98.830	93.619	5.6	98.888	93.749	5.5
3	97.960	89.527	9.4	98.058	89.725	9.3	98.152	89.919	9.2	98.241	90.111	9.0
4	97.141	85.322	13.9	97.274	85.579	13.7	97.402	85.832	13.5	97.525	86.082	13.3
5	96.241	80.699	19.3	96.411	81.009	19.0	96.574	81.317	18.8	96.731	81.620	18.5
6	95.251	75.617	26.0	95.459	75.974	25.6	95.660	76.329	25.3	95.852	76.679	25.0
7	94.163	70.031	34.5	94.411	70.426	34.1	94.649	70.818	33.7	94.879	71.207	33.2
8	92.967	63.890	45.5	93.255	64.312	45.0	93.533	64.731	44.5	93.801	65.147	44.0
9	91.653	57.140	60.4	91.982	57.574	59.8	92.300	58.006	59.1	92.608	58.436	58.5
10	90.208	49.721	81.4	90.579	50.149	80.6	90.938	50.577	79.8	91.286	51.003	79.0
11	88.619	41.564	113.2	89.032	41.967	112.1	89.433	42.370	111.1	89.822	42.772	110.0
12	86.873	32.598	166.5	87.328	32.951	165.0	87.771	33.303	163.5	88.201	33.656	162.1
13	84.954	22.743	273.5	85.451	23.015	271.3	85.934	23.288	269.0	86.405	23.561	266.7
14	82.844	11.909	595.6	83.381	12.066	591.1	83.906	12.223	586.5	84.417	12.381	581.8
15	80.524	---	---	81.101	---	---	81.665	---	---	82.215	---	---

Total Interest Paid

Year	30	15	Var	30	15	Var	30	15	Var	30	15	Var
1	9.474	9.364	1.2	9.724	9.614	1.1	9.975	9.864	1.1	10.226	10.113	1.1
2	18.886	18.415	2.6	19.389	18.912	2.5	19.892	19.410	2.5	20.395	19.908	2.4
3	28.231	27.120	4.1	28.988	27.862	4.0	29.744	28.605	4.0	30.501	29.349	3.9
4	37.502	35.445	5.8	38.514	36.428	5.7	39.526	37.413	5.6	40.538	38.400	5.6
5	46.692	43.352	7.7	47.960	44.571	7.6	49.229	45.793	7.5	50.497	47.017	7.4
6	55.793	50.801	9.8	57.319	52.249	9.7	58.845	53.700	9.6	60.372	55.156	9.5
7	64.795	57.746	12.2	66.580	59.412	12.1	68.365	61.085	11.9	70.152	62.763	11.8
8	73.689	64.136	14.9	75.734	66.011	14.7	77.780	67.893	14.6	79.827	69.782	14.4
9	82.465	69.917	17.9	84.771	71.985	17.8	87.078	74.063	17.6	89.387	76.150	17.4
10	91.110	75.028	21.4	93.677	77.273	21.2	96.247	79.529	21.0	98.818	81.797	20.8
11	99.612	79.402	25.5	102.441	81.803	25.2	105.273	84.218	25.0	108.107	86.646	24.8
12	107.956	82.967	30.1	111.047	85.499	29.9	114.141	88.046	29.6	117.239	90.609	29.4
13	116.127	85.642	35.6	119.479	88.275	35.3	122.836	90.926	35.1	126.197	93.594	34.8
14	124.107	87.339	42.1	127.719	90.039	41.8	131.338	92.757	41.6	134.962	95.493	41.3
15	131.878	87.960	49.9	135.749	90.685	49.7	139.627	93.429	49.4	143.513	96.191	49.2

Monthly Payment

	10.50%			10.75%			11.00%			11.25%		
	30 Year 0.9147	15 Year 1.1054	Percent Variance 20.8	30 Year 0.9335	15 Year 1.1209	Percent Variance 20.1	30 Year 0.9523	15 Year 1.1366	Percent Variance 19.3	30 Year 0.9713	15 Year 1.1523	Percent Variance 18.6

Mortgage Balance

	30	15	Var	30	15	Var	30	15	Var	30	15	Var
1	99.499	97.098	2.5	99.525	97.161	2.4	99.550	97.224	2.4	99.573	97.285	2.4
2	98.944	93.877	5.4	98.997	94.002	5.3	99.048	94.126	5.2	99.096	94.248	5.1
3	98.327	90.300	8.9	98.409	90.486	8.8	98.487	90.670	8.6	98.562	90.851	8.5
4	97.642	86.329	13.1	97.754	86.573	12.9	97.862	86.814	12.7	97.965	87.051	12.5
5	96.882	81.921	18.3	97.026	82.218	18.0	97.165	82.512	17.8	97.297	82.802	17.5
6	96.038	77.027	24.7	96.215	77.371	24.4	96.386	77.711	24.0	96.551	78.049	23.7
7	95.100	71.593	32.8	95.313	71.976	32.4	95.518	72.356	32.0	95.715	72.733	31.6
8	94.060	65.561	43.5	94.309	65.972	43.0	94.549	66.381	42.4	94.781	66.786	41.9
9	92.905	58.864	57.8	93.192	59.290	57.2	93.468	59.714	56.5	93.736	60.136	55.9
10	91.622	51.428	78.2	91.948	51.853	77.3	92.263	52.276	76.5	92.567	52.697	75.7
11	90.199	43.174	108.9	90.564	43.575	107.8	90.917	43.977	106.7	91.259	44.377	105.6
12	88.618	34.010	160.6	89.023	34.363	159.1	89.416	34.717	157.6	89.797	35.071	156.0
13	86.863	23.836	264.4	87.308	24.111	262.1	87.741	24.386	259.8	88.161	24.663	257.5
14	84.915	12.540	577.1	85.400	12.700	572.5	85.872	12.860	567.7	86.332	13.021	563.0
15	82.752	---	---	83.276	---	---	83.787	---	---	84.286	---	---

Total Interest Paid

Year	30	15	Var	30	15	Var	30	15	Var	30	15	Var
1	10.476	10.363	1.1	10.727	10.613	1.1	10.978	10.863	1.1	11.228	11.113	1.0
2	20.898	20.406	2.4	21.401	20.905	2.4	21.903	21.404	2.3	22.406	21.904	2.3
3	31.258	30.094	3.9	32.014	30.840	3.8	32.771	31.587	3.7	33.528	32.335	3.7
4	41.550	39.388	5.5	42.562	40.379	5.4	43.574	41.370	5.3	44.586	42.364	5.2
5	51.766	48.245	7.3	53.035	49.475	7.2	54.304	50.707	7.1	55.573	51.943	7.0
6	61.899	56.615	9.3	63.426	58.079	9.2	64.954	59.546	9.1	66.481	61.018	9.0
7	71.938	64.447	11.6	73.726	66.136	11.5	75.513	67.830	11.3	77.301	69.530	11.2
8	81.875	71.679	14.2	83.923	73.583	14.1	85.972	75.494	13.9	88.022	77.412	13.7
9	91.697	78.247	17.2	94.008	80.352	17.0	96.319	82.466	16.8	98.632	84.589	16.6
10	101.391	84.076	20.6	103.966	86.366	20.4	106.541	88.667	20.2	109.118	90.978	19.9
11	110.944	89.087	24.5	113.783	91.541	24.3	116.624	94.007	24.1	119.466	96.487	23.8
12	120.340	93.187	29.1	123.444	95.780	28.9	126.550	98.387	28.6	129.659	101.009	28.4
13	129.562	96.278	34.6	132.931	98.979	34.3	136.303	101.696	34.0	139.678	104.429	33.8
14	138.591	98.247	41.1	142.225	101.019	40.8	145.863	103.808	40.5	149.504	106.615	40.2
15	147.405	98.972	48.9	151.303	101.771	48.7	155.205	104.587	48.4	159.113	107.422	48.1

Entries are percentages of original loan amount.

Comparison of 15-Year vs 30-Year Amortization

Monthly Payment

	11.50%			11.75%			12.00%			12.25%		
	30 Year	15 Year	Percent Variance	30 Year	15 Year	Percent Variance	30 Year	15 Year	Percent Variance	30 Year	15 Year	Percent Variance
	0.9903	1.1682	18.0	1.0094	1.1841	17.3	1.0286	1.2002	16.7	1.0479	1.2163	16.1

Mortgage Balance

	30	15	%	30	15	%	30	15	%	30	15	%
1	99.596	97.345	2.3	99.617	97.404	2.3	99.637	97.461	2.2	99.656	97.518	2.2
2	99.142	94.367	5.1	99.186	94.485	5.0	99.228	94.601	4.9	99.268	94.715	4.8
3	98.634	91.029	8.4	98.702	91.205	8.2	98.767	91.377	8.1	98.830	91.548	8.0
4	98.064	87.286	12.3	98.158	87.517	12.2	98.248	87.745	12.0	98.334	87.970	11.8
5	97.425	83.089	17.3	97.547	83.372	17.0	97.663	83.652	16.7	97.775	83.929	16.5
6	96.708	78.383	23.4	96.859	78.713	23.1	97.004	79.040	22.7	97.143	79.364	22.4
7	95.904	73.106	31.2	96.086	73.476	30.8	96.261	73.844	30.4	96.429	74.207	29.9
8	95.003	67.190	41.4	95.218	67.590	40.9	95.424	67.988	40.4	95.622	68.382	39.8
9	93.993	60.556	55.2	94.242	60.973	54.6	94.481	61.389	53.9	94.711	61.802	53.2
10	92.860	53.117	74.8	93.144	53.536	74.0	93.418	53.954	73.1	93.682	54.369	72.3
11	91.590	44.777	104.5	91.911	45.176	103.4	92.220	45.575	102.3	92.520	45.973	101.2
12	90.166	35.425	154.5	90.524	35.780	153.0	90.871	36.134	151.5	91.207	36.488	150.0
13	88.569	24.940	255.1	88.966	25.217	252.8	89.350	25.496	250.5	89.723	25.774	248.1
14	86.779	13.183	558.3	87.214	13.345	553.5	87.637	13.508	548.8	88.047	13.672	544.0
15	84.771	---	---	85.245	---	---	85.706	---	---	86.155	---	---

Total Interest Paid

Year	30	15	%	30	15	%	30	15	%	30	15	%
1	11.479	11.363	1.0	11.730	11.613	1.0	11.980	11.863	1.0	12.231	12.114	1.0
2	22.909	22.404	2.3	23.412	22.904	2.2	23.915	23.405	2.2	24.418	23.906	2.1
3	34.284	33.084	3.6	35.041	33.833	3.6	35.798	34.583	3.5	36.554	35.334	3.5
4	45.598	43.359	5.2	46.610	44.355	5.1	47.622	45.353	5.0	48.633	46.353	4.9
5	56.842	53.180	6.9	58.111	54.420	6.8	59.380	55.662	6.7	60.649	56.907	6.6
6	68.009	62.492	8.8	69.537	63.971	8.7	71.064	65.453	8.6	72.591	66.938	8.4
7	79.089	71.234	11.0	80.877	72.943	10.9	82.665	74.658	10.7	84.452	76.377	10.6
8	90.071	79.336	13.5	92.121	81.267	13.4	94.171	83.204	13.2	96.220	85.147	13.0
9	100.945	86.720	16.4	103.258	88.860	16.2	105.571	91.007	16.0	107.884	93.163	15.8
10	111.695	93.300	19.7	114.273	95.632	19.5	116.852	97.974	19.3	119.430	100.325	19.0
11	122.309	98.978	23.6	125.153	101.482	23.3	127.997	103.997	23.1	130.842	106.525	22.8
12	132.768	103.645	28.1	135.879	106.295	27.8	138.991	108.958	27.6	142.104	111.635	27.3
13	143.055	107.177	33.5	146.434	109.942	33.2	149.814	112.722	32.9	153.195	115.517	32.6
14	153.148	109.439	39.9	156.795	112.279	39.6	160.443	115.136	39.4	164.094	118.010	39.1
15	163.024	110.274	47.8	166.938	113.144	47.5	170.856	116.030	47.3	174.776	118.934	47.0

Monthly Payment

	12.50%			12.75%			13.00%			13.25%		
	30 Year	15 Year	Percent Variance	30 Year	15 Year	Percent Variance	30 Year	15 Year	Percent Variance	30 Year	15 Year	Percent Variance
	1.0673	1.2325	15.5	1.0867	1.2488	14.9	1.1062	1.2652	14.4	1.1258	1.2817	13.9

Mortgage Balance

	30	15	%	30	15	%	30	15	%	30	15	%
1	99.675	97.574	2.2	99.692	97.629	2.1	99.709	97.682	2.1	99.724	97.735	2.0
2	99.306	94.826	4.7	99.343	94.936	4.6	99.377	95.045	4.6	99.410	95.151	4.5
3	98.889	91.715	7.8	98.946	91.880	7.7	99.000	92.043	7.6	99.051	92.203	7.4
4	98.417	88.192	11.6	98.495	88.411	11.4	98.570	88.627	11.2	98.642	88.839	11.0
5	97.882	84.202	16.2	97.984	84.472	16.0	98.082	84.739	15.7	98.175	85.002	15.5
6	97.276	79.684	22.1	97.403	80.001	21.8	97.526	80.315	21.4	97.642	80.624	21.1
7	96.590	74.568	29.5	96.744	74.925	29.1	96.893	75.280	28.7	97.035	75.630	28.3
8	95.813	68.774	39.3	95.996	69.163	38.8	96.172	69.550	38.3	96.341	69.933	37.8
9	94.933	62.213	52.6	95.147	62.622	51.9	95.353	63.029	51.3	95.550	63.433	50.6
10	93.937	54.784	71.5	94.183	55.196	70.6	94.420	55.608	69.8	94.648	56.017	69.0
11	92.809	46.370	100.1	93.088	46.767	99.0	93.358	47.162	98.0	93.619	47.557	96.9
12	91.531	36.843	148.4	91.846	37.197	146.9	92.150	37.551	145.4	92.444	37.905	143.9
13	90.085	26.054	245.8	90.435	26.333	243.4	90.775	26.613	241.1	91.104	26.894	238.8
14	88.447	13.836	539.3	88.834	14.000	534.5	89.211	14.166	529.8	89.576	14.332	525.0
15	86.591	---	---	87.016	---	---	87.430	---	---	87.832	---	---

Total Interest Paid

Year	30	15	%	30	15	%	30	15	%	30	15	%
1	12.482	12.364	1.0	12.732	12.615	0.9	12.983	12.865	0.9	13.234	13.116	0.9
2	24.920	24.407	2.1	25.423	24.909	2.1	25.926	25.410	2.0	26.428	25.912	2.0
3	37.310	36.086	3.4	38.067	36.838	3.3	38.823	37.591	3.3	39.579	38.345	3.2
4	49.645	47.353	4.8	50.657	48.355	4.8	51.668	49.358	4.7	52.679	50.363	4.6
5	61.917	58.154	6.5	63.186	59.403	6.4	64.454	60.653	6.3	65.721	61.906	6.2
6	74.119	68.426	8.3	75.645	69.917	8.2	77.172	71.412	8.1	78.698	72.909	7.9
7	86.240	78.100	10.4	88.027	79.828	10.3	89.813	81.560	10.1	91.600	83.296	10.0
8	98.270	87.097	12.8	100.319	89.052	12.7	102.367	91.013	12.5	104.416	92.979	12.3
9	110.197	95.326	15.6	112.510	97.497	15.4	114.822	99.675	15.2	117.134	101.860	15.0
10	122.008	102.686	18.8	124.586	105.057	18.6	127.164	107.437	18.4	129.741	109.825	18.1
11	133.687	109.063	22.6	136.532	111.613	22.3	139.377	114.174	22.1	142.221	116.746	21.8
12	145.217	114.326	27.0	148.330	117.029	26.7	151.443	119.746	26.5	154.556	122.475	26.2
13	156.577	118.327	32.3	159.960	121.152	32.0	163.342	123.991	31.7	166.725	126.845	31.4
14	167.746	120.899	38.7	171.399	123.805	38.4	175.052	126.726	38.1	178.706	129.663	37.8
15	178.698	121.854	46.6	182.621	124.791	46.3	186.546	127.744	46.0	190.471	130.713	45.7

Entries are percentages of original loan amount.

BiWeekly & Weekly Payments Compared to Monthly Payments

Interest Rate	Normal Payment	BiWeekly Payment	New Term	Interest Savings in First Year	5 yrs	10 yrs	Total	Weekly Payment	New Term	Interest Savings in First Year	5 Yrs	10 Yrs	Total
5.50%	567.79	283.90	24Y46wks	$17	436	1910	20,750	141.95	24Y46wks	$18	$442	1927	$20,865
.625	575.66	287.84	24Y41wks	18	452	1988	21,723	143.92	24Y41wks	19	459	2006	21,815
.75	583.58	291.79	24Y36wks	18	469	2069	22,722	145.90	24Y36wks	19	476	2087	22,824
.875	591.54	295.78	24Y31wks	19	487	2152	23,745	147.89	24Y31wks	20	494	2171	23,877
6.00%	599.56	299.78	24Y26wks	19	504	2237	24,817	149.89	24Y26wks	20	512	2256	24,906
.125	607.62	303.81	24Y21wks	20	523	2324	25,913	151.91	24Y21wks	21	530	2343	26,022
.25	615.72	307.87	24Y16wks	21	541	2413	27,027	153.94	24Y16wks	22	549	2433	27,129
.375	623.87	311.94	24Y11wks	21	560	2504	28,184	155.97	24Y11wks	22	568	2525	28,308
6.50%	632.07	316.04	24Y 6wks	22	580	2598	29,384	158.02	24Y 6wks	23	587	2619	29,506
.625	640.32	320.16	24Y 1wks	22	599	2694	30,597	160.08	24Y 1wks	24	607	2715	30,712
.75	648.60	324.31	23Y47wks	23	620	2792	31,860	162.16	23Y47wks	24	627	2814	31,983
.875	656.93	328.47	23Y42wks	24	640	2892	33,144	164.24	23Y42wks	25	648	2915	33,282
7.00%	665.31	332.66	23Y37wks	25	661	2996	34,468	166.33	23Y37wks	26	669	3018	34,602
.125	673.72	336.87	23Y31wks	25	683	3101	35,827	168.44	23Y31wks	26	691	3124	35,969
.25	682.18	341.10	23Y26wks	26	704	3209	37,208	170.55	23Y26wks	27	713	3233	37,377
.375	690.68	345.35	23Y20wks	27	727	3319	38,639	172.68	23Y20wks	28	735	3344	38,788
7.50%	699.22	349.61	23Y15wks	27	749	3432	40,106	174.81	23Y15wks	29	758	3457	40,266
.625	707.80	353.90	23Y 9wks	28	773	3548	41,593	176.95	23Y 9wks	29	781	3573	41,772
.75	716.42	358.21	23Y 3wks	29	796	3666	43,136	179.11	23Y 3wks	30	805	3692	43,296
.875	725.07	362.54	22Y49wks	30	820	3787	44,703	181.27	22Y49wks	31	829	3813	44,874
8.00%	733.77	366.89	22Y44wks	30	845	3911	46,295	183.45	22Y44wks	32	854	3938	46,493
.125	742.50	371.26	22Y38wks	31	870	4037	47,942	185.63	22Y38wks	33	879	4064	48,113
.25	751.27	375.64	22Y32wks	32	895	4166	49,615	187.82	22Y32wks	33	904	4194	49,810
.375	760.08	380.04	22Y26wks	33	921	4298	51,326	190.02	22Y26wks	34	930	4327	51,491
8.50%	768.92	384.46	22Y20wks	34	947	4433	53,081	192.23	22Y20wks	35	957	4462	53,265
.625	777.79	388.90	22Y14wks	35	974	4571	54,856	194.45	22Y14wks	36	984	4601	55,053
.75	786.71	393.36	22Y 8wks	35	1001	4711	56,676	196.68	22Y 8wks	37	1011	4742	56,871
.875	795.65	397.83	22Y 2wks	36	1029	4855	58,529	198.92	22Y 2wks	38	1039	4886	58,742
9.00%	804.63	402.32	21Y48wks	37	1057	5002	60,423	201.16	21Y48wks	39	1067	5034	60,626
.125	813.64	406.82	21Y41wks	38	1086	5152	62,350	203.41	21Y41wks	40	1096	5184	62,558
.25	822.68	411.35	21Y35wks	39	1115	5305	64,308	205.68	21Y35wks	40	1126	5338	64,525
.375	831.75	415.88	21Y29wks	40	1145	5461	66,307	207.94	21Y29wks	41	1155	5495	66,538
9.50%	840.86	420.43	21Y23wks	41	1175	5620	68,347	210.22	21Y23wks	42	1186	5655	68,555
.625	849.99	425.00	21Y17wks	42	1206	5783	70,414	212.50	21Y17wks	43	1217	5818	70,634
.75	859.16	429.58	21Y10wks	43	1237	5949	72,508	214.79	21Y10wks	44	1248	5985	72,732
.875	868.35	434.18	21Y 4wks	44	1269	6118	74,651	217.09	21Y 4wks	45	1280	6155	74,875
10.00%	877.58	438.79	20Y50wks	45	1301	6291	76,828	219.40	20Y50wks	46	1312	6328	77,063
.125	886.83	443.42	20Y44wks	46	1334	6467	79,031	221.71	20Y44wks	47	1345	6505	79,275
.25	896.11	448.06	20Y37wks	47	1367	6646	81,266	224.03	20Y37wks	48	1379	6686	81,506
.375	905.41	452.71	20Y31wks	48	1401	6830	83,548	226.36	20Y31wks	49	1413	6870	83,786
10.50%	914.74	457.38	20Y25wks	49	1435	7016	85,855	228.69	20Y25wks	51	1448	7057	86,099
.625	924.10	462.06	20Y18wks	50	1470	7207	88,193	231.03	20Y18wks	52	1483	7248	88,460
.75	933.49	466.75	20Y12wks	51	1506	7401	90,569	233.38	20Y12wks	53	1518	7443	90,834
.875	942.90	471.45	20Y 6wks	52	1542	7598	92,972	235.73	20Y 6wks	54	1554	7642	93,235
11.00%	952.33	476.17	19Y51wks	53	1578	7800	95,407	238.09	19Y51wks	55	1591	7845	95,668
.125	961.79	480.90	19Y45wks	54	1615	8005	97,879	240.45	19Y45wks	56	1628	8051	98,147
.25	971.27	485.64	19Y39wks	56	1653	8215	100,377	242.82	19Y39wks	57	1666	8261	100,648
.375	980.77	490.39	19Y32wks	57	1691	8428	102,903	245.20	19Y32wks	58	1705	8475	103,184
11.50%	990.30	495.15	19Y26wks	58	1730	8645	105,462	247.58	19Y26wks	60	1744	8694	105,746
.625	999.84	499.93	19Y20wks	59	1769	8866	108,057	249.97	19Y20wks	61	1783	8916	108,337
.75	1009.41	504.71	19Y13wks	60	1809	9091	110,678	252.36	19Y13wks	62	1824	9142	110,953
.875	1019.01	509.51	19Y 7wks	61	1850	9321	113,323	254.76	19Y 7wks	63	1864	9373	113,612
12.00%	1028.62	514.31	19Y 1wks	63	1891	9554	116,003	257.16	19Y 1wks	64	1906	9608	116,299
.125	1038.25	519.13	18Y47wks	64	1933	9792	118,704	259.57	18Y47wks	66	1947	9847	119,005
.25	1047.90	523.96	18Y40wks	65	1975	10034	121,435	261.98	18Y40wks	67	1990	10090	121,747
.375	1057.57	528.79	18Y34wks	66	2018	10281	124,197	264.40	18Y34wks	68	2033	10338	124,498
12.50%	1067.26	533.64	18Y28wks	$ 68	$2061	10532	$126,977	266.82	18Y28wks	$70	$2077	10590	$127,285

Entries are per $100,000 of loan. Biweekly payments equal 1/2 normal and are paid every two weeks. Weekly payments equal 1/4 normal and are paid every week.

Rising Rate Mortgages
(a) Monthly Payments

Rate Rises 1/4% per year

Interest Rate	Payment per $100,000 in Year									
	1 same	2 +1/4%	3 +1/2%	4 +3/4%	5 +1.00%	6 +1.25%	7 +1.50%	8 +1.75%	9 +2.00%	10 +2.25%
5.50	567.79	583.22	598.47	613.52	628.36	642.98	657.35	671.45	685.26	698.78
.75	583.58	599.20	614.65	629.90	644.94	659.75	674.31	688.61	702.63	716.33
6.00	599.56	615.37	631.01	646.45	661.69	676.69	691.45	705.94	720.15	734.05
.25	615.72	631.73	647.55	663.19	678.61	693.80	708.75	723.43	737.83	751.92
.50	632.07	648.26	664.27	680.09	695.70	711.08	726.21	741.08	755.67	769.95
.75	648.60	664.97	681.16	697.16	712.95	728.51	743.83	758.88	773.65	788.12
7.00	665.31	681.85	698.22	714.39	730.36	746.10	761.59	776.83	791.78	806.42
.25	682.18	698.89	715.43	731.78	747.92	763.83	779.50	794.91	810.04	824.86
.50	699.22	716.10	732.80	749.31	765.62	781.71	797.55	813.13	828.43	843.43
.75	716.42	733.46	750.32	767.00	783.47	799.72	815.73	831.48	846.95	862.13
8.00	733.77	750.96	767.99	784.82	801.45	817.87	834.04	849.96	865.60	880.94
.25	751.27	768.62	785.79	802.78	819.57	836.14	852.47	868.55	884.36	899.86
.50	768.92	786.41	803.73	820.87	837.81	854.54	871.03	887.26	903.23	918.89
.75	786.71	804.34	821.81	839.09	856.18	873.05	889.69	906.08	922.20	938.03
9.00	804.63	822.40	840.00	857.43	874.66	891.68	908.47	925.01	941.29	957.27
.25	822.68	840.58	858.32	875.89	893.26	910.42	927.35	944.04	960.46	976.60
.50	840.86	858.89	876.76	894.46	911.96	929.26	946.34	963.17	979.74	996.02
.75	859.16	877.31	895.31	913.13	930.77	948.20	965.42	982.39	999.10	1015.53
10.00	877.58	895.85	913.97	931.92	949.68	967.24	984.59	1001.70	1018.54	1035.11
.25	896.11	914.50	932.73	950.80	968.69	986.38	1003.85	1021.09	1038.07	1054.78
.50	914.74	933.24	951.59	969.78	987.78	1005.60	1023.19	1040.56	1057.68	1074.52
.75	933.49	952.09	970.55	988.85	1006.97	1024.90	1042.62	1060.11	1077.36	1094.33
11.00	952.33	971.04	989.60	1008.01	1026.24	1044.28	1062.12	1079.74	1097.11	1114.21
.25	971.27	990.07	1008.74	1027.25	1045.59	1063.75	1081.70	1099.43	1116.92	1134.15
.50	990.30	1009.20	1027.96	1046.57	1065.02	1083.28	1101.34	1119.19	1136.80	1154.15
.75	1009.41	1028.41	1047.27	1065.97	1084.52	1102.89	1121.06	1139.01	1156.74	1174.20
12.00	1028.62	1047.70	1066.65	1085.45	1104.09	1122.56	1140.83	1158.90	1176.73	1194.31
.25	1047.90	1067.07	1086.10	1104.99	1123.73	1142.29	1160.67	1178.84	1196.78	1214.47
.50	1067.26	1086.51	1105.63	1124.60	1143.43	1162.09	1180.56	1198.83	1216.88	1234.68

(b) Remaining Balances

Interest Rate	Balance at End of Year									
	1	2	3	4	5	6	7	8	9	10
5.50	98,653	97,291	95,910	94,502	93,062	91,582	90,057	88,476	86,833	85,118
.75	98,714	97,410	96,085	94,732	93,345	91,917	90,441	88,909	87,312	85,640
6.00	98,772	97,525	96,255	94,955	93,619	92,241	90,814	89,328	87,777	86,149
.25	98,828	97,636	96,419	95,170	93,885	92,555	91,175	89,736	88,229	86,644
.50	98,882	97,743	96,577	95,378	94,141	92,859	91,525	90,131	88,668	87,126
.75	98,934	97,845	96,729	95,578	94,389	93,153	91,864	90,514	89,094	87,595
7.00	98,984	97,944	96,875	95,772	94,628	93,437	92,192	90,886	89,508	88,050
.25	99,032	98,039	97,016	95,958	94,858	93,711	92,510	91,245	89,909	88,492
.50	99,078	98,130	97,152	96,137	95,081	93,976	92,817	91,594	90,298	88,921
.75	99,122	98,218	97,282	96,310	95,295	94,232	93,113	91,930	90,675	89,337
8.00	99,165	98,302	97,407	96,476	95,502	94,479	93,400	92,256	91,040	89,741
.25	99,205	98,383	97,528	96,636	95,701	94,717	93,676	92,571	91,393	90,132
.50	99,244	98,460	97,643	96,789	95,892	94,946	93,943	92,876	91,735	90,511
.75	99,281	98,534	97,754	96,937	96,076	95,166	94,200	93,169	92,065	90,877
9.00	99,317	98,605	97,861	97,079	96,253	95,379	94,448	93,453	92,385	91,232
.25	99,351	98,673	97,963	97,215	96,424	95,583	94,687	93,727	92,693	91,576
.50	99,383	98,738	98,060	97,345	96,587	95,780	94,917	93,990	92,991	91,908
.75	99,414	98,800	98,154	97,470	96,744	95,969	95,139	94,245	93,278	92,229
10.00	99,444	98,860	98,243	97,590	96,894	96,151	95,352	94,490	93,556	92,539
.25	99,472	98,917	98,329	97,705	97,039	96,325	95,557	94,726	93,823	92,838
.50	99,499	98,971	98,411	97,815	97,177	96,493	95,754	94,953	94,081	93,127
.75	99,525	99,023	98,490	97,920	97,310	96,653	95,943	95,171	94,329	93,406
11.00	99,550	99,073	98,565	98,021	97,437	96,807	96,125	95,381	94,568	93,675
.25	99,573	99,120	98,636	98,118	97,559	96,955	96,299	95,583	94,799	93,934
.50	99,596	99,165	98,704	98,210	97,676	97,097	96,467	95,778	95,020	94,184
.75	99,617	99,208	98,770	98,298	97,787	97,233	96,628	95,964	95,233	94,425
12.00	99,637	99,249	98,832	98,382	97,894	97,363	96,782	96,143	95,438	94,657
.25	99,656	99,288	98,891	98,462	97,996	97,487	96,930	96,315	95,636	94,880
.50	99,675	99,325	98,948	98,539	98,094	97,607	97,071	96,480	95,825	95,095

Entries are per $100,000 of loan. Payment in first year equals normal 30-year payment.

Rising Rate Mortgages
(a) Monthly Payments

Rate rises 1/2% per year

Interest Rate	1 same	2 +1/2%	3 +1.00%	4 +1.50%	5 +2.00%	6 +2.50%	7 +3.00%	8 +3.50%	9 +4.00%	10 +4.50%
5.50	567.79	598.83	629.88	660.87	691.76	722.49	753.00	783.25	813.17	842.73
.75	583.58	615.01	646.44	677.81	709.07	740.16	771.03	801.64	831.92	861.83
6.00	599.56	631.37	663.17	694.91	726.53	757.98	789.21	820.17	850.80	881.06
.25	615.72	647.91	680.08	712.17	744.15	775.95	807.52	838.82	869.80	900.41
.50	632.07	664.62	697.15	729.59	761.91	794.05	825.97	857.61	888.93	919.87
.75	648.60	681.51	714.38	747.17	779.82	812.30	844.54	876.51	908.16	939.43
7.00	665.31	698.56	731.77	764.89	797.87	830.67	863.24	895.54	927.50	959.10
.25	682.18	715.77	749.30	782.75	816.05	849.17	882.06	914.67	946.95	978.86
.50	699.22	733.13	766.99	800.75	834.36	867.79	900.99	933.90	966.49	998.71
.75	716.42	750.64	784.81	818.88	852.80	886.53	920.02	953.24	986.13	1018.65
8.00	733.77	768.30	802.77	837.14	871.35	905.37	939.16	972.67	1005.85	1038.67
.25	751.27	786.10	820.87	855.52	890.02	924.33	958.40	992.19	1025.66	1058.76
.50	768.92	804.04	839.08	874.02	908.80	943.38	977.73	1011.80	1045.55	1078.93
.75	786.71	822.10	857.42	892.63	927.68	962.53	997.15	1031.49	1065.51	1099.17
9.00	804.63	840.30	875.88	911.35	946.66	981.77	1016.65	1051.26	1085.55	1119.47
.25	822.68	858.61	894.45	930.18	965.74	1001.11	1036.24	1071.10	1105.64	1139.83
.50	840.86	877.04	913.13	949.10	984.91	1020.52	1055.90	1091.01	1125.81	1160.24
.75	859.16	895.58	931.92	968.12	1004.17	1040.02	1075.64	1110.99	1146.03	1180.71
10.00	877.58	914.23	950.80	987.24	1023.51	1059.60	1095.45	1131.03	1166.30	1201.23
.25	896.11	932.99	969.78	1006.44	1042.94	1079.24	1115.32	1151.13	1186.63	1221.79
.50	914.74	951.85	988.85	1025.72	1062.44	1098.96	1135.25	1171.28	1207.01	1242.40
.75	933.49	970.80	1008.01	1045.09	1082.01	1118.74	1155.25	1191.49	1227.43	1263.04
11.00	952.33	989.84	1027.25	1064.53	1101.66	1138.59	1175.30	1211.75	1247.90	1283.72
.25	971.27	1008.97	1046.58	1084.05	1121.37	1158.49	1195.40	1232.05	1268.41	1304.43
.50	990.30	1028.19	1065.98	1103.64	1141.14	1178.45	1215.55	1252.39	1288.95	1325.18
.75	1009.41	1047.49	1085.45	1123.29	1160.97	1198.47	1235.75	1272.78	1309.52	1345.95
12.00	1028.62	1066.86	1105.00	1143.01	1180.86	1218.53	1255.99	1293.20	1330.13	1366.75
.25	1047.90	1086.31	1124.61	1162.79	1200.81	1238.64	1276.27	1313.66	1350.77	1387.57
.50	1067.26	1105.83	1144.29	1182.62	1220.80	1258.80	1296.60	1334.15	1371.44	1408.41

(b) Remaining Balances

Interest Rate	1	2	3	4	5	6	7	8	9	10
5.50	98,653	97,351	96,083	94,838	93,608	92,383	91,152	89,906	88,635	87,327
.75	98,714	97,468	96,252	95,058	93,875	92,693	91,505	90,299	89,066	87,794
6.00	98,772	97,581	96,416	95,270	94,132	92,994	91,846	90,679	89,484	88,249
.25	98,828	97,689	96,574	95,474	94,380	93,284	92,176	91,048	89,889	88,690
.50	98,882	97,794	96,727	95,671	94,620	93,565	92,496	91,405	90,282	89,118
.75	98,934	97,895	96,873	95,862	94,852	93,836	92,805	91,750	90,663	89,533
7.00	98,984	97,992	97,014	96,045	95,075	94,097	93,103	92,085	91,032	89,935
.25	99,032	98,085	97,150	96,221	95,290	94,350	93,392	92,408	91,389	90,324
.50	99,078	98,174	97,281	96,391	95,498	94,593	93,670	92,720	91,734	90,702
.75	99,122	98,260	97,406	96,554	95,697	94,828	93,938	93,021	92,067	91,067
8.00	99,165	98,342	97,527	96,711	95,889	95,054	94,197	93,312	92,390	91,420
.25	99,205	98,421	97,643	96,862	96,074	95,271	94,447	93,593	92,701	91,762
.50	99,244	98,497	97,754	97,007	96,252	95,481	94,687	93,864	93,002	92,092
.75	99,281	98,570	97,860	97,146	96,422	95,682	94,919	94,125	93,292	92,411
9.00	99,317	98,639	97,962	97,280	96,586	95,876	95,141	94,376	93,572	92,719
.25	99,351	98,706	98,060	97,408	96,744	96,062	95,356	94,618	93,842	93,016
.50	99,383	98,770	98,154	97,531	96,895	96,241	95,562	94,851	94,101	93,303
.75	99,414	98,830	98,243	97,648	97,040	96,412	95,760	95,076	94,352	93,579
10.00	99,444	98,889	98,329	97,761	97,179	96,577	95,950	95,291	94,593	93,846
.25	99,472	98,944	98,411	97,869	97,312	96,735	96,133	95,499	94,825	94,103
.50	99,499	98,997	98,490	97,972	97,439	96,887	96,308	95,698	95,048	94,350
.75	99,525	99,048	98,565	98,071	97,561	97,032	96,477	95,890	95,263	94,588
11.00	99,550	99,097	98,636	98,165	97,678	97,171	96,638	96,073	95,469	94,817
.25	99,573	99,143	98,705	98,255	97,790	97,305	96,793	96,250	95,667	95,038
.50	99,596	99,187	98,770	98,342	97,897	97,432	96,942	96,419	95,858	95,250
.75	99,617	99,229	98,832	98,424	97,999	97,554	97,084	96,582	96,041	95,454
12.00	99,637	99,269	98,892	98,503	98,097	97,671	97,220	96,737	96,217	95,650
.25	99,656	99,307	98,948	98,578	98,191	97,783	97,350	96,887	96,385	95,838
.50	99,675	99,343	99,002	98,649	98,280	97,890	97,475	97,030	96,547	96,019

Entries are per $100,000 of loan. Payment in first year equals normal 30-year payment.

Rate rises 3/4% per year

Rising Rate Mortgages
(a) Monthly Payments

Interest Rate	1 same	2 +3/4%	3 +1.50%	4 +2.25%	5 +3.00%	6 +3.75%	7 +4.50%	8 +5.25%	9 +6.00%	10 +6.75%
5.50	567.79	614.63	662.00	709.75	757.75	805.89	854.05	902.14	950.04	997.68
.75	583.58	630.99	678.92	727.20	775.73	824.37	873.02	921.59	969.97	1018.09
6.00	599.56	647.54	696.00	744.81	793.84	842.97	892.11	941.15	990.00	1038.58
.25	615.72	664.26	713.25	762.57	812.09	861.70	911.31	960.81	1010.12	1059.14
.50	632.07	681.15	730.66	780.47	830.47	880.55	930.61	980.56	1030.31	1079.79
.75	648.60	698.20	748.22	798.51	848.98	899.51	950.02	1000.41	1050.59	1100.49
7.00	665.31	715.42	765.92	816.68	867.60	918.58	969.52	1020.34	1070.95	1121.27
.25	682.18	732.79	783.76	834.98	886.35	937.75	989.12	1040.35	1091.37	1142.10
.50	699.22	750.31	801.74	853.41	905.20	957.03	1008.80	1060.43	1111.86	1162.99
.75	716.42	767.97	819.86	871.95	924.16	976.39	1028.56	1080.59	1132.40	1183.92
8.00	733.77	785.78	838.10	890.61	943.22	995.85	1048.40	1100.82	1153.01	1204.91
.25	751.27	803.72	856.46	909.37	962.38	1015.39	1068.32	1121.10	1173.67	1225.93
.50	768.92	821.80	874.94	928.25	981.63	1035.01	1088.31	1141.45	1194.37	1247.00
.75	786.71	839.99	893.53	947.22	1000.97	1054.71	1108.36	1161.85	1215.12	1268.10
9.00	804.63	858.32	912.23	966.29	1020.39	1074.48	1128.47	1182.31	1235.91	1289.23
.25	822.68	876.75	931.04	985.45	1039.90	1094.32	1148.65	1202.81	1256.74	1310.38
.50	840.86	895.30	949.94	1004.69	1059.48	1114.23	1168.88	1223.36	1277.61	1331.57
.75	859.16	913.96	968.94	1024.03	1079.13	1134.20	1189.16	1243.95	1298.51	1352.77
10.00	877.58	932.72	988.04	1043.44	1098.86	1154.23	1209.48	1264.57	1319.43	1374.00
.25	896.11	951.59	1007.22	1062.93	1118.65	1174.31	1229.86	1285.24	1340.38	1395.24
.50	914.74	970.55	1026.48	1082.49	1138.50	1194.44	1250.27	1305.93	1361.36	1416.50
.75	933.49	989.60	1045.83	1102.12	1158.41	1214.63	1270.73	1326.66	1382.36	1437.77
11.00	952.33	1008.74	1065.25	1121.82	1178.37	1234.86	1291.22	1347.41	1403.37	1459.05
.25	971.27	1027.96	1084.75	1141.58	1198.39	1255.14	1311.75	1368.19	1424.41	1480.34
.50	990.30	1047.26	1104.32	1161.40	1218.47	1275.45	1332.31	1389.00	1445.45	1501.63
.75	1009.41	1066.64	1123.95	1181.28	1238.58	1295.81	1352.90	1409.82	1466.52	1522.93
12.00	1028.62	1086.10	1143.65	1201.22	1258.75	1316.20	1373.52	1430.66	1487.59	1544.24
.25	1047.90	1105.62	1163.41	1221.20	1278.95	1336.62	1394.16	1451.53	1508.67	1565.54
.50	1067.26	1125.22	1183.22	1241.23	1299.20	1357.08	1414.83	1472.40	1529.76	1586.85

(b) Remaining Balances

Interest Rate	1	2	3	4	5	6	7	8	9	10
5.50	98,653	97,408	96,246	95,149	94,104	93,096	92,112	91,142	90,173	89,193
.75	98,714	97,523	96,410	95,358	94,354	93,383	92,435	91,497	90,559	89,609
6.00	98,772	97,634	96,568	95,560	94,595	93,661	92,747	91,842	90,934	90,012
.25	98,828	97,741	96,721	95,754	94,828	93,929	93,049	92,174	91,296	90,403
.50	98,882	97,843	96,868	95,941	95,052	94,188	93,340	92,496	91,647	90,781
.75	98,934	97,942	97,009	96,122	95,268	94,438	93,621	92,807	91,986	91,147
7.00	98,984	98,037	97,145	96,295	95,477	94,679	93,892	93,107	92,313	91,501
.25	99,032	98,129	97,276	96,463	95,678	94,911	94,154	93,397	92,630	91,844
.50	99,078	98,216	97,402	96,623	95,871	95,135	94,406	93,676	92,935	92,174
.75	99,122	98,300	97,522	96,778	96,057	95,350	94,649	93,946	93,230	92,494
8.00	99,165	98,381	97,638	96,926	96,235	95,557	94,883	94,205	93,515	92,802
.25	99,205	98,459	97,750	97,069	96,407	95,756	95,108	94,455	93,789	93,100
.50	99,244	98,533	97,856	97,206	96,572	95,948	95,325	94,696	94,053	93,387
.75	99,281	98,604	97,959	97,337	96,730	96,132	95,533	94,928	94,307	93,663
9.00	99,317	98,672	98,057	97,463	96,882	96,308	95,733	95,151	94,552	93,930
.25	99,351	98,737	98,151	97,583	97,028	96,478	95,926	95,365	94,788	94,187
.50	99,383	98,800	98,241	97,699	97,168	96,641	96,111	95,571	95,015	94,434
.75	99,414	98,859	98,327	97,810	97,302	96,797	96,288	95,769	95,233	94,672
10.00	99,444	98,916	98,409	97,916	97,430	96,946	96,458	95,959	95,443	94,901
.25	99,472	98,971	98,487	98,017	97,553	97,090	96,621	96,142	95,644	95,121
.50	99,499	99,022	98,563	98,114	97,670	97,227	96,778	96,317	95,837	95,333
.75	99,525	99,072	98,634	98,207	97,783	97,358	96,928	96,485	96,023	95,536
11.00	99,550	99,119	98,703	98,295	97,891	97,484	97,071	96,646	96,201	95,731
.25	99,573	99,165	98,768	98,380	97,993	97,605	97,209	96,800	96,372	95,919
.50	99,596	99,208	98,831	98,460	98,092	97,720	97,341	96,948	96,536	96,099
.75	99,617	99,249	98,890	98,538	98,186	97,830	97,467	97,090	96,694	96,272
12.00	99,637	99,288	98,947	98,611	98,275	97,936	97,587	97,225	96,844	96,438
.25	99,656	99,325	99,001	98,681	98,361	98,036	97,702	97,355	96,989	96,597
.50	99,675	99,360	99,053	98,748	98,443	98,132	97,813	97,479	97,127	96,750

Entries are per $100,000 of loan. Payment in first year equals normal 30-year payment.

Rate rises 1% per year

Rising Rate Mortgages
(a) Monthly Payments

Payment per $100,000 in Year

Interest Rate	1 same	2 +1.00%	3 +2.00%	4 +3.00%	5 +4.00%	6 +5.00%	7 +6.00%	8 +7.00%	9 +8.00%	10 +9.00%
5.50	567.79	630.61	694.79	760.04	826.10	892.74	959.77	1027.03	1094.34	1161.59
.75	583.58	647.16	712.05	777.98	844.67	911.93	979.55	1047.38	1115.25	1183.05
6.00	599.56	663.88	729.48	796.06	863.38	931.23	999.42	1067.80	1136.22	1204.55
.25	615.72	680.78	747.05	814.27	882.20	950.63	1019.38	1088.30	1157.25	1226.10
.50	632.07	697.84	764.77	832.62	901.13	970.12	1039.41	1108.86	1178.32	1247.68
.75	648.60	715.06	782.64	851.08	920.17	989.71	1059.53	1129.48	1199.45	1269.30
7.00	665.31	732.43	800.64	869.67	939.31	1009.38	1079.71	1150.16	1220.61	1290.94
.25	682.18	749.96	818.77	888.38	958.56	1029.14	1099.96	1170.90	1241.82	1312.61
.50	699.22	767.63	837.04	907.19	977.89	1048.97	1120.28	1191.68	1263.06	1334.30
.75	716.42	785.45	855.42	926.11	997.32	1068.88	1140.65	1212.51	1284.33	1356.02
8.00	733.77	803.39	873.92	945.13	1016.83	1088.86	1161.08	1233.38	1305.63	1377.74
.25	751.27	821.47	892.54	964.25	1036.42	1108.91	1181.57	1254.29	1326.96	1399.48
.50	768.92	839.68	911.26	983.45	1056.09	1129.01	1202.10	1275.23	1348.30	1421.22
.75	786.71	858.01	930.09	1002.75	1075.83	1149.18	1222.67	1296.20	1369.67	1442.98
9.00	804.63	876.45	949.02	1022.13	1095.64	1169.40	1243.29	1317.20	1391.05	1464.73
.25	822.68	895.01	968.04	1041.60	1115.52	1189.67	1263.94	1338.23	1412.44	1486.49
.50	840.86	913.68	987.16	1061.14	1135.45	1209.99	1284.63	1359.28	1433.85	1508.25
.75	859.16	932.45	1006.36	1080.75	1155.45	1230.35	1305.35	1380.35	1455.26	1530.00
10.00	877.58	951.32	1025.65	1100.43	1175.50	1250.76	1326.10	1401.44	1476.68	1551.75
.25	896.11	970.28	1045.02	1120.18	1195.61	1271.21	1346.88	1422.54	1498.10	1573.49
.50	914.74	989.34	1064.47	1139.99	1215.76	1291.70	1367.69	1443.66	1519.53	1595.22
.75	933.49	1008.49	1083.99	1159.86	1235.96	1312.21	1388.52	1464.79	1540.96	1616.95
11.00	952.33	1027.72	1103.58	1179.78	1256.21	1332.77	1409.37	1485.93	1562.38	1638.66
.25	971.27	1047.03	1123.24	1199.76	1276.50	1353.35	1430.23	1507.08	1583.81	1660.36
.50	990.30	1066.42	1142.95	1219.79	1296.82	1373.96	1451.12	1528.23	1605.23	1682.05
.75	1009.41	1085.88	1162.74	1239.87	1317.18	1394.59	1472.02	1549.39	1626.65	1703.73
12.00	1028.62	1105.41	1182.57	1259.99	1337.58	1415.25	1492.93	1570.55	1648.06	1725.39
.25	1047.90	1125.01	1202.47	1280.16	1358.01	1435.93	1513.86	1591.72	1669.47	1747.03
.50	1067.26	1144.67	1222.41	1300.37	1378.47	1456.63	1534.79	1612.89	1690.87	1768.66

(b) Remaining Balances

Balance at End of Year

Interest Rate	1	2	3	4	5	6	7	8	9	10
5.50	98,653	97,463	96,399	95,436	94,551	93,727	92,948	92,201	91,472	90,749
.75	98,714	97,576	96,558	95,635	94,786	93,994	93,244	92,523	91,818	91,119
6.00	98,772	97,685	96,711	95,826	95,012	94,251	93,529	92,833	92,153	91,476
.25	98,828	97,790	96,858	96,011	95,230	94,499	93,804	93,134	92,477	91,821
.50	98,882	97,891	97,000	96,189	95,440	94,738	94,069	93,424	92,789	92,155
.75	98,934	97,988	97,136	96,360	95,642	94,968	94,325	93,703	93,091	92,478
7.00	98,984	98,081	97,268	96,525	95,837	95,190	94,572	93,973	93,382	92,789
.25	99,032	98,171	97,394	96,683	96,024	95,403	94,810	94,232	93,662	93,090
.50	99,078	98,257	97,515	96,836	96,204	95,609	95,038	94,483	93,933	93,379
.75	99,122	98,339	97,631	96,982	96,377	95,806	95,258	94,724	94,193	93,659
8.00	99,165	98,418	97,743	97,122	96,544	95,996	95,470	94,955	94,444	93,928
.25	99,205	98,494	97,850	97,257	96,704	96,179	95,673	95,178	94,686	94,187
.50	99,244	98,567	97,952	97,386	96,857	96,354	95,869	95,393	94,918	94,437
.75	99,281	98,637	98,051	97,510	97,004	96,522	96,056	95,599	95,142	94,677
9.00	99,317	98,703	98,145	97,629	97,145	96,684	96,237	95,797	95,356	94,908
.25	99,351	98,767	98,235	97,743	97,280	96,838	96,410	95,987	95,563	95,130
.50	99,383	98,828	98,321	97,852	97,409	96,987	96,576	96,169	95,761	95,344
.75	99,414	98,887	98,404	97,956	97,533	97,129	96,735	96,344	95,951	95,549
10.00	99,444	98,942	98,483	98,056	97,652	97,265	96,887	96,512	96,134	95,746
.25	99,472	98,996	98,558	98,151	97,766	97,395	97,033	96,673	96,309	95,935
.50	99,499	99,046	98,630	98,242	97,874	97,520	97,173	96,827	96,478	96,117
.75	99,525	99,095	98,699	98,329	97,978	97,639	97,307	96,975	96,639	96,291
11.00	99,550	99,141	98,765	98,412	98,077	97,753	97,435	97,117	96,793	96,458
.25	99,573	99,185	98,827	98,492	98,172	97,862	97,558	97,252	96,941	96,618
.50	99,596	99,227	98,887	98,568	98,263	97,967	97,675	97,382	97,083	96,772
.75	99,617	99,267	98,944	98,640	98,349	98,066	97,787	97,506	97,218	96,919
12.00	99,637	99,306	98,998	98,709	98,431	98,161	97,894	97,625	97,348	97,060
.25	99,656	99,342	99,050	98,775	98,510	98,252	97,996	97,738	97,473	97,195
.50	99,675	99,377	99,099	98,837	98,585	98,339	98,094	97,846	97,591	97,324

Entries are per $100,000 of loan. Payment in first year equals normal 30-year payment.

Growing Equity Mortgage

Payment rises 2.0% per year   (a) Monthly Payments

Interest Rate					Payment in Year					
	1	2	3	4	5	6	7	8	9	10
5.50	567.79	579.15	590.74	602.56	614.62	626.92	639.46	652.25	665.30	678.61
.75	583.58	595.25	607.16	619.31	631.70	644.34	657.23	670.38	683.80	697.48
6.00	599.56	611.55	623.79	636.27	649.00	661.98	675.23	688.74	702.52	716.57
.25	615.72	628.04	640.61	653.42	666.50	679.83	693.43	707.31	721.46	735.89
.50	632.07	644.72	657.62	670.78	684.20	697.89	˥11.85	726.09	740.62	755.43
.75	648.60	661.58	674.82	688.32	702.09	716.14	730.46	745.08	759.98	775.19
7.00	665.31	678.62	692.20	706.04	720.17	734.58	749.28	764.27	779.56	795.15
.25	682.18	695.83	709.75	723.95	738.44	753.21	768.28	783.65	799.33	815.32
.50	699.22	713.21	727.48	742.03	756.88	772.02	787.47	803.22	819.29	835.68
.75	716.42	730.75	745.37	760.28	775.49	791.01	806.83	822.98	839.44	856.23
8.00	733.77	748.45	763.42	778.70	794.28	810.17	826.38	842.91	859.77	876.97
.25	751.27	766.30	781.63	797.27	813.22	829.49	846.09	863.01	880.28	897.89
.50	768.92	784.30	799.99	816.00	832.32	848.97	865.96	883.28	900.95	918.98
.75	786.71	802.44	818.50	834.87	851.58	868.61	885.99	903.71	921.79	940.23
9.00	804.63	820.73	837.14	853.89	870.98	888.40	906.17	924.30	942.79	961.65
.25	822.68	839.14	855.93	873.05	890.52	908.33	926.50	945.04	963.94	983.23
.50	840.86	857.68	874.84	892.34	910.19	928.40	946.98	965.92	985.24	1004.95
.75	859.16	876.35	893.88	911.76	930.00	948.61	967.58	986.94	1006.68	1026.82
10.00	877.58	895.13	913.04	931.31	949.94	968.94	988.33	1008.10	1028.26	1048.83
.25	896.11	914.03	932.32	950.97	969.99	989.40	1009.19	1029.38	1049.97	1070.98
.50	914.74	933.04	951.71	970.75	990.17	1009.98	1030.18	1050.79	1071.81	1093.25
.75	933.49	952.16	971.21	990.64	1010.46	1030.67	1051.29	1072.32	1093.77	1115.65
11.00	952.33	971.38	990.81	1010.63	1030.85	1051.47	1072.51	1093.96	1115.85	1138.17
.25	971.27	990.70	1010.52	1030.73	1051.35	1072.38	1093.84	1115.72	1138.04	1160.80
.50	990.30	1010.11	1030.31	1050.93	1071.95	1093.39	1115.27	1137.58	1160.33	1183.54
.75	1009.41	1029.61	1050.21	1071.21	1092.64	1114.50	1136.80	1159.54	1182.73	1206.39
12.00	1028.62	1049.19	1070.18	1091.59	1113.43	1135.70	1158.42	1181.60	1205.23	1229.34
.25	1047.90	1068.86	1090.25	1112.06	1134.30	1156.99	1180.14	1203.75	1227.83	1252.39
.50	1067.26	1088.61	1110.39	1132.60	1155.26	1178.37	1201.94	1225.99	1250.51	1275.53

Entries are per $100,000 of loan. Entry in first year equals standard mortgage payment.

(b) Overall Maturity of GEM

Interest Rate				If Payment Continues at Rate in Column						
	1	2	3	4	5	6	7	8	9	10
5.50	30Y 0m	28Y 8m	27Y 6m	26Y 6m	25Y 8m	24Y11m	24Y 3m	23Y 9m	23Y 3m	22Y10m
.75	30Y 0m	28Y 7m	27Y 5m	26Y 5m	25Y 6m	24Y 9m	24Y 1m	23Y 7m	23Y 1m	22Y 8m
6.00	30Y 0m	28Y 6m	27Y 4m	26Y 3m	25Y 4m	24Y 7m	23Y11m	23Y 5m	22Y11m	22Y 6m
.25	30Y 0m	28Y 6m	27Y 2m	26Y 2m	25Y 3m	24Y 5m	23Y 9m	23Y 2m	22Y 9m	22Y 4m
.50	30Y 0m	28Y 5m	27Y 1m	26Y 0m	25Y 1m	24Y 3m	23Y 7m	23Y 0m	22Y 6m	22Y 1m
.75	30Y 0m	28Y 4m	27Y 0m	25Y10m	24Y11m	24Y 1m	23Y 5m	22Y10m	22Y 4m	21Y11m
7.00	30Y 0m	28Y 3m	26Y10m	25Y 8m	24Y 9m	23Y11m	23Y 3m	22Y 8m	22Y 2m	21Y 9m
.25	30Y 0m	28Y 2m	26Y 9m	25Y 7m	24Y 7m	23Y 9m	23Y 1m	22Y 6m	22Y 0m	21Y 7m
.50	30Y 0m	28Y 1m	26Y 7m	25Y 5m	24Y 5m	23Y 7m	22Y10m	22Y 3m	21Y10m	21Y 5m
.75	30Y 0m	28Y 0m	26Y 6m	25Y 3m	24Y 3m	23Y 5m	22Y 8m	22Y 1m	21Y 7m	21Y 2m
8.00	30Y 0m	27Y11m	26Y 4m	25Y 1m	24Y 1m	23Y 2m	22Y 6m	21Y11m	21Y 5m	21Y 0m
.25	30Y 0m	27Y10m	26Y 2m	24Y11m	23Y10m	23Y 0m	22Y 4m	21Y 9m	21Y 3m	20Y10m
.50	30Y 0m	27Y 9m	26Y 1m	24Y 9m	23Y 8m	22Y10m	22Y 1m	21Y 6m	21Y 0m	20Y 8m
.75	30Y 0m	27Y 8m	25Y11m	24Y 7m	23Y 6m	22Y 7m	21Y11m	21Y 4m	20Y10m	20Y 5m
9.00	30Y 0m	27Y 7m	25Y 9m	24Y 5m	23Y 4m	22Y 5m	21Y 9m	21Y 2m	20Y 8m	20Y 3m
.25	30Y 0m	27Y 5m	25Y 7m	24Y 3m	23Y 1m	22Y 3m	21Y 6m	20Y11m	20Y 5m	20Y 1m
.50	30Y 0m	27Y 4m	25Y 5m	24Y 0m	22Y11m	22Y 0m	21Y 4m	20Y 9m	20Y 3m	19Y11m
.75	30Y 0m	27Y 3m	25Y 3m	23Y10m	22Y 9m	21Y10m	21Y 1m	20Y 6m	20Y 1m	19Y 8m
10.00	30Y 0m	27Y 1m	25Y 1m	23Y 8m	22Y 6m	21Y 8m	20Y11m	20Y 4m	19Y11m	19Y 6m
.25	30Y 0m	27Y 0m	24Y11m	23Y 5m	22Y 4m	21Y 5m	20Y 9m	20Y 2m	19Y 8m	19Y 4m
.50	30Y 0m	26Y10m	24Y 9m	23Y 3m	22Y 1m	21Y 3m	20Y 6m	19Y11m	19Y 6m	19Y 2m
.75	30Y 0m	26Y 9m	24Y 7m	23Y 1m	21Y11m	21Y 0m	20Y 4m	19Y 9m	19Y 4m	18Y11m
11.00	30Y 0m	26Y 7m	24Y 5m	22Y10m	21Y 9m	20Y10m	20Y 1m	19Y 7m	19Y 1m	18Y 9m
.25	30Y 0m	26Y 6m	24Y 3m	22Y 8m	21Y 6m	20Y 7m	19Y11m	19Y 4m	18Y11m	18Y 7m
.50	30Y 0m	26Y 4m	24Y 1m	22Y 6m	21Y 4m	20Y 5m	19Y 9m	19Y 2m	18Y 9m	18Y 5m
.75	30Y 0m	26Y 2m	23Y10m	22Y 3m	21Y 1m	20Y 3m	19Y 6m	19Y 0m	18Y 7m	18Y 3m
12.00	30Y 0m	26Y 0m	23Y 8m	22Y 1m	20Y11m	20Y 0m	19Y 4m	18Y 9m	18Y 4m	18Y 0m
.25	30Y 0m	25Y11m	23Y 6m	21Y10m	20Y 8m	19Y10m	19Y 2m	18Y 7m	18Y 2m	17Y10m
.50	30Y 0m	25Y 9m	23Y 3m	21Y 8m	20Y 6m	19Y 7m	18Y11m	18Y 5m	18Y 0m	17Y 8m

Growing Equity Mortgage

Payment rises 3.0% per year   (a) Monthly Payments

Interest Rate	1	2	3	4	Payment in Year 5	6	7	8	9	10
5.50	567.79	584.83	602.38	620.46	639.08	658.26	678.01	698.35	719.31	740.89
.75	583.58	601.09	619.13	637.71	656.84	676.55	696.85	717.77	739.30	761.49
6.00	599.56	617.55	636.08	655.17	674.83	695.08	715.93	737.42	759.54	782.33
.25	615.72	634.20	653.23	672.83	693.02	713.82	735.24	757.30	780.02	803.43
.50	632.07	651.04	670.58	690.70	711.42	732.77	754.76	777.41	800.74	824.76
.75	648.60	668.07	688.11	708.76	730.03	751.94	774.50	797.74	821.68	846.33
7.00	665.31	685.27	705.83	727.01	748.83	771.30	794.44	818.28	842.84	868.13
.25	682.18	702.65	723.74	745.45	767.82	790.86	814.59	839.04	864.21	890.14
.50	699.22	720.20	741.81	764.07	787.00	810.61	834.94	859.99	885.79	912.37
.75	716.42	737.91	760.06	782.86	806.35	830.55	855.47	881.14	907.58	934.81
8.00	733.77	755.79	778.47	801.83	825.88	850.67	876.19	902.48	929.56	957.45
.25	751.27	773.81	797.03	820.95	845.58	870.96	897.09	924.01	951.73	980.29
.50	768.92	791.99	815.76	840.23	865.45	891.41	918.16	945.71	974.09	1003.31
.75	786.71	810.31	834.63	859.67	885.46	912.03	939.40	967.59	996.62	1026.52
9.00	804.63	828.77	853.64	879.25	905.64	932.81	960.80	989.63	1019.32	1049.91
.25	822.68	847.37	872.79	898.98	925.95	953.74	982.36	1011.83	1042.19	1073.46
.50	840.86	866.09	892.08	918.84	946.42	974.81	1004.06	1034.19	1065.22	1097.18
.75	859.16	884.94	911.49	938.84	967.01	996.03	1025.91	1056.70	1088.40	1121.06
10.00	877.58	903.91	931.03	958.97	987.74	1017.38	1047.90	1079.35	1111.73	1145.09
.25	896.11	922.99	950.69	979.21	1008.60	1038.86	1070.03	1102.14	1135.20	1169.27
.50	914.74	942.19	970.46	999.58	1029.57	1060.47	1092.28	1125.06	1158.82	1193.58
.75	933.49	961.50	990.35	1020.06	1050.67	1082.19	1114.66	1148.11	1182.56	1218.04
11.00	952.33	980.90	1010.34	1040.65	1071.87	1104.04	1137.16	1171.28	1206.43	1242.62
.25	971.27	1000.41	1030.43	1061.34	1093.19	1125.99	1159.77	1194.57	1230.42	1267.33
.50	990.30	1020.01	1050.62	1082.14	1114.61	1148.05	1182.50	1217.98	1254.52	1292.16
.75	1009.41	1039.70	1070.90	1103.03	1136.13	1170.21	1205.33	1241.49	1278.74	1317.11
12.00	1028.62	1059.48	1091.27	1124.01	1157.74	1192.48	1228.26	1265.11	1303.07	1342.16
.25	1047.90	1079.34	1111.73	1145.09	1179.44	1214.83	1251.28	1288.82	1327.49	1367.32
.50	1067.26	1099.29	1132.27	1166.24	1201.23	1237.28	1274.40	1312.64	1352.02	1392.59

Entries are per $100,000 of loan. Entry in first year equals standard mortgage payment.

(b) Overall Maturity of GEM

Interest Rate	1	2	3	4	If Payment Continues at Rate in Column 5	6	7	8	9	10
5.50	30Y 0m	28Y 0m	26Y 5m	25Y 1m	24Y 0m	23Y 0m	22Y 3m	21Y 6m	20Y11m	20Y 6m
.75	30Y 0m	27Y11m	26Y 3m	24Y11m	23Y 9m	22Y10m	22Y 0m	21Y 4m	20Y 9m	20Y 3m
6.00	30Y 0m	27Y10m	26Y 2m	24Y 9m	23Y 7m	22Y 8m	21Y10m	21Y 2m	20Y 7m	20Y 1m
.25	30Y 0m	27Y 9m	26Y 0m	24Y 7m	23Y 5m	22Y 5m	21Y 7m	20Y11m	20Y 4m	19Y11m
.50	30Y 0m	27Y 8m	25Y10m	24Y 5m	23Y 3m	22Y 3m	21Y 5m	20Y 9m	20Y 2m	19Y 8m
.75	30Y 0m	27Y 7m	25Y 9m	24Y 3m	23Y 0m	22Y 0m	21Y 3m	20Y 6m	20Y 0m	19Y 6m
7.00	30Y 0m	27Y 6m	25Y 7m	24Y 1m	22Y10m	21Y10m	21Y 0m	20Y 4m	19Y 9m	19Y 4m
.25	30Y 0m	27Y 5m	25Y 5m	23Y10m	22Y 8m	21Y 8m	20Y10m	20Y 2m	19Y 7m	19Y 2m
.50	30Y 0m	27Y 3m	25Y 3m	23Y 8m	22Y 5m	21Y 5m	20Y 7m	19Y11m	19Y 5m	18Y11m
.75	30Y 0m	27Y 2m	25Y 1m	23Y 6m	22Y 3m	21Y 3m	20Y 5m	19Y 9m	19Y 2m	18Y 9m
8.00	30Y 0m	27Y 1m	24Y11m	23Y 4m	22Y 0m	21Y 0m	20Y 2m	19Y 6m	19Y 0m	18Y 7m
.25	30Y 0m	26Y11m	24Y 9m	23Y 1m	21Y10m	20Y10m	20Y 0m	19Y 4m	18Y10m	18Y 4m
.50	30Y 0m	26Y10m	24Y 7m	22Y11m	21Y 7m	20Y 7m	19Y 9m	19Y 2m	18Y 7m	18Y 2m
.75	30Y 0m	26Y 8m	24Y 5m	22Y 8m	21Y 5m	20Y 5m	19Y 7m	18Y11m	18Y 5m	18Y 0m
9.00	30Y 0m	26Y 7m	24Y 2m	22Y 6m	21Y 2m	20Y 2m	19Y 4m	18Y 9m	18Y 3m	17Y10m
.25	30Y 0m	26Y 5m	24Y 0m	22Y 3m	21Y 0m	20Y 0m	19Y 2m	18Y 6m	18Y 0m	17Y 7m
.50	30Y 0m	26Y 3m	23Y10m	22Y 1m	20Y 9m	19Y 9m	19Y 0m	18Y 4m	17Y10m	17Y 5m
.75	30Y 0m	26Y 1m	23Y 8m	21Y10m	20Y 7m	19Y 7m	18Y 9m	18Y 2m	17Y 8m	17Y 3m
10.00	30Y 0m	26Y 0m	23Y 5m	21Y 8m	20Y 4m	19Y 4m	18Y 7m	17Y11m	17Y 5m	17Y 1m
.25	30Y 0m	25Y10m	23Y 3m	21Y 5m	20Y 1m	19Y 2m	18Y 4m	17Y 9m	17Y 3m	16Y11m
.50	30Y 0m	25Y 8m	23Y 0m	21Y 3m	19Y11m	18Y11m	18Y 2m	17Y 7m	17Y 1m	16Y 9m
.75	30Y 0m	25Y 6m	22Y10m	21Y 0m	19Y 8m	18Y 9m	17Y11m	17Y 4m	16Y11m	16Y 7m
11.00	30Y 0m	25Y 4m	22Y 7m	20Y10m	19Y 6m	18Y 6m	17Y 9m	17Y 2m	16Y 9m	16Y 5m
.25	30Y 0m	25Y 2m	22Y 5m	20Y 7m	19Y 3m	18Y 4m	17Y 7m	17Y 0m	16Y 7m	16Y 3m
.50	30Y 0m	25Y 0m	22Y 2m	20Y 4m	19Y 1m	18Y 1m	17Y 4m	16Y10m	16Y 5m	16Y 1m
.75	30Y 0m	24Y10m	22Y 0m	20Y 2m	18Y10m	17Y11m	17Y 2m	16Y 8m	16Y 2m	15Y11m
12.00	30Y 0m	24Y 7m	21Y 9m	19Y11m	18Y 8m	17Y 8m	17Y 0m	16Y 5m	16Y 0m	15Y 9m
.25	30Y 0m	24Y 5m	21Y 7m	19Y 9m	18Y 5m	17Y 6m	16Y10m	16Y 3m	15Y10m	15Y 7m
.50	30Y 0m	24Y 3m	21Y 4m	19Y 6m	18Y 3m	17Y 4m	16Y 8m	16Y 1m	15Y 8m	15Y 5m

Growing Equity Mortgage

Payment rises 4.0% per year   (a) Monthly Payments

Interest Rate					Payment in Year					
	1	2	3	4	5	6	7	8	9	10
5.50	567.79	590.51	614.14	638.71	664.26	690.84	718.47	747.22	777.11	808.20
.75	583.58	606.93	631.21	656.46	682.72	710.04	738.45	767.99	798.71	830.67
6.00	599.56	623.54	648.49	674.43	701.42	729.48	758.66	789.01	820.58	853.41
.25	615.72	640.36	665.98	692.62	720.33	749.15	779.12	810.29	842.70	876.42
.50	632.07	657.36	683.66	711.01	739.46	769.04	799.81	831.80	865.08	899.69
.75	648.60	674.55	701.54	729.61	758.79	789.15	820.72	853.56	887.70	923.22
7.00	665.31	691.92	719.61	748.40	778.34	809.48	841.86	875.54	910.56	946.99
.25	682.18	709.47	737.86	767.38	798.08	830.00	863.21	897.74	933.66	971.01
.50	699.22	727.19	756.29	786.54	818.01	850.73	884.77	920.16	956.98	995.26
.75	716.42	745.08	774.89	805.89	838.13	871.66	906.53	942.80	980.51	1019.74
8.00	733.77	763.13	793.66	825.41	858.43	892.77	928.49	965.63	1004.26	1044.44
.25	751.27	781.33	812.59	845.09	878.90	914.06	950.63	988.66	1028.21	1069.35
.50	768.92	799.68	831.67	864.94	899.55	935.53	972.96	1011.88	1052.36	1094.46
.75	786.71	818.18	850.91	884.95	920.36	957.17	995.47	1035.29	1076.71	1119.78
9.00	804.63	836.82	870.30	905.11	941.32	978.98	1018.14	1058.87	1101.23	1145.29
.25	822.68	855.59	889.82	925.42	962.44	1000.94	1040.99	1082.63	1125.94	1170.98
.50	840.86	874.50	909.48	945.87	983.71	1023.06	1063.99	1106.55	1150.82	1196.86
.75	859.16	893.53	929.28	966.45	1005.12	1045.33	1087.14	1130.63	1175.86	1222.90
10.00	877.58	912.68	949.20	987.17	1026.66	1067.73	1110.45	1154.87	1201.07	1249.12
.25	896.11	931.96	969.24	1008.01	1048.34	1090.28	1133.89	1179.25	1226.43	1275.49
.50	914.74	951.34	989.40	1028.98	1070.14	1112.95	1157.48	1203.78	1251.94	1302.02
.75	933.49	970.83	1009.67	1050.06	1092.07	1135.76	1181.19	1228.44	1277.59	1328.69
11.00	952.33	990.43	1030.05	1071.26	1114.11	1158.68	1205.03	1253.24	1303.37	1355.51
.25	971.27	1010.12	1050.53	1092.56	1136.27	1181.72	1228.99	1278.16	1329.29	1382.47
.50	990.30	1029.91	1071.11	1113.96	1158.53	1204.87	1253.07	1303.20	1355.33	1409.55
.75	1009.41	1049.80	1091.79	1135.47	1180.89	1228.13	1277.26	1328.36	1381.50	1436.76
12.00	1028.62	1069.77	1112.56	1157.07	1203.36	1251.50	1301.56	1353.63	1407.78	1464.10
.25	1047.90	1089.82	1133.42	1178.76	1225.92	1274.96	1325.96	1379.01	1434.17	1491.54
.50	1067.26	1109.96	1154.36	1200.54	1248.57	1298.52	1350.46	1404.48	1460.67	1519.10

Entries are per $100,000 of loan. Entry in first year equals standard mortgage payment.

(b) Overall Maturity of GEM

Interest Rate					If Payment Continues at Rate in Column					
	1	2	3	4	5	6	7	8	9	10
5.50	30Y 0m	27Y 5m	25Y 5m	23Y10m	22Y 6m	21Y 5m	20Y 6m	19Y 9m	19Y 1m	18Y 7m
.75	30Y 0m	27Y 4m	25Y 3m	23Y 7m	22Y 3m	21Y 2m	20Y 3m	19Y 6m	18Y11m	18Y 5m
6.00	30Y 0m	27Y 3m	25Y 1m	23Y 5m	22Y 1m	21Y 0m	20Y 1m	19Y 4m	18Y 8m	18Y 2m
.25	30Y 0m	27Y 2m	24Y11m	23Y 3m	21Y10m	20Y 9m	19Y10m	19Y 1m	18Y 6m	18Y 0m
.50	30Y 0m	27Y 0m	24Y 9m	23Y 0m	21Y 8m	20Y 7m	19Y 8m	18Y11m	18Y 4m	17Y10m
.75	30Y 0m	26Y11m	24Y 7m	22Y10m	21Y 5m	20Y 4m	19Y 5m	18Y 8m	18Y 1m	17Y 8m
7.00	30Y 0m	26Y 9m	24Y 5m	22Y 8m	21Y 3m	20Y 1m	19Y 3m	18Y 6m	17Y11m	17Y 5m
.25	30Y 0m	26Y 8m	24Y 3m	22Y 5m	21Y 0m	19Y11m	19Y 0m	18Y 3m	17Y 9m	17Y 3m
.50	30Y 0m	26Y 6m	24Y 1m	22Y 3m	20Y10m	19Y 8m	18Y10m	18Y 1m	17Y 6m	17Y 1m
.75	30Y 0m	26Y 5m	23Y10m	22Y 0m	20Y 7m	19Y 6m	18Y 7m	17Y11m	17Y 4m	16Y11m
8.00	30Y 0m	26Y 3m	23Y 8m	21Y 9m	20Y 4m	19Y 3m	18Y 5m	17Y 8m	17Y 2m	16Y 8m
.25	30Y 0m	26Y 1m	23Y 6m	21Y 7m	20Y 2m	19Y 0m	18Y 2m	17Y 6m	16Y11m	16Y 6m
.50	30Y 0m	25Y11m	23Y 3m	21Y 4m	19Y11m	18Y10m	18Y 0m	17Y 4m	16Y 9m	16Y 4m
.75	30Y 0m	25Y 9m	23Y 1m	21Y 2m	19Y 9m	18Y 7m	17Y 9m	17Y 1m	16Y 7m	16Y 2m
9.00	30Y 0m	25Y 8m	22Y10m	20Y11m	19Y 6m	18Y 5m	17Y 7m	16Y11m	16Y 5m	16Y 0m
.25	30Y 0m	25Y 6m	22Y 8m	20Y 8m	19Y 3m	18Y 2m	17Y 4m	16Y 9m	16Y 3m	15Y10m
.50	30Y 0m	25Y 4m	22Y 5m	20Y 6m	19Y 1m	18Y 0m	17Y 2m	16Y 6m	16Y 0m	15Y 8m
.75	30Y 0m	25Y 2m	22Y 3m	20Y 3m	18Y10m	17Y 9m	17Y 0m	16Y 4m	15Y10m	15Y 6m
10.00	30Y 0m	24Y11m	22Y 0m	20Y 1m	18Y 8m	17Y 7m	16Y 9m	16Y 2m	15Y 8m	15Y 4m
.25	30Y 0m	24Y 9m	21Y10m	19Y10m	18Y 5m	17Y 4m	16Y 7m	16Y 0m	15Y 6m	15Y 2m
.50	30Y 0m	24Y 7m	21Y 7m	19Y 7m	18Y 2m	17Y 2m	16Y 5m	15Y 9m	15Y 4m	15Y 0m
.75	30Y 0m	24Y 5m	21Y 4m	19Y 5m	18Y 0m	17Y 0m	16Y 2m	15Y 7m	15Y 2m	14Y10m
11.00	30Y 0m	24Y 3m	21Y 2m	19Y 2m	17Y 9m	16Y 9m	16Y 0m	15Y 5m	15Y 0m	14Y 8m
.25	30Y 0m	24Y 0m	20Y11m	18Y11m	17Y 7m	16Y 7m	15Y10m	15Y 3m	14Y10m	14Y 6m
.50	30Y 0m	23Y10m	20Y 9m	18Y 9m	17Y 4m	16Y 5m	15Y 8m	15Y 1m	14Y 8m	14Y 5m
.75	30Y 0m	23Y 8m	20Y 6m	18Y 6m	17Y 2m	16Y 2m	15Y 6m	14Y11m	14Y 6m	14Y 3m
12.00	30Y 0m	23Y 5m	20Y 3m	18Y 4m	17Y 0m	16Y 0m	15Y 4m	14Y 9m	14Y 4m	14Y 1m
.25	30Y 0m	23Y 3m	20Y 1m	18Y 1m	16Y 9m	15Y10m	15Y 1m	14Y 7m	14Y 3m	13Y11m
.50	30Y 0m	23Y 0m	19Y10m	17Y11m	16Y 7m	15Y 8m	14Y11m	14Y 5m	14Y 1m	13Y10m

Growing Equity Mortgage

Payment rises 5.0% per year   (a) Monthly Payments

Interest Rate	1	2	3	4	Payment in Year 5	6	7	8	9	10
5.50	567.79	596.19	626.00	657.31	690.18	724.69	760.93	798.98	838.94	880.89
.75	583.58	612.76	643.40	675.58	709.36	744.84	782.08	821.19	862.26	905.38
6.00	599.56	629.54	661.02	694.08	728.78	765.23	803.50	843.68	885.86	930.16
.25	615.72	646.51	678.84	712.79	748.44	785.86	825.16	866.42	909.75	955.24
.50	632.07	663.68	696.87	731.72	768.31	806.73	847.07	889.43	933.91	980.61
.75	648.60	681.04	715.10	750.85	788.40	827.83	869.22	912.69	958.33	1006.25
7.00	665.31	698.58	733.51	770.19	808.71	849.15	891.61	936.19	983.01	1032.17
.25	682.18	716.30	752.11	789.73	829.22	870.68	914.22	959.94	1007.94	1058.34
.50	699.22	734.19	770.90	809.45	849.93	892.43	937.05	983.91	1033.11	1084.77
.75	716.42	752.24	789.86	829.36	870.83	914.38	960.10	1008.11	1058.52	1111.45
8.00	733.77	770.46	808.99	849.45	891.92	936.52	983.36	1032.53	1084.16	1138.37
.25	751.27	788.84	828.29	869.71	913.20	958.86	1006.81	1057.16	1110.02	1165.52
.50	768.92	807.37	847.74	890.13	934.65	981.38	1030.46	1081.99	1136.09	1192.90
.75	786.71	826.05	867.35	910.73	956.27	1004.09	1054.29	1107.01	1162.37	1220.49
9.00	804.63	844.86	887.11	931.47	978.05	1026.96	1078.31	1132.23	1188.85	1248.30
.25	822.68	863.82	907.02	952.37	999.99	1050.00	1102.50	1157.63	1215.52	1276.30
.50	840.86	882.91	927.06	973.42	1022.09	1073.20	1126.87	1183.21	1242.38	1304.50
.75	859.16	902.12	947.23	994.60	1044.34	1096.56	1151.39	1208.96	1269.42	1332.89
10.00	877.58	921.46	967.54	1015.92	1066.72	1120.06	1176.07	1234.88	1296.63	1361.46
.25	896.11	940.92	987.97	1037.37	1089.24	1143.71	1200.90	1260.95	1324.00	1390.21
.50	914.74	960.49	1008.52	1058.95	1111.90	1167.50	1225.88	1287.18	1351.54	1419.12
.75	933.49	980.17	1029.18	1080.64	1134.68	1191.42	1250.99	1313.55	1379.23	1448.20
11.00	952.33	999.95	1049.95	1102.45	1157.58	1215.47	1276.24	1340.06	1407.07	1477.43
.25	971.27	1019.83	1070.83	1124.38	1180.60	1239.64	1301.62	1366.71	1435.05	1506.81
.50	990.30	1039.82	1091.81	1146.41	1203.73	1263.92	1327.13	1393.49	1463.17	1536.33
.75	1009.41	1059.89	1112.89	1168.54	1226.97	1288.32	1352.75	1420.39	1491.41	1565.99
12.00	1028.62	1080.05	1134.06	1190.77	1250.31	1312.83	1378.48	1447.41	1519.78	1595.78
.25	1047.90	1100.30	1155.32	1213.09	1273.75	1337.44	1404.32	1474.54	1548.27	1625.69
.50	1067.26	1120.63	1176.67	1235.51	1297.29	1362.16	1430.27	1501.79	1576.88	1655.73

Entries are per $100,000 of loan. Entry in first year equals standard mortgage payment.

(b) Overall Maturity of GEM

Interest Rate	1	2	3	If Payment Continues at Rate in Column 4	5	6	7	8	9	10
5.50	30Y 0m	26Y11m	24Y 6m	22Y 8m	21Y 2m	20Y 0m	19Y 0m	18Y 2m	17Y 7m	17Y 1m
.75	30Y 0m	26Y 9m	24Y 4m	22Y 5m	20Y11m	19Y 9m	18Y 9m	18Y 0m	17Y 4m	16Y10m
6.00	30Y 0m	26Y 8m	24Y 2m	22Y 3m	20Y 9m	19Y 6m	18Y 7m	17Y10m	17Y 2m	16Y 8m
.25	30Y 0m	26Y 6m	24Y 0m	22Y 0m	20Y 6m	19Y 4m	18Y 4m	17Y 7m	17Y 0m	16Y 6m
.50	30Y 0m	26Y 5m	23Y 9m	21Y10m	20Y 4m	19Y 1m	18Y 2m	17Y 5m	16Y 9m	16Y 4m
.75	30Y 0m	26Y 3m	23Y 7m	21Y 7m	20Y 1m	18Y11m	17Y11m	17Y 2m	16Y 7m	16Y 2m
7.00	30Y 0m	26Y 1m	23Y 5m	21Y 5m	19Y10m	18Y 8m	17Y 9m	17Y 0m	16Y 5m	15Y11m
.25	30Y 0m	25Y11m	23Y 2m	21Y 2m	19Y 8m	18Y 5m	17Y 6m	16Y 9m	16Y 3m	15Y 9m
.50	30Y 0m	25Y10m	23Y 0m	20Y11m	19Y 5m	18Y 3m	17Y 4m	16Y 7m	16Y 0m	15Y 7m
.75	30Y 0m	25Y 8m	22Y 9m	20Y 9m	19Y 2m	18Y 0m	17Y 1m	16Y 5m	15Y10m	15Y 5m
8.00	30Y 0m	25Y 6m	22Y 7m	20Y 6m	19Y 0m	17Y10m	16Y11m	16Y 2m	15Y 8m	15Y 3m
.25	30Y 0m	25Y 4m	22Y 4m	20Y 3m	18Y 9m	17Y 7m	16Y 8m	16Y 0m	15Y 6m	15Y 1m
.50	30Y 0m	25Y 2m	22Y 2m	20Y 1m	18Y 6m	17Y 5m	16Y 6m	15Y10m	15Y 4m	14Y11m
.75	30Y 0m	25Y 0m	21Y11m	19Y10m	18Y 4m	17Y 2m	16Y 4m	15Y 8m	15Y 2m	14Y 9m
9.00	30Y 0m	24Y10m	21Y 8m	19Y 7m	18Y 1m	17Y 0m	16Y 1m	15Y 5m	15Y 0m	14Y 7m
.25	30Y 0m	24Y 7m	21Y 6m	19Y 5m	17Y10m	16Y 9m	15Y11m	15Y 3m	14Y10m	14Y 5m
.50	30Y 0m	24Y 5m	21Y 3m	19Y 2m	17Y 8m	16Y 7m	15Y 9m	15Y 1m	14Y 8m	14Y 3m
.75	30Y 0m	24Y 3m	21Y 0m	18Y11m	17Y 5m	16Y 4m	15Y 6m	14Y11m	14Y 6m	14Y 2m
10.00	30Y 0m	24Y 1m	20Y10m	18Y 9m	17Y 3m	16Y 2m	15Y 4m	14Y 9m	14Y 4m	14Y 0m
.25	30Y 0m	23Y10m	20Y 7m	18Y 6m	17Y 0m	16Y 0m	15Y 2m	14Y 7m	14Y 2m	13Y10m
.50	30Y 0m	23Y 8m	20Y 4m	18Y 3m	16Y10m	15Y 9m	15Y 0m	14Y 5m	14Y 0m	13Y 8m
.75	30Y 0m	23Y 6m	20Y 2m	18Y 1m	16Y 7m	15Y 7m	14Y10m	14Y 3m	13Y10m	13Y 6m
11.00	30Y 0m	23Y 3m	19Y11m	17Y10m	16Y 5m	15Y 5m	14Y 8m	14Y 1m	13Y 8m	13Y 5m
.25	30Y 0m	23Y 1m	19Y 8m	17Y 8m	16Y 3m	15Y 2m	14Y 6m	13Y11m	13Y 6m	13Y 3m
.50	30Y 0m	22Y10m	19Y 6m	17Y 5m	16Y 0m	15Y 0m	14Y 4m	13Y 9m	13Y 5m	13Y 2m
.75	30Y 0m	22Y 8m	19Y 3m	17Y 2m	15Y10m	14Y10m	14Y 2m	13Y 7m	13Y 3m	13Y 0m
12.00	30Y 0m	22Y 5m	19Y 0m	17Y 0m	15Y 8m	14Y 8m	14Y 0m	13Y 6m	13Y 1m	12Y10m
.25	30Y 0m	22Y 2m	18Y10m	16Y10m	15Y 5m	14Y 6m	13Y10m	13Y 4m	13Y 0m	12Y 9m
.50	30Y 0m	22Y 0m	18Y 7m	16Y 7m	15Y 3m	14Y 4m	13Y 8m	13Y 2m	12Y10m	12Y 7m

Growing Equity Mortgage

Payment rises 7.5% per year   (a) Monthly Payments

Interest Rate	1	2	3	4	Payment in Year 5	6	7	8	9	10
5.50	567.79	610.38	656.17	705.39	758.29	815.17	876.31	942.04	1012.70	1088.66
.75	583.58	627.35	674.41	724.99	779.37	837.83	900.67	968.23	1040.85	1118.92
6.00	599.56	644.53	692.87	744.84	800.71	860.77	925.33	994.74	1069.35	1149.55
.25	615.72	661.91	711.55	764.93	822.30	883.98	950.28	1021.56	1098.18	1180.55
.50	632.07	679.48	730.45	785.24	844.14	907.45	975.52	1048.68	1127.34	1211.90
.75	648.60	697.25	749.55	805.77	866.21	931.18	1001.03	1076.11	1156.82	1243.59
7.00	665.31	715.21	768.86	826.53	888.52	955.16	1026.81	1103.82	1186.61	1275.61
.25	682.18	733.35	788.36	847.49	911.05	979.39	1052.85	1131.82	1216.71	1307.97
.50	699.22	751.67	808.05	868.65	933.81	1003.85	1079.14	1160.08	1247.10	1340.63
.75	716.42	770.15	827.92	890.02	956.78	1028.54	1105.68	1188.62	1277.77	1373.60
8.00	733.77	788.81	847.97	911.58	979.95	1053.45	1132.46	1217.40	1308.71	1406.87
.25	751.27	807.62	868.20	933.32	1003.32	1078.58	1159.48	1246.44	1339.93	1440.43
.50	768.92	826.59	888.59	955.24	1026.89	1103.91	1186.71	1275.72	1371.40	1474.26
.75	786.71	845.71	909.15	977.34	1050.64	1129.45	1214.16	1305.23	1403.12	1508.36
9.00	804.63	864.98	929.86	999.60	1074.58	1155.18	1241.82	1334.96	1435.09	1542.72
.25	822.68	884.39	950.72	1022.03	1098.69	1181.09	1269.68	1364.91	1467.29	1577.34
.50	840.86	903.93	971.73	1044.61	1122.96	1207.19	1297.74	1395.07	1499.71	1612.19
.75	859.16	923.60	992.88	1067.35	1147.40	1233.46	1325.98	1425.43	1532.34	1647.28
10.00	877.58	943.40	1014.16	1090.23	1172.00	1259.90	1354.40	1455.99	1565.19	1682.59
.25	896.11	963.32	1035.57	1113.25	1196.74	1286.51	1383.00	1486.73	1598.24	1718.11
.50	914.74	983.36	1057.11	1136.40	1221.64	1313.26	1411.76	1517.65	1631.48	1753.85
.75	933.49	1003.50	1078.77	1159.68	1246.66	1340.17	1440.69	1548.74	1664.91	1789.78
11.00	952.33	1023.76	1100.54	1183.09	1271.83	1367.22	1469.77	1580.00	1698.51	1825.90
.25	971.27	1044.12	1122.43	1206.62	1297.12	1394.41	1498.99	1611.42	1732.28	1862.21
.50	990.30	1064.57	1144.42	1230.26	1322.53	1421.73	1528.36	1642.99	1766.22	1898.70
.75	1009.41	1085.13	1166.52	1254.01	1348.06	1449.17	1557.87	1674.71	1800.32	1935.35
12.00	1028.62	1105.77	1188.71	1277.86	1373.71	1476.74	1587.50	1706.57	1834.57	1972.17
.25	1047.90	1126.50	1210.99	1301.82	1399.46	1504.43	1617.26	1738.56	1868.96	2009.14
.50	1067.26	1147.31	1233.37	1325.87	1425.32	1532.22	1647.15	1770.69	1903.49	2046.26

Entries are per $100,000 of loan. Entry in first year equals standard mortgage payment.

(b) Overall Maturity of GEM

Interest Rate	1	2	3	If Payment Continues at Rate in Column 4	5	6	7	8	9	10
5.50	30Y 0m	25Y 7m	22Y 6m	20Y 3m	18Y 6m	17Y 2m	16Y 1m	15Y 4m	14Y 8m	14Y 3m
.75	30Y 0m	25Y 5m	22Y 4m	20Y 0m	18Y 3m	16Y11m	15Y11m	15Y 1m	14Y 6m	14Y 1m
6.00	30Y 0m	25Y 3m	22Y 1m	19Y 9m	18Y 0m	16Y 8m	15Y 8m	14Y11m	14Y 4m	13Y11m
.25	30Y 0m	25Y 1m	21Y10m	19Y 6m	17Y10m	16Y 6m	15Y 6m	14Y 9m	14Y 2m	13Y 9m
.50	30Y 0m	24Y11m	21Y 8m	19Y 4m	17Y 7m	16Y 3m	15Y 3m	14Y 7m	14Y 0m	13Y 7m
.75	30Y 0m	24Y 9m	21Y 5m	19Y 1m	17Y 4m	16Y 1m	15Y 1m	14Y 4m	13Y10m	13Y 5m
7.00	30Y 0m	24Y 7m	21Y 2m	18Y10m	17Y 2m	15Y10m	14Y11m	14Y 2m	13Y 8m	13Y 3m
.25	30Y 0m	24Y 5m	21Y 0m	18Y 7m	16Y11m	15Y 8m	14Y 8m	14Y 0m	13Y 6m	13Y 2m
.50	30Y 0m	24Y 3m	20Y 9m	18Y 5m	16Y 8m	15Y 5m	14Y 6m	13Y10m	13Y 4m	13Y 0m
.75	30Y 0m	24Y 0m	20Y 6m	18Y 2m	16Y 6m	15Y 3m	14Y 4m	13Y 8m	13Y 2m	12Y10m
8.00	30Y 0m	23Y10m	20Y 3m	17Y11m	16Y 3m	15Y 1m	14Y 2m	13Y 6m	13Y 0m	12Y 8m
.25	30Y 0m	23Y 8m	20Y 1m	17Y 8m	16Y 0m	14Y10m	14Y 0m	13Y 4m	12Y10m	12Y 7m
.50	30Y 0m	23Y 5m	19Y10m	17Y 6m	15Y10m	14Y 8m	13Y10m	13Y 2m	12Y 9m	12Y 5m
.75	30Y 0m	23Y 3m	19Y 7m	17Y 3m	15Y 7m	14Y 6m	13Y 7m	13Y 0m	12Y 7m	12Y 4m
9.00	30Y 0m	23Y 0m	19Y 4m	17Y 0m	15Y 5m	14Y 3m	13Y 5m	12Y10m	12Y 5m	12Y 2m
.25	30Y 0m	22Y10m	19Y 1m	16Y10m	15Y 3m	14Y 1m	13Y 3m	12Y 8m	12Y 4m	12Y 0m
.50	30Y 0m	22Y 7m	18Y11m	16Y 7m	15Y 0m	13Y11m	13Y 1m	12Y 7m	12Y 2m	11Y11m
.75	30Y 0m	22Y 5m	18Y 8m	16Y 4m	14Y10m	13Y 9m	13Y 0m	12Y 5m	12Y 0m	11Y 9m
10.00	30Y 0m	22Y 2m	18Y 5m	16Y 2m	14Y 8m	13Y 7m	12Y10m	12Y 3m	11Y11m	11Y 8m
.25	30Y 0m	21Y11m	18Y 2m	15Y11m	14Y 5m	13Y 5m	12Y 8m	12Y 2m	11Y 9m	11Y 7m
.50	30Y 0m	21Y 9m	18Y 0m	15Y 9m	14Y 3m	13Y 3m	12Y 6m	12Y 0m	11Y 8m	11Y 5m
.75	30Y 0m	21Y 6m	17Y 9m	15Y 6m	14Y 1m	13Y 1m	12Y 4m	11Y10m	11Y 6m	11Y 4m
11.00	30Y 0m	21Y 3m	17Y 6m	15Y 4m	13Y11m	12Y11m	12Y 2m	11Y 9m	11Y 5m	11Y 3m
.25	30Y 0m	21Y 1m	17Y 4m	15Y 2m	13Y 8m	12Y 9m	12Y 1m	11Y 7m	11Y 4m	11Y 1m
.50	30Y 0m	20Y10m	17Y 1m	14Y11m	13Y 6m	12Y 7m	11Y11m	11Y 6m	11Y 2m	11Y 0m
.75	30Y 0m	20Y 7m	16Y11m	14Y 9m	13Y 4m	12Y 5m	11Y 9m	11Y 4m	11Y 1m	10Y11m
12.00	30Y 0m	20Y 4m	16Y 8m	14Y 7m	13Y 2m	12Y 3m	11Y 8m	11Y 3m	10Y11m	10Y10m
.25	30Y 0m	20Y 2m	16Y 6m	14Y 4m	13Y 0m	12Y 2m	11Y 6m	11Y 1m	10Y10m	10Y 8m
.50	30Y 0m	19Y11m	16Y 3m	14Y 2m	12Y10m	12Y 0m	11Y 5m	11Y 0m	10Y 9m	10Y 7m

----

Number of Points to Buy Down a Loan

Market Interest Rate 9.00% Buydown Credit Rate 5.50%							Market Interest Rate 9.25% Buydown Credit Rate 5.50%						

Desired Buydown	____ Years of Buydown ____						Desired Buydown	____ Years of Buydown ____					
	1	2	3	4	5	6	7	1	2	3	4	5	6	7

Desired Buydown	1	2	3	4	5	6	7	Desired Buydown	1	2	3	4	5	6	7
8.50%	0.416	0.810	1.183	1.535	1.869	2.186	2.485	8.75%	0.419	0.816	1.191	1.547	1.883	2.202	2.503
8.25%	0.622	1.210	1.767	2.294	2.793	3.266	3.713	8.50%	0.626	1.219	1.780	2.312	2.815	3.291	3.741
8.00%	0.825	1.607	2.347	3.047	3.710	4.337	4.931	8.25%	0.832	1.619	2.365	3.070	3.738	4.371	4.969
7.75%	1.028	2.000	2.921	3.793	4.618	5.399	6.138	8.00%	1.036	2.016	2.944	3.823	4.655	5.442	6.187
7.50%	1.228	2.390	3.491	4.532	5.518	6.452	7.335	7.75%	1.238	2.410	3.519	4.569	5.563	6.504	7.395
7.25%	1.427	2.777	4.055	5.265	6.410	7.495	8.521	7.50%	1.438	2.800	4.089	5.309	6.464	7.557	8.592
7.00%	1.623	3.159	4.614	5.991	7.294	8.527	9.695	7.25%	1.637	3.186	4.653	6.041	7.356	8.600	9.777
6.75%	1.818	3.538	5.167	6.709	8.168	9.550	10.858	7.00%	1.833	3.569	5.212	6.767	8.239	9.632	10.951
6.50%	2.010	3.913	5.715	7.420	9.034	10.562	12.008	6.75%	2.028	3.948	5.765	7.485	9.113	10.655	12.114
6.25%	2.201	4.284	6.256	8.123	9.890	11.562	13.146	6.50%	2.221	4.323	6.312	8.196	9.979	11.667	13.264
6.00%	2.389	4.651	6.791	8.818	10.736	12.552	14.271	6.25%	2.411	4.693	6.854	8.899	10.835	12.667	14.402
5.75%	2.575	5.013	7.321	9.505	11.573	13.530	15.383	6.00%	2.599	5.060	7.389	9.594	11.681	13.657	15.527
5.50%	2.759	5.371	7.843	10.184	12.399	14.496	16.481	5.75%	2.786	5.422	7.918	10.281	12.518	14.635	16.639
5.25%	2.941	5.724	8.359	10.854	13.215	15.450	17.566	5.50%	2.969	5.780	8.441	10.960	13.344	15.601	17.737
3-2-1	---	---	4.625	---	---	---	---	3-2-1	---	---	4.665	---	---	---	---

Buydown Credit Rate 9.00%								Buydown Credit Rate 9.25%							
8.50%	0.408	0.782	1.123	1.435	1.720	1.981	2.219	8.75%	0.411	0.785	1.127	1.439	1.723	1.982	2.218
8.25%	0.610	1.168	1.678	2.144	2.570	2.960	3.316	8.50%	0.614	1.174	1.684	2.150	2.575	2.962	3.315
8.00%	0.810	1.551	2.228	2.847	3.413	3.931	4.404	8.25%	0.815	1.559	2.237	2.856	3.420	3.934	4.404
7.75%	1.009	1.931	2.774	3.545	4.249	4.894	5.483	8.00%	1.015	1.941	2.786	3.556	4.258	4.899	5.483
7.50%	1.205	2.307	3.315	4.236	5.078	5.848	6.552	7.75%	1.214	2.320	3.329	4.250	5.089	5.855	6.553
7.25%	1.400	2.680	3.851	4.920	5.899	6.793	7.611	7.50%	1.410	2.696	3.868	4.938	5.913	6.802	7.613
7.00%	1.593	3.050	4.381	5.599	6.712	7.729	8.659	7.25%	1.604	3.068	4.402	5.619	6.729	7.741	8.664
6.75%	1.784	3.415	4.906	6.270	7.516	8.656	9.698	7.00%	1.797	3.436	4.931	6.294	7.537	8.671	9.705
6.50%	1.973	3.777	5.426	6.934	8.313	9.573	10.725	6.75%	1.988	3.801	5.454	6.962	8.337	9.591	10.735
6.25%	2.160	4.135	5.940	7.591	9.100	10.480	11.741	6.50%	2.177	4.162	5.972	7.623	9.129	10.502	11.754
6.00%	2.345	4.489	6.449	8.241	9.879	11.377	12.746	6.25%	2.363	4.519	6.484	8.277	9.912	11.403	12.762
5.75%	2.528	4.839	6.951	8.883	10.649	12.263	13.739	6.00%	2.548	4.872	6.991	8.924	10.686	12.293	13.759
5.50%	2.708	5.184	7.448	9.517	11.409	13.139	14.720	5.75%	2.730	5.221	7.492	9.563	11.451	13.174	14.745
5.25%	2.886	5.525	7.938	10.143	12.160	14.003	15.689	5.50%	2.911	5.565	7.986	10.194	12.207	14.043	15.718
3-2-1	---	---	4.417	---	---	---	---	3-2-1	---	---	4.442	---	---	---	---

Buydown Credit Rate 0.00%								Buydown Credit Rate 0.00%							
8.50%	0.429	0.857	1.286	1.714	2.143	2.571	3.000	8.75%	0.432	0.863	1.295	1.727	2.159	2.590	3.022
8.25%	0.640	1.281	1.921	2.561	3.201	3.842	4.482	8.50%	0.645	1.290	1.935	2.581	3.226	3.871	4.516
8.00%	0.850	1.701	2.551	3.401	4.251	5.102	5.952	8.25%	0.857	1.714	2.571	3.428	4.285	5.141	5.998
7.75%	1.059	2.117	3.176	4.234	5.293	6.351	7.410	8.00%	1.067	2.134	3.201	4.268	5.335	6.402	7.469
7.50%	1.265	2.530	3.795	5.060	6.324	7.589	8.854	7.75%	1.275	2.550	3.825	5.101	6.376	7.651	8.926
7.25%	1.469	2.939	4.408	5.877	7.347	8.816	10.285	7.50%	1.482	2.963	4.445	5.926	7.408	8.889	10.371
7.00%	1.672	3.344	5.016	6.687	8.359	10.031	11.703	7.25%	1.686	3.372	5.058	6.744	8.430	10.116	11.802
6.75%	1.872	3.745	5.617	7.489	9.361	11.234	13.106	7.00%	1.888	3.777	5.665	7.554	9.442	11.331	13.219
6.50%	2.071	4.141	6.212	8.283	10.353	12.424	14.495	6.75%	2.089	4.178	6.267	8.356	10.445	12.534	14.622
6.25%	2.267	4.534	6.801	9.067	11.334	13.601	15.868	6.50%	2.287	4.575	6.862	9.149	11.436	13.724	16.011
6.00%	2.461	4.922	7.383	9.843	12.304	14.765	17.226	6.25%	2.483	4.967	7.450	9.934	12.417	14.901	17.384
5.75%	2.653	5.305	7.958	10.610	13.263	15.916	18.568	6.00%	2.677	5.355	8.032	10.710	13.387	16.065	18.742
5.50%	2.842	5.684	8.526	11.368	14.210	17.052	19.894	5.75%	2.869	5.738	8.608	11.477	14.346	17.215	20.085
5.25%	3.029	6.058	9.087	12.116	15.145	18.174	21.203	5.50%	3.059	6.117	9.176	12.235	15.293	18.352	21.410
3-2-1	---	---	4.983	---	---	---	---	3-2-1	---	---	5.026	---	---	---	---

Buydown Credit Rate 8.00%								Buydown Credit Rate 8.25%							
8.50%	0.411	0.790	1.140	1.463	1.761	2.037	2.291	8.75%	0.413	0.793	1.144	1.467	1.764	2.038	2.290
8.25%	0.613	1.180	1.703	2.186	2.631	3.043	3.423	8.50%	0.617	1.186	1.709	2.192	2.636	3.045	3.422
8.00%	0.815	1.567	2.261	2.902	3.495	4.041	4.546	8.25%	0.820	1.575	2.270	2.911	3.501	4.045	4.545
7.75%	1.014	1.950	2.815	3.613	4.350	5.031	5.660	8.00%	1.021	1.961	2.827	3.625	4.359	5.036	5.659
7.50%	1.212	2.331	3.364	4.318	5.199	6.012	6.763	7.75%	1.220	2.344	3.379	4.332	5.210	6.019	6.764
7.25%	1.408	2.707	3.907	5.016	6.039	6.984	7.856	7.50%	1.417	2.723	3.925	5.033	6.053	6.993	7.858
7.00%	1.602	3.080	4.446	5.707	6.871	7.946	8.939	7.25%	1.613	3.099	4.467	5.728	6.888	7.958	8.943
6.75%	1.794	3.450	4.979	6.391	7.695	8.899	10.010	7.00%	1.807	3.471	5.004	6.415	7.716	8.914	10.017
6.50%	1.984	3.815	5.507	7.068	8.510	9.842	11.071	6.75%	1.998	3.839	5.535	7.096	8.535	9.860	11.080
6.25%	2.172	4.177	6.028	7.738	9.317	10.774	12.120	6.50%	2.188	4.204	6.060	7.770	9.345	10.796	12.132
6.00%	2.357	4.534	6.544	8.400	10.114	11.696	13.157	6.25%	2.376	4.564	6.580	8.437	10.147	11.722	13.173
5.75%	2.541	4.888	7.054	9.055	10.902	12.607	14.182	6.00%	2.562	4.921	7.094	9.096	10.940	12.638	14.202
5.50%	2.723	5.237	7.558	9.701	11.680	13.508	15.195	5.75%	2.745	5.273	7.602	9.747	11.723	13.543	15.219
5.25%	2.902	5.581	8.055	10.340	12.449	14.397	16.195	5.50%	2.926	5.621	8.104	10.391	12.497	14.437	16.223
3-2-1	---	---	4.475	---	---	---	---	3-2-1	---	---	4.500	---	---	---	---

Entry is number of points paid at closing; 3-2-1 is a 3-year buydown of 3% 1st year, 2% 2nd year and 1% 3rd year.

Number of Points to Buy Down a Loan

```
Market Interest Rate  9.50%                          Market Interest Rate  9.75%
Buydown Credit Rate   5.50%                          Buydown Credit Rate   5.50%
------------------------------------------------     ------------------------------------------------
Desired            Years of Buydown                  Desired            Years of Buydown
Buydown   1      2      3      4      5      6      7 Buydown   1      2      3      4      5      6      7
------------------------------------------------     ------------------------------------------------
 9.00%  0.422  0.822  1.200  1.558  1.897  2.218  2.521  9.25%  0.425  0.827  1.208  1.569  1.910  2.233  2.539
 8.75%  0.631  1.228  1.793  2.329  2.835  3.315  3.769  9.00%  0.635  1.237  1.806  2.345  2.855  3.338  3.795
 8.50%  0.838  1.631  2.382  3.093  3.766  4.403  5.006  8.75%  0.844  1.643  2.399  3.115  3.793  4.435  5.042
 8.25%  1.044  2.032  2.967  3.852  4.690  5.483  6.234  8.50%  1.051  2.046  2.989  3.880  4.724  5.523  6.280

 8.00%  1.248  2.429  3.546  4.605  5.606  6.555  7.452  8.25%  1.257  2.447  3.573  4.639  5.648  6.604  7.508
 7.75%  1.450  2.822  4.121  5.351  6.515  7.617  8.660  8.00%  1.461  2.844  4.153  5.392  6.565  7.675  8.726
 7.50%  1.650  3.212  4.691  6.090  7.415  8.669  9.857  7.75%  1.663  3.237  4.727  6.138  7.473  8.737  9.933
 7.25%  1.849  3.598  5.255  6.823  8.307  9.712 11.042  7.50%  1.863  3.627  5.297  6.877  8.373  9.790 11.130

 7.00%  2.045  3.981  5.814  7.549  9.191 10.745 12.217  7.25%  2.062  4.014  5.861  7.610  9.265 10.832 12.316
 6.75%  2.240  4.360  6.367  8.267 10.065 11.768 13.379  7.00%  2.258  4.396  6.420  8.335 10.149 11.865 13.490
 6.50%  2.432  4.735  6.914  8.978 10.931 12.779 14.529  6.75%  2.453  4.775  6.973  9.054 11.023 12.888 14.652
 6.25%  2.623  5.106  7.456  9.681 11.787 13.780 15.667  6.50%  2.646  5.150  7.520  9.764 11.889 13.899 15.803

 6.00%  2.811  5.472  7.991 10.376 12.633 14.770 16.792  6.25%  2.836  5.521  8.062 10.468 12.745 14.900 16.941
 5.75%  2.997  5.835  8.520 11.063 13.469 15.748 17.904  6.00%  3.024  5.887  8.597 11.163 13.591 15.890 18.066
 3-2-1   ---    ---   4.704   ---    ---    ---    ---   3-2-1   ---    ---   4.742   ---    ---    ---    ---
------------------------------------------------     ------------------------------------------------
Buydown Credit Rate  9.50%                           Buydown Credit Rate  9.75%
------------------------------------------------     ------------------------------------------------
 9.00%  0.413  0.789  1.131  1.442  1.725  1.983  2.217  9.25%  0.415  0.793  1.135  1.445  1.727  1.983  2.215
 8.75%  0.618  1.179  1.691  2.156  2.579  2.963  3.313  9.00%  0.621  1.185  1.696  2.160  2.581  2.964  3.311
 8.50%  0.820  1.567  2.246  2.864  3.425  3.937  4.402  8.75%  0.825  1.574  2.254  2.870  3.430  3.938  4.399
 8.25%  1.022  1.951  2.797  3.566  4.266  4.902  5.481  8.50%  1.028  1.960  2.807  3.575  4.272  4.904  5.478

 8.00%  1.221  2.332  3.343  4.263  5.099  5.860  6.552  8.25%  1.229  2.344  3.356  4.274  5.107  5.863  6.550
 7.75%  1.419  2.710  3.885  4.953  5.925  6.810  7.614  8.00%  1.428  2.724  3.900  4.967  5.936  6.815  7.612
 7.50%  1.615  3.085  4.422  5.638  6.744  7.751  8.666  7.75%  1.626  3.101  4.440  5.655  6.757  7.758  8.666
 7.25%  1.810  3.456  4.954  6.316  7.555  8.683  9.709  7.50%  1.822  3.475  4.975  6.336  7.571  8.692  9.710

 7.00%  2.002  3.823  5.480  6.988  8.359  9.606 10.741  7.25%  2.016  3.845  5.505  7.011  8.378  9.618 10.744
 6.75%  2.193  4.187  6.002  7.653  9.154 10.520 11.763  7.00%  2.208  4.211  6.030  7.680  9.177 10.535 11.768
 6.50%  2.381  4.547  6.518  8.311  9.941 11.425 12.774  6.75%  2.398  4.574  6.549  8.341  9.968 11.443 12.782
 6.25%  2.568  4.903  7.028  8.961 10.720 12.320 13.775  6.50%  2.586  4.933  7.063  8.996 10.750 12.342 13.786

 6.00%  2.752  5.256  7.533  9.605 11.490 13.204 14.764  6.25%  2.773  5.289  7.572  9.644 11.524 13.230 14.779
 5.75%  2.934  5.603  8.032 10.241 12.250 14.079 15.742  6.00%  2.957  5.640  8.075 10.284 12.289 14.109 15.760
 3-2-1   ---    ---   4.464   ---    ---    ---    ---   3-2-1   ---    ---   4.486   ---    ---    ---    ---
------------------------------------------------     ------------------------------------------------
Buydown Credit Rate  0.00%                           Buydown Credit Rate  0.00%
------------------------------------------------     ------------------------------------------------
 9.00%  0.435  0.870  1.304  1.739  2.174  2.609  3.043  9.25%  0.438  0.875  1.313  1.751  2.189  2.626  3.064
 8.75%  0.650  1.300  1.950  2.599  3.249  3.899  4.549  9.00%  0.654  1.309  1.963  2.618  3.272  3.926  4.581
 8.50%  0.863  1.727  2.590  3.453  4.316  5.180  6.043  8.75%  0.869  1.739  2.608  3.478  4.347  5.217  6.086
 8.25%  1.075  2.150  3.225  4.300  5.375  6.450  7.525  8.50%  1.083  2.166  3.249  4.332  5.414  6.497  7.580

 8.00%  1.285  2.570  3.855  5.140  6.425  7.710  8.996  8.25%  1.295  2.589  3.884  5.179  6.473  7.768  9.063
 7.75%  1.493  2.987  4.480  5.973  7.467  8.960 10.453  8.00%  1.505  3.009  4.514  6.019  7.523  9.028 10.533
 7.50%  1.700  3.399  5.099  6.799  8.498 10.198 11.898  7.75%  1.713  3.426  5.139  6.852  8.565 10.277 11.990
 7.25%  1.904  3.808  5.712  7.617  9.521 11.425 13.329  7.50%  1.919  3.839  5.758  7.677  9.596 11.516 13.435

 7.00%  2.107  4.213  6.320  8.426 10.533 12.640 14.746  7.25%  2.124  4.247  6.371  8.495 10.619 12.742 14.866
 6.75%  2.307  4.614  6.921  9.228 11.535 13.842 16.150  7.00%  2.326  4.652  6.979  9.305 11.631 13.957 16.284
 6.50%  2.505  5.011  7.516 10.022 12.527 15.033 17.538  6.75%  2.527  5.053  7.580 10.107 12.633 15.160 17.687
 6.25%  2.702  5.403  8.105 10.807 13.508 16.210 18.912  6.50%  2.725  5.450  8.175 10.900 13.625 16.350 19.075

 6.00%  2.896  5.791  8.687 11.583 14.478 17.374 20.270  6.25%  2.921  5.842  8.764 11.685 14.606 17.527 20.449
 5.75%  3.087  6.175  9.262 12.350 15.437 18.524 21.612  6.00%  3.115  6.230  9.346 12.461 15.576 18.691 21.807
 3-2-1   ---    ---   5.068   ---    ---    ---    ---   3-2-1   ---    ---   5.109   ---    ---    ---    ---
------------------------------------------------     ------------------------------------------------
Buydown Credit Rate  8.50%                           Buydown Credit Rate  8.75%
------------------------------------------------     ------------------------------------------------
 9.00%  0.415  0.797  1.148  1.470  1.766  2.038  2.288  9.25%  0.418  0.801  1.151  1.473  1.768  2.038  2.285
 8.75%  0.621  1.191  1.715  2.197  2.640  3.046  3.420  9.00%  0.624  1.197  1.721  2.202  2.642  3.046  3.416
 8.50%  0.825  1.583  2.279  2.919  3.506  4.047  4.543  8.75%  0.830  1.590  2.287  2.925  3.511  4.047  4.539
 8.25%  1.027  1.971  2.838  3.635  4.367  5.039  5.657  8.50%  1.033  1.980  2.848  3.644  4.373  5.041  5.653

 8.00%  1.228  2.356  3.392  4.345  5.220  6.024  6.762  8.25%  1.235  2.368  3.405  4.356  5.228  6.027  6.759
 7.75%  1.427  2.738  3.942  5.049  6.065  7.000  7.858  8.00%  1.436  2.752  3.958  5.063  6.076  7.004  7.855
 7.50%  1.624  3.116  4.487  5.746  6.904  7.967  8.944  7.75%  1.634  3.132  4.505  5.764  6.917  7.974  8.942
 7.25%  1.819  3.491  5.027  6.438  7.734  8.925 10.020  7.50%  1.831  3.510  5.048  6.458  7.750  8.934 10.020

 7.00%  2.013  3.862  5.561  7.122  8.557  9.874 11.085  7.25%  2.026  3.884  5.586  7.146  8.576  9.886 11.087
 6.75%  2.204  4.230  6.090  7.800  9.371 10.814 12.140  7.00%  2.220  4.254  6.118  7.827  9.393 10.829 12.144
 6.50%  2.394  4.593  6.614  8.471 10.176 11.744 13.184  6.75%  2.411  4.620  6.646  8.502 10.203 11.762 13.191
 6.25%  2.581  4.953  7.132  9.134 10.973 12.664 14.216  6.50%  2.600  4.983  7.167  9.169 11.004 12.685 14.226

 6.00%  2.767  5.309  7.644  9.790 11.761 13.573 15.237  6.25%  2.787  5.342  7.683  9.829 11.796 13.599 15.251
 5.75%  2.950  5.660  8.150 10.438 12.540 14.472 16.246  6.00%  2.972  5.697  8.194 10.482 12.579 14.502 16.263
 3-2-1   ---    ---   4.523   ---    ---    ---    ---   3-2-1   ---    ---   4.544   ---    ---    ---    ---
------------------------------------------------     ------------------------------------------------
```

Entry is number of points paid at closing; 3-2-1 is a 3-year buydown of 3% 1st year, 2% 2nd year and 1% 3rd year.

Number of Points to Buy Down a Loan

Market Interest Rate 10.00%
Buydown Credit Rate 5.50%

Desired Buydown	1	2	3	4	5	6	7
9.50%	0.428	0.833	1.216	1.579	1.922	2.247	2.555
9.25%	0.640	1.245	1.818	2.360	2.874	3.360	3.820
9.00%	0.850	1.654	2.416	3.137	3.819	4.465	5.076
8.75%	1.059	2.061	3.009	3.907	4.757	5.562	6.324
8.50%	1.266	2.464	3.598	4.672	5.689	6.651	7.561
8.25%	1.471	2.864	4.183	5.431	6.612	7.731	8.789
8.00%	1.675	3.261	4.762	6.184	7.529	8.802	10.007
7.75%	1.878	3.655	5.337	6.930	8.437	9.864	11.215
7.50%	2.078	4.045	5.907	7.669	9.337	10.917	12.412
7.25%	2.276	4.431	6.471	8.402	10.229	11.960	13.597
7.00%	2.473	4.814	7.030	9.127	11.113	12.992	14.772
6.75%	2.668	5.193	7.583	9.846	11.987	14.015	15.934
6.50%	2.860	5.568	8.130	10.556	12.853	15.027	17.084
6.25%	3.051	5.938	8.672	11.259	13.709	16.027	18.222
3-2-1	---	---	4.779	---	---	---	---

Market Interest Rate 10.25%
Buydown Credit Rate 5.50%

Desired Buydown	1	2	3	4	5	6	7
9.75%	0.430	0.838	1.224	1.589	1.934	2.261	2.571
9.50%	0.644	1.253	1.830	2.376	2.892	3.382	3.845
9.25%	0.855	1.665	2.432	3.157	3.844	4.494	5.110
9.00%	1.066	2.075	3.030	3.933	4.789	5.599	6.366
8.75%	1.275	2.481	3.623	4.704	5.727	6.696	7.613
8.50%	1.482	2.884	4.212	5.469	6.659	7.785	8.851
8.25%	1.687	3.285	4.797	6.228	7.583	8.865	10.079
8.00%	1.891	3.681	5.376	6.980	8.499	9.936	11.297
7.75%	2.093	4.075	5.951	7.726	9.407	10.998	12.504
7.50%	2.294	4.465	6.520	8.466	10.308	12.051	13.701
7.25%	2.492	4.851	7.085	9.199	11.200	13.094	14.887
7.00%	2.689	5.234	7.643	9.924	12.083	14.127	16.061
6.75%	2.883	5.613	8.197	10.642	12.957	15.149	17.224
6.50%	3.076	5.988	8.744	11.353	13.823	16.161	18.374
3-2-1	---	---	4.814	---	---	---	---

Buydown Credit Rate 10.00%

Desired Buydown	1	2	3	4	5	6	7
9.50%	0.418	0.796	1.138	1.448	1.728	1.982	2.212
9.25%	0.624	1.190	1.701	2.164	2.584	2.963	3.307
9.00%	0.830	1.581	2.261	2.876	3.433	3.938	4.394
8.75%	1.034	1.969	2.816	3.583	4.277	4.905	5.474
8.50%	1.236	2.355	3.367	4.284	5.114	5.865	6.545
8.25%	1.437	2.737	3.914	4.980	5.945	6.818	7.608
8.00%	1.636	3.116	4.457	5.670	6.768	7.763	8.662
7.75%	1.833	3.492	4.995	6.354	7.585	8.699	9.708
7.50%	2.029	3.865	5.528	7.032	8.394	9.627	10.744
7.25%	2.223	4.234	6.056	7.704	9.196	10.547	11.770
7.00%	2.414	4.600	6.578	8.369	9.991	11.458	12.786
6.75%	2.604	4.962	7.096	9.028	10.777	12.360	13.793
6.50%	2.792	5.320	7.608	9.680	11.555	13.252	14.788
6.25%	2.978	5.675	8.115	10.324	12.324	14.135	15.773
3-2-1	---	---	4.506	---	---	---	---

Buydown Credit Rate 10.25%

Desired Buydown	1	2	3	4	5	6	7
9.75%	0.420	0.799	1.141	1.450	1.729	1.981	2.208
9.50%	0.628	1.194	1.706	2.168	2.585	2.962	3.302
9.25%	0.834	1.587	2.267	2.881	3.436	3.937	4.389
9.00%	1.039	1.977	2.825	3.590	4.281	4.904	5.468
8.75%	1.243	2.365	3.378	4.293	5.119	5.865	6.539
8.50%	1.445	2.749	3.927	4.991	5.952	6.819	7.602
8.25%	1.645	3.131	4.472	5.684	6.777	7.765	8.657
8.00%	1.844	3.509	5.013	6.370	7.596	8.703	9.703
7.75%	2.041	3.884	5.549	7.051	8.408	9.634	10.740
7.50%	2.237	4.256	6.080	7.726	9.213	10.556	11.768
7.25%	2.430	4.624	6.606	8.395	10.010	11.469	12.786
7.00%	2.622	4.989	7.127	9.057	10.800	12.374	13.795
6.75%	2.812	5.350	7.643	9.713	11.582	13.269	14.793
6.50%	2.999	5.708	8.153	10.361	12.355	14.156	15.781
3-2-1	---	---	4.525	---	---	---	---

Buydown Credit Rate 0.00%

Desired Buydown	1	2	3	4	5	6	7
9.50%	0.441	0.881	1.322	1.762	2.203	2.644	3.084
9.25%	0.659	1.318	1.976	2.635	3.294	3.953	4.611
9.00%	0.875	1.751	2.626	3.502	4.377	5.252	6.128
8.75%	1.090	2.181	3.271	4.362	5.452	6.543	7.633
8.50%	1.304	2.608	3.912	5.216	6.519	7.823	9.127
8.25%	1.516	3.031	4.547	6.063	7.578	9.094	10.610
8.00%	1.726	3.451	5.177	6.903	8.628	10.354	12.080
7.75%	1.934	3.868	5.802	7.736	9.670	11.603	13.537
7.50%	2.140	4.281	6.421	8.561	10.701	12.842	14.982
7.25%	2.345	4.689	7.034	9.379	11.724	14.068	16.413
7.00%	2.547	5.094	7.642	10.189	12.736	15.283	17.831
6.75%	2.748	5.495	8.243	10.991	13.738	16.486	19.234
6.50%	2.946	5.892	8.838	11.784	14.730	17.676	20.622
6.25%	3.142	6.285	9.427	12.569	15.711	18.854	21.996
3-2-1	---	---	5.148	---	---	---	---

Buydown Credit Rate 0.00%

Desired Buydown	1	2	3	4	5	6	7
9.75%	0.443	0.887	1.330	1.773	2.217	2.660	3.104
9.50%	0.663	1.326	1.989	2.652	3.315	3.978	4.641
9.25%	0.881	1.762	2.643	3.524	4.406	5.287	6.168
9.00%	1.098	2.195	3.293	4.391	5.489	6.586	7.684
8.75%	1.313	2.626	3.938	5.251	6.564	7.877	9.190
8.50%	1.526	3.053	4.579	6.105	7.631	9.158	10.684
8.25%	1.738	3.476	5.214	6.952	8.690	10.428	12.166
8.00%	1.948	3.896	5.844	7.792	9.740	11.688	13.636
7.75%	2.156	4.313	6.469	8.625	10.781	12.938	15.094
7.50%	2.363	4.725	7.088	9.451	11.813	14.176	16.538
7.25%	2.567	5.134	7.701	10.268	12.836	15.403	17.970
7.00%	2.770	5.539	8.309	11.078	13.848	16.618	19.387
6.75%	2.970	5.940	8.910	11.880	14.850	17.820	20.790
6.50%	3.168	6.337	9.505	12.674	15.842	19.010	22.179
3-2-1	---	---	5.186	---	---	---	---

Buydown Credit Rate 9.00%

Desired Buydown	1	2	3	4	5	6	7
9.50%	0.420	0.804	1.155	1.475	1.769	2.037	2.282
9.25%	0.628	1.202	1.726	2.206	2.645	3.045	3.412
9.00%	0.834	1.597	2.294	2.931	3.514	4.047	4.534
8.75%	1.039	1.989	2.858	3.652	4.378	5.041	5.648
8.50%	1.242	2.378	3.417	4.366	5.234	6.028	6.754
8.25%	1.444	2.765	3.972	5.076	6.085	7.007	7.850
8.00%	1.644	3.148	4.522	5.779	6.928	7.978	8.938
7.75%	1.843	3.528	5.068	6.476	7.764	8.941	10.017
7.50%	2.039	3.904	5.609	7.167	8.592	9.895	11.086
7.25%	2.234	4.277	6.145	7.852	9.413	10.840	12.145
7.00%	2.427	4.646	6.675	8.530	10.226	11.776	13.193
6.75%	2.618	5.012	7.200	9.201	11.030	12.703	14.232
6.50%	2.807	5.374	7.720	9.866	11.827	13.620	15.259
6.25%	2.994	5.732	8.234	10.523	12.614	14.527	16.275
3-2-1	---	---	4.564	---	---	---	---

Buydown Credit Rate 9.25%

Desired Buydown	1	2	3	4	5	6	7
9.75%	0.422	0.807	1.158	1.478	1.769	2.036	2.278
9.50%	0.631	1.206	1.731	2.210	2.646	3.044	3.407
9.25%	0.839	1.603	2.301	2.937	3.517	4.046	4.528
9.00%	1.045	1.997	2.866	3.659	4.381	5.040	5.641
8.75%	1.249	2.389	3.428	4.375	5.240	6.028	6.746
8.50%	1.452	2.777	3.985	5.087	6.091	7.008	7.843
8.25%	1.654	3.162	4.538	5.792	6.937	7.980	8.931
8.00%	1.854	3.545	5.086	6.492	7.775	8.944	10.011
7.75%	2.052	3.923	5.630	7.186	8.606	9.900	11.081
7.50%	2.248	4.299	6.169	7.874	9.429	10.848	12.141
7.25%	2.443	4.671	6.703	8.556	10.246	11.787	13.192
7.00%	2.636	5.039	7.231	9.231	11.054	12.716	14.233
6.75%	2.826	5.404	7.755	9.899	11.854	13.637	15.263
6.50%	3.015	5.765	8.273	10.560	12.645	14.547	16.282
3-2-1	---	---	4.583	---	---	---	---

Entry is number of points paid at closing; 3-2-1 is a 3-year buydown of 3% 1st year, 2% 2nd year and 1% 3rd year.

Number of Points to Buy Down a Loan

| Market Interest Rate 10.50% | | | | | | | | Market Interest Rate 10.75% | | | | | | |
| Buydown Credit Rate 5.50% | | | | | | | | Buydown Credit Rate 5.50% | | | | | | |

Desired Buydown	1	2	Years of Buydown 3	4	5	6	7	Desired Buydown	1	2	Years of Buydown 3	4	5	6	7
10.00%	0.433	0.843	1.231	1.598	1.946	2.275	2.586	10.25%	0.435	0.848	1.238	1.607	1.957	2.288	2.601
9.75%	0.648	1.261	1.841	2.390	2.910	3.402	3.868	10.00%	0.651	1.268	1.852	2.404	2.927	3.422	3.891
9.50%	0.861	1.676	2.447	3.177	3.868	4.522	5.142	9.75%	0.866	1.686	2.461	3.196	3.891	4.549	5.172
9.25%	1.073	2.088	3.049	3.959	4.820	5.635	6.407	9.50%	1.079	2.101	3.068	3.983	4.849	5.669	6.446
9.00%	1.283	2.497	3.647	4.735	5.765	6.740	7.663	9.25%	1.291	2.513	3.670	4.765	5.801	6.782	7.711
8.75%	1.492	2.904	4.240	5.506	6.703	7.837	8.910	9.00%	1.501	2.922	4.267	5.541	6.746	7.887	8.967
8.50%	1.699	3.307	4.829	6.270	7.634	8.926	10.148	8.75%	1.710	3.329	4.861	6.311	7.684	8.984	10.214
8.25%	1.904	3.707	5.414	7.029	8.558	10.006	11.376	8.50%	1.917	3.732	5.450	7.076	8.616	10.073	11.452
8.00%	2.108	4.104	5.993	7.782	9.475	11.077	12.594	8.25%	2.123	4.132	6.034	7.835	9.539	11.153	12.680
7.75%	2.311	4.498	6.568	8.528	10.383	12.139	13.801	8.00%	2.327	4.529	6.614	8.588	10.456	12.224	13.898
7.50%	2.511	4.888	7.138	9.267	11.283	13.192	14.998	7.75%	2.529	4.923	7.189	9.334	11.364	13.286	15.106
7.25%	2.709	5.274	7.702	10.000	12.175	14.235	16.184	7.50%	2.729	5.313	7.758	10.073	12.265	14.339	16.302
7.00%	2.906	5.657	8.261	10.725	13.059	15.267	17.358	7.25%	2.928	5.699	8.322	10.806	13.157	15.382	17.488
6.75%	3.101	6.036	8.814	11.444	13.933	16.290	18.521	7.00%	3.124	6.082	8.881	11.531	14.040	16.415	18.662
3-2-1	---	---	4.848	---	---	---	---	3-2-1	---	---	4.881	---	---	---	---

Buydown Credit Rate 10.50%								Buydown Credit Rate 10.75%						
10.00%	0.422	0.801	1.144	1.452	1.729	1.979	2.204	10.25%	0.423	0.804	1.146	1.453	1.729	1.977	2.200
9.75%	0.631	1.199	1.710	2.171	2.586	2.960	3.297	10.00%	0.633	1.203	1.714	2.173	2.586	2.957	3.291
9.50%	0.838	1.593	2.273	2.886	3.437	3.934	4.382	9.75%	0.842	1.599	2.279	2.889	3.438	3.931	4.374
9.25%	1.044	1.985	2.833	3.596	4.283	4.902	5.460	9.50%	1.049	1.992	2.840	3.601	4.285	4.899	5.451
9.00%	1.249	2.374	3.388	4.301	5.123	5.864	6.531	9.25%	1.255	2.383	3.397	4.307	5.126	5.861	6.521
8.75%	1.453	2.761	3.939	5.001	5.957	6.818	7.594	9.00%	1.460	2.772	3.950	5.009	5.961	6.816	7.584
8.50%	1.654	3.144	4.487	5.696	6.785	7.765	8.649	8.75%	1.663	3.157	4.500	5.706	6.790	7.764	8.639
8.25%	1.855	3.525	5.030	6.385	7.606	8.705	9.696	8.50%	1.864	3.540	5.045	6.397	7.613	8.704	9.685
8.00%	2.053	3.902	5.568	7.068	8.420	9.637	10.734	8.25%	2.064	3.919	5.586	7.083	8.429	9.638	10.724
7.75%	2.250	4.276	6.102	7.746	9.227	10.561	11.763	8.00%	2.263	4.296	6.122	7.764	9.238	10.564	11.754
7.50%	2.445	4.647	6.631	8.418	10.027	11.477	12.783	7.75%	2.459	4.669	6.654	8.438	10.041	11.481	12.775
7.25%	2.638	5.015	7.155	9.083	10.820	12.384	13.793	7.50%	2.654	5.039	7.182	9.107	10.837	12.391	13.787
7.00%	2.830	5.379	7.674	9.742	11.605	13.283	14.794	7.25%	2.847	5.405	7.704	9.769	11.625	13.292	14.790
6.75%	3.019	5.739	8.188	10.395	12.382	14.172	15.785	7.00%	3.038	5.768	8.221	10.425	12.405	14.185	15.783
3-2-1	---	---	4.542	---	---	---	---	3-2-1	---	---	4.558	---	---	---	---

Buydown Credit Rate 0.00%								Buydown Credit Rate 0.00%						
10.00%	0.446	0.892	1.338	1.784	2.230	2.676	3.122	10.25%	0.449	0.897	1.346	1.794	2.243	2.691	3.140
9.75%	0.667	1.334	2.001	2.668	3.335	4.002	4.669	10.00%	0.671	1.342	2.013	2.684	3.355	4.026	4.696
9.50%	0.887	1.773	2.660	3.546	4.433	5.320	6.206	9.75%	0.892	1.784	2.676	3.568	4.460	5.352	6.243
9.25%	1.105	2.210	3.314	4.419	5.524	6.629	7.733	9.50%	1.112	2.223	3.335	4.446	5.558	6.669	7.781
9.00%	1.321	2.643	3.964	5.286	6.607	7.928	9.250	9.25%	1.330	2.659	3.989	5.319	6.648	7.978	9.308
8.75%	1.536	3.073	4.609	6.146	7.682	9.219	10.755	9.00%	1.546	3.093	4.639	6.185	7.732	9.278	10.824
8.50%	1.750	3.500	5.250	7.000	8.750	10.499	12.249	8.75%	1.761	3.523	5.284	7.045	8.807	10.568	12.330
8.25%	1.962	3.923	5.885	7.847	9.808	11.770	13.732	8.50%	1.975	3.950	5.924	7.899	9.874	11.849	13.824
8.00%	2.172	4.343	6.515	8.687	10.858	13.030	15.202	8.25%	2.187	4.373	6.560	8.746	10.933	13.119	15.306
7.75%	2.380	4.760	7.140	9.520	11.900	14.280	16.659	8.00%	2.397	4.793	7.190	9.586	11.983	14.380	16.776
7.50%	2.586	5.173	7.759	10.345	12.931	15.518	18.104	7.75%	2.605	5.210	7.814	10.419	13.024	15.629	18.234
7.25%	2.791	5.582	8.372	11.163	13.954	16.745	19.535	7.50%	2.811	5.622	8.434	11.245	14.056	16.867	19.678
7.00%	2.993	5.986	8.980	11.973	14.966	17.959	20.953	7.25%	3.016	6.031	9.047	12.063	15.078	18.094	21.110
6.75%	3.194	6.387	9.581	12.775	15.968	19.162	22.356	7.00%	3.218	6.436	9.654	12.873	16.091	19.309	22.527
3-2-1	---	---	5.223	---	---	---	---	3-2-1	---	---	5.258	---	---	---	---

Buydown Credit Rate 9.50%								Buydown Credit Rate 9.75%						
10.00%	0.424	0.809	1.160	1.479	1.770	2.034	2.274	10.25%	0.426	0.812	1.163	1.481	1.770	2.032	2.269
9.75%	0.634	1.211	1.735	2.212	2.647	3.042	3.401	10.00%	0.637	1.215	1.739	2.215	2.647	3.039	3.394
9.50%	0.843	1.609	2.307	2.941	3.518	4.043	4.521	9.75%	0.847	1.615	2.312	2.944	3.519	4.040	4.512
9.25%	1.050	2.005	2.874	3.665	4.384	5.038	5.633	9.50%	1.055	2.012	2.881	3.669	4.385	5.034	5.623
9.00%	1.256	2.398	3.438	4.383	5.243	6.026	6.737	9.25%	1.262	2.407	3.447	4.390	5.245	6.022	6.727
8.75%	1.460	2.789	3.997	5.096	6.097	7.006	7.834	9.00%	1.468	2.799	4.008	5.105	6.100	7.003	7.823
8.50%	1.663	3.176	4.552	5.804	6.943	7.980	8.922	8.75%	1.672	3.189	4.566	5.815	6.948	7.977	8.911
8.25%	1.864	3.560	5.103	6.507	7.784	8.945	10.002	8.50%	1.874	3.575	5.119	6.519	7.790	8.944	9.991
8.00%	2.064	3.942	5.650	7.204	8.617	9.903	11.073	8.25%	2.075	3.959	5.668	7.219	8.626	9.903	11.062
7.75%	2.262	4.319	6.191	7.894	9.443	10.853	12.135	8.00%	2.275	4.339	6.212	7.912	9.454	10.854	12.124
7.50%	2.458	4.694	6.728	8.579	10.262	11.794	13.187	7.75%	2.472	4.716	6.752	8.599	10.276	11.797	13.178
7.25%	2.652	5.065	7.260	9.257	11.073	12.726	14.229	7.50%	2.668	5.089	7.287	9.281	11.090	12.732	14.222
7.00%	2.845	5.433	7.787	9.929	11.877	13.649	15.262	7.25%	2.862	5.460	7.817	9.956	11.897	13.658	15.256
6.75%	3.035	5.796	8.308	10.593	12.672	14.563	16.284	7.00%	3.054	5.826	8.342	10.624	12.695	14.575	16.281
3-2-1	---	---	4.601	---	---	---	---	3-2-1	---	---	4.617	---	---	---	---

Entry is number of points paid at closing; 3-2-1 is a 3-year buydown of 3% 1st year, 2% 2nd year and 1% 3rd year.

Number of Points to Buy Down a Loan

Market Interest Rate 11.00% — Buydown Credit Rate 5.50%

Desired Buydown	1	2	3	4	5	6	7
10.50%	0.438	0.852	1.245	1.616	1.968	2.300	2.615
10.25%	0.655	1.275	1.862	2.417	2.943	3.441	3.912
10.00%	0.871	1.695	2.476	3.214	3.913	4.575	5.202
9.75%	1.085	2.113	3.085	4.006	4.878	5.703	6.484
9.50%	1.299	2.528	3.692	4.793	5.836	6.823	7.757
9.25%	1.510	2.940	4.294	5.575	6.787	7.935	9.022
9.00%	1.721	3.350	4.891	6.351	7.733	9.040	10.278
8.75%	1.930	3.756	5.485	7.122	8.671	10.137	11.526
8.50%	2.137	4.159	6.074	7.886	9.602	11.226	12.763
8.25%	2.342	4.560	6.658	8.645	10.526	12.306	13.991
8.00%	2.546	4.956	7.238	9.398	11.442	13.377	15.209
7.75%	2.748	5.350	7.813	10.144	12.351	14.440	16.417
7.50%	2.949	5.740	8.382	10.883	13.251	15.492	17.614
7.25%	3.147	6.126	8.946	11.616	14.143	16.535	18.799
3-2-1	---	---	4.912	---	---	---	---

Market Interest Rate 11.25% — Buydown Credit Rate 5.50%

Desired Buydown	1	2	3	4	5	6	7
10.75%	0.440	0.857	1.251	1.624	1.978	2.312	2.629
10.50%	0.658	1.282	1.872	2.430	2.959	3.460	3.933
10.25%	0.876	1.704	2.489	3.232	3.935	4.600	5.230
10.00%	1.091	2.125	3.103	4.029	4.905	5.735	6.520
9.75%	1.306	2.542	3.713	4.820	5.869	6.862	7.801
9.50%	1.519	2.957	4.319	5.607	6.827	7.982	9.075
9.25%	1.731	3.370	4.921	6.389	7.779	9.095	10.340
9.00%	1.941	3.779	5.519	7.165	8.724	10.200	11.596
8.75%	2.150	4.185	6.112	7.936	9.662	11.297	12.843
8.50%	2.357	4.589	6.701	8.701	10.593	12.385	14.081
8.25%	2.563	4.989	7.286	9.460	11.517	13.465	15.309
8.00%	2.767	5.386	7.865	10.212	12.434	14.537	16.527
7.75%	2.969	5.779	8.440	10.958	13.342	15.599	17.735
7.50%	3.169	6.169	9.009	11.698	14.242	16.651	18.932
3-2-1	---	---	4.943	---	---	---	---

Buydown Credit Rate 11.00%

Desired Buydown	1	2	3	4	5	6	7
10.50%	0.425	0.806	1.148	1.454	1.729	1.975	2.195
10.25%	0.636	1.206	1.717	2.175	2.586	2.954	3.284
10.00%	0.846	1.604	2.283	2.892	3.438	3.927	4.366
9.75%	1.054	1.999	2.846	3.605	4.285	4.895	5.441
9.50%	1.261	2.392	3.405	4.313	5.127	5.856	6.510
9.25%	1.467	2.782	3.960	5.016	5.963	6.811	7.572
9.00%	1.671	3.169	4.512	5.715	6.793	7.760	8.626
8.75%	1.874	3.554	5.059	6.408	7.618	8.701	9.673
8.50%	2.075	3.935	5.602	7.096	8.436	9.636	10.712
8.25%	2.275	4.314	6.141	7.779	9.247	10.563	11.742
8.00%	2.473	4.689	6.676	8.456	10.052	11.483	12.764
7.75%	2.669	5.062	7.206	9.128	10.850	12.394	13.778
7.50%	2.864	5.431	7.731	9.793	11.641	13.298	14.782
7.25%	3.057	5.796	8.252	10.452	12.425	14.193	15.777
3-2-1	---	---	4.573	---	---	---	---

Buydown Credit Rate 11.25%

Desired Buydown	1	2	3	4	5	6	7
10.75%	0.427	0.809	1.150	1.455	1.728	1.972	2.190
10.50%	0.639	1.210	1.720	2.177	2.585	2.950	3.276
10.25%	0.849	1.609	2.287	2.894	3.437	3.922	4.356
10.00%	1.059	2.005	2.851	3.608	4.284	4.889	5.430
9.75%	1.267	2.399	3.412	4.317	5.127	5.850	6.497
9.50%	1.474	2.791	3.969	5.022	5.964	6.805	7.558
9.25%	1.679	3.180	4.522	5.722	6.795	7.754	8.612
9.00%	1.883	3.566	5.072	6.417	7.620	8.696	9.658
8.75%	2.085	3.950	5.617	7.107	8.440	9.631	10.697
8.50%	2.286	4.331	6.158	7.792	9.253	10.560	11.727
8.25%	2.486	4.708	6.695	8.472	10.060	11.481	12.750
8.00%	2.684	5.083	7.228	9.146	10.861	12.394	13.765
7.75%	2.880	5.454	7.756	9.814	11.654	13.299	14.770
7.50%	3.074	5.822	8.280	10.477	12.441	14.197	15.767
3-2-1	---	---	4.587	---	---	---	---

Buydown Credit Rate 0.00%

Desired Buydown	1	2	3	4	5	6	7
10.50%	0.451	0.902	1.353	1.804	2.255	2.706	3.157
10.25%	0.675	1.349	2.024	2.699	3.373	4.048	4.723
10.00%	0.897	1.794	2.691	3.588	4.485	5.382	6.279
9.75%	1.118	2.236	3.354	4.472	5.590	6.708	7.826
9.50%	1.338	2.675	4.013	5.351	6.688	8.026	9.363
9.25%	1.556	3.112	4.667	6.223	7.779	9.335	10.890
9.00%	1.772	3.545	5.317	7.090	8.862	10.634	12.407
8.75%	1.987	3.975	5.962	7.950	9.937	11.925	13.912
8.50%	2.201	4.402	6.603	8.804	11.005	13.206	15.406
8.25%	2.413	4.825	7.238	9.651	12.063	14.476	16.889
8.00%	2.623	5.245	7.868	10.491	13.114	15.736	18.359
7.75%	2.831	5.662	8.493	11.324	14.155	16.986	19.817
7.50%	3.037	6.075	9.112	12.149	15.187	18.224	21.261
7.25%	3.242	6.484	9.725	12.967	16.209	19.451	22.692
3-2-1	---	---	5.292	---	---	---	---

Buydown Credit Rate 0.00%

Desired Buydown	1	2	3	4	5	6	7
10.75%	0.453	0.907	1.360	1.813	2.267	2.720	3.174
10.50%	0.678	1.357	2.035	2.713	3.391	4.070	4.748
10.25%	0.902	1.804	2.706	3.608	4.510	5.412	6.313
10.00%	1.124	2.249	3.373	4.497	5.621	6.746	7.870
9.75%	1.345	2.691	4.036	5.381	6.726	8.072	9.417
9.50%	1.565	3.130	4.695	6.260	7.824	9.389	10.954
9.25%	1.783	3.566	5.349	7.132	8.915	10.698	12.481
9.00%	2.000	3.999	5.999	7.999	9.998	11.998	13.998
8.75%	2.215	4.429	6.644	8.859	11.074	13.288	15.503
8.50%	2.428	4.856	7.285	9.713	12.141	14.569	16.997
8.25%	2.640	5.280	7.920	10.560	13.200	15.840	18.480
8.00%	2.850	5.700	8.550	11.400	14.250	17.100	19.950
7.75%	3.058	6.116	9.175	12.233	15.291	18.349	21.407
7.50%	3.265	6.529	9.794	13.058	16.323	19.587	22.852
3-2-1	---	---	5.325	---	---	---	---

Buydown Credit Rate 10.00%

Desired Buydown	1	2	3	4	5	6	7
10.50%	0.428	0.814	1.165	1.482	1.769	2.029	2.264
10.25%	0.639	1.218	1.742	2.217	2.646	3.035	3.387
10.00%	0.850	1.620	2.317	2.947	3.518	4.035	4.503
9.75%	1.060	2.019	2.887	3.673	4.385	5.029	5.612
9.50%	1.268	2.416	3.455	4.395	5.246	6.017	6.715
9.25%	1.475	2.810	4.018	5.112	6.102	6.998	7.810
9.00%	1.680	3.201	4.577	5.824	6.952	7.973	8.897
8.75%	1.884	3.589	5.133	6.530	7.795	8.940	9.977
8.50%	2.086	3.975	5.684	7.232	8.632	9.900	11.048
8.25%	2.287	4.357	6.231	7.927	9.463	10.853	12.111
8.00%	2.486	4.736	6.773	8.617	10.287	11.798	13.165
7.75%	2.683	5.112	7.311	9.302	11.103	12.734	14.211
7.50%	2.879	5.485	7.844	9.980	11.913	13.662	15.246
7.25%	3.073	5.854	8.372	10.651	12.715	14.582	16.273
3-2-1	---	---	4.632	---	---	---	---

Buydown Credit Rate 10.25%

Desired Buydown	1	2	3	4	5	6	7
10.75%	0.429	0.817	1.167	1.483	1.768	2.026	2.258
10.50%	0.642	1.222	1.745	2.218	2.645	3.030	3.378
10.25%	0.854	1.625	2.321	2.949	3.517	4.030	4.492
10.00%	1.064	2.025	2.893	3.677	4.384	5.023	5.600
9.75%	1.273	2.423	3.462	4.399	5.246	6.010	6.701
9.50%	1.481	2.819	4.027	5.117	6.102	6.992	7.795
9.25%	1.688	3.212	4.588	5.831	6.953	7.966	8.881
9.00%	1.893	3.602	5.146	6.539	7.798	8.934	9.960
8.75%	2.097	3.990	5.699	7.243	8.636	9.895	11.031
8.50%	2.299	4.374	6.248	7.941	9.469	10.848	12.094
8.25%	2.499	4.756	6.793	8.633	10.294	11.795	13.149
8.00%	2.698	5.134	7.334	9.320	11.113	12.733	14.195
7.75%	2.895	5.509	7.869	10.001	11.925	13.663	15.232
7.50%	3.090	5.881	8.400	10.676	12.730	14.585	16.260
3-2-1	---	---	4.646	---	---	---	---

Entry is number of points paid at closing; 3-2-1 is a 3-year buydown of 3% 1st year, 2% 2nd year and 1% 3rd year.

Number of Points to Buy Down a Loan

Market Interest Rate 11.50%   Market Interest Rate 11.75%
Buydown Credit Rate 5.50%   Buydown Credit Rate 5.50%

Desired Buydown	1	2	3	Years of Buydown 4	5	6	7	Desired Buydown	1	2	3	Years of Buydown 4	5	6	7
11.00%	0.442	0.861	1.257	1.633	1.988	2.324	2.642	11.25%	0.444	0.865	1.263	1.640	1.997	2.335	2.655
10.75%	0.662	1.288	1.881	2.443	2.974	3.477	3.953	11.00%	0.665	1.295	1.891	2.455	2.989	3.494	3.973
10.50%	0.880	1.713	2.502	3.249	3.955	4.624	5.258	10.75%	0.885	1.722	2.515	3.265	3.975	4.647	5.284
10.25%	1.097	2.136	3.119	4.050	4.931	5.765	6.555	10.50%	1.103	2.147	3.135	4.071	4.956	5.795	6.588
10.00%	1.313	2.556	3.733	4.847	5.901	6.899	7.844	10.25%	1.320	2.570	3.752	4.872	5.932	6.935	7.885
9.75%	1.528	2.974	4.343	5.639	6.865	8.027	9.126	10.00%	1.536	2.990	4.366	5.669	6.902	8.069	9.175
9.50%	1.741	3.389	4.949	6.426	7.823	9.147	10.399	9.75%	1.750	3.407	4.976	6.461	7.866	9.197	10.456
9.25%	1.953	3.801	5.551	7.207	8.775	10.259	11.664	9.50%	1.964	3.822	5.582	7.248	8.824	10.317	11.730
9.00%	2.163	4.211	6.149	7.984	9.720	11.364	12.921	9.25%	2.175	4.235	6.184	8.029	9.776	11.430	12.995
8.75%	2.372	4.617	6.742	8.754	10.659	12.461	14.168	9.00%	2.386	4.644	6.782	8.806	10.721	12.534	14.251
8.50%	2.579	5.020	7.331	9.519	11.590	13.550	15.406	8.75%	2.595	5.051	7.375	9.576	11.659	13.631	15.498
8.25%	2.785	5.421	7.916	10.278	12.514	14.630	16.634	8.50%	2.802	5.454	7.965	10.341	12.591	14.720	16.736
8.00%	2.989	5.818	8.495	11.030	13.430	15.701	17.852	8.25%	3.007	5.854	8.549	11.100	13.515	15.800	17.964
7.75%	3.191	6.211	9.070	11.776	14.338	16.763	19.059	8.00%	3.211	6.251	9.129	11.852	14.431	16.872	19.182
3-2-1	---	---	4.972	---	---	---	---	3-2-1	---	---	5.000	---	---	---	---

Buydown Credit Rate 11.50%   Buydown Credit Rate 11.75%

Desired Buydown	1	2	3	4	5	6	7	Desired Buydown	1	2	3	4	5	6	7
11.00%	0.428	0.811	1.151	1.455	1.726	1.968	2.184	11.25%	0.430	0.812	1.153	1.455	1.725	1.964	2.178
10.75%	0.641	1.213	1.723	2.178	2.583	2.945	3.267	11.00%	0.643	1.216	1.725	2.178	2.581	2.939	3.258
10.50%	0.853	1.613	2.291	2.896	3.435	3.916	4.345	10.75%	0.856	1.617	2.294	2.897	3.433	3.910	4.334
10.25%	1.063	2.011	2.856	3.610	4.283	4.883	5.417	10.50%	1.067	2.016	2.861	3.612	4.280	4.875	5.404
10.00%	1.272	2.406	3.418	4.321	5.125	5.843	6.483	10.25%	1.277	2.413	3.424	4.323	5.123	5.834	6.468
9.75%	1.480	2.800	3.977	5.027	5.963	6.798	7.542	10.00%	1.486	2.808	3.984	5.030	5.961	6.789	7.525
9.50%	1.686	3.190	4.532	5.728	6.795	7.746	8.595	9.75%	1.693	3.200	4.540	5.732	6.793	7.737	8.577
9.25%	1.892	3.578	5.083	6.425	7.621	8.689	9.641	9.50%	1.900	3.590	5.093	6.431	7.621	8.679	9.621
9.00%	2.095	3.964	5.630	7.117	8.442	9.625	10.679	9.25%	2.104	3.977	5.642	7.124	8.443	9.615	10.659
8.75%	2.297	4.346	6.174	7.804	9.257	10.554	11.710	9.00%	2.308	4.361	6.188	7.813	9.259	10.545	11.689
8.50%	2.498	4.726	6.713	8.485	10.066	11.476	12.733	8.75%	2.510	4.743	6.729	8.497	10.069	11.468	12.712
8.25%	2.697	5.103	7.248	9.162	10.868	12.390	13.748	8.50%	2.710	5.122	7.267	9.175	10.873	12.384	13.727
8.00%	2.895	5.477	7.779	9.833	11.664	13.298	14.754	8.25%	2.909	5.497	7.800	9.849	11.671	13.292	14.735
7.75%	3.091	5.847	8.305	10.498	12.453	14.197	15.752	8.00%	3.106	5.870	8.329	10.516	12.462	14.194	15.734
3-2-1	---	---	4.600	---	---	---	---	3-2-1	---	---	4.611	---	---	---	---

Buydown Credit Rate 0.00%   Buydown Credit Rate 0.00%

Desired Buydown	1	2	3	4	5	6	7	Desired Buydown	1	2	3	4	5	6	7
11.00%	0.456	0.911	1.367	1.822	2.278	2.734	3.189	11.25%	0.458	0.916	1.373	1.831	2.289	2.747	3.204
10.75%	0.682	1.363	2.045	2.727	3.409	4.090	4.772	11.00%	0.685	1.370	2.055	2.740	3.425	4.110	4.795
10.50%	0.907	1.813	2.720	3.627	4.533	5.440	6.346	10.75%	0.911	1.822	2.733	3.645	4.556	5.467	6.378
10.25%	1.130	2.261	3.391	4.521	5.651	6.782	7.912	10.50%	1.136	2.272	3.408	4.544	5.680	6.816	7.952
10.00%	1.353	2.705	4.058	5.411	6.763	8.116	9.468	10.25%	1.360	2.719	4.079	5.439	6.799	8.158	9.518
9.75%	1.574	3.147	4.721	6.295	7.868	9.442	11.016	10.00%	1.582	3.164	4.746	6.328	7.910	9.492	11.074
9.50%	1.793	3.586	5.380	7.173	8.966	10.759	12.553	9.75%	1.803	3.606	5.409	7.212	9.015	10.818	12.621
9.25%	2.011	4.023	6.034	8.046	10.057	12.068	14.080	9.50%	2.023	4.045	6.068	8.091	10.113	12.136	14.159
9.00%	2.228	4.456	6.684	8.912	11.140	13.368	15.596	9.25%	2.241	4.482	6.722	8.963	11.204	13.445	15.686
8.75%	2.443	4.886	7.329	9.772	12.215	14.659	17.102	9.00%	2.457	4.915	7.372	9.830	12.287	14.745	17.202
8.50%	2.657	5.313	7.970	10.626	13.283	15.939	18.596	8.75%	2.673	5.345	8.018	10.690	13.363	16.035	18.708
8.25%	2.868	5.737	8.605	11.473	14.341	17.210	20.078	8.50%	2.886	5.772	8.658	11.544	14.430	17.316	20.202
8.00%	3.078	6.157	9.235	12.313	15.392	18.470	21.548	8.25%	3.098	6.195	9.293	12.391	15.489	18.586	21.684
7.75%	3.287	6.573	9.860	13.146	16.433	19.719	23.006	8.00%	3.308	6.615	9.923	13.231	16.539	19.846	23.154
3-2-1	---	---	5.356	---	---	---	---	3-2-1	---	---	5.387	---	---	---	---

Buydown Credit Rate 10.50%   Buydown Credit Rate 10.75%

Desired Buydown	1	2	3	4	5	6	7	Desired Buydown	1	2	3	4	5	6	7
11.00%	0.431	0.819	1.168	1.483	1.766	2.022	2.252	11.25%	0.432	0.821	1.169	1.483	1.765	2.018	2.245
10.75%	0.644	1.225	1.748	2.219	2.643	3.025	3.369	11.00%	0.647	1.228	1.750	2.219	2.641	3.019	3.360
10.50%	0.857	1.629	2.325	2.951	3.515	4.023	4.481	10.75%	0.860	1.633	2.328	2.952	3.512	4.016	4.469
10.25%	1.069	2.031	2.898	3.679	4.382	5.016	5.586	10.50%	1.073	2.036	2.902	3.680	4.379	5.007	5.572
10.00%	1.279	2.431	3.468	4.403	5.244	6.002	6.685	10.25%	1.284	2.437	3.474	4.405	5.241	5.993	6.669
9.75%	1.488	2.828	4.035	5.122	6.101	6.983	7.778	10.00%	1.494	2.836	4.042	5.125	6.099	6.973	7.759
9.50%	1.695	3.222	4.598	5.837	6.953	7.958	8.863	9.75%	1.702	3.232	4.606	5.841	6.950	7.947	8.843
9.25%	1.902	3.614	5.157	6.547	7.798	8.926	9.941	9.50%	1.910	3.625	5.167	6.552	7.797	8.915	9.920
9.00%	2.106	4.004	5.712	7.252	8.638	9.887	11.012	9.25%	2.116	4.016	5.724	7.259	8.638	9.877	10.990
8.75%	2.310	4.390	6.264	7.952	9.472	10.841	12.075	9.00%	2.320	4.405	6.278	7.961	9.473	10.832	12.052
8.50%	2.511	4.774	6.811	8.646	10.300	11.789	13.130	8.75%	2.523	4.790	6.827	8.658	10.302	11.780	13.107
8.25%	2.712	5.154	7.354	9.336	11.121	12.728	14.176	8.50%	2.725	5.173	7.373	9.349	11.125	12.720	14.154
8.00%	2.910	5.531	7.893	10.019	11.935	13.660	15.215	8.25%	2.925	5.552	7.914	10.035	11.941	13.654	15.193
7.75%	3.107	5.906	8.426	10.697	12.742	14.584	16.244	8.00%	3.123	5.929	8.450	10.715	12.751	14.580	16.223
3-2-1	---	---	4.659	---	---	---	---	3-2-1	---	---	4.670	---	---	---	---

Entry is number of points paid at closing; 3-2-1 is a 3-year buydown of 3% 1st year, 2% 2nd year and 1% 3rd year.

Number of Points to Buy Down a Loan

Market Interest Rate 12.00% — Buydown Credit Rate 5.50%

Desired Buydown	1	2	3	4	5	6	7
11.50%	0.446	0.869	1.269	1.648	2.006	2.346	2.667
11.25%	0.668	1.301	1.899	2.466	3.002	3.510	3.991
11.00%	0.889	1.730	2.526	3.280	3.994	4.669	5.309
10.75%	1.108	2.157	3.150	4.091	4.980	5.823	6.620
10.50%	1.327	2.582	3.771	4.896	5.962	6.970	7.924
10.25%	1.544	3.005	4.388	5.698	6.937	8.111	9.221
10.00%	1.760	3.425	5.002	6.495	7.907	9.245	10.511
9.75%	1.974	3.843	5.612	7.286	8.872	10.372	11.792
9.50%	2.187	4.258	6.218	8.073	9.830	11.492	13.066
9.25%	2.399	4.670	6.820	8.855	10.781	12.605	14.331
9.00%	2.609	5.080	7.418	9.631	11.727	13.710	15.587
8.75%	2.818	5.486	8.011	10.402	12.665	14.807	16.834
8.50%	3.025	5.889	8.600	11.167	13.596	15.896	18.072
8.25%	3.231	6.290	9.185	11.926	14.520	16.976	19.300
3-2-1	---	---	5.028	---	---	---	---

Market Interest Rate 12.50% — Buydown Credit Rate 5.50%

Desired Buydown	1	2	3	4	5	6	7
12.00%	0.450	0.876	1.280	1.662	2.023	2.365	2.689
11.75%	0.674	1.312	1.916	2.487	3.029	3.541	4.026
11.50%	0.897	1.745	2.549	3.309	4.029	4.711	5.356
11.25%	1.118	2.177	3.179	4.128	5.026	5.876	6.680
11.00%	1.339	2.606	3.806	4.942	6.017	7.035	7.998
10.75%	1.558	3.034	4.430	5.752	7.004	8.188	9.309
10.50%	1.777	3.459	5.051	6.558	7.985	9.335	10.614
10.25%	1.994	3.881	5.668	7.360	8.961	10.476	11.911
10.00%	2.210	4.302	6.282	8.156	9.931	11.610	13.200
9.75%	2.424	4.719	6.892	8.948	10.895	12.737	14.482
9.50%	2.638	5.134	7.498	9.735	11.853	13.858	15.755
9.25%	2.849	5.547	8.100	10.517	12.805	14.970	17.020
9.00%	3.060	5.956	8.698	11.293	13.750	16.075	18.277
8.75%	3.268	6.362	9.291	12.064	14.688	17.172	19.524
3-2-1	---	---	5.079	---	---	---	---

Buydown Credit Rate 12.00% (Market 12.00%)

Desired Buydown	1	2	3	4	5	6	7
11.50%	0.431	0.814	1.154	1.455	1.723	1.960	2.171
11.25%	0.645	1.218	1.727	2.178	2.578	2.934	3.249
11.00%	0.859	1.621	2.297	2.897	3.430	3.902	4.322
10.75%	1.071	2.021	2.864	3.613	4.277	4.866	5.389
10.50%	1.282	2.419	3.428	4.324	5.119	5.825	6.451
10.25%	1.491	2.815	3.990	5.032	5.957	6.778	7.507
10.00%	1.700	3.209	4.547	5.736	6.790	7.726	8.556
9.75%	1.907	3.600	5.102	6.435	7.618	8.668	9.600
9.50%	2.113	3.989	5.653	7.130	8.441	9.604	10.636
9.25%	2.318	4.375	6.200	7.820	9.258	10.534	11.666
9.00%	2.521	4.758	6.744	8.506	10.069	11.457	12.689
8.75%	2.723	5.139	7.283	9.186	10.875	12.374	13.704
8.50%	2.923	5.517	7.819	9.862	11.675	13.284	14.712
8.25%	3.122	5.892	8.350	10.532	12.468	14.186	15.711
3-2-1	---	---	4.622	---	---	---	---

Buydown Credit Rate 12.50% (Market 12.50%)

Desired Buydown	1	2	3	4	5	6	7
12.00%	0.434	0.817	1.155	1.454	1.718	1.951	2.156
11.75%	0.649	1.223	1.729	2.176	2.571	2.920	3.228
11.50%	0.864	1.627	2.301	2.896	3.421	3.885	4.295
11.25%	1.078	2.029	2.870	3.612	4.267	4.846	5.357
11.00%	1.290	2.430	3.436	4.324	5.109	5.801	6.413
10.75%	1.502	2.828	3.999	5.033	5.946	6.753	7.465
10.50%	1.712	3.224	4.559	5.738	6.779	7.699	8.510
10.25%	1.921	3.618	5.116	6.439	7.608	8.639	9.550
10.00%	2.129	4.010	5.670	7.136	8.431	9.575	10.584
9.75%	2.336	4.399	6.221	7.829	9.250	10.504	11.612
9.50%	2.541	4.786	6.768	8.518	10.063	11.428	12.633
9.25%	2.746	5.170	7.311	9.202	10.871	12.346	13.648
9.00%	2.948	5.552	7.851	9.881	11.674	13.257	14.655
8.75%	3.149	5.931	8.386	10.555	12.470	14.162	15.655
3-2-1	---	---	4.640	---	---	---	---

Buydown Credit Rate 0.00% (Market 12.00%)

Desired Buydown	1	2	3	4	5	6	7
11.50%	0.460	0.920	1.380	1.839	2.299	2.759	3.219
11.25%	0.688	1.376	2.065	2.753	3.441	4.129	4.818
11.00%	0.915	1.831	2.746	3.662	4.577	5.493	6.408
10.75%	1.142	2.283	3.425	4.566	5.708	6.849	7.991
10.50%	1.366	2.733	4.099	5.466	6.832	8.199	9.565
10.25%	1.590	3.180	4.770	6.361	7.951	9.541	11.131
10.00%	1.812	3.625	5.437	7.250	9.062	10.875	12.687
9.75%	2.033	4.067	6.100	8.134	10.167	12.201	14.234
9.50%	2.253	4.506	6.759	9.012	11.266	13.519	15.772
9.25%	2.471	4.942	7.414	9.885	12.356	14.827	17.299
9.00%	2.688	5.376	8.064	10.752	13.439	16.127	18.815
8.75%	2.903	5.806	8.709	11.612	14.515	17.418	20.321
8.50%	3.116	6.233	9.349	12.466	15.582	18.698	21.815
8.25%	3.328	6.656	9.984	13.313	16.641	19.969	23.297
3-2-1	---	---	5.416	---	---	---	---

Buydown Credit Rate 0.00% (Market 12.50%)

Desired Buydown	1	2	3	4	5	6	7
12.00%	0.464	0.927	1.391	1.855	2.319	2.782	3.246
11.75%	0.694	1.388	2.083	2.777	3.471	4.165	4.859
11.50%	0.924	1.847	2.771	3.694	4.618	5.542	6.465
11.25%	1.152	2.304	3.456	4.608	5.760	6.912	8.064
11.00%	1.379	2.758	4.138	5.517	6.896	8.275	9.654
10.75%	1.605	3.211	4.816	6.421	8.027	9.632	11.237
10.50%	1.830	3.660	5.491	7.321	9.151	10.981	12.812
10.25%	2.054	4.108	6.162	8.216	10.269	12.323	14.377
10.00%	2.276	4.552	6.829	9.105	11.381	13.657	15.934
9.75%	2.497	4.994	7.492	9.989	12.486	14.983	17.481
9.50%	2.717	5.434	8.151	10.867	13.584	16.301	19.018
9.25%	2.935	5.870	8.805	11.740	14.675	17.610	20.545
9.00%	3.152	6.303	9.455	12.606	15.758	18.910	22.061
8.75%	3.367	6.733	10.100	13.467	16.833	20.200	23.567
3-2-1	---	---	5.471	---	---	---	---

Buydown Credit Rate 11.00% (Market 12.00%)

Desired Buydown	1	2	3	4	5	6	7
11.50%	0.434	0.822	1.171	1.483	1.763	2.013	2.238
11.25%	0.649	1.231	1.752	2.219	2.638	3.013	3.349
11.00%	0.863	1.637	2.330	2.952	3.509	4.008	4.456
10.75%	1.076	2.041	2.906	3.681	4.375	4.998	5.556
10.50%	1.288	2.443	3.478	4.406	5.237	5.983	6.651
10.25%	1.499	2.843	4.048	5.127	6.095	6.962	7.739
10.00%	1.709	3.241	4.614	5.844	6.947	7.935	8.821
9.75%	1.917	3.636	5.176	6.557	7.794	8.903	9.897
9.50%	2.124	4.028	5.735	7.265	8.636	9.864	10.966
9.25%	2.330	4.419	6.290	7.968	9.472	10.819	12.027
9.00%	2.534	4.806	6.842	8.666	10.302	11.768	13.082
8.75%	2.737	5.190	7.389	9.360	11.126	12.709	14.128
8.50%	2.938	5.572	7.932	10.048	11.944	13.644	15.167
8.25%	3.138	5.951	8.471	10.731	12.756	14.571	16.198
3-2-1	---	---	4.681	---	---	---	---

Buydown Credit Rate 11.50% (Market 12.50%)

Desired Buydown	1	2	3	4	5	6	7
12.00%	0.436	0.825	1.172	1.481	1.757	2.003	2.223
11.75%	0.653	1.235	1.754	2.217	2.630	2.999	3.327
11.50%	0.869	1.643	2.334	2.950	3.500	3.990	4.427
11.25%	1.083	2.049	2.911	3.680	4.365	4.976	5.521
11.00%	1.297	2.454	3.485	4.405	5.226	5.958	6.611
10.75%	1.510	2.856	4.057	5.128	6.083	6.935	7.694
10.50%	1.721	3.256	4.625	5.846	6.935	7.906	8.772
10.25%	1.931	3.654	5.190	6.560	7.782	8.872	9.844
10.00%	2.141	4.050	5.752	7.271	8.625	9.833	10.910
9.75%	2.348	4.443	6.311	7.977	9.462	10.788	11.969
9.50%	2.555	4.834	6.866	8.678	10.295	11.736	13.022
9.25%	2.760	5.222	7.417	9.375	11.121	12.678	14.067
9.00%	2.964	5.607	7.964	10.067	11.942	13.614	15.106
8.75%	3.166	5.990	8.508	10.754	12.757	14.543	16.137
3-2-1	---	---	4.699	---	---	---	---

Entry is number of points paid at closing; 3-2-1 is a 3-year buydown of 3% 1st year, 2% 2nd year and 1% 3rd year.

Yield on Mortgage Loan When Points Are Paid

Interest Rate   5.50%   25 Year Schedule   Annual Constant   7.369050%

Yield to end of Year	1.0 Point	1.5 Point	2.0 Points	2.5 Points	3.0 Points	3.5 Points	4.0 Points	5.0 Points	6.0 Points	7.0 Points	8.0 Points	10.0 Points
1	6.544	7.071	7.601	8.134	8.669	9.208	9.750	10.844	11.950	13.069	14.202	16.509
2	6.042	6.315	6.589	6.866	7.143	7.423	7.704	8.270	8.844	9.424	10.011	11.205
3	5.874	6.063	6.253	6.444	6.637	6.830	7.024	7.417	7.813	8.215	8.621	9.448
4	5.792	5.939	6.086	6.235	6.385	6.535	6.686	6.992	7.301	7.614	7.930	8.575
5	5.742	5.864	5.987	6.110	6.234	6.359	6.485	6.739	6.996	7.256	7.519	8.055
6	5.709	5.814	5.921	6.028	6.135	6.243	6.352	6.572	6.794	7.019	7.247	7.712
7	5.686	5.780	5.874	5.969	6.065	6.161	6.258	6.454	6.652	6.852	7.055	7.470
8	5.669	5.754	5.840	5.926	6.013	6.101	6.189	6.366	6.546	6.729	6.914	7.291
9	5.656	5.734	5.813	5.893	5.973	6.054	6.135	6.300	6.466	6.634	6.805	7.154
10	5.646	5.719	5.793	5.867	5.942	6.018	6.094	6.247	6.403	6.561	6.720	7.047
11	5.638	5.706	5.776	5.847	5.918	5.989	6.061	6.206	6.353	6.502	6.653	6.961
12	5.631	5.697	5.763	5.830	5.897	5.965	6.034	6.172	6.312	6.454	6.598	6.892
13	5.625	5.689	5.752	5.816	5.881	5.946	6.012	6.144	6.278	6.415	6.553	6.836
14	5.621	5.682	5.744	5.805	5.867	5.930	5.993	6.121	6.251	6.383	6.516	6.789
15	5.617	5.676	5.736	5.796	5.856	5.917	5.978	6.102	6.228	6.356	6.486	6.751
16	5.614	5.671	5.729	5.788	5.847	5.906	5.966	6.087	6.210	6.334	6.461	6.719
17	5.612	5.667	5.724	5.781	5.839	5.897	5.956	6.074	6.194	6.316	6.440	6.693
18	5.609	5.664	5.720	5.776	5.833	5.890	5.947	6.063	6.181	6.301	6.423	6.672
19	5.607	5.662	5.717	5.772	5.828	5.884	5.940	6.055	6.171	6.289	6.409	6.655
20	5.606	5.660	5.714	5.769	5.824	5.879	5.935	6.048	6.163	6.279	6.398	6.641
21	5.605	5.658	5.712	5.766	5.820	5.875	5.931	6.043	6.156	6.272	6.390	6.630
22	5.604	5.657	5.710	5.764	5.818	5.873	5.928	6.039	6.152	6.267	6.383	6.623
23	5.604	5.656	5.709	5.763	5.816	5.871	5.925	6.036	6.148	6.263	6.379	6.617
24	5.603	5.656	5.709	5.762	5.815	5.870	5.924	6.034	6.147	6.261	6.376	6.614
25	5.603	5.656	5.708	5.762	5.815	5.869	5.924	6.034	6.146	6.260	6.376	6.613

Interest Rate   5.50%   30 Year Schedule   Annual Constant   6.813468%

Yield to end of Year	1.0 Point	1.5 Point	2.0 Points	2.5 Points	3.0 Points	3.5 Points	4.0 Points	5.0 Points	6.0 Points	7.0 Points	8.0 Points	10.0 Points
1	6.542	7.067	7.595	8.127	8.661	9.199	9.739	10.830	11.933	13.049	14.179	16.480
2	6.039	6.310	6.583	6.858	7.134	7.412	7.691	8.255	8.825	9.402	9.985	11.173
3	5.871	6.059	6.247	6.436	6.627	6.819	7.011	7.400	7.793	8.191	8.594	9.414
4	5.788	5.933	6.079	6.226	6.374	6.523	6.673	6.974	7.280	7.589	7.901	8.538
5	5.738	5.859	5.980	6.101	6.223	6.347	6.470	6.720	6.973	7.229	7.488	8.016
6	5.706	5.809	5.913	6.018	6.124	6.230	6.337	6.552	6.770	6.991	7.215	7.671
7	5.682	5.774	5.867	5.959	6.053	6.147	6.242	6.433	6.627	6.823	7.021	7.426
8	5.664	5.748	5.831	5.915	6.000	6.085	6.171	6.344	6.520	6.697	6.877	7.245
9	5.652	5.728	5.804	5.882	5.960	6.038	6.117	6.276	6.438	6.601	6.767	7.105
10	5.641	5.712	5.784	5.856	5.928	6.001	6.074	6.223	6.373	6.526	6.680	6.995
11	5.633	5.699	5.766	5.834	5.902	5.971	6.040	6.180	6.321	6.465	6.610	6.907
12	5.626	5.689	5.752	5.817	5.881	5.946	6.012	6.144	6.279	6.415	6.553	6.835
13	5.619	5.680	5.741	5.802	5.864	5.926	5.989	6.115	6.243	6.373	6.505	6.775
14	5.615	5.673	5.731	5.790	5.849	5.909	5.969	6.091	6.214	6.339	6.466	6.725
15	5.611	5.667	5.723	5.780	5.837	5.895	5.953	6.070	6.189	6.310	6.433	6.683
16	5.607	5.661	5.716	5.771	5.827	5.883	5.939	6.053	6.168	6.285	6.404	6.648
17	5.604	5.657	5.710	5.764	5.818	5.872	5.927	6.038	6.150	6.265	6.381	6.618
18	5.602	5.654	5.705	5.758	5.810	5.864	5.917	6.025	6.135	6.247	6.360	6.592
19	5.600	5.651	5.702	5.753	5.805	5.856	5.909	6.015	6.122	6.232	6.343	6.570
20	5.598	5.648	5.697	5.748	5.799	5.850	5.901	6.006	6.111	6.219	6.328	6.552
21	5.597	5.646	5.694	5.744	5.794	5.844	5.895	5.998	6.102	6.208	6.316	6.536
22	5.595	5.644	5.692	5.741	5.790	5.840	5.890	5.991	6.094	6.199	6.305	6.523
23	5.594	5.642	5.690	5.738	5.787	5.836	5.886	5.986	6.088	6.191	6.297	6.512
24	5.593	5.641	5.688	5.736	5.784	5.833	5.882	5.981	6.082	6.185	6.289	6.503
25	5.593	5.640	5.687	5.734	5.782	5.830	5.879	5.978	6.078	6.180	6.284	6.496
26	5.592	5.639	5.686	5.733	5.781	5.828	5.877	5.975	6.075	6.176	6.279	6.491
27	5.592	5.638	5.685	5.732	5.780	5.827	5.876	5.973	6.072	6.173	6.276	6.486
28	5.591	5.638	5.684	5.731	5.779	5.826	5.874	5.971	6.070	6.171	6.274	6.484
29	5.591	5.637	5.684	5.731	5.778	5.826	5.874	5.971	6.069	6.170	6.272	6.482
30	5.591	5.637	5.684	5.731	5.778	5.826	5.874	5.970	6.069	6.170	6.272	6.481

Yield on Mortgage Loan When Points Are Paid

Interest Rate   5.75% 25 Year Schedule   Annual Constant   7.549277%

Yield to end of Year	1.0 Point	1.5 Point	2.0 Points	2.5 Points	3.0 Points	3.5 Points	4.0 Points	5.0 Points	6.0 Points	7.0 Points	8.0 Points	10.0 Points
1	6.795	7.323	7.853	8.386	8.923	9.462	10.005	11.099	12.207	13.327	14.461	16.771
2	6.292	6.566	6.841	7.118	7.396	7.676	7.958	8.526	9.100	9.681	10.269	11.467
3	6.126	6.315	6.505	6.697	6.890	7.084	7.278	7.672	8.070	8.472	8.880	9.709
4	6.043	6.190	6.338	6.488	6.638	6.789	6.941	7.247	7.557	7.871	8.189	8.836
5	5.993	6.115	6.239	6.363	6.488	6.613	6.739	6.994	7.252	7.513	7.778	8.317
6	5.960	6.066	6.173	6.280	6.388	6.497	6.606	6.827	7.051	7.277	7.506	7.974
7	5.937	6.031	6.126	6.222	6.318	6.415	6.513	6.709	6.908	7.110	7.315	7.731
8	5.920	6.006	6.092	6.179	6.266	6.354	6.443	6.622	6.803	6.987	7.173	7.553
9	5.907	5.986	6.066	6.146	6.227	6.308	6.390	6.555	6.723	6.893	7.065	7.416
10	5.897	5.970	6.045	6.120	6.196	6.272	6.348	6.503	6.660	6.819	6.980	7.309
11	5.888	5.958	6.029	6.100	6.171	6.243	6.315	6.461	6.610	6.760	6.912	7.224
12	5.882	5.948	6.015	6.083	6.151	6.219	6.288	6.428	6.569	6.712	6.858	7.155
13	5.877	5.940	6.004	6.069	6.134	6.200	6.266	6.400	6.536	6.673	6.813	7.099
14	5.872	5.933	5.995	6.058	6.121	6.184	6.248	6.377	6.508	6.641	6.776	7.052
15	5.868	5.928	5.988	6.049	6.110	6.171	6.233	6.359	6.486	6.615	6.746	7.014
16	5.865	5.923	5.982	6.041	6.101	6.161	6.221	6.343	6.467	6.593	6.721	6.983
17	5.862	5.919	5.977	6.035	6.093	6.152	6.211	6.330	6.452	6.575	6.700	6.957
18	5.861	5.916	5.973	6.029	6.087	6.144	6.202	6.320	6.439	6.560	6.684	6.936
19	5.859	5.914	5.969	6.025	6.082	6.138	6.196	6.311	6.429	6.548	6.670	6.919
20	5.857	5.912	5.966	6.022	6.077	6.134	6.190	6.305	6.421	6.539	6.659	6.905
21	5.856	5.910	5.964	6.019	6.074	6.130	6.186	6.299	6.415	6.532	6.651	6.895
22	5.855	5.909	5.963	6.017	6.072	6.127	6.183	6.295	6.410	6.526	6.644	6.887
23	5.855	5.908	5.962	6.016	6.070	6.125	6.181	6.293	6.407	6.522	6.640	6.881
24	5.855	5.908	5.961	6.015	6.069	6.124	6.179	6.291	6.405	6.520	6.638	6.878
25	5.854	5.907	5.961	6.015	6.069	6.124	6.179	6.291	6.404	6.520	6.637	6.877

Interest Rate   5.75% 30 Year Schedule   Annual Constant   7.002874%

Yield to end of Year	1.0 Point	1.5 Point	2.0 Points	2.5 Points	3.0 Points	3.5 Points	4.0 Points	5.0 Points	6.0 Points	7.0 Points	8.0 Points	10.0 Points
1	6.793	7.319	7.848	8.380	8.915	9.453	9.994	11.085	12.190	13.307	14.438	16.742
2	6.289	6.562	6.835	7.111	7.387	7.666	7.946	8.510	9.082	9.659	10.244	11.435
3	6.123	6.310	6.499	6.689	6.880	7.072	7.266	7.655	8.050	8.449	8.853	9.675
4	6.039	6.185	6.332	6.479	6.627	6.777	6.927	7.230	7.536	7.847	8.160	8.800
5	5.989	6.110	6.232	6.354	6.477	6.600	6.725	6.976	7.230	7.487	7.748	8.278
6	5.956	6.060	6.165	6.271	6.377	6.484	6.591	6.808	7.027	7.249	7.474	7.933
7	5.933	6.025	6.118	6.212	6.306	6.401	6.496	6.689	6.884	7.081	7.281	7.688
8	5.916	5.999	6.084	6.168	6.254	6.339	6.426	6.600	6.777	6.956	7.137	7.507
9	5.902	5.979	6.057	6.135	6.213	6.292	6.372	6.532	6.695	6.860	7.027	7.368
10	5.892	5.963	6.036	6.108	6.181	6.255	6.329	6.479	6.630	6.784	6.940	7.258
11	5.884	5.951	6.019	6.087	6.156	6.225	6.295	6.436	6.579	6.723	6.870	7.170
12	5.877	5.940	6.005	6.070	6.135	6.201	6.267	6.401	6.536	6.674	6.813	7.098
13	5.871	5.932	5.993	6.055	6.118	6.180	6.244	6.371	6.501	6.632	6.766	7.038
14	5.866	5.925	5.984	6.043	6.103	6.164	6.224	6.347	6.472	6.598	6.726	6.989
15	5.862	5.918	5.976	6.033	6.091	6.149	6.208	6.327	6.447	6.569	6.693	6.947
16	5.858	5.913	5.969	6.024	6.081	6.137	6.194	6.309	6.426	6.545	6.665	6.912
17	5.855	5.909	5.963	6.017	6.072	6.127	6.182	6.295	6.409	6.524	6.641	6.882
18	5.853	5.905	5.958	6.011	6.064	6.118	6.172	6.282	6.393	6.506	6.621	6.856
19	5.851	5.902	5.954	6.006	6.058	6.111	6.164	6.271	6.381	6.491	6.604	6.835
20	5.849	5.899	5.950	6.001	6.053	6.104	6.157	6.262	6.370	6.479	6.590	6.816
21	5.848	5.897	5.947	5.997	6.048	6.099	6.151	6.255	6.361	6.468	6.577	6.801
22	5.846	5.895	5.944	5.994	6.044	6.095	6.145	6.248	6.353	6.459	6.567	6.788
23	5.846	5.894	5.942	5.991	6.041	6.091	6.141	6.243	6.346	6.451	6.558	6.777
24	5.844	5.892	5.941	5.989	6.038	6.088	6.138	6.238	6.341	6.445	6.551	6.768
25	5.844	5.891	5.939	5.987	6.036	6.085	6.135	6.235	6.337	6.440	6.545	6.761
26	5.843	5.890	5.938	5.986	6.034	6.083	6.133	6.232	6.333	6.436	6.541	6.756
27	5.843	5.890	5.937	5.985	6.033	6.082	6.131	6.230	6.331	6.433	6.538	6.752
28	5.842	5.889	5.937	5.984	6.032	6.081	6.130	6.229	6.329	6.431	6.535	6.749
29	5.842	5.889	5.936	5.984	6.032	6.080	6.129	6.228	6.328	6.430	6.534	6.747
30	5.842	5.889	5.936	5.984	6.032	6.080	6.129	6.228	6.328	6.430	6.534	6.747

Yield on Mortgage Loan When Points Are Paid

Interest Rate   6.00%   25 Year Schedule   Annual Constant   7.731617%

Yield to end of Year	1.0 Point	1.5 Point	2.0 Points	2.5 Points	3.0 Points	3.5 Points	4.0 Points	5.0 Points	6.0 Points	7.0 Points	8.0 Points	10.0 Points
1	7.046	7.574	8.105	8.639	9.176	9.716	10.259	11.355	12.463	13.585	14.720	17.032
2	6.543	6.818	7.093	7.371	7.650	7.930	8.212	8.781	9.357	9.939	10.528	11.728
3	6.376	6.566	6.757	6.950	7.143	7.337	7.533	7.927	8.326	8.730	9.138	9.971
4	6.293	6.441	6.590	6.740	6.891	7.042	7.195	7.503	7.814	8.129	8.448	9.098
5	6.244	6.367	6.491	6.615	6.741	6.867	6.994	7.250	7.509	7.771	8.037	8.578
6	6.211	6.318	6.425	6.533	6.642	6.751	6.861	7.083	7.307	7.535	7.765	8.235
7	6.188	6.283	6.379	6.475	6.572	6.669	6.767	6.965	7.165	7.368	7.574	7.993
8	6.171	6.257	6.344	6.432	6.520	6.608	6.698	6.878	7.060	7.245	7.432	7.815
9	6.158	6.238	6.318	6.399	6.480	6.562	6.645	6.811	6.980	7.151	7.324	7.678
10	6.147	6.222	6.297	6.373	6.449	6.526	6.603	6.759	6.917	7.077	7.240	7.572
11	6.139	6.210	6.281	6.352	6.424	6.497	6.570	6.717	6.867	7.019	7.172	7.486
12	6.133	6.200	6.268	6.336	6.404	6.474	6.543	6.684	6.826	6.971	7.118	7.418
13	6.127	6.192	6.257	6.322	6.388	6.454	6.521	6.656	6.793	6.932	7.073	7.362
14	6.123	6.185	6.248	6.311	6.375	6.439	6.503	6.634	6.766	6.900	7.037	7.316
15	6.119	6.180	6.240	6.302	6.364	6.426	6.488	6.615	6.744	6.874	7.007	7.278
16	6.116	6.175	6.234	6.294	6.354	6.415	6.476	6.600	6.725	6.852	6.982	7.246
17	6.114	6.171	6.229	6.288	6.347	6.406	6.466	6.587	6.710	6.834	6.961	7.221
18	6.111	6.168	6.225	6.283	6.340	6.399	6.458	6.576	6.697	6.820	6.944	7.200
19	6.110	6.166	6.222	6.278	6.335	6.393	6.451	6.568	6.687	6.808	6.931	7.183
20	6.108	6.164	6.219	6.275	6.331	6.388	6.445	6.561	6.679	6.799	6.920	7.169
21	6.107	6.162	6.217	6.272	6.328	6.385	6.441	6.556	6.673	6.791	6.912	7.159
22	6.107	6.161	6.215	6.270	6.326	6.382	6.438	6.552	6.668	6.786	6.906	7.151
23	6.106	6.160	6.214	6.269	6.324	6.380	6.436	6.550	6.665	6.782	6.901	7.146
24	6.106	6.160	6.214	6.268	6.323	6.379	6.435	6.548	6.663	6.780	6.899	7.143
25	6.106	6.159	6.214	6.268	6.323	6.379	6.434	6.548	6.662	6.779	6.898	7.142

Interest Rate   6.00%   30 Year Schedule   Annual Constant   7.194606%

Yield to end of Year	1.0 Point	1.5 Point	2.0 Points	2.5 Points	3.0 Points	3.5 Points	4.0 Points	5.0 Points	6.0 Points	7.0 Points	8.0 Points	10.0 Points
1	7.044	7.570	8.100	8.632	9.168	9.707	10.248	11.341	12.447	13.566	14.698	17.004
2	6.541	6.813	7.088	7.363	7.641	7.920	8.200	8.766	9.338	9.917	10.503	11.696
3	6.373	6.562	6.751	6.942	7.133	7.326	7.520	7.911	8.307	8.707	9.112	9.937
4	6.290	6.436	6.584	6.732	6.881	7.031	7.181	7.485	7.793	8.105	8.420	9.062
5	6.240	6.362	6.484	6.607	6.730	6.854	6.979	7.232	7.487	7.745	8.007	8.540
6	6.207	6.312	6.418	6.524	6.630	6.738	6.846	7.063	7.284	7.507	7.734	8.195
7	6.184	6.277	6.371	6.465	6.560	6.655	6.751	6.945	7.141	7.339	7.540	7.951
8	6.167	6.251	6.336	6.421	6.507	6.594	6.681	6.856	7.034	7.214	7.397	7.769
9	6.153	6.231	6.309	6.388	6.467	6.546	6.627	6.788	6.952	7.118	7.287	7.630
10	6.143	6.215	6.288	6.361	6.435	6.509	6.584	6.735	6.888	7.043	7.200	7.521
11	6.134	6.203	6.271	6.340	6.410	6.479	6.550	6.692	6.836	6.982	7.130	7.433
12	6.128	6.192	6.257	6.323	6.389	6.455	6.522	6.657	6.794	6.933	7.073	7.361
13	6.122	6.184	6.246	6.308	6.371	6.435	6.499	6.628	6.759	6.892	7.026	7.302
14	6.117	6.176	6.236	6.296	6.357	6.418	6.479	6.604	6.730	6.857	6.987	7.252
15	6.113	6.170	6.228	6.286	6.345	6.404	6.463	6.583	6.705	6.829	6.954	7.211
16	6.110	6.165	6.221	6.278	6.335	6.392	6.449	6.566	6.684	6.804	6.926	7.176
17	6.107	6.161	6.215	6.270	6.326	6.382	6.438	6.551	6.667	6.784	6.903	7.146
18	6.104	6.157	6.211	6.264	6.318	6.373	6.428	6.539	6.652	6.766	6.883	7.121
19	6.102	6.154	6.206	6.259	6.312	6.366	6.419	6.528	6.639	6.751	6.866	7.099
20	6.100	6.151	6.203	6.255	6.307	6.359	6.412	6.519	6.628	6.739	6.851	7.081
21	6.099	6.149	6.200	6.251	6.302	6.354	6.406	6.512	6.619	6.728	6.839	7.066
22	6.098	6.147	6.197	6.248	6.298	6.349	6.401	6.505	6.611	6.719	6.829	7.053
23	6.097	6.146	6.195	6.245	6.295	6.346	6.397	6.500	6.605	6.712	6.820	7.042
24	6.096	6.144	6.193	6.243	6.293	6.343	6.393	6.496	6.600	6.706	6.813	7.034
25	6.095	6.143	6.192	6.241	6.290	6.340	6.390	6.492	6.596	6.701	6.807	7.027
26	6.094	6.142	6.191	6.240	6.289	6.338	6.388	6.489	6.592	6.697	6.803	7.021
27	6.094	6.142	6.190	6.239	6.288	6.337	6.387	6.487	6.590	6.694	6.800	7.017
28	6.094	6.141	6.189	6.238	6.287	6.336	6.386	6.486	6.588	6.692	6.798	7.015
29	6.094	6.141	6.189	6.237	6.286	6.335	6.385	6.485	6.587	6.691	6.796	7.013
30	6.093	6.141	6.189	6.237	6.286	6.335	6.385	6.485	6.587	6.690	6.796	7.012

Yield on Mortgage Loan When Points Are Paid

Interest Rate   6.25%   25 Year Schedule   Annual Constant   7.916033%

Yield to end of Year	1.0 Point	1.5 Point	2.0 Points	2.5 Points	3.0 Points	3.5 Points	4.0 Points	5.0 Points	6.0 Points	7.0 Points	8.0 Points	10.0 Points
1	7.298	7.826	8.357	8.892	9.429	9.970	10.513	11.610	12.720	13.843	14.979	17.294
2	6.794	7.069	7.346	7.623	7.903	8.184	8.466	9.036	9.613	10.196	10.787	11.989
3	6.627	6.818	7.010	7.202	7.396	7.591	7.787	8.182	8.583	8.987	9.397	10.232
4	6.544	6.693	6.842	6.993	7.144	7.296	7.449	7.758	8.070	8.387	8.707	9.359
5	6.495	6.618	6.743	6.868	6.994	7.121	7.248	7.505	7.765	8.029	8.296	8.840
6	6.462	6.569	6.677	6.786	6.895	7.005	7.115	7.338	7.564	7.793	8.025	8.497
7	6.439	6.535	6.631	6.728	6.825	6.923	7.021	7.221	7.422	7.626	7.833	8.255
8	6.422	6.509	6.596	6.685	6.773	6.862	6.952	7.134	7.317	7.503	7.692	8.077
9	6.409	6.489	6.570	6.652	6.734	6.816	6.899	7.067	7.237	7.409	7.584	7.941
10	6.399	6.474	6.550	6.626	6.703	6.780	6.858	7.015	7.174	7.336	7.500	7.834
11	6.390	6.462	6.533	6.605	6.678	6.751	6.825	6.974	7.124	7.277	7.432	7.749
12	6.384	6.452	6.520	6.589	6.658	6.728	6.798	6.940	7.084	7.230	7.378	7.681
13	6.378	6.444	6.509	6.575	6.642	6.709	6.776	6.913	7.051	7.191	7.334	7.625
14	6.374	6.437	6.500	6.564	6.628	6.693	6.758	6.890	7.024	7.159	7.297	7.579
15	6.370	6.431	6.493	6.555	6.617	6.680	6.743	6.871	7.001	7.133	7.267	7.541
16	6.367	6.427	6.487	6.547	6.608	6.669	6.731	6.856	6.983	7.112	7.242	7.510
17	6.365	6.423	6.482	6.541	6.601	6.661	6.721	6.843	6.968	7.094	7.222	7.485
18	6.363	6.420	6.478	6.536	6.594	6.653	6.713	6.833	6.955	7.079	7.206	7.464
19	6.361	6.418	6.474	6.532	6.589	6.648	6.706	6.825	6.945	7.068	7.192	7.447
20	6.360	6.416	6.472	6.528	6.585	6.643	6.701	6.818	6.937	7.058	7.181	7.434
21	6.359	6.414	6.470	6.526	6.582	6.639	6.697	6.813	6.931	7.051	7.173	7.423
22	6.358	6.413	6.468	6.524	6.580	6.637	6.694	6.809	6.926	7.046	7.167	7.416
23	6.357	6.412	6.467	6.523	6.578	6.635	6.692	6.807	6.923	7.042	7.163	7.411
24	6.357	6.412	6.466	6.522	6.578	6.634	6.690	6.805	6.922	7.040	7.161	7.408
25	6.357	6.411	6.466	6.522	6.577	6.633	6.690	6.805	6.921	7.039	7.160	7.407

Interest Rate   6.25%   30 Year Schedule   Annual Constant   7.388606%

Yield to end of Year	1.0 Point	1.5 Point	2.0 Points	2.5 Points	3.0 Points	3.5 Points	4.0 Points	5.0 Points	6.0 Points	7.0 Points	8.0 Points	10.0 Points
1	7.295	7.822	8.352	8.885	9.421	9.961	10.503	11.597	12.704	13.824	14.957	17.266
2	6.792	7.065	7.340	7.616	7.894	8.174	8.455	9.022	9.595	10.175	10.763	11.958
3	6.624	6.813	7.003	7.195	7.387	7.580	7.774	8.167	8.563	8.965	9.371	10.199
4	6.541	6.688	6.836	6.985	7.134	7.285	7.436	7.741	8.050	8.363	8.679	9.324
5	6.491	6.613	6.736	6.859	6.983	7.108	7.234	7.487	7.744	8.003	8.266	8.802
6	6.458	6.564	6.670	6.776	6.884	6.992	7.100	7.319	7.541	7.766	7.993	8.457
7	6.435	6.529	6.623	6.718	6.813	6.909	7.006	7.200	7.398	7.598	7.800	8.213
8	6.418	6.503	6.588	6.674	6.761	6.848	6.935	7.112	7.291	7.473	7.657	8.032
9	6.405	6.483	6.561	6.641	6.720	6.801	6.881	7.045	7.210	7.377	7.547	7.893
10	6.394	6.467	6.540	6.614	6.689	6.764	6.839	6.991	7.145	7.302	7.460	7.784
11	6.386	6.454	6.524	6.593	6.663	6.734	6.805	6.948	7.094	7.241	7.391	7.696
12	6.379	6.444	6.510	6.576	6.642	6.709	6.777	6.913	7.052	7.192	7.334	7.625
13	6.373	6.435	6.498	6.562	6.625	6.689	6.754	6.884	7.017	7.151	7.287	7.566
14	6.368	6.428	6.489	6.550	6.611	6.673	6.735	6.860	6.988	7.117	7.248	7.516
15	6.364	6.422	6.481	6.540	6.599	6.658	6.718	6.840	6.963	7.088	7.215	7.475
16	6.361	6.417	6.474	6.531	6.589	6.646	6.705	6.823	6.943	7.064	7.187	7.440
17	6.358	6.413	6.468	6.524	6.580	6.636	6.693	6.808	6.925	7.044	7.164	7.411
18	6.356	6.409	6.463	6.518	6.572	6.628	6.683	6.796	6.910	7.026	7.144	7.386
19	6.354	6.406	6.459	6.512	6.566	6.620	6.675	6.785	6.898	7.011	7.127	7.364
20	6.352	6.403	6.456	6.508	6.561	6.614	6.668	6.776	6.887	6.999	7.113	7.346
21	6.350	6.401	6.453	6.504	6.556	6.609	6.662	6.769	6.878	6.988	7.101	7.331
22	6.349	6.399	6.450	6.501	6.553	6.604	6.657	6.763	6.870	6.979	7.091	7.318
23	6.348	6.398	6.448	6.498	6.549	6.601	6.653	6.757	6.864	6.972	7.082	7.308
24	6.347	6.396	6.446	6.496	6.547	6.598	6.649	6.753	6.859	6.966	7.075	7.299
25	6.346	6.395	6.445	6.495	6.545	6.595	6.646	6.750	6.854	6.961	7.070	7.292
26	6.346	6.395	6.444	6.493	6.543	6.593	6.644	6.747	6.851	6.957	7.065	7.287
27	6.345	6.394	6.443	6.492	6.542	6.592	6.643	6.745	6.849	6.955	7.062	7.283
28	6.345	6.394	6.442	6.491	6.541	6.591	6.641	6.743	6.847	6.953	7.060	7.280
29	6.345	6.393	6.442	6.491	6.541	6.590	6.641	6.743	6.846	6.952	7.059	7.279
30	6.345	6.393	6.442	6.491	6.540	6.590	6.641	6.742	6.846	6.951	7.058	7.278

Yield on Mortgage Loan When Points Are Paid

Interest Rate   6.50%   25 Year Schedule   Annual Constant   8.102486%

Yield to end of Year	1.0 Point	1.5 Point	2.0 Points	2.5 Points	3.0 Points	3.5 Points	4.0 Points	5.0 Points	6.0 Points	7.0 Points	8.0 Points	10.0 Points
1	7.549	8.078	8.610	9.145	9.683	10.224	10.768	11.866	12.977	14.101	15.239	17.556
2	7.046	7.321	7.598	7.876	8.156	8.438	8.721	9.292	9.870	10.454	11.046	12.250
3	6.878	7.070	7.262	7.455	7.649	7.845	8.041	8.438	8.839	9.245	9.656	10.493
4	6.795	6.945	7.095	7.245	7.397	7.550	7.704	8.013	8.327	8.645	8.966	9.621
5	6.746	6.870	6.995	7.121	7.247	7.374	7.502	7.761	8.022	8.287	8.555	9.101
6	6.713	6.821	6.929	7.038	7.148	7.259	7.370	7.594	7.821	8.051	8.284	8.759
7	6.690	6.786	6.883	6.980	7.078	7.177	7.276	7.476	7.679	7.885	8.093	8.517
8	6.673	6.761	6.849	6.937	7.027	7.116	7.207	7.389	7.574	7.762	7.952	8.339
9	6.660	6.741	6.823	6.905	6.987	7.070	7.154	7.323	7.494	7.668	7.844	8.203
10	6.650	6.726	6.802	6.879	6.956	7.034	7.113	7.271	7.432	7.595	7.760	8.097
11	6.642	6.713	6.786	6.858	6.932	7.005	7.080	7.230	7.382	7.536	7.693	8.012
12	6.635	6.704	6.772	6.842	6.912	6.982	7.053	7.196	7.342	7.489	7.638	7.944
13	6.630	6.695	6.762	6.828	6.896	6.963	7.031	7.169	7.309	7.450	7.594	7.888
14	6.625	6.689	6.753	6.817	6.882	6.948	7.013	7.147	7.282	7.419	7.558	7.843
15	6.622	6.683	6.745	6.808	6.871	6.935	6.999	7.128	7.259	7.393	7.528	7.805
16	6.619	6.679	6.739	6.801	6.862	6.924	6.986	7.113	7.241	7.371	7.503	7.774
17	6.616	6.675	6.734	6.794	6.855	6.915	6.976	7.100	7.226	7.354	7.483	7.749
18	6.614	6.672	6.730	6.789	6.848	6.908	6.968	7.090	7.214	7.339	7.467	7.728
19	6.612	6.670	6.727	6.785	6.843	6.902	6.962	7.082	7.204	7.327	7.453	7.712
20	6.611	6.668	6.724	6.782	6.839	6.898	6.956	7.075	7.196	7.318	7.443	7.698
21	6.610	6.666	6.722	6.779	6.836	6.894	6.952	7.070	7.190	7.311	7.435	7.688
22	6.609	6.665	6.721	6.777	6.834	6.891	6.949	7.066	7.185	7.306	7.429	7.681
23	6.609	6.664	6.720	6.776	6.833	6.890	6.947	7.064	7.182	7.302	7.425	7.676
24	6.608	6.664	6.719	6.775	6.832	6.889	6.946	7.062	7.180	7.300	7.422	7.673
25	6.608	6.663	6.719	6.775	6.831	6.888	6.946	7.062	7.180	7.299	7.421	7.672

Interest Rate   6.50%   30 Year Schedule   Annual Constant   7.584816%

Yield to end of Year	1.0 Point	1.5 Point	2.0 Points	2.5 Points	3.0 Points	3.5 Points	4.0 Points	5.0 Points	6.0 Points	7.0 Points	8.0 Points	10.0 Points
1	7.546	8.074	8.604	9.138	9.675	10.215	10.758	11.853	12.961	14.082	15.217	17.528
2	7.043	7.317	7.592	7.869	8.147	8.427	8.709	9.277	9.852	10.434	11.022	12.220
3	6.875	7.065	7.256	7.447	7.640	7.834	8.029	8.422	8.820	9.223	9.631	10.461
4	6.792	6.940	7.088	7.237	7.388	7.539	7.690	7.997	8.307	8.621	8.939	9.586
5	6.742	6.865	6.988	7.112	7.237	7.362	7.488	7.743	8.001	8.262	8.526	9.064
6	6.710	6.816	6.922	7.029	7.137	7.246	7.355	7.575	7.798	8.024	8.253	8.720
7	6.686	6.780	6.875	6.971	7.067	7.163	7.260	7.456	7.655	7.856	8.060	8.476
8	6.669	6.755	6.841	6.927	7.014	7.102	7.190	7.368	7.549	7.732	7.917	8.295
9	6.656	6.735	6.814	6.894	6.974	7.055	7.136	7.301	7.467	7.636	7.807	8.156
10	6.645	6.719	6.793	6.867	6.942	7.018	7.094	7.248	7.403	7.561	7.721	8.047
11	6.637	6.706	6.776	6.846	6.917	6.988	7.060	7.205	7.352	7.500	7.651	7.960
12	6.630	6.696	6.762	6.829	6.896	6.964	7.032	7.170	7.309	7.451	7.595	7.888
13	6.624	6.687	6.751	6.815	6.879	6.944	7.009	7.141	7.275	7.410	7.548	7.830
14	6.620	6.680	6.741	6.803	6.865	6.927	6.990	7.117	7.246	7.376	7.509	7.781
15	6.616	6.674	6.733	6.793	6.853	6.913	6.974	7.097	7.221	7.348	7.476	7.739
16	6.612	6.669	6.727	6.784	6.843	6.901	6.960	7.080	7.201	7.324	7.449	7.705
17	6.609	6.665	6.721	6.777	6.834	6.891	6.949	7.065	7.183	7.304	7.426	7.675
18	6.607	6.661	6.716	6.771	6.827	6.883	6.939	7.053	7.169	7.286	7.406	7.651
19	6.605	6.658	6.712	6.766	6.820	6.875	6.931	7.043	7.156	7.272	7.389	7.629
20	6.603	6.656	6.708	6.761	6.815	6.869	6.924	7.034	7.146	7.259	7.375	7.612
21	6.602	6.653	6.705	6.758	6.811	6.864	6.918	7.026	7.137	7.249	7.363	7.597
22	6.600	6.651	6.703	6.755	6.807	6.860	6.913	7.020	7.129	7.240	7.353	7.584
23	6.599	6.650	6.701	6.752	6.804	6.856	6.908	7.015	7.123	7.233	7.344	7.574
24	6.598	6.649	6.699	6.750	6.801	6.853	6.905	7.010	7.118	7.227	7.338	7.565
25	6.598	6.648	6.698	6.748	6.799	6.850	6.902	7.007	7.114	7.222	7.332	7.558
26	6.597	6.647	6.697	6.747	6.798	6.849	6.900	7.004	7.110	7.218	7.328	7.553
27	6.597	6.646	6.696	6.746	6.796	6.847	6.899	7.002	7.108	7.215	7.325	7.549
28	6.597	6.646	6.695	6.745	6.796	6.846	6.897	7.001	7.106	7.214	7.323	7.547
29	6.596	6.645	6.695	6.745	6.795	6.846	6.897	7.000	7.105	7.212	7.321	7.545
30	6.596	6.645	6.695	6.745	6.795	6.846	6.897	7.000	7.105	7.212	7.321	7.544

Yield on Mortgage Loan When Points Are Paid

Interest Rate   6.75%   25 Year Schedule   Annual Constant   8.290938%

Yield to end of Year	1.0 Point	1.5 Point	2.0 Points	2.5 Points	3.0 Points	3.5 Points	4.0 Points	5.0 Points	6.0 Points	7.0 Points	8.0 Points	10.0 Points
1	7.800	8.329	8.862	9.397	9.936	10.478	11.022	12.122	13.234	14.359	15.498	17.818
2	7.297	7.572	7.850	8.129	8.409	8.691	8.975	9.547	10.126	10.712	11.305	12.512
3	7.130	7.321	7.514	7.708	7.902	8.099	8.296	8.693	9.096	9.503	9.915	10.755
4	7.046	7.196	7.347	7.498	7.651	7.804	7.958	8.269	8.584	8.902	9.225	9.882
5	6.997	7.122	7.247	7.374	7.501	7.628	7.757	8.016	8.279	8.545	8.814	9.363
6	6.964	7.073	7.182	7.291	7.402	7.513	7.624	7.850	8.078	8.309	8.543	9.021
7	6.941	7.038	7.135	7.233	7.332	7.431	7.531	7.732	7.936	8.143	8.352	8.780
8	6.924	7.012	7.101	7.190	7.280	7.371	7.462	7.645	7.832	8.020	8.211	8.602
9	6.911	6.993	7.075	7.158	7.241	7.325	7.409	7.579	7.752	7.927	8.104	8.466
10	6.901	6.977	7.054	7.132	7.210	7.288	7.368	7.527	7.689	7.853	8.020	8.360
11	6.893	6.965	7.038	7.112	7.185	7.260	7.335	7.486	7.639	7.795	7.953	8.276
12	6.886	6.955	7.025	7.095	7.166	7.237	7.308	7.453	7.599	7.748	7.899	8.208
13	6.881	6.947	7.014	7.082	7.149	7.218	7.286	7.425	7.566	7.710	7.855	8.152
14	6.877	6.941	7.005	7.070	7.136	7.202	7.269	7.403	7.540	7.678	7.819	8.107
15	6.873	6.935	6.998	7.061	7.125	7.189	7.254	7.385	7.517	7.652	7.789	8.069
16	6.870	6.931	6.992	7.054	7.116	7.179	7.242	7.370	7.499	7.631	7.765	8.039
17	6.867	6.927	6.987	7.048	7.109	7.170	7.232	7.357	7.484	7.613	7.745	8.013
18	6.865	6.924	6.983	7.042	7.102	7.163	7.224	7.347	7.472	7.599	7.728	7.993
19	6.864	6.922	6.980	7.038	7.098	7.157	7.217	7.339	7.462	7.587	7.715	7.976
20	6.862	6.920	6.977	7.035	7.094	7.152	7.212	7.332	7.454	7.578	7.705	7.963
21	6.861	6.918	6.975	7.033	7.091	7.149	7.208	7.327	7.448	7.571	7.696	7.953
22	6.861	6.917	6.974	7.031	7.088	7.146	7.205	7.323	7.444	7.566	7.691	7.946
23	6.860	6.916	6.973	7.029	7.087	7.145	7.203	7.321	7.441	7.563	7.686	7.941
24	6.860	6.916	6.972	7.029	7.086	7.144	7.202	7.319	7.439	7.560	7.684	7.938
25	6.860	6.916	6.972	7.028	7.086	7.143	7.201	7.319	7.438	7.560	7.683	7.937

Interest Rate   6.75%   30 Year Schedule   Annual Constant   7.783177%

Yield to end of Year	1.0 Point	1.5 Point	2.0 Points	2.5 Points	3.0 Points	3.5 Points	4.0 Points	5.0 Points	6.0 Points	7.0 Points	8.0 Points	10.0 Points
1	7.797	8.325	8.857	9.391	9.928	10.469	11.012	12.109	13.218	14.341	15.477	17.791
2	7.294	7.568	7.844	8.122	8.401	8.681	8.964	9.533	10.109	10.692	11.281	12.482
3	7.127	7.317	7.508	7.700	7.893	8.088	8.284	8.678	9.077	9.481	9.890	10.723
4	7.043	7.191	7.340	7.490	7.641	7.793	7.945	8.253	8.564	8.879	9.198	9.848
5	6.994	7.117	7.241	7.365	7.490	7.616	7.743	7.999	8.258	8.520	8.786	9.327
6	6.961	7.067	7.174	7.282	7.391	7.500	7.610	7.831	8.056	8.283	8.513	8.982
7	6.937	7.032	7.128	7.224	7.320	7.417	7.515	7.713	7.912	8.115	8.320	8.739
8	6.920	7.006	7.093	7.180	7.268	7.356	7.445	7.625	7.806	7.991	8.177	8.558
9	6.907	6.986	7.066	7.147	7.228	7.309	7.391	7.557	7.725	7.895	8.068	8.420
10	6.896	6.971	7.045	7.121	7.196	7.272	7.349	7.504	7.661	7.820	7.981	8.311
11	6.888	6.958	7.029	7.099	7.171	7.243	7.315	7.461	7.609	7.760	7.912	8.224
12	6.881	6.948	7.015	7.082	7.150	7.219	7.287	7.426	7.568	7.711	7.856	8.152
13	6.876	6.939	7.003	7.068	7.133	7.199	7.264	7.398	7.533	7.670	7.809	8.094
14	6.871	6.932	6.994	7.056	7.119	7.182	7.245	7.374	7.504	7.636	7.770	8.045
15	6.867	6.926	6.986	7.046	7.107	7.168	7.229	7.354	7.480	7.608	7.738	8.004
16	6.864	6.921	6.979	7.038	7.097	7.156	7.216	7.337	7.459	7.584	7.711	7.970
17	6.861	6.917	6.974	7.031	7.088	7.146	7.204	7.322	7.442	7.564	7.687	7.940
18	6.858	6.913	6.969	7.025	7.081	7.137	7.195	7.310	7.427	7.547	7.668	7.916
19	6.856	6.910	6.965	7.019	7.075	7.130	7.186	7.300	7.415	7.532	7.651	7.895
20	6.855	6.908	6.961	7.015	7.069	7.124	7.179	7.291	7.404	7.520	7.637	7.877
21	6.853	6.905	6.958	7.011	7.065	7.119	7.173	7.284	7.396	7.509	7.625	7.862
22	6.852	6.904	6.956	7.008	7.061	7.115	7.168	7.277	7.388	7.501	7.615	7.850
23	6.851	6.902	6.954	7.006	7.058	7.111	7.164	7.272	7.382	7.494	7.607	7.840
24	6.850	6.901	6.952	7.004	7.056	7.108	7.161	7.268	7.377	7.488	7.600	7.831
25	6.849	6.900	6.951	7.002	7.054	7.106	7.158	7.265	7.373	7.483	7.595	7.825
26	6.849	6.899	6.950	7.001	7.052	7.104	7.156	7.262	7.370	7.479	7.591	7.819
27	6.848	6.898	6.949	7.000	7.051	7.103	7.155	7.260	7.367	7.477	7.588	7.816
28	6.848	6.898	6.948	6.999	7.050	7.102	7.154	7.259	7.366	7.475	7.585	7.813
29	6.848	6.898	6.948	6.999	7.050	7.101	7.153	7.258	7.365	7.474	7.584	7.811
30	6.848	6.898	6.948	6.998	7.049	7.101	7.153	7.258	7.365	7.473	7.584	7.811

Yield on Mortgage Loan When Points Are Paid

Interest Rate   7.00%   25 Year Schedule   Annual Constant   8.481350%

Yield to end of Year	1.0 Point	1.5 Point	2.0 Points	2.5 Points	3.0 Points	3.5 Points	4.0 Points	5.0 Points	6.0 Points	7.0 Points	8.0 Points	10.0 Points
1	8.051	8.581	9.114	9.650	10.189	10.732	11.277	12.377	13.491	14.617	15.758	18.080
2	7.548	7.824	8.102	8.381	8.662	8.945	9.229	9.803	10.383	10.970	11.564	12.774
3	7.381	7.573	7.766	7.960	8.156	8.352	8.550	8.949	9.353	9.761	10.174	11.017
4	7.297	7.448	7.599	7.751	7.904	8.058	8.212	8.525	8.841	9.161	9.484	10.144
5	7.248	7.373	7.499	7.626	7.754	7.882	8.011	8.272	8.536	8.803	9.074	9.625
6	7.215	7.324	7.434	7.544	7.655	7.767	7.879	8.106	8.335	8.568	8.803	9.283
7	7.192	7.290	7.388	7.486	7.585	7.685	7.785	7.988	8.193	8.401	8.612	9.042
8	7.175	7.264	7.353	7.443	7.534	7.625	7.716	7.901	8.089	8.279	8.471	8.865
9	7.162	7.245	7.327	7.411	7.494	7.579	7.664	7.835	8.009	8.185	8.364	8.729
10	7.152	7.229	7.307	7.385	7.464	7.543	7.622	7.784	7.947	8.112	8.280	8.623
11	7.144	7.217	7.291	7.365	7.439	7.514	7.590	7.742	7.897	8.054	8.213	8.539
12	7.138	7.207	7.277	7.348	7.419	7.491	7.563	7.709	7.857	8.007	8.160	8.471
13	7.132	7.199	7.267	7.335	7.403	7.472	7.542	7.682	7.824	7.969	8.116	8.416
14	7.128	7.193	7.258	7.324	7.390	7.457	7.524	7.660	7.798	7.938	8.080	8.371
15	7.124	7.187	7.251	7.315	7.379	7.444	7.509	7.641	7.776	7.912	8.050	8.334
16	7.121	7.183	7.245	7.307	7.370	7.433	7.497	7.626	7.758	7.891	8.026	8.303
17	7.119	7.179	7.240	7.301	7.363	7.425	7.487	7.614	7.743	7.873	8.006	8.278
18	7.117	7.176	7.236	7.296	7.357	7.418	7.479	7.604	7.730	7.859	7.990	8.258
19	7.115	7.174	7.232	7.292	7.352	7.412	7.473	7.596	7.721	7.848	7.977	8.241
20	7.114	7.172	7.230	7.289	7.348	7.407	7.468	7.589	7.713	7.839	7.966	8.228
21	7.113	7.170	7.228	7.286	7.345	7.404	7.464	7.584	7.707	7.832	7.958	8.219
22	7.112	7.169	7.226	7.284	7.343	7.401	7.461	7.581	7.702	7.826	7.953	8.211
23	7.112	7.168	7.225	7.283	7.341	7.400	7.459	7.578	7.699	7.823	7.949	8.206
24	7.111	7.168	7.225	7.282	7.340	7.399	7.457	7.577	7.698	7.821	7.946	8.203
25	7.111	7.168	7.225	7.282	7.340	7.398	7.457	7.576	7.697	7.820	7.945	8.202

Interest Rate   7.00%   30 Year Schedule   Annual Constant   7.983630%

Yield to end of Year	1.0 Point	1.5 Point	2.0 Points	2.5 Points	3.0 Points	3.5 Points	4.0 Points	5.0 Points	6.0 Points	7.0 Points	8.0 Points	10.0 Points
1	8.048	8.577	9.109	9.644	10.182	10.723	11.267	12.365	13.475	14.599	15.737	18.053
2	7.545	7.820	8.097	8.375	8.654	8.935	9.218	9.789	10.366	10.950	11.541	12.744
3	7.378	7.568	7.760	7.953	8.147	8.342	8.538	8.934	9.334	9.740	10.150	10.985
4	7.294	7.443	7.593	7.743	7.894	8.047	8.200	8.509	8.821	9.138	9.458	10.110
5	7.245	7.368	7.493	7.618	7.744	7.871	7.998	8.255	8.515	8.779	9.046	9.589
6	7.212	7.319	7.427	7.535	7.644	7.754	7.864	8.087	8.313	8.542	8.773	9.245
7	7.189	7.284	7.380	7.477	7.574	7.672	7.770	7.969	8.170	8.374	8.580	9.002
8	7.171	7.258	7.345	7.433	7.522	7.611	7.700	7.881	8.064	8.250	8.438	8.821
9	7.158	7.238	7.319	7.400	7.482	7.564	7.646	7.813	7.983	8.154	8.328	8.683
10	7.148	7.223	7.298	7.374	7.450	7.527	7.604	7.760	7.919	8.079	8.242	8.575
11	7.139	7.210	7.281	7.353	7.425	7.497	7.570	7.718	7.868	8.019	8.173	8.488
12	7.133	7.200	7.267	7.336	7.404	7.473	7.543	7.683	7.826	7.970	8.117	8.417
13	7.127	7.191	7.256	7.321	7.387	7.453	7.520	7.655	7.791	7.930	8.071	8.358
14	7.122	7.184	7.247	7.310	7.373	7.437	7.501	7.631	7.762	7.896	8.032	8.310
15	7.118	7.178	7.239	7.300	7.361	7.423	7.485	7.611	7.738	7.868	8.000	8.269
16	7.115	7.173	7.232	7.291	7.351	7.411	7.471	7.594	7.718	7.844	7.972	8.235
17	7.112	7.169	7.226	7.284	7.342	7.401	7.460	7.580	7.701	7.824	7.949	8.206
18	7.110	7.165	7.222	7.278	7.335	7.393	7.450	7.567	7.686	7.807	7.930	8.181
19	7.108	7.162	7.217	7.273	7.329	7.385	7.442	7.557	7.674	7.793	7.913	8.161
20	7.106	7.160	7.214	7.269	7.324	7.379	7.435	7.548	7.664	7.780	7.899	8.143
21	7.104	7.158	7.211	7.265	7.319	7.374	7.429	7.541	7.655	7.770	7.888	8.128
22	7.103	7.156	7.209	7.262	7.316	7.370	7.424	7.535	7.647	7.762	7.878	8.116
23	7.102	7.154	7.207	7.259	7.313	7.366	7.420	7.530	7.641	7.755	7.870	8.106
24	7.101	7.153	7.205	7.257	7.310	7.363	7.417	7.526	7.636	7.749	7.863	8.098
25	7.101	7.152	7.204	7.256	7.308	7.361	7.414	7.522	7.632	7.744	7.858	8.091
26	7.100	7.151	7.203	7.254	7.307	7.359	7.412	7.520	7.629	7.740	7.854	8.086
27	7.100	7.151	7.202	7.253	7.305	7.358	7.411	7.518	7.627	7.738	7.851	8.082
28	7.100	7.150	7.201	7.253	7.305	7.357	7.410	7.517	7.625	7.736	7.849	8.080
29	7.099	7.150	7.201	7.252	7.304	7.356	7.409	7.516	7.624	7.735	7.847	8.078
30	7.099	7.150	7.201	7.252	7.304	7.356	7.409	7.516	7.624	7.735	7.847	8.078

Yield on Mortgage Loan When Points Are Paid

Interest Rate   7.25%   25 Year Schedule   Annual Constant   8.673682%

Yield to end of Year	1.0 Point	1.5 Point	2.0 Points	2.5 Points	3.0 Points	3.5 Points	4.0 Points	5.0 Points	6.0 Points	7.0 Points	8.0 Points	10.0 Points
1	8.302	8.833	9.366	9.903	10.443	10.986	11.532	12.633	13.748	14.876	16.017	18.342
2	7.799	8.076	8.354	8.634	8.916	9.199	9.484	10.058	10.640	11.228	11.823	13.035
3	7.632	7.824	8.018	8.213	8.409	8.606	8.805	9.205	9.609	10.019	10.434	11.278
4	7.549	7.699	7.851	8.004	8.157	8.312	8.467	8.780	9.098	9.419	9.744	10.406
5	7.499	7.625	7.752	7.879	8.007	8.136	8.266	8.528	8.793	9.061	9.333	9.888
6	7.467	7.576	7.686	7.797	7.908	8.021	8.134	8.361	8.592	8.826	9.063	9.546
7	7.444	7.541	7.640	7.739	7.839	7.939	8.040	8.244	8.451	8.660	8.872	9.305
8	7.427	7.516	7.606	7.696	7.787	7.879	7.971	8.158	8.346	8.538	8.732	9.127
9	7.414	7.496	7.580	7.664	7.748	7.833	7.919	8.091	8.267	8.444	8.624	8.992
10	7.403	7.481	7.559	7.638	7.717	7.797	7.878	8.040	8.204	8.371	8.541	8.887
11	7.395	7.469	7.543	7.618	7.693	7.769	7.845	7.999	8.155	8.313	8.474	8.803
12	7.389	7.459	7.530	7.601	7.673	7.746	7.818	7.966	8.115	8.267	8.420	8.735
13	7.383	7.451	7.519	7.588	7.657	7.727	7.797	7.939	8.083	8.229	8.377	8.680
14	7.379	7.445	7.511	7.577	7.644	7.711	7.779	7.917	8.056	8.197	8.341	8.635
15	7.375	7.439	7.503	7.568	7.633	7.699	7.765	7.898	8.034	8.172	8.312	8.598
16	7.373	7.435	7.497	7.560	7.624	7.688	7.753	7.883	8.016	8.151	8.288	8.568
17	7.370	7.431	7.492	7.554	7.617	7.680	7.743	7.871	8.001	8.133	8.268	8.543
18	7.368	7.428	7.488	7.549	7.611	7.673	7.735	7.861	7.989	8.119	8.252	8.523
19	7.366	7.426	7.485	7.545	7.606	7.667	7.728	7.853	7.979	8.108	8.239	8.507
20	7.365	7.424	7.483	7.542	7.602	7.662	7.723	7.846	7.972	8.099	8.228	8.494
21	7.364	7.422	7.481	7.540	7.599	7.659	7.719	7.842	7.966	8.092	8.220	8.484
22	7.363	7.421	7.479	7.538	7.597	7.656	7.716	7.838	7.961	8.087	8.215	8.477
23	7.363	7.420	7.478	7.537	7.595	7.655	7.714	7.835	7.958	8.083	8.211	8.472
24	7.363	7.420	7.478	7.536	7.594	7.654	7.713	7.834	7.957	8.082	8.208	8.469
25	7.363	7.420	7.477	7.536	7.594	7.653	7.713	7.833	7.956	8.081	8.208	8.468

Interest Rate   7.25%   30 Year Schedule   Annual Constant   8.186115%

Yield to end of Year	1.0 Point	1.5 Point	2.0 Points	2.5 Points	3.0 Points	3.5 Points	4.0 Points	5.0 Points	6.0 Points	7.0 Points	8.0 Points	10.0 Points
1	8.300	8.829	9.361	9.897	10.435	10.977	11.522	12.621	13.733	14.858	15.997	18.316
2	7.796	8.072	8.349	8.627	8.908	9.190	9.473	10.045	10.623	11.208	11.801	13.006
3	7.629	7.820	8.012	8.206	8.400	8.596	8.793	9.190	9.592	9.998	10.409	11.247
4	7.546	7.695	7.845	7.996	8.148	8.301	8.454	8.765	9.078	9.396	9.718	10.373
5	7.496	7.620	7.745	7.871	7.997	8.125	8.253	8.511	8.773	9.037	9.306	9.852
6	7.463	7.571	7.679	7.788	7.898	8.008	8.119	8.344	8.570	8.800	9.033	9.508
7	7.440	7.536	7.632	7.730	7.828	7.926	8.025	8.225	8.428	8.633	8.841	9.265
8	7.423	7.510	7.598	7.686	7.775	7.865	7.955	8.137	8.322	8.509	8.698	9.085
9	7.409	7.490	7.571	7.653	7.735	7.818	7.902	8.070	8.241	8.414	8.589	8.947
10	7.399	7.475	7.550	7.627	7.704	7.781	7.859	8.017	8.177	8.339	8.503	8.839
11	7.391	7.462	7.534	7.606	7.679	7.752	7.826	7.975	8.126	8.279	8.434	8.752
12	7.384	7.452	7.520	7.589	7.658	7.728	7.798	7.940	8.084	8.230	8.378	8.681
13	7.378	7.443	7.509	7.575	7.641	7.708	7.775	7.912	8.050	8.190	8.332	8.623
14	7.374	7.436	7.499	7.563	7.627	7.691	7.756	7.888	8.021	8.156	8.294	8.575
15	7.370	7.430	7.491	7.553	7.615	7.678	7.741	7.868	7.997	8.128	8.261	8.534
16	7.366	7.425	7.485	7.545	7.605	7.666	7.727	7.851	7.977	8.105	8.234	8.500
17	7.364	7.421	7.479	7.538	7.597	7.656	7.716	7.837	7.960	8.085	8.211	8.471
18	7.361	7.418	7.474	7.532	7.589	7.648	7.706	7.825	7.945	8.068	8.192	8.447
19	7.359	7.415	7.470	7.527	7.583	7.641	7.698	7.815	7.933	8.053	8.176	8.427
20	7.357	7.412	7.467	7.522	7.578	7.635	7.691	7.806	7.923	8.041	8.162	8.409
21	7.356	7.410	7.464	7.519	7.574	7.629	7.685	7.799	7.914	8.031	8.150	8.395
22	7.355	7.408	7.462	7.516	7.570	7.625	7.681	7.793	7.907	8.023	8.141	8.383
23	7.354	7.406	7.460	7.513	7.567	7.622	7.677	7.788	7.901	8.016	8.133	8.373
24	7.353	7.405	7.458	7.511	7.565	7.619	7.673	7.784	7.896	8.010	8.126	8.364
25	7.352	7.404	7.457	7.510	7.563	7.617	7.671	7.780	7.892	8.005	8.121	8.358
26	7.352	7.403	7.456	7.508	7.561	7.615	7.669	7.778	7.889	8.002	8.117	8.353
27	7.351	7.403	7.455	7.507	7.560	7.613	7.667	7.776	7.887	7.999	8.114	8.349
28	7.351	7.403	7.454	7.507	7.559	7.612	7.666	7.775	7.885	7.997	8.112	8.347
29	7.351	7.402	7.454	7.506	7.559	7.612	7.665	7.774	7.884	7.996	8.111	8.345
30	7.351	7.402	7.454	7.506	7.559	7.612	7.665	7.774	7.884	7.996	8.110	8.345

Yield on Mortgage Loan When Points Are Paid

Interest Rate   7.50%   25 Year Schedule   Annual Constant   8.867894%

Yield to end of Year	1.0 Point	1.5 Point	2.0 Points	2.5 Points	3.0 Points	3.5 Points	4.0 Points	5.0 Points	6.0 Points	7.0 Points	8.0 Points	10.0 Points
1	8.554	9.084	9.619	10.156	10.696	11.240	11.786	12.889	14.005	15.134	16.277	18.604
2	8.050	8.327	8.606	8.887	9.169	9.453	9.738	10.314	10.897	11.486	12.083	13.297
3	7.883	8.076	8.270	8.466	8.662	8.860	9.059	9.460	9.866	10.277	10.693	11.540
4	7.800	7.951	8.103	8.257	8.411	8.566	8.722	9.036	9.355	9.677	10.003	10.668
5	7.751	7.877	8.004	8.132	8.261	8.390	8.521	8.784	9.050	9.320	9.593	10.150
6	7.718	7.828	7.938	8.050	8.162	8.275	8.388	8.617	8.849	9.084	9.323	9.808
7	7.695	7.793	7.892	7.992	8.092	8.193	8.295	8.500	8.708	8.919	9.132	9.568
8	7.678	7.768	7.858	7.949	8.041	8.133	8.226	8.414	8.604	8.796	8.992	9.391
9	7.665	7.748	7.832	7.917	8.002	8.087	8.174	8.348	8.524	8.703	8.885	9.256
10	7.655	7.733	7.812	7.891	7.971	8.052	8.133	8.296	8.462	8.631	8.801	9.150
11	7.647	7.721	7.796	7.871	7.947	8.023	8.100	8.255	8.413	8.573	8.735	9.067
12	7.640	7.711	7.783	7.855	7.927	8.000	8.074	8.222	8.373	8.526	8.681	8.999
13	7.635	7.703	7.772	7.841	7.911	7.981	8.052	8.195	8.341	8.488	8.638	8.945
14	7.630	7.697	7.763	7.830	7.898	7.966	8.035	8.173	8.314	8.457	8.602	8.900
15	7.627	7.691	7.756	7.821	7.887	7.953	8.020	8.155	8.292	8.432	8.573	8.863
16	7.624	7.687	7.750	7.814	7.878	7.943	8.008	8.140	8.275	8.411	8.549	8.833
17	7.621	7.683	7.745	7.808	7.871	7.934	7.999	8.128	8.260	8.394	8.530	8.808
18	7.619	7.680	7.741	7.803	7.865	7.928	7.991	8.118	8.248	8.380	8.514	8.788
19	7.618	7.678	7.738	7.799	7.860	7.922	7.984	8.110	8.238	8.368	8.501	8.772
20	7.617	7.676	7.736	7.796	7.856	7.917	7.979	8.104	8.231	8.359	8.491	8.760
21	7.616	7.674	7.734	7.793	7.853	7.914	7.975	8.099	8.225	8.353	8.483	8.750
22	7.615	7.673	7.732	7.791	7.851	7.911	7.972	8.095	8.220	8.348	8.477	8.743
23	7.614	7.673	7.731	7.790	7.850	7.910	7.970	8.093	8.217	8.344	8.473	8.738
24	7.614	7.672	7.731	7.789	7.849	7.909	7.969	8.091	8.216	8.342	8.471	8.735
25	7.614	7.672	7.730	7.789	7.849	7.908	7.969	8.091	8.215	8.342	8.470	8.734

Interest Rate   7.50%   30 Year Schedule   Annual Constant   8.390574%

Yield to end of Year	1.0 Point	1.5 Point	2.0 Points	2.5 Points	3.0 Points	3.5 Points	4.0 Points	5.0 Points	6.0 Points	7.0 Points	8.0 Points	10.0 Points
1	8.551	9.081	9.614	10.150	10.689	11.231	11.777	12.877	13.990	15.117	16.257	18.579
2	8.047	8.323	8.601	8.880	9.161	9.444	9.728	10.301	10.880	11.467	12.060	13.269
3	7.880	8.072	8.265	8.459	8.654	8.850	9.048	9.446	9.849	10.256	10.669	11.510
4	7.797	7.947	8.097	8.249	8.401	8.555	8.709	9.021	9.336	9.655	9.978	10.636
5	7.747	7.872	7.998	8.124	8.251	8.379	8.508	8.767	9.030	9.296	9.566	10.115
6	7.714	7.823	7.932	8.041	8.152	8.263	8.374	8.600	8.828	9.059	9.293	9.771
7	7.691	7.788	7.885	7.983	8.081	8.180	8.280	8.481	8.685	8.892	9.101	9.528
8	7.674	7.762	7.850	7.940	8.029	8.119	8.210	8.394	8.580	8.768	8.959	9.348
9	7.661	7.742	7.824	7.906	7.989	8.073	8.157	8.327	8.499	8.673	8.850	9.211
10	7.651	7.726	7.803	7.880	7.958	8.036	8.115	8.274	8.435	8.598	8.764	9.103
11	7.642	7.714	7.786	7.859	7.933	8.007	8.081	8.231	8.384	8.539	8.696	9.016
12	7.635	7.704	7.773	7.842	7.912	7.983	8.054	8.197	8.342	8.490	8.640	8.946
13	7.630	7.695	7.762	7.828	7.895	7.963	8.031	8.169	8.308	8.450	8.594	8.888
14	7.625	7.688	7.752	7.816	7.881	7.946	8.012	8.145	8.280	8.417	8.555	8.840
15	7.621	7.682	7.744	7.807	7.869	7.933	7.996	8.125	8.256	8.389	8.523	8.800
16	7.618	7.677	7.738	7.798	7.859	7.921	7.983	8.108	8.236	8.365	8.497	8.766
17	7.615	7.673	7.732	7.791	7.851	7.911	7.972	8.094	8.219	8.345	8.474	8.737
18	7.613	7.670	7.727	7.785	7.844	7.903	7.962	8.082	8.204	8.329	8.455	8.713
19	7.611	7.667	7.723	7.780	7.838	7.896	7.954	8.072	8.192	8.314	8.438	8.693
20	7.609	7.664	7.720	7.776	7.833	7.890	7.947	8.064	8.182	8.302	8.425	8.676
21	7.607	7.662	7.717	7.773	7.828	7.885	7.942	8.057	8.174	8.292	8.413	8.661
22	7.606	7.660	7.715	7.770	7.825	7.881	7.937	8.051	8.166	8.284	8.404	8.649
23	7.605	7.659	7.713	7.767	7.822	7.877	7.933	8.046	8.160	8.277	8.396	8.639
24	7.604	7.658	7.711	7.765	7.819	7.874	7.930	8.042	8.156	8.271	8.389	8.631
25	7.604	7.657	7.710	7.763	7.818	7.872	7.927	8.038	8.152	8.267	8.384	8.625
26	7.603	7.656	7.709	7.762	7.816	7.870	7.925	8.036	8.149	8.263	8.380	8.620
27	7.603	7.655	7.708	7.761	7.815	7.869	7.924	8.034	8.146	8.261	8.377	8.616
28	7.603	7.655	7.707	7.761	7.814	7.868	7.922	8.033	8.145	8.259	8.375	8.614
29	7.602	7.655	7.707	7.760	7.814	7.868	7.922	8.032	8.144	8.258	8.374	8.613
30	7.602	7.655	7.707	7.760	7.813	7.867	7.922	8.032	8.144	8.258	8.374	8.612

Yield on Mortgage Loan When Points Are Paid

Interest Rate   7.75%   25 Year Schedule   Annual Constant   9.063945%

Yield to end of Year	1.0 Point	1.5 Point	2.0 Points	2.5 Points	3.0 Points	3.5 Points	4.0 Points	5.0 Points	6.0 Points	7.0 Points	8.0 Points	10.0 Points
1	8.805	9.336	9.871	10.409	10.950	11.494	12.041	13.145	14.262	15.393	16.537	18.867
2	8.301	8.579	8.859	9.140	9.423	9.707	9.993	10.570	11.154	11.744	12.342	13.559
3	8.134	8.328	8.523	8.719	8.916	9.114	9.314	9.716	10.123	10.535	10.953	11.802
4	8.051	8.203	8.356	8.509	8.664	8.820	8.976	9.292	9.612	9.935	10.263	10.931
5	8.001	8.128	8.256	8.385	8.514	8.644	8.775	9.040	9.307	9.578	9.853	10.412
6	7.969	8.079	8.191	8.303	8.416	8.529	8.643	8.873	9.107	9.343	9.583	10.071
7	7.946	8.045	8.145	8.245	8.346	8.448	8.550	8.756	8.966	9.178	9.392	9.831
8	7.929	8.019	8.111	8.202	8.295	8.388	8.481	8.670	8.861	9.055	9.252	9.654
9	7.916	8.000	8.085	8.170	8.256	8.342	8.429	8.604	8.782	8.962	9.145	9.519
10	7.906	7.985	8.064	8.144	8.225	8.306	8.388	8.553	8.720	8.890	9.062	9.414
11	7.898	7.973	8.048	8.124	8.201	8.278	8.355	8.512	8.671	8.832	8.996	9.331
12	7.891	7.963	8.035	8.108	8.181	8.255	8.329	8.479	8.631	8.786	8.943	9.264
13	7.886	7.955	8.025	8.095	8.165	8.236	8.308	8.452	8.599	8.748	8.899	9.209
14	7.882	7.949	8.016	8.084	8.152	8.221	8.290	8.430	8.573	8.717	8.864	9.165
15	7.878	7.943	8.009	8.075	8.141	8.208	8.276	8.412	8.551	8.692	8.835	9.128
16	7.875	7.939	8.003	8.067	8.132	8.198	8.264	8.398	8.533	8.671	8.811	9.098
17	7.873	7.935	7.998	8.061	8.125	8.189	8.254	8.385	8.519	8.654	8.792	9.074
18	7.871	7.932	7.994	8.056	8.119	8.183	8.246	8.376	8.507	8.640	8.776	9.054
19	7.869	7.930	7.991	8.052	8.114	8.177	8.240	8.368	8.497	8.629	8.763	9.038
20	7.868	7.928	7.988	8.049	8.111	8.173	8.235	8.361	8.490	8.620	8.753	9.025
21	7.867	7.927	7.986	8.047	8.108	8.169	8.231	8.356	8.484	8.613	8.745	9.016
22	7.866	7.925	7.985	8.045	8.106	8.167	8.228	8.353	8.480	8.608	8.740	9.009
23	7.866	7.925	7.984	8.044	8.104	8.165	8.226	8.350	8.477	8.605	8.736	9.004
24	7.866	7.924	7.983	8.043	8.103	8.164	8.225	8.349	8.475	8.603	8.734	9.001
25	7.865	7.924	7.983	8.043	8.103	8.164	8.225	8.349	8.474	8.603	8.733	9.000

Interest Rate   7.75%   30 Year Schedule   Annual Constant   8.596947%

Yield to end of Year	1.0 Point	1.5 Point	2.0 Points	2.5 Points	3.0 Points	3.5 Points	4.0 Points	5.0 Points	6.0 Points	7.0 Points	8.0 Points	10.0 Points
1	8.802	9.333	9.866	10.403	10.943	11.486	12.032	13.133	14.248	15.376	16.517	18.842
2	8.298	8.575	8.853	9.133	9.415	9.698	9.982	10.557	11.138	11.725	12.320	13.531
3	8.131	8.324	8.517	8.712	8.907	9.104	9.302	9.702	10.106	10.515	10.929	11.772
4	8.048	8.198	8.350	8.502	8.655	8.809	8.964	9.277	9.593	9.913	10.238	10.898
5	7.998	8.124	8.250	8.377	8.505	8.633	8.762	9.023	9.288	9.555	9.826	10.378
6	7.965	8.074	8.184	8.294	8.405	8.517	8.629	8.856	9.086	9.318	9.554	10.034
7	7.942	8.040	8.137	8.236	8.335	8.435	8.535	8.738	8.943	9.151	9.362	9.792
8	7.925	8.014	8.103	8.193	8.283	8.374	8.465	8.650	8.838	9.027	9.220	9.612
9	7.912	7.994	8.077	8.160	8.243	8.327	8.412	8.583	8.757	8.933	9.111	9.475
10	7.902	7.978	8.056	8.134	8.212	8.291	8.370	8.531	8.693	8.858	9.025	9.367
11	7.893	7.966	8.039	8.113	8.187	8.261	8.337	8.488	8.642	8.799	8.957	9.281
12	7.887	7.956	8.025	8.096	8.166	8.237	8.309	8.454	8.601	8.750	8.901	9.211
13	7.881	7.947	8.014	8.082	8.149	8.218	8.287	8.426	8.567	8.710	8.856	9.153
14	7.876	7.940	8.005	8.070	8.135	8.201	8.268	8.402	8.539	8.677	8.817	9.105
15	7.872	7.935	7.997	8.060	8.124	8.188	8.252	8.382	8.515	8.649	8.786	9.065
16	7.869	7.930	7.991	8.052	8.114	8.176	8.239	8.366	8.495	8.626	8.759	9.032
17	7.866	7.925	7.985	8.045	8.105	8.166	8.228	8.352	8.478	8.606	8.736	9.003
18	7.864	7.922	7.980	8.039	8.098	8.158	8.218	8.340	8.464	8.590	8.717	8.979
19	7.862	7.919	7.976	8.034	8.092	8.151	8.210	8.330	8.452	8.575	8.701	8.959
20	7.860	7.916	7.973	8.030	8.087	8.145	8.204	8.322	8.442	8.564	8.688	8.942
21	7.859	7.914	7.970	8.026	8.083	8.140	8.198	8.315	8.433	8.554	8.676	8.928
22	7.858	7.913	7.968	8.023	8.080	8.136	8.193	8.309	8.426	8.545	8.667	8.916
23	7.857	7.911	7.966	8.021	8.077	8.133	8.189	8.304	8.420	8.539	8.659	8.907
24	7.856	7.910	7.964	8.019	8.074	8.130	8.186	8.300	8.415	8.533	8.653	8.899
25	7.855	7.909	7.963	8.017	8.072	8.128	8.183	8.297	8.412	8.529	8.648	8.892
26	7.855	7.908	7.962	8.016	8.071	8.126	8.181	8.294	8.409	8.525	8.644	8.888
27	7.854	7.908	7.961	8.015	8.070	8.125	8.180	8.292	8.406	8.523	8.641	8.884
28	7.854	7.907	7.961	8.015	8.069	8.124	8.179	8.291	8.405	8.521	8.639	8.882
29	7.854	7.907	7.960	8.014	8.068	8.123	8.178	8.290	8.404	8.520	8.638	8.880
30	7.854	7.907	7.960	8.014	8.068	8.123	8.178	8.290	8.404	8.520	8.637	8.880

Yield on Mortgage Loan When Points Are Paid

Interest Rate 8.00% 25 Year Schedule   Annual Constant 9.261795%

Yield to end of Year	1.0 Point	1.5 Point	2.0 Points	2.5 Points	3.0 Points	3.5 Points	4.0 Points	5.0 Points	6.0 Points	7.0 Points	8.0 Points	10.0 Points
1	9.056	9.588	10.123	10.662	11.203	11.748	12.296	13.401	14.519	15.651	16.796	19.129
2	8.553	8.831	9.111	9.393	9.676	9.961	10.247	10.826	11.411	12.002	12.601	13.821
3	8.385	8.579	8.775	8.971	9.169	9.368	9.568	9.972	10.380	10.794	11.212	12.065
4	8.302	8.455	8.608	8.762	8.918	9.074	9.231	9.548	9.869	10.194	10.523	11.193
5	8.253	8.380	8.509	8.638	8.768	8.899	9.030	9.296	9.565	9.837	10.113	10.675
6	8.220	8.331	8.443	8.556	8.669	8.783	8.898	9.130	9.364	9.602	9.843	10.334
7	8.197	8.297	8.397	8.498	8.600	8.702	8.805	9.013	9.223	9.436	9.653	10.094
8	8.180	8.271	8.363	8.455	8.548	8.642	8.736	8.926	9.119	9.315	9.513	9.917
9	8.168	8.252	8.337	8.423	8.509	8.596	8.684	8.861	9.040	9.222	9.406	9.783
10	8.158	8.237	8.317	8.398	8.479	8.561	8.643	8.809	8.978	9.149	9.323	9.678
11	8.149	8.225	8.301	8.377	8.455	8.532	8.611	8.769	8.929	9.092	9.257	9.595
12	8.143	8.215	8.288	8.361	8.435	8.509	8.584	8.736	8.890	9.046	9.204	9.528
13	8.137	8.207	8.277	8.348	8.419	8.491	8.563	8.709	8.858	9.008	9.161	9.474
14	8.133	8.201	8.269	8.337	8.406	8.476	8.546	8.687	8.831	8.977	9.126	9.430
15	8.130	8.195	8.262	8.328	8.395	8.463	8.531	8.669	8.810	8.952	9.097	9.393
16	8.127	8.191	8.256	8.321	8.387	8.453	8.520	8.655	8.792	8.931	9.073	9.364
17	8.124	8.187	8.251	8.315	8.379	8.445	8.510	8.643	8.778	8.915	9.054	9.339
18	8.122	8.184	8.247	8.310	8.374	8.438	8.502	8.633	8.766	8.901	9.038	9.320
19	8.121	8.182	8.244	8.306	8.369	8.432	8.496	8.625	8.756	8.890	9.025	9.304
20	8.119	8.180	8.241	8.303	8.365	8.428	8.491	8.619	8.749	8.881	9.015	9.291
21	8.119	8.179	8.239	8.301	8.362	8.424	8.487	8.614	8.743	8.874	9.008	9.282
22	8.118	8.178	8.238	8.299	8.360	8.422	8.484	8.611	8.739	8.869	9.002	9.275
23	8.118	8.177	8.237	8.298	8.359	8.420	8.482	8.608	8.736	8.866	8.999	9.270
24	8.118	8.177	8.236	8.297	8.358	8.419	8.481	8.607	8.734	8.864	8.996	9.268
25	8.117	8.176	8.236	8.297	8.358	8.419	8.481	8.606	8.734	8.864	8.996	9.267

Interest Rate 8.00% 30 Year Schedule   Annual Constant 8.805175%

Yield to end of Year	1.0 Point	1.5 Point	2.0 Points	2.5 Points	3.0 Points	3.5 Points	4.0 Points	5.0 Points	6.0 Points	7.0 Points	8.0 Points	10.0 Points
1	9.054	9.584	10.119	10.656	11.196	11.740	12.287	13.389	14.505	15.634	16.777	19.105
2	8.550	8.827	9.106	9.386	9.668	9.952	10.237	10.813	11.395	11.984	12.580	13.794
3	8.382	8.575	8.769	8.965	9.161	9.358	9.557	9.958	10.363	10.774	11.189	12.035
4	8.299	8.450	8.602	8.755	8.909	9.063	9.219	9.533	9.851	10.172	10.498	11.161
5	8.249	8.376	8.502	8.630	8.758	8.888	9.017	9.280	9.545	9.814	10.086	10.641
6	8.217	8.326	8.437	8.547	8.659	8.771	8.884	9.112	9.343	9.577	9.814	10.298
7	8.194	8.291	8.390	8.489	8.589	8.689	8.790	8.994	9.201	9.410	9.623	10.056
8	8.176	8.266	8.356	8.446	8.537	8.629	8.721	8.907	9.096	9.287	9.481	9.876
9	8.164	8.246	8.329	8.413	8.497	8.582	8.667	8.840	9.015	9.192	9.372	9.739
10	8.153	8.230	8.308	8.387	8.466	8.546	8.626	8.787	8.952	9.118	9.287	9.632
11	8.145	8.218	8.292	8.366	8.441	8.516	8.592	8.745	8.901	9.059	9.219	9.546
12	8.138	8.208	8.278	8.349	8.421	8.492	8.565	8.711	8.860	9.010	9.163	9.476
13	8.132	8.199	8.267	8.335	8.404	8.473	8.542	8.683	8.826	8.971	9.118	9.418
14	8.128	8.193	8.258	8.324	8.390	8.456	8.524	8.660	8.797	8.938	9.080	9.371
15	8.124	8.187	8.250	8.314	8.378	8.443	8.508	8.640	8.774	8.910	9.048	9.331
16	8.121	8.182	8.244	8.306	8.368	8.431	8.495	8.623	8.754	8.887	9.022	9.298
17	8.118	8.178	8.238	8.299	8.360	8.422	8.484	8.610	8.737	8.867	8.999	9.270
18	8.116	8.174	8.233	8.293	8.353	8.413	8.474	8.598	8.723	8.851	8.980	9.246
19	8.114	8.171	8.229	8.288	8.347	8.407	8.467	8.588	8.711	8.837	8.964	9.226
20	8.112	8.169	8.226	8.284	8.342	8.401	8.460	8.580	8.701	8.825	8.951	9.209
21	8.111	8.167	8.223	8.280	8.338	8.396	8.454	8.573	8.693	8.815	8.940	9.195
22	8.110	8.165	8.221	8.277	8.334	8.392	8.450	8.567	8.686	8.807	8.930	9.184
23	8.108	8.164	8.219	8.275	8.331	8.388	8.446	8.562	8.680	8.800	8.923	9.174
24	8.108	8.162	8.217	8.273	8.329	8.386	8.443	8.558	8.675	8.795	8.916	9.166
25	8.107	8.161	8.216	8.271	8.327	8.383	8.440	8.555	8.672	8.790	8.911	9.160
26	8.107	8.161	8.215	8.270	8.326	8.382	8.438	8.552	8.669	8.787	8.908	9.155
27	8.107	8.160	8.214	8.269	8.325	8.380	8.437	8.551	8.667	8.785	8.905	9.152
28	8.106	8.160	8.214	8.269	8.324	8.379	8.436	8.549	8.665	8.783	8.903	9.149
29	8.106	8.160	8.214	8.268	8.323	8.379	8.435	8.549	8.664	8.782	8.902	9.148
30	8.106	8.160	8.214	8.268	8.323	8.379	8.435	8.548	8.664	8.782	8.901	9.147

Yield on Mortgage Loan When Points Are Paid

Interest Rate   8.25%   25 Year Schedule   Annual Constant   9.461402%

Yield to end of Year	1.0 Point	1.5 Point	2.0 Points	2.5 Points	3.0 Points	3.5 Points	4.0 Points	5.0 Points	6.0 Points	7.0 Points	8.0 Points	10.0 Points
1	9.307	9.840	10.376	10.915	11.457	12.002	12.551	13.657	14.777	15.910	17.056	19.392
2	8.804	9.082	9.363	9.645	9.929	10.215	10.502	11.081	11.668	12.261	12.861	14.084
3	8.636	8.831	9.027	9.224	9.423	9.622	9.823	10.228	10.637	11.052	11.472	12.327
4	8.553	8.706	8.860	9.015	9.171	9.328	9.486	9.804	10.126	10.452	10.782	11.455
5	8.504	8.632	8.761	8.891	9.021	9.153	9.285	9.552	9.822	10.096	10.373	10.938
6	8.471	8.583	8.696	8.809	8.923	9.037	9.153	9.386	9.622	9.861	10.103	10.597
7	8.448	8.549	8.650	8.751	8.853	8.956	9.060	9.269	9.481	9.695	9.913	10.357
8	8.432	8.523	8.616	8.709	8.802	8.896	8.991	9.183	9.377	9.574	9.773	10.181
9	8.418	·8.504	8.590	8.676	8.763	8.851	8.939	9.117	9.298	9.481	9.667	10.047
10	8.409	8.489	8.570	8.651	8.733	8.815	8.898	9.066	9.236	9.409	9.584	9.942
11	8.401	8.477	8.553	8.631	8.709	8.787	8.866	9.026	9.187	9.352	9.518	9.859
12	8.394	8.467	8.541	8.615	8.689	8.764	8.840	8.993	9.148	9.306	9.465	9.793
13	8.389	8.459	8.530	8.601	8.673	8.746	8.819	8.966	9.116	9.268	9.423	9.739
14	8.384	8.453	8.521	8.591	8.660	8.731	8.801	8.945	9.090	9.238	9.388	9.695
15	8.381	8.447	8.514	8.582	8.650	8.718	8.787	8.927	9.069	9.213	9.359	9.659
16	8.378	8.443	8.509	8.575	8.641	8.708	8.776	8.912	9.051	9.192	9.335	9.629
17	8.376	8.439	8.504	8.569	8.634	8.700	8.766	8.900	9.037	9.175	9.316	9.605
18	8.374	8.437	8.500	8.564	8.628	8.693	8.758	8.890	9.025	9.162	9.301	9.586
19	8.372	8.434	8.497	8.560	8.623	8.687	8.752	8.883	9.016	9.151	9.288	9.570
20	8.371	8.432	8.494	8.557	8.620	8.683	8.747	8.877	9.008	9.142	9.278	9.558
21	8.370	8.431	8.493	8.554	8.617	8.680	8.743	8.872	9.002	9.135	9.271	9.548
22	8.370	8.430	8.491	8.553	8.615	8.677	8.740	8.868	8.998	9.131	9.265	9.542
23	8.369	8.429	8.490	8.551	8.613	8.676	8.739	8.866	8.996	9.127	9.261	9.537
24	8.369	8.429	8.490	8.551	8.612	8.675	8.737	8.865	8.994	9.125	9.259	9.534
25	8.368	8.429	8.489	8.550	8.612	8.674	8.737	8.864	8.993	9.125	9.259	9.533

Interest Rate   8.25%   30 Year Schedule   Annual Constant   9.015199%

Yield to end of Year	1.0 Point	1.5 Point	2.0 Points	2.5 Points	3.0 Points	3.5 Points	4.0 Points	5.0 Points	6.0 Points	7.0 Points	8.0 Points	10.0 Points
1	9.305	9.836	10.371	10.909	11.450	11.994	12.541	13.646	14.763	15.893	17.037	19.368
2	8.801	9.079	9.358	9.639	9.922	10.206	10.492	11.069	11.652	12.243	12.840	14.057
3	8.633	8.827	9.022	9.218	9.415	9.613	9.812	10.214	10.621	11.033	11.449	12.298
4	8.551	8.702	8.855	9.008	9.162	9.318	9.474	9.789	10.108	10.431	10.758	11.424
5	8.501	8.627	8.755	8.883	9.012	9.142	9.273	9.536	9.803	10.073	10.347	10.905
6	8.468	8.578	8.689	8.801	8.913	9.026	9.140	9.369	9.601	9.837	10.075	10.562
7	8.445	8.543	8.643	8.742	8.843	8.944	9.046	9.251	9.459	9.670	9.883	10.319
8	8.428	8.518	8.608	8.699	8.791	8.883	8.976	9.164	9.354	9.546	9.742	10.141
9	8.415	8.498	8.582	8.666	8.751	8.837	8.923	9.097	9.273	9.452	9.633	10.004
10	8.405	8.482	8.561	8.640	8.720	8.800	8.881	9.044	9.210	9.378	9.548	9.897
11	8.396	8.470	8.545	8.620	8.695	8.771	8.848	9.003	9.160	9.319	9.480	9.811
12	8.389	8.460	8.531	8.603	8.675	8.747	8.821	8.968	9.118	9.271	9.425	9.741
13	8.384	8.452	8.520	8.589	8.658	8.728	8.798	8.940	9.085	9.231	9.380	9.684
14	8.379	8.445	8.511	8.577	8.644	8.712	8.780	8.917	9.057	9.198	9.342	9.637
15	8.376	8.439	8.503	8.568	8.633	8.698	8.764	8.898	9.033	9.171	9.311	9.597
16	8.372	8.434	8.497	8.559	8.623	8.687	8.751	8.881	9.013	9.148	9.284	9.564
17	8.370	8.430	8.491	8.553	8.615	8.677	8.740	8.867	8.997	9.128	9.262	9.536
18	8.368	8.426	8.486	8.547	8.608	8.669	8.731	8.856	8.983	9.112	9.243	9.513
19	8.366	8.424	8.482	8.542	8.602	8.662	8.723	8.846	8.971	9.098	9.228	9.493
20	8.364	8.421	8.479	8.538	8.597	8.656	8.716	8.838	8.961	9.087	9.214	9.476
21	8.363	8.419	8.476	8.534	8.593	8.651	8.711	8.831	8.953	9.077	9.203	9.463
22	8.361	8.418	8.474	8.531	8.589	8.647	8.706	8.825	8.946	9.069	9.194	9.451
23	8.360	8.416	8.472	8.529	8.586	8.644	8.702	8.820	8.940	9.062	9.186	9.442
24	8.360	8.415	8.471	8.527	8.584	8.641	8.699	8.816	8.936	9.057	9.180	9.434
25	8.359	8.414	8.470	8.525	8.582	8.639	8.697	8.813	8.932	9.053	9.175	9.428
26	8.359	8.413	8.468	8.524	8.581	8.637	8.695	8.811	8.929	9.049	9.172	9.423
27	8.358	8.412	8.468	8.523	8.580	8.636	8.693	8.809	8.927	9.047	9.169	9.420
28	8.358	8.413	8.468	8.523	8.579	8.636	8.692	8.808	8.925	9.045	9.167	9.417
29	8.358	8.412	8.467	8.523	8.578	8.635	8.692	8.807	8.925	9.044	9.166	9.416
30	8.358	8.412	8.467	8.523	8.578	8.635	8.692	8.807	8.924	9.044	9.165	9.416

Yield on Mortgage Loan When Points Are Paid

Interest Rate   8.50%   25 Year Schedule   Annual Constant   9.662725%

Yield to end of Year	1.0 Point	1.5 Point	2.0 Points	2.5 Points	3.0 Points	3.5 Points	4.0 Points	5.0 Points	6.0 Points	7.0 Points	8.0 Points	10.0 Points
1	9.558	10.091	10.628	11.168	11.710	12.256	12.805	13.913	15.034	16.168	17.316	19.655
2	9.055	9.334	9.615	9.898	10.183	10.469	10.757	11.337	11.925	12.519	13.121	14.346
3	8.887	9.083	9.279	9.477	9.676	9.876	10.078	10.484	10.895	11.311	11.732	12.589
4	8.804	8.958	9.113	9.268	9.425	9.582	9.740	10.060	10.383	10.711	11.042	11.718
5	8.755	8.884	9.013	9.144	9.275	9.407	9.540	9.808	10.079	10.354	10.633	11.201
6	8.722	8.835	8.948	9.062	9.176	9.292	9.408	9.642	9.879	10.120	10.363	10.860
7	8.700	8.801	8.902	9.004	9.107	9.211	9.315	9.525	9.739	9.955	10.174	10.621
8	8.683	8.775	8.868	8.962	9.056	9.151	9.246	9.439	9.635	9.833	10.034	10.445
9	8.670	8.756	8.842	8.929	9.017	9.105	9.194	9.374	9.556	9.741	9.928	10.311
10	8.660	8.741	8.822	8.904	8.987	9.070	9.154	9.323	9.495	9.669	9.845	10.207
11	8.652	8.729	8.806	8.884	8.963	9.042	9.121	9.282	9.446	9.612	9.780	10.124
12	8.646	8.719	8.793	8.868	8.943	9.019	9.095	9.250	9.407	9.566	9.727	10.058
13	8.640	8.711	8.783	8.855	8.928	9.001	9.074	9.223	9.375	9.528	9.684	10.004
14	8.636	8.705	8.774	8.844	8.915	8.986	9.057	9.202	9.349	9.498	9.650	9.960
15	8.632	8.700	8.767	8.835	8.904	8.973	9.043	9.184	9.327	9.473	9.621	9.924
16	8.630	8.695	8.761	8.828	8.895	8.963	9.031	9.170	9.310	9.453	9.598	9.895
17	8.628	8.692	8.757	8.822	8.888	8.955	9.022	9.158	9.296	9.436	9.579	9.871
18	8.626	8.689	8.753	8.817	8.883	8.948	9.014	9.148	9.284	9.423	9.563	9.852
19	8.624	8.686	8.750	8.814	8.878	8.943	9.008	9.140	9.275	9.412	9.551	9.836
20	8.623	8.685	8.747	8.810	8.874	8.938	9.003	9.134	9.268	9.403	9.541	9.824
21	8.622	8.684	8.745	8.808	8.871	8.935	8.999	9.130	9.262	9.397	9.534	9.815
22	8.621	8.682	8.745	8.806	8.869	8.933	8.997	9.126	9.258	9.392	9.528	9.808
23	8.621	8.682	8.743	8.805	8.868	8.931	8.995	9.124	9.255	9.389	9.525	9.804
24	8.621	8.682	8.743	8.805	8.867	8.930	8.994	9.123	9.254	9.387	9.522	9.801
25	8.620	8.681	8.743	8.804	8.867	8.930	8.993	9.122	9.253	9.386	9.522	9.800

Interest Rate   8.50%   30 Year Schedule   Annual Constant   9.226962%

Yield to end of Year	1.0 Point	1.5 Point	2.0 Points	2.5 Points	3.0 Points	3.5 Points	4.0 Points	5.0 Points	6.0 Points	7.0 Points	8.0 Points	10.0 Points
1	9.556	10.088	10.624	11.162	11.704	12.249	12.796	13.902	15.020	16.152	17.298	19.631
2	9.052	9.330	9.611	9.892	10.176	10.460	10.747	11.325	11.910	12.501	13.100	14.320
3	8.885	9.079	9.274	9.471	9.668	9.867	10.067	10.470	10.878	11.291	11.709	12.561
4	8.801	8.954	9.107	9.261	9.416	9.572	9.729	10.045	10.366	10.690	11.019	11.688
5	8.752	8.879	9.007	9.136	9.266	9.396	9.528	9.793	10.061	10.332	10.607	11.168
6	8.719	8.830	8.942	9.054	9.167	9.280	9.395	9.626	9.859	10.096	10.336	10.825
7	8.696	8.795	8.895	8.996	9.097	9.198	9.301	9.508	9.717	9.929	10.145	10.584
8	8.680	8.770	8.861	8.953	9.045	9.138	9.232	9.421	9.612	9.806	10.003	10.405
9	8.666	8.750	8.835	8.920	9.005	9.092	9.178	9.354	9.532	9.712	9.895	10.269
10	8.656	8.735	8.814	8.894	8.974	9.055	9.137	9.302	9.469	9.638	9.810	10.162
11	8.647	8.722	8.797	8.873	8.949	9.026	9.103	9.260	9.418	9.579	9.742	10.076
12	8.641	8.712	8.784	8.856	8.929	9.002	9.076	9.226	9.377	9.531	9.687	10.007
13	8.636	8.704	8.773	8.842	8.912	8.983	9.054	9.198	9.344	9.492	9.642	9.950
14	8.631	8.697	8.764	8.831	8.899	8.967	9.036	9.175	9.316	9.459	9.605	9.903
15	8.627	8.691	8.756	8.821	8.887	8.953	9.020	9.155	9.292	9.432	9.573	9.864
16	8.624	8.686	8.750	8.813	8.877	8.942	9.007	9.139	9.273	9.409	9.547	9.831
17	8.621	8.682	8.745	8.806	8.869	8.932	8.996	9.125	9.256	9.390	9.525	9.803
18	8.619	8.679	8.739	8.801	8.862	8.924	8.987	9.114	9.243	9.374	9.507	9.780
19	8.617	8.676	8.736	8.796	8.856	8.918	8.979	9.104	9.231	9.360	9.491	9.760
20	8.616	8.674	8.732	8.792	8.852	8.912	8.973	9.096	9.221	9.348	9.478	9.744
21	8.614	8.671	8.730	8.788	8.847	8.907	8.967	9.089	9.213	9.339	9.467	9.730
22	8.613	8.670	8.727	8.785	8.844	8.903	8.963	9.083	9.206	9.331	9.458	9.719
23	8.612	8.669	8.725	8.783	8.841	8.900	8.959	9.079	9.200	9.324	9.450	9.709
24	8.611	8.668	8.724	8.781	8.839	8.897	8.956	9.075	9.196	9.319	9.444	9.702
25	8.611	8.667	8.723	8.780	8.837	8.895	8.953	9.072	9.192	9.315	9.440	9.696
26	8.610	8.666	8.722	8.779	8.836	8.893	8.952	9.069	9.189	9.311	9.436	9.691
27	8.610	8.665	8.721	8.778	8.835	8.892	8.950	9.068	9.187	9.309	9.433	9.688
28	8.610	8.665	8.721	8.777	8.834	8.891	8.949	9.066	9.186	9.307	9.431	9.686
29	8.609	8.664	8.720	8.777	8.833	8.891	8.949	9.066	9.185	9.307	9.430	9.684
30	8.609	8.664	8.720	8.777	8.833	8.891	8.948	9.066	9.185	9.306	9.430	9.684

Yield on Mortgage Loan When Points Are Paid

Interest Rate   8.75%   25 Year Schedule   Annual Constant   9.865724%

Yield to end of Year	1.0 Point	1.5 Point	2.0 Points	2.5 Points	3.0 Points	3.5 Points	4.0 Points	5.0 Points	6.0 Points	7.0 Points	8.0 Points	10.0 Points
1	9.809	10.343	10.880	11.421	11.964	12.510	13.060	14.169	15.291	16.427	17.576	19.917
2	9.305	9.586	9.868	10.151	10.436	10.723	11.011	11.593	12.182	12.778	13.381	14.608
3	9.138	9.335	9.532	9.730	9.930	10.130	10.332	10.740	11.152	11.569	11.991	12.852
4	9.055	9.210	9.365	9.521	9.678	9.836	9.995	10.316	10.641	10.969	11.302	11.981
5	9.006	9.136	9.266	9.397	9.529	9.661	9.795	10.064	10.337	10.613	10.893	11.464
6	8.974	9.087	9.201	9.315	9.430	9.546	9.663	9.898	10.137	10.379	10.624	11.123
7	8.951	9.052	9.155	9.257	9.361	9.465	9.570	9.782	9.996	10.214	10.434	10.884
8	8.934	9.027	9.121	9.215	9.310	9.405	9.502	9.696	9.893	10.093	10.295	10.709
9	8.921	9.008	9.095	9.183	9.271	9.360	9.450	9.631	9.814	10.000	10.189	10.575
10	8.911	8.993	9.075	9.158	9.241	9.325	9.409	9.580	9.753	9.929	10.107	10.471
11	8.903	8.981	9.059	9.138	9.217	9.297	9.377	9.539	9.704	9.872	10.041	10.389
12	8.897	8.971	9.046	9.121	9.197	9.274	9.351	9.507	9.665	9.826	9.989	10.323
13	8.892	8.963	9.036	9.108	9.182	9.256	9.330	9.481	9.634	9.789	9.946	10.269
14	8.887	8.957	9.027	9.098	9.169	9.241	9.313	9.459	9.608	9.759	9.912	10.226
15	8.884	8.952	9.020	9.089	9.158	9.228	9.299	9.442	9.587	9.734	9.883	10.190
16	8.881	8.947	9.014	9.082	9.150	9.218	9.287	9.427	9.569	9.714	9.860	10.161
17	8.879	8.944	9.010	9.076	9.143	9.210	9.278	9.415	9.555	9.697	9.841	10.137
18	8.877	8.941	9.006	9.071	9.137	9.203	9.270	9.406	9.544	9.684	9.826	10.118
19	8.875	8.939	9.003	9.067	9.132	9.198	9.264	9.398	9.534	9.673	9.814	10.103
20	8.874	8.937	9.000	9.064	9.129	9.194	9.259	9.392	9.527	9.664	9.804	10.091
21	8.873	8.935	8.998	9.062	9.126	9.191	9.256	9.388	9.522	9.658	9.797	10.082
22	8.872	8.934	8.997	9.060	9.124	9.188	9.253	9.384	9.518	9.653	9.792	10.075
23	8.872	8.934	8.996	9.059	9.123	9.187	9.251	9.382	9.515	9.650	9.788	10.071
24	8.872	8.933	8.996	9.058	9.122	9.186	9.250	9.381	9.513	9.648	9.786	10.068
25	8.871	8.933	8.995	9.058	9.122	9.185	9.250	9.380	9.513	9.648	9.785	10.067

Interest Rate   8.75%   30 Year Schedule   Annual Constant   9.440405%

Yield to end of Year	1.0 Point	1.5 Point	2.0 Points	2.5 Points	3.0 Points	3.5 Points	4.0 Points	5.0 Points	6.0 Points	7.0 Points	8.0 Points	10.0 Points
1	9.807	10.340	10.876	11.415	11.958	12.503	13.052	14.158	15.278	16.411	17.558	19.894
2	9.303	9.582	9.863	10.145	10.429	10.715	11.002	11.581	12.167	12.760	13.360	14.583
3	9.136	9.331	9.527	9.724	9.922	10.121	10.322	10.726	11.136	11.550	11.970	12.824
4	9.053	9.206	9.359	9.514	9.670	9.826	9.984	10.302	10.624	10.949	11.279	11.951
5	9.003	9.131	9.260	9.389	9.520	9.651	9.783	10.049	10.319	10.592	10.868	11.432
6	8.970	9.082	9.194	9.307	9.421	9.535	9.650	9.882	10.117	10.356	10.597	11.089
7	8.947	9.047	9.148	9.249	9.351	9.453	9.556	9.764	9.975	10.189	10.406	10.848
8	8.930	9.022	9.113	9.206	9.299	9.393	9.487	9.677	9.870	10.066	10.264	10.670
9	8.917	9.002	9.087	9.173	9.259	9.346	9.434	9.611	9.790	9.972	10.157	10.533
10	8.907	8.987	9.067	9.147	9.228	9.310	9.392	9.559	9.727	9.898	10.072	10.427
11	8.899	8.974	9.050	9.127	9.204	9.281	9.359	9.517	9.677	9.840	10.004	10.342
12	8.892	8.964	9.037	9.110	9.183	9.258	9.332	9.483	9.636	9.792	9.950	10.273
13	8.887	8.956	9.026	9.096	9.167	9.238	9.310	9.455	9.603	9.753	9.905	10.216
14	8.882	8.949	9.017	9.085	9.153	9.222	9.292	9.432	9.575	9.720	9.867	10.169
15	8.878	8.943	9.009	9.075	9.142	9.209	9.276	9.413	9.552	9.693	9.836	10.130
16	8.875	8.939	9.003	9.067	9.132	9.197	9.263	9.397	9.533	9.670	9.810	10.097
17	8.872	8.935	8.997	9.060	9.124	9.188	9.253	9.383	9.516	9.651	9.789	10.070
18	8.870	8.931	8.993	9.055	9.117	9.180	9.243	9.372	9.502	9.635	9.770	10.047
19	8.868	8.928	8.989	9.050	9.111	9.173	9.236	9.362	9.491	9.622	9.755	10.028
20	8.867	8.926	8.986	9.046	9.106	9.168	9.229	9.354	9.481	9.610	9.742	10.012
21	8.865	8.924	8.983	9.042	9.102	9.163	9.224	9.347	9.473	9.601	9.731	9.998
22	8.864	8.922	8.981	9.040	9.099	9.159	9.219	9.342	9.466	9.593	9.722	9.987
23	8.863	8.921	8.979	9.037	9.096	9.156	9.216	9.337	9.461	9.587	9.715	9.978
24	8.862	8.920	8.977	9.035	9.094	9.153	9.213	9.333	9.456	9.581	9.709	9.970
25	8.862	8.919	8.976	9.034	9.092	9.151	9.210	9.330	9.453	9.577	9.704	9.964
26	8.861	8.918	8.975	9.033	9.091	9.149	9.208	9.328	9.450	9.574	9.700	9.960
27	8.861	8.917	8.974	9.032	9.090	9.148	9.207	9.326	9.448	9.572	9.698	9.957
28	8.861	8.917	8.974	9.031	9.089	9.147	9.206	9.325	9.447	9.570	9.696	9.954
29	8.861	8.917	8.974	9.031	9.089	9.147	9.206	9.325	9.446	9.569	9.695	9.953
30	8.861	8.917	8.974	9.031	9.088	9.147	9.205	9.324	9.445	9.569	9.694	9.953

Yield on Mortgage Loan When Points Are Paid

Interest Rate   9.00%   25 Year Schedule   Annual Constant   10.070356%

Yield to end of Year	1.0 Point	1.5 Point	2.0 Points	2.5 Points	3.0 Points	3.5 Points	4.0 Points	5.0 Points	6.0 Points	7.0 Points	8.0 Points	10.0 Points
1	10.061	10.595	11.133	11.674	12.218	12.765	13.315	14.425	15.549	16.686	17.836	20.180
2	9.557	9.838	10.120	10.404	10.690	10.977	11.266	11.849	12.439	13.036	13.640	14.871
3	9.390	9.586	9.784	9.983	10.183	10.385	10.587	10.996	11.409	11.828	12.251	13.115
4	9.307	9.462	9.617	9.774	9.932	10.090	10.250	10.572	10.898	11.228	11.562	12.244
5	9.257	9.387	9.518	9.650	9.782	9.916	10.050	10.320	10.595	10.872	11.153	11.727
6	9.225	9.339	9.453	9.568	9.684	9.801	9.918	10.155	10.395	10.638	10.884	11.387
7	9.202	9.304	9.407	9.511	9.615	9.720	9.825	10.038	10.254	10.473	10.695	11.148
8	9.185	9.279	9.373	9.468	9.564	9.660	9.757	9.953	10.151	10.352	10.556	10.973
9	9.172	9.260	9.348	9.436	9.525	9.615	9.705	9.887	10.072	10.260	10.450	10.839
10	9.162	9.245	9.328	9.411	9.495	9.579	9.665	9.837	10.011	10.188	10.368	10.736
11	9.154	9.233	9.312	9.391	9.471	9.551	9.633	9.797	9.963	10.132	10.303	10.654
12	9.148	9.223	9.299	9.375	9.452	9.529	9.607	9.764	9.924	10.086	10.251	10.588
13	9.143	9.215	9.288	9.362	9.436	9.511	9.586	9.738	9.892	10.049	10.209	10.535
14	9.139	9.209	9.280	9.351	9.423	9.496	9.569	9.717	9.867	10.019	10.174	10.492
15	9.135	9.204	9.273	9.343	9.413	9.484	9.555	9.699	9.846	9.995	10.146	10.456
16	9.132	9.200	9.267	9.336	9.404	9.474	9.543	9.685	9.829	9.975	10.123	10.427
17	9.130	9.196	9.263	9.330	9.397	9.465	9.534	9.673	9.814	9.958	10.104	10.404
18	9.128	9.193	9.259	9.325	9.392	9.459	9.527	9.664	9.803	9.945	10.089	10.385
19	9.127	9.191	9.256	9.321	9.387	9.454	9.521	9.656	9.794	9.934	10.077	10.370
20	9.125	9.189	9.253	9.318	9.384	9.449	9.516	9.650	9.787	9.926	10.067	10.358
21	9.125	9.188	9.252	9.316	9.381	9.446	9.512	9.646	9.781	9.920	10.060	10.349
22	9.124	9.187	9.250	9.314	9.379	9.444	9.509	9.642	9.777	9.915	10.055	10.342
23	9.123	9.186	9.249	9.313	9.377	9.442	9.508	9.640	9.775	9.912	10.051	10.338
24	9.123	9.186	9.249	9.312	9.377	9.441	9.507	9.639	9.773	9.910	10.049	10.336
25	9.123	9.186	9.249	9.312	9.376	9.441	9.506	9.638	9.773	9.909	10.049	10.335

Interest Rate   9.00%   30 Year Schedule   Annual Constant   9.655471%

Yield to end of Year	1.0 Point	1.5 Point	2.0 Points	2.5 Points	3.0 Points	3.5 Points	4.0 Points	5.0 Points	6.0 Points	7.0 Points	8.0 Points	10.0 Points
1	10.059	10.592	11.129	11.668	12.211	12.757	13.307	14.415	15.536	16.671	17.819	20.158
2	9.554	9.834	10.115	10.398	10.683	10.969	11.257	11.837	12.425	13.019	13.621	14.846
3	9.387	9.583	9.779	9.977	10.176	10.376	10.577	10.983	11.394	11.809	12.230	13.088
4	9.304	9.458	9.612	9.767	9.924	10.081	10.239	10.558	10.881	11.208	11.540	12.215
5	9.254	9.383	9.512	9.643	9.774	9.905	10.038	10.306	10.577	10.851	11.129	11.696
6	9.222	9.334	9.447	9.560	9.675	9.790	9.905	10.139	10.375	10.615	10.858	11.353
7	9.199	9.299	9.400	9.502	9.605	9.708	9.812	10.021	10.234	10.449	10.667	11.112
8	9.182	9.274	9.366	9.459	9.553	9.648	9.743	9.934	10.129	10.326	10.526	10.934
9	9.169	9.254	9.340	9.427	9.514	9.601	9.690	9.868	10.049	10.232	10.418	10.798
10	9.158	9.239	9.319	9.401	9.483	9.565	9.648	9.816	9.986	10.159	10.334	10.692
11	9.150	9.226	9.303	9.380	9.458	9.536	9.615	9.774	9.936	10.100	10.267	10.607
12	9.144	9.216	9.290	9.364	9.438	9.513	9.588	9.741	9.896	10.053	10.212	10.539
13	9.138	9.208	9.279	9.350	9.421	9.494	9.566	9.713	9.862	10.014	10.167	10.482
14	9.134	9.201	9.270	9.338	9.408	9.478	9.548	9.690	9.835	9.981	10.130	10.436
15	9.130	9.196	9.262	9.329	9.396	9.464	9.533	9.671	9.812	9.954	10.100	10.397
16	9.127	9.191	9.256	9.321	9.387	9.453	9.520	9.655	9.792	9.932	10.074	10.365
17	9.124	9.187	9.250	9.314	9.379	9.444	9.509	9.642	9.776	9.913	10.052	10.337
18	9.122	9.184	9.246	9.309	9.372	9.436	9.500	9.630	9.763	9.897	10.034	10.315
19	9.120	9.181	9.242	9.304	9.366	9.429	9.492	9.621	9.751	9.884	10.019	10.295
20	9.118	9.178	9.239	9.300	9.361	9.423	9.486	9.613	9.741	9.872	10.006	10.279
21	9.117	9.176	9.236	9.297	9.357	9.419	9.481	9.606	9.733	9.863	9.995	10.266
22	9.116	9.175	9.234	9.294	9.354	9.415	9.476	9.600	9.727	9.855	9.986	10.255
23	9.115	9.173	9.232	9.291	9.351	9.412	9.473	9.596	9.721	9.849	9.979	10.246
24	9.114	9.172	9.231	9.290	9.349	9.409	9.470	9.592	9.717	9.844	9.973	10.239
25	9.113	9.171	9.229	9.288	9.347	9.407	9.467	9.589	9.713	9.840	9.968	10.233
26	9.113	9.171	9.228	9.287	9.346	9.405	9.465	9.587	9.711	9.837	9.965	10.229
27	9.113	9.170	9.228	9.286	9.345	9.404	9.464	9.585	9.709	9.834	9.962	10.225
28	9.112	9.170	9.227	9.286	9.344	9.403	9.463	9.584	9.707	9.833	9.960	10.223
29	9.112	9.169	9.227	9.285	9.344	9.403	9.463	9.583	9.707	9.832	9.959	10.222
30	9.112	9.169	9.227	9.285	9.344	9.403	9.462	9.583	9.706	9.832	9.959	10.222

Yield on Mortgage Loan When Points Are Paid

Interest Rate   9.25%   25 Year Schedule   Annual Constant   10.276582%

Yield to end of Year	1.0 Point	1.5 Point	2.0 Points	2.5 Points	3.0 Points	3.5 Points	4.0 Points	5.0 Points	6.0 Points	7.0 Points	8.0 Points	10.0 Points
1	10.312	10.847	11.385	11.927	12.471	13.019	13.570	14.682	15.806	16.945	18.097	20.443
2	9.808	10.089	10.372	10.657	10.943	11.231	11.521	12.105	12.697	13.295	13.900	15.134
3	9.641	9.838	10.037	10.236	10.437	10.639	10.842	11.252	11.667	12.086	12.511	13.377
4	9.558	9.713	9.870	10.027	10.185	10.345	10.505	10.828	11.156	11.487	11.823	12.507
5	9.509	9.639	9.771	9.903	10.036	10.170	10.305	10.577	10.852	11.131	11.414	11.990
6	9.476	9.590	9.706	9.821	9.938	10.055	10.173	10.411	10.653	10.897	11.145	11.651
7	9.453	9.556	9.660	9.764	9.869	9.974	10.080	10.295	10.512	10.733	10.956	11.412
8	9.436	9.531	9.626	9.722	9.818	9.915	10.012	10.209	10.409	10.612	10.817	11.237
9	9.424	9.512	9.600	9.689	9.779	9.870	9.961	10.144	10.331	10.520	10.712	11.104
10	9.414	9.497	9.580	9.664	9.749	9.834	9.920	10.094	10.270	10.449	10.630	11.001
11	9.406	9.485	9.564	9.644	9.725	9.806	9.888	10.054	10.222	10.392	10.565	10.919
12	9.399	9.475	9.552	9.629	9.706	9.784	9.863	10.022	10.183	10.347	10.513	10.854
13	9.394	9.468	9.541	9.616	9.690	9.766	9.842	9.995	10.151	10.310	10.471	10.801
14	9.390	9.461	9.533	9.605	9.678	9.751	9.825	9.974	10.126	10.280	10.437	10.758
15	9.387	9.456	9.526	9.596	9.667	9.739	9.811	9.957	10.105	10.256	10.409	10.722
16	9.384	9.452	9.520	9.589	9.659	9.729	9.800	9.943	10.088	10.236	10.386	10.694
17	9.382	9.448	9.516	9.584	9.652	9.721	9.790	9.931	10.074	10.219	10.367	10.671
18	9.380	9.446	9.512	9.579	9.646	9.714	9.783	9.922	10.063	10.206	10.352	10.652
19	9.378	9.443	9.509	9.575	9.642	9.709	9.777	9.914	10.054	10.196	10.340	10.637
20	9.377	9.442	9.507	9.572	9.638	9.705	9.772	9.908	10.047	10.188	10.331	10.625
21	9.376	9.440	9.505	9.570	9.636	9.702	9.769	9.904	10.041	10.181	10.324	10.616
22	9.375	9.439	9.503	9.568	9.634	9.699	9.766	9.900	10.037	10.177	10.319	10.610
23	9.375	9.438	9.503	9.567	9.632	9.698	9.764	9.898	10.035	10.174	10.315	10.606
24	9.375	9.438	9.502	9.566	9.631	9.697	9.763	9.897	10.033	10.172	10.313	10.603
25	9.375	9.438	9.502	9.566	9.631	9.697	9.763	9.897	10.033	10.171	10.312	10.602

Interest Rate   9.25%   30 Year Schedule   Annual Constant   9.872105%

Yield to end of Year	1.0 Point	1.5 Point	2.0 Points	2.5 Points	3.0 Points	3.5 Points	4.0 Points	5.0 Points	6.0 Points	7.0 Points	8.0 Points	10.0 Points
1	10.309	10.844	11.381	11.922	12.465	13.012	13.562	14.671	15.794	16.930	18.079	20.421
2	9.806	10.086	10.368	10.651	10.937	11.223	11.512	12.094	12.682	13.278	13.881	15.109
3	9.638	9.834	10.032	10.230	10.429	10.630	10.832	11.239	11.651	12.068	12.491	13.351
4	9.555	9.709	9.865	10.021	10.177	10.335	10.494	10.815	11.139	11.468	11.800	12.478
5	9.506	9.635	9.765	9.896	10.028	10.160	10.293	10.562	10.835	11.110	11.390	11.960
6	9.473	9.586	9.699	9.814	9.929	10.044	10.161	10.396	10.634	10.875	11.119	11.618
7	9.450	9.551	9.653	9.756	9.859	9.963	10.067	10.278	10.492	10.709	10.928	11.377
8	9.433	9.526	9.619	9.713	9.807	9.902	9.998	10.192	10.388	10.586	10.788	11.199
9	9.420	9.506	9.593	9.680	9.768	9.856	9.945	10.125	10.308	10.493	10.680	11.064
10	9.410	9.491	9.572	9.654	9.737	9.820	9.904	10.073	10.245	10.419	10.596	10.958
11	9.402	9.479	9.556	9.634	9.712	9.791	9.871	10.032	10.195	10.361	10.529	10.873
12	9.395	9.469	9.543	9.617	9.692	9.768	9.844	9.998	10.155	10.314	10.475	10.805
13	9.390	9.460	9.532	9.604	9.676	9.749	9.822	9.971	10.122	10.275	10.430	10.749
14	9.385	9.454	9.523	9.592	9.662	9.733	9.804	9.948	10.094	10.243	10.393	10.702
15	9.381	9.448	9.515	9.583	9.651	9.720	9.789	9.929	10.071	10.216	10.363	10.664
16	9.378	9.443	9.509	9.575	9.642	9.709	9.776	9.913	10.052	10.194	10.337	10.632
17	9.376	9.439	9.504	9.568	9.634	9.699	9.766	9.900	10.036	10.175	10.316	10.605
18	9.373	9.436	9.499	9.563	9.627	9.691	9.757	9.889	10.023	10.159	10.298	10.582
19	9.371	9.433	9.495	9.558	9.621	9.685	9.749	9.879	10.011	10.146	10.283	10.563
20	9.370	9.431	9.492	9.554	9.616	9.679	9.743	9.871	10.002	10.135	10.270	10.548
21	9.369	9.429	9.489	9.551	9.612	9.675	9.737	9.865	9.994	10.125	10.259	10.535
22	9.367	9.427	9.487	9.548	9.609	9.671	9.733	9.859	9.987	10.118	10.251	10.524
23	9.367	9.426	9.485	9.546	9.606	9.668	9.729	9.855	9.982	10.112	10.244	10.515
24	9.366	9.425	9.484	9.544	9.604	9.665	9.727	9.851	9.978	10.107	10.238	10.508
25	9.366	9.424	9.483	9.542	9.602	9.663	9.724	9.848	9.974	10.102	10.233	10.502
26	9.365	9.423	9.482	9.541	9.601	9.662	9.722	9.846	9.971	10.099	10.230	10.498
27	9.364	9.423	9.481	9.540	9.600	9.660	9.721	9.844	9.970	10.097	10.227	10.494
28	9.364	9.422	9.481	9.540	9.599	9.660	9.720	9.843	9.968	10.096	10.225	10.492
29	9.364	9.422	9.481	9.540	9.599	9.659	9.720	9.842	9.967	10.095	10.224	10.491
30	9.364	9.422	9.480	9.539	9.599	9.659	9.720	9.842	9.967	10.094	10.224	10.491

Yield on Mortgage Loan When Points Are Paid

Interest Rate   9.50%   25 Year Schedule   Annual Constant   10.484360%

Yield to end of Year	1.0 Point	1.5 Point	2.0 Points	2.5 Points	3.0 Points	3.5 Points	4.0 Points	5.0 Points	6.0 Points	7.0 Points	8.0 Points	10.0 Points
1	10.563	11.098	11.638	12.180	12.725	13.273	13.825	14.938	16.064	17.203	18.357	20.706
2	10.059	10.341	10.625	10.910	11.197	11.486	11.776	12.361	12.954	13.554	14.160	15.396
3	9.892	10.090	10.289	10.489	10.691	10.893	11.097	11.508	11.924	12.345	12.772	13.640
4	9.809	9.965	10.122	10.280	10.439	10.599	10.760	11.085	11.413	11.746	12.083	12.770
5	9.760	9.891	10.023	10.156	10.290	10.424	10.560	10.833	11.110	11.390	11.674	12.254
6	9.727	9.842	9.958	10.074	10.192	10.310	10.428	10.668	10.911	11.157	11.406	11.914
7	9.705	9.808	9.912	10.017	10.123	10.229	10.336	10.552	10.770	10.992	11.217	11.676
8	9.688	9.783	9.879	9.975	10.072	10.169	10.268	10.466	10.668	10.872	11.079	11.501
9	9.676	9.764	9.853	9.943	10.033	10.124	10.216	10.401	10.589	10.780	10.973	11.369
10	9.666	9.749	9.833	9.918	10.003	10.089	10.176	10.351	10.529	10.709	10.892	11.266
11	9.658	9.737	9.817	9.898	9.979	10.061	10.144	10.311	10.480	10.652	10.827	11.184
12	9.651	9.727	9.805	9.882	9.960	10.039	10.118	10.279	10.442	10.607	10.775	11.119
13	9.646	9.720	9.794	9.869	9.945	10.021	10.098	10.253	10.411	10.571	10.733	11.067
14	9.642	9.713	9.786	9.859	9.932	10.006	10.081	10.232	10.385	10.541	10.699	11.024
15	9.638	9.708	9.779	9.850	9.922	9.994	10.067	10.215	10.364	10.517	10.672	10.989
16	9.635	9.704	9.773	9.843	9.913	9.984	10.056	10.200	10.348	10.497	10.649	10.961
17	9.633	9.701	9.769	9.837	9.907	9.976	10.047	10.189	10.334	10.481	10.630	10.938
18	9.631	9.698	9.765	9.833	9.901	9.970	10.039	10.180	10.323	10.468	10.616	10.919
19	9.630	9.696	9.762	9.829	9.897	9.965	10.033	10.172	10.314	10.457	10.604	10.904
20	9.629	9.694	9.760	9.826	9.893	9.961	10.029	10.166	10.307	10.449	10.595	10.893
21	9.628	9.693	9.758	9.824	9.890	9.957	10.025	10.162	10.301	10.443	10.587	10.884
22	9.627	9.692	9.757	9.822	9.888	9.955	10.022	10.159	10.297	10.439	10.582	10.878
23	9.627	9.691	9.756	9.821	9.887	9.954	10.021	10.157	10.295	10.436	10.579	10.873
24	9.626	9.691	9.755	9.821	9.886	9.953	10.020	10.155	10.293	10.434	10.577	10.871
25	9.626	9.690	9.755	9.820	9.886	9.952	10.019	10.155	10.293	10.433	10.576	10.870

Interest Rate   9.50%   30 Year Schedule   Annual Constant   10.090250%

Yield to end of Year	1.0 Point	1.5 Point	2.0 Points	2.5 Points	3.0 Points	3.5 Points	4.0 Points	5.0 Points	6.0 Points	7.0 Points	8.0 Points	10.0 Points
1	10.561	11.096	11.634	12.175	12.719	13.266	13.817	14.928	16.052	17.189	18.340	20.685
2	10.057	10.338	10.620	10.905	11.190	11.478	11.767	12.350	12.940	13.537	14.142	15.373
3	9.890	10.086	10.284	10.483	10.683	10.885	11.087	11.496	11.909	12.328	12.751	13.614
4	9.806	9.961	10.117	10.274	10.431	10.590	10.749	11.071	11.397	11.727	12.061	12.742
5	9.757	9.887	10.018	10.149	10.281	10.415	10.549	10.819	11.093	11.370	11.651	12.224
6	9.724	9.838	9.952	10.067	10.183	10.299	10.416	10.652	10.892	11.135	11.380	11.882
7	9.701	9.803	9.906	10.009	10.113	10.217	10.323	10.535	10.751	10.969	11.190	11.642
8	9.684	9.778	9.872	9.966	10.061	10.157	10.254	10.449	10.646	10.846	11.050	11.464
9	9.672	9.758	9.846	9.934	10.022	10.111	10.201	10.383	10.567	10.753	10.942	11.329
10	9.662	9.743	9.825	9.908	9.991	10.075	10.160	10.331	10.504	10.680	10.859	11.223
11	9.654	9.731	9.809	9.888	9.967	10.047	10.127	10.290	10.454	10.622	10.792	11.139
12	9.647	9.721	9.796	9.871	9.947	10.023	10.100	10.256	10.414	10.575	10.738	11.071
13	9.641	9.713	9.785	9.857	9.931	10.004	10.079	10.229	10.381	10.536	10.693	11.015
14	9.637	9.706	9.776	9.846	9.917	9.988	10.060	10.206	10.354	10.504	10.657	10.969
15	9.633	9.700	9.768	9.837	9.906	9.975	10.045	10.187	10.331	10.478	10.626	10.931
16	9.630	9.696	9.762	9.829	9.896	9.964	10.033	10.171	10.312	10.455	10.601	10.899
17	9.627	9.692	9.757	9.822	9.888	9.955	10.022	10.158	10.296	10.437	10.580	10.873
18	9.625	9.688	9.752	9.817	9.882	9.947	10.013	10.147	10.283	10.421	10.562	10.850
19	9.623	9.686	9.749	9.812	9.876	9.941	10.006	10.138	10.272	10.408	10.547	10.832
20	9.622	9.683	9.745	9.808	9.871	9.935	10.000	10.130	10.262	10.397	10.534	10.816
21	9.620	9.681	9.743	9.805	9.868	9.931	9.994	10.123	10.255	10.388	10.524	10.803
22	9.619	9.680	9.741	9.802	9.864	9.927	9.990	10.118	10.248	10.381	10.515	10.792
23	9.618	9.678	9.739	9.800	9.862	9.924	9.986	10.114	10.243	10.374	10.508	10.784
24	9.618	9.677	9.737	9.798	9.859	9.921	9.984	10.110	10.238	10.369	10.503	10.777
25	9.617	9.676	9.736	9.797	9.858	9.919	9.981	10.107	10.235	10.365	10.498	10.771
26	9.616	9.676	9.735	9.796	9.856	9.918	9.980	10.105	10.232	10.362	10.495	10.767
27	9.616	9.675	9.735	9.795	9.855	9.917	9.978	10.103	10.231	10.360	10.492	10.764
28	9.616	9.675	9.734	9.794	9.855	9.916	9.977	10.102	10.229	10.359	10.491	10.762
29	9.616	9.675	9.734	9.794	9.854	9.915	9.977	10.102	10.229	10.358	10.490	10.761
30	9.616	9.675	9.734	9.794	9.854	9.915	9.977	10.101	10.228	10.358	10.489	10.760

Yield on Mortgage Loan When Points Are Paid

Interest Rate   9.75%   25 Year Schedule   Annual Constant   10.693649%

Yield to end of Year	1.0 Point	1.5 Point	2.0 Points	2.5 Points	3.0 Points	3.5 Points	4.0 Points	5.0 Points	6.0 Points	7.0 Points	8.0 Points	10.0 Points
1	10.814	11.350	11.890	12.433	12.979	13.528	14.080	15.194	16.321	17.462	18.617	20.969
2	10.311	10.593	10.877	11.163	11.451	11.740	12.031	12.618	13.211	13.812	14.420	15.659
3	10.143	10.342	10.541	10.742	10.944	11.147	11.352	11.764	12.182	12.604	13.032	13.903
4	10.060	10.217	10.375	10.533	10.693	10.853	11.015	11.341	11.671	12.005	12.343	13.033
5	10.011	10.143	10.276	10.409	10.544	10.679	10.815	11.090	11.368	11.650	11.935	12.517
6	9.979	10.094	10.211	10.328	10.446	10.564	10.683	10.924	11.169	11.416	11.667	12.178
7	9.956	10.060	10.165	10.270	10.377	10.483	10.591	10.808	11.029	11.252	11.478	11.941
8	9.939	10.035	10.131	10.228	10.326	10.424	10.523	10.723	10.926	11.131	11.340	11.766
9	9.926	10.016	10.106	10.196	10.287	10.379	10.472	10.658	10.848	11.040	11.235	11.634
10	9.916	10.001	10.086	10.171	10.257	10.344	10.432	10.608	10.787	10.969	11.154	11.531
11	9.909	9.989	10.070	10.152	10.234	10.316	10.400	10.568	10.739	10.913	11.089	11.450
12	9.903	9.980	10.057	10.136	10.215	10.294	10.374	10.536	10.701	10.868	11.038	11.385
13	9.897	9.972	10.047	10.123	10.199	10.276	10.354	10.511	10.670	10.832	10.996	11.333
14	9.893	9.966	10.039	10.113	10.187	10.262	10.337	10.490	10.645	10.802	10.962	11.290
15	9.890	9.961	10.032	10.104	10.177	10.250	10.323	10.472	10.624	10.778	10.935	11.256
16	9.887	9.956	10.026	10.097	10.168	10.240	10.312	10.458	10.607	10.758	10.912	11.228
17	9.885	9.953	10.022	10.091	10.161	10.232	10.303	10.447	10.594	10.742	10.894	11.205
18	9.883	9.950	10.018	10.087	10.156	10.225	10.296	10.438	10.582	10.730	10.879	11.186
19	9.881	9.948	10.015	10.083	10.151	10.220	10.290	10.431	10.574	10.719	10.867	11.172
20	9.880	9.946	10.013	10.080	10.148	10.216	10.285	10.425	10.567	10.711	10.858	11.160
21	9.879	9.945	10.011	10.078	10.145	10.213	10.282	10.420	10.562	10.705	10.851	11.152
22	9.879	9.944	10.010	10.076	10.143	10.211	10.279	10.417	10.558	10.701	10.846	11.145
23	9.878	9.943	10.009	10.075	10.142	10.209	10.277	10.415	10.555	10.698	10.843	11.141
24	9.878	9.943	10.009	10.075	10.141	10.209	10.276	10.414	10.554	10.696	10.841	11.139
25	9.878	9.943	10.008	10.074	10.141	10.208	10.277	10.413	10.553	10.695	10.840	11.138

Interest Rate   9.75%   30 Year Schedule   Annual Constant   10.309853%

Yield to end of Year	1.0 Point	1.5 Point	2.0 Points	2.5 Points	3.0 Points	3.5 Points	4.0 Points	5.0 Points	6.0 Points	7.0 Points	8.0 Points	10.0 Points
1	10.812	11.348	11.886	12.428	12.973	13.521	14.072	15.184	16.309	17.448	18.601	20.949
2	10.309	10.590	10.873	11.158	11.444	11.732	12.022	12.606	13.198	13.796	14.402	15.636
3	10.141	10.338	10.537	10.736	10.937	11.139	11.342	11.752	12.167	12.587	13.012	13.878
4	10.058	10.213	10.370	10.527	10.685	10.844	11.005	11.328	11.655	11.986	12.322	13.006
5	10.009	10.139	10.270	10.402	10.535	10.669	10.804	11.076	11.351	11.630	11.912	12.488
6	9.976	10.090	10.205	10.320	10.437	10.554	10.672	10.909	11.150	11.394	11.642	12.147
7	9.953	10.055	10.159	10.263	10.367	10.472	10.578	10.792	11.009	11.229	11.452	11.907
8	9.936	10.030	10.125	10.220	10.316	10.412	10.510	10.706	10.905	11.107	11.311	11.730
9	9.923	10.010	10.099	10.187	10.277	10.366	10.457	10.640	10.826	11.014	11.205	11.595
10	9.913	9.995	10.078	10.162	10.246	10.331	10.416	10.588	10.763	10.941	11.121	11.489
11	9.905	9.983	10.062	10.141	10.221	10.302	10.383	10.547	10.714	10.883	11.054	11.406
12	9.898	9.973	10.049	10.125	10.202	10.279	10.357	10.514	10.674	10.836	11.001	11.338
13	9.893	9.965	10.038	10.111	10.185	10.260	10.335	10.487	10.641	10.797	10.957	11.282
14	9.888	9.958	10.029	10.100	10.172	10.244	10.317	10.464	10.614	10.766	10.920	11.237
15	9.884	9.953	10.022	10.091	10.161	10.231	10.302	10.445	10.591	10.739	10.890	11.199
16	9.881	9.948	10.015	10.083	10.151	10.220	10.289	10.430	10.572	10.717	10.865	11.167
17	9.879	9.944	10.010	10.076	10.143	10.211	10.279	10.417	10.557	10.699	10.844	11.141
18	9.877	9.941	10.006	10.071	10.137	10.203	10.270	10.406	10.543	10.684	10.826	11.119
19	9.875	9.938	10.002	10.066	10.131	10.197	10.263	10.396	10.532	10.671	10.811	11.100
20	9.873	9.936	9.999	10.062	10.127	10.191	10.257	10.389	10.523	10.660	10.799	11.085
21	9.872	9.934	9.996	10.059	10.123	10.187	10.251	10.382	10.515	10.651	10.789	11.072
22	9.871	9.932	9.994	10.057	10.120	10.183	10.247	10.377	10.509	10.643	10.780	11.061
23	9.870	9.931	9.992	10.054	10.117	10.180	10.244	10.373	10.504	10.637	10.773	11.053
24	9.869	9.930	9.991	10.053	10.115	10.178	10.241	10.369	10.500	10.632	10.768	11.046
25	9.869	9.929	9.990	10.051	10.113	10.176	10.239	10.366	10.496	10.629	10.763	11.041
26	9.868	9.928	9.989	10.050	10.112	10.174	10.237	10.364	10.494	10.626	10.760	11.036
27	9.868	9.928	9.988	10.049	10.111	10.173	10.236	10.362	10.492	10.623	10.757	11.033
28	9.868	9.928	9.988	10.049	10.110	10.172	10.235	10.361	10.490	10.622	10.756	11.031
29	9.868	9.927	9.988	10.048	10.110	10.172	10.234	10.361	10.490	10.621	10.755	11.030
30	9.868	9.927	9.988	10.048	10.110	10.172	10.235	10.361	10.490	10.621	10.755	11.030

Yield on Mortgage Loan When Points Are Paid

Interest Rate 10.00% 25 Year Schedule   Annual Constant 10.904409%

Yield to end of Year	1.0 Point	1.5 Point	2.0 Points	2.5 Points	3.0 Points	3.5 Points	4.0 Points	5.0 Points	6.0 Points	7.0 Points	8.0 Points	10.0 Points
1	11.065	11.603	12.143	12.686	13.233	13.782	14.335	15.451	16.580	17.721	18.877	21.233
2	10.562	10.845	11.130	11.416	11.704	11.994	12.286	12.874	13.469	14.071	14.681	15.922
3	10.394	10.593	10.794	10.995	11.198	11.402	11.607	12.020	12.439	12.863	13.292	14.167
4	10.312	10.469	10.627	10.786	10.947	11.108	11.270	11.597	11.929	12.264	12.604	13.297
5	10.263	10.395	10.528	10.662	10.798	10.933	11.070	11.346	11.626	11.909	12.196	12.781
6	10.230	10.346	10.463	10.581	10.699	10.819	10.939	11.181	11.427	11.676	11.928	12.443
7	10.208	10.313	10.418	10.524	10.631	10.738	10.846	11.065	11.287	11.512	11.740	12.205
8	10.191	10.287	10.384	10.482	10.580	10.679	10.779	10.980	11.184	11.392	11.602	12.031
9	10.178	10.268	10.358	10.450	10.542	10.634	10.727	10.916	11.107	11.300	11.497	11.899
10	10.168	10.253	10.339	10.425	10.512	10.599	10.687	10.865	11.046	11.230	11.416	11.797
11	10.161	10.242	10.323	10.405	10.488	10.572	10.656	10.826	10.998	11.174	11.352	11.716
12	10.154	10.232	10.311	10.389	10.469	10.549	10.630	10.794	10.960	11.129	11.300	11.651
13	10.149	10.224	10.300	10.377	10.454	10.532	10.610	10.768	10.929	11.093	11.259	11.599
14	10.145	10.218	10.292	10.366	10.441	10.517	10.593	10.747	10.904	11.063	11.225	11.557
15	10.142	10.213	10.285	10.358	10.431	10.505	10.580	10.730	10.884	11.039	11.198	11.523
16	10.138	10.209	10.280	10.351	10.423	10.495	10.569	10.717	10.867	11.020	11.175	11.495
17	10.137	10.206	10.276	10.345	10.416	10.488	10.560	10.705	10.853	11.004	11.157	11.472
18	10.134	10.203	10.271	10.341	10.411	10.481	10.552	10.696	10.843	10.991	11.143	11.454
19	10.133	10.201	10.269	10.337	10.406	10.476	10.546	10.689	10.834	10.981	11.131	11.440
20	10.132	10.199	10.267	10.335	10.403	10.472	10.542	10.683	10.827	10.973	11.122	11.428
21	10.131	10.198	10.265	10.333	10.401	10.470	10.539	10.679	10.822	10.967	11.115	11.420
22	10.131	10.196	10.264	10.331	10.399	10.467	10.536	10.676	10.818	10.963	11.110	11.414
23	10.130	10.196	10.263	10.330	10.398	10.466	10.535	10.674	10.816	10.960	11.107	11.409
24	10.130	10.196	10.262	10.329	10.397	10.464	10.534	10.672	10.814	10.958	11.105	11.407
25	10.130	10.196	10.262	10.329	10.397	10.464	10.533	10.672	10.814	10.958	11.105	11.406

Interest Rate 10.00% 30 Year Schedule   Annual Constant 10.530859%

Yield to end of Year	1.0 Point	1.5 Point	2.0 Points	2.5 Points	3.0 Points	3.5 Points	4.0 Points	5.0 Points	6.0 Points	7.0 Points	8.0 Points	10.0 Points
1	11.064	11.600	12.139	12.681	13.227	13.775	14.327	15.441	16.567	17.708	18.862	21.212
2	10.560	10.842	11.125	11.411	11.698	11.987	12.277	12.863	13.456	14.056	14.663	15.899
3	10.392	10.590	10.789	10.989	11.191	11.394	11.597	12.009	12.425	12.846	13.273	14.142
4	10.309	10.466	10.622	10.780	10.939	11.099	11.260	11.585	11.913	12.246	12.583	13.270
5	10.260	10.391	10.523	10.656	10.789	10.924	11.059	11.332	11.609	11.889	12.173	12.752
6	10.228	10.342	10.457	10.574	10.691	10.809	10.927	11.166	11.409	11.654	11.903	12.411
7	10.205	10.308	10.412	10.517	10.622	10.727	10.834	11.049	11.268	11.489	11.714	12.172
8	10.188	10.282	10.377	10.473	10.570	10.667	10.765	10.963	11.164	11.367	11.574	11.995
9	10.175	10.263	10.351	10.441	10.531	10.622	10.713	10.897	11.085	11.274	11.467	11.861
10	10.165	10.247	10.331	10.415	10.500	10.586	10.672	10.846	11.023	11.202	11.384	11.756
11	10.157	10.236	10.315	10.396	10.476	10.558	10.639	10.805	10.973	11.144	11.317	11.672
12	10.150	10.226	10.302	10.379	10.456	10.534	10.613	10.772	10.933	11.097	11.264	11.605
13	10.144	10.217	10.291	10.365	10.440	10.515	10.591	10.745	10.901	11.059	11.220	11.549
14	10.140	10.211	10.283	10.355	10.427	10.500	10.573	10.722	10.874	11.028	11.184	11.504
15	10.137	10.206	10.275	10.345	10.416	10.487	10.559	10.704	10.851	11.001	11.154	11.466
16	10.133	10.201	10.269	10.337	10.406	10.476	10.546	10.688	10.833	10.980	11.129	11.435
17	10.131	10.197	10.263	10.331	10.398	10.467	10.536	10.675	10.817	10.961	11.108	11.409
18	10.129	10.194	10.260	10.326	10.392	10.460	10.528	10.665	10.804	10.946	11.091	11.387
19	10.127	10.191	10.256	10.321	10.387	10.453	10.520	10.655	10.793	10.933	11.076	11.369
20	10.125	10.188	10.253	10.317	10.382	10.448	10.514	10.648	10.784	10.923	11.064	11.354
21	10.124	10.187	10.250	10.314	10.378	10.443	10.509	10.641	10.776	10.914	11.054	11.341
22	10.123	10.185	10.248	10.311	10.375	10.439	10.504	10.636	10.770	10.906	11.045	11.331
23	10.122	10.184	10.246	10.309	10.372	10.436	10.501	10.632	10.765	10.900	11.038	11.322
24	10.121	10.183	10.245	10.308	10.371	10.434	10.499	10.628	10.761	10.896	11.033	11.316
25	10.121	10.182	10.244	10.306	10.369	10.432	10.496	10.625	10.757	10.892	11.029	11.310
26	10.120	10.181	10.243	10.305	10.368	10.431	10.495	10.623	10.755	10.889	11.025	11.306
27	10.120	10.181	10.242	10.304	10.367	10.430	10.493	10.622	10.753	10.887	11.023	11.303
28	10.120	10.181	10.242	10.303	10.366	10.429	10.492	10.621	10.752	10.885	11.021	11.301
29	10.120	10.181	10.242	10.303	10.366	10.428	10.492	10.620	10.751	10.885	11.020	11.300
30	10.120	10.180	10.242	10.303	10.366	10.429	10.492	10.620	10.751	10.884	11.020	11.300

Yield on Mortgage Loan When Points Are Paid

Interest Rate 10.25% 25 Year Schedule   Annual Constant 11.116599%

Yield to end of Year	1.0 Point	1.5 Point	2.0 Points	2.5 Points	3.0 Points	3.5 Points	4.0 Points	5.0 Points	6.0 Points	7.0 Points	8.0 Points	10.0 Points
1	11.317	11.854	12.395	12.939	13.486	14.036	14.590	15.707	16.837	17.980	19.138	21.496
2	10.813	11.096	11.382	11.669	11.958	12.248	12.541	13.130	13.726	14.330	14.941	16.185
3	10.646	10.845	11.046	11.248	11.452	11.656	11.862	12.277	12.697	13.122	13.553	14.430
4	10.563	10.721	10.880	11.040	11.200	11.362	11.525	11.854	12.186	12.523	12.865	13.560
5	10.514	10.647	10.781	10.916	11.051	11.188	11.325	11.603	11.884	12.168	12.457	13.045
6	10.481	10.598	10.716	10.834	10.953	11.073	11.194	11.438	11.685	11.935	12.189	12.707
7	10.459	10.565	10.671	10.778	10.885	10.993	11.102	11.322	11.545	11.772	12.001	12.470
8	10.442	10.539	10.637	10.735	10.834	10.934	11.034	11.237	11.443	11.652	11.863	12.296
9	10.430	10.520	10.611	10.703	10.796	10.889	10.983	11.173	11.365	11.561	11.759	12.164
10	10.420	10.505	10.592	10.679	10.766	10.854	10.943	11.123	11.305	11.490	11.678	12.062
11	10.412	10.494	10.576	10.659	10.743	10.827	10.912	11.083	11.258	11.434	11.614	11.982
12	10.406	10.485	10.564	10.644	10.724	10.805	10.886	11.052	11.219	11.390	11.563	11.917
13	10.401	10.477	10.554	10.631	10.708	10.787	10.866	11.026	11.189	11.354	11.522	11.866
14	10.396	10.470	10.545	10.620	10.696	10.772	10.850	11.005	11.164	11.325	11.488	11.824
15	10.393	10.465	10.538	10.612	10.686	10.761	10.836	10.988	11.143	11.301	11.461	11.790
16	10.390	10.462	10.533	10.605	10.678	10.751	10.825	10.975	11.127	11.282	11.439	11.762
17	10.388	10.458	10.528	10.599	10.671	10.743	10.816	10.964	11.113	11.266	11.421	11.740
18	10.386	10.455	10.525	10.595	10.666	10.737	10.809	10.955	11.103	11.253	11.407	11.722
19	10.385	10.453	10.522	10.591	10.661	10.732	10.803	10.947	11.094	11.243	11.395	11.707
20	10.384	10.451	10.519	10.588	10.658	10.728	10.799	10.942	11.087	11.236	11.386	11.696
21	10.383	10.450	10.518	10.586	10.655	10.725	10.795	10.937	11.082	11.230	11.380	11.688
22	10.382	10.449	10.517	10.585	10.653	10.723	10.793	10.934	11.079	11.225	11.375	11.682
23	10.382	10.448	10.516	10.584	10.652	10.721	10.791	10.932	11.076	11.222	11.371	11.678
24	10.382	10.448	10.515	10.583	10.651	10.720	10.790	10.931	11.075	11.221	11.370	11.676
25	10.382	10.448	10.515	10.583	10.651	10.720	10.790	10.931	11.074	11.220	11.369	11.675

Interest Rate 10.25% 30 Year Schedule   Annual Constant 10.753216%

Yield to end of Year	1.0 Point	1.5 Point	2.0 Points	2.5 Points	3.0 Points	3.5 Points	4.0 Points	5.0 Points	6.0 Points	7.0 Points	8.0 Points	10.0 Points
1	11.315	11.851	12.391	12.934	13.481	14.030	14.582	15.697	16.825	17.967	19.122	21.476
2	10.811	11.094	11.378	11.664	11.952	12.241	12.532	13.119	13.714	14.315	14.923	16.163
3	10.643	10.842	11.042	11.243	11.445	11.648	11.853	12.265	12.683	13.106	13.534	14.406
4	10.561	10.717	10.875	11.034	11.193	11.354	11.515	11.841	12.171	12.506	12.844	13.534
5	10.511	10.643	10.776	10.909	11.044	11.179	11.315	11.589	11.868	12.149	12.435	13.017
6	10.478	10.594	10.710	10.827	10.945	11.063	11.183	11.423	11.667	11.915	12.165	12.676
7	10.456	10.560	10.665	10.770	10.876	10.982	11.090	11.307	11.527	11.749	11.975	12.437
8	10.439	10.534	10.630	10.727	10.824	10.922	11.021	11.221	11.423	11.628	11.836	12.261
9	10.426	10.515	10.604	10.695	10.785	10.877	10.969	11.155	11.344	11.535	11.729	12.127
10	10.416	10.500	10.584	10.669	10.755	10.841	10.928	11.104	11.282	11.463	11.646	12.022
11	10.408	10.487	10.568	10.649	10.731	10.813	10.896	11.063	11.233	11.405	11.580	11.939
12	10.402	10.478	10.555	10.633	10.711	10.790	10.869	11.030	11.193	11.359	11.527	11.872
13	10.396	10.470	10.544	10.619	10.695	10.771	10.848	11.003	11.161	11.321	11.483	11.817
14	10.392	10.463	10.535	10.608	10.682	10.755	10.830	10.981	11.134	11.289	11.448	11.772
15	10.388	10.458	10.528	10.599	10.671	10.743	10.815	10.962	11.112	11.264	11.418	11.734
16	10.385	10.453	10.522	10.591	10.661	10.732	10.803	10.947	11.093	11.242	11.393	11.703
17	10.382	10.449	10.517	10.585	10.654	10.723	10.793	10.934	11.078	11.224	11.372	11.678
18	10.380	10.446	10.513	10.580	10.648	10.716	10.784	10.923	11.065	11.209	11.355	11.656
19	10.378	10.444	10.509	10.575	10.642	10.709	10.777	10.915	11.054	11.196	11.341	11.638
20	10.377	10.441	10.506	10.572	10.637	10.704	10.771	10.907	11.045	11.185	11.329	11.623
21	10.376	10.440	10.503	10.568	10.634	10.700	10.766	10.900	11.037	11.177	11.319	11.611
22	10.374	10.437	10.501	10.565	10.630	10.696	10.762	10.895	11.031	11.170	11.310	11.600
23	10.374	10.436	10.499	10.563	10.628	10.693	10.758	10.891	11.026	11.164	11.304	11.592
24	10.373	10.436	10.499	10.562	10.626	10.690	10.755	10.888	11.022	11.159	11.298	11.585
25	10.373	10.434	10.497	10.560	10.624	10.688	10.753	10.885	11.019	11.155	11.294	11.580
26	10.372	10.434	10.497	10.560	10.623	10.687	10.752	10.883	11.016	11.152	11.291	11.576
27	10.372	10.434	10.496	10.558	10.622	10.686	10.750	10.881	11.015	11.150	11.289	11.573
28	10.372	10.433	10.496	10.558	10.622	10.686	10.750	10.880	11.013	11.149	11.287	11.571
29	10.372	10.433	10.495	10.558	10.621	10.685	10.749	10.880	11.013	11.148	11.286	11.570
30	10.372	10.433	10.495	10.558	10.621	10.685	10.749	10.879	11.012	11.148	11.286	11.570

Yield on Mortgage Loan When Points Are Paid

Interest Rate 10.50% 25 Year Schedule   Annual Constant 11.330180%

Yield to end of Year	1.0 Point	1.5 Point	2.0 Points	2.5 Points	3.0 Points	3.5 Points	4.0 Points	5.0 Points	6.0 Points	7.0 Points	8.0 Points	10.0 Points
1	11.568	12.106	12.647	13.192	13.740	14.291	14.845	15.963	17.095	18.240	19.398	21.759
2	11.064	11.348	11.634	11.922	12.212	12.503	12.796	13.386	13.984	14.589	15.201	16.448
3	10.897	11.097	11.299	11.501	11.705	11.910	12.117	12.533	12.955	13.382	13.813	14.694
4	10.814	10.973	11.132	11.293	11.454	11.617	11.780	12.110	12.444	12.783	13.125	13.824
5	10.765	10.899	11.033	11.169	11.305	11.443	11.581	11.859	12.142	12.428	12.718	13.309
6	10.733	10.850	10.968	11.088	11.207	11.328	11.450	11.695	11.943	12.195	12.450	12.971
7	10.710	10.817	10.923	11.031	11.139	11.248	11.358	11.579	11.804	12.032	12.263	12.734
8	10.694	10.791	10.889	10.989	11.088	11.189	11.290	11.494	11.702	11.912	12.125	12.561
9	10.681	10.773	10.865	10.957	11.050	11.144	11.239	11.430	11.624	11.821	12.021	12.430
10	10.671	10.758	10.845	10.933	11.020	11.109	11.199	11.380	11.564	11.751	11.940	12.328
11	10.663	10.746	10.829	10.913	10.997	11.082	11.168	11.341	11.517	11.695	11.877	12.248
12	10.657	10.737	10.817	10.897	10.978	11.060	11.143	11.309	11.479	11.651	11.826	12.184
13	10.652	10.729	10.807	10.885	10.964	11.043	11.122	11.284	11.448	11.615	11.785	12.132
14	10.648	10.723	10.799	10.874	10.951	11.028	11.106	11.263	11.424	11.586	11.752	12.091
15	10.645	10.718	10.791	10.866	10.941	11.016	11.092	11.247	11.403	11.563	11.725	12.057
16	10.642	10.714	10.786	10.859	10.933	11.007	11.082	11.233	11.387	11.544	11.703	12.030
17	10.640	10.711	10.782	10.853	10.926	10.999	11.073	11.222	11.374	11.528	11.685	12.007
18	10.638	10.707	10.778	10.849	10.921	10.993	11.066	11.213	11.363	11.516	11.671	11.990
19	10.637	10.706	10.776	10.846	10.917	10.988	11.060	11.206	11.354	11.506	11.659	11.976
20	10.636	10.704	10.773	10.843	10.913	10.984	11.055	11.200	11.348	11.498	11.644	11.965
21	10.635	10.703	10.771	10.840	10.911	10.981	11.052	11.196	11.343	11.492	11.644	11.956
22	10.634	10.702	10.770	10.839	10.908	10.979	11.050	11.193	11.339	11.488	11.639	11.950
23	10.634	10.701	10.769	10.838	10.907	10.977	11.048	11.191	11.337	11.485	11.636	11.947
24	10.633	10.701	10.769	10.837	10.907	10.976	11.047	11.190	11.335	11.483	11.634	11.944
25	10.633	10.701	10.769	10.838	10.907	10.977	11.047	11.189	11.335	11.483	11.634	11.944

Interest Rate 10.50% 30 Year Schedule   Annual Constant 10.976872%

Yield to end of Year	1.0 Point	1.5 Point	2.0 Points	2.5 Points	3.0 Points	3.5 Points	4.0 Points	5.0 Points	6.0 Points	7.0 Points	8.0 Points	10.0 Points
1	11.566	12.104	12.644	13.188	13.735	14.285	14.838	15.954	17.084	18.227	19.384	21.741
2	11.062	11.346	11.630	11.917	12.206	12.496	12.787	13.376	13.972	14.574	15.184	16.427
3	10.895	11.094	11.294	11.496	11.699	11.903	12.108	12.522	12.941	13.365	13.794	14.670
4	10.812	10.970	11.128	11.287	11.447	11.608	11.771	12.098	12.430	12.765	13.105	13.798
5	10.763	10.895	11.028	11.163	11.298	11.434	11.570	11.846	12.126	12.409	12.696	13.281
6	10.730	10.846	10.963	11.081	11.199	11.318	11.438	11.681	11.926	12.175	12.427	12.941
7	10.707	10.812	10.918	11.024	11.130	11.237	11.346	11.564	11.785	12.010	12.237	12.702
8	10.691	10.787	10.883	10.981	11.079	11.178	11.277	11.478	11.682	11.889	12.098	12.526
9	10.678	10.767	10.857	10.948	11.040	11.132	11.225	11.413	11.603	11.796	11.992	12.393
10	10.668	10.752	10.838	10.923	11.009	11.097	11.184	11.362	11.541	11.724	11.909	12.288
11	10.660	10.740	10.822	10.903	10.986	11.069	11.152	11.321	11.493	11.667	11.844	12.206
12	10.653	10.731	10.809	10.887	10.966	11.045	11.126	11.288	11.453	11.620	11.791	12.139
13	10.648	10.723	10.798	10.874	10.950	11.027	11.105	11.261	11.421	11.583	11.747	12.084
14	10.643	10.716	10.789	10.862	10.936	11.011	11.087	11.239	11.394	11.552	11.712	12.040
15	10.640	10.711	10.782	10.853	10.926	10.998	11.072	11.221	11.372	11.526	11.682	12.003
16	10.637	10.706	10.776	10.846	10.917	10.988	11.060	11.206	11.354	11.504	11.658	11.972
17	10.634	10.702	10.771	10.840	10.909	10.979	11.050	11.193	11.338	11.486	11.637	11.946
18	10.632	10.699	10.766	10.834	10.903	10.971	11.041	11.182	11.326	11.471	11.620	11.925
19	10.630	10.696	10.763	10.830	10.897	10.966	11.034	11.173	11.315	11.459	11.606	11.907
20	10.629	10.694	10.760	10.826	10.892	10.960	11.028	11.166	11.306	11.449	11.594	11.892
21	10.628	10.692	10.757	10.823	10.889	10.956	11.023	11.160	11.298	11.440	11.584	11.880
22	10.627	10.691	10.755	10.820	10.886	10.952	11.019	11.155	11.293	11.433	11.576	11.870
23	10.626	10.689	10.754	10.818	10.884	10.950	11.016	11.151	11.287	11.427	11.569	11.862
24	10.625	10.688	10.752	10.816	10.882	10.947	11.013	11.147	11.283	11.422	11.564	11.855
25	10.624	10.688	10.751	10.815	10.880	10.945	11.011	11.145	11.280	11.419	11.560	11.850
26	10.624	10.687	10.750	10.814	10.879	10.944	11.010	11.143	11.278	11.416	11.557	11.846
27	10.624	10.686	10.750	10.814	10.878	10.943	11.008	11.141	11.276	11.414	11.554	11.844
28	10.624	10.686	10.749	10.813	10.877	10.942	11.007	11.140	11.275	11.413	11.553	11.842
29	10.623	10.686	10.749	10.813	10.876	10.941	11.007	11.139	11.274	11.412	11.552	11.841
30	10.623	10.686	10.749	10.813	10.877	10.942	11.007	11.140	11.274	11.412	11.552	11.840

Yield on Mortgage Loan When Points Are Paid

Interest Rate 10.75% 25 Year Schedule   Annual Constant 11.545113%

Yield to end of Year	1.0 Point	1.5 Point	2.0 Points	2.5 Points	3.0 Points	3.5 Points	4.0 Points	5.0 Points	6.0 Points	7.0 Points	8.0 Points	10.0 Points
1	11.819	12.358	12.900	13.445	13.994	14.546	15.101	16.220	17.353	18.499	19.660	22.023
2	11.315	11.600	11.887	12.175	12.465	12.757	13.051	13.643	14.242	14.848	15.462	16.712
3	11.148	11.349	11.551	11.755	11.959	12.165	12.372	12.790	13.212	13.640	14.074	14.957
4	11.066	11.225	11.385	11.546	11.709	11.871	12.035	12.367	12.702	13.042	13.386	14.088
5	11.017	11.151	11.286	11.422	11.559	11.697	11.836	12.116	12.400	12.688	12.979	13.573
6	10.984	11.102	11.221	11.341	11.462	11.583	11.705	11.952	12.202	12.455	12.712	13.236
7	10.962	11.069	11.176	11.284	11.393	11.503	11.613	11.836	12.062	12.292	12.524	12.999
8	10.945	11.043	11.142	11.242	11.343	11.444	11.546	11.752	11.960	12.172	12.387	12.826
9	10.932	11.025	11.117	11.210	11.304	11.399	11.495	11.688	11.883	12.082	12.283	12.695
10	10.923	11.009	11.097	11.186	11.275	11.365	11.455	11.638	11.823	12.012	12.203	12.594
11	10.915	10.998	11.082	11.166	11.252	11.337	11.424	11.599	11.776	11.956	12.139	12.514
12	10.909	10.989	11.070	11.151	11.233	11.316	11.399	11.567	11.738	11.912	12.089	12.451
13	10.904	10.981	11.059	11.138	11.218	11.298	11.379	11.542	11.708	11.877	12.048	12.399
14	10.899	10.975	11.051	11.128	11.206	11.284	11.362	11.522	11.683	11.848	12.015	12.358
15	10.896	10.970	11.045	11.120	11.196	11.272	11.349	11.505	11.663	11.824	11.988	12.325
16	10.894	10.966	11.039	11.113	11.187	11.262	11.338	11.491	11.647	11.806	11.967	12.297
17	10.891	10.963	11.035	11.107	11.181	11.255	11.329	11.480	11.634	11.790	11.949	12.275
18	10.890	10.960	11.032	11.104	11.176	11.249	11.322	11.472	11.623	11.778	11.935	12.258
19	10.888	10.958	11.028	11.100	11.171	11.244	11.317	11.465	11.615	11.768	11.924	12.244
20	10.887	10.956	11.026	11.097	11.168	11.240	11.312	11.459	11.608	11.760	11.915	12.233
21	10.886	10.955	11.024	11.095	11.165	11.237	11.309	11.455	11.603	11.755	11.909	12.225
22	10.886	10.954	11.023	11.093	11.164	11.235	11.307	11.452	11.600	11.750	11.904	12.219
23	10.885	10.953	11.022	11.092	11.162	11.233	11.305	11.450	11.597	11.748	11.901	12.215
24	10.885	10.953	11.022	11.092	11.162	11.233	11.304	11.449	11.596	11.746	11.899	12.213
25	10.885	10.953	11.022	11.091	11.162	11.232	11.304	11.448	11.596	11.746	11.898	12.212

Interest Rate 10.75% 30 Year Schedule   Annual Constant 11.201776%

Yield to end of Year	1.0 Point	1.5 Point	2.0 Points	2.5 Points	3.0 Points	3.5 Points	4.0 Points	5.0 Points	6.0 Points	7.0 Points	8.0 Points	10.0 Points
1	11.817	12.356	12.896	13.441	13.988	14.539	15.093	16.211	17.342	18.486	19.644	22.004
2	11.314	11.597	11.883	12.170	12.459	12.750	13.043	13.633	14.230	14.834	15.445	16.691
3	11.146	11.346	11.547	11.749	11.953	12.157	12.363	12.779	13.199	13.625	14.056	14.934
4	11.063	11.221	11.380	11.540	11.701	11.863	12.026	12.355	12.688	13.025	13.367	14.063
5	11.014	11.147	11.281	11.416	11.552	11.688	11.826	12.103	12.384	12.669	12.958	13.546
6	10.982	11.098	11.216	11.334	11.453	11.573	11.694	11.938	12.185	12.435	12.689	13.207
7	10.959	11.064	11.170	11.277	11.384	11.492	11.601	11.821	12.044	12.270	12.500	12.968
8	10.942	11.039	11.136	11.234	11.333	11.433	11.533	11.736	11.941	12.149	12.361	12.792
9	10.929	11.019	11.110	11.202	11.294	11.387	11.481	11.670	11.862	12.057	12.255	12.659
10	10.919	11.005	11.090	11.177	11.264	11.352	11.441	11.619	11.801	11.985	12.172	12.555
11	10.911	10.993	11.075	11.157	11.240	11.324	11.408	11.579	11.752	11.928	12.107	12.473
12	10.905	10.983	11.062	11.141	11.220	11.301	11.382	11.546	11.713	11.882	12.054	12.406
13	10.899	10.975	11.051	11.127	11.205	11.282	11.361	11.520	11.681	11.845	12.011	12.352
14	10.895	10.968	11.042	11.116	11.191	11.267	11.343	11.498	11.654	11.814	11.976	12.308
15	10.891	10.963	11.035	11.107	11.181	11.254	11.329	11.479	11.633	11.788	11.946	12.271
16	10.888	10.959	11.029	11.100	11.172	11.244	11.317	11.464	11.614	11.767	11.922	12.241
17	10.886	10.955	11.024	11.093	11.164	11.235	11.307	11.452	11.599	11.749	11.902	12.215
18	10.884	10.951	11.019	11.088	11.158	11.228	11.298	11.441	11.587	11.734	11.885	12.194
19	10.882	10.949	11.016	11.084	11.152	11.221	11.291	11.432	11.576	11.722	11.871	12.177
20	10.881	10.947	11.013	11.080	11.148	11.216	11.285	11.425	11.567	11.712	11.859	12.162
21	10.879	10.945	11.010	11.078	11.144	11.212	11.280	11.419	11.560	11.703	11.849	12.150
22	10.878	10.943	11.009	11.075	11.141	11.208	11.276	11.414	11.554	11.696	11.842	12.140
23	10.878	10.942	11.007	11.073	11.139	11.206	11.274	11.410	11.549	11.691	11.835	12.132
24	10.877	10.941	11.006	11.071	11.137	11.204	11.271	11.407	11.545	11.686	11.830	12.126
25	10.876	10.940	11.004	11.070	11.136	11.202	11.269	11.404	11.542	11.683	11.826	12.121
26	10.876	10.940	11.004	11.068	11.134	11.201	11.267	11.402	11.540	11.680	11.823	12.117
27	10.876	10.939	11.003	11.068	11.134	11.200	11.266	11.400	11.538	11.678	11.821	12.114
28	10.875	10.939	11.003	11.068	11.133	11.199	11.265	11.399	11.537	11.677	11.819	12.112
29	10.875	10.939	11.003	11.067	11.132	11.198	11.264	11.399	11.536	11.676	11.818	12.111
30	10.875	10.939	11.003	11.067	11.132	11.198	11.264	11.399	11.536	11.676	11.818	12.111

Yield on Mortgage Loan When Points Are Paid

Interest Rate 11.00% 25 Year Schedule   Annual Constant 11.761357%

Yield to end of Year	1.0 Point	1.5 Point	2.0 Points	2.5 Points	3.0 Points	3.5 Points	4.0 Points	5.0 Points	6.0 Points	7.0 Points	8.0 Points	10.0 Points
1	12.070	12.610	13.153	13.699	14.247	14.800	15.356	16.477	17.610	18.758	19.920	22.287
2	11.567	11.852	12.139	12.428	12.719	13.011	13.306	13.899	14.499	15.107	15.722	16.975
3	11.400	11.601	11.804	12.008	12.213	12.419	12.627	13.046	13.471	13.900	14.335	15.221
4	11.317	11.477	11.638	11.800	11.963	12.126	12.291	12.623	12.960	13.302	13.648	14.352
5	11.268	11.403	11.539	11.676	11.813	11.952	12.091	12.373	12.658	12.947	13.240	13.838
6	11.236	11.354	11.474	11.594	11.716	11.838	11.960	12.209	12.460	12.715	12.973	13.500
7	11.213	11.321	11.429	11.537	11.647	11.758	11.869	12.093	12.321	12.552	12.786	13.264
8	11.196	11.296	11.395	11.496	11.597	11.699	11.801	12.009	12.219	12.433	12.649	13.092
9	11.184	11.277	11.370	11.464	11.559	11.654	11.751	11.945	12.142	12.342	12.546	12.961
10	11.174	11.262	11.351	11.439	11.529	11.620	11.711	11.895	12.083	12.273	12.465	12.860
11	11.166	11.251	11.335	11.421	11.506	11.593	11.680	11.856	12.036	12.218	12.402	12.781
12	11.160	11.241	11.323	11.405	11.488	11.571	11.655	11.825	11.998	12.174	12.352	12.717
13	11.155	11.234	11.313	11.393	11.473	11.554	11.635	11.800	11.968	12.138	12.311	12.667
14	11.151	11.228	11.305	11.383	11.461	11.540	11.619	11.780	11.943	12.110	12.279	12.626
15	11.148	11.223	11.298	11.374	11.451	11.528	11.606	11.763	11.924	12.086	12.252	12.592
16	11.145	11.219	11.293	11.367	11.443	11.519	11.595	11.750	11.907	12.068	12.231	12.565
17	11.143	11.216	11.289	11.362	11.436	11.511	11.586	11.739	11.894	12.052	12.213	12.544
18	11.141	11.213	11.285	11.358	11.431	11.505	11.580	11.731	11.884	12.040	12.199	12.526
19	11.140	11.211	11.282	11.354	11.427	11.500	11.574	11.723	11.876	12.031	12.188	12.513
20	11.139	11.209	11.280	11.352	11.424	11.496	11.570	11.718	11.869	12.023	12.180	12.502
21	11.138	11.208	11.278	11.349	11.421	11.493	11.566	11.714	11.864	12.017	12.173	12.494
22	11.137	11.207	11.277	11.348	11.419	11.491	11.564	11.711	11.861	12.013	12.169	12.488
23	11.137	11.206	11.276	11.347	11.418	11.490	11.562	11.709	11.858	12.011	12.166	12.484
24	11.137	11.206	11.276	11.346	11.418	11.489	11.562	11.708	11.857	12.009	12.164	12.482
25	11.137	11.206	11.276	11.346	11.417	11.489	11.561	11.707	11.857	12.008	12.163	12.482

Interest Rate 11.00% 30 Year Schedule   Annual Constant 11.427881%

Yield to end of Year	1.0 Point	1.5 Point	2.0 Points	2.5 Points	3.0 Points	3.5 Points	4.0 Points	5.0 Points	6.0 Points	7.0 Points	8.0 Points	10.0 Points
1	12.069	12.608	13.149	13.694	14.242	14.794	15.349	16.467	17.600	18.746	19.905	22.268
2	11.565	11.850	12.136	12.424	12.713	13.005	13.298	13.889	14.488	15.094	15.707	16.955
3	11.398	11.598	11.800	12.002	12.207	12.412	12.618	13.036	13.458	13.885	14.317	15.198
4	11.315	11.473	11.633	11.794	11.955	12.118	12.282	12.612	12.946	13.285	13.628	14.327
5	11.266	11.399	11.534	11.669	11.806	11.943	12.081	12.360	12.643	12.929	13.219	13.811
6	11.233	11.350	11.469	11.588	11.708	11.828	11.950	12.195	12.444	12.695	12.951	13.472
7	11.210	11.316	11.423	11.530	11.639	11.748	11.857	12.079	12.303	12.531	12.762	13.234
8	11.193	11.291	11.389	11.488	11.588	11.688	11.789	11.993	12.200	12.410	12.623	13.059
9	11.181	11.272	11.363	11.456	11.549	11.643	11.737	11.928	12.122	12.318	12.518	12.926
10	11.171	11.257	11.344	11.431	11.519	11.607	11.697	11.877	12.061	12.247	12.436	12.822
11	11.163	11.245	11.328	11.411	11.495	11.579	11.665	11.837	12.012	12.190	12.370	12.740
12	11.156	11.235	11.315	11.395	11.476	11.557	11.639	11.805	11.973	12.144	12.318	12.674
13	11.151	11.227	11.304	11.382	11.460	11.539	11.618	11.778	11.941	12.107	12.275	12.620
14	11.147	11.221	11.296	11.371	11.447	11.523	11.600	11.756	11.915	12.076	12.240	12.576
15	11.143	11.216	11.289	11.362	11.436	11.510	11.586	11.738	11.893	12.051	12.211	12.540
16	11.140	11.211	11.283	11.355	11.427	11.500	11.574	11.723	11.875	12.030	12.187	12.509
17	11.138	11.207	11.278	11.348	11.420	11.492	11.564	11.711	11.860	12.012	12.167	12.484
18	11.136	11.204	11.273	11.343	11.413	11.484	11.556	11.700	11.848	11.998	12.150	12.464
19	11.134	11.202	11.270	11.339	11.408	11.478	11.548	11.692	11.837	11.985	12.136	12.446
20	11.132	11.199	11.267	11.335	11.404	11.473	11.543	11.684	11.828	11.975	12.125	12.432
21	11.131	11.198	11.265	11.332	11.400	11.469	11.538	11.678	11.821	11.967	12.115	12.420
22	11.130	11.196	11.263	11.330	11.397	11.466	11.534	11.673	11.815	11.960	12.107	12.410
23	11.129	11.195	11.261	11.328	11.395	11.463	11.531	11.669	11.811	11.954	12.101	12.403
24	11.129	11.194	11.260	11.326	11.393	11.460	11.529	11.667	11.807	11.950	12.096	12.396
25	11.128	11.193	11.259	11.325	11.391	11.459	11.526	11.664	11.804	11.946	12.092	12.391
26	11.128	11.193	11.258	11.324	11.390	11.457	11.525	11.662	11.802	11.944	12.089	12.388
27	11.127	11.192	11.257	11.323	11.389	11.456	11.524	11.661	11.800	11.942	12.087	12.385
28	11.127	11.192	11.257	11.322	11.389	11.456	11.523	11.659	11.799	11.941	12.085	12.383
29	11.127	11.192	11.257	11.322	11.388	11.455	11.523	11.659	11.798	11.940	12.084	12.382
30	11.127	11.192	11.257	11.322	11.388	11.455	11.522	11.659	11.798	11.940	12.084	12.382

Yield on Mortgage Loan When Points Are Paid

Interest Rate 11.25% 25 Year Schedule   Annual Constant 11.978875%

Yield to end of Year	1.0 Point	1.5 Point	2.0 Points	2.5 Points	3.0 Points	3.5 Points	4.0 Points	5.0 Points	6.0 Points	7.0 Points	8.0 Points	10.0 Points
1	12.322	12.862	13.405	13.952	14.501	15.054	15.611	16.733	17.869	19.017	20.180	22.550
2	11.818	12.104	12.392	12.682	12.973	13.266	13.561	14.155	14.757	15.366	15.983	17.239
3	11.651	11.853	12.056	12.261	12.467	12.674	12.882	13.303	13.729	14.159	14.595	15.484
4	11.568	11.729	11.890	12.052	12.216	12.380	12.546	12.880	13.218	13.561	13.908	14.616
5	11.519	11.655	11.791	11.929	12.067	12.207	12.347	12.630	12.917	13.207	13.501	14.102
6	11.487	11.606	11.727	11.848	11.970	12.092	12.216	12.466	12.718	12.975	13.235	13.765
7	11.464	11.572	11.681	11.791	11.901	12.013	12.124	12.351	12.580	12.812	13.048	13.530
8	11.448	11.548	11.648	11.750	11.852	11.954	12.057	12.266	12.478	12.693	12.911	13.357
9	11.435	11.528	11.623	11.718	11.813	11.910	12.007	12.203	12.401	12.603	12.808	13.227
10	11.426	11.514	11.603	11.693	11.784	11.875	11.967	12.153	12.342	12.534	12.728	13.126
11	11.418	11.503	11.588	11.674	11.761	11.848	11.936	12.114	12.295	12.479	12.665	13.047
12	11.412	11.494	11.576	11.659	11.742	11.827	11.911	12.083	12.258	12.435	12.615	12.984
13	11.407	11.486	11.566	11.646	11.727	11.809	11.892	12.058	12.228	12.400	12.575	12.934
14	11.403	11.480	11.558	11.636	11.715	11.795	11.875	12.038	12.203	12.372	12.543	12.893
15	11.400	11.475	11.552	11.628	11.705	11.783	11.862	12.022	12.184	12.349	12.516	12.860
16	11.397	11.471	11.546	11.622	11.698	11.775	11.852	12.008	12.168	12.330	12.495	12.834
17	11.394	11.468	11.541	11.616	11.691	11.767	11.843	11.998	12.155	12.315	12.478	12.812
18	11.393	11.465	11.538	11.612	11.686	11.761	11.836	11.989	12.145	12.303	12.464	12.795
19	11.392	11.463	11.536	11.608	11.682	11.756	11.831	11.982	12.136	12.293	12.453	12.781
20	11.391	11.462	11.534	11.605	11.678	11.752	11.826	11.977	12.130	12.286	12.445	12.771
21	11.390	11.461	11.532	11.603	11.676	11.749	11.823	11.973	12.125	12.280	12.438	12.763
22	11.389	11.459	11.531	11.602	11.675	11.747	11.821	11.970	12.122	12.276	12.434	12.757
23	11.389	11.459	11.530	11.601	11.673	11.746	11.820	11.968	12.119	12.273	12.431	12.754
24	11.389	11.459	11.529	11.601	11.673	11.745	11.818	11.967	12.118	12.272	12.429	12.752
25	11.388	11.459	11.529	11.601	11.673	11.745	11.818	11.966	12.118	12.271	12.428	12.751

Interest Rate 11.25% 30 Year Schedule   Annual Constant 11.655137%

Yield to end of Year	1.0 Point	1.5 Point	2.0 Points	2.5 Points	3.0 Points	3.5 Points	4.0 Points	5.0 Points	6.0 Points	7.0 Points	8.0 Points	10.0 Points
1	12.320	12.859	13.402	13.947	14.496	15.048	15.604	16.725	17.858	19.005	20.167	22.533
2	11.816	12.102	12.388	12.677	12.967	13.259	13.553	14.146	14.746	15.353	15.967	17.219
3	11.649	11.850	12.052	12.256	12.461	12.667	12.874	13.292	13.716	14.144	14.578	15.463
4	11.566	11.725	11.886	12.047	12.209	12.373	12.537	12.869	13.205	13.545	13.889	14.592
5	11.517	11.652	11.787	11.923	12.060	12.198	12.337	12.618	12.902	13.189	13.481	14.076
6	11.484	11.602	11.721	11.841	11.962	12.083	12.206	12.452	12.702	12.956	13.213	13.737
7	11.462	11.569	11.676	11.784	11.893	12.003	12.113	12.336	12.562	12.792	13.024	13.499
8	11.445	11.543	11.642	11.742	11.842	11.943	12.045	12.251	12.460	12.671	12.886	13.325
9	11.432	11.524	11.616	11.710	11.804	11.898	11.993	12.186	12.381	12.580	12.781	13.192
10	11.422	11.509	11.597	11.685	11.774	11.863	11.953	12.136	12.321	12.508	12.699	13.089
11	11.414	11.497	11.580	11.665	11.750	11.835	11.921	12.095	12.272	12.452	12.634	13.007
12	11.408	11.488	11.568	11.649	11.731	11.813	11.895	12.063	12.233	12.406	12.582	12.942
13	11.403	11.480	11.558	11.636	11.715	11.794	11.874	12.037	12.202	12.369	12.539	12.888
14	11.398	11.473	11.549	11.625	11.702	11.780	11.857	12.015	12.175	12.339	12.504	12.845
15	11.394	11.468	11.541	11.616	11.691	11.767	11.843	11.997	12.154	12.313	12.476	12.808
16	11.392	11.463	11.536	11.608	11.682	11.756	11.831	11.982	12.136	12.293	12.452	12.779
17	11.389	11.459	11.531	11.603	11.675	11.748	11.821	11.970	12.121	12.275	12.432	12.754
18	11.387	11.457	11.526	11.597	11.668	11.740	11.813	11.959	12.109	12.261	12.415	12.733
19	11.386	11.454	11.523	11.593	11.663	11.734	11.806	11.951	12.099	12.249	12.402	12.716
20	11.384	11.452	11.521	11.589	11.659	11.729	11.800	11.944	12.090	12.239	12.390	12.702
21	11.383	11.450	11.518	11.586	11.655	11.725	11.795	11.938	12.083	12.231	12.381	12.690
22	11.382	11.449	11.516	11.584	11.653	11.722	11.791	11.933	12.077	12.224	12.373	12.681
23	11.381	11.448	11.515	11.582	11.651	11.719	11.788	11.929	12.072	12.218	12.367	12.673
24	11.381	11.447	11.513	11.581	11.648	11.717	11.786	11.926	12.069	12.214	12.362	12.667
25	11.380	11.446	11.512	11.579	11.647	11.715	11.784	11.923	12.066	12.211	12.358	12.662
26	11.380	11.445	11.512	11.578	11.645	11.713	11.782	11.921	12.063	12.208	12.355	12.659
27	11.379	11.445	11.511	11.577	11.645	11.713	11.781	11.920	12.062	12.206	12.353	12.656
28	11.379	11.445	11.511	11.577	11.644	11.712	11.780	11.919	12.061	12.205	12.352	12.654
29	11.379	11.444	11.510	11.577	11.644	11.712	11.780	11.919	12.060	12.204	12.351	12.653
30	11.379	11.444	11.510	11.577	11.644	11.711	11.780	11.918	12.060	12.204	12.351	12.653

Yield on Mortgage Loan When Points Are Paid

Interest Rate 11.50%   25 Year Schedule   Annual Constant 12.197628%

Yield to end of Year	1.0 Point	1.5 Point	2.0 Points	2.5 Points	3.0 Points	3.5 Points	4.0 Points	5.0 Points	6.0 Points	7.0 Points	8.0 Points	10.0 Points
1	12.573	13.114	13.658	14.205	14.756	15.309	15.866	16.990	18.126	19.277	20.442	22.814
2	12.069	12.356	12.645	12.935	13.227	13.521	13.816	14.412	15.015	15.626	16.244	17.503
3	11.902	12.105	12.309	12.515	12.721	12.929	13.138	13.560	13.986	14.419	14.856	15.748
4	11.820	11.981	12.143	12.306	12.470	12.636	12.802	13.137	13.477	13.821	14.170	14.880
5	11.771	11.907	12.044	12.182	12.321	12.461	12.602	12.887	13.175	13.467	13.763	14.366
6	11.738	11.859	11.979	12.101	12.224	12.347	12.472	12.723	12.977	13.235	13.497	14.031
7	11.716	11.825	11.935	12.045	12.156	12.268	12.380	12.608	12.839	13.073	13.310	13.795
8	11.699	11.800	11.901	12.003	12.106	12.209	12.313	12.524	12.737	12.954	13.174	13.623
9	11.687	11.781	11.876	11.972	12.068	12.165	12.263	12.460	12.661	12.864	13.071	13.494
10	11.677	11.767	11.856	11.947	12.038	12.131	12.223	12.411	12.601	12.795	12.991	13.393
11	11.669	11.755	11.841	11.928	12.016	12.104	12.192	12.372	12.555	12.740	12.929	13.315
12	11.663	11.746	11.829	11.913	11.997	12.082	12.168	12.341	12.518	12.697	12.879	13.252
13	11.658	11.739	11.819	11.901	11.983	12.065	12.148	12.317	12.488	12.662	12.839	13.202
14	11.654	11.733	11.811	11.890	11.970	12.051	12.132	12.296	12.464	12.634	12.806	13.162
15	11.651	11.728	11.805	11.883	11.961	12.040	12.119	12.281	12.444	12.611	12.781	13.129
16	11.649	11.724	11.800	11.876	11.953	12.031	12.109	12.268	12.429	12.592	12.760	13.102
17	11.646	11.721	11.795	11.871	11.947	12.023	12.100	12.256	12.416	12.577	12.743	13.081
18	11.645	11.718	11.791	11.866	11.941	12.017	12.093	12.248	12.405	12.566	12.729	13.064
19	11.643	11.716	11.789	11.863	11.937	12.012	12.088	12.242	12.398	12.557	12.718	13.051
20	11.642	11.714	11.787	11.860	11.934	12.008	12.084	12.236	12.391	12.549	12.710	13.041
21	11.641	11.713	11.785	11.858	11.931	12.005	12.080	12.232	12.386	12.543	12.703	13.032
22	11.641	11.712	11.784	11.857	11.930	12.003	12.078	12.229	12.383	12.540	12.699	13.027
23	11.641	11.712	11.783	11.856	11.929	12.002	12.076	12.227	12.380	12.537	12.696	13.024
24	11.640	11.711	11.783	11.855	11.928	12.002	12.076	12.226	12.379	12.536	12.695	13.022
25	11.640	11.711	11.783	11.855	11.928	12.002	12.076	12.226	12.379	12.535	12.694	13.021

Interest Rate 11.50%   30 Year Schedule   Annual Constant 11.883497%

Yield to end of Year	1.0 Point	1.5 Point	2.0 Points	2.5 Points	3.0 Points	3.5 Points	4.0 Points	5.0 Points	6.0 Points	7.0 Points	8.0 Points	10.0 Points
1	12.571	13.112	13.655	14.201	14.751	15.304	15.860	16.981	18.117	19.265	20.428	22.797
2	12.067	12.354	12.641	12.931	13.222	13.514	13.809	14.403	15.004	15.613	16.229	17.483
3	11.900	12.102	12.305	12.509	12.715	12.922	13.130	13.549	13.974	14.404	14.840	15.727
4	11.817	11.978	12.139	12.301	12.464	12.628	12.793	13.126	13.464	13.805	14.151	14.857
5	11.768	11.904	12.040	12.176	12.314	12.453	12.593	12.875	13.160	13.450	13.743	14.341
6	11.736	11.855	11.974	12.095	12.216	12.338	12.461	12.710	12.961	13.216	13.475	14.003
7	11.713	11.821	11.929	12.038	12.147	12.258	12.369	12.594	12.822	13.053	13.287	13.765
8	11.696	11.796	11.895	11.996	12.097	12.199	12.301	12.509	12.719	12.933	13.149	13.592
9	11.684	11.777	11.869	11.964	12.058	12.154	12.250	12.444	12.641	12.841	13.044	13.459
10	11.674	11.762	11.850	11.939	12.028	12.119	12.210	12.394	12.580	12.770	12.962	13.356
11	11.666	11.750	11.834	11.919	12.005	12.091	12.178	12.354	12.532	12.714	12.898	13.276
12	11.660	11.740	11.821	11.903	11.986	12.068	12.152	12.322	12.494	12.668	12.846	13.210
13	11.654	11.732	11.811	11.890	11.970	12.051	12.132	12.296	12.462	12.631	12.804	13.157
14	11.650	11.726	11.803	11.880	11.957	12.036	12.114	12.274	12.437	12.602	12.769	13.113
15	11.647	11.721	11.795	11.871	11.947	12.023	12.100	12.256	12.415	12.576	12.741	13.078
16	11.644	11.716	11.790	11.863	11.937	12.013	12.089	12.242	12.398	12.556	12.717	13.048
17	11.641	11.713	11.785	11.857	11.930	12.004	12.078	12.229	12.382	12.539	12.698	13.024
18	11.639	11.710	11.781	11.852	11.924	11.997	12.070	12.219	12.370	12.524	12.681	13.003
19	11.637	11.707	11.777	11.848	11.919	11.991	12.064	12.210	12.360	12.512	12.667	12.986
20	11.636	11.705	11.774	11.844	11.915	11.986	12.058	12.203	12.352	12.503	12.656	12.972
21	11.635	11.703	11.771	11.841	11.911	11.982	12.053	12.197	12.345	12.494	12.647	12.961
22	11.634	11.702	11.770	11.839	11.909	11.978	12.049	12.193	12.339	12.488	12.639	12.952
23	11.633	11.700	11.768	11.837	11.906	11.976	12.047	12.189	12.334	12.482	12.633	12.944
24	11.632	11.700	11.767	11.835	11.904	11.974	12.044	12.186	12.331	12.478	12.628	12.938
25	11.632	11.699	11.766	11.834	11.903	11.972	12.042	12.183	12.328	12.475	12.625	12.933
26	11.632	11.698	11.765	11.833	11.902	11.971	12.041	12.181	12.325	12.472	12.622	12.930
27	11.631	11.698	11.765	11.833	11.901	11.970	12.039	12.181	12.324	12.470	12.620	12.927
28	11.631	11.698	11.765	11.832	11.900	11.969	12.039	12.179	12.323	12.469	12.618	12.926
29	11.631	11.697	11.764	11.832	11.900	11.968	12.038	12.179	12.322	12.468	12.618	12.925
30	11.631	11.697	11.764	11.832	11.900	11.969	12.038	12.179	12.322	12.468	12.617	12.924

Yield on Mortgage Loan When Points Are Paid

Interest Rate 11.75% 25 Year Schedule   Annual Constant 12.417578%

Yield to end of Year	1.0 Point	1.5 Point	2.0 Points	2.5 Points	3.0 Points	3.5 Points	4.0 Points	5.0 Points	6.0 Points	7.0 Points	8.0 Points	10.0 Points
1	12.824	13.366	13.911	14.458	15.009	15.564	16.121	17.246	18.384	19.536	20.702	23.078
2	12.320	12.608	12.897	13.188	13.481	13.775	14.071	14.669	15.273	15.885	16.504	17.766
3	12.153	12.357	12.561	12.768	12.975	13.183	13.393	13.816	14.244	14.678	15.117	16.012
4	12.070	12.232	12.395	12.559	12.724	12.890	13.057	13.394	13.735	14.081	14.431	15.145
5	12.021	12.159	12.297	12.436	12.575	12.716	12.858	13.144	13.433	13.727	14.024	14.631
6	11.989	12.110	12.232	12.355	12.478	12.602	12.727	12.980	13.236	13.495	13.758	14.295
7	11.967	12.076	12.187	12.298	12.410	12.523	12.636	12.865	13.097	13.333	13.572	14.060
8	11.951	12.052	12.154	12.257	12.360	12.464	12.569	12.782	12.997	13.215	13.437	13.889
9	11.938	12.033	12.129	12.225	12.322	12.420	12.519	12.718	12.920	13.125	13.333	13.759
10	11.929	12.018	12.109	12.201	12.293	12.386	12.480	12.669	12.861	13.056	13.254	13.660
11	11.921	12.007	12.094	12.182	12.270	12.359	12.449	12.630	12.815	13.002	13.192	13.581
12	11.915	11.998	12.082	12.166	12.252	12.338	12.424	12.600	12.778	12.959	13.142	13.519
13	11.910	11.991	12.073	12.155	12.237	12.321	12.405	12.575	12.748	12.924	13.103	13.469
14	11.906	11.985	12.064	12.144	12.225	12.307	12.389	12.555	12.724	12.896	13.071	13.429
15	11.903	11.980	12.058	12.136	12.215	12.295	12.376	12.539	12.705	12.873	13.045	13.397
16	11.900	11.976	12.053	12.130	12.208	12.286	12.365	12.526	12.689	12.855	13.024	13.371
17	11.898	11.973	12.048	12.124	12.201	12.279	12.357	12.515	12.676	12.840	13.007	13.350
18	11.896	11.970	12.045	12.120	12.196	12.273	12.350	12.507	12.666	12.828	12.993	13.333
19	11.895	11.968	12.042	12.117	12.192	12.268	12.345	12.500	12.658	12.819	12.983	13.320
20	11.894	11.966	12.040	12.114	12.189	12.264	12.341	12.495	12.652	12.812	12.975	13.310
21	11.893	11.965	12.038	12.112	12.187	12.262	12.337	12.491	12.647	12.806	12.968	13.302
22	11.892	11.964	12.037	12.111	12.185	12.260	12.335	12.488	12.644	12.802	12.964	13.296
23	11.892	11.964	12.037	12.110	12.184	12.258	12.334	12.486	12.642	12.800	12.961	13.293
24	11.892	11.963	12.036	12.109	12.183	12.258	12.333	12.485	12.640	12.798	12.959	13.291
25	11.891	11.963	12.036	12.109	12.183	12.257	12.333	12.485	12.640	12.798	12.959	13.291

Interest Rate 11.75% 30 Year Schedule   Annual Constant 12.112917%

Yield to end of Year	1.0 Point	1.5 Point	2.0 Points	2.5 Points	3.0 Points	3.5 Points	4.0 Points	5.0 Points	6.0 Points	7.0 Points	8.0 Points	10.0 Points
1	12.823	13.363	13.907	14.455	15.005	15.558	16.115	17.238	18.375	19.525	20.689	23.061
2	12.319	12.605	12.894	13.184	13.476	13.769	14.064	14.660	15.262	15.872	16.490	17.747
3	12.151	12.354	12.558	12.763	12.969	13.177	13.385	13.806	14.233	14.664	15.101	15.991
4	12.068	12.229	12.391	12.554	12.718	12.882	13.048	13.383	13.722	14.065	14.413	15.122
5	12.019	12.155	12.292	12.430	12.569	12.708	12.848	13.132	13.419	13.710	14.005	14.607
6	11.987	12.107	12.227	12.349	12.471	12.594	12.717	12.967	13.220	13.477	13.737	14.269
7	11.964	12.072	12.182	12.291	12.402	12.513	12.625	12.852	13.081	13.314	13.550	14.032
8	11.947	12.048	12.148	12.250	12.352	12.455	12.558	12.767	12.979	13.194	13.412	13.858
9	11.935	12.028	12.123	12.217	12.313	12.409	12.506	12.702	12.901	13.103	13.307	13.726
10	11.925	12.013	12.103	12.193	12.283	12.374	12.466	12.652	12.840	13.032	13.226	13.624
11	11.918	12.002	12.087	12.173	12.259	12.347	12.434	12.612	12.792	12.976	13.162	13.543
12	11.911	11.993	12.075	12.157	12.240	12.324	12.409	12.580	12.754	12.931	13.110	13.478
13	11.906	11.985	12.064	12.144	12.225	12.306	12.388	12.554	12.723	12.894	13.068	13.426
14	11.902	11.979	12.056	12.133	12.212	12.291	12.371	12.533	12.697	12.864	13.034	13.383
15	11.898	11.973	12.048	12.125	12.201	12.279	12.357	12.515	12.676	12.839	13.006	13.347
16	11.895	11.968	12.043	12.117	12.193	12.269	12.345	12.501	12.659	12.819	12.983	13.318
17	11.892	11.965	12.038	12.111	12.185	12.260	12.336	12.488	12.644	12.802	12.963	13.294
18	11.890	11.962	12.034	12.106	12.179	12.253	12.328	12.478	12.632	12.788	12.947	13.273
19	11.889	11.959	12.030	12.102	12.174	12.247	12.321	12.470	12.622	12.776	12.933	13.257
20	11.887	11.957	12.028	12.099	12.170	12.242	12.315	12.463	12.613	12.766	12.922	13.243
21	11.886	11.955	12.026	12.096	12.167	12.238	12.311	12.457	12.606	12.758	12.913	13.232
22	11.886	11.954	12.023	12.093	12.164	12.235	12.307	12.453	12.601	12.752	12.906	13.223
23	11.884	11.953	12.022	12.091	12.162	12.232	12.304	12.449	12.596	12.747	12.900	13.216
24	11.884	11.952	12.021	12.090	12.160	12.230	12.301	12.446	12.593	12.742	12.895	13.209
25	11.883	11.951	12.020	12.089	12.158	12.229	12.299	12.443	12.590	12.739	12.891	13.205
26	11.883	11.951	12.019	12.088	12.157	12.227	12.298	12.441	12.588	12.737	12.888	13.201
27	11.883	11.951	12.018	12.087	12.156	12.226	12.297	12.440	12.586	12.735	12.886	13.199
28	11.883	11.950	12.018	12.087	12.156	12.226	12.296	12.439	12.585	12.734	12.885	13.197
29	11.882	11.950	12.018	12.086	12.155	12.225	12.296	12.439	12.584	12.733	12.884	13.196
30	11.882	11.950	12.018	12.086	12.155	12.225	12.296	12.439	12.584	12.733	12.884	13.196

Yield on Mortgage Loan When Points Are Paid

Interest Rate 12.00% 25 Year Schedule   Annual Constant 12.638690%

Yield to end of Year	1.0 Point	1.5 Point	2.0 Points	2.5 Points	3.0 Points	3.5 Points	4.0 Points	5.0 Points	6.0 Points	7.0 Points	8.0 Points	10.0 Points
1	13.075	13.618	14.163	14.712	15.263	15.818	16.376	17.503	18.642	19.796	20.963	23.342
2	12.572	12.860	13.150	13.442	13.735	14.030	14.327	14.925	15.531	16.144	16.765	18.030
3	12.404	12.609	12.814	13.021	13.229	13.438	13.648	14.073	14.503	14.938	15.378	16.276
4	12.322	12.484	12.648	12.812	12.978	13.145	13.313	13.651	13.994	14.341	14.692	15.409
5	12.273	12.411	12.549	12.689	12.830	12.971	13.113	13.401	13.692	13.987	14.286	14.896
6	12.241	12.362	12.485	12.608	12.732	12.857	12.983	13.237	13.494	13.755	14.020	14.560
7	12.218	12.329	12.440	12.552	12.664	12.778	12.892	13.123	13.356	13.594	13.834	14.326
8	12.202	12.304	12.407	12.510	12.614	12.719	12.826	13.039	13.256	13.476	13.699	14.155
9	12.189	12.285	12.382	12.479	12.577	12.675	12.775	12.976	13.179	13.386	13.596	14.026
10	12.180	12.271	12.362	12.455	12.548	12.641	12.736	12.927	13.121	13.317	13.517	13.927
11	12.173	12.259	12.347	12.436	12.525	12.615	12.705	12.888	13.074	13.263	13.455	13.849
12	12.167	12.250	12.335	12.421	12.507	12.593	12.681	12.858	13.038	13.220	13.406	13.787
13	12.162	12.243	12.325	12.408	12.492	12.576	12.661	12.833	13.008	13.186	13.367	13.737
14	12.158	12.238	12.318	12.398	12.480	12.563	12.646	12.814	12.984	13.158	13.335	13.697
15	12.155	12.232	12.311	12.390	12.471	12.551	12.633	12.798	12.966	13.136	13.310	13.666
16	12.152	12.228	12.306	12.384	12.463	12.542	12.622	12.785	12.950	13.118	13.289	13.640
17	12.149	12.225	12.302	12.379	12.457	12.535	12.614	12.774	12.937	13.103	13.272	13.619
18	12.148	12.223	12.298	12.375	12.451	12.529	12.607	12.766	12.927	13.091	13.258	13.602
19	12.146	12.221	12.296	12.371	12.448	12.524	12.602	12.759	12.919	13.082	13.249	13.590
20	12.145	12.219	12.294	12.369	12.444	12.521	12.598	12.755	12.914	13.076	13.240	13.580
21	12.145	12.218	12.292	12.367	12.442	12.518	12.595	12.750	12.909	13.070	13.234	13.572
22	12.144	12.217	12.291	12.365	12.440	12.516	12.593	12.747	12.906	13.066	13.230	13.567
23	12.144	12.217	12.290	12.364	12.439	12.515	12.591	12.746	12.904	13.064	13.227	13.563
24	12.143	12.216	12.290	12.364	12.439	12.514	12.590	12.745	12.902	13.062	13.225	13.561
25	12.143	12.216	12.290	12.364	12.438	12.514	12.590	12.744	12.901	13.061	13.224	13.560

Interest Rate 12.00% 30 Year Schedule   Annual Constant 12.343351%

Yield to end of Year	1.0 Point	1.5 Point	2.0 Points	2.5 Points	3.0 Points	3.5 Points	4.0 Points	5.0 Points	6.0 Points	7.0 Points	8.0 Points	10.0 Points
1	13.074	13.615	14.160	14.708	15.259	15.813	16.370	17.495	18.633	19.785	20.951	23.326
2	12.570	12.857	13.147	13.437	13.730	14.024	14.320	14.917	15.521	16.132	16.751	18.012
3	12.403	12.606	12.810	13.016	13.223	13.431	13.641	14.063	14.491	14.924	15.362	16.256
4	12.320	12.481	12.644	12.808	12.972	13.138	13.304	13.640	13.981	14.326	14.675	15.387
5	12.271	12.407	12.545	12.683	12.823	12.963	13.104	13.389	13.678	13.971	14.267	14.872
6	12.238	12.359	12.480	12.602	12.725	12.849	12.973	13.225	13.480	13.738	14.000	14.534
7	12.216	12.325	12.435	12.545	12.656	12.768	12.881	13.109	13.340	13.575	13.812	14.298
8	12.199	12.300	12.401	12.503	12.606	12.710	12.814	13.024	13.238	13.455	13.675	14.125
9	12.186	12.281	12.376	12.471	12.568	12.665	12.763	12.960	13.161	13.364	13.571	13.994
10	12.177	12.266	12.356	12.447	12.538	12.630	12.723	12.910	13.100	13.294	13.490	13.891
11	12.169	12.254	12.340	12.427	12.514	12.602	12.691	12.871	13.053	13.238	13.426	13.811
12	12.163	12.245	12.328	12.411	12.495	12.580	12.666	12.839	13.014	13.193	13.374	13.746
13	12.158	12.237	12.317	12.398	12.480	12.562	12.645	12.813	12.983	13.157	13.333	13.695
14	12.154	12.231	12.309	12.388	12.467	12.547	12.628	12.792	12.958	13.127	13.299	13.651
15	12.150	12.226	12.302	12.379	12.457	12.535	12.614	12.774	12.937	13.102	13.271	13.617
16	12.147	12.221	12.296	12.372	12.448	12.525	12.603	12.760	12.920	13.082	13.248	13.588
17	12.144	12.218	12.291	12.366	12.441	12.517	12.593	12.748	12.906	13.066	13.229	13.564
18	12.142	12.215	12.287	12.361	12.435	12.510	12.585	12.738	12.894	13.052	13.213	13.544
19	12.141	12.212	12.284	12.357	12.430	12.504	12.578	12.730	12.883	13.040	13.200	13.528
20	12.139	12.210	12.281	12.353	12.426	12.499	12.573	12.723	12.875	13.031	13.189	13.514
21	12.138	12.208	12.279	12.350	12.422	12.495	12.568	12.717	12.868	13.023	13.180	13.503
22	12.137	12.207	12.277	12.348	12.420	12.492	12.565	12.712	12.863	13.016	13.173	13.494
23	12.136	12.206	12.276	12.346	12.417	12.489	12.562	12.709	12.858	13.011	13.166	13.487
24	12.136	12.205	12.274	12.345	12.416	12.487	12.559	12.706	12.855	13.007	13.162	13.481
25	12.135	12.204	12.273	12.344	12.415	12.485	12.557	12.703	12.852	13.004	13.158	13.477
26	12.135	12.204	12.273	12.343	12.413	12.484	12.556	12.702	12.850	13.001	13.155	13.473
27	12.135	12.203	12.272	12.342	12.412	12.483	12.555	12.700	12.848	12.999	13.153	13.470
28	12.134	12.203	12.272	12.342	12.412	12.483	12.554	12.699	12.847	12.998	13.152	13.469
29	12.134	12.203	12.272	12.341	12.411	12.482	12.554	12.699	12.847	12.998	13.151	13.468
30	12.134	12.203	12.272	12.341	12.411	12.482	12.554	12.699	12.847	12.997	13.151	13.468

Yield on Mortgage Loan When Points Are Paid

Interest Rate 12.25% 25 Year Schedule   Annual Constant 12.860925%

Yield to end of Year	1.0 Point	1.5 Point	2.0 Points	2.5 Points	3.0 Points	3.5 Points	4.0 Points	5.0 Points	6.0 Points	7.0 Points	8.0 Points	10.0 Points
1	13.327	13.870	14.416	14.965	15.517	16.073	16.632	17.759	18.900	20.055	21.224	23.606
2	12.823	13.112	13.402	13.695	13.989	14.284	14.582	15.182	15.789	16.404	17.026	18.294
3	12.656	12.861	13.067	13.274	13.483	13.693	13.904	14.330	14.761	15.197	15.639	16.540
4	12.574	12.737	12.901	13.066	13.232	13.400	13.568	13.908	14.252	14.600	14.953	15.674
5	12.525	12.663	12.803	12.943	13.084	13.226	13.369	13.658	13.950	14.247	14.548	15.161
6	12.492	12.614	12.738	12.862	12.987	13.112	13.239	13.495	13.754	14.016	14.282	14.826
7	12.470	12.581	12.693	12.806	12.919	13.033	13.148	13.381	13.616	13.855	14.097	14.592
8	12.453	12.556	12.660	12.764	12.869	12.975	13.082	13.297	13.515	13.737	13.962	14.422
9	12.441	12.538	12.635	12.733	12.832	12.931	13.032	13.234	13.439	13.648	13.860	14.293
10	12.432	12.523	12.615	12.709	12.802	12.897	12.992	13.185	13.380	13.579	13.781	14.194
11	12.424	12.512	12.600	12.690	12.780	12.870	12.962	13.147	13.334	13.525	13.719	14.116
12	12.418	12.503	12.589	12.675	12.762	12.850	12.938	13.117	13.298	13.483	13.670	14.055
13	12.413	12.495	12.579	12.662	12.747	12.832	12.918	13.092	13.269	13.448	13.631	14.005
14	12.409	12.490	12.571	12.653	12.735	12.818	12.902	13.072	13.245	13.421	13.599	13.966
15	12.406	12.485	12.564	12.645	12.726	12.807	12.890	13.056	13.226	13.399	13.574	13.934
16	12.404	12.481	12.560	12.638	12.718	12.798	12.879	13.044	13.210	13.380	13.553	13.909
17	12.402	12.478	12.556	12.634	12.712	12.792	12.872	13.034	13.199	13.366	13.537	13.888
18	12.399	12.475	12.552	12.630	12.707	12.786	12.865	13.025	13.189	13.355	13.524	13.872
19	12.398	12.473	12.550	12.626	12.703	12.781	12.860	13.019	13.181	13.346	13.514	13.859
20	12.397	12.472	12.548	12.624	12.700	12.778	12.856	13.014	13.175	13.339	13.506	13.849
21	12.396	12.471	12.546	12.622	12.698	12.775	12.853	13.010	13.170	13.334	13.500	13.842
22	12.396	12.470	12.545	12.620	12.696	12.773	12.850	13.007	13.167	13.330	13.496	13.837
23	12.396	12.469	12.544	12.619	12.695	12.771	12.849	13.006	13.165	13.327	13.493	13.833
24	12.396	12.469	12.544	12.618	12.695	12.771	12.848	13.005	13.164	13.326	13.491	13.831
25	12.396	12.469	12.544	12.618	12.694	12.771	12.848	13.004	13.163	13.325	13.491	13.831

Interest Rate 12.25% 30 Year Schedule   Annual Constant 12.574757%

Yield to end of Year	1.0 Point	1.5 Point	2.0 Points	2.5 Points	3.0 Points	3.5 Points	4.0 Points	5.0 Points	6.0 Points	7.0 Points	8.0 Points	10.0 Points
1	13.325	13.867	14.413	14.961	15.513	16.068	16.626	17.752	18.891	20.045	21.212	23.590
2	12.821	13.109	13.399	13.691	13.984	14.279	14.575	15.173	15.779	16.392	17.012	18.276
3	12.654	12.858	13.063	13.270	13.477	13.686	13.896	14.320	14.749	15.184	15.624	16.521
4	12.572	12.734	12.897	13.061	13.226	13.393	13.560	13.898	14.240	14.586	14.937	15.652
5	12.522	12.660	12.798	12.938	13.078	13.218	13.360	13.647	13.937	14.231	14.529	15.138
6	12.490	12.611	12.733	12.856	12.980	13.104	13.229	13.482	13.739	13.999	14.263	14.801
7	12.467	12.577	12.688	12.799	12.911	13.024	13.138	13.367	13.600	13.836	14.076	14.565
8	12.451	12.552	12.655	12.758	12.861	12.966	13.071	13.283	13.498	13.717	13.939	14.392
9	12.438	12.534	12.629	12.726	12.823	12.921	13.019	13.218	13.421	13.626	13.835	14.261
10	12.429	12.518	12.609	12.701	12.793	12.886	12.979	13.169	13.361	13.556	13.754	14.159
11	12.421	12.507	12.594	12.682	12.769	12.858	12.948	13.130	13.313	13.500	13.690	14.079
12	12.415	12.497	12.581	12.665	12.751	12.836	12.923	13.098	13.276	13.456	13.639	14.015
13	12.409	12.490	12.571	12.653	12.735	12.818	12.902	13.072	13.244	13.419	13.598	13.963
14	12.405	12.483	12.562	12.642	12.723	12.804	12.885	13.051	13.219	13.390	13.564	13.921
15	12.402	12.479	12.556	12.634	12.713	12.792	12.872	13.034	13.199	13.366	13.537	13.886
16	12.398	12.474	12.550	12.626	12.704	12.782	12.861	13.020	13.181	13.346	13.514	13.858
17	12.396	12.471	12.545	12.620	12.697	12.774	12.851	13.008	13.167	13.330	13.495	13.834
18	12.394	12.467	12.541	12.616	12.691	12.766	12.843	12.997	13.155	13.316	13.479	13.815
19	12.392	12.465	12.538	12.611	12.686	12.761	12.836	12.989	13.146	13.304	13.466	13.798
20	12.392	12.463	12.536	12.608	12.682	12.756	12.831	12.983	13.137	13.295	13.455	13.785
21	12.390	12.462	12.533	12.606	12.679	12.752	12.826	12.977	13.130	13.287	13.447	13.774
22	12.389	12.460	12.532	12.603	12.676	12.749	12.823	12.972	13.125	13.281	13.439	13.765
23	12.388	12.459	12.530	12.602	12.673	12.746	12.820	12.969	13.121	13.275	13.433	13.758
24	12.388	12.458	12.528	12.600	12.672	12.744	12.817	12.966	13.117	13.271	13.429	13.753
25	12.388	12.458	12.528	12.598	12.670	12.743	12.816	12.964	13.115	13.268	13.425	13.748
26	12.387	12.456	12.527	12.598	12.669	12.741	12.814	12.962	13.112	13.266	13.423	13.745
27	12.387	12.456	12.526	12.597	12.668	12.740	12.813	12.961	13.111	13.264	13.421	13.743
28	12.386	12.456	12.526	12.597	12.668	12.740	12.812	12.960	13.110	13.263	13.419	13.741
29	12.386	12.456	12.526	12.596	12.668	12.739	12.812	12.959	13.109	13.262	13.419	13.740
30	12.386	12.456	12.526	12.596	12.667	12.739	12.812	12.959	13.109	13.262	13.419	13.740

Yield on Mortgage Loan When Points Are Paid

Interest Rate 12.50% 25 Year Schedule   Annual Constant 13.084250%

Yield to end of Year	1.0 Point	1.5 Point	2.0 Points	2.5 Points	3.0 Points	3.5 Points	4.0 Points	5.0 Points	6.0 Points	7.0 Points	8.0 Points	10.0 Points
1	13.578	14.121	14.668	15.218	15.771	16.328	16.887	18.016	19.159	20.315	21.485	23.870
2	13.074	13.363	13.655	13.947	14.243	14.539	14.837	15.439	16.047	16.663	17.287	18.557
3	12.907	13.113	13.320	13.528	13.737	13.947	14.159	14.586	15.019	15.457	15.900	16.804
4	12.824	12.988	13.154	13.320	13.487	13.654	13.824	14.165	14.510	14.860	15.215	15.938
5	12.776	12.915	13.055	13.196	13.338	13.481	13.625	13.915	14.209	14.507	14.809	15.426
6	12.743	12.867	12.991	13.115	13.241	13.368	13.495	13.752	14.013	14.277	14.545	15.092
7	12.721	12.833	12.946	13.059	13.173	13.289	13.404	13.638	13.875	14.116	14.360	14.858
8	12.705	12.809	12.913	13.018	13.124	13.231	13.338	13.555	13.775	13.998	14.225	14.688
9	12.692	12.790	12.888	12.987	13.086	13.186	13.287	13.491	13.699	13.909	14.123	14.560
10	12.683	12.775	12.869	12.963	13.057	13.153	13.249	13.443	13.640	13.841	14.044	14.461
11	12.676	12.764	12.854	12.944	13.035	13.126	13.218	13.405	13.594	13.787	13.983	14.384
12	12.669	12.755	12.842	12.929	13.017	13.105	13.194	13.375	13.558	13.745	13.934	14.323
13	12.664	12.748	12.832	12.917	13.002	13.088	13.175	13.351	13.530	13.710	13.896	14.274
14	12.661	12.742	12.824	12.907	12.990	13.074	13.159	13.331	13.506	13.683	13.864	14.234
15	12.658	12.737	12.818	12.899	12.981	13.063	13.147	13.316	13.487	13.662	13.839	14.203
16	12.655	12.734	12.813	12.893	12.974	13.055	13.137	13.303	13.472	13.644	13.819	14.178
17	12.653	12.730	12.809	12.888	12.967	13.047	13.128	13.292	13.459	13.629	13.802	14.158
18	12.652	12.728	12.806	12.884	12.963	13.042	13.122	13.285	13.450	13.618	13.790	14.142
19	12.650	12.727	12.803	12.881	12.959	13.038	13.117	13.278	13.442	13.609	13.779	14.129
20	12.649	12.724	12.801	12.878	12.956	13.034	13.113	13.273	13.436	13.602	13.772	14.119
21	12.648	12.723	12.799	12.876	12.954	13.032	13.110	13.270	13.432	13.597	13.766	14.112
22	12.648	12.723	12.798	12.874	12.951	13.030	13.108	13.267	13.429	13.593	13.761	14.107
23	12.647	12.722	12.798	12.874	12.951	13.028	13.107	13.265	13.427	13.591	13.759	14.104
24	12.647	12.722	12.798	12.874	12.950	13.028	13.106	13.264	13.425	13.590	13.757	14.102
25	12.647	12.722	12.797	12.873	12.950	13.027	13.105	13.263	13.425	13.589	13.757	14.101

Interest Rate 12.50% 30 Year Schedule   Annual Constant 12.807093%

Yield to end of Year	1.0 Point	1.5 Point	2.0 Points	2.5 Points	3.0 Points	3.5 Points	4.0 Points	5.0 Points	6.0 Points	7.0 Points	8.0 Points	10.0 Points
1	13.577	14.119	14.665	15.215	15.767	16.323	16.881	18.009	19.150	20.305	21.473	23.855
2	13.072	13.361	13.652	13.944	14.237	14.533	14.831	15.430	16.037	16.652	17.273	18.540
3	12.906	13.110	13.316	13.523	13.731	13.941	14.152	14.577	15.008	15.444	15.885	16.785
4	12.822	12.985	13.149	13.315	13.481	13.648	13.816	14.155	14.498	14.846	15.198	15.917
5	12.773	12.912	13.051	13.191	13.332	13.473	13.616	13.904	14.196	14.492	14.792	15.403
6	12.741	12.863	12.986	13.110	13.234	13.359	13.485	13.740	13.998	14.260	14.525	15.067
7	12.719	12.830	12.941	13.053	13.166	13.280	13.394	13.625	13.860	14.097	14.339	14.831
8	12.703	12.805	12.908	13.011	13.115	13.221	13.327	13.541	13.758	13.978	14.202	14.659
9	12.689	12.785	12.882	12.979	13.077	13.176	13.276	13.477	13.681	13.888	14.098	14.528
10	12.680	12.771	12.862	12.955	13.048	13.142	13.236	13.427	13.621	13.818	14.018	14.427
11	12.672	12.759	12.847	12.935	13.024	13.114	13.205	13.388	13.574	13.763	13.954	14.347
12	12.666	12.750	12.834	12.920	13.006	13.092	13.180	13.357	13.536	13.719	13.904	14.284
13	12.661	12.742	12.824	12.907	12.990	13.075	13.159	13.331	13.505	13.682	13.863	14.232
14	12.657	12.736	12.816	12.897	12.978	13.060	13.143	13.310	13.480	13.653	13.829	14.190
15	12.653	12.731	12.810	12.889	12.968	13.049	13.129	13.293	13.460	13.630	13.802	14.156
16	12.651	12.727	12.804	12.882	12.960	13.039	13.118	13.279	13.443	13.610	13.779	14.128
17	12.648	12.723	12.799	12.876	12.953	13.030	13.109	13.267	13.429	13.593	13.761	14.105
18	12.646	12.720	12.795	12.870	12.946	13.023	13.100	13.257	13.417	13.580	13.745	14.085
19	12.644	12.718	12.792	12.866	12.941	13.017	13.094	13.249	13.408	13.569	13.732	14.069
20	12.643	12.716	12.789	12.863	12.937	13.013	13.089	13.243	13.399	13.559	13.721	14.056
21	12.642	12.714	12.787	12.860	12.934	13.009	13.084	13.237	13.393	13.552	13.713	14.046
22	12.641	12.713	12.785	12.858	12.931	13.006	13.081	13.233	13.387	13.545	13.706	14.037
23	12.640	12.712	12.783	12.856	12.929	13.003	13.078	13.229	13.383	13.540	13.700	14.030
24	12.640	12.711	12.782	12.855	12.928	13.001	13.075	13.226	13.380	13.536	13.696	14.025
25	12.639	12.710	12.782	12.853	12.926	13.000	13.074	13.224	13.377	13.533	13.693	14.020
26	12.639	12.709	12.781	12.853	12.925	12.998	13.072	13.222	13.375	13.531	13.690	14.017
27	12.639	12.709	12.780	12.852	12.924	12.998	13.071	13.221	13.374	13.530	13.688	14.015
28	12.638	12.709	12.780	12.852	12.924	12.997	13.071	13.220	13.373	13.528	13.686	14.013
29	12.638	12.709	12.780	12.851	12.924	12.997	13.070	13.220	13.372	13.528	13.686	14.013
30	12.638	12.709	12.780	12.851	12.924	12.997	13.070	13.220	13.372	13.528	13.686	14.012

Yield on Mortgage Loan When Points Are Paid

Interest Rate 15.00% 25 Year Schedule   Annual Constant 15.369967%

Yield to end of Year	1.0 Point	1.5 Point	2.0 Points	2.5 Points	3.0 Points	3.5 Points	4.0 Points	5.0 Points	6.0 Points	7.0 Points	8.0 Points	10.0 Points
1	16.091	16.641	17.195	17.752	18.311	18.875	19.441	20.584	21.741	22.912	24.098	26.513
2	15.587	15.884	16.182	16.481	16.783	17.086	17.391	18.007	18.630	19.260	19.899	21.200
3	15.421	15.633	15.847	16.062	16.278	16.495	16.714	17.156	17.603	18.056	18.515	19.451
4	15.339	15.510	15.682	15.855	16.029	16.204	16.380	16.737	17.097	17.463	17.833	18.590
5	15.290	15.437	15.584	15.733	15.882	16.032	16.184	16.490	16.799	17.114	17.432	18.083
6	15.259	15.389	15.521	15.653	15.786	15.921	16.056	16.329	16.605	16.886	17.171	17.753
7	15.237	15.356	15.477	15.598	15.720	15.843	15.967	16.217	16.471	16.728	16.990	17.525
8	15.221	15.332	15.445	15.558	15.672	15.786	15.902	16.136	16.373	16.614	16.859	17.359
9	15.209	15.314	15.420	15.528	15.635	15.744	15.854	16.075	16.300	16.529	16.761	17.236
10	15.200	15.300	15.402	15.505	15.608	15.712	15.817	16.029	16.244	16.463	16.686	17.142
11	15.192	15.290	15.387	15.486	15.586	15.686	15.788	15.993	16.201	16.412	16.628	17.069
12	15.187	15.281	15.376	15.472	15.569	15.667	15.765	15.964	16.167	16.373	16.582	17.012
13	15.182	15.274	15.367	15.461	15.555	15.651	15.747	15.941	16.139	16.341	16.546	16.967
14	15.179	15.269	15.360	15.452	15.544	15.638	15.732	15.923	16.118	16.316	16.517	16.931
15	15.176	15.265	15.355	15.445	15.536	15.628	15.721	15.909	16.101	16.296	16.494	16.903
16	15.174	15.261	15.350	15.439	15.530	15.620	15.712	15.898	16.087	16.280	16.476	16.880
17	15.172	15.259	15.346	15.435	15.524	15.614	15.705	15.889	16.077	16.268	16.462	16.863
18	15.170	15.256	15.343	15.431	15.519	15.609	15.699	15.881	16.068	16.258	16.451	16.849
19	15.169	15.255	15.341	15.428	15.516	15.605	15.695	15.876	16.062	16.250	16.442	16.838
20	15.168	15.253	15.339	15.426	15.514	15.602	15.691	15.872	16.056	16.244	16.435	16.829
21	15.168	15.252	15.338	15.425	15.512	15.600	15.689	15.869	16.053	16.240	16.431	16.824
22	15.167	15.252	15.337	15.423	15.511	15.598	15.687	15.867	16.050	16.237	16.427	16.820
23	15.167	15.251	15.337	15.423	15.510	15.597	15.686	15.865	16.048	16.235	16.425	16.817
24	15.167	15.251	15.336	15.422	15.509	15.597	15.685	15.865	16.047	16.234	16.424	16.816
25	15.167	15.251	15.336	15.422	15.509	15.597	15.685	15.864	16.047	16.233	16.423	16.815

Interest Rate 15.00% 30 Year Schedule   Annual Constant 15.173328%

Yield to end of Year	1.0 Point	1.5 Point	2.0 Points	2.5 Points	3.0 Points	3.5 Points	4.0 Points	5.0 Points	6.0 Points	7.0 Points	8.0 Points	10.0 Points
1	16.090	16.640	17.193	17.749	18.308	18.871	19.437	20.579	21.735	22.905	24.089	26.502
2	15.586	15.882	16.179	16.478	16.779	17.082	17.386	18.001	18.622	19.252	19.889	21.188
3	15.420	15.631	15.844	16.058	16.274	16.491	16.709	17.149	17.595	18.047	18.504	19.437
4	15.337	15.507	15.679	15.851	16.024	16.199	16.375	16.729	17.088	17.452	17.821	18.574
5	15.289	15.434	15.581	15.729	15.877	16.027	16.177	16.481	16.790	17.102	17.419	18.066
6	15.257	15.387	15.517	15.649	15.781	15.914	16.049	16.320	16.595	16.873	17.156	17.734
7	15.235	15.353	15.473	15.593	15.714	15.836	15.959	16.207	16.459	16.714	16.974	17.504
8	15.219	15.329	15.440	15.552	15.665	15.779	15.894	16.125	16.360	16.599	16.841	17.337
9	15.206	15.311	15.416	15.522	15.629	15.736	15.844	16.063	16.286	16.512	16.741	17.212
10	15.197	15.297	15.397	15.498	15.600	15.703	15.807	16.016	16.229	16.445	16.665	17.116
11	15.190	15.286	15.382	15.480	15.578	15.677	15.777	15.979	16.184	16.393	16.605	17.041
12	15.184	15.276	15.370	15.465	15.560	15.656	15.753	15.949	16.148	16.351	16.557	16.981
13	15.179	15.270	15.361	15.453	15.546	15.640	15.734	15.925	16.120	16.318	16.520	16.933
14	15.175	15.264	15.354	15.444	15.535	15.626	15.719	15.907	16.097	16.291	16.489	16.895
15	15.172	15.260	15.348	15.436	15.526	15.616	15.706	15.891	16.079	16.270	16.464	16.864
16	15.170	15.256	15.342	15.430	15.518	15.607	15.697	15.879	16.064	16.253	16.445	16.840
17	15.168	15.253	15.338	15.425	15.512	15.600	15.689	15.868	16.052	16.238	16.428	16.820
18	15.166	15.250	15.335	15.420	15.507	15.594	15.682	15.860	16.042	16.227	16.415	16.803
19	15.165	15.248	15.332	15.416	15.502	15.589	15.676	15.853	16.033	16.217	16.404	16.790
20	15.163	15.246	15.329	15.414	15.499	15.585	15.671	15.847	16.027	16.209	16.395	16.779
21	15.162	15.245	15.328	15.411	15.496	15.581	15.668	15.843	16.021	16.203	16.388	16.770
22	15.162	15.244	15.326	15.410	15.494	15.579	15.665	15.839	16.017	16.198	16.382	16.763
23	15.161	15.243	15.325	15.408	15.492	15.577	15.662	15.836	16.013	16.194	16.378	16.757
24	15.161	15.242	15.324	15.407	15.491	15.575	15.661	15.834	16.010	16.190	16.374	16.753
25	15.160	15.242	15.324	15.406	15.490	15.574	15.659	15.832	16.008	16.189	16.372	16.750
26	15.160	15.241	15.323	15.405	15.489	15.573	15.658	15.831	16.007	16.186	16.370	16.748
27	15.160	15.241	15.323	15.405	15.489	15.572	15.657	15.830	16.006	16.185	16.368	16.746
28	15.160	15.241	15.322	15.405	15.488	15.572	15.657	15.830	16.005	16.185	16.368	16.745
29	15.160	15.241	15.322	15.405	15.488	15.572	15.657	15.829	16.005	16.184	16.367	16.745
30	15.160	15.241	15.322	15.405	15.487	15.572	15.656	15.829	16.005	16.184	16.367	16.744

Yield on Construction Loan When Points Are Paid

Points Paid	Yield at Month	5.50% Interest Rate Average Balance							5.75% Interest Rate Average Balance						
		50%	55%	60%	70%	80%	90%	100%	50%	55%	60%	70%	80%	90%	100%
	3	13.683	12.930	12.304	11.322	10.588	10.019	9.564	13.937	13.183	12.557	11.575	10.841	10.271	9.816
	6	9.613	9.235	8.920	8.428	8.059	7.773	7.544	9.866	9.488	9.173	8.680	8.311	8.024	7.796
	9	8.259	8.006	7.795	7.464	7.217	7.025	6.872	8.512	8.258	8.047	7.716	7.469	7.277	7.123
	12	7.583	7.392	7.233	6.983	6.796	6.652	6.536	7.836	7.644	7.485	7.235	7.048	6.903	6.787
1 Point	15	7.178	7.023	6.895	6.694	6.544	6.427	6.334	7.430	7.276	7.148	6.946	6.796	6.679	6.585
	18	6.907	6.778	6.671	6.502	6.376	6.278	6.200	7.160	7.031	6.923	6.754	6.628	6.530	6.451
	24	6.570	6.472	6.390	6.262	6.166	6.091	6.032	6.823	6.724	6.642	6.514	6.418	6.343	6.283
	30	6.367	6.288	6.222	6.118	6.040	5.979	5.931	6.620	6.540	6.474	6.370	6.292	6.231	6.183
	36	6.233	6.165	6.109	6.022	5.956	5.905	5.864	6.485	6.418	6.362	6.274	6.208	6.156	6.116
	48	6.064	6.013	5.969	5.902	5.851	5.812	5.781	6.317	6.265	6.222	6.154	6.103	6.063	6.032
	60	5.963	5.921	5.886	5.830	5.788	5.756	5.730	6.216	6.173	6.138	6.082	6.040	6.008	5.982
	72	5.897	5.860	5.830	5.782	5.747	5.719	5.697	6.149	6.113	6.082	6.034	5.998	5.971	5.948
	3	17.859	16.714	15.764	14.276	13.165	12.304	11.616	18.114	16.969	16.018	14.530	13.418	12.557	11.869
	6	11.706	11.133	10.657	9.910	9.353	8.920	8.575	11.961	11.387	10.910	10.164	9.606	9.173	8.828
	9	9.663	9.278	8.959	8.459	8.085	7.795	7.563	9.917	9.532	9.212	8.712	8.338	8.047	7.816
	12	8.642	8.352	8.111	7.734	7.451	7.233	7.058	8.896	8.606	8.365	7.987	7.704	7.485	7.310
1.5 Points	15	8.030	7.797	7.603	7.299	7.072	6.895	6.755	8.285	8.051	7.856	7.552	7.324	7.148	7.007
	18	7.623	7.427	7.264	7.009	6.818	6.671	6.553	7.877	7.681	7.518	7.262	7.071	6.923	6.805
	24	7.114	6.965	6.841	6.647	6.502	6.390	6.300	7.368	7.218	7.094	6.900	6.755	6.642	6.552
	30	6.808	6.688	6.587	6.430	6.313	6.222	6.149	7.062	6.941	6.841	6.683	6.565	6.474	6.401
	36	6.605	6.503	6.418	6.286	6.186	6.109	6.048	6.859	6.757	6.672	6.538	6.439	6.362	6.300
	48	6.351	6.273	6.207	6.105	6.029	5.969	5.922	6.605	6.526	6.461	6.358	6.281	6.222	6.174
	60	6.199	6.135	6.081	5.997	5.934	5.886	5.847	6.453	6.389	6.335	6.250	6.187	6.138	6.099
	72	6.098	6.043	5.997	5.925	5.871	5.830	5.797	6.353	6.297	6.251	6.178	6.124	6.082	6.049
	3	22.093	20.546	19.264	17.259	15.764	14.606	13.683	22.350	20.803	19.519	17.514	16.018	14.860	13.937
	6	13.826	13.052	12.410	11.406	10.657	10.076	9.613	14.082	13.308	12.665	11.660	10.910	10.329	9.866
	9	11.083	10.564	10.134	9.461	8.959	8.570	8.259	11.338	10.820	10.389	9.715	9.212	8.823	8.512
	12	9.713	9.322	8.998	8.490	8.111	7.817	7.583	9.969	9.578	9.253	8.744	8.365	8.070	7.836
2 Points	15	8.893	8.578	8.317	7.908	7.603	7.366	7.178	9.149	8.833	8.571	8.162	7.856	7.619	7.430
	18	8.346	8.082	7.863	7.520	7.264	7.066	6.907	8.602	8.337	8.118	7.774	7.518	7.319	7.160
	24	7.663	7.463	7.296	7.036	6.841	6.690	6.570	7.919	7.718	7.551	7.289	7.094	6.943	6.823
	30	7.254	7.091	6.956	6.745	6.587	6.465	6.367	7.510	7.347	7.211	6.999	6.841	6.718	6.620
	36	6.982	6.844	6.730	6.552	6.418	6.315	6.233	7.237	7.099	6.985	6.805	6.672	6.568	6.485
	48	6.641	6.535	6.448	6.310	6.207	6.128	6.064	6.897	6.791	6.702	6.564	6.461	6.381	6.317
	60	6.438	6.351	6.278	6.165	6.081	6.016	5.963	6.693	6.606	6.533	6.419	6.335	6.269	6.216
	72	6.302	6.228	6.166	6.069	5.997	5.941	5.897	6.558	6.483	6.421	6.323	6.251	6.194	6.149
	3	30.740	28.357	26.386	23.313	21.029	19.264	17.859	31.001	28.617	26.645	23.571	21.285	19.519	18.114
	6	18.143	16.955	15.971	14.436	13.293	12.410	11.706	18.402	17.213	16.229	14.692	13.549	12.665	11.961
	9	13.973	13.178	12.519	11.491	10.726	10.134	9.663	14.232	13.436	12.777	11.748	10.981	10.389	9.917
	12	11.893	11.294	10.797	10.022	9.445	8.998	8.642	12.152	11.552	11.054	10.278	9.700	9.253	8.896
3 Points	15	10.648	10.165	9.765	9.141	8.676	8.317	8.030	10.906	10.423	10.022	9.397	8.932	8.571	8.285
	18	9.818	9.413	9.078	8.554	8.165	7.863	7.623	10.077	9.671	9.335	8.810	8.420	8.118	7.877
	24	8.782	8.474	8.220	7.822	7.525	7.296	7.114	9.041	8.732	8.477	8.078	7.781	7.551	7.368
	30	8.161	7.912	7.705	7.383	7.142	6.956	6.808	8.420	8.169	7.962	7.639	7.397	7.211	7.062
	36	7.748	7.537	7.362	7.090	6.887	6.730	6.605	8.006	7.795	7.620	7.346	7.142	6.985	6.859
	48	7.232	7.069	6.935	6.725	6.568	6.448	6.351	7.490	7.327	7.192	6.981	6.824	6.702	6.605
	60	6.923	6.789	6.679	6.506	6.378	6.278	6.199	7.182	7.047	6.936	6.762	6.633	6.533	6.453
	72	6.718	6.603	6.509	6.361	6.251	6.166	6.098	6.977	6.861	6.766	6.617	6.506	6.421	6.353
	3	39.637	36.372	33.677	29.490	26.386	23.993	22.093	39.901	36.635	33.939	29.772	26.645	24.251	22.350
	6	22.570	20.947	19.606	17.520	15.971	14.776	13.826	22.832	21.208	19.866	17.778	16.229	15.033	14.082
	9	16.933	15.849	14.952	13.556	12.519	11.719	11.083	17.195	16.109	15.212	13.814	12.777	11.976	11.338
	12	14.125	13.308	12.631	11.579	10.797	10.194	9.713	14.387	13.568	12.891	11.837	11.054	10.450	9.969
4 Points	15	12.444	11.786	11.242	10.394	9.765	9.279	8.893	12.705	12.046	11.501	10.653	10.022	9.536	9.149
	18	11.324	10.772	10.316	9.606	9.078	8.670	8.346	11.586	11.033	10.576	9.864	9.335	8.927	8.602
	24	9.927	9.507	9.161	8.621	8.220	7.910	7.663	10.188	9.768	9.420	8.879	8.477	8.166	7.919
	30	9.089	8.749	8.468	8.030	7.705	7.454	7.254	9.351	9.010	8.728	8.288	7.962	7.710	7.510
	36	8.532	8.245	8.007	7.637	7.362	7.150	6.982	8.793	8.505	8.267	7.895	7.620	7.407	7.237
	48	7.836	7.615	7.432	7.147	6.935	6.771	6.641	8.098	7.875	7.691	7.405	7.192	7.028	6.897
	60	7.420	7.238	7.087	6.853	6.679	6.545	6.438	7.682	7.499	7.347	7.111	6.936	6.801	6.693
	72	7.143	6.987	6.858	6.658	6.509	6.394	6.302	7.405	7.248	7.118	6.916	6.766	6.650	6.558
	3	48.796	44.600	41.145	35.793	31.838	28.797	26.386	49.065	44.898	41.410	37.243	33.077	29.057	26.645
	6	27.111	25.032	23.318	20.659	18.690	17.174	15.971	27.377	25.297	23.582	20.920	18.950	17.433	16.229
	9	19.967	18.559	17.434	15.656	14.333	13.325	12.519	20.232	18.843	17.696	15.917	14.598	13.583	12.777
	12	16.411	15.365	14.502	13.162	12.170	11.405	10.797	16.676	15.629	14.765	13.423	12.429	11.663	11.054
5 Points	15	14.283	13.441	12.747	11.669	10.870	10.254	9.765	14.548	13.705	13.009	11.929	11.129	10.512	10.022
	18	12.866	12.161	11.579	10.674	10.004	9.488	9.078	13.131	12.424	11.841	10.935	10.263	9.746	9.335
	24	11.098	10.562	10.120	9.433	8.924	8.531	8.220	11.363	10.826	10.382	9.693	9.183	8.789	8.477
	30	10.039	9.605	9.246	8.689	8.276	7.958	7.705	10.304	9.868	9.508	8.949	8.535	8.216	7.962
	36	9.335	8.967	8.664	8.194	7.845	7.576	7.362	9.599	9.231	8.926	8.454	8.104	7.834	7.620
	48	8.455	8.172	7.938	7.575	7.307	7.099	6.935	8.720	8.435	8.201	7.836	7.566	7.357	7.192
	60	7.929	7.696	7.504	7.205	6.984	6.814	6.679	8.194	7.960	7.766	7.466	7.244	7.072	6.936
	72	7.579	7.380	7.215	6.960	6.770	6.625	6.509	7.845	7.644	7.478	7.220	7.030	6.883	6.766

Yield on Construction Loan When Points Are Paid

Points Paid	Yield at Month	6.00% Interest Rate — Average Balance							6.25% Interest Rate — Average Balance						
		50%	55%	60%	70%	80%	90%	100%	50%	55%	60%	70%	80%	90%	100%
	3	14.190	13.436	12.809	11.827	11.093	10.523	10.067	14.443	13.689	13.062	12.080	11.345	10.774	10.319
	6	10.119	9.740	9.425	8.932	8.563	8.276	8.047	10.372	9.993	9.678	9.184	8.815	8.528	8.299
	9	8.765	8.511	8.300	7.968	7.721	7.528	7.375	9.018	8.764	8.552	8.220	7.972	7.780	7.626
	12	8.089	7.897	7.737	7.487	7.300	7.155	7.038	8.341	8.149	7.990	7.739	7.552	7.406	7.290
1 Point	15	7.683	7.529	7.400	7.198	7.048	6.930	6.837	7.936	7.781	7.652	7.450	7.299	7.182	7.088
	18	7.413	7.283	7.175	7.006	6.879	6.781	6.702	7.666	7.536	7.427	7.258	7.131	7.033	6.954
	24	7.075	6.977	6.894	6.766	6.669	6.594	6.535	7.328	7.229	7.147	7.018	6.921	6.846	6.786
	30	6.873	6.793	6.726	6.622	6.543	6.483	6.434	7.126	7.045	6.978	6.873	6.795	6.734	6.685
	36	6.738	6.670	6.614	6.526	6.459	6.408	6.367	6.991	6.923	6.866	6.777	6.711	6.660	6.618
	48	6.570	6.517	6.474	6.406	6.355	6.315	6.283	6.823	6.770	6.726	6.658	6.606	6.567	6.535
	60	6.469	6.426	6.390	6.334	6.292	6.259	6.233	6.722	6.679	6.643	6.586	6.544	6.511	6.485
	72	6.402	6.365	6.335	6.286	6.250	6.222	6.200	6.655	6.618	6.587	6.538	6.502	6.474	6.451
	3	18.369	17.224	16.272	14.783	13.672	12.809	12.122	18.624	17.478	16.527	15.037	13.925	13.062	12.374
	6	12.215	11.641	11.164	10.417	9.858	9.425	9.080	12.470	11.895	11.418	10.670	10.111	9.678	9.332
	9	10.171	9.786	9.466	8.965	8.590	8.300	8.068	10.426	10.040	9.720	9.218	8.843	8.552	8.320
	12	9.151	8.860	8.618	8.240	7.957	7.737	7.562	9.405	9.114	8.872	8.493	8.209	7.990	7.814
1.5 Points	15	8.539	8.304	8.110	7.805	7.577	7.400	7.259	8.793	8.558	8.363	8.058	7.829	7.652	7.511
	18	8.131	7.934	7.771	7.515	7.324	7.175	7.057	8.385	8.188	8.024	7.768	7.576	7.427	7.309
	24	7.622	7.472	7.348	7.153	7.007	6.894	6.804	7.876	7.726	7.601	7.406	7.260	7.147	7.056
	30	7.317	7.195	7.094	6.936	6.818	6.726	6.653	7.571	7.449	7.348	7.189	7.070	6.978	6.905
	36	7.113	7.011	6.925	6.791	6.691	6.614	6.552	7.368	7.264	7.179	7.044	6.944	6.866	6.804
	48	6.860	6.780	6.714	6.611	6.534	6.474	6.426	7.114	7.034	6.968	6.864	6.786	6.726	6.678
	60	6.708	6.642	6.588	6.503	6.440	6.390	6.351	6.962	6.896	6.842	6.756	6.692	6.643	6.603
	72	6.607	6.551	6.504	6.431	6.377	6.335	6.301	6.861	6.805	6.758	6.684	6.630	6.587	6.553
	3	22.607	21.059	19.775	17.769	16.272	15.114	14.190	22.864	21.315	20.031	18.024	16.527	15.368	14.443
	6	14.338	13.563	12.920	11.914	11.164	10.583	10.119	14.594	13.819	13.175	12.169	11.418	10.836	10.372
	9	11.594	11.075	10.644	9.969	9.466	9.076	8.765	11.850	11.330	10.899	10.224	9.720	9.329	9.018
	12	10.225	9.833	9.507	8.998	8.618	8.324	8.089	10.481	10.088	9.762	9.252	8.872	8.577	8.341
2 Points	15	9.404	9.088	8.826	8.416	8.110	7.872	7.683	9.660	9.343	9.081	8.670	8.363	8.125	7.936
	18	8.857	8.592	8.372	8.028	7.771	7.572	7.413	9.113	8.847	8.627	8.282	8.024	7.825	7.666
	24	8.175	7.973	7.805	7.543	7.348	7.196	7.075	8.430	8.228	8.060	7.797	7.601	7.449	7.328
	30	7.765	7.602	7.466	7.253	7.094	6.971	6.873	8.021	7.857	7.720	7.507	7.348	7.224	7.126
	36	7.493	7.354	7.239	7.059	6.925	6.821	6.738	7.748	7.609	7.494	7.313	7.179	7.074	6.991
	48	7.153	7.046	6.957	6.818	6.714	6.634	6.570	7.408	7.301	7.212	7.072	6.968	6.887	6.823
	60	6.949	6.861	6.788	6.674	6.588	6.522	6.469	7.205	7.116	7.043	6.928	6.842	6.775	6.722
	72	6.814	6.738	6.676	6.578	6.504	6.447	6.402	7.070	6.994	6.931	6.832	6.758	6.701	6.655
	3	31.261	28.877	26.903	23.828	21.542	19.775	18.369	31.522	29.136	27.162	24.086	21.798	20.031	18.624
	6	18.662	17.472	16.486	14.949	13.805	12.920	12.215	18.921	17.730	16.744	15.206	14.061	13.175	12.470
	9	14.491	13.694	13.034	12.004	11.237	10.644	10.171	14.750	13.952	13.291	12.260	11.492	10.899	10.426
	12	12.411	11.810	11.312	10.534	9.955	9.507	9.151	12.670	12.068	11.569	10.790	10.211	9.762	9.405
3 Points	15	11.165	10.681	10.279	9.653	9.187	8.826	8.539	11.424	10.938	10.537	9.909	9.442	9.081	8.793
	18	10.335	9.929	9.592	9.067	8.675	8.372	8.131	10.594	10.187	9.849	9.323	8.930	8.627	8.385
	24	9.299	8.990	8.734	8.334	8.036	7.805	7.622	9.558	9.248	8.991	8.590	8.291	8.060	7.876
	30	8.678	8.427	8.219	7.895	7.653	7.466	7.317	8.937	8.685	8.476	8.151	7.908	7.720	7.571
	36	8.265	8.053	7.877	7.602	7.398	7.239	7.113	8.524	8.310	8.134	7.858	7.653	7.494	7.368
	48	7.749	7.585	7.449	7.237	7.079	6.957	6.860	8.008	7.843	7.706	7.493	7.334	7.212	7.114
	60	7.441	7.305	7.193	7.019	6.889	6.788	6.708	7.699	7.563	7.451	7.275	7.144	7.043	6.962
	72	7.236	7.120	7.024	6.874	6.762	6.676	6.607	7.495	7.378	7.281	7.130	7.017	6.931	6.861
	3	40.166	36.898	34.201	30.010	26.903	24.509	22.607	40.430	37.161	34.463	30.296	27.162	24.767	22.864
	6	23.095	21.470	20.127	18.037	16.486	15.289	14.338	23.358	21.731	20.387	18.296	16.744	15.546	14.594
	9	17.457	16.370	15.472	14.073	13.034	12.232	11.594	17.720	16.631	15.732	14.331	13.291	12.489	11.850
	12	14.649	13.829	13.151	12.095	11.312	10.706	10.225	14.911	14.090	13.411	12.354	11.569	10.963	10.481
4 Points	15	12.967	12.307	11.761	10.911	10.279	9.792	9.404	13.229	12.567	12.021	11.169	10.537	10.048	9.660
	18	11.847	11.293	10.835	10.122	9.592	9.183	8.857	12.109	11.554	11.095	10.380	9.849	9.439	9.113
	24	10.450	10.028	9.680	9.137	8.734	8.422	8.175	10.711	10.289	9.939	9.395	8.991	8.679	8.430
	30	9.613	9.270	8.987	8.547	8.219	7.966	7.765	9.874	9.531	9.247	8.805	8.476	8.223	8.021
	36	9.055	8.766	8.526	8.154	7.877	7.663	7.493	9.317	9.026	8.786	8.412	8.134	7.919	7.748
	48	8.360	8.136	7.951	7.663	7.449	7.284	7.153	8.622	8.397	8.211	7.921	7.706	7.540	7.408
	60	7.944	7.759	7.607	7.370	7.193	7.057	6.949	8.206	8.020	7.867	7.628	7.451	7.314	7.205
	72	7.668	7.509	7.378	7.175	7.024	6.907	6.814	7.930	7.770	7.638	7.433	7.281	7.163	7.070
	3	49.333	45.133	41.675	36.318	32.360	29.317	26.903	49.601	45.435	41.940	37.773	33.607	29.577	27.162
	6	27.643	25.561	23.845	21.181	19.210	17.691	16.486	27.909	25.826	24.108	21.442	19.469	17.950	16.744
	9	20.498	19.107	17.959	16.177	14.858	13.841	13.034	20.763	19.370	18.222	16.438	15.117	14.099	13.291
	12	16.941	15.892	15.027	13.683	12.688	11.921	11.312	17.206	16.156	15.289	13.944	12.947	12.179	11.569
5 Points	15	14.813	13.968	13.272	12.189	11.388	10.770	10.279	15.078	14.232	13.534	12.450	11.647	11.028	10.537
	18	13.396	12.687	12.103	11.195	10.522	10.004	9.592	13.661	12.951	12.365	11.455	10.781	10.262	9.849
	24	11.628	11.089	10.644	9.953	9.441	9.047	8.734	11.893	11.352	10.906	10.214	9.700	9.305	8.991
	30	10.569	10.131	9.770	9.209	8.794	8.474	8.219	10.834	10.395	10.033	9.470	9.053	8.732	8.476
	36	9.864	9.494	9.189	8.714	8.363	8.092	7.877	10.129	9.758	9.451	8.975	8.622	8.350	8.134
	48	8.985	8.699	8.463	8.096	7.825	7.615	7.449	9.250	8.963	8.725	8.357	8.084	7.873	7.706
	60	8.460	8.224	8.029	7.727	7.503	7.330	7.193	8.725	8.487	8.292	7.987	7.762	7.589	7.451
	72	8.110	7.908	7.741	7.481	7.289	7.141	7.024	8.376	8.172	8.003	7.742	7.548	7.399	7.281

Yield on Construction Loan When Points Are Paid

Points Paid	Yield at Month	6.50% Interest Rate Average Balance							6.75% Interest Rate Average Balance						
		50%	55%	60%	70%	80%	90%	100%	50%	55%	60%	70%	80%	90%	100%
1 Point	3	14.697	13.942	13.315	12.332	11.597	11.026	10.571	14.950	14.195	13.568	12.585	11.849	11.278	10.822
	6	10.625	10.246	9.930	9.436	9.067	8.779	8.550	10.878	10.498	10.183	9.688	9.318	9.031	8.802
	9	9.271	9.016	8.804	8.473	8.224	8.031	7.877	9.523	9.269	9.057	8.725	8.476	8.283	8.129
	12	8.594	8.402	8.242	7.991	7.803	7.658	7.541	8.847	8.654	8.494	8.243	8.055	7.909	7.793
	15	8.189	8.034	7.905	7.702	7.551	7.433	7.340	8.441	8.286	8.157	7.954	7.803	7.685	7.591
	18	7.918	7.788	7.680	7.510	7.383	7.284	7.205	8.171	8.041	7.932	7.762	7.635	7.536	7.457
	24	7.581	7.482	7.399	7.270	7.173	7.097	7.037	7.834	7.734	7.651	7.521	7.424	7.349	7.289
	30	7.378	7.298	7.231	7.125	7.047	6.986	6.937	7.631	7.550	7.483	7.377	7.298	7.237	7.188
	36	7.244	7.175	7.119	7.029	6.963	6.911	6.870	7.496	7.428	7.371	7.281	7.215	7.163	7.121
	48	7.075	7.023	6.979	6.910	6.858	6.818	6.786	7.328	7.275	7.231	7.162	7.110	7.070	7.037
	60	6.975	6.931	6.895	6.838	6.795	6.762	6.736	7.228	7.184	7.147	7.090	7.047	7.014	6.987
	72	6.908	6.871	6.839	6.790	6.754	6.725	6.703	7.161	7.123	7.092	7.043	7.006	6.977	6.954
1.5 Points	3	18.880	17.733	16.781	15.291	14.178	13.315	12.627	19.135	17.988	17.035	15.544	14.431	13.568	12.879
	6	12.725	12.149	11.671	10.923	10.364	9.930	9.584	12.979	12.403	11.925	11.176	10.617	10.183	9.837
	9	10.680	10.294	9.973	9.471	9.096	8.804	8.572	10.934	10.548	10.227	9.724	9.348	9.057	8.824
	12	9.659	9.368	9.125	8.746	8.462	8.242	8.066	9.913	9.621	9.379	8.999	8.715	8.494	8.318
	15	9.047	8.812	8.617	8.311	8.082	7.905	7.763	9.302	9.066	8.870	8.564	8.335	8.157	8.015
	18	8.639	8.442	8.278	8.021	7.829	7.680	7.561	8.894	8.696	8.531	8.274	8.081	7.932	7.813
	24	8.130	7.980	7.855	7.659	7.513	7.399	7.308	8.384	8.234	8.108	7.912	7.765	7.651	7.560
	30	7.825	7.703	7.601	7.442	7.323	7.231	7.157	8.079	7.957	7.855	7.695	7.576	7.483	7.409
	36	7.622	7.518	7.432	7.297	7.197	7.119	7.056	7.876	7.772	7.686	7.550	7.449	7.371	7.308
	48	7.368	7.288	7.221	7.117	7.039	6.979	6.930	7.622	7.542	7.475	7.370	7.292	7.231	7.182
	60	7.216	7.150	7.095	7.009	6.945	6.895	6.855	7.471	7.404	7.349	7.262	7.198	7.147	7.107
	72	7.116	7.059	7.012	6.938	6.882	6.839	6.805	7.370	7.313	7.265	7.191	7.135	7.092	7.057
2 Points	3	23.120	21.572	20.287	18.278	16.781	15.621	14.697	23.377	21.828	20.542	18.533	17.035	15.875	14.950
	6	14.850	14.074	13.430	12.423	11.671	11.089	10.625	15.106	14.330	13.685	12.677	11.925	11.343	10.878
	9	12.106	11.585	11.154	10.478	9.973	9.582	9.271	12.362	11.841	11.408	10.732	10.227	9.836	9.523
	12	10.736	10.343	10.017	9.506	9.125	8.830	8.594	10.992	10.598	10.272	9.760	9.379	9.083	8.847
	15	9.915	9.599	9.336	8.924	8.617	8.379	8.189	10.171	9.854	9.590	9.178	8.870	8.632	8.441
	18	9.369	9.103	8.882	8.536	8.278	8.078	7.918	9.624	9.358	9.136	8.790	8.531	8.331	8.171
	24	8.686	8.483	8.315	8.051	7.855	7.702	7.581	8.941	8.738	8.569	8.305	8.108	7.955	7.834
	30	8.277	8.112	7.975	7.761	7.601	7.477	7.378	8.532	8.367	8.230	8.015	7.855	7.730	7.631
	36	8.004	7.865	7.749	7.567	7.432	7.327	7.244	8.260	8.120	8.003	7.821	7.686	7.580	7.496
	48	7.664	7.556	7.466	7.326	7.221	7.140	7.075	7.920	7.811	7.721	7.580	7.475	7.393	7.328
	60	7.461	7.372	7.298	7.182	7.095	7.028	6.975	7.717	7.627	7.552	7.436	7.349	7.281	7.228
	72	7.326	7.249	7.185	7.086	7.012	6.954	6.908	7.582	7.504	7.440	7.340	7.265	7.207	7.161
3 Points	3	31.782	29.396	27.421	24.343	22.055	20.287	18.880	32.043	29.655	27.680	24.600	22.311	20.542	19.135
	6	19.180	17.989	17.002	15.462	14.316	13.430	12.725	19.439	18.247	17.259	15.719	14.572	13.685	12.979
	9	15.009	14.210	13.549	12.516	11.748	11.154	10.680	15.267	14.468	13.806	12.773	12.003	11.408	10.934
	12	12.928	12.325	11.826	11.046	10.466	10.017	9.659	13.187	12.583	12.083	11.303	10.721	10.272	9.913
	15	11.682	11.196	10.794	10.165	9.697	9.336	9.047	11.941	11.454	11.051	10.421	9.953	9.590	9.301
	18	10.852	10.444	10.106	9.579	9.186	8.882	8.639	11.111	10.702	10.363	9.835	9.441	9.136	8.894
	24	9.816	9.505	9.248	8.846	8.546	8.315	8.130	10.075	9.763	9.505	9.102	8.802	8.569	8.384
	30	9.195	8.943	8.733	8.407	8.163	7.975	7.825	9.454	9.201	8.991	8.663	8.419	8.230	8.079
	36	8.782	8.568	8.391	8.114	7.908	7.749	7.622	9.041	8.826	8.648	8.370	8.163	8.003	7.876
	48	8.267	8.101	7.964	7.749	7.590	7.466	7.368	8.525	8.359	8.221	8.006	7.845	7.721	7.622
	60	7.958	7.822	7.708	7.531	7.399	7.298	7.216	8.217	8.080	7.965	7.787	7.655	7.552	7.471
	72	7.754	7.636	7.538	7.386	7.273	7.185	7.116	8.013	7.894	7.796	7.643	7.529	7.440	7.370
4 Points	3	40.694	37.424	34.725	30.530	27.421	25.024	23.120	40.959	37.687	34.987	30.820	27.680	25.282	23.377
	6	23.620	21.993	20.648	18.555	17.002	15.803	14.850	23.883	22.254	20.908	18.814	17.259	16.060	15.106
	9	17.982	16.892	15.992	14.590	13.549	12.754	12.106	18.244	17.153	16.252	14.848	13.806	13.002	12.362
	12	15.173	14.350	13.671	12.612	11.826	11.219	10.736	15.434	14.611	13.930	12.870	12.083	11.475	10.992
	15	13.491	12.828	12.280	11.427	10.794	10.305	9.915	13.752	13.089	12.540	11.686	11.051	10.561	10.171
	18	12.371	11.814	11.355	10.638	10.106	9.695	9.369	12.632	12.075	11.614	10.896	10.363	9.952	9.624
	24	10.973	10.549	10.199	9.653	9.248	8.935	8.686	11.235	10.810	10.458	9.911	9.505	9.191	8.941
	30	10.136	9.791	9.507	9.063	8.733	8.479	8.277	10.398	10.052	9.766	9.321	8.991	8.735	8.532
	36	9.579	9.287	9.046	8.670	8.391	8.175	8.004	9.840	9.547	9.305	8.928	8.648	8.432	8.260
	48	8.884	8.658	8.471	8.180	7.964	7.797	7.664	9.146	8.918	8.730	8.438	8.221	8.053	7.920
	60	8.468	8.281	8.127	7.887	7.708	7.570	7.461	8.730	8.542	8.387	8.145	7.965	7.827	7.717
	72	8.192	8.031	7.899	7.692	7.538	7.420	7.326	8.454	8.293	8.159	7.951	7.796	7.677	7.582
5 Points	3	49.870	45.666	42.205	36.844	32.882	29.836	27.421	50.138	45.972	42.470	38.304	34.137	30.096	27.680
	6	28.175	26.090	24.371	21.704	19.729	18.209	17.002	28.441	26.355	24.634	21.965	19.989	18.467	17.259
	9	21.029	19.634	18.484	16.699	15.376	14.358	13.549	21.294	19.898	18.747	16.959	15.636	14.616	13.806
	12	17.471	16.420	15.552	14.204	13.206	12.437	11.826	17.737	16.683	15.814	14.465	13.465	12.695	12.083
	15	15.342	14.495	13.796	12.710	11.906	11.286	10.794	15.607	14.759	14.058	12.971	12.165	11.544	11.051
	18	13.926	13.214	12.627	11.716	11.040	10.520	10.106	14.191	13.478	12.890	11.976	11.299	10.778	10.363
	24	12.158	11.616	11.169	10.474	9.959	9.563	9.248	12.422	11.879	11.431	10.734	10.218	9.821	9.505
	30	11.099	10.658	10.295	9.730	9.312	8.989	8.733	11.364	10.922	10.557	9.991	9.571	9.247	8.991
	36	10.394	10.021	9.713	9.235	8.881	8.608	8.391	10.659	10.285	9.975	9.495	9.140	8.866	8.648
	48	9.516	9.226	8.988	8.617	8.343	8.132	7.964	9.781	9.490	9.250	8.878	8.602	8.390	8.221
	60	8.990	8.751	8.554	8.248	8.021	7.847	7.708	9.256	9.015	8.817	8.509	8.281	8.105	7.965
	72	8.642	8.436	8.266	8.003	7.808	7.658	7.538	8.907	8.700	8.529	8.264	8.067	7.916	7.796

Yield on Construction Loan When Points Are Paid

Points Paid	Yield at Month	7.00% Interest Rate Average Balance							7.25% Interest Rate Average Balance						
		50%	55%	60%	70%	80%	90%	100%	50%	55%	60%	70%	80%	90%	100%
	3	15.204	14.449	13.821	12.837	12.101	11.530	11.074	15.457	14.702	14.074	13.089	12.353	11.782	11.326
	6	11.131	10.751	10.435	9.940	9.570	9.283	9.053	11.384	11.004	10.688	10.193	9.822	9.534	9.305
	9	9.776	9.521	9.309	8.977	8.728	8.535	8.380	10.029	9.774	9.562	9.229	8.980	8.786	8.632
	12	9.100	8.907	8.747	8.495	8.307	8.161	8.044	9.353	9.160	8.999	8.747	8.559	8.412	8.295
1 Point	15	8.694	8.539	8.409	8.206	8.054	7.937	7.842	8.947	8.791	8.662	8.458	8.306	8.188	8.094
	18	8.424	8.293	8.184	8.014	7.886	7.787	7.708	8.677	8.546	8.437	8.266	8.138	8.039	7.959
	24	8.086	7.987	7.904	7.773	7.676	7.601	7.540	8.339	8.239	8.156	8.025	7.928	7.852	7.791
	30	7.884	7.803	7.735	7.629	7.550	7.489	7.439	8.137	8.055	7.988	7.881	7.802	7.740	7.691
	36	7.749	7.680	7.623	7.533	7.466	7.414	7.372	8.002	7.933	7.875	7.785	7.718	7.666	7.624
	48	7.581	7.528	7.483	7.414	7.362	7.321	7.289	7.834	7.780	7.736	7.666	7.613	7.573	7.540
	60	7.481	7.436	7.400	7.342	7.299	7.266	7.239	7.733	7.689	7.652	7.594	7.551	7.517	7.490
	72	7.414	7.376	7.344	7.295	7.257	7.229	7.206	7.667	7.628	7.597	7.547	7.509	7.480	7.457
	3	19.390	18.242	17.290	15.798	14.684	13.821	13.132	19.645	18.497	17.544	16.052	14.937	14.074	13.384
	6	13.234	12.658	12.179	11.430	10.870	10.435	10.089	13.488	12.912	12.433	11.683	11.122	10.688	10.341
	9	11.189	10.802	10.480	9.977	9.601	9.309	9.076	11.443	11.056	10.734	10.230	9.854	9.562	9.328
	12	10.168	9.875	9.632	9.252	8.967	8.747	8.570	10.422	10.129	9.886	9.505	9.220	8.999	8.823
1.5 Points	15	9.556	9.320	9.124	8.817	8.587	8.409	8.267	9.810	9.574	9.377	9.070	8.840	8.662	8.519
	18	9.148	8.950	8.785	8.527	8.334	8.184	8.065	9.402	9.203	9.038	8.780	8.587	8.437	8.317
	24	8.639	8.487	8.362	8.165	8.018	7.904	7.812	8.893	8.741	8.615	8.418	8.270	8.156	8.065
	30	8.333	8.210	8.108	7.948	7.828	7.735	7.661	8.588	8.464	8.362	8.201	8.081	7.988	7.913
	36	8.130	8.026	7.939	7.803	7.702	7.623	7.560	8.384	8.280	8.193	8.056	7.954	7.875	7.812
	48	7.877	7.796	7.728	7.623	7.544	7.483	7.435	8.131	8.050	7.982	7.876	7.797	7.736	7.687
	60	7.725	7.658	7.603	7.515	7.450	7.400	7.359	7.979	7.912	7.856	7.768	7.703	7.652	7.612
	72	7.625	7.567	7.519	7.444	7.388	7.344	7.309	7.879	7.821	7.773	7.697	7.640	7.597	7.562
	3	23.634	22.084	20.798	18.788	17.290	16.129	15.204	23.891	22.340	21.054	19.043	17.544	16.383	15.457
	6	15.362	14.585	13.940	12.932	12.179	11.596	11.131	15.618	14.841	14.195	13.186	12.433	11.849	11.384
	9	12.618	12.096	11.663	10.986	10.480	10.089	9.776	12.873	12.351	11.918	11.240	10.734	10.342	10.029
	12	11.248	10.854	10.526	10.014	9.632	9.336	9.100	11.504	11.109	10.781	10.268	9.886	9.589	9.353
2 Points	15	10.427	10.109	9.845	9.432	9.124	8.885	8.694	10.683	10.364	10.100	9.686	9.377	9.138	8.947
	18	9.880	9.613	9.391	9.044	8.785	8.584	8.424	10.136	9.868	9.646	9.298	9.038	8.837	8.677
	24	9.197	8.993	8.824	8.559	8.362	8.208	8.086	9.453	9.248	9.079	8.813	8.615	8.462	8.339
	30	8.788	8.622	8.484	8.269	8.108	7.983	7.884	9.044	8.877	8.739	8.523	8.362	8.236	8.137
	36	8.515	8.375	8.258	8.075	7.939	7.833	7.749	8.771	8.630	8.513	8.330	8.193	8.087	8.002
	48	8.176	8.067	7.976	7.834	7.728	7.646	7.581	8.431	8.322	8.231	8.088	7.982	7.900	7.834
	60	7.973	7.882	7.807	7.690	7.603	7.535	7.481	8.228	8.138	8.062	7.944	7.856	7.788	7.733
	72	7.838	7.760	7.695	7.594	7.519	7.460	7.414	8.094	8.015	7.950	7.849	7.773	7.714	7.667
	3	32.304	29.915	27.938	24.858	22.568	20.798	19.390	32.564	30.175	28.197	25.115	22.824	21.054	19.645
	6	19.699	18.505	17.517	15.975	14.828	13.940	13.234	19.958	18.764	17.775	16.232	15.083	14.195	13.488
	9	15.526	14.726	14.063	13.029	12.259	11.663	11.189	15.785	14.984	14.321	13.285	12.514	11.918	11.443
	12	13.446	12.841	12.340	11.559	10.977	10.526	10.168	13.705	13.099	12.598	11.815	11.232	10.781	10.422
3 Points	15	12.199	11.712	11.308	10.678	10.208	9.845	9.556	12.458	11.970	11.565	10.934	10.463	10.100	9.810
	18	11.370	10.960	10.620	10.091	9.696	9.391	9.148	11.628	11.218	10.878	10.347	9.951	9.646	9.402
	24	10.333	10.021	9.762	9.358	9.057	8.824	8.639	10.592	10.279	10.019	9.614	9.312	9.079	8.893
	30	9.713	9.458	9.248	8.919	8.674	8.484	8.333	9.971	9.716	9.505	9.175	8.929	8.739	8.588
	36	9.300	9.084	8.905	8.626	8.419	8.258	8.130	9.558	9.342	9.162	8.883	8.674	8.513	8.384
	48	8.784	8.617	8.478	8.262	8.101	7.976	7.877	9.043	8.875	8.735	8.518	8.356	8.231	8.131
	60	8.476	8.338	8.223	8.044	7.910	7.807	7.725	8.735	8.596	8.480	8.300	8.166	8.062	7.979
	72	8.272	8.152	8.053	7.899	7.784	7.695	7.625	8.531	8.411	8.311	8.156	8.040	7.950	7.879
	3	41.223	37.950	35.248	31.050	27.938	25.540	23.634	41.488	38.213	35.510	31.344	28.197	25.798	23.891
	6	24.145	22.515	21.169	19.073	17.517	16.317	15.362	24.408	22.777	21.429	19.332	17.775	16.573	15.618
	9	18.506	17.414	16.512	15.107	14.063	13.258	12.618	18.768	17.675	16.772	15.365	14.321	13.515	12.873
	12	15.696	14.872	14.190	13.129	12.340	11.732	11.248	15.958	15.133	14.450	13.387	12.598	11.988	11.504
4 Points	15	14.014	13.349	12.800	11.944	11.308	10.817	10.427	14.276	13.610	13.059	12.202	11.565	11.074	10.683
	18	12.894	12.336	11.874	11.155	10.620	10.208	9.880	13.156	12.596	12.134	11.413	10.878	10.464	10.136
	24	11.496	11.070	10.718	10.169	9.762	9.447	9.197	11.758	11.331	10.978	10.428	10.019	9.704	9.453
	30	10.659	10.313	10.026	9.579	9.248	8.992	8.788	10.921	10.573	10.285	9.838	9.505	9.248	9.044
	36	10.102	9.808	9.565	9.186	8.905	8.688	8.515	10.364	10.069	9.825	9.445	9.162	8.945	8.771
	48	9.407	9.179	8.990	8.696	8.478	8.310	8.176	9.670	9.440	9.250	8.955	8.735	8.566	8.431
	60	8.992	8.803	8.647	8.404	8.223	8.083	7.973	9.255	9.064	8.907	8.662	8.480	8.340	8.228
	72	8.717	8.554	8.419	8.209	8.053	7.933	7.838	8.979	8.815	8.679	8.468	8.311	8.190	8.094
	3	50.407	46.199	42.735	37.369	33.405	30.356	27.938	50.675	46.508	43.000	38.834	34.667	30.616	28.197
	6	28.708	26.619	24.898	22.226	20.249	18.726	17.517	28.974	26.884	25.161	22.487	20.508	18.984	17.775
	9	21.560	20.162	19.010	17.220	15.895	14.874	14.063	21.825	20.426	19.272	17.481	16.154	15.132	14.321
	12	18.002	16.947	16.077	14.725	13.724	12.953	12.340	18.267	17.211	16.339	14.986	13.983	13.211	12.598
5 Points	15	15.872	15.022	14.321	13.231	12.424	11.802	11.308	16.137	15.286	14.583	13.492	12.683	12.060	11.565
	18	14.455	13.741	13.152	12.236	11.558	11.036	10.620	14.720	14.005	13.414	12.497	11.817	11.294	10.878
	24	12.687	12.142	11.693	10.995	10.477	10.079	9.762	12.952	12.406	11.955	11.255	10.736	10.337	10.019
	30	11.629	11.185	10.819	10.251	9.830	9.505	9.248	11.894	11.449	11.082	10.511	10.089	9.763	9.505
	36	10.924	10.548	10.238	9.756	9.399	9.124	8.905	11.189	10.812	10.500	10.016	9.658	9.382	9.162
	48	10.046	9.754	9.513	9.139	8.861	8.648	8.478	10.311	10.018	9.775	9.399	9.121	8.906	8.735
	60	9.521	9.279	9.080	8.770	8.540	8.363	8.223	9.787	9.543	9.342	9.030	8.799	8.622	8.480
	72	9.173	8.964	8.792	8.525	8.327	8.174	8.053	9.439	9.229	9.055	8.786	8.586	8.433	8.311

Yield on Construction Loan When Points Are Paid

Points Paid	Yield at Month	7.50% Interest Rate Average Balance							7.75% Interest Rate Average Balance						
		50%	55%	60%	70%	80%	90%	100%	50%	55%	60%	70%	80%	90%	100%
	3	15.710	14.955	14.326	13.342	12.605	12.034	11.577	15.964	15.208	14.579	13.594	12.858	12.286	11.829
	6	11.637	11.257	10.940	10.445	10.074	9.786	9.556	11.890	11.509	11.193	10.697	10.326	10.038	9.807
	9	10.282	10.027	9.814	9.481	9.231	9.038	8.883	10.535	10.279	10.066	9.733	9.483	9.289	9.134
	12	9.605	9.412	9.251	8.999	8.810	8.664	8.547	9.858	9.665	9.504	9.251	9.062	8.915	8.798
1 Point	15	9.200	9.044	8.914	8.710	8.558	8.440	8.345	9.453	9.296	9.166	8.962	8.810	8.691	8.597
	18	8.929	8.798	8.689	8.518	8.390	8.290	8.211	9.182	9.051	8.941	8.770	8.641	8.542	8.462
	24	8.592	8.492	8.408	8.277	8.180	8.104	8.043	8.845	8.744	8.660	8.529	8.431	8.355	8.294
	30	8.390	8.308	8.240	8.133	8.054	7.992	7.942	8.642	8.560	8.492	8.385	8.305	8.243	8.194
	36	8.255	8.185	8.128	8.037	7.970	7.917	7.875	8.508	8.438	8.380	8.289	8.221	8.169	8.127
	48	8.087	8.033	7.988	7.918	7.865	7.824	7.792	8.340	8.285	8.240	8.170	8.117	8.076	8.043
	60	7.986	7.942	7.905	7.846	7.803	7.769	7.742	8.239	8.194	8.157	8.098	8.054	8.020	7.993
	72	7.920	7.881	7.849	7.799	7.761	7.732	7.709	8.173	8.134	8.102	8.051	8.013	7.984	7.960
	3	19.900	18.752	17.798	16.305	15.191	14.326	13.637	20.155	19.006	18.052	16.559	15.444	14.579	13.889
	6	13.743	13.166	12.687	11.936	11.375	10.940	10.593	13.997	13.420	12.940	12.189	11.628	11.193	10.846
	9	11.697	11.310	10.988	10.483	10.106	9.814	9.581	11.952	11.564	11.241	10.736	10.359	10.066	9.833
	12	10.676	10.383	10.139	9.758	9.472	9.251	9.075	10.930	10.637	10.393	10.011	9.725	9.504	9.327
1.5 Points	15	10.064	9.827	9.631	9.323	9.092	8.914	8.771	10.318	10.081	9.884	9.576	9.345	9.166	9.023
	18	9.656	9.457	9.292	9.033	8.839	8.689	8.569	9.910	9.711	9.545	9.286	9.092	8.941	8.821
	24	9.147	8.995	8.869	8.671	8.523	8.408	8.317	9.401	9.249	9.122	8.924	8.775	8.660	8.569
	30	8.842	8.718	8.615	8.454	8.333	8.240	8.165	9.096	8.972	8.869	8.707	8.586	8.492	8.417
	36	8.639	8.534	8.446	8.309	8.207	8.128	8.064	8.893	8.787	8.700	8.562	8.460	8.380	8.317
	48	8.385	8.304	8.236	8.129	8.050	7.988	7.939	8.640	8.557	8.489	8.382	8.302	8.240	8.191
	60	8.234	8.166	8.110	8.022	7.956	7.905	7.864	8.488	8.420	8.363	8.275	8.208	8.157	8.116
	72	8.133	8.075	8.026	7.950	7.893	7.849	7.814	8.388	8.329	8.280	8.203	8.146	8.102	8.066
	3	24.148	22.597	21.310	19.298	17.798	16.636	15.710	24.405	22.853	21.565	19.553	18.052	16.890	15.964
	6	15.874	15.096	14.450	13.440	12.687	12.103	11.637	16.131	15.352	14.706	13.695	12.940	12.356	11.890
	9	13.129	12.607	12.173	11.494	10.988	10.595	10.282	13.385	12.862	12.428	11.748	11.241	10.848	10.535
	12	11.759	11.364	11.036	10.523	10.139	9.842	9.605	12.015	11.619	11.291	10.777	10.393	10.096	9.858
2 Points	15	10.938	10.619	10.354	9.940	9.631	9.391	9.200	11.194	10.874	10.609	10.194	9.884	9.644	9.453
	18	10.391	10.123	9.900	9.552	9.292	9.090	8.929	10.647	10.378	10.155	9.806	9.545	9.343	9.182
	24	9.708	9.504	9.333	9.067	8.869	8.715	8.592	9.964	9.759	9.588	9.321	9.122	8.968	8.845
	30	9.299	9.132	8.994	8.777	8.615	8.490	8.390	9.555	9.387	9.248	9.031	8.869	8.743	8.642
	36	9.027	8.885	8.768	8.584	8.446	8.340	8.255	9.283	9.140	9.022	8.838	8.700	8.593	8.508
	48	8.687	8.577	8.486	8.342	8.236	8.153	8.087	8.943	8.832	8.740	8.597	8.489	8.406	8.340
	60	8.484	8.393	8.317	8.198	8.110	8.041	7.986	8.740	8.648	8.572	8.453	8.363	8.294	8.239
	72	8.350	8.271	8.205	8.103	8.026	7.967	7.920	8.606	8.526	8.460	8.357	8.280	8.220	8.173
	3	32.825	30.434	28.456	25.373	23.081	21.310	19.900	33.085	30.694	28.715	25.630	23.337	21.565	20.155
	6	20.217	19.022	18.032	16.488	15.339	14.450	13.743	20.477	19.281	18.290	16.745	15.595	14.706	13.997
	9	16.044	15.242	14.578	13.542	12.770	12.173	11.697	16.303	15.500	14.836	13.798	13.025	12.428	11.952
	12	13.963	13.357	12.855	12.071	11.487	11.036	10.676	14.222	13.615	13.112	12.327	11.743	11.291	10.930
3 Points	15	12.717	12.228	11.822	11.190	10.719	10.354	10.064	12.976	12.486	12.080	11.446	10.974	10.609	10.318
	18	11.887	11.476	11.135	10.603	10.207	9.900	9.656	12.145	11.733	11.392	10.859	10.462	10.155	9.910
	24	10.851	10.537	10.276	9.870	9.567	9.333	9.147	11.109	10.794	10.533	10.126	9.823	9.588	9.401
	30	10.230	9.974	9.762	9.431	9.184	8.994	8.842	10.489	10.232	10.019	9.687	9.440	9.248	9.096
	36	9.817	9.600	9.420	9.139	8.929	8.768	8.639	10.076	9.858	9.677	9.395	9.185	9.022	8.893
	48	9.302	9.133	8.993	8.774	8.611	8.486	8.385	9.561	9.391	9.250	9.030	8.867	8.740	8.640
	60	8.994	8.854	8.738	8.556	8.421	8.317	8.234	9.253	9.112	8.995	8.813	8.677	8.572	8.488
	72	8.790	8.669	8.569	8.412	8.295	8.205	8.133	9.050	8.927	8.826	8.668	8.551	8.460	8.388
	3	41.752	38.476	35.772	31.570	28.456	26.055	24.148	42.017	38.739	36.034	31.867	28.715	26.313	24.405
	6	24.671	23.038	21.689	19.590	18.032	16.830	15.874	24.933	23.300	21.950	19.849	18.290	17.087	16.131
	9	19.030	17.936	17.032	15.624	14.558	13.771	13.129	19.292	18.197	17.292	15.882	14.835	14.028	13.385
	12	16.220	15.393	14.710	13.645	12.855	12.245	11.759	16.482	15.654	14.970	13.904	13.112	12.501	12.015
4 Points	15	14.538	13.871	13.319	12.460	11.822	11.330	10.938	14.799	14.131	13.579	12.719	12.080	11.586	11.194
	18	13.418	12.857	12.393	11.671	11.135	10.721	10.391	13.679	13.117	12.653	11.929	11.392	10.977	10.647
	24	12.020	11.592	11.237	10.686	10.276	9.960	9.708	12.282	11.852	11.497	10.944	10.533	10.216	9.964
	30	11.183	10.834	10.545	10.096	9.762	9.504	9.299	11.445	11.094	10.805	10.354	10.019	9.761	9.555
	36	10.626	10.329	10.084	9.703	9.420	9.201	9.027	10.888	10.590	10.344	9.961	9.677	9.457	9.283
	48	9.932	9.701	9.510	9.213	8.993	8.823	8.687	10.194	9.962	9.770	9.472	9.250	9.079	8.943
	60	9.517	9.325	9.167	8.921	8.738	8.597	8.484	9.779	9.586	9.427	9.179	8.995	8.853	8.740
	72	9.242	9.076	8.940	8.727	8.569	8.447	8.350	9.504	9.338	9.200	8.985	8.826	8.703	8.606
	3	50.943	46.732	43.265	37.895	33.927	30.875	28.456	51.212	47.045	43.530	39.364	35.197	31.135	28.715
	6	29.240	27.148	25.424	22.748	20.768	19.243	18.032	29.506	27.413	25.687	23.010	21.028	19.502	18.290
	9	22.090	20.690	19.535	17.742	16.414	15.390	14.578	22.356	20.954	19.798	18.002	16.673	15.649	14.836
	12	18.532	17.474	16.602	15.246	14.243	13.469	12.855	18.797	17.738	16.864	15.507	14.502	13.727	13.112
5 Points	15	16.402	15.549	14.845	13.752	12.942	12.318	11.822	16.668	15.813	15.108	14.013	13.201	12.576	12.080
	18	14.985	14.268	13.676	12.757	12.076	11.552	11.135	15.250	14.532	13.939	13.018	12.335	11.809	11.392
	24	13.217	12.669	12.217	11.515	10.995	10.595	10.276	13.482	12.933	12.480	11.776	11.254	10.853	10.533
	30	12.159	11.712	11.344	10.772	10.348	10.021	9.762	12.424	11.976	11.606	11.032	10.607	10.279	10.019
	36	11.454	11.075	10.763	10.277	9.917	9.640	9.420	11.720	11.339	11.025	10.537	10.176	9.898	9.677
	48	10.577	10.282	10.038	9.660	9.380	9.164	8.993	10.842	10.545	10.301	9.921	9.639	9.422	9.250
	60	10.053	9.807	9.605	9.291	9.059	8.880	8.738	10.318	10.072	9.868	9.552	9.318	9.138	8.995
	72	9.705	9.493	9.318	9.047	8.846	8.691	8.569	9.971	9.758	9.581	9.308	9.106	8.950	8.826

Yield on Construction Loan When Points Are Paid

Points Paid	Yield at Month	8.00% Interest Rate Average Balance							8.25% Interest Rate Average Balance						
		50%	55%	60%	70%	80%	90%	100%	50%	55%	60%	70%	80%	90%	100%
	3	16.217	15.461	14.832	13.847	13.110	12.538	12.081	16.471	15.714	15.085	14.099	13.362	12.790	12.332
	6	12.143	11.762	11.445	10.949	10.578	10.289	10.059	12.396	12.015	11.698	11.201	10.829	10.541	10.310
	9	10.788	10.532	10.319	9.985	9.735	9.541	9.386	11.041	10.784	10.571	10.237	9.987	9.792	9.637
	12	10.111	9.917	9.756	9.503	9.314	9.167	9.050	10.364	10.170	10.008	9.755	9.566	9.419	9.301
1 Point	15	9.705	9.549	9.418	9.214	9.061	8.943	8.848	9.958	9.801	9.671	9.466	9.313	9.194	9.099
	18	9.435	9.303	9.194	9.022	8.893	8.793	8.713	9.688	9.556	9.446	9.274	9.145	9.045	8.965
	24	9.097	8.997	8.913	8.781	8.683	8.607	8.546	9.350	9.249	9.165	9.033	8.935	8.858	8.797
	30	8.895	8.813	8.745	8.637	8.557	8.495	8.445	9.148	9.065	8.997	8.889	8.809	8.746	8.696
	36	8.760	8.691	8.632	8.541	8.473	8.420	8.378	9.013	8.943	8.885	8.793	8.725	8.672	8.629
	48	8.593	8.538	8.493	8.422	8.369	8.327	8.295	8.845	8.791	8.745	8.674	8.620	8.579	8.546
	60	8.492	8.447	8.409	8.350	8.306	8.272	8.245	8.745	8.700	8.662	8.602	8.558	8.524	8.496
	72	8.426	8.387	8.354	8.303	8.265	8.235	8.212	8.679	8.639	8.607	8.555	8.517	8.487	8.463
	3	20.411	19.261	18.307	16.813	15.697	14.832	14.142	20.666	19.516	18.561	17.066	15.950	15.085	14.395
	6	14.252	13.674	13.194	12.442	11.881	11.445	11.098	14.506	13.928	13.448	12.696	12.134	11.698	11.350
	9	12.206	11.818	11.495	10.989	10.612	10.319	10.085	12.460	12.072	11.749	11.243	10.864	10.571	10.337
	12	11.185	10.891	10.646	10.264	9.978	9.756	9.579	11.439	11.145	10.900	10.517	10.230	10.008	9.831
1.5 Points	15	10.573	10.335	10.138	9.829	9.598	9.418	9.275	10.827	10.589	10.391	10.082	9.850	9.671	9.528
	18	10.165	9.965	9.799	9.539	9.344	9.194	9.073	10.419	10.219	10.052	9.792	9.597	9.446	9.325
	24	9.655	9.503	9.376	9.177	9.028	8.913	8.821	9.910	9.756	9.629	9.430	9.281	9.165	9.073
	30	9.350	9.226	9.122	8.960	8.839	8.745	8.669	9.605	9.479	9.376	9.213	9.091	8.997	8.922
	36	9.147	9.041	8.953	8.815	8.712	8.632	8.569	9.402	9.295	9.207	9.068	8.965	8.885	8.821
	48	8.894	8.811	8.743	8.635	8.555	8.493	8.443	9.148	9.065	8.996	8.888	8.808	8.745	8.695
	60	8.743	8.674	8.617	8.528	8.461	8.409	8.368	8.997	8.928	8.871	8.781	8.714	8.662	8.620
	72	8.642	8.583	8.534	8.457	8.399	8.354	8.318	8.897	8.837	8.788	8.710	8.652	8.607	8.571
	3	24.662	23.109	21.821	19.808	18.307	17.144	16.217	24.919	23.366	22.077	20.063	18.561	17.398	16.471
	6	16.387	15.607	14.961	13.949	13.194	12.609	12.143	16.643	15.863	15.216	14.203	13.448	12.863	12.396
	9	13.641	13.117	12.682	12.002	11.495	11.102	10.788	13.897	13.373	12.937	12.257	11.749	11.355	11.041
	12	12.271	11.874	11.545	11.031	10.646	10.349	10.111	12.526	12.130	11.800	11.285	10.900	10.602	10.364
2 Points	15	11.450	11.129	10.864	10.448	10.138	9.897	9.705	11.705	11.385	11.118	10.702	10.391	10.150	9.958
	18	10.903	10.633	10.410	10.060	9.799	9.596	9.435	11.158	10.888	10.664	10.314	10.052	9.850	9.688
	24	10.220	10.014	9.843	9.575	9.376	9.221	9.097	10.475	10.269	10.097	9.829	9.629	9.474	9.350
	30	9.811	9.643	9.503	9.285	9.122	8.996	8.895	10.066	9.898	9.758	9.539	9.376	9.249	9.148
	36	9.538	9.396	9.277	9.092	8.953	8.846	8.760	9.794	9.651	9.532	9.346	9.207	9.099	9.013
	48	9.199	9.088	8.995	8.851	8.743	8.659	8.593	9.455	9.343	9.250	9.105	8.996	8.912	8.845
	60	8.996	8.904	8.827	8.707	8.617	8.548	8.492	9.252	9.159	9.082	8.961	8.871	8.801	8.745
	72	8.862	8.782	8.715	8.611	8.534	8.474	8.426	9.118	9.037	8.970	8.866	8.788	8.727	8.679
	3	33.346	30.953	28.973	25.888	23.594	21.821	20.411	33.607	31.213	29.232	26.145	23.850	22.077	20.666
	6	20.736	19.539	18.548	17.001	15.851	14.961	14.252	20.995	19.798	18.806	17.258	16.106	15.216	14.506
	9	16.562	15.759	15.093	14.054	13.281	12.682	12.206	16.821	16.017	15.350	14.310	13.536	12.937	12.461
	12	14.481	13.873	13.369	12.583	11.998	11.545	11.185	14.740	14.131	13.627	12.840	12.254	11.800	11.439
3 Points	15	13.234	12.743	12.337	11.702	11.229	10.864	10.573	13.493	13.001	12.594	11.958	11.485	11.118	10.827
	18	12.404	11.991	11.649	11.115	10.717	10.410	10.165	12.663	12.249	11.906	11.371	10.973	10.664	10.419
	24	11.368	11.052	10.791	10.382	10.078	9.843	9.655	11.627	11.310	11.048	10.638	10.333	10.097	9.910
	30	10.747	10.490	10.276	9.943	9.695	9.503	9.350	11.006	10.748	10.533	10.199	9.950	9.758	9.605
	36	10.334	10.116	9.934	9.651	9.440	9.277	9.147	10.593	10.373	10.191	9.907	9.696	9.532	9.401
	48	9.820	9.649	9.508	9.287	9.122	8.995	8.894	10.079	9.907	9.765	9.543	9.378	9.250	9.148
	60	9.512	9.370	9.253	9.069	8.933	8.827	8.743	9.772	9.629	9.510	9.326	9.188	9.082	8.997
	72	9.309	9.186	9.084	8.925	8.807	8.715	8.642	9.568	9.444	9.342	9.182	9.062	8.970	8.897
	3	42.281	39.002	36.296	32.090	28.973	26.571	24.662	42.545	39.265	36.558	32.391	29.232	26.829	24.919
	6	25.196	23.561	22.210	20.108	18.548	17.344	16.387	25.459	23.823	22.471	20.367	18.806	17.601	16.643
	9	19.554	18.458	17.552	16.141	15.093	14.284	13.641	19.817	18.719	17.812	16.399	15.350	14.541	13.897
	12	16.744	15.915	15.229	14.162	13.369	12.758	12.271	17.006	16.176	15.489	14.420	13.627	13.014	12.527
4 Points	15	15.061	14.392	13.839	12.977	12.337	11.843	11.450	15.323	14.653	14.098	13.235	12.594	12.099	11.705
	18	13.941	13.378	12.913	12.188	11.649	11.233	10.903	14.203	13.639	13.172	12.446	11.906	11.490	11.158
	24	12.543	12.113	11.757	11.202	10.791	10.473	10.220	12.805	12.373	12.016	11.461	11.048	10.729	10.475
	30	11.706	11.355	11.065	10.612	10.276	10.017	9.811	11.968	11.616	11.324	10.871	10.533	10.273	10.066
	36	11.150	10.851	10.604	10.220	9.934	9.714	9.538	11.412	11.112	10.864	10.478	10.191	9.970	9.794
	48	10.456	10.223	10.030	9.730	9.508	9.336	9.199	10.718	10.484	10.290	9.989	9.765	9.592	9.455
	60	10.042	9.848	9.687	9.438	9.253	9.110	8.996	10.304	10.109	9.948	9.697	9.510	9.367	9.252
	72	9.767	9.599	9.460	9.244	9.084	8.960	8.862	10.030	9.861	9.721	9.503	9.342	9.217	9.118
	3	51.480	47.265	43.795	38.420	34.449	31.395	28.973	51.748	47.582	44.061	39.894	35.727	31.655	29.232
	6	29.772	27.677	25.951	23.271	21.287	19.760	18.548	30.038	27.942	26.214	23.532	21.547	20.019	18.806
	9	22.621	21.218	20.060	18.263	16.932	15.907	15.093	22.887	21.482	20.323	18.524	17.192	16.165	15.350
	12	19.062	18.002	17.126	15.768	14.761	13.985	13.369	19.328	18.265	17.389	16.028	15.020	14.243	13.627
5 Points	15	16.933	16.076	15.370	14.273	13.460	12.834	12.337	17.198	16.340	15.632	14.533	13.719	13.092	12.594
	18	15.515	14.795	14.201	13.278	12.594	12.067	11.649	15.780	15.059	14.463	13.538	12.853	12.326	11.906
	24	13.747	13.196	12.742	12.036	11.513	11.111	10.791	14.012	13.460	13.004	12.297	11.772	11.369	11.048
	30	12.689	12.239	11.869	11.293	10.866	10.537	10.276	12.954	12.503	12.131	11.553	11.125	10.795	10.533
	36	11.985	11.603	11.287	10.798	10.435	10.156	9.934	12.250	11.866	11.550	11.058	10.694	10.414	10.191
	48	11.108	10.809	10.563	10.181	9.898	9.681	9.508	11.373	11.073	10.826	10.442	10.158	9.939	9.765
	60	10.584	10.336	10.131	9.813	9.578	9.397	9.253	10.850	10.600	10.394	10.074	9.837	9.655	9.510
	72	10.237	10.022	9.845	9.569	9.365	9.209	9.084	10.504	10.287	10.108	9.831	9.625	9.467	9.342

Yield on Construction Loan When Points Are Paid

Points Paid	Yield at Month	8.50% Interest Rate — Average Balance							8.75% Interest Rate — Average Balance						
		50%	55%	60%	70%	80%	90%	100%	50%	55%	60%	70%	80%	90%	100%
1 Point	3	16.724	15.967	15.338	14.352	13.614	13.041	12.584	16.977	16.220	15.591	14.604	13.866	13.293	12.836
	6	12.649	12.267	11.950	11.453	11.081	10.793	10.562	12.902	12.520	12.203	11.705	11.333	11.044	10.813
	9	11.294	11.037	10.824	10.489	10.238	10.044	9.889	11.547	11.290	11.076	10.741	10.490	10.296	10.140
	12	10.617	10.422	10.261	10.007	9.817	9.670	9.552	10.870	10.675	10.513	10.259	10.069	9.922	9.804
	15	10.211	10.054	9.923	9.718	9.565	9.446	9.351	10.464	10.306	10.175	9.970	9.817	9.697	9.602
	18	9.941	9.808	9.698	9.526	9.397	9.296	9.216	10.193	10.061	9.951	9.778	9.648	9.548	9.468
	24	9.603	9.502	9.417	9.285	9.186	9.110	9.048	9.856	9.754	9.670	9.537	9.438	9.361	9.300
	30	9.401	9.318	9.249	9.141	9.061	8.998	8.948	9.654	9.571	9.502	9.393	9.312	9.249	9.199
	36	9.266	9.196	9.137	9.045	8.977	8.923	8.881	9.519	9.448	9.390	9.297	9.228	9.175	9.132
	48	9.098	9.043	8.998	8.926	8.872	8.831	8.797	9.351	9.296	9.250	9.178	9.124	9.082	9.049
	60	8.998	8.952	8.914	8.855	8.810	8.775	8.748	9.251	9.205	9.167	9.107	9.062	9.027	8.999
	72	8.932	8.892	8.859	8.807	8.769	8.739	8.715	9.185	9.145	9.112	9.059	9.020	8.990	8.966
1.5 Points	3	20.921	19.771	18.815	17.320	16.203	15.338	14.647	21.176	20.025	19.069	17.574	16.457	15.591	14.900
	6	14.761	14.182	13.702	12.949	12.387	11.950	11.602	15.015	14.437	13.955	13.202	12.639	12.203	11.855
	9	12.715	12.326	12.002	11.496	11.117	10.824	10.589	12.969	12.580	12.256	11.749	11.370	11.076	10.841
	12	11.693	11.398	11.154	10.770	10.483	10.261	10.083	11.948	11.652	11.407	11.023	10.736	10.513	10.335
	15	11.081	10.843	10.645	10.335	10.103	9.923	9.780	11.335	11.097	10.898	10.588	10.356	10.175	10.032
	18	10.673	10.473	10.306	10.045	9.850	9.698	9.577	10.927	10.726	10.559	10.298	10.102	9.951	9.830
	24	10.164	10.010	9.883	9.683	9.533	9.417	9.325	10.418	10.264	10.136	9.936	9.786	9.670	9.577
	30	9.859	9.733	9.629	9.466	9.344	9.249	9.174	10.113	9.987	9.883	9.719	9.596	9.502	9.426
	36	9.656	9.549	9.460	9.321	9.218	9.137	9.073	9.910	9.803	9.714	9.575	9.470	9.390	9.325
	48	9.403	9.319	9.250	9.142	9.061	8.998	8.947	9.657	9.573	9.504	9.395	9.313	9.250	9.200
	60	9.252	9.182	9.124	9.034	8.967	8.914	8.872	9.506	9.436	9.378	9.287	9.219	9.167	9.125
	72	9.152	9.091	9.041	8.963	8.904	8.859	8.823	9.406	9.345	9.295	9.216	9.157	9.112	9.075
2 Points	3	25.176	23.622	22.333	20.318	18.815	17.652	16.724	25.433	23.878	22.588	20.573	19.069	17.905	16.977
	6	16.899	16.118	15.471	14.458	13.702	13.116	12.649	17.155	16.374	15.726	14.712	13.955	13.369	12.902
	9	14.153	13.628	13.192	12.511	12.002	11.608	11.294	14.409	13.883	13.447	12.765	12.256	11.861	11.547
	12	12.782	12.385	12.055	11.539	11.154	10.855	10.617	13.038	12.640	12.310	11.793	11.407	11.108	10.870
	15	11.961	11.640	11.373	10.956	10.645	10.403	10.211	12.217	11.895	11.628	11.210	10.898	10.657	10.464
	18	11.414	11.144	10.919	10.568	10.306	10.103	9.941	11.670	11.399	11.174	10.822	10.559	10.356	10.193
	24	10.731	10.524	10.352	10.083	9.883	9.727	9.603	10.987	10.779	10.607	10.337	10.136	9.980	9.856
	30	10.322	10.153	10.013	9.793	9.629	9.502	9.401	10.578	10.408	10.267	10.047	9.883	9.755	9.654
	36	10.050	9.906	9.787	9.600	9.460	9.352	9.266	10.306	10.161	10.041	9.854	9.714	9.605	9.519
	48	9.711	9.598	9.505	9.359	9.250	9.166	9.098	9.967	9.854	9.760	9.613	9.504	9.419	9.351
	60	9.508	9.415	9.337	9.215	9.124	9.054	8.998	9.764	9.670	9.592	9.469	9.378	9.307	9.251
	72	9.374	9.293	9.225	9.120	9.041	8.980	8.932	9.630	9.548	9.480	9.374	9.295	9.234	9.185
3 Points	3	33.867	31.473	29.491	26.403	24.107	22.333	20.921	34.128	31.732	29.750	26.660	24.363	22.588	21.176
	6	21.255	20.056	19.063	17.515	16.362	15.471	14.761	21.514	20.315	19.321	17.771	16.618	15.726	15.015
	9	17.080	16.275	15.608	14.567	13.792	13.192	12.715	17.339	16.533	15.865	14.823	14.047	13.447	12.969
	12	14.999	14.389	13.884	13.096	12.509	12.055	11.693	15.257	14.647	14.141	13.352	12.764	12.310	11.948
	15	13.752	13.259	12.851	12.214	11.740	11.373	11.081	14.010	13.517	13.108	12.470	11.995	11.628	11.335
	18	12.922	12.507	12.163	11.627	11.228	10.919	10.673	13.180	12.765	12.421	11.883	11.483	11.174	10.927
	24	11.885	11.568	11.305	10.894	10.589	10.352	10.164	12.144	11.826	11.562	11.150	10.844	10.607	10.418
	30	11.265	11.006	10.791	10.455	10.206	10.013	9.859	11.524	11.263	11.048	10.712	10.461	10.267	10.113
	36	10.852	10.631	10.449	10.163	9.951	9.787	9.656	11.111	10.889	10.706	10.420	10.206	10.041	9.910
	48	10.338	10.165	10.022	9.799	9.633	9.505	9.403	10.597	10.423	10.280	10.056	9.889	9.760	9.657
	60	10.031	9.887	9.768	9.582	9.444	9.337	9.252	10.290	10.145	10.025	9.839	9.699	9.592	9.506
	72	9.828	9.703	9.599	9.438	9.318	9.225	9.152	10.087	9.961	9.857	9.695	9.574	9.480	9.406
4 Points	3	42.810	39.528	36.820	32.611	29.491	27.086	25.176	43.074	39.791	37.081	32.915	29.750	27.344	25.433
	6	25.722	24.084	22.731	20.626	19.063	17.858	16.899	25.984	24.346	22.992	20.885	19.321	18.114	17.155
	9	20.079	18.980	18.072	16.658	15.608	14.797	14.153	20.341	19.241	18.332	16.916	15.865	15.054	14.409
	12	17.268	16.436	15.749	14.679	13.884	13.270	12.782	17.530	16.697	16.009	14.937	14.141	13.527	13.038
	15	15.585	14.913	14.358	13.493	12.851	12.355	11.961	15.847	15.174	14.618	13.752	13.108	12.612	12.217
	18	14.465	13.899	13.432	12.704	12.163	11.746	11.414	14.727	14.160	13.692	12.962	12.421	12.002	11.670
	24	13.067	12.634	12.276	11.719	11.305	10.985	10.731	13.329	12.895	12.536	11.977	11.562	11.242	10.987
	30	12.230	11.876	11.584	11.129	10.791	10.530	10.322	12.492	12.137	11.844	11.387	11.048	10.786	10.578
	36	11.674	11.373	11.124	10.736	10.449	10.226	10.050	11.936	11.633	11.384	10.995	10.706	10.483	10.306
	48	10.980	10.745	10.550	10.247	10.022	9.849	9.711	11.242	11.006	10.810	10.506	10.280	10.105	9.967
	60	10.567	10.370	10.208	9.955	9.768	9.623	9.508	10.829	10.631	10.468	10.214	10.025	9.880	9.764
	72	10.293	10.122	9.981	9.762	9.599	9.474	9.374	10.555	10.384	10.242	10.021	9.857	9.731	9.630
5 Points	3	52.017	47.798	44.326	38.946	34.971	31.915	29.491	52.285	48.119	44.591	40.424	36.258	32.174	29.750
	6	30.304	28.207	26.477	23.793	21.807	20.277	19.063	30.571	28.471	26.740	24.055	22.067	20.536	19.321
	9	23.152	21.746	20.586	18.785	17.451	16.423	15.608	23.418	22.010	20.848	19.045	17.710	16.682	15.865
	12	19.593	18.529	17.651	16.289	15.279	14.502	13.884	19.858	18.793	17.914	16.549	15.538	14.760	14.141
	15	17.463	16.604	15.895	14.794	13.979	13.350	12.851	17.728	16.867	16.157	15.054	14.238	13.608	13.108
	18	16.045	15.322	14.726	13.799	13.113	12.583	12.163	16.310	15.586	14.988	14.059	13.372	12.842	12.421
	24	14.277	13.724	13.267	12.557	12.032	11.627	11.305	14.542	13.987	13.529	12.818	12.291	11.885	11.562
	30	13.219	12.767	12.393	11.814	11.384	11.054	10.791	13.484	13.030	12.656	12.074	11.643	11.312	11.048
	36	12.515	12.130	11.812	11.319	10.954	10.672	10.449	12.781	12.394	12.075	11.580	11.213	10.930	10.706
	48	11.639	11.337	11.089	10.703	10.417	10.197	10.022	11.904	11.601	11.352	10.964	10.677	10.455	10.280
	60	11.116	10.864	10.657	10.335	10.097	9.914	9.768	11.382	11.129	10.920	10.596	10.357	10.172	10.025
	72	10.770	10.551	10.371	10.092	9.885	9.726	9.599	11.036	10.816	10.635	10.353	10.145	9.984	9.857

Yield on Construction Loan When Points Are Paid

Points Paid	Yield at Month	9.00% Interest Rate Average Balance							9.25% Interest Rate Average Balance						
		50%	55%	60%	70%	80%	90%	100%	50%	55%	60%	70%	80%	90%	100%
1 Point	3	17.231	16.473	15.843	14.856	14.118	13.545	13.088	17.484	16.726	16.096	15.109	14.370	13.797	13.339
	6	13.155	12.773	12.455	11.958	11.585	11.296	11.065	13.408	13.026	12.708	12.210	11.837	11.548	11.316
	9	11.799	11.542	11.328	10.993	10.742	10.547	10.392	12.052	11.795	11.581	11.245	10.994	10.799	10.643
	12	11.122	10.927	10.765	10.511	10.321	10.173	10.055	11.375	11.180	11.018	10.763	10.573	10.425	10.307
	15	10.717	10.559	10.428	10.222	10.068	9.949	9.853	10.969	10.811	10.680	10.474	10.320	10.200	10.105
	18	10.446	10.313	10.203	10.030	9.900	9.799	9.719	10.699	10.566	10.455	10.282	10.152	10.051	9.970
	24	10.109	10.007	9.922	9.789	9.690	9.613	9.551	10.361	10.259	10.174	10.041	9.942	9.864	9.803
	30	9.906	9.823	9.754	9.645	9.564	9.501	9.451	10.159	10.076	10.006	9.897	9.816	9.753	9.702
	36	9.772	9.701	9.642	9.549	9.480	9.427	9.384	10.025	9.953	9.894	9.801	9.732	9.678	9.635
	48	9.604	9.549	9.502	9.430	9.376	9.334	9.300	9.857	9.801	9.755	9.682	9.628	9.585	9.552
	60	9.504	9.458	9.419	9.359	9.314	9.278	9.251	9.757	9.710	9.672	9.611	9.565	9.530	9.502
	72	9.438	9.398	9.364	9.312	9.272	9.242	9.218	9.691	9.650	9.617	9.564	9.524	9.494	9.469
1.5 Points	3	21.431	20.280	19.324	17.827	16.710	15.843	15.152	21.686	20.535	19.578	18.081	16.963	16.096	15.405
	6	15.270	14.691	14.209	13.455	12.892	12.455	12.107	15.524	14.945	14.463	13.709	13.145	12.708	12.359
	9	13.224	12.833	12.509	12.002	11.623	11.328	11.093	13.478	13.088	12.763	12.255	11.875	11.581	11.346
	12	12.202	11.906	11.661	11.276	10.988	10.765	10.587	12.456	12.160	11.914	11.529	11.241	11.018	10.839
	15	11.589	11.350	11.152	10.841	10.608	10.428	10.284	11.844	11.604	11.405	11.094	10.861	10.680	10.536
	18	11.182	10.980	10.813	10.551	10.355	10.203	10.082	11.436	11.234	11.066	10.804	10.607	10.455	10.334
	24	10.672	10.518	10.390	10.189	10.039	9.922	9.829	10.927	10.772	10.643	10.442	10.291	10.174	10.081
	30	10.367	10.241	10.136	9.972	9.849	9.754	9.678	10.622	10.495	10.390	10.225	10.102	10.006	9.930
	36	10.164	10.057	9.967	9.828	9.723	9.642	9.577	10.419	10.311	10.221	10.081	9.976	9.894	9.829
	48	9.911	9.827	9.757	9.648	9.566	9.502	9.452	10.166	10.081	10.011	9.901	9.819	9.755	9.704
	60	9.761	9.690	9.632	9.540	9.472	9.419	9.377	10.015	9.944	9.886	9.794	9.725	9.672	9.629
	72	9.661	9.600	9.549	9.469	9.410	9.364	9.327	9.915	9.854	9.803	9.723	9.663	9.617	9.580
2 Points	3	25.690	24.134	22.844	20.828	19.324	18.159	17.231	25.947	24.391	23.100	21.082	19.578	18.413	17.484
	6	17.411	16.630	15.981	14.966	14.209	13.623	13.155	17.667	16.885	16.236	15.221	14.463	13.876	13.408
	9	14.664	14.139	13.702	13.019	12.509	12.114	11.799	14.920	14.394	13.957	13.273	12.763	12.368	12.052
	12	13.294	12.895	12.564	12.047	11.661	11.361	11.122	13.550	13.151	12.819	12.301	11.914	11.614	11.375
	15	12.472	12.150	11.883	11.464	11.152	10.910	10.717	12.728	12.405	12.137	11.718	11.405	11.163	10.969
	18	11.925	11.654	11.429	11.076	10.813	10.609	10.446	12.181	11.909	11.683	11.330	11.066	10.862	10.699
	24	11.242	11.034	10.862	10.591	10.390	10.233	10.109	11.498	11.290	11.116	10.845	10.643	10.486	10.361
	30	10.834	10.663	10.522	10.301	10.136	10.008	9.906	11.089	10.919	10.777	10.555	10.390	10.261	10.159
	36	10.562	10.416	10.296	10.108	9.967	9.859	9.772	10.817	10.672	10.551	10.362	10.221	10.112	10.025
	48	10.222	10.109	10.015	9.867	9.757	9.672	9.604	10.478	10.364	10.270	10.121	10.011	9.925	9.857
	60	10.020	9.925	9.847	9.724	9.632	9.561	9.504	10.276	10.181	10.102	9.978	9.886	9.814	9.757
	72	9.886	9.804	9.736	9.629	9.549	9.487	9.438	10.143	10.060	9.991	9.883	9.803	9.740	9.691
3 Points	3	34.388	31.992	30.009	26.918	24.620	22.844	21.431	34.649	32.251	30.267	27.175	24.876	23.100	21.686
	6	21.773	20.573	19.579	18.028	16.873	15.981	15.270	22.033	20.831	19.836	18.284	17.129	16.236	15.525
	9	17.598	16.791	16.122	15.079	14.303	13.702	13.224	17.857	17.049	16.380	15.336	14.558	13.957	13.478
	12	15.516	14.905	14.398	13.608	13.020	12.564	12.202	15.775	15.163	14.656	13.864	13.275	12.819	12.456
	15	14.269	13.775	13.366	12.727	12.251	11.883	11.589	14.528	14.033	13.623	12.983	12.506	12.138	11.844
	18	13.439	13.023	12.678	12.139	11.739	11.429	11.182	13.698	13.281	12.935	12.396	11.994	11.683	11.436
	24	12.403	12.084	11.819	11.407	11.099	10.862	10.672	12.661	12.342	12.076	11.663	11.355	11.116	10.927
	30	11.782	11.521	11.305	10.968	10.717	10.522	10.367	12.041	11.779	11.562	11.224	10.972	10.777	10.622
	36	11.370	11.147	10.963	10.676	10.462	10.296	10.164	11.629	11.405	11.220	10.932	10.717	10.551	10.419
	48	10.856	10.682	10.537	10.312	10.144	10.015	9.911	11.115	10.940	10.795	10.568	10.400	10.270	10.166
	60	10.549	10.404	10.283	10.095	9.955	9.847	9.761	10.808	10.662	10.541	10.352	10.211	10.102	10.015
	72	10.346	10.220	10.115	9.951	9.830	9.736	9.661	10.606	10.478	10.373	10.208	10.086	9.991	9.915
4 Points	3	43.339	40.054	37.343	33.131	30.009	27.602	25.690	43.603	40.317	37.605	33.439	30.267	27.860	25.947
	6	26.247	24.607	23.252	21.144	19.579	18.371	17.411	26.510	24.869	23.512	21.402	19.836	18.628	17.667
	9	20.603	19.502	18.592	17.175	16.122	15.310	14.664	20.865	19.763	18.852	17.433	16.380	15.567	14.920
	12	17.792	16.958	16.269	15.195	14.398	13.783	13.294	18.054	17.219	16.528	15.454	14.656	14.040	13.550
	15	16.109	15.435	14.878	14.010	13.366	12.868	12.472	16.371	15.695	15.137	14.268	13.623	13.125	12.728
	18	14.988	14.421	13.951	13.221	12.678	12.259	11.925	15.250	14.681	14.211	13.479	12.935	12.515	12.181
	24	13.591	13.155	12.796	12.235	11.819	11.498	11.242	13.853	13.416	13.055	12.494	12.076	11.754	11.498
	30	12.754	12.398	12.104	11.645	11.305	11.042	10.834	13.016	12.659	12.364	11.904	11.562	11.299	11.089
	36	12.198	11.894	11.643	11.253	10.963	10.739	10.562	12.460	12.155	11.903	11.511	11.220	10.996	10.817
	48	11.505	11.267	11.070	10.764	10.537	10.362	10.222	11.767	11.528	11.330	11.023	10.795	10.618	10.478
	60	11.092	10.893	10.728	10.473	10.283	10.137	10.020	11.354	11.154	10.989	10.732	10.541	10.393	10.276
	72	10.818	10.645	10.502	10.280	10.115	9.988	9.886	11.081	10.907	10.763	10.539	10.373	10.245	10.143
5 Points	3	52.554	48.331	44.856	39.471	35.493	32.434	30.009	52.822	48.655	45.121	40.954	36.788	32.694	30.267
	6	30.837	28.736	27.004	24.316	22.326	20.795	19.579	31.103	29.000	27.267	24.577	22.586	21.053	19.836
	9	23.683	22.274	21.111	19.306	17.970	16.940	16.122	23.949	22.538	21.374	19.567	18.229	17.198	16.380
	12	20.123	19.056	18.176	16.810	15.798	15.018	14.398	20.388	19.320	18.439	17.070	16.057	15.276	14.656
	15	17.993	17.131	16.420	15.315	14.497	13.866	13.366	18.258	17.394	16.682	15.575	14.756	14.124	13.623
	18	16.575	15.849	15.250	14.320	13.631	13.100	12.678	16.841	16.113	15.513	14.580	13.890	13.358	12.935
	24	14.807	14.251	13.791	13.078	12.550	12.143	11.819	15.073	14.514	14.054	13.339	12.809	12.401	12.077
	30	13.749	13.294	12.918	12.335	11.903	11.570	11.305	14.015	13.558	13.181	12.595	12.162	11.828	11.562
	36	13.046	12.658	12.337	11.840	11.472	11.188	10.963	13.311	12.922	12.600	12.101	11.731	11.447	11.220
	48	12.170	11.865	11.614	11.225	10.936	10.714	10.537	12.436	12.130	11.877	11.485	11.195	10.972	10.795
	60	11.648	11.393	11.183	10.857	10.616	10.431	10.283	11.914	11.658	11.446	11.119	10.876	10.689	10.541
	72	11.303	11.081	10.898	10.615	10.405	10.243	10.115	11.569	11.346	11.162	10.876	10.665	10.502	10.373

Yield on Construction Loan When Points Are Paid

Points Paid	Yield at Month	9.50% Interest Rate Average Balance							9.75% Interest Rate Average Balance						
		50%	55%	60%	70%	80%	90%	100%	50%	55%	60%	70%	80%	90%	100%
	3	17.738	16.980	16.349	15.361	14.622	14.049	13.591	17.991	17.233	16.602	15.614	14.874	14.301	13.843
	6	13.661	13.278	12.960	12.462	12.089	11.799	11.568	13.914	13.531	13.213	12.714	12.341	12.051	11.820
	9	12.305	12.047	11.833	11.497	11.246	11.051	10.894	12.558	12.300	12.086	11.749	11.497	11.302	11.146
	12	11.628	11.433	11.270	11.015	10.824	10.676	10.558	11.881	11.685	11.522	11.267	11.076	10.928	10.809
1 Point	15	11.222	11.064	10.932	10.726	10.572	10.452	10.356	11.475	11.317	11.185	10.978	10.824	10.704	10.608
	18	10.952	10.818	10.708	10.534	10.404	10.303	10.222	11.205	11.071	10.960	10.786	10.655	10.554	10.473
	24	10.614	10.512	10.427	10.293	10.193	10.116	10.054	10.867	10.764	10.679	10.545	10.445	10.367	10.305
	30	10.412	10.328	10.259	10.149	10.068	10.004	9.953	10.665	10.581	10.511	10.401	10.319	10.256	10.205
	36	10.277	10.206	10.147	10.053	9.984	9.930	9.886	10.530	10.459	10.399	10.306	10.236	10.181	10.138
	48	10.110	10.054	10.007	9.934	9.879	9.837	9.803	10.363	10.306	10.260	10.186	10.131	10.089	10.055
	60	10.010	9.963	9.924	9.863	9.817	9.782	9.753	10.263	10.216	10.177	10.115	10.069	10.033	10.005
	72	9.944	9.903	9.869	9.816	9.776	9.745	9.721	10.197	10.156	10.122	10.068	10.028	9.997	9.972
	3	21.941	20.789	19.832	18.335	17.216	16.349	15.657	22.197	21.044	20.087	18.588	17.469	16.602	15.910
	6	15.779	15.199	14.717	13.962	13.398	12.960	12.611	16.034	15.453	14.971	14.215	13.651	13.213	12.864
	9	13.732	13.341	13.017	12.508	12.128	11.833	11.598	13.987	13.595	13.270	12.761	12.381	12.086	11.850
	12	12.711	12.414	12.168	11.782	11.494	11.270	11.092	12.965	12.668	12.421	12.035	11.746	11.522	11.344
1.5 Points	15	12.098	11.858	11.659	11.347	11.113	10.932	10.788	12.352	12.112	11.912	11.600	11.366	11.185	11.040
	18	11.690	11.488	11.320	11.057	10.860	10.708	10.586	11.944	11.742	11.573	11.310	11.113	10.960	10.838
	24	11.181	11.026	10.897	10.695	10.544	10.427	10.333	11.435	11.279	11.150	10.948	10.796	10.679	10.585
	30	10.876	10.749	10.643	10.478	10.354	10.259	10.182	11.130	11.003	10.897	10.731	10.607	10.511	10.434
	36	10.673	10.565	10.475	10.334	10.228	10.147	10.081	10.927	10.819	10.728	10.587	10.481	10.399	10.334
	48	10.420	10.335	10.265	10.154	10.071	10.007	9.956	10.675	10.589	10.518	10.407	10.324	10.260	10.208
	60	10.270	10.198	10.139	10.047	9.978	9.924	9.881	10.524	10.453	10.393	10.300	10.231	10.177	10.134
	72	10.170	10.108	10.057	9.976	9.916	9.869	9.832	10.425	10.362	10.310	10.229	10.169	10.122	10.084
	3	26.204	24.647	23.356	21.337	19.832	18.667	17.738	26.461	24.903	23.611	21.592	20.087	18.921	17.991
	6	17.923	17.141	16.491	15.475	14.717	14.129	13.661	18.180	17.396	16.746	15.729	14.971	14.383	13.914
	9	15.176	14.649	14.212	13.527	13.017	12.621	12.305	15.432	14.905	14.467	13.782	13.270	12.874	12.558
	12	13.805	13.406	13.074	12.555	12.168	11.868	11.628	14.061	13.661	13.329	12.809	12.421	12.121	11.881
2 Points	15	12.984	12.661	12.392	11.972	11.659	11.416	11.222	13.240	12.916	12.647	12.226	11.912	11.669	11.475
	18	12.437	12.164	11.938	11.584	11.320	11.115	10.952	12.693	12.419	12.193	11.838	11.573	11.368	11.205
	24	11.754	11.545	11.371	11.099	10.897	10.740	10.614	12.010	11.800	11.626	11.354	11.150	10.993	10.867
	30	11.345	11.174	11.032	10.809	10.643	10.515	10.412	11.601	11.429	11.286	11.063	10.897	10.768	10.665
	36	11.073	10.927	10.806	10.616	10.475	10.365	10.277	11.329	11.182	11.061	10.870	10.728	10.618	10.530
	48	10.734	10.620	10.525	10.376	10.265	10.179	10.110	10.990	10.875	10.779	10.630	10.518	10.432	10.363
	60	10.532	10.436	10.357	10.232	10.139	10.067	10.010	10.788	10.692	10.612	10.487	10.393	10.321	10.263
	72	10.399	10.315	10.246	10.137	10.057	9.994	9.944	10.655	10.571	10.501	10.392	10.310	10.247	10.197
	3	34.910	32.511	30.526	27.433	25.133	23.356	21.941	35.170	32.771	30.785	27.690	25.389	23.611	22.197
	6	22.292	21.090	20.094	18.541	17.385	16.491	15.779	22.552	21.348	20.352	18.797	17.641	16.746	16.034
	9	18.116	17.307	16.637	15.592	14.814	14.212	13.732	18.375	17.565	16.895	15.848	15.069	14.467	13.987
	12	16.034	15.421	14.913	14.121	13.530	13.074	12.711	16.293	15.679	15.170	14.377	13.786	13.329	12.965
3 Points	15	14.787	14.291	13.880	13.239	12.761	12.392	12.098	15.045	14.549	14.137	13.495	13.017	12.647	12.352
	18	13.956	13.538	13.192	12.652	12.249	11.938	11.690	14.215	13.796	13.449	12.908	12.505	12.193	11.944
	24	12.920	12.599	12.334	11.919	11.610	11.371	11.181	13.179	12.857	12.591	12.175	11.865	11.626	11.435
	30	12.300	12.037	11.820	11.480	11.227	11.032	10.876	12.559	12.295	12.077	11.736	11.483	11.286	11.130
	36	11.887	11.663	11.478	11.188	10.973	10.806	10.673	12.146	11.921	11.735	11.444	11.228	11.061	10.927
	48	11.374	11.198	11.052	10.825	10.656	10.525	10.420	11.633	11.456	11.310	11.081	10.911	10.779	10.675
	60	11.068	10.920	10.798	10.608	10.466	10.357	10.270	11.327	11.179	11.056	10.865	10.722	10.612	10.524
	72	10.865	10.737	10.631	10.465	10.341	10.246	10.170	11.125	10.996	10.889	10.721	10.597	10.501	10.425
	3	43.868	40.580	37.867	33.651	30.526	28.117	26.204	44.132	40.843	38.129	33.962	30.785	28.375	26.461
	6	26.772	25.130	23.773	21.661	20.094	18.885	17.923	27.035	25.391	24.033	21.920	20.352	19.142	18.180
	9	21.128	20.024	19.112	17.692	16.637	15.823	15.176	21.390	20.285	19.372	17.950	16.895	16.080	15.432
	12	18.316	17.480	16.788	15.712	14.913	14.296	13.805	18.578	17.740	17.048	15.971	15.170	14.553	14.061
4 Points	15	16.632	15.956	15.397	14.527	13.880	13.381	12.984	16.894	16.217	15.657	14.785	14.137	13.637	13.240
	18	15.512	14.942	14.471	13.737	13.192	12.771	12.437	15.774	15.203	14.731	13.995	13.449	13.028	12.693
	24	14.114	13.677	13.315	12.752	12.334	12.011	11.754	14.376	13.938	13.575	13.010	12.591	12.267	12.010
	30	13.278	12.920	12.623	12.162	11.820	11.555	11.345	13.540	13.180	12.883	12.421	12.077	11.812	11.601
	36	12.722	12.416	12.163	11.770	11.478	11.252	11.073	12.984	12.677	12.423	12.028	11.735	11.509	11.329
	48	12.029	11.789	11.591	11.282	11.052	10.875	10.734	12.292	12.050	11.851	11.540	11.310	11.132	10.990
	60	11.617	11.416	11.249	10.990	10.798	10.650	10.532	11.880	11.677	11.510	11.249	11.056	10.907	10.788
	72	11.344	11.169	11.024	10.798	10.631	10.502	10.399	11.607	11.430	11.284	11.057	10.889	10.758	10.655
	3	53.090	48.865	45.386	39.997	36.015	32.954	30.526	53.359	49.192	45.651	41.484	37.318	33.214	30.785
	6	31.369	29.265	27.530	24.838	22.846	21.312	20.094	31.635	29.529	27.794	25.100	23.106	21.571	20.352
	9	24.214	22.802	21.637	19.828	18.488	17.457	16.637	24.480	23.066	21.899	20.089	18.748	17.715	16.895
	12	20.654	19.584	18.701	17.331	16.316	15.534	14.913	20.919	19.848	18.964	17.592	16.575	15.792	15.170
5 Points	15	18.523	17.658	16.944	15.836	15.015	14.382	13.880	18.788	17.922	17.207	16.097	15.274	14.641	14.137
	18	17.106	16.376	15.775	14.841	14.149	13.616	13.192	17.371	16.640	16.037	15.101	14.408	13.874	13.449
	24	15.338	14.778	14.316	13.599	13.068	12.659	12.334	15.603	15.042	14.579	13.860	13.327	12.917	12.591
	30	14.280	13.821	13.443	12.856	12.421	12.086	11.820	14.545	14.085	13.706	13.117	12.680	12.344	12.077
	36	13.577	13.185	12.863	12.362	11.991	11.705	11.478	13.842	13.449	13.125	12.622	12.250	11.963	11.735
	48	12.702	12.394	12.140	11.746	11.455	11.230	11.052	12.967	12.658	12.403	12.007	11.714	11.489	11.310
	60	12.180	11.922	11.710	11.380	11.136	10.948	10.798	12.446	12.187	11.973	11.641	11.395	11.206	11.056
	72	11.836	11.611	11.425	11.137	10.925	10.761	10.631	12.102	11.876	11.689	11.399	11.185	11.020	10.889

Yield on Construction Loan When Points Are Paid

Points Paid	Yield at Month	10.00% Interest Rate Average Balance							10.25% Interest Rate Average Balance						
		50%	55%	60%	70%	80%	90%	100%	50%	55%	60%	70%	80%	90%	100%
1 Point	3	18.244	17.486	16.855	15.866	15.127	14.553	14.094	18.498	17.739	17.108	16.118	15.379	14.805	14.346
	6	14.167	13.784	13.465	12.966	12.593	12.303	12.071	14.420	14.037	13.718	13.218	12.844	12.554	12.322
	9	12.811	12.553	12.338	12.001	11.749	11.554	11.397	13.064	12.805	12.590	12.253	12.001	11.805	11.649
	12	12.134	11.938	11.775	11.519	11.328	11.179	11.061	12.387	12.190	12.027	11.771	11.580	11.431	11.312
	15	11.728	11.569	11.437	11.230	11.075	10.955	10.859	11.981	11.822	11.689	11.482	11.327	11.207	11.110
	18	11.457	11.324	11.212	11.038	10.907	10.806	10.725	11.710	11.576	11.465	11.290	11.159	11.057	10.976
	24	11.120	11.017	10.931	10.797	10.697	10.619	10.557	11.373	11.270	11.184	11.049	10.949	10.871	10.808
	30	10.918	10.833	10.763	10.653	10.571	10.507	10.456	11.170	11.086	11.016	10.905	10.823	10.759	10.708
	36	10.783	10.711	10.651	10.558	10.487	10.433	10.389	11.036	10.964	10.904	10.810	10.739	10.684	10.641
	48	10.616	10.559	10.512	10.438	10.383	10.340	10.306	10.869	10.812	10.765	10.690	10.635	10.592	10.557
	60	10.516	10.469	10.429	10.367	10.321	10.285	10.256	10.769	10.721	10.682	10.619	10.573	10.537	10.508
	72	10.450	10.409	10.374	10.320	10.280	10.249	10.224	10.703	10.661	10.627	10.572	10.532	10.500	10.475
1.5 Points	3	22.452	21.299	20.341	18.842	17.723	16.855	16.162	22.707	21.553	20.595	19.096	17.976	17.108	16.415
	6	16.288	15.707	15.224	14.468	13.904	13.465	13.116	16.543	15.961	15.478	14.722	14.156	13.718	13.368
	9	14.241	13.849	13.524	13.014	12.633	12.338	12.102	14.495	14.103	13.778	13.267	12.886	12.590	12.354
	12	13.219	12.922	12.675	12.288	11.999	11.775	11.596	13.473	13.176	12.929	12.541	12.252	12.027	11.848
	15	12.607	12.366	12.166	11.853	11.619	11.437	11.292	12.861	12.620	12.419	12.106	11.871	11.689	11.544
	18	12.199	11.996	11.827	11.563	11.365	11.212	11.090	12.453	12.249	12.080	11.816	11.618	11.465	11.342
	24	11.689	11.533	11.404	11.201	11.049	10.931	10.837	11.944	11.787	11.657	11.454	11.302	11.184	11.090
	30	11.384	11.257	11.150	10.984	10.860	10.763	10.686	11.639	11.510	11.404	11.237	11.112	11.016	10.938
	36	11.182	11.072	10.982	10.840	10.734	10.651	10.586	11.436	11.326	11.235	11.093	10.986	10.904	10.838
	48	10.929	10.843	10.772	10.660	10.577	10.512	10.460	11.184	11.097	11.026	10.913	10.830	10.765	10.713
	60	10.779	10.707	10.647	10.553	10.483	10.429	10.386	11.033	10.961	10.901	10.807	10.736	10.682	10.638
	72	10.679	10.616	10.564	10.483	10.422	10.374	10.336	10.934	10.871	10.818	10.736	10.674	10.627	10.589
2 Points	3	26.718	25.160	23.867	21.847	20.341	19.174	18.244	26.975	25.416	24.123	22.102	20.595	19.428	18.498
	6	18.436	17.652	17.001	15.984	15.224	14.636	14.167	18.692	17.907	17.256	16.238	15.478	14.889	14.420
	9	15.688	15.160	14.721	14.036	13.524	13.127	12.811	15.944	15.415	14.976	14.290	13.778	13.381	13.064
	12	14.317	13.916	13.584	13.063	12.675	12.374	12.134	14.573	14.172	13.838	13.317	12.929	12.627	12.387
	15	13.495	13.171	12.902	12.480	12.166	11.922	11.728	13.751	13.426	13.157	12.735	12.420	12.175	11.981
	18	12.948	12.675	12.448	12.092	11.827	11.621	11.457	13.204	12.930	12.702	12.346	12.081	11.875	11.710
	24	12.265	12.055	11.881	11.608	11.404	11.246	11.120	12.521	12.310	12.135	11.862	11.657	11.499	11.373
	30	11.857	11.684	11.541	11.317	11.150	11.021	10.918	12.112	11.939	11.796	11.571	11.404	11.274	11.170
	36	11.585	11.438	11.315	11.124	10.982	10.871	10.783	11.841	11.693	11.570	11.379	11.235	11.125	11.036
	48	11.246	11.130	11.034	10.884	10.772	10.685	10.616	11.502	11.386	11.289	11.138	11.026	10.938	10.869
	60	11.045	10.948	10.867	10.741	10.647	10.574	10.516	11.301	11.203	11.122	10.995	10.901	10.827	10.769
	72	10.911	10.827	10.756	10.646	10.564	10.501	10.450	11.168	11.082	11.012	10.901	10.818	10.754	10.703
3 Points	3	35.431	33.030	31.044	27.947	25.646	23.867	22.452	35.692	33.290	31.302	28.205	25.902	24.123	22.707
	6	22.811	21.607	20.610	19.054	17.896	17.001	16.288	23.070	21.865	20.867	19.311	18.152	17.256	16.543
	9	18.634	17.823	17.152	16.105	15.325	14.721	14.241	18.893	18.082	17.410	16.361	15.580	14.976	14.495
	12	16.551	15.937	15.428	14.633	14.041	13.584	13.219	16.810	16.195	15.685	14.889	14.297	13.838	13.473
	15	15.304	14.807	14.395	13.751	13.272	12.902	12.607	15.563	15.065	14.652	14.007	13.528	13.157	12.861
	18	14.474	14.054	13.707	13.164	12.760	12.448	12.199	14.733	14.312	13.964	13.420	13.015	12.702	12.453
	24	13.438	13.115	12.848	12.431	12.121	11.881	11.689	13.697	13.373	13.105	12.687	12.376	12.135	11.944
	30	12.818	12.553	12.334	11.992	11.738	11.541	11.384	13.077	12.811	12.592	12.249	11.993	11.796	11.639
	36	12.405	12.180	11.993	11.701	11.483	11.315	11.182	12.664	12.438	12.250	11.957	11.739	11.570	11.436
	48	11.892	11.714	11.567	11.338	11.167	11.034	10.929	12.151	11.973	11.825	11.594	11.422	11.289	11.184
	60	11.586	11.437	11.314	11.121	10.978	10.867	10.779	11.846	11.696	11.572	11.378	11.234	11.122	11.033
	72	11.385	11.254	11.146	10.978	10.853	10.756	10.679	11.644	11.513	11.404	11.235	11.109	11.012	10.934
4 Points	3	44.396	41.106	38.391	34.171	31.044	28.633	26.718	44.661	41.369	38.653	34.486	31.302	28.891	26.975
	6	27.298	25.653	24.294	22.179	20.610	19.399	18.436	27.560	25.914	24.554	22.438	20.867	19.655	18.692
	9	21.652	20.546	19.632	18.209	17.152	16.337	15.688	21.914	20.807	19.892	18.467	17.410	16.593	15.944
	12	18.840	18.001	17.308	16.229	15.428	14.809	14.317	19.102	18.262	17.568	16.487	15.685	15.065	14.573
	15	17.156	16.478	15.917	15.043	14.395	13.894	13.495	17.418	16.738	16.176	15.302	14.652	14.150	13.751
	18	16.036	15.464	14.990	14.254	13.707	13.284	12.948	16.298	15.724	15.250	14.512	13.964	13.541	13.204
	24	14.638	14.198	13.835	13.269	12.848	12.524	12.265	14.900	14.459	14.095	13.527	13.105	12.780	12.521
	30	13.802	13.441	13.143	12.679	12.334	12.068	11.857	14.064	13.702	13.403	12.937	12.592	12.325	12.112
	36	13.246	12.938	12.683	12.287	11.993	11.765	11.585	13.508	13.199	12.943	12.545	12.250	12.022	11.841
	48	12.554	12.312	12.111	11.799	11.567	11.388	11.246	12.817	12.573	12.371	12.058	11.825	11.645	11.502
	60	12.142	11.939	11.770	11.508	11.314	11.164	11.045	12.405	12.200	12.031	11.767	11.572	11.421	11.301
	72	11.870	11.692	11.545	11.316	11.146	11.015	10.911	12.133	11.954	11.806	11.575	11.404	11.273	11.168
5 Points	3	53.627	49.398	45.916	40.522	36.538	33.473	31.044	53.896	49.729	46.181	42.015	37.848	33.733	31.302
	6	31.902	29.794	28.057	25.361	23.366	21.829	20.610	32.168	30.059	28.320	25.622	23.625	22.088	20.867
	9	24.745	23.330	22.162	20.349	19.007	17.973	17.152	25.011	23.594	22.425	20.610	19.267	18.231	17.410
	12	21.184	20.111	19.226	17.852	16.834	16.050	15.428	21.450	20.375	19.489	18.113	17.094	16.308	15.685
	15	19.054	18.185	17.469	16.357	15.533	14.899	14.395	19.319	18.449	17.732	16.618	15.792	15.157	14.652
	18	17.636	16.904	16.300	15.362	14.667	14.132	13.707	17.901	17.167	16.562	15.622	14.926	14.390	13.964
	24	15.868	15.305	14.841	14.120	13.586	13.175	12.848	16.133	15.569	15.104	14.381	13.845	13.433	13.105
	30	14.810	14.349	13.968	13.377	12.939	12.602	12.334	15.076	14.613	14.231	13.638	13.199	12.860	12.592
	36	14.108	13.713	13.388	12.883	12.509	12.221	11.993	14.373	13.977	13.651	13.144	12.769	12.479	12.250
	48	13.233	12.922	12.666	12.268	11.974	11.747	11.567	13.499	13.187	12.929	12.530	12.234	12.006	11.825
	60	12.713	12.452	12.236	11.902	11.655	11.465	11.314	12.979	12.716	12.500	12.164	11.915	11.724	11.572
	72	12.369	12.141	11.952	11.661	11.445	11.278	11.146	12.636	12.406	12.216	11.922	11.705	11.537	11.404

Yield on Construction Loan When Points Are Paid

Points Paid	Yield at Month	10.50% Interest Rate Average Balance							10.75% Interest Rate Average Balance						
		50%	55%	60%	70%	80%	90%	100%	50%	55%	60%	70%	80%	90%	100%
	3	18.751	17.992	17.360	16.371	15.631	15.056	14.598	19.005	18.245	17.613	16.623	15.883	15.308	14.849
	6	14.673	14.289	13.970	13.470	13.096	12.806	12.574	14.926	14.542	14.223	13.723	13.348	13.058	12.825
	9	13.317	13.058	12.843	12.505	12.253	12.057	11.900	13.570	13.311	13.095	12.757	12.505	12.308	12.152
	12	12.639	12.443	12.279	12.023	11.831	11.683	11.564	12.892	12.696	12.532	12.275	12.083	11.934	11.815
1 Point	15	12.233	12.074	11.942	11.734	11.579	11.458	11.362	12.486	12.327	12.194	11.986	11.831	11.710	11.613
	18	11.963	11.829	11.717	11.542	11.411	11.309	11.227	12.216	12.081	11.969	11.794	11.662	11.560	11.479
	24	11.625	11.522	11.436	11.301	11.201	11.122	11.060	11.878	11.775	11.688	11.553	11.452	11.374	11.311
	30	11.423	11.339	11.268	11.157	11.075	11.010	10.959	11.676	11.591	11.520	11.409	11.326	11.262	11.210
	36	11.289	11.216	11.156	11.062	10.991	10.936	10.892	11.542	11.469	11.409	11.314	11.243	11.188	11.144
	48	11.122	11.064	11.017	10.942	10.887	10.843	10.809	11.375	11.317	11.269	11.195	11.139	11.095	11.060
	60	11.022	10.974	10.934	10.872	10.825	10.788	10.759	11.275	11.227	11.187	11.124	11.077	11.040	11.011
	72	10.956	10.914	10.879	10.825	10.784	10.752	10.727	11.209	11.167	11.132	11.077	11.036	11.004	10.978
	3	22.962	21.808	20.849	19.349	18.229	17.360	16.667	23.217	22.063	21.104	19.603	18.482	17.613	16.920
	6	16.797	16.215	15.732	14.975	14.409	13.970	13.620	17.052	16.470	15.986	15.228	14.662	14.223	13.873
	9	14.750	14.357	14.031	13.521	13.139	12.843	12.607	15.004	14.611	14.285	13.774	13.392	13.095	12.859
	12	13.728	13.430	13.182	12.794	12.504	12.279	12.100	13.982	13.684	13.436	13.047	12.757	12.532	12.352
1.5 Points	15	13.115	12.874	12.673	12.359	12.124	11.942	11.796	13.369	13.128	12.927	12.612	12.377	12.194	12.049
	18	12.707	12.503	12.334	12.069	11.871	11.717	11.594	12.961	12.757	12.588	12.322	12.123	11.969	11.846
	24	12.198	12.041	11.911	11.707	11.554	11.436	11.342	12.452	12.295	12.164	11.960	11.807	11.688	11.594
	30	11.893	11.764	11.658	11.490	11.365	11.268	11.191	12.147	12.018	11.911	11.743	11.618	11.520	11.443
	36	11.690	11.580	11.489	11.346	11.239	11.156	11.090	11.945	11.834	11.743	11.599	11.492	11.409	11.342
	48	11.438	11.351	11.279	11.167	11.082	11.017	10.965	11.692	11.605	11.533	11.420	11.335	11.269	11.217
	60	11.288	11.215	11.155	11.060	10.989	10.934	10.890	11.542	11.469	11.408	11.313	11.242	11.187	11.143
	72	11.189	11.125	11.072	10.989	10.927	10.879	10.841	11.443	11.379	11.326	11.243	11.180	11.132	11.093
	3	27.232	25.672	24.379	22.357	20.849	19.682	18.751	27.489	25.929	24.634	22.612	21.104	19.936	19.005
	6	18.948	18.163	17.511	16.492	15.732	15.143	14.673	19.204	18.418	17.766	16.747	15.986	15.396	14.926
	9	16.200	15.671	15.231	14.544	14.031	13.634	13.317	16.456	15.926	15.486	14.798	14.285	13.887	13.570
	12	14.829	14.427	14.093	13.572	13.182	12.880	12.639	15.084	14.682	14.348	13.826	13.436	13.133	12.892
2 Points	15	14.007	13.681	13.411	12.989	12.673	12.429	12.233	14.263	13.937	13.666	13.243	12.927	12.682	12.486
	18	13.460	13.185	12.957	12.600	12.334	12.128	11.963	13.716	13.440	13.212	12.854	12.588	12.381	12.216
	24	12.777	12.566	12.390	12.116	11.911	11.752	11.625	13.033	12.821	12.645	12.370	12.164	12.005	11.878
	30	12.368	12.195	12.051	11.826	11.658	11.527	11.423	12.624	12.450	12.306	12.080	11.911	11.780	11.676
	36	12.096	11.948	11.825	11.633	11.489	11.378	11.289	12.352	12.203	12.080	11.887	11.743	11.631	11.542
	48	11.758	11.641	11.544	11.393	11.279	11.192	11.122	12.014	11.897	11.799	11.647	11.533	11.445	11.375
	60	11.557	11.459	11.377	11.250	11.155	11.081	11.022	11.813	11.714	11.632	11.504	11.408	11.334	11.275
	72	11.424	11.338	11.267	11.155	11.072	11.008	10.956	11.680	11.594	11.522	11.410	11.326	11.261	11.209
	3	35.952	33.549	31.561	28.462	26.159	24.379	22.962	36.213	33.809	31.820	28.720	26.415	24.634	23.217
	6	23.330	22.124	21.125	19.567	18.408	17.511	16.797	23.589	22.382	21.383	19.824	18.664	17.766	17.052
	9	19.152	18.340	17.667	16.617	15.836	15.231	14.750	19.411	18.598	17.924	16.874	16.091	15.486	15.004
	12	17.069	16.453	15.942	15.145	14.552	14.093	13.728	17.328	16.711	16.200	15.402	14.808	14.348	13.982
3 Points	15	15.822	15.323	14.909	14.264	13.783	13.411	13.115	16.081	15.580	15.166	14.520	14.038	13.666	13.369
	18	14.991	14.570	14.221	13.676	13.271	12.957	12.707	15.250	14.828	14.478	13.933	13.526	13.212	12.961
	24	13.955	13.631	13.363	12.944	12.632	12.390	12.198	14.214	13.889	13.620	13.200	12.887	12.645	12.452
	30	13.335	13.069	12.849	12.505	12.249	12.051	11.893	13.594	13.327	13.106	12.761	12.504	12.306	12.147
	36	12.923	12.696	12.507	12.213	11.994	11.825	11.690	13.182	12.954	12.765	12.470	12.250	12.080	11.945
	48	12.410	12.231	12.082	11.850	11.678	11.544	11.438	12.670	12.489	12.340	12.107	11.933	11.799	11.692
	60	12.105	11.954	11.829	11.634	11.489	11.377	11.288	12.365	12.213	12.087	11.891	11.745	11.632	11.542
	72	11.904	11.772	11.663	11.492	11.365	11.267	11.189	12.164	12.031	11.920	11.749	11.621	11.522	11.443
	3	44.925	41.632	38.915	34.691	31.561	29.148	27.232	45.190	41.895	39.176	35.010	31.820	29.406	27.489
	6	27.823	26.176	24.815	22.697	21.125	19.912	18.948	28.086	26.437	25.075	22.956	21.383	20.169	19.204
	9	22.176	21.068	20.152	18.726	17.667	16.850	16.200	22.439	21.329	20.412	18.984	17.924	17.106	16.456
	12	19.364	18.523	17.828	16.746	15.942	15.322	14.829	19.626	18.784	18.088	17.004	16.200	15.578	15.084
4 Points	15	17.680	16.999	16.436	15.560	14.909	14.407	14.007	17.942	17.260	16.696	15.818	15.166	14.663	14.263
	18	16.560	15.985	15.510	14.770	14.221	13.797	13.460	16.822	16.246	15.770	15.029	14.478	14.053	13.716
	24	15.162	14.720	14.354	13.785	13.363	13.036	12.777	15.424	14.981	14.614	14.044	13.620	13.293	13.033
	30	14.326	13.963	13.663	13.196	12.849	12.581	12.368	14.588	14.224	13.923	13.454	13.106	12.838	12.624
	36	13.770	13.460	13.203	12.804	12.507	12.278	12.096	14.033	13.721	13.463	13.063	12.765	12.535	12.352
	48	13.079	12.834	12.632	12.316	12.082	11.902	11.758	13.342	13.095	12.892	12.575	12.340	12.159	12.014
	60	12.668	12.462	12.291	12.026	11.829	11.678	11.557	12.931	12.723	12.552	12.285	12.087	11.935	11.813
	72	12.397	12.216	12.067	11.835	11.663	11.530	11.424	12.660	12.478	12.328	12.094	11.920	11.787	11.680
	3	54.164	49.931	46.446	41.048	37.060	33.993	31.561	54.432	50.266	46.711	42.545	38.378	34.253	31.820
	6	32.434	30.323	28.583	25.883	23.885	22.346	21.125	32.700	30.588	28.847	26.145	24.145	22.605	21.383
	9	25.277	23.858	22.688	20.871	19.526	18.490	17.667	25.542	24.122	22.950	21.132	19.785	18.748	17.924
	12	21.715	20.639	19.752	18.374	17.353	16.567	15.942	21.980	20.903	20.014	18.634	17.612	16.825	16.200
5 Points	15	19.584	18.713	17.994	16.878	16.052	15.415	14.909	19.849	18.976	18.257	17.139	16.311	15.673	15.166
	18	18.166	17.431	16.825	15.883	15.185	14.648	14.221	18.431	17.695	17.087	16.144	15.445	14.906	14.478
	24	16.398	15.833	15.366	14.641	14.105	13.691	13.363	16.664	16.096	15.629	14.902	14.364	13.949	13.620
	30	15.341	14.877	14.493	13.899	13.458	13.119	12.849	15.607	15.140	14.756	14.159	13.717	13.377	13.106
	36	14.639	14.241	13.914	13.405	13.028	12.738	12.507	14.904	14.505	14.176	13.666	13.287	12.996	12.765
	48	13.765	13.451	13.192	12.791	12.493	12.264	12.082	14.031	13.716	13.455	13.052	12.753	12.523	12.340
	60	13.245	12.981	12.763	12.425	12.175	11.982	11.829	13.512	13.246	13.027	12.687	12.435	12.241	12.087
	72	12.903	12.671	12.480	12.184	11.965	11.796	11.663	13.170	12.936	12.744	12.446	12.225	12.055	11.920

Yield on Construction Loan When Points Are Paid

Points Paid	Yield at Month	11.00% Interest Rate Average Balance							11.25% Interest Rate Average Balance						
		50%	55%	60%	70%	80%	90%	100%	50%	55%	60%	70%	80%	90%	100%
1 Point	3	19.258	18.498	17.866	16.876	16.135	15.560	15.101	19.512	18.751	18.119	17.128	16.387	15.812	15.353
	6	15.179	14.795	14.475	13.975	13.600	13.309	13.077	15.432	15.048	14.728	14.227	13.852	13.561	13.328
	9	13.823	13.563	13.348	13.009	12.757	12.560	12.403	14.075	13.816	13.600	13.262	13.008	12.812	12.655
	12	13.145	12.948	12.784	12.527	12.335	12.186	12.066	13.398	13.201	13.037	12.779	12.587	12.437	12.318
	15	12.739	12.579	12.447	12.238	12.082	11.961	11.865	12.992	12.832	12.699	12.490	12.334	12.213	12.116
	18	12.469	12.334	12.222	12.046	11.914	11.812	11.730	12.722	12.586	12.474	12.298	12.166	12.063	11.982
	24	12.131	12.027	11.941	11.805	11.704	11.625	11.562	12.384	12.280	12.193	12.057	11.956	11.877	11.814
	30	11.929	11.844	11.773	11.661	11.578	11.513	11.462	12.182	12.096	12.025	11.913	11.830	11.765	11.713
	36	11.795	11.722	11.661	11.566	11.495	11.439	11.395	12.048	11.974	11.913	11.818	11.746	11.691	11.646
	48	11.628	11.570	11.522	11.447	11.390	11.347	11.312	11.881	11.823	11.774	11.699	11.642	11.598	11.563
	60	11.528	11.480	11.439	11.376	11.328	11.292	11.262	11.781	11.732	11.692	11.628	11.580	11.543	11.514
	72	11.462	11.420	11.385	11.329	11.288	11.255	11.230	11.716	11.673	11.637	11.581	11.540	11.507	11.481
1.5 Points	3	23.472	22.317	21.358	19.857	18.735	17.866	17.173	23.728	22.572	21.612	20.110	18.989	18.119	17.425
	6	17.306	16.724	16.239	15.481	14.915	14.475	14.125	17.561	16.978	16.493	15.735	15.168	14.728	14.377
	9	15.259	14.865	14.538	14.027	13.644	13.348	13.111	15.513	15.119	14.792	14.280	13.897	13.600	13.363
	12	14.236	13.938	13.689	13.300	13.010	12.784	12.604	14.491	14.191	13.943	13.553	13.262	13.037	12.856
	15	13.624	13.381	13.180	12.865	12.629	12.447	12.301	13.878	13.635	13.434	13.118	12.882	12.699	12.553
	18	13.216	13.011	12.841	12.575	12.376	12.222	12.098	13.470	13.265	13.095	12.828	12.629	12.474	12.351
	24	12.707	12.549	12.418	12.213	12.060	11.941	11.846	12.961	12.803	12.672	12.466	12.312	12.193	12.098
	30	12.402	12.272	12.165	11.996	11.870	11.773	11.695	12.656	12.526	12.418	12.249	12.123	12.025	11.947
	36	12.199	12.088	11.996	11.852	11.744	11.661	11.594	12.453	12.342	12.250	12.105	11.997	11.913	11.846
	48	11.947	11.859	11.787	11.673	11.588	11.522	11.469	12.201	12.114	12.041	11.926	11.841	11.774	11.721
	60	11.797	11.723	11.662	11.566	11.495	11.439	11.395	12.052	11.978	11.916	11.820	11.748	11.692	11.647
	72	11.698	11.634	11.580	11.496	11.433	11.385	11.346	11.953	11.888	11.834	11.749	11.686	11.637	11.598
2 Points	3	27.746	26.185	24.890	22.867	21.358	20.190	19.258	28.002	26.441	25.146	23.122	21.612	20.443	19.512
	6	19.460	18.674	18.021	17.001	16.239	15.649	15.179	19.716	18.929	18.277	17.255	16.493	15.903	15.432
	9	16.712	16.181	15.741	15.052	14.538	14.140	13.823	16.967	16.437	15.996	15.307	14.792	14.393	14.075
	12	15.340	14.937	14.603	14.080	13.689	13.387	13.145	15.596	15.193	14.858	14.334	13.943	13.640	13.398
	15	14.518	14.192	13.921	13.497	13.180	12.935	12.739	14.774	14.447	14.176	13.751	13.434	13.188	12.992
	18	13.971	13.696	13.467	13.109	12.841	12.634	12.469	14.227	13.951	13.721	13.363	13.095	12.887	12.722
	24	13.289	13.076	12.900	12.624	12.418	12.258	12.131	13.544	13.331	13.155	12.878	12.672	12.512	12.384
	30	12.880	12.705	12.560	12.334	12.165	12.034	11.929	13.136	12.961	12.815	12.588	12.418	12.287	12.182
	36	12.608	12.459	12.335	12.141	11.996	11.884	11.795	12.864	12.714	12.590	12.395	12.250	12.137	12.048
	48	12.270	12.152	12.054	11.901	11.787	11.698	11.628	12.526	12.408	12.309	12.155	12.041	11.952	11.881
	60	12.069	11.970	11.887	11.758	11.662	11.588	11.528	12.326	12.226	12.143	12.013	11.916	11.841	11.781
	72	11.937	11.850	11.777	11.664	11.580	11.515	11.462	12.193	12.105	12.033	11.919	11.834	11.768	11.716
3 Points	3	36.473	34.069	32.079	28.977	26.672	24.890	23.472	36.734	34.328	32.337	29.235	26.928	25.146	23.728
	6	23.848	22.641	21.641	20.080	18.919	18.021	17.306	24.108	22.899	21.898	20.337	19.175	18.277	17.561
	9	19.670	18.856	18.182	17.130	16.347	15.741	15.259	19.929	19.114	18.439	17.386	16.602	15.996	15.513
	12	17.587	16.969	16.457	15.658	15.063	14.603	14.236	17.846	17.227	16.714	15.914	15.318	14.858	14.491
	15	16.339	15.838	15.424	14.776	14.294	13.921	13.624	16.598	16.096	15.681	15.032	14.549	14.176	13.878
	18	15.509	15.086	14.736	14.189	13.782	13.467	13.216	15.768	15.344	14.993	14.445	14.037	13.721	13.470
	24	14.473	14.147	13.877	13.456	13.142	12.900	12.707	14.732	14.405	14.135	13.712	13.398	13.155	12.961
	30	13.853	13.585	13.364	13.018	12.760	12.560	12.402	14.112	13.844	13.621	13.274	13.015	12.815	12.656
	36	13.441	13.212	13.022	12.726	12.506	12.335	12.199	13.700	13.470	13.280	12.982	12.761	12.590	12.454
	48	12.929	12.748	12.598	12.363	12.189	12.054	11.947	13.188	13.006	12.855	12.620	12.445	12.309	12.201
	60	12.624	12.472	12.345	12.148	12.001	11.887	11.797	12.884	12.730	12.603	12.405	12.257	12.143	12.052
	72	12.423	12.289	12.178	12.005	11.877	11.777	11.698	12.683	12.548	12.437	12.262	12.133	12.033	11.953
4 Points	3	45.454	42.158	39.438	35.211	32.079	29.664	27.746	45.719	42.422	39.700	35.534	32.337	29.922	28.002
	6	28.349	26.699	25.336	23.215	21.641	20.426	19.460	28.611	26.960	25.596	23.474	21.898	20.683	19.716
	9	22.701	21.590	20.672	19.243	18.182	17.363	16.712	22.963	21.851	20.932	19.501	18.439	17.619	16.967
	12	19.888	19.045	18.348	17.263	16.457	15.835	15.340	20.150	19.305	18.608	17.521	16.714	16.091	15.596
	15	18.204	17.521	16.956	16.077	15.424	14.919	14.518	18.466	17.782	17.216	16.335	15.681	15.176	14.774
	18	17.083	16.507	16.030	15.287	14.736	14.310	13.971	17.345	16.767	16.289	15.545	14.993	14.566	14.227
	24	15.686	15.241	14.874	14.302	13.877	13.549	13.289	15.948	15.502	15.134	14.560	14.134	13.806	13.544
	30	14.850	14.485	14.183	13.713	13.364	13.094	12.880	15.112	14.746	14.443	13.971	13.621	13.351	13.136
	36	14.295	13.982	13.723	13.321	13.022	12.792	12.608	14.557	14.243	13.984	13.580	13.280	13.048	12.864
	48	13.604	13.357	13.152	12.834	12.598	12.415	12.270	13.867	13.618	13.413	13.093	12.855	12.672	12.526
	60	13.194	12.985	12.813	12.544	12.345	12.191	12.069	13.457	13.247	13.073	12.803	12.603	12.448	12.326
	72	12.923	12.740	12.589	12.353	12.178	12.044	11.937	13.187	13.002	12.850	12.613	12.437	12.301	12.193
5 Points	3	54.701	50.464	46.977	41.574	37.582	34.513	32.079	54.969	50.803	47.242	43.075	38.908	34.772	32.337
	6	32.966	30.853	29.110	26.406	24.405	22.864	21.641	33.233	31.117	29.373	26.667	24.664	23.122	21.898
	9	25.808	24.386	23.213	21.393	20.045	19.006	18.182	26.073	24.650	23.476	21.654	20.304	19.265	18.439
	12	22.246	21.167	20.277	18.895	17.871	17.083	16.457	22.511	21.430	20.539	19.155	18.131	17.341	16.714
	15	20.114	19.240	18.519	17.399	16.570	15.931	15.424	20.380	19.504	18.782	17.660	16.829	16.189	15.681
	18	18.697	17.958	17.350	16.404	15.704	15.164	14.736	18.962	18.222	17.612	16.665	15.963	15.422	14.993
	24	16.929	16.360	15.891	15.163	14.623	14.207	13.877	17.194	16.624	16.154	15.424	14.882	14.466	14.135
	30	15.872	15.404	15.019	14.420	13.977	13.635	13.364	16.137	15.668	15.281	14.681	14.236	13.893	13.621
	36	15.170	14.769	14.439	13.926	13.547	13.254	13.022	15.435	15.033	14.702	14.187	13.806	13.513	13.280
	48	14.297	13.980	13.719	13.313	13.013	12.781	12.598	14.563	14.244	13.982	13.574	13.272	13.040	12.855
	60	13.778	13.511	13.290	12.948	12.695	12.500	12.345	14.045	13.776	13.554	13.209	12.955	12.759	12.603
	72	13.437	13.202	13.008	12.707	12.485	12.314	12.178	13.704	13.467	13.272	12.969	12.746	12.573	12.437

Yield on Construction Loan When Points Are Paid

Points Paid	Yield at Month	11.50% Interest Rate Average Balance							11.75% Interest Rate Average Balance						
		50%	55%	60%	70%	80%	90%	100%	50%	55%	60%	70%	80%	90%	100%
	3	19.765	19.004	18.372	17.381	16.639	16.064	15.604	20.018	19.257	18.625	17.633	16.891	16.316	15.856
	6	15.685	15.300	14.980	14.479	14.104	13.813	13.580	15.938	15.553	15.233	14.731	14.356	14.064	13.831
	9	14.328	14.069	13.852	13.514	13.260	13.063	12.906	14.581	14.321	14.105	13.766	13.512	13.315	13.157
	12	13.651	13.453	13.289	13.031	12.839	12.689	12.569	13.904	13.706	13.541	13.283	13.090	12.941	12.821
1 Point	15	13.245	13.085	12.951	12.742	12.586	12.464	12.367	13.498	13.337	13.204	12.994	12.838	12.716	12.619
	18	12.974	12.839	12.726	12.550	12.418	12.315	12.233	13.227	13.092	12.979	12.802	12.669	12.567	12.484
	24	12.637	12.532	12.446	12.309	12.207	12.128	12.065	12.890	12.785	12.698	12.561	12.459	12.380	12.317
	30	12.435	12.349	12.277	12.165	12.082	12.017	11.965	12.688	12.602	12.530	12.418	12.333	12.268	12.216
	36	12.300	12.227	12.166	12.070	11.998	11.942	11.898	12.553	12.480	12.418	12.322	12.250	12.194	12.149
	48	12.133	12.075	12.027	11.951	11.894	11.850	11.815	12.386	12.328	12.279	12.203	12.146	12.102	12.066
	60	12.034	11.985	11.944	11.880	11.832	11.795	11.765	12.287	12.238	12.197	12.132	12.084	12.047	12.017
	72	11.969	11.926	11.890	11.834	11.792	11.759	11.733	12.222	12.178	12.142	12.086	12.043	12.011	11.984
	3	23.983	22.827	21.867	20.364	19.242	18.372	17.678	24.238	23.081	22.121	20.618	19.495	18.625	17.930
	6	17.816	17.232	16.747	15.988	15.420	14.980	14.629	18.070	17.486	17.001	16.241	15.673	15.233	14.882
	9	15.767	15.373	15.046	14.533	14.150	13.852	13.615	16.022	15.627	15.299	14.786	14.402	14.105	13.867
	12	14.745	14.445	14.196	13.806	13.515	13.289	13.109	14.999	14.699	14.450	14.060	13.768	13.541	13.361
1.5 Points	15	14.132	13.889	13.687	13.371	13.135	12.951	12.805	14.387	14.143	13.941	13.624	13.387	13.204	13.057
	18	13.724	13.519	13.348	13.081	12.881	12.726	12.603	13.979	13.773	13.602	13.334	13.134	12.979	12.855
	24	13.215	13.057	12.925	12.719	12.565	12.446	12.350	13.469	13.311	13.179	12.972	12.818	12.698	12.602
	30	12.910	12.780	12.672	12.502	12.376	12.277	12.199	13.165	13.034	12.926	12.756	12.629	12.530	12.451
	36	12.708	12.596	12.504	12.358	12.250	12.166	12.099	12.962	12.850	12.757	12.612	12.503	12.418	12.351
	48	12.456	12.368	12.294	12.179	12.093	12.027	11.974	12.711	12.622	12.548	12.433	12.346	12.279	12.226
	60	12.306	12.232	12.170	12.073	12.001	11.944	11.899	12.561	12.486	12.424	12.326	12.253	12.197	12.152
	72	12.208	12.142	12.088	12.003	11.939	11.890	11.850	12.462	12.396	12.342	12.256	12.192	12.142	12.103
	3	28.259	26.697	25.402	23.377	21.867	20.697	19.765	28.516	26.954	25.658	23.632	22.121	20.951	20.018
	6	19.972	19.185	18.532	17.510	16.747	16.156	15.685	20.229	19.441	18.787	17.764	17.001	16.410	15.938
	9	17.223	16.692	16.251	15.561	15.046	14.647	14.328	17.479	16.947	16.506	15.815	15.299	14.900	14.581
	12	15.852	15.448	15.112	14.588	14.196	13.893	13.651	16.108	15.703	15.367	14.842	14.450	14.146	13.904
2 Points	15	15.030	14.702	14.430	14.005	13.687	13.441	13.245	15.286	14.958	14.685	14.259	13.941	13.694	13.498
	18	14.483	14.206	13.976	13.617	13.348	13.140	12.974	14.739	14.461	14.231	13.871	13.602	13.394	13.227
	24	13.800	13.587	13.409	13.132	12.925	12.765	12.637	14.056	13.842	13.664	13.386	13.179	13.018	12.890
	30	13.392	13.216	13.070	12.842	12.672	12.540	12.435	13.647	13.471	13.325	13.096	12.926	12.793	12.688
	36	13.120	12.970	12.845	12.649	12.504	12.391	12.300	13.376	13.225	13.100	12.904	12.757	12.644	12.554
	48	12.782	12.663	12.564	12.410	12.294	12.205	12.133	13.039	12.919	12.820	12.664	12.548	12.458	12.386
	60	12.582	12.481	12.398	12.267	12.170	12.094	12.034	12.838	12.737	12.653	12.522	12.424	12.348	12.287
	72	12.450	12.361	12.288	12.173	12.088	12.022	11.969	12.706	12.617	12.543	12.428	12.342	12.275	12.222
	3	36.995	34.588	32.596	29.492	27.185	25.402	23.983	37.255	34.847	32.855	29.750	27.441	25.658	24.238
	6	24.367	23.158	22.156	20.594	19.431	18.532	17.816	24.627	23.416	22.414	20.850	19.686	18.787	18.070
	9	20.188	19.372	18.697	17.643	16.858	16.251	15.767	20.447	19.630	18.954	17.899	17.113	16.506	16.022
	12	18.105	17.485	16.971	16.170	15.574	15.112	14.745	18.363	17.743	17.229	16.427	15.829	15.367	14.999
3 Points	15	16.857	16.354	15.938	15.288	14.805	14.430	14.132	17.116	16.612	16.195	15.545	15.060	14.685	14.387
	18	16.027	15.602	15.250	14.701	14.292	13.976	13.724	16.285	15.860	15.507	14.957	14.548	14.231	13.979
	24	14.991	14.663	14.392	13.968	13.653	13.409	13.215	15.250	14.921	14.649	14.225	13.909	13.664	13.469
	30	14.371	14.102	13.878	13.530	13.271	13.070	12.910	14.630	14.360	14.136	13.786	13.526	13.325	13.165
	36	13.959	13.728	13.537	13.239	13.017	12.845	12.708	14.218	13.987	13.795	13.495	13.272	13.100	12.962
	48	13.448	13.265	13.113	12.877	12.701	12.564	12.456	13.707	13.523	13.371	13.133	12.956	12.820	12.711
	60	13.144	12.989	12.861	12.661	12.513	12.398	12.306	13.403	13.248	13.119	12.918	12.769	12.653	12.561
	72	12.943	12.807	12.695	12.519	12.389	12.288	12.208	13.203	13.066	12.953	12.776	12.645	12.543	12.462
	3	45.983	42.685	39.962	35.732	32.596	30.179	28.259	46.248	42.948	40.224	36.057	32.855	30.437	28.516
	6	28.874	27.222	25.857	23.733	22.156	20.940	19.972	29.137	27.483	26.117	23.991	22.414	21.196	20.229
	9	23.225	22.112	21.192	19.760	18.697	17.876	17.223	23.488	22.373	21.452	20.019	18.954	18.133	17.479
	12	20.412	19.566	18.867	17.779	16.971	16.348	15.852	20.674	19.827	19.127	18.038	17.229	16.604	16.108
4 Points	15	18.728	18.042	17.476	16.593	15.938	15.432	15.030	18.990	18.303	17.735	16.852	16.195	15.689	15.286
	18	17.607	17.028	16.549	15.804	15.250	14.823	14.483	17.869	17.289	16.809	16.062	15.507	15.079	14.739
	24	16.210	15.763	15.394	14.819	14.392	14.062	13.800	16.472	16.024	15.654	15.077	14.649	14.319	14.056
	30	15.374	15.007	14.703	14.230	13.878	13.607	13.392	15.637	15.268	14.963	14.488	14.136	13.864	13.647
	36	14.819	14.504	14.244	13.838	13.537	13.305	13.120	15.082	14.765	14.504	14.097	13.795	13.561	13.376
	48	14.130	13.880	13.673	13.352	13.113	12.929	12.782	14.392	14.141	13.933	13.610	13.371	13.186	13.039
	60	13.720	13.509	13.334	13.062	12.861	12.705	12.582	13.983	13.770	13.595	13.322	13.119	12.962	12.838
	72	13.450	13.264	13.111	12.872	12.695	12.558	12.450	13.713	13.526	13.372	13.131	12.953	12.815	12.706
	3	55.238	50.997	47.507	42.099	38.104	35.032	32.596	55.506	51.340	47.772	43.605	39.439	35.292	32.855
	6	33.499	31.382	29.637	26.928	24.924	23.381	22.156	33.765	31.646	29.900	27.190	25.184	23.640	22.414
	9	26.339	24.914	23.739	21.914	20.564	19.523	18.697	26.605	25.178	24.002	22.175	20.823	19.781	18.954
	12	22.776	21.694	20.802	19.416	18.390	17.599	16.971	23.042	21.958	21.064	19.677	18.649	17.857	17.229
5 Points	15	20.645	19.768	19.044	17.921	17.088	16.447	15.938	20.910	20.031	19.307	18.181	17.348	16.705	16.195
	18	19.227	18.486	17.875	16.925	16.222	15.680	15.250	19.492	18.750	18.137	17.186	16.481	15.938	15.507
	24	17.460	16.888	16.416	15.684	15.141	14.724	14.392	17.725	17.152	16.679	15.945	15.401	14.982	14.649
	30	16.403	15.932	15.544	14.941	14.495	14.151	13.878	16.668	16.196	15.807	15.202	14.755	14.410	14.136
	36	15.701	15.298	14.965	14.448	14.066	13.771	13.537	15.967	15.562	15.228	14.709	14.325	14.029	13.795
	48	14.829	14.509	14.245	13.835	13.532	13.298	13.113	15.096	14.773	14.508	14.096	13.792	13.557	13.371
	60	14.312	14.041	13.817	13.471	13.215	13.017	12.861	14.578	14.306	14.081	13.733	13.475	13.276	13.119
	72	13.971	13.732	13.536	13.231	13.006	12.832	12.695	14.238	13.998	13.800	13.493	13.266	13.091	12.953

Yield on Construction Loan When Points Are Paid

Points Paid	Yield at Month	12.00% Interest Rate Average Balance							12.25% Interest Rate Average Balance						
		50%	55%	60%	70%	80%	90%	100%	50%	55%	60%	70%	80%	90%	100%
1 Point	3	20.272	19.510	18.878	17.885	17.144	16.568	16.108	20.525	19.764	19.130	18.138	17.396	16.820	16.360
	6	16.191	15.806	15.485	14.983	14.608	14.316	14.083	16.444	16.058	15.738	15.235	14.859	14.567	14.334
	9	14.834	14.574	14.357	14.018	13.764	13.566	13.409	15.087	14.826	14.610	14.270	14.016	13.818	13.660
	12	14.157	13.959	13.794	13.535	13.342	13.192	13.072	14.410	14.211	14.046	13.787	13.594	13.444	13.324
	15	13.751	13.590	13.456	13.246	13.089	12.968	12.870	14.003	13.842	13.708	13.498	13.341	13.219	13.122
	18	13.480	13.344	13.231	13.054	12.921	12.818	12.736	13.733	13.597	13.483	13.306	13.173	13.070	12.987
	24	13.143	13.038	12.950	12.814	12.711	12.631	12.568	13.395	13.290	13.203	13.066	12.963	12.883	12.819
	30	12.941	12.854	12.782	12.670	12.585	12.520	12.468	13.194	13.107	13.035	12.922	12.837	12.772	12.719
	36	12.806	12.732	12.671	12.574	12.502	12.446	12.401	13.059	12.985	12.923	12.826	12.754	12.697	12.652
	48	12.639	12.581	12.532	12.455	12.398	12.353	12.318	12.892	12.833	12.784	12.707	12.650	12.605	12.569
	60	12.540	12.491	12.449	12.385	12.336	12.299	12.268	12.793	12.743	12.702	12.637	12.588	12.550	12.520
	72	12.475	12.431	12.395	12.338	12.295	12.262	12.236	12.728	12.684	12.648	12.590	12.548	12.514	12.488
1.5 Points	3	24.493	23.336	22.375	20.871	19.748	18.878	18.183	24.748	23.591	22.630	21.125	20.001	19.130	18.435
	6	18.325	17.740	17.255	16.494	15.926	15.485	15.134	18.579	17.994	17.508	16.747	16.179	15.738	15.386
	9	16.276	15.881	15.553	15.039	14.655	14.357	14.119	16.531	16.135	15.807	15.292	14.908	14.610	14.372
	12	15.254	14.953	14.704	14.313	14.020	13.794	13.613	15.508	15.207	14.957	14.566	14.273	14.046	13.865
	15	14.641	14.397	14.194	13.877	13.640	13.456	13.309	14.895	14.651	14.448	14.130	13.893	13.708	13.561
	18	14.233	14.027	13.855	13.587	13.387	13.231	13.107	14.487	14.281	14.109	13.840	13.639	13.483	13.359
	24	13.724	13.565	13.432	13.225	13.070	12.950	12.855	13.978	13.819	13.686	13.478	13.323	13.203	13.107
	30	13.419	13.288	13.179	13.009	12.881	12.782	12.703	13.674	13.542	13.433	13.262	13.134	13.035	12.956
	36	13.217	13.104	13.011	12.865	12.755	12.671	12.603	13.471	13.358	13.265	13.118	13.008	12.923	12.855
	48	12.965	12.876	12.802	12.686	12.599	12.532	12.478	13.220	13.130	13.056	12.939	12.852	12.784	12.730
	60	12.816	12.740	12.678	12.579	12.506	12.449	12.404	13.070	12.995	12.932	12.833	12.759	12.702	12.656
	72	12.717	12.651	12.596	12.509	12.445	12.395	12.355	12.972	12.905	12.850	12.763	12.698	12.648	12.608
2 Points	3	28.773	27.210	25.913	23.887	22.375	21.205	20.272	29.030	27.466	26.169	24.141	22.630	21.459	20.525
	6	20.485	19.696	19.042	18.018	17.255	16.663	16.191	20.741	19.952	19.297	18.273	17.508	16.916	16.444
	9	17.735	17.203	16.761	16.069	15.553	15.153	14.834	17.991	17.458	17.015	16.323	15.807	15.406	15.087
	12	16.363	15.958	15.622	15.096	14.704	14.399	14.157	16.619	16.214	15.877	15.350	14.957	14.653	14.410
	15	15.542	15.213	14.940	14.513	14.194	13.948	13.751	15.797	15.468	15.195	14.767	14.448	14.201	14.003
	18	14.994	14.716	14.486	14.125	13.855	13.647	13.480	15.250	14.972	14.741	14.379	14.109	13.900	13.733
	24	14.312	14.097	13.919	13.640	13.432	13.271	13.143	14.568	14.352	14.174	13.894	13.686	13.524	13.395
	30	13.903	13.727	13.580	13.350	13.179	13.046	12.941	14.159	13.982	13.835	13.605	13.433	13.300	13.194
	36	13.632	13.480	13.355	13.158	13.011	12.897	12.806	13.888	13.736	13.610	13.412	13.265	13.150	13.059
	48	13.295	13.174	13.075	12.918	12.802	12.711	12.639	13.551	13.430	13.330	13.173	13.056	12.965	12.893
	60	13.094	12.993	12.908	12.776	12.678	12.601	12.540	13.351	13.248	13.163	13.031	12.932	12.855	12.794
	72	12.963	12.873	12.799	12.682	12.596	12.529	12.475	13.219	13.129	13.054	12.937	12.850	12.782	12.728
3 Points	3	37.516	35.107	33.114	30.007	27.698	25.913	24.493	37.777	35.367	33.373	30.265	27.954	26.169	24.748
	6	24.886	23.675	22.672	21.107	19.942	19.042	18.325	25.145	23.933	22.929	21.363	20.198	19.297	18.579
	9	20.706	19.889	19.212	18.155	17.369	16.761	16.276	20.965	20.147	19.469	18.412	17.624	17.015	16.531
	12	18.622	18.001	17.486	16.683	16.085	15.622	15.254	18.881	18.259	17.743	16.939	16.340	15.877	15.508
	15	17.375	16.870	16.453	15.801	15.315	14.940	14.641	17.633	17.128	16.710	16.057	15.571	15.195	14.895
	18	16.544	16.118	15.765	15.214	14.803	14.486	14.233	16.803	16.376	16.022	15.470	15.058	14.740	14.487
	24	15.508	15.179	14.907	14.481	14.164	13.919	13.724	15.767	15.437	15.164	14.737	14.420	14.174	13.978
	30	14.889	14.618	14.393	14.043	13.782	13.580	13.419	15.148	14.876	14.651	14.299	14.037	13.835	13.674
	36	14.478	14.245	14.052	13.752	13.528	13.355	13.217	14.737	14.503	14.310	14.008	13.783	13.610	13.471
	48	13.966	13.781	13.628	13.390	13.212	13.075	12.965	14.226	14.040	13.886	13.646	13.468	13.330	13.220
	60	13.663	13.506	13.377	13.175	13.024	12.908	12.816	13.922	13.765	13.635	13.432	13.280	13.163	13.070
	72	13.463	13.325	13.211	13.033	12.901	12.799	12.717	13.723	13.584	13.469	13.290	13.157	13.054	12.972
4 Points	3	46.512	43.211	40.486	36.252	33.114	30.695	28.773	46.777	43.474	40.748	36.581	33.373	30.953	29.030
	6	29.400	27.745	26.378	24.250	22.672	21.453	20.485	29.662	28.006	26.638	24.509	22.929	21.710	20.741
	9	23.750	22.634	21.712	20.277	19.212	18.389	17.735	24.012	22.895	21.972	20.536	19.469	18.646	17.991
	12	20.936	20.088	19.387	18.296	17.486	16.861	16.363	21.198	20.349	19.647	18.555	17.743	17.117	16.619
	15	19.252	18.564	17.995	17.110	16.453	15.945	15.542	19.514	18.825	18.255	17.368	16.710	16.202	15.797
	18	18.131	17.550	17.069	16.321	15.765	15.336	14.994	18.393	17.811	17.329	16.579	16.022	15.592	15.250
	24	16.734	16.285	15.914	15.336	14.907	14.575	14.312	16.996	16.546	16.174	15.594	15.164	14.832	14.568
	30	15.899	15.529	15.223	14.747	14.393	14.120	13.903	16.161	15.790	15.483	15.005	14.651	14.377	14.159
	36	15.344	15.026	14.764	14.355	14.052	13.818	13.632	15.606	15.288	15.024	14.614	14.310	14.075	13.888
	48	14.655	14.403	14.194	13.869	13.628	13.443	13.295	14.918	14.664	14.454	14.128	13.886	13.699	13.551
	60	14.246	14.032	13.855	13.581	13.377	13.219	13.094	14.509	14.294	14.116	13.840	13.635	13.477	13.351
	72	13.977	13.788	13.633	13.391	13.211	13.073	12.963	14.241	14.051	13.894	13.650	13.469	13.330	13.219
5 Points	3	55.775	51.530	48.037	42.625	38.626	35.552	33.114	56.043	51.876	48.302	44.135	39.969	35.812	33.373
	6	34.031	31.911	30.163	27.451	25.444	23.898	22.672	34.298	32.176	30.427	27.712	25.704	24.157	22.929
	9	26.870	25.442	24.264	22.436	21.082	20.040	19.212	27.136	25.706	24.527	22.697	21.342	20.298	19.469
	12	23.307	22.222	21.327	19.938	18.908	18.116	17.486	23.572	22.486	21.590	20.198	19.168	18.374	17.743
	15	21.175	20.295	19.569	18.442	17.607	16.964	16.453	21.441	20.559	19.832	18.702	17.866	17.222	16.710
	18	19.758	19.013	18.400	17.446	16.741	16.197	15.765	20.023	19.277	18.662	17.707	17.000	16.455	16.022
	24	17.990	17.416	16.941	16.205	15.660	15.240	14.907	18.256	17.679	17.204	16.466	15.919	15.498	15.164
	30	16.934	16.460	16.070	15.463	15.014	14.668	14.393	17.200	16.724	16.332	15.724	15.273	14.926	14.651
	36	16.233	15.826	15.491	14.970	14.585	14.288	14.052	16.498	16.090	15.754	15.231	14.844	14.546	14.310
	48	15.362	15.038	14.772	14.358	14.051	13.816	13.628	15.628	15.303	15.035	14.619	14.311	14.074	13.886
	60	14.845	14.571	14.345	13.994	13.735	13.535	13.377	15.112	14.836	14.608	14.256	13.995	13.794	13.635
	72	14.505	14.263	14.064	13.755	13.526	13.351	13.211	14.773	14.529	14.328	14.017	13.787	13.610	13.469

Yield on Construction Loan When Points Are Paid

Points Paid	Yield at Month	12.50% Interest Rate Average Balance							15.00% Interest Rate Average Balance						
		50%	55%	60%	70%	80%	90%	100%	50%	55%	60%	70%	80%	90%	100%
1 Point	3	20.779	20.017	19.383	18.390	17.648	17.071	16.611	23.313	22.548	21.912	20.915	20.169	19.590	19.128
	6	16.697	16.311	15.991	15.488	15.111	14.819	14.586	19.227	18.839	18.516	18.009	17.630	17.336	17.101
	9	15.340	15.079	14.862	14.522	14.267	14.070	13.912	17.869	17.606	17.386	17.043	16.785	16.586	16.426
	12	14.662	14.464	14.299	14.040	13.846	13.695	13.575	17.191	16.990	16.822	16.560	16.363	16.211	16.089
	15	14.256	14.095	13.961	13.750	13.593	13.471	13.373	16.785	16.621	16.484	16.271	16.111	15.986	15.887
	18	13.986	13.849	13.736	13.558	13.425	13.321	13.239	16.514	16.375	16.260	16.078	15.942	15.837	15.753
	24	13.648	13.543	13.455	13.318	13.215	13.135	13.071	16.177	16.069	15.979	15.838	15.733	15.651	15.585
	30	13.446	13.359	13.287	13.174	13.089	13.023	12.970	15.976	15.886	15.811	15.695	15.607	15.539	15.485
	36	13.312	13.238	13.176	13.078	13.005	12.949	12.904	15.842	15.765	15.700	15.599	15.524	15.465	15.418
	48	13.146	13.086	13.037	12.960	12.902	12.857	12.821	15.676	15.614	15.562	15.481	15.421	15.374	15.336
	60	13.047	12.996	12.955	12.889	12.840	12.802	12.772	15.578	15.525	15.481	15.412	15.360	15.319	15.287
	72	12.982	12.937	12.900	12.843	12.799	12.766	12.739	15.514	15.467	15.428	15.366	15.320	15.284	15.255
1.5 Points	3	25.004	23.845	22.884	21.379	20.255	19.383	18.688	27.555	26.392	25.427	23.915	22.787	21.912	21.213
	6	18.834	18.249	17.762	17.001	16.432	15.991	15.638	21.380	20.790	20.300	19.533	18.960	18.516	18.161
	9	16.785	16.389	16.060	15.545	15.161	14.862	14.624	19.329	18.929	18.597	18.077	17.688	17.386	17.146
	12	15.762	15.461	15.211	14.819	14.526	14.299	14.117	18.306	18.000	17.747	17.350	17.053	16.822	16.639
	15	15.149	14.905	14.702	14.383	14.145	13.961	13.813	17.693	17.444	17.237	16.914	16.672	16.485	16.335
	18	14.741	14.534	14.363	14.093	13.892	13.736	13.611	17.285	17.074	16.898	16.624	16.419	16.259	16.132
	24	14.232	14.072	13.940	13.731	13.576	13.455	13.359	16.776	16.612	16.476	16.262	16.103	15.979	15.880
	30	13.928	13.796	13.686	13.515	13.387	13.287	13.208	16.472	16.336	16.223	16.046	15.914	15.811	15.729
	36	13.726	13.612	13.518	13.371	13.261	13.176	13.107	16.270	16.153	16.056	15.903	15.789	15.700	15.630
	48	13.474	13.384	13.309	13.192	13.105	13.037	12.983	16.021	15.926	15.848	15.725	15.633	15.562	15.506
	60	13.325	13.249	13.185	13.086	13.012	12.955	12.909	15.873	15.792	15.725	15.620	15.542	15.481	15.432
	72	13.227	13.160	13.104	13.016	12.951	12.900	12.860	15.776	15.705	15.645	15.551	15.482	15.428	15.384
2 Points	3	29.287	27.723	26.425	24.396	22.884	21.712	20.779	31.857	30.286	28.983	26.946	25.427	24.251	23.313
	6	20.997	20.207	19.552	18.527	17.762	17.170	16.697	23.559	22.763	22.103	21.071	20.300	19.703	19.227
	9	18.247	17.713	17.270	16.577	16.060	15.660	15.340	20.806	20.267	19.819	19.119	18.597	18.192	17.869
	12	16.875	16.469	16.132	15.604	15.211	14.906	14.662	19.433	19.022	18.680	18.146	17.747	17.438	17.191
	15	16.053	15.723	15.450	15.021	14.702	14.454	14.256	18.611	18.276	17.998	17.562	17.237	16.986	16.785
	18	15.506	15.227	14.995	14.633	14.363	14.153	13.986	18.064	17.780	17.544	17.174	16.898	16.685	16.514
	24	14.823	14.608	14.429	14.148	13.940	13.778	13.648	17.382	17.161	16.977	16.690	16.476	16.310	16.177
	30	14.415	14.237	14.090	13.859	13.686	13.553	13.446	16.975	16.791	16.639	16.401	16.223	16.085	15.976
	36	14.144	13.991	13.864	13.666	13.518	13.404	13.312	16.704	16.546	16.414	16.209	16.056	15.937	15.842
	48	13.807	13.686	13.585	13.427	13.309	13.218	13.146	16.369	16.242	16.136	15.971	15.848	15.752	15.676
	60	13.607	13.504	13.419	13.285	13.185	13.108	13.047	16.172	16.063	15.972	15.831	15.725	15.643	15.578
	72	13.476	13.385	13.310	13.192	13.104	13.036	12.982	16.042	15.945	15.865	15.739	15.645	15.572	15.514
3 Points	3	38.037	35.626	33.631	30.522	28.211	26.425	25.004	40.644	38.223	36.219	33.097	30.776	28.983	27.555
	6	25.405	24.192	23.187	21.620	20.454	19.552	18.834	27.999	26.777	25.765	24.186	23.011	22.103	21.380
	9	21.224	20.405	19.727	18.668	17.880	17.270	16.785	23.815	22.987	22.301	21.232	20.435	19.819	19.329
	12	19.140	18.517	18.001	17.195	16.596	16.132	15.762	21.729	21.098	20.575	19.758	19.150	18.680	18.306
	15	17.892	17.386	16.967	16.313	15.826	15.450	15.149	20.481	19.967	19.541	18.876	18.381	17.998	17.693
	18	17.062	16.634	16.279	15.726	15.314	14.995	14.741	19.651	19.214	18.853	18.289	17.868	17.544	17.285
	24	16.026	15.695	15.421	14.993	14.675	14.429	14.232	18.616	18.277	17.995	17.557	17.230	16.977	16.776
	30	15.407	15.134	14.908	14.555	14.293	14.090	13.928	17.998	17.716	17.483	17.119	16.848	16.639	16.472
	36	14.996	14.761	14.567	14.264	14.039	13.864	13.726	17.588	17.345	17.143	16.829	16.595	16.414	16.270
	48	14.485	14.298	14.144	13.903	13.723	13.585	13.474	17.081	16.885	16.723	16.470	16.282	16.136	16.021
	60	14.182	14.024	13.893	13.688	13.536	13.419	13.325	16.781	16.613	16.474	16.258	16.097	15.972	15.873
	72	13.983	13.843	13.728	13.547	13.413	13.310	13.227	16.585	16.436	16.312	16.119	15.976	15.865	15.776
4 Points	3	47.041	43.737	41.010	36.772	33.631	31.210	29.287	49.686	46.367	43.629	39.462	36.219	33.788	31.857
	6	29.925	28.268	26.899	24.768	23.187	21.967	20.997	32.553	30.883	29.504	27.358	25.765	24.536	23.559
	9	24.274	23.156	22.232	20.794	19.727	18.902	18.247	26.897	25.768	24.834	23.380	22.301	21.469	20.806
	12	21.460	20.610	19.907	18.813	18.001	17.374	16.875	24.082	23.220	22.507	21.398	20.575	19.939	19.433
	15	19.776	19.086	18.515	17.627	16.967	16.458	16.053	22.397	21.695	21.115	20.211	19.541	19.023	18.611
	18	18.655	18.071	17.589	16.837	16.279	15.849	15.506	21.276	20.681	20.188	19.422	18.853	18.413	18.064
	24	17.258	16.807	16.434	15.853	15.421	15.088	14.823	19.880	19.417	19.034	18.438	17.995	17.654	17.382
	30	16.423	16.051	15.743	15.264	14.908	14.633	14.415	19.047	18.662	18.345	17.850	17.483	17.200	16.975
	36	15.869	15.549	15.284	14.873	14.567	14.331	14.144	18.494	18.162	17.888	17.461	17.143	16.899	16.704
	48	15.181	14.926	14.715	14.387	14.144	13.956	13.807	17.810	17.543	17.322	16.978	16.723	16.526	16.369
	60	14.772	14.556	14.377	14.099	13.893	13.734	13.607	17.407	17.177	16.988	16.693	16.474	16.306	16.172
	72	14.504	14.313	14.155	13.910	13.728	13.587	13.476	17.143	16.938	16.769	16.507	16.312	16.162	16.042
5 Points	3	56.311	52.064	48.567	43.150	39.149	36.071	33.631	58.996	54.829	51.218	47.052	42.885	38.719	36.219
	6	34.564	32.440	30.690	27.974	25.963	24.416	23.187	37.227	35.087	33.324	30.587	28.562	27.002	25.765
	9	27.401	25.970	24.790	22.958	21.601	20.556	19.727	30.058	28.612	27.419	25.567	24.196	23.140	22.301
	12	23.838	22.750	21.852	20.459	19.427	18.632	18.001	26.492	25.389	24.479	23.066	22.020	21.214	20.575
	15	21.706	20.823	20.094	18.963	18.125	17.480	16.967	24.360	23.462	22.721	21.570	20.718	20.062	19.541
	18	20.288	19.541	18.925	17.968	17.259	16.713	16.279	22.942	22.180	21.551	20.575	19.852	19.295	18.853
	24	18.521	17.943	17.467	16.727	16.179	15.756	15.421	21.177	20.583	20.094	19.335	18.772	18.339	17.995
	30	17.465	16.988	16.595	15.985	15.533	15.184	14.908	20.123	19.630	19.224	18.594	18.128	17.768	17.483
	36	16.764	16.354	16.017	15.492	15.104	14.805	14.567	19.425	18.999	18.648	18.103	17.700	17.390	17.143
	48	15.894	15.568	15.298	14.880	14.571	14.333	14.144	18.560	18.217	17.934	17.495	17.171	16.921	16.723
	60	15.379	15.101	14.872	14.517	14.255	14.053	13.893	18.051	17.756	17.513	17.136	16.858	16.644	16.474
	72	15.040	14.795	14.592	14.279	14.047	13.869	13.728	17.718	17.455	17.238	16.902	16.654	16.463	16.312

Yield on Loan When Prepayment Premium Is Paid
Yield on Loan from Points Paid in Back

Interest Rate 5.500%   30 Year Schedule

Years to Payoff	1	1.5	2	2.5	Number of Points at Loan Payoff 3	3.5	4	5	6	7	8	10
1.0	6.464	6.943	7.419	7.893	8.366	8.836	9.304	10.234	11.157	12.072	12.979	14.771
2.0	5.965	6.196	6.426	6.655	6.883	7.109	7.335	7.784	8.228	8.669	9.106	9.970
3.0	5.799	5.948	6.095	6.242	6.389	6.535	6.680	6.968	7.254	7.538	7.819	8.374
4.0	5.716	5.823	5.930	6.036	6.142	6.247	6.352	6.561	6.767	6.972	7.176	7.577
5.0	5.666	5.749	5.831	5.913	5.994	6.075	6.156	6.316	6.476	6.633	6.790	7.099
7.5	5.600	5.650	5.699	5.748	5.797	5.846	5.894	5.991	6.087	6.182	6.276	6.463
10.0	5.567	5.600	5.633	5.666	5.699	5.731	5.764	5.829	5.893	5.957	6.020	6.145
12.5	5.547	5.571	5.594	5.617	5.640	5.663	5.686	5.731	5.776	5.821	5.866	5.955
15.0	5.534	5.551	5.567	5.584	5.601	5.617	5.634	5.666	5.699	5.731	5.763	5.827

Interest Rate 5.750%   30 Year Schedule

Years to Payoff	1	1.5	2	2.5	3	3.5	4	5	6	7	8	10
1.0	6.713	7.191	7.667	8.141	8.613	9.083	9.551	10.481	11.402	12.316	13.223	15.014
2.0	6.215	6.445	6.674	6.903	7.130	7.357	7.582	8.030	8.474	8.914	9.350	10.212
3.0	6.048	6.196	6.344	6.490	6.636	6.782	6.927	7.214	7.499	7.782	8.063	8.616
4.0	5.965	6.072	6.179	6.284	6.390	6.495	6.599	6.807	7.013	7.217	7.419	7.820
5.0	5.916	5.998	6.079	6.161	6.242	6.323	6.403	6.563	6.721	6.878	7.034	7.342
7.5	5.849	5.899	5.948	5.996	6.045	6.093	6.142	6.238	6.333	6.427	6.521	6.706
10.0	5.816	5.849	5.882	5.914	5.947	5.979	6.011	6.075	6.139	6.202	6.265	6.389
12.5	5.797	5.820	5.843	5.865	5.888	5.911	5.933	5.978	6.023	6.068	6.112	6.199
15.0	5.784	5.800	5.816	5.833	5.849	5.865	5.882	5.914	5.946	5.978	6.010	6.073

Interest Rate 6.000%   30 Year Schedule

Years to Payoff	1	1.5	2	2.5	3	3.5	4	5	6	7	8	10
1.0	6.962	7.440	7.916	8.389	8.861	9.330	9.798	10.727	11.648	12.561	13.467	15.256
2.0	6.464	6.694	6.923	7.151	7.378	7.604	7.829	8.276	8.719	9.158	9.594	10.454
3.0	6.298	6.445	6.592	6.738	6.884	7.029	7.173	7.460	7.745	8.027	8.306	8.859
4.0	6.215	6.321	6.427	6.532	6.637	6.742	6.846	7.053	7.258	7.462	7.663	8.062
5.0	6.165	6.247	6.328	6.409	6.490	6.570	6.650	6.809	6.967	7.123	7.278	7.585
7.5	6.099	6.148	6.196	6.245	6.293	6.341	6.389	6.484	6.579	6.672	6.765	6.950
10.0	6.066	6.098	6.131	6.163	6.195	6.227	6.259	6.322	6.385	6.448	6.510	6.633
12.5	6.046	6.069	6.091	6.114	6.136	6.159	6.181	6.226	6.270	6.314	6.357	6.444
15.0	6.033	6.049	6.065	6.081	6.098	6.114	6.130	6.161	6.193	6.224	6.256	6.318

Interest Rate 6.250%   30 Year Schedule

Years to Payoff	1	1.5	2	2.5	3	3.5	4	5	6	7	8	10
1.0	7.212	7.689	8.164	8.637	9.109	9.578	10.045	10.973	11.893	12.806	13.711	15.499
2.0	6.713	6.942	7.171	7.399	7.625	7.851	8.075	8.522	8.964	9.403	9.838	10.696
3.0	6.547	6.694	6.840	6.986	7.132	7.276	7.420	7.706	7.990	8.271	8.550	9.101
4.0	6.464	6.570	6.675	6.780	6.885	6.989	7.093	7.299	7.503	7.706	7.907	8.304
5.0	6.414	6.495	6.576	6.657	6.737	6.817	6.897	7.055	7.212	7.368	7.522	7.827
7.5	6.348	6.396	6.445	6.493	6.541	6.588	6.636	6.731	6.824	6.918	7.010	7.193
10.0	6.315	6.347	6.379	6.411	6.443	6.475	6.506	6.569	6.632	6.693	6.755	6.877
12.5	6.296	6.318	6.340	6.363	6.385	6.407	6.429	6.473	6.516	6.560	6.603	6.688
15.0	6.283	6.298	6.314	6.330	6.346	6.362	6.378	6.409	6.440	6.471	6.502	6.563

Interest Rate 6.500%   30 Year Schedule

Years to Payoff	1	1.5	2	2.5	3	3.5	4	5	6	7	8	10
1.0	7.461	7.938	8.413	8.885	9.356	9.825	10.292	11.219	12.138	13.050	13.955	15.741
2.0	6.962	7.191	7.419	7.647	7.873	8.098	8.322	8.768	9.209	9.647	10.081	10.939
3.0	6.796	6.943	7.089	7.234	7.379	7.523	7.667	7.952	8.235	8.515	8.794	9.343
4.0	6.713	6.819	6.924	7.028	7.133	7.236	7.340	7.545	7.749	7.951	8.151	8.547
5.0	6.663	6.744	6.825	6.905	6.985	7.064	7.144	7.301	7.457	7.612	7.766	8.070
7.5	6.597	6.645	6.693	6.741	6.789	6.836	6.883	6.977	7.070	7.163	7.254	7.436
10.0	6.565	6.596	6.628	6.660	6.691	6.722	6.754	6.816	6.878	6.939	7.000	7.121
12.5	6.545	6.567	6.589	6.611	6.633	6.655	6.677	6.720	6.763	6.806	6.848	6.933
15.0	6.532	6.548	6.563	6.579	6.595	6.610	6.626	6.657	6.687	6.718	6.748	6.808

Interest Rate 6.750%   30 Year Schedule

Years to Payoff	1	1.5	2	2.5	3	3.5	4	5	6	7	8	10
1.0	7.710	8.186	8.661	9.133	9.604	10.072	10.538	11.465	12.384	13.295	14.198	15.983
2.0	7.211	7.440	7.668	7.894	8.120	8.345	8.569	9.013	9.454	9.891	10.325	11.180
3.0	7.045	7.191	7.337	7.482	7.627	7.770	7.914	8.198	8.480	8.760	9.037	9.585
4.0	6.962	7.067	7.172	7.276	7.380	7.483	7.586	7.791	7.994	8.195	8.395	8.789
5.0	6.913	6.993	7.073	7.153	7.233	7.312	7.391	7.547	7.703	7.857	8.010	8.312
7.5	6.847	6.894	6.942	6.989	7.036	7.083	7.130	7.223	7.316	7.408	7.499	7.679
10.0	6.814	6.845	6.877	6.908	6.939	6.970	7.001	7.063	7.124	7.185	7.245	7.364
12.5	6.794	6.816	6.838	6.860	6.881	6.903	6.924	6.967	7.010	7.052	7.094	7.177
15.0	6.782	6.797	6.812	6.828	6.843	6.858	6.874	6.904	6.934	6.964	6.994	7.054

Entry is percentage annual yield with no points in front and selected number of points in back.

Yield on Loan When Prepayment Premium Is Paid
Yield on Loan from Points Paid in Back

Interest Rate 7.000%   30 Year Schedule

Years to Payoff	1	1.5	2	2.5	3	3.5	4	5	6	7	8	10
					Number of Points at Loan Payoff							
1.0	7.959	8.435	8.909	9.381	9.851	10.319	10.785	11.711	12.629	13.539	14.442	16.225
2.0	7.460	7.689	7.916	8.142	8.368	8.592	8.815	9.259	9.699	10.135	10.568	11.422
3.0	7.294	7.440	7.585	7.730	7.874	8.017	8.160	8.444	8.725	9.004	9.281	9.827
4.0	7.211	7.316	7.420	7.524	7.628	7.731	7.833	8.037	8.239	8.440	8.638	9.031
5.0	7.162	7.242	7.322	7.401	7.480	7.559	7.637	7.793	7.948	8.102	8.254	8.555
7.5	7.096	7.143	7.190	7.237	7.284	7.331	7.377	7.470	7.562	7.653	7.743	7.922
10.0	7.063	7.094	7.125	7.156	7.187	7.218	7.249	7.310	7.370	7.430	7.490	7.608
12.5	7.044	7.065	7.087	7.108	7.130	7.151	7.172	7.214	7.256	7.298	7.340	7.422
15.0	7.031	7.046	7.061	7.077	7.092	7.107	7.122	7.152	7.181	7.211	7.240	7.299

Interest Rate 7.250%   30 Year Schedule

Years to Payoff	1	1.5	2	2.5	3	3.5	4	5	6	7	8	10
1.0	8.208	8.684	9.158	9.629	10.099	10.566	11.032	11.957	12.874	13.784	14.686	16.467
2.0	7.709	7.937	8.164	8.390	8.615	8.839	9.062	9.505	9.944	10.380	10.811	11.664
3.0	7.543	7.689	7.834	7.978	8.121	8.264	8.407	8.690	8.970	9.248	9.524	10.069
4.0	7.461	7.565	7.669	7.772	7.875	7.978	8.080	8.283	8.484	8.684	8.882	9.273
5.0	7.411	7.491	7.570	7.649	7.728	7.806	7.884	8.039	8.193	8.346	8.498	8.797
7.5	7.345	7.392	7.439	7.486	7.532	7.578	7.625	7.716	7.807	7.898	7.988	8.165
10.0	7.313	7.343	7.374	7.405	7.435	7.466	7.496	7.556	7.616	7.676	7.735	7.852
12.5	7.293	7.315	7.336	7.357	7.378	7.399	7.420	7.462	7.503	7.544	7.585	7.666
15.0	7.281	7.296	7.310	7.325	7.340	7.355	7.370	7.399	7.428	7.458	7.487	7.544

Interest Rate 7.500%   30 Year Schedule

Years to Payoff	1	1.5	2	2.5	3	3.5	4	5	6	7	8	10
1.0	8.457	8.933	9.406	9.877	10.346	10.813	11.278	12.203	13.119	14.028	14.929	16.710
2.0	7.959	8.186	8.412	8.638	8.862	9.086	9.308	9.751	10.189	10.624	11.055	11.906
3.0	7.793	7.938	8.082	8.226	8.369	8.511	8.653	8.935	9.215	9.492	9.767	10.311
4.0	7.710	7.814	7.917	8.020	8.123	8.225	8.327	8.529	8.729	8.928	9.125	9.515
5.0	7.660	7.739	7.818	7.897	7.975	8.053	8.131	8.285	8.439	8.591	8.741	9.039
7.5	7.594	7.641	7.687	7.734	7.780	7.826	7.872	7.963	8.053	8.143	8.232	8.408
10.0	7.562	7.592	7.623	7.653	7.683	7.713	7.743	7.803	7.862	7.921	7.980	8.096
12.5	7.543	7.564	7.585	7.605	7.626	7.647	7.668	7.709	7.750	7.790	7.831	7.911
15.0	7.530	7.545	7.559	7.574	7.589	7.603	7.618	7.647	7.676	7.704	7.733	7.789

Interest Rate 7.750%   30 Year Schedule

Years to Payoff	1	1.5	2	2.5	3	3.5	4	5	6	7	8	10
1.0	8.707	9.181	9.654	10.125	10.594	11.060	11.525	12.448	13.364	14.272	15.172	16.951
2.0	8.208	8.435	8.661	8.886	9.110	9.333	9.555	9.996	10.434	10.868	11.298	12.148
3.0	8.042	8.186	8.330	8.474	8.616	8.758	8.900	9.181	9.460	9.737	10.011	10.553
4.0	7.959	8.062	8.165	8.268	8.370	8.472	8.573	8.775	8.974	9.173	9.369	9.757
5.0	7.909	7.988	8.067	8.145	8.223	8.300	8.378	8.531	8.684	8.835	8.985	9.282
7.5	7.844	7.890	7.936	7.982	8.028	8.073	8.119	8.209	8.299	8.388	8.476	8.651
10.0	7.811	7.841	7.871	7.901	7.931	7.961	7.991	8.050	8.109	8.167	8.225	8.340
12.5	7.792	7.813	7.833	7.854	7.874	7.895	7.915	7.956	7.996	8.036	8.076	8.155
15.0	7.780	7.794	7.809	7.823	7.837	7.852	7.866	7.894	7.923	7.951	7.979	8.035

Interest Rate 8.000%   30 Year Schedule

Years to Payoff	1	1.5	2	2.5	3	3.5	4	5	6	7	8	10
1.0	8.956	9.430	9.902	10.373	10.841	11.307	11.772	12.694	13.609	14.516	15.416	17.193
2.0	8.457	8.683	8.909	9.134	9.357	9.580	9.801	10.242	10.679	11.112	11.541	12.389
3.0	8.291	8.435	8.578	8.721	8.864	9.005	9.146	9.427	9.705	9.981	10.254	10.794
4.0	8.208	8.311	8.414	8.516	8.618	8.719	8.820	9.020	9.219	9.417	9.612	9.999
5.0	8.158	8.237	8.315	8.393	8.470	8.548	8.625	8.777	8.929	9.080	9.229	9.524
7.5	8.093	8.139	8.185	8.230	8.276	8.321	8.366	8.455	8.544	8.633	8.721	8.894
10.0	8.061	8.090	8.120	8.150	8.179	8.209	8.238	8.297	8.355	8.412	8.470	8.583
12.5	8.042	8.062	8.082	8.103	8.123	8.143	8.163	8.203	8.243	8.282	8.322	8.400
15.0	8.029	8.043	8.058	8.072	8.086	8.100	8.114	8.142	8.170	8.198	8.225	8.280

Interest Rate 8.250%   30 Year Schedule

Years to Payoff	1	1.5	2	2.5	3	3.5	4	5	6	7	8	10
1.0	9.205	9.679	10.151	10.621	11.088	11.554	12.018	12.940	13.854	14.760	15.659	17.435
2.0	8.706	8.932	9.157	9.381	9.604	9.827	10.048	10.488	10.923	11.356	11.784	12.631
3.0	8.540	8.684	8.827	8.969	9.111	9.252	9.393	9.673	9.950	10.225	10.497	11.036
4.0	8.457	8.560	8.662	8.764	8.865	8.966	9.066	9.266	9.464	9.661	9.856	10.241
5.0	8.408	8.486	8.563	8.641	8.718	8.795	8.871	9.023	9.174	9.324	9.472	9.766
7.5	8.342	8.388	8.433	8.478	8.523	8.568	8.613	8.702	8.790	8.878	8.965	9.137
10.0	8.310	8.339	8.369	8.398	8.427	8.457	8.486	8.543	8.601	8.658	8.715	8.827
12.5	8.291	8.311	8.331	8.351	8.371	8.391	8.411	8.450	8.490	8.529	8.567	8.644
15.0	8.279	8.293	8.307	8.321	8.334	8.348	8.362	8.390	8.417	8.444	8.471	8.525

Entry is percentage annual yield with no points in front and selected number of points in back.

Yield on Loan When Prepayment Premium Is Paid
Yield on Loan from Points Paid in Back

Interest Rate 8.500%   30 Year Schedule

Years to Payoff	Number of Points at Loan Payoff											
	1	1.5	2	2.5	3	3.5	4	5	6	7	8	10
1.0	9.454	9.927	10.399	10.868	11.336	11.801	12.265	13.186	14.099	15.004	15.902	17.677
2.0	8.955	9.181	9.405	9.629	9.852	10.074	10.294	10.733	11.168	11.599	12.027	12.872
3.0	8.789	8.932	9.075	9.217	9.358	9.499	9.640	9.918	10.195	10.469	10.741	11.278
4.0	8.706	8.808	8.910	9.012	9.112	9.213	9.313	9.512	9.709	9.905	10.099	10.483
5.0	8.657	8.734	8.812	8.889	8.966	9.042	9.118	9.269	9.419	9.568	9.716	10.008
7.5	8.591	8.637	8.682	8.726	8.771	8.816	8.860	8.948	9.036	9.123	9.209	9.380
10.0	8.559	8.588	8.618	8.647	8.676	8.704	8.733	8.790	8.847	8.904	8.960	9.071
12.5	8.540	8.560	8.580	8.600	8.619	8.639	8.659	8.698	8.736	8.775	8.813	8.889
15.0	8.528	8.542	8.556	8.569	8.583	8.597	8.610	8.637	8.664	8.691	8.718	8.771

Interest Rate 8.750%   30 Year Schedule

Years to Payoff	1	1.5	2	2.5	3	3.5	4	5	6	7	8	10
1.0	9.703	10.176	10.647	11.116	11.583	12.048	12.511	13.431	14.344	15.248	16.146	17.918
2.0	9.204	9.429	9.653	9.877	10.099	10.320	10.541	10.979	11.413	11.843	12.270	13.113
3.0	9.038	9.181	9.323	9.465	9.606	9.746	9.886	10.164	10.439	10.713	10.984	11.519
4.0	8.955	9.057	9.158	9.259	9.360	9.460	9.560	9.758	9.954	10.149	10.343	10.725
5.0	8.906	8.983	9.060	9.137	9.213	9.289	9.365	9.515	9.665	9.813	9.960	10.250
7.5	8.841	8.885	8.930	8.975	9.019	9.063	9.107	9.195	9.281	9.368	9.453	9.623
10.0	8.809	8.837	8.866	8.895	8.924	8.952	8.980	9.037	9.093	9.149	9.205	9.314
12.5	8.790	8.809	8.829	8.848	8.868	8.887	8.906	8.945	8.983	9.021	9.059	9.134
15.0	8.778	8.791	8.805	8.818	8.832	8.845	8.858	8.885	8.911	8.938	8.964	9.016

Interest Rate 9.000%   30 Year Schedule

Years to Payoff	1	1.5	2	2.5	3	3.5	4	5	6	7	8	10
1.0	9.952	10.425	10.895	11.364	11.830	12.295	12.758	13.677	14.588	15.492	16.389	18.160
2.0	9.453	9.678	9.902	10.124	10.346	10.567	10.787	11.224	11.657	12.087	12.513	13.355
3.0	9.287	9.430	9.571	9.712	9.853	9.993	10.132	10.409	10.684	10.957	11.227	11.761
4.0	9.204	9.306	9.407	9.507	9.607	9.707	9.806	10.004	10.199	10.393	10.586	10.967
5.0	9.155	9.232	9.308	9.385	9.461	9.536	9.611	9.761	9.910	10.057	10.203	10.492
7.5	9.090	9.134	9.179	9.223	9.267	9.310	9.354	9.441	9.527	9.613	9.698	9.866
10.0	9.058	9.086	9.115	9.143	9.172	9.200	9.228	9.284	9.339	9.395	9.449	9.558
12.5	9.039	9.058	9.078	9.097	9.116	9.135	9.154	9.192	9.230	9.267	9.304	9.378
15.0	9.027	9.040	9.054	9.067	9.080	9.093	9.106	9.133	9.159	9.184	9.210	9.261

Interest Rate 9.250%   30 Year Schedule

Years to Payoff	1	1.5	2	2.5	3	3.5	4	5	6	7	8	10
1.0	10.201	10.673	11.144	11.612	12.078	12.542	13.004	13.922	14.833	15.736	16.632	18.401
2.0	9.702	9.926	10.150	10.372	10.594	10.814	11.033	11.470	11.902	12.331	12.756	13.596
3.0	9.536	9.678	9.820	9.960	10.100	10.240	10.379	10.655	10.929	11.200	11.470	12.002
4.0	9.454	9.554	9.655	9.755	9.855	9.954	10.053	10.249	10.444	10.637	10.829	11.208
5.0	9.404	9.481	9.557	9.633	9.708	9.783	9.858	10.007	10.155	10.301	10.447	10.734
7.5	9.339	9.383	9.427	9.471	9.514	9.558	9.601	9.687	9.773	9.858	9.942	10.109
10.0	9.307	9.335	9.364	9.392	9.420	9.448	9.475	9.531	9.586	9.640	9.694	9.802
12.5	9.289	9.308	9.327	9.346	9.364	9.383	9.402	9.439	9.476	9.513	9.550	9.623
15.0	9.277	9.290	9.303	9.316	9.329	9.342	9.355	9.380	9.406	9.431	9.457	9.507

Interest Rate 9.500%   30 Year Schedule

Years to Payoff	1	1.5	2	2.5	3	3.5	4	5	6	7	8	10
1.0	10.450	10.922	11.392	11.859	12.325	12.789	13.250	14.168	15.078	15.980	16.875	18.643
2.0	9.951	10.175	10.398	10.620	10.841	11.061	11.280	11.715	12.147	12.575	12.999	13.837
3.0	9.785	9.927	10.068	10.208	10.348	10.487	10.625	10.901	11.174	11.444	11.713	12.243
4.0	9.703	9.803	9.903	10.003	10.102	10.201	10.299	10.495	10.689	10.882	11.073	11.450
5.0	9.653	9.729	9.805	9.880	9.955	10.030	10.105	10.253	10.400	10.546	10.690	10.976
7.5	9.588	9.632	9.676	9.719	9.762	9.805	9.848	9.933	10.018	10.102	10.186	10.351
10.0	9.557	9.584	9.612	9.640	9.668	9.695	9.723	9.777	9.832	9.886	9.939	10.046
12.5	9.538	9.557	9.575	9.594	9.613	9.631	9.650	9.686	9.723	9.759	9.796	9.867
15.0	9.526	9.539	9.552	9.565	9.577	9.590	9.603	9.628	9.653	9.678	9.703	9.752

Interest Rate 9.750%   30 Year Schedule

Years to Payoff	1	1.5	2	2.5	3	3.5	4	5	6	7	8	10
1.0	10.699	11.171	11.640	12.107	12.572	13.035	13.497	14.413	15.322	16.224	17.118	18.884
2.0	10.200	10.424	10.646	10.867	11.088	11.307	11.526	11.960	12.391	12.818	13.242	14.078
3.0	10.034	10.175	10.316	10.456	10.595	10.734	10.872	11.146	11.418	11.688	11.956	12.485
4.0	9.952	10.052	10.151	10.251	10.349	10.448	10.546	10.741	10.934	11.126	11.316	11.692
5.0	9.903	9.978	10.053	10.128	10.203	10.277	10.351	10.499	10.645	10.790	10.934	11.218
7.5	9.838	9.881	9.924	9.967	10.010	10.053	10.095	10.180	10.264	10.347	10.430	10.594
10.0	9.806	9.834	9.861	9.888	9.916	9.943	9.970	10.024	10.078	10.131	10.184	10.289
12.5	9.788	9.806	9.824	9.843	9.861	9.879	9.897	9.934	9.970	10.006	10.041	10.112
15.0	9.776	9.788	9.801	9.813	9.826	9.838	9.851	9.876	9.900	9.925	9.949	9.998

Entry is percentage annual yield with no points in front and selected number of points in back.

Yield on Loan When Prepayment Premium Is Paid
Yield on Loan from Points Paid in Back

Interest Rate 10.000%   30 Year Schedule

Years to Payoff	Number of Points at Loan Payoff											
	1	1.5	2	2.5	3	3.5	4	5	6	7	8	10
1.0	10.948	11.419	11.888	12.355	12.819	13.282	13.743	14.659	15.567	16.467	17.361	19.125
2.0	10.449	10.672	10.894	11.115	11.335	11.554	11.772	12.206	12.636	13.062	13.485	14.320
3.0	10.283	10.424	10.564	10.703	10.842	10.980	11.118	11.392	11.663	11.932	12.199	12.726
4.0	10.201	10.301	10.400	10.498	10.597	10.695	10.792	10.986	11.179	11.370	11.559	11.933
5.0	10.152	10.227	10.302	10.376	10.450	10.524	10.596	10.745	10.890	11.034	11.177	11.460
7.5	10.087	10.130	10.173	10.215	10.258	10.300	10.342	10.426	10.509	10.592	10.674	10.837
10.0	10.055	10.083	10.110	10.137	10.164	10.191	10.218	10.271	10.324	10.377	10.429	10.533
12.5	10.037	10.055	10.073	10.091	10.109	10.127	10.145	10.181	10.216	10.252	10.287	10.357
15.0	10.025	10.038	10.050	10.062	10.075	10.087	10.099	10.123	10.148	10.172	10.196	10.243

Interest Rate 10.250%   30 Year Schedule

Years to Payoff	1	1.5	2	2.5	3	3.5	4	5	6	7	8	10
1.0	11.197	11.668	12.136	12.602	13.067	13.529	13.989	14.904	15.811	16.711	17.603	19.366
2.0	10.698	10.921	11.142	11.363	11.582	11.801	12.019	12.451	12.880	13.305	13.727	14.561
3.0	10.533	10.673	10.812	10.951	11.089	11.227	11.364	11.637	11.907	12.176	12.442	12.967
4.0	10.450	10.549	10.648	10.746	10.844	10.942	11.039	11.232	11.423	11.614	11.802	12.175
5.0	10.401	10.476	10.550	10.624	10.698	10.771	10.845	10.990	11.135	11.278	11.421	11.702
7.5	10.336	10.379	10.421	10.463	10.505	10.547	10.589	10.672	10.755	10.837	10.919	11.080
10.0	10.305	10.332	10.358	10.385	10.412	10.438	10.465	10.518	10.570	10.622	10.674	10.777
12.5	10.286	10.304	10.322	10.340	10.358	10.375	10.393	10.428	10.463	10.498	10.533	10.601
15.0	10.275	10.287	10.299	10.311	10.323	10.335	10.347	10.371	10.395	10.419	10.442	10.489

Interest Rate 10.500%   30 Year Schedule

Years to Payoff	1	1.5	2	2.5	3	3.5	4	5	6	7	8	10
1.0	11.446	11.916	12.384	12.850	13.314	13.776	14.236	15.150	16.056	16.955	17.846	19.607
2.0	10.947	11.169	11.390	11.610	11.829	12.048	12.265	12.697	13.125	13.549	13.970	14.802
3.0	10.782	10.921	11.060	11.199	11.337	11.474	11.611	11.883	12.152	12.419	12.685	13.209
4.0	10.699	10.798	10.896	10.994	11.092	11.189	11.285	11.478	11.668	11.858	12.045	12.416
5.0	10.650	10.724	10.798	10.872	10.945	11.018	11.091	11.236	11.380	11.523	11.664	11.944
7.5	10.585	10.628	10.670	10.711	10.753	10.795	10.836	10.919	11.001	11.082	11.163	11.323
10.0	10.554	10.581	10.607	10.634	10.660	10.686	10.712	10.765	10.816	10.868	10.919	11.021
12.5	10.536	10.553	10.571	10.589	10.606	10.623	10.641	10.675	10.710	10.744	10.778	10.846
15.0	10.524	10.536	10.548	10.560	10.572	10.584	10.595	10.619	10.642	10.665	10.689	10.735

Interest Rate 10.750%   30 Year Schedule

Years to Payoff	1	1.5	2	2.5	3	3.5	4	5	6	7	8	10
1.0	11.695	12.165	12.632	13.098	13.561	14.022	14.482	15.395	16.300	17.198	18.089	19.848
2.0	11.196	11.418	11.638	11.858	12.077	12.294	12.511	12.942	13.369	13.793	14.213	15.043
3.0	11.031	11.170	11.308	11.446	11.584	11.721	11.857	12.128	12.397	12.663	12.927	13.450
4.0	10.948	11.046	11.144	11.242	11.339	11.436	11.532	11.723	11.913	12.101	12.288	12.658
5.0	10.899	10.973	11.047	11.120	11.193	11.266	11.338	11.482	11.625	11.767	11.908	12.186
7.5	10.835	10.876	10.918	10.960	11.001	11.042	11.083	11.165	11.246	11.327	11.407	11.566
10.0	10.803	10.830	10.856	10.882	10.908	10.934	10.960	11.011	11.063	11.114	11.164	11.265
12.5	10.785	10.803	10.820	10.837	10.854	10.872	10.889	10.923	10.957	10.990	11.024	11.091
15.0	10.774	10.786	10.797	10.809	10.820	10.832	10.844	10.867	10.890	10.912	10.935	10.980

Interest Rate 11.000%   30 Year Schedule

Years to Payoff	1	1.5	2	2.5	3	3.5	4	5	6	7	8	10
1.0	11.945	12.413	12.880	13.345	13.808	14.269	14.728	15.640	16.545	17.442	18.332	20.090
2.0	11.445	11.666	11.887	12.106	12.324	12.541	12.757	13.187	13.613	14.036	14.455	15.284
3.0	11.280	11.418	11.557	11.694	11.831	11.968	12.103	12.373	12.641	12.907	13.170	13.691
4.0	11.197	11.295	11.393	11.490	11.586	11.682	11.778	11.969	12.158	12.345	12.532	12.899
5.0	11.148	11.222	11.295	11.368	11.440	11.513	11.585	11.728	11.870	12.011	12.151	12.428
7.5	11.084	11.125	11.167	11.208	11.249	11.290	11.330	11.411	11.492	11.572	11.651	11.808
10.0	11.053	11.079	11.105	11.130	11.156	11.182	11.207	11.258	11.309	11.359	11.409	11.508
12.5	11.035	11.052	11.069	11.086	11.103	11.120	11.137	11.170	11.204	11.237	11.270	11.335
15.0	11.023	11.035	11.046	11.058	11.069	11.081	11.092	11.114	11.137	11.159	11.182	11.226

Interest Rate 11.250%   30 Year Schedule

Years to Payoff	1	1.5	2	2.5	3	3.5	4	5	6	7	8	10
1.0	12.194	12.662	13.128	13.593	14.055	14.516	14.974	15.886	16.789	17.685	18.574	20.331
2.0	11.694	11.915	12.135	12.353	12.571	12.788	13.003	13.432	13.858	14.280	14.698	15.524
3.0	11.529	11.667	11.805	11.942	12.078	12.214	12.350	12.619	12.886	13.150	13.413	13.932
4.0	11.446	11.544	11.641	11.737	11.833	11.929	12.025	12.214	12.403	12.589	12.775	13.141
5.0	11.397	11.470	11.543	11.616	11.688	11.760	11.831	11.974	12.115	12.255	12.394	12.670
7.5	11.333	11.374	11.415	11.456	11.496	11.537	11.577	11.658	11.737	11.817	11.895	12.051
10.0	11.302	11.328	11.353	11.379	11.404	11.429	11.455	11.505	11.555	11.605	11.654	11.752
12.5	11.284	11.301	11.318	11.335	11.351	11.368	11.384	11.417	11.450	11.483	11.516	11.580
15.0	11.273	11.284	11.295	11.307	11.318	11.329	11.340	11.362	11.384	11.406	11.428	11.472

Entry is percentage annual yield with no points in front and selected number of points in back.

Yield on Loan When Prepayment Premium Is Paid
Yield on Loan from Points Paid in Back

Interest Rate 11.500%   30 Year Schedule

| Years to Payoff | 1 | 1.5 | 2 | 2.5 | Number of Points at Loan Payoff ||||||||
					3	3.5	4	5	6	7	8	10
1.0	12.443	12.911	13.377	13.841	14.302	14.763	15.221	16.131	17.034	17.929	18.817	20.571
2.0	11.943	12.164	12.383	12.601	12.818	13.034	13.250	13.678	14.102	14.523	14.940	15.765
3.0	11.778	11.916	12.053	12.189	12.326	12.461	12.596	12.864	13.130	13.394	13.656	14.173
4.0	11.696	11.792	11.889	11.985	12.081	12.176	12.271	12.460	12.647	12.833	13.018	13.382
5.0	11.647	11.719	11.791	11.863	11.935	12.007	12.078	12.219	12.360	12.499	12.638	12.912
7.5	11.582	11.623	11.664	11.704	11.744	11.784	11.824	11.904	11.983	12.062	12.140	12.294
10.0	11.551	11.577	11.602	11.627	11.652	11.677	11.702	11.752	11.801	11.850	11.899	11.996
12.5	11.534	11.550	11.567	11.583	11.600	11.616	11.632	11.665	11.697	11.729	11.761	11.825
15.0	11.523	11.534	11.545	11.556	11.567	11.577	11.588	11.610	11.632	11.653	11.675	11.717

Interest Rate 11.750%   30 Year Schedule

Years to Payoff	1	1.5	2	2.5	3	3.5	4	5	6	7	8	10
1.0	12.692	13.159	13.625	14.088	14.550	15.009	15.467	16.376	17.278	18.172	19.060	20.812
2.0	12.193	12.412	12.631	12.848	13.065	13.281	13.496	13.923	14.346	14.766	15.183	16.006
3.0	12.027	12.164	12.301	12.437	12.573	12.708	12.842	13.110	13.375	13.638	13.899	14.414
4.0	11.945	12.041	12.137	12.233	12.328	12.423	12.518	12.706	12.892	13.077	13.261	13.624
5.0	11.896	11.968	12.040	12.111	12.183	12.254	12.324	12.465	12.605	12.744	12.881	13.153
7.5	11.832	11.872	11.912	11.952	11.992	12.032	12.071	12.150	12.229	12.307	12.384	12.537
10.0	11.801	11.826	11.851	11.876	11.900	11.925	11.950	11.999	12.048	12.096	12.144	12.240
12.5	11.783	11.799	11.816	11.832	11.848	11.864	11.880	11.912	11.944	11.976	12.007	12.070
15.0	11.772	11.783	11.794	11.805	11.815	11.826	11.837	11.858	11.879	11.900	11.921	11.963

Interest Rate 12.000%   30 Year Schedule

Years to Payoff	1	1.5	2	2.5	3	3.5	4	5	6	7	8	10
1.0	12.941	13.408	13.873	14.336	14.797	15.256	15.713	16.621	17.522	18.416	19.302	21.053
2.0	12.442	12.661	12.879	13.096	13.312	13.528	13.742	14.168	14.591	15.010	15.426	16.247
3.0	12.276	12.413	12.549	12.685	12.820	12.954	13.089	13.355	13.619	13.881	14.141	14.655
4.0	12.194	12.290	12.385	12.481	12.575	12.670	12.764	12.951	13.137	13.321	13.504	13.865
5.0	12.145	12.216	12.288	12.359	12.430	12.501	12.571	12.711	12.850	12.988	13.125	13.395
7.5	12.081	12.121	12.161	12.200	12.240	12.279	12.318	12.397	12.474	12.551	12.628	12.780
10.0	12.050	12.075	12.099	12.124	12.148	12.173	12.197	12.246	12.294	12.342	12.389	12.484
12.5	12.033	12.049	12.065	12.081	12.096	12.112	12.128	12.160	12.191	12.222	12.253	12.315
15.0	12.022	12.032	12.043	12.053	12.064	12.074	12.085	12.106	12.127	12.147	12.168	12.209

Interest Rate 12.250%   30 Year Schedule

Years to Payoff	1	1.5	2	2.5	3	3.5	4	5	6	7	8	10
1.0	13.190	13.656	14.121	14.583	15.044	15.502	15.959	16.867	17.767	18.659	19.545	21.294
2.0	12.691	12.909	13.127	13.343	13.559	13.774	13.988	14.413	14.835	15.253	15.668	16.488
3.0	12.525	12.661	12.797	12.932	13.067	13.201	13.335	13.600	13.864	14.125	14.384	14.896
4.0	12.443	12.538	12.633	12.728	12.823	12.917	13.010	13.197	13.381	13.565	13.747	14.107
5.0	12.394	12.465	12.536	12.607	12.677	12.748	12.818	12.957	13.095	13.232	13.368	13.637
7.5	12.330	12.370	12.409	12.448	12.488	12.527	12.566	12.643	12.720	12.796	12.872	13.023
10.0	12.299	12.324	12.348	12.372	12.397	12.421	12.445	12.492	12.540	12.587	12.634	12.728
12.5	12.282	12.298	12.314	12.329	12.345	12.360	12.376	12.407	12.438	12.469	12.499	12.560
15.0	12.271	12.282	12.292	12.302	12.313	12.323	12.333	12.354	12.374	12.394	12.415	12.455

Interest Rate 12.500%   30 Year Schedule

Years to Payoff	1	1.5	2	2.5	3	3.5	4	5	6	7	8	10
1.0	13.439	13.905	14.369	14.831	15.291	15.749	16.205	17.112	18.011	18.903	19.787	21.535
2.0	12.940	13.158	13.375	13.591	13.806	14.021	14.234	14.659	15.079	15.497	15.911	16.728
3.0	12.774	12.910	13.045	13.180	13.314	13.448	13.581	13.846	14.108	14.369	14.627	15.137
4.0	12.692	12.787	12.882	12.976	13.070	13.164	13.257	13.442	13.626	13.809	13.990	14.348
5.0	12.643	12.714	12.784	12.855	12.925	12.995	13.064	13.202	13.340	13.476	13.611	13.879
7.5	12.579	12.618	12.658	12.697	12.735	12.774	12.813	12.889	12.966	13.041	13.117	13.266
10.0	12.549	12.573	12.597	12.621	12.645	12.668	12.692	12.739	12.786	12.833	12.880	12.972
12.5	12.532	12.547	12.563	12.578	12.593	12.609	12.624	12.654	12.685	12.715	12.745	12.805
15.0	12.521	12.531	12.541	12.551	12.561	12.572	12.582	12.602	12.622	12.642	12.661	12.701

Interest Rate 15.000%   30 Year Schedule

Years to Payoff	1	1.5	2	2.5	3	3.5	4	5	6	7	8	10
1.0	15.929	16.390	16.849	17.306	17.761	18.214	18.666	19.563	20.453	21.335	22.211	23.941
2.0	15.430	15.643	15.855	16.066	16.277	16.486	16.695	17.110	17.521	17.929	18.334	19.134
3.0	15.264	15.396	15.526	15.656	15.786	15.915	16.043	16.299	16.552	16.804	17.053	17.547
4.0	15.183	15.273	15.363	15.453	15.543	15.632	15.721	15.898	16.073	16.247	16.420	16.762
5.0	15.134	15.201	15.267	15.333	15.399	15.465	15.530	15.660	15.790	15.918	16.045	16.297
7.5	15.072	15.107	15.143	15.178	15.214	15.249	15.284	15.353	15.423	15.492	15.560	15.696
10.0	15.043	15.064	15.085	15.106	15.126	15.147	15.168	15.209	15.251	15.291	15.332	15.413
12.5	15.027	15.040	15.053	15.066	15.079	15.091	15.104	15.130	15.156	15.181	15.206	15.257
15.0	15.017	15.025	15.033	15.042	15.050	15.058	15.066	15.082	15.099	15.115	15.131	15.163

Entry is percentage annual yield with no points in front and selected number of points in back.

Yield on Wraparound Mortgage Loan

| 20% New Money | 80% Old Money | | | | | | | | | | | 9.00% Overall Interest Rate |

New Term	Old Term	5.75%	6.00%	6.25%	6.50%	6.75%	7.00%	7.25%	7.50%	7.75%	8.00%	8.25%	8.50%
						Interest Rate on Old Money							
15	5.0	10.566	10.443	10.319	10.197	10.075	9.953	9.832	9.712	9.592	9.472	9.354	9.235
	7.5	11.857	11.629	11.401	11.176	10.952	10.729	10.508	10.288	10.070	9.853	9.637	9.423
	10.0	13.763	13.382	13.003	12.626	12.252	11.880	11.511	11.144	10.780	10.419	10.060	9.704
	12.5	16.502	15.929	15.353	14.777	14.200	13.622	13.044	12.465	11.886	11.308	10.730	10.152
	15.0	19.911	19.179	18.433	17.672	16.897	16.105	15.295	14.467	13.619	12.748	11.854	10.933
20	5.0	10.188	10.094	10.001	9.907	9.815	9.722	9.631	9.539	9.448	9.358	9.268	9.178
	7.5	11.049	10.884	10.720	10.558	10.397	10.237	10.078	9.920	9.764	9.609	9.455	9.302
	10.0	12.189	11.928	11.670	11.415	11.162	10.912	10.664	10.419	10.176	9.936	9.698	9.463
	12.5	13.693	13.308	12.927	12.549	12.176	11.806	11.441	11.080	10.722	10.369	10.021	9.676
	15.0	15.591	15.063	14.538	14.015	13.496	12.979	12.466	11.957	11.453	10.952	10.457	9.966
25	5.0	9.999	9.920	9.841	9.763	9.685	9.607	9.530	9.453	9.376	9.300	9.225	9.149
	7.5	10.677	10.542	10.407	10.274	10.142	10.011	9.881	9.752	9.624	9.497	9.371	9.246
	10.0	11.530	11.321	11.115	10.911	10.710	10.511	10.314	10.120	9.928	9.738	9.550	9.365
	12.5	12.599	12.298	12.000	11.707	11.418	11.133	10.852	10.576	10.303	10.035	9.770	9.510
	15.0	13.912	13.499	13.091	12.689	12.292	11.902	11.518	11.140	10.768	10.402	10.042	9.689
30	5.0	9.891	9.820	9.749	9.679	9.610	9.541	9.472	9.403	9.335	9.267	9.200	9.133
	7.5	10.473	10.354	10.235	10.118	10.002	9.886	9.772	9.659	9.547	9.435	9.325	9.216
	10.0	11.185	11.003	10.825	10.648	10.474	10.302	10.132	9.964	9.798	9.634	9.473	9.313
	12.5	12.053	11.794	11.540	11.289	11.043	10.801	10.562	10.328	10.097	9.871	9.647	9.428
	15.0	13.097	12.744	12.398	12.058	11.724	11.397	11.076	10.761	10.453	10.150	9.854	9.563

| 25% New Money | 75% Old Money | | | | | | | | | | | 9.00% Overall Interest Rate |

New Term	Old Term	5.75%	6.00%	6.25%	6.50%	6.75%	7.00%	7.25%	7.50%	7.75%	8.00%	8.25%	8.50%
15	5.0	10.417	10.306	10.195	10.085	9.975	9.865	9.755	9.646	9.538	9.429	9.322	9.214
	7.5	11.510	11.312	11.115	10.918	10.722	10.527	10.333	10.140	9.948	9.756	9.566	9.376
	10.0	13.013	12.698	12.385	12.072	11.760	11.449	11.138	10.829	10.521	10.215	9.909	9.605
	12.5	15.007	14.556	14.103	13.648	13.191	12.731	12.270	11.807	11.343	10.877	10.409	9.941
	15.0	17.378	16.809	16.231	15.641	15.040	14.427	13.802	13.164	12.511	11.843	11.160	10.459
20	5.0	10.083	9.998	9.913	9.829	9.744	9.660	9.577	9.493	9.410	9.328	9.245	9.163
	7.5	10.829	10.684	10.539	10.395	10.252	10.110	9.968	9.827	9.687	9.548	9.410	9.273
	10.0	11.770	11.548	11.327	11.108	10.890	10.674	10.460	10.247	10.035	9.825	9.616	9.409
	12.5	12.936	12.622	12.310	11.999	11.690	11.383	11.078	10.774	10.473	10.174	9.877	9.583
	15.0	14.320	13.907	13.494	13.081	12.668	12.256	11.844	11.433	11.024	10.616	10.209	9.804
25	5.0	9.914	9.842	9.770	9.699	9.628	9.557	9.486	9.416	9.346	9.276	9.207	9.137
	7.5	10.509	10.388	10.268	10.149	10.031	9.913	9.797	9.681	9.565	9.451	9.337	9.224
	10.0	11.226	11.046	10.867	10.690	10.514	10.340	10.168	9.996	9.827	9.658	9.492	9.326
	12.5	12.082	11.831	11.582	11.336	11.091	10.849	10.610	10.372	10.137	9.905	9.675	9.448
	15.0	13.077	12.746	12.417	12.091	11.768	11.448	11.131	10.816	10.505	10.197	9.893	9.592
30	5.0	9.817	9.752	9.688	9.624	9.560	9.497	9.434	9.371	9.308	9.246	9.184	9.123
	7.5	10.330	10.224	10.118	10.012	9.908	9.804	9.701	9.599	9.497	9.396	9.296	9.197
	10.0	10.936	10.778	10.622	10.467	10.314	10.162	10.012	9.863	9.716	9.570	9.425	9.282
	12.5	11.642	11.424	11.209	10.996	10.785	10.577	10.372	10.168	9.967	9.769	9.573	9.380
	15.0	12.451	12.164	11.881	11.602	11.326	11.053	10.784	10.518	10.256	9.997	9.743	9.491

| 33% New Money | 67% Old Money | | | | | | | | | | | 9.00% Overall Interest Rate |

New Term	Old Term	5.75%	6.00%	6.25%	6.50%	6.75%	7.00%	7.25%	7.50%	7.75%	8.00%	8.25%	8.50%
15	5.0	10.192	10.099	10.007	9.914	9.822	9.730	9.638	9.546	9.455	9.363	9.272	9.181
	7.5	11.025	10.867	10.710	10.553	10.396	10.240	10.084	9.928	9.773	9.618	9.463	9.308
	10.0	12.069	11.834	11.598	11.362	11.127	10.890	10.654	10.418	10.181	9.945	9.709	9.472
	12.5	13.330	13.010	12.688	12.363	12.037	11.708	11.377	11.043	10.708	10.370	10.031	9.689
	15.0	14.742	14.346	13.944	13.534	13.117	12.694	12.262	11.823	11.375	10.919	10.454	9.979
20	5.0	9.921	9.849	9.778	9.706	9.635	9.563	9.492	9.422	9.351	9.280	9.210	9.140
	7.5	10.509	10.391	10.273	10.155	10.038	9.921	9.805	9.689	9.573	9.458	9.343	9.228
	10.0	11.202	11.029	10.857	10.686	10.515	10.344	10.174	10.005	9.836	9.667	9.500	9.332
	12.5	11.998	11.766	11.534	11.302	11.070	10.838	10.607	10.376	10.146	9.915	9.686	9.456
	15.0	12.879	12.586	12.292	11.997	11.700	11.403	11.105	10.806	10.506	10.206	9.905	9.603
25	5.0	9.782	9.721	9.660	9.599	9.538	9.478	9.417	9.357	9.297	9.238	9.178	9.118
	7.5	10.258	10.159	10.060	9.962	9.864	9.766	9.669	9.572	9.476	9.380	9.284	9.189
	10.0	10.801	10.659	10.517	10.376	10.235	10.095	9.956	9.817	9.679	9.542	9.405	9.270
	12.5	11.409	11.219	11.029	10.840	10.652	10.465	10.279	10.093	9.909	9.725	9.542	9.360
	15.0	12.070	11.830	11.591	11.351	11.113	10.874	10.637	10.400	10.164	9.929	9.695	9.462
30	5.0	9.701	9.646	9.591	9.536	9.482	9.428	9.374	9.320	9.266	9.212	9.159	9.106
	7.5	10.116	10.028	9.940	9.852	9.765	9.679	9.592	9.507	9.421	9.336	9.251	9.167
	10.0	10.581	10.455	10.330	10.205	10.082	9.958	9.836	9.714	9.594	9.473	9.354	9.235
	12.5	11.093	10.926	10.760	10.595	10.430	10.267	10.105	9.944	9.784	9.625	9.467	9.310
	15.0	11.645	11.434	11.225	11.016	10.809	10.602	10.397	10.193	9.991	9.790	9.590	9.392

Entry is the annual percentage yield on the new money.

Yield on Wraparound Mortgage Loan

40% New Money   60% Old Money   9.00% Overall Interest Rate

New Term	Old Term	5.75%	6.00%	6.25%	6.50%	6.75%	7.00%	7.25%	7.50%	7.75%	8.00%	8.25%	8.50%
				Interest Rate on Old Money										
15	5.0	10.029	9.949	9.870	9.790	9.711	9.632	9.552	9.473	9.394	9.315	9.236	9.157
	7.5	10.699	10.568	10.437	10.306	10.176	10.045	9.914	9.783	9.653	9.522	9.391	9.261
	10.0	11.493	11.304	11.114	10.924	10.733	10.542	10.351	10.159	9.967	9.774	9.581	9.388
	12.5	12.399	12.149	11.897	11.644	11.388	11.130	10.871	10.609	10.346	10.080	9.813	9.544
	15.0	13.376	13.070	12.761	12.446	12.126	11.801	11.471	11.136	10.795	10.448	10.096	9.737
20	5.0	9.802	9.740	9.677	9.615	9.553	9.492	9.430	9.368	9.306	9.245	9.184	9.122
	7.5	10.286	10.186	10.086	9.987	9.887	9.788	9.689	9.590	9.491	9.393	9.294	9.196
	10.0	10.831	10.690	10.548	10.407	10.266	10.124	9.983	9.842	9.702	9.561	9.420	9.280
	12.5	11.431	11.245	11.060	10.873	10.687	10.500	10.313	10.126	9.938	9.751	9.563	9.376
	15.0	12.067	11.839	11.609	11.377	11.144	10.910	10.675	10.439	10.202	9.963	9.724	9.483
25	5.0	9.683	9.630	9.577	9.524	9.471	9.419	9.366	9.313	9.261	9.208	9.156	9.104
	7.5	10.080	9.996	9.912	9.828	9.744	9.660	9.577	9.494	9.411	9.329	9.246	9.164
	10.0	10.515	10.397	10.279	10.161	10.044	9.927	9.810	9.693	9.577	9.461	9.345	9.230
	12.5	10.984	10.830	10.676	10.522	10.369	10.216	10.063	9.910	9.757	9.605	9.453	9.302
	15.0	11.475	11.285	11.095	10.905	10.714	10.523	10.333	10.142	9.951	9.761	9.570	9.380
30	5.0	9.614	9.566	9.518	9.470	9.423	9.376	9.328	9.281	9.234	9.187	9.140	9.093
	7.5	9.962	9.886	9.811	9.736	9.662	9.587	9.513	9.439	9.365	9.292	9.218	9.145
	10.0	10.338	10.233	10.128	10.024	9.920	9.816	9.713	9.610	9.507	9.405	9.303	9.202
	12.5	10.738	10.602	10.466	10.331	10.196	10.061	9.927	9.793	9.659	9.526	9.394	9.262
	15.0	11.155	10.987	10.819	10.652	10.484	10.318	10.151	9.985	9.819	9.654	9.490	9.326

50% New Money   50% Old Money   9.00% Overall Interest Rate

New Term	Old Term	5.75%	6.00%	6.25%	6.50%	6.75%	7.00%	7.25%	7.50%	7.75%	8.00%	8.25%	8.50%
15	5.0	9.808	9.746	9.684	9.622	9.560	9.498	9.436	9.373	9.311	9.249	9.187	9.124
	7.5	10.288	10.190	10.091	9.993	9.894	9.795	9.696	9.597	9.498	9.399	9.299	9.200
	10.0	10.817	10.681	10.544	10.407	10.268	10.130	9.990	9.850	9.710	9.569	9.427	9.285
	12.5	11.384	11.210	11.034	10.856	10.677	10.497	10.315	10.132	9.947	9.760	9.572	9.383
	15.0	11.968	11.759	11.546	11.330	11.112	10.890	10.665	10.437	10.206	9.972	9.734	9.493
20	5.0	9.637	9.588	9.539	9.490	9.441	9.392	9.343	9.294	9.245	9.196	9.147	9.098
	7.5	9.994	9.917	9.841	9.765	9.688	9.612	9.535	9.459	9.382	9.306	9.230	9.153
	10.0	10.374	10.269	10.164	10.059	9.954	9.849	9.743	9.637	9.531	9.425	9.319	9.213
	12.5	10.770	10.637	10.504	10.369	10.235	10.099	9.964	9.827	9.690	9.553	9.415	9.277
	15.0	11.172	11.012	10.851	10.688	10.524	10.359	10.193	10.026	9.857	9.688	9.517	9.346
25	5.0	9.546	9.504	9.462	9.420	9.377	9.335	9.293	9.251	9.209	9.167	9.126	9.084
	7.5	9.842	9.777	9.713	9.648	9.583	9.518	9.453	9.388	9.323	9.259	9.194	9.129
	10.0	10.153	10.064	9.976	9.887	9.799	9.710	9.621	9.532	9.444	9.355	9.266	9.177
	12.5	10.472	10.360	10.247	10.135	10.022	9.909	9.796	9.682	9.569	9.455	9.342	9.228
	15.0	10.792	10.657	10.521	10.385	10.249	10.112	9.974	9.836	9.698	9.559	9.420	9.280
30	5.0	9.492	9.454	9.416	9.378	9.340	9.302	9.264	9.226	9.188	9.151	9.113	9.075
	7.5	9.754	9.696	9.638	9.579	9.521	9.463	9.405	9.347	9.289	9.231	9.173	9.115
	10.0	10.026	9.947	9.868	9.789	9.710	9.630	9.551	9.472	9.393	9.315	9.236	9.157
	12.5	10.303	10.203	10.103	10.003	9.902	9.802	9.702	9.601	9.501	9.401	9.300	9.200
	15.0	10.579	10.459	10.338	10.217	10.096	9.975	9.853	9.732	9.610	9.488	9.366	9.244

67% New Money   33% Old Money   9.00% Overall Interest Rate

New Term	Old Term	5.75%	6.00%	6.25%	6.50%	6.75%	7.00%	7.25%	7.50%	7.75%	8.00%	8.25%	8.50%
15	5.0	9.493	9.455	9.418	9.380	9.342	9.305	9.267	9.229	9.191	9.153	9.115	9.076
	7.5	9.748	9.692	9.635	9.579	9.522	9.464	9.407	9.349	9.292	9.234	9.176	9.117
	10.0	10.007	9.932	9.857	9.781	9.705	9.628	9.551	9.474	9.396	9.317	9.239	9.160
	12.5	10.264	10.171	10.078	9.984	9.889	9.794	9.697	9.600	9.502	9.403	9.303	9.203
	15.0	10.513	10.404	10.294	10.183	10.071	9.957	9.842	9.726	9.608	9.489	9.369	9.247
20	5.0	9.394	9.364	9.334	9.304	9.274	9.244	9.213	9.183	9.152	9.122	9.092	9.061
	7.5	9.592	9.547	9.502	9.457	9.412	9.367	9.321	9.276	9.230	9.184	9.138	9.092
	10.0	9.789	9.730	9.670	9.611	9.551	9.490	9.430	9.369	9.308	9.247	9.186	9.124
	12.5	9.981	9.908	9.835	9.761	9.687	9.612	9.537	9.462	9.386	9.310	9.233	9.156
	15.0	10.165	10.080	9.994	9.907	9.820	9.731	9.642	9.553	9.462	9.371	9.279	9.187
25	5.0	9.341	9.315	9.289	9.263	9.237	9.210	9.184	9.158	9.132	9.105	9.079	9.053
	7.5	9.509	9.470	9.431	9.393	9.354	9.315	9.276	9.236	9.197	9.158	9.119	9.079
	10.0	9.674	9.623	9.572	9.521	9.470	9.418	9.366	9.315	9.262	9.210	9.158	9.105
	12.5	9.834	9.772	9.709	9.646	9.583	9.519	9.455	9.391	9.327	9.262	9.197	9.131
	15.0	9.987	9.914	9.840	9.766	9.692	9.617	9.541	9.465	9.389	9.312	9.234	9.157
30	5.0	9.309	9.285	9.261	9.238	9.214	9.190	9.167	9.143	9.119	9.095	9.072	9.048
	7.5	9.459	9.424	9.389	9.354	9.319	9.284	9.248	9.213	9.178	9.142	9.107	9.071
	10.0	9.606	9.560	9.514	9.468	9.422	9.375	9.329	9.282	9.235	9.189	9.142	9.095
	12.5	9.748	9.692	9.635	9.579	9.522	9.465	9.407	9.350	9.292	9.234	9.176	9.117
	15.0	9.883	9.817	9.751	9.684	9.618	9.550	9.483	9.415	9.346	9.278	9.209	9.139

Entry is the annual percentage yield on the new money.

Yield on Wraparound Mortgage Loan

20% New Money   80% Old Money   **9.50% Overall Interest Rate**

New Term	Old Term	6.25%	6.50%	6.75%	7.00%	7.25%	7.50%	7.75%	8.00%	8.25%	8.50%	8.75%	9.00%
	5.0	11.091	10.965	10.840	10.715	10.591	10.468	10.345	10.223	10.101	9.980	9.859	9.739
	7.5	12.402	12.169	11.938	11.709	11.481	11.255	11.030	10.807	10.585	10.365	10.147	9.930
15	10.0	14.332	13.944	13.559	13.177	12.797	12.420	12.045	11.673	11.304	10.937	10.574	10.213
	12.5	17.086	16.505	15.922	15.339	14.754	14.170	13.585	12.999	12.414	11.830	11.246	10.663
	15.0	20.474	19.734	18.981	18.214	17.431	16.633	15.818	14.984	14.131	13.256	12.359	11.435
	5.0	10.714	10.618	10.522	10.427	10.332	10.238	10.144	10.051	9.958	9.865	9.773	9.682
	7.5	11.595	11.426	11.259	11.093	10.928	10.764	10.602	10.440	10.281	10.122	9.965	9.809
20	10.0	12.762	12.494	12.230	11.968	11.710	11.453	11.200	10.949	10.701	10.456	10.213	9.973
	12.5	14.295	13.901	13.510	13.124	12.742	12.364	11.990	11.621	11.257	10.896	10.541	10.189
	15.0	16.214	15.676	15.139	14.606	14.076	13.549	13.027	12.508	11.994	11.485	10.980	10.481
	5.0	10.527	10.446	10.365	10.284	10.204	10.124	10.044	9.965	9.887	9.809	9.731	9.654
	7.5	11.226	11.087	10.948	10.811	10.675	10.540	10.406	10.273	10.141	10.011	9.882	9.753
25	10.0	12.106	11.891	11.678	11.468	11.260	11.055	10.852	10.652	10.454	10.259	10.066	9.875
	12.5	13.209	12.897	12.590	12.287	11.989	11.695	11.406	11.121	10.840	10.563	10.291	10.023
	15.0	14.555	14.129	13.708	13.293	12.885	12.482	12.087	11.698	11.315	10.939	10.569	10.206
	5.0	10.421	10.347	10.275	10.202	10.130	10.059	9.987	9.917	9.846	9.776	9.707	9.637
	7.5	11.025	10.902	10.779	10.657	10.537	10.417	10.299	10.182	10.065	9.950	9.836	9.723
30	10.0	11.766	11.577	11.391	11.208	11.027	10.848	10.672	10.498	10.326	10.157	9.989	9.824
	12.5	12.669	12.400	12.135	11.874	11.618	11.366	11.119	10.875	10.636	10.401	10.170	9.943
	15.0	13.753	13.385	13.025	12.671	12.324	11.984	11.650	11.324	11.003	10.690	10.383	10.082

25% New Money   75% Old Money   **9.50% Overall Interest Rate**

New Term	Old Term	6.25%	6.50%	6.75%	7.00%	7.25%	7.50%	7.75%	8.00%	8.25%	8.50%	8.75%	9.00%
	5.0	10.939	10.826	10.713	10.601	10.489	10.378	10.267	10.156	10.046	9.936	9.826	9.717
	7.5	12.047	11.846	11.645	11.445	11.247	11.049	10.852	10.656	10.461	10.267	10.074	9.882
15	10.0	13.565	13.246	12.928	12.611	12.294	11.979	11.665	11.352	11.040	10.729	10.420	10.112
	12.5	15.566	15.110	14.651	14.191	13.729	13.265	12.799	12.332	11.863	11.392	10.921	10.448
	15.0	17.920	17.346	16.762	16.168	15.563	14.946	14.316	13.674	13.019	12.349	11.663	10.960
	5.0	10.606	10.519	10.433	10.346	10.260	10.174	10.089	10.004	9.919	9.834	9.750	9.667
	7.5	11.369	11.220	11.072	10.925	10.778	10.633	10.488	10.345	10.202	10.060	9.918	9.778
20	10.0	12.328	12.101	11.876	11.652	11.429	11.208	10.989	10.772	10.556	10.341	10.128	9.917
	12.5	13.513	13.192	12.873	12.556	12.241	11.927	11.616	11.307	11.000	10.695	10.393	10.093
	15.0	14.908	14.487	14.066	13.646	13.226	12.806	12.388	11.970	11.554	11.140	10.727	10.316
	5.0	10.439	10.365	10.291	10.218	10.145	10.072	9.999	9.927	9.855	9.783	9.712	9.641
	7.5	11.051	10.927	10.804	10.681	10.559	10.439	10.318	10.199	10.081	9.963	9.846	9.730
25	10.0	11.789	11.604	11.420	11.237	11.056	10.877	10.699	10.523	10.349	10.176	10.005	9.835
	12.5	12.668	12.409	12.153	11.899	11.648	11.399	11.152	10.908	10.667	10.429	10.193	9.959
	15.0	13.683	13.343	13.005	12.670	12.338	12.009	11.683	11.361	11.042	10.726	10.414	10.106
	5.0	10.344	10.277	10.210	10.144	10.079	10.013	9.948	9.883	9.818	9.754	9.690	9.626
	7.5	10.876	10.765	10.656	10.547	10.439	10.331	10.225	10.119	10.014	9.909	9.806	9.703
30	10.0	11.504	11.340	11.178	11.018	10.859	10.702	10.546	10.392	10.240	10.089	9.939	9.791
	12.5	12.235	12.009	11.786	11.565	11.346	11.131	10.918	10.707	10.500	10.295	10.092	9.892
	15.0	13.069	12.772	12.479	12.189	11.903	11.621	11.342	11.067	10.796	10.529	10.266	10.007

33% New Money   67% Old Money   **9.50% Overall Interest Rate**

New Term	Old Term	6.25%	6.50%	6.75%	7.00%	7.25%	7.50%	7.75%	8.00%	8.25%	8.50%	8.75%	9.00%
	5.0	10.709	10.615	10.521	10.427	10.334	10.240	10.147	10.054	9.961	9.869	9.776	9.684
	7.5	11.552	11.392	11.233	11.074	10.915	10.756	10.598	10.440	10.283	10.125	9.969	9.812
15	10.0	12.604	12.366	12.127	11.889	11.650	11.411	11.172	10.933	10.694	10.455	10.216	9.977
	12.5	13.865	13.542	13.217	12.890	12.560	12.228	11.894	11.558	11.220	10.880	10.537	10.193
	15.0	15.266	14.867	14.461	14.049	13.630	13.203	12.770	12.328	11.879	11.421	10.955	10.480
	5.0	10.440	10.367	10.293	10.220	10.148	10.075	10.002	9.930	9.858	9.786	9.714	9.643
	7.5	11.039	10.919	10.798	10.678	10.559	10.439	10.321	10.202	10.084	9.966	9.849	9.732
20	10.0	11.743	11.567	11.392	11.217	11.043	10.869	10.696	10.523	10.351	10.179	10.009	9.838
	12.5	12.549	12.312	12.076	11.840	11.604	11.368	11.133	10.898	10.664	10.430	10.196	9.964
	15.0	13.433	13.136	12.837	12.537	12.236	11.934	11.632	11.329	11.025	10.721	10.416	10.111
	5.0	10.303	10.240	10.177	10.115	10.052	9.990	9.928	9.867	9.805	9.744	9.682	9.621
	7.5	10.791	10.690	10.588	10.487	10.386	10.286	10.187	10.087	9.988	9.890	9.792	9.694
25	10.0	11.348	11.201	11.056	10.911	10.766	10.623	10.480	10.338	10.196	10.055	9.915	9.776
	12.5	11.968	11.773	11.579	11.385	11.192	11.000	10.809	10.619	10.430	10.242	10.055	9.869
	15.0	12.639	12.393	12.148	11.903	11.659	11.415	11.172	10.930	10.689	10.449	10.210	9.972
	5.0	10.223	10.166	10.110	10.053	9.997	9.941	9.885	9.830	9.774	9.719	9.664	9.609
	7.5	10.652	10.561	10.470	10.380	10.290	10.200	10.111	10.023	9.934	9.847	9.759	9.672
30	10.0	11.132	11.002	10.872	10.744	10.616	10.489	10.362	10.237	10.112	9.988	9.865	9.742
	12.5	11.659	11.487	11.315	11.144	10.975	10.806	10.639	10.472	10.307	10.143	9.981	9.819
	15.0	12.224	12.007	11.791	11.576	11.362	11.149	10.938	10.728	10.519	10.312	10.107	9.903

Entry is the annual percentage yield on the new money.

Yield on Wraparound Mortgage Loan

| 40% New Money | | 60% Old Money | | | | | | | | 9.50% Overall Interest Rate | | | |

New Term	Old Term	6.25%	6.50%	6.75%	7.00%	7.25%	7.50%	7.75%	8.00%	8.25%	8.50%	8.75%	9.00%
						Interest Rate on Old Money							
15	5.0	10.543	10.462	10.382	10.301	10.221	10.140	10.060	9.980	9.899	9.819	9.739	9.659
	7.5	11.220	11.088	10.955	10.823	10.690	10.558	10.425	10.293	10.160	10.028	9.896	9.764
	10.0	12.018	11.827	11.636	11.443	11.251	11.058	10.864	10.670	10.476	10.281	10.087	9.891
	12.5	12.923	12.671	12.418	12.162	11.904	11.645	11.383	11.120	10.854	10.587	10.318	10.047
	15.0	13.891	13.584	13.272	12.956	12.634	12.308	11.976	11.640	11.298	10.950	10.596	10.237
20	5.0	10.318	10.254	10.191	10.127	10.064	10.001	9.938	9.875	9.812	9.750	9.687	9.625
	7.5	10.810	10.708	10.607	10.505	10.404	10.303	10.202	10.101	10.000	9.900	9.800	9.700
	10.0	11.363	11.219	11.075	10.931	10.788	10.644	10.500	10.357	10.213	10.070	9.927	9.785
	12.5	11.968	11.780	11.591	11.402	11.212	11.022	10.833	10.642	10.452	10.262	10.071	9.881
	15.0	12.606	12.374	12.140	11.906	11.670	11.433	11.195	10.955	10.715	10.474	10.232	9.988
25	5.0	10.201	10.146	10.092	10.038	9.983	9.929	9.875	9.821	9.767	9.714	9.660	9.607
	7.5	10.607	10.521	10.434	10.348	10.263	10.177	10.092	10.006	9.921	9.837	9.752	9.668
	10.0	11.052	10.931	10.810	10.689	10.569	10.449	10.329	10.210	10.090	9.972	9.853	9.735
	12.5	11.529	11.371	11.214	11.056	10.899	10.743	10.586	10.430	10.274	10.118	9.963	9.808
	15.0	12.025	11.831	11.637	11.443	11.248	11.053	10.859	10.664	10.470	10.275	10.081	9.887
30	5.0	10.133	10.083	10.034	9.985	9.936	9.887	9.838	9.790	9.741	9.693	9.644	9.596
	7.5	10.492	10.414	10.336	10.259	10.182	10.105	10.029	9.953	9.876	9.801	9.725	9.650
	10.0	10.879	10.771	10.663	10.555	10.448	10.341	10.234	10.128	10.022	9.917	9.812	9.708
	12.5	11.289	11.149	11.009	10.869	10.730	10.591	10.453	10.315	10.178	10.041	9.905	9.769
	15.0	11.714	11.541	11.369	11.196	11.024	10.853	10.682	10.511	10.341	10.171	10.003	9.834

| 50% New Money | | 50% Old Money | | | | | | | | 9.50% Overall Interest Rate | | | |

New Term	Old Term	6.25%	6.50%	6.75%	7.00%	7.25%	7.50%	7.75%	8.00%	8.25%	8.50%	8.75%	9.00%
15	5.0	10.319	10.256	10.193	10.130	10.067	10.004	9.941	9.878	9.815	9.752	9.689	9.626
	7.5	10.803	10.703	10.604	10.504	10.404	10.304	10.204	10.104	10.004	9.903	9.803	9.702
	10.0	11.334	11.196	11.058	10.919	10.780	10.639	10.499	10.358	10.216	10.074	9.931	9.788
	12.5	11.899	11.724	11.546	11.367	11.187	11.005	10.822	10.638	10.452	10.264	10.075	9.885
	15.0	12.477	12.266	12.052	11.836	11.616	11.394	11.168	10.939	10.708	10.473	10.235	9.993
20	5.0	10.149	10.099	10.049	9.999	9.949	9.899	9.849	9.799	9.749	9.699	9.649	9.600
	7.5	10.511	10.434	10.356	10.278	10.200	10.123	10.045	9.967	9.889	9.811	9.733	9.656
	10.0	10.896	10.789	10.683	10.576	10.469	10.362	10.255	10.147	10.040	9.932	9.824	9.716
	12.5	11.295	11.159	11.024	10.888	10.751	10.614	10.476	10.338	10.199	10.060	9.921	9.781
	15.0	11.696	11.534	11.370	11.206	11.040	10.873	10.705	10.536	10.366	10.194	10.022	9.849
25	5.0	10.059	10.016	9.973	9.930	9.887	9.844	9.801	9.758	9.715	9.672	9.629	9.586
	7.5	10.362	10.296	10.229	10.163	10.096	10.030	9.964	9.897	9.831	9.765	9.698	9.632
	10.0	10.679	10.588	10.497	10.407	10.316	10.225	10.135	10.044	9.953	9.863	9.772	9.681
	12.5	11.002	10.887	10.773	10.658	10.542	10.427	10.312	10.196	10.080	9.964	9.848	9.732
	15.0	11.324	11.187	11.049	10.910	10.771	10.631	10.491	10.350	10.210	10.068	9.927	9.785
30	5.0	10.007	9.967	9.928	9.889	9.850	9.811	9.772	9.733	9.694	9.655	9.616	9.578
	7.5	10.276	10.216	10.156	10.096	10.036	9.977	9.917	9.857	9.797	9.738	9.678	9.619
	10.0	10.555	10.474	10.392	10.311	10.229	10.148	10.067	9.986	9.904	9.823	9.742	9.661
	12.5	10.838	10.735	10.632	10.529	10.426	10.323	10.220	10.117	10.014	9.911	9.808	9.705
	15.0	11.118	10.995	10.871	10.747	10.623	10.498	10.374	10.249	10.124	10.000	9.875	9.750

| 67% New Money | | 33% Old Money | | | | | | | | 9.50% Overall Interest Rate | | | |

New Term	Old Term	6.25%	6.50%	6.75%	7.00%	7.25%	7.50%	7.75%	8.00%	8.25%	8.50%	8.75%	9.00%
15	5.0	9.999	9.961	9.923	9.885	9.846	9.808	9.770	9.731	9.693	9.655	9.616	9.577
	7.5	10.256	10.199	10.142	10.084	10.027	9.969	9.911	9.853	9.794	9.736	9.677	9.618
	10.0	10.515	10.439	10.364	10.287	10.210	10.133	10.055	9.977	9.899	9.820	9.740	9.661
	12.5	10.770	10.677	10.583	10.489	10.393	10.297	10.200	10.102	10.004	9.905	9.805	9.704
	15.0	11.016	10.907	10.797	10.685	10.573	10.459	10.343	10.227	10.109	9.990	9.869	9.747
20	5.0	9.901	9.871	9.840	9.809	9.779	9.748	9.717	9.686	9.655	9.624	9.593	9.562
	7.5	10.102	10.056	10.010	9.965	9.919	9.873	9.826	9.780	9.734	9.687	9.641	9.594
	10.0	10.300	10.240	10.180	10.119	10.058	9.997	9.936	9.874	9.812	9.750	9.688	9.626
	12.5	10.492	10.419	10.344	10.270	10.195	10.119	10.043	9.967	9.890	9.813	9.735	9.657
	15.0	10.676	10.590	10.503	10.415	10.327	10.237	10.148	10.057	9.966	9.874	9.782	9.688
25	5.0	9.849	9.822	9.795	9.769	9.742	9.715	9.688	9.662	9.635	9.608	9.581	9.554
	7.5	10.020	9.980	9.941	9.901	9.861	9.822	9.782	9.742	9.701	9.661	9.621	9.581
	10.0	10.187	10.136	10.083	10.031	9.979	9.926	9.874	9.821	9.768	9.714	9.661	9.607
	12.5	10.349	10.285	10.222	10.157	10.093	10.028	9.963	9.898	9.832	9.766	9.700	9.634
	15.0	10.502	10.428	10.353	10.278	10.202	10.126	10.049	9.972	9.894	9.816	9.738	9.659
30	5.0	9.817	9.793	9.769	9.744	9.720	9.696	9.671	9.647	9.622	9.598	9.574	9.549
	7.5	9.971	9.936	9.900	9.864	9.827	9.791	9.755	9.719	9.682	9.646	9.610	9.573
	10.0	10.122	10.074	10.027	9.980	9.932	9.885	9.837	9.789	9.741	9.693	9.645	9.597
	12.5	10.266	10.208	10.150	10.092	10.034	9.975	9.917	9.858	9.799	9.739	9.680	9.620
	15.0	10.402	10.335	10.267	10.199	10.130	10.062	9.992	9.923	9.853	9.783	9.713	9.642

Entry is the annual percentage yield on the new money.

Yield on Wraparound Mortgage Loan

20% New Money   80% Old Money — 10.00% Overall Interest Rate

New Term	Old Term	6.75%	7.00%	7.25%	7.50%	7.75%	8.00%	8.25%	8.50%	8.75%	9.00%	9.25%	9.50%
15	5.0	11.616	11.488	11.361	11.234	11.108	10.983	10.858	10.734	10.610	10.487	10.364	10.242
	7.5	12.948	12.711	12.476	12.243	12.012	11.782	11.553	11.327	11.102	10.878	10.656	10.436
	10.0	14.902	14.509	14.117	13.729	13.343	12.960	12.580	12.202	11.828	11.456	11.088	10.722
	12.5	17.671	17.082	16.492	15.901	15.310	14.718	14.126	13.534	12.943	12.352	11.762	11.173
	15.0	21.037	20.289	19.529	18.754	17.965	17.161	16.340	15.501	14.643	13.765	12.863	11.937
20	5.0	11.241	11.143	11.045	10.947	10.851	10.754	10.658	10.563	10.468	10.373	10.279	10.186
	7.5	12.143	11.970	11.799	11.628	11.459	11.292	11.126	10.961	10.798	10.636	10.475	10.315
	10.0	13.336	13.063	12.792	12.524	12.259	11.996	11.737	11.481	11.227	10.976	10.728	10.482
	12.5	14.900	14.496	14.096	13.701	13.310	12.923	12.542	12.164	11.792	11.424	11.061	10.703
	15.0	16.841	16.290	15.743	15.199	14.658	14.121	13.588	13.060	12.536	12.018	11.505	10.997
25	5.0	11.056	10.972	10.889	10.806	10.723	10.641	10.560	10.478	10.397	10.317	10.237	10.158
	7.5	11.777	11.633	11.491	11.349	11.209	11.070	10.932	10.795	10.660	10.525	10.392	10.260
	10.0	12.685	12.463	12.243	12.026	11.812	11.601	11.392	11.185	10.982	10.780	10.582	10.385
	12.5	13.822	13.500	13.183	12.870	12.562	12.259	11.961	11.667	11.378	11.093	10.813	10.538
	15.0	15.203	14.763	14.329	13.901	13.480	13.065	12.658	12.257	11.864	11.477	11.097	10.725
30	5.0	10.952	10.876	10.801	10.726	10.651	10.577	10.504	10.430	10.358	10.285	10.213	10.142
	7.5	11.580	11.451	11.324	11.198	11.073	10.949	10.827	10.705	10.585	10.466	10.348	10.231
	10.0	12.350	12.154	11.961	11.770	11.582	11.397	11.214	11.033	10.855	10.680	10.506	10.335
	12.5	13.290	13.009	12.734	12.463	12.196	11.934	11.677	11.425	11.177	10.933	10.693	10.458
	15.0	14.414	14.032	13.656	13.288	12.927	12.574	12.227	11.888	11.556	11.231	10.913	10.602

25% New Money   75% Old Money — 10.00% Overall Interest Rate

New Term	Old Term	6.75%	7.00%	7.25%	7.50%	7.75%	8.00%	8.25%	8.50%	8.75%	9.00%	9.25%	9.50%
15	5.0	11.461	11.346	11.232	11.118	11.004	10.891	10.778	10.666	10.554	10.442	10.331	10.220
	7.5	12.585	12.380	12.176	11.974	11.772	11.571	11.371	11.173	10.975	10.778	10.582	10.387
	10.0	14.119	13.795	13.472	13.151	12.830	12.510	12.192	11.875	11.559	11.244	10.931	10.619
	12.5	16.125	15.664	15.200	14.735	14.268	13.799	13.328	12.856	12.383	11.908	11.432	10.956
	15.0	18.461	17.882	17.293	16.694	16.085	15.464	14.831	14.185	13.526	12.854	12.166	11.462
20	5.0	11.130	11.041	10.953	10.864	10.776	10.688	10.601	10.514	10.428	10.341	10.256	10.170
	7.5	11.910	11.757	11.606	11.455	11.306	11.157	11.009	10.862	10.716	10.571	10.427	10.284
	10.0	12.888	12.656	12.425	12.196	11.969	11.744	11.520	11.297	11.077	10.858	10.641	10.426
	12.5	14.092	13.764	13.438	13.115	12.793	12.473	12.156	11.840	11.527	11.217	10.909	10.603
	15.0	15.498	15.069	14.640	14.212	13.784	13.358	12.932	12.508	12.085	11.664	11.245	10.827
25	5.0	10.965	10.889	10.813	10.738	10.662	10.587	10.513	10.439	10.365	10.291	10.218	10.145
	7.5	11.595	11.467	11.340	11.214	11.089	10.965	10.841	10.718	10.597	10.476	10.355	10.236
	10.0	12.355	12.163	11.974	11.786	11.600	11.415	11.233	11.051	10.872	10.694	10.518	10.344
	12.5	13.257	12.990	12.726	12.465	12.206	11.950	11.696	11.446	11.198	10.953	10.710	10.471
	15.0	14.292	13.942	13.595	13.251	12.909	12.572	12.237	11.906	11.579	11.256	10.936	10.620
30	5.0	10.872	10.803	10.734	10.666	10.598	10.530	10.463	10.395	10.329	10.262	10.196	10.131
	7.5	11.423	11.309	11.195	11.082	10.970	10.859	10.749	10.639	10.531	10.423	10.316	10.210
	10.0	12.074	11.904	11.736	11.570	11.406	11.243	11.082	10.922	10.764	10.608	10.454	10.301
	12.5	12.832	12.597	12.365	12.136	11.910	11.686	11.466	11.248	11.033	10.821	10.611	10.405
	15.0	13.691	13.383	13.079	12.779	12.483	12.191	11.902	11.618	11.338	11.062	10.790	10.523

33% New Money   67% Old Money — 10.00% Overall Interest Rate

New Term	Old Term	6.75%	7.00%	7.25%	7.50%	7.75%	8.00%	8.25%	8.50%	8.75%	9.00%	9.25%	9.50%
15	5.0	11.226	11.131	11.036	10.940	10.845	10.751	10.656	10.562	10.468	10.374	10.280	10.186
	7.5	12.079	11.917	11.756	11.594	11.433	11.273	11.112	10.952	10.793	10.633	10.475	10.316
	10.0	13.139	12.898	12.657	12.415	12.174	11.932	11.690	11.448	11.207	10.965	10.724	10.482
	12.5	14.401	14.075	13.746	13.416	13.083	12.748	12.411	12.073	11.732	11.389	11.044	10.698
	15.0	15.789	15.387	14.978	14.563	14.142	13.713	13.277	12.834	12.383	11.924	11.457	10.980
20	5.0	10.960	10.885	10.810	10.735	10.661	10.587	10.513	10.439	10.365	10.292	10.218	10.145
	7.5	11.571	11.447	11.324	11.202	11.080	10.958	10.837	10.716	10.595	10.475	10.356	10.237
	10.0	12.286	12.107	11.928	11.749	11.572	11.394	11.218	11.042	10.866	10.692	10.518	10.344
	12.5	13.101	12.860	12.619	12.379	12.139	11.899	11.660	11.421	11.182	10.945	10.707	10.471
	15.0	13.988	13.686	13.382	13.078	12.772	12.466	12.160	11.852	11.544	11.236	10.927	10.618
25	5.0	10.824	10.759	10.695	10.631	10.567	10.503	10.440	10.376	10.313	10.250	10.187	10.125
	7.5	11.326	11.221	11.117	11.013	10.910	10.807	10.704	10.602	10.501	10.400	10.299	10.199
	10.0	11.896	11.745	11.596	11.447	11.299	11.151	11.005	10.859	10.714	10.569	10.426	10.283
	12.5	12.529	12.329	12.129	11.931	11.733	11.536	11.340	11.146	10.952	10.759	10.568	10.377
	15.0	13.210	12.958	12.707	12.456	12.206	11.957	11.708	11.461	11.214	10.969	10.725	10.482
30	5.0	10.746	10.688	10.629	10.571	10.513	10.455	10.398	10.340	10.283	10.226	10.169	10.113
	7.5	11.189	11.095	11.001	10.908	10.815	10.723	10.631	10.539	10.448	10.358	10.268	10.178
	10.0	11.684	11.550	11.416	11.283	11.151	11.020	10.890	10.760	10.631	10.503	10.376	10.250
	12.5	12.227	12.049	11.872	11.695	11.520	11.346	11.174	11.002	10.832	10.663	10.495	10.329
	15.0	12.806	12.581	12.358	12.137	11.916	11.697	11.479	11.263	11.048	10.835	10.624	10.414

Entry is the annual percentage yield on the new money.

Yield on Wraparound Mortgage Loan

40% New Money   60% Old Money   10.00% Overall Interest Rate

New Term	Old Term	6.75%	7.00%	7.25%	7.50%	7.75%	8.00%	8.25%	8.50%	8.75%	9.00%	9.25%	9.50%
						Interest Rate on Old Money							
15	5.0	11.057	10.976	10.894	10.812	10.730	10.649	10.567	10.486	10.405	10.324	10.243	10.162
	7.5	11.742	11.607	11.473	11.339	11.205	11.071	10.936	10.802	10.668	10.535	10.401	10.267
	10.0	12.544	12.351	12.157	11.963	11.768	11.573	11.378	11.182	10.986	10.789	10.592	10.395
	12.5	13.448	13.194	12.938	12.680	12.420	12.159	11.895	11.630	11.363	11.094	10.823	10.550
	15.0	14.406	14.097	13.783	13.465	13.142	12.814	12.481	12.143	11.800	11.452	11.097	10.738
20	5.0	10.834	10.769	10.704	10.640	10.575	10.511	10.447	10.383	10.319	10.255	10.191	10.127
	7.5	11.335	11.232	11.128	11.024	10.921	10.818	10.715	10.612	10.510	10.407	10.305	10.203
	10.0	11.896	11.750	11.603	11.456	11.310	11.164	11.017	10.871	10.726	10.580	10.435	10.289
	12.5	12.506	12.315	12.123	11.930	11.738	11.545	11.352	11.159	10.966	10.773	10.580	10.386
	15.0	13.145	12.909	12.673	12.435	12.196	11.956	11.714	11.472	11.229	10.985	10.740	10.494
25	5.0	10.719	10.663	10.607	10.551	10.496	10.440	10.385	10.329	10.274	10.219	10.164	10.109
	7.5	11.135	11.046	10.958	10.870	10.782	10.694	10.606	10.519	10.432	10.345	10.258	10.172
	10.0	11.590	11.466	11.342	11.218	11.095	10.972	10.849	10.726	10.604	10.483	10.361	10.241
	12.5	12.075	11.913	11.752	11.591	11.431	11.270	11.110	10.950	10.791	10.632	10.473	10.315
	15.0	12.577	12.379	12.180	11.981	11.783	11.584	11.385	11.187	10.988	10.790	10.592	10.394
30	5.0	10.653	10.602	10.551	10.500	10.450	10.399	10.349	10.299	10.249	10.199	10.149	10.099
	7.5	11.022	10.942	10.862	10.783	10.703	10.624	10.545	10.466	10.388	10.310	10.232	10.154
	10.0	11.421	11.309	11.198	11.087	10.976	10.866	10.756	10.647	10.538	10.429	10.321	10.214
	12.5	11.842	11.697	11.553	11.409	11.266	11.123	10.980	10.838	10.697	10.556	10.416	10.277
	15.0	12.274	12.097	11.919	11.742	11.565	11.389	11.213	11.038	10.863	10.689	10.516	10.343

50% New Money   50% Old Money   10.00% Overall Interest Rate

New Term	Old Term	6.75%	7.00%	7.25%	7.50%	7.75%	8.00%	8.25%	8.50%	8.75%	9.00%	9.25%	9.50%
15	5.0	10.830	10.766	10.702	10.638	10.574	10.511	10.447	10.383	10.319	10.255	10.192	10.128
	7.5	11.317	11.217	11.116	11.015	10.915	10.813	10.712	10.611	10.509	10.408	10.306	10.204
	10.0	11.851	11.712	11.572	11.432	11.291	11.150	11.008	10.865	10.722	10.579	10.435	10.290
	12.5	12.415	12.237	12.059	11.879	11.697	11.514	11.330	11.144	10.957	10.768	10.578	10.387
	15.0	12.986	12.774	12.559	12.341	12.121	11.897	11.671	11.441	11.209	10.974	10.735	10.493
20	5.0	10.661	10.610	10.559	10.508	10.457	10.407	10.356	10.305	10.254	10.203	10.152	10.101
	7.5	11.029	10.950	10.871	10.792	10.713	10.634	10.554	10.475	10.396	10.317	10.238	10.158
	10.0	11.418	11.310	11.202	11.093	10.984	10.876	10.766	10.657	10.548	10.439	10.329	10.219
	12.5	11.819	11.682	11.544	11.406	11.268	11.129	10.989	10.849	10.708	10.567	10.426	10.284
	15.0	12.220	12.056	11.890	11.724	11.556	11.387	11.217	11.046	10.874	10.701	10.527	10.352
25	5.0	10.573	10.529	10.485	10.440	10.396	10.352	10.308	10.264	10.220	10.176	10.132	10.088
	7.5	10.883	10.815	10.747	10.679	10.611	10.543	10.475	10.407	10.339	10.271	10.203	10.135
	10.0	11.205	11.112	11.020	10.927	10.834	10.741	10.649	10.556	10.463	10.370	10.278	10.185
	12.5	11.532	11.415	11.298	11.181	11.063	10.946	10.828	10.710	10.592	10.473	10.355	10.237
	15.0	11.857	11.717	11.576	11.435	11.293	11.151	11.008	10.865	10.722	10.578	10.434	10.289
30	5.0	10.522	10.482	10.441	10.401	10.361	10.320	10.280	10.240	10.200	10.160	10.120	10.080
	7.5	10.799	10.737	10.676	10.614	10.552	10.490	10.429	10.367	10.306	10.245	10.183	10.122
	10.0	11.085	11.001	10.917	10.833	10.750	10.666	10.583	10.499	10.416	10.332	10.249	10.166
	12.5	11.373	11.268	11.162	11.056	10.950	10.844	10.739	10.633	10.527	10.422	10.316	10.211
	15.0	11.658	11.531	11.404	11.277	11.150	11.022	10.895	10.767	10.639	10.511	10.383	10.256

67% New Money   33% Old Money   10.00% Overall Interest Rate

New Term	Old Term	6.75%	7.00%	7.25%	7.50%	7.75%	8.00%	8.25%	8.50%	8.75%	9.00%	9.25%	9.50%
15	5.0	10.505	10.466	10.428	10.389	10.350	10.312	10.273	10.234	10.195	10.156	10.117	10.078
	7.5	10.764	10.706	10.648	10.590	10.532	10.474	10.415	10.356	10.297	10.238	10.179	10.119
	10.0	11.023	10.947	10.870	10.793	10.716	10.638	10.559	10.481	10.402	10.322	10.242	10.162
	12.5	11.277	11.183	11.089	10.994	10.898	10.801	10.703	10.605	10.506	10.406	10.306	10.205
	15.0	11.520	11.410	11.300	11.188	11.074	10.960	10.844	10.727	10.609	10.490	10.369	10.247
20	5.0	10.408	10.377	10.346	10.315	10.284	10.252	10.221	10.189	10.158	10.126	10.095	10.063
	7.5	10.611	10.565	10.519	10.472	10.425	10.379	10.332	10.285	10.237	10.190	10.143	10.095
	10.0	10.811	10.750	10.689	10.627	10.566	10.504	10.442	10.379	10.317	10.254	10.191	10.127
	12.5	11.004	10.929	10.854	10.779	10.703	10.626	10.549	10.472	10.394	10.316	10.238	10.159
	15.0	11.187	11.100	11.012	10.923	10.834	10.744	10.653	10.562	10.470	10.377	10.284	10.190
25	5.0	10.357	10.330	10.302	10.275	10.248	10.220	10.193	10.165	10.138	10.110	10.083	10.055
	7.5	10.531	10.491	10.450	10.410	10.369	10.328	10.288	10.247	10.206	10.165	10.124	10.083
	10.0	10.701	10.648	10.595	10.542	10.488	10.435	10.381	10.327	10.273	10.218	10.164	10.110
	12.5	10.864	10.799	10.734	10.669	10.603	10.537	10.471	10.405	10.338	10.271	10.203	10.136
	15.0	11.018	10.942	10.866	10.789	10.712	10.635	10.557	10.479	10.400	10.321	10.241	10.161
30	5.0	10.326	10.301	10.276	10.251	10.226	10.201	10.176	10.151	10.126	10.101	10.076	10.050
	7.5	10.484	10.447	10.410	10.373	10.336	10.299	10.262	10.225	10.187	10.150	10.113	10.075
	10.0	10.637	10.589	10.541	10.492	10.443	10.395	10.346	10.297	10.247	10.198	10.149	10.099
	12.5	10.783	10.724	10.665	10.606	10.546	10.486	10.426	10.366	10.305	10.245	10.184	10.123
	15.0	10.921	10.852	10.783	10.713	10.643	10.573	10.503	10.432	10.360	10.289	10.217	10.145

Entry is the annual percentage yield on the new money.

Yield on Wraparound Mortgage Loan

20% New Money   80% Old Money   10.50% Overall Interest Rate

New Term	Old Term	7.25%	7.50%	7.75%	8.00%	8.25%	8.50%	8.75%	9.00%	9.25%	9.50%	9.75%	10.00%
15	5.0	12.142	12.012	11.883	11.754	11.626	11.498	11.371	11.245	11.120	10.994	10.870	10.746
	7.5	13.494	13.254	13.015	12.778	12.543	12.309	12.077	11.847	11.618	11.391	11.166	10.942
	10.0	15.474	15.074	14.677	14.282	13.890	13.502	13.116	12.733	12.353	11.976	11.602	11.232
	12.5	18.257	17.660	17.063	16.464	15.866	15.267	14.668	14.069	13.472	12.875	12.279	11.684
	15.0	21.599	20.844	20.076	19.294	18.499	17.688	16.862	16.018	15.155	14.272	13.368	12.439
20	5.0	11.769	11.668	11.568	11.468	11.369	11.271	11.173	11.075	10.978	10.881	10.785	10.690
	7.5	12.692	12.515	12.340	12.165	11.992	11.821	11.651	11.482	11.315	11.149	10.985	10.822
	10.0	13.914	13.633	13.355	13.081	12.809	12.541	12.275	12.013	11.753	11.497	11.243	10.993
	12.5	15.508	15.094	14.684	14.280	13.880	13.485	13.094	12.709	12.328	11.953	11.582	11.216
	15.0	17.469	16.907	16.348	15.793	15.241	14.694	14.151	13.613	13.079	12.552	12.030	11.514
25	5.0	11.586	11.500	11.414	11.328	11.244	11.159	11.075	10.992	10.908	10.826	10.744	10.662
	7.5	12.330	12.182	12.034	11.888	11.744	11.601	11.459	11.318	11.178	11.040	10.903	10.768
	10.0	13.268	13.038	12.811	12.587	12.366	12.148	11.932	11.720	11.510	11.303	11.098	10.896
	12.5	14.440	14.106	13.779	13.456	13.138	12.825	12.518	12.215	11.917	11.624	11.336	11.053
	15.0	15.855	15.401	14.953	14.512	14.078	13.651	13.231	12.819	12.414	12.016	11.626	11.243
30	5.0	11.484	11.406	11.328	11.250	11.173	11.097	11.020	10.945	10.870	10.795	10.720	10.647
	7.5	12.136	12.003	11.871	11.740	11.611	11.482	11.355	11.230	11.105	10.982	10.859	10.738
	10.0	12.938	12.734	12.533	12.335	12.140	11.947	11.757	11.570	11.385	11.203	11.024	10.847
	12.5	13.916	13.624	13.336	13.054	12.777	12.505	12.238	11.976	11.718	11.466	11.218	10.974
	15.0	15.082	14.683	14.293	13.910	13.534	13.167	12.807	12.455	12.111	11.774	11.445	11.123

25% New Money   75% Old Money   10.50% Overall Interest Rate

New Term	Old Term	7.25%	7.50%	7.75%	8.00%	8.25%	8.50%	8.75%	9.00%	9.25%	9.50%	9.75%	10.00%
15	5.0	11.983	11.867	11.750	11.635	11.519	11.404	11.290	11.176	11.062	10.949	10.836	10.724
	7.5	13.123	12.915	12.709	12.503	12.298	12.094	11.891	11.689	11.489	11.289	11.090	10.892
	10.0	14.673	14.345	14.018	13.691	13.366	13.042	12.719	12.398	12.078	11.759	11.442	11.127
	12.5	16.685	16.218	15.750	15.279	14.807	14.333	13.858	13.381	12.903	12.424	11.944	11.463
	15.0	19.002	18.418	17.824	17.220	16.606	15.981	15.344	14.696	14.034	13.358	12.668	11.963
20	5.0	11.655	11.564	11.473	11.383	11.293	11.203	11.114	11.025	10.937	10.849	10.761	10.674
	7.5	12.451	12.296	12.141	11.987	11.834	11.682	11.531	11.381	11.232	11.083	10.936	10.790
	10.0	13.450	13.212	12.977	12.743	12.510	12.280	12.051	11.824	11.599	11.375	11.154	10.934
	12.5	14.673	14.338	14.005	13.674	13.346	13.020	12.696	12.374	12.055	11.739	11.425	11.114
	15.0	16.088	15.651	15.215	14.779	14.344	13.910	13.477	13.046	12.616	12.188	11.763	11.339
25	5.0	11.492	11.414	11.335	11.258	11.180	11.103	11.027	10.950	10.875	10.799	10.724	10.649
	7.5	12.140	12.009	11.878	11.748	11.619	11.491	11.364	11.238	11.113	10.989	10.865	10.743
	10.0	12.922	12.725	12.530	12.336	12.145	11.955	11.767	11.580	11.396	11.213	11.032	10.853
	12.5	13.848	13.573	13.301	13.032	12.766	12.502	12.242	11.984	11.729	11.478	11.229	10.983
	15.0	14.904	14.544	14.187	13.833	13.483	13.136	12.793	12.453	12.118	11.786	11.458	11.135
30	5.0	11.400	11.329	11.258	11.187	11.117	11.047	10.978	10.908	10.839	10.771	10.703	10.635
	7.5	11.972	11.853	11.736	11.619	11.503	11.388	11.274	11.161	11.048	10.937	10.827	10.717
	10.0	12.647	12.471	12.297	12.125	11.954	11.785	11.619	11.454	11.290	11.129	10.969	10.811
	12.5	13.431	13.188	12.947	12.710	12.475	12.244	12.015	11.790	11.567	11.348	11.132	10.918
	15.0	14.317	13.998	13.683	13.372	13.065	12.763	12.464	12.170	11.881	11.596	11.315	11.039

33% New Money   67% Old Money   10.50% Overall Interest Rate

New Term	Old Term	7.25%	7.50%	7.75%	8.00%	8.25%	8.50%	8.75%	9.00%	9.25%	9.50%	9.75%	10.00%
15	5.0	11.744	11.647	11.551	11.454	11.358	11.262	11.166	11.070	10.974	10.879	10.784	10.689
	7.5	12.607	12.443	12.279	12.116	11.952	11.790	11.627	11.465	11.303	11.142	10.981	10.820
	10.0	13.675	13.431	13.187	12.942	12.698	12.453	12.209	11.964	11.720	11.475	11.231	10.987
	12.5	14.937	14.608	14.276	13.942	13.607	13.269	12.929	12.588	12.244	11.899	11.552	11.203
	15.0	16.312	15.906	15.495	15.078	14.653	14.222	13.785	13.340	12.887	12.427	11.958	11.481
20	5.0	11.479	11.403	11.326	11.250	11.174	11.099	11.023	10.948	10.873	10.798	10.723	10.648
	7.5	12.102	11.976	11.851	11.726	11.601	11.477	11.353	11.230	11.107	10.985	10.863	10.741
	10.0	12.830	12.647	12.464	12.282	12.101	11.920	11.740	11.561	11.382	11.204	11.027	10.851
	12.5	13.654	13.408	13.163	12.919	12.674	12.430	12.187	11.944	11.701	11.460	11.219	10.978
	15.0	14.543	14.236	13.928	13.619	13.309	12.999	12.687	12.376	12.064	11.751	11.438	11.126
25	5.0	11.346	11.280	11.213	11.148	11.082	11.016	10.951	10.886	10.821	10.757	10.692	10.628
	7.5	11.861	11.753	11.646	11.540	11.434	11.328	11.223	11.118	11.014	10.910	10.807	10.704
	10.0	12.445	12.291	12.137	11.984	11.832	11.681	11.530	11.380	11.232	11.084	10.936	10.790
	12.5	13.091	12.886	12.681	12.478	12.275	12.073	11.872	11.673	11.474	11.277	11.081	10.886
	15.0	13.781	13.524	13.266	13.010	12.754	12.499	12.245	11.992	11.740	11.489	11.240	10.992
30	5.0	11.270	11.210	11.149	11.089	11.029	10.970	10.910	10.851	10.792	10.733	10.675	10.616
	7.5	11.728	11.630	11.534	11.437	11.341	11.246	11.151	11.056	10.962	10.869	10.776	10.683
	10.0	12.239	12.100	11.962	11.824	11.688	11.552	11.418	11.284	11.151	11.019	10.888	10.758
	12.5	12.797	12.613	12.430	12.248	12.067	11.888	11.709	11.533	11.357	11.183	11.010	10.839
	15.0	13.389	13.158	12.928	12.699	12.472	12.246	12.021	11.799	11.578	11.359	11.141	10.926

Entry is the annual percentage yield on the new money.

Yield on Wraparound Mortgage Loan

| 40% New Money | 60% Old Money | | | | | | | | | | 10.50% Overall Interest Rate | |

New Term	Old Term	7.25%	7.50%	7.75%	8.00%	8.25%	8.50%	8.75%	9.00%	9.25%	9.50%	9.75%	10.00%
						Interest Rate on Old Money							
15	5.0	11.572	11.489	11.406	11.323	11.241	11.158	11.075	10.993	10.910	10.828	10.746	10.664
	7.5	12.264	12.128	11.992	11.856	11.720	11.584	11.448	11.312	11.177	11.041	10.906	10.770
	10.0	13.071	12.875	12.679	12.483	12.286	12.089	11.891	11.694	11.495	11.297	11.098	10.899
	12.5	13.973	13.717	13.459	13.199	12.937	12.673	12.407	12.140	11.871	11.600	11.328	11.053
	15.0	14.921	14.610	14.294	13.974	13.650	13.320	12.986	12.647	12.303	11.953	11.598	11.238
20	5.0	11.351	11.285	11.219	11.153	11.087	11.021	10.956	10.890	10.825	10.760	10.695	10.630
	7.5	11.861	11.755	11.649	11.544	11.439	11.333	11.229	11.124	11.019	10.915	10.811	10.707
	10.0	12.430	12.280	12.131	11.982	11.833	11.684	11.535	11.386	11.238	11.090	10.942	10.794
	12.5	13.045	12.850	12.655	12.460	12.264	12.068	11.872	11.676	11.480	11.284	11.088	10.892
	15.0	13.684	13.445	13.205	12.964	12.722	12.478	12.234	11.989	11.743	11.496	11.248	10.999
25	5.0	11.238	11.180	11.123	11.066	11.008	10.951	10.895	10.838	10.781	10.725	10.668	10.612
	7.5	11.664	11.573	11.482	11.392	11.301	11.211	11.121	11.032	10.943	10.854	10.765	10.676
	10.0	12.129	12.001	11.874	11.747	11.621	11.495	11.369	11.244	11.119	10.994	10.870	10.746
	12.5	12.622	12.457	12.292	12.127	11.962	11.798	11.634	11.471	11.308	11.145	10.983	10.822
	15.0	13.129	12.926	12.724	12.521	12.318	12.115	11.912	11.710	11.507	11.305	11.103	10.902
30	5.0	11.173	11.120	11.068	11.016	10.964	10.911	10.860	10.808	10.756	10.705	10.653	10.602
	7.5	11.554	11.471	11.389	11.307	11.225	11.143	11.062	10.981	10.900	10.819	10.739	10.659
	10.0	11.964	11.849	11.734	11.620	11.506	11.392	11.279	11.166	11.054	10.942	10.831	10.720
	12.5	12.395	12.246	12.098	11.949	11.802	11.655	11.508	11.362	11.217	11.072	10.928	10.785
	15.0	12.836	12.653	12.471	12.288	12.107	11.926	11.745	11.565	11.386	11.207	11.029	10.852

| 50% New Money | 50% Old Money | | | | | | | | | | 10.50% Overall Interest Rate | |

New Term	Old Term	7.25%	7.50%	7.75%	8.00%	8.25%	8.50%	8.75%	9.00%	9.25%	9.50%	9.75%	10.00%
15	5.0	11.341	11.276	11.211	11.147	11.082	11.017	10.953	10.888	10.823	10.759	10.694	10.629
	7.5	11.833	11.731	11.629	11.527	11.425	11.323	11.220	11.118	11.015	10.912	10.809	10.706
	10.0	12.368	12.227	12.086	11.945	11.802	11.660	11.516	11.373	11.228	11.084	10.938	10.793
	12.5	12.930	12.751	12.571	12.390	12.207	12.023	11.837	11.650	11.462	11.272	11.081	10.889
	15.0	13.494	13.281	13.065	12.846	12.625	12.401	12.173	11.943	11.710	11.475	11.236	10.994
20	5.0	11.174	11.122	11.070	11.018	10.966	10.914	10.862	10.811	10.759	10.707	10.655	10.603
	7.5	11.548	11.467	11.386	11.306	11.225	11.145	11.064	10.983	10.903	10.822	10.742	10.661
	10.0	11.941	11.831	11.721	11.610	11.500	11.389	11.279	11.168	11.057	10.945	10.834	10.723
	12.5	12.344	12.205	12.065	11.925	11.785	11.643	11.502	11.360	11.218	11.075	10.932	10.788
	15.0	12.744	12.578	12.410	12.241	12.072	11.901	11.729	11.556	11.383	11.208	11.032	10.856
25	5.0	11.087	11.042	10.997	10.951	10.906	10.861	10.816	10.770	10.725	10.680	10.635	10.590
	7.5	11.404	11.334	11.264	11.195	11.125	11.055	10.986	10.916	10.847	10.777	10.708	10.638
	10.0	11.732	11.637	11.542	11.448	11.353	11.258	11.163	11.068	10.973	10.879	10.784	10.689
	12.5	12.064	11.944	11.825	11.705	11.585	11.464	11.344	11.224	11.103	10.983	10.862	10.741
	15.0	12.390	12.247	12.104	11.960	11.816	11.671	11.525	11.380	11.234	11.088	10.941	10.794
30	5.0	11.038	10.996	10.954	10.913	10.871	10.830	10.788	10.747	10.706	10.665	10.623	10.582
	7.5	11.323	11.259	11.195	11.132	11.068	11.005	10.941	10.878	10.815	10.752	10.689	10.626
	10.0	11.615	11.529	11.443	11.357	11.271	11.185	11.099	11.013	10.927	10.841	10.756	10.670
	12.5	11.909	11.801	11.692	11.584	11.475	11.366	11.258	11.149	11.041	10.932	10.824	10.716
	15.0	12.198	12.068	11.938	11.807	11.677	11.546	11.416	11.285	11.154	11.023	10.892	10.761

| 67% New Money | 33% Old Money | | | | | | | | | | 10.50% Overall Interest Rate | |

New Term	Old Term	7.25%	7.50%	7.75%	8.00%	8.25%	8.50%	8.75%	9.00%	9.25%	9.50%	9.75%	10.00%
15	5.0	11.011	10.972	10.933	10.894	10.855	10.816	10.776	10.737	10.698	10.658	10.619	10.579
	7.5	11.271	11.213	11.155	11.096	11.037	10.978	10.919	10.860	10.800	10.741	10.681	10.621
	10.0	11.531	11.454	11.377	11.299	11.221	11.142	11.064	10.984	10.904	10.824	10.744	10.663
	12.5	11.783	11.689	11.594	11.498	11.402	11.305	11.207	11.108	11.008	10.908	10.807	10.705
	15.0	12.023	11.913	11.802	11.690	11.576	11.461	11.345	11.228	11.110	10.990	10.870	10.748
20	5.0	10.916	10.884	10.852	10.820	10.789	10.757	10.725	10.693	10.661	10.629	10.597	10.564
	7.5	11.121	11.074	11.027	10.980	10.932	10.885	10.837	10.789	10.741	10.693	10.645	10.597
	10.0	11.322	11.261	11.199	11.136	11.074	11.011	10.948	10.884	10.821	10.757	10.693	10.629
	12.5	11.516	11.440	11.364	11.287	11.211	11.133	11.055	10.977	10.899	10.820	10.740	10.661
	15.0	11.697	11.609	11.520	11.431	11.341	11.250	11.158	11.066	10.973	10.880	10.786	10.691
25	5.0	10.865	10.837	10.809	10.781	10.753	10.725	10.697	10.669	10.641	10.613	10.585	10.556
	7.5	11.043	11.001	10.960	10.919	10.877	10.836	10.794	10.752	10.710	10.668	10.626	10.584
	10.0	11.215	11.161	11.107	11.052	10.998	10.943	10.888	10.833	10.778	10.723	10.667	10.612
	12.5	11.379	11.313	11.247	11.180	11.114	11.047	10.979	10.911	10.844	10.775	10.707	10.638
	15.0	11.533	11.456	11.379	11.301	11.223	11.144	11.065	10.986	10.906	10.825	10.745	10.663
30	5.0	10.836	10.810	10.784	10.758	10.733	10.707	10.681	10.655	10.629	10.604	10.578	10.552
	7.5	10.997	10.959	10.921	10.883	10.845	10.807	10.769	10.731	10.692	10.654	10.616	10.577
	10.0	11.153	11.104	11.054	11.004	10.954	10.904	10.854	10.804	10.753	10.703	10.652	10.602
	12.5	11.301	11.241	11.180	11.120	11.059	10.997	10.936	10.874	10.812	10.750	10.688	10.625
	15.0	11.440	11.370	11.299	11.228	11.156	11.085	11.013	10.940	10.868	10.795	10.721	10.648

Entry is the annual percentage yield on the new money.

Yield on Wraparound Mortgage Loan

20% New Money   80% Old Money   11.00% Overall Interest Rate

New Term	Old Term	7.75%	8.00%	8.25%	8.50%	8.75%	9.00%	9.25%	9.50%	9.75%	10.00%	10.25%	10.50%
						Interest Rate on Old Money							
15	5.0	12.668	12.536	12.405	12.274	12.144	12.014	11.885	11.757	11.629	11.502	11.376	11.250
	7.5	14.043	13.798	13.555	13.314	13.075	12.837	12.602	12.368	12.135	11.905	11.676	11.449
	10.0	16.048	15.641	15.238	14.837	14.439	14.044	13.652	13.264	12.878	12.496	12.117	11.741
	12.5	18.844	18.239	17.634	17.028	16.422	15.816	15.210	14.605	14.001	13.398	12.796	12.195
	15.0	22.160	21.397	20.622	19.834	19.032	18.215	17.383	16.534	15.667	14.780	13.872	12.941
20	5.0	12.297	12.194	12.092	11.990	11.889	11.788	11.687	11.588	11.488	11.390	11.292	11.194
	7.5	13.243	13.062	12.882	12.703	12.526	12.351	12.177	12.004	11.833	11.664	11.496	11.329
	10.0	14.494	14.206	13.921	13.640	13.362	13.087	12.815	12.546	12.281	12.019	11.759	11.503
	12.5	16.118	15.694	15.275	14.861	14.452	14.047	13.648	13.254	12.865	12.482	12.104	11.730
	15.0	18.099	17.525	16.955	16.389	15.826	15.268	14.715	14.166	13.624	13.086	12.555	12.030
25	5.0	12.117	12.028	11.940	11.852	11.764	11.678	11.591	11.505	11.420	11.335	11.250	11.167
	7.5	12.885	12.731	12.580	12.429	12.280	12.133	11.986	11.841	11.698	11.556	11.415	11.275
	10.0	13.853	13.616	13.381	13.150	12.922	12.697	12.475	12.255	12.039	11.826	11.615	11.407
	12.5	15.061	14.717	14.378	14.045	13.717	13.394	13.076	12.764	12.458	12.156	11.859	11.568
	15.0	16.512	16.043	15.581	15.126	14.678	14.239	13.807	13.382	12.965	12.557	12.156	11.763
30	5.0	12.017	11.936	11.855	11.775	11.696	11.616	11.538	11.460	11.382	11.304	11.228	11.151
	7.5	12.695	12.556	12.419	12.284	12.149	12.017	11.885	11.755	11.626	11.498	11.372	11.247
	10.0	13.529	13.317	13.108	12.902	12.699	12.499	12.302	12.108	11.917	11.728	11.542	11.359
	12.5	14.547	14.242	13.943	13.650	13.362	13.079	12.801	12.529	12.262	12.000	11.743	11.490
	15.0	15.755	15.340	14.933	14.535	14.145	13.763	13.390	13.024	12.667	12.318	11.977	11.644

25% New Money   75% Old Money   11.00% Overall Interest Rate

New Term	Old Term	7.75%	8.00%	8.25%	8.50%	8.75%	9.00%	9.25%	9.50%	9.75%	10.00%	10.25%	10.50%
15	5.0	12.506	12.388	12.270	12.152	12.035	11.918	11.802	11.686	11.571	11.456	11.341	11.227
	7.5	13.663	13.451	13.241	13.032	12.824	12.617	12.411	12.207	12.003	11.800	11.598	11.398
	10.0	15.229	14.896	14.564	14.233	13.903	13.575	13.248	12.922	12.598	12.275	11.954	11.634
	12.5	17.246	16.773	16.299	15.824	15.346	14.868	14.387	13.906	13.424	12.940	12.456	11.971
	15.0	19.542	18.953	18.354	17.746	17.127	16.498	15.858	15.206	14.541	13.863	13.171	12.464
20	5.0	12.180	12.087	11.994	11.902	11.810	11.718	11.627	11.536	11.446	11.356	11.266	11.177
	7.5	12.994	12.835	12.676	12.519	12.363	12.207	12.053	11.899	11.747	11.596	11.445	11.296
	10.0	14.014	13.771	13.529	13.290	13.052	12.817	12.583	12.351	12.121	11.893	11.667	11.443
	12.5	15.255	14.913	14.573	14.236	13.901	13.568	13.237	12.909	12.584	12.262	11.942	11.625
	15.0	16.680	16.235	15.791	15.347	14.904	14.463	14.023	13.585	13.148	12.713	12.281	11.851
25	5.0	12.019	11.939	11.858	11.779	11.699	11.620	11.541	11.463	11.385	11.307	11.230	11.153
	7.5	12.687	12.552	12.417	12.283	12.151	12.019	11.888	11.759	11.630	11.502	11.375	11.249
	10.0	13.492	13.289	13.088	12.888	12.691	12.495	12.302	12.110	11.920	11.733	11.547	11.363
	12.5	14.442	14.159	13.879	13.602	13.328	13.057	12.789	12.524	12.262	12.003	11.748	11.495
	15.0	15.517	15.148	14.781	14.418	14.058	13.702	13.350	13.001	12.657	12.317	11.981	11.650
30	5.0	11.930	11.856	11.783	11.710	11.637	11.565	11.493	11.422	11.350	11.280	11.209	11.139
	7.5	12.523	12.400	12.278	12.157	12.037	11.918	11.800	11.683	11.567	11.452	11.337	11.224
	10.0	13.222	13.040	12.859	12.681	12.504	12.329	12.157	11.986	11.817	11.650	11.485	11.321
	12.5	14.034	13.782	13.532	13.286	13.043	12.803	12.567	12.333	12.103	11.876	11.652	11.432
	15.0	14.946	14.616	14.289	13.967	13.650	13.337	13.028	12.724	12.425	12.131	11.841	11.556

33% New Money   67% Old Money   11.00% Overall Interest Rate

New Term	Old Term	7.75%	8.00%	8.25%	8.50%	8.75%	9.00%	9.25%	9.50%	9.75%	10.00%	10.25%	10.50%
15	5.0	12.263	12.164	12.066	11.968	11.870	11.773	11.675	11.578	11.481	11.385	11.288	11.192
	7.5	13.136	12.969	12.803	12.637	12.472	12.307	12.142	11.978	11.814	11.650	11.487	11.324
	10.0	14.212	13.965	13.717	13.470	13.222	12.975	12.728	12.480	12.233	11.986	11.739	11.492
	12.5	15.473	15.141	14.806	14.469	14.130	13.790	13.447	13.103	12.756	12.408	12.059	11.707
	15.0	16.834	16.426	16.012	15.591	15.165	14.732	14.292	13.845	13.391	12.929	12.460	11.982
20	5.0	12.000	11.922	11.844	11.766	11.688	11.611	11.534	11.457	11.380	11.304	11.227	11.151
	7.5	12.635	12.507	12.378	12.251	12.123	11.997	11.870	11.745	11.619	11.494	11.370	11.246
	10.0	13.375	13.188	13.002	12.816	12.631	12.447	12.264	12.081	11.899	11.717	11.537	11.357
	12.5	14.207	13.958	13.708	13.459	13.210	12.962	12.714	12.467	12.221	11.975	11.730	11.486
	15.0	15.099	14.787	14.475	14.161	13.846	13.531	13.216	12.900	12.583	12.267	11.950	11.633
25	5.0	11.868	11.800	11.732	11.665	11.597	11.530	11.463	11.396	11.330	11.263	11.197	11.131
	7.5	12.397	12.287	12.177	12.067	11.958	11.850	11.742	11.634	11.527	11.421	11.315	11.209
	10.0	12.996	12.837	12.679	12.522	12.366	12.211	12.056	11.903	11.750	11.598	11.447	11.297
	12.5	13.655	13.444	13.234	13.026	12.818	12.611	12.405	12.201	11.997	11.795	11.594	11.395
	15.0	14.354	14.090	13.827	13.564	13.303	13.042	12.782	12.524	12.266	12.010	11.755	11.502
30	5.0	11.794	11.732	11.670	11.608	11.546	11.485	11.423	11.362	11.301	11.240	11.180	11.120
	7.5	12.267	12.167	12.067	11.967	11.868	11.770	11.671	11.574	11.477	11.381	11.285	11.189
	10.0	12.795	12.651	12.508	12.367	12.226	12.086	11.947	11.809	11.671	11.535	11.400	11.266
	12.5	13.369	13.179	12.989	12.802	12.615	12.430	12.246	12.064	11.883	11.703	11.525	11.349
	15.0	13.973	13.735	13.498	13.262	13.028	12.796	12.565	12.336	12.108	11.883	11.659	11.437

Entry is the annual percentage yield on the new money.

Yield on Wraparound Mortgage Loan

40% New Money   60% Old Money   **11.00% Overall Interest Rate**

New Term	Old Term	7.75%	8.00%	8.25%	8.50%	8.75%	9.00%	9.25%	9.50%	9.75%	10.00%	10.25%	10.50%
							Interest Rate on Old Money						
15	5.0	12.087	12.003	11.919	11.835	11.751	11.667	11.583	11.500	11.416	11.333	11.249	11.166
	7.5	12.786	12.648	12.510	12.373	12.235	12.097	11.960	11.822	11.685	11.548	11.411	11.274
	10.0	13.598	13.400	13.202	13.003	12.804	12.605	12.405	12.205	12.005	11.805	11.604	11.403
	12.5	14.499	14.240	13.979	13.717	13.453	13.187	12.920	12.651	12.380	12.107	11.833	11.557
	15.0	15.436	15.123	14.805	14.484	14.157	13.826	13.491	13.150	12.805	12.455	12.099	11.738
20	5.0	11.868	11.800	11.733	11.666	11.599	11.532	11.465	11.398	11.331	11.265	11.198	11.132
	7.5	12.387	12.279	12.172	12.064	11.957	11.849	11.742	11.636	11.529	11.423	11.317	11.211
	10.0	12.964	12.812	12.660	12.508	12.356	12.204	12.053	11.902	11.751	11.600	11.449	11.299
	12.5	13.585	13.386	13.188	12.989	12.791	12.592	12.393	12.194	11.995	11.795	11.596	11.397
	15.0	14.223	13.981	13.738	13.493	13.248	13.001	12.754	12.506	12.257	12.007	11.756	11.504
25	5.0	11.757	11.698	11.639	11.580	11.521	11.463	11.405	11.346	11.288	11.230	11.173	11.115
	7.5	12.194	12.100	12.007	11.914	11.822	11.729	11.637	11.545	11.454	11.362	11.271	11.181
	10.0	12.668	12.538	12.407	12.278	12.148	12.019	11.890	11.761	11.633	11.506	11.379	11.252
	12.5	13.170	13.001	12.832	12.663	12.495	12.327	12.159	11.992	11.826	11.659	11.494	11.329
	15.0	13.682	13.475	13.268	13.061	12.854	12.647	12.440	12.233	12.027	11.820	11.615	11.409
30	5.0	11.694	11.639	11.585	11.532	11.478	11.424	11.371	11.317	11.264	11.211	11.158	11.105
	7.5	12.087	12.001	11.916	11.831	11.747	11.663	11.579	11.495	11.412	11.329	11.246	11.164
	10.0	12.508	12.390	12.271	12.153	12.036	11.919	11.802	11.686	11.570	11.455	11.341	11.227
	12.5	12.950	12.796	12.643	12.491	12.339	12.187	12.037	11.886	11.737	11.588	11.440	11.292
	15.0	13.398	13.210	13.023	12.836	12.649	12.463	12.277	12.093	11.908	11.725	11.542	11.361

50% New Money   50% Old Money   **11.00% Overall Interest Rate**

New Term	Old Term	7.75%	8.00%	8.25%	8.50%	8.75%	9.00%	9.25%	9.50%	9.75%	10.00%	10.25%	10.50%
15	5.0	11.852	11.786	11.721	11.655	11.590	11.524	11.459	11.393	11.328	11.262	11.197	11.131
	7.5	12.348	12.245	12.142	12.039	11.936	11.832	11.728	11.625	11.521	11.417	11.313	11.209
	10.0	12.885	12.743	12.601	12.458	12.314	12.170	12.025	11.880	11.735	11.589	11.442	11.295
	12.5	13.445	13.265	13.084	12.901	12.717	12.531	12.344	12.156	11.967	11.776	11.584	11.391
	15.0	14.003	13.788	13.571	13.351	13.129	12.904	12.676	12.445	12.212	11.975	11.736	11.494
20	5.0	11.687	11.634	11.581	11.528	11.475	11.422	11.369	11.316	11.264	11.211	11.158	11.105
	7.5	12.066	11.984	11.902	11.820	11.738	11.656	11.574	11.492	11.410	11.328	11.246	11.164
	10.0	12.464	12.352	12.240	12.128	12.016	11.903	11.791	11.678	11.565	11.452	11.339	11.226
	12.5	12.869	12.728	12.586	12.444	12.302	12.159	12.015	11.871	11.727	11.582	11.437	11.292
	15.0	13.268	13.100	12.930	12.760	12.588	12.415	12.241	12.067	11.891	11.715	11.537	11.359
25	5.0	11.602	11.555	11.509	11.462	11.416	11.370	11.323	11.277	11.231	11.184	11.138	11.092
	7.5	11.926	11.854	11.783	11.711	11.640	11.568	11.497	11.426	11.355	11.284	11.213	11.142
	10.0	12.260	12.163	12.066	11.969	11.872	11.775	11.678	11.581	11.484	11.387	11.290	11.193
	12.5	12.595	12.473	12.351	12.229	12.106	11.984	11.861	11.738	11.615	11.492	11.369	11.246
	15.0	12.924	12.778	12.632	12.485	12.338	12.191	12.043	11.895	11.746	11.597	11.448	11.299
30	5.0	11.554	11.511	11.468	11.425	11.382	11.340	11.297	11.254	11.212	11.169	11.127	11.085
	7.5	11.847	11.781	11.715	11.650	11.585	11.519	11.454	11.389	11.324	11.259	11.194	11.129
	10.0	12.146	12.058	11.969	11.880	11.792	11.703	11.615	11.527	11.439	11.351	11.263	11.175
	12.5	12.446	12.335	12.223	12.112	12.000	11.889	11.777	11.666	11.555	11.443	11.332	11.221
	15.0	12.738	12.605	12.472	12.338	12.205	12.071	11.937	11.803	11.669	11.535	11.401	11.267

67% New Money   33% Old Money   **11.00% Overall Interest Rate**

New Term	Old Term	7.75%	8.00%	8.25%	8.50%	8.75%	9.00%	9.25%	9.50%	9.75%	10.00%	10.25%	10.50%
15	5.0	11.517	11.478	11.438	11.399	11.359	11.319	11.280	11.240	11.200	11.160	11.120	11.080
	7.5	11.779	11.720	11.661	11.602	11.543	11.483	11.423	11.363	11.303	11.243	11.182	11.122
	10.0	12.039	11.961	11.884	11.805	11.726	11.647	11.568	11.488	11.407	11.327	11.246	11.164
	12.5	12.290	12.195	12.099	12.003	11.906	11.808	11.710	11.610	11.510	11.410	11.308	11.206
	15.0	12.527	12.416	12.304	12.192	12.078	11.963	11.846	11.729	11.610	11.491	11.370	11.248
20	5.0	11.423	11.391	11.359	11.326	11.294	11.261	11.229	11.196	11.164	11.131	11.098	11.066
	7.5	11.631	11.583	11.535	11.487	11.439	11.391	11.342	11.294	11.245	11.196	11.147	11.098
	10.0	11.834	11.771	11.708	11.645	11.581	11.518	11.454	11.390	11.325	11.261	11.196	11.131
	12.5	12.027	11.951	11.874	11.796	11.719	11.640	11.562	11.483	11.403	11.323	11.243	11.162
	15.0	12.208	12.119	12.029	11.939	11.848	11.756	11.664	11.571	11.477	11.383	11.288	11.193
25	5.0	11.374	11.345	11.317	11.288	11.259	11.231	11.202	11.173	11.144	11.115	11.087	11.058
	7.5	11.555	11.512	11.470	11.428	11.385	11.343	11.300	11.257	11.215	11.172	11.129	11.086
	10.0	11.729	11.674	11.619	11.563	11.508	11.452	11.396	11.340	11.283	11.227	11.170	11.114
	12.5	11.895	11.827	11.760	11.692	11.624	11.556	11.487	11.418	11.349	11.280	11.210	11.140
	15.0	12.049	11.971	11.892	11.813	11.734	11.654	11.573	11.493	11.411	11.330	11.248	11.166
30	5.0	11.345	11.319	11.292	11.266	11.239	11.213	11.186	11.160	11.133	11.107	11.080	11.053
	7.5	11.511	11.472	11.433	11.394	11.354	11.315	11.276	11.237	11.197	11.158	11.119	11.079
	10.0	11.670	11.619	11.568	11.517	11.466	11.414	11.363	11.311	11.260	11.208	11.156	11.104
	12.5	11.820	11.758	11.696	11.634	11.571	11.508	11.445	11.382	11.319	11.256	11.192	11.128
	15.0	11.959	11.887	11.815	11.742	11.670	11.596	11.523	11.449	11.375	11.300	11.226	11.151

Entry is the annual percentage yield on the new money.

Yield on Wraparound Mortgage Loan

20% New Money   80% Old Money   11.50% Overall Interest Rate

New Term	Old Term	8.25%	8.50%	8.75%	9.00%	9.25%	9.50%	9.75%	10.00%	10.25%	10.50%	10.75%	11.00%
						Interest Rate on Old Money							
15	5.0	13.195	13.061	12.927	12.794	12.662	12.530	12.399	12.269	12.139	12.010	11.882	11.754
	7.5	14.592	14.343	14.096	13.851	13.608	13.366	13.127	12.889	12.653	12.419	12.186	11.956
	10.0	16.623	16.210	15.800	15.392	14.988	14.587	14.190	13.795	13.404	13.016	12.632	12.251
	12.5	19.432	18.819	18.206	17.593	16.979	16.366	15.753	15.141	14.531	13.921	13.313	12.706
	15.0	22.721	21.950	21.168	20.373	19.564	18.742	17.904	17.050	16.178	15.288	14.377	13.443
20	5.0	12.826	12.721	12.616	12.512	12.408	12.305	12.203	12.101	11.999	11.898	11.798	11.698
	7.5	13.796	13.610	13.425	13.242	13.061	12.882	12.703	12.527	12.352	12.179	12.007	11.836
	10.0	15.076	14.781	14.489	14.200	13.915	13.634	13.356	13.081	12.809	12.541	12.276	12.014
	12.5	16.732	16.297	15.868	15.444	15.025	14.612	14.204	13.801	13.404	13.012	12.626	12.245
	15.0	18.730	18.145	17.564	16.986	16.413	15.844	15.280	14.721	14.168	13.621	13.081	12.547
25	5.0	12.649	12.557	12.466	12.376	12.286	12.197	12.108	12.019	11.932	11.844	11.757	11.671
	7.5	13.441	13.283	13.126	12.971	12.818	12.666	12.515	12.366	12.218	12.072	11.927	11.783
	10.0	14.441	14.196	13.954	13.715	13.480	13.247	13.018	12.792	12.570	12.350	12.133	11.919
	12.5	15.686	15.331	14.981	14.636	14.298	13.965	13.637	13.316	12.999	12.689	12.384	12.084
	15.0	17.171	16.688	16.211	15.743	15.282	14.829	14.384	13.947	13.519	13.098	12.686	12.283
30	5.0	12.551	12.468	12.384	12.301	12.219	12.137	12.056	11.975	11.894	11.815	11.735	11.656
	7.5	13.255	13.112	12.969	12.829	12.690	12.552	12.416	12.281	12.147	12.015	11.884	11.755
	10.0	14.123	13.903	13.686	13.472	13.261	13.054	12.849	12.648	12.449	12.254	12.061	11.871
	12.5	15.182	14.865	14.554	14.249	13.949	13.655	13.367	13.084	12.807	12.535	12.269	12.007
	15.0	16.433	16.001	15.579	15.165	14.759	14.363	13.975	13.596	13.226	12.864	12.510	12.166

25% New Money   75% Old Money   11.50% Overall Interest Rate

New Term	Old Term	8.25%	8.50%	8.75%	9.00%	9.25%	9.50%	9.75%	10.00%	10.25%	10.50%	10.75%	11.00%
15	5.0	13.030	12.909	12.790	12.670	12.551	12.432	12.314	12.197	12.079	11.963	11.846	11.730
	7.5	14.203	13.988	13.775	13.563	13.351	13.141	12.932	12.724	12.517	12.312	12.107	11.904
	10.0	15.786	15.448	15.111	14.775	14.441	14.108	13.776	13.446	13.118	12.791	12.466	12.142
	12.5	17.806	17.329	16.849	16.369	15.886	15.402	14.917	14.431	13.944	13.457	12.968	12.479
	15.0	20.082	19.487	18.884	18.271	17.648	17.015	16.371	15.716	15.049	14.368	13.674	12.965
20	5.0	12.706	12.611	12.516	12.421	12.327	12.234	12.141	12.048	11.956	11.864	11.772	11.681
	7.5	13.539	13.375	13.213	13.052	12.892	12.733	12.576	12.419	12.263	12.108	11.955	11.802
	10.0	14.579	14.330	14.083	13.839	13.596	13.355	13.116	12.879	12.644	12.411	12.180	11.952
	12.5	15.839	15.490	15.143	14.798	14.456	14.117	13.779	13.445	13.114	12.785	12.459	12.136
	15.0	17.272	16.819	16.367	15.916	15.466	15.017	14.569	14.124	13.680	13.239	12.800	12.364
25	5.0	12.548	12.465	12.382	12.300	12.218	12.137	12.056	11.975	11.895	11.815	11.736	11.657
	7.5	13.236	13.096	12.957	12.820	12.683	12.548	12.413	12.280	12.147	12.016	11.885	11.756
	10.0	14.064	13.854	13.647	13.442	13.238	13.037	12.838	12.641	12.446	12.253	12.062	11.872
	12.5	15.038	14.747	14.458	14.173	13.891	13.612	13.337	13.065	12.796	12.530	12.267	12.008
	15.0	16.134	15.754	15.377	15.004	14.635	14.269	13.908	13.550	13.197	12.849	12.505	12.165
30	5.0	12.461	12.384	12.309	12.233	12.158	12.083	12.009	11.935	11.862	11.789	11.716	11.644
	7.5	13.075	12.947	12.821	12.696	12.572	12.449	12.327	12.206	12.086	11.967	11.848	11.731
	10.0	13.800	13.611	13.424	13.239	13.056	12.875	12.696	12.519	12.344	12.171	12.001	11.832
	12.5	14.640	14.378	14.120	13.865	13.613	13.364	13.119	12.878	12.640	12.405	12.174	11.946
	15.0	15.578	15.236	14.898	14.565	14.237	13.913	13.594	13.280	12.971	12.667	12.367	12.073

33% New Money   67% Old Money   11.50% Overall Interest Rate

New Term	Old Term	8.25%	8.50%	8.75%	9.00%	9.25%	9.50%	9.75%	10.00%	10.25%	10.50%	10.75%	11.00%
15	5.0	12.781	12.681	12.582	12.482	12.383	12.284	12.185	12.086	11.988	11.890	11.792	11.695
	7.5	13.665	13.496	13.328	13.160	12.992	12.824	12.657	12.491	12.324	12.159	11.993	11.828
	10.0	14.749	14.499	14.248	13.998	13.747	13.497	13.247	12.996	12.746	12.497	12.247	11.998
	12.5	16.010	15.674	15.336	14.996	14.654	14.311	13.965	13.618	13.269	12.918	12.566	12.212
	15.0	17.356	16.945	16.528	16.105	15.676	15.241	14.799	14.350	13.895	13.432	12.961	12.482
20	5.0	12.521	12.441	12.361	12.282	12.203	12.124	12.045	11.966	11.888	11.810	11.732	11.655
	7.5	13.169	13.037	12.906	12.776	12.646	12.517	12.388	12.260	12.132	12.004	11.877	11.751
	10.0	13.920	13.730	13.540	13.351	13.162	12.974	12.787	12.601	12.415	12.231	12.047	11.864
	12.5	14.762	14.508	14.254	14.000	13.747	13.494	13.242	12.991	12.740	12.491	12.242	11.993
	15.0	15.656	15.339	15.021	14.703	14.384	14.064	13.744	13.424	13.103	12.782	12.462	12.141
25	5.0	12.391	12.321	12.252	12.182	12.113	12.044	11.975	11.907	11.838	11.770	11.702	11.635
	7.5	12.935	12.821	12.708	12.596	12.484	12.372	12.261	12.151	12.041	11.932	11.823	11.715
	10.0	13.548	13.385	13.223	13.062	12.901	12.742	12.583	12.426	12.269	12.113	11.959	11.805
	12.5	14.221	14.004	13.789	13.575	13.361	13.149	12.939	12.729	12.521	12.314	12.108	11.904
	15.0	14.928	14.658	14.389	14.120	13.852	13.586	13.320	13.056	12.793	12.531	12.271	12.012
30	5.0	12.320	12.255	12.191	12.127	12.063	12.000	11.936	11.873	11.811	11.748	11.686	11.624
	7.5	12.808	12.704	12.601	12.498	12.396	12.294	12.193	12.092	11.992	11.893	11.794	11.695
	10.0	13.352	13.204	13.056	12.910	12.764	12.620	12.476	12.334	12.192	12.052	11.912	11.774
	12.5	13.942	13.746	13.551	13.357	13.164	12.973	12.784	12.596	12.409	12.224	12.041	11.859
	15.0	14.560	14.314	14.070	13.827	13.586	13.347	13.109	12.873	12.639	12.407	12.177	11.949

Entry is the annual percentage yield on the new money.

Yield on Wraparound Mortgage Loan

40% New Money   60% Old Money   11.50% Overall Interest Rate

New Term	Old Term	8.25%	8.50%	8.75%	9.00%	9.25%	9.50%	9.75%	10.00%	10.25%	10.50%	10.75%	11.00%
						Interest Rate on Old Money							
15	5.0	12.603	12.517	12.432	12.347	12.261	12.176	12.091	12.007	11.922	11.837	11.753	11.668
	7.5	13.309	13.169	13.030	12.890	12.751	12.611	12.472	12.333	12.193	12.055	11.916	11.777
	10.0	14.125	13.925	13.725	13.524	13.323	13.121	12.920	12.717	12.515	12.312	12.110	11.907
	12.5	15.024	14.763	14.500	14.236	13.970	13.702	13.432	13.161	12.888	12.614	12.338	12.060
	15.0	15.951	15.636	15.316	14.993	14.665	14.332	13.995	13.654	13.308	12.956	12.600	12.239
20	5.0	12.385	12.316	12.248	12.179	12.111	12.042	11.974	11.906	11.838	11.770	11.702	11.635
	7.5	12.914	12.804	12.694	12.584	12.475	12.366	12.257	12.148	12.039	11.931	11.823	11.715
	10.0	13.499	13.344	13.189	13.034	12.880	12.725	12.571	12.417	12.264	12.110	11.957	11.804
	12.5	14.125	13.923	13.722	13.520	13.318	13.116	12.913	12.711	12.509	12.307	12.105	11.903
	15.0	14.763	14.518	14.271	14.023	13.774	13.525	13.274	13.023	12.771	12.518	12.264	12.010
25	5.0	12.276	12.216	12.155	12.095	12.035	11.975	11.915	11.855	11.796	11.736	11.677	11.618
	7.5	12.724	12.628	12.533	12.437	12.342	12.248	12.153	12.059	11.965	11.871	11.778	11.685
	10.0	13.209	13.075	12.942	12.808	12.676	12.543	12.411	12.280	12.148	12.018	11.888	11.758
	12.5	13.719	13.546	13.373	13.200	13.028	12.856	12.685	12.514	12.344	12.174	12.004	11.836
	15.0	14.235	14.024	13.813	13.601	13.390	13.178	12.967	12.757	12.546	12.336	12.126	11.917
30	5.0	12.215	12.159	12.103	12.048	11.992	11.937	11.882	11.827	11.772	11.717	11.663	11.608
	7.5	12.620	12.532	12.444	12.357	12.270	12.183	12.096	12.010	11.924	11.839	11.754	11.669
	10.0	13.054	12.931	12.809	12.688	12.566	12.446	12.326	12.206	12.087	11.968	11.851	11.733
	12.5	13.506	13.348	13.190	13.033	12.877	12.721	12.566	12.411	12.257	12.104	11.952	11.801
	15.0	13.962	13.768	13.576	13.384	13.192	13.001	12.810	12.621	12.432	12.243	12.056	11.870

50% New Money   50% Old Money   11.50% Overall Interest Rate

New Term	Old Term	8.25%	8.50%	8.75%	9.00%	9.25%	9.50%	9.75%	10.00%	10.25%	10.50%	10.75%	11.00%
15	5.0	12.363	12.297	12.230	12.164	12.097	12.031	11.965	11.898	11.832	11.765	11.699	11.633
	7.5	12.864	12.760	12.655	12.551	12.446	12.342	12.237	12.132	12.027	11.922	11.816	11.711
	10.0	13.403	13.259	13.115	12.971	12.826	12.681	12.535	12.388	12.241	12.094	11.946	11.798
	12.5	13.960	13.779	13.596	13.412	13.227	13.040	12.852	12.663	12.472	12.280	12.087	11.893
	15.0	14.511	14.295	14.077	13.857	13.633	13.407	13.179	12.947	12.713	12.476	12.237	11.994
20	5.0	12.200	12.146	12.092	12.038	11.984	11.930	11.876	11.822	11.769	11.715	11.661	11.607
	7.5	12.586	12.502	12.418	12.335	12.251	12.168	12.084	12.001	11.917	11.834	11.750	11.667
	10.0	12.988	12.874	12.760	12.646	12.532	12.418	12.303	12.189	12.074	11.959	11.845	11.730
	12.5	13.395	13.252	13.108	12.964	12.819	12.674	12.528	12.382	12.236	12.090	11.943	11.795
	15.0	13.793	13.622	13.450	13.278	13.104	12.929	12.754	12.577	12.400	12.221	12.042	11.862
25	5.0	12.117	12.069	12.022	11.974	11.926	11.879	11.831	11.784	11.736	11.689	11.642	11.594
	7.5	12.448	12.374	12.301	12.228	12.155	12.082	12.009	11.936	11.863	11.790	11.718	11.645
	10.0	12.788	12.688	12.589	12.490	12.391	12.292	12.192	12.093	11.994	11.895	11.796	11.697
	12.5	13.128	13.003	12.878	12.753	12.628	12.503	12.378	12.252	12.127	12.002	11.876	11.751
	15.0	13.458	13.310	13.161	13.011	12.861	12.711	12.561	12.410	12.259	12.107	11.956	11.804
30	5.0	12.070	12.026	11.982	11.938	11.894	11.850	11.806	11.762	11.718	11.674	11.631	11.587
	7.5	12.371	12.304	12.236	12.169	12.101	12.034	11.967	11.900	11.833	11.766	11.699	11.633
	10.0	12.678	12.587	12.496	12.405	12.314	12.223	12.132	12.041	11.951	11.860	11.770	11.680
	12.5	12.984	12.869	12.755	12.640	12.526	12.411	12.297	12.183	12.069	11.954	11.841	11.727
	15.0	13.279	13.143	13.006	12.869	12.732	12.595	12.458	12.321	12.184	12.047	11.910	11.773

67% New Money   33% Old Money   11.50% Overall Interest Rate

New Term	Old Term	8.25%	8.50%	8.75%	9.00%	9.25%	9.50%	9.75%	10.00%	10.25%	10.50%	10.75%	11.00%
15	5.0	12.023	11.983	11.943	11.903	11.863	11.823	11.783	11.743	11.702	11.662	11.622	11.581
	7.5	12.287	12.228	12.168	12.108	12.048	11.988	11.928	11.867	11.806	11.745	11.684	11.623
	10.0	12.547	12.469	12.390	12.311	12.232	12.152	12.072	11.991	11.910	11.829	11.747	11.665
	12.5	12.797	12.701	12.605	12.508	12.410	12.312	12.213	12.113	12.013	11.911	11.810	11.707
	15.0	13.030	12.919	12.807	12.694	12.579	12.464	12.347	12.230	12.111	11.991	11.870	11.748
20	5.0	11.931	11.898	11.865	11.832	11.799	11.766	11.733	11.700	11.666	11.633	11.600	11.567
	7.5	12.141	12.093	12.044	11.995	11.946	11.897	11.848	11.798	11.749	11.699	11.650	11.600
	10.0	12.346	12.282	12.218	12.154	12.090	12.025	11.960	11.895	11.830	11.764	11.698	11.632
	12.5	12.539	12.462	12.384	12.305	12.227	12.147	12.068	11.988	11.907	11.827	11.746	11.664
	15.0	12.719	12.629	12.538	12.447	12.355	12.262	12.169	12.075	11.981	11.886	11.790	11.694
25	5.0	11.882	11.853	11.824	11.795	11.765	11.736	11.706	11.677	11.648	11.618	11.589	11.559
	7.5	12.066	12.023	11.980	11.937	11.894	11.850	11.807	11.763	11.719	11.676	11.632	11.588
	10.0	12.243	12.187	12.131	12.074	12.017	11.961	11.903	11.846	11.789	11.731	11.674	11.616
	12.5	12.410	12.342	12.273	12.204	12.135	12.065	11.996	11.925	11.855	11.785	11.714	11.643
	15.0	12.564	12.485	12.405	12.325	12.244	12.163	12.081	12.000	11.917	11.834	11.751	11.668
30	5.0	11.855	11.828	11.800	11.773	11.746	11.719	11.691	11.664	11.637	11.609	11.582	11.555
	7.5	12.024	11.984	11.944	11.904	11.864	11.824	11.783	11.743	11.703	11.662	11.622	11.581
	10.0	12.186	12.134	12.082	12.029	11.977	11.924	11.872	11.819	11.766	11.713	11.660	11.607
	12.5	12.338	12.275	12.211	12.148	12.084	12.020	11.955	11.891	11.826	11.761	11.696	11.631
	15.0	12.478	12.405	12.331	12.257	12.183	12.108	12.033	11.958	11.882	11.806	11.730	11.654

Entry is the annual percentage yield on the new money.

Yield on Wraparound Mortgage Loan

20% New Money   80% Old Money   12.00% Overall Interest Rate

New Term	Old Term	8.75%	9.00%	9.25%	9.50%	9.75%	10.00%	10.25%	10.50%	10.75%	11.00%	11.25%	11.50%
						Interest Rate on Old Money							
15	5.0	13.723	13.586	13.451	13.315	13.181	13.047	12.914	12.781	12.649	12.518	12.388	12.258
	7.5	15.143	14.889	14.638	14.389	14.141	13.896	13.652	13.411	13.171	12.933	12.697	12.463
	10.0	17.200	16.780	16.363	15.949	15.539	15.131	14.728	14.327	13.931	13.537	13.148	12.761
	12.5	20.020	19.400	18.779	18.158	17.537	16.917	16.297	15.678	15.061	14.444	13.830	13.218
	15.0	23.280	22.502	21.713	20.911	20.096	19.268	18.424	17.565	16.690	15.795	14.881	13.946
20	5.0	13.357	13.249	13.142	13.035	12.929	12.823	12.718	12.614	12.510	12.407	12.304	12.202
	7.5	14.350	14.159	13.970	13.783	13.597	13.413	13.231	13.050	12.871	12.694	12.518	12.344
	10.0	15.660	15.357	15.058	14.763	14.471	14.182	13.897	13.616	13.338	13.064	12.793	12.525
	12.5	17.348	16.903	16.463	16.029	15.601	15.178	14.760	14.349	13.943	13.543	13.148	12.760
	15.0	19.364	18.767	18.174	17.585	17.000	16.420	15.846	15.277	14.714	14.157	13.607	13.064
25	5.0	13.181	13.087	12.994	12.901	12.808	12.716	12.625	12.534	12.444	12.354	12.265	12.176
	7.5	13.999	13.836	13.675	13.515	13.357	13.200	13.045	12.891	12.739	12.588	12.439	12.291
	10.0	15.033	14.779	14.529	14.283	14.039	13.800	13.564	13.331	13.101	12.874	12.651	12.431
	12.5	16.316	15.948	15.586	15.231	14.881	14.538	14.200	13.868	13.543	13.223	12.909	12.600
	15.0	17.835	17.336	16.845	16.362	15.888	15.421	14.963	14.514	14.073	13.641	13.218	12.803
30	5.0	13.087	13.000	12.914	12.828	12.743	12.658	12.574	12.490	12.407	12.325	12.243	12.161
	7.5	13.818	13.669	13.521	13.376	13.231	13.089	12.948	12.808	12.670	12.533	12.398	12.264
	10.0	14.721	14.492	14.266	14.044	13.825	13.610	13.397	13.189	12.983	12.780	12.581	12.384
	12.5	15.822	15.492	15.168	14.851	14.539	14.234	13.935	13.641	13.354	13.072	12.796	12.525
	15.0	17.115	16.667	16.228	15.798	15.377	14.965	14.563	14.170	13.786	13.411	13.045	12.688

25% New Money   75% Old Money   12.00% Overall Interest Rate

New Term	Old Term	8.75%	9.00%	9.25%	9.50%	9.75%	10.00%	10.25%	10.50%	10.75%	11.00%	11.25%	11.50%
15	5.0	13.554	13.432	13.310	13.188	13.067	12.947	12.827	12.707	12.588	12.470	12.352	12.234
	7.5	14.744	14.526	14.309	14.094	13.879	13.666	13.453	13.242	13.032	12.824	12.616	12.409
	10.0	16.343	16.000	15.658	15.318	14.979	14.642	14.305	13.971	13.638	13.307	12.978	12.650
	12.5	18.368	17.885	17.400	16.914	16.426	15.938	15.448	14.957	14.465	13.973	13.480	12.987
	15.0	20.621	20.021	19.413	18.796	18.169	17.532	16.885	16.226	15.556	14.873	14.177	13.467
20	5.0	13.232	13.135	13.038	12.941	12.845	12.750	12.655	12.560	12.465	12.372	12.278	12.185
	7.5	14.084	13.917	13.751	13.587	13.423	13.260	13.099	12.939	12.779	12.621	12.464	12.309
	10.0	15.146	14.891	14.639	14.389	14.140	13.894	13.650	13.408	13.168	12.930	12.694	12.461
	12.5	16.425	16.068	15.714	15.362	15.013	14.666	14.323	13.982	13.644	13.309	12.977	12.648
	15.0	17.866	17.405	16.945	16.485	16.027	15.571	15.116	14.664	14.213	13.765	13.319	12.876
25	5.0	13.077	12.991	12.907	12.822	12.738	12.654	12.571	12.488	12.406	12.324	12.242	12.161
	7.5	13.785	13.641	13.499	13.357	13.217	13.077	12.939	12.802	12.665	12.530	12.396	12.263
	10.0	14.638	14.422	14.208	13.997	13.788	13.581	13.376	13.173	12.972	12.773	12.577	12.382
	12.5	15.637	15.337	15.040	14.747	14.456	14.170	13.886	13.606	13.330	13.057	12.787	12.521
	15.0	16.752	16.362	15.975	15.592	15.213	14.838	14.467	14.101	13.739	13.381	13.029	12.681
30	5.0	12.992	12.913	12.835	12.757	12.680	12.602	12.526	12.449	12.373	12.298	12.223	12.148
	7.5	13.629	13.497	13.366	13.237	13.108	12.981	12.854	12.729	12.605	12.482	12.360	12.239
	10.0	14.381	14.184	13.990	13.799	13.609	13.422	13.237	13.054	12.873	12.694	12.517	12.343
	12.5	15.249	14.978	14.710	14.445	14.184	13.927	13.674	13.424	13.177	12.935	12.696	12.460
	15.0	16.213	15.859	15.510	15.165	14.825	14.491	14.161	13.837	13.517	13.203	12.894	12.591

33% New Money   67% Old Money   12.00% Overall Interest Rate

New Term	Old Term	8.75%	9.00%	9.25%	9.50%	9.75%	10.00%	10.25%	10.50%	10.75%	11.00%	11.25%	11.50%
15	5.0	13.300	13.199	13.098	12.997	12.896	12.795	12.695	12.595	12.495	12.396	12.296	12.197
	7.5	14.195	14.024	13.853	13.682	13.512	13.342	13.173	13.004	12.835	12.667	12.500	12.333
	10.0	15.287	15.033	14.780	14.526	14.273	14.019	13.766	13.513	13.260	13.008	12.755	12.503
	12.5	16.547	16.207	15.866	15.523	15.178	14.832	14.483	14.133	13.781	13.428	13.073	12.717
	15.0	17.877	17.464	17.044	16.619	16.187	15.750	15.306	14.856	14.398	13.934	13.462	12.983
20	5.0	13.042	12.960	12.879	12.798	12.717	12.637	12.556	12.476	12.396	12.316	12.237	12.158
	7.5	13.703	13.569	13.435	13.302	13.169	13.037	12.906	12.775	12.644	12.514	12.385	12.256
	10.0	14.467	14.273	14.079	13.886	13.694	13.502	13.312	13.122	12.933	12.744	12.557	12.370
	12.5	15.317	15.059	14.800	14.542	14.284	14.027	13.771	13.515	13.261	13.007	12.753	12.501
	15.0	16.212	15.891	15.568	15.245	14.922	14.598	14.273	13.948	13.623	13.298	12.973	12.649
25	5.0	12.915	12.843	12.772	12.700	12.629	12.558	12.488	12.417	12.347	12.277	12.208	12.138
	7.5	13.473	13.356	13.240	13.125	13.010	12.895	12.781	12.668	12.555	12.443	12.331	12.220
	10.0	14.101	13.934	13.768	13.602	13.437	13.274	13.111	12.949	12.788	12.629	12.470	12.312
	12.5	14.787	14.565	14.344	14.125	13.906	13.689	13.473	13.258	13.045	12.833	12.623	12.414
	15.0	15.503	15.227	14.951	14.676	14.403	14.130	13.859	13.588	13.320	13.052	12.787	12.523
30	5.0	12.846	12.779	12.713	12.647	12.581	12.515	12.450	12.385	12.320	12.256	12.191	12.127
	7.5	13.350	13.243	13.136	13.030	12.924	12.819	12.715	12.611	12.507	12.405	12.303	12.201
	10.0	13.911	13.758	13.606	13.454	13.304	13.155	13.007	12.860	12.714	12.569	12.425	12.282
	12.5	14.517	14.315	14.113	13.913	13.715	13.518	13.322	13.129	12.936	12.746	12.557	12.369
	15.0	15.147	14.894	14.643	14.393	14.145	13.899	13.654	13.412	13.171	12.932	12.696	12.462

Entry is the annual percentage yield on the new money.

Yield on Wraparound Mortgage Loan

| 40% New Money | 60% Old Money | | | | | | | | 12.00% Overall Interest Rate | | | |

New Term	Old Term	8.75%	9.00%	9.25%	9.50%	Interest Rate on Old Money 9.75%	10.00%	10.25%	10.50%	10.75%	11.00%	11.25%	11.50%
15	5.0	13.118	13.032	12.945	12.859	12.772	12.686	12.600	12.514	12.428	12.342	12.256	12.171
	7.5	13.832	13.691	13.549	13.408	13.266	13.125	12.984	12.843	12.702	12.561	12.421	12.280
	10.0	14.653	14.451	14.248	14.045	13.842	13.638	13.434	13.230	13.025	12.821	12.616	12.411
	12.5	15.549	15.286	15.021	14.755	14.486	14.217	13.945	13.672	13.397	13.121	12.843	12.563
	15.0	16.465	16.148	15.827	15.501	15.172	14.838	14.500	14.157	13.810	13.458	13.101	12.739
20	5.0	12.903	12.833	12.763	12.693	12.623	12.553	12.484	12.414	12.345	12.275	12.206	12.137
	7.5	13.442	13.329	13.217	13.105	12.994	12.882	12.771	12.660	12.549	12.439	12.329	12.219
	10.0	14.035	13.877	13.719	13.562	13.404	13.247	13.090	12.933	12.777	12.621	12.465	12.310
	12.5	14.665	14.460	14.255	14.050	13.845	13.640	13.434	13.229	13.024	12.819	12.614	12.409
	15.0	15.303	15.054	14.804	14.553	14.301	14.048	13.794	13.540	13.285	13.029	12.772	12.515
25	5.0	12.796	12.734	12.672	12.610	12.549	12.487	12.426	12.364	12.303	12.242	12.182	12.121
	7.5	13.255	13.157	13.059	12.961	12.863	12.766	12.669	12.573	12.477	12.381	12.285	12.190
	10.0	13.751	13.613	13.476	13.340	13.204	13.068	12.933	12.798	12.664	12.530	12.397	12.264
	12.5	14.269	14.091	13.915	13.738	13.562	13.386	13.211	13.036	12.862	12.688	12.515	12.343
	15.0	14.789	14.574	14.358	14.142	13.926	13.711	13.495	13.281	13.066	12.852	12.638	12.425
30	5.0	12.737	12.679	12.622	12.565	12.507	12.450	12.394	12.337	12.280	12.224	12.168	12.112
	7.5	13.154	13.064	12.973	12.883	12.793	12.704	12.614	12.526	12.437	12.349	12.261	12.174
	10.0	13.600	13.474	13.348	13.223	13.098	12.974	12.850	12.727	12.604	12.482	12.361	12.240
	12.5	14.063	13.900	13.738	13.576	13.415	13.255	13.095	12.936	12.778	12.621	12.464	12.309
	15.0	14.526	14.327	14.129	13.932	13.735	13.539	13.344	13.149	12.955	12.762	12.570	12.379

| 50% New Money | 50% Old Money | | | | | | | | 12.00% Overall Interest Rate | | | |

New Term	Old Term	8.75%	9.00%	9.25%	9.50%	9.75%	10.00%	10.25%	10.50%	10.75%	11.00%	11.25%	11.50%
15	5.0	12.875	12.807	12.740	12.673	12.605	12.538	12.471	12.404	12.336	12.269	12.202	12.134
	7.5	13.380	13.274	13.169	13.063	12.957	12.851	12.745	12.639	12.533	12.426	12.320	12.213
	10.0	13.920	13.776	13.630	13.484	13.338	13.191	13.044	12.896	12.748	12.599	12.450	12.300
	12.5	14.476	14.293	14.109	13.923	13.737	13.549	13.359	13.169	12.977	12.784	12.590	12.395
	15.0	15.019	14.802	14.583	14.362	14.137	13.911	13.681	13.449	13.215	12.977	12.737	12.494
20	5.0	12.714	12.659	12.603	12.548	12.493	12.438	12.384	12.329	12.274	12.219	12.164	12.109
	7.5	13.105	13.020	12.935	12.850	12.765	12.680	12.595	12.510	12.425	12.340	12.255	12.170
	10.0	13.512	13.396	13.280	13.165	13.048	12.932	12.816	12.699	12.583	12.467	12.350	12.233
	12.5	13.921	13.775	13.630	13.483	13.337	13.189	13.042	12.894	12.746	12.597	12.448	12.299
	15.0	14.317	14.144	13.971	13.796	13.620	13.444	13.266	13.088	12.908	12.728	12.547	12.366
25	5.0	12.632	12.583	12.534	12.486	12.437	12.388	12.339	12.291	12.242	12.194	12.145	12.097
	7.5	12.970	12.895	12.820	12.745	12.670	12.596	12.521	12.446	12.372	12.297	12.223	12.148
	10.0	13.316	13.215	13.113	13.012	12.910	12.809	12.707	12.606	12.505	12.404	12.303	12.202
	12.5	13.660	13.533	13.406	13.278	13.151	13.023	12.895	12.767	12.639	12.511	12.383	12.256
	15.0	13.992	13.841	13.689	13.537	13.384	13.232	13.078	12.925	12.771	12.617	12.463	12.309
30	5.0	12.587	12.541	12.496	12.450	12.405	12.360	12.315	12.270	12.224	12.179	12.134	12.090
	7.5	12.896	12.827	12.757	12.688	12.619	12.549	12.480	12.411	12.342	12.274	12.205	12.137
	10.0	13.211	13.117	13.023	12.929	12.836	12.742	12.649	12.556	12.463	12.370	12.277	12.185
	12.5	13.521	13.404	13.286	13.169	13.052	12.934	12.817	12.700	12.583	12.466	12.349	12.233
	15.0	13.820	13.680	13.541	13.401	13.261	13.120	12.980	12.840	12.700	12.559	12.419	12.279

| 67% New Money | 33% Old Money | | | | | | | | 12.00% Overall Interest Rate | | | |

New Term	Old Term	8.75%	9.00%	9.25%	9.50%	9.75%	10.00%	10.25%	10.50%	10.75%	11.00%	11.25%	11.50%
15	5.0	12.530	12.489	12.449	12.408	12.368	12.327	12.286	12.246	12.205	12.164	12.123	12.082
	7.5	12.795	12.735	12.675	12.614	12.554	12.493	12.432	12.371	12.309	12.248	12.186	12.124
	10.0	13.055	12.976	12.897	12.818	12.737	12.657	12.576	12.495	12.413	12.331	12.249	12.166
	12.5	13.303	13.207	13.110	13.013	12.915	12.816	12.716	12.616	12.515	12.413	12.311	12.208
	15.0	13.533	13.422	13.309	13.196	13.081	12.965	12.848	12.730	12.611	12.491	12.370	12.248
20	5.0	12.438	12.405	12.371	12.338	12.304	12.271	12.237	12.203	12.169	12.136	12.102	12.068
	7.5	12.652	12.602	12.553	12.503	12.453	12.403	12.353	12.303	12.253	12.202	12.152	12.101
	10.0	12.857	12.793	12.728	12.663	12.598	12.532	12.466	12.400	12.334	12.268	12.201	12.134
	12.5	13.051	12.973	12.894	12.814	12.735	12.655	12.574	12.493	12.412	12.330	12.248	12.166
	15.0	13.230	13.139	13.047	12.955	12.862	12.769	12.675	12.580	12.485	12.389	12.292	12.196
25	5.0	12.391	12.361	12.331	12.301	12.271	12.241	12.211	12.181	12.151	12.121	12.091	12.060
	7.5	12.579	12.535	12.490	12.446	12.402	12.358	12.313	12.269	12.224	12.179	12.135	12.090
	10.0	12.758	12.701	12.643	12.585	12.527	12.469	12.411	12.353	12.294	12.236	12.177	12.118
	12.5	12.926	12.856	12.786	12.716	12.646	12.575	12.504	12.433	12.361	12.289	12.217	12.145
	15.0	13.080	12.999	12.918	12.837	12.755	12.672	12.590	12.507	12.423	12.339	12.255	12.170
30	5.0	12.364	12.337	12.309	12.281	12.253	12.225	12.197	12.169	12.141	12.112	12.084	12.056
	7.5	12.538	12.497	12.456	12.414	12.373	12.332	12.291	12.249	12.208	12.166	12.125	12.083
	10.0	12.703	12.649	12.596	12.542	12.488	12.435	12.381	12.327	12.272	12.218	12.164	12.109
	12.5	12.857	12.792	12.727	12.662	12.597	12.531	12.465	12.399	12.333	12.267	12.200	12.134
	15.0	12.998	12.923	12.848	12.772	12.696	12.620	12.543	12.466	12.389	12.312	12.234	12.156

Entry is the annual percentage yield on the new money.

Yield on Wraparound Mortgage Loan

20% New Money   80% Old Money   12.50% Overall Interest Rate

New Term	Old Term	9.25%	9.50%	9.75%	10.00%	Interest Rate on Old Money 10.25%	10.50%	10.75%	11.00%	11.25%	11.50%	11.75%	12.00%
15	5.0	14.251	14.112	13.974	13.837	13.700	13.564	13.429	13.294	13.160	13.027	12.894	12.762
	7.5	15.695	15.437	15.181	14.928	14.676	14.426	14.179	13.933	13.689	13.448	13.208	12.970
	10.0	17.779	17.352	16.928	16.507	16.090	15.677	15.267	14.860	14.458	14.059	13.663	13.272
	12.5	20.609	19.981	19.352	18.724	18.095	17.468	16.841	16.215	15.591	14.968	14.348	13.729
	15.0	23.838	23.053	22.257	21.448	20.627	19.793	18.944	18.081	17.201	16.303	15.386	14.448
20	5.0	13.888	13.777	13.667	13.558	13.450	13.342	13.234	13.128	13.022	12.916	12.811	12.707
	7.5	14.906	14.710	14.516	14.324	14.134	13.946	13.759	13.574	13.391	13.210	13.030	12.852
	10.0	16.247	15.937	15.630	15.327	15.028	14.732	14.440	14.152	13.868	13.587	13.310	13.037
	12.5	17.966	17.511	17.061	16.617	16.178	15.745	15.318	14.898	14.483	14.074	13.672	13.275
	15.0	19.998	19.390	18.785	18.184	17.588	16.998	16.412	15.833	15.260	14.694	14.134	13.582
25	5.0	13.715	13.618	13.522	13.426	13.331	13.236	13.142	13.049	12.956	12.864	12.772	12.681
	7.5	14.560	14.391	14.225	14.060	13.897	13.735	13.575	13.417	13.260	13.105	12.952	12.799
	10.0	15.627	15.365	15.107	14.852	14.601	14.354	14.110	13.870	13.633	13.400	13.170	12.944
	12.5	16.949	16.569	16.195	15.828	15.467	15.113	14.765	14.423	14.087	13.758	13.434	13.117
	15.0	18.501	17.988	17.482	16.985	16.496	16.016	15.544	15.082	14.629	14.185	13.750	13.324
30	5.0	13.623	13.533	13.444	13.355	13.267	13.180	13.093	13.007	12.921	12.836	12.751	12.667
	7.5	14.382	14.228	14.075	13.924	13.774	13.627	13.480	13.336	13.193	13.051	12.911	12.773
	10.0	15.322	15.084	14.849	14.619	14.391	14.168	13.948	13.731	13.518	13.308	13.101	12.897
	12.5	16.467	16.123	15.787	15.456	15.133	14.815	14.505	14.200	13.902	13.610	13.324	13.043
	15.0	17.803	17.337	16.881	16.434	15.997	15.570	15.153	14.745	14.347	13.959	13.581	13.211

25% New Money   75% Old Money   12.50% Overall Interest Rate

New Term	Old Term	9.25%	9.50%	9.75%	10.00%	10.25%	10.50%	10.75%	11.00%	11.25%	11.50%	11.75%	12.00%
15	5.0	14.079	13.954	13.830	13.707	13.584	13.462	13.340	13.218	13.097	12.977	12.857	12.737
	7.5	15.286	15.065	14.845	14.625	14.407	14.191	13.975	13.761	13.548	13.336	13.125	12.915
	10.0	16.902	16.554	16.207	15.862	15.518	15.176	14.835	14.496	14.159	13.823	13.490	13.158
	12.5	18.930	18.441	17.951	17.460	16.967	16.473	15.978	15.483	14.987	14.490	13.993	13.495
	15.0	21.159	20.555	19.942	19.320	18.689	18.048	17.397	16.736	16.063	15.377	14.680	13.968
20	5.0	13.760	13.660	13.561	13.462	13.364	13.266	13.169	13.072	12.976	12.880	12.784	12.689
	7.5	14.631	14.460	14.290	14.122	13.954	13.788	13.623	13.459	13.296	13.135	12.974	12.815
	10.0	15.714	15.454	15.196	14.940	14.686	14.434	14.185	13.937	13.692	13.449	13.209	12.970
	12.5	17.013	16.648	16.287	15.927	15.571	15.217	14.867	14.519	14.174	13.833	13.495	13.160
	15.0	18.460	17.991	17.522	17.055	16.590	16.126	15.664	15.204	14.746	14.291	13.838	13.389
25	5.0	13.607	13.519	13.432	13.345	13.258	13.172	13.087	13.002	12.917	12.833	12.749	12.666
	7.5	14.336	14.188	14.041	13.896	13.751	13.607	13.465	13.324	13.184	13.045	12.907	12.770
	10.0	15.214	14.992	14.771	14.554	14.338	14.125	13.914	13.705	13.499	13.295	13.093	12.893
	12.5	16.238	15.929	15.624	15.322	15.023	14.728	14.437	14.149	13.865	13.585	13.308	13.035
	15.0	17.372	16.971	16.574	16.181	15.792	15.408	15.027	14.652	14.281	13.914	13.553	13.197
30	5.0	13.525	13.443	13.362	13.282	13.202	13.122	13.043	12.964	12.885	12.808	12.730	12.653
	7.5	14.184	14.047	13.912	13.778	13.645	13.514	13.383	13.253	13.125	12.998	12.872	12.747
	10.0	14.963	14.760	14.559	14.360	14.164	13.970	13.778	13.589	13.402	13.217	13.034	12.854
	12.5	15.861	15.580	15.302	15.028	14.758	14.492	14.229	13.971	13.716	13.465	13.218	12.975
	15.0	16.850	16.484	16.123	15.767	15.416	15.070	14.730	14.395	14.065	13.741	13.422	13.109

33% New Money   67% Old Money   12.50% Overall Interest Rate

New Term	Old Term	9.25%	9.50%	9.75%	10.00%	10.25%	10.50%	10.75%	11.00%	11.25%	11.50%	11.75%	12.00%
15	5.0	13.820	13.717	13.614	13.511	13.409	13.307	13.205	13.104	13.003	12.902	12.801	12.700
	7.5	14.726	14.552	14.378	14.205	14.033	13.861	13.689	13.518	13.347	13.176	13.007	12.837
	10.0	15.825	15.568	15.312	15.055	14.799	14.542	14.286	14.030	13.774	13.519	13.263	13.009
	12.5	17.083	16.741	16.396	16.050	15.702	15.353	15.001	14.649	14.294	13.938	13.581	13.222
	15.0	18.399	17.982	17.560	17.132	16.698	16.259	15.813	15.361	14.902	14.436	13.964	13.484
20	5.0	13.564	13.481	13.398	13.315	13.232	13.150	13.068	12.986	12.904	12.823	12.742	12.661
	7.5	14.238	14.101	13.965	13.829	13.693	13.559	13.424	13.291	13.157	13.025	12.893	12.761
	10.0	15.015	14.817	14.619	14.422	14.226	14.031	13.836	13.643	13.450	13.258	13.067	12.877
	12.5	15.874	15.610	15.347	15.084	14.822	14.561	14.300	14.040	13.781	13.523	13.265	13.009
	15.0	16.769	16.443	16.116	15.788	15.460	15.131	14.802	14.473	14.144	13.815	13.485	13.157
25	5.0	13.440	13.366	13.292	13.219	13.146	13.073	13.001	12.928	12.856	12.784	12.713	12.642
	7.5	14.012	13.892	13.773	13.654	13.536	13.419	13.302	13.185	13.070	12.955	12.840	12.726
	10.0	14.656	14.484	14.313	14.143	13.974	13.806	13.639	13.473	13.308	13.145	12.982	12.820
	12.5	15.355	15.127	14.901	14.676	14.452	14.229	14.008	13.788	13.570	13.353	13.137	12.923
	15.0	16.079	15.796	15.514	15.233	14.953	14.675	14.398	14.122	13.847	13.574	13.303	13.034
30	5.0	13.372	13.303	13.235	13.167	13.099	13.031	12.964	12.897	12.830	12.764	12.697	12.631
	7.5	13.893	13.782	13.672	13.562	13.453	13.345	13.237	13.130	13.023	12.917	12.812	12.708
	10.0	14.472	14.313	14.156	14.000	13.845	13.691	13.538	13.386	13.236	13.086	12.938	12.791
	12.5	15.094	14.885	14.677	14.471	14.266	14.063	13.862	13.662	13.464	13.268	13.073	12.880
	15.0	15.735	15.475	15.217	14.960	14.704	14.451	14.200	13.950	13.703	13.458	13.215	12.974

Entry is the annual percentage yield on the new money.

Yield on Wraparound Mortgage Loan

40% New Money   60% Old Money   12.50% Overall Interest Rate

New Term	Old Term	9.25%	9.50%	9.75%	10.00%	10.25%	10.50%	10.75%	11.00%	11.25%	11.50%	11.75%	12.00%
						Interest Rate on Old Money							
15	5.0	13.634	13.546	13.459	13.371	13.283	13.196	13.108	13.021	12.934	12.847	12.760	12.673
	7.5	14.356	14.213	14.069	13.926	13.783	13.640	13.497	13.354	13.211	13.069	12.926	12.784
	10.0	15.181	14.976	14.771	14.566	14.360	14.155	13.948	13.742	13.535	13.329	13.122	12.915
	12.5	16.075	15.809	15.542	15.274	15.003	14.731	14.458	14.182	13.906	13.628	13.348	13.067
	15.0	16.979	16.660	16.337	16.010	15.679	15.344	15.004	14.661	14.312	13.960	13.602	13.240
20	5.0	13.422	13.350	13.278	13.207	13.136	13.064	12.993	12.922	12.852	12.781	12.711	12.640
	7.5	13.970	13.855	13.741	13.627	13.513	13.399	13.286	13.173	13.060	12.947	12.835	12.723
	10.0	14.572	14.411	14.250	14.089	13.929	13.769	13.609	13.449	13.290	13.132	12.973	12.815
	12.5	15.206	14.998	14.790	14.581	14.373	14.164	13.956	13.747	13.539	13.331	13.123	12.915
	15.0	15.843	15.590	15.337	15.083	14.828	14.572	14.315	14.057	13.799	13.540	13.281	13.021
25	5.0	13.317	13.253	13.189	13.126	13.063	12.999	12.937	12.874	12.811	12.748	12.686	12.624
	7.5	13.787	13.686	13.586	13.485	13.385	13.286	13.186	13.087	12.988	12.890	12.792	12.694
	10.0	14.293	14.152	14.012	13.872	13.733	13.594	13.455	13.317	13.180	13.043	12.906	12.770
	12.5	14.819	14.638	14.457	14.276	14.096	13.916	13.737	13.559	13.381	13.203	13.026	12.850
	15.0	15.344	15.123	14.903	14.683	14.463	14.243	14.024	13.805	13.586	13.368	13.150	12.933
30	5.0	13.259	13.200	13.141	13.082	13.023	12.964	12.906	12.847	12.789	12.731	12.673	12.615
	7.5	13.689	13.596	13.503	13.410	13.317	13.225	13.133	13.041	12.950	12.859	12.769	12.679
	10.0	14.147	14.017	13.888	13.759	13.630	13.502	13.375	13.248	13.122	12.996	12.871	12.747
	12.5	14.620	14.453	14.286	14.120	13.954	13.789	13.625	13.462	13.300	13.138	12.977	12.817
	15.0	15.090	14.887	14.683	14.481	14.279	14.078	13.878	13.678	13.479	13.281	13.084	12.888

50% New Money   50% Old Money   12.50% Overall Interest Rate

New Term	Old Term	9.25%	9.50%	9.75%	10.00%	10.25%	10.50%	10.75%	11.00%	11.25%	11.50%	11.75%	12.00%
15	5.0	13.386	13.318	13.250	13.182	13.114	13.045	12.977	12.909	12.841	12.773	12.704	12.636
	7.5	13.896	13.789	13.682	13.576	13.468	13.361	13.254	13.146	13.039	12.931	12.824	12.716
	10.0	14.438	14.292	14.145	13.998	13.850	13.702	13.553	13.404	13.254	13.104	12.954	12.803
	12.5	14.991	14.807	14.621	14.435	14.247	14.057	13.867	13.675	13.482	13.288	13.093	12.896
	15.0	15.527	15.309	15.089	14.866	14.641	14.414	14.184	13.951	13.716	13.478	13.238	12.994
20	5.0	13.227	13.171	13.115	13.059	13.003	12.947	12.891	12.835	12.779	12.723	12.667	12.612
	7.5	13.625	13.538	13.452	13.365	13.279	13.192	13.105	13.019	12.932	12.846	12.759	12.673
	10.0	14.036	13.919	13.801	13.683	13.565	13.447	13.329	13.211	13.092	12.974	12.855	12.737
	12.5	14.447	14.299	14.151	14.003	13.854	13.705	13.556	13.406	13.255	13.105	12.954	12.803
	15.0	14.841	14.667	14.491	14.314	14.136	13.958	13.778	13.598	13.417	13.235	13.052	12.869
25	5.0	13.148	13.098	13.048	12.997	12.948	12.898	12.848	12.798	12.748	12.698	12.649	12.599
	7.5	13.493	13.416	13.340	13.263	13.186	13.110	13.033	12.957	12.880	12.804	12.728	12.652
	10.0	13.845	13.741	13.638	13.534	13.430	13.327	13.223	13.119	13.016	12.913	12.809	12.706
	12.5	14.193	14.063	13.933	13.803	13.673	13.543	13.412	13.282	13.152	13.021	12.891	12.761
	15.0	14.526	14.372	14.218	14.063	13.908	13.752	13.596	13.440	13.284	13.128	12.971	12.814
30	5.0	13.104	13.057	13.010	12.964	12.917	12.870	12.824	12.777	12.731	12.685	12.638	12.592
	7.5	13.422	13.350	13.279	13.207	13.136	13.065	12.994	12.923	12.852	12.782	12.711	12.641
	10.0	13.743	13.647	13.551	13.454	13.358	13.262	13.166	13.071	12.975	12.880	12.785	12.689
	12.5	14.060	13.939	13.819	13.698	13.578	13.458	13.337	13.217	13.097	12.977	12.858	12.738
	15.0	14.361	14.218	14.075	13.932	13.789	13.645	13.502	13.358	13.215	13.072	12.929	12.786

67% New Money   33% Old Money   12.50% Overall Interest Rate

New Term	Old Term	9.25%	9.50%	9.75%	10.00%	10.25%	10.50%	10.75%	11.00%	11.25%	11.50%	11.75%	12.00%
15	5.0	13.036	12.995	12.954	12.913	12.872	12.831	12.790	12.749	12.708	12.666	12.625	12.583
	7.5	13.304	13.243	13.182	13.121	13.059	12.998	12.936	12.874	12.813	12.750	12.688	12.626
	10.0	13.564	13.484	13.404	13.324	13.243	13.162	13.081	12.999	12.917	12.834	12.751	12.668
	12.5	13.810	13.713	13.616	13.518	13.419	13.319	13.219	13.119	13.017	12.915	12.812	12.709
	15.0	14.036	13.925	13.812	13.698	13.583	13.466	13.349	13.231	13.112	12.992	12.870	12.748
20	5.0	12.946	12.912	12.878	12.844	12.810	12.775	12.741	12.707	12.672	12.638	12.604	12.569
	7.5	13.162	13.112	13.062	13.011	12.961	12.910	12.859	12.808	12.757	12.706	12.654	12.603
	10.0	13.370	13.304	13.238	13.172	13.106	13.039	12.973	12.906	12.839	12.771	12.704	12.636
	12.5	13.563	13.484	13.404	13.324	13.243	13.162	13.080	12.998	12.916	12.834	12.751	12.668
	15.0	13.740	13.649	13.556	13.463	13.369	13.275	13.180	13.085	12.988	12.892	12.795	12.697
25	5.0	12.900	12.870	12.839	12.808	12.778	12.747	12.716	12.685	12.655	12.624	12.593	12.562
	7.5	13.091	13.046	13.001	12.956	12.911	12.865	12.820	12.774	12.729	12.683	12.637	12.592
	10.0	13.273	13.214	13.156	13.097	13.038	12.978	12.919	12.860	12.800	12.740	12.680	12.620
	12.5	13.442	13.371	13.300	13.228	13.157	13.085	13.012	12.940	12.867	12.794	12.721	12.647
	15.0	13.596	13.514	13.431	13.349	13.265	13.182	13.098	13.014	12.929	12.844	12.758	12.672
30	5.0	12.874	12.846	12.817	12.788	12.760	12.731	12.702	12.673	12.644	12.616	12.587	12.558
	7.5	13.052	13.010	12.967	12.925	12.883	12.841	12.798	12.756	12.713	12.671	12.628	12.585
	10.0	13.220	13.165	13.110	13.055	13.000	12.945	12.890	12.834	12.779	12.723	12.668	12.612
	12.5	13.376	13.309	13.243	13.176	13.110	13.042	12.975	12.908	12.840	12.772	12.705	12.637
	15.0	13.517	13.441	13.364	13.287	13.209	13.132	13.054	12.975	12.897	12.818	12.739	12.659

Entry is the annual percentage yield on the new money.

Yield on Shared Appreciation Mortgage

Growth Rate 3%   Loan to Value Ratio 67%
Interest Rate 5.50% 30 Year Schedule

Years to Payoff	Share of Profit on Sale									
	10%	20%	30%	40%	50%	60%	70%	80%	90%	100%
1.0	5.940	6.379	6.816	7.251	7.685	8.116	8.546	8.975	9.401	9.826
2.0	5.936	6.370	6.799	7.225	7.648	8.067	8.482	8.894	9.303	9.709
3.0	5.933	6.360	6.783	7.200	7.611	8.018	8.420	8.817	9.209	9.597
4.0	5.929	6.351	6.766	7.174	7.576	7.971	8.360	8.742	9.119	9.490
5.0	5.925	6.342	6.750	7.150	7.541	7.925	8.301	8.670	9.033	9.388
7.5	5.917	6.320	6.711	7.090	7.458	7.815	8.163	8.501	8.830	9.151
10.0	5.908	6.298	6.673	7.033	7.379	7.712	8.034	8.345	8.646	8.937
12.5	5.899	6.277	6.636	6.978	7.304	7.616	7.915	8.201	8.477	8.743
15.0	5.891	6.257	6.601	6.926	7.234	7.526	7.804	8.069	8.323	8.566

Interest Rate 6.00% 30 Year Schedule

Years to Payoff	10%	20%	30%	40%	50%	60%	70%	80%	90%	100%
1.0	6.439	6.876	7.312	7.746	8.178	8.609	9.038	9.465	9.890	10.314
2.0	6.434	6.864	7.291	7.715	8.135	8.551	8.965	9.375	9.781	10.185
3.0	6.429	6.853	7.271	7.684	8.092	8.496	8.894	9.288	9.677	10.062
4.0	6.424	6.841	7.251	7.654	8.051	8.441	8.826	9.204	9.577	9.944
5.0	6.419	6.829	7.231	7.625	8.010	8.389	8.760	9.124	9.481	9.832
7.5	6.407	6.801	7.183	7.553	7.913	8.263	8.604	8.935	9.258	9.572
10.0	6.395	6.773	7.136	7.486	7.822	8.146	8.460	8.762	9.056	9.340
12.5	6.383	6.746	7.092	7.421	7.736	8.037	8.327	8.604	8.872	9.130
15.0	6.371	6.720	7.049	7.360	7.655	7.936	8.203	8.459	8.704	8.940

Interest Rate 6.50% 30 Year Schedule

Years to Payoff	10%	20%	30%	40%	50%	60%	70%	80%	90%	100%
1.0	6.938	7.374	7.808	8.241	8.672	9.102	9.529	9.955	10.380	10.802
2.0	6.931	7.359	7.784	8.205	8.622	9.037	9.448	9.855	10.260	10.661
3.0	6.925	7.345	7.760	8.169	8.574	8.974	9.369	9.759	10.145	10.526
4.0	6.919	7.331	7.736	8.134	8.527	8.913	9.293	9.667	10.035	10.399
5.0	6.912	7.317	7.712	8.100	8.480	8.853	9.219	9.578	9.931	10.277
7.5	6.897	7.282	7.656	8.018	8.370	8.713	9.046	9.371	9.688	9.996
10.0	6.882	7.249	7.601	7.940	8.267	8.583	8.888	9.183	9.469	9.746
12.5	6.867	7.217	7.549	7.867	8.171	8.462	8.742	9.011	9.270	9.521
15.0	6.853	7.186	7.500	7.797	8.080	8.350	8.607	8.854	9.090	9.318

Interest Rate 7.00% 30 Year Schedule

Years to Payoff	10%	20%	30%	40%	50%	60%	70%	80%	90%	100%
1.0	7.436	7.871	8.305	8.736	9.166	9.595	10.021	10.446	10.869	11.291
2.0	7.429	7.854	8.276	8.695	9.110	9.522	9.931	10.336	10.738	11.137
3.0	7.421	7.837	8.248	8.655	9.056	9.452	9.844	10.231	10.614	10.992
4.0	7.414	7.821	8.221	8.615	9.003	9.384	9.760	10.130	10.495	10.854
5.0	7.406	7.804	8.194	8.576	8.951	9.319	9.680	10.034	10.381	10.723
7.5	7.388	7.764	8.129	8.484	8.829	9.164	9.491	9.809	10.119	10.422
10.0	7.370	7.725	8.067	8.397	8.715	9.021	9.318	9.606	9.884	10.155
12.5	7.352	7.688	8.009	8.315	8.608	8.890	9.160	9.421	9.673	9.915
15.0	7.336	7.653	7.953	8.238	8.509	8.768	9.016	9.253	9.481	9.700

Interest Rate 7.50% 30 Year Schedule

Years to Payoff	10%	20%	30%	40%	50%	60%	70%	80%	90%	100%
1.0	7.935	8.369	8.801	9.232	9.660	10.088	10.513	10.937	11.359	11.779
2.0	7.926	8.349	8.769	9.185	9.598	10.008	10.414	10.817	11.217	11.614
3.0	7.917	8.330	8.738	9.140	9.538	9.931	10.319	10.703	11.083	11.458
4.0	7.909	8.311	8.707	9.096	9.479	9.857	10.228	10.595	10.955	11.311
5.0	7.900	8.292	8.676	9.053	9.423	9.785	10.141	10.490	10.833	11.170
7.5	7.879	8.246	8.604	8.951	9.288	9.617	9.937	10.249	10.553	10.850
10.0	7.858	8.203	8.535	8.855	9.163	9.462	9.751	10.031	10.303	10.566
12.5	7.838	8.161	8.469	8.765	9.048	9.320	9.582	9.835	10.078	10.314
15.0	7.819	8.121	8.408	8.681	8.941	9.189	9.428	9.656	9.876	10.088

Interest Rate 8.00% 30 Year Schedule

Years to Payoff	10%	20%	30%	40%	50%	60%	70%	80%	90%	100%
1.0	8.434	8.867	9.298	9.727	10.155	10.581	11.005	11.427	11.848	12.268
2.0	8.424	8.845	9.262	9.676	10.086	10.494	10.898	11.299	11.697	12.092
3.0	8.414	8.823	9.227	9.626	10.021	10.410	10.796	11.176	11.553	11.925
4.0	8.404	8.801	9.193	9.578	9.957	10.330	10.697	11.060	11.416	11.768
5.0	8.394	8.780	9.159	9.531	9.895	10.252	10.603	10.948	11.286	11.619
7.5	8.370	8.729	9.079	9.418	9.749	10.071	10.384	10.690	10.988	11.280
10.0	8.347	8.681	9.003	9.314	9.614	9.905	10.186	10.459	10.724	10.981
12.5	8.325	8.635	8.932	9.217	9.490	9.753	10.007	10.251	10.487	10.716
15.0	8.303	8.592	8.865	9.126	9.376	9.614	9.843	10.064	10.275	10.480

Entry is annual percentage yield from interest plus selected share of price appreciation.

Yield on Shared Appreciation Mortgage

Growth Rate 3%   Loan to Value Ratio 67%
Interest Rate 8.50% 30 Year Schedule

Years to Payoff	10%	20%	30%	Share of Profit on Sale 40%	50%	60%	70%	80%	90%	100%
1.0	8.933	9.364	9.794	10.222	10.649	11.074	11.497	11.918	12.338	12.757
2.0	8.921	9.340	9.755	10.167	10.575	10.980	11.382	11.781	12.177	12.569
3.0	8.910	9.316	9.716	10.112	10.503	10.890	11.272	11.650	12.023	12.393
4.0	8.899	9.292	9.679	10.060	10.434	10.803	11.167	11.525	11.878	12.226
5.0	8.888	9.269	9.642	10.008	10.368	10.720	11.066	11.406	11.741	12.069
7.5	8.861	9.213	9.555	9.887	10.211	10.526	10.833	11.133	11.426	11.711
10.0	8.836	9.160	9.473	9.775	10.067	10.349	10.623	10.889	11.147	11.398
12.5	8.812	9.110	9.396	9.671	9.935	10.189	10.434	10.671	10.900	11.121
15.0	8.789	9.063	9.325	9.574	9.813	10.043	10.263	10.475	10.679	10.876

Interest Rate 9.00% 30 Year Schedule

Years to Payoff	10%	20%	30%	40%	50%	60%	70%	80%	90%	100%
1.0	9.432	9.862	10.291	10.718	11.143	11.567	11.989	12.410	12.828	13.246
2.0	9.419	9.835	10.248	10.657	11.064	11.466	11.866	12.263	12.657	13.047
3.0	9.407	9.809	10.206	10.599	10.987	11.370	11.749	12.124	12.494	12.861
4.0	9.394	9.783	10.165	10.542	10.912	11.277	11.637	11.992	12.341	12.685
5.0	9.382	9.758	10.126	10.487	10.841	11.189	11.530	11.866	12.196	12.520
7.5	9.353	9.697	10.031	10.356	10.673	10.982	11.283	11.577	11.864	12.145
10.0	9.326	9.640	9.943	10.237	10.520	10.795	11.062	11.321	11.573	11.818
12.5	9.299	9.586	9.862	10.126	10.381	10.627	10.864	11.093	11.315	11.530
15.0	9.274	9.536	9.786	10.025	10.254	10.474	10.685	10.889	11.086	11.276

Interest Rate 9.50% 30 Year Schedule

Years to Payoff	10%	20%	30%	40%	50%	60%	70%	80%	90%	100%
1.0	9.931	10.360	10.788	11.214	11.638	12.060	12.481	12.901	13.319	13.735
2.0	9.917	10.331	10.741	11.148	11.552	11.953	12.351	12.745	13.137	13.526
3.0	9.903	10.302	10.696	11.085	11.470	11.850	12.226	12.598	12.966	13.329
4.0	9.890	10.274	10.652	11.024	11.391	11.752	12.108	12.459	12.804	13.145
5.0	9.877	10.247	10.609	10.965	11.315	11.658	11.995	12.326	12.652	12.972
7.5	9.845	10.181	10.508	10.827	11.137	11.440	11.735	12.023	12.305	12.580
10.0	9.815	10.120	10.415	10.700	10.976	11.243	11.503	11.755	12.001	12.239
12.5	9.787	10.063	10.329	10.584	10.830	11.067	11.296	11.518	11.733	11.942
15.0	9.761	10.011	10.249	10.478	10.697	10.908	11.111	11.307	11.497	11.680

Interest Rate 10.00% 30 Year Schedule

Years to Payoff	10%	20%	30%	40%	50%	60%	70%	80%	90%	100%
1.0	10.429	10.858	11.284	11.709	12.132	12.554	12.974	13.392	13.809	14.224
2.0	10.414	10.826	11.234	11.639	12.041	12.440	12.836	13.228	13.618	14.004
3.0	10.400	10.795	11.186	11.572	11.954	12.331	12.704	13.073	13.438	13.798
4.0	10.385	10.765	11.139	11.507	11.870	12.227	12.579	12.926	13.268	13.606
5.0	10.371	10.736	11.094	11.445	11.789	12.128	12.460	12.787	13.108	13.424
7.5	10.337	10.666	10.986	11.298	11.602	11.898	12.188	12.470	12.746	13.016
10.0	10.306	10.601	10.887	11.164	11.433	11.693	11.946	12.192	12.431	12.664
12.5	10.276	10.541	10.797	11.043	11.280	11.509	11.731	11.946	12.154	12.356
15.0	10.248	10.486	10.714	10.933	11.143	11.345	11.540	11.729	11.911	12.087

Interest Rate 10.50% 30 Year Schedule

Years to Payoff	10%	20%	30%	40%	50%	60%	70%	80%	90%	100%
1.0	10.928	11.356	11.781	12.205	12.627	13.047	13.466	13.884	14.299	14.713
2.0	10.912	11.322	11.728	12.131	12.530	12.927	13.320	13.711	14.099	14.483
3.0	10.896	11.289	11.676	12.059	12.438	12.812	13.182	13.548	13.910	14.268
4.0	10.881	11.257	11.626	11.990	12.349	12.703	13.051	13.394	13.733	14.067
5.0	10.866	11.225	11.578	11.924	12.264	12.598	12.926	13.249	13.566	13.878
7.5	10.830	11.151	11.465	11.770	12.067	12.358	12.641	12.918	13.189	13.454
10.0	10.796	11.083	11.361	11.630	11.891	12.144	12.390	12.630	12.863	13.090
12.5	10.765	11.020	11.266	11.503	11.732	11.954	12.168	12.376	12.578	12.774
15.0	10.736	10.963	11.180	11.389	11.591	11.785	11.972	12.153	12.328	12.498

Interest Rate 11.00% 30 Year Schedule

Years to Payoff	10%	20%	30%	40%	50%	60%	70%	80%	90%	100%
1.0	11.427	11.853	12.278	12.700	13.122	13.541	13.959	14.375	14.790	15.203
2.0	11.410	11.817	12.221	12.622	13.020	13.414	13.806	14.194	14.580	14.962
3.0	11.393	11.782	12.167	12.546	12.922	13.293	13.661	14.024	14.383	14.738
4.0	11.377	11.748	12.114	12.474	12.829	13.178	13.523	13.863	14.198	14.528
5.0	11.361	11.715	12.063	12.404	12.740	13.069	13.393	13.711	14.024	14.332
7.5	11.323	11.637	11.943	12.242	12.534	12.818	13.096	13.368	13.634	13.894
10.0	11.287	11.565	11.835	12.096	12.350	12.597	12.836	13.069	13.297	13.518
12.5	11.255	11.500	11.737	11.965	12.186	12.400	12.608	12.809	13.004	13.194
15.0	11.225	11.441	11.648	11.848	12.041	12.227	12.407	12.581	12.749	12.913

Entry is annual percentage yield from interest plus selected share of price appreciation.

Yield on Shared Appreciation Mortgage

Growth Rate 3%　　　　　　　　　　　　　　　　　　　　　　　Loan to Value Ratio 67%
Interest Rate 11.50% 30 Year Schedule

Years to Payoff	10%	20%	30%	Share of Profit on Sale 40%	50%	60%	70%	80%	90%	100%
1.0	11.926	12.351	12.775	13.196	13.616	14.035	14.451	14.867	15.280	15.692
2.0	11.908	12.313	12.715	13.113	13.509	13.901	14.291	14.677	15.061	15.442
3.0	11.890	12.276	12.657	13.034	13.406	13.775	14.139	14.499	14.856	15.208
4.0	11.872	12.240	12.601	12.958	13.309	13.655	13.996	14.332	14.664	14.991
5.0	11.856	12.205	12.548	12.885	13.215	13.541	13.860	14.174	14.484	14.788
7.5	11.815	12.123	12.423	12.715	13.001	13.280	13.552	13.819	14.079	14.335
10.0	11.778	12.048	12.310	12.564	12.811	13.050	13.284	13.511	13.732	13.948
12.5	11.744	11.981	12.209	12.429	12.642	12.849	13.049	13.244	13.433	13.617
15.0	11.714	11.920	12.118	12.309	12.493	12.671	12.844	13.011	13.173	13.331

Interest Rate 12.00% 30 Year Schedule

Years to Payoff	10%	20%	30%	40%	50%	60%	70%	80%	90%	100%
1.0	12.425	12.849	13.271	13.692	14.111	14.528	14.944	15.358	15.771	16.182
2.0	12.406	12.809	13.208	13.605	13.998	14.389	14.776	15.161	15.543	15.921
3.0	12.387	12.769	13.148	13.521	13.891	14.257	14.618	14.976	15.329	15.679
4.0	12.368	12.731	13.089	13.442	13.789	14.131	14.469	14.802	15.130	15.454
5.0	12.350	12.695	13.033	13.365	13.692	14.013	14.328	14.638	14.943	15.244
7.5	12.308	12.609	12.903	13.189	13.469	13.742	14.009	14.271	14.526	14.777
10.0	12.270	12.532	12.786	13.033	13.272	13.506	13.733	13.954	14.170	14.380
12.5	12.235	12.462	12.681	12.894	13.099	13.299	13.492	13.681	13.864	14.042
15.0	12.203	12.399	12.588	12.771	12.947	13.118	13.284	13.444	13.600	13.751

Interest Rate 12.50% 30 Year Schedule

Years to Payoff	10%	20%	30%	40%	50%	60%	70%	80%	90%	100%
1.0	12.924	13.347	13.768	14.188	14.606	15.022	15.437	15.850	16.262	16.672
2.0	12.904	13.304	13.702	14.097	14.488	14.876	15.262	15.645	16.024	16.401
3.0	12.884	13.263	13.638	14.009	14.376	14.739	15.097	15.452	15.803	16.150
4.0	12.864	13.223	13.577	13.926	14.270	14.608	14.942	15.272	15.597	15.917
5.0	12.846	13.185	13.519	13.846	14.168	14.485	14.796	15.103	15.404	15.700
7.5	12.801	13.096	13.383	13.664	13.938	14.205	14.467	14.723	14.974	15.220
10.0	12.762	13.016	13.262	13.502	13.735	13.962	14.183	14.399	14.609	14.814
12.5	12.725	12.944	13.155	13.360	13.558	13.751	13.938	14.120	14.297	14.469
15.0	12.693	12.880	13.060	13.235	13.404	13.567	13.726	13.880	14.030	14.175

Interest Rate 13.00% 30 Year Schedule

Years to Payoff	10%	20%	30%	40%	50%	60%	70%	80%	90%	100%
1.0	13.423	13.845	14.265	14.684	15.101	15.516	15.930	16.342	16.753	17.162
2.0	13.401	13.800	14.196	14.588	14.978	15.364	15.748	16.128	16.506	16.881
3.0	13.380	13.757	14.129	14.497	14.861	15.221	15.577	15.929	16.277	16.622
4.0	13.360	13.715	14.065	14.410	14.750	15.086	15.416	15.742	16.064	16.381
5.0	13.341	13.676	14.005	14.328	14.646	14.958	15.265	15.567	15.865	16.158
7.5	13.295	13.583	13.864	14.139	14.407	14.669	14.926	15.177	15.423	15.664
10.0	13.253	13.500	13.739	13.972	14.199	14.420	14.635	14.845	15.050	15.250
12.5	13.217	13.426	13.630	13.827	14.018	14.204	14.385	14.561	14.732	14.899
15.0	13.184	13.362	13.534	13.700	13.862	14.018	14.170	14.318	14.462	14.602

Interest Rate 13.50% 30 Year Schedule

Years to Payoff	10%	20%	30%	40%	50%	60%	70%	80%	90%	100%
1.0	13.922	14.343	14.762	15.180	15.596	16.010	16.423	16.834	17.244	17.652
2.0	13.899	14.296	14.689	15.080	15.468	15.852	16.234	16.612	16.988	17.362
3.0	13.877	14.251	14.620	14.985	15.346	15.703	16.057	16.406	16.752	17.094
4.0	13.856	14.208	14.554	14.895	15.232	15.563	15.890	16.213	16.532	16.846
5.0	13.836	14.166	14.491	14.809	15.123	15.431	15.735	16.033	16.327	16.616
7.5	13.788	14.070	14.345	14.614	14.877	15.134	15.386	15.632	15.873	16.110
10.0	13.746	13.985	14.217	14.444	14.664	14.879	15.088	15.292	15.492	15.687
12.5	13.708	13.910	14.105	14.295	14.480	14.659	14.834	15.004	15.170	15.331
15.0	13.675	13.844	14.008	14.167	14.322	14.471	14.617	14.759	14.897	15.031

Interest Rate 14.00% 30 Year Schedule

Years to Payoff	10%	20%	30%	40%	50%	60%	70%	80%	90%	100%
1.0	14.421	14.841	15.259	15.676	16.090	16.504	16.916	17.326	17.735	18.142
2.0	14.397	14.792	15.183	15.572	15.957	16.340	16.720	17.097	17.471	17.842
3.0	14.374	14.745	15.111	15.473	15.832	16.186	16.536	16.883	17.226	17.566
4.0	14.352	14.700	15.042	15.380	15.713	16.041	16.365	16.684	17.000	17.311
5.0	14.331	14.657	14.977	15.291	15.601	15.905	16.204	16.499	16.789	17.074
7.5	14.282	14.558	14.827	15.090	15.348	15.600	15.846	16.088	16.324	16.556
10.0	14.238	14.470	14.696	14.916	15.130	15.339	15.542	15.741	15.936	16.126
12.5	14.200	14.394	14.582	14.765	14.943	15.116	15.284	15.449	15.609	15.765
15.0	14.166	14.328	14.484	14.636	14.783	14.927	15.066	15.202	15.334	15.464

Entry is annual percentage yield from interest plus selected share of price appreciation.

Yield on Shared Appreciation Mortgage

Growth Rate 3%   Loan to Value Ratio 75%
Interest Rate 5.50% 30 Year Schedule

Years to Payoff	10%	20%	30%	Share of Profit on Sale 40%	50%	60%	70%	80%	90%	100%
1.0	5.891	6.281	6.670	7.058	7.444	7.829	8.212	8.594	8.975	9.354
2.0	5.888	6.274	6.656	7.036	7.413	7.788	8.159	8.528	8.894	9.258
3.0	5.885	6.266	6.642	7.015	7.383	7.747	8.108	8.464	8.817	9.166
4.0	5.882	6.258	6.629	6.994	7.354	7.708	8.058	8.402	8.742	9.078
5.0	5.879	6.250	6.615	6.973	7.325	7.670	8.009	8.343	8.670	8.993
7.5	5.871	6.232	6.582	6.923	7.255	7.578	7.893	8.201	8.501	8.794
10.0	5.863	6.213	6.550	6.875	7.188	7.491	7.785	8.069	8.345	8.613
12.5	5.856	6.195	6.519	6.828	7.125	7.410	7.683	7.947	8.201	8.447
15.0	5.849	6.178	6.489	6.784	7.065	7.333	7.588	7.834	8.069	8.295

Interest Rate 6.00% 30 Year Schedule

Years to Payoff	10%	20%	30%	40%	50%	60%	70%	80%	90%	100%
1.0	6.390	6.779	7.167	7.553	7.938	8.322	8.704	9.085	9.465	9.843
2.0	6.386	6.769	7.149	7.527	7.902	8.274	8.644	9.010	9.375	9.736
3.0	6.381	6.759	7.132	7.501	7.866	8.227	8.585	8.938	9.288	9.634
4.0	6.377	6.749	7.115	7.476	7.831	8.182	8.527	8.868	9.204	9.536
5.0	6.373	6.739	7.098	7.451	7.797	8.137	8.472	8.800	9.124	9.442
7.5	6.362	6.714	7.057	7.390	7.715	8.031	8.340	8.641	8.935	9.222
10.0	6.352	6.690	7.017	7.332	7.637	7.931	8.217	8.494	8.762	9.024
12.5	6.341	6.667	6.979	7.277	7.563	7.838	8.103	8.358	8.604	8.843
15.0	6.331	6.645	6.942	7.224	7.493	7.750	7.996	8.232	8.459	8.678

Interest Rate 6.50% 30 Year Schedule

Years to Payoff	10%	20%	30%	40%	50%	60%	70%	80%	90%	100%
1.0	6.889	7.277	7.664	8.049	8.433	8.816	9.197	9.577	9.955	10.333
2.0	6.883	7.264	7.643	8.018	8.391	8.761	9.128	9.493	9.855	10.215
3.0	6.878	7.252	7.622	7.988	8.350	8.708	9.062	9.412	9.759	10.102
4.0	6.872	7.240	7.601	7.958	8.309	8.656	8.998	9.334	9.667	9.995
5.0	6.867	7.227	7.581	7.929	8.270	8.606	8.935	9.259	9.578	9.892
7.5	6.853	7.198	7.532	7.858	8.176	8.486	8.788	9.083	9.371	9.653
10.0	6.840	7.169	7.485	7.791	8.087	8.374	8.651	8.921	9.183	9.437
12.5	6.827	7.141	7.440	7.728	8.004	8.269	8.525	8.772	9.011	9.242
15.0	6.815	7.113	7.397	7.667	7.925	8.172	8.408	8.635	8.854	9.065

Interest Rate 7.00% 30 Year Schedule

Years to Payoff	10%	20%	30%	40%	50%	60%	70%	80%	90%	100%
1.0	7.388	7.775	8.161	8.545	8.928	9.309	9.689	10.068	10.446	10.822
2.0	7.381	7.760	8.136	8.509	8.880	9.248	9.613	9.976	10.336	10.694
3.0	7.374	7.745	8.112	8.475	8.833	9.188	9.540	9.887	10.231	10.571
4.0	7.368	7.731	8.088	8.441	8.788	9.131	9.468	9.802	10.130	10.455
5.0	7.361	7.716	8.065	8.407	8.744	9.075	9.400	9.719	10.034	10.343
7.5	7.345	7.681	8.009	8.327	8.638	8.941	9.237	9.526	9.809	10.085
10.0	7.329	7.648	7.955	8.252	8.539	8.818	9.088	9.351	9.606	9.854
12.5	7.314	7.615	7.903	8.180	8.447	8.703	8.951	9.190	9.421	9.645
15.0	7.299	7.584	7.854	8.113	8.360	8.597	8.824	9.042	9.253	9.456

Interest Rate 7.50% 30 Year Schedule

Years to Payoff	10%	20%	30%	40%	50%	60%	70%	80%	90%	100%
1.0	7.887	8.273	8.657	9.041	9.422	9.803	10.182	10.560	10.937	11.312
2.0	7.879	8.256	8.630	9.001	9.369	9.735	10.098	10.459	10.817	11.173
3.0	7.871	8.239	8.602	8.962	9.318	9.669	10.018	10.362	10.703	11.041
4.0	7.863	8.222	8.575	8.924	9.267	9.606	9.940	10.269	10.595	10.915
5.0	7.856	8.206	8.549	8.887	9.218	9.544	9.865	10.180	10.490	10.796
7.5	7.837	8.166	8.486	8.798	9.102	9.399	9.689	9.972	10.249	10.520
10.0	7.819	8.127	8.425	8.714	8.993	9.264	9.527	9.783	10.031	10.273
12.5	7.801	8.091	8.368	8.635	8.892	9.140	9.379	9.611	9.835	10.052
15.0	7.784	8.056	8.314	8.561	8.798	9.025	9.243	9.454	9.656	9.852

Interest Rate 8.00% 30 Year Schedule

Years to Payoff	10%	20%	30%	40%	50%	60%	70%	80%	90%	100%
1.0	8.386	8.771	9.154	9.536	9.917	10.297	10.675	11.052	11.427	11.802
2.0	8.377	8.751	9.123	9.492	9.859	10.223	10.584	10.943	11.299	11.653
3.0	8.368	8.732	9.093	9.449	9.802	10.151	10.496	10.838	11.176	11.511
4.0	8.359	8.714	9.063	9.407	9.747	10.082	10.412	10.738	11.060	11.377
5.0	8.351	8.695	9.034	9.366	9.693	10.015	10.331	10.642	10.948	11.249
7.5	8.329	8.651	8.963	9.269	9.566	9.857	10.141	10.419	10.690	10.956
10.0	8.309	8.608	8.897	9.177	9.449	9.712	9.968	10.217	10.459	10.695
12.5	8.289	8.567	8.834	9.092	9.340	9.579	9.810	10.034	10.251	10.462
15.0	8.270	8.529	8.776	9.012	9.239	9.456	9.666	9.868	10.064	10.252

Entry is annual percentage yield from interest plus selected share of price appreciation.

Yield on Shared Appreciation Mortgage

Growth Rate 3%   Loan to Value Ratio 75%
Interest Rate 8.50% 30 Year Schedule

Years to Payoff	10%	20%	30%	Share of Profit on Sale 40%	50%	60%	70%	80%	90%	100%
1.0	8.885	9.269	9.651	10.032	10.412	10.791	11.168	11.544	11.918	12.292
2.0	8.875	9.247	9.617	9.984	10.348	10.710	11.070	11.426	11.781	12.133
3.0	8.865	9.226	9.583	9.937	10.287	10.633	10.975	11.314	11.650	11.982
4.0	8.855	9.205	9.551	9.891	10.227	10.558	10.885	11.207	11.525	11.839
5.0	8.845	9.185	9.519	9.846	10.169	10.486	10.798	11.104	11.406	11.704
7.5	8.822	9.136	9.442	9.740	10.032	10.317	10.595	10.867	11.133	11.393
10.0	8.799	9.089	9.370	9.642	9.906	10.162	10.411	10.653	10.889	11.119
12.5	8.778	9.045	9.302	9.550	9.789	10.020	10.244	10.461	10.671	10.875
15.0	8.757	9.003	9.239	9.465	9.682	9.891	10.092	10.287	10.475	10.656

Interest Rate 9.00% 30 Year Schedule

Years to Payoff	10%	20%	30%	40%	50%	60%	70%	80%	90%	100%
1.0	9.384	9.767	10.148	10.528	10.907	11.285	11.661	12.036	12.410	12.782
2.0	9.373	9.743	10.111	10.476	10.838	11.198	11.556	11.911	12.263	12.613
3.0	9.362	9.720	10.074	10.425	10.772	11.115	11.455	11.791	12.124	12.453
4.0	9.351	9.697	10.039	10.375	10.707	11.035	11.358	11.677	11.992	12.302
5.0	9.340	9.675	10.004	10.327	10.645	10.958	11.265	11.568	11.866	12.159
7.5	9.314	9.621	9.921	10.213	10.498	10.777	11.050	11.316	11.577	11.833
10.0	9.290	9.571	9.843	10.107	10.364	10.613	10.855	11.091	11.321	11.545
12.5	9.267	9.524	9.771	10.010	10.241	10.464	10.680	10.890	11.093	11.291
15.0	9.245	9.479	9.704	9.920	10.128	10.328	10.522	10.708	10.889	11.064

Interest Rate 9.50% 30 Year Schedule

Years to Payoff	10%	20%	30%	40%	50%	60%	70%	80%	90%	100%
1.0	9.883	10.265	10.645	11.024	11.402	11.779	12.154	12.528	12.901	13.272
2.0	9.871	10.239	10.605	10.968	11.328	11.686	12.042	12.395	12.745	13.094
3.0	9.859	10.214	10.565	10.913	11.257	11.597	11.934	12.268	12.598	12.925
4.0	9.847	10.189	10.527	10.860	11.188	11.512	11.832	12.147	12.459	12.766
5.0	9.835	10.165	10.489	10.808	11.122	11.430	11.733	12.032	12.326	12.616
7.5	9.807	10.107	10.400	10.686	10.966	11.239	11.506	11.767	12.023	12.274
10.0	9.781	10.053	10.318	10.574	10.824	11.066	11.302	11.532	11.755	11.974
12.5	9.756	10.003	10.241	10.471	10.694	10.910	11.119	11.321	11.518	11.710
15.0	9.733	9.956	10.171	10.377	10.576	10.768	10.954	11.133	11.307	11.476

Interest Rate 10.00% 30 Year Schedule

Years to Payoff	10%	20%	30%	40%	50%	60%	70%	80%	90%	100%
1.0	10.382	10.763	11.142	11.520	11.897	12.273	12.647	13.020	13.392	13.763
2.0	10.369	10.735	11.099	11.460	11.818	12.174	12.528	12.879	13.228	13.574
3.0	10.356	10.708	11.056	11.401	11.742	12.080	12.414	12.745	13.073	13.397
4.0	10.343	10.681	11.015	11.344	11.669	11.990	12.306	12.618	12.926	13.230
5.0	10.330	10.655	10.975	11.289	11.599	11.903	12.202	12.497	12.787	13.073
7.5	10.300	10.594	10.880	11.160	11.434	11.701	11.963	12.219	12.470	12.716
10.0	10.272	10.537	10.793	11.042	11.285	11.520	11.750	11.974	12.192	12.405
12.5	10.246	10.483	10.713	10.935	11.149	11.357	11.559	11.755	11.946	12.131
15.0	10.221	10.434	10.639	10.836	11.027	11.211	11.389	11.561	11.729	11.891

Interest Rate 10.50% 30 Year Schedule

Years to Payoff	10%	20%	30%	40%	50%	60%	70%	80%	90%	100%
1.0	10.881	11.261	11.639	12.017	12.393	12.767	13.141	13.513	13.884	14.253
2.0	10.867	11.231	11.593	11.952	12.309	12.663	13.015	13.364	13.711	14.056
3.0	10.853	11.202	11.547	11.890	12.228	12.563	12.895	13.223	13.548	13.870
4.0	10.839	11.174	11.504	11.829	12.151	12.468	12.780	13.089	13.394	13.695
5.0	10.826	11.146	11.461	11.771	12.076	12.376	12.672	12.962	13.249	13.531
7.5	10.794	11.081	11.361	11.635	11.903	12.165	12.421	12.672	12.918	13.160
10.0	10.764	11.020	11.269	11.511	11.747	11.976	12.199	12.417	12.630	12.837
12.5	10.736	10.964	11.185	11.399	11.606	11.807	12.002	12.192	12.376	12.556
15.0	10.710	10.913	11.109	11.297	11.480	11.656	11.827	11.992	12.153	12.309

Interest Rate 11.00% 30 Year Schedule

Years to Payoff	10%	20%	30%	40%	50%	60%	70%	80%	90%	100%
1.0	11.380	11.759	12.136	12.513	12.888	13.262	13.634	14.005	14.375	14.744
2.0	11.365	11.727	12.087	12.444	12.799	13.151	13.501	13.849	14.194	14.537
3.0	11.350	11.696	12.039	12.378	12.714	13.046	13.375	13.701	14.024	14.343
4.0	11.335	11.666	11.992	12.314	12.632	12.946	13.255	13.561	13.863	14.161
5.0	11.321	11.637	11.948	12.253	12.554	12.850	13.142	13.429	13.711	13.990
7.5	11.287	11.568	11.842	12.110	12.373	12.629	12.881	13.127	13.368	13.605
10.0	11.256	11.504	11.746	11.981	12.210	12.433	12.650	12.862	13.069	13.272
12.5	11.227	11.446	11.659	11.865	12.065	12.258	12.447	12.630	12.809	12.983
15.0	11.200	11.393	11.580	11.760	11.935	12.103	12.267	12.426	12.581	12.731

Entry is annual percentage yield from interest plus selected share of price appreciation.

Yield on Shared Appreciation Mortgage

Growth Rate 3%   Loan to Value Ratio 75%
Interest Rate 11.50% 30 Year Schedule

Years to Payoff	10%	20%	30%	Share of Profit on Sale 40%	50%	60%	70%	80%	90%	100%
1.0	11.879	12.257	12.634	13.009	13.383	13.756	14.127	14.498	14.867	15.234
2.0	11.863	12.223	12.581	12.937	13.290	13.640	13.988	14.334	14.677	15.019
3.0	11.847	12.190	12.530	12.867	13.200	13.530	13.856	14.179	14.499	14.816
4.0	11.831	12.159	12.481	12.800	13.114	13.425	13.731	14.033	14.332	14.627
5.0	11.816	12.128	12.434	12.736	13.032	13.324	13.612	13.895	14.174	14.449
7.5	11.781	12.055	12.324	12.586	12.843	13.095	13.341	13.582	13.819	14.051
10.0	11.748	11.989	12.224	12.452	12.674	12.891	13.103	13.309	13.511	13.708
12.5	11.718	11.929	12.133	12.332	12.524	12.712	12.894	13.071	13.244	13.412
15.0	11.690	11.875	12.052	12.225	12.391	12.553	12.710	12.863	13.011	13.155

Interest Rate 12.00% 30 Year Schedule

Years to Payoff	10%	20%	30%	40%	50%	60%	70%	80%	90%	100%
1.0	12.378	12.755	13.131	13.505	13.878	14.250	14.621	14.990	15.358	15.725
2.0	12.361	12.719	13.075	13.429	13.780	14.129	14.475	14.819	15.161	15.500
3.0	12.344	12.685	13.022	13.356	13.686	14.013	14.337	14.658	14.976	15.290
4.0	12.328	12.651	12.971	13.286	13.597	13.904	14.207	14.506	14.802	15.094
5.0	12.312	12.619	12.921	13.218	13.511	13.799	14.083	14.363	14.638	14.910
7.5	12.274	12.543	12.806	13.063	13.314	13.561	13.802	14.039	14.271	14.498
10.0	12.240	12.474	12.702	12.924	13.140	13.351	13.557	13.758	13.954	14.146
12.5	12.209	12.412	12.609	12.800	12.986	13.166	13.342	13.514	13.681	13.844
15.0	12.181	12.356	12.526	12.691	12.850	13.005	13.155	13.302	13.444	13.583

Interest Rate 12.50% 30 Year Schedule

Years to Payoff	10%	20%	30%	40%	50%	60%	70%	80%	90%	100%
1.0	12.877	13.253	13.628	14.002	14.374	14.745	15.114	15.483	15.850	16.216
2.0	12.859	13.216	13.570	13.922	14.271	14.618	14.962	15.305	15.645	15.982
3.0	12.841	13.179	13.514	13.845	14.173	14.497	14.819	15.137	15.452	15.764
4.0	12.824	13.144	13.460	13.772	14.079	14.383	14.683	14.979	15.272	15.561
5.0	12.807	13.110	13.408	13.702	13.990	14.275	14.555	14.831	15.103	15.371
7.5	12.768	13.031	13.288	13.540	13.786	14.027	14.264	14.496	14.723	14.947
10.0	12.733	12.960	13.181	13.396	13.606	13.811	14.012	14.207	14.399	14.586
12.5	12.701	12.896	13.085	13.270	13.449	13.623	13.793	13.958	14.120	14.277
15.0	12.672	12.839	13.001	13.158	13.311	13.459	13.603	13.743	13.880	14.013

Interest Rate 13.00% 30 Year Schedule

Years to Payoff	10%	20%	30%	40%	50%	60%	70%	80%	90%	100%
1.0	13.376	13.751	14.125	14.498	14.869	15.239	15.608	15.976	16.342	16.707
2.0	13.357	13.712	14.064	14.414	14.762	15.107	15.450	15.790	16.128	16.464
3.0	13.338	13.674	14.006	14.334	14.659	14.981	15.300	15.616	15.929	16.239
4.0	13.320	13.637	13.949	14.258	14.562	14.863	15.159	15.453	15.742	16.028
5.0	13.303	13.602	13.896	14.185	14.470	14.750	15.027	15.299	15.567	15.832
7.5	13.262	13.519	13.771	14.017	14.259	14.495	14.727	14.954	15.177	15.396
10.0	13.226	13.446	13.660	13.870	14.074	14.273	14.468	14.658	14.845	15.027
12.5	13.193	13.380	13.563	13.740	13.913	14.081	14.245	14.405	14.561	14.713
15.0	13.164	13.323	13.477	13.627	13.773	13.914	14.052	14.187	14.318	14.446

Interest Rate 13.50% 30 Year Schedule

Years to Payoff	10%	20%	30%	40%	50%	60%	70%	80%	90%	100%
1.0	13.875	14.249	14.622	14.994	15.365	15.734	16.102	16.468	16.834	17.198
2.0	13.855	14.208	14.559	14.907	15.253	15.596	15.937	16.276	16.612	16.947
3.0	13.836	14.168	14.498	14.823	15.146	15.466	15.782	16.096	16.406	16.713
4.0	13.817	14.130	14.439	14.744	15.045	15.343	15.636	15.926	16.213	16.496
5.0	13.799	14.093	14.383	14.668	14.949	15.226	15.499	15.768	16.033	16.294
7.5	13.757	14.008	14.254	14.495	14.732	14.963	15.190	15.413	15.632	15.847
10.0	13.719	13.932	14.141	14.344	14.542	14.736	14.926	15.111	15.292	15.470
12.5	13.685	13.865	14.041	14.212	14.378	14.540	14.698	14.853	15.004	15.151
15.0	13.656	13.807	13.954	14.097	14.236	14.372	14.504	14.633	14.759	14.882

Interest Rate 14.00% 30 Year Schedule

Years to Payoff	10%	20%	30%	40%	50%	60%	70%	80%	90%	100%
1.0	14.374	14.748	15.120	15.491	15.860	16.228	16.595	16.961	17.326	17.689
2.0	14.353	14.704	15.053	15.400	15.744	16.085	16.425	16.762	17.097	17.429
3.0	14.333	14.663	14.990	15.313	15.633	15.950	16.264	16.575	16.883	17.188
4.0	14.313	14.623	14.929	15.231	15.529	15.823	16.113	16.401	16.684	16.965
5.0	14.295	14.585	14.871	15.152	15.430	15.703	15.972	16.237	16.499	16.757
7.5	14.251	14.497	14.738	14.974	15.205	15.432	15.655	15.873	16.088	16.298
10.0	14.212	14.419	14.621	14.819	15.011	15.200	15.384	15.565	15.741	15.914
12.5	14.178	14.351	14.520	14.684	14.845	15.001	15.154	15.303	15.449	15.591
15.0	14.148	14.292	14.432	14.569	14.702	14.831	14.958	15.081	15.202	15.320

Entry is annual percentage yield from interest plus selected share of price appreciation.

Yield on Shared Appreciation Mortgage

Growth Rate 4%   Loan to Value Ratio 67%
Interest Rate 5.50% 30 Year Schedule

Years to Payoff	10%	20%	30%	Share of Profit on Sale 40%	50%	60%	70%	80%	90%	100%
1.0	6.086	6.670	7.251	7.829	8.403	8.975	9.543	10.109	10.671	11.231
2.0	6.084	6.662	7.233	7.799	8.358	8.911	9.458	9.999	10.535	11.065
3.0	6.082	6.654	7.216	7.769	8.313	8.848	9.375	9.894	10.405	10.908
4.0	6.079	6.645	7.199	7.740	8.270	8.788	9.296	9.793	10.281	10.759
5.0	6.077	6.637	7.182	7.711	8.227	8.729	9.219	9.696	10.163	10.618
7.5	6.071	6.617	7.140	7.642	8.125	8.590	9.038	9.471	9.890	10.295
10.0	6.065	6.597	7.099	7.576	8.028	8.460	8.872	9.267	9.645	10.009
12.5	6.059	6.577	7.060	7.512	7.937	8.339	8.719	9.080	9.424	9.753
15.0	6.053	6.558	7.022	7.452	7.852	8.226	8.578	8.910	9.225	9.523

Interest Rate 6.00% 30 Year Schedule

Years to Payoff	10%	20%	30%	40%	50%	60%	70%	80%	90%	100%
1.0	6.585	7.167	7.746	8.322	8.895	9.465	10.032	10.596	11.157	11.715
2.0	6.581	7.155	7.723	8.285	8.841	9.391	9.935	10.473	11.006	11.533
3.0	6.576	7.143	7.701	8.249	8.788	9.319	9.841	10.356	10.862	11.361
4.0	6.572	7.131	7.678	8.213	8.737	9.249	9.751	10.243	10.726	11.199
5.0	6.568	7.120	7.656	8.178	8.686	9.182	9.665	10.136	10.596	11.045
7.5	6.557	7.091	7.602	8.094	8.567	9.022	9.462	9.887	10.297	10.695
10.0	6.547	7.062	7.550	8.013	8.454	8.874	9.276	9.662	10.031	10.387
12.5	6.536	7.035	7.500	7.937	8.349	8.738	9.107	9.458	9.792	10.112
15.0	6.526	7.008	7.452	7.865	8.250	8.611	8.951	9.272	9.577	9.867

Interest Rate 6.50% 30 Year Schedule

Years to Payoff	10%	20%	30%	40%	50%	60%	70%	80%	90%	100%
1.0	7.083	7.664	8.241	8.816	9.387	9.955	10.521	11.083	11.643	12.200
2.0	7.077	7.648	8.213	8.772	9.324	9.871	10.412	10.948	11.477	12.002
3.0	7.071	7.633	8.185	8.729	9.264	9.790	10.308	10.818	11.321	11.816
4.0	7.065	7.618	8.158	8.687	9.204	9.711	10.208	10.695	11.172	11.640
5.0	7.059	7.603	8.131	8.646	9.147	9.635	10.112	10.577	11.031	11.475
7.5	7.044	7.565	8.066	8.547	9.010	9.457	9.888	10.305	10.708	11.099
10.0	7.029	7.529	8.003	8.453	8.882	9.292	9.684	10.060	10.421	10.768
12.5	7.015	7.494	7.943	8.365	8.763	9.140	9.498	9.839	10.165	10.476
15.0	7.000	7.460	7.886	8.282	8.652	9.000	9.328	9.639	9.934	10.215

Interest Rate 7.00% 30 Year Schedule

Years to Payoff	10%	20%	30%	40%	50%	60%	70%	80%	90%	100%
1.0	7.582	8.161	8.736	9.309	9.879	10.446	11.010	11.571	12.129	12.684
2.0	7.574	8.142	8.703	9.259	9.808	10.352	10.890	11.422	11.949	12.471
3.0	7.566	8.123	8.671	9.209	9.740	10.262	10.775	11.281	11.780	12.271
4.0	7.558	8.104	8.638	9.161	9.673	10.174	10.666	11.147	11.620	12.083
5.0	7.550	8.086	8.607	9.114	9.608	10.090	10.560	11.019	11.468	11.906
7.5	7.531	8.041	8.531	9.002	9.455	9.893	10.316	10.725	11.121	11.504
10.0	7.512	7.998	8.458	8.895	9.313	9.712	10.094	10.461	10.814	11.154
12.5	7.494	7.955	8.388	8.796	9.181	9.546	9.894	10.225	10.541	10.844
15.0	7.476	7.915	8.322	8.702	9.058	9.394	9.711	10.011	10.297	10.570

Interest Rate 7.50% 30 Year Schedule

Years to Payoff	10%	20%	30%	40%	50%	60%	70%	80%	90%	100%
1.0	8.080	8.657	9.232	9.803	10.371	10.937	11.499	12.059	12.615	13.169
2.0	8.070	8.635	9.194	9.746	10.292	10.833	11.368	11.898	12.422	12.941
3.0	8.061	8.613	9.156	9.690	10.216	10.734	11.243	11.745	12.240	12.727
4.0	8.052	8.591	9.119	9.636	10.142	10.638	11.124	11.601	12.068	12.527
5.0	8.042	8.570	9.083	9.583	10.071	10.546	11.010	11.463	11.906	12.338
7.5	8.019	8.517	8.996	9.457	9.902	10.331	10.746	11.147	11.536	11.913
10.0	7.996	8.467	8.914	9.340	9.746	10.135	10.508	10.866	11.210	11.542
12.5	7.974	8.418	8.836	9.229	9.602	9.956	10.293	10.614	10.922	11.217
15.0	7.953	8.372	8.762	9.126	9.469	9.792	10.098	10.388	10.665	10.929

Interest Rate 8.00% 30 Year Schedule

Years to Payoff	10%	20%	30%	40%	50%	60%	70%	80%	90%	100%
1.0	8.578	9.154	9.727	10.297	10.864	11.427	11.988	12.546	13.102	13.654
2.0	8.567	9.129	9.684	10.233	10.777	11.315	11.847	12.374	12.895	13.411
3.0	8.556	9.103	9.642	10.172	10.693	11.206	11.712	12.210	12.701	13.184
4.0	8.545	9.079	9.601	10.112	10.612	11.103	11.583	12.055	12.518	12.972
5.0	8.534	9.054	9.560	10.053	10.534	11.003	11.461	11.908	12.345	12.772
7.5	8.507	8.994	9.463	9.915	10.350	10.771	11.177	11.571	11.953	12.323
10.0	8.481	8.937	9.372	9.785	10.181	10.560	10.924	11.273	11.610	11.934
12.5	8.455	8.883	9.285	9.665	10.026	10.369	10.695	11.008	11.307	11.594
15.0	8.431	8.831	9.204	9.554	9.883	10.194	10.489	10.770	11.038	11.293

Entry is annual percentage yield from interest plus selected share of price appreciation.

Yield on Shared Appreciation Mortgage

Growth Rate 4%   Loan to Value Ratio 67%
Interest Rate 8.50% 30 Year Schedule

Years				Share of Profit on Sale						
to Payoff	10%	20%	30%	40%	50%	60%	70%	80%	90%	100%
1.0	9.077	9.651	10.222	10.791	11.356	11.918	12.478	13.035	13.588	14.139
2.0	9.064	9.622	10.175	10.721	11.262	11.796	12.326	12.850	13.368	13.882
3.0	9.051	9.594	10.128	10.653	11.170	11.680	12.181	12.675	13.162	13.642
4.0	9.039	9.566	10.082	10.588	11.083	11.568	12.044	12.510	12.968	13.418
5.0	9.026	9.539	10.038	10.524	10.998	11.461	11.913	12.354	12.785	13.207
7.5	8.996	9.472	9.931	10.373	10.800	11.212	11.611	11.997	12.372	12.736
10.0	8.966	9.409	9.831	10.233	10.618	10.988	11.342	11.683	12.012	12.329
12.5	8.937	9.349	9.737	10.104	10.453	10.785	11.101	11.405	11.695	11.974
15.0	8.910	9.292	9.649	9.984	10.301	10.601	10.885	11.156	11.415	11.662

Interest Rate 9.00% 30 Year Schedule

	10%	20%	30%	40%	50%	60%	70%	80%	90%	100%
1.0	9.575	10.148	10.718	11.285	11.849	12.410	12.968	13.523	14.075	14.625
2.0	9.561	10.116	10.665	11.209	11.746	12.279	12.805	13.326	13.842	14.353
3.0	9.547	10.085	10.614	11.135	11.648	12.153	12.651	13.141	13.624	14.100
4.0	9.532	10.054	10.564	11.064	11.554	12.034	12.505	12.966	13.420	13.864
5.0	9.518	10.024	10.516	10.995	11.463	11.919	12.365	12.801	13.227	13.644
7.5	9.484	9.950	10.399	10.832	11.251	11.655	12.046	12.426	12.793	13.151
10.0	9.451	9.881	10.291	10.683	11.058	11.417	11.763	12.096	12.417	12.727
12.5	9.420	9.816	10.190	10.545	10.882	11.203	11.511	11.805	12.087	12.358
15.0	9.390	9.754	10.096	10.418	10.722	11.011	11.285	11.546	11.797	12.036

Interest Rate 9.50% 30 Year Schedule

	10%	20%	30%	40%	50%	60%	70%	80%	90%	100%
1.0	10.074	10.645	11.214	11.779	12.341	12.901	13.457	14.011	14.562	15.110
2.0	10.058	10.610	11.156	11.697	12.232	12.761	13.285	13.803	14.317	14.825
3.0	10.042	10.576	11.101	11.617	12.126	12.628	13.121	13.608	14.087	14.559
4.0	10.026	10.542	11.047	11.541	12.025	12.500	12.966	13.423	13.872	14.312
5.0	10.011	10.509	10.994	11.467	11.928	12.379	12.819	13.249	13.670	14.082
7.5	9.973	10.429	10.869	11.293	11.703	12.099	12.483	12.855	13.217	13.568
10.0	9.938	10.355	10.753	11.134	11.499	11.849	12.186	12.511	12.825	13.127
12.5	9.903	10.285	10.645	10.988	11.314	11.625	11.923	12.208	12.483	12.746
15.0	9.871	10.219	10.546	10.854	11.146	11.424	11.688	11.941	12.182	12.414

Interest Rate 10.00% 30 Year Schedule

	10%	20%	30%	40%	50%	60%	70%	80%	90%	100%
1.0	10.572	11.142	11.709	12.273	12.834	13.392	13.947	14.500	15.049	15.596
2.0	10.555	11.104	11.647	12.185	12.717	13.243	13.765	14.280	14.791	15.297
3.0	10.537	11.067	11.587	12.100	12.605	13.102	13.592	14.075	14.550	15.019
4.0	10.520	11.030	11.529	12.018	12.498	12.967	13.429	13.881	14.325	14.761
5.0	10.503	10.994	11.473	11.939	12.395	12.839	13.274	13.699	14.114	14.521
7.5	10.463	10.909	11.339	11.754	12.156	12.545	12.921	13.287	13.642	13.986
10.0	10.424	10.829	11.216	11.586	11.941	12.283	12.612	12.929	13.235	13.531
12.5	10.388	10.754	11.102	11.433	11.748	12.049	12.338	12.615	12.881	13.138
15.0	10.353	10.685	10.998	11.293	11.574	11.841	12.096	12.339	12.573	12.797

Interest Rate 10.50% 30 Year Schedule

	10%	20%	30%	40%	50%	60%	70%	80%	90%	100%
1.0	11.071	11.639	12.205	12.767	13.327	13.884	14.437	14.988	15.537	16.082
2.0	11.052	11.598	12.139	12.673	13.203	13.726	14.245	14.758	15.266	15.769
3.0	11.033	11.558	12.074	12.583	13.084	13.577	14.063	14.542	15.014	15.479
4.0	11.014	11.518	12.012	12.496	12.970	13.435	13.891	14.339	14.779	15.211
5.0	10.996	11.480	11.952	12.412	12.862	13.300	13.729	14.149	14.559	14.961
7.5	10.952	11.389	11.810	12.217	12.610	12.992	13.361	13.720	14.068	14.407
10.0	10.911	11.304	11.680	12.040	12.386	12.719	13.039	13.348	13.647	13.936
12.5	10.872	11.225	11.561	11.880	12.185	12.476	12.756	13.025	13.283	13.532
15.0	10.836	11.153	11.452	11.735	12.004	12.261	12.506	12.741	12.966	13.183

Interest Rate 11.00% 30 Year Schedule

	10%	20%	30%	40%	50%	60%	70%	80%	90%	100%
1.0	11.569	12.136	12.700	13.262	13.820	14.375	14.928	15.477	16.024	16.568
2.0	11.549	12.092	12.630	13.162	13.688	14.209	14.725	15.236	15.741	16.242
3.0	11.528	12.049	12.561	13.066	13.563	14.052	14.535	15.010	15.478	15.940
4.0	11.509	12.007	12.495	12.974	13.443	13.903	14.355	14.798	15.234	15.661
5.0	11.489	11.966	12.432	12.886	13.329	13.762	14.186	14.600	15.005	15.402
7.5	11.442	11.869	12.282	12.680	13.066	13.440	13.802	14.154	14.496	14.829
10.0	11.399	11.780	12.145	12.495	12.832	13.156	13.469	13.770	14.062	14.344
12.5	11.358	11.697	12.021	12.329	12.624	12.906	13.177	13.437	13.688	13.930
15.0	11.320	11.622	11.908	12.179	12.438	12.685	12.921	13.147	13.364	13.573

Entry is annual percentage yield from interest plus selected share of price appreciation.

Yield on Shared Appreciation Mortgage

Growth Rate 4%   Loan to Value Ratio 67%
Interest Rate 11.50% 30 Year Schedule

Years to Payoff	10%	20%	30%	Share of Profit on Sale 40%	50%	60%	70%	80%	90%	100%
1.0	12.068	12.634	13.196	13.756	14.313	14.867	15.418	15.966	16.512	17.055
2.0	12.046	12.586	13.121	13.650	14.174	14.693	15.206	15.714	16.217	16.715
3.0	12.024	12.540	13.049	13.549	14.042	14.528	15.006	15.478	15.943	16.402
4.0	12.003	12.496	12.979	13.452	13.917	14.372	14.819	15.258	15.689	16.112
5.0	11.982	12.453	12.912	13.360	13.797	14.225	14.643	15.052	15.452	15.844
7.5	11.933	12.350	12.754	13.144	13.523	13.889	14.245	14.590	14.926	15.253
10.0	11.886	12.256	12.611	12.952	13.280	13.595	13.900	14.194	14.479	14.755
12.5	11.844	12.171	12.482	12.780	13.064	13.338	13.600	13.853	14.096	14.331
15.0	11.804	12.093	12.366	12.626	12.874	13.111	13.338	13.556	13.766	13.968

Interest Rate 12.00% 30 Year Schedule

Years to Payoff	10%	20%	30%	40%	50%	60%	70%	80%	90%	100%
1.0	12.567	13.131	13.692	14.250	14.806	15.358	15.908	16.455	16.999	17.541
2.0	12.543	13.081	13.613	14.139	14.660	15.176	15.687	16.192	16.693	17.188
3.0	12.520	13.032	13.536	14.033	14.522	15.004	15.479	15.947	16.409	16.864
4.0	12.497	12.985	13.463	13.931	14.391	14.841	15.284	15.718	16.145	16.564
5.0	12.475	12.939	13.392	13.834	14.266	14.688	15.101	15.505	15.900	16.287
7.5	12.423	12.832	13.227	13.610	13.980	14.340	14.688	15.028	15.357	15.678
10.0	12.375	12.734	13.078	13.410	13.729	14.036	14.333	14.620	14.898	15.168
12.5	12.330	12.645	12.945	13.232	13.507	13.772	14.026	14.271	14.507	14.735
15.0	12.290	12.564	12.826	13.075	13.312	13.540	13.759	13.969	14.171	14.366

Interest Rate 12.50% 30 Year Schedule

Years to Payoff	10%	20%	30%	40%	50%	60%	70%	80%	90%	100%
1.0	13.065	13.628	14.188	14.745	15.299	15.850	16.399	16.944	17.487	18.028
2.0	13.040	13.575	14.104	14.628	15.146	15.660	16.168	16.671	17.169	17.662
3.0	13.016	13.524	14.024	14.517	15.002	15.480	15.952	16.416	16.874	17.326
4.0	12.992	13.474	13.947	14.410	14.865	15.311	15.749	16.179	16.602	17.017
5.0	12.969	13.426	13.873	14.309	14.735	15.152	15.559	15.958	16.349	16.731
7.5	12.914	13.314	13.701	14.075	14.439	14.791	15.133	15.466	15.790	16.105
10.0	12.863	13.212	13.547	13.869	14.179	14.479	14.768	15.048	15.320	15.583
12.5	12.817	13.120	13.409	13.686	13.952	14.208	14.454	14.691	14.920	15.142
15.0	12.775	13.038	13.287	13.525	13.753	13.972	14.182	14.384	14.579	14.767

Interest Rate 13.00% 30 Year Schedule

Years to Payoff	10%	20%	30%	40%	50%	60%	70%	80%	90%	100%
1.0	13.564	14.125	14.684	15.239	15.792	16.342	16.889	17.434	17.975	18.514
2.0	13.537	14.069	14.596	15.117	15.633	16.143	16.649	17.149	17.645	18.136
3.0	13.511	14.015	14.512	15.001	15.482	15.957	16.425	16.886	17.340	17.789
4.0	13.486	13.963	14.431	14.890	15.340	15.781	16.215	16.641	17.059	17.470
5.0	13.462	13.913	14.354	14.784	15.205	15.616	16.018	16.412	16.798	17.176
7.5	13.405	13.796	14.175	14.542	14.898	15.244	15.579	15.906	16.224	16.534
10.0	13.352	13.690	14.016	14.329	14.631	14.923	15.205	15.478	15.743	16.000
12.5	13.305	13.596	13.875	14.142	14.399	14.646	14.884	15.114	15.336	15.551
15.0	13.262	13.512	13.750	13.978	14.197	14.407	14.609	14.803	14.991	15.172

Interest Rate 13.50% 30 Year Schedule

Years to Payoff	10%	20%	30%	40%	50%	60%	70%	80%	90%	100%
1.0	14.062	14.622	15.180	15.734	16.285	16.834	17.380	17.923	18.463	19.001
2.0	14.034	14.564	15.088	15.606	16.119	16.627	17.130	17.628	18.122	18.610
3.0	14.007	14.507	15.000	15.485	15.963	16.434	16.898	17.356	17.807	18.252
4.0	13.981	14.453	14.915	15.369	15.815	16.252	16.681	17.102	17.517	17.924
5.0	13.955	14.400	14.835	15.260	15.675	16.081	16.478	16.867	17.248	17.622
7.5	13.896	14.279	14.650	15.009	15.358	15.697	16.027	16.347	16.659	16.963
10.0	13.841	14.170	14.486	14.790	15.084	15.368	15.643	15.910	16.168	16.419
12.5	13.793	14.073	14.341	14.599	14.847	15.086	15.317	15.539	15.755	15.963
15.0	13.749	13.987	14.215	14.433	14.643	14.844	15.038	15.225	15.405	15.580

Interest Rate 14.00% 30 Year Schedule

Years to Payoff	10%	20%	30%	40%	50%	60%	70%	80%	90%	100%
1.0	14.561	15.120	15.676	16.228	16.779	17.326	17.870	18.412	18.951	19.488
2.0	14.532	15.058	15.579	16.095	16.606	17.111	17.612	18.108	18.598	19.084
3.0	14.503	14.999	15.488	15.969	16.443	16.911	17.371	17.826	18.274	18.716
4.0	14.476	14.942	15.400	15.849	16.290	16.722	17.147	17.565	17.975	18.378
5.0	14.449	14.888	15.317	15.736	16.145	16.546	16.938	17.323	17.699	18.068
7.5	14.387	14.762	15.125	15.477	15.819	16.152	16.475	16.789	17.096	17.394
10.0	14.331	14.650	14.957	15.253	15.539	15.815	16.083	16.343	16.595	16.840
12.5	14.281	14.551	14.809	15.058	15.297	15.528	15.751	15.967	16.176	16.378
15.0	14.237	14.464	14.681	14.890	15.090	15.283	15.470	15.649	15.823	15.992

Entry is annual percentage yield from interest plus selected share of price appreciation.

Yield on Shared Appreciation Mortgage

Growth Rate 4%   Loan to Value Ratio 75%
Interest Rate 5.50% 30 Year Schedule

Years to Payoff	Share of Profit on Sale									
	10%	20%	30%	40%	50%	60%	70%	80%	90%	100%
1.0	6.021	6.541	7.058	7.572	8.084	8.594	9.101	9.606	10.109	10.609
2.0	6.019	6.534	7.044	7.548	8.048	8.543	9.033	9.518	9.999	10.476
3.0	6.017	6.527	7.030	7.524	8.012	8.492	8.966	9.433	9.894	10.348
4.0	6.015	6.521	7.016	7.501	7.977	8.444	8.902	9.351	9.793	10.227
5.0	6.013	6.514	7.002	7.478	7.942	8.396	8.839	9.272	9.696	10.111
7.5	6.008	6.497	6.968	7.421	7.859	8.282	8.691	9.087	9.471	9.844
10.0	6.004	6.481	6.935	7.367	7.780	8.174	8.553	8.917	9.267	9.604
12.5	5.999	6.465	6.903	7.315	7.704	8.074	8.425	8.760	9.080	9.387
15.0	5.994	6.450	6.871	7.265	7.633	7.979	8.306	8.616	8.910	9.191

Interest Rate 6.00% 30 Year Schedule

Years to Payoff	10%	20%	30%	40%	50%	60%	70%	80%	90%	100%
1.0	6.520	7.038	7.553	8.066	8.577	9.085	9.591	10.095	10.596	11.095
2.0	6.516	7.028	7.534	8.036	8.533	9.025	9.512	9.995	10.473	10.947
3.0	6.513	7.018	7.516	8.006	8.490	8.966	9.436	9.899	10.356	10.806
4.0	6.509	7.008	7.497	7.977	8.447	8.909	9.362	9.806	10.243	10.673
5.0	6.505	6.998	7.479	7.948	8.406	8.853	9.290	9.718	10.136	10.545
7.5	6.496	6.974	7.434	7.878	8.306	8.720	9.121	9.510	9.887	10.252
10.0	6.487	6.950	7.391	7.810	8.212	8.596	8.965	9.320	9.662	9.991
12.5	6.479	6.927	7.348	7.746	8.123	8.481	8.821	9.147	9.458	9.756
15.0	6.470	6.904	7.308	7.685	8.039	8.372	8.688	8.987	9.272	9.544

Interest Rate 6.50% 30 Year Schedule

Years to Payoff	10%	20%	30%	40%	50%	60%	70%	80%	90%	100%
1.0	7.018	7.535	8.049	8.561	9.070	9.577	10.081	10.583	11.083	11.581
2.0	7.013	7.522	8.026	8.524	9.018	9.507	9.992	10.472	10.948	11.419
3.0	7.008	7.509	8.002	8.488	8.968	9.440	9.906	10.365	10.818	11.265
4.0	7.003	7.496	7.979	8.453	8.918	9.375	9.823	10.263	10.695	11.120
5.0	6.998	7.483	7.957	8.419	8.870	9.311	9.742	10.164	10.577	10.981
7.5	6.985	7.451	7.901	8.335	8.755	9.161	9.554	9.935	10.305	10.664
10.0	6.972	7.421	7.848	8.256	8.647	9.021	9.381	9.727	10.060	10.382
12.5	6.959	7.390	7.797	8.181	8.545	8.891	9.221	9.537	9.839	10.129
15.0	6.947	7.361	7.747	8.109	8.449	8.770	9.075	9.364	9.639	9.902

Interest Rate 7.00% 30 Year Schedule

Years to Payoff	10%	20%	30%	40%	50%	60%	70%	80%	90%	100%
1.0	7.517	8.032	8.545	9.055	9.563	10.068	10.571	11.072	11.571	12.067
2.0	7.510	8.016	8.517	9.013	9.504	9.990	10.472	10.949	11.422	11.891
3.0	7.503	8.000	8.489	8.971	9.446	9.915	10.376	10.832	11.281	11.725
4.0	7.497	7.984	8.462	8.930	9.390	9.841	10.284	10.720	11.147	11.567
5.0	7.490	7.968	8.435	8.890	9.335	9.770	10.196	10.612	11.019	11.418
7.5	7.473	7.930	8.370	8.794	9.205	9.603	9.988	10.362	10.725	11.077
10.0	7.457	7.892	8.307	8.704	9.083	9.448	9.799	10.136	10.461	10.776
12.5	7.441	7.856	8.247	8.618	8.970	9.305	9.625	9.931	10.225	10.507
15.0	7.425	7.820	8.190	8.536	8.863	9.172	9.466	9.745	10.011	10.266

Interest Rate 7.50% 30 Year Schedule

Years to Payoff	10%	20%	30%	40%	50%	60%	70%	80%	90%	100%
1.0	8.016	8.529	9.041	9.549	10.056	10.560	11.062	11.561	12.059	12.553
2.0	8.007	8.510	9.008	9.501	9.990	10.473	10.953	11.427	11.898	12.364
3.0	7.999	8.491	8.976	9.454	9.925	10.390	10.848	11.300	11.745	12.185
4.0	7.991	8.472	8.945	9.408	9.862	10.309	10.747	11.178	11.601	12.017
5.0	7.983	8.454	8.914	9.363	9.802	10.231	10.650	11.061	11.463	11.857
7.5	7.962	8.408	8.839	9.255	9.657	10.047	10.424	10.791	11.147	11.493
10.0	7.943	8.364	8.767	9.153	9.522	9.878	10.219	10.548	10.866	11.173
12.5	7.923	8.322	8.699	9.057	9.397	9.722	10.032	10.329	10.614	10.888
15.0	7.904	8.281	8.635	8.967	9.281	9.579	9.861	10.131	10.388	10.635

Interest Rate 8.00% 30 Year Schedule

Years to Payoff	10%	20%	30%	40%	50%	60%	70%	80%	90%	100%
1.0	8.514	9.027	9.536	10.044	10.549	11.052	11.552	12.051	12.546	13.040
2.0	8.504	9.004	9.500	9.990	10.476	10.957	11.433	11.906	12.374	12.837
3.0	8.495	8.983	9.463	9.937	10.404	10.865	11.319	11.768	12.210	12.646
4.0	8.485	8.961	9.428	9.886	10.335	10.777	11.210	11.636	12.055	12.467
5.0	8.475	8.940	9.393	9.836	10.268	10.692	11.106	11.511	11.908	12.297
7.5	8.452	8.888	9.309	9.716	10.110	10.492	10.862	11.222	11.571	11.911
10.0	8.429	8.838	9.229	9.604	9.964	10.309	10.642	10.963	11.273	11.573
12.5	8.406	8.790	9.154	9.499	9.828	10.142	10.443	10.731	11.008	11.274
15.0	8.384	8.744	9.082	9.401	9.702	9.989	10.261	10.521	10.770	11.009

Entry is annual percentage yield from interest plus selected share of price appreciation.

Yield on Shared Appreciation Mortgage

Growth Rate 4%   Loan to Value Ratio 75%
Interest Rate 8.50% 30 Year Schedule

Years to Payoff	10%	20%	30%	40%	50%	60%	70%	80%	90%	100%
				Share of Profit on Sale						
1.0	9.013	9.524	10.032	10.539	11.042	11.544	12.043	12.540	13.035	13.527
2.0	9.002	9.499	9.991	10.479	10.962	11.441	11.915	12.384	12.850	13.311
3.0	8.990	9.474	9.951	10.421	10.884	11.341	11.792	12.236	12.675	13.108
4.0	8.979	9.450	9.911	10.364	10.809	11.246	11.674	12.096	12.510	12.918
5.0	8.968	9.426	9.873	10.309	10.736	11.154	11.562	11.962	12.354	12.738
7.5	8.941	9.368	9.780	10.178	10.564	10.939	11.302	11.655	11.997	12.331
10.0	8.915	9.312	9.692	10.057	10.406	10.743	11.068	11.381	11.683	11.976
12.5	8.890	9.259	9.610	9.943	10.261	10.565	10.856	11.136	11.405	11.663
15.0	8.866	9.209	9.532	9.838	10.127	10.403	10.665	10.916	11.156	11.387

Interest Rate 9.00% 30 Year Schedule

Years to Payoff	10%	20%	30%	40%	50%	60%	70%	80%	90%	100%
1.0	9.512	10.021	10.528	11.033	11.536	12.036	12.534	13.029	13.523	14.014
2.0	9.499	9.993	10.483	10.968	11.448	11.924	12.396	12.863	13.326	13.785
3.0	9.486	9.966	10.439	10.905	11.364	11.817	12.265	12.706	13.141	13.571
4.0	9.474	9.939	10.395	10.843	11.283	11.715	12.139	12.556	12.966	13.370
5.0	9.461	9.912	10.353	10.783	11.204	11.616	12.019	12.414	12.801	13.180
7.5	9.431	9.848	10.252	10.642	11.020	11.387	11.743	12.089	12.426	12.753
10.0	9.402	9.788	10.157	10.511	10.851	11.179	11.495	11.801	12.096	12.382
12.5	9.375	9.730	10.068	10.389	10.697	10.991	11.273	11.544	11.805	12.056
15.0	9.348	9.676	9.985	10.277	10.555	10.820	11.073	11.315	11.546	11.769

Interest Rate 9.50% 30 Year Schedule

Years to Payoff	10%	20%	30%	40%	50%	60%	70%	80%	90%	100%
1.0	10.010	10.518	11.024	11.528	12.029	12.528	13.025	13.519	14.011	14.501
2.0	9.996	10.488	10.975	11.457	11.935	12.409	12.878	13.343	13.803	14.260
3.0	9.982	10.458	10.927	11.389	11.845	12.294	12.738	13.176	13.608	14.034
4.0	9.968	10.428	10.879	11.322	11.757	12.185	12.605	13.017	13.423	13.822
5.0	9.955	10.399	10.834	11.258	11.673	12.080	12.478	12.867	13.249	13.624
7.5	9.922	10.330	10.724	11.106	11.477	11.836	12.185	12.525	12.855	13.177
10.0	9.890	10.264	10.622	10.966	11.298	11.617	11.925	12.223	12.511	12.790
12.5	9.860	10.202	10.527	10.838	11.135	11.419	11.692	11.955	12.208	12.453
15.0	9.831	10.144	10.439	10.719	10.986	11.241	11.484	11.717	11.941	12.156

Interest Rate 10.00% 30 Year Schedule

Years to Payoff	10%	20%	30%	40%	50%	60%	70%	80%	90%	100%
1.0	10.509	11.016	11.520	12.023	12.523	13.020	13.516	14.009	14.500	14.988
2.0	10.493	10.982	11.467	11.947	12.422	12.893	13.360	13.822	14.280	14.735
3.0	10.478	10.950	11.415	11.873	12.325	12.771	13.212	13.646	14.075	14.498
4.0	10.463	10.918	11.364	11.802	12.232	12.655	13.071	13.479	13.881	14.276
5.0	10.448	10.886	11.315	11.733	12.143	12.544	12.937	13.321	13.699	14.068
7.5	10.412	10.811	11.197	11.572	11.935	12.287	12.629	12.963	13.287	13.603
10.0	10.378	10.741	11.089	11.423	11.746	12.057	12.357	12.647	12.929	13.201
12.5	10.346	10.675	10.988	11.288	11.575	11.850	12.115	12.369	12.615	12.852
15.0	10.315	10.613	10.896	11.164	11.420	11.664	11.899	12.123	12.339	12.547

Interest Rate 10.50% 30 Year Schedule

Years to Payoff	10%	20%	30%	40%	50%	60%	70%	80%	90%	100%
1.0	11.008	11.513	12.017	12.518	13.016	13.513	14.007	14.499	14.988	15.476
2.0	10.991	11.477	11.959	12.436	12.909	13.378	13.842	14.302	14.758	15.210
3.0	10.974	11.442	11.903	12.358	12.806	13.249	13.686	14.117	14.542	14.962
4.0	10.958	11.407	11.849	12.282	12.708	13.126	13.537	13.942	14.339	14.731
5.0	10.942	11.374	11.796	12.209	12.613	13.009	13.397	13.776	14.149	14.514
7.5	10.903	11.293	11.671	12.038	12.393	12.739	13.075	13.402	13.720	14.030
10.0	10.866	11.218	11.556	11.882	12.195	12.498	12.791	13.074	13.348	13.615
12.5	10.832	11.148	11.451	11.740	12.017	12.283	12.540	12.786	13.025	13.255
15.0	10.800	11.084	11.354	11.611	11.857	12.091	12.317	12.533	12.741	12.942

Interest Rate 11.00% 30 Year Schedule

Years to Payoff	10%	20%	30%	40%	50%	60%	70%	80%	90%	100%
1.0	11.506	12.011	12.513	13.013	13.510	14.005	14.498	14.989	15.477	15.964
2.0	11.488	11.972	12.451	12.926	13.396	13.863	14.324	14.782	15.236	15.685
3.0	11.470	11.934	12.392	12.843	13.288	13.727	14.160	14.588	15.010	15.427
4.0	11.453	11.897	12.334	12.762	13.184	13.598	14.005	14.405	14.798	15.186
5.0	11.435	11.861	12.278	12.685	13.084	13.475	13.857	14.232	14.600	14.961
7.5	11.394	11.776	12.146	12.505	12.853	13.192	13.521	13.842	14.154	14.459
10.0	11.355	11.697	12.025	12.341	12.646	12.941	13.227	13.503	13.770	14.030
12.5	11.319	11.623	11.915	12.194	12.461	12.719	12.967	13.206	13.437	13.661
15.0	11.285	11.556	11.814	12.060	12.296	12.521	12.738	12.946	13.147	13.341

Entry is annual percentage yield from interest plus selected share of price appreciation.

Yield on Shared Appreciation Mortgage

Growth Rate 4%   Loan to Value Ratio 75%
Interest Rate 11.50% 30 Year Schedule

Years to Payoff	10%	20%	30%	Share of Profit on Sale 40%	50%	60%	70%	80%	90%	100%
1.0	12.005	12.508	13.009	13.508	14.004	14.498	14.989	15.479	15.966	16.451
2.0	11.985	12.467	12.944	13.416	13.884	14.348	14.807	15.262	15.714	16.161
3.0	11.966	12.426	12.880	13.328	13.769	14.205	14.635	15.059	15.478	15.892
4.0	11.947	12.387	12.819	13.243	13.660	14.069	14.472	14.868	15.258	15.641
5.0	11.929	12.349	12.760	13.162	13.555	13.941	14.318	14.689	15.052	15.408
7.5	11.885	12.259	12.621	12.973	13.314	13.646	13.969	14.284	14.590	14.889
10.0	11.844	12.176	12.495	12.802	13.099	13.386	13.664	13.933	14.194	14.448
12.5	11.806	12.099	12.380	12.649	12.908	13.157	13.397	13.629	13.853	14.070
15.0	11.771	12.030	12.276	12.512	12.737	12.954	13.162	13.363	13.556	13.743

Interest Rate 12.00% 30 Year Schedule

Years to Payoff	10%	20%	30%	40%	50%	60%	70%	80%	90%	100%
1.0	12.504	13.006	13.505	14.003	14.498	14.990	15.481	15.969	16.455	16.939
2.0	12.483	12.962	13.436	13.906	14.371	14.833	15.290	15.743	16.192	16.637
3.0	12.462	12.919	13.369	13.813	14.251	14.683	15.110	15.531	15.947	16.358
4.0	12.442	12.877	13.304	13.724	14.136	14.542	14.940	15.333	15.718	16.098
5.0	12.423	12.837	13.242	13.639	14.027	14.407	14.780	15.146	15.505	15.856
7.5	12.377	12.742	13.097	13.441	13.776	14.101	14.418	14.727	15.028	15.321
10.0	12.334	12.655	12.965	13.264	13.553	13.832	14.103	14.366	14.620	14.868
12.5	12.294	12.576	12.846	13.106	13.356	13.597	13.829	14.053	14.271	14.481
15.0	12.258	12.505	12.740	12.965	13.182	13.389	13.589	13.782	13.969	14.149

Interest Rate 12.50% 30 Year Schedule

Years to Payoff	10%	20%	30%	40%	50%	60%	70%	80%	90%	100%
1.0	13.003	13.503	14.002	14.498	14.991	15.483	15.972	16.459	16.944	17.427
2.0	12.980	13.457	13.928	14.396	14.859	15.318	15.773	16.224	16.671	17.114
3.0	12.959	13.411	13.858	14.299	14.733	15.162	15.586	16.003	16.416	16.824
4.0	12.938	13.368	13.790	14.205	14.613	15.015	15.409	15.797	16.179	16.555
5.0	12.917	13.325	13.725	14.116	14.499	14.875	15.243	15.604	15.958	16.306
7.5	12.868	13.226	13.573	13.910	14.238	14.557	14.868	15.171	15.466	15.754
10.0	12.824	13.136	13.436	13.727	14.008	14.280	14.544	14.800	15.048	15.290
12.5	12.783	13.054	13.314	13.565	13.806	14.038	14.263	14.481	14.691	14.895
15.0	12.746	12.980	13.205	13.421	13.628	13.827	14.019	14.205	14.384	14.558

Interest Rate 13.00% 30 Year Schedule

Years to Payoff	10%	20%	30%	40%	50%	60%	70%	80%	90%	100%
1.0	13.501	14.001	14.498	14.993	15.485	15.976	16.464	16.950	17.434	17.915
2.0	13.478	13.952	14.421	14.886	15.347	15.804	16.256	16.705	17.149	17.590
3.0	13.455	13.904	14.347	14.784	15.215	15.641	16.061	16.476	16.886	17.290
4.0	13.433	13.858	14.276	14.687	15.091	15.488	15.878	16.262	16.641	17.013
5.0	13.411	13.814	14.208	14.594	14.972	15.343	15.706	16.062	16.412	16.756
7.5	13.360	13.710	14.050	14.380	14.702	15.014	15.319	15.616	15.906	16.189
10.0	13.314	13.616	13.909	14.191	14.465	14.729	14.986	15.236	15.478	15.714
12.5	13.271	13.532	13.783	14.025	14.257	14.482	14.700	14.910	15.114	15.312
15.0	13.234	13.457	13.672	13.878	14.077	14.268	14.452	14.630	14.803	14.970

Interest Rate 13.50% 30 Year Schedule

Years to Payoff	10%	20%	30%	40%	50%	60%	70%	80%	90%	100%
1.0	14.000	14.498	14.994	15.488	15.979	16.468	16.955	17.440	17.923	18.403
2.0	13.975	14.447	14.914	15.376	15.835	16.289	16.740	17.186	17.628	18.067
3.0	13.951	14.397	14.836	15.270	15.698	16.120	16.537	16.949	17.356	17.757
4.0	13.928	14.349	14.762	15.169	15.568	15.961	16.348	16.728	17.102	17.471
5.0	13.905	14.303	14.691	15.072	15.445	15.811	16.170	16.522	16.867	17.206
7.5	13.852	14.195	14.527	14.851	15.166	15.472	15.771	16.063	16.347	16.625
10.0	13.804	14.098	14.382	14.656	14.922	15.180	15.430	15.673	15.910	16.140
12.5	13.761	14.012	14.253	14.486	14.711	14.928	15.138	15.342	15.539	15.731
15.0	13.722	13.935	14.140	14.337	14.527	14.710	14.888	15.059	15.225	15.386

Interest Rate 14.00% 30 Year Schedule

Years to Payoff	10%	20%	30%	40%	50%	60%	70%	80%	90%	100%
1.0	14.499	14.996	15.491	15.983	16.473	16.961	17.447	17.931	18.412	18.892
2.0	14.473	14.942	15.406	15.867	16.323	16.775	17.223	17.667	18.108	18.544
3.0	14.448	14.890	15.326	15.756	16.181	16.600	17.014	17.422	17.826	18.224
4.0	14.423	14.840	15.249	15.651	16.046	16.435	16.818	17.194	17.565	17.930
5.0	14.400	14.791	15.175	15.551	15.919	16.280	16.634	16.981	17.323	17.658
7.5	14.344	14.680	15.005	15.322	15.631	15.931	16.224	16.510	16.789	17.062
10.0	14.295	14.580	14.855	15.122	15.381	15.632	15.876	16.112	16.343	16.567
12.5	14.250	14.492	14.724	14.949	15.165	15.375	15.579	15.776	15.967	16.153
15.0	14.211	14.414	14.610	14.798	14.980	15.156	15.325	15.490	15.649	15.804

Entry is annual percentage yield from interest plus selected share of price appreciation.

Yield on Shared Appreciation Mortgage

Growth Rate 5%   Loan to Value Ratio 67%
Interest Rate 5.50% 30 Year Schedule

Years to Payoff	10%	20%	30%	Share of Profit on Sale 40%	50%	60%	70%	80%	90%	100%
1.0	6.233	6.961	7.685	8.403	9.117	9.826	10.531	11.231	11.927	12.618
2.0	6.233	6.955	7.668	8.371	9.065	9.749	10.424	11.091	11.749	12.399
3.0	6.233	6.950	7.652	8.340	9.014	9.674	10.322	10.957	11.581	12.193
4.0	6.233	6.944	7.636	8.309	8.964	9.602	10.223	10.830	11.422	12.000
5.0	6.233	6.939	7.620	8.278	8.915	9.531	10.129	10.708	11.271	11.819
7.5	6.233	6.925	7.581	8.204	8.798	9.365	9.908	10.428	10.928	11.409
10.0	6.233	6.911	7.542	8.133	8.688	9.211	9.707	10.177	10.624	11.051
12.5	6.233	6.897	7.505	8.065	8.584	9.069	9.523	9.950	10.354	10.737
15.0	6.234	6.884	7.469	8.000	8.487	8.937	9.355	9.746	10.112	10.458

Interest Rate 6.00% 30 Year Schedule

1.0	6.731	7.457	8.178	8.895	9.607	10.314	11.017	11.715	12.409	13.098
2.0	6.728	7.447	8.155	8.854	9.544	10.224	10.896	11.559	12.213	12.859
3.0	6.726	7.437	8.133	8.815	9.483	10.138	10.780	11.410	12.029	12.636
4.0	6.724	7.427	8.110	8.775	9.423	10.054	10.669	11.269	11.855	12.427
5.0	6.721	7.417	8.088	8.737	9.365	9.973	10.563	11.135	11.691	12.231
7.5	6.715	7.392	8.034	8.644	9.226	9.783	10.315	10.826	11.317	11.790
10.0	6.709	7.368	7.981	8.556	9.097	9.608	10.091	10.551	10.989	11.407
12.5	6.704	7.343	7.930	8.472	8.976	9.446	9.888	10.305	10.698	11.072
15.0	6.698	7.320	7.881	8.392	8.863	9.298	9.703	10.082	10.439	10.775

Interest Rate 6.50% 30 Year Schedule

1.0	7.229	7.953	8.672	9.387	10.097	10.802	11.503	12.200	12.891	13.579
2.0	7.224	7.938	8.643	9.338	10.024	10.700	11.368	12.027	12.678	13.321
3.0	7.219	7.924	8.614	9.290	9.952	10.602	11.239	11.864	12.478	13.081
4.0	7.215	7.910	8.585	9.243	9.883	10.507	11.116	11.710	12.290	12.856
5.0	7.210	7.895	8.557	9.197	9.816	10.416	10.998	11.563	12.112	12.646
7.5	7.199	7.860	8.488	9.086	9.657	10.202	10.725	11.227	11.710	12.175
10.0	7.187	7.826	8.422	8.982	9.509	10.007	10.480	10.929	11.358	11.768
12.5	7.176	7.792	8.358	8.883	9.371	9.828	10.258	10.663	11.047	11.412
15.0	7.164	7.759	8.297	8.790	9.243	9.664	10.057	10.425	10.771	11.099

Interest Rate 7.00% 30 Year Schedule

1.0	7.727	8.449	9.166	9.879	10.587	11.291	11.990	12.684	13.374	14.060
2.0	7.720	8.430	9.131	9.822	10.504	11.176	11.841	12.496	13.144	13.783
3.0	7.713	8.411	9.095	9.766	10.423	11.067	11.699	12.319	12.928	13.526
4.0	7.706	8.393	9.061	9.711	10.344	10.962	11.564	12.152	12.726	13.287
5.0	7.699	8.375	9.027	9.658	10.268	10.861	11.435	11.993	12.535	13.063
7.5	7.682	8.329	8.944	9.530	10.089	10.624	11.138	11.631	12.105	12.562
10.0	7.665	8.285	8.865	9.410	9.923	10.410	10.872	11.311	11.730	12.132
12.5	7.649	8.242	8.789	9.297	9.770	10.214	10.632	11.027	11.401	11.757
15.0	7.632	8.201	8.717	9.191	9.629	10.035	10.416	10.773	11.109	11.428

Interest Rate 7.50% 30 Year Schedule

1.0	8.225	8.945	9.660	10.371	11.077	11.779	12.476	13.169	13.857	14.541
2.0	8.216	8.922	9.619	10.306	10.984	11.653	12.314	12.966	13.610	14.246
3.0	8.207	8.899	9.577	10.242	10.894	11.533	12.160	12.775	13.379	13.973
4.0	8.198	8.877	9.537	10.180	10.806	11.417	12.013	12.595	13.163	13.718
5.0	8.189	8.854	9.497	10.119	10.722	11.306	11.873	12.424	12.960	13.481
7.5	8.167	8.799	9.401	9.975	10.523	11.049	11.552	12.037	12.503	12.953
10.0	8.145	8.746	9.310	9.840	10.341	10.816	11.267	11.696	12.107	12.499
12.5	8.123	8.695	9.223	9.714	10.173	10.604	11.010	11.395	11.759	12.106
15.0	8.102	8.645	9.141	9.597	10.019	10.412	10.780	11.126	11.453	11.762

Interest Rate 8.00% 30 Year Schedule

1.0	8.723	9.441	10.155	10.864	11.568	12.268	12.963	13.654	14.341	15.023
2.0	8.712	9.414	10.107	10.790	11.465	12.130	12.787	13.436	14.077	14.710
3.0	8.701	9.387	10.060	10.719	11.365	11.999	12.621	13.232	13.831	14.420
4.0	8.690	9.361	10.013	10.649	11.269	11.873	12.463	13.039	13.602	14.151
5.0	8.679	9.334	9.968	10.582	11.176	11.753	12.313	12.857	13.386	13.901
7.5	8.651	9.270	9.859	10.422	10.959	11.475	11.969	12.445	12.903	13.345
10.0	8.625	9.209	9.757	10.273	10.761	11.224	11.665	12.085	12.486	12.871
12.5	8.598	9.149	9.659	10.135	10.579	10.998	11.393	11.767	12.122	12.460
15.0	8.573	9.092	9.568	10.006	10.413	10.793	11.149	11.484	11.801	12.102

Entry is annual percentage yield from interest plus selected share of price appreciation.

Yield on Shared Appreciation Mortgage

Growth Rate 5%   Loan to Value Ratio 67%
Interest Rate 8.50% 30 Year Schedule

Years to Payoff	10%	20%	30%	Share of Profit on Sale 40%	50%	60%	70%	80%	90%	100%
1.0	9.221	9.937	10.649	11.356	12.059	12.757	13.450	14.139	14.824	15.505
2.0	9.208	9.906	10.595	11.275	11.946	12.608	13.261	13.907	14.544	15.174
3.0	9.195	9.875	10.542	11.196	11.837	12.466	13.083	13.689	14.284	14.869
4.0	9.182	9.845	10.490	11.119	11.732	12.330	12.914	13.484	14.041	14.586
5.0	9.169	9.815	10.440	11.045	11.632	12.201	12.754	13.291	13.814	14.323
7.5	9.137	9.742	10.319	10.870	11.397	11.903	12.388	12.856	13.306	13.741
10.0	9.105	9.672	10.205	10.708	11.183	11.635	12.066	12.476	12.869	13.245
12.5	9.075	9.606	10.098	10.558	10.989	11.395	11.779	12.143	12.489	12.819
15.0	9.045	9.542	9.998	10.419	10.811	11.178	11.522	11.847	12.155	12.447

Interest Rate 9.00% 30 Year Schedule

Years to Payoff	10%	20%	30%	40%	50%	60%	70%	80%	90%	100%
1.0	9.719	10.433	11.143	11.849	12.549	13.246	13.937	14.625	15.308	15.987
2.0	9.704	10.398	11.083	11.760	12.427	13.086	13.736	14.378	15.012	15.639
3.0	9.689	10.364	11.025	11.673	12.309	12.933	13.546	14.147	14.738	15.318
4.0	9.674	10.329	10.968	11.590	12.197	12.788	13.366	13.930	14.482	15.021
5.0	9.659	10.296	10.912	11.509	12.088	12.650	13.196	13.727	14.243	14.746
7.5	9.622	10.215	10.779	11.319	11.836	12.333	12.809	13.269	13.711	14.139
10.0	9.587	10.137	10.655	11.145	11.608	12.049	12.469	12.871	13.255	13.623
12.5	9.552	10.064	10.539	10.984	11.401	11.795	12.168	12.522	12.859	13.181
15.0	9.519	9.994	10.431	10.836	11.214	11.567	11.901	12.215	12.514	12.797

Interest Rate 9.50% 30 Year Schedule

Years to Payoff	10%	20%	30%	40%	50%	60%	70%	80%	90%	100%
1.0	10.217	10.930	11.638	12.341	13.040	13.735	14.425	15.110	15.792	16.469
2.0	10.200	10.891	11.572	12.245	12.908	13.564	14.211	14.849	15.480	16.104
3.0	10.183	10.852	11.508	12.151	12.782	13.401	14.009	14.606	15.192	15.768
4.0	10.166	10.814	11.446	12.061	12.661	13.247	13.819	14.378	14.924	15.458
5.0	10.149	10.777	11.385	11.974	12.546	13.100	13.640	14.164	14.674	15.171
7.5	10.108	10.688	11.241	11.770	12.277	12.764	13.232	13.683	14.118	14.539
10.0	10.069	10.603	11.107	11.583	12.035	12.465	12.876	13.268	13.644	14.005
12.5	10.031	10.523	10.982	11.412	11.817	12.199	12.562	12.906	13.234	13.547
15.0	9.994	10.448	10.867	11.256	11.620	11.961	12.283	12.588	12.877	13.152

Interest Rate 10.00% 30 Year Schedule

Years to Payoff	10%	20%	30%	40%	50%	60%	70%	80%	90%	100%
1.0	10.715	11.426	12.132	12.834	13.531	14.224	14.912	15.596	16.276	16.951
2.0	10.696	11.383	12.061	12.730	13.390	14.042	14.686	15.321	15.949	16.569
3.0	10.677	11.341	11.992	12.630	13.256	13.870	14.473	15.065	15.647	16.219
4.0	10.658	11.300	11.924	12.533	13.127	13.707	14.273	14.826	15.367	15.896
5.0	10.640	11.259	11.859	12.440	13.004	13.552	14.084	14.602	15.106	15.597
7.5	10.595	11.162	11.704	12.222	12.719	13.197	13.657	14.100	14.528	14.941
10.0	10.551	11.070	11.560	12.024	12.464	12.884	13.285	13.668	14.036	14.389
12.5	10.510	10.984	11.428	11.843	12.235	12.606	12.958	13.293	13.612	13.918
15.0	10.471	10.904	11.305	11.679	12.029	12.359	12.670	12.965	13.245	13.511

Interest Rate 10.50% 30 Year Schedule

Years to Payoff	10%	20%	30%	40%	50%	60%	70%	80%	90%	100%
1.0	11.213	11.922	12.627	13.327	14.022	14.713	15.400	16.082	16.760	17.434
2.0	11.192	11.876	12.550	13.215	13.872	14.521	15.161	15.794	16.418	17.035
3.0	11.171	11.830	12.475	13.108	13.729	14.339	14.937	15.525	16.103	16.670
4.0	11.151	11.785	12.403	13.005	13.593	14.167	14.727	15.275	15.810	16.335
5.0	11.131	11.741	12.333	12.906	13.463	14.004	14.529	15.041	15.539	16.025
7.5	11.082	11.637	12.167	12.675	13.163	13.632	14.083	14.519	14.939	15.345
10.0	11.035	11.539	12.015	12.466	12.896	13.305	13.696	14.071	14.430	14.776
12.5	10.990	11.447	11.875	12.277	12.657	13.016	13.358	13.683	13.994	14.292
15.0	10.948	11.362	11.747	12.106	12.443	12.760	13.061	13.346	13.617	13.876

Interest Rate 11.00% 30 Year Schedule

Years to Payoff	10%	20%	30%	40%	50%	60%	70%	80%	90%	100%
1.0	11.711	12.419	13.122	13.820	14.513	15.203	15.888	16.568	17.245	17.917
2.0	11.689	12.368	13.039	13.701	14.355	15.000	15.637	16.266	16.888	17.502
3.0	11.666	12.319	12.959	13.587	14.203	14.808	15.402	15.986	16.559	17.123
4.0	11.644	12.271	12.882	13.478	14.060	14.627	15.182	15.725	16.255	16.774
5.0	11.622	12.224	12.807	13.373	13.923	14.456	14.976	15.481	15.973	16.453
7.5	11.569	12.112	12.632	13.130	13.608	14.068	14.511	14.939	15.352	15.751
10.0	11.518	12.008	12.471	12.910	13.329	13.728	14.110	14.476	14.827	15.165
12.5	11.471	11.911	12.324	12.713	13.080	13.429	13.761	14.077	14.379	14.669
15.0	11.427	11.822	12.190	12.535	12.859	13.165	13.455	13.731	13.993	14.244

Entry is annual percentage yield from interest plus selected share of price appreciation.

Yield on Shared Appreciation Mortgage

Growth Rate 5%   Loan to Value Ratio 67%
Interest Rate 11.50% 30 Year Schedule

Years to Payoff	10%	20%	30%	Share of Profit on Sale 40%	50%	60%	70%	80%	90%	100%
1.0	12.210	12.915	13.616	14.313	15.005	15.692	16.376	17.055	17.729	18.400
2.0	12.185	12.861	13.528	14.187	14.837	15.479	16.113	16.739	17.358	17.969
3.0	12.160	12.808	13.443	14.066	14.678	15.278	15.868	16.447	17.016	17.575
4.0	12.136	12.757	13.361	13.951	14.527	15.089	15.638	16.175	16.701	17.215
5.0	12.113	12.707	13.282	13.841	14.383	14.910	15.423	15.922	16.409	16.883
7.5	12.056	12.588	13.097	13.585	14.054	14.505	14.941	15.361	15.767	16.160
10.0	12.003	12.478	12.928	13.356	13.764	14.153	14.526	14.883	15.227	15.558
12.5	11.953	12.376	12.775	13.151	13.507	13.844	14.166	14.474	14.768	15.050
15.0	11.906	12.284	12.636	12.967	13.279	13.574	13.853	14.120	14.374	14.616

Interest Rate 12.00% 30 Year Schedule

Years to Payoff	10%	20%	30%	40%	50%	60%	70%	80%	90%	100%
1.0	12.708	13.412	14.111	14.806	15.496	16.182	16.864	17.541	18.214	18.883
2.0	12.681	13.354	14.018	14.673	15.320	15.959	16.589	17.212	17.828	18.436
3.0	12.655	13.298	13.928	14.546	15.153	15.749	16.334	16.908	17.473	18.029
4.0	12.629	13.243	13.841	14.425	14.994	15.551	16.095	16.627	17.147	17.656
5.0	12.604	13.190	13.758	14.309	14.844	15.365	15.871	16.364	16.845	17.314
7.5	12.544	13.064	13.563	14.041	14.501	14.944	15.372	15.784	16.183	16.570
10.0	12.487	12.949	13.386	13.803	14.200	14.580	14.944	15.293	15.629	15.952
12.5	12.435	12.843	13.228	13.591	13.935	14.263	14.575	14.874	15.159	15.434
15.0	12.387	12.747	13.085	13.402	13.702	13.985	14.255	14.512	14.758	14.993

Interest Rate 12.50% 30 Year Schedule

Years to Payoff	10%	20%	30%	40%	50%	60%	70%	80%	90%	100%
1.0	13.206	13.908	14.606	15.299	15.988	16.672	17.352	18.028	18.699	19.366
2.0	13.178	13.847	14.507	15.159	15.803	16.438	17.066	17.686	18.299	18.904
3.0	13.150	13.787	14.412	15.026	15.628	16.219	16.800	17.371	17.931	18.483
4.0	13.122	13.729	14.321	14.899	15.462	16.013	16.552	17.078	17.594	18.098
5.0	13.096	13.673	14.233	14.777	15.306	15.820	16.320	16.808	17.283	17.746
7.5	13.032	13.541	14.030	14.499	14.950	15.384	15.804	16.209	16.601	16.981
10.0	12.973	13.421	13.846	14.251	14.639	15.009	15.364	15.705	16.033	16.350
12.5	12.918	13.311	13.682	14.033	14.366	14.683	14.986	15.276	15.554	15.821
15.0	12.868	13.212	13.535	13.839	14.127	14.401	14.661	14.909	15.146	15.374

Interest Rate 13.00% 30 Year Schedule

Years to Payoff	10%	20%	30%	40%	50%	60%	70%	80%	90%	100%
1.0	13.704	14.405	15.101	15.792	16.479	17.162	17.840	18.514	19.184	19.850
2.0	13.674	14.340	14.997	15.645	16.286	16.918	17.543	18.160	18.769	19.372
3.0	13.644	14.277	14.897	15.506	16.103	16.690	17.267	17.833	18.390	18.937
4.0	13.615	14.216	14.801	15.373	15.931	16.476	17.010	17.531	18.042	18.541
5.0	13.587	14.157	14.710	15.246	15.768	16.276	16.770	17.251	17.721	18.179
7.5	13.520	14.019	14.497	14.957	15.399	15.826	16.238	16.636	17.021	17.395
10.0	13.458	13.893	14.307	14.701	15.078	15.440	15.786	16.119	16.440	16.750
12.5	13.402	13.780	14.138	14.477	14.799	15.107	15.400	15.682	15.952	16.212
15.0	13.350	13.679	13.987	14.279	14.556	14.819	15.069	15.309	15.538	15.758

Interest Rate 13.50% 30 Year Schedule

Years to Payoff	10%	20%	30%	40%	50%	60%	70%	80%	90%	100%
1.0	14.203	14.901	15.596	16.285	16.971	17.652	18.328	19.001	19.669	20.334
2.0	14.171	14.833	15.487	16.132	16.769	17.398	18.020	18.634	19.240	19.840
3.0	14.139	14.767	15.382	15.986	16.579	17.161	17.734	18.296	18.849	19.392
4.0	14.109	14.703	15.282	15.848	16.400	16.940	17.468	17.984	18.490	18.985
5.0	14.079	14.641	15.186	15.716	16.231	16.732	17.220	17.696	18.160	18.613
7.5	14.009	14.497	14.965	15.416	15.850	16.268	16.673	17.064	17.442	17.809
10.0	13.944	14.367	14.769	15.153	15.520	15.872	16.210	16.536	16.849	17.151
12.5	13.886	14.250	14.595	14.923	15.234	15.532	15.817	16.090	16.353	16.605
15.0	13.833	14.146	14.442	14.722	14.987	15.240	15.481	15.712	15.934	16.146

Interest Rate 14.00% 30 Year Schedule

Years to Payoff	10%	20%	30%	40%	50%	60%	70%	80%	90%	100%
1.0	14.701	15.398	16.090	16.779	17.462	18.142	18.817	19.488	20.155	20.817
2.0	14.667	15.326	15.976	16.618	17.252	17.879	18.497	19.108	19.712	20.309
3.0	14.634	15.256	15.867	16.467	17.055	17.633	18.201	18.759	19.308	19.848
4.0	14.602	15.190	15.763	16.323	16.869	17.404	17.927	18.438	18.939	19.429
5.0	14.571	15.125	15.663	16.186	16.695	17.190	17.672	18.142	18.600	19.048
7.5	14.498	14.975	15.434	15.876	16.301	16.712	17.109	17.493	17.865	18.226
10.0	14.431	14.841	15.232	15.605	15.963	16.306	16.636	16.954	17.260	17.556
12.5	14.371	14.721	15.054	15.370	15.672	15.960	16.236	16.501	16.756	17.001
15.0	14.317	14.616	14.898	15.166	15.421	15.664	15.896	16.119	16.333	16.538

Entry is annual percentage yield from interest plus selected share of price appreciation.

Yield on Shared Appreciation Mortgage

Growth Rate 5%   Loan to Value Ratio 75%
Interest Rate 5.50% 30 Year Schedule

Years to Payoff	Share of Profit on Sale									
	10%	20%	30%	40%	50%	60%	70%	80%	90%	100%
1.0	6.152	6.800	7.444	8.084	8.721	9.354	9.983	10.609	11.231	11.850
2.0	6.152	6.796	7.432	8.060	8.681	9.294	9.900	10.499	11.091	11.676
3.0	6.152	6.792	7.420	8.036	8.641	9.235	9.819	10.393	10.957	11.512
4.0	6.152	6.788	7.408	8.012	8.602	9.178	9.741	10.291	10.830	11.357
5.0	6.152	6.784	7.396	7.988	8.564	9.123	9.666	10.194	10.708	11.210
7.5	6.153	6.774	7.366	7.931	8.471	8.990	9.488	9.967	10.428	10.873
10.0	6.154	6.765	7.337	7.875	8.384	8.866	9.324	9.760	10.177	10.576
12.5	6.155	6.755	7.308	7.821	8.300	8.749	9.172	9.572	9.950	10.310
15.0	6.156	6.746	7.280	7.770	8.221	8.641	9.032	9.400	9.746	10.073

Interest Rate 6.00% 30 Year Schedule

1.0	6.650	7.296	7.938	8.577	9.212	9.843	10.471	11.095	11.715	12.332
2.0	6.648	7.288	7.920	8.545	9.162	9.772	10.374	10.970	11.559	12.141
3.0	6.646	7.280	7.902	8.513	9.113	9.702	10.281	10.851	11.410	11.961
4.0	6.644	7.272	7.885	8.482	9.065	9.635	10.192	10.736	11.269	11.791
5.0	6.642	7.264	7.867	8.451	9.019	9.570	10.106	10.627	11.135	11.630
7.5	6.638	7.245	7.824	8.377	8.906	9.414	9.903	10.373	10.826	11.264
10.0	6.633	7.225	7.781	8.305	8.800	9.270	9.717	10.144	10.551	10.942
12.5	6.629	7.206	7.740	8.236	8.700	9.136	9.547	9.936	10.305	10.656
15.0	6.624	7.187	7.700	8.171	8.606	9.011	9.390	9.746	10.082	10.400

Interest Rate 6.50% 30 Year Schedule

1.0	7.148	7.792	8.433	9.070	9.703	10.333	10.959	11.581	12.200	12.815
2.0	7.144	7.780	8.409	9.030	9.644	10.250	10.849	11.442	12.027	12.606
3.0	7.140	7.769	8.386	8.991	9.586	10.170	10.745	11.309	11.864	12.410
4.0	7.136	7.757	8.362	8.953	9.529	10.093	10.644	11.183	11.710	12.226
5.0	7.132	7.745	8.339	8.915	9.475	10.018	10.547	11.062	11.563	12.052
7.5	7.123	7.716	8.282	8.824	9.343	9.841	10.320	10.782	11.227	11.657
10.0	7.113	7.688	8.228	8.737	9.220	9.678	10.114	10.531	10.929	11.311
12.5	7.104	7.659	8.175	8.654	9.104	9.527	9.926	10.304	10.663	11.006
15.0	7.094	7.632	8.123	8.576	8.996	9.387	9.754	10.099	10.425	10.734

Interest Rate 7.00% 30 Year Schedule

1.0	7.646	8.289	8.928	9.563	10.194	10.822	11.446	12.067	12.684	13.298
2.0	7.640	8.273	8.898	9.516	10.126	10.729	11.325	11.914	12.496	13.072
3.0	7.634	8.257	8.869	9.469	10.059	10.639	11.208	11.768	12.319	12.861
4.0	7.629	8.242	8.840	9.424	9.994	10.552	11.097	11.630	12.152	12.663
5.0	7.623	8.227	8.812	9.380	9.931	10.468	10.990	11.498	11.993	12.476
7.5	7.608	8.188	8.743	9.273	9.781	10.270	10.740	11.193	11.631	12.053
10.0	7.594	8.151	8.676	9.172	9.642	10.089	10.514	10.921	11.311	11.685
12.5	7.579	8.115	8.612	9.076	9.511	9.921	10.309	10.677	11.027	11.360
15.0	7.565	8.079	8.550	8.985	9.390	9.767	10.122	10.456	10.773	11.073

Interest Rate 7.50% 30 Year Schedule

1.0	8.144	8.785	9.422	10.056	10.686	11.312	11.934	12.553	13.169	13.781
2.0	8.137	8.766	9.387	10.001	10.608	11.208	11.801	12.387	12.966	13.539
3.0	8.129	8.746	9.353	9.948	10.533	11.108	11.673	12.229	12.775	13.313
4.0	8.121	8.727	9.319	9.896	10.460	11.012	11.551	12.078	12.595	13.100
5.0	8.113	8.708	9.285	9.845	10.389	10.919	11.434	11.935	12.424	12.901
7.5	8.094	8.662	9.204	9.723	10.222	10.701	11.162	11.607	12.037	12.452
10.0	8.075	8.616	9.126	9.608	10.066	10.502	10.918	11.315	11.696	12.062
12.5	8.056	8.572	9.051	9.500	9.922	10.320	10.696	11.054	11.395	11.720
15.0	8.038	8.529	8.980	9.398	9.788	10.153	10.496	10.819	11.126	11.417

Interest Rate 8.00% 30 Year Schedule

1.0	8.643	9.282	9.917	10.549	11.177	11.802	12.423	13.040	13.654	14.264
2.0	8.633	9.259	9.877	10.487	11.091	11.687	12.277	12.860	13.436	14.006
3.0	8.623	9.236	9.837	10.427	11.007	11.578	12.138	12.689	13.232	13.765
4.0	8.614	9.213	9.798	10.369	10.927	11.472	12.006	12.528	13.039	13.540
5.0	8.604	9.191	9.759	10.312	10.848	11.371	11.879	12.374	12.857	13.328
7.5	8.581	9.135	9.666	10.175	10.664	11.134	11.586	12.023	12.445	12.853
10.0	8.557	9.082	9.578	10.047	10.493	10.918	11.324	11.712	12.085	12.442
12.5	8.534	9.031	9.493	9.927	10.336	10.722	11.087	11.435	11.767	12.083
15.0	8.512	8.981	9.414	9.815	10.190	10.542	10.874	11.187	11.484	11.767

Entry is annual percentage yield from interest plus selected share of price appreciation.

Yield on Shared Appreciation Mortgage

Growth Rate 5%
Interest Rate 8.50% 30 Year Schedule

Loan to Value Ratio 75%

Years to Payoff	10%	20%	30%	Share of Profit on Sale 40%	50%	60%	70%	80%	90%	100%
1.0	9.141	9.778	10.412	11.042	11.669	12.292	12.911	13.527	14.139	14.748
2.0	9.129	9.752	10.366	10.974	11.574	12.167	12.754	13.334	13.907	14.474
3.0	9.118	9.725	10.321	10.907	11.482	12.048	12.604	13.151	13.689	14.218
4.0	9.107	9.699	10.277	10.842	11.394	11.933	12.461	12.978	13.484	13.980
5.0	9.095	9.673	10.234	10.779	11.308	11.824	12.325	12.815	13.291	13.757
7.5	9.067	9.610	10.130	10.628	11.107	11.568	12.012	12.441	12.856	13.257
10.0	9.040	9.549	10.031	10.488	10.922	11.337	11.733	12.112	12.476	12.826
12.5	9.013	9.491	9.938	10.357	10.753	11.127	11.482	11.820	12.143	12.451
15.0	8.987	9.435	9.850	10.236	10.597	10.936	11.256	11.560	11.847	12.122

Interest Rate 9.00% 30 Year Schedule

Years to Payoff	10%	20%	30%	40%	50%	60%	70%	80%	90%	100%
1.0	9.639	10.275	10.907	11.536	12.161	12.782	13.400	14.014	14.625	15.232
2.0	9.626	10.245	10.856	11.460	12.057	12.647	13.231	13.808	14.378	14.942
3.0	9.613	10.215	10.806	11.387	11.958	12.519	13.070	13.613	14.147	14.673
4.0	9.600	10.185	10.757	11.316	11.862	12.396	12.918	13.429	13.930	14.421
5.0	9.587	10.156	10.709	11.246	11.769	12.278	12.773	13.256	13.727	14.187
7.5	9.555	10.085	10.594	11.082	11.552	12.004	12.440	12.861	13.269	13.663
10.0	9.523	10.018	10.486	10.930	11.354	11.758	12.144	12.515	12.871	13.213
12.5	9.493	9.953	10.384	10.790	11.173	11.535	11.880	12.209	12.522	12.823
15.0	9.464	9.892	10.289	10.659	11.007	11.334	11.643	11.936	12.215	12.481

Interest Rate 9.50% 30 Year Schedule

Years to Payoff	10%	20%	30%	40%	50%	60%	70%	80%	90%	100%
1.0	10.137	10.772	11.402	12.029	12.652	13.272	13.888	14.501	15.110	15.716
2.0	10.122	10.738	11.346	11.947	12.541	13.128	13.708	14.282	14.849	15.411
3.0	10.108	10.705	11.291	11.867	12.433	12.990	13.537	14.076	14.606	15.127
4.0	10.093	10.672	11.237	11.790	12.330	12.858	13.375	13.882	14.378	14.864
5.0	10.078	10.640	11.185	11.715	12.230	12.732	13.222	13.699	14.164	14.618
7.5	10.042	10.562	11.059	11.538	11.998	12.442	12.870	13.283	13.683	14.071
10.0	10.007	10.487	10.942	11.375	11.787	12.181	12.558	12.920	13.268	13.603
12.5	9.974	10.417	10.833	11.225	11.595	11.947	12.281	12.601	12.906	13.198
15.0	9.942	10.350	10.731	11.086	11.420	11.736	12.034	12.318	12.588	12.845

Interest Rate 10.00% 30 Year Schedule

Years to Payoff	10%	20%	30%	40%	50%	60%	70%	80%	90%	100%
1.0	10.636	11.268	11.897	12.523	13.144	13.763	14.377	14.988	15.596	16.201
2.0	10.619	11.231	11.836	12.434	13.024	13.608	14.186	14.757	15.321	15.880
3.0	10.602	11.195	11.776	12.348	12.909	13.462	14.005	14.539	15.065	15.583
4.0	10.586	11.159	11.718	12.264	12.799	13.322	13.834	14.335	14.826	15.307
5.0	10.570	11.123	11.661	12.184	12.693	13.188	13.671	14.142	14.602	15.051
7.5	10.530	11.038	11.526	11.994	12.446	12.881	13.301	13.707	14.100	14.481
10.0	10.492	10.958	11.400	11.821	12.222	12.607	12.975	13.328	13.668	13.995
12.5	10.455	10.882	11.283	11.662	12.020	12.361	12.686	12.996	13.293	13.577
15.0	10.420	10.811	11.175	11.516	11.838	12.141	12.429	12.703	12.965	13.214

Interest Rate 10.50% 30 Year Schedule

Years to Payoff	10%	20%	30%	40%	50%	60%	70%	80%	90%	100%
1.0	11.134	11.765	12.393	13.016	13.636	14.253	14.866	15.476	16.082	16.685
2.0	11.116	11.725	12.326	12.921	13.508	14.089	14.664	15.232	15.794	16.349
3.0	11.097	11.685	12.262	12.828	13.386	13.934	14.473	15.003	15.525	16.039
4.0	11.079	11.646	12.199	12.739	13.268	13.786	14.292	14.789	15.275	15.752
5.0	11.062	11.607	12.138	12.654	13.156	13.645	14.122	14.587	15.041	15.484
7.5	11.018	11.515	11.993	12.452	12.894	13.321	13.734	14.132	14.519	14.893
10.0	10.977	11.429	11.859	12.268	12.660	13.034	13.393	13.738	14.071	14.391
12.5	10.937	11.348	11.735	12.101	12.448	12.779	13.094	13.395	13.683	13.960
15.0	10.900	11.273	11.621	11.949	12.258	12.550	12.828	13.093	13.346	13.587

Interest Rate 11.00% 30 Year Schedule

Years to Payoff	10%	20%	30%	40%	50%	60%	70%	80%	90%	100%
1.0	11.633	12.262	12.888	13.510	14.129	14.744	15.355	15.964	16.568	17.170
2.0	11.612	12.218	12.816	13.408	13.993	14.571	15.142	15.707	16.266	16.819
3.0	11.592	12.175	12.747	13.310	13.863	14.406	14.941	15.468	15.986	16.496
4.0	11.573	12.133	12.680	13.215	13.738	14.250	14.752	15.243	15.725	16.197
5.0	11.554	12.092	12.615	13.124	13.619	14.102	14.573	15.033	15.481	15.919
7.5	11.507	11.993	12.461	12.911	13.345	13.763	14.168	14.559	14.939	15.307
10.0	11.462	11.901	12.319	12.718	13.099	13.464	13.814	14.151	14.476	14.789
12.5	11.420	11.816	12.189	12.543	12.879	13.199	13.504	13.796	14.077	14.346
15.0	11.381	11.737	12.070	12.384	12.681	12.963	13.231	13.486	13.731	13.965

Entry is annual percentage yield from interest plus selected share of price appreciation.

Yield on Shared Appreciation Mortgage

Growth Rate 5%   Loan to Value Ratio 75%
Interest Rate 11.50% 30 Year Schedule

Years to Payoff	10%	20%	30%	Share of Profit on Sale 40%	50%	60%	70%	80%	90%	100%
1.0	12.131	12.759	13.383	14.004	14.621	15.234	15.845	16.451	17.055	17.655
2.0	12.109	12.712	13.307	13.895	14.477	15.052	15.621	16.183	16.739	17.289
3.0	12.088	12.665	13.233	13.791	14.340	14.879	15.410	15.933	16.447	16.953
4.0	12.066	12.620	13.161	13.691	14.209	14.716	15.212	15.698	16.175	16.643
5.0	12.046	12.576	13.092	13.595	14.084	14.560	15.025	15.479	15.922	16.355
7.5	11.996	12.472	12.929	13.370	13.796	14.206	14.604	14.988	15.361	15.722
10.0	11.948	12.374	12.780	13.168	13.539	13.895	14.237	14.566	14.883	15.189
12.5	11.904	12.285	12.645	12.986	13.311	13.621	13.917	14.201	14.474	14.736
15.0	11.862	12.202	12.521	12.823	13.108	13.379	13.637	13.884	14.120	14.346

Interest Rate 12.00% 30 Year Schedule
1.0	12.629	13.256	13.878	14.498	15.113	15.725	16.334	16.939	17.541	18.140
2.0	12.606	13.205	13.797	14.383	14.961	15.534	16.099	16.659	17.212	17.760
3.0	12.583	13.156	13.719	14.273	14.817	15.353	15.879	16.398	16.908	17.411
4.0	12.560	13.108	13.643	14.167	14.680	15.181	15.673	16.154	16.627	17.090
5.0	12.538	13.061	13.570	14.066	14.549	15.019	15.478	15.927	16.364	16.792
7.5	12.485	12.951	13.399	13.831	14.248	14.651	15.041	15.418	15.784	16.140
10.0	12.435	12.848	13.243	13.620	13.982	14.329	14.662	14.983	15.293	15.592
12.5	12.388	12.755	13.102	13.432	13.746	14.046	14.333	14.609	14.874	15.128
15.0	12.345	12.669	12.974	13.263	13.537	13.798	14.047	14.284	14.512	14.731

Interest Rate 12.50% 30 Year Schedule
1.0	13.128	13.753	14.374	14.991	15.605	16.216	16.823	17.427	18.028	18.625
2.0	13.103	13.699	14.288	14.870	15.446	16.015	16.578	17.135	17.686	18.231
3.0	13.078	13.647	14.205	14.755	15.295	15.826	16.349	16.864	17.371	17.870
4.0	13.054	13.596	14.125	14.644	15.151	15.648	16.134	16.611	17.078	17.537
5.0	13.030	13.546	14.049	14.538	15.014	15.479	15.932	16.375	16.808	17.230
7.5	12.974	13.430	13.869	14.292	14.701	15.096	15.479	15.850	16.209	16.559
10.0	12.921	13.323	13.707	14.074	14.426	14.764	15.089	15.403	15.705	15.998
12.5	12.873	13.226	13.561	13.879	14.183	14.474	14.752	15.019	15.276	15.524
15.0	12.828	13.138	13.430	13.706	13.969	14.220	14.459	14.689	14.909	15.120

Interest Rate 13.00% 30 Year Schedule
1.0	13.626	14.250	14.869	15.485	16.098	16.707	17.313	17.915	18.514	19.110
2.0	13.600	14.193	14.779	15.358	15.931	16.497	17.058	17.612	18.160	18.702
3.0	13.573	14.137	14.692	15.237	15.773	16.300	16.819	17.330	17.833	18.328
4.0	13.548	14.084	14.608	15.121	15.623	16.114	16.596	17.068	17.531	17.985
5.0	13.523	14.032	14.527	15.010	15.480	15.939	16.387	16.824	17.251	17.669
7.5	13.463	13.910	14.340	14.755	15.155	15.543	15.919	16.283	16.636	16.979
10.0	13.409	13.799	14.171	14.528	14.871	15.201	15.518	15.824	16.119	16.405
12.5	13.358	13.698	14.021	14.328	14.622	14.903	15.173	15.432	15.682	15.922
15.0	13.312	13.607	13.887	14.152	14.404	14.645	14.875	15.096	15.309	15.513

Interest Rate 13.50% 30 Year Schedule
1.0	14.125	14.747	15.365	15.979	16.590	17.198	17.802	18.403	19.001	19.595
2.0	14.096	14.686	15.270	15.846	16.416	16.980	17.537	18.088	18.634	19.173
3.0	14.069	14.628	15.178	15.719	16.251	16.774	17.289	17.797	18.296	18.788
4.0	14.042	14.572	15.090	15.598	16.095	16.581	17.058	17.526	17.984	18.434
5.0	14.016	14.518	15.006	15.482	15.947	16.400	16.842	17.274	17.696	18.109
7.5	13.953	14.390	14.811	15.218	15.611	15.991	16.359	16.717	17.064	17.401
10.0	13.896	14.275	14.637	14.984	15.318	15.639	15.948	16.247	16.536	16.815
12.5	13.844	14.171	14.482	14.779	15.063	15.335	15.597	15.848	16.090	16.324
15.0	13.797	14.078	14.345	14.599	14.841	15.073	15.294	15.507	15.712	15.909

Interest Rate 14.00% 30 Year Schedule
1.0	14.623	15.243	15.860	16.473	17.083	17.689	18.292	18.892	19.488	20.081
2.0	14.593	15.180	15.760	16.334	16.901	17.462	18.017	18.565	19.108	19.645
3.0	14.564	15.119	15.665	16.201	16.729	17.249	17.760	18.264	18.759	19.248
4.0	14.536	15.060	15.573	16.075	16.567	17.049	17.521	17.984	18.438	18.884
5.0	14.508	15.003	15.486	15.956	16.414	16.861	17.298	17.724	18.142	18.550
7.5	14.443	14.871	15.283	15.682	16.067	16.440	16.801	17.152	17.493	17.824
10.0	14.384	14.752	15.104	15.441	15.766	16.079	16.381	16.672	16.954	17.226
12.5	14.330	14.645	14.945	15.232	15.506	15.769	16.022	16.266	16.501	16.728
15.0	14.283	14.551	14.806	15.049	15.281	15.503	15.717	15.922	16.119	16.309

Entry is annual percentage yield from interest plus selected share of price appreciation.

Yield on Participating Mortgage Loan

Growth Rate   3%   Loan to Value Ratio 67%
Interest Rate 5.50%   30 Year Schedule

Debt Coverage	Years to Payoff	10%	20%	30%	40%	50%	60%	70%	80%	90%	100%
				Share of Increase in Income & Profit on Sale							
1.150	1.0	5.944	6.388	6.831	7.272	7.713	8.152	8.591	9.028	9.465	9.900
	2.0	5.941	6.379	6.815	7.248	7.678	8.105	8.530	8.952	9.371	9.788
	3.0	5.938	6.371	6.799	7.224	7.643	8.059	8.471	8.878	9.282	9.682
	4.0	5.934	6.362	6.784	7.200	7.610	8.015	8.414	8.808	9.197	9.581
	5.0	5.931	6.354	6.769	7.177	7.578	7.972	8.359	8.740	9.115	9.485
	7.5	5.922	6.333	6.732	7.119	7.497	7.865	8.225	8.576	8.919	9.254
	10.0	5.915	6.315	6.699	7.071	7.429	7.777	8.114	8.442	8.760	9.071
	12.5	5.908	6.296	6.666	7.020	7.360	7.687	8.003	8.308	8.603	8.890
	15.0	5.901	6.280	6.638	6.978	7.303	7.615	7.914	8.203	8.482	8.752
1.200	1.0	5.944	6.388	6.831	7.273	7.714	8.154	8.593	9.030	9.467	9.904
	2.0	5.941	6.380	6.816	7.249	7.679	8.107	8.532	8.954	9.374	9.792
	3.0	5.938	6.371	6.800	7.225	7.645	8.061	8.473	8.881	9.285	9.686
	4.0	5.934	6.363	6.785	7.201	7.612	8.017	8.416	8.811	9.200	9.585
	5.0	5.931	6.355	6.770	7.178	7.579	7.974	8.361	8.743	9.119	9.489
	7.5	5.923	6.333	6.732	7.121	7.499	7.868	8.227	8.579	8.923	9.259
	10.0	5.916	6.315	6.701	7.072	7.432	7.780	8.118	8.446	8.765	9.077
	12.5	5.908	6.296	6.667	7.022	7.362	7.690	8.007	8.313	8.609	8.897
	15.0	5.902	6.281	6.639	6.981	7.306	7.619	7.919	8.209	8.489	8.761
1.250	1.0	5.945	6.389	6.832	7.274	7.715	8.155	8.595	9.033	9.470	9.907
	2.0	5.941	6.380	6.816	7.250	7.680	8.108	8.534	8.957	9.377	9.795
	3.0	5.938	6.372	6.801	7.226	7.646	8.063	8.475	8.884	9.288	9.689
	4.0	5.935	6.363	6.786	7.202	7.613	8.018	8.418	8.813	9.203	9.589
	5.0	5.931	6.355	6.771	7.180	7.581	7.976	8.364	8.746	9.123	9.493
	7.5	5.923	6.334	6.733	7.122	7.501	7.870	8.230	8.582	8.927	9.264
	10.0	5.916	6.316	6.702	7.074	7.434	7.783	8.121	8.450	8.771	9.083
	12.5	5.908	6.297	6.668	7.024	7.365	7.694	8.011	8.317	8.615	8.904
	15.0	5.902	6.281	6.641	6.983	7.310	7.623	7.924	8.215	8.496	8.769

Interest Rate 6.00%   30 Year Schedule

Debt Coverage	Years to Payoff	10%	20%	30%	40%	50%	60%	70%	80%	90%	100%
1.150	1.0	6.444	6.887	7.329	7.770	8.210	8.649	9.088	9.525	9.961	10.397
	2.0	6.439	6.876	7.309	7.741	8.169	8.595	9.018	9.439	9.857	10.273
	3.0	6.434	6.865	7.290	7.712	8.129	8.542	8.951	9.357	9.758	10.157
	4.0	6.430	6.854	7.272	7.684	8.090	8.491	8.887	9.278	9.664	10.046
	5.0	6.425	6.843	7.253	7.656	8.052	8.442	8.826	9.203	9.575	9.941
	7.5	6.414	6.816	7.207	7.588	7.959	8.321	8.675	9.021	9.359	9.690
	10.0	6.404	6.792	7.168	7.530	7.881	8.222	8.552	8.874	9.188	9.494
	12.5	6.393	6.768	7.127	7.471	7.802	8.121	8.430	8.728	9.019	9.301
	15.0	6.384	6.748	7.093	7.422	7.738	8.041	8.334	8.617	8.891	9.157
1.200	1.0	6.444	6.887	7.330	7.771	8.212	8.651	9.090	9.527	9.964	10.400
	2.0	6.439	6.876	7.310	7.742	8.171	8.597	9.020	9.442	9.861	10.277
	3.0	6.435	6.865	7.291	7.713	8.131	8.544	8.954	9.360	9.762	10.161
	4.0	6.430	6.854	7.273	7.685	8.092	8.493	8.890	9.281	9.668	10.050
	5.0	6.426	6.844	7.254	7.658	8.054	8.444	8.828	9.206	9.579	9.946
	7.5	6.414	6.816	7.208	7.589	7.961	8.324	8.678	9.024	9.364	9.696
	10.0	6.404	6.793	7.169	7.532	7.884	8.225	8.557	8.879	9.194	9.501
	12.5	6.393	6.769	7.128	7.473	7.805	8.125	8.434	8.734	9.025	9.308
	15.0	6.385	6.749	7.095	7.425	7.742	8.046	8.340	8.624	8.899	9.167
1.250	1.0	6.444	6.888	7.330	7.772	8.213	8.653	9.092	9.530	9.967	10.404
	2.0	6.439	6.877	7.311	7.743	8.172	8.599	9.023	9.445	9.864	10.281
	3.0	6.435	6.866	7.292	7.714	8.132	8.546	8.956	9.363	9.766	10.165
	4.0	6.430	6.855	7.273	7.686	8.094	8.496	8.893	9.285	9.672	10.055
	5.0	6.426	6.844	7.255	7.659	8.056	8.447	8.831	9.210	9.583	9.951
	7.5	6.414	6.817	7.209	7.591	7.963	8.326	8.681	9.028	9.368	9.701
	10.0	6.404	6.794	7.170	7.534	7.886	8.228	8.561	8.884	9.200	9.508
	12.5	6.394	6.770	7.130	7.475	7.808	8.128	8.439	8.740	9.032	9.316
	15.0	6.385	6.750	7.097	7.428	7.746	8.051	8.346	8.631	8.908	9.177

Entry is annual yield from interest, growth in income and selected share of price appreciation.

Yield on Participating Mortgage Loan

Growth Rate　3%
Interest Rate　6.50%

Loan to Value Ratio 67%
30 Year Schedule

Debt Coverage	Years to Payoff	10%	20%	30%	40%	50%	60%	70%	80%	90%	100%
				Share of Increase in Income & Profit on Sale							
1.150	1.0	6.943	7.386	7.828	8.268	8.708	9.147	9.585	10.022	10.459	10.894
	2.0	6.937	7.372	7.804	8.234	8.661	9.086	9.508	9.927	10.345	10.760
	3.0	6.931	7.359	7.782	8.201	8.615	9.026	9.433	9.837	10.237	10.633
	4.0	6.926	7.345	7.760	8.168	8.571	8.969	9.362	9.750	10.134	10.513
	5.0	6.920	7.333	7.738	8.137	8.528	8.914	9.294	9.668	10.037	10.400
	7.5	6.905	7.300	7.684	8.058	8.423	8.779	9.128	9.469	9.803	10.130
	10.0	6.893	7.272	7.638	7.992	8.336	8.670	8.995	9.312	9.621	9.923
	12.5	6.879	7.242	7.590	7.925	8.248	8.560	8.862	9.155	9.440	9.718
	15.0	6.868	7.218	7.552	7.872	8.179	8.475	8.761	9.039	9.309	9.573
1.200	1.0	6.943	7.386	7.828	8.270	8.710	9.149	9.588	10.025	10.462	10.898
	2.0	6.937	7.373	7.805	8.235	8.663	9.088	9.510	9.930	10.348	10.764
	3.0	6.932	7.359	7.783	8.202	8.617	9.029	9.436	9.840	10.241	10.638
	4.0	6.926	7.346	7.761	8.170	8.573	8.972	9.365	9.754	10.138	10.518
	5.0	6.920	7.333	7.739	8.138	8.531	8.917	9.297	9.672	10.041	10.406
	7.5	6.906	7.300	7.685	8.059	8.425	8.782	9.132	9.473	9.808	10.136
	10.0	6.893	7.273	7.639	7.995	8.339	8.674	9.000	9.318	9.628	9.931
	12.5	6.880	7.243	7.592	7.928	8.251	8.564	8.867	9.162	9.448	9.727
	15.0	6.869	7.220	7.554	7.875	8.183	8.480	8.768	9.047	9.319	9.585
1.250	1.0	6.944	7.387	7.829	8.271	8.711	9.151	9.590	10.028	10.466	10.902
	2.0	6.938	7.373	7.806	8.237	8.664	9.090	9.513	9.934	10.352	10.768
	3.0	6.932	7.360	7.784	8.203	8.619	9.031	9.439	9.844	10.245	10.642
	4.0	6.926	7.347	7.762	8.171	8.575	8.974	9.368	9.758	10.143	10.523
	5.0	6.920	7.334	7.740	8.140	8.533	8.920	9.301	9.676	10.046	10.411
	7.5	6.906	7.301	7.686	8.061	8.427	8.785	9.135	9.478	9.813	10.142
	10.0	6.894	7.274	7.641	7.997	8.342	8.678	9.005	9.323	9.635	9.939
	12.5	6.880	7.245	7.594	7.930	8.255	8.568	8.873	9.168	9.456	9.736
	15.0	6.870	7.221	7.557	7.878	8.187	8.486	8.775	9.056	9.329	9.596

Interest Rate　7.00%　　　　30 Year Schedule

Debt Coverage	Years to Payoff	10%	20%	30%	40%	50%	60%	70%	80%	90%	100%
1.150	1.0	7.443	7.885	8.326	8.767	9.207	9.645	10.083	10.520	10.957	11.392
	2.0	7.436	7.869	8.300	8.728	9.154	9.577	9.998	10.417	10.833	11.247
	3.0	7.428	7.853	8.274	8.690	9.103	9.511	9.916	10.318	10.716	11.111
	4.0	7.422	7.838	8.248	8.653	9.053	9.448	9.839	10.224	10.606	10.983
	5.0	7.415	7.823	8.223	8.618	9.006	9.388	9.764	10.135	10.501	10.862
	7.5	7.397	7.784	8.161	8.529	8.889	9.240	9.584	9.920	10.250	10.574
	10.0	7.382	7.752	8.110	8.457	8.794	9.122	9.442	9.754	10.059	10.358
	12.5	7.367	7.719	8.057	8.383	8.698	9.003	9.300	9.588	9.869	10.144
	15.0	7.354	7.692	8.015	8.326	8.625	8.915	9.196	9.470	9.737	9.999
1.200	1.0	7.443	7.886	8.327	8.768	9.208	9.647	10.086	10.524	10.961	11.397
	2.0	7.436	7.870	8.301	8.729	9.156	9.579	10.001	10.420	10.837	11.252
	3.0	7.429	7.854	8.275	8.692	9.105	9.514	9.920	10.322	10.721	11.116
	4.0	7.422	7.838	8.249	8.655	9.056	9.451	9.842	10.228	10.610	10.988
	5.0	7.415	7.823	8.225	8.620	9.008	9.391	9.768	10.140	10.506	10.868
	7.5	7.398	7.785	8.163	8.531	8.891	9.243	9.588	9.925	10.256	10.581
	10.0	7.383	7.753	8.112	8.460	8.798	9.127	9.448	9.761	10.067	10.367
	12.5	7.367	7.720	8.059	8.386	8.702	9.009	9.306	9.596	9.878	10.154
	15.0	7.355	7.693	8.018	8.330	8.630	8.922	9.205	9.480	9.749	10.013
1.250	1.0	7.443	7.886	8.328	8.770	9.210	9.650	10.089	10.527	10.964	11.401
	2.0	7.436	7.870	8.302	8.731	9.157	9.582	10.004	10.424	10.841	11.257
	3.0	7.429	7.855	8.276	8.693	9.107	9.517	9.923	10.326	10.725	11.121
	4.0	7.422	7.839	8.251	8.657	9.058	9.454	9.845	10.233	10.615	10.994
	5.0	7.415	7.824	8.226	8.621	9.011	9.394	9.772	10.144	10.512	10.874
	7.5	7.398	7.786	8.164	8.533	8.894	9.247	9.592	9.930	10.262	10.588
	10.0	7.383	7.754	8.114	8.462	8.801	9.131	9.453	9.767	10.075	10.376
	12.5	7.368	7.721	8.061	8.389	8.706	9.014	9.312	9.603	9.887	10.165
	15.0	7.355	7.695	8.020	8.333	8.636	8.928	9.213	9.490	9.761	10.027

Entry is annual yield from interest, growth in income and selected share of price appreciation.

Yield on Participating Mortgage Loan

Growth Rate   3%
Interest Rate 7.50%

Loan to Value Ratio 67%
30 Year Schedule

| Debt Coverage | Years to Payoff | Share of Increase in Income & Profit on Sale | | | | | | | | | |
		10%	20%	30%	40%	50%	60%	70%	80%	90%	100%
1.150	1.0	7.942	8.384	8.825	9.266	9.705	10.144	10.582	11.019	11.456	11.891
	2.0	7.934	8.366	8.795	9.222	9.647	10.069	10.489	10.907	11.323	11.736
	3.0	7.926	8.348	8.766	9.180	9.591	9.997	10.401	10.801	11.197	11.591
	4.0	7.918	8.330	8.738	9.140	9.537	9.929	10.317	10.700	11.079	11.454
	5.0	7.910	8.313	8.710	9.100	9.485	9.863	10.236	10.605	10.968	11.326
	7.5	7.890	8.270	8.641	9.003	9.357	9.703	10.042	10.375	10.701	11.022
	10.0	7.873	8.234	8.584	8.924	9.256	9.578	9.893	10.201	10.503	10.799
	12.5	7.855	8.197	8.526	8.844	9.153	9.452	9.744	10.028	10.306	10.577
	15.0	7.841	8.168	8.482	8.785	9.078	9.363	9.640	9.911	10.176	10.437
1.200	1.0	7.943	8.385	8.827	9.267	9.707	10.146	10.585	11.023	11.460	11.896
	2.0	7.934	8.367	8.796	9.224	9.649	10.072	10.492	10.911	11.327	11.742
	3.0	7.926	8.349	8.767	9.182	9.593	10.000	10.404	10.805	11.202	11.596
	4.0	7.918	8.331	8.739	9.141	9.539	9.932	10.320	10.705	11.084	11.460
	5.0	7.910	8.314	8.711	9.102	9.487	9.867	10.241	10.610	10.974	11.333
	7.5	7.890	8.271	8.642	9.005	9.360	9.707	10.047	10.381	10.708	11.029
	10.0	7.873	8.235	8.586	8.928	9.260	9.583	9.900	10.209	10.512	10.809
	12.5	7.856	8.198	8.529	8.848	9.157	9.458	9.751	10.037	10.316	10.590
	15.0	7.842	8.170	8.485	8.789	9.084	9.370	9.650	9.923	10.190	10.454
1.250	1.0	7.943	8.386	8.828	9.269	9.709	10.149	10.588	11.026	11.464	11.901
	2.0	7.935	8.367	8.798	9.226	9.651	10.075	10.496	10.915	11.332	11.747
	3.0	7.927	8.349	8.769	9.184	9.595	10.003	10.408	10.809	11.207	11.602
	4.0	7.919	8.332	8.740	9.143	9.542	9.935	10.324	10.709	11.090	11.467
	5.0	7.911	8.315	8.713	9.104	9.490	9.870	10.245	10.615	10.980	11.340
	7.5	7.891	8.272	8.644	9.007	9.363	9.711	10.052	10.386	10.715	11.037
	10.0	7.874	8.237	8.589	8.931	9.264	9.589	9.906	10.217	10.521	10.820
	12.5	7.857	8.200	8.531	8.851	9.162	9.464	9.758	10.046	10.327	10.602
	15.0	7.843	8.172	8.488	8.794	9.090	9.378	9.659	9.935	10.205	10.471

Interest Rate 8.00%   30 Year Schedule

Debt Coverage	Years to Payoff	10%	20%	30%	40%	50%	60%	70%	80%	90%	100%
1.150	1.0	8.442	8.884	9.325	9.765	10.204	10.643	11.081	11.519	11.955	12.391
	2.0	8.433	8.863	9.291	9.717	10.141	10.562	10.981	11.398	11.813	12.226
	3.0	8.423	8.843	9.259	9.671	10.080	10.485	10.886	11.285	11.680	12.072
	4.0	8.414	8.823	9.227	9.627	10.021	10.411	10.796	11.177	11.554	11.928
	5.0	8.405	8.804	9.197	9.584	9.965	10.340	10.711	11.076	11.437	11.793
	7.5	8.383	8.756	9.121	9.478	9.827	10.169	10.504	10.833	11.156	11.474
	10.0	8.364	8.717	9.061	9.395	9.720	10.038	10.349	10.654	10.953	11.246
	12.5	8.344	8.677	8.998	9.310	9.612	9.906	10.194	10.474	10.750	11.020
	15.0	8.329	8.647	8.953	9.249	9.537	9.818	10.092	10.362	10.627	10.888
1.200	1.0	8.442	8.885	9.326	9.767	10.207	10.646	11.085	11.523	11.960	12.397
	2.0	8.433	8.864	9.293	9.719	10.143	10.565	10.985	11.403	11.818	12.232
	3.0	8.424	8.844	9.260	9.673	10.082	10.488	10.890	11.289	11.685	12.079
	4.0	8.415	8.824	9.229	9.629	10.024	10.414	10.800	11.182	11.561	11.935
	5.0	8.406	8.805	9.199	9.586	9.968	10.344	10.715	11.082	11.443	11.801
	7.5	8.383	8.758	9.123	9.481	9.830	10.173	10.509	10.839	11.163	11.482
	10.0	8.365	8.719	9.063	9.398	9.725	10.044	10.357	10.663	10.963	11.258
	12.5	8.345	8.679	9.001	9.314	9.617	9.913	10.202	10.485	10.762	11.034
	15.0	8.331	8.649	8.956	9.254	9.544	9.827	10.104	10.376	10.644	10.908
1.250	1.0	8.443	8.885	9.327	9.768	10.209	10.649	11.088	11.527	11.965	12.402
	2.0	8.433	8.865	9.294	9.721	10.145	10.568	10.989	11.407	11.824	12.238
	3.0	8.424	8.845	9.262	9.675	10.085	10.491	10.894	11.294	11.691	12.085
	4.0	8.415	8.825	9.230	9.631	10.027	10.418	10.805	11.188	11.567	11.942
	5.0	8.406	8.806	9.200	9.588	9.971	10.348	10.720	11.087	11.450	11.809
	7.5	8.384	8.759	9.125	9.483	9.834	10.178	10.515	10.846	11.171	11.491
	10.0	8.365	8.721	9.066	9.402	9.730	10.050	10.364	10.671	10.973	11.270
	12.5	8.346	8.681	9.004	9.318	9.623	9.920	10.211	10.495	10.774	11.048
	15.0	8.332	8.651	8.960	9.260	9.552	9.836	10.116	10.390	10.660	10.928

Entry is annual yield from interest, growth in income and selected share of price appreciation.

Yield on Participating Mortgage Loan

Growth Rate   3%
Interest Rate 8.50%

Loan to Value Ratio 67%
30 Year Schedule

Debt Coverage	Years to Payoff	Share of Increase in Income & Profit on Sale									
		10%	20%	30%	40%	50%	60%	70%	80%	90%	100%
	1.0	8.942	9.383	9.824	10.265	10.704	11.143	11.581	12.019	12.456	12.892
	2.0	8.931	9.361	9.788	10.213	10.635	11.056	11.474	11.891	12.305	12.718
1.150	3.0	8.921	9.338	9.752	10.163	10.569	10.973	11.373	11.770	12.164	12.555
	4.0	8.911	9.317	9.718	10.114	10.506	10.894	11.277	11.656	12.032	12.404
	5.0	8.901	9.296	9.685	10.068	10.446	10.819	11.187	11.550	11.908	12.263
	7.5	8.876	9.244	9.603	9.955	10.299	10.637	10.969	11.294	11.614	11.929
	10.0	8.856	9.202	9.539	9.867	10.188	10.502	10.810	11.112	11.408	11.700
	12.5	8.835	9.159	9.473	9.778	10.076	10.366	10.650	10.928	11.202	11.471
	15.0	8.819	9.128	9.428	9.719	10.003	10.281	10.554	10.824	11.090	11.354
	1.0	8.942	9.384	9.826	10.266	10.707	11.146	11.585	12.023	12.461	12.898
	2.0	8.932	9.362	9.789	10.215	10.638	11.059	11.478	11.895	12.311	12.724
1.200	3.0	8.921	9.339	9.754	10.165	10.572	10.976	11.377	11.775	12.170	12.562
	4.0	8.911	9.318	9.720	10.117	10.509	10.898	11.282	11.662	12.039	12.412
	5.0	8.901	9.297	9.687	10.071	10.450	10.823	11.192	11.556	11.916	12.272
	7.5	8.877	9.245	9.605	9.958	10.303	10.642	10.975	11.301	11.623	11.939
	10.0	8.857	9.204	9.542	9.872	10.194	10.509	10.818	11.122	11.420	11.714
	12.5	8.836	9.161	9.477	9.783	10.082	10.374	10.660	10.940	11.216	11.487
	15.0	8.821	9.131	9.432	9.725	10.011	10.292	10.568	10.840	11.110	11.378
	1.0	8.943	9.385	9.827	10.268	10.709	11.149	11.589	12.028	12.466	12.904
	2.0	8.932	9.362	9.791	10.217	10.640	11.062	11.482	11.900	12.316	12.731
1.250	3.0	8.922	9.340	9.755	10.167	10.575	10.980	11.382	11.781	12.176	12.570
	4.0	8.912	9.319	9.721	10.119	10.513	10.902	11.287	11.668	12.046	12.420
	5.0	8.902	9.298	9.689	10.074	10.453	10.828	11.197	11.562	11.923	12.280
	7.5	8.877	9.246	9.607	9.961	10.307	10.647	10.981	11.309	11.631	11.949
	10.0	8.858	9.206	9.545	9.876	10.199	10.516	10.827	11.132	11.432	11.728
	12.5	8.837	9.163	9.480	9.788	10.088	10.382	10.670	10.952	11.230	11.504
	15.0	8.822	9.134	9.437	9.732	10.020	10.303	10.582	10.857	11.130	11.401

Interest Rate 9.00%   30 Year Schedule

Debt Coverage	Years to Payoff	10%	20%	30%	40%	50%	60%	70%	80%	90%	100%
	1.0	9.442	9.883	10.324	10.764	11.204	11.643	12.082	12.520	12.957	13.394
	2.0	9.430	9.858	10.284	10.708	11.130	11.550	11.968	12.384	12.798	13.210
1.150	3.0	9.419	9.834	10.246	10.655	11.060	11.462	11.861	12.257	12.650	13.040
	4.0	9.408	9.811	10.209	10.603	10.993	11.378	11.760	12.137	12.511	12.882
	5.0	9.397	9.788	10.174	10.554	10.929	11.299	11.665	12.026	12.383	12.736
	7.5	9.370	9.732	10.086	10.433	10.774	11.108	11.436	11.759	12.076	12.389
	10.0	9.349	9.688	10.020	10.343	10.660	10.970	11.275	11.575	11.870	12.161
	12.5	9.326	9.643	9.951	10.251	10.544	10.831	11.113	11.390	11.662	11.932
	15.0	9.311	9.613	9.907	10.194	10.476	10.753	11.027	11.298	11.567	11.836
	1.0	9.442	9.884	10.326	10.767	11.207	11.647	12.086	12.524	12.963	13.401
	2.0	9.431	9.859	10.286	10.711	11.133	11.554	11.972	12.389	12.804	13.218
1.200	3.0	9.419	9.835	10.248	10.657	11.063	11.466	11.866	12.262	12.657	13.048
	4.0	9.408	9.812	10.211	10.606	10.996	11.383	11.765	12.144	12.519	12.891
	5.0	9.398	9.790	10.176	10.557	10.933	11.304	11.671	12.033	12.391	12.745
	7.5	9.371	9.733	10.089	10.437	10.778	11.113	11.443	11.767	12.086	12.401
	10.0	9.350	9.690	10.023	10.348	10.666	10.978	11.285	11.587	11.884	12.177
	12.5	9.327	9.646	9.955	10.257	10.552	10.841	11.124	11.403	11.679	11.951
	15.0	9.312	9.616	9.912	10.202	10.486	10.766	11.043	11.317	11.591	11.864
	1.0	9.443	9.885	10.327	10.769	11.209	11.650	12.090	12.529	12.968	13.407
	2.0	9.431	9.860	10.288	10.713	11.136	11.557	11.977	12.395	12.811	13.225
1.250	3.0	9.420	9.836	10.250	10.660	11.066	11.470	11.871	12.268	12.663	13.056
	4.0	9.409	9.813	10.213	10.609	11.000	11.387	11.770	12.150	12.527	12.900
	5.0	9.398	9.791	10.178	10.560	10.937	11.309	11.677	12.040	12.399	12.755
	7.5	9.371	9.735	10.091	10.440	10.783	11.119	11.450	11.775	12.096	12.412
	10.0	9.351	9.692	10.026	10.353	10.672	10.986	11.295	11.598	11.898	12.193
	12.5	9.329	9.648	9.959	10.262	10.559	10.850	11.136	11.417	11.695	11.970
	15.0	9.314	9.620	9.918	10.210	10.496	10.779	11.059	11.337	11.615	11.893

Entry is annual yield from interest, growth in income and selected share of price appreciation.

Yield on Participating Mortgage Loan

Growth Rate   3%
Interest Rate 9.50%

Loan to Value Ratio 67%
30 Year Schedule

Debt Coverage	Years to Payoff	Share of Increase in Income & Profit on Sale									
		10%	20%	30%	40%	50%	60%	70%	80%	90%	100%
1.150	1.0	9.942	10.383	10.824	11.265	11.705	12.144	12.583	13.021	13.459	13.897
	2.0	9.929	10.356	10.782	11.205	11.626	12.045	12.463	12.878	13.292	13.704
	3.0	9.917	10.330	10.741	11.147	11.551	11.952	12.350	12.745	13.137	13.527
	4.0	9.905	10.305	10.701	11.093	11.480	11.864	12.244	12.620	12.993	13.363
	5.0	9.893	10.281	10.664	11.041	11.413	11.781	12.145	12.504	12.859	13.211
	7.5	9.864	10.221	10.571	10.914	11.250	11.581	11.906	12.227	12.543	12.854
	10.0	9.842	10.176	10.502	10.822	11.135	11.443	11.746	12.044	12.339	12.630
	12.5	9.819	10.129	10.432	10.728	11.018	11.303	11.583	11.859	12.133	12.404
	15.0	9.804	10.101	10.391	10.676	10.957	11.235	11.510	11.785	12.060	12.336
1.200	1.0	9.942	10.384	10.826	11.267	11.708	12.148	12.587	13.027	13.465	13.904
	2.0	9.930	10.357	10.783	11.207	11.629	12.049	12.468	12.884	13.299	13.712
	3.0	9.917	10.332	10.742	11.150	11.555	11.956	12.355	12.751	13.145	13.535
	4.0	9.905	10.307	10.703	11.096	11.484	11.869	12.250	12.627	13.001	13.372
	5.0	9.894	10.283	10.666	11.044	11.418	11.787	12.151	12.512	12.869	13.222
	7.5	9.865	10.223	10.573	10.917	11.255	11.587	11.914	12.236	12.553	12.866
	10.0	9.843	10.178	10.506	10.827	11.142	11.452	11.757	12.057	12.354	12.648
	12.5	9.820	10.132	10.437	10.734	11.026	11.313	11.596	11.875	12.152	12.426
	15.0	9.806	10.105	10.397	10.685	10.969	11.250	11.530	11.809	12.089	12.370
1.250	1.0	9.943	10.385	10.828	11.269	11.710	12.151	12.592	13.032	13.472	13.911
	2.0	9.930	10.359	10.785	11.210	11.632	12.053	12.473	12.890	13.306	13.720
	3.0	9.918	10.333	10.744	11.153	11.558	11.961	12.361	12.758	13.152	13.544
	4.0	9.906	10.308	10.705	11.099	11.488	11.874	12.256	12.634	13.010	13.382
	5.0	9.895	10.284	10.668	11.048	11.422	11.792	12.158	12.520	12.878	13.233
	7.5	9.866	10.225	10.576	10.921	11.260	11.594	11.922	12.245	12.564	12.879
	10.0	9.844	10.181	10.510	10.833	11.149	11.461	11.768	12.071	12.370	12.667
	12.5	9.822	10.135	10.441	10.741	11.035	11.324	11.609	11.891	12.171	12.448
	15.0	9.808	10.109	10.404	10.694	10.981	11.266	11.549	11.833	12.117	12.405

Interest Rate 10.00%   30 Year Schedule

Debt Coverage	Years to Payoff	10%	20%	30%	40%	50%	60%	70%	80%	90%	100%
1.150	1.0	10.442	10.883	11.325	11.765	12.206	12.645	13.085	13.524	13.962	14.400
	2.0	10.428	10.855	11.279	11.702	12.122	12.541	12.958	13.374	13.788	14.200
	3.0	10.415	10.827	11.235	11.641	12.044	12.443	12.840	13.234	13.626	14.015
	4.0	10.402	10.800	11.194	11.583	11.969	12.351	12.730	13.105	13.477	13.845
	5.0	10.390	10.774	11.154	11.529	11.899	12.265	12.627	12.985	13.339	13.690
	7.5	10.359	10.711	11.057	11.396	11.729	12.057	12.380	12.698	13.013	13.323
	10.0	10.336	10.665	10.987	11.303	11.614	11.920	12.222	12.520	12.814	13.107
	12.5	10.312	10.618	10.916	11.209	11.497	11.780	12.060	12.338	12.613	12.887
	15.0	10.299	10.592	10.880	11.164	11.446	11.727	12.007	12.288	12.572	12.859
1.200	1.0	10.442	10.885	11.326	11.768	12.209	12.649	13.090	13.529	13.969	14.408
	2.0	10.429	10.856	11.281	11.704	12.126	12.546	12.964	13.380	13.795	14.208
	3.0	10.415	10.828	11.238	11.644	12.047	12.448	12.846	13.241	13.634	14.025
	4.0	10.403	10.802	11.196	11.587	11.973	12.357	12.736	13.113	13.486	13.856
	5.0	10.391	10.776	11.157	11.533	11.904	12.271	12.634	12.993	13.349	13.702
	7.5	10.360	10.713	11.060	11.400	11.735	12.064	12.389	12.709	13.025	13.337
	10.0	10.337	10.668	10.992	11.310	11.622	11.930	12.234	12.535	12.832	13.128
	12.5	10.314	10.621	10.921	11.216	11.507	11.793	12.076	12.356	12.635	12.913
	15.0	10.301	10.596	10.887	11.175	11.461	11.745	12.030	12.316	12.606	12.900
1.250	1.0	10.443	10.886	11.328	11.770	12.212	12.653	13.094	13.535	13.976	14.416
	2.0	10.429	10.857	11.283	11.707	12.129	12.550	12.969	13.387	13.803	14.217
	3.0	10.416	10.830	11.240	11.647	12.051	12.453	12.852	13.249	13.643	14.034
	4.0	10.403	10.803	11.199	11.590	11.978	12.362	12.743	13.121	13.495	13.867
	5.0	10.391	10.778	11.159	11.536	11.909	12.277	12.641	13.002	13.360	13.714
	7.5	10.361	10.715	11.063	11.404	11.740	12.071	12.397	12.719	13.037	13.351
	10.0	10.339	10.671	10.996	11.316	11.630	11.941	12.247	12.550	12.850	13.149
	12.5	10.316	10.624	10.927	11.224	11.517	11.805	12.091	12.375	12.657	12.939
	15.0	10.303	10.601	10.895	11.186	11.475	11.764	12.053	12.345	12.640	12.941

Entry is annual yield from interest, growth in income and selected share of price appreciation.

Yield on Participating Mortgage Loan

Growth Rate 3%
Interest Rate 10.50%

Loan to Value Ratio 67%
30 Year Schedule

Debt Coverage	Years to Payoff	Share of Increase in Income & Profit on Sale									
		10%	20%	30%	40%	50%	60%	70%	80%	90%	100%
1.150	1.0	10.942	11.384	11.825	12.266	12.707	13.147	13.587	14.027	14.466	14.905
	2.0	10.927	11.353	11.777	12.199	12.619	13.038	13.455	13.870	14.284	14.697
	3.0	10.913	11.324	11.731	12.135	12.537	12.935	13.332	13.725	14.116	14.505
	4.0	10.900	11.295	11.687	12.075	12.459	12.840	13.217	13.591	13.962	14.331
	5.0	10.887	11.268	11.646	12.018	12.386	12.750	13.111	13.468	13.821	14.171
	7.5	10.854	11.202	11.544	11.880	12.210	12.536	12.857	13.174	13.487	13.796
	10.0	10.831	11.156	11.475	11.788	12.097	12.402	12.703	13.002	13.298	13.592
	12.5	10.807	11.108	11.404	11.694	11.981	12.265	12.546	12.826	13.105	13.383
	15.0	10.795	11.086	11.374	11.660	11.945	12.231	12.518	12.809	13.105	13.407
1.200	1.0	10.942	11.385	11.827	12.269	12.710	13.152	13.592	14.033	14.473	14.913
	2.0	10.928	11.354	11.779	12.202	12.623	13.043	13.461	13.877	14.292	14.706
	3.0	10.914	11.325	11.733	12.139	12.541	12.941	13.338	13.733	14.126	14.516
	4.0	10.900	11.297	11.690	12.079	12.464	12.846	13.224	13.600	13.973	14.342
	5.0	10.887	11.270	11.648	12.022	12.392	12.757	13.119	13.477	13.832	14.185
	7.5	10.855	11.204	11.547	11.885	12.217	12.544	12.867	13.185	13.500	13.812
	10.0	10.833	11.159	11.480	11.795	12.106	12.414	12.718	13.019	13.318	13.616
	12.5	10.809	11.112	11.410	11.703	11.993	12.280	12.564	12.848	13.130	13.413
	15.0	10.798	11.092	11.383	11.673	11.962	12.253	12.546	12.843	13.146	13.457
1.250	1.0	10.943	11.386	11.829	12.272	12.714	13.156	13.598	14.039	14.481	14.922
	2.0	10.929	11.356	11.781	12.205	12.627	13.048	13.467	13.884	14.301	14.715
	3.0	10.915	11.327	11.736	12.142	12.545	12.946	13.345	13.741	14.135	14.527
	4.0	10.901	11.299	11.692	12.082	12.469	12.852	13.232	13.609	13.983	14.354
	5.0	10.888	11.272	11.651	12.026	12.397	12.764	13.127	13.487	13.844	14.198
	7.5	10.856	11.207	11.551	11.889	12.223	12.552	12.876	13.197	13.514	13.828
	10.0	10.834	11.162	11.485	11.802	12.116	12.426	12.732	13.037	13.339	13.640
	12.5	10.811	11.116	11.416	11.712	12.004	12.294	12.582	12.869	13.156	13.444
	15.0	10.800	11.097	11.392	11.685	11.979	12.275	12.573	12.877	13.188	13.508

Interest Rate 11.00%   30 Year Schedule

Debt Coverage	Years to Payoff	10%	20%	30%	40%	50%	60%	70%	80%	90%	100%
1.150	1.0	11.442	11.884	12.326	12.768	13.209	13.650	14.090	14.530	14.971	15.411
	2.0	11.427	11.852	12.275	12.697	13.117	13.535	13.952	14.368	14.782	15.195
	3.0	11.412	11.821	12.227	12.630	13.031	13.429	13.824	14.218	14.609	14.998
	4.0	11.397	11.791	12.181	12.567	12.950	13.330	13.706	14.079	14.450	14.818
	5.0	11.384	11.763	12.138	12.508	12.875	13.238	13.597	13.953	14.306	14.656
	7.5	11.350	11.694	12.032	12.365	12.694	13.017	13.337	13.653	13.966	14.275
	10.0	11.327	11.648	11.964	12.276	12.584	12.889	13.191	13.491	13.789	14.087
	12.5	11.303	11.601	11.895	12.185	12.472	12.757	13.041	13.325	13.609	13.894
	15.0	11.293	11.584	11.874	12.164	12.455	12.748	13.046	13.351	13.663	13.987
1.200	1.0	11.443	11.886	12.328	12.771	13.213	13.654	14.096	14.537	14.979	15.420
	2.0	11.427	11.853	12.278	12.700	13.121	13.541	13.959	14.375	14.791	15.205
	3.0	11.412	11.822	12.229	12.634	13.035	13.435	13.832	14.226	14.619	15.009
	4.0	11.398	11.793	12.184	12.571	12.955	13.336	13.714	14.089	14.461	14.831
	5.0	11.385	11.765	12.141	12.513	12.881	13.245	13.606	13.964	14.319	14.671
	7.5	11.351	11.696	12.036	12.371	12.701	13.026	13.348	13.666	13.981	14.293
	10.0	11.329	11.652	11.970	12.284	12.595	12.902	13.207	13.511	13.813	14.114
	12.5	11.305	11.605	11.902	12.195	12.485	12.774	13.062	13.350	13.638	13.929
	15.0	11.296	11.591	11.884	12.179	12.475	12.774	13.079	13.391	13.714	14.049
1.250	1.0	11.443	11.887	12.330	12.773	13.216	13.659	14.102	14.544	14.987	15.429
	2.0	11.428	11.855	12.280	12.703	13.125	13.546	13.965	14.383	14.800	15.215
	3.0	11.413	11.824	12.232	12.637	13.040	13.441	13.839	14.235	14.629	15.021
	4.0	11.399	11.795	12.187	12.575	12.961	13.343	13.722	14.099	14.473	14.844
	5.0	11.386	11.767	12.144	12.518	12.887	13.253	13.615	13.975	14.331	14.685
	7.5	11.352	11.699	12.040	12.376	12.708	13.035	13.359	13.679	13.996	14.310
	10.0	11.330	11.656	11.976	12.292	12.606	12.916	13.224	13.531	13.837	14.142
	12.5	11.307	11.610	11.909	12.205	12.498	12.791	13.083	13.375	13.669	13.965
	15.0	11.299	11.597	11.895	12.193	12.495	12.800	13.112	13.433	13.765	14.113

Entry is annual yield from interest, growth in income and selected share of price appreciation.

Yield on Participating Mortgage Loan

Growth Rate   3%
Interest Rate 11.50%

Loan to Value Ratio 67%
30 Year Schedule

Debt Coverage	Years to Payoff	Share of Increase in Income & Profit on Sale									
		10%	20%	30%	40%	50%	60%	70%	80%	90%	100%
	1.0	11.942	12.385	12.827	13.269	13.711	14.153	14.594	15.035	15.476	15.917
	2.0	11.926	12.351	12.774	13.195	13.615	14.034	14.451	14.866	15.281	15.694
1.150	3.0	11.910	12.318	12.723	13.126	13.526	13.923	14.318	14.711	15.103	15.492
	4.0	11.895	12.287	12.676	13.061	13.442	13.821	14.197	14.570	14.940	15.309
	5.0	11.881	12.258	12.631	13.000	13.365	13.727	14.085	14.441	14.794	15.144
	7.5	11.846	12.187	12.522	12.853	13.180	13.502	13.821	14.136	14.449	14.759
	10.0	11.823	12.142	12.457	12.768	13.076	13.381	13.685	13.988	14.290	14.592
	12.5	11.800	12.096	12.389	12.680	12.969	13.257	13.546	13.835	14.126	14.421
	15.0	11.793	12.087	12.380	12.676	12.976	13.281	13.594	13.917	14.254	14.608
	1.0	11.943	12.386	12.830	13.272	13.715	14.158	14.600	15.042	15.485	15.927
	2.0	11.927	12.352	12.776	13.199	13.620	14.039	14.458	14.875	15.291	15.705
1.200	3.0	11.911	12.320	12.726	13.130	13.531	13.930	14.326	14.721	15.114	15.504
	4.0	11.896	12.289	12.679	13.065	13.448	13.828	14.206	14.580	14.953	15.323
	5.0	11.882	12.261	12.635	13.005	13.372	13.735	14.096	14.453	14.808	15.160
	7.5	11.847	12.190	12.527	12.859	13.188	13.512	13.833	14.151	14.466	14.778
	10.0	11.825	12.146	12.463	12.777	13.088	13.397	13.704	14.011	14.317	14.624
	12.5	11.802	12.101	12.398	12.692	12.984	13.277	13.570	13.864	14.161	14.462
	15.0	11.797	12.094	12.393	12.694	13.000	13.312	13.633	13.967	14.316	14.686
	1.0	11.944	12.388	12.832	13.276	13.719	14.163	14.606	15.050	15.493	15.937
	2.0	11.928	12.354	12.779	13.202	13.625	14.045	14.465	14.883	15.300	15.717
1.250	3.0	11.912	12.322	12.729	13.134	13.536	13.936	14.334	14.730	15.125	15.517
	4.0	11.897	12.291	12.682	13.070	13.454	13.836	14.215	14.591	14.965	15.337
	5.0	11.883	12.263	12.638	13.010	13.378	13.744	14.106	14.465	14.822	15.176
	7.5	11.849	12.192	12.531	12.865	13.196	13.522	13.845	14.165	14.483	14.798
	10.0	11.827	12.151	12.470	12.786	13.100	13.412	13.723	14.033	14.344	14.655
	12.5	11.805	12.107	12.406	12.703	13.000	13.296	13.594	13.894	14.197	14.504
	15.0	11.800	12.102	12.405	12.712	13.024	13.343	13.674	14.017	14.380	14.767

Interest Rate 12.00%   30 Year Schedule

Debt Coverage	Years to Payoff	10%	20%	30%	40%	50%	60%	70%	80%	90%	100%
	1.0	12.443	12.886	13.329	13.771	14.214	14.656	15.098	15.540	15.982	16.425
	2.0	12.426	12.850	13.273	13.694	14.114	14.533	14.950	15.366	15.781	16.195
1.150	3.0	12.409	12.816	13.220	13.622	14.021	14.419	14.814	15.207	15.598	15.988
	4.0	12.394	12.784	13.171	13.555	13.936	14.314	14.689	15.062	15.433	15.801
	5.0	12.379	12.754	13.125	13.493	13.857	14.218	14.576	14.932	15.285	15.635
	7.5	12.343	12.681	13.014	13.343	13.668	13.990	14.308	14.624	14.937	15.248
	10.0	12.321	12.638	12.952	13.263	13.572	13.880	14.187	14.493	14.800	15.109
	12.5	12.298	12.594	12.888	13.181	13.474	13.767	14.062	14.359	14.660	14.967
	15.0	12.296	12.593	12.894	13.199	13.511	13.832	14.165	14.514	14.884	15.282
	1.0	12.444	12.887	13.331	13.775	14.218	14.662	15.105	15.548	15.992	16.435
	2.0	12.426	12.852	13.276	13.698	14.119	14.539	14.958	15.375	15.792	16.207
1.200	3.0	12.410	12.818	13.223	13.626	14.027	14.426	14.822	15.217	15.610	16.001
	4.0	12.395	12.786	13.175	13.560	13.942	14.322	14.699	15.074	15.446	15.817
	5.0	12.380	12.757	13.129	13.498	13.864	14.227	14.587	14.945	15.300	15.653
	7.5	12.344	12.684	13.019	13.350	13.677	14.001	14.322	14.640	14.956	15.270
	10.0	12.323	12.643	12.960	13.274	13.586	13.897	14.208	14.519	14.831	15.145
	12.5	12.301	12.600	12.898	13.194	13.491	13.789	14.089	14.393	14.701	15.016
	15.0	12.300	12.602	12.908	13.220	13.539	13.869	14.213	14.575	14.962	15.383
	1.0	12.444	12.889	13.334	13.778	14.223	14.667	15.112	15.556	16.001	16.446
	2.0	12.427	12.854	13.278	13.702	14.124	14.545	14.965	15.384	15.802	16.219
1.250	3.0	12.411	12.820	13.227	13.631	14.033	14.433	14.831	15.228	15.622	16.015
	4.0	12.396	12.789	13.178	13.565	13.949	14.330	14.709	15.086	15.460	15.833
	5.0	12.381	12.759	13.133	13.504	13.872	14.236	14.598	14.958	15.316	15.671
	7.5	12.346	12.687	13.024	13.357	13.686	14.012	14.335	14.656	14.975	15.292
	10.0	12.325	12.648	12.967	13.284	13.600	13.915	14.230	14.545	14.862	15.181
	12.5	12.304	12.606	12.907	13.208	13.509	13.812	14.118	14.427	14.743	15.065
	15.0	12.304	12.611	12.923	13.241	13.568	13.907	14.262	14.638	15.043	15.489

Entry is annual yield from interest, growth in income and selected share of price appreciation.

Yield on Participating Mortgage Loan

Growth Rate   3%
Interest Rate 5.50%

Loan to Value Ratio 75%
30 Year Schedule

Debt Coverage	Years to Payoff	10%	20%	30%	40%	50%	60%	70%	80%	90%	100%
				Share of Increase in Income & Profit on Sale							
1.150	1.0	5.944	6.388	6.831	7.272	7.713	8.152	8.591	9.028	9.465	9.900
	2.0	5.941	6.379	6.815	7.248	7.678	8.105	8.530	8.952	9.371	9.788
	3.0	5.938	6.371	6.799	7.224	7.643	8.059	8.471	8.878	9.282	9.682
	4.0	5.934	6.362	6.784	7.200	7.610	8.015	8.414	8.808	9.197	9.581
	5.0	5.931	6.354	6.769	7.177	7.578	7.972	8.359	8.740	9.115	9.485
	7.5	5.922	6.333	6.732	7.119	7.497	7.865	8.225	8.576	8.919	9.254
	10.0	5.915	6.315	6.699	7.071	7.429	7.777	8.114	8.442	8.760	9.071
	12.5	5.908	6.296	6.666	7.020	7.360	7.687	8.003	8.308	8.603	8.890
	15.0	5.901	6.280	6.638	6.978	7.303	7.615	7.914	8.203	8.482	8.752
1.200	1.0	5.944	6.388	6.831	7.273	7.714	8.154	8.593	9.030	9.467	9.904
	2.0	5.941	6.380	6.816	7.249	7.679	8.107	8.532	8.954	9.374	9.792
	3.0	5.938	6.371	6.800	7.225	7.645	8.061	8.473	8.881	9.285	9.686
	4.0	5.934	6.363	6.785	7.201	7.612	8.017	8.416	8.811	9.200	9.585
	5.0	5.931	6.355	6.770	7.178	7.579	7.974	8.361	8.743	9.119	9.489
	7.5	5.923	6.333	6.732	7.121	7.499	7.868	8.227	8.579	8.923	9.259
	10.0	5.916	6.315	6.701	7.072	7.432	7.780	8.118	8.446	8.765	9.077
	12.5	5.908	6.296	6.667	7.022	7.362	7.690	8.007	8.313	8.609	8.897
	15.0	5.902	6.281	6.639	6.981	7.306	7.619	7.919	8.209	8.489	8.761
1.250	1.0	5.945	6.389	6.832	7.274	7.715	8.155	8.595	9.033	9.470	9.907
	2.0	5.941	6.380	6.816	7.250	7.680	8.108	8.534	8.957	9.377	9.795
	3.0	5.938	6.372	6.801	7.226	7.646	8.063	8.475	8.884	9.288	9.689
	4.0	5.935	6.363	6.786	7.202	7.613	8.018	8.418	8.813	9.203	9.589
	5.0	5.931	6.355	6.771	7.180	7.581	7.976	8.364	8.746	9.123	9.493
	7.5	5.923	6.334	6.733	7.122	7.501	7.870	8.230	8.582	8.927	9.264
	10.0	5.916	6.316	6.702	7.074	7.434	7.783	8.121	8.450	8.771	9.083
	12.5	5.908	6.297	6.668	7.024	7.365	7.694	8.011	8.317	8.615	8.904
	15.0	5.902	6.281	6.641	6.983	7.310	7.623	7.924	8.215	8.496	8.769

Interest Rate 6.00%   30 Year Schedule

Debt Coverage	Years to Payoff	10%	20%	30%	40%	50%	60%	70%	80%	90%	100%
1.150	1.0	6.444	6.887	7.329	7.770	8.210	8.649	9.088	9.525	9.961	10.397
	2.0	6.439	6.876	7.309	7.741	8.169	8.595	9.018	9.439	9.857	10.273
	3.0	6.434	6.865	7.290	7.712	8.129	8.542	8.951	9.357	9.758	10.157
	4.0	6.430	6.854	7.272	7.684	8.090	8.491	8.887	9.278	9.664	10.046
	5.0	6.425	6.843	7.253	7.656	8.052	8.442	8.826	9.203	9.575	9.941
	7.5	6.414	6.816	7.207	7.588	7.959	8.321	8.675	9.021	9.359	9.690
	10.0	6.404	6.792	7.168	7.530	7.881	8.222	8.552	8.874	9.188	9.494
	12.5	6.393	6.768	7.127	7.471	7.802	8.121	8.430	8.728	9.019	9.301
	15.0	6.384	6.748	7.093	7.422	7.738	8.041	8.334	8.617	8.891	9.157
1.200	1.0	6.444	6.887	7.330	7.771	8.212	8.651	9.090	9.527	9.964	10.400
	2.0	6.439	6.876	7.310	7.742	8.171	8.597	9.020	9.442	9.861	10.277
	3.0	6.435	6.865	7.291	7.713	8.131	8.544	8.954	9.360	9.762	10.161
	4.0	6.430	6.854	7.273	7.685	8.092	8.493	8.890	9.281	9.668	10.050
	5.0	6.426	6.844	7.254	7.658	8.054	8.444	8.828	9.206	9.579	9.946
	7.5	6.414	6.816	7.208	7.589	7.961	8.324	8.678	9.024	9.364	9.696
	10.0	6.404	6.793	7.169	7.532	7.884	8.225	8.557	8.879	9.194	9.501
	12.5	6.393	6.769	7.128	7.473	7.805	8.125	8.434	8.734	9.025	9.308
	15.0	6.385	6.749	7.095	7.425	7.742	8.046	8.340	8.624	8.899	9.167
1.250	1.0	6.444	6.888	7.330	7.772	8.213	8.653	9.092	9.530	9.967	10.404
	2.0	6.439	6.877	7.311	7.743	8.172	8.599	9.023	9.445	9.864	10.281
	3.0	6.435	6.866	7.292	7.714	8.132	8.546	8.956	9.363	9.766	10.165
	4.0	6.430	6.855	7.273	7.686	8.094	8.496	8.893	9.285	9.672	10.055
	5.0	6.426	6.844	7.255	7.659	8.056	8.447	8.831	9.210	9.583	9.951
	7.5	6.414	6.817	7.209	7.591	7.963	8.326	8.681	9.028	9.368	9.701
	10.0	6.404	6.794	7.170	7.534	7.886	8.228	8.561	8.884	9.200	9.508
	12.5	6.394	6.770	7.130	7.475	7.808	8.128	8.439	8.740	9.032	9.316
	15.0	6.385	6.750	7.097	7.428	7.746	8.051	8.346	8.631	8.908	9.177

Entry is annual yield from interest, growth in income and selected share of price appreciation.

Yield on Participating Mortgage Loan

Growth Rate   3%
Interest Rate 6.50%

Loan to Value Ratio 75%
30 Year Schedule

Debt Coverage	Years to Payoff	10%	20%	30%	40%	50%	60%	70%	80%	90%	100%
				Share of Increase in Income & Profit on Sale							
1.150	1.0	6.943	7.386	7.828	8.268	8.708	9.147	9.585	10.022	10.459	10.894
	2.0	6.937	7.372	7.804	8.234	8.661	9.086	9.508	9.927	10.345	10.760
	3.0	6.931	7.359	7.782	8.201	8.615	9.026	9.433	9.837	10.237	10.633
	4.0	6.926	7.345	7.760	8.168	8.571	8.969	9.362	9.750	10.134	10.513
	5.0	6.920	7.333	7.738	8.137	8.528	8.914	9.294	9.668	10.037	10.400
	7.5	6.905	7.300	7.684	8.058	8.423	8.779	9.128	9.469	9.803	10.130
	10.0	6.893	7.272	7.638	7.992	8.336	8.670	8.995	9.312	9.621	9.923
	12.5	6.879	7.242	7.590	7.925	8.248	8.560	8.862	9.155	9.440	9.718
	15.0	6.868	7.218	7.552	7.872	8.179	8.475	8.761	9.039	9.309	9.573
1.200	1.0	6.943	7.386	7.828	8.270	8.710	9.149	9.588	10.025	10.462	10.898
	2.0	6.937	7.373	7.805	8.235	8.663	9.088	9.510	9.930	10.348	10.764
	3.0	6.932	7.359	7.783	8.202	8.617	9.029	9.436	9.840	10.241	10.638
	4.0	6.926	7.346	7.761	8.170	8.573	8.972	9.365	9.754	10.138	10.518
	5.0	6.920	7.333	7.739	8.138	8.531	8.917	9.297	9.672	10.041	10.406
	7.5	6.906	7.300	7.685	8.059	8.425	8.782	9.132	9.473	9.808	10.136
	10.0	6.893	7.273	7.639	7.995	8.339	8.674	9.000	9.318	9.628	9.931
	12.5	6.880	7.243	7.592	7.928	8.251	8.564	8.867	9.162	9.448	9.727
	15.0	6.869	7.220	7.554	7.875	8.183	8.480	8.768	9.047	9.319	9.585
1.250	1.0	6.944	7.387	7.829	8.271	8.711	9.151	9.590	10.028	10.466	10.902
	2.0	6.938	7.373	7.806	8.237	8.664	9.090	9.513	9.934	10.352	10.768
	3.0	6.932	7.360	7.784	8.203	8.619	9.031	9.439	9.844	10.245	10.642
	4.0	6.926	7.347	7.762	8.171	8.575	8.974	9.368	9.758	10.143	10.523
	5.0	6.920	7.334	7.740	8.140	8.533	8.920	9.301	9.676	10.046	10.411
	7.5	6.906	7.301	7.686	8.061	8.427	8.785	9.135	9.478	9.813	10.142
	10.0	6.894	7.274	7.641	7.997	8.342	8.678	9.005	9.323	9.635	9.939
	12.5	6.880	7.245	7.594	7.930	8.255	8.568	8.873	9.168	9.456	9.736
	15.0	6.870	7.221	7.557	7.878	8.187	8.486	8.775	9.056	9.329	9.596

Interest Rate 7.00%   30 Year Schedule

Debt Coverage	Years to Payoff	10%	20%	30%	40%	50%	60%	70%	80%	90%	100%
1.150	1.0	7.443	7.885	8.326	8.767	9.207	9.645	10.083	10.520	10.957	11.392
	2.0	7.436	7.869	8.300	8.728	9.154	9.577	9.998	10.417	10.833	11.247
	3.0	7.428	7.853	8.274	8.690	9.103	9.511	9.916	10.318	10.716	11.111
	4.0	7.422	7.838	8.248	8.653	9.053	9.448	9.839	10.224	10.606	10.983
	5.0	7.415	7.823	8.223	8.618	9.006	9.388	9.764	10.135	10.501	10.862
	7.5	7.397	7.784	8.161	8.529	8.889	9.240	9.584	9.920	10.250	10.574
	10.0	7.382	7.752	8.110	8.457	8.794	9.122	9.442	9.754	10.059	10.358
	12.5	7.367	7.719	8.057	8.383	8.698	9.003	9.300	9.588	9.869	10.144
	15.0	7.354	7.692	8.015	8.326	8.625	8.915	9.196	9.470	9.737	9.999
1.200	1.0	7.443	7.886	8.327	8.768	9.208	9.647	10.086	10.524	10.961	11.397
	2.0	7.436	7.870	8.301	8.729	9.156	9.579	10.001	10.420	10.837	11.252
	3.0	7.429	7.854	8.275	8.692	9.105	9.514	9.920	10.322	10.721	11.116
	4.0	7.422	7.838	8.249	8.655	9.056	9.451	9.842	10.228	10.610	10.988
	5.0	7.415	7.823	8.225	8.620	9.008	9.391	9.768	10.140	10.506	10.868
	7.5	7.398	7.785	8.163	8.531	8.891	9.243	9.588	9.925	10.256	10.581
	10.0	7.383	7.753	8.112	8.460	8.798	9.127	9.448	9.761	10.067	10.367
	12.5	7.367	7.720	8.059	8.386	8.702	9.009	9.306	9.596	9.878	10.154
	15.0	7.355	7.693	8.018	8.330	8.630	8.922	9.205	9.480	9.749	10.013
1.250	1.0	7.443	7.886	8.328	8.770	9.210	9.650	10.089	10.527	10.964	11.401
	2.0	7.436	7.870	8.302	8.731	9.157	9.582	10.004	10.424	10.841	11.257
	3.0	7.429	7.855	8.276	8.693	9.107	9.517	9.923	10.326	10.725	11.121
	4.0	7.422	7.839	8.251	8.657	9.058	9.454	9.845	10.233	10.615	10.994
	5.0	7.415	7.824	8.226	8.621	9.011	9.394	9.772	10.144	10.512	10.874
	7.5	7.398	7.786	8.164	8.533	8.894	9.247	9.592	9.930	10.262	10.588
	10.0	7.383	7.754	8.114	8.462	8.801	9.131	9.453	9.767	10.075	10.376
	12.5	7.368	7.721	8.061	8.389	8.706	9.014	9.312	9.603	9.887	10.165
	15.0	7.355	7.695	8.020	8.333	8.636	8.928	9.213	9.490	9.761	10.027

Entry is annual yield from interest, growth in income and selected share of price appreciation.

Yield on Participating Mortgage Loan

Growth Rate   3%
Interest Rate 7.50%

Loan to Value Ratio 75%
30 Year Schedule

Debt Coverage	Years to Payoff	Share of Increase in Income & Profit on Sale									
		10%	20%	30%	40%	50%	60%	70%	80%	90%	100%
1.150	1.0	7.942	8.384	8.825	9.266	9.705	10.144	10.582	11.019	11.456	11.891
	2.0	7.934	8.366	8.795	9.222	9.647	10.069	10.489	10.907	11.323	11.736
	3.0	7.926	8.348	8.766	9.180	9.591	9.997	10.401	10.801	11.197	11.591
	4.0	7.918	8.330	8.738	9.140	9.537	9.929	10.317	10.700	11.079	11.454
	5.0	7.910	8.313	8.710	9.100	9.485	9.863	10.236	10.605	10.968	11.326
	7.5	7.890	8.270	8.641	9.003	9.357	9.703	10.042	10.375	10.701	11.022
	10.0	7.873	8.234	8.584	8.924	9.256	9.578	9.893	10.201	10.503	10.799
	12.5	7.855	8.197	8.526	8.844	9.153	9.452	9.744	10.028	10.306	10.577
	15.0	7.841	8.168	8.482	8.785	9.078	9.363	9.640	9.911	10.176	10.437
1.200	1.0	7.943	8.385	8.827	9.267	9.707	10.146	10.585	11.023	11.460	11.896
	2.0	7.934	8.367	8.796	9.224	9.649	10.072	10.492	10.911	11.327	11.742
	3.0	7.926	8.349	8.767	9.182	9.593	10.000	10.404	10.805	11.202	11.596
	4.0	7.918	8.331	8.739	9.141	9.539	9.932	10.320	10.705	11.084	11.460
	5.0	7.910	8.314	8.711	9.102	9.487	9.867	10.241	10.610	10.974	11.333
	7.5	7.890	8.271	8.642	9.005	9.360	9.707	10.047	10.381	10.708	11.029
	10.0	7.873	8.235	8.586	8.928	9.260	9.583	9.900	10.209	10.512	10.809
	12.5	7.856	8.198	8.529	8.848	9.157	9.458	9.751	10.037	10.316	10.590
	15.0	7.842	8.170	8.485	8.789	9.084	9.370	9.650	9.923	10.190	10.454
1.250	1.0	7.943	8.386	8.828	9.269	9.709	10.149	10.588	11.026	11.464	11.901
	2.0	7.935	8.367	8.798	9.226	9.651	10.075	10.496	10.915	11.332	11.747
	3.0	7.927	8.349	8.769	9.184	9.595	10.003	10.408	10.809	11.207	11.602
	4.0	7.919	8.332	8.740	9.143	9.542	9.935	10.324	10.709	11.090	11.467
	5.0	7.911	8.315	8.713	9.104	9.490	9.870	10.245	10.615	10.980	11.340
	7.5	7.891	8.272	8.644	9.007	9.363	9.711	10.052	10.386	10.715	11.037
	10.0	7.874	8.237	8.589	8.931	9.264	9.589	9.906	10.217	10.521	10.820
	12.5	7.857	8.200	8.531	8.851	9.162	9.464	9.758	10.046	10.327	10.602
	15.0	7.843	8.172	8.488	8.794	9.090	9.378	9.659	9.935	10.205	10.471

Interest Rate 8.00%   30 Year Schedule

Debt Coverage	Years to Payoff	10%	20%	30%	40%	50%	60%	70%	80%	90%	100%
1.150	1.0	8.442	8.884	9.325	9.765	10.204	10.643	11.081	11.519	11.955	12.391
	2.0	8.433	8.863	9.291	9.717	10.141	10.562	10.981	11.398	11.813	12.226
	3.0	8.423	8.843	9.259	9.671	10.080	10.485	10.886	11.285	11.680	12.072
	4.0	8.414	8.823	9.227	9.627	10.021	10.411	10.796	11.177	11.554	11.928
	5.0	8.405	8.804	9.197	9.584	9.965	10.340	10.711	11.076	11.437	11.793
	7.5	8.383	8.756	9.121	9.478	9.827	10.169	10.504	10.833	11.156	11.474
	10.0	8.364	8.717	9.061	9.395	9.720	10.038	10.349	10.654	10.953	11.246
	12.5	8.344	8.677	8.998	9.310	9.612	9.906	10.194	10.474	10.750	11.020
	15.0	8.329	8.647	8.953	9.249	9.537	9.818	10.092	10.362	10.627	10.888
1.200	1.0	8.442	8.885	9.326	9.767	10.207	10.646	11.085	11.523	11.960	12.397
	2.0	8.433	8.864	9.293	9.719	10.143	10.565	10.985	11.403	11.818	12.232
	3.0	8.424	8.844	9.260	9.673	10.082	10.488	10.890	11.289	11.685	12.079
	4.0	8.415	8.824	9.229	9.629	10.024	10.414	10.800	11.182	11.561	11.935
	5.0	8.406	8.805	9.199	9.586	9.968	10.344	10.715	11.082	11.443	11.801
	7.5	8.383	8.758	9.123	9.481	9.830	10.173	10.509	10.839	11.163	11.482
	10.0	8.365	8.719	9.063	9.398	9.725	10.044	10.357	10.663	10.963	11.258
	12.5	8.345	8.679	9.001	9.314	9.617	9.913	10.202	10.485	10.762	11.034
	15.0	8.331	8.649	8.956	9.254	9.544	9.827	10.104	10.376	10.644	10.908
1.250	1.0	8.443	8.885	9.327	9.768	10.209	10.649	11.088	11.527	11.965	12.402
	2.0	8.433	8.865	9.294	9.721	10.145	10.568	10.989	11.407	11.824	12.238
	3.0	8.424	8.845	9.262	9.675	10.085	10.491	10.894	11.294	11.691	12.085
	4.0	8.415	8.825	9.230	9.631	10.027	10.418	10.805	11.188	11.567	11.942
	5.0	8.406	8.806	9.200	9.588	9.971	10.348	10.720	11.087	11.450	11.809
	7.5	8.384	8.759	9.125	9.483	9.834	10.178	10.515	10.846	11.171	11.491
	10.0	8.365	8.721	9.066	9.402	9.730	10.050	10.364	10.671	10.973	11.270
	12.5	8.346	8.681	9.004	9.318	9.623	9.920	10.211	10.495	10.774	11.048
	15.0	8.332	8.651	8.960	9.260	9.552	9.836	10.116	10.390	10.660	10.928

Entry is annual yield from interest, growth in income and selected share of price appreciation.

Yield on Participating Mortgage Loan

Growth Rate   3%   Loan to Value Ratio 75%
Interest Rate 8.50%   30 Year Schedule

Debt Coverage	Years to Payoff	Share of Increase in Income & Profit on Sale									
		10%	20%	30%	40%	50%	60%	70%	80%	90%	100%
1.150	1.0	8.942	9.383	9.824	10.265	10.704	11.143	11.581	12.019	12.456	12.892
	2.0	8.931	9.361	9.788	10.213	10.635	11.056	11.474	11.891	12.305	12.718
	3.0	8.921	9.338	9.752	10.163	10.569	10.973	11.373	11.770	12.164	12.555
	4.0	8.911	9.317	9.718	10.114	10.506	10.894	11.277	11.656	12.032	12.404
	5.0	8.901	9.296	9.685	10.068	10.446	10.819	11.187	11.550	11.908	12.263
	7.5	8.876	9.244	9.603	9.955	10.299	10.637	10.969	11.294	11.614	11.929
	10.0	8.856	9.202	9.539	9.867	10.188	10.502	10.810	11.112	11.408	11.700
	12.5	8.835	9.159	9.473	9.778	10.076	10.366	10.650	10.928	11.202	11.471
	15.0	8.819	9.128	9.428	9.719	10.003	10.281	10.554	10.824	11.090	11.354
1.200	1.0	8.942	9.384	9.826	10.266	10.707	11.146	11.585	12.023	12.461	12.898
	2.0	8.932	9.362	9.789	10.215	10.638	11.059	11.478	11.895	12.311	12.724
	3.0	8.921	9.339	9.754	10.165	10.572	10.976	11.377	11.775	12.170	12.562
	4.0	8.911	9.318	9.720	10.117	10.509	10.898	11.282	11.662	12.039	12.412
	5.0	8.901	9.297	9.687	10.071	10.450	10.823	11.192	11.556	11.916	12.272
	7.5	8.877	9.245	9.605	9.958	10.303	10.642	10.975	11.301	11.623	11.939
	10.0	8.857	9.204	9.542	9.872	10.194	10.509	10.818	11.122	11.420	11.714
	12.5	8.836	9.161	9.477	9.783	10.082	10.374	10.660	10.940	11.216	11.487
	15.0	8.821	9.131	9.432	9.725	10.011	10.292	10.568	10.840	11.110	11.378
1.250	1.0	8.943	9.385	9.827	10.268	10.709	11.149	11.589	12.028	12.466	12.904
	2.0	8.932	9.362	9.791	10.217	10.640	11.062	11.482	11.900	12.316	12.731
	3.0	8.922	9.340	9.755	10.167	10.575	10.980	11.382	11.781	12.176	12.570
	4.0	8.912	9.319	9.721	10.119	10.513	10.902	11.287	11.668	12.046	12.420
	5.0	8.902	9.298	9.689	10.074	10.453	10.828	11.197	11.562	11.923	12.280
	7.5	8.877	9.246	9.607	9.961	10.307	10.647	10.981	11.309	11.631	11.949
	10.0	8.858	9.206	9.545	9.876	10.199	10.516	10.827	11.132	11.432	11.728
	12.5	8.837	9.163	9.480	9.788	10.088	10.382	10.670	10.952	11.230	11.504
	15.0	8.822	9.134	9.437	9.732	10.020	10.303	10.582	10.857	11.130	11.401

Interest Rate 9.00%   30 Year Schedule

Debt Coverage	Years to Payoff	10%	20%	30%	40%	50%	60%	70%	80%	90%	100%
1.150	1.0	9.442	9.883	10.324	10.764	11.204	11.643	12.082	12.520	12.957	13.394
	2.0	9.430	9.858	10.284	10.708	11.130	11.550	11.968	12.384	12.798	13.210
	3.0	9.419	9.834	10.246	10.655	11.060	11.462	11.861	12.257	12.650	13.040
	4.0	9.408	9.811	10.209	10.603	10.993	11.378	11.760	12.137	12.511	12.882
	5.0	9.397	9.788	10.174	10.554	10.929	11.299	11.665	12.026	12.383	12.736
	7.5	9.370	9.732	10.086	10.433	10.774	11.108	11.436	11.759	12.076	12.389
	10.0	9.349	9.688	10.020	10.343	10.660	10.970	11.275	11.575	11.870	12.161
	12.5	9.326	9.643	9.951	10.251	10.544	10.831	11.113	11.390	11.662	11.932
	15.0	9.311	9.613	9.907	10.194	10.476	10.753	11.027	11.298	11.567	11.836
1.200	1.0	9.442	9.884	10.326	10.767	11.207	11.647	12.086	12.524	12.963	13.401
	2.0	9.431	9.859	10.286	10.711	11.133	11.554	11.972	12.389	12.804	13.218
	3.0	9.419	9.835	10.248	10.657	11.063	11.466	11.866	12.262	12.657	13.048
	4.0	9.408	9.812	10.211	10.606	10.996	11.383	11.765	12.144	12.519	12.891
	5.0	9.398	9.790	10.176	10.557	10.933	11.304	11.671	12.033	12.391	12.745
	7.5	9.371	9.733	10.089	10.437	10.778	11.113	11.443	11.767	12.086	12.401
	10.0	9.350	9.690	10.023	10.348	10.666	10.978	11.285	11.587	11.884	12.177
	12.5	9.327	9.646	9.955	10.257	10.552	10.841	11.124	11.403	11.679	11.951
	15.0	9.312	9.616	9.912	10.202	10.486	10.766	11.043	11.317	11.591	11.864
1.250	1.0	9.443	9.885	10.327	10.769	11.209	11.650	12.090	12.529	12.968	13.407
	2.0	9.431	9.860	10.288	10.713	11.136	11.557	11.977	12.395	12.811	13.225
	3.0	9.420	9.836	10.250	10.660	11.066	11.470	11.871	12.268	12.663	13.056
	4.0	9.409	9.813	10.213	10.609	11.000	11.387	11.770	12.150	12.527	12.900
	5.0	9.398	9.791	10.178	10.560	10.937	11.309	11.677	12.040	12.399	12.755
	7.5	9.371	9.735	10.091	10.440	10.783	11.119	11.450	11.775	12.096	12.412
	10.0	9.351	9.692	10.026	10.353	10.672	10.986	11.295	11.598	11.898	12.193
	12.5	9.329	9.648	9.959	10.262	10.559	10.850	11.136	11.417	11.695	11.970
	15.0	9.314	9.620	9.918	10.210	10.496	10.779	11.059	11.337	11.615	11.893

Entry is annual yield from interest, growth in income and selected share of price appreciation.

Yield on Participating Mortgage Loan

Growth Rate   3%   Loan to Value Ratio 75%
Interest Rate 9.50%   30 Year Schedule

Debt Coverage	Years to Payoff	10%	20%	30%	40%	50%	60%	70%	80%	90%	100%
					Share of Increase in Income & Profit on Sale						
	1.0	9.942	10.383	10.824	11.265	11.705	12.144	12.583	13.021	13.459	13.897
	2.0	9.929	10.356	10.782	11.205	11.626	12.045	12.463	12.878	13.292	13.704
1.150	3.0	9.917	10.330	10.741	11.147	11.551	11.952	12.350	12.745	13.137	13.527
	4.0	9.905	10.305	10.701	11.093	11.480	11.864	12.244	12.620	12.993	13.363
	5.0	9.893	10.281	10.664	11.041	11.413	11.781	12.145	12.504	12.859	13.211
	7.5	9.864	10.221	10.571	10.914	11.250	11.581	11.906	12.227	12.543	12.854
	10.0	9.842	10.176	10.502	10.822	11.135	11.443	11.746	12.044	12.339	12.630
	12.5	9.819	10.129	10.432	10.728	11.018	11.303	11.583	11.859	12.133	12.404
	15.0	9.804	10.101	10.391	10.676	10.957	11.235	11.510	11.785	12.060	12.336
	1.0	9.942	10.384	10.826	11.267	11.708	12.148	12.587	13.027	13.465	13.904
	2.0	9.930	10.357	10.783	11.207	11.629	12.049	12.468	12.884	13.299	13.712
1.200	3.0	9.917	10.332	10.742	11.150	11.555	11.956	12.355	12.751	13.145	13.535
	4.0	9.905	10.307	10.703	11.096	11.484	11.869	12.250	12.627	13.001	13.372
	5.0	9.894	10.283	10.666	11.044	11.418	11.787	12.151	12.512	12.869	13.222
	7.5	9.865	10.223	10.573	10.917	11.255	11.587	11.914	12.236	12.553	12.866
	10.0	9.843	10.178	10.506	10.827	11.142	11.452	11.757	12.057	12.354	12.648
	12.5	9.820	10.132	10.437	10.734	11.026	11.313	11.596	11.875	12.152	12.426
	15.0	9.806	10.105	10.397	10.685	10.969	11.250	11.530	11.809	12.089	12.370
	1.0	9.943	10.385	10.828	11.269	11.710	12.151	12.592	13.032	13.472	13.911
	2.0	9.930	10.359	10.785	11.210	11.632	12.053	12.473	12.890	13.306	13.720
1.250	3.0	9.918	10.333	10.744	11.153	11.558	11.961	12.361	12.758	13.152	13.544
	4.0	9.906	10.308	10.705	11.099	11.488	11.874	12.256	12.634	13.010	13.382
	5.0	9.895	10.284	10.668	11.048	11.422	11.792	12.158	12.520	12.878	13.233
	7.5	9.866	10.225	10.576	10.921	11.260	11.594	11.922	12.245	12.564	12.879
	10.0	9.844	10.181	10.510	10.833	11.149	11.461	11.768	12.071	12.370	12.667
	12.5	9.822	10.135	10.441	10.741	11.035	11.324	11.609	11.891	12.171	12.448
	15.0	9.808	10.109	10.404	10.694	10.981	11.266	11.549	11.833	12.117	12.405

Interest Rate 10.00%   30 Year Schedule

Debt Coverage	Years to Payoff	10%	20%	30%	40%	50%	60%	70%	80%	90%	100%
	1.0	10.442	10.883	11.325	11.765	12.206	12.645	13.085	13.524	13.962	14.400
	2.0	10.428	10.855	11.279	11.702	12.122	12.541	12.958	13.374	13.788	14.200
1.150	3.0	10.415	10.827	11.235	11.641	12.044	12.443	12.840	13.234	13.626	14.015
	4.0	10.402	10.800	11.194	11.583	11.969	12.351	12.730	13.105	13.477	13.845
	5.0	10.390	10.774	11.154	11.529	11.899	12.265	12.627	12.985	13.339	13.690
	7.5	10.359	10.711	11.057	11.396	11.729	12.057	12.380	12.698	13.013	13.323
	10.0	10.336	10.665	10.987	11.303	11.614	11.920	12.222	12.520	12.814	13.107
	12.5	10.312	10.618	10.916	11.209	11.497	11.780	12.060	12.338	12.613	12.887
	15.0	10.299	10.592	10.880	11.164	11.446	11.727	12.007	12.288	12.572	12.859
	1.0	10.442	10.885	11.326	11.768	12.209	12.649	13.090	13.529	13.969	14.408
	2.0	10.429	10.856	11.281	11.704	12.126	12.546	12.964	13.380	13.795	14.208
1.200	3.0	10.415	10.828	11.238	11.644	12.047	12.448	12.846	13.241	13.634	14.025
	4.0	10.403	10.802	11.196	11.587	11.973	12.357	12.736	13.113	13.486	13.856
	5.0	10.391	10.776	11.157	11.533	11.904	12.271	12.634	12.993	13.349	13.702
	7.5	10.360	10.713	11.060	11.400	11.735	12.064	12.389	12.709	13.025	13.337
	10.0	10.337	10.668	10.992	11.310	11.622	11.930	12.234	12.535	12.832	13.128
	12.5	10.314	10.621	10.921	11.216	11.507	11.793	12.076	12.356	12.635	12.913
	15.0	10.301	10.596	10.887	11.175	11.461	11.745	12.030	12.316	12.606	12.900
	1.0	10.443	10.886	11.328	11.770	12.212	12.653	13.094	13.535	13.976	14.416
	2.0	10.429	10.857	11.283	11.707	12.129	12.550	12.969	13.387	13.803	14.217
1.250	3.0	10.416	10.830	11.240	11.647	12.051	12.453	12.852	13.249	13.643	14.034
	4.0	10.403	10.803	11.199	11.590	11.978	12.362	12.743	13.121	13.495	13.867
	5.0	10.391	10.778	11.159	11.536	11.909	12.277	12.641	13.002	13.360	13.714
	7.5	10.361	10.715	11.063	11.404	11.740	12.071	12.397	12.719	13.037	13.351
	10.0	10.339	10.671	10.996	11.316	11.630	11.941	12.247	12.550	12.850	13.149
	12.5	10.316	10.624	10.927	11.224	11.517	11.805	12.091	12.375	12.657	12.939
	15.0	10.303	10.601	10.895	11.186	11.475	11.764	12.053	12.345	12.640	12.941

Entry is annual yield from interest, growth in income and selected share of price appreciation.

Yield on Participating Mortgage Loan

Growth Rate   3%   Loan to Value Ratio 75%
Interest Rate 10.50%   30 Year Schedule

Debt Coverage	Years to Payoff	Share of Increase in Income & Profit on Sale 10%	20%	30%	40%	50%	60%	70%	80%	90%	100%
	1.0	10.942	11.384	11.825	12.266	12.707	13.147	13.587	14.027	14.466	14.905
	2.0	10.927	11.353	11.777	12.199	12.619	13.038	13.455	13.870	14.284	14.697
1.150	3.0	10.913	11.324	11.731	12.135	12.537	12.935	13.332	13.725	14.116	14.505
	4.0	10.900	11.295	11.687	12.075	12.459	12.840	13.217	13.591	13.962	14.331
	5.0	10.887	11.268	11.646	12.018	12.386	12.750	13.111	13.468	13.821	14.171
	7.5	10.854	11.202	11.544	11.880	12.210	12.536	12.857	13.174	13.487	13.796
	10.0	10.831	11.156	11.475	11.788	12.097	12.402	12.703	13.002	13.298	13.592
	12.5	10.807	11.108	11.404	11.694	11.981	12.265	12.546	12.826	13.105	13.383
	15.0	10.795	11.086	11.374	11.660	11.945	12.231	12.518	12.809	13.105	13.407
	1.0	10.942	11.385	11.827	12.269	12.710	13.152	13.592	14.033	14.473	14.913
	2.0	10.928	11.354	11.779	12.202	12.623	13.043	13.461	13.877	14.292	14.706
1.200	3.0	10.914	11.325	11.733	12.139	12.541	12.941	13.338	13.733	14.126	14.516
	4.0	10.900	11.297	11.690	12.079	12.464	12.846	13.224	13.600	13.973	14.342
	5.0	10.887	11.270	11.648	12.022	12.392	12.757	13.119	13.477	13.832	14.185
	7.5	10.855	11.204	11.547	11.885	12.217	12.544	12.867	13.185	13.500	13.812
	10.0	10.833	11.159	11.480	11.795	12.106	12.414	12.718	13.019	13.318	13.616
	12.5	10.809	11.112	11.410	11.703	11.993	12.280	12.564	12.848	13.130	13.413
	15.0	10.798	11.092	11.383	11.673	11.962	12.253	12.546	12.843	13.146	13.457
	1.0	10.943	11.386	11.829	12.272	12.714	13.156	13.598	14.039	14.481	14.922
	2.0	10.929	11.356	11.781	12.205	12.627	13.048	13.467	13.884	14.301	14.715
1.250	3.0	10.915	11.327	11.736	12.142	12.545	12.946	13.345	13.741	14.135	14.527
	4.0	10.901	11.299	11.692	12.082	12.469	12.852	13.232	13.609	13.983	14.354
	5.0	10.888	11.272	11.651	12.026	12.397	12.764	13.127	13.487	13.844	14.198
	7.5	10.856	11.207	11.551	11.889	12.223	12.552	12.876	13.197	13.514	13.828
	10.0	10.834	11.162	11.485	11.802	12.116	12.426	12.732	13.037	13.339	13.640
	12.5	10.811	11.116	11.416	11.712	12.004	12.294	12.582	12.869	13.156	13.444
	15.0	10.800	11.097	11.392	11.685	11.979	12.275	12.573	12.877	13.188	13.508

Interest Rate 11.00%   30 Year Schedule

Debt Coverage	Years to Payoff	10%	20%	30%	40%	50%	60%	70%	80%	90%	100%
	1.0	11.442	11.884	12.326	12.768	13.209	13.650	14.090	14.530	14.971	15.411
	2.0	11.427	11.852	12.275	12.697	13.117	13.535	13.952	14.368	14.782	15.195
1.150	3.0	11.412	11.821	12.227	12.630	13.031	13.429	13.824	14.218	14.609	14.998
	4.0	11.397	11.791	12.181	12.567	12.950	13.330	13.706	14.079	14.450	14.818
	5.0	11.384	11.763	12.138	12.508	12.875	13.238	13.597	13.953	14.306	14.656
	7.5	11.350	11.694	12.032	12.365	12.694	13.017	13.337	13.653	13.966	14.275
	10.0	11.327	11.648	11.964	12.276	12.584	12.889	13.191	13.491	13.789	14.087
	12.5	11.303	11.601	11.895	12.185	12.472	12.757	13.041	13.325	13.609	13.894
	15.0	11.293	11.584	11.874	12.164	12.455	12.748	13.046	13.351	13.663	13.987
	1.0	11.443	11.886	12.328	12.771	13.213	13.654	14.096	14.537	14.979	15.420
	2.0	11.427	11.853	12.278	12.700	13.121	13.541	13.959	14.375	14.791	15.205
1.200	3.0	11.412	11.822	12.229	12.634	13.035	13.435	13.832	14.226	14.619	15.009
	4.0	11.398	11.793	12.184	12.571	12.955	13.336	13.714	14.089	14.461	14.831
	5.0	11.385	11.765	12.141	12.513	12.881	13.245	13.606	13.964	14.319	14.671
	7.5	11.351	11.696	12.036	12.371	12.701	13.026	13.348	13.666	13.981	14.293
	10.0	11.329	11.652	11.970	12.284	12.595	12.902	13.207	13.511	13.813	14.114
	12.5	11.305	11.605	11.902	12.195	12.485	12.774	13.062	13.350	13.638	13.929
	15.0	11.296	11.591	11.884	12.179	12.475	12.774	13.079	13.391	13.714	14.049
	1.0	11.443	11.887	12.330	12.773	13.216	13.659	14.102	14.544	14.987	15.429
	2.0	11.428	11.855	12.280	12.703	13.125	13.546	13.965	14.383	14.800	15.215
1.250	3.0	11.413	11.824	12.232	12.637	13.040	13.441	13.839	14.235	14.629	15.021
	4.0	11.399	11.795	12.187	12.575	12.961	13.343	13.722	14.099	14.473	14.844
	5.0	11.386	11.767	12.144	12.518	12.887	13.253	13.615	13.975	14.331	14.685
	7.5	11.352	11.699	12.040	12.376	12.708	13.035	13.359	13.679	13.996	14.310
	10.0	11.330	11.656	11.976	12.292	12.606	12.916	13.224	13.531	13.837	14.142
	12.5	11.307	11.610	11.909	12.205	12.498	12.791	13.083	13.375	13.669	13.965
	15.0	11.299	11.597	11.895	12.193	12.495	12.800	13.112	13.433	13.765	14.113

Entry is annual yield from interest, growth in income and selected share of price appreciation.

Yield on Participating Mortgage Loan

Growth Rate   3%   Loan to Value Ratio 75%
Interest Rate 11.50%   30 Year Schedule

Debt Coverage	Years to Payoff	10%	20%	30%	40%	50%	60%	70%	80%	90%	100%
				Share of Increase in Income & Profit on Sale							
1.150	1.0	11.942	12.385	12.827	13.269	13.711	14.153	14.594	15.035	15.476	15.917
	2.0	11.926	12.351	12.774	13.195	13.615	14.034	14.451	14.866	15.281	15.694
	3.0	11.910	12.318	12.723	13.126	13.526	13.923	14.318	14.711	15.103	15.492
	4.0	11.895	12.287	12.676	13.061	13.442	13.821	14.197	14.570	14.940	15.309
	5.0	11.881	12.258	12.631	13.000	13.365	13.727	14.085	14.441	14.794	15.144
	7.5	11.846	12.187	12.522	12.853	13.180	13.502	13.821	14.136	14.449	14.759
	10.0	11.823	12.142	12.457	12.768	13.076	13.381	13.685	13.988	14.290	14.592
	12.5	11.800	12.096	12.389	12.680	12.969	13.257	13.546	13.835	14.126	14.421
	15.0	11.793	12.087	12.380	12.676	12.976	13.281	13.594	13.917	14.254	14.608
1.200	1.0	11.943	12.386	12.830	13.272	13.715	14.158	14.600	15.042	15.485	15.927
	2.0	11.927	12.352	12.776	13.199	13.620	14.039	14.458	14.875	15.291	15.705
	3.0	11.911	12.320	12.726	13.130	13.531	13.930	14.326	14.721	15.114	15.504
	4.0	11.896	12.289	12.679	13.065	13.448	13.828	14.206	14.580	14.953	15.323
	5.0	11.882	12.261	12.635	13.005	13.372	13.735	14.096	14.453	14.808	15.160
	7.5	11.847	12.190	12.527	12.859	13.188	13.512	13.833	14.151	14.466	14.778
	10.0	11.825	12.146	12.463	12.777	13.088	13.397	13.704	14.011	14.317	14.624
	12.5	11.802	12.101	12.398	12.692	12.984	13.277	13.570	13.864	14.161	14.462
	15.0	11.797	12.094	12.393	12.694	13.000	13.312	13.633	13.967	14.316	14.686
1.250	1.0	11.944	12.388	12.832	13.276	13.719	14.163	14.606	15.050	15.493	15.937
	2.0	11.928	12.354	12.779	13.202	13.625	14.045	14.465	14.883	15.300	15.717
	3.0	11.912	12.322	12.729	13.134	13.536	13.936	14.334	14.730	15.125	15.517
	4.0	11.897	12.291	12.682	13.070	13.454	13.836	14.215	14.591	14.965	15.337
	5.0	11.883	12.263	12.638	13.010	13.378	13.744	14.106	14.465	14.822	15.176
	7.5	11.849	12.192	12.531	12.865	13.196	13.522	13.845	14.165	14.483	14.798
	10.0	11.827	12.151	12.470	12.786	13.100	13.412	13.723	14.033	14.344	14.655
	12.5	11.805	12.107	12.406	12.703	13.000	13.296	13.594	13.894	14.197	14.504
	15.0	11.800	12.102	12.405	12.712	13.024	13.343	13.674	14.017	14.380	14.767

Interest Rate 12.00%   30 Year Schedule

Debt Coverage	Years to Payoff	10%	20%	30%	40%	50%	60%	70%	80%	90%	100%
1.150	1.0	12.443	12.886	13.329	13.771	14.214	14.656	15.098	15.540	15.982	16.425
	2.0	12.426	12.850	13.273	13.694	14.114	14.533	14.950	15.366	15.781	16.195
	3.0	12.409	12.816	13.220	13.622	14.021	14.419	14.814	15.207	15.598	15.988
	4.0	12.394	12.784	13.171	13.555	13.936	14.314	14.689	15.062	15.433	15.801
	5.0	12.379	12.754	13.125	13.493	13.857	14.218	14.576	14.932	15.285	15.635
	7.5	12.343	12.681	13.014	13.343	13.668	13.990	14.308	14.624	14.937	15.248
	10.0	12.321	12.638	12.952	13.263	13.572	13.880	14.187	14.493	14.800	15.109
	12.5	12.298	12.594	12.888	13.181	13.474	13.767	14.062	14.359	14.660	14.967
	15.0	12.296	12.593	12.894	13.199	13.511	13.832	14.165	14.514	14.884	15.282
1.200	1.0	12.444	12.887	13.331	13.775	14.218	14.662	15.105	15.548	15.992	16.435
	2.0	12.426	12.852	13.276	13.698	14.119	14.539	14.958	15.375	15.792	16.207
	3.0	12.410	12.818	13.223	13.626	14.027	14.426	14.822	15.217	15.610	16.001
	4.0	12.395	12.786	13.175	13.560	13.942	14.322	14.699	15.074	15.446	15.817
	5.0	12.380	12.757	13.129	13.498	13.864	14.227	14.587	14.945	15.300	15.653
	7.5	12.344	12.684	13.019	13.350	13.677	14.001	14.322	14.640	14.956	15.270
	10.0	12.323	12.643	12.960	13.274	13.586	13.897	14.208	14.519	14.831	15.145
	12.5	12.301	12.600	12.898	13.194	13.491	13.789	14.089	14.393	14.701	15.016
	15.0	12.300	12.602	12.908	13.220	13.539	13.869	14.213	14.575	14.962	15.383
1.250	1.0	12.444	12.889	13.334	13.778	14.223	14.667	15.112	15.556	16.001	16.446
	2.0	12.427	12.854	13.278	13.702	14.124	14.545	14.965	15.384	15.802	16.219
	3.0	12.411	12.820	13.227	13.631	14.033	14.433	14.831	15.228	15.622	16.015
	4.0	12.396	12.789	13.178	13.565	13.949	14.330	14.709	15.086	15.460	15.833
	5.0	12.381	12.759	13.133	13.504	13.872	14.236	14.598	14.958	15.316	15.671
	7.5	12.346	12.687	13.024	13.357	13.686	14.012	14.335	14.656	14.975	15.292
	10.0	12.325	12.648	12.967	13.284	13.600	13.915	14.230	14.545	14.862	15.181
	12.5	12.304	12.606	12.907	13.208	13.509	13.812	14.118	14.427	14.743	15.065
	15.0	12.304	12.611	12.923	13.241	13.568	13.907	14.262	14.638	15.043	15.489

Entry is annual yield from interest, growth in income and selected share of price appreciation.

Yield on Participating Mortgage Loan

Growth Rate   5%
Interest Rate 5.50%

Loan to Value Ratio 67%
30 Year Schedule

Debt Coverage	Years to Payoff	Share of Increase in Income & Profit on Sale									
		10%	20%	30%	40%	50%	60%	70%	80%	90%	100%
1.150	1.0	6.237	6.971	7.701	8.428	9.151	9.871	10.587	11.300	12.009	12.716
	2.0	6.237	6.966	7.686	8.398	9.101	9.796	10.484	11.164	11.837	12.504
	3.0	6.238	6.961	7.671	8.368	9.053	9.725	10.386	11.036	11.676	12.306
	4.0	6.238	6.957	7.657	8.339	9.006	9.656	10.292	10.915	11.524	12.121
	5.0	6.238	6.952	7.642	8.311	8.960	9.590	10.203	10.800	11.381	11.949
	7.5	6.239	6.939	7.605	8.240	8.847	9.429	9.988	10.527	11.046	11.549
	10.0	6.241	6.929	7.574	8.179	8.751	9.294	9.812	10.306	10.780	11.236
	12.5	6.242	6.918	7.540	8.116	8.655	9.161	9.639	10.094	10.527	10.941
	15.0	6.245	6.910	7.512	8.065	8.576	9.054	9.503	9.928	10.333	10.720
1.200	1.0	6.237	6.972	7.702	8.429	9.152	9.872	10.589	11.303	12.013	12.720
	2.0	6.238	6.967	7.687	8.399	9.103	9.799	10.487	11.168	11.841	12.508
	3.0	6.238	6.962	7.672	8.370	9.054	9.727	10.389	11.040	11.680	12.311
	4.0	6.238	6.957	7.658	8.341	9.007	9.659	10.296	10.919	11.529	12.127
	5.0	6.239	6.952	7.643	8.312	8.962	9.593	10.206	10.804	11.386	11.955
	7.5	6.239	6.940	7.606	8.241	8.849	9.431	9.991	10.531	11.052	11.555
	10.0	6.241	6.930	7.575	8.181	8.754	9.298	9.816	10.312	10.787	11.245
	12.5	6.242	6.919	7.541	8.118	8.658	9.165	9.645	10.100	10.534	10.950
	15.0	6.245	6.911	7.514	8.067	8.580	9.059	9.510	9.937	10.343	10.733
1.250	1.0	6.238	6.972	7.703	8.430	9.154	9.874	10.592	11.306	12.016	12.724
	2.0	6.238	6.967	7.688	8.400	9.104	9.801	10.489	11.171	11.845	12.513
	3.0	6.238	6.962	7.673	8.371	9.056	9.730	10.392	11.043	11.684	12.316
	4.0	6.238	6.958	7.659	8.342	9.009	9.661	10.299	10.922	11.533	12.132
	5.0	6.239	6.953	7.644	8.314	8.964	9.595	10.209	10.808	11.391	11.961
	7.5	6.239	6.940	7.607	8.243	8.851	9.434	9.995	10.535	11.057	11.562
	10.0	6.241	6.931	7.576	8.183	8.757	9.302	9.821	10.318	10.794	11.253
	12.5	6.243	6.920	7.543	8.121	8.661	9.169	9.650	10.106	10.542	10.960
	15.0	6.246	6.912	7.516	8.070	8.584	9.064	9.516	9.945	10.354	10.745

Interest Rate 6.00%   30 Year Schedule

Debt Coverage	Years to Payoff	10%	20%	30%	40%	50%	60%	70%	80%	90%	100%
1.150	1.0	6.736	7.468	8.197	8.923	9.645	10.364	11.079	11.791	12.500	13.206
	2.0	6.734	7.459	8.176	8.884	9.585	10.278	10.963	11.641	12.312	12.976
	3.0	6.732	7.450	8.155	8.847	9.527	10.195	10.852	11.499	12.135	12.762
	4.0	6.730	7.441	8.134	8.810	9.470	10.116	10.747	11.364	11.969	12.563
	5.0	6.728	7.432	8.114	8.774	9.416	10.039	10.646	11.237	11.814	12.377
	7.5	6.723	7.409	8.062	8.685	9.282	9.855	10.406	10.938	11.451	11.948
	10.0	6.719	7.389	8.017	8.609	9.170	9.703	10.211	10.699	11.166	11.617
	12.5	6.714	7.368	7.971	8.532	9.057	9.553	10.022	10.469	10.895	11.305
	15.0	6.711	7.351	7.933	8.468	8.967	9.434	9.875	10.294	10.694	11.078
1.200	1.0	6.736	7.469	8.198	8.924	9.647	10.366	11.082	11.794	12.504	13.211
	2.0	6.734	7.460	8.177	8.886	9.587	10.280	10.966	11.644	12.316	12.981
	3.0	6.732	7.451	8.156	8.848	9.529	10.197	10.855	11.502	12.140	12.767
	4.0	6.730	7.442	8.135	8.812	9.472	10.118	10.750	11.368	11.974	12.569
	5.0	6.728	7.433	8.115	8.776	9.418	10.042	10.650	11.242	11.819	12.383
	7.5	6.723	7.409	8.063	8.687	9.284	9.858	10.410	10.942	11.457	11.955
	10.0	6.719	7.390	8.019	8.612	9.173	9.707	10.217	10.705	11.174	11.627
	12.5	6.715	7.369	7.973	8.534	9.061	9.557	10.028	10.476	10.904	11.316
	15.0	6.712	7.352	7.935	8.472	8.972	9.440	9.883	10.303	10.706	11.092
1.250	1.0	6.736	7.469	8.199	8.925	9.648	10.368	11.084	11.798	12.508	13.216
	2.0	6.734	7.460	8.178	8.887	9.588	10.282	10.969	11.648	12.320	12.986
	3.0	6.732	7.451	8.157	8.850	9.531	10.200	10.858	11.506	12.144	12.773
	4.0	6.730	7.442	8.136	8.813	9.475	10.121	10.753	11.373	11.980	12.575
	5.0	6.729	7.433	8.116	8.778	9.420	10.045	10.654	11.246	11.825	12.390
	7.5	6.723	7.410	8.064	8.689	9.287	9.861	10.414	10.947	11.463	11.962
	10.0	6.720	7.391	8.021	8.614	9.176	9.711	10.222	10.712	11.182	11.636
	12.5	6.715	7.370	7.974	8.537	9.065	9.562	10.034	10.483	10.913	11.326
	15.0	6.713	7.353	7.937	8.475	8.976	9.446	9.891	10.313	10.718	11.107

Entry is annual yield from interest, growth in income and selected share of price appreciation.

Yield on Participating Mortgage Loan

Growth Rate   5%   Loan to Value Ratio 67%
Interest Rate 6.50%   30 Year Schedule

Debt Coverage	Years to Payoff	10%	20%	30%	40%	50%	60%	70%	80%	90%	100%
					Share of Increase in Income & Profit on Sale						
1.150	1.0	7.234	7.966	8.694	9.418	10.139	10.857	11.572	12.283	12.992	13.698
	2.0	7.230	7.952	8.666	9.372	10.069	10.760	11.442	12.118	12.787	13.449
	3.0	7.226	7.939	8.639	9.326	10.002	10.666	11.319	11.963	12.596	13.220
	4.0	7.222	7.926	8.612	9.282	9.937	10.577	11.203	11.816	12.417	13.006
	5.0	7.218	7.913	8.586	9.239	9.874	10.491	11.092	11.678	12.250	12.808
	7.5	7.207	7.879	8.520	9.133	9.720	10.284	10.828	11.353	11.860	12.352
	10.0	7.198	7.851	8.464	9.043	9.593	10.116	10.617	11.097	11.559	12.005
	12.5	7.188	7.820	8.406	8.952	9.466	9.951	10.411	10.851	11.272	11.678
	15.0	7.180	7.795	8.358	8.879	9.365	9.822	10.256	10.669	11.066	11.448
1.200	1.0	7.235	7.966	8.695	9.420	10.141	10.860	11.575	12.287	12.996	13.703
	2.0	7.231	7.953	8.667	9.373	10.071	10.762	11.446	12.122	12.792	13.455
	3.0	7.226	7.940	8.640	9.328	10.004	10.669	11.323	11.967	12.601	13.226
	4.0	7.222	7.927	8.613	9.284	9.939	10.580	11.207	11.821	12.423	13.013
	5.0	7.218	7.914	8.587	9.241	9.876	10.494	11.096	11.683	12.256	12.816
	7.5	7.207	7.880	8.522	9.135	9.723	10.288	10.832	11.358	11.867	12.360
	10.0	7.199	7.852	8.466	9.046	9.596	10.121	10.623	11.104	11.568	12.016
	12.5	7.189	7.822	8.408	8.955	9.470	9.956	10.418	10.860	11.283	11.690
	15.0	7.181	7.797	8.361	8.883	9.370	9.830	10.265	10.681	11.079	11.464
1.250	1.0	7.235	7.967	8.696	9.421	10.143	10.862	11.578	12.291	13.001	13.708
	2.0	7.231	7.954	8.668	9.375	10.073	10.765	11.449	12.126	12.797	13.461
	3.0	7.227	7.940	8.641	9.329	10.006	10.672	11.326	11.971	12.606	13.232
	4.0	7.223	7.927	8.615	9.286	9.941	10.583	11.210	11.825	12.428	13.020
	5.0	7.219	7.914	8.589	9.243	9.879	10.497	11.100	11.688	12.262	12.823
	7.5	7.208	7.881	8.523	9.137	9.726	10.292	10.837	11.364	11.873	12.368
	10.0	7.199	7.853	8.468	9.049	9.600	10.126	10.629	11.112	11.577	12.027
	12.5	7.189	7.823	8.410	8.958	9.474	9.962	10.425	10.868	11.293	11.702
	15.0	7.182	7.798	8.363	8.887	9.376	9.837	10.274	10.692	11.093	11.481

Interest Rate 7.00%   30 Year Schedule

Debt Coverage	Years to Payoff	10%	20%	30%	40%	50%	60%	70%	80%	90%	100%
1.150	1.0	7.733	8.464	9.190	9.914	10.634	11.351	12.065	12.777	13.485	14.190
	2.0	7.727	8.446	9.157	9.859	10.555	11.242	11.923	12.597	13.264	13.925
	3.0	7.721	8.429	9.124	9.807	10.478	11.138	11.788	12.428	13.059	13.680
	4.0	7.715	8.411	9.091	9.755	10.404	11.039	11.661	12.270	12.867	13.453
	5.0	7.708	8.395	9.060	9.706	10.333	10.945	11.540	12.121	12.688	13.243
	7.5	7.692	8.351	8.981	9.583	10.161	10.717	11.253	11.772	12.274	12.760
	10.0	7.679	8.315	8.914	9.481	10.020	10.534	11.027	11.501	11.958	12.400
	12.5	7.664	8.276	8.845	9.377	9.879	10.355	10.808	11.241	11.658	12.060
	15.0	7.651	8.244	8.789	9.295	9.770	10.219	10.647	11.055	11.449	11.830
1.200	1.0	7.734	8.464	9.191	9.915	10.636	11.354	12.069	12.781	13.490	14.196
	2.0	7.727	8.447	9.158	9.861	10.557	11.245	11.927	12.601	13.269	13.931
	3.0	7.721	8.429	9.125	9.808	10.480	11.142	11.792	12.433	13.064	13.686
	4.0	7.715	8.412	9.093	9.757	10.407	11.043	11.665	12.275	12.873	13.461
	5.0	7.709	8.395	9.061	9.708	10.336	10.948	11.545	12.127	12.695	13.251
	7.5	7.693	8.352	8.982	9.585	10.164	10.721	11.259	11.778	12.281	12.769
	10.0	7.679	8.316	8.916	9.484	10.024	10.540	11.034	11.510	11.969	12.413
	12.5	7.664	8.277	8.847	9.381	9.884	10.361	10.816	11.251	11.670	12.074
	15.0	7.652	8.246	8.792	9.300	9.777	10.228	10.657	11.069	11.465	11.850
1.250	1.0	7.734	8.465	9.192	9.917	10.638	11.357	12.072	12.785	13.494	14.201
	2.0	7.728	8.447	9.159	9.863	10.559	11.248	11.930	12.606	13.275	13.937
	3.0	7.721	8.430	9.126	9.810	10.483	11.145	11.796	12.438	13.070	13.693
	4.0	7.715	8.413	9.094	9.759	10.410	11.046	11.669	12.280	12.880	13.468
	5.0	7.709	8.396	9.063	9.710	10.339	10.952	11.549	12.132	12.702	13.259
	7.5	7.693	8.353	8.984	9.588	10.167	10.725	11.264	11.784	12.289	12.778
	10.0	7.680	8.317	8.918	9.487	10.028	10.545	11.041	11.519	11.979	12.425
	12.5	7.665	8.279	8.849	9.384	9.889	10.368	10.824	11.261	11.682	12.088
	15.0	7.653	8.248	8.795	9.305	9.783	10.236	10.668	11.082	11.482	11.870

Entry is annual yield from interest, growth in income and selected share of price appreciation.

Yield on Participating Mortgage Loan

Growth Rate   5%   Loan to Value Ratio 67%
Interest Rate 7.50%   30 Year Schedule

Debt Coverage	Years to Payoff	10%	20%	30%	40%	50%	60%	70%	80%	90%	100%
				Share of Increase in Income & Profit on Sale							
1.150	1.0	8.232	8.961	9.687	10.410	11.130	11.846	12.560	13.271	13.978	14.684
	2.0	8.224	8.940	9.648	10.348	11.041	11.726	12.405	13.077	13.742	14.402
	3.0	8.215	8.918	9.609	10.288	10.955	11.612	12.259	12.896	13.523	14.142
	4.0	8.207	8.898	9.571	10.230	10.873	11.504	12.121	12.726	13.320	13.903
	5.0	8.199	8.877	9.535	10.173	10.795	11.400	11.991	12.567	13.130	13.682
	7.5	8.178	8.825	9.443	10.035	10.605	11.153	11.683	12.195	12.692	13.174
	10.0	8.160	8.780	9.366	9.921	10.451	10.957	11.443	11.912	12.364	12.803
	12.5	8.141	8.734	9.287	9.807	10.298	10.765	11.212	11.640	12.052	12.451
	15.0	8.125	8.696	9.225	9.718	10.184	10.625	11.047	11.453	11.846	12.227
1.200	1.0	8.232	8.962	9.688	10.412	11.132	11.849	12.563	13.275	13.984	14.690
	2.0	8.224	8.941	9.649	10.350	11.043	11.729	12.409	13.082	13.748	14.408
	3.0	8.216	8.919	9.610	10.290	10.958	11.616	12.263	12.901	13.530	14.149
	4.0	8.208	8.898	9.573	10.232	10.876	11.507	12.126	12.732	13.327	13.911
	5.0	8.200	8.878	9.536	10.176	10.798	11.404	11.996	12.573	13.138	13.690
	7.5	8.179	8.826	9.445	10.038	10.608	11.158	11.688	12.202	12.700	13.184
	10.0	8.161	8.782	9.368	9.925	10.456	10.964	11.451	11.922	12.376	12.817
	12.5	8.141	8.736	9.290	9.811	10.304	10.773	11.221	11.651	12.066	12.467
	15.0	8.126	8.698	9.228	9.724	10.191	10.635	11.060	11.468	11.864	12.250
1.250	1.0	8.233	8.963	9.690	10.413	11.134	11.852	12.567	13.279	13.989	14.696
	2.0	8.224	8.941	9.650	10.352	11.046	11.733	12.413	13.087	13.754	14.415
	3.0	8.216	8.920	9.612	10.292	10.961	11.619	12.267	12.906	13.536	14.157
	4.0	8.208	8.899	9.574	10.234	10.879	11.511	12.130	12.738	13.334	13.919
	5.0	8.200	8.879	9.538	10.178	10.801	11.409	12.001	12.580	13.146	13.699
	7.5	8.179	8.827	9.446	10.041	10.612	11.162	11.694	12.209	12.708	13.194
	10.0	8.161	8.783	9.371	9.929	10.461	10.970	11.459	11.931	12.388	12.831
	12.5	8.142	8.737	9.293	9.815	10.310	10.780	11.230	11.662	12.079	12.484
	15.0	8.127	8.701	9.232	9.729	10.199	10.645	11.072	11.484	11.884	12.273

Interest Rate 8.00%   30 Year Schedule

Debt Coverage	Years to Payoff	10%	20%	30%	40%	50%	60%	70%	80%	90%	100%
1.150	1.0	8.731	9.459	10.184	10.907	11.626	12.342	13.055	13.765	14.473	15.178
	2.0	8.721	9.434	10.139	10.837	11.527	12.211	12.888	13.558	14.222	14.880
	3.0	8.710	9.409	10.095	10.770	11.434	12.087	12.731	13.365	13.990	14.606
	4.0	8.700	9.384	10.052	10.705	11.344	11.970	12.583	13.184	13.775	14.355
	5.0	8.690	9.360	10.010	10.643	11.258	11.858	12.444	13.016	13.575	14.123
	7.5	8.665	9.299	9.907	10.490	11.051	11.592	12.115	12.622	13.114	13.592
	10.0	8.643	9.248	9.821	10.366	10.886	11.385	11.865	12.329	12.777	13.213
	12.5	8.619	9.195	9.734	10.242	10.723	11.183	11.623	12.046	12.456	12.853
	15.0	8.600	9.152	9.666	10.148	10.605	11.040	11.458	11.862	12.255	12.640
1.200	1.0	8.731	9.460	10.186	10.908	11.628	12.345	13.059	13.770	14.479	15.185
	2.0	8.721	9.435	10.141	10.839	11.530	12.215	12.892	13.563	14.228	14.887
	3.0	8.711	9.410	10.097	10.772	11.437	12.091	12.735	13.371	13.997	14.615
	4.0	8.701	9.385	10.054	10.707	11.347	11.974	12.588	13.191	13.782	14.364
	5.0	8.691	9.361	10.012	10.645	11.262	11.863	12.449	13.023	13.584	14.133
	7.5	8.665	9.301	9.909	10.493	11.055	11.597	12.122	12.630	13.124	13.603
	10.0	8.643	9.250	9.824	10.370	10.892	11.392	11.874	12.340	12.791	13.229
	12.5	8.620	9.197	9.737	10.246	10.730	11.191	11.633	12.059	12.471	12.871
	15.0	8.601	9.155	9.670	10.155	10.613	11.052	11.473	11.881	12.278	12.667
1.250	1.0	8.732	9.461	10.187	10.910	11.631	12.348	13.063	13.775	14.485	15.192
	2.0	8.722	9.436	10.142	10.841	11.533	12.218	12.897	13.569	14.235	14.895
	3.0	8.711	9.411	10.098	10.774	11.440	12.095	12.740	13.376	14.004	14.623
	4.0	8.701	9.386	10.055	10.710	11.350	11.978	12.593	13.197	13.790	14.373
	5.0	8.691	9.362	10.014	10.648	11.265	11.867	12.455	13.030	13.592	14.143
	7.5	8.666	9.302	9.911	10.496	11.059	11.603	12.128	12.638	13.133	13.615
	10.0	8.644	9.251	9.827	10.374	10.897	11.400	11.883	12.351	12.804	13.245
	12.5	8.621	9.199	9.740	10.251	10.736	11.199	11.644	12.072	12.487	12.890
	15.0	8.602	9.158	9.675	10.161	10.622	11.063	11.488	11.899	12.300	12.694

Entry is annual yield from interest, growth in income and selected share of price appreciation.

Yield on Participating Mortgage Loan

Growth Rate 5%								Loan to Value Ratio 67%			
Interest Rate 8.50%								30 Year Schedule			

| Debt Coverage | Years to Payoff | Share of Increase in Income & Profit on Sale | | | | | | | | | |
		10%	20%	30%	40%	50%	60%	70%	80%	90%	100%
	1.0	9.230	9.958	10.682	11.403	12.122	12.838	13.551	14.261	14.969	15.674
	2.0	9.218	9.928	10.631	11.327	12.015	12.697	13.372	14.040	14.703	15.360
1.150	3.0	9.206	9.900	10.582	11.253	11.913	12.563	13.204	13.835	14.458	15.073
	4.0	9.194	9.871	10.534	11.182	11.816	12.437	13.047	13.645	14.232	14.810
	5.0	9.182	9.844	10.487	11.113	11.723	12.318	12.899	13.467	14.023	14.568
	7.5	9.152	9.775	10.373	10.947	11.500	12.035	12.552	13.054	13.541	14.016
	10.0	9.126	9.718	10.279	10.814	11.326	11.818	12.293	12.752	13.198	13.632
	12.5	9.099	9.658	10.184	10.681	11.154	11.606	12.041	12.462	12.869	13.265
	15.0	9.078	9.612	10.113	10.585	11.034	11.465	11.881	12.285	12.680	13.070
	1.0	9.231	9.958	10.683	11.405	12.125	12.841	13.555	14.266	14.975	15.681
	2.0	9.218	9.929	10.633	11.329	12.018	12.701	13.377	14.046	14.710	15.368
1.200	3.0	9.206	9.901	10.583	11.255	11.916	12.568	13.209	13.842	14.466	15.082
	4.0	9.194	9.873	10.536	11.184	11.819	12.442	13.052	13.652	14.241	14.820
	5.0	9.182	9.845	10.489	11.116	11.727	12.323	12.906	13.475	14.033	14.579
	7.5	9.152	9.777	10.375	10.950	11.505	12.040	12.559	13.062	13.552	14.028
	10.0	9.127	9.720	10.282	10.819	11.332	11.826	12.303	12.765	13.213	13.650
	12.5	9.100	9.661	10.188	10.686	11.161	11.616	12.054	12.476	12.887	13.287
	15.0	9.079	9.615	10.118	10.592	11.044	11.478	11.898	12.306	12.707	13.101
	1.0	9.231	9.959	10.685	11.408	12.127	12.845	13.559	14.272	14.981	15.689
	2.0	9.219	9.930	10.634	11.331	12.021	12.704	13.381	14.052	14.717	15.376
1.250	3.0	9.207	9.902	10.585	11.258	11.920	12.572	13.215	13.848	14.474	15.091
	4.0	9.195	9.874	10.538	11.187	11.823	12.447	13.058	13.659	14.249	14.830
	5.0	9.183	9.847	10.491	11.119	11.731	12.328	12.912	13.483	14.042	14.590
	7.5	9.153	9.778	10.377	10.954	11.509	12.046	12.566	13.071	13.562	14.041
	10.0	9.128	9.722	10.285	10.823	11.339	11.835	12.313	12.777	13.228	13.668
	12.5	9.101	9.663	10.191	10.692	11.169	11.626	12.066	12.491	12.905	13.308
	15.0	9.080	9.619	10.123	10.600	11.055	11.492	11.915	12.328	12.733	13.134

Interest Rate 9.00%   30 Year Schedule

Debt Coverage	Years to Payoff	10%	20%	30%	40%	50%	60%	70%	80%	90%	100%
	1.0	9.729	10.456	11.180	11.901	12.619	13.334	14.047	14.757	15.465	16.171
	2.0	9.715	10.423	11.123	11.817	12.503	13.183	13.857	14.524	15.186	15.841
1.150	3.0	9.701	10.391	11.069	11.736	12.393	13.041	13.679	14.308	14.929	15.541
	4.0	9.687	10.359	11.016	11.659	12.289	12.907	13.512	14.107	14.692	15.267
	5.0	9.674	10.329	10.965	11.585	12.190	12.780	13.357	13.922	14.475	15.017
	7.5	9.640	10.252	10.840	11.406	11.952	12.480	12.992	13.489	13.973	14.444
	10.0	9.611	10.189	10.739	11.265	11.770	12.256	12.726	13.182	13.626	14.059
	12.5	9.580	10.125	10.638	11.125	11.590	12.037	12.468	12.886	13.292	13.689
	15.0	9.557	10.076	10.565	11.028	11.472	11.900	12.316	12.722	13.122	13.519
	1.0	9.730	10.457	11.181	11.903	12.622	13.338	14.052	14.763	15.472	16.179
	2.0	9.716	10.424	11.125	11.819	12.507	13.187	13.862	14.531	15.193	15.850
1.200	3.0	9.702	10.392	11.071	11.739	12.397	13.046	13.685	14.315	14.937	15.551
	4.0	9.688	10.361	11.018	11.662	12.293	12.912	13.519	14.115	14.702	15.278
	5.0	9.675	10.330	10.968	11.589	12.194	12.786	13.364	13.930	14.485	15.029
	7.5	9.640	10.254	10.843	11.410	11.957	12.487	13.000	13.499	13.985	14.458
	10.0	9.612	10.191	10.743	11.271	11.777	12.266	12.738	13.196	13.643	14.079
	12.5	9.582	10.127	10.642	11.131	11.599	12.048	12.482	12.903	13.313	13.714
	15.0	9.559	10.080	10.571	11.037	11.484	11.916	12.336	12.747	13.153	13.557
	1.0	9.730	10.458	11.183	11.905	12.625	13.342	14.057	14.769	15.479	16.187
	2.0	9.716	10.425	11.127	11.822	12.510	13.192	13.867	14.537	15.201	15.859
1.250	3.0	9.702	10.393	11.073	11.742	12.401	13.050	13.691	14.322	14.946	15.561
	4.0	9.689	10.362	11.020	11.665	12.297	12.917	13.525	14.123	14.711	15.289
	5.0	9.675	10.332	10.970	11.592	12.199	12.792	13.371	13.939	14.495	15.041
	7.5	9.641	10.255	10.845	11.414	11.962	12.493	13.008	13.509	13.997	14.472
	10.0	9.613	10.194	10.747	11.276	11.785	12.275	12.750	13.211	13.660	14.100
	12.5	9.583	10.130	10.647	11.138	11.608	12.059	12.496	12.920	13.334	13.739
	15.0	9.560	10.084	10.577	11.046	11.496	11.932	12.356	12.773	13.185	13.596

Entry is annual yield from interest, growth in income and selected share of price appreciation.

Yield on Participating Mortgage Loan

Growth Rate   5%   Loan to Value Ratio 67%
Interest Rate   9.50%   30 Year Schedule

Debt Coverage	Years to Payoff	Share of Increase in Income & Profit on Sale 10%	20%	30%	40%	50%	60%	70%	80%	90%	100%
	1.0	10.228	10.955	11.678	12.398	13.116	13.831	14.544	15.255	15.963	16.668
	2.0	10.212	10.918	11.616	12.308	12.992	13.671	14.343	15.009	15.670	16.325
1.150	3.0	10.197	10.882	11.557	12.221	12.875	13.520	14.155	14.782	15.401	16.012
	4.0	10.181	10.848	11.500	12.138	12.764	13.378	13.980	14.572	15.155	15.728
	5.0	10.166	10.814	11.445	12.059	12.659	13.244	13.817	14.379	14.929	15.469
	7.5	10.128	10.730	11.309	11.867	12.407	12.929	13.436	13.929	14.409	14.878
	10.0	10.096	10.663	11.203	11.721	12.219	12.700	13.166	13.619	14.061	14.494
	12.5	10.063	10.594	11.096	11.574	12.033	12.475	12.903	13.320	13.727	14.126
	15.0	10.039	10.544	11.023	11.480	11.919	12.346	12.764	13.175	13.583	13.991
	1.0	10.229	10.956	11.680	12.401	13.119	13.836	14.549	15.261	15.970	16.677
	2.0	10.213	10.919	11.618	12.310	12.996	13.675	14.349	15.016	15.678	16.334
1.200	3.0	10.197	10.884	11.559	12.224	12.879	13.525	14.162	14.790	15.410	16.023
	4.0	10.182	10.849	11.502	12.141	12.768	13.383	13.987	14.581	15.165	15.740
	5.0	10.167	10.816	11.447	12.063	12.664	13.251	13.825	14.388	14.940	15.482
	7.5	10.129	10.732	11.312	11.872	12.413	12.936	13.445	13.940	14.423	14.894
	10.0	10.097	10.665	11.207	11.727	12.227	12.710	13.179	13.635	14.081	14.518
	12.5	10.065	10.597	11.101	11.582	12.043	12.488	12.919	13.339	13.751	14.155
	15.0	10.041	10.548	11.030	11.490	11.934	12.365	12.788	13.205	13.620	14.037
	1.0	10.229	10.957	11.681	12.403	13.123	13.840	14.555	15.267	15.978	16.686
	2.0	10.214	10.920	11.620	12.313	13.000	13.680	14.354	15.023	15.686	16.344
1.250	3.0	10.198	10.885	11.561	12.227	12.883	13.530	14.168	14.798	15.420	16.034
	4.0	10.183	10.851	11.504	12.145	12.773	13.389	13.995	14.590	15.175	15.752
	5.0	10.168	10.817	11.450	12.066	12.669	13.257	13.833	14.398	14.952	15.496
	7.5	10.130	10.734	11.315	11.876	12.418	12.944	13.454	13.951	14.436	14.910
	10.0	10.099	10.668	11.211	11.733	12.235	12.721	13.193	13.652	14.101	14.541
	12.5	10.066	10.600	11.106	11.589	12.053	12.501	12.935	13.359	13.775	14.183
	15.0	10.043	10.553	11.037	11.500	11.948	12.384	12.811	13.235	13.657	14.083

Interest Rate 10.00%   30 Year Schedule

Debt Coverage	Years to Payoff	10%	20%	30%	40%	50%	60%	70%	80%	90%	100%
	1.0	10.728	11.453	12.176	12.896	13.614	14.329	15.042	15.753	16.461	17.167
	2.0	10.710	11.413	12.110	12.799	13.482	14.159	14.830	15.495	16.155	16.809
1.150	3.0	10.693	11.374	12.045	12.706	13.357	14.000	14.633	15.258	15.875	16.485
	4.0	10.676	11.337	11.984	12.618	13.240	13.850	14.450	15.040	15.620	16.191
	5.0	10.659	11.300	11.925	12.534	13.129	13.711	14.280	14.839	15.386	15.925
	7.5	10.617	11.210	11.780	12.331	12.864	13.381	13.884	14.373	14.851	15.318
	10.0	10.583	11.138	11.669	12.180	12.672	13.149	13.612	14.064	14.506	14.940
	12.5	10.548	11.065	11.558	12.029	12.482	12.921	13.348	13.764	14.173	14.576
	15.0	10.523	11.016	11.487	11.939	12.377	12.805	13.227	13.646	14.066	14.491
	1.0	10.728	11.455	12.178	12.899	13.618	14.334	15.048	15.759	16.469	17.177
	2.0	10.711	11.415	12.112	12.802	13.486	14.164	14.836	15.503	16.164	16.820
1.200	3.0	10.693	11.376	12.048	12.710	13.362	14.005	14.640	15.267	15.885	16.497
	4.0	10.676	11.338	11.986	12.622	13.245	13.857	14.458	15.049	15.631	16.204
	5.0	10.660	11.302	11.928	12.538	13.134	13.718	14.289	14.849	15.399	15.939
	7.5	10.618	11.212	11.784	12.336	12.871	13.389	13.894	14.386	14.865	15.335
	10.0	10.584	11.141	11.674	12.187	12.681	13.161	13.627	14.082	14.528	14.966
	12.5	10.549	11.069	11.564	12.037	12.494	12.936	13.366	13.787	14.201	14.609
	15.0	10.525	11.021	11.495	11.951	12.393	12.827	13.255	13.682	14.110	14.546
	1.0	10.729	11.456	12.180	12.902	13.621	14.338	15.053	15.766	16.477	17.186
	2.0	10.711	11.416	12.114	12.805	13.490	14.169	14.843	15.510	16.173	16.831
1.250	3.0	10.694	11.377	12.050	12.713	13.366	14.011	14.647	15.275	15.896	16.509
	4.0	10.677	11.340	11.989	12.625	13.250	13.863	14.466	15.059	15.642	16.218
	5.0	10.661	11.304	11.931	12.542	13.140	13.725	14.298	14.860	15.412	15.954
	7.5	10.619	11.214	11.787	12.341	12.877	13.398	13.904	14.398	14.880	15.352
	10.0	10.586	11.144	11.679	12.194	12.691	13.173	13.642	14.101	14.550	14.993
	12.5	10.551	11.073	11.569	12.046	12.505	12.950	13.384	13.810	14.228	14.643
	15.0	10.527	11.026	11.503	11.963	12.410	12.849	13.283	13.717	14.155	14.602

Entry is annual yield from interest, growth in income and selected share of price appreciation.

Yield on Participating Mortgage Loan

Growth Rate   5%
Interest Rate 10.50%

Loan to Value Ratio 67%
30 Year Schedule

Debt Coverage	Years to Payoff	Share of Increase in Income & Profit on Sale									
		10%	20%	30%	40%	50%	60%	70%	80%	90%	100%
1.150	1.0	11.227	11.952	12.675	13.395	14.112	14.828	15.541	16.251	16.960	17.667
	2.0	11.208	11.909	12.603	13.291	13.973	14.648	15.318	15.983	16.642	17.296
	3.0	11.189	11.867	12.535	13.192	13.841	14.481	15.112	15.736	16.352	16.960
	4.0	11.170	11.826	12.469	13.099	13.717	14.325	14.922	15.509	16.087	16.657
	5.0	11.152	11.787	12.406	13.010	13.601	14.179	14.746	15.302	15.847	16.384
	7.5	11.107	11.690	12.253	12.797	13.325	13.837	14.335	14.822	15.297	15.763
	10.0	11.070	11.616	12.139	12.642	13.130	13.603	14.065	14.516	14.959	15.395
	12.5	11.033	11.540	12.024	12.489	12.938	13.375	13.801	14.220	14.633	15.042
	15.0	11.009	11.493	11.957	12.406	12.845	13.278	13.708	14.139	14.575	15.023
1.200	1.0	11.228	11.954	12.677	13.398	14.116	14.833	15.547	16.259	16.969	17.678
	2.0	11.208	11.910	12.606	13.294	13.977	14.654	15.325	15.991	16.651	17.307
	3.0	11.189	11.868	12.537	13.196	13.846	14.487	15.120	15.745	16.363	16.973
	4.0	11.171	11.828	12.472	13.103	13.723	14.332	14.930	15.520	16.100	16.672
	5.0	11.153	11.789	12.409	13.015	13.607	14.187	14.755	15.313	15.861	16.400
	7.5	11.108	11.693	12.257	12.803	13.332	13.846	14.347	14.836	15.314	15.782
	10.0	11.072	11.619	12.144	12.650	13.141	13.617	14.082	14.537	14.984	15.425
	12.5	11.035	11.544	12.031	12.498	12.951	13.392	13.822	14.246	14.664	15.080
	15.0	11.011	11.498	11.967	12.420	12.865	13.303	13.741	14.181	14.629	15.090
1.250	1.0	11.228	11.955	12.679	13.401	14.120	14.838	15.553	16.266	16.978	17.688
	2.0	11.209	11.912	12.608	13.298	13.981	14.660	15.332	15.999	16.661	17.319
	3.0	11.190	11.870	12.540	13.200	13.851	14.493	15.128	15.754	16.374	16.986
	4.0	11.172	11.830	12.475	13.107	13.728	14.339	14.939	15.530	16.112	16.686
	5.0	11.154	11.791	12.412	13.020	13.613	14.195	14.765	15.325	15.875	16.417
	7.5	11.109	11.695	12.261	12.808	13.339	13.855	14.358	14.849	15.330	15.801
	10.0	11.074	11.622	12.150	12.658	13.151	13.631	14.099	14.558	15.010	15.456
	12.5	11.037	11.548	12.037	12.508	12.964	13.409	13.844	14.272	14.697	15.119
	15.0	11.014	11.504	11.976	12.435	12.884	13.329	13.774	14.224	14.683	15.160

Interest Rate 11.00%   30 Year Schedule

Debt Coverage	Years to Payoff	10%	20%	30%	40%	50%	60%	70%	80%	90%	100%
1.150	1.0	11.727	12.451	13.174	13.894	14.611	15.327	16.040	16.751	17.461	18.168
	2.0	11.706	12.405	13.097	13.784	14.464	15.138	15.807	16.471	17.130	17.784
	3.0	11.685	12.360	13.024	13.680	14.326	14.963	15.593	16.215	16.830	17.438
	4.0	11.665	12.316	12.955	13.581	14.196	14.801	15.395	15.981	16.558	17.126
	5.0	11.645	12.275	12.888	13.488	14.075	14.650	15.214	15.767	16.311	16.847
	7.5	11.597	12.172	12.728	13.266	13.788	14.296	14.791	15.275	15.749	16.213
	10.0	11.559	12.095	12.611	13.109	13.593	14.064	14.525	14.977	15.422	15.862
	12.5	11.521	12.018	12.494	12.954	13.401	13.837	14.265	14.688	15.107	15.525
	15.0	11.497	11.974	12.434	12.883	13.326	13.766	14.207	14.655	15.116	15.596
1.200	1.0	11.727	12.453	13.176	13.897	14.615	15.332	16.047	16.759	17.470	18.179
	2.0	11.706	12.406	13.100	13.787	14.469	15.145	15.815	16.480	17.140	17.796
	3.0	11.686	12.361	13.027	13.684	14.331	14.970	15.601	16.225	16.842	17.452
	4.0	11.666	12.318	12.958	13.586	14.202	14.808	15.405	15.992	16.571	17.142
	5.0	11.646	12.277	12.892	13.493	14.082	14.659	15.224	15.780	16.327	16.865
	7.5	11.598	12.175	12.732	13.272	13.796	14.306	14.804	15.290	15.767	16.235
	10.0	11.561	12.099	12.617	13.118	13.605	14.079	14.544	15.000	15.451	15.896
	12.5	11.523	12.022	12.502	12.965	13.416	13.857	14.290	14.718	15.143	15.569
	15.0	11.500	11.980	12.445	12.900	13.349	13.796	14.247	14.706	15.181	15.681
1.250	1.0	11.728	12.454	13.178	13.900	14.620	15.337	16.053	16.767	17.480	18.190
	2.0	11.707	12.408	13.102	13.791	14.474	15.151	15.823	16.489	17.151	17.809
	3.0	11.687	12.363	13.030	13.688	14.337	14.977	15.610	16.235	16.854	17.466
	4.0	11.667	12.320	12.961	13.590	14.208	14.816	15.414	16.004	16.585	17.158
	5.0	11.647	12.279	12.896	13.498	14.089	14.667	15.235	15.793	16.342	16.883
	7.5	11.599	12.177	12.736	13.278	13.804	14.316	14.816	15.306	15.785	16.256
	10.0	11.563	12.103	12.623	13.127	13.617	14.095	14.564	15.024	15.480	15.931
	12.5	11.525	12.027	12.510	12.977	13.431	13.876	14.314	14.748	15.181	15.615
	15.0	11.503	11.987	12.457	12.917	13.372	13.827	14.287	14.758	15.249	15.768

Entry is annual yield from interest, growth in income and selected share of price appreciation.

Yield on Participating Mortgage Loan

Growth Rate   5%   Loan to Value Ratio 67%
Interest Rate 11.50%   30 Year Schedule

Debt Coverage	Years to Payoff	Share of Increase in Income & Profit on Sale									
		10%	20%	30%	40%	50%	60%	70%	80%	90%	100%
	1.0	12.226	12.951	13.673	14.393	15.111	15.826	16.540	17.252	17.962	18.670
	2.0	12.204	12.901	13.592	14.277	14.956	15.630	16.298	16.961	17.619	18.273
1.150	3.0	12.181	12.853	13.515	14.167	14.811	15.447	16.075	16.696	17.310	17.917
	4.0	12.160	12.807	13.441	14.064	14.676	15.278	15.871	16.455	17.031	17.599
	5.0	12.139	12.763	13.372	13.968	14.551	15.123	15.684	16.236	16.779	17.314
	7.5	12.088	12.655	13.204	13.736	14.254	14.758	15.251	15.733	16.205	16.670
	10.0	12.049	12.577	13.086	13.580	14.061	14.531	14.992	15.446	15.895	16.341
	12.5	12.010	12.498	12.969	13.426	13.872	14.309	14.741	15.169	15.597	16.027
	15.0	11.988	12.459	12.919	13.371	13.820	14.271	14.730	15.202	15.696	16.224
	1.0	12.227	12.952	13.675	14.396	15.115	15.832	16.547	17.261	17.972	18.682
	2.0	12.204	12.903	13.595	14.281	14.961	15.636	16.306	16.971	17.631	18.287
1.200	3.0	12.182	12.855	13.518	14.172	14.817	15.455	16.084	16.707	17.323	17.933
	4.0	12.161	12.809	13.445	14.069	14.683	15.287	15.881	16.467	17.045	17.616
	5.0	12.140	12.765	13.376	13.973	14.558	15.132	15.696	16.250	16.796	17.334
	7.5	12.089	12.658	13.209	13.743	14.263	14.770	15.265	15.750	16.226	16.694
	10.0	12.051	12.581	13.093	13.590	14.075	14.549	15.014	15.473	15.928	16.380
	12.5	12.012	12.504	12.978	13.439	13.889	14.331	14.769	15.204	15.640	16.079
	15.0	11.992	12.467	12.932	13.390	13.847	14.308	14.778	15.264	15.778	16.333
	1.0	12.228	12.954	13.678	14.400	15.120	15.838	16.554	17.269	17.982	18.694
	2.0	12.205	12.904	13.598	14.285	14.966	15.643	16.314	16.981	17.643	18.300
1.250	3.0	12.183	12.857	13.521	14.176	14.823	15.462	16.094	16.718	17.336	17.948
	4.0	12.162	12.811	13.448	14.074	14.690	15.295	15.892	16.480	17.060	17.633
	5.0	12.141	12.768	13.380	13.979	14.566	15.142	15.708	16.264	16.813	17.353
	7.5	12.090	12.661	13.213	13.750	14.272	14.781	15.279	15.767	16.246	16.718
	10.0	12.053	12.586	13.101	13.601	14.088	14.566	15.036	15.500	15.961	16.419
	12.5	12.015	12.509	12.987	13.451	13.906	14.354	14.797	15.240	15.683	16.132
	15.0	11.995	12.475	12.945	13.410	13.874	14.344	14.826	15.328	15.862	16.447

Interest Rate 12.00%   30 Year Schedule

Debt Coverage	Years to Payoff	10%	20%	30%	40%	50%	60%	70%	80%	90%	100%
	1.0	12.726	13.450	14.172	14.892	15.610	16.326	17.041	17.753	18.464	19.173
	2.0	12.702	13.397	14.087	14.771	15.449	16.122	16.789	17.452	18.110	18.764
1.150	3.0	12.678	13.347	14.006	14.656	15.298	15.932	16.559	17.179	17.792	18.399
	4.0	12.655	13.298	13.929	14.549	15.158	15.758	16.349	16.931	17.506	18.074
	5.0	12.633	13.252	13.857	14.448	15.029	15.598	16.157	16.708	17.250	17.785
	7.5	12.579	13.139	13.682	14.209	14.723	15.224	15.715	16.196	16.668	17.133
	10.0	12.540	13.061	13.565	14.056	14.535	15.005	15.468	15.925	16.380	16.833
	12.5	12.500	12.982	13.449	13.904	14.351	14.791	15.229	15.666	16.105	16.551
	15.0	12.481	12.950	13.411	13.869	14.330	14.798	15.280	15.786	16.329	16.929
	1.0	12.727	13.452	14.175	14.896	15.615	16.333	17.049	17.763	18.475	19.186
	2.0	12.703	13.399	14.090	14.775	15.454	16.129	16.798	17.463	18.123	18.779
1.200	3.0	12.679	13.349	14.009	14.661	15.305	15.940	16.569	17.191	17.806	18.416
	4.0	12.656	13.300	13.933	14.554	15.165	15.767	16.360	16.945	17.522	18.093
	5.0	12.635	13.255	13.861	14.455	15.037	15.608	16.170	16.723	17.269	17.806
	7.5	12.581	13.143	13.687	14.217	14.733	15.237	15.730	16.214	16.690	17.159
	10.0	12.542	13.066	13.573	14.067	14.550	15.025	15.493	15.956	16.417	16.877
	12.5	12.503	12.988	13.459	13.919	14.370	14.817	15.261	15.706	16.156	16.613
	15.0	12.486	12.960	13.427	13.892	14.362	14.841	15.338	15.863	16.433	17.074
	1.0	12.728	13.454	14.178	14.900	15.620	16.339	17.056	17.772	18.486	19.199
	2.0	12.703	13.401	14.093	14.779	15.460	16.136	16.807	17.473	18.136	18.794
1.250	3.0	12.680	13.351	14.013	14.666	15.311	15.949	16.579	17.203	17.821	18.432
	4.0	12.657	13.303	13.937	14.560	15.173	15.776	16.372	16.959	17.539	18.112
	5.0	12.636	13.257	13.865	14.461	15.045	15.619	16.183	16.739	17.287	17.828
	7.5	12.582	13.146	13.693	14.224	14.743	15.250	15.746	16.234	16.713	17.186
	10.0	12.544	13.071	13.581	14.079	14.566	15.045	15.518	15.987	16.455	16.923
	12.5	12.506	12.994	13.469	13.933	14.390	14.843	15.294	15.748	16.207	16.676
	15.0	12.490	12.969	13.442	13.915	14.394	14.885	15.397	15.943	16.542	17.231

Entry is annual yield from interest, growth in income and selected share of price appreciation.

Yield on Participating Mortgage Loan

Growth Rate   5%   Loan to Value Ratio 75%
Interest Rate 5.50%   30 Year Schedule

Debt Coverage	Years to Payoff	10%	20%	Share of Increase in Income & Profit on Sale 30%	40%	50%	60%	70%	80%	90%	100%
1.150	1.0	6.237	6.971	7.701	8.428	9.151	9.871	10.587	11.300	12.009	12.716
	2.0	6.237	6.966	7.686	8.398	9.101	9.796	10.484	11.164	11.837	12.504
	3.0	6.238	6.961	7.671	8.368	9.053	9.725	10.386	11.036	11.676	12.306
	4.0	6.238	6.957	7.657	8.339	9.006	9.656	10.292	10.915	11.524	12.121
	5.0	6.238	6.952	7.642	8.311	8.960	9.590	10.203	10.800	11.381	11.949
	7.5	6.239	6.939	7.605	8.240	8.847	9.429	9.988	10.527	11.046	11.549
	10.0	6.241	6.929	7.574	8.179	8.751	9.294	9.812	10.306	10.780	11.236
	12.5	6.242	6.918	7.540	8.116	8.655	9.161	9.639	10.094	10.527	10.941
	15.0	6.245	6.910	7.512	8.065	8.576	9.054	9.503	9.928	10.333	10.720
1.200	1.0	6.237	6.972	7.702	8.429	9.152	9.872	10.589	11.303	12.013	12.720
	2.0	6.238	6.967	7.687	8.399	9.103	9.799	10.487	11.168	11.841	12.508
	3.0	6.238	6.962	7.672	8.370	9.054	9.727	10.389	11.040	11.680	12.311
	4.0	6.238	6.957	7.658	8.341	9.007	9.659	10.296	10.919	11.529	12.127
	5.0	6.239	6.952	7.643	8.312	8.962	9.593	10.206	10.804	11.386	11.955
	7.5	6.239	6.940	7.606	8.241	8.849	9.431	9.991	10.531	11.052	11.555
	10.0	6.241	6.930	7.575	8.181	8.754	9.298	9.816	10.312	10.787	11.245
	12.5	6.242	6.919	7.541	8.118	8.658	9.165	9.645	10.100	10.534	10.950
	15.0	6.245	6.911	7.514	8.067	8.580	9.059	9.510	9.937	10.343	10.733
1.250	1.0	6.238	6.972	7.703	8.430	9.154	9.874	10.592	11.306	12.016	12.724
	2.0	6.238	6.967	7.688	8.400	9.104	9.801	10.489	11.171	11.845	12.513
	3.0	6.238	6.962	7.673	8.371	9.056	9.730	10.392	11.043	11.684	12.316
	4.0	6.238	6.958	7.659	8.342	9.009	9.661	10.299	10.922	11.533	12.132
	5.0	6.239	6.953	7.644	8.314	8.964	9.595	10.209	10.808	11.391	11.961
	7.5	6.239	6.940	7.607	8.243	8.851	9.434	9.995	10.535	11.057	11.562
	10.0	6.241	6.931	7.576	8.183	8.757	9.302	9.821	10.318	10.794	11.253
	12.5	6.243	6.920	7.543	8.121	8.661	9.169	9.650	10.106	10.542	10.960
	15.0	6.246	6.912	7.516	8.070	8.584	9.064	9.516	9.945	10.354	10.745

Interest Rate 6.00%   30 Year Schedule

Debt Coverage	Years to Payoff	10%	20%	30%	40%	50%	60%	70%	80%	90%	100%
1.150	1.0	6.736	7.468	8.197	8.923	9.645	10.364	11.079	11.791	12.500	13.206
	2.0	6.734	7.459	8.176	8.884	9.585	10.278	10.963	11.641	12.312	12.976
	3.0	6.732	7.450	8.155	8.847	9.527	10.195	10.852	11.499	12.135	12.762
	4.0	6.730	7.441	8.134	8.810	9.470	10.116	10.747	11.364	11.969	12.563
	5.0	6.728	7.432	8.114	8.774	9.416	10.039	10.646	11.237	11.814	12.377
	7.5	6.723	7.409	8.062	8.685	9.282	9.855	10.406	10.938	11.451	11.948
	10.0	6.719	7.389	8.017	8.609	9.170	9.703	10.211	10.699	11.166	11.617
	12.5	6.714	7.368	7.971	8.532	9.057	9.553	10.022	10.469	10.895	11.305
	15.0	6.711	7.351	7.933	8.468	8.967	9.434	9.875	10.294	10.694	11.078
1.200	1.0	6.736	7.469	8.198	8.924	9.647	10.366	11.082	11.794	12.504	13.211
	2.0	6.734	7.460	8.177	8.886	9.587	10.280	10.966	11.644	12.316	12.981
	3.0	6.732	7.451	8.156	8.848	9.529	10.197	10.855	11.502	12.140	12.767
	4.0	6.730	7.442	8.135	8.812	9.472	10.118	10.750	11.368	11.974	12.569
	5.0	6.728	7.433	8.115	8.776	9.418	10.042	10.650	11.242	11.819	12.383
	7.5	6.723	7.409	8.063	8.687	9.284	9.858	10.410	10.942	11.457	11.955
	10.0	6.719	7.390	8.019	8.612	9.173	9.707	10.217	10.705	11.174	11.627
	12.5	6.715	7.369	7.973	8.534	9.061	9.557	10.028	10.476	10.904	11.316
	15.0	6.712	7.352	7.935	8.472	8.972	9.440	9.883	10.303	10.706	11.092
1.250	1.0	6.736	7.469	8.199	8.925	9.648	10.368	11.084	11.798	12.508	13.216
	2.0	6.734	7.460	8.178	8.887	9.588	10.282	10.969	11.648	12.320	12.986
	3.0	6.732	7.451	8.157	8.850	9.531	10.200	10.858	11.506	12.144	12.773
	4.0	6.730	7.442	8.136	8.813	9.475	10.121	10.753	11.373	11.980	12.575
	5.0	6.729	7.433	8.116	8.778	9.420	10.045	10.654	11.246	11.825	12.390
	7.5	6.723	7.410	8.064	8.689	9.287	9.861	10.414	10.947	11.463	11.962
	10.0	6.720	7.391	8.021	8.614	9.176	9.711	10.222	10.712	11.182	11.636
	12.5	6.715	7.370	7.974	8.537	9.065	9.562	10.034	10.483	10.913	11.326
	15.0	6.713	7.353	7.937	8.475	8.976	9.446	9.891	10.313	10.718	11.107

Entry is annual yield from interest, growth in income and selected share of price appreciation.

Yield on Participating Mortgage Loan

Growth Rate   5%   Loan to Value Ratio 75%
Interest Rate 6.50%   30 Year Schedule

| Debt Coverage | Years to Payoff | Share of Increase in Income & Profit on Sale | | | | | | | | | |
		10%	20%	30%	40%	50%	60%	70%	80%	90%	100%
1.150	1.0	7.234	7.966	8.694	9.418	10.139	10.857	11.572	12.283	12.992	13.698
	2.0	7.230	7.952	8.666	9.372	10.069	10.760	11.442	12.118	12.787	13.449
	3.0	7.226	7.939	8.639	9.326	10.002	10.666	11.319	11.963	12.596	13.220
	4.0	7.222	7.926	8.612	9.282	9.937	10.577	11.203	11.816	12.417	13.006
	5.0	7.218	7.913	8.586	9.239	9.874	10.491	11.092	11.678	12.250	12.808
	7.5	7.207	7.879	8.520	9.133	9.720	10.284	10.828	11.353	11.860	12.352
	10.0	7.198	7.851	8.464	9.043	9.593	10.116	10.617	11.097	11.559	12.005
	12.5	7.188	7.820	8.406	8.952	9.466	9.951	10.411	10.851	11.272	11.678
	15.0	7.180	7.795	8.358	8.879	9.365	9.822	10.256	10.669	11.066	11.448
1.200	1.0	7.235	7.966	8.695	9.420	10.141	10.860	11.575	12.287	12.996	13.703
	2.0	7.231	7.953	8.667	9.373	10.071	10.762	11.446	12.122	12.792	13.455
	3.0	7.226	7.940	8.640	9.328	10.004	10.669	11.323	11.967	12.601	13.226
	4.0	7.222	7.927	8.613	9.284	9.939	10.580	11.207	11.821	12.423	13.013
	5.0	7.218	7.914	8.587	9.241	9.876	10.494	11.096	11.683	12.256	12.816
	7.5	7.207	7.880	8.522	9.135	9.723	10.288	10.832	11.358	11.867	12.360
	10.0	7.199	7.852	8.466	9.046	9.596	10.121	10.623	11.104	11.568	12.016
	12.5	7.189	7.822	8.408	8.955	9.470	9.956	10.418	10.860	11.283	11.690
	15.0	7.181	7.797	8.361	8.883	9.370	9.830	10.265	10.681	11.079	11.464
1.250	1.0	7.235	7.967	8.696	9.421	10.143	10.862	11.578	12.291	13.001	13.708
	2.0	7.231	7.954	8.668	9.375	10.073	10.765	11.449	12.126	12.797	13.461
	3.0	7.227	7.940	8.641	9.329	10.006	10.672	11.326	11.971	12.606	13.232
	4.0	7.223	7.927	8.615	9.286	9.941	10.583	11.210	11.825	12.428	13.020
	5.0	7.219	7.914	8.589	9.243	9.879	10.497	11.100	11.688	12.262	12.823
	7.5	7.208	7.881	8.523	9.137	9.726	10.292	10.837	11.364	11.873	12.368
	10.0	7.199	7.853	8.468	9.049	9.600	10.126	10.629	11.112	11.577	12.027
	12.5	7.189	7.823	8.410	8.958	9.474	9.962	10.425	10.868	11.293	11.702
	15.0	7.182	7.798	8.363	8.887	9.376	9.837	10.274	10.692	11.093	11.481

Interest Rate 7.00%   30 Year Schedule

Debt Coverage	Years to Payoff	10%	20%	30%	40%	50%	60%	70%	80%	90%	100%
1.150	1.0	7.733	8.464	9.190	9.914	10.634	11.351	12.065	12.777	13.485	14.190
	2.0	7.727	8.446	9.157	9.859	10.555	11.242	11.923	12.597	13.264	13.925
	3.0	7.721	8.429	9.124	9.807	10.478	11.138	11.788	12.428	13.059	13.680
	4.0	7.715	8.411	9.091	9.755	10.404	11.039	11.661	12.270	12.867	13.453
	5.0	7.708	8.395	9.060	9.706	10.333	10.945	11.540	12.121	12.688	13.243
	7.5	7.692	8.351	8.981	9.583	10.161	10.717	11.253	11.772	12.274	12.760
	10.0	7.679	8.315	8.914	9.481	10.020	10.534	11.027	11.501	11.958	12.400
	12.5	7.664	8.276	8.845	9.377	9.879	10.355	10.808	11.241	11.658	12.060
	15.0	7.651	8.244	8.789	9.295	9.770	10.219	10.647	11.055	11.449	11.830
1.200	1.0	7.734	8.464	9.191	9.915	10.636	11.354	12.069	12.781	13.490	14.196
	2.0	7.727	8.447	9.158	9.861	10.557	11.245	11.927	12.601	13.269	13.931
	3.0	7.721	8.429	9.125	9.808	10.480	11.142	11.792	12.433	13.064	13.686
	4.0	7.715	8.412	9.093	9.757	10.407	11.043	11.665	12.275	12.873	13.461
	5.0	7.709	8.395	9.061	9.708	10.336	10.948	11.545	12.127	12.695	13.251
	7.5	7.693	8.352	8.982	9.585	10.164	10.721	11.259	11.778	12.281	12.769
	10.0	7.679	8.316	8.916	9.484	10.024	10.540	11.034	11.510	11.969	12.413
	12.5	7.664	8.277	8.847	9.381	9.884	10.361	10.816	11.251	11.670	12.074
	15.0	7.652	8.246	8.792	9.300	9.777	10.228	10.657	11.069	11.465	11.850
1.250	1.0	7.734	8.465	9.192	9.917	10.638	11.357	12.072	12.785	13.494	14.201
	2.0	7.728	8.447	9.159	9.863	10.559	11.248	11.930	12.606	13.275	13.937
	3.0	7.721	8.430	9.126	9.810	10.483	11.145	11.796	12.438	13.070	13.693
	4.0	7.715	8.413	9.094	9.759	10.410	11.046	11.669	12.280	12.880	13.468
	5.0	7.709	8.396	9.063	9.710	10.339	10.952	11.549	12.132	12.702	13.259
	7.5	7.693	8.353	8.984	9.588	10.167	10.725	11.264	11.784	12.289	12.778
	10.0	7.680	8.317	8.918	9.487	10.028	10.545	11.041	11.519	11.979	12.425
	12.5	7.665	8.279	8.849	9.384	9.889	10.368	10.824	11.261	11.682	12.088
	15.0	7.653	8.248	8.795	9.305	9.783	10.236	10.668	11.082	11.482	11.870

Entry is annual yield from interest, growth in income and selected share of price appreciation.

Yield on Participating Mortgage Loan

Growth Rate 5%
Interest Rate 7.50%

Loan to Value Ratio 75%
30 Year Schedule

Debt Coverage	Years to Payoff	Share of Increase in Income & Profit on Sale									
		10%	20%	30%	40%	50%	60%	70%	80%	90%	100%
1.150	1.0	8.232	8.961	9.687	10.410	11.130	11.846	12.560	13.271	13.978	14.684
	2.0	8.224	8.940	9.648	10.348	11.041	11.726	12.405	13.077	13.742	14.402
	3.0	8.215	8.918	9.609	10.288	10.955	11.612	12.259	12.896	13.523	14.142
	4.0	8.207	8.898	9.571	10.230	10.873	11.504	12.121	12.726	13.320	13.903
	5.0	8.199	8.877	9.535	10.173	10.795	11.400	11.991	12.567	13.130	13.682
	7.5	8.178	8.825	9.443	10.035	10.605	11.153	11.683	12.195	12.692	13.174
	10.0	8.160	8.780	9.366	9.921	10.451	10.957	11.443	11.912	12.364	12.803
	12.5	8.141	8.734	9.287	9.807	10.298	10.765	11.212	11.640	12.052	12.451
	15.0	8.125	8.696	9.225	9.718	10.184	10.625	11.047	11.453	11.846	12.227
1.200	1.0	8.232	8.962	9.688	10.412	11.132	11.849	12.563	13.275	13.984	14.690
	2.0	8.224	8.941	9.649	10.350	11.043	11.729	12.409	13.082	13.748	14.408
	3.0	8.216	8.919	9.610	10.290	10.958	11.616	12.263	12.901	13.530	14.149
	4.0	8.208	8.898	9.573	10.232	10.876	11.507	12.126	12.732	13.327	13.911
	5.0	8.200	8.878	9.536	10.176	10.798	11.404	11.996	12.573	13.138	13.690
	7.5	8.179	8.826	9.445	10.038	10.608	11.158	11.688	12.202	12.700	13.184
	10.0	8.161	8.782	9.368	9.925	10.456	10.964	11.451	11.922	12.376	12.817
	12.5	8.141	8.736	9.290	9.811	10.304	10.773	11.221	11.651	12.066	12.467
	15.0	8.126	8.698	9.228	9.724	10.191	10.635	11.060	11.468	11.864	12.250
1.250	1.0	8.233	8.963	9.690	10.413	11.134	11.852	12.567	13.279	13.989	14.696
	2.0	8.224	8.941	9.650	10.352	11.046	11.733	12.413	13.087	13.754	14.415
	3.0	8.216	8.920	9.612	10.292	10.961	11.619	12.267	12.906	13.536	14.157
	4.0	8.208	8.899	9.574	10.234	10.879	11.511	12.130	12.738	13.334	13.919
	5.0	8.200	8.879	9.538	10.178	10.801	11.409	12.001	12.580	13.146	13.699
	7.5	8.179	8.827	9.446	10.041	10.612	11.162	11.694	12.209	12.708	13.194
	10.0	8.161	8.783	9.371	9.929	10.461	10.970	11.459	11.931	12.388	12.831
	12.5	8.142	8.737	9.293	9.815	10.310	10.780	11.230	11.662	12.079	12.484
	15.0	8.127	8.701	9.232	9.729	10.199	10.645	11.072	11.484	11.884	12.273

Interest Rate 8.00%   30 Year Schedule

Debt Coverage	Years to Payoff	10%	20%	30%	40%	50%	60%	70%	80%	90%	100%
1.150	1.0	8.731	9.459	10.184	10.907	11.626	12.342	13.055	13.765	14.473	15.178
	2.0	8.721	9.434	10.139	10.837	11.527	12.211	12.888	13.558	14.222	14.880
	3.0	8.710	9.409	10.095	10.770	11.434	12.087	12.731	13.365	13.990	14.606
	4.0	8.700	9.384	10.052	10.705	11.344	11.970	12.583	13.184	13.775	14.355
	5.0	8.690	9.360	10.010	10.643	11.258	11.858	12.444	13.016	13.575	14.123
	7.5	8.665	9.299	9.907	10.490	11.051	11.592	12.115	12.622	13.114	13.592
	10.0	8.643	9.248	9.821	10.366	10.886	11.385	11.865	12.329	12.777	13.213
	12.5	8.619	9.195	9.734	10.242	10.723	11.183	11.623	12.046	12.456	12.853
	15.0	8.600	9.152	9.666	10.148	10.605	11.040	11.458	11.862	12.255	12.640
1.200	1.0	8.731	9.460	10.186	10.908	11.628	12.345	13.059	13.770	14.479	15.185
	2.0	8.721	9.435	10.141	10.839	11.530	12.215	12.892	13.563	14.228	14.887
	3.0	8.711	9.410	10.097	10.772	11.437	12.091	12.735	13.371	13.997	14.615
	4.0	8.701	9.385	10.054	10.707	11.347	11.974	12.588	13.191	13.782	14.364
	5.0	8.691	9.361	10.012	10.645	11.262	11.863	12.449	13.023	13.584	14.133
	7.5	8.665	9.301	9.909	10.493	11.055	11.597	12.122	12.630	13.124	13.603
	10.0	8.643	9.250	9.824	10.370	10.892	11.392	11.874	12.340	12.791	13.229
	12.5	8.620	9.197	9.737	10.246	10.730	11.191	11.633	12.059	12.471	12.871
	15.0	8.601	9.155	9.670	10.155	10.613	11.052	11.473	11.881	12.278	12.667
1.250	1.0	8.732	9.461	10.187	10.910	11.631	12.348	13.063	13.775	14.485	15.192
	2.0	8.722	9.436	10.142	10.841	11.533	12.218	12.897	13.569	14.235	14.895
	3.0	8.711	9.411	10.098	10.774	11.440	12.095	12.740	13.376	14.004	14.623
	4.0	8.701	9.386	10.055	10.710	11.350	11.978	12.593	13.197	13.790	14.373
	5.0	8.691	9.362	10.014	10.648	11.265	11.867	12.455	13.030	13.592	14.143
	7.5	8.666	9.302	9.911	10.496	11.059	11.603	12.128	12.638	13.133	13.615
	10.0	8.644	9.251	9.827	10.374	10.897	11.400	11.883	12.351	12.804	13.245
	12.5	8.621	9.199	9.740	10.251	10.736	11.199	11.644	12.072	12.487	12.890
	15.0	8.602	9.158	9.675	10.161	10.622	11.063	11.488	11.899	12.300	12.694

Entry is annual yield from interest, growth in income and selected share of price appreciation.

Yield on Participating Mortgage Loan

Growth Rate   5%   Loan to Value Ratio 75%
Interest Rate   8.50%   30 Year Schedule

Debt Coverage	Years to Payoff	10%	20%	30%	40%	50%	60%	70%	80%	90%	100%
				Share of Increase in Income & Profit on Sale							
	1.0	9.230	9.958	10.682	11.403	12.122	12.838	13.551	14.261	14.969	15.674
	2.0	9.218	9.928	10.631	11.327	12.015	12.697	13.372	14.040	14.703	15.360
1.150	3.0	9.206	9.900	10.582	11.253	11.913	12.563	13.204	13.835	14.458	15.073
	4.0	9.194	9.871	10.534	11.182	11.816	12.437	13.047	13.645	14.232	14.810
	5.0	9.182	9.844	10.487	11.113	11.723	12.318	12.899	13.467	14.023	14.568
	7.5	9.152	9.775	10.373	10.947	11.500	12.035	12.552	13.054	13.541	14.016
	10.0	9.126	9.718	10.279	10.814	11.326	11.818	12.293	12.752	13.198	13.632
	12.5	9.099	9.658	10.184	10.681	11.154	11.606	12.041	12.462	12.869	13.265
	15.0	9.078	9.612	10.113	10.585	11.034	11.465	11.881	12.285	12.680	13.070
	1.0	9.231	9.958	10.683	11.405	12.125	12.841	13.555	14.266	14.975	15.681
	2.0	9.218	9.929	10.633	11.329	12.018	12.701	13.377	14.046	14.710	15.368
1.200	3.0	9.206	9.901	10.583	11.255	11.916	12.568	13.209	13.842	14.466	15.082
	4.0	9.194	9.873	10.536	11.184	11.819	12.442	13.052	13.652	14.241	14.820
	5.0	9.182	9.845	10.489	11.116	11.727	12.323	12.906	13.475	14.033	14.579
	7.5	9.152	9.777	10.375	10.950	11.505	12.040	12.559	13.062	13.552	14.028
	10.0	9.127	9.720	10.282	10.819	11.332	11.826	12.303	12.765	13.213	13.650
	12.5	9.100	9.661	10.188	10.686	11.161	11.616	12.054	12.476	12.887	13.287
	15.0	9.079	9.615	10.118	10.592	11.044	11.478	11.898	12.306	12.707	13.101
	1.0	9.231	9.959	10.685	11.408	12.127	12.845	13.559	14.272	14.981	15.689
	2.0	9.219	9.930	10.634	11.331	12.021	12.704	13.381	14.052	14.717	15.376
1.250	3.0	9.207	9.902	10.585	11.258	11.920	12.572	13.215	13.848	14.474	15.091
	4.0	9.195	9.874	10.538	11.187	11.823	12.447	13.058	13.659	14.249	14.830
	5.0	9.183	9.847	10.491	11.119	11.731	12.328	12.912	13.483	14.042	14.590
	7.5	9.153	9.778	10.377	10.954	11.509	12.046	12.566	13.071	13.562	14.041
	10.0	9.128	9.722	10.285	10.823	11.339	11.835	12.313	12.777	13.228	13.668
	12.5	9.101	9.663	10.191	10.692	11.169	11.626	12.066	12.491	12.905	13.308
	15.0	9.080	9.619	10.123	10.600	11.055	11.492	11.915	12.328	12.733	13.134

Interest Rate   9.00%   30 Year Schedule

Debt Coverage	Years to Payoff	10%	20%	30%	40%	50%	60%	70%	80%	90%	100%
	1.0	9.729	10.456	11.180	11.901	12.619	13.334	14.047	14.757	15.465	16.171
	2.0	9.715	10.423	11.123	11.817	12.503	13.183	13.857	14.524	15.186	15.841
1.150	3.0	9.701	10.391	11.069	11.736	12.393	13.041	13.679	14.308	14.929	15.541
	4.0	9.687	10.359	11.016	11.659	12.289	12.907	13.512	14.107	14.692	15.267
	5.0	9.674	10.329	10.965	11.585	12.190	12.780	13.357	13.922	14.475	15.017
	7.5	9.640	10.252	10.840	11.406	11.952	12.480	12.992	13.489	13.973	14.444
	10.0	9.611	10.189	10.739	11.265	11.770	12.256	12.726	13.182	13.626	14.059
	12.5	9.580	10.125	10.638	11.125	11.590	12.037	12.468	12.886	13.292	13.689
	15.0	9.557	10.076	10.565	11.028	11.472	11.900	12.316	12.722	13.122	13.519
	1.0	9.730	10.457	11.181	11.903	12.622	13.338	14.052	14.763	15.472	16.179
	2.0	9.716	10.424	11.125	11.819	12.507	13.187	13.862	14.531	15.193	15.850
1.200	3.0	9.702	10.392	11.071	11.739	12.397	13.046	13.685	14.315	14.937	15.551
	4.0	9.688	10.361	11.018	11.662	12.293	12.912	13.519	14.115	14.702	15.278
	5.0	9.675	10.330	10.968	11.589	12.194	12.786	13.364	13.930	14.485	15.029
	7.5	9.640	10.254	10.843	11.410	11.957	12.487	13.000	13.499	13.985	14.458
	10.0	9.612	10.191	10.743	11.271	11.777	12.266	12.738	13.196	13.643	14.079
	12.5	9.582	10.127	10.642	11.131	11.599	12.048	12.482	12.903	13.313	13.714
	15.0	9.559	10.080	10.571	11.037	11.484	11.916	12.336	12.747	13.153	13.557
	1.0	9.730	10.458	11.183	11.905	12.625	13.342	14.057	14.769	15.479	16.187
	2.0	9.716	10.425	11.127	11.822	12.510	13.192	13.867	14.537	15.201	15.859
1.250	3.0	9.702	10.393	11.073	11.742	12.401	13.050	13.691	14.322	14.946	15.561
	4.0	9.689	10.362	11.020	11.665	12.297	12.917	13.525	14.123	14.711	15.289
	5.0	9.675	10.332	10.970	11.592	12.199	12.792	13.371	13.939	14.495	15.041
	7.5	9.641	10.255	10.845	11.414	11.962	12.493	13.008	13.509	13.997	14.472
	10.0	9.613	10.194	10.747	11.276	11.785	12.275	12.750	13.211	13.660	14.100
	12.5	9.583	10.130	10.647	11.138	11.608	12.059	12.496	12.920	13.334	13.739
	15.0	9.560	10.084	10.577	11.046	11.496	11.932	12.356	12.773	13.185	13.596

Entry is annual yield from interest, growth in income and selected share of price appreciation.

Yield on Participating Mortgage Loan

Growth Rate   5%   Loan to Value Ratio 75%
Interest Rate   9.50%   30 Year Schedule

Debt Coverage	Years to Payoff	10%	20%	30%	40%	50%	60%	70%	80%	90%	100%
				Share of Increase in Income & Profit on Sale							
1.150	1.0	10.228	10.955	11.678	12.398	13.116	13.831	14.544	15.255	15.963	16.668
	2.0	10.212	10.918	11.616	12.308	12.992	13.671	14.343	15.009	15.670	16.325
	3.0	10.197	10.882	11.557	12.221	12.875	13.520	14.155	14.782	15.401	16.012
	4.0	10.181	10.848	11.500	12.138	12.764	13.378	13.980	14.572	15.155	15.728
	5.0	10.166	10.814	11.445	12.059	12.659	13.244	13.817	14.379	14.929	15.469
	7.5	10.128	10.730	11.309	11.867	12.407	12.929	13.436	13.929	14.409	14.878
	10.0	10.096	10.663	11.203	11.721	12.219	12.700	13.166	13.619	14.061	14.494
	12.5	10.063	10.594	11.096	11.574	12.033	12.475	12.903	13.320	13.727	14.126
	15.0	10.039	10.544	11.023	11.480	11.919	12.346	12.764	13.175	13.583	13.991
1.200	1.0	10.229	10.956	11.680	12.401	13.119	13.836	14.549	15.261	15.970	16.677
	2.0	10.213	10.919	11.618	12.310	12.996	13.675	14.349	15.016	15.678	16.334
	3.0	10.197	10.884	11.559	12.224	12.879	13.525	14.162	14.790	15.410	16.023
	4.0	10.182	10.849	11.502	12.141	12.768	13.383	13.987	14.581	15.165	15.740
	5.0	10.167	10.816	11.447	12.063	12.664	13.251	13.825	14.388	14.940	15.482
	7.5	10.129	10.732	11.312	11.872	12.413	12.936	13.445	13.940	14.423	14.894
	10.0	10.097	10.665	11.207	11.727	12.227	12.710	13.179	13.635	14.081	14.518
	12.5	10.065	10.597	11.101	11.582	12.043	12.488	12.919	13.339	13.751	14.155
	15.0	10.041	10.548	11.030	11.490	11.934	12.365	12.788	13.205	13.620	14.037
1.250	1.0	10.229	10.957	11.681	12.403	13.123	13.840	14.555	15.267	15.978	16.686
	2.0	10.214	10.920	11.620	12.313	13.000	13.680	14.354	15.023	15.686	16.344
	3.0	10.198	10.885	11.561	12.227	12.883	13.530	14.168	14.798	15.420	16.034
	4.0	10.183	10.851	11.504	12.145	12.773	13.389	13.995	14.590	15.175	15.752
	5.0	10.168	10.817	11.450	12.066	12.669	13.257	13.833	14.398	14.952	15.496
	7.5	10.130	10.734	11.315	11.876	12.418	12.944	13.454	13.951	14.436	14.910
	10.0	10.099	10.668	11.211	11.733	12.235	12.721	13.193	13.652	14.101	14.541
	12.5	10.066	10.600	11.106	11.589	12.053	12.501	12.935	13.359	13.775	14.183
	15.0	10.043	10.553	11.037	11.500	11.948	12.384	12.811	13.235	13.657	14.083

Interest Rate 10.00%   30 Year Schedule

Debt Coverage	Years to Payoff	10%	20%	30%	40%	50%	60%	70%	80%	90%	100%
1.150	1.0	10.728	11.453	12.176	12.896	13.614	14.329	15.042	15.753	16.461	17.167
	2.0	10.710	11.413	12.110	12.799	13.482	14.159	14.830	15.495	16.155	16.809
	3.0	10.693	11.374	12.045	12.706	13.357	14.000	14.633	15.258	15.875	16.485
	4.0	10.676	11.337	11.984	12.618	13.240	13.850	14.450	15.040	15.620	16.191
	5.0	10.659	11.300	11.925	12.534	13.129	13.711	14.280	14.839	15.386	15.925
	7.5	10.617	11.210	11.780	12.331	12.864	13.381	13.884	14.373	14.851	15.318
	10.0	10.583	11.138	11.669	12.180	12.672	13.149	13.612	14.064	14.506	14.940
	12.5	10.548	11.065	11.558	12.029	12.482	12.921	13.348	13.764	14.173	14.576
	15.0	10.523	11.016	11.487	11.939	12.377	12.805	13.227	13.646	14.066	14.491
1.200	1.0	10.728	11.455	12.178	12.899	13.618	14.334	15.048	15.759	16.469	17.177
	2.0	10.711	11.415	12.112	12.802	13.486	14.164	14.836	15.503	16.164	16.820
	3.0	10.693	11.376	12.048	12.710	13.362	14.005	14.640	15.267	15.885	16.497
	4.0	10.676	11.338	11.986	12.622	13.245	13.857	14.458	15.049	15.631	16.204
	5.0	10.660	11.302	11.928	12.538	13.134	13.718	14.289	14.849	15.399	15.939
	7.5	10.618	11.212	11.784	12.336	12.871	13.389	13.894	14.386	14.865	15.335
	10.0	10.584	11.141	11.674	12.187	12.681	13.161	13.627	14.082	14.528	14.966
	12.5	10.549	11.069	11.564	12.037	12.494	12.936	13.366	13.787	14.201	14.609
	15.0	10.525	11.021	11.495	11.951	12.393	12.827	13.255	13.682	14.110	14.546
1.250	1.0	10.729	11.456	12.180	12.902	13.621	14.338	15.053	15.766	16.477	17.186
	2.0	10.711	11.416	12.114	12.805	13.490	14.169	14.843	15.510	16.173	16.831
	3.0	10.694	11.377	12.050	12.713	13.366	14.011	14.647	15.275	15.896	16.509
	4.0	10.677	11.340	11.989	12.625	13.250	13.863	14.466	15.059	15.642	16.218
	5.0	10.661	11.304	11.931	12.542	13.140	13.725	14.298	14.860	15.412	15.954
	7.5	10.619	11.214	11.787	12.341	12.877	13.398	13.904	14.398	14.880	15.352
	10.0	10.586	11.144	11.679	12.194	12.691	13.173	13.642	14.101	14.550	14.993
	12.5	10.551	11.073	11.569	12.046	12.505	12.950	13.384	13.810	14.228	14.643
	15.0	10.527	11.026	11.503	11.963	12.410	12.849	13.283	13.717	14.155	14.602

Entry is annual yield from interest, growth in income and selected share of price appreciation.

Yield on Participating Mortgage Loan

Growth Rate   5%   Loan to Value Ratio 75%
Interest Rate 10.50%   30 Year Schedule

Debt Coverage	Years to Payoff	10%	20%	30%	40%	Share of Increase in Income & Profit on Sale 50%	60%	70%	80%	90%	100%
	1.0	11.227	11.952	12.675	13.395	14.112	14.828	15.541	16.251	16.960	17.667
	2.0	11.208	11.909	12.603	13.291	13.973	14.648	15.318	15.983	16.642	17.296
1.150	3.0	11.189	11.867	12.535	13.192	13.841	14.481	15.112	15.736	16.352	16.960
	4.0	11.170	11.826	12.469	13.099	13.717	14.325	14.922	15.509	16.087	16.657
	5.0	11.152	11.787	12.406	13.010	13.601	14.179	14.746	15.302	15.847	16.384
	7.5	11.107	11.690	12.253	12.797	13.325	13.837	14.335	14.822	15.297	15.763
	10.0	11.070	11.616	12.139	12.642	13.130	13.603	14.065	14.516	14.959	15.395
	12.5	11.033	11.540	12.024	12.489	12.938	13.375	13.801	14.220	14.633	15.042
	15.0	11.009	11.493	11.957	12.406	12.845	13.278	13.708	14.139	14.575	15.023
	1.0	11.228	11.954	12.677	13.398	14.116	14.833	15.547	16.259	16.969	17.678
	2.0	11.208	11.910	12.606	13.294	13.977	14.654	15.325	15.991	16.651	17.307
1.200	3.0	11.189	11.868	12.537	13.196	13.846	14.487	15.120	15.745	16.363	16.973
	4.0	11.171	11.828	12.472	13.103	13.723	14.332	14.930	15.520	16.100	16.672
	5.0	11.153	11.789	12.409	13.015	13.607	14.187	14.755	15.313	15.861	16.400
	7.5	11.108	11.693	12.257	12.803	13.332	13.846	14.347	14.836	15.314	15.782
	10.0	11.072	11.619	12.144	12.650	13.141	13.617	14.082	14.537	14.984	15.425
	12.5	11.035	11.544	12.031	12.498	12.951	13.392	13.822	14.246	14.664	15.080
	15.0	11.011	11.498	11.967	12.420	12.865	13.303	13.741	14.181	14.629	15.090
	1.0	11.228	11.955	12.679	13.401	14.120	14.838	15.553	16.266	16.978	17.688
	2.0	11.209	11.912	12.608	13.298	13.981	14.660	15.332	15.999	16.661	17.319
1.250	3.0	11.190	11.870	12.540	13.200	13.851	14.493	15.128	15.754	16.374	16.986
	4.0	11.172	11.830	12.475	13.107	13.728	14.339	14.939	15.530	16.112	16.686
	5.0	11.154	11.791	12.412	13.020	13.613	14.195	14.765	15.325	15.875	16.417
	7.5	11.109	11.695	12.261	12.808	13.339	13.855	14.358	14.849	15.330	15.801
	10.0	11.074	11.622	12.150	12.658	13.151	13.631	14.099	14.558	15.010	15.456
	12.5	11.037	11.548	12.037	12.508	12.964	13.409	13.844	14.272	14.697	15.119
	15.0	11.014	11.504	11.976	12.435	12.884	13.329	13.774	14.224	14.683	15.160

Interest Rate 11.00%   30 Year Schedule

Debt Coverage	Years to Payoff	10%	20%	30%	40%	50%	60%	70%	80%	90%	100%
	1.0	11.727	12.451	13.174	13.894	14.611	15.327	16.040	16.751	17.461	18.168
	2.0	11.706	12.405	13.097	13.784	14.464	15.138	15.807	16.471	17.130	17.784
1.150	3.0	11.685	12.360	13.024	13.680	14.326	14.963	15.593	16.215	16.830	17.438
	4.0	11.665	12.316	12.955	13.581	14.196	14.801	15.395	15.981	16.558	17.126
	5.0	11.645	12.275	12.888	13.488	14.075	14.650	15.214	15.767	16.311	16.847
	7.5	11.597	12.172	12.728	13.266	13.788	14.296	14.791	15.275	15.749	16.213
	10.0	11.559	12.095	12.611	13.109	13.593	14.064	14.525	14.977	15.422	15.862
	12.5	11.521	12.018	12.494	12.954	13.401	13.837	14.265	14.688	15.107	15.525
	15.0	11.497	11.974	12.434	12.883	13.326	13.766	14.207	14.655	15.116	15.596
	1.0	11.727	12.453	13.176	13.897	14.615	15.332	16.047	16.759	17.470	18.179
	2.0	11.706	12.406	13.100	13.787	14.469	15.145	15.815	16.480	17.140	17.796
1.200	3.0	11.686	12.361	13.027	13.684	14.331	14.970	15.601	16.225	16.842	17.452
	4.0	11.666	12.318	12.958	13.586	14.202	14.808	15.405	15.992	16.571	17.142
	5.0	11.646	12.277	12.892	13.493	14.082	14.659	15.224	15.780	16.327	16.865
	7.5	11.598	12.175	12.732	13.272	13.796	14.306	14.804	15.290	15.767	16.235
	10.0	11.561	12.099	12.617	13.118	13.605	14.079	14.544	15.000	15.451	15.896
	12.5	11.523	12.022	12.502	12.965	13.416	13.857	14.290	14.718	15.143	15.569
	15.0	11.500	11.980	12.445	12.900	13.349	13.796	14.247	14.706	15.181	15.681
	1.0	11.728	12.454	13.178	13.900	14.620	15.337	16.053	16.767	17.480	18.190
	2.0	11.707	12.408	13.102	13.791	14.474	15.151	15.823	16.489	17.151	17.809
1.250	3.0	11.687	12.363	13.030	13.688	14.337	14.977	15.610	16.235	16.854	17.466
	4.0	11.667	12.320	12.961	13.590	14.208	14.816	15.414	16.004	16.585	17.158
	5.0	11.647	12.279	12.896	13.498	14.089	14.667	15.235	15.793	16.342	16.883
	7.5	11.599	12.177	12.736	13.278	13.804	14.316	14.816	15.306	15.785	16.256
	10.0	11.563	12.103	12.623	13.127	13.617	14.095	14.564	15.024	15.480	15.931
	12.5	11.525	12.027	12.510	12.977	13.431	13.876	14.314	14.748	15.181	15.615
	15.0	11.503	11.987	12.457	12.917	13.372	13.827	14.287	14.758	15.249	15.768

Entry is annual yield from interest, growth in income and selected share of price appreciation.

Yield on Participating Mortgage Loan

Growth Rate   5%

Loan to Value Ratio 75%

Interest Rate 11.50%

30 Year Schedule

Debt Coverage	Years to Payoff	10%	20%	30%	40%	50%	60%	70%	80%	90%	100%
					Share of Increase in Income & Profit on Sale						
	1.0	12.226	12.951	13.673	14.393	15.111	15.826	16.540	17.252	17.962	18.670
	2.0	12.204	12.901	13.592	14.277	14.956	15.630	16.298	16.961	17.619	18.273
1.150	3.0	12.181	12.853	13.515	14.167	14.811	15.447	16.075	16.696	17.310	17.917
	4.0	12.160	12.807	13.441	14.064	14.676	15.278	15.871	16.455	17.031	17.599
	5.0	12.139	12.763	13.372	13.968	14.551	15.123	15.684	16.236	16.779	17.314
	7.5	12.088	12.655	13.204	13.736	14.254	14.758	15.251	15.733	16.205	16.670
	10.0	12.049	12.577	13.086	13.580	14.061	14.531	14.992	15.446	15.895	16.341
	12.5	12.010	12.498	12.969	13.426	13.872	14.309	14.741	15.169	15.597	16.027
	15.0	11.988	12.459	12.919	13.371	13.820	14.271	14.730	15.202	15.696	16.224
	1.0	12.227	12.952	13.675	14.396	15.115	15.832	16.547	17.261	17.972	18.682
	2.0	12.204	12.903	13.595	14.281	14.961	15.636	16.306	16.971	17.631	18.287
1.200	3.0	12.182	12.855	13.518	14.172	14.817	15.455	16.084	16.707	17.323	17.933
	4.0	12.161	12.809	13.445	14.069	14.683	15.287	15.881	16.467	17.045	17.616
	5.0	12.140	12.765	13.376	13.973	14.558	15.132	15.696	16.250	16.796	17.334
	7.5	12.089	12.658	13.209	13.743	14.263	14.770	15.265	15.750	16.226	16.694
	10.0	12.051	12.581	13.093	13.590	14.075	14.549	15.014	15.473	15.928	16.380
	12.5	12.012	12.504	12.978	13.439	13.889	14.331	14.769	15.204	15.640	16.079
	15.0	11.992	12.467	12.932	13.390	13.847	14.308	14.778	15.264	15.778	16.333
	1.0	12.228	12.954	13.678	14.400	15.120	15.838	16.554	17.269	17.982	18.694
	2.0	12.205	12.904	13.598	14.285	14.966	15.643	16.314	16.981	17.643	18.300
1.250	3.0	12.183	12.857	13.521	14.176	14.823	15.462	16.094	16.718	17.336	17.948
	4.0	12.162	12.811	13.448	14.074	14.690	15.295	15.892	16.480	17.060	17.633
	5.0	12.141	12.768	13.380	13.979	14.566	15.142	15.708	16.264	16.813	17.353
	7.5	12.090	12.661	13.213	13.750	14.272	14.781	15.279	15.767	16.246	16.718
	10.0	12.053	12.586	13.101	13.601	14.088	14.566	15.036	15.500	15.961	16.419
	12.5	12.015	12.509	12.987	13.451	13.906	14.354	14.797	15.240	15.683	16.132
	15.0	11.995	12.475	12.945	13.410	13.874	14.344	14.826	15.328	15.862	16.447

Interest Rate 12.00%   30 Year Schedule

Debt Coverage	Years to Payoff	10%	20%	30%	40%	50%	60%	70%	80%	90%	100%
	1.0	12.726	13.450	14.172	14.892	15.610	16.326	17.041	17.753	18.464	19.173
	2.0	12.702	13.397	14.087	14.771	15.449	16.122	16.789	17.452	18.110	18.764
1.150	3.0	12.678	13.347	14.006	14.656	15.298	15.932	16.559	17.179	17.792	18.399
	4.0	12.655	13.298	13.929	14.549	15.158	15.758	16.349	16.931	17.506	18.074
	5.0	12.633	13.252	13.857	14.448	15.029	15.598	16.157	16.708	17.250	17.785
	7.5	12.579	13.139	13.682	14.209	14.723	15.224	15.715	16.196	16.668	17.133
	10.0	12.540	13.061	13.565	14.056	14.535	15.005	15.468	15.925	16.380	16.833
	12.5	12.500	12.982	13.449	13.904	14.351	14.791	15.229	15.666	16.105	16.551
	15.0	12.481	12.950	13.411	13.869	14.330	14.798	15.280	15.786	16.329	16.929
	1.0	12.727	13.452	14.175	14.896	15.615	16.333	17.049	17.763	18.475	19.186
	2.0	12.703	13.399	14.090	14.775	15.454	16.129	16.798	17.463	18.123	18.779
1.200	3.0	12.679	13.349	14.009	14.661	15.305	15.940	16.569	17.191	17.806	18.416
	4.0	12.656	13.300	13.933	14.554	15.165	15.767	16.360	16.945	17.522	18.093
	5.0	12.635	13.255	13.861	14.455	15.037	15.608	16.170	16.723	17.269	17.806
	7.5	12.581	13.143	13.687	14.217	14.733	15.237	15.730	16.214	16.690	17.159
	10.0	12.542	13.066	13.573	14.067	14.550	15.025	15.493	15.956	16.417	16.877
	12.5	12.503	12.988	13.459	13.919	14.370	14.817	15.261	15.706	16.156	16.613
	15.0	12.486	12.960	13.427	13.892	14.362	14.841	15.338	15.863	16.433	17.074
	1.0	12.728	13.454	14.178	14.900	15.620	16.339	17.056	17.772	18.486	19.199
	2.0	12.703	13.401	14.093	14.779	15.460	16.136	16.807	17.473	18.136	18.794
1.250	3.0	12.680	13.351	14.013	14.666	15.311	15.949	16.579	17.203	17.821	18.432
	4.0	12.657	13.303	13.937	14.560	15.173	15.776	16.372	16.959	17.539	18.112
	5.0	12.636	13.257	13.865	14.461	15.045	15.619	16.183	16.739	17.287	17.828
	7.5	12.582	13.146	13.693	14.224	14.743	15.250	15.746	16.234	16.713	17.186
	10.0	12.544	13.071	13.581	14.079	14.566	15.045	15.518	15.987	16.455	16.923
	12.5	12.506	12.994	13.469	13.933	14.390	14.843	15.294	15.748	16.207	16.676
	15.0	12.490	12.969	13.442	13.915	14.394	14.885	15.397	15.943	16.542	17.231

Entry is annual yield from interest, growth in income and selected share of price appreciation.

Yield on Loan with Compensating Balances

Interest Rate on Loan

Compensating Balance Required	Average Loan Balance	5.50%	5.75%	6.00%	6.25%	6.50%	6.75%	7.00%	7.25%	7.50%	7.75%	8.00%
5% of Loan	Any	5.789	6.053	6.316	6.579	6.842	7.105	7.368	7.632	7.895	8.158	8.421
10% of Loan	Any	6.111	6.389	6.667	6.944	7.222	7.500	7.778	8.056	8.333	8.611	8.889
15% of Loan	Any	6.471	6.765	7.059	7.353	7.647	7.941	8.235	8.529	8.824	9.118	9.412
20% of Loan	Any	6.875	7.187	7.500	7.812	8.125	8.437	8.750	9.062	9.375	9.687	10.000
25% of Loan	Any	7.333	7.667	8.000	8.333	8.667	9.000	9.333	9.667	10.000	10.333	10.667
10% of Line plus 5% of Loan	25%	8.105	8.474	8.842	9.211	9.579	9.947	10.316	10.684	11.053	11.421	11.789
	40%	7.237	7.566	7.895	8.224	8.553	8.882	9.211	9.539	9.868	10.197	10.526
	50%	6.947	7.263	7.579	7.895	8.211	8.526	8.842	9.158	9.474	9.789	10.105
	55%	6.842	7.153	7.464	7.775	8.086	8.397	8.708	9.019	9.330	9.641	9.952
	75%	6.561	6.860	7.158	7.456	7.754	8.053	8.351	8.649	8.947	9.246	9.544
	100%	6.368	6.658	6.947	7.237	7.526	7.816	8.105	8.395	8.684	8.974	9.263
10% of Line plus 10% of Loan	25%	8.556	8.944	9.333	9.722	10.111	10.500	10.889	11.278	11.667	12.056	12.444
	40%	7.639	7.986	8.333	8.681	9.028	9.375	9.722	10.069	10.417	10.764	11.111
	50%	7.333	7.667	8.000	8.333	8.667	9.000	9.333	9.667	10.000	10.333	10.667
	55%	7.222	7.551	7.879	8.207	8.535	8.864	9.192	9.520	9.848	10.177	10.505
	75%	6.926	7.241	7.556	7.870	8.185	8.500	8.815	9.130	9.444	9.759	10.074
	100%	6.722	7.028	7.333	7.639	7.944	8.250	8.556	8.861	9.167	9.472	9.778
10% of Line plus 15% of Loan	25%	9.059	9.471	9.882	10.294	10.706	11.118	11.529	11.941	12.353	12.765	13.176
	40%	8.088	8.456	8.824	9.191	9.559	9.926	10.294	10.662	11.029	11.397	11.765
	50%	7.765	8.118	8.471	8.824	9.176	9.529	9.882	10.235	10.588	10.941	11.294
	55%	7.647	7.995	8.342	8.690	9.037	9.385	9.733	10.080	10.428	10.775	11.123
	75%	7.333	7.667	8.000	8.333	8.667	9.000	9.333	9.667	10.000	10.333	10.667
	100%	7.118	7.441	7.765	8.088	8.412	8.735	9.059	9.382	9.706	10.029	10.353
15% of Line plus 5% of Loan	25%	9.263	9.684	10.105	10.526	10.947	11.368	11.789	12.211	12.632	13.053	13.474
	40%	7.961	8.322	8.684	9.046	9.408	9.770	10.132	10.493	10.855	11.217	11.579
	50%	7.526	7.868	8.211	8.553	8.895	9.237	9.579	9.921	10.263	10.605	10.947
	55%	7.368	7.703	8.038	8.373	8.708	9.043	9.378	9.713	10.048	10.383	10.718
	75%	6.947	7.263	7.579	7.895	8.211	8.526	8.842	9.158	9.474	9.789	10.105
	100%	6.658	6.961	7.263	7.566	7.868	8.171	8.474	8.776	9.079	9.382	9.684
15% of Line plus 10% of Loan	25%	9.778	10.222	10.667	11.111	11.556	12.000	12.444	12.889	13.333	13.778	14.222
	40%	8.403	8.785	9.167	9.549	9.931	10.313	10.694	11.076	11.458	11.840	12.222
	50%	7.944	8.306	8.667	9.028	9.389	9.750	10.111	10.472	10.833	11.194	11.556
	55%	7.778	8.131	8.485	8.838	9.192	9.545	9.899	10.253	10.606	10.960	11.313
	75%	7.333	7.667	8.000	8.333	8.667	9.000	9.333	9.667	10.000	10.333	10.667
	100%	7.028	7.347	7.667	7.986	8.306	8.625	8.944	9.264	9.583	9.903	10.222

Interest Rate on Loan

Balance Required	Average Balance	8.25%	8.50%	8.75%	9.00%	9.25%	9.50%	9.75%	10.00%	10.25%	10.50%	10.75%
5% of Loan	Any	8.684	8.947	9.211	9.474	9.737	10.000	10.263	10.526	10.789	11.053	11.316
10% of Loan	Any	9.167	9.444	9.722	10.000	10.278	10.556	10.833	11.111	11.389	11.667	11.944
15% of Loan	Any	9.706	10.000	10.294	10.588	10.882	11.176	11.471	11.765	12.059	12.353	12.647
20% of Loan	Any	10.312	10.625	10.937	11.250	11.562	11.875	12.187	12.500	12.812	13.125	13.437
25% of Loan	Any	11.000	11.333	11.667	12.000	12.333	12.667	13.000	13.333	13.667	14.000	14.333
10% of Line plus 5% of Loan	25%	12.158	12.526	12.895	13.263	13.632	14.000	14.368	14.737	15.105	15.474	15.842
	40%	10.855	11.184	11.513	11.842	12.171	12.500	12.829	13.158	13.487	13.816	14.145
	50%	10.421	10.737	11.053	11.368	11.684	12.000	12.316	12.632	12.947	13.263	13.579
	55%	10.263	10.574	10.885	11.196	11.507	11.818	12.129	12.440	12.751	13.062	13.373
	75%	9.842	10.140	10.439	10.737	11.035	11.333	11.632	11.930	12.228	12.526	12.825
	100%	9.553	9.842	10.132	10.421	10.711	11.000	11.289	11.579	11.868	12.158	12.447
10% of Line plus 10% of Loan	25%	12.833	13.222	13.611	14.000	14.389	14.778	15.167	15.556	15.944	16.333	16.722
	40%	11.458	11.806	12.153	12.500	12.847	13.194	13.542	13.889	14.236	14.583	14.931
	50%	11.000	11.333	11.667	12.000	12.333	12.667	13.000	13.333	13.667	14.000	14.333
	55%	10.833	11.162	11.490	11.818	12.146	12.475	12.803	13.131	13.460	13.788	14.116
	75%	10.389	10.704	11.019	11.333	11.648	11.963	12.278	12.593	12.907	13.222	13.537
	100%	10.083	10.389	10.694	11.000	11.306	11.611	11.917	12.222	12.528	12.833	13.139
10% of Line plus 15% of Loan	25%	13.588	14.000	14.412	14.824	15.235	15.647	16.059	16.471	16.882	17.294	17.706
	40%	12.132	12.500	12.868	13.235	13.603	13.971	14.338	14.706	15.074	15.441	15.809
	50%	11.647	12.000	12.353	12.706	13.059	13.412	13.765	14.118	14.471	14.824	15.176
	55%	11.471	11.818	12.166	12.513	12.861	13.209	13.556	13.904	14.251	14.599	14.947
	75%	11.000	11.333	11.667	12.000	12.333	12.667	13.000	13.333	13.667	14.000	14.333
	100%	10.676	11.000	11.324	11.647	11.971	12.294	12.618	12.941	13.265	13.588	13.912
15% of Line plus 5% of Loan	25%	13.895	14.316	14.737	15.158	15.579	16.000	16.421	16.842	17.263	17.684	18.105
	40%	11.941	12.303	12.664	13.026	13.388	13.750	14.112	14.474	14.836	15.197	15.559
	50%	11.289	11.632	11.974	12.316	12.658	13.000	13.342	13.684	14.026	14.368	14.711
	55%	11.053	11.388	11.722	12.057	12.392	12.727	13.062	13.397	13.732	14.067	14.402
	75%	10.421	10.737	11.053	11.368	11.684	12.000	12.316	12.632	12.947	13.263	13.579
	100%	9.987	10.289	10.592	10.895	11.197	11.500	11.803	12.105	12.408	12.711	13.013
15% of Line plus 10% of Loan	25%	14.667	15.111	15.556	16.000	16.444	16.889	17.333	17.778	18.222	18.667	19.111
	40%	12.604	12.986	13.368	13.750	14.132	14.514	14.896	15.278	15.660	16.042	16.424
	50%	11.917	12.278	12.639	13.000	13.361	13.722	14.083	14.444	14.806	15.167	15.528
	55%	11.667	12.020	12.374	12.727	13.081	13.434	13.788	14.141	14.495	14.848	15.202
	75%	11.000	11.333	11.667	12.000	12.333	12.667	13.000	13.333	13.667	14.000	14.333
	100%	10.542	10.861	11.181	11.500	11.819	12.139	12.458	12.778	13.097	13.417	13.736

Yield on Loan with Compensating Balances

Compensating Balance Required	Average Loan Balance	Interest Rate on Loan 11.00%	11.25%	11.50%	11.75%	12.00%	12.25%	12.50%	12.75%	13.00%	13.25%	13.50%
5% of Loan	Any	11.579	11.842	12.105	12.368	12.632	12.895	13.158	13.421	13.684	13.947	14.211
10% of Loan	Any	12.222	12.500	12.778	13.056	13.333	13.611	13.889	14.167	14.444	14.722	15.000
15% of Loan	Any	12.941	13.235	13.529	13.824	14.118	14.412	14.706	15.000	15.294	15.588	15.882
20% of Loan	Any	13.750	14.062	14.375	14.687	15.000	15.312	15.625	15.937	16.250	16.562	16.875
25% of Loan	Any	14.667	15.000	15.333	15.667	16.000	16.333	16.667	17.000	17.333	17.667	18.000
10% of Line plus 5% of Loan	25%	16.211	16.579	16.947	17.316	17.684	18.053	18.421	18.789	19.158	19.526	19.895
	40%	14.474	14.803	15.132	15.461	15.789	16.118	16.447	16.776	17.105	17.434	17.763
	50%	13.895	14.211	14.526	14.842	15.158	15.474	15.789	16.105	16.421	16.737	17.053
	55%	13.684	13.995	14.306	14.617	14.928	15.239	15.550	15.861	16.172	16.483	16.794
	75%	13.123	13.421	13.719	14.018	14.316	14.614	14.912	15.211	15.509	15.807	16.105
	100%	12.737	13.026	13.316	13.605	13.895	14.184	14.474	14.763	15.053	15.342	15.632
10% of Line plus 10% of Loan	25%	17.111	17.500	17.889	18.278	18.667	19.056	19.444	19.833	20.222	20.611	21.000
	40%	15.278	15.625	15.972	16.319	16.667	17.014	17.361	17.708	18.056	18.403	18.750
	50%	14.667	15.000	15.333	15.667	16.000	16.333	16.667	17.000	17.333	17.667	18.000
	55%	14.444	14.773	15.101	15.429	15.758	16.086	16.414	16.742	17.071	17.399	17.727
	75%	13.852	14.167	14.481	14.796	15.111	15.426	15.741	16.056	16.370	16.685	17.000
	100%	13.444	13.750	14.056	14.361	14.667	14.972	15.278	15.583	15.889	16.194	16.500
10% of Line plus 15% of Loan	25%	18.118	18.529	18.941	19.353	19.765	20.176	20.588	21.000	21.412	21.824	22.235
	40%	16.176	16.544	16.912	17.279	17.647	18.015	18.382	18.750	19.118	19.485	19.853
	50%	15.529	15.882	16.235	16.588	16.941	17.294	17.647	18.000	18.353	18.706	19.059
	55%	15.294	15.642	15.989	16.337	16.684	17.032	17.380	17.727	18.075	18.422	18.770
	75%	14.667	15.000	15.333	15.667	16.000	16.333	16.667	17.000	17.333	17.667	18.000
	100%	14.235	14.559	14.882	15.206	15.529	15.853	16.176	16.500	16.824	17.147	17.471
15% of Line plus 5% of Loan	25%	18.526	18.947	19.368	19.789	20.211	20.632	21.053	21.474	21.895	22.316	22.737
	40%	15.921	16.283	16.645	17.007	17.368	17.730	18.092	18.454	18.816	19.178	19.539
	50%	15.053	15.395	15.737	16.079	16.421	16.763	17.105	17.447	17.789	18.132	18.474
	55%	14.737	15.072	15.407	15.742	16.077	16.411	16.746	17.081	17.416	17.751	18.086
	75%	13.895	14.211	14.526	14.842	15.158	15.474	15.789	16.105	16.421	16.737	17.053
	100%	13.316	13.618	13.921	14.224	14.526	14.829	15.132	15.434	15.737	16.039	16.342
15% of Line plus 10% of Loan	25%	19.556	20.000	20.444	20.889	21.333	21.778	22.222	22.667	23.111	23.556	24.000
	40%	16.806	17.188	17.569	17.951	18.333	18.715	19.097	19.479	19.861	20.243	20.625
	50%	15.889	16.250	16.611	16.972	17.333	17.694	18.056	18.417	18.778	19.139	19.500
	55%	15.556	15.909	16.263	16.616	16.970	17.323	17.677	18.030	18.384	18.737	19.091
	75%	14.667	15.000	15.333	15.667	16.000	16.333	16.667	17.000	17.333	17.667	18.000
	100%	14.056	14.375	14.694	15.014	15.333	15.653	15.972	16.292	16.611	16.931	17.250

Balance Required	Average Balance	Interest Rate on Loan 13.75%	14.00%	14.25%	14.50%	14.75%	15.00%	15.50%	16.00%	16.50%	17.00%	18.00%
5% of Loan	Any	14.474	14.737	15.000	15.263	15.526	15.789	16.316	16.842	17.368	17.895	18.947
10% of Loan	Any	15.278	15.556	15.833	16.111	16.389	16.667	17.222	17.778	18.333	18.889	20.000
15% of Loan	Any	16.176	16.471	16.765	17.059	17.353	17.647	18.235	18.824	19.412	20.000	21.176
20% of Loan	Any	17.187	17.500	17.812	18.125	18.437	18.750	19.375	20.000	20.625	21.250	22.500
25% of Loan	Any	18.333	18.667	19.000	19.333	19.667	20.000	20.667	21.333	22.000	22.667	24.000
10% of Line plus 5% of Loan	25%	20.263	20.632	21.000	21.368	21.737	22.105	22.842	23.579	24.316	25.053	26.526
	40%	18.092	18.421	18.750	19.079	19.408	19.737	20.395	21.053	21.711	22.368	23.684
	50%	17.368	17.684	18.000	18.316	18.632	18.947	19.579	20.211	20.842	21.474	22.737
	55%	17.105	17.416	17.727	18.038	18.349	18.660	19.282	19.904	20.526	21.148	22.392
	75%	16.404	16.702	17.000	17.298	17.596	17.895	18.491	19.088	19.684	20.281	21.474
	100%	15.921	16.211	16.500	16.789	17.079	17.368	17.947	18.526	19.105	19.684	20.842
10% of Line plus 10% of Loan	25%	21.389	21.778	22.167	22.556	22.944	23.333	24.111	24.889	25.667	26.444	28.000
	40%	19.097	19.444	19.792	20.139	20.486	20.833	21.528	22.222	22.917	23.611	25.000
	50%	18.333	18.667	19.000	19.333	19.667	20.000	20.667	21.333	22.000	22.667	24.000
	55%	18.056	18.384	18.712	19.040	19.369	19.697	20.354	21.010	21.667	22.323	23.636
	75%	17.315	17.630	17.944	18.259	18.574	18.889	19.519	20.148	20.778	21.407	22.667
	100%	16.806	17.111	17.417	17.722	18.028	18.333	18.944	19.556	20.167	20.778	22.000
10% of Line plus 15% of Loan	25%	22.647	23.059	23.471	23.882	24.294	24.706	25.529	26.353	27.176	28.000	29.647
	40%	20.221	20.588	20.956	21.324	21.691	22.059	22.794	23.529	24.265	25.000	26.471
	50%	19.412	19.765	20.118	20.471	20.824	21.176	21.882	22.588	23.294	24.000	25.412
	55%	19.118	19.465	19.813	20.160	20.508	20.856	21.551	22.246	22.941	23.636	25.027
	75%	18.333	18.667	19.000	19.333	19.667	20.000	20.667	21.333	22.000	22.667	24.000
	100%	17.794	18.118	18.441	18.765	19.088	19.412	20.059	20.706	21.353	22.000	23.294
15% of Line plus 5% of Loan	25%	23.158	23.579	24.000	24.421	24.842	25.263	26.105	26.947	27.789	28.632	30.316
	40%	19.901	20.263	20.625	20.987	21.349	21.711	22.434	23.158	23.882	24.605	26.053
	50%	18.816	19.158	19.500	19.842	20.184	20.526	21.211	21.895	22.579	23.263	24.632
	55%	18.421	18.756	19.091	19.426	19.761	20.096	20.766	21.435	22.105	22.775	24.115
	75%	17.368	17.684	18.000	18.316	18.632	18.947	19.579	20.211	20.842	21.474	22.737
	100%	16.645	16.947	17.250	17.553	17.855	18.158	18.763	19.368	19.974	20.579	21.789
15% of Line plus 10% of Loan	25%	24.444	24.889	25.333	25.778	26.222	26.667	27.556	28.444	29.333	30.222	32.000
	40%	21.007	21.389	21.771	22.153	22.535	22.917	23.681	24.444	25.208	25.972	27.500
	50%	19.861	20.222	20.583	20.944	21.306	21.667	22.389	23.111	23.833	24.556	26.000
	55%	19.444	19.798	20.152	20.505	20.859	21.212	21.919	22.626	23.333	24.040	25.455
	75%	18.333	18.667	19.000	19.333	19.667	20.000	20.667	21.333	22.000	22.667	24.000
	100%	17.569	17.889	18.208	18.528	18.847	19.167	19.806	20.444	21.083	21.722	23.000

Yield from Add-on Interest Loan

Term Months	Add-on Interest Rate 2.90%	3.00%	3.25%	3.50%	3.75%	3.90%	4.00%	4.25%	4.50%	4.75%
3	4.345	4.495	4.869	5.243	5.617	5.841	5.991	6.364	6.738	7.111
6	4.955	5.125	5.551	5.976	6.401	6.656	6.825	7.250	7.674	8.098
9	5.191	5.369	5.813	6.257	6.701	6.967	7.144	7.587	8.029	8.471
12	5.311	5.493	5.947	6.400	6.852	7.123	7.304	7.755	8.206	8.656
15	5.382	5.565	6.024	6.482	6.938	7.212	7.395	7.850	8.304	8.758
18	5.426	5.611	6.072	6.532	6.991	7.266	7.449	7.906	8.362	8.818
21	5.454	5.640	6.102	6.563	7.023	7.298	7.482	7.940	8.396	8.852
24	5.473	5.658	6.121	6.583	7.043	7.318	7.501	7.959	8.415	8.870
27	5.485	5.670	6.133	6.594	7.054	7.329	7.512	7.969	8.424	8.878
30	5.492	5.677	6.139	6.600	7.059	7.333	7.516	7.971	8.425	8.878
33	5.496	5.681	6.142	6.602	7.059	7.333	7.515	7.969	8.422	8.873
36	5.497	5.682	6.142	6.600	7.057	7.330	7.511	7.964	8.415	8.864
39	5.497	5.681	6.140	6.597	7.052	7.324	7.505	7.955	8.405	8.852
42	5.494	5.678	6.136	6.591	7.045	7.316	7.496	7.945	8.392	8.837
45	5.491	5.674	6.130	6.584	7.036	7.306	7.486	7.933	8.378	8.821
48	5.486	5.669	6.124	6.576	7.027	7.295	7.474	7.920	8.363	8.804
51	5.481	5.663	6.117	6.568	7.016	7.284	7.462	7.905	8.346	8.785
54	5.475	5.657	6.109	6.558	7.005	7.271	7.449	7.890	8.329	8.766
57	5.469	5.650	6.100	6.548	6.993	7.258	7.435	7.874	8.311	8.746
60	5.462	5.642	6.091	6.537	6.980	7.245	7.421	7.858	8.293	8.725
63	5.455	5.634	6.082	6.526	6.967	7.231	7.406	7.841	8.274	8.704
66	5.447	5.626	6.072	6.515	6.954	7.217	7.391	7.824	8.255	8.683
69	5.439	5.618	6.062	6.503	6.941	7.202	7.376	7.807	8.236	8.662
72	5.431	5.609	6.052	6.491	6.927	7.187	7.360	7.790	8.216	8.640
75	5.423	5.601	6.042	6.479	6.914	7.173	7.345	7.772	8.197	8.619

Term Months	Add-on Interest Rate 4.90%	5.00%	5.25%	5.50%	5.75%	5.90%	6.00%	6.25%	6.50%	6.75%
3	7.336	7.485	7.858	8.232	8.605	8.829	8.978	9.351	9.724	10.097
6	8.352	8.522	8.945	9.368	9.791	10.045	10.214	10.637	11.059	11.481
9	8.736	8.913	9.354	9.794	10.235	10.499	10.674	11.114	11.553	11.992
12	8.925	9.105	9.554	10.002	10.450	10.718	10.897	11.343	11.789	12.235
15	9.030	9.211	9.663	10.115	10.566	10.836	11.016	11.465	11.914	12.361
18	9.090	9.272	9.726	10.178	10.630	10.900	11.081	11.530	11.979	12.427
21	9.125	9.306	9.760	10.212	10.664	10.934	11.114	11.563	12.011	12.458
24	9.143	9.324	9.777	10.228	10.678	10.948	11.127	11.575	12.022	12.467
27	9.150	9.330	9.782	10.232	10.680	10.949	11.127	11.573	12.018	12.461
30	9.149	9.329	9.779	10.227	10.673	10.941	11.118	11.562	12.004	12.445
33	9.143	9.322	9.770	10.216	10.660	10.926	11.103	11.544	11.984	12.422
36	9.132	9.311	9.757	10.200	10.643	10.907	11.083	11.522	11.959	12.394
39	9.119	9.297	9.740	10.182	10.621	10.884	11.059	11.496	11.930	12.363
42	9.103	9.280	9.721	10.161	10.598	10.859	11.033	11.467	11.898	12.328
45	9.086	9.262	9.701	10.138	10.572	10.832	11.005	11.436	11.865	12.292
48	9.067	9.242	9.679	10.113	10.545	10.804	10.975	11.403	11.830	12.254
51	9.047	9.221	9.656	10.087	10.517	10.774	10.945	11.370	11.793	12.215
54	9.026	9.200	9.632	10.061	10.488	10.743	10.913	11.336	11.756	12.175
57	9.005	9.178	9.607	10.034	10.459	10.712	10.881	11.301	11.719	12.135
60	8.983	9.155	9.582	10.007	10.429	10.681	10.848	11.266	11.681	12.094
63	8.961	9.132	9.556	9.979	10.398	10.649	10.816	11.230	11.643	12.053
66	8.939	9.108	9.531	9.951	10.368	10.617	10.783	11.195	11.605	12.012
69	8.916	9.085	9.505	9.922	10.337	10.585	10.750	11.159	11.567	11.971
72	8.893	9.061	9.479	9.894	10.307	10.553	10.716	11.124	11.528	11.931
75	8.870	9.037	9.453	9.866	10.276	10.521	10.683	11.088	11.490	11.890

Entry is the nominal annual percentage yield from add-on interest.

Yield from Add-on Interest Loan

Term Months	Add-on Interest Rate									
	6.90%	7.00%	7.25%	7.50%	7.75%	7.90%	8.00%	8.25%	8.50%	8.75%
3	10.321	10.470	10.843	11.216	11.588	11.812	11.961	12.333	12.706	13.078
6	11.734	11.903	12.324	12.745	13.167	13.419	13.587	14.008	14.428	14.848
9	12.255	12.430	12.868	13.305	13.742	14.004	14.179	14.615	15.050	15.486
12	12.502	12.679	13.124	13.567	14.010	14.276	14.453	14.895	15.336	15.777
15	12.630	12.808	13.255	13.700	14.145	14.412	14.589	15.033	15.476	15.918
18	12.696	12.875	13.321	13.766	14.211	14.477	14.655	15.098	15.540	15.981
21	12.726	12.904	13.350	13.794	14.237	14.502	14.679	15.120	15.560	16.000
24	12.734	12.911	13.355	13.797	14.238	14.502	14.678	15.116	15.554	15.991
27	12.727	12.903	13.344	13.784	14.222	14.485	14.659	15.095	15.530	15.963
30	12.709	12.885	13.323	13.760	14.195	14.456	14.629	15.062	15.494	15.924
33	12.685	12.859	13.295	13.728	14.161	14.420	14.592	15.021	15.450	15.876
36	12.655	12.828	13.261	13.692	14.121	14.378	14.549	14.975	15.400	15.823
39	12.622	12.794	13.223	13.651	14.077	14.332	14.501	14.924	15.346	15.765
42	12.585	12.756	13.183	13.607	14.030	14.283	14.451	14.871	15.289	15.705
45	12.547	12.717	13.140	13.562	13.981	14.232	14.399	14.815	15.230	15.643
48	12.507	12.676	13.096	13.515	13.931	14.180	14.346	14.759	15.170	15.579
51	12.466	12.634	13.051	13.467	13.880	14.127	14.291	14.701	15.109	15.515
54	12.425	12.591	13.006	13.418	13.828	14.073	14.236	14.643	15.047	15.450
57	12.383	12.548	12.959	13.369	13.776	14.019	14.181	14.585	14.986	15.385
60	12.341	12.505	12.913	13.319	13.724	13.965	14.126	14.526	14.924	15.321
63	12.298	12.461	12.867	13.270	13.671	13.911	14.071	14.468	14.863	15.256
66	12.256	12.417	12.820	13.221	13.619	13.857	14.016	14.410	14.802	15.192
69	12.213	12.374	12.774	13.172	13.568	13.804	13.961	14.352	14.742	15.129
72	12.171	12.330	12.728	13.123	13.516	13.751	13.907	14.295	14.682	15.066
75	12.129	12.287	12.682	13.075	13.465	13.698	13.853	14.239	14.622	15.004

Term Months	Add-on Interest Rate									
	8.90%	9.00%	9.25%	9.50%	9.75%	9.90%	10.00%	10.25%	10.50%	10.75%
3	13.302	13.451	13.823	14.195	14.567	14.790	14.939	15.311	15.683	16.054
6	15.100	15.268	15.688	16.107	16.526	16.778	16.945	17.364	17.783	18.201
9	15.747	15.921	16.355	16.790	17.223	17.483	17.657	18.090	18.522	18.955
12	16.041	16.217	16.657	17.096	17.534	17.797	17.972	18.410	18.847	19.283
15	16.183	16.359	16.800	17.240	17.679	17.942	18.118	18.556	18.993	19.429
18	16.245	16.421	16.861	17.300	17.738	18.000	18.175	18.611	19.047	19.481
21	16.263	16.438	16.875	17.312	17.747	18.008	18.182	18.615	19.048	19.480
24	16.252	16.426	16.860	17.294	17.726	17.985	18.158	18.588	19.017	19.445
27	16.223	16.396	16.827	17.257	17.686	17.943	18.114	18.540	18.966	19.390
30	16.182	16.353	16.781	17.207	17.632	17.887	18.056	18.479	18.901	19.321
33	16.132	16.302	16.726	17.149	17.570	17.822	17.990	18.409	18.827	19.243
36	16.076	16.245	16.665	17.084	17.502	17.752	17.918	18.333	18.747	19.159
39	16.017	16.184	16.600	17.016	17.430	17.677	17.842	18.253	18.662	19.071
42	15.954	16.120	16.533	16.945	17.355	17.600	17.763	18.170	18.576	18.980
45	15.890	16.054	16.464	16.871	17.278	17.521	17.683	18.086	18.487	18.888
48	15.824	15.987	16.393	16.797	17.200	17.441	17.601	18.001	18.398	18.795
51	15.758	15.919	16.322	16.723	17.122	17.360	17.519	17.915	18.309	18.702
54	15.691	15.851	16.250	16.648	17.043	17.280	17.437	17.829	18.220	18.609
57	15.624	15.783	16.179	16.573	16.965	17.199	17.355	17.744	18.131	18.517
60	15.558	15.715	16.108	16.498	16.887	17.120	17.274	17.660	18.043	18.425
63	15.491	15.648	16.037	16.424	16.810	17.040	17.194	17.576	17.956	18.335
66	15.425	15.580	15.967	16.351	16.733	16.962	17.114	17.493	17.870	18.245
69	15.360	15.514	15.897	16.278	16.658	16.885	17.035	17.411	17.785	18.157
72	15.296	15.448	15.828	16.207	16.583	16.808	16.958	17.330	17.701	18.070
75	15.232	15.383	15.761	16.136	16.509	16.733	16.881	17.251	17.619	17.985

Entry is the nominal annual percentage yield from add-on interest.

Nominal Annual Rate Converted to Effective Rate

Nominal Annual Rate	Bi-weekly	Monthly	Quarterly	Semi-annual	Nominal Annual Rate	Bi-weekly	Monthly	Quarterly	Semi-annual	Nominal Annual Rate	Bi-weekly	Monthly	Quarterly	Semi-annual
5.00%	5.122	5.116	5.095	5.063										
5.01	5.133	5.127	5.105	5.073	5.34	5.479	5.473	5.448	5.411	5.67	5.827	5.820	5.792	5.750
5.02	5.143	5.137	5.115	5.083	5.35	5.490	5.483	5.458	5.422	5.68	5.838	5.830	5.802	5.761
5.03	5.154	5.148	5.126	5.093	5.36	5.500	5.494	5.469	5.432	5.6875	5.846	5.838	5.810	5.768
5.04	5.164	5.158	5.136	5.104	5.37	5.511	5.504	5.479	5.442	5.69	5.848	5.841	5.813	5.771
5.05	5.175	5.169	5.146	5.114	5.3750	5.516	5.509	5.484	5.447	5.70	5.859	5.851	5.823	5.781
5.06	5.185	5.179	5.157	5.124	5.38	5.521	5.515	5.490	5.452	5.71	5.870	5.862	5.833	5.792
5.0625	5.188	5.182	5.159	5.127	5.39	5.532	5.525	5.500	5.463	5.72	5.880	5.872	5.844	5.802
5.07	5.196	5.189	5.167	5.134	5.40	5.543	5.536	5.510	5.473	5.73	5.891	5.883	5.854	5.812
5.08	5.206	5.200	5.178	5.145	5.41	5.553	5.546	5.521	5.483	5.74	5.901	5.893	5.865	5.822
5.09	5.217	5.210	5.188	5.155	5.42	5.564	5.557	5.531	5.493	5.7500	5.912	5.904	5.875	5.833
5.10	5.227	5.221	5.198	5.165	5.43	5.574	5.567	5.542	5.504	5.76	5.922	5.915	5.886	5.843
5.11	5.238	5.231	5.209	5.175	5.4375	5.582	5.575	5.549	5.511	5.77	5.933	5.925	5.896	5.853
5.12	5.248	5.242	5.219	5.186	5.44	5.585	5.578	5.552	5.514	5.78	5.944	5.936	5.906	5.864
5.1250	5.253	5.247	5.224	5.191	5.45	5.595	5.588	5.562	5.524	5.79	5.954	5.946	5.917	5.874
5.13	5.259	5.252	5.230	5.196	5.46	5.606	5.599	5.573	5.535	5.80	5.965	5.957	5.927	5.884
5.14	5.269	5.263	5.240	5.206	5.47	5.616	5.609	5.583	5.545	5.81	5.975	5.967	5.938	5.894
5.15	5.280	5.273	5.250	5.216	5.48	5.627	5.620	5.594	5.555	5.8125	5.978	5.970	5.940	5.897
5.16	5.290	5.284	5.261	5.227	5.49	5.637	5.630	5.604	5.565	5.82	5.986	5.978	5.948	5.905
5.17	5.301	5.294	5.271	5.237	5.5000	5.648	5.641	5.614	5.576	5.83	5.996	5.988	5.959	5.915
5.18	5.311	5.305	5.281	5.247	5.51	5.658	5.651	5.625	5.586	5.84	6.007	5.999	5.969	5.925
5.1875	5.319	5.313	5.289	5.255	5.52	5.669	5.662	5.635	5.596	5.85	6.018	6.009	5.980	5.936
5.19	5.322	5.315	5.292	5.257	5.53	5.680	5.672	5.646	5.606	5.86	6.028	6.020	5.990	5.946
5.20	5.332	5.326	5.302	5.268	5.54	5.690	5.683	5.656	5.617	5.87	6.039	6.031	6.000	5.956
5.21	5.343	5.336	5.313	5.278	5.55	5.701	5.693	5.667	5.627	5.8750	6.044	6.036	6.006	5.961
5.22	5.353	5.347	5.323	5.288	5.56	5.711	5.704	5.677	5.637	5.88	6.049	6.041	6.011	5.966
5.23	5.364	5.357	5.333	5.298	5.5625	5.714	5.707	5.680	5.640	5.89	6.060	6.052	6.021	5.977
5.24	5.374	5.368	5.344	5.309	5.57	5.722	5.714	5.687	5.648	5.90	6.070	6.062	6.032	5.987
5.2500	5.385	5.378	5.354	5.319	5.58	5.732	5.725	5.698	5.658	5.91	6.081	6.073	6.042	5.997
5.26	5.395	5.389	5.365	5.329	5.59	5.743	5.735	5.708	5.668	5.92	6.092	6.083	6.053	6.008
5.27	5.406	5.399	5.375	5.339	5.60	5.753	5.746	5.719	5.678	5.93	6.102	6.094	6.063	6.018
5.28	5.416	5.410	5.385	5.350	5.61	5.764	5.757	5.729	5.689	5.9375	6.110	6.102	6.071	6.026
5.29	5.427	5.420	5.396	5.360	5.62	5.775	5.767	5.740	5.699	5.94	6.113	6.104	6.074	6.028
5.30	5.437	5.431	5.406	5.370	5.6250	5.780	5.772	5.745	5.704	5.95	6.123	6.115	6.084	6.039
5.31	5.448	5.441	5.417	5.380	5.63	5.785	5.778	5.750	5.709	5.96	6.134	6.126	6.095	6.049
5.3125	5.450	5.444	5.419	5.383	5.64	5.796	5.788	5.760	5.720	5.97	6.145	6.136	6.105	6.059
5.32	5.458	5.452	5.427	5.391	5.65	5.806	5.799	5.771	5.730	5.98	6.155	6.147	6.115	6.069
5.33	5.469	5.462	5.437	5.401	5.66	5.817	5.809	5.781	5.740	5.99	6.166	6.157	6.126	6.080
6.00%	6.176	6.168	6.136	6.090										
6.01	6.187	6.178	6.147	6.100	6.34	6.537	6.528	6.492	6.440	6.67	6.888	6.878	6.839	6.781
6.02	6.198	6.189	6.157	6.111	6.35	6.548	6.538	6.503	6.451	6.68	6.899	6.888	6.849	6.792
6.03	6.208	6.199	6.168	6.121	6.36	6.558	6.549	6.513	6.461	6.6875	6.907	6.896	6.857	6.799
6.04	6.219	6.210	6.178	6.131	6.37	6.569	6.559	6.524	6.471	6.69	6.910	6.899	6.860	6.802
6.05	6.229	6.221	6.189	6.142	6.3750	6.574	6.565	6.529	6.477	6.70	6.920	6.910	6.870	6.812
6.06	6.240	6.231	6.199	6.152	6.38	6.580	6.570	6.534	6.482	6.71	6.931	6.920	6.881	6.823
6.0625	6.243	6.234	6.202	6.154	6.39	6.590	6.581	6.545	6.492	6.72	6.942	6.931	6.891	6.833
6.07	6.250	6.242	6.210	6.162	6.40	6.601	6.591	6.555	6.502	6.73	6.952	6.942	6.902	6.843
6.08	6.261	6.252	6.220	6.172	6.41	6.611	6.602	6.566	6.513	6.74	6.963	6.952	6.912	6.854
6.09	6.272	6.263	6.230	6.183	6.42	6.622	6.612	6.576	6.523	6.7500	6.974	6.963	6.923	6.864
6.10	6.282	6.273	6.241	6.193	6.43	6.633	6.623	6.587	6.533	6.76	6.984	6.973	6.933	6.874
6.11	6.293	6.284	6.251	6.203	6.4375	6.641	6.631	6.595	6.541	6.77	6.995	6.984	6.944	6.885
6.12	6.304	6.295	6.262	6.214	6.44	6.643	6.634	6.597	6.544	6.78	7.006	6.995	6.954	6.895
6.1250	6.309	6.300	6.267	6.219	6.45	6.654	6.644	6.608	6.554	6.79	7.016	7.005	6.965	6.905
6.13	6.314	6.305	6.272	6.224	6.46	6.665	6.655	6.618	6.564	6.80	7.027	7.016	6.975	6.916
6.14	6.325	6.316	6.283	6.234	6.47	6.675	6.665	6.629	6.575	6.81	7.038	7.027	6.986	6.926
6.15	6.335	6.326	6.293	6.245	6.48	6.686	6.676	6.639	6.585	6.8125	7.040	7.029	6.989	6.929
6.16	6.346	6.337	6.304	6.255	6.49	6.697	6.687	6.650	6.595	6.82	7.048	7.037	6.996	6.936
6.17	6.357	6.348	6.314	6.265	6.5000	6.707	6.697	6.660	6.606	6.83	7.059	7.048	7.007	6.947
6.18	6.367	6.358	6.325	6.275	6.51	6.718	6.708	6.671	6.616	6.84	7.070	7.059	7.017	6.957
6.1875	6.375	6.366	6.333	6.283	6.52	6.729	6.718	6.681	6.626	6.85	7.080	7.069	7.028	6.967
6.19	6.378	6.369	6.335	6.286	6.53	6.739	6.729	6.692	6.637	6.86	7.091	7.080	7.039	6.978
6.20	6.388	6.379	6.346	6.296	6.54	6.750	6.740	6.702	6.647	6.87	7.102	7.091	7.049	6.988
6.21	6.399	6.390	6.356	6.306	6.55	6.760	6.750	6.713	6.657	6.8750	7.107	7.096	7.054	6.993
6.22	6.410	6.400	6.367	6.317	6.56	6.771	6.761	6.723	6.668	6.88	7.112	7.101	7.060	6.998
6.23	6.420	6.411	6.377	6.327	6.5625	6.774	6.764	6.726	6.670	6.89	7.123	7.112	7.070	7.009
6.24	6.431	6.422	6.388	6.337	6.57	6.782	6.771	6.734	6.678	6.90	7.134	7.122	7.081	7.019
6.2500	6.441	6.432	6.398	6.348	6.58	6.792	6.782	6.744	6.688	6.91	7.145	7.133	7.091	7.029
6.26	6.452	6.443	6.408	6.358	6.59	6.803	6.793	6.755	6.699	6.92	7.155	7.144	7.102	7.040
6.27	6.463	6.453	6.419	6.368	6.60	6.814	6.803	6.765	6.709	6.93	7.166	7.154	7.112	7.050
6.28	6.473	6.464	6.429	6.379	6.61	6.824	6.814	6.776	6.719	6.9375	7.174	7.162	7.120	7.058
6.29	6.484	6.475	6.440	6.389	6.62	6.835	6.825	6.786	6.730	6.94	7.177	7.165	7.123	7.060
6.30	6.495	6.485	6.450	6.399	6.6250	6.840	6.830	6.791	6.735	6.95	7.187	7.176	7.133	7.071
6.31	6.505	6.496	6.461	6.410	6.63	6.846	6.835	6.797	6.740	6.96	7.198	7.186	7.144	7.081
6.3125	6.508	6.498	6.464	6.412	6.64	6.856	6.846	6.807	6.750	6.97	7.209	7.197	7.154	7.091
6.32	6.516	6.506	6.471	6.420	6.65	6.867	6.856	6.818	6.761	6.98	7.219	7.208	7.165	7.102
6.33	6.526	6.517	6.482	6.430	6.66	6.878	6.867	6.828	6.771	6.99	7.230	7.218	7.175	7.112

Nominal Annual Rate Converted to Effective Rate

Nominal Annual Rate	Bi-weekly	Monthly	Quarterly	Semi-annual
7.00%	7.241	7.229	7.186	7.123
7.01	7.251	7.240	7.196	7.133
7.02	7.262	7.250	7.207	7.143
7.03	7.273	7.261	7.218	7.154
7.04	7.284	7.272	7.228	7.164
7.05	7.294	7.282	7.239	7.174
7.06	7.305	7.293	7.249	7.185
7.0625	7.308	7.296	7.252	7.187
7.07	7.316	7.304	7.260	7.195
7.08	7.326	7.314	7.270	7.205
7.09	7.337	7.325	7.281	7.216
7.10	7.348	7.336	7.291	7.226
7.11	7.358	7.346	7.302	7.236
7.12	7.369	7.357	7.312	7.247
7.1250	7.375	7.362	7.318	7.252
7.13	7.380	7.368	7.323	7.257
7.14	7.391	7.378	7.333	7.267
7.15	7.401	7.389	7.344	7.278
7.16	7.412	7.400	7.355	7.288
7.17	7.423	7.410	7.365	7.299
7.18	7.433	7.421	7.376	7.309
7.1875	7.441	7.429	7.384	7.317
7.19	7.444	7.432	7.386	7.319
7.20	7.455	7.442	7.397	7.330
7.21	7.466	7.453	7.407	7.340
7.22	7.476	7.464	7.418	7.350
7.23	7.487	7.474	7.428	7.361
7.24	7.498	7.485	7.439	7.371
7.2500	7.508	7.496	7.450	7.381
7.26	7.519	7.507	7.460	7.392
7.27	7.530	7.517	7.471	7.402
7.28	7.541	7.528	7.481	7.412
7.29	7.551	7.539	7.492	7.423
7.30	7.562	7.549	7.502	7.433
7.31	7.573	7.560	7.513	7.444
7.3125	7.575	7.563	7.515	7.446
7.32	7.584	7.571	7.523	7.454
7.33	7.594	7.581	7.534	7.464
7.34	7.605	7.592	7.545	7.475
7.35	7.616	7.603	7.555	7.485
7.36	7.626	7.613	7.566	7.495
7.37	7.637	7.624	7.576	7.506
7.3750	7.643	7.629	7.581	7.511
7.38	7.648	7.635	7.587	7.516
7.39	7.659	7.646	7.597	7.527
7.40	7.669	7.656	7.608	7.537
7.41	7.680	7.667	7.618	7.547
7.42	7.691	7.678	7.629	7.558
7.43	7.702	7.688	7.640	7.568
7.4375	7.710	7.696	7.648	7.576
7.44	7.712	7.699	7.650	7.578
7.45	7.723	7.710	7.661	7.589
7.46	7.734	7.720	7.671	7.599
7.47	7.745	7.731	7.682	7.610
7.48	7.755	7.742	7.692	7.620
7.49	7.766	7.753	7.703	7.630
7.5000	7.777	7.763	7.714	7.641
7.51	7.788	7.774	7.724	7.651
7.52	7.798	7.785	7.735	7.661
7.53	7.809	7.795	7.745	7.672
7.54	7.820	7.806	7.756	7.682
7.55	7.831	7.817	7.766	7.693
7.56	7.841	7.828	7.777	7.703
7.5625	7.844	7.830	7.780	7.705
7.57	7.852	7.838	7.788	7.713
7.58	7.863	7.849	7.798	7.724
7.59	7.874	7.860	7.809	7.734
7.60	7.884	7.870	7.819	7.744
7.61	7.895	7.881	7.830	7.755
7.62	7.906	7.892	7.841	7.765
7.6250	7.911	7.897	7.846	7.770
7.63	7.917	7.903	7.851	7.776
7.64	7.927	7.913	7.862	7.786
7.65	7.938	7.924	7.872	7.796
7.66	7.949	7.935	7.883	7.807
7.67	7.960	7.945	7.893	7.817
7.68	7.970	7.956	7.904	7.827
7.6875	7.978	7.964	7.912	7.835
7.69	7.981	7.967	7.915	7.838
7.70	7.992	7.978	7.925	7.848
7.71	8.003	7.988	7.936	7.859
7.72	8.013	7.999	7.946	7.869
7.73	8.024	8.010	7.957	7.879
7.74	8.035	8.021	7.968	7.890
7.7500	8.046	8.031	7.978	7.900
7.76	8.057	8.042	7.989	7.911
7.77	8.067	8.053	7.999	7.921
7.78	8.078	8.064	8.010	7.931
7.79	8.089	8.074	8.021	7.942
7.80	8.100	8.085	8.031	7.952
7.81	8.110	8.096	8.042	7.962
7.8125	8.113	8.098	8.044	7.965
7.82	8.121	8.106	8.052	7.973
7.83	8.132	8.117	8.063	7.983
7.84	8.143	8.128	8.074	7.994
7.85	8.154	8.139	8.084	8.004
7.86	8.164	8.149	8.095	8.014
7.87	8.175	8.160	8.105	8.025
7.8750	8.181	8.166	8.111	8.030
7.88	8.186	8.171	8.116	8.035
7.89	8.197	8.182	8.127	8.046
7.90	8.207	8.192	8.137	8.056
7.91	8.218	8.203	8.148	8.066
7.92	8.229	8.214	8.158	8.077
7.93	8.240	8.225	8.169	8.087
7.9375	8.248	8.233	8.177	8.095
7.94	8.251	8.235	8.180	8.098
7.95	8.261	8.246	8.190	8.108
7.96	8.272	8.257	8.201	8.118
7.97	8.283	8.268	8.211	8.129
7.98	8.294	8.278	8.222	8.139
7.99	8.305	8.289	8.233	8.150
8.00%	8.315	8.300	8.243	8.160
8.01	8.326	8.311	8.254	8.170
8.02	8.337	8.321	8.264	8.181
8.03	8.348	8.332	8.275	8.191
8.04	8.359	8.343	8.286	8.202
8.05	8.369	8.354	8.296	8.212
8.06	8.380	8.365	8.307	8.222
8.0625	8.383	8.367	8.310	8.225
8.07	8.391	8.375	8.318	8.233
8.08	8.402	8.386	8.328	8.243
8.09	8.413	8.397	8.339	8.254
8.10	8.423	8.408	8.349	8.264
8.11	8.434	8.418	8.360	8.274
8.12	8.445	8.429	8.371	8.285
8.1250	8.450	8.435	8.376	8.290
8.13	8.456	8.440	8.381	8.295
8.14	8.467	8.451	8.392	8.306
8.15	8.477	8.461	8.402	8.316
8.16	8.488	8.472	8.413	8.326
8.17	8.499	8.483	8.424	8.337
8.18	8.510	8.494	8.434	8.347
8.1875	8.518	8.502	8.442	8.355
8.19	8.521	8.505	8.445	8.358
8.20	8.532	8.515	8.456	8.368
8.21	8.542	8.526	8.466	8.379
8.22	8.553	8.537	8.477	8.389
8.23	8.564	8.548	8.488	8.399
8.24	8.575	8.558	8.498	8.410
8.2500	8.586	8.569	8.509	8.420
8.26	8.597	8.580	8.519	8.431
8.27	8.607	8.591	8.530	8.441
8.28	8.618	8.602	8.541	8.451
8.29	8.629	8.612	8.551	8.462
8.30	8.640	8.623	8.562	8.472
8.31	8.651	8.634	8.573	8.483
8.3125	8.653	8.637	8.575	8.485
8.32	8.661	8.645	8.583	8.493
8.33	8.672	8.656	8.594	8.503
8.34	8.683	8.666	8.604	8.514
8.35	8.694	8.677	8.615	8.524
8.36	8.705	8.688	8.626	8.535
8.37	8.716	8.699	8.636	8.545
8.3750	8.721	8.704	8.642	8.550
8.38	8.726	8.709	8.647	8.556
8.39	8.737	8.720	8.658	8.566
8.40	8.748	8.731	8.668	8.576
8.41	8.759	8.742	8.679	8.587
8.42	8.770	8.753	8.690	8.597
8.43	8.781	8.763	8.700	8.608
8.4375	8.789	8.772	8.708	8.615
8.44	8.792	8.774	8.711	8.618
8.45	8.802	8.785	8.722	8.629
8.46	8.813	8.796	8.732	8.639
8.47	8.824	8.807	8.743	8.649
8.48	8.835	8.817	8.753	8.660
8.49	8.846	8.828	8.764	8.670
8.5000	8.857	8.839	8.775	8.681
8.51	8.867	8.850	8.785	8.691
8.52	8.878	8.861	8.796	8.701
8.53	8.889	8.872	8.807	8.712
8.54	8.900	8.882	8.817	8.722
8.55	8.911	8.893	8.828	8.733
8.56	8.922	8.904	8.839	8.743
8.5625	8.924	8.907	8.841	8.746
8.57	8.933	8.915	8.849	8.754
8.58	8.943	8.926	8.860	8.764
8.59	8.954	8.936	8.871	8.774
8.60	8.965	8.947	8.881	8.785
8.61	8.976	8.958	8.892	8.795
8.62	8.987	8.969	8.903	8.806
8.6250	8.992	8.974	8.908	8.811
8.63	8.998	8.980	8.913	8.816
8.64	9.009	8.990	8.924	8.827
8.65	9.019	9.001	8.935	8.837
8.66	9.030	9.012	8.945	8.847
8.67	9.041	9.023	8.956	8.858
8.68	9.052	9.034	8.967	8.868
8.6875	9.060	9.042	8.975	8.876
8.69	9.063	9.045	8.977	8.879
8.70	9.074	9.055	8.988	8.889
8.71	9.085	9.066	8.999	8.900
8.72	9.096	9.077	9.009	8.910
8.73	9.106	9.088	9.020	8.921
8.74	9.117	9.099	9.031	8.931
8.7500	9.128	9.110	9.041	8.941
8.76	9.139	9.120	9.052	8.952
8.77	9.150	9.131	9.063	8.962
8.78	9.161	9.142	9.073	8.973
8.79	9.172	9.153	9.084	8.983
8.80	9.183	9.164	9.095	8.994
8.81	9.193	9.175	9.105	9.004
8.8125	9.196	9.177	9.108	9.007
8.82	9.204	9.185	9.116	9.014
8.83	9.215	9.196	9.127	9.025
8.84	9.226	9.207	9.137	9.035
8.85	9.237	9.218	9.148	9.046
8.86	9.248	9.229	9.159	9.056
8.87	9.259	9.240	9.169	9.067
8.8750	9.264	9.245	9.175	9.072
8.88	9.270	9.250	9.180	9.077
8.89	9.281	9.261	9.191	9.088
8.90	9.291	9.272	9.201	9.098
8.91	9.302	9.283	9.212	9.108
8.92	9.313	9.294	9.223	9.119
8.93	9.324	9.305	9.234	9.129
8.9375	9.332	9.313	9.242	9.137
8.94	9.335	9.316	9.244	9.140
8.95	9.346	9.326	9.255	9.150
8.96	9.357	9.337	9.266	9.161
8.97	9.368	9.348	9.276	9.171
8.98	9.379	9.359	9.287	9.182
8.99	9.390	9.370	9.298	9.192

Nominal Annual Rate Converted to Effective Rate

Nominal Annual Rate	Effective rate Bi-weekly	Monthly	Quarterly	Semi-annual	Nominal Annual Rate	Effective rate Bi-weekly	Monthly	Quarterly	Semi-annual	Nominal Annual Rate	Effective rate Bi-weekly	Monthly	Quarterly	Semi-annual
9.00%	9.400	9.381	9.308	9.203										
9.01	9.411	9.392	9.319	9.213	9.34	9.772	9.750	9.672	9.558	9.67	10.133	10.110	10.026	9.904
9.02	9.422	9.402	9.330	9.223	9.35	9.783	9.761	9.683	9.569	9.68	10.144	10.121	10.037	9.914
9.03	9.433	9.413	9.340	9.234	9.36	9.794	9.772	9.694	9.579	9.6875	10.152	10.129	10.045	9.922
9.04	9.444	9.424	9.351	9.244	9.37	9.805	9.783	9.704	9.589	9.69	10.155	10.132	10.048	9.925
9.05	9.455	9.435	9.362	9.255	9.3750	9.810	9.789	9.710	9.595	9.70	10.166	10.143	10.059	9.935
9.06	9.466	9.446	9.372	9.265	9.38	9.815	9.794	9.715	9.600	9.71	10.177	10.154	10.069	9.946
9.0625	9.469	9.449	9.375	9.268	9.39	9.826	9.805	9.726	9.610	9.72	10.188	10.165	10.080	9.956
9.07	9.477	9.457	9.383	9.276	9.40	9.837	9.816	9.737	9.621	9.73	10.199	10.176	10.091	9.967
9.08	9.488	9.468	9.394	9.286	9.41	9.848	9.827	9.747	9.631	9.74	10.210	10.187	10.102	9.977
9.09	9.499	9.478	9.405	9.297	9.42	9.859	9.838	9.758	9.642	9.7500	10.221	10.198	10.112	9.988
9.10	9.510	9.489	9.415	9.307	9.43	9.870	9.848	9.769	9.652	9.76	10.232	10.209	10.123	9.998
9.11	9.520	9.500	9.426	9.317	9.4375	9.878	9.857	9.777	9.660	9.77	10.243	10.220	10.134	10.009
9.12	9.531	9.511	9.437	9.328	9.44	9.881	9.859	9.779	9.663	9.78	10.254	10.231	10.145	10.019
9.1250	9.537	9.516	9.442	9.333	9.45	9.892	9.870	9.790	9.673	9.79	10.265	10.241	10.155	10.030
9.13	9.542	9.522	9.447	9.338	9.46	9.903	9.881	9.801	9.684	9.80	10.276	10.252	10.166	10.040
9.14	9.553	9.533	9.458	9.349	9.47	9.914	9.892	9.812	9.694	9.81	10.287	10.263	10.177	10.051
9.15	9.564	9.544	9.469	9.359	9.48	9.925	9.903	9.822	9.705	9.8125	10.290	10.266	10.180	10.053
9.16	9.575	9.555	9.479	9.370	9.49	9.936	9.914	9.833	9.715	9.82	10.298	10.274	10.188	10.061
9.17	9.586	9.565	9.490	9.380	9.5000	9.947	9.925	9.844	9.726	9.83	10.309	10.285	10.198	10.072
9.18	9.597	9.576	9.501	9.391	9.51	9.958	9.936	9.855	9.736	9.84	10.320	10.296	10.209	10.082
9.1875	9.605	9.584	9.509	9.399	9.52	9.969	9.947	9.865	9.747	9.85	10.331	10.307	10.220	10.093
9.19	9.608	9.587	9.512	9.401	9.53	9.980	9.957	9.876	9.757	9.86	10.342	10.318	10.231	10.103
9.20	9.619	9.598	9.522	9.412	9.54	9.991	9.968	9.887	9.768	9.87	10.353	10.329	10.241	10.114
9.21	9.630	9.609	9.533	9.422	9.55	10.002	9.979	9.897	9.778	9.8750	10.358	10.334	10.247	10.119
9.22	9.641	9.620	9.544	9.433	9.56	10.013	9.990	9.908	9.788	9.88	10.364	10.340	10.252	10.124
9.23	9.651	9.631	9.554	9.443	9.5625	10.015	9.993	9.911	9.791	9.89	10.375	10.351	10.263	10.135
9.24	9.662	9.642	9.565	9.453	9.57	10.024	10.001	9.919	9.799	9.90	10.386	10.362	10.274	10.145
9.2500	9.673	9.652	9.576	9.464	9.58	10.035	10.012	9.930	9.809	9.91	10.397	10.373	10.284	10.156
9.26	9.684	9.663	9.587	9.474	9.59	10.045	10.023	9.940	9.820	9.92	10.408	10.384	10.295	10.166
9.27	9.695	9.674	9.597	9.485	9.60	10.056	10.034	9.951	9.830	9.93	10.419	10.395	10.306	10.177
9.28	9.706	9.685	9.608	9.495	9.61	10.067	10.045	9.962	9.841	9.9375	10.427	10.403	10.314	10.184
9.29	9.717	9.696	9.619	9.506	9.62	10.078	10.056	9.973	9.851	9.94	10.430	10.406	10.317	10.187
9.30	9.728	9.707	9.629	9.516	9.6250	10.084	10.061	9.978	9.857	9.95	10.441	10.417	10.327	10.198
9.31	9.739	9.718	9.640	9.527	9.63	10.089	10.067	9.983	9.862	9.96	10.452	10.427	10.338	10.208
9.3125	9.742	9.720	9.643	9.529	9.64	10.100	10.078	9.994	9.872	9.97	10.463	10.438	10.349	10.219
9.32	9.750	9.729	9.651	9.537	9.65	10.111	10.088	10.005	9.883	9.98	10.474	10.449	10.360	10.229
9.33	9.761	9.739	9.662	9.548	9.66	10.122	10.099	10.016	9.893	9.99	10.485	10.460	10.371	10.240
10.00%	10.496	10.471	10.381	10.250										
10.01	10.507	10.482	10.392	10.261	10.34	10.871	10.844	10.748	10.607	10.67	11.236	11.208	11.105	10.955
10.02	10.518	10.493	10.403	10.271	10.35	10.882	10.855	10.759	10.618	10.68	11.247	11.219	11.115	10.965
10.03	10.529	10.504	10.414	10.282	10.36	10.893	10.866	10.769	10.628	10.6875	11.255	11.227	11.124	10.973
10.04	10.540	10.515	10.424	10.292	10.37	10.904	10.877	10.780	10.639	10.69	11.258	11.230	11.126	10.976
10.05	10.551	10.526	10.435	10.303	10.3750	10.909	10.883	10.786	10.644	10.70	11.269	11.241	11.137	10.986
10.06	10.562	10.537	10.446	10.313	10.38	10.915	10.888	10.791	10.649	10.71	11.280	11.252	11.148	10.997
10.0625	10.565	10.540	10.449	10.316	10.39	10.926	10.899	10.802	10.660	10.72	11.291	11.263	11.159	11.007
10.07	10.573	10.548	10.457	10.324	10.40	10.937	10.910	10.813	10.670	10.73	11.302	11.274	11.170	11.018
10.08	10.584	10.559	10.467	10.334	10.41	10.948	10.921	10.823	10.681	10.74	11.313	11.285	11.180	11.028
10.09	10.595	10.570	10.478	10.345	10.42	10.959	10.932	10.834	10.691	10.7500	11.324	11.296	11.191	11.039
10.10	10.606	10.581	10.489	10.355	10.43	10.970	10.943	10.845	10.702	10.76	11.335	11.307	11.202	11.049
10.11	10.617	10.592	10.500	10.366	10.4375	10.978	10.952	10.853	10.710	10.77	11.347	11.318	11.213	11.060
10.12	10.628	10.603	10.511	10.376	10.44	10.981	10.954	10.856	10.712	10.78	11.358	11.329	11.224	11.071
10.1250	10.634	10.608	10.516	10.381	10.45	10.992	10.965	10.867	10.723	10.79	11.369	11.340	11.234	11.081
10.13	10.639	10.614	10.521	10.387	10.46	11.003	10.976	10.877	10.734	10.80	11.380	11.351	11.245	11.092
10.14	10.650	10.625	10.532	10.397	10.47	11.014	10.987	10.888	10.744	10.81	11.391	11.362	11.256	11.102
10.15	10.661	10.636	10.543	10.408	10.48	11.025	10.998	10.899	10.755	10.8125	11.394	11.365	11.259	11.105
10.16	10.672	10.647	10.554	10.418	10.49	11.037	11.009	10.910	10.765	10.82	11.402	11.373	11.267	11.113
10.17	10.683	10.658	10.564	10.429	10.5000	11.048	11.020	10.921	10.776	10.83	11.413	11.384	11.278	11.123
10.18	10.694	10.669	10.575	10.439	10.51	11.059	11.031	10.932	10.786	10.84	11.424	11.395	11.289	11.134
10.1875	10.702	10.677	10.583	10.447	10.52	11.070	11.042	10.942	10.797	10.85	11.435	11.406	11.299	11.144
10.19	10.705	10.680	10.586	10.450	10.53	11.081	11.053	10.953	10.807	10.86	11.446	11.417	11.310	11.155
10.20	10.716	10.691	10.597	10.460	10.54	11.092	11.064	10.964	10.818	10.87	11.458	11.428	11.321	11.165
10.21	10.727	10.702	10.608	10.471	10.55	11.103	11.075	10.975	10.828	10.8750	11.463	11.434	11.327	11.171
10.22	10.738	10.713	10.618	10.481	10.56	11.114	11.086	10.986	10.839	10.88	11.469	11.439	11.332	11.176
10.23	10.749	10.724	10.629	10.492	10.5625	11.117	11.089	10.988	10.841	10.89	11.480	11.450	11.343	11.186
10.24	10.760	10.735	10.640	10.502	10.57	11.125	11.097	10.996	10.849	10.90	11.491	11.461	11.354	11.197
10.2500	10.771	10.746	10.651	10.513	10.58	11.136	11.108	11.007	10.860	10.91	11.502	11.472	11.365	11.208
10.26	10.782	10.756	10.662	10.523	10.59	11.147	11.119	11.018	10.870	10.92	11.513	11.483	11.375	11.218
10.27	10.793	10.767	10.672	10.534	10.60	11.158	11.130	11.029	10.881	10.93	11.524	11.495	11.386	11.229
10.28	10.805	10.778	10.683	10.544	10.61	11.169	11.141	11.040	10.891	10.9375	11.532	11.503	11.394	11.237
10.29	10.816	10.789	10.694	10.555	10.62	11.180	11.152	11.050	10.902	10.94	11.535	11.506	11.397	11.239
10.30	10.827	10.800	10.705	10.565	10.6250	11.186	11.158	11.056	10.907	10.95	11.546	11.517	11.408	11.250
10.31	10.838	10.811	10.716	10.576	10.63	11.191	11.164	11.061	10.912	10.96	11.557	11.528	11.419	11.260
10.3125	10.840	10.814	10.718	10.578	10.64	11.203	11.175	11.072	10.923	10.97	11.569	11.539	11.430	11.271
10.32	10.849	10.822	10.726	10.586	10.65	11.214	11.186	11.083	10.934	10.98	11.580	11.550	11.440	11.281
10.33	10.860	10.833	10.737	10.597	10.66	11.225	11.197	11.094	10.944	10.99	11.591	11.561	11.451	11.292

Nominal Annual Rate Converted to Effective Rate

Nominal Annual Rate	Bi-weekly	Monthly	Quarterly	Semi-annual
11.00%	11.602	11.572	11.462	11.303
11.01	11.613	11.583	11.473	11.313
11.02	11.624	11.594	11.484	11.324
11.03	11.635	11.605	11.495	11.334
11.04	11.646	11.616	11.506	11.345
11.05	11.657	11.627	11.516	11.355
11.06	11.669	11.638	11.527	11.366
11.0625	11.671	11.641	11.530	11.368
11.07	11.680	11.649	11.538	11.376
11.08	11.691	11.660	11.549	11.387
11.09	11.702	11.671	11.560	11.397
11.10	11.713	11.682	11.571	11.408
11.11	11.724	11.694	11.582	11.419
11.12	11.735	11.705	11.592	11.429
11.1250	11.741	11.710	11.598	11.434
11.13	11.746	11.716	11.603	11.440
11.14	11.758	11.727	11.614	11.450
11.15	11.769	11.738	11.625	11.461
11.16	11.780	11.749	11.636	11.471
11.17	11.791	11.760	11.647	11.482
11.18	11.802	11.771	11.658	11.492
11.1875	11.810	11.779	11.666	11.500
11.19	11.813	11.782	11.668	11.503
11.20	11.824	11.793	11.679	11.514
11.21	11.836	11.804	11.690	11.524
11.22	11.847	11.815	11.701	11.535
11.23	11.858	11.826	11.712	11.545
11.24	11.869	11.838	11.723	11.556
11.2500	11.880	11.849	11.734	11.566
11.26	11.891	11.860	11.744	11.577
11.27	11.902	11.871	11.755	11.588
11.28	11.913	11.882	11.766	11.598
11.29	11.925	11.893	11.777	11.609
11.30	11.936	11.904	11.788	11.619
11.31	11.947	11.915	11.799	11.630
11.3125	11.950	11.918	11.802	11.632
11.32	11.958	11.926	11.810	11.640
11.33	11.969	11.937	11.821	11.651
11.34	11.980	11.948	11.831	11.661
11.35	11.992	11.959	11.842	11.672
11.36	12.003	11.971	11.853	11.683
11.37	12.014	11.982	11.864	11.693
11.3750	12.019	11.987	11.869	11.698
11.38	12.025	11.993	11.875	11.704
11.39	12.036	12.004	11.886	11.714
11.40	12.047	12.015	11.897	11.725
11.41	12.058	12.026	11.908	11.735
11.42	12.070	12.037	11.918	11.746
11.43	12.081	12.048	11.929	11.757
11.4375	12.089	12.057	11.937	11.765
11.44	12.092	12.059	11.940	11.767
11.45	12.103	12.070	11.951	11.778
11.46	12.114	12.082	11.962	11.788
11.47	12.125	12.093	11.973	11.799
11.48	12.137	12.104	11.984	11.809
11.49	12.148	12.115	11.995	11.820
11.5000	12.159	12.126	12.006	11.831
11.51	12.170	12.137	12.016	11.841
11.52	12.181	12.148	12.027	11.852
11.53	12.192	12.159	12.038	11.862
11.54	12.204	12.170	12.049	11.873
11.55	12.215	12.181	12.060	11.884
11.56	12.226	12.193	12.071	11.894
11.5625	12.229	12.195	12.074	11.897
11.57	12.237	12.204	12.082	11.905
11.58	12.248	12.215	12.093	11.915
11.59	12.259	12.226	12.104	11.926
11.60	12.271	12.237	12.114	11.936
11.61	12.282	12.248	12.125	11.947
11.62	12.293	12.259	12.136	11.958
11.6250	12.299	12.265	12.142	11.963
11.63	12.304	12.270	12.147	11.968
11.64	12.315	12.282	12.158	11.979
11.65	12.327	12.293	12.169	11.989
11.66	12.338	12.304	12.180	12.000
11.67	12.349	12.315	12.191	12.010
11.68	12.360	12.326	12.202	12.021
11.6875	12.368	12.334	12.210	12.029
11.69	12.371	12.337	12.213	12.032
11.70	12.382	12.348	12.223	12.042
11.71	12.394	12.359	12.234	12.053
11.72	12.405	12.371	12.245	12.063
11.73	12.416	12.382	12.256	12.074
11.74	12.427	12.393	12.267	12.085
11.7500	12.438	12.404	12.278	12.095
11.76	12.450	12.415	12.289	12.106
11.77	12.461	12.426	12.300	12.116
11.78	12.472	12.437	12.311	12.127
11.79	12.483	12.448	12.322	12.138
11.80	12.494	12.460	12.332	12.148
11.81	12.506	12.471	12.343	12.159
11.8125	12.508	12.473	12.346	12.161
11.82	12.517	12.482	12.354	12.169
11.83	12.528	12.493	12.365	12.180
11.84	12.539	12.504	12.376	12.190
11.85	12.550	12.515	12.387	12.201
11.86	12.562	12.526	12.398	12.212
11.87	12.573	12.538	12.409	12.222
11.8750	12.578	12.543	12.414	12.228
11.88	12.584	12.549	12.420	12.233
11.89	12.595	12.560	12.431	12.243
11.90	12.606	12.571	12.442	12.254
11.91	12.618	12.582	12.453	12.265
11.92	12.629	12.593	12.463	12.275
11.93	12.640	12.604	12.474	12.286
11.9375	12.648	12.613	12.483	12.294
11.94	12.651	12.616	12.485	12.296
11.95	12.662	12.627	12.496	12.307
11.96	12.674	12.638	12.507	12.318
11.97	12.685	12.649	12.518	12.328
11.98	12.696	12.660	12.529	12.339
11.99	12.707	12.671	12.540	12.349
12.00%	12.719	12.683	12.551	12.360
12.01	12.730	12.694	12.562	12.371
12.02	12.741	12.705	12.573	12.381
12.03	12.752	12.716	12.584	12.392
12.04	12.763	12.727	12.595	12.402
12.05	12.775	12.738	12.606	12.413
12.06	12.786	12.749	12.616	12.424
12.0625	12.789	12.752	12.619	12.426
12.07	12.797	12.761	12.627	12.434
12.08	12.808	12.772	12.638	12.445
12.09	12.820	12.783	12.649	12.455
12.10	12.831	12.794	12.660	12.466
12.11	12.842	12.805	12.671	12.477
12.12	12.853	12.816	12.682	12.487
12.1250	12.859	12.822	12.688	12.493
12.13	12.865	12.828	12.693	12.498
12.14	12.876	12.839	12.704	12.508
12.15	12.887	12.850	12.715	12.519
12.16	12.898	12.861	12.726	12.530
12.17	12.909	12.872	12.737	12.540
12.18	12.921	12.883	12.748	12.551
12.1875	12.929	12.892	12.756	12.559
12.19	12.932	12.895	12.759	12.561
12.20	12.943	12.906	12.770	12.572
12.21	12.954	12.917	12.781	12.583
12.22	12.966	12.928	12.791	12.593
12.23	12.977	12.939	12.802	12.604
12.24	12.988	12.951	12.813	12.615
12.2500	12.999	12.962	12.824	12.625
12.26	13.011	12.973	12.835	12.636
12.27	13.022	12.984	12.846	12.646
12.28	13.033	12.995	12.857	12.657
12.29	13.044	13.006	12.868	12.668
12.30	13.056	13.018	12.879	12.678
12.31	13.067	13.029	12.890	12.689
12.3125	13.070	13.032	12.893	12.691
12.32	13.078	13.040	12.901	12.699
12.33	13.089	13.051	12.912	12.710
12.34	13.101	13.062	12.923	12.721
12.35	13.112	13.074	12.934	12.731
12.36	13.123	13.085	12.945	12.742
12.37	13.134	13.096	12.956	12.753
12.3750	13.140	13.102	12.961	12.758
12.38	13.146	13.107	12.967	12.763
12.39	13.157	13.118	12.978	12.774
12.40	13.168	13.130	12.989	12.784
12.41	13.179	13.141	13.000	12.795
12.42	13.191	13.152	13.011	12.806
12.43	13.202	13.163	13.021	12.816
12.4375	13.210	13.172	13.030	12.824
12.44	13.213	13.174	13.032	12.827
12.45	13.225	13.186	13.043	12.838
12.46	13.236	13.197	13.054	12.848
12.47	13.247	13.208	13.065	12.859
12.48	13.258	13.219	13.076	12.869
12.49	13.270	13.230	13.087	12.880
12.5000	13.281	13.242	13.098	12.891
12.51	13.292	13.253	13.109	12.901
12.52	13.303	13.264	13.120	12.912
12.53	13.315	13.275	13.131	12.923
12.54	13.326	13.286	13.142	12.933
12.55	13.337	13.298	13.153	12.944
12.56	13.349	13.309	13.164	12.954
12.5625	13.351	13.312	13.167	12.957
12.57	13.360	13.320	13.175	12.965
12.58	13.371	13.331	13.186	12.976
12.59	13.382	13.343	13.197	12.986
12.60	13.394	13.354	13.208	12.997
12.61	13.405	13.365	13.219	13.008
12.62	13.416	13.376	13.230	13.018
12.6250	13.422	13.382	13.235	13.023
12.63	13.428	13.387	13.241	13.029
12.64	13.439	13.399	13.252	13.039
12.65	13.450	13.410	13.263	13.050
12.66	13.461	13.421	13.274	13.061
12.67	13.473	13.432	13.285	13.071
12.68	13.484	13.444	13.296	13.082
12.6875	13.492	13.452	13.304	13.090
12.69	13.495	13.455	13.307	13.093
12.70	13.507	13.466	13.318	13.103
12.71	13.518	13.477	13.329	13.114
12.72	13.529	13.488	13.340	13.124
12.73	13.540	13.500	13.351	13.135
12.74	13.552	13.511	13.362	13.146
12.7500	13.563	13.522	13.373	13.156
12.76	13.574	13.533	13.384	13.167
12.77	13.586	13.545	13.395	13.178
12.78	13.597	13.556	13.406	13.188
12.79	13.608	13.567	13.417	13.199
12.80	13.620	13.578	13.428	13.210
12.81	13.631	13.590	13.439	13.220
12.8125	13.634	13.592	13.441	13.223
12.82	13.642	13.601	13.450	13.231
12.83	13.654	13.612	13.461	13.242
12.84	13.665	13.623	13.472	13.252
12.85	13.676	13.634	13.483	13.263
12.86	13.687	13.646	13.494	13.273
12.87	13.699	13.657	13.505	13.284
12.8750	13.704	13.663	13.510	13.289
12.88	13.710	13.668	13.516	13.295
12.89	13.721	13.679	13.527	13.305
12.90	13.733	13.691	13.538	13.316
12.91	13.744	13.702	13.549	13.327
12.92	13.755	13.713	13.560	13.337
12.93	13.767	13.724	13.571	13.348
12.9375	13.775	13.733	13.579	13.356
12.94	13.778	13.736	13.582	13.359
12.95	13.789	13.747	13.593	13.369
12.96	13.801	13.758	13.604	13.380
12.97	13.812	13.769	13.615	13.391
12.98	13.823	13.781	13.626	13.401
12.99	13.835	13.792	13.637	13.412

Effective Annual Rate Converted to Nominal Rate

Effective Annual Rate	Bi-weekly	Monthly	Quarterly	Semi-annual	Effective Annual Rate	Bi-weekly	Monthly	Quarterly	Semi-annual	Effective Annual Rate	Bi-weekly	Monthly	Quarterly	Semi-annual
5.00%	4.884	4.889	4.909	4.939										
5.01	4.893	4.899	4.919	4.949	5.34	5.208	5.214	5.236	5.271	5.67	5.521	5.528	5.553	5.592
5.02	4.903	4.908	4.928	4.959	5.35	5.217	5.223	5.246	5.280	5.68	5.530	5.537	5.563	5.602
5.03	4.912	4.918	4.938	4.968	5.36	5.227	5.233	5.256	5.290	5.69	5.540	5.547	5.572	5.611
5.04	4.922	4.927	4.947	4.978	5.37	5.236	5.242	5.265	5.300	5.70	5.549	5.556	5.582	5.621
5.05	4.931	4.937	4.957	4.988	5.38	5.246	5.252	5.275	5.310	5.71	5.559	5.566	5.592	5.631
5.06	4.941	4.946	4.967	4.998	5.39	5.255	5.261	5.284	5.319	5.72	5.568	5.575	5.601	5.640
5.07	4.950	4.956	4.976	5.007	5.40	5.265	5.271	5.294	5.329	5.73	5.578	5.585	5.611	5.650
5.08	4.960	4.965	4.986	5.017	5.41	5.274	5.280	5.304	5.339	5.74	5.587	5.594	5.620	5.660
5.09	4.969	4.975	4.996	5.027	5.42	5.284	5.290	5.313	5.348	5.75	5.597	5.604	5.630	5.670
5.10	4.979	4.985	5.005	5.037	5.43	5.293	5.299	5.323	5.358	5.76	5.606	5.613	5.640	5.679
5.11	4.989	4.994	5.015	5.046	5.44	5.303	5.309	5.332	5.368	5.77	5.616	5.623	5.649	5.689
5.12	4.998	5.004	5.025	5.056	5.45	5.312	5.318	5.342	5.378	5.78	5.625	5.632	5.659	5.699
5.13	5.008	5.013	5.034	5.066	5.46	5.322	5.328	5.352	5.387	5.79	5.635	5.642	5.668	5.709
5.14	5.017	5.023	5.044	5.076	5.47	5.331	5.337	5.361	5.397	5.80	5.644	5.651	5.678	5.718
5.15	5.027	5.032	5.053	5.085	5.48	5.341	5.347	5.371	5.407	5.81	5.654	5.661	5.688	5.728
5.16	5.036	5.042	5.063	5.095	5.49	5.350	5.357	5.380	5.417	5.82	5.663	5.670	5.697	5.738
5.17	5.046	5.051	5.073	5.105	5.50	5.360	5.366	5.390	5.426	5.83	5.673	5.680	5.707	5.747
5.18	5.055	5.061	5.082	5.115	5.51	5.369	5.376	5.400	5.436	5.84	5.682	5.689	5.716	5.757
5.19	5.065	5.070	5.092	5.124	5.52	5.379	5.385	5.409	5.446	5.85	5.692	5.699	5.726	5.767
5.20	5.074	5.080	5.102	5.134	5.53	5.388	5.395	5.419	5.456	5.86	5.701	5.708	5.735	5.777
5.21	5.084	5.090	5.111	5.144	5.54	5.398	5.404	5.429	5.465	5.87	5.710	5.718	5.745	5.786
5.22	5.093	5.099	5.121	5.154	5.55	5.407	5.414	5.438	5.475	5.88	5.720	5.727	5.755	5.796
5.23	5.103	5.109	5.130	5.163	5.56	5.417	5.423	5.448	5.485	5.89	5.729	5.737	5.764	5.806
5.24	5.112	5.118	5.140	5.173	5.57	5.426	5.433	5.457	5.495	5.90	5.739	5.746	5.774	5.815
5.25	5.122	5.128	5.150	5.183	5.58	5.436	5.442	5.467	5.504	5.91	5.748	5.756	5.783	5.825
5.26	5.131	5.137	5.159	5.193	5.59	5.445	5.452	5.477	5.514	5.92	5.758	5.765	5.793	5.835
5.27	5.141	5.147	5.169	5.202	5.60	5.455	5.461	5.486	5.524	5.93	5.767	5.775	5.803	5.845
5.28	5.150	5.156	5.179	5.212	5.61	5.464	5.471	5.496	5.533	5.94	5.777	5.784	5.812	5.854
5.29	5.160	5.166	5.188	5.222	5.62	5.474	5.480	5.505	5.543	5.95	5.786	5.794	5.822	5.864
5.30	5.169	5.175	5.198	5.232	5.63	5.483	5.490	5.515	5.553	5.96	5.796	5.803	5.831	5.874
5.31	5.179	5.185	5.207	5.241	5.64	5.492	5.499	5.524	5.563	5.97	5.805	5.813	5.841	5.883
5.32	5.188	5.195	5.217	5.251	5.65	5.502	5.509	5.534	5.572	5.98	5.815	5.822	5.850	5.893
5.33	5.198	5.204	5.227	5.261	5.66	5.511	5.518	5.544	5.582	5.99	5.824	5.832	5.860	5.903
6.00%	5.833	5.841	5.870	5.913										
6.01	5.843	5.851	5.879	5.922	6.34	6.154	6.163	6.195	6.243	6.67	6.465	6.474	6.509	6.562
6.02	5.852	5.860	5.889	5.932	6.35	6.164	6.172	6.204	6.252	6.68	6.474	6.484	6.519	6.572
6.03	5.862	5.869	5.898	5.942	6.36	6.173	6.182	6.214	6.262	6.69	6.484	6.493	6.528	6.582
6.04	5.871	5.879	5.908	5.951	6.37	6.183	6.191	6.223	6.272	6.70	6.493	6.503	6.538	6.591
6.05	5.881	5.888	5.917	5.961	6.38	6.192	6.201	6.233	6.281	6.71	6.503	6.512	6.547	6.601
6.06	5.890	5.898	5.927	5.971	6.39	6.202	6.210	6.242	6.291	6.72	6.512	6.521	6.557	6.611
6.07	5.900	5.907	5.937	5.981	6.40	6.211	6.220	6.252	6.301	6.73	6.521	6.531	6.567	6.620
6.08	5.909	5.917	5.946	5.990	6.41	6.220	6.229	6.261	6.310	6.74	6.531	6.540	6.576	6.630
6.09	5.918	5.926	5.956	6.000	6.42	6.230	6.238	6.271	6.320	6.75	6.540	6.550	6.586	6.640
6.10	5.928	5.936	5.965	6.010	6.43	6.239	6.248	6.281	6.330	6.76	6.550	6.559	6.595	6.649
6.11	5.937	5.945	5.975	6.019	6.44	6.249	6.257	6.290	6.340	6.77	6.559	6.569	6.605	6.659
6.12	5.947	5.955	5.984	6.029	6.45	6.258	6.267	6.300	6.349	6.78	6.568	6.578	6.614	6.669
6.13	5.956	5.964	5.994	6.039	6.46	6.267	6.276	6.309	6.359	6.79	6.578	6.587	6.624	6.678
6.14	5.966	5.974	6.003	6.049	6.47	6.277	6.286	6.319	6.369	6.80	6.587	6.597	6.633	6.688
6.15	5.975	5.983	6.013	6.058	6.48	6.286	6.295	6.328	6.378	6.81	6.596	6.606	6.643	6.698
6.16	5.985	5.993	6.023	6.068	6.49	6.296	6.305	6.338	6.388	6.82	6.606	6.616	6.652	6.708
6.17	5.994	6.002	6.032	6.078	6.50	6.305	6.314	6.347	6.398	6.83	6.615	6.625	6.662	6.717
6.18	6.003	6.012	6.042	6.087	6.51	6.315	6.323	6.357	6.407	6.84	6.625	6.634	6.671	6.727
6.19	6.013	6.021	6.051	6.097	6.52	6.324	6.333	6.366	6.417	6.85	6.634	6.644	6.681	6.737
6.20	6.022	6.030	6.061	6.107	6.53	6.333	6.342	6.376	6.427	6.86	6.643	6.653	6.690	6.746
6.21	6.032	6.040	6.070	6.116	6.54	6.343	6.352	6.385	6.436	6.87	6.653	6.663	6.700	6.756
6.22	6.041	6.049	6.080	6.126	6.55	6.352	6.361	6.395	6.446	6.88	6.662	6.672	6.709	6.766
6.23	6.051	6.059	6.090	6.136	6.56	6.362	6.371	6.405	6.456	6.89	6.672	6.682	6.719	6.775
6.24	6.060	6.068	6.099	6.146	6.57	6.371	6.380	6.414	6.465	6.90	6.681	6.691	6.728	6.785
6.25	6.070	6.078	6.109	6.155	6.58	6.380	6.390	6.424	6.475	6.91	6.690	6.700	6.738	6.795
6.26	6.079	6.087	6.118	6.165	6.59	6.390	6.399	6.433	6.485	6.92	6.700	6.710	6.747	6.804
6.27	6.088	6.097	6.128	6.175	6.60	6.399	6.408	6.443	6.495	6.93	6.709	6.719	6.757	6.814
6.28	6.098	6.106	6.137	6.184	6.61	6.409	6.418	6.452	6.504	6.94	6.718	6.729	6.766	6.824
6.29	6.107	6.116	6.147	6.194	6.62	6.418	6.427	6.462	6.514	6.95	6.728	6.738	6.776	6.833
6.30	6.117	6.125	6.156	6.204	6.63	6.427	6.437	6.471	6.524	6.96	6.737	6.747	6.785	6.843
6.31	6.126	6.135	6.166	6.213	6.64	6.437	6.446	6.481	6.533	6.97	6.747	6.757	6.795	6.853
6.32	6.136	6.144	6.176	6.223	6.65	6.446	6.456	6.490	6.543	6.98	6.756	6.766	6.804	6.862
6.33	6.145	6.153	6.185	6.233	6.66	6.456	6.465	6.500	6.553	6.99	6.765	6.776	6.814	6.872

Entry is nominal annual percentage rate from which this effective rate is derived.

Effective Annual Rate Converted to Nominal Rate

Effective Annual Rate	Bi-weekly	Monthly	Quarterly	Semi-annual	Effective Annual Rate	Bi-weekly	Monthly	Quarterly	Semi-annual	Effective Annual Rate	Bi-weekly	Monthly	Quarterly	Semi-annual
7.00%	6.775	6.785	6.823	6.882										
7.01	6.784	6.794	6.833	6.891	7.34	7.093	7.104	7.146	7.210	7.67	7.401	7.413	7.459	7.528
7.02	6.793	6.804	6.842	6.901	7.35	7.102	7.113	7.156	7.220	7.68	7.410	7.422	7.468	7.538
7.03	6.803	6.813	6.852	6.911	7.36	7.111	7.123	7.165	7.229	7.69	7.419	7.432	7.478	7.548
7.04	6.812	6.823	6.861	6.920	7.37	7.121	7.132	7.175	7.239	7.70	7.429	7.441	7.487	7.557
7.05	6.822	6.832	6.871	6.930	7.38	7.130	7.142	7.184	7.249	7.71	7.438	7.450	7.497	7.567
7.06	6.831	6.841	6.880	6.940	7.39	7.139	7.151	7.194	7.258	7.72	7.447	7.460	7.506	7.576
7.07	6.840	6.851	6.890	6.949	7.40	7.149	7.160	7.203	7.268	7.73	7.456	7.469	7.516	7.586
7.08	6.850	6.860	6.899	6.959	7.41	7.158	7.170	7.213	7.278	7.74	7.466	7.478	7.525	7.596
7.09	6.859	6.870	6.909	6.969	7.42	7.167	7.179	7.222	7.287	7.75	7.475	7.488	7.534	7.605
7.10	6.868	6.879	6.918	6.978	7.43	7.177	7.188	7.232	7.297	7.76	7.484	7.497	7.544	7.615
7.11	6.878	6.888	6.928	6.988	7.44	7.186	7.198	7.241	7.307	7.77	7.494	7.506	7.553	7.625
7.12	6.887	6.898	6.937	6.998	7.45	7.195	7.207	7.250	7.316	7.78	7.503	7.516	7.563	7.634
7.13	6.896	6.907	6.947	7.007	7.46	7.205	7.216	7.260	7.326	7.79	7.512	7.525	7.572	7.644
7.14	6.906	6.916	6.956	7.017	7.47	7.214	7.226	7.269	7.335	7.80	7.522	7.534	7.582	7.654
7.15	6.915	6.926	6.966	7.027	7.48	7.223	7.235	7.279	7.345	7.81	7.531	7.544	7.591	7.663
7.16	6.924	6.935	6.975	7.036	7.49	7.233	7.245	7.288	7.355	7.82	7.540	7.553	7.601	7.673
7.17	6.934	6.945	6.985	7.046	7.50	7.242	7.254	7.298	7.364	7.83	7.550	7.562	7.610	7.682
7.18	6.943	6.954	6.994	7.056	7.51	7.251	7.263	7.307	7.374	7.84	7.559	7.572	7.620	7.692
7.19	6.953	6.963	7.004	7.065	7.52	7.261	7.273	7.317	7.384	7.85	7.568	7.581	7.629	7.702
7.20	6.962	6.973	7.013	7.075	7.53	7.270	7.282	7.326	7.393	7.86	7.577	7.590	7.638	7.711
7.21	6.971	6.982	7.023	7.085	7.54	7.279	7.291	7.336	7.403	7.87	7.587	7.600	7.648	7.721
7.22	6.981	6.992	7.032	7.094	7.55	7.289	7.301	7.345	7.413	7.88	7.596	7.609	7.657	7.731
7.23	6.990	7.001	7.042	7.104	7.56	7.298	7.310	7.355	7.422	7.89	7.605	7.618	7.667	7.740
7.24	6.999	7.010	7.051	7.113	7.57	7.307	7.319	7.364	7.432	7.90	7.615	7.628	7.676	7.750
7.25	7.009	7.020	7.061	7.123	7.58	7.317	7.329	7.374	7.442	7.91	7.624	7.637	7.686	7.759
7.26	7.018	7.029	7.070	7.133	7.59	7.326	7.338	7.383	7.451	7.92	7.633	7.646	7.695	7.769
7.27	7.027	7.038	7.080	7.142	7.60	7.335	7.347	7.393	7.461	7.93	7.642	7.656	7.705	7.779
7.28	7.037	7.048	7.089	7.152	7.61	7.345	7.357	7.402	7.470	7.94	7.652	7.665	7.714	7.788
7.29	7.046	7.057	7.099	7.162	7.62	7.354	7.366	7.411	7.480	7.95	7.661	7.674	7.723	7.798
7.30	7.055	7.067	7.108	7.171	7.63	7.363	7.375	7.421	7.490	7.96	7.670	7.684	7.733	7.808
7.31	7.065	7.076	7.118	7.181	7.64	7.373	7.385	7.430	7.499	7.97	7.680	7.693	7.742	7.817
7.32	7.074	7.085	7.127	7.191	7.65	7.382	7.394	7.440	7.509	7.98	7.689	7.702	7.752	7.827
7.33	7.083	7.095	7.137	7.200	7.66	7.391	7.404	7.449	7.519	7.99	7.698	7.712	7.761	7.836
8.00%	7.708	7.721	7.771	7.846										
8.01	7.717	7.730	7.780	7.856	8.34	8.023	8.037	8.091	8.173	8.67	8.328	8.343	8.402	8.490
8.02	7.726	7.739	7.790	7.865	8.35	8.032	8.047	8.101	8.183	8.68	8.337	8.353	8.411	8.499
8.03	7.735	7.749	7.799	7.875	8.36	8.041	8.056	8.110	8.192	8.69	8.346	8.362	8.420	8.509
8.04	7.745	7.758	7.808	7.885	8.37	8.051	8.065	8.119	8.202	8.70	8.356	8.371	8.430	8.519
8.05	7.754	7.767	7.818	7.894	8.38	8.060	8.074	8.129	8.211	8.71	8.365	8.380	8.439	8.528
8.06	7.763	7.777	7.827	7.904	8.39	8.069	8.084	8.138	8.221	8.72	8.374	8.390	8.449	8.538
8.07	7.772	7.786	7.837	7.913	8.40	8.078	8.093	8.148	8.231	8.73	8.383	8.399	8.458	8.547
8.08	7.782	7.795	7.846	7.923	8.41	8.088	8.102	8.157	8.240	8.74	8.392	8.408	8.467	8.557
8.09	7.791	7.805	7.856	7.933	8.42	8.097	8.112	8.167	8.250	8.75	8.402	8.418	8.477	8.567
8.10	7.800	7.814	7.865	7.942	8.43	8.106	8.121	8.176	8.259	8.76	8.411	8.427	8.486	8.576
8.11	7.810	7.823	7.874	7.952	8.44	8.115	8.130	8.185	8.269	8.77	8.420	8.436	8.495	8.586
8.12	7.819	7.833	7.884	7.962	8.45	8.125	8.139	8.195	8.279	8.78	8.429	8.445	8.505	8.595
8.13	7.828	7.842	7.893	7.971	8.46	8.134	8.149	8.204	8.288	8.79	8.439	8.455	8.514	8.605
8.14	7.837	7.851	7.903	7.981	8.47	8.143	8.158	8.214	8.298	8.80	8.448	8.464	8.524	8.614
8.15	7.847	7.861	7.912	7.990	8.48	8.152	8.167	8.223	8.307	8.81	8.457	8.473	8.533	8.624
8.16	7.856	7.870	7.922	8.000	8.49	8.162	8.177	8.232	8.317	8.82	8.466	8.482	8.542	8.634
8.17	7.865	7.879	7.931	8.010	8.50	8.171	8.186	8.242	8.327	8.83	8.475	8.492	8.552	8.643
8.18	7.875	7.888	7.940	8.019	8.51	8.180	8.195	8.251	8.336	8.84	8.485	8.501	8.561	8.653
8.19	7.884	7.898	7.950	8.029	8.52	8.189	8.204	8.261	8.346	8.85	8.494	8.510	8.571	8.662
8.20	7.893	7.907	7.959	8.038	8.53	8.199	8.214	8.270	8.355	8.86	8.503	8.519	8.580	8.672
8.21	7.902	7.916	7.969	8.048	8.54	8.208	8.223	8.279	8.365	8.87	8.512	8.529	8.589	8.682
8.22	7.912	7.926	7.978	8.058	8.55	8.217	8.232	8.289	8.375	8.88	8.522	8.538	8.599	8.691
8.23	7.921	7.935	7.988	8.067	8.56	8.226	8.241	8.298	8.384	8.89	8.531	8.547	8.608	8.701
8.24	7.930	7.944	7.997	8.077	8.57	8.236	8.251	8.308	8.394	8.90	8.540	8.556	8.617	8.710
8.25	7.939	7.954	8.006	8.087	8.58	8.245	8.260	8.317	8.403	8.91	8.549	8.566	8.627	8.720
8.26	7.949	7.963	8.016	8.096	8.59	8.254	8.269	8.326	8.413	8.92	8.558	8.575	8.636	8.729
8.27	7.958	7.972	8.025	8.106	8.60	8.263	8.279	8.336	8.423	8.93	8.568	8.584	8.646	8.739
8.28	7.967	7.981	8.035	8.115	8.61	8.272	8.288	8.345	8.432	8.94	8.577	8.593	8.655	8.749
8.29	7.976	7.991	8.044	8.125	8.62	8.282	8.297	8.355	8.442	8.95	8.586	8.603	8.664	8.758
8.30	7.986	8.000	8.053	8.135	8.63	8.291	8.306	8.364	8.451	8.96	8.595	8.612	8.674	8.768
8.31	7.995	8.009	8.063	8.144	8.64	8.300	8.316	8.373	8.461	8.97	8.604	8.621	8.683	8.777
8.32	8.004	8.019	8.072	8.154	8.65	8.309	8.325	8.383	8.471	8.98	8.614	8.630	8.693	8.787
8.33	8.014	8.028	8.082	8.163	8.66	8.319	8.334	8.392	8.480	8.99	8.623	8.640	8.702	8.797

Entry is nominal annual percentage rate from which this effective rate is derived.

Effective Annual Rate Converted to Nominal Rate

Effective Annual Rate	Bi-weekly	Monthly	Quarterly	Semi-annual	Effective Annual Rate	Bi-weekly	Monthly	Quarterly	Semi-annual	Effective Annual Rate	Bi-weekly	Monthly	Quarterly	Semi-annual
9.00%	8.632	8.649	8.711	8.806										
9.01	8.641	8.658	8.721	8.816	9.34	8.945	8.963	9.030	9.132	9.67	9.247	9.266	9.338	9.447
9.02	8.650	8.667	8.730	8.825	9.35	8.954	8.972	9.039	9.141	9.68	9.256	9.275	9.347	9.456
9.03	8.660	8.677	8.739	8.835	9.36	8.963	8.981	9.048	9.151	9.69	9.265	9.285	9.357	9.466
9.04	8.669	8.686	8.749	8.844	9.37	8.972	8.990	9.058	9.160	9.70	9.274	9.294	9.366	9.476
9.05	8.678	8.695	8.758	8.854	9.38	8.981	8.999	9.067	9.170	9.71	9.284	9.303	9.375	9.485
9.06	8.687	8.704	8.768	8.864	9.39	8.990	9.009	9.076	9.179	9.72	9.293	9.312	9.385	9.495
9.07	8.696	8.713	8.777	8.873	9.40	9.000	9.018	9.086	9.189	9.73	9.302	9.321	9.394	9.504
9.08	8.706	8.723	8.786	8.883	9.41	9.009	9.027	9.095	9.198	9.74	9.311	9.330	9.403	9.514
9.09	8.715	8.732	8.796	8.892	9.42	9.018	9.036	9.104	9.208	9.75	9.320	9.340	9.413	9.523
9.10	8.724	8.741	8.805	8.902	9.43	9.027	9.045	9.114	9.218	9.76	9.329	9.349	9.422	9.533
9.11	8.733	8.750	8.814	8.911	9.44	9.036	9.055	9.123	9.227	9.77	9.338	9.358	9.431	9.542
9.12	8.742	8.760	8.824	8.921	9.45	9.045	9.064	9.132	9.237	9.78	9.348	9.367	9.441	9.552
9.13	8.752	8.769	8.833	8.931	9.46	9.055	9.073	9.142	9.246	9.79	9.357	9.376	9.450	9.561
9.14	8.761	8.778	8.842	8.940	9.47	9.064	9.082	9.151	9.256	9.80	9.366	9.386	9.459	9.571
9.15	8.770	8.787	8.852	8.950	9.48	9.073	9.091	9.160	9.265	9.81	9.375	9.395	9.468	9.581
9.16	8.779	8.797	8.861	8.959	9.49	9.082	9.101	9.170	9.275	9.82	9.384	9.404	9.478	9.590
9.17	8.788	8.806	8.871	8.969	9.50	9.091	9.110	9.179	9.284	9.83	9.393	9.413	9.487	9.600
9.18	8.798	8.815	8.880	8.978	9.51	9.100	9.119	9.189	9.294	9.84	9.402	9.422	9.496	9.609
9.19	8.807	8.824	8.889	8.988	9.52	9.110	9.128	9.198	9.304	9.85	9.412	9.431	9.506	9.619
9.20	8.816	8.833	8.899	8.998	9.53	9.119	9.137	9.207	9.313	9.86	9.421	9.441	9.515	9.628
9.21	8.825	8.843	8.908	9.007	9.54	9.128	9.147	9.217	9.323	9.87	9.430	9.450	9.524	9.638
9.22	8.834	8.852	8.917	9.017	9.55	9.137	9.156	9.226	9.332	9.88	9.439	9.459	9.534	9.647
9.23	8.844	8.861	8.927	9.026	9.56	9.146	9.165	9.235	9.342	9.89	9.448	9.468	9.543	9.657
9.24	8.853	8.870	8.936	9.036	9.57	9.155	9.174	9.245	9.351	9.90	9.457	9.477	9.552	9.666
9.25	8.862	8.880	8.945	9.045	9.58	9.165	9.183	9.254	9.361	9.91	9.466	9.486	9.562	9.676
9.26	8.871	8.889	8.955	9.055	9.59	9.174	9.193	9.263	9.370	9.92	9.475	9.496	9.571	9.685
9.27	8.880	8.898	8.964	9.065	9.60	9.183	9.202	9.273	9.380	9.93	9.485	9.505	9.580	9.695
9.28	8.889	8.907	8.974	9.074	9.61	9.192	9.211	9.282	9.390	9.94	9.494	9.514	9.590	9.705
9.29	8.899	8.916	8.983	9.084	9.62	9.201	9.220	9.291	9.399	9.95	9.503	9.523	9.599	9.714
9.30	8.908	8.926	8.992	9.093	9.63	9.210	9.229	9.301	9.409	9.96	9.512	9.532	9.608	9.724
9.31	8.917	8.935	9.002	9.103	9.64	9.220	9.239	9.310	9.418	9.97	9.521	9.541	9.618	9.733
9.32	8.926	8.944	9.011	9.112	9.65	9.229	9.248	9.319	9.428	9.98	9.530	9.551	9.627	9.743
9.33	8.935	8.953	9.020	9.122	9.66	9.238	9.257	9.329	9.437	9.99	9.539	9.560	9.636	9.752
10.00%	9.549	9.569	9.645	9.762										
10.01	9.558	9.578	9.655	9.771	10.34	9.858	9.880	9.962	10.086	10.67	10.158	10.181	10.268	10.400
10.02	9.567	9.587	9.664	9.781	10.35	9.867	9.889	9.971	10.095	10.68	10.167	10.190	10.277	10.409
10.03	9.576	9.596	9.673	9.790	10.36	9.876	9.898	9.980	10.105	10.69	10.176	10.199	10.286	10.419
10.04	9.585	9.606	9.683	9.800	10.37	9.886	9.907	9.990	10.114	10.70	10.185	10.209	10.296	10.428
10.05	9.594	9.615	9.692	9.809	10.38	9.895	9.917	9.999	10.124	10.71	10.194	10.218	10.305	10.438
10.06	9.603	9.624	9.701	9.819	10.39	9.904	9.926	10.008	10.133	10.72	10.203	10.227	10.314	10.447
10.07	9.612	9.633	9.711	9.829	10.40	9.913	9.935	10.017	10.143	10.73	10.212	10.236	10.323	10.457
10.08	9.621	9.642	9.720	9.838	10.41	9.922	9.944	10.027	10.152	10.74	10.222	10.245	10.333	10.466
10.09	9.631	9.651	9.729	9.848	10.42	9.931	9.953	10.036	10.162	10.75	10.231	10.254	10.342	10.476
10.10	9.640	9.661	9.739	9.857	10.43	9.940	9.962	10.045	10.171	10.76	10.240	10.263	10.351	10.485
10.11	9.649	9.670	9.748	9.867	10.44	9.949	9.971	10.054	10.181	10.77	10.249	10.272	10.360	10.495
10.12	9.658	9.679	9.757	9.876	10.45	9.958	9.981	10.064	10.190	10.78	10.258	10.281	10.370	10.504
10.13	9.667	9.688	9.766	9.886	10.46	9.967	9.990	10.073	10.200	10.79	10.267	10.291	10.379	10.514
10.14	9.676	9.697	9.776	9.895	10.47	9.976	9.999	10.082	10.209	10.80	10.276	10.300	10.388	10.523
10.15	9.685	9.706	9.785	9.905	10.48	9.986	10.008	10.092	10.219	10.81	10.285	10.309	10.398	10.533
10.16	9.694	9.715	9.794	9.914	10.49	9.995	10.017	10.101	10.228	10.82	10.294	10.318	10.407	10.542
10.17	9.704	9.725	9.804	9.924	10.50	10.004	10.026	10.110	10.238	10.83	10.303	10.327	10.416	10.552
10.18	9.713	9.734	9.813	9.933	10.51	10.013	10.035	10.119	10.247	10.84	10.312	10.336	10.425	10.561
10.19	9.722	9.743	9.822	9.943	10.52	10.022	10.044	10.129	10.257	10.85	10.321	10.345	10.435	10.571
10.20	9.731	9.752	9.832	9.952	10.53	10.031	10.054	10.138	10.266	10.86	10.330	10.354	10.444	10.580
10.21	9.740	9.761	9.841	9.962	10.54	10.040	10.063	10.147	10.276	10.87	10.339	10.363	10.453	10.590
10.22	9.749	9.770	9.850	9.971	10.55	10.049	10.072	10.157	10.286	10.88	10.348	10.372	10.462	10.599
10.23	9.758	9.780	9.859	9.981	10.56	10.058	10.081	10.166	10.295	10.89	10.357	10.382	10.472	10.609
10.24	9.767	9.789	9.869	9.990	10.57	10.067	10.090	10.175	10.305	10.90	10.366	10.391	10.481	10.618
10.25	9.776	9.798	9.878	10.000	10.58	10.076	10.099	10.184	10.314	10.91	10.376	10.400	10.490	10.628
10.26	9.785	9.807	9.887	10.010	10.59	10.085	10.108	10.194	10.324	10.92	10.385	10.409	10.499	10.637
10.27	9.795	9.816	9.897	10.019	10.60	10.095	10.117	10.203	10.333	10.93	10.394	10.418	10.509	10.647
10.28	9.804	9.825	9.906	10.029	10.61	10.104	10.127	10.212	10.343	10.94	10.403	10.427	10.518	10.656
10.29	9.813	9.834	9.915	10.038	10.62	10.113	10.136	10.221	10.352	10.95	10.412	10.436	10.527	10.666
10.30	9.822	9.844	9.925	10.048	10.63	10.122	10.145	10.231	10.362	10.96	10.421	10.445	10.536	10.675
10.31	9.831	9.853	9.934	10.057	10.64	10.131	10.154	10.240	10.371	10.97	10.430	10.454	10.546	10.685
10.32	9.840	9.862	9.943	10.067	10.65	10.140	10.163	10.249	10.381	10.98	10.439	10.463	10.555	10.694
10.33	9.849	9.871	9.952	10.076	10.66	10.149	10.172	10.259	10.390	10.99	10.448	10.472	10.564	10.704

Entry is nominal annual percentage rate from which this effective rate is derived.

Effective Annual Rate Converted to Nominal Rate

Effective Annual Rate	Bi-weekly	Monthly	Quarterly	Semi-annual	Effective Annual Rate	Bi-weekly	Monthly	Quarterly	Semi-annual	Effective Annual Rate	Bi-weekly	Monthly	Quarterly	Semi-annual
11.00%	10.457	10.482	10.573	10.713										
11.01	10.466	10.491	10.583	10.723	11.34	10.764	10.790	10.887	11.036	11.67	11.061	11.089	11.192	11.348
11.02	10.475	10.500	10.592	10.732	11.35	10.773	10.799	10.897	11.045	11.68	11.070	11.098	11.201	11.358
11.03	10.484	10.509	10.601	10.742	11.36	10.782	10.808	10.906	11.054	11.69	11.079	11.107	11.210	11.367
11.04	10.493	10.518	10.610	10.751	11.37	10.791	10.817	10.915	11.064	11.70	11.088	11.116	11.219	11.376
11.05	10.502	10.527	10.620	10.761	11.38	10.800	10.826	10.924	11.073	11.71	11.097	11.125	11.228	11.386
11.06	10.511	10.536	10.629	10.770	11.39	10.809	10.835	10.933	11.083	11.72	11.106	11.134	11.238	11.395
11.07	10.520	10.545	10.638	10.780	11.40	10.818	10.844	10.943	11.092	11.73	11.115	11.143	11.247	11.405
11.08	10.529	10.554	10.647	10.789	11.41	10.827	10.853	10.952	11.102	11.74	11.124	11.152	11.256	11.414
11.09	10.538	10.563	10.657	10.798	11.42	10.836	10.863	10.961	11.111	11.75	11.133	11.161	11.265	11.424
11.10	10.547	10.572	10.666	10.808	11.43	10.845	10.872	10.970	11.121	11.76	11.142	11.170	11.274	11.433
11.11	10.556	10.581	10.675	10.817	11.44	10.854	10.881	10.980	11.130	11.77	11.151	11.179	11.283	11.443
11.12	10.565	10.591	10.684	10.827	11.45	10.863	10.890	10.989	11.140	11.78	11.160	11.188	11.293	11.452
11.13	10.574	10.600	10.694	10.836	11.46	10.872	10.899	10.998	11.149	11.79	11.169	11.197	11.302	11.462
11.14	10.584	10.609	10.703	10.846	11.47	10.881	10.908	11.007	11.159	11.80	11.178	11.206	11.311	11.471
11.15	10.593	10.618	10.712	10.855	11.48	10.890	10.917	11.016	11.168	11.81	11.187	11.215	11.320	11.480
11.16	10.602	10.627	10.721	10.865	11.49	10.899	10.926	11.026	11.178	11.82	11.196	11.224	11.330	11.490
11.17	10.611	10.636	10.730	10.874	11.50	10.908	10.935	11.035	11.187	11.83	11.205	11.233	11.339	11.499
11.18	10.620	10.645	10.740	10.884	11.51	10.917	10.944	11.044	11.197	11.84	11.214	11.242	11.348	11.509
11.19	10.629	10.654	10.749	10.893	11.52	10.926	10.953	11.053	11.206	11.85	11.223	11.251	11.357	11.518
11.20	10.638	10.663	10.758	10.903	11.53	10.935	10.962	11.063	11.216	11.86	11.232	11.260	11.366	11.528
11.21	10.647	10.672	10.767	10.912	11.54	10.944	10.971	11.072	11.225	11.87	11.241	11.269	11.375	11.537
11.22	10.656	10.681	10.777	10.922	11.55	10.953	10.980	11.081	11.234	11.88	11.250	11.278	11.385	11.547
11.23	10.665	10.690	10.786	10.931	11.56	10.962	10.989	11.090	11.244	11.89	11.259	11.287	11.394	11.556
11.24	10.674	10.699	10.795	10.941	11.57	10.971	10.998	11.099	11.253	11.90	11.268	11.296	11.403	11.566
11.25	10.683	10.708	10.804	10.950	11.58	10.980	11.007	11.109	11.263	11.91	11.277	11.305	11.412	11.575
11.26	10.692	10.718	10.814	10.960	11.59	10.989	11.016	11.118	11.272	11.92	11.286	11.314	11.421	11.584
11.27	10.701	10.727	10.823	10.969	11.60	10.998	11.025	11.127	11.282	11.93	11.295	11.323	11.431	11.594
11.28	10.710	10.736	10.832	10.979	11.61	11.007	11.034	11.136	11.291	11.94	11.304	11.332	11.440	11.603
11.29	10.719	10.745	10.841	10.988	11.62	11.016	11.044	11.145	11.301	11.95	11.313	11.341	11.449	11.613
11.30	10.728	10.754	10.850	10.998	11.63	11.025	11.053	11.155	11.310	11.96	11.322	11.350	11.458	11.622
11.31	10.737	10.763	10.860	11.007	11.64	11.034	11.062	11.164	11.320	11.97	11.331	11.360	11.467	11.632
11.32	10.746	10.772	10.869	11.017	11.65	11.043	11.071	11.173	11.329	11.98	11.340	11.369	11.477	11.641
11.33	10.755	10.781	10.878	11.026	11.66	11.052	11.080	11.182	11.339	11.99	11.349	11.378	11.486	11.651
12.00%	11.358	11.387	11.495	11.660										
12.01	11.367	11.396	11.504	11.670	12.34	11.662	11.693	11.807	11.981	12.67	11.957	11.989	12.109	12.292
12.02	11.376	11.405	11.513	11.679	12.35	11.671	11.702	11.816	11.991	12.68	11.966	11.998	12.118	12.302
12.03	11.385	11.414	11.522	11.688	12.36	11.680	11.711	11.825	12.000	12.69	11.975	12.007	12.127	12.311
12.04	11.393	11.423	11.532	11.698	12.37	11.689	11.720	11.834	12.009	12.70	11.983	12.016	12.136	12.321
12.05	11.402	11.432	11.541	11.707	12.38	11.698	11.729	11.844	12.019	12.71	11.992	12.025	12.146	12.330
12.06	11.411	11.441	11.550	11.717	12.39	11.707	11.738	11.853	12.028	12.72	12.001	12.034	12.155	12.339
12.07	11.420	11.450	11.559	11.726	12.40	11.716	11.746	11.862	12.038	12.73	12.010	12.043	12.164	12.349
12.08	11.429	11.459	11.568	11.736	12.41	11.725	11.755	11.871	12.047	12.74	12.019	12.052	12.173	12.358
12.09	11.438	11.468	11.578	11.745	12.42	11.734	11.764	11.880	12.057	12.75	12.028	12.060	12.182	12.368
12.10	11.447	11.477	11.587	11.755	12.43	11.742	11.773	11.889	12.066	12.76	12.037	12.069	12.191	12.377
12.11	11.456	11.486	11.596	11.764	12.44	11.751	11.782	11.898	12.075	12.77	12.046	12.078	12.200	12.386
12.12	11.465	11.495	11.605	11.773	12.45	11.760	11.791	11.908	12.085	12.78	12.055	12.087	12.210	12.396
12.13	11.474	11.504	11.614	11.783	12.46	11.769	11.800	11.917	12.094	12.79	12.064	12.096	12.219	12.405
12.14	11.483	11.513	11.623	11.792	12.47	11.778	11.809	11.926	12.104	12.80	12.073	12.105	12.228	12.415
12.15	11.492	11.522	11.633	11.802	12.48	11.787	11.818	11.935	12.113	12.81	12.081	12.114	12.237	12.424
12.16	11.501	11.531	11.642	11.811	12.49	11.796	11.827	11.944	12.123	12.82	12.090	12.123	12.246	12.434
12.17	11.510	11.540	11.651	11.821	12.50	11.805	11.836	11.953	12.132	12.83	12.099	12.132	12.255	12.443
12.18	11.519	11.549	11.660	11.830	12.51	11.814	11.845	11.963	12.141	12.84	12.108	12.141	12.264	12.452
12.19	11.528	11.558	11.669	11.840	12.52	11.823	11.854	11.972	12.151	12.85	12.117	12.150	12.273	12.462
12.20	11.537	11.567	11.679	11.849	12.53	11.832	11.863	11.981	12.160	12.86	12.126	12.159	12.283	12.471
12.21	11.546	11.576	11.688	11.858	12.54	11.841	11.872	11.990	12.170	12.87	12.135	12.168	12.292	12.481
12.22	11.555	11.585	11.697	11.868	12.55	11.850	11.881	11.999	12.179	12.88	12.144	12.177	12.301	12.490
12.23	11.564	11.594	11.706	11.877	12.56	11.859	11.890	12.008	12.189	12.89	12.153	12.186	12.310	12.499
12.24	11.573	11.603	11.715	11.887	12.57	11.868	11.899	12.017	12.198	12.90	12.162	12.195	12.319	12.509
12.25	11.582	11.612	11.724	11.896	12.58	11.876	11.908	12.027	12.207	12.91	12.170	12.204	12.328	12.518
12.26	11.591	11.621	11.734	11.906	12.59	11.885	11.917	12.036	12.217	12.92	12.179	12.213	12.337	12.528
12.27	11.599	11.630	11.743	11.915	12.60	11.894	11.926	12.045	12.226	12.93	12.188	12.222	12.347	12.537
12.28	11.608	11.639	11.752	11.925	12.61	11.903	11.935	12.054	12.236	12.94	12.197	12.231	12.356	12.546
12.29	11.617	11.648	11.761	11.934	12.62	11.912	11.944	12.063	12.245	12.95	12.206	12.240	12.365	12.556
12.30	11.626	11.657	11.770	11.943	12.63	11.921	11.953	12.072	12.255	12.96	12.215	12.248	12.374	12.565
12.31	11.635	11.666	11.779	11.953	12.64	11.930	11.962	12.082	12.264	12.97	12.224	12.257	12.383	12.575
12.32	11.644	11.675	11.789	11.962	12.65	11.939	11.971	12.091	12.273	12.98	12.233	12.266	12.392	12.584
12.33	11.653	11.684	11.798	11.972	12.66	11.948	11.980	12.100	12.283	12.99	12.242	12.275	12.401	12.594

Entry is nominal annual percentage rate from which this effective rate is derived.

The Interest Rate Yield Curve

1 Year Forward Rate

One Year	If the Two Year Rate is													
	4.500%	4.625%	4.750%	4.875%	5.000%	5.125%	5.250%	5.375%	5.500%	5.625%	5.750%	5.875%	6.000%	6.125%
4.500%	4.500	4.750	5.001	5.251	5.502	5.754	6.005	6.257	6.510	6.762	7.015	7.268	7.522	7.775
4.625%	4.375	4.625	4.875	5.126	5.376	5.627	5.879	6.130	6.382	6.635	6.887	7.140	7.393	7.646
4.750%	4.251	4.500	4.750	5.000	5.251	5.501	5.752	6.004	6.255	6.507	6.760	7.012	7.265	7.518
4.875%	4.126	4.376	4.625	4.875	5.125	5.376	5.626	5.877	6.129	6.380	6.632	6.885	7.137	7.390
5.000%	4.002	4.251	4.501	4.750	5.000	5.250	5.501	5.751	6.002	6.254	6.505	6.757	7.010	7.262
5.125%	3.879	4.127	4.376	4.626	4.875	5.125	5.375	5.626	5.876	6.127	6.379	6.630	6.882	7.135
5.250%	3.755	4.004	4.252	4.501	4.751	5.000	5.250	5.500	5.751	6.001	6.252	6.504	6.755	7.007
5.375%	3.632	3.880	4.129	4.377	4.626	4.876	5.125	5.375	5.625	5.876	6.126	6.377	6.629	6.880
5.500%	3.509	3.757	4.005	4.254	4.502	4.751	5.001	5.250	5.500	5.750	6.001	6.251	6.502	6.754
5.625%	3.387	3.634	3.882	4.130	4.379	4.627	4.876	5.126	5.375	5.625	5.875	6.126	6.376	6.627
5.750%	3.265	3.512	3.759	4.007	4.255	4.504	4.752	5.001	5.251	5.500	5.750	6.000	6.251	6.501
5.875%	3.143	3.390	3.637	3.884	4.132	4.380	4.629	4.877	5.126	5.376	5.625	5.875	6.125	6.376

1 Year Forward Rate

One Year	If the Two Year Rate Is													
	5.500%	5.625%	5.750%	5.875%	6.000%	6.125%	6.250%	6.375%	6.500%	6.625%	6.750%	6.875%	7.000%	7.125%
5.500%	5.500	5.750	6.001	6.251	6.502	6.754	7.005	7.257	7.509	7.762	8.015	8.268	8.521	8.775
5.625%	5.375	5.625	5.875	6.126	6.376	6.627	6.879	7.130	7.382	7.634	7.887	8.140	8.393	8.646
5.750%	5.251	5.500	5.750	6.000	6.251	6.501	6.752	7.004	7.255	7.507	7.759	8.012	8.265	8.518
5.875%	5.126	5.376	5.625	5.875	6.125	6.376	6.626	6.877	7.129	7.380	7.632	7.884	8.137	8.390
6.000%	5.002	5.251	5.501	5.750	6.000	6.250	6.501	6.751	7.002	7.254	7.505	7.757	8.009	8.262
6.125%	4.879	5.127	5.376	5.626	5.875	6.125	6.375	6.626	6.876	7.127	7.379	7.630	7.882	8.134
6.250%	4.755	5.004	5.252	5.501	5.751	6.000	6.250	6.500	6.751	7.001	7.252	7.504	7.755	8.007
6.375%	4.632	4.880	5.129	5.377	5.626	5.876	6.125	6.375	6.625	6.876	7.126	7.377	7.629	7.880
6.500%	4.509	4.757	5.005	5.254	5.502	5.751	6.001	6.250	6.500	6.750	7.001	7.251	7.502	7.754
6.625%	4.387	4.634	4.882	5.130	5.379	5.627	5.876	6.126	6.375	6.625	6.875	7.126	7.376	7.627
6.750%	4.265	4.512	4.759	5.007	5.255	5.504	5.752	6.001	6.251	6.500	6.750	7.000	7.251	7.501
6.875%	4.143	4.390	4.637	4.884	5.132	5.380	5.629	5.877	6.126	6.376	6.625	6.875	7.125	7.376

1 Year Forward Rate

One Year	If the Two Year Rate is													
	6.500%	6.625%	6.750%	6.875%	7.000%	7.125%	7.250%	7.375%	7.500%	7.625%	7.750%	7.875%	8.000%	8.125%
6.500%	6.500	6.750	7.001	7.251	7.502	7.754	8.005	8.257	8.509	8.762	9.015	9.268	9.521	9.775
6.625%	6.375	6.625	6.875	7.126	7.376	7.627	7.879	8.130	8.382	8.634	8.887	9.140	9.393	9.646
6.750%	6.251	6.500	6.750	7.000	7.251	7.501	7.752	8.004	8.255	8.507	8.759	9.012	9.265	9.518
6.875%	6.126	6.376	6.625	6.875	7.125	7.376	7.626	7.877	8.129	8.380	8.632	8.884	9.137	9.390
7.000%	6.002	6.251	6.501	6.750	7.000	7.250	7.501	7.751	8.002	8.254	8.505	8.757	9.009	9.262
7.125%	5.879	6.127	6.376	6.626	6.875	7.125	7.375	7.626	7.876	8.127	8.379	8.630	8.882	9.134
7.250%	5.755	6.004	6.252	6.501	6.751	7.000	7.250	7.500	7.751	8.001	8.252	8.504	8.755	9.007
7.375%	5.632	5.880	6.129	6.377	6.626	6.876	7.125	7.375	7.625	7.876	8.126	8.377	8.629	8.880
7.500%	5.509	5.757	6.005	6.254	6.502	6.751	7.001	7.250	7.500	7.750	8.001	8.251	8.502	8.754
7.625%	5.387	5.634	5.882	6.130	6.379	6.627	6.876	7.126	7.375	7.625	7.875	8.126	8.376	8.627
7.750%	5.265	5.512	5.759	6.007	6.255	6.504	6.752	7.001	7.251	7.500	7.750	8.000	8.251	8.501
7.875%	5.143	5.389	5.637	5.884	6.132	6.380	6.629	6.877	7.126	7.376	7.625	7.875	8.125	8.376

1 Year Forward Rate

One Year	If the Two Year Rate is													
	7.500%	7.625%	7.750%	7.875%	8.000%	8.125%	8.250%	8.375%	8.500%	8.625%	8.750%	8.875%	9.000%	9.125%
7.500%	7.500	7.750	8.001	8.251	8.502	8.754	9.005	9.257	9.509	9.762	10.015	10.268	10.521	10.775
7.625%	7.375	7.625	7.875	8.126	8.376	8.627	8.879	9.130	9.382	9.634	9.887	10.140	10.393	10.646
7.750%	7.251	7.500	7.750	8.000	8.251	8.501	8.752	9.004	9.255	9.507	9.759	10.012	10.265	10.518
7.875%	7.126	7.376	7.625	7.875	8.125	8.376	8.626	8.877	9.129	9.380	9.632	9.884	10.137	10.389
8.000%	7.002	7.251	7.501	7.750	8.000	8.250	8.501	8.751	9.002	9.254	9.505	9.757	10.009	10.262
8.125%	6.879	7.127	7.376	7.626	7.875	8.125	8.375	8.626	8.876	9.127	9.379	9.630	9.882	10.134
8.250%	6.755	7.004	7.252	7.501	7.751	8.000	8.250	8.500	8.751	9.001	9.252	9.504	9.755	10.007
8.375%	6.632	6.880	7.129	7.377	7.626	7.876	8.125	8.375	8.625	8.876	9.126	9.377	9.629	9.880
8.500%	6.509	6.757	7.005	7.254	7.502	7.751	8.001	8.250	8.500	8.750	9.001	9.251	9.502	9.754
8.625%	6.387	6.634	6.882	7.130	7.379	7.627	7.876	8.126	8.375	8.625	8.875	9.126	9.376	9.627
8.750%	6.264	6.512	6.759	7.007	7.255	7.504	7.752	8.001	8.251	8.500	8.750	9.000	9.251	9.501
8.875%	6.142	6.389	6.637	6.884	7.132	7.380	7.629	7.877	8.126	8.376	8.625	8.875	9.125	9.376

Entry is the interest rate forecast for the forward rate year

The Interest Rate Yield Curve

2 Year Forward Rate

Two Year	\					If the Three Year Rate Is								
	4.500%	4.625%	4.750%	4.875%	5.000%	5.125%	5.250%	5.375%	5.500%	5.625%	5.750%	5.875%	6.000%	6.125%
4.500%	4.500	4.875	5.252	5.629	6.007	6.386	6.766	7.147	7.529	7.911	8.295	8.680	9.065	9.451
4.625%	4.250	4.625	5.000	5.377	5.754	6.132	6.511	6.891	7.272	7.654	8.036	8.420	8.804	9.190
4.750%	4.002	4.375	4.750	5.125	5.502	5.879	6.257	6.636	7.016	7.397	7.779	8.161	8.545	8.929
4.875%	3.754	4.127	4.500	4.875	5.250	5.627	6.004	6.382	6.761	7.141	7.522	7.904	8.286	8.670
5.000%	3.507	3.879	4.252	4.625	5.000	5.375	5.752	6.129	6.507	6.886	7.266	7.647	8.029	8.411
5.125%	3.261	3.632	4.004	4.377	4.750	5.125	5.500	5.877	6.254	6.632	7.011	7.391	7.772	8.154
5.250%	3.016	3.386	3.757	4.129	4.502	4.875	5.250	5.625	6.002	6.379	6.757	7.136	7.516	7.897
5.375%	2.772	3.141	3.511	3.882	4.254	4.627	5.000	5.375	5.750	6.127	6.504	6.882	7.261	7.641
5.500%	2.528	2.897	3.266	3.636	4.007	4.379	4.752	5.125	5.500	5.875	6.252	6.629	7.007	7.386
5.625%	2.286	2.653	3.022	3.391	3.761	4.132	4.504	4.877	5.250	5.625	6.000	6.377	6.754	7.132
5.750%	2.044	2.411	2.778	3.147	3.516	3.886	4.257	4.629	5.002	5.375	5.750	6.125	6.502	6.879
5.875%	1.803	2.169	2.536	2.903	3.272	3.641	4.011	4.382	4.754	5.127	5.500	5.875	6.250	6.627

2 Year Forward Rate

Two Year						If the Three Year Rate Is								
	5.500%	5.625%	5.750%	5.875%	6.000%	6.125%	6.250%	6.375%	6.500%	6.625%	6.750%	6.875%	7.000%	7.125%
5.500%	5.500	5.875	6.252	6.629	7.007	7.386	7.766	8.147	8.529	8.911	9.295	9.679	10.064	10.450
5.625%	5.250	5.625	6.000	6.377	6.754	7.132	7.511	7.891	8.272	8.653	9.036	9.420	9.804	10.189
5.750%	5.002	5.375	5.750	6.125	6.502	6.879	7.257	7.636	8.016	8.397	8.778	9.161	9.545	9.929
5.875%	4.754	5.127	5.500	5.875	6.252	6.627	7.004	7.382	7.761	8.141	8.522	8.903	9.286	9.669
6.000%	4.507	4.879	5.252	5.625	6.000	6.375	6.752	7.129	7.507	7.886	8.266	8.647	9.028	9.411
6.125%	4.261	4.632	5.004	5.377	5.750	6.125	6.500	6.877	7.254	7.632	8.011	8.391	8.772	9.153
6.250%	4.016	4.386	4.757	5.129	5.502	5.875	6.250	6.625	7.002	7.379	7.757	8.136	8.516	8.897
6.375%	3.771	4.141	4.511	4.882	5.254	5.627	6.000	6.375	6.750	7.127	7.504	7.882	8.261	8.641
6.500%	3.528	3.896	4.266	4.636	5.007	5.379	5.752	6.125	6.500	6.875	7.252	7.629	8.007	8.386
6.625%	3.285	3.653	4.021	4.391	4.761	5.132	5.504	5.877	6.250	6.625	7.000	7.377	7.754	8.132
6.750%	3.044	3.410	3.778	4.146	4.516	4.886	5.257	5.629	6.002	6.375	6.750	7.125	7.502	7.879
6.875%	2.803	3.169	3.535	3.903	4.271	4.641	5.011	5.382	5.754	6.127	6.500	6.875	7.250	7.627

2 Year Forward Rate

Two Year						If the Three Year Rate Is								
	6.500%	6.625%	6.750%	6.875%	7.000%	7.125%	7.250%	7.375%	7.500%	7.625%	7.750%	7.875%	8.000%	8.125%
6.500%	6.500	6.875	7.252	7.629	8.007	8.386	8.766	9.147	9.528	9.911	10.294	10.678	11.064	11.450
6.625%	6.250	6.625	7.000	7.377	7.754	8.132	8.511	8.891	9.272	9.653	10.036	10.419	10.803	11.189
6.750%	6.002	6.375	6.750	7.125	7.502	7.879	8.257	8.636	9.016	9.397	9.778	10.161	10.544	10.928
6.875%	5.754	6.127	6.500	6.875	7.250	7.627	8.004	8.382	8.761	9.141	9.522	9.903	10.286	10.669
7.000%	5.507	5.879	6.252	6.625	7.000	7.375	7.752	8.129	8.507	8.886	9.266	9.647	10.028	10.411
7.125%	5.261	5.632	6.004	6.377	6.750	7.125	7.500	7.877	8.254	8.632	9.011	9.391	9.772	10.153
7.250%	5.016	5.386	5.757	6.129	6.502	6.875	7.250	7.625	8.002	8.379	8.757	9.136	9.516	9.896
7.375%	4.771	5.141	5.511	5.882	6.254	6.627	7.000	7.375	7.750	8.127	8.504	8.882	9.261	9.641
7.500%	4.528	4.896	5.266	5.636	6.007	6.379	6.752	7.125	7.500	7.875	8.252	8.629	9.007	9.386
7.625%	4.285	4.653	5.021	5.391	5.761	6.132	6.504	6.877	7.250	7.625	8.000	8.377	8.754	9.132
7.750%	4.043	4.410	4.778	5.146	5.516	5.886	6.257	6.629	7.002	7.375	7.750	8.125	8.502	8.879
7.875%	3.802	4.168	4.535	4.903	5.271	5.641	6.011	6.382	6.754	7.127	7.500	7.875	8.250	8.627

2 Year Forward Rate

Two Year						If the Three Year Rate Is								
	7.500%	7.625%	7.750%	7.875%	8.000%	8.125%	8.250%	8.375%	8.500%	8.625%	8.750%	8.875%	9.000%	9.125%
7.500%	7.500	7.875	8.252	8.629	9.007	9.386	9.766	10.146	10.528	10.910	11.294	11.678	12.063	12.449
7.625%	7.250	7.625	8.000	8.377	8.754	9.132	9.511	9.891	10.271	10.653	11.035	11.419	11.803	12.188
7.750%	7.002	7.375	7.750	8.125	8.502	8.879	9.257	9.636	10.016	10.396	10.778	11.160	11.544	11.928
7.875%	6.754	7.127	7.500	7.875	8.250	8.627	9.004	9.382	9.761	10.141	10.521	10.903	11.285	11.669
8.000%	6.507	6.879	7.252	7.625	8.000	8.375	8.752	9.129	9.507	9.886	10.266	10.646	11.028	11.410
8.125%	6.261	6.632	7.004	7.377	7.750	8.125	8.500	8.877	9.254	9.632	10.011	10.391	10.771	11.153
8.250%	6.016	6.386	6.757	7.129	7.502	7.875	8.250	8.625	9.002	9.379	9.757	10.136	10.516	10.896
8.375%	5.771	6.141	6.511	6.882	7.254	7.627	8.000	8.375	8.750	9.127	9.504	9.882	10.261	10.641
8.500%	5.528	5.896	6.266	6.636	7.007	7.379	7.752	8.125	8.500	8.875	9.252	9.629	10.007	10.386
8.625%	5.285	5.653	6.021	6.391	6.761	7.132	7.504	7.877	8.250	8.625	9.000	9.377	9.754	10.132
8.750%	5.043	5.410	5.778	6.146	6.515	6.886	7.257	7.629	8.002	8.375	8.750	9.125	9.502	9.879
8.875%	4.802	5.168	5.535	5.902	6.271	6.640	7.011	7.382	7.754	8.127	8.500	8.875	9.250	9.627

Entry is the interest rate forecast for the forward rate year

The Interest Rate Yield Curve

3 Year Forward Rate

Three Year	4.500%	4.625%	4.750%	4.875%	5.000%	5.125%	If the Four Year Rate Is 5.250%	5.375%	5.500%	5.625%	5.750%	5.875%	6.000%	6.125%
4.500%	4.500	5.001	5.504	6.008	6.514	7.023	7.532	8.044	8.558	9.073	9.590	10.110	10.630	11.153
4.625%	4.126	4.625	5.126	5.629	6.133	6.639	7.148	7.657	8.169	8.683	9.198	9.715	10.234	10.755
4.750%	3.754	4.251	4.750	5.251	5.754	6.258	6.764	7.272	7.782	8.294	8.808	9.323	9.840	10.359
4.875%	3.383	3.879	4.376	4.875	5.376	5.879	6.383	6.889	7.397	7.907	8.419	8.933	9.448	9.965
5.000%	3.014	3.508	4.004	4.501	5.000	5.501	6.004	6.508	7.014	7.522	8.032	8.544	9.058	9.573
5.125%	2.647	3.139	3.633	4.129	4.626	5.125	5.626	6.129	6.633	7.139	7.647	8.157	8.669	9.182
5.250%	2.282	2.772	3.264	3.758	4.254	4.751	5.250	5.751	6.254	6.758	7.264	7.772	8.282	8.794
5.375%	1.918	2.407	2.897	3.389	3.883	4.379	4.876	5.375	5.876	6.379	6.883	7.389	7.897	8.407
5.500%	1.557	2.043	2.532	3.022	3.514	4.008	4.504	5.001	5.500	6.001	6.504	7.008	7.514	8.022
5.625%	1.196	1.681	2.168	2.657	3.147	3.639	4.133	4.629	5.126	5.625	6.126	6.629	7.133	7.639
5.750%	0.838	1.321	1.806	2.293	2.782	3.272	3.764	4.258	4.754	5.251	5.750	6.251	6.754	7.258
5.875%	0.481	0.963	1.446	1.931	2.418	2.907	3.397	3.889	4.383	4.879	5.376	5.875	6.376	6.879

3 Year Forward Rate

Three Year	5.500%	5.625%	5.750%	5.875%	6.000%	6.125%	If the Four Year Rate Is 6.250%	6.375%	6.500%	6.625%	6.750%	6.875%	7.000%	7.125%
5.500%	5.500	6.001	6.504	7.008	7.514	8.022	8.532	9.044	9.557	10.073	10.590	11.108	11.629	12.152
5.625%	5.126	5.625	6.126	6.629	7.133	7.639	8.147	8.657	9.169	9.682	10.197	10.714	11.233	11.754
5.750%	4.754	5.251	5.750	6.251	6.754	7.258	7.764	8.272	8.782	9.294	9.807	10.322	10.839	11.358
5.875%	4.383	4.879	5.376	5.875	6.376	6.879	7.383	7.889	8.397	8.907	9.419	9.932	10.447	10.964
6.000%	4.014	4.508	5.004	5.501	6.000	6.501	7.004	7.508	8.014	8.522	9.032	9.544	10.057	10.572
6.125%	3.647	4.139	4.633	5.129	5.626	6.125	6.626	7.129	7.633	8.139	8.647	9.157	9.669	10.182
6.250%	3.282	3.772	4.264	4.758	5.254	5.751	6.250	6.751	7.254	7.758	8.264	8.772	9.282	9.793
6.375%	2.918	3.407	3.897	4.389	4.883	5.378	5.876	6.375	6.876	7.379	7.883	8.389	8.897	9.407
6.500%	2.556	3.043	3.532	4.022	4.514	5.008	5.503	6.001	6.500	7.001	7.503	8.008	8.514	9.022
6.625%	2.196	2.681	3.168	3.657	4.147	4.639	5.133	5.629	6.126	6.625	7.126	7.629	8.133	8.639
6.750%	1.837	2.321	2.806	3.293	3.781	4.272	4.764	5.258	5.754	6.251	6.750	7.251	7.754	8.258
6.875%	1.480	1.962	2.446	2.931	3.418	3.906	4.397	4.889	5.383	5.878	6.376	6.875	7.376	7.878

3 Year Forward Rate

Three Year	6.500%	6.625%	6.750%	6.875%	7.000%	7.125%	If the Four Year Rate Is 7.250%	7.375%	7.500%	7.625%	7.750%	7.875%	8.000%	8.125%
6.500%	6.500	7.001	7.503	8.008	8.514	9.022	9.532	10.043	10.557	11.072	11.589	12.107	12.628	13.150
6.625%	6.126	6.625	7.126	7.629	8.133	8.639	9.147	9.657	10.168	10.682	11.197	11.714	12.232	12.753
6.750%	5.754	6.251	6.750	7.251	7.754	8.258	8.764	9.272	9.782	10.293	10.807	11.322	11.839	12.357
6.875%	5.383	5.878	6.376	6.875	7.376	7.878	8.383	8.889	9.397	9.907	10.418	10.931	11.447	11.963
7.000%	5.014	5.508	6.003	6.501	7.000	7.501	8.003	8.508	9.014	9.522	10.032	10.543	11.056	11.571
7.125%	4.647	5.139	5.633	6.129	6.626	7.125	7.626	8.129	8.633	9.139	9.647	10.157	10.668	11.181
7.250%	4.281	4.772	5.264	5.758	6.254	6.751	7.250	7.751	8.254	8.758	9.264	9.772	10.282	10.793
7.375%	3.918	4.406	4.897	5.389	5.883	6.378	6.876	7.375	7.876	8.378	8.883	9.389	9.897	10.407
7.500%	3.555	4.042	4.531	5.022	5.514	6.008	6.503	7.001	7.500	8.001	8.503	9.008	9.514	10.022
7.625%	3.195	3.680	4.167	4.656	5.147	5.639	6.133	6.628	7.126	7.625	8.126	8.628	9.133	9.639
7.750%	2.836	3.320	3.805	4.292	4.781	5.272	5.764	6.258	6.753	7.251	7.750	8.251	8.754	9.258
7.875%	2.479	2.961	3.445	3.930	4.417	4.906	5.397	5.889	6.383	6.878	7.376	7.875	8.376	8.878

3 Year Forward Rate

Three Year	7.500%	7.625%	7.750%	7.875%	8.000%	8.125%	If the Four Year Rate Is 8.250%	8.375%	8.500%	8.625%	8.750%	8.875%	9.000%	9.125%
7.500%	7.500	8.001	8.503	9.008	9.514	10.022	10.532	11.043	11.556	12.071	12.588	13.106	13.627	14.149
7.625%	7.126	7.625	8.126	8.628	9.133	9.639	10.147	10.657	11.168	11.681	12.196	12.713	13.231	13.752
7.750%	6.753	7.251	7.750	8.251	8.754	9.258	9.764	10.272	10.781	11.293	11.806	12.321	12.838	13.356
7.875%	6.383	6.878	7.376	7.875	8.376	8.878	9.383	9.889	10.397	10.906	11.418	11.931	12.446	12.963
8.000%	6.014	6.508	7.003	7.501	8.000	8.501	9.003	9.508	10.014	10.522	11.031	11.543	12.056	12.571
8.125%	5.647	6.139	6.633	7.128	7.626	8.125	8.626	9.128	9.633	10.139	10.647	11.156	11.668	12.181
8.250%	5.281	5.772	6.264	6.758	7.253	7.751	8.250	8.751	9.254	9.758	10.264	10.772	11.281	11.793
8.375%	4.917	5.406	5.897	6.389	6.883	7.378	7.876	8.375	8.876	9.378	9.883	10.389	10.897	11.406
8.500%	4.555	5.042	5.531	6.022	6.514	7.008	7.503	8.001	8.500	9.001	9.503	10.008	10.514	11.022
8.625%	4.194	4.680	5.167	5.656	6.147	6.639	7.133	7.628	8.126	8.625	9.126	9.628	10.133	10.639
8.750%	3.836	4.319	4.805	5.292	5.781	6.271	6.764	7.258	7.753	8.251	8.750	9.251	9.753	10.258
8.875%	3.478	3.960	4.444	4.930	5.417	5.906	6.396	6.889	7.383	7.878	8.376	8.875	9.376	9.878

Entry is the interest rate forecast for the forward rate year

The Interest Rate Yield Curve

4 Year Forward Rate

Four Year	4.500%	4.625%	4.750%	4.875%	5.000%	5.125%	If the Five Year Rate Is 5.250%	5.375%	5.500%	5.625%	5.750%	5.875%	6.000%	6.125%
4.500%	4.500	5.127	5.756	6.389	7.024	7.663	8.304	8.949	9.597	10.247	10.901	11.558	12.218	12.882
4.625%	4.001	4.625	5.252	5.881	6.513	7.149	7.788	8.429	9.074	9.721	10.372	11.026	11.683	12.343
4.750%	3.506	4.126	4.750	5.376	6.006	6.638	7.274	7.913	8.554	9.199	9.846	10.497	11.151	11.808
4.875%	3.013	3.631	4.251	4.875	5.501	6.131	6.763	7.399	8.037	8.679	9.324	9.971	10.622	11.276
5.000%	2.524	3.138	3.756	4.377	5.000	5.627	6.256	6.888	7.524	8.162	8.804	9.449	10.096	10.747
5.125%	2.037	2.649	3.263	3.881	4.501	5.125	5.752	6.381	7.013	7.649	8.287	8.929	9.573	10.221
5.250%	1.553	2.162	2.774	3.388	4.006	4.626	5.250	5.877	6.506	7.138	7.774	8.412	9.054	9.698
5.375%	1.072	1.678	2.287	2.899	3.513	4.131	4.751	5.375	6.001	6.631	7.263	7.899	8.537	9.179
5.500%	0.594	1.197	1.803	2.412	3.024	3.638	4.256	4.877	5.500	6.127	6.756	7.388	8.024	8.662
5.625%	0.119	0.719	1.322	1.928	2.537	3.149	3.763	4.381	5.001	5.625	6.251	6.881	7.513	8.149
5.750%	-0.354	0.243	0.844	1.447	2.053	2.662	3.274	3.888	4.506	5.126	5.750	6.376	7.006	7.638
5.875%	-0.824	-0.229	0.368	0.969	1.572	2.178	2.787	3.399	4.013	4.631	5.251	5.875	6.501	7.131

4 Year Forward Rate

Four Year	5.500%	5.625%	5.750%	5.875%	6.000%	6.125%	If the Five Year Rate Is 6.250%	6.375%	6.500%	6.625%	6.750%	6.875%	7.000%	7.125%
5.500%	5.500	6.127	6.756	7.388	8.024	8.662	9.304	9.948	10.596	11.246	11.900	12.557	13.216	13.879
5.625%	5.001	5.625	6.251	6.881	7.513	8.149	8.787	9.429	10.073	10.721	11.371	12.025	12.681	13.341
5.750%	4.506	5.126	5.750	6.376	7.006	7.638	8.274	8.912	9.554	10.198	10.845	11.496	12.150	12.806
5.875%	4.013	4.631	5.251	5.875	6.501	7.131	7.763	8.399	9.037	9.678	10.323	10.970	11.621	12.274
6.000%	3.523	4.138	4.756	5.377	6.000	6.626	7.256	7.888	8.524	9.162	9.803	10.448	11.095	11.746
6.125%	3.037	3.648	4.263	4.881	5.501	6.125	6.751	7.381	8.013	8.649	9.287	9.928	10.573	11.220
6.250%	2.553	3.162	3.773	4.388	5.006	5.626	6.250	6.876	7.506	8.138	8.774	9.412	10.053	10.698
6.375%	2.071	2.677	3.287	3.898	4.513	5.131	5.751	6.375	7.001	7.631	8.263	8.899	9.537	10.178
6.500%	1.593	2.196	2.802	3.411	4.023	4.638	5.256	5.876	6.500	7.126	7.756	8.388	9.024	9.662
6.625%	1.117	1.718	2.321	2.927	3.536	4.148	4.763	5.381	6.002	6.625	7.251	7.881	8.513	9.149
6.750%	0.645	1.242	1.843	2.446	3.052	3.661	4.273	4.888	5.506	6.126	6.750	7.376	8.006	8.638
6.875%	0.175	0.769	1.367	1.968	2.571	3.177	3.786	4.398	5.013	5.631	6.251	6.875	7.501	8.131

4 Year Forward Rate

Four Year	6.500%	6.625%	6.750%	6.875%	7.000%	7.125%	If the Five Year Rate Is 7.250%	7.375%	7.500%	7.625%	7.750%	7.875%	8.000%	8.125%
6.500%	6.500	7.126	7.756	8.388	9.024	9.662	10.303	10.947	11.595	12.245	12.898	13.555	14.214	14.877
6.625%	6.002	6.625	7.251	7.881	8.513	9.149	9.787	10.428	11.072	11.720	12.370	13.023	13.680	14.339
6.750%	5.506	6.126	6.750	7.376	8.006	8.638	9.274	9.912	10.553	11.197	11.845	12.495	13.148	13.804
6.875%	5.013	5.631	6.251	6.875	7.501	8.131	8.763	9.398	10.037	10.678	11.322	11.969	12.620	13.273
7.000%	4.523	5.138	5.756	6.376	7.000	7.626	8.256	8.888	9.523	10.162	10.803	11.447	12.094	12.744
7.125%	4.036	4.648	5.263	5.881	6.501	7.125	7.751	8.381	9.013	9.648	10.287	10.928	11.572	12.219
7.250%	3.552	4.161	4.773	5.388	6.006	6.626	7.250	7.876	8.506	9.138	9.773	10.412	11.053	11.697
7.375%	3.071	3.677	4.286	4.898	5.513	6.131	6.751	7.375	8.001	8.631	9.263	9.898	10.537	11.178
7.500%	2.592	3.196	3.802	4.411	5.023	5.638	6.256	6.876	7.500	8.126	8.756	9.388	10.023	10.662
7.625%	2.116	2.717	3.321	3.927	4.536	5.148	5.763	6.381	7.001	7.625	8.251	8.881	9.513	10.148
7.750%	1.643	2.241	2.842	3.445	4.052	4.661	5.273	5.888	6.506	7.126	7.750	8.376	9.006	9.638
7.875%	1.173	1.768	2.366	2.967	3.570	4.177	4.786	5.398	6.013	6.631	7.251	7.875	8.501	9.131

4 Year Forward Rate

Four Year	7.500%	7.625%	7.750%	7.875%	8.000%	8.125%	If the Five Year Rate Is 8.250%	8.375%	8.500%	8.625%	8.750%	8.875%	9.000%	9.125%
7.500%	7.500	8.126	8.756	9.388	10.023	10.662	11.303	11.947	12.594	13.244	13.897	14.553	15.212	15.874
7.625%	7.001	7.625	8.251	8.881	9.513	10.148	10.787	11.428	12.072	12.719	13.369	14.022	14.678	15.337
7.750%	6.506	7.126	7.750	8.376	9.006	9.638	10.273	10.911	11.553	12.197	12.844	13.494	14.147	14.803
7.875%	6.013	6.631	7.251	7.875	8.501	9.131	9.763	10.398	11.036	11.677	12.322	12.969	13.619	14.272
8.000%	5.523	6.138	6.756	7.376	8.000	8.626	9.256	9.888	10.523	11.161	11.802	12.446	13.093	13.743
8.125%	5.036	5.648	6.263	6.881	7.501	8.125	8.751	9.381	10.013	10.648	11.286	11.927	12.571	13.218
8.250%	4.552	5.161	5.773	6.388	7.006	7.626	8.250	8.876	9.506	10.138	10.773	11.411	12.052	12.696
8.375%	4.070	4.677	5.286	5.898	6.513	7.131	7.751	8.375	9.001	9.631	10.263	10.898	11.536	12.177
8.500%	3.591	4.195	4.801	5.411	6.023	6.638	7.256	7.876	8.500	9.126	9.756	10.388	11.023	11.661
8.625%	3.115	3.716	4.320	4.926	5.536	6.148	6.763	7.381	8.001	8.625	9.251	9.881	10.513	11.148
8.750%	2.642	3.240	3.841	4.445	5.051	5.661	6.273	6.888	7.506	8.126	8.750	9.376	10.006	10.638
8.875%	2.171	2.767	3.365	3.966	4.570	5.176	5.786	6.398	7.013	7.631	8.251	8.875	9.501	10.131

Entry is the interest rate forecast for the forward rate year

The Interest Rate Yield Curve

1 Year Forward Rate

One Year	|	|	|	|	If the Two Year Rate Is									
	9.000%	9.125%	9.250%	9.375%	9.500%	9.625%	9.750%	9.875%	10.000%	10.125%	10.250%	10.375%	10.500%	10.625%
9.000%	9.000	9.250	9.501	9.751	10.002	10.254	10.505	10.757	11.009	11.262	11.514	11.767	12.021	12.274
9.125%	8.875	9.125	9.375	9.626	9.876	10.127	10.379	10.630	10.882	11.134	11.387	11.639	11.892	12.146
9.250%	8.751	9.000	9.250	9.500	9.751	10.001	10.252	10.504	10.755	11.007	11.259	11.512	11.764	12.017
9.375%	8.626	8.876	9.125	9.375	9.625	9.876	10.126	10.377	10.629	10.880	11.132	11.384	11.637	11.889
9.500%	8.502	8.751	9.001	9.250	9.500	9.750	10.001	10.251	10.502	10.754	11.005	11.257	11.509	11.762
9.625%	8.379	8.627	8.876	9.126	9.375	9.625	9.875	10.126	10.376	10.627	10.879	11.130	11.382	11.634
9.750%	8.255	8.504	8.752	9.001	9.251	9.500	9.750	10.000	10.251	10.501	10.752	11.004	11.255	11.507
9.875%	8.132	8.380	8.629	8.877	9.126	9.376	9.625	9.875	10.125	10.376	10.626	10.877	11.129	11.380
10.000%	8.009	8.257	8.505	8.754	9.002	9.251	9.501	9.750	10.000	10.250	10.501	10.751	11.002	11.254
10.125%	7.886	8.134	8.382	8.630	8.879	9.127	9.376	9.626	9.875	10.125	10.375	10.626	10.876	11.127
10.250%	7.764	8.011	8.259	8.507	8.755	9.004	9.252	9.501	9.751	10.000	10.250	10.500	10.751	11.001
10.375%	7.642	7.889	8.136	8.384	8.632	8.880	9.129	9.377	9.626	9.876	10.125	10.375	10.625	10.876

1 Year Forward Rate

One Year	|	|	|	|	If the Two Year Rate Is									
	10.000%	10.125%	10.250%	10.375%	10.500%	10.625%	10.750%	10.875%	11.000%	11.125%	11.250%	11.375%	11.500%	11.625%
10.000%	10.000	10.250	10.501	10.751	11.002	11.254	11.505	11.757	12.009	12.262	12.514	12.767	13.020	13.274
10.125%	9.875	10.125	10.375	10.626	10.876	11.127	11.379	11.630	11.882	12.134	12.386	12.639	12.892	13.145
10.250%	9.751	10.000	10.250	10.500	10.751	11.001	11.252	11.504	11.755	12.007	12.259	12.511	12.764	13.017
10.375%	9.626	9.876	10.125	10.375	10.625	10.876	11.126	11.377	11.629	11.880	12.132	12.384	12.636	12.889
10.500%	9.502	9.751	10.001	10.250	10.500	10.750	11.001	11.251	11.502	11.754	12.005	12.257	12.509	12.761
10.625%	9.379	9.627	9.876	10.126	10.375	10.625	10.875	11.126	11.376	11.627	11.879	12.130	12.382	12.634
10.750%	9.255	9.504	9.752	10.001	10.251	10.500	10.750	11.000	11.251	11.501	11.752	12.004	12.255	12.507
10.875%	9.132	9.380	9.629	9.877	10.126	10.376	10.625	10.875	11.125	11.376	11.626	11.877	12.129	12.380
11.000%	9.009	9.257	9.505	9.754	10.002	10.251	10.501	10.750	11.000	11.250	11.501	11.751	12.002	12.254
11.125%	8.886	9.134	9.382	9.630	9.879	10.127	10.376	10.626	10.875	11.125	11.375	11.626	11.876	12.127
11.250%	8.764	9.011	9.259	9.507	9.755	10.004	10.252	10.501	10.751	11.000	11.250	11.500	11.751	12.001
11.375%	8.642	8.889	9.136	9.384	9.632	9.880	10.129	10.377	10.626	10.876	11.125	11.375	11.625	11.876

1 Year Forward Rate

One Year	|	|	|	|	If the Two Year Rate Is									
	11.000%	11.125%	11.250%	11.375%	11.500%	11.625%	11.750%	11.875%	12.000%	12.125%	12.250%	12.375%	12.500%	12.625%
11.000%	11.000	11.250	11.501	11.751	12.002	12.254	12.505	12.757	13.009	13.261	13.514	13.767	14.020	14.274
11.125%	10.875	11.125	11.375	11.626	11.876	12.127	12.378	12.630	12.882	13.134	13.386	13.639	13.892	14.145
11.250%	10.751	11.000	11.250	11.500	11.751	12.001	12.252	12.504	12.755	13.007	13.259	13.511	13.764	14.017
11.375%	10.626	10.876	11.125	11.375	11.625	11.876	12.126	12.377	12.629	12.880	13.132	13.384	13.636	13.889
11.500%	10.502	10.751	11.001	11.250	11.500	11.750	12.001	12.251	12.502	12.754	13.005	13.257	13.509	13.761
11.625%	10.378	10.627	10.876	11.126	11.375	11.625	11.875	12.126	12.376	12.627	12.878	13.130	13.382	13.634
11.750%	10.255	10.504	10.752	11.001	11.251	11.500	11.750	12.000	12.251	12.501	12.752	13.003	13.255	13.507
11.875%	10.132	10.380	10.628	10.877	11.126	11.376	11.625	11.875	12.125	12.376	12.626	12.877	13.128	13.380
12.000%	10.009	10.257	10.505	10.753	11.002	11.251	11.501	11.750	12.000	12.250	12.501	12.751	13.002	13.253
12.125%	9.886	10.134	10.382	10.630	10.878	11.127	11.376	11.626	11.875	12.125	12.375	12.626	12.876	13.127
12.250%	9.764	10.011	10.259	10.507	10.755	11.003	11.252	11.501	11.751	12.000	12.250	12.500	12.751	13.001
12.375%	9.642	9.889	10.136	10.384	10.632	10.880	11.128	11.377	11.626	11.876	12.125	12.375	12.625	12.876

1 Year Forward Rate

One Year	|	|	|	|	If the Two Year Rate Is									
	12.000%	12.125%	12.250%	12.375%	12.500%	12.625%	12.750%	12.875%	13.000%	13.125%	13.250%	13.375%	13.500%	13.625%
12.000%	12.000	12.250	12.501	12.751	13.002	13.253	13.505	13.757	14.009	14.261	14.514	14.767	15.020	15.274
12.125%	11.875	12.125	12.375	12.626	12.876	13.127	13.378	13.630	13.882	14.134	14.386	14.639	14.892	15.145
12.250%	11.751	12.000	12.250	12.500	12.751	13.001	13.252	13.503	13.755	14.007	14.259	14.511	14.764	15.017
12.375%	11.626	11.876	12.125	12.375	12.625	12.876	13.126	13.377	13.628	13.880	14.132	14.384	14.636	14.889
12.500%	11.502	11.751	12.001	12.250	12.500	12.750	13.001	13.251	13.502	13.753	14.005	14.257	14.509	14.761
12.625%	11.378	11.627	11.876	12.126	12.375	12.625	12.875	13.126	13.376	13.627	13.878	14.130	14.382	14.634
12.750%	11.255	11.503	11.752	12.001	12.251	12.500	12.750	13.000	13.251	13.501	13.752	14.003	14.255	14.507
12.875%	11.132	11.380	11.628	11.877	12.126	12.376	12.625	12.875	13.125	13.376	13.626	13.877	14.128	14.380
13.000%	11.009	11.257	11.505	11.753	12.002	12.251	12.501	12.750	13.000	13.250	13.501	13.751	14.002	14.253
13.125%	10.886	11.134	11.382	11.630	11.878	12.127	12.376	12.626	12.875	13.125	13.375	13.626	13.876	14.127
13.250%	10.764	11.011	11.259	11.507	11.755	12.003	12.252	12.501	12.751	13.000	13.250	13.500	13.751	14.001
13.375%	10.642	10.889	11.136	11.384	11.632	11.880	12.128	12.377	12.626	12.876	13.125	13.375	13.625	13.876

Entry is the interest rate forecast for the forward year

The Interest Rate Yield Curve

2 Year Forward Rate

Two Year	\multicolumn{14}{c}{If the Three Year Rate Is}

Two Year	9.000%	9.125%	9.250%	9.375%	9.500%	9.625%	9.750%	9.875%	10.000%	10.125%	10.250%	10.375%	10.500%	10.625%
9.000%	9.000	9.375	9.752	10.129	10.507	10.886	11.265	11.646	12.028	12.410	12.793	13.177	13.562	13.948
9.125%	8.750	9.125	9.500	9.877	10.254	10.632	11.011	11.391	11.771	12.153	12.535	12.918	13.302	13.687
9.250%	8.502	8.875	9.250	9.625	10.002	10.379	10.757	11.136	11.515	11.896	12.278	12.660	13.043	13.427
9.375%	8.254	8.627	9.000	9.375	9.750	10.127	10.504	10.882	11.261	11.640	12.021	12.403	12.785	13.168
9.500%	8.007	8.379	8.752	9.125	9.500	9.875	10.252	10.629	11.007	11.386	11.765	12.146	12.527	12.910
9.625%	7.761	8.132	8.504	8.877	9.250	9.625	10.000	10.377	10.754	11.132	11.511	11.890	12.271	12.652
9.750%	7.515	7.886	8.257	8.629	9.002	9.375	9.750	10.125	10.502	10.879	11.257	11.636	12.015	12.396
9.875%	7.271	7.640	8.011	8.382	8.754	9.127	9.500	9.875	10.250	10.627	11.004	11.382	11.761	12.140
10.000%	7.027	7.396	7.765	8.136	8.507	8.879	9.252	9.625	10.000	10.375	10.752	11.129	11.507	11.886
10.125%	6.784	7.152	7.521	7.890	8.261	8.632	9.004	9.377	9.750	10.125	10.500	10.877	11.254	11.632
10.250%	6.542	6.909	7.277	7.646	8.015	8.386	8.757	9.129	9.502	9.875	10.250	10.625	11.002	11.379
10.375%	6.301	6.667	7.034	7.402	7.771	8.140	8.511	8.882	9.254	9.627	10.000	10.375	10.750	11.127

2 Year Forward Rate

Two Year	\multicolumn{14}{c}{If the Three Year Rate Is}

Two Year	10.000%	10.125%	10.250%	10.375%	10.500%	10.625%	10.750%	10.875%	11.000%	11.125%	11.250%	11.375%	11.500%	11.625%
10.000%	10.000	10.375	10.752	11.129	11.507	11.886	12.265	12.646	13.027	13.410	13.793	14.177	14.562	14.947
10.125%	9.750	10.125	10.500	10.877	11.254	11.632	12.011	12.390	12.771	13.152	13.535	13.918	14.302	14.687
10.250%	9.502	9.875	10.250	10.625	11.002	11.379	11.757	12.136	12.515	12.896	13.277	13.660	14.043	14.427
10.375%	9.254	9.627	10.000	10.375	10.750	11.127	11.504	11.882	12.261	12.640	13.021	13.402	13.785	14.168
10.500%	9.007	9.379	9.752	10.125	10.500	10.875	11.252	11.629	12.007	12.386	12.765	13.146	13.527	13.909
10.625%	8.761	9.132	9.504	9.877	10.250	10.625	11.000	11.377	11.754	12.132	12.511	12.890	13.271	13.652
10.750%	8.515	8.886	9.257	9.629	10.002	10.375	10.750	11.125	11.502	11.879	12.257	12.636	13.015	13.396
10.875%	8.271	8.640	9.011	9.382	9.754	10.127	10.500	10.875	11.250	11.627	12.004	12.382	12.761	13.140
11.000%	8.027	8.396	8.765	9.136	9.507	9.879	10.252	10.625	11.000	11.375	11.752	12.129	12.507	12.886
11.125%	7.784	8.152	8.521	8.890	9.261	9.632	10.004	10.377	10.750	11.125	11.500	11.877	12.254	12.632
11.250%	7.542	7.909	8.277	8.646	9.015	9.386	9.757	10.129	10.502	10.875	11.250	11.625	12.002	12.379
11.375%	7.301	7.667	8.034	8.402	8.771	9.140	9.510	9.882	10.254	10.627	11.000	11.375	11.750	12.127

2 Year Forward Rate

Two Year	\multicolumn{14}{c}{If the Three Year Rate Is}

Two Year	11.000%	11.125%	11.250%	11.375%	11.500%	11.625%	11.750%	11.875%	12.000%	12.125%	12.250%	12.375%	12.500%	12.625%
11.000%	11.000	11.375	11.752	12.129	12.507	12.886	13.265	13.646	14.027	14.409	14.792	15.176	15.561	15.947
11.125%	10.750	11.125	11.500	11.877	12.254	12.632	13.011	13.390	13.771	14.152	14.534	14.917	15.301	15.686
11.250%	10.502	10.875	11.250	11.625	12.002	12.379	12.757	13.136	13.515	13.896	14.277	14.659	15.042	15.426
11.375%	10.254	10.627	11.000	11.375	11.750	12.127	12.504	12.882	13.261	13.640	14.021	14.402	14.784	15.167
11.500%	10.007	10.379	10.752	11.125	11.500	11.875	12.252	12.629	13.007	13.386	13.765	14.146	14.527	14.909
11.625%	9.760	10.132	10.504	10.877	11.250	11.625	12.000	12.377	12.754	13.132	13.510	13.890	14.271	14.652
11.750%	9.515	9.885	10.257	10.629	11.002	11.375	11.750	12.125	12.502	12.879	13.257	13.636	14.015	14.396
11.875%	9.270	9.640	10.010	10.382	10.754	11.127	11.500	11.875	12.250	12.627	13.004	13.382	13.761	14.140
12.000%	9.027	9.395	9.765	10.135	10.507	10.879	11.252	11.625	12.000	12.375	12.752	13.129	13.507	13.885
12.125%	8.784	9.152	9.520	9.890	10.260	10.632	11.004	11.377	11.750	12.125	12.500	12.877	13.254	13.632
12.250%	8.542	8.909	9.277	9.645	10.015	10.385	10.757	11.129	11.502	11.875	12.250	12.625	13.002	13.379
12.375%	8.300	8.667	9.034	9.402	9.770	10.140	10.510	10.882	11.254	11.627	12.000	12.375	12.750	13.127

2 Year Forward Rate

Two Year	\multicolumn{14}{c}{If the Three Year Rate Is}

Two Year	12.000%	12.125%	12.250%	12.375%	12.500%	12.625%	12.750%	12.875%	13.000%	13.125%	13.250%	13.375%	13.500%	13.625%
12.000%	12.000	12.375	12.752	13.129	13.507	13.885	14.265	14.646	15.027	15.409	15.792	16.176	16.561	16.946
12.125%	11.750	12.125	12.500	12.877	13.254	13.632	14.010	14.390	14.771	15.152	15.534	15.917	16.301	16.685
12.250%	11.502	11.875	12.250	12.625	13.002	13.379	13.757	14.135	14.515	14.896	15.277	15.659	16.042	16.426
12.375%	11.254	11.627	12.000	12.375	12.750	13.127	13.504	13.882	14.260	14.640	15.021	15.402	15.784	16.167
12.500%	11.007	11.379	11.752	12.125	12.500	12.875	13.252	13.629	14.007	14.385	14.765	15.145	15.527	15.909
12.625%	10.760	11.132	11.504	11.877	12.250	12.625	13.000	13.377	13.754	14.132	14.510	14.890	15.270	15.652
12.750%	10.515	10.885	11.257	11.629	12.002	12.375	12.750	13.125	13.502	13.879	14.257	14.635	15.015	15.395
12.875%	10.270	10.640	11.010	11.382	11.754	12.127	12.500	12.875	13.250	13.627	14.004	14.382	14.760	15.140
13.000%	10.026	10.395	10.765	11.135	11.507	11.879	12.252	12.625	13.000	13.375	13.752	14.129	14.507	14.888
13.125%	9.783	10.151	10.520	10.890	11.260	11.632	12.004	12.377	12.750	13.125	13.500	13.877	14.254	14.632
13.250%	9.541	9.908	10.276	10.645	11.015	11.385	11.757	12.129	12.502	12.875	13.250	13.625	14.002	14.379
13.375%	9.300	9.666	10.033	10.401	10.770	11.140	11.510	11.882	12.254	12.627	13.000	13.375	13.750	14.127

Entry is the interest rate forecast for the forward year

The Interest Rate Yield Curve

3 Year Forward Rate

Three Year	If the Four Year Rate Is													
	9.000%	9.125%	9.250%	9.375%	9.500%	9.625%	9.750%	9.875%	10.000%	10.125%	10.250%	10.375%	10.500%	10.625%
9.000%	9.000	9.501	10.003	10.508	11.014	11.522	12.031	12.542	13.055	13.570	14.087	14.605	15.125	15.647
9.125%	8.626	9.125	9.626	10.128	10.633	11.139	11.647	12.156	12.667	13.180	13.695	14.212	14.730	15.250
9.250%	8.253	8.751	9.250	9.751	10.253	10.758	11.264	11.772	12.281	12.792	13.305	13.820	14.336	14.855
9.375%	7.883	8.378	8.876	9.375	9.876	10.378	10.883	11.389	11.897	12.406	12.917	13.430	13.945	14.461
9.500%	7.514	8.008	8.503	9.001	9.500	10.001	10.503	11.008	11.514	12.021	12.531	13.042	13.555	14.070
9.625%	7.146	7.639	8.133	8.628	9.126	9.625	10.126	10.628	11.133	11.639	12.146	12.656	13.167	13.680
9.750%	6.781	7.271	7.764	8.258	8.753	9.251	9.750	10.251	10.753	11.258	11.764	12.271	12.781	13.292
9.875%	6.417	6.906	7.396	7.889	8.383	8.878	9.376	9.875	10.376	10.878	11.383	11.889	12.396	12.906
10.000%	6.054	6.542	7.031	7.521	8.014	8.508	9.003	9.501	10.000	10.501	11.003	11.508	12.014	12.521
10.125%	5.693	6.179	6.666	7.155	7.646	8.139	8.633	9.128	9.626	10.125	10.626	11.128	11.633	12.139
10.250%	5.334	5.818	6.304	6.791	7.280	7.771	8.264	8.758	9.253	9.751	10.250	10.751	11.253	11.758
10.375%	4.977	5.459	5.943	6.429	6.916	7.405	7.896	8.389	8.883	9.378	9.876	10.375	10.876	11.378

3 Year Forward Rate

Three Year	If the Four Year Rate Is													
	10.000%	10.125%	10.250%	10.375%	10.500%	10.625%	10.750%	10.875%	11.000%	11.125%	11.250%	11.375%	11.500%	11.625%
10.000%	10.000	10.501	11.003	11.508	12.014	12.521	13.031	13.542	14.055	14.570	15.086	15.604	16.124	16.645
10.125%	9.626	10.125	10.626	11.128	11.633	12.139	12.646	13.156	13.667	14.180	14.694	15.211	15.729	16.249
10.250%	9.253	9.751	10.250	10.751	11.253	11.758	12.264	12.771	13.281	13.792	14.305	14.819	15.336	15.854
10.375%	8.883	9.378	9.876	10.375	10.876	11.378	11.883	12.389	12.896	13.406	13.917	14.430	14.944	15.461
10.500%	8.514	9.008	9.503	10.001	10.500	11.001	11.503	12.008	12.514	13.021	13.531	14.042	14.555	15.069
10.625%	8.146	8.639	9.133	9.628	10.126	10.625	11.126	11.628	12.133	12.639	13.146	13.656	14.167	14.680
10.750%	7.780	8.271	8.763	9.258	9.753	10.251	10.750	11.251	11.753	12.258	12.764	13.271	13.781	14.292
10.875%	7.416	7.905	8.396	8.888	9.383	9.878	10.376	10.875	11.376	11.878	12.383	12.889	13.396	13.906
11.000%	7.054	7.541	8.030	8.521	9.013	9.508	10.003	10.501	11.000	11.501	12.003	12.508	13.014	13.521
11.125%	6.693	7.179	7.666	8.155	8.646	9.138	9.633	10.128	10.626	11.125	11.626	12.128	12.633	13.139
11.250%	6.334	6.818	7.304	7.791	8.280	8.771	9.263	9.758	10.253	10.751	11.250	11.751	12.253	12.758
11.375%	5.976	6.459	6.943	7.429	7.916	8.405	8.896	9.388	9.883	10.378	10.876	11.375	11.876	12.378

3 Year Forward Rate

Three Year	If the Four Year Rate Is													
	11.000%	11.125%	11.250%	11.375%	11.500%	11.625%	11.750%	11.875%	12.000%	12.125%	12.250%	12.375%	12.500%	12.625%
11.000%	11.000	11.501	12.003	12.508	13.014	13.521	14.031	14.542	15.054	15.569	16.085	16.603	17.123	17.644
11.125%	10.626	11.125	11.626	12.128	12.633	13.139	13.646	14.155	14.667	15.179	15.694	16.210	16.728	17.248
11.250%	10.253	10.751	11.250	11.751	12.253	12.758	13.264	13.771	14.280	14.792	15.304	15.819	16.335	16.853
11.375%	9.883	10.378	10.876	11.375	11.876	12.378	12.883	13.388	13.896	14.405	14.916	15.429	15.944	16.460
11.500%	9.513	10.008	10.503	11.001	11.500	12.001	12.503	13.008	13.513	14.021	14.530	15.041	15.554	16.069
11.625%	9.146	9.638	10.133	10.628	11.126	11.625	12.125	12.628	13.133	13.638	14.146	14.665	15.166	15.679
11.750%	8.780	9.271	9.763	10.258	10.753	11.251	11.750	12.251	12.753	13.258	13.763	14.271	14.780	15.291
11.875%	8.416	8.905	9.396	9.888	10.383	10.878	11.376	11.875	12.376	12.878	13.383	13.888	14.396	14.905
12.000%	8.053	8.541	9.030	9.521	10.013	10.508	11.003	11.501	12.000	12.501	13.003	13.508	14.013	14.521
12.125%	7.692	8.178	8.666	9.155	9.646	10.138	10.632	11.128	11.626	12.125	12.626	13.128	13.633	14.138
12.250%	7.333	7.817	8.303	8.791	9.280	9.771	10.263	10.758	11.253	11.751	12.250	12.751	13.253	13.758
12.375%	6.975	7.458	7.942	8.428	8.916	9.405	9.896	10.388	10.882	11.378	11.876	12.375	12.876	13.378

3 Year Forward Rate

Three Year	If the Four Year Rate Is													
	12.000%	12.125%	12.250%	12.375%	12.500%	12.625%	12.750%	12.875%	13.000%	13.125%	13.250%	13.375%	13.500%	13.625%
12.000%	12.000	12.501	13.003	13.508	14.013	14.521	15.030	15.541	16.054	16.568	17.084	17.602	18.122	18.643
12.125%	11.626	12.125	12.626	13.128	13.633	14.138	14.646	15.155	15.666	16.179	16.693	17.209	17.727	18.246
12.250%	11.253	11.751	12.250	12.751	13.253	13.758	14.263	14.771	15.280	15.791	16.304	16.818	17.334	17.852
12.375%	10.882	11.378	11.876	12.375	12.876	13.378	13.883	14.388	14.896	15.405	15.916	16.429	16.943	17.459
12.500%	10.513	11.008	11.503	12.001	12.500	13.001	13.503	14.008	14.513	15.021	15.530	16.041	16.554	17.068
12.625%	10.146	10.638	11.132	11.628	12.126	12.625	13.126	13.628	14.132	14.638	15.146	15.655	16.166	16.679
12.750%	9.780	10.271	10.763	11.257	11.753	12.251	12.750	13.251	13.753	14.257	14.763	15.271	15.780	16.291
12.875%	9.416	9.905	10.396	10.888	11.382	11.878	12.376	12.875	13.376	13.878	14.383	14.888	15.396	15.905
13.000%	9.053	9.540	10.030	10.521	11.013	11.507	12.003	12.501	13.000	13.501	14.003	14.507	15.013	15.521
13.125%	8.692	9.178	9.665	10.155	10.646	11.138	11.632	12.128	12.626	13.125	13.626	14.128	14.632	15.138
13.250%	8.332	8.817	9.303	9.790	10.280	10.771	11.263	11.757	12.253	12.751	13.250	13.751	14.253	14.757
13.375%	7.974	8.457	8.942	9.428	9.915	10.405	10.896	11.388	11.882	12.378	12.876	13.375	13.876	14.378

Entry is the interest rate forecast for the forward year

The Interest Rate Yield Curve

4 Year Forward Rate

Four Year	If the Five Year Rate Is													
	9.000%	9.125%	9.250%	9.375%	9.500%	9.625%	9.750%	9.875%	10.000%	10.125%	10.250%	10.375%	10.500%	10.625%
9.000%	9.000	9.626	10.256	10.888	11.523	12.161	12.802	13.446	14.093	14.742	15.395	16.051	16.709	17.371
9.125%	8.501	9.125	9.751	10.381	11.013	11.648	12.286	12.927	13.571	14.218	14.867	15.520	16.175	16.834
9.250%	8.006	8.626	9.250	9.876	10.506	11.138	11.773	12.411	13.052	13.696	14.342	14.992	15.645	16.300
9.375%	7.513	8.131	8.751	9.375	10.001	10.631	11.263	11.898	12.536	13.177	13.821	14.467	15.117	15.770
9.500%	7.023	7.638	8.256	8.876	9.500	10.126	10.756	11.388	12.023	12.661	13.302	13.945	14.592	15.242
9.625%	6.535	7.148	7.763	8.381	9.001	9.625	10.251	10.881	11.513	12.148	12.786	13.427	14.070	14.717
9.750%	6.051	6.660	7.273	7.888	8.506	9.126	9.750	10.376	11.006	11.638	12.273	12.911	13.552	14.195
9.875%	5.569	6.176	6.785	7.398	8.013	8.631	9.251	9.875	10.501	11.131	11.763	12.398	13.036	13.677
10.000%	5.090	5.694	6.301	6.910	7.523	8.138	8.756	9.376	10.000	10.626	11.256	11.888	12.523	13.161
10.125%	4.614	5.215	5.819	6.426	7.035	7.648	8.263	8.881	9.501	10.125	10.751	11.381	12.013	12.648
10.250%	4.140	4.739	5.340	5.944	6.551	7.160	7.773	8.388	9.006	9.626	10.250	10.876	11.506	12.138
10.375%	3.669	4.265	4.864	5.465	6.069	6.676	7.285	7.898	8.513	9.131	9.751	10.375	11.001	11.631

4 Year Forward Rate

Four Year	If the Five Year Rate Is													
	10.000%	10.125%	10.250%	10.375%	10.500%	10.625%	10.750%	10.875%	11.000%	11.125%	11.250%	11.375%	11.500%	11.625%
10.000%	10.000	10.626	11.256	11.888	12.523	13.161	13.801	14.445	15.092	15.741	16.394	17.049	17.707	18.369
10.125%	9.501	10.125	10.751	11.381	12.013	12.648	13.286	13.926	14.570	15.217	15.866	16.518	17.174	17.832
10.250%	9.006	9.626	10.250	10.876	11.506	12.138	12.773	13.411	14.051	14.695	15.342	15.991	16.643	17.299
10.375%	8.513	9.131	9.751	10.375	11.001	11.631	12.263	12.898	13.536	14.176	14.820	15.466	16.116	16.768
10.500%	8.023	8.638	9.256	9.876	10.500	11.126	11.756	12.388	13.023	13.661	14.301	14.945	15.591	16.241
10.625%	7.535	8.147	8.763	9.381	10.001	10.625	11.251	11.881	12.513	13.148	13.785	14.426	15.070	15.716
10.750%	7.050	7.660	8.272	8.888	9.506	10.126	10.750	11.376	12.006	12.638	13.273	13.910	14.551	15.195
10.875%	6.569	7.175	7.785	8.397	9.013	9.631	10.251	10.875	11.501	12.131	12.763	13.398	14.035	14.676
11.000%	6.089	6.693	7.300	7.910	8.522	9.138	9.756	10.376	11.000	11.626	12.256	12.888	13.523	14.160
11.125%	5.613	6.214	6.818	7.425	8.035	8.647	9.263	9.881	10.501	11.125	11.751	12.381	13.013	13.648
11.250%	5.139	5.738	6.339	6.943	7.550	8.160	8.772	9.388	10.006	10.626	11.250	11.876	12.506	13.138
11.375%	4.668	5.264	5.862	6.464	7.068	7.675	8.285	8.897	9.513	10.131	10.751	11.375	12.001	12.631

4 Year Forward Rate

Four Year	If the Five Year Rate Is													
	11.000%	11.125%	11.250%	11.375%	11.500%	11.625%	11.750%	11.875%	12.000%	12.125%	12.250%	12.375%	12.500%	12.625%
11.000%	11.000	11.626	12.256	12.888	13.523	14.160	14.801	15.444	16.091	16.740	17.392	18.047	18.705	19.366
11.125%	10.501	11.125	11.751	12.381	13.013	13.648	14.285	14.926	15.569	16.216	16.865	17.517	18.172	18.830
11.250%	10.006	10.626	11.250	11.876	12.506	13.138	13.773	14.410	15.051	15.694	16.341	16.990	17.642	18.297
11.375%	9.513	10.131	10.751	11.375	12.001	12.631	13.263	13.898	14.535	15.176	15.819	16.466	17.115	17.767
11.500%	9.022	9.638	10.256	10.876	11.500	12.126	12.756	13.388	14.023	14.660	15.301	15.944	16.591	17.240
11.625%	8.535	9.147	9.763	10.381	11.001	11.625	12.251	12.881	13.513	14.148	14.785	15.426	16.069	16.715
11.750%	8.050	8.660	9.272	9.888	10.506	11.126	11.750	12.376	13.006	13.638	14.272	14.910	15.551	16.194
11.875%	7.568	8.175	8.785	9.397	10.013	10.631	11.251	11.875	12.501	13.131	13.763	14.397	15.035	15.676
12.000%	7.088	7.693	8.300	8.910	9.522	10.138	10.756	11.376	12.000	12.626	13.256	13.888	14.522	15.160
12.125%	6.612	7.213	7.818	8.425	9.035	9.647	10.262	10.881	11.501	12.125	12.751	13.381	14.013	14.647
12.250%	6.138	6.737	7.338	7.943	8.550	9.160	9.772	10.387	11.006	11.626	12.250	12.876	13.506	14.138
12.375%	5.666	6.263	6.861	7.463	8.068	8.675	9.285	9.897	10.512	11.131	11.751	12.375	13.001	13.631

4 Year Forward Rate

Four Year	If the Five Year Rate Is													
	12.000%	12.125%	12.250%	12.375%	12.500%	12.625%	12.750%	12.875%	13.000%	13.125%	13.250%	13.375%	13.500%	13.625%
12.000%	12.000	12.626	13.256	13.888	14.522	15.160	15.801	16.444	17.090	17.739	18.391	19.046	19.704	20.364
12.125%	11.501	12.125	12.751	13.381	14.013	14.647	15.285	15.925	16.569	17.215	17.864	18.516	19.171	19.828
12.250%	11.006	11.626	12.250	12.876	13.506	14.138	14.772	15.410	16.050	16.694	17.340	17.989	18.641	19.296
12.375%	10.512	11.131	11.751	12.375	13.001	13.631	14.263	14.897	15.535	16.175	16.819	17.465	18.114	18.766
12.500%	10.022	10.637	11.256	11.876	12.500	13.126	13.756	14.388	15.022	15.660	16.300	16.944	17.590	18.239
12.625%	9.534	10.147	10.762	11.381	12.001	12.625	13.251	13.881	14.513	15.147	15.785	16.425	17.068	17.715
12.750%	9.050	9.659	10.272	10.887	11.506	12.126	12.750	13.376	14.006	14.638	15.272	15.910	16.550	17.193
12.875%	8.567	9.175	9.784	10.397	11.012	11.631	12.251	12.875	13.501	14.131	14.763	15.397	16.035	16.675
13.000%	8.088	8.692	9.299	9.909	10.522	11.137	11.756	12.376	13.000	13.626	14.256	14.887	15.522	16.160
13.125%	7.611	8.213	8.817	9.424	10.034	10.647	11.262	11.880	12.501	13.125	13.751	14.381	15.012	15.647
13.250%	7.136	7.736	8.337	8.942	9.549	10.159	10.772	11.387	12.005	12.626	13.250	13.876	14.506	15.137
13.375%	6.665	7.261	7.861	8.462	9.067	9.674	10.284	10.897	11.512	12.131	12.751	13.375	14.001	14.631

Entry is the interest rate forecast for the forward year

Annual Mortgage Constant for Monthly Payment Loans

Loan Term	5.00%	5.0625%	5.10%	5.125%	Annual Interest Rate 5.1875%	5.20%	5.25%	5.30%	5.3125%	5.375%	5.40%
1	102.728978	102.763351	102.783978	102.797730	102.832116	102.838994	102.866508	102.894027	102.900907	102.935312	102.949076
2	52.645668	52.679262	52.699426	52.712870	52.746491	52.753216	52.780124	52.807040	52.813771	52.847430	52.860897
3	35.965077	35.998760	36.018979	36.032462	36.066184	36.072930	36.099925	36.126931	36.133685	36.167465	36.180982
4	27.635152	27.669139	27.689544	27.703152	27.737191	27.744002	27.771255	27.798525	27.805345	27.839461	27.853115
5	22.645480	22.679857	22.700499	22.714266	22.748707	22.755599	22.783181	22.810782	22.817686	22.852223	22.866047
6	19.325919	19.360728	19.381632	19.395575	19.430461	19.437442	19.465384	19.493351	19.500347	19.535348	19.549359
7	16.960691	16.995955	17.017134	17.031263	17.066616	17.073692	17.102014	17.130364	17.137456	17.172943	17.187151
8	15.191904	15.227636	15.249100	15.263420	15.299254	15.306427	15.335139	15.363883	15.371074	15.407061	15.421470
9	13.820728	13.856937	13.878690	13.893203	13.929527	13.936798	13.965907	13.995052	14.002344	14.038838	14.053451
10	12.727862	12.764553	12.786598	12.801307	12.838124	12.845495	12.875004	12.904554	12.911947	12.948953	12.963773
11	11.837386	11.874561	11.896900	11.911806	11.949120	11.956590	11.986502	12.016457	12.023953	12.061473	12.076500
12	11.098685	11.136346	11.158979	11.174082	11.211893	11.219464	11.249779	11.280141	11.287739	11.325773	11.341008
13	10.476716	10.514863	10.537790	10.553091	10.591399	10.599070	10.629787	10.660555	10.668256	10.706804	10.722246
14	9.946449	9.985080	10.008301	10.023798	10.062602	10.070373	10.101492	10.132666	10.140468	10.179529	10.195178
15	9.489524	9.528638	9.552151	9.567845	9.607143	9.615014	9.646533	9.678110	9.686013	9.725585	9.741439
16	9.092172	9.131768	9.155572	9.171461	9.211251	9.219220	9.251137	9.283116	9.291120	9.331200	9.347258
17	8.743863	8.783938	8.808032	8.824114	8.864393	8.872461	8.904774	8.937151	8.945256	8.985839	9.002101
18	8.436406	8.476956	8.501338	8.517613	8.558377	8.566543	8.599249	8.632022	8.640226	8.681310	8.697773
19	8.163333	8.204355	8.229022	8.245489	8.286735	8.294998	8.328093	8.361259	8.369562	8.411142	8.427805
20	7.919469	7.960959	7.985909	8.002566	8.044290	8.052649	8.086130	8.119686	8.128086	8.170158	8.187019
21	7.700624	7.742578	7.767809	7.784654	7.826851	7.835305	7.869169	7.903111	7.911608	7.954167	7.971224
22	7.503369	7.545783	7.571293	7.588324	7.630969	7.639538	7.673781	7.708104	7.716697	7.759737	7.776988
23	7.324872	7.367741	7.393526	7.410742	7.453871	7.462513	7.497131	7.531831	7.540519	7.584035	7.601478
24	7.162770	7.206091	7.232147	7.249545	7.293134	7.301868	7.336856	7.371929	7.380711	7.424698	7.442330
25	7.015080	7.058847	7.085173	7.102751	7.146793	7.155618	7.190973	7.226414	7.235288	7.279740	7.297559
26	6.880123	6.924330	6.950923	6.968679	7.013169	7.022084	7.057800	7.093606	7.102571	7.147482	7.165485
27	6.756468	6.801110	6.827965	6.845898	6.890830	6.899834	6.935907	6.972071	6.981127	7.026490	7.044675
28	6.642887	6.687959	6.715074	6.733180	6.778549	6.787641	6.824065	6.860584	6.869728	6.915537	6.933901
29	6.538324	6.583820	6.611190	6.629468	6.675267	6.684445	6.721217	6.758085	6.767317	6.813565	6.832106
30	6.441859	6.487774	6.515397	6.533844	6.580067	6.589331	6.626444	6.663656	6.672974	6.719655	6.738370
31	6.352696	6.399023	6.426895	6.445508	6.492150	6.501497	6.538948	6.576497	6.585900	6.633007	6.651893
32	6.270133	6.316867	6.344984	6.363761	6.410815	6.420244	6.458027	6.495910	6.505396	6.552922	6.571976
33	6.193556	6.240691	6.269049	6.287988	6.335447	6.344958	6.383066	6.421277	6.430845	6.478783	6.498002
34	6.122423	6.169952	6.198548	6.217645	6.265503	6.275094	6.313523	6.352056	6.361705	6.410048	6.429429
35	6.056252	6.104169	6.132999	6.152253	6.200502	6.210172	6.248917	6.287766	6.297494	6.346234	6.365775
36	5.994616	6.042914	6.071975	6.091382	6.140017	6.149764	6.188818	6.227978	6.237785	6.286915	6.306612
37	5.937133	5.985807	6.015093	6.034651	6.083665	6.093488	6.132846	6.172311	6.182194	6.231707	6.251558
38	5.883462	5.932504	5.962013	5.981719	6.031105	6.041002	6.080659	6.120424	6.130382	6.180270	6.200272
39	5.833296	5.882701	5.912427	5.932279	5.982030	5.992000	6.031951	6.072009	6.082040	6.132293	6.152446
40	5.786359	5.836120	5.866061	5.886056	5.936164	5.946207	5.986444	6.026790	6.036894	6.087511	6.107805

Loan Term	5.4375%	5.50%	5.5625%	5.60%	Annual Interest Rate 5.625%	5.70%	5.75%	5.80%	5.875%	5.90%	5.9375%
1	102.969724	103.004141	103.038566	103.059223	103.072997	103.114322	103.141877	103.169437	103.210784	103.224568	103.245246
2	52.881102	52.914787	52.948485	52.968710	52.982196	53.022666	53.049657	53.076655	53.117169	53.130677	53.150944
3	36.201264	36.235082	36.268920	36.289232	36.302777	36.343431	36.370549	36.397679	36.438398	36.451977	36.472352
4	27.873603	27.907770	27.941963	27.962492	27.976182	28.017279	28.044697	28.072132	28.113314	28.127050	28.147662
5	22.886793	22.921395	22.956028	22.976824	22.990694	23.032335	23.060122	23.087929	23.129678	23.143604	23.164504
6	19.570387	19.605465	19.640580	19.661668	19.675735	19.717971	19.746158	19.774371	19.816735	19.830869	19.852081
7	17.208475	17.244051	17.279672	17.301066	17.315338	17.358195	17.386802	17.415438	17.458445	17.472795	17.494333
8	15.443098	15.479187	15.515326	15.537033	15.551515	15.595010	15.624046	15.653116	15.696780	15.711351	15.733223
9	14.075389	14.111996	14.148661	14.170687	14.185382	14.229523	14.258995	14.288503	14.332834	14.347629	14.369839
10	12.986022	13.023153	13.060348	13.082694	13.097605	13.142396	13.172306	13.202257	13.247258	13.262279	13.284828
11	12.099062	12.136719	12.174445	12.197113	12.212239	12.257683	12.288034	12.318428	12.364101	12.379347	12.402237
12	11.363883	11.402066	11.440324	11.463314	11.478656	11.524752	11.555542	11.586380	11.632725	11.648197	11.671427
13	10.745433	10.784142	10.822931	10.846264	10.861800	10.908547	10.939776	10.971055	11.018070	11.033767	11.057336
14	10.218676	10.257908	10.297226	10.320858	10.336629	10.384025	10.415691	10.447410	10.495092	10.511013	10.534919
15	9.765248	9.805001	9.844846	9.868796	9.884780	9.932822	9.964921	9.997078	10.045422	10.061565	10.085807
16	9.371375	9.411647	9.452014	9.476281	9.492477	9.541159	9.573690	9.606281	9.655282	9.671647	9.696221
17	9.026524	9.067310	9.108197	9.132777	9.149184	9.198501	9.231460	9.264482	9.314135	9.330718	9.355623
18	8.722500	8.763796	8.805198	8.830090	8.846705	8.896652	8.930035	8.963484	9.013783	9.030583	9.055813
19	8.452833	8.494635	8.536547	8.561747	8.578569	8.629140	8.662942	8.696813	8.747752	8.764768	8.790320
20	8.212345	8.254648	8.297065	8.322570	8.339597	8.390785	8.425002	8.459292	8.510862	8.528088	8.553961
21	7.996845	8.039643	8.082560	8.108367	8.125596	8.177395	8.212022	8.246724	8.298919	8.316354	8.342543
22	7.802901	7.846189	7.889600	7.915706	7.933134	7.985537	8.020569	8.055679	8.108490	8.126132	8.152631
23	7.627680	7.671452	7.715351	7.741752	7.759377	7.812315	7.847807	7.883320	7.936738	7.954584	7.981390
24	7.468817	7.513067	7.557449	7.584140	7.601960	7.655545	7.691372	7.727281	7.781299	7.799346	7.826454
25	7.324328	7.369050	7.413907	7.440885	7.458897	7.513061	7.549277	7.585577	7.640185	7.658430	7.685836
26	7.192531	7.237719	7.283044	7.310305	7.328507	7.383242	7.419840	7.456525	7.511714	7.530154	7.557852
27	7.071995	7.117641	7.163429	7.190968	7.209356	7.264653	7.301629	7.338693	7.394453	7.413084	7.441071
28	6.961491	7.007590	7.053832	7.081646	7.100217	7.156067	7.193414	7.230850	7.287173	7.305991	7.334261
29	6.859961	6.906505	6.953195	6.981279	7.000030	7.056424	7.094135	7.131938	7.188812	7.207816	7.236363
30	6.766487	6.813468	6.860598	6.888948	6.907877	6.964805	7.002874	7.041036	7.098453	7.117638	7.146458
31	6.680267	6.727679	6.775243	6.803853	6.822956	6.880410	6.918831	6.957346	7.015294	7.034657	7.063745
32	6.600603	6.648438	6.696427	6.725294	6.744568	6.802537	6.841303	6.880165	6.938633	6.958172	6.987522
33	6.526878	6.575129	6.623536	6.652654	6.672097	6.730571	6.769676	6.808877	6.867858	6.887567	6.917173
34	6.458549	6.507209	6.556025	6.585390	6.604998	6.663969	6.703405	6.742939	6.802421	6.822296	6.852154
35	6.395135	6.444195	6.493414	6.523021	6.542790	6.602247	6.642009	6.681869	6.741841	6.761880	6.791984
36	6.336207	6.385661	6.435274	6.465118	6.485046	6.544979	6.585059	6.625238	6.685690	6.705889	6.736233
37	6.281384	6.331223	6.381223	6.411299	6.431382	6.491781	6.532173	6.572664	6.633585	6.653941	6.684520
38	6.230324	6.280540	6.330919	6.361223	6.381457	6.442313	6.483009	6.523805	6.585185	6.605693	6.636502
39	6.182719	6.233306	6.284055	6.314581	6.334965	6.396267	6.437261	6.478355	6.540182	6.560840	6.591873
40	6.138295	6.189243	6.240355	6.271100	6.291628	6.353366	6.394652	6.436037	6.498301	6.519105	6.550357

Annual Mortgage Constant for Monthly Payment Loans

Loan Term	6.00%	6.0625%	6.10%	6.125%	Annual Interest Rate 6.1875%	6.20%	6.25%	6.30%	6.3125%	6.375%	6.40%
1	103.279716	103.314191	103.334880	103.348673	103.383162	103.390060	103.417657	103.445257	103.452158	103.486666	103.500471
2	53.184732	53.218533	53.238820	53.252347	53.286174	53.292941	53.320014	53.347095	53.353867	53.387732	53.401282
3	36.506325	36.540317	36.560722	36.574329	36.608360	36.615168	36.642410	36.669664	36.676479	36.710568	36.724209
4	28.182035	28.216434	28.237085	28.250858	28.285308	28.292201	28.319784	28.347383	28.354285	28.388812	28.402630
5	23.199362	23.234252	23.255201	23.269174	23.304128	23.311123	23.339114	23.367126	23.374132	23.409182	23.423211
6	19.887465	19.922888	19.944160	19.958349	19.993848	20.000952	20.029385	20.057842	20.064960	20.100574	20.114830
7	17.530265	17.566242	17.587850	17.602264	17.638330	17.645548	17.674440	17.703360	17.710594	17.746793	17.761285
8	15.769716	15.806260	15.828211	15.842854	15.879499	15.886834	15.916194	15.945587	15.952940	15.989736	16.004469
9	14.406900	14.444017	14.466315	14.481191	14.518421	14.525874	14.555708	14.585578	14.593051	14.630451	14.645426
10	13.322460	13.360155	13.382801	13.397911	13.435730	13.443302	13.473612	13.503961	13.511555	13.549560	13.564780
11	12.440442	12.478714	12.501710	12.517054	12.555462	12.563152	12.593939	12.624768	12.632483	12.671094	12.686558
12	11.710203	11.749052	11.772397	11.787975	11.826971	11.834780	11.866041	11.897350	11.905184	11.944401	11.960108
13	11.096681	11.136106	11.159798	11.175609	11.215191	11.223117	11.254852	11.286638	11.294592	11.334410	11.350360
14	10.574831	10.614827	10.638866	10.654908	10.695073	10.703116	10.735321	10.767581	10.775654	10.816070	10.832260
15	10.126282	10.166846	10.191228	10.207500	10.248243	10.256402	10.289074	10.321804	10.329995	10.371004	10.387433
16	9.737254	9.778382	9.803104	9.819604	9.860920	9.869194	9.902330	9.935525	9.943833	9.985430	10.002095
17	9.397209	9.438895	9.463954	9.480680	9.522563	9.530952	9.564545	9.598201	9.606625	9.648804	9.665702
18	9.097948	9.140186	9.165579	9.182528	9.224973	9.233474	9.267520	9.301632	9.310171	9.352924	9.370053
19	8.832996	8.875780	8.901503	8.918672	8.961672	8.970285	9.004779	9.039341	9.047993	9.091313	9.108671
20	8.597173	8.640497	8.666545	8.683933	8.727480	8.736203	8.771138	8.806145	8.814908	8.858788	8.876371
21	8.386283	8.430140	8.456509	8.474112	8.518200	8.527031	8.562402	8.597847	8.606720	8.651151	8.668956
22	8.196893	8.241275	8.267962	8.285776	8.330397	8.339335	8.375136	8.411012	8.419993	8.464967	8.482990
23	8.026166	8.071066	8.098065	8.116088	8.161233	8.170277	8.206500	8.242801	8.251888	8.297397	8.315634
24	7.871737	7.917146	7.944452	7.962681	8.008342	8.017490	8.054128	8.090847	8.100039	8.146073	8.164522
25	7.731617	7.777528	7.805136	7.823568	7.869736	7.878985	7.916033	7.953161	7.962456	8.009007	8.027663
26	7.604124	7.650528	7.678434	7.697064	7.743731	7.753080	7.790529	7.828061	7.837457	7.884514	7.903373
27	7.487824	7.534713	7.562911	7.581736	7.628893	7.638341	7.676183	7.714111	7.723606	7.771160	7.790218
28	7.381488	7.428853	7.457337	7.476354	7.523992	7.533536	7.571765	7.610080	7.619672	7.667713	7.686967
29	7.284055	7.331887	7.360653	7.379858	7.427966	7.437605	7.476212	7.514907	7.524595	7.573113	7.592558
30	7.194606	7.242896	7.271937	7.291326	7.339897	7.349628	7.388606	7.427673	7.437454	7.486439	7.506071
31	7.112340	7.161078	7.190390	7.209960	7.258982	7.268804	7.308145	7.347576	7.357448	7.406889	7.426704
32	7.036555	7.085733	7.115309	7.135055	7.184520	7.194431	7.234127	7.273914	7.283875	7.333763	7.353757
33	6.966635	7.016241	7.046079	7.065997	7.115895	7.125892	7.165938	7.206071	7.216119	7.266442	7.286611
34	6.902036	6.952066	6.982154	7.002241	7.052562	7.062644	7.103027	7.143501	7.153634	7.204383	7.224722
35	6.842276	6.892717	6.923053	6.943305	6.994039	7.004204	7.044918	7.085724	7.095939	7.147103	7.167608
36	6.786927	6.837770	6.868347	6.888761	6.939898	6.950143	6.991180	7.032309	7.042606	7.094174	7.114841
37	6.735606	6.786842	6.817654	6.838225	6.889756	6.900080	6.941432	6.982876	6.993252	7.045214	7.066039
38	6.687971	6.739590	6.770633	6.791357	6.843271	6.853672	6.895331	6.937082	6.947534	6.999880	7.020858
39	6.643716	6.695708	6.726975	6.747849	6.800137	6.810612	6.852571	6.894621	6.905148	6.957867	6.978994
40	6.602564	6.654921	6.686406	6.707426	6.760078	6.770626	6.812875	6.855216	6.865815	6.918898	6.940170

Loan Term	6.4375%	6.50%	6.5625%	6.60%	Annual Interest Rate 6.625%	6.70%	6.75%	6.80%	6.875%	6.90%	6.9375%
1	103.521180	103.555700	103.590227	103.610947	103.624761	103.666209	103.693847	103.721488	103.762958	103.776784	103.797524
2	53.421610	53.455502	53.489406	53.509754	53.523323	53.564040	53.591195	53.618359	53.659119	53.672710	53.693101
3	36.744676	36.778803	36.812950	36.833447	36.847116	36.888141	36.915506	36.942883	36.983972	36.997675	37.018235
4	28.423365	28.457944	28.492548	28.513322	28.527177	28.568767	28.596514	28.624277	28.665952	28.679852	28.700710
5	23.444264	23.479378	23.514524	23.535627	23.549701	23.591957	23.620153	23.648369	23.690732	23.704863	23.726069
6	20.136226	20.171916	20.207644	20.229099	20.243410	20.286380	20.315057	20.343738	20.386866	20.401234	20.422813
7	17.783036	17.819324	17.855656	17.877476	17.892032	17.935741	17.964916	17.994120	18.037978	18.052611	18.074575
8	16.026582	16.063479	16.100426	16.122618	16.137423	16.181886	16.211568	16.241283	16.285914	16.300807	16.323162
9	14.667906	14.705418	14.742986	14.765554	14.780610	14.825833	14.856027	14.886256	14.931668	14.946823	14.969572
10	13.587628	13.625757	13.663949	13.686893	13.702202	13.748187	13.778894	13.809640	13.855832	13.871250	13.894394
11	12.709774	12.748521	12.787335	12.810656	12.826217	12.872964	12.904183	12.935445	12.982418	12.998097	13.021636
12	11.983690	12.023053	12.062489	12.086185	12.101997	12.149503	12.181232	12.213008	12.260758	12.276698	12.300629
13	11.374307	11.414282	11.454336	11.478405	11.494467	11.542728	11.574964	11.607250	11.655772	11.671970	11.696292
14	10.856570	10.897153	10.937820	10.962259	10.978569	11.027579	11.060318	11.093110	11.142397	11.158853	11.183561
15	10.412102	10.453288	10.494563	10.519370	10.535925	10.585676	10.618914	10.652207	10.702252	10.718962	10.744052
16	10.027126	10.068903	10.110779	10.135949	10.152748	10.203233	10.236963	10.270752	10.321546	10.338507	10.363975
17	9.691080	9.733453	9.775924	9.801453	9.818492	9.869702	9.903919	9.938198	9.989732	10.006940	10.032782
18	9.395779	9.438735	9.481794	9.507678	9.524954	9.576879	9.611576	9.646338	9.698601	9.716054	9.742264
19	9.134739	9.178272	9.221910	9.248143	9.265653	9.318284	9.353455	9.388693	9.441674	9.459368	9.485940
20	8.902778	8.946878	8.991087	9.017665	9.035405	9.088731	9.124368	9.160074	9.213763	9.231694	9.258622
21	8.695696	8.740355	8.785127	8.812044	8.830011	8.884021	8.920116	8.956283	9.010667	9.028831	9.056109
22	8.510059	8.555268	8.600593	8.627844	8.646034	8.700716	8.737262	8.773882	8.828948	8.847340	8.874962
23	8.343027	8.388776	8.434645	8.462224	8.480633	8.535975	8.572964	8.610028	8.665764	8.684380	8.712340
24	8.192231	8.238512	8.284915	8.312815	8.331440	8.387430	8.424853	8.462353	8.518746	8.537582	8.565871
25	8.055684	8.102486	8.149413	8.177629	8.196465	8.253090	8.290938	8.328865	8.385902	8.404953	8.433566
26	7.931700	7.979014	8.026455	8.054980	8.074023	8.131270	8.169535	8.207880	8.265546	8.284808	8.313737
27	7.818845	7.866660	7.914604	7.943433	7.962678	8.020534	8.059207	8.097961	8.156243	8.175711	8.204949
28	7.715887	7.764193	7.812630	7.841756	7.861198	7.919651	7.958723	7.997877	8.056760	8.076428	8.105969
29	7.621765	7.670552	7.719472	7.748887	7.768523	7.827559	7.867020	7.906564	7.966035	7.985899	8.015734
30	7.535560	7.584816	7.634207	7.663906	7.683732	7.743336	7.783177	7.823102	7.883146	7.903202	7.933324
31	7.456468	7.506184	7.556035	7.586011	7.606021	7.666180	7.706393	7.746689	7.807291	7.827533	7.857936
32	7.383789	7.433953	7.484254	7.514499	7.534690	7.595391	7.635964	7.676623	7.737769	7.758192	7.788867
33	7.316905	7.367507	7.418245	7.448754	7.469121	7.530349	7.571275	7.612286	7.673961	7.694562	7.725501
34	7.255272	7.306300	7.357466	7.388232	7.408769	7.470512	7.511780	7.553135	7.615324	7.636096	7.667293
35	7.198408	7.249852	7.301434	7.332449	7.353153	7.415396	7.456998	7.498686	7.561376	7.582314	7.613761
36	7.145884	7.197733	7.249720	7.280978	7.301845	7.364573	7.406500	7.448511	7.511687	7.532788	7.564477
37	7.097318	7.149561	7.201942	7.233437	7.254461	7.317662	7.359903	7.402229	7.465877	7.487134	7.519059
38	7.052368	7.104994	7.157759	7.189483	7.210660	7.274320	7.316867	7.359499	7.423603	7.445013	7.477166
39	7.010727	7.063726	7.116863	7.148811	7.170136	7.234242	7.277085	7.320013	7.384560	7.406117	7.438492
40	6.972120	7.025482	7.078980	7.111144	7.132614	7.197151	7.240282	7.283496	7.348473	7.370173	7.402761

Annual Mortgage Constant for Monthly Payment Loans

Loan Term	7.00%	7.0625%	7.10%	7.125%	Annual Interest Rate 7.1875%	7.20%	7.25%	7.30%	7.3125%	7.375%	7.40%
1	103.832095	103.866674	103.887424	103.901258	103.935849	103.942768	103.970447	103.998129	104.005050	104.039661	104.053506
2	53.727095	53.761102	53.781512	53.795122	53.829155	53.835963	53.863200	53.890446	53.897259	53.931330	53.944962
3	37.052516	37.086817	37.107407	37.121137	37.155476	37.162347	37.189835	37.217336	37.224213	37.258610	37.272374
4	28.735494	28.770303	28.791200	28.805137	28.839997	28.846973	28.874883	28.902810	28.909795	28.944732	28.958714
5	23.761438	23.796839	23.818095	23.832272	23.867737	23.874834	23.903234	23.931654	23.938762	23.974322	23.988555
6	20.458808	20.494841	20.516479	20.530912	20.567020	20.574247	20.603167	20.632112	20.639352	20.675575	20.690075
7	18.111216	18.147901	18.169934	18.184631	18.221404	18.228764	18.258221	18.287707	18.295083	18.331988	18.346763
8	16.360460	16.397809	16.420242	16.435207	16.472655	16.480151	16.510153	16.540188	16.547701	16.585299	16.600352
9	15.007532	15.045548	15.068384	15.083620	15.121747	15.129379	15.159930	15.190517	15.198169	15.236464	15.251797
10	13.933018	13.971702	13.994943	14.010448	14.049256	14.057025	14.088125	14.119264	14.127055	14.166046	14.181660
11	13.060921	13.100273	13.123917	13.139692	13.179178	13.187083	13.218730	13.250420	13.258350	13.298035	13.313928
12	12.340573	12.380589	12.404633	12.420677	12.460838	12.468878	12.501070	12.533307	12.541374	12.581749	12.597920
13	11.736890	11.777565	11.802007	11.818317	11.859146	11.867321	11.900053	11.932833	11.941036	11.982096	11.998541
14	11.224807	11.266135	11.290971	11.307545	11.349037	11.357345	11.390610	11.423928	11.432266	11.474003	11.490720
15	10.785939	10.827913	10.853139	10.869974	10.912121	10.920561	10.954355	10.988203	10.996674	11.039080	11.056066
16	10.406496	10.449108	10.474719	10.491811	10.534605	10.543175	10.577490	10.611863	10.620465	10.663530	10.680782
17	10.075928	10.119169	10.145160	10.162506	10.205938	10.214635	10.249464	10.284353	10.293085	10.336800	10.354313
18	9.786026	9.829888	9.856252	9.873849	9.917908	9.926732	9.962067	9.997464	10.006323	10.050678	10.068447
19	9.530309	9.574781	9.601513	9.619355	9.664033	9.672981	9.708812	9.744709	9.753694	9.798677	9.816698
20	9.303587	9.348659	9.375754	9.393838	9.439122	9.448192	9.484512	9.520899	9.530007	9.575606	9.593875
21	9.101661	9.147322	9.174772	9.193093	9.238973	9.248162	9.284961	9.321830	9.331058	9.377262	9.395774
22	8.921089	8.967329	8.995127	9.013681	9.060145	9.069451	9.106720	9.144060	9.153406	9.200203	9.218952
23	8.759031	8.805837	8.833976	8.852759	8.899794	8.909215	8.946944	8.984746	8.994207	9.041583	9.060565
24	8.613115	8.660477	8.688950	8.707955	8.755551	8.765084	8.803263	8.841515	8.851090	8.899032	8.918241
25	8.481350	8.529255	8.558055	8.577279	8.625422	8.635064	8.673682	8.712376	8.722061	8.770556	8.789986
26	8.362051	8.410486	8.439606	8.459043	8.507720	8.517470	8.556517	8.595640	8.605433	8.654467	8.674114
27	8.253779	8.302733	8.332164	8.351809	8.401008	8.410862	8.450328	8.489871	8.499768	8.549329	8.569186
28	8.155303	8.204763	8.234498	8.254347	8.304054	8.314010	8.353883	8.393835	8.403835	8.453907	8.473969
29	8.065561	8.115513	8.145545	8.165591	8.215794	8.225849	8.266120	8.306469	8.316568	8.367138	8.387400
30	7.983630	8.034063	8.064384	8.084622	8.135307	8.145459	8.186115	8.226851	8.237047	8.288102	8.308558
31	7.908709	7.959609	7.990211	8.010637	8.061790	8.072036	8.113068	8.154180	8.164470	8.215994	8.236638
32	7.840094	7.891450	7.922324	7.942933	7.994541	8.004878	8.046275	8.087751	8.098133	8.150114	8.170940
33	7.777170	7.828968	7.860107	7.880893	7.932944	7.943369	7.985120	8.026950	8.037420	8.089843	8.110846
34	7.719391	7.771618	7.803015	7.823972	7.876452	7.886964	7.929058	7.971231	7.981786	8.034638	8.055813
35	7.666276	7.718920	7.750567	7.771690	7.824586	7.835180	7.877607	7.920112	7.930751	7.984017	8.005358
36	7.617397	7.670444	7.702333	7.723618	7.776917	7.787591	7.830340	7.873167	7.883886	7.937553	7.959054
37	7.572370	7.625809	7.657933	7.679374	7.733063	7.743815	7.786875	7.830013	7.840810	7.894865	7.916520
38	7.530857	7.584674	7.617025	7.638617	7.692684	7.703512	7.746873	7.790311	7.801182	7.855612	7.877417
39	7.492550	7.546734	7.579305	7.601043	7.655474	7.666375	7.710026	7.753755	7.764699	7.819490	7.841439
40	7.457175	7.511714	7.544497	7.566376	7.621159	7.632131	7.676063	7.720071	7.731085	7.786225	7.808313

Loan Term	7.4375%	7.50%	7.5625%	7.60%	Annual Interest Rate 7.625%	7.70%	7.75%	7.80%	7.875%	7.90%	7.9375%
1	104.074277	104.108900	104.143530	104.164310	104.178166	104.219737	104.247456	104.275180	104.316773	104.330639	104.351441
2	53.965414	53.999511	54.033621	54.054093	54.067744	54.108708	54.136028	54.163356	54.204363	54.218036	54.238550
3	37.293026	37.327462	37.361917	37.382599	37.396391	37.437785	37.465396	37.493020	37.534479	37.548305	37.569049
4	28.979694	29.014682	29.049696	29.070716	29.084735	29.126816	29.154890	29.182981	29.225147	29.239211	29.260314
5	24.000914	24.045538	24.081194	24.102603	24.116881	24.159768	24.188352	24.216915	24.259949	24.274284	24.295795
6	20.711836	20.748135	20.784471	20.806292	20.820846	20.864546	20.893709	20.922896	20.966723	20.981344	21.003287
7	18.368938	18.405931	18.442968	18.465212	18.480050	18.524605	18.554344	18.584110	18.628813	18.643728	18.666113
8	16.622947	16.660645	16.698392	16.721064	16.736189	16.781611	16.811933	16.842286	16.887875	16.903087	16.925920
9	15.274814	15.313219	15.351681	15.374784	15.390197	15.436490	15.467396	15.498338	15.544817	15.560327	15.583610
10	14.205099	14.244212	14.283387	14.306921	14.322622	14.369785	14.401276	14.432805	14.480172	14.495981	14.519712
11	13.337788	13.377606	13.417491	13.441454	13.457442	13.505471	13.537543	13.569657	13.617908	13.634013	13.658189
12	12.622197	12.662716	12.703306	12.727695	12.743968	12.792856	12.825505	12.858199	12.907326	12.923725	12.948343
13	12.023232	12.064445	12.105734	12.130544	12.147100	12.196839	12.230059	12.263328	12.313322	12.330010	12.355066
14	11.515821	11.557720	11.599700	11.624927	11.641762	11.692342	11.726126	11.759962	11.810812	11.827788	11.853275
15	11.081571	11.124148	11.166811	11.192449	11.209559	11.260968	11.295309	11.329704	11.381398	11.398657	11.424570
16	10.706686	10.749931	10.793266	10.819310	10.836690	10.888917	10.923806	10.958752	11.011276	11.028813	11.055144
17	10.380610	10.424513	10.468509	10.494952	10.512599	10.565630	10.601057	10.636544	10.689886	10.707696	10.734438
18	10.095130	10.139680	10.184327	10.211162	10.229071	10.282891	10.318848	10.354866	10.409009	10.427087	10.454233
19	9.843761	9.888946	9.934231	9.961451	9.979617	10.034212	10.070688	10.107227	10.162155	10.180496	10.208037
20	9.621310	9.667118	9.713030	9.740627	9.759045	9.814398	9.851383	9.888432	9.944129	9.962727	9.990655
21	9.423574	9.469992	9.516517	9.544483	9.563148	9.619244	9.656726	9.694275	9.750723	9.769572	9.797878
22	9.247109	9.294125	9.341250	9.369577	9.388483	9.445306	9.483273	9.521310	9.578492	9.597587	9.626261
23	9.089071	9.136671	9.184382	9.213062	9.232204	9.289736	9.328178	9.366690	9.424588	9.443922	9.472956
24	8.947088	8.995259	9.043542	9.072567	9.091939	9.150162	9.189067	9.228043	9.286639	9.306206	9.335590
25	8.819167	8.867894	8.916736	8.946096	8.965692	9.024590	9.063945	9.103372	9.162648	9.182442	9.212166
26	8.703620	8.752889	8.802275	8.831962	8.851777	8.911330	8.951124	8.990991	9.050926	9.070941	9.100996
27	8.599008	8.648806	8.698721	8.728727	8.748754	8.808945	8.849165	8.889459	8.950036	8.970264	9.000641
28	8.504099	8.554411	8.604841	8.635156	8.655389	8.716201	8.756835	8.797543	8.858742	8.879178	8.909866
29	8.417830	8.468641	8.519571	8.550187	8.570620	8.632034	8.673069	8.714179	8.775982	8.796619	8.827609
30	8.339278	8.390574	8.441990	8.472897	8.493525	8.555522	8.596947	8.638446	8.700833	8.721665	8.752947
31	8.267641	8.319408	8.371295	8.402484	8.423301	8.485863	8.527665	8.569541	8.632493	8.653513	8.685078
32	8.202216	8.254440	8.306783	8.338246	8.359245	8.422355	8.464521	8.506762	8.570260	8.591463	8.623301
33	8.142388	8.195053	8.247838	8.279566	8.300742	8.364381	8.406900	8.449492	8.513518	8.534897	8.566998
34	8.087611	8.140704	8.193916	8.225900	8.247247	8.311397	8.354257	8.397189	8.461725	8.483272	8.515628
35	8.037404	8.090911	8.144536	8.176768	8.198279	8.262923	8.306111	8.349372	8.414398	8.436109	8.468709
36	7.991341	8.045247	8.099271	8.131742	8.153412	8.218532	8.262037	8.305614	8.371113	8.392982	8.425817
37	7.949039	8.003332	8.057741	8.090441	8.112265	8.177843	8.221654	8.265536	8.331490	8.353510	8.386572
38	7.910160	7.964824	8.019604	8.052527	8.074499	8.140521	8.184624	8.228798	8.295190	8.317355	8.350635
39	7.874398	7.929421	7.984559	8.017696	8.039809	8.106257	8.150643	8.195099	8.261911	8.284216	8.317705
40	7.841480	7.896849	7.952331	7.985673	8.007924	8.074781	8.119438	8.164165	8.231381	8.253820	8.287509

Annual Mortgage Constant for Monthly Payment Loans

Loan Term	8.00%	8.0625%	8.10%	8.125%	8.1875%	8.20%	8.25%	8.30%	8.3125%	8.375%	8.40%
					Annual Interest Rate						
1	104.386115	104.420796	104.441607	104.455483	104.490176	104.497115	104.524876	104.552640	104.559582	104.594295	104.608181
2	54.272750	54.306962	54.327496	54.341188	54.375426	54.382275	54.409677	54.437087	54.443941	54.478218	54.491932
3	37.603639	37.638247	37.659022	37.672875	37.707522	37.714454	37.742188	37.769935	37.776874	37.811578	37.825465
4	29.295507	29.330725	29.351868	29.365968	29.401237	29.408294	29.436532	29.464785	29.471851	29.507197	29.521342
5	24.331673	24.367583	24.389144	24.403524	24.439497	24.446696	24.475502	24.504329	24.511538	24.547606	24.562043
6	21.039889	21.076528	21.098530	21.113205	21.149921	21.157268	21.186673	21.216103	21.223464	21.260292	21.275034
7	18.703457	18.740845	18.763299	18.778277	18.815752	18.823252	18.853271	18.883317	18.890833	18.928440	18.943494
8	16.964015	17.002160	17.025070	17.040354	17.078597	17.086252	17.116890	17.147560	17.155232	17.193623	17.208994
9	15.622458	15.661361	15.684730	15.700320	15.739333	15.747142	15.778401	15.809695	15.817524	15.856703	15.872389
10	14.559311	14.598972	14.622797	14.638692	14.678474	14.686437	14.718315	14.750232	14.758217	14.798179	14.814180
11	13.698536	13.738949	13.763228	13.779427	13.819971	13.828088	13.860580	13.893115	13.901255	13.941995	13.958309
12	12.989431	13.030589	13.055318	13.071818	13.113118	13.121386	13.154487	13.187633	13.195927	13.237437	13.254061
13	12.396887	12.438782	12.463956	12.480753	12.522799	12.531217	12.564920	12.598670	12.607115	12.649385	12.666314
14	11.895818	11.938441	11.964053	11.981144	12.023926	12.032492	12.066787	12.101133	12.109728	12.152747	12.169977
15	11.467825	11.511164	11.537208	11.554587	11.598094	11.606806	11.641684	11.676616	11.685358	11.729114	11.746640
16	11.099100	11.143144	11.169613	11.187276	11.231494	11.240349	11.275801	11.311308	11.320194	11.364673	11.382489
17	10.779082	10.823818	10.850703	10.868644	10.913562	10.922556	10.958570	10.994642	11.003669	11.048858	11.066959
18	10.499551	10.544965	10.572259	10.590473	10.636076	10.645207	10.681772	10.718396	10.727562	10.773445	10.791824
19	10.254017	10.300094	10.327788	10.346269	10.392541	10.401808	10.438910	10.476075	10.485376	10.531938	10.550589
20	10.037281	10.084008	10.112092	10.130835	10.177762	10.187159	10.224788	10.262480	10.271913	10.319137	10.338054
21	9.845135	9.892496	9.920962	9.939960	9.987526	9.997051	10.035193	10.073400	10.082962	10.130831	10.150007
22	9.674135	9.722114	9.750952	9.770198	9.818387	9.828037	9.866679	9.905387	9.915074	9.963572	9.983000
23	9.521431	9.570013	9.599214	9.618702	9.667496	9.677268	9.716396	9.755591	9.765401	9.814510	9.834182
24	9.384649	9.433818	9.463371	9.483094	9.532478	9.542368	9.581969	9.621638	9.631566	9.681268	9.701179
25	9.261795	9.311533	9.341429	9.361381	9.411337	9.421342	9.461402	9.501530	9.511573	9.561851	9.581992
26	9.151177	9.201469	9.231698	9.251872	9.302384	9.312499	9.353004	9.393578	9.403733	9.454569	9.474933
27	9.051358	9.102187	9.132738	9.153127	9.204177	9.214400	9.255337	9.296342	9.306605	9.357980	9.378561
28	8.961104	9.012453	9.043316	9.063914	9.115485	9.125812	9.167165	9.208588	9.218955	9.270853	9.291642
29	8.879350	8.931203	8.962368	8.983167	9.035242	9.045670	9.087427	9.129253	9.139720	9.192122	9.213112
30	8.805175	8.857515	8.888972	8.909966	8.962528	8.973053	9.015199	9.057415	9.067979	9.120867	9.142052
31	8.737777	8.790587	8.822327	8.843509	8.896540	8.907160	8.949681	8.992272	9.002930	9.056286	9.077658
32	8.676454	8.729718	8.761730	8.783093	8.836578	8.847288	8.890171	8.933123	8.943872	8.997679	9.019231
33	8.620589	8.674292	8.706566	8.728104	8.782025	8.792822	8.836054	8.879354	8.890189	8.944430	8.966156
34	8.569642	8.623766	8.656293	8.677999	8.732340	8.743221	8.786788	8.830422	8.841341	8.895999	8.917891
35	8.523131	8.577661	8.610431	8.632299	8.687043	8.698005	8.741894	8.785849	8.796848	8.851906	8.873958
36	8.480630	8.535551	8.568554	8.590578	8.645710	8.656749	8.700947	8.745211	8.756287	8.811728	8.833933
37	8.441761	8.497057	8.530285	8.552458	8.607963	8.619076	8.663570	8.708129	8.719279	8.775088	8.797440
38	8.406186	8.461842	8.495286	8.517602	8.573464	8.584648	8.629426	8.674269	8.685489	8.741650	8.764142
39	8.373603	8.429604	8.463254	8.485708	8.541912	8.553164	8.598215	8.643328	8.654616	8.711114	8.733740
40	8.343740	8.400073	8.433921	8.456506	8.513037	8.524355	8.569666	8.615038	8.626391	8.683210	8.705964

Loan Term	8.4375%	8.50%	8.5625%	8.60%	8.625%	8.70%	8.75%	8.80%	8.875%	8.90%	8.9375%
					Annual Interest Rate						
1	104.629014	104.663739	104.698471	104.719313	104.733209	104.774903	104.802704	104.830510	104.872225	104.886133	104.906996
2	54.512507	54.546810	54.581125	54.601720	54.615453	54.656664	54.684148	54.711640	54.752894	54.766649	54.787286
3	37.846302	37.881045	37.915807	37.936674	37.950588	37.992351	38.020209	38.048078	38.089906	38.103854	38.124783
4	29.542568	29.577964	29.613386	29.634651	29.648833	29.691403	29.719804	29.748221	29.790877	29.805103	29.826451
5	24.583706	24.619838	24.656001	24.677714	24.692195	24.735670	24.764679	24.793708	24.837290	24.851827	24.873642
6	21.297158	21.334062	21.371003	21.393186	21.407982	21.452406	21.482052	21.511723	21.556273	21.571136	21.593440
7	18.966089	19.003783	19.041519	19.064182	19.079300	19.124693	19.154991	19.185316	19.230856	19.246049	19.268853
8	17.232064	17.270554	17.309094	17.332241	17.347682	17.394053	17.425006	17.455991	17.502527	17.518055	17.541361
9	15.895936	15.935223	15.974566	15.998197	16.013963	16.061311	16.092921	16.124565	16.172097	16.187958	16.211766
10	14.838201	14.878283	14.918425	14.942539	14.958627	15.006948	15.039210	15.071510	15.120032	15.136225	15.160533
11	13.982800	14.023670	14.064605	14.089198	14.105606	14.154891	14.187800	14.220751	14.270253	14.286775	14.311577
12	13.279017	13.320667	13.362386	13.387452	13.404176	13.454415	13.487963	13.521555	13.572027	13.588873	13.614178
13	12.691730	12.734149	12.776643	12.802175	12.819211	12.870390	12.904568	12.938793	12.990220	13.007386	13.033156
14	12.195845	12.239022	12.282278	12.308269	12.325612	12.377715	12.412514	12.447362	12.499727	12.517207	12.543450
15	11.772953	11.816875	11.860879	11.887321	11.904965	11.957977	11.993384	12.028843	12.082129	12.099917	12.126623
16	11.409240	11.453892	11.498631	11.525515	11.543455	11.597357	11.633360	11.669418	11.723606	11.741696	11.768856
17	11.094137	11.139505	11.184963	11.212280	11.230510	11.285283	11.321870	11.358513	11.413583	11.431968	11.459571
18	10.819421	10.865489	10.911651	10.939391	10.957904	11.013528	11.050685	11.087899	11.143830	11.162503	11.190539
19	10.578595	10.625348	10.672195	10.700349	10.719138	10.775593	10.813305	10.851077	10.907848	10.926801	10.955258
20	10.366459	10.413879	10.461396	10.489953	10.509010	10.566275	10.604529	10.642843	10.700430	10.719656	10.748523
21	10.178801	10.226870	10.275040	10.303989	10.323308	10.381360	10.420140	10.458982	10.517362	10.536853	10.566119
22	10.012172	10.060874	10.109677	10.139007	10.158581	10.217398	10.256689	10.296043	10.355194	10.374942	10.404594
23	9.863722	9.913038	9.962457	9.992157	10.011978	10.071537	10.111324	10.151175	10.211072	10.231069	10.261095
24	9.731076	9.780988	9.831004	9.861063	9.881123	9.941401	9.981668	10.022000	10.082619	10.102858	10.133246
25	9.612235	9.662725	9.713319	9.743726	9.764017	9.824992	9.865724	9.906521	9.967838	9.988310	10.019047
26	9.505511	9.556560	9.607714	9.638456	9.658970	9.720619	9.761800	9.803046	9.865038	9.885734	9.916809
27	9.409463	9.461052	9.512747	9.543814	9.564547	9.626844	9.668458	9.710137	9.772779	9.793692	9.825092
28	9.322857	9.374969	9.427186	9.458566	9.479507	9.542431	9.584462	9.626560	9.689827	9.710949	9.742661
29	9.244630	9.297245	9.349966	9.381648	9.402791	9.466318	9.508752	9.551251	9.615121	9.636443	9.668456
30	9.173861	9.226962	9.280167	9.312141	9.333477	9.397585	9.440405	9.483290	9.547739	9.569254	9.601556
31	9.109748	9.163316	9.216988	9.249241	9.270764	9.335430	9.378622	9.421878	9.486882	9.508582	9.541161
32	9.051591	9.105609	9.159729	9.192251	9.213953	9.279154	9.322703	9.366315	9.431851	9.453728	9.486573
33	8.998776	9.053225	9.107776	9.140556	9.162429	9.228145	9.272035	9.315988	9.382035	9.404081	9.437179
34	8.950760	9.005623	9.060588	9.093615	9.115653	9.181861	9.226079	9.270358	9.336893	9.359101	9.392442
35	8.907066	8.962327	9.017688	9.050951	9.073147	9.139827	9.184358	9.228949	9.295950	9.318314	9.351887
36	8.867210	8.922912	8.978652	9.012143	9.034489	9.101620	9.146450	9.191340	9.258786	9.281297	9.315092
37	8.830997	8.887003	8.943105	8.976813	8.999303	9.066865	9.111981	9.157156	9.225026	9.247679	9.281684
38	8.797909	8.854263	8.910713	8.944627	8.967255	9.035229	9.080617	9.126063	9.194339	9.217126	9.251332
39	8.767707	8.824395	8.881175	8.915287	8.938047	9.006413	9.052061	9.097766	9.166427	9.189342	9.223739
40	8.740124	8.797129	8.854225	8.888526	8.911411	8.980150	9.026046	9.071997	9.141025	9.164061	9.198640

Annual Mortgage Constant for Monthly Payment Loans

Loan Term	9.00%	9.0625%	9.10%	9.125%	9.1875%	9.20%	9.25%	9.30%	9.3125%	9.375%	9.40%
1	104.941772	104.976555	104.997428	105.011344	105.046140	105.053100	105.080942	105.108788	105.115750	105.150565	105.164493
2	54.821691	54.856109	54.876765	54.890539	54.924983	54.931873	54.959439	54.987013	54.993908	55.028390	55.042186
3	38.159679	38.194595	38.215553	38.229529	38.264483	38.271476	38.299456	38.327448	38.334448	38.369460	38.383470
4	29.862051	29.897676	29.919063	29.933327	29.969003	29.976141	30.004704	30.033284	30.040431	30.076183	30.090491
5	24.910026	24.946442	24.968306	24.982889	25.019368	25.026667	25.055878	25.085109	25.092420	25.128993	25.143631
6	21.630645	21.667887	21.690250	21.705166	21.742483	21.749951	21.779837	21.809748	21.817229	21.854658	21.869640
7	19.306894	19.344978	19.367849	19.383106	19.421276	19.428916	19.459490	19.490093	19.497747	19.536048	19.551380
8	17.580244	17.619176	17.642558	17.658156	17.697186	17.704998	17.736264	17.767562	17.775391	17.814567	17.830251
9	16.251490	16.291269	16.315162	16.331101	16.370988	16.378972	16.410929	16.442921	16.450924	16.490973	16.507008
10	15.201093	15.241712	15.266112	15.282391	15.323129	15.331284	15.363927	15.396607	15.404783	15.445699	15.462082
11	14.352965	14.394417	14.419319	14.435933	14.477514	14.485837	14.519158	14.552520	14.560867	14.602639	14.619366
12	13.656368	13.698642	13.724040	13.740985	13.783396	13.791887	13.825876	13.859909	13.868424	13.911041	13.928107
13	13.076166	13.119249	13.145134	13.162405	13.205634	13.214288	13.248935	13.283629	13.292309	13.335756	13.353155
14	12.587250	12.631128	12.657491	12.675082	12.719113	12.727929	12.763221	12.798563	12.807406	12.851666	12.869392
15	12.171199	12.215855	12.242688	12.260592	12.305410	12.314383	12.350307	12.386283	12.395285	12.440343	12.458388
16	11.814190	11.859609	11.886900	11.905111	11.950697	11.959824	11.996367	12.032962	12.042120	12.087955	12.106313
17	11.505647	11.551810	11.579549	11.598060	11.644396	11.653674	11.690819	11.728019	11.737328	11.783922	11.802584
18	11.237338	11.284227	11.312403	11.331205	11.378273	11.387697	11.425429	11.463218	11.472674	11.520007	11.538965
19	11.002761	11.050357	11.078958	11.098044	11.145823	11.155389	11.193693	11.232054	11.241653	11.289704	11.308950
20	10.796711	10.844994	10.874008	10.893370	10.941839	10.951545	10.990402	11.029319	11.039057	11.087805	11.107329
21	10.614972	10.663921	10.693336	10.712966	10.762105	10.771944	10.811339	10.850794	10.860668	10.910089	10.929884
22	10.454092	10.503687	10.533491	10.553379	10.603167	10.613137	10.653052	10.693027	10.703031	10.753105	10.773161
23	10.311218	10.361438	10.391618	10.411757	10.462173	10.472267	10.512685	10.553164	10.563294	10.613998	10.634306
24	10.183972	10.234797	10.265340	10.285721	10.336742	10.346958	10.387661	10.428826	10.439077	10.490389	10.510940
25	10.070356	10.121765	10.152658	10.173273	10.224879	10.235211	10.276582	10.318015	10.328383	10.380280	10.401065
26	9.968681	10.020652	10.051882	10.072722	10.124891	10.135336	10.177157	10.219040	10.229520	10.281980	10.302991
27	9.877505	9.930018	9.961573	9.982629	10.035339	10.045893	10.088147	10.130462	10.141051	10.194051	10.215278
28	9.795596	9.848629	9.880497	9.901761	9.954991	9.965649	10.008318	10.051049	10.061741	10.115260	10.136694
29	9.721891	9.775425	9.807592	9.829057	9.882785	9.893543	9.936611	9.979739	9.990531	10.044546	10.066179
30	9.655471	9.709485	9.741940	9.763596	9.817803	9.828656	9.872105	9.915615	9.926502	9.980992	10.002814
31	9.595537	9.650011	9.682741	9.704580	9.759245	9.770189	9.814004	9.857878	9.868856	9.923801	9.945804
32	9.541390	9.596304	9.629298	9.651313	9.706415	9.717447	9.761610	9.805832	9.816897	9.872275	9.894452
33	9.492419	9.547754	9.581000	9.603182	9.658702	9.669817	9.714314	9.758868	9.770016	9.825807	9.848149
34	9.448086	9.503823	9.537309	9.559651	9.615570	9.626764	9.671579	9.716450	9.727676	9.783861	9.806360
35	9.407916	9.464036	9.497751	9.520246	9.576545	9.587815	9.632932	9.678104	9.689406	9.745966	9.768614
36	9.371488	9.427974	9.461907	9.484547	9.541208	9.552551	9.597955	9.643414	9.654787	9.711703	9.734493
37	9.338431	9.395264	9.429406	9.452184	9.509189	9.520600	9.566278	9.612010	9.623451	9.680705	9.703629
38	9.308412	9.365576	9.399916	9.422825	9.480158	9.491634	9.537572	9.583561	9.595067	9.652642	9.675694
39	9.281135	9.338615	9.373142	9.396177	9.453819	9.465357	9.511542	9.557776	9.569343	9.627222	9.650395
40	9.256338	9.314116	9.348822	9.371975	9.429912	9.441509	9.487927	9.534394	9.546018	9.604184	9.627472

Loan Term	9.4375%	9.50%	9.5625%	9.60%	9.625%	9.70%	9.75%	9.80%	9.875%	9.90%	9.9375%
1	105.185387	105.220214	105.255048	105.275952	105.289888	105.331705	105.359588	105.387475	105.429314	105.443262	105.464186
2	55.062884	55.097392	55.131912	55.152630	55.166445	55.207901	55.235549	55.263205	55.304705	55.318542	55.339302
3	38.404490	38.439540	38.474608	38.495659	38.509696	38.551827	38.579929	38.608044	38.650239	38.664310	38.685422
4	30.111961	30.147764	30.183592	30.205102	30.219446	30.262504	30.291229	30.319971	30.363114	30.377503	30.399094
5	25.165597	25.202234	25.238901	25.260917	25.275600	25.319680	25.349092	25.378524	25.422710	25.437449	25.459566
6	21.892125	21.929629	21.967170	21.989713	22.004749	22.049893	22.080019	22.110168	22.155438	22.170539	22.193203
7	19.574391	19.612778	19.651208	19.674286	19.689681	19.735905	19.766755	19.797634	19.844002	19.859472	19.882690
8	17.853792	17.893065	17.932387	17.956003	17.971757	18.019065	18.050643	18.082252	18.129723	18.145563	18.169336
9	16.531076	16.571233	16.611444	16.635596	16.651708	16.700097	16.732399	16.764735	16.813304	16.829511	16.853837
10	15.486673	15.527707	15.568799	15.593483	15.609951	15.659410	15.692429	15.725486	15.775142	15.791713	15.816586
11	14.644475	14.686375	14.728338	14.753546	14.770365	14.820880	14.854608	14.888377	14.939105	14.956034	14.981447
12	13.953726	13.996479	14.039300	14.065025	14.082188	14.133744	14.168169	14.202637	14.254420	14.271702	14.297646
13	13.379275	13.422866	13.466530	13.492762	13.510265	13.562842	13.597950	13.633104	13.685921	13.703550	13.730014
14	12.896003	12.940416	12.984905	13.011634	13.029469	13.083046	13.118823	13.154649	13.208478	13.226445	13.253418
15	12.485480	12.530696	12.575992	12.603207	12.621367	12.675920	12.712352	12.748834	12.803651	12.821948	12.849417
16	12.133874	12.179875	12.225958	12.253647	12.272123	12.327630	12.364699	12.401820	12.457599	12.476218	12.504171
17	11.830602	11.877368	11.924218	11.952369	11.971153	12.027587	12.065276	12.103019	12.159734	12.178666	12.207088
18	11.567429	11.614937	11.662534	11.691133	11.710217	11.767551	11.805843	11.844190	11.901813	11.921048	11.949926
19	11.337845	11.386076	11.434396	11.463431	11.482805	11.541013	11.579889	11.618821	11.677324	11.696852	11.726172
20	11.136644	11.185574	11.234596	11.264052	11.283708	11.342761	11.382202	11.421700	11.481054	11.500867	11.530613
21	10.959604	11.009212	11.058912	11.088777	11.108704	11.168575	11.208562	11.248607	11.308782	11.328869	11.359026
22	10.803274	10.853536	10.903892	10.934150	10.954340	11.015000	11.055513	11.096085	11.157052	11.177403	11.207957
23	10.664797	10.715691	10.766679	10.797317	10.817760	10.879180	10.920201	10.961280	11.023009	11.043614	11.074549
24	10.541796	10.593298	10.644895	10.675898	10.696586	10.758737	10.800245	10.841813	10.904273	10.925123	10.956424
25	10.432272	10.484360	10.536542	10.567896	10.588818	10.651672	10.693649	10.735685	10.798848	10.819931	10.851583
26	10.334535	10.387185	10.439930	10.471621	10.492768	10.556296	10.598722	10.641207	10.705042	10.726350	10.758338
27	10.247146	10.300336	10.353620	10.385635	10.406997	10.471171	10.514026	10.556941	10.621420	10.642942	10.675252
28	10.168873	10.222580	10.276380	10.308705	10.330273	10.395065	10.438332	10.481657	10.546751	10.568478	10.601094
29	10.098655	10.152857	10.207151	10.239772	10.261537	10.326919	10.370579	10.414296	10.479977	10.501899	10.534808
30	10.035575	10.090250	10.145017	10.177920	10.199873	10.265818	10.309853	10.353944	10.420184	10.442291	10.475479
31	9.978837	10.033963	10.089180	10.122352	10.144485	10.210967	10.255359	10.299805	10.366577	10.388862	10.422314
32	9.927743	9.983301	10.038946	10.072376	10.094679	10.161673	10.206404	10.251188	10.318466	10.340919	10.374622
33	9.881687	9.937655	9.993709	10.027383	10.049849	10.117328	10.162381	10.207488	10.275246	10.297857	10.331800
34	9.840133	9.896491	9.952934	9.986840	10.009460	10.077401	10.122761	10.168172	10.236385	10.259148	10.293316
35	9.802611	9.859339	9.916151	9.950277	9.973044	10.041423	10.087073	10.132773	10.201417	10.224323	10.258705
36	9.768702	9.825783	9.882945	9.917280	9.940186	10.008980	10.054904	10.100878	10.169930	10.192971	10.227556
37	9.738040	9.795454	9.852948	9.887481	9.910519	9.979705	10.025890	10.072123	10.141560	10.164729	10.199504
38	9.710295	9.768026	9.825834	9.860555	9.883717	9.953275	9.999705	10.046182	10.115983	10.139273	10.174228
39	9.685177	9.743207	9.801312	9.836210	9.859490	9.929399	9.976062	10.022769	10.092914	10.116317	10.151442
40	9.662425	9.720739	9.779124	9.814190	9.837581	9.907821	9.954703	10.001628	10.072095	10.095606	10.130891

Annual Mortgage Constant for Monthly Payment Loans

Loan Term	10.00%	10.0625%	10.10%	10.125%	10.1875%	10.20%	10.25%	10.30%	10.3125%	10.375%	10.40%
1	105.499065	105.533950	105.554884	105.568841	105.603739	105.610719	105.638643	105.666571	105.673554	105.708471	105.722439
2	55.373912	55.408534	55.429314	55.443170	55.477818	55.484749	55.512479	55.540216	55.547152	55.581839	55.595717
3	38.720625	38.755846	38.776988	38.791087	38.826347	38.833401	38.861626	38.889863	38.896924	38.932241	38.946373
4	30.435100	30.471131	30.492762	30.507187	30.543269	30.550488	30.579376	30.608279	30.615508	30.651665	30.666135
5	25.496454	25.533372	25.555539	25.570322	25.607304	25.614704	25.644317	25.673949	25.681361	25.718436	25.733275
6	22.231005	22.268845	22.291567	22.306722	22.344636	22.352223	22.382587	22.412975	22.420576	22.458602	22.473822
7	19.921421	19.960194	19.983479	19.999011	20.037870	20.045647	20.076772	20.107925	20.115717	20.154705	20.170312
8	18.208997	18.248706	18.272555	18.288464	18.328269	18.336236	18.368123	18.400041	18.408025	18.447975	18.463969
9	16.894423	16.935063	16.959473	16.975757	17.016503	17.024659	17.057303	17.089981	17.098156	17.139062	17.155439
10	15.858088	15.899649	15.924614	15.941268	15.982945	15.991288	16.024680	16.058110	16.066473	16.108324	16.125081
11	15.023853	15.066321	15.091833	15.108853	15.151446	15.159973	15.194103	15.228273	15.236821	15.279602	15.296732
12	14.340939	14.384300	14.410348	14.427727	14.471221	14.479928	14.514781	14.549678	14.558409	14.602102	14.619598
13	13.774177	13.818411	13.844986	13.862716	13.907092	13.915976	13.951538	13.987146	13.996054	14.040641	14.058495
14	13.298432	13.343521	13.370610	13.388684	13.433920	13.442977	13.479231	13.515533	13.524615	13.570073	13.588277
15	12.895261	12.941183	12.968773	12.987182	13.033258	13.042483	13.079411	13.116389	13.125641	13.171947	13.190490
16	12.550823	12.597556	12.625633	12.644368	12.691260	12.700648	12.738232	12.775866	12.785283	12.832413	12.851287
17	12.254525	12.302045	12.330597	12.349647	12.397332	12.406878	12.445098	12.483369	12.492945	12.540874	12.560069
18	11.998124	12.046407	12.075418	12.094775	12.143226	12.152927	12.191761	12.230650	12.240380	12.289082	12.308584
19	11.775107	11.824128	11.853583	11.873236	11.922429	11.932278	11.971708	12.011191	12.021071	12.070519	12.090322
20	11.580260	11.629994	11.659877	11.679816	11.729725	11.739717	11.779721	11.819779	11.829802	11.879969	11.900060
21	11.409360	11.459782	11.490078	11.510293	11.560891	11.571021	11.611577	11.652188	11.662350	11.713208	11.733576
22	11.258952	11.310036	11.340729	11.361209	11.412471	11.422733	11.463820	11.504962	11.515256	11.566780	11.587413
23	11.126180	11.177900	11.208975	11.229709	11.281607	11.291998	11.333593	11.375245	11.385667	11.437827	11.458716
24	11.008665	11.060995	11.092436	11.113415	11.165923	11.176435	11.218519	11.260659	11.271202	11.323972	11.345105
25	10.904409	10.957324	10.989116	11.010328	11.063420	11.074049	11.116599	11.159206	11.169866	11.223219	11.244584
26	10.811724	10.865198	10.897325	10.918760	10.972410	10.983151	11.026147	11.069199	11.079970	11.133879	11.155466
27	10.729172	10.783180	10.815627	10.837276	10.891458	10.902305	10.945727	10.989203	11.000080	11.054519	11.076318
28	10.655525	10.710043	10.742795	10.764647	10.819336	10.830284	10.874111	10.917991	10.928970	10.983912	11.005912
29	10.589725	10.644728	10.677771	10.699816	10.754988	10.766033	10.810244	10.854508	10.865583	10.921003	10.943194
30	10.530859	10.586323	10.619642	10.641872	10.697503	10.708639	10.753216	10.797844	10.809010	10.864884	10.887256
31	10.478134	10.534037	10.567618	10.590022	10.646088	10.657311	10.702235	10.747209	10.758461	10.814765	10.837309
32	10.430860	10.487179	10.521009	10.543579	10.600057	10.611362	10.656614	10.701916	10.713249	10.769961	10.792667
33	10.388434	10.445147	10.479213	10.501939	10.558808	10.570191	10.615753	10.661364	10.672774	10.729870	10.752730
34	10.350325	10.407412	10.441700	10.464574	10.521812	10.533269	10.579125	10.625028	10.636511	10.693970	10.716974
35	10.316069	10.373508	10.408008	10.431022	10.488608	10.500134	10.546267	10.592446	10.603998	10.661799	10.684938
36	10.285255	10.343027	10.377725	10.400872	10.458787	10.470379	10.516773	10.563211	10.574827	10.632950	10.656218
37	10.257520	10.315607	10.350492	10.373763	10.431988	10.443641	10.490281	10.536964	10.548641	10.607067	10.630455
38	10.232543	10.290926	10.325988	10.349376	10.407892	10.419604	10.466475	10.513387	10.525121	10.583832	10.607333
39	10.210038	10.268699	10.303928	10.327426	10.386217	10.397982	10.445071	10.492199	10.503987	10.562964	10.586572
40	10.189751	10.248675	10.284059	10.307661	10.366709	10.378526	10.425818	10.473149	10.484987	10.544215	10.567922

Loan Term	10.4375%	10.50%	10.5625%	10.60%	10.625%	10.70%	10.75%	10.80%	10.875%	10.90%	10.9375%
1	105.743394	105.778323	105.813260	105.834224	105.848202	105.890141	105.918106	105.946075	105.988035	106.002024	106.023010
2	55.616538	55.651250	55.685975	55.706816	55.720712	55.762414	55.790226	55.818045	55.859790	55.873709	55.894592
3	38.967577	39.002932	39.038307	39.059540	39.073700	39.116197	39.144544	39.172903	39.215464	39.229657	39.250953
4	30.687848	30.724056	30.760289	30.782041	30.796547	30.840091	30.869140	30.898205	30.941833	30.956384	30.978217
5	25.755543	25.792680	25.829850	25.852166	25.867050	25.911732	25.941544	25.971377	26.016164	26.031103	26.053520
6	22.496664	22.534764	22.572901	22.595801	22.611075	22.656932	22.687534	22.718158	22.764140	22.779479	22.802499
7	20.193735	20.232808	20.271923	20.295413	20.311082	20.358128	20.389526	20.420951	20.468140	20.483883	20.507511
8	18.487973	18.528019	18.568113	18.592193	18.608255	18.656489	18.688683	18.720907	18.769301	18.785448	18.809682
9	17.180021	17.221033	17.262099	17.286763	17.303217	17.352628	17.385611	17.418628	17.468217	17.484764	17.509599
10	16.150233	16.192200	16.234224	16.259466	16.276306	16.326880	16.360642	16.394440	16.445207	16.462148	16.487576
11	15.322446	15.365351	15.408319	15.434129	15.451348	15.503065	15.537592	15.572159	15.624083	15.641410	15.667420
12	14.645862	14.689698	14.733580	14.759947	14.777538	14.830375	14.865651	14.900970	14.954027	14.971733	14.998312
13	14.085297	14.130024	14.174819	14.201730	14.219685	14.273615	14.309624	14.345676	14.399838	14.417914	14.445049
14	13.615604	13.661208	13.706885	13.734326	13.752635	13.807630	13.844352	13.881120	13.936358	13.954793	13.982468
15	13.218329	13.264787	13.311321	13.339278	13.357931	13.413962	13.451376	13.488838	13.545121	13.563905	13.592105
16	12.879622	12.926909	12.974275	13.002732	13.021719	13.078754	13.116839	13.154974	13.212268	13.231391	13.260098
17	12.588884	12.636975	12.685146	12.714087	12.733397	12.791403	12.830138	12.868923	12.927195	12.946645	12.975842
18	12.337866	12.386733	12.435682	12.465091	12.484713	12.543657	12.583018	12.622431	12.681647	12.701411	12.731081
19	12.120051	12.169667	12.219366	12.249226	12.269149	12.328997	12.368961	12.408978	12.469101	12.489169	12.519294
20	11.930221	11.980559	12.030980	12.061274	12.081486	12.142203	12.182747	12.223345	12.284340	12.304698	12.335260
21	11.764153	11.815184	11.866299	11.897009	11.917499	11.979051	12.020152	12.061306	12.123137	12.143774	12.174753
22	11.618389	11.670005	11.721866	11.752975	11.773742	11.836082	11.877716	11.919403	11.982034	12.002937	12.034317
23	11.490074	11.542407	11.594825	11.626316	11.647328	11.710442	11.752586	11.794782	11.858177	11.879334	11.911095
24	11.376829	11.429771	11.482797	11.514654	11.535909	11.599753	11.642383	11.685065	11.749188	11.770588	11.802713
25	11.276657	11.330180	11.383788	11.415991	11.437480	11.502020	11.545113	11.588258	11.653073	11.674704	11.707175
26	11.187872	11.241950	11.296112	11.328648	11.350356	11.415558	11.459091	11.502676	11.568150	11.590000	11.622799
27	11.109041	11.163646	11.218334	11.251186	11.273104	11.338934	11.382886	11.426888	11.492987	11.515045	11.548156
28	11.038936	11.094043	11.149231	11.182382	11.204499	11.270926	11.315274	11.359672	11.426363	11.448618	11.482023
29	10.976505	11.032088	11.087750	11.121185	11.143491	11.210483	11.255206	11.299979	11.367229	11.389670	11.423354
30	10.920839	10.976872	11.032983	11.066686	11.089171	11.156698	11.201776	11.246903	11.314682	11.337298	11.371245
31	10.871148	10.927608	10.984143	11.018101	11.040754	11.108786	11.154200	11.199660	11.267938	11.290720	11.324914
32	10.826748	10.883611	10.940548	10.974745	10.997558	11.066066	11.111796	11.157571	11.226317	11.249255	11.283683
33	10.787040	10.844283	10.901599	10.936022	10.958985	11.027942	11.073969	11.120040	11.189229	11.212313	11.246960
34	10.751501	10.809102	10.866774	10.901410	10.924515	10.993894	11.040201	11.086550	11.156153	11.179375	11.214228
35	10.719669	10.777608	10.835615	10.870452	10.893689	10.963465	11.010035	11.056645	11.126638	11.149989	11.185034
36	10.691140	10.749397	10.807719	10.842744	10.866106	10.936255	10.983071	11.029926	11.100283	11.123755	11.158981
37	10.665558	10.724113	10.782731	10.817932	10.841411	10.911909	10.958956	11.006041	11.076739	11.100324	11.135718
38	10.642605	10.701439	10.760335	10.795701	10.819291	10.890115	10.937378	10.984678	11.055696	11.079386	11.114938
39	10.622002	10.681099	10.740254	10.775775	10.799468	10.870598	10.918063	10.965564	11.036879	11.060668	11.096367
40	10.603501	10.662843	10.722242	10.757908	10.781696	10.853113	10.900767	10.948454	11.020048	11.043929	11.079765

Annual Mortgage Constant for Monthly Payment Loans

Loan Term	11.00%	11.0625%	11.10%	11.125%	11.1875%	11.20%	11.25%	11.30%	11.3125%	11.375%	11.40%
					Annual Interest Rate						
1	106.057990	106.092977	106.113973	106.127971	106.162970	106.169971	106.197976	106.225986	106.232989	106.268008	106.282017
2	55.929406	55.964233	55.985135	55.999072	56.033925	56.040897	56.068790	56.096691	56.103668	56.138559	56.152519
3	39.286461	39.321987	39.343313	39.357533	39.393098	39.400213	39.428682	39.457163	39.464285	39.499907	39.514161
4	31.014627	31.051062	31.072935	31.087522	31.124007	31.131307	31.160518	31.189744	31.197053	31.233614	31.248245
5	26.090908	26.128326	26.150793	26.165776	26.203257	26.210757	26.240769	26.270802	26.278313	26.315887	26.330925
6	22.840895	22.879327	22.902405	22.917797	22.956303	22.964009	22.994847	23.025708	23.033427	23.072043	23.087500
7	20.546924	20.586379	20.610073	20.625877	20.665418	20.673331	20.705000	20.736697	20.744625	20.784292	20.800171
8	18.850111	18.890587	18.914895	18.931111	18.971682	18.979802	19.012300	19.044829	19.052966	19.093680	19.109978
9	17.551033	17.592520	17.617437	17.634059	17.675651	17.683975	17.717295	17.750648	17.758991	17.800739	17.817453
10	16.530001	16.572484	16.598001	16.615024	16.657620	16.666146	16.700274	16.734437	16.742984	16.785750	16.802873
11	15.710819	15.754279	15.780384	15.797800	15.841382	15.850106	15.885025	15.919983	15.928729	15.972494	15.990016
12	15.042663	15.087079	15.113759	15.131560	15.176105	15.185022	15.220715	15.256449	15.265390	15.310129	15.328042
13	14.490328	14.535676	14.562917	14.581092	14.626576	14.635681	14.672128	14.708618	14.717748	14.763435	14.781729
14	14.028651	14.074904	14.102691	14.121229	14.167625	14.176913	14.214092	14.251317	14.260630	14.307238	14.325901
15	13.639163	13.686296	13.714611	13.733502	13.780782	13.790247	13.828135	13.866071	13.875562	13.923061	13.942081
16	13.308005	13.355987	13.384814	13.404046	13.452181	13.461817	13.500390	13.539013	13.548676	13.597036	13.616401
17	13.024568	13.073371	13.102690	13.122252	13.171211	13.181012	13.220247	13.259530	13.269359	13.318548	13.338245
18	12.780596	12.830190	12.859984	12.879862	12.929614	12.939574	12.979444	13.019365	13.029353	13.079339	13.099355
19	12.569567	12.619920	12.650171	12.670354	12.720867	12.730979	12.771460	12.811991	12.822132	12.872882	12.893204
20	12.386261	12.437343	12.468031	12.488506	12.539749	12.550007	12.591072	12.632188	12.642475	12.693957	12.714571
21	12.226451	12.278231	12.309338	12.330092	12.382033	12.392431	12.434054	12.475729	12.486155	12.538336	12.559230
22	12.086681	12.139128	12.170634	12.191655	12.244262	12.254793	12.296950	12.339157	12.349717	12.402562	12.423723
23	11.964096	12.017178	12.049065	12.070340	12.123582	12.134240	12.176904	12.219618	12.230305	12.283784	12.305198
24	11.856319	11.910005	11.942256	11.963772	12.017618	12.028397	12.071543	12.114739	12.125546	12.179626	12.201280
25	11.761357	11.815618	11.848213	11.869959	11.924378	11.935271	11.978875	12.022528	12.033449	12.088099	12.109981
26	11.677528	11.732335	11.765256	11.787219	11.842181	11.853183	11.897220	11.941305	11.952334	12.007524	12.029621
27	11.603402	11.658725	11.691956	11.714125	11.769601	11.780705	11.825152	11.869646	11.880777	11.936476	11.958776
28	11.537759	11.593571	11.627095	11.649458	11.705419	11.716620	11.761454	11.806334	11.817561	11.873740	11.896232
29	11.479553	11.535826	11.569625	11.592173	11.648591	11.659883	11.705081	11.750325	11.761643	11.818274	11.840947
30	11.427881	11.484589	11.518648	11.541368	11.598217	11.609596	11.655137	11.700722	11.712125	11.769182	11.792023
31	11.381961	11.439078	11.473382	11.496265	11.553520	11.564979	11.610842	11.656748	11.668232	11.725687	11.748688
32	11.341117	11.398619	11.433152	11.456188	11.513823	11.525358	11.571524	11.617732	11.629290	11.687120	11.710269
33	11.304757	11.362620	11.397370	11.420548	11.478541	11.490147	11.536596	11.583086	11.594714	11.652894	11.676183
34	11.272366	11.330568	11.365519	11.388832	11.447159	11.458831	11.505546	11.552299	11.563994	11.622501	11.645920
35	11.243492	11.302011	11.337151	11.360590	11.419229	11.430964	11.477927	11.524926	11.536682	11.595495	11.619035
36	11.217738	11.276553	11.311871	11.335427	11.394358	11.406151	11.453345	11.500575	11.512388	11.571485	11.595139
37	11.194755	11.253848	11.289330	11.312996	11.372199	11.384046	11.431456	11.478900	11.490767	11.550129	11.573889
38	11.174236	11.233587	11.269223	11.292992	11.352449	11.364346	11.411957	11.459601	11.471517	11.531126	11.554984
39	11.155908	11.215501	11.251281	11.275144	11.334837	11.346782	11.394580	11.442409	11.454371	11.514210	11.538158
40	11.139533	11.199350	11.235263	11.259215	11.319128	11.331116	11.379088	11.427089	11.439094	11.499146	11.523179

Loan Term	11.4375%	11.50%	11.5625%	11.60%	11.625%	11.70%	11.75%	11.80%	11.875%	11.90%	11.9375%
					Annual Interest Rate						
1	106.303033	106.338065	106.373103	106.394128	106.408147	106.450208	106.478255	106.506305	106.548388	106.562417	106.583464
2	56.173462	56.208378	56.243307	56.264271	56.278249	56.320196	56.348171	56.376154	56.418143	56.432144	56.453149
3	39.535548	39.571208	39.606887	39.628303	39.642585	39.685447	39.714038	39.742640	39.785567	39.799882	39.821360
4	31.270200	31.306811	31.343447	31.365441	31.380108	31.424135	31.453608	31.482893	31.527004	31.541716	31.563791
5	26.353492	26.391129	26.428796	26.451412	26.466495	26.511774	26.541985	26.572216	26.617599	26.632737	26.655453
6	23.110697	23.149387	23.188115	23.211368	23.226878	23.273443	23.304516	23.335612	23.382300	23.397875	23.421247
7	20.824001	20.863753	20.903546	20.927443	20.943382	20.991241	21.023180	21.055146	21.103146	21.119159	21.143192
8	19.134441	19.175249	19.216104	19.240640	19.257006	19.306152	19.338953	19.371784	19.421087	19.437537	19.462225
9	17.842540	17.884392	17.926297	17.951464	17.968253	18.018670	18.052322	18.086007	18.136597	18.153477	18.178812
10	16.828574	16.871453	16.914389	16.940178	16.957382	17.009047	17.043535	17.078059	17.129913	17.147215	17.173185
11	16.016319	16.060204	16.104150	16.130547	16.148157	16.201044	16.236350	16.271694	16.324783	16.342498	16.369089
12	15.354932	15.399799	15.444730	15.471720	15.489725	15.543804	15.579907	15.616050	15.670342	15.688459	15.715654
13	14.809190	14.855012	14.900902	14.928468	14.946858	15.002094	15.038971	15.075891	15.131351	15.149858	15.177640
14	14.353917	14.400665	14.447483	14.475608	14.494372	14.550729	14.588356	14.626028	14.682618	14.701503	14.729852
15	13.970633	14.018278	14.065995	14.094659	14.113783	14.171225	14.209576	14.247974	14.305655	14.324904	14.353800
16	13.645470	13.693980	13.742563	13.771748	13.791220	13.849706	13.888755	13.927852	13.986583	14.006184	14.035606
17	13.367814	13.417155	13.466572	13.496259	13.516065	13.575555	13.615275	13.655042	13.714783	13.734720	13.764648
18	13.129402	13.179543	13.229760	13.259928	13.280054	13.340507	13.380870	13.421281	13.481988	13.502247	13.532659
19	12.923711	12.974617	13.025601	13.056228	13.076662	13.138037	13.179014	13.220040	13.281670	13.302238	13.333112
20	12.745517	12.797156	12.848872	12.879939	12.900666	12.962921	13.004485	13.046098	13.108608	13.129469	13.160756
21	12.590595	12.642932	12.695347	12.726833	12.747840	12.810932	12.853055	12.895227	12.958575	12.979715	13.011448
22	12.455487	12.508489	12.561569	12.593454	12.614727	12.678616	12.721270	12.763972	12.828116	12.849521	12.881651
23	12.337341	12.390976	12.444687	12.476951	12.498475	12.563121	12.606278	12.649484	12.714381	12.736037	12.768543
24	12.233784	12.288010	12.342328	12.374951	12.396714	12.462076	12.505710	12.549391	12.615001	12.636894	12.669756
25	12.142826	12.197628	12.252504	12.285466	12.307456	12.373494	12.417578	12.461709	12.527991	12.550108	12.583305
26	12.062788	12.118127	12.173539	12.206821	12.229024	12.295701	12.340210	12.384764	12.451680	12.474008	12.507520
27	11.992248	12.048093	12.104010	12.137594	12.159998	12.227227	12.272185	12.317138	12.384650	12.407175	12.440984
28	11.929991	11.986313	12.042705	12.076573	12.099166	12.167010	12.212294	12.257621	12.325692	12.348404	12.382491
29	11.874976	11.931746	11.988584	12.022719	12.045490	12.113865	12.159502	12.205180	12.273775	12.296661	12.331009
30	11.826306	11.883497	11.940755	11.975140	11.998077	12.066950	12.112917	12.158924	12.228010	12.251058	12.285650
31	11.783209	11.840795	11.898445	11.933065	11.956158	12.025497	12.071772	12.118086	12.187631	12.210831	12.245650
32	11.745013	11.802968	11.860986	11.895825	11.919064	11.988838	12.035401	12.082003	12.151975	12.175317	12.210348
33	11.711135	11.769436	11.827796	11.862841	11.886216	11.956396	12.003228	12.050097	12.120467	12.143942	12.179170
34	11.681066	11.739690	11.798371	11.833607	11.857109	11.927667	11.974750	12.021867	12.092608	12.116205	12.151617
35	11.654363	11.713288	11.772267	11.807681	11.831301	11.902211	11.949527	11.996876	12.067961	12.091673	12.127254
36	11.630636	11.689841	11.749098	11.784677	11.808407	11.879645	11.927177	11.974741	12.046145	12.069962	12.105702
37	11.609544	11.669009	11.728524	11.764257	11.788089	11.859631	11.907364	11.955127	12.026827	12.050742	12.086628
38	11.590785	11.650492	11.710247	11.746123	11.770049	11.841873	11.889792	11.937738	12.009714	12.033719	12.069740
39	11.574095	11.634027	11.694005	11.730013	11.754027	11.826111	11.874202	11.922321	11.994549	12.018638	12.054784
40	11.559242	11.619382	11.679566	11.715696	11.739792	11.812118	11.860368	11.908644	11.981106	12.005272	12.041533

Annual Mortgage Constant for Monthly Payment Loans

Loan Term	12.00%	12.0625%	12.10%	12.125%	12.1875%	12.20%	12.25%	12.30%	12.3125%	12.375%	12.40%
1	106.618546	106.653635	106.674692	106.688730	106.723832	106.730853	106.758940	106.787031	106.794054	106.829175	106.843225
2	56.488167	56.523198	56.544222	56.558241	56.593297	56.600310	56.628366	56.656451	56.663448	56.698543	56.712584
3	39.857172	39.893003	39.914510	39.928853	39.964722	39.971898	40.000610	40.029333	40.036516	40.072442	40.086818
4	31.600603	31.637439	31.659554	31.674301	31.711188	31.718569	31.748100	31.777648	31.785037	31.821999	31.836791
5	26.693337	26.731253	26.754017	26.769199	26.807176	26.814775	26.845184	26.875613	26.883224	26.921293	26.936530
6	23.460231	23.499251	23.522681	23.538308	23.577401	23.585224	23.616531	23.647861	23.655697	23.694900	23.710591
7	21.183279	21.223409	21.247507	21.263580	21.303794	21.311841	21.344049	21.376283	21.384346	21.424684	21.440831
8	19.503410	19.544641	19.569403	19.585920	19.627245	19.635515	19.668617	19.701748	19.710035	19.751500	19.768099
9	18.221079	18.263397	18.288813	18.305767	18.348188	18.356678	18.390660	18.424675	18.433184	18.475759	18.492803
10	17.216514	17.259898	17.285955	17.303338	17.346833	17.355539	17.390384	17.425265	17.433990	17.477652	17.495132
11	16.413455	16.457880	16.484564	16.502365	16.546909	16.555825	16.591512	16.627237	16.636174	16.680896	16.698801
12	15.761030	15.806468	15.833761	15.851969	15.897533	15.906653	15.943159	15.979705	15.988848	16.034599	16.052917
13	15.223995	15.270416	15.298300	15.316902	15.363454	15.372773	15.410072	15.447413	15.456755	15.503503	15.522220
14	14.777154	14.824525	14.852981	14.871964	14.919471	14.928981	14.967046	15.005155	15.014689	15.062399	15.081502
15	14.402017	14.450304	14.479309	14.498661	14.547088	14.556781	14.595584	14.634432	14.644151	14.692787	14.712260
16	14.084702	14.133869	14.163404	14.183108	14.232419	14.242290	14.281801	14.321358	14.331254	14.380778	14.400608
17	13.814586	13.864598	13.894640	13.914683	13.964841	13.974881	14.015071	14.055307	14.065373	14.115747	14.135917
18	13.583405	13.634224	13.664752	13.685118	13.736085	13.746287	13.787125	13.828010	13.838238	13.889424	13.909918
19	13.384628	13.436219	13.467209	13.487884	13.539622	13.549979	13.591434	13.632937	13.643320	13.695278	13.716081
20	13.213034	13.265358	13.296789	13.317757	13.370230	13.380733	13.422776	13.464866	13.475395	13.528087	13.549184
21	13.064396	13.117418	13.149267	13.170514	13.223683	13.234326	13.276926	13.319572	13.330240	13.383628	13.405002
22	12.935260	12.988943	13.021188	13.042700	13.096529	13.107303	13.150430	13.193603	13.204403	13.258448	13.280086
23	12.822779	12.877087	12.909707	12.931468	12.985920	12.996819	13.040444	13.084114	13.095039	13.149703	13.171589
24	12.724583	12.779481	12.812455	12.834451	12.889492	12.900508	12.944602	12.988740	12.999782	13.055031	13.077150
25	12.638690	12.694145	12.727451	12.749669	12.805263	12.816390	12.860925	12.905504	12.916656	12.972454	12.994792
26	12.563430	12.619408	12.653027	12.675454	12.731567	12.742798	12.787748	12.832740	12.843995	12.900307	12.922851
27	12.497387	12.553856	12.587769	12.610391	12.666992	12.678320	12.723658	12.769038	12.780389	12.837183	12.859919
28	12.439356	12.496285	12.530474	12.553279	12.610336	12.621755	12.667457	12.713198	12.724639	12.781884	12.804799
29	12.388306	12.445666	12.480112	12.503088	12.560572	12.572076	12.618116	12.664196	12.675721	12.733386	12.756469
30	12.343351	12.401113	12.435799	12.458935	12.516817	12.528400	12.574757	12.621151	12.632756	12.690811	12.714050
31	12.303729	12.361866	12.396776	12.420061	12.478313	12.489970	12.536621	12.583308	12.594986	12.653405	12.676788
32	12.268778	12.327264	12.362383	12.385806	12.444403	12.456129	12.503054	12.550013	12.561758	12.620515	12.644033
33	12.237927	12.296738	12.332050	12.355602	12.414519	12.426308	12.473487	12.520699	12.532507	12.591577	12.615219
34	12.210678	12.269791	12.305282	12.328954	12.388167	12.400016	12.447430	12.494876	12.506742	12.566102	12.589859
35	12.186597	12.245989	12.281648	12.305430	12.364918	12.376821	12.424453	12.472115	12.484035	12.543663	12.567527
36	12.165306	12.224957	12.260770	12.284654	12.344397	12.356351	12.404184	12.452045	12.464015	12.523890	12.547853
37	12.146474	12.206364	12.242320	12.266298	12.326276	12.338276	12.386295	12.434341	12.446357	12.506459	12.530512
38	12.129810	12.189921	12.226008	12.250074	12.310268	12.322312	12.370502	12.418718	12.430776	12.491088	12.515224
39	12.115060	12.175375	12.211583	12.235730	12.296124	12.308207	12.356555	12.404927	12.417024	12.477529	12.501742
40	12.101999	12.162503	12.198823	12.223044	12.283621	12.295741	12.344234	12.392750	12.404883	12.465566	12.489848

Loan Term	12.4375%	12.50%	12.5625%	12.60%	12.625%	12.70%	12.75%	12.80%	12.875%	12.90%	12.9375%
1	106.864302	106.899435	106.934575	106.955662	106.969721	107.011905	107.040032	107.068164	107.110369	107.124439	107.145547
2	56.733650	56.768770	56.803903	56.824988	56.839048	56.881239	56.909377	56.937523	56.979757	56.993839	57.014965
3	40.108387	40.144351	40.180333	40.201932	40.216335	40.259562	40.288395	40.317240	40.360531	40.374967	40.396627
4	31.858987	31.895999	31.933036	31.955270	31.970098	32.014605	32.044297	32.074005	32.118596	32.133468	32.155783
5	26.959394	26.997526	27.035688	27.058601	27.073882	27.119754	27.150361	27.180987	27.226963	27.242298	27.265310
6	23.734139	23.773414	23.812726	23.836331	23.852075	23.899340	23.930880	23.962443	24.009831	24.025638	24.049360
7	21.465064	21.505486	21.545950	21.570248	21.586455	21.635115	21.667589	21.700090	21.748890	21.765170	21.789602
8	19.793012	19.834570	19.876175	19.901160	19.917826	19.967826	20.001268	20.034696	20.084895	20.101642	20.126777
9	18.518384	18.561061	18.603789	18.629450	18.646568	18.697969	18.732278	18.766618	18.818190	18.835397	18.861222
10	17.521368	17.565140	17.608967	17.635290	17.652849	17.705579	17.740777	17.776010	17.828924	17.846579	17.873079
11	16.725676	16.770515	16.815412	16.842379	16.860369	16.914393	16.950456	16.986557	17.040777	17.058869	17.086024
12	16.080412	16.126287	16.172224	16.199816	16.218223	16.273503	16.310405	16.347346	16.402832	16.421347	16.449137
13	15.550315	15.597193	15.644135	15.672331	15.691141	15.747634	15.785347	15.823101	15.879808	15.898731	15.927134
14	15.110176	15.158020	15.205931	15.234710	15.253909	15.311570	15.350063	15.388599	15.446482	15.465797	15.494790
15	14.741491	14.790265	14.839107	14.868446	14.888018	14.946801	14.986044	15.025330	15.084340	15.104032	15.133590
16	14.430373	14.480038	14.529772	14.559647	14.579577	14.639434	14.679394	14.719399	14.779487	14.799539	14.829637
17	14.166193	14.216710	14.267297	14.297684	14.317956	14.378839	14.419483	14.460173	14.521290	14.541685	14.572297
18	13.940681	13.992010	14.043411	14.074286	14.094883	14.156743	14.198039	14.239380	14.301476	14.322197	14.353299
19	13.747308	13.799410	13.851584	13.882923	13.903829	13.966617	14.008532	14.050491	14.113515	14.134545	14.166111
20	13.580851	13.633687	13.686594	13.718372	13.739572	13.803239	13.845739	13.888285	13.952186	13.973508	14.005513
21	13.437086	13.490616	13.544217	13.576412	13.597888	13.662386	13.705440	13.748539	13.813269	13.834867	13.867286
22	13.312563	13.366749	13.421005	13.453592	13.475330	13.540612	13.584188	13.627807	13.693318	13.715176	13.747984
23	13.204438	13.259242	13.314115	13.347072	13.369056	13.435075	13.479142	13.523251	13.589495	13.611597	13.644770
24	13.110349	13.165734	13.221187	13.254491	13.276707	13.343418	13.387945	13.432514	13.499445	13.521776	13.555291
25	13.028318	13.084250	13.140247	13.173876	13.196309	13.263669	13.308627	13.353626	13.421200	13.443745	13.477581
26	12.956685	13.013128	13.069634	13.103568	13.126204	13.194171	13.239532	13.284933	13.353107	13.375851	13.409986
27	12.894041	12.950962	13.007944	13.042163	13.064988	13.133521	13.179259	13.225034	13.293768	13.316698	13.351112
28	12.839190	12.896557	12.953983	12.988468	13.011469	13.080530	13.126617	13.172741	13.241996	13.265099	13.299770
29	12.791110	12.848892	12.906732	12.941464	12.964630	13.034181	13.080594	13.127042	13.196779	13.220043	13.254954
30	12.748924	12.807093	12.865318	12.900279	12.923597	12.993604	13.040319	13.087067	13.157253	13.180664	13.215798
31	12.711879	12.770407	12.828988	12.864163	12.887622	12.958052	13.005046	13.052072	13.122672	13.146221	13.181560
32	12.679324	12.738185	12.797097	12.832469	12.856059	12.926879	12.974132	13.021416	13.092399	13.116075	13.151603
33	12.650697	12.709866	12.769084	12.804638	12.828350	12.899531	12.947022	12.994543	13.065879	13.089672	13.125375
34	12.625509	12.684963	12.744463	12.780185	12.804009	12.875523	12.923235	12.970975	13.042636	13.066537	13.102401
35	12.603335	12.663053	12.722814	12.758691	12.782618	12.854439	12.902354	12.950295	13.022255	13.046255	13.082267
36	12.583808	12.643767	12.703769	12.739789	12.763811	12.835915	12.884016	12.932142	13.004377	13.028468	13.064615
37	12.566603	12.626786	12.687008	12.723160	12.747269	12.819633	12.867905	12.916201	12.988688	13.012862	13.049134
38	12.551439	12.611828	12.672253	12.708526	12.732715	12.805317	12.853746	12.902198	12.974916	12.999167	13.035552
39	12.538071	12.598648	12.659260	12.695644	12.719907	12.792727	12.841300	12.889894	12.962824	12.987144	13.023634
40	12.526282	12.587033	12.647816	12.684301	12.708631	12.781651	12.830356	12.879081	12.952204	12.976588	13.013173

Annual Mortgage Constant for Monthly Payment Loans

Loan Term	13.00%	13.0625%	13.10%	13.125%	13.1875%	13.20%	13.25%	13.30%	13.3125%	13.375%	13.40%
1	107.180731	107.215921	107.237039	107.251118	107.286322	107.293363	107.321531	107.349703	107.356747	107.391969	107.406060
2	57.050187	57.085421	57.106568	57.120668	57.155928	57.162982	57.191201	57.219428	57.226486	57.261784	57.275906
3	40.432742	40.468877	40.490566	40.505030	40.541202	40.548438	40.577392	40.606359	40.613602	40.649831	40.664328
4	32.192995	32.230232	32.252586	32.267494	32.304780	32.312241	32.342092	32.371959	32.379429	32.416790	32.431742
5	27.303688	27.342096	27.365156	27.380536	27.419006	27.426703	27.457506	27.488329	27.496037	27.534599	27.550033
6	24.088926	24.128528	24.152307	24.168167	24.207841	24.215780	24.247552	24.279346	24.287298	24.327081	24.343004
7	21.830356	21.871151	21.895648	21.911988	21.952865	21.961046	21.993784	22.026549	22.034744	22.075745	22.092158
8	20.168706	20.210681	20.235888	20.252702	20.294769	20.303188	20.336882	20.370605	20.379040	20.421245	20.438140
9	18.904305	18.947438	18.973342	18.990622	19.033856	19.042509	19.077140	19.111803	19.120474	19.163858	19.181226
10	17.917289	17.961553	17.988137	18.005871	18.050243	18.059124	18.094670	18.130250	18.139150	18.183685	18.201514
11	17.131329	17.176692	17.203938	17.222113	17.267591	17.276694	17.313127	17.349597	17.358720	17.404370	17.422646
12	16.495503	16.541930	16.569815	16.588417	16.634965	16.644282	16.681573	16.718903	16.728241	16.774970	16.793678
13	15.974523	16.021976	16.050478	16.069491	16.117070	16.126593	16.164711	16.202869	16.212415	16.260181	16.279305
14	15.543163	15.591602	15.620696	15.640105	15.688674	15.698395	15.737307	15.776260	15.786004	15.834766	15.854289
15	15.182906	15.232289	15.261951	15.281739	15.331255	15.341166	15.380837	15.420550	15.430485	15.480199	15.500103
16	14.879854	14.930139	14.960343	14.980493	15.030913	15.041005	15.081400	15.121839	15.131955	15.182576	15.202843
17	14.623373	14.674518	14.705237	14.725731	14.777012	14.787276	14.828360	14.869488	14.879776	14.931259	14.951871
18	14.405190	14.457151	14.488360	14.509180	14.561278	14.571705	14.613443	14.655223	14.665675	14.717975	14.738914
19	14.218775	14.271509	14.303182	14.324311	14.377181	14.387763	14.430118	14.472517	14.483123	14.536195	14.557442
20	14.058909	14.112372	14.144483	14.165904	14.219503	14.230231	14.273169	14.316150	14.326902	14.380701	14.402239
21	13.921370	13.975522	14.008046	14.029741	14.084027	14.094892	14.138378	14.181907	14.192796	14.247279	14.269090
22	13.802716	13.857515	13.890426	13.912380	13.967310	13.978304	14.022306	14.066348	14.077365	14.132489	14.154556
23	13.700111	13.755517	13.788791	13.810987	13.866522	13.877636	13.922119	13.966643	13.977780	14.033504	14.055811
24	13.611202	13.667176	13.700790	13.723212	13.779312	13.790539	13.835472	13.880445	13.891695	13.947978	13.970508
25	13.534024	13.590528	13.624460	13.647093	13.703719	13.715052	13.760405	13.805797	13.817151	13.873955	13.896693
26	13.466925	13.523924	13.558152	13.580982	13.638098	13.649528	13.695272	13.741053	13.752504	13.809793	13.832724
27	13.408512	13.465971	13.500473	13.523486	13.581058	13.592579	13.638686	13.684828	13.696369	13.754107	13.777218
28	13.357600	13.415486	13.450244	13.473426	13.531421	13.543026	13.589469	13.635946	13.647571	13.705724	13.729001
29	13.313182	13.371463	13.406457	13.429797	13.488183	13.499866	13.546620	13.593406	13.605108	13.663646	13.687075
30	13.274394	13.333042	13.368254	13.391739	13.450486	13.462241	13.509282	13.556354	13.568127	13.627019	13.650590
31	13.240497	13.299483	13.334897	13.358516	13.417596	13.429418	13.476723	13.524058	13.535897	13.595115	13.618816
32	13.210854	13.270151	13.305751	13.329494	13.388881	13.400764	13.448313	13.495890	13.507789	13.567307	13.591127
33	13.184916	13.244500	13.280271	13.304127	13.363797	13.375736	13.423508	13.471308	13.483262	13.543056	13.566985
34	13.162207	13.222055	13.257984	13.281944	13.341873	13.353863	13.401841	13.449845	13.461849	13.521896	13.545925
35	13.142318	13.202408	13.238480	13.262536	13.322703	13.334741	13.382907	13.431097	13.443148	13.503425	13.527546
36	13.124890	13.185202	13.221407	13.245551	13.305935	13.318016	13.366354	13.414715	13.426808	13.487296	13.511501
37	13.109614	13.170130	13.206455	13.230679	13.291262	13.303383	13.351878	13.400395	13.412527	13.473208	13.497489
38	13.096221	13.156922	13.193358	13.217655	13.278420	13.290577	13.339216	13.387874	13.400042	13.460898	13.485249
39	13.084474	13.145345	13.181882	13.206246	13.267177	13.279366	13.328136	13.376924	13.389124	13.450140	13.474554
40	13.074170	13.135196	13.171825	13.196250	13.257331	13.269551	13.318440	13.367345	13.379575	13.440736	13.465207

Loan Term	13.4375%	13.50%	13.5625%	13.60%	13.625%	13.70%	13.75%	13.80%	13.875%	13.90%	13.9375%
1	107.427198	107.462433	107.497674	107.518822	107.532922	107.575227	107.603436	107.631649	107.673976	107.688087	107.709255
2	57.297094	57.332417	57.367753	57.388961	57.403102	57.445537	57.473837	57.502146	57.544623	57.558786	57.580035
3	40.686078	40.722345	40.758630	40.780410	40.794934	40.838524	40.867599	40.896686	40.940340	40.954897	40.976738
4	32.454176	32.491588	32.529024	32.551497	32.566485	32.611470	32.641481	32.671507	32.716577	32.731608	32.754162
5	27.573192	27.611815	27.650469	27.673676	27.689153	27.735615	27.766614	27.797632	27.844196	27.859728	27.883033
6	24.366960	24.406755	24.446645	24.470597	24.486572	24.534532	24.566534	24.598559	24.646639	24.662677	24.686745
7	22.116788	22.157871	22.198996	22.223690	22.240161	22.289614	22.322615	22.355643	22.405233	22.421776	22.446603
8	20.463495	20.505792	20.548133	20.573560	20.590521	20.641446	20.675433	20.709448	20.760526	20.777567	20.803141
9	19.207292	19.250777	19.294311	19.320456	19.337895	19.390262	19.425212	19.460195	19.512728	19.530255	19.556560
10	18.228273	18.272915	18.317610	18.344453	18.362359	18.416128	18.452017	18.487940	18.541889	18.559888	18.586904
11	17.450077	17.495842	17.541663	17.569183	17.587541	17.642669	17.679466	17.716300	17.771617	17.790075	17.817777
12	16.821758	16.868606	16.915514	16.943687	16.962481	17.018920	17.056593	17.094304	17.150941	17.169839	17.198204
13	16.308010	16.355900	16.403853	16.432564	16.451867	16.509565	16.548080	16.586634	16.644537	16.663858	16.692858
14	15.883592	15.932482	15.981435	16.010838	16.030452	16.089356	16.128676	16.168036	16.227151	16.246876	16.276482
15	15.529978	15.579823	15.629732	15.659709	15.679706	15.739760	15.779847	15.819976	15.880245	15.900355	15.930539
16	15.233263	15.284016	15.334836	15.365359	15.385720	15.446846	15.487685	15.528544	15.589909	15.610385	15.641118
17	14.982809	15.034425	15.086108	15.117149	15.137856	15.200041	15.241550	15.283100	15.345503	15.366325	15.397577
18	14.770342	14.822775	14.875275	14.906806	14.927840	14.991005	15.033167	15.075371	15.138753	15.159902	15.191643
19	14.589333	14.642537	14.695808	14.727801	14.749143	14.813232	14.856010	14.898828	14.963133	14.984589	15.016791
20	14.434566	14.488496	14.542492	14.574920	14.596552	14.661509	14.704865	14.748261	14.813432	14.835175	14.867809
21	14.301826	14.356438	14.411114	14.443950	14.465854	14.531625	14.575523	14.619460	14.685441	14.707454	14.740492
22	14.187676	14.242927	14.298240	14.331458	14.353616	14.420148	14.464552	14.508995	14.575732	14.597997	14.631413
23	14.089289	14.145136	14.201045	14.234619	14.257014	14.324256	14.369132	14.414046	14.481488	14.503987	14.537754
24	14.004321	14.060725	14.117188	14.151094	14.173709	14.241612	14.286928	14.332280	14.400376	14.423093	14.457185
25	13.930818	13.987739	14.044717	14.078931	14.101752	14.170269	14.215992	14.261750	14.330453	14.353372	14.387766
26	13.867138	13.924539	13.981996	14.016496	14.039507	14.108593	14.154693	14.200827	14.270092	14.293197	14.327870
27	13.811900	13.869746	13.927645	13.962410	13.985597	14.055208	14.101657	14.148138	14.217921	14.241198	14.276129
28	13.763930	13.822188	13.880496	13.915505	13.938855	14.008951	14.055722	14.102523	14.172784	14.196219	14.231387
29	13.722234	13.780871	13.839556	13.874791	13.898290	13.968833	14.015900	14.062996	14.133695	14.157277	14.192662
30	13.685959	13.744946	13.803979	13.839421	13.863058	13.934012	13.981350	14.028717	14.099819	14.123534	14.159119
31	13.654379	13.713688	13.773040	13.808672	13.832435	13.903767	13.951355	13.998969	14.070441	14.094278	14.130045
32	13.626869	13.686472	13.746117	13.781924	13.805803	13.877480	13.925297	13.973138	14.044948	14.068896	14.104831
33	13.602890	13.662764	13.722678	13.758644	13.782630	13.854623	13.902648	13.950697	14.022815	14.046866	14.082953
34	13.581980	13.642102	13.702260	13.738373	13.762456	13.834737	13.882953	13.931192	14.003591	14.027734	14.063960
35	13.563738	13.624086	13.684469	13.720715	13.744886	13.817431	13.865821	13.914232	13.986887	14.011115	14.047467
36	13.547818	13.608373	13.668960	13.705328	13.729579	13.802364	13.850912	13.899480	13.972368	13.996673	14.033140
37	13.533920	13.594663	13.655436	13.691915	13.716240	13.789243	13.837935	13.886645	13.959744	13.984119	14.020690
38	13.521783	13.582698	13.643641	13.680220	13.704612	13.777813	13.826635	13.875475	13.948766	13.973204	14.009870
39	13.511183	13.572253	13.633350	13.670021	13.694473	13.767854	13.816793	13.865752	13.939216	13.963712	14.000463
40	13.501922	13.563134	13.624370	13.661124	13.685631	13.759175	13.808224	13.857287	13.930908	13.955456	13.992283

Annual Mortgage Constant for Monthly Payment Loans

Loan Term	14.00%	14.0625%	14.10%	14.125%	14.1875%	14.20%	14.25%	14.30%	14.3125%	14.375%	14.40%
1	107.744541	107.779833	107.801011	107.815132	107.850436	107.857498	107.885747	107.914001	107.921065	107.956389	107.970520
2	57.615460	57.650897	57.672166	57.686347	57.721810	57.728904	57.757285	57.785675	57.792773	57.828274	57.842478
3	41.013156	41.049592	41.071463	41.086047	41.122521	41.129818	41.159014	41.188221	41.195525	41.232056	41.246673
4	32.791772	32.829407	32.851999	32.867066	32.904750	32.912290	32.942459	32.972645	32.980193	33.017952	33.033062
5	27.921901	27.960799	27.984152	27.999728	28.038686	28.046482	28.077676	28.108889	28.116696	28.155746	28.171374
6	24.726887	24.767065	24.791189	24.807279	24.847529	24.855583	24.887814	24.920068	24.928135	24.968492	24.984644
7	22.488014	22.529446	22.554356	22.570958	22.612491	22.620802	22.654065	22.687353	22.695679	22.737334	22.754007
8	20.845801	20.888507	20.914152	20.931257	20.974053	20.982618	21.016894	21.051200	21.059780	21.102711	21.119897
9	19.600441	19.644372	19.670754	19.688352	19.732381	19.741193	19.776460	19.811758	19.820587	19.864763	19.882448
10	18.631972	18.677093	18.704191	18.722267	18.767494	18.776546	18.812773	18.849035	18.858105	18.903489	18.921658
11	17.863993	17.910265	17.938055	17.956593	18.002977	18.012260	18.049416	18.086607	18.095910	18.142460	18.161096
12	17.245525	17.292905	17.321360	17.340343	17.387839	17.397345	17.435393	17.473478	17.483005	17.530675	17.549759
13	16.741239	16.789680	16.818774	16.838182	16.886744	16.896464	16.935366	16.974307	16.984048	17.032789	17.052303
14	16.325875	16.375331	16.405034	16.424848	16.474428	16.484351	16.524068	16.563825	16.573770	16.623533	16.643455
15	15.980897	16.031317	16.061600	16.081801	16.132347	16.142464	16.182956	16.223488	16.233627	16.284360	16.304670
16	15.692390	15.743726	15.774558	15.795126	15.846589	15.856889	15.898114	15.939380	15.949703	16.001353	16.022031
17	15.449715	15.501916	15.533268	15.554182	15.606510	15.616983	15.658901	15.700860	15.711356	15.763872	15.784896
18	15.244597	15.297614	15.329455	15.350695	15.403839	15.414475	15.457045	15.499655	15.510313	15.563644	15.584993
19	15.070512	15.124296	15.156596	15.178142	15.232051	15.242841	15.286022	15.329243	15.340054	15.394148	15.415803
20	14.922250	14.976752	15.009483	15.031316	15.085941	15.096874	15.140627	15.184420	15.195374	15.250181	15.272120
21	14.795605	14.850779	14.883912	14.906013	14.961307	14.972373	15.016661	15.060986	15.072073	15.127545	15.149750
22	14.687153	14.742952	14.776460	14.798810	14.854727	14.865917	14.910702	14.955523	14.966734	15.022823	15.045275
23	14.594077	14.650459	14.684315	14.706897	14.763392	14.774698	14.819943	14.865224	14.876550	14.933212	14.955893
24	14.514050	14.570971	14.605150	14.627947	14.684978	14.696391	14.742063	14.787770	14.799202	14.856394	14.879286
25	14.445133	14.502553	14.537031	14.560026	14.617552	14.629064	14.675130	14.721230	14.732760	14.790441	14.813528
26	14.385700	14.443581	14.478335	14.501514	14.559496	14.571099	14.617529	14.663991	14.675611	14.733742	14.757008
27	14.334386	14.392693	14.427700	14.451048	14.509451	14.521137	14.567901	14.614696	14.626399	14.684944	14.708375
28	14.290037	14.348734	14.383974	14.407477	14.466267	14.478030	14.525101	14.572201	14.583980	14.642904	14.666486
29	14.251673	14.310729	14.346183	14.369828	14.428971	14.440805	14.488157	14.535537	14.547386	14.606656	14.630376
30	14.218461	14.277845	14.313496	14.337271	14.396738	14.408636	14.456245	14.503880	14.515793	14.575380	14.599226
31	14.189690	14.249375	14.285204	14.309099	14.368861	14.380818	14.428662	14.476530	14.488500	14.548376	14.572337
32	14.164752	14.224711	14.260704	14.284707	14.344739	14.356750	14.404807	14.452887	14.464911	14.525049	14.549114
33	14.143126	14.203335	14.239477	14.263578	14.323856	14.335915	14.384167	14.432440	14.444512	14.504889	14.529049
34	14.124364	14.184800	14.221077	14.245268	14.305769	14.317873	14.366301	14.414749	14.426864	14.487458	14.511704
35	14.108079	14.168722	14.205122	14.229395	14.290098	14.302243	14.350831	14.399438	14.411592	14.472382	14.496706
36	14.093942	14.154772	14.191284	14.215631	14.276517	14.288698	14.337431	14.386181	14.398372	14.459339	14.483733
37	14.081664	14.142664	14.179277	14.203691	14.264743	14.276957	14.325821	14.374702	14.386924	14.448052	14.472510
38	14.070999	14.132153	14.168857	14.193332	14.254534	14.266777	14.315760	14.364758	14.377010	14.438282	14.462797
39	14.061733	14.123026	14.159813	14.184342	14.245680	14.257950	14.307040	14.356143	14.368421	14.429823	14.454390
40	14.053681	14.115099	14.151961	14.176539	14.237999	14.250294	14.299479	14.348678	14.360980	14.422499	14.447112

Loan Term	14.4375%	14.50%	14.5625%	14.60%	14.625%	14.70%	14.75%	14.80%	14.875%	14.90%	14.9375%
1	107.991719	108.027055	108.062398	108.083607	108.097747	108.140174	108.168464	108.196758	108.239207	108.253358	108.274588
2	57.863788	57.899314	57.934852	57.956182	57.970404	58.013082	58.041544	58.070015	58.112736	58.126980	58.148350
3	41.268605	41.305173	41.341760	41.363721	41.378365	41.422317	41.451633	41.480961	41.524769	41.539654	41.561676
4	33.055735	33.093543	33.131376	33.154088	33.169234	33.214696	33.245023	33.275366	33.320911	33.336101	33.358892
5	28.194826	28.233937	28.273079	28.296578	28.312250	28.359296	28.390684	28.422092	28.469240	28.484965	28.508563
6	25.008884	25.049312	25.089776	25.114071	25.130275	25.178921	25.211380	25.243862	25.292627	25.308894	25.333304
7	22.779029	22.820765	22.862541	22.887627	22.904358	22.954592	22.988113	23.021660	23.072029	23.088831	23.114047
8	21.145688	21.188708	21.231774	21.257635	21.274885	21.326677	21.361240	21.395832	21.447774	21.465102	21.491108
9	19.908989	19.953263	19.997586	20.024203	20.041957	20.095267	20.130846	20.166456	20.219929	20.237768	20.264543
10	18.948926	18.994415	19.039956	19.067305	19.085549	19.140329	19.176891	19.213485	19.268440	19.286774	19.314291
11	18.189066	18.235726	18.282441	18.310497	18.329212	18.385408	18.422916	18.460459	18.516839	18.535650	18.563882
12	17.578403	17.626188	17.674030	17.702763	17.721930	17.779485	17.817900	17.856352	17.914098	17.933364	17.962281
13	17.081590	17.130451	17.179370	17.208750	17.228349	17.287201	17.326482	17.365801	17.424850	17.444551	17.474121
14	16.673357	16.723241	16.773186	16.803182	16.823191	16.883277	16.923382	16.963525	17.023811	17.043925	17.074114
15	16.335154	16.386010	16.436928	16.467507	16.487906	16.549160	16.590045	16.630968	16.692425	16.712930	16.743706
16	16.053066	16.104841	16.156677	16.187809	16.208575	16.270933	16.312554	16.354213	16.416774	16.437647	16.468975
17	15.816845	15.869091	15.921793	15.953444	15.974556	16.037952	16.080265	16.122616	16.186216	16.207434	16.239281
18	15.617036	15.670490	15.724004	15.756142	15.777580	15.841950	15.884911	15.927911	15.992482	16.014024	16.046356
19	15.448302	15.502518	15.556793	15.589387	15.611128	15.676408	15.719976	15.763581	15.829060	15.850904	15.883689
20	15.305047	15.359973	15.414958	15.447977	15.470002	15.536131	15.580264	15.624433	15.690756	15.712881	15.746087
21	15.183075	15.238662	15.294308	15.327723	15.350011	15.416929	15.461586	15.506279	15.573385	15.595772	15.629368
22	15.078969	15.135172	15.191430	15.225212	15.247744	15.315393	15.360537	15.405715	15.473546	15.496174	15.530131
23	14.989929	15.046701	15.103527	15.137648	15.160406	15.228731	15.274324	15.319949	15.388450	15.411301	15.445591
24	14.913639	14.970936	15.028286	15.062720	15.085687	15.154635	15.200642	15.246680	15.315797	15.338852	15.373450
25	14.848173	14.905955	14.963787	14.998510	15.021668	15.091190	15.137577	15.183994	15.253678	15.276921	15.311799
26	14.791922	14.850150	14.908425	14.943413	14.966747	15.036795	15.083531	15.130296	15.200498	15.223914	15.259050
27	14.743535	14.802171	14.860853	14.896083	14.919579	14.990110	15.037165	15.084248	15.154924	15.178497	15.213868
28	14.701871	14.760882	14.819936	14.855389	14.879032	14.950003	14.997350	15.044724	15.115832	15.139548	15.175134
29	14.665968	14.725321	14.784715	14.820370	14.844148	14.915521	14.963134	15.010772	15.082274	15.106121	15.141901
30	14.635006	14.694671	14.754374	14.790214	14.814115	14.885854	14.933709	14.981587	15.053447	15.077412	15.113370
31	14.608289	14.668238	14.728223	14.764231	14.788243	14.860314	14.908389	14.956485	15.028671	15.052743	15.088861
32	14.585222	14.645430	14.705671	14.741831	14.765945	14.838317	14.886591	14.934885	15.007364	15.031534	15.067798
33	14.565299	14.625740	14.686213	14.722512	14.746717	14.819362	14.867816	14.916289	14.989034	15.013292	15.049687
34	14.548082	14.608736	14.669419	14.705843	14.730131	14.803023	14.851640	14.900275	14.973259	14.997596	15.034109
35	14.533200	14.594046	14.654919	14.691456	14.715819	14.788934	14.837698	14.886478	14.959679	14.984087	15.020707
36	14.520333	14.581352	14.642396	14.679035	14.703466	14.776781	14.825678	14.874589	14.947985	14.972457	15.009173
37	14.509204	14.570379	14.631579	14.668309	14.692801	14.766297	14.815313	14.864342	14.937912	14.962457	14.999244
38	14.499576	14.560893	14.622231	14.659045	14.683591	14.757250	14.806372	14.855508	14.929235	14.953817	14.990695
39	14.491246	14.552690	14.614153	14.651041	14.675636	14.749442	14.798660	14.847890	14.921758	14.946386	14.983334
40	14.484038	14.545595	14.607171	14.644125	14.668765	14.742701	14.792006	14.841321	14.915315	14.939985	14.976994

Annual Mortgage Constant for Monthly Payment Loans

Loan Term	15.00%	15.25%	15.50%	15.75%	16.00%	16.25%	16.50%	16.75%	17.0000%	17.250%	17.50%
1	108.309975	108.451587	108.593300	108.735114	108.877029	109.019046	109.161164	109.303383	109.445702	109.588123	109.730645
2	58.183978	58.326613	58.469451	58.612491	58.755733	58.899176	59.042822	59.186669	59.330717	59.474967	59.619418
3	41.598394	41.745456	41.892817	42.040479	42.188440	42.336700	42.485259	42.634117	42.783273	42.932727	43.082479
4	33.396898	33.549167	33.701831	33.854887	34.008337	34.162179	34.316412	34.471036	34.626051	34.781455	34.937248
5	28.547916	28.705631	28.863829	29.022509	29.181669	29.341308	29.501425	29.662020	29.823091	29.984637	30.146656
6	25.374016	25.537219	25.700986	25.865317	26.030209	26.195661	26.361670	26.528237	26.695357	26.863031	27.031255
7	23.156106	23.324741	23.494016	23.663929	23.834477	24.005657	24.177467	24.349904	24.522966	24.696650	24.870953
8	21.534486	21.708443	21.883107	22.058475	22.234543	22.411308	22.588765	22.766912	22.945745	23.125259	23.305452
9	20.309205	20.488334	20.668230	20.848887	21.030301	21.212467	21.395379	21.579034	21.763426	21.948550	22.134401
10	19.360195	19.544321	19.729264	19.915017	20.101575	20.288929	20.477076	20.666008	20.855718	21.046202	21.237451
11	18.610979	18.799908	18.989694	19.180329	19.371807	19.564119	19.757258	19.951216	20.145985	20.341557	20.537925
12	18.010521	18.204041	18.398451	18.593742	18.789904	18.986927	19.184803	19.383522	19.583075	19.783452	19.984644
13	17.523450	17.721341	17.920147	18.119855	18.320454	18.521933	18.724282	18.927489	19.131543	19.336434	19.542149
14	17.124477	17.326513	17.529479	17.733360	17.938145	18.143820	18.350373	18.557790	18.766059	18.975168	19.185103
15	16.795045	17.000997	17.207884	17.415693	17.624409	17.834017	18.044503	18.255853	18.468051	18.681085	18.894939
16	16.521235	16.730870	16.941440	17.152930	17.365324	17.578605	17.792756	18.007763	18.223609	18.440278	18.657754
17	16.292405	16.505493	16.719510	16.934438	17.150259	17.366955	17.584509	17.802904	18.022121	18.242143	18.462954
18	16.100289	16.316603	16.533834	16.751961	16.970965	17.190827	17.411527	17.633047	17.855368	18.078472	18.302340
19	15.938376	16.157695	16.377912	16.599006	16.820956	17.043740	17.267340	17.491734	17.716902	17.942826	18.169486
20	15.801475	16.023584	16.246568	16.470405	16.695071	16.920546	17.146808	17.373835	17.601607	17.830103	18.059303
21	15.685406	15.910098	16.135637	16.362001	16.589166	16.817109	17.045807	17.275239	17.505382	17.736216	17.967721
22	15.586770	15.813846	16.041739	16.270425	16.499880	16.730080	16.961002	17.192622	17.424920	17.657873	17.891459
23	15.502783	15.732054	15.962109	16.192923	16.424472	16.656730	16.889674	17.123282	17.357530	17.592396	17.827859
24	15.431151	15.662436	15.894471	16.127230	16.360687	16.594818	16.829598	17.065003	17.301012	17.537602	17.774751
25	15.369967	15.603098	15.836943	16.071474	16.306667	16.542495	16.778936	17.015965	17.253559	17.491697	17.730356
26	15.317645	15.552462	15.787956	16.024099	16.260866	16.498231	16.736170	16.974661	17.213679	17.453204	17.693213
27	15.272854	15.509209	15.746202	15.983807	16.221998	16.460751	16.700040	16.939843	17.180137	17.420901	17.662114
28	15.234475	15.472229	15.710583	15.949512	16.188989	16.428991	16.669493	16.910472	17.151907	17.393776	17.636059
29	15.201566	15.440589	15.680176	15.920301	16.160937	16.402061	16.643650	16.885682	17.128133	17.370986	17.614218
30	15.173328	15.413502	15.654203	15.895405	16.137084	16.379215	16.621777	16.864747	17.108104	17.351829	17.595903
31	15.149085	15.390300	15.632005	15.874178	16.116792	16.359825	16.603255	16.847061	17.091222	17.335721	17.580538
32	15.128262	15.370415	15.613026	15.856070	16.099522	16.343361	16.587565	16.832114	17.076989	17.322171	17.567644
33	15.110368	15.353368	15.596793	15.840617	16.084819	16.329377	16.574270	16.819478	17.064985	17.310771	17.556821
34	15.094986	15.338749	15.582903	15.827427	16.072298	16.317496	16.563001	16.808794	17.054858	17.301177	17.547734
35	15.081760	15.326207	15.571016	15.816165	16.061633	16.307400	16.553447	16.799757	17.046314	17.293101	17.540104
36	15.070383	15.315445	15.560840	15.806547	16.052546	16.298818	16.545346	16.792113	17.039103	17.286302	17.533696
37	15.060597	15.306208	15.552127	15.798331	16.044802	16.291523	16.538476	16.785646	17.033018	17.280578	17.528313
38	15.052175	15.298280	15.544665	15.791312	16.038203	16.285320	16.532649	16.780174	17.027881	17.275758	17.523792
39	15.044928	15.291472	15.538274	15.785315	16.032577	16.280046	16.527706	16.775543	17.023544	17.271698	17.519993
40	15.038690	15.285627	15.532799	15.780190	16.027781	16.275560	16.523512	16.771623	17.019883	17.268279	17.516801

Loan Term	17.75%	18.00%	18.25%	18.50%	18.75%	19.00%	20.00%	21.00%	22.000%	23.00%	24.00%
1	109.873268	110.015991	110.158816	110.301741	110.444767	110.587894	111.161407	111.736529	112.313256	112.891586	113.471516
2	59.764069	59.908922	60.053976	60.199230	60.344685	60.490341	61.074963	61.662781	62.253786	62.847967	63.445317
3	43.232528	43.382875	43.533518	43.684457	43.835693	43.987224	44.596300	45.210081	45.828544	46.451666	47.079423
4	35.093430	35.250000	35.406956	35.564299	35.722028	35.880142	36.516435	37.158834	37.807293	38.461766	39.122203
5	30.309149	30.472113	30.635547	30.799451	30.963823	31.128661	31.792660	32.464032	33.142694	33.828565	34.521559
6	27.200029	27.369349	27.539215	27.709625	27.880576	28.052068	28.743391	29.443196	30.151353	30.867731	31.592197
7	25.045872	25.221406	25.397550	25.574303	25.751662	25.929623	26.647439	27.374672	28.111133	28.856632	29.610974
8	23.486319	23.667857	23.850062	24.032929	24.216456	24.400638	25.143840	25.897212	26.660495	27.433430	28.215753
9	22.320974	22.508265	22.696268	22.884978	23.074391	23.264500	24.031802	24.809841	25.598282	26.396787	27.205018
10	21.429461	21.622224	21.815734	22.009985	22.204970	22.400683	23.190681	23.991801	24.803625	25.625736	26.457716
11	20.735080	20.933014	21.131721	21.331191	21.531417	21.732391	22.543608	23.366160	24.199543	25.043257	25.896809
12	20.186641	20.389434	20.593014	20.797370	21.002493	21.208377	22.039303	22.881614	23.734722	24.598050	25.471031
13	19.748678	19.956010	20.164134	20.373040	20.582715	20.793150	21.642266	22.502675	23.373706	24.254709	25.145053
14	19.395853	19.607404	19.819744	20.032861	20.246742	20.461375	21.327185	22.204066	23.091276	23.988099	24.893847
15	19.109599	19.325052	19.541284	19.758280	19.976028	20.194512	21.075588	21.967347	22.869072	23.779962	24.699284
16	18.876023	19.095068	19.314875	19.535428	19.756712	19.978713	20.873593	21.778800	22.693472	23.616794	24.548003
17	18.684537	18.906874	19.129951	19.353750	19.578255	19.803450	20.710831	21.628053	22.554212	23.488463	24.430020
18	18.526954	18.752297	18.978351	19.205100	19.432525	19.660611	20.579235	21.507165	22.443464	23.387270	24.337788
19	18.396863	18.624938	18.853694	19.083112	19.313174	19.543863	20.472558	21.409986	22.355196	23.307315	24.265553
20	18.289188	18.519738	18.750935	18.982759	19.215193	19.448218	20.385895	21.331715	22.284719	23.244040	24.208898
21	18.199875	18.432659	18.666053	18.900039	19.134598	19.369712	20.315371	21.268575	22.228369	23.193901	24.164412
22	18.125659	18.360453	18.595819	18.831741	19.068197	19.305172	20.257898	21.217575	22.183264	23.154132	24.129450
23	18.063898	18.300494	18.537625	18.775273	19.013419	19.252045	20.211008	21.176340	22.147126	23.122563	24.101954
24	18.012439	18.250644	18.489349	18.728533	18.968178	19.208267	20.172716	21.142973	22.118152	23.097486	24.080318
25	17.969517	18.209159	18.449263	18.689810	18.930781	19.172160	20.141421	21.115954	22.094908	23.077558	24.063285
26	17.933687	18.174606	18.415591	18.657703	18.899845	19.142360	20.115830	21.094064	22.076253	23.061714	24.049872
27	17.903756	18.145807	18.388250	18.631066	18.874238	19.117750	20.094891	21.076321	22.061275	23.049114	24.039307
28	17.878736	18.121790	18.365201	18.608954	18.853030	19.097416	20.077752	21.061935	22.049246	23.039091	24.030982
29	17.857813	18.101751	18.346015	18.590590	18.835459	19.080608	20.063718	21.050267	22.039582	23.031116	24.024423
30	17.840307	18.085024	18.330039	18.575334	18.820896	19.066710	20.052224	21.040801	22.031817	23.024770	24.019253
31	17.825656	18.071058	18.316730	18.562656	18.808822	19.055215	20.042808	21.033121	22.025578	23.019719	24.015178
32	17.813390	18.059394	18.305641	18.552118	18.798810	19.045706	20.035093	21.026888	22.020563	23.015699	24.011966
33	17.803119	18.049650	18.296400	18.543356	18.790506	19.037808	20.028770	21.021829	22.016532	23.012499	24.009434
34	17.794516	18.041508	18.288697	18.536070	18.783617	19.031326	20.023587	21.017723	22.013292	23.009951	24.007438
35	17.787309	18.034703	18.282274	18.530011	18.777901	19.025937	20.019339	21.014390	22.010687	23.007923	24.005865
36	17.781271	18.029016	18.276920	18.524970	18.773159	19.021475	20.015857	21.011684	22.008593	23.006308	24.004624
37	17.776212	18.024262	18.272454	18.520778	18.769223	19.017782	20.013002	21.009487	22.006909	23.005023	24.003646
38	17.771972	18.020288	18.268730	18.517289	18.765957	19.014725	20.010662	21.007703	22.005555	23.003999	24.002875
39	17.768419	18.016966	18.265625	18.514387	18.763246	19.012193	20.008743	21.006255	22.004467	23.003184	24.002267
40	17.765441	18.014188	18.263034	18.511973	18.760996	19.010097	20.007169	21.005079	22.003592	23.002536	24.001787

Annual Mortgage Constant for Monthly Payment Loans

5.50% Interest Rate   5.50% Interest Rate

Years	0	1	2	3	Number of Months 4	5	6	7	8	9	10	11
2	52.914787	50.912302	49.064015	47.352793	45.763951	44.284829	42.904454	41.613270	40.402917	39.266044	38.196170	37.187551
3	36.235082	35.334211	34.480865	33.671386	32.902487	32.171196	31.474828	30.810947	30.177337	29.571980	28.993034	28.438812
4	27.907770	27.398489	26.909662	26.440086	25.988651	25.554331	25.136173	24.733297	24.344883	23.970171	23.608452	23.259066
5	22.921395	22.594863	22.278931	21.973096	21.676882	21.389847	21.111573	20.841667	20.579761	20.325506	20.078576	19.838659
6	19.605465	19.378716	19.158151	18.943524	18.734599	18.531154	18.332979	18.139874	17.951648	17.768120	17.589119	17.414482
7	17.244051	17.077679	16.915225	16.756552	16.601533	16.450043	16.301966	16.157188	16.015603	15.877106	15.741601	15.608991
8	15.479187	15.352101	15.227651	15.105757	14.986342	14.869332	14.754656	14.642247	14.532040	14.423970	14.317978	14.214006
9	14.111996	14.011897	13.913654	13.817218	13.722541	13.629576	13.538277	13.448602	13.360508	13.273954	13.188903	13.105314
10	13.023153	12.942384	12.862972	12.784884	12.708089	12.632554	12.558251	12.485150	12.413223	12.342442	12.272782	12.204216
11	12.136719	12.070268	12.004839	11.940409	11.876956	11.814459	11.752896	11.692249	11.632497	11.573621	11.515602	11.458423
12	11.402066	11.346514	11.291751	11.237759	11.184525	11.132032	11.080266	11.029211	10.978855	10.929183	10.880182	10.831840
13	10.784142	10.737078	10.690634	10.644800	10.599563	10.554913	10.510839	10.467330	10.424376	10.381966	10.340092	10.298742
14	10.257908	10.217581	10.177752	10.138411	10.099551	10.061163	10.023239	9.985771	9.948751	9.912171	9.876024	9.840304
15	9.805001	9.770111	9.735626	9.701538	9.667843	9.634533	9.601602	9.569044	9.536854	9.505024	9.473550	9.442426
16	9.411647	9.381206	9.351100	9.321322	9.291867	9.262732	9.233910	9.205397	9.177189	9.149280	9.121667	9.094345
17	9.067310	9.040557	9.014083	8.987883	8.961953	8.936290	8.910889	8.885748	8.860861	8.836226	8.811840	8.787697
18	8.763796	8.740133	8.716704	8.693507	8.670538	8.647794	8.625271	8.602968	8.580881	8.559007	8.537343	8.515886
19	8.494635	8.473585	8.452735	8.432081	8.411622	8.391355	8.371277	8.351385	8.331678	8.312153	8.292808	8.273640
20	8.254648	8.235828	8.217180	8.198700	8.180387	8.162238	8.144253	8.126427	8.108761	8.091251	8.073896	8.056694
21	8.039643	8.022741	8.005987	7.989379	7.972915	7.956593	7.940412	7.924370	7.908465	7.892696	7.877062	7.861560
22	7.846189	7.830948	7.815836	7.800850	7.785989	7.771253	7.756639	7.742146	7.727773	7.713518	7.699380	7.685359
23	7.671452	7.657658	7.643977	7.630406	7.616945	7.603593	7.590348	7.577209	7.564175	7.551245	7.538418	7.525692
24	7.513067	7.500542	7.488116	7.475786	7.463554	7.451417	7.439374	7.427425	7.415569	7.403804	7.392130	7.380545
25	7.369050	7.357642	7.346322	7.335088	7.323939	7.312874	7.301893	7.290995	7.280179	7.269444	7.258790	7.248215
26	7.237719	7.227301	7.216960	7.206695	7.196507	7.186394	7.176354	7.166389	7.156496	7.146676	7.136927	7.127249
27	7.117641	7.108103	7.098634	7.089233	7.079899	7.070632	7.061432	7.052298	7.043228	7.034223	7.025282	7.016405
28	7.007590	6.998837	6.990146	6.981516	6.972947	6.964437	6.955987	6.947596	6.939263	6.930988	6.922770	6.914609
29	6.906505	6.898456	6.890463	6.882524	6.874640	6.866810	6.859033	6.851309	6.843638	6.836018	6.828451	6.820934
30	6.813468	6.806052	6.798687	6.791370	6.784103	6.776884	6.769714	6.762591	6.755515	6.748487	6.741505	6.734569
31	6.727679	6.720835	6.714035	6.707281	6.700570	6.693904	6.687281	6.680701	6.674164	6.667670	6.661218	6.654807
32	6.648438	6.642111	6.635824	6.629577	6.623371	6.617205	6.611078	6.604990	6.598941	6.592931	6.586959	6.581026
33	6.575129	6.569270	6.563449	6.557664	6.551915	6.546203	6.540527	6.534886	6.529281	6.523711	6.518176	6.512675
34	6.507209	6.501777	6.496378	6.491013	6.485681	6.480383	6.475117	6.469883	6.464682	6.459513	6.454376	6.449270
35	6.444195	6.439152	6.434139	6.429157	6.424206	6.419285	6.414393	6.409531	6.404699	6.399896	6.395122	6.390377
36	6.385661	6.380973	6.376313	6.371681	6.367077	6.362501	6.357952	6.353430	6.348936	6.344468	6.340026	6.335612
37	6.331223	6.326860	6.322524	6.318213	6.313927	6.309667	6.305432	6.301222	6.297037	6.292876	6.288740	6.284628
38	6.280540	6.276476	6.272436	6.268420	6.264426	6.260457	6.256510	6.252586	6.248685	6.244807	6.240951	6.237117
39	6.233306	6.229516	6.225749	6.222003	6.218279	6.214576	6.210894	6.207234	6.203594	6.199976	6.196378	6.192800
40	6.189243	6.185707	6.182190	6.178694	6.175217	6.171760	6.168323	6.164905	6.161507	6.158127	6.154767	6.151426

5.75% Interest Rate   5.75% Interest Rate

Years	0	1	2	3	4	5	6	7	8	9	10	11
2	53.049657	51.047158	49.198873	47.487668	45.898855	44.419773	43.039449	41.748326	40.538040	39.401244	38.331453	37.322923
3	36.370549	35.469778	34.616537	33.807169	33.038383	32.307210	31.610964	30.947207	30.313725	29.708499	29.129686	28.575601
4	28.044697	27.535556	27.046871	26.577441	26.126152	25.691980	25.273972	24.871247	24.482986	24.108429	23.746865	23.397635
5	23.060122	22.733742	22.417978	22.112303	21.816251	21.529279	21.251268	20.981527	20.719787	20.465698	20.218934	19.979185
6	19.746158	19.519578	19.299183	19.084725	18.875971	18.672697	18.474693	18.281760	18.093706	17.910351	17.731523	17.557059
7	17.386802	17.220605	17.058324	16.899827	16.744982	16.593668	16.445766	16.301165	16.159755	16.021435	15.886106	15.753673
8	15.624046	15.497138	15.372866	15.251149	15.131912	15.015080	14.900583	14.788352	14.678323	14.570432	14.464619	14.360825
9	14.258995	14.159074	14.061011	13.964754	13.870256	13.777470	13.686351	13.596856	13.508941	13.422568	13.337696	13.254288
10	13.172306	13.091717	13.012485	12.934577	12.857962	12.782608	12.708485	12.635564	12.563817	12.493216	12.423736	12.355350
11	12.288034	12.221763	12.156514	12.092264	12.028991	11.966674	11.905292	11.844825	11.785253	11.726557	11.668718	11.611719
12	11.555542	11.500170	11.445587	11.391776	11.338721	11.286408	11.234821	11.183947	11.133770	11.084278	11.035457	10.987294
13	10.939776	10.892891	10.846626	10.800971	10.755914	10.711443	10.667548	10.624218	10.581443	10.539213	10.497517	10.456346
14	10.415691	10.375542	10.335891	10.296729	10.258048	10.219838	10.182092	10.144801	10.107959	10.071557	10.035589	10.000046
15	9.964921	9.930208	9.895900	9.861990	9.828472	9.795339	9.762585	9.730204	9.698190	9.666538	9.635240	9.604293
16	9.573690	9.543425	9.513495	9.483893	9.454614	9.425654	9.397008	9.368671	9.340638	9.312905	9.285467	9.258320
17	9.231460	9.204882	9.178582	9.152556	9.126801	9.101312	9.076086	9.051118	9.026405	9.001944	8.977731	8.953762
18	8.930035	8.906544	8.883289	8.860264	8.837468	8.814896	8.792547	8.770416	8.748500	8.726798	8.705306	8.684022
19	8.662942	8.642064	8.621385	8.600902	8.580614	8.560518	8.540610	8.520889	8.501352	8.481998	8.462823	8.443825
20	8.425002	8.406352	8.387873	8.369563	8.351419	8.333439	8.315622	8.297966	8.280468	8.263126	8.245939	8.228905
21	8.212022	8.195288	8.178701	8.162260	8.145963	8.129808	8.113794	8.097919	8.082181	8.066578	8.051110	8.035774
22	8.020569	8.005494	7.990546	7.975726	7.961030	7.946459	7.932009	7.917681	7.903472	7.889382	7.875408	7.861550
23	7.847807	7.834177	7.820659	7.807251	7.793953	7.780763	7.767681	7.754704	7.741832	7.729064	7.716399	7.703835
24	7.691372	7.679008	7.666742	7.654574	7.642502	7.630526	7.618643	7.606854	7.595158	7.583553	7.572038	7.560613
25	7.549277	7.538028	7.526867	7.515791	7.504800	7.493894	7.483071	7.472331	7.461672	7.451095	7.440597	7.430179
26	7.419840	7.409579	7.399394	7.389286	7.379254	7.369296	7.359412	7.349602	7.339865	7.330199	7.320605	7.311082
27	7.301629	7.292245	7.282929	7.273682	7.264502	7.255389	7.246341	7.237360	7.228443	7.219591	7.210802	7.202077
28	7.193414	7.184813	7.176273	7.167794	7.159376	7.151017	7.142718	7.134477	7.126294	7.118169	7.110101	7.102090
29	7.094135	7.086236	7.078391	7.070601	7.062866	7.055184	7.047555	7.039977	7.032455	7.024983	7.017563	7.010193
30	7.002874	6.995605	6.988386	6.981216	6.974094	6.967021	6.959996	6.953019	6.946088	6.939205	6.932368	6.925576
31	6.918831	6.912130	6.905474	6.898863	6.892296	6.885773	6.879293	6.872856	6.866461	6.860109	6.853799	6.847530
32	6.841303	6.835117	6.828971	6.822866	6.816800	6.810774	6.804788	6.798840	6.792931	6.787060	6.781228	6.775433
33	6.769676	6.763956	6.758273	6.752626	6.747015	6.741441	6.735902	6.730399	6.724931	6.719498	6.714099	6.708735
34	6.703405	6.698109	6.692846	6.687617	6.682420	6.677257	6.672126	6.667027	6.661960	6.656925	6.651922	6.646950
35	6.642009	6.637099	6.632219	6.627370	6.622551	6.617762	6.613003	6.608273	6.603573	6.598901	6.594258	6.589644
36	6.585059	6.580501	6.575972	6.571470	6.566996	6.562550	6.558130	6.553738	6.549372	6.545033	6.540720	6.536433
37	6.532173	6.527938	6.523729	6.519546	6.515387	6.511254	6.507146	6.503062	6.499003	6.494969	6.490958	6.486972
38	6.483009	6.479070	6.475155	6.471263	6.467395	6.463549	6.459726	6.455926	6.452148	6.448393	6.444661	6.440950
39	6.437261	6.433594	6.429948	6.426324	6.422722	6.419140	6.415580	6.412041	6.408522	6.405024	6.401546	6.398089
40	6.394652	6.391235	6.387837	6.384460	6.381102	6.377764	6.374445	6.371146	6.367865	6.364604	6.361361	6.358138

Annual Mortgage Constant for Monthly Payment Loans

6.00% Interest Rate

Years	0	1	2	3	4	5	6	7	8	9	10	11
2	53.184732	51.182228	49.333955	47.622775	46.034000	44.554967	43.174702	41.883647	40.673439	39.536727	38.467027	37.458595
3	36.506325	35.605663	34.752536	33.943286	33.174622	32.443576	31.747460	31.083836	30.450490	29.845403	29.266733	28.712792
4	28.182035	27.673043	27.184510	26.715232	26.264098	25.830082	25.412233	25.009668	24.621568	24.247173	23.885774	23.536709
5	23.199362	22.873156	22.557554	22.252048	21.956167	21.669466	21.391527	21.121959	20.860392	20.606478	20.359889	20.120316
6	19.887465	19.661062	19.440844	19.226565	19.017989	18.814894	18.617070	18.424317	18.236443	18.053269	17.874623	17.700340
7	17.530265	17.364250	17.202153	17.043838	16.889177	16.738046	16.590328	16.445911	16.304686	16.166550	16.031406	15.899158
8	15.769716	15.642994	15.518907	15.397376	15.278324	15.161678	15.047367	14.935323	14.825480	14.717716	14.612150	14.508543
9	14.406900	14.307166	14.209289	14.113220	14.018910	13.926311	13.835379	13.746071	13.658345	13.572159	13.487474	13.404254
10	13.322460	13.242059	13.163014	13.085294	13.008867	12.933701	12.859765	12.787032	12.715473	12.645061	12.575768	12.507570
11	12.440442	12.374358	12.309297	12.245235	12.182150	12.120021	12.058827	11.998547	11.939163	11.880654	11.823003	11.766192
12	11.710203	11.655018	11.600622	11.546998	11.494131	11.442005	11.390605	11.339918	11.289929	11.240623	11.191989	11.144013
13	11.096681	11.049983	11.003905	10.958437	10.913566	10.869282	10.825573	10.782429	10.739840	10.697795	10.656285	10.615300
14	10.574831	10.534868	10.495403	10.456426	10.417930	10.379905	10.342344	10.305239	10.268582	10.232365	10.196581	10.161222
15	10.126282	10.091753	10.057630	10.023904	9.990570	9.957620	9.925050	9.892853	9.861023	9.829553	9.798439	9.767675
16	9.737254	9.707173	9.677425	9.648006	9.618910	9.590132	9.561668	9.533513	9.505662	9.478110	9.450854	9.423888
17	9.397209	9.370812	9.344694	9.318849	9.293274	9.267966	9.242920	9.218132	9.193600	9.169319	9.145285	9.121496
18	9.097948	9.074637	9.051561	9.028715	9.006097	8.983705	8.961533	8.939581	8.917844	8.896320	8.875005	8.853898
19	8.832996	8.812295	8.791793	8.771488	8.751377	8.731457	8.711726	8.692181	8.672820	8.653642	8.634642	8.615820
20	8.597173	8.578698	8.560394	8.542258	8.524289	8.506484	8.488841	8.471359	8.454035	8.436867	8.419854	8.402993
21	8.386283	8.369722	8.353308	8.337040	8.320915	8.304933	8.289090	8.273387	8.257820	8.242389	8.227092	8.211927
22	8.196893	8.181989	8.167212	8.152562	8.138036	8.123634	8.109355	8.095196	8.081156	8.067235	8.053430	8.039741
23	8.026166	8.012705	7.999354	7.986115	7.972984	7.959962	7.947047	7.934237	7.921532	7.908931	7.896432	7.884034
24	7.871737	7.859539	7.847439	7.835436	7.823529	7.811717	7.800000	7.788375	7.776843	7.765402	7.754051	7.742790
25	7.731617	7.720531	7.709533	7.698620	7.687792	7.677048	7.666387	7.655808	7.645312	7.634896	7.624559	7.614303
26	7.604124	7.594023	7.583999	7.574051	7.564178	7.554380	7.544656	7.535005	7.525427	7.515920	7.506485	7.497120
27	7.487824	7.478598	7.469440	7.460350	7.451327	7.442371	7.433481	7.424656	7.415895	7.407199	7.398566	7.389996
28	7.381488	7.373042	7.364658	7.356333	7.348069	7.339865	7.331719	7.323632	7.315603	7.307631	7.299716	7.291858
29	7.284055	7.276308	7.268616	7.260978	7.253394	7.245863	7.238385	7.230960	7.223587	7.216266	7.208995	7.201776
30	7.194606	7.187487	7.180417	7.173395	7.166423	7.159498	7.152621	7.145792	7.139009	7.132273	7.125583	7.118939
31	7.112340	7.105786	7.099277	7.092812	7.086390	7.080012	7.073678	7.067386	7.061136	7.054929	7.048763	7.042638
32	7.036555	7.030512	7.024510	7.018548	7.012625	7.006742	7.000898	6.995092	6.989325	6.983596	6.977905	6.972252
33	6.966635	6.961056	6.955513	6.950006	6.944536	6.939101	6.933702	6.928338	6.923009	6.917715	6.912454	6.907229
34	6.902036	6.896878	6.891753	6.886660	6.881601	6.876574	6.871580	6.866617	6.861686	6.856787	6.851919	6.847082
35	6.842276	6.837501	6.832756	6.828041	6.823356	6.818701	6.814075	6.809479	6.804911	6.800373	6.795862	6.791381
36	6.786927	6.782501	6.778104	6.773733	6.769390	6.765074	6.760785	6.756523	6.752287	6.748078	6.743895	6.739737
37	6.735606	6.731500	6.727420	6.723364	6.719334	6.715329	6.711348	6.707391	6.703459	6.699552	6.695668	6.691808
38	6.687971	6.684158	6.680368	6.676602	6.672858	6.669137	6.665439	6.661763	6.658110	6.654478	6.650869	6.647282
39	6.643716	6.640171	6.636649	6.633147	6.629666	6.626207	6.622768	6.619350	6.615952	6.612575	6.609218	6.605881
40	6.602564	6.599266	6.595989	6.592731	6.589492	6.586273	6.583073	6.579891	6.576729	6.573585	6.570460	6.567354

6.25% Interest Rate

Years	0	1	2	3	4	5	6	7	8	9	10	11
2	53.320014	51.317514	49.469259	47.758113	46.169384	44.690409	43.310213	42.019235	40.809112	39.672494	38.602894	37.594568
3	36.642410	35.741866	34.888860	34.079737	33.311205	32.580293	31.884315	31.220834	30.587633	29.982694	29.404173	28.850385
4	28.319784	27.810949	27.322576	26.853459	26.402489	25.968638	25.550955	25.148559	24.760629	24.386405	24.025178	23.676286
5	23.339114	23.013084	22.697658	22.392331	22.096628	21.810107	21.532349	21.262962	21.001577	20.747845	20.501400	20.262050
6	20.029385	19.803167	19.583135	19.369042	19.160652	18.957745	18.760109	18.567544	18.379859	18.196874	18.018417	17.844324
7	17.674440	17.508615	17.346708	17.188585	17.034115	16.883176	16.735650	16.591425	16.450392	16.312449	16.177498	16.045443
8	15.916194	15.789665	15.665716	15.544435	15.425577	15.309125	15.195008	15.083159	14.973510	14.866000	14.760569	14.657157
9	14.555708	14.456169	14.358488	14.262614	14.168498	14.076095	13.985359	13.896246	13.808714	13.722724	13.638235	13.555210
10	13.473612	13.393405	13.314557	13.237032	13.160800	13.085829	13.012090	12.939552	12.868189	12.797971	12.728874	12.660872
11	12.593939	12.528051	12.463185	12.399318	12.336429	12.274495	12.213495	12.153411	12.094222	12.035908	11.978452	11.921836
12	11.866041	11.811052	11.756850	11.703421	11.650748	11.598817	11.547612	11.497119	11.447324	11.398212	11.349772	11.301990
13	11.254785	11.208348	11.162464	11.117189	11.072512	11.028421	10.984906	10.941955	10.899559	10.857707	10.816390	10.775598
14	10.735321	10.695551	10.656278	10.617494	10.579189	10.541357	10.503988	10.467074	10.430609	10.394583	10.358991	10.323823
15	10.289074	10.254737	10.220804	10.187269	10.154125	10.121367	10.088987	10.056980	10.025339	9.994060	9.963135	9.932560
16	9.902350	9.872437	9.842879	9.813648	9.784741	9.756152	9.727876	9.699909	9.672247	9.644883	9.617815	9.591037
17	9.564545	9.538336	9.512404	9.486746	9.461359	9.436237	9.411377	9.386776	9.362430	9.338334	9.314487	9.290883
18	9.267520	9.244395	9.221503	9.198843	9.176410	9.154201	9.132214	9.110446	9.088893	9.067552	9.046422	9.025498
19	9.004779	8.984261	8.963942	8.943819	8.923890	8.904153	8.884603	8.865241	8.846062	8.827064	8.808246	8.789605
20	8.771138	8.752844	8.734721	8.716765	8.698976	8.681351	8.663888	8.646585	8.629440	8.612451	8.595616	8.578934
21	8.562402	8.546019	8.529784	8.513693	8.497746	8.481940	8.466275	8.450748	8.435358	8.420104	8.404983	8.389994
22	8.375136	8.360406	8.345805	8.331330	8.316979	8.302752	8.288647	8.274662	8.260796	8.247049	8.233417	8.219902
23	8.206500	8.193211	8.180033	8.166966	8.154007	8.141157	8.128413	8.115775	8.103241	8.090811	8.078483	8.066255
24	8.054128	8.042100	8.030170	8.018336	8.006599	7.994956	7.983408	7.971952	7.960588	7.949315	7.938132	7.927038
25	7.916033	7.905114	7.894282	7.883536	7.872874	7.862297	7.851802	7.841389	7.831058	7.820807	7.810635	7.800543
26	7.790529	7.780592	7.770732	7.760948	7.751239	7.741604	7.732043	7.722554	7.713138	7.703794	7.694520	7.685317
27	7.676183	7.667118	7.658121	7.649192	7.640330	7.631533	7.622803	7.614137	7.605536	7.596999	7.588525	7.580114
28	7.571765	7.563477	7.555250	7.547083	7.538977	7.530929	7.522941	7.515010	7.507137	7.499322	7.491563	7.483860
29	7.476212	7.468620	7.461083	7.453599	7.446169	7.438793	7.431469	7.424197	7.416977	7.409809	7.402691	7.395624
30	7.388606	7.381639	7.374720	7.367850	7.361029	7.354255	7.347529	7.340850	7.334217	7.327631	7.321090	7.314595
31	7.308145	7.301740	7.295379	7.289062	7.282789	7.276559	7.270371	7.264226	7.258124	7.252063	7.246043	7.240065
32	7.234127	7.228230	7.222373	7.216556	7.210778	7.205039	7.199339	7.193677	7.188054	7.182469	7.176921	7.171410
33	7.165936	7.160499	7.155098	7.149733	7.144404	7.139111	7.133853	7.128629	7.123441	7.118286	7.113166	7.108080
34	7.103027	7.098007	7.093021	7.088067	7.083146	7.078257	7.073400	7.068575	7.063782	7.059019	7.054288	7.049588
35	7.044918	7.040278	7.035669	7.031089	7.026539	7.022019	7.017527	7.013065	7.008631	7.004226	6.999850	6.995501
36	6.991180	6.986887	6.982621	6.978383	6.974172	6.969987	6.965830	6.961698	6.957593	6.953514	6.949461	6.945434
37	6.941432	6.937455	6.933504	6.929577	6.925675	6.921798	6.917945	6.914117	6.910312	6.906532	6.902775	6.899041
38	6.895331	6.891644	6.887980	6.884339	6.880721	6.877125	6.873551	6.870000	6.866470	6.862963	6.859477	6.856013
39	6.852571	6.849149	6.845749	6.842370	6.839011	6.835673	6.832356	6.829059	6.825782	6.822526	6.819289	6.816072
40	6.812875	6.809697	6.806539	6.803400	6.800280	6.797179	6.794098	6.791034	6.787990	6.784964	6.781956	6.778966

Annual Mortgage Constant for Monthly Payment Loans

6.50% Interest Rate --- 6.50% Interest Rate

Years	0	1	2	3	4	5	6	7	8	9	10	11
						Number of Months						
2	53.455502	51.453013	49.604787	47.893683	46.305010	44.826101	43.445981	42.155089	40.945060	39.808543	38.739052	37.730841
3	36.778803	35.878385	35.025511	34.216523	33.448130	32.717362	32.021531	31.358200	30.725152	30.120369	29.542008	28.988381
4	28.457944	27.949275	27.461069	26.992123	26.541325	26.107647	25.690140	25.287919	24.900168	24.526123	24.165077	23.816367
5	23.479378	23.153532	22.838291	22.533150	22.237635	21.951301	21.673732	21.404534	21.143339	20.889799	20.643585	20.404388
6	20.171916	19.945891	19.726053	19.512155	19.303960	19.101249	18.903809	18.711440	18.523952	18.341164	18.162905	17.989010
7	17.819324	17.653698	17.491990	17.334065	17.179795	17.029056	16.881730	16.737705	16.596873	16.459131	16.324380	16.192527
8	16.063479	15.937151	15.813460	15.692324	15.573668	15.457419	15.343504	15.231856	15.122410	15.015103	14.909873	14.806664
9	14.705418	14.606082	14.508603	14.412932	14.319020	14.226819	14.136286	14.047376	13.960048	13.874260	13.789974	13.707152
10	13.625757	13.545754	13.467109	13.389787	13.313758	13.238991	13.165454	13.093119	13.021959	12.951945	12.883051	12.815251
11	12.748521	12.682836	12.618172	12.554508	12.491821	12.430090	12.369294	12.309412	12.250425	12.192314	12.135060	12.078646
12	12.023053	11.968265	11.914266	11.861039	11.808568	11.756838	11.705834	11.655543	11.605949	11.557039	11.508800	11.461219
13	11.414282	11.367979	11.322295	11.277221	11.232744	11.188854	11.145539	11.102788	11.060592	11.018940	10.977823	10.937230
14	10.897153	10.857582	10.818508	10.779923	10.741817	10.704184	10.667013	10.630298	10.594031	10.558204	10.522809	10.487840
15	10.453288	10.419148	10.385413	10.352075	10.319128	10.286567	10.254384	10.222573	10.191129	10.160046	10.129317	10.098938
16	10.068910	10.039207	10.009843	9.980808	9.952096	9.923702	9.895621	9.867848	9.840379	9.813210	9.786336	9.759751
17	9.733453	9.707437	9.681699	9.656234	9.631039	9.606110	9.581442	9.557033	9.532879	9.508975	9.485319	9.461907
18	9.438735	9.415801	9.393100	9.370630	9.348387	9.326369	9.304572	9.282993	9.261630	9.240479	9.219537	9.198802
19	9.178272	9.157942	9.137811	9.117877	9.098135	9.078585	9.059223	9.040048	9.021056	9.002245	8.983613	8.965158
20	8.946878	8.928769	8.910831	8.893061	8.875457	8.858016	8.840738	8.823619	8.806658	8.789853	8.773202	8.756704
21	8.740355	8.724155	8.708102	8.692194	8.676429	8.660805	8.645322	8.629977	8.614768	8.599694	8.584754	8.569946
22	8.555268	8.540719	8.526297	8.512001	8.497830	8.483782	8.469855	8.456049	8.442362	8.428792	8.415339	8.402001
23	8.388776	8.375664	8.362663	8.349772	8.336990	8.324316	8.311748	8.299285	8.286927	8.274671	8.262518	8.250465
24	8.238512	8.226658	8.214901	8.203241	8.191677	8.180207	8.168831	8.157547	8.146356	8.135254	8.124243	8.113321
25	8.102486	8.091738	8.081077	8.070501	8.060009	8.049601	8.039276	8.029032	8.018869	8.008787	7.998784	7.988860
26	7.979014	7.969244	7.959551	7.949934	7.940392	7.930923	7.921528	7.912206	7.902955	7.893776	7.884668	7.875629
27	7.866660	7.857759	7.848926	7.840160	7.831461	7.822828	7.814260	7.805757	7.797319	7.788943	7.780631	7.772381
28	7.764193	7.756066	7.748000	7.739994	7.732047	7.724159	7.716330	7.708558	7.700844	7.693187	7.685587	7.678042
29	7.670552	7.663117	7.655737	7.648410	7.641137	7.633917	7.626749	7.619633	7.612568	7.605555	7.598592	7.591679
30	7.584816	7.578003	7.571238	7.564521	7.557853	7.551232	7.544658	7.538131	7.531651	7.525216	7.518827	7.512483
31	7.506184	7.499929	7.493719	7.487551	7.481428	7.475347	7.469309	7.463313	7.457358	7.451446	7.445574	7.439743
32	7.433953	7.428203	7.422492	7.416822	7.411190	7.405597	7.400042	7.394526	7.389048	7.383607	7.378203	7.372837
33	7.367507	7.362213	7.356955	7.351734	7.346547	7.341396	7.336280	7.331198	7.326151	7.321138	7.316159	7.311213
34	7.306300	7.301421	7.296574	7.291760	7.286978	7.282228	7.277509	7.272822	7.268167	7.263542	7.258948	7.254385
35	7.249852	7.245349	7.240876	7.236432	7.232018	7.227632	7.223276	7.218948	7.214649	7.210378	7.206135	7.201920
36	7.197733	7.193573	7.189440	7.185334	7.181254	7.177202	7.173176	7.169175	7.165201	7.161253	7.157330	7.153433
37	7.149561	7.145714	7.141891	7.138094	7.134320	7.130571	7.126847	7.123146	7.119469	7.115815	7.112185	7.108578
38	7.104994	7.101433	7.097895	7.094379	7.090886	7.087415	7.083966	7.080539	7.077133	7.073750	7.070387	7.067046
39	7.063726	7.060427	7.057149	7.053892	7.050655	7.047439	7.044242	7.041066	7.037910	7.034773	7.031657	7.028560
40	7.025482	7.022423	7.019384	7.016363	7.013362	7.010379	7.007414	7.004469	7.001541	6.998632	6.995740	6.992867

6.75% Interest Rate --- 6.75% Interest Rate

Years	0	1	2	3	4	5	6	7	8	9	10	11
2	53.591195	51.588728	49.740539	48.029485	46.440875	44.962041	43.582006	42.291208	41.081282	39.944876	38.875501	37.867414
3	36.915506	36.015222	35.162487	34.353643	33.585398	32.854782	32.159106	31.495934	30.863048	30.258430	29.680236	29.126779
4	28.596514	28.088019	27.599990	27.131222	26.680604	26.247109	25.829784	25.427749	25.040184	24.666327	24.305470	23.956951
5	23.620153	23.294500	22.979452	22.674505	22.379185	22.093048	21.815676	21.546676	21.285680	21.032339	20.786325	20.547328
6	20.315057	20.089234	19.869599	19.655903	19.447912	19.245404	19.048168	18.856046	18.668721	18.486138	18.308085	18.134396
7	17.964916	17.799497	17.637996	17.480279	17.326216	17.175685	17.028567	16.884750	16.744127	16.606593	16.472051	16.340407
8	16.211568	16.085450	15.961968	15.841042	15.722596	15.606556	15.492851	15.381413	15.272177	15.165080	15.060061	14.957062
9	14.856027	14.756901	14.659633	14.564172	14.470471	14.378481	14.288158	14.199459	14.112341	14.026764	13.942689	13.860078
10	13.778894	13.699101	13.620666	13.543556	13.467737	13.393180	13.319854	13.247730	13.176780	13.106976	13.038292	12.970703
11	12.904183	12.838708	12.774255	12.710801	12.648324	12.586803	12.526216	12.466544	12.407766	12.349865	12.292821	12.236616
12	12.181232	12.126654	12.072863	12.019845	11.967583	11.916062	11.865267	11.815184	11.765798	11.717097	11.669066	11.621692
13	11.574964	11.528868	11.483392	11.438525	11.394256	11.350572	11.307464	11.264921	11.222931	11.181486	11.140575	11.100189
14	11.060318	11.020953	10.982085	10.943705	10.905805	10.868376	10.831411	10.794901	10.758839	10.723216	10.688026	10.653261
15	10.618914	10.584977	10.551446	10.518311	10.485568	10.453210	10.421229	10.389622	10.358380	10.327499	10.296973	10.266796
16	10.236963	10.207468	10.178306	10.149472	10.120961	10.092767	10.064887	10.037315	10.010047	9.983077	9.956402	9.930018
17	9.903919	9.878102	9.852563	9.827296	9.802300	9.777569	9.753100	9.728889	9.704932	9.681226	9.657767	9.634551
18	9.611576	9.588838	9.566334	9.544060	9.522013	9.500190	9.478588	9.457205	9.436036	9.415079	9.394332	9.373792
19	9.353455	9.333319	9.313382	9.293640	9.274092	9.254734	9.235565	9.216581	9.197781	9.179162	9.160722	9.142458
20	9.124368	9.106451	9.088703	9.071123	9.053708	9.036458	9.019368	9.002439	8.985667	8.969050	8.952588	8.936277
21	8.920116	8.904104	8.888238	8.872517	8.856939	8.841502	8.826205	8.811045	8.796022	8.781134	8.766379	8.751755
22	8.737262	8.722897	8.708660	8.694548	8.680560	8.666695	8.652951	8.639328	8.625823	8.612435	8.599164	8.586007
23	8.572964	8.560033	8.547212	8.534502	8.521900	8.509406	8.497017	8.484734	8.472554	8.460477	8.448502	8.436628
24	8.424853	8.413176	8.401597	8.390114	8.378726	8.367433	8.356233	8.345125	8.334109	8.323183	8.312346	8.301599
25	8.290938	8.280365	8.269877	8.259475	8.249156	8.238921	8.228768	8.218697	8.208706	8.198795	8.188964	8.179211
26	8.169535	8.159936	8.150414	8.140966	8.131593	8.122294	8.113068	8.103915	8.094833	8.085821	8.076881	8.068010
27	8.059207	8.050473	8.041807	8.033208	8.024674	8.016207	8.007805	7.999467	7.991193	7.982982	7.974834	7.966748
28	7.958723	7.950759	7.942856	7.935012	7.927228	7.919502	7.911834	7.904224	7.896671	7.889175	7.881734	7.874350
29	7.867020	7.859744	7.852523	7.845355	7.838241	7.831179	7.824169	7.817210	7.810303	7.803447	7.796640	7.789884
30	7.783177	7.776519	7.769910	7.763348	7.756835	7.750368	7.743949	7.737576	7.731249	7.724967	7.718731	7.712540
31	7.706393	7.700290	7.694231	7.688215	7.682243	7.676312	7.670425	7.664579	7.658774	7.653011	7.647288	7.641606
32	7.635964	7.630362	7.624800	7.619277	7.613792	7.608346	7.602938	7.597568	7.592236	7.586940	7.581682	7.576460
33	7.571275	7.566126	7.561012	7.555934	7.550891	7.545883	7.540910	7.535971	7.531066	7.526194	7.521357	7.516552
34	7.511780	7.507041	7.502335	7.497661	7.493018	7.488407	7.483828	7.479280	7.474763	7.470276	7.465820	7.461394
35	7.456998	7.452632	7.448295	7.443987	7.439709	7.435459	7.431238	7.427045	7.422881	7.418744	7.414635	7.410554
36	7.406500	7.402472	7.398472	7.394499	7.390552	7.386631	7.382736	7.378867	7.375024	7.371206	7.367413	7.363646
37	7.359903	7.356185	7.352492	7.348823	7.345178	7.341557	7.337960	7.334386	7.330836	7.327309	7.323806	7.320325
38	7.316867	7.313431	7.310018	7.306628	7.303259	7.299912	7.296587	7.293284	7.290002	7.286741	7.283501	7.280283
39	7.277085	7.273908	7.270751	7.267615	7.264499	7.261403	7.258327	7.255271	7.252235	7.249218	7.246220	7.243241
40	7.240282	7.237342	7.234420	7.231517	7.228633	7.225767	7.222919	7.220090	7.217278	7.214485	7.211709	7.208951

Annual Mortgage Constant for Monthly Payment Loans

7.00% Interest Rate   7.00% Interest Rate

Years	0	1	2	3	4	5	6	7	8	9	10	11
						Number of Months						
2	53.727095	51.724657	49.876513	48.165519	46.576981	45.098230	43.718289	42.427594	41.217779	40.081491	39.012242	38.004287
3	37.052516	36.152376	35.299788	34.491097	33.723009	32.992553	32.297041	31.634036	31.001320	30.396875	29.818857	29.265578
4	28.735494	28.227182	27.739338	27.270757	26.820327	26.387022	25.969890	25.568048	25.180678	24.807017	24.446357	24.098036
5	23.761438	23.435986	23.121140	22.816396	22.521280	22.235347	21.958180	21.689386	21.428597	21.175463	20.929657	20.690870
6	20.458808	20.233195	20.013770	19.800285	19.592506	19.390209	19.193186	19.001234	18.814164	18.631796	18.453956	18.280481
7	18.111216	17.946011	17.784726	17.627224	17.473377	17.323061	17.176159	17.032558	16.892151	16.754835	16.620509	16.489082
8	16.360460	16.234559	16.111294	15.990586	15.872357	15.756535	15.643048	15.531828	15.422810	15.315931	15.211130	15.108349
9	15.007532	14.908624	14.811575	14.716332	14.622848	14.531077	14.440972	14.352492	14.265592	14.180234	14.096377	14.013984
10	13.933018	13.853443	13.775226	13.698334	13.622733	13.548394	13.475286	13.403380	13.332648	13.263062	13.194596	13.127224
11	13.060921	12.995664	12.931428	12.868191	12.805931	12.744627	12.684257	12.624802	12.566241	12.508556	12.451729	12.395740
12	12.340573	12.286211	12.232636	12.179834	12.127788	12.076482	12.025903	11.976035	11.926865	11.878378	11.830562	11.783404
13	11.736890	11.691008	11.645747	11.601094	11.557039	11.513569	11.470675	11.428345	11.386569	11.345336	11.304639	11.264465
14	11.224807	11.185654	11.146998	11.108831	11.071143	11.033926	10.997172	10.960873	10.925022	10.889610	10.854631	10.820076
15	10.785939	10.752213	10.718891	10.685967	10.653433	10.621284	10.589513	10.558114	10.527081	10.496409	10.466091	10.436122
16	10.406496	10.377209	10.348254	10.319627	10.291323	10.263336	10.235662	10.208296	10.181234	10.154470	10.128001	10.101822
17	10.075928	10.050316	10.024981	9.999919	9.975126	9.950599	9.926333	9.902326	9.878572	9.855068	9.831812	9.808799
18	9.786026	9.763490	9.741187	9.719114	9.697268	9.675646	9.654245	9.633061	9.612093	9.591336	9.570788	9.550446
19	9.530309	9.510371	9.490632	9.471089	9.451738	9.432578	9.413606	9.394820	9.376216	9.357793	9.339549	9.321481
20	9.303587	9.285865	9.268312	9.250927	9.233707	9.216651	9.199755	9.183019	9.166440	9.150017	9.133747	9.117629
21	9.101661	9.085840	9.070166	9.054636	9.039249	9.024002	9.008895	8.993926	8.979093	8.964394	8.949828	8.935394
22	8.921089	8.906913	8.892863	8.878939	8.865138	8.851461	8.837904	8.824467	8.811148	8.797946	8.784861	8.771889
23	8.759031	8.746284	8.733648	8.721122	8.708704	8.696393	8.684187	8.672087	8.660090	8.648195	8.636402	8.624709
24	8.613115	8.601619	8.590220	8.578918	8.567710	8.556596	8.545576	8.534647	8.523809	8.513062	8.502403	8.491833
25	8.481350	8.470954	8.460643	8.450417	8.440274	8.430215	8.420238	8.410341	8.400526	8.390789	8.381132	8.371553
26	8.362051	8.352625	8.343275	8.334000	8.324800	8.315672	8.306618	8.297635	8.288724	8.279884	8.271113	8.262412
27	8.253779	8.245214	8.236717	8.228286	8.219921	8.211622	8.203387	8.195216	8.187109	8.179065	8.171083	8.163162
28	8.155303	8.147505	8.139766	8.132087	8.124467	8.116905	8.109401	8.101954	8.094564	8.087230	8.079952	8.072729
29	8.065561	8.058447	8.051386	8.044379	8.037424	8.030522	8.023672	8.016872	8.010124	8.003426	7.996778	7.990179
30	7.983630	7.977129	7.970676	7.964271	7.957914	7.951603	7.945339	7.939121	7.932949	7.926822	7.920740	7.914702
31	7.908709	7.902759	7.896853	7.890989	7.885168	7.879390	7.873653	7.867958	7.862305	7.856692	7.851119	7.845587
32	7.840094	7.834641	7.829227	7.823852	7.818516	7.813217	7.807957	7.802733	7.797548	7.792399	7.787286	7.782210
33	7.777170	7.772166	7.767197	7.762263	7.757364	7.752499	7.747669	7.742873	7.738110	7.733381	7.728685	7.724022
34	7.719391	7.714793	7.710227	7.705693	7.701190	7.696719	7.692279	7.687869	7.683491	7.679142	7.674824	7.670535
35	7.666276	7.662047	7.657846	7.653675	7.649532	7.645418	7.641332	7.637274	7.633244	7.629241	7.625266	7.621318
36	7.617397	7.613502	7.609634	7.605793	7.601977	7.598188	7.594424	7.590686	7.586973	7.583285	7.579622	7.575984
37	7.572370	7.568781	7.565216	7.561675	7.558158	7.554665	7.551194	7.547748	7.544324	7.540923	7.537545	7.534190
38	7.530857	7.527546	7.524257	7.520991	7.517746	7.514522	7.511320	7.508140	7.504980	7.501842	7.498724	7.495627
39	7.492550	7.489494	7.486458	7.483442	7.480445	7.477469	7.474512	7.471575	7.468657	7.465758	7.462878	7.460017
40	7.457175	7.454352	7.451547	7.448760	7.445992	7.443242	7.440509	7.437795	7.435098	7.432419	7.429757	7.427112

7.25% Interest Rate   7.25% Interest Rate

Years	0	1	2	3	4	5	6	7	8	9	10	11
2	53.863200	51.860800	50.012710	48.301784	46.713326	45.234668	43.854828	42.564245	41.354550	40.218389	39.149274	38.141459
3	37.189835	36.289846	35.437415	34.628884	33.860961	33.130674	32.435335	31.772505	31.139968	30.535705	29.957871	29.404779
4	28.874883	28.366763	27.879112	27.410726	26.960494	26.527387	26.110455	25.708815	25.321648	24.948192	24.587737	24.239624
5	23.900234	23.577990	23.263355	22.958822	22.663917	22.378197	22.101244	21.832664	21.572090	21.319172	21.073583	20.835012
6	20.603167	20.377773	20.158566	19.945300	19.737740	19.535664	19.338861	19.147130	18.960282	18.778135	18.600517	18.427264
7	18.258221	18.093239	17.932177	17.774898	17.621275	17.471183	17.324505	17.181128	17.040945	16.903853	16.769753	16.638550
8	16.510153	16.384477	16.261437	16.140954	16.022951	15.907354	15.794092	15.683098	15.574306	15.467652	15.363077	15.260522
9	15.159930	15.061249	14.964425	14.869408	14.776150	14.684604	14.594726	14.506471	14.419797	14.334654	14.251033	14.168865
10	14.088125	14.008776	13.930785	13.854118	13.778743	13.704629	13.631746	13.560065	13.489558	13.420197	13.351955	13.284808
11	13.218730	13.153698	13.089686	13.026674	12.964638	12.903558	12.843412	12.784181	12.725844	12.668383	12.611779	12.556013
12	12.501070	12.446930	12.393579	12.340999	12.289175	12.238092	12.187735	12.138090	12.089141	12.040877	11.993282	11.946345
13	11.900053	11.854392	11.809352	11.764920	11.721085	11.677836	11.635162	11.593051	11.551495	11.510483	11.470004	11.430050
14	11.390610	11.351677	11.313239	11.275290	11.237820	11.200821	11.164285	11.128204	11.092570	11.057376	11.022613	10.988275
15	10.954355	10.920845	10.887739	10.855030	10.822712	10.790778	10.759222	10.728038	10.697219	10.666761	10.636657	10.606902
16	10.577490	10.548416	10.519674	10.491260	10.463168	10.435394	10.407932	10.380778	10.353927	10.327375	10.301116	10.275148
17	10.249464	10.224062	10.198937	10.174085	10.149502	10.125184	10.101127	10.077328	10.053782	10.030487	10.007438	9.984632
18	9.962067	9.939737	9.917643	9.895774	9.874134	9.852718	9.831523	9.810544	9.789780	9.769228	9.748884	9.728747
19	9.708812	9.689079	9.669543	9.650202	9.631054	9.612096	9.593326	9.574741	9.556339	9.538117	9.520073	9.502206
20	9.484512	9.466989	9.449636	9.432450	9.415429	9.398571	9.381874	9.365335	9.348954	9.332728	9.316655	9.300734
21	9.284961	9.269337	9.253858	9.238523	9.223331	9.208280	9.193367	9.178592	9.163952	9.149447	9.135074	9.120832
22	9.106720	9.092736	9.078878	9.065145	9.051536	9.038048	9.024682	9.011435	8.998306	8.985294	8.972397	8.959614
23	8.946944	8.934386	8.921938	8.909599	8.897367	8.885243	8.873224	8.861309	8.849498	8.837789	8.826180	8.814672
24	8.803263	8.791951	8.780736	8.769616	8.758591	8.747660	8.736822	8.726075	8.715419	8.704852	8.694375	8.683985
25	8.673682	8.663466	8.653334	8.643287	8.633323	8.623442	8.613643	8.603924	8.594286	8.584727	8.575246	8.565843
26	8.556517	8.547267	8.538092	8.528992	8.519966	8.511012	8.502132	8.493323	8.484584	8.475917	8.467318	8.458789
27	8.450328	8.441934	8.433608	8.425347	8.417153	8.409023	8.400958	8.392956	8.385018	8.377142	8.369328	8.361575
28	8.353883	8.346252	8.338680	8.331167	8.323712	8.316316	8.308977	8.301695	8.294469	8.287299	8.280185	8.273125
29	8.266120	8.259168	8.252270	8.245424	8.238631	8.231890	8.225200	8.218561	8.211973	8.205435	8.198946	8.192506
30	8.186115	8.179773	8.173478	8.167230	8.161030	8.154876	8.148768	8.142706	8.136689	8.130718	8.124790	8.118907
31	8.113068	8.107272	8.101519	8.095809	8.090141	8.084515	8.078930	8.073387	8.067884	8.062422	8.057000	8.051618
32	8.046275	8.040971	8.035707	8.030480	8.025292	8.020141	8.015028	8.009952	8.004913	7.999911	7.994945	7.990014
33	7.985120	7.980260	7.975436	7.970647	7.965891	7.961171	7.956483	7.951830	7.947210	7.942623	7.938069	7.933547
34	7.929058	7.924600	7.920174	7.915780	7.911417	7.907085	7.902784	7.898513	7.894272	7.890062	7.885881	7.881729
35	7.877607	7.873514	7.869449	7.865414	7.861406	7.857427	7.853475	7.849552	7.845655	7.841786	7.837944	7.834129
36	7.830340	7.826578	7.822841	7.819131	7.815447	7.811788	7.808154	7.804546	7.800963	7.797404	7.793870	7.790361
37	7.786875	7.783414	7.779976	7.776563	7.773172	7.769805	7.766461	7.763140	7.759842	7.756566	7.753313	7.750082
38	7.746873	7.743685	7.740520	7.737376	7.734254	7.731153	7.728073	7.725014	7.721975	7.718958	7.715960	7.712983
39	7.710026	7.707090	7.704173	7.701275	7.698398	7.695539	7.692700	7.689881	7.687080	7.684298	7.681534	7.678789
40	7.676063	7.673355	7.670665	7.667993	7.665339	7.662703	7.660084	7.657483	7.654899	7.652333	7.649783	7.647251

Annual Mortgage Constant for Monthly Payment Loans

7.50% Interest Rate   7.50% Interest Rate

                                              Number of Months
Years	0	1	2	3	4	5	6	7	8	9	10	11
2	53.999511	51.997157	50.149129	48.438280	46.849912	45.371354	43.991625	42.701161	41.491594	40.355569	39.286597	38.278931
3	37.327462	36.427633	35.575367	34.767005	33.999255	33.269146	32.573987	31.911342	31.278992	30.674919	30.097277	29.544381
4	29.014682	28.506762	28.019313	27.551130	27.101103	26.668204	26.251480	25.850050	25.463094	25.089851	24.729611	24.381712
5	24.045538	23.720513	23.406095	23.101781	22.807097	22.521598	22.244866	21.976509	21.716158	21.463464	21.218099	20.979754
6	20.748135	20.522966	20.303986	20.090948	19.883616	19.681768	19.485193	19.293691	19.107071	18.925154	18.747766	18.574743
7	18.405931	18.241180	18.080348	17.923301	17.769909	17.620048	17.473602	17.330458	17.190507	17.053647	16.919779	16.788808
8	16.660645	16.535201	16.412394	16.292144	16.174374	16.059010	15.945982	15.835221	15.726662	15.620241	15.515899	15.413577
9	15.313219	15.214771	15.118180	15.023397	14.930372	14.839060	14.749415	14.661393	14.574952	14.490052	14.406654	14.324720
10	14.244212	14.165096	14.087338	14.010903	13.935761	13.861880	13.789229	13.717781	13.647505	13.578377	13.510367	13.443452
11	13.377606	13.312805	13.249025	13.186244	13.124440	13.063591	13.003676	12.944675	12.886569	12.829338	12.772964	12.717429
12	12.662716	12.608806	12.555684	12.503334	12.451740	12.400886	12.350758	12.301341	12.252621	12.204585	12.157219	12.110510
13	12.064445	12.019012	11.974199	11.929995	11.886387	11.843364	11.800916	11.759033	11.717703	11.676916	11.636663	11.596934
14	11.557720	11.519011	11.480799	11.443074	11.405829	11.369054	11.332742	11.296884	11.261473	11.226502	11.191962	11.157846
15	11.124148	11.090861	11.057976	11.025489	10.993392	10.961679	10.930344	10.899380	10.868782	10.838544	10.808660	10.779124
16	10.749931	10.721076	10.692553	10.664357	10.636483	10.608926	10.581682	10.554745	10.528111	10.501775	10.475733	10.449980
17	10.424513	10.399326	10.374416	10.349779	10.325410	10.301306	10.277463	10.253878	10.230545	10.207463	10.184627	10.162034
18	10.139680	10.117562	10.095677	10.074022	10.052593	10.031387	10.010401	9.989633	9.969079	9.948735	9.928601	9.908672
19	9.888946	9.869420	9.850092	9.830958	9.812017	9.793266	9.774702	9.756323	9.738126	9.720110	9.702271	9.684608
20	9.667118	9.649800	9.632650	9.615667	9.598849	9.582193	9.565698	9.549362	9.533182	9.517157	9.501285	9.485564
21	9.469992	9.454567	9.439288	9.424153	9.409159	9.394306	9.379591	9.365014	9.350572	9.336263	9.322087	9.308041
22	9.294125	9.280336	9.266673	9.253135	9.239720	9.226427	9.213254	9.200201	9.187265	9.174445	9.161740	9.149150
23	9.136671	9.124304	9.112047	9.099898	9.087857	9.075922	9.064092	9.052367	9.040744	9.029223	9.017802	9.006481
24	8.995259	8.984134	8.973105	8.962171	8.951332	8.940586	8.929932	8.919370	8.908898	8.898515	8.888221	8.878014
25	8.867894	8.857860	8.847910	8.838044	8.828262	8.818561	8.808942	8.799403	8.789944	8.780564	8.771262	8.762038
26	8.752889	8.743817	8.734819	8.725896	8.717046	8.708269	8.699564	8.690930	8.682367	8.673874	8.665449	8.657094
27	8.648806	8.640585	8.632431	8.624343	8.616320	8.608362	8.600468	8.592637	8.584868	8.577162	8.569518	8.561934
28	8.554411	8.546948	8.539544	8.532198	8.524911	8.517681	8.510509	8.503392	8.496332	8.489327	8.482378	8.475482
29	8.468641	8.461853	8.455118	8.448435	8.441805	8.435225	8.428697	8.422220	8.415792	8.409414	8.403086	8.396806
30	8.390574	8.384390	8.378254	8.372165	8.366122	8.360125	8.354174	8.348269	8.342408	8.336592	8.330821	8.325092
31	8.319408	8.313766	8.308167	8.302610	8.297095	8.291622	8.286189	8.280798	8.275447	8.270136	8.264864	8.259633
32	8.254440	8.249286	8.244170	8.239092	8.234052	8.229050	8.224084	8.219156	8.214263	8.209407	8.204587	8.199803
33	8.195053	8.190339	8.185659	8.181013	8.176402	8.171824	8.167280	8.162769	8.158292	8.153846	8.149434	8.145053
34	8.140704	8.136387	8.132101	8.127846	8.123622	8.119429	8.115266	8.111133	8.107030	8.102956	8.098912	8.094897
35	8.090911	8.086954	8.083025	8.079124	8.075251	8.071406	8.067588	8.063797	8.060034	8.056298	8.052588	8.048904
36	8.045247	8.041616	8.038011	8.034431	8.030876	8.027347	8.023843	8.020364	8.016909	8.013478	8.010072	8.006690
37	8.003332	7.999997	7.996686	7.993398	7.990133	7.986891	7.983672	7.980475	7.977301	7.974149	7.971019	7.967911
38	7.964824	7.961759	7.958716	7.955694	7.952692	7.949712	7.946752	7.943813	7.940895	7.937996	7.935118	7.932260
39	7.929421	7.926602	7.923803	7.921023	7.918262	7.915520	7.912797	7.910093	7.907407	7.904740	7.902092	7.899461
40	7.896849	7.894254	7.891678	7.889119	7.886577	7.884053	7.881546	7.879057	7.876584	7.874128	7.871689	7.869267

7.75% Interest Rate   7.75% Interest Rate

Years	0	1	2	3	4	5	6	7	8	9	10	11
2	54.136028	52.133729	50.285772	48.575008	46.986737	45.508288	44.128678	42.838343	41.628913	40.493032	39.424211	38.416703
3	37.465396	36.565736	35.713643	34.905459	34.137891	33.407967	32.712998	32.050545	31.418391	30.814516	30.237076	29.684383
4	29.154890	28.647178	28.159939	27.691968	27.242155	26.809470	26.392964	25.991752	25.605016	25.231994	24.871976	24.524301
5	24.188352	23.863551	23.549361	23.245274	22.950818	22.665548	22.389047	22.120921	21.860801	21.608339	21.363206	21.125094
6	20.893709	20.668775	20.450030	20.237226	20.030130	19.828518	19.632179	19.440914	19.254532	19.072852	18.895702	18.722918
7	18.554344	18.389831	18.229238	18.072430	17.919277	17.769656	17.623449	17.480545	17.340834	17.204214	17.070586	16.939856
8	16.811933	16.686730	16.564163	16.444154	16.326624	16.211501	16.098714	15.988193	15.879875	15.773696	15.669595	15.567513
9	15.467396	15.369189	15.272839	15.178296	15.085512	14.994441	14.905036	14.817254	14.731054	14.646395	14.563237	14.481543
10	14.401276	14.322400	14.244881	14.168687	14.093784	14.020143	13.947732	13.876522	13.806487	13.737597	13.669827	13.603150
11	13.537543	13.472981	13.409439	13.346897	13.285330	13.224719	13.165042	13.106279	13.048410	12.991417	12.935280	12.879982
12	12.825505	12.771832	12.718947	12.666832	12.615474	12.564856	12.514963	12.465782	12.417297	12.369494	12.322364	12.275890
13	12.230059	12.184860	12.140281	12.096310	12.052935	12.010146	11.967931	11.926280	11.885182	11.844627	11.804606	11.765109
14	11.726126	11.687648	11.649667	11.612172	11.575157	11.538612	11.502530	11.466902	11.431720	11.396977	11.362666	11.328779
15	11.295309	11.262249	11.229592	11.197332	11.165462	11.133976	11.102867	11.072129	11.041757	11.011744	10.982085	10.952774
16	10.923806	10.895175	10.866876	10.838903	10.811253	10.783919	10.756897	10.730183	10.703771	10.677657	10.651836	10.626304
17	10.601057	10.576091	10.551401	10.526984	10.502834	10.478950	10.455326	10.431958	10.408844	10.385980	10.363361	10.340985
18	10.318848	10.296947	10.275278	10.253838	10.232624	10.211634	10.190863	10.170308	10.149968	10.129839	10.109917	10.090201
19	10.070688	10.051374	10.032258	10.013336	9.994606	9.976065	9.957711	9.939542	9.921556	9.903748	9.886119	9.868664
20	9.851383	9.834272	9.817330	9.800554	9.783942	9.767493	9.751204	9.735074	9.719099	9.703279	9.687611	9.672094
21	9.656726	9.641505	9.626428	9.611495	9.596704	9.582053	9.567539	9.553163	9.538921	9.524813	9.510837	9.496991
22	9.483273	9.469683	9.456219	9.442878	9.429661	9.416565	9.403589	9.390732	9.377992	9.365368	9.352858	9.340462
23	9.328178	9.316005	9.303941	9.291986	9.280137	9.268395	9.256757	9.245223	9.233791	9.222461	9.211231	9.200100
24	9.189067	9.178131	9.167291	9.156546	9.145894	9.135336	9.124869	9.114494	9.104208	9.094011	9.083902	9.073881
25	9.063945	9.054095	9.044329	9.034647	9.025047	9.015529	9.006092	8.996735	8.987458	8.978259	8.969137	8.960093
26	8.951124	8.942231	8.933413	8.924668	8.915996	8.907396	8.898869	8.890412	8.882025	8.873707	8.865459	8.857278
27	8.849165	8.841119	8.833139	8.825224	8.817375	8.809589	8.801867	8.794208	8.786611	8.779076	8.771602	8.764188
28	8.756835	8.749541	8.742306	8.735129	8.728010	8.720948	8.713942	8.706993	8.700099	8.693261	8.686476	8.679746
29	8.673069	8.666446	8.659875	8.653356	8.646888	8.640471	8.634106	8.627790	8.621524	8.615307	8.609139	8.603019
30	8.596947	8.590922	8.584945	8.579014	8.573129	8.567291	8.561497	8.555748	8.550044	8.544384	8.538768	8.533195
31	8.527665	8.522177	8.516732	8.511329	8.505967	8.500646	8.495366	8.490126	8.484927	8.479767	8.474646	8.469564
32	8.464521	8.459516	8.454550	8.449621	8.444729	8.439874	8.435056	8.430274	8.425528	8.420818	8.416144	8.411504
33	8.406900	8.402330	8.397794	8.393292	8.388824	8.384389	8.379987	8.375618	8.371282	8.366978	8.362706	8.358465
34	8.354257	8.350079	8.345932	8.341816	8.337730	8.333675	8.329650	8.325654	8.321687	8.317750	8.313842	8.309962
35	8.306111	8.302288	8.298494	8.294727	8.290987	8.287275	8.283590	8.279932	8.276301	8.272696	8.269117	8.265564
36	8.262037	8.258536	8.255060	8.251609	8.248184	8.244783	8.241406	8.238055	8.234727	8.231423	8.228143	8.224887
37	8.221654	8.218445	8.215259	8.212095	8.208954	8.205836	8.202740	8.199666	8.196615	8.193585	8.190576	8.187590
38	8.184624	8.181680	8.178757	8.175854	8.172972	8.170111	8.167270	8.164449	8.161649	8.158868	8.156107	8.153365
39	8.150643	8.147940	8.145256	8.142591	8.139945	8.137318	8.134709	8.132119	8.129547	8.126993	8.124457	8.121939
40	8.119438	8.116955	8.114490	8.112042	8.109611	8.107197	8.104800	8.102420	8.100056	8.097709	8.095378	8.093064

Annual Mortgage Constant for Monthly Payment Loans

8.00% Interest Rate   8.00% Interest Rate

Years	0	1	2	3	4	5	6	7	8	9	10	11
2	54.272750	52.270514	50.422637	48.711966	47.123802	45.645470	44.265989	42.975790	41.766505	40.630777	39.562116	38.554773
3	37.603639	36.704155	35.852244	35.044246	34.276869	33.547139	32.852367	32.190115	31.558165	30.954497	30.377266	29.824785
4	29.295507	28.788011	28.300990	27.833240	27.383648	26.951188	26.534906	26.133921	25.747413	25.374620	25.014833	24.667390
5	24.331673	24.007107	23.693151	23.389300	23.095080	22.810048	22.533784	22.265897	22.006017	21.753795	21.508903	21.271032
6	21.039889	20.815197	20.596695	20.384134	20.177282	19.975914	19.779820	19.588800	19.402663	19.221228	19.044323	18.871785
7	18.703457	18.539191	18.378845	18.222284	18.069378	17.920004	17.774045	17.631388	17.491925	17.355552	17.222172	17.091690
8	16.964015	16.839060	16.716742	16.596981	16.479700	16.364825	16.252285	16.142013	16.033943	15.928012	15.824160	15.722327
9	15.622458	15.524499	15.428397	15.334102	15.241566	15.150743	15.061586	14.974052	14.888100	14.803688	14.720778	14.639331
10	14.559311	14.480683	14.403411	14.327464	14.252808	14.179413	14.107249	14.036286	13.966496	13.897853	13.830328	13.763898
11	13.698536	13.634219	13.570923	13.508626	13.447304	13.386938	13.327505	13.268987	13.211362	13.154612	13.098719	13.043665
12	12.989431	12.936001	12.883359	12.831487	12.780371	12.729995	12.680344	12.631405	12.583161	12.535601	12.488711	12.442477
13	12.396887	12.351928	12.307589	12.263857	12.220722	12.178172	12.136196	12.094783	12.053924	12.013607	11.973824	11.934564
14	11.895818	11.857577	11.819833	11.782575	11.745795	11.709486	11.673639	11.638246	11.603300	11.568792	11.534715	11.501061
15	11.467825	11.434998	11.402575	11.370547	11.338910	11.307655	11.276778	11.246272	11.216131	11.186348	11.156920	11.127839
16	11.099100	11.070699	11.042629	11.014885	10.987463	10.960357	10.933563	10.907076	10.880891	10.855003	10.829409	10.804103
17	10.779082	10.754341	10.729876	10.705683	10.681758	10.658097	10.634696	10.611552	10.588661	10.566018	10.543622	10.521467
18	10.499551	10.477871	10.456423	10.435203	10.414209	10.393438	10.372886	10.352550	10.332428	10.312516	10.292812	10.273313
19	10.254017	10.234919	10.216018	10.197312	10.178797	10.160471	10.142332	10.124377	10.106604	10.089010	10.071593	10.054350
20	10.037281	10.020382	10.003650	9.987085	9.970684	9.954445	9.938365	9.922444	9.906678	9.891066	9.875606	9.860297
21	9.845135	9.830121	9.815251	9.800523	9.785937	9.771491	9.757182	9.743010	9.728972	9.715067	9.701294	9.687650
22	9.674135	9.660746	9.647483	9.634344	9.621327	9.608431	9.595654	9.582996	9.570455	9.558029	9.545717	9.533518
23	9.521431	9.509454	9.497587	9.485827	9.474174	9.462626	9.451183	9.439842	9.428604	9.417467	9.406430	9.395491
24	9.384649	9.373905	9.363256	9.352701	9.342240	9.331871	9.321593	9.311406	9.301309	9.291300	9.281378	9.271544
25	9.261795	9.252130	9.242550	9.233053	9.223638	9.214305	9.205052	9.195878	9.186784	9.177767	9.168828	9.159965
26	9.151177	9.142465	9.133827	9.125262	9.116769	9.108349	9.100000	9.091721	9.083512	9.075371	9.067300	9.059295
27	9.051358	9.043488	9.035682	9.027942	9.020266	9.012654	9.005106	8.997619	8.990195	8.982832	8.975529	8.968287
28	8.961104	8.953980	8.946914	8.939907	8.932956	8.926062	8.919225	8.912443	8.905716	8.899044	8.892426	8.885861
29	8.879350	8.872891	8.866484	8.860129	8.853825	8.847571	8.841368	8.835214	8.829109	8.823054	8.817046	8.811087
30	8.805175	8.799310	8.793491	8.787719	8.781992	8.776311	8.770675	8.765083	8.759535	8.754031	8.748570	8.743152
31	8.737777	8.732443	8.727152	8.721902	8.716693	8.711524	8.706396	8.701308	8.696259	8.691250	8.686279	8.681347
32	8.676454	8.671598	8.666779	8.661998	8.657254	8.652546	8.647875	8.643239	8.638639	8.634075	8.629545	8.625050
33	8.620589	8.616163	8.611770	8.607411	8.603086	8.598793	8.594532	8.590305	8.586109	8.581945	8.577813	8.573712
34	8.569642	8.565603	8.561594	8.557616	8.553667	8.549749	8.545859	8.542000	8.538169	8.534367	8.530593	8.526848
35	8.523131	8.519441	8.515779	8.512145	8.508538	8.504957	8.501404	8.497876	8.494375	8.490901	8.487451	8.484028
36	8.480630	8.477257	8.473909	8.470586	8.467288	8.464013	8.460764	8.457538	8.454335	8.451157	8.448002	8.444870
37	8.441761	8.438675	8.435612	8.432571	8.429552	8.426556	8.423582	8.420629	8.417698	8.414788	8.411900	8.409033
38	8.406186	8.403361	8.400556	8.397771	8.395007	8.392262	8.389538	8.386834	8.384149	8.381484	8.378838	8.376211
39	8.373603	8.371014	8.368444	8.365892	8.363359	8.360844	8.358347	8.355869	8.353408	8.350965	8.348539	8.346131
40	8.343740	8.341367	8.339010	8.336671	8.334348	8.332042	8.329752	8.327479	8.325222	8.322981	8.320757	8.318548

8.25% Interest Rate   8.25% Interest Rate

Years	0	1	2	3	4	5	6	7	8	9	10	11
2	54.409677	52.407514	50.559724	48.849156	47.261106	45.782901	44.403555	43.113502	41.904371	40.768804	39.700311	38.693143
3	37.742188	36.842890	35.991169	35.183366	34.416187	33.686660	32.992095	32.330052	31.698314	31.094861	30.517848	29.965587
4	29.436532	28.929260	28.442466	27.974944	27.525583	27.093354	26.677306	26.276556	25.890285	25.517730	25.158181	24.810977
5	24.475502	24.151178	23.837465	23.533858	23.239883	22.955095	22.679078	22.411438	22.151805	21.899831	21.655188	21.417567
6	21.186673	20.962232	20.743980	20.531671	20.325070	20.123954	19.928113	19.737345	19.551461	19.370280	19.193629	19.021345
7	18.853271	18.689259	18.529167	18.372861	18.220209	18.071091	17.925387	17.782985	17.643777	17.507660	17.374536	17.244309
8	17.116890	16.992190	16.870128	16.750623	16.633597	16.518978	16.406695	16.296678	16.188864	16.083189	15.979592	15.878015
9	15.778401	15.680697	15.584861	15.490812	15.398532	15.307963	15.219061	15.131783	15.046085	14.961928	14.879273	14.798081
10	14.718315	14.639941	14.562923	14.487230	14.412828	14.339687	14.267776	14.197066	14.127530	14.059139	13.991868	13.925690
11	13.860580	13.796515	13.733471	13.671426	13.610356	13.550241	13.491059	13.432792	13.375418	13.318919	13.263276	13.208471
12	13.154487	13.101307	13.048913	12.997291	12.946424	12.896296	12.846894	12.798202	12.750206	12.702894	12.656250	12.610263
13	12.564920	12.520207	12.476144	12.432628	12.389738	12.347433	12.305702	12.264534	12.223919	12.183846	12.144307	12.105290
14	12.066787	12.028789	11.991286	11.954271	11.917733	11.881665	11.846059	11.810907	11.776201	11.741933	11.708095	11.674682
15	11.641684	11.609096	11.576911	11.545122	11.513721	11.482704	11.452064	11.421794	11.391889	11.362343	11.333150	11.304304
16	11.275801	11.247633	11.219797	11.192287	11.165099	11.138226	11.111664	11.085409	11.059456	11.033800	11.008436	10.983361
17	10.958570	10.934059	10.909824	10.885860	10.862163	10.838731	10.815558	10.792641	10.769977	10.747561	10.725391	10.703462
18	10.681772	10.660316	10.639093	10.618097	10.597327	10.576779	10.556450	10.536337	10.516437	10.496747	10.477265	10.457987
19	10.438910	10.420033	10.401352	10.382865	10.364569	10.346461	10.328540	10.310803	10.293246	10.275869	10.258668	10.241642
20	10.224788	10.208104	10.191587	10.175236	10.159048	10.143022	10.127156	10.111446	10.095892	10.080492	10.065243	10.050141
21	10.035193	10.020388	10.005727	9.991209	9.976831	9.962592	9.948491	9.934526	9.920695	9.906996	9.893428	9.879989
22	9.866679	9.853494	9.840435	9.827499	9.814685	9.801991	9.789417	9.776960	9.764620	9.752395	9.740283	9.728284
23	9.716396	9.704618	9.692949	9.681387	9.669931	9.658580	9.647333	9.636189	9.625146	9.614204	9.603361	9.592617
24	9.581969	9.571418	9.560961	9.550599	9.540329	9.530152	9.520065	9.510068	9.500161	9.490341	9.480609	9.470963
25	9.461402	9.451925	9.442532	9.433221	9.423993	9.414845	9.405777	9.396788	9.387878	9.379045	9.370289	9.361609
26	9.353004	9.344474	9.336017	9.327633	9.319321	9.311080	9.302911	9.294811	9.286780	9.278818	9.270924	9.263097
27	9.255337	9.247642	9.240013	9.232448	9.224947	9.217509	9.210134	9.202821	9.195569	9.188379	9.181248	9.174177
28	9.167165	9.160212	9.153317	9.146478	9.139697	9.132972	9.126303	9.119688	9.113129	9.106623	9.100172	9.093773
29	9.087427	9.081133	9.074890	9.068699	9.062558	9.056468	9.050427	9.044435	9.038492	9.032598	9.026751	9.020952
30	9.015199	9.009493	9.003834	8.998220	8.992651	8.987127	8.981647	8.976212	8.970820	8.965471	8.960166	8.954902
31	8.949681	8.944501	8.939363	8.934266	8.929209	8.924192	8.919215	8.914278	8.909380	8.904520	8.899699	8.894916
32	8.890117	8.885463	8.880792	8.876158	8.871561	8.866999	8.862474	8.857983	8.853528	8.849108	8.844723	8.840371
33	8.836054	8.831770	8.827520	8.823302	8.819118	8.814966	8.810846	8.806758	8.802701	8.798677	8.794683	8.790720
34	8.786788	8.782886	8.779014	8.775172	8.771359	8.767576	8.763822	8.760097	8.756400	8.752731	8.749091	8.745479
35	8.741894	8.738336	8.734806	8.731302	8.727826	8.724376	8.720952	8.717554	8.714182	8.710835	8.707514	8.704218
36	8.700947	8.697701	8.694479	8.691282	8.688109	8.684960	8.681834	8.678733	8.675654	8.672599	8.669567	8.666557
37	8.663570	8.660606	8.657664	8.654743	8.651845	8.648969	8.646114	8.643280	8.640468	8.637676	8.634906	8.632156
38	8.629426	8.626717	8.624029	8.621360	8.618711	8.616081	8.613472	8.610881	8.608310	8.605758	8.603225	8.600711
39	8.598215	8.595738	8.593279	8.590838	8.588415	8.586010	8.583623	8.581254	8.578902	8.576567	8.574250	8.571949
40	8.569666	8.567399	8.565149	8.562916	8.560699	8.558498	8.556313	8.554144	8.551992	8.549855	8.547733	8.545628

Annual Mortgage Constant for Monthly Payment Loans

8.50% Interest Rate ····· 8.50% Interest Rate

Years	0	1	2	3	4	5	6	7	8	9	10	11
					Number	of Months						
2	54.546810	52.544727	50.697034	48.986576	47.398650	45.920579	44.541378	43.251479	42.042510	40.907113	39.838797	38.831811
3	37.881045	36.981940	36.130418	35.322818	34.555847	33.826530	33.132179	32.470354	31.838837	31.235608	30.658821	30.106789
4	29.577964	29.070926	28.584366	28.117081	27.667959	27.235971	26.820164	26.419658	26.033630	25.661321	25.302019	24.955064
5	24.619838	24.295763	23.982301	23.678946	23.385224	23.100691	22.824928	22.557542	22.298165	22.046448	21.802062	21.564697
6	21.334062	21.109878	20.891886	20.679836	20.473494	20.272638	20.077057	19.886550	19.700927	19.520007	19.343617	19.171594
7	19.003783	18.840033	18.680203	18.524159	18.371770	18.222914	18.077473	17.935334	17.796389	17.660535	17.527674	17.397711
8	17.270554	17.146118	17.024319	16.905077	16.788315	16.673959	16.561938	16.452185	16.344634	16.239222	16.135888	16.034574
9	15.935223	15.837782	15.742199	15.648422	15.556404	15.466098	15.377458	15.290442	15.205006	15.121111	15.038718	14.957787
10	14.878283	14.800170	14.723413	14.647981	14.573839	14.500958	14.429308	14.358859	14.289582	14.221451	14.154439	14.088521
11	14.023670	13.959864	13.897079	13.835291	13.774480	13.714622	13.655699	13.597688	13.540571	13.484329	13.428943	13.374395
12	13.320667	13.267742	13.215604	13.164237	13.113625	13.063752	13.014604	12.966166	12.918424	12.871365	12.824975	12.779241
13	12.734149	12.689689	12.645848	12.602614	12.559975	12.517921	12.476441	12.435523	12.395158	12.355335	12.316044	12.277277
14	12.239022	12.201272	12.164018	12.127249	12.090959	12.055138	12.019779	11.984873	11.950412	11.916389	11.882797	11.849628
15	11.816875	11.784531	11.752589	11.721042	11.689885	11.659110	11.628712	11.598684	11.569020	11.539715	11.510762	11.482156
16	11.453892	11.425964	11.398367	11.371095	11.344144	11.317509	11.291185	11.265166	11.239450	11.214029	11.188902	11.164062
17	11.139505	11.115228	11.091227	11.067496	11.044033	11.020832	10.997892	10.975207	10.952774	10.930589	10.908649	10.886950
18	10.865489	10.844263	10.823268	10.802501	10.781959	10.761638	10.741536	10.721649	10.701975	10.682511	10.663253	10.644200
19	10.625348	10.606694	10.588236	10.569972	10.551898	10.534012	10.516313	10.498796	10.481460	10.464303	10.447322	10.430514
20	10.413879	10.397413	10.381114	10.364980	10.349009	10.333199	10.317548	10.302054	10.286715	10.271529	10.256494	10.241609
21	10.226870	10.212278	10.197829	10.183522	10.169355	10.155327	10.141436	10.127680	10.114058	10.100568	10.087208	10.073977
22	10.060874	10.047896	10.035043	10.022313	10.009704	9.997215	9.984844	9.972591	9.960454	9.948432	9.936523	9.924725
23	9.913038	9.901461	9.889992	9.878630	9.867373	9.856221	9.845173	9.834226	9.823381	9.812636	9.801989	9.791440
24	9.780988	9.770631	9.760369	9.750200	9.740124	9.730139	9.720245	9.710440	9.700724	9.691095	9.681553	9.672097
25	9.662725	9.653437	9.644232	9.635110	9.626068	9.617107	9.608225	9.599423	9.590697	9.582049	9.573478	9.564981
26	9.556560	9.548212	9.539937	9.531735	9.523605	9.515545	9.507555	9.499635	9.491784	9.484001	9.476285	9.468636
27	9.461052	9.453534	9.446081	9.438692	9.431366	9.424103	9.416903	9.409763	9.402685	9.395667	9.388709	9.381809
28	9.374969	9.368186	9.361461	9.354792	9.348180	9.341624	9.335123	9.328676	9.322284	9.315945	9.309659	9.303426
29	9.297245	9.291116	9.285038	9.279010	9.273033	9.267105	9.261226	9.255396	9.249615	9.243881	9.238194	9.232555
30	9.226962	9.221415	9.215913	9.210457	9.205046	9.199678	9.194355	9.189076	9.183839	9.178645	9.173494	9.168384
31	9.163316	9.158289	9.153304	9.148358	9.143453	9.138587	9.133760	9.128973	9.124224	9.119514	9.114841	9.110206
32	9.105609	9.101048	9.096524	9.092036	9.087584	9.083168	9.078787	9.074441	9.070129	9.065852	9.061609	9.057400
33	9.053225	9.049082	9.044973	9.040896	9.036851	9.032838	9.028857	9.024908	9.020990	9.017102	9.013246	9.009419
34	9.005623	9.001857	8.998120	8.994413	8.990735	8.987085	8.983465	8.979872	8.976308	8.972771	8.969263	8.965781
35	8.962327	8.958900	8.955499	8.952125	8.948777	8.945455	8.942159	8.938888	8.935643	8.932423	8.929228	8.926058
36	8.922912	8.919791	8.916693	8.913620	8.910570	8.907544	8.904541	8.901561	8.898604	8.895670	8.892759	8.889870
37	8.887003	8.884158	8.881334	8.878533	8.875753	8.872994	8.870256	8.867539	8.864843	8.862168	8.859513	8.856878
38	8.854263	8.851668	8.849093	8.846538	8.844002	8.841485	8.838988	8.836509	8.834049	8.831608	8.829185	8.826781
39	8.824395	8.822027	8.819676	8.817344	8.815029	8.812732	8.810452	8.808189	8.805944	8.803715	8.801503	8.799308
40	8.797129	8.794966	8.792820	8.790690	8.788576	8.786478	8.784396	8.782329	8.780278	8.778242	8.776221	8.774216

8.75% Interest Rate ····· 8.75% Interest Rate

Years	0	1	2	3	4	5	6	7	8	9	10	11
2	54.684148	52.682154	50.834566	49.124227	47.536433	46.058505	44.679458	43.389721	42.180922	41.045703	39.977572	38.970778
3	38.020209	37.121306	36.269991	35.462603	34.695847	33.966750	33.272622	32.611023	31.979735	31.376737	30.800185	30.248390
4	29.719804	29.213007	28.726691	28.259651	27.810775	27.379035	26.963479	26.563224	26.177449	25.805394	25.446347	25.099648
5	24.764679	24.440863	24.127661	23.824566	23.531104	23.246832	22.971332	22.704209	22.445096	22.193642	21.949521	21.712422
6	21.482052	21.258135	21.040409	20.828627	20.622552	20.421964	20.226651	20.036413	19.851058	19.670407	19.494286	19.322533
7	19.154991	18.991511	18.831951	18.676177	18.524058	18.375473	18.230302	18.088433	17.949756	17.814156	17.681585	17.551892
8	17.425006	17.300841	17.179313	17.060341	16.943849	16.829764	16.718014	16.608532	16.501251	16.396109	16.293045	16.192001
9	16.092921	15.995750	15.900436	15.806929	15.715181	15.625144	15.536774	15.450026	15.364860	15.281233	15.199108	15.118446
10	15.039210	14.961365	14.884877	14.809712	14.735838	14.663224	14.591841	14.521658	14.452648	14.384784	14.318038	14.252385
11	14.187800	14.124259	14.061739	14.000216	13.939669	13.880076	13.821417	13.763670	13.706817	13.650838	13.595714	13.541428
12	13.487963	13.435300	13.383424	13.332318	13.281967	13.232355	13.183467	13.135289	13.087807	13.041007	12.994876	12.949401
13	12.904568	12.860066	12.816782	12.773805	12.731424	12.689626	12.648402	12.607740	12.567630	12.528063	12.489027	12.450514
14	12.412514	12.375017	12.338016	12.301500	12.265462	12.229894	12.194786	12.160131	12.125921	12.092149	12.058807	12.025888
15	11.993384	11.961289	11.929595	11.898297	11.867387	11.836860	11.806708	11.776927	11.747509	11.718449	11.689741	11.661380
16	11.633360	11.605676	11.578322	11.551294	11.524585	11.498192	11.472109	11.446332	11.420856	11.395676	11.370788	11.346187
17	11.321870	11.297831	11.274068	11.250575	11.227348	11.204385	11.181680	11.159231	11.137033	11.115083	11.093377	11.071912
18	11.050685	11.029691	11.008929	10.988393	10.968082	10.947993	10.928121	10.908464	10.889020	10.869784	10.850755	10.831930
19	10.813305	10.794879	10.776648	10.758609	10.740761	10.723101	10.705625	10.688333	10.671220	10.654286	10.637528	10.620943
20	10.604529	10.588283	10.572205	10.556291	10.540540	10.524949	10.509517	10.494241	10.479120	10.464151	10.449332	10.434662
21	10.420140	10.405762	10.391528	10.377435	10.363481	10.349666	10.335988	10.322445	10.309033	10.295753	10.282604	10.269583
22	10.256689	10.243920	10.231275	10.218752	10.206350	10.194068	10.181904	10.169857	10.157925	10.146107	10.134401	10.122808
23	10.111324	10.099949	10.088682	10.077521	10.066466	10.055514	10.044665	10.033918	10.023272	10.012724	10.002275	9.991924
24	9.981668	9.971508	9.961441	9.951467	9.941586	9.931795	9.922094	9.912482	9.902958	9.893521	9.884171	9.874905
25	9.865724	9.856626	9.847610	9.838676	9.829823	9.821049	9.812355	9.803738	9.795199	9.786737	9.778350	9.770038
26	9.761800	9.753636	9.745544	9.737524	9.729575	9.721697	9.713888	9.706148	9.698476	9.690872	9.683334	9.675863
27	9.668458	9.661117	9.653840	9.646627	9.639476	9.632388	9.625362	9.618396	9.611491	9.604646	9.597859	9.591132
28	9.584462	9.577850	9.571295	9.564796	9.558353	9.551965	9.545632	9.539353	9.533128	9.526955	9.520835	9.514768
29	9.508752	9.502787	9.496872	9.491008	9.485193	9.479427	9.473710	9.468042	9.462421	9.456847	9.451320	9.445839
30	9.440405	9.435016	9.429672	9.424373	9.419118	9.413906	9.408739	9.403614	9.398532	9.393492	9.388494	9.383537
31	9.378622	9.373747	9.368912	9.364117	9.359362	9.354646	9.349969	9.345331	9.340730	9.336168	9.331642	9.327154
32	9.322703	9.318288	9.313909	9.309566	9.305258	9.300986	9.296748	9.292545	9.288375	9.284240	9.280139	9.276070
33	9.272035	9.268032	9.264062	9.260124	9.256217	9.252343	9.248499	9.244686	9.240905	9.237153	9.233432	9.229741
34	9.226079	9.222446	9.218843	9.215269	9.211723	9.208206	9.204716	9.201255	9.197821	9.194415	9.191036	9.187683
35	9.184358	9.181059	9.177786	9.174539	9.171318	9.168122	9.164952	9.161806	9.158686	9.155591	9.152520	9.149473
36	9.146450	9.143451	9.140476	9.137524	9.134596	9.131690	9.128807	9.125947	9.123110	9.120295	9.117502	9.114730
37	9.111981	9.109253	9.106547	9.103861	9.101197	9.098553	9.095930	9.093328	9.090746	9.088184	9.085642	9.083120
38	9.080617	9.078134	9.075670	9.073226	9.070800	9.068394	9.066005	9.063636	9.061285	9.058952	9.056637	9.054340
39	9.052061	9.049800	9.047555	9.045329	9.043119	9.040927	9.038751	9.036593	9.034451	9.032325	9.030216	9.028123
40	9.026046	9.023985	9.021940	9.019911	9.017897	9.015899	9.013916	9.011949	9.009996	9.008059	9.006136	9.004228

Annual Mortgage Constant for Monthly Payment Loans

9.00% Interest Rate   9.00% Interest Rate

Years	0	1	2	3	4	5	6	7	8	9	10	11
					Number of Months							
2	54.821691	52.819795	50.972320	49.262109	47.674455	46.196679	44.817793	43.528227	42.319608	41.184575	40.116638	39.110043
3	38.159679	37.260987	36.409888	35.602719	34.836187	34.107318	33.413421	32.752056	32.121006	31.518249	30.941939	30.390389
4	29.862051	29.355503	28.869439	28.402652	27.954032	27.522548	27.107250	26.707255	26.321741	25.949948	25.591164	25.244730
5	24.910026	24.586477	24.273541	23.970714	23.677522	23.393520	23.118289	22.851438	22.592596	22.341415	22.097567	21.860741
6	21.630645	21.407002	21.189550	20.978043	20.772244	20.571931	20.376894	20.186932	20.001853	19.821479	19.645635	19.474159
7	19.306894	19.143691	18.984409	18.828912	18.677072	18.528764	18.383871	18.242280	18.103884	17.968579	17.836266	17.706852
8	17.580244	17.456357	17.335106	17.216412	17.100199	16.986391	16.874919	16.765715	16.658711	16.553847	16.451060	16.350294
9	16.251490	16.154596	16.059559	15.966329	15.874857	15.785097	15.697003	15.610532	15.525641	15.442291	15.360441	15.280054
10	15.201093	15.123523	15.047309	14.972418	14.898818	14.826479	14.755369	14.685460	14.616723	14.549131	14.482658	14.417277
11	14.352965	14.289696	14.227447	14.166195	14.105919	14.046597	13.988207	13.930731	13.874147	13.818437	13.763583	13.709566
12	13.656368	13.603974	13.552365	13.501527	13.451442	13.402097	13.353475	13.305563	13.258347	13.211812	13.165946	13.120735
13	13.076166	13.032228	12.988907	12.946194	12.904074	12.862539	12.821576	12.781176	12.741327	12.702020	12.663244	12.624991
14	12.587250	12.550013	12.513270	12.477012	12.441232	12.405921	12.371070	12.336671	12.302717	12.269201	12.236113	12.203449
15	12.171199	12.139358	12.107917	12.076872	12.046215	12.015939	11.986039	11.956508	11.927341	11.898531	11.870073	11.841961
16	11.814190	11.786754	11.759648	11.732867	11.706405	11.680258	11.654421	11.628890	11.603658	11.578723	11.554079	11.529721
17	11.505647	11.481851	11.458329	11.435077	11.412092	11.389369	11.366904	11.344694	11.322735	11.301024	11.279556	11.258329
18	11.237338	11.216581	11.196054	11.175754	11.155678	11.135823	11.116185	11.096761	11.077550	11.058547	11.039749	11.021155
19	11.002761	10.984565	10.966563	10.948754	10.931134	10.913702	10.896454	10.879389	10.862503	10.845795	10.829262	10.812901
20	10.796711	10.780690	10.764835	10.749144	10.733615	10.718246	10.703034	10.687979	10.673078	10.658328	10.643728	10.629277
21	10.614972	10.600812	10.586794	10.572917	10.559180	10.545580	10.532115	10.518785	10.505588	10.492521	10.479584	10.466775
22	10.454092	10.441534	10.429099	10.416785	10.404593	10.392519	10.380563	10.368722	10.356997	10.345385	10.333886	10.322497
23	10.311218	10.300047	10.288983	10.278025	10.267172	10.256422	10.245774	10.235228	10.224781	10.214433	10.204183	10.194030
24	10.183972	10.174009	10.164139	10.154361	10.144675	10.135079	10.125572	10.116154	10.106824	10.097580	10.088421	10.079347
25	10.070356	10.061449	10.052623	10.043878	10.035214	10.026628	10.018121	10.009692	10.001339	9.993063	9.984861	9.976734
26	9.968681	9.960700	9.952791	9.944954	9.937187	9.929490	9.921862	9.914302	9.906810	9.899385	9.892026	9.884733
27	9.877505	9.870341	9.863240	9.856203	9.849228	9.842314	9.835462	9.828670	9.821938	9.815265	9.808651	9.802094
28	9.795596	9.789154	9.782768	9.776439	9.770164	9.763944	9.757778	9.751666	9.745607	9.739601	9.733646	9.727743
29	9.721891	9.716090	9.710338	9.704636	9.698984	9.693379	9.687823	9.682315	9.676853	9.671439	9.666071	9.660748
30	9.655471	9.650239	9.645052	9.639909	9.634809	9.629753	9.624739	9.619769	9.614840	9.609952	9.605107	9.600302
31	9.595537	9.590813	9.586128	9.581483	9.576877	9.572310	9.567781	9.563289	9.558836	9.554419	9.550040	9.545697
32	9.541390	9.537120	9.532885	9.528685	9.524520	9.520389	9.516293	9.512231	9.508203	9.504208	9.500246	9.496316
33	9.492419	9.488555	9.484722	9.480921	9.477151	9.473412	9.469704	9.466027	9.462379	9.458762	9.455174	9.451615
34	9.448086	9.444586	9.441114	9.437671	9.434255	9.430868	9.427508	9.424176	9.420870	9.417592	9.414340	9.411115
35	9.407916	9.404743	9.401595	9.398473	9.395377	9.392305	9.389258	9.386236	9.383239	9.380265	9.377316	9.374390
36	9.371488	9.368609	9.365754	9.362921	9.360112	9.357324	9.354560	9.351817	9.349097	9.346398	9.343721	9.341065
37	9.338431	9.335817	9.333225	9.330653	9.328102	9.325571	9.323060	9.320570	9.318099	9.315648	9.313217	9.310804
38	9.308412	9.306038	9.303683	9.301346	9.299028	9.296729	9.294448	9.292185	9.289940	9.287712	9.285502	9.283310
39	9.281135	9.278978	9.276837	9.274713	9.272606	9.270516	9.268442	9.266385	9.264343	9.262318	9.260309	9.258316
40	9.256338	9.254376	9.252429	9.250498	9.248581	9.246680	9.244794	9.242922	9.241066	9.239223	9.237396	9.235582

9.25% Interest Rate   9.25% Interest Rate

Years	0	1	2	3	4	5	6	7	8	9	10	11
2	54.959439	52.957649	51.110296	49.400222	47.812716	46.335100	44.956384	43.666998	42.458566	41.323729	40.255993	39.249606
3	38.299456	37.400983	36.550108	35.743168	34.976868	34.248235	33.554577	32.893455	32.262651	31.660142	31.084083	30.532787
4	30.004704	29.498415	29.012610	28.546085	28.097728	27.666509	27.251478	26.851750	26.466505	26.094982	25.736470	25.390308
5	25.055878	24.732603	24.419943	24.117392	23.824477	23.540752	23.265800	22.999228	22.740665	22.489764	22.246196	22.000652
6	21.779837	21.556476	21.339307	21.128082	20.922566	20.722537	20.527784	20.338105	20.153311	19.973221	19.797662	19.626470
7	19.459490	19.296573	19.137576	18.982364	18.830809	18.682786	18.538179	18.396873	18.258763	18.123743	17.991716	17.862586
8	17.736264	17.612662	17.491697	17.373289	17.257360	17.143838	17.032651	16.923731	16.817012	16.712432	16.609937	16.509448
9	16.410929	16.314319	16.219566	16.126619	16.035431	15.945954	15.858143	15.771954	15.687347	15.604278	15.522711	15.442606
10	15.363927	15.286638	15.210705	15.136096	15.062777	14.990716	14.919888	14.850258	14.781801	14.714489	14.648294	14.583192
11	14.519158	14.456167	14.394196	14.333222	14.273223	14.214177	14.156064	14.098863	14.042555	13.987121	13.932542	13.878799
12	13.825876	13.773755	13.722420	13.671855	13.622043	13.572970	13.524621	13.476981	13.430035	13.383771	13.338175	13.293234
13	13.248935	13.205266	13.162215	13.119769	13.077918	13.036650	12.995954	12.955820	12.916238	12.877196	12.838686	12.800698
14	12.763221	12.726248	12.689768	12.653774	12.618256	12.583207	12.548618	12.514480	12.480787	12.447531	12.414704	12.382298
15	12.350307	12.318724	12.287542	12.256754	12.226354	12.196335	12.166691	12.137415	12.108503	12.079948	12.051744	12.023885
16	11.996367	11.969183	11.942329	11.915799	11.889588	11.863692	11.838105	11.812822	11.787840	11.763153	11.738756	11.714646
17	11.690819	11.667269	11.643993	11.620986	11.598245	11.575766	11.553545	11.531578	11.509862	11.488392	11.467166	11.446179
18	11.425429	11.404912	11.384624	11.364563	11.344725	11.325107	11.305706	11.286519	11.267543	11.248775	11.230213	11.211853
19	11.193693	11.175729	11.157960	11.140383	11.122995	11.105793	11.088775	11.071939	11.055283	11.038803	11.022498	11.006365
20	10.990402	10.974607	10.958977	10.943511	10.928207	10.913062	10.898074	10.883241	10.868562	10.854034	10.839655	10.825424
21	10.811339	10.797398	10.783599	10.769940	10.756420	10.743037	10.729789	10.716675	10.703693	10.690841	10.678118	10.665522
22	10.653052	10.640705	10.628482	10.616380	10.604398	10.592534	10.580787	10.569155	10.557638	10.546234	10.534941	10.523759
23	10.512685	10.501719	10.490860	10.480106	10.469456	10.458909	10.448463	10.438118	10.427873	10.417725	10.407675	10.397721
24	10.387861	10.378096	10.368423	10.358843	10.349353	10.339952	10.330641	10.321417	10.312280	10.303229	10.294263	10.285381
25	10.276582	10.267865	10.259230	10.250675	10.242199	10.233802	10.225483	10.217241	10.209075	10.200984	10.192968	10.185026
26	10.177157	10.169360	10.161634	10.153979	10.146394	10.138879	10.131431	10.124052	10.116739	10.109493	10.102313	10.095198
27	10.088147	10.081159	10.074235	10.067373	10.060573	10.053833	10.047155	10.040536	10.033976	10.027475	10.021032	10.014647
28	10.008318	10.002046	9.995829	9.989668	9.983561	9.977509	9.971510	9.965564	9.959670	9.953829	9.948038	9.942299
29	9.936611	9.930972	9.925382	9.919842	9.914350	9.908906	9.903510	9.898161	9.892858	9.887602	9.882391	9.877226
30	9.872105	9.867029	9.861997	9.857008	9.852063	9.847160	9.842300	9.837481	9.832704	9.827968	9.823273	9.818619
31	9.814004	9.809429	9.804893	9.800395	9.795937	9.791516	9.787133	9.782788	9.778480	9.774208	9.769973	9.765774
32	9.761610	9.757482	9.753389	9.749330	9.745306	9.741316	9.737360	9.733437	9.729547	9.725690	9.721866	9.718074
33	9.714314	9.710585	9.706888	9.703222	9.699586	9.695982	9.692407	9.688862	9.685347	9.681862	9.678405	9.674978
34	9.671579	9.668208	9.664865	9.661551	9.658264	9.655004	9.651771	9.648566	9.645387	9.642234	9.639107	9.636007
35	9.632932	9.629882	9.626858	9.623859	9.620884	9.617935	9.615009	9.612108	9.609230	9.606376	9.603546	9.600739
36	9.597955	9.595194	9.592456	9.589740	9.587047	9.584375	9.581726	9.579098	9.576492	9.573907	9.571343	9.568800
37	9.566278	9.563777	9.561296	9.558835	9.556395	9.553974	9.551573	9.549191	9.546829	9.544487	9.542163	9.539858
38	9.537572	9.535304	9.533055	9.530824	9.528611	9.526416	9.524239	9.522080	9.519938	9.517813	9.515706	9.513615
39	9.511542	9.509485	9.507445	9.505421	9.503414	9.501423	9.499448	9.497488	9.495545	9.493617	9.491705	9.489808
40	9.487927	9.486060	9.484209	9.482372	9.480551	9.478743	9.476951	9.475172	9.473408	9.471658	9.469923	9.468201

Annual Mortgage Constant for Monthly Payment Loans

9.50% Interest Rate .... 9.50% Interest Rate

Years	0	1	2	3	4	Number of Months 5	6	7	8	9	10	11
2	55.097392	53.095716	51.248495	49.538564	47.951216	46.473768	45.095231	43.806033	42.597797	41.463163	40.395637	39.389467
3	38.439540	37.541294	36.690651	35.883947	35.117888	34.389499	33.696090	33.035219	32.404668	31.802416	31.226617	30.675582
4	30.147764	29.641740	29.156204	28.689949	28.241863	27.810917	27.396160	26.996708	26.611741	26.240496	25.882264	25.536382
5	25.202234	24.879241	24.566864	24.264598	23.971967	23.688528	23.413862	23.147577	22.889302	22.638689	22.395410	22.159154
6	21.929629	21.706558	21.489679	21.278744	21.073520	20.873782	20.679319	20.489932	20.305430	20.125632	19.950365	19.779466
7	19.612778	19.450153	19.291449	19.136530	18.985267	18.837537	18.693223	18.552210	18.414392	18.279665	18.147931	18.019094
8	17.893065	17.769755	17.649083	17.530967	17.415331	17.302100	17.191205	17.082577	16.976151	16.871863	16.769652	16.669461
9	16.571233	16.474914	16.380451	16.287796	16.196897	16.107710	16.020189	15.934291	15.849972	15.767193	15.685914	15.606098
10	15.527707	15.450706	15.375061	15.300739	15.227707	15.155935	15.085392	15.016049	14.947877	14.880850	14.814941	14.750124
11	14.686375	14.623668	14.561981	14.501290	14.441574	14.382811	14.324980	14.268062	14.212035	14.156882	14.102584	14.049122
12	13.996479	13.944638	13.893582	13.843295	13.793762	13.744967	13.696895	13.649532	13.602864	13.556876	13.511556	13.466890
13	13.422866	13.379472	13.336694	13.294522	13.252944	13.211949	13.171526	13.131664	13.092352	13.053582	13.015342	12.977623
14	12.940416	12.903711	12.867500	12.831774	12.796524	12.761741	12.727419	12.693547	12.660120	12.627128	12.594565	12.562424
15	12.530696	12.499396	12.468456	12.437930	12.407791	12.378032	12.348649	12.319633	12.290980	12.262683	12.234737	12.207136
16	12.179875	12.152948	12.126349	12.100075	12.074119	12.048477	12.023144	11.998114	11.973384	11.948949	11.924804	11.900945
17	11.877368	11.854068	11.831041	11.808283	11.785790	11.763559	11.741584	11.719864	11.698393	11.677169	11.656187	11.635444
18	11.614937	11.594663	11.574618	11.554798	11.535201	11.515824	11.496663	11.477715	11.458978	11.440448	11.422123	11.404000
19	11.386076	11.368348	11.350815	11.333472	11.316317	11.299349	11.282564	11.265960	11.249535	11.233286	11.217211	11.201308
20	11.185574	11.170008	11.154606	11.139367	11.124289	11.109370	11.094607	11.080000	11.065544	11.051240	11.037084	11.023076
21	11.009212	10.995492	10.981913	10.968475	10.955174	10.942009	10.928979	10.916082	10.903317	10.890681	10.878173	10.865792
22	10.853536	10.841404	10.829393	10.817503	10.805733	10.794080	10.782543	10.771122	10.759814	10.748618	10.737533	10.726558
23	10.715691	10.704931	10.694277	10.683728	10.673282	10.662939	10.652696	10.642553	10.632509	10.622563	10.612713	10.602959
24	10.593298	10.583732	10.574257	10.564873	10.555580	10.546376	10.537260	10.528231	10.519288	10.510430	10.501657	10.492967
25	10.484360	10.475834	10.467389	10.459024	10.450737	10.442529	10.434397	10.426343	10.418363	10.410459	10.402628	10.394871
26	10.387185	10.379572	10.372029	10.364556	10.357153	10.349818	10.342551	10.335352	10.328218	10.321151	10.314148	10.307210
27	10.300336	10.293525	10.286776	10.280089	10.273463	10.266897	10.260391	10.253945	10.247557	10.241227	10.234955	10.228739
28	10.222580	10.216477	10.210428	10.204434	10.198495	10.192608	10.186775	10.180994	10.175265	10.169587	10.163960	10.158384
29	10.152857	10.147380	10.141951	10.136571	10.131239	10.125954	10.120717	10.115525	10.110380	10.105280	10.100226	10.095216
30	10.090250	10.085329	10.080450	10.075615	10.070822	10.066071	10.061363	10.056695	10.052068	10.047482	10.042936	10.038430
31	10.033963	10.029535	10.025146	10.020795	10.016483	10.012207	10.007969	10.003767	9.999603	9.995474	9.991381	9.987323
32	9.983301	9.979313	9.975360	9.971441	9.967556	9.963704	9.959886	9.956100	9.952347	9.948626	9.944938	9.941281
33	9.937655	9.934060	9.930496	9.926963	9.923460	9.919987	9.916544	9.913130	9.909745	9.906389	9.903061	9.899762
34	9.896491	9.893248	9.890032	9.886844	9.883683	9.880549	9.877441	9.874360	9.871304	9.868275	9.865271	9.862292
35	9.859339	9.856411	9.853507	9.850628	9.847773	9.844943	9.842136	9.839352	9.836593	9.833856	9.831142	9.828451
36	9.825783	9.823137	9.820513	9.817912	9.815332	9.812773	9.810237	9.807721	9.805226	9.802752	9.800299	9.797867
37	9.795454	9.793062	9.790690	9.788337	9.786004	9.783691	9.781397	9.779121	9.776865	9.774628	9.772409	9.770208
38	9.768026	9.765862	9.763716	9.761587	9.759477	9.757383	9.755307	9.753249	9.751207	9.749182	9.747174	9.745182
39	9.743207	9.741249	9.739306	9.737379	9.735469	9.733574	9.731694	9.729830	9.727982	9.726149	9.724330	9.722527
40	9.720739	9.718965	9.717206	9.715461	9.713731	9.712014	9.710312	9.708624	9.706950	9.705289	9.703642	9.702009

9.75% Interest Rate .... 9.75% Interest Rate

Years	0	1	2	3	4	Number of Months 5	6	7	8	9	10	11
2	55.235549	53.233997	51.386914	49.677137	48.089955	46.612684	45.234334	43.945331	42.737300	41.602878	40.535571	39.529626
3	38.579929	37.681920	36.831517	36.025058	35.259248	34.531112	33.837959	33.177347	32.547059	31.945072	31.369541	30.818776
4	30.291229	29.785480	29.300219	28.834242	28.386436	27.955772	27.541297	27.142129	26.757447	26.386489	26.028544	25.682951
5	25.349092	25.026390	24.714305	24.412330	24.119993	23.836847	23.562476	23.296485	23.038506	22.788189	22.545206	22.309247
6	22.080019	21.857245	21.640664	21.430028	21.225102	21.025662	20.831499	20.642411	20.458209	20.278710	20.103743	19.933143
7	19.766755	19.604430	19.446026	19.291407	19.140445	18.993016	18.849001	18.708289	18.570771	18.436344	18.304910	18.176373
8	18.050643	17.927634	17.807261	17.689444	17.574107	17.461177	17.350581	17.242252	17.136124	17.032134	16.930222	16.830329
9	16.732399	16.636378	16.542213	16.449854	16.359253	16.270363	16.183138	16.097536	16.013513	15.931030	15.850046	15.770525
10	15.692429	15.615723	15.540372	15.466344	15.393605	15.322126	15.251876	15.182825	15.114946	15.048211	14.982593	14.918067
11	14.854608	14.792192	14.730794	14.670393	14.610966	14.552492	14.494950	14.438319	14.382580	14.327714	14.273702	14.220526
12	14.168169	14.116613	14.065842	14.015840	13.966591	13.918079	13.870291	13.823210	13.776824	13.731118	13.686079	13.641694
13	13.597950	13.554835	13.512337	13.470444	13.429144	13.388426	13.348280	13.308695	13.269660	13.231165	13.193200	13.155756
14	13.118823	13.082393	13.046455	13.011001	12.976023	12.941512	12.907460	12.873859	12.840701	12.807979	12.775685	12.743812
15	12.712352	12.681299	12.650646	12.620385	12.590512	12.561018	12.531899	12.503147	12.474757	12.446723	12.419039	12.391699
16	12.364699	12.338032	12.311693	12.285678	12.259981	12.234596	12.209520	12.184748	12.160274	12.136094	12.112204	12.088600
17	12.065276	12.042229	12.019455	11.996949	11.974707	11.952726	11.931002	11.909531	11.888309	11.867333	11.846599	11.826103
18	11.805843	11.785814	11.766014	11.746439	11.727085	11.707951	11.689033	11.670327	11.651831	11.633542	11.615458	11.597574
19	11.579889	11.562399	11.545103	11.527997	11.511079	11.494346	11.477796	11.461427	11.445235	11.429219	11.413377	11.397705
20	11.382202	11.366866	11.351694	11.336684	11.321835	11.307144	11.292608	11.278227	11.263997	11.249918	11.235987	11.222202
21	11.208562	11.195065	11.181708	11.168490	11.155410	11.142465	11.129655	11.116976	11.104429	11.092010	11.079719	11.067554
22	11.055513	11.043596	11.031799	11.020123	11.008565	10.997124	10.985799	10.974588	10.963490	10.952504	10.941627	10.930860
23	10.920201	10.909648	10.899200	10.888856	10.878615	10.868476	10.858436	10.848496	10.838655	10.828910	10.819261	10.809706
24	10.800245	10.790877	10.781601	10.772415	10.763318	10.754310	10.745389	10.736555	10.727807	10.719143	10.710563	10.702065
25	10.693649	10.685314	10.677059	10.668883	10.660786	10.652766	10.644822	10.636954	10.629161	10.621442	10.613797	10.606223
26	10.598722	10.591291	10.583931	10.576640	10.569418	10.562264	10.555177	10.548156	10.541201	10.534312	10.527486	10.520725
27	10.514026	10.507390	10.500816	10.494303	10.487850	10.481458	10.475124	10.468849	10.462632	10.456472	10.450369	10.444323
28	10.438332	10.432396	10.426515	10.420687	10.414913	10.409192	10.403523	10.397906	10.392340	10.386825	10.381360	10.375945
29	10.370579	10.365262	10.359993	10.354772	10.349598	10.344471	10.339390	10.334355	10.329366	10.324421	10.319521	10.314665
30	10.309853	10.305084	10.300358	10.295674	10.291032	10.286432	10.281872	10.277354	10.272876	10.268437	10.264039	10.259679
31	10.255359	10.251076	10.246832	10.242626	10.238456	10.234324	10.230228	10.226169	10.222146	10.218158	10.214205	10.210287
32	10.206404	10.202554	10.198739	10.194957	10.191209	10.187494	10.183811	10.180160	10.176542	10.172955	10.169399	10.165875
33	10.162381	10.158918	10.155486	10.152083	10.148710	10.145366	10.142052	10.138766	10.135509	10.132280	10.129079	10.125906
34	10.122761	10.119642	10.116551	10.113487	10.110449	10.107438	10.104452	10.101492	10.098558	10.095649	10.092766	10.089907
35	10.087073	10.084263	10.081477	10.078716	10.075978	10.073264	10.070573	10.067905	10.065260	10.062637	10.060037	10.057460
36	10.054904	10.052371	10.049859	10.047369	10.044899	10.042451	10.040024	10.037618	10.035232	10.032866	10.030521	10.028196
37	10.025890	10.023604	10.021338	10.019090	10.016862	10.014653	10.012463	10.010291	10.008138	10.006003	10.003886	10.001787
38	9.999705	9.997642	9.995596	9.993567	9.991555	9.989560	9.987583	9.985622	9.983677	9.981749	9.979837	9.977941
39	9.976062	9.974198	9.972350	9.970517	9.968700	9.966898	9.965112	9.963340	9.961583	9.959841	9.958114	9.956401
40	9.954703	9.953019	9.951349	9.949693	9.948050	9.946422	9.944807	9.943206	9.941618	9.940044	9.938483	9.936935

Annual Mortgage Constant for Monthly Payment Loans

10.00% Interest Rate   10.00% Interest Rate

Years	0	1	2	3	4	5	6	7	8	9	10	11
						Number of Months						
2	55.373912	53.372491	51.525556	49.815940	48.228932	46.751847	45.373692	44.084894	42.877076	41.742874	40.675794	39.670083
3	38.720625	37.822859	36.972705	36.166500	35.400947	34.673072	33.980183	33.319840	32.689822	32.088108	31.512853	30.962366
4	30.435100	29.929633	29.444657	28.978966	28.531447	28.101073	27.686889	27.288013	26.903624	26.532960	26.175311	25.830015
5	25.496454	25.174050	24.862264	24.560589	24.268553	23.985709	23.711639	23.445951	23.188275	22.938262	22.695583	22.459928
6	22.231005	22.008537	21.792262	21.581931	21.377311	21.178178	20.984322	20.795541	20.611645	20.432453	20.257793	20.087501
7	19.921421	19.759403	19.601306	19.446995	19.296340	19.149218	19.005511	18.865106	18.727896	18.593776	18.462649	18.334420
8	18.208997	18.086294	17.966228	17.848718	17.733688	17.621063	17.510773	17.402750	17.296928	17.193244	17.091637	16.992049
9	16.894423	16.798707	16.704846	16.612791	16.522494	16.433907	16.346986	16.261686	16.177966	16.095785	16.015103	15.935883
10	15.858088	15.781683	15.706633	15.632905	15.560466	15.489286	15.419335	15.350583	15.283002	15.216564	15.151244	15.087015
11	15.023853	14.961733	14.900631	14.840525	14.781393	14.723214	14.665965	14.609628	14.554182	14.499609	14.445889	14.393005
12	14.340939	14.289674	14.239194	14.189481	14.140521	14.092299	14.044798	13.998006	13.951907	13.906487	13.861735	13.817636
13	13.774177	13.731347	13.689133	13.647523	13.606507	13.566072	13.526208	13.486904	13.448150	13.409936	13.372251	13.335086
14	13.298432	13.262280	13.226619	13.191443	13.156741	13.122506	13.088729	13.055403	13.022520	12.990071	12.958050	12.926449
15	12.895261	12.864480	12.834097	12.804107	12.774503	12.745278	12.716427	12.687942	12.659819	12.632052	12.604633	12.577559
16	12.550823	12.524420	12.498345	12.472592	12.447157	12.422034	12.397219	12.372706	12.348492	12.324571	12.300939	12.277592
17	12.254525	12.231735	12.209216	12.186965	12.164978	12.143251	12.121780	12.100561	12.079591	12.058866	12.038382	12.018136
18	11.998124	11.978344	11.958791	11.939463	11.920357	11.901468	11.882795	11.864334	11.846082	11.828036	11.810193	11.792551
19	11.775107	11.757858	11.740801	11.723934	11.707254	11.690759	11.674446	11.658313	11.642357	11.626576	11.610968	11.595530
20	11.580260	11.565156	11.550215	11.535436	11.520817	11.506355	11.492048	11.477895	11.463893	11.450040	11.436335	11.422776
21	11.409360	11.396086	11.382953	11.369958	11.357099	11.344376	11.331786	11.319327	11.306998	11.294798	11.282725	11.270776
22	11.258952	11.247250	11.235668	11.224206	11.212861	11.201633	11.190520	11.179521	11.168633	11.157857	11.147190	11.136631
23	11.126180	11.115834	11.105593	11.095455	11.085419	11.075484	11.065648	11.055911	11.046272	11.036728	11.027280	11.017926
24	11.008665	10.999496	10.990417	10.981429	10.972529	10.963717	10.954992	10.946352	10.937798	10.929327	10.920939	10.912634
25	10.904409	10.896265	10.888200	10.880213	10.872304	10.864472	10.856715	10.849034	10.841426	10.833893	10.826431	10.819042
26	10.811724	10.804475	10.797297	10.790187	10.783145	10.776170	10.769262	10.762420	10.755643	10.748930	10.742281	10.735695
27	10.729172	10.722710	10.716310	10.709969	10.703689	10.697468	10.691305	10.685200	10.679153	10.673162	10.667228	10.661349
28	10.655525	10.649755	10.644039	10.638377	10.632767	10.627210	10.621704	10.616249	10.610845	10.605491	10.600187	10.594932
29	10.589725	10.584566	10.579455	10.574391	10.569374	10.564403	10.559477	10.554597	10.549762	10.544971	10.540223	10.535520
30	10.530859	10.526241	10.521665	10.517131	10.512638	10.508186	10.503774	10.499403	10.495071	10.490779	10.486526	10.482311
31	10.478134	10.473995	10.469894	10.465830	10.461802	10.457811	10.453855	10.449936	10.446051	10.442202	10.438387	10.434607
32	10.430860	10.427147	10.423468	10.419821	10.416207	10.412625	10.409076	10.405558	10.402071	10.398616	10.395191	10.391797
33	10.388434	10.385100	10.381796	10.378521	10.375275	10.372058	10.368870	10.365710	10.362578	10.359474	10.356397	10.353348
34	10.350325	10.347329	10.344360	10.341417	10.338500	10.335608	10.332742	10.329902	10.327086	10.324295	10.321529	10.318787
35	10.316069	10.313375	10.310705	10.308058	10.305434	10.302833	10.300256	10.297700	10.295167	10.292656	10.290168	10.287701
36	10.285255	10.282831	10.280428	10.278046	10.275685	10.273344	10.271024	10.268724	10.266444	10.264183	10.261943	10.259722
37	10.257520	10.255338	10.253174	10.251029	10.248903	10.246795	10.244705	10.242634	10.240580	10.238545	10.236527	10.234526
38	10.232543	10.230577	10.228627	10.226695	10.224780	10.222880	10.220998	10.219131	10.217281	10.215447	10.213628	10.211825
39	10.210038	10.208266	10.206509	10.204767	10.203041	10.201329	10.199632	10.197949	10.196281	10.194627	10.192988	10.191362
40	10.189751	10.188153	10.186569	10.184999	10.183442	10.181898	10.180368	10.178851	10.177346	10.175855	10.174376	10.172910

10.25% Interest Rate   10.25% Interest Rate

Years	0	1	2	3	4	5	6	7	8	9	10	11
2	55.512479	53.511198	51.664419	49.954974	48.368148	46.891256	45.513306	44.224721	43.017123	41.883151	40.816306	39.810836
3	38.861626	37.964113	37.114216	36.308272	35.542985	34.815379	34.122763	33.462696	32.832957	32.231525	31.656553	31.106353
4	30.579376	30.074199	29.589516	29.124119	28.676896	28.246819	27.832934	27.434358	27.050271	26.679910	26.322564	25.977572
5	25.644317	25.322219	25.010740	24.709374	24.417646	24.135111	23.861352	23.595974	23.338609	23.088907	22.846540	22.611198
6	22.382587	22.160432	21.944470	21.734453	21.530147	21.331328	21.137785	20.949319	20.765738	20.586860	20.412515	20.242538
7	20.076772	19.915069	19.757287	19.603291	19.452951	19.306144	19.162751	19.022661	18.885765	18.751960	18.621147	18.493232
8	18.368123	18.245734	18.125982	18.008785	17.894068	17.781757	17.671780	17.564070	17.458560	17.355188	17.253893	17.154617
9	17.057103	16.961897	16.868347	16.776603	16.686616	16.598339	16.511727	16.426737	16.343326	16.261453	16.181080	16.102168
10	16.024680	15.948582	15.873838	15.800416	15.728284	15.657409	15.587763	15.519316	15.452039	15.385905	15.320889	15.256963
11	15.194103	15.132284	15.071484	15.011680	14.952848	14.894969	14.838020	14.781982	14.726835	14.672560	14.619138	14.566551
12	14.514781	14.463813	14.413628	14.364210	14.315545	14.267617	14.220410	14.173910	14.128103	14.082976	14.038515	13.994706
13	13.951538	13.908998	13.867073	13.825752	13.785023	13.744876	13.705298	13.666281	13.627813	13.589883	13.552483	13.515602
14	13.479231	13.443361	13.407983	13.373087	13.338667	13.304712	13.271215	13.238168	13.205562	13.173392	13.141648	13.110323
15	13.079411	13.048904	13.018796	12.989080	12.959749	12.930797	12.902218	12.874005	12.846152	12.818654	12.791506	12.764700
16	12.738232	12.712096	12.686288	12.660801	12.635631	12.610773	12.586221	12.561972	12.538021	12.514362	12.490991	12.467905
17	12.445098	12.422566	12.400306	12.378313	12.356583	12.335112	12.313897	12.292933	12.272217	12.251746	12.231515	12.211521
18	12.191761	12.172232	12.152930	12.133851	12.114993	12.096353	12.077927	12.059712	12.041706	12.023905	12.006307	11.988909
19	11.971708	11.954701	11.937886	11.921259	11.904820	11.888564	11.872490	11.856595	11.840876	11.825332	11.809959	11.794756
20	11.779721	11.764850	11.750143	11.735596	11.721208	11.706977	11.692900	11.678976	11.665203	11.651578	11.638100	11.624767
21	11.611577	11.598528	11.585619	11.572847	11.560211	11.547710	11.535341	11.523103	11.510994	11.499013	11.487158	11.475427
22	11.463820	11.452334	11.440968	11.429720	11.418589	11.407574	11.396674	11.385886	11.375210	11.364644	11.354186	11.343837
23	11.333593	11.323455	11.313420	11.303488	11.293657	11.283927	11.274295	11.264761	11.255324	11.245982	11.236735	11.227581
24	11.218519	11.209548	11.200668	11.191876	11.183173	11.174557	11.166027	11.157582	11.149221	11.140943	11.132747	11.124633
25	11.116599	11.108645	11.100769	11.092971	11.085250	11.077605	11.070035	11.062539	11.055117	11.047767	11.040490	11.033283
26	11.026147	11.019080	11.012083	11.005153	10.998290	10.991494	10.984764	10.978099	10.971499	10.964962	10.958488	10.952077
27	10.945727	10.939438	10.933210	10.927041	10.920932	10.914881	10.908888	10.902952	10.897073	10.891250	10.885482	10.879769
28	10.874111	10.868506	10.862955	10.857456	10.852009	10.846613	10.841269	10.835975	10.830731	10.825536	10.820391	10.815294
29	10.810244	10.805242	10.800287	10.795379	10.790516	10.785699	10.780927	10.776200	10.771516	10.766877	10.762280	10.757727
30	10.753216	10.748746	10.744319	10.739932	10.735586	10.731280	10.727014	10.722788	10.718601	10.714452	10.710342	10.706270
31	10.702235	10.698237	10.694276	10.690352	10.686464	10.682611	10.678794	10.675012	10.671264	10.667551	10.663872	10.660226
32	10.656614	10.653035	10.649489	10.645975	10.642493	10.639042	10.635623	10.632236	10.628879	10.625552	10.622256	10.618990
33	10.615753	10.612546	10.609368	10.606218	10.603098	10.600005	10.596940	10.593903	10.590894	10.587911	10.584956	10.582027
34	10.579125	10.576249	10.573399	10.570574	10.567775	10.565001	10.562252	10.559527	10.556827	10.554151	10.551500	10.548872
35	10.546267	10.543686	10.541128	10.538593	10.536081	10.533591	10.531123	10.528677	10.526254	10.523851	10.521471	10.519111
36	10.516773	10.514455	10.512158	10.509881	10.507625	10.505389	10.503172	10.500976	10.498798	10.496641	10.494502	10.492382
37	10.490281	10.488199	10.486135	10.484089	10.482062	10.480052	10.478061	10.476087	10.474130	10.472191	10.470268	10.468363
38	10.466475	10.464603	10.462748	10.460909	10.459086	10.457279	10.455489	10.453714	10.451954	10.450211	10.448482	10.446769
39	10.445071	10.443387	10.441719	10.440065	10.438426	10.436801	10.435190	10.433594	10.432011	10.430442	10.428887	10.427346
40	10.425818	10.424304	10.422803	10.421315	10.419840	10.418378	10.416929	10.415492	10.414068	10.412656	10.411257	10.409870

Annual Mortgage Constant for Monthly Payment Loans

10.50% Interest Rate | 10.50% Interest Rate

Years	0	1	2	3	4	5	6	7	8	9	10	11
						Number of Months						
2	55.651250	53.650118	51.803503	50.094237	48.507602	47.030913	45.653174	44.364811	43.157443	42.023708	40.957107	39.951887
3	39.002932	38.105680	37.256049	36.450375	35.685362	34.958034	34.265699	33.605915	32.976463	32.375321	31.800642	31.250736
4	30.724056	30.219178	29.734795	29.269701	28.822782	28.393010	27.979432	27.581164	27.197387	26.827336	26.470302	26.125623
5	25.792680	25.470897	25.159734	24.858683	24.567272	24.285054	24.011612	23.746553	23.489506	23.240124	22.998076	22.763054
6	22.534764	22.312929	22.097288	21.887592	21.683607	21.485110	21.291889	21.103744	20.920485	20.741930	20.567907	20.398251
7	20.232808	20.071427	19.913967	19.760293	19.610275	19.463790	19.320719	19.180951	19.044376	18.910893	18.780401	18.652807
8	18.528019	18.405951	18.286520	18.169644	18.055247	17.943255	17.833598	17.726207	17.621017	17.517964	17.416987	17.318029
9	17.221033	17.125945	17.032713	16.941286	16.851615	16.763655	16.677359	16.592684	16.509588	16.428030	16.347971	16.269373
10	16.192200	16.116415	16.041984	15.968874	15.897053	15.826490	15.757155	15.689018	15.622052	15.556228	15.491520	15.427903
11	15.365351	15.303841	15.243348	15.183850	15.125325	15.067751	15.011107	14.955374	14.900531	14.846559	14.793440	14.741156
12	14.689688	14.639021	14.589137	14.540020	14.491654	14.444025	14.397116	14.350914	14.305405	14.260575	14.216410	14.172897
13	14.130024	14.087777	14.046146	14.005118	13.964682	13.924827	13.885541	13.846814	13.808636	13.770996	13.733884	13.697291
14	13.661208	13.625625	13.590533	13.555923	13.521787	13.488117	13.454903	13.422139	13.389816	13.357927	13.326464	13.295420
15	13.264787	13.234559	13.204729	13.175291	13.146237	13.117561	13.089257	13.061319	13.033740	13.006516	12.979640	12.953106
16	12.926909	12.901044	12.875505	12.850288	12.825386	12.800796	12.776511	12.752529	12.728842	12.705448	12.682342	12.659519
17	12.636975	12.614705	12.592706	12.570973	12.549503	12.528292	12.507334	12.486628	12.466169	12.445954	12.425978	12.406239
18	12.386733	12.367457	12.348407	12.329580	12.310973	12.292582	12.274405	12.256439	12.238681	12.221127	12.203776	12.186623
19	12.169667	12.152904	12.136332	12.119949	12.103751	12.087736	12.071902	12.056247	12.040767	12.025460	12.010325	11.995359
20	11.980559	11.965923	11.951450	11.937137	11.922981	11.908982	11.895136	11.881443	11.867899	11.854503	11.841253	11.828147
21	11.815184	11.802361	11.789676	11.777129	11.764717	11.752438	11.740291	11.728274	11.716386	11.704624	11.692988	11.681475
22	11.670085	11.658815	11.647665	11.636633	11.625716	11.614915	11.604227	11.593651	11.583186	11.572830	11.562583	11.552442
23	11.542407	11.532476	11.522648	11.512921	11.503296	11.493769	11.484341	11.475010	11.465775	11.456634	11.447587	11.438633
24	11.429771	11.420998	11.412315	11.403721	11.395213	11.386792	11.378457	11.370205	11.362037	11.353952	11.345948	11.338024
25	11.330180	11.322415	11.314728	11.307118	11.299584	11.292125	11.284740	11.277429	11.270191	11.263025	11.255930	11.248905
26	11.241950	11.235064	11.228246	11.221495	11.214810	11.208192	11.201638	11.195149	11.188724	11.182362	11.176062	11.169824
27	11.163646	11.157529	11.151472	11.145473	11.139534	11.133651	11.127826	11.122058	11.116345	11.110688	11.105086	11.099538
28	11.094043	11.088601	11.083212	11.077875	11.072589	11.067354	11.062169	11.057034	11.051948	11.046911	11.041922	11.036981
29	11.032088	11.027240	11.022440	11.017684	11.012975	11.008310	11.003689	10.999112	10.994579	10.990089	10.985641	10.981235
30	10.976872	10.972549	10.968267	10.964026	10.959825	10.955663	10.951541	10.947457	10.943412	10.939405	10.935435	10.931503
31	10.927608	10.923749	10.919926	10.916139	10.912388	10.908672	10.904990	10.901343	10.897730	10.894150	10.890604	10.887091
32	10.883611	10.880163	10.876747	10.873363	10.870010	10.866688	10.863398	10.860137	10.856907	10.853707	10.850537	10.847395
33	10.844283	10.841200	10.838145	10.835118	10.832119	10.829148	10.826205	10.823288	10.820398	10.817535	10.814698	10.811887
34	10.809102	10.806343	10.803609	10.800900	10.798216	10.795556	10.792921	10.790310	10.787723	10.785159	10.782619	10.780102
35	10.777608	10.775137	10.772689	10.770262	10.767858	10.765476	10.763116	10.760777	10.758459	10.756162	10.753887	10.751632
36	10.749397	10.747183	10.744989	10.742815	10.740660	10.738525	10.736410	10.734313	10.732236	10.730177	10.728137	10.726116
37	10.724113	10.722127	10.720160	10.718211	10.716279	10.714365	10.712468	10.710588	10.708725	10.706879	10.705049	10.703236
38	10.701439	10.699659	10.697894	10.696146	10.694413	10.692696	10.690994	10.689307	10.687636	10.685979	10.684338	10.682711
39	10.681099	10.679501	10.677918	10.676348	10.674793	10.673252	10.671725	10.670211	10.668711	10.667224	10.665751	10.664291
40	10.662843	10.661409	10.659988	10.658579	10.657183	10.655799	10.654428	10.653069	10.651722	10.650387	10.649064	10.647753

10.75% Interest Rate | 10.75% Interest Rate

Years	0	1	2	3	4	5	6	7	8	9	10	11
2	55.790226	53.789251	51.942809	50.233729	48.647294	47.170816	45.793298	44.505165	43.298035	42.164545	41.098197	40.093235
3	39.144544	38.247561	37.398204	36.592808	35.828077	35.101035	34.408989	33.749498	33.120341	32.519497	31.945118	31.395515
4	30.869140	30.364569	29.880495	29.415711	28.969104	28.539646	28.126383	27.728431	27.344971	26.975238	26.618524	26.274165
5	25.941544	25.620084	25.309243	25.008516	24.717429	24.435536	24.162420	23.897686	23.640966	23.391910	23.150190	22.915496
6	22.687534	22.466027	22.250714	22.041347	21.837691	21.639522	21.446631	21.258815	21.075885	20.897659	20.723966	20.554640
7	20.389526	20.228474	20.071344	19.917999	19.768310	19.622154	19.479412	19.339972	19.203727	19.070572	18.940409	18.813143
8	18.688683	18.566943	18.447838	18.331289	18.217220	18.105555	17.996224	17.889159	17.784295	17.681567	17.580916	17.482283
9	17.385611	17.290848	17.197939	17.106835	17.017488	16.929850	16.843876	16.759523	16.676749	16.595512	16.515774	16.437496
10	16.360642	16.285176	16.211064	16.138272	16.066770	15.996524	15.927506	15.859685	15.793034	15.727526	15.663133	15.599830
11	15.537592	15.476395	15.416215	15.357029	15.298815	15.241552	15.185219	15.129796	15.075262	15.021599	14.968789	14.916812
12	14.865651	14.815290	14.765712	14.716900	14.668839	14.621514	14.574909	14.529010	14.483803	14.439274	14.395410	14.352197
13	14.309624	14.267676	14.226344	14.185613	14.145474	14.105915	14.066925	14.028493	13.990609	13.953263	13.916444	13.880144
14	13.844352	13.809060	13.774258	13.739938	13.706091	13.672708	13.639782	13.607305	13.575268	13.543664	13.512485	13.481725
15	13.451376	13.421430	13.391882	13.362725	13.333951	13.305554	13.277529	13.249869	13.222568	13.195620	13.169020	13.142761
16	13.116839	13.091247	13.065982	13.041036	13.016406	12.992086	12.968071	12.944358	12.920940	12.897813	12.874974	12.852417
17	12.830138	12.808132	12.786397	12.764927	12.743719	12.722769	12.702072	12.681626	12.661426	12.641469	12.621751	12.602268
18	12.583018	12.563997	12.545201	12.526628	12.508273	12.490135	12.472209	12.454494	12.436985	12.419680	12.402576	12.385671
19	12.368961	12.352444	12.336117	12.319977	12.304023	12.288251	12.272658	12.257243	12.242003	12.226936	12.212039	12.197310
20	12.182747	12.168348	12.154110	12.140031	12.126109	12.112343	12.098729	12.085267	12.071953	12.058787	12.045766	12.032888
21	12.020152	12.007555	11.995096	11.982773	11.970585	11.958529	11.946605	11.934809	11.923142	11.911600	11.900183	11.888889
22	11.877716	11.866663	11.855729	11.844911	11.834209	11.823621	11.813146	11.802782	11.792528	11.782383	11.772345	11.762413
23	11.752586	11.742862	11.733240	11.723719	11.714298	11.704976	11.695751	11.686622	11.677589	11.668649	11.659802	11.651047
24	11.642383	11.633808	11.625322	11.616923	11.608611	11.600385	11.592243	11.584185	11.576209	11.568315	11.560501	11.552767
25	11.545113	11.537536	11.530036	11.522613	11.515264	11.507991	11.500791	11.493663	11.486608	11.479624	11.472710	11.465866
26	11.459091	11.452384	11.445744	11.439170	11.432663	11.426220	11.419842	11.413528	11.407276	11.401087	11.394959	11.388892
27	11.382886	11.376939	11.371051	11.365221	11.359449	11.353734	11.348075	11.342472	11.336925	11.331432	11.325993	11.320607
28	11.315274	11.309994	11.304765	11.299588	11.294461	11.289384	11.284357	11.279379	11.274449	11.269568	11.264734	11.259947
29	11.255206	11.250512	11.245863	11.241259	11.236700	11.232185	11.227713	11.223285	11.218900	11.214556	11.210255	11.205995
30	11.201776	11.197598	11.193460	11.189362	11.185303	11.181283	11.177301	11.173358	11.169452	11.165584	11.161753	11.157958
31	11.154200	11.150477	11.146790	11.143139	11.139521	11.135939	11.132390	11.128875	11.125394	11.121946	11.118530	11.115147
32	11.111796	11.108476	11.105188	11.101931	11.098705	11.095510	11.092344	11.089209	11.086103	11.083026	11.079978	11.076960
33	11.073969	11.071007	11.068072	11.065165	11.062286	11.059433	11.056607	11.053808	11.051035	11.048288	11.045567	11.042871
34	11.040201	11.037555	11.034934	11.032338	11.029766	11.027218	11.024694	11.022193	11.019716	11.017261	11.014830	11.012421
35	11.010035	11.007671	11.005328	11.003008	11.000709	10.998432	10.996176	10.993940	10.991726	10.989532	10.987358	10.985204
36	10.983071	10.980957	10.978863	10.976788	10.974732	10.972695	10.970677	10.968678	10.966698	10.964735	10.962791	10.960864
37	10.958956	10.957065	10.955191	10.953335	10.951496	10.949673	10.947868	10.946079	10.944307	10.942550	10.940811	10.939087
38	10.937378	10.935686	10.934009	10.932348	10.930701	10.929070	10.927454	10.925853	10.924266	10.922694	10.921136	10.919593
39	10.918063	10.916548	10.915047	10.913559	10.912085	10.910624	10.909177	10.907743	10.906322	10.904914	10.903519	10.902137
40	10.900767	10.899410	10.898065	10.896732	10.895412	10.894103	10.892807	10.891522	10.890249	10.888988	10.887738	10.886500

Annual Mortgage Constant for Monthly Payment Loans

11.00% Interest Rate   11.00% Interest Rate

Years	0	1	2	3	4	Number of Months 5	6	7	8	9	10	11
2	55.929406	53.928597	52.082336	50.373452	48.787224	47.310965	45.933677	44.645781	43.438898	42.305662	41.239574	40.234879
3	39.286461	38.389755	37.540680	36.735571	35.971130	35.244382	34.552634	33.893443	33.264590	32.664052	32.089982	31.540690
4	31.014627	30.510371	30.026614	29.562148	29.115862	28.686725	28.273785	27.876157	27.493022	27.123617	26.767230	26.423199
5	26.090908	25.769777	25.459267	25.158871	24.868116	24.586556	24.313773	24.049374	23.792987	23.544266	23.302881	23.068521
6	22.840895	22.619724	22.404747	22.195716	21.992396	21.794564	21.602009	21.414530	21.231937	21.054048	20.880690	20.711701
7	20.546924	20.386209	20.229415	20.076406	19.927054	19.781234	19.638828	19.499724	19.363814	19.230995	19.101167	18.974236
8	18.850111	18.728705	18.609935	18.493720	18.379984	18.268653	18.159655	18.052923	17.948390	17.845995	17.745675	17.647374
9	17.551033	17.456600	17.364021	17.273247	17.184229	17.096920	17.011275	16.927250	16.844803	16.763893	16.684482	16.606530
10	16.530001	16.454861	16.381073	16.308606	16.237427	16.167504	16.098808	16.031310	15.964981	15.899793	15.835721	15.772738
11	15.710819	15.649940	15.590078	15.531210	15.473313	15.416367	15.360349	15.305241	15.251022	15.197673	15.145176	15.093511
12	15.042663	14.992613	14.943346	14.894844	14.847093	14.800076	14.753779	14.708188	14.663287	14.619065	14.575506	14.532598
13	14.490328	14.448684	14.407654	14.367226	14.327388	14.288130	14.249439	14.211307	14.173721	14.136672	14.100151	14.064147
14	14.028651	13.993653	13.959146	13.925119	13.891564	13.858474	13.825839	13.793652	13.761904	13.730589	13.699699	13.669226
15	13.639163	13.609504	13.580241	13.551367	13.522877	13.494763	13.467020	13.439641	13.412620	13.385952	13.359630	13.333650
16	13.308005	13.282690	13.257699	13.233029	13.208673	13.184626	13.160884	13.137442	13.114295	13.091438	13.068868	13.046579
17	13.024568	13.002829	12.981360	12.960155	12.939212	12.918525	12.898091	12.877907	12.857968	12.838271	12.818812	12.799588
18	12.780596	12.761831	12.743292	12.724973	12.706874	12.688989	12.671316	12.653852	12.636595	12.619540	12.602686	12.586029
19	12.569567	12.553296	12.537216	12.521321	12.505611	12.490082	12.474733	12.459560	12.444561	12.429734	12.415076	12.400586
20	12.386261	12.372098	12.358096	12.344252	12.330565	12.317032	12.303651	12.290420	12.277338	12.264401	12.251610	12.238960
21	12.226451	12.214082	12.201849	12.189751	12.177787	12.165955	12.154252	12.142679	12.131232	12.119910	12.108712	12.097637
22	12.086681	12.075845	12.065127	12.054524	12.044036	12.033662	12.023399	12.013247	12.003204	11.993268	11.983440	11.973716
23	11.964096	11.954579	11.945163	11.935847	11.926630	11.917511	11.908489	11.899562	11.890729	11.881990	11.873342	11.864786
24	11.856319	11.847941	11.839651	11.831447	11.823330	11.815297	11.807348	11.799481	11.791697	11.783993	11.776369	11.768824
25	11.761357	11.753967	11.746654	11.739416	11.732252	11.725162	11.718145	11.711200	11.704327	11.697523	11.690790	11.684125
26	11.677528	11.670998	11.664535	11.658137	11.651805	11.645537	11.639333	11.633191	11.627112	11.621094	11.615136	11.609239
27	11.603402	11.597623	11.591903	11.586240	11.580633	11.575084	11.569589	11.564150	11.558766	11.553435	11.548157	11.542932
28	11.537759	11.532638	11.527568	11.522548	11.517578	11.512658	11.507786	11.502963	11.498187	11.493459	11.488778	11.484143
29	11.479553	11.475009	11.470510	11.466055	11.461644	11.457276	11.452952	11.448670	11.444429	11.440231	11.436074	11.431957
30	11.427881	11.423844	11.419847	11.415890	11.411970	11.408090	11.404246	11.400441	11.396672	11.392941	11.389245	11.385585
31	11.381961	11.378372	11.374818	11.371299	11.367813	11.364362	11.360944	11.357558	11.354206	11.350886	11.347598	11.344342
32	11.341117	11.337923	11.334760	11.331628	11.328526	11.325453	11.322410	11.319397	11.316412	11.313456	11.310528	11.307629
33	11.304757	11.301913	11.299096	11.296306	11.293543	11.290806	11.288095	11.285410	11.282751	11.280118	11.277509	11.274925
34	11.272366	11.269831	11.267321	11.264834	11.262371	11.259932	11.257515	11.255122	11.252751	11.250403	11.248077	11.245774
35	11.243492	11.241232	11.238993	11.236775	11.234579	11.232403	11.230248	11.228113	11.225998	11.223904	11.221829	11.219774
36	11.217738	11.215721	11.213724	11.211745	11.209785	11.207843	11.205920	11.204015	11.202128	11.200258	11.198406	11.196572
37	11.194755	11.192955	11.191172	11.189405	11.187655	11.185922	11.184205	11.182504	11.180819	11.179150	11.177496	11.175858
38	11.174236	11.172628	11.171036	11.169458	11.167895	11.166347	11.164814	11.163294	11.161789	11.160298	11.158821	11.157358
39	11.155908	11.154472	11.153050	11.151640	11.150244	11.148861	11.147490	11.146133	11.144788	11.143456	11.142136	11.140828
40	11.139533	11.138249	11.136978	11.135718	11.134471	11.133234	11.132010	11.130796	11.129594	11.128403	11.127223	11.126055

11.25% Interest Rate   11.25% Interest Rate

Years	0	1	2	3	4	5	6	7	8	9	10	11
2	56.068790	54.068155	52.222084	50.513403	48.927392	47.451361	46.074310	44.786661	43.580033	42.447059	41.381240	40.376820
3	39.428682	38.532262	37.683477	36.878663	36.114521	35.388075	34.696633	34.037751	33.409209	32.808986	32.235232	31.686259
4	31.160518	30.656585	30.173152	29.709013	29.263055	28.834248	28.421638	28.024343	27.641541	27.272470	26.916418	26.572724
5	26.242069	25.919977	25.609805	25.309749	25.019334	24.738114	24.465672	24.201613	23.945569	23.697190	23.456147	23.222130
6	22.994847	22.774019	22.559386	22.350698	22.147722	21.950234	21.758022	21.570887	21.388638	21.211092	21.038079	20.869434
7	20.705000	20.544629	20.388179	20.235513	20.086504	19.941027	19.798965	19.660203	19.524636	19.392159	19.262673	19.136084
8	19.012300	18.891236	18.772806	18.656932	18.543537	18.432545	18.323887	18.217494	18.113301	18.011243	17.911262	17.813298
9	17.717295	17.623198	17.530956	17.440518	17.351835	17.264861	17.179551	17.095860	17.013746	16.933169	16.854090	16.776471
10	16.700274	16.625464	16.552007	16.479870	16.409020	16.339426	16.271058	16.203887	16.137885	16.073024	16.009277	15.946619
11	15.885025	15.824471	15.764932	15.706386	15.648812	15.592187	15.536490	15.481702	15.427803	15.374772	15.322593	15.271246
12	15.220715	15.170982	15.122029	15.073843	15.026405	14.979702	14.933718	14.888438	14.843849	14.799937	14.756688	14.714089
13	14.672128	14.630792	14.590069	14.549946	14.510414	14.471460	14.433074	14.395244	14.357961	14.321214	14.284993	14.249289
14	14.214092	14.179394	14.145184	14.111454	14.078195	14.045400	14.013060	13.981167	13.949712	13.918690	13.888091	13.857908
15	13.828135	13.798765	13.769790	13.741204	13.713000	13.685172	13.657714	13.630619	13.603881	13.577495	13.551455	13.525756
16	13.500390	13.475355	13.450642	13.426249	13.402170	13.378399	13.354931	13.331763	13.308889	13.286305	13.264006	13.241988
17	13.220247	13.198777	13.177576	13.156638	13.135961	13.115540	13.095370	13.075450	13.055774	13.036338	13.017141	12.998177
18	12.979444	12.960939	12.942656	12.924595	12.906751	12.889121	12.871703	12.854492	12.837487	12.820684	12.804080	12.787673
19	12.771460	12.755438	12.739604	12.723956	12.708491	12.693207	12.678101	12.663171	12.648414	12.633828	12.619410	12.605159
20	12.591072	12.577147	12.563382	12.549774	12.536321	12.523022	12.509874	12.496875	12.484024	12.471318	12.458756	12.446335
21	12.434054	12.421911	12.409905	12.398032	12.386292	12.374683	12.363204	12.351852	12.340626	12.329524	12.318545	12.307688
22	12.296950	12.286330	12.275827	12.265439	12.255165	12.245003	12.234953	12.225012	12.215179	12.205453	12.195833	12.186317
23	12.176904	12.167593	12.158382	12.149271	12.140257	12.131341	12.122520	12.113794	12.105161	12.096621	12.088172	12.079813
24	12.071543	12.063361	12.055265	12.047256	12.039332	12.031491	12.023734	12.016058	12.008463	12.000948	11.993513	11.986155
25	11.978875	11.971671	11.964542	11.957488	11.950508	11.943600	11.936765	11.930001	11.923307	11.916683	11.910127	11.903640
26	11.897220	11.890866	11.884578	11.878355	11.872196	11.866101	11.860068	11.854097	11.848188	11.842340	11.836551	11.830822
27	11.825152	11.819539	11.813984	11.808486	11.803044	11.797657	11.792325	11.787046	11.781824	11.776653	11.771535	11.766469
28	11.761454	11.756489	11.751575	11.746711	11.741896	11.737129	11.732411	11.727740	11.723116	11.718539	11.714008	11.709522
29	11.705081	11.700685	11.696333	11.692025	11.687760	11.683537	11.679357	11.675218	11.671121	11.667065	11.663049	11.659073
30	11.655137	11.651240	11.647381	11.643561	11.639779	11.636035	11.632327	11.628657	11.625023	11.621425	11.617862	11.614335
31	11.610842	11.607384	11.603960	11.600570	11.597214	11.593890	11.590600	11.587341	11.584115	11.580921	11.577757	11.574625
32	11.571524	11.568453	11.565413	11.562402	11.559420	11.556468	11.553545	11.550650	11.547784	11.544946	11.542135	11.539352
33	11.536596	11.533867	11.531165	11.528489	11.525839	11.523214	11.520616	11.518042	11.515494	11.512971	11.510472	11.507997
34	11.505546	11.503119	11.500716	11.498336	11.495979	11.493645	11.491333	11.489044	11.486777	11.484532	11.482309	11.480107
35	11.477927	11.475767	11.473629	11.471511	11.469413	11.467336	11.465279	11.463241	11.461223	11.459225	11.457246	11.455286
36	11.453345	11.451422	11.449518	11.447633	11.445765	11.443916	11.442084	11.440270	11.438473	11.436693	11.434931	11.433185
37	11.431456	11.429744	11.428048	11.426369	11.424705	11.423057	11.421426	11.419809	11.418209	11.416623	11.415053	11.413498
38	11.411957	11.410431	11.408920	11.407424	11.405941	11.404473	11.403019	11.401578	11.400152	11.398739	11.397339	11.395953
39	11.394580	11.393220	11.391873	11.390539	11.389217	11.387908	11.386612	11.385328	11.384056	11.382796	11.381548	11.380312
40	11.379088	11.377876	11.376674	11.375485	11.374306	11.373139	11.371983	11.370838	11.369704	11.368580	11.367467	11.366365

Annual Mortgage Constant for Monthly Payment Loans

11.50% Interest Rate   11.50% Interest Rate

Years	0	1	2	3	4	5	6	7	8	9	10	11
2	56.208378	54.207926	52.362053	50.653585	49.067798	47.592002	46.215198	44.927804	43.721438	42.588735	41.523193	40.519057
3	39.571208	38.675082	37.826596	37.022085	36.258250	35.532114	34.840986	34.182421	33.554199	32.954298	32.380869	31.832223
4	31.306811	30.803209	30.320109	29.856305	29.410683	28.982213	28.569942	28.172987	27.790526	27.421797	27.066089	26.722739
5	26.391129	26.070682	25.760856	25.461147	25.171079	24.890208	24.618114	24.354405	24.098709	23.850680	23.609987	23.376321
6	23.149387	22.928911	22.714628	22.506291	22.303666	22.106529	21.914669	21.727885	21.545986	21.368792	21.196130	21.027836
7	20.863753	20.703733	20.547633	20.395318	20.246659	20.101532	19.959819	19.821408	19.686190	19.554061	19.424924	19.298684
8	19.175249	19.054532	18.936450	18.820923	18.707874	18.597229	18.488917	18.382870	18.279022	18.177309	18.077672	17.980052
9	17.884392	17.790639	17.698739	17.608643	17.520302	17.433669	17.348699	17.265348	17.183574	17.103336	17.024595	16.947313
10	16.871453	16.796980	16.723859	16.652057	16.581542	16.512283	16.444249	16.377411	16.311741	16.247212	16.183796	16.121469
11	16.060204	15.999979	15.940769	15.882551	15.825304	15.769005	15.713634	15.659171	15.605596	15.552890	15.501033	15.450009
12	15.399799	15.350386	15.301754	15.253887	15.206768	15.160382	15.114715	15.069752	15.025479	14.981881	14.938946	14.896661
13	14.855012	14.813988	14.773576	14.733764	14.694541	14.655895	14.617817	14.580294	14.543317	14.506875	14.470959	14.435559
14	14.400665	14.366268	14.332360	14.298930	14.265971	14.233475	14.201433	14.169836	14.138678	14.107951	14.077647	14.047758
15	14.018278	13.989199	13.960515	13.932219	13.904305	13.876766	13.849595	13.822787	13.796335	13.770235	13.744479	13.719062
16	13.693980	13.669225	13.644794	13.620680	13.596879	13.573386	13.550196	13.527304	13.504706	13.482396	13.460371	13.438625
17	13.417155	13.395957	13.375025	13.354357	13.333947	13.313793	13.293890	13.274235	13.254823	13.235652	13.216717	13.198015
18	13.179543	13.161297	13.143274	13.125471	13.107884	13.090510	13.073347	13.056391	13.039639	13.023089	13.006737	12.990580
19	12.974617	12.958844	12.943258	12.927857	12.912638	12.897599	12.882738	12.868051	12.853536	12.839192	12.825015	12.811004
20	12.797156	12.783468	12.769940	12.756568	12.743350	12.730285	12.717371	12.704605	12.691985	12.679510	12.667177	12.654985
21	12.642932	12.631016	12.619235	12.607587	12.596072	12.584686	12.573429	12.562298	12.551293	12.540411	12.529650	12.519010
22	12.508489	12.498086	12.487798	12.477624	12.467563	12.457614	12.447775	12.438044	12.428421	12.418904	12.409492	12.400183
23	12.390976	12.381870	12.372863	12.363955	12.355145	12.346430	12.337810	12.329284	12.320850	12.312507	12.304255	12.296093
24	12.288010	12.280031	12.272129	12.264313	12.256580	12.248931	12.241363	12.233877	12.226471	12.219143	12.211895	12.204723
25	12.197628	12.190608	12.183663	12.176791	12.169992	12.163266	12.156610	12.150025	12.143510	12.137063	12.130684	12.124372
26	12.118121	12.111947	12.105832	12.099782	12.093794	12.087870	12.082007	12.076206	12.070465	12.064784	12.059162	12.053599
27	12.048093	12.042645	12.037253	12.031918	12.026637	12.021412	12.016240	12.011122	12.006057	12.001044	11.996082	11.991172
28	11.986313	11.981503	11.976743	11.972032	11.967369	11.962754	11.958187	11.953666	11.949191	11.944762	11.940379	11.936040
29	11.931746	11.927495	11.923288	11.919123	11.915001	11.910921	11.906883	11.902885	11.898928	11.895011	11.891134	11.887296
30	11.883497	11.879737	11.876014	11.872329	11.868682	11.865071	11.861497	11.857958	11.854456	11.850989	11.847556	11.844158
31	11.840795	11.837465	11.834168	11.830905	11.827674	11.824476	11.821310	11.818176	11.815073	11.812001	11.808960	11.805949
32	11.802968	11.800017	11.797096	11.794204	11.791340	11.788505	11.785699	11.782920	11.780169	11.777445	11.774749	11.772079
33	11.769436	11.766819	11.764228	11.761663	11.759123	11.756608	11.754119	11.751654	11.749213	11.746797	11.744404	11.742036
34	11.739690	11.737368	11.735069	11.732792	11.730538	11.728306	11.726097	11.723909	11.721742	11.719597	11.717473	11.715370
35	11.713288	11.711226	11.709185	11.707163	11.705162	11.703180	11.701217	11.699274	11.697350	11.695445	11.693559	11.691691
36	11.689841	11.688010	11.686196	11.684400	11.682622	11.680861	11.679118	11.677391	11.675682	11.673989	11.672312	11.670653
37	11.669009	11.667381	11.665769	11.664173	11.662593	11.661028	11.659478	11.657944	11.656424	11.654919	11.653429	11.651953
38	11.650492	11.649045	11.647612	11.646193	11.644788	11.643396	11.642018	11.640654	11.639303	11.637964	11.636639	11.635327
39	11.634027	11.632740	11.631466	11.630204	11.628954	11.627716	11.626491	11.625277	11.624075	11.622885	11.621706	11.620538
40	11.619382	11.618238	11.617104	11.615981	11.614869	11.613768	11.612677	11.611597	11.610528	11.609469	11.608420	11.607381

11.75% Interest Rate   11.75% Interest Rate

Years	0	1	2	3	4	5	6	7	8	9	10	11
2	56.348171	54.347909	52.502243	50.793995	49.208442	47.732890	46.356340	45.069209	43.863115	42.730691	41.665435	40.661590
3	39.714038	38.818214	37.970035	37.165835	36.402315	35.676499	34.985692	34.327452	33.699558	33.099987	32.526892	31.978581
4	31.453506	30.950243	30.467484	30.004023	29.558744	29.130620	28.718696	28.322089	27.939977	27.571598	27.216240	26.873242
5	26.541985	26.221891	25.912426	25.613065	25.323353	25.042837	24.771099	24.507746	24.252408	24.004736	23.764400	23.531091
6	23.304516	23.084397	22.870473	22.662494	22.460227	22.263449	22.071947	21.885521	21.703981	21.527145	21.354841	21.186905
7	21.023180	20.863517	20.707775	20.555818	20.407516	20.262746	20.121390	19.983335	19.848473	19.716700	19.587919	19.462033
8	19.338459	19.218590	19.100683	18.985689	18.872994	18.762701	18.654742	18.549046	18.445550	18.344189	18.244902	18.147632
9	18.052322	17.958917	17.867366	17.777618	17.689625	17.603338	17.518715	17.435709	17.354280	17.274387	17.195991	17.119052
10	17.043535	16.969404	16.896625	16.825164	16.754989	16.686069	16.618374	16.551875	16.486543	16.422350	16.359271	16.297279
11	16.236350	16.176458	16.117582	16.059697	16.002782	15.946814	15.891774	15.837641	15.784395	15.732017	15.680488	15.629791
12	15.579907	15.530819	15.482512	15.434968	15.388172	15.342109	15.296763	15.252121	15.208167	15.164888	15.122272	15.080304
13	15.038971	14.998263	14.958165	14.918667	14.879757	14.841424	14.803657	14.766445	14.729778	14.693645	14.658037	14.622944
14	14.588356	14.554265	14.520661	14.487535	14.454879	14.422685	14.390944	14.359648	14.328789	14.298360	14.268353	14.238761
15	14.209576	14.180793	14.152403	14.124400	14.096777	14.069529	14.042649	14.016130	13.989967	13.964154	13.938684	13.913553
16	13.888755	13.864285	13.840136	13.816305	13.792785	13.769572	13.746661	13.724047	13.701726	13.679692	13.657942	13.636471
17	13.615275	13.594349	13.573689	13.553291	13.533151	13.513266	13.493631	13.474242	13.455096	13.436190	13.417519	13.399080
18	13.380870	13.362885	13.345122	13.327578	13.310250	13.293133	13.276226	13.259526	13.243028	13.226731	13.210632	13.194727
19	13.179014	13.163491	13.148153	13.133000	13.118028	13.103235	13.088618	13.074175	13.059904	13.045801	13.031865	13.018094
20	13.004485	12.991036	12.977744	12.964608	12.951626	12.938796	12.926114	12.913580	12.901192	12.888947	12.876844	12.864881
21	12.853055	12.841366	12.829810	12.818388	12.807096	12.795933	12.784898	12.773988	12.763202	12.752539	12.741997	12.731575
22	12.721270	12.711081	12.701008	12.691048	12.681199	12.671462	12.661833	12.652312	12.642898	12.633589	12.624383	12.615280
23	12.606278	12.597376	12.588573	12.579868	12.571258	12.562744	12.554323	12.545996	12.537760	12.529614	12.521558	12.513590
24	12.505710	12.497915	12.490206	12.482581	12.475039	12.467579	12.460201	12.452902	12.445683	12.438541	12.431478	12.424490
25	12.417578	12.410741	12.403977	12.397287	12.390668	12.384120	12.377643	12.371235	12.364896	12.358624	12.352420	12.346282
26	12.340210	12.334202	12.328259	12.322378	12.316560	12.310804	12.305110	12.299475	12.293900	12.288385	12.282927	12.277528
27	12.272185	12.266899	12.261668	12.256493	12.251372	12.246305	12.241291	12.236330	12.231421	12.226564	12.221757	12.217001
28	12.212294	12.207637	12.203028	12.198468	12.193955	12.189489	12.185069	12.180696	12.176368	12.172085	12.167847	12.163652
29	12.159502	12.155394	12.151328	12.147305	12.143324	12.139383	12.135484	12.131624	12.127805	12.124025	12.120284	12.116581
30	12.112917	12.109290	12.105701	12.102148	12.098632	12.095152	12.091708	12.088299	12.084925	12.081586	12.078281	12.075010
31	12.071772	12.068567	12.065395	12.062256	12.059148	12.056072	12.053028	12.050014	12.047032	12.044079	12.041157	12.038265
32	12.035401	12.032567	12.029762	12.026985	12.024237	12.021516	12.018823	12.016158	12.013519	12.010907	12.008321	12.005762
33	12.003228	12.000720	11.998238	11.995780	11.993348	11.990940	11.988556	11.986196	11.983860	11.981548	11.979259	11.976993
34	11.974750	11.972529	11.970331	11.968155	11.966000	11.963868	11.961757	11.959667	11.957598	11.955549	11.953522	11.951514
35	11.949527	11.947560	11.945612	11.943684	11.941776	11.939886	11.938015	11.936163	11.934330	11.932514	11.930717	11.928938
36	11.927177	11.925433	11.923707	11.921998	11.920306	11.918631	11.916973	11.915331	11.913705	11.912096	11.910503	11.908925
37	11.907364	11.905817	11.904287	11.902771	11.901271	11.899785	11.898314	11.896858	11.895417	11.893989	11.892576	11.891177
38	11.889792	11.888420	11.887062	11.885718	11.884387	11.883069	11.881764	11.880472	11.879193	11.877927	11.876673	11.875432
39	11.874202	11.872986	11.871781	11.870588	11.869406	11.868237	11.867079	11.865933	11.864797	11.863673	11.862561	11.861459
40	11.860368	11.859288	11.858218	11.857159	11.856111	11.855073	11.854045	11.853027	11.852019	11.851022	11.850034	11.849056

Annual Mortgage Constant for Monthly Payment Loans

12.00% Interest Rate   12.00% Interest Rate

| | | | | | | Number of Months | | | | | | |
Years	0	1	2	3	4	5	6	7	8	9	10	11
2	56.488167	54.488104	52.642653	50.934634	49.349323	47.874024	46.497736	45.210877	44.005063	42.872925	41.807963	40.804418
3	39.857172	38.961659	38.113795	37.309914	36.546718	35.821228	35.130751	34.472845	33.845287	33.246055	32.673300	32.125332
4	31.600603	31.097687	30.615277	30.152166	29.707239	29.279468	28.867899	28.471648	28.089893	27.721871	27.366873	27.024234
5	26.693337	26.373604	26.064495	25.765502	25.476153	25.196000	24.924626	24.661637	24.406663	24.159355	23.919385	23.686441
6	23.460231	23.240478	23.026918	22.819306	22.617404	22.420991	22.229855	22.043795	21.862620	21.686150	21.514211	21.346639
7	21.183279	21.023981	20.868604	20.717010	20.569072	20.424666	20.283673	20.145981	20.011482	19.880072	19.751653	19.626129
8	19.503410	19.383408	19.266041	19.151228	19.038892	18.928959	18.821358	18.716020	18.612881	18.511877	18.412948	18.316034
9	18.221079	18.128030	18.036833	17.947439	17.859799	17.773865	17.689594	17.606940	17.525862	17.446319	17.368272	17.291682
10	17.216514	17.142731	17.070298	16.999184	16.929354	16.860780	16.793429	16.727273	16.662283	16.598433	16.535695	16.474044
11	16.413455	16.353902	16.295364	16.237817	16.181238	16.125607	16.070902	16.017104	15.964191	15.912146	15.860949	15.810583
12	15.761030	15.712272	15.664293	15.617078	15.570609	15.524872	15.479852	15.435534	15.391904	15.348948	15.306654	15.265007
13	15.223995	15.183605	15.143826	15.104646	15.066053	15.028036	14.990584	14.953686	14.917332	14.881512	14.846215	14.811432
14	14.777154	14.743372	14.710075	14.677256	14.644906	14.613017	14.581580	14.550587	14.520030	14.489902	14.460196	14.430903
15	14.402017	14.373530	14.345437	14.317730	14.290402	14.263447	14.236859	14.210632	14.184760	14.159236	14.134056	14.109213
16	14.084702	14.060517	14.036653	14.013105	13.989868	13.966937	13.944307	13.921974	13.899931	13.878176	13.856703	13.835508
17	13.814586	13.793934	13.773547	13.753422	13.733553	13.713938	13.694572	13.675451	13.656573	13.637932	13.619526	13.601352
18	13.583405	13.565682	13.548180	13.530896	13.513827	13.496968	13.480319	13.463874	13.447632	13.431589	13.415742	13.400090
19	13.384628	13.369354	13.354266	13.339361	13.324636	13.310089	13.295717	13.281519	13.267490	13.253630	13.239935	13.226404
20	13.213034	13.199823	13.186768	13.173869	13.161122	13.148525	13.136077	13.123775	13.111618	13.099603	13.087729	13.075994
21	13.064396	13.052932	13.041603	13.030404	13.019335	13.008395	12.997581	12.986891	12.976325	12.965881	12.955556	12.945350
22	12.935260	12.925286	12.915426	12.905678	12.896042	12.886515	12.877096	12.867784	12.858577	12.849474	12.840475	12.831577
23	12.822779	12.814080	12.805478	12.796974	12.788564	12.780249	12.772027	12.763896	12.755857	12.747907	12.740045	12.732271
24	12.724583	12.716980	12.709461	12.702026	12.694673	12.687401	12.680209	12.673097	12.666063	12.659106	12.652225	12.645420
25	12.638690	12.632033	12.625449	12.618937	12.612496	12.606126	12.599824	12.593592	12.587427	12.581329	12.575297	12.569331
26	12.563430	12.557592	12.551817	12.546105	12.540455	12.534865	12.529336	12.523866	12.518455	12.513102	12.507807	12.502569
27	12.497387	12.492260	12.487188	12.482171	12.477207	12.472296	12.467438	12.462631	12.457876	12.453171	12.448517	12.443912
28	12.439356	12.434848	12.430388	12.425976	12.421610	12.417290	12.413017	12.408788	12.404604	12.400464	12.396369	12.392316
29	12.388306	12.384338	12.380412	12.376527	12.372684	12.368880	12.365117	12.361393	12.357708	12.354062	12.350454	12.346884
30	12.343350	12.339855	12.336396	12.332973	12.329586	12.326234	12.322917	12.319634	12.316386	12.313172	12.309991	12.306844
31	12.303729	12.300646	12.297596	12.294577	12.291589	12.288633	12.285707	12.282812	12.279946	12.277110	12.274304	12.271527
32	12.268778	12.266058	12.263366	12.260702	12.258065	12.255455	12.252873	12.250317	12.247787	12.245284	12.242806	12.240354
33	12.237927	12.235525	12.233148	12.230795	12.228466	12.226162	12.223881	12.221623	12.219389	12.217177	12.214989	12.212822
34	12.210678	12.208556	12.206455	12.204377	12.202319	12.200282	12.198267	12.196271	12.194297	12.192342	12.190407	12.188493
35	12.186597	12.184721	12.182865	12.181027	12.179208	12.177407	12.175625	12.173861	12.172115	12.170386	12.168676	12.166982
36	12.165306	12.163647	12.162005	12.160380	12.158771	12.157178	12.155602	12.154041	12.152497	12.150968	12.149455	12.147957
37	12.146474	12.145006	12.143553	12.142115	12.140692	12.139282	12.137888	12.136507	12.135140	12.133787	12.132448	12.131122
38	12.129810	12.128511	12.127225	12.125952	12.124692	12.123445	12.122210	12.120988	12.119778	12.118580	12.117395	12.116221
39	12.115060	12.113910	12.112771	12.111644	12.110529	12.109424	12.108331	12.107249	12.106178	12.105117	12.104067	12.103028
40	12.101999	12.100981	12.099973	12.098975	12.097987	12.097009	12.096041	12.095082	12.094134	12.093194	12.092264	12.091344

12.25% Interest Rate   12.25% Interest Rate

Years	0	1	2	3	4	5	6	7	8	9	10	11
2	56.628366	54.628512	52.783284	51.075503	49.490441	48.015403	46.639386	45.352807	44.147281	43.015439	41.950779	40.947542
3	40.000610	39.105415	38.257875	37.454322	36.691456	35.966302	35.276163	34.618598	33.991385	33.392494	32.820093	32.272477
4	31.748100	31.245540	30.763487	30.300734	29.856167	29.428725	29.017551	28.621663	28.240273	27.872617	27.517985	27.175713
5	26.845184	26.525820	26.217080	25.918458	25.629478	25.349696	25.078693	24.816076	24.561474	24.314538	24.074940	23.842368
6	23.616531	23.397150	23.183964	22.976724	22.775195	22.579155	22.388391	22.202704	22.021901	21.845803	21.674236	21.507037
7	21.344049	21.185122	21.030116	20.878894	20.731326	20.587290	20.446668	20.309346	20.175216	20.044175	19.916124	19.790968
8	19.668617	19.548983	19.431982	19.317535	19.205565	19.095997	18.988761	18.883788	18.781013	18.680372	18.581805	18.485253
9	18.390660	18.297972	18.207136	18.118101	18.030820	17.945245	17.861331	17.779034	17.698313	17.619126	17.541434	17.465199
10	17.390384	17.316954	17.244874	17.174111	17.104632	17.036408	16.969406	16.903599	16.838957	16.775454	16.713062	16.651757
11	16.591512	16.532304	16.474108	16.416903	16.360666	16.305376	16.251011	16.197551	16.144977	16.093269	16.042409	15.992378
12	15.943159	15.894736	15.847090	15.800206	15.754069	15.708662	15.663971	15.619982	15.576680	15.534051	15.492082	15.450760
13	15.410072	15.370006	15.330549	15.291690	15.253417	15.215719	15.178586	15.142005	15.105968	15.070463	15.035481	15.001012
14	14.967046	14.933575	14.900590	14.868081	14.836039	14.804455	14.773327	14.742640	14.712388	14.682564	14.653161	14.624170
15	14.595584	14.567398	14.539603	14.512194	14.485163	14.458504	14.432211	14.406278	14.380698	14.355467	14.330577	14.306024
16	14.281801	14.257904	14.234327	14.211065	14.188113	14.165466	14.143118	14.121066	14.099304	14.077828	14.056634	14.035716
17	14.015071	13.994694	13.974582	13.954729	13.935133	13.915789	13.896693	13.877842	13.859231	13.840858	13.822718	13.804808
18	13.787125	13.769665	13.752425	13.735402	13.718592	13.701993	13.685601	13.669413	13.653426	13.637638	13.622045	13.606645
19	13.591434	13.576411	13.561572	13.546916	13.532438	13.518137	13.504011	13.490056	13.476271	13.462652	13.449199	13.435907
20	13.422776	13.409803	13.396986	13.384322	13.371810	13.359447	13.347232	13.335162	13.323235	13.311450	13.299805	13.288297
21	13.276926	13.265688	13.254582	13.243608	13.232761	13.222042	13.211449	13.200979	13.190631	13.180404	13.170296	13.160305
22	13.150430	13.140670	13.131022	13.121486	13.112059	13.102742	13.093531	13.084427	13.075426	13.066529	13.057734	13.049039
23	13.040444	13.031947	13.023546	13.015241	13.007030	12.998912	12.990887	12.982952	12.975107	12.967351	12.959682	12.952099
24	12.944602	12.937189	12.929860	12.922612	12.915446	12.908360	12.901354	12.894425	12.887575	12.880800	12.874101	12.867476
25	12.860925	12.854447	12.848041	12.841706	12.835441	12.829245	12.823118	12.817058	12.811066	12.805139	12.799278	12.793481
26	12.787748	12.782078	12.776470	12.770924	12.765438	12.760013	12.754647	12.749339	12.744090	12.738898	12.733762	12.728683
27	12.723658	12.718689	12.713773	12.708911	12.704102	12.699345	12.694639	12.689985	12.685381	12.680826	12.676321	12.671865
28	12.667457	12.663096	12.658782	12.654515	12.650294	12.646118	12.641987	12.637900	12.633858	12.629859	12.625902	12.621988
29	12.618116	12.614286	12.610496	12.606747	12.603038	12.599369	12.595739	12.592148	12.588595	12.585080	12.581602	12.578161
30	12.574757	12.571389	12.568057	12.564761	12.561499	12.558272	12.555079	12.551921	12.548795	12.545703	12.542643	12.539616
31	12.536621	12.533658	12.530726	12.527825	12.524954	12.522114	12.519304	12.516523	12.513772	12.511050	12.508356	12.505691
32	12.503054	12.500444	12.497862	12.495307	12.492779	12.490278	12.487803	12.485354	12.482930	12.480532	12.478159	12.475811
33	12.473487	12.471188	12.468913	12.466662	12.464434	12.462230	12.460048	12.457890	12.455754	12.453640	12.451548	12.449478
34	12.447430	12.445403	12.443397	12.441413	12.439448	12.437505	12.435581	12.433678	12.431794	12.429930	12.428085	12.426260
35	12.424453	12.422666	12.420897	12.419146	12.417413	12.415699	12.414002	12.412323	12.410661	12.409016	12.407389	12.405778
36	12.404184	12.402606	12.401045	12.399500	12.397971	12.396458	12.394961	12.393479	12.392012	12.390561	12.389124	12.387702
37	12.386295	12.384903	12.383525	12.382161	12.380811	12.379475	12.378153	12.376845	12.375550	12.374268	12.373000	12.371745
38	12.370502	12.369273	12.368056	12.366852	12.365660	12.364480	12.363312	12.362157	12.361013	12.359881	12.358761	12.357652
39	12.356555	12.355469	12.354394	12.353330	12.352278	12.351235	12.350204	12.349183	12.348173	12.347173	12.346183	12.345204
40	12.344234	12.343275	12.342325	12.341385	12.340455	12.339534	12.338623	12.337721	12.336828	12.335945	12.335070	12.334205

Annual Mortgage Constant for Monthly Payment Loans

12.50% Interest Rate   12.50% Interest Rate

Years	0	1	2	3	4	5	6	7	8	9	10	11
						Number of Months						
2	56.768770	54.769131	52.924135	51.216600	49.631796	48.157028	46.781290	45.495000	44.289770	43.158232	42.093882	41.090961
3	40.144351	39.249483	38.402274	37.599057	36.836531	36.111720	35.421928	34.764712	34.137851	33.539320	32.967271	32.420014
4	31.895999	31.393801	30.912113	30.449726	30.005528	29.578487	29.167650	28.772134	28.391116	28.023833	27.669575	27.327679
5	26.997526	26.678538	26.370175	26.071930	25.783328	25.503924	25.233300	24.971062	24.716839	24.470282	24.231064	23.998872
6	23.773414	23.554413	23.341607	23.134747	22.933598	22.737937	22.547554	22.362246	22.181823	22.006104	21.834916	21.668096
7	21.505486	21.346938	21.192310	21.041465	20.894275	20.750616	20.610370	20.473424	20.339670	20.209005	20.081329	19.956548
8	19.834570	19.715310	19.598683	19.484608	19.373010	19.263814	19.156949	19.052346	18.949941	18.849669	18.751471	18.655287
9	18.561061	18.468739	18.378269	18.289600	18.202684	18.117473	18.033922	17.951988	17.871629	17.792803	17.715471	17.639596
10	17.565140	17.492068	17.420346	17.349939	17.280817	17.212947	17.146300	17.080846	17.016558	16.953406	16.891366	16.830410
11	16.770515	16.711655	16.653808	16.596949	16.541058	16.486113	16.432092	16.378976	16.326744	16.275378	16.224858	16.175167
12	16.126287	16.078201	16.030893	15.984345	15.938543	15.893470	15.849113	15.805456	15.762485	15.720186	15.678547	15.637553
13	15.597193	15.557453	15.518322	15.479788	15.441838	15.404463	15.367651	15.331391	15.295673	15.260487	15.225822	15.191670
14	15.158020	15.124864	15.092192	15.059995	15.028265	14.996994	14.966173	14.935794	14.905850	14.876332	14.847234	14.818547
15	14.790265	14.762381	14.734887	14.707778	14.681046	14.654685	14.628689	14.603051	14.577767	14.552829	14.528231	14.503970
16	14.480038	14.456430	14.433141	14.410167	14.387501	14.365138	14.343075	14.321306	14.299826	14.278631	14.257716	14.237077
17	14.216710	14.196609	14.176772	14.157194	14.137871	14.118799	14.099975	14.081393	14.063052	14.044946	14.027073	14.009429
18	13.992010	13.974814	13.957837	13.941075	13.924525	13.908185	13.892051	13.876120	13.860389	13.844856	13.829516	13.814369
19	13.799410	13.784637	13.770048	13.755640	13.741409	13.727355	13.713473	13.699762	13.686220	13.672843	13.659631	13.646579
20	13.633687	13.620951	13.608370	13.595942	13.583664	13.571534	13.559551	13.547713	13.536016	13.524460	13.513043	13.501762
21	13.490616	13.479603	13.468722	13.457970	13.447345	13.436847	13.426473	13.416221	13.406091	13.396080	13.386187	13.376411
22	13.366749	13.357201	13.347764	13.338438	13.329221	13.320112	13.311108	13.302210	13.293415	13.284722	13.276129	13.267637
23	13.259242	13.250945	13.242743	13.234636	13.226622	13.218700	13.210870	13.203129	13.195477	13.187913	13.180435	13.173042
24	13.165734	13.158509	13.151367	13.144305	13.137324	13.130423	13.123599	13.116853	13.110183	13.103589	13.097069	13.090623
25	13.084250	13.077948	13.071717	13.065557	13.059465	13.053442	13.047487	13.041598	13.035775	13.030017	13.024324	13.018694
26	13.013128	13.007623	13.002179	12.996796	12.991473	12.986210	12.981004	12.975857	12.970766	12.965732	12.960754	12.955830
27	12.950962	12.946147	12.941385	12.936675	12.932018	12.927412	12.922857	12.918351	12.913896	12.909489	12.905131	12.900820
28	12.896557	12.892340	12.888170	12.884045	12.879966	12.875931	12.871940	12.867992	12.864088	12.860227	12.856407	12.852629
29	12.848892	12.845196	12.841540	12.837924	12.834347	12.830809	12.827309	12.823847	12.820423	12.817036	12.813686	12.810371
30	12.807093	12.803850	12.800642	12.797469	12.794330	12.791225	12.788154	12.785115	12.782110	12.779136	12.776195	12.773286
31	12.770407	12.767560	12.764743	12.761957	12.759200	12.756473	12.753775	12.751106	12.748466	12.745854	12.743270	12.740714
32	12.738185	12.735684	12.733209	12.730760	12.728337	12.725941	12.723570	12.721224	12.718904	12.716608	12.714337	12.712089
33	12.709866	12.707667	12.705491	12.703338	12.701208	12.699100	12.697015	12.694953	12.692912	12.690893	12.688895	12.686918
34	12.684963	12.683028	12.681114	12.679220	12.677346	12.675492	12.673658	12.671843	12.670047	12.668271	12.666513	12.664774
35	12.663053	12.661350	12.659665	12.657999	12.656349	12.654717	12.653103	12.651505	12.649925	12.648361	12.646813	12.645282
36	12.643767	12.642268	12.640785	12.639317	12.637865	12.636429	12.635007	12.633600	12.632208	12.630831	12.629468	12.628120
37	12.626786	12.625466	12.624159	12.622867	12.621588	12.620322	12.619070	12.617831	12.616605	12.615391	12.614191	12.613003
38	12.611828	12.610665	12.609514	12.608375	12.607248	12.606133	12.605030	12.603938	12.602858	12.601789	12.600731	12.599684
39	12.598648	12.597623	12.596609	12.595606	12.594612	12.593630	12.592657	12.591695	12.590743	12.589801	12.588868	12.587946
40	12.587033	12.586129	12.585235	12.584351	12.583475	12.582609	12.581752	12.580904	12.580064	12.579234	12.578412	12.577598

12.75% Interest Rate   12.75% Interest Rate

Years	0	1	2	3	4	5	6	7	8	9	10	11
2	56.909377	54.909962	53.065207	51.357926	49.773389	48.298898	46.923448	45.637454	44.432529	43.301303	42.237272	41.234676
3	40.288395	39.393863	38.546994	37.744220	36.981942	36.257482	35.568045	34.911186	34.284685	33.686517	33.114833	32.567943
4	32.044297	31.542471	31.061155	30.599142	30.155319	29.728655	29.318197	28.923059	28.542422	28.175520	27.821644	27.480130
5	27.150361	26.831757	26.523778	26.225918	25.937701	25.658683	25.388445	25.126593	24.872757	24.626587	24.387755	24.155951
6	23.930880	23.712266	23.499847	23.293374	23.092612	22.897338	22.707341	22.522419	22.342383	22.167050	21.996249	21.829814
7	21.667589	21.509426	21.355182	21.204722	21.057916	20.914641	20.774778	20.638215	20.504843	20.374560	20.247265	20.122865
8	20.001268	19.882387	19.766139	19.652444	19.541224	19.432405	19.325917	19.221691	19.119661	19.019764	18.921940	18.826130
9	18.732278	18.640328	18.550230	18.461932	18.375385	18.290544	18.207362	18.125796	18.045804	17.967345	17.890379	17.814869
10	17.740777	17.668068	17.596708	17.526664	17.457902	17.390393	17.324105	17.259009	17.195078	17.132283	17.070598	17.009998
11	16.950456	16.891950	16.834454	16.777948	16.722407	16.667811	16.614139	16.561370	16.509484	16.458464	16.408289	16.358942
12	16.310405	16.262661	16.215693	16.169485	16.124022	16.079287	16.035266	15.991945	15.949309	15.907345	15.866038	15.825376
13	15.785347	15.745937	15.707134	15.668928	15.631305	15.594256	15.557768	15.521832	15.486437	15.451572	15.417228	15.383395
14	15.350063	15.317224	15.284868	15.252987	15.221571	15.190613	15.160103	15.130035	15.100401	15.071192	15.042401	15.014020
15	14.986044	14.958464	14.931273	14.904466	14.878035	14.851974	14.826276	14.800937	14.775948	14.751306	14.727003	14.703034
16	14.679394	14.656078	14.633079	14.610393	14.588014	14.565938	14.544160	14.522675	14.501479	14.480565	14.459931	14.439572
17	14.419483	14.399661	14.380100	14.360797	14.341748	14.322949	14.304396	14.286085	14.268013	14.250176	14.232571	14.215193
18	14.198039	14.181107	14.164392	14.147892	14.131603	14.115522	14.099646	14.083972	14.068498	14.053219	14.038134	14.023239
19	14.008532	13.994009	13.979669	13.965509	13.951526	13.937717	13.924080	13.910613	13.897313	13.884178	13.871206	13.858394
20	13.845739	13.833241	13.820896	13.808702	13.796658	13.784761	13.773010	13.761401	13.749934	13.738606	13.727416	13.716361
21	13.705440	13.694651	13.683995	13.673462	13.663058	13.652779	13.642623	13.632589	13.622675	13.612880	13.603201	13.593638
22	13.584188	13.574850	13.565624	13.556506	13.547497	13.538594	13.529796	13.521102	13.512511	13.504020	13.495629	13.487337
23	13.479142	13.471043	13.463038	13.455127	13.447308	13.439581	13.431943	13.424395	13.416934	13.409559	13.402270	13.395066
24	13.387945	13.380906	13.373949	13.367071	13.360273	13.353554	13.346911	13.340345	13.333855	13.327438	13.321096	13.314826
25	13.308627	13.302500	13.296442	13.290454	13.284534	13.278681	13.272895	13.267174	13.261519	13.255928	13.250400	13.244935
26	13.239532	13.234190	13.228908	13.223686	13.218523	13.213419	13.208371	13.203381	13.198447	13.193568	13.188744	13.183975
27	13.179259	13.174595	13.169984	13.165425	13.160917	13.156459	13.152051	13.147692	13.143382	13.139120	13.134906	13.130738
28	13.126617	13.122542	13.118512	13.114527	13.110586	13.106689	13.102836	13.099025	13.095256	13.091529	13.087843	13.084198
29	13.080594	13.077029	13.073503	13.070017	13.066569	13.063159	13.059787	13.056452	13.053153	13.049891	13.046665	13.043474
30	13.040319	13.037198	13.034111	13.031058	13.028039	13.025053	13.022099	13.019178	13.016289	13.013432	13.010606	13.007810
31	13.005046	13.002311	12.999607	12.996932	12.994286	12.991669	12.989081	12.986520	12.983988	12.981484	12.979006	12.976556
32	12.974132	12.971735	12.969363	12.967018	12.964698	12.962403	12.960133	12.957888	12.955667	12.953471	12.951298	12.949148
33	12.947022	12.944919	12.942839	12.940781	12.938746	12.936732	12.934741	12.932771	12.930822	12.928894	12.926987	12.925101
34	12.923235	12.921389	12.919564	12.917757	12.915971	12.914203	12.912455	12.910726	12.909015	12.907322	12.905648	12.903992
35	12.902354	12.900733	12.899130	12.897544	12.895975	12.894423	12.892888	12.891369	12.889866	12.888380	12.886909	12.885455
36	12.884016	12.882592	12.881184	12.879790	12.878412	12.877049	12.875700	12.874365	12.873045	12.871739	12.870447	12.869169
37	12.867905	12.866654	12.865416	12.864192	12.862981	12.861783	12.860597	12.859425	12.858264	12.857117	12.855981	12.854858
38	12.853746	12.852647	12.851559	12.850483	12.849418	12.848365	12.847323	12.846292	12.845272	12.844263	12.843265	12.842277
39	12.841300	12.840333	12.839377	12.838431	12.837495	12.836569	12.835653	12.834746	12.833849	12.832962	12.832084	12.831216
40	12.830356	12.829506	12.828665	12.827833	12.827010	12.826196	12.825390	12.824593	12.823804	12.823023	12.822251	12.821488

Annual Mortgage Constant to Amortize Part of a Loan by a Given Date

5.50% Interest Rate

Years to Balloon	Percentage to be amortized										
	10%	20%	25%	30%	40%	50%	60%	70%	75%	80%	90%
3	8.57244	11.64595	13.18270	14.71945	17.79296	20.86647	23.93998	27.01349	28.55024	30.08700	33.16050
	(18Y 8m)	(11Y 8m)	(9Y10m)	(8Y 6m)	(6Y 9m)	(5Y 7m)	(4Y 9m)	(4Y 2m)	(3Y11m)	(3Y 8m)	(3Y 4m)
5	7.24196	8.98410	9.85517	10.72624	12.46838	14.21051	15.95265	17.69479	18.56586	19.43693	21.17907
	(25Y12m)	(17Y 3m)	(14Y11m)	(13Y 1m)	(10Y 7m)	(8Y11m)	(7Y 8m)	(6Y 9m)	(6Y 5m)	(6Y 1m)	(5Y 6m)
7.5	6.57904	7.65924	8.19934	8.73944	9.81963	10.89983	11.98003	13.06022	13.60032	14.14042	15.22062
	(32Y11m)	(23Y 1m)	(20Y 3m)	(18Y 1m)	(14Y12m)	(12Y10m)	(11Y 2m)	(9Y12m)	(9Y 5m)	(8Y12m)	(8Y 2m)
10	6.25157	7.00389	7.38005	7.75620	8.50852	9.26084	10.01315	10.76547	11.14162	11.51778	12.27010
	(38Y 7m)	(28Y 0m)	(24Y11m)	(22Y 6m)	(18Y11m)	(16Y 5m)	(14Y 6m)	(13Y 0m)	(12Y 5m)	(11Y10m)	(10Y10m)
12.5	6.05737	6.61540	6.89441	7.17343	7.73145	8.28948	8.84751	9.40553	9.68455	9.96356	10.52159
	(43Y 6m)	(32Y 5m)	(29Y 2m)	(26Y 6m)	(22Y 8m)	(19Y10m)	(17Y 9m)	(16Y 0m)	(15Y 4m)	(14Y 8m)	(13Y 6m)
15	5.92951	6.36001	6.57526	6.79051	7.22101	7.65151	8.08201	8.51251	8.72776	8.94301	9.37351
	(47Y10m)	(36Y 6m)	(32Y12m)	(30Y 3m)	(26Y 2m)	(23Y 1m)	(20Y10m)	(18Y11m)	(18Y 2m)	(17Y 5m)	(16Y 1m)
20	5.77443	6.04989	6.18763	6.32536	6.60082	6.87629	7.15175	7.42722	7.56495	7.70268	7.97815
	(55Y 6m)	(43Y 8m)	(40Y 0m)	(37Y 1m)	(32Y 8m)	(29Y 4m)	(26Y 8m)	(24Y 7m)	(23Y 8m)	(22Y11m)	(21Y 4m)
25	5.68587	5.87277	5.96622	6.05968	6.24658	6.43349	6.62039	6.80730	6.90075	6.99420	7.18111
	(62Y 4m)	(50Y 3m)	(46Y 5m)	(43Y 5m)	(38Y 9m)	(35Y 2m)	(32Y 4m)	(30Y 1m)	(29Y 1m)	(28Y 2m)	(26Y 6m)
30	5.63029	5.76164	5.82731	5.89298	6.02433	6.15568	6.28702	6.41837	6.48404	6.54972	6.68107
	(68Y 8m)	(56Y 4m)	(52Y 6m)	(49Y 4m)	(44Y 6m)	(40Y10m)	(37Y10m)	(35Y 5m)	(34Y 4m)	(33Y 4m)	(31Y 7m)

5.75% Interest Rate

Years to Balloon	10%	20%	25%	30%	40%	50%	60%	70%	75%	80%	90%
3	8.81112	11.87317	13.40420	14.93523	17.99728	21.05934	24.12139	27.18345	28.71447	30.24550	33.30756
	(18Y 5m)	(11Y 7m)	(9Y 9m)	(8Y 6m)	(6Y 9m)	(5Y 7m)	(4Y 9m)	(4Y 2m)	(3Y11m)	(3Y 8m)	(3Y 4m)
5	7.48010	9.21111	10.07662	10.94213	12.67314	14.40415	16.13516	17.86618	18.73168	19.59719	21.32820
	(25Y 6m)	(17Y 1m)	(14Y 9m)	(12Y12m)	(10Y 6m)	(8Y11m)	(7Y 8m)	(6Y 9m)	(6Y 5m)	(6Y 1m)	(5Y 6m)
7.5	6.81862	7.88820	8.42299	8.95778	10.02735	11.09693	12.16651	13.23608	13.77087	14.30566	15.37524
	(32Y 4m)	(22Y 9m)	(20Y 0m)	(17Y11m)	(14Y10m)	(12Y 9m)	(11Y 2m)	(9Y11m)	(9Y 5m)	(8Y12m)	(8Y 2m)
10	6.49114	7.23337	7.60448	7.97560	8.71783	9.46006	10.20229	10.94452	11.31564	11.68675	12.42898
	(37Y10m)	(27Y 7m)	(24Y 7m)	(22Y 3m)	(18Y 9m)	(16Y 4m)	(14Y 5m)	(12Y12m)	(12Y 4m)	(11Y10m)	(10Y10m)
12.5	6.29807	6.84655	7.12080	7.39504	7.94352	8.49200	9.04048	9.58897	9.86321	10.13745	10.68593
	(42Y 7m)	(31Y11m)	(28Y 9m)	(26Y 2m)	(22Y 5m)	(19Y 8m)	(17Y 7m)	(15Y11m)	(15Y 3m)	(14Y 7m)	(13Y 6m)
15	6.17138	6.59288	6.80362	7.01437	7.43586	7.85735	8.27884	8.70034	8.91108	9.12183	9.54332
	(46Y10m)	(35Y10m)	(32Y 6m)	(29Y10m)	(25Y10m)	(22Y11m)	(20Y 8m)	(18Y10m)	(18Y 1m)	(17Y 4m)	(16Y 1m)
20	6.01651	6.28401	6.41776	6.55151	6.81901	7.08651	7.35401	7.62151	7.75526	7.88901	8.15651
	(54Y 4m)	(42Y12m)	(39Y 5m)	(36Y 8m)	(32Y 4m)	(29Y 1m)	(26Y 7m)	(24Y 6m)	(23Y 7m)	(22Y 9m)	(21Y 3m)
25	5.92986	6.10979	6.19975	6.28972	6.46965	6.64957	6.82950	7.00943	7.09939	7.18936	7.36928
	(60Y11m)	(49Y 4m)	(45Y 9m)	(42Y12m)	(38Y 3m)	(34Y10m)	(32Y 2m)	(29Y11m)	(28Y11m)	(28Y 0m)	(26Y 5m)
30	5.87443	5.99971	6.06236	6.12500	6.25029	6.37557	6.50086	6.62615	6.68879	6.75144	6.87672
	(67Y 2m)	(55Y 5m)	(51Y 8m)	(48Y 8m)	(44Y 0m)	(40Y 6m)	(37Y 8m)	(35Y 3m)	(34Y 3m)	(33Y 3m)	(31Y 6m)

6.00% Interest Rate

Years to Balloon	10%	20%	25%	30%	40%	50%	60%	70%	75%	80%	90%
3	9.04952	12.10015	13.62547	15.15078	18.20142	21.25205	24.30268	27.35331	28.87863	30.40395	33.45458
	(18Y 2m)	(11Y 5m)	(9Y 8m)	(8Y 5m)	(6Y 9m)	(5Y 7m)	(4Y 9m)	(4Y 2m)	(3Y11m)	(3Y 8m)	(3Y 4m)
5	7.71899	9.43892	10.29889	11.15886	12.87879	14.59873	16.31867	18.03860	18.89857	19.75854	21.47848
	(25Y 1m)	(16Y10m)	(14Y 7m)	(12Y11m)	(10Y 6m)	(8Y10m)	(7Y 8m)	(6Y 9m)	(6Y 5m)	(6Y 1m)	(5Y 6m)
7.5	7.05872	8.11775	8.64727	9.17678	10.23582	11.29485	12.35388	13.41291	13.94243	14.47195	15.53098
	(31Y 8m)	(22Y 5m)	(19Y 9m)	(17Y 9m)	(14Y 9m)	(12Y 8m)	(11Y 1m)	(9Y11m)	(9Y 5m)	(8Y11m)	(8Y 2m)
10	6.73220	7.46444	7.83057	8.19669	8.92894	9.66118	10.39343	11.12567	11.49180	11.85792	12.59017
	(37Y 1m)	(27Y 3m)	(24Y 3m)	(22Y 0m)	(18Y 7m)	(16Y 3m)	(14Y 5m)	(12Y11m)	(12Y 4m)	(11Y 9m)	(10Y10m)
12.5	6.53887	7.07793	7.34746	7.61699	8.15605	8.69511	9.23417	9.77323	10.04276	10.31229	10.85135
	(41Y 8m)	(31Y 5m)	(28Y 4m)	(25Y11m)	(22Y 3m)	(19Y 7m)	(17Y 6m)	(15Y11m)	(15Y 2m)	(14Y 7m)	(13Y 5m)
15	6.41196	6.82459	7.03090	7.23721	7.64984	8.06247	8.47510	8.88773	9.09404	9.30036	9.71298
	(45Y10m)	(35Y 4m)	(32Y 1m)	(29Y 6m)	(25Y 8m)	(22Y 9m)	(20Y 7m)	(18Y 9m)	(18Y 0m)	(17Y 4m)	(16Y 1m)
20	6.25936	6.51907	6.64893	6.77879	7.03851	7.29823	7.55794	7.81766	7.94752	8.07738	8.33709
	(53Y 2m)	(42Y 3m)	(38Y11m)	(36Y 2m)	(31Y12m)	(28Y10m)	(26Y 5m)	(24Y 4m)	(23Y 6m)	(22Y 8m)	(21Y 3m)
25	6.17316	6.34632	6.43290	6.51948	6.69264	6.86580	7.03897	7.21213	7.29871	7.38529	7.55845
	(59Y 9m)	(48Y 7m)	(45Y 1m)	(42Y 3m)	(37Y11m)	(34Y 7m)	(31Y12m)	(29Y10m)	(28Y11m)	(27Y12m)	(26Y 5m)
30	6.11887	6.23833	6.29806	6.35779	6.47725	6.59671	6.71617	6.83563	6.89536	6.95509	7.07455
	(65Y10m)	(54Y 7m)	(50Y12m)	(48Y 1m)	(43Y 7m)	(40Y 2m)	(37Y 5m)	(35Y 1m)	(34Y 1m)	(33Y 2m)	(31Y 6m)

6.25% Interest Rate

Years to Balloon	10%	20%	25%	30%	40%	50%	60%	70%	75%	80%	90%
3	9.28884	12.32808	13.84770	15.36733	18.40657	21.44581	24.48505	27.52429	29.04391	30.56353	33.60277
	(17Y11m)	(11Y 4m)	(9Y 8m)	(8Y 4m)	(6Y 8m)	(5Y 6m)	(4Y 9m)	(4Y 2m)	(3Y11m)	(3Y 8m)	(3Y 4m)
5	7.95861	9.66752	10.52198	11.37643	13.08534	14.79425	16.50317	18.21208	19.06653	19.92099	21.62990
	(24Y 8m)	(16Y 8m)	(14Y 6m)	(12Y 9m)	(10Y 5m)	(8Y10m)	(7Y 8m)	(6Y 9m)	(6Y 4m)	(6Y 0m)	(5Y 6m)
7.5	7.29813	8.34669	8.87097	9.39526	10.44382	11.49239	12.54095	13.58952	14.11380	14.63808	15.68665
	(31Y 2m)	(22Y 2m)	(19Y 7m)	(17Y 7m)	(14Y 8m)	(12Y 7m)	(11Y 1m)	(9Y11m)	(9Y 5m)	(8Y11m)	(8Y 2m)
10	6.97116	7.69352	8.05470	8.41588	9.13825	9.86061	10.58297	11.30533	11.66651	12.02769	12.75005
	(36Y 5m)	(26Y10m)	(23Y12m)	(21Y 9m)	(18Y 6m)	(16Y 1m)	(14Y 4m)	(12Y11m)	(12Y 4m)	(11Y 9m)	(10Y10m)
12.5	6.77856	7.30832	7.57320	7.83808	8.36784	8.89761	9.42737	9.95713	10.22201	10.48689	11.01665
	(40Y11m)	(30Y12m)	(27Y12m)	(25Y 7m)	(22Y 0m)	(19Y 5m)	(17Y 5m)	(15Y10m)	(15Y 2m)	(14Y 6m)	(13Y 5m)
15	6.65365	7.05755	7.25951	7.46146	7.86537	8.26927	8.67318	9.07709	9.27904	9.48100	9.88490
	(44Y11m)	(34Y 9m)	(31Y 8m)	(29Y 2m)	(25Y 5m)	(22Y 7m)	(20Y 5m)	(18Y 9m)	(17Y12m)	(17Y 3m)	(16Y 1m)
20	6.50179	6.75390	6.87996	7.00602	7.25813	7.51024	7.76236	8.01447	8.14053	8.26658	8.51870
	(52Y 2m)	(41Y 8m)	(38Y 4m)	(35Y 9m)	(31Y 8m)	(28Y 8m)	(26Y 3m)	(24Y 3m)	(23Y 5m)	(22Y 8m)	(21Y 3m)
25	6.41578	6.58239	6.66569	6.74899	6.91559	7.08220	7.24880	7.41540	7.49870	7.58201	7.74861
	(58Y 8m)	(47Y11m)	(44Y 6m)	(41Y 9m)	(37Y 7m)	(34Y 4m)	(31Y10m)	(29Y 9m)	(28Y 9m)	(27Y11m)	(26Y 4m)
30	6.36367	6.47753	6.53446	6.59139	6.70525	6.81911	6.93297	7.04683	7.10376	7.16069	7.27455
	(64Y 7m)	(53Y 9m)	(50Y 3m)	(47Y 6m)	(43Y 2m)	(39Y10m)	(37Y 2m)	(34Y12m)	(33Y12m)	(33Y 1m)	(31Y 5m)

Upper entry is the sum of 12 monthly payments; lower entry is term to amortize a loan fully.

Annual Mortgage Constant to Amortize Part of a Loan by a Given Date

6.50% Interest Rate

Years to Balloon	Percentage to be amortized										
	10%	20%	25%	30%	40%	50%	60%	70%	75%	80%	90%
3	9.52669	12.55457	14.06851	15.58245	18.61033	21.63821	24.66609	27.69397	29.20791	30.72185	33.74973
	(17Y 8m)	(11Y 3m)	(9Y 7m)	(8Y 4m)	(6Y 8m)	(5Y 6m)	(4Y 9m)	(4Y 2m)	(3Y11m)	(3Y 8m)	(3Y 4m)
5	8.19777	9.89571	10.74468	11.59365	13.29159	14.98952	16.68746	18.38540	19.23437	20.08334	21.78127
	(24Y 3m)	(16Y 6m)	(14Y 4m)	(12Y 8m)	(10Y 4m)	(8Y 9m)	(7Y 7m)	(6Y 9m)	(6Y 4m)	(6Y 0m)	(5Y 6m)
7.5	7.53805	8.57623	9.09531	9.61440	10.65257	11.69075	12.72892	13.76709	14.28618	14.80527	15.84344
	(30Y 7m)	(21Y11m)	(19Y 4m)	(17Y 5m)	(14Y 6m)	(12Y 6m)	(11Y 0m)	(9Y10m)	(9Y 4m)	(8Y11m)	(8Y 2m)
10	7.21163	7.92421	8.28049	8.63678	9.34936	10.06193	10.77451	11.48708	11.84337	12.19966	12.91224
	(35Y 9m)	(26Y 6m)	(23Y 9m)	(21Y 7m)	(18Y 4m)	(16Y 0m)	(14Y 3m)	(12Y10m)	(12Y 3m)	(11Y 9m)	(10Y10m)
12.5	7.01956	7.54014	7.80044	8.06073	8.58131	9.10189	9.62248	10.14306	10.40335	10.66365	11.18423
	(40Y 2m)	(30Y 7m)	(27Y 8m)	(25Y 4m)	(21Y10m)	(19Y 4m)	(17Y 4m)	(15Y10m)	(15Y 1m)	(14Y 6m)	(13Y 5m)
15	6.89525	7.29058	7.48825	7.68591	8.08124	8.47657	8.87190	9.26723	9.46489	9.66255	10.05788
	(44Y 1m)	(34Y 3m)	(31Y 3m)	(28Y10m)	(25Y 2m)	(22Y 6m)	(20Y 4m)	(18Y 8m)	(17Y11m)	(17Y 3m)	(16Y 0m)
20	6.74382	6.98851	7.11085	7.23320	7.47789	7.72257	7.96726	8.21195	8.33429	8.45664	8.70132
	(51Y 3m)	(41Y 1m)	(37Y10m)	(35Y 4m)	(31Y 5m)	(28Y 5m)	(26Y 1m)	(24Y 2m)	(23Y 4m)	(22Y 7m)	(21Y 2m)
25	6.66017	6.82042	6.90055	6.98067	7.14092	7.30117	7.46142	7.62167	7.70179	7.78191	7.94216
	(57Y 6m)	(47Y 2m)	(43Y11m)	(41Y 3m)	(37Y 2m)	(34Y 1m)	(31Y 7m)	(29Y 7m)	(28Y 8m)	(27Y10m)	(26Y 4m)
30	6.60768	6.71616	6.77040	6.82464	6.93312	7.04160	7.15009	7.25857	7.31281	7.36705	7.47553
	(63Y 6m)	(53Y 0m)	(49Y 8m)	(46Y12m)	(42Y 9m)	(39Y 7m)	(36Y12m)	(34Y10m)	(33Y11m)	(33Y 0m)	(31Y 5m)

6.75% Interest Rate

Years to Balloon	10%	20%	25%	30%	40%	50%	60%	70%	75%	80%	90%
3	9.76546	12.78201	14.29028	15.79856	18.81511	21.83166	24.84821	27.86476	29.37304	30.88131	33.89786
	(17Y 5m)	(11Y 2m)	(9Y 6m)	(8Y 3m)	(6Y 7m)	(5Y 6m)	(4Y 9m)	(4Y 1m)	(3Y11m)	(3Y 8m)	(3Y 4m)
5	8.43647	10.12349	10.96700	11.81051	13.49752	15.18454	16.87155	18.55857	19.40207	20.24558	21.93260
	(23Y11m)	(16Y 4m)	(14Y 2m)	(12Y 7m)	(10Y 4m)	(8Y 9m)	(7Y 7m)	(6Y 9m)	(6Y 4m)	(6Y 0m)	(5Y 6m)
7.5	7.77730	8.80516	9.31909	9.83302	10.86087	11.88873	12.91659	13.94444	14.45837	14.97230	16.00016
	(30Y 1m)	(21Y 7m)	(19Y 2m)	(17Y 3m)	(14Y 5m)	(12Y 6m)	(10Y12m)	(9Y10m)	(9Y 4m)	(8Y11m)	(8Y 2m)
10	7.45241	8.15530	8.50674	8.85819	9.56108	10.26397	10.96685	11.66974	12.02119	12.37263	13.07552
	(35Y 1m)	(26Y 1m)	(23Y 5m)	(21Y 4m)	(18Y 2m)	(15Y11m)	(14Y 2m)	(12Y10m)	(12Y 3m)	(11Y 9m)	(10Y 9m)
12.5	7.26067	7.77220	8.02796	8.28373	8.79525	9.30678	9.81831	10.32983	10.58560	10.84136	11.35289
	(39Y 5m)	(30Y 2m)	(27Y 4m)	(25Y 1m)	(21Y 8m)	(19Y 2m)	(17Y 3m)	(15Y 9m)	(15Y 1m)	(14Y 6m)	(13Y 5m)
15	7.13679	7.52368	7.71713	7.91057	8.29746	8.68436	9.07125	9.45814	9.65158	9.84503	10.23192
	(43Y 4m)	(33Y10m)	(30Y10m)	(28Y 6m)	(24Y11m)	(22Y 4m)	(20Y 3m)	(18Y 7m)	(17Y10m)	(17Y 2m)	(16Y 0m)
20	6.98668	7.22412	7.34284	7.46155	7.69899	7.93643	8.17386	8.41130	8.53002	8.64874	8.88618
	(50Y 3m)	(40Y 6m)	(37Y 5m)	(34Y11m)	(31Y 1m)	(28Y 3m)	(25Y12m)	(24Y 1m)	(23Y 3m)	(22Y 6m)	(21Y 2m)
25	6.90397	7.05806	7.13511	7.21216	7.36625	7.52034	7.67444	7.82853	7.90558	7.98262	8.13672
	(56Y 6m)	(46Y 6m)	(43Y 4m)	(40Y10m)	(36Y10m)	(33Y10m)	(31Y 5m)	(29Y 5m)	(28Y 7m)	(27Y 9m)	(26Y 3m)
30	6.85215	6.95547	7.00713	7.05879	7.16211	7.26542	7.36874	7.47206	7.52372	7.57538	7.67869
	(62Y 6m)	(52Y 4m)	(49Y 1m)	(46Y 6m)	(42Y 5m)	(39Y 4m)	(36Y10m)	(34Y 9m)	(33Y10m)	(32Y11m)	(31Y 5m)

7.00% Interest Rate

Years to Balloon	10%	20%	25%	30%	40%	50%	60%	70%	75%	80%	90%
3	10.00515	13.01040	14.51302	16.01565	19.02090	22.02615	25.03141	28.03666	29.53928	31.04191	34.04716
	(17Y 3m)	(11Y 1m)	(9Y 5m)	(8Y 3m)	(6Y 7m)	(5Y 6m)	(4Y 8m)	(4Y 1m)	(3Y10m)	(3Y 8m)	(3Y 4m)
5	8.67592	10.35206	11.19013	12.02821	13.70435	15.38049	17.05664	18.73278	19.57085	20.40892	22.08507
	(23Y 7m)	(16Y 2m)	(14Y 1m)	(12Y 6m)	(10Y 3m)	(8Y 9m)	(7Y 7m)	(6Y 9m)	(6Y 4m)	(6Y 0m)	(5Y 6m)
7.5	8.01707	9.03468	9.54349	10.05230	11.06992	12.08753	13.10515	14.12276	14.63157	15.14038	16.15800
	(29Y 7m)	(21Y 4m)	(18Y11m)	(17Y 1m)	(14Y 4m)	(12Y 5m)	(10Y11m)	(9Y10m)	(9Y 4m)	(8Y11m)	(8Y 2m)
10	7.69230	8.38560	8.73225	9.07890	9.77220	10.46550	11.15880	11.85211	12.19876	12.54541	13.23871
	(34Y 6m)	(25Y10m)	(23Y 2m)	(21Y 1m)	(18Y 1m)	(15Y10m)	(14Y 2m)	(12Y10m)	(12Y 3m)	(11Y 8m)	(10Y 9m)
12.5	7.50190	8.00449	8.25578	8.50708	9.00967	9.51226	10.01485	10.51744	10.76874	11.02003	11.52262
	(38Y 9m)	(29Y 9m)	(26Y12m)	(24Y10m)	(21Y 6m)	(19Y 1m)	(17Y 2m)	(15Y 8m)	(15Y 1m)	(14Y 5m)	(13Y 5m)
15	7.37827	7.75686	7.94616	8.13545	8.51405	8.89264	9.27124	9.64983	9.83913	10.02842	10.40702
	(42Y 7m)	(33Y 4m)	(30Y 6m)	(28Y 3m)	(24Y 9m)	(22Y 2m)	(20Y 2m)	(18Y 6m)	(17Y10m)	(17Y 2m)	(15Y12m)
20	7.22918	7.45954	7.57472	7.68990	7.92026	8.15062	8.38098	8.61134	8.72652	8.84169	9.07205
	(49Y 5m)	(39Y11m)	(36Y11m)	(34Y 7m)	(30Y10m)	(28Y 1m)	(25Y10m)	(24Y 0m)	(23Y 3m)	(22Y 6m)	(21Y 2m)
25	7.14720	7.29533	7.36940	7.44347	7.59160	7.73974	7.88787	8.03601	8.11007	8.18414	8.33228
	(55Y 8m)	(45Y11m)	(42Y11m)	(40Y 5m)	(36Y 7m)	(33Y 8m)	(31Y 4m)	(29Y 4m)	(28Y 6m)	(27Y 8m)	(26Y 3m)
30	7.09835	7.19671	7.24589	7.29507	7.39343	7.49180	7.59016	7.68852	7.73770	7.78689	7.88525
	(61Y 4m)	(51Y 7m)	(48Y 6m)	(45Y12m)	(42Y 0m)	(39Y 0m)	(36Y 7m)	(34Y 7m)	(33Y 8m)	(32Y10m)	(31Y 4m)

7.25% Interest Rate

Years to Balloon	10%	20%	25%	30%	40%	50%	60%	70%	75%	80%	90%
3	10.24336	13.23734	14.73434	16.23133	19.22531	22.21929	25.21328	28.20726	29.70425	31.20124	34.19523
	(17Y 0m)	(10Y12m)	(9Y 4m)	(8Y 2m)	(6Y 7m)	(5Y 6m)	(4Y 8m)	(4Y 1m)	(3Y10m)	(3Y 8m)	(3Y 4m)
5	8.91490	10.58023	11.41289	12.24555	13.91087	15.57620	17.24152	18.90684	19.73950	20.57217	22.23749
	(23Y 3m)	(15Y11m)	(13Y11m)	(12Y 5m)	(10Y 2m)	(8Y 8m)	(7Y 7m)	(6Y 9m)	(6Y 4m)	(6Y 0m)	(5Y 6m)
7.5	8.25736	9.26481	9.76853	10.27226	11.27971	12.28716	13.29461	14.30206	14.80579	15.30951	16.31696
	(29Y 1m)	(21Y 1m)	(18Y 9m)	(16Y11m)	(14Y 3m)	(12Y 4m)	(10Y11m)	(9Y 9m)	(9Y 4m)	(8Y11m)	(8Y 2m)
10	7.93370	8.61751	8.95942	9.30132	9.98514	10.66895	11.35276	12.03657	12.37848	12.72039	13.40420
	(33Y11m)	(25Y 6m)	(22Y11m)	(20Y11m)	(17Y11m)	(15Y 9m)	(14Y 1m)	(12Y 9m)	(12Y 2m)	(11Y 8m)	(10Y 9m)
12.5	7.74325	8.23702	8.48391	8.73080	9.22457	9.71834	10.21212	10.70589	10.95278	11.19966	11.69344
	(38Y 1m)	(29Y 4m)	(26Y 8m)	(24Y 7m)	(21Y 4m)	(18Y12m)	(17Y 1m)	(15Y 8m)	(15Y 0m)	(14Y 5m)	(13Y 5m)
15	7.61969	7.99013	8.17535	8.36056	8.73100	9.10143	9.47187	9.84231	10.02752	10.21274	10.58318
	(41Y10m)	(32Y11m)	(30Y 2m)	(27Y11m)	(24Y 7m)	(22Y 0m)	(20Y 1m)	(18Y 5m)	(17Y 9m)	(17Y 1m)	(15Y12m)
20	7.47255	7.69600	7.80773	7.91945	8.14290	8.36636	8.58981	8.81326	8.92498	9.03671	9.26016
	(48Y 7m)	(39Y 5m)	(36Y 6m)	(34Y 2m)	(30Y 7m)	(27Y10m)	(25Y11m)	(23Y11m)	(23Y 2m)	(22Y 5m)	(21Y 2m)
25	7.39230	7.53467	7.60585	7.67703	7.81940	7.96177	8.10414	8.24651	8.31769	8.38888	8.53124
	(54Y 8m)	(45Y 4m)	(42Y 4m)	(39Y12m)	(36Y 3m)	(33Y 5m)	(31Y 2m)	(29Y 3m)	(28Y 5m)	(27Y 8m)	(26Y 3m)
30	7.34271	7.43632	7.48313	7.52993	7.62354	7.71715	7.81077	7.90438	7.95118	7.99799	8.09160
	(60Y 6m)	(51Y 0m)	(47Y12m)	(45Y 7m)	(41Y 9m)	(38Y10m)	(36Y 5m)	(34Y 6m)	(33Y 7m)	(32Y 9m)	(31Y 4m)

Upper entry is the sum of 12 monthly payments; lower entry is term to amortize a loan fully.

Annual Mortgage Constant to Amortize Part of a Loan by a Given Date

7.50% Interest Rate

Years to Balloon	10%	20%	25%	30%	Percentage to be amortized 40%	50%	60%	70%	75%	80%	90%
3	10.48250	13.46524	14.95662	16.44799	19.43073	22.41348	25.39623	28.37897	29.87035	31.36172	34.34447
	(16Y10m)	(10Y11m)	(9Y 4m)	(8Y 2m)	(6Y 6m)	(5Y 5m)	(4Y 8m)	(4Y 1m)	(3Y10m)	(3Y 8m)	(3Y 4m)
5	9.15343	10.80798	11.63526	12.46254	14.11709	15.77164	17.42620	19.08075	19.90803	20.73530	22.38986
	(22Y11m)	(15Y10m)	(13Y10m)	(12Y 4m)	(10Y 2m)	(8Y 8m)	(7Y 6m)	(6Y 8m)	(6Y 4m)	(6Y 0m)	(5Y 5m)
7.5	8.49697	9.49433	9.99301	10.49169	11.48905	12.48641	13.48377	14.48113	14.97981	15.47849	16.47585
	(28Y 8m)	(20Y10m)	(18Y 7m)	(16Y 9m)	(14Y 2m)	(12Y 3m)	(10Y10m)	(9Y 9m)	(9Y 3m)	(8Y10m)	(8Y 1m)
10	8.17422	8.84864	9.18585	9.52306	10.19748	10.87191	11.54633	12.22075	12.55796	12.89517	13.56959
	(33Y 4m)	(25Y 2m)	(22Y 8m)	(20Y 9m)	(17Y 9m)	(15Y 8m)	(14Y 0m)	(12Y 9m)	(12Y 2m)	(11Y 8m)	(10Y 9m)
12.5	7.98473	8.46981	8.71234	8.95488	9.43996	9.92503	10.41011	10.89518	11.13772	11.38026	11.86534
	(37Y 6m)	(28Y12m)	(26Y 5m)	(24Y 4m)	(21Y 2m)	(18Y10m)	(17Y 1m)	(15Y 7m)	(14Y12m)	(14Y 5m)	(13Y 4m)
15	7.86228	8.22469	8.40590	8.58711	8.94952	9.31194	9.67435	10.03677	10.21797	10.39918	10.76160
	(41Y 2m)	(32Y 6m)	(29Y10m)	(27Y 8m)	(24Y 4m)	(21Y11m)	(19Y12m)	(18Y 5m)	(17Y 9m)	(17Y 1m)	(15Y12m)
20	7.71561	7.93232	8.04067	8.14903	8.36574	8.58245	8.79916	9.01588	9.12423	9.23259	9.44930
	(47Y10m)	(38Y11m)	(36Y 1m)	(33Y10m)	(30Y 4m)	(27Y 8m)	(25Y 7m)	(23Y10m)	(23Y 1m)	(22Y 5m)	(21Y 1m)
25	7.63571	7.77250	7.84089	7.90929	8.04608	8.18286	8.31965	8.45644	8.52484	8.59323	8.73002
	(53Y11m)	(44Y10m)	(41Y11m)	(39Y 7m)	(35Y12m)	(33Y 3m)	(30Y12m)	(29Y 2m)	(28Y 4m)	(27Y 7m)	(26Y 3m)
30	7.58890	7.67795	7.72248	7.76701	7.85607	7.94512	8.03418	8.12324	8.16777	8.21230	8.30135
	(59Y 6m)	(50Y 4m)	(47Y 5m)	(45Y 1m)	(41Y 5m)	(38Y 7m)	(36Y 3m)	(34Y 4m)	(33Y 6m)	(32Y 8m)	(31Y 3m)

7.75% Interest Rate

	10%	20%	25%	30%	40%	50%	60%	70%	75%	80%	90%
3	10.72136	13.69289	15.17866	16.66443	19.63597	22.60751	25.57905	28.55059	30.03636	31.52213	34.49367
	(16Y 7m)	(10Y10m)	(9Y 3m)	(8Y 1m)	(6Y 6m)	(5Y 5m)	(4Y 8m)	(4Y 1m)	(3Y10m)	(3Y 8m)	(3Y 4m)
5	9.39270	11.03653	11.85845	12.68037	14.32420	15.96804	17.61187	19.25571	20.07762	20.89954	22.54338
	(22Y 7m)	(15Y 8m)	(13Y 9m)	(12Y 3m)	(10Y 1m)	(8Y 7m)	(7Y 6m)	(6Y 8m)	(6Y 4m)	(5Y12m)	(5Y 5m)
7.5	8.73711	9.72445	10.21812	10.71180	11.69914	12.68649	13.67383	14.66118	15.15485	15.64852	16.63587
	(28Y 3m)	(20Y 8m)	(18Y 5m)	(16Y 8m)	(14Y 1m)	(12Y 3m)	(10Y10m)	(9Y 9m)	(9Y 3m)	(8Y10m)	(8Y 1m)
10	8.41506	9.08019	9.41276	9.74532	10.41045	11.07557	11.74070	12.40583	12.73839	13.07096	13.73608
	(32Y10m)	(24Y10m)	(22Y 5m)	(20Y 6m)	(17Y 8m)	(15Y 7m)	(13Y12m)	(12Y 8m)	(12Y 2m)	(11Y 8m)	(10Y 9m)
12.5	8.22634	8.70284	8.94109	9.17934	9.65583	10.13233	10.60883	11.08532	11.32357	11.56182	12.03832
	(36Y11m)	(28Y 8m)	(26Y 1m)	(24Y 1m)	(21Y 0m)	(18Y 9m)	(16Y12m)	(15Y 7m)	(14Y11m)	(14Y 4m)	(13Y 4m)
15	8.10363	8.45816	8.63543	8.81270	9.16723	9.52176	9.87629	10.23082	10.40808	10.58535	10.93988
	(40Y 6m)	(32Y 1m)	(29Y 6m)	(27Y 5m)	(24Y 2m)	(21Y 9m)	(19Y11m)	(18Y 4m)	(17Y 7m)	(17Y 1m)	(15Y11m)
20	7.95957	8.16971	8.27477	8.37984	8.58998	8.80012	9.01026	9.22040	9.32547	9.43054	9.64067
	(47Y 1m)	(38Y 5m)	(35Y 8m)	(33Y 6m)	(30Y 1m)	(27Y 6m)	(25Y 6m)	(23Y 9m)	(23Y 0m)	(22Y 4m)	(21Y 1m)
25	7.88106	8.01246	8.07815	8.14385	8.27524	8.40664	8.53803	8.66943	8.73513	8.80082	8.93222
	(53Y 0m)	(44Y 3m)	(41Y 6m)	(39Y 3m)	(35Y 4m)	(33Y 0m)	(30Y10m)	(29Y 1m)	(28Y 3m)	(27Y 6m)	(26Y 2m)
30	7.83456	7.91925	7.96160	8.00395	8.08864	8.17334	8.25803	8.34273	8.38508	8.42742	8.51212
	(58Y 8m)	(49Y 9m)	(46Y12m)	(44Y 8m)	(41Y 1m)	(38Y 2m)	(36Y 1m)	(34Y 3m)	(33Y 5m)	(32Y 8m)	(31Y 3m)

8.00% Interest Rate

	10%	20%	25%	30%	40%	50%	60%	70%	75%	80%	90%
3	10.95994	13.92030	15.40048	16.88066	19.84103	22.80139	25.76176	28.72212	30.20230	31.68248	34.64285
	(16Y 5m)	(10Y 9m)	(9Y 2m)	(8Y 1m)	(6Y 6m)	(5Y 5m)	(4Y 8m)	(4Y 1m)	(3Y10m)	(3Y 8m)	(3Y 4m)
5	9.63271	11.26587	12.08246	12.89904	14.53221	16.16538	17.79854	19.43171	20.24829	21.06488	22.69804
	(22Y 3m)	(15Y 6m)	(13Y 7m)	(12Y 2m)	(10Y 0m)	(8Y 7m)	(7Y 6m)	(6Y 8m)	(6Y 4m)	(5Y12m)	(5Y 5m)
7.5	8.97657	9.95398	10.44268	10.93138	11.90878	12.88619	13.86359	14.84100	15.32970	15.81840	16.79581
	(27Y10m)	(20Y 5m)	(18Y 3m)	(16Y 6m)	(13Y12m)	(12Y 2m)	(10Y10m)	(9Y 9m)	(9Y 3m)	(8Y10m)	(8Y 1m)
10	8.65503	9.31096	9.63893	9.96689	10.62283	11.27876	11.93469	12.59062	12.91858	13.24655	13.90248
	(32Y 4m)	(24Y 7m)	(22Y 3m)	(20Y 4m)	(17Y 7m)	(15Y 6m)	(13Y11m)	(12Y 8m)	(12Y 1m)	(11Y 7m)	(10Y 9m)
12.5	8.46690	8.93494	9.16895	9.40297	9.87101	10.33904	10.80707	11.27511	11.50913	11.74314	12.21118
	(36Y 4m)	(28Y 4m)	(25Y10m)	(23Y10m)	(20Y10m)	(18Y 8m)	(16Y11m)	(15Y 6m)	(14Y11m)	(14Y 4m)	(13Y 4m)
15	8.34617	8.69295	8.86634	9.03973	9.38652	9.73330	10.08008	10.42686	10.60026	10.77365	11.12043
	(39Y11m)	(31Y 9m)	(29Y 2m)	(27Y 1m)	(23Y12m)	(21Y 8m)	(19Y10m)	(18Y 3m)	(17Y 7m)	(17Y 0m)	(15Y11m)
20	8.20326	8.40699	8.50885	8.61072	8.81444	9.01817	9.22190	9.42563	9.52749	9.62936	9.83308
	(46Y 5m)	(37Y12m)	(35Y 4m)	(33Y 2m)	(29Y10m)	(27Y 4m)	(25Y 4m)	(23Y 8m)	(22Y11m)	(22Y 3m)	(21Y 1m)
25	8.12600	8.25218	8.31527	8.37836	8.50454	8.63071	8.75689	8.88307	8.94616	9.00925	9.13543
	(52Y 3m)	(43Y 9m)	(41Y 0m)	(38Y10m)	(35Y 5m)	(32Y10m)	(30Y 8m)	(28Y11m)	(28Y 2m)	(27Y 5m)	(26Y 2m)
30	8.07975	8.16027	8.20053	8.24079	8.32131	8.40182	8.48234	8.56286	8.60312	8.64338	8.72389
	(57Y11m)	(49Y 3m)	(46Y 7m)	(44Y 4m)	(40Y10m)	(38Y 2m)	(35Y11m)	(34Y 2m)	(33Y 4m)	(32Y 7m)	(31Y 3m)

8.25% Interest Rate

	10%	20%	25%	30%	40%	50%	60%	70%	75%	80%	90%
3	11.19824	14.14746	15.62207	17.09668	20.04590	22.99512	25.94434	28.89356	30.36816	31.84277	34.79199
	(16Y 3m)	(10Y 8m)	(9Y 2m)	(8Y 0m)	(6Y 5m)	(5Y 5m)	(4Y 8m)	(4Y 1m)	(3Y10m)	(3Y 8m)	(3Y 4m)
5	9.87226	11.49481	12.30609	13.11736	14.73991	16.36246	17.98501	19.60756	20.41884	21.23011	22.85266
	(21Y12m)	(15Y 5m)	(13Y 6m)	(12Y 1m)	(9Y12m)	(8Y 6m)	(7Y 6m)	(6Y 8m)	(6Y 4m)	(5Y12m)	(5Y 5m)
7.5	9.21656	10.18410	10.66787	11.15164	12.11918	13.08672	14.05426	15.02180	15.50557	15.98933	16.95687
	(27Y 5m)	(20Y 2m)	(18Y 1m)	(16Y 4m)	(13Y11m)	(12Y 1m)	(10Y 9m)	(9Y 8m)	(9Y 3m)	(8Y10m)	(8Y 1m)
10	8.89653	9.54336	9.86678	10.19019	10.83702	11.48385	12.13069	12.77752	13.10093	13.42435	14.07118
	(31Y11m)	(24Y 4m)	(21Y12m)	(20Y 2m)	(17Y 5m)	(15Y 5m)	(13Y10m)	(12Y 7m)	(12Y 1m)	(11Y 7m)	(10Y 9m)
12.5	8.70881	9.16850	9.39834	9.62819	10.08788	10.54757	11.00725	11.46694	11.69679	11.92663	12.38632
	(35Y10m)	(27Y12m)	(25Y 7m)	(23Y 8m)	(20Y 9m)	(18Y 6m)	(16Y10m)	(15Y 6m)	(14Y10m)	(14Y 4m)	(13Y 4m)
15	8.58870	8.92786	9.09745	9.26703	9.60620	9.94537	10.28454	10.62371	10.79329	10.96288	11.30204
	(39Y 4m)	(31Y 4m)	(28Y10m)	(26Y10m)	(23Y10m)	(21Y 6m)	(19Y 8m)	(18Y 3m)	(17Y 7m)	(16Y12m)	(15Y11m)
20	8.44670	8.64418	8.74292	8.84166	9.03914	9.23662	9.43410	9.63158	9.73032	9.82905	10.02653
	(45Y 9m)	(37Y 7m)	(34Y12m)	(32Y11m)	(29Y 8m)	(27Y 2m)	(25Y 3m)	(23Y 7m)	(22Y11m)	(22Y 3m)	(21Y 1m)
25	8.37055	8.49169	8.55226	8.61283	8.73397	8.85511	8.97625	9.09739	9.15796	9.21853	9.33967
	(51Y 7m)	(43Y 3m)	(40Y 8m)	(38Y 6m)	(35Y 2m)	(32Y 7m)	(30Y 7m)	(28Y10m)	(28Y 1m)	(27Y 5m)	(26Y 2m)
30	8.32573	8.40225	8.44051	8.47877	8.55529	8.63181	8.70833	8.78485	8.82311	8.86137	8.93789
	(57Y 2m)	(48Y 9m)	(46Y 1m)	(43Y11m)	(40Y 6m)	(37Y11m)	(35Y10m)	(34Y 0m)	(33Y 3m)	(32Y 6m)	(31Y 2m)

Upper entry is the sum of 12 monthly payments; lower entry is term to amortize a loan fully.

Annual Mortgage Constant to Amortize Part of a Loan by a Given Date

8.50% Interest Rate

Years to Balloon	10%	20%	25%	30%	40% Percentage to be amortized	50%	60%	70%	75%	80%	90%
3	11.43747	14.37558	15.84463	17.31368	20.25179	23.18989	26.12799	29.06610	30.53515	32.00420	34.94231
	(16Y 1m)	(10Y 7m)	(9Y 1m)	(7Y12m)	(6Y 5m)	(5Y 5m)	(4Y 8m)	(4Y 1m)	(3Y10m)	(3Y 8m)	(3Y 3m)
5	10.11136	11.72334	12.52933	13.33533	14.94731	16.55929	18.17128	19.78326	20.58925	21.39524	23.00723
	(21Y 8m)	(15Y 3m)	(13Y 5m)	(11Y12m)	(9Y11m)	(8Y 6m)	(7Y 5m)	(6Y 8m)	(6Y 3m)	(5Y12m)	(5Y 5m)
7.5	9.45709	10.41483	10.89371	11.37258	12.33033	13.28808	14.24582	15.20357	15.68244	16.16132	17.11906
	(27Y 1m)	(19Y12m)	(17Y11m)	(16Y 3m)	(13Y10m)	(12Y 1m)	(10Y 9m)	(9Y 8m)	(9Y 3m)	(8Y10m)	(8Y 1m)
10	9.13716	9.77499	10.09390	10.41281	11.05064	11.68847	12.32630	12.96413	13.28304	13.60196	14.23978
	(31Y 5m)	(24Y 1m)	(21Y 9m)	(20Y 0m)	(17Y 4m)	(15Y 4m)	(13Y10m)	(12Y 7m)	(12Y 1m)	(11Y 7m)	(10Y 9m)
12.5	8.95087	9.40233	9.62806	9.85379	10.30525	10.75671	11.20817	11.65963	11.88536	12.11109	12.56255
	(35Y 3m)	(27Y 8m)	(25Y 4m)	(23Y 5m)	(20Y 7m)	(18Y 5m)	(16Y 9m)	(15Y 5m)	(14Y10m)	(14Y 3m)	(13Y 4m)
15	8.83122	9.16291	9.32876	9.49460	9.82629	10.15797	10.48966	10.82135	10.98719	11.15304	11.48472
	(38Y 9m)	(31Y 0m)	(28Y 7m)	(26Y 8m)	(23Y 8m)	(21Y 5m)	(19Y 8m)	(18Y 2m)	(17Y 6m)	(16Y11m)	(15Y11m)
20	8.69112	8.88251	8.97820	9.07390	9.26528	9.45667	9.64806	9.83945	9.93514	10.03084	10.22222
	(45Y 1m)	(37Y 2m)	(34Y 7m)	(32Y 7m)	(29Y 5m)	(27Y 1m)	(25Y 2m)	(23Y 7m)	(22Y10m)	(22Y 2m)	(21Y 0m)
25	8.61596	8.73037	8.79037	8.84850	8.96478	9.08105	9.19732	9.31359	9.37173	9.42987	9.54614
	(50Y10m)	(42Y10m)	(40Y 3m)	(38Y 2m)	(34Y11m)	(32Y 5m)	(30Y 5m)	(28Y 9m)	(28Y 0m)	(27Y 4m)	(26Y 1m)
30	8.57255	8.64524	8.68159	8.71794	8.79063	8.86333	8.93603	9.00872	9.04507	9.08142	9.15412
	(56Y 4m)	(48Y 3m)	(45Y 8m)	(43Y 7m)	(40Y 3m)	(37Y 9m)	(35Y 8m)	(33Y11m)	(33Y 2m)	(32Y 5m)	(31Y 2m)

8.75% Interest Rate

Years to Balloon	10%	20%	25%	30%	40%	50%	60%	70%	75%	80%	90%
3	11.67642	14.60345	16.06696	17.53047	20.45749	23.38451	26.31153	29.23855	30.70206	32.16557	35.09259
	(15Y10m)	(10Y 6m)	(9Y 0m)	(7Y11m)	(6Y 5m)	(5Y 5m)	(4Y 8m)	(4Y 1m)	(3Y10m)	(3Y 8m)	(3Y 3m)
5	10.35120	11.95267	12.75340	13.55414	15.15560	16.75707	18.35854	19.96001	20.76074	21.56148	23.16294
	(21Y 5m)	(15Y 1m)	(13Y 3m)	(11Y11m)	(9Y11m)	(8Y 6m)	(7Y 5m)	(6Y 7m)	(6Y 3m)	(5Y12m)	(5Y 5m)
7.5	9.69694	10.64497	11.11899	11.59300	12.54103	13.48906	14.43709	15.38512	15.85914	16.33315	17.28118
	(26Y 8m)	(19Y10m)	(17Y 9m)	(16Y 1m)	(13Y 9m)	(11Y12m)	(10Y 8m)	(9Y 8m)	(9Y 2m)	(8Y10m)	(8Y 1m)
10	9.37812	10.00704	10.32150	10.63596	11.26489	11.89381	12.52273	13.15165	13.46611	13.78057	14.40949
	(31Y 0m)	(23Y10m)	(21Y 7m)	(19Y10m)	(17Y 2m)	(15Y 3m)	(13Y 9m)	(12Y 7m)	(12Y 0m)	(11Y 7m)	(10Y 9m)
12.5	9.19309	9.63644	9.85811	10.07979	10.52313	10.96648	11.40983	11.85317	12.07485	12.29652	12.73987
	(34Y 9m)	(27Y 4m)	(25Y 1m)	(23Y 3m)	(20Y 5m)	(18Y 4m)	(16Y 8m)	(15Y 4m)	(14Y10m)	(14Y 3m)	(13Y 4m)
15	9.07377	9.39810	9.56027	9.72244	10.04678	10.37112	10.69546	11.01980	11.18197	11.34414	11.66847
	(38Y 3m)	(30Y 8m)	(28Y 4m)	(26Y 5m)	(23Y 6m)	(21Y 3m)	(19Y 7m)	(18Y 1m)	(17Y 7m)	(16Y11m)	(15Y11m)
20	8.93534	9.12079	9.21352	9.30624	9.49169	9.67715	9.86260	10.04805	10.14078	10.23351	10.41896
	(44Y 5m)	(36Y 9m)	(34Y 3m)	(32Y 4m)	(29Y 3m)	(26Y11m)	(25Y 0m)	(23Y 6m)	(22Y 9m)	(22Y 2m)	(21Y 0m)
25	8.86106	8.97263	9.02842	9.08421	9.19578	9.30735	9.41892	9.53049	9.58628	9.64207	9.75364
	(50Y 3m)	(42Y 5m)	(39Y11m)	(37Y11m)	(34Y 4m)	(32Y 4m)	(30Y 4m)	(28Y 8m)	(27Y12m)	(27Y 4m)	(26Y 1m)
30	8.81785	8.88689	8.92141	8.95593	9.02497	9.09401	9.16305	9.23209	9.26661	9.30113	9.37017
	(55Y10m)	(47Y10m)	(45Y 4m)	(43Y 3m)	(40Y 1m)	(37Y 7m)	(35Y 7m)	(33Y10m)	(33Y 1m)	(32Y 5m)	(31Y 2m)

9.00% Interest Rate

Years to Balloon	10%	20%	25%	30%	40%	50%	60%	70%	75%	80%	90%
3	11.91510	14.83107	16.28905	17.74704	20.66300	23.57897	26.49494	29.41091	30.86889	32.32688	35.24284
	(15Y 8m)	(10Y 5m)	(8Y12m)	(7Y11m)	(6Y 5m)	(5Y 4m)	(4Y 8m)	(4Y 1m)	(3Y10m)	(3Y 8m)	(3Y 3m)
5	10.59059	12.18159	12.97709	13.77259	15.36360	16.95460	18.54560	20.13660	20.93211	21.72761	23.31861
	(21Y 2m)	(14Y12m)	(13Y 2m)	(11Y10m)	(9Y10m)	(8Y 5m)	(7Y 5m)	(6Y 7m)	(6Y 3m)	(5Y12m)	(5Y 5m)
7.5	9.93733	10.87572	11.34491	11.81410	12.75249	13.69088	14.62926	15.56765	16.03684	16.50604	17.44442
	(26Y 4m)	(19Y 7m)	(17Y 7m)	(16Y 0m)	(13Y 8m)	(11Y11m)	(10Y 8m)	(9Y 8m)	(9Y 2m)	(8Y 9m)	(8Y 1m)
10	9.61943	10.23954	10.54959	10.85965	11.47976	12.09987	12.71997	13.34008	13.65014	13.96019	14.58030
	(30Y 7m)	(23Y 7m)	(21Y 5m)	(19Y 8m)	(17Y 1m)	(15Y 2m)	(13Y 9m)	(12Y 6m)	(12Y 0m)	(11Y 6m)	(10Y 9m)
12.5	9.43428	9.86963	10.08731	10.30498	10.74033	11.17567	11.61102	12.04637	12.26404	12.48172	12.91706
	(34Y 4m)	(27Y 1m)	(24Y10m)	(23Y 1m)	(20Y 4m)	(18Y 3m)	(16Y 8m)	(15Y 4m)	(14Y 9m)	(14Y 3m)	(13Y 4m)
15	9.31633	9.63345	9.79201	9.95057	10.26769	10.58481	10.90193	11.21905	11.37761	11.53617	11.85329
	(37Y 9m)	(30Y 4m)	(28Y 1m)	(26Y 2m)	(23Y 4m)	(21Y 2m)	(19Y 6m)	(18Y 1m)	(17Y 6m)	(16Y11m)	(15Y11m)
20	9.17937	9.35904	9.44888	9.53871	9.71839	9.89806	10.07773	10.25740	10.34723	10.43707	10.61674
	(43Y11m)	(36Y 4m)	(33Y12m)	(32Y 1m)	(29Y 1m)	(26Y 9m)	(24Y11m)	(23Y 5m)	(22Y 9m)	(22Y 1m)	(20Y12m)
25	9.10589	9.21293	9.26644	9.31996	9.42700	9.53403	9.64107	9.74811	9.80162	9.85514	9.96218
	(49Y 8m)	(42Y 0m)	(39Y 7m)	(37Y 7m)	(34Y 6m)	(32Y 2m)	(30Y 3m)	(28Y 8m)	(27Y11m)	(27Y 3m)	(26Y 1m)
30	9.06529	9.13083	9.16361	9.19638	9.26193	9.32748	9.39302	9.45857	9.49134	9.52412	9.58966
	(55Y 0m)	(47Y 4m)	(44Y11m)	(42Y11m)	(39Y 9m)	(37Y 4m)	(35Y 5m)	(33Y 9m)	(33Y 0m)	(32Y 4m)	(31Y 1m)

9.25% Interest Rate

Years to Balloon	10%	20%	25%	30%	40%	50%	60%	70%	75%	80%	90%
3	12.15470	15.05965	16.51212	17.96459	20.86954	23.77448	26.67943	29.58438	31.03685	32.48932	35.39427
	(15Y 6m)	(10Y 4m)	(8Y11m)	(7Y10m)	(6Y 4m)	(5Y 4m)	(4Y 7m)	(4Y 1m)	(3Y10m)	(3Y 8m)	(3Y 3m)
5	10.82952	12.41011	13.20040	13.99070	15.57129	17.15187	18.73246	20.31305	21.10334	21.89364	23.47422
	(20Y11m)	(14Y10m)	(13Y 1m)	(11Y 9m)	(9Y 9m)	(8Y 5m)	(7Y 5m)	(6Y 7m)	(6Y 3m)	(5Y12m)	(5Y 5m)
7.5	10.17825	11.10707	11.57148	12.03589	12.96470	13.89352	14.82234	15.75116	16.21557	16.67998	17.60879
	(25Y12m)	(19Y 5m)	(17Y 5m)	(15Y11m)	(13Y 7m)	(11Y11m)	(10Y 7m)	(9Y 7m)	(9Y 2m)	(8Y 9m)	(8Y 1m)
10	9.86108	10.47247	10.77817	11.08386	11.69526	12.30665	12.91804	13.52943	13.83513	14.14083	14.75222
	(30Y 2m)	(23Y 4m)	(21Y 2m)	(19Y 6m)	(16Y12m)	(15Y 1m)	(13Y 8m)	(12Y 6m)	(11Y12m)	(11Y 6m)	(10Y 8m)
12.5	9.67685	10.10432	10.31805	10.53178	10.95924	11.38670	11.81416	12.24163	12.45536	12.66909	13.09655
	(33Y10m)	(26Y10m)	(24Y 7m)	(22Y10m)	(20Y 2m)	(18Y 2m)	(16Y 7m)	(15Y 3m)	(14Y 9m)	(14Y 3m)	(13Y 4m)
15	9.55894	9.86897	10.02398	10.17900	10.48903	10.79906	11.10909	11.41912	11.57414	11.72915	12.03918
	(37Y 3m)	(30Y 1m)	(27Y10m)	(25Y12m)	(23Y 2m)	(21Y 1m)	(19Y 5m)	(18Y 0m)	(17Y 5m)	(16Y10m)	(15Y10m)
20	9.42325	9.59729	9.68431	9.77133	9.94537	10.11941	10.29345	10.46749	10.55451	10.64153	10.81557
	(43Y 4m)	(36Y 0m)	(33Y 8m)	(31Y10m)	(28Y10m)	(26Y 8m)	(24Y10m)	(23Y 4m)	(22Y 8m)	(22Y 1m)	(20Y12m)
25	9.35169	9.45435	9.50568	9.55700	9.65966	9.76232	9.86498	9.96764	10.01897	10.07030	10.17295
	(49Y 1m)	(41Y 7m)	(39Y 3m)	(37Y 4m)	(34Y 4m)	(31Y12m)	(30Y 1m)	(28Y 7m)	(27Y10m)	(27Y 3m)	(26Y 1m)
30	9.31132	9.37353	9.40463	9.43574	9.49795	9.56016	9.62237	9.68458	9.71569	9.74679	9.80900
	(54Y 6m)	(46Y12m)	(44Y 7m)	(42Y 8m)	(39Y 7m)	(37Y 2m)	(35Y 3m)	(33Y 8m)	(32Y12m)	(32Y 4m)	(31Y 1m)

Upper entry is the sum of 12 monthly payments; lower entry is term to amortize a loan fully.

Annual Mortgage Constant to Amortize Part of a Loan by a Given Date

9.50% Interest Rate
```
--------------------------------------------------------------------------------------------------
Years to                                Percentage to be amortized
Balloon  10%      20%      25%      30%      40%      50%      60%      70%      75%      80%      90%
--------------------------------------------------------------------------------------------------
  3     12.39283 15.28678 16.73376 18.18073 21.07469 23.96864 26.86260 29.75655 31.20353 32.65050 35.54446
        (15Y 5m) (10Y 3m) ( 8Y10m) ( 7Y10m) ( 6Y 4m) ( 5Y 4m) ( 4Y 7m) ( 4Y 1m) ( 3Y10m) ( 3Y 8m) ( 3Y 3m)
  5     11.06920 12.63943 13.42454 14.20965 15.77987 17.35010 18.92032 20.49054 21.27565 22.06077 23.63099
        (20Y 8m) (14Y 9m) (12Y12m) (11Y 8m) ( 9Y 9m) ( 8Y 5m) ( 7Y 4m) ( 6Y 7m) ( 6Y 3m) ( 5Y11m) ( 5Y 5m)
  7.5   10.41851 11.33783 11.79749 12.25716 13.17648 14.09580 15.01512 15.93445 16.39411 16.85377 17.77309
        (25Y 8m) (19Y 3m) (17Y 3m) (15Y 9m) (13Y 6m) (11Y10m) (10Y 7m) ( 9Y 7m) ( 9Y 2m) ( 8Y 9m) ( 8Y 1m)
 10     10.10188 10.70465 11.00603 11.30742 11.91019 12.51296 13.11573 13.71850 14.01989 14.32127 14.92404
        (29Y10m) (23Y 1m) (21Y 0m) (19Y 5m) (16Y11m) (15Y 1m) (13Y 7m) (12Y 6m) (11Y12m) (11Y 6m) (10Y 8m)
 12.5    9.91961 10.33930 10.54914 10.75899 11.17867 11.59836 12.01805 12.43774 12.64759 12.85743 13.27712
        (33Y 5m) (26Y 6m) (24Y 5m) (22Y 8m) (20Y 0m) (18Y 1m) (16Y 6m) (15Y 3m) (14Y 8m) (14Y 2m) (13Y 3m)
 15      9.80279 10.10586 10.25739 10.40892 10.71199 11.01506 11.31813 11.62120 11.77274 11.92427 12.22734
        (36Y 9m) (29Y 9m) (27Y 6m) (25Y 9m) (23Y 0m) (20Y12m) (19Y 4m) (17Y12m) (17Y 5m) (16Y10m) (15Y10m)
 20      9.66820  9.83675  9.92103 10.00531 10.17387 10.34242 10.51098 10.67954 10.76382 10.84810 11.01665
        (42Y10m) (35Y 8m) (33Y 5m) (31Y 7m) (28Y 8m) (26Y 6m) (24Y 9m) (23Y 3m) (22Y 8m) (22Y 0m) (20Y11m)
 25      9.59729  9.69572  9.74494  9.79416  9.89260  9.99103 10.08947 10.18790 10.23712 10.28634 10.38478
        (48Y 6m) (41Y 3m) (38Y11m) (37Y 1m) (34Y 1m) (31Y12m) (30Y 0m) (28Y 6m) (27Y10m) (27Y 2m) (26Y 0m)
 30      9.55839  9.61741  9.64692  9.67644  9.73546  9.79449  9.85351  9.91254  9.94205  9.97156 10.03059
        (53Y11m) (46Y 7m) (44Y 3m) (42Y 4m) (39Y 4m) (37Y 0m) (35Y 2m) (33Y 7m) (32Y11m) (32Y 3m) (31Y 1m)
```

9.75% Interest Rate
```
         10%      20%      25%      30%      40%      50%      60%      70%      75%      80%      90%
--------------------------------------------------------------------------------------------------
  3     12.63188 15.51487 16.95637 18.39786 21.28085 24.16385 27.04684 29.92983 31.37133 32.81283 35.69582
        (15Y 3m) (10Y 2m) ( 8Y10m) ( 7Y 9m) ( 6Y 4m) ( 5Y 4m) ( 4Y 7m) ( 4Y 1m) ( 3Y10m) ( 3Y 8m) ( 3Y 3m)
  5     11.30963 12.86954 13.64949 14.42945 15.98936 17.54927 19.10918 20.66908 21.44904 22.22899 23.78890
        (20Y 5m) (14Y 7m) (12Y11m) (11Y 7m) ( 9Y 8m) ( 8Y 4m) ( 7Y 4m) ( 6Y 7m) ( 6Y 3m) ( 5Y11m) ( 5Y 5m)
  7.5   10.65931 11.56921 12.02416 12.47911 13.38901 14.29891 15.20881 16.11871 16.57366 17.02861 17.93851
        (25Y 4m) (19Y 1m) (17Y 2m) (15Y 8m) (13Y 5m) (11Y10m) (10Y 7m) ( 9Y 7m) ( 9Y 2m) ( 8Y 9m) ( 8Y 1m)
 10     10.34423 10.93847 11.23559 11.53271 12.12695 12.72120 13.31544 13.90968 14.20680 14.50393 15.09817
        (29Y 5m) (22Y10m) (20Y10m) (19Y 3m) (16Y 9m) (14Y12m) (13Y 7m) (12Y 5m) (11Y11m) (11Y 6m) (10Y 8m)
 12.5   10.16135 10.57338 10.77939 10.98541 11.39744 11.80947 12.22150 12.63352 12.83954 13.04555 13.45758
        (33Y 0m) (26Y 3m) (24Y 2m) (22Y 6m) (19Y11m) (17Y12m) (16Y 6m) (15Y 3m) (14Y 8m) (14Y 2m) (13Y 3m)
 15     10.04550 10.34173 10.48985 10.63797 10.93420 11.23044 11.52667 11.82291 11.97102 12.11914 12.41538
        (36Y 4m) (29Y 6m) (27Y 4m) (25Y 7m) (22Y11m) (20Y10m) (19Y 3m) (17Y11m) (17Y 4m) (16Y10m) (15Y10m)
 20      9.91303 10.07625 10.15786 10.23947 10.40269 10.56591 10.72913 10.89235 10.97396 11.05557 11.21879
        (42Y 4m) (35Y 4m) (33Y 1m) (31Y 4m) (28Y 6m) (26Y 4m) (24Y 8m) (23Y 3m) (22Y 7m) (21Y12m) (20Y11m)
 25      9.84393  9.93829  9.98548 10.03266 10.12702 10.22139 10.31575 10.41012 10.45730 10.50448 10.59885
        (47Y11m) (40Y10m) (38Y 7m) (36Y 9m) (33Y11m) (31Y 8m) (29Y11m) (28Y 5m) (27Y 9m) (27Y 1m) (25Y12m)
 30      9.80534  9.86133  9.88932  9.91731  9.97330 10.02929 10.08527 10.14126 10.16925 10.19724 10.25323
        (53Y 4m) (46Y 2m) (43Y11m) (42Y 0m) (39Y 1m) (36Y11m) (35Y 1m) (33Y 6m) (32Y10m) (32Y 2m) (31Y 0m)
```

10.00% Interest Rate
```
         10%      20%      25%      30%      40%      50%      60%      70%      75%      80%      90%
--------------------------------------------------------------------------------------------------
  3     12.87185 15.74391 17.17994 18.61597 21.48804 24.36010 27.23216 30.10422 31.54026 32.97629 35.84835
        (15Y 1m) (10Y 2m) ( 8Y 9m) ( 7Y 9m) ( 6Y 3m) ( 5Y 4m) ( 4Y 7m) ( 4Y 1m) ( 3Y10m) ( 3Y 8m) ( 3Y 3m)
  5     11.54960 13.09925 13.87407 14.64889 16.19854 17.74819 19.29783 20.84748 21.62230 22.39712 23.94677
        (20Y 2m) (14Y 6m) (12Y10m) (11Y 6m) ( 9Y 8m) ( 8Y 4m) ( 7Y 4m) ( 6Y 7m) ( 6Y 3m) ( 5Y11m) ( 5Y 5m)
  7.5   10.89945 11.80000 12.25028 12.70055 13.60111 14.50166 15.40221 16.30276 16.75303 17.20331 18.10386
        (25Y 1m) (18Y11m) (17Y 0m) (15Y 7m) (13Y 4m) (11Y 9m) (10Y 6m) ( 9Y 7m) ( 9Y 1m) ( 8Y 9m) ( 8Y 1m)
 10     10.58573 11.17154 11.46445 11.75735 12.34316 12.92897 13.51478 14.10059 14.39349 14.68639 15.27220
        (29Y 1m) (22Y 8m) (20Y 8m) (19Y 1m) (16Y 8m) (14Y11m) (13Y 6m) (12Y 5m) (11Y11m) (11Y 6m) (10Y 8m)
 12.5   10.40329 10.80777 11.01001 11.21225 11.61673 12.02121 12.42569 12.83017 13.03241 13.23465 13.63913
        (32Y 8m) (26Y 1m) (23Y12m) (22Y 4m) (19Y10m) (17Y11m) (16Y 5m) (15Y 2m) (14Y 8m) (14Y 2m) (13Y 3m)
 15     10.28948 10.57900 10.72377 10.86853 11.15806 11.44758 11.73711 12.02663 12.17140 12.31616 12.60569
        (35Y10m) (29Y 2m) (27Y 1m) (25Y 4m) (22Y 9m) (20Y 9m) (19Y 2m) (17Y11m) (17Y 4m) (16Y 9m) (15Y10m)
 20     10.15778 10.31580 10.39482 10.47383 10.63186 10.78988 10.94791 11.10593 11.18495 11.26396 11.42199
        (41Y10m) (35Y 0m) (32Y10m) (31Y 1m) (28Y 4m) (26Y 3m) (24Y 7m) (23Y 2m) (22Y 7m) (21Y12m) (20Y11m)
 25     10.08924 10.17968 10.22491 10.27013 10.36057 10.45101 10.54145 10.63189 10.67711 10.72233 10.81277
        (47Y 6m) (40Y 6m) (38Y 4m) (36Y 6m) (33Y 9m) (31Y 7m) (29Y10m) (28Y 4m) (27Y 8m) (27Y 1m) (25Y12m)
 30     10.05224 10.10532 10.13187 10.15841 10.21150 10.26458 10.31767 10.37075 10.39730 10.42384 10.47693
        (52Y10m) (45Y10m) (43Y 7m) (41Y 9m) (38Y11m) (36Y 9m) (34Y11m) (33Y 5m) (32Y 9m) (32Y 2m) (31Y 0m)
```

10.25% Interest Rate
```
         10%      20%      25%      30%      40%      50%      60%      70%      75%      80%      90%
--------------------------------------------------------------------------------------------------
  3     13.11035 15.97151 17.40209 18.83267 21.69384 24.55500 27.41616 30.27732 31.70791 33.13849 35.99965
        (14Y11m) (10Y 1m) ( 8Y 9m) ( 7Y 8m) ( 6Y 3m) ( 5Y 4m) ( 4Y 7m) ( 4Y 1m) ( 3Y10m) ( 3Y 8m) ( 3Y 3m)
  5     11.78913 13.32856 14.09827 14.86799 16.40742 17.94685 19.48629 21.02572 21.79543 22.56515 24.10458
        (19Y11m) (14Y 4m) (12Y 9m) (11Y 5m) ( 9Y 7m) ( 8Y 4m) ( 7Y 4m) ( 6Y 7m) ( 6Y 3m) ( 5Y11m) ( 5Y 5m)
  7.5   11.14014 12.03141 12.47705 12.92269 13.81396 14.70524 15.59651 16.48779 16.93342 17.37906 18.27034
        (24Y 9m) (18Y 9m) (16Y11m) (15Y 5m) (13Y 3m) (11Y 8m) (10Y 6m) ( 9Y 6m) ( 9Y 1m) ( 8Y 9m) ( 8Y 1m)
 10     10.82640 11.40387 11.69260 11.98134 12.55880 13.13627 13.71374 14.29121 14.57994 14.86868 15.44614
        (28Y 9m) (22Y 5m) (20Y 6m) (18Y11m) (16Y 7m) (14Y10m) (13Y 6m) (12Y 5m) (11Y11m) (11Y 5m) (10Y 8m)
 12.5   10.64664 11.04368 11.24220 11.44073 11.83777 12.23481 12.63185 13.02889 13.22741 13.42593 13.82297
        (32Y 3m) (25Y10m) (23Y 9m) (22Y 2m) (19Y 8m) (17Y10m) (16Y 4m) (15Y 2m) (14Y 7m) (14Y 1m) (13Y 3m)
 15     10.53234 10.81528 10.95675 11.09822 11.38117 11.66411 11.94705 12.22999 12.37146 12.51293 12.79587
        (35Y 6m) (28Y11m) (26Y10m) (25Y 2m) (22Y 7m) (20Y 8m) (19Y 1m) (17Y10m) (17Y 3m) (16Y 9m) (15Y10m)
 20     10.40246 10.55544 10.63192 10.70841 10.86138 11.01435 11.16732 11.32030 11.39678 11.47327 11.62624
        (41Y 4m) (34Y 9m) (32Y 7m) (30Y10m) (28Y 2m) (26Y 1m) (24Y 6m) (23Y 1m) (22Y 6m) (21Y11m) (20Y11m)
 25     10.33567 10.42233 10.46566 10.50899 10.59565 10.68231 10.76897 10.85563 10.89896 10.94229 11.02895
        (46Y12m) (40Y 2m) (38Y 0m) (36Y 3m) (33Y 6m) (31Y 5m) (29Y 9m) (28Y 3m) (27Y 8m) (27Y 1m) (25Y12m)
 30     10.30032 10.35064 10.37580 10.40096 10.45128 10.50160 10.55193 10.60225 10.62741 10.65257 10.70289
        (52Y 2m) (45Y 5m) (43Y 3m) (41Y 6m) (38Y 8m) (36Y 7m) (34Y10m) (33Y 4m) (32Y 8m) (32Y 1m) (30Y12m)
```
Upper entry is the sum of 12 monthly payments; lower entry is term to amortize a loan fully.

Annual Mortgage Constant to Amortize Part of a Loan by a Given Date

10.50% Interest Rate

Years to Balloon	10%	20%	25%	30%	Percentage to be amortized 40%	50%	60%	70%	75%	80%	90%
3	13.34977	16.20007	17.62521	19.05036	21.90065	24.75095	27.60124	30.45153	31.87668	33.30183	36.15212
	(14Y 9m)	(9Y12m)	(8Y 8m)	(7Y 8m)	(6Y 3m)	(5Y 3m)	(4Y 7m)	(4Y 1m)	(3Y10m)	(3Y 7m)	(3Y 3m)
5	12.02820	13.55747	14.32210	15.08674	16.61600	18.14527	19.67454	21.20381	21.96844	22.73308	24.26234
	(19Y 9m)	(14Y 3m)	(12Y 8m)	(11Y 5m)	(9Y 7m)	(8Y 3m)	(7Y 4m)	(6Y 6m)	(6Y 3m)	(5Y11m)	(5Y 5m)
7.5	11.38136	12.26344	12.70447	13.14551	14.02758	14.90965	15.79172	16.67380	17.11483	17.55587	18.43794
	(24Y 6m)	(18Y 7m)	(16Y 9m)	(15Y 4m)	(13Y 2m)	(11Y 8m)	(10Y 5m)	(9Y 6m)	(9Y 1m)	(8Y 9m)	(8Y 1m)
10	11.06863	11.63785	11.92246	12.20707	12.77629	13.34551	13.91473	14.48395	14.76856	15.05317	15.62239
	(28Y 5m)	(22Y 3m)	(20Y 4m)	(18Y10m)	(16Y 6m)	(14Y 9m)	(13Y 5m)	(12Y 4m)	(11Y10m)	(11Y 5m)	(10Y 8m)
12.5	10.88901	11.27872	11.47357	11.66843	12.05814	12.44785	12.83757	13.22728	13.42213	13.61699	14.00670
	(31Y10m)	(25Y 7m)	(23Y 7m)	(22Y 0m)	(19Y 7m)	(17Y 9m)	(16Y 4m)	(15Y 1m)	(14Y 7m)	(14Y 1m)	(13Y 3m)
15	10.77530	11.05178	11.19002	11.32826	11.60474	11.88122	12.15770	12.43418	12.57242	12.71065	12.98713
	(35Y 1m)	(28Y 8m)	(26Y 8m)	(25Y 0m)	(22Y 6m)	(20Y 7m)	(19Y 1m)	(17Y10m)	(17Y 3m)	(16Y 9m)	(15Y10m)
20	10.64711	10.79517	10.86919	10.94322	11.09128	11.23933	11.38739	11.53544	11.60947	11.68350	11.83156
	(40Y11m)	(34Y 5m)	(32Y 4m)	(30Y 8m)	(28Y 1m)	(26Y 0m)	(24Y 5m)	(23Y 1m)	(22Y 6m)	(21Y11m)	(20Y11m)
25	10.58205	10.66507	10.70658	10.74809	10.83110	10.91412	10.99714	11.08016	11.12167	11.16318	11.24619
	(46Y 6m)	(39Y10m)	(37Y 9m)	(36Y 1m)	(33Y 4m)	(31Y 4m)	(29Y 7m)	(28Y 3m)	(27Y 7m)	(27Y 0m)	(25Y11m)
30	10.54723	10.59491	10.61876	10.64260	10.69029	10.73798	10.78566	10.83335	10.85719	10.88104	10.92872
	(51Y 9m)	(45Y 1m)	(42Y12m)	(41Y 3m)	(38Y 6m)	(36Y 5m)	(34Y 9m)	(33Y 4m)	(32Y 8m)	(32Y 1m)	(30Y12m)

10.75% Interest Rate

Years to Balloon	10%	20%	25%	30%	40%	50%	60%	70%	75%	80%	90%
3	13.58892	16.42838	17.84810	19.26783	22.10729	24.94674	27.78619	30.62565	32.04538	33.46510	36.30456
	(14Y 8m)	(9Y11m)	(8Y 7m)	(7Y 8m)	(6Y 3m)	(5Y 3m)	(4Y 7m)	(4Y 0m)	(3Y10m)	(3Y 7m)	(3Y 3m)
5	12.26802	13.78718	14.54675	15.30633	16.82549	18.34464	19.86379	21.38295	22.14253	22.90210	24.42126
	(19Y 6m)	(14Y 2m)	(12Y 7m)	(11Y 4m)	(9Y 6m)	(8Y 3m)	(7Y 3m)	(6Y 6m)	(6Y 3m)	(5Y11m)	(5Y 5m)
7.5	11.62194	12.49488	12.93135	13.36782	14.24076	15.11371	15.98665	16.85959	17.29606	17.73253	18.60547
	(24Y 2m)	(18Y 5m)	(16Y 8m)	(15Y 3m)	(13Y 2m)	(11Y 7m)	(10Y 5m)	(9Y 6m)	(9Y 1m)	(8Y 9m)	(8Y 1m)
10	11.31003	11.87110	12.15163	12.43216	12.99323	13.55429	14.11536	14.67642	14.95695	15.23748	15.79855
	(28Y 1m)	(22Y 1m)	(20Y 2m)	(18Y 8m)	(16Y 5m)	(14Y 9m)	(13Y 5m)	(12Y 4m)	(11Y10m)	(11Y 5m)	(10Y 8m)
12.5	11.13159	11.51408	11.70533	11.89658	12.27907	12.66156	13.04405	13.42654	13.61778	13.80903	14.19152
	(31Y 6m)	(25Y 4m)	(23Y 5m)	(21Y10m)	(19Y 6m)	(17Y 8m)	(16Y 3m)	(15Y 1m)	(14Y 7m)	(14Y 1m)	(13Y 3m)
15	11.01957	11.28971	11.42478	11.55985	11.82999	12.10012	12.37026	12.64040	12.77547	12.91054	13.18067
	(34Y 8m)	(28Y 5m)	(26Y 5m)	(24Y10m)	(22Y 4m)	(20Y 6m)	(18Y12m)	(17Y 9m)	(17Y 3m)	(16Y 8m)	(15Y10m)
20	10.89294	11.03621	11.10785	11.17949	11.32276	11.46604	11.60931	11.75259	11.82423	11.89586	12.03914
	(40Y 6m)	(34Y 2m)	(32Y 1m)	(30Y 5m)	(27Y11m)	(25Y11m)	(24Y 4m)	(22Y12m)	(22Y 5m)	(21Y10m)	(20Y11m)
25	10.82841	10.90792	10.94768	10.98743	11.06694	11.14646	11.22597	11.30548	11.34523	11.38499	11.46450
	(46Y 1m)	(39Y 7m)	(37Y 6m)	(35Y10m)	(33Y 2m)	(31Y 2m)	(29Y 6m)	(28Y 2m)	(27Y 7m)	(26Y12m)	(25Y11m)
30	10.79421	10.83939	10.86198	10.88457	10.92975	10.97492	11.02010	11.06528	11.08787	11.11046	11.15563
	(51Y 4m)	(44Y10m)	(42Y 9m)	(41Y 1m)	(38Y 5m)	(36Y 4m)	(34Y 8m)	(33Y 3m)	(32Y 7m)	(32Y 0m)	(30Y12m)

11.00% Interest Rate

Years to Balloon	10%	20%	25%	30%	40%	50%	60%	70%	75%	80%	90%
3	13.82780	16.65644	18.07077	19.48509	22.31374	25.14238	27.97103	30.79967	32.21400	33.62832	36.45697
	(14Y 6m)	(9Y10m)	(8Y 7m)	(7Y 7m)	(6Y 2m)	(5Y 3m)	(4Y 7m)	(4Y 0m)	(3Y10m)	(3Y 7m)	(3Y 3m)
5	12.50860	14.01769	14.77223	15.52678	17.03587	18.54496	20.05405	21.56314	22.31769	23.07223	24.58132
	(19Y 4m)	(14Y 0m)	(12Y 6m)	(11Y 3m)	(9Y 6m)	(8Y 3m)	(7Y 3m)	(6Y 6m)	(6Y 2m)	(5Y11m)	(5Y 5m)
7.5	11.86307	12.72695	13.15889	13.59083	14.45472	15.31860	16.18248	17.04636	17.47830	17.91025	18.77413
	(23Y11m)	(18Y 3m)	(16Y 6m)	(15Y 2m)	(13Y 1m)	(11Y 7m)	(10Y 5m)	(9Y 5m)	(9Y 1m)	(8Y 8m)	(8Y 1m)
10	11.55181	12.10481	12.38131	12.65781	13.21081	13.76381	14.31681	14.86981	15.14631	15.42281	15.97581
	(27Y 9m)	(21Y10m)	(20Y 0m)	(18Y 7m)	(16Y 4m)	(14Y 8m)	(13Y 4m)	(12Y 4m)	(11Y10m)	(11Y 5m)	(10Y 8m)
12.5	11.37441	11.74979	11.93748	12.12517	12.50054	12.87592	13.25130	13.62668	13.81437	14.00206	14.37743
	(31Y 2m)	(25Y 2m)	(23Y 3m)	(21Y 9m)	(19Y 4m)	(17Y 7m)	(16Y 2m)	(15Y 0m)	(14Y 6m)	(14Y 1m)	(13Y 3m)
15	11.26277	11.52668	11.65864	11.79060	12.05451	12.31843	12.58235	12.84626	12.97822	13.11018	13.37410
	(34Y 4m)	(28Y 2m)	(26Y 3m)	(24Y 8m)	(22Y 3m)	(20Y 5m)	(18Y11m)	(17Y 9m)	(17Y 2m)	(16Y 8m)	(15Y 9m)
20	11.13758	11.27620	11.34552	11.41483	11.55346	11.69208	11.83071	11.96933	12.03865	12.10796	12.24659
	(40Y 2m)	(33Y11m)	(31Y11m)	(30Y 3m)	(27Y 9m)	(25Y10m)	(24Y 3m)	(22Y11m)	(22Y 5m)	(21Y10m)	(20Y10m)
25	11.07599	11.15213	11.19019	11.22826	11.30440	11.38053	11.45667	11.53280	11.57087	11.60894	11.68508
	(45Y 6m)	(39Y 3m)	(37Y 3m)	(35Y 7m)	(33Y 0m)	(31Y 0m)	(29Y 5m)	(28Y 1m)	(27Y 6m)	(26Y11m)	(25Y11m)
30	11.04252	11.08531	11.10670	11.12810	11.17088	11.21367	11.25646	11.29925	11.32064	11.34204	11.38482
	(50Y 9m)	(44Y 5m)	(42Y 5m)	(40Y 9m)	(38Y 2m)	(36Y 2m)	(34Y 6m)	(33Y 2m)	(32Y 7m)	(31Y12m)	(30Y11m)

11.25% Interest Rate

Years to Balloon	10%	20%	25%	30%	40%	50%	60%	70%	75%	80%	90%
3	14.06760	16.88547	18.29440	19.70333	22.52120	25.33907	28.15694	30.97481	32.38374	33.79268	36.61054
	(14Y 4m)	(9Y10m)	(8Y 6m)	(7Y 7m)	(6Y 2m)	(5Y 3m)	(4Y 7m)	(4Y 0m)	(3Y10m)	(3Y 7m)	(3Y 3m)
5	12.74872	14.24780	14.99733	15.74687	17.24595	18.74503	20.24410	21.74318	22.49272	23.24226	24.74134
	(19Y 1m)	(13Y11m)	(12Y 5m)	(11Y 2m)	(9Y 5m)	(8Y 2m)	(7Y 3m)	(6Y 6m)	(6Y 2m)	(5Y11m)	(5Y 5m)
7.5	12.10474	12.95964	13.38709	13.81454	14.66943	15.52433	16.37923	17.23412	17.66157	18.08902	18.94392
	(23Y 8m)	(18Y 1m)	(16Y 5m)	(15Y 0m)	(13Y 0m)	(11Y 6m)	(10Y 4m)	(9Y 5m)	(9Y 1m)	(8Y 8m)	(8Y 1m)
10	11.79397	12.33899	12.61151	12.88402	13.42905	13.97408	14.51910	15.06413	15.33664	15.60916	16.15418
	(27Y 6m)	(21Y 8m)	(19Y11m)	(18Y 5m)	(16Y 3m)	(14Y 7m)	(13Y 4m)	(12Y 3m)	(11Y10m)	(11Y 5m)	(10Y 8m)
12.5	11.61747	11.98584	12.17002	12.35421	12.72258	13.09095	13.45932	13.82770	14.01188	14.19607	14.56444
	(30Y10m)	(24Y11m)	(23Y 1m)	(21Y 7m)	(19Y 3m)	(17Y 6m)	(16Y 2m)	(15Y 0m)	(14Y 6m)	(14Y 1m)	(13Y 3m)
15	11.50729	11.76510	11.89401	12.02292	12.28073	12.53854	12.79636	13.05417	13.18308	13.31198	13.56980
	(33Y11m)	(27Y11m)	(26Y 1m)	(24Y 6m)	(22Y 2m)	(20Y 4m)	(18Y10m)	(17Y 8m)	(17Y 2m)	(16Y 8m)	(15Y 9m)
20	11.38345	11.51755	11.58461	11.65166	11.78577	11.91988	12.05398	12.18809	12.25514	12.32220	12.45630
	(39Y 8m)	(33Y 7m)	(31Y 8m)	(30Y 1m)	(27Y 7m)	(25Y 9m)	(24Y 2m)	(22Y11m)	(22Y 4m)	(21Y10m)	(20Y10m)
25	11.32242	11.39531	11.43176	11.46820	11.54109	11.61397	11.68686	11.75975	11.79619	11.83264	11.90552
	(45Y 1m)	(38Y11m)	(36Y12m)	(35Y 5m)	(32Y10m)	(30Y11m)	(29Y 4m)	(28Y 0m)	(27Y 5m)	(26Y11m)	(25Y11m)
30	11.28979	11.33030	11.35056	11.37082	11.41133	11.45184	11.49236	11.53287	11.55313	11.57338	11.61390
	(50Y 5m)	(44Y 2m)	(42Y 2m)	(40Y 7m)	(38Y 0m)	(36Y 1m)	(34Y 6m)	(33Y 1m)	(32Y 6m)	(31Y11m)	(30Y11m)

Upper entry is the sum of 12 monthly payments; lower entry is term to amortize a loan fully.

Annual Mortgage Constant to Amortize Part of a Loan by a Given Date

11.50% Interest Rate

Years to Balloon	Percentage to be amortized										
	10%	20%	25%	30%	40%	50%	60%	70%	75%	80%	90%
3	14.30593 (14Y 3m)	17.11305 (9Y 9m)	18.51661 (8Y 6m)	19.92017 (7Y 6m)	22.72729 (6Y 2m)	25.53441 (5Y 3m)	28.34153 (4Y 7m)	31.14865 (4Y 0m)	32.55221 (3Y10m)	33.95577 (3Y 7m)	36.76289 (3Y 3m)
5	12.98840 (18Y11m)	14.47751 (13Y10m)	15.22207 (12Y 4m)	15.96662 (11Y 2m)	17.45573 (9Y 5m)	18.94485 (8Y 2m)	20.43396 (7Y 3m)	21.92307 (6Y 6m)	22.66763 (6Y 2m)	23.41219 (5Y11m)	24.90130 (5Y 5m)
7.5	12.34577 (23Y 5m)	13.19176 (17Y11m)	13.61475 (16Y 3m)	14.03774 (14Y11m)	14.88372 (12Y11m)	15.72970 (11Y 6m)	16.57568 (10Y 4m)	17.42167 (9Y 5m)	17.84466 (9Y 0m)	18.26765 (8Y 8m)	19.11363 (8Y 1m)
10	12.03650 (27Y 2m)	12.57365 (21Y 6m)	12.84222 (19Y 9m)	13.11079 (18Y 4m)	13.64794 (16Y 2m)	14.18509 (14Y 7m)	14.72223 (13Y 3m)	15.25938 (12Y 3m)	15.52795 (11Y 9m)	15.79652 (11Y 5m)	16.33367 (10Y 8m)
12.5	11.86077 (30Y 6m)	12.22224 (24Y 9m)	12.40298 (22Y11m)	12.58371 (21Y 5m)	12.94518 (19Y 2m)	13.30665 (17Y 5m)	13.66813 (16Y 1m)	14.02960 (14Y12m)	14.21033 (14Y 6m)	14.39107 (14Y 0m)	14.75254 (13Y 3m)
15	11.75076 (33Y 7m)	12.00259 (27Y 9m)	12.12850 (25Y10m)	12.25442 (24Y 4m)	12.50625 (22Y 0m)	12.75807 (20Y 3m)	13.00990 (18Y10m)	13.26173 (17Y 8m)	13.38764 (17Y 1m)	13.51356 (16Y 8m)	13.76538 (15Y 9m)
20	11.62937 (39Y 4m)	11.75909 (33Y 4m)	11.82395 (31Y 5m)	11.88880 (29Y11m)	12.01852 (27Y 6m)	12.14823 (25Y 7m)	12.27795 (24Y 1m)	12.40767 (22Y10m)	12.47252 (22Y 4m)	12.53738 (21Y 9m)	12.66710 (20Y10m)
25	11.56895 (44Y 9m)	11.63871 (38Y 8m)	11.67359 (36Y 9m)	11.70847 (35Y 2m)	11.77824 (32Y 9m)	11.84800 (30Y10m)	11.91776 (29Y 3m)	11.98752 (27Y12m)	12.02241 (27Y 5m)	12.05729 (26Y10m)	12.12705 (25Y11m)
30	11.53726 (50Y 1m)	11.57561 (43Y11m)	11.59479 (41Y12m)	11.61396 (40Y 5m)	11.65231 (37Y11m)	11.69066 (35Y12m)	11.72901 (34Y 5m)	11.76736 (33Y 1m)	11.78654 (32Y 6m)	11.80571 (31Y11m)	11.84406 (30Y11m)

11.75% Interest Rate

Years to Balloon	10%	20%	25%	30%	40%	50%	60%	70%	75%	80%	90%
3	14.54638 (14Y 1m)	17.34278 (9Y 8m)	18.74098 (8Y 5m)	20.13919 (7Y 6m)	22.93559 (6Y 2m)	25.73199 (5Y 3m)	28.52840 (4Y 7m)	31.32480 (4Y 0m)	32.72300 (3Y10m)	34.12120 (3Y 7m)	36.91761 (3Y 3m)
5	13.22883 (18Y 9m)	14.70802 (13Y 9m)	15.44762 (12Y 3m)	16.18722 (11Y 1m)	17.66642 (9Y 4m)	19.14562 (8Y 2m)	20.62482 (7Y 3m)	22.10402 (6Y 6m)	22.84362 (6Y 2m)	23.58321 (5Y11m)	25.06241 (5Y 5m)
7.5	12.58616 (23Y 2m)	13.42330 (17Y10m)	13.84187 (16Y 2m)	14.26044 (14Y10m)	15.09758 (12Y11m)	15.93472 (11Y 5m)	16.77186 (10Y 4m)	17.60900 (9Y 5m)	18.02756 (9Y 0m)	18.44613 (8Y 8m)	19.28327 (8Y 0m)
10	12.27823 (26Y11m)	12.80758 (21Y 4m)	13.07226 (19Y 7m)	13.33694 (18Y 2m)	13.86629 (16Y 1m)	14.39564 (14Y 6m)	14.92500 (13Y 3m)	15.45435 (12Y 3m)	15.71903 (11Y 9m)	15.98370 (11Y 4m)	16.51306 (10Y 8m)
12.5	12.10433 (30Y 2m)	12.45900 (24Y 6m)	12.63634 (22Y 9m)	12.81368 (21Y 3m)	13.16835 (19Y 1m)	13.52303 (17Y 5m)	13.87771 (16Y 0m)	14.23238 (14Y11m)	14.40972 (14Y 5m)	14.58706 (14Y 0m)	14.94174 (13Y 2m)
15	11.99559 (33Y 3m)	12.24155 (27Y 6m)	12.36453 (25Y 8m)	12.48751 (24Y 2m)	12.73347 (21Y11m)	12.97942 (20Y 2m)	13.22538 (18Y 9m)	13.47134 (17Y 7m)	13.59432 (17Y 1m)	13.71730 (16Y 7m)	13.96325 (15Y 9m)
20	11.87538 (38Y11m)	12.00082 (33Y 1m)	12.06355 (31Y 3m)	12.12627 (29Y 8m)	12.25172 (27Y 4m)	12.37717 (25Y 6m)	12.50262 (24Y 0m)	12.62807 (22Y10m)	12.69079 (22Y 3m)	12.75352 (21Y 9m)	12.87896 (20Y10m)
25	11.81559 (44Y 5m)	11.88235 (38Y 6m)	11.91573 (36Y 7m)	11.94911 (35Y 0m)	12.01587 (32Y 7m)	12.08262 (30Y 9m)	12.14938 (29Y 2m)	12.21614 (27Y11m)	12.24952 (27Y 4m)	12.28290 (26Y10m)	12.34965 (25Y10m)
30	11.78619 (49Y 6m)	11.82248 (43Y 7m)	11.84062 (41Y 8m)	11.85877 (40Y 1m)	11.89506 (37Y 8m)	11.93135 (35Y10m)	11.96765 (34Y 3m)	12.00394 (32Y12m)	12.02208 (32Y 5m)	12.04023 (31Y10m)	12.07652 (30Y11m)

12.00% Interest Rate

Years to Balloon	10%	20%	25%	30%	40%	50%	60%	70%	75%	80%	90%
3	14.78536 (13Y12m)	17.57107 (9Y 7m)	18.96393 (8Y 5m)	20.35679 (7Y 5m)	23.14251 (6Y 1m)	25.92823 (5Y 2m)	28.71394 (4Y 6m)	31.49966 (4Y 0m)	32.89252 (3Y10m)	34.28538 (3Y 7m)	37.07109 (3Y 3m)
5	13.46881 (18Y 7m)	14.93814 (13Y 7m)	15.67281 (12Y 2m)	16.40748 (11Y 0m)	17.87681 (9Y 4m)	19.34614 (8Y 1m)	20.81548 (7Y 2m)	22.28481 (6Y 6m)	23.01948 (6Y 2m)	23.75414 (5Y11m)	25.22348 (5Y 5m)
7.5	12.82831 (22Y11m)	13.65667 (17Y 8m)	14.07086 (16Y 1m)	14.48504 (14Y 9m)	15.31341 (12Y10m)	16.14178 (11Y 5m)	16.97014 (10Y 3m)	17.79851 (9Y 5m)	18.21269 (9Y 0m)	18.62688 (8Y 8m)	19.45524 (8Y 0m)
10	12.52155 (26Y 7m)	13.04320 (21Y 2m)	13.30403 (19Y 5m)	13.56485 (18Y 1m)	14.08650 (15Y12m)	14.60816 (14Y 5m)	15.12981 (13Y 2m)	15.65146 (12Y 2m)	15.91228 (11Y 9m)	16.17311 (11Y 4m)	16.69476 (10Y 7m)
12.5	12.34695 (29Y11m)	12.69493 (24Y 4m)	12.86892 (22Y 7m)	13.04292 (21Y 2m)	13.39090 (18Y12m)	13.73889 (17Y 4m)	14.08687 (15Y12m)	14.43486 (14Y11m)	14.60885 (14Y 5m)	14.78284 (13Y12m)	15.13083 (13Y 2m)
15	12.23940 (32Y11m)	12.47960 (27Y 4m)	12.59970 (25Y 6m)	12.71980 (24Y 1m)	12.96000 (21Y10m)	13.20020 (20Y 1m)	13.44041 (18Y 8m)	13.68061 (17Y 7m)	13.80071 (17Y 1m)	13.92081 (16Y 7m)	14.16101 (15Y 9m)
20	12.12028 (38Y 8m)	12.24159 (32Y10m)	12.30224 (31Y 0m)	12.36289 (29Y 7m)	12.48419 (27Y 3m)	12.60550 (25Y 5m)	12.72680 (23Y12m)	12.84810 (22Y 9m)	12.90875 (22Y 3m)	12.96941 (21Y 9m)	13.09071 (20Y10m)
25	12.06359 (43Y11m)	12.12746 (38Y 2m)	12.15939 (36Y 4m)	12.19133 (34Y10m)	12.25520 (32Y 5m)	12.31907 (30Y 7m)	12.38294 (29Y 1m)	12.44681 (27Y10m)	12.47874 (27Y 4m)	12.51067 (26Y 9m)	12.57454 (25Y10m)
30	12.03420 (49Y 1m)	12.06853 (43Y 4m)	12.08570 (41Y 5m)	12.10287 (39Y11m)	12.13720 (37Y 6m)	12.17154 (35Y 8m)	12.20587 (34Y 2m)	12.24021 (32Y11m)	12.25737 (32Y 4m)	12.27454 (31Y10m)	12.30888 (30Y10m)

12.50% Interest Rate

Years to Balloon	10%	20%	25%	30%	40%	50%	60%	70%	75%	80%	90%
3	15.26370 (13Y 9m)	18.02813 (9Y 6m)	19.41035 (8Y 4m)	20.79257 (7Y 5m)	23.55700 (6Y 1m)	26.32144 (5Y 2m)	29.08587 (4Y 6m)	31.85031 (4Y 0m)	33.23252 (3Y10m)	34.61474 (3Y 7m)	37.37918 (3Y 3m)
5	13.94864 (18Y 3m)	15.39839 (13Y 5m)	16.12327 (12Y 0m)	16.84814 (10Y11m)	18.29790 (9Y 3m)	19.74765 (8Y 1m)	21.19740 (7Y 2m)	22.64715 (6Y 5m)	23.37203 (6Y 2m)	24.09691 (5Y11m)	25.54666 (5Y 5m)
7.5	13.31068 (22Y 6m)	14.12172 (17Y 5m)	14.52723 (15Y10m)	14.93275 (14Y 7m)	15.74379 (12Y 8m)	16.55483 (11Y 4m)	17.36586 (10Y 3m)	18.17690 (9Y 4m)	18.58242 (9Y 0m)	18.98794 (8Y 7m)	19.79897 (8Y 0m)
10	13.00579 (26Y 1m)	13.51230 (20Y10m)	13.76556 (19Y 2m)	14.01881 (17Y10m)	14.52533 (15Y10m)	15.03184 (14Y 4m)	15.53836 (13Y 1m)	16.04487 (12Y 2m)	16.29813 (11Y 9m)	16.55138 (11Y 4m)	17.05790 (10Y 7m)
12.5	12.83421 (29Y 4m)	13.16912 (23Y12m)	13.33658 (22Y 3m)	13.50403 (20Y11m)	13.83894 (18Y 9m)	14.17386 (17Y 2m)	14.50877 (15Y11m)	14.84368 (14Y10m)	15.01113 (14Y 5m)	15.17859 (13Y11m)	15.51350 (13Y 2m)
15	12.72877 (32Y 4m)	12.95780 (26Y11m)	13.07231 (25Y 2m)	13.18683 (23Y 9m)	13.41585 (21Y 7m)	13.64488 (19Y11m)	13.87391 (18Y 7m)	14.10293 (17Y 6m)	14.21745 (16Y12m)	14.33196 (16Y 7m)	14.56099 (15Y 9m)
20	12.61289 (37Y11m)	12.72626 (32Y 5m)	12.78295 (30Y 8m)	12.83963 (29Y 3m)	12.95300 (26Y12m)	13.06637 (25Y 3m)	13.17974 (23Y10m)	13.29311 (22Y 8m)	13.34979 (22Y 2m)	13.40647 (21Y 8m)	13.51984 (20Y 9m)
25	12.55779 (43Y 3m)	12.61621 (37Y 8m)	12.64542 (35Y11m)	12.67464 (34Y 5m)	12.73306 (32Y 1m)	12.79149 (30Y 4m)	12.84991 (28Y12m)	12.90834 (27Y 9m)	12.93755 (27Y 3m)	12.96676 (26Y 9m)	13.02519 (25Y10m)
30	12.53003 (48Y 6m)	12.56074 (42Y11m)	12.57609 (41Y 1m)	12.59145 (39Y 7m)	12.62216 (37Y 4m)	12.65287 (35Y 6m)	12.68357 (34Y 1m)	12.71428 (32Y10m)	12.72964 (32Y 3m)	12.74499 (31Y 9m)	12.77570 (30Y10m)

Upper entry is the sum of 12 monthly payments; lower entry is term to amortize a loan fully.

Annual Mortgage Constant for Annual, Semiannual & Quarterly Payments

Term of Loan Years	Interest Rate 5.50%			5.75%			6.00%			6.25%		
	annual	semiannual	quarterly	annual	semiannual	quarterly	annual	semiannual	quarterly	annual	semiannual	quarterly
1	105.50000	104.14365	103.46097	105.75000	104.33287	103.61939	106.00000	104.52217	103.77791	106.25000	104.71154	103.93653
2	54.16180	53.48412	53.14303	54.35267	53.64467	53.28822	54.54369	53.80541	53.43361	54.73485	53.96633	53.57920
3	37.06541	36.61417	36.38705	37.23807	36.76669	36.52937	37.41098	36.91950	36.67200	37.58415	37.07260	36.81492
4	28.52945	28.19159	28.02155	28.69412	28.34124	28.16359	28.85915	28.49128	28.30603	29.02453	28.64171	28.44888
5	23.41764	23.14794	23.01221	23.57841	23.29678	23.15500	23.73964	23.44610	23.29829	23.90132	23.59591	23.44209
6	20.01789	19.79374	19.68094	20.17680	19.94279	19.82499	20.33626	20.09242	19.96964	20.49627	20.24263	20.11490
7	17.59644	17.40491	17.30854	17.75465	17.55475	17.45413	17.91350	17.70527	17.60043	18.07300	17.85647	17.74743
8	15.78640	15.61942	15.53540	15.94463	15.77041	15.68272	16.10359	15.92217	15.83084	16.26330	16.07471	15.97975
9	14.38395	14.23613	14.16175	14.54267	14.38850	14.31091	14.70222	14.54174	14.46096	14.86260	14.69585	14.61190
10	13.26678	13.13435	13.06772	13.42633	13.28826	13.21879	13.58680	13.44314	13.37084	13.74818	13.59898	13.52388
11	12.35707	12.23728	12.17703	12.51768	12.39285	12.33005	12.67929	12.54948	12.48415	12.84191	12.70715	12.63933
12	11.60292	11.49373	11.43880	11.76477	11.65103	11.59382	11.92770	11.80948	11.75000	12.09172	11.96907	11.90734
13	10.96843	10.86823	10.81784	11.13163	11.02733	10.97487	11.29601	11.18766	11.13315	11.46156	11.34920	11.29267
14	10.42791	10.33548	10.28900	10.59257	10.49641	10.44804	10.75849	10.65865	10.60843	10.92565	10.82219	10.77014
15	9.96256	9.87688	9.83381	10.12875	10.03967	9.99488	10.29628	10.20385	10.15737	10.46512	10.36941	10.32127
16	9.55825	9.47853	9.43845	9.72603	9.64319	9.60154	9.89521	9.80932	9.76614	10.06580	9.97692	9.93222
17	9.20420	9.12975	9.09233	9.37360	9.29630	9.25744	9.54448	9.46439	9.42413	9.71683	9.63402	9.59239
18	8.89199	8.82226	8.78722	9.06305	8.99070	8.95434	9.23565	9.16076	9.12312	9.40980	9.33242	9.29353
19	8.61501	8.54953	8.51663	8.78773	8.71985	8.68574	8.96209	8.89187	8.85658	9.13804	9.06555	9.02913
20	8.36793	8.30630	8.27534	8.54235	8.47851	8.44644	8.71846	8.65248	8.61933	8.89623	8.82818	8.79399
21	8.14648	8.08835	8.05916	8.32259	8.26243	8.23222	8.50045	8.43833	8.40714	8.68004	8.61603	8.58389
22	7.94712	7.89220	7.86462	8.12493	8.06814	8.03963	8.30456	8.24597	8.21655	8.48596	8.42565	8.39537
23	7.76696	7.71499	7.68889	7.94647	7.89278	7.86582	8.12785	8.07251	8.04473	8.31106	8.25415	8.22558
24	7.60358	7.55432	7.52959	7.78478	7.73394	7.70842	7.96790	7.91555	7.88929	8.15291	8.09913	8.07215
25	7.45494	7.40818	7.38472	7.63782	7.58962	7.56543	7.82267	7.77310	7.74823	8.00946	7.95854	7.93307
26	7.31931	7.27489	7.25260	7.50386	7.45811	7.43517	7.69043	7.64344	7.61987	7.87899	7.83081	7.80666
27	7.19523	7.15298	7.13179	7.38144	7.33798	7.31618	7.56972	7.52512	7.50276	7.76001	7.71435	7.69146
28	7.08144	7.04122	7.02106	7.26929	7.22797	7.20725	7.45926	7.41689	7.39566	7.65128	7.60796	7.58625
29	6.97686	6.93854	6.91933	7.16634	7.12701	7.10729	7.35796	7.31770	7.29752	7.55168	7.51056	7.48996
30	6.88054	6.84400	6.82569	7.07162	7.03417	7.01540	7.26489	7.22659	7.20741	7.46028	7.42122	7.40166

Term of Loan Years	Interest Rate 6.50%			6.75%			7.00%			7.25%		
	annual	semiannual	quarterly	annual	semiannual	quarterly	annual	semiannual	quarterly	annual	semiannual	quarterly
1	106.50000	104.90098	104.09524	106.75000	105.09050	104.25405	107.00000	105.28010	104.41295	107.25000	105.46977	104.57194
2	54.92615	54.12745	53.72499	55.11759	54.28874	53.87098	55.30918	54.45023	54.01717	55.50090	54.61190	54.16356
3	37.75757	37.22599	36.95815	37.93124	37.37967	37.10168	38.10517	37.53364	37.24551	38.27934	37.68790	37.38964
4	29.19027	28.79253	28.59213	29.35637	28.94373	28.73578	29.52281	29.09533	28.87983	29.68961	29.24731	29.02429
5	24.06345	23.74621	23.58639	24.22604	23.89700	23.73119	24.38907	24.04827	23.87649	24.55255	24.20003	24.02229
6	20.65683	20.39344	20.26075	20.81793	20.54482	20.40721	20.97958	20.69679	20.55426	21.14177	20.84934	20.70191
7	18.23314	18.00835	17.89513	18.39391	18.16091	18.04352	18.55532	18.31415	18.19261	18.71736	18.46805	18.34239
8	16.42373	16.22803	16.12946	16.58489	16.38211	16.27996	16.74678	16.53697	16.43125	16.90938	16.69258	16.58332
9	15.02380	14.85083	14.76372	15.18582	15.00667	14.91644	15.34865	15.16337	15.07003	15.51228	15.32092	15.22450
10	13.91047	13.75578	13.67789	14.07366	13.91352	13.83288	14.23775	14.07222	13.98884	14.40273	14.23185	14.14576
11	13.00552	12.86587	12.79557	13.17012	13.02563	12.95288	13.33569	13.18641	13.11124	13.50224	13.34823	13.27066
12	12.25682	12.12978	12.06584	12.42298	12.29162	12.22549	12.59020	12.45457	12.38628	12.75847	12.61862	12.54820
13	11.62826	11.51596	11.45344	11.79610	11.67592	11.61544	11.96508	11.84108	11.77866	12.13519	12.00742	11.94310
14	11.09405	10.98702	10.93318	11.26367	11.15314	11.09753	11.43449	11.32053	11.26318	11.60652	11.48918	11.43013
15	10.63528	10.53634	10.48658	10.80673	10.70463	10.65327	10.97946	10.87427	10.82134	11.15347	11.04523	10.99078
16	10.23776	10.14595	10.09978	10.41109	10.31642	10.26881	10.58576	10.48830	10.43928	10.76178	10.66159	10.61120
17	9.89763	9.80516	9.76219	10.06587	9.97780	9.93353	10.24252	10.15193	10.10639	10.42057	10.32753	10.28075
18	9.58546	9.50566	9.46555	9.76262	9.68047	9.63918	9.94126	9.85683	9.81440	10.12136	10.03472	9.99118
19	9.31558	9.24089	9.20336	9.49467	9.41785	9.37926	9.67530	9.59643	9.55680	9.85745	9.77659	9.73597
20	9.07564	9.00559	8.97040	9.25667	9.18469	9.14853	9.43929	9.36546	9.32837	9.62348	9.54787	9.50998
21	8.86133	8.79551	8.76245	9.04429	8.97672	8.94279	9.22890	9.15966	9.12489	9.41512	9.34428	9.30872
22	8.66912	8.60716	8.57605	8.85400	8.79046	8.75857	9.04058	8.97554	8.94290	9.22882	9.16235	9.12900
23	8.49608	8.43767	8.40836	8.68287	8.62304	8.59302	8.87139	8.81022	8.77953	9.06162	8.99918	8.96786
24	8.33977	8.28464	8.25698	8.52845	8.47204	8.44375	8.71890	8.66129	8.63240	8.91110	8.85236	8.82292
25	8.19815	8.14605	8.11993	8.38869	8.33545	8.30876	8.58105	8.52674	8.49952	8.77519	8.71989	8.69218
26	8.06948	8.02021	7.99550	8.26187	8.21157	8.18636	8.45610	8.40486	8.37918	8.65215	8.60003	8.57393
27	7.95229	7.90564	7.88226	8.14649	8.09893	8.07511	8.34257	8.29418	8.26995	8.54049	8.49134	8.46674
28	7.84531	7.80111	7.77897	8.04129	7.99629	7.97376	8.23919	8.19346	8.17057	8.43895	8.39256	8.36936
29	7.74744	7.70553	7.68455	7.94519	7.90257	7.88125	8.14487	8.10162	8.07999	8.34642	8.30262	8.28072
30	7.65774	7.61799	7.59809	7.85722	7.81684	7.79664	8.05864	8.01772	7.99727	8.26196	8.22058	8.19990

Entry is annual mortgage constant in percent of loan amount.

Annual Mortgage Constant for Annual, Semiannual & Quarterly Payments

Interest Rate

Term of Loan Years	7.50% annual	semiannual	quarterly	7.75% annual	semiannual	quarterly	8.00% annual	semiannual	quarterly	8.25% annual	semiannual	quarterly
1	107.50000	105.65951	104.73103	107.75000	105.84933	104.89022	108.00000	106.03922	105.04950	108.25000	106.22918	105.20888
2	55.69277	54.77375	54.31015	55.88478	54.93579	54.45693	56.07692	55.09801	54.60392	56.26921	55.26041	54.75110
3	38.45376	37.84244	37.53407	38.62843	37.99727	37.67881	38.80335	38.15238	37.82384	38.97852	38.30778	37.96917
4	29.85675	29.39968	29.16914	30.02424	29.55243	29.31440	30.19208	29.70557	29.46005	30.36026	29.85909	29.60610
5	24.71647	24.35227	24.16859	24.88084	24.50499	24.31539	25.04565	24.65819	24.46269	25.21089	24.81187	24.61048
6	21.30449	21.00246	20.85016	21.46775	21.15616	20.99900	21.63154	21.31043	21.14844	21.79586	21.46528	21.29847
7	18.88003	18.62263	18.49286	19.04333	18.77788	18.64402	19.20724	18.93379	18.79587	19.37177	19.09037	18.94840
8	17.07270	16.84897	16.73618	17.23674	17.00610	16.88982	17.40148	17.16400	17.04424	17.56692	17.32265	17.19944
9	15.67672	15.47932	15.37984	15.84195	15.63857	15.53606	16.00797	15.79867	15.69314	16.17478	15.95960	15.85109
10	14.56859	14.39242	14.30365	14.73533	14.55392	14.46250	14.90295	14.71635	14.62230	15.07143	14.87970	14.78305
11	13.66975	13.51106	13.43112	13.83822	13.67491	13.59263	14.00763	13.83976	13.75518	14.17800	14.00562	13.91875
12	12.92778	12.78378	12.71126	13.09813	12.95003	12.87544	13.26950	13.11737	13.04073	13.44189	13.28578	13.20714
13	12.30642	12.17494	12.10875	12.47875	12.34363	12.27559	12.65218	12.51348	12.44363	12.82670	12.68447	12.61286
14	11.77974	11.65908	11.59836	11.95413	11.83022	11.76786	12.12969	12.00260	11.93863	12.30639	12.17619	12.11065
15	11.32872	11.21752	11.16158	11.50522	11.39112	11.33372	11.68295	11.56602	11.50719	11.86190	11.74220	11.68198
16	10.93912	10.83626	10.78453	11.11776	11.01231	10.95928	11.29769	11.18972	11.13542	11.47889	11.36847	11.31294
17	10.60000	10.50457	10.45660	10.78080	10.68306	10.63392	10.96294	10.86295	10.81269	11.14642	11.04425	10.99290
18	10.30290	10.21412	10.16951	10.48585	10.39501	10.34936	10.67021	10.57738	10.53073	10.85595	10.76119	10.71359
19	10.04109	9.95832	9.91674	10.22620	10.14159	10.09909	10.41276	10.32638	10.28301	10.60075	10.51268	10.46846
20	9.80922	9.73189	9.69306	9.99647	9.91751	9.87787	10.18522	10.10470	10.06428	10.37544	10.29343	10.25228
21	9.60294	9.53057	9.49425	9.79231	9.71850	9.68147	9.98323	9.90804	9.87032	10.17564	10.09916	10.06081
22	9.41869	9.35087	9.31685	9.61016	9.54106	9.50641	9.80321	9.73291	9.69767	9.99779	9.92637	9.89057
23	9.25353	9.18989	9.15798	9.44707	9.38231	9.34985	9.64222	9.57641	9.54344	9.83894	9.77216	9.73871
24	9.10501	9.04522	9.01526	9.30058	9.23982	9.20938	9.49780	9.43613	9.40525	9.69661	9.63411	9.60283
25	8.97107	8.91484	8.88668	9.16864	9.11158	9.08300	9.36788	9.31004	9.28110	9.56873	9.51020	9.48092
26	8.84996	8.79705	8.77056	9.04950	8.99586	8.96902	9.25071	9.19642	9.16928	9.45357	9.39870	9.37128
27	8.74020	8.69037	8.66543	8.94166	8.89121	8.86598	9.14481	9.09382	9.06834	9.34961	9.29816	9.27246
28	8.64052	8.59355	8.57007	8.84385	8.79637	8.77265	9.04889	9.00097	8.97704	9.25559	9.20731	9.18321
29	8.54981	8.50552	8.48339	8.75497	8.71027	8.68794	8.96185	8.91680	8.89432	9.17041	9.12508	9.10247
30	8.46712	8.42534	8.40447	8.67407	8.63196	8.61094	8.88274	8.84037	8.81924	9.09309	9.05052	9.02931

Interest Rate

Term of Loan Years	8.50% annual	semiannual	quarterly	8.75% annual	semiannual	quarterly	9.00% annual	semiannual	quarterly	9.25% annual	semiannual	quarterly
1	108.50000	106.41922	105.36835	108.75000	106.60933	105.52791	109.00000	106.79951	105.68757	109.25000	106.98977	105.84732
2	56.46163	55.42300	54.89849	56.65419	55.58578	55.04607	56.84689	55.74873	55.19385	57.03973	55.91187	55.34182
3	39.15392	38.46346	38.11480	39.32958	38.61943	38.26073	39.50548	38.77568	38.40696	39.68162	38.93221	38.55349
4	30.52879	30.01299	29.75256	30.69766	30.16727	29.89941	30.86687	30.32193	30.04665	31.03641	30.47697	30.19429
5	25.37658	24.96602	24.75877	25.54269	25.12066	24.90755	25.70925	25.27576	25.05683	25.87623	25.43135	25.20660
6	21.96071	21.62070	21.44909	22.12608	21.77668	21.60030	22.29198	21.93324	21.75209	22.45839	22.09036	21.90447
7	19.53692	19.24761	19.10162	19.70268	19.40551	19.25552	19.86905	19.56406	19.41010	20.03603	19.72327	19.56536
8	17.73307	17.48204	17.35541	17.89991	17.64219	17.51215	18.06744	17.80307	17.66966	18.23566	17.96470	17.82793
9	16.34237	16.12136	16.00090	16.51074	16.28396	16.16957	16.67988	16.44738	16.33009	16.84979	16.61162	16.49146
10	15.24077	15.04397	14.94474	15.41097	15.20914	15.10738	15.58201	15.37523	15.27095	15.75389	15.54221	15.43545
11	14.34929	14.17247	14.08335	14.52152	14.34031	14.24897	14.69467	14.50913	14.41560	14.86873	14.67893	14.58324
12	13.61529	13.45526	13.37464	13.78968	13.62581	13.54324	13.96507	13.79741	13.71293	14.14143	13.97005	13.88370
13	13.00229	12.85661	12.78325	13.17894	13.02988	12.95482	13.35666	13.20427	13.12753	13.53541	13.37978	13.30140
14	12.48424	12.35098	12.28391	12.66322	12.52698	12.45840	12.84332	12.70416	12.63412	13.02452	12.88252	12.81105
15	12.04205	11.91965	11.85807	12.22338	12.09836	12.03546	12.40589	12.27831	12.21413	12.58956	12.45949	12.39407
16	11.66135	11.54855	11.49183	11.84506	11.72995	11.67207	12.02999	11.91264	11.85364	12.21613	12.09662	12.03654
17	11.33120	11.22694	11.17454	11.51727	11.41099	11.35758	11.70462	11.59638	11.54200	11.89323	11.78311	11.72779
18	11.04300	10.94644	10.89792	11.23148	11.13310	11.08370	11.42123	11.32116	11.27091	11.61228	11.51058	11.45953
19	10.79014	10.70045	10.65543	10.98091	10.88968	10.84389	11.17304	11.08034	11.03383	11.36651	11.27241	11.22521
20	10.56710	10.48368	10.44183	10.76018	10.67542	10.63291	10.95465	10.86863	10.82550	11.15049	11.06328	11.01958
21	10.36954	10.29184	10.25288	10.56489	10.48604	10.44652	10.76166	10.68174	10.64169	10.95983	10.87890	10.83838
22	10.19389	10.12142	10.08511	10.39147	10.31802	10.28123	10.59050	10.51614	10.47892	10.79095	10.71576	10.67814
23	10.03719	9.96952	9.93564	10.23695	10.16846	10.13418	10.43819	10.36894	10.33431	10.64086	10.57094	10.53598
24	9.89698	9.83373	9.80209	10.09887	10.03494	10.00298	10.30226	10.23772	10.20546	10.50709	10.44201	10.40951
25	9.77117	9.71201	9.68244	9.97515	9.91543	9.88560	10.18063	10.12043	10.09037	10.38757	10.32696	10.29672
26	9.65802	9.60264	9.57499	9.86402	9.80821	9.78035	10.07154	10.01536	9.98734	10.28052	10.22404	10.19589
27	9.55603	9.50417	9.47829	9.76400	9.71181	9.68578	9.97349	9.92104	9.89490	10.18446	10.13180	10.10558
28	9.46391	9.41533	9.39110	9.67380	9.62498	9.60065	9.88520	9.83621	9.81182	10.09808	10.04898	10.02455
29	9.38058	9.33503	9.31234	9.59232	9.54662	9.52388	9.80557	9.75979	9.73702	10.02030	9.97449	9.95173
30	9.30506	9.26236	9.24110	9.51859	9.47582	9.45454	9.73364	9.69085	9.66959	9.95014	9.90740	9.88619

Entry is annual mortgage constant in percent of loan amount.

Annual Mortgage Constant for Annual, Semiannual & Quarterly Payments

Term of Loan Years	Interest Rate 9.50% annual	semiannual	quarterly	9.75% annual	semiannual	quarterly	10.00% annual	semiannual	quarterly	10.25% annual	semiannual	quarterly
1	109.50000	107.18010	106.00717	109.75000	107.37050	106.16711	110.00000	107.56098	106.32715	110.25000	107.75152	106.48728
2	57.23270	56.07518	55.49000	57.42580	56.23869	55.63837	57.61905	56.40237	55.78694	57.81243	56.56623	55.93570
3	39.85800	39.08902	38.70031	40.03462	39.24612	38.84743	40.21148	39.40349	38.99485	40.38858	39.56115	39.14257
4	31.20630	30.63239	30.34233	31.37652	30.78819	30.49077	31.54708	30.94436	30.63960	31.71797	31.10091	30.78882
5	26.04364	25.58740	25.35686	26.21148	25.74392	25.50761	26.37975	25.90091	25.65885	26.54844	26.05838	25.81058
6	22.62533	22.24804	22.05744	22.79278	22.40628	22.21099	22.96074	22.56508	22.36513	23.12921	22.72444	22.51984
7	20.20360	19.88313	19.72129	20.37178	20.04364	19.87790	20.54055	20.20479	20.03517	20.70991	20.36659	20.19312
8	18.40456	18.12706	17.98697	18.57414	18.29016	18.14677	18.74440	18.45398	18.30732	18.91533	18.61853	18.46863
9	17.02045	16.77669	16.65367	17.19188	16.94256	16.81673	17.36405	17.10924	16.98063	17.53698	17.27673	17.14536
10	15.92662	15.71009	15.60088	16.10017	15.87886	15.76723	16.27454	16.04852	15.93449	16.44973	16.21905	16.10267
11	15.04369	14.84969	14.75189	15.21956	15.02142	14.92152	15.39631	15.19410	15.09215	15.57395	15.36773	15.26375
12	14.31877	14.14373	14.05554	14.49707	14.31845	14.22844	14.67633	14.49418	14.40240	14.85653	14.67093	14.57740
13	13.71521	13.55638	13.47640	13.89602	13.73408	13.65254	14.07785	13.91286	13.82979	14.26069	14.09272	14.00814
14	13.20681	13.06203	12.98917	13.39018	13.24270	13.16848	13.57462	13.42451	13.34897	13.76012	13.60744	13.53062
15	12.77437	12.64189	12.57526	12.96031	12.82549	12.75770	13.14738	13.01029	12.94136	13.33554	13.19626	13.12623
16	12.40347	12.28186	12.22074	12.59198	12.46835	12.40623	12.78166	12.65608	12.59299	12.97249	12.84503	12.78102
17	12.08308	11.97115	11.91494	12.27414	12.16048	12.10341	12.46641	12.35109	12.29320	12.65987	12.54296	12.48429
18	11.80461	11.70136	11.64955	11.99820	11.89347	11.84093	12.19302	12.08689	12.03367	12.38906	12.28160	12.22773
19	11.56128	11.46586	11.41802	11.75735	11.66068	11.61223	11.95469	11.85685	11.80782	12.15327	12.05432	12.00477
20	11.34767	11.25935	11.21510	11.54617	11.45681	11.41206	11.74596	11.65563	11.61042	11.94702	11.85580	11.81015
21	11.15937	11.07751	11.03654	11.36025	11.27754	11.23616	11.56244	11.47894	11.43719	11.76592	11.68171	11.63962
22	10.99278	10.91684	10.87886	11.19598	11.11934	11.08104	11.40051	11.32325	11.28466	11.60633	11.52853	11.48969
23	10.84494	10.77441	10.73917	11.05039	10.97932	10.94383	11.25718	11.18564	11.14995	11.46528	11.39334	11.35747
24	10.71335	10.64780	10.61508	10.92099	10.85504	10.82214	11.12998	11.06369	11.03065	11.34028	11.27371	11.24056
25	10.59594	10.53498	10.50459	10.80570	10.74446	10.71395	11.01681	10.95535	10.92475	11.22923	11.16761	11.13697
26	10.49094	10.43422	10.40597	10.70275	10.64586	10.61754	10.91590	10.85890	10.83056	11.13037	11.07331	11.04497
27	10.39685	10.34406	10.31779	10.61064	10.55717	10.53149	10.82576	10.77288	10.74661	11.04220	10.98935	10.96313
28	10.31239	10.26324	10.23881	10.52808	10.47893	10.45453	10.74510	10.69602	10.67168	10.96342	10.91445	10.89020
29	10.23644	10.19067	10.16794	10.45396	10.40827	10.38561	10.67281	10.62725	10.60469	10.89293	10.84756	10.82512
30	10.16806	10.12542	10.10428	10.38734	10.34485	10.32380	10.60792	10.56564	10.54472	10.82978	10.78774	10.76697

Term of Loan Years	Interest Rate 10.50% annual	semiannual	quarterly	10.75% annual	semiannual	quarterly	11.00% annual	semiannual	quarterly	11.25% annual	semiannual	quarterly
1	110.50000	107.94214	106.64751	110.75000	108.13284	106.80782	111.00000	108.32360	106.96824	111.25000	108.51444	107.12874
2	58.00594	56.73027	56.08467	58.19958	56.89449	56.23382	58.39336	57.05890	56.38318	58.58728	57.22348	56.53273
3	40.56592	39.71908	39.29058	40.74350	39.87730	39.43888	40.92131	40.03579	39.58748	41.09935	40.19456	39.73638
4	31.88920	31.25784	30.93843	32.06075	31.41513	31.08844	32.23264	31.57280	31.23884	32.40485	31.73084	31.38963
5	26.71755	26.21630	25.96280	26.88708	26.37470	26.11550	27.05703	26.53355	26.26869	27.22740	26.69287	26.42237
6	23.29819	22.88436	22.67514	23.46767	23.04483	22.83101	23.63766	23.20585	22.98745	23.80814	23.36742	23.14447
7	20.87987	20.52903	20.35173	21.05041	20.69211	20.51101	21.22153	20.85582	20.67095	21.39323	21.02017	20.83155
8	19.08693	18.78381	18.63069	19.25919	18.94980	18.79350	19.43211	19.11651	18.95705	19.60568	19.28393	19.12135
9	17.71064	17.44502	17.31093	17.88504	17.61411	17.47732	18.06017	17.78398	17.64453	18.23602	17.95465	17.81256
10	16.62573	16.39046	16.27175	16.80254	16.56273	16.44173	16.98014	16.73587	16.61261	17.15854	16.90966	16.78437
11	15.75247	15.54231	15.43634	15.93186	15.71781	15.60989	16.11210	15.89425	15.78440	16.29320	16.07160	15.95987
12	15.03767	14.84868	14.75345	15.21974	15.02743	14.93053	15.40273	15.20716	15.10863	15.58662	15.38787	15.28775
13	14.44451	14.27363	14.18760	14.62932	14.45560	14.36815	14.81510	14.63861	14.54978	15.00184	14.82266	14.73247
14	13.94666	13.79149	13.71343	14.13423	13.97664	13.89737	14.32282	14.16288	14.08245	14.51242	14.35020	14.26864
15	13.52480	13.38339	13.31231	13.71513	13.57167	13.49957	13.90652	13.76108	13.68801	14.09896	13.95161	13.87760
16	13.16444	13.03519	12.97028	13.35751	13.22653	13.16077	13.55167	13.41904	13.35247	13.74692	13.61270	13.54537
17	12.85449	12.73606	12.67665	13.05025	12.93039	12.87028	13.24715	13.12592	13.06514	13.44516	13.32263	13.26123
18	12.58630	12.47758	12.42310	12.78472	12.67481	12.61976	12.98429	12.87327	12.81768	13.18499	13.07293	13.01685
19	12.35307	12.25310	12.20305	12.55407	12.45314	12.40264	12.75625	12.65443	12.60351	12.95959	12.85695	12.80565
20	12.14933	12.05727	12.01124	12.35285	12.26004	12.21366	12.55756	12.46407	12.41737	12.76345	12.66934	12.62236
21	11.97065	11.88580	11.84342	12.17662	12.09119	12.04855	12.38379	12.29785	12.25499	12.59214	12.50576	12.46270
22	11.81343	11.73514	11.69608	12.02176	11.94306	11.90382	12.23131	12.15226	12.11287	12.44204	12.36270	12.32321
23	11.67466	11.60238	11.56636	11.88528	11.81273	11.77660	12.09712	12.02435	11.98815	12.31014	12.23722	12.20098
24	11.55186	11.48508	11.45186	11.76468	11.69776	11.66449	11.97872	11.91171	11.87842	12.19394	12.12689	12.09362
25	11.44293	11.38122	11.35055	11.65787	11.59612	11.56546	11.87402	11.81229	11.78167	12.09134	12.02968	11.99913
26	11.34611	11.28906	11.26074	11.56309	11.50609	11.47783	11.78126	11.72437	11.69620	12.00059	11.94387	11.91581
27	11.25989	11.20713	11.18099	11.47881	11.42619	11.40015	11.69892	11.64649	11.62057	11.92016	11.86798	11.84221
28	11.18299	11.13419	11.11004	11.40377	11.35519	11.33117	11.62571	11.57740	11.55354	11.84879	11.80077	11.77710
29	11.11429	11.06916	11.04685	11.33685	11.29199	11.26985	11.56055	11.51601	11.49406	11.78536	11.74118	11.71944
30	11.05285	11.01110	10.99050	11.27709	11.23567	11.21526	11.50246	11.46141	11.44122	11.72891	11.68828	11.66831

Entry is annual mortgage constant in percent of loan amount.

Annual Mortgage Constant for Annual, Semiannual & Quarterly Payments

Term of Loan Years	11.50% annual	11.50% semiannual	11.50% quarterly	11.75% annual	11.75% semiannual	11.75% quarterly	12.00% annual	12.00% semiannual	12.00% quarterly	12.25% annual	12.25% semiannual	12.25% quarterly
1	111.50000	108.70535	107.28934	111.75000	108.89633	107.45003	112.00000	109.08738	107.61082	112.25000	109.27850	107.77170
2	58.78132	57.38824	56.68248	58.97550	57.55318	56.83242	59.16981	57.71830	56.98256	59.36425	57.88359	57.13289
3	41.27764	40.35361	39.88557	41.45615	40.51293	40.03506	41.63490	40.67253	40.18483	41.81388	40.83240	40.33491
4	32.57739	31.88926	31.54081	32.75025	32.04804	31.69238	32.92344	32.20719	31.84434	33.09696	32.36671	31.99669
5	27.39818	26.85265	26.57652	27.56937	27.01289	26.73116	27.74097	27.17359	26.88628	27.91299	27.33475	27.04188
6	23.97912	23.52953	23.30207	24.15060	23.69220	23.46023	24.32257	23.85541	23.61897	24.49503	24.01916	23.77827
7	21.56550	21.18515	20.99281	21.73835	21.35075	21.15473	21.91177	21.51698	21.31729	22.08576	21.68383	21.48051
8	19.77990	19.45206	19.28638	19.95477	19.62089	19.45215	20.13028	19.79043	19.61865	20.30643	19.96066	19.78588
9	18.41260	18.12609	17.98140	18.58989	18.29831	18.15106	18.76789	18.47131	18.32152	18.94659	18.64507	18.49278
10	17.33772	17.08470	16.95702	17.51768	17.26039	17.13055	17.69842	17.43691	17.30495	17.87992	17.61427	17.48022
11	16.47514	16.24987	16.13629	16.65793	16.42904	16.31365	16.84154	16.60911	16.49194	17.02598	16.79008	16.67116
12	15.77142	15.56956	15.46787	15.95711	15.75220	15.64900	16.14368	15.93580	15.83111	16.33113	16.12034	16.01420
13	15.18953	15.00772	14.91623	15.37816	15.19379	15.10103	15.56772	15.38087	15.28687	15.75820	15.56893	15.47374
14	14.70301	14.53859	14.45593	14.89458	14.72803	14.64432	15.08712	14.91851	14.83379	15.28063	15.11002	15.02432
15	14.29244	14.14325	14.06834	14.48693	14.33598	14.26020	14.68242	14.52978	14.45318	14.87891	14.72465	14.64727
16	13.94324	13.80751	13.73944	14.14060	14.00343	13.93467	14.33900	14.20047	14.13104	14.53842	14.39859	14.32854
17	13.64426	13.52051	13.45852	13.84444	13.71953	13.65699	14.04567	13.91969	13.85663	14.24795	14.12095	14.05742
18	13.38682	13.27379	13.21724	13.58974	13.47580	13.41884	13.79373	13.67897	13.62162	13.99878	13.88325	13.82556
19	13.16405	13.06067	13.00902	13.36963	13.26557	13.21361	13.57630	13.47162	13.41940	13.78404	13.67881	13.62635
20	12.97048	12.87581	12.82859	13.17863	13.08348	13.03605	13.38788	13.29231	13.24470	13.59820	13.50227	13.45452
21	12.80165	12.71489	12.67167	13.01228	12.92521	12.88187	13.22401	13.13668	13.09325	13.43681	13.34930	13.30581
22	12.65393	12.57436	12.53479	12.86694	12.78721	12.74758	13.08105	13.00121	12.96157	13.29623	13.21635	13.17672
23	12.52431	12.45130	12.41504	12.73961	12.66656	12.63032	12.95600	12.88297	12.84678	13.17345	13.10050	13.06438
24	12.41030	12.34328	12.31006	12.62778	12.56084	12.52768	12.84634	12.77953	12.74648	13.06596	12.99933	12.96640
25	12.30980	12.24827	12.21781	12.52936	12.46800	12.43767	12.75000	12.68886	12.65867	12.97167	12.91080	12.88078
26	12.22104	12.16453	12.13661	12.44259	12.38633	12.35857	12.66519	12.60923	12.58166	12.88880	12.83320	12.80582
27	12.14252	12.09062	12.06502	12.36595	12.31437	12.28897	12.59041	12.53920	12.51402	12.81587	12.76507	12.74012
28	12.07295	12.02528	12.00182	12.29816	12.25088	12.22764	12.52439	12.47753	12.45453	12.75159	12.70519	12.68244
29	12.01123	11.96746	11.94594	12.23813	12.19479	12.17352	12.46602	12.42315	12.40214	12.69486	12.65248	12.63176
30	11.95641	11.91621	11.89649	12.18491	12.14518	12.12573	12.41437	12.37514	12.35597	12.64475	12.60605	12.58717

Term of Loan Years	12.50% annual	12.50% semiannual	12.50% quarterly	13.00% annual	13.00% semiannual	13.00% quarterly	15.00% annual	15.00% semiannual	15.00% quarterly	18.00% annual	18.00% semiannual	18.00% quarterly
1	112.50000	109.46970	107.93267	113.00000	109.85230	108.25489	115.00000	111.38554	109.54750	118.00000	113.69378	111.49746
2	59.55882	58.04907	57.28342	59.94836	58.38055	57.58505	61.51163	59.71350	58.79936	63.87156	61.73373	60.64386
3	41.99309	40.99255	40.48527	42.35220	41.31366	40.78688	43.79770	42.60898	42.00492	45.99239	44.58396	43.86648
4	33.27079	32.52659	32.14942	33.61942	32.84746	32.45605	35.02654	34.14540	33.69793	37.17387	36.13488	35.60615
5	28.08540	27.49636	27.19796	28.43145	27.82094	27.51155	29.83156	29.13719	28.78484	31.97778	31.16402	30.75046
6	24.66798	24.18344	23.93814	25.01532	24.51363	24.25956	26.42369	25.85557	25.56756	28.59101	27.93013	27.59481
7	22.26031	21.85131	21.64428	22.61108	22.18810	21.97405	24.03604	23.55947	23.31816	26.23620	25.68663	25.40832
8	20.48322	20.13159	19.95383	20.83867	20.47551	20.29190	22.28501	21.87823	21.67252	24.52444	24.05998	23.82528
9	19.12600	18.81960	18.66484	19.48689	19.17092	19.01133	20.95740	20.60579	20.42824	23.23948	22.84246	22.64231
10	18.06218	17.79245	17.65635	18.42896	18.15128	18.01118	19.92521	19.61844	19.46378	22.25146	21.90930	21.73726
11	17.21123	16.97192	16.85130	17.58415	17.33824	17.21432	19.10690	18.83737	18.70173	21.47764	21.18100	21.03228
12	16.51943	16.30582	16.19827	16.89861	16.67954	16.56928	18.44808	18.21002	18.09044	20.86278	20.60451	20.47543
13	15.94958	15.75798	15.66163	16.33503	16.13896	16.04041	17.91005	17.69992	17.59549	20.36862	20.14307	20.03072
14	15.47507	15.30255	15.21592	15.86675	15.69061	15.60221	17.46885	17.28104	17.18710	19.96781	19.77041	19.67242
15	15.07638	14.92057	14.84243	15.47418	15.31549	15.23597	17.10171	16.93425	16.85068	19.64028	19.46727	19.38170
16	14.73884	14.59778	14.52716	15.14262	14.99933	14.92765	16.79477	16.64520	16.57074	19.37101	19.21924	19.14446
17	14.45125	14.32331	14.25934	14.86084	14.73122	14.66649	16.53669	16.40292	16.33650	19.14853	19.01532	18.94995
18	14.20487	14.08865	14.03064	14.62009	14.50266	14.44413	16.31863	16.19889	16.13959	18.96395	18.84701	18.78986
19	13.99282	13.88711	13.83444	14.41344	14.30696	14.25398	16.13364	16.02639	15.97342	18.81028	18.70764	18.65769
20	13.80957	13.71335	13.66549	14.23538	14.13875	14.09076	15.97615	15.88006	15.83274	18.68200	18.59192	18.54828
21	13.65067	13.56302	13.51950	14.08143	13.99368	13.95020	15.84168	15.75558	15.71329	18.57464	18.49563	18.45751
22	13.51246	13.43258	13.39300	13.94795	13.86824	13.82882	15.72658	15.64942	15.61164	18.48463	18.41535	18.38209
23	13.39194	13.31911	13.28310	13.83191	13.75949	13.72375	15.62784	15.55871	15.52496	18.40902	18.34832	18.31931
24	13.28660	13.22019	13.18742	13.73083	13.66501	13.63261	15.54298	15.48105	15.45092	18.34543	18.29228	18.26700
25	13.19434	13.13379	13.10396	13.64259	13.58279	13.55340	15.46994	15.41448	15.38758	18.29188	18.24537	18.22336
26	13.11341	13.05818	13.03104	13.56545	13.51111	13.48447	15.40698	15.35734	15.33333	18.24675	18.20608	18.18692
27	13.04230	12.99194	12.96724	13.49791	13.44853	13.42439	15.35265	15.30822	15.28681	18.20867	18.17314	18.15648
28	12.97973	12.93382	12.91135	13.43869	13.39385	13.37197	15.30571	15.26598	15.24690	18.17653	18.14551	18.13104
29	12.92461	12.88276	12.86233	13.38672	13.34600	13.32618	15.26513	15.22961	15.21261	18.14938	18.12231	18.10975
30	12.87602	12.83788	12.81929	13.34107	13.30409	13.28615	15.23002	15.19828	15.18314	18.12643	18.10284	18.09195

Entry is annual mortgage constant in percent of loan amount.

Annual Mortgage Constant, Payments In Advance
Annual Rent Constant

Year	Interest Rate 5.50%				Interest Rate 5.75%			
	Monthly Arrears	Monthly Advance	Quarterly Advance	Semiannual Advance	Monthly Arrears	Monthly Advance	Quarterly Advance	Semiannual Advance
1	103.004141	102.534193	102.057678	101.356350	103.141877	102.650013	102.150974	101.417129
2	52.914787	52.673368	52.422225	52.052669	53.049657	52.796673	52.533057	52.145487
3	36.235082	36.069762	35.893519	35.634224	36.370549	36.197105	36.011706	35.739186
4	27.907770	27.780443	27.641480	27.437070	28.044697	27.910957	27.764474	27.549199
5	22.921395	22.816818	22.700088	22.528413	23.060122	22.950152	22.826866	22.645713
6	19.605465	19.516016	19.413998	19.263982	19.746158	19.651993	19.544043	19.385454
7	17.244051	17.165377	17.073771	16.939088	17.386802	17.303888	17.206785	17.064154
8	15.479187	15.408564	15.324686	15.201382	15.624046	15.549538	15.460476	15.329677
9	14.111996	14.047612	13.969670	13.855110	14.258995	14.190996	14.108105	13.986387
10	13.023153	12.963736	12.890479	12.782819	13.172306	13.109490	13.031461	12.916901
11	12.136719	12.081346	12.011863	11.909763	12.288034	12.229434	12.155318	12.046516
12	11.402066	11.350045	11.283654	11.186109	11.555542	11.500436	11.429519	11.325428
13	10.784142	10.734940	10.671117	10.577355	10.939776	10.887606	10.819341	10.719156
14	10.257908	10.211108	10.149440	10.058857	10.415691	10.366020	10.299978	10.203068
15	9.805001	9.760267	9.700428	9.612539	9.964921	9.917400	9.853239	9.759098
16	9.411647	9.368707	9.310429	9.224843	9.573690	9.528034	9.465475	9.373696
17	9.067310	9.025941	8.969006	8.885401	9.231460	9.187437	9.126252	9.036498
18	8.763796	8.723812	8.668038	8.586145	8.930035	8.887449	8.827449	8.739443
19	8.494635	8.455879	8.401113	8.320708	8.662942	8.621630	8.562656	8.476163
20	8.254648	8.216987	8.163100	8.083993	8.425002	8.384825	8.326743	8.241566
21	8.039643	8.002963	7.949845	7.871874	8.212022	8.172860	8.115555	8.031525
22	7.846189	7.810392	7.757949	7.680974	8.020569	7.982320	7.925694	7.842667
23	7.671452	7.636452	7.584601	7.508502	7.847807	7.810382	7.754350	7.672200
24	7.513067	7.478790	7.427461	7.352133	7.691372	7.654693	7.599182	7.517800
25	7.369050	7.335429	7.284560	7.209911	7.549277	7.513276	7.458220	7.377514
26	7.237719	7.204697	7.154233	7.080184	7.419840	7.384456	7.329801	7.249686
27	7.117641	7.085168	7.035061	6.961540	7.301629	7.266809	7.212503	7.132907
28	7.007590	6.975618	6.925826	6.852772	7.193414	7.159109	7.105111	7.025970
29	6.906505	6.874994	6.825480	6.752837	7.094135	7.060304	7.006575	6.927831
30	6.813468	6.782382	6.733112	6.660831	7.002874	6.969479	6.915983	6.837587
35	6.444195	6.414794	6.366357	6.295315	6.642009	6.610334	6.557615	6.480375
40	6.189243	6.161005	6.112965	6.042516	6.394652	6.364157	6.311773	6.235038

Year	Interest Rate 6.00%				Interest Rate 6.25%			
1	103.279716	102.765886	102.244251	101.477833	103.417657	102.881814	102.337506	101.538462
2	53.184732	52.920132	52.643951	52.238261	53.320014	53.043744	52.754904	52.330991
3	36.506325	36.324701	36.130046	35.844175	36.642410	36.452553	36.248539	35.949190
4	28.182035	28.041826	27.887715	27.661435	28.319784	28.173049	28.011202	27.773777
5	23.199362	23.083942	22.953985	22.763205	23.339114	23.218186	23.081442	22.880886
6	19.887465	19.788523	19.674523	19.507201	20.029385	19.925606	19.805435	19.629222
7	17.530265	17.443050	17.340326	17.189580	17.674440	17.582862	17.474391	17.315364
8	15.769716	15.691260	15.596886	15.458417	15.916194	15.833727	15.733911	15.587599
9	14.406900	14.335223	14.247249	14.118193	14.555708	14.480290	14.387099	14.250523
10	13.322460	13.256179	13.173242	13.051594	13.473612	13.403800	13.315816	13.186891
11	12.440442	12.378549	12.299657	12.183960	12.593939	12.528685	12.444876	12.322089
12	11.710203	11.651943	11.576355	11.465518	11.866041	11.804559	11.724153	11.606369
13	11.096681	11.041474	10.968619	10.861804	11.254852	11.196537	11.118941	11.005289
14	10.574831	10.522220	10.451651	10.348201	10.735321	10.679698	10.604446	10.494244
15	10.126282	10.075902	10.007262	9.906652	10.289074	10.235763	10.162485	10.055188
16	9.737254	9.688810	9.621810	9.523615	9.902330	9.851022	9.779418	9.674584
17	9.397209	9.350457	9.284859	9.188731	9.564545	9.514988	9.444811	9.342079
18	9.097948	9.052684	8.988292	8.893941	9.267520	9.219502	9.150548	9.049618
19	8.832996	8.789051	8.725699	8.632882	9.004779	8.958122	8.890220	8.790840
20	8.597173	8.554401	8.491950	8.400462	8.771138	8.725692	8.658697	8.560655
21	8.386283	8.344560	8.282892	8.192558	8.562402	8.518038	8.451827	8.354942
22	8.196893	8.156113	8.095125	8.005796	8.375136	8.331741	8.266210	8.170328
23	8.026166	7.986235	7.925840	7.837386	8.206500	8.163979	8.099037	8.004024
24	7.871737	7.832574	7.772695	7.685005	8.054128	8.012397	7.947965	7.853706
25	7.731617	7.693151	7.633723	7.546698	7.916033	7.875017	7.811027	7.717422
26	7.604124	7.566292	7.507256	7.420812	7.790529	7.750164	7.686556	7.593517
27	7.487824	7.450571	7.391877	7.305939	7.676183	7.636410	7.573133	7.480584
28	7.381488	7.344764	7.286367	7.200868	7.571765	7.532533	7.469541	7.377414
29	7.284055	7.247816	7.189676	7.104560	7.476212	7.437475	7.374728	7.282964
30	7.194606	7.158812	7.100895	7.016108	7.388606	7.350323	7.287785	7.196332
35	6.842276	6.808235	6.751030	6.667306	7.044918	7.008416	6.946518	6.856023
40	6.602564	6.569715	6.512780	6.429465	6.812875	6.777575	6.715879	6.625692

Annual Mortgage Constant, Payments In Advance
Annual Rent Constant

	Interest Rate 6.50%				Interest Rate 6.75%			
Year	Monthly Arrears	Monthly Advance	Quarterly Advance	Semiannual Advance	Monthly Arrears	Monthly Advance	Quarterly Advance	Semiannual Advance
1	103.555700	102.997796	102.430741	101.599016	103.693847	103.113831	102.523954	101.659496
2	53.455502	53.167511	52.865919	52.423677	53.591195	53.291431	52.976993	52.516319
3	36.778803	36.580658	36.367183	36.054231	36.915506	36.709017	36.485978	36.159298
4	28.457944	28.304627	28.134933	27.886224	28.596514	28.436558	28.258908	27.998776
5	23.479378	23.352883	23.209238	22.998755	23.620153	23.488033	23.337370	23.116809
6	20.171916	20.063240	19.936778	19.751513	20.315057	20.201424	20.068549	19.874073
7	17.819324	17.723322	17.608979	17.441502	17.964916	17.864429	17.744087	17.567991
8	16.063479	15.976937	15.871548	15.717217	16.211568	16.120888	16.009795	15.847267
9	14.705418	14.626193	14.527650	14.383370	14.856027	14.772929	14.668897	14.516730
10	13.625757	13.552349	13.459177	13.322786	13.778894	13.701821	13.603321	13.459273
11	12.748521	12.679838	12.590967	12.460893	12.904183	12.832003	12.737924	12.600365
12	12.023053	11.958279	11.872906	11.747972	12.181232	12.113096	12.022606	11.890318
13	11.414282	11.352788	11.270297	11.149600	11.574964	11.510219	11.422680	11.294726
14	10.897153	10.838445	10.758354	10.641185	11.060318	10.998451	10.913364	10.789011
15	10.453288	10.396971	10.318896	10.204691	10.618914	10.559516	10.476481	10.355146
16	10.068903	10.014657	9.938285	9.826587	10.236963	10.179702	10.098397	9.979606
17	9.733453	9.681014	9.606091	9.496525	9.903919	9.848521	9.768682	9.652048
18	9.438735	9.387884	9.314198	9.206453	9.611576	9.557814	9.479222	9.364424
19	9.178272	9.128824	9.056197	8.950014	9.353455	9.301136	9.223609	9.110379
20	8.946878	8.898676	8.826961	8.722119	9.124368	9.073331	8.996714	8.884827
21	8.740355	8.693267	8.622335	8.518649	8.920116	8.870221	8.794385	8.683648
22	8.555268	8.509177	8.438920	8.336231	8.737262	8.688390	8.613222	8.503471
23	8.388776	8.343582	8.273907	8.172077	8.572964	8.525011	8.450415	8.341510
24	8.238512	8.194127	8.124954	8.023865	8.424853	8.377728	8.303623	8.195442
25	8.102486	8.058834	7.990092	7.889642	8.290938	8.244563	8.170876	8.063315
26	7.979014	7.936027	7.867655	7.767754	8.169535	8.123839	8.050509	7.943475
27	7.866660	7.824278	7.756224	7.656793	8.059207	8.014128	7.941100	7.834515
28	7.764193	7.722364	7.654580	7.555551	7.958723	7.914205	7.841433	7.735227
29	7.670552	7.629227	7.561674	7.462986	7.867020	7.823015	7.750456	7.644568
30	7.584816	7.543953	7.476594	7.378195	7.783177	7.739642	7.667260	7.561636
35	7.249852	7.210793	7.143998	7.046444	7.456998	7.415287	7.343386	7.238486
40	7.025482	6.987632	6.920965	6.823613	7.240282	7.199783	7.127935	7.023127

	Interest Rate 7.00%				Interest Rate 7.25%			
1	103.832095	103.229921	102.617147	101.719902	103.970447	103.346064	102.710318	101.780233
2	53.727095	53.415504	53.088127	52.608916	53.863200	53.539731	53.199321	52.701468
3	37.052516	36.837630	36.604923	36.264388	37.189835	36.966496	36.724018	36.369502
4	28.735494	28.568842	28.383126	28.111429	28.874883	28.701479	28.507585	28.224184
5	23.761438	23.623634	23.465838	23.235047	23.903234	23.759686	23.594638	23.353467
6	20.458808	20.340157	20.200747	19.996898	20.603167	20.479437	20.333370	20.119987
7	18.111216	18.006180	17.879711	17.694827	18.258221	18.148574	18.015849	17.822006
8	16.360460	16.265578	16.148647	15.977745	16.510153	16.411003	16.288102	16.108646
9	15.007532	14.920496	14.810837	14.650597	15.159930	15.068889	14.953465	14.784966
10	13.933018	13.852213	13.748242	13.596343	14.088125	14.003520	13.893935	13.733992
11	13.060921	12.985174	12.885741	12.740497	13.218730	13.139347	13.034410	12.881282
12	12.340573	12.269004	12.173246	12.033397	12.501070	12.425996	12.324817	12.177200
13	11.736890	11.668822	11.576079	11.440656	11.900053	11.828588	11.730485	11.587379
14	11.224807	11.159708	11.069464	10.937709	11.390610	11.322205	11.226642	11.087266
15	10.785939	10.723386	10.635227	10.506538	10.954355	10.888569	10.795122	10.658851
16	10.406496	10.346144	10.259738	10.133624	10.577490	10.513968	10.422292	10.288624
17	10.075928	10.017492	9.932567	9.808630	10.249464	10.187912	10.097726	9.966250
18	9.786026	9.729272	9.645601	9.523510	9.962067	9.902241	9.813313	9.683688
19	9.530309	9.475037	9.392432	9.271911	9.708812	9.650507	9.562644	9.434586
20	9.303587	9.249631	9.167934	9.048750	9.484512	9.427554	9.340592	9.213863
21	9.101661	9.048875	8.967951	8.849909	9.284961	9.229202	9.143004	9.017401
22	8.921089	8.869351	8.789086	8.672016	9.106720	9.052031	8.966480	8.841831
23	8.759031	8.708233	8.628528	8.512286	8.946944	8.893214	8.808210	8.684369
24	8.613115	8.563163	8.483935	8.368398	8.803263	8.750396	8.665851	8.542691
25	8.481350	8.432163	8.353338	8.238398	8.673682	8.621594	8.537435	8.414848
26	8.362051	8.313555	8.235070	8.120635	8.556517	8.505132	8.421295	8.299186
27	8.253779	8.205911	8.127712	8.013700	8.450328	8.399580	8.316011	8.194297
28	8.155303	8.108007	8.030045	7.916386	8.353883	8.303715	8.220363	8.098975
29	8.065561	8.018784	7.941018	7.827652	8.266120	8.216478	8.133303	8.012179
30	7.983630	7.937329	7.859722	7.746593	8.186115	8.136955	8.053919	7.933005
35	7.666276	7.621816	7.544601	7.432068	7.877607	7.830299	7.747563	7.627109
40	7.457175	7.413927	7.336688	7.224133	7.676063	7.629965	7.547125	7.426534

Annual Mortgage Constant, Payments In Advance
Annual Rent Constant

Year	Interest Rate 7.50%				Interest Rate 7.75%			
	Monthly Arrears	Monthly Advance	Quarterly Advance	Semiannual Advance	Monthly Arrears	Monthly Advance	Quarterly Advance	Semiannual Advance
1	104.108900	103.462261	102.803469	101.840491	104.247456	103.578512	102.896599	101.900674
2	53.999511	53.664110	53.310573	52.793976	54.136028	53.788643	53.421885	52.886438
3	37.327462	37.095614	36.843262	36.474640	37.465396	37.224985	36.962655	36.579800
4	29.014682	28.834467	28.632285	28.337039	29.154890	28.967807	28.757224	28.449993
5	24.045538	23.896187	23.723771	23.472066	24.188352	24.033138	23.853234	23.590843
6	20.748135	20.619264	20.466415	20.243335	20.893709	20.759636	20.599880	20.366941
7	18.405931	18.291608	18.152499	17.949526	18.554343	18.435282	18.289658	18.077382
8	16.660645	16.557162	16.428155	16.239967	16.811933	16.704052	16.568803	16.371701
9	15.313219	15.218106	15.096777	14.919830	15.467396	15.368144	15.240767	15.055185
10	14.244212	14.155739	14.040394	13.872212	14.401276	14.308864	14.187613	14.010995
11	13.377606	13.294515	13.183925	13.022709	13.537543	13.450674	13.334280	13.164773
12	12.662716	12.584065	12.477311	12.321716	12.825505	12.743205	12.630719	12.466937
13	12.064445	11.989511	11.885887	11.734883	12.230059	12.151580	12.042276	11.883156
14	11.557720	11.485933	11.384888	11.237668	11.726126	11.650881	11.544190	11.388903
15	11.124148	11.055054	10.956150	10.812072	11.295309	11.222828	11.118299	10.966184
16	10.749931	10.683161	10.586044	10.444590	10.923806	10.853709	10.750978	10.601502
17	10.424513	10.359764	10.264144	10.124890	10.601057	10.533032	10.431801	10.284530
18	10.139680	10.076701	9.982339	9.844936	10.318848	10.252633	10.152657	10.007232
19	9.888946	9.827524	9.734221	9.598378	10.070688	10.006065	9.907141	9.763263
20	9.667118	9.607074	9.514664	9.380136	9.851383	9.788168	9.690124	9.547543
21	9.469992	9.411172	9.319514	9.186094	9.656726	9.594760	9.497452	9.355958
22	9.294125	9.236397	9.145371	9.012884	9.483273	9.422420	9.325727	9.185140
23	9.136671	9.079922	8.989425	8.857721	9.328178	9.268320	9.172137	9.032306
24	8.995259	8.939388	8.849333	8.718283	9.189067	9.130102	9.034340	8.895133
25	8.867894	8.812814	8.723126	8.592620	9.063945	9.005783	8.910366	8.771673
26	8.752889	8.698524	8.609137	8.479080	8.951124	8.893686	8.798549	8.660273
27	8.648806	8.595087	8.505946	8.376256	8.849165	8.792381	8.697469	8.559526
28	8.554411	8.501278	8.412335	8.282940	8.756835	8.700643	8.605906	8.468227
29	8.468641	8.416041	8.327253	8.198092	8.673069	8.617415	8.522811	8.385334
30	8.390574	8.338459	8.249790	8.120809	8.596947	8.541781	8.447275	8.309946
35	8.090911	8.040657	7.952191	7.823530	8.306111	8.252812	8.158408	8.021254
40	7.896849	7.847800	7.759150	7.630234	8.119438	8.067337	7.972668	7.835142

Year	Interest Rate 8.00%				Interest Rate 8.25%			
1	104.386115	103.694816	102.989707	101.960784	104.524876	103.811174	103.082794	102.020821
2	54.272750	53.913328	53.533255	52.978855	54.409677	54.038165	53.644683	53.071226
3	37.603639	37.354608	37.082195	36.684981	37.742188	37.484482	37.201882	36.790184
4	29.295507	29.101497	28.882402	28.563045	29.436532	29.235537	29.007818	28.676192
5	24.331673	24.170536	23.983027	23.709797	24.475502	24.308382	24.113146	23.828925
6	21.039889	20.900552	20.733764	20.490802	21.186673	21.042009	20.868063	20.614916
7	18.703457	18.579593	18.427322	18.205572	18.853271	18.724540	18.565490	18.334091
8	16.964015	16.851671	16.710042	16.503846	17.116890	17.000015	16.851869	16.636396
9	15.622458	15.518998	15.385432	15.191025	15.778401	15.670655	15.530767	15.327344
10	14.559311	14.462892	14.335587	14.150337	14.718315	14.617818	14.484311	14.290228
11	13.698536	13.607817	13.485466	13.307464	13.860580	13.765940	13.637478	13.450774
12	12.989431	12.903408	12.785034	12.612852	13.154487	13.064668	12.940246	12.759452
13	12.396887	12.314788	12.199641	12.032189	12.564920	12.479126	12.357974	12.181967
14	11.895818	11.817038	11.704535	11.540957	12.066787	11.984395	11.865912	11.693816
15	11.467825	11.391879	11.281555	11.121173	11.641684	11.562194	11.445904	11.277022
16	11.099100	11.025596	10.917077	10.759344	11.275801	11.198809	11.084326	10.918098
17	10.779082	10.707697	10.600678	10.445148	10.958570	10.883745	10.770758	10.606727
18	10.499551	10.430018	10.324247	10.170553	10.681772	10.608836	10.497088	10.334878
19	10.254017	10.186109	10.081378	9.929215	10.438910	10.367633	10.256910	10.096210
20	10.037281	9.970809	9.866943	9.716056	10.224788	10.154972	10.045097	9.885646
21	9.845135	9.779936	9.676789	9.526962	10.035193	9.966672	9.857495	9.699074
22	9.674135	9.610068	9.507515	9.358566	9.866679	9.799309	9.690703	9.533128
23	9.521431	9.458375	9.356311	9.208086	9.716396	9.650052	9.541911	9.385026
24	9.384649	9.322499	9.220834	9.073201	9.581969	9.516543	9.408776	9.252448
25	9.261795	9.200458	9.099115	8.951962	9.461402	9.396799	9.289329	9.133444
26	9.151177	9.090574	8.989487	8.842716	9.353004	9.289141	9.181903	9.026364
27	9.051358	8.991416	8.890529	8.744058	9.255337	9.192141	9.085077	8.929802
28	8.961104	8.901759	8.801024	8.654782	9.167165	9.104571	8.997635	8.842553
29	8.879350	8.820546	8.719921	8.573848	9.087427	9.025377	8.918527	8.763578
30	8.805175	8.746862	8.646313	8.500355	9.015199	8.953643	8.846844	8.691977
35	8.523131	8.466686	8.366136	8.220204	8.741894	8.682204	8.575300	8.420307
40	8.343740	8.288484	8.187589	8.041168	8.569666	8.511152	8.403824	8.248226

Annual Mortgage Constant, Payments In Advance
Annual Rent Constant

	Interest Rate	8.50%			Interest Rate	8.75%		
Year	Monthly Arrears	Monthly Advance	Quarterly Advance	Semiannual Advance	Monthly Arrears	Monthly Advance	Quarterly Advance	Semiannual Advance
1	104.663739	103.927585	103.175860	102.080783	104.802704	104.044050	103.268904	102.140673
2	54.546810	54.163154	53.756169	53.163552	54.684148	54.288296	53.867712	53.255832
3	37.881045	37.614608	37.321716	36.895407	38.020209	37.744985	37.441695	37.000650
4	29.577964	29.369927	29.133470	28.789435	29.719804	29.504666	29.259357	28.902772
5	24.619838	24.446674	24.243592	23.948225	24.764679	24.585411	24.374362	24.067695
6	21.334062	21.184008	21.002777	20.739279	21.482052	21.326546	21.137903	20.863890
7	19.003783	18.870119	18.704158	18.462936	19.154991	19.016330	18.843323	18.592104
8	17.270554	17.149082	16.994281	16.769347	17.425006	17.298869	17.137272	16.902695
9	15.935223	15.823143	15.676767	15.464136	16.092921	15.976426	15.823428	15.601396
10	14.878283	14.773636	14.633777	14.430664	15.039210	14.930343	14.783981	14.571636
11	14.023670	13.925035	13.790307	13.594694	14.187800	14.085096	13.943947	13.739217
12	13.320667	13.226976	13.096346	12.906726	13.487963	13.390325	13.253327	13.054665
13	12.734149	12.644584	12.517262	12.332482	12.904568	12.811153	12.677496	12.483719
14	12.239022	12.152939	12.028308	11.847467	12.412514	12.322661	12.191710	12.001897
15	11.816875	11.733761	11.611330	11.433716	11.993384	11.906565	11.777821	11.591240
16	11.453892	11.373331	11.252708	11.077747	11.633360	11.549148	11.422207	11.238271
17	11.139505	11.061155	10.942021	10.769244	11.321870	11.239912	11.114448	10.932681
18	10.865489	10.789067	10.671157	10.500183	11.050685	10.970690	10.846434	10.666445
19	10.625348	10.550614	10.433712	10.264221	10.813305	10.735029	10.611760	10.433225
20	10.413879	10.340633	10.224557	10.056286	10.604529	10.527764	10.405297	10.227947
21	10.226870	10.154940	10.039539	9.872264	10.420140	10.344710	10.222892	10.046502
22	10.060874	9.990111	9.875257	9.708792	10.256689	10.182442	10.061145	9.885525
23	9.913038	9.843315	9.728900	9.563088	10.111324	10.038129	9.917243	9.742236
24	9.780988	9.712193	9.598126	9.432832	9.981668	9.909412	9.788845	9.614315
25	9.662725	9.594762	9.480966	9.316076	9.865724	9.794307	9.673982	9.499816
26	9.556560	9.489344	9.375752	9.211170	9.761800	9.691136	9.570988	9.397089
27	9.461052	9.394508	9.281065	9.116709	9.668458	9.598469	9.478442	9.304729
28	9.374969	9.309030	9.195688	9.031488	9.584462	9.515082	9.395129	9.221534
29	9.297245	9.231853	9.118572	8.954469	9.508752	9.439919	9.320002	9.146466
30	9.226962	9.162064	9.048810	8.884754	9.440405	9.372067	9.252152	9.078627
35	8.962327	8.899290	8.785826	8.621490	9.184358	9.117873	8.997642	8.823683
40	8.797129	8.735254	8.621288	8.456233	9.026046	8.960708	8.839898	8.665107

	Interest Rate	9.00%			Interest Rate	9.25%		
1	104.941772	104.160568	103.361928	102.200489	105.080942	104.277139	103.454929	102.260232
2	54.821691	54.413589	53.979313	53.348067	54.959439	54.539034	54.090970	53.440255
3	38.159679	37.875612	37.561820	37.105911	38.299456	38.006490	37.682089	37.211192
4	29.862051	29.639753	29.385479	29.016202	30.004704	29.775187	29.511834	29.129722
5	24.910026	24.724592	24.505456	24.187334	25.055878	24.864216	24.636870	24.307140
6	21.630645	21.469622	21.273439	20.988744	21.779837	21.613235	21.409383	21.113841
7	19.306894	19.163170	18.982983	18.721592	19.459490	19.310637	19.123135	18.851394
8	17.580244	17.449374	17.280841	17.036434	17.736264	17.600593	17.424982	17.170561
9	16.251490	16.130512	15.970744	15.739119	16.410929	16.285396	16.118711	15.877298
10	15.201093	15.087933	14.934916	14.713138	15.363927	15.246402	15.086576	14.855162
11	14.352965	14.246119	14.098390	13.884334	14.519158	14.408096	14.253629	14.030037
12	13.656368	13.554708	13.411180	13.203259	13.825876	13.720117	13.569894	13.352498
13	13.076166	12.978825	12.838664	12.635668	13.248935	13.147589	13.000757	12.788318
14	12.587250	12.493548	12.356108	12.157092	12.763221	12.665591	12.521486	12.313038
15	12.171199	12.080595	11.945360	11.749578	12.350307	12.255835	12.113935	11.908713
16	11.814190	11.726243	11.592804	11.399655	11.996367	11.904602	11.764485	11.561879
17	11.505647	11.419997	11.288019	11.097017	11.690819	11.601391	11.462717	11.262231
18	11.237338	11.153685	11.022897	10.833642	11.425429	11.338032	11.200523	11.001751
19	11.002761	10.920855	10.791029	10.603195	11.193693	11.108068	10.971496	10.774106
20	10.796711	10.716339	10.587290	10.400602	10.990402	10.906332	10.770508	10.574223
21	10.614972	10.535953	10.407524	10.221756	10.811339	10.728639	10.593405	10.397996
22	10.454092	10.376270	10.248332	10.063293	10.653052	10.571562	10.436787	10.242062
23	10.311218	10.234459	10.106903	9.922433	10.512685	10.432270	10.297844	10.103643
24	10.183972	10.108161	9.980894	9.796858	10.387861	10.308401	10.174234	9.980420
25	10.070356	9.995391	9.868337	9.684621	10.276582	10.197973	10.063987	9.870450
26	9.968681	9.894472	9.767565	9.584075	10.177157	10.099308	9.965439	9.772084
27	9.877505	9.803975	9.677161	9.493816	10.088147	10.010979	9.877173	9.683921
28	9.795596	9.722676	9.595909	9.412641	10.008318	9.931761	9.797975	9.604759
29	9.721891	9.649520	9.522762	9.339516	9.936611	9.860602	9.726797	9.533564
30	9.655471	9.583594	9.456814	9.273542	9.872105	9.796590	9.662737	9.469441
35	9.407916	9.337882	9.210677	9.026816	9.632932	9.559246	9.424863	9.230823
40	9.256338	9.187432	9.059575	8.874774	9.487927	9.415350	9.280242	9.085158

Annual Mortgage Constant, Payments In Advance
Annual Rent Constant

	Interest Rate	9.50%			Interest Rate	9.75%		
Year	Monthly Arrears	Monthly Advance	Quarterly Advance	Semiannual Advance	Monthly Arrears	Monthly Advance	Quarterly Advance	Semiannual Advance
1	105.220214	104.393764	103.547910	102.319902	105.359588	104.510441	103.640869	102.379500
2	55.097392	54.664630	54.202684	53.532396	55.235549	54.790377	54.314455	53.624491
3	38.439540	38.137617	37.802502	37.316490	38.579929	38.268994	37.923058	37.421805
4	30.147764	29.910969	29.638421	29.243334	30.291229	30.047097	29.765240	29.357034
5	25.202234	25.004283	24.768604	24.427110	25.349092	25.144791	24.900657	24.547244
6	21.929629	21.757383	21.545732	21.239176	22.080019	21.902064	21.682484	21.364748
7	19.612778	19.458730	19.263775	18.981509	19.766755	19.607445	19.404901	19.111933
8	17.893065	17.752524	17.569692	17.305071	18.050643	17.905164	17.714968	17.439959
9	16.571233	16.441074	16.267325	16.015929	16.732399	16.597544	16.416579	16.155004
10	15.527707	15.405745	15.238955	14.997703	15.692429	15.565956	15.392048	15.140752
11	14.686375	14.571021	14.409657	14.176316	14.854608	14.734887	14.566465	14.323165
12	13.996479	13.886544	13.729462	13.502371	14.168169	14.053980	13.889873	13.652869
13	13.422866	13.317437	13.163764	12.941655	13.597950	13.488357	13.327673	13.095669
14	12.940416	12.838776	12.687834	12.469721	13.118823	13.013092	12.855138	12.627127
15	12.530696	12.432274	12.283529	12.068631	12.712352	12.609897	12.454127	12.229315
16	12.179875	12.084208	11.937230	11.724925	12.364699	12.265045	12.111024	11.888776
17	11.877368	11.784077	11.638520	11.428303	12.065276	11.968036	11.815410	11.595214
18	11.614937	11.523708	11.379290	11.170750	11.805843	11.710693	11.559177	11.340616
19	11.386076	11.296644	11.153134	10.945933	11.579889	11.486560	11.335920	11.118651
20	11.185574	11.097717	10.954923	10.748782	11.382202	11.290467	11.140509	10.924251
21	11.009212	10.922741	10.780504	10.575191	11.208562	11.118227	10.968791	10.753312
22	10.853536	10.768287	10.626477	10.421800	11.055513	10.966411	10.817367	10.602473
23	10.715691	10.631525	10.490031	10.285829	10.920201	10.832189	10.683426	10.468957
24	10.593298	10.510094	10.368825	10.164965	10.800245	10.713201	10.564628	10.350452
25	10.484360	10.402011	10.260891	10.057261	10.693649	10.607463	10.459007	10.245012
26	10.387185	10.305599	10.164565	9.961072	10.598722	10.513301	10.364899	10.150994
27	10.300336	10.219432	10.078432	9.874998	10.514026	10.429289	10.280889	10.067000
28	10.222580	10.142287	10.001277	9.797838	10.438332	10.354204	10.205765	9.991829
29	10.152857	10.073112	9.932056	9.728560	10.370579	10.286997	10.138485	9.924453
30	10.090250	10.010997	9.869867	9.666271	10.309853	10.226761	10.078149	9.863979
35	9.859339	9.781899	9.640134	9.435641	10.087073	10.005776	9.856425	9.641206
40	9.720739	9.644387	9.501828	9.296190	9.954703	9.874473	9.724262	9.507801

	Interest Rate	10.00%			Interest Rate	10.25%		
1	105.499065	104.627172	103.733806	102.439024	105.638643	104.743955	103.826722	102.498477
2	55.373912	54.916276	54.426281	53.716540	55.512479	55.042325	54.538163	53.808541
3	38.720625	38.400619	38.043757	37.527137	38.861626	38.532494	38.164598	37.632484
4	30.435100	30.183570	29.892288	29.470822	30.579376	30.320389	30.019566	29.584696
5	25.496454	25.285739	25.033026	24.667538	25.644317	25.427127	25.165710	24.787992
6	22.231005	22.047278	21.819637	21.490554	22.382587	22.193022	21.957189	21.616591
7	19.921421	19.756781	19.546510	19.242661	20.076772	19.906736	19.688599	19.373691
8	18.208997	18.058509	17.860805	17.575221	18.368123	18.212558	18.007199	17.710851
9	16.894423	16.754800	16.566469	16.294519	17.057303	16.912839	16.716990	16.434467
10	15.858088	15.727030	15.545847	15.284302	16.024680	15.888962	15.700347	15.428348
11	15.023853	14.899689	14.724046	14.470573	15.194103	15.065419	14.882393	14.618533
12	14.340939	14.222419	14.051120	13.803981	14.514781	14.391851	14.213191	13.955698
13	13.774177	13.660341	13.492474	13.250347	13.951538	13.833378	13.658155	13.405677
14	13.298432	13.188528	13.023386	12.785244	13.479231	13.365071	13.192563	12.944056
15	12.895261	12.788689	12.625715	12.390750	13.079411	12.968637	12.798278	12.552919
16	12.550823	12.447097	12.285849	12.053413	12.738232	12.630348	12.461687	12.218819
17	12.254525	12.153248	11.993367	11.762942	12.445098	12.339696	12.172371	11.931468
18	11.998124	11.898966	11.740162	11.511325	12.191761	12.088505	11.922222	11.682856
19	11.775107	11.677792	11.519828	11.292234	11.971018	11.870315	11.704834	11.466658
20	11.580260	11.484555	11.327237	11.100602	11.779721	11.679954	11.515081	11.277808
21	11.409360	11.315068	11.158236	10.932326	11.611577	11.513235	11.348809	11.112206
22	11.258952	11.165903	11.009425	10.784048	11.463820	11.366729	11.202618	10.966493
23	11.126180	11.034228	10.877995	10.652991	11.333593	11.237605	11.073702	10.837896
24	11.008665	10.917684	10.761607	10.536844	11.218519	11.123506	10.959721	10.724104
25	10.904409	10.814290	10.658294	10.433664	11.116599	11.022449	10.858712	10.623176
26	10.811724	10.722370	10.566396	10.341809	11.026147	10.932763	10.769013	10.533473
27	10.729172	10.640501	10.484498	10.259881	10.945727	10.853024	10.689214	10.453598
28	10.655525	10.567463	10.411391	10.186685	10.874111	10.782014	10.618107	10.382359
29	10.589725	10.502206	10.346034	10.121192	10.810244	10.718689	10.554653	10.318728
30	10.530859	10.443827	10.287529	10.062511	10.753216	10.662143	10.497955	10.261819
35	10.316069	10.230812	10.073673	9.847458	10.546267	10.456948	10.291818	10.054339
40	10.189751	10.105538	9.947477	9.719928	10.425818	10.337519	10.171409	9.932510

Annual Mortgage Constant, Payments In Advance
Annual Rent Constant

	Interest Rate 10.50%				Interest Rate 10.75%			
Year	Monthly Arrears	Monthly Advance	Quarterly Advance	Semiannual Advance	Monthly Arrears	Monthly Advance	Quarterly Advance	Semiannual Advance
1	105.778323	104.860792	103.919616	102.557856	105.918106	104.977681	104.012488	102.617164
2	55.651250	55.168525	54.650101	53.900496	55.790226	55.294876	54.762093	53.992403
3	39.002932	38.664617	38.285580	37.737847	39.144544	38.796988	38.406702	37.843224
4	30.724056	30.457552	30.147072	29.698656	30.869140	30.595059	30.274804	29.812700
5	25.792680	25.568952	25.298708	24.908602	25.941544	25.711215	25.432017	25.029368
6	22.534764	22.339295	22.095138	21.742857	22.687533	22.486096	22.233482	21.869348
7	20.232808	20.057306	19.831165	19.505018	20.389526	20.208491	19.974204	19.636640
8	18.528019	18.367306	18.154147	17.846847	18.688683	18.522750	18.301644	17.983202
9	17.221033	17.071656	16.868138	16.574843	17.385611	17.231248	17.019906	16.715641
10	16.192200	16.051747	15.855541	15.572880	16.360642	16.215379	16.011423	15.717894
11	15.365351	15.232071	15.041497	14.767036	15.537592	15.399637	15.201351	14.916073
12	14.689688	14.562268	14.376079	14.108008	14.865651	14.733662	14.539774	14.260902
13	14.130024	14.007458	13.824705	13.561648	14.309624	14.182571	13.992113	13.718248
14	13.661208	13.542709	13.362658	13.103551	13.844352	13.721431	13.533656	13.263714
15	13.264787	13.149727	12.971800	12.715807	13.451376	13.331944	13.146267	12.879398
16	12.926909	12.814780	12.638521	12.384975	13.116839	13.000377	12.816333	12.551864
17	12.636975	12.527360	12.352401	12.100770	12.830138	12.716221	12.533440	12.270830
18	12.386733	12.279289	12.105334	11.855186	12.583018	12.471296	12.289477	12.028292
19	12.169667	12.064106	11.890914	11.641897	12.368961	12.259140	12.078041	11.817927
20	11.980559	11.876638	11.704013	11.455842	12.182747	12.074579	11.894005	11.634676
21	11.815184	11.712698	11.540479	11.292920	12.020152	11.913427	11.733218	11.474439
22	11.670085	11.568858	11.396914	11.149775	11.877716	11.772256	11.592281	11.333863
23	11.542407	11.442287	11.270512	11.023636	11.752586	11.648237	11.468390	11.210178
24	11.429771	11.330628	11.158935	10.912194	11.642383	11.539012	11.359209	11.101077
25	11.330180	11.231901	11.060219	10.813509	11.545113	11.442606	11.262777	11.004624
26	11.241950	11.144436	10.972708	10.725945	11.459091	11.357348	11.177439	10.919183
27	11.163646	11.066812	10.894992	10.648107	11.382886	11.281819	11.101787	10.843364
28	11.094043	10.997812	10.825864	10.578805	11.315274	11.214808	11.034618	10.775978
29	11.032088	10.936394	10.764291	10.517014	11.255206	11.155274	10.974900	10.716004
30	10.976872	10.881657	10.709377	10.461851	11.201776	11.102318	10.921743	10.662560
35	10.777608	10.684122	10.510803	10.261793	11.010035	10.912279	10.730571	10.469766
40	10.662843	10.570353	10.395998	10.145488	10.900767	10.803981	10.621187	10.358807

	Interest Rate 11.00%				Interest Rate 11.25%			
1	106.057990	105.094623	104.105339	102.676399	106.197976	105.211618	104.198167	102.735562
2	55.929406	55.421377	54.874140	54.084263	56.068790	55.548025	54.986242	54.176075
3	39.286461	38.929606	38.527965	37.948616	39.428682	39.062471	38.649367	38.054020
4	31.014627	30.732909	30.402763	29.926827	31.160518	30.871101	30.530946	30.041036
5	26.090908	25.853913	25.565637	25.150288	26.240769	25.997047	25.699566	25.271359
6	22.840895	22.633422	22.372217	21.996063	22.994847	22.781272	22.511343	22.122998
7	20.546924	20.360288	20.117715	19.768553	20.705000	20.512694	20.261693	19.900753
8	18.850111	18.678888	18.449686	18.119912	19.012300	18.835715	18.598271	18.256974
9	17.551033	17.391610	17.172290	16.856856	17.717295	17.552738	17.325285	16.998481
10	16.530001	16.379853	16.167986	15.863380	16.700274	16.545163	16.325224	16.009333
11	15.710819	15.568111	15.361947	15.065636	15.885025	15.737486	15.523277	15.215717
12	15.042663	14.906025	14.704265	14.414370	15.220715	15.079346	14.869544	14.568402
13	14.490328	14.358707	14.160368	13.875464	14.672128	14.535854	14.329458	14.033284
14	14.028651	13.901223	13.705544	13.424531	14.214092	14.082073	13.878310	13.585988
15	13.639163	13.515273	13.321661	13.043676	13.828135	13.699701	13.497969	13.208625
16	13.308005	13.187123	12.995107	12.719467	13.500390	13.375000	13.174824	12.887767
17	13.024568	12.906260	12.715465	12.441626	13.220247	13.097458	12.898458	12.613139
18	12.780596	12.664504	12.474629	12.202151	12.974944	12.858892	12.660766	12.376743
19	12.569567	12.455392	12.266193	11.994723	12.771460	12.652840	12.455343	12.172261
20	12.386261	12.273751	12.085031	11.814283	12.591072	12.474127	12.277064	11.994637
21	12.226451	12.115394	11.926994	11.656734	12.434054	12.318568	12.121780	11.839776
22	12.086681	11.976893	11.788685	11.518725	12.296950	12.182736	11.986096	11.704330
23	11.964096	11.855421	11.667301	11.397488	12.176904	12.063806	11.867212	11.585533
24	11.856319	11.748623	11.560508	11.290719	12.071543	11.959423	11.762794	11.481083
25	11.761357	11.654524	11.466346	11.196483	11.978875	11.867616	11.670887	11.389049
26	11.677528	11.571456	11.383164	11.113149	11.897220	11.786719	11.589842	11.307802
27	11.603402	11.498004	11.309556	11.039328	11.825152	11.715321	11.518256	11.235957
28	11.537759	11.432957	11.244323	10.973834	11.761454	11.652214	11.454933	11.172331
29	11.479553	11.375280	11.186435	10.915651	11.705081	11.596366	11.398848	11.115911
30	11.427881	11.324077	11.135005	10.863899	11.655137	11.546885	11.349115	11.065823
35	11.243492	11.141363	10.951067	10.678207	11.477927	11.371320	11.172241	10.887066
40	11.139533	11.038348	10.846919	10.572414	11.379088	11.273400	11.073144	10.786261

Annual Mortgage Constant, Payments In Advance
Annual Rent Constant

	Interest Rate 11.50%				Interest Rate 11.75%			
Year	Monthly Arrears	Monthly Advance	Quarterly Advance	Semiannual Advance	Monthly Arrears	Monthly Advance	Quarterly Advance	Semiannual Advance
1	106.338065	105.328665	104.290974	102.794654	106.478255	105.445765	104.383759	102.853673
2	56.208378	55.674828	55.098397	54.267840	56.348171	55.801778	55.210607	54.359556
3	39.571208	39.195583	38.770907	38.159437	39.714038	39.328942	38.892586	38.264867
4	31.306811	31.009635	30.659354	30.155325	31.453506	31.148510	30.787983	30.269693
5	26.391129	26.140615	25.833801	25.392580	26.541985	26.284615	25.968343	25.513949
6	23.149387	22.929645	22.650856	22.250151	23.304516	23.078539	22.790754	22.377519
7	20.863753	20.665707	20.406135	20.033236	21.023180	20.819324	20.551039	20.165999
8	19.175249	18.993230	18.747392	18.394381	19.338953	19.151428	18.897047	18.532130
9	17.884392	17.714627	17.478885	17.140511	18.052322	17.877273	17.633086	17.282940
10	16.871453	16.711303	16.483131	16.155744	17.043535	16.878269	16.641700	16.302608
11	16.060204	15.907755	15.685333	15.366306	16.236350	16.078910	15.848107	15.517395
12	15.399799	15.253618	15.035601	14.722986	15.579907	15.428833	15.202426	14.878114
13	14.855012	14.714003	14.499372	14.191698	15.038971	14.893143	14.670098	14.350692
14	14.400665	14.263969	14.051940	13.748073	14.588356	14.446897	14.226420	13.910770
15	14.018278	13.885211	13.675175	13.374230	14.209576	14.071790	13.853263	13.540474
16	13.693980	13.563991	13.355466	13.056745	13.888755	13.754080	13.537016	13.226385
17	13.417155	13.289795	13.082399	12.785349	13.615275	13.483251	13.267267	12.958235
18	13.179543	13.054438	12.847867	12.552044	13.380870	13.251120	13.035910	12.728032
19	12.974617	12.851457	12.645467	12.350516	13.179014	13.051221	12.836541	12.529463
20	12.797156	12.675680	12.470076	12.175710	13.004485	12.878384	12.664040	12.357478
21	12.642932	12.522921	12.317544	12.023536	12.853055	12.728423	12.514260	12.207986
22	12.508489	12.389754	12.184481	11.890647	12.721270	12.597915	12.383810	12.077644
23	12.390976	12.273356	12.068087	11.774279	12.606278	12.484039	12.269894	11.963694
24	12.288018	12.171376	11.966032	11.672134	12.505710	12.384445	12.170186	11.863838
25	12.197628	12.081843	11.876363	11.582284	12.417578	12.297169	12.082735	11.776153
26	12.118127	12.003097	11.797433	11.503103	12.340210	12.220550	12.005899	11.699016
27	12.048093	11.933728	11.727845	11.433211	12.272185	12.153185	11.938283	11.631050
28	11.986313	11.872534	11.666406	11.371427	12.212294	12.093875	11.878700	11.571081
29	11.931746	11.818485	11.612094	11.316743	12.159502	12.041594	11.826130	11.518102
30	11.883497	11.770695	11.564029	11.268287	12.112917	11.995461	11.779700	11.471248
35	11.713288	11.602101	11.394041	11.096295	11.949527	11.833656	11.616421	11.305849
40	11.619382	11.509087	11.299813	11.000300	11.860368	11.745361	11.526878	11.214487

	Interest Rate 12.00%				Interest Rate 12.25%			
1	106.618546	105.562917	104.476522	102.912621	106.758940	105.680122	104.569264	102.971498
2	56.488167	55.928878	55.322869	54.451225	56.628366	56.056127	55.435185	54.542845
3	39.857172	39.462546	39.014402	38.370307	40.000610	39.596396	39.136355	38.475759
4	31.600603	31.287725	30.916835	30.384140	31.748100	31.427280	31.045906	30.498664
5	26.693337	26.429047	26.103187	25.635464	26.845184	26.573909	26.238335	25.757123
6	23.460231	23.227951	22.931035	22.505100	23.616531	23.377882	23.071697	22.632891
7	21.183279	20.973544	20.696401	20.299039	21.344049	21.128363	20.842219	20.432352
8	19.503410	19.310307	19.047230	18.670216	19.668617	19.469862	19.197939	18.808634
9	18.221079	18.040672	17.787881	17.425762	18.390660	18.204819	17.943266	17.568972
10	17.216514	17.046053	16.800923	16.449916	17.390384	17.214651	16.960796	16.597662
11	16.413455	16.250945	16.011591	15.668975	16.591512	16.423852	16.175777	15.821038
12	15.761030	15.604980	15.370009	15.033775	15.943159	15.782051	15.538341	15.189957
13	15.223995	15.073262	14.841625	14.510254	15.410072	15.254350	15.013941	14.670373
14	14.777154	14.630846	14.401737	14.074066	14.967046	14.815802	14.577877	14.237948
15	14.402017	14.259423	14.032217	13.707342	14.595584	14.448094	14.212023	13.874818
16	14.084702	13.945249	13.719457	13.396667	14.281801	14.137481	13.902770	13.567575
17	13.814586	13.677808	13.453044	13.131778	14.015071	13.873446	13.639708	13.305959
18	13.583405	13.448915	13.224872	12.904686	13.787125	13.647804	13.414731	13.081983
19	13.384628	13.252107	13.028541	12.709080	13.591434	13.454091	13.221442	12.889342
20	13.213034	13.082211	12.858930	12.539912	13.422776	13.287137	13.054720	12.722989
21	13.064396	12.935045	12.711896	12.393097	13.276925	13.142760	12.910426	12.578842
22	12.935260	12.807188	12.584051	12.265294	13.150430	13.017543	12.785173	12.453565
23	12.822779	12.695820	12.472600	12.153746	13.040444	12.908668	12.676172	12.344404
24	12.724583	12.598597	12.375221	12.056161	12.944602	12.813795	12.581102	12.249071
25	12.638690	12.513554	12.289967	11.970620	12.860925	12.730963	12.498023	12.165651
26	12.563430	12.439039	12.215200	11.895503	12.787748	12.658525	12.425300	12.092528
27	12.497387	12.373650	12.149530	11.829438	12.723658	12.595084	12.361546	12.028336
28	12.439356	12.316194	12.091772	11.771254	12.667457	12.539450	12.305583	11.971907
29	12.388306	12.265649	12.040914	11.719950	12.618116	12.490608	12.256403	11.922247
30	12.343351	12.221140	11.996084	11.674664	12.574757	12.447687	12.213141	11.878497
35	12.186597	12.065938	11.839335	11.515685	12.424453	12.298902	12.062738	11.725760
40	12.101999	11.982178	11.754296	11.428781	12.344234	12.219494	11.982025	11.643142

Annual Mortgage Constant, Payments In Advance
Annual Rent Constant

	Interest Rate 12.50%				Interest Rate 12.75%			
Year	Monthly Arrears	Monthly Advance	Quarterly Advance	Semiannual Advance	Monthly Arrears	Monthly Advance	Quarterly Advance	Semiannual Advance
1	106.899435	105.797379	104.661983	103.030303	107.040032	105.914689	104.754680	103.089037
2	56.768770	56.183525	55.547554	54.634418	56.909377	56.311072	55.659975	54.725941
3	40.144351	39.730491	39.258444	38.581220	40.288395	39.864831	39.380668	38.686691
4	31.895999	31.567174	31.175198	30.613263	32.044297	31.707406	31.304707	30.727937
5	26.997526	26.719201	26.373782	25.878924	27.150361	26.864921	26.509529	26.000866
6	23.773414	23.528328	23.212738	22.760889	23.930880	23.679288	23.354154	22.889091
7	21.505486	21.283780	20.988488	20.565935	21.667589	21.439791	21.135207	20.699783
8	19.834570	19.630090	19.349169	18.947380	20.001268	19.790989	19.500915	19.086448
9	18.561061	18.369710	18.099236	17.712563	18.732278	18.535340	18.255784	17.856529
10	17.565140	17.384056	17.121310	16.745839	17.740777	17.554263	17.282460	16.894439
11	16.770515	16.597623	16.340656	15.973576	16.950456	16.772251	16.506220	16.126579
12	16.126287	15.960037	15.707412	15.346653	16.310405	16.138929	15.877211	15.503850
13	15.597193	15.436397	15.187034	14.831038	15.785347	15.619391	15.360894	14.992235
14	15.158020	15.001752	14.754827	14.402401	15.350063	15.188683	14.932573	14.567412
15	14.790265	14.637788	14.392664	14.042887	14.986044	14.828491	14.574125	14.211533
16	14.480038	14.330759	14.086939	13.739091	14.679394	14.525065	14.271944	13.911198
17	14.216710	14.070146	13.827240	13.480758	14.419483	14.267887	14.015621	13.656155
18	13.992010	13.847763	13.605466	13.259903	14.198039	14.048771	13.797054	13.438424
19	13.799410	13.657148	13.415219	13.070226	14.008532	13.861256	13.609850	13.251708
20	13.633687	13.493133	13.251383	12.906682	13.845739	13.700175	13.448894	13.090966
21	13.490616	13.351538	13.109820	12.765194	13.705440	13.561351	13.310051	12.952126
22	13.366749	13.228948	12.987147	12.642428	13.584188	13.441373	13.189942	12.831856
23	13.259242	13.122549	12.880578	12.535636	13.479142	13.337432	13.085786	12.727414
24	13.165734	13.030005	12.787797	12.442534	13.387945	13.247193	12.995271	12.636520
25	13.084250	12.949360	12.706868	12.361211	13.308627	13.168710	12.916466	12.557268
26	13.013128	12.878972	12.636160	12.290056	13.239532	13.100341	12.847745	12.488053
27	12.950962	12.817447	12.574293	12.227707	13.179258	13.040701	12.787734	12.427518
28	12.896557	12.763603	12.520094	12.173004	13.126617	12.988613	12.735265	12.374507
29	12.848892	12.716429	12.472559	12.124954	13.080594	12.943073	12.689341	12.328035
30	12.807093	12.675061	12.430829	12.082706	13.040319	12.903222	12.649108	12.287255
35	12.663053	12.532506	12.286590	11.936036	12.902354	12.766708	12.510849	12.146475
40	12.587033	12.457270	12.210026	11.857534	12.830356	12.695467	12.438263	12.071921

	Interest Rate 13.00%				Interest Rate 13.25%			
1	107.180731	106.032050	104.847354	103.147700	107.321531	106.149464	104.940007	103.206292
2	57.050187	56.438767	55.772449	54.817416	57.191201	56.566611	55.884974	54.908842
3	40.432742	39.999415	39.503027	38.792171	40.577392	40.134243	39.625520	38.897660
4	32.192995	31.847975	31.434434	30.842685	32.342092	31.988881	31.564376	30.957505
5	27.303688	27.011068	26.645572	26.122946	27.457506	27.157641	26.781912	26.245164
6	24.088926	23.830760	23.495944	23.017496	24.247552	23.982742	23.638106	23.146100
7	21.830356	21.596395	21.282371	20.833893	21.993784	21.753588	21.429977	20.968262
8	20.168706	19.952553	19.653174	19.225835	20.336882	20.114781	19.805941	19.365536
9	18.904305	18.701703	18.412906	18.000866	19.077140	18.868797	18.570596	18.145566
10	17.917289	17.725265	17.444238	17.043455	18.094670	17.897057	17.606638	17.192880
11	17.131329	16.947729	16.672461	16.280038	17.313127	17.124049	16.839371	16.433947
12	16.495503	16.318717	16.047730	15.661539	16.681573	16.499392	16.218958	15.819711
13	15.974523	15.803320	15.535508	15.153953	16.164711	15.988175	15.710864	15.316180
14	15.543163	15.376583	15.111102	14.732968	15.737307	15.565438	15.290400	14.899054
15	15.182906	15.020187	14.756390	14.380740	15.380837	15.212862	14.939445	14.550494
16	14.879854	14.720383	14.457769	14.083878	15.081400	14.916695	14.644397	14.257113
17	14.623373	14.466651	14.204830	13.832131	14.828360	14.666419	14.394849	14.008667
18	14.405190	14.250807	13.989475	13.617525	14.613443	14.453848	14.182706	13.797185
19	14.218775	14.066390	13.805310	13.433765	14.430118	14.272526	14.001576	13.616375
20	14.058909	13.908236	13.647226	13.275817	14.273169	14.117291	13.846355	13.461210
21	13.921370	13.772172	13.511090	13.139610	14.138378	13.983972	13.712912	13.327621
22	13.802716	13.654789	13.393529	13.021819	14.022306	13.869167	13.597880	13.212291
23	13.700111	13.553284	13.291765	12.919706	13.922119	13.770075	13.498485	13.112484
24	13.611202	13.465328	13.203492	12.830996	13.835472	13.684374	13.412428	13.025933
25	13.534024	13.388976	13.126784	12.753789	13.760405	13.610127	13.337788	12.950743
26	13.466925	13.322597	13.060020	12.686485	13.695272	13.545705	13.272951	12.885320
27	13.408512	13.264810	13.001833	12.627732	13.638686	13.489737	13.216555	12.828318
28	13.357600	13.214444	12.951061	12.576382	13.589469	13.441058	13.167445	12.778595
29	13.313182	13.170502	12.906713	12.531454	13.546620	13.398676	13.124637	12.735176
30	13.274394	13.132129	12.867941	12.492108	13.509282	13.361746	13.087289	12.697229
35	13.142318	13.001468	12.735478	12.357040	13.382907	13.236751	12.960441	12.567698
40	13.074170	12.934051	12.666701	12.286272	13.318440	13.172988	12.895307	12.500555

Daily Interest on a Loan of $100,000

360 Day Year

Number of Days	Interest Rate							
	5.500%	5.625%	5.750%	5.875%	6.000%	6.125%	6.250%	6.375%
1	15.2778	15.6250	15.9722	16.3194	16.6667	17.0139	17.3611	17.7083
2	30.5556	31.2500	31.9444	32.6389	33.3333	34.0278	34.7222	35.4167
3	45.8333	46.8750	47.9167	48.9583	50.0000	51.0417	52.0833	53.1250
4	61.1111	62.5000	63.8889	65.2778	66.6667	68.0556	69.4444	70.8333
5	76.3889	78.1250	79.8611	81.5972	83.3333	85.0694	86.8056	88.5417
6	91.6667	93.7500	95.8333	97.9167	100.0000	102.0833	104.1667	106.2500
7	106.9444	109.3750	111.8056	114.2361	116.6667	119.0972	121.5278	123.9583
8	122.2222	125.0000	127.7778	130.5556	133.3333	136.1111	138.8889	141.6667
9	137.5000	140.6250	143.7500	146.8750	150.0000	153.1250	156.2500	159.3750
10	152.7778	156.2500	159.7222	163.1944	166.6667	170.1389	173.6111	177.0833
11	168.0556	171.8750	175.6944	179.5139	183.3333	187.1528	190.9722	194.7917
12	183.3333	187.5000	191.6667	195.8333	200.0000	204.1667	208.3333	212.5000
13	198.6111	203.1250	207.6389	212.1528	216.6667	221.1806	225.6944	230.2083
14	213.8889	218.7500	223.6111	228.4722	233.3333	238.1944	243.0556	247.9167
15	229.1667	234.3750	239.5833	244.7917	250.0000	255.2083	260.4167	265.6250
16	244.4444	250.0000	255.5556	261.1111	266.6667	272.2222	277.7778	283.3333
17	259.7222	265.6250	271.5278	277.4306	283.3333	289.2361	295.1389	301.0417
18	275.0000	281.2500	287.5000	293.7500	300.0000	306.2500	312.5000	318.7500
19	290.2778	296.8750	303.4722	310.0694	316.6667	323.2639	329.8611	336.4583
20	305.5556	312.5000	319.4444	326.3889	333.3333	340.2778	347.2222	354.1667
21	320.8333	328.1250	335.4167	342.7083	350.0000	357.2917	364.5833	371.8750
22	336.1111	343.7500	351.3889	359.0278	366.6667	374.3056	381.9444	389.5833
23	351.3889	359.3750	367.3611	375.3472	383.3333	391.3194	399.3056	407.2917
24	366.6667	375.0000	383.3333	391.6667	400.0000	408.3333	416.6667	425.0000
25	381.9444	390.6250	399.3056	407.9861	416.6667	425.3472	434.0278	442.7083
26	397.2222	406.2500	415.2778	424.3056	433.3333	442.3611	451.3889	460.4167
27	412.5000	421.8750	431.2500	440.6250	450.0000	459.3750	468.7500	478.1250
28	427.7778	437.5000	447.2222	456.9444	466.6667	476.3889	486.1111	495.8333
29	443.0556	453.1250	463.1944	473.2639	483.3333	493.4028	503.4722	513.5417
30	458.3333	468.7500	479.1667	489.5833	500.0000	510.4167	520.8333	531.2500
31	473.6111	484.3750	495.1389	505.9028	516.6667	527.4306	538.1944	548.9583

Number of Days	Interest Rate							
	6.500%	6.625%	6.750%	6.875%	7.000%	7.125%	7.250%	7.375%
1	18.0556	18.4028	18.7500	19.0972	19.4444	19.7917	20.1389	20.4861
2	36.1111	36.8056	37.5000	38.1944	38.8889	39.5833	40.2778	40.9722
3	54.1667	55.2083	56.2500	57.2917	58.3333	59.3750	60.4167	61.4583
4	72.2222	73.6111	75.0000	76.3889	77.7778	79.1667	80.5556	81.9444
5	90.2778	92.0139	93.7500	95.4861	97.2222	98.9583	100.6944	102.4306
6	108.3333	110.4167	112.5000	114.5833	116.6667	118.7500	120.8333	122.9167
7	126.3889	128.8194	131.2500	133.6806	136.1111	138.5417	140.9722	143.4028
8	144.4444	147.2222	150.0000	152.7778	155.5556	158.3333	161.1111	163.8889
9	162.5000	165.6250	168.7500	171.8750	175.0000	178.1250	181.2500	184.3750
10	180.5556	184.0278	187.5000	190.9722	194.4444	197.9167	201.3889	204.8611
11	198.6111	202.4306	206.2500	210.0694	213.8889	217.7083	221.5278	225.3472
12	216.6667	220.8333	225.0000	229.1667	233.3333	237.5000	241.6667	245.8333
13	234.7222	239.2361	243.7500	248.2639	252.7778	257.2917	261.8056	266.3194
14	252.7778	257.6389	262.5000	267.3611	272.2222	277.0833	281.9444	286.8056
15	270.8333	276.0417	281.2500	286.4583	291.6667	296.8750	302.0833	307.2917
16	288.8889	294.4444	300.0000	305.5556	311.1111	316.6667	322.2222	327.7778
17	306.9444	312.8472	318.7500	324.6528	330.5556	336.4583	342.3611	348.2639
18	325.0000	331.2500	337.5000	343.7500	350.0000	356.2500	362.5000	368.7500
19	343.0556	349.6528	356.2500	362.8472	369.4444	376.0417	382.6389	389.2361
20	361.1111	368.0556	375.0000	381.9444	388.8889	395.8333	402.7778	409.7222
21	379.1667	386.4583	393.7500	401.0417	408.3333	415.6250	422.9167	430.2083
22	397.2222	404.8611	412.5000	420.1389	427.7778	435.4167	443.0556	450.6944
23	415.2778	423.2639	431.2500	439.2361	447.2222	455.2083	463.1944	471.1806
24	433.3333	441.6667	450.0000	458.3333	466.6667	475.0000	483.3333	491.6667
25	451.3889	460.0694	468.7500	477.4306	486.1111	494.7917	503.4722	512.1528
26	469.4444	478.4722	487.5000	496.5278	505.5556	514.5833	523.6111	532.6389
27	487.5000	496.8750	506.2500	515.6250	525.0000	534.3750	543.7500	553.1250
28	505.5556	515.2778	525.0000	534.7222	544.4444	554.1667	563.8889	573.6111
29	523.6111	533.6806	543.7500	553.8194	563.8889	573.9583	584.0278	594.0972
30	541.6667	552.0833	562.5000	572.9167	583.3333	593.7500	604.1667	614.5833
31	559.7222	570.4861	581.2500	592.0139	602.7778	613.5417	624.3056	635.0694

Entry is in dollars per $100,000 of loan amount.

Daily Interest on a Loan of $100,000

360 Day Year

Number of Days	Interest Rate 7.500%	7.625%	7.750%	7.875%	8.000%	8.125%	8.250%	8.375%
1	20.8333	21.1806	21.5278	21.8750	22.2222	22.5694	22.9167	23.2639
2	41.6667	42.3611	43.0556	43.7500	44.4444	45.1389	45.8333	46.5278
3	62.5000	63.5417	64.5833	65.6250	66.6667	67.7083	68.7500	69.7917
4	83.3333	84.7222	86.1111	87.5000	88.8889	90.2778	91.6667	93.0556
5	104.1667	105.9028	107.6389	109.3750	111.1111	112.8472	114.5833	116.3194
6	125.0000	127.0833	129.1667	131.2500	133.3333	135.4167	137.5000	139.5833
7	145.8333	148.2639	150.6944	153.1250	155.5556	157.9861	160.4167	162.8472
8	166.6667	169.4444	172.2222	175.0000	177.7778	180.5556	183.3333	186.1111
9	187.5000	190.6250	193.7500	196.8750	200.0000	203.1250	206.2500	209.3750
10	208.3333	211.8056	215.2778	218.7500	222.2222	225.6944	229.1667	232.6389
11	229.1667	232.9861	236.8056	240.6250	244.4444	248.2639	252.0833	255.9028
12	250.0000	254.1667	258.3333	262.5000	266.6667	270.8333	275.0000	279.1667
13	270.8333	275.3472	279.8611	284.3750	288.8889	293.4028	297.9167	302.4306
14	291.6667	296.5278	301.3889	306.2500	311.1111	315.9722	320.8333	325.6944
15	312.5000	317.7083	322.9167	328.1250	333.3333	338.5417	343.7500	348.9583
16	333.3333	338.8889	344.4444	350.0000	355.5556	361.1111	366.6667	372.2222
17	354.1667	360.0694	365.9722	371.8750	377.7778	383.6806	389.5833	395.4861
18	375.0000	381.2500	387.5000	393.7500	400.0000	406.2500	412.5000	418.7500
19	395.8333	402.4306	409.0278	415.6250	422.2222	428.8194	435.4167	442.0139
20	416.6667	423.6111	430.5556	437.5000	444.4444	451.3889	458.3333	465.2778
21	437.5000	444.7917	452.0833	459.3750	466.6667	473.9583	481.2500	488.5417
22	458.3333	465.9722	473.6111	481.2500	488.8889	496.5278	504.1667	511.8056
23	479.1667	487.1528	495.1389	503.1250	511.1111	519.0972	527.0833	535.0694
24	500.0000	508.3333	516.6667	525.0000	533.3333	541.6667	550.0000	558.3333
25	520.8333	529.5139	538.1944	546.8750	555.5556	564.2361	572.9167	581.5972
26	541.6667	550.6944	559.7222	568.7500	577.7778	586.8056	595.8333	604.8611
27	562.5000	571.8750	581.2500	590.6250	600.0000	609.3750	618.7500	628.1250
28	583.3333	593.0556	602.7778	612.5000	622.2222	631.9444	641.6667	651.3889
29	604.1667	614.2361	624.3056	634.3750	644.4444	654.5139	664.5833	674.6528
30	625.0000	635.4167	645.8333	656.2500	666.6667	677.0833	687.5000	697.9167
31	645.8333	656.5972	667.3611	678.1250	688.8889	699.6528	710.4167	721.1806

Number of Days	Interest Rate 8.500%	8.625%	8.750%	8.875%	9.000%	9.125%	9.250%	9.375%
1	23.6111	23.9583	24.3056	24.6528	25.0000	25.3472	25.6944	26.0417
2	47.2222	47.9167	48.6111	49.3056	50.0000	50.6944	51.3889	52.0833
3	70.8333	71.8750	72.9167	73.9583	75.0000	76.0417	77.0833	78.1250
4	94.4444	95.8333	97.2222	98.6111	100.0000	101.3889	102.7778	104.1667
5	118.0556	119.7917	121.5278	123.2639	125.0000	126.7361	128.4722	130.2083
6	141.6667	143.7500	145.8333	147.9167	150.0000	152.0833	154.1667	156.2500
7	165.2778	167.7083	170.1389	172.5694	175.0000	177.4306	179.8611	182.2917
8	188.8889	191.6667	194.4444	197.2222	200.0000	202.7778	205.5556	208.3333
9	212.5000	215.6250	218.7500	221.8750	225.0000	228.1250	231.2500	234.3750
10	236.1111	239.5833	243.0556	246.5278	250.0000	253.4722	256.9444	260.4167
11	259.7222	263.5417	267.3611	271.1806	275.0000	278.8194	282.6389	286.4583
12	283.3333	287.5000	291.6667	295.8333	300.0000	304.1667	308.3333	312.5000
13	306.9444	311.4583	315.9722	320.4861	325.0000	329.5139	334.0278	338.5417
14	330.5556	335.4167	340.2778	345.1389	350.0000	354.8611	359.7222	364.5833
15	354.1667	359.3750	364.5833	369.7917	375.0000	380.2083	385.4167	390.6250
16	377.7778	383.3333	388.8889	394.4444	400.0000	405.5556	411.1111	416.6667
17	401.3889	407.2917	413.1944	419.0972	425.0000	430.9028	436.8056	442.7083
18	425.0000	431.2500	437.5000	443.7500	450.0000	456.2500	462.5000	468.7500
19	448.6111	455.2083	461.8056	468.4028	475.0000	481.5972	488.1944	494.7917
20	472.2222	479.1667	486.1111	493.0556	500.0000	506.9444	513.8889	520.8333
21	495.8333	503.1250	510.4167	517.7083	525.0000	532.2917	539.5833	546.8750
22	519.4444	527.0833	534.7222	542.3611	550.0000	557.6389	565.2778	572.9167
23	543.0556	551.0417	559.0278	567.0139	575.0000	582.9861	590.9722	598.9583
24	566.6667	575.0000	583.3333	591.6667	600.0000	608.3333	616.6667	625.0000
25	590.2778	598.9583	607.6389	616.3194	625.0000	633.6806	642.3611	651.0417
26	613.8889	622.9167	631.9444	640.9722	650.0000	659.0278	668.0556	677.0833
27	637.5000	646.8750	656.2500	665.6250	675.0000	684.3750	693.7500	703.1250
28	661.1111	670.8333	680.5556	690.2778	700.0000	709.7222	719.4444	729.1667
29	684.7222	694.7917	704.8611	714.9306	725.0000	735.0694	745.1389	755.2083
30	708.3333	718.7500	729.1667	739.5833	750.0000	760.4167	770.8333	781.2500
31	731.9444	742.7083	753.4722	764.2361	775.0000	785.7639	796.5278	807.2917

Entry is in dollars per $100,000 of loan amount.

Daily Interest on a Loan of $100,000

360 Day Year

Number of Days	9.500%	9.625%	9.750%	9.875%	Interest Rate 10.000%	10.125%	10.250%	10.375%
1	26.3889	26.7361	27.0833	27.4306	27.7778	28.1250	28.4722	28.8194
2	52.7778	53.4722	54.1667	54.8611	55.5556	56.2500	56.9444	57.6389
3	79.1667	80.2083	81.2500	82.2917	83.3333	84.3750	85.4167	86.4583
4	105.5556	106.9444	108.3333	109.7222	111.1111	112.5000	113.8889	115.2778
5	131.9444	133.6806	135.4167	137.1528	138.8889	140.6250	142.3611	144.0972
6	158.3333	160.4167	162.5000	164.5833	166.6667	168.7500	170.8333	172.9167
7	184.7222	187.1528	189.5833	192.0139	194.4444	196.8750	199.3056	201.7361
8	211.1111	213.8889	216.6667	219.4444	222.2222	225.0000	227.7778	230.5556
9	237.5000	240.6250	243.7500	246.8750	250.0000	253.1250	256.2500	259.3750
10	263.8889	267.3611	270.8333	274.3056	277.7778	281.2500	284.7222	288.1944
11	290.2778	294.0972	297.9167	301.7361	305.5556	309.3750	313.1944	317.0139
12	316.6667	320.8333	325.0000	329.1667	333.3333	337.5000	341.6667	345.8333
13	343.0556	347.5694	352.0833	356.5972	361.1111	365.6250	370.1389	374.6528
14	369.4444	374.3056	379.1667	384.0278	388.8889	393.7500	398.6111	403.4722
15	395.8333	401.0417	406.2500	411.4583	416.6667	421.8750	427.0833	432.2917
16	422.2222	427.7778	433.3333	438.8889	444.4444	450.0000	455.5556	461.1111
17	448.6111	454.5139	460.4167	466.3194	472.2222	478.1250	484.0278	489.9306
18	475.0000	481.2500	487.5000	493.7500	500.0000	506.2500	512.5000	518.7500
19	501.3889	507.9861	514.5833	521.1806	527.7778	534.3750	540.9722	547.5694
20	527.7778	534.7222	541.6667	548.6111	555.5556	562.5000	569.4444	576.3889
21	554.1667	561.4583	568.7500	576.0417	583.3333	590.6250	597.9167	605.2083
22	580.5556	588.1944	595.8333	603.4722	611.1111	618.7500	626.3889	634.0278
23	606.9444	614.9305	622.9167	630.9028	638.8889	646.8750	654.8611	662.8472
24	633.3333	641.6667	650.0000	658.3333	666.6667	675.0000	683.3333	691.6667
25	659.7222	668.4028	677.0833	685.7639	694.4444	703.1250	711.8055	720.4861
26	686.1111	695.1389	704.1667	713.1944	722.2222	731.2500	740.2778	749.3055
27	712.5000	721.8750	731.2500	740.6250	750.0000	759.3750	768.7500	778.1250
28	738.8889	748.6111	758.3333	768.0555	777.7778	787.5000	797.2222	806.9444
29	765.2778	775.3472	785.4167	795.4861	805.5555	815.6250	825.6944	835.7639
30	791.6667	802.0833	812.5000	822.9167	833.3333	843.7500	854.1667	864.5833
31	818.0555	828.8194	839.5833	850.3472	861.1111	871.8750	882.6389	893.4028

Number of Days	10.500%	10.625%	10.750%	10.875%	Interest Rate 11.000%	11.125%	11.250%	11.375%
1	29.1667	29.5139	29.8611	30.2083	30.5556	30.9028	31.2500	31.5972
2	58.3333	59.0278	59.7222	60.4167	61.1111	61.8056	62.5000	63.1944
3	87.5000	88.5417	89.5833	90.6250	91.6667	92.7083	93.7500	94.7917
4	116.6667	118.0556	119.4444	120.8333	122.2222	123.6111	125.0000	126.3889
5	145.8333	147.5694	149.3056	151.0417	152.7778	154.5139	156.2500	157.9861
6	175.0000	177.0833	179.1667	181.2500	183.3333	185.4167	187.5000	189.5833
7	204.1667	206.5972	209.0278	211.4583	213.8889	216.3194	218.7500	221.1806
8	233.3333	236.1111	238.8889	241.6667	244.4444	247.2222	250.0000	252.7778
9	262.5000	265.6250	268.7500	271.8750	275.0000	278.1250	281.2500	284.3750
10	291.6667	295.1389	298.6111	302.0833	305.5556	309.0278	312.5000	315.9722
11	320.8333	324.6528	328.4722	332.2917	336.1111	339.9306	343.7500	347.5694
12	350.0000	354.1667	358.3333	362.5000	366.6667	370.8333	375.0000	379.1667
13	379.1667	383.6806	388.1944	392.7083	397.2222	401.7361	406.2500	410.7639
14	408.3333	413.1944	418.0556	422.9167	427.7778	432.6389	437.5000	442.3611
15	437.5000	442.7083	447.9167	453.1250	458.3333	463.5417	468.7500	473.9583
16	466.6667	472.2222	477.7778	483.3333	488.8889	494.4444	500.0000	505.5556
17	495.8333	501.7361	507.6389	513.5417	519.4444	525.3472	531.2500	537.1528
18	525.0000	531.2500	537.5000	543.7500	550.0000	556.2500	562.5000	568.7500
19	554.1667	560.7639	567.3611	573.9583	580.5555	587.1528	593.7500	600.3472
20	583.3333	590.2778	597.2222	604.1667	611.1111	618.0555	625.0000	631.9444
21	612.5000	619.7917	627.0833	634.3750	641.6667	648.9583	656.2500	663.5417
22	641.6667	649.3055	656.9444	664.5833	672.2222	679.8611	687.5000	695.1389
23	670.8333	678.8194	686.8055	694.7917	702.7778	710.7639	718.7500	726.7361
24	700.0000	708.3333	716.6667	725.0000	733.3333	741.6667	750.0000	758.3333
25	729.1667	737.8472	746.5278	755.2083	763.8889	772.5694	781.2500	789.9305
26	758.3333	767.3611	776.3889	785.4167	794.4444	803.4722	812.5000	821.5278
27	787.5000	796.8750	806.2500	815.6250	825.0000	834.3750	843.7500	853.1250
28	816.6667	826.3889	836.1111	845.8333	855.5555	865.2778	875.0000	884.7222
29	845.8333	855.9028	865.9722	876.0417	886.1111	896.1805	906.2500	916.3194
30	875.0000	885.4167	895.8333	906.2500	916.6667	927.0833	937.5000	947.9167
31	904.1667	914.9305	925.6944	936.4583	947.2222	957.9861	968.7500	979.5139

Entry is in dollars per $100,000 of loan amount.

Daily Interest on a Loan of $100,000

360 Day Year

Number of Days	Interest Rate 11.500%	11.625%	11.750%	11.875%	12.000%	12.125%	12.250%	12.375%
1	31.9444	32.2917	32.6389	32.9861	33.3333	33.6806	34.0278	34.3750
2	63.8889	64.5833	65.2778	65.9722	66.6667	67.3611	68.0556	68.7500
3	95.8333	96.8750	97.9167	98.9583	100.0000	101.0417	102.0833	103.1250
4	127.7778	129.1667	130.5556	131.9444	133.3333	134.7222	136.1111	137.5000
5	159.7222	161.4583	163.1944	164.9306	166.6667	168.4028	170.1389	171.8750
6	191.6667	193.7500	195.8333	197.9167	200.0000	202.0833	204.1667	206.2500
7	223.6111	226.0417	228.4722	230.9028	233.3333	235.7639	238.1944	240.6250
8	255.5556	258.3333	261.1111	263.8889	266.6667	269.4444	272.2222	275.0000
9	287.5000	290.6250	293.7500	296.8750	300.0000	303.1250	306.2500	309.3750
10	319.4444	322.9167	326.3889	329.8611	333.3333	336.8056	340.2778	343.7500
11	351.3889	355.2083	359.0278	362.8472	366.6667	370.4861	374.3056	378.1250
12	383.3333	387.5000	391.6667	395.8333	400.0000	404.1667	408.3333	412.5000
13	415.2778	419.7917	424.3056	428.8194	433.3333	437.8472	442.3611	446.8750
14	447.2222	452.0833	456.9444	461.8056	466.6667	471.5278	476.3889	481.2500
15	479.1667	484.3750	489.5833	494.7917	500.0000	505.2083	510.4167	515.6250
16	511.1111	516.6667	522.2222	527.7778	533.3333	538.8889	544.4444	550.0000
17	543.0555	548.9583	554.8611	560.7639	566.6667	572.5694	578.4722	584.3750
18	575.0000	581.2500	587.5000	593.7500	600.0000	606.2500	612.5000	618.7500
19	606.9444	613.5417	620.1389	626.7361	633.3333	639.9305	646.5278	653.1250
20	638.8889	645.8333	652.7778	659.7222	666.6667	673.6111	680.5555	687.5000
21	670.8333	678.1250	685.4167	692.7083	700.0000	707.2917	714.5833	721.8750
22	702.7778	710.4167	718.0555	725.6944	733.3333	740.9722	748.6111	756.2500
23	734.7222	742.7083	750.6944	758.6805	766.6667	774.6528	782.6389	790.6250
24	766.6667	775.0000	783.3333	791.6667	800.0000	808.3333	816.6667	825.0000
25	798.6111	807.2917	815.9722	824.6528	833.3333	842.0139	850.6944	859.3750
26	830.5555	839.5833	848.6111	857.6389	866.6667	875.6944	884.7222	893.7500
27	862.5000	871.8750	881.2500	890.6250	900.0000	909.3750	918.7500	928.1250
28	894.4444	904.1667	913.8889	923.6111	933.3333	943.0555	952.7778	962.5000
29	926.3889	936.4583	946.5278	956.5972	966.6667	976.7361	986.8055	996.8750
30	958.3333	968.7500	979.1667	989.5833	1000.0000	1010.4167	1020.8333	1031.2500
31	990.2778	1001.0417	1011.8055	1022.5694	1033.3333	1044.0972	1054.8611	1065.6250

Number of Days	Interest Rate 12.500%	12.625%	12.750%	12.875%	13.000%	13.125%	13.250%	13.375%
1	34.7222	35.0694	35.4167	35.7639	36.1111	36.4583	36.8056	37.1528
2	69.4444	70.1389	70.8333	71.5278	72.2222	72.9167	73.6111	74.3056
3	104.1667	105.2083	106.2500	107.2917	108.3333	109.3750	110.4167	111.4583
4	138.8889	140.2778	141.6667	143.0556	144.4444	145.8333	147.2222	148.6111
5	173.6111	175.3472	177.0833	178.8194	180.5556	182.2917	184.0278	185.7639
6	208.3333	210.4167	212.5000	214.5833	216.6667	218.7500	220.8333	222.9167
7	243.0556	245.4861	247.9167	250.3472	252.7778	255.2083	257.6389	260.0694
8	277.7778	280.5556	283.3333	286.1111	288.8889	291.6667	294.4444	297.2222
9	312.5000	315.6250	318.7500	321.8750	325.0000	328.1250	331.2500	334.3750
10	347.2222	350.6944	354.1667	357.6389	361.1111	364.5833	368.0556	371.5278
11	381.9444	385.7639	389.5833	393.4028	397.2222	401.0417	404.8611	408.6806
12	416.6667	420.8333	425.0000	429.1667	433.3333	437.5000	441.6667	445.8333
13	451.3889	455.9028	460.4167	464.9305	469.4444	473.9583	478.4722	482.9861
14	486.1111	490.9722	495.8333	500.6944	505.5555	510.4167	515.2778	520.1389
15	520.8333	526.0417	531.2500	536.4583	541.6667	546.8750	552.0833	557.2917
16	555.5555	561.1111	566.6667	572.2222	577.7778	583.3333	588.8889	594.4444
17	590.2778	596.1805	602.0833	607.9861	613.8889	619.7917	625.6944	631.5972
18	625.0000	631.2500	637.5000	643.7500	650.0000	656.2500	662.5000	668.7500
19	659.7222	666.3194	672.9167	679.5139	686.1111	692.7083	699.3055	705.9028
20	694.4444	701.3889	708.3333	715.2778	722.2222	729.1667	736.1111	743.0555
21	729.1667	736.4583	743.7500	751.0417	758.3333	765.6250	772.9167	780.2083
22	763.8889	771.5278	779.1667	786.8055	794.4444	802.0833	809.7222	817.3611
23	798.6111	806.5972	814.5833	822.5694	830.5555	838.5417	846.5278	854.5139
24	833.3333	841.6667	850.0000	858.3333	866.6667	875.0000	883.3333	891.6667
25	868.0555	876.7361	885.4167	894.0972	902.7778	911.4583	920.1389	928.8194
26	902.7778	911.8055	920.8333	929.8611	938.8889	947.9167	956.9444	965.9722
27	937.5000	946.8750	956.2500	965.6250	975.0000	984.3750	993.7500	1003.1250
28	972.2222	981.9444	991.6667	1001.3889	1011.1111	1020.8333	1030.5555	1040.2778
29	1006.9444	1017.0139	1027.0833	1037.1528	1047.2222	1057.2917	1067.3611	1077.4305
30	1041.6667	1052.0833	1062.5000	1072.9167	1083.3333	1093.7500	1104.1667	1114.5833
31	1076.3889	1087.1528	1097.9167	1108.6805	1119.4444	1130.2083	1140.9722	1151.7361

Entry is in dollars per $100,000 of loan amount.

Daily Interest on a Loan of $100,000

365 Day Year

Number of Days		Interest Rate						
	5.500%	5.625%	5.750%	5.875%	6.000%	6.125%	6.250%	6.375%
1	15.0685	15.4110	15.7534	16.0959	16.4384	16.7808	17.1233	17.4658
2	30.1370	30.8219	31.5068	32.1918	32.8767	33.5616	34.2466	34.9315
3	45.2055	46.2329	47.2603	48.2877	49.3151	50.3425	51.3699	52.3973
4	60.2740	61.6438	63.0137	64.3836	65.7534	67.1233	68.4932	69.8630
5	75.3425	77.0548	78.7671	80.4795	82.1918	83.9041	85.6164	87.3288
6	90.4110	92.4658	94.5205	96.5753	98.6301	100.6849	102.7397	104.7945
7	105.4795	107.8767	110.2740	112.6712	115.0685	117.4658	119.8630	122.2603
8	120.5479	123.2877	126.0274	128.7671	131.5068	134.2466	136.9863	139.7260
9	135.6164	138.6986	141.7808	144.8630	147.9452	151.0274	154.1096	157.1918
10	150.6849	154.1096	157.5342	160.9589	164.3836	167.8082	171.2329	174.6575
11	165.7534	169.5205	173.2877	177.0548	180.8219	184.5890	188.3562	192.1233
12	180.8219	184.9315	189.0411	193.1507	197.2603	201.3699	205.4795	209.5890
13	195.8904	200.3425	204.7945	209.2466	213.6986	218.1507	222.6027	227.0548
14	210.9589	215.7534	220.5479	225.3425	230.1370	234.9315	239.7260	244.5205
15	226.0274	231.1644	236.3014	241.4384	246.5753	251.7123	256.8493	261.9863
16	241.0959	246.5753	252.0548	257.5342	263.0137	268.4932	273.9726	279.4521
17	256.1644	261.9863	267.8082	273.6301	279.4521	285.2740	291.0959	296.9178
18	271.2329	277.3973	283.5616	289.7260	295.8904	302.0548	308.2192	314.3836
19	286.3014	292.8082	299.3151	305.8219	312.3288	318.8356	325.3425	331.8493
20	301.3699	308.2192	315.0685	321.9178	328.7671	335.6164	342.4658	349.3151
21	316.4384	323.6301	330.8219	338.0137	345.2055	352.3973	359.5890	366.7808
22	331.5068	339.0411	346.5753	354.1096	361.6438	369.1781	376.7123	384.2466
23	346.5753	354.4521	362.3288	370.2055	378.0822	385.9589	393.8356	401.7123
24	361.6438	369.8630	378.0822	386.3014	394.5205	402.7397	410.9589	419.1781
25	376.7123	385.2740	393.8356	402.3973	410.9589	419.5205	428.0822	436.6438
26	391.7808	400.6849	409.5890	418.4932	427.3973	436.3014	445.2055	454.1096
27	406.8493	416.0959	425.3425	434.5890	443.8356	453.0822	462.3288	471.5753
28	421.9178	431.5068	441.0959	450.6849	460.2740	469.8630	479.4521	489.0411
29	436.9863	446.9178	456.8493	466.7808	476.7123	486.6438	496.5753	506.5068
30	452.0548	462.3288	472.6027	482.8767	493.1507	503.4247	513.6986	523.9726
31	467.1233	477.7397	488.3562	498.9726	509.5890	520.2055	530.8219	541.4384

Number of Days		Interest Rate						
	6.500%	6.625%	6.750%	6.875%	7.000%	7.125%	7.250%	7.375%
1	17.8082	18.1507	18.4932	18.8356	19.1781	19.5205	19.8630	20.2055
2	35.6164	36.3014	36.9863	37.6712	38.3562	39.0411	39.7260	40.4110
3	53.4247	54.4521	55.4795	56.5068	57.5342	58.5616	59.5890	60.6164
4	71.2329	72.6027	73.9726	75.3425	76.7123	78.0822	79.4521	80.8219
5	89.0411	90.7534	92.4658	94.1781	95.8904	97.6027	99.3151	101.0274
6	106.8493	108.9041	110.9589	113.0137	115.0685	117.1233	119.1781	121.2329
7	124.6575	127.0548	129.4521	131.8493	134.2466	136.6438	139.0411	141.4384
8	142.4658	145.2055	147.9452	150.6849	153.4247	156.1644	158.9041	161.6438
9	160.2740	163.3562	166.4384	169.5205	172.6027	175.6849	178.7671	181.8493
10	178.0822	181.5068	184.9315	188.3562	191.7808	195.2055	198.6301	202.0548
11	195.8904	199.6575	203.4247	207.1918	210.9589	214.7260	218.4932	222.2603
12	213.6986	217.8082	221.9178	226.0274	230.1370	234.2466	238.3562	242.4658
13	231.5068	235.9589	240.4110	244.8630	249.3151	253.7671	258.2192	262.6712
14	249.3151	254.1096	258.9041	263.6986	268.4931	273.2877	278.0822	282.8767
15	267.1233	272.2603	277.3973	282.5342	287.6712	292.8082	297.9452	303.0822
16	284.9315	290.4110	295.8904	301.3699	306.8493	312.3288	317.8082	323.2877
17	302.7397	308.5616	314.3836	320.2055	326.0274	331.8493	337.6712	343.4931
18	320.5479	326.7123	332.8767	339.0411	345.2055	351.3699	357.5342	363.6986
19	338.3562	344.8630	351.3699	357.8767	364.3836	370.8904	377.3973	383.9041
20	356.1644	363.0137	369.8630	376.7123	383.5616	390.4110	397.2603	404.1096
21	373.9726	381.1644	388.3562	395.5479	402.7397	409.9315	417.1233	424.3151
22	391.7808	399.3151	406.8493	414.3836	421.9178	429.4521	436.9863	444.5205
23	409.5890	417.4658	425.3425	433.2192	441.0959	448.9726	456.8493	464.7260
24	427.3973	435.6164	443.8356	452.0548	460.2740	468.4931	476.7123	484.9315
25	445.2055	453.7671	462.3288	470.8904	479.4521	488.0137	496.5753	505.1370
26	463.0137	471.9178	480.8219	489.7260	498.6301	507.5342	516.4384	525.3425
27	480.8219	490.0685	499.3151	508.5616	517.8082	527.0548	536.3014	545.5479
28	498.6301	508.2192	517.8082	527.3973	536.9863	546.5753	556.1644	565.7534
29	516.4384	526.3699	536.3014	546.2329	556.1644	566.0959	576.0274	585.9589
30	534.2466	544.5205	554.7945	565.0685	575.3425	585.6164	595.8904	606.1644
31	552.0548	562.6712	573.2877	583.9041	594.5205	605.1370	615.7534	626.3699

Entry is in dollars per $100,000 of loan amount.

Daily Interest on a Loan of $100,000

365 Day Year

Number of Days	Interest Rate 7.500%	7.625%	7.750%	7.875%	8.000%	8.125%	8.250%	8.375%
1	20.5479	20.8904	21.2329	21.5753	21.9178	22.2603	22.6027	22.9452
2	41.0959	41.7808	42.4658	43.1507	43.8356	44.5205	45.2055	45.8904
3	61.6438	62.6712	63.6986	64.7260	65.7534	66.7808	67.8082	68.8356
4	82.1918	83.5616	84.9315	86.3014	87.6712	89.0411	90.4110	91.7808
5	102.7397	104.4521	106.1644	107.8767	109.5890	111.3014	113.0137	114.7260
6	123.2877	125.3425	127.3973	129.4521	131.5068	133.5616	135.6164	137.6712
7	143.8356	146.2329	148.6301	151.0274	153.4247	155.8219	158.2192	160.6164
8	164.3836	167.1233	169.8630	172.6027	175.3425	178.0822	180.8219	183.5616
9	184.9315	188.0137	191.0959	194.1781	197.2603	200.3425	203.4247	206.5068
10	205.4795	208.9041	212.3288	215.7534	219.1781	222.6027	226.0274	229.4521
11	226.0274	229.7945	233.5616	237.3288	241.0959	244.8630	248.6301	252.3973
12	246.5753	250.6849	254.7945	258.9041	263.0137	267.1233	271.2329	275.3425
13	267.1233	271.5753	276.0274	280.4795	284.9315	289.3836	293.8356	298.2877
14	287.6712	292.4658	297.2603	302.0548	306.8493	311.6438	316.4384	321.2329
15	308.2192	313.3562	318.4931	323.6301	328.7671	333.9041	339.0411	344.1781
16	328.7671	334.2466	339.7260	345.2055	350.6849	356.1644	361.6438	367.1233
17	349.3151	355.1370	360.9589	366.7808	372.6027	378.4247	384.2466	390.0685
18	369.8630	376.0274	382.1918	388.3562	394.5205	400.6849	406.8493	413.0137
19	390.4110	396.9178	403.4247	409.9315	416.4384	422.9452	429.4521	435.9589
20	410.9589	417.8082	424.6575	431.5068	438.3562	445.2055	452.0548	458.9041
21	431.5068	438.6986	445.8904	453.0822	460.2740	467.4658	474.6575	481.8493
22	452.0548	459.5890	467.1233	474.6575	482.1918	489.7260	497.2603	504.7945
23	472.6027	480.4794	488.3562	496.2329	504.1096	511.9863	519.8630	527.7397
24	493.1507	501.3699	509.5890	517.8082	526.0274	534.2466	542.4658	550.6849
25	513.6986	522.2603	530.8219	539.3836	547.9452	556.5068	565.0685	573.6301
26	534.2466	543.1507	552.0548	560.9589	569.8630	578.7671	587.6712	596.5753
27	554.7945	564.0411	573.2877	582.5342	591.7808	601.0274	610.2740	619.5205
28	575.3425	584.9315	594.5205	604.1096	613.6986	623.2877	632.8767	642.4657
29	595.8904	605.8219	615.7534	625.6849	635.6164	645.5479	655.4794	665.4110
30	616.4384	626.7123	636.9863	647.2603	657.5342	667.8082	678.0822	688.3562
31	636.9863	647.6027	658.2192	668.8356	679.4521	690.0685	700.6849	711.3014

Number of Days	Interest Rate 8.500%	8.625%	8.750%	8.875%	9.000%	9.125%	9.250%	9.375%
1	23.2877	23.6301	23.9726	24.3151	24.6575	25.0000	25.3425	25.6849
2	46.5753	47.2603	47.9452	48.6301	49.3151	50.0000	50.6849	51.3699
3	69.8630	70.8904	71.9178	72.9452	73.9726	75.0000	76.0274	77.0548
4	93.1507	94.5205	95.8904	97.2603	98.6301	100.0000	101.3699	102.7397
5	116.4384	118.1507	119.8630	121.5753	123.2877	125.0000	126.7123	128.4247
6	139.7260	141.7808	143.8356	145.8904	147.9452	150.0000	152.0548	154.1096
7	163.0137	165.4110	167.8082	170.2055	172.6027	175.0000	177.3973	179.7945
8	186.3014	189.0411	191.7808	194.5205	197.2603	200.0000	202.7397	205.4795
9	209.5890	212.6712	215.7534	218.8356	221.9178	225.0000	228.0822	231.1644
10	232.8767	236.3014	239.7260	243.1507	246.5753	250.0000	253.4247	256.8493
11	256.1644	259.9315	263.6986	267.4658	271.2329	275.0000	278.7671	282.5342
12	279.4521	283.5616	287.6712	291.7808	295.8904	300.0000	304.1096	308.2192
13	302.7397	307.1918	311.6438	316.0959	320.5479	325.0000	329.4521	333.9041
14	326.0274	330.8219	335.6164	340.4110	345.2055	350.0000	354.7945	359.5890
15	349.3151	354.4521	359.5890	364.7260	369.8630	375.0000	380.1370	385.2740
16	372.6027	378.0822	383.5616	389.0411	394.5205	400.0000	405.4794	410.9589
17	395.8904	401.7123	407.5342	413.3562	419.1781	425.0000	430.8219	436.6438
18	419.1781	425.3425	431.5068	437.6712	443.8356	450.0000	456.1644	462.3288
19	442.4657	448.9726	455.4794	461.9863	468.4931	475.0000	481.5068	488.0137
20	465.7534	472.6027	479.4521	486.3014	493.1507	500.0000	506.8493	513.6986
21	489.0411	496.2329	503.4247	510.6164	517.8082	525.0000	532.1918	539.3836
22	512.3288	519.8630	527.3973	534.9315	542.4657	550.0000	557.5342	565.0685
23	535.6164	543.4931	551.3699	559.2466	567.1233	575.0000	582.8767	590.7534
24	558.9041	567.1233	575.3425	583.5616	591.7808	600.0000	608.2192	616.4384
25	582.1918	590.7534	599.3151	607.8767	616.4384	625.0000	633.5616	642.1233
26	605.4794	614.3836	623.2877	632.1918	641.0959	650.0000	658.9041	667.8082
27	628.7671	638.0137	647.2603	656.5068	665.7534	675.0000	684.2466	693.4931
28	652.0548	661.6438	671.2329	680.8219	690.4110	700.0000	709.5890	719.1781
29	675.3425	685.2740	695.2055	705.1370	715.0685	725.0000	734.9315	744.8630
30	698.6301	708.9041	719.1781	729.4520	739.7260	750.0000	760.2740	770.5479
31	721.9178	732.5342	743.1507	753.7671	764.3836	775.0000	785.6164	796.2329

Entry is in dollars per $100,000 of loan amount.

Daily Interest on a Loan of $100,000

365 Day Year

Number of Days	Interest Rate							
	9.500%	9.625%	9.750%	9.875%	10.000%	10.125%	10.250%	10.375%
1	26.0274	26.3699	26.7123	27.0548	27.3973	27.7397	28.0822	28.4247
2	52.0548	52.7397	53.4247	54.1096	54.7945	55.4795	56.1644	56.8493
3	78.0822	79.1096	80.1370	81.1644	82.1918	83.2192	84.2466	85.2740
4	104.1096	105.4795	106.8493	108.2192	109.5890	110.9589	112.3288	113.6986
5	130.1370	131.8493	133.5616	135.2740	136.9863	138.6986	140.4110	142.1233
6	156.1644	158.2192	160.2740	162.3288	164.3836	166.4384	168.4931	170.5479
7	182.1918	184.5890	186.9863	189.3836	191.7808	194.1781	196.5753	198.9726
8	208.2192	210.9589	213.6986	216.4384	219.1781	221.9178	224.6575	227.3973
9	234.2466	237.3288	240.4110	243.4931	246.5753	249.6575	252.7397	255.8219
10	260.2740	263.6986	267.1233	270.5479	273.9726	277.3973	280.8219	284.2466
11	286.3014	290.0685	293.8356	297.6027	301.3699	305.1370	308.9041	312.6712
12	312.3288	316.4384	320.5479	324.6575	328.7671	332.8767	336.9863	341.0959
13	338.3562	342.8082	347.2603	351.7123	356.1644	360.6164	365.0685	369.5205
14	364.3836	369.1781	373.9726	378.7671	383.5616	388.3562	393.1507	397.9452
15	390.4110	395.5479	400.6849	405.8219	410.9589	416.0959	421.2329	426.3699
16	416.4384	421.9178	427.3973	432.8767	438.3562	443.8356	449.3151	454.7945
17	442.4657	448.2877	454.1096	459.9315	465.7534	471.5753	477.3973	483.2192
18	468.4931	474.6575	480.8219	486.9863	493.1507	499.3151	505.4794	511.6438
19	494.5205	501.0274	507.5342	514.0411	520.5479	527.0548	533.5616	540.0685
20	520.5479	527.3973	534.2466	541.0959	547.9452	554.7945	561.6438	568.4931
21	546.5753	553.7671	560.9589	568.1507	575.3425	582.5342	589.7260	596.9178
22	572.6027	580.1370	587.6712	595.2055	602.7397	610.2740	617.8082	625.3425
23	598.6301	606.5068	614.3836	622.2603	630.1370	638.0137	645.8904	653.7671
24	624.6575	632.8767	641.0959	649.3151	657.5342	665.7534	673.9726	682.1918
25	650.6849	659.2466	667.8082	676.3699	684.9315	693.4931	702.0548	710.6164
26	676.7123	685.6164	694.5205	703.4247	712.3288	721.2329	730.1370	739.0411
27	702.7397	711.9863	721.2329	730.4794	739.7260	748.9726	758.2192	767.4657
28	728.7671	738.3562	747.9452	757.5342	767.1233	776.7123	786.3014	795.8904
29	754.7945	764.7260	774.6575	784.5890	794.5205	804.4520	814.3836	824.3151
30	780.8219	791.0959	801.3699	811.6438	821.9178	832.1918	842.4657	852.7397
31	806.8493	817.4657	828.0822	838.6986	849.3151	859.9315	870.5479	881.1644

Number of Days	Interest Rate							
	10.500%	10.625%	10.750%	10.875%	11.000%	11.125%	11.250%	11.375%
1	28.7671	29.1096	29.4521	29.7945	30.1370	30.4795	30.8219	31.1644
2	57.5342	58.2192	58.9041	59.5890	60.2740	60.9589	61.6438	62.3288
3	86.3014	87.3288	88.3562	89.3836	90.4110	91.4384	92.4658	93.4931
4	115.0685	116.4384	117.8082	119.1781	120.5479	121.9178	123.2877	124.6575
5	143.8356	145.5479	147.2603	148.9726	150.6849	152.3973	154.1096	155.8219
6	172.6027	174.6575	176.7123	178.7671	180.8219	182.8767	184.9315	186.9863
7	201.3699	203.7671	206.1644	208.5616	210.9589	213.3562	215.7534	218.1507
8	230.1370	232.8767	235.6164	238.3562	241.0959	243.8356	246.5753	249.3151
9	258.9041	261.9863	265.0685	268.1507	271.2329	274.3151	277.3973	280.4794
10	287.6712	291.0959	294.5205	297.9452	301.3699	304.7945	308.2192	311.6438
11	316.4384	320.2055	323.9726	327.7397	331.5068	335.2740	339.0411	342.8082
12	345.2055	349.3151	353.4247	357.5342	361.6438	365.7534	369.8630	373.9726
13	373.9726	378.4247	382.8767	387.3288	391.7808	396.2329	400.6849	405.1370
14	402.7397	407.5342	412.3288	417.1233	421.9178	426.7123	431.5068	436.3014
15	431.5068	436.6438	441.7808	446.9178	452.0548	457.1918	462.3288	467.4657
16	460.2740	465.7534	471.2329	476.7123	482.1918	487.6712	493.1507	498.6301
17	489.0411	494.8630	500.6849	506.5068	512.3288	518.1507	523.9726	529.7945
18	517.8082	523.9726	530.1370	536.3014	542.4657	548.6301	554.7945	560.9589
19	546.5753	553.0822	559.5890	566.0959	572.6027	579.1096	585.6164	592.1233
20	575.3425	582.1918	589.0411	595.8904	602.7397	609.5890	616.4384	623.2877
21	604.1096	611.3014	618.4931	625.6849	632.8767	640.0685	647.2603	654.4520
22	632.8767	640.4110	647.9452	655.4794	663.0137	670.5479	678.0822	685.6164
23	661.6438	669.5205	677.3973	685.2740	693.1507	701.0274	708.9041	716.7808
24	690.4110	698.6301	706.8493	715.0685	723.2877	731.5068	739.7260	747.9452
25	719.1781	727.7397	736.3014	744.8630	753.4246	761.9863	770.5479	779.1096
26	747.9452	756.8493	765.7534	774.6575	783.5616	792.4657	801.3699	810.2740
27	776.7123	785.9589	795.2055	804.4520	813.6986	822.9452	832.1918	841.4383
28	805.4794	815.0685	824.6575	834.2466	843.8356	853.4246	863.0137	872.6027
29	834.2466	844.1781	854.1096	864.0411	873.9726	883.9041	893.8356	903.7671
30	863.0137	873.2877	883.5616	893.8356	904.1096	914.3836	924.6575	934.9315
31	891.7808	902.3973	913.0137	923.6301	934.2466	944.8630	955.4794	966.0959

Entry is in dollars per $100,000 of loan amount.

Daily Interest on a Loan of $100,000

365 Day Year

Number of Days	11.500%	11.625%	11.750%	Interest Rate 11.875%	12.000%	12.125%	12.250%	12.375%
1	31.5068	31.8493	32.1918	32.5342	32.8767	33.2192	33.5616	33.9041
2	63.0137	63.6986	64.3836	65.0685	65.7534	66.4384	67.1233	67.8082
3	94.5205	95.5479	96.5753	97.6027	98.6301	99.6575	100.6849	101.7123
4	126.0274	127.3973	128.7671	130.1370	131.5068	132.8767	134.2466	135.6164
5	157.5342	159.2466	160.9589	162.6712	164.3836	166.0959	167.8082	169.5205
6	189.0411	191.0959	193.1507	195.2055	197.2603	199.3151	201.3699	203.4247
7	220.5479	222.9452	225.3425	227.7397	230.1370	232.5342	234.9315	237.3288
8	252.0548	254.7945	257.5342	260.2740	263.0137	265.7534	268.4931	271.2329
9	283.5616	286.6438	289.7260	292.8082	295.8904	298.9726	302.0548	305.1370
10	315.0685	318.4931	321.9178	325.3425	328.7671	332.1918	335.6164	339.0411
11	346.5753	350.3425	354.1096	357.8767	361.6438	365.4110	369.1781	372.9452
12	378.0822	382.1918	386.3014	390.4110	394.5205	398.6301	402.7397	406.8493
13	409.5890	414.0411	418.4931	422.9452	427.3973	431.8493	436.3014	440.7534
14	441.0959	445.8904	450.6849	455.4794	460.2740	465.0685	469.8630	474.6575
15	472.6027	477.7397	482.8767	488.0137	493.1507	498.2877	503.4247	508.5616
16	504.1096	509.5890	515.0685	520.5479	526.0274	531.5068	536.9863	542.4657
17	535.6164	541.4383	547.2603	553.0822	558.9041	564.7260	570.5479	576.3699
18	567.1233	573.2877	579.4520	585.6164	591.7808	597.9452	604.1096	610.2740
19	598.6301	605.1370	611.6438	618.1507	624.6575	631.1644	637.6712	644.1781
20	630.1370	636.9863	643.8356	650.6849	657.5342	664.3836	671.2329	678.0822
21	661.6438	668.8356	676.0274	683.2192	690.4110	697.6027	704.7945	711.9863
22	693.1507	700.6849	708.2192	715.7534	723.2877	730.8219	738.3562	745.8904
23	724.6575	732.5342	740.4110	748.2877	756.1644	764.0411	771.9178	779.7945
24	756.1644	764.3836	772.6027	780.8219	789.0411	797.2603	805.4794	813.6986
25	787.6712	796.2329	804.7945	813.3562	821.9178	830.4794	839.0411	847.6027
26	819.1781	828.0822	836.9863	845.8904	854.7945	863.6986	872.6027	881.5068
27	850.6849	859.9315	869.1781	878.4246	887.6712	896.9178	906.1644	915.4109
28	882.1918	891.7808	901.3699	910.9589	920.5479	930.1370	939.7260	949.3151
29	913.6986	923.6301	933.5616	943.4931	953.4246	963.3562	973.2877	983.2192
30	945.2055	955.4794	965.7534	976.0274	986.3014	996.5753	1006.8493	1017.1233
31	976.7123	987.3288	997.9452	1008.5616	1019.1781	1029.7945	1040.4109	1051.0274

Number of Days	12.500%	12.625%	12.750%	Interest Rate 12.875%	13.000%	13.125%	13.250%	13.375%
1	34.2466	34.5890	34.9315	35.2740	35.6164	35.9589	36.3014	36.6438
2	68.4931	69.1781	69.8630	70.5479	71.2329	71.9178	72.6027	73.2877
3	102.7397	103.7671	104.7945	105.8219	106.8493	107.8767	108.9041	109.9315
4	136.9863	138.3562	139.7260	141.0959	142.4658	143.8356	145.2055	146.5753
5	171.2329	172.9452	174.6575	176.3699	178.0822	179.7945	181.5068	183.2192
6	205.4794	207.5342	209.5890	211.6438	213.6986	215.7534	217.8082	219.8630
7	239.7260	242.1233	244.5205	246.9178	249.3151	251.7123	254.1096	256.5068
8	273.9726	276.7123	279.4521	282.1918	284.9315	287.6712	290.4110	293.1507
9	308.2192	311.3014	314.3836	317.4657	320.5479	323.6301	326.7123	329.7945
10	342.4657	345.8904	349.3151	352.7397	356.1644	359.5890	363.0137	366.4384
11	376.7123	380.4794	384.2466	388.0137	391.7808	395.5479	399.3151	403.0822
12	410.9589	415.0685	419.1781	423.2877	427.3973	431.5068	435.6164	439.7260
13	445.2055	449.6575	454.1096	458.5616	463.0137	467.4657	471.9178	476.3699
14	479.4520	484.2466	489.0411	493.8356	498.6301	503.4247	508.2192	513.0137
15	513.6986	518.8356	523.9726	529.1096	534.2466	539.3836	544.5205	549.6575
16	547.9452	553.4247	558.9041	564.3836	569.8630	575.3425	580.8219	586.3014
17	582.1918	588.0137	593.8356	599.6575	605.4794	611.3014	617.1233	622.9452
18	616.4383	622.6027	628.7671	634.9315	641.0959	647.2603	653.4246	659.5890
19	650.6849	657.1918	663.6986	670.2055	676.7123	683.2192	689.7260	696.2329
20	684.9315	691.7808	698.6301	705.4794	712.3288	719.1781	726.0274	732.8767
21	719.1781	726.3699	733.5616	740.7534	747.9452	755.1370	762.3288	769.5205
22	753.4246	760.9589	768.4931	776.0274	783.5616	791.0959	798.6301	806.1644
23	787.6712	795.5479	803.4246	811.3014	819.1781	827.0548	834.9315	842.8082
24	821.9178	830.1370	838.3562	846.5753	854.7945	863.0137	871.2329	879.4520
25	856.1644	864.7260	873.2877	881.8493	890.4109	898.9726	907.5342	916.0959
26	890.4109	899.3151	908.2192	917.1233	926.0274	934.9315	943.8356	952.7397
27	924.6575	933.9041	943.1507	952.3972	961.6438	970.8904	980.1370	989.3836
28	958.9041	968.4931	978.0822	987.6712	997.2603	1006.8493	1016.4383	1026.0274
29	993.1507	1003.0822	1013.0137	1022.9452	1032.8767	1042.8082	1052.7397	1062.6712
30	1027.3972	1037.6712	1047.9452	1058.2192	1068.4931	1078.7671	1089.0411	1099.3151
31	1061.6438	1072.2603	1082.8767	1093.4931	1104.1096	1114.7260	1125.3425	1135.9589

Entry is in dollars per $100,000 of loan amount.

Interest Payment on Constant Principal Repayment Loans

5.50% Interest Rate   Monthly Payments

		1.00%			Constant Principal Repayment 2.00%			2.50%		3.00%	3.33%	4.00%	5.00%
Year	1/120	1/100	1/84	1/72	1/60	1/50	1/48	1/40	1/36	1/33	1/30	1/25	1/20
1	5.2479	5.1975	5.1399	5.0799	4.9958	4.8950	4.8698	4.7438	4.6597	4.5833	4.4917	4.2900	3.9875
2	4.6979	4.5375	4.3542	4.1632	3.8958	3.5750	3.4948	3.0938	2.8264	2.5833	2.2917	1.6500	0.8250
3	4.1479	3.8775	3.5685	3.2465	2.7958	2.2550	2.1198	1.4438	0.9931	0.6250	0.3208	0.0183	----
4	3.5979	3.2175	2.7827	2.3299	1.6958	0.9350	0.7448	0.1146	0.0000	----	----	----	----
5	3.0479	2.5575	1.9970	1.4132	0.5958	0.0275	----	----	----	----	----	----	----
6	2.4979	1.8975	1.2113	0.4965	0.0000	----	----	----	----	----	----	----	----
7	1.9479	1.2375	0.4256	0.0000	----	----	----	----	----	----	----	----	----
8	1.3979	0.5775	----	----	----	----	----	----	----	----	----	----	----
9	0.8479	0.0458	----	----	----	----	----	----	----	----	----	----	----
10	0.2979	----	----	----	----	----	----	----	----	----	----	----	----

5.75% Interest Rate   Monthly Payments

Year	1/120	1/100	1/84	1/72	1/60	1/50	1/48	1/40	1/36	1/33	1/30	1/25	1/20
1	5.4865	5.4338	5.3735	5.3108	5.2229	5.1175	5.0911	4.9594	4.8715	4.7917	4.6958	4.4850	4.1687
2	4.9115	4.7438	4.5521	4.3524	4.0729	3.7375	3.6536	3.2344	2.9549	2.7008	2.3958	1.7250	0.8625
3	4.3365	4.0537	3.7307	3.3941	2.9229	2.3575	2.2161	1.5094	1.0382	0.6534	0.3354	0.0192	----
4	3.7615	3.3637	2.9092	2.4358	1.7729	0.9775	0.7786	0.1198	0.0000	----	----	----	----
5	3.1865	2.6738	2.0878	1.4774	0.6229	0.0288	----	----	----	----	----	----	----
6	2.6115	1.9838	1.2664	0.5191	0.0000	----	----	----	----	----	----	----	----
7	2.0365	1.2938	0.4449	0.0000	----	----	----	----	----	----	----	----	----
8	1.4615	0.6038	----	----	----	----	----	----	----	----	----	----	----
9	0.8865	0.0479	----	----	----	----	----	----	----	----	----	----	----
10	0.3115	----	----	----	----	----	----	----	----	----	----	----	----

6.00% Interest Rate   Monthly Payments

Year	1/120	1/100	1/84	1/72	1/60	1/50	1/48	1/40	1/36	1/33	1/30	1/25	1/20
1	5.7250	5.6700	5.6071	5.5417	5.4500	5.3400	5.3125	5.1750	5.0833	5.0000	4.9000	4.6800	4.3500
2	5.1250	4.9500	4.7500	4.5417	4.2500	3.9000	3.8125	3.3750	3.0833	2.8182	2.5000	1.8000	0.9000
3	4.5250	4.2300	3.8929	3.5417	3.0500	2.4600	2.3125	1.5750	1.0833	0.6818	0.3500	0.0200	----
4	3.9250	3.5100	3.0357	2.5417	1.8500	1.0200	0.8125	0.1250	0.0000	----	----	----	----
5	3.3250	2.7900	2.1786	1.5417	0.6500	0.0300	----	----	----	----	----	----	----
6	2.7250	2.0700	1.3214	0.5417	0.0000	----	----	----	----	----	----	----	----
7	2.1250	1.3500	0.4643	0.0000	----	----	----	----	----	----	----	----	----
8	1.5250	0.6300	----	----	----	----	----	----	----	----	----	----	----
9	0.9250	0.0500	----	----	----	----	----	----	----	----	----	----	----
10	0.3250	----	----	----	----	----	----	----	----	----	----	----	----

6.25% Interest Rate   Monthly Payments

Year	1/120	1/100	1/84	1/72	1/60	1/50	1/48	1/40	1/36	1/33	1/30	1/25	1/20
1	5.9635	5.9063	5.8408	5.7726	5.6771	5.5625	5.5339	5.3906	5.2951	5.2083	5.1042	4.8750	4.5313
2	5.3385	5.1563	4.9479	4.7309	4.4271	4.0625	3.9714	3.5156	3.2118	2.9356	2.6042	1.8750	0.9375
3	4.7135	4.4063	4.0551	3.6892	3.1771	2.5625	2.4089	1.6406	1.1285	0.7102	0.3646	0.0208	----
4	4.0885	3.6563	3.1622	2.6476	1.9271	1.0625	0.8464	0.1302	0.0000	----	----	----	----
5	3.4635	2.9063	2.2693	1.6059	0.6771	0.0312	----	----	----	----	----	----	----
6	2.8385	2.1563	1.3765	0.5642	0.0000	----	----	----	----	----	----	----	----
7	2.2135	1.4063	0.4836	0.0000	----	----	----	----	----	----	----	----	----
8	1.5885	0.6563	----	----	----	----	----	----	----	----	----	----	----
9	0.9635	0.0521	----	----	----	----	----	----	----	----	----	----	----
10	0.3385	----	----	----	----	----	----	----	----	----	----	----	----

6.50% Interest Rate   Monthly Payments

Year	1/120	1/100	1/84	1/72	1/60	1/50	1/48	1/40	1/36	1/33	1/30	1/25	1/20
1	6.2021	6.1425	6.0744	6.0035	5.9042	5.7850	5.7552	5.6063	5.5069	5.4167	5.3083	5.0700	4.7125
2	5.5521	5.3625	5.1458	4.9201	4.6042	4.2250	4.1302	3.6562	3.3403	3.0530	2.7083	1.9500	0.9750
3	4.9021	4.5825	4.2173	3.8368	3.3042	2.6650	2.5052	1.7062	1.1736	0.7386	0.3792	0.0217	----
4	4.2521	3.8025	3.2887	2.7535	2.0042	1.1050	0.8802	0.1354	0.0000	----	----	----	----
5	3.6021	3.0225	2.3601	1.6701	0.7042	0.0325	----	----	----	----	----	----	----
6	2.9521	2.2425	1.4315	0.5868	0.0000	----	----	----	----	----	----	----	----
7	2.3021	1.4625	0.5030	0.0000	----	----	----	----	----	----	----	----	----
8	1.6521	0.6825	----	----	----	----	----	----	----	----	----	----	----
9	1.0021	0.0542	----	----	----	----	----	----	----	----	----	----	----
10	0.3521	----	----	----	----	----	----	----	----	----	----	----	----

6.75% Interest Rate   Monthly Payments

Year	1/120	1/100	1/84	1/72	1/60	1/50	1/48	1/40	1/36	1/33	1/30	1/25	1/20
1	6.4406	6.3787	6.3080	6.2344	6.1313	6.0075	5.9766	5.8219	5.7188	5.6250	5.5125	5.2650	4.8937
2	5.7656	5.5687	5.3437	5.1094	4.7813	4.3875	4.2891	3.7969	3.4688	3.1705	2.8125	2.0250	1.0125
3	5.0906	4.7587	4.3795	3.9844	3.4313	2.7675	2.6016	1.7719	1.2188	0.7670	0.3937	0.0225	----
4	4.4156	3.9487	3.4152	2.8594	2.0813	1.1475	0.9141	0.1406	0.0000	----	----	----	----
5	3.7406	3.1387	2.4509	1.7344	0.7313	0.0337	----	----	----	----	----	----	----
6	3.0656	2.3287	1.4866	0.6094	0.0000	----	----	----	----	----	----	----	----
7	2.3906	1.5187	0.5223	0.0000	----	----	----	----	----	----	----	----	----
8	1.7156	0.7087	----	----	----	----	----	----	----	----	----	----	----
9	1.0406	0.0562	----	----	----	----	----	----	----	----	----	----	----
10	0.3656	----	----	----	----	----	----	----	----	----	----	----	----

Entry is percentage of original principal paid as interest in selected year.

Interest Payment on Constant Principal Repayment Loans

7.00% Interest Rate — Monthly Payments

	1.00%					Constant Principal Repayment 2.00%		2.50%		3.00%	3.33%	4.00%	5.00%
Year	1/120	1/100	1/84	1/72	1/60	1/50	1/48	1/40	1/36	1/33	1/30	1/25	1/20
1	6.6792	6.6150	6.5417	6.4653	6.3583	6.2300	6.1979	6.0375	5.9306	5.8333	5.7167	5.4600	5.0750
2	5.9792	5.7750	5.5417	5.2986	4.9583	4.5500	4.4479	3.9375	3.5972	3.2879	2.9167	2.1000	1.0500
3	5.2792	4.9350	4.5417	4.1319	3.5583	2.8700	2.6979	1.8375	1.2639	0.7955	0.4083	0.0233	----
4	4.5792	4.0950	3.5417	2.9653	2.1583	1.1900	0.9479	0.1458	0.0000	----	----	----	----
5	3.8792	3.2550	2.5417	1.7986	0.7583	0.0350	----	----	----	----	----	----	----
6	3.1792	2.4150	1.5417	0.6319	0.0000	----	----	----	----	----	----	----	----
7	2.4792	1.5750	0.5417	0.0000	----	----	----	----	----	----	----	----	----
8	1.7792	0.7350	----	----	----	----	----	----	----	----	----	----	----
9	1.0792	0.0583	----	----	----	----	----	----	----	----	----	----	----
10	0.3792	----	----	----	----	----	----	----	----	----	----	----	----

7.25% Interest Rate — Monthly Payments

Year	1/120	1/100	1/84	1/72	1/60	1/50	1/48	1/40	1/36	1/33	1/30	1/25	1/20
1	6.9177	6.8513	6.7753	6.6962	6.5854	6.4525	6.4193	6.2531	6.1424	6.0417	5.9208	5.6550	5.2563
2	6.1927	5.9813	5.7396	5.4878	5.1354	4.7125	4.6068	4.0781	3.7257	3.4053	3.0208	2.1750	1.0875
3	5.4677	5.1113	4.7039	4.2795	3.6854	2.9725	2.7943	1.9031	1.3090	0.8239	0.4229	0.0242	----
4	4.7427	4.2413	3.6682	3.0712	2.2354	1.2325	0.9818	0.1510	0.0000	----	----	----	----
5	4.0177	3.3713	2.6324	1.8628	0.7854	0.0363	----	----	----	----	----	----	----
6	3.2927	2.5013	1.5967	0.6545	0.0000	----	----	----	----	----	----	----	----
7	2.5677	1.6313	0.5610	0.0000	----	----	----	----	----	----	----	----	----
8	1.8427	0.7613	----	----	----	----	----	----	----	----	----	----	----
9	1.1177	0.0604	----	----	----	----	----	----	----	----	----	----	----
10	0.3927	----	----	----	----	----	----	----	----	----	----	----	----

7.50% Interest Rate — Monthly Payments

Year	1/120	1/100	1/84	1/72	1/60	1/50	1/48	1/40	1/36	1/33	1/30	1/25	1/20
1	7.1562	7.0875	7.0089	6.9271	6.8125	6.6750	6.6406	6.4688	6.3542	6.2500	6.1250	5.8500	5.4375
2	6.4062	6.1875	5.9375	5.6771	5.3125	4.8750	4.7656	4.2188	3.8542	3.5227	3.1250	2.2500	1.1250
3	5.6562	5.2875	4.8661	4.4271	3.8125	3.0750	2.8906	1.9688	1.3542	0.8523	0.4375	0.0250	----
4	4.9062	4.3875	3.7946	3.1771	2.3125	1.2750	1.0156	0.1563	0.0000	----	----	----	----
5	4.1562	3.4875	2.7232	1.9271	0.8125	0.0375	----	----	----	----	----	----	----
6	3.4062	2.5875	1.6518	0.6771	0.0000	----	----	----	----	----	----	----	----
7	2.6562	1.6875	0.5804	0.0000	----	----	----	----	----	----	----	----	----
8	1.9062	0.7875	----	----	----	----	----	----	----	----	----	----	----
9	1.1562	0.0625	----	----	----	----	----	----	----	----	----	----	----
10	0.4062	----	----	----	----	----	----	----	----	----	----	----	----

7.75% Interest Rate — Monthly Payments

Year	1/120	1/100	1/84	1/72	1/60	1/50	1/48	1/40	1/36	1/33	1/30	1/25	1/20
1	7.3948	7.3238	7.2426	7.1580	7.0396	6.8975	6.8620	6.6844	6.5660	6.4583	6.3292	6.0450	5.6188
2	6.6198	6.3938	6.1354	5.8663	5.4896	5.0375	4.9245	4.3594	3.9826	3.6402	3.2292	2.3250	1.1625
3	5.8448	5.4638	5.0283	4.5747	3.9396	3.1775	2.9870	2.0344	1.3993	0.8807	0.4521	0.0258	----
4	5.0698	4.5337	3.9211	3.2830	2.3896	1.3175	1.0495	0.1615	0.0000	----	----	----	----
5	4.2948	3.6038	2.8140	1.9913	0.8396	0.0388	----	----	----	----	----	----	----
6	3.5198	2.6738	1.7068	0.6997	0.0000	----	----	----	----	----	----	----	----
7	2.7448	1.7438	0.5997	0.0000	----	----	----	----	----	----	----	----	----
8	1.9698	0.8138	----	----	----	----	----	----	----	----	----	----	----
9	1.1948	0.0646	----	----	----	----	----	----	----	----	----	----	----
10	0.4198	----	----	----	----	----	----	----	----	----	----	----	----

8.00% Interest Rate — Monthly Payments

Year	1/120	1/100	1/84	1/72	1/60	1/50	1/48	1/40	1/36	1/33	1/30	1/25	1/20
1	7.6333	7.5600	7.4762	7.3889	7.2667	7.1200	7.0833	6.9000	6.7778	6.6667	6.5333	6.2400	5.8000
2	6.8333	6.6000	6.3333	6.0556	5.6667	5.2000	5.0833	4.5000	4.1111	3.7576	3.3333	2.4000	1.2000
3	6.0333	5.6400	5.1905	4.7222	4.0667	3.2800	3.0833	2.1000	1.4444	0.9091	0.4667	0.0267	----
4	5.2333	4.6800	4.0476	3.3889	2.4667	1.3600	1.0833	0.1667	0.0000	----	----	----	----
5	4.4333	3.7200	2.9048	2.0556	0.8667	0.0400	----	----	----	----	----	----	----
6	3.6333	2.7600	1.7619	0.7222	0.0000	----	----	----	----	----	----	----	----
7	2.8333	1.8000	0.6190	0.0000	----	----	----	----	----	----	----	----	----
8	2.0333	0.8400	----	----	----	----	----	----	----	----	----	----	----
9	1.2333	0.0667	----	----	----	----	----	----	----	----	----	----	----
10	0.4333	----	----	----	----	----	----	----	----	----	----	----	----

8.25% Interest Rate — Monthly Payments

Year	1/120	1/100	1/84	1/72	1/60	1/50	1/48	1/40	1/36	1/33	1/30	1/25	1/20
1	7.8719	7.7963	7.7098	7.6198	7.4938	7.3425	7.3047	7.1156	6.9896	6.8750	6.7375	6.4350	5.9813
2	7.0469	6.8063	6.5312	6.2448	5.8438	5.3625	5.2422	4.6406	4.2396	3.8750	3.4375	2.4750	1.2375
3	6.2219	5.8163	5.3527	4.8698	4.1938	3.3825	3.1797	2.1656	1.4896	0.9375	0.4812	0.0275	----
4	5.3969	4.8263	4.1741	3.4948	2.5438	1.4025	1.1172	0.1719	0.0000	----	----	----	----
5	4.5719	3.8363	2.9955	2.1198	0.8938	0.0413	----	----	----	----	----	----	----
6	3.7469	2.8463	1.8170	0.7448	0.0000	----	----	----	----	----	----	----	----
7	2.9219	1.8563	0.6384	0.0000	----	----	----	----	----	----	----	----	----
8	2.0969	0.8663	----	----	----	----	----	----	----	----	----	----	----
9	1.2719	0.0688	----	----	----	----	----	----	----	----	----	----	----
10	0.4469	----	----	----	----	----	----	----	----	----	----	----	----

Entry is percentage of original principal paid as interest in selected year.

Interest Payment on Constant Principal Repayment Loans

| | | | | | | Constant Principal Repayment | | | | | | | |
| | 1.00% | | | | | 2.00% | | 2.50% | | 3.00% | 3.33% | 4.00% | 5.00% |
Year	1/120	1/100	1/84	1/72	1/60	1/50	1/48	1/40	1/36	1/33	1/30	1/25	1/20
1	8.1104	8.0325	7.9435	7.8507	7.7208	7.5650	7.5260	7.3313	7.2014	7.0833	6.9417	6.6300	6.1625
2	7.2604	7.0125	6.7292	6.4340	6.0208	5.5250	5.4010	4.7813	4.3681	3.9924	3.5417	2.5500	1.2750
3	6.4104	5.9925	5.5149	5.0174	4.3208	3.4850	3.2760	2.2313	1.5347	0.9659	0.4958	0.0283	----
4	5.5604	4.9725	4.3006	3.6007	2.6208	1.4450	1.1510	0.1771	0.0000	----	----	----	----
5	4.7104	3.9525	3.0863	2.1840	0.9208	0.0425	----	----	----	----	----	----	----
6	3.8604	2.9325	1.8720	0.7674	0.0000	----	----	----	----	----	----	----	----
7	3.0104	1.9125	0.6577	0.0000	----	----	----	----	----	----	----	----	----
8	2.1604	0.8925	----	----	----	----	----	----	----	----	----	----	----
9	1.3104	0.0708	----	----	----	----	----	----	----	----	----	----	----
10	0.4604	----	----	----	----	----	----	----	----	----	----	----	----

Year	1/120	1/100	1/84	1/72	1/60	1/50	1/48	1/40	1/36	1/33	1/30	1/25	1/20
1	8.3490	8.2688	8.1771	8.0816	7.9479	7.7875	7.7474	7.5469	7.4132	7.2917	7.1458	6.8250	6.3438
2	7.4740	7.2188	6.9271	6.6233	6.1979	5.6875	5.5599	4.9219	4.4965	4.1098	3.6458	2.6250	1.3125
3	6.5990	6.1688	5.6771	5.1649	4.4479	3.5875	3.3724	2.2969	1.5799	0.9943	0.5104	0.0292	----
4	5.7240	5.1188	4.4271	3.7066	2.6979	1.4875	1.1849	0.1823	0.0000	----	----	----	----
5	4.8490	4.0688	3.1771	2.2483	0.9479	0.0438	----	----	----	----	----	----	----
6	3.9740	3.0188	1.9271	0.7899	0.0000	----	----	----	----	----	----	----	----
7	3.0990	1.9688	0.6771	0.0000	----	----	----	----	----	----	----	----	----
8	2.2240	0.9188	----	----	----	----	----	----	----	----	----	----	----
9	1.3490	0.0729	----	----	----	----	----	----	----	----	----	----	----
10	0.4740	----	----	----	----	----	----	----	----	----	----	----	----

Year	1/120	1/100	1/84	1/72	1/60	1/50	1/48	1/40	1/36	1/33	1/30	1/25	1/20
1	8.5875	8.5050	8.4107	8.3125	8.1750	8.0100	7.9688	7.7625	7.6250	7.5000	7.3500	7.0200	6.5250
2	7.6875	7.4250	7.1250	6.8125	6.3750	5.8500	5.7187	5.0625	4.6250	4.2273	3.7500	2.7000	1.3500
3	6.7875	6.3450	5.8393	5.3125	4.5750	3.6900	3.4687	2.3625	1.6250	1.0227	0.5250	0.0300	----
4	5.8875	5.2650	4.5536	3.8125	2.7750	1.5300	1.2187	0.1875	0.0000	----	----	----	----
5	4.9875	4.1850	3.2679	2.3125	0.9750	0.0450	----	----	----	----	----	----	----
6	4.0875	3.1050	1.9821	0.8125	0.0000	----	----	----	----	----	----	----	----
7	3.1875	2.0250	0.6964	0.0000	----	----	----	----	----	----	----	----	----
8	2.2875	0.9450	----	----	----	----	----	----	----	----	----	----	----
9	1.3875	0.0750	----	----	----	----	----	----	----	----	----	----	----
10	0.4875	----	----	----	----	----	----	----	----	----	----	----	----

Year	1/120	1/100	1/84	1/72	1/60	1/50	1/48	1/40	1/36	1/33	1/30	1/25	1/20
1	8.8260	8.7413	8.6443	8.5434	8.4021	8.2325	8.1901	7.9781	7.8368	7.7083	7.5542	7.2150	6.7063
2	7.9010	7.6313	7.3229	7.0017	6.5521	6.0125	5.8776	5.2031	4.7535	4.3447	3.8542	2.7750	1.3875
3	6.9760	6.5213	6.0015	5.4601	4.7021	3.7925	3.5651	2.4281	1.6701	1.0511	0.5396	0.0308	----
4	6.0510	5.4113	4.6801	3.9184	2.8521	1.5725	1.2526	0.1927	0.0000	----	----	----	----
5	5.1260	4.3013	3.3586	2.3767	1.0021	0.0463	----	----	----	----	----	----	----
6	4.2010	3.1913	2.0372	0.8351	0.0000	----	----	----	----	----	----	----	----
7	3.2760	2.0813	0.7158	0.0000	----	----	----	----	----	----	----	----	----
8	2.3510	0.9713	----	----	----	----	----	----	----	----	----	----	----
9	1.4260	0.0771	----	----	----	----	----	----	----	----	----	----	----
10	0.5010	----	----	----	----	----	----	----	----	----	----	----	----

Year	1/120	1/100	1/84	1/72	1/60	1/50	1/48	1/40	1/36	1/33	1/30	1/25	1/20
1	9.0646	8.9775	8.8780	8.7743	8.6292	8.4550	8.4115	8.1938	8.0486	7.9167	7.7583	7.4100	6.8875
2	8.1146	7.8375	7.5208	7.1910	6.7292	6.1750	6.0365	5.3438	4.8819	4.4621	3.9583	2.8500	1.4250
3	7.1646	6.6975	6.1637	5.6076	4.8292	3.8950	3.6615	2.4938	1.7153	1.0795	0.5542	0.0317	----
4	6.2146	5.5575	4.8065	4.0243	2.9292	1.6150	1.2865	0.1979	0.0000	----	----	----	----
5	5.2646	4.4175	3.4494	2.4410	1.0292	0.0475	----	----	----	----	----	----	----
6	4.3146	3.2775	2.0923	0.8576	0.0000	----	----	----	----	----	----	----	----
7	3.3646	2.1375	0.7351	0.0000	----	----	----	----	----	----	----	----	----
8	2.4146	0.9975	----	----	----	----	----	----	----	----	----	----	----
9	1.4646	0.0792	----	----	----	----	----	----	----	----	----	----	----
10	0.5146	----	----	----	----	----	----	----	----	----	----	----	----

Year	1/120	1/100	1/84	1/72	1/60	1/50	1/48	1/40	1/36	1/33	1/30	1/25	1/20
1	9.3031	9.2138	9.1116	9.0052	8.8563	8.6775	8.6328	8.4094	8.2604	8.1250	7.9625	7.6050	7.0688
2	8.3281	8.0438	7.7187	7.3802	6.9063	6.3375	6.1953	5.4844	5.0104	4.5795	4.0625	2.9250	1.4625
3	7.3531	6.8738	6.3259	5.7552	4.9563	3.9975	3.7578	2.5594	1.7604	1.1080	0.5687	0.0325	----
4	6.3781	5.7038	4.9330	4.1302	3.0063	1.6575	1.3203	0.2031	0.0000	----	----	----	----
5	5.4031	4.5338	3.5402	2.5052	1.0563	0.0488	----	----	----	----	----	----	----
6	4.4281	3.3638	2.1473	0.8802	0.0000	----	----	----	----	----	----	----	----
7	3.4531	2.1938	0.7545	0.0000	----	----	----	----	----	----	----	----	----
8	2.4781	1.0238	----	----	----	----	----	----	----	----	----	----	----
9	1.5031	0.0813	----	----	----	----	----	----	----	----	----	----	----
10	0.5281	----	----	----	----	----	----	----	----	----	----	----	----

Entry is percentage of original principal paid as interest in selected year.

Interest Payment on Constant Principal Repayment Loans

10.00% Interest Rate   Monthly Payments

| | | | | | Constant Principal Repayment | | | | | | | | |
| | | 1.00% | | | | 2.00% | | 2.50% | | 3.00% | 3.33% | 4.00% | 5.00% |
Year	1/120	1/100	1/84	1/72	1/60	1/50	1/48	1/40	1/36	1/33	1/30	1/25	1/20
1	9.5417	9.4500	9.3452	9.2361	9.0833	8.9000	8.8542	8.6250	8.4722	8.3333	8.1667	7.8000	7.2500
2	8.5417	8.2500	7.9167	7.5694	7.0833	6.5000	6.3542	5.6250	5.1389	4.6970	4.1667	3.0000	1.5000
3	7.5417	7.0500	6.4881	5.9028	5.0833	4.1000	3.8542	2.6250	1.8056	1.1364	0.5833	0.0333	----
4	6.5417	5.8500	5.0595	4.2361	3.0833	1.7000	1.3542	0.2083	0.0000	----	----	----	----
5	5.5417	4.6500	3.6310	2.5694	1.0833	0.0500	----	----	----	----	----	----	----
6	4.5417	3.4500	2.2024	0.9028	0.0000	----	----	----	----	----	----	----	----
7	3.5417	2.2500	0.7738	0.0000	----	----	----	----	----	----	----	----	----
8	2.5417	1.0500	----	----	----	----	----	----	----	----	----	----	----
9	1.5417	0.0833	----	----	----	----	----	----	----	----	----	----	----
10	0.5417	----	----	----	----	----	----	----	----	----	----	----	----

10.25% Interest Rate   Monthly Payments

Year	1/120	1/100	1/84	1/72	1/60	1/50	1/48	1/40	1/36	1/33	1/30	1/25	1/20
1	9.7802	9.6863	9.5789	9.4670	9.3104	9.1225	9.0755	8.8406	8.6840	8.5417	8.3708	7.9950	7.4313
2	8.7552	8.4563	8.1146	7.7587	7.2604	6.6625	6.5130	5.7656	5.2674	4.8144	4.2708	3.0750	1.5375
3	7.7302	7.2263	6.6503	6.0503	5.2104	4.2025	3.9505	2.6906	1.8507	1.1648	0.5979	0.0342	----
4	6.7052	5.9963	5.1860	4.3420	3.1604	1.7425	1.3880	0.2135	0.0000	----	----	----	----
5	5.6802	4.7663	3.7217	2.6337	1.1104	0.0513	----	----	----	----	----	----	----
6	4.6552	3.5363	2.2574	0.9253	0.0000	----	----	----	----	----	----	----	----
7	3.6302	2.3063	0.7932	0.0000	----	----	----	----	----	----	----	----	----
8	2.6052	1.0763	----	----	----	----	----	----	----	----	----	----	----
9	1.5802	0.0854	----	----	----	----	----	----	----	----	----	----	----
10	0.5552	----	----	----	----	----	----	----	----	----	----	----	----

10.50% Interest Rate   Monthly Payments

Year	1/120	1/100	1/84	1/72	1/60	1/50	1/48	1/40	1/36	1/33	1/30	1/25	1/20
1	10.0188	9.9225	9.8125	9.6979	9.5375	9.3450	9.2969	9.0563	8.8958	8.7500	8.5750	8.1900	7.6125
2	8.9687	8.6625	8.3125	7.9479	7.4375	6.8250	6.6719	5.9063	5.3958	4.9318	4.3750	3.1500	1.5750
3	7.9187	7.4025	6.8125	6.1979	5.3375	4.3050	4.0469	2.7563	1.8958	1.1932	0.6125	0.0350	----
4	6.8687	6.1425	5.3125	4.4479	3.2375	1.7850	1.4219	0.2188	0.0000	----	----	----	----
5	5.8187	4.8825	3.8125	2.6979	1.1375	0.0525	----	----	----	----	----	----	----
6	4.7687	3.6225	2.3125	0.9479	0.0000	----	----	----	----	----	----	----	----
7	3.7187	2.3625	0.8125	0.0000	----	----	----	----	----	----	----	----	----
8	2.6687	1.1025	----	----	----	----	----	----	----	----	----	----	----
9	1.6187	0.0875	----	----	----	----	----	----	----	----	----	----	----
10	0.5687	----	----	----	----	----	----	----	----	----	----	----	----

10.75% Interest Rate   Monthly Payments

Year	1/120	1/100	1/84	1/72	1/60	1/50	1/48	1/40	1/36	1/33	1/30	1/25	1/20
1	10.2573	10.1588	10.0461	9.9288	9.7646	9.5675	9.5182	9.2719	9.1076	8.9583	8.7792	8.3850	7.7938
2	9.1823	8.8688	8.5104	8.1372	7.6146	6.9875	6.8307	6.0469	5.5243	5.0492	4.4792	3.2250	1.6125
3	8.1073	7.5788	6.9747	6.3455	5.4646	4.4075	4.1432	2.8219	1.9410	1.2216	0.6271	0.0358	----
4	7.0323	6.2888	5.4390	4.5538	3.3146	1.8275	1.4557	0.2240	0.0000	----	----	----	----
5	5.9573	4.9988	3.9033	2.7622	1.1646	0.0538	----	----	----	----	----	----	----
6	4.8823	3.7088	2.3676	0.9705	0.0000	----	----	----	----	----	----	----	----
7	3.8073	2.4188	0.8318	0.0000	----	----	----	----	----	----	----	----	----
8	2.7323	1.1288	----	----	----	----	----	----	----	----	----	----	----
9	1.6573	0.0896	----	----	----	----	----	----	----	----	----	----	----
10	0.5823	----	----	----	----	----	----	----	----	----	----	----	----

11.00% Interest Rate   Monthly Payments

Year	1/120	1/100	1/84	1/72	1/60	1/50	1/48	1/40	1/36	1/33	1/30	1/25	1/20
1	10.4958	10.3950	10.2798	10.1597	9.9917	9.7900	9.7396	9.4875	9.3194	9.1667	8.9833	8.5800	7.9750
2	9.3958	9.0750	8.7083	8.3264	7.7917	7.1500	6.9896	6.1875	5.6528	5.1667	4.5833	3.3000	1.6500
3	8.2958	7.7550	7.1369	6.4931	5.5917	4.5100	4.2396	2.8875	1.9861	1.2500	0.6417	0.0367	----
4	7.1958	6.4350	5.5655	4.6597	3.3917	1.8700	1.4896	0.2292	0.0000	----	----	----	----
5	6.0958	5.1150	3.9940	2.8264	1.1917	0.0550	----	----	----	----	----	----	----
6	4.9958	3.7950	2.4226	0.9931	0.0000	----	----	----	----	----	----	----	----
7	3.8958	2.4750	0.8512	0.0000	----	----	----	----	----	----	----	----	----
8	2.7958	1.1550	----	----	----	----	----	----	----	----	----	----	----
9	1.6958	0.0917	----	----	----	----	----	----	----	----	----	----	----
10	0.5958	----	----	----	----	----	----	----	----	----	----	----	----

11.25% Interest Rate   Monthly Payments

Year	1/120	1/100	1/84	1/72	1/60	1/50	1/48	1/40	1/36	1/33	1/30	1/25	1/20
1	10.7344	10.6313	10.5134	10.3906	10.2188	10.0125	9.9609	9.7031	9.5313	9.3750	9.1875	8.7750	8.1563
2	9.6094	9.2813	8.9063	8.5156	7.9688	7.3125	7.1484	6.3281	5.7813	5.2841	4.6875	3.3750	1.6875
3	8.4844	7.9313	7.2991	6.6406	5.7188	4.6125	4.3359	2.9531	2.0313	1.2784	0.6562	0.0375	----
4	7.3594	6.5813	5.6920	4.7656	3.4688	1.9125	1.5234	0.2344	0.0000	----	----	----	----
5	6.2344	5.2313	4.0848	2.8906	1.2188	0.0563	----	----	----	----	----	----	----
6	5.1094	3.8813	2.4777	1.0156	0.0000	----	----	----	----	----	----	----	----
7	3.9844	2.5313	0.8705	0.0000	----	----	----	----	----	----	----	----	----
8	2.8594	1.1813	----	----	----	----	----	----	----	----	----	----	----
9	1.7344	0.0938	----	----	----	----	----	----	----	----	----	----	----
10	0.6094	----	----	----	----	----	----	----	----	----	----	----	----

Entry is percentage of original principal paid as interest in selected year.

Interest Payment on Constant Principal Repayment Loans

| | | | | | Constant Principal Repayment | | | | | | | | |
| | 1.00% | | | | 2.00% | | 2.50% | | 3.00% | 3.33% | 4.00% | 5.00% |
Year	1/120	1/100	1/84	1/72	1/60	1/50	1/48	1/40	1/36	1/33	1/30	1/25	1/20
1	10.9729	10.8675	10.7470	10.6215	10.4458	10.2350	10.1823	9.9188	9.7431	9.5833	9.3917	8.9700	8.3375
2	9.8229	9.4875	9.1042	8.7049	8.1458	7.4750	7.3073	6.4688	5.9097	5.4015	4.7917	3.4500	1.7250
3	8.6729	8.1075	7.4613	6.7882	5.8458	4.7150	4.4323	3.0188	2.0764	1.3068	0.6708	0.0383	----
4	7.5229	6.7275	5.8185	4.8715	3.5458	1.9550	1.5573	0.2396	0.0000	----	----	----	----
5	6.3729	5.3475	4.1756	2.9549	1.2458	0.0575	----	----	----	----	----	----	----
6	5.2229	3.9675	2.5327	1.0382	0.0000	----	----	----	----	----	----	----	----
7	4.0729	2.5875	0.8899	0.0000	----	----	----	----	----	----	----	----	----
8	2.9229	1.2075	----	----	----	----	----	----	----	----	----	----	----
9	1.7729	0.0958	----	----	----	----	----	----	----	----	----	----	----
10	0.6229	----	----	----	----	----	----	----	----	----	----	----	----

Year	1/120	1/100	1/84	1/72	1/60	1/50	1/48	1/40	1/36	1/33	1/30	1/25	1/20
1	11.2115	11.1038	10.9807	10.8524	10.6729	10.4575	10.4036	10.1344	9.9549	9.7917	9.5958	9.1650	8.5188
2	10.0365	9.6938	9.3021	8.8941	8.3229	7.6375	7.4661	6.6094	6.0382	5.5189	4.8958	3.5250	1.7625
3	8.8615	8.2838	7.6235	6.9358	5.9729	4.8175	4.5286	3.0844	2.1215	1.3352	0.6854	0.0392	----
4	7.6865	6.8738	5.9449	4.9774	3.6229	1.9975	1.5911	0.2448	0.0000	----	----	----	----
5	6.5115	5.4638	4.2664	3.0191	1.2729	0.0588	----	----	----	----	----	----	----
6	5.3365	4.0538	2.5878	1.0608	0.0000	----	----	----	----	----	----	----	----
7	4.1615	2.6438	0.9092	0.0000	----	----	----	----	----	----	----	----	----
8	2.9865	1.2338	----	----	----	----	----	----	----	----	----	----	----
9	1.8115	0.0979	----	----	----	----	----	----	----	----	----	----	----
10	0.6365	----	----	----	----	----	----	----	----	----	----	----	----

Year	1/120	1/100	1/84	1/72	1/60	1/50	1/48	1/40	1/36	1/33	1/30	1/25	1/20
1	11.4500	11.3400	11.2143	11.0833	10.9000	10.6800	10.6250	10.3500	10.1667	10.0000	9.8000	9.3600	8.7000
2	10.2500	9.9000	9.5000	9.0833	8.5000	7.8000	7.6250	6.7500	6.1667	5.6364	5.0000	3.6000	1.8000
3	9.0500	8.4600	7.7857	7.0833	6.1000	4.9200	4.6250	3.1500	2.1667	1.3636	0.7000	0.0400	----
4	7.8500	7.0200	6.0714	5.0833	3.7000	2.0400	1.6250	0.2500	0.0000	----	----	----	----
5	6.6500	5.5800	4.3571	3.0833	1.3000	0.0600	----	----	----	----	----	----	----
6	5.4500	4.1400	2.6429	1.0833	0.0000	----	----	----	----	----	----	----	----
7	4.2500	2.7000	0.9286	0.0000	----	----	----	----	----	----	----	----	----
8	3.0500	1.2600	----	----	----	----	----	----	----	----	----	----	----
9	1.8500	0.1000	----	----	----	----	----	----	----	----	----	----	----
10	0.6500	----	----	----	----	----	----	----	----	----	----	----	----

Year	1/120	1/100	1/84	1/72	1/60	1/50	1/48	1/40	1/36	1/33	1/30	1/25	1/20
1	11.6885	11.5763	11.4479	11.3142	11.1271	10.9025	10.8464	10.5656	10.3785	10.2083	10.0042	9.5550	8.8813
2	10.4635	10.1063	9.6979	9.2726	8.6771	7.9625	7.7839	6.8906	6.2951	5.7538	5.1042	3.6750	1.8375
3	9.2385	8.6363	7.9479	7.2309	6.2271	5.0225	4.7214	3.2156	2.2118	1.3920	0.7146	0.0408	----
4	8.0135	7.1663	6.1979	5.1892	3.7771	2.0825	1.6589	0.2552	0.0000	----	----	----	----
5	6.7885	5.6963	4.4479	3.1476	1.3271	0.0613	----	----	----	----	----	----	----
6	5.5635	4.2263	2.6979	1.1059	0.0000	----	----	----	----	----	----	----	----
7	4.3385	2.7563	0.9479	0.0000	----	----	----	----	----	----	----	----	----
8	3.1135	1.2863	----	----	----	----	----	----	----	----	----	----	----
9	1.8885	0.1021	----	----	----	----	----	----	----	----	----	----	----
10	0.6635	----	----	----	----	----	----	----	----	----	----	----	----

Year	1/120	1/100	1/84	1/72	1/60	1/50	1/48	1/40	1/36	1/33	1/30	1/25	1/20
1	11.9271	11.8125	11.6815	11.5451	11.3542	11.1250	11.0677	10.7813	10.5903	10.4167	10.2083	9.7500	9.0625
2	10.6771	10.3125	9.8958	9.4618	8.8542	8.1250	7.9427	7.0313	6.4236	5.8712	5.2083	3.7500	1.8750
3	9.4271	8.8125	8.1101	7.3785	6.3542	5.1250	4.8177	3.2813	2.2569	1.4205	0.7292	0.0417	----
4	8.1771	7.3125	6.3244	5.2951	3.8542	2.1250	1.6927	0.2604	0.0000	----	----	----	----
5	6.9271	5.8125	4.5387	3.2118	1.3542	0.0625	----	----	----	----	----	----	----
6	5.6771	4.3125	2.7530	1.1285	0.0000	----	----	----	----	----	----	----	----
7	4.4271	2.8125	0.9673	0.0000	----	----	----	----	----	----	----	----	----
8	3.1771	1.3125	----	----	----	----	----	----	----	----	----	----	----
9	1.9271	0.1042	----	----	----	----	----	----	----	----	----	----	----
10	0.6771	----	----	----	----	----	----	----	----	----	----	----	----

Year	1/120	1/100	1/84	1/72	1/60	1/50	1/48	1/40	1/36	1/33	1/30	1/25	1/20
1	12.1656	12.0488	11.9152	11.7760	11.5813	11.3475	11.2891	10.9969	10.8021	10.6250	10.4125	9.9450	9.2438
2	10.8906	10.5188	10.0937	9.6510	9.0313	8.2875	8.1016	7.1719	6.5521	5.9886	5.3125	3.8250	1.9125
3	9.6156	8.9888	8.2723	7.5260	6.4813	5.2275	4.9141	3.3469	2.3021	1.4489	0.7437	0.0425	----
4	8.3406	7.4588	6.4509	5.4010	3.9313	2.1675	1.7266	0.2656	0.0000	----	----	----	----
5	7.0656	5.9288	4.6295	3.2760	1.3813	0.0638	----	----	----	----	----	----	----
6	5.7906	4.3988	2.8080	1.1510	0.0000	----	----	----	----	----	----	----	----
7	4.5156	2.8688	0.9866	0.0000	----	----	----	----	----	----	----	----	----
8	3.2406	1.3388	----	----	----	----	----	----	----	----	----	----	----
9	1.9656	0.1063	----	----	----	----	----	----	----	----	----	----	----
10	0.6906	----	----	----	----	----	----	----	----	----	----	----	----

Entry is percentage of original principal paid as interest in selected year.

Interest Payment on Constant Principal Repayment Loans

5.50% Interest Rate   Annual Payments

Repayment Period in Years

Year	15.0	12.0	10.0	9.0	8.0	7.5	7.0	6.0	5.0	4.0	3.0	2.0
1	5.5000	5.5000	5.5000	5.5000	5.5000	5.5000	5.5000	5.5000	5.5000	5.5000	5.5000	5.5000
2	5.1333	5.0417	4.9500	4.8889	4.8125	4.7667	4.7143	4.5833	4.4000	4.1250	3.6667	2.7500
3	4.7667	4.5833	4.4000	4.2778	4.1250	4.0333	3.9286	3.6667	3.3000	2.7500	1.8333	0.0000
4	4.4000	4.1250	3.8500	3.6667	3.4375	3.3000	3.1429	2.7500	2.2000	1.3750	----	----
5	4.0333	3.6667	3.3000	3.0556	2.7500	2.5667	2.3571	1.8333	1.1000	0.0000	----	----
6	3.6667	3.2083	2.7500	2.4444	2.0625	1.8333	1.5714	0.9167	0.0000	----	----	----
7	3.3000	2.7500	2.2000	1.8333	1.3750	1.1000	0.7857	----	----	----	----	----
8	2.9333	2.2917	1.6500	1.2222	0.6875	0.3667	0.0000	----	----	----	----	----
9	2.5667	1.8333	1.1000	0.6111	0.0000	----	----	----	----	----	----	----
10	2.2000	1.3750	0.5500	----	----	----	----	----	----	----	----	----
11	1.8333	0.9167	0.0000	----	----	----	----	----	----	----	----	----
12	1.4667	0.4583	----	----	----	----	----	----	----	----	----	----
13	1.1000	----	----	----	----	----	----	----	----	----	----	----
14	0.7333	----	----	----	----	----	----	----	----	----	----	----
15	0.3667	----	----	----	----	----	----	----	----	----	----	----

5.75% Interest Rate   Annual Payments

Year	15.0	12.0	10.0	9.0	8.0	7.5	7.0	6.0	5.0	4.0	3.0	2.0
1	5.7500	5.7500	5.7500	5.7500	5.7500	5.7500	5.7500	5.7500	5.7500	5.7500	5.7500	5.7500
2	5.3667	5.2708	5.1750	5.1111	5.0313	4.9833	4.9286	4.7917	4.6000	4.3125	3.8333	2.8750
3	4.9833	4.7917	4.6000	4.4722	4.3125	4.2167	4.1071	3.8333	3.4500	2.8750	1.9167	0.0000
4	4.6000	4.3125	4.0250	3.8333	3.5938	3.4500	3.2857	2.8750	2.3000	1.4375	----	----
5	4.2167	3.8333	3.4500	3.1944	2.8750	2.6833	2.4643	1.9167	1.1500	0.0000	----	----
6	3.8333	3.3542	2.8750	2.5556	2.1563	1.9167	1.6429	0.9583	0.0000	----	----	----
7	3.4500	2.8750	2.3000	1.9167	1.4375	1.1500	0.8214	----	----	----	----	----
8	3.0667	2.3958	1.7250	1.2778	0.7188	0.3833	0.0000	----	----	----	----	----
9	2.6833	1.9167	1.1500	0.6389	0.0000	----	----	----	----	----	----	----
10	2.3000	1.4375	0.5750	----	----	----	----	----	----	----	----	----
11	1.9167	0.9583	0.0000	----	----	----	----	----	----	----	----	----
12	1.5333	0.4792	----	----	----	----	----	----	----	----	----	----
13	1.1500	----	----	----	----	----	----	----	----	----	----	----
14	0.7667	----	----	----	----	----	----	----	----	---c	----	----
15	0.3833	----	----	----	----	----	----	----	----	----	----	----

6.00% Interest Rate   Annual Payments

Year	15.0	12.0	10.0	9.0	8.0	7.5	7.0	6.0	5.0	4.0	3.0	2.0
1	6.0000	6.0000	6.0000	6.0000	6.0000	6.0000	6.0000	6.0000	6.0000	6.0000	6.0000	6.0000
2	5.6000	5.5000	5.4000	5.3333	5.2500	5.2000	5.1429	5.0000	4.8000	4.5000	4.0000	3.0000
3	5.2000	5.0000	4.8000	4.6667	4.5000	4.4000	4.2857	4.0000	3.6000	3.0000	2.0000	0.0000
4	4.8000	4.5000	4.2000	4.0000	3.7500	3.6000	3.4286	3.0000	2.4000	1.5000	----	----
5	4.4000	4.0000	3.6000	3.3333	3.0000	2.8000	2.5714	2.0000	1.2000	0.0000	----	----
6	4.0000	3.5000	3.0000	2.6667	2.2500	2.0000	1.7143	1.0000	0.0000	----	----	----
7	3.6000	3.0000	2.4000	2.0000	1.5000	1.2000	0.8571	----	----	----	----	----
8	3.2000	2.5000	1.8000	1.3333	0.7500	0.4000	0.0000	----	----	----	----	----
9	2.8000	2.0000	1.2000	0.6667	0.0000	----	----	----	----	----	----	----
10	2.4000	1.5000	0.6000	----	----	----	----	----	----	----	----	----
11	2.0000	1.0000	0.0000	----	----	----	----	----	----	----	----	----
12	1.6000	0.5000	----	----	----	----	----	----	----	----	----	----
13	1.2000	----	----	----	----	----	----	----	----	----	----	----
14	0.8000	----	----	----	----	----	----	----	----	----	----	----
15	0.4000	----	----	----	----	----	----	----	----	----	----	----

6.25% Interest Rate   Annual Payments

Year	15.0	12.0	10.0	9.0	8.0	7.5	7.0	6.0	5.0	4.0	3.0	2.0
1	6.2500	6.2500	6.2500	6.2500	6.2500	6.2500	6.2500	6.2500	6.2500	6.2500	6.2500	6.2500
2	5.8333	5.7292	5.6250	5.5556	5.4687	5.4167	5.3571	5.2083	5.0000	4.6875	4.1667	3.1250
3	5.4167	5.2083	5.0000	4.8611	4.6875	4.5833	4.4643	4.1667	3.7500	3.1250	2.0833	0.0000
4	5.0000	4.6875	4.3750	4.1667	3.9062	3.7500	3.5714	3.1250	2.5000	1.5625	----	----
5	4.5833	4.1667	3.7500	3.4722	3.1250	2.9167	2.6786	2.0833	1.2500	0.0000	----	----
6	4.1667	3.6458	3.1250	2.7778	2.3437	2.0833	1.7857	1.0417	0.0000	----	----	----
7	3.7500	3.1250	2.5000	2.0833	1.5625	1.2500	0.8929	----	----	----	----	----
8	3.3333	2.6042	1.8750	1.3889	0.7812	0.4167	0.0000	----	----	----	----	----
9	2.9167	2.0833	1.2500	0.6944	0.0000	----	----	----	----	----	----	----
10	2.5000	1.5625	0.6250	----	----	----	----	----	----	----	----	----
11	2.0833	1.0417	0.0000	----	----	----	----	----	----	----	----	----
12	1.6667	0.5208	----	----	----	----	----	----	----	----	----	----
13	1.2500	----	----	----	----	----	----	----	----	----	----	----
14	0.8333	----	----	----	----	----	----	----	----	----	----	----
15	0.4167	----	----	----	----	----	----	----	----	----	----	----

Entry is percentage of original principal paid as interest in selected year.

Interest Payment on Constant Principal Repayment Loans

6.50% Interest Rate   Annual Payments

Repayment Period in Years

Year	15.0	12.0	10.0	9.0	8.0	7.5	7.0	6.0	5.0	4.0	3.0	2.0
1	6.5000	6.5000	6.5000	6.5000	6.5000	6.5000	6.5000	6.5000	6.5000	6.5000	6.5000	6.5000
2	6.0667	5.9583	5.8500	5.7778	5.6875	5.6333	5.5714	5.4167	5.2000	4.8750	4.3333	3.2500
3	5.6333	5.4167	5.2000	5.0556	4.8750	4.7667	4.6429	4.3333	3.9000	3.2500	2.1667	0.0000
4	5.2000	4.8750	4.5500	4.3333	4.0625	3.9000	3.7143	3.2500	2.6000	1.6250	----	----
5	4.7667	4.3333	3.9000	3.6111	3.2500	3.0333	2.7857	2.1667	1.3000	0.0000	----	----
6	4.3333	3.7917	3.2500	2.8889	2.4375	2.1667	1.8571	1.0833	0.0000	----	----	----
7	3.9000	3.2500	2.6000	2.1667	1.6250	1.3000	0.9286	----	----	----	----	----
8	3.4667	2.7083	1.9500	1.4444	0.8125	0.4333	0.0000	----	----	----	----	----
9	3.0333	2.1667	1.3000	0.7222	0.0000	----	----	----	----	----	----	----
10	2.6000	1.6250	0.6500	----	----	----	----	----	----	----	----	----
11	2.1667	1.0833	0.0000	----	----	----	----	----	----	----	----	----
12	1.7333	0.5417	----	----	----	----	----	----	----	----	----	----
13	1.3000	----	----	----	----	----	----	----	----	----	----	----
14	0.8667	----	----	----	----	----	----	----	----	----	----	----
15	0.4333	----	----	----	----	----	----	----	----	----	----	----

6.75% Interest Rate   Annual Payments

Year	15.0	12.0	10.0	9.0	8.0	7.5	7.0	6.0	5.0	4.0	3.0	2.0
1	6.7500	6.7500	6.7500	6.7500	6.7500	6.7500	6.7500	6.7500	6.7500	6.7500	6.7500	6.7500
2	6.3000	6.1875	6.0750	6.0000	5.9062	5.8500	5.7857	5.6250	5.4000	5.0625	4.5000	3.3750
3	5.8500	5.6250	5.4000	5.2500	5.0625	4.9500	4.8214	4.5000	4.0500	3.3750	2.2500	0.0000
4	5.4000	5.0625	4.7250	4.5000	4.2188	4.0500	3.8571	3.3750	2.7000	1.6875	----	----
5	4.9500	4.5000	4.0500	3.7500	3.3750	3.1500	2.8929	2.2500	1.3500	0.0000	----	----
6	4.5000	3.9375	3.3750	3.0000	2.5312	2.2500	1.9286	1.1250	0.0000	----	----	----
7	4.0500	3.3750	2.7000	2.2500	1.6875	1.3500	0.9643	----	----	----	----	----
8	3.6000	2.8125	2.0250	1.5000	0.8437	0.4500	0.0000	----	----	----	----	----
9	3.1500	2.2500	1.3500	0.7500	0.0000	----	----	----	----	----	----	----
10	2.7000	1.6875	0.6750	----	----	----	----	----	----	----	----	----
11	2.2500	1.1250	0.0000	----	----	----	----	----	----	----	----	----
12	1.8000	0.5625	----	----	----	----	----	----	----	----	----	----
13	1.3500	----	----	----	----	----	----	----	----	----	----	----
14	0.9000	----	----	----	----	----	----	----	----	----	----	----
15	0.4500	----	----	----	----	----	----	----	----	----	----	----

7.00% Interest Rate   Annual Payments

Year	15.0	12.0	10.0	9.0	8.0	7.5	7.0	6.0	5.0	4.0	3.0	2.0
1	7.0000	7.0000	7.0000	7.0000	7.0000	7.0000	7.0000	7.0000	7.0000	7.0000	7.0000	7.0000
2	6.5333	6.4167	6.3000	6.2222	6.1250	6.0667	6.0000	5.8333	5.6000	5.2500	4.6667	3.5000
3	6.0667	5.8333	5.6000	5.4444	5.2500	5.1333	5.0000	4.6667	4.2000	3.5000	2.3333	0.0000
4	5.6000	5.2500	4.9000	4.6667	4.3750	4.2000	4.0000	3.5000	2.8000	1.7500	----	----
5	5.1333	4.6667	4.2000	3.8889	3.5000	3.2667	3.0000	2.3333	1.4000	0.0000	----	----
6	4.6667	4.0833	3.5000	3.1111	2.6250	2.3333	2.0000	1.1667	0.0000	----	----	----
7	4.2000	3.5000	2.8000	2.3333	1.7500	1.4000	1.0000	----	----	----	----	----
8	3.7333	2.9167	2.1000	1.5556	0.8750	0.4667	0.0000	----	----	----	----	----
9	3.2667	2.3333	1.4000	0.7778	0.0000	----	----	----	----	----	----	----
10	2.8000	1.7500	0.7000	----	----	----	----	----	----	----	----	----
11	2.3333	1.1667	0.0000	----	----	----	----	----	----	----	----	----
12	1.8667	0.5833	----	----	----	----	----	----	----	----	----	----
13	1.4000	----	----	----	----	----	----	----	----	----	----	----
14	0.9333	----	----	----	----	----	----	----	----	----	----	----
15	0.4667	----	----	----	----	----	----	----	----	----	----	----

7.25% Interest Rate   Annual Payments

Year	15.0	12.0	10.0	9.0	8.0	7.5	7.0	6.0	5.0	4.0	3.0	2.0
1	7.2500	7.2500	7.2500	7.2500	7.2500	7.2500	7.2500	7.2500	7.2500	7.2500	7.2500	7.2500
2	6.7667	6.6458	6.5250	6.4444	6.3438	6.2833	6.2143	6.0417	5.8000	5.4375	4.8333	3.6250
3	6.2833	6.0417	5.8000	5.6389	5.4375	5.3167	5.1786	4.8333	4.3500	3.6250	2.4167	0.0000
4	5.8000	5.4375	5.0750	4.8333	4.5313	4.3500	4.1429	3.6250	2.9000	1.8125	----	----
5	5.3167	4.8333	4.3500	4.0278	3.6250	3.3833	3.1071	2.4167	1.4500	0.0000	----	----
6	4.8333	4.2292	3.6250	3.2222	2.7188	2.4167	2.0714	1.2083	0.0000	----	----	----
7	4.3500	3.6250	2.9000	2.4167	1.8125	1.4500	1.0357	----	----	----	----	----
8	3.8667	3.0208	2.1750	1.6111	0.9063	0.4833	0.0000	----	----	----	----	----
9	3.3833	2.4167	1.4500	0.8056	0.0000	----	----	----	----	----	----	----
10	2.9000	1.8125	0.7250	----	----	----	----	----	----	----	----	----
11	2.4167	1.2083	0.0000	----	----	----	----	----	----	----	----	----
12	1.9333	0.6042	----	----	----	----	----	----	----	----	----	----
13	1.4500	----	----	----	----	----	----	----	----	----	----	----
14	0.9667	----	----	----	----	----	----	----	----	----	----	----
15	0.4833	----	----	----	----	----	----	----	----	----	----	----

Entry is percentage of original principal paid as interest in selected year.

Interest Payment on Constant Principal Repayment Loans

7.50% Interest Rate   Annual Payments

Repayment Period in Years

Year	15.0	12.0	10.0	9.0	8.0	7.5	7.0	6.0	5.0	4.0	3.0	2.0
1	7.5000	7.5000	7.5000	7.5000	7.5000	7.5000	7.5000	7.5000	7.5000	7.5000	7.5000	7.5000
2	7.0000	6.8750	6.7500	6.6667	6.5625	6.5000	6.4286	6.2500	6.0000	5.6250	5.0000	3.7500
3	6.5000	6.2500	6.0000	5.8333	5.6250	5.5000	5.3571	5.0000	4.5000	3.7500	2.5000	0.0000
4	6.0000	5.6250	5.2500	5.0000	4.6875	4.5000	4.2857	3.7500	3.0000	1.8750	----	----
5	5.5000	5.0000	4.5000	4.1667	3.7500	3.5000	3.2143	2.5000	1.5000	0.0000	----	----
6	5.0000	4.3750	3.7500	3.3333	2.8125	2.5000	2.1429	1.2500	0.0000	----	----	----
7	4.5000	3.7500	3.0000	2.5000	1.8750	1.5000	1.0714	----	----	----	----	----
8	4.0000	3.1250	2.2500	1.6667	0.9375	0.5000	0.0000	----	----	----	----	----
9	3.5000	2.5000	1.5000	0.8333	0.0000	----	----	----	----	----	----	----
10	3.0000	1.8750	0.7500	----	----	----	----	----	----	----	----	----
11	2.5000	1.2500	0.0000	----	----	----	----	----	----	----	----	----
12	2.0000	0.6250	----	----	----	----	----	----	----	----	----	----
13	1.5000	----	----	----	----	----	----	----	----	----	----	----
14	1.0000	----	----	----	----	----	----	----	----	----	----	----
15	0.5000	----	----	----	----	----	----	----	----	----	----	----

7.75% Interest Rate   Annual Payments

Year	15.0	12.0	10.0	9.0	8.0	7.5	7.0	6.0	5.0	4.0	3.0	2.0
1	7.7500	7.7500	7.7500	7.7500	7.7500	7.7500	7.7500	7.7500	7.7500	7.7500	7.7500	7.7500
2	7.2333	7.1042	6.9750	6.8889	6.7813	6.7167	6.6429	6.4583	6.2000	5.8125	5.1667	3.8750
3	6.7167	6.4583	6.2000	6.0278	5.8125	5.6833	5.5357	5.1667	4.6500	3.8750	2.5833	0.0000
4	6.2000	5.8125	5.4250	5.1667	4.8438	4.6500	4.4286	3.8750	3.1000	1.9375	----	----
5	5.6833	5.1667	4.6500	4.3056	3.8750	3.6167	3.3214	2.5833	1.5500	0.0000	----	----
6	5.1667	4.5208	3.8750	3.4444	2.9063	2.5833	2.2143	1.2917	0.0000	----	----	----
7	4.6500	3.8750	3.1000	2.5833	1.9375	1.5500	1.1071	----	----	----	----	----
8	4.1333	3.2292	2.3250	1.7222	0.9688	0.5167	0.0000	----	----	----	----	----
9	3.6167	2.5833	1.5500	0.8611	0.0000	----	----	----	----	----	----	----
10	3.1000	1.9375	0.7750	----	----	----	----	----	----	----	----	----
11	2.5833	1.2917	0.0000	----	----	----	----	----	----	----	----	----
12	2.0667	0.6458	----	----	----	----	----	----	----	----	----	----
13	1.5500	----	----	----	----	----	----	----	----	----	----	----
14	1.0333	----	----	----	----	----	----	----	----	----	----	----
15	0.5167	----	----	----	----	----	----	----	----	----	----	----

8.00% Interest Rate   Annual Payments

Year	15.0	12.0	10.0	9.0	8.0	7.5	7.0	6.0	5.0	4.0	3.0	2.0
1	8.0000	8.0000	8.0000	8.0000	8.0000	8.0000	8.0000	8.0000	8.0000	8.0000	8.0000	8.0000
2	7.4667	7.3333	7.2000	7.1111	7.0000	6.9333	6.8571	6.6667	6.4000	6.0000	5.3333	4.0000
3	6.9333	6.6667	6.4000	6.2222	6.0000	5.8667	5.7143	5.3333	4.8000	4.0000	2.6667	0.0000
4	6.4000	6.0000	5.6000	5.3333	5.0000	4.8000	4.5714	4.0000	3.2000	2.0000	----	----
5	5.8667	5.3333	4.8000	4.4444	4.0000	3.7333	3.4286	2.6667	1.6000	0.0000	----	----
6	5.3333	4.6667	4.0000	3.5556	3.0000	2.6667	2.2857	1.3333	0.0000	----	----	----
7	4.8000	4.0000	3.2000	2.6667	2.0000	1.6000	1.1429	----	----	----	----	----
8	4.2667	3.3333	2.4000	1.7778	1.0000	0.5333	0.0000	----	----	----	----	----
9	3.7333	2.6667	1.6000	0.8889	0.0000	----	----	----	----	----	----	----
10	3.2000	2.0000	0.8000	----	----	----	----	----	----	----	----	----
11	2.6667	1.3333	0.0000	----	----	----	----	----	----	----	----	----
12	2.1333	0.6667	----	----	----	----	----	----	----	----	----	----
13	1.6000	----	----	----	----	----	----	----	----	----	----	----
14	1.0667	----	----	----	----	----	----	----	----	----	----	----
15	0.5333	----	----	----	----	----	----	----	----	----	----	----

8.25% Interest Rate   Annual Payments

Year	15.0	12.0	10.0	9.0	8.0	7.5	7.0	6.0	5.0	4.0	3.0	2.0
1	8.2500	8.2500	8.2500	8.2500	8.2500	8.2500	8.2500	8.2500	8.2500	8.2500	8.2500	8.2500
2	7.7000	7.5625	7.4250	7.3333	7.2188	7.1500	7.0714	6.8750	6.6000	6.1875	5.5000	4.1250
3	7.1500	6.8750	6.6000	6.4167	6.1875	6.0500	5.8929	5.5000	4.9500	4.1250	2.7500	0.0000
4	6.6000	6.1875	5.7750	5.5000	5.1563	4.9500	4.7143	4.1250	3.3000	2.0625	----	----
5	6.0500	5.5000	4.9500	4.5833	4.1250	3.8500	3.5357	2.7500	1.6500	0.0000	----	----
6	5.5000	4.8125	4.1250	3.6667	3.0938	2.7500	2.3571	1.3750	0.0000	----	----	----
7	4.9500	4.1250	3.3000	2.7500	2.0625	1.6500	1.1786	----	----	----	----	----
8	4.4000	3.4375	2.4750	1.8333	1.0313	0.5500	0.0000	----	----	----	----	----
9	3.8500	2.7500	1.6500	0.9167	0.0000	----	----	----	----	----	----	----
10	3.3000	2.0625	0.8250	----	----	----	----	----	----	----	----	----
11	2.7500	1.3750	0.0000	----	----	----	----	----	----	----	----	----
12	2.2000	0.6875	----	----	----	----	----	----	----	----	----	----
13	1.6500	----	----	----	----	----	----	----	----	----	----	----
14	1.1000	----	----	----	----	----	----	----	----	----	----	----
15	0.5500	----	----	----	----	----	----	----	----	----	----	----

Entry is percentage of original principal paid as interest in selected year.

Interest Payment on Constant Principal Repayment Loans

8.50% Interest Rate
Annual Payments

Repayment Period in Years

Year	15.0	12.0	10.0	9.0	8.0	7.5	7.0	6.0	5.0	4.0	3.0	2.0
1	8.5000	8.5000	8.5000	8.5000	8.5000	8.5000	8.5000	8.5000	8.5000	8.5000	8.5000	8.5000
2	7.9333	7.7917	7.6500	7.5556	7.4375	7.3667	7.2857	7.0833	6.8000	6.3750	5.6667	4.2500
3	7.3667	7.0833	6.8000	6.6111	6.3750	6.2333	6.0714	5.6667	5.1000	4.2500	2.8333	0.0000
4	6.8000	6.3750	5.9500	5.6667	5.3125	5.1000	4.8571	4.2500	3.4000	2.1250	----	----
5	6.2333	5.6667	5.1000	4.7222	4.2500	3.9667	3.6429	2.8333	1.7000	0.0000	----	----
6	5.6667	4.9583	4.2500	3.7778	3.1875	2.8333	2.4286	1.4167	0.0000	----	----	----
7	5.1000	4.2500	3.4000	2.8333	2.1250	1.7000	1.2143	----	----	----	----	----
8	4.5333	3.5417	2.5500	1.8889	1.0625	0.5667	0.0000	----	----	----	----	----
9	3.9667	2.8333	1.7000	0.9444	0.0000	----	----	----	----	----	----	----
10	3.4000	2.1250	0.8500	----	----	----	----	----	----	----	----	----
11	2.8333	1.4167	0.0000	----	----	----	----	----	----	----	----	----
12	2.2667	0.7083	----	----	----	----	----	----	----	----	----	----
13	1.7000	----	----	----	----	----	----	----	----	----	----	----
14	1.1333	----	----	----	----	----	----	----	----	----	----	----
15	0.5667	----	----	----	----	----	----	----	----	----	----	----

8.75% Interest Rate
Annual Payments

Year	15.0	12.0	10.0	9.0	8.0	7.5	7.0	6.0	5.0	4.0	3.0	2.0
1	8.7500	8.7500	8.7500	8.7500	8.7500	8.7500	8.7500	8.7500	8.7500	8.7500	8.7500	8.7500
2	8.1667	8.0208	7.8750	7.7778	7.6563	7.5833	7.5000	7.2917	7.0000	6.5625	5.8333	4.3750
3	7.5833	7.2917	7.0000	6.8056	6.5625	6.4167	6.2500	5.8333	5.2500	4.3750	2.9167	0.0000
4	7.0000	6.5625	6.1250	5.8333	5.4688	5.2500	5.0000	4.3750	3.5000	2.1875	----	----
5	6.4167	5.8333	5.2500	4.8611	4.3750	4.0833	3.7500	2.9167	1.7500	0.0000	----	----
6	5.8333	5.1042	4.3750	3.8889	3.2813	2.9167	2.5000	1.4583	0.0000	----	----	----
7	5.2500	4.3750	3.5000	2.9167	2.1875	1.7500	1.2500	----	----	----	----	----
8	4.6667	3.6458	2.6250	1.9444	1.0938	0.5833	0.0000	----	----	----	----	----
9	4.0833	2.9167	1.7500	0.9722	0.0000	----	----	----	----	----	----	----
10	3.5000	2.1875	0.8750	----	----	----	----	----	----	----	----	----
11	2.9167	1.4583	0.0000	----	----	----	----	----	----	----	----	----
12	2.3333	0.7292	----	----	----	----	----	----	----	----	----	----
13	1.7500	----	----	----	----	----	----	----	----	----	----	----
14	1.1667	----	----	----	----	----	----	----	----	----	----	----
15	0.5833	----	----	----	----	----	----	----	----	----	----	----

9.00% Interest Rate
Annual Payments

Year	15.0	12.0	10.0	9.0	8.0	7.5	7.0	6.0	5.0	4.0	3.0	2.0
1	9.0000	9.0000	9.0000	9.0000	9.0000	9.0000	9.0000	9.0000	9.0000	9.0000	9.0000	9.0000
2	8.4000	8.2500	8.1000	8.0000	7.8750	7.8000	7.7143	7.5000	7.2000	6.7500	6.0000	4.5000
3	7.8000	7.5000	7.2000	7.0000	6.7500	6.6000	6.4286	6.0000	5.4000	4.5000	3.0000	0.0000
4	7.2000	6.7500	6.3000	6.0000	5.6250	5.4000	5.1429	4.5000	3.6000	2.2500	----	----
5	6.6000	6.0000	5.4000	5.0000	4.5000	4.2000	3.8571	3.0000	1.8000	0.0000	----	----
6	6.0000	5.2500	4.5000	4.0000	3.3750	3.0000	2.5714	1.5000	0.0000	----	----	----
7	5.4000	4.5000	3.6000	3.0000	2.2500	1.8000	1.2857	----	----	----	----	----
8	4.8000	3.7500	2.7000	2.0000	1.1250	0.6000	0.0000	----	----	----	----	----
9	4.2000	3.0000	1.8000	1.0000	0.0000	----	----	----	----	----	----	----
10	3.6000	2.2500	0.9000	----	----	----	----	----	----	----	----	----
11	3.0000	1.5000	0.0000	----	----	----	----	----	----	----	----	----
12	2.4000	0.7500	----	----	----	----	----	----	----	----	----	----
13	1.8000	----	----	----	----	----	----	----	----	----	----	----
14	1.2000	----	----	----	----	----	----	----	----	----	----	----
15	0.6000	----	----	----	----	----	----	----	----	----	----	----

9.25% Interest Rate
Annual Payments

Year	15.0	12.0	10.0	9.0	8.0	7.5	7.0	6.0	5.0	4.0	3.0	2.0
1	9.2500	9.2500	9.2500	9.2500	9.2500	9.2500	9.2500	9.2500	9.2500	9.2500	9.2500	9.2500
2	8.6333	8.4792	8.3250	8.2222	8.0938	8.0167	7.9286	7.7083	7.4000	6.9375	6.1667	4.6250
3	8.0167	7.7083	7.4000	7.1944	6.9375	6.7833	6.6071	6.1667	5.5500	4.6250	3.0833	0.0000
4	7.4000	6.9375	6.4750	6.1667	5.7813	5.5500	5.2857	4.6250	3.7000	2.3125	----	----
5	6.7833	6.1667	5.5500	5.1389	4.6250	4.3167	3.9643	3.0833	1.8500	0.0000	----	----
6	6.1667	5.3958	4.6250	4.1111	3.4688	3.0833	2.6429	1.5417	0.0000	----	----	----
7	5.5500	4.6250	3.7000	3.0833	2.3125	1.8500	1.3214	----	----	----	----	----
8	4.9333	3.8542	2.7750	2.0556	1.1563	0.6167	0.0000	----	----	----	----	----
9	4.3167	3.0833	1.8500	1.0278	0.0000	----	----	----	----	----	----	----
10	3.7000	2.3125	0.9250	----	----	----	----	----	----	----	----	----
11	3.0833	1.5417	0.0000	----	----	----	----	----	----	----	----	----
12	2.4667	0.7708	----	----	----	----	----	----	----	----	----	----
13	1.8500	----	----	----	----	----	----	----	----	----	----	----
14	1.2333	----	----	----	----	----	----	----	----	----	----	----
15	0.6167	----	----	----	----	----	----	----	----	----	----	----

Entry is percentage of original principal paid as interest in selected year.

Interest Payment on Constant Principal Repayment Loans

9.50% Interest Rate   Annual Payments

Repayment Period in Years

Year	15.0	12.0	10.0	9.0	8.0	7.5	7.0	6.0	5.0	4.0	3.0	2.0
1	9.5000	9.5000	9.5000	9.5000	9.5000	9.5000	9.5000	9.5000	9.5000	9.5000	9.5000	9.5000
2	8.8667	8.7083	8.5500	8.4444	8.3125	8.2333	8.1429	7.9167	7.6000	7.1250	6.3333	4.7500
3	8.2333	7.9167	7.6000	7.3889	7.1250	6.9667	6.7857	6.3333	5.7000	4.7500	3.1667	0.0000
4	7.6000	7.1250	6.6500	6.3333	5.9375	5.7000	5.4286	4.7500	3.8000	2.3750	----	----
5	6.9667	6.3333	5.7000	5.2778	4.7500	4.4333	4.0714	3.1667	1.9000	0.0000	----	----
6	6.3333	5.5417	4.7500	4.2222	3.5625	3.1667	2.7143	1.5833	0.0000	----	----	----
7	5.7000	4.7500	3.8000	3.1667	2.3750	1.9000	1.3571	----	----	----	----	----
8	5.0667	3.9583	2.8500	2.1111	1.1875	0.6333	0.0000	----	----	----	----	----
9	4.4333	3.1667	1.9000	1.0556	0.0000	----	----	----	----	----	----	----
10	3.8000	2.3750	0.9500	----	----	----	----	----	----	----	----	----
11	3.1667	1.5833	0.0000	----	----	----	----	----	----	----	----	----
12	2.5333	0.7917	----	----	----	----	----	----	----	----	----	----
13	1.9000	----	----	----	----	----	----	----	----	----	----	----
14	1.2667	----	----	----	----	----	----	----	----	----	----	----
15	0.6333	----	----	----	----	----	----	----	----	----	----	----

9.75% Interest Rate   Annual Payments

Year	15.0	12.0	10.0	9.0	8.0	7.5	7.0	6.0	5.0	4.0	3.0	2.0
1	9.7500	9.7500	9.7500	9.7500	9.7500	9.7500	9.7500	9.7500	9.7500	9.7500	9.7500	9.7500
2	9.1000	8.9375	8.7750	8.6667	8.5313	8.4500	8.3571	8.1250	7.8000	7.3125	6.5000	4.8750
3	8.4500	8.1250	7.8000	7.5833	7.3125	7.1500	6.9643	6.5000	5.8500	4.8750	3.2500	0.0000
4	7.8000	7.3125	6.8250	6.5000	6.0938	5.8500	5.5714	4.8750	3.9000	2.4375	----	----
5	7.1500	6.5000	5.8500	5.4167	4.8750	4.5500	4.1786	3.2500	1.9500	0.0000	----	----
6	6.5000	5.6875	4.8750	4.3333	3.6563	3.2500	2.7857	1.6250	0.0000	----	----	----
7	5.8500	4.8750	3.9000	3.2500	2.4375	1.9500	1.3929	----	----	----	----	----
8	5.2000	4.0625	2.9250	2.1667	1.2188	0.6500	0.0000	----	----	----	----	----
9	4.5500	3.2500	1.9500	1.0833	0.0000	----	----	----	----	----	----	----
10	3.9000	2.4375	0.9750	----	----	----	----	----	----	----	----	----
11	3.2500	1.6250	0.0000	----	----	----	----	----	----	----	----	----
12	2.6000	0.8125	----	----	----	----	----	----	----	----	----	----
13	1.9500	----	----	----	----	----	----	----	----	----	----	----
14	1.3000	----	----	----	----	----	----	----	----	----	----	----
15	0.6500	----	----	----	----	----	----	----	----	----	----	----

10.00% Interest Rate   Annual Payments

Year	15.0	12.0	10.0	9.0	8.0	7.5	7.0	6.0	5.0	4.0	3.0	2.0
1	10.0000	10.0000	10.0000	10.0000	10.0000	10.0000	10.0000	10.0000	10.0000	10.0000	10.0000	10.0000
2	9.3333	9.1667	9.0000	8.8889	8.7500	8.6667	8.5714	8.3333	8.0000	7.5000	6.6667	5.0000
3	8.6667	8.3333	8.0000	7.7778	7.5000	7.3333	7.1429	6.6667	6.0000	5.0000	3.3333	0.0000
4	8.0000	7.5000	7.0000	6.6667	6.2500	6.0000	5.7143	5.0000	4.0000	2.5000	----	----
5	7.3333	6.6667	6.0000	5.5556	5.0000	4.6667	4.2857	3.3333	2.0000	0.0000	----	----
6	6.6667	5.8333	5.0000	4.4444	3.7500	3.3333	2.8571	1.6667	0.0000	----	----	----
7	6.0000	5.0000	4.0000	3.3333	2.5000	2.0000	1.4286	----	----	----	----	----
8	5.3333	4.1667	3.0000	2.2222	1.2500	0.6667	0.0000	----	----	----	----	----
9	4.6667	3.3333	2.0000	1.1111	0.0000	----	----	----	----	----	----	----
10	4.0000	2.5000	1.0000	----	----	----	----	----	----	----	----	----
11	3.3333	1.6667	0.0000	----	----	----	----	----	----	----	----	----
12	2.6667	0.8333	----	----	----	----	----	----	----	----	----	----
13	2.0000	----	----	----	----	----	----	----	----	----	----	----
14	1.3333	----	----	----	----	----	----	----	----	----	----	----
15	0.6667	----	----	----	----	----	----	----	----	----	----	----

10.25% Interest Rate   Annual Payments

Year	15.0	12.0	10.0	9.0	8.0	7.5	7.0	6.0	5.0	4.0	3.0	2.0
1	10.2500	10.2500	10.2500	10.2500	10.2500	10.2500	10.2500	10.2500	10.2500	10.2500	10.2500	10.2500
2	9.5667	9.3958	9.2250	9.1111	8.9688	8.8833	8.7857	8.5417	8.2000	7.6875	6.8333	5.1250
3	8.8833	8.5417	8.2000	7.9722	7.6875	7.5167	7.3214	6.8333	6.1500	5.1250	3.4167	0.0000
4	8.2000	7.6875	7.1750	6.8333	6.4063	6.1500	5.8571	5.1250	4.1000	2.5625	----	----
5	7.5167	6.8333	6.1500	5.6944	5.1250	4.7833	4.3929	3.4167	2.0500	0.0000	----	----
6	6.8333	5.9792	5.1250	4.5556	3.8438	3.4167	2.9286	1.7083	0.0000	----	----	----
7	6.1500	5.1250	4.1000	3.4167	2.5625	2.0500	1.4643	----	----	----	----	----
8	5.4667	4.2708	3.0750	2.2778	1.2813	0.6833	0.0000	----	----	----	----	----
9	4.7833	3.4167	2.0500	1.1389	0.0000	----	----	----	----	----	----	----
10	4.1000	2.5625	1.0250	----	----	----	----	----	----	----	----	----
11	3.4167	1.7083	0.0000	----	----	----	----	----	----	----	----	----
12	2.7333	0.8542	----	----	----	----	----	----	----	----	----	----
13	2.0500	----	----	----	----	----	----	----	----	----	----	----
14	1.3667	----	----	----	----	----	----	----	----	----	----	----
15	0.6833	----	----	----	----	----	----	----	----	----	----	----

Entry is percentage of original principal paid as interest in selected year.

Interest Payment on Constant Principal Repayment Loans

10.50% Interest Rate Annual Payments

Repayment Period in Years

Year	15.0	12.0	10.0	9.0	8.0	7.5	7.0	6.0	5.0	4.0	3.0	2.0
1	10.5000	10.5000	10.5000	10.5000	10.5000	10.5000	10.5000	10.5000	10.5000	10.5000	10.5000	10.5000
2	9.8000	9.6250	9.4500	9.3333	9.1875	9.1000	9.0000	8.7500	8.4000	7.8750	7.0000	5.2500
3	9.1000	8.7500	8.4000	8.1667	7.8750	7.7000	7.5000	7.0000	6.3000	5.2500	3.5000	0.0000
4	8.4000	7.8750	7.3500	7.0000	6.5625	6.3000	6.0000	5.2500	4.2000	2.6250	----	----
5	7.7000	7.0000	6.3000	5.8333	5.2500	4.9000	4.5000	3.5000	2.1000	0.0000	----	----
6	7.0000	6.1250	5.2500	4.6667	3.9375	3.5000	3.0000	1.7500	0.0000	----	----	----
7	6.3000	5.2500	4.2000	3.5000	2.6250	2.1000	1.5000	----	----	----	----	----
8	5.6000	4.3750	3.1500	2.3333	1.3125	0.7000	0.0000	----	----	----	----	----
9	4.9000	3.5000	2.1000	1.1667	0.0000	----	----	----	----	----	----	----
10	4.2000	2.6250	1.0500	----	----	----	----	----	----	----	----	----
11	3.5000	1.7500	0.0000	----	----	----	----	----	----	----	----	----
12	2.8000	0.8750	----	----	----	----	----	----	----	----	----	----
13	2.1000	----	----	----	----	----	----	----	----	----	----	----
14	1.4000	----	----	----	----	----	----	----	----	----	----	----
15	0.7000	----	----	----	----	----	----	----	----	----	----	----

10.75% Interest Rate Annual Payments

Year	15.0	12.0	10.0	9.0	8.0	7.5	7.0	6.0	5.0	4.0	3.0	2.0
1	10.7500	10.7500	10.7500	10.7500	10.7500	10.7500	10.7500	10.7500	10.7500	10.7500	10.7500	10.7500
2	10.0333	9.8542	9.6750	9.5556	9.4063	9.3167	9.2143	8.9583	8.6000	8.0625	7.1667	5.3750
3	9.3167	8.9583	8.6000	8.3611	8.0625	7.8833	7.6786	7.1667	6.4500	5.3750	3.5833	0.0000
4	8.6000	8.0625	7.5250	7.1667	6.7188	6.4500	6.1429	5.3750	4.3000	2.6875	----	----
5	7.8833	7.1667	6.4500	5.9722	5.3750	5.0167	4.6071	3.5833	2.1500	0.0000	----	----
6	7.1667	6.2708	5.3750	4.7778	4.0313	3.5833	3.0714	1.7917	0.0000	----	----	----
7	6.4500	5.3750	4.3000	3.5833	2.6875	2.1500	1.5357	----	----	----	----	----
8	5.7333	4.4792	3.2250	2.3889	1.3438	0.7167	0.0000	----	----	----	----	----
9	5.0167	3.5833	2.1500	1.1944	0.0000	----	----	----	----	----	----	----
10	4.3000	2.6875	1.0750	----	----	----	----	----	----	----	----	----
11	3.5833	1.7917	0.0000	----	----	----	----	----	----	----	----	----
12	2.8667	0.8958	----	----	----	----	----	----	----	----	----	----
13	2.1500	----	----	----	----	----	----	----	----	----	----	----
14	1.4333	----	----	----	----	----	----	----	----	----	----	----
15	0.7167	----	----	----	----	----	----	----	----	----	----	----

11.00% Interest Rate Annual Payments

Year	15.0	12.0	10.0	9.0	8.0	7.5	7.0	6.0	5.0	4.0	3.0	2.0
1	11.0000	11.0000	11.0000	11.0000	11.0000	11.0000	11.0000	11.0000	11.0000	11.0000	11.0000	11.0000
2	10.2667	10.0833	9.9000	9.7778	9.6250	9.5333	9.4286	9.1667	8.8000	8.2500	7.3333	5.5000
3	9.5333	9.1667	8.8000	8.5556	8.2500	8.0667	7.8571	7.3333	6.6000	5.5000	3.6667	0.0000
4	8.8000	8.2500	7.7000	7.3333	6.8750	6.6000	6.2857	5.5000	4.4000	2.7500	----	----
5	8.0667	7.3333	6.6000	6.1111	5.5000	5.1333	4.7143	3.6667	2.2000	0.0000	----	----
6	7.3333	6.4167	5.5000	4.8889	4.1250	3.6667	3.1429	1.8333	0.0000	----	----	----
7	6.6000	5.5000	4.4000	3.6667	2.7500	2.2000	1.5714	----	----	----	----	----
8	5.8667	4.5833	3.3000	2.4444	1.3750	0.7333	0.0000	----	----	----	----	----
9	5.1333	3.6667	2.2000	1.2222	0.0000	----	----	----	----	----	----	----
10	4.4000	2.7500	1.1000	----	----	----	----	----	----	----	----	----
11	3.6667	1.8333	0.0000	----	----	----	----	----	----	----	----	----
12	2.9333	0.9167	----	----	----	----	----	----	----	----	----	----
13	2.2000	----	----	----	----	----	----	----	----	----	----	----
14	1.4667	----	----	----	----	----	----	----	----	----	----	----
15	0.7333	----	----	----	----	----	----	----	----	----	----	----

11.25% Interest Rate Annual Payments

Year	15.0	12.0	10.0	9.0	8.0	7.5	7.0	6.0	5.0	4.0	3.0	2.0
1	11.2500	11.2500	11.2500	11.2500	11.2500	11.2500	11.2500	11.2500	11.2500	11.2500	11.2500	11.2500
2	10.5000	10.3125	10.1250	10.0000	9.8438	9.7500	9.6429	9.3750	9.0000	8.4375	7.5000	5.6250
3	9.7500	9.3750	9.0000	8.7500	8.4375	8.2500	8.0357	7.5000	6.7500	5.6250	3.7500	0.0000
4	9.0000	8.4375	7.8750	7.5000	7.0313	6.7500	6.4286	5.6250	4.5000	2.8125	----	----
5	8.2500	7.5000	6.7500	6.2500	5.6250	5.2500	4.8214	3.7500	2.2500	0.0000	----	----
6	7.5000	6.5625	5.6250	5.0000	4.2188	3.7500	3.2143	1.8750	0.0000	----	----	----
7	6.7500	5.6250	4.5000	3.7500	2.8125	2.2500	1.6071	----	----	----	----	----
8	6.0000	4.6875	3.3750	2.5000	1.4063	0.7500	0.0000	----	----	----	----	----
9	5.2500	3.7500	2.2500	1.2500	0.0000	----	----	----	----	----	----	----
10	4.5000	2.8125	1.1250	----	----	----	----	----	----	----	----	----
11	3.7500	1.8750	0.0000	----	----	----	----	----	----	----	----	----
12	3.0000	0.9375	----	----	----	----	----	----	----	----	----	----
13	2.2500	----	----	----	----	----	----	----	----	----	----	----
14	1.5000	----	----	----	----	----	----	----	----	----	----	----
15	0.7500	----	----	----	----	----	----	----	----	----	----	----

Entry is percentage of original principal paid as interest in selected year.

Interest Payment on Constant Principal Repayment Loans

11.50% Interest Rate Annual Payments

Repayment Period in Years

Year	15.0	12.0	10.0	9.0	8.0	7.5	7.0	6.0	5.0	4.0	3.0	2.0
1	11.5000	11.5000	11.5000	11.5000	11.5000	11.5000	11.5000	11.5000	11.5000	11.5000	11.5000	11.5000
2	10.7333	10.5417	10.3500	10.2222	10.0625	9.9667	9.8571	9.5833	9.2000	8.6250	7.6667	5.7500
3	9.9667	9.5833	9.2000	8.9444	8.6250	8.4333	8.2143	7.6667	6.9000	5.7500	3.8333	0.0000
4	9.2000	8.6250	8.0500	7.6667	7.1875	6.9000	6.5714	5.7500	4.6000	2.8750	----	----
5	8.4333	7.6667	6.9000	6.3889	5.7500	5.3667	4.9286	3.8333	2.3000	0.0000	----	----
6	7.6667	6.7083	5.7500	5.1111	4.3125	3.8333	3.2857	1.9167	0.0000	----	----	----
7	6.9000	5.7500	4.6000	3.8333	2.8750	2.3000	1.6429	----	----	----	----	----
8	6.1333	4.7917	3.4500	2.5556	1.4375	0.7667	0.0000	----	----	----	----	----
9	5.3667	3.8333	2.3000	1.2778	0.0000	----	----	----	----	----	----	----
10	4.6000	2.8750	1.1500	----	----	----	----	----	----	----	----	----
11	3.8333	1.9167	0.0000	----	----	----	----	----	----	----	----	----
12	3.0667	0.9583	----	----	----	----	----	----	----	----	----	----
13	2.3000	----	----	----	----	----	----	----	----	----	----	----
14	1.5333	----	----	----	----	----	----	----	----	----	----	----
15	0.7667	----	----	----	----	----	----	----	----	----	----	----

11.75% Interest Rate Annual Payments

Year	15.0	12.0	10.0	9.0	8.0	7.5	7.0	6.0	5.0	4.0	3.0	2.0
1	11.7500	11.7500	11.7500	11.7500	11.7500	11.7500	11.7500	11.7500	11.7500	11.7500	11.7500	11.7500
2	10.9667	10.7708	10.5750	10.4444	10.2813	10.1833	10.0714	9.7917	9.4000	8.8125	7.8333	5.8750
3	10.1833	9.7917	9.4000	9.1389	8.8125	8.6167	8.3929	7.8333	7.0500	5.8750	3.9167	0.0000
4	9.4000	8.8125	8.2250	7.8333	7.3438	7.0500	6.7143	5.8750	4.7000	2.9375	----	----
5	8.6167	7.8333	7.0500	6.5278	5.8750	5.4833	5.0357	3.9167	2.3500	0.0000	----	----
6	7.8333	6.8542	5.8750	5.2222	4.4063	3.9167	3.3571	1.9583	0.0000	----	----	----
7	7.0500	5.8750	4.7000	3.9167	2.9375	2.3500	1.6786	----	----	----	----	----
8	6.2667	4.8958	3.5250	2.6111	1.4688	0.7833	0.0000	----	----	----	----	----
9	5.4833	3.9167	2.3500	1.3056	0.0000	----	----	----	----	----	----	----
10	4.7000	2.9375	1.1750	----	----	----	----	----	----	----	----	----
11	3.9167	1.9583	0.0000	----	----	----	----	----	----	----	----	----
12	3.1333	0.9792	----	----	----	----	----	----	----	----	----	----
13	2.3500	----	----	----	----	----	----	----	----	----	----	----
14	1.5667	----	----	----	----	----	----	----	----	----	----	----
15	0.7833	----	----	----	----	----	----	----	----	----	----	----

12.00% Interest Rate Annual Payments

Year	15.0	12.0	10.0	9.0	8.0	7.5	7.0	6.0	5.0	4.0	3.0	2.0
1	12.0000	12.0000	12.0000	12.0000	12.0000	12.0000	12.0000	12.0000	12.0000	12.0000	12.0000	12.0000
2	11.2000	11.0000	10.8000	10.6667	10.5000	10.4000	10.2857	10.0000	9.6000	9.0000	8.0000	6.0000
3	10.4000	10.0000	9.6000	9.3333	9.0000	8.8000	8.5714	8.0000	7.2000	6.0000	4.0000	0.0000
4	9.6000	9.0000	8.4000	8.0000	7.5000	7.2000	6.8571	6.0000	4.8000	3.0000	----	----
5	8.8000	8.0000	7.2000	6.6667	6.0000	5.6000	5.1429	4.0000	2.4000	0.0000	----	----
6	8.0000	7.0000	6.0000	5.3333	4.5000	4.0000	3.4286	2.0000	0.0000	----	----	----
7	7.2000	6.0000	4.8000	4.0000	3.0000	2.4000	1.7143	----	----	----	----	----
8	6.4000	5.0000	3.6000	2.6667	1.5000	0.8000	0.0000	----	----	----	----	----
9	5.6000	4.0000	2.4000	1.3333	0.0000	----	----	----	----	----	----	----
10	4.8000	3.0000	1.2000	----	----	----	----	----	----	----	----	----
11	4.0000	2.0000	0.0000	----	----	----	----	----	----	----	----	----
12	3.2000	1.0000	----	----	----	----	----	----	----	----	----	----
13	2.4000	----	----	----	----	----	----	----	----	----	----	----
14	1.6000	----	----	----	----	----	----	----	----	----	----	----
15	0.8000	----	----	----	----	----	----	----	----	----	----	----

12.25% Interest Rate Annual Payments

Year	15.0	12.0	10.0	9.0	8.0	7.5	7.0	6.0	5.0	4.0	3.0	2.0
1	12.2500	12.2500	12.2500	12.2500	12.2500	12.2500	12.2500	12.2500	12.2500	12.2500	12.2500	12.2500
2	11.4333	11.2292	11.0250	10.8889	10.7188	10.6167	10.5000	10.2083	9.8000	9.1875	8.1667	6.1250
3	10.6167	10.2083	9.8000	9.5278	9.1875	8.9833	8.7500	8.1667	7.3500	6.1250	4.0833	0.0000
4	9.8000	9.1875	8.5750	8.1667	7.6563	7.3500	7.0000	6.1250	4.9000	3.0625	----	----
5	8.9833	8.1667	7.3500	6.8056	6.1250	5.7167	5.2500	4.0833	2.4500	0.0000	----	----
6	8.1667	7.1458	6.1250	5.4444	4.5938	4.0833	3.5000	2.0417	0.0000	----	----	----
7	7.3500	6.1250	4.9000	4.0833	3.0625	2.4500	1.7500	----	----	----	----	----
8	6.5333	5.1042	3.6750	2.7222	1.5313	0.8167	0.0000	----	----	----	----	----
9	5.7167	4.0833	2.4500	1.3611	0.0000	----	----	----	----	----	----	----
10	4.9000	3.0625	1.2250	----	----	----	----	----	----	----	----	----
11	4.0833	2.0417	0.0000	----	----	----	----	----	----	----	----	----
12	3.2667	1.0208	----	----	----	----	----	----	----	----	----	----
13	2.4500	----	----	----	----	----	----	----	----	----	----	----
14	1.6333	----	----	----	----	----	----	----	----	----	----	----
15	0.8167	----	----	----	----	----	----	----	----	----	----	----

Entry is percentage of original principal paid as interest in selected year.

Discounted Amount of a Loan

Zero interest rate on note   Actual/365 Basis

Term of Loan	6.00%	6.125%	6.25%	6.375%	Desired Yield (Nominal Rate) 6.50%	6.625%	6.75%	6.875%	7.00%	7.125%	7.25%
1 Day	99.98356	99.98322	99.98288	99.98254	99.98219	99.98185	99.98151	99.98117	99.98083	99.98048	99.98014
2 Days	99.96713	99.96645	99.96577	99.96508	99.96440	99.96371	99.96303	99.96234	99.96166	99.96097	99.96029
3	99.95071	99.94968	99.94866	99.94763	99.94660	99.94558	99.94455	99.94353	99.94250	99.94147	99.94045
4	99.93429	99.93292	99.93155	99.93019	99.92882	99.92745	99.92608	99.92471	99.92335	99.92198	99.92061
5	99.91788	99.91617	99.91446	99.91275	99.91104	99.90933	99.90762	99.90591	99.90420	99.90249	99.90078
6	99.90147	99.89942	99.89737	99.89532	99.89326	99.89121	99.88916	99.88711	99.88506	99.88301	99.88096
7	99.88506	99.88267	99.88028	99.87789	99.87550	99.87311	99.87072	99.86832	99.86593	99.86354	99.86115
8	99.86867	99.86593	99.86320	99.86047	99.85774	99.85501	99.85227	99.84954	99.84681	99.84408	99.84135
9	99.85227	99.84920	99.84613	99.84305	99.83998	99.83691	99.83384	99.83077	99.82769	99.82462	99.82155
10	99.83589	99.83247	99.82906	99.82565	99.82223	99.81882	99.81541	99.81200	99.80859	99.80517	99.80176
11	99.81950	99.81575	99.81200	99.80825	99.80449	99.80074	99.79699	99.79324	99.78949	99.78573	99.78198
12	99.80313	99.79903	99.79494	99.79085	99.78676	99.78267	99.77857	99.77448	99.77039	99.76630	99.76221
13	99.78676	99.78232	99.77789	99.77346	99.76903	99.76460	99.76017	99.75574	99.75130	99.74688	99.74245
14	99.77039	99.76562	99.76085	99.75608	99.75130	99.74653	99.74176	99.73699	99.73223	99.72746	99.72269
15	99.75403	99.74892	99.74381	99.73870	99.73359	99.72848	99.72337	99.71826	99.71315	99.70805	99.70294
16	99.73768	99.73223	99.72678	99.72133	99.71588	99.71043	99.70498	99.69954	99.69409	99.68864	99.68320
17	99.72133	99.71554	99.70975	99.70396	99.69817	99.69239	99.68660	99.68082	99.67503	99.66925	99.66347
18	99.70498	99.69885	99.69273	99.68660	99.68048	99.67435	99.66823	99.66210	99.65598	99.64986	99.64374
19	99.68864	99.68218	99.67571	99.66925	99.66278	99.65632	99.64986	99.64340	99.63694	99.63048	99.62402
20	99.67231	99.66551	99.65870	99.65190	99.64510	99.63830	99.63150	99.62470	99.61790	99.61111	99.60431
21	99.65598	99.64884	99.64170	99.63456	99.62742	99.62028	99.61315	99.60601	99.59888	99.59174	99.58461
22	99.63966	99.63218	99.62470	99.61722	99.60975	99.60227	99.59480	99.58733	99.57985	99.57238	99.56491
23	99.62334	99.61553	99.60771	99.59989	99.59208	99.58427	99.57646	99.56865	99.56084	99.55303	99.54523
24	99.60703	99.59888	99.59072	99.58257	99.57442	99.56627	99.55813	99.54998	99.54183	99.53369	99.52555
25	99.59072	99.58223	99.57374	99.56525	99.55677	99.54828	99.53980	99.53132	99.52284	99.51436	99.50588
26	99.57442	99.56559	99.55677	99.54794	99.53912	99.53030	99.52148	99.51266	99.50384	99.49503	99.48622
27	99.55813	99.54896	99.53980	99.53064	99.52148	99.51232	99.50317	99.49401	99.48486	99.47571	99.46656
28	99.54183	99.53233	99.52284	99.51334	99.50384	99.49435	99.48486	99.47537	99.46588	99.45640	99.44691
29	99.52555	99.51571	99.50588	99.49605	99.48622	99.47639	99.46656	99.45673	99.44691	99.43709	99.42727
30 Days	99.50927	99.49910	99.48893	99.47876	99.46859	99.45843	99.44827	99.43811	99.42795	99.41779	99.40764
60	99.02095	99.00070	98.98047	98.96023	98.94001	98.91979	98.89958	98.87937	98.85917	98.83898	98.81879
90	98.53502	98.50481	98.47460	98.44441	98.41423	98.38407	98.35391	98.32377	98.29364	98.26353	98.23342
120	98.05148	98.01139	97.97133	97.93128	97.89125	97.85125	97.81126	97.77130	97.73135	97.69143	97.65153
150	97.57031	97.52045	97.47062	97.42082	97.37105	97.32131	97.27161	97.22193	97.17228	97.12267	97.07308
180	97.09150	97.03197	96.97247	96.91302	96.85361	96.79425	96.73493	96.67564	96.61641	96.55721	96.49806
210	96.61505	96.54593	96.47687	96.40787	96.33893	96.27004	96.20121	96.13243	96.06371	95.99505	95.92644
240	96.14093	96.06233	95.98381	95.90535	95.82698	95.74867	95.67043	95.59227	95.51418	95.43616	95.35821
270	95.66913	95.58115	95.49326	95.40546	95.31774	95.23012	95.14259	95.05514	94.96779	94.88052	94.79334
300	95.19966	95.10238	95.00522	94.90816	94.81122	94.71438	94.61765	94.52103	94.42452	94.32812	94.23183
330	94.73248	94.62601	94.51967	94.41346	94.30738	94.20143	94.09562	93.98993	93.88437	93.77894	93.67363
360	94.26760	94.15203	94.03661	93.92134	93.80623	93.69127	93.57646	93.46180	93.34730	93.23295	93.11875
390	93.80500	93.68042	93.55601	93.43178	93.30773	93.18386	93.06017	92.93665	92.81331	92.69014	92.56715
420	93.34467	93.21117	93.07787	92.94478	92.81189	92.67920	92.54672	92.41444	92.28237	92.15049	92.01882
450	92.88660	92.74427	92.60218	92.46031	92.31868	92.17728	92.03611	91.89517	91.75446	91.61398	91.47374
480	92.43078	92.27971	92.12891	91.97837	91.82809	91.67807	91.52832	91.37882	91.22958	91.08060	90.93188
510	91.97719	91.81748	91.65806	91.49894	91.34011	91.18157	91.02332	90.86537	90.70770	90.55032	90.39324
540	91.52583	91.35756	91.18962	91.02201	90.85472	90.68776	90.52112	90.35480	90.18881	90.02313	89.85778
570	91.07668	90.89995	90.72358	90.54757	90.37191	90.19662	90.02168	89.84710	89.67288	89.49901	89.32550
600	90.62974	90.44463	90.25991	90.07559	89.89167	89.70814	89.52500	89.34226	89.15991	88.97794	88.79637
630	90.18500	89.99159	89.79862	89.60608	89.41398	89.22231	89.03106	88.84025	88.64987	88.45991	88.27038
660	89.74243	89.54082	89.33968	89.13902	88.93883	88.73910	88.53985	88.34106	88.14274	87.94489	87.74750
690	89.30204	89.09231	88.88309	88.67439	88.46620	88.25852	88.05134	87.84468	87.63852	87.43287	87.22772
720	88.86380	88.64604	88.42883	88.21218	87.99608	87.78053	87.56554	87.35109	87.13718	86.92383	86.71101

Entry is discounted amount in percent at selected rate, compounded each 30 days.

Discounted Amount of a Loan

Zero interest rate on note   Actual/365 Basis

Term of Loan	7.375%	7.50%	7.625%	7.75%	7.875%	8.00%	8.125%	8.25%	8.375%	8.50%	8.625%
					Desired Yield (Nominal Rate)						
1 Day	99.97980	99.97946	99.97911	99.97877	99.97843	99.97809	99.97774	99.97740	99.97706	99.97672	99.97638
2 Days	99.95961	99.95892	99.95824	99.95755	99.95687	99.95618	99.95550	99.95481	99.95413	99.95345	99.95276
3	99.93942	99.93839	99.93737	99.93634	99.93532	99.93429	99.93326	99.93224	99.93121	99.93019	99.92916
4	99.91924	99.91788	99.91651	99.91514	99.91377	99.91241	99.91104	99.90967	99.90830	99.90694	99.90557
5	99.89907	99.89737	99.89566	99.89395	99.89224	99.89053	99.88882	99.88711	99.88541	99.88370	99.88199
6	99.87891	99.87686	99.87481	99.87276	99.87072	99.86867	99.86662	99.86457	99.86252	99.86047	99.85842
7	99.85876	99.85637	99.85398	99.85159	99.84920	99.84681	99.84442	99.84203	99.83964	99.83725	99.83486
8	99.83862	99.83589	99.83316	99.83043	99.82769	99.82496	99.82223	99.81950	99.81677	99.81405	99.81132
9	99.81848	99.81541	99.81234	99.80927	99.80620	99.80313	99.80006	99.79699	99.79392	99.79085	99.78778
10	99.79835	99.79494	99.79153	99.78812	99.78471	99.78130	99.77789	99.77448	99.77107	99.76766	99.76426
11	99.77823	99.77448	99.77073	99.76698	99.76323	99.75948	99.75574	99.75199	99.74824	99.74449	99.74074
12	99.75812	99.75403	99.74994	99.74585	99.74176	99.73768	99.73359	99.72950	99.72541	99.72133	99.71724
13	99.73802	99.73359	99.72916	99.72473	99.72031	99.71588	99.71145	99.70703	99.70260	99.69817	99.69375
14	99.71792	99.71315	99.70839	99.70362	99.69885	99.69409	99.68932	99.68456	99.67980	99.67503	99.67027
15	99.69783	99.69273	99.68762	99.68252	99.67741	99.67231	99.66721	99.66210	99.65700	99.65190	99.64680
16	99.67775	99.67231	99.66687	99.66142	99.65598	99.65054	99.64510	99.63966	99.63422	99.62878	99.62334
17	99.65768	99.65190	99.64612	99.64034	99.63456	99.62878	99.62300	99.61722	99.61145	99.60567	99.59989
18	99.63762	99.63150	99.62538	99.61926	99.61315	99.60703	99.60091	99.59480	99.58869	99.58257	99.57646
19	99.61756	99.61111	99.60465	99.59820	99.59174	99.58529	99.57884	99.57238	99.56593	99.55948	99.55303
20	99.59752	99.59072	99.58393	99.57714	99.57035	99.56356	99.55677	99.54998	99.54319	99.53641	99.52962
21	99.57748	99.57035	99.56322	99.55609	99.54896	99.54183	99.53471	99.52758	99.52046	99.51334	99.50622
22	99.55745	99.54998	99.54251	99.53505	99.52758	99.52012	99.51266	99.50520	99.49774	99.49028	99.48283
23	99.53742	99.52962	99.52182	99.51402	99.50622	99.49842	99.49062	99.48283	99.47503	99.46724	99.45944
24	99.51741	99.50927	99.50113	99.49299	99.48486	99.47673	99.46859	99.46046	99.45233	99.44420	99.43607
25	99.49740	99.48893	99.48045	99.47198	99.46351	99.45504	99.44657	99.43811	99.42964	99.42118	99.41272
26	99.47740	99.46859	99.45978	99.45098	99.44217	99.43337	99.42456	99.41576	99.40696	99.39816	99.38937
27	99.45741	99.44827	99.43912	99.42998	99.42084	99.41170	99.40256	99.39343	99.38429	99.37516	99.36603
28	99.43743	99.42795	99.41847	99.40899	99.39952	99.39004	99.38057	99.37110	99.36164	99.35217	99.34271
29	99.41745	99.40764	99.39783	99.38801	99.37821	99.36840	99.35859	99.34879	99.33899	99.32919	99.31939
30 Days	99.39749	99.38734	99.37719	99.36705	99.35690	99.34676	99.33662	99.32648	99.31635	99.30622	99.29609
60	98.79861	98.77843	98.75826	98.73810	98.71794	98.69779	98.67764	98.65751	98.63737	98.61725	98.59713
90	98.20333	98.17325	98.14319	98.11313	98.08309	98.05306	98.02304	97.99303	97.96304	97.93306	97.90309
120	97.61165	97.57178	97.53194	97.49212	97.45232	97.41254	97.37278	97.33303	97.29331	97.25361	97.21393
150	97.02352	96.97400	96.92450	96.87504	96.82560	96.77620	96.72683	96.67748	96.62817	96.57888	96.52963
180	96.43894	96.37988	96.32085	96.26186	96.20292	96.14402	96.08516	96.02634	95.96757	95.90884	95.85015
210	95.85789	95.78939	95.72095	95.65257	95.58424	95.51597	95.44775	95.37959	95.31149	95.24344	95.17544
240	95.28033	95.20253	95.12479	95.04713	94.96954	94.89202	94.81457	94.73720	94.65989	94.58265	94.50549
270	94.70626	94.61926	94.53235	94.44553	94.35879	94.27215	94.18559	94.09913	94.01275	93.92646	93.84025
300	94.13564	94.03956	93.94359	93.84773	93.75198	93.65633	93.56079	93.46535	93.37003	93.27481	93.17970
330	93.56846	93.46342	93.35850	93.25372	93.14906	93.04453	92.94013	92.83585	92.73170	92.62769	92.52379
360	93.00470	92.89080	92.77706	92.66346	92.55002	92.43672	92.32358	92.21059	92.09774	91.98505	91.87251
390	92.44434	92.32170	92.19923	92.07695	91.95483	91.83289	91.71113	91.58954	91.46812	91.34687	91.22580
420	91.88735	91.75608	91.62501	91.49414	91.36347	91.23300	91.10274	90.97267	90.84280	90.71312	90.58365
450	91.33371	91.19392	91.05436	90.91502	90.77592	90.63703	90.49838	90.35995	90.22175	90.08377	89.94602
480	90.78342	90.63521	90.48726	90.33957	90.19214	90.04496	89.89803	89.75136	89.60495	89.45879	89.31288
510	90.23644	90.07993	89.92370	89.76776	89.61211	89.45675	89.30167	89.14687	88.99236	88.83814	88.68419
540	89.69275	89.52804	89.36365	89.19958	89.03582	88.87238	88.70926	88.54646	88.38397	88.22179	88.05993
570	89.15234	88.97954	88.80708	88.63498	88.46323	88.29183	88.12078	87.95008	87.77973	87.60972	87.44006
600	88.61519	88.43439	88.25399	88.07396	87.89433	87.71508	87.53621	87.35773	87.17962	87.00190	86.82456
630	88.08127	87.89259	87.70433	87.51650	87.32908	87.14209	86.95551	86.76936	86.58362	86.39830	86.21339
660	87.55057	87.35411	87.15810	86.96256	86.76747	86.57284	86.37867	86.18495	85.99169	85.79888	85.60652
690	87.02307	86.81892	86.61527	86.41212	86.20947	86.00731	85.80565	85.60448	85.40381	85.20362	85.00393
720	86.49874	86.28701	86.07582	85.86517	85.65506	85.44548	85.23644	85.02793	84.81994	84.61249	84.40557

Entry is discounted amount in percent at selected rate, compounded each 30 days.

Discounted Amount of a Loan

Zero interest rate on note　　　　　　　　　　　　　　　　　　　　　　　　　　　　　Actual/365 Basis

Term of Loan	Desired Yield (Nominal Rate)										
	8.75%	8.875%	9.00%	9.125%	9.25%	9.375%	9.50%	9.625%	9.75%	9.875%	10.00%
1 Day	99.97603	99.97569	99.97535	99.97501	99.97466	99.97432	99.97398	99.97364	99.97329	99.97295	99.97261
2 Days	99.95208	99.95139	99.95071	99.95002	99.94934	99.94866	99.94797	99.94729	99.94660	99.94592	99.94524
3	99.92813	99.92711	99.92608	99.92506	99.92403	99.92300	99.92198	99.92095	99.91993	99.91890	99.91788
4	99.90420	99.90283	99.90147	99.90010	99.89873	99.89737	99.89600	99.89463	99.89326	99.89190	99.89053
5	99.88028	99.87857	99.87686	99.87516	99.87345	99.87174	99.87003	99.86832	99.86662	99.86491	99.86320
6	99.85637	99.85432	99.85227	99.85022	99.84818	99.84613	99.84408	99.84203	99.83998	99.83793	99.83589
7	99.83247	99.83008	99.82769	99.82531	99.82292	99.82053	99.81814	99.81575	99.81336	99.81097	99.80859
8	99.80859	99.80586	99.80313	99.80040	99.79767	99.79494	99.79221	99.78949	99.78676	99.78403	99.78130
9	99.78471	99.78164	99.77857	99.77551	99.77244	99.76937	99.76630	99.76323	99.76017	99.75710	99.75403
10	99.76085	99.75744	99.75403	99.75062	99.74722	99.74381	99.74040	99.73699	99.73359	99.73018	99.72678
11	99.73699	99.73325	99.72950	99.72575	99.72201	99.71826	99.71452	99.71077	99.70703	99.70328	99.69954
12	99.71315	99.70907	99.70498	99.70090	99.69681	99.69273	99.68864	99.68456	99.68048	99.67639	99.67231
13	99.68932	99.68490	99.68048	99.67605	99.67163	99.66721	99.66278	99.65836	99.65394	99.64952	99.64510
14	99.66551	99.66074	99.65598	99.65122	99.64646	99.64170	99.63694	99.63218	99.62742	99.62266	99.61790
15	99.64170	99.63660	99.63150	99.62640	99.62130	99.61620	99.61111	99.60601	99.60091	99.59582	99.59072
16	99.61790	99.61247	99.60703	99.60159	99.59616	99.59072	99.58529	99.57985	99.57442	99.56899	99.56356
17	99.59412	99.58835	99.58257	99.57680	99.57103	99.56525	99.55948	99.55371	99.54794	99.54217	99.53641
18	99.57035	99.56424	99.55813	99.55202	99.54591	99.53980	99.53369	99.52758	99.52148	99.51537	99.50927
19	99.54659	99.54014	99.53369	99.52725	99.52080	99.51436	99.50791	99.50147	99.49503	99.48859	99.48215
20	99.52284	99.51605	99.50927	99.50249	99.49571	99.48893	99.48215	99.47537	99.46859	99.46182	99.45504
21	99.49910	99.49198	99.48486	99.47774	99.47063	99.46351	99.45640	99.44928	99.44217	99.43506	99.42795
22	99.47537	99.46791	99.46046	99.45301	99.44556	99.43811	99.43066	99.42321	99.41576	99.40832	99.40087
23	99.45165	99.44386	99.43607	99.42829	99.42050	99.41272	99.40493	99.39715	99.38937	99.38159	99.37381
24	99.42795	99.41982	99.41170	99.40358	99.39546	99.38734	99.37922	99.37110	99.36299	99.35487	99.34676
25	99.40426	99.39580	99.38734	99.37888	99.37043	99.36197	99.35352	99.34507	99.33662	99.32817	99.31973
26	99.38057	99.37178	99.36299	99.35420	99.34541	99.33662	99.32784	99.31905	99.31027	99.30149	99.29271
27	99.35690	99.34778	99.33865	99.32953	99.32040	99.31128	99.30216	99.29305	99.28393	99.27482	99.26571
28	99.33324	99.32378	99.31432	99.30487	99.29541	99.28596	99.27651	99.26706	99.25761	99.24816	99.23872
29	99.30959	99.29980	99.29001	99.28022	99.27043	99.26064	99.25086	99.24108	99.23130	99.22152	99.21174
30 Days	99.28596	99.27583	99.26571	99.25558	99.24546	99.23534	99.22523	99.21511	99.20500	99.19489	99.18478
60	98.57701	98.55691	98.53680	98.51671	98.49662	98.47654	98.45646	98.43639	98.41632	98.39626	98.37621
90	97.87313	97.84319	97.81325	97.78333	97.75342	97.72353	97.69364	97.66377	97.63391	97.60407	97.57423
120	97.17427	97.13464	97.09502	97.05542	97.01584	96.97628	96.93674	96.89722	96.85772	96.81825	96.77879
150	96.48041	96.43122	96.38205	96.33292	96.28382	96.23474	96.18570	96.13669	96.08771	96.03875	95.98983
180	95.79150	95.73289	95.67433	95.61580	95.55732	95.49888	95.44048	95.38213	95.32381	95.26554	95.20731
210	95.10750	95.03962	94.97179	94.90402	94.83630	94.76864	94.70104	94.63348	94.56599	94.49855	94.43116
240	94.42840	94.35137	94.27442	94.19754	94.12073	94.04399	93.96732	93.89072	93.81419	93.73773	93.66134
270	93.75414	93.66811	93.58217	93.49632	93.41055	93.32488	93.23929	93.15378	93.06837	92.98304	92.89780
300	93.08469	92.98979	92.89500	92.80032	92.70574	92.61126	92.51689	92.42263	92.32847	92.23442	92.14048
330	92.42003	92.31639	92.21288	92.10949	92.00624	91.90310	91.80010	91.69722	91.59446	91.49184	91.38933
360	91.76011	91.64786	91.53576	91.42382	91.31201	91.20036	91.08886	90.97750	90.86629	90.75523	90.64431
390	91.10490	90.98418	90.86362	90.74324	90.62303	90.50299	90.38313	90.26343	90.14390	90.02455	89.90536
420	90.45437	90.32530	90.19642	90.06773	89.93925	89.81096	89.68286	89.55496	89.42726	89.29975	89.17244
450	89.80849	89.67119	89.53411	89.39725	89.26062	89.12421	88.98802	88.85206	88.71631	88.58079	88.44549
480	89.16722	89.02182	88.87667	88.73177	88.58712	88.44272	88.29857	88.15467	88.01102	87.86762	87.72447
510	88.53053	88.37715	88.22405	88.07123	87.91869	87.76644	87.61446	87.46276	87.31133	87.16019	87.00932
540	87.89838	87.73715	87.57623	87.41561	87.25531	87.09532	86.93564	86.77627	86.61721	86.45845	86.30001
570	87.27075	87.10178	86.93316	86.76488	86.59694	86.42934	86.26209	86.09518	85.92860	85.76237	85.59647
600	86.64760	86.47102	86.29481	86.11899	85.94353	85.76846	85.59376	85.41943	85.24547	85.07189	84.89868
630	86.02890	85.84482	85.66116	85.47790	85.29506	85.11262	84.93060	84.74898	84.56777	84.38697	84.20657
660	85.41462	85.22316	85.03215	84.84159	84.65147	84.46181	84.27258	84.08380	83.89546	83.70756	83.52010
690	84.80472	84.60600	84.40776	84.21001	84.01275	83.81596	83.61966	83.42384	83.22849	83.03362	82.83923
720	84.19918	83.99331	83.78796	83.58314	83.37884	83.17506	82.97180	82.76905	82.56682	82.36511	82.16391

Entry is discounted amount in percent at selected rate, compounded each 30 days.

Discounted Amount of a Loan

Zero interest rate on note   Actual/365 Basis

Term of Loan	10.125%	10.25%	10.375%	10.50%	Desired Yield (Nominal Rate) 10.625%	10.75%	10.875%	11.00%	11.125%	11.25%	11.375%
1 Day	99.97227	99.97193	99.97158	99.97124	99.97090	99.97056	99.97021	99.96987	99.96953	99.96919	99.96885
2 Days	99.94455	99.94387	99.94318	99.94250	99.94181	99.94113	99.94045	99.93976	99.93908	99.93839	99.93771
3	99.91685	99.91582	99.91480	99.91377	99.91275	99.91172	99.91070	99.90967	99.90865	99.90762	99.90659
4	99.88916	99.88780	99.88643	99.88506	99.88370	99.88233	99.88096	99.87960	99.87823	99.87686	99.87550
5	99.86149	99.85979	99.85808	99.85637	99.85466	99.85296	99.85125	99.84954	99.84783	99.84613	99.84442
6	99.83384	99.83179	99.82974	99.82769	99.82565	99.82360	99.82155	99.81950	99.81746	99.81541	99.81336
7	99.80620	99.80381	99.80142	99.79903	99.79665	99.79426	99.79187	99.78949	99.78710	99.78471	99.78232
8	99.77857	99.77585	99.77312	99.77039	99.76766	99.76494	99.76221	99.75948	99.75676	99.75403	99.75130
9	99.75096	99.74790	99.74483	99.74176	99.73870	99.73563	99.73257	99.72950	99.72644	99.72337	99.72031
10	99.72337	99.71996	99.71656	99.71315	99.70975	99.70634	99.70294	99.69954	99.69613	99.69273	99.68932
11	99.69579	99.69205	99.68830	99.68456	99.68082	99.67707	99.67333	99.66959	99.66585	99.66210	99.65836
12	99.66823	99.66415	99.66006	99.65598	99.65190	99.64782	99.64374	99.63966	99.63558	99.63150	99.62742
13	99.64068	99.63626	99.63184	99.62742	99.62300	99.61858	99.61417	99.60975	99.60533	99.60091	99.59650
14	99.61315	99.60839	99.60363	99.59888	99.59412	99.58936	99.58461	99.57985	99.57510	99.57035	99.56559
15	99.58563	99.58053	99.57544	99.57035	99.56525	99.56016	99.55507	99.54998	99.54489	99.53980	99.53471
16	99.55813	99.55269	99.54726	99.54183	99.53641	99.53098	99.52555	99.52012	99.51470	99.50927	99.50384
17	99.53064	99.52487	99.51910	99.51334	99.50757	99.50181	99.49605	99.49028	99.48452	99.47876	99.47300
18	99.50317	99.49706	99.49096	99.48486	99.47876	99.47266	99.46656	99.46046	99.45436	99.44827	99.44217
19	99.47571	99.46927	99.46283	99.45640	99.44996	99.44352	99.43709	99.43066	99.42422	99.41779	99.41136
20	99.44827	99.44149	99.43472	99.42795	99.42118	99.41441	99.40764	99.40087	99.39410	99.38734	99.38057
21	99.42084	99.41373	99.40662	99.39952	99.39241	99.38531	99.37821	99.37110	99.36400	99.35690	99.34980
22	99.39343	99.38599	99.37854	99.37110	99.36366	99.35623	99.34879	99.34135	99.33392	99.32648	99.31905
23	99.36603	99.35825	99.35048	99.34271	99.33493	99.32716	99.31939	99.31162	99.30385	99.29609	99.28832
24	99.33865	99.33054	99.32243	99.31432	99.30622	99.29811	99.29001	99.28191	99.27381	99.26571	99.25761
25	99.31128	99.30284	99.29440	99.28596	99.27752	99.26908	99.26064	99.25221	99.24378	99.23534	99.22691
26	99.28393	99.27516	99.26638	99.25761	99.24884	99.24007	99.23130	99.22253	99.21376	99.20500	99.19624
27	99.25660	99.24749	99.23838	99.22927	99.22017	99.21107	99.20197	99.19287	99.18377	99.17468	99.16558
28	99.22927	99.21983	99.21039	99.20096	99.19152	99.18209	99.17266	99.16323	99.15380	99.14437	99.13495
29	99.20197	99.19220	99.18242	99.17266	99.16289	99.15312	99.14336	99.13360	99.12384	99.11408	99.10433
30 Days	99.17468	99.16457	99.15447	99.14437	99.13427	99.12418	99.11408	99.10399	99.09390	99.08381	99.07373
60	98.35616	98.33612	98.31609	98.29606	98.27604	98.25602	98.23601	98.21601	98.19601	98.17602	98.15604
90	97.54441	97.51460	97.48480	97.45501	97.42524	97.39548	97.36573	97.33599	97.30626	97.27655	97.24685
120	96.73935	96.69993	96.66054	96.62116	96.58180	96.54246	96.50315	96.46385	96.42457	96.38531	96.34608
150	95.94094	95.89208	95.84324	95.79444	95.74567	95.69692	95.64821	95.59952	95.55087	95.50224	95.45365
180	95.14912	95.09097	95.03286	94.97479	94.91677	94.85879	94.80084	94.74294	94.68508	94.62727	94.56949
210	94.36383	94.29655	94.22933	94.16216	94.09505	94.02799	93.96099	93.89404	93.82714	93.76030	93.69352
240	93.58502	93.50877	93.43259	93.35648	93.28044	93.20447	93.12857	93.05274	92.97698	92.90129	92.82566
270	92.81264	92.72757	92.64259	92.55770	92.47289	92.38817	92.30353	92.21898	92.13452	92.05014	91.96585
300	92.04664	91.95290	91.85927	91.76575	91.67232	91.57901	91.48580	91.39269	91.29969	91.20679	91.11399
330	91.28695	91.18470	91.08257	90.98057	90.87869	90.77694	90.67531	90.57380	90.47242	90.37116	90.27003
360	90.53354	90.42292	90.31244	90.20211	90.09193	89.98189	89.87200	89.76225	89.65265	89.54320	89.43388
390	89.78635	89.66750	89.54883	89.43032	89.31198	89.19381	89.07581	88.95798	88.84031	88.72281	88.60548
420	89.04532	88.91839	88.79166	88.66513	88.53878	88.41263	88.28667	88.16090	88.03533	87.90995	87.78476
450	88.31041	88.17555	88.04090	87.90648	87.77228	87.63829	87.50452	87.37098	87.23764	87.10453	86.97163
480	87.58156	87.43890	87.29649	87.15433	87.01241	86.87074	86.72931	86.58812	86.44718	86.30649	86.16604
510	86.85873	86.70841	86.55837	86.40861	86.25912	86.10990	85.96096	85.81229	85.66389	85.51576	85.36791
540	86.14186	85.98403	85.82650	85.66927	85.51235	85.35573	85.19941	85.04340	84.88769	84.73228	84.57717
570	85.43091	85.26569	85.10081	84.93626	84.77205	84.60817	84.44462	84.28140	84.11852	83.95597	83.79375
600	84.72583	84.55336	84.38126	84.20952	84.03815	83.86715	83.69651	83.52624	83.35633	83.18678	83.01759
630	84.02657	83.84698	83.66779	83.48900	83.31061	83.13262	82.95503	82.77783	82.60104	82.42463	82.24863
660	83.33308	83.14650	82.96035	82.77464	82.58937	82.40452	82.22012	82.03614	81.85259	81.66947	81.48678
690	82.64531	82.45187	82.25890	82.06640	81.87437	81.68281	81.49171	81.30109	81.11092	80.92123	80.73199
720	81.96322	81.76304	81.56337	81.36421	81.16556	80.96741	80.76976	80.57262	80.37598	80.17984	79.98419

Entry is discounted amount in percent at selected rate, compounded each 30 days.

Discounted Amount of a Loan

Zero interest rate on note   Actual/365 Basis

Term   Desired Yield (Nominal Rate)
of Loan 11.50%   11.625%   11.75%   11.875%   12.00%   12.125%   12.25%   12.375%   12.50%   12.625%   12.75%

Term of Loan	11.50%	11.625%	11.75%	11.875%	12.00%	12.125%	12.25%	12.375%	12.50%	12.625%	12.75%
1 Day	99.96850	99.96816	99.96782	99.96748	99.96713	99.96679	99.96645	99.96611	99.96577	99.96542	99.96508
2 Days	99.93703	99.93634	99.93566	99.93497	99.93429	99.93361	99.93292	99.93224	99.93155	99.93087	99.93019
3	99.90557	99.90454	99.90352	99.90249	99.90147	99.90044	99.89942	99.89839	99.89737	99.89634	99.89532
4	99.87413	99.87276	99.87140	99.87003	99.86867	99.86730	99.86593	99.86457	99.86320	99.86183	99.86047
5	99.84271	99.84101	99.83930	99.83759	99.83589	99.83418	99.83247	99.83077	99.82906	99.82735	99.82565
6	99.81132	99.80927	99.80722	99.80517	99.80313	99.80108	99.79903	99.79699	99.79494	99.79290	99.79085
7	99.77994	99.77755	99.77516	99.77278	99.77039	99.76801	99.76562	99.76323	99.76085	99.75846	99.75608
8	99.74858	99.74585	99.74313	99.74040	99.73768	99.73495	99.73223	99.72950	99.72678	99.72405	99.72133
9	99.71724	99.71418	99.71111	99.70805	99.70498	99.70192	99.69885	99.69579	99.69273	99.68966	99.68660
10	99.68592	99.68252	99.67912	99.67571	99.67231	99.66891	99.66551	99.66210	99.65870	99.65530	99.65190
11	99.65462	99.65088	99.64714	99.64340	99.63966	99.63592	99.63218	99.62844	99.62470	99.62096	99.61722
12	99.62334	99.61926	99.61519	99.61111	99.60703	99.60295	99.59888	99.59480	99.59072	99.58665	99.58257
13	99.59208	99.58767	99.58325	99.57884	99.57442	99.57001	99.56559	99.56118	99.55677	99.55236	99.54794
14	99.56084	99.55609	99.55134	99.54659	99.54183	99.53708	99.53233	99.52758	99.52284	99.51809	99.51334
15	99.52962	99.52453	99.51944	99.51436	99.50927	99.50418	99.49910	99.49401	99.48893	99.48384	99.47876
16	99.49842	99.49299	99.48757	99.48215	99.47673	99.47130	99.46588	99.46046	99.45504	99.44962	99.44420
17	99.46724	99.46148	99.45572	99.44996	99.44420	99.43845	99.43269	99.42693	99.42118	99.41542	99.40967
18	99.43607	99.42998	99.42389	99.41779	99.41170	99.40561	99.39952	99.39343	99.38734	99.38125	99.37516
19	99.40493	99.39850	99.39207	99.38565	99.37922	99.37279	99.36637	99.35995	99.35352	99.34710	99.34068
20	99.37381	99.36705	99.36028	99.35352	99.34676	99.34000	99.33324	99.32648	99.31973	99.31297	99.30622
21	99.34271	99.33561	99.32851	99.32142	99.31432	99.30723	99.30014	99.29305	99.28596	99.27887	99.27178
22	99.31162	99.30419	99.29676	99.28933	99.28191	99.27448	99.26706	99.25963	99.25221	99.24479	99.23737
23	99.28056	99.27279	99.26503	99.25727	99.24951	99.24175	99.23400	99.22624	99.21848	99.21073	99.20298
24	99.24951	99.24141	99.23332	99.22523	99.21714	99.20905	99.20096	99.19287	99.18478	99.17670	99.16861
25	99.21848	99.21006	99.20163	99.19321	99.18478	99.17636	99.16794	99.15952	99.15110	99.14269	99.13427
26	99.18748	99.17872	99.16996	99.16120	99.15245	99.14370	99.13495	99.12620	99.11745	99.10870	99.09996
27	99.15649	99.14740	99.13831	99.12922	99.12014	99.11106	99.10197	99.09289	99.08381	99.07474	99.06566
28	99.12552	99.11610	99.10668	99.09726	99.08785	99.07843	99.06902	99.05961	99.05020	99.04080	99.03139
29	99.09457	99.08482	99.07507	99.06533	99.05558	99.04584	99.03609	99.02635	99.01662	99.00688	98.99715
30 Days	99.06364	99.05356	99.04348	99.03341	99.02333	99.01326	99.00319	98.99312	98.98305	98.97299	98.96292
60	98.13606	98.11608	98.09612	98.07616	98.05620	98.03625	98.01631	97.99637	97.97644	97.95652	97.93660
90	97.21716	97.18748	97.15781	97.12816	97.09852	97.06889	97.03927	97.00967	96.98007	96.95049	96.92092
120	96.30686	96.26766	96.22848	96.18933	96.15019	96.11107	96.07197	96.03289	95.99383	95.95480	95.91578
150	95.40508	95.35655	95.30804	95.25957	95.21112	95.16270	95.11431	95.06596	95.01763	94.96933	94.92106
180	94.51175	94.45406	94.39641	94.33879	94.28122	94.22369	94.16620	94.10875	94.05135	93.99398	93.93665
210	93.62679	93.56011	93.49349	93.42692	93.36041	93.29395	93.22754	93.16119	93.09489	93.02865	92.96246
240	92.75011	92.67462	92.59921	92.52386	92.44859	92.37338	92.29824	92.22317	92.14816	92.07323	91.99836
270	91.88164	91.79752	91.71348	91.62953	91.54567	91.46189	91.37820	91.29459	91.21106	91.12762	91.04427
300	91.02130	90.92871	90.83623	90.74385	90.65157	90.55940	90.46733	90.37536	90.28349	90.19173	90.10007
330	90.16902	90.06813	89.96737	89.86672	89.76621	89.66581	89.56554	89.46539	89.36536	89.26545	89.16566
360	89.32472	89.21569	89.10681	88.99808	88.88949	88.78104	88.67274	88.56457	88.45656	88.34868	88.24095
390	88.48832	88.37132	88.25449	88.13783	88.02133	87.90500	87.78883	87.67283	87.55700	87.44133	87.32582
420	87.65975	87.53494	87.41032	87.28590	87.16166	87.03761	86.91374	86.79007	86.66659	86.54329	86.42018
450	86.83895	86.70648	86.57423	86.44220	86.31038	86.17877	86.04738	85.91620	85.78523	85.65448	85.52394
480	86.02583	85.88586	85.74614	85.60665	85.46741	85.32841	85.18965	85.05112	84.91284	84.77480	84.63699
510	85.22032	85.07301	84.92596	84.77918	84.63268	84.48644	84.34046	84.19476	84.04932	83.90415	83.75924
540	84.42236	84.26784	84.11363	83.95971	83.80609	83.65277	83.49975	83.34702	83.19458	83.04244	82.89059
570	83.63186	83.47030	83.30907	83.14816	82.98759	82.82734	82.66741	82.50781	82.34853	82.18958	82.03095
600	82.84877	82.68031	82.51220	82.34446	82.17707	82.01004	81.84337	81.67705	81.51109	81.34548	81.18023
630	82.07301	81.89779	81.72296	81.54852	81.37448	81.20082	81.02755	80.85466	80.68217	80.51005	80.33833
660	81.30452	81.12268	80.94127	80.76028	80.57972	80.39957	80.21985	80.04055	79.86167	79.68320	79.50516
690	80.54322	80.35491	80.16705	79.97966	79.79272	79.60624	79.42021	79.23464	79.04952	78.86485	78.68063
720	79.78905	79.59440	79.40024	79.20658	79.01341	78.82073	78.62854	78.43684	78.24562	78.05489	77.86465

Discounted Amount of a Loan

Zero interest rate on note

30/360 Basis

Term of Loan		5.500%	5.625%	5.750%	5.875%	6.00%	6.125%	6.250%	6.375%	6.500%	6.625%
						Desired Yield (Nominal Rate)					
1	Day	99.98479	99.98445	99.98410	99.98376	99.98342	99.98307	99.98273	99.98239	99.98204	99.98170
2	Days	99.96958	99.96890	99.96821	99.96752	99.96683	99.96615	99.96546	99.96477	99.96408	99.96340
3	"	99.95438	99.95334	99.95231	99.95128	99.95025	99.94922	99.94819	99.94716	99.94613	99.94509
4	"	99.93917	99.93779	99.93642	99.93504	99.93367	99.93229	99.93092	99.92954	99.92817	99.92679
5	"	99.92396	99.92224	99.92052	99.91880	99.91708	99.91536	99.91364	99.91193	99.91021	99.90849
6	"	99.90875	99.90669	99.90462	99.90256	99.90050	99.89844	99.89637	99.89431	99.89225	99.89019
7	"	99.89354	99.89114	99.88873	99.88632	99.88391	99.88151	99.87910	99.87670	99.87429	99.87189
8	"	99.87834	99.87558	99.87283	99.87008	99.86733	99.86458	99.86183	99.85908	99.85633	99.85359
9	"	99.86313	99.86003	99.85694	99.85384	99.85075	99.84765	99.84456	99.84147	99.83838	99.83528
10	"	99.84792	99.84448	99.84104	99.83760	99.83416	99.83073	99.82729	99.82385	99.82042	99.81698
11	"	99.83271	99.82893	99.82514	99.82136	99.81758	99.81380	99.81002	99.80624	99.80246	99.79868
12	"	99.81750	99.81337	99.80925	99.80512	99.80100	99.79687	99.79275	99.78862	99.78450	99.78038
13	"	99.80230	99.79782	99.79335	99.78888	99.78441	99.77994	99.77547	99.77101	99.76654	99.76208
14	"	99.78709	99.78227	99.77746	99.77264	99.76783	99.76302	99.75820	99.75339	99.74858	99.74378
15	"	99.77188	99.76672	99.76156	99.75640	99.75124	99.74609	99.74093	99.73578	99.73063	99.72547
16	"	99.75667	99.75117	99.74566	99.74016	99.73466	99.72916	99.72366	99.71816	99.71267	99.70717
17	"	99.74146	99.73561	99.72977	99.72392	99.71808	99.71223	99.70639	99.70055	99.69471	99.68887
18	"	99.72625	99.72006	99.71387	99.70768	99.70149	99.69531	99.68912	99.68293	99.67675	99.67057
19	"	99.71105	99.70451	99.69797	99.69144	99.68491	99.67838	99.67185	99.66532	99.65879	99.65227
20	"	99.69584	99.68896	99.68208	99.67520	99.66833	99.66145	99.65458	99.64770	99.64083	99.63397
21	"	99.68063	99.67341	99.66618	99.65896	99.65174	99.64452	99.63731	99.63009	99.62288	99.61566
22	"	99.66542	99.65785	99.65029	99.64272	99.63516	99.62760	99.62003	99.61248	99.60492	99.59736
23	"	99.65021	99.64230	99.63439	99.62648	99.61857	99.61067	99.60276	99.59486	99.58696	99.57906
24	"	99.63501	99.62675	99.61849	99.61024	99.60199	99.59374	99.58549	99.57725	99.56900	99.56076
25	"	99.61980	99.61120	99.60260	99.59400	99.58541	99.57681	99.56822	99.55963	99.55104	99.54246
26	"	99.60459	99.59565	99.58670	99.57776	99.56882	99.55989	99.55095	99.54202	99.53308	99.52415
27	"	99.58938	99.58009	99.57081	99.56152	99.55224	99.54296	99.53368	99.52440	99.51513	99.50585
28	"	99.57417	99.56454	99.55491	99.54528	99.53566	99.52603	99.51641	99.50679	99.49717	99.48755
29	"	99.55897	99.54899	99.53901	99.52904	99.51907	99.50910	99.49914	99.48917	99.47921	99.46925
1	Month	99.54376	99.53344	99.52312	99.51280	99.50249	99.49218	99.48187	99.47156	99.46125	99.45095
2	Months	99.08960	99.06905	99.04851	99.02798	99.00745	98.98693	98.96642	98.94591	98.92541	98.90491
3		98.63751	98.60683	98.57617	98.54552	98.51488	98.48425	98.45364	98.42303	98.39245	98.36187
4		98.18748	98.14677	98.10608	98.06540	98.02475	97.98412	97.94351	97.90293	97.86236	97.82181
5		97.73951	97.68885	97.63823	97.58763	97.53707	97.48653	97.43603	97.38556	97.33513	97.28472
6		97.29358	97.23307	97.17261	97.11219	97.05181	96.99147	96.93118	96.87094	96.81074	96.75058
7		96.84969	96.77942	96.70921	96.63906	96.56896	96.49893	96.42895	96.35903	96.28917	96.21937
8		96.40782	96.32788	96.24802	96.16823	96.08852	96.00888	95.92932	95.84983	95.77041	95.69107
9		95.96796	95.87845	95.78903	95.69970	95.61047	95.52133	95.43228	95.34332	95.25445	95.16568
10		95.53012	95.43112	95.33223	95.23346	95.13479	95.03624	94.93781	94.83948	94.74127	94.64317
11		95.09427	94.98587	94.87761	94.76948	94.66149	94.55363	94.44590	94.33831	94.23085	94.12353
12	Months	94.66041	94.54270	94.42515	94.30777	94.19053	94.07346	93.95654	93.83979	93.72318	93.60674
13		94.22853	94.10160	93.97486	93.84830	93.72192	93.59573	93.46972	93.34390	93.21825	93.09279
14		93.79862	93.66256	93.52671	93.39107	93.25565	93.12043	92.98542	92.85063	92.71604	92.58166
15		93.37067	93.22556	93.08070	92.93607	92.79169	92.64754	92.50363	92.35997	92.21653	92.07334
16		92.94467	92.79061	92.63681	92.48329	92.33004	92.17705	92.02434	91.87190	91.71972	91.56781
17		92.52062	92.35768	92.19505	92.03271	91.87068	91.70896	91.54753	91.38641	91.22558	91.06506
18		92.09850	91.92677	91.75538	91.58433	91.41362	91.24324	91.07319	90.90348	90.73410	90.56506
19		91.67831	91.49788	91.31782	91.13813	90.95882	90.77988	90.60131	90.42311	90.24528	90.06781
20		91.26003	91.07098	90.88234	90.69411	90.50629	90.31888	90.13187	89.94527	89.75908	89.57329
21		90.84367	90.64608	90.44894	90.25225	90.05601	89.86022	89.66487	89.46996	89.27551	89.08149
22		90.42920	90.22316	90.01761	89.81254	89.60797	89.40388	89.20028	88.99717	88.79453	88.59238
23		90.01662	89.80221	89.58833	89.37498	89.16216	88.94987	88.73811	88.52687	88.31616	88.10597
24	Months	89.60593	89.38323	89.16110	88.93955	88.71857	88.49816	88.27832	88.05905	87.84035	87.62222
2.5	Years	87.18082	86.91006	86.64016	86.37114	86.10297	85.83567	85.56922	85.30363	85.03889	84.77500
3		84.82134	84.50532	84.19051	83.87690	83.56449	83.25328	82.94326	82.63443	82.32678	82.02030
3.5		82.52572	82.16712	81.81011	81.45469	81.10085	80.74858	80.39789	80.04875	79.70116	79.35512
4		80.29223	79.89361	79.49701	79.10243	78.70984	78.31924	77.93062	77.54397	77.15928	76.77653
4.5		78.11918	77.68301	77.24932	76.81810	76.38932	75.96299	75.53908	75.11757	74.69846	74.28174
5	Years	76.00495	75.53358	75.06518	74.59973	74.13722	73.67762	73.22092	72.76710	72.31613	71.86801
6		71.94660	71.41149	70.88041	70.35334	69.83024	69.31109	68.79585	68.28449	67.77698	67.27330
7		68.10494	67.51435	66.92894	66.34866	65.77348	65.20334	64.63820	64.07802	63.52275	62.97234
8		64.46842	63.82989	63.19775	62.57194	61.95239	61.33904	60.73182	60.13067	59.53554	58.94636
9		61.02607	60.34650	59.67458	59.01020	58.35329	57.70376	57.06152	56.42650	55.79860	55.17776
10		57.76752	57.05322	56.34781	55.65120	54.96327	54.28392	53.61303	52.95050	52.29623	51.65011
11		54.68298	53.93965	53.20651	52.48340	51.77020	51.06676	50.37295	49.68864	49.01369	48.34798
12	Years	51.76313	50.99600	50.24033	49.49593	48.76263	48.04027	47.32868	46.62771	45.93719	45.25697

Entry is percentage value today which, compounded monthly, will give 100% at term of note.

Discounted Amount of a Loan

Zero interest rate on note   30/360 Basis

Term of Loan		6.750%	6.875%	7.00%	7.125%	Desired Yield (Nominal Rate) 7.250%	7.375%	7.500%	7.625%	7.750%	7.875%
1 Day		99.98135	99.98101	99.98067	99.98033	99.97998	99.97964	99.97930	99.97895	99.97861	99.97827
2 Days		99.96271	99.96202	99.96134	99.96065	99.95996	99.95928	99.95859	99.95791	99.95722	99.95654
3	"	99.94406	99.94303	99.94200	99.94098	99.93995	99.93892	99.93789	99.93686	99.93583	99.93480
4	"	99.92542	99.92405	99.92267	99.92130	99.91993	99.91856	99.91718	99.91581	99.91444	99.91307
5	"	99.90677	99.90506	99.90334	99.90163	99.89991	99.89820	99.89648	99.89477	99.89305	99.89134
6	"	99.88813	99.88607	99.88401	99.88195	99.87989	99.87783	99.87578	99.87372	99.87166	99.86961
7	"	99.86948	99.86708	99.86468	99.86228	99.85987	99.85747	99.85507	99.85267	99.85027	99.84787
8	"	99.85084	99.84809	99.84535	99.84260	99.83986	99.83711	99.83437	99.83163	99.82888	99.82614
9	"	99.83219	99.82910	99.82601	99.82293	99.81984	99.81675	99.81366	99.81058	99.80749	99.80441
10	"	99.81355	99.81012	99.80668	99.80325	99.79982	99.79639	99.79296	99.78953	99.78610	99.78268
11	"	99.79490	99.79113	99.78735	99.78358	99.77980	99.77603	99.77226	99.76848	99.76471	99.76094
12	"	99.77626	99.77214	99.76802	99.76390	99.75978	99.75567	99.75155	99.74744	99.74332	99.73921
13	"	99.75761	99.75315	99.74869	99.74423	99.73977	99.73531	99.73085	99.72639	99.72193	99.71748
14	"	99.73897	99.73416	99.72936	99.72455	99.71975	99.71495	99.71014	99.70534	99.70055	99.69575
15	"	99.72032	99.71517	99.71002	99.70488	99.69973	99.69459	99.68944	99.68430	99.67916	99.67401
16	"	99.70168	99.69619	99.69069	99.68520	99.67971	99.67422	99.66874	99.66325	99.65777	99.65228
17	"	99.68303	99.67720	99.67136	99.66553	99.65969	99.65386	99.64803	99.64220	99.63638	99.63055
18	"	99.66439	99.65821	99.65203	99.64585	99.63968	99.63350	99.62733	99.62116	99.61499	99.60882
19	"	99.64574	99.63922	99.63270	99.62618	99.61966	99.61314	99.60663	99.60011	99.59360	99.58708
20	"	99.62710	99.62023	99.61337	99.60650	99.59964	99.59278	99.58592	99.57906	99.57221	99.56535
21	"	99.60845	99.60124	99.59403	99.58683	99.57962	99.57242	99.56522	99.55802	99.55082	99.54362
22	"	99.58981	99.58225	99.57470	99.56715	99.55961	99.55206	99.54451	99.53697	99.52943	99.52189
23	"	99.57116	99.56327	99.55537	99.54748	99.53959	99.53170	99.52381	99.51592	99.50804	99.50016
24	"	99.55252	99.54428	99.53604	99.52780	99.51957	99.51134	99.50311	99.49488	99.48665	99.47842
25	"	99.53387	99.52529	99.51671	99.50813	99.49955	99.49098	99.48240	99.47383	99.46526	99.45669
26	"	99.51523	99.50630	99.49738	99.48845	99.47953	99.47061	99.46170	99.45278	99.44387	99.43496
27	"	99.49658	99.48731	99.47804	99.46878	99.45952	99.45025	99.44099	99.43174	99.42248	99.41323
28	"	99.47794	99.46832	99.45871	99.44910	99.43950	99.42989	99.42029	99.41069	99.40109	99.39149
29	"	99.45929	99.44934	99.43938	99.42943	99.41948	99.40953	99.39959	99.38964	99.37970	99.36976
1 Month		99.44065	99.43035	99.42005	99.40975	99.39946	99.38917	99.37888	99.36860	99.35831	99.34803
2 Months		98.88442	98.86394	98.84346	98.82299	98.80253	98.78207	98.76162	98.74118	98.72074	98.70031
3		98.33131	98.30076	98.27022	98.23969	98.20918	98.17868	98.14820	98.11772	98.08726	98.05681
4		97.78129	97.74078	97.70030	97.65984	97.61940	97.57898	97.53858	97.49820	97.45784	97.41751
5		97.23434	97.18400	97.13369	97.08341	97.03316	96.98294	96.93275	96.88259	96.83247	96.78237
6		96.69046	96.63039	96.57036	96.51038	96.45044	96.39054	96.33068	96.27087	96.21110	96.15138
7		96.14962	96.07993	96.01030	95.94073	95.87121	95.80176	95.73236	95.66301	95.59373	95.52450
8		95.61180	95.53261	95.45349	95.37444	95.29547	95.21657	95.13774	95.05899	94.98031	94.90171
9		95.07700	94.98840	94.89991	94.81150	94.72318	94.63496	94.54683	94.45879	94.37084	94.28298
10		94.54518	94.44730	94.34953	94.25188	94.15433	94.05690	93.95958	93.86237	93.76527	93.66828
11		94.01634	93.90928	93.80235	93.69556	93.58890	93.48237	93.37598	93.26972	93.16359	93.05759
12 Months		93.49045	93.37432	93.25835	93.14253	93.02686	92.91136	92.79600	92.68081	92.56577	92.45088
13		92.96751	92.84241	92.71749	92.59276	92.46820	92.34383	92.21963	92.09562	91.97178	91.84813
14		92.44749	92.31353	92.17978	92.04623	91.91290	91.77976	91.64684	91.51412	91.38161	91.24930
15		91.93038	91.78767	91.64518	91.50294	91.36092	91.21915	91.07760	90.93630	90.79522	90.65438
16		91.41617	91.26479	91.11369	90.96284	90.81227	90.66195	90.51191	90.36212	90.21260	90.06334
17		90.90483	90.74490	90.58527	90.42594	90.26690	90.10816	89.94972	89.79157	89.63372	89.47615
18		90.39635	90.22797	90.05992	89.89220	89.72482	89.55776	89.39103	89.22462	89.05855	88.89280
19		89.89071	89.71398	89.53762	89.36162	89.18598	89.01071	88.83580	88.66125	88.48707	88.31324
20		89.38791	89.20293	89.01835	88.83417	88.65039	88.46701	88.28403	88.10144	87.91925	87.73746
21		88.88791	88.69478	88.50208	88.30983	88.11801	87.92663	87.73568	87.54517	87.35509	87.16544
22		88.39072	88.18953	87.98882	87.78858	87.58883	87.38954	87.19074	86.99240	86.79454	86.59715
23		87.89630	87.68715	87.47852	87.27041	87.06282	86.85574	86.64918	86.44313	86.23759	86.03256
24 Months		87.40465	87.18764	86.97119	86.75530	86.53998	86.32520	86.11099	85.89732	85.68421	85.47165
2.5 Years		84.51196	84.24976	83.98839	83.72787	83.46818	83.20933	82.95130	82.69410	82.43772	82.18217
3		81.71500	81.41087	81.10790	80.80608	80.50543	80.20592	79.90755	79.61033	79.31425	79.01929
3.5		79.01061	78.66764	78.32619	77.98626	77.64783	77.31091	76.97549	76.64156	76.30911	75.97814
4		76.39572	76.01684	75.63988	75.26483	74.89167	74.52041	74.15102	73.78350	73.41784	73.05403
4.5		73.86738	73.45537	73.04571	72.63837	72.23334	71.83062	71.43018	71.03202	70.63611	70.24246
5 Years		71.42271	70.98021	70.54050	70.10356	69.66938	69.23792	68.80918	68.38314	67.95978	67.53909
6		66.77341	66.27729	65.78491	65.29623	64.81124	64.32989	63.85217	63.37805	62.90750	62.44048
7		62.42677	61.88597	61.34992	60.81856	60.29186	59.76978	59.25226	58.73929	58.23080	57.72677
8		58.36307	57.78561	57.21392	56.64794	56.08763	55.53291	54.98373	54.44005	53.90179	53.36891
9		54.56389	53.95692	53.35675	52.76333	52.17656	51.59638	51.02271	50.45548	49.89460	49.34003
10		51.01203	50.38191	49.75963	49.14510	48.53822	47.93890	47.34704	46.76254	46.18532	45.61529
11		47.69138	47.04376	46.40501	45.77499	45.15358	44.54068	43.93616	43.33990	42.75180	42.17173
12 Years		44.58689	43.92679	43.27654	42.63598	42.00496	41.38335	40.77100	40.16777	39.57353	38.98814

Entry is percentage value today which, compounded monthly, will give 100% at term of note.

Discounted Amount of a Loan

Zero interest rate on note   30/360 Basis

Term of Loan		8.000%	8.125%	8.250%	8.375%	8.500%	8.625%	8.750%	8.875%	9.000%	9.125%
						Desired Yield (Nominal Rate)					
1	Day	99.97792	99.97758	99.97724	99.97690	99.97655	99.97621	99.97587	99.97553	99.97519	99.97484
2	Days	99.95585	99.95516	99.95448	99.95379	99.95311	99.95243	99.95174	99.95106	99.95037	99.94969
3	"	99.93377	99.93275	99.93172	99.93069	99.92966	99.92864	99.92761	99.92658	99.92556	99.92453
4	"	99.91170	99.91033	99.90896	99.90759	99.90622	99.90485	99.90348	99.90211	99.90074	99.89938
5	"	99.88962	99.88791	99.88620	99.88449	99.88277	99.88106	99.87935	99.87764	99.87593	99.87422
6	"	99.86755	99.86549	99.86344	99.86138	99.85933	99.85728	99.85522	99.85317	99.85112	99.84906
7	"	99.84547	99.84308	99.84068	99.83828	99.83588	99.83349	99.83109	99.82870	99.82630	99.82391
8	"	99.82340	99.82066	99.81792	99.81518	99.81244	99.80970	99.80696	99.80423	99.80149	99.79875
9	"	99.80132	99.79824	99.79516	99.79208	99.78899	99.78591	99.78283	99.77975	99.77667	99.77360
10	"	99.77925	99.77582	99.77240	99.76897	99.76555	99.76213	99.75870	99.75528	99.75186	99.74844
11	"	99.75717	99.75341	99.74964	99.74587	99.74210	99.73834	99.73457	99.73081	99.72705	99.72328
12	"	99.73510	99.73099	99.72688	99.72277	99.71866	99.71455	99.71044	99.70634	99.70223	99.69813
13	"	99.71302	99.70857	99.70412	99.69967	99.69521	99.69076	99.68632	99.68187	99.67742	99.67297
14	"	99.69095	99.68615	99.68136	99.67656	99.67177	99.66698	99.66219	99.65739	99.65261	99.64782
15	"	99.66887	99.66374	99.65860	99.65346	99.64832	99.64319	99.63806	99.63292	99.62779	99.62266
16	"	99.64680	99.64132	99.63584	99.63036	99.62488	99.61940	99.61393	99.60845	99.60298	99.59751
17	"	99.62472	99.61890	99.61308	99.60725	99.60143	99.59561	99.58980	99.58398	99.57816	99.57235
18	"	99.60265	99.59648	99.59032	99.58415	99.57799	99.57183	99.56567	99.55951	99.55335	99.54719
19	"	99.58057	99.57406	99.56756	99.56105	99.55454	99.54804	99.54154	99.53504	99.52854	99.52204
20	"	99.55850	99.55165	99.54480	99.53795	99.53110	99.52425	99.51741	99.51056	99.50372	99.49688
21	"	99.53642	99.52923	99.52204	99.51484	99.50765	99.50047	99.49328	99.48609	99.47891	99.47173
22	"	99.51435	99.50681	99.49928	99.49174	99.48421	99.47668	99.46915	99.46162	99.45409	99.44657
23	"	99.49227	99.48439	99.47652	99.46864	99.46076	99.45289	99.44502	99.43715	99.42928	99.42141
24	"	99.47020	99.46198	99.45376	99.44554	99.43732	99.42910	99.42089	99.41268	99.40447	99.39626
25	"	99.44812	99.43956	99.43100	99.42243	99.41387	99.40532	99.39676	99.38821	99.37965	99.37110
26	"	99.42605	99.41714	99.40824	99.39933	99.39043	99.38153	99.37263	99.36373	99.35484	99.34595
27	"	99.40397	99.39472	99.38547	99.37623	99.36698	99.35774	99.34850	99.33926	99.33002	99.32079
28	"	99.38190	99.37231	99.36271	99.35313	99.34354	99.33395	99.32437	99.31479	99.30521	99.29563
29	"	99.35982	99.34989	99.33995	99.33002	99.32009	99.31017	99.30024	99.29032	99.28040	99.27048
1	Month	99.33775	99.32747	99.31719	99.30692	99.29665	99.28638	99.27611	99.26585	99.25558	99.24532
2	Months	98.67988	98.65946	98.63905	98.61864	98.59824	98.57785	98.55746	98.53708	98.51671	98.49634
3		98.02637	97.99595	97.96554	97.93514	97.90475	97.87438	97.84402	97.81367	97.78333	97.75301
4		97.37719	97.33690	97.29662	97.25637	97.21614	97.17593	97.13574	97.09557	97.05542	97.01529
5		96.73231	96.68228	96.63228	96.58231	96.53237	96.48246	96.43258	96.38274	96.33292	96.28314
6		96.09170	96.03206	95.97247	95.91291	95.85341	95.79394	95.73452	95.67514	95.61580	95.55651
7		95.45533	95.38622	95.31716	95.24816	95.17922	95.11033	95.04151	94.97274	94.90402	94.83536
8		94.82318	94.74472	94.66633	94.58802	94.50978	94.43161	94.35351	94.27549	94.19754	94.11966
9		94.19521	94.10753	94.01994	93.93245	93.84504	93.75772	93.67050	93.58336	93.49632	93.40936
10		93.57140	93.47463	93.37797	93.28142	93.18498	93.08865	92.99243	92.89632	92.80032	92.70442
11		92.95172	92.84598	92.74038	92.63490	92.52956	92.42435	92.31927	92.21432	92.10949	92.00480
12	Months	92.33615	92.22157	92.10714	91.99287	91.87875	91.76479	91.65098	91.53732	91.42382	91.31046
13		91.72465	91.60135	91.47823	91.35529	91.23252	91.10994	90.98753	90.86530	90.74324	90.62136
14		91.11720	90.98530	90.85361	90.72212	90.59084	90.45976	90.32888	90.19821	90.06773	89.93746
15		90.51377	90.37340	90.23326	90.09335	89.95367	89.81422	89.67500	89.53601	89.39725	89.25873
16		89.91435	89.76561	89.61714	89.46893	89.32098	89.17328	89.02585	88.87868	88.73177	88.58511
17		89.31889	89.16191	89.00523	88.84884	88.69274	88.53693	88.38141	88.22617	88.07123	87.91658
18		88.72737	88.56227	88.39750	88.23304	88.06891	87.90511	87.74162	87.57846	87.41561	87.25309
19		88.13977	87.96666	87.79391	87.62152	87.44948	87.27780	87.10647	86.93550	86.76488	86.59461
20		87.55607	87.37506	87.19445	87.01423	86.83440	86.65497	86.47592	86.29726	86.11899	85.94110
21		86.97622	86.78744	86.59908	86.41115	86.22365	86.03658	85.84993	85.66370	85.47790	85.29252
22		86.40022	86.20377	86.00778	85.81226	85.61720	85.42260	85.22847	85.03480	84.84159	84.64884
23		85.82804	85.62402	85.42051	85.21751	85.01501	84.81301	84.61151	84.41051	84.21001	84.01001
24	Months	85.25964	85.04817	84.83726	84.62688	84.41705	84.20777	83.99902	83.79081	83.58314	83.37601
2.5	Years	81.92743	81.67351	81.42041	81.16811	80.91662	80.66594	80.41606	80.16697	79.91869	79.67120
3		78.72546	78.43276	78.14117	77.85070	77.56134	77.27308	76.98592	76.69986	76.41490	76.13102
3.5		75.64863	75.32059	74.99401	74.66887	74.34518	74.02293	73.70210	73.38270	73.06472	72.74814
4		72.69206	72.33192	71.97360	71.61709	71.26239	70.90948	70.55835	70.20900	69.86141	69.51558
4.5		69.85103	69.46183	69.07484	68.69004	68.30743	67.92698	67.54870	67.17256	66.79855	66.42666
5	Years	67.12104	66.70563	66.29283	65.88262	65.47500	65.06993	64.66742	64.26744	63.86997	63.47500
6		61.97699	61.51698	61.06043	60.60731	60.15761	59.71129	59.26832	58.82869	58.39236	57.95932
7		57.22716	56.73192	56.24101	55.75441	55.27206	54.79394	54.32000	53.85021	53.38453	52.92292
8		52.84135	52.31906	51.80199	51.29008	50.78328	50.28154	49.78481	49.29304	48.80617	48.32416
9		48.79167	48.24946	47.71333	47.18322	46.65905	46.14075	45.62827	45.12153	44.62046	44.12502
10		45.05235	44.49641	43.94739	43.40520	42.86975	42.34096	41.81875	41.30304	40.79373	40.29076
11		41.59960	41.03529	40.47868	39.92969	39.38819	38.85410	38.32730	37.80769	37.29518	36.78968
12	Years	38.41147	37.84338	37.28376	36.73247	36.18938	35.65438	35.12734	34.60815	34.09668	33.59282

Entry is percentage value today which, compounded monthly, will give 100% at term of note.

Discounted Amount of a Loan

Zero interest rate on note   30/360 Basis

Term of Loan	9.250%	9.375%	9.500%	9.625%	Desired Yield (Nominal Rate) 9.750%	9.875%	10.000%	10.125%	10.250%	10.375%
1 Day	99.97450	99.97416	99.97382	99.97348	99.97313	99.97279	99.97245	99.97211	99.97177	99.97143
2 Days	99.94900	99.94832	99.94764	99.94695	99.94627	99.94559	99.94490	99.94422	99.94354	99.94286
3 "	99.92351	99.92248	99.92146	99.92043	99.91940	99.91838	99.91736	99.91633	99.91531	99.91428
4 "	99.89801	99.89664	99.89527	99.89391	99.89254	99.89117	99.88981	99.88844	99.88708	99.88571
5 "	99.87251	99.87080	99.86909	99.86738	99.86567	99.86397	99.86226	99.86055	99.85884	99.85714
6 "	99.84701	99.84496	99.84291	99.84086	99.83881	99.83676	99.83471	99.83266	99.83061	99.82857
7 "	99.82151	99.81912	99.81673	99.81434	99.81194	99.80955	99.80716	99.80477	99.80238	99.79999
8 "	99.79602	99.79328	99.79055	99.78781	99.78508	99.78235	99.77961	99.77688	99.77415	99.77142
9 "	99.77052	99.76744	99.76437	99.76129	99.75821	99.75514	99.75207	99.74899	99.74592	99.74285
10 "	99.74502	99.74160	99.73818	99.73477	99.73135	99.72793	99.72452	99.72110	99.71769	99.71428
11 "	99.71952	99.71576	99.71200	99.70824	99.70448	99.70073	99.69697	99.69321	99.68946	99.68570
12 "	99.69403	99.68992	99.68582	99.68172	99.67762	99.67352	99.66942	99.66532	99.66123	99.65713
13 "	99.66853	99.66408	99.65964	99.65520	99.65075	99.64631	99.64187	99.63743	99.63300	99.62856
14 "	99.64303	99.63824	99.63346	99.62867	99.62389	99.61911	99.61433	99.60954	99.60476	99.59999
15 "	99.61753	99.61240	99.60728	99.60215	99.59702	99.59190	99.58678	99.58165	99.57653	99.57141
16 "	99.59203	99.58656	99.58109	99.57563	99.57016	99.56469	99.55923	99.55377	99.54830	99.54284
17 "	99.56654	99.56072	99.55491	99.54910	99.54329	99.53749	99.53168	99.52588	99.52007	99.51427
18 "	99.54104	99.53488	99.52873	99.52258	99.51643	99.51028	99.50413	99.49799	99.49184	99.48570
19 "	99.51554	99.50904	99.50255	99.49606	99.48956	99.48307	99.47658	99.47010	99.46361	99.45712
20 "	99.49004	99.48320	99.47637	99.46953	99.46270	99.45587	99.44904	99.44221	99.43538	99.42855
21 "	99.46454	99.45736	99.45019	99.44301	99.43583	99.42866	99.42149	99.41432	99.40715	99.39998
22 "	99.43905	99.43152	99.42400	99.41649	99.40897	99.40145	99.39394	99.38643	99.37892	99.37141
23 "	99.41355	99.40568	99.39782	99.38996	99.38210	99.37425	99.36639	99.35854	99.35069	99.34283
24 "	99.38805	99.37984	99.37164	99.36344	99.35524	99.34704	99.33884	99.33065	99.32245	99.31426
25 "	99.36255	99.35401	99.34546	99.33692	99.32837	99.31983	99.31129	99.30276	99.29422	99.28569
26 "	99.33705	99.32817	99.31928	99.31039	99.30151	99.29263	99.28375	99.27487	99.26599	99.25712
27 "	99.31156	99.30233	99.29310	99.28387	99.27464	99.26542	99.25620	99.24698	99.23776	99.22854
28 "	99.28606	99.27649	99.26691	99.25735	99.24778	99.23821	99.22865	99.21909	99.20953	99.19997
29 "	99.26056	99.25065	99.24073	99.23082	99.22091	99.21101	99.20110	99.19120	99.18130	99.17140
1 Month	99.23506	99.22481	99.21455	99.20430	99.19405	99.18380	99.17355	99.16331	99.15307	99.14283
2 Months	98.47598	98.45562	98.43527	98.41493	98.39459	98.37426	98.35394	98.33362	98.31331	98.29300
3	97.72270	97.69240	97.66211	97.63184	97.60158	97.57133	97.54110	97.51087	97.48066	97.45046
4	96.97518	96.93509	96.89503	96.85498	96.81496	96.77495	96.73497	96.69501	96.65507	96.61514
5	96.23338	96.18366	96.13397	96.08431	96.03468	95.98508	95.93551	95.88597	95.83646	95.78699
6	95.49726	95.43805	95.37888	95.31976	95.26068	95.20165	95.14265	95.08370	95.02479	94.96593
7	94.76676	94.69822	94.62973	94.56130	94.49293	94.42461	94.35635	94.28814	94.22000	94.15190
8	94.04186	93.96413	93.88646	93.80888	93.73136	93.65392	93.57654	93.49924	93.42202	93.34486
9	93.32250	93.23572	93.14904	93.06244	92.97593	92.88951	92.80319	92.71695	92.63080	92.54473
10	92.60864	92.51296	92.41740	92.32194	92.22659	92.13135	92.03622	91.94119	91.84627	91.75147
11	91.90024	91.79581	91.69151	91.58733	91.48329	91.37937	91.27559	91.17193	91.06840	90.96500
12 Months	91.19726	91.08421	90.97132	90.85857	90.74598	90.63353	90.52124	90.40910	90.29711	90.18527
13	90.49966	90.37813	90.25678	90.13561	90.01461	89.89378	89.77313	89.65266	89.53236	89.41223
14	89.80740	89.67753	89.54786	89.41840	89.28913	89.16007	89.03121	88.90254	88.77408	88.64581
15	89.12043	88.98235	88.84451	88.70690	88.56951	88.43235	88.29541	88.15870	88.02222	87.88596
16	88.43871	88.29257	88.14668	88.00105	87.85568	87.71056	87.56570	87.42109	87.27673	87.13263
17	87.76221	87.60813	87.45434	87.30083	87.14761	86.99467	86.84201	86.68964	86.53756	86.38575
18	87.09088	86.92900	86.76743	86.60617	86.44524	86.28462	86.12431	85.96432	85.80464	85.64528
19	86.42469	86.25513	86.08591	85.91705	85.74853	85.58036	85.41254	85.24506	85.07793	84.91115
20	85.76360	85.58648	85.40975	85.23341	85.05744	84.88186	84.70665	84.53183	84.35738	84.18332
21	85.10756	84.92302	84.73890	84.55520	84.37192	84.18905	84.00660	83.82456	83.64293	83.46172
22	84.45654	84.26471	84.07332	83.88240	83.69192	83.50190	83.31233	83.12321	82.93453	82.74631
23	83.81050	83.61149	83.41297	83.21494	83.01740	82.82036	82.62380	82.42772	82.23213	82.03703
24 Months	83.16941	82.96334	82.75780	82.55280	82.34832	82.14438	81.94095	81.73806	81.53568	81.33383
2.5 Years	79.42450	79.17859	78.93347	78.68913	78.44558	78.20280	77.96080	77.71957	77.47911	77.23943
3	75.84822	75.56651	75.28586	75.00629	74.72779	74.45035	74.17397	73.89864	73.62437	73.35114
3.5	72.43297	72.11920	71.80682	71.49582	71.18621	70.87796	70.57108	70.26556	69.96140	69.65859
4	69.17150	68.82916	68.48854	68.14965	67.81247	67.47699	67.14320	66.81110	66.48068	66.15192
4.5	66.05689	65.68920	65.32361	64.96008	64.59862	64.23920	63.88182	63.52647	63.17312	62.82178
5 Years	63.08251	62.69250	62.30493	61.91980	61.53708	61.15678	60.77886	60.40332	60.03013	59.65929
6	57.52953	57.10297	56.67961	56.25944	55.84243	55.42855	55.01778	54.61009	54.20547	53.80389
7	52.46535	52.01179	51.56219	51.11653	50.67476	50.23685	49.80278	49.37250	48.94598	48.52318
8	47.84697	47.37453	46.90680	46.44374	45.98530	45.53144	45.08209	44.63723	44.19680	43.76077
9	43.63512	43.15072	42.67174	42.19812	41.72981	41.26675	40.80887	40.35612	39.90844	39.46577
10	39.79404	39.30349	38.81904	38.34061	37.86813	37.40151	36.94070	36.48560	36.03617	35.59231
11	36.29107	35.79928	35.31419	34.83573	34.36380	33.89831	33.43918	32.98631	32.53962	32.09902
12 Years	33.09646	32.60749	32.12579	31.65125	31.18377	30.72324	30.26956	29.82262	29.38233	28.94859

Entry is percentage value today which, compounded monthly, will give 100% at term of note.

Discounted Amount of a Loan

Zero interest rate on note   30/360 Basis

Term of Loan	10.500%	10.625%	10.750%	10.875%	Desired Yield (Nominal Rate) 11.000%	11.125%	11.250%	13.00%	15.000%	18.00%
1 Day	99.97109	99.97075	99.97040	99.97006	99.96972	99.96938	99.96904	99.96428	99.95885	99.95074
2 Days	99.94217	99.94149	99.94081	99.94013	99.93944	99.93876	99.93808	99.92855	99.91770	99.90148
3 "	99.91326	99.91224	99.91121	99.91019	99.90917	99.90814	99.90712	99.89283	99.87654	99.85222
4 "	99.88435	99.88298	99.88162	99.88025	99.87889	99.87752	99.87616	99.85710	99.83539	99.80296
5 "	99.85543	99.85373	99.85202	99.85031	99.84861	99.84691	99.84520	99.82138	99.79424	99.75369
6 "	99.82652	99.82447	99.82242	99.82038	99.81833	99.81629	99.81424	99.78566	99.75309	99.70443
7 "	99.79760	99.79522	99.79283	99.79044	99.78805	99.78567	99.78328	99.74993	99.71193	99.65517
8 "	99.76869	99.76596	99.76323	99.76050	99.75778	99.75505	99.75232	99.71421	99.67078	99.60591
9 "	99.73978	99.73671	99.73364	99.73057	99.72750	99.72443	99.72136	99.67848	99.62963	99.55665
10 "	99.71086	99.70745	99.70404	99.70063	99.69722	99.69381	99.69040	99.64276	99.58848	99.50739
11 "	99.68195	99.67820	99.67444	99.67069	99.66694	99.66319	99.65944	99.60703	99.54733	99.45813
12 "	99.65304	99.64894	99.64485	99.64076	99.63666	99.63257	99.62848	99.57131	99.50617	99.40887
13 "	99.62412	99.61969	99.61525	99.61082	99.60639	99.60195	99.59752	99.53559	99.46502	99.35961
14 "	99.59521	99.59043	99.58566	99.58088	99.57611	99.57134	99.56656	99.49986	99.42387	99.31034
15 "	99.56629	99.56118	99.55606	99.55094	99.54583	99.54072	99.53560	99.46414	99.38272	99.26108
16 "	99.53738	99.53192	99.52646	99.52101	99.51555	99.51010	99.50464	99.42841	99.34156	99.21182
17 "	99.50847	99.50267	99.49687	99.49107	99.48527	99.47948	99.47368	99.39269	99.30041	99.16256
18 "	99.47955	99.47341	99.46727	99.46113	99.45500	99.44886	99.44272	99.35697	99.25926	99.11330
19 "	99.45064	99.44416	99.43768	99.43120	99.42472	99.41824	99.41176	99.32124	99.21811	99.06404
20 "	99.42173	99.41490	99.40808	99.40126	99.39444	99.38762	99.38080	99.28552	99.17695	99.01478
21 "	99.39281	99.38565	99.37848	99.37132	99.36416	99.35700	99.34985	99.24979	99.13580	98.96552
22 "	99.36390	99.35639	99.34889	99.34139	99.33388	99.32638	99.31889	99.21407	99.09465	98.91626
23 "	99.33499	99.32714	99.31929	99.31145	99.30361	99.29576	99.28793	99.17835	99.05350	98.86700
24 "	99.30607	99.29788	99.28970	99.28151	99.27333	99.26515	99.25697	99.14262	99.01235	98.81773
25 "	99.27716	99.26863	99.26010	99.25157	99.24305	99.23453	99.22601	99.10690	98.97119	98.76847
26 "	99.24824	99.23937	99.23050	99.22164	99.21277	99.20391	99.19505	99.07117	98.93004	98.71921
27 "	99.21933	99.21012	99.20091	99.19170	99.18249	99.17329	99.16409	99.03545	98.88889	98.66995
28 "	99.19042	99.18086	99.17131	99.16176	99.15222	99.14267	99.13313	98.99973	98.84774	98.62069
29 "	99.16150	99.15161	99.14172	99.13183	99.12194	99.11205	99.10217	98.96400	98.80658	98.57143
1 Month	99.13259	99.12235	99.11212	99.10189	99.09166	99.08143	99.07121	98.92828	98.76543	98.52217
2 Months	98.27270	98.25241	98.23212	98.21184	98.19157	98.17130	98.15104	97.86804	97.54611	97.06617
3	97.42028	97.39010	97.35994	97.32979	97.29966	97.26953	97.23942	96.81917	96.34183	95.63170
4	96.57524	96.53536	96.49550	96.45566	96.41584	96.37605	96.33627	95.78153	95.15243	94.21842
5	95.73754	95.68812	95.63874	95.58938	95.54006	95.49077	95.44151	94.75502	93.97771	92.82603
6	94.90710	94.84832	94.78958	94.73089	94.67223	94.61362	94.55505	93.73951	92.81749	91.45422
7	94.08387	94.01589	93.94797	93.88010	93.81229	93.74453	93.67683	92.73488	91.67159	90.10268
8	93.26778	93.19076	93.11382	93.03695	92.96015	92.88342	92.80677	91.74102	90.53984	88.77111
9	92.45876	92.37288	92.28708	92.20138	92.11576	92.03023	91.94479	90.75781	89.42207	87.45922
10	91.65676	91.56217	91.46768	91.37330	91.27903	91.18487	91.09081	89.78514	88.31809	86.16672
11	90.86172	90.75858	90.65556	90.55267	90.44991	90.34727	90.24476	88.82289	87.22775	84.89332
12 Months	90.07358	89.96204	89.85065	89.73941	89.62832	89.51737	89.40658	87.87095	86.15086	83.63874
13	89.29227	89.17249	89.05288	88.93345	88.81419	88.69509	88.57618	86.92922	85.08727	82.40270
14	88.51774	88.38987	88.26220	88.13473	88.00745	87.88037	87.75349	85.99758	84.03681	81.18493
15	87.74993	87.61412	87.47854	87.34318	87.20804	87.07313	86.93844	85.07592	82.99932	79.98515
16	86.98878	86.84518	86.70184	86.55874	86.41590	86.27330	86.13096	84.16415	81.97463	78.80310
17	86.23423	86.08299	85.93203	85.78135	85.63095	85.48083	85.33098	83.26214	80.96260	77.63853
18	85.48623	85.32748	85.16906	85.01094	84.85313	84.69563	84.53844	82.36980	79.96306	76.49116
19	84.74471	84.57861	84.41286	84.24744	84.08237	83.91764	83.75325	81.48702	78.97587	75.36075
20	84.00962	83.83631	83.66337	83.49081	83.31862	83.14680	82.97536	80.61371	78.00085	74.24704
21	83.28092	83.10053	82.92054	82.74097	82.56180	82.38304	82.20469	79.74975	77.03788	73.14979
22	82.55853	82.37120	82.18431	81.99786	81.81186	81.62630	81.44118	78.89506	76.08680	72.06876
23	81.84241	81.64827	81.45461	81.26143	81.06873	80.87650	80.68476	78.04952	75.14745	71.00371
24 Months	81.13250	80.93169	80.73139	80.53161	80.33235	80.13360	79.93536	77.21305	74.21971	69.95439
2.5 Years	77.00050	76.76235	76.52495	76.28831	76.05243	75.81730	75.58292	72.37913	68.88887	63.97624
3	73.07895	72.80780	72.53768	72.26859	72.00053	71.73349	71.46747	67.84784	63.94092	58.50897
3.5	69.35711	69.05697	68.75816	68.46068	68.16451	67.86965	67.57610	63.60023	59.34835	53.50892
4	65.82482	65.49938	65.17558	64.85341	64.53286	64.21394	63.89662	59.61854	55.08565	48.93617
4.5	62.47243	62.12506	61.77966	61.43621	61.09470	60.75513	60.41748	55.88613	51.12912	44.75419
5 Years	59.29078	58.92458	58.56068	58.19906	57.83972	57.48263	57.12778	52.38738	47.45676	40.92960
6	53.40533	53.00975	52.61715	52.22750	51.84077	51.45694	51.07599	46.03329	40.88441	34.23300
7	48.10409	47.68865	47.27685	46.86864	46.46401	46.06290	45.66530	40.44989	35.22227	28.63205
8	43.32908	42.90169	42.47856	42.05964	41.64491	41.23430	40.82778	35.54371	30.34429	23.94749
9	39.02805	38.59523	38.16726	37.74408	37.32563	36.91186	36.50272	31.23260	26.14186	20.02938
10	35.15396	34.72106	34.29353	33.87131	33.45433	33.04253	32.63583	27.44438	22.52144	16.75232
11	31.66443	31.23577	30.81296	30.39591	29.98455	29.57880	29.17858	24.11564	19.40242	14.01143
12 Years	28.52129	28.10034	27.68564	27.27711	26.87465	26.47817	26.08757	21.19064	16.71535	11.71898

Entry is percentage value today which, compounded monthly, will give 100% at term of note.

The Most Commonly Needed Mortgage Balances

30 Year Amortization Schedule

Interest Rate	1	2	3	4	Balance at End of Year 5	6	7	8	10	12	15	20	25
6.000%	98.7720	97.4682	96.0841	94.6145	93.0544	91.3980	89.6394	87.7724	83.6857	79.0794	71.0488	54.0036	31.0121
6.125%	98.8004	97.5252	96.1696	94.7287	93.1970	91.5687	89.8379	87.9981	83.9634	79.4044	71.4311	54.4214	31.3347
6.250%	98.8282	97.5810	96.2536	94.8409	93.3372	91.7369	90.0336	88.2207	84.2377	79.7258	71.8102	54.8376	31.6576
6.375%	98.8555	97.6359	96.3362	94.9512	93.4752	91.9024	90.2264	88.4403	84.5086	80.0438	72.1862	55.2523	31.9808
6.500%	98.8823	97.6897	96.4172	95.0596	93.6110	92.0654	90.4162	88.6567	84.7761	80.3584	72.5591	55.6653	32.3042
6.625%	98.9085	97.7425	96.4968	95.1661	93.7445	92.2257	90.6033	88.8700	85.0403	80.6695	72.9289	56.0766	32.6277
6.750%	98.9343	97.7943	96.5750	95.2707	93.8757	92.3835	90.7875	89.0803	85.3010	80.9771	73.2954	56.4862	32.9514
6.875%	98.9595	97.8451	96.6517	95.3736	94.0047	92.5388	90.9688	89.2875	85.5584	81.2813	73.6588	56.8941	33.2752
7.000%	98.9842	97.8949	96.7270	95.4745	94.1316	92.6916	91.1474	89.4917	85.8124	81.5819	74.0189	57.3001	33.5991
7.125%	99.0084	97.9438	96.8008	95.5737	94.2563	92.8418	91.3232	89.6928	86.0630	81.8791	74.3757	57.7042	33.9230
7.250%	99.0321	97.9917	96.8733	95.6711	94.3788	92.9896	91.4962	89.8909	86.3104	82.1729	74.7293	58.1065	34.2469
7.375%	99.0554	98.0387	96.9445	95.7667	94.4992	93.1349	91.6665	90.0861	86.5543	82.4631	75.0796	58.5068	34.5707
7.500%	99.0782	98.0848	97.0142	95.8606	94.6174	93.2777	91.8340	90.2783	86.7950	82.7499	75.4267	58.9051	34.8945
7.625%	99.1005	98.1299	97.0827	95.9528	94.7336	93.4182	91.9989	90.4675	87.0323	83.0332	75.7704	59.3015	35.2182
7.750%	99.1223	98.1741	97.1498	96.0432	94.8477	93.5563	92.1611	90.6538	87.2664	83.3131	76.1108	59.6957	35.5417
7.875%	99.1437	98.2175	97.2156	96.1320	94.9598	93.6919	92.3206	90.8372	87.4972	83.5894	76.4478	60.0879	35.8650
8.000%	99.1646	98.2599	97.2801	96.2190	95.0699	93.8253	92.4774	91.0177	87.7247	83.8624	76.7816	60.4780	36.1881
8.125%	99.1851	98.3015	97.3434	96.3045	95.1779	93.9563	92.6317	91.1953	87.9490	84.1319	77.1119	60.8659	36.5110
8.250%	99.2052	98.3423	97.4054	96.3883	95.2840	94.0850	92.7834	91.3702	88.1700	84.3980	77.4390	61.2516	36.8336
8.375%	99.2248	98.3822	97.4662	96.4705	95.3881	94.2115	92.9325	91.5421	88.3879	84.6606	77.7626	61.6351	37.1558
8.500%	99.2440	98.4213	97.5257	96.5511	95.4903	94.3357	93.0790	91.7113	88.6025	84.9199	78.0829	62.0163	37.4778
8.625%	99.2628	98.4595	97.5841	96.6301	95.5905	94.4577	93.2231	91.8778	88.8140	85.1758	78.3999	62.3953	37.7993
8.750%	99.2812	98.4970	97.6413	96.7076	95.6889	94.5774	93.3647	92.0414	89.0224	85.4282	78.7134	62.7719	38.1204
8.875%	99.2992	98.5336	97.6973	96.7836	95.7854	94.6950	93.5038	92.2024	89.2276	85.6774	79.0236	63.1463	38.4411
9.000%	99.3168	98.5695	97.7521	96.8581	95.8801	94.8105	93.6405	92.3607	89.4297	85.9231	79.3305	63.5183	38.7614
9.125%	99.3340	98.6046	97.8059	96.9311	95.9730	94.9238	93.7747	92.5163	89.6288	86.1656	79.6340	63.8879	39.0811
9.250%	99.3508	98.6390	97.8585	97.0026	96.0641	95.0350	93.9066	92.6693	89.8248	86.4047	79.9341	64.2551	39.4004
9.375%	99.3673	98.6726	97.9100	97.0727	96.1534	95.1442	94.0361	92.8196	90.0178	86.6405	80.2308	64.6199	39.7190
9.500%	99.3834	98.7055	97.9604	97.1413	96.2410	95.2513	94.1633	92.9674	90.2077	86.8731	80.5243	64.9822	40.0371
9.625%	99.3991	98.7377	98.0098	97.2086	96.3268	95.3563	94.2882	93.1126	90.3947	87.1023	80.8143	65.3421	40.3546
9.750%	99.4144	98.7692	98.0581	97.2745	96.4110	95.4594	94.4108	93.2553	90.5787	87.3284	81.1011	65.6995	40.6715
9.875%	99.4295	98.7999	98.1054	97.3390	96.4935	95.5606	94.5312	93.3955	90.7598	87.5512	81.3845	66.0545	40.9877
10.000%	99.4441	98.8300	98.1516	97.4022	96.5743	95.6597	94.6494	93.5332	90.9380	87.7709	81.6646	66.4069	41.3032
10.125%	99.4585	98.8595	98.1969	97.4641	96.6535	95.7570	94.7653	93.6685	91.1133	87.9873	81.9413	66.7567	41.6181
10.250%	99.4725	98.8882	98.2412	97.5247	96.7312	95.8524	94.8791	93.8013	91.2858	88.2007	82.2148	67.1041	41.9322
10.375%	99.4861	98.9163	98.2846	97.5840	96.8072	95.9459	94.9908	93.9318	91.4555	88.4109	82.4850	67.4489	42.2455
10.500%	99.4995	98.9438	98.3269	97.6421	96.8817	96.0375	95.1004	94.0599	91.6224	88.6180	82.7520	67.7911	42.5581
10.625%	99.5125	98.9707	98.3684	97.6989	96.9547	96.1274	95.2079	94.1857	91.7865	88.8220	83.0156	68.1308	42.8699
10.750%	99.5253	98.9969	98.4089	97.7545	97.0261	96.2155	95.3133	94.3092	91.9479	89.0230	83.2761	68.4678	43.1808
10.875%	99.5377	99.0226	98.4486	97.8089	97.0961	96.3018	95.4167	94.4304	92.1065	89.2209	83.5333	68.8023	43.4910
11.000%	99.5499	99.0477	98.4873	97.8622	97.1646	96.3864	95.5181	94.5494	92.2626	89.4159	83.7873	69.1342	43.8002
11.125%	99.5617	99.0721	98.5252	97.9143	97.2317	96.4693	95.6176	94.6661	92.4159	89.6078	84.0381	69.4634	44.1086
11.250%	99.5733	99.0961	98.5623	97.9652	97.2974	96.5505	95.7151	94.7807	92.5667	89.7969	84.2857	69.7901	44.4161
11.375%	99.5846	99.1194	98.5985	98.0151	97.3617	96.6301	95.8107	94.8931	92.7148	89.9830	84.5301	70.1141	44.7227
11.500%	99.5956	99.1422	98.6338	98.0638	97.4247	96.7080	95.9044	95.0035	92.8605	90.1662	84.7714	70.4355	45.0284
11.625%	99.6064	99.1645	98.6684	98.1115	97.4863	96.7843	95.9963	95.1117	93.0035	90.3466	85.0096	70.7543	45.3331
11.750%	99.6169	99.1863	98.7022	98.1581	97.5465	96.8591	96.0864	95.2178	93.1442	90.5241	85.2447	71.0704	45.6368
11.875%	99.6271	99.2075	98.7352	98.2037	97.6055	96.9323	96.1746	95.3219	93.2823	90.6989	85.4768	71.3840	45.9396
12.000%	99.6371	99.2282	98.7675	98.2483	97.6632	97.0040	96.2611	95.4241	93.4180	90.8708	85.7057	71.6948	46.2413
12.125%	99.6469	99.2485	98.7990	98.2918	97.7197	97.0742	96.3459	95.5242	93.5513	91.0400	85.9316	72.0031	46.5421
12.250%	99.6564	99.2682	98.8297	98.3344	97.7749	97.1429	96.4289	95.6224	93.6822	91.2065	86.1545	72.3087	46.8418
12.375%	99.6656	99.2875	98.8598	98.3760	97.8289	97.2101	96.5102	95.7187	93.8108	91.3703	86.3744	72.6117	47.1404
12.500%	99.6747	99.3063	98.8891	98.4167	97.8818	97.2760	96.5899	95.8131	93.9371	91.5315	86.5914	72.9120	47.4380
12.750%	99.6921	99.3426	98.9458	98.4953	97.9839	97.4034	96.7444	95.9963	94.1829	91.8459	87.0164	73.5048	48.0300
15.000%	99.8142	99.5986	99.3484	99.0578	98.7206	98.3292	97.8749	97.3475	96.0248	94.2426	90.3441	78.3738	53.1504
18.000%	99.9076	99.7971	99.6650	99.5071	99.3183	99.0925	98.8226	98.4999	97.6527	96.4416	93.5833	83.6409	59.3494

Remaining Balance Tables

Term of 3 Years
Interest Rate 5.50%   Interest Rate 5.75%
Monthly Payment 3.019590%   Annual Constant 36.23508%   Monthly Payment 3.030879%   Annual Constant 36.37055%

Year End	Principal Paid in Year	Interest Paid in Year	Total Interest Paid	Remaining Balance Year End	Curtail First Month	Principal Paid in Year	Interest Paid in Year	Total Interest Paid	Remaining Balance Year End	Curtail First Month	Year End
1	31.521822	4.713260	4.713260	68.478178	2.549571	31.440557	4.929992	4.929992	68.559443	2.676652	1
2	33.299901	2.935181	7.648441	35.178277	2.693387	33.296803	3.073746	8.003738	35.262640	2.834681	2
3	35.178277	1.056805	8.705246	0.000000	2.845315	35.262640	1.107909	9.111647	0.000000	3.002041	3

Term of 4 Years
Interest Rate 5.50%   Interest Rate 5.75%
Monthly Payment 2.325648%   Annual Constant 27.90777%   Monthly Payment 2.337058%   Annual Constant 28.04470%

Year End	Principal Paid in Year	Interest Paid in Year	Total Interest Paid	Remaining Balance Year End	Curtail First Month	Principal Paid in Year	Interest Paid in Year	Total Interest Paid	Remaining Balance Year End	Curtail First Month	Year End
1	22.981352	4.926418	4.926418	77.018648	1.858795	22.891742	5.152955	5.152955	77.108258	1.948860	1
2	24.277681	3.630089	8.556507	52.740966	1.963645	24.243266	3.801431	8.954386	52.864992	2.063920	2
3	25.647133	2.260637	10.817144	27.093833	2.074410	25.674585	2.370112	11.324498	27.190408	2.185774	3
4	27.093833	0.813937	11.631081	0.000000	2.191423	27.190408	0.854289	12.178788	0.000000	2.314821	4

Term of 5 Years
Interest Rate 5.50%   Interest Rate 5.75%
Monthly Payment 1.910116%   Annual Constant 22.92139%   Monthly Payment 1.921677%   Annual Constant 23.06012%

Year End	Principal Paid in Year	Interest Paid in Year	Total Interest Paid	Remaining Balance Year End	Curtail First Month	Principal Paid in Year	Interest Paid in Year	Total Interest Paid	Remaining Balance Year End	Curtail First Month	Year End
1	17.867338	5.054057	5.054057	82.132662	1.445159	17.773681	5.286441	5.286441	82.226319	1.513140	1
2	18.875196	4.046198	9.100255	63.257466	1.526678	18.823036	4.237085	9.523526	63.403282	1.602476	2
3	19.939906	2.981489	12.081743	43.317560	1.612794	19.934345	3.125777	12.649303	43.468937	1.697085	3
4	21.064673	1.856721	13.938465	22.252886	1.703768	21.111266	1.948856	14.598159	22.357671	1.797281	4
5	22.252886	0.668508	14.606973	0.000000	1.799874	22.357671	0.702451	15.300609	0.000000	1.903392	5

Term of 7 Years
Interest Rate 5.50%   Interest Rate 5.75%
Monthly Payment 1.437004%   Annual Constant 17.24405%   Monthly Payment 1.448900%   Annual Constant 17.38680%

Year End	Principal Paid in Year	Interest Paid in Year	Total Interest Paid	Remaining Balance Year End	Curtail First Month	Principal Paid in Year	Interest Paid in Year	Total Interest Paid	Remaining Balance Year End	Curtail First Month	Year End
1	12.044669	5.199382	5.199382	87.955331	0.974206	11.948432	5.438370	5.438370	88.051568	1.017215	1
2	12.724083	4.519968	9.719350	75.231248	1.029159	12.653865	4.732937	10.171307	75.397703	1.077271	2
3	13.441821	3.802230	13.521580	61.789426	1.087211	13.400947	3.985855	14.157162	61.996755	1.140873	3
4	14.200046	3.044005	16.565585	47.589381	1.148539	14.192137	3.194665	17.351827	47.804618	1.208230	4
5	15.001040	2.243011	18.808597	32.588341	1.213325	15.030038	2.356764	19.708591	32.774580	1.279563	5
6	15.847217	1.396835	20.205431	16.741124	1.281766	15.917409	1.469393	21.177983	16.857171	1.355109	6
7	16.741124	0.502927	20.708358	0.000000	1.354068	16.857171	0.529632	21.707615	0.000000	1.435114	7

Term of 10 Years
Interest Rate 5.50%   Interest Rate 5.75%
Monthly Payment 1.085263%   Annual Constant 13.02315%   Monthly Payment 1.097692%   Annual Constant 13.17231%

Year End	Principal Paid in Year	Interest Paid in Year	Total Interest Paid	Remaining Balance Year End	Curtail First Month	Principal Paid in Year	Interest Paid in Year	Total Interest Paid	Remaining Balance Year End	Curtail First Month	Year End
1	7.715727	5.307426	5.307426	92.284273	0.624069	7.621073	5.551233	5.551233	92.378927	0.648811	1
2	8.150955	4.872199	10.179625	84.133318	0.659272	8.071020	5.101286	10.652519	84.307906	0.687116	2
3	8.610733	4.412421	14.592046	75.522586	0.696460	8.547532	4.624774	15.277294	75.760374	0.727683	3
4	9.096446	3.926708	18.518754	66.426140	0.735745	9.052177	4.120130	19.397423	66.708198	0.770646	4
5	9.609557	3.413597	21.932350	56.816584	0.777247	9.586616	3.585691	22.983114	57.121582	0.816144	5
6	10.151611	2.871542	24.803893	46.664973	0.821090	10.152608	3.019698	26.002813	46.968974	0.864330	6
7	10.724242	2.298912	27.102804	35.940731	0.867406	10.752016	2.420290	28.423103	36.216958	0.915359	7
8	11.329173	1.693980	28.796784	24.611558	0.916335	11.386813	1.785493	30.208596	24.830144	0.969402	8
9	11.968228	1.054926	29.851710	12.643330	0.968023	12.059089	1.113217	31.321813	12.771056	1.026635	9
10	12.643330	0.379824	30.231534	0.000000	1.022627	12.771056	0.401251	31.723064	0.000000	1.087248	10

Term of 15 Years
Interest Rate 5.50%   Interest Rate 5.75%
Monthly Payment 0.817083%   Annual Constant 9.80500%   Monthly Payment 0.830410%   Annual Constant 9.96492%

Year End	Principal Paid in Year	Interest Paid in Year	Total Interest Paid	Remaining Balance Year End	Curtail First Month	Principal Paid in Year	Interest Paid in Year	Total Interest Paid	Remaining Balance Year End	Curtail First Month	Year End
1	4.415199	5.389803	5.389803	95.584801	0.357113	4.327795	5.637126	5.637126	95.672205	0.368441	1
2	4.664250	5.140751	10.530554	90.920551	0.377257	4.583308	5.381613	11.018739	91.088897	0.390194	2
3	4.927351	4.877651	15.408204	85.993200	0.398538	4.853905	5.111016	16.129755	86.234992	0.413231	3
4	5.205292	4.599709	20.007914	80.787908	0.421018	5.140479	4.824442	20.954197	81.094513	0.437628	4
5	5.498912	4.306090	24.314004	75.288996	0.444767	5.443972	4.520949	25.475146	75.650541	0.463466	5
6	5.809093	3.995908	28.309912	69.479903	0.469855	5.765383	4.199538	29.674684	69.885158	0.490829	6
7	6.136772	3.668230	31.978141	63.343131	0.496359	6.105770	3.859151	33.533835	63.779387	0.519807	7
8	6.482934	3.322067	35.300209	56.860197	0.524357	6.466254	3.498667	37.032501	57.313133	0.550496	8
9	6.848623	2.956379	38.256587	50.011574	0.553935	6.848021	3.116900	40.149402	50.465112	0.582998	9
10	7.234939	2.570063	40.826650	42.776636	0.585182	7.252327	2.712594	42.861996	43.212786	0.617418	10
11	7.643046	2.161955	42.988606	35.133590	0.618191	7.680503	2.284418	45.146414	35.532283	0.653870	11
12	8.074174	1.730827	44.719433	27.059416	0.653061	8.133958	1.830963	46.977377	27.398325	0.692474	12
13	8.529621	1.275381	45.994814	18.529795	0.689899	8.614186	1.350735	48.328112	18.784139	0.733358	13
14	9.010759	0.794243	46.789057	9.519036	0.728815	9.122766	0.842155	49.170267	9.661373	0.776655	14
15	9.519036	0.285965	47.075022	0.000000	0.769926	9.661373	0.303548	49.473816	0.000000	0.822509	15

Monthly Factors for 5.500% Interest:				Monthly Factors for 5.750% Interest:		
Month	This Month	Year-to-date		Month	This Month	Year-to-date
1	1.004583	1.004583		1	1.004792	1.004792
2	1.009188	2.013771		2	1.009606	2.014398
3	1.013813	3.027584		3	1.014444	3.028842
4	1.018460	4.046044		4	1.019305	4.048147
5	1.023128	5.069172		5	1.024189	5.072336
6	1.027817	6.096989		6	1.029097	6.101432
7	1.032528	7.129516		7	1.034028	7.135460
8	1.037260	8.166777		8	1.038982	8.174443
9	1.042014	9.208791		9	1.043961	9.218403
10	1.046790	10.255581		10	1.048963	10.267367
11	1.051588	11.307170		11	1.053989	11.321356

Entries are percentages of the original loan amount.

Remaining Balance Tables

Term of 25 Years				
Interest Rate 5.50%			Interest Rate 5.75%	
Monthly Payment 0.614087%	Annual Constant 7.36905%		Monthly Payment 0.629106%	Annual Constant 7.54928%

Year End	Principal Paid in Year	Interest Paid in Year	Total Interest Paid	Remaining Balance Year End	Curtail First Month	Principal Paid in Year	Interest Paid in Year	Total Interest Paid	Remaining Balance Year End	Curtail First Month	Year End
1	1.916893	5.452157	5.452157	98.083107	0.155044	1.847461	5.701816	5.701816	98.152539	0.157281	1
2	2.025021	5.344029	10.796186	96.058086	0.163789	1.956535	5.592742	11.294558	96.196004	0.166567	2
3	2.139248	5.229802	16.025988	93.918839	0.173028	2.072048	5.477229	16.771787	94.123956	0.176401	3
4	2.259918	5.109132	21.135120	91.658921	0.182788	2.194382	5.354895	22.126682	91.929575	0.186816	4
5	2.387395	4.981655	26.116775	89.271525	0.193099	2.323937	5.225339	27.352022	89.605637	0.197845	5
6	2.522063	4.846987	30.963762	86.749462	0.203991	2.461142	5.088135	32.440156	87.144495	0.209526	6
7	2.664327	4.704723	35.668484	84.085135	0.215498	2.606448	4.942829	37.382985	84.538047	0.221897	7
8	2.814616	4.554434	40.222918	81.270519	0.227654	2.760332	4.788945	42.171930	81.777715	0.234997	8
9	2.973383	4.395667	44.618585	78.297136	0.240495	2.923301	4.625975	46.797905	78.854414	0.248872	9
10	3.141105	4.227945	48.846530	75.156031	0.254061	3.095893	4.453384	51.251290	75.758521	0.263565	10
11	3.318288	4.050762	52.897292	71.837743	0.268392	3.278674	4.270603	55.521893	72.479848	0.279126	11
12	3.505466	3.863584	56.760876	68.332277	0.283532	3.472246	4.077031	59.598923	69.007602	0.295605	12
13	3.703201	3.665849	60.426725	64.629076	0.299525	3.677247	3.872030	63.470953	65.330355	0.313058	13
14	3.912091	3.456959	63.883684	60.716985	0.316421	3.894351	3.654926	67.125879	61.436004	0.331541	14
15	4.132764	3.236286	67.119970	56.584221	0.334269	4.124273	3.425004	70.550884	57.311731	0.351115	15
16	4.365884	3.003166	70.123136	52.218337	0.353125	4.367769	3.181508	73.732391	52.943962	0.371845	16
17	4.612154	2.756896	72.880031	47.606183	0.373044	4.625641	2.923635	76.656027	48.318321	0.393798	17
18	4.872316	2.496734	75.376765	42.733867	0.394086	4.898739	2.650538	79.306565	43.419582	0.417048	18
19	5.147153	2.221897	77.598662	37.586714	0.416316	5.187959	2.361318	81.667883	38.231623	0.441670	19
20	5.437493	1.931557	79.530220	32.149221	0.439799	5.494255	2.055021	83.722904	32.737367	0.467747	20
21	5.744210	1.624840	81.155059	26.405011	0.464607	5.818635	1.730641	85.453546	26.918732	0.495362	21
22	6.068229	1.300821	82.455881	20.336783	0.490815	6.162167	1.387110	86.840656	20.756566	0.524608	22
23	6.410524	0.958525	83.414406	13.926258	0.518501	6.525980	1.023297	87.863953	14.230586	0.555581	23
24	6.772128	0.596921	84.011328	7.154130	0.547748	6.911273	0.638004	88.501957	7.319313	0.588383	24
25	7.154130	0.214920	84.226248	0.000000	0.578646	7.319313	0.229964	88.731921	0.000000	0.623121	25

Term of 30 Years				
Interest Rate 5.50%			Interest Rate 5.75%	
Monthly Payment 0.567789%	Annual Constant 6.81347%		Monthly Payment 0.583573%	Annual Constant 7.00287%

Year End	Principal Paid in Year	Interest Paid in Year	Total Interest Paid	Remaining Balance Year End	Curtail First Month	Principal Paid in Year	Interest Paid in Year	Total Interest Paid	Remaining Balance Year End	Curtail First Month	Year End
1	1.347089	5.466379	5.466379	98.652911	0.108956	1.286426	5.716448	5.716448	98.713574	0.109518	1
2	1.423076	5.390392	10.856771	97.229835	0.115102	1.362376	5.640498	11.356947	97.351198	0.115984	2
3	1.503349	5.310119	16.166890	95.726486	0.121595	1.442811	5.560064	16.917010	95.908387	0.122832	3
4	1.588149	5.225319	21.392209	94.138337	0.128454	1.527994	5.474880	22.391890	94.380393	0.130084	4
5	1.677733	5.135735	26.527944	92.460603	0.135700	1.618206	5.384668	27.776558	92.762187	0.137764	5
6	1.772371	5.041097	31.569041	90.688233	0.143354	1.713745	5.289129	33.065687	91.048442	0.145898	6
7	1.872346	4.941122	36.510163	88.815886	0.151440	1.814924	5.187950	38.253637	89.233517	0.154511	7
8	1.977961	4.835507	41.345669	86.837925	0.159983	1.922077	5.080797	43.334434	87.311440	0.163634	8
9	2.089534	4.723934	46.069603	84.748391	0.169007	2.035556	4.967318	48.301752	85.275884	0.173295	9
10	2.207400	4.606068	50.675671	82.540991	0.178541	2.155735	4.847139	53.148892	83.120149	0.183526	10
11	2.331915	4.481553	55.157224	80.209076	0.188612	2.283009	4.719865	57.868756	80.837139	0.194361	11
12	2.463453	4.350015	59.507239	77.745623	0.199251	2.417798	4.585076	62.453833	78.419341	0.205836	12
13	2.602411	4.211057	63.718296	75.143212	0.210490	2.560544	4.442330	66.896163	75.858797	0.217989	13
14	2.749208	4.064260	67.782556	72.394004	0.222363	2.711718	4.291156	71.187319	73.147079	0.230859	14
15	2.904285	3.909183	71.691740	69.489720	0.234906	2.871818	4.131056	75.318375	70.275261	0.244489	15
16	3.068109	3.745359	75.437099	66.421610	0.248157	3.041369	3.961505	79.279880	67.233892	0.258923	16
17	3.241175	3.572293	79.009392	63.180436	0.262155	3.220931	3.781943	83.061823	64.012960	0.274210	17
18	3.424002	3.389466	82.398858	59.756434	0.276943	3.411095	3.591780	86.653603	60.601866	0.290399	18
19	3.617143	3.196325	85.595183	56.139291	0.292564	3.612485	3.390389	90.043992	56.989381	0.307544	19
20	3.821178	2.992290	88.587473	52.318112	0.309067	3.825766	3.177109	93.221101	53.163615	0.325702	20
21	4.036723	2.776745	91.364218	48.281390	0.326501	4.051638	2.951236	96.172337	49.111977	0.344931	21
22	4.264426	2.549042	93.913260	44.016964	0.344918	4.290846	2.712028	98.884365	44.821131	0.365296	22
23	4.504973	2.308495	96.221756	39.511991	0.364375	4.544177	2.458697	101.343062	40.276954	0.386863	23
24	4.759089	2.054379	98.276135	34.752903	0.384928	4.812464	2.190410	103.533472	35.464489	0.409703	24
25	5.027539	1.785929	100.062065	29.725364	0.406641	5.096591	1.906283	105.439755	30.367898	0.433892	25
26	5.311131	1.502337	101.564401	24.414233	0.429579	5.397493	1.605381	107.045136	24.970405	0.459509	26
27	5.610721	1.202747	102.767148	18.803512	0.453810	5.716160	1.286714	108.331850	19.254244	0.486638	27
28	5.927210	0.886258	103.653407	12.876302	0.479409	6.053642	0.949233	109.281082	13.200602	0.515369	28
29	6.261551	0.551917	104.205324	6.614752	0.506651	6.411048	0.591827	109.872909	6.789555	0.545796	29
30	6.614752	0.198716	104.404040	0.000000	0.535019	6.789555	0.213319	110.086228	0.000000	0.578020	30

Monthly Factors for 5.500% Interest:			Monthly Factors for 5.750% Interest:		
Month	This Month	Year-to-date	Month	This Month	Year-to-date
1	1.004583	1.004583	1	1.004792	1.004792
2	1.009188	2.013771	2	1.009606	2.014398
3	1.013813	3.027584	3	1.014444	3.028842
4	1.018460	4.046044	4	1.019305	4.048147
5	1.023128	5.069172	5	1.024189	5.072336
6	1.027817	6.096989	6	1.029097	6.101432
7	1.032528	7.129516	7	1.034028	7.135460
8	1.037260	8.166777	8	1.038982	8.174443
9	1.042014	9.208791	9	1.043961	9.218403
10	1.046790	10.255581	10	1.048963	10.267367
11	1.051588	11.307170	11	1.053989	11.321356

Entries are percentages of the original loan amount.

Remaining Balance Tables

Term of 3 Years

	Interest Rate 6.00%					Interest Rate 6.25%					
	Monthly Payment 3.042194%		Annual Constant 36.50632%			Monthly Payment 3.053534%		Annual Constant 36.64241%			
Year End	Principal Paid in Year	Interest Paid in Year	Total Interest Paid	Remaining Balance Year End	Curtail First Month	Principal Paid in Year	Interest Paid in Year	Total Interest Paid	Remaining Balance Year End	Curtail First Month	Year End
1	31.359390	5.146935	5.146935	68.640610	2.529546	31.278319	5.364091	5.364091	68.721681	2.667747	1
2	33.293568	3.212757	8.359692	35.347042	2.685563	33.290197	3.352212	8.716303	35.431483	2.839342	2
3	35.347042	1.159282	9.518975	0.000000	2.851203	35.431483	1.210926	9.927229	0.000000	3.021973	3

Term of 4 Years

	Interest Rate 6.00%					Interest Rate 6.25%					
	Monthly Payment 2.348503%		Annual Constant 28.18203%			Monthly Payment 2.359982%		Annual Constant 28.31978%			
Year End	Principal Paid in Year	Interest Paid in Year	Total Interest Paid	Remaining Balance Year End	Curtail First Month	Principal Paid in Year	Interest Paid in Year	Total Interest Paid	Remaining Balance Year End	Curtail First Month	Year End
1	22.802323	5.379712	5.379712	77.197677	1.839306	22.713097	5.606687	5.606687	77.286903	1.937214	1
2	24.208720	3.973315	9.353027	52.988957	1.952751	24.174044	4.145740	9.752427	53.112859	2.061819	2
3	25.701861	2.480174	11.833200	27.287096	2.073192	25.728963	2.590821	12.343248	27.383896	2.194439	3
4	27.287096	0.894939	12.728139	0.000000	2.201062	27.383896	0.935888	13.279135	0.000000	2.335590	4

Term of 5 Years

	Interest Rate 6.00%					Interest Rate 6.25%					
	Monthly Payment 1.933280%		Annual Constant 23.19936%			Monthly Payment 1.944926%		Annual Constant 23.33911%			
Year End	Principal Paid in Year	Interest Paid in Year	Total Interest Paid	Remaining Balance Year End	Curtail First Month	Principal Paid in Year	Interest Paid in Year	Total Interest Paid	Remaining Balance Year End	Curtail First Month	Year End
1	17.680317	5.519045	5.519045	82.319683	1.426149	17.587245	5.751869	5.751869	82.412755	1.500027	1
2	18.770800	4.428562	9.947607	63.548883	1.514111	18.718489	4.620625	10.372494	63.694266	1.596512	2
3	19.928542	3.270820	13.218427	43.620341	1.607498	19.922496	3.416618	13.789112	43.771770	1.699202	3
4	21.157691	2.041671	15.260098	22.462651	1.706645	21.203947	2.135167	15.924279	22.567823	1.808498	4
5	22.462651	0.736711	15.996809	0.000000	1.811907	22.567823	0.771291	16.695570	0.000000	1.924824	5

Term of 7 Years

	Interest Rate 6.00%					Interest Rate 6.25%					
	Monthly Payment 1.460855%		Annual Constant 17.53027%			Monthly Payment 1.472870%		Annual Constant 17.67444%			
Year End	Principal Paid in Year	Interest Paid in Year	Total Interest Paid	Remaining Balance Year End	Curtail First Month	Principal Paid in Year	Interest Paid in Year	Total Interest Paid	Remaining Balance Year End	Curtail First Month	Year End
1	11.852692	5.677573	5.677573	88.147308	0.956075	11.757451	5.916989	5.916989	88.242549	1.002800	1
2	12.583740	4.946525	10.624098	75.563567	1.015044	12.513712	5.160728	11.077717	75.728837	1.067302	2
3	13.359878	4.170387	14.794485	62.203689	1.077649	13.318616	4.355823	15.433540	62.410221	1.135953	3
4	14.183886	3.346379	18.140865	48.019803	1.144116	14.175294	3.499146	18.932686	48.234927	1.209020	4
5	15.058717	2.471548	20.612413	32.961086	1.214683	15.087074	2.587365	21.520051	33.147853	1.286786	5
6	15.987506	1.542760	22.155172	16.973580	1.289602	16.057502	1.616937	23.136988	17.090350	1.369554	6
7	16.973580	0.556685	22.711858	0.000000	1.369142	17.090350	0.584089	23.721078	0.000000	1.457647	7

Term of 10 Years

	Interest Rate 6.00%					Interest Rate 6.25%					
	Monthly Payment 1.110205%		Annual Constant 13.32246%			Monthly Payment 1.122801%		Annual Constant 13.47361%			
Year End	Principal Paid in Year	Interest Paid in Year	Total Interest Paid	Remaining Balance Year End	Curtail First Month	Principal Paid in Year	Interest Paid in Year	Total Interest Paid	Remaining Balance Year End	Curtail First Month	Year End
1	7.527222	5.795238	5.795238	92.472778	0.607169	7.434173	6.039439	6.039439	92.565827	0.634065	1
2	7.991485	5.330976	11.126214	84.481293	0.644618	7.912352	5.561259	11.600698	84.653475	0.674849	2
3	8.484382	4.838078	15.964292	75.996911	0.684377	8.421289	5.052322	16.653020	76.232185	0.718257	3
4	9.007680	4.314780	20.279072	66.989231	0.726588	8.962962	4.510650	21.163670	67.269223	0.764457	4
5	9.563254	3.759206	24.038278	57.425977	0.771402	9.539476	3.934136	25.097806	57.729748	0.813628	5
6	10.153095	3.169366	27.207644	47.272883	0.818980	10.153072	3.320539	28.418345	47.576675	0.865962	6
7	10.779315	2.543145	29.750789	36.493567	0.869493	10.806136	2.667475	31.085820	36.770539	0.921662	7
8	11.444160	1.878300	31.629089	25.049407	0.923122	11.501207	1.972405	33.058225	25.269332	0.980945	8
9	12.150011	1.172450	32.801539	12.899397	0.980058	12.240985	1.232627	34.290852	13.028347	1.044041	9
10	12.899397	0.423064	33.224602	0.000000	1.040506	13.028347	0.445264	34.736116	0.000000	1.111196	10

Term of 15 Years

	Interest Rate 6.00%					Interest Rate 6.25%					
	Monthly Payment 0.843857%		Annual Constant 10.12628%			Monthly Payment 0.857423%		Annual Constant 10.28907%			
Year End	Principal Paid in Year	Interest Paid in Year	Total Interest Paid	Remaining Balance Year End	Curtail First Month	Principal Paid in Year	Interest Paid in Year	Total Interest Paid	Remaining Balance Year End	Curtail First Month	Year End
1	4.241667	5.884615	5.884615	95.758333	0.342146	4.156810	6.132265	6.132265	95.843190	0.354537	1
2	4.503254	5.622998	11.507612	91.255049	0.363249	4.424183	5.864891	11.997156	91.419007	0.377341	2
3	4.781037	5.345245	16.852858	86.474012	0.385653	4.708755	5.580320	17.577476	86.710253	0.401613	3
4	5.075921	5.050361	21.903219	81.398091	0.409440	5.011630	5.277444	22.854920	81.698623	0.427445	4
5	5.388992	4.737290	26.640508	76.009099	0.434693	5.333987	4.955087	27.810007	76.364635	0.454959	5
6	5.721374	4.404908	31.045417	70.287725	0.461504	5.677079	4.611995	32.422003	70.687556	0.484202	6
7	6.074255	4.052026	35.097443	64.213470	0.489968	6.042239	4.246835	36.668838	64.645317	0.515346	7
8	6.448902	3.677380	38.774823	57.764567	0.520189	6.430887	3.858188	40.527026	58.214430	0.548494	8
9	6.846656	3.279626	42.054448	50.917911	0.552273	6.844533	3.444541	43.971567	51.369897	0.583774	9
10	7.268943	2.857339	44.911787	43.648968	0.586336	7.284786	3.004288	46.975855	44.085111	0.621324	10
11	7.717276	2.409006	47.320793	35.931692	0.622499	7.753357	2.535718	49.511573	36.331755	0.661289	11
12	8.193260	1.933022	49.253815	27.738431	0.660894	8.252067	2.037008	51.548581	28.079688	0.703824	12
13	8.698603	1.427679	50.681494	19.039829	0.701656	8.782854	1.506220	53.054801	19.296834	0.749095	13
14	9.235114	0.891168	51.572662	9.804715	0.744933	9.347784	0.941291	53.996092	9.949050	0.797278	14
15	9.804715	0.321567	51.894229	0.000000	0.790879	9.949050	0.340024	54.336116	0.000000	0.848561	15

Monthly Factors for 6.000% Interest:				Monthly Factors for 6.250% Interest:		
Month	This Month	Year-to-date		Month	This Month	Year-to-date
1	1.005000	1.005000		1	1.005208	1.005208
2	1.010025	2.015025		2	1.010444	2.015652
3	1.015075	3.030100		3	1.015707	3.031359
4	1.020151	4.050251		4	1.020997	4.052355
5	1.025251	5.075502		5	1.026314	5.078670
6	1.030378	6.105879		6	1.031660	6.110329
7	1.035529	7.141409		7	1.037033	7.147362
8	1.040707	8.182116		8	1.042434	8.189797
9	1.045911	9.228026		9	1.047864	9.237660
10	1.051140	10.279167		10	1.053321	10.290981
11	1.056396	11.335562		11	1.058807	11.349788

Entries are percentages of the original loan amount.

Remaining Balance Tables

Term of 25 Years
Interest Rate   6.00%   Interest Rate   6.25%
Monthly Payment 0.644301%   Annual Constant 7.73162%   Monthly Payment 0.659669%   Annual Constant 7.91603%

Year End	Principal Paid in Year	Interest Paid in Year	Total Interest Paid	Remaining Balance Year End	Curtail First Month	Principal Paid in Year	Interest Paid in Year	Total Interest Paid	Remaining Balance Year End	Curtail First Month	Year End
1	1.780039	5.951578	5.951578	98.219961	0.143583	1.714596	6.201437	6.201437	98.285404	0.146239	1
2	1.889828	5.841789	11.793367	96.330133	0.152439	1.824882	6.091151	12.292588	96.460523	0.155645	2
3	2.006388	5.725229	17.518595	94.323745	0.161842	1.942261	5.973771	18.266359	94.518261	0.165657	3
4	2.130138	5.601479	23.120074	92.193607	0.171824	2.067191	5.848841	24.115200	92.451070	0.176312	4
5	2.261520	5.470097	28.590171	89.932087	0.182421	2.200157	5.715876	29.831076	90.250913	0.187653	5
6	2.401006	5.330611	33.920782	87.531081	0.193673	2.341675	5.574358	35.405434	87.909239	0.199723	6
7	2.549095	5.182522	39.103304	84.981986	0.205618	2.492295	5.423737	40.829171	85.416943	0.212569	7
8	2.706317	5.025300	44.128604	82.275669	0.218300	2.652604	5.263428	46.092599	82.764339	0.226242	8
9	2.873237	4.858380	48.986984	79.402432	0.231764	2.823225	5.092808	51.185407	79.941114	0.240795	9
10	3.050452	4.681165	53.668149	76.351981	0.246059	3.004820	4.911213	56.096620	76.936294	0.256283	10
11	3.238597	4.493020	58.161169	73.113384	0.261235	3.198095	4.717937	60.814557	73.738199	0.272768	11
12	3.438347	4.293270	62.454439	69.675037	0.277348	3.403802	4.512230	65.326787	70.334396	0.290312	12
13	3.650416	4.081201	66.535639	66.024621	0.294454	3.622741	4.293291	69.620078	66.711655	0.308986	13
14	3.875566	3.856051	70.391690	62.149055	0.312615	3.855763	4.060270	73.680348	62.855893	0.328860	14
15	4.114602	3.617014	74.008704	58.034452	0.331897	4.103772	3.812260	77.492609	58.752121	0.350013	15
16	4.368382	3.363235	77.371939	53.666070	0.352367	4.367734	3.548298	81.040907	54.384386	0.372527	16
17	4.637814	3.093802	80.465742	49.028256	0.374101	4.648675	3.267358	84.308265	49.735711	0.396488	17
18	4.923865	2.807752	83.273494	44.104391	0.397174	4.947686	2.968347	87.276611	44.788025	0.421991	18
19	5.227558	2.504059	85.777553	38.876833	0.421671	5.265930	2.650102	89.926714	39.522095	0.449134	19
20	5.549982	2.181635	87.959188	33.326851	0.447679	5.604644	2.311388	92.238102	33.917451	0.478024	20
21	5.892293	1.839324	89.798512	27.434558	0.475291	5.965145	1.950887	94.188989	27.952306	0.508771	21
22	6.255717	1.475900	91.274412	21.178842	0.504606	6.348834	1.567198	95.756187	21.603471	0.541496	22
23	6.641556	1.090061	92.364473	14.537286	0.535729	6.757203	1.158830	96.915017	14.846269	0.576326	23
24	7.051192	0.680045	93.044898	7.486094	0.568771	7.191838	0.724194	97.639211	7.654430	0.613396	24
25	7.486094	0.245523	93.290420	0.000000	0.603852	7.654430	0.261602	97.900813	0.000000	0.652851	25

Term of 30 Years
Interest Rate   6.00%   Interest Rate   6.25%
Monthly Payment 0.599551%   Annual Constant 7.19461%   Monthly Payment 0.615717%   Annual Constant 7.38861%

Year End	Principal Paid in Year	Interest Paid in Year	Total Interest Paid	Remaining Balance Year End	Curtail First Month	Principal Paid in Year	Interest Paid in Year	Total Interest Paid	Remaining Balance Year End	Curtail First Month	Year End
1	1.228012	5.966595	5.966595	98.771988	0.099055	1.171796	6.216811	6.216811	98.828204	0.099943	1
2	1.303753	5.890854	11.857448	97.468236	0.105165	1.247168	6.141439	12.358249	97.581037	0.106372	2
3	1.384165	5.810441	17.667889	96.084070	0.111651	1.327388	6.061219	18.419468	96.253649	0.113214	3
4	1.469538	5.725069	23.392958	94.614532	0.118537	1.412768	5.975839	24.395307	94.840881	0.120496	4
5	1.560176	5.634431	29.027388	93.054357	0.125849	1.503640	5.884967	30.280273	93.337241	0.128246	5
6	1.656404	5.538203	34.565591	91.397953	0.133611	1.600356	5.788250	36.068523	91.736885	0.136495	6
7	1.758567	5.436039	40.001630	89.639386	0.141852	1.703294	5.685312	41.753836	90.033591	0.145275	7
8	1.867032	5.327575	45.329205	87.772354	0.150601	1.812853	5.575753	47.329589	88.220738	0.154619	8
9	1.982186	5.212420	50.541625	85.790168	0.159889	1.929459	5.459147	52.788736	86.291278	0.164565	9
10	2.104443	5.090163	55.631788	83.685725	0.169751	2.053566	5.335041	58.123777	84.237713	0.175150	10
11	2.234240	4.960366	60.592154	81.451484	0.180221	2.185655	5.202952	63.326729	82.052058	0.186416	11
12	2.372044	4.822563	65.414717	79.079441	0.191336	2.326240	5.062367	68.389095	79.725818	0.198406	12
13	2.518346	4.676260	70.090977	76.561095	0.203138	2.475868	4.912739	73.301834	77.249951	0.211168	13
14	2.673672	4.520934	74.611911	73.887423	0.215667	2.635120	4.753486	78.055320	74.614830	0.224751	14
15	2.838578	4.356028	78.967939	71.048844	0.228969	2.804616	4.583991	82.639311	71.810215	0.239207	15
16	3.013656	4.180951	83.148890	68.035189	0.243091	2.985014	4.403593	87.042903	68.825201	0.254594	16
17	3.199531	3.995075	87.143965	64.835657	0.258084	3.177015	4.211591	91.254494	65.648185	0.270970	17
18	3.396871	3.797735	90.941700	61.438786	0.274002	3.381367	4.007240	95.261734	62.266819	0.288399	18
19	3.606383	3.588223	94.529923	57.832403	0.290902	3.598862	3.789744	99.051478	58.667956	0.306949	19
20	3.828817	3.365789	97.895712	54.003586	0.308844	3.830348	3.558259	102.609737	54.837609	0.326693	20
21	4.064970	3.129636	101.025349	49.938616	0.327893	4.076723	3.311884	105.921620	50.760886	0.347706	21
22	4.315688	2.878918	103.904267	45.622928	0.348117	4.338945	3.049662	108.971282	46.421941	0.370071	22
23	4.581871	2.612736	106.517002	41.041058	0.369588	4.618034	2.770573	111.741855	41.803907	0.393875	23
24	4.864470	2.330136	108.847139	36.176587	0.392383	4.915074	2.473532	114.215387	36.888833	0.419210	24
25	5.164500	2.030106	110.877245	31.012087	0.416585	5.231220	2.157386	116.372773	31.657613	0.446174	25
26	5.483035	1.711571	112.588816	25.529052	0.442279	5.567702	1.820904	118.193678	26.089911	0.474873	26
27	5.821217	1.373389	113.962205	19.707835	0.469557	5.925827	1.462780	119.656457	20.164084	0.505417	27
28	6.180257	1.014350	114.976555	13.527578	0.498519	6.306987	1.081620	120.738077	13.857098	0.537927	28
29	6.561441	0.633165	115.609720	6.966137	0.529266	6.712663	0.675943	121.414020	7.144434	0.572527	29
30	6.966137	0.228469	115.838189	0.000000	0.561910	7.144434	0.244172	121.658192	0.000000	0.609353	30

| Monthly Factors for 6.000% Interest: | | | | Monthly Factors for 6.250% Interest: | | |
Month	This Month	Year-to-date		Month	This Month	Year-to-date
1	1.005000	1.005000		1	1.005208	1.005208
2	1.010025	2.015025		2	1.010444	2.015652
3	1.015075	3.030100		3	1.015707	3.031359
4	1.020151	4.050251		4	1.020997	4.052355
5	1.025251	5.075502		5	1.026314	5.078670
6	1.030378	6.105879		6	1.031660	6.110329
7	1.035529	7.141409		7	1.037033	7.147362
8	1.040707	8.182116		8	1.042434	8.189797
9	1.045911	9.228026		9	1.047864	9.237660
10	1.051140	10.279167		10	1.053321	10.290981
11	1.056396	11.335562		11	1.058807	11.349788

Entries are percentages of the original loan amount.

Remaining Balance Tables

Term of 3 Years
Interest Rate   6.50%   Interest Rate   6.75%
Monthly Payment 3.064900%   Annual Constant 36.77880%   Monthly Payment 3.076292%   Annual Constant 36.91551%

Year End	Principal Paid in Year	Interest Paid in Year	Total Interest Paid	Remaining Balance Year End	Curtail First Month	Principal Paid in Year	Interest Paid in Year	Total Interest Paid	Remaining Balance Year End	Curtail First Month	Year End
1	31.197347	5.581457	5.581457	68.802653	2.509640	31.116473	5.799033	5.799033	68.883527	2.658826	1
2	33.286691	3.492113	9.073569	35.515962	2.677715	33.283049	3.632457	9.431490	35.600479	2.843955	2
3	35.515962	1.262841	10.336410	0.000000	2.857046	35.600479	1.315027	10.746517	0.000000	3.041974	3

Term of 4 Years
Interest Rate   6.50%   Interest Rate   6.75%
Monthly Payment 2.371495%   Annual Constant 28.45794%   Monthly Payment 2.383043%   Annual Constant 28.59651%

Year End	Principal Paid in Year	Interest Paid in Year	Total Interest Paid	Remaining Balance Year End	Curtail First Month	Principal Paid in Year	Interest Paid in Year	Total Interest Paid	Remaining Balance Year End	Curtail First Month	Year End
1	22.624064	5.833880	5.833880	77.375936	1.819970	22.535225	6.061289	6.061289	77.464775	1.925580	1
2	24.139239	4.318704	10.152584	53.236697	1.941857	24.104306	4.492208	10.553497	53.360470	2.059654	2
3	25.755889	2.702055	12.854639	27.480808	2.071907	25.782639	2.813875	13.367371	27.577831	2.203063	3
4	27.480808	0.977135	13.831774	0.000000	2.210666	27.577831	1.018683	14.386054	0.000000	2.356458	4

Term of 5 Years
Interest Rate   6.50%   Interest Rate   6.75%
Monthly Payment 1.956615%   Annual Constant 23.47938%   Monthly Payment 1.968346%   Annual Constant 23.62015%

Year End	Principal Paid in Year	Interest Paid in Year	Total Interest Paid	Remaining Balance Year End	Curtail First Month	Principal Paid in Year	Interest Paid in Year	Total Interest Paid	Remaining Balance Year End	Curtail First Month	Year End
1	17.494467	5.984910	5.984910	82.505533	1.407325	17.401984	6.218169	6.218169	82.598016	1.486957	1
2	18.666104	4.813274	10.798184	63.839428	1.501576	18.613648	5.006504	11.224673	63.984367	1.590491	2
3	19.916208	3.563170	14.361354	43.923220	1.602140	19.909678	3.710474	14.935148	44.074689	1.701233	3
4	21.250033	2.229345	16.590699	22.673187	1.709438	21.259948	2.324205	17.259352	22.778741	1.819687	4
5	22.673187	0.806191	17.396889	0.000000	1.823922	22.778741	0.841412	18.100764	0.000000	1.946388	5

Term of 7 Years
Interest Rate   6.50%   Interest Rate   6.75%
Monthly Payment 1.484944%   Annual Constant 17.81932%   Monthly Payment 1.497076%   Annual Constant 17.96492%

Year End	Principal Paid in Year	Interest Paid in Year	Total Interest Paid	Remaining Balance Year End	Curtail First Month	Principal Paid in Year	Interest Paid in Year	Total Interest Paid	Remaining Balance Year End	Curtail First Month	Year End
1	11.662709	6.156615	6.156615	88.337291	0.938195	11.568466	6.396450	6.396450	88.431534	0.988497	1
2	12.443782	5.375542	11.532157	75.893509	1.001028	12.373955	5.590961	11.987411	76.057579	1.057324	2
3	13.277165	4.542159	16.074315	62.616344	1.068068	13.235528	4.729389	16.716800	62.822051	1.130943	3
4	14.166362	3.652962	19.727277	48.449982	1.139599	14.157090	3.807826	20.524626	48.664961	1.209689	4
5	15.115109	2.704215	22.431492	33.334873	1.215920	15.142819	2.822097	23.346723	33.522141	1.293917	5
6	16.127396	1.691928	24.123420	17.207477	1.297352	16.197183	1.767734	25.114457	17.324959	1.384010	6
7	17.207477	0.611846	24.735266	0.000000	1.384239	17.324959	0.639957	25.754414	0.000000	1.480375	7

Term of 10 Years
Interest Rate   6.50%   Interest Rate   6.75%
Monthly Payment 1.135480%   Annual Constant 13.62576%   Monthly Payment 1.148241%   Annual Constant 13.77889%

Year End	Principal Paid in Year	Interest Paid in Year	Total Interest Paid	Remaining Balance Year End	Curtail First Month	Principal Paid in Year	Interest Paid in Year	Total Interest Paid	Remaining Balance Year End	Curtail First Month	Year End
1	7.341926	6.283832	6.283832	92.658074	0.590614	7.250480	6.528414	6.528414	92.749520	0.619536	1
2	7.833628	5.792129	12.075961	84.824447	0.630168	7.755315	6.023578	12.551993	84.994205	0.662673	2
3	8.358260	5.267497	17.343458	76.466186	0.672372	8.295302	5.483592	18.035584	76.698903	0.708813	3
4	8.918029	4.707729	22.051186	67.548157	0.717402	8.872887	4.906007	22.941591	67.826016	0.758166	4
5	9.515286	4.110472	26.161658	58.032872	0.765448	9.490688	4.288206	27.229797	58.335329	0.810956	5
6	10.152542	3.473215	29.634874	47.880330	0.816711	10.151505	3.627389	30.857186	48.183824	0.867421	6
7	10.832476	2.793281	32.428154	37.047854	0.871408	10.858333	2.920561	33.777747	37.325491	0.927818	7
8	11.557647	2.067810	34.495964	25.489906	0.929768	11.614376	2.164517	35.942265	25.711115	0.992420	8
9	12.332005	1.293753	35.789717	13.157902	0.992036	12.423061	1.355832	37.298097	13.288053	1.061520	9
10	13.157902	0.467856	36.257573	0.000000	1.058474	13.288053	0.490840	37.788937	0.000000	1.135432	10

Term of 15 Years
Interest Rate   6.50%   Interest Rate   6.75%
Monthly Payment 0.871107%   Annual Constant 10.45329%   Monthly Payment 0.884909%   Annual Constant 10.61891%

Year End	Principal Paid in Year	Interest Paid in Year	Total Interest Paid	Remaining Balance Year End	Curtail First Month	Principal Paid in Year	Interest Paid in Year	Total Interest Paid	Remaining Balance Year End	Curtail First Month	Year End
1	4.073216	6.380072	6.380072	95.926784	0.327666	3.990881	6.628033	6.628033	96.009119	0.341011	1
2	4.346007	6.107281	12.487354	91.580777	0.349610	4.268758	6.350156	12.978188	91.740361	0.364755	2
3	4.637067	5.816221	18.303575	86.943710	0.373024	4.565983	6.052931	19.031119	87.174379	0.390152	3
4	4.947620	5.505668	23.809244	81.996090	0.398006	4.883903	5.735011	24.766130	82.290476	0.417318	4
5	5.278971	5.174317	28.983561	76.717119	0.424662	5.223959	5.394955	30.161085	77.066517	0.446374	5
6	5.632514	4.820775	33.804335	71.084605	0.453102	5.587692	5.031221	35.192307	71.478825	0.477455	6
7	6.009734	4.443555	38.247890	65.074871	0.483447	5.976752	4.642162	39.834469	65.502074	0.510699	7
8	6.412217	4.041072	42.288962	58.662655	0.515824	6.392900	4.226013	44.060482	59.109173	0.546258	8
9	6.841655	3.611634	45.900596	51.821000	0.550370	6.838025	3.780889	47.841371	52.271149	0.584292	9
10	7.299853	3.153435	49.054031	44.521147	0.587229	7.314142	3.304771	51.146142	44.957006	0.624976	10
11	7.788738	2.664551	51.718582	36.732410	0.626557	7.823411	2.795502	53.941644	37.133595	0.668491	11
12	8.310364	2.142925	53.861506	28.422046	0.668519	8.368139	2.250774	56.192419	28.765456	0.715037	12
13	8.866924	1.586364	55.447871	19.555122	0.713291	8.950795	1.668118	57.860537	19.814661	0.764824	13
14	9.460759	0.992530	56.440400	10.094363	0.761061	9.574021	1.044893	58.905430	10.240640	0.818077	14
15	10.094363	0.358925	56.799326	0.000000	0.812031	10.240640	0.378274	59.283703	0.000000	0.875038	15

Monthly Factors for 6.500% Interest:				Monthly Factors for 6.750% Interest:		
Month	This Month	Year-to-date		Month	This Month	Year-to-date
1	1.005417	1.005417		1	1.005625	1.005625
2	1.010863	2.016279		2	1.011282	2.016907
3	1.016338	3.032618		3	1.016970	3.033877
4	1.021843	4.054461		4	1.022691	4.056567
5	1.027378	5.081839		5	1.028443	5.085010
6	1.032943	6.114782		6	1.034228	6.119239
7	1.038538	7.153321		7	1.040046	7.159284
8	1.044164	8.197485		8	1.045896	8.205180
9	1.049820	9.247304		9	1.051779	9.256960
10	1.055506	10.302811		10	1.057695	10.314655
11	1.061224	11.364034		11	1.063645	11.378300

Entries are percentages of the original loan amount.

Remaining Balance Tables

Term of 25 Years

	Interest Rate 6.50%					Interest Rate 6.75%					
	Monthly Payment 0.675207%		Annual Constant 8.10249%			Monthly Payment 0.690912%		Annual Constant 8.29094%			
Year End	Principal Paid in Year	Interest Paid in Year	Total Interest Paid	Remaining Balance Year End	Curtail First Month	Principal Paid in Year	Interest Paid in Year	Total Interest Paid	Remaining Balance Year End	Curtail First Month	Year End
1	1.651099	6.451387	6.451387	98.348901	0.132821	1.589516	6.701422	6.701422	98.410484	0.135820	1
2	1.761676	6.340810	12.792196	96.587224	0.141716	1.700191	6.590747	13.292169	96.710293	0.145277	2
3	1.879659	6.222827	19.015023	94.707565	0.151207	1.818572	6.472366	19.764536	94.891721	0.155393	3
4	2.005543	6.096943	25.111966	92.702022	0.161334	1.945195	6.345743	26.110279	92.946525	0.166212	4
5	2.139858	5.962628	31.074593	90.562163	0.172139	2.080635	6.210303	32.320582	90.865890	0.177785	5
6	2.283169	5.819317	36.893910	88.278995	0.183667	2.225506	6.065433	38.386014	88.640384	0.190164	6
7	2.436077	5.666409	42.560320	85.842918	0.195968	2.380463	5.910475	44.296490	86.259922	0.203405	7
8	2.599225	5.503261	48.063580	83.243693	0.209092	2.546210	5.744729	50.041218	83.713712	0.217567	8
9	2.773300	5.329186	53.392766	80.470393	0.223095	2.723497	5.567441	55.608660	80.990215	0.232716	9
10	2.959033	5.143453	58.536219	77.511359	0.238037	2.913128	5.377810	60.986469	78.077086	0.248920	10
11	3.157205	4.945281	63.481500	74.354154	0.253978	3.115964	5.174975	66.161444	74.961123	0.266251	11
12	3.368649	4.733837	68.215337	70.985505	0.270988	3.332922	4.958017	71.119461	71.628201	0.284790	12
13	3.594254	4.508232	72.723569	67.391252	0.289136	3.564986	4.725952	75.845413	68.063215	0.304619	13
14	3.834968	4.267518	76.991087	63.556284	0.308500	3.813209	4.477729	80.323142	64.250006	0.325829	14
15	4.091802	4.010684	81.001771	59.464382	0.329161	4.078715	4.212224	84.535366	60.171291	0.348516	15
16	4.365838	3.736648	84.738419	55.098644	0.351206	4.362707	3.928231	88.463597	55.808584	0.372783	16
17	4.658226	3.444260	88.182678	50.440417	0.374726	4.666473	3.624465	92.088062	51.142111	0.398739	17
18	4.970196	3.132290	91.314968	45.470221	0.399823	4.991390	3.299548	95.387610	46.150720	0.426502	18
19	5.303060	2.799426	94.114394	40.167162	0.426599	5.338931	2.952008	98.339618	40.811790	0.456199	19
20	5.658215	2.444271	96.558665	34.508946	0.455170	5.710669	2.580269	100.919887	35.101121	0.487963	20
21	6.037156	2.065330	98.623995	28.471790	0.485653	6.108291	2.182647	103.102533	28.992829	0.521939	21
22	6.441476	1.661010	100.285005	22.030314	0.518178	6.533599	1.757339	104.859873	22.459230	0.558280	22
23	6.872874	1.229612	101.514617	15.157441	0.552882	6.988520	1.302418	106.162291	15.470710	0.597152	23
24	7.333163	0.769323	102.283941	7.824278	0.589909	7.475116	0.815822	106.978113	7.995593	0.638730	24
25	7.824278	0.278208	102.562148	0.000000	0.629416	7.995593	0.295345	107.273458	0.000000	0.683204	25

Term of 30 Years

	Interest Rate 6.50%					Interest Rate 6.75%					
	Monthly Payment 0.632068%		Annual Constant 7.58482%			Monthly Payment 0.648598%		Annual Constant 7.78318%			
1	1.117725	6.467091	6.467091	98.882275	0.089914	1.065748	6.717429	6.717429	98.934252	0.091066	1
2	1.192582	6.392235	12.859325	97.689693	0.095936	1.139954	6.643223	13.360652	97.794298	0.097406	2
3	1.272451	6.312365	19.171691	96.417242	0.102361	1.219327	6.563851	19.924503	96.574972	0.104188	3
4	1.357669	6.227147	25.398838	95.059572	0.109216	1.304226	6.478951	26.403454	95.270746	0.111443	4
5	1.448595	6.136221	31.535059	93.610977	0.116531	1.395036	6.388141	32.791595	93.875710	0.119202	5
6	1.545610	6.039206	37.574265	92.065367	0.124335	1.492170	6.291007	39.082603	92.383540	0.127502	6
7	1.649123	5.935694	43.509959	90.416245	0.132662	1.596066	6.187111	45.269713	90.787473	0.136380	7
8	1.759567	5.825249	49.335208	88.656677	0.141547	1.707197	6.075980	51.345693	89.080276	0.145876	8
9	1.877409	5.707407	55.042615	86.779269	0.151026	1.826066	5.957111	57.302805	87.254210	0.156033	9
10	2.003142	5.581674	60.624289	84.776126	0.161141	1.953211	5.829966	63.132771	85.300999	0.166897	10
11	2.137296	5.447520	66.071809	82.638830	0.171933	2.089209	5.693968	68.826739	83.211790	0.178518	11
12	2.280435	5.304381	71.376190	80.358395	0.183447	2.234676	5.548501	74.375239	80.977113	0.190948	12
13	2.433160	5.151656	76.527846	77.925235	0.195733	2.390272	5.392905	79.768144	78.586841	0.204243	13
14	2.596113	4.988703	81.516549	75.329121	0.208842	2.556702	5.226475	84.994619	76.030139	0.218464	14
15	2.769980	4.814836	86.331385	72.559141	0.222828	2.734720	5.048457	90.043076	73.295419	0.233675	15
16	2.955491	4.629326	90.960711	69.603651	0.237752	2.925133	4.858044	94.901120	70.370286	0.249945	16
17	3.153425	4.431391	95.392102	66.450225	0.253674	3.128804	4.654373	99.555494	67.241482	0.267349	17
18	3.364616	4.220200	99.612302	63.085609	0.270663	3.346656	4.436521	103.992015	63.894826	0.285964	18
19	3.589951	3.994866	103.607168	59.495659	0.288790	3.579677	4.203500	108.195515	60.315149	0.305875	19
20	3.830376	3.754440	107.361608	55.665283	0.308131	3.828922	3.954255	112.149770	56.486227	0.327172	20
21	4.086904	3.497913	110.859521	51.578379	0.328767	4.095522	3.687655	115.837425	52.390704	0.349952	21
22	4.360611	3.224205	114.083726	47.217768	0.350785	4.380685	3.402492	119.239917	48.010019	0.374319	22
23	4.652649	2.932167	117.015893	42.565119	0.374278	4.685703	3.097474	122.337391	43.324316	0.400382	23
24	4.964246	2.620570	119.636463	37.600873	0.399344	5.011959	2.771218	125.108609	38.312357	0.428260	24
25	5.296711	2.288106	121.924569	32.304162	0.426089	5.360931	2.422246	127.530855	32.951426	0.458078	25
26	5.651441	1.933375	123.857944	26.652721	0.454625	5.734202	2.048975	129.579830	27.217224	0.489974	26
27	6.029929	1.554888	125.412832	20.622792	0.485072	6.133463	1.649715	131.229545	21.083761	0.524089	27
28	6.433764	1.151052	126.563884	14.189028	0.517558	6.560523	1.222654	132.452199	14.523239	0.560581	28
29	6.864645	0.720171	127.284055	7.324383	0.552220	7.017319	0.765859	133.218058	7.505920	0.599613	29
30	7.324383	0.260433	127.544488	0.000000	0.589203	7.505920	0.277257	133.495315	0.000000	0.641362	30

Monthly Factors for 6.500% Interest:			Monthly Factors for 6.750% Interest:		
Month	This Month	Year-to-date	Month	This Month	Year-to-date
1	1.005417	1.005417	1	1.005625	1.005625
2	1.010863	2.016279	2	1.011282	2.016907
3	1.016338	3.032618	3	1.016970	3.033877
4	1.021843	4.054461	4	1.022691	4.056567
5	1.027378	5.081839	5	1.028443	5.085010
6	1.032943	6.114782	6	1.034228	6.119239
7	1.038538	7.153321	7	1.040046	7.159284
8	1.044164	8.197485	8	1.045896	8.205180
9	1.049820	9.247304	9	1.051779	9.256960
10	1.055506	10.302811	10	1.057695	10.314655
11	1.061224	11.364034	11	1.063645	11.378300

Entries are percentages of the original loan amount.

Remaining Balance Tables

Term of 3 Years
Interest Rate 7.00%
Monthly Payment 3.087710%   Annual Constant 37.05252%

Interest Rate 7.25%
Monthly Payment 3.099153%   Annual Constant 37.18984%

Year End	Principal Paid in Year	Interest Paid in Year	Total Interest Paid	Remaining Balance Year End	Curtail First Month	Principal Paid in Year	Interest Paid in Year	Total Interest Paid	Remaining Balance Year End	Curtail First Month	Year End
1	31.035698	6.016819	6.016819	68.964302	2.489852	30.955021	6.234814	6.234814	69.044979	2.649890	1
2	33.279271	3.773246	9.790064	35.685032	2.669844	33.275357	3.914478	10.149291	35.769621	2.848521	2
3	35.685032	1.367484	11.157549	0.000000	2.862847	35.769621	1.420214	11.569505	0.000000	3.062041	3

Term of 4 Years
Interest Rate 7.00%
Monthly Payment 2.394624%   Annual Constant 28.73549%

Interest Rate 7.25%
Monthly Payment 2.406240%   Annual Constant 28.87488%

1	22.446580	6.288914	6.288914	77.553420	1.800787	22.358130	6.516753	6.516753	77.641870	1.913957	1
2	24.069245	4.666249	10.955162	53.484175	1.930966	24.034058	4.840826	11.357579	53.607812	2.057424	2
3	25.809213	2.926281	13.881443	27.674963	2.070555	25.835610	3.039274	14.396853	27.772203	2.211645	3
4	27.674963	1.060531	14.941974	0.000000	2.220236	27.772203	1.102680	15.499533	0.000000	2.377426	4

Term of 5 Years
Interest Rate 7.00%
Monthly Payment 1.980120%   Annual Constant 23.76144%

Interest Rate 7.25%
Monthly Payment 1.991936%   Annual Constant 23.90323%

1	17.309796	6.451642	6.451642	82.690204	1.388686	17.217904	6.685330	6.685330	82.782096	1.473931	1
2	18.561123	5.200316	11.651958	64.129081	1.489074	18.508529	5.394705	12.080035	64.273567	1.584414	2
3	19.902908	3.858531	15.510488	44.226174	1.596719	19.895897	4.007337	16.087372	44.377671	1.703179	3
4	21.341691	2.419748	17.930236	22.884483	1.712146	21.387259	2.515975	18.603346	22.990412	1.830846	4
5	22.884483	0.876955	18.807191	0.000000	1.835918	22.990412	0.912822	19.516168	0.000000	1.968083	5

Term of 7 Years
Interest Rate 7.00%
Monthly Payment 1.509268%   Annual Constant 18.11122%

Interest Rate 7.25%
Monthly Payment 1.521518%   Annual Constant 18.25822%

1	11.474274	6.636492	6.636492	88.525276	0.920565	11.381483	6.876738	6.876738	88.618517	0.974306	1
2	12.304233	5.806983	12.443475	76.221043	0.987112	12.234620	6.023602	12.900340	76.383897	1.047339	2
3	13.193707	4.917509	17.360984	63.027336	1.058471	13.151706	5.106515	18.006855	63.232191	1.125846	3
4	14.147481	3.963735	21.324718	48.879854	1.134988	14.137536	4.120686	22.127541	49.094655	1.210237	4
5	15.170204	2.941012	24.265730	33.709651	1.217036	15.197261	3.060960	25.188501	33.897394	1.300954	5
6	16.266859	1.844357	26.110087	17.442792	1.305016	16.336422	1.921799	27.110300	17.560972	1.398472	6
7	17.442792	0.668424	26.778512	0.000000	1.399355	17.560972	0.697249	27.807550	0.000000	1.503299	7

Term of 10 Years
Interest Rate 7.00%
Monthly Payment 1.161085%   Annual Constant 13.93302%

Interest Rate 7.25%
Monthly Payment 1.174010%   Annual Constant 14.08812%

1	7.159834	6.773183	6.773183	92.840166	0.574401	7.069989	7.018136	7.018136	92.930011	0.605223	1
2	7.677419	6.255598	13.028782	85.162747	0.615924	7.599943	6.488182	13.506318	85.330068	0.650590	2
3	8.232420	5.700597	18.729379	76.930326	0.660449	8.169622	5.918503	19.424820	77.160445	0.699357	3
4	8.827543	5.105475	23.834853	68.102783	0.708193	8.782003	5.306122	24.730942	68.378442	0.751779	4
5	9.465687	4.467331	28.302184	58.637097	0.759389	9.440287	4.647838	29.378780	58.938155	0.808131	5
6	10.149962	3.783056	32.085240	48.487135	0.814285	10.147915	3.940210	33.318990	48.790240	0.868707	6
7	10.883703	3.049314	35.134554	37.603431	0.873150	10.908585	3.179540	36.498529	37.881655	0.933824	7
8	11.670487	2.262530	37.397084	25.932944	0.936270	11.726274	2.361851	38.860380	26.155380	1.003822	8
9	12.514148	1.418870	38.815954	13.418796	1.003953	12.605256	1.482869	40.343249	13.550124	1.079067	9
10	13.418796	0.514221	39.330175	0.000000	1.076529	13.550124	0.538000	40.881249	0.000000	1.159952	10

Term of 15 Years
Interest Rate 7.00%
Monthly Payment 0.898828%   Annual Constant 10.78594%

Interest Rate 7.25%
Monthly Payment 0.912863%   Annual Constant 10.95435%

1	3.909798	6.876141	6.876141	96.090202	0.313665	3.829960	7.124394	7.124394	96.170040	0.327862	1
2	4.192438	6.593502	13.469643	91.897765	0.336340	4.117047	6.837307	13.961702	92.052992	0.352438	2
3	4.495509	6.290430	19.760073	87.402255	0.360654	4.425654	6.528700	20.490402	87.627338	0.378856	3
4	4.820490	5.965449	25.725522	82.581765	0.386726	4.757394	6.196961	26.687363	82.869944	0.407254	4
5	5.168964	5.616976	31.342498	77.412802	0.414682	5.114000	5.840355	32.527717	77.755944	0.437782	5
6	5.542628	5.243311	36.585809	71.870174	0.444660	5.497337	5.457018	37.984735	72.258608	0.470597	6
7	5.943305	4.842634	41.428443	65.926868	0.476804	5.909408	5.044947	43.029682	66.349200	0.505872	7
8	6.372947	4.412992	45.841435	59.553921	0.511272	6.352367	4.601988	47.631670	59.996833	0.543791	8
9	6.833648	3.952291	49.793726	52.720273	0.548232	6.828529	4.125825	51.757495	53.168304	0.584553	9
10	7.327653	3.458286	53.252012	45.392619	0.587864	7.340384	3.613970	55.371465	45.827919	0.628370	10
11	7.857370	2.928569	56.180581	37.535250	0.630361	7.890607	3.063747	58.435212	37.937312	0.675472	11
12	8.425380	2.360559	58.541141	29.109870	0.675930	8.482074	2.472281	60.907493	29.455238	0.726104	12
13	9.034451	1.751488	60.292629	20.075419	0.724793	9.117875	1.836479	62.743972	20.337363	0.780531	13
14	9.687552	1.098387	61.391016	10.387866	0.777188	9.801336	1.153019	63.896991	10.536027	0.839039	14
15	10.387866	0.398073	61.789089	0.000000	0.833371	10.536027	0.418327	64.315319	0.000000	0.901932	15

Month	Monthly Factors for 7.000% Interest: This Month	Year-to-date	Month	Monthly Factors for 7.250% Interest: This Month	Year-to-date
1	1.005833	1.005833	1	1.006042	1.006042
2	1.011701	2.017534	2	1.012120	2.018162
3	1.017602	3.035136	3	1.018235	3.036396
4	1.023538	4.058675	4	1.024387	4.060783
5	1.029509	5.088184	5	1.030576	5.091358
6	1.035514	6.123698	6	1.036802	6.128160
7	1.041555	7.165253	7	1.043066	7.171226
8	1.047631	8.212883	8	1.049368	8.220594
9	1.053742	9.266625	9	1.055708	9.276302
10	1.059889	10.326514	10	1.062086	10.338388
11	1.066071	11.392585	11	1.068503	11.406891

Entries are percentages of the original loan amount.

Remaining Balance Tables

Term of 25 Years
Interest Rate 7.00%
Monthly Payment 0.706779%   Annual Constant 8.48135%

Interest Rate 7.25%
Monthly Payment 0.722807%   Annual Constant 8.67368%

Year End	Principal Paid in Year	Interest Paid in Year	Total Interest Paid	Remaining Balance Year End	Curtail First Month	Principal Paid in Year	Interest Paid in Year	Total Interest Paid	Remaining Balance Year End	Curtail First Month	Year End
1	1.529813	6.951537	6.951537	98.470187	0.122730	1.471956	7.201726	7.201726	98.528044	0.126006	1
2	1.640404	6.840947	13.792484	96.829783	0.131602	1.582291	7.091391	14.293118	96.945753	0.135451	2
3	1.758989	6.722362	20.514845	95.070794	0.141116	1.700897	6.972785	21.265903	95.244856	0.145604	3
4	1.886146	6.595204	27.110050	93.184648	0.151317	1.828393	6.845289	28.111192	93.416462	0.156519	4
5	2.022496	6.458855	33.568904	91.162152	0.162256	1.965447	6.708236	34.819427	91.451015	0.168251	5
6	2.168702	6.312648	39.881552	88.993450	0.173985	2.112773	6.560909	41.380336	89.338242	0.180863	6
7	2.325478	6.155873	46.037425	86.667973	0.186562	2.271143	6.402539	47.782876	87.067099	0.194420	7
8	2.493587	5.987764	52.025189	84.174386	0.200049	2.441384	6.232298	54.015174	84.625715	0.208994	8
9	2.673848	5.807502	57.832691	81.500537	0.214511	2.624386	6.049296	60.064470	82.001329	0.224659	9
10	2.867141	5.614209	63.446900	78.633396	0.230018	2.821106	5.852577	65.917047	79.180223	0.241499	10
11	3.074407	5.406943	68.853844	75.558990	0.246646	3.032571	5.641111	71.558158	76.147652	0.259602	11
12	3.296656	5.184694	74.038538	72.262333	0.264476	3.259887	5.413795	76.971953	72.887765	0.279061	12
13	3.534972	4.946379	78.984917	68.727362	0.283595	3.504243	5.169439	82.141392	69.383522	0.299979	13
14	3.790515	4.690835	83.675752	64.936847	0.304096	3.766915	4.906767	87.048160	65.616607	0.322465	14
15	4.064532	4.416819	88.092571	60.872315	0.326079	4.049277	4.624406	91.672566	61.567330	0.346636	15
16	4.358357	4.122993	92.215564	56.513959	0.349651	4.352803	4.320879	95.993444	57.214527	0.372620	16
17	4.673423	3.807928	96.023492	51.840536	0.374927	4.679082	3.994600	99.988045	52.535444	0.400551	17
18	5.011265	3.470085	99.493577	46.829271	0.402031	5.029818	3.643864	103.631909	47.505626	0.430575	18
19	5.373530	3.107821	102.601398	41.455741	0.431094	5.406845	3.266838	106.898746	42.098781	0.462850	19
20	5.761983	2.719368	105.320766	35.693758	0.462258	5.812133	2.861550	109.760296	36.286649	0.497545	20
21	6.178517	2.302834	107.623599	29.515242	0.495674	6.247800	2.425882	112.186178	30.038848	0.534840	21
22	6.625162	1.856188	109.479787	22.890079	0.531506	6.716125	1.957558	114.143736	23.322723	0.574931	22
23	7.104096	1.377255	110.857042	15.785984	0.569929	7.219554	1.454128	115.597864	16.103169	0.618027	23
24	7.617651	0.863699	111.720741	8.168332	0.611129	7.760720	0.912963	116.510827	8.342450	0.664353	24
25	8.168332	0.313018	112.033759	0.000000	0.655308	8.342450	0.331233	116.842059	0.000000	0.714151	25

Term of 30 Years
Interest Rate 7.00%
Monthly Payment 0.665302%   Annual Constant 7.98363%

Interest Rate 7.25%
Monthly Payment 0.682176%   Annual Constant 8.18612%

Year End	Principal Paid in Year	Interest Paid in Year	Total Interest Paid	Remaining Balance Year End	Curtail First Month	Principal Paid in Year	Interest Paid in Year	Total Interest Paid	Remaining Balance Year End	Curtail First Month	Year End
1	1.015810	6.967820	6.967820	98.984190	0.081494	0.967857	7.218259	7.218259	99.032143	0.082853	1
2	1.089243	6.894387	13.862207	97.894947	0.087385	1.040406	7.145710	14.363968	97.991738	0.089063	2
3	1.167984	6.815646	20.677853	96.726963	0.093702	1.118393	7.067723	21.431691	96.873345	0.095739	3
4	1.252418	6.731212	27.409065	95.474545	0.100476	1.202225	6.983890	28.415581	95.671119	0.102916	4
5	1.342955	6.640675	34.049740	94.131590	0.107739	1.292342	6.893773	35.309354	94.378777	0.110630	5
6	1.440038	6.543592	40.593332	92.691552	0.115528	1.389214	6.796901	42.106255	92.989563	0.118923	6
7	1.544138	6.439492	47.032824	91.147414	0.123879	1.493347	6.692768	48.799024	91.496216	0.127837	7
8	1.655764	6.327866	53.360690	89.491650	0.132834	1.605286	6.580829	55.379853	89.890930	0.137420	8
9	1.775459	6.208171	59.568860	87.716191	0.142437	1.725615	6.460500	61.840353	88.165315	0.147720	9
10	1.903807	6.079823	65.648683	85.812383	0.152734	1.854965	6.331151	68.171504	86.310350	0.158793	10
11	2.041434	5.942196	71.590879	83.770950	0.163775	1.994010	6.192106	74.363610	84.316341	0.170696	11
12	2.189009	5.794621	77.385500	81.581940	0.175614	2.143477	6.042638	80.406248	82.172863	0.183491	12
13	2.347253	5.636377	83.021877	79.234688	0.188309	2.304149	5.881967	86.288215	79.868715	0.197246	13
14	2.516936	5.466904	88.488571	76.717752	0.201922	2.476804	5.709252	91.997466	77.391851	0.212031	14
15	2.698885	5.284744	93.773315	74.018866	0.216519	2.662525	5.523590	97.521057	74.729326	0.227924	15
16	2.893988	5.089642	98.862957	71.124878	0.232171	2.862103	5.324012	102.845069	71.867223	0.245009	16
17	3.103195	4.880435	103.743392	68.021683	0.248955	3.076642	5.109474	107.954542	68.790581	0.263374	17
18	3.327525	4.656105	108.399497	64.694158	0.266952	3.307262	4.878854	112.833396	65.483319	0.283117	18
19	3.568072	4.415558	112.815055	61.126086	0.286250	3.555168	4.630947	117.464343	61.928151	0.304339	19
20	3.826008	4.157622	116.972677	57.300078	0.306943	3.821658	4.364458	121.828800	58.106493	0.327151	20
21	4.102591	3.881039	120.853716	53.197488	0.329132	4.108123	4.077993	125.906793	53.998371	0.351674	21
22	4.399167	3.584463	124.438179	48.798320	0.352925	4.416061	3.770055	129.676848	49.582310	0.378035	22
23	4.717183	3.266447	127.704626	44.081137	0.378438	4.747081	3.439034	133.115882	44.835229	0.406372	23
24	5.058189	2.925441	130.630067	39.022948	0.405795	5.102914	3.083201	136.199084	39.732315	0.436833	24
25	5.423846	2.559784	133.189851	33.599102	0.435130	5.485420	2.700696	138.899779	34.246895	0.469577	25
26	5.815936	2.167694	135.357545	27.783166	0.466586	5.896598	2.289518	141.189297	28.350298	0.504775	26
27	6.236371	1.747259	137.104804	21.546796	0.500316	6.338596	1.847519	143.036816	22.011701	0.542613	27
28	6.687198	1.296432	138.401236	14.859597	0.536483	6.813727	1.372389	144.409204	15.197974	0.583286	28
29	7.170616	0.813014	139.214249	7.688981	0.575266	7.324472	0.861643	145.270848	7.873502	0.627008	29
30	7.688981	0.294649	139.508898	0.000000	0.616852	7.873502	0.312613	145.583461	0.000000	0.674007	30

Month	Monthly Factors for 7.000% Interest: This Month	Year-to-date		Month	Monthly Factors for 7.250% Interest: This Month	Year-to-date
1	1.005833	1.005833		1	1.006042	1.006042
2	1.011701	2.017534		2	1.012120	2.018162
3	1.017602	3.035136		3	1.018235	3.036396
4	1.023538	4.058675		4	1.024387	4.060783
5	1.029509	5.088184		5	1.030576	5.091358
6	1.035514	6.123698		6	1.036802	6.128160
7	1.041555	7.165253		7	1.043066	7.171226
8	1.047631	8.212883		8	1.049368	8.220594
9	1.053742	9.266625		9	1.055708	9.276302
10	1.059889	10.326514		10	1.062086	10.338388
11	1.066071	11.392585		11	1.068503	11.406891

Entries are percentages of the original loan amount.

Remaining Balance Tables

Term of 3 Years
Interest Rate 7.50%   Interest Rate 7.75%
Monthly Payment 3.110622%   Annual Constant 37.32746%   Monthly Payment 3.122116%   Annual Constant 37.46540%

Year End	Principal Paid in Year	Interest Paid in Year	Total Interest Paid	Remaining Balance Year End	Curtail First Month	Principal Paid in Year	Interest Paid in Year	Total Interest Paid	Remaining Balance Year End	Curtail First Month	Year End
1	30.874445	6.453017	6.453017	69.125555	2.470183	30.793969	6.671428	6.671428	69.206031	2.640938	1
2	33.271308	4.056153	10.509170	35.854247	2.661950	33.267124	4.198272	10.869700	35.938907	2.853040	2
3	35.854247	1.473215	11.982385	0.000000	2.868604	35.938907	1.526489	12.396189	0.000000	3.082176	3

Term of 4 Years
Interest Rate 7.50%   Interest Rate 7.75%
Monthly Payment 2.417890%   Annual Constant 29.01468%   Monthly Payment 2.429574%   Annual Constant 29.15489%

1	22.269876	6.744806	6.744806	77.730124	1.781754	22.181818	6.973072	6.973072	77.818182	1.902347	1
2	23.998744	5.015938	11.760744	53.731380	1.920076	23.963306	5.191584	12.164656	53.854875	2.055130	2
3	25.861829	3.152853	14.913597	27.869550	2.069137	25.887871	3.267019	15.431675	27.967004	2.220184	3
4	27.869550	1.145132	16.058729	0.000000	2.229769	27.967004	1.187886	16.619561	0.000000	2.398494	4

Term of 5 Years
Interest Rate 7.50%   Interest Rate 7.75%
Monthly Payment 2.003795%   Annual Constant 24.04554%   Monthly Payment 2.015696%   Annual Constant 24.18835%

1	17.126309	6.919230	6.919230	82.873691	1.370231	17.035010	7.153341	7.153341	82.964990	1.460949	1
2	18.455868	5.589670	12.508900	64.417823	1.476606	18.403143	5.785209	12.938550	64.561847	1.578282	2
3	19.888645	4.156893	16.665793	44.529178	1.591238	19.881155	4.307197	17.245747	44.680692	1.705039	3
4	21.432653	2.612886	19.278678	23.096525	1.714770	21.477870	2.710482	19.956229	23.202822	1.841975	4
5	23.096525	0.949013	20.227692	0.000000	1.847892	23.202822	0.985530	20.941759	0.000000	1.989910	5

Term of 7 Years
Interest Rate 7.50%   Interest Rate 7.75%
Monthly Payment 1.533828%   Annual Constant 18.40593%   Monthly Payment 1.546195%   Annual Constant 18.55434%

1	11.288744	7.117187	7.117187	88.711256	0.903183	11.196506	7.357837	7.357837	88.803494	0.960230	1
2	12.165118	6.240813	13.358000	76.546138	0.973299	12.095731	6.458613	13.816450	76.707763	1.037349	2
3	13.109528	5.296403	18.654404	63.436611	1.048859	13.067175	5.487168	19.303618	63.640588	1.120661	3
4	14.127255	4.278676	22.933080	49.309356	1.130284	14.116639	4.437704	23.741322	49.523948	1.210665	4
5	15.223990	3.181941	26.115021	34.085366	1.218031	15.250389	3.303954	27.045277	34.273559	1.307897	5
6	16.405868	2.000063	28.115084	17.679498	1.312590	16.475194	2.079150	29.124427	17.798366	1.412938	6
7	17.679498	0.726433	28.841517	0.000000	1.414490	17.798366	0.755978	29.880405	0.000000	1.526415	7

Term of 10 Years
Interest Rate 7.50%   Interest Rate 7.75%
Monthly Payment 1.187018%   Annual Constant 14.24421%   Monthly Payment 1.200106%   Annual Constant 14.40128%

1	6.980943	7.263269	7.263269	93.019057	0.558527	6.892695	7.508580	7.508580	93.107305	0.591128	1
2	7.522892	6.721321	13.984590	85.496165	0.601887	7.446268	6.955007	14.463588	85.661036	0.638604	2
3	8.106913	6.137299	20.121889	77.389252	0.648613	8.044301	6.356975	20.820563	77.616736	0.689892	3
4	8.736274	5.507938	25.629827	68.652978	0.698966	8.690362	5.710913	26.531476	68.926373	0.745299	4
5	9.414494	4.829718	30.459545	59.238484	0.753229	9.388312	5.012964	31.544440	59.538062	0.805156	5
6	10.145365	4.098847	34.558392	49.093118	0.811704	10.142315	4.258961	35.803401	49.395747	0.869821	6
7	10.932977	3.311236	37.869628	38.160142	0.874719	10.956875	3.444401	39.247802	38.438872	0.939679	7
8	11.781732	2.462480	40.332108	26.378410	0.942625	11.836854	2.564422	41.812224	26.602018	1.015147	8
9	12.696378	1.547834	41.879942	13.682031	1.015804	12.787507	1.613768	43.425992	13.814510	1.096676	9
10	13.682031	0.562181	42.442123	0.000000	1.094663	13.814510	0.586765	44.012757	0.000000	1.184754	10

Term of 15 Years
Interest Rate 7.50%   Interest Rate 7.75%
Monthly Payment 0.927012%   Annual Constant 11.12415%   Monthly Payment 0.941276%   Annual Constant 11.29531%

1	3.751361	7.372788	7.372788	96.248639	0.300137	3.673992	7.621317	7.621317	96.326008	0.315087	1
2	4.042589	7.081560	14.454347	92.206051	0.323437	3.969062	7.326247	14.947564	92.356946	0.340393	2
3	4.356425	6.767723	21.222070	87.849625	0.348546	4.287829	7.007480	21.955045	88.069117	0.367731	3
4	4.694626	6.429522	27.651593	83.155000	0.375605	4.632197	6.663112	28.618156	83.436920	0.397264	4
5	5.059082	6.065066	33.716659	78.095918	0.404764	5.004223	6.291086	34.909243	78.432698	0.429170	5
6	5.451832	5.672317	39.388976	72.644086	0.436187	5.406127	5.889182	40.798425	73.026571	0.463638	6
7	5.875071	5.249077	44.638053	66.769015	0.470049	5.840309	5.455000	46.253425	67.186261	0.500874	7
8	6.331168	4.792980	49.431033	60.437846	0.506540	6.309362	4.985947	51.239372	60.876899	0.541101	8
9	6.822674	4.301475	53.732508	53.615173	0.545864	6.816086	4.479223	55.718595	54.060814	0.584558	9
10	7.352335	3.771813	57.504321	46.262838	0.588241	7.363506	3.931803	59.650398	46.697308	0.631506	10
11	7.923116	3.201032	60.705353	38.339721	0.633908	7.954891	3.340418	62.990816	38.742417	0.682224	11
12	8.538208	2.585940	63.291293	29.801513	0.683120	8.593772	2.701537	65.692353	30.148644	0.737015	12
13	9.201052	1.923097	65.214389	20.600461	0.736152	9.283964	2.011345	67.703698	20.864680	0.796207	13
14	9.915353	1.208795	66.423184	10.685108	0.793301	10.029581	1.265722	68.969420	10.835093	0.860153	14
15	10.685108	0.439040	66.862225	0.000000	0.854887	10.835093	0.460216	69.429636	0.000000	0.929234	15

Monthly Factors for 7.500% Interest:			Monthly Factors for 7.750% Interest:		
Month	This Month	Year-to-date	Month	This Month	Year-to-date
1	1.006250	1.006250	1	1.006458	1.006458
2	1.012539	2.018789	2	1.012958	2.019417
3	1.018867	3.037656	3	1.019500	3.038917
4	1.025235	4.062892	4	1.026085	4.065002
5	1.031643	5.094535	5	1.032711	5.097713
6	1.038091	6.132626	6	1.039381	6.137094
7	1.044579	7.177205	7	1.046094	7.183188
8	1.051108	8.228312	8	1.052850	8.236038
9	1.057677	9.285989	9	1.059649	9.295687
10	1.064287	10.350277	10	1.066493	10.362180
11	1.070939	11.421216	11	1.073381	11.435561

Entries are percentages of the original loan amount.

Remaining Balance Tables

Term of 25 Years

	Interest Rate 7.50% Monthly Payment 0.738991% Annual Constant 8.86789%					Interest Rate 7.75% Monthly Payment 0.755329% Annual Constant 9.06395%					
Year End	Principal Paid in Year	Interest Paid in Year	Total Interest Paid	Remaining Balance Year End	Curtail First Month	Principal Paid in Year	Interest Paid in Year	Total Interest Paid	Remaining Balance Year End	Curtail First Month	Year End
1	1.415909	7.451985	7.451985	98.584091	0.113283	1.361637	7.702308	7.702308	98.638363	0.116776	1
2	1.525830	7.342064	14.794050	97.058261	0.122078	1.470994	7.592951	15.295259	97.167369	0.126155	2
3	1.644284	7.223610	22.017660	95.413977	0.131555	1.589134	7.474811	22.770070	95.578234	0.136287	3
4	1.771934	7.095960	29.113620	93.642044	0.141768	1.716762	7.347183	30.117253	93.861472	0.147232	4
5	1.909494	6.958400	36.072021	91.732550	0.152774	1.854641	7.209304	37.326557	92.006832	0.159057	5
6	2.057733	6.810161	42.882182	89.674817	0.164634	2.003592	7.060353	44.386910	90.003239	0.171831	6
7	2.217480	6.650414	49.532596	87.457337	0.177415	2.164507	6.899438	51.286348	87.838732	0.185631	7
8	2.389629	6.478266	56.010862	85.067709	0.191188	2.338345	6.725600	58.011948	85.500387	0.200540	8
9	2.575142	6.292753	62.303614	82.492567	0.206030	2.526144	6.537801	64.549749	82.974243	0.216646	9
10	2.775057	6.092838	68.396452	79.717511	0.222025	2.729027	6.334918	70.884668	80.245216	0.234046	10
11	2.990491	5.877403	74.273855	76.727019	0.239261	2.948203	6.115742	77.000410	77.297013	0.252842	11
12	3.222651	5.645243	79.919098	73.504368	0.257836	3.184982	5.878963	82.879373	74.112031	0.273149	12
13	3.472834	5.395060	85.314158	70.031535	0.277852	3.440777	5.623168	88.502541	70.671254	0.295086	13
14	3.742439	5.125455	90.439614	66.289096	0.299423	3.717117	5.346829	93.849369	66.954137	0.318786	14
15	4.032974	4.834920	95.274534	62.256122	0.322668	4.015649	5.048296	98.897665	62.938488	0.344388	15
16	4.346064	4.521830	99.796363	57.910057	0.347717	4.338158	4.725787	103.623452	58.600329	0.372047	16
17	4.683461	4.184433	103.980797	53.226597	0.374711	4.686569	4.377376	108.000828	53.913761	0.401927	17
18	5.047050	3.820844	107.801641	48.179547	0.403801	5.062961	4.000984	112.001812	48.850800	0.434207	18
19	5.438865	3.429029	111.230670	42.740681	0.435149	5.469583	3.594362	115.596175	43.381217	0.469080	19
20	5.861099	3.006795	114.237465	36.879582	0.468931	5.908861	3.155084	118.751258	37.472356	0.506753	20
21	6.316111	2.551783	116.789248	30.563471	0.505335	6.383420	2.680525	121.431784	31.088936	0.547452	21
22	6.806447	2.061441	118.850695	23.757024	0.544566	6.896091	2.167854	123.599638	24.192845	0.591419	22
23	7.334849	1.533045	120.383740	16.422175	0.586842	7.449937	1.614008	125.213646	16.742908	0.638918	23
24	7.904273	0.963621	121.347361	8.517902	0.632400	8.048264	1.015681	126.229327	8.694644	0.690232	24
25	8.517902	0.349992	121.697353	0.000000	0.681495	8.694644	0.369301	126.598629	0.000000	0.745666	25

Term of 30 Years

	Interest Rate 7.50% Monthly Payment 0.699215% Annual Constant 8.39057%					Interest Rate 7.75% Monthly Payment 0.716412% Annual Constant 8.59695%					
1	0.921834	7.468740	7.468740	99.078166	0.073754	0.877688	7.719259	7.719259	99.122312	0.075272	1
2	0.993399	7.397175	14.865915	98.084767	0.079479	0.948178	7.648769	15.368027	98.174133	0.081317	2
3	1.070519	7.320055	22.185970	97.014248	0.085649	1.024329	7.572618	22.940645	97.149804	0.087848	3
4	1.153626	7.236948	29.422918	95.860622	0.092299	1.106596	7.490351	30.430996	96.043208	0.094903	4
5	1.243185	7.147389	36.570307	94.617437	0.099464	1.195470	7.401477	37.832473	94.847738	0.102525	5
6	1.339697	7.050877	43.621184	93.277740	0.107186	1.291482	7.305465	45.137938	93.556256	0.110759	6
7	1.443701	6.946873	50.568057	91.834039	0.115507	1.395205	7.201742	52.339680	92.161051	0.119655	7
8	1.555779	6.834795	57.402852	90.278260	0.124474	1.507258	7.089689	59.429369	90.653793	0.129265	8
9	1.676558	6.714016	64.116868	88.601701	0.134137	1.628310	6.968637	66.398006	89.025483	0.139646	9
10	1.806714	6.583860	70.700728	86.794987	0.144550	1.759085	6.837862	73.235868	87.266399	0.150862	10
11	1.946974	6.443600	77.144328	84.848013	0.155772	1.900362	6.696585	79.932453	85.366036	0.162978	11
12	2.098123	6.292452	83.436780	82.749891	0.167865	2.052986	6.543961	86.476414	83.313051	0.176067	12
13	2.261005	6.129569	89.566349	80.488885	0.180897	2.217867	6.379080	92.855444	81.095183	0.190208	13
14	2.436533	5.954041	95.520390	78.052352	0.194941	2.395991	6.200956	99.056450	78.699192	0.205484	14
15	2.625687	5.764887	101.285277	75.426665	0.210074	2.588420	6.008527	105.064977	76.110772	0.221987	15
16	2.829526	5.561048	106.846325	72.597139	0.226383	2.796304	5.800643	110.865620	73.314468	0.239815	16
17	3.049190	5.341384	112.187709	69.547949	0.243958	3.020883	5.576064	116.441683	70.293585	0.259076	17
18	3.285906	5.104668	117.292377	66.262043	0.262897	3.263500	5.333447	121.775131	67.030086	0.279883	18
19	3.541000	4.849574	122.141951	62.721043	0.283306	3.525601	5.071346	126.846476	63.504484	0.302361	19
20	3.815897	4.574677	126.716628	58.905146	0.305300	3.808753	4.788194	131.634671	59.695732	0.326645	20
21	4.112135	4.278439	130.995068	54.793012	0.329001	4.114645	4.482302	136.116973	55.581087	0.352878	21
22	4.431370	3.959204	134.954271	50.361641	0.354542	4.445104	4.151843	140.268815	51.135982	0.381219	22
23	4.775389	3.615185	138.569456	45.586252	0.382066	4.802104	3.794843	144.063658	46.333878	0.411836	23
24	5.146115	3.244459	141.813915	40.440137	0.411727	5.187775	3.409171	147.472830	41.146103	0.444912	24
25	5.545621	2.844953	144.658868	34.894516	0.443691	5.604421	2.992526	150.465355	35.541682	0.480644	25
26	5.976142	2.414432	147.073300	28.918373	0.478135	6.054529	2.542418	153.007773	29.487152	0.519246	26
27	6.440086	1.950488	149.023788	22.478287	0.515254	6.540787	2.056160	155.063933	22.946366	0.560948	27
28	6.940046	1.450528	150.474316	15.538241	0.555255	7.066097	1.530850	156.594784	15.880269	0.605999	28
29	7.478820	0.911754	151.386070	8.059421	0.598361	7.633596	0.963351	157.558135	8.246673	0.654669	29
30	8.059421	0.331154	151.717223	0.000000	0.644813	8.246673	0.350274	157.908408	0.000000	0.707247	30

Monthly Factors for 7.500% Interest:			Monthly Factors for 7.750% Interest:		
Month	This Month	Year-to-date	Month	This Month	Year-to-date
1	1.006250	1.006250	1	1.006458	1.006458
2	1.012539	2.018789	2	1.012958	2.019417
3	1.018867	3.037656	3	1.019500	3.038917
4	1.025235	4.062892	4	1.026085	4.065002
5	1.031643	5.094535	5	1.032711	5.097713
6	1.038091	6.132626	6	1.039381	6.137094
7	1.044579	7.177205	7	1.046094	7.183188
8	1.051108	8.228312	8	1.052850	8.236038
9	1.057677	9.285989	9	1.059649	9.295687
10	1.064287	10.350277	10	1.066493	10.362180
11	1.070939	11.421216	11	1.073381	11.435561

Entries are percentages of the original loan amount.

Remaining Balance Tables

Term of 3 Years

Interest Rate 8.00% — Monthly Payment 3.133637% — Annual Constant 37.60364%
Interest Rate 8.25% — Monthly Payment 3.145182% — Annual Constant 37.74219%

Year End	Principal Paid in Year	Interest Paid in Year	Total Interest Paid	Remaining Balance Year End	Curtail First Month	Principal Paid in Year	Interest Paid in Year	Total Interest Paid	Remaining Balance Year End	Curtail First Month	Year End
1	30.713592	6.890046	6.890046	69.286408	2.450632	30.633317	7.108871	7.108871	69.366683	2.631972	1
2	33.262806	4.340833	11.230879	36.023602	2.654034	33.258352	4.483836	11.592707	36.108331	2.857512	2
3	36.023602	1.580037	12.810916	0.000000	2.874317	36.108331	1.633857	13.226564	0.000000	3.102378	3

Term of 4 Years

Interest Rate 8.00% — Monthly Payment 2.441292% — Annual Constant 29.29551%
Interest Rate 8.25% — Monthly Payment 2.453044% — Annual Constant 29.43653%

Year End	Principal Paid in Year	Interest Paid in Year	Total Interest Paid	Remaining Balance Year End	Curtail First Month	Principal Paid in Year	Interest Paid in Year	Total Interest Paid	Remaining Balance Year End	Curtail First Month	Year End
1	22.093957	7.201550	7.201550	77.906043	1.762873	22.006293	7.430238	7.430238	77.993707	1.890750	1
2	23.927745	5.367762	12.569312	53.978298	1.909191	23.892060	5.544472	12.974710	54.101647	2.052773	2
3	25.913736	3.381771	15.951083	28.064563	2.067653	25.939421	3.497110	16.471820	28.162226	2.228679	3
4	28.064563	1.230944	17.182027	0.000000	2.239267	28.162226	1.274306	17.746126	0.000000	2.419660	4

Term of 5 Years

Interest Rate 8.00% — Monthly Payment 2.027639% — Annual Constant 24.33167%
Interest Rate 8.25% — Monthly Payment 2.039625% — Annual Constant 24.47550%

Year End	Principal Paid in Year	Interest Paid in Year	Total Interest Paid	Remaining Balance Year End	Curtail First Month	Principal Paid in Year	Interest Paid in Year	Total Interest Paid	Remaining Balance Year End	Curtail First Month	Year End
1	16.944010	7.387663	7.387663	83.055990	1.351960	16.853309	7.622193	7.622193	83.146691	1.448013	1
2	18.350355	5.981318	13.368981	64.705635	1.464172	18.297505	6.177997	13.800191	64.849187	1.572096	2
3	19.873425	4.458248	17.827229	44.832210	1.585697	19.865457	4.610045	18.410236	44.983730	1.706813	3
4	21.522910	2.808764	20.635993	23.309300	1.717309	21.567771	2.907731	21.317967	23.415959	1.853073	4
5	23.309300	1.022373	21.658366	0.000000	1.859845	23.415959	1.059543	22.377510	0.000000	2.011867	5

Term of 7 Years

Interest Rate 8.00% — Monthly Payment 1.558621% — Annual Constant 18.70346%
Interest Rate 8.25% — Monthly Payment 1.571106% — Annual Constant 18.85327%

Year End	Principal Paid in Year	Interest Paid in Year	Total Interest Paid	Remaining Balance Year End	Curtail First Month	Principal Paid in Year	Interest Paid in Year	Total Interest Paid	Remaining Balance Year End	Curtail First Month	Year End
1	11.104771	7.598686	7.598686	88.895229	0.886048	11.013539	7.839732	7.839732	88.986461	0.946268	1
2	12.026461	6.676996	14.275682	76.868768	0.959589	11.957313	6.895958	14.735690	77.029149	1.027356	2
3	13.024652	5.678805	19.954488	63.844116	1.039235	12.981960	5.871311	20.607001	64.047188	1.115392	3
4	14.105692	4.597766	24.552253	49.738424	1.125491	14.094412	4.758859	25.365860	49.952776	1.210972	4
5	15.276457	3.427000	27.979254	34.461967	1.218906	15.302192	3.551078	28.916938	34.650584	1.314743	5
6	16.544395	2.159062	30.138316	17.917572	1.320074	16.613470	2.239801	31.156739	18.037114	1.427406	6
7	17.917572	0.785885	30.924201	0.000000	1.429640	18.037114	0.816157	31.972896	0.000000	1.549724	7

Term of 10 Years

Interest Rate 8.00% — Monthly Payment 1.213276% — Annual Constant 14.55931%
Interest Rate 8.25% — Monthly Payment 1.226526% — Annual Constant 14.71832%

Year End	Principal Paid in Year	Interest Paid in Year	Total Interest Paid	Remaining Balance Year End	Curtail First Month	Principal Paid in Year	Interest Paid in Year	Total Interest Paid	Remaining Balance Year End	Curtail First Month	Year End
1	6.805245	7.754066	7.754066	93.194755	0.542989	6.718591	7.999724	7.999724	93.281409	0.577252	1
2	7.370077	7.189234	14.943301	85.824678	0.588057	7.294321	7.423994	15.423718	85.987088	0.626718	2
3	7.981790	6.577522	21.520822	77.842888	0.636866	7.919387	6.798928	22.222646	78.067701	0.680423	3
4	8.644274	5.915037	27.435859	69.198614	0.689725	8.598017	6.120299	28.342944	69.469684	0.738730	4
5	9.361745	5.197566	32.633425	59.836869	0.746972	9.334799	5.383516	33.726460	60.134885	0.802033	5
6	10.138765	4.420546	37.053972	49.698104	0.808970	10.134718	4.583597	38.310057	50.000167	0.870761	6
7	10.980278	3.579034	40.633005	38.717826	0.876114	11.003183	3.715132	42.025189	38.996984	0.945378	7
8	11.891635	2.667676	43.300681	26.826191	0.948832	11.946070	2.772245	44.797434	27.050914	1.026390	8
9	12.878635	1.680676	44.981357	13.947556	1.027584	12.969754	1.748561	46.545995	14.081160	1.114343	9
10	13.947556	0.611756	45.593113	0.000000	1.112873	14.081160	0.637155	47.183150	0.000000	1.209834	10

Term of 15 Years

Interest Rate 8.00% — Monthly Payment 0.955652% — Annual Constant 11.46783%
Interest Rate 8.25% — Monthly Payment 0.970140% — Annual Constant 11.64168%

Year End	Principal Paid in Year	Interest Paid in Year	Total Interest Paid	Remaining Balance Year End	Curtail First Month	Principal Paid in Year	Interest Paid in Year	Total Interest Paid	Remaining Balance Year End	Curtail First Month	Year End
1	3.597847	7.869978	7.869978	96.402153	0.287072	3.522917	8.118767	8.118767	96.477083	0.302684	1
2	3.896467	7.571358	15.441336	92.505686	0.310898	3.824804	7.816881	15.935648	92.652279	0.328622	2
3	4.219871	7.247954	22.689290	88.285815	0.336703	4.152559	7.489125	23.424773	88.499720	0.356782	3
4	4.570119	6.897706	29.586996	83.715696	0.364649	4.508401	7.133283	30.558056	83.991319	0.387356	4
5	4.949436	6.518389	36.105385	78.766260	0.394915	4.894735	6.746949	37.305005	79.096583	0.420549	5
6	5.360237	6.107588	42.212973	73.406023	0.427692	5.314176	6.327508	43.632513	73.782407	0.456587	6
7	5.805134	5.662691	47.875664	67.600889	0.463191	5.769559	5.872125	49.504639	68.012849	0.495713	7
8	6.286957	5.180868	53.056532	61.313932	0.501635	6.263965	5.377720	54.882358	61.748884	0.538191	8
9	6.808772	4.659053	57.715585	54.505160	0.543271	6.800737	4.840947	59.723305	54.948147	0.584310	9
10	7.373896	4.093929	61.809514	47.131264	0.588362	7.383507	4.258177	63.981482	47.564640	0.634381	10
11	7.985926	3.481899	65.291413	39.145337	0.637196	8.016216	3.625469	67.606951	39.548424	0.688742	11
12	8.648754	2.819071	68.110484	30.496583	0.690083	8.703142	2.938542	70.545493	30.845282	0.747762	12
13	9.366596	2.101229	70.211712	21.129987	0.747359	9.448933	2.192751	72.738245	21.396349	0.811839	13
14	10.144019	1.323806	71.535518	10.985968	0.809390	10.258632	1.383052	74.121297	11.137716	0.881408	14
15	10.985968	0.481857	72.017375	0.000000	0.876569	11.137716	0.503968	74.625264	0.000000	0.956937	15

Month	Monthly Factors for 8.000% Interest: This Month	Year-to-date	Month	Monthly Factors for 8.250% Interest: This Month	Year-to-date
1	1.006667	1.006667	1	1.006875	1.006875
2	1.013378	2.020044	2	1.013797	2.020672
3	1.020134	3.040178	3	1.020767	3.041439
4	1.026935	4.067113	4	1.027785	4.069224
5	1.033781	5.100893	5	1.034851	5.104075
6	1.040673	6.141566	6	1.041966	6.146041
7	1.047610	7.189176	7	1.049129	7.195170
8	1.054595	8.243771	8	1.056342	8.251512
9	1.061625	9.305396	9	1.063604	9.315116
10	1.068703	10.374099	10	1.070916	10.386032
11	1.075827	11.449926	11	1.078279	11.464311

Entries are percentages of the original loan amount.

Remaining Balance Tables

Term of 25 Years
Interest Rate   8.00%
Monthly Payment   0.771816%   Annual Constant   9.26179%

Interest Rate   8.25%
Monthly Payment   0.788450%   Annual Constant   9.46140%

Year End	Principal Paid in Year	Interest Paid in Year	Total Interest Paid	Remaining Balance Year End	Curtail First Month	Principal Paid in Year	Interest Paid in Year	Total Interest Paid	Remaining Balance Year End	Curtail First Month	Year End
1	1.309104	7.952690	7.952690	98.690896	0.104453	1.258274	8.203128	8.203128	98.741726	0.108109	1
2	1.417759	7.844035	15.796726	97.273137	0.113123	1.366098	8.095304	16.298431	97.375628	0.117373	2
3	1.535432	7.726362	23.523088	95.737704	0.122512	1.483162	7.978240	24.276671	95.892466	0.127431	3
4	1.662873	7.598922	31.122010	94.074832	0.132680	1.610257	7.851144	32.127815	94.282209	0.138351	4
5	1.800890	7.460904	38.582915	92.273941	0.143693	1.748244	7.713158	39.840973	92.533965	0.150207	5
6	1.950363	7.311431	45.894346	90.323578	0.155619	1.898054	7.563347	47.404321	90.635911	0.163078	6
7	2.112242	7.149552	53.043898	88.211336	0.168535	2.060703	7.400699	54.805020	88.575208	0.177053	7
8	2.287557	6.974237	60.018135	85.923778	0.182524	2.237289	7.224113	62.029132	86.337919	0.192225	8
9	2.477424	6.784371	66.802506	83.446355	0.197673	2.429007	7.032395	69.061527	83.908913	0.208697	9
10	2.683049	6.578746	73.381253	80.763306	0.214080	2.637154	6.824248	75.885775	81.271759	0.226581	10
11	2.905740	6.356054	79.737307	77.857566	0.231849	2.863137	6.598265	82.484040	78.408622	0.245997	11
12	3.146915	6.114879	85.852186	74.710651	0.251092	3.108485	6.352916	88.836956	75.300137	0.267077	12
13	3.408108	5.853687	91.705873	71.302543	0.271932	3.374858	6.086544	94.923500	71.925279	0.289963	13
14	3.690979	5.570816	97.276689	67.611564	0.294503	3.664057	5.797345	100.720845	68.261222	0.314811	14
15	3.997328	5.264466	102.541155	63.614236	0.318946	3.978038	5.483364	106.204209	64.283185	0.341788	15
16	4.329105	4.932690	107.473845	59.285131	0.345419	4.318924	5.142477	111.346686	59.964260	0.371076	16
17	4.688418	4.573376	112.047222	54.596713	0.374088	4.689022	4.772380	116.119066	55.275238	0.402874	17
18	5.077555	4.184240	116.231462	49.519158	0.405137	5.090834	4.370567	120.489633	50.184404	0.437397	18
19	5.498989	3.762806	119.994267	44.020169	0.438763	5.527079	3.934323	124.423956	44.657325	0.474879	19
20	5.955402	3.306392	123.300659	38.064767	0.475181	6.000706	3.460696	127.884652	38.656619	0.515572	20
21	6.449698	2.812097	126.112756	31.615069	0.514620	6.514919	2.946482	130.831134	32.141700	0.559753	21
22	6.985020	2.276775	128.389531	24.630049	0.557392	7.073197	2.388205	133.219339	25.068503	0.607719	22
23	7.564773	1.697022	130.086553	17.065276	0.603592	7.679314	1.782088	135.001426	17.389189	0.659796	23
24	8.192645	1.069149	131.155702	8.872631	0.653690	8.337371	1.124031	136.125457	9.051818	0.716335	24
25	8.872631	0.389164	131.544866	0.000000	0.707946	9.051818	0.409584	136.535040	0.000000	0.777720	25

Term of 30 Years
Interest Rate   8.00%
Monthly Payment   0.733765%   Annual Constant   8.80517%

Interest Rate   8.25%
Monthly Payment   0.751267%   Annual Constant   9.01520%

Year End	Principal Paid in Year	Interest Paid in Year	Total Interest Paid	Remaining Balance Year End	Curtail First Month	Principal Paid in Year	Interest Paid in Year	Total Interest Paid	Remaining Balance Year End	Curtail First Month	Year End
1	0.835364	7.969811	7.969811	99.164636	0.066654	0.794807	8.220392	8.220392	99.205193	0.068289	1
2	0.904699	7.900476	15.870287	98.259937	0.072186	0.862915	8.152284	16.372676	98.342278	0.074141	2
3	0.979788	7.825387	23.695674	97.280149	0.078177	0.936861	8.078339	24.451015	97.405417	0.080494	3
4	1.061110	7.744065	31.439738	96.219039	0.084666	1.017142	7.998057	32.449072	96.388275	0.087391	4
5	1.149182	7.655993	39.095731	95.069857	0.091693	1.104303	7.910896	40.359968	95.283972	0.094880	5
6	1.244563	7.560611	46.656343	93.825293	0.099304	1.198933	7.816266	48.176234	94.085038	0.103011	6
7	1.347862	7.457313	54.113656	92.477432	0.107546	1.301672	7.713527	55.889761	92.783366	0.111838	7
8	1.459763	7.345441	61.459097	91.017698	0.116477	1.413216	7.601984	63.491744	91.370150	0.121422	8
9	1.580891	7.224284	68.683382	89.436808	0.126139	1.534317	7.480882	70.972627	89.835833	0.131826	9
10	1.712104	7.093071	75.776453	87.724704	0.136608	1.665796	7.349403	78.322030	88.170037	0.143123	10
11	1.854208	6.950967	82.727420	85.870496	0.147947	1.808542	7.206658	85.528688	86.361496	0.155387	11
12	2.008106	6.797069	89.524489	83.862391	0.160226	1.963519	7.051680	92.580367	84.397976	0.168703	12
13	2.174778	6.630397	96.154887	81.687613	0.173525	2.131778	6.883422	99.463789	82.266199	0.183159	13
14	2.355283	6.449892	102.604778	79.332330	0.187928	2.314454	6.700745	106.164534	79.951745	0.198855	14
15	2.550770	6.254404	108.859183	76.781560	0.203526	2.512785	6.502415	112.666949	77.438960	0.215895	15
16	2.762483	6.042692	114.901875	74.019076	0.220418	2.728111	6.287089	118.954037	74.710849	0.234395	16
17	2.991768	5.813407	120.715282	71.027309	0.238712	2.961888	6.053311	125.007349	71.748961	0.254481	17
18	3.240083	5.565092	126.280373	67.787226	0.258526	3.215699	5.799501	130.806849	68.533263	0.276288	18
19	3.509008	5.296167	131.576540	64.278217	0.279983	3.491259	5.523940	136.330790	65.042004	0.299964	19
20	3.800254	5.004921	136.581461	60.477963	0.303222	3.790432	5.224767	141.555557	61.251572	0.325669	20
21	4.115674	4.689501	141.270962	56.362289	0.328389	4.115242	4.899957	146.455513	57.136329	0.353576	21
22	4.457272	4.347902	145.618864	51.905017	0.355645	4.467886	4.547313	151.002826	52.668443	0.383875	22
23	4.827224	3.977951	149.596815	47.077793	0.385163	4.850749	4.164450	155.167276	47.817693	0.416770	23
24	5.227881	3.577294	153.174109	41.849912	0.417132	5.266420	3.748779	158.916055	42.551273	0.452484	24
25	5.661793	3.143382	156.317491	36.188119	0.451753	5.717711	3.297488	162.213543	36.833562	0.491258	25
26	6.131719	2.673456	158.990948	30.056401	0.489249	6.207674	2.807525	165.021069	30.625888	0.533355	26
27	6.640648	2.164527	161.155474	23.415752	0.529856	6.739623	2.275576	167.296645	23.886265	0.579059	27
28	7.191819	1.613356	162.768830	16.223934	0.573834	7.317155	1.698044	168.994689	16.569110	0.628680	28
29	7.788736	1.016439	163.785269	8.435197	0.621462	7.944178	1.071021	170.065710	8.624932	0.682553	29
30	8.435197	0.369977	164.155247	0.000000	0.673043	8.624932	0.390267	170.455977	0.000000	0.741042	30

	Monthly Factors for 8.000% Interest:				Monthly Factors for 8.250% Interest:	
Month	This Month	Year-to-date		Month	This Month	Year-to-date
1	1.006667	1.006667		1	1.006875	1.006875
2	1.013378	2.020044		2	1.013797	2.020672
3	1.020134	3.040178		3	1.020767	3.041439
4	1.026935	4.067113		4	1.027785	4.069224
5	1.033781	5.100893		5	1.034851	5.104075
6	1.040673	6.141566		6	1.041966	6.146041
7	1.047610	7.189176		7	1.049129	7.195170
8	1.054595	8.243771		8	1.056342	8.251512
9	1.061625	9.305396		9	1.063604	9.315116
10	1.068703	10.374099		10	1.070916	10.386032
11	1.075827	11.449926		11	1.078279	11.464311

Entries are percentages of the original loan amount.

Remaining Balance Tables

Term of 3 Years										
Interest Rate 8.50%						Interest Rate 8.75%				
Monthly Payment 3.156754%			Annual Constant 37.88104%			Monthly Payment 3.168351%			Annual Constant 38.02021%	

Year End	Principal Paid in Year	Interest Paid in Year	Total Interest Paid	Remaining Balance Year End	Curtail First Month	Principal Paid in Year	Interest Paid in Year	Total Interest Paid	Remaining Balance Year End	Curtail First Month	Year End
1	30.553143	7.327902	7.327902	69.446857	2.431199	30.473071	7.547138	7.547138	69.526929	2.622992	1
2	33.253763	4.627282	11.955183	36.193094	2.646095	33.249040	4.771168	12.318306	36.277889	2.861936	2
3	36.193094	1.687951	13.643135	0.000000	2.879986	36.277889	1.742320	14.060626	0.000000	3.122646	3

Term of 4 Years										
Interest Rate 8.50%						Interest Rate 8.75%				
Monthly Payment 2.464830%			Annual Constant 29.57796%			Monthly Payment 2.476650%			Annual Constant 29.71980%	

1	21.918827	7.659137	7.659137	78.081173	1.744143	21.831560	7.888244	7.888244	78.168440	1.879168	1
2	23.856252	5.721712	13.380848	54.224920	1.898309	23.820324	5.899480	13.787724	54.348116	2.050352	2
3	25.964928	3.613036	16.993884	28.259992	2.066102	25.990256	3.729548	17.517272	28.357860	2.237131	3
4	28.259992	1.317972	18.311856	0.000000	2.248727	28.357860	1.361944	18.879216	0.000000	2.440924	4

Term of 5 Years										
Interest Rate 8.50%						Interest Rate 8.75%				
Monthly Payment 2.051653%			Annual Constant 24.61984%			Monthly Payment 2.063723%			Annual Constant 24.76468%	

1	16.762906	7.856931	7.856931	83.237094	1.333872	16.672804	8.091875	8.091875	83.327196	1.435124	1
2	18.244595	6.375243	14.232174	64.992499	1.451774	18.191627	6.573052	14.664927	65.135569	1.565858	2
3	19.857251	4.762586	18.994760	45.135247	1.580097	19.848808	4.915871	19.580799	45.286761	1.708501	3
4	21.612452	3.007386	22.002146	23.522796	1.719763	21.656952	3.107728	22.688526	23.629809	1.864138	4
5	23.522796	1.097042	23.099188	0.000000	1.871775	23.629809	1.134870	23.823396	0.000000	2.033953	5

Term of 7 Years										
Interest Rate 8.50%						Interest Rate 8.75%				
Monthly Payment 1.583649%			Annual Constant 19.00378%			Monthly Payment 1.596249%			Annual Constant 19.15499%	

1	10.922810	8.080972	8.080972	89.077190	0.869159	10.832585	8.322406	8.322406	89.167415	0.932423	1
2	11.888287	7.115495	15.196468	77.188903	0.945984	11.819388	7.335603	15.658008	77.348027	1.017363	2
3	12.939104	6.064679	21.261147	64.249799	1.029601	12.896085	6.258906	21.916914	64.451942	1.110040	3
4	14.082803	4.920980	26.182127	50.166997	1.120608	14.070864	5.084126	27.001041	50.381077	1.211160	4
5	15.327594	3.676188	29.858315	34.839402	1.219660	15.352661	3.802329	30.803370	35.028416	1.321492	5
6	16.682414	2.321368	32.179683	18.156988	1.327467	16.751225	2.403766	33.207136	18.277191	1.441874	6
7	18.156988	0.846795	33.026478	0.000000	1.444803	18.277191	0.877799	34.084935	0.000000	1.573223	7

Term of 10 Years										
Interest Rate 8.50%						Interest Rate 8.75%				
Monthly Payment 1.239857%			Annual Constant 14.87828%			Monthly Payment 1.253268%			Annual Constant 15.03921%	

1	6.632732	8.245551	8.245551	93.367268	0.527785	6.547666	8.491544	8.491544	93.452334	0.563595	1
2	7.219005	7.659278	15.904826	86.148264	0.574436	7.144131	7.895079	16.386624	86.308203	0.614936	2
3	7.857099	7.021184	22.926013	78.291165	0.625211	7.794931	7.244279	23.630902	78.513272	0.670954	3
4	8.551595	6.326687	29.252700	69.739569	0.680474	8.505017	6.534193	30.165096	70.008255	0.732076	4
5	9.307478	5.570804	34.823504	60.432091	0.740622	9.279788	5.759422	35.924517	60.728467	0.798765	5
6	10.130175	4.748108	39.571612	50.301916	0.806086	10.125138	4.914072	40.838589	50.603329	0.871529	6
7	11.025590	3.852692	43.424305	39.276326	0.877337	11.047496	3.991714	44.830303	39.555832	0.950921	7
8	12.000152	2.878131	46.302435	27.276174	0.954886	12.053877	2.985333	47.815636	27.501956	1.037546	8
9	13.060856	1.817426	48.119861	14.215317	1.039289	13.151935	1.887275	49.702911	14.350021	1.132063	9
10	14.215317	0.662965	48.782827	0.000000	1.131153	14.350021	0.689189	50.392101	0.000000	1.235189	10

Term of 15 Years										
Interest Rate 8.50%						Interest Rate 8.75%				
Monthly Payment 0.984740%			Annual Constant 11.81687%			Monthly Payment 0.999449%			Annual Constant 11.99338%	

1	3.449195	8.367680	8.367680	96.550805	0.274462	3.376671	8.616713	8.616713	96.623329	0.290649	1
2	3.754072	8.062802	16.430482	92.796733	0.298722	3.684272	8.309112	16.925825	92.939057	0.317126	2
3	4.085898	7.730977	24.161459	88.710835	0.325126	4.019893	7.973490	24.899315	88.919164	0.346015	3
4	4.447054	7.369820	31.531279	84.263780	0.353865	4.386089	7.607295	32.506610	84.533075	0.377536	4
5	4.840134	6.976741	38.508020	79.423647	0.385143	4.785643	7.207741	39.714351	79.747432	0.411928	5
6	5.267957	6.548917	45.056938	74.155690	0.419186	5.221595	6.771788	46.486140	74.525837	0.449453	6
7	5.733597	6.083278	51.140216	68.422093	0.456238	5.697261	6.296123	52.782263	68.828576	0.490396	7
8	6.240395	5.576480	56.716696	62.181698	0.496566	6.216257	5.777126	58.559389	62.612318	0.535069	8
9	6.791989	5.024886	61.741582	55.389709	0.540458	6.782533	5.210851	63.770240	55.829786	0.583812	9
10	7.392339	4.424536	66.166118	47.997371	0.588229	7.400393	4.592991	68.363231	48.429393	0.636994	10
11	8.045754	3.771120	69.937238	39.951616	0.640223	8.074538	3.918846	72.282077	40.354855	0.695022	11
12	8.756926	3.059949	72.997187	31.194690	0.696813	8.810094	3.183289	75.465366	31.544761	0.758335	12
13	9.530958	2.285916	75.283103	21.663732	0.758405	9.612657	2.380727	77.846093	21.932103	0.827417	13
14	10.373409	1.443466	76.726569	11.290323	0.825441	10.488330	1.505054	79.351147	11.443773	0.902791	14
15	11.290323	0.526551	77.253120	0.000000	0.898403	11.443773	0.549611	79.900757	0.000000	0.985031	15

Monthly Factors for 8.500% Interest:			Monthly Factors for 8.750% Interest:		
Month	This Month	Year-to-date	Month	This Month	Year-to-date
1	1.007083	1.007083	1	1.007292	1.007292
2	1.014217	2.021300	2	1.014637	2.021928
3	1.021401	3.042701	3	1.022035	3.043963
4	1.028636	4.071337	4	1.029487	4.073450
5	1.035922	5.107259	5	1.036994	5.110444
6	1.043260	6.150519	6	1.044555	6.155000
7	1.050650	7.201168	7	1.052172	7.207171
8	1.058092	8.259260	8	1.059844	8.267015
9	1.065586	9.324846	9	1.067572	9.334587
10	1.073134	10.397980	10	1.075356	10.409944
11	1.080736	11.478716	11	1.083198	11.493141

Entries are percentages of the original loan amount.

Remaining Balance Tables

Term of 25 Years
| Interest Rate 8.50% | | | | | | Interest Rate 8.75% | | | | | |
| Monthly Payment 0.805227% | | Annual Constant 9.66273% | | | | Monthly Payment 0.822144% | | Annual Constant 9.86572% | | | |

Year End	Principal Paid in Year	Interest Paid in Year	Total Interest Paid	Remaining Balance Year End	Curtail First Month	Principal Paid in Year	Interest Paid in Year	Total Interest Paid	Remaining Balance Year End	Curtail First Month	Year End
1	1.209110	8.453615	8.453615	98.790890	0.096212	1.161574	8.704149	8.704149	98.838426	0.099983	1
2	1.315984	8.346741	16.800357	97.474907	0.104717	1.267389	8.598335	17.302484	97.571037	0.109091	2
3	1.432305	8.230420	25.030777	96.042602	0.113973	1.382843	8.482881	25.785365	96.188194	0.119029	3
4	1.558908	8.103817	33.134594	94.483694	0.124047	1.508814	8.356910	34.142274	94.679380	0.129872	4
5	1.696701	7.966024	41.100618	92.786993	0.135011	1.646261	8.219463	42.361737	93.033119	0.141703	5
6	1.846674	7.816051	48.916669	90.940319	0.146945	1.796228	8.069495	50.431233	91.236891	0.154612	6
7	2.009903	7.652822	56.569491	88.930416	0.159934	1.959857	7.905867	58.337099	89.277034	0.168696	7
8	2.187560	7.475165	64.044656	86.742856	0.174070	2.138392	7.727332	66.064431	87.138642	0.184064	8
9	2.380921	7.281804	71.326461	84.361936	0.189457	2.333190	7.532533	73.596964	84.805452	0.200831	9
10	2.591372	7.071353	78.397813	81.770563	0.206203	2.545734	7.319989	80.916954	82.259717	0.219126	10
11	2.820426	6.842299	85.240112	78.950137	0.224429	2.777640	7.088084	88.005037	79.482077	0.239087	11
12	3.069726	6.592999	91.833111	75.880411	0.244267	3.030671	6.835052	94.840090	76.451406	0.260867	12
13	3.341062	6.321663	98.154774	72.539349	0.265858	3.306753	6.558971	101.399060	73.144653	0.284631	13
14	3.636381	6.026344	104.181118	68.902968	0.289357	3.607984	6.257739	107.656800	69.536669	0.310560	14
15	3.957804	5.704921	109.886039	64.945163	0.314934	3.936657	5.929067	113.585867	65.600012	0.338851	15
16	4.307638	5.355087	115.241125	60.637525	0.342771	4.295270	5.570454	119.156321	61.304743	0.369719	16
17	4.688394	4.974331	120.215456	55.949131	0.373069	4.686551	5.179173	124.335494	56.618192	0.403398	17
18	5.102806	4.559919	124.775375	50.846325	0.406045	5.113476	4.752248	129.087742	51.504716	0.440146	18
19	5.553847	4.108878	128.884252	45.292477	0.441935	5.579292	4.286432	133.374173	45.925424	0.480242	19
20	6.044757	3.617968	132.502220	39.247720	0.480998	6.087542	3.778181	137.152354	39.837882	0.523990	20
21	6.579509	3.083666	135.585887	32.668662	0.523514	6.642092	3.223632	140.375986	33.195790	0.571723	21
22	7.160588	2.502137	138.088024	25.508074	0.569788	7.247159	2.618565	142.994551	25.948631	0.623805	22
23	7.793518	1.869207	139.957231	17.714556	0.620152	7.907345	1.958379	144.952930	18.041286	0.680631	23
24	8.482395	1.180330	141.137561	9.232161	0.674968	8.627671	1.238053	146.190983	9.413616	0.742633	24
25	9.232161	0.430564	141.568125	0.000000	0.734629	9.413616	0.452108	146.643091	0.000000	0.810284	25

Term of 30 Years
| Interest Rate 8.50% | | | | | | Interest Rate 8.75% | | | | | |
| Monthly Payment 0.768913% | | Annual Constant 9.22696% | | | | Monthly Payment 0.786700% | | Annual Constant 9.44040% | | | |

Year End	Principal Paid in Year	Interest Paid in Year	Total Interest Paid	Remaining Balance Year End	Curtail First Month	Principal Paid in Year	Interest Paid in Year	Total Interest Paid	Remaining Balance Year End	Curtail First Month	Year End
1	0.755962	8.470999	8.470999	99.244038	0.060154	0.718777	8.721628	8.721628	99.281223	0.061869	1
2	0.822783	8.404179	16.875178	98.421255	0.065471	0.784255	8.656150	17.377778	98.496968	0.067505	2
3	0.895509	8.331453	25.206631	97.525746	0.071258	0.855697	8.584708	25.962486	97.641271	0.073655	3
4	0.974664	8.252298	33.458929	96.551081	0.077557	0.933647	8.506757	34.469243	96.707624	0.080364	4
5	1.060816	8.166146	41.625075	95.490266	0.084412	1.018699	8.421706	42.890949	95.688925	0.087685	5
6	1.154582	8.072380	49.697455	94.335684	0.091873	1.111498	8.328907	51.219856	94.577427	0.095673	6
7	1.256637	7.970325	57.667780	93.079047	0.099994	1.212751	8.227654	59.447510	93.364676	0.104388	7
8	1.367712	7.859250	65.527030	91.711336	0.108833	1.323227	8.117177	67.564687	92.041448	0.113898	8
9	1.488605	7.738357	73.265387	90.222731	0.118452	1.443768	7.996637	75.561324	90.597680	0.124273	9
10	1.620184	7.606778	80.872164	88.602546	0.128923	1.575289	7.865116	83.426440	89.022391	0.135594	10
11	1.763394	7.463568	88.335733	86.839153	0.140318	1.718791	7.721613	91.148053	87.303600	0.147946	11
12	1.919262	7.307700	95.643433	84.919891	0.152721	1.875366	7.565039	98.713092	85.428234	0.161424	12
13	2.088907	7.138055	102.781487	82.830984	0.166220	2.046204	7.394201	106.107293	83.382030	0.176129	13
14	2.273547	6.953414	109.734902	80.557437	0.180913	2.232605	7.207800	113.315093	81.149425	0.192173	14
15	2.474508	6.752454	116.487355	78.082928	0.196904	2.435986	7.004419	120.319512	78.713439	0.209679	15
16	2.693232	6.533729	123.021085	75.389696	0.214308	2.657894	6.782511	127.102023	76.055545	0.228780	16
17	2.931290	6.295672	129.316757	72.458406	0.233251	2.900017	6.540388	133.642411	73.155528	0.249621	17
18	3.190389	6.036573	135.353330	69.268018	0.253868	3.164196	6.276209	139.918620	69.991332	0.272361	18
19	3.472390	5.754572	141.107902	65.795627	0.276308	3.452441	5.987963	145.906563	66.538891	0.297171	19
20	3.779318	5.447644	146.555545	62.016309	0.300731	3.766944	5.673461	151.580044	62.771946	0.324243	20
21	4.113375	5.113586	151.669132	57.902934	0.327313	4.110097	5.330308	156.910351	58.661849	0.353780	21
22	4.476960	4.750002	156.419133	53.425974	0.356244	4.484510	4.955895	161.866246	54.177339	0.386008	22
23	4.872683	4.354279	160.773412	48.553291	0.387733	4.893030	4.547375	166.413621	49.284309	0.421171	23
24	5.303384	3.923578	164.696990	43.249907	0.422005	5.338765	4.101640	170.515261	43.945544	0.459538	24
25	5.772155	3.454807	168.151798	37.477753	0.459307	5.825104	3.615301	174.130562	38.120441	0.501400	25
26	6.282361	2.944601	171.096399	31.195392	0.499905	6.355746	3.084658	177.215221	31.764694	0.547076	26
27	6.837664	2.389298	173.485696	24.357728	0.544092	6.934728	2.505677	179.720897	24.829966	0.596912	27
28	7.442051	1.784910	175.270607	16.915676	0.592185	7.566453	1.873952	181.594849	17.263513	0.651288	28
29	8.099861	1.127101	176.397707	8.815815	0.644529	8.255725	1.184679	182.779529	9.007787	0.710618	29
30	8.815815	0.411147	176.808854	0.000000	0.701499	9.007787	0.432617	183.212146	0.000000	0.775352	30

Monthly Factors for 8.500% Interest:				Monthly Factors for 8.750% Interest:		
Month	This Month	Year-to-date		Month	This Month	Year-to-date
1	1.007083	1.007083		1	1.007292	1.007292
2	1.014217	2.021300		2	1.014637	2.021928
3	1.021401	3.042701		3	1.022035	3.043963
4	1.028636	4.071337		4	1.029487	4.073450
5	1.035922	5.107259		5	1.036994	5.110444
6	1.043260	6.150519		6	1.044555	6.155000
7	1.050650	7.201168		7	1.052172	7.207171
8	1.058092	8.259260		8	1.059844	8.267015
9	1.065586	9.324846		9	1.067572	9.334587
10	1.073134	10.397980		10	1.075356	10.409944
11	1.080736	11.478716		11	1.083198	11.493141

Entries are percentages of the original loan amount.

Remaining Balance Tables

Term of 3 Years
Interest Rate 9.00%   Interest Rate 9.25%
Monthly Payment 3.179973%   Annual Constant 38.15968%   Monthly Payment 3.191621%   Annual Constant 38.29946%

Year End	Principal Paid in Year	Interest Paid in Year	Total Interest Paid	Remaining Balance Year End	Curtail First Month	Principal Paid in Year	Interest Paid in Year	Total Interest Paid	Remaining Balance Year End	Curtail First Month	Year End
1	30.393100	7.766579	7.766579	69.606900	2.411884	30.313233	7.986224	7.986224	69.686767	2.613998	1
2	33.244183	4.915496	12.682075	36.362717	2.638136	33.239191	5.060265	13.046489	36.447576	2.866312	2
3	36.362717	1.796963	14.479038	0.000000	2.885611	36.447576	1.851880	14.898369	0.000000	3.142980	3

Term of 4 Years
Interest Rate 9.00%   Interest Rate 9.25%
Monthly Payment 2.488504%   Annual Constant 29.86205%   Monthly Payment 2.500392%   Annual Constant 30.00470%

Year End	Principal Paid in Year	Interest Paid in Year	Total Interest Paid	Remaining Balance Year End	Curtail First Month	Principal Paid in Year	Interest Paid in Year	Total Interest Paid	Remaining Balance Year End	Curtail First Month	Year End
1	21.744492	8.117559	8.117559	78.255508	1.725563	21.657623	8.347081	8.347081	78.342377	1.867600	1
2	23.784275	6.077776	14.195335	54.471233	1.887432	23.748107	6.256598	14.603679	54.594270	2.047868	2
3	26.015404	3.846647	18.041981	28.455829	2.064486	26.040373	3.964332	18.568010	28.553897	2.245537	3
4	28.455829	1.406222	19.448203	0.000000	2.258149	28.553897	1.450807	20.018817	0.000000	2.462285	4

Term of 5 Years
Interest Rate 9.00%   Interest Rate 9.25%
Monthly Payment 2.075836%   Annual Constant 24.91003%   Monthly Payment 2.087990%   Annual Constant 25.05588%

Year End	Principal Paid in Year	Interest Paid in Year	Total Interest Paid	Remaining Balance Year End	Curtail First Month	Principal Paid in Year	Interest Paid in Year	Total Interest Paid	Remaining Balance Year End	Curtail First Month	Year End
1	16.583002	8.327024	8.327024	83.416998	1.315966	16.493502	8.562376	8.562376	83.506498	1.422283	1
2	18.138602	6.771424	15.098448	65.278395	1.439412	18.085523	6.970355	15.532732	65.420976	1.559567	2
3	19.840128	5.069898	20.168346	45.438267	1.574439	19.831212	5.224666	20.757397	45.589763	1.710103	3
4	21.701269	3.208757	23.377103	23.736998	1.722133	21.745403	3.310475	24.067872	23.844360	1.875169	4
5	23.736998	1.173028	24.550131	0.000000	1.883680	23.844360	1.211518	25.279390	0.000000	2.056168	5

Term of 7 Years
Interest Rate 9.00%   Interest Rate 9.25%
Monthly Payment 1.608908%   Annual Constant 19.30689%   Monthly Payment 1.621624%   Annual Constant 19.45949%

Year End	Principal Paid in Year	Interest Paid in Year	Total Interest Paid	Remaining Balance Year End	Curtail First Month	Principal Paid in Year	Interest Paid in Year	Total Interest Paid	Remaining Balance Year End	Curtail First Month	Year End
1	10.742864	8.564030	8.564030	89.257136	0.852514	10.653647	8.805843	8.805843	89.346353	0.918695	1
2	11.750619	7.556275	16.120305	77.506518	0.932486	11.681981	7.777509	16.583352	77.664372	1.007371	2
3	12.852908	6.453986	22.574292	64.653610	1.019959	12.809574	6.649916	23.233268	64.854797	1.104607	3
4	14.058599	5.248295	27.822587	50.595011	1.115638	14.046008	5.413483	28.646751	50.808790	1.211228	4
5	15.377393	3.929501	31.752088	35.217619	1.220293	15.401787	4.057704	32.704454	35.407003	1.328141	5
6	16.819898	2.486996	34.239084	18.397720	1.334765	16.888431	2.571059	35.275514	18.518572	1.456338	6
7	18.397720	0.909173	35.148257	0.000000	1.459975	18.518572	0.940918	36.216432	0.000000	1.596910	7

Term of 10 Years
Interest Rate 9.00%   Interest Rate 9.25%
Monthly Payment 1.266758%   Annual Constant 15.20109%   Monthly Payment 1.280327%   Annual Constant 15.36393%

Year End	Principal Paid in Year	Interest Paid in Year	Total Interest Paid	Remaining Balance Year End	Curtail First Month	Principal Paid in Year	Interest Paid in Year	Total Interest Paid	Remaining Balance Year End	Curtail First Month	Year End
1	6.463392	8.737701	8.737701	93.536608	0.512911	6.379909	8.984018	8.984018	93.620091	0.550158	1
2	7.069703	8.131390	16.869091	86.466905	0.561025	6.995724	8.368203	17.352221	86.624367	0.603262	2
3	7.732890	7.468203	24.337294	78.734016	0.613654	7.670980	7.692946	25.045167	78.953387	0.661491	3
4	8.458288	6.742805	31.080099	70.275727	0.671218	8.411415	6.952512	31.997678	70.541972	0.725341	4
5	9.251734	5.949359	37.029458	61.023994	0.734183	9.223320	6.140607	38.138285	61.318652	0.795354	5
6	10.119610	5.081483	42.110940	50.904383	0.803055	10.113593	5.250334	43.388619	51.205059	0.872124	6
7	11.068900	4.132193	46.243134	39.835484	0.878387	11.089799	4.274128	47.662747	40.115260	0.956306	7
8	12.107239	3.093854	49.336988	27.728245	0.960786	12.160232	3.203694	50.866441	27.955028	1.048612	8
9	13.242981	1.958112	51.295100	14.485264	1.050914	13.333988	2.029938	52.896380	14.621040	1.149829	9
10	14.485264	0.715829	52.010929	0.000000	1.149497	14.621040	0.742887	53.639266	0.000000	1.260815	10

Term of 15 Years
Interest Rate 9.00%   Interest Rate 9.25%
Monthly Payment 1.014267%   Annual Constant 12.17120%   Monthly Payment 1.029192%   Annual Constant 12.35031%

Year End	Principal Paid in Year	Interest Paid in Year	Total Interest Paid	Remaining Balance Year End	Curtail First Month	Principal Paid in Year	Interest Paid in Year	Total Interest Paid	Remaining Balance Year End	Curtail First Month	Year End
1	3.305337	8.865862	8.865862	96.694663	0.262299	3.235184	9.115123	9.115123	96.764816	0.278979	1
2	3.615401	8.555798	17.421660	93.079262	0.286905	3.547458	8.802850	17.917973	93.217358	0.305908	2
3	3.954550	8.216649	25.638309	89.124712	0.313818	3.889873	8.460435	26.378408	89.327485	0.335435	3
4	4.325514	7.845685	33.483994	84.799198	0.343257	4.265340	8.084968	34.463376	85.062146	0.367813	4
5	4.731277	7.439922	40.923916	80.067921	0.375457	4.677048	7.673260	42.136635	80.385098	0.403315	5
6	5.175104	6.996095	47.920011	74.892817	0.410677	5.128496	7.221812	49.358447	75.256602	0.442245	6
7	5.660564	6.510635	54.430646	69.232253	0.449201	5.623520	6.726788	56.085235	69.633082	0.484932	7
8	6.191564	5.979635	60.410281	63.040689	0.491340	6.166325	6.183982	62.269217	63.466757	0.531740	8
9	6.772375	5.398824	65.809105	56.268314	0.537431	6.761524	5.588783	67.858001	56.705233	0.583066	9
10	7.407671	4.763528	70.572633	48.860643	0.587845	7.414175	4.936133	72.794133	49.291059	0.639346	10
11	8.102562	4.068637	74.641271	40.758081	0.642989	8.129822	4.220486	77.014619	41.161237	0.701058	11
12	8.862638	3.308561	77.949832	31.895444	0.703306	8.914546	3.435762	80.450381	32.246691	0.768727	12
13	9.694014	2.477185	80.427017	22.201429	0.769281	9.775015	2.575293	83.025674	22.471677	0.842928	13
14	10.603380	1.567819	81.994836	11.598050	0.841445	10.718539	1.631768	84.657442	11.753137	0.924291	14
15	11.598050	0.573149	82.567985	0.000000	0.920378	11.753137	0.597170	85.254612	0.000000	1.013507	15

Monthly Factors for 9.000% Interest:			Monthly Factors for 9.250% Interest:		
Month	This Month	Year-to-date	Month	This Month	Year-to-date
1	1.007500	1.007500	1	1.007708	1.007708
2	1.015056	2.022556	2	1.015476	2.023184
3	1.022669	3.045225	3	1.023304	3.046488
4	1.030339	4.075565	4	1.031192	4.077680
5	1.038067	5.113631	5	1.039140	5.116820
6	1.045852	6.159484	6	1.047150	6.163971
7	1.053696	7.213180	7	1.055222	7.219193
8	1.061599	8.274779	8	1.063356	8.282549
9	1.069561	9.344339	9	1.071553	9.354102
10	1.077583	10.421922	10	1.079813	10.433915
11	1.085664	11.507586	11	1.088136	11.522052

Entries are percentages of the original loan amount.

Remaining Balance Tables

Term of 25 Years
Interest Rate   9.00%   Interest Rate   9.25%
Monthly Payment 0.839196%   Annual Constant 10.07036%   Monthly Payment 0.856382%   Annual Constant 10.27658%

Year End	Principal Paid in Year	Interest Paid in Year	Total Interest Paid	Remaining Balance Year End	Curtail First Month	Principal Paid in Year	Interest Paid in Year	Total Interest Paid	Remaining Balance Year End	Curtail First Month	Year End
1	1.115631	8.954725	8.954725	98.884369	0.088532	1.071243	9.205339	9.205339	98.928757	0.092376	1
2	1.220285	8.850071	17.804796	97.664084	0.096837	1.174644	9.101938	18.307278	97.754114	0.101293	2
3	1.334756	8.735600	26.540396	96.329327	0.105921	1.288025	8.988557	27.295835	96.466088	0.111070	3
4	1.459966	8.610391	35.150787	94.869362	0.115857	1.412351	8.864231	36.160066	95.053738	0.121791	4
5	1.596920	8.473436	43.624223	93.272441	0.126726	1.548677	8.727906	44.887972	93.505061	0.133547	5
6	1.746723	8.323634	51.947857	91.525719	0.138613	1.698161	8.578421	53.466393	91.806900	0.146437	6
7	1.910577	8.159779	60.107636	89.615141	0.151616	1.862075	8.414507	61.880900	89.944825	0.160572	7
8	2.089803	7.980554	68.088190	87.525339	0.165839	2.041810	8.234772	70.115672	87.903015	0.176071	8
9	2.285840	7.784516	75.872706	85.239498	0.181396	2.238894	8.037688	78.153360	85.664121	0.193066	9
10	2.500268	7.570088	83.442794	82.739230	0.198412	2.455001	7.821581	85.974941	83.209120	0.211702	10
11	2.734810	7.335546	90.778340	80.004420	0.217024	2.691968	7.584614	93.559555	80.517151	0.232136	11
12	2.991355	7.079002	97.857341	77.013065	0.237383	2.951808	7.324774	100.884328	77.565343	0.254543	12
13	3.271964	6.798392	104.655734	73.741101	0.259651	3.236729	7.039853	107.924182	74.328614	0.279113	13
14	3.578897	6.491459	111.147193	70.162204	0.284008	3.549151	6.727431	114.651612	70.779463	0.306054	14
15	3.914622	6.155734	117.302927	66.247581	0.310650	3.891730	6.384852	121.036464	66.887732	0.335595	15
16	4.281841	5.788515	123.091442	61.965741	0.339791	4.267376	6.009206	127.045670	62.620356	0.367988	16
17	4.683507	5.386849	128.478292	57.282233	0.371666	4.679281	5.597301	132.642971	57.941075	0.403508	17
18	5.122852	4.947504	133.425796	52.159381	0.406531	5.130945	5.145637	137.788608	52.810130	0.442456	18
19	5.603411	4.466945	137.892741	46.555970	0.444666	5.626205	4.650377	142.438985	47.183925	0.485164	19
20	6.129050	3.941306	141.834047	40.426920	0.486379	6.169269	4.107313	146.546298	41.014656	0.531994	20
21	6.703997	3.366359	145.200406	33.722923	0.532004	6.764753	3.511829	150.058127	34.249903	0.583344	21
22	7.332878	2.737478	147.937885	26.390045	0.581910	7.417715	2.858867	152.916994	26.832188	0.639651	22
23	8.020753	2.049604	149.987488	18.369292	0.636497	8.133704	2.142879	155.059873	18.698484	0.701393	23
24	8.773155	1.297202	151.284690	9.596137	0.696205	8.918802	1.357780	156.417653	9.779682	0.769094	24
25	9.596137	0.474219	151.758909	0.000000	0.761514	9.779682	0.496900	156.914553	0.000000	0.843330	25

Term of 30 Years
Interest Rate   9.00%   Interest Rate   9.25%
Monthly Payment 0.804623%   Annual Constant 9.65547%   Monthly Payment 0.822675%   Annual Constant 9.87211%

Year End	Principal Paid in Year	Interest Paid in Year	Total Interest Paid	Remaining Balance Year End	Curtail First Month	Principal Paid in Year	Interest Paid in Year	Total Interest Paid	Remaining Balance Year End	Curtail First Month	Year End
1	0.683197	8.972274	8.972274	99.316803	0.054216	0.649169	9.222936	9.222936	99.350831	0.055980	1
2	0.747286	8.908186	17.880460	98.569517	0.059302	0.711830	9.160275	18.383211	98.639001	0.061283	2
3	0.817386	8.838085	26.718545	97.752131	0.064865	0.780539	9.091566	27.474777	97.858462	0.067308	3
4	0.894063	8.761409	35.479954	96.858068	0.070950	0.855879	9.016226	36.491003	97.002583	0.073805	4
5	0.977932	8.677539	44.157493	95.880136	0.077605	0.938493	8.933613	45.424616	96.064090	0.080929	5
6	1.069669	8.585803	52.743296	94.810468	0.084885	1.029080	8.843025	54.267641	95.035010	0.088741	6
7	1.170011	8.485460	61.228756	93.640456	0.092848	1.128411	8.743694	63.011335	93.906600	0.097306	7
8	1.279766	8.375705	69.604462	92.360690	0.101558	1.237330	8.634775	71.646111	92.669270	0.106699	8
9	1.399817	8.255654	77.860116	90.960873	0.111084	1.356762	8.515343	80.161454	91.312508	0.116998	9
10	1.531130	8.124342	85.984458	89.429744	0.121505	1.487722	8.384383	88.545837	89.824786	0.128291	10
11	1.674760	7.980711	93.965169	87.754984	0.132903	1.631323	8.240782	96.786619	88.193463	0.140674	11
12	1.831864	7.823607	101.788776	85.923120	0.145370	1.788785	8.083320	104.869939	86.404678	0.154252	12
13	2.003706	7.651766	109.440542	83.919414	0.159007	1.961446	7.910659	112.780598	84.443232	0.169141	13
14	2.191667	7.463804	116.904347	81.727747	0.173923	2.150773	7.721332	120.501930	82.292458	0.185467	14
15	2.397260	7.258211	124.162558	79.330487	0.190238	2.358375	7.513730	128.015660	79.934084	0.203370	15
16	2.622140	7.033331	131.195889	76.708347	0.208083	2.586015	7.286090	135.301750	77.348069	0.223000	16
17	2.868115	6.787357	137.983246	73.840232	0.227603	2.835628	7.036477	142.338228	74.512441	0.244524	17
18	3.137164	6.518308	144.501553	70.703068	0.248954	3.109334	6.762771	149.100999	71.403107	0.268127	18
19	3.431451	6.224020	150.725573	67.271617	0.272307	3.409460	6.462645	155.563644	67.993647	0.294008	19
20	3.753345	5.902126	156.627699	63.518271	0.297852	3.738555	6.133550	161.697194	64.255091	0.322386	20
21	4.105435	5.550037	162.177736	59.412836	0.325792	4.099416	5.772689	167.469882	60.155675	0.353505	21
22	4.490553	5.164918	167.342654	54.922283	0.356354	4.495109	5.376996	172.846879	55.660566	0.387626	22
23	4.911798	4.743674	172.086328	50.010486	0.389782	4.928995	4.943110	177.789988	50.731571	0.425042	23
24	5.372558	4.282913	176.369241	44.637927	0.426346	5.404762	4.467343	182.257331	45.326809	0.466068	24
25	5.876541	3.778930	180.148171	38.761386	0.466341	5.926453	3.945653	186.202984	39.400356	0.511055	25
26	6.427802	3.227670	183.375841	32.333584	0.510087	6.498498	3.373607	189.576590	32.901858	0.560384	26
27	7.030774	2.624698	186.000539	25.302811	0.557936	7.125760	2.746345	192.322935	25.776097	0.614475	27
28	7.690309	1.965163	187.965701	17.612502	0.610274	7.813568	2.058537	194.381472	17.962529	0.673787	28
29	8.411713	1.243759	189.209460	9.200789	0.667522	8.567766	1.304339	195.685811	9.394763	0.738823	29
30	9.200789	0.454682	189.664142	0.000000	0.730141	9.394763	0.477342	196.163153	0.000000	0.810138	30

| Monthly Factors for 9.000% Interest: | | | Monthly Factors for 9.250% Interest: | | |
Month	This Month	Year-to-date	Month	This Month	Year-to-date
1	1.007500	1.007500	1	1.007708	1.007708
2	1.015056	2.022556	2	1.015476	2.023184
3	1.022669	3.045225	3	1.023304	3.046488
4	1.030339	4.075565	4	1.031192	4.077680
5	1.038067	5.113631	5	1.039140	5.116820
6	1.045852	6.159484	6	1.047150	6.163971
7	1.053696	7.213180	7	1.055222	7.219193
8	1.061599	8.274779	8	1.063356	8.282549
9	1.069561	9.344339	9	1.071553	9.354102
10	1.077583	10.421922	10	1.079813	10.433915
11	1.085664	11.507586	11	1.088136	11.522052

Entries are percentages of the original loan amount.

Remaining Balance Tables

Term of 3 Years

	Interest Rate 9.50%					Interest Rate 9.75%					
	Monthly Payment 3.203295%		Annual Constant 38.43954%			Monthly Payment 3.214994%		Annual Constant 38.57993%			
Year End	Principal Paid in Year	Interest Paid in Year	Total Interest Paid	Remaining Balance Year End	Curtail First Month	Principal Paid in Year	Interest Paid in Year	Total Interest Paid	Remaining Balance Year End	Curtail First Month	Year End
1	30.233467	8.206072	8.206072	69.766533	2.392686	30.153805	8.426124	8.426124	69.846195	2.604991	1
2	33.234066	5.205474	13.411546	36.532467	2.630155	33.228807	5.351123	13.777246	36.617388	2.870640	2
3	36.532467	1.907073	15.318619	0.000000	2.891191	36.617388	1.962541	15.739788	0.000000	3.163380	3

Term of 4 Years

	Interest Rate 9.50%					Interest Rate 9.75%					
	Monthly Payment 2.512314%		Annual Constant 30.14776%			Monthly Payment 2.524269%		Annual Constant 30.29123%			
Year End	Principal Paid in Year	Interest Paid in Year	Total Interest Paid	Remaining Balance Year End	Curtail First Month	Principal Paid in Year	Interest Paid in Year	Total Interest Paid	Remaining Balance Year End	Curtail First Month	Year End
1	21.570955	8.576809	8.576809	78.429045	1.707132	21.484487	8.806743	8.806743	78.515513	1.856047	1
2	23.711820	6.435944	15.012754	54.717226	1.876561	23.675415	6.615814	15.422557	54.840098	2.045322	2
3	26.065161	4.082603	19.095357	28.652065	2.062805	26.089768	4.201461	19.624018	28.750330	2.253898	3
4	28.652065	1.495699	20.591056	0.000000	2.267534	28.750330	1.540899	21.164918	0.000000	2.483744	4

Term of 5 Years

	Interest Rate 9.50%					Interest Rate 9.75%					
	Monthly Payment 2.100186%		Annual Constant 25.20223%			Monthly Payment 2.112424%		Annual Constant 25.34909%			
Year End	Principal Paid in Year	Interest Paid in Year	Total Interest Paid	Remaining Balance Year End	Curtail First Month	Principal Paid in Year	Interest Paid in Year	Total Interest Paid	Remaining Balance Year End	Curtail First Month	Year End
1	16.404303	8.797931	8.797931	83.595697	1.298242	16.315406	9.033687	9.033687	83.684594	1.409490	1
2	18.032390	7.169844	15.967775	65.563307	1.427089	17.979206	7.369887	16.403573	65.705389	1.553226	2
3	19.822061	5.380172	21.347947	45.741246	1.568724	19.812675	5.536417	21.939991	45.892714	1.711619	3
4	21.789353	3.412881	24.760828	23.951893	1.724416	21.833117	3.515976	25.455967	24.059597	1.886165	4
5	23.951893	1.250340	26.011168	0.000000	1.895560	24.059597	1.289495	26.745462	0.000000	2.078511	5

Term of 7 Years

	Interest Rate 9.50%					Interest Rate 9.75%					
	Monthly Payment 1.634398%		Annual Constant 19.61278%			Monthly Payment 1.647230%		Annual Constant 19.76676%			
Year End	Principal Paid in Year	Interest Paid in Year	Total Interest Paid	Remaining Balance Year End	Curtail First Month	Principal Paid in Year	Interest Paid in Year	Total Interest Paid	Remaining Balance Year End	Curtail First Month	Year End
1	10.564935	9.047843	9.047843	89.435065	0.836112	10.476727	9.290029	9.290029	89.523273	0.905086	1
2	11.613479	7.999209	17.047143	77.821587	0.919094	11.545114	8.221641	17.511670	77.978159	0.997384	2
3	12.766089	6.846689	23.893832	65.055498	1.010312	12.722453	7.044302	24.555972	65.255706	1.099094	3
4	14.033092	5.579686	29.473518	51.022406	1.110583	14.019853	5.746902	30.302874	51.235852	1.211177	4
5	15.425842	4.186936	33.660454	35.596564	1.220806	15.449559	4.317196	34.620070	35.786293	1.334689	5
6	16.956820	2.655958	36.316412	18.639743	1.341968	17.025062	2.741693	37.361764	18.761231	1.470797	6
7	18.639743	0.973035	37.289446	0.000000	1.475155	18.761231	1.005525	38.367288	0.000000	1.620785	7

Term of 10 Years

	Interest Rate 9.50%					Interest Rate 9.75%					
	Monthly Payment 1.293976%		Annual Constant 15.52771%			Monthly Payment 1.307702%		Annual Constant 15.69243%			
Year End	Principal Paid in Year	Interest Paid in Year	Total Interest Paid	Remaining Balance Year End	Curtail First Month	Principal Paid in Year	Interest Paid in Year	Total Interest Paid	Remaining Balance Year End	Curtail First Month	Year End
1	6.297214	9.230493	9.230493	93.702786	0.498364	6.215307	9.477122	9.477122	93.784693	0.536941	1
2	6.922197	8.605509	17.836002	86.780588	0.547825	6.849126	8.843303	18.320425	86.935567	0.591697	2
3	7.609209	7.918498	25.754500	79.171379	0.602195	7.547581	8.144848	26.465273	79.387986	0.652036	3
4	8.364404	7.163302	32.917803	70.806975	0.661962	8.317262	7.375167	33.840440	71.070723	0.718529	4
5	9.194551	6.333156	39.250958	61.612424	0.727660	9.165434	6.526995	40.367435	61.905290	0.791803	5
6	10.107088	5.420619	44.671577	51.505335	0.799878	10.100099	5.592330	45.959765	51.805190	0.872549	6
7	11.110193	4.417514	49.089091	40.395143	0.879264	11.130079	4.562350	50.522115	40.675111	0.961529	7
8	12.212852	3.314855	52.403946	28.182290	0.966529	12.265094	3.427335	53.949450	28.410017	1.059583	8
9	13.424948	2.102759	54.506704	14.757342	1.062455	13.515854	2.176575	56.126025	14.894163	1.167636	9
10	14.757342	0.770365	55.277069	0.000000	1.167901	14.894163	0.798266	56.924291	0.000000	1.286708	10

Term of 15 Years

	Interest Rate 9.50%					Interest Rate 9.75%					
	Monthly Payment 1.044225%		Annual Constant 12.53070%			Monthly Payment 1.059363%		Annual Constant 12.71235%			
Year End	Principal Paid in Year	Interest Paid in Year	Total Interest Paid	Remaining Balance Year End	Curtail First Month	Principal Paid in Year	Interest Paid in Year	Total Interest Paid	Remaining Balance Year End	Curtail First Month	Year End
1	3.166203	9.364493	9.364493	96.833797	0.250574	3.098384	9.613968	9.613968	96.901616	0.267670	1
2	3.480441	9.050255	18.414749	93.353356	0.275443	3.414348	9.298004	18.911972	93.487268	0.294966	2
3	3.825866	8.704830	27.119579	89.527490	0.302780	3.762534	8.949818	27.861790	89.724734	0.325046	3
4	4.205158	8.325122	35.444701	85.321916	0.332830	4.146227	8.566125	36.427915	85.578507	0.358193	4
5	4.622967	7.907729	43.352429	80.698948	0.365863	4.569048	8.143304	44.571219	81.009459	0.394721	5
6	5.081786	7.448911	50.801340	75.617163	0.402174	5.034986	7.677366	52.248585	75.974473	0.434973	6
7	5.586141	6.944556	57.745896	70.031022	0.442089	5.548440	7.163912	59.412497	70.426033	0.479330	7
8	6.140552	6.390145	64.136040	63.890471	0.485965	6.114255	6.598097	66.010594	64.311778	0.528211	8
9	6.749986	5.780710	69.916750	57.140484	0.534196	6.737769	5.974583	71.985177	57.574009	0.582077	9
10	7.419906	5.110790	75.027540	49.720578	0.587214	7.424868	5.287484	77.272660	50.149141	0.641435	10
11	8.156314	4.374382	79.401922	41.564264	0.645493	8.182036	4.530316	81.802976	41.967105	0.706847	11
12	8.965809	3.564888	82.966810	32.598455	0.709557	9.016417	3.695935	85.498911	32.950688	0.778929	12
13	9.855643	2.675053	85.641863	22.742812	0.779979	9.935886	2.776466	88.275377	23.014801	0.858362	13
14	10.833792	1.696904	87.338767	11.909020	0.857390	10.949120	1.763232	90.038609	12.065681	0.945896	14
15	11.909020	0.621676	87.960443	0.000000	0.942484	12.065681	0.646671	90.685279	0.000000	1.042356	15

Monthly Factors for 9.500% Interest:				Monthly Factors for 9.750% Interest:		
Month	This Month	Year-to-date		Month	This Month	Year-to-date
1	1.007917	1.007917		1	1.008125	1.008125
2	1.015896	2.023813		2	1.016316	2.024441
3	1.023939	3.047751		3	1.024574	3.049015
4	1.032045	4.079796		4	1.032898	4.081913
5	1.040215	5.120011		5	1.041291	5.123203
6	1.048450	6.168461		6	1.049751	6.172954
7	1.056750	7.225211		7	1.058280	7.231235
8	1.065116	8.290328		8	1.066879	8.298113
9	1.073548	9.363876		9	1.075547	9.373661
10	1.082047	10.445923		10	1.084286	10.457947
11	1.090614	11.536537		11	1.093096	11.551042

Entries are percentages of the original loan amount.

514   **Table 42b, page 18**

Remaining Balance Tables

Term of 25 Years
Interest Rate 9.50%
Monthly Payment 0.873697%   Annual Constant 10.48436%

Interest Rate 9.75%
Monthly Payment 0.891137%   Annual Constant 10.69365%

Year End	Principal Paid in Year	Interest Paid in Year	Total Interest Paid	Remaining Balance Year End	Curtail First Month	Principal Paid in Year	Interest Paid in Year	Total Interest Paid	Remaining Balance Year End	Curtail First Month	Year End
1	1.028372	9.455988	9.455988	98.971628	0.081386	0.986982	9.706667	9.706667	99.013018	0.085265	1
2	1.130435	9.353924	18.809912	97.841192	0.089463	1.087631	9.606018	19.312685	97.925387	0.093961	2
3	1.242628	9.241731	28.051644	96.598564	0.098342	1.198545	9.495104	28.807789	96.726842	0.103542	3
4	1.365956	9.118404	37.170047	95.232608	0.108102	1.320769	9.372880	38.180669	95.406073	0.114101	4
5	1.501524	8.982836	46.152883	93.731083	0.118831	1.455457	9.238192	47.418861	93.950616	0.125737	5
6	1.650547	8.833813	54.986696	92.080536	0.130625	1.603881	9.089768	56.508629	92.346735	0.138559	6
7	1.814360	8.670000	63.656696	90.266177	0.143589	1.767440	8.926209	65.434838	90.579294	0.152689	7
8	1.994430	8.489929	72.146626	88.271746	0.157840	1.947679	8.745970	74.180808	88.631615	0.168260	8
9	2.192373	8.291987	80.438613	86.079373	0.173505	2.146298	8.547351	82.728159	86.485318	0.185419	9
10	2.409961	8.074399	88.513012	83.669413	0.190725	2.365171	8.328478	91.056637	84.120146	0.204327	10
11	2.649143	7.835217	96.348229	81.020269	0.209654	2.606365	8.087284	99.143921	81.513781	0.225164	11
12	2.912064	7.572295	103.920524	78.108205	0.230462	2.872155	7.821494	106.965415	78.641626	0.248126	12
13	3.201080	7.283280	111.203804	74.907125	0.253334	3.165049	7.528600	114.494015	75.476577	0.273429	13
14	3.518779	6.965581	118.169385	71.388346	0.278477	3.487812	7.205837	121.699852	71.988765	0.301312	14
15	3.868010	6.616350	124.785735	67.520336	0.306116	3.843489	6.850160	128.550011	68.145276	0.332039	15
16	4.251900	6.232460	131.018195	63.268436	0.336497	4.235438	6.458211	135.008223	63.909838	0.365900	16
17	4.673891	5.810469	136.828664	58.594545	0.369893	4.667356	6.026293	141.034516	59.242482	0.403213	17
18	5.137763	5.346597	142.175260	53.456782	0.406604	5.143320	5.550329	146.584845	54.099162	0.444332	18
19	5.647674	4.836686	147.011946	47.809108	0.446959	5.667821	5.025828	151.610672	48.431340	0.489644	19
20	6.208192	4.276168	151.288114	41.600916	0.491318	6.245810	4.447839	156.058511	42.185530	0.539576	20
21	6.824340	3.660020	154.948134	34.776576	0.540080	6.882740	3.810909	159.869420	35.302790	0.594601	21
22	7.501639	2.982721	157.930855	27.274936	0.593682	7.584623	3.109026	162.978446	27.718167	0.655236	22
23	8.246159	2.238201	160.169056	19.028777	0.652604	8.358082	2.335567	165.314013	19.360085	0.722056	23
24	9.064570	1.419107	161.588845	9.964207	0.717373	9.210416	1.483233	166.797246	10.149669	0.795689	24
25	9.964207	0.520153	162.108998	0.000000	0.788571	10.149669	0.543980	167.341226	0.000000	0.876831	25

Term of 30 Years
Interest Rate 9.50%
Monthly Payment 0.840854%   Annual Constant 10.09025%

Interest Rate 9.75%
Monthly Payment 0.859154%   Annual Constant 10.30985%

Year End	Principal Paid in Year	Interest Paid in Year	Total Interest Paid	Remaining Balance Year End	Curtail First Month	Principal Paid in Year	Interest Paid in Year	Total Interest Paid	Remaining Balance Year End	Curtail First Month	Year End
1	0.616641	9.473609	9.473609	99.383359	0.048801	0.585562	9.724291	9.724291	99.414438	0.050587	1
2	0.677842	9.412409	18.886018	98.705517	0.053645	0.645275	9.664578	19.388869	98.769163	0.055745	2
3	0.745116	9.345135	28.231153	97.960401	0.058969	0.711079	9.598774	28.987643	98.058084	0.061430	3
4	0.819067	9.271184	37.502337	97.141335	0.064821	0.783593	9.526260	38.513903	97.274492	0.067695	4
5	0.900357	9.189893	46.692230	96.240978	0.071255	0.863501	9.446352	47.960255	96.410990	0.074598	5
6	0.989715	9.100535	55.792765	95.251262	0.078326	0.951559	9.358294	57.318549	95.459432	0.082205	6
7	1.087942	9.002308	64.795073	94.163320	0.086100	1.048596	9.261257	66.579806	94.410835	0.090588	7
8	1.195918	8.894333	73.689406	92.967402	0.094645	1.155529	9.154324	75.734130	93.255307	0.099826	8
9	1.314610	8.775641	82.465047	91.652793	0.104039	1.273367	9.036486	84.770616	91.981940	0.110006	9
10	1.445082	8.645169	91.110216	90.207711	0.114364	1.403221	8.906632	93.677248	90.578719	0.121224	10
11	1.588502	8.501748	99.611964	88.619208	0.125715	1.546318	8.763535	102.440784	89.032401	0.133587	11
12	1.746157	8.344093	107.956057	86.873051	0.138191	1.704007	8.605846	111.046630	87.328395	0.147209	12
13	1.919459	8.170791	116.126848	84.953592	0.151907	1.877777	8.432076	119.478706	85.450618	0.162221	13
14	2.109961	7.980289	124.107137	82.843630	0.166983	2.069267	8.240586	127.719292	83.381351	0.178764	14
15	2.319370	7.770881	131.878018	80.524261	0.183556	2.280285	8.029568	135.748860	81.101066	0.196994	15
16	2.549561	7.540689	139.418707	77.974699	0.201773	2.512822	7.797031	143.545891	78.588244	0.217083	16
17	2.802599	7.287651	146.706358	75.172100	0.221799	2.769073	7.540780	151.086671	75.819171	0.239221	17
18	3.080751	7.009500	153.715858	72.091350	0.243812	3.051455	7.258398	158.345069	72.767716	0.263616	18
19	3.386508	6.703743	160.419601	68.704842	0.268009	3.362634	6.947219	165.292287	69.405081	0.290498	19
20	3.722610	6.367640	166.787241	64.982232	0.294609	3.705546	6.604307	171.896594	65.699535	0.320123	20
21	4.092070	5.998180	172.785422	60.890161	0.323848	4.083428	6.226425	178.123019	61.616108	0.352768	21
22	4.498198	5.592052	178.377474	56.391963	0.355989	4.499844	5.810009	183.933028	57.116263	0.388742	22
23	4.944634	5.145617	183.523090	51.447329	0.391320	4.958726	5.351127	189.284155	52.157538	0.428385	23
24	5.435377	4.654874	188.177964	46.011953	0.430157	5.464403	4.845450	194.129606	46.693135	0.472070	24
25	5.974825	4.115426	192.293390	40.037128	0.472850	6.021647	4.288206	198.417811	40.671488	0.520211	25
26	6.567812	3.522439	195.815829	33.469316	0.519779	6.635718	3.674135	202.091946	34.035769	0.573260	26
27	7.219661	2.870599	198.686428	26.249665	0.571365	7.312410	2.997443	205.089388	26.723359	0.631720	27
28	7.936184	2.154067	200.840495	18.313481	0.628072	8.058110	2.251743	207.341132	18.665249	0.696141	28
29	8.723831	1.366419	202.206914	9.589650	0.690407	8.879853	1.430000	208.771131	9.785396	0.767132	29
30	9.589650	0.500600	202.707515	0.000000	0.758928	9.785396	0.524457	209.295588	0.000000	0.845361	30

Month	Monthly Factors for 9.500% Interest: This Month	Year-to-date	Month	Monthly Factors for 9.750% Interest: This Month	Year-to-date
1	1.007917	1.007917	1	1.008125	1.008125
2	1.015896	2.023813	2	1.016316	2.024441
3	1.023939	3.047751	3	1.024574	3.049015
4	1.032045	4.079796	4	1.032898	4.081913
5	1.040215	5.120011	5	1.041291	5.123203
6	1.048450	6.168461	6	1.049751	6.172954
7	1.056750	7.225211	7	1.058280	7.231235
8	1.065116	8.290328	8	1.066879	8.298113
9	1.073548	9.363876	9	1.075547	9.373661
10	1.082047	10.445923	10	1.084286	10.457947
11	1.090614	11.536537	11	1.093096	11.551042

Entries are percentages of the original loan amount.

Remaining Balance Tables

Term of 3 Years
Interest Rate 10.00%
Monthly Payment 3.226719%   Annual Constant 38.72062%

Interest Rate 10.25%
Monthly Payment 3.238469%   Annual Constant 38.86163%

Year End	Principal Paid in Year	Interest Paid in Year	Total Interest Paid	Remaining Balance Year End	Curtail First Month	Principal Paid in Year	Interest Paid in Year	Total Interest Paid	Remaining Balance Year End	Curtail First Month	Year End
1	30.074247	8.646378	8.646378	69.925753	2.373605	29.994793	8.866833	8.866833	70.005207	2.595970	1
2	33.223414	5.497211	14.143589	36.702339	2.622153	33.217887	5.643738	14.510571	36.787320	2.874921	2
3	36.702339	2.018285	16.161874	0.000000	2.896727	36.787320	2.074306	16.584877	0.000000	3.183846	3

Term of 4 Years
Interest Rate 10.00%
Monthly Payment 2.536258%   Annual Constant 30.43510%

Interest Rate 10.25%
Monthly Payment 2.548281%   Annual Constant 30.57938%

Year End	Principal Paid in Year	Interest Paid in Year	Total Interest Paid	Remaining Balance Year End	Curtail First Month	Principal Paid in Year	Interest Paid in Year	Total Interest Paid	Remaining Balance Year End	Curtail First Month	Year End
1	21.398220	9.036880	9.036880	78.601780	1.688851	21.312155	9.267220	9.267220	78.687845	1.844511	1
2	23.638893	6.796207	15.833087	54.962886	1.865696	23.602256	6.977120	16.244340	55.085589	2.042713	2
3	26.114194	4.320906	20.153992	28.848692	2.061059	26.138440	4.440936	20.685276	28.947149	2.262213	3
4	28.848692	1.586408	21.740400	0.000000	2.276879	28.947149	1.632226	22.317503	0.000000	2.505300	4

Term of 5 Years
Interest Rate 10.00%
Monthly Payment 2.124704%   Annual Constant 25.49645%

Interest Rate 10.25%
Monthly Payment 2.137026%   Annual Constant 25.64432%

Year End	Principal Paid in Year	Interest Paid in Year	Total Interest Paid	Remaining Balance Year End	Curtail First Month	Principal Paid in Year	Interest Paid in Year	Total Interest Paid	Remaining Balance Year End	Curtail First Month	Year End
1	16.226812	9.269642	9.269642	83.773188	1.280699	16.138521	9.505795	9.505795	83.861479	1.396747	1
2	17.925971	7.570482	16.840124	65.847217	1.414805	17.872689	7.771628	17.277423	65.988790	1.546834	2
3	19.803055	5.693399	22.533523	46.044162	1.562953	19.793201	5.851116	23.128539	46.195589	1.713049	3
4	21.876693	3.619760	26.153284	24.167469	1.726615	21.920082	3.724235	26.852774	24.275507	1.897125	4
5	24.167469	1.328985	27.482268	0.000000	1.907414	24.275507	1.368809	28.221583	0.000000	2.100981	5

Term of 7 Years
Interest Rate 10.00%
Monthly Payment 1.660118%   Annual Constant 19.92142%

Interest Rate 10.25%
Monthly Payment 1.673064%   Annual Constant 20.07677%

Year End	Principal Paid in Year	Interest Paid in Year	Total Interest Paid	Remaining Balance Year End	Curtail First Month	Principal Paid in Year	Interest Paid in Year	Total Interest Paid	Remaining Balance Year End	Curtail First Month	Year End
1	10.389024	9.532397	9.532397	89.610976	0.819952	10.301826	9.774946	9.774946	89.698174	0.891596	1
2	11.476891	8.444530	17.976927	78.134085	0.905812	11.408810	8.667962	18.442908	78.289363	0.987403	2
3	12.678671	7.242750	25.219677	65.455414	1.000662	12.634746	7.442027	25.884934	65.654618	1.093504	3
4	14.006294	5.915127	31.134804	51.449121	1.105445	13.992414	6.084358	31.969293	51.662204	1.211007	4
5	15.472936	4.448485	35.583289	35.976185	1.221199	15.495971	4.580801	36.550094	36.166233	1.341136	5
6	17.093154	2.828267	38.411556	18.883031	1.349075	17.161093	2.915680	39.465774	19.005140	1.485247	6
7	18.883031	1.038390	39.449946	0.000000	1.490340	19.005140	1.071632	40.537406	0.000000	1.644845	7

Term of 10 Years
Interest Rate 10.00%
Monthly Payment 1.321507%   Annual Constant 15.85809%

Interest Rate 10.25%
Monthly Payment 1.335390%   Annual Constant 16.02468%

Year End	Principal Paid in Year	Interest Paid in Year	Total Interest Paid	Remaining Balance Year End	Curtail First Month	Principal Paid in Year	Interest Paid in Year	Total Interest Paid	Remaining Balance Year End	Curtail First Month	Year End
1	6.134184	9.723904	9.723904	93.865816	0.484140	6.053845	9.970836	9.970836	93.946155	0.523944	1
2	6.776513	9.081575	18.805479	87.089303	0.534835	6.704361	9.320319	19.291155	87.241794	0.580245	2
3	7.486103	8.371986	27.177465	79.603200	0.590840	7.424779	8.599901	27.891055	79.817015	0.642595	3
4	8.269996	7.588093	34.765558	71.333204	0.652708	8.222610	7.802070	35.693125	71.594405	0.711645	4
5	9.135972	6.722116	41.487674	62.197232	0.721055	9.106172	6.918508	42.611634	62.488233	0.788115	5
6	10.092628	5.765461	47.253135	52.104604	0.796559	10.084677	5.940003	48.551637	52.403556	0.872802	6
7	11.149458	4.708631	51.961765	40.955146	0.879969	11.168327	4.856353	53.407990	41.235229	0.966589	7
8	12.316952	3.541137	55.502902	28.638194	0.972114	12.368421	3.656259	57.064249	28.866807	1.070454	8
9	13.606698	2.251391	57.754293	15.031497	1.073907	13.697472	2.327208	59.391458	15.169336	1.185480	9
10	15.031497	0.826592	58.580884	0.000000	1.186359	15.169336	0.855345	60.246802	0.000000	1.312866	10

Term of 15 Years
Interest Rate 10.00%
Monthly Payment 1.074605%   Annual Constant 12.89526%

Interest Rate 10.25%
Monthly Payment 1.089951%   Annual Constant 13.07941%

Year End	Principal Paid in Year	Interest Paid in Year	Total Interest Paid	Remaining Balance Year End	Curtail First Month	Principal Paid in Year	Interest Paid in Year	Total Interest Paid	Remaining Balance Year End	Curtail First Month	Year End
1	3.031717	9.863544	9.863544	96.968283	0.239278	2.966193	10.113218	10.113218	97.033807	0.256716	1
2	3.349177	9.546084	19.409628	93.619106	0.264333	3.284925	9.794486	19.907704	93.748882	0.284302	2
3	3.699880	9.195381	28.605010	89.919225	0.292012	3.637908	9.441503	29.349207	90.110974	0.314851	3
4	4.087306	8.807956	37.412965	85.831920	0.322590	4.028819	9.050592	38.399799	86.082155	0.348684	4
5	4.515300	8.379961	45.792926	81.316619	0.356369	4.461737	8.617674	47.017473	81.620418	0.386152	5
6	4.988111	7.907150	53.700077	76.328508	0.393686	4.941173	8.138238	55.155711	76.679245	0.427646	6
7	5.510432	7.384830	61.084907	70.818077	0.434910	5.472128	7.607283	62.762994	71.207117	0.473598	7
8	6.087446	6.807816	67.892722	64.730631	0.480451	6.060136	7.019275	69.782269	65.146981	0.524489	8
9	6.724881	6.170381	74.063103	58.005750	0.530760	6.711329	6.368082	76.150351	58.435652	0.580848	9
10	7.429064	5.466198	79.529301	50.576686	0.586338	7.432496	5.646915	81.797267	51.003157	0.643263	10
11	8.206984	4.688278	84.217578	42.369703	0.647735	8.231155	4.848256	86.645523	42.772001	0.712385	11
12	9.066362	3.828899	88.046477	33.303340	0.715561	9.115635	3.963776	90.609298	33.656366	0.788934	12
13	10.015729	2.879533	90.926010	23.287612	0.790490	10.095157	2.984254	93.593552	23.561209	0.873709	13
14	11.064507	1.830755	92.756765	12.223105	0.873264	11.179934	1.899477	95.493029	12.381275	0.967594	14
15	12.223105	0.672156	93.428921	0.000000	0.964707	12.381275	0.698136	96.191165	0.000000	1.071567	15

Monthly Factors for 10.000% Interest:			Monthly Factors for 10.250% Interest:		
Month	This Month	Year-to-date	Month	This Month	Year-to-date
1	1.008333	1.008333	1	1.008542	1.008542
2	1.016736	2.025069	2	1.017156	2.025698
3	1.025209	3.050278	3	1.025845	3.051542
4	1.033752	4.084031	4	1.034607	4.086149
5	1.042367	5.126398	5	1.043444	5.129594
6	1.051053	6.177451	6	1.052357	6.181951
7	1.059812	7.237263	7	1.061346	7.243296
8	1.068644	8.305907	8	1.070411	8.313708
9	1.077549	9.383456	9	1.079555	9.393262
10	1.086529	10.469985	10	1.088776	10.482038
11	1.095583	11.565568	11	1.098076	11.580114

Entries are percentages of the original loan amount.

Remaining Balance Tables

Term of 25 Years
Interest Rate 10.00%
Monthly Payment 0.908701%   Annual Constant 10.90441%

Interest Rate 10.25%
Monthly Payment 0.926383%   Annual Constant 11.11660%

Year End	Principal Paid in Year	Interest Paid in Year	Total Interest Paid	Remaining Balance Year End	Curtail First Month	Principal Paid in Year	Interest Paid in Year	Total Interest Paid	Remaining Balance Year End	Curtail First Month	Year End
1	0.947034	9.957375	9.957375	99.052966	0.074745	0.908493	10.208106	10.208106	99.091507	0.078628	1
2	1.046201	9.858208	19.815582	98.006764	0.082571	1.006116	10.110484	20.318590	98.085391	0.087077	2
3	1.155752	9.748657	29.564239	96.851012	0.091218	1.114228	10.002372	30.320962	96.971163	0.096433	3
4	1.276775	9.627634	39.191874	95.574238	0.100769	1.233957	9.882642	40.203604	95.737206	0.106796	4
5	1.410469	9.493939	48.685813	94.163768	0.111321	1.366552	9.750047	49.953651	94.370654	0.118272	5
6	1.558164	9.346245	58.032058	92.605604	0.122978	1.513395	9.603204	59.556855	92.857258	0.130980	6
7	1.721324	9.183085	67.215143	90.884280	0.135855	1.676018	9.440582	68.997436	91.181241	0.145055	7
8	1.901569	9.002840	76.217982	88.982711	0.150081	1.856114	9.260485	78.257922	89.325127	0.160642	8
9	2.100689	8.803720	85.021703	86.882022	0.165797	2.055563	9.061036	87.318958	87.269563	0.177904	9
10	2.320658	8.583751	93.605454	84.561364	0.183158	2.276444	8.840155	96.159113	84.993119	0.197020	10
11	2.563661	8.340748	101.946201	81.997703	0.202337	2.521060	8.595540	104.754653	82.472059	0.218191	11
12	2.832110	8.072299	110.018500	79.165593	0.223524	2.791961	8.324639	113.079291	79.680099	0.241637	12
13	3.128669	7.775740	117.794240	76.036924	0.246930	3.091971	8.024628	121.103920	76.588128	0.267602	13
14	3.456282	7.448127	125.242367	72.580642	0.272786	3.424219	7.692380	128.796300	73.163908	0.296357	14
15	3.818199	7.086210	132.328577	68.762443	0.301351	3.792169	7.324430	136.120730	69.371739	0.328202	15
16	4.218015	6.686394	139.014971	64.544428	0.332906	4.199657	6.916942	143.037672	65.172082	0.363469	16
17	4.659696	6.244713	145.259684	59.884732	0.367766	4.650932	6.465667	149.503339	60.521150	0.402526	17
18	5.147627	5.756782	151.016466	54.737105	0.406276	5.150699	5.965901	155.469240	55.370451	0.445779	18
19	5.686651	5.217758	156.234224	49.050454	0.448818	5.704168	5.412432	160.881672	49.666284	0.493681	19
20	6.282118	4.622291	160.856515	42.768336	0.495815	6.317110	4.799490	165.681161	43.349174	0.546729	20
21	6.939937	3.964471	164.820986	35.828398	0.547734	6.995916	4.120684	169.801845	36.353258	0.605478	21
22	7.666640	3.237769	168.058756	28.161759	0.605088	7.747663	3.368937	173.170782	28.605595	0.670540	22
23	8.469437	2.434972	170.493728	19.692322	0.668449	8.580189	2.536410	175.707192	20.025406	0.742593	23
24	9.356298	1.548111	172.041839	10.336024	0.738444	9.502174	1.614425	177.321617	10.523232	0.822388	24
25	10.336024	0.568385	172.610224	0.000000	0.815769	10.523232	0.593367	177.914985	0.000000	0.910758	25

Term of 30 Years
Interest Rate 10.00%
Monthly Payment 0.877572%   Annual Constant 10.53086%

Interest Rate 10.25%
Monthly Payment 0.896101%   Annual Constant 10.75322%

Year End	Principal Paid in Year	Interest Paid in Year	Total Interest Paid	Remaining Balance Year End	Curtail First Month	Principal Paid in Year	Interest Paid in Year	Total Interest Paid	Remaining Balance Year End	Curtail First Month	Year End
1	0.555879	9.974980	9.974980	99.444121	0.043873	0.527542	10.225673	10.225673	99.472458	0.045657	1
2	0.614086	9.916773	19.891753	98.830035	0.048467	0.584230	10.168986	20.394659	98.888228	0.050564	2
3	0.678389	9.852470	29.744222	98.151646	0.053542	0.647008	10.106208	30.500867	98.241220	0.055997	3
4	0.749425	9.781433	39.525656	97.402221	0.059148	0.716532	10.036683	40.537550	97.524688	0.062014	4
5	0.827900	9.702959	49.228615	96.574320	0.065342	0.793527	9.959688	50.497238	96.731160	0.068678	5
6	0.914592	9.616267	58.844882	95.659728	0.072184	0.878796	9.874419	60.371657	95.852364	0.076057	6
7	1.010362	9.520497	68.365379	94.649367	0.079743	0.973227	9.779988	70.151646	94.879137	0.084230	7
8	1.116160	9.414699	77.780078	93.533207	0.088093	1.077805	9.675410	79.827056	93.801331	0.093281	8
9	1.233036	9.297823	87.077900	92.300171	0.097317	1.193621	9.559594	89.386650	92.607710	0.103305	9
10	1.362151	9.168708	96.246608	90.938019	0.107508	1.321882	9.431334	98.817984	91.285828	0.114405	10
11	1.504786	9.026072	105.272680	89.433233	0.118765	1.463925	9.289291	108.107274	89.821903	0.126699	11
12	1.662357	8.868502	114.141182	87.770876	0.131201	1.621231	9.131984	117.239259	88.200672	0.140313	12
13	1.836428	8.694431	122.835613	85.934448	0.144940	1.795441	8.957775	126.197033	86.405231	0.155391	13
14	2.028726	8.502133	131.337746	83.905722	0.160117	1.988370	8.764845	134.961879	84.416861	0.172088	14
15	2.241160	8.289699	139.627445	81.664563	0.176883	2.202031	8.551185	143.513063	82.214830	0.190580	15
16	2.475838	8.055020	147.682466	79.188724	0.195405	2.438650	8.314565	151.827629	79.776180	0.211059	16
17	2.735091	7.795768	155.478233	76.453633	0.215867	2.700696	8.052520	159.880148	77.075484	0.233738	17
18	3.021491	7.509368	162.987601	73.432142	0.238471	2.990899	7.762316	167.642464	74.084585	0.258854	18
19	3.337880	7.192978	170.180580	70.094262	0.263442	3.312287	7.440929	175.083393	70.772297	0.286670	19
20	3.687400	6.843459	177.024038	66.406862	0.291027	3.668209	7.085006	182.168399	67.104088	0.317474	20
21	4.073519	6.457340	183.481378	62.333343	0.321502	4.062377	6.690838	188.859238	63.041711	0.351588	21
22	4.500070	6.030789	189.512167	57.833273	0.355167	4.498901	6.254315	195.113553	58.542810	0.389368	22
23	4.971286	5.559573	195.071740	52.861987	0.392358	4.982331	5.770885	200.884438	53.560480	0.431208	23
24	5.491845	5.039014	200.110754	47.370142	0.433443	5.517708	5.235508	206.119946	48.042772	0.477543	24
25	6.066912	4.463946	204.574701	41.303230	0.478830	6.110614	4.642602	210.762548	41.932159	0.528858	25
26	6.702197	3.828661	208.403362	34.601032	0.528970	6.767230	3.985985	214.748533	35.164928	0.585686	26
27	7.404005	3.126854	211.530216	27.197027	0.584360	7.494404	3.258811	218.007344	27.670524	0.648621	27
28	8.179301	2.351558	213.881774	19.017726	0.645550	8.299716	2.453499	220.460843	19.370808	0.718319	28
29	9.035781	1.495078	215.376852	9.981945	0.713148	9.191564	1.561652	222.022495	10.179244	0.795506	29
30	9.981945	0.548914	215.925765	0.000000	0.787823	10.179244	0.573971	222.596467	0.000000	0.880987	30

Monthly Factors for 10.000% Interest:			Monthly Factors for 10.250% Interest:		
Month	This Month	Year-to-date	Month	This Month	Year-to-date
1	1.008333	1.008333	1	1.008542	1.008542
2	1.016736	2.025069	2	1.017156	2.025698
3	1.025209	3.050278	3	1.025845	3.051542
4	1.033752	4.084031	4	1.034607	4.086149
5	1.042367	5.126398	5	1.043444	5.129594
6	1.051053	6.177451	6	1.052357	6.181951
7	1.059812	7.237263	7	1.061346	7.243296
8	1.068644	8.305907	8	1.070411	8.313708
9	1.077549	9.383456	9	1.079555	9.393262
10	1.086529	10.469985	10	1.088776	10.482038
11	1.095583	11.565568	11	1.098076	11.580114

Entries are percentages of the original loan amount.

Remaining Balance Tables

Term of 3 Years
Interest Rate 10.50%
Monthly Payment 3.250244%   Annual Constant 39.00293%   Interest Rate 10.75%
Monthly Payment 3.262045%   Annual Constant 39.14454%

Year End	Principal Paid in Year	Interest Paid in Year	Total Interest Paid	Remaining Balance Year End	Curtail First Month	Principal Paid in Year	Interest Paid in Year	Total Interest Paid	Remaining Balance Year End	Curtail First Month	Year End
1	29.915443	9.087490	9.087490	70.084557	2.354641	29.836197	9.308347	9.308347	70.163803	2.586938	1
2	33.212228	5.790705	14.878194	36.872330	2.614131	33.206435	5.938109	15.246456	36.957368	2.879153	2
3	36.872330	2.130602	17.008797	0.000000	2.902217	36.957368	2.187176	17.433632	0.000000	3.204376	3

Term of 4 Years
Interest Rate 10.50%
Monthly Payment 2.560338%   Annual Constant 30.72406%   Interest Rate 10.75%
Monthly Payment 2.572428%   Annual Constant 30.86914%

1	21.226293	9.497763	9.497763	78.773707	1.670719	21.140633	9.728507	9.728507	78.859367	1.832992	1
2	23.565503	7.158552	16.656316	55.208204	1.854838	23.528636	7.340503	17.069010	55.330731	2.040043	2
3	26.162503	4.561553	21.217868	29.045701	2.059248	26.186384	4.682755	21.751765	29.144346	2.270482	3
4	29.045701	1.678355	22.896223	0.000000	2.286184	29.144346	1.724793	23.476559	0.000000	2.526951	4

Term of 5 Years
Interest Rate 10.50%
Monthly Payment 2.149390%   Annual Constant 25.79268%   Interest Rate 10.75%
Monthly Payment 2.161795%   Annual Constant 25.94154%

1	16.050535	9.742146	9.742146	83.949465	1.263336	15.962853	9.978692	9.978692	84.037147	1.384054	1
2	17.819359	7.973321	17.715467	66.130106	1.402560	17.765985	8.175560	18.154252	66.271163	1.540394	2
3	19.783114	6.009566	23.725034	46.346992	1.557127	19.772795	6.168749	24.323001	46.498368	1.714394	3
4	21.963281	3.829399	27.554433	24.383711	1.728727	22.006291	3.935254	28.258255	24.492077	1.908048	4
5	24.383711	1.408970	28.963402	0.000000	1.919239	24.492077	1.449467	29.707722	0.000000	2.123578	5

Term of 7 Years
Interest Rate 10.50%
Monthly Payment 1.686067%   Annual Constant 20.23281%   Interest Rate 10.75%
Monthly Payment 1.699127%   Annual Constant 20.38953%

1	10.215133	10.017674	10.017674	89.784867	0.804032	10.128946	10.260580	10.260580	89.871054	0.878227	1
2	11.340876	8.891932	18.909606	78.443990	0.892639	11.273091	9.116435	19.377015	78.597963	0.977430	2
3	12.590680	7.642128	26.551734	65.853310	0.991011	12.546477	7.843049	27.220063	66.051486	1.087838	3
4	13.978216	6.254591	32.806325	51.875094	1.100224	13.963702	6.425823	33.645887	52.087784	1.210718	4
5	15.518664	4.714144	37.520469	36.356430	1.221472	15.541014	4.848511	38.494398	36.546770	1.347479	5
6	17.228874	3.003933	40.524402	19.127556	1.356083	17.296496	3.093029	41.587428	19.250274	1.499687	6
7	19.127556	1.105252	41.629654	0.000000	1.505528	19.250274	1.139252	42.726679	0.000000	1.669089	7

Term of 10 Years
Interest Rate 10.50%
Monthly Payment 1.349350%   Annual Constant 16.19220%   Interest Rate 10.75%
Monthly Payment 1.363387%   Annual Constant 16.36064%

1	5.974286	10.217914	10.217914	94.025714	0.470235	5.895506	10.465135	10.465135	94.104494	0.511168	1
2	6.632673	9.559527	19.777440	87.393041	0.522057	6.561451	9.799191	20.264326	87.543043	0.568908	2
3	7.363616	8.828583	28.606023	80.029424	0.579589	7.302619	9.058022	29.322348	80.240423	0.633171	3
4	8.175112	8.017087	36.623110	71.854312	0.643462	8.127509	8.233133	37.555481	72.112915	0.704693	4
5	9.076038	7.116162	43.739272	62.778274	0.714374	9.045576	7.315066	44.870547	63.067339	0.784294	5
6	10.076249	6.115951	49.855223	52.702025	0.793100	10.067346	6.293295	51.163842	52.999992	0.872886	6
7	11.186686	5.005514	54.860737	41.515339	0.880503	11.204534	5.156108	56.319950	41.795459	0.971485	7
8	12.419497	3.772702	58.633439	29.095842	0.977537	12.470176	3.890466	60.210416	29.325283	1.081222	8
9	13.788169	2.404031	61.037469	15.307673	1.085265	13.878782	2.481860	62.692276	15.446501	1.203355	9
10	15.307673	0.884527	61.921996	0.000000	1.204865	15.446501	0.914140	63.606417	0.000000	1.339284	10

Term of 15 Years
Interest Rate 10.50%
Monthly Payment 1.105399%   Annual Constant 13.26479%   Interest Rate 10.75%
Monthly Payment 1.120948%   Annual Constant 13.45138%

1	2.901801	10.362986	10.362986	97.098199	0.228400	2.838531	10.612845	10.612845	97.161469	0.246114	1
2	3.221589	10.043198	20.406184	93.876610	0.253571	3.159165	10.292210	20.905056	94.002304	0.273914	2
3	3.576619	9.688168	30.094352	90.299991	0.281515	3.516018	9.935357	30.840413	90.486286	0.304855	3
4	3.970775	9.294012	39.388364	86.329215	0.312539	3.913181	9.538195	40.378608	86.573105	0.339291	4
5	4.408368	8.856419	48.244783	81.920847	0.346982	4.355206	9.096170	49.474778	82.217899	0.377617	5
6	4.894186	8.370601	56.615384	77.026661	0.385221	4.847161	8.604214	58.078992	77.370737	0.420272	6
7	5.433542	7.831245	64.446629	71.593119	0.427673	5.394687	8.056689	66.135681	71.976050	0.467745	7
8	6.032337	7.232450	71.679079	65.560782	0.474805	6.004060	7.447316	73.582997	65.971990	0.520580	8
9	6.697121	6.567666	78.246745	58.863661	0.527130	6.682267	6.769109	80.352105	59.289723	0.579384	9
10	7.435167	5.829620	84.076365	51.428494	0.585221	7.437083	6.014293	86.366399	51.852641	0.644830	10
11	8.254548	5.010239	89.086603	43.173946	0.649715	8.277161	5.174215	91.540614	43.575480	0.717668	11
12	9.164228	4.100559	93.187163	34.009718	0.721315	9.212132	4.239244	95.779858	34.363348	0.798735	12
13	10.174158	3.090630	96.277792	23.835560	0.800807	10.252716	3.198660	98.978517	24.110632	0.888958	13
14	11.295385	1.969402	98.247194	12.540175	0.889059	11.410843	2.040533	101.019050	12.699789	0.989373	14
15	12.540175	0.724612	98.971806	0.000000	0.987036	12.699789	0.751587	101.770637	0.000000	1.101131	15

Monthly Factors for 10.500% Interest:			Monthly Factors for 10.750% Interest:		
Month	This Month	Year-to-date	Month	This Month	Year-to-date
1	1.008750	1.008750	1	1.008958	1.008958
2	1.017577	2.026327	2	1.017997	2.026955
3	1.026480	3.052807	3	1.027116	3.054072
4	1.035462	4.088269	4	1.036318	4.090389
5	1.044522	5.132791	5	1.045601	5.135991
6	1.053662	6.186453	6	1.054968	6.190959
7	1.062881	7.249335	7	1.064419	7.255378
8	1.072182	8.321516	8	1.073954	8.329333
9	1.081563	9.403080	9	1.083575	9.412908
10	1.091027	10.494107	10	1.093282	10.506190
11	1.100573	11.594680	11	1.103076	11.609266

Entries are percentages of the original loan amount.

Remaining Balance Tables

Term of 25 Years
Interest Rate 10.50%
Monthly Payment 0.944182%   Annual Constant 11.33018%

Interest Rate 10.75%
Monthly Payment 0.962093%   Annual Constant 11.54511%

Year End	Principal Paid in Year	Interest Paid in Year	Total Interest Paid	Remaining Balance Year End	Curtail First Month	Principal Paid in Year	Interest Paid in Year	Total Interest Paid	Remaining Balance Year End	Curtail First Month	Year End
1	0.871321	10.458859	10.458859	99.128679	0.068582	0.835482	10.709630	10.709630	99.164518	0.072440	1
2	0.967344	10.362836	20.821695	98.161334	0.076140	0.929857	10.615256	21.324886	98.234661	0.080623	2
3	1.073949	10.256232	31.077927	97.087386	0.084530	1.034891	10.510221	31.835108	97.199770	0.089730	3
4	1.192302	10.137879	41.215806	95.895084	0.093846	1.151791	10.393322	42.228429	96.047979	0.099866	4
5	1.323697	10.006483	51.222289	94.571387	0.104188	1.281895	10.263218	52.491647	94.766084	0.111146	5
6	1.469573	9.860607	61.082896	93.101814	0.115670	1.426695	10.118418	62.610065	93.339389	0.123701	6
7	1.631525	9.698655	70.781551	91.470288	0.128417	1.587852	9.957261	72.567326	91.751537	0.137674	7
8	1.811325	9.518855	80.300407	89.658963	0.142569	1.767212	9.777900	82.345226	89.984325	0.153226	8
9	2.010939	9.319241	89.619648	87.648024	0.158281	1.966833	9.578280	91.923506	88.017492	0.170534	9
10	2.232552	9.097629	98.717276	85.415472	0.175724	2.189003	9.356110	101.279616	85.828490	0.189797	10
11	2.478587	8.851594	107.568870	82.936885	0.195089	2.436268	9.108845	110.388461	83.392222	0.211236	11
12	2.751736	8.578445	116.147315	80.185149	0.216589	2.711464	8.833649	119.222110	80.680758	0.235097	12
13	3.054986	8.275194	124.422509	77.130163	0.240458	3.017745	8.527367	127.749477	77.663012	0.261653	13
14	3.391656	7.938524	132.361033	73.738507	0.266957	3.358624	8.186489	135.935966	74.304388	0.291208	14
15	3.765429	7.564752	139.925785	69.973078	0.296376	3.738008	7.807105	143.743071	70.566381	0.324103	15
16	4.180392	7.149789	147.075574	65.792686	0.329038	4.160245	7.384867	151.127938	66.406135	0.360713	16
17	4.641085	6.689095	153.764669	61.151601	0.365299	4.630178	6.914934	158.042872	61.775957	0.401458	17
18	5.152549	6.177631	159.942300	55.999052	0.405557	5.153194	6.391918	164.434791	56.622763	0.446806	18
19	5.720378	5.609803	165.552103	50.278674	0.450250	5.735289	5.809824	170.244615	50.887474	0.497276	19
20	6.350783	4.979397	170.531500	43.927891	0.499869	6.383136	5.161977	175.406592	44.504338	0.553448	20
21	7.050661	4.279519	174.811019	36.877229	0.554957	7.104162	4.440951	179.847542	37.400176	0.615964	21
22	7.827669	3.502512	178.313531	29.049561	0.616115	7.906634	3.638479	183.486021	29.493542	0.685542	22
23	8.690350	2.639876	180.953407	20.359256	0.684013	8.799752	2.745361	186.231382	20.693791	0.762980	23
24	9.648006	1.682174	182.635581	10.711250	0.759394	9.793754	1.751359	187.982741	10.900037	0.849164	24
25	10.711250	0.618931	183.254512	0.000000	0.843081	10.900037	0.645076	188.627817	0.000000	0.945084	25

Term of 30 Years
Interest Rate 10.50%
Monthly Payment 0.914739%   Annual Constant 10.97687%

Interest Rate 10.75%
Monthly Payment 0.933481%   Annual Constant 11.20178%

Year End	Principal Paid in Year	Interest Paid in Year	Total Interest Paid	Remaining Balance Year End	Curtail First Month	Principal Paid in Year	Interest Paid in Year	Total Interest Paid	Remaining Balance Year End	Curtail First Month	Year End
1	0.500504	10.476368	10.476368	99.499496	0.039395	0.474714	10.727062	10.727062	99.525286	0.041160	1
2	0.555661	10.421211	20.897578	98.943835	0.043736	0.528337	10.673440	21.400502	98.996949	0.045809	2
3	0.616897	10.359975	31.257553	98.326939	0.048556	0.588017	10.613760	32.014262	98.408933	0.050984	3
4	0.684881	10.291991	41.549544	97.642058	0.053907	0.654438	10.547339	42.561600	97.754495	0.056744	4
5	0.760357	10.216514	51.766058	96.881701	0.059848	0.728362	10.473415	53.035015	97.026133	0.063152	5
6	0.844151	10.132721	61.898779	96.037550	0.066443	0.810636	10.391140	63.426155	96.215497	0.070286	6
7	0.937179	10.039692	71.938471	95.100370	0.073765	0.902204	10.299572	73.725727	95.313293	0.078225	7
8	1.040460	9.936412	81.874883	94.059911	0.081894	1.004115	10.197661	83.923388	94.309177	0.087061	8
9	1.155122	9.821749	91.696632	92.904789	0.090920	1.117538	10.084238	94.007627	93.191639	0.096896	9
10	1.282420	9.694451	101.391083	91.622368	0.100939	1.243773	9.958003	103.965630	91.947867	0.107841	10
11	1.423748	9.553124	110.944207	90.198620	0.112063	1.384267	9.817509	113.783139	90.563600	0.120022	11
12	1.580650	9.396222	120.340429	88.617971	0.124413	1.540631	9.661145	123.444285	89.022968	0.133580	12
13	1.754843	9.222029	129.562458	86.863128	0.138123	1.714658	9.487119	132.931403	87.308311	0.148669	13
14	1.948232	9.028639	138.591097	84.914896	0.153345	1.908342	9.293434	142.224838	85.399969	0.165462	14
15	2.162934	8.813937	147.405035	82.751962	0.170244	2.123905	9.077872	151.302710	83.276064	0.184152	15
16	2.401297	8.575575	155.980609	80.350665	0.189006	2.363817	8.837960	160.140669	80.912248	0.204954	16
17	2.665928	8.310943	164.291553	77.684736	0.209835	2.630829	8.570948	168.711617	78.281419	0.228105	17
18	2.959723	8.017149	172.308701	74.725014	0.232959	2.928002	8.273775	176.985392	75.353417	0.253871	18
19	3.285894	7.690977	179.999678	71.439119	0.258632	3.258743	7.943033	184.928425	72.094674	0.282548	19
20	3.648011	7.328860	187.328539	67.791108	0.287135	3.626844	7.574932	192.503357	68.467830	0.314464	20
21	4.050035	6.926837	194.255376	63.741073	0.318778	4.036525	7.165251	199.668608	64.431305	0.349986	21
22	4.496363	6.480509	200.735885	59.244711	0.353908	4.492483	6.709293	206.377902	59.938822	0.389519	22
23	4.991877	5.984994	206.720879	54.252834	0.392910	4.999945	6.201831	212.579733	54.938877	0.433519	23
24	5.541999	5.434872	212.155751	48.710834	0.436210	5.564729	5.637047	218.216780	49.374148	0.482488	24
25	6.152747	4.824125	216.979876	42.558088	0.484282	6.193310	5.008467	223.225247	43.180838	0.536989	25
26	6.830801	4.146071	221.125947	35.727287	0.537652	6.892894	4.308883	227.534130	36.287945	0.597646	26
27	7.583578	3.393293	224.519240	28.143708	0.596903	7.671501	3.530275	231.064405	28.616444	0.665155	27
28	8.419315	2.557557	227.076796	19.724394	0.662683	8.538059	2.663718	233.728123	20.078385	0.740290	28
29	9.347153	1.629719	228.706515	10.377241	0.735713	9.502501	1.699276	235.427399	10.575884	0.823911	29
30	10.377241	0.599631	229.306146	0.000000	0.816792	10.575884	0.625892	236.053291	0.000000	0.916979	30

Month	Monthly Factors for 10.500% Interest: This Month	Year-to-date	Month	Monthly Factors for 10.750% Interest: This Month	Year-to-date
1	1.008750	1.008750	1	1.008958	1.008958
2	1.017577	2.026327	2	1.017997	2.026955
3	1.026480	3.052807	3	1.027116	3.054072
4	1.035462	4.088269	4	1.036318	4.090389
5	1.044522	5.132791	5	1.045601	5.135991
6	1.053662	6.186453	6	1.054968	6.190959
7	1.062881	7.249335	7	1.064419	7.255378
8	1.072182	8.321516	8	1.073954	8.329333
9	1.081563	9.403080	9	1.083575	9.412908
10	1.091027	10.494107	10	1.093282	10.506190
11	1.100573	11.594680	11	1.103076	11.609266

Entries are percentages of the original loan amount.

Remaining Balance Tables

Term of 3 Years

Interest Rate 11.00%					Interest Rate 11.25%					
Monthly Payment 3.273872%		Annual Constant 39.28646%			Monthly Payment 3.285723%		Annual Constant 39.42868%			

Year End	Principal Paid in Year	Interest Paid in Year	Total Interest Paid	Remaining Balance Year End	Curtail First Month	Principal Paid in Year	Interest Paid in Year	Total Interest Paid	Remaining Balance Year End	Curtail First Month	Year End
1	29.757057	9.529403	9.529403	70.242943	2.335794	29.678023	9.750659	9.750659	70.321977	2.577893	1
2	33.200509	6.085951	15.615355	37.042434	2.606089	33.194451	6.234231	15.984890	37.127527	2.883337	2
3	37.042434	2.244027	17.859382	0.000000	2.907662	37.127527	2.301155	18.286046	0.000000	3.224972	3

Term of 4 Years

Interest Rate 11.00%					Interest Rate 11.25%					
Monthly Payment 2.584552%		Annual Constant 31.01463%			Monthly Payment 2.596710%		Annual Constant 31.16052%			

Year End	Principal Paid in Year	Interest Paid in Year	Total Interest Paid	Remaining Balance Year End	Curtail First Month	Principal Paid in Year	Interest Paid in Year	Total Interest Paid	Remaining Balance Year End	Curtail First Month	Year End
1	21.055176	9.959451	9.959451	78.944824	1.652736	20.969534	10.190595	10.190595	79.030077	1.821490	1
2	23.491656	7.522971	17.482422	55.453168	1.843988	23.454564	7.705954	17.896548	55.575513	2.037311	2
3	26.210084	4.804544	22.286965	29.243084	2.057372	26.233600	4.926918	22.823466	29.341913	2.278703	3
4	29.243084	1.771543	24.058509	0.000000	2.295449	29.341913	1.818605	24.642071	0.000000	2.548698	4

Term of 5 Years

Interest Rate 11.00%					Interest Rate 11.25%					
Monthly Payment 2.174242%		Annual Constant 26.09091%			Monthly Payment 2.186731%		Annual Constant 26.24077%			

Year End	Principal Paid in Year	Interest Paid in Year	Total Interest Paid	Remaining Balance Year End	Curtail First Month	Principal Paid in Year	Interest Paid in Year	Total Interest Paid	Remaining Balance Year End	Curtail First Month	Year End
1	15.875475	10.215432	10.215432	84.124525	1.246153	15.788403	10.452366	10.452366	84.211597	1.371413	1
2	17.712567	8.378341	18.593773	66.411958	1.390356	17.659107	8.581662	19.034029	66.552490	1.533906	2
3	19.762244	6.328663	24.922437	46.649714	1.551246	19.751463	6.489307	25.523335	46.801027	1.715652	3
4	22.049108	4.041799	28.964236	24.600605	1.730755	22.091734	4.149036	29.672371	24.709293	1.918933	4
5	24.600605	1.490302	30.454538	0.000000	1.931036	24.709293	1.531476	31.203847	0.000000	2.146299	5

Term of 7 Years

Interest Rate 11.00%					Interest Rate 11.25%					
Monthly Payment 1.712244%		Annual Constant 20.54692%			Monthly Payment 1.725417%		Annual Constant 20.70500%			

Year End	Principal Paid in Year	Interest Paid in Year	Total Interest Paid	Remaining Balance Year End	Curtail First Month	Principal Paid in Year	Interest Paid in Year	Total Interest Paid	Remaining Balance Year End	Curtail First Month	Year End
1	10.043263	10.503661	10.503661	89.956737	0.788350	9.958085	10.746915	10.746915	90.041915	0.864979	1
2	11.205457	9.341466	19.845127	78.751280	0.879577	11.137978	9.567022	20.313937	78.903937	0.967467	2
3	12.502140	8.044784	27.889911	66.249140	0.981361	12.457672	8.247328	28.561266	66.446265	1.082098	3
4	13.948873	6.598051	34.487962	52.300267	1.094923	13.933731	6.771269	35.332535	52.512535	1.210312	4
5	15.563020	4.983903	39.471865	36.737247	1.221626	15.584682	5.120318	40.452854	36.927853	1.353717	5
6	17.363955	3.182969	42.654834	19.373292	1.362991	17.431247	3.273753	43.726606	19.496605	1.514113	6
7	19.373292	1.173632	43.828466	0.000000	1.520715	19.496605	1.208395	44.935001	0.000000	1.693514	7

Term of 10 Years

Interest Rate 11.00%					Interest Rate 11.25%					
Monthly Payment 1.377500%		Annual Constant 16.53000%			Monthly Payment 1.391689%		Annual Constant 16.70027%			

Year End	Principal Paid in Year	Interest Paid in Year	Total Interest Paid	Remaining Balance Year End	Curtail First Month	Principal Paid in Year	Interest Paid in Year	Total Interest Paid	Remaining Balance Year End	Curtail First Month	Year End
1	5.817503	10.712498	10.712498	94.182497	0.456648	5.740274	10.960000	10.960000	94.259726	0.498612	1
2	6.490698	10.039304	20.751802	87.691799	0.509490	6.420415	10.279858	21.239858	87.839311	0.557690	2
3	7.241794	9.288208	30.040010	80.450006	0.568448	7.181144	9.519129	30.758988	80.658167	0.623769	3
4	8.079805	8.450196	38.490206	72.370200	0.634228	8.032009	8.668265	39.427253	72.626158	0.697676	4
5	9.014791	7.515210	46.005416	63.355409	0.707620	8.983689	7.716585	47.143837	63.642469	0.780341	5
6	10.057972	6.472029	52.477445	53.297437	0.789505	10.048130	6.652144	53.795981	53.594340	0.872801	6
7	11.221869	5.308132	57.785577	42.075568	0.880866	11.238692	5.461582	59.257563	42.355648	0.976215	7
8	12.520451	4.009551	61.795128	29.555117	0.982798	12.570319	4.129955	63.387518	29.785329	1.091883	8
9	13.969303	2.560699	64.355826	15.585814	1.096527	14.059725	2.640549	66.028067	15.725604	1.221256	9
10	15.585814	0.944187	65.300014	0.000000	1.223416	15.725604	0.974669	67.002736	0.000000	1.365958	10

Term of 15 Years

Interest Rate 11.00%					Interest Rate 11.25%					
Monthly Payment 1.136597%		Annual Constant 13.63916%			Monthly Payment 1.152345%		Annual Constant 13.82814%			

Year End	Principal Paid in Year	Interest Paid in Year	Total Interest Paid	Remaining Balance Year End	Curtail First Month	Principal Paid in Year	Interest Paid in Year	Total Interest Paid	Remaining Balance Year End	Curtail First Month	Year End
1	2.776372	10.862791	10.862791	97.223628	0.217933	2.715314	11.112822	11.112822	97.284686	0.235858	1
2	3.097650	10.541513	21.404304	94.125978	0.243151	3.037040	10.791095	21.903917	94.247646	0.263803	2
3	3.456107	10.183056	31.587361	90.669871	0.271289	3.396887	10.431249	32.335166	90.850760	0.295060	3
4	3.856043	9.783120	41.370481	86.813828	0.302682	3.799370	10.028765	42.363931	87.051390	0.330021	4
5	4.302260	9.336903	50.707384	82.511567	0.337708	4.249542	9.578594	51.942525	82.801848	0.369124	5
6	4.800113	8.839050	59.546434	77.711455	0.376787	4.753053	9.075083	61.017607	78.048796	0.412860	6
7	5.355576	8.283587	67.830021	72.355878	0.420388	5.316223	8.511913	69.529520	72.732573	0.461778	7
8	5.975317	7.663846	75.493867	66.380561	0.469035	5.946120	7.882015	77.411535	66.786453	0.516492	8
9	6.666774	6.972389	82.466256	59.713787	0.523311	6.650652	7.177483	84.589019	60.135801	0.577689	9
10	7.438245	6.200918	88.667173	52.275541	0.583868	7.438660	6.389475	90.978493	52.697141	0.646137	10
11	8.298991	5.340173	94.007346	43.976551	0.651433	8.320037	5.508098	96.486592	44.377104	0.722695	11
12	9.259340	4.379823	98.387169	34.717211	0.726816	9.305845	4.522291	101.008882	35.071259	0.808324	12
13	10.330820	3.308343	101.695512	24.386390	0.810922	10.408456	3.419679	104.428561	24.662803	0.904099	13
14	11.526291	2.112873	103.808385	12.860100	0.904761	11.641712	2.186423	106.614985	13.021091	1.011223	14
15	12.860100	0.779064	104.587448	0.000000	1.009459	13.021091	0.807044	107.422029	0.000000	1.131038	15

Monthly Factors for 11.000% Interest:				Monthly Factors for 11.250% Interest:		
Month	This Month	Year-to-date		Month	This Month	Year-to-date
1	1.009167	1.009167		1	1.009375	1.009375
2	1.018417	2.027584		2	1.018838	2.028213
3	1.027753	3.055337		3	1.028389	3.056602
4	1.037174	4.092511		4	1.038031	4.094633
5	1.046681	5.139192		5	1.047762	5.142395
6	1.056276	6.195468		6	1.057585	6.199980
7	1.065958	7.261427		7	1.067500	7.267480
8	1.075730	8.337156		8	1.077508	8.344988
9	1.085591	9.422747		9	1.087609	9.432597
10	1.095542	10.518289		10	1.097806	10.530402
11	1.105584	11.623873		11	1.108098	11.638500

Entries are percentages of the original loan amount.

Remaining Balance Tables

Term of 25 Years
Interest Rate 11.00%
Monthly Payment 0.980113%   Annual Constant 11.76136%

Interest Rate 11.25%
Monthly Payment 0.998240%   Annual Constant 11.97887%

Year End	Principal Paid in Year	Interest Paid in Year	Total Interest Paid	Remaining Balance Year End	Curtail First Month	Principal Paid in Year	Interest Paid in Year	Total Interest Paid	Remaining Balance Year End	Curtail First Month	Year End
1	0.800939	10.960417	10.960417	99.199061	0.062870	0.767657	11.211218	11.211218	99.232343	0.066680	1
2	0.893623	10.867734	21.828151	98.305437	0.070145	0.858613	11.120261	22.331479	98.373730	0.074581	2
3	0.997032	10.764325	32.592476	97.308405	0.078262	0.960347	11.018528	33.350007	97.413383	0.083418	3
4	1.112408	10.648949	43.241425	96.195997	0.087319	1.074135	10.904740	44.254747	96.339248	0.093301	4
5	1.241134	10.520223	53.761648	94.954863	0.097423	1.201404	10.777470	55.032217	95.137844	0.104356	5
6	1.384757	10.376600	64.138248	93.570107	0.108697	1.343754	10.635121	65.667338	93.794090	0.116721	6
7	1.544999	10.216358	74.354606	92.025107	0.121275	1.502970	10.475905	76.143242	92.291120	0.130551	7
8	1.723785	10.037572	84.392178	90.301323	0.135309	1.681051	10.297824	86.441066	90.610070	0.146019	8
9	1.923259	9.838098	94.230276	88.378063	0.150967	1.880232	10.098643	96.539709	88.729838	0.163321	9
10	2.145816	9.615541	103.845816	86.232247	0.168437	2.103013	9.875862	106.415572	86.626826	0.182672	10
11	2.394128	9.367229	113.213045	83.838119	0.187928	2.352190	9.626685	116.042256	84.274636	0.204316	11
12	2.671173	9.090183	122.303229	81.166946	0.209675	2.630891	9.347983	125.390239	81.643744	0.228525	12
13	2.980279	8.781078	131.084307	78.186667	0.233938	2.942615	9.036260	134.426499	78.701129	0.255601	13
14	3.325153	8.436204	139.520511	74.861514	0.261009	3.291273	8.687601	143.114100	75.409856	0.285887	14
15	3.709936	8.051421	147.571933	71.151579	0.291213	3.681243	8.297632	151.411732	71.728613	0.319760	15
16	4.139245	7.622112	155.194044	67.012334	0.324912	4.117419	7.861456	159.273188	67.611194	0.357647	16
17	4.618234	7.143123	162.337167	62.394100	0.362510	4.605275	7.373600	166.646788	63.005919	0.400023	17
18	5.152650	6.608706	168.945874	57.241449	0.404460	5.150935	6.827939	173.474727	57.854984	0.447421	18
19	5.748909	6.012448	174.958322	51.492540	0.451263	5.761248	6.217626	179.692353	52.093736	0.500434	19
20	6.414166	5.347191	180.305512	45.078374	0.503483	6.443875	5.534999	185.227352	45.649860	0.559728	20
21	7.156406	4.604951	184.910463	37.921968	0.561745	7.207384	4.771491	189.998843	38.442476	0.626048	21
22	7.984537	3.776820	188.687283	29.937431	0.626750	8.061358	3.917517	193.916360	30.381119	0.700226	22
23	8.908498	2.852859	191.540142	21.028932	0.699277	9.016515	2.962359	196.878719	21.364603	0.783193	23
24	9.939379	1.821977	193.362119	11.089553	0.780196	10.084845	1.894029	198.772748	11.279758	0.875990	24
25	11.089553	0.671804	194.033923	0.000000	0.870479	11.279758	0.699117	199.471865	0.000000	0.979783	25

Term of 30 Years
Interest Rate 11.00%
Monthly Payment 0.952323%   Annual Constant 11.42788%

Interest Rate 11.25%
Monthly Payment 0.971261%   Annual Constant 11.65514%

Year End	Principal Paid in Year	Interest Paid in Year	Total Interest Paid	Remaining Balance Year End	Curtail First Month	Principal Paid in Year	Interest Paid in Year	Total Interest Paid	Remaining Balance Year End	Curtail First Month	Year End
1	0.450126	10.977755	10.977755	99.549874	0.035333	0.426693	11.228443	11.228443	99.573307	0.037063	1
2	0.502214	10.925667	21.903421	99.047660	0.039422	0.477250	11.177886	22.406330	99.096056	0.041455	2
3	0.560330	10.867551	32.770972	98.487330	0.043983	0.533798	11.121339	33.527668	98.562258	0.046367	3
4	0.625170	10.802710	43.573683	97.862160	0.049073	0.597045	11.058091	44.585759	97.965213	0.051861	4
5	0.697514	10.730366	54.304049	97.164645	0.054752	0.667787	10.987350	55.573109	97.297426	0.058005	5
6	0.778230	10.649651	64.953700	96.386415	0.061088	0.746910	10.908226	66.481336	96.550516	0.064878	6
7	0.868286	10.559595	75.513295	95.518130	0.068156	0.835409	10.819728	77.301063	95.715107	0.072565	7
8	0.968763	10.459118	85.972413	94.549367	0.076043	0.934393	10.720744	88.021807	94.780704	0.081163	8
9	1.080867	10.347014	96.319427	93.468500	0.084843	1.045105	10.610031	98.631839	93.735609	0.090780	9
10	1.205944	10.221937	106.541364	92.262556	0.094661	1.168936	10.486201	109.118040	92.566673	0.101536	10
11	1.345494	10.082387	116.623750	90.917062	0.105615	1.307438	10.347699	119.465738	91.259235	0.113567	11
12	1.501193	9.926688	126.550438	89.415869	0.117837	1.462351	10.192786	129.658524	89.796884	0.127023	12
13	1.674909	9.752971	136.303410	87.740960	0.131473	1.635619	10.019518	139.678042	88.161265	0.142073	13
14	1.868728	9.559153	145.862562	85.872232	0.146687	1.829417	9.825720	149.503761	86.331848	0.158907	14
15	2.084975	9.342906	155.205468	83.787257	0.163661	2.046177	9.608960	159.112721	84.285671	0.177735	15
16	2.326246	9.101635	164.307103	81.461011	0.182600	2.288620	9.366516	168.479238	81.997051	0.198794	16
17	2.595436	8.832445	173.139548	78.865575	0.203732	2.559790	9.095347	177.574585	79.437262	0.222348	17
18	2.895777	8.532104	181.671651	75.969798	0.227305	2.863089	8.792048	186.366633	76.574173	0.248694	18
19	3.230873	8.197008	189.868659	72.738925	0.253609	3.202324	8.452812	194.819445	73.371849	0.278160	19
20	3.604746	7.823135	197.691794	69.134179	0.282956	3.581755	8.073382	202.892827	69.790094	0.311118	20
21	4.021883	7.405998	205.097792	65.112296	0.315700	4.006142	7.648994	210.541821	65.783952	0.347982	21
22	4.487290	6.940590	212.038382	60.625006	0.352232	4.480814	7.174323	217.716144	61.303138	0.389213	22
23	5.006555	6.421326	218.459708	55.618451	0.392992	5.011727	6.643409	224.359553	56.291410	0.435329	23
24	5.585907	5.841974	224.301682	50.032544	0.438468	5.605546	6.049590	230.409143	50.685864	0.486909	24
25	6.232302	5.195579	229.497261	43.800242	0.489207	6.269725	5.385412	235.794555	44.416139	0.544601	25
26	6.953497	4.474384	233.971645	36.846746	0.545818	7.012599	4.642537	240.437093	37.403540	0.609129	26
27	7.758147	3.669734	237.641379	29.088598	0.608979	7.843494	3.811643	244.248736	29.560046	0.681302	27
28	8.655911	2.771970	240.413348	20.432688	0.679450	8.772837	2.882299	247.131035	20.787209	0.762026	28
29	9.657563	1.770318	242.183666	10.775125	0.758075	9.812295	1.842842	248.973877	10.974914	0.852316	29
30	10.775125	0.652756	242.836422	0.000000	0.845798	10.974914	0.680223	249.654099	0.000000	0.953303	30

Monthly Factors for 11.000% Interest:			Monthly Factors for 11.250% Interest:		
Month	This Month	Year-to-date	Month	This Month	Year-to-date
1	1.009167	1.009167	1	1.009375	1.009375
2	1.018417	2.027584	2	1.018838	2.028213
3	1.027753	3.055337	3	1.028389	3.056602
4	1.037174	4.092511	4	1.038031	4.094633
5	1.046681	5.139192	5	1.047762	5.142395
6	1.056276	6.195468	6	1.057585	6.199980
7	1.065958	7.261427	7	1.067500	7.267480
8	1.075730	8.337156	8	1.077508	8.344988
9	1.085591	9.422747	9	1.087609	9.432597
10	1.095542	10.518289	10	1.097806	10.530402
11	1.105584	11.623873	11	1.108098	11.638500

Entries are percentages of the original loan amount.

Remaining Balance Tables

Term of 3 Years

	Interest Rate 11.50%					Interest Rate 11.75%					
	Monthly Payment 3.297601%		Annual Constant 39.57121%			Monthly Payment 3.309503%		Annual Constant 39.71404%			
Year End	Principal Paid in Year	Interest Paid in Year	Total Interest Paid	Remaining Balance Year End	Curtail First Month	Principal Paid in Year	Interest Paid in Year	Total Interest Paid	Remaining Balance Year End	Curtail First Month	Year End
1	29.599094	9.972114	9.972114	70.400906	2.317062	29.520271	10.193766	10.193766	70.479729	2.568836	1
2	33.188260	6.382948	16.355062	37.212646	2.598028	33.181937	6.532101	16.725867	37.297792	2.887472	2
3	37.212646	2.358562	18.713623	0.000000	2.913063	37.297792	2.416246	19.142113	0.000000	3.245632	3

Term of 4 Years

	Interest Rate 11.50%					Interest Rate 11.75%					
	Monthly Payment 2.608901%		Annual Constant 31.30681%			Monthly Payment 2.621125%		Annual Constant 31.45351%			
1	20.884874	10.421936	10.421936	79.115126	1.634900	20.800030	10.653475	10.653475	79.199970	1.810006	1
2	23.417360	7.889450	18.311387	55.697765	1.833147	23.380046	8.073460	18.726935	55.819924	2.034518	2
3	26.256934	5.049877	23.361264	29.440832	2.055433	26.280084	5.173422	23.900357	29.539840	2.286877	3
4	29.440832	1.865979	25.227243	0.000000	2.304673	29.539840	1.913666	25.814023	0.000000	2.570539	4

Term of 5 Years

	Interest Rate 11.50%					Interest Rate 11.75%					
	Monthly Payment 2.199261%		Annual Constant 26.39113%			Monthly Payment 2.211832%		Annual Constant 26.54199%			
1	15.701637	10.689492	10.689492	84.298363	1.229148	15.615177	10.926808	10.926808	84.384823	1.358823	1
2	17.605607	8.785522	19.475013	66.692756	1.378194	17.552069	8.989916	19.916724	66.832754	1.527371	2
3	19.740451	6.650678	26.125691	46.952304	1.545313	19.729210	6.812775	26.729499	47.103544	1.716824	3
4	22.134165	4.256964	30.382655	24.818139	1.732696	22.176402	4.365583	31.095082	24.927141	1.929777	4
5	24.818139	1.572990	31.955644	0.000000	1.942802	24.927141	1.614844	32.709925	0.000000	2.169145	5

Term of 7 Years

	Interest Rate 11.50%					Interest Rate 11.75%					
	Monthly Payment 1.738646%		Annual Constant 20.86375%			Monthly Payment 1.751932%		Annual Constant 21.02318%			
1	9.873412	10.990341	10.990341	90.126588	0.772906	9.789244	11.233936	11.233936	90.210756	0.851854	1
2	11.070655	9.793098	20.783438	79.055932	0.866628	11.003492	10.019688	21.253624	79.207264	0.957517	2
3	12.413076	8.450677	29.234116	66.642857	0.971714	12.368355	8.654825	29.908449	66.838909	1.076287	3
4	13.918277	6.945476	36.179592	52.724580	1.089544	13.902513	7.120667	37.029116	52.936395	1.209788	4
5	15.605998	5.257755	41.437347	37.118582	1.221661	15.626968	5.396213	42.425328	37.309428	1.359849	5
6	17.498371	3.365382	44.802729	19.620211	1.369799	17.565321	3.457859	45.883187	19.744107	1.528524	6
7	19.620211	1.243542	46.046271	0.000000	1.535900	19.744107	1.279073	47.162260	0.000000	1.718120	7

Term of 10 Years

	Interest Rate 11.50%					Interest Rate 11.75%					
	Monthly Payment 1.405954%		Annual Constant 16.87145%			Monthly Payment 1.420295%		Annual Constant 17.04354%			
1	5.663816	11.207637	11.207637	94.336184	0.443372	5.588127	11.455408	11.455408	94.411873	0.486275	1
2	6.350606	10.520847	21.728484	87.985578	0.497135	6.281273	10.762262	22.217671	88.130600	0.546593	2
3	7.120677	9.750777	31.479261	80.864901	0.557417	7.060396	9.983139	32.200810	81.070205	0.614391	3
4	7.984125	8.887328	40.366590	72.880776	0.625009	7.936160	9.107375	41.308185	73.134044	0.690600	4
5	8.952275	7.919179	48.285768	63.928502	0.700798	8.920554	8.122981	49.431166	64.213491	0.776261	5
6	10.037821	6.833632	55.119400	53.890680	0.785776	10.027051	7.016485	56.447651	54.186440	0.872548	6
7	11.255001	5.616452	60.735852	42.635679	0.881059	11.270796	5.772739	62.220390	42.915644	0.980778	7
8	12.619775	4.251679	64.987531	30.015905	0.987895	12.668815	4.374721	66.595110	30.246830	1.102433	8
9	14.150040	2.721413	67.708944	15.865865	1.107687	14.240242	2.803293	69.398404	16.006588	1.239177	9
10	15.865865	1.005589	68.714533	0.000000	1.242004	16.006588	1.036948	70.435351	0.000000	1.392884	10

Term of 15 Years

	Interest Rate 11.50%					Interest Rate 11.75%					
	Monthly Payment 1.168190%		Annual Constant 14.01828%			Monthly Payment 1.184131%		Annual Constant 14.20958%			
1	2.655345	11.362933	11.362933	97.344655	0.207864	2.596455	11.613122	11.613122	97.403545	0.225942	1
2	2.977330	11.040947	22.403880	94.367325	0.233070	2.918517	11.291060	22.904181	94.485029	0.253968	2
3	3.338359	10.679918	33.083799	91.028966	0.261332	3.280526	10.929050	33.833231	91.204502	0.285469	3
4	3.743167	10.275111	43.358910	87.285799	0.293021	3.687440	10.522137	44.355368	87.517062	0.320879	4
5	4.197060	9.821217	53.180127	83.088739	0.328552	4.144826	10.064750	54.420118	83.372236	0.360680	5
6	4.705993	9.312285	62.492412	78.382746	0.368392	4.658946	9.550630	63.970748	78.713290	0.405419	6
7	5.276639	8.741639	71.234051	73.106107	0.413063	5.236838	8.972739	72.943487	73.476452	0.455706	7
8	5.916480	8.101797	79.335848	67.189627	0.463151	5.886410	8.323167	81.266653	67.590043	0.512232	8
9	6.633909	7.384369	86.720217	60.555718	0.519312	6.616554	7.593022	88.859675	60.973488	0.575769	9
10	7.438332	6.579946	93.300163	53.117386	0.582284	7.437265	6.772311	95.631987	53.536223	0.647186	10
11	8.340299	5.677979	98.978141	44.777087	0.652891	8.359776	5.849800	101.481787	45.176447	0.727463	11
12	9.351638	4.666639	103.644781	35.425448	0.732060	9.396715	4.812862	106.294648	35.779732	0.817697	12
13	10.485612	3.532666	107.177447	24.939837	0.820830	10.562274	3.647302	109.941951	25.217458	0.919123	13
14	11.757090	2.261188	109.438635	13.182747	0.920363	11.872408	2.337168	112.279119	13.345050	1.033130	14
15	13.182747	0.835531	110.274166	0.000000	1.031965	13.345050	0.864526	113.143645	0.000000	1.161278	15

Monthly Factors for 11.500% Interest:			Monthly Factors for 11.750% Interest:		
Month	This Month	Year-to-date	Month	This Month	Year-to-date
1	1.009583	1.009583	1	1.009792	1.009792
2	1.019259	2.028842	2	1.019679	2.029471
3	1.029026	3.057868	3	1.029664	3.059134
4	1.038888	4.096756	4	1.039746	4.098880
5	1.048844	5.145600	5	1.049927	5.148807
6	1.058895	6.204495	6	1.060207	6.209014
7	1.069043	7.273538	7	1.070588	7.279602
8	1.079288	8.352827	8	1.081071	8.360673
9	1.089631	9.442458	9	1.091657	9.452330
10	1.100074	10.542531	10	1.102346	10.554675
11	1.110616	11.653147	11	1.113140	11.667815

Entries are percentages of the original loan amount.

Remaining Balance Tables

Term of 25 Years
Interest Rate 11.50%
Monthly Payment 1.016469%   Annual Constant 12.19763%

Interest Rate 11.75%
Monthly Payment 1.034798%   Annual Constant 12.41758%

Year End	Principal Paid in Year	Interest Paid in Year	Total Interest Paid	Remaining Balance Year End	Curtail First Month	Principal Paid in Year	Interest Paid in Year	Total Interest Paid	Remaining Balance Year End	Curtail First Month	Year End
1	0.735599	11.462029	11.462029	99.264401	0.057584	0.704730	11.712848	11.712848	99.295270	0.061325	1
2	0.824797	11.372831	22.834860	98.439604	0.064566	0.792144	11.625434	23.338283	98.503126	0.068932	2
3	0.924811	11.272816	34.107676	97.514793	0.072396	0.890401	11.527178	34.865461	97.612726	0.077482	3
4	1.036953	11.160674	45.268350	96.477840	0.081174	1.000845	11.416733	46.282194	96.611881	0.087093	4
5	1.162693	11.034934	56.303284	95.315146	0.091017	1.124989	11.292595	57.574783	95.486892	0.097896	5
6	1.303681	10.893947	67.197231	94.011466	0.102054	1.264531	11.153047	68.727830	94.222360	0.110039	6
7	1.461764	10.735863	77.933094	92.549701	0.114429	1.421383	10.996196	79.724026	92.800978	0.123688	7
8	1.639017	10.558611	88.491705	90.910684	0.128305	1.597690	10.819889	90.543915	91.203288	0.139030	8
9	1.837763	10.359865	98.851569	89.072921	0.143863	1.795865	10.621713	101.165628	89.407423	0.156275	9
10	2.060609	10.137019	108.988588	87.012312	0.161308	2.018623	10.398955	111.564583	87.388800	0.175659	10
11	2.310477	9.887151	118.875739	84.701835	0.180868	2.269011	10.148568	121.713151	85.119790	0.197448	11
12	2.590644	9.606984	128.482722	82.111191	0.202800	2.550457	9.867122	131.580272	82.569333	0.221939	12
13	2.904784	9.292844	137.775566	79.206408	0.227391	2.866813	9.550766	141.131038	79.702520	0.249468	13
14	3.257016	8.940612	146.716178	75.949392	0.254964	3.222409	9.195169	150.326207	76.480111	0.280412	14
15	3.651959	8.545668	155.261846	72.297433	0.285881	3.622114	8.795464	159.121671	72.857997	0.315194	15
16	4.094793	8.102834	163.364681	68.202639	0.320547	4.071397	8.346181	167.467852	68.786600	0.354291	16
17	4.591325	7.606302	170.970983	63.611314	0.359416	4.576409	7.841169	175.309021	64.210190	0.398236	17
18	5.148066	7.049061	178.020544	58.463248	0.402998	5.144063	7.273515	182.582536	59.066127	0.447633	18
19	5.772317	6.425310	184.445854	52.690930	0.451866	5.782127	6.635451	189.217987	53.284000	0.503157	19
20	6.472265	5.725363	190.171217	46.218666	0.506659	6.499337	5.918241	195.136229	46.784663	0.565568	20
21	7.257087	4.940540	195.111758	38.961578	0.568096	7.305508	5.112070	200.248299	39.479155	0.635721	21
22	8.137077	4.060551	199.172308	30.824502	0.636983	8.211676	4.205902	204.454201	31.267479	0.714575	22
23	9.123773	3.073854	202.246163	21.700728	0.714223	9.230245	3.187334	207.641535	22.037234	0.803210	23
24	10.230116	1.967512	204.213675	11.470613	0.800829	10.375155	2.042423	209.683958	11.662079	0.902840	24
25	11.470613	0.727015	204.940689	0.000000	0.897937	11.662079	0.755499	210.439457	0.000000	1.014827	25

Term of 30 Years
Interest Rate 11.50%
Monthly Payment 0.990291%   Annual Constant 11.88350%

Interest Rate 11.75%
Monthly Payment 1.009410%   Annual Constant 12.11292%

	Principal Paid in Year	Interest Paid in Year	Total Interest Paid	Remaining Balance Year End	Curtail First Month	Principal Paid in Year	Interest Paid in Year	Total Interest Paid	Remaining Balance Year End	Curtail First Month	
1	0.404371	11.479127	11.479127	99.595629	0.031655	0.383114	11.729803	11.729803	99.616886	0.033338	1
2	0.453404	11.430093	22.909220	99.142225	0.035493	0.430655	11.682282	23.412085	99.186252	0.037474	2
3	0.508384	11.375113	34.284333	98.633841	0.039797	0.484050	11.628867	35.040952	98.702202	0.042122	3
4	0.570030	11.313467	45.597800	98.063811	0.044623	0.544091	11.568826	46.609778	98.158110	0.047346	4
5	0.639151	11.244346	56.842146	97.424660	0.050034	0.611580	11.501337	58.111115	97.546531	0.053219	5
6	0.716655	11.166843	68.008989	96.708005	0.056101	0.687440	11.425477	69.536592	96.859091	0.059821	6
7	0.803556	11.079942	79.088930	95.904450	0.062904	0.772709	11.340208	80.876800	96.086382	0.067241	7
8	0.900994	10.982503	90.071433	95.003456	0.070531	0.868555	11.244362	92.121162	95.217827	0.075581	8
9	1.010248	10.873249	100.944682	93.993208	0.079084	0.976290	11.136627	103.257789	94.241538	0.084956	9
10	1.132750	10.750747	111.695429	92.860457	0.088673	1.097388	11.015529	114.273318	93.144150	0.095494	10
11	1.270107	10.613391	122.308820	91.590351	0.099426	1.233506	10.879410	125.152729	91.910644	0.107339	11
12	1.424119	10.459378	132.768198	90.166232	0.111482	1.386509	10.726407	135.879136	90.524134	0.120653	12
13	1.596807	10.286661	143.054889	88.569425	0.125000	1.558491	10.554426	146.433562	88.965644	0.135619	13
14	1.790434	10.093063	153.147951	86.778991	0.140158	1.751804	10.361110	156.794675	87.213839	0.152441	14
15	2.007541	9.875956	163.023907	84.771449	0.157153	1.969096	10.143820	166.938495	85.244743	0.171350	15
16	2.250974	9.632523	172.656430	82.520475	0.176210	2.213341	9.899576	176.838071	83.031402	0.192604	16
17	2.523926	9.359571	182.016001	79.996549	0.197577	2.487882	9.625035	186.463106	80.543520	0.216494	17
18	2.829976	9.053522	191.069523	77.166573	0.221535	2.796476	9.316440	195.779546	77.747043	0.243348	18
19	3.173137	8.710361	199.779884	73.993437	0.248398	3.143349	8.969568	204.749114	74.603695	0.273532	19
20	3.557909	8.325588	208.105472	70.435528	0.278519	3.533246	8.579670	213.328785	71.070448	0.307461	20
21	3.989339	7.894159	215.999631	66.446189	0.312291	3.971507	8.141410	221.470195	67.098941	0.345598	21
22	4.473083	7.410414	223.410045	61.973106	0.350160	4.464129	7.648788	229.118983	62.634813	0.388466	22
23	5.015486	6.868011	230.278056	56.957620	0.392620	5.017855	7.095062	236.214045	57.616958	0.436651	23
24	5.623661	6.259837	236.537892	51.333960	0.440229	5.640265	6.472652	242.686697	51.976693	0.490812	24
25	6.305582	5.577915	242.115808	45.028378	0.493611	6.339878	5.773039	248.459736	45.636816	0.551692	25
26	7.070193	4.813305	246.929112	37.958185	0.553465	7.126270	4.986647	253.446383	38.510546	0.620124	26
27	7.927519	3.955978	250.885090	30.030666	0.620578	8.010205	4.102712	257.549095	30.500341	0.697043	27
28	8.888805	2.994692	253.879782	21.141861	0.695829	9.003783	3.109133	260.658228	21.496557	0.783504	28
29	9.966656	1.916842	255.796624	11.175205	0.780205	10.120604	1.992313	262.650541	11.375954	0.880689	29
30	11.175205	0.708292	256.504916	0.000000	0.874812	11.375954	0.736963	263.387504	0.000000	0.989929	30

Month	Monthly Factors for 11.500% Interest: This Month	Year-to-date		Month	Monthly Factors for 11.750% Interest: This Month	Year-to-date
1	1.009583	1.009583		1	1.009792	1.009792
2	1.019259	2.028842		2	1.019679	2.029471
3	1.029026	3.057868		3	1.029664	3.059134
4	1.038888	4.096756		4	1.039746	4.098880
5	1.048844	5.145600		5	1.049927	5.148807
6	1.058895	6.204495		6	1.060207	6.209014
7	1.069043	7.273538		7	1.070588	7.279602
8	1.079288	8.352827		8	1.081071	8.360673
9	1.089631	9.442458		9	1.091657	9.452330
10	1.100074	10.542531		10	1.102346	10.554675
11	1.110616	11.653147		11	1.113140	11.667815

Entries are percentages of the original loan amount.

Remaining Balance Tables

Term of 3 Years
Interest Rate 12.00%
Monthly Payment 3.321431%   Annual Constant 39.85717%

Interest Rate 12.25%
Monthly Payment 3.333384%   Annual Constant 40.00061%

Year End	Principal Paid in Year	Interest Paid in Year	Total Interest Paid	Remaining Balance Year End	Curtail First Month	Principal Paid in Year	Interest Paid in Year	Total Interest Paid	Remaining Balance Year End	Curtail First Month	Year End
1	29.441555	10.415616	10.415616	70.558445	2.298447	29.362947	10.637663	10.637663	70.637053	2.559769	1
2	33.175482	6.681690	17.097307	37.382963	2.589947	33.168894	6.831715	17.469378	37.468159	2.891559	2
3	37.382963	2.474209	19.571515	0.000000	2.918417	37.468159	2.532450	20.001829	0.000000	3.266356	3

Term of 4 Years
Interest Rate 12.00%
Monthly Payment 2.633384%   Annual Constant 31.60060%

Interest Rate 12.25%
Monthly Payment 2.645675%   Annual Constant 31.74810%

1	20.715392	10.885211	10.885211	79.284608	1.617211	20.630959	11.117142	11.117142	79.369041	1.798542	1
2	23.342622	8.257981	19.143191	55.941986	1.822314	23.305089	8.443011	19.560153	56.063952	2.031664	2
3	26.303051	5.297552	24.440743	29.638936	2.053429	26.325833	5.422267	24.982420	29.738119	2.295003	3
4	29.638936	1.961667	26.402410	0.000000	2.313856	29.738119	2.009982	26.992401	0.000000	2.592475	4

Term of 5 Years
Interest Rate 12.00%
Monthly Payment 2.224445%   Annual Constant 26.69334%

Interest Rate 12.25%
Monthly Payment 2.237099%   Annual Constant 26.84518%

1	15.529024	11.164313	11.164313	84.470976	1.212322	15.443179	11.402006	11.402006	84.556821	1.346287	1
2	17.498493	9.194844	20.359157	66.972482	1.366074	17.444883	9.400302	20.802307	67.111939	1.520790	2
3	19.717740	6.975597	27.334753	47.254742	1.539327	19.706043	7.139142	27.941449	47.405896	1.717910	3
4	22.218443	4.474894	31.809647	25.036298	1.734552	22.260288	4.584896	32.526346	25.145608	1.940582	4
5	25.036298	1.657039	33.466686	0.000000	1.954536	25.145608	1.699577	34.225922	0.000000	2.192115	5

Term of 7 Years
Interest Rate 12.00%
Monthly Payment 1.765273%   Annual Constant 21.18328%

Interest Rate 12.25%
Monthly Payment 1.778671%   Annual Constant 21.34405%

1	9.705581	11.477699	11.477699	90.294419	0.757696	9.622422	11.721627	11.721627	90.377578	0.838852	1
2	10.936491	10.246788	21.724487	79.357928	0.853791	10.869655	10.474394	22.196021	79.507924	0.947582	2
3	12.323512	8.859767	30.584254	67.034416	0.962073	12.278551	9.065498	31.261519	67.229373	1.070405	3
4	13.886442	7.296837	37.881092	53.147974	1.084088	13.870064	7.473985	38.735504	53.359309	1.209148	4
5	15.647590	5.535689	43.416781	37.500384	1.221578	15.667865	5.676183	44.411687	37.691443	1.365875	5
6	17.632096	3.551183	46.967964	19.868288	1.376504	17.698693	3.645356	48.057043	19.992751	1.542916	6
7	19.868288	1.314992	48.282955	0.000000	1.551080	19.992751	1.351298	49.408341	0.000000	1.742905	7

Term of 10 Years
Interest Rate 12.00%
Monthly Payment 1.434709%   Annual Constant 17.21651%

Interest Rate 12.25%
Monthly Payment 1.449199%   Annual Constant 17.39038%

1	5.513204	11.703309	11.703309	94.486796	0.430405	5.439045	11.951339	11.951339	94.560955	0.474159	1
2	6.212417	11.004097	22.707407	88.274379	0.484992	6.144040	11.246344	23.197683	88.416915	0.535618	2
3	7.000307	10.216207	32.923614	81.274072	0.546501	6.940414	10.449970	33.647653	81.476501	0.605043	3
4	7.888121	9.328393	42.252007	73.385952	0.615811	7.840012	9.550372	43.198024	73.636488	0.683467	4
5	8.888532	8.327982	50.579989	64.497420	0.693911	8.856214	8.534170	51.732194	64.780274	0.772057	5
6	10.015820	7.200694	57.780683	54.481600	0.781916	10.004133	7.386251	59.118444	54.776140	0.872129	6
7	11.286077	5.930437	63.711120	43.195523	0.881083	11.300843	6.089541	65.207986	43.475298	0.985172	7
8	12.717434	4.499080	68.210200	30.478089	0.992826	12.765628	4.624756	69.832741	30.709669	1.112867	8
9	14.330323	2.886191	71.096391	16.147766	1.118741	14.420276	2.970108	72.802850	16.289394	1.257114	9
10	16.147766	1.068747	72.165138	0.000000	1.260626	16.289394	1.100990	73.903840	0.000000	1.420058	10

Term of 15 Years
Interest Rate 12.00%
Monthly Payment 1.200168%   Annual Constant 14.40202%

Interest Rate 12.25%
Monthly Payment 1.216299%   Annual Constant 14.59558%

1	2.538632	11.863385	11.863385	97.461368	0.198186	2.481865	12.113719	12.113719	97.518135	0.216361	1
2	2.860594	11.541423	23.404807	94.600774	0.223321	2.803558	11.792026	23.905746	94.714577	0.244405	2
3	3.223389	11.178628	34.583435	91.377385	0.251644	3.166948	11.428637	35.334382	91.547629	0.276084	3
4	3.632195	10.769821	45.353256	87.745189	0.283559	3.577439	11.018145	46.352528	87.970190	0.311870	4
5	4.092849	10.309168	55.662424	83.652340	0.319521	4.041138	10.554447	56.906975	83.929052	0.352294	5
6	4.611924	9.790092	65.452516	79.040416	0.360044	4.564939	10.030645	66.937620	79.364113	0.397957	6
7	5.196832	9.205185	74.657701	73.843584	0.405707	5.156635	9.438950	76.376570	74.207479	0.449539	7
8	5.855920	8.546096	83.203798	67.987664	0.457161	5.825024	8.770561	85.147130	68.382455	0.507807	8
9	6.598598	7.803419	91.007217	61.389066	0.515140	6.580048	8.015536	93.162667	61.802407	0.573628	9
10	7.435465	6.966552	97.973769	53.953601	0.580473	7.432937	7.162648	100.325315	54.369470	0.647980	10
11	8.378468	6.023549	103.997318	45.575133	0.654091	8.396374	6.199210	106.524525	45.973095	0.731969	11
12	9.441067	4.960949	108.958267	36.134066	0.737046	9.484690	5.110894	111.635419	36.488405	0.826845	12
13	10.638431	3.763586	112.721853	25.495605	0.830522	10.714071	3.881514	115.516922	25.774334	0.934019	13
14	11.987650	2.414366	115.136219	13.507985	0.935853	12.102801	2.492784	118.009716	13.671534	1.055084	14
15	13.507985	0.894032	116.030251	0.000000	1.054543	13.671534	0.924051	118.933767	0.000000	1.191841	15

Monthly Factors for 12.000% Interest:			Monthly Factors for 12.250% Interest:		
Month	This Month	Year-to-date	Month	This Month	Year-to-date
1	1.010000	1.010000	1	1.010208	1.010208
2	1.020100	2.030100	2	1.020521	2.030729
3	1.030301	3.060401	3	1.030939	3.061668
4	1.040604	4.101005	4	1.041463	4.103131
5	1.051010	5.152015	5	1.052094	5.155225
6	1.061520	6.213535	6	1.062835	6.218060
7	1.072135	7.285671	7	1.073684	7.291744
8	1.082857	8.368527	8	1.084645	8.376389
9	1.093685	9.462213	9	1.095717	9.472106
10	1.104622	10.566835	10	1.106903	10.579009
11	1.115668	11.682503	11	1.118202	11.697212

Entries are percentages of the original loan amount.

Remaining Balance Tables

Term of 25 Years
Interest Rate 12.00%
Monthly Payment 1.053224%   Annual Constant 12.63869%

Interest Rate 12.25%
Monthly Payment 1.071744%   Annual Constant 12.86093%

Year End	Principal Paid in Year	Interest Paid in Year	Total Interest Paid	Remaining Balance Year End	Curtail First Month	Principal Paid in Year	Interest Paid in Year	Total Interest Paid	Remaining Balance Year End	Curtail First Month	Year End
1	0.675015	11.963674	11.963674	99.324985	0.052697	0.646421	12.214505	12.214505	99.353579	0.056353	1
2	0.760624	11.878066	23.841740	98.564360	0.059380	0.730208	12.130717	24.345222	98.623371	0.063657	2
3	0.857090	11.781599	35.623339	97.707270	0.066911	0.824856	12.036070	36.381292	97.798515	0.071908	3
4	0.965791	11.672899	47.296238	96.741479	0.075397	0.931771	11.929154	48.310446	96.866744	0.081229	4
5	1.088277	11.550412	58.846650	95.653202	0.084960	1.052545	11.808380	60.118826	95.814199	0.091758	5
6	1.226298	11.412392	70.259042	94.426904	0.095735	1.188973	11.671952	71.790778	94.625225	0.103651	6
7	1.381823	11.256866	81.515908	93.045080	0.107876	1.343085	11.517841	83.308618	93.282140	0.117086	7
8	1.557073	11.081616	92.597525	91.488007	0.121558	1.517172	11.343753	94.652372	91.764968	0.132262	8
9	1.754549	10.884141	103.481665	89.733458	0.136974	1.713824	11.147102	105.799473	90.051145	0.149406	9
10	1.977070	10.661620	114.143285	87.756388	0.154346	1.935965	10.924960	116.724434	88.115179	0.168771	10
11	2.227812	10.410878	124.554163	85.528576	0.173921	2.186900	10.674025	127.398459	85.928279	0.190647	11
12	2.510354	10.128336	134.682499	83.018222	0.195979	2.470360	10.390565	137.789024	83.457919	0.215358	12
13	2.828730	9.809960	144.492459	80.189492	0.220834	2.790562	10.070364	147.859388	80.667357	0.243272	13
14	3.187484	9.451206	153.943665	77.002009	0.248841	3.152267	9.708658	157.568046	77.515090	0.274805	14
15	3.591736	9.046953	162.990618	73.410273	0.280400	3.560856	9.300070	166.868116	73.954235	0.310424	15
16	4.047258	8.591431	171.582049	69.363014	0.315962	4.022404	8.838521	175.706637	69.931831	0.350660	16
17	4.560552	8.078138	179.660187	64.802462	0.356034	4.543778	8.317148	184.023785	65.388053	0.396112	17
18	5.138944	7.499746	187.159933	59.663518	0.401188	5.132730	7.728195	191.751980	60.255323	0.447455	18
19	5.790691	6.847999	194.007932	53.872827	0.452068	5.798021	7.062904	198.814884	54.457301	0.505453	19
20	6.525095	6.113594	200.121526	47.347732	0.509402	6.549545	6.311380	205.126264	47.907756	0.570969	20
21	7.352641	5.286049	205.407575	39.995091	0.574007	7.398480	5.462445	210.588709	40.509276	0.644976	21
22	8.285140	4.353550	209.761125	31.709951	0.646805	8.357452	4.503474	215.092183	32.151824	0.728576	22
23	9.335903	3.302787	213.063912	22.374048	0.728836	9.440723	3.420203	218.512386	22.711101	0.823012	23
24	10.519929	2.118761	215.182672	11.854119	0.821271	10.664404	2.196521	220.708907	12.046696	0.929689	24
25	11.854119	0.784570	215.967243	0.000000	0.925429	12.046696	0.814229	221.523136	0.000000	1.050193	25

Term of 30 Years
Interest Rate 12.00%
Monthly Payment 1.028613%   Annual Constant 12.34335%

Interest Rate 12.25%
Monthly Payment 1.047896%   Annual Constant 12.57476%

Year End	Principal Paid in Year	Interest Paid in Year	Total Interest Paid	Remaining Balance Year End	Curtail First Month	Principal Paid in Year	Interest Paid in Year	Total Interest Paid	Remaining Balance Year End	Curtail First Month	Year End
1	0.362879	11.980472	11.980472	99.637121	0.028329	0.343626	12.231131	12.231131	99.656374	0.029956	1
2	0.408902	11.934450	23.914921	99.228219	0.031922	0.388166	12.186591	24.417723	99.268208	0.033839	2
3	0.460760	11.882591	35.797512	98.767459	0.035971	0.438479	12.136278	36.554001	98.829730	0.038225	3
4	0.519196	11.824155	47.621667	98.248262	0.040533	0.495313	12.079444	48.633445	98.334416	0.043180	4
5	0.585044	11.758308	59.379974	97.663219	0.045673	0.559514	12.015243	60.648688	97.774902	0.048777	5
6	0.659242	11.684109	71.064084	97.003977	0.051466	0.632037	11.942720	72.591408	97.142864	0.055099	6
7	0.742850	11.600501	82.664585	96.261127	0.057993	0.713960	11.860797	84.452205	96.428904	0.062241	7
8	0.837062	11.506289	94.170874	95.424065	0.065348	0.806502	11.768255	96.220460	95.622402	0.070308	8
9	0.943222	11.400129	105.571003	94.480842	0.073636	0.911039	11.663719	107.884178	94.711364	0.079421	9
10	1.062847	11.280504	116.851507	93.417996	0.082974	1.029125	11.545632	119.429811	93.682239	0.089716	10
11	1.197642	11.145709	127.997216	92.220353	0.093498	1.162517	11.412240	130.842050	92.519721	0.101345	11
12	1.349533	10.993818	138.991034	90.870820	0.105356	1.313200	11.261557	142.103608	91.206521	0.114481	12
13	1.520688	10.822663	149.813697	89.350132	0.118717	1.483413	11.091344	153.194951	89.723108	0.129319	13
14	1.713549	10.629802	160.443500	87.636583	0.133774	1.675690	10.899068	164.094019	88.047418	0.146081	14
15	1.930870	10.412481	170.855981	85.705713	0.150739	1.892888	10.681869	174.775888	86.154530	0.165016	15
16	2.175753	10.167598	181.023579	83.529960	0.169857	2.138239	10.436518	185.212406	84.016291	0.186405	16
17	2.451693	9.891659	190.915238	81.078268	0.191399	2.415392	10.159365	195.371771	81.600898	0.210566	17
18	2.762629	9.580723	200.495960	78.315639	0.215673	2.728469	9.846288	205.218059	78.872429	0.237859	18
19	3.112999	9.230352	209.726312	75.202640	0.243026	3.082126	9.492631	214.710690	75.790303	0.268690	19
20	3.507805	8.835546	218.561858	71.694835	0.273848	3.481623	9.093134	223.803824	72.308680	0.303517	20
21	3.952683	8.390668	226.952527	67.742152	0.308578	3.932902	8.641855	232.445680	68.375779	0.342858	21
22	4.453982	7.889369	234.841896	63.288170	0.347714	4.442674	8.132083	240.577763	63.933104	0.387298	22
23	5.018858	7.324493	242.166389	58.269312	0.391813	5.018522	7.556235	248.133999	58.914582	0.437499	23
24	5.655375	6.687976	248.854365	52.613937	0.441504	5.669010	6.905748	255.039746	53.245573	0.494206	24
25	6.372618	5.970733	254.825098	46.241319	0.497498	6.403812	6.170946	261.210691	46.841761	0.558264	25
26	7.180826	5.162525	259.987623	39.060493	0.560593	7.233857	5.340900	266.551591	39.607904	0.630625	26
27	8.091534	4.251817	264.239440	30.968959	0.631691	8.171490	4.403267	270.954858	31.436414	0.712365	27
28	9.117743	3.225608	267.465048	21.851216	0.711805	9.230657	3.344100	274.298958	22.205757	0.804700	28
29	10.274101	2.069250	269.534298	11.577114	0.802080	10.427111	2.147646	276.446604	11.778646	0.909003	29
30	11.577114	0.766237	270.300535	0.000000	0.903803	11.778646	0.796112	277.242716	0.000000	1.026825	30

Month	Monthly Factors for 12.000% Interest: This Month	Year-to-date		Month	Monthly Factors for 12.250% Interest: This Month	Year-to-date
1	1.010000	1.010000		1	1.010208	1.010208
2	1.020100	2.030100		2	1.020521	2.030729
3	1.030301	3.060401		3	1.030939	3.061668
4	1.040604	4.101005		4	1.041463	4.103131
5	1.051010	5.152015		5	1.052094	5.155225
6	1.061520	6.213535		6	1.062835	6.218060
7	1.072135	7.285671		7	1.073684	7.291744
8	1.082857	8.368527		8	1.084645	8.376389
9	1.093685	9.462213		9	1.095717	9.472106
10	1.104622	10.566835		10	1.106903	10.579009
11	1.115668	11.682503		11	1.118202	11.697212

Entries are percentages of the original loan amount.

Remaining Balance Tables

Term of 3 Years

| | Interest Rate 12.50% | | | | | Interest Rate 12.75% | | | | | |
Year End	Principal Paid in Year	Interest Paid in Year	Total Interest Paid	Remaining Balance Year End	Curtail First Month	Principal Paid in Year	Interest Paid in Year	Total Interest Paid	Remaining Balance Year End	Curtail First Month	Year End
	Monthly Payment 3.345363% — Annual Constant 40.14435%					Monthly Payment 3.357366% — Annual Constant 40.28840%					
1	29.284445	10.859906	10.859906	70.715555	2.279946	29.206051	11.082344	11.082344	70.793949	2.550690	1
2	33.162175	6.982175	17.842081	37.553380	2.581848	33.155325	7.133070	18.215414	37.638624	2.895598	2
3	37.553380	2.590971	20.433052	0.000000	2.923726	37.638624	2.649771	20.865185	0.000000	3.287143	3

Term of 4 Years

| | Interest Rate 12.50% | | | | | Interest Rate 12.75% | | | | | |
Year End	Principal Paid in Year	Interest Paid in Year	Total Interest Paid	Remaining Balance Year End	Curtail First Month	Principal Paid in Year	Interest Paid in Year	Total Interest Paid	Remaining Balance Year End	Curtail First Month	Year End
	Monthly Payment 2.658000% — Annual Constant 31.89600%					Monthly Payment 2.670358% — Annual Constant 32.04430%					
1	20.546732	11.349267	11.349267	79.453268	1.599670	20.462711	11.581586	11.581586	79.537289	1.787097	1
2	23.267449	8.628550	19.977817	56.185820	1.811492	23.229701	8.814596	20.396182	56.307587	2.028750	2
3	26.348432	5.547566	25.525383	29.837387	2.051363	26.370847	5.673451	26.069632	29.936741	2.303080	3
4	29.837387	2.058611	27.583995	0.000000	2.322996	29.936741	2.107556	28.177188	0.000000	2.614505	4

Term of 5 Years

| | Interest Rate 12.50% | | | | | Interest Rate 12.75% | | | | | |
Year End	Principal Paid in Year	Interest Paid in Year	Total Interest Paid	Remaining Balance Year End	Curtail First Month	Principal Paid in Year	Interest Paid in Year	Total Interest Paid	Remaining Balance Year End	Curtail First Month	Year End
	Monthly Payment 2.249794% — Annual Constant 26.99753%					Monthly Payment 2.262530% — Annual Constant 27.15036%					
1	15.357640	11.639885	11.639885	84.642360	1.195672	15.272410	11.877950	11.877950	84.727590	1.333805	1
2	17.391239	9.606287	21.246173	67.251121	1.353998	17.337562	9.812798	21.690749	67.390028	1.514164	2
3	19.694118	7.303408	28.549581	47.557003	1.533290	19.681966	7.468395	29.159143	47.708062	1.718911	3
4	22.301935	4.695591	33.245172	25.255069	1.736322	22.343383	4.806978	33.966121	25.364679	1.951344	4
5	25.255069	1.742457	34.987629	0.000000	1.966239	25.364679	1.785682	35.751803	0.000000	2.215207	5

Term of 7 Years

| | Interest Rate 12.50% | | | | | Interest Rate 12.75% | | | | | |
Year End	Principal Paid in Year	Interest Paid in Year	Total Interest Paid	Remaining Balance Year End	Curtail First Month	Principal Paid in Year	Interest Paid in Year	Total Interest Paid	Remaining Balance Year End	Curtail First Month	Year End
	Monthly Payment 1.792124% — Annual Constant 21.50549%					Monthly Payment 1.805632% — Annual Constant 21.66759%					
1	9.539767	11.965719	11.965719	90.460233	0.742721	9.457616	12.209973	12.209973	90.542384	0.825974	1
2	10.802985	10.702501	22.668220	79.657248	0.841069	10.736485	10.931104	23.141077	79.805899	0.937664	2
3	12.233474	9.272012	31.940233	67.423774	0.952440	12.188284	9.479305	32.620382	67.617614	1.064455	3
4	13.853382	7.652104	39.592337	53.570392	1.078558	13.836397	7.831192	40.451574	53.781217	1.208392	4
5	15.687792	5.817694	45.410031	37.882600	1.221376	15.707370	5.960219	46.411794	38.073847	1.371792	5
6	17.765107	3.740379	49.150409	20.117493	1.383106	17.831337	3.836252	50.248046	20.242510	1.557288	6
7	20.117493	1.387993	50.538403	0.000000	1.566252	20.242510	1.425079	51.673125	0.000000	1.767866	7

Term of 10 Years

| | Interest Rate 12.50% | | | | | Interest Rate 12.75% | | | | | |
Year End	Principal Paid in Year	Interest Paid in Year	Total Interest Paid	Remaining Balance Year End	Curtail First Month	Principal Paid in Year	Interest Paid in Year	Total Interest Paid	Remaining Balance Year End	Curtail First Month	Year End
	Monthly Payment 1.463762% — Annual Constant 17.56514%					Monthly Payment 1.478398% — Annual Constant 17.74078%					
1	5.365647	12.199493	12.199493	94.634353	0.417744	5.293006	12.447771	12.447771	94.706994	0.462261	1
2	6.076144	11.488996	23.688489	88.558209	0.473059	6.008732	11.732045	24.179816	88.698262	0.524768	2
3	6.880724	10.684417	34.372906	81.677485	0.535700	6.821239	10.919538	35.099354	81.877023	0.595728	3
4	7.791842	9.773299	44.146204	73.885643	0.606635	7.743615	9.997163	45.096517	74.133408	0.676283	4
5	8.823607	8.741534	52.887738	65.062037	0.686964	8.790714	8.950063	54.046570	65.342694	0.767731	5
6	9.991994	7.573147	60.460885	55.070043	0.777929	9.979404	7.761373	61.807952	55.363290	0.871544	6
7	11.315094	6.250046	66.710931	43.754949	0.880939	11.328830	6.411947	68.219899	44.034460	0.989396	7
8	12.813394	4.751746	71.462677	30.941555	0.997589	12.860727	4.880050	73.099949	31.173733	1.123183	8
9	14.510093	3.055047	74.517724	16.431462	1.129686	14.599768	3.141009	76.240958	16.573965	1.275061	9
10	16.431462	1.133678	75.651402	0.000000	1.279275	16.573965	1.166812	77.407770	0.000000	1.447476	10

Term of 15 Years

| | Interest Rate 12.50% | | | | | Interest Rate 12.75% | | | | | |
Year End	Principal Paid in Year	Interest Paid in Year	Total Interest Paid	Remaining Balance Year End	Curtail First Month	Principal Paid in Year	Interest Paid in Year	Total Interest Paid	Remaining Balance Year End	Curtail First Month	Year End
	Monthly Payment 1.232522% — Annual Constant 14.79026%					Monthly Payment 1.248837% — Annual Constant 14.98604%					
1	2.426143	12.364122	12.364122	97.573857	0.188888	2.371453	12.614591	12.614591	97.628547	0.207109	1
2	2.747403	12.042862	24.406984	94.826454	0.213900	2.692123	12.293920	24.908511	94.936424	0.235115	2
3	3.111203	11.679062	36.086046	91.715251	0.242223	3.056155	11.929889	36.838400	91.880269	0.266907	3
4	3.523176	11.267089	47.353135	88.192075	0.274298	3.469412	11.516632	48.355032	88.410857	0.302999	4
5	3.989701	10.800564	58.153698	84.202373	0.310619	3.938549	11.047494	59.402526	84.472307	0.343971	5
6	4.518002	10.272263	68.425962	79.684372	0.351750	4.471124	10.514919	69.917445	80.001183	0.390483	6
7	5.116258	9.674007	78.099969	74.568114	0.398327	5.075715	9.910329	79.827775	74.925469	0.443284	7
8	5.793733	8.996532	87.096501	68.774381	0.451072	5.762058	9.223986	89.051760	69.163411	0.503225	8
9	6.560916	8.229349	95.325850	62.213465	0.510801	6.541210	8.444834	97.496594	62.622201	0.571272	9
10	7.429686	7.360579	102.686429	54.783779	0.578440	7.425719	7.560324	105.056919	55.196481	0.648520	10
11	8.413496	6.376769	109.063198	46.370283	0.655034	8.429833	6.556211	111.613129	46.766648	0.736214	11
12	9.527578	5.262687	114.325886	36.842706	0.741772	9.569724	5.416319	117.029449	37.196924	0.835765	12
13	10.789182	4.001083	118.326969	26.053524	0.839994	10.863753	4.122291	121.151740	26.333171	0.948778	13
14	12.217843	2.572422	120.899391	13.835681	0.951223	12.332761	2.653283	123.805022	14.000410	1.077073	14
15	13.835681	0.954584	121.853975	0.000000	1.077180	14.000410	0.985633	124.790656	0.000000	1.222716	15

| Monthly Factors for 12.500% Interest: | | | Monthly Factors for 12.750% Interest: | | |
Month	This Month	Year-to-date	Month	This Month	Year-to-date
1	1.010417	1.010417	1	1.010625	1.010625
2	1.020942	2.031359	2	1.021363	2.031988
3	1.031577	3.062935	3	1.032215	3.064203
4	1.042322	4.105257	4	1.043182	4.107385
5	1.053180	5.158437	5	1.054266	5.161651
6	1.064150	6.222588	6	1.065468	6.227118
7	1.075235	7.297823	7	1.076788	7.303907
8	1.086436	8.384258	8	1.088229	8.392136
9	1.097753	9.482011	9	1.099791	9.491927
10	1.109188	10.591199	10	1.111477	10.603404
11	1.120742	11.711940	11	1.123286	11.726690

Entries are percentages of the original loan amount.

Remaining Balance Tables

Term of 25 Years
Interest Rate 12.50%
Monthly Payment 1.090354%   Annual Constant 13.08425%

Interest Rate 12.75%
Monthly Payment 1.109052%   Annual Constant 13.30863%

Year End	Principal Paid in Year	Interest Paid in Year	Total Interest Paid	Remaining Balance Year End	Curtail First Month	Principal Paid in Year	Interest Paid in Year	Total Interest Paid	Remaining Balance Year End	Curtail First Month	Year End
1	0.618912	12.465337	12.465337	99.381088	0.048186	0.592456	12.716171	12.716171	99.407544	0.051742	1
2	0.700866	12.383384	24.848721	98.680222	0.054566	0.672569	12.636058	25.352229	98.734975	0.058738	2
3	0.793672	12.290578	37.139299	97.886550	0.061791	0.763514	12.545113	37.897342	97.971461	0.066681	3
4	0.898767	12.185483	49.324781	96.987783	0.069974	0.866758	12.441870	50.339212	97.104703	0.075698	4
5	1.017778	12.066472	61.391253	95.970004	0.079239	0.983961	12.324666	62.663878	96.120742	0.085934	5
6	1.152548	11.931701	73.322954	94.817456	0.089732	1.117014	12.191613	74.855491	95.003728	0.097554	6
7	1.305164	11.779085	85.102040	93.512292	0.101614	1.268058	12.040570	86.896061	93.735670	0.110745	7
8	1.477989	11.606261	96.708300	92.034303	0.115069	1.439526	11.869101	98.765162	92.296144	0.125720	8
9	1.673698	11.410551	108.118852	90.360605	0.130306	1.634180	11.674447	110.439609	90.661964	0.142720	9
10	1.895323	11.188927	119.307778	88.465282	0.147561	1.855156	11.453472	121.893081	88.806809	0.162019	10
11	2.146294	10.937956	130.245734	86.318988	0.167100	2.106012	11.202616	133.095697	86.700797	0.183927	11
12	2.430498	10.653752	140.899486	83.888490	0.189227	2.390789	10.917838	144.013535	84.310008	0.208798	12
13	2.752335	10.331915	151.231401	81.136156	0.214284	2.714074	10.594553	154.608088	81.595935	0.237032	13
14	3.116788	9.967462	161.198863	78.019368	0.242658	3.081074	10.227553	164.835642	78.514861	0.269083	14
15	3.529501	9.554749	170.753612	74.489867	0.274790	3.497700	9.810927	174.646569	75.017161	0.305469	15
16	3.996863	9.087386	179.840998	70.493004	0.311177	3.970663	9.337964	183.984533	71.046498	0.346775	16
17	4.526112	8.558138	188.399136	65.966892	0.352381	4.507580	8.801047	192.785580	66.538918	0.393666	17
18	5.125442	7.958808	196.357944	60.841450	0.399042	5.117100	8.191527	200.977108	61.421818	0.446898	18
19	5.804133	7.280117	203.638061	55.037318	0.451882	5.809040	7.499587	208.476695	55.612778	0.507328	19
20	6.572693	6.511557	210.149618	48.464625	0.511718	6.594544	6.714083	215.190778	49.018234	0.575930	20
21	7.443023	5.641227	215.790844	41.021602	0.579478	7.486266	5.822361	221.013139	41.531968	0.653808	21
22	8.428599	4.655651	220.446496	32.593004	0.656210	8.498567	4.810060	225.823200	33.033401	0.742216	22
23	9.544680	3.539569	223.986065	23.048323	0.743103	9.647752	3.660875	229.484075	23.385649	0.842580	23
24	10.808549	2.275701	226.261766	12.239774	0.841502	10.952332	2.356296	231.840371	12.433318	0.956514	24
25	12.239774	0.844475	227.106241	0.000000	0.952930	12.433318	0.875310	232.715680	0.000000	1.085855	25

Term of 30 Years
Interest Rate 12.50%
Monthly Payment 1.067258%   Annual Constant 12.80709%

Interest Rate 12.75%
Monthly Payment 1.086693%   Annual Constant 13.04032%

Year End	Principal Paid in Year	Interest Paid in Year	Total Interest Paid	Remaining Balance Year End	Curtail First Month	Principal Paid in Year	Interest Paid in Year	Total Interest Paid	Remaining Balance Year End	Curtail First Month	Year End
1	0.325312	12.481781	12.481781	99.674688	0.025327	0.307900	12.732419	12.732419	99.692100	0.026890	1
2	0.368389	12.438704	24.920485	99.306298	0.028681	0.349534	12.690785	25.423204	99.342566	0.030526	2
3	0.417170	12.389923	37.310408	98.889129	0.032479	0.396798	12.643520	38.066724	98.945768	0.034654	3
4	0.472410	12.334683	49.645092	98.416719	0.036780	0.450454	12.589865	50.656588	98.495314	0.039340	4
5	0.534964	12.272129	61.917221	97.881755	0.041650	0.511365	12.528954	63.185542	97.983949	0.044660	5
6	0.605802	12.201291	74.118512	97.275953	0.047165	0.580512	12.459806	75.645349	97.403437	0.050699	6
7	0.686020	12.121073	86.239585	96.589933	0.053410	0.659010	12.381309	88.026658	96.744428	0.057554	7
8	0.776860	12.030233	98.269818	95.813072	0.060483	0.748121	12.292197	100.318855	95.996306	0.065337	8
9	0.879729	11.927364	110.197182	94.933344	0.068491	0.849283	12.191035	112.509890	95.147023	0.074172	9
10	0.996219	11.810874	122.008056	93.937124	0.077561	0.964124	12.076194	124.586084	94.182899	0.084201	10
11	1.128134	11.678959	133.687015	92.808990	0.087831	1.094494	11.945824	136.531909	93.088405	0.095587	11
12	1.277518	11.529576	145.216590	91.531472	0.099461	1.242493	11.797826	148.329734	91.845912	0.108512	12
13	1.446681	11.360412	156.577002	90.084791	0.112632	1.410504	11.629814	159.959549	90.435407	0.123185	13
14	1.638245	11.168848	167.745850	88.446546	0.127546	1.601234	11.439085	171.398633	88.834173	0.139843	14
15	1.855175	10.951918	178.697768	86.591370	0.144435	1.817755	11.222564	182.621197	87.016419	0.158752	15
16	2.100830	10.706263	189.404031	84.490540	0.163561	2.063553	10.976765	193.597962	84.952865	0.180219	16
17	2.379014	10.428079	199.832110	82.111526	0.185219	2.342589	10.697729	204.295691	82.610276	0.204588	17
18	2.694033	10.113060	209.945170	79.417493	0.209754	2.659357	10.380962	214.676653	79.950919	0.232253	18
19	3.050767	9.756326	219.701496	76.366726	0.237518	3.018958	10.021361	224.698014	76.931961	0.263659	19
20	3.454737	9.352356	229.053852	72.911989	0.268969	3.427185	9.613134	234.311148	73.504777	0.299311	20
21	3.912200	8.894893	237.948745	68.999789	0.304585	3.890612	9.149706	243.460854	69.614165	0.339784	21
22	4.430238	8.376855	246.325601	64.569552	0.344917	4.416705	8.623614	252.084468	65.197460	0.385730	22
23	5.016872	7.790221	254.115822	59.552679	0.390590	5.013937	8.026382	260.110850	60.183523	0.437889	23
24	5.681187	7.125906	261.241728	53.871492	0.442310	5.691927	7.348392	267.459242	54.491596	0.497100	24
25	6.433467	6.373626	267.615354	47.438025	0.500879	6.461595	6.578724	274.037965	48.030001	0.564319	25
26	7.285361	5.521732	273.137086	40.152664	0.567203	7.335339	5.704980	279.742945	40.694662	0.640627	26
27	8.250060	4.557033	277.694119	31.902604	0.642310	8.327231	4.713087	284.456032	32.367431	0.727253	27
28	9.342500	3.464593	281.158711	22.560103	0.727362	9.453249	3.587070	288.043102	22.914183	0.825593	28
29	10.579597	2.227496	283.386207	11.980506	0.823677	10.731527	2.308792	290.351894	12.182656	0.937231	29
30	11.980506	0.826587	284.212794	0.000000	0.932745	12.182656	0.857663	291.209557	0.000000	1.063964	30

	Monthly Factors for 12.500% Interest:			Monthly Factors for 12.750% Interest:	
Month	This Month	Year-to-date	Month	This Month	Year-to-date
1	1.010417	1.010417	1	1.010625	1.010625
2	1.020942	2.031359	2	1.021363	2.031988
3	1.031577	3.062935	3	1.032215	3.064203
4	1.042322	4.105257	4	1.043182	4.107385
5	1.053180	5.158437	5	1.054266	5.161651
6	1.064150	6.222588	6	1.065468	6.227118
7	1.075235	7.297823	7	1.076788	7.303907
8	1.086436	8.384258	8	1.088229	8.392136
9	1.097753	9.482011	9	1.099791	9.491927
10	1.109188	10.591199	10	1.111477	10.603404
11	1.120742	11.711940	11	1.123286	11.726690

Entries are percentages of the original loan amount.

Prepayment Premium to Maintain Yield

9.00% Interest Rate   15 Year Amortization Schedule

Prepaid in Year	Market Rate at Time of Prepayment									
	5.50%	6.00%	6.50%	7.00%	7.25%	7.50%	7.75%	8.00%	8.25%	8.50%
1	18.5056	15.9878	13.4271	10.8240	9.5068	8.1791	6.8412	5.4931	4.1348	2.7665
2	17.5283	15.1381	12.7093	10.2421	8.9943	7.7371	6.4706	5.1948	3.9098	2.6156
3	16.5073	14.2510	11.9601	9.6350	8.4598	7.2761	6.0841	4.8837	3.6751	2.4582
4	15.4410	13.3249	11.1785	9.0019	7.9024	6.7955	5.6812	4.5595	3.4305	2.2943
5	14.3275	12.3585	10.3633	8.3420	7.3216	6.2948	5.2616	4.2219	3.1759	2.1236
6	13.1649	11.3503	9.5134	7.6544	6.7167	5.7734	4.8248	3.8706	2.9111	1.9461
7	11.9512	10.2986	8.6277	6.9384	6.0869	5.2309	4.3703	3.5052	2.6357	1.7616
8	10.6845	9.2020	7.7049	6.1930	5.4316	4.6665	3.8978	3.1255	2.3495	1.5700
9	9.3626	8.0588	6.7438	5.4175	4.7501	4.0799	3.4069	2.7311	2.0525	1.3711
10	7.9833	6.8674	5.7433	4.6109	4.0417	3.4704	2.8971	2.3218	1.7444	1.1649
11	6.5444	5.6259	4.7020	3.7725	3.3058	2.8376	2.3681	1.8972	1.4250	0.9513
12	5.0435	4.3327	3.6187	2.9014	2.5415	2.1809	1.8194	1.4571	1.0941	0.7302
13	3.4784	2.9860	2.4921	1.9966	1.7484	1.4997	1.2507	1.0013	0.7516	0.5014
14	1.8464	1.5838	1.3208	1.0574	0.9256	0.7937	0.6616	0.5295	0.3973	0.2649

9.25% Interest Rate   15 Year Amortization Schedule

Prepaid in Year	Market Rate at Time of Prepayment									
	5.75%	6.25%	6.75%	7.25%	7.50%	7.75%	8.00%	8.25%	8.50%	8.75%
1	18.3929	15.8886	13.3423	10.7544	9.4451	8.1257	6.7961	5.4566	4.1071	2.7478
2	17.4290	15.0509	12.6348	10.1811	8.9403	7.6903	6.4311	5.1628	3.8855	2.5992
3	16.4209	14.1751	11.8954	9.5821	8.4124	7.2355	6.0499	4.8560	3.6541	2.4441
4	15.3668	13.2599	11.1231	8.9566	7.8624	6.7608	5.6520	4.5359	3.4126	2.2822
5	14.2647	12.3036	10.3166	8.3039	7.2879	6.2657	5.2370	4.2021	3.1609	2.1135
6	13.1128	11.3048	9.4748	7.6230	6.6889	5.7494	4.8045	3.8543	2.8987	1.9378
7	11.9090	10.2619	8.5965	6.9130	6.0645	5.2115	4.3541	3.4921	2.6257	1.7549
8	10.6513	9.1732	7.6804	6.1732	5.4141	4.6514	3.8852	3.1153	2.3418	1.5648
9	9.3374	8.0370	6.7254	5.4026	4.7370	4.0686	3.3974	2.7235	2.0467	1.3673
10	7.9652	6.8517	5.7301	4.6003	4.0323	3.4624	2.8904	2.3163	1.7403	1.1622
11	6.5323	5.6155	4.6932	3.7655	3.2996	2.8323	2.3636	1.8936	1.4222	0.9495
12	5.0364	4.3266	3.6135	2.8972	2.5379	2.1777	1.8168	1.4550	1.0925	0.7291
13	3.4749	2.9830	2.4896	1.9946	1.7466	1.4982	1.2494	1.0003	0.7508	0.5009
14	1.8453	1.5829	1.3200	1.0568	0.9250	0.7932	0.6612	0.5292	0.3970	0.2648

9.50% Interest Rate   15 Year Amortization Schedule

Prepaid in Year	Market Rate at Time of Prepayment									
	6.00%	6.50%	7.00%	7.50%	7.75%	8.00%	8.25%	8.50%	8.75%	9.00%
1	18.2806	15.7898	13.2578	10.6851	9.3837	8.0724	6.7512	5.4202	4.0795	2.7292
2	17.3300	14.9639	12.5605	10.1202	8.8864	7.6435	6.3917	5.1309	3.8613	2.5829
3	16.3347	14.0994	11.8309	9.5293	8.3662	7.1950	6.0157	4.8284	3.6332	2.4300
4	15.2926	13.1949	11.0678	8.9114	7.8224	6.7262	5.6229	4.5124	3.3948	2.2702
5	14.2020	12.2487	10.2700	8.2658	7.2543	6.2366	5.2126	4.1824	3.1460	2.1034
6	13.0608	11.2594	9.4362	7.5916	6.6612	5.7254	4.7844	3.8380	2.8864	1.9295
7	11.8669	10.2251	8.5654	6.8877	6.0422	5.1922	4.3379	3.4791	2.6159	1.7483
8	10.6181	9.1443	7.6560	6.1534	5.3967	4.6364	3.8725	3.1051	2.3341	1.5596
9	9.3123	8.0152	6.7070	5.3877	4.7238	4.0573	3.3879	2.7158	2.0410	1.3634
10	7.9472	6.8361	5.7169	4.5897	4.0230	3.4543	2.8836	2.3109	1.7362	1.1595
11	6.5203	5.6051	4.6845	3.7584	3.2934	2.8269	2.3592	1.8900	1.4195	0.9477
12	5.0292	4.3204	3.6083	2.8931	2.5342	2.1746	1.8142	1.4529	1.0909	0.7281
13	3.4714	2.9800	2.4870	1.9926	1.7448	1.4967	1.2482	0.9993	0.7500	0.5004
14	1.8442	1.5819	1.3193	1.0562	0.9245	0.7927	0.6608	0.5289	0.3968	0.2646

9.75% Interest Rate   15 Year Amortization Schedule

Prepaid in Year	Market Rate at Time of Prepayment									
	6.25%	6.75%	7.25%	7.75%	8.00%	8.25%	8.50%	8.75%	9.00%	9.25%
1	18.1686	15.6912	13.1735	10.6160	9.3225	8.0193	6.7064	5.3839	4.0520	2.7106
2	17.2313	14.8771	12.4864	10.0595	8.8327	7.5970	6.3524	5.0992	3.8372	2.5667
3	16.2486	14.0239	11.7665	9.4766	8.3196	7.1546	5.9817	4.8009	3.6123	2.4159
4	15.2186	13.1301	11.0126	8.8664	7.7826	6.6917	5.5938	4.4889	3.3770	2.2582
5	14.1394	12.1940	10.2234	8.2279	7.2208	6.2075	5.1881	4.1626	3.1310	2.0934
6	13.0088	11.2140	9.3977	7.5602	6.6335	5.7015	4.7643	3.8218	2.8741	1.9212
7	11.8248	10.1884	8.5343	6.8624	6.0199	5.1730	4.3217	3.4660	2.6060	1.7417
8	10.5850	9.1155	7.6317	6.1336	5.3792	4.6213	3.8599	3.0949	2.3264	1.5545
9	9.2873	7.9935	6.6886	5.3728	4.7107	4.0459	3.3784	2.7082	2.0352	1.3595
10	7.9292	6.8205	5.7038	4.5790	4.0136	3.4462	2.8768	2.3055	1.7321	1.1567
11	6.5083	5.5947	4.6758	3.7514	3.2872	2.8216	2.3547	1.8864	1.4168	0.9459
12	5.0221	4.3142	3.6032	2.8889	2.5306	2.1714	1.8115	1.4508	1.0893	0.7270
13	3.4679	2.9770	2.4845	1.9906	1.7431	1.4952	1.2469	0.9983	0.7493	0.4999
14	1.8431	1.5810	1.3185	1.0556	0.9240	0.7923	0.6605	0.5286	0.3966	0.2645

Entries are the points to raise the yield on prepaid funds to that of the original loan.

Prepayment Premium to Maintain Yield

10.00% Interest Rate   15 Year Amortization Schedule

Prepaid in Year	6.50%	7.00%	7.50%	Market Rate at Time of Prepayment 8.00%	8.25%	8.50%	8.75%	9.00%	9.25%	9.50%
1	18.0569	15.5930	13.0896	10.5472	9.2616	7.9664	6.6618	5.3479	4.0246	2.6922
2	17.1327	14.7906	12.4126	9.9991	8.7792	7.5506	6.3133	5.0675	3.8132	2.5505
3	16.1627	13.9486	11.7023	9.4241	8.2732	7.1144	5.9478	4.7735	3.5916	2.4019
4	15.1448	13.0654	10.9576	8.8214	7.7428	6.6573	5.5648	4.4655	3.3593	2.2463
5	14.0769	12.1394	10.1770	8.1900	7.1873	6.1786	5.1638	4.1430	3.1161	2.0834
6	12.9570	11.1687	9.3593	7.5289	6.6059	5.6776	4.7442	3.8056	2.8619	1.9130
7	11.7827	10.1518	8.5032	6.8372	5.9976	5.1537	4.3055	3.4530	2.5961	1.7350
8	10.5519	9.0867	7.6073	6.1138	5.3618	4.6063	3.8473	3.0848	2.3188	1.5493
9	9.2622	7.9717	6.6703	5.3579	4.6976	4.0347	3.3690	2.7006	2.0295	1.3557
10	7.9112	6.8049	5.6907	4.5684	4.0043	3.4382	2.8701	2.3000	1.7280	1.1540
11	6.4963	5.5844	4.6670	3.7443	3.2810	2.8163	2.3502	1.8829	1.4141	0.9441
12	5.0150	4.3081	3.5980	2.8847	2.5269	2.1683	1.8089	1.4487	1.0877	0.7259
13	3.4645	2.9740	2.4820	1.9886	1.7413	1.4937	1.2456	0.9973	0.7485	0.4994
14	1.8421	1.5801	1.3177	1.0549	0.9234	0.7918	0.6601	0.5282	0.3963	0.2643

10.25% Interest Rate   15 Year Amortization Schedule

Prepaid in Year	6.75%	7.25%	7.75%	Market Rate at Time of Prepayment 8.25%	8.50%	8.75%	9.00%	9.25%	9.50%	9.75%
1	17.9455	15.4951	13.0060	10.4787	9.2009	7.9138	6.6174	5.3119	3.9974	2.6738
2	17.0345	14.7044	12.3390	9.9388	8.7258	7.5043	6.2744	5.0360	3.7893	2.5344
3	16.0771	13.8735	11.6383	9.3718	8.2269	7.0743	5.9141	4.7462	3.5709	2.3880
4	15.0711	13.0009	10.9026	8.7766	7.7032	6.6230	5.5360	4.4421	3.3416	2.2344
5	14.0145	12.0848	10.1307	8.1522	7.1539	6.1497	5.1395	4.1233	3.1013	2.0734
6	12.9052	11.1235	9.3210	7.4977	6.5783	5.6538	4.7241	3.7894	2.8496	1.9048
7	11.7407	10.1152	8.4722	6.8120	5.9754	5.1345	4.2894	3.4400	2.5863	1.7284
8	10.5189	9.0580	7.5830	6.0941	5.3441	4.5913	3.8347	3.0746	2.3111	1.5442
9	9.2372	7.9500	6.6520	5.3431	4.6846	4.0234	3.3595	2.6929	2.0237	1.3518
10	7.8932	6.7894	5.6775	4.5578	3.9950	3.4301	2.8634	2.2946	1.7239	1.1512
11	6.4843	5.5740	4.6583	3.7373	3.2748	2.8110	2.3458	1.8793	1.4114	0.9423
12	5.0078	4.3019	3.5928	2.8806	2.5233	2.1652	1.8063	1.4466	1.0861	0.7249
13	3.4610	2.9710	2.4795	1.9866	1.7396	1.4922	1.2444	0.9962	0.7477	0.4989
14	1.8410	1.5792	1.3169	1.0543	0.9229	0.7913	0.6597	0.5279	0.3961	0.2642

10.50% Interest Rate   15 Year Amortization Schedule

Prepaid in Year	7.00%	7.50%	8.00%	Market Rate at Time of Prepayment 8.50%	8.75%	9.00%	9.25%	9.50%	9.75%	10.00%
1	17.8345	15.3975	12.9226	10.4104	9.1404	7.8614	6.5733	5.2762	3.9703	2.6555
2	16.9365	14.6184	12.2656	9.8788	8.6727	7.4583	6.2356	5.0046	3.7656	2.5184
3	15.9916	13.7986	11.5745	9.3196	8.1807	7.0343	5.8804	4.7190	3.5502	2.3741
4	14.9976	12.9365	10.8479	8.7319	7.6637	6.5888	5.5072	4.4189	3.3240	2.2225
5	13.9523	12.0304	10.0844	8.1145	7.1206	6.1209	5.1153	4.1038	3.0865	2.0634
6	12.8535	11.0784	9.2827	7.4665	6.5508	5.6300	4.7042	3.7733	2.8374	1.8966
7	11.6988	10.0787	8.4413	6.7868	5.9532	5.1154	4.2733	3.4270	2.5765	1.7218
8	10.4859	9.0293	7.5588	6.0744	5.3271	4.5763	3.8221	3.0645	2.3034	1.5390
9	9.2122	7.9283	6.6336	5.3282	4.6715	4.0121	3.3501	2.6853	2.0180	1.3480
10	7.8753	6.7738	5.6644	4.5472	3.9856	3.4221	2.8566	2.2892	1.7198	1.1485
11	6.4723	5.5636	4.6496	3.7303	3.2686	2.8056	2.3413	1.8757	1.4088	0.9405
12	5.0007	4.2958	3.5877	2.8764	2.5196	2.1620	1.8036	1.4445	1.0845	0.7238
13	3.4575	2.9680	2.4770	1.9846	1.7378	1.4906	1.2431	0.9952	0.7470	0.4984
14	1.8399	1.5782	1.3162	1.0537	0.9223	0.7909	0.6593	0.5276	0.3959	0.2640

10.75% Interest Rate   15 Year Amortization Schedule

Prepaid in Year	7.25%	7.75%	8.25%	Market Rate at Time of Prepayment 8.75%	9.00%	9.25%	9.50%	9.75%	10.00%	10.25%
1	17.7238	15.3003	12.8396	10.3424	9.0803	7.8092	6.5293	5.2406	3.9433	2.6373
2	16.8388	14.5326	12.1925	9.8190	8.6198	7.4124	6.1969	4.9734	3.7419	2.5024
3	15.9063	13.7239	11.5109	9.2676	8.1347	6.9945	5.8469	4.6919	3.5297	2.3603
4	14.9242	12.8723	10.7933	8.6873	7.6243	6.5546	5.4784	4.3957	3.3064	2.2107
5	13.8901	11.9761	10.0383	8.0769	7.0874	6.0922	5.0911	4.0843	3.0717	2.0535
6	12.8019	11.0333	9.2445	7.4354	6.5233	5.6063	4.6842	3.7572	2.8253	1.8884
7	11.6569	10.0422	8.4104	6.7617	5.9311	5.0962	4.2572	3.4140	2.5667	1.7153
8	10.4529	9.0006	7.5345	6.0548	5.3097	4.5613	3.8095	3.0544	2.2958	1.5339
9	9.1873	7.9067	6.6154	5.3134	4.6585	4.0009	3.3406	2.6777	2.0122	1.3441
10	7.8573	6.7582	5.6513	4.5366	3.9763	3.4141	2.8499	2.2838	1.7157	1.1458
11	6.4604	5.5533	4.6409	3.7233	3.2624	2.8003	2.3369	1.8721	1.4061	0.9387
12	4.9936	4.2896	3.5825	2.8723	2.5160	2.1589	1.8010	1.4424	1.0830	0.7228
13	3.4541	2.9650	2.4745	1.9826	1.7360	1.4891	1.2419	0.9942	0.7462	0.4978
14	1.8388	1.5773	1.3154	1.0531	0.9218	0.7904	0.6589	0.5273	0.3956	0.2638

Entries are the points to raise the yield on prepaid funds to that of the original loan.

Prepayment Premium to Maintain Yield

11.00% Interest Rate   15 Year Amortization Schedule

Prepaid in Year	Market Rate at Time of Prepayment									
	7.50%	8.00%	8.50%	9.00%	9.25%	9.50%	9.75%	10.00%	10.25%	10.50%
1	17.6135	15.2034	12.7570	10.2747	9.0203	7.7572	6.4855	5.2052	3.9164	2.6192
2	16.7414	14.4472	12.1197	9.7594	8.5670	7.3667	6.1584	4.9423	3.7183	2.4865
3	15.8213	13.6494	11.4474	9.2158	8.0889	6.9548	5.8134	4.6649	3.5092	2.3465
4	14.8510	12.8083	10.7388	8.6428	7.5850	6.5206	5.4498	4.3726	3.2889	2.1989
5	13.8281	11.9219	9.9922	8.0394	7.0543	6.0635	5.0670	4.0648	3.0570	2.0436
6	12.7503	10.9884	9.2064	7.4044	6.4959	5.5826	4.6643	3.7411	2.8131	1.8802
7	11.6151	10.0058	8.3796	6.7367	5.9090	5.0771	4.2412	3.4011	2.5569	1.7087
8	10.4200	8.9720	7.5103	6.0351	5.2924	4.5464	3.7970	3.0443	2.2882	1.5288
9	9.1623	7.8850	6.5971	5.2986	4.6454	3.9896	3.3312	2.6702	2.0065	1.3403
10	7.8394	6.7427	5.6382	4.5260	3.9670	3.4061	2.8432	2.2784	1.7117	1.1430
11	6.4484	5.5429	4.6322	3.7162	3.2563	2.7950	2.3324	1.8686	1.4034	0.9369
12	4.9864	4.2835	3.5774	2.8681	2.5123	2.1558	1.7984	1.4403	1.0814	0.7217
13	3.4506	2.9620	2.4720	1.9806	1.7343	1.4876	1.2406	0.9932	0.7455	0.4973
14	1.8378	1.5764	1.3146	1.0525	0.9212	0.7899	0.6585	0.5270	0.3954	0.2637

11.25% Interest Rate   15 Year Amortization Schedule

Prepaid in Year	Market Rate at Time of Prepayment									
	7.75%	8.25%	8.75%	9.25%	9.50%	9.75%	10.00%	10.25%	10.50%	10.75%
1	17.5035	15.1069	12.6746	10.2073	8.9607	7.7055	6.4419	5.1699	3.8897	2.6012
2	16.6443	14.3620	12.0471	9.7000	8.5145	7.3212	6.1201	4.9113	3.6948	2.4707
3	15.7365	13.5751	11.3842	9.1641	8.0432	6.9152	5.7801	4.6380	3.4888	2.3328
4	14.7780	12.7444	10.6844	8.5985	7.5458	6.4867	5.4213	4.3495	3.2715	2.1872
5	13.7662	11.8678	9.9463	8.0019	7.0212	6.0349	5.0429	4.0454	3.0423	2.0337
6	12.6989	10.9435	9.1683	7.3734	6.4686	5.5590	4.6445	3.7251	2.8010	1.8721
7	11.5734	9.9694	8.3488	6.7116	5.8869	5.0581	4.2252	3.3882	2.5472	1.7021
8	10.3871	8.9434	7.4862	6.0155	5.2752	4.5315	3.7845	3.0342	2.2806	1.5237
9	9.1374	7.8634	6.5788	5.2838	4.6324	3.9784	3.3218	2.6626	2.0008	1.3364
10	7.8215	6.7272	5.6252	4.5155	3.9577	3.3981	2.8365	2.2730	1.7076	1.1403
11	6.4364	5.5326	4.6235	3.7092	3.2501	2.7897	2.3280	1.8650	1.4007	0.9351
12	4.9793	4.2773	3.5722	2.8640	2.5087	2.1526	1.7958	1.4382	1.0798	0.7206
13	3.4471	2.9591	2.4695	1.9786	1.7325	1.4861	1.2393	0.9922	0.7447	0.4968
14	1.8367	1.5755	1.3138	1.0518	0.9207	0.7895	0.6581	0.5267	0.3952	0.2635

11.50% Interest Rate   15 Year Amortization Schedule

Prepaid in Year	Market Rate at Time of Prepayment									
	8.00%	8.50%	9.00%	9.50%	9.75%	10.00%	10.25%	10.50%	10.75%	11.00%
1	17.3940	15.0107	12.5926	10.1401	8.9013	7.6540	6.3986	5.1349	3.8631	2.5833
2	16.5474	14.2771	11.9747	9.6408	8.4622	7.2759	6.0819	4.8804	3.6714	2.4550
3	15.6519	13.5010	11.3211	9.1126	7.9977	6.8758	5.7469	4.6112	3.4685	2.3191
4	14.7051	12.6806	10.6302	8.5542	7.5067	6.4529	5.3928	4.3266	3.2541	2.1755
5	13.7045	11.8139	9.9005	7.9646	6.9883	6.0064	5.0190	4.0261	3.0277	2.0238
6	12.6475	10.8987	9.1303	7.3425	6.4413	5.5354	4.6246	3.7091	2.7889	1.8640
7	11.5317	9.9331	8.3180	6.6867	5.8649	5.0391	4.2092	3.3753	2.5375	1.6956
8	10.3543	8.9148	7.4620	5.9959	5.2579	4.5166	3.7720	3.0241	2.2730	1.5186
9	9.1125	7.8418	6.5606	5.2691	4.6194	3.9672	3.3124	2.6550	1.9951	1.3326
10	7.8036	6.7117	5.6121	4.5049	3.9484	3.3901	2.8298	2.2676	1.7035	1.1376
11	6.4245	5.5223	4.6148	3.7022	3.2440	2.7844	2.3236	1.8614	1.3980	0.9333
12	4.9722	4.2712	3.5671	2.8598	2.5050	2.1495	1.7932	1.4361	1.0782	0.7196
13	3.4437	2.9561	2.4670	1.9766	1.7308	1.4846	1.2381	0.9912	0.7439	0.4963
14	1.8356	1.5745	1.3131	1.0512	0.9202	0.7890	0.6577	0.5264	0.3949	0.2634

11.75% Interest Rate   15 Year Amortization Schedule

Prepaid in Year	Market Rate at Time of Prepayment									
	8.25%	8.75%	9.25%	9.75%	10.00%	10.25%	10.50%	10.75%	11.00%	11.25%
1	17.2848	14.9149	12.5109	10.0733	8.8421	7.6028	6.3554	5.1000	3.8367	2.5655
2	16.4509	14.1925	11.9026	9.5819	8.4101	7.2308	6.0439	4.8497	3.6481	2.4393
3	15.5676	13.4272	11.2583	9.0613	7.9523	6.8365	5.7139	4.5845	3.4483	2.3055
4	14.6324	12.6171	10.5762	8.5102	7.4678	6.4192	5.3645	4.3037	3.2368	2.1638
5	13.6428	11.7600	9.8548	7.9274	6.9554	5.9780	4.9951	4.0068	3.0131	2.0140
6	12.5963	10.8540	9.0924	7.3117	6.4141	5.5119	4.6049	3.6932	2.7769	1.8559
7	11.4901	9.8968	8.2874	6.6617	5.8429	5.0201	4.1933	3.3625	2.5278	1.6891
8	10.3215	8.8863	7.4379	5.9764	5.2407	4.5017	3.7595	3.0141	2.2654	1.5135
9	9.0877	7.8202	6.5424	5.2543	4.6064	3.9560	3.3030	2.6475	1.9894	1.3288
10	7.7857	6.6962	5.5991	4.4944	3.9392	3.3821	2.8231	2.2622	1.6995	1.1349
11	6.4126	5.5120	4.6062	3.6952	3.2378	2.7791	2.3191	1.8579	1.3953	0.9315
12	4.9651	4.2651	3.5619	2.8557	2.5014	2.1464	1.7906	1.4340	1.0766	0.7185
13	3.4402	2.9531	2.4646	1.9745	1.7290	1.4831	1.2368	0.9902	0.7432	0.4958
14	1.8345	1.5736	1.3123	1.0506	0.9196	0.7885	0.6573	0.5261	0.3947	0.2632

Entries are the points to raise the yield on prepaid funds to that of the original loan.

Prepayment Premium to Maintain Yield

12.00% Interest Rate   15 Year Amortization Schedule

Prepaid in Year	Market Rate at Time of Prepayment									
	8.50%	9.00%	9.50%	10.00%	10.25%	10.50%	10.75%	11.00%	11.25%	11.50%
1	17.1761	14.8195	12.4296	10.0068	8.7833	7.5518	6.3125	5.0653	3.8104	2.5478
2	16.3547	14.1082	11.8309	9.5232	8.3582	7.1858	6.0061	4.8191	3.6250	2.4237
3	15.4835	13.3536	11.1957	9.0101	7.9071	6.7974	5.6810	4.5579	3.4282	2.2919
4	14.5599	12.5537	10.5223	8.4662	7.4290	6.3856	5.3362	4.2809	3.2195	2.1522
5	13.5813	11.7063	9.8092	7.8902	6.9226	5.9496	4.9712	3.9875	2.9985	2.0042
6	12.5451	10.8094	9.0546	7.2809	6.3870	5.4884	4.5852	3.6773	2.7648	1.8478
7	11.4485	9.8607	8.2567	6.6369	5.8210	5.0011	4.1774	3.3497	2.5181	1.6826
8	10.2888	8.8579	7.4139	5.9569	5.2235	4.4869	3.7471	3.0040	2.2578	1.5084
9	9.0629	7.7987	6.5242	5.2396	4.5935	3.9448	3.2936	2.6399	1.9837	1.3250
10	7.7679	6.6807	5.5861	4.4838	3.9299	3.3741	2.8164	2.2569	1.6954	1.1321
11	6.4006	5.5016	4.5975	3.6882	3.2317	2.7738	2.3147	1.8543	1.3926	0.9297
12	4.9580	4.2589	3.5568	2.8515	2.4978	2.1433	1.7880	1.4319	1.0751	0.7175
13	3.4367	2.9501	2.4621	1.9725	1.7272	1.4816	1.2356	0.9892	0.7424	0.4953
14	1.8335	1.5727	1.3115	1.0500	0.9191	0.7881	0.6570	0.5258	0.3945	0.2631

12.25% Interest Rate   15 Year Amortization Schedule

Prepaid in Year	Market Rate at Time of Prepayment									
	8.75%	9.25%	9.75%	10.25%	10.50%	10.75%	11.00%	11.25%	11.50%	11.75%
1	17.0677	14.7245	12.3486	9.9406	8.7248	7.5011	6.2697	5.0307	3.7842	2.5302
2	16.2589	14.0242	11.7593	9.4648	8.3066	7.1411	5.9685	4.7887	3.6019	2.4082
3	15.3997	13.2802	11.1332	8.9592	7.8621	6.7584	5.6482	4.5314	3.4081	2.2784
4	14.4876	12.4904	10.4686	8.4224	7.3903	6.3522	5.3081	4.2581	3.2023	2.1406
5	13.5200	11.6527	9.7638	7.8532	6.8899	5.9213	4.9475	3.9683	2.9840	1.9945
6	12.4941	10.7649	9.0169	7.2502	6.3599	5.4650	4.5655	3.6615	2.7529	1.8397
7	11.4071	9.8245	8.2262	6.6120	5.7991	4.9822	4.1615	3.3369	2.5084	1.6761
8	10.2561	8.8294	7.3899	5.9374	5.2063	4.4721	3.7346	2.9940	2.2503	1.5033
9	9.0381	7.7772	6.5061	5.2249	4.5805	3.9337	3.2843	2.6324	1.9780	1.3212
10	7.7500	6.6653	5.5730	4.4733	3.9206	3.3661	2.8097	2.2515	1.6914	1.1294
11	6.3887	5.4913	4.5888	3.6812	3.2255	2.7685	2.3103	1.8508	1.3900	0.9279
12	4.9509	4.2528	3.5516	2.8474	2.4942	2.1401	1.7853	1.4298	1.0735	0.7164
13	3.4333	2.9472	2.4596	1.9705	1.7255	1.4801	1.2343	0.9882	0.7417	0.4948
14	1.8324	1.5718	1.3108	1.0494	0.9185	0.7876	0.6566	0.5254	0.3942	0.2629

12.50% Interest Rate   15 Year Amortization Schedule

Prepaid in Year	Market Rate at Time of Prepayment									
	9.00%	9.50%	10.00%	10.50%	10.75%	11.00%	11.25%	11.50%	11.75%	12.00%
1	16.9598	14.6299	12.2680	9.8747	8.6665	7.4506	6.2272	4.9964	3.7582	2.5126
2	16.1633	13.9405	11.6881	9.4066	8.2551	7.0966	5.9310	4.7584	3.5790	2.3927
3	15.3161	13.2071	11.0710	8.9084	7.8173	6.7196	5.6155	4.5050	3.3881	2.2650
4	14.4155	12.4274	10.4151	8.3788	7.3517	6.3188	5.2800	4.2355	3.1851	2.1291
5	13.4587	11.5993	9.7184	7.8163	6.8573	5.8931	4.9238	3.9492	2.9695	1.9848
6	12.4431	10.7204	8.9792	7.2196	6.3329	5.4417	4.5459	3.6456	2.7409	1.8317
7	11.3656	9.7885	8.1957	6.5872	5.7772	4.9634	4.1456	3.3241	2.4988	1.6696
8	10.2234	8.8010	7.3659	5.9179	5.1892	4.4573	3.7222	2.9840	2.2427	1.4983
9	9.0133	7.7557	6.4880	5.2102	4.5676	3.9225	3.2750	2.6249	1.9724	1.3174
10	7.7322	6.6498	5.5600	4.4628	3.9114	3.3582	2.8031	2.2461	1.6873	1.1267
11	6.3768	5.4810	4.5802	3.6743	3.2194	2.7633	2.3059	1.8472	1.3873	0.9261
12	4.9438	4.2467	3.5465	2.8433	2.4905	2.1370	1.7827	1.4277	1.0719	0.7154
13	3.4298	2.9442	2.4571	1.9685	1.7237	1.4786	1.2330	0.9871	0.7409	0.4943
14	1.8313	1.5708	1.3100	1.0488	0.9180	0.7871	0.6562	0.5251	0.3940	0.2628

12.75% Interest Rate   15 Year Amortization Schedule

Prepaid in Year	Market Rate at Time of Prepayment									
	9.25%	9.75%	10.25%	10.75%	11.00%	11.25%	11.50%	11.75%	12.00%	12.25%
1	16.8523	14.5357	12.1878	9.8092	8.6085	7.4004	6.1850	4.9622	3.7323	2.4952
2	16.0681	13.8571	11.6172	9.3487	8.2039	7.0522	5.8937	4.7283	3.5562	2.3774
3	15.2328	13.1342	11.0091	8.8579	7.7726	6.6809	5.5830	4.4787	3.3682	2.2516
4	14.3436	12.3646	10.3617	8.3353	7.3133	6.2856	5.2521	4.2129	3.1681	2.1176
5	13.3977	11.5460	9.6732	7.7795	6.8248	5.8650	4.9001	3.9302	2.9551	1.9751
6	12.3922	10.6761	8.9417	7.1890	6.3059	5.4184	4.5263	3.6299	2.7290	1.8237
7	11.3243	9.7525	8.1652	6.5625	5.7554	4.9445	4.1298	3.3114	2.4891	1.6632
8	10.1908	8.7727	7.3419	5.8985	5.1721	4.4425	3.7099	2.9741	2.2352	1.4932
9	8.9886	7.7342	6.4699	5.1956	4.5547	3.9114	3.2656	2.6174	1.9667	1.3136
10	7.7144	6.6344	5.5470	4.4523	3.9022	3.3502	2.7964	2.2408	1.6833	1.1240
11	6.3649	5.4708	4.5716	3.6673	3.2133	2.7580	2.3015	1.8437	1.3846	0.9243
12	4.9368	4.2406	3.5414	2.8392	2.4869	2.1339	1.7801	1.4256	1.0703	0.7143
13	3.4264	2.9412	2.4546	1.9665	1.7220	1.4771	1.2318	0.9861	0.7401	0.4938
14	1.8302	1.5699	1.3092	1.0481	0.9175	0.7867	0.6558	0.5248	0.3938	0.2626

Entries are the points to raise the yield on prepaid funds to that of the original loan.

Prepayment Premium to Maintain Yield

13.00% Interest Rate   15 Year Amortization Schedule

Prepaid in Year	Market Rate at Time of Prepayment									
	9.50%	10.00%	10.50%	11.00%	11.25%	11.50%	11.75%	12.00%	12.25%	12.50%
1	16.7453	14.4419	12.1079	9.7439	8.5508	7.3505	6.1429	4.9283	3.7066	2.4779
2	15.9733	13.7741	11.5465	9.2910	8.1530	7.0081	5.8565	4.6983	3.5334	2.3621
3	15.1497	13.0615	10.9473	8.8075	7.7281	6.6424	5.5506	4.4526	3.3484	2.2383
4	14.2718	12.3019	10.3085	8.2919	7.2750	6.2524	5.2242	4.1904	3.1511	2.1062
5	13.3367	11.4928	9.6281	7.7427	6.7924	5.8370	4.8766	3.9112	2.9408	1.9654
6	12.3415	10.6319	8.9042	7.1585	6.2790	5.3951	4.5068	3.6141	2.7171	1.8157
7	11.2830	9.7166	8.1348	6.5378	5.7337	4.9257	4.1141	3.2987	2.4795	1.6567
8	10.1582	8.7444	7.3180	5.8791	5.1550	4.4278	3.6975	2.9641	2.2277	1.4882
9	8.9639	7.7128	6.4518	5.1809	4.5418	3.9003	3.2563	2.6099	1.9610	1.3098
10	7.6966	6.6190	5.5341	4.4418	3.8929	3.3423	2.7897	2.2354	1.6793	1.1213
11	6.3530	5.4605	4.5629	3.6603	3.2071	2.7527	2.2971	1.8401	1.3820	0.9225
12	4.9297	4.2345	3.5363	2.8350	2.4833	2.1308	1.7775	1.4235	1.0688	0.7133
13	3.4229	2.9382	2.4521	1.9646	1.7202	1.4756	1.2305	0.9851	0.7394	0.4933
14	1.8292	1.5690	1.3085	1.0475	0.9169	0.7862	0.6554	0.5245	0.3935	0.2624

13.25% Interest Rate   15 Year Amortization Schedule

Prepaid in Year	Market Rate at Time of Prepayment									
	9.75%	10.25%	10.75%	11.25%	11.50%	11.75%	12.00%	12.25%	12.50%	12.75%
1	16.6387	14.3486	12.0285	9.6790	8.4935	7.3008	6.1011	4.8945	3.6810	2.4607
2	15.8788	13.6914	11.4762	9.2336	8.1022	6.9642	5.8196	4.6684	3.5108	2.3469
3	15.0669	12.9891	10.8858	8.7573	7.6838	6.6041	5.5183	4.4265	3.3287	2.2250
4	14.2003	12.2394	10.2554	8.2487	7.2368	6.2194	5.1965	4.1680	3.1341	2.0948
5	13.2760	11.4398	9.5831	7.7061	6.7601	5.8091	4.8531	3.8922	2.9264	1.9558
6	12.2908	10.5877	8.8668	7.1281	6.2522	5.3720	4.4874	3.5984	2.7052	1.8077
7	11.2418	9.6807	8.1045	6.5132	5.7120	4.9070	4.0983	3.2860	2.4700	1.6503
8	10.1257	8.7162	7.2941	5.8598	5.1380	4.4131	3.6852	2.9542	2.2202	1.4831
9	8.9392	7.6914	6.4337	5.1663	4.5290	3.8892	3.2470	2.6024	1.9554	1.3060
10	7.6788	6.6036	5.5211	4.4313	3.8837	3.3343	2.7831	2.2301	1.6752	1.1186
11	6.3412	5.4502	4.5543	3.6534	3.2010	2.7475	2.2926	1.8366	1.3793	0.9208
12	4.9226	4.2284	3.5311	2.8309	2.4797	2.1277	1.7749	1.4214	1.0672	0.7122
13	3.4195	2.9353	2.4496	1.9626	1.7185	1.4741	1.2293	0.9841	0.7386	0.4928
14	1.8281	1.5681	1.3077	1.0469	0.9164	0.7857	0.6550	0.5242	0.3933	0.2623

13.50% Interest Rate   15 Year Amortization Schedule

Prepaid in Year	Market Rate at Time of Prepayment									
	10.00%	10.50%	11.00%	11.50%	11.75%	12.00%	12.25%	12.50%	12.75%	13.00%
1	16.5326	14.2556	11.9494	9.6144	8.4364	7.2514	6.0595	4.8609	3.6555	2.4436
2	15.7847	13.6090	11.4061	9.1764	8.0517	6.9205	5.7828	4.6387	3.4884	2.3317
3	14.9844	12.9170	10.8245	8.7073	7.6396	6.5659	5.4862	4.4006	3.3091	2.2118
4	14.1290	12.1771	10.2026	8.2056	7.1988	6.1865	5.1688	4.1457	3.1172	2.0834
5	13.2153	11.3869	9.5382	7.6696	6.7279	5.7812	4.8297	3.8734	2.9122	1.9462
6	12.2403	10.5437	8.8295	7.0978	6.2255	5.3489	4.4680	3.5828	2.6934	1.7998
7	11.2007	9.6449	8.0742	6.4886	5.6903	4.8883	4.0826	3.2733	2.4604	1.6439
8	10.0933	8.6879	7.2703	5.8404	5.1209	4.3984	3.6728	2.9443	2.2127	1.4781
9	8.9145	7.6700	6.4157	5.1517	4.5163	3.8781	3.2377	2.5949	1.9498	1.3022
10	7.6611	6.5882	5.5082	4.4209	3.8745	3.3264	2.7765	2.2247	1.6712	1.1159
11	6.3293	5.4400	4.5457	3.6464	3.1949	2.7422	2.2882	1.8331	1.3766	0.9190
12	4.9155	4.2223	3.5260	2.8268	2.4761	2.1246	1.7723	1.4194	1.0656	0.7112
13	3.4161	2.9323	2.4472	1.9606	1.7167	1.4726	1.2280	0.9831	0.7379	0.4923
14	1.8270	1.5672	1.3069	1.0463	0.9158	0.7853	0.6546	0.5239	0.3931	0.2621

13.75% Interest Rate   15 Year Amortization Schedule

Prepaid in Year	Market Rate at Time of Prepayment									
	10.25%	10.75%	11.25%	11.75%	12.00%	12.25%	12.50%	12.75%	13.00%	13.25%
1	16.4269	14.1631	11.8707	9.5502	8.3796	7.2023	6.0182	4.8275	3.6303	2.4265
2	15.6909	13.5270	11.3364	9.1195	8.0014	6.8770	5.7462	4.6092	3.4660	2.3167
3	14.9022	12.8451	10.7635	8.6576	7.5957	6.5279	5.4542	4.3748	3.2896	2.1987
4	14.0579	12.1150	10.1499	8.1627	7.1609	6.1538	5.1413	4.1235	3.1004	2.0721
5	13.1549	11.3341	9.4935	7.6332	6.6958	5.7535	4.8064	3.8545	2.8979	1.9366
6	12.1899	10.4998	8.7923	7.0676	6.1988	5.3258	4.4486	3.5672	2.6816	1.7919
7	11.1597	9.6092	8.0440	6.4641	5.6687	4.8696	4.0670	3.2607	2.4509	1.6375
8	10.0608	8.6598	7.2465	5.8212	5.1040	4.3837	3.6605	2.9344	2.2052	1.4731
9	8.8899	7.6486	6.3977	5.1371	4.5033	3.8671	3.2285	2.5875	1.9441	1.2984
10	7.6433	6.5729	5.4952	4.4104	3.8653	3.3185	2.7698	2.2194	1.6672	1.1132
11	6.3174	5.4297	4.5371	3.6395	3.1888	2.7369	2.2838	1.8295	1.3740	0.9172
12	4.9085	4.2162	3.5209	2.8227	2.4724	2.1215	1.7697	1.4173	1.0641	0.7101
13	3.4126	2.9294	2.4447	1.9586	1.7150	1.4711	1.2268	0.9821	0.7371	0.4918
14	1.8260	1.5662	1.3061	1.0457	0.9153	0.7848	0.6543	0.5236	0.3928	0.2620

Entries are the points to raise the yield on prepaid funds to that of the original loan.

Prepayment Premium to Maintain Yield

9.00% Interest Rate   30 Year Amortization Schedule

Prepaid in Year	Market Rate at Time of Prepayment									
	5.50%	6.00%	6.50%	7.00%	7.25%	7.50%	7.75%	8.00%	8.25%	8.50%
1	28.9592	25.0757	21.1002	17.0371	14.9742	12.8910	10.7882	8.6664	6.5261	4.3679
2	28.4618	24.6448	20.7379	16.7452	14.7180	12.6708	10.6044	8.5191	6.4154	4.2940
3	27.9409	24.1932	20.3578	16.4386	14.4488	12.4394	10.4109	8.3639	6.2988	4.2162
4	27.3954	23.7199	19.9592	16.1168	14.1660	12.1961	10.2075	8.2007	6.1761	4.1342
5	26.8243	23.2240	19.5412	15.7790	13.8692	11.9406	9.9938	8.0291	6.0470	4.0478
6	26.2266	22.7046	19.1032	15.4248	13.5577	11.6724	9.7693	7.8488	5.9113	3.9570
7	25.6009	22.1608	18.6442	15.0534	13.2310	11.3910	9.5337	7.6595	5.7687	3.8616
8	24.9462	21.5915	18.1635	14.6641	12.8885	11.0958	9.2865	7.4608	5.6190	3.7614
9	24.2613	20.9957	17.6601	14.2564	12.5296	10.7865	9.0273	7.2524	5.4619	3.6562
10	23.5448	20.3723	17.1333	13.8294	12.1537	10.4624	8.7557	7.0339	5.2972	3.5458
11	22.7954	19.7202	16.5821	13.3826	11.7602	10.1231	8.4713	6.8051	5.1246	3.4302
12	22.0118	19.0382	16.0056	12.9151	11.3485	9.7680	8.1736	6.5655	4.9439	3.3090
13	21.1925	18.3252	15.4028	12.4262	10.9180	9.3966	7.8621	6.3149	4.7549	3.1823
14	20.3361	17.5800	14.7728	11.9153	10.4679	9.0083	7.5366	6.0528	4.5571	3.0497
15	19.4410	16.8013	14.1146	11.3815	9.9977	8.6027	7.1964	5.7790	4.3506	2.9112
16	18.5056	15.9878	13.4271	10.8240	9.5068	8.1791	6.8412	5.4931	4.1348	2.7665
17	17.5283	15.1381	12.7093	10.2421	8.9943	7.7371	6.4706	5.1948	3.9098	2.6156
18	16.5073	14.2510	11.9601	9.6350	8.4598	7.2761	6.0841	4.8837	3.6751	2.4582
19	15.4410	13.3249	11.1785	9.0019	7.9024	6.7955	5.6812	4.5595	3.4305	2.2943
20	14.3275	12.3585	10.3633	8.3420	7.3216	6.2948	5.2616	4.2219	3.1759	2.1236
21	13.1649	11.3503	9.5134	7.6544	6.7167	5.7734	4.8248	3.8706	2.9111	1.9461
22	11.9512	10.2986	8.6277	6.9384	6.0869	5.2309	4.3703	3.5052	2.6357	1.7616
23	10.6845	9.2020	7.7049	6.1930	5.4316	4.6665	3.8978	3.1255	2.3495	1.5700
24	9.3626	8.0588	6.7438	5.4175	4.7501	4.0799	3.4069	2.7311	2.0525	1.3711
25	7.9833	6.8674	5.7433	4.6109	4.0417	3.4704	2.8971	2.3218	1.7444	1.1649
26	6.5444	5.6259	4.7020	3.7725	3.3058	2.8376	2.3681	1.8972	1.4250	0.9513
27	5.0435	4.3327	3.6187	2.9014	2.5415	2.1809	1.8194	1.4571	1.0941	0.7302
28	3.4784	2.9860	2.4921	1.9966	1.7484	1.4997	1.2507	1.0013	0.7516	0.5014
29	1.8464	1.5838	1.3208	1.0574	0.9256	0.7937	0.6616	0.5295	0.3973	0.2649

9.25% Interest Rate   30 Year Amortization Schedule

Prepaid in Year	Market Rate at Time of Prepayment									
	5.75%	6.25%	6.75%	7.25%	7.50%	7.75%	8.00%	8.25%	8.50%	8.75%
1	28.6061	24.7609	20.8279	16.8115	14.7733	12.7160	10.6401	8.5460	6.4344	4.3059
2	28.1257	24.3453	20.4789	16.5306	14.5270	12.5044	10.4634	8.4045	6.3282	4.2350
3	27.6217	23.9089	20.1121	16.2351	14.2676	12.2816	10.2773	8.2553	6.2161	4.1602
4	27.0932	23.4508	19.7267	15.9243	13.9947	12.0469	10.0812	8.0981	6.0979	4.0813
5	26.5390	22.9702	19.3220	15.5976	13.7077	11.8000	9.8748	7.9324	5.9734	3.9980
6	25.9581	22.4660	18.8971	15.2543	13.4061	11.5403	9.6575	7.7580	5.8421	3.9103
7	25.3492	21.9372	18.4512	14.8938	13.0891	11.2674	9.4291	7.5746	5.7040	3.8179
8	24.7111	21.3828	17.9835	14.5154	12.7562	10.9807	9.1891	7.3817	5.5588	3.7207
9	24.0425	20.8017	17.4930	14.1183	12.4069	10.6797	8.9369	7.1790	5.4061	3.6184
10	23.3422	20.1927	16.9788	13.7019	12.0404	10.3638	8.6723	6.9662	5.2457	3.5110
11	22.6087	19.5549	16.4400	13.2653	11.6561	10.0325	8.3947	6.7429	5.0774	3.3982
12	21.8407	18.8869	15.8756	12.8079	11.2534	9.6852	8.1037	6.5088	4.9008	3.2799
13	21.0367	18.1876	15.2846	12.3289	10.8316	9.3215	7.7987	6.2634	4.7158	3.1559
14	20.1951	17.4556	14.6661	11.8276	10.3901	8.9407	7.4795	6.0065	4.5220	3.0260
15	19.3144	16.6897	14.0190	11.3030	9.9282	8.5423	7.1454	5.7377	4.3192	2.8900
16	18.3929	15.8886	13.3423	10.7544	9.4451	8.1257	6.7961	5.4566	4.1071	2.7478
17	17.4290	15.0509	12.6348	10.1811	8.9403	7.6903	6.4311	5.1628	3.8855	2.5992
18	16.4209	14.1751	11.8954	9.5821	8.4129	7.2355	6.0499	4.8560	3.6541	2.4441
19	15.3668	13.2599	11.1231	8.9566	7.8624	6.7608	5.6520	4.5359	3.4126	2.2822
20	14.2647	12.3036	10.3166	8.3039	7.2879	6.2657	5.2370	4.2021	3.1609	2.1135
21	13.1128	11.3048	9.4748	7.6230	6.6889	5.7494	4.8045	3.8543	2.8987	1.9378
22	11.9090	10.2619	8.5965	6.9130	6.0645	5.2115	4.3541	3.4921	2.6257	1.7549
23	10.6513	9.1732	7.6804	6.1732	5.4141	4.6514	3.8852	3.1153	2.3418	1.5648
24	9.3374	8.0370	6.7254	5.4026	4.7370	4.0686	3.3974	2.7235	2.0467	1.3673
25	7.9652	6.8517	5.7301	4.6003	4.0323	3.4624	2.8904	2.3163	1.7403	1.1622
26	6.5323	5.6155	4.6932	3.7655	3.2996	2.8323	2.3636	1.8936	1.4222	0.9495
27	5.0364	4.3266	3.6135	2.8972	2.5379	2.1777	1.8168	1.4550	1.0925	0.7291
28	3.4749	2.9830	2.4896	1.9946	1.7466	1.4982	1.2494	1.0003	0.7508	0.5009
29	1.8453	1.5829	1.3200	1.0568	0.9250	0.7932	0.6612	0.5292	0.3970	0.2648

Entries are the points to raise the yield on prepaid funds to that of the original loan.

Prepayment Premium to Maintain Yield

9.50% Interest Rate   30 Year Amortization Schedule

Prepaid in Year	Market Rate at Time of Prepayment									
	6.00%	6.50%	7.00%	7.50%	7.75%	8.00%	8.25%	8.50%	8.75%	9.00%
1	28.2561	24.4493	20.5587	16.5886	14.5751	12.5433	10.4939	8.4273	6.3441	4.2448
2	27.7923	24.0486	20.2227	16.3185	14.3383	12.3401	10.3243	8.2916	6.2422	4.1769
3	27.3050	23.6272	19.8688	16.0337	14.0886	12.1256	10.1453	8.1481	6.1345	4.1050
4	26.7932	23.1841	19.4965	15.7338	13.8253	11.8994	9.9563	7.9966	6.0207	4.0290
5	26.2557	22.7184	19.1047	15.4179	13.5479	11.6608	9.7570	7.8368	5.9006	3.9488
6	25.6914	22.2290	18.6928	15.0854	13.2558	11.4096	9.5469	7.6682	5.7737	3.8640
7	25.0989	21.7150	18.2598	14.7356	12.9484	11.1450	9.3255	7.4904	5.6400	3.7746
8	24.4772	21.1753	17.8048	14.3678	12.6250	10.8665	9.0925	7.3033	5.4991	3.6803
9	23.8249	20.6087	17.3269	13.9812	12.2850	10.5737	8.8473	7.1062	5.3507	3.5810
10	23.1405	20.0141	16.8251	13.5751	11.9278	10.2658	8.5895	6.8990	5.1946	3.4765
11	22.4228	19.3904	16.2986	13.1488	11.5526	9.9425	8.3186	6.6812	5.0304	3.3665
12	21.6703	18.7362	15.7462	12.7014	11.1588	9.6030	8.0342	6.4524	4.8580	3.2510
13	20.8814	18.0504	15.1670	12.2321	10.7457	9.2469	7.7357	6.2123	4.6769	3.1297
14	20.0546	17.3316	14.5599	11.7402	10.3127	8.8734	7.4227	5.9605	4.4870	3.0024
15	19.1882	16.5786	13.9239	11.2248	9.8589	8.4821	7.0947	5.6966	4.2880	2.8689
16	18.2806	15.7898	13.2578	10.6851	9.3837	8.0724	6.7512	5.4202	4.0795	2.7292
17	17.3300	14.9639	12.5605	10.1202	8.8864	7.6435	6.3917	5.1309	3.8613	2.5829
18	16.3347	14.0994	11.8309	9.5293	8.3662	7.1950	6.0157	4.8284	3.6332	2.4300
19	15.2926	13.1949	11.0678	8.9114	7.8224	6.7262	5.6229	4.5124	3.3948	2.2702
20	14.2020	12.2487	10.2700	8.2658	7.2543	6.2366	5.2126	4.1824	3.1460	2.1034
21	13.0608	11.2594	9.4362	7.5916	6.6612	5.7254	4.7844	3.8380	2.8864	1.9295
22	11.8669	10.2251	8.5654	6.8877	6.0422	5.1922	4.3379	3.4791	2.6159	1.7483
23	10.6181	9.1443	7.6560	6.1534	5.3967	4.6364	3.8725	3.1051	2.3341	1.5596
24	9.3123	8.0152	6.7070	5.3877	4.7238	4.0573	3.3879	2.7158	2.0410	1.3634
25	7.9472	6.8361	5.7169	4.5897	4.0230	3.4543	2.8836	2.3109	1.7362	1.1595
26	6.5203	5.6051	4.6845	3.7584	3.2934	2.8269	2.3592	1.8900	1.4195	0.9477
27	5.0292	4.3204	3.6083	2.8931	2.5342	2.1746	1.8142	1.4529	1.0909	0.7281
28	3.4714	2.9800	2.4870	1.9926	1.7448	1.4967	1.2482	0.9993	0.7500	0.5004
29	1.8442	1.5819	1.3193	1.0562	0.9245	0.7927	0.6608	0.5289	0.3968	0.2646

9.75% Interest Rate   30 Year Amortization Schedule

Prepaid in Year	Market Rate at Time of Prepayment									
	6.25%	6.75%	7.25%	7.75%	8.00%	8.25%	8.50%	8.75%	9.00%	9.25%
1	27.9094	24.1410	20.2926	16.3685	14.3794	12.3730	10.3498	8.3103	6.2551	4.1846
2	27.4619	23.7548	19.9692	16.1089	14.1520	12.1779	10.1871	8.1801	6.1575	4.1196
3	26.9910	23.3480	19.6281	15.8347	13.9116	11.9715	10.0149	8.0423	6.0540	4.0506
4	26.4956	22.9196	19.2684	15.5452	13.6577	11.7535	9.8329	7.8964	5.9445	3.9775
5	25.9744	22.4686	18.8894	15.2399	13.3898	11.5232	9.6405	7.7422	5.8286	3.9001
6	25.4264	21.9939	18.4902	14.9180	13.1071	11.2801	9.4374	7.5792	5.7061	3.8183
7	24.8503	21.4945	18.0698	14.5787	12.8090	11.0237	9.2229	7.4072	5.5767	3.7318
8	24.2447	20.9692	17.6273	14.2213	12.4949	10.7533	8.9968	7.2256	5.4400	3.6404
9	23.6084	20.4169	17.1619	13.8451	12.1642	10.4685	8.7584	7.0341	5.2959	3.5439
10	22.9399	19.8365	16.6724	13.4492	11.8160	10.1686	8.5073	6.8324	5.1439	3.4422
11	22.2378	19.2267	16.1580	13.0329	11.4498	9.8531	8.2431	6.6200	4.9839	3.3351
12	21.5006	18.5863	15.6175	12.5954	11.0648	9.5213	7.9652	6.3965	4.8155	3.2222
13	20.7267	17.9139	15.0499	12.1358	10.6603	9.1727	7.6730	6.1615	4.6383	3.1036
14	19.9145	17.2081	14.4541	11.6533	10.2356	8.8065	7.3662	5.9147	4.4523	2.9789
15	19.0624	16.4678	13.8290	11.1470	9.7899	8.4223	7.0442	5.6557	4.2569	2.8480
16	18.1686	15.6912	13.1735	10.6160	9.3225	8.0193	6.7064	5.3839	4.0520	2.7106
17	17.2313	14.8771	12.4864	10.0595	8.8327	7.5970	6.3524	5.0992	3.8372	2.5667
18	16.2486	14.0239	11.7665	9.4766	8.3196	7.1546	5.9817	4.8009	3.6123	2.4159
19	15.2186	13.1301	11.0126	8.8664	7.7826	6.6917	5.5938	4.4889	3.3770	2.2582
20	14.1394	12.1940	10.2234	8.2279	7.2208	6.2075	5.1881	4.1626	3.1310	2.0934
21	13.0088	11.2140	9.3977	7.5602	6.6335	5.7015	4.7643	3.8218	2.8741	1.9212
22	11.8248	10.1884	8.5343	6.8624	6.0199	5.1730	4.3217	3.4660	2.6060	1.7417
23	10.5850	9.1155	7.6317	6.1336	5.3792	4.6213	3.8599	3.0949	2.3264	1.5545
24	9.2873	7.9935	6.6886	5.3728	4.7107	4.0459	3.3784	2.7082	2.0352	1.3595
25	7.9292	6.8205	5.7038	4.5790	4.0136	3.4462	2.8768	2.3055	1.7321	1.1567
26	6.5083	5.5947	4.6758	3.7514	3.2872	2.8216	2.3547	1.8864	1.4168	0.9459
27	5.0221	4.3142	3.6032	2.8889	2.5306	2.1714	1.8115	1.4508	1.0893	0.7270
28	3.4679	2.9770	2.4845	1.9906	1.7431	1.4952	1.2469	0.9983	0.7493	0.4999
29	1.8431	1.5810	1.3185	1.0556	0.9240	0.7923	0.6605	0.5286	0.3966	0.2645

Entries are the points to raise the yield on prepaid funds to that of the original loan.

Prepayment Premium to Maintain Yield

10.00% Interest Rate   30 Year Amortization Schedule

Prepaid in Year	6.50%	7.00%	7.50%	8.00%	8.25%	8.50%	8.75%	9.00%	9.25%	9.50%
				Market Rate at Time of Prepayment						
1	27.5661	23.8360	20.0296	16.1513	14.1864	12.2050	10.2078	8.1951	6.1674	4.1254
2	27.1346	23.4641	19.7185	15.9018	13.9680	12.0178	10.0517	8.0703	6.0739	4.0631
3	26.6797	23.0716	19.3898	15.6379	13.7367	11.8194	9.8863	7.9379	5.9746	3.9969
4	26.2004	22.6576	19.0426	15.3588	13.4920	11.6093	9.7110	7.7975	5.8692	3.9266
5	25.6953	22.2209	18.6761	15.0638	13.2332	11.3870	9.5254	7.6488	5.7576	3.8521
6	25.1634	21.7606	18.2893	14.7522	12.9598	11.1519	9.3290	7.4913	5.6392	3.7731
7	24.6033	21.2755	17.8813	14.4232	12.6709	10.9035	9.1213	7.3247	5.5140	3.6894
8	24.0136	20.7645	17.4512	14.0761	12.3659	10.6411	8.9019	7.1486	5.3815	3.6008
9	23.3931	20.2264	16.9980	13.7100	12.0442	10.3642	8.6703	6.9626	5.2415	3.5072
10	22.7403	19.6599	16.5207	13.3242	11.7050	10.0721	8.4258	6.7662	5.0936	3.4083
11	22.0536	19.0639	16.0182	12.9178	11.3476	9.7643	8.1681	6.5591	4.9377	3.3038
12	21.3316	18.4370	15.4895	12.4901	10.9713	9.4401	7.8966	6.3409	4.7732	3.1937
13	20.5726	17.7779	14.9334	12.0400	10.5753	9.0988	7.6107	6.1110	4.6000	3.0777
14	19.7750	17.0851	14.3488	11.5668	10.1589	8.7399	7.3100	5.8692	4.4177	2.9556
15	18.9370	16.3573	13.7346	11.0695	9.7212	8.3627	6.9939	5.6149	4.2260	2.8271
16	18.0569	15.5930	13.0896	10.5472	9.2616	7.9664	6.6618	5.3479	4.0246	2.6922
17	17.1327	14.7906	12.4126	9.9991	8.7792	7.5506	6.3133	5.0675	3.8132	2.5505
18	16.1627	13.9486	11.7023	9.4241	8.2732	7.1144	5.9478	4.7735	3.5916	2.4019
19	15.1448	13.0654	10.9576	8.8214	7.7428	6.6573	5.5648	4.4655	3.3593	2.2463
20	14.0769	12.1394	10.1770	8.1900	7.1873	6.1786	5.1638	4.1430	3.1161	2.0834
21	12.9570	11.1687	9.3593	7.5289	6.6059	5.6776	4.7442	3.8056	2.8619	1.9130
22	11.7827	10.1518	8.5032	6.8372	5.9976	5.1537	4.3055	3.4530	2.5961	1.7350
23	10.5519	9.0867	7.6073	6.1138	5.3618	4.6063	3.8473	3.0848	2.3188	1.5493
24	9.2622	7.9717	6.6703	5.3579	4.6976	4.0347	3.3690	2.7006	2.0295	1.3557
25	7.9112	6.8049	5.6907	4.5684	4.0043	3.4382	2.8701	2.3000	1.7280	1.1540
26	6.4963	5.5844	4.6670	3.7443	3.2810	2.8163	2.3502	1.8829	1.4141	0.9441
27	5.0150	4.3081	3.5980	2.8847	2.5269	2.1683	1.8089	1.4487	1.0877	0.7259
28	3.4645	2.9740	2.4820	1.9886	1.7413	1.4937	1.2456	0.9973	0.7485	0.4994
29	1.8421	1.5801	1.3177	1.0549	0.9234	0.7918	0.6601	0.5282	0.3963	0.2643

10.25% Interest Rate   30 Year Amortization Schedule

Prepaid in Year	6.75%	7.25%	7.75%	8.25%	8.50%	8.75%	9.00%	9.25%	9.50%	9.75%
				Market Rate at Time of Prepayment						
1	27.2263	23.5344	19.7699	15.9369	13.9960	12.0394	10.0678	8.0815	6.0811	4.0671
2	26.8104	23.1764	19.4708	15.6973	13.7863	11.8598	9.9182	7.9620	5.9916	4.0075
3	26.3712	22.7979	19.1542	15.4434	13.5640	11.6691	9.7593	7.8348	5.8963	3.9440
4	25.9076	22.3979	18.8191	15.1743	13.3282	11.4668	9.5905	7.6998	5.7950	3.8765
5	25.4184	21.9754	18.4648	14.8894	13.0784	11.2523	9.4115	7.5564	5.6873	3.8047
6	24.9023	21.5292	18.0902	14.5879	12.8139	11.0251	9.2218	7.4043	5.5731	3.7284
7	24.3579	21.0582	17.6944	14.2691	12.5340	10.7845	9.0208	7.2431	5.4520	3.6475
8	23.7840	20.5612	17.2765	13.9320	12.2380	10.5299	8.8080	7.0724	5.3236	3.5617
9	23.1791	20.0370	16.8354	13.5760	11.9252	10.2608	8.5829	6.8917	5.1876	3.4708
10	22.5417	19.4844	16.3700	13.2001	11.5949	9.9764	8.3449	6.7007	5.0438	3.3746
11	21.8703	18.9020	15.8793	12.8035	11.2462	9.6762	8.0936	6.4988	4.8918	3.2729
12	21.1633	18.2885	15.3621	12.3853	10.8784	9.3594	7.8284	6.2857	4.7313	3.1654
13	20.4191	17.6426	14.8174	11.9447	10.4908	9.0255	7.5488	6.0609	4.5619	3.0520
14	19.6359	16.9627	14.2439	11.4806	10.0826	8.6737	7.2541	5.8239	4.3833	2.9324
15	18.8120	16.2473	13.6405	10.9923	9.6529	8.3033	6.9438	5.5744	4.1953	2.8064
16	17.9455	15.4951	13.0060	10.4787	9.2009	7.9138	6.6174	5.3119	3.9974	2.6738
17	17.0345	14.7044	12.3390	9.9388	8.7258	7.5043	6.2744	5.0360	3.7893	2.5344
18	16.0771	13.8735	11.6383	9.3718	8.2269	7.0743	5.9141	4.7462	3.5709	2.3880
19	15.0711	13.0009	10.9026	8.7766	7.7032	6.6230	5.5360	4.4421	3.3416	2.2344
20	14.0145	12.0848	10.1307	8.1522	7.1539	6.1497	5.1395	4.1233	3.1013	2.0734
21	12.9052	11.1235	9.3210	7.4977	6.5783	5.6538	4.7241	3.7894	2.8496	1.9048
22	11.7407	10.1152	8.4722	6.8120	5.9754	5.1345	4.2894	3.4400	2.5863	1.7284
23	10.5189	9.0580	7.5830	6.0941	5.3444	4.5913	3.8347	3.0746	2.3111	1.5442
24	9.2372	7.9500	6.6520	5.3431	4.6846	4.0234	3.3595	2.6929	2.0237	1.3518
25	7.8932	6.7894	5.6775	4.5578	3.9950	3.4301	2.8634	2.2946	1.7239	1.1512
26	6.4843	5.5740	4.6583	3.7373	3.2748	2.8110	2.3458	1.8793	1.4114	0.9423
27	5.0078	4.3019	3.5928	2.8806	2.5233	2.1652	1.8063	1.4466	1.0861	0.7249
28	3.4610	2.9710	2.4795	1.9866	1.7396	1.4922	1.2444	0.9962	0.7477	0.4989
29	1.8410	1.5792	1.3169	1.0543	0.9229	0.7913	0.6597	0.5279	0.3961	0.2642

Entries are the points to raise the yield on prepaid funds to that of the original loan.

Prepayment Premium to Maintain Yield

10.50% Interest Rate   30 Year Amortization Schedule

Prepaid in Year	7.00%	7.50%	8.00%	8.50%	8.75%	9.00%	9.25%	9.50%	9.75%	10.00%
				Market Rate at Time of Prepayment						
1	26.8900	23.2363	19.5134	15.7254	13.8082	11.8762	9.9299	7.9698	5.9962	4.0098
2	26.4893	22.8919	19.2260	15.4955	13.6071	11.7040	9.7866	7.8552	5.9105	3.9527
3	26.0656	22.5271	18.9211	15.2512	13.3934	11.5208	9.6339	7.7332	5.8191	3.8919
4	25.6174	22.1408	18.5980	14.9920	13.1663	11.3261	9.4716	7.6034	5.7217	3.8270
5	25.1437	21.7321	18.2555	14.7169	12.9253	11.1192	9.2990	7.4652	5.6180	3.7579
6	24.6432	21.2997	17.8929	14.4253	12.6696	10.8996	9.1157	7.3184	5.5078	3.6843
7	24.1143	20.8426	17.5091	14.1164	12.3985	10.6667	8.9212	7.1624	5.3906	3.6061
8	23.5559	20.3594	17.1031	13.7892	12.1113	10.4197	8.7149	6.9969	5.2662	3.5230
9	22.9664	19.8490	16.6739	13.4430	11.8072	10.1582	8.4962	6.8215	5.1343	3.4348
10	22.3443	19.3100	16.2203	13.0769	11.4855	9.8814	8.2647	6.6356	4.9944	3.3412
11	21.6880	18.7410	15.7412	12.6899	11.1454	9.5886	8.0197	6.4389	4.8463	3.2422
12	20.9959	18.1408	15.2355	12.2812	10.7861	9.2792	7.7608	6.2308	4.6896	3.1373
13	20.2663	17.5078	14.7020	11.8499	10.4068	8.9525	7.4872	6.0110	4.5240	3.0264
14	19.4974	16.8407	14.1396	11.3950	10.0066	8.6078	7.1985	5.7789	4.3491	2.9093
15	18.6874	16.1378	13.5469	10.9155	9.5848	8.2443	6.8940	5.5341	4.1647	2.7858
16	17.8345	15.3975	12.9226	10.4104	9.1404	7.8614	6.5733	5.2762	3.9703	2.6555
17	16.9365	14.6184	12.2656	9.8788	8.6727	7.4583	6.2356	5.0046	3.7656	2.5184
18	15.9916	13.7986	11.5745	9.3196	8.1807	7.0343	5.8804	4.7190	3.5502	2.3741
19	14.9976	12.9365	10.8479	8.7319	7.6637	6.5888	5.5072	4.4189	3.3240	2.2225
20	13.9523	12.0304	10.0844	8.1145	7.1206	6.1209	5.1153	4.1038	3.0865	2.0634
21	12.8535	11.0784	9.2827	7.4665	6.5508	5.6300	4.7042	3.7733	2.8374	1.8966
22	11.6988	10.0787	8.4413	6.7868	5.9532	5.1154	4.2733	3.4270	2.5765	1.7218
23	10.4859	9.0293	7.5588	6.0744	5.3271	4.5763	3.8221	3.0645	2.3034	1.5390
24	9.2122	7.9283	6.6336	5.3282	4.6715	4.0121	3.3501	2.6853	2.0180	1.3480
25	7.8753	6.7738	5.6644	4.5472	3.9856	3.4221	2.8566	2.2892	1.7198	1.1485
26	6.4723	5.5636	4.6496	3.7303	3.2686	2.8056	2.3413	1.8757	1.4088	0.9405
27	5.0007	4.2958	3.5877	2.8764	2.5196	2.1620	1.8036	1.4445	1.0845	0.7238
28	3.4575	2.9680	2.4770	1.9846	1.7378	1.4906	1.2431	0.9952	0.7470	0.4984
29	1.8399	1.5782	1.3162	1.0537	0.9223	0.7909	0.6593	0.5276	0.3959	0.2640

10.75% Interest Rate   30 Year Amortization Schedule

Prepaid in Year	7.25%	7.75%	8.25%	8.75%	9.00%	9.25%	9.50%	9.75%	10.00%	10.25%
				Market Rate at Time of Prepayment						
1	26.5574	22.9417	19.2602	15.5169	13.6232	11.7154	9.7941	7.8597	5.9127	3.9534
2	26.1716	22.6105	18.9842	15.2962	13.4303	11.5504	9.6568	7.7501	5.8306	3.8988
3	25.7629	22.2590	18.6908	15.0615	13.2250	11.3744	9.5103	7.6330	5.7430	3.8405
4	25.3299	21.8863	18.3792	14.8117	13.0064	11.1870	9.3542	7.5082	5.6494	3.7782
5	24.8714	21.4911	18.0484	14.5463	12.7739	10.9876	9.1879	7.3751	5.5496	3.7116
6	24.3861	21.0723	17.6975	14.2644	12.5267	10.7755	9.0109	7.2334	5.4432	3.6407
7	23.8725	20.6287	17.3255	13.9651	12.2643	10.5500	8.8227	7.0826	5.3299	3.5651
8	23.3294	20.1591	16.9312	13.6476	11.9857	10.3106	8.6227	6.9222	5.2095	3.4846
9	22.7550	19.6622	16.5136	13.3111	11.6902	10.0565	8.4104	6.7519	5.0814	3.3991
10	22.1480	19.1366	16.0716	12.9545	11.3770	9.7872	8.1851	6.5711	4.9454	3.3082
11	21.5066	18.5810	15.6040	12.5771	11.0454	9.5018	7.9464	6.3795	4.8012	3.2117
12	20.8293	17.9939	15.1096	12.1778	10.6944	9.1996	7.6936	6.1764	4.6483	3.1094
13	20.1142	17.3738	14.5873	11.7557	10.3233	8.8800	7.4260	5.9614	4.4864	3.0011
14	19.3595	16.7192	14.0357	11.3097	9.9311	8.5422	7.1432	5.7342	4.3152	2.8864
15	18.5633	16.0286	13.4536	10.8390	9.5171	8.1855	6.8445	5.4940	4.1343	2.7653
16	17.7238	15.3003	12.8396	10.3424	9.0803	7.8092	6.5293	5.2406	3.9433	2.6373
17	16.8388	14.5326	12.1925	9.8190	8.6198	7.4124	6.1969	4.9734	3.7419	2.5024
18	15.9063	13.7239	11.5109	9.2676	8.1347	6.9945	5.8469	4.6919	3.5297	2.3603
19	14.9242	12.8723	10.7933	8.6873	7.6243	6.5546	5.4784	4.3957	3.3064	2.2107
20	13.8901	11.9761	10.0383	8.0769	7.0874	6.0922	5.0911	4.0843	3.0717	2.0535
21	12.8019	11.0333	9.2445	7.4354	6.5233	5.6063	4.6842	3.7572	2.8253	1.8884
22	11.6569	10.0422	8.4104	6.7617	5.9311	5.0962	4.2572	3.4140	2.5667	1.7153
23	10.4529	9.0006	7.5345	6.0548	5.3097	4.5613	3.8095	3.0544	2.2958	1.5339
24	9.1873	7.9067	6.6154	5.3134	4.6585	4.0009	3.3406	2.6777	2.0122	1.3441
25	7.8573	6.7582	5.6513	4.5366	3.9763	3.4141	2.8499	2.2838	1.7157	1.1458
26	6.4604	5.5533	4.6409	3.7233	3.2624	2.8003	2.3369	1.8721	1.4061	0.9387
27	4.9936	4.2896	3.5825	2.8723	2.5160	2.1589	1.8010	1.4424	1.0830	0.7228
28	3.4541	2.9650	2.4745	1.9826	1.7360	1.4891	1.2419	0.9942	0.7462	0.4978
29	1.8388	1.5773	1.3154	1.0531	0.9218	0.7904	0.6589	0.5273	0.3956	0.2638

Entries are the points to raise the yield on prepaid funds to that of the original loan.

Prepayment Premium to Maintain Yield

11.00% Interest Rate   30 Year Amortization Schedule

Prepaid in Year	Market Rate at Time of Prepayment									
	7.50%	8.00%	8.50%	9.00%	9.25%	9.50%	9.75%	10.00%	10.25%	10.50%
1	26.2285	22.6507	19.0104	15.3112	13.4408	11.5570	9.6604	7.7514	5.8304	3.8979
2	25.8573	22.3324	18.7453	15.0997	13.2560	11.3989	9.5290	7.6465	5.7520	3.8458
3	25.4632	21.9939	18.4631	14.8741	13.0587	11.2300	9.3884	7.5343	5.6680	3.7899
4	25.0450	21.6343	18.1628	14.6336	12.8484	11.0498	9.2383	7.4143	5.5781	3.7300
5	24.6014	21.2523	17.8435	14.3776	12.6242	10.8576	9.0781	7.2861	5.4820	3.6660
6	24.1311	20.8469	17.5040	14.1051	12.3854	10.6527	8.9073	7.1494	5.3794	3.5976
7	23.6326	20.4166	17.1434	13.8153	12.1314	10.4346	8.7252	7.0036	5.2700	3.5246
8	23.1044	19.9604	16.7607	13.5073	11.8612	10.2025	8.5314	6.8483	5.1533	3.4467
9	22.5450	19.4768	16.3545	13.1803	11.5742	9.9558	8.3253	6.6830	5.0291	3.3638
10	21.9529	18.9644	15.9239	12.8332	11.2694	9.6937	8.1062	6.5072	4.8969	3.2754
11	21.3263	18.4219	15.4677	12.4651	10.9461	9.4155	7.8736	6.3205	4.7564	3.1815
12	20.6635	17.8477	14.9845	12.0750	10.6033	9.1205	7.6268	6.1223	4.6073	3.0817
13	19.9627	17.2404	14.4731	11.6620	10.2403	8.8080	7.3652	5.9122	4.4491	2.9759
14	19.2221	16.5983	13.9323	11.2249	9.8560	8.4771	7.0883	5.6897	4.2814	2.8637
15	18.4397	15.9199	13.3607	10.7629	9.4497	8.1271	6.7952	5.4542	4.1040	2.7449
16	17.6135	15.2034	12.7570	10.2747	9.0203	7.7572	6.4855	5.2052	3.9164	2.6192
17	16.7414	14.4472	12.1197	9.7594	8.5670	7.3667	6.1584	4.9423	3.7183	2.4865
18	15.8213	13.6494	11.4474	9.2158	8.0889	6.9548	5.8134	4.6649	3.5092	2.3465
19	14.8510	12.8083	10.7388	8.6428	7.5850	6.5206	5.4498	4.3726	3.2889	2.1989
20	13.8281	11.9219	9.9922	8.0394	7.0543	6.0635	5.0670	4.0648	3.0570	2.0436
21	12.7503	10.9884	9.2064	7.4044	6.4959	5.5826	4.6643	3.7411	2.8131	1.8802
22	11.6151	10.0058	8.3796	6.7367	5.9090	5.0771	4.2412	3.4011	2.5569	1.7087
23	10.4200	8.9720	7.5103	6.0351	5.2924	4.5464	3.7970	3.0443	2.2882	1.5288
24	9.1623	7.8850	6.5971	5.2986	4.6454	3.9896	3.3312	2.6702	2.0065	1.3403
25	7.8394	6.7427	5.6382	4.5260	3.9670	3.4061	2.8432	2.2784	1.7117	1.1430
26	6.4484	5.5429	4.6322	3.7162	3.2563	2.7950	2.3324	1.8686	1.4034	0.9369
27	4.9864	4.2835	3.5774	2.8681	2.5123	2.1558	1.7984	1.4403	1.0814	0.7217
28	3.4506	2.9620	2.4720	1.9806	1.7343	1.4876	1.2406	0.9932	0.7455	0.4973
29	1.8378	1.5764	1.3146	1.0525	0.9212	0.7899	0.6585	0.5270	0.3954	0.2637

11.25% Interest Rate   30 Year Amortization Schedule

Prepaid in Year	Market Rate at Time of Prepayment									
	7.75%	8.25%	8.75%	9.25%	9.50%	9.75%	10.00%	10.25%	10.50%	10.75%
1	25.9034	22.3634	18.7639	15.1086	13.2611	11.4011	9.5288	7.6449	5.7496	3.8434
2	25.5463	22.0575	18.5095	14.9058	13.0840	11.2496	9.4030	7.5445	5.6746	3.7936
3	25.1666	21.7318	18.2382	14.6891	12.8947	11.0876	9.2682	7.4369	5.5941	3.7400
4	24.7629	21.3850	17.9489	14.4577	12.6923	10.9143	9.1239	7.3216	5.5078	3.6826
5	24.3339	21.0159	17.6406	14.2108	12.4763	10.7291	8.9697	7.1983	5.4153	3.6211
6	23.8783	20.6235	17.3124	13.9475	12.2457	10.5314	8.8048	7.0664	5.3164	3.5551
7	23.3945	20.2064	16.9631	13.6670	11.9999	10.3204	8.6288	6.9255	5.2107	3.4846
8	22.8811	19.7632	16.5916	13.3683	11.7380	10.0955	8.4411	6.7751	5.0977	3.4092
9	22.3365	19.2927	16.1968	13.0506	11.4592	9.8559	8.2410	6.6147	4.9772	3.3288
10	21.7590	18.7934	15.7774	12.7127	11.1627	9.6010	8.0280	6.4439	4.8488	3.2430
11	21.1469	18.2638	15.3323	12.3539	10.8475	9.3300	7.8014	6.2620	4.7120	3.1515
12	20.4985	17.7024	14.8601	11.9729	10.5128	9.0420	7.5606	6.0687	4.5665	3.0543
13	19.8120	17.1077	14.3596	11.5688	10.1577	8.7364	7.3049	5.8633	4.4120	2.9508
14	19.0853	16.4780	13.8295	11.1406	9.7813	8.4123	7.0336	5.6455	4.2479	2.8410
15	18.3165	15.8116	13.2682	10.6871	9.3826	8.0689	6.7462	5.4145	4.0739	2.7246
16	17.5035	15.1069	12.6746	10.2073	8.9607	7.7055	6.4419	5.1699	3.8897	2.6012
17	16.6443	14.3620	12.0471	9.7000	8.5145	7.3212	6.1201	4.9113	3.6948	2.4707
18	15.7365	13.5751	11.3842	9.1641	8.0432	6.9152	5.7801	4.6380	3.4888	2.3328
19	14.7780	12.7444	10.6844	8.5985	7.5458	6.4867	5.4213	4.3495	3.2715	2.1872
20	13.7662	11.8678	9.9463	8.0019	7.0212	6.0349	5.0429	4.0454	3.0423	2.0337
21	12.6989	10.9435	9.1683	7.3734	6.4686	5.5590	4.6445	3.7251	2.8010	1.8721
22	11.5734	9.9694	8.3488	6.7116	5.8869	5.0581	4.2252	3.3882	2.5472	1.7021
23	10.3871	8.9434	7.4862	6.0155	5.2752	4.5315	3.7845	3.0342	2.2806	1.5237
24	9.1374	7.8634	6.5788	5.2838	4.6324	3.9784	3.3218	2.6626	2.0008	1.3364
25	7.8215	6.7272	5.6252	4.5155	3.9577	3.3981	2.8365	2.2730	1.7076	1.1403
26	6.4364	5.5326	4.6235	3.7092	3.2501	2.7897	2.3280	1.8650	1.4007	0.9351
27	4.9793	4.2773	3.5722	2.8640	2.5087	2.1526	1.7958	1.4382	1.0798	0.7206
28	3.4471	2.9591	2.4695	1.9786	1.7325	1.4861	1.2393	0.9922	0.7447	0.4968
29	1.8367	1.5755	1.3138	1.0518	0.9207	0.7895	0.6581	0.5267	0.3952	0.2635

Entries are the points to raise the yield on prepaid funds to that of the original loan.

Prepayment Premium to Maintain Yield

11.50% Interest Rate   30 Year Amortization Schedule

Prepaid in Year	8.00%	8.50%	9.00%	Market Rate at Time of Prepayment 9.50%	9.75%	10.00%	10.25%	10.50%	10.75%	11.00%
1	25.5821	22.0798	18.5208	14.9089	13.0841	11.2475	9.3993	7.5400	5.6701	3.7898
2	25.2389	21.7861	18.2768	14.7146	12.9146	11.1026	9.2789	7.4441	5.5984	3.7422
3	24.8731	21.4726	18.0160	14.5065	12.7329	10.9471	9.1497	7.3410	5.5213	3.6910
4	24.4836	21.1383	17.7374	14.2839	12.5383	10.7806	9.0111	7.2303	5.4384	3.6359
5	24.0689	20.7819	17.4400	14.0459	12.3301	10.6022	8.8626	7.1116	5.3495	3.5767
6	23.6276	20.4022	17.1227	13.7916	12.1075	10.4114	8.7036	6.9844	5.2542	3.5132
7	23.1583	19.9979	16.7845	13.5202	11.8697	10.2074	8.5335	6.8483	5.1521	3.4451
8	22.6594	19.5676	16.4240	13.2306	11.6159	9.9895	8.3517	6.7027	5.0428	3.3722
9	22.1293	19.1100	16.0403	12.9220	11.3452	9.7570	8.1576	6.5471	4.9259	3.2942
10	21.5663	18.6235	15.6319	12.5933	11.0568	9.5091	7.9505	6.3811	4.8011	3.2108
11	20.9686	18.1067	15.1978	12.2435	10.7497	9.2451	7.7298	6.2040	4.6680	3.1219
12	20.3345	17.5579	14.7365	11.8715	10.4230	8.9640	7.4948	6.0155	4.5261	3.0270
13	19.6619	16.9757	14.2467	11.4763	10.0758	8.6652	7.2449	5.8148	4.3751	2.9260
14	18.9491	16.3582	13.7271	11.0567	9.7070	8.3479	6.9793	5.6015	4.2146	2.8186
15	18.1938	15.7038	13.1762	10.6117	9.3159	8.0111	6.6974	5.3751	4.0440	2.7044
16	17.3940	15.0107	12.5926	10.1401	8.9013	7.6540	6.3986	5.1349	3.8631	2.5833
17	16.5474	14.2771	11.9747	9.6408	8.4622	7.2759	6.0819	4.8804	3.6714	2.4550
18	15.6519	13.5010	11.3211	9.1126	7.9977	6.8758	5.7469	4.6112	3.4685	2.3191
19	14.7051	12.6806	10.6302	8.5542	7.5067	6.4529	5.3928	4.3266	3.2541	2.1755
20	13.7045	11.8139	9.9005	7.9646	6.9883	6.0064	5.0190	4.0261	3.0277	2.0238
21	12.6475	10.8987	9.1303	7.3425	6.4413	5.5354	4.6246	3.7091	2.7889	1.8640
22	11.5317	9.9331	8.3180	6.6867	5.8649	5.0391	4.2092	3.3753	2.5375	1.6956
23	10.3543	8.9148	7.4620	5.9959	5.2579	4.5166	3.7720	3.0241	2.2730	1.5186
24	9.1125	7.8418	6.5606	5.2691	4.6194	3.9672	3.3124	2.6550	1.9951	1.3326
25	7.8036	6.7117	5.6121	4.5049	3.9484	3.3901	2.8298	2.2676	1.7035	1.1376
26	6.4245	5.5223	4.6148	3.7022	3.2440	2.7844	2.3236	1.8614	1.3980	0.9333
27	4.9722	4.2712	3.5671	2.8598	2.5050	2.1495	1.7932	1.4361	1.0782	0.7196
28	3.4437	2.9561	2.4670	1.9766	1.7308	1.4846	1.2381	0.9912	0.7439	0.4963
29	1.8356	1.5745	1.3131	1.0512	0.9202	0.7890	0.6577	0.5264	0.3949	0.2634

11.75% Interest Rate   30 Year Amortization Schedule

Prepaid in Year	8.25%	8.75%	9.25%	Market Rate at Time of Prepayment 9.75%	10.00%	10.25%	10.50%	10.75%	11.00%	11.25%
1	25.2648	21.7998	18.2811	14.7121	12.9099	11.0963	9.2719	7.4369	5.5919	3.7372
2	24.9349	21.5179	18.0472	14.5260	12.7476	10.9577	9.1568	7.3452	5.5234	3.6917
3	24.5828	21.2165	17.7967	14.3264	12.5733	10.8087	9.0329	7.2465	5.4496	3.6427
4	24.2071	20.8944	17.5285	14.1123	12.3862	10.6486	8.8998	7.1402	5.3701	3.5898
5	23.8064	20.5503	17.2417	13.8830	12.1857	10.4769	8.7569	7.0261	5.2846	3.5329
6	23.3792	20.1831	16.9351	13.6375	11.9709	10.2928	8.6036	6.9035	5.1928	3.4718
7	22.9242	19.7914	16.6075	13.3749	11.7410	10.0956	8.4392	6.7720	5.0941	3.4060
8	22.4395	19.3737	16.2580	13.0943	11.4951	9.8846	8.2632	6.6311	4.9884	3.3355
9	21.9237	18.9287	15.8851	12.7946	11.2323	9.6590	8.0749	6.4802	4.8751	3.2599
10	21.3749	18.4548	15.4876	12.4748	10.9518	9.4180	7.8736	6.3189	4.7539	3.1790
11	20.7914	17.9506	15.0643	12.1339	10.6526	9.1608	7.6587	6.1465	4.6244	3.0924
12	20.1713	17.4143	14.6137	11.7707	10.3338	8.8866	7.4295	5.9626	4.4861	3.0000
13	19.5127	16.8444	14.1345	11.3843	9.9943	8.5946	7.1853	5.7666	4.3386	2.9014
14	18.8135	16.2390	13.6253	10.9733	9.6332	8.2838	6.9254	5.5579	4.1814	2.7963
15	18.0716	15.5965	13.0846	10.5367	9.2495	7.9535	6.6490	5.3358	4.0143	2.6844
16	17.2848	14.9149	12.5109	10.0733	8.8421	7.6028	6.3554	5.1000	3.8367	2.5655
17	16.4509	14.1925	11.9026	9.5819	8.4101	7.2308	6.0439	4.8497	3.6481	2.4393
18	15.5676	13.4272	11.2583	9.0613	7.9523	6.8365	5.7139	4.5845	3.4483	2.3055
19	14.6324	12.6171	10.5762	8.5102	7.4678	6.4192	5.3645	4.3037	3.2368	2.1638
20	13.6428	11.7600	9.8548	7.9274	6.9554	5.9780	4.9951	4.0068	3.0131	2.0140
21	12.5963	10.8540	9.0924	7.3117	6.4141	5.5119	4.6049	3.6932	2.7769	1.8559
22	11.4901	9.8968	8.2874	6.6617	5.8429	5.0201	4.1933	3.3625	2.5278	1.6891
23	10.3215	8.8863	7.4379	5.9764	5.2407	4.5017	3.7595	3.0141	2.2654	1.5135
24	9.0877	7.8202	6.5424	5.2543	4.6064	3.9560	3.3030	2.6475	1.9894	1.3288
25	7.7857	6.6962	5.5991	4.4944	3.9392	3.3821	2.8231	2.2622	1.6995	1.1349
26	6.4126	5.5120	4.6062	3.6952	3.2378	2.7791	2.3191	1.8579	1.3953	0.9315
27	4.9651	4.2651	3.5619	2.8557	2.5014	2.1464	1.7906	1.4340	1.0766	0.7185
28	3.4402	2.9531	2.4646	1.9745	1.7290	1.4831	1.2368	0.9902	0.7432	0.4958
29	1.8345	1.5736	1.3123	1.0506	0.9196	0.7885	0.6573	0.5261	0.3947	0.2632

Entries are the points to raise the yield on prepaid funds to that of the original loan.

Prepayment Premium to Maintain Yield

12.00% Interest Rate 30 Year Amortization Schedule

Prepaid in Year	Market Rate at Time of Prepayment									
	8.50%	9.00%	9.50%	10.00%	10.25%	10.50%	10.75%	11.00%	11.25%	11.50%
1	24.9514	21.5236	18.0448	14.5184	12.7383	10.9476	9.1465	7.3356	5.5151	3.6854
2	24.6346	21.2532	17.8207	14.3402	12.5830	10.8150	9.0365	7.2479	5.4497	3.6420
3	24.2958	20.9634	17.5801	14.1487	12.4159	10.6722	8.9179	7.1534	5.3790	3.5951
4	23.9335	20.6532	17.3221	13.9429	12.2362	10.5185	8.7901	7.0514	5.3028	3.5444
5	23.5465	20.3212	17.0455	13.7220	12.0431	10.3532	8.6526	6.9416	5.2206	3.4898
6	23.1331	19.9662	16.7493	13.4851	11.8359	10.1757	8.5048	6.8235	5.1321	3.4309
7	22.6920	19.5867	16.4324	13.2311	11.6136	9.9851	8.3460	6.6965	5.0369	3.3675
8	22.2213	19.1814	16.0934	12.9592	11.3754	9.7808	8.1757	6.5602	4.9347	3.2993
9	21.7195	18.7488	15.7312	12.6683	11.1204	9.5620	7.9931	6.4140	4.8249	3.2260
10	21.1848	18.2874	15.3444	12.3573	10.8477	9.3277	7.7975	6.2573	4.7072	3.1475
11	20.6153	17.7955	14.9317	12.0251	10.5563	9.0773	7.5883	6.0895	4.5811	3.0633
12	20.0091	17.2716	14.4917	11.6707	10.2452	8.8098	7.3648	5.9102	4.4463	2.9732
13	19.3642	16.7138	14.0230	11.2929	9.9134	8.5244	7.1262	5.7187	4.3023	2.8769
14	18.6785	16.1204	13.5241	10.8904	9.5598	8.2202	6.8717	5.5145	4.1486	2.7741
15	17.9499	15.4896	12.9935	10.4621	9.1835	7.8963	6.6007	5.2969	3.9847	2.6645
16	17.1761	14.8195	12.4296	10.0068	8.7833	7.5518	6.3125	5.0653	3.8104	2.5478
17	16.3547	14.1082	11.8309	9.5232	8.3582	7.1858	6.0061	4.8191	3.6250	2.4237
18	15.4835	13.3536	11.1957	9.0101	7.9071	6.7974	5.6810	4.5579	3.4282	2.2919
19	14.5599	12.5537	10.5223	8.4662	7.4290	6.3856	5.3362	4.2809	3.2195	2.1522
20	13.5813	11.7063	9.8092	7.8902	6.9226	5.9496	4.9712	3.9875	2.9985	2.0042
21	12.5451	10.8094	9.0546	7.2809	6.3870	5.4884	4.5852	3.6773	2.7648	1.8478
22	11.4485	9.8607	8.2567	6.6369	5.8210	5.0011	4.1774	3.3497	2.5181	1.6826
23	10.2888	8.8579	7.4139	5.9569	5.2235	4.4869	3.7471	3.0040	2.2578	1.5084
24	9.0629	7.7987	6.5242	5.2396	4.5935	3.9448	3.2936	2.6399	1.9837	1.3250
25	7.7679	6.6807	5.5861	4.4838	3.9299	3.3741	2.8164	2.2569	1.6954	1.1321
26	6.4006	5.5016	4.5975	3.6882	3.2317	2.7738	2.3147	1.8543	1.3926	0.9297
27	4.9580	4.2589	3.5568	2.8515	2.4978	2.1433	1.7880	1.4319	1.0751	0.7175
28	3.4367	2.9501	2.4621	1.9725	1.7272	1.4816	1.2356	0.9892	0.7424	0.4953
29	1.8335	1.5727	1.3115	1.0500	0.9191	0.7881	0.6570	0.5258	0.3945	0.2631

12.25% Interest Rate 30 Year Amortization Schedule

Prepaid in Year	Market Rate at Time of Prepayment									
	8.75%	9.25%	9.75%	10.25%	10.50%	10.75%	11.00%	11.25%	11.50%	11.75%
1	24.6421	21.2512	17.8120	14.3276	12.5695	10.8012	9.0232	7.2359	5.4396	3.6346
2	24.3379	20.9919	17.5973	14.1571	12.4209	10.6745	8.9181	7.1522	5.3771	3.5932
3	24.0120	20.7135	17.3663	13.9734	12.2607	10.5376	8.8045	7.0617	5.3095	3.5483
4	23.6629	20.4148	17.1181	13.7757	12.0881	10.3901	8.6819	6.9639	5.2364	3.4997
5	23.2892	20.0945	16.8516	13.5630	11.9023	10.2311	8.5497	6.8584	5.1575	3.4472
6	22.8893	19.7514	16.5656	13.3344	11.7024	10.0599	8.4072	6.7446	5.0723	3.3905
7	22.4618	19.3840	16.2590	13.0889	11.4876	9.8759	8.2539	6.6220	4.9804	3.3294
8	22.0049	18.9909	15.9304	12.8255	11.2570	9.6781	8.0891	6.4901	4.8815	3.2635
9	21.5169	18.5705	15.5786	12.5432	11.0096	9.4659	7.9120	6.3484	4.7752	3.1925
10	20.9960	18.1212	15.2023	12.2408	10.7446	9.2382	7.7221	6.1962	4.6609	3.1163
11	20.4403	17.6416	14.8001	11.9173	10.4608	8.9944	7.5185	6.0330	4.5383	3.0344
12	19.8478	17.1297	14.3705	11.5714	10.1572	8.7336	7.3005	5.8582	4.4069	2.9466
13	19.2165	16.5839	13.9121	11.2020	9.8330	8.4547	7.0674	5.6712	4.2662	2.8526
14	18.5442	16.0024	13.4234	10.8079	9.4868	8.1570	6.8184	5.4714	4.1159	2.7521
15	17.8287	15.3833	12.9028	10.3879	9.1178	7.8394	6.5528	5.2581	3.9554	2.6447
16	17.0677	14.7245	12.3486	9.9406	8.7248	7.5011	6.2697	5.0307	3.7842	2.5302
17	16.2589	14.0242	11.7593	9.4648	8.3066	7.1411	5.9685	4.7887	3.6019	2.4082
18	15.3997	13.2802	11.1332	8.9592	7.8621	6.7584	5.6482	4.5314	3.4081	2.2784
19	14.4876	12.4904	10.4686	8.4224	7.3903	6.3522	5.3081	4.2581	3.2023	2.1406
20	13.5200	11.6527	9.7638	7.8532	6.8899	5.9213	4.9475	3.9683	2.9840	1.9945
21	12.4941	10.7649	9.0169	7.2502	6.3599	5.4650	4.5655	3.6615	2.7529	1.8397
22	11.4071	9.8245	8.2262	6.6120	5.7991	4.9822	4.1615	3.3369	2.5084	1.6761
23	10.2561	8.8294	7.3899	5.9374	5.2063	4.4721	3.7346	2.9940	2.2503	1.5033
24	9.0381	7.7772	6.5061	5.2249	4.5805	3.9337	3.2843	2.6324	1.9780	1.3212
25	7.7500	6.6653	5.5730	4.4733	3.9206	3.3661	2.8097	2.2515	1.6914	1.1294
26	6.3887	5.4913	4.5888	3.6812	3.2255	2.7685	2.3103	1.8508	1.3900	0.9279
27	4.9509	4.2528	3.5516	2.8474	2.4942	2.1401	1.7853	1.4298	1.0735	0.7164
28	3.4333	2.9472	2.4596	1.9705	1.7255	1.4801	1.2343	0.9882	0.7417	0.4948
29	1.8324	1.5718	1.3108	1.0494	0.9185	0.7876	0.6566	0.5254	0.3942	0.2629

Entries are the points to raise the yield on prepaid funds to that of the original loan.

Prepayment Premium to Maintain Yield

12.50% Interest Rate   30 Year Amortization Schedule

Prepaid in Year	9.00%	9.50%	10.00%	10.50%	10.75%	11.00%	11.25%	11.50%	11.75%	12.00%
				Market Rate at Time of Prepayment						
1	24.3367	20.9826	17.5826	14.1398	12.4033	10.6573	8.9020	7.1379	5.3654	3.5846
2	24.0449	20.7340	17.3770	13.9767	12.2613	10.5361	8.8016	7.0580	5.3058	3.5451
3	23.7315	20.4666	17.1554	13.8006	12.1078	10.4051	8.6929	6.9714	5.2411	3.5022
4	23.3952	20.1792	16.9168	13.6107	11.9421	10.2635	8.5752	6.8777	5.1711	3.4557
5	23.0345	19.8704	16.6600	13.4060	11.7633	10.1106	8.4481	6.7763	5.0952	3.4053
6	22.6479	19.5389	16.3840	13.1855	11.5706	9.9456	8.3109	6.6667	5.0132	3.3508
7	22.2337	19.1832	16.0874	12.9482	11.3631	9.7679	8.1629	6.5484	4.9246	3.2918
8	21.7903	18.8020	15.7690	12.6932	11.1398	9.5765	8.0034	6.4209	4.8290	3.2281
9	21.3159	18.3936	15.4274	12.4192	10.8999	9.3707	7.8318	6.2835	4.7260	3.1594
10	20.8086	17.9563	15.0614	12.1253	10.6423	9.1496	7.6473	6.1358	4.6151	3.0854
11	20.2664	17.4887	14.6695	11.8102	10.3660	8.9123	7.4492	5.9770	4.4958	3.0058
12	19.6875	16.9888	14.2502	11.4728	10.0700	8.6579	7.2367	5.8067	4.3678	2.9203
13	19.0696	16.4549	13.8020	11.1118	9.7531	8.3855	7.0091	5.6240	4.2305	2.8285
14	18.4105	15.8851	13.3233	10.7260	9.4143	8.0941	6.7655	5.4286	4.0834	2.7302
15	17.7080	15.2774	12.8125	10.3141	9.0525	7.7828	6.5052	5.2196	3.9262	2.6250
16	16.9598	14.6299	12.2680	9.8747	8.6665	7.4506	6.2272	4.9964	3.7582	2.5126
17	16.1633	13.9405	11.6881	9.4066	8.2551	7.0966	5.9310	4.7584	3.5790	2.3927
18	15.3161	13.2071	11.0710	8.9084	7.8173	6.7196	5.6155	4.5050	3.3881	2.2650
19	14.4155	12.4274	10.4151	8.3788	7.3517	6.3188	5.2800	4.2355	3.1851	2.1291
20	13.4587	11.5993	9.7184	7.8163	6.8573	5.8931	4.9238	3.9492	2.9695	1.9848
21	12.4431	10.7204	8.9792	7.2196	6.3329	5.4417	4.5459	3.6456	2.7409	1.8317
22	11.3656	9.7885	8.1957	6.5872	5.7772	4.9634	4.1456	3.3241	2.4988	1.6696
23	10.2234	8.8010	7.3659	5.9179	5.1892	4.4573	3.7222	2.9840	2.2427	1.4983
24	9.0133	7.7557	6.4880	5.2102	4.5676	3.9225	3.2750	2.6249	1.9724	1.3174
25	7.7322	6.6498	5.5600	4.4628	3.9114	3.3582	2.8031	2.2461	1.6873	1.1267
26	6.3768	5.4810	4.5802	3.6743	3.2194	2.7633	2.3059	1.8472	1.3873	0.9261
27	4.9438	4.2467	3.5465	2.8433	2.4905	2.1370	1.7827	1.4277	1.0719	0.7154
28	3.4298	2.9442	2.4571	1.9685	1.7237	1.4786	1.2330	0.9871	0.7409	0.4943
29	1.8313	1.5708	1.3100	1.0488	0.9180	0.7871	0.6562	0.5251	0.3940	0.2628

12.75% Interest Rate   30 Year Amortization Schedule

Prepaid in Year	9.25%	9.75%	10.25%	10.75%	11.00%	11.25%	11.50%	11.75%	12.00%	12.25%
				Market Rate at Time of Prepayment						
1	24.0355	20.7178	17.3566	13.9549	12.2398	10.5157	8.7828	7.0417	5.2925	3.5356
2	23.7555	20.4797	17.1598	13.7990	12.1041	10.4000	8.6870	6.9654	5.2356	3.4979
3	23.4544	20.2229	16.9473	13.6303	11.9571	10.2745	8.5829	6.8826	5.1738	3.4569
4	23.1305	19.9464	16.7180	13.4479	11.7980	10.1387	8.4701	6.7927	5.1067	3.4124
5	22.7826	19.6487	16.4707	13.2509	11.6261	9.9917	8.3480	6.6953	5.0339	3.3640
6	22.4088	19.3286	16.2043	13.0383	11.4403	9.8327	8.2158	6.5898	4.9549	3.3115
7	22.0078	18.9844	15.9175	12.8091	11.2399	9.6611	8.0730	6.4757	4.8695	3.2546
8	21.5776	18.6148	15.6091	12.5622	11.0239	9.4760	7.9188	6.3524	4.7771	3.1931
9	21.1164	18.2182	15.2776	12.2965	10.7913	9.2765	7.7525	6.2193	4.6773	3.1266
10	20.6225	17.7927	14.9217	12.0109	10.5410	9.0618	7.5733	6.0759	4.5697	3.0548
11	20.0937	17.3369	14.5399	11.7041	10.2721	8.8308	7.3806	5.9215	4.4537	2.9775
12	19.5281	16.8488	14.1307	11.3750	9.9834	8.5828	7.1735	5.7555	4.3290	2.8942
13	18.9235	16.3266	13.6925	11.0222	9.6738	8.3168	6.9512	5.5772	4.1950	2.8046
14	18.2775	15.7683	13.2237	10.6445	9.3423	8.0317	6.7129	5.3860	4.0512	2.7085
15	17.5879	15.1721	12.7227	10.2406	8.9876	7.7266	6.4578	5.1813	3.8971	2.6055
16	16.8523	14.5357	12.1878	9.8092	8.6085	7.4004	6.1850	4.9622	3.7323	2.4952
17	16.0681	13.8571	11.6172	9.3487	8.2039	7.0522	5.8937	4.7283	3.5562	2.3774
18	15.2328	13.1342	11.0091	8.8579	7.7726	6.6809	5.5830	4.4787	3.3682	2.2516
19	14.3436	12.3646	10.3617	8.3353	7.3133	6.2856	5.2521	4.2129	3.1681	2.1176
20	13.3977	11.5460	9.6732	7.7795	6.8248	5.8650	4.9001	3.9302	2.9551	1.9751
21	12.3922	10.6761	8.9417	7.1890	6.3059	5.4184	4.5263	3.6299	2.7290	1.8237
22	11.3243	9.7525	8.1652	6.5625	5.7554	4.9445	4.1298	3.3114	2.4891	1.6632
23	10.1908	8.7727	7.3419	5.8985	5.1721	4.4425	3.7099	2.9741	2.2352	1.4932
24	8.9886	7.7342	6.4699	5.1956	4.5547	3.9114	3.2656	2.6174	1.9667	1.3136
25	7.7144	6.6344	5.5470	4.4523	3.9022	3.3502	2.7964	2.2408	1.6833	1.1240
26	6.3649	5.4708	4.5716	3.6673	3.2133	2.7580	2.3015	1.8437	1.3846	0.9243
27	4.9368	4.2406	3.5414	2.8392	2.4869	2.1339	1.7801	1.4256	1.0703	0.7143
28	3.4264	2.9412	2.4546	1.9665	1.7220	1.4771	1.2318	0.9861	0.7401	0.4938
29	1.8302	1.5699	1.3092	1.0481	0.9175	0.7867	0.6558	0.5248	0.3938	0.2626

Entries are the points to raise the yield on prepaid funds to that of the original loan.

Prepayment Premium to Maintain Yield

13.00% Interest Rate 30 Year Amortization Schedule

Prepaid in Year	\ Market Rate at Time of Prepayment									
	9.50%	10.00%	10.50%	11.00%	11.25%	11.50%	11.75%	12.00%	12.25%	12.50%
1	23.7383	20.4568	17.1341	13.7730	12.0790	10.3765	8.6657	6.9471	5.2209	3.4874
2	23.4699	20.2288	16.9458	13.6240	11.9494	10.2660	8.5742	6.8743	5.1667	3.4515
3	23.1806	19.9824	16.7421	13.4624	11.8086	10.1459	8.4747	6.7951	5.1076	3.4124
4	22.8689	19.7165	16.5218	13.2874	11.6560	10.0156	8.3665	6.7090	5.0433	3.3697
5	22.5333	19.4297	16.2837	13.0979	11.4907	9.8743	8.2492	6.6154	4.9734	3.3233
6	22.1722	19.1206	16.0267	12.8929	11.3117	9.7213	8.1219	6.5139	4.8974	3.2728
7	21.7839	18.7877	15.7495	12.6715	11.1182	9.5557	7.9841	6.4038	4.8150	3.2180
8	21.3667	18.4294	15.4508	12.4326	10.9092	9.3766	7.8350	6.2847	4.7258	3.1586
9	20.9186	18.0443	15.1292	12.1749	10.6837	9.1833	7.6739	6.1558	4.6292	3.0942
10	20.4378	17.6304	14.7832	11.8974	10.4406	8.9748	7.5000	6.0166	4.5248	3.0246
11	19.9222	17.1862	14.4113	11.5988	10.1789	8.7501	7.3126	5.8665	4.4121	2.9494
12	19.3698	16.7097	14.0120	11.2778	9.8974	8.5084	7.1108	5.7048	4.2906	2.8683
13	18.7782	16.1991	13.5837	10.9332	9.5951	8.2486	6.8937	5.5308	4.1598	2.7809
14	18.1452	15.6522	13.1248	10.5636	9.2707	7.9697	6.6607	5.3438	4.0192	2.6870
15	17.4684	15.0672	12.6334	10.1676	8.9230	7.6707	6.4107	5.1432	3.8683	2.5861
16	16.7453	14.4419	12.1079	9.7439	8.5508	7.3505	6.1429	4.9283	3.7066	2.4779
17	15.9733	13.7741	11.5465	9.2910	8.1530	7.0081	5.8565	4.6983	3.5334	2.3621
18	15.1497	13.0615	10.9473	8.8075	7.7281	6.6424	5.5506	4.4526	3.3484	2.2383
19	14.2718	12.3019	10.3085	8.2919	7.2750	6.2524	5.2242	4.1904	3.1511	2.1062
20	13.3367	11.4928	9.6281	7.7427	6.7924	5.8370	4.8766	3.9112	2.9408	1.9654
21	12.3415	10.6319	8.9042	7.1585	6.2790	5.3951	4.5068	3.6141	2.7171	1.8157
22	11.2830	9.7166	8.1348	6.5378	5.7337	4.9257	4.1141	3.2987	2.4795	1.6567
23	10.1582	8.7444	7.3180	5.8791	5.1550	4.4278	3.6975	2.9641	2.2277	1.4882
24	8.9639	7.7128	6.4518	5.1809	4.5418	3.9003	3.2563	2.6099	1.9610	1.3098
25	7.6966	6.6190	5.5341	4.4418	3.8929	3.3423	2.7897	2.2354	1.6793	1.1213
26	6.3530	5.4605	4.5629	3.6603	3.2071	2.7527	2.2971	1.8401	1.3820	0.9225
27	4.9297	4.2345	3.5363	2.8350	2.4833	2.1308	1.7775	1.4235	1.0688	0.7133
28	3.4229	2.9382	2.4521	1.9646	1.7202	1.4756	1.2305	0.9851	0.7394	0.4933
29	1.8292	1.5690	1.3085	1.0475	0.9169	0.7862	0.6554	0.5245	0.3935	0.2624

13.25% Interest Rate 30 Year Amortization Schedule

Prepaid in Year	\ Market Rate at Time of Prepaymen									
	9.75%	10.25%	10.75%	11.25%	11.50%	11.75%	12.00%	12.25%	12.50%	12.75%
1	23.4453	20.1997	16.9150	13.5941	11.9209	10.2396	8.5506	6.8541	5.1506	3.4402
2	23.1881	19.9813	16.7350	13.4517	11.7970	10.1341	8.4633	6.7848	5.0989	3.4060
3	22.9103	19.7450	16.5397	13.2970	11.6624	10.0193	8.3681	6.7091	5.0425	3.3686
4	22.6104	19.4894	16.3281	13.1290	11.5160	9.8944	8.2645	6.6266	4.9809	3.3277
5	22.2868	19.2131	16.0990	12.9468	11.3571	9.7586	8.1518	6.5367	4.9138	3.2832
6	21.9380	18.9148	15.8512	12.7493	11.1847	9.6113	8.0293	6.4390	4.8407	3.2346
7	21.5622	18.5929	15.5834	12.5356	10.9979	9.4514	7.8964	6.3329	4.7613	3.1818
8	21.1577	18.2458	15.2941	12.3044	10.7958	9.2783	7.7523	6.2178	4.6751	3.1244
9	20.7224	17.8719	14.9821	12.0546	10.5772	9.0910	7.5962	6.0930	4.5816	3.0621
10	20.2546	17.4695	14.6458	11.7850	10.3412	8.8886	7.4275	5.9580	4.4803	2.9946
11	19.7520	17.0367	14.2837	11.4944	10.0866	8.6701	7.2452	5.8120	4.3708	2.9216
12	19.2124	16.5716	13.8942	11.1815	9.8122	8.4345	7.0486	5.6545	4.2525	2.8426
13	18.6338	16.0723	13.4757	10.8449	9.5169	8.1808	6.8367	5.4847	4.1249	2.7574
14	18.0136	15.5368	13.0264	10.4832	9.1995	7.9081	6.6088	5.3019	3.9874	2.6656
15	17.3494	14.9629	12.5446	10.0950	8.8588	7.6151	6.3639	5.1054	3.8397	2.5668
16	16.6387	14.3486	12.0285	9.6790	8.4935	7.3008	6.1011	4.8945	3.6810	2.4607
17	15.8788	13.6914	11.4762	9.2336	8.1022	6.9642	5.8196	4.6684	3.5108	2.3469
18	15.0669	12.9891	10.8858	8.7573	7.6838	6.6041	5.5183	4.4265	3.3287	2.2250
19	14.2003	12.2394	10.2554	8.2487	7.2368	6.2194	5.1965	4.1680	3.1341	2.0948
20	13.2760	11.4398	9.5831	7.7061	6.7601	5.8091	4.8531	3.8922	2.9264	1.9558
21	12.2908	10.5877	8.8668	7.1281	6.2522	5.3720	4.4874	3.5984	2.7052	1.8077
22	11.2418	9.6807	8.1045	6.5132	5.7120	4.9070	4.0983	3.2860	2.4700	1.6503
23	10.1257	8.7162	7.2941	5.8598	5.1380	4.4131	3.6852	2.9542	2.2202	1.4831
24	8.9392	7.6914	6.4337	5.1663	4.5290	3.8892	3.2470	2.6024	1.9554	1.3060
25	7.6788	6.6036	5.5211	4.4313	3.8837	3.3343	2.7831	2.2301	1.6752	1.1186
26	6.3412	5.4502	4.5543	3.6534	3.2010	2.7475	2.2926	1.8366	1.3793	0.9208
27	4.9226	4.2284	3.5311	2.8309	2.4797	2.1277	1.7749	1.4214	1.0672	0.7122
28	3.4195	2.9353	2.4496	1.9626	1.7185	1.4741	1.2293	0.9841	0.7386	0.4928
29	1.8281	1.5681	1.3077	1.0469	0.9164	0.7857	0.6550	0.5242	0.3933	0.2623

Entries are the points to raise the yield on prepaid funds to that of the original loan.

Prepayment Premium to Maintain Yield

13.50% Interest Rate   30 Year Amortization Schedule

Prepaid in Year	\multicolumn{10}{c}{Market Rate at Time of Prepayment}									
	10.00%	10.50%	11.00%	11.50%	11.75%	12.00%	12.25%	12.50%	12.75%	13.00%
1	23.1563	19.9464	16.6994	13.4181	11.7654	10.1051	8.4375	6.7628	5.0815	3.3938
2	22.9100	19.7374	16.5273	13.2821	11.6472	10.0044	8.3542	6.6967	5.0323	3.3612
3	22.6433	19.5108	16.3402	13.1340	11.5183	9.8946	8.2632	6.6244	4.9784	3.3255
4	22.3549	19.2652	16.1371	12.9729	11.3780	9.7749	8.1639	6.5454	4.9194	3.2864
5	22.0431	18.9992	15.9167	12.7977	11.2253	9.6445	8.0557	6.4591	4.8550	3.2437
6	21.7063	18.7114	15.6778	12.6075	11.0593	9.5027	7.9379	6.3652	4.7848	3.1970
7	21.3427	18.4002	15.4190	12.4012	10.8791	9.3485	7.8097	6.2629	4.7083	3.1461
8	20.9506	18.0640	15.1391	12.1775	10.6836	9.1812	7.6705	6.1517	4.6250	3.0907
9	20.5279	17.7011	14.8365	11.9355	10.4718	8.9997	7.5194	6.0309	4.5345	3.0305
10	20.0727	17.3099	14.5097	11.6737	10.2427	8.8033	7.3556	5.8999	4.4363	2.9650
11	19.5829	16.8883	14.1572	11.3909	9.9950	8.5908	7.1784	5.7581	4.3299	2.8940
12	19.0562	16.4345	13.7773	11.0859	9.7276	8.3613	6.9869	5.6047	4.2147	2.8172
13	18.4902	15.9464	13.3684	10.7571	9.4393	8.1136	6.7801	5.4390	4.0902	2.7341
14	17.8827	15.4220	12.9286	10.4033	9.1289	7.8469	6.5573	5.2603	3.9559	2.6443
15	17.2310	14.8592	12.4562	10.0229	8.7950	7.5598	6.3174	5.0678	3.8112	2.5476
16	16.5326	14.2556	11.9494	9.6144	8.4364	7.2514	6.0595	4.8609	3.6555	2.4436
17	15.7847	13.6090	11.4061	9.1764	8.0517	6.9205	5.7828	4.6387	3.4884	2.3317
18	14.9844	12.9170	10.8245	8.7073	7.6396	6.5659	5.4862	4.4006	3.3091	2.2118
19	14.1290	12.1771	10.2026	8.2056	7.1988	6.1865	5.1688	4.1457	3.1172	2.0834
20	13.2153	11.3869	9.5382	7.6696	6.7279	5.7812	4.8297	3.8734	2.9122	1.9462
21	12.2403	10.5437	8.8295	7.0978	6.2255	5.3489	4.4680	3.5828	2.6934	1.7998
22	11.2007	9.6449	8.0742	6.4886	5.6903	4.8883	4.0826	3.2733	2.4604	1.6439
23	10.0933	8.6879	7.2703	5.8404	5.1209	4.3984	3.6728	2.9443	2.2127	1.4781
24	8.9145	7.6700	6.4157	5.1517	4.5161	3.8781	3.2377	2.5949	1.9498	1.3022
25	7.6611	6.5882	5.5082	4.4209	3.8745	3.3264	2.7765	2.2247	1.6712	1.1159
26	6.3293	5.4400	4.5457	3.6464	3.1949	2.7422	2.2882	1.8331	1.3766	0.9190
27	4.9155	4.2223	3.5260	2.8268	2.4761	2.1246	1.7723	1.4194	1.0656	0.7112
28	3.4161	2.9323	2.4472	1.9606	1.7167	1.4726	1.2280	0.9831	0.7379	0.4923
29	1.8270	1.5672	1.3069	1.0463	0.9158	0.7853	0.6546	0.5239	0.3931	0.2621

13.75% Interest Rate   30 Year Amortization Schedule

Prepaid in Year	\multicolumn{10}{c}{Market Rate at Time of Prepayment}									
	10.25%	10.75%	11.25%	11.75%	12.00%	12.25%	12.50%	12.75%	13.00%	13.25%
1	22.8716	19.6969	16.4871	13.2449	11.6125	9.9728	8.3263	6.6732	5.0137	3.3482
2	22.6357	19.4970	16.3227	13.1151	11.4997	9.8769	8.2469	6.6102	4.9668	3.3172
3	22.3799	19.2798	16.1435	12.9735	11.3765	9.7719	8.1600	6.5411	4.9153	3.2831
4	22.1025	19.0439	15.9486	12.8189	11.2419	9.6572	8.0649	6.4654	4.8589	3.2457
5	21.8022	18.7878	15.7366	12.6506	11.0953	9.5320	7.9610	6.3827	4.7972	3.2047
6	21.4770	18.5102	15.5064	12.4675	10.9355	9.3955	7.8477	6.2923	4.7297	3.1599
7	21.1254	18.2095	15.2565	12.2683	10.7616	9.2468	7.7241	6.1938	4.6560	3.1109
8	20.7454	17.8840	14.9856	12.0521	10.5727	9.0851	7.5896	6.0864	4.5756	3.0574
9	20.3351	17.5319	14.6922	11.8175	10.3676	8.9094	7.4433	5.9695	4.4880	2.9992
10	19.8924	17.1516	14.3748	11.5634	10.1452	8.7188	7.2845	5.8425	4.3928	2.9357
11	19.4151	16.7410	14.0317	11.2883	9.9043	8.5122	7.1123	5.7046	4.2894	2.8668
12	18.9009	16.2983	13.6613	10.9910	9.6438	8.2886	6.9257	5.5552	4.1773	2.7920
13	18.3476	15.8213	13.2618	10.6700	9.3623	8.0469	6.7240	5.3936	4.0559	2.7109
14	17.7525	15.3079	12.8315	10.3239	9.0587	7.7861	6.5061	5.2189	3.9246	2.6233
15	17.1132	14.7560	12.3684	9.9511	8.7316	7.5049	6.2712	5.0305	3.7829	2.5286
16	16.4269	14.1631	11.8707	9.5502	8.3796	7.2023	6.0182	4.8275	3.6303	2.4265
17	15.6909	13.5270	11.3364	9.1195	8.0014	6.8770	5.7462	4.6092	3.4660	2.3167
18	14.9022	12.8451	10.7635	8.6576	7.5957	6.5279	5.4542	4.3748	3.2896	2.1987
19	14.0579	12.1150	10.1499	8.1627	7.1609	6.1538	5.1413	4.1235	3.1004	2.0721
20	13.1549	11.3341	9.4935	7.6332	6.6958	5.7535	4.8064	3.8545	2.8979	1.9366
21	12.1899	10.4998	8.7923	7.0676	6.1988	5.3258	4.4486	3.5672	2.6816	1.7919
22	11.1597	9.6092	8.0440	6.4641	5.6687	4.8696	4.0670	3.2607	2.4509	1.6375
23	10.0608	8.6598	7.2465	5.8212	5.1040	4.3837	3.6605	2.9344	2.2052	1.4731
24	8.8899	7.6486	6.3977	5.1371	4.5033	3.8671	3.2285	2.5875	1.9441	1.2984
25	7.6433	6.5729	5.4952	4.4104	3.8653	3.3185	2.7698	2.2194	1.6672	1.1132
26	6.3174	5.4297	4.5371	3.6395	3.1888	2.7369	2.2838	1.8295	1.3740	0.9172
27	4.9085	4.2162	3.5209	2.8227	2.4724	2.1215	1.7697	1.4173	1.0641	0.7101
28	3.4126	2.9294	2.4447	1.9586	1.7150	1.4711	1.2268	0.9821	0.7371	0.4918
29	1.8260	1.5662	1.3061	1.0457	0.9153	0.7848	0.6543	0.5236	0.3928	0.2620

Entries are the points to raise the yield on prepaid funds to that of the original loan.

Months' Interest Prepayment Premium Converted to Percentage

Percentage Premium	6.00%	6.25%	6.50%	6.75%	7.00%	7.25%	7.50%	7.75%	8.00%	8.25%	8.50%	8.75%
1.00%	2.00	1.92	1.85	1.78	1.71	1.66	1.60	1.55	1.50	1.45	1.41	1.37
1.25%	2.50	2.40	2.31	2.22	2.14	2.07	2.00	1.94	1.88	1.82	1.76	1.71
1.50%	3.00	2.88	2.77	2.67	2.57	2.48	2.40	2.32	2.25	2.18	2.12	2.06
1.75%	3.50	3.36	3.23	3.11	3.00	2.90	2.80	2.71	2.63	2.55	2.47	2.40
2.00%	4.00	3.84	3.69	3.56	3.43	3.31	3.20	3.10	3.00	2.91	2.82	2.74
2.25%	4.50	4.32	4.15	4.00	3.86	3.72	3.60	3.48	3.38	3.27	3.18	3.09
2.50%	5.00	4.80	4.62	4.44	4.29	4.14	4.00	3.87	3.75	3.64	3.53	3.43
2.75%	5.50	5.28	5.08	4.89	4.71	4.55	4.40	4.26	4.13	4.00	3.88	3.77
3.00%	6.00	5.76	5.54	5.33	5.14	4.97	4.80	4.65	4.50	4.36	4.24	4.11
3.25%	6.50	6.24	6.00	5.78	5.57	5.38	5.20	5.03	4.88	4.73	4.59	4.46
3.50%	7.00	6.72	6.46	6.22	6.00	5.79	5.60	5.42	5.25	5.09	4.94	4.80
3.75%	7.50	7.20	6.92	6.67	6.43	6.21	6.00	5.81	5.63	5.45	5.29	5.14
4.00%	8.00	7.68	7.38	7.11	6.86	6.62	6.40	6.19	6.00	5.82	5.65	5.49
4.25%	8.50	8.16	7.85	7.56	7.29	7.03	6.80	6.58	6.38	6.18	6.00	5.83
4.50%	9.00	8.64	8.31	8.00	7.71	7.45	7.20	6.97	6.75	6.55	6.35	6.17
4.75%	9.50	9.12	8.77	8.44	8.14	7.86	7.60	7.35	7.13	6.91	6.71	6.51
5.00%	10.00	9.60	9.23	8.89	8.57	8.28	8.00	7.74	7.50	7.27	7.06	6.86
5.25%	10.50	10.08	9.69	9.33	9.00	8.69	8.40	8.13	7.88	7.64	7.41	7.20
5.50%	11.00	10.56	10.15	9.78	9.43	9.10	8.80	8.52	8.25	8.00	7.76	7.54
5.75%	11.50	11.04	10.62	10.22	9.86	9.52	9.20	8.90	8.63	8.36	8.12	7.89
6.00%	12.00	11.52	11.08	10.67	10.29	9.93	9.60	9.29	9.00	8.73	8.47	8.23
6.25%	12.50	12.00	11.54	11.11	10.71	10.34	10.00	9.68	9.38	9.09	8.82	8.57
6.50%	13.00	12.48	12.00	11.56	11.14	10.76	10.40	10.06	9.75	9.45	9.18	8.91
6.75%	13.50	12.96	12.46	12.00	11.57	11.17	10.80	10.45	10.13	9.82	9.53	9.26
7.00%	14.00	13.44	12.92	12.44	12.00	11.59	11.20	10.84	10.50	10.18	9.88	9.60
7.25%	14.50	13.92	13.38	12.89	12.43	12.00	11.60	11.23	10.88	10.55	10.24	9.94
7.50%	15.00	14.40	13.85	13.33	12.86	12.41	12.00	11.61	11.25	10.91	10.59	10.29
7.75%	15.50	14.88	14.31	13.78	13.29	12.83	12.40	12.00	11.63	11.27	10.94	10.63
8.00%	16.00	15.36	14.77	14.22	13.71	13.24	12.80	12.39	12.00	11.64	11.29	10.97

Percentage Premium	9.00%	9.25%	9.50%	9.75%	10.00%	10.25%	10.50%	10.75%	11.00%	11.25%	11.50%	11.75%
1.00%	1.33	1.30	1.26	1.23	1.20	1.17	1.14	1.12	1.09	1.07	1.04	1.02
1.25%	1.67	1.62	1.58	1.54	1.50	1.46	1.43	1.40	1.36	1.33	1.30	1.28
1.50%	2.00	1.95	1.89	1.85	1.80	1.76	1.71	1.67	1.64	1.60	1.57	1.53
1.75%	2.33	2.27	2.21	2.15	2.10	2.05	2.00	1.95	1.91	1.87	1.83	1.79
2.00%	2.67	2.59	2.53	2.46	2.40	2.34	2.29	2.23	2.18	2.13	2.09	2.04
2.25%	3.00	2.92	2.84	2.77	2.70	2.63	2.57	2.51	2.45	2.40	2.35	2.30
2.50%	3.33	3.24	3.16	3.08	3.00	2.93	2.86	2.79	2.73	2.67	2.61	2.55
2.75%	3.67	3.57	3.47	3.38	3.30	3.22	3.14	3.07	3.00	2.93	2.87	2.81
3.00%	4.00	3.89	3.79	3.69	3.60	3.51	3.43	3.35	3.27	3.20	3.13	3.06
3.25%	4.33	4.22	4.11	4.00	3.90	3.80	3.71	3.63	3.55	3.47	3.39	3.32
3.50%	4.67	4.54	4.42	4.31	4.20	4.10	4.00	3.91	3.82	3.73	3.65	3.57
3.75%	5.00	4.86	4.74	4.62	4.50	4.39	4.29	4.19	4.09	4.00	3.91	3.83
4.00%	5.33	5.19	5.05	4.92	4.80	4.68	4.57	4.47	4.36	4.27	4.17	4.09
4.25%	5.67	5.51	5.37	5.23	5.10	4.98	4.86	4.74	4.64	4.53	4.43	4.34
4.50%	6.00	5.84	5.68	5.54	5.40	5.27	5.14	5.02	4.91	4.80	4.70	4.60
4.75%	6.33	6.16	6.00	5.85	5.70	5.56	5.43	5.30	5.18	5.07	4.96	4.85
5.00%	6.67	6.49	6.32	6.15	6.00	5.85	5.71	5.58	5.45	5.33	5.22	5.11
5.25%	7.00	6.81	6.63	6.46	6.30	6.15	6.00	5.86	5.73	5.60	5.48	5.36
5.50%	7.33	7.14	6.95	6.77	6.60	6.44	6.29	6.14	6.00	5.87	5.74	5.62
5.75%	7.67	7.46	7.26	7.08	6.90	6.73	6.57	6.42	6.27	6.13	6.00	5.87
6.00%	8.00	7.78	7.58	7.38	7.20	7.02	6.86	6.70	6.55	6.40	6.26	6.13
6.25%	8.33	8.11	7.89	7.69	7.50	7.32	7.14	6.98	6.82	6.67	6.52	6.38
6.50%	8.67	8.43	8.21	8.00	7.80	7.61	7.43	7.26	7.09	6.93	6.78	6.64
6.75%	9.00	8.76	8.53	8.31	8.10	7.90	7.71	7.53	7.36	7.20	7.04	6.89
7.00%	9.33	9.08	8.84	8.62	8.40	8.20	8.00	7.81	7.64	7.47	7.30	7.15
7.25%	9.67	9.41	9.16	8.92	8.70	8.49	8.29	8.09	7.91	7.73	7.57	7.40
7.50%	10.00	9.73	9.47	9.23	9.00	8.78	8.57	8.37	8.18	8.00	7.83	7.66
7.75%	10.33	10.05	9.79	9.54	9.30	9.07	8.86	8.65	8.45	8.27	8.09	7.91
8.00%	10.67	10.38	10.11	9.85	9.60	9.37	9.14	8.93	8.73	8.53	8.35	8.17

Entry is the months of interest on the amount prepaid equal to the selected percentage.

Interest Rebate by Rule of 78s

Loan Term	Payments Left	Add-on Interest Rate											
		4.00%	4.25%	4.50%	4.75%	5.00%	5.25%	5.50%	5.75%	6.00%	6.25%	6.50%	6.75%
12	3	0.30769	0.32692	0.34615	0.36538	0.38462	0.40385	0.42308	0.44231	0.46154	0.48077	0.50000	0.51923
	6	1.07692	1.14423	1.21154	1.27885	1.34615	1.41346	1.48077	1.54808	1.61538	1.68269	1.75000	1.81731
	9	2.30769	2.45192	2.59615	2.74038	2.88462	3.02885	3.17308	3.31731	3.46154	3.60577	3.75000	3.89423
18	3	0.21053	0.22368	0.23684	0.25000	0.26316	0.27632	0.28947	0.30263	0.31579	0.32895	0.34211	0.35526
	6	0.73684	0.78289	0.82895	0.87500	0.92105	0.96711	1.01316	1.05921	1.10526	1.15132	1.19737	1.24342
	9	1.57895	1.67763	1.77632	1.87500	1.97368	2.07237	2.17105	2.26974	2.36842	2.46711	2.56579	2.66447
	12	2.73684	2.90789	3.07895	3.25000	3.42105	3.59211	3.76316	3.93421	4.10526	4.27632	4.44737	4.61842
	15	4.21053	4.47368	4.73684	5.00000	5.26316	5.52632	5.78947	6.05263	6.31579	6.57895	6.84211	7.10526
24	3	0.16000	0.17000	0.18000	0.19000	0.20000	0.21000	0.22000	0.23000	0.24000	0.25000	0.26000	0.27000
	6	0.56000	0.59500	0.63000	0.66500	0.70000	0.73500	0.77000	0.80500	0.84000	0.87500	0.91000	0.94500
	9	1.20000	1.27500	1.35000	1.42500	1.50000	1.57500	1.65000	1.72500	1.80000	1.87500	1.95000	2.02500
	12	2.08000	2.21000	2.34000	2.47000	2.60000	2.73000	2.86000	2.99000	3.12000	3.25000	3.38000	3.51000
	15	3.20000	3.40000	3.60000	3.80000	4.00000	4.20000	4.40000	4.60000	4.80000	5.00000	5.20000	5.40000
	18	4.56000	4.84500	5.13000	5.41500	5.70000	5.98500	6.27000	6.55500	6.84000	7.12500	7.41000	7.69500
	21	6.16000	6.54500	6.93000	7.31500	7.70000	8.08500	8.47000	8.85500	9.24000	9.62500	10.01000	10.39500
30	3	0.12903	0.13710	0.14516	0.15323	0.16129	0.16935	0.17742	0.18548	0.19355	0.20161	0.20968	0.21774
	6	0.45161	0.47984	0.50806	0.53629	0.56452	0.59274	0.62097	0.64919	0.67742	0.70565	0.73387	0.76210
	9	0.96774	1.02823	1.08871	1.14919	1.20968	1.27016	1.33065	1.39113	1.45161	1.51210	1.57258	1.63306
	12	1.67742	1.78226	1.88710	1.99194	2.09677	2.20161	2.30645	2.41129	2.51613	2.62097	2.72581	2.83065
	15	2.58065	2.74194	2.90323	3.06452	3.22581	3.38710	3.54839	3.70968	3.87097	4.03226	4.19355	4.35484
	18	3.67742	3.90726	4.13710	4.36694	4.59677	4.82661	5.05645	5.28629	5.51613	5.74597	5.97581	6.20565
	21	4.96774	5.27823	5.58871	5.89919	6.20968	6.52016	6.83065	7.14113	7.45161	7.76210	8.07258	8.38306
	24	6.45161	6.85484	7.25806	7.66129	8.06452	8.46774	8.87097	9.27419	9.67742	10.08065	10.48387	10.88710
	27	8.12903	8.63710	9.14516	9.65323	10.16129	10.66935	11.17742	11.68548	12.19355	12.70161	13.20968	13.71774
36	3	0.10811	0.11486	0.12162	0.12838	0.13514	0.14189	0.14865	0.15541	0.16216	0.16892	0.17568	0.18243
	6	0.37838	0.40203	0.42568	0.44932	0.47297	0.49662	0.52027	0.54392	0.56757	0.59122	0.61486	0.63851
	9	0.81081	0.86149	0.91216	0.96284	1.01351	1.06419	1.11486	1.16554	1.21622	1.26689	1.31757	1.36824
	12	1.40541	1.49324	1.58108	1.66892	1.75676	1.84459	1.93243	2.02027	2.10811	2.19595	2.28378	2.37162
	15	2.16216	2.29730	2.43243	2.56757	2.70270	2.83784	2.97297	3.10811	3.24324	3.37838	3.51351	3.64865
	18	3.08108	3.27365	3.46622	3.65878	3.85135	4.04392	4.23649	4.42905	4.62162	4.81419	5.00676	5.19932
	21	4.16216	4.42230	4.68243	4.94257	5.20270	5.46284	5.72297	5.98311	6.24324	6.50338	6.76351	7.02365
	24	5.40541	5.74324	6.08108	6.41892	6.75676	7.09459	7.43243	7.77027	8.10811	8.44595	8.78378	9.12162
	27	6.81081	7.23649	7.66216	8.08784	8.51351	8.93919	9.36486	9.79054	10.21622	10.64189	11.06757	11.49324
	30	8.37838	8.90203	9.42568	9.94932	10.47297	10.99662	11.52027	12.04392	12.56757	13.09122	13.61486	14.13851
	33	10.10811	10.73986	11.37162	12.00338	12.63514	13.26689	13.89865	14.53041	15.16216	15.79392	16.42568	17.05743
48	3	0.08163	0.08673	0.09184	0.09694	0.10204	0.10714	0.11224	0.11735	0.12245	0.12755	0.13265	0.13776
	6	0.28571	0.30357	0.32143	0.33929	0.35714	0.37500	0.39286	0.41071	0.42857	0.44643	0.46429	0.48214
	9	0.61224	0.65051	0.68878	0.72704	0.76531	0.80357	0.84184	0.88010	0.91837	0.95663	0.99490	1.03316
	12	1.06122	1.12755	1.19388	1.26020	1.32653	1.39286	1.45918	1.52551	1.59184	1.65816	1.72449	1.79082
	15	1.63265	1.73469	1.83673	1.93878	2.04082	2.14286	2.24490	2.34694	2.44898	2.55102	2.65306	2.75510
	18	2.32653	2.47194	2.61735	2.76276	2.90816	3.05357	3.19898	3.34439	3.48980	3.63520	3.78061	3.92602
	21	3.14286	3.33929	3.53571	3.73214	3.92857	4.12500	4.32143	4.51786	4.71429	4.91071	5.10714	5.30357
	24	4.08163	4.33673	4.59184	4.84694	5.10204	5.35714	5.61224	5.86735	6.12245	6.37755	6.63265	6.88776
	27	5.14286	5.46429	5.78571	6.10714	6.42857	6.75000	7.07143	7.39286	7.71429	8.03571	8.35714	8.67857
	30	6.32653	6.72194	7.11735	7.51276	7.90816	8.30357	8.69898	9.09439	9.48980	9.88520	10.28061	10.67602
	33	7.63265	8.10969	8.58673	9.06378	9.54082	10.01786	10.49490	10.97194	11.44898	11.92602	12.40306	12.88010
	36	9.06122	9.62755	10.19388	10.76020	11.32653	11.89286	12.45918	13.02551	13.59184	14.15816	14.72449	15.29082
	39	10.61224	11.27551	11.93878	12.60204	13.26531	13.92857	14.59184	15.25510	15.91837	16.58163	17.24490	17.90816
	42	12.28571	13.05357	13.82143	14.58929	15.35714	16.12500	16.89286	17.66071	18.42857	19.19643	19.96429	20.73214
	45	14.08163	14.96173	15.84184	16.72194	17.60204	18.48214	19.36224	20.24235	21.12245	22.00255	22.88265	23.76276
60	3	0.06557	0.06967	0.07377	0.07787	0.08197	0.08607	0.09016	0.09426	0.09836	0.10246	0.10656	0.11066
	6	0.22951	0.24385	0.25820	0.27254	0.28689	0.30123	0.31557	0.32992	0.34426	0.35861	0.37295	0.38730
	9	0.49180	0.52254	0.55328	0.58402	0.61475	0.64549	0.67623	0.70697	0.73770	0.76844	0.79918	0.82992
	12	0.85246	0.90574	0.95902	1.01230	1.06557	1.11885	1.17213	1.22541	1.27869	1.33197	1.38525	1.43852
	15	1.31148	1.39344	1.47541	1.55738	1.63934	1.72131	1.80328	1.88525	1.96721	2.04918	2.13115	2.21311
	18	1.86885	1.98566	2.10246	2.21926	2.33607	2.45287	2.56967	2.68648	2.80328	2.92008	3.03689	3.15369
	21	2.52459	2.68238	2.84016	2.99795	3.15574	3.31352	3.47131	3.62910	3.78689	3.94467	4.10246	4.26025
	24	3.27869	3.48361	3.68852	3.89344	4.09836	4.30328	4.50820	4.71311	4.91803	5.12295	5.32787	5.53279
	27	4.13115	4.38934	4.64754	4.90574	5.16393	5.42213	5.68033	5.93852	6.19672	6.45492	6.71311	6.97131
	30	5.08197	5.39959	5.71721	6.03484	6.35246	6.67008	6.98770	7.30533	7.62295	7.94057	8.25820	8.57582
	33	6.13115	6.51434	6.89754	7.28074	7.66393	8.04713	8.43033	8.81352	9.19672	9.57992	9.96311	10.34631
	36	7.27869	7.73361	8.18852	8.64344	9.09836	9.55328	10.00820	10.46311	10.91803	11.37295	11.82787	12.28279
	39	8.52459	9.05738	9.59016	10.12295	10.65574	11.18852	11.72131	12.25410	12.78689	13.31967	13.85246	14.38525
	42	9.86885	10.48566	11.10246	11.71926	12.33607	12.95287	13.56967	14.18648	14.80328	15.42008	16.03689	16.65369
	45	11.31148	12.01844	12.72541	13.43238	14.13934	14.84631	15.55328	16.26025	16.96721	17.67418	18.38115	19.08811
	48	12.85246	13.65574	14.45902	15.26230	16.06557	16.86885	17.67213	18.47541	19.27869	20.08197	20.88525	21.68852
	51	14.49180	15.39754	16.30328	17.20902	18.11475	19.02049	19.92623	20.83197	21.73770	22.64344	23.54918	24.45492
	54	16.22951	17.24385	18.25820	19.27254	20.28689	21.30123	22.31557	23.32992	24.34426	25.35861	26.37295	27.38730
	57	18.06557	19.19467	20.32377	21.45287	22.58197	23.71107	24.84016	25.96926	27.09836	28.22746	29.35656	30.48566

Entry is percent of original loan proceeds to be rebated on prepayment.

Interest Rebate by Rule of 78s

Loan Term	Payments Left	7.00%	7.25%	7.50%	7.75%	8.00%	8.25%	8.50%	8.75%	9.00%	9.25%	9.50%	9.75%
12	3	0.53846	0.55769	0.57692	0.59615	0.61538	0.63462	0.65385	0.67308	0.69231	0.71154	0.73077	0.75000
	6	1.88462	1.95192	2.01923	2.08654	2.15385	2.22115	2.28846	2.35577	2.42308	2.49038	2.55769	2.62500
	9	4.03846	4.18269	4.32692	4.47115	4.61538	4.75962	4.90385	5.04808	5.19231	5.33654	5.48077	5.62500
18	3	0.36842	0.38158	0.39474	0.40789	0.42105	0.43421	0.44737	0.46053	0.47368	0.48684	0.50000	0.51316
	6	1.28947	1.33553	1.38158	1.42763	1.47368	1.51974	1.56579	1.61184	1.65789	1.70395	1.75000	1.79605
	9	2.76316	2.86184	2.96053	3.05921	3.15789	3.25658	3.35526	3.45395	3.55263	3.65132	3.75000	3.84868
	12	4.78947	4.96053	5.13158	5.30263	5.47368	5.64474	5.81579	5.98684	6.15789	6.32895	6.50000	6.67105
	15	7.36842	7.63158	7.89474	8.15789	8.42105	8.68421	8.94737	9.21053	9.47368	9.73684	10.00000	10.26316
24	3	0.28000	0.29000	0.30000	0.31000	0.32000	0.33000	0.34000	0.35000	0.36000	0.37000	0.38000	0.39000
	6	0.98000	1.01500	1.05000	1.08500	1.12000	1.15500	1.19000	1.22500	1.26000	1.29500	1.33000	1.36500
	9	2.10000	2.17500	2.25000	2.32500	2.40000	2.47500	2.55000	2.62500	2.70000	2.77500	2.85000	2.92500
	12	3.64000	3.77000	3.90000	4.03000	4.16000	4.29000	4.42000	4.55000	4.68000	4.81000	4.94000	5.07000
	15	5.60000	5.80000	6.00000	6.20000	6.40000	6.60000	6.80000	7.00000	7.20000	7.40000	7.60000	7.80000
	18	7.98000	8.26500	8.55000	8.83500	9.12000	9.40500	9.69000	9.97500	10.26000	10.54500	10.83000	11.11500
	21	10.78000	11.16500	11.55000	11.93500	12.32000	12.70500	13.09000	13.47500	13.86000	14.24500	14.63000	15.01500
30	3	0.22581	0.23387	0.24194	0.25000	0.25806	0.26613	0.27419	0.28226	0.29032	0.29839	0.30645	0.31452
	6	0.79032	0.81855	0.84677	0.87500	0.90323	0.93145	0.95968	0.98790	1.01613	1.04435	1.07258	1.10081
	9	1.69355	1.75403	1.81452	1.87500	1.93548	1.99597	2.05645	2.11694	2.17742	2.23790	2.29839	2.35887
	12	2.93548	3.04032	3.14516	3.25000	3.35484	3.45968	3.56452	3.66935	3.77419	3.87903	3.98387	4.08871
	15	4.51613	4.67742	4.83871	5.00000	5.16129	5.32258	5.48387	5.64516	5.80645	5.96774	6.12903	6.29032
	18	6.43548	6.66532	6.89516	7.12500	7.35484	7.58468	7.81452	8.04435	8.27419	8.50403	8.73387	8.96371
	21	8.69355	9.00403	9.31452	9.62500	9.93548	10.24597	10.55645	10.86694	11.17742	11.48790	11.79839	12.10887
	24	11.29032	11.69355	12.09677	12.50000	12.90323	13.30645	13.70968	14.11290	14.51613	14.91935	15.32258	15.72581
	27	14.22581	14.73387	15.24194	15.75000	16.25806	16.76613	17.27419	17.78226	18.29032	18.79839	19.30645	19.81452
36	3	0.18919	0.19595	0.20270	0.20946	0.21622	0.22297	0.22973	0.23649	0.24324	0.25000	0.25676	0.26351
	6	0.66216	0.68581	0.70946	0.73311	0.75676	0.78041	0.80405	0.82770	0.85135	0.87500	0.89865	0.92230
	9	1.41892	1.46959	1.52027	1.57095	1.62162	1.67230	1.72297	1.77365	1.82432	1.87500	1.92568	1.97635
	12	2.45946	2.54730	2.63514	2.72297	2.81081	2.89865	2.98649	3.07432	3.16216	3.25000	3.33784	3.42568
	15	3.78378	3.91892	4.05405	4.18919	4.32432	4.45946	4.59459	4.72973	4.86486	5.00000	5.13514	5.27027
	18	5.39189	5.58446	5.77703	5.96959	6.16216	6.35473	6.54730	6.73986	6.93243	7.12500	7.31757	7.51014
	21	7.28378	7.54392	7.80405	8.06419	8.32432	8.58446	8.84459	9.10473	9.36486	9.62500	9.88514	10.14527
	24	9.45946	9.79730	10.13514	10.47297	10.81081	11.14865	11.48649	11.82432	12.16216	12.50000	12.83784	13.17568
	27	11.91892	12.34459	12.77027	13.19595	13.62162	14.04730	14.47297	14.89865	15.32432	15.75000	16.17568	16.60135
	30	14.66216	15.18581	15.70946	16.23311	16.75676	17.28041	17.80405	18.32770	18.85135	19.37500	19.89865	20.42230
	33	17.68919	18.32095	18.95270	19.58446	20.21622	20.84797	21.47973	22.11149	22.74324	23.37500	24.00676	24.63851
48	3	0.14286	0.14796	0.15306	0.15816	0.16327	0.16837	0.17347	0.17857	0.18367	0.18878	0.19388	0.19898
	6	0.50000	0.51786	0.53571	0.55357	0.57143	0.58929	0.60714	0.62500	0.64286	0.66071	0.67857	0.69643
	9	1.07143	1.10969	1.14796	1.18622	1.22449	1.26276	1.30102	1.33929	1.37755	1.41582	1.45408	1.49235
	12	1.85714	1.92347	1.98980	2.05612	2.12245	2.18878	2.25510	2.32143	2.38776	2.45408	2.52041	2.58673
	15	2.85714	2.95918	3.06122	3.16327	3.26531	3.36735	3.46939	3.57143	3.67347	3.77551	3.87755	3.97959
	18	4.07143	4.21684	4.36224	4.50765	4.65306	4.79847	4.94388	5.08929	5.23469	5.38010	5.52551	5.67092
	21	5.50000	5.69643	5.89286	6.08929	6.28571	6.48214	6.67857	6.87500	7.07143	7.26786	7.46429	7.66071
	24	7.14286	7.39796	7.65306	7.90816	8.16327	8.41837	8.67347	8.92857	9.18367	9.43878	9.69388	9.94898
	27	9.00000	9.32143	9.64286	9.96429	10.28571	10.60714	10.92857	11.25000	11.57143	11.89286	12.21429	12.53571
	30	11.07143	11.46684	11.86224	12.25765	12.65306	13.04847	13.44388	13.83929	14.23469	14.63010	15.02551	15.42092
	33	13.35714	13.83418	14.31122	14.78827	15.26531	15.74235	16.21939	16.69643	17.17347	17.65051	18.12755	18.60459
	36	15.85714	16.42347	16.98980	17.55612	18.12245	18.68878	19.25510	19.82143	20.38776	20.95408	21.52041	22.08673
	39	18.57143	19.23469	19.89796	20.56122	21.22449	21.88776	22.55102	23.21429	23.87755	24.54082	25.20408	25.86735
	42	21.50000	22.26786	23.03571	23.80357	24.57143	25.33929	26.10714	26.87500	27.64286	28.41071	29.17857	29.94643
	45	24.64286	25.52296	26.40306	27.28316	28.16327	29.04337	29.92347	30.80357	31.68367	32.56378	33.44388	34.32398
60	3	0.11475	0.11885	0.12295	0.12705	0.13115	0.13525	0.13934	0.14344	0.14754	0.15164	0.15574	0.15984
	6	0.40164	0.41598	0.43033	0.44467	0.45902	0.47336	0.48770	0.50205	0.51639	0.53074	0.54508	0.55943
	9	0.86066	0.89139	0.92213	0.95287	0.98361	1.01434	1.04508	1.07582	1.10656	1.13730	1.16803	1.19877
	12	1.49180	1.54508	1.59836	1.65164	1.70492	1.75820	1.81148	1.86475	1.91803	1.97131	2.02459	2.07787
	15	2.29508	2.37705	2.45902	2.54098	2.62295	2.70492	2.78689	2.86885	2.95082	3.03279	3.11475	3.19672
	18	3.27049	3.38730	3.50410	3.62090	3.73770	3.85451	3.97131	4.08811	4.20492	4.32172	4.43852	4.55533
	21	4.41803	4.57582	4.73361	4.89139	5.04918	5.20697	5.36475	5.52254	5.68033	5.83811	5.99590	6.15369
	24	5.73770	5.94262	6.14754	6.35246	6.55738	6.76230	6.96721	7.17213	7.37705	7.58197	7.78689	7.99180
	27	7.22951	7.48770	7.74590	8.00410	8.26230	8.52049	8.77869	9.03689	9.29508	9.55328	9.81148	10.06967
	30	8.89344	9.21107	9.52869	9.84631	10.16393	10.48156	10.79918	11.11680	11.43443	11.75205	12.06967	12.38730
	33	10.72951	11.11270	11.49590	11.87910	12.26230	12.64549	13.02869	13.41189	13.79508	14.17828	14.56148	14.94467
	36	12.73770	13.19262	13.64754	14.10246	14.55738	15.01230	15.46721	15.92213	16.37705	16.83197	17.28689	17.74180
	39	14.91803	15.45082	15.98361	16.51639	17.04918	17.58197	18.11475	18.64754	19.18033	19.71311	20.24590	20.77869
	42	17.27049	17.88730	18.50410	19.12090	19.73770	20.35451	20.97131	21.58811	22.20492	22.82172	23.43852	24.05533
	45	19.79508	20.50205	21.20902	21.91598	22.62295	23.32992	24.03689	24.74385	25.45082	26.15779	26.86475	27.57172
	48	22.49180	23.29508	24.09836	24.90164	25.70492	26.50820	27.31148	28.11475	28.91803	29.72131	30.52459	31.32787
	51	25.36066	26.26639	27.17213	28.07787	28.98361	29.88934	30.79508	31.70082	32.60656	33.51230	34.41803	35.32377
	54	28.40164	29.41598	30.43033	31.44467	32.45902	33.47336	34.48770	35.50205	36.51639	37.53074	38.54508	39.55943
	57	31.61475	32.74385	33.87295	35.00205	36.13115	37.26025	38.38934	39.51844	40.64754	41.77664	42.90574	44.03484

Entry is percent of original loan proceeds to be rebated on prepayment.

Present and Future Value

5.500% Discount Rate   5.500% Discount Rate

	Annual Payments				Monthly Payments				
Years	Present Value	Future Value	Present Value of 1 per Period	Future Value of 1 per Period	Present Value	Future Value	Present Value of 1 per Period	Future Value of 1 per Period	Months
					.9954376	1.0045833	0.9954376	1.0000000	1
					.9908960	1.0091877	1.9863335	2.0045833	2
					.9863751	1.0138131	2.9727086	3.0137710	3
					.9818748	1.0184598	3.9545835	4.0275841	4
					.9773951	1.0231277	4.9319786	5.0460439	5
					.9729358	1.0278170	5.9049144	6.0691716	6
					.9684969	1.0325279	6.8734112	7.0969886	7
					.9640782	1.0372603	7.8374894	8.1295165	8
					.9596796	1.0420144	8.7971690	9.1667768	9
					.9553012	1.0467903	9.7524702	10.2087912	10
					.9509427	1.0515881	10.7034129	11.2555815	11
1	.9478673	1.0550000	0.9478673	1.0000000	.9466041	1.0564079	11.6500170	12.3071695	12
2	.8984524	1.1130250	1.8463197	2.0550000	.8960593	1.1159976	22.6779707	25.3085602	24
3	.8516137	1.1742414	2.6979334	3.1680250	.8482134	1.1789486	33.1170768	39.0433314	36
4	.8072167	1.2388247	3.5051501	4.3422664	.8029223	1.2454506	42.9987773	53.5528518	48
5	.7651344	1.3069600	4.2702845	5.5810910	.7600495	1.3157038	52.3528354	68.8808231	60
6	.7252458	1.3788428	4.9955303	6.8880510	.7194660	1.3899198	61.2074251	85.0734125	72
7	.6874368	1.4546792	5.6829671	8.2668938	.6810494	1.4683222	69.5892159	102.1793912	84
8	.6515989	1.5346865	6.3345660	9.7215730	.6446842	1.5511471	77.5234533	120.2502816	96
9	.6176293	1.6190943	6.9521952	11.2562595	.6102607	1.6386440	85.0340348	139.3405122	108
10	.5854306	1.7081445	7.5376258	12.8753538	.5776752	1.7310764	92.1435821	159.5075819	120
11	.5549105	1.8020924	8.0925363	14.5834982	.5468298	1.8287227	98.8735085	180.8122329	132
12	.5259815	1.9012075	8.6185178	16.3855907	.5176313	1.9318771	105.2440845	203.3186336	144
13	.4985607	2.0057739	9.1170785	18.2867981	.4899919	2.0408501	111.2744977	227.0945722	156
14	.4725694	2.1160915	9.5896479	20.2925720	.4638283	2.1559701	116.9829115	252.2116607	168
15	.4479330	2.2324765	10.0375809	22.4086635	.4390618	2.2775838	122.3865193	278.7455504	180
16	.4245811	2.3552627	10.4621620	24.6411400	.4156177	2.4060574	127.5015966	306.7761600	192
17	.4024465	2.4848021	10.8646086	26.9964027	.3934254	2.5417779	132.3435497	336.3879163	204
18	.3814659	2.6214663	11.2460745	29.4812048	.3724181	2.6851542	136.9269622	367.6700085	216
19	.3615791	2.7656469	11.6076535	32.1026711	.3525325	2.8366180	141.2656393	400.7166565	228
20	.3427290	2.9177575	11.9503825	34.8683180	.3337087	2.9966256	145.3726488	435.6273953	240
21	.3248616	3.0782342	12.2752441	37.7860755	.3158900	3.1656588	149.2603607	472.5073741	252
22	.3079257	3.2475370	12.5831697	40.8643097	.2990228	3.3442268	152.9404847	511.4676736	264
23	.2918727	3.4261516	12.8750424	44.1118467	.2830562	3.5328675	156.4241052	552.6256403	276
24	.2766566	3.6145899	13.1516990	47.5379983	.2679421	3.7321490	159.7217146	596.1052398	288
25	.2622337	3.8133923	13.4139327	51.1525882	.2536351	3.9426716	162.8432451	642.0374305	300
26	.2485628	4.0231289	13.6624954	54.9659805	.2400920	4.1650692	165.7980986	690.5605578	312
27	.2356045	4.2444010	13.8980999	58.9891094	.2272721	4.4000119	168.5951751	741.8207708	324
28	.2233218	4.4778431	14.1214217	63.2335105	.2151367	4.6482071	171.2428990	795.9724629	336
29	.2116794	4.7241244	14.3331012	67.7113535	.2036493	4.9104025	173.7492454	853.1787360	348
30	.2006440	4.9839513	14.5337452	72.4354780	.1927753	5.1873878	176.1217631	913.6118925	360
31	.1901839	5.2580686	14.7239291	77.4194293	.1824818	5.4799973	178.3675981	977.4539541	372
32	.1802691	5.5472624	14.9041982	82.6774979	.1727381	5.7891122	180.4935147	1044.8972098	384
33	.1708712	5.8523618	15.0750694	88.2247603	.1635146	6.1156636	182.5059160	1116.1447953	396
34	.1619632	6.1742417	15.2370326	94.0771221	.1547835	6.4606351	184.4108633	1191.4113046	408
35	.1535196	6.5138250	15.3905522	100.2513638	.1465187	6.8250658	186.2140942	1270.9234367	420
36	.1455162	6.8720854	15.5360684	106.7651888	.1386952	7.2100531	187.9210399	1354.9206780	432
37	.1379301	7.2500501	15.6739985	113.6372742	.1312895	7.6167568	189.5368418	1443.6560240	444
38	.1307394	7.6488028	15.8047379	120.8873242	.1242792	8.0464017	191.0663664	1537.3967410	456
39	.1239236	8.0694870	15.9286615	128.5361271	.1176432	8.5002820	192.5142206	1636.4251713	468
40	.1174631	8.5133088	16.0461247	136.6056141	.1113615	8.9797648	193.8847654	1741.0395834	480
41	.1113395	8.9815408	16.1574642	145.1189228	.1054152	9.4862941	195.1821287	1851.5550707	492
42	.1055350	9.4755255	16.2629992	154.1004636	.0997865	10.0213956	196.4102181	1968.3045001	504
43	.1000332	9.9966794	16.3630324	163.5759891	.0944583	10.5866811	197.5727325	2091.6395151	516
44	.0948182	10.5464968	16.4578506	173.5726685	.0894146	11.1838531	198.6731734	2221.9315944	528
45	.0898751	11.1265541	16.5477257	184.1191653	.0846402	11.8147104	199.7148553	2359.5731711	540
46	.0851897	11.7385146	16.6329154	195.2457194	.0801208	12.4811529	200.7009156	2504.9788146	552
47	.0807485	12.3841329	16.7136639	206.9842339	.0758427	13.1851880	201.6343243	2658.5864794	564
48	.0765389	13.0652602	16.7902027	219.3683668	.0717930	13.9289363	202.5178928	2820.8588239	576
49	.0725487	13.7838495	16.8627514	232.4336270	.0679595	14.7146378	203.3542824	2992.2846042	588
50	.0687665	14.5419612	16.9315179	246.2174764	.0643308	15.5446590	204.1460122	3173.3801459	600

Present and Future Value

5.750% Discount Rate   5.750% Discount Rate

	Annual Payments					Monthly Payments			
	Present Value	Future Value	Present Value of 1 per Period	Future Value of 1 per Period	Present Value	Future Value	Present Value of 1 per Period	Future Value of 1 per Period	
Years									Months
					.9952312	1.0047917	0.9952312	1.0000000	1
					.9904851	1.0096063	1.9857163	2.0047917	2
					.9857617	1.0144440	2.9714780	3.0143980	3
					.9810608	1.0193049	3.9525387	4.0288420	4
					.9763823	1.0241890	4.9289210	5.0481468	5
					.9717261	1.0290966	5.9006470	6.0723359	6
					.9670921	1.0340277	6.8677391	7.1014325	7
					.9624802	1.0389824	7.8302193	8.1354602	8
					.9578903	1.0439609	8.7881096	9.1744426	9
					.9533223	1.0489632	9.7414319	10.2184034	10
					.9487761	1.0539895	10.6902080	11.2673666	11
1	.9456265	1.0575000	0.9456265	1.0000000	.9442515	1.0590398	11.6344596	12.3213561	12
2	.8942094	1.1183063	1.8398359	2.0575000	.8916110	1.1215654	22.6203160	25.3701630	24
3	.8455881	1.1826089	2.6854240	3.1758062	.8419051	1.1877824	32.9937280	39.1893692	36
4	.7996105	1.2506089	3.4850345	4.3584151	.7949701	1.2579089	42.7888383	53.8244590	48
5	.7561329	1.3225189	4.2411674	5.6090240	.7506518	1.3321756	52.0378863	69.3236021	60
6	.7150193	1.3985637	4.9561867	6.9315429	.7088041	1.4108270	60.7713143	85.7378120	72
7	.6761411	1.4789811	5.6323278	8.3301066	.6692894	1.4941220	69.0178672	103.1211140	84
8	.6393770	1.5640225	6.2717048	9.8090877	.6319775	1.5823347	76.8046875	121.5307233	96
9	.6046118	1.6539538	6.8763166	11.3731102	.5967458	1.6757555	84.1574046	141.0272328	108
10	.5717369	1.7490562	7.4480535	13.0270641	.5634781	1.7746918	91.1002191	161.6748129	120
11	.5406496	1.8496269	7.9887031	14.7761203	.5320651	1.8794693	97.6559825	183.5414227	132
12	.5112526	1.9559805	8.4999556	16.6257472	.5024033	1.9904329	103.8462722	206.6990334	144
13	.4834539	2.0684493	8.9834096	18.5817276	.4743951	2.1079477	109.6914628	231.2238656	156
14	.4571669	2.1873852	9.4405764	20.6501770	.4479483	2.2324006	115.2107931	257.1966397	168
15	.4323091	2.3131598	9.8728855	22.8375622	.4229759	2.3642011	120.4224293	284.7028420	180
16	.4088029	2.4461665	10.2816884	25.1507220	.3993956	2.5037832	125.3435248	313.8330058	192
17	.3865749	2.5868211	10.6682633	27.5968885	.3771299	2.6516061	129.9902769	344.6830096	204
18	.3655554	2.7355633	11.0338187	30.1837096	.3561055	2.8081565	134.3779798	377.3543925	216
19	.3456789	2.8928582	11.3794976	32.9192729	.3362532	2.9739495	138.5210750	411.9546882	228
20	.3268831	3.0591975	11.7063807	35.8121311	.3175076	3.1495310	142.4331990	448.5977796	240
21	.3091093	3.2351014	12.0154900	38.8713286	.2998070	3.3354788	146.1272282	487.4042729	252
22	.2923020	3.4211197	12.3077920	42.1064300	.2830933	3.5324049	149.6153210	528.5018950	264
23	.2764085	3.6178341	12.5842005	45.5275497	.2673112	3.7409575	152.9089580	572.0259139	276
24	.2613792	3.8258596	12.8455796	49.1453838	.2524091	3.9618230	156.0189799	618.1195834	288
25	.2471671	4.0458465	13.0927467	52.9712434	.2383376	4.1957284	158.9556228	666.9346154	300
26	.2337277	4.2784827	13.3264744	57.0170899	.2250507	4.4434435	161.7285524	718.6316787	312
27	.2210191	4.5244954	13.5474936	61.2955726	.2125045	4.7057836	164.3468955	773.3809278	324
28	.2090015	4.7846539	13.7564951	65.8200680	.2006577	4.9836123	166.8192701	831.3625634	336
29	.1976374	5.0597715	13.9541325	70.6047219	.1894713	5.2778439	169.1538136	892.7674250	348
30	.1868911	5.3507084	14.1410236	75.6644934	.1789086	5.5894469	171.3582099	957.7976192	360
31	.1767292	5.6583741	14.3177528	81.0152018	.1689347	5.9194469	173.4397145	1026.6671852	372
32	.1671198	5.9837306	14.4848726	86.6735759	.1595169	6.2689301	175.4051784	1099.6027986	384
33	.1580329	6.3277951	14.6429056	92.6573065	.1506240	6.6390467	177.2610708	1176.8445184	396
34	.1494401	6.6916433	14.7923457	98.9851016	.1422270	7.0310148	179.0135001	1258.6465763	408
35	.1413145	7.0764128	14.9336602	105.6767450	.1342980	7.4461248	180.6682341	1345.2782140	420
36	.1336308	7.4833066	15.0672910	112.7531578	.1268111	7.8857427	182.2307193	1437.0245688	432
37	.1263648	7.9135967	15.1936558	120.2364644	.1197416	8.3513156	183.7060983	1534.1876130	444
38	.1194939	8.3686285	15.3131497	128.1500611	.1130662	8.8443759	185.0992273	1637.0871469	456
39	.1129966	8.8498247	15.4261463	136.5186896	.1067629	9.3665464	186.4146914	1746.0618520	468
40	.1068526	9.3586896	15.5329988	145.3685143	.1008111	9.9195457	187.6568205	1861.4704052	480
41	.1010426	9.8968142	15.6340415	154.7272038	.0951910	10.5051940	188.8297028	1983.6926600	492
42	.0955486	10.4658810	15.7295900	164.6240181	.0898843	11.1254189	189.9371987	2113.1308960	504
43	.0903533	11.0676692	15.8199433	175.0898991	.0848733	11.7822617	190.9829535	2250.2111437	516
44	.0854404	11.7040602	15.9053837	186.1575683	.0801418	12.4778845	191.9704090	2395.3845861	528
45	.0807947	12.3770436	15.9861785	197.8616285	.0756740	13.2145767	192.9028154	2549.1290440	540
46	.0764016	13.0887236	16.0625801	210.2386721	.0714545	13.9947630	193.7832416	2711.9505487	552
47	.0722474	13.8413253	16.1348275	223.3273958	.0674718	14.8210115	194.6145854	2884.3850077	564
48	.0683191	14.6372015	16.2031466	237.1687210	.0637103	15.6960415	195.3995831	3066.9999680	576
49	.0646043	15.4788405	16.2677509	251.8059225	.0601586	16.6227332	196.1408184	3260.3964847	588
50	.0610916	16.3688739	16.3288425	267.2847630	.0568048	17.6041365	196.8407309	3465.2110992	600

Present and Future Value

6.000% Discount Rate

6.000% Discount Rate

Annual Payments

Monthly Payments

Years	Present Value	Future Value	Present Value of 1 per Period	Future Value of 1 per Period	Present Value	Future Value	Present Value of 1 per Period	Future Value of 1 per Period	Months
					.9950249	1.0050000	0.9950249	1.0000000	1
					.9900745	1.0100250	1.9850994	2.0050000	2
					.9851488	1.0150751	2.9702481	3.0150250	3
					.9802475	1.0201505	3.9504957	4.0301001	4
					.9753707	1.0252513	4.9258663	5.0502506	5
					.9705181	1.0303775	5.8963844	6.0755019	6
					.9656896	1.0355294	6.8620740	7.1058794	7
					.9608852	1.0407070	7.8229592	8.1414088	8
					.9561047	1.0459106	8.7790639	9.1821158	9
					.9513479	1.0511401	9.7304119	10.2280264	10
					.9466149	1.0563958	10.6770267	11.2791665	11
1	.9433962	1.0600000	0.9433962	1.0000000	.9419053	1.0616778	11.6189321	12.3355624	12
2	.8899964	1.1236000	1.8333927	2.0600000	.8871857	1.1271598	22.5628662	25.4319552	24
3	.8396193	1.1910160	2.6730119	3.1836000	.8356449	1.1966805	32.8710162	39.3361050	36
4	.7920937	1.2624770	3.4651056	4.3746160	.7870984	1.2704892	42.5803178	54.0978322	48
5	.7472582	1.3382256	4.2123638	5.6370930	.7413722	1.3488502	51.7255608	69.7700305	60
6	.7049605	1.4185191	4.9173243	6.9753185	.6983024	1.4320443	60.3395139	86.4088557	72
7	.6650571	1.5036303	5.5823814	8.3938376	.6577348	1.5203696	68.4530424	104.0739272	84
8	.6274124	1.5938481	6.2097938	9.8974679	.6195239	1.6141427	76.0952183	122.8285417	96
9	.5918985	1.6894790	6.8016923	11.4913160	.5835329	1.7136995	83.2934245	142.7398998	108
10	.5583948	1.7908477	7.3600871	13.1807949	.5496327	1.8193967	90.0734533	163.8793468	120
11	.5267875	1.8982986	7.8868746	14.9716426	.5177020	1.9316131	96.4595987	186.3226287	132
12	.4969694	2.0121965	8.3838439	16.8699412	.4876263	2.0507508	102.4747432	210.1501631	144
13	.4688390	2.1329283	8.8526830	18.8821377	.4592978	2.1772366	108.1404398	235.4473277	156
14	.4423010	2.2609040	9.2949839	21.0150659	.4326151	2.3115238	113.4769898	262.3047661	168
15	.4172651	2.3965582	9.7122490	23.2759699	.4074824	2.4540936	118.5035147	290.8187124	180
16	.3936463	2.5403517	10.1058953	25.6725281	.3838099	2.6054567	123.2380253	321.0913067	192
17	.3713644	2.6927728	10.4772597	28.2128798	.3615126	2.7661556	127.6974861	353.2311101	204
18	.3503438	2.8543392	10.8276035	30.9056525	.3405106	2.9367660	131.8978761	387.3531944	216
19	.3305130	3.0255995	11.1581165	33.7599917	.3207288	3.1178993	135.8542459	423.5798542	228
20	.3118047	3.2071355	11.4699212	36.7855912	.3020961	3.3102045	139.5807717	462.0408952	240
21	.2941554	3.3995636	11.7640766	39.9927267	.2845460	3.5143706	143.0908062	502.8741289	252
22	.2775051	3.6035374	12.0415817	43.3922903	.2680154	3.7311293	146.3969265	546.2258672	264
23	.2617973	3.8197497	12.3033790	46.9958277	.2524451	3.9612572	149.5109789	592.2514459	276
24	.2469785	4.0489346	12.5503575	50.8155774	.2377794	4.2055789	152.4441214	641.1157815	288
25	.2329986	4.2918707	12.7833562	54.8645120	.2239657	4.4649698	155.2068640	692.9939624	300
26	.2198100	4.5493830	13.0031662	59.1563827	.2109545	4.7403594	157.8095039	748.0718760	312
27	.2073680	4.8223459	13.2105341	63.7057657	.1986991	5.0327344	160.2601717	806.5468748	324
28	.1956301	5.1116867	13.4061643	68.5281116	.1871558	5.3431424	162.5688435	868.6284836	336
29	.1845567	5.4183879	13.5907210	73.6397983	.1762830	5.6726958	164.7433938	934.5391502	348
30	.1741101	5.7434912	13.7648312	79.0581862	.1660419	6.0225752	166.7916144	1004.5150425	360
31	.1642548	6.0881006	13.9290860	84.8016774	.1563958	6.3940345	168.7208443	1078.8068946	372
32	.1549574	6.4533867	14.0840434	90.8897780	.1473100	6.7884045	170.5379962	1157.6809057	384
33	.1461862	6.8405899	14.2302296	97.3431647	.1387521	7.2070985	172.2495813	1241.4196932	396
34	.1379115	7.2510253	14.3681411	104.1837546	.1306913	7.6516165	173.8617325	1330.3233058	408
35	.1301052	7.6860868	14.4982464	111.4347799	.1230989	8.1235515	175.3802262	1424.7102988	420
36	.1227408	8.1472520	14.6209871	119.1208667	.1159475	8.6245944	176.8105036	1524.9188749	432
37	.1157932	8.6360871	14.7367803	127.2681187	.1092116	9.1565405	178.1576895	1631.3080967	444
38	.1092389	9.1542523	14.8460192	135.9042058	.1028669	9.7212959	179.4266111	1744.2591730	456
39	.1030555	9.7035075	14.9490747	145.0584581	.0968909	10.3208841	180.6218152	1864.1768245	468
40	.0972222	10.2857179	15.0462969	154.7619656	.0912621	10.9574537	181.7475842	1991.4907343	480
41	.0917190	10.9028610	15.1380159	165.0476836	.0859602	11.6332854	182.8079521	2126.6570875	492
42	.0865274	11.5570327	15.2245433	175.9505446	.0809664	12.3508010	183.8067183	2270.1602057	504
43	.0816296	12.2504546	15.3061729	187.5075772	.0762627	13.1125714	184.7474615	2422.5142821	516
44	.0770091	12.9854819	15.3831820	199.7580319	.0718322	13.9213261	185.6335526	2584.2652246	528
45	.0726501	13.7646108	15.4558321	212.7435138	.0676592	14.7799631	186.4681664	2755.9926113	540
46	.0685378	14.5904875	15.5243699	226.5081246	.0637285	15.6915588	187.2542937	2938.3117675	552
47	.0646583	15.4659167	15.5890282	241.0986121	.0600262	16.6593799	187.9947512	3131.8759702	564
48	.0609984	16.3938717	15.6500266	256.5645288	.0565390	17.6868939	188.6921920	3337.3787895	576
49	.0575457	17.3775040	15.7075723	272.9584006	.0532544	18.7777829	189.3491153	3555.5565730	588
50	.0542884	18.4201543	15.7618606	290.3359046	.0501606	19.9359554	189.9678748	3787.1910847	600

Present and Future Value

	Annual Payments				Monthly Payments				
Years	Present Value	Future Value	Present Value of 1 per Period	Future Value of 1 per Period	Present Value	Future Value	Present Value of 1 per Period	Future Value of 1 per Period	Months
					.9948187	1.0052083	0.9948187	1.0000000	1
					.9896642	1.0104438	1.9844828	2.0052083	2
					.9845364	1.0157065	2.9690192	3.0156521	3
					.9794351	1.0209967	3.9484543	4.0313586	4
					.9743603	1.0263144	4.9228146	5.0523553	5
					.9693118	1.0316597	5.8921265	6.0786697	6
					.9642895	1.0370330	6.8564160	7.1103294	7
					.9592932	1.0424342	7.8157092	8.1473624	8
					.9543228	1.0478635	8.7700319	9.1897965	9
					.9493781	1.0533211	9.7194100	10.2376601	10
					.9444590	1.0588072	10.6638690	11.2909812	11
1	.9411765	1.0625000	0.9411765	1.0000000	.9395654	1.0643218	11.6034344	12.3497884	12
2	.8858131	1.1289063	1.8269896	2.0625000	.8827832	1.1327809	22.5056205	25.4939376	24
3	.8337065	1.1994629	2.6606961	3.1914063	.8294326	1.2056434	32.7489378	39.4835423	36
4	.7846649	1.2744293	3.4453610	4.3908691	.7793062	1.2831926	42.3732048	54.3729838	48
5	.7385082	1.3540812	4.1838692	5.6652985	.7322092	1.3657299	51.4158335	70.2201412	60
6	.6950665	1.4387112	4.8789357	7.0193796	.6879585	1.4535761	59.9119749	87.0866165	72
7	.6541803	1.5286307	5.5331160	8.4580908	.6463820	1.5470728	67.8946559	105.0379741	84
8	.6156991	1.6241701	6.1488150	9.9867215	.6073182	1.6465833	75.3949070	124.1439956	96
9	.5794815	1.7256807	6.7282965	11.6108916	.5706152	1.7524945	82.4418839	144.4789511	108
10	.5453943	1.8335358	7.2736908	13.3365723	.5361303	1.8652182	89.0629798	166.1218878	120
11	.5133123	1.9481318	7.7870031	15.1701081	.5037295	1.9851924	95.2839328	189.1569375	132
12	.4831175	2.0698900	8.2701206	17.1182399	.4732868	2.1128836	101.1289252	213.6736434	144
13	.4546988	2.1992581	8.7248194	19.1881299	.4446840	2.2487881	106.6206781	239.7673083	156
14	.4279518	2.3367117	9.1527712	21.3873880	.4178097	2.3934342	111.7805394	267.5393650	168
15	.4027782	2.4827562	9.5555494	23.7240997	.3925595	2.5473842	116.6285667	297.0977709	180
16	.3790853	2.6379285	9.9346347	26.2068560	.3688354	2.7112366	121.1836057	328.5574270	192
17	.3567862	2.8027990	10.2914209	28.8447845	.3465450	2.8856283	125.4633629	362.0406253	204
18	.3357988	2.9779740	10.6272197	31.6475835	.3256017	3.0712371	129.4844750	397.6775237	216
19	.3160459	3.1640973	10.9432656	34.6255575	.3059241	3.2687846	133.2625729	435.6066521	228
20	.2974550	3.3618534	11.2407205	37.7896548	.2874357	3.4790388	136.8123431	475.9754508	240
21	.2799576	3.5719693	11.5206781	41.1515082	.2700647	3.7028169	140.1475845	518.9408439	252
22	.2634895	3.7952173	11.7841677	44.7234775	.2537434	3.9409888	143.2812622	564.6698490	264
23	.2479901	4.0324184	12.0321578	48.5186948	.2384086	4.1944803	146.2255574	613.3402268	276
24	.2334025	4.2844446	12.2655603	52.5511132	.2240004	4.4642769	148.9919154	665.1411716	288
25	.2196729	4.5522224	12.4852332	56.8355578	.2104631	4.7514273	151.5910899	720.2740471	300
26	.2067510	4.8367363	12.6919842	61.3877802	.1977438	5.0570478	154.0331843	778.9531692	312
27	.1945892	5.1390323	12.8865734	66.2245165	.1857933	5.3823262	156.3276919	841.4066390	324
28	.1831427	5.4602218	13.0697161	71.3635487	.1745649	5.7285272	158.4835320	907.8772292	336
29	.1723696	5.8014857	13.2420857	76.8237705	.1640152	6.0969965	160.5090848	978.6233284	348
30	.1622303	6.1640785	13.4043160	82.6252562	.1541030	6.4891664	162.4122242	1053.9199451	360
31	.1526873	6.5493334	13.5570033	88.7893347	.1447899	6.9065613	164.2003482	1134.0597769	372
32	.1437057	6.9586668	13.7007090	95.3386681	.1360395	7.3508039	165.8804078	1219.3543480	384
33	.1352524	7.3935834	13.8359614	102.2973349	.1278181	7.8236209	167.4589337	1310.1352207	396
34	.1272964	7.8556824	13.9632578	109.6909183	.1200934	8.3268504	168.9420621	1406.7552839	408
35	.1198084	8.3466625	14.0830661	117.5466007	.1128356	8.8624486	170.3355583	1509.5901248	420
36	.1127608	8.8683290	14.1958270	125.8932632	.1060165	9.4324973	171.6448392	1619.0394894	432
37	.1061278	9.4225995	14.3019548	134.7615922	.0996094	10.0392127	172.8749943	1735.5288357	444
38	.0998850	10.0115120	14.4018398	144.1841917	.0935896	10.6849531	174.0308055	1859.5109881	456
39	.0940094	10.6372315	14.4958492	154.1957037	.0879335	11.3722286	175.1167657	1991.4678975	468
40	.0884795	11.3020584	14.5843287	164.8329352	.0826193	12.1037110	176.1370965	2131.9125148	480
41	.0832748	12.0084371	14.6676035	176.1349936	.0776262	12.8822437	177.0957640	2281.3907848	492
42	.0783763	12.7589644	14.7459797	188.1434307	.0729349	13.7108530	177.9964949	2440.4837683	504
43	.0737659	13.5563597	14.8197456	200.9023951	.0685271	14.5927599	178.8427904	2609.8099012	516
44	.0694267	14.4036747	14.8891724	214.4587948	.0643857	15.5313927	179.6379405	2790.0273982	528
45	.0653428	15.3039043	14.9545152	228.8624695	.0604946	16.5304001	180.3850361	2981.8368116	540
46	.0614991	16.2603984	15.0160143	244.1663739	.0568386	17.5936654	181.0869813	3185.9837546	552
47	.0578815	17.2766733	15.0738958	260.4267722	.0534036	18.7253219	181.7465047	3403.2617994	564
48	.0544767	18.3564653	15.1283725	277.7034455	.0501762	19.9297686	182.3661701	3634.5155624	576
49	.0512722	19.5037444	15.1796447	296.0599108	.0471438	21.2116874	182.9483863	3880.6439870	588
50	.0482562	20.7227285	15.2279009	315.5636552	.0442947	22.5760617	183.4954166	4142.6038384	600

Present and Future Value

6.500% Discount Rate   6.500% Discount Rate

| | Annual Payments | | | | | Monthly Payments | | | |
Years	Present Value	Future Value	Present Value of 1 per Period	Future Value of 1 per Period	Present Value	Future Value	Present Value of 1 per Period	Future Value of 1 per Period	Months
					.9946125	1.0054167	0.9946125	1.0000000	1
					.9892541	1.0108627	1.9838666	2.0054167	2
					.9839245	1.0163382	2.9677910	3.0162793	3
					.9786236	1.0218433	3.9464146	4.0326175	4
					.9733513	1.0273783	4.9197659	5.0544609	5
					.9681074	1.0329433	5.8878732	6.0818392	6
					.9628917	1.0385384	6.8507649	7.1147825	7
					.9577041	1.0441638	7.8084691	8.1533209	8
					.9525445	1.0498197	8.7610136	9.1974847	9
					.9474127	1.0555062	9.7084263	10.2473044	10
					.9423085	1.0612236	10.6507348	11.3028107	11
1	.9389671	1.0650000	0.9389671	1.0000000	.9372318	1.0669719	11.5879666	12.3640342	12
2	.8816593	1.1342250	1.8206264	2.0650000	.8784035	1.1384289	22.4485780	25.5561107	24
3	.8278491	1.2079496	2.6484755	3.1992250	.8232678	1.2146716	32.6274889	39.6316850	36
4	.7773231	1.2864664	3.4257986	4.4071746	.7715928	1.2960204	42.1674883	54.6499265	48
5	.7298808	1.3700867	4.1556794	5.6936410	.7231613	1.3828173	51.1086796	70.6739675	60
6	.6853341	1.4591423	4.8410136	7.0637276	.6777698	1.4754272	59.4886488	87.7711683	72
7	.6435062	1.5539865	5.4845198	8.5228699	.6352275	1.5742393	67.3426229	106.0134002	84
8	.6042312	1.6549957	6.0887510	10.0768565	.5953554	1.6796690	74.7036175	125.4773481	96
9	.5673532	1.7625704	6.6561042	11.7318522	.5579860	1.7921595	81.6025760	146.2448327	108
10	.5327260	1.8771375	7.1888302	13.4944225	.5229623	1.9121838	88.0684997	168.4031542	120
11	.5002122	1.9991514	7.6890425	15.3715600	.4901369	2.0402462	94.1285693	192.0454596	132
12	.4696829	2.1290962	8.1587253	17.3707114	.4593737	2.1768853	99.8082596	217.2711339	144
13	.4410168	2.2674875	8.5997421	19.4998076	.4305380	2.3226753	105.1314461	244.1862183	156
14	.4141002	2.4148742	9.0138423	21.7672951	.4035139	2.4782292	110.1205061	272.9038558	168
15	.3888265	2.5718410	9.4026689	24.1821693	.3781861	2.6442008	114.7964120	303.5447667	180
16	.3650953	2.7390107	9.7677642	26.7540103	.3544481	2.8212878	119.1788199	336.2377561	192
17	.3428125	2.9170464	10.1105767	29.4930210	.3322000	3.0102347	123.2861522	371.1202555	204
18	.3218897	3.1066544	10.4324664	32.4100674	.3113484	3.2118357	127.1356748	408.3389006	216
19	.3022438	3.3085869	10.7347102	35.5167218	.2918057	3.4269383	130.7435700	448.0501472	228
20	.2837970	3.5236451	11.0185072	38.8253087	.2734896	3.6564467	134.1250043	490.4209296	240
21	.2664761	3.7526820	11.2849833	42.3489537	.2563231	3.9013257	137.2941922	535.6293617	252
22	.2502123	3.9966063	11.5351956	46.1016357	.2402342	4.1626047	140.2644560	583.8654863	264
23	.2349411	4.2563857	11.7701367	50.0982420	.2251551	4.4413821	143.0482819	635.3320734	276
24	.2206020	4.5330508	11.9907387	54.3546278	.2110226	4.7388296	145.6573721	690.2454732	288
25	.2071380	4.8276991	12.1978767	58.8876596	.1977771	5.0561978	148.1026946	748.8365251	300
26	.1944958	5.1414996	12.3923725	63.7153777	.1853630	5.3948208	150.3945287	811.3515283	312
27	.1826252	5.4756970	12.5749977	68.8568772	.1737281	5.7561219	152.5425086	878.0532770	324
28	.1714790	5.8316173	12.7464767	74.3325743	.1628235	6.1416201	154.5556638	949.2221653	336
29	.1610132	6.2106725	12.9074898	80.1641916	.1526034	6.5529357	156.4424569	1025.1573659	348
30	.1511861	6.6143662	13.0586759	86.3748640	.1430247	6.9917980	158.2108195	1106.1780875	360
31	.1419587	7.0443000	13.2006347	92.9892302	.1340473	7.4600516	159.8681853	1192.6249169	372
32	.1332940	7.5021795	13.3339292	100.0335302	.1256334	7.9596651	161.4215213	1284.8612505	384
33	.1251592	7.9898211	13.4590885	107.5357096	.1177476	8.4927386	162.8773572	1383.2748222	396
34	.1175204	8.5091595	13.5766089	115.5255308	.1103568	9.0615131	164.2418131	1488.2793331	408
35	.1103478	9.0622549	13.6869567	124.0346903	.1034300	9.6683794	165.5206245	1600.3161906	420
36	.1036130	9.6513014	13.7905697	133.0969451	.0969378	10.3158886	166.7191673	1719.8563639	432
37	.0972892	10.2786360	13.8878589	142.7482466	.0908532	11.0067628	167.8424798	1847.4023639	444
38	.0913513	10.9467474	13.9792102	153.0268826	.0851505	11.7439061	168.8952841	1983.4903559	456
39	.0857759	11.6582859	14.0649861	163.9736300	.0798058	12.5304172	169.8820057	2128.6924126	468
40	.0805408	12.4160745	14.1455269	175.6319159	.0747965	13.3696025	170.8067927	2283.6189201	480
41	.0756251	13.2231194	14.2211520	188.0479904	.0701017	14.2649895	171.6735325	2448.9211426	492
42	.0710095	14.0826221	14.2921615	201.2711098	.0657015	15.2203423	172.4858687	2625.2939612	504
43	.0666756	14.9979926	14.3588371	215.3537320	.0615776	16.2396768	173.2472160	2813.4787940	516
44	.0626062	15.9728621	14.4214433	230.3517245	.0577125	17.3272780	173.9607749	3014.2667137	528
45	.0587852	17.0110981	14.4802284	246.3245866	.0540900	18.4877179	174.6295451	3228.5017721	540
46	.0551973	18.1168396	14.5354257	263.3356848	.0506948	19.7258746	175.2563378	3457.0845492	552
47	.0518285	19.2944128	14.5872542	281.4525043	.0475128	21.0469530	175.8437879	3700.9759382	564
48	.0486652	20.5485496	14.6359195	300.7469170	.0445305	22.4565064	176.3943648	3961.2011852	576
49	.0456951	21.8842053	14.6816145	321.2954666	.0417354	23.9604602	176.9103830	4238.8541990	588
50	.0429062	23.3066787	14.7245207	343.1796720	.0391158	25.5651366	177.3940117	4535.1021493	600

Present and Future Value

	Annual Payments				Monthly Payments				
Years	Present Value	Future Value	Present Value of 1 per Period	Future Value of 1 per Period	Present Value	Future Value	Present Value of 1 per Period	Future Value of 1 per Period	Months
					.9944065	1.0056250	0.9944065	1.0000000	1
					.9888442	1.0112816	1.9832507	2.0056250	2
					.9833131	1.0169701	2.9665638	3.0169066	3
					.9778129	1.0226906	3.9443766	4.0338767	4
					.9723434	1.0284432	4.9167201	5.0565673	5
					.9669046	1.0342282	5.8836247	6.0850105	6
					.9614962	1.0400457	6.8451209	7.1192387	7
					.9561180	1.0458960	7.8012389	8.1592844	8
					.9507700	1.0517791	8.7520089	9.2051804	9
					.9454518	1.0576954	9.6974607	10.2569595	10
					.9401634	1.0636449	10.6376240	11.3146549	11
1	.9367681	1.0675000	0.9367681	1.0000000	.9349045	1.0696279	11.5725286	12.3782998	12
2	.8775346	1.1395563	1.8143027	2.0675000	.8740465	1.1441039	22.3917379	25.6184751	24
3	.8220464	1.2164763	2.6363491	3.2070563	.8171500	1.2237655	32.5066657	39.7805365	36
4	.7700669	1.2985884	3.4064161	4.4235325	.7639572	1.3089738	41.9631574	54.9286731	48
5	.7213742	1.3862432	4.1277902	5.7221210	.7142271	1.4001149	50.8040744	71.1315431	60
6	.6757603	1.4798146	4.8035506	7.1083642	.6677341	1.4976020	59.0694877	88.4625855	72
7	.6330308	1.5797021	5.4365813	8.5881787	.6242677	1.6018770	66.7968600	107.0003526	84
8	.5930031	1.6863320	6.0295844	10.1678808	.5836307	1.7134124	74.0212153	126.8288662	96
9	.5555064	1.8001594	6.5850908	11.8542128	.5456389	1.8327137	80.7752979	148.0379983	108
10	.5203807	1.9216701	7.1054714	13.6543721	.5101203	1.9603218	87.0897202	170.7238784	120
11	.4874760	2.0513829	7.5929475	15.5760422	.4769138	2.0968150	92.9931022	194.9893297	132
12	.4566520	2.1898512	8.0495995	17.6274251	.4458689	2.2428119	98.5122008	220.9443342	144
13	.4277771	2.3376661	8.4773766	19.8172763	.4168448	2.3989742	103.6720310	248.7065321	156
14	.4007279	2.4954586	8.8781045	22.1549424	.3897101	2.5660099	108.4959796	278.4017546	168
15	.3753892	2.6639021	9.2534937	24.6504010	.3643418	2.7446758	113.0059111	310.1645941	180
16	.3516526	2.8437155	9.6051463	27.3143031	.3406248	2.9357820	117.2222664	344.1390146	192
17	.3294170	3.0356663	9.9345633	30.1580186	.3184516	3.1401944	121.1641560	380.4790040	204
18	.3085873	3.2405737	10.2431506	33.1936848	.2977219	3.3588397	124.8494465	419.3492717	216
19	.2890748	3.4593125	10.5322254	36.4342586	.2783415	3.5927087	128.2948413	460.9259961	228
20	.2707961	3.6928160	10.8030215	39.8935710	.2602227	3.8428616	131.5159565	505.3976219	240
21	.2536731	3.9420811	11.0566946	43.5863871	.2432834	4.1104321	134.5273916	552.9657153	252
22	.2376329	4.2081716	11.2943275	47.5284682	.2274468	4.3966331	137.3427960	603.8458769	264
23	.2226069	4.4922232	11.5169344	51.7366398	.2126410	4.7027615	139.9749302	658.2687192	276
24	.2085311	4.7954483	11.7254655	56.2288630	.1987990	5.0302051	142.4357245	716.4809116	288
25	.1953453	5.1191410	11.9208108	61.0243112	.1858581	5.3804479	144.7363322	778.7462989	300
26	.1829932	5.4646830	12.1038040	66.1434522	.1737596	5.7550774	146.8871807	845.3470967	312
27	.1714222	5.8335491	12.2752262	71.6081353	.1624486	6.1557916	148.8980187	916.5851705	324
28	.1605829	6.2273137	12.4358091	77.4416844	.1518740	6.5844067	150.7779603	992.7834045	336
29	.1504289	6.6476574	12.5862380	83.6689981	.1419877	7.0428653	152.5355262	1074.2871642	348
30	.1409170	7.0963742	12.7271551	90.3166555	.1327449	7.5332455	154.1786825	1161.4658626	360
31	.1320066	7.5753795	12.8591617	97.4130297	.1241038	8.0577698	155.7148768	1254.7146339	372
32	.1236596	8.0867176	12.9828212	104.9884092	.1160252	8.6188157	157.1510717	1354.4561246	384
33	.1158403	8.6325711	13.0986616	113.0751268	.1084725	9.2189261	158.4937769	1461.1424096	396
34	.1085155	9.2152696	13.2071771	121.7076979	.1014114	9.8608209	159.7490781	1575.2570405	408
35	.1016539	9.8373003	13.3088310	130.9229675	.0948100	10.5474095	160.9226648	1697.3172376	420
36	.0952261	10.5013181	13.4040572	140.7602678	.0886383	11.2818038	162.0198564	1827.8762344	432
37	.0892048	11.2101570	13.4932620	151.2615859	.0828684	12.0673325	163.0456257	1967.5257847	444
38	.0835642	11.9668426	13.5768262	162.4717429	.0774740	12.9075560	164.0046221	2116.8988451	456
39	.0782803	12.7746045	13.6551065	174.4385856	.0724308	13.8062825	164.9011922	2276.6724435	468
40	.0733305	13.6368903	13.7284370	187.2131901	.0677159	14.7675855	165.7393996	2447.5707478	480
41	.0686937	14.5573804	13.7971307	200.8500804	.0633079	15.7958220	166.5230436	2630.3683484	492
42	.0643500	15.5400036	13.8614807	215.4074608	.0591868	16.8956524	167.2556758	2825.8937688	504
43	.0602811	16.5889539	13.9217618	230.9474645	.0553340	18.0720169	167.9406170	3035.0332207	516
44	.0564694	17.7087082	13.9782312	247.5364183	.0517320	19.3303822	168.5809717	3258.7346211	528
45	.0528987	18.9040460	14.0311299	265.2451265	.0483645	20.6763169	169.1796421	3498.0118884	540
46	.0495538	20.1800691	14.0806338	284.1491726	.0452162	22.1159662	169.7393418	3753.9495382	552
47	.0464205	21.5422238	14.1271043	304.3292417	.0422728	23.6558552	170.2626076	4027.7075985	564
48	.0434852	22.9963239	14.1705895	325.8714655	.0395211	25.3029636	170.7518112	4320.5268674	576
49	.0407356	24.5485758	14.2113250	348.8677895	.0369484	27.0647568	171.2091698	4633.7345379	588
50	.0381598	26.2056047	14.2494848	373.4163653	.0345432	28.9492199	171.6367564	4968.7502122	600

Present and Future Value

7.000% Discount Rate   7.000% Discount Rate

	Annual Payments				Monthly Payments				
Years	Present Value	Future Value	Present Value of 1 per Period	Future Value of 1 per Period	Present Value	Future Value	Present Value of 1 per Period	Future Value of 1 per Period	Months
					.9942005	1.0058333	0.9942005	1.0000000	1
					.9884346	1.0117007	1.9826351	2.0058333	2
					.9827022	1.0176023	2.9653373	3.0175340	3
					.9770030	1.0235383	3.9423403	4.0351363	4
					.9713369	1.0295089	4.9136772	5.0586746	5
					.9657036	1.0355144	5.8793808	6.0881835	6
					.9601030	1.0415549	6.8394838	7.1236979	7
					.9545349	1.0476306	7.7940187	8.1652528	8
					.9489991	1.0537418	8.7430178	9.2128835	9
					.9434953	1.0598886	9.6865131	10.2666253	10
					.9380235	1.0660713	10.6245367	11.3265140	11
1	.9345794	1.0700000	0.9345794	1.0000000	.9325835	1.0722901	11.5571201	12.3925853	12
2	.8734387	1.1449000	1.8080182	2.0700000	.8697119	1.1498060	22.3350993	25.6810316	24
3	.8162979	1.2250430	2.6243160	3.2149000	.8110790	1.2329256	32.3864645	39.9301007	36
4	.7628952	1.3107960	3.3872113	4.4399430	.7563988	1.3220539	41.7602014	55.2092362	48
5	.7129862	1.4025517	4.1001974	5.7507390	.7054050	1.4176253	50.5019935	71.5929016	60
6	.6663422	1.5007304	4.7665397	7.1532907	.6578491	1.5201055	58.6544443	89.1609436	72
7	.6227497	1.6057815	5.3892894	8.6540211	.6134992	1.6299941	66.2572851	107.9989807	84
8	.5820091	1.7181862	5.9712985	10.2598026	.5721392	1.7478265	73.3475687	128.1988210	96
9	.5439337	1.8384592	6.5152322	11.9779887	.5335675	1.8741770	79.9598500	149.8589095	108
10	.5083493	1.9671514	7.0235815	13.8164480	.4975963	2.0096614	86.1263541	173.0848074	120
11	.4750928	2.1048520	7.4986743	15.7835993	.4640501	2.1549400	91.8771340	197.9897074	132
12	.4440120	2.2521916	7.9426863	17.8884513	.4327654	2.3107207	97.2402162	224.6949847	144
13	.4149644	2.4098450	8.3576507	20.1406429	.4035899	2.4777629	102.2417380	253.3307886	156
14	.3878172	2.5785342	8.7454680	22.5504879	.3763812	2.6568806	106.9060745	284.0366771	168
15	.3624460	2.7590315	9.1079140	25.1290220	.3510069	2.8489467	111.2559576	316.9622967	180
16	.3387346	2.9521637	9.4466486	27.8880536	.3273432	3.0548973	115.3125867	352.2681121	192
17	.3165744	3.1588152	9.7632230	30.8402173	.3052749	3.2757361	119.0957319	390.1261877	204
18	.2958639	3.3799323	10.0590869	33.9990325	.2846943	3.5125393	122.6238306	430.7210266	216
19	.2765083	3.6165275	10.3355952	37.3789648	.2655012	3.7664611	125.9140770	474.2504697	228
20	.2584190	3.8696845	10.5940142	40.9954923	.2476020	4.0387388	128.9825065	520.9266598	240
21	.2415131	4.1405624	10.8355273	44.8651768	.2309096	4.3306996	131.8440731	570.9770755	252
22	.2257132	4.4304017	11.0612405	49.0057392	.2153425	4.6437662	134.5127228	624.6456397	264
23	.2109469	4.7405299	11.2721874	53.4361409	.2008248	4.9794645	137.0014613	682.1939088	276
24	.1971466	5.0723670	11.4693340	58.1766708	.1872859	5.3394304	139.3224178	743.9023469	288
25	.1842490	5.4274326	11.6535832	63.2490377	.1746597	5.7254182	141.4869034	810.0716930	300
26	.1721955	5.8073529	11.8257787	68.6764704	.1628848	6.1393092	143.5054669	881.0244265	312
27	.1609304	6.2138676	11.9867090	74.4838233	.1519036	6.5831203	145.3879458	957.1063388	324
28	.1504022	6.6488384	12.1371113	80.6976909	.1416628	7.0590146	147.1435145	1038.6882187	336
29	.1405628	7.1142570	12.2776741	87.3465293	.1321124	7.5693113	148.7807289	1126.1676593	348
30	.1313671	7.6122550	12.4090412	94.4607863	.1232059	8.1164975	150.3075679	1219.9709958	360
31	.1227730	8.1451129	12.5318142	102.0730414	.1148997	8.7032397	151.7314728	1320.5553830	372
32	.1147411	8.7152708	12.6465553	110.2181543	.1071536	9.3323976	153.0593829	1428.4110237	384
33	.1072347	9.3253398	12.7537900	118.9334251	.0999297	10.0070374	154.2977699	1544.0635574	396
34	.1002193	9.9781135	12.8540094	128.2587648	.0931928	10.7304470	155.4526692	1668.0766221	408
35	.0936629	10.6765815	12.9476723	138.2368784	.0869100	11.5061518	156.5297092	1801.0546013	420
36	.0875355	11.4239422	13.0352078	148.9134598	.0810509	12.3379325	157.5341388	1943.6455693	432
37	.0818088	12.2236181	13.1170166	160.3374020	.0755867	13.2298426	158.4708533	2096.5444499	444
38	.0764569	13.0792714	13.1934735	172.5610202	.0704909	14.1862290	159.3444178	2260.4964030	456
39	.0714550	13.9948204	13.2649285	185.6402916	.0657386	15.2117527	160.1590895	2436.3004561	468
40	.0667804	14.9744578	13.3317088	199.6351120	.0613068	16.3114115	160.9188389	2624.8133983	480
41	.0624116	16.0226699	13.3941204	214.6095698	.0571737	17.4905647	161.6273687	2826.9539564	492
42	.0583286	17.1442568	13.4524490	230.6322397	.0533192	18.7549700	162.2881318	3043.7072718	504
43	.0545127	18.3443548	13.5069617	247.7764965	.0497246	20.1107566	162.9043486	3276.1297019	516
44	.0509464	19.6284596	13.5579081	266.1208513	.0463724	21.5645648	163.4790221	3525.3539682	528
45	.0476135	21.0024518	13.6055216	285.7493108	.0432461	23.1234689	164.0149532	3792.5946769	540
46	.0444986	22.4726234	13.6500202	306.7517626	.0403306	24.7950664	164.5147536	4079.1542380	552
47	.0415875	24.0457070	13.6916076	329.2243860	.0376117	26.5875037	164.9808593	4386.4292130	564
48	.0388668	25.7289065	13.7304744	353.2700930	.0350760	28.5095165	165.4155417	4715.9171208	576
49	.0363241	27.5299300	13.7667985	378.9989995	.0327113	30.5704718	165.8209193	5069.2237361	588
50	.0339478	29.4570251	13.8007463	406.5289295	.0305060	32.7804137	166.1989678	5448.0709151	600

Present and Future Value

| 7.250% Discount Rate | | | | 7.250% Discount Rate | | | | |
| Annual Payments | | | | Monthly Payments | | | | |
Years	Present Value	Future Value	Present Value of 1 per Period	Future Value of 1 per Period	Present Value	Future Value	Present Value of 1 per Period	Future Value of 1 per Period	Months
					.9939946	1.0060417	0.9939946	1.0000000	1
					.9880253	1.0121198	1.9820199	2.0060417	2
					.9820918	1.0182347	2.9641117	3.0181615	3
					.9761940	1.0243866	3.9403057	4.0363962	4
					.9703316	1.0305756	4.9106373	5.0607828	5
					.9645044	1.0368020	5.8751416	6.0913584	6
					.9587121	1.0430660	6.8338538	7.1281603	7
					.9529547	1.0493678	7.7868085	8.1712263	8
					.9472318	1.0557078	8.7340403	9.2205941	9
					.9415433	1.0620860	9.6755837	10.2763019	10
					.9358890	1.0685028	10.6114727	11.3383878	11
1	.9324009	1.0725000	0.9324009	1.0000000	.9302686	1.0749583	11.5417413	12.4068906	12
2	.8693715	1.1502563	1.8017724	2.0725000	.8653998	1.1555353	22.2786614	25.7437806	24
3	.8106028	1.2336498	2.6123752	3.2227563	.8050543	1.2421523	32.2668815	40.0803812	36
4	.7558068	1.3230894	3.3681820	4.4564061	.7489167	1.3352619	41.5586095	55.4916289	48
5	.7047150	1.4190134	4.0728970	5.7794955	.6966938	1.4353509	50.2024127	72.0580776	60
6	.6570769	1.5218919	4.7299739	7.1985089	.6481124	1.5429423	58.2434719	89.8663190	72
7	.6126591	1.6322291	5.3426330	8.7204008	.6029186	1.6585987	65.7238170	109.0094358	84
8	.5712439	1.7505657	5.9138769	10.3526299	.5608763	1.7829244	72.6825476	129.5874882	96
9	.5326284	1.8774817	6.4465053	12.1031956	.5217656	1.9165694	79.1560365	151.7080363	108
10	.4966232	2.0135991	6.9431285	13.9806773	.4853822	2.0602322	85.1781202	175.4867030	120
11	.4630519	2.1595850	7.4061804	15.9942764	.4515358	2.2146637	90.7802759	201.0477780	132
12	.4317500	2.3161550	7.8379304	18.1538614	.4200496	2.3806711	95.9917857	228.5248678	144
13	.4025641	2.4840762	8.2404946	20.4700163	.3907590	2.5591221	100.8398899	258.0615934	156
14	.3753512	2.6641717	8.6158458	22.9540925	.3635108	2.7509490	105.3499291	289.8123417	168
15	.3499778	2.8573242	8.9658236	25.6182642	.3381627	2.9571561	109.5454773	323.9430720	180
16	.3263196	3.0644802	9.2921432	28.4755884	.3145822	3.1788194	113.4484642	360.6321838	192
17	.3042607	3.2866550	9.5964039	31.5400685	.2926460	3.4170983	117.0792905	400.0714489	204
18	.2836930	3.5249375	9.8800969	34.8267235	.2722394	3.6732382	120.4569344	442.4670141	216
19	.2645156	3.7804954	10.1446125	38.3516610	.2532557	3.9485779	123.5990506	488.0404788	228
20	.2466346	4.0545813	10.3912471	42.1321564	.2355959	4.2445566	126.5210628	537.0300527	240
21	.2299623	4.3485385	10.6212094	46.1867377	.2191675	4.5627213	129.2412494	589.6918018	252
22	.2144171	4.6638075	10.8356265	50.5352762	.2038846	4.9047351	131.7708234	646.3009858	264
23	.1999227	5.0019336	11.0355491	55.1990837	.1896675	5.2723857	134.1240068	707.1534980	276
24	.1864081	5.3645738	11.2219572	60.2010173	.1764417	5.6675948	136.3130996	772.5674108	288
25	.1738071	5.7535054	11.3957643	65.5655911	.1641382	6.0924280	138.3495439	842.8846392	300
26	.1620579	6.1706345	11.5578222	71.3190964	.1526926	6.5491061	140.2439843	918.4727272	312
27	.1511029	6.6180055	11.7089251	77.4897309	.1420451	7.0400159	142.0063227	999.7267697	324
28	.1408885	7.0978104	11.8498137	84.1077364	.1321401	7.5677235	143.6457709	1087.0714769	336
29	.1313646	7.6124022	11.9811782	91.2055473	.1229258	8.1349872	145.1708981	1180.9633945	348
30	.1224845	8.1643013	12.1036627	98.8179495	.1143540	8.7447720	146.5896762	1281.8932905	360
31	.1142046	8.7562132	12.2178703	106.9822508	.1063800	9.4002652	147.9095209	1390.3887197	372
32	.1064845	9.3910386	12.3243518	115.7384640	.0989620	10.1048931	149.1373311	1507.0167814	384
33	.0992862	10.0718889	12.4236380	125.1295026	.0920612	10.8623386	150.2795244	1632.3870842	396
34	.0925746	10.8021009	12.5162126	135.2013916	.0856417	11.6765610	151.3420711	1767.1549313	408
35	.0863166	11.5852532	12.6025293	146.0034924	.0796697	12.5518162	152.3305249	1912.0247469	420
36	.0804817	12.4251841	12.6830110	157.5887456	.0741143	13.4926789	153.2500525	2067.7537572	432
37	.0750412	13.3260099	12.7580522	170.0139297	.0689462	14.5040672	154.1054602	2235.1559489	444
38	.0699685	14.2921456	12.8280207	183.3399396	.0641385	15.5912674	154.9012191	2415.1063239	456
39	.0652387	15.3283262	12.8932594	197.6320852	.0596660	16.7599622	155.6414887	2608.5454726	468
40	.0608286	16.4396298	12.9540880	212.9604114	.0555054	18.0162605	156.3301383	2816.4844906	480
41	.0567167	17.6315030	13.0108047	229.4000412	.0516349	19.3667287	156.9707675	3040.0102633	492
42	.0528827	18.9097870	13.0636873	247.0315442	.0480344	20.8184257	157.5667247	3280.2911474	504
43	.0493078	20.2807465	13.1129952	265.9413312	.0446849	22.3789394	158.1211250	3538.5830775	516
44	.0459747	21.7511006	13.1589699	286.2220777	.0415689	24.0564266	158.6368662	3816.2361309	528
45	.0428668	23.3280543	13.2018367	307.9731783	.0386703	25.8596554	159.1166440	4114.7015844	540
46	.0399691	25.0193394	13.2418058	331.3012338	.0359737	27.7980511	159.5629664	4435.5395002	552
47	.0372672	26.8332416	13.2790730	356.3205732	.0334652	29.8817457	159.9781660	4780.4268799	564
48	.0347480	28.7786516	13.3138210	383.1538148	.0311317	32.1216305	160.3644132	5151.1664303	576
49	.0323990	30.8651038	13.3462200	411.9324663	.0289608	34.5294133	160.7237269	5549.6959863	588
50	.0302089	33.1028238	13.3764289	442.7975701	.0269413	37.1176793	161.0579852	5978.0986393	600

Present and Future Value

7.500% Discount Rate   7.500% Discount Rate

	Annual Payments				Monthly Payments				
Years	Present Value	Future Value	Present Value of 1 per Period	Future Value of 1 per Period	Present Value	Future Value	Present Value of 1 per Period	Future Value of 1 per Period	Months
					.9937888	1.0062500	0.9937888	1.0000000	1
					.9876162	1.0125391	1.9814050	2.0062500	2
					.9814820	1.0188674	2.9628870	3.0187891	3
					.9753858	1.0252354	3.9382728	4.0376565	4
					.9693275	1.0316431	4.9076003	5.0628918	5
					.9633068	1.0380908	5.8709071	6.0945349	6
					.9573236	1.0445789	6.8282307	7.1326258	7
					.9513774	1.0511075	7.7796081	8.1772047	8
					.9454683	1.0576770	8.7250764	9.2283122	9
					.9395958	1.0642874	9.6646722	10.2859892	10
					.9337598	1.0709392	10.5984320	11.3502766	11
1	.9302326	1.0750000	0.9302326	1.0000000	.9279600	1.0776326	11.5263920	12.4212158	12
2	.8653326	1.1556250	1.7955652	2.0750000	.8611099	1.1612920	22.2224234	25.8067229	24
3	.8049606	1.2422969	2.6005257	3.2306250	.7990755	1.2514461	32.1479132	40.2313817	36
4	.7488005	1.3354691	3.3493263	4.4729219	.7415102	1.3485992	41.3583711	55.7758642	48
5	.6965586	1.4356293	4.0458849	5.8083910	.6880918	1.4532944	49.9053082	72.5271053	60
6	.6479615	1.5433015	4.6938464	7.2440203	.6385217	1.5661174	57.8365243	90.5787888	72
7	.6027549	1.6590491	5.2966013	8.7873219	.5925226	1.6876992	65.1963760	110.0318714	84
8	.5607022	1.7834778	5.8573036	10.4463710	.5498373	1.8187197	72.0260244	130.9951474	96
9	.5215835	1.9172387	6.3788870	12.2298488	.5102271	1.9599116	78.3636652	153.5858569	108
10	.4851939	2.0610316	6.8640810	14.1470875	.4734704	2.1120646	84.2447427	177.9303419	120
11	.4513432	2.2156089	7.3154241	16.2081191	.4393616	2.2760297	89.7021477	204.1647526	132
12	.4198541	2.3817796	7.7352783	18.4237280	.4077100	2.4527238	94.7664015	232.4358088	144
13	.3905620	2.5604131	8.1258403	20.8055076	.3783386	2.6431351	99.4658267	262.9016205	156
14	.3633135	2.7524440	8.4891537	23.3659207	.3510831	2.8483286	103.8267055	295.7325724	168
15	.3379660	2.9588774	8.8271197	26.1183647	.3257911	3.0694517	107.8734268	331.1122763	180
16	.3143870	3.1807932	9.1415067	29.0772421	.3023211	3.3077412	111.6286226	369.2385987	192
17	.2924530	3.4193526	9.4339598	32.2580352	.2805419	3.5645298	115.1132942	410.3247665	204
18	.2720493	3.6758041	9.7060091	35.6773879	.2603317	3.8412535	118.3469303	454.6005603	216
19	.2530691	3.9514894	9.9590782	39.3531919	.2415774	4.1394600	121.3476153	502.3135991	228
20	.2354131	4.2478511	10.1944914	43.3046813	.2241742	4.4608170	124.1321312	553.7307250	240
21	.2189890	4.5664399	10.4134803	47.5525324	.2080247	4.8071219	126.7160507	609.1394961	252
22	.2037107	4.9089229	10.6171910	52.1189724	.1930386	5.1803112	129.1138247	668.8497941	264
23	.1894983	5.2770921	10.8066893	57.0278953	.1791321	5.5824722	131.3388633	733.1955576	276
24	.1762775	5.6728741	10.9829668	62.3049874	.1662274	6.0158541	133.4036101	802.5366501	288
25	.1639791	6.0983396	11.1469459	67.9778615	.1542524	6.4828804	135.3196127	877.2608717	300
26	.1525387	6.5557151	11.2994845	74.0762011	.1431401	6.9861633	137.0975866	957.7861289	312
27	.1418964	7.0473937	11.4413810	80.6319162	.1328283	7.5285173	138.7474753	1044.5627710	324
28	.1319967	7.5759482	11.5733776	87.6793099	.1232593	8.1129757	140.2785062	1138.0761094	336
29	.1227876	8.1441444	11.6961652	95.2552582	.1143797	8.7428071	141.6992416	1238.8491313	348
30	.1142210	8.7549552	11.8103863	103.3994025	.1061398	9.4215339	143.0176273	1347.4454248	360
31	.1062521	9.4115768	11.9166384	112.1543577	.0984935	10.1529521	144.2410366	1464.4723307	372
32	.0988392	10.1174451	12.0154776	121.5659345	.0913981	10.9411521	145.3763115	1590.5843395	384
33	.0919434	10.8762535	12.1074210	131.6833796	.0848137	11.7905422	146.4298013	1726.4867513	396
34	.0855288	11.6919725	12.1929498	142.5596331	.0787038	12.7058726	147.4073978	1872.9396205	408
35	.0795616	12.5688704	12.2725114	154.2516056	.0730339	13.6922625	148.3145682	2030.7620066	420
36	.0740108	13.5115357	12.3465222	166.8204760	.0677726	14.7552285	149.1563861	2200.8365546	432
37	.0688473	14.5249009	12.4153695	180.3320117	.0628903	15.9007152	149.9375595	2384.1144318	444
38	.0640440	15.6142684	12.4794135	194.8569126	.0583596	17.1351290	150.6624572	2581.6206470	456
39	.0595758	16.7853386	12.5389893	210.4711810	.0541554	18.4653736	151.3351334	2794.4597829	468
40	.0554194	18.0442390	12.5944087	227.2565196	.0502541	19.8988886	151.9593499	3023.8221740	480
41	.0515529	19.3975569	12.6459615	245.3007586	.0466338	21.4436910	152.5385980	3270.9905637	492
42	.0479562	20.8523737	12.6939177	264.6983155	.0432743	23.1084205	153.0761170	3537.3472778	504
43	.0446104	22.4163017	12.7385221	285.5506891	.0401568	24.9023872	153.5749132	3824.3819559	516
44	.0414980	24.0975243	12.7800261	307.9669908	.0372639	26.8356243	154.0377761	4133.6998819	528
45	.0386028	25.9048386	12.8186290	332.0645151	.0345794	28.9189435	154.4672944	4467.0309625	540
46	.0359096	27.8477015	12.8545386	357.9693537	.0320883	31.1639963	154.8658703	4826.2394011	552
47	.0334043	29.9362791	12.8879429	385.8170553	.0297767	33.5833383	155.2357327	5213.3341243	564
48	.0310738	32.1815001	12.9190166	415.7533344	.0276316	36.1905001	155.5789503	5630.4800169	576
49	.0289058	34.5951126	12.9479224	447.9348345	.0256410	39.0000627	155.8974425	6080.0100292	588
50	.0268891	37.1897460	12.9748116	482.5299471	.0237938	42.0277389	156.1929905	6564.4382247	600

Present and Future Value

7.750% Discount Rate   7.750% Discount Rate

Annual Payments   Monthly Payments

Years	Present Value	Future Value	Present Value of 1 per Period	Future Value of 1 per Period	Present Value	Future Value	Present Value of 1 per Period	Future Value of 1 per Period	Months
					.9935831	1.0064583	0.9935831	1.0000000	1
					.9872074	1.0129584	1.9807905	2.0064583	2
					.9808726	1.0195004	2.9616631	3.0194167	3
					.9745784	1.0260847	3.9362415	4.0389171	4
					.9683247	1.0327115	4.9045662	5.0650018	5
					.9621110	1.0393811	5.8666773	6.0977133	6
					.9559373	1.0460937	6.8226145	7.1370943	7
					.9498031	1.0528498	7.7724177	8.1831881	8
					.9437084	1.0596494	8.7161260	9.2360378	9
					.9376527	1.0664930	9.6537787	10.2956872	10
					.9316359	1.0733807	10.5854146	11.3621802	11
1	.9280742	1.0775000	0.9280742	1.0000000	.9256577	1.0803130	11.5110722	12.4355609	12
2	.8613218	1.1610063	1.7893961	2.0775000	.8568421	1.1670762	22.1663844	25.8698591	24
3	.7993706	1.2509842	2.5887666	3.2385063	.7931425	1.2608076	32.0295557	40.3831059	36
4	.7418753	1.3479355	3.3306419	4.4894905	.7341784	1.3620668	41.1594758	56.0619552	48
5	.6885153	1.4524005	4.0191572	5.8374260	.6795978	1.4714585	49.6106562	73.0000198	60
6	.6389933	1.5649616	4.6581505	7.2898265	.6290750	1.5896357	57.4335561	91.2984312	72
7	.5930333	1.6862461	5.2511838	8.8547881	.5823080	1.7173041	64.6748833	111.0664428	84
8	.5503789	1.8169301	5.8015627	10.5410341	.5390179	1.8552260	71.3778732	132.4220828	96
9	.5107925	1.9577422	6.3123552	12.3579643	.4989460	2.0042247	77.5825472	155.4928581	108
10	.4740533	2.1094673	6.7864085	14.3157065	.4618532	2.1651900	83.3259512	180.4165167	120
11	.4399567	2.2729510	7.2263652	16.4251738	.4275180	2.3390829	88.6423772	207.3418689	132
12	.4083125	2.4491047	7.6346777	18.6981247	.3957353	2.5269417	93.5635675	236.4296769	144
13	.3789443	2.6389103	8.0136220	21.1472294	.3663154	2.7298879	98.1189051	267.8536140	156
14	.3516884	2.8434258	8.3653104	23.7861397	.3390827	2.9491334	102.3355881	301.8013016	168
15	.3263930	3.0637913	8.6917034	26.6295655	.3138745	3.1859872	106.2387931	338.4754298	180
16	.3029169	3.3012352	8.9946203	29.6933568	.2905403	3.4418633	109.8518247	378.0949672	192
17	.2811294	3.5570809	9.2757497	32.9945920	.2689409	3.7182897	113.1962551	420.8964684	204
18	.2609090	3.8327546	9.5366587	36.5516729	.2489472	4.0169167	116.2920527	467.1354865	216
19	.2421429	4.1297931	9.7788016	40.3844275	.2304398	4.3395273	119.1577014	517.0880987	228
20	.2247266	4.4498521	10.0035281	44.5142207	.2133084	4.6880478	121.8103111	571.0525550	240
21	.2085629	4.7947156	10.2120911	48.9640728	.1974506	5.0645589	124.2657196	629.3510585	252
22	.1935619	5.1663061	10.4056530	53.7587884	.1827716	5.4713088	126.5385873	692.3316896	264
23	.1796398	5.5666948	10.5852928	58.9250945	.1691840	5.9107260	128.6424846	760.3704840	276
24	.1667191	5.9981137	10.7520119	64.4917893	.1566064	6.3854342	130.5899733	833.8736780	288
25	.1547277	6.4629675	10.9067395	70.4899030	.1449639	6.8982675	132.3926812	913.2801337	300
26	.1435988	6.9638475	11.0503383	76.9528705	.1341870	7.4522881	134.0613715	999.0639600	312
27	.1332703	7.5035456	11.1836087	83.9167179	.1242112	8.0508037	135.6060075	1091.7373426	324
28	.1236848	8.0850704	11.3072934	91.4202636	.1149771	8.6973878	137.0358116	1191.8536023	336
29	.1147886	8.7116634	11.4220821	99.5053340	.1064294	9.3959011	138.3593207	1300.0104989	348
30	.1065324	9.3868173	11.5286144	108.2169974	.0985172	10.1505141	139.5844371	1416.8538002	360
31	.0988700	10.1142956	11.6274844	117.6038147	.0911932	10.9657323	140.7184754	1543.0811372	372
32	.0917587	10.8981536	11.7192431	127.7181103	.0844137	11.8464232	141.7682067	1679.4461701	384
33	.0851589	11.7427605	11.8044019	138.6162639	.0781382	12.7978449	142.7398985	1826.7630876	396
34	.0790337	12.6528244	11.8834356	150.3590243	.0723292	13.8256782	143.6393524	1985.9114683	408
35	.0733492	13.6334183	11.9567848	163.0118487	.0669521	14.9360599	144.4719389	2157.8415326	420
36	.0680735	14.6900082	12.0248583	176.6452670	.0619747	16.1356196	145.2426289	2343.5798157	432
37	.0631772	15.8284838	12.0880355	191.3352752	.0573673	17.4315196	145.9560240	2544.2352972	444
38	.0586332	17.0551913	12.1466687	207.1637590	.0531025	18.8314972	146.6163837	2761.0060219	456
39	.0544159	18.3769687	12.2010847	224.2189503	.0491548	20.3439112	147.2276506	2995.1862533	468
40	.0505020	19.8011837	12.2515867	242.5959190	.0455005	21.9777917	147.7934746	3248.1742012	480
41	.0468696	21.3357755	12.2984563	262.3971027	.0421179	23.7428941	148.3172338	3521.4803695	492
42	.0434985	22.9892961	12.3419206	283.7328782	.0389867	25.6497571	148.8020556	3816.7365755	504
43	.0403698	24.7709687	12.3823247	306.7221762	.0360884	27.7097659	149.2508346	4135.7056926	516
44	.0374662	26.6907187	12.4197909	331.4931449	.0334055	29.9352203	149.6662503	4480.2921756	528
45	.0347714	28.7592494	12.4545623	358.1838636	.0309220	32.3394076	150.0507831	4852.5534320	540
46	.0322705	30.9880913	12.4868328	386.9431130	.0286232	34.9366824	150.4067268	5254.7121060	552
47	.0299494	33.3896683	12.5167821	417.9312043	.0264953	37.7425520	150.7362126	5689.1693486	564
48	.0277953	35.9773676	12.5445774	451.3208726	.0245256	40.7737695	151.0412018	6158.5191547	576
49	.0257961	38.7656136	12.5703735	487.2982403	.0227023	44.0484332	151.3235175	6665.5638508	588
50	.0239407	41.7699487	12.5943141	526.0638539	.0210145	47.5860949	151.5848451	7213.3308265	600

Present and Future Value

8.000% Discount Rate   8.000% Discount Rate

	Annual Payments				Monthly Payments				
Years	Present Value	Future Value	Present Value of 1 per Period	Future Value of 1 per Period	Present Value	Future Value	Present Value of 1 per Period	Future Value of 1 per Period	Months
					.9933775	1.0066667	0.9933775	1.0000000	1
					.9867988	1.0133778	1.9801763	2.0066667	2
					.9802637	1.0201336	2.9604400	3.0200444	3
					.9737719	1.0269345	3.9342120	4.0401781	4
					.9673231	1.0337808	4.9015351	5.0671126	5
					.9609170	1.0406726	5.8624520	6.1008933	6
					.9545533	1.0476104	6.8170053	7.1415660	7
					.9482318	1.0545945	7.7652371	8.1891764	8
					.9419521	1.0616251	8.7071892	9.2437709	9
					.9357140	1.0687026	9.6429031	10.3053961	10
					.9295172	1.0758273	10.5724203	11.3740987	11
1	.9259259	1.0800000	0.9259259	1.0000000	.9233615	1.0829995	11.4957818	12.4499260	12
2	.8573388	1.1664000	1.7832647	2.0800000	.8525964	1.1728879	22.1105436	25.9331898	24
3	.7938322	1.2597120	2.5770970	3.2464000	.7872546	1.2702371	31.9118055	40.5355577	36
4	.7350299	1.3604890	3.3121268	4.5061120	.7269206	1.3756661	40.9619130	56.3499151	48
5	.6805832	1.4693281	3.9927100	5.8666010	.6712104	1.4898457	49.3184333	73.4768562	60
6	.6301696	1.5868743	4.6228797	7.3359290	.6197699	1.6135022	57.0345221	92.0253251	72
7	.5834904	1.7138243	5.2063701	8.9228034	.5722716	1.7474221	64.1592611	112.1133077	84
8	.5402689	1.8509302	5.7466389	10.6366276	.5284135	1.8924572	70.7379705	133.8685830	96
9	.5002490	1.9990046	6.2468879	12.4875578	.4879167	2.0495302	76.8124971	157.4295354	108
10	.4631935	2.1589250	6.7100814	14.4865625	.4505235	2.2196402	82.4214809	182.9460352	120
11	.4288829	2.3316390	7.1389643	16.6454875	.4159960	2.4038693	87.6006003	210.5803919	132
12	.3971138	2.5181701	7.5360780	18.9771265	.3841147	2.6033892	92.3827995	240.5083866	144
13	.3676979	2.7196237	7.9037759	21.4952966	.3546767	2.8194693	96.7984979	272.9203901	156
14	.3404610	2.9371936	8.2442370	24.2149203	.3274948	3.0534838	100.8757837	308.0225739	168
15	.3152417	3.1721691	8.5594787	27.1521139	.3023961	3.3069215	104.6405922	346.0382216	180
16	.2918905	3.4259426	8.8513692	30.3242830	.2792209	3.5813943	108.1168712	387.2091494	192
17	.2702690	3.7000181	9.1216381	33.7502257	.2578218	3.8786483	111.3267333	431.7972438	204
18	.2502490	3.9960195	9.3718871	37.4502437	.2380627	4.2005742	114.2905962	480.0861281	216
19	.2317121	4.3157011	9.6035992	41.4462632	.2198179	4.5492198	117.0273129	532.3829660	228
20	.2145482	4.6609571	9.8181474	45.7619643	.2029714	4.9268028	119.5542917	589.0204156	240
21	.1986557	5.0338337	10.0168032	50.4229214	.1874160	5.3357250	121.8876065	650.3587456	252
22	.1839405	5.4365404	10.2007437	55.4567552	.1730527	5.7785875	124.0420994	716.7881268	264
23	.1703153	5.8714636	10.3710589	60.8932956	.1597902	6.2582074	126.0314752	788.7311138	276
24	.1576993	6.3411807	10.5287583	66.7647592	.1475441	6.7776356	127.8683881	866.6453333	288
25	.1460179	6.8484752	10.6747762	73.1059400	.1362365	7.3401760	129.5645226	951.0263946	300
26	.1352018	7.3963532	10.8099780	79.9544151	.1257955	7.9494069	131.1306679	1042.4110423	312
27	.1251868	7.9880615	10.9351648	87.3507684	.1161548	8.6092038	132.5767860	1141.3805707	324
28	.1159137	8.6271064	11.0510785	95.3388298	.1072528	9.3237635	133.9120758	1248.5645212	336
29	.1073275	9.3172749	11.1584060	103.9659362	.0990331	10.0976312	135.1450309	1364.6446867	348
30	.0993773	10.0626569	11.2577833	113.2832111	.0914434	10.9357297	136.2834941	1490.3594487	360
31	.0920160	10.8676694	11.3497994	123.3458680	.0844353	11.8433898	137.3347072	1626.5084739	372
32	.0852000	11.7370830	11.4349994	134.2135374	.0779643	12.8263853	138.3053568	1773.9578011	384
33	.0788889	12.6760496	11.5138884	145.9506204	.0719892	13.8909690	139.2016173	1933.6453497	396
34	.0730453	13.6901336	11.5869337	158.6266701	.0664721	15.0439126	140.0291896	2106.5868861	408
35	.0676345	14.7853443	11.6545682	172.3168037	.0613777	16.2925499	140.7933380	2293.8824847	420
36	.0626246	15.9681718	11.7171928	187.1021480	.0566738	17.6448235	141.4989232	2496.7235256	432
37	.0579857	17.2456256	11.7751785	203.0703198	.0523304	19.1093352	142.1504333	2716.4002729	444
38	.0536905	18.6252756	11.8288690	220.3159454	.0483199	20.6954005	142.7520127	2954.3100818	456
39	.0497134	20.1152977	11.8785824	238.9412210	.0446167	22.4131086	143.3074879	3211.9662876	468
40	.0460309	21.7245215	11.9246133	259.0565187	.0411974	24.2733855	143.8203923	3491.0078314	480
41	.0426212	23.4624832	11.9672346	280.7810402	.0380401	26.2880646	144.2939885	3793.2096857	492
42	.0394641	25.3394819	12.0066987	304.2435234	.0351247	28.4699610	144.7312889	4120.4941448	504
43	.0365408	27.3666404	12.0432395	329.5830053	.0324328	30.8329537	145.1350752	4474.9430526	516
44	.0338341	29.5559717	12.0770736	356.9496457	.0299472	33.3920736	145.5079160	4858.8110450	528
45	.0313279	31.9204494	12.1084015	386.5056174	.0276521	36.1635993	145.8521828	5274.5398915	540
46	.0290073	34.4740853	12.1374088	418.4260668	.0255329	39.1651602	146.1700655	5724.7740271	552
47	.0268586	37.2320122	12.1642674	452.9001521	.0235761	42.4158492	146.4635861	6212.3773740	564
48	.0248691	40.2105731	12.1891365	490.1321643	.0217693	45.9363437	146.7346117	6740.4515581	576
49	.0230269	43.4274190	12.2121634	530.3427374	.0201009	49.7490376	146.9848663	7312.3556391	588
50	.0213212	46.9016125	12.2334846	573.7701564	.0185604	53.8781832	147.2159418	7931.7274768	600

Present and Future Value

8.250% Discount Rate   8.250% Discount Rate

	Annual Payments				Monthly Payments				
Years	Present Value	Future Value	Present Value of 1 per Period	Future Value of 1 per Period	Present Value	Future Value	Present Value of 1 per Period	Future Value of 1 per Period	Months
					.9931719	1.0068750	0.9931719	1.0000000	1
					.9863905	1.0137973	1.9795625	2.0068750	2
					.9796554	1.0207671	2.9592178	3.0206723	3
					.9729662	1.0277849	3.9321841	4.0414394	4
					.9663228	1.0348509	4.8985068	5.0692243	5
					.9597247	1.0419655	5.8582315	6.1040752	6
					.9531716	1.0491290	6.8114031	7.1460407	7
					.9466633	1.0563418	7.7580664	8.1951697	8
					.9401994	1.0636041	8.6982658	9.2515115	9
					.9337797	1.0709164	9.6320455	10.3151157	10
					.9274038	1.0782790	10.5594493	11.3860321	11
1	.9237875	1.0825000	0.9237875	1.0000000	.9210714	1.0856921	11.4805207	12.4643111	12
2	.8533834	1.1718062	1.7771709	2.0825000	.8483726	1.1787274	22.0549002	25.9967156	24
3	.7883449	1.2684803	2.5655159	3.2543062	.7814117	1.2797351	31.7946590	40.6887408	36
4	.7282632	1.3731299	3.2937791	4.5227865	.7197360	1.3893983	40.7656724	56.6397571	48
5	.6727605	1.4864131	3.9665396	5.8959164	.6629283	1.5084588	49.0286165	73.9576501	60
6	.6214877	1.6090422	4.5880273	7.3823295	.6106043	1.6377219	56.6393781	92.7595504	72
7	.5741226	1.7417882	5.1621500	8.9913717	.5624101	1.7780618	63.6494331	113.1726257	84
8	.5303673	1.8854857	5.6925173	10.7331599	.5180199	1.9304277	70.1061945	135.3349411	96
9	.4899467	2.0410383	6.1824640	12.6186455	.4771333	2.0958502	76.0533328	159.3963927	108
10	.4526067	2.2094239	6.6350707	14.6596838	.4394739	2.2754481	81.5310719	185.5197216	120
11	.4181124	2.3917014	7.0531831	16.8691077	.4047868	2.4704361	86.5764609	213.8816144	132
12	.3862470	2.5890168	7.4394301	19.2608091	.3728376	2.6821331	91.2236245	244.6738984	144
13	.3568102	2.8026106	7.7962403	21.8498259	.3434100	2.9119708	95.5039941	278.1048391	156
14	.3296168	3.0338260	8.1258571	24.6524365	.3163052	3.1615038	99.4465202	314.4005486	168
15	.3044959	3.2841167	8.4303529	27.6862625	.2913397	3.4324198	103.0778683	353.8065150	180
16	.2812895	3.5550563	8.7116424	30.9703791	.2683446	3.7265512	106.4225992	396.5892630	192
17	.2598517	3.8483484	8.9714942	34.5254354	.2471646	4.0458873	109.5033353	443.0381562	204
18	.2400478	4.1658372	9.2115420	38.3737839	.2276562	4.3925881	112.3409133	493.4673544	216
19	.2217532	4.5095187	9.4332951	42.5396210	.2096876	4.7689983	114.9545252	548.2179384	228
20	.2048528	4.8815540	9.6381479	47.0491398	.1931373	5.1776640	117.3618485	607.6602170	240
21	.1892405	5.2842822	9.8273884	51.9306938	.1778932	5.6213491	119.5791652	672.1962317	252
22	.1748180	5.7202355	10.0022063	57.2149760	.1638524	6.1030545	121.6214722	742.2624754	264
23	.1614947	6.1921550	10.1637010	62.9352115	.1509197	6.6260383	123.5025828	818.3328454	276
24	.1491868	6.7030077	10.3128878	69.1273665	.1390079	7.1938377	125.2352201	900.9218481	288
25	.1378169	7.2560059	10.4507046	75.8303742	.1280362	7.8102930	126.8311027	990.5880791	300
26	.1273135	7.8546264	10.5780181	83.0863801	.1179305	8.4795738	128.3010246	1087.9380011	312
27	.1176106	8.5026330	10.6956288	90.9410065	.1086224	9.2062066	129.6549276	1193.6300462	324
28	.1086472	9.2041003	10.8042760	99.4436395	.1000490	9.9951061	130.9019690	1308.3790686	336
29	.1003670	9.9634385	10.9046430	108.6477398	.0921522	10.8516081	132.0505832	1432.9611802	348
30	.0927177	10.7854222	10.9973607	118.6111783	.0848788	11.7815056	133.1085389	1568.2189994	360
31	.0856515	11.6752195	11.0830122	129.3966005	.0781794	12.7910880	134.0829917	1715.0673504	372
32	.0791238	12.6384252	11.1621360	141.0718200	.0720088	13.8871837	134.9805323	1874.4994506	384
33	.0730936	13.6810952	11.2352295	153.7102452	.0663253	15.0772062	135.8072313	2047.5936284	396
34	.0675229	14.8097856	11.3027525	167.3913404	.0610903	16.3692042	136.5686801	2235.5206165	408
35	.0623768	16.0315929	11.3651293	182.2011260	.0562686	17.7719164	137.2700288	2439.5514701	420
36	.0576229	17.3541993	11.4227522	198.2327189	.0518274	19.2948299	137.9160211	2661.0661640	432
37	.0532314	18.7859208	11.4759836	215.5869182	.0477367	20.9482451	138.5110261	2901.5629256	444
38	.0491745	20.3357592	11.5251580	234.3728390	.0439689	22.7433450	139.0590682	3162.6683691	456
39	.0454268	22.0134593	11.5705848	254.7085982	.0404985	24.6922709	139.5638542	3446.1484965	468
40	.0419647	23.8295697	11.6125495	276.7220575	.0373020	26.8082044	140.0287981	3753.9206422	480
41	.0387664	25.7955092	11.6513159	300.5516273	.0343578	29.1054568	140.4570446	4088.0664413	492
42	.0358120	27.9236388	11.6871279	326.3471365	.0316460	31.5995656	140.8514902	4450.8459086	504
43	.0330826	30.2273390	11.7202105	354.2707753	.0291482	34.3074000	141.2148028	4844.7127242	516
44	.0305613	32.7210944	11.7507718	384.4981142	.0268476	37.2472745	141.5494397	5272.3308297	528
45	.0282322	35.4205847	11.7790040	417.2192087	.0247286	40.4390731	141.8576642	5736.5924450	540
46	.0260805	38.3427830	11.8050845	452.6397934	.0227768	43.9043837	142.1415609	6240.6376311	552
47	.0240929	41.5060625	11.8291774	490.9825763	.0209790	47.6666442	142.4030501	6787.8755271	564
48	.0222567	44.9303127	11.8514341	532.4886389	.0193232	51.7513009	142.6439003	7382.0074088	576
49	.0205605	48.6370635	11.8719945	577.4189516	.0177980	56.1859806	142.8657405	8027.0517221	588
50	.0189935	52.6496212	11.8909880	626.0560151	.0163933	61.0006774	143.0700712	8727.3712620	600

Present and Future Value

8.500% Discount Rate

8.500% Discount Rate

	Annual Payments				Monthly Payments				
Years	Present Value	Future Value	Present Value of 1 per Period	Future Value of 1 per Period	Present Value	Future Value	Present Value of 1 per Period	Future Value of 1 per Period	Months
					.9929665	1.0070833	0.9929665	1.0000000	1
					.9859824	1.0142168	1.9789489	2.0070833	2
					.9790475	1.0214009	2.9579965	3.0213002	3
					.9721614	1.0286358	3.9301578	4.0427010	4
					.9653237	1.0359220	4.8954815	5.0713368	5
					.9585341	1.0432597	5.8540156	6.1072588	6
					.9517922	1.0506495	6.8058078	7.1505186	7
					.9450978	1.0580916	7.7509055	8.2011681	8
					.9384504	1.0655864	8.6893559	9.2592597	9
					.9318498	1.0731343	9.6212057	10.3248461	10
					.9252956	1.0807357	10.5465013	11.3979804	11
1	.9216590	1.0850000	0.9216590	1.0000000	.9187875	1.0883909	11.4652889	12.4787161	12
2	.8494553	1.1772250	1.7711143	2.0850000	.8441705	1.1845948	21.9994534	26.0604373	24
3	.7829081	1.2772891	2.5540224	3.2622250	.7756134	1.2893022	31.6781124	40.8426591	36
4	.7215743	1.3858587	3.2755967	4.5395141	.7126239	1.4032648	40.5707438	56.9314948	48
5	.6650454	1.5036567	3.9406421	5.9253728	.6547500	1.5273006	48.7411826	74.4424373	60
6	.6129451	1.6314675	4.5535872	7.4290295	.6015761	1.6623001	56.2480800	93.5011879	72
7	.5649264	1.7701422	5.1185135	9.0604970	.5527206	1.8092323	63.1453238	114.2445588	84
8	.5206694	1.9206043	5.6391830	10.8306393	.5078328	1.9691520	69.4824254	136.8214549	96
9	.4798797	2.0838557	6.1190626	12.7512436	.4665905	2.1432071	75.3048753	161.3939434	108
10	.4422854	2.2609834	6.5613481	14.8350993	.4286975	2.3326471	80.6544698	188.1384164	120
11	.4076363	2.4531670	6.9689844	17.0960828	.3938819	2.5388319	85.5696105	217.2468576	132
12	.3757017	2.6616862	7.3446861	19.5492498	.3618938	2.7632416	90.0855806	248.9282203	144
13	.3462688	2.8879296	7.6909549	22.2109360	.3325035	3.0074870	94.2347976	283.4099273	156
14	.3191418	3.1334036	8.0100967	25.0988656	.3055001	3.2733215	98.0470465	320.9395036	168
15	.2941399	3.3997429	8.3042366	28.2322692	.2806897	3.5626533	101.5496932	361.7863532	180
16	.2710967	3.6887210	8.5753332	31.6320120	.2578942	3.8775595	104.7678814	406.2436928	192
17	.2498587	4.0022623	8.8251919	35.3207331	.2369500	4.2203005	107.7247126	454.6306570	204
18	.2302845	4.3424546	9.0554764	39.3229954	.2177067	4.5933367	110.4414122	507.2945887	216
19	.2122438	4.7115632	9.2677202	43.6654500	.2000262	4.9993459	112.9374820	564.6135331	228
20	.1956164	5.1120461	9.4633366	48.3770132	.1837816	5.4412426	115.2308398	626.9989509	240
21	.1802916	5.5465700	9.6436282	53.4890594	.1688562	5.9221989	117.3379484	694.8986723	252
22	.1661674	6.0180285	9.8097956	59.0356294	.1551430	6.4456675	119.2739335	768.8001116	264
23	.1531497	6.5295609	9.9629452	65.0536579	.1425434	7.0154058	121.0526925	849.2337660	276
24	.1411518	7.0845736	10.1040970	71.5832188	.1309671	7.6355039	122.6869941	936.7770240	288
25	.1300938	7.6867624	10.2341908	78.6677924	.1203310	8.3104130	124.1885700	1032.0583099	300
26	.1199021	8.3401372	10.3540929	86.3545548	.1105586	9.0449780	125.5681992	1135.7615950	312
27	.1105089	9.0490488	10.4646017	94.6946919	.1015799	9.8444718	126.8357854	1248.6313074	324
28	.1018515	9.8182180	10.5664532	103.7437407	.0933303	10.7146335	128.0004277	1371.4776759	336
29	.0938723	10.6527665	10.6603255	113.5619587	.0857507	11.6617097	129.0704866	1505.1825462	348
30	.0865183	11.5582516	10.7468438	124.2147252	.0787867	12.6924988	130.0536434	1650.7057111	360
31	.0797403	12.5407030	10.8265842	135.7729768	.0723882	13.8144003	130.9569556	1809.0918004	372
32	.0734934	13.6066628	10.9000776	148.3136799	.0665094	15.0354676	131.7869070	1981.4777796	384
33	.0677359	14.7632291	10.9678134	161.9203427	.0611080	16.3644662	132.5494571	2169.1011117	396
34	.0624294	16.0181036	11.0302428	176.6835718	.0561453	17.8109362	133.2500781	2373.3086401	408
35	.0575386	17.3796424	11.0877814	192.7016754	.0515856	19.3852610	133.8938000	2595.5662568	420
36	.0530310	18.8569120	11.1408123	210.0813178	.0473462	21.0987418	134.4852436	2837.4694257	432
37	.0488765	20.4597495	11.1896888	228.9382298	.0435470	22.9636787	135.0286546	3100.7546348	444
38	.0450474	22.1988282	11.2347362	249.3979793	.0400105	24.9934590	135.5279339	3387.3118621	456
39	.0415184	24.0857286	11.2762546	271.5968076	.0367611	27.2026535	135.9866655	3699.1981422	468
40	.0382658	26.1330156	11.3145203	295.6825362	.0337757	29.6071207	136.4081423	4038.6523332	480
41	.0352680	28.3543219	11.3497883	321.8155518	.0310327	32.2241209	136.7953900	4408.1111877	492
42	.0325051	30.7644393	11.3822934	350.1698737	.0285124	35.0724402	137.1511883	4810.2268449	504
43	.0299586	33.3794166	11.4122520	380.9343130	.0261965	38.1725249	137.4780914	5247.8858694	516
44	.0276116	36.2166670	11.4398636	414.3137296	.0240693	41.5466290	137.7784459	5724.2299716	528
45	.0254485	39.2950837	11.4653120	450.5303966	.0221146	45.2189731	138.0544079	6242.6785604	540
46	.0234548	42.6351658	11.4887669	489.8254803	.0203186	49.2159191	138.3079583	6806.9532897	552
47	.0216173	46.2591549	11.5103642	532.4606461	.0186665	53.5661588	138.5409172	7421.1047735	564
48	.0199238	50.1911831	11.5303080	578.7198011	.0171524	58.3009201	138.7549570	8089.5416633	576
49	.0183630	54.4574337	11.5486710	628.9109842	.0157594	63.4541913	138.9516141	8817.0622953	588
50	.0169244	59.0863155	11.5655954	683.3684178	.0144795	69.0629647	139.1323002	9608.8891350	600

Present and Future Value

8.750% Discount Rate   8.750% Discount Rate

8.750% Discount Rate

	Annual Payments				Monthly Payments				
Years	Present Value	Future Value	Present Value of 1 per Period	Future Value of 1 per Period	Present Value	Future Value	Present Value of 1 per Period	Future Value of 1 per Period	Months
					.9927611	1.0072917	0.9927611	1.0000000	1
					.9855746	1.0146365	1.9783358	2.0072917	2
					.9784402	1.0220349	2.9567759	3.0219282	3
					.9713574	1.0294872	3.9281333	4.0439631	4
					.9643258	1.0369939	4.8924591	5.0734503	5
					.9573452	1.0445553	5.8498043	6.1104442	6
					.9504151	1.0521719	6.8002194	7.1549995	7
					.9435351	1.0598440	7.7437545	8.2071714	8
					.9367050	1.0675720	8.6804595	9.2670154	9
					.9299243	1.0753564	9.6103837	10.3345873	10
					.9231927	1.0831975	10.5335764	11.4099437	11
1	.9195402	1.0875000	0.9195402	1.0000000	.9165098	1.0910958	11.4500862	12.4931412	12
2	.8455542	1.1826563	1.7650945	2.0875000	.8399902	1.1904901	21.9442023	26.1243554	24
3	.7775211	1.2861387	2.5426156	3.2701562	.7698592	1.2989388	31.5621624	40.9973162	36
4	.7149620	1.3986758	3.2575776	4.5562949	.7055835	1.4172667	40.3771170	57.2251416	48
5	.6574363	1.5210599	3.9150139	5.9549707	.6466742	1.5463737	48.4561091	74.9312541	60
6	.6045391	1.6541527	4.5195530	7.4760307	.5926832	1.6872419	55.8605845	94.2503194	72
7	.5558980	1.7988910	5.0754510	9.1301833	.5432000	1.8409426	62.6468587	115.3292709	84
8	.5111706	1.9562940	5.5866216	10.9290744	.4978481	2.0086448	68.8665454	138.3284268	96
9	.4700419	2.1274697	6.0566636	12.8853684	.4562827	2.1916239	74.5669491	163.4227096	108
10	.4322225	2.3136233	6.4888860	15.0128381	.4181875	2.3912717	79.7914249	190.8029768	120
11	.3974460	2.5160654	6.8863320	17.3264615	.3832730	2.6091066	84.5797082	220.6774719	132
12	.3654675	2.7362211	7.2517995	19.8425269	.3512734	2.8467853	88.9682166	253.2734087	144
13	.3360621	2.9756404	7.5878616	22.5787400	.3219455	3.1061155	92.9903276	288.8386991	156
14	.3090226	3.2360090	7.8968843	25.5543884	.2950662	3.3890697	96.6766316	327.6438388	168
15	.2841587	3.5191598	8.1810430	28.7903974	.2704311	3.6977997	100.0551654	369.9839646	180
16	.2612954	3.8270863	8.4423384	32.3095572	.2478527	4.0346538	103.1516246	416.1810990	192
17	.2402716	4.1619563	8.6826100	36.1366434	.2271595	4.4021940	105.9895598	466.5865992	204
18	.2209394	4.5261275	8.9035494	40.2985997	.2081939	4.8032154	108.5905552	521.5838299	216
19	.2031627	4.9221636	9.1067121	44.8247272	.1908117	5.2407683	110.9743929	581.5910785	228
20	.1868163	5.3528529	9.2935284	49.7468908	.1748808	5.7181804	113.1592036	647.0647367	240
21	.1717851	5.8212276	9.4653135	55.0997438	.1602800	6.2390827	115.1616039	718.5027715	252
22	.1579633	6.3305850	9.6232767	60.9209713	.1468982	6.8074371	116.9968234	796.4485129	264
23	.1452536	6.8845112	9.7685303	67.2515563	.1346336	7.4275661	118.6788200	881.4947855	276
24	.1335665	7.4869059	9.9020969	74.1360675	.1233930	8.1041864	120.2203864	974.2884182	288
25	.1228198	8.1420102	10.0249167	81.6229734	.1130909	8.8424439	121.6332470	1075.5351631	300
26	.1129377	8.8544361	10.1378544	89.7649836	.1036489	9.6479536	122.9281477	1186.0050633	312
27	.1038508	9.6291992	10.2417052	98.6194196	.0949953	10.5268418	124.1149368	1306.5383099	324
28	.0954950	10.4717542	10.3372002	108.2486189	.0870641	11.4857931	125.2026406	1438.0516316	336
29	.0878115	11.3880326	10.4250117	118.7203730	.0797951	12.5321009	126.1995318	1581.5452673	348
30	.0807462	12.3844855	10.5057578	130.1084056	.0731330	13.6737229	127.1131924	1738.1105736	360
31	.0742494	13.4681280	10.5800072	142.4928911	.0670271	14.9193420	127.9505712	1908.9383250	372
32	.0682753	14.6465892	10.6482825	155.9610191	.0614310	16.2784317	128.7180371	2095.3277708	384
33	.0627819	15.9281657	10.7110644	170.6076083	.0563021	17.7613288	129.4214271	2298.6965163	396
34	.0577305	17.3218802	10.7687948	186.5357740	.0516014	19.3793116	130.0660910	2520.5913047	408
35	.0530855	18.8375447	10.8218803	203.8576542	.0472932	21.1446859	130.6569317	2762.6997810	420
36	.0488142	20.4858299	10.8706945	222.6951990	.0433447	23.0708784	131.1984430	3026.8633279	432
37	.0448866	22.2783400	10.9155812	243.1810289	.0397258	25.1725391	131.6947434	3315.0910700	444
38	.0412751	24.2276948	10.9568562	265.4593689	.0364091	27.4656522	132.1496075	3629.5751550	456
39	.0379541	26.3476181	10.9948103	289.6870637	.0333693	29.9676583	132.5664950	3972.7074261	468
40	.0349003	28.6530347	11.0297107	316.0346818	.0305833	32.6975868	132.9485764	4347.0976132	480
41	.0320922	31.1601752	11.0618029	344.6877164	.0280299	35.6762003	133.2987578	4755.5931819	492
42	.0295101	33.8866905	11.0913130	375.8478916	.0256897	38.9261531	133.6197025	5201.3009899	504
43	.0271357	36.8517759	11.1184488	409.7345821	.0235448	42.4721629	133.9138514	5687.6109168	516
44	.0249524	40.0763063	11.1434012	446.5863581	.0215791	46.3411995	134.1834418	6218.2216459	528
45	.0229447	43.5829831	11.1663459	486.6626644	.0197774	50.5626891	134.4305240	6797.1687952	540
46	.0210986	47.3964942	11.1874445	530.2456476	.0181262	55.1687388	134.6569773	7428.8556105	552
47	.0194010	51.5436874	11.2068455	577.6421417	.0166128	60.1943804	134.8645239	8118.0864552	564
48	.0178400	56.0537600	11.2246855	629.1858291	.0152258	65.6778369	135.0547425	8870.1033497	576
49	.0164046	60.9584641	11.2410901	685.2395892	.0139546	71.6608134	135.2290796	9690.6258408	588
50	.0150847	66.2923297	11.2561748	746.1980532	.0127896	78.1888141	135.3888613	10585.8945022	600

Present and Future Value

9.000% Discount Rate   9.000% Discount Rate

	Annual Payments				Monthly Payments				
Years	Present Value	Future Value	Present Value of 1 per Period	Future Value of 1 per Period	Present Value	Future Value	Present Value of 1 per Period	Future Value of 1 per Period	Months
					.9925558	1.0075000	0.9925558	1.0000000	1
					.9851671	1.0150563	1.9777229	2.0075000	2
					.9778333	1.0226692	2.9555562	3.0225563	3
					.9705542	1.0303392	3.9261104	4.0452254	4
					.9633292	1.0380667	4.8894396	5.0755646	5
					.9561580	1.0458522	5.8455976	6.1136313	6
					.9490402	1.0536961	6.7946378	7.1594836	7
					.9419754	1.0615988	7.7366132	8.2131797	8
					.9349632	1.0695608	8.6715764	9.2747786	9
					.9280032	1.0775825	9.5995796	10.3443394	10
					.9210949	1.0856644	10.5206745	11.4219219	11
1	.9174312	1.0900000	0.9174312	1.0000000	.9142382	1.0938069	11.4349127	12.5075864	12
2	.8416800	1.1881000	1.7591112	2.0900000	.8358314	1.1964135	21.8891461	26.1884706	24
3	.7721835	1.2950290	2.5312947	3.2781000	.7641490	1.3086454	31.4468053	41.1527161	36
4	.7084252	1.4115816	3.2397199	4.5731290	.6986141	1.4314053	40.1847819	57.5207111	48
5	.6499314	1.5386240	3.8896513	5.9847106	.6386997	1.5656810	48.1733735	75.4241369	60
6	.5962673	1.6771001	4.4859186	7.5233346	.5839236	1.7125527	55.4768488	95.0070276	72
7	.5470342	1.8280391	5.0329528	9.2004347	.5338453	1.8732020	62.1539646	116.4269284	84
8	.5018663	1.9925626	5.5348191	11.0284738	.4880617	2.0489212	68.2584386	139.8561638	96
9	.4604278	2.1718933	5.9952469	13.0210364	.4462046	2.2411242	73.8393816	165.4832230	108
10	.4224108	2.3673637	6.4176577	15.1929297	.4079373	2.4513571	78.9416927	193.5142771	120
11	.3875329	2.5804264	6.8051906	17.5602934	.3729518	2.6813113	83.6064201	224.1748374	132
12	.3555347	2.8126648	7.1607253	20.1407198	.3409668	2.9328368	87.8710920	257.7115698	144
13	.3261786	3.0658046	7.4869039	22.9533846	.3117249	3.2079577	91.7700177	294.3942790	156
14	.2992465	3.3417270	7.7861504	26.0191892	.2849908	3.5088856	95.3345643	334.5180794	168
15	.2745380	3.6424825	8.0606884	29.3609162	.2605494	3.8380433	98.5934088	378.4057690	180
16	.2518698	3.9703059	8.3125582	33.0033987	.2382042	4.1980782	101.5727689	426.4104266	192
17	.2310732	4.3276334	8.5436314	36.9737046	.2177754	4.5918869	104.2966135	478.9182522	204
18	.2119937	4.7171204	8.7556251	41.3013380	.1990986	5.0226376	106.7868561	536.3516740	216
19	.1944897	5.1416613	8.9501148	46.0184584	.1820235	5.4937956	109.0635310	599.1727470	228
20	.1784309	5.6044108	9.1285457	51.1601196	.1664128	6.0091515	111.1449540	667.8868699	240
21	.1636981	6.1088077	9.2922437	56.7645304	.1521410	6.5728514	113.0478704	743.0468515	252
22	.1501817	6.6586004	9.4424254	62.8733381	.1390931	7.1894302	114.7875891	825.2573579	264
23	.1377814	7.2578745	9.5802068	69.5319386	.1271642	7.8638483	116.3781063	915.1797768	276
24	.1264049	7.9110832	9.7066118	76.7898131	.1162584	8.6015315	117.8322179	1013.5375388	288
25	.1159678	8.6230807	9.8225796	84.7008962	.1062878	9.4084145	119.1616222	1121.1219373	300
26	.1063925	9.3991579	9.9289721	93.3239769	.0971724	10.2909887	120.3770143	1238.7984945	312
27	.0976078	10.2450821	10.0265799	102.7231348	.0888387	11.2563544	121.4881721	1367.5139245	324
28	.0895484	11.1671395	10.1161284	112.9682169	.0812197	12.3122781	122.5040350	1508.3037496	336
29	.0821545	12.1721821	10.1982829	124.1353565	.0742542	13.4672547	123.4327756	1662.3006315	348
30	.0753711	13.2676785	10.2736540	136.3075385	.0678860	14.7305761	124.2818657	1830.7434831	360
31	.0691478	14.4617695	10.3428019	149.5752170	.0620640	16.1124058	125.0581362	2014.9874360	372
32	.0634384	15.7633288	10.4062403	164.0369865	.0567413	17.6238606	125.7678324	2216.5147426	384
33	.0582003	17.1820284	10.4644406	179.8003153	.0518750	19.2771003	126.4166637	2436.9467006	396
34	.0533948	18.7284109	10.5178354	196.9823437	.0474261	21.0854252	127.0098501	2678.0566967	408
35	.0489861	20.4139679	10.5668215	215.7107547	.0433588	23.0633836	127.5521637	2941.7844736	420
36	.0449413	22.2512250	10.6117628	236.1247226	.0396402	25.2268880	128.0479674	3230.2517350	432
37	.0412306	24.2538353	10.6529934	258.3759476	.0362406	27.5933441	128.5012502	3545.7792153	444
38	.0378262	26.4366805	10.6908196	282.6297829	.0331326	30.1817901	128.9156585	3890.9053497	456
39	.0347030	28.8159817	10.7255226	309.0664633	.0302911	33.0130502	129.2945265	4268.4066960	468
40	.0318376	31.4094201	10.7573602	337.8824450	.0276932	36.1099020	129.6409020	4681.3202725	480
41	.0292088	34.2362679	10.7865690	369.2918651	.0253182	39.4972599	129.9575717	5132.9679907	492
42	.0267971	37.3175320	10.8133660	403.5281330	.0231469	43.2023754	130.2470833	5626.9833801	504
43	.0245845	40.6761098	10.8379505	440.8456649	.0211618	47.2550562	130.5117658	6167.3408206	516
44	.0225545	44.3369597	10.8605050	481.5217748	.0193469	51.6879064	130.7537486	6758.3875162	528
45	.0206922	48.3272861	10.8811973	525.8587345	.0176877	56.5365885	130.9749786	7404.8784687	540
46	.0189837	52.6767419	10.9001810	574.1860206	.0161707	61.8401105	131.1772354	8112.0147318	552
47	.0174162	57.4176486	10.9175072	626.8627625	.0147839	67.6411394	131.3621464	8885.4852540	564
48	.0159782	62.5852370	10.9335755	684.2804111	.0135160	73.9863448	131.5311990	9731.5126464	576
49	.0146589	68.2179083	10.9482344	746.8656481	.0123568	80.9267743	131.6857534	10656.9032437	588
50	.0134485	74.3575201	10.9616829	815.0835564	.0112971	88.5182640	131.8270529	11669.1018622	600

Present and Future Value

9.250% Discount Rate

	Annual Payments				Monthly Payments				
Years	Present Value	Future Value	Present Value of 1 per Period	Future Value of 1 per Period	Present Value	Future Value	Present Value of 1 per Period	Future Value of 1 per Period	Months
					.9923506	1.0077083	0.9923506	1.0000000	1
					.9847598	1.0154761	1.9771104	2.0077083	2
					.9772270	1.0233037	2.9543374	3.0231844	3
					.9697518	1.0311917	3.9240892	4.0464881	4
					.9623338	1.0391404	4.8864230	5.0776798	5
					.9549726	1.0471505	5.8413956	6.1168203	6
					.9476676	1.0552223	6.7890632	7.1639707	7
					.9404186	1.0633563	7.7294818	8.2191930	8
					.9332250	1.0715530	8.6627068	9.2825493	9
					.9260864	1.0798129	9.5887932	10.3541023	10
					.9190024	1.0881364	10.5077956	11.4339152	11
1	.9153318	1.0925000	0.9153318	1.0000000	.9119726	1.0965241	11.4197682	12.5220516	12
2	.8378323	1.1935562	1.7531641	2.0925000	.8316941	1.2023652	21.8342841	26.2527835	24
3	.7668946	1.3039602	2.5200587	3.2860562	.7584822	1.3184225	31.3320375	41.3088627	36
4	.7019630	1.4245765	3.2220217	4.5900165	.6917150	1.4456821	39.9937285	57.8182170	48
5	.6425291	1.5563499	3.8645507	6.0145930	.6308251	1.5852253	47.8929536	75.9211227	60
6	.5881273	1.7003122	4.4526780	7.5709428	.5752953	1.7382378	55.0968306	95.7713960	72
7	.5383316	1.8575911	4.9910096	9.2712550	.5246535	1.9060198	61.6665691	117.5376999	84
8	.4927520	2.0294183	5.4837617	11.1288461	.4784697	2.0899967	67.6579908	141.4049778	96
9	.4510316	2.2171395	5.9347933	13.1582644	.4363512	2.2917319	73.1220034	167.5760244	108
10	.4128436	2.4222249	6.3476369	15.3754039	.3979404	2.5129393	78.1050332	196.2732089	120
11	.3778889	2.6462807	6.7255258	17.7976287	.3629107	2.7554986	82.6494200	227.7403647	132
12	.3458937	2.8910616	7.0714195	20.4439094	.3309646	3.0214708	86.7937763	262.2448609	144
13	.3166075	3.1584848	7.3880270	23.3349710	.3018307	3.3131197	90.5733158	300.0798741	156
14	.2898009	3.4506447	7.6778279	26.4934558	.2752613	3.6329114	94.0201523	341.5668798	168
15	.2652640	3.7698293	7.9430919	29.9441005	.2510308	3.9835750	97.1635728	387.0583833	180
16	.2428046	4.1185385	8.1858965	33.7139297	.2289332	4.3680862	100.0302863	436.9409154	192
17	.2222468	4.4995033	8.4081432	37.8324682	.2087808	4.7897120	102.6446505	491.6383165	204
18	.2034295	4.9157074	8.6115727	42.3319716	.1904024	5.2520349	105.0288790	551.6153375	216
19	.1862055	5.3704103	8.7977782	47.2476789	.1736418	5.7589831	107.2032302	617.3815894	228
20	.1704398	5.8671733	8.9682181	52.6180892	.1583565	6.3148640	109.1861789	689.4958727	240
21	.1560090	6.4098868	9.1242271	58.4852625	.1444168	6.9244009	110.9945739	768.5709257	252
22	.1428000	7.0028013	9.2670271	64.8951493	.1317042	7.5927728	112.6437806	855.2786308	264
23	.1307094	7.6505604	9.3977364	71.8979506	.1201106	8.3256587	114.1478119	950.3557232	276
24	.1196425	8.3582373	9.5173789	79.5485110	.1095376	9.1292858	115.5194473	1054.6100510	288
25	.1095125	9.1313742	9.6268914	87.9067483	.0998953	10.0104823	116.7703412	1168.9274389	300
26	.1002403	9.9760263	9.7271318	97.0381225	.0911018	10.9767356	117.9111222	1294.2792152	312
27	.0917531	10.8988088	9.8188849	107.0141488	.0830823	12.0362557	118.9514833	1431.7304648	324
28	.0839846	11.9069486	9.9028695	117.9129576	.0757688	13.1980450	119.9002641	1582.4490792	336
29	.0768738	13.0083413	9.9797432	129.8199062	.0690991	14.4719750	120.7655262	1747.7156794	348
30	.0703650	14.2116129	10.0501082	142.8282475	.0630165	15.8688701	121.5546215	1928.9344973	360
31	.0644073	15.5261871	10.1145155	157.0398604	.0574693	17.4005992	122.2742549	2127.6453071	372
32	.0589541	16.9623594	10.1734696	172.5660474	.0524104	19.0801773	122.9305408	2345.5365085	384
33	.0539625	18.5313776	10.2274321	189.5284068	.0477969	20.9218751	123.5290556	2584.4594724	396
34	.0493936	20.2455301	10.2768257	208.0597845	.0435894	22.9413413	124.0748847	2846.4442717	408
35	.0452116	22.1182416	10.3220373	228.3053145	.0397524	25.1557347	124.5726659	3133.7169305	420
36	.0413836	24.1641789	10.3634209	250.4235561	.0362531	27.5838705	125.0266287	3448.7183378	432
37	.0378797	26.3993655	10.4013006	274.5877351	.0330618	30.2463801	125.4406304	3794.1249875	444
38	.0346725	28.8413068	10.4359731	300.9871006	.0301515	33.1658862	125.8181885	4172.8717196	456
39	.0317368	31.5091277	10.4677099	329.8284074	.0274973	36.3671951	126.1625113	4588.1766572	468
40	.0290497	34.4237220	10.4967596	361.3375350	.0250768	39.8775076	126.4765242	5043.5685500	480
41	.0265901	37.6079163	10.5233498	395.7612570	.0228693	43.7266500	126.7628953	5542.9167570	492
42	.0243388	41.0866485	10.5476886	433.3691733	.0208562	47.9473276	127.0240580	6090.4641241	504
43	.0222781	44.8871635	10.5699423	474.4558218	.0190203	52.5754026	127.2622312	6690.8630341	516
44	.0203918	49.0392261	10.5903585	519.3429854	.0173460	57.6501985	127.4794386	7349.2149372	528
45	.0186653	53.5753546	10.6090238	568.3822115	.0158191	63.2148347	127.6775258	8071.1136966	540
46	.0170849	58.5310749	10.6261087	621.9575661	.0144266	69.3165928	127.8581760	8862.6931184	552
47	.0156384	63.9451993	10.6417471	680.4886409	.0131566	76.0073178	128.0229239	9730.6790693	564
48	.0143143	69.8601302	10.6560614	744.4338402	.0119985	83.3438594	128.1731696	10682.4466242	576
49	.0131023	76.3221923	10.6691638	814.2939704	.0109423	91.3885544	128.3101895	11726.0827311	588
50	.0119930	83.3819951	10.6811568	890.6161627	.0099791	100.2097567	128.4351479	12870.4549237	600

Present and Future Value

9.500% Discount Rate   9.500% Discount Rate

| | Annual Payments | | | | Monthly Payments | | | | |
Years	Present Value	Future Value	Present Value of 1 per Period	Future Value of 1 per Period	Present Value	Future Value	Present Value of 1 per Period	Future Value of 1 per Period	Months
					.9921455	1.0079167	0.9921455	1.0000000	1
					.9843527	1.0158960	1.9764982	2.0079167	2
					.9766211	1.0239385	2.9531194	3.0238127	3
					.9689503	1.0320447	3.9220697	4.0477512	4
					.9613397	1.0402151	4.8834093	5.0797959	5
					.9537888	1.0484501	5.8371982	6.1200109	6
					.9462973	1.0567503	6.7834955	7.1684610	7
					.9388646	1.0651163	7.7223602	8.2252113	8
					.9314904	1.0735484	8.6538505	9.2903276	9
					.9241740	1.0820474	9.5780245	10.3638760	10
					.9169151	1.0906136	10.4949395	11.4459234	11
1	.9132420	1.0950000	0.9132420	1.0000000	.9097132	1.0992476	11.4046527	12.5365369	12
2	.8340110	1.1990250	1.7472530	2.0950000	.8275780	1.2083453	21.7796154	26.3172949	24
3	.7616539	1.3129324	2.5089068	3.2940250	.7528586	1.3282706	31.2178556	41.4657597	36
4	.6955743	1.4376610	3.2044811	4.6069574	.6848854	1.4600982	39.8039470	58.1176732	48
5	.6352277	1.5742387	3.8397088	6.0446183	.6230493	1.6050095	47.6148273	76.4222488	60
6	.5801166	1.7237914	4.4198254	7.6188571	.5667961	1.7643028	54.7204880	96.5435092	72
7	.5297868	1.8875516	4.9496122	9.3426485	.5156219	1.9394056	61.1846011	118.6617562	84
8	.4838236	2.0668690	5.4334358	11.2302001	.4690680	2.1318869	67.0650899	142.9751858	96
9	.4418480	2.2632216	5.8752838	13.2970691	.4267174	2.3434715	72.4146480	169.7016645	108
10	.4035142	2.4782276	6.2787980	15.5602907	.3881904	2.5760554	77.2812114	199.0806817	120
11	.3685061	2.7136592	6.6473041	18.0385183	.3531419	2.8317227	81.7083882	231.3754953	132
12	.3365353	2.9714569	6.9838394	20.7521775	.3212579	3.1127643	85.7358492	266.8754912	144
13	.3073381	3.2537453	7.2911775	23.7236344	.2922525	3.4216986	89.3996836	305.8987758	156
14	.2806741	3.5628511	7.5718516	26.9773796	.2658660	3.7612940	92.7327219	348.7950273	168
15	.2563234	3.9013219	7.8281750	30.5402307	.2418618	4.1345933	95.7648307	395.9486280	180
16	.2340853	4.2719475	8.0622603	34.4415526	.2200248	4.5449417	98.5231801	447.7821097	192
17	.2137765	4.6777825	8.2760368	38.7135001	.2001595	4.9960162	101.0324868	504.7599392	204
18	.1952297	5.1221719	8.4712665	43.3912826	.1820877	5.4918587	103.3152361	567.3926806	216
19	.1782920	5.6087782	8.6495584	48.5134545	.1656476	6.0369124	105.3918833	636.2415703	228
20	.1628237	6.1416121	8.8123821	54.1222327	.1506918	6.6360614	107.2810365	711.9235460	240
21	.1486974	6.7250653	8.9610796	60.2638448	.1370863	7.2946745	108.9996241	795.1167750	252
22	.1357968	7.3639465	9.0968763	66.9889100	.1247092	8.0186533	110.5630458	886.5667309	264
23	.1240153	8.0635214	9.2208916	74.3528565	.1134496	8.8144853	111.9853112	987.0928740	276
24	.1132560	8.8295559	9.3341476	82.4163779	.1032066	9.6893016	113.2791647	1097.5959939	288
25	.1034301	9.6683637	9.4375777	91.2459337	.0938884	10.6509414	114.4562003	1219.0662815	300
26	.0944567	10.5868583	9.5320344	100.9142975	.0854115	11.7080216	115.5269650	1352.5922018	312
27	.0862619	11.5926098	9.6182963	111.5011557	.0777000	12.8700145	116.5010538	1499.3702470	324
28	.0787779	12.6939077	9.6970742	123.0937655	.0706847	14.1473323	117.3871952	1660.7156586	336
29	.0719433	13.8998290	9.7690176	135.7876732	.0643028	15.5514208	118.1933298	1838.0742124	348
30	.0657017	15.2203127	9.8347192	149.6875022	.0584971	17.0948618	118.9266809	2033.0351743	360
31	.0600015	16.6662424	9.8947208	164.9078149	.0532156	18.7914855	119.5938201	2247.3455407	372
32	.0547959	18.2495354	9.9495167	181.5740573	.0484109	20.6564951	120.2007255	2482.9256931	384
33	.0500419	19.9832413	9.9995986	199.8235928	.0440401	22.7066023	120.7528352	2741.8866065	396
34	.0457004	21.8816492	10.0452590	219.8068341	.0400638	24.9601777	121.2550968	3026.5487650	408
35	.0417355	23.9604059	10.0869945	241.6884833	.0364466	27.4374151	121.7120107	3339.4629550	420
36	.0381146	26.2366445	10.1251092	265.6488892	.0331559	30.1605122	122.1276713	3683.4331223	432
37	.0348079	28.7291257	10.1599170	291.8855337	.0301624	33.1538702	122.5058032	4061.5414978	444
38	.0317880	31.4583926	10.1917051	320.6146594	.0274391	36.4443117	122.8497948	4477.1762160	456
39	.0290302	34.4469399	10.2207352	352.0730520	.0249617	40.0613216	123.1627285	4934.0616759	468
40	.0265116	37.7193992	10.2472468	386.5199920	.0227080	44.0373110	123.4474084	5436.2919139	480
41	.0242115	41.3027422	10.2714582	424.2393912	.0206578	48.4079077	123.7063854	5988.3672896	492
42	.0221109	45.2265027	10.2935692	465.5421334	.0187927	53.2122756	123.9419803	6595.2348126	504
43	.0201926	49.5230204	10.3137618	510.7686360	.0170769	58.4934654	124.1563040	7262.3324712	516
44	.0184408	54.2277074	10.3322026	560.2916565	.0155524	64.2988005	124.3512771	7995.6379607	528
45	.0168409	59.3793396	10.3490434	614.5193638	.0141482	70.6803011	124.5286467	8801.7222484	540
46	.0153798	65.0203768	10.3644232	673.8987034	.0128708	77.6951503	124.6900022	9687.8084542	552
47	.0140455	71.1973126	10.3784692	738.9190802	.0117088	85.4062062	124.8367894	10661.8365753	564
48	.0128269	77.9610573	10.3912956	810.1163928	.0106516	93.8825659	124.9703236	11732.5346342	576
49	.0117141	85.3673578	10.4030097	888.0774502	.0096899	103.2001837	125.0918014	12909.4968887	588
50	.0106978	93.4772568	10.4137075	973.4448079	.0088150	113.4425526	125.2023114	14203.2698035	600

Present and Future Value

9.750% Discount Rate   9.750% Discount Rate

	Annual Payments				Monthly Payments				
Years	Present Value	Future Value	Present Value of 1 per Period	Future Value of 1 per Period	Present Value	Future Value	Present Value of 1 per Period	Future Value of 1 per Period	Months
					.9919405	1.0081250	0.9919405	1.0000000	1
					.9839459	1.0163160	1.9758864	2.0081250	2
					.9760158	1.0245736	2.9519022	3.0244410	3
					.9681496	1.0328982	3.9200518	4.0490146	4
					.9603468	1.0412905	4.8803985	5.0819128	5
					.9526068	1.0497510	5.8330054	6.1232034	6
					.9449293	1.0582803	6.7779347	7.1729544	7
					.9373136	1.0668788	7.7152483	8.2312347	8
					.9297593	1.0755472	8.6450076	9.2981134	9
					.9222659	1.0842860	9.5672735	10.3736606	10
					.9148329	1.0930958	10.4821064	11.4579466	11
1	.9111617	1.0975000	0.9111617	1.0000000	.9074598	1.1019772	11.3895661	12.5510424	12
2	.8302157	1.2045063	1.7413774	2.0975000	.8234832	1.2143538	21.7251393	26.3820053	24
3	.7564608	1.3219456	2.4978382	3.3020063	.7472779	1.3381902	31.1042561	41.6234112	36
4	.6892581	1.4508353	3.1870963	4.6239519	.6781247	1.4746551	39.6154274	58.4190934	48
5	.6280256	1.5922917	3.8151219	6.0747872	.6153708	1.6250364	47.3389730	76.9275526	60
6	.5722329	1.7475402	4.3873548	7.6670789	.5584243	1.7907531	54.3477799	97.3234529	72
7	.5213967	1.9179254	4.9087516	9.4146191	.5067476	1.9733691	60.7079903	119.7992705	84
8	.4750767	2.1049231	5.3838283	11.3325445	.4598530	2.1746078	66.4796254	144.5671095	96
9	.4328717	2.3101531	5.8167000	13.4374676	.4172981	2.3963682	71.7171520	171.8607038	108
10	.3944162	2.5353930	6.2111162	15.7476206	.3786813	2.6407432	76.4699968	201.9376230	120
11	.3593769	2.7825938	6.5704931	18.2830137	.3436380	2.9100388	80.7830122	235.0817028	132
12	.3274505	3.0538967	6.8979436	21.0656075	.3118377	3.2067965	84.6969002	271.6057237	144
13	.2983604	3.3516517	7.1963040	24.1195042	.2829802	3.5338167	88.2485962	311.8543626	156
14	.2718545	3.6784377	7.4681585	27.4711559	.2567931	3.8941855	91.4716174	356.2074459	168
15	.2477035	4.0370854	7.7158620	31.1495936	.2330294	4.2913037	94.3963795	405.0835333	180
16	.2256979	4.4307012	7.9415599	35.1866790	.2114648	4.7289189	97.0504834	458.9438683	192
17	.2056473	4.8626946	8.1472072	39.6173802	.1918958	5.2111609	99.4589760	518.2967304	204
18	.1873779	5.3368073	8.3345851	44.4800747	.1741377	5.7425806	101.6445861	583.7022324	216
19	.1707316	5.8571460	8.5053168	49.8168820	.1580230	6.3281930	103.6279394	655.7776056	228
20	.1555641	6.4282177	8.6608809	55.6740280	.1433995	6.9735246	105.4277527	735.2030250	240
21	.1417441	7.0549690	8.8026249	62.1022457	.1301293	7.6846652	107.0610109	822.7280279	252
22	.1291518	7.7428284	8.9317767	69.1572147	.1180871	8.4683260	108.5431271	919.1785872	264
23	.1176782	8.4977542	9.0494549	76.9000431	.1071593	9.3319024	109.8880878	1025.4649064	276
24	.1072238	9.3262852	9.1566787	85.3977973	.0972427	10.2835438	111.1085856	1142.5900089	288
25	.0976982	10.2355980	9.2543769	94.7240826	.0882439	11.3322310	112.2161382	1271.6592038	300
26	.0890189	11.2335689	9.3433958	104.9596806	.0800778	12.4878604	113.2211977	1413.8905162	312
27	.0811106	12.3288418	9.4245065	116.1932495	.0726674	13.7613377	114.1332487	1570.6261825	324
28	.0739049	13.5309039	9.4984114	128.5220913	.0659427	15.1646807	114.9608984	1743.3453163	336
29	.0673393	14.8501670	9.5657507	142.0529952	.0598403	16.7111327	115.7119571	1933.6778671	348
30	.0613570	16.2980583	9.6271077	156.9031622	.0543027	18.4152875	116.3935127	2143.4200023	360
31	.0559062	17.8871190	9.6830138	173.2012205	.0492775	20.2932273	117.0119970	2374.5510572	372
32	.0509395	19.6311131	9.7339534	191.0883395	.0447174	22.3626742	117.5732467	2629.2522146	384
33	.0464142	21.5451466	9.7803675	210.7194526	.0405792	24.6431576	118.0825581	2909.9270878	396
34	.0422908	23.6457984	9.8226583	232.2645993	.0368240	27.1561983	118.5447378	3219.2244043	408
35	.0385338	25.9512638	9.8611921	255.9103977	.0334163	29.9255119	118.9641472	3560.0630012	420
36	.0351105	28.4815120	9.8963026	281.8616615	.0303240	32.9772324	119.3447444	3935.6593705	432
37	.0319913	31.2584594	9.9282939	310.3431735	.0275178	36.3401589	119.6901211	4349.5580134	444
38	.0291493	34.3061592	9.9574432	341.6016329	.0249713	40.0460272	120.0035365	4805.6648891	456
39	.0265597	37.6510097	9.9840029	375.9077921	.0226604	44.1298097	120.2879484	5308.2842759	468
40	.0242002	41.3219832	10.0082031	413.5588018	.0205634	48.6300450	120.5460407	5862.1593903	480
41	.0220503	45.3508765	10.0302534	454.8807850	.0186605	53.5892018	120.7802491	6472.5171490	492
42	.0200914	49.7725870	10.0503448	500.2316615	.0169336	59.0540796	120.9927839	7145.1174949	504
43	.0183065	54.6254142	10.0686513	550.0042485	.0153666	65.0762505	121.1856506	7886.3077542	516
44	.0166802	59.9513921	10.0853215	604.6296628	.0139446	71.7125456	121.3606694	8703.0825315	528
45	.0151983	65.7966529	10.1005298	664.5810549	.0126541	79.0255916	121.5194919	9603.1497378	540
46	.0138481	72.2118265	10.1143780	730.3777077	.0114831	87.0844017	121.6636169	10595.0032912	552
47	.0126179	79.2524796	10.1269959	802.5895342	.0104205	95.9650269	121.7944046	11688.0033123	564
48	.0114969	86.9795963	10.1384928	881.8420138	.0094562	105.7512735	121.9130891	12892.4644367	576
49	.0104756	95.4601070	10.1489684	968.8216102	.0085811	116.5354944	122.0207906	14219.7531579	588
50	.0095449	104.7674674	10.1585134	1064.2817172	.0077870	128.4194601	122.1185253	15682.3950927	600

Present and Future Value

10.000% Discount Rate

10.000% Discount Rate

Annual Payments

Monthly Payments

Years	Present Value	Future Value	Present Value of 1 per Period	Future Value of 1 per Period	Present Value	Future Value	Present Value of 1 per Period	Future Value of 1 per Period	Months
					.9917355	1.0083333	0.9917355	1.0000000	1
					.9835394	1.0167361	1.9752749	2.0083333	2
					.9754110	1.0252089	2.9506859	3.0250694	3
					.9673497	1.0337523	3.9180356	4.0502784	4
					.9593551	1.0423669	4.8773906	5.0840307	5
					.9514265	1.0510533	5.8288172	6.1263976	6
					.9435635	1.0598121	6.7723807	7.1774509	7
					.9357654	1.0686439	7.7081461	8.2372630	8
					.9280319	1.0775492	8.6361780	9.3059069	9
					.9203622	1.0865288	9.5565401	10.3834561	10
					.9127559	1.0955832	10.4692960	11.4699849	11
1	.9090909	1.1000000	0.9090909	1.0000000	.9052124	1.1047131	11.3745084	12.5655681	12
2	.8264463	1.2100000	1.7355372	2.1000000	.8194095	1.2203910	21.6708548	26.4469154	24
3	.7513148	1.3310000	2.4868520	3.3100000	.7417397	1.3481818	30.9912356	41.7818211	36
4	.6830135	1.4641000	3.1698654	4.6410000	.6714320	1.4893541	39.4281601	58.7224918	48
5	.6209213	1.6105100	3.7907868	6.1051000	.6077886	1.6453089	47.0653690	77.4370722	60
6	.5644739	1.7715610	4.3552607	7.7156100	.5501778	1.8175943	53.9786655	98.1113136	72
7	.5131581	1.9487171	4.8684188	9.4871710	.4980278	2.0079202	60.2366674	120.9504183	84
8	.4665074	2.1435888	5.3349262	11.4358881	.4508209	2.2181756	65.9014884	146.1810757	96
9	.4240976	2.3579477	5.7590238	13.5794769	.4080887	2.4504476	71.0293549	174.0537127	108
10	.3855433	2.5937425	6.1445671	15.9374246	.3694070	2.7070415	75.6711634	204.8449789	120
11	.3504939	2.8531167	6.4950610	18.5311671	.3343918	2.9905041	79.8729861	238.8604931	132
12	.3186308	3.1384284	6.8136918	21.3842808	.3026956	3.3036490	83.6765282	276.4378761	144
13	.2896644	3.4522712	7.1033562	24.5227121	.2740038	3.6495842	87.1195419	317.9501022	156
14	.2633313	3.7974983	7.3666875	27.9749834	.2480317	4.0317433	90.2362006	363.8092007	168
15	.2393920	4.1772482	7.6060795	31.7724817	.2245213	4.4539196	93.0574388	414.4703462	180
16	.2176291	4.5949730	7.8237086	35.9497299	.2032395	4.9203031	95.6112587	470.4363756	192
17	.1978447	5.0544703	8.0215533	40.5447028	.1839749	5.4355232	97.9230083	532.2627796	204
18	.1798588	5.5599173	8.2014121	45.5991731	.1665364	6.0046935	100.0156327	600.5632161	216
19	.1635080	6.1159090	8.3649201	51.1590904	.1507508	6.6334633	101.9099023	676.0156007	228
20	.1486436	6.7274999	8.5135637	57.2749995	.1364615	7.3280736	103.6246187	759.3688360	240
21	.1351306	7.4002499	8.6486943	64.0024994	.1235267	8.0954187	105.1768013	851.4502442	252
22	.1228460	8.1402749	8.7715403	71.4027494	.1118179	8.9431148	106.5818563	953.1737792	264
23	.1116782	8.9543024	8.8832184	79.5430243	.1012189	9.8795758	107.8537295	1065.5490975	276
24	.1015256	9.8497327	8.9847440	88.4973268	.0916246	10.9140965	109.0050450	1189.6915801	288
25	.0922960	10.8347059	9.0770400	98.3470594	.0829397	12.0569450	110.0472301	1326.8334028	300
26	.0839055	11.9181765	9.1609455	109.1817654	.0750781	13.3194647	110.9906289	1478.3357665	312
27	.0762777	13.1099942	9.2372232	121.0999419	.0679616	14.7141867	111.8446053	1645.7024074	324
28	.0693433	14.4209936	9.3065665	134.2099361	.0615197	16.2549544	112.6176354	1830.5945227	336
29	.0630394	15.8630930	9.3696059	148.6309297	.0556884	17.9570605	113.3173918	2034.8472585	348
30	.0573086	17.4494023	9.4269145	164.4940227	.0504098	19.8373994	113.9508200	2260.4879248	360
31	.0520987	19.1943425	9.4790132	181.9434250	.0456316	21.9146343	114.5242071	2509.7561174	372
32	.0473624	21.1137767	9.5263756	201.1377675	.0413063	24.2093829	115.0432442	2785.1259471	384
33	.0430568	23.2251544	9.5694324	222.2515442	.0373910	26.7444216	115.5130830	3089.3305963	396
34	.0391425	25.5476699	9.6085749	245.4766986	.0338468	29.5449121	115.9383870	3425.3894475	408
35	.0355841	28.1024368	9.6441590	271.0243685	.0306385	32.6386504	116.3233774	3796.6380518	420
36	.0323492	30.9126805	9.6765082	299.1268053	.0277344	36.0563436	116.6718655	4206.7612363	432
37	.0294083	34.0039486	9.7059165	330.0394859	.0251055	39.8319140	116.9873404	4659.8296774	444
38	.0267349	37.4043434	9.7326514	364.0434344	.0227258	44.0028359	117.2729030	5160.3403048	456
39	.0243044	41.1447778	9.7569558	401.4477779	.0205717	48.6105078	117.5313979	5713.2609352	468
40	.0220949	45.2592556	9.7790507	442.5925557	.0186217	53.7006632	117.7653907	6324.0795809	480
41	.0200863	49.7851811	9.7991370	487.8518112	.0168566	59.3238243	117.9772039	6998.8589207	492
42	.0182603	54.7636992	9.8173973	537.6369924	.0152588	65.5358040	118.1689398	7744.2964749	504
43	.0166002	60.2400692	9.8339975	592.4006916	.0138125	72.3982590	118.3425016	8567.7910821	516
44	.0150911	66.2640761	9.8490887	652.6407608	.0125032	79.9793028	118.4996118	9477.5163356	528
45	.0137192	72.8904837	9.8628079	718.9048369	.0113181	88.3541809	118.6418300	10482.5017109	540
46	.0124720	80.1795321	9.8752799	791.7953205	.0102453	97.6060082	118.7705676	11592.7221876	552
47	.0113382	88.1974853	9.8866181	871.9748526	.0092741	107.8266438	118.8871025	12819.1972560	564
48	.0103074	97.0172338	9.8969255	960.1723378	.0083951	119.1175024	118.9925914	14174.1002909	576
49	.0093704	106.7189572	9.9062959	1057.1895716	.0075993	131.5906615	119.0880812	15670.8793786	588
50	.0085186	117.3908529	9.9148145	1163.9085288	.0068790	145.3699233	119.1745198	17324.3907960	600

Present and Future Value

10.250% Discount Rate   10.250% Discount Rate

| | Annual Payments | | | | Monthly Payments | | | | |
Years	Present Value	Future Value	Present Value of 1 per Period	Future Value of 1 per Period	Present Value	Future Value	Present Value of 1 per Period	Future Value of 1 per Period	Months
					.9915307	1.0085417	0.9915307	1.0000000	1
					.9831331	1.0171563	1.9746638	2.0085417	2
					.9748066	1.0258445	2.9494704	3.0256980	3
					.9665507	1.0346069	3.9160210	4.0515425	4
					.9583646	1.0434442	4.8743856	5.0861494	5
					.9502479	1.0523569	5.8246336	6.1295936	6
					.9422000	1.0613458	6.7668335	7.1819505	7
					.9342202	1.0704115	7.7010537	8.2432964	8
					.9263080	1.0795546	8.6273616	9.3137078	9
					.9184627	1.0887758	9.5458244	10.3932624	10
					.9106840	1.0980757	10.4565084	11.4820382	11
1	.9070295	1.1025000	0.9070295	1.0000000	.9029711	1.1074551	11.3594795	12.5801140	12
2	.8227025	1.2155063	1.7297320	2.1025000	.8153568	1.2264569	21.6167613	26.5120258	24
3	.7462154	1.3400956	2.4759473	3.3180063	.7362437	1.3582460	30.8787905	41.9409932	36
4	.6768394	1.4774554	3.1527867	4.6581019	.6648068	1.5041965	39.2421353	59.0278825	48
5	.6139133	1.6288946	3.7667000	6.1355573	.6003013	1.6658301	46.7939941	77.9508458	60
6	.5568374	1.7958563	4.3235374	7.7644520	.5420547	1.8448322	53.6131044	98.9071788	72
7	.5050680	1.9799316	4.8286053	9.5603083	.4894598	2.0430688	59.7705640	122.1153776	84
8	.4581115	2.1828746	5.2867169	11.5402399	.4419680	2.2626071	65.3305722	147.8174165	96
9	.4155207	2.4066192	5.7022375	13.7231145	.3990844	2.5057359	70.3510990	176.2812717	108
10	.3768895	2.6532977	6.0791270	16.1297337	.3603617	2.7749901	74.8844896	207.8037144	120
11	.3418499	2.9252607	6.4209769	18.7830314	.3253962	3.0731770	78.9780104	242.7134055	132
12	.3100679	3.2250999	6.7310448	21.7082921	.2938233	3.4034057	82.6743414	281.3743225	144
13	.2812407	3.5556727	7.0122855	24.9333921	.2653140	3.7691191	86.0120216	324.1895537	156
14	.2550936	3.9201291	7.2673791	28.4890648	.2395709	4.1741303	89.0258503	371.6055015	168
15	.2313774	4.3219424	7.4987566	32.4091939	.2163256	4.6226261	91.7472506	424.1165367	180
16	.2098662	4.7649415	7.7086228	36.7311363	.1953357	5.1193909	94.2045965	482.2701525	192
17	.1903548	5.2533480	7.8989776	41.4960777	.1763825	5.6694958	96.4235088	546.6726732	204
18	.1726574	5.7918161	8.0716350	46.7494257	.1592683	6.2787122	98.4271225	617.9955759	216
19	.1566054	6.3854773	8.2282403	52.5412419	.1438147	6.9533921	100.2363278	696.9824910	228
20	.1420457	7.0399887	8.3702860	58.9267191	.1298605	7.7005698	101.8699879	784.4569561	240
21	.1288396	7.7615876	8.4991256	65.9667079	.1172603	8.5280356	103.3451359	881.3310022	252
22	.1168613	8.5571503	8.6159870	73.7282954	.1058827	9.4444169	104.6771518	988.6146624	264
23	.1059967	9.4342582	8.7219837	82.2854457	.0956090	10.4592680	105.8799237	1107.4265034	276
24	.0961421	10.4012696	8.8181245	91.7197039	.0863322	11.5831702	106.9659920	1239.0052874	288
25	.0872037	11.4673998	8.9053295	102.1209780	.0779554	12.8278413	107.9466803	1384.7228880	300
26	.0790964	12.6428083	8.9844258	113.5883733	.0703915	14.2062588	108.8322135	1546.0985938	312
27	.0717427	13.9386961	9.0561686	126.2311816	.0635615	15.7327944	109.6318245	1724.8149487	324
28	.0650728	15.3674125	9.1212413	140.1698777	.0573942	17.4233640	110.3538500	1922.7352946	336
29	.0590229	16.9425722	9.1802642	155.5372901	.0518253	19.2955940	111.0058182	2141.9231989	348
30	.0535355	18.6791859	9.2337998	172.4798624	.0467968	21.3690047	111.5945267	2384.6639702	360
31	.0485583	20.5938024	9.2823581	191.1590483	.0422561	23.6652141	112.1261134	2653.4884851	372
32	.0440438	22.7046672	9.3264019	211.7528507	.0381561	26.2081630	112.6061209	2951.1995758	384
33	.0399490	25.0318956	9.3663509	234.4575179	.0344538	29.0243649	113.0395538	3280.9012535	396
34	.0362349	27.5976649	9.4025859	259.4894135	.0311108	32.1431821	113.4309311	3646.0310712	408
35	.0328662	30.4264255	9.4354520	287.0870784	.0280922	35.5971322	113.7843336	4050.3959646	420
36	.0298106	33.5451342	9.4652626	317.5135039	.0253664	39.4222270	114.1034458	4498.2119442	432
37	.0270391	36.9835104	9.4923017	351.0586381	.0229051	43.6583479	114.3915949	4994.1480526	444
38	.0245252	40.7743202	9.5168269	388.0421485	.0206827	48.3496618	114.6517852	5543.3750450	456
39	.0222451	44.9536880	9.5390720	428.8164687	.0186759	53.5450815	114.8867296	6151.6193008	468
40	.0201770	49.5614411	9.5592490	473.7701567	.0168638	59.2987758	115.0988775	6825.2225283	480
41	.0183011	54.6414888	9.5775501	523.3315978	.0152275	65.6707340	115.2904410	7571.2078850	492
42	.0165996	60.2422414	9.5941498	577.9730866	.0137500	72.7273919	115.4634173	8397.3532026	504
43	.0150564	66.4170711	9.6092061	638.2153280	.0124158	80.5423240	115.6196099	9312.2720811	516
44	.0136566	73.2248209	9.6228627	704.6323991	.0112111	89.1970107	115.7606473	10325.5036958	528
45	.0123869	80.7303650	9.6352496	777.8572200	.0101233	98.7816880	115.8879999	11447.6122555	540
46	.0112353	89.0052275	9.6464849	858.5875850	.0091411	109.3962881	116.0029957	12690.2971477	552
47	.0101907	98.1282633	9.6566757	947.5928125	.0082541	121.1514816	116.1068336	14066.5149190	564
48	.0092433	108.1864103	9.6659190	1045.7210758	.0074532	134.1698310	116.2005963	15590.6143637	576
49	.0083840	119.2755173	9.6743029	1153.9074861	.0067301	148.5870690	116.2852612	17278.4861277	588
50	.0076045	131.5012578	9.6819074	1273.1830034	.0060771	164.5535133	116.3617112	19147.7283884	600

Present and Future Value

10.500% Discount Rate   10.500% Discount Rate

| | Annual Payments | | | | | Monthly Payments | | | |
Years	Present Value	Future Value	Present Value of 1 per Period	Future Value of 1 per Period	Present Value	Future Value	Present Value of 1 per Period	Future Value of 1 per Period	Months
					.9913259	1.0087500	0.9913259	1.0000000	1
					.9827270	1.0175766	1.9740529	2.0087500	2
					.9742028	1.0264804	2.9482557	3.0263266	3
					.9657524	1.0354621	3.9140081	4.0528069	4
					.9573754	1.0445224	4.8713835	5.0882690	5
					.9490710	1.0536619	5.8204545	6.1327913	6
					.9408387	1.0628815	6.7612932	7.1864533	7
					.9326778	1.0721817	7.6939710	8.2493347	8
					.9245876	1.0815633	8.6185586	9.3215164	9
					.9165676	1.0910269	9.5351262	10.4030797	10
					.9086172	1.1005734	10.4437435	11.4941066	11
1	.9049774	1.1050000	0.9049774	1.0000000	.9007358	1.1102035	11.3444793	12.5946801	12
2	.8189841	1.2210250	1.7239614	2.1050000	.8113250	1.2325517	21.5628580	26.5773373	24
3	.7411620	1.3492326	2.4651235	3.3260250	.7307895	1.3683832	30.7669176	42.1009316	36
4	.6707349	1.4909021	3.1358583	4.6752576	.6582482	1.5191837	39.0573436	59.3352796	48
5	.6069999	1.6474468	3.7428582	6.1661597	.5929078	1.6866030	46.5248272	78.4689122	60
6	.5493212	1.8204287	4.2921794	7.8136064	.5340533	1.8724724	53.2510570	99.7111371	72
7	.4971232	2.0115737	4.7893026	9.6340351	.4810409	2.0788254	59.3096130	123.2943286	84
8	.4498853	2.2227889	5.2391879	11.6456088	.4332908	2.3079191	64.7667714	149.4764690	96
9	.4071360	2.4561818	5.6463239	13.8683977	.3902805	2.5622598	69.6822293	178.5439717	108
10	.3684489	2.7140808	6.0147727	16.3245795	.3515396	2.8446296	74.1097583	210.8148135	120
11	.3334379	2.9990593	6.3482106	19.0386603	.3166443	3.1581176	78.0977922	246.6420134	132
12	.3017537	3.3139606	6.6499644	22.0377197	.2852129	3.5061531	81.6899571	286.4174944	144
13	.2730803	3.6619264	6.9230447	25.3516802	.2569014	3.8925432	84.9255487	330.5763706	156
14	.2471315	4.0464287	7.1701762	29.0136067	.2314003	4.3215149	87.8399618	379.6017073	168
15	.2236484	4.4713037	7.3938246	33.0600354	.2084306	4.7977608	90.4650781	434.0298053	180
16	.2023968	4.9407906	7.5962214	37.5313391	.1877409	5.3264906	92.8296144	494.4560675	192
17	.1831645	5.4595736	7.7793858	42.4721297	.1691049	5.9134882	94.9594368	561.5415123	204
18	.1657597	6.0328288	7.9451456	47.9317033	.1523189	6.5651750	96.8778442	636.0200046	216
19	.1500088	6.6662759	8.0951543	53.9645321	.1371991	7.2886800	98.6058224	718.7062837	228
20	.1357546	7.3662348	8.2309089	60.6308080	.1235801	8.0919177	100.1622742	810.5048761	240
21	.1228548	8.1396895	8.3537637	67.9970429	.1113130	8.9836749	101.5642261	912.4199901	252
22	.1111808	8.9943569	8.4649445	76.1367324	.1002636	9.9737069	102.8270144	1025.5665013	264
23	.1006161	9.9387644	8.5655607	85.1310893	.0903110	11.0728438	103.9644530	1151.1821485	276
24	.0910553	10.9823346	8.6566160	95.0698536	.0813464	12.2931094	104.9889847	1290.6410734	288
25	.0824030	12.1354798	8.7390190	106.0521883	.0732716	13.6647525	105.9118170	1445.4688530	300
26	.0745729	13.4097051	8.8135919	118.1876680	.0659984	15.1518929	106.7430452	1617.3591882	312
27	.0674867	14.8177242	8.8810786	131.5973732	.0594471	16.8216838	107.4917622	1808.1924314	324
28	.0610740	16.3735852	8.9421526	146.4150974	.0535461	18.6754914	108.1661583	2020.0561565	336
29	.0552706	18.0928117	8.9974232	162.7886826	.0482309	20.7335950	108.7736111	2255.2679951	348
30	.0500186	19.9925569	9.0474418	180.8814942	.0434433	23.0185087	109.3207656	2516.4009899	360
31	.0452657	22.0917754	9.0927075	200.8740591	.0391309	25.5552277	109.8136072	2806.3117418	372
32	.0409644	24.4114118	9.1336719	222.9658265	.0352466	28.3715020	110.2575273	3128.1716588	384
33	.0370719	26.9746100	9.1707438	247.3772383	.0317479	31.4981394	110.6573821	3485.5016492	396
34	.0335492	29.8069441	9.2042931	274.3518483	.0285965	34.9693431	111.0175455	3882.2106376	408
35	.0303613	32.9366732	9.2346543	304.1587924	.0257579	38.8230853	111.3419577	4322.6383253	420
36	.0274763	36.3950239	9.2621306	337.0954656	.0232010	43.1015233	111.6341673	4811.6026638	432
37	.0248654	40.2165014	9.2869960	373.4904895	.0208980	47.8514599	111.8973710	5354.4525597	444
38	.0225026	44.4392340	9.3094987	413.7069909	.0188236	53.1248559	112.1344479	5957.1263871	456
39	.0203644	49.1053536	9.3298631	458.1462249	.0169551	58.9793983	112.3479917	6626.2169497	468
40	.0184293	54.2614157	9.3482924	507.2515785	.0152720	65.4791315	112.5403381	7369.0436011	480
41	.0166781	59.9588644	9.3649705	561.5129943	.0137561	72.6951577	112.7135915	8193.7323125	492
42	.0150933	66.2545452	9.3800638	621.4718587	.0123906	80.7064149	112.8696470	9109.3045655	504
43	.0136591	73.2112724	9.3937229	687.7264038	.0111606	89.6005403	113.0102118	10125.7760399	516
44	.0123612	80.8984560	9.4060840	760.9376762	.0100528	99.4748291	113.1368235	11254.2661780	528
45	.0111866	89.3927939	9.4172706	841.8361323	.0090549	110.4372985	113.2508672	12507.1198232	540
46	.0101236	98.7790372	9.4273942	931.2289261	.0081561	122.6078698	113.3535905	13898.0422630	552
47	.0091616	109.1508362	9.4365559	1030.0079634	.0073465	136.1196801	113.4461170	15442.2491549	564
48	.0082911	120.6116740	9.4448469	1139.1587995	.0066172	151.1205385	113.5294589	17156.6329746	576
49	.0075032	133.2758997	9.4523502	1259.7704735	.0059604	167.7745433	113.6045280	19059.9478066	588
50	.0067903	147.2698692	9.4591404	1393.0463732	.0053687	186.2638769	113.6721454	21173.0145004	600

Present and Future Value

10.750% Discount Rate

10.750% Discount Rate

	Annual Payments				Monthly Payments				
Years	Present Value	Future Value	Present Value of 1 per Period	Future Value of 1 per Period	Present Value	Future Value	Present Value of 1 per Period	Future Value of 1 per Period	Months
					.9911212	1.0089583	0.9911212	1.0000000	1
					.9823212	1.0179969	1.9734425	2.0089583	2
					.9735994	1.0271165	2.9470419	3.0269553	3
					.9649550	1.0363177	3.9119969	4.0540717	4
					.9563874	1.0456014	4.8683843	5.0903895	5
					.9478958	1.0549683	5.8162801	6.1359909	6
					.9394797	1.0644190	6.7557598	7.1909591	7
					.9311382	1.0739544	7.6868980	8.2553781	8
					.9228708	1.0835753	8.6097688	9.3293325	9
					.9146768	1.0932823	9.5244456	10.4129078	10
					.9065556	1.1030763	10.4310012	11.5061901	11
1	.9029345	1.1075000	0.9029345	1.0000000	.8985065	1.1129580	11.3295077	12.6092664	12
2	.8152908	1.2265563	1.7182253	2.1075000	.8073139	1.2386755	21.5091440	26.6428505	24
3	.7361542	1.3584110	2.4543795	3.3340563	.7253768	1.3785939	30.6556133	42.2616403	36
4	.6646991	1.5044402	3.1190786	4.6924673	.6517558	1.5343171	38.8737753	59.6446975	48
5	.6001797	1.6661676	3.7192583	6.1969075	.5856068	1.7076305	46.2578473	78.9913104	60
6	.5419230	1.8452806	4.2611813	7.8630751	.5261715	1.9005210	52.8924839	100.5232781	72
7	.4893210	2.0436482	4.7505023	9.7083557	.4727685	2.1152001	58.8537479	124.4874541	84
8	.4418248	2.2633404	5.1923271	11.7520039	.4247856	2.3541289	64.2099824	151.1585758	96
9	.3989389	2.5066495	5.5912660	14.0153443	.3816726	2.6200466	69.0225939	180.8424144	108
10	.3602157	2.7761143	5.9514818	16.5219938	.3429353	2.9160019	73.3467565	213.8792803	120
11	.3252512	3.0745466	6.2767330	19.2981082	.3081296	3.2453877	77.2320447	250.6479249	132
12	.2936805	3.4050604	6.5704135	22.3726548	.2768564	3.6119802	80.7230014	291.5698825	144
13	.2651743	3.7711044	6.8355878	25.7777152	.2487573	4.0199823	83.8596486	337.1143030	156
14	.2394350	4.1764981	7.0750229	29.5488196	.2235101	4.4740715	86.6779466	387.8033308	168
15	.2161942	4.6254716	7.2912170	33.7253177	.2008252	4.9794537	89.2102055	444.2180903	180
16	.1952092	5.1227099	7.4864262	38.3507893	.1804428	5.5419229	91.4854567	507.0053488	192
17	.1762611	5.6734012	7.6626873	43.4734992	.1621290	6.1679275	93.5297846	576.8849313	204
18	.1591522	6.2832918	7.8218396	49.1469003	.1456740	6.8646443	95.3666265	654.6579724	216
19	.1437041	6.9587457	7.9655436	55.4301921	.1308890	7.6400609	97.0170409	741.2161016	228
20	.1297554	7.7068108	8.0952990	62.3889378	.1176046	8.5030670	98.4999489	837.5516649	240
21	.1171606	8.5352930	8.2124596	70.0957486	.1056685	9.4635565	99.8323514	944.7691019	252
22	.1057883	9.4528370	8.3182479	78.6310416	.0949439	10.5325411	101.0295237	1064.0976075	264
23	.0955200	10.4690169	8.4137679	88.0838785	.0853077	11.7222760	102.1051908	1196.9052237	276
24	.0862483	11.5944363	8.5000161	98.5528955	.0766495	13.0464009	103.0716847	1344.7145241	288
25	.0778765	12.8408382	8.5778927	110.1473317	.0688701	14.5200965	103.9400857	1509.2200692	300
26	.0703174	14.2212283	8.6482101	122.9881699	.0618802	16.1602577	104.7203496	1692.3078336	312
27	.0634920	15.7500103	8.7117021	137.2093981	.0555998	17.9856882	105.4214218	1896.0768278	324
28	.0573291	17.4431364	8.7690313	152.9594084	.0499567	20.0173158	106.0513398	2122.8631623	336
29	.0517645	19.3182736	8.8207957	170.4025449	.0448865	22.2784320	106.6173251	2375.2668303	348
30	.0467399	21.3949880	8.8675356	189.7208184	.0403308	24.7949594	107.1258667	2656.1815147	360
31	.0422031	23.6949492	8.9097387	211.1158064	.0362375	27.5957487	107.5827945	2968.8277632	372
32	.0381066	26.2421562	8.9478454	234.8107556	.0325596	30.7129096	107.9933472	3316.7899103	384
33	.0344078	29.0631880	8.9822531	261.0529118	.0292550	34.1821788	108.3622314	3704.0571696	396
34	.0310680	32.1874807	9.0133211	290.1160998	.0262858	38.0433298	108.6936763	4135.0693685	408
35	.0280524	35.6476349	9.0413735	322.3035806	.0236180	42.3406286	108.9914816	4614.7678483	420
36	.0253294	39.4797557	9.0667029	357.9512155	.0212209	47.1233419	109.2590617	5148.6521145	432
37	.0228708	43.7238294	9.0895737	397.4309712	.0190671	52.4463009	109.4994841	5742.8428858	444
38	.0206509	48.4241411	9.1102246	441.1548006	.0171319	58.3705307	109.7155052	6404.1522650	456
39	.0186464	53.6297362	9.1288710	489.5789416	.0153932	64.9639498	109.9096016	7140.1618368	468
40	.0168365	59.3949329	9.1457074	543.2086778	.0138308	72.3021484	110.0839984	7959.3095862	480
41	.0152022	65.7798882	9.1609096	602.6036107	.0124271	80.4692553	110.2406951	8870.9866366	492
42	.0137266	72.8512261	9.1746362	668.3834989	.0111658	89.5589024	110.3814881	9885.6449138	504
43	.0123942	80.6827329	9.1870305	741.2347250	.0100326	99.6752979	110.5079915	11014.9169722	516
44	.0111912	89.3561267	9.1982216	821.9174579	.0090143	110.9344213	110.6216557	12271.7493569	528
45	.0101049	98.9619104	9.2083265	911.2735847	.0080994	123.4653530	110.7237836	13670.5510286	540
46	.0091241	109.6003157	9.2174506	1010.2354950	.0072774	137.4117537	110.8155463	15227.3585557	552
47	.0082384	121.3823497	9.2256890	1119.8358107	.0065388	152.9335122	110.8979956	16960.0199653	564
48	.0074388	134.4309522	9.2331278	1241.2181604	.0058751	170.2085776	110.9720769	18888.3993624	576
49	.0067167	148.8822796	9.2398445	1375.6491126	.0052789	189.4350001	111.0386394	21034.6046616	588
50	.0060648	164.8871247	9.2459093	1524.5313922	.0047431	210.8332010	111.0984462	23423.2410438	600

Present and Future Value

11.000% Discount Rate   11.000% Discount Rate

	Annual Payments				Monthly Payments				
Years	Present Value	Future Value	Present Value of 1 per Period	Future Value of 1 per Period	Present Value	Future Value	Present Value of 1 per Period	Future Value of 1 per Period	Months
					.9909166	1.0091667	0.9909166	1.0000000	1
					.9819157	1.0184174	1.9728323	2.0091667	2
					.9729966	1.0277529	2.9458289	3.0275840	3
					.9641584	1.0371739	3.9099873	4.0553369	4
					.9554006	1.0466813	4.8653879	5.0925108	5
					.9467223	1.0562759	5.8121103	6.1391922	6
					.9381229	1.0659585	6.7502331	7.1954681	7
					.9296015	1.0757297	7.6798346	8.2614265	8
					.9211576	1.0855906	8.6009922	9.3371563	9
					.9127903	1.0955418	9.5137825	10.4227469	10
					.9044991	1.1055843	10.4182816	11.5182887	11
1	.9009009	1.1100000	0.9009009	1.0000000	.8962832	1.1157188	11.3145648	12.6238730	12
2	.8116224	1.2321000	1.7125233	2.1100000	.8033235	1.2448285	21.4556186	26.7085660	24
3	.7311914	1.3676310	2.4437147	3.3421000	.7200053	1.3888786	30.5448743	42.4231232	36
4	.6587310	1.5180704	3.1024457	4.7097310	.6453286	1.5495980	38.6914211	59.9561507	48
5	.5934513	1.6850582	3.6958970	6.2278014	.5783972	1.7289157	45.9930338	79.5180797	60
6	.5346408	1.8704146	4.2305379	7.9128596	.5184077	1.9289838	52.5373463	101.3436924	72
7	.4816584	2.0761602	4.7121963	9.7832741	.4646401	2.1522036	58.4029033	125.6949395	84
8	.4339265	2.3045378	5.1461228	11.8594343	.4164491	2.4012541	63.6601033	152.8640847	96
9	.3909248	2.5580369	5.5370475	14.1639720	.3732563	2.6791244	68.3720431	183.1772117	108
10	.3521845	2.8394210	5.8892320	16.7220090	.3345433	2.9891496	72.5952754	216.9981385	120
11	.3172833	3.1517573	6.2065153	19.5614300	.2998455	3.3350505	76.3804873	254.7327836	132
12	.2858408	3.4984506	6.4923561	22.7131872	.2687065	3.7209787	79.7731090	296.8340379	144
13	.2575143	3.8832802	6.7498704	26.2116378	.2408730	4.1515660	82.8138587	343.8072003	156
14	.2319948	4.3104410	6.9818652	30.0949180	.2158904	4.6319804	85.5392314	396.2160425	168
15	.2090043	4.7845895	7.1908696	34.4053590	.1934989	5.1679878	87.9819371	454.6895748	180
16	.1882922	5.3108943	7.3791618	39.1899485	.1734298	5.7660213	90.1712930	519.9295963	192
17	.1696326	5.8950927	7.5487944	44.5008428	.1554422	6.4332586	92.1335759	592.7191171	204
18	.1528222	6.5435529	7.7016166	50.3959355	.1393202	7.1777078	93.8923370	673.9317566	216
19	.1376776	7.2633437	7.8392942	56.9394884	.1248704	8.0083038	95.4686849	764.5422282	228
20	.1240339	8.0623115	7.9633281	64.2028321	.1119192	8.9350153	96.8815390	865.6380381	240
21	.1117423	8.9491658	8.0750704	72.2651437	.1003113	9.9689649	98.1478563	978.4325375	252
22	.1006687	9.9335740	8.1757390	81.2143095	.0899073	11.1225619	99.2828352	1104.2794850	264
23	.0906925	11.0262672	8.2664316	91.1478835	.0805824	12.4096519	100.3000977	1244.6892949	276
24	.0817050	12.2391566	8.3481366	102.1741507	.0722247	13.8456823	101.2118529	1401.3471646	288
25	.0736081	13.5854638	8.4217447	114.4133073	.0647338	15.4478886	102.0290437	1576.1333006	300
26	.0663136	15.0798648	8.4880583	127.9987711	.0580198	17.2355003	102.7614781	1771.1454849	312
27	.0597420	16.7386500	8.5478002	143.0786359	.0520022	19.2299723	103.4179467	1988.7242522	324
28	.0538216	18.5799014	8.6016218	159.8172859	.0466087	21.4552423	104.0063285	2231.4809812	336
29	.0484879	20.6236906	8.6501098	178.3971873	.0417746	23.9380180	104.5336851	2502.3292364	348
30	.0436828	22.8922966	8.6937926	199.0208779	.0374418	26.7080976	105.0063460	2804.5197364	360
31	.0393539	25.4104492	8.7331465	221.9131745	.0335585	29.7987276	105.4299840	3141.6793694	372
32	.0354540	28.2055986	8.7686004	247.3236237	.0300779	33.2470016	105.8096836	3517.8547228	384
33	.0319405	31.3082145	8.8005409	275.5292223	.0269583	37.0943060	106.1500020	3937.5606503	396
34	.0287752	34.7521180	8.8293161	306.8374368	.0241623	41.3868159	106.4550236	4405.8344592	408
35	.0259236	38.5748510	8.8552398	341.5895548	.0216562	46.1760500	106.7284093	4928.2963684	420
36	.0233546	42.8180846	8.8785944	380.1644058	.0194101	51.5194888	106.9734403	5511.2169616	432
37	.0210402	47.5280740	8.8996346	422.9824905	.0173970	57.4812641	107.1930575	6161.5924474	444
38	.0189551	52.7561621	8.9185897	470.5105644	.0155926	64.1329291	107.3898967	6887.2286276	456
39	.0170767	58.5593399	8.9356664	523.2667265	.0139754	71.5543170	107.5663203	7696.8345820	468
40	.0153844	65.0008673	8.9510508	581.8260664	.0125259	79.8344993	107.7244458	8600.1271953	480
41	.0138598	72.1509627	8.9649106	646.8269337	.0112268	89.0728546	107.8661711	9607.9477785	492
42	.0124863	80.0875686	8.9773970	718.9778964	.0100624	99.3802617	107.9931971	10732.3921867	504
43	.0112489	88.8972012	8.9886459	799.0654650	.0090187	110.8804299	108.1070483	11986.9559931	516
44	.0101342	98.6758933	8.9987801	887.9626662	.0080833	123.7113842	108.2090912	13386.6964632	528
45	.0091299	109.5302415	9.0079100	986.6385595	.0072450	138.0271217	108.3005506	14948.4132715	540
46	.0082251	121.5785681	9.0161351	1096.1688010	.0064935	153.9994595	108.3825241	16690.8501313	552
47	.0074100	134.9522106	9.0235452	1217.7473691	.0058200	171.8200978	108.4559955	18634.9197566	564
48	.0066757	149.7969538	9.0302209	1352.6995797	.0052164	191.7029195	108.5218468	20803.9548565	576
49	.0060141	166.2746187	9.0362350	1502.4965335	.0046754	213.8865583	108.5808681	23223.9881737	588
50	.0054182	184.5648267	9.0416532	1668.7711522	.0041905	238.6372619	108.6337680	25924.0649301	600

Present and Future Value

11.250% Discount Rate   11.250% Discount Rate

	Annual Payments				Monthly Payments				
Years	Present Value	Future Value	Present Value of 1 per Period	Future Value of 1 per Period	Present Value	Future Value	Present Value of 1 per Period	Future Value of 1 per Period	Months
					.9907121	1.0093750	0.9907121	1.0000000	1
					.9815104	1.0188379	1.9722225	2.0093750	2
					.9723942	1.0283895	2.9446167	3.0282129	3
					.9633627	1.0380306	3.9079794	4.0566024	4
					.9544151	1.0477622	4.8623945	5.0946330	5
					.9455505	1.0575850	5.8079450	6.1423952	6
					.9367683	1.0674998	6.7447133	7.1999802	7
					.9280677	1.0775076	7.6727810	8.2674800	8
					.9194479	1.0876093	8.5922288	9.3449876	9
					.9109081	1.0978056	9.5031369	10.4325969	10
					.9024476	1.1080975	10.4055846	11.5304025	11
1	.8988764	1.1125000	0.8988764	1.0000000	.8940658	1.1184859	11.2996503	12.6385000	12
2	.8079788	1.2376563	1.7068552	2.1125000	.7993536	1.2510108	21.4022810	26.7744845	24
3	.7262731	1.3768926	2.4331283	3.3501562	.7146747	1.3992380	30.4346973	42.5853844	36
4	.6528297	1.5317930	3.0859580	4.7270488	.6389662	1.5650280	38.5102717	60.2696536	48
5	.5868132	1.7041197	3.6727712	6.2588418	.5712778	1.7504618	45.7303664	80.0492600	60
6	.5274726	1.8958332	4.2002438	7.9629615	.5107599	1.9578669	52.1856059	102.1724715	72
7	.4741326	2.1091144	4.6743764	9.8587947	.4566530	2.1898466	57.9570147	126.9169726	84
8	.4261867	2.3463898	5.1005631	11.9679091	.4082778	2.4493126	63.1170338	154.5933491	96
9	.3830891	2.6103586	5.4836522	14.3142989	.3650272	2.7395218	67.7304302	185.5489869	108
10	.3443498	2.9040240	5.8280020	16.9246575	.3263583	3.0641166	71.8551101	220.1724326	120
11	.3095279	3.2307267	6.1375299	19.8286815	.2917858	3.4271713	75.5428453	258.8982696	132
12	.2782273	3.5941834	6.4157572	23.0594081	.2608757	3.8332429	78.8399231	302.2125738	144
13	.2500920	3.9985290	6.6658492	26.6535915	.2332401	4.2874283	81.7877275	350.6590139	156
14	.2248018	4.4483636	6.8906509	30.6521206	.2085320	4.7954282	84.4232586	404.8456759	168
15	.2020690	4.9488045	7.0927199	35.1004842	.1864413	5.3636190	86.7795967	465.4526953	180
16	.1816351	5.5055450	7.2743550	40.0492886	.1666908	5.9991324	88.8863180	533.2407942	192
17	.1632675	6.1249188	7.4376225	45.5548336	.1490325	6.7099453	90.7698654	609.0608295	204
18	.1467573	6.8139721	7.5843798	51.6797524	.1332449	7.5049794	92.4538807	693.8644729	216
19	.1319167	7.5805440	7.7162964	58.4937245	.1191297	8.3942140	93.9595011	788.7161553	228
20	.1185768	8.4333552	7.8348732	66.0742685	.1065098	9.3888103	95.3056248	894.8064283	240
21	.1065859	9.3821077	7.9414590	74.5076237	.0952267	10.5012523	96.5091479	1013.4669068	252
22	.0958075	10.4375948	8.0372665	83.8897314	.0851390	11.7455030	97.5851768	1146.1869833	264
23	.0861191	11.6118242	8.1233857	94.3273262	.0761198	13.1371799	98.5472173	1294.6325224	276
24	.0774104	12.9181544	8.2007961	105.9391504	.0680561	14.6937510	99.4073449	1460.6667704	288
25	.0695824	14.3714468	8.2703785	118.8573048	.0608467	16.4347538	100.1763555	1646.3737420	300
26	.0625460	15.9882346	8.3329245	133.2287516	.0544009	18.3820410	100.8639015	1854.0843781	312
27	.0562211	17.7869109	8.3891456	149.2169862	.0486380	20.5600544	101.4786130	2086.4058037	324
28	.0505358	19.7879384	8.4396815	167.0038971	.0434856	22.9961317	102.0282054	2346.2540511	336
29	.0454255	22.0140815	8.4851069	186.7918355	.0388790	25.7208500	102.5195772	2636.8906618	348
30	.0408319	24.4906657	8.5259388	208.8059170	.0347604	28.7684090	102.9588959	2961.9636237	360
31	.0367028	27.2458656	8.5626416	233.2965827	.0310780	32.1770609	103.3516757	3325.5531602	372
32	.0329913	30.3110254	8.5956329	260.5424483	.0277858	35.9895901	103.7028467	3732.2229438	384
33	.0296551	33.7210158	8.6252880	290.8534737	.0248423	40.2538504	104.0168166	4187.0773779	396
34	.0266563	37.5146301	8.6519443	324.5744896	.0222107	45.0233656	104.2975264	4695.8256660	408
35	.0239607	41.7350259	8.6759050	362.0891195	.0198578	50.3580013	104.5484995	5264.8534719	420
36	.0215377	46.4302164	8.6974427	403.8241455	.0177542	56.3247163	104.7728859	5901.3030709	432
37	.0193597	51.6536157	8.7168024	450.2543619	.0158734	62.9984031	104.9735021	6613.1629972	444
38	.0174020	57.4646475	8.7342044	501.9079776	.0141919	70.4628279	105.1528661	7409.3683141	456
39	.0156423	63.9294203	8.7498467	559.3726250	.0126885	78.8116822	105.3132294	8299.9127644	468
40	.0140604	71.1214801	8.7639071	623.3020454	.0113443	88.1497582	105.4566047	9295.9742087	480
41	.0126386	79.1226466	8.7765457	694.4235255	.0101426	98.5942469	105.5847917	10410.0549270	492
42	.0113605	88.0239444	8.7879063	773.5461721	.0090681	110.2762988	105.6993993	11656.1385435	504
43	.0102117	97.9266381	8.7981180	861.5701164	.0081075	123.3424895	105.8018660	13049.8655454	516
44	.0091791	108.9433849	8.8072971	959.4967545	.0072486	137.9568400	105.8934780	14608.7295976	528
45	.0082509	121.1995157	8.8155479	1068.4401394	.0064808	154.3027855	105.9753851	16352.2971183	540
46	.0074165	134.8344612	8.8229644	1189.6396551	.0057942	172.5854957	106.0486155	18302.4528711	552
47	.0066665	150.0033381	8.8296309	1324.4741163	.0051804	193.0344499	106.1140883	20483.6746565	564
48	.0059924	166.8787136	8.8356233	1474.4774544	.0046316	215.9063177	106.1726252	22923.3405497	576
49	.0053864	185.6525689	8.8410097	1641.3561680	.0041410	241.4881801	106.2249611	25652.0725433	588
50	.0048417	206.5384829	8.8458514	1827.0087369	.0037023	270.1011335	106.2717529	28704.1209051	600

Present and Future Value

11.500% Discount Rate   11.500% Discount Rate

	Annual Payments				Monthly Payments				
Years	Present Value	Future Value	Present Value of 1 per Period	Future Value of 1 per Period	Present Value	Future Value	Present Value of 1 per Period	Future Value of 1 per Period	Months
					.9905076	1.0095833	0.9905076	1.0000000	1
					.9811054	1.0192585	1.9716130	2.0095833	2
					.9717924	1.0290264	2.9434054	3.0288418	3
					.9625678	1.0388879	3.9059731	4.0578682	4
					.9534307	1.0488439	4.8594038	5.0967561	5
					.9443804	1.0588953	5.8037842	6.1456001	6
					.9354160	1.0690431	6.7392002	7.2044954	7
					.9265367	1.0792881	7.6657369	8.2735385	8
					.9177417	1.0896313	8.5834786	9.3528266	9
					.9090301	1.1000736	9.4925087	10.4424578	10
					.9004013	1.1106159	10.3929100	11.5425314	11
1	.8968610	1.1150000	0.8968610	1.0000000	.8918543	1.1212593	11.2847643	12.6531473	12
2	.8043596	1.2432250	1.7012206	2.1150000	.7954042	1.2572225	21.3491304	26.8406067	24
3	.7213988	1.3861959	2.4226194	3.3582250	.7093847	1.4096724	30.3250790	42.7484279	36
4	.6469944	1.5456084	3.0696138	4.7444209	.6326678	1.5806084	38.3303177	60.5852209	48
5	.5802640	1.7233534	3.6498778	6.2900293	.5642475	1.7722719	45.4698246	80.5848913	60
6	.5204162	1.9215390	4.1702940	8.0133826	.5032266	1.9871764	51.8372248	103.0097084	72
7	.4667410	2.1425160	4.6370350	9.9349216	.4488048	2.2281400	57.5160184	128.1537437	84
8	.4186018	2.3889053	5.0556368	12.0774376	.4002685	2.4983228	62.5806750	156.3467278	96
9	.3754276	2.6636294	5.4310644	14.4663430	.3569812	2.8012678	67.0976111	187.9583743	108
10	.3367064	2.9699468	5.7677707	17.1299724	.3183753	3.1409476	71.1260601	223.4032278	120
11	.3019788	3.3114907	6.0697495	20.0999192	.2839444	3.5218168	74.7188499	263.1461004	132
12	.2708330	3.6923121	6.3405825	23.4114099	.2532370	3.9488699	77.9230950	307.7081670	144
13	.2428996	4.1169280	6.5834821	27.1037221	.2258505	4.4277072	80.7808149	357.6737998	156
14	.2178471	4.5903748	6.8013292	31.2206501	.2014258	4.9646081	83.3294849	413.6982318	168
15	.1953786	5.1182679	6.9967078	35.8110249	.1796424	5.5666131	85.6025272	476.5161487	180
16	.1752274	5.7068687	7.1719353	40.9292928	.1602149	6.2416169	87.6297499	546.9513240	192
17	.1571547	6.3631586	7.3290899	46.6361614	.1428884	6.9984711	89.4377373	625.9274214	204
18	.1409459	7.0949218	7.4700358	52.9993200	.1274356	7.8471010	91.0501986	714.4801073	216
19	.1264089	7.9108378	7.5964447	60.0942418	.1136540	8.7986352	92.4882793	813.7706323	228
20	.1133712	8.8205842	7.7098159	68.0050796	.1013628	9.8655518	93.7708378	925.1010597	240
21	.1016782	9.8349513	7.8114940	76.8256637	.0904009	11.0618420	94.9146932	1049.9313400	252
22	.0911912	10.9659707	7.9026852	86.6606151	.0806244	12.4031935	95.9348455	1189.8984562	264
23	.0817858	12.2270574	7.9844711	97.6265858	.0719052	13.9071965	96.8446728	1346.8378908	276
24	.0733505	13.6331690	8.0578216	109.8536432	.0641290	15.5935738	97.6561063	1522.8076958	288
25	.0657852	15.2009834	8.1236068	123.4868121	.0571937	17.4844400	98.3797867	1720.1154812	300
26	.0590002	16.9490965	8.1826070	138.6877955	.0510085	19.6045915	99.0252043	1941.3486760	312
27	.0529150	18.8982426	8.2355220	155.6368920	.0454921	21.9818311	99.6008227	2189.4084594	324
28	.0474574	21.0715405	8.2829793	174.5351346	.0405723	24.6473331	100.1141905	2467.5478055	336
29	.0425627	23.4947676	8.3255420	195.6066751	.0361846	27.6360522	100.5720398	2779.4141419	348
30	.0381728	26.1966659	8.3637148	219.1014427	.0322714	30.9871813	100.9803747	3129.0971806	360
31	.0342357	29.2092825	8.3979505	245.2981086	.0287814	34.7446661	101.3445500	3521.1825497	372
32	.0307047	32.5683500	8.4286552	274.5073911	.0256688	38.9577810	101.6693412	3960.8119272	384
33	.0275378	36.3137102	8.4561930	307.0757411	.0228928	43.6817753	101.9590077	4453.7504677	396
34	.0246976	40.4897869	8.4808906	343.3894513	.0204171	48.9785980	102.2173481	5006.4624044	408
35	.0221503	45.1461124	8.5030409	383.8792382	.0182091	54.9177099	102.4477500	5626.1958191	420
36	.0198657	50.3379153	8.5229066	429.0253506	.0162398	61.5769945	102.6532350	6321.0776914	432
37	.0178168	56.1267756	8.5407234	479.3632659	.0144836	69.0437795	102.8364977	7100.2204727	444
38	.0159792	62.5813548	8.5567026	535.4900415	.0129172	77.4159818	102.9999413	7973.8415841	456
39	.0143311	69.7782106	8.5710337	598.0713963	.0115203	86.8033918	103.1457092	8953.3974046	468
40	.0128530	77.8027048	8.5838868	667.8496068	.0102744	97.3291128	103.2757129	10051.7335057	480
41	.0115274	86.7500158	8.5954141	745.6523116	.0091633	109.1311756	103.3916573	11283.2531045	492
42	.0103385	96.7262677	8.6057524	832.4023275	.0081723	122.3643486	103.4950628	12664.1059424	504
43	.0092722	107.8497884	8.6150247	929.1285951	.0072885	137.2021673	103.5872854	14212.4000678	516
44	.0083158	120.2525141	8.6233406	1036.9783836	.0065003	153.8392099	103.6695346	15948.4392985	528
45	.0074581	134.0815532	8.6307987	1157.2308977	.0057973	172.4936492	103.7428889	17894.9894800	540
46	.0066889	149.5009319	8.6374876	1291.3124509	.0051704	193.4101132	103.8083102	20077.5770286	552
47	.0059990	166.6935390	8.6434867	1440.8133828	.0046112	216.8628936	103.8666565	22524.8236771	564
48	.0053803	185.8632960	8.6488670	1607.5069218	.0041125	243.1595423	103.9186929	25268.8218098	576
49	.0048254	207.2375750	8.6536923	1793.3702178	.0036678	272.6449051	103.9651018	28345.5553126	588
50	.0043277	231.0698962	8.6580200	2000.6077928	.0032711	305.7056431	104.0064918	31795.3714528	600

Present and Future Value

11.750% Discount Rate   11.750% Discount Rate

| | Annual Payments | | | | Monthly Payments | | | | |
Years	Present Value	Future Value	Present Value of 1 per Period	Future Value of 1 per Period	Present Value	Future Value	Present Value of 1 per Period	Future Value of 1 per Period	Months
					.9903033	1.0097917	0.9903033	1.0000000	1
					.9807006	1.0196792	1.9710039	2.0097917	2
					.9711910	1.0296636	2.9421949	3.0294709	3
					.9617736	1.0397457	3.9039685	4.0591344	4
					.9524476	1.0499265	4.8564161	5.0988801	5
					.9432120	1.0602071	5.7996281	6.1488067	6
					.9340659	1.0705883	6.7336940	7.2090137	7
					.9250085	1.0810711	7.6587025	8.2796020	8
					.9160390	1.0916566	8.5747415	9.3606731	9
					.9071564	1.1023457	9.4818979	10.4523297	10
					.8983600	1.1131395	10.3802579	11.5546754	11
1	.8948546	1.1175000	0.8948546	1.0000000	.8896488	1.1240390	11.2699067	12.6678149	12
2	.8007647	1.2488062	1.6956193	2.1175000	.7914750	1.2634637	21.2961661	26.9069333	24
3	.7165680	1.3955410	2.4121873	3.3663062	.7041348	1.4201825	30.2160160	42.9122579	36
4	.6412242	1.5595171	3.0534115	4.7618472	.6264327	1.5963406	38.1515500	60.9028673	48
5	.5738024	1.7427603	3.6272138	6.3213643	.5573052	1.7943491	45.2113886	81.1250143	60
6	.5134697	1.9475346	4.1406835	8.0641246	.4958059	2.0169184	51.4921657	103.8554966	72
7	.4594807	2.1763700	4.6001642	10.0116592	.4410931	2.2670950	57.0798517	129.4054458	84
8	.4111684	2.4320934	5.0113326	12.1880292	.3924180	2.5483032	62.0509300	158.1245856	96
9	.3679359	2.7178644	5.3792686	14.6201226	.3491142	2.8643923	66.4734440	190.4060194	108
10	.3292492	3.0372135	5.7085177	17.3379870	.3105890	3.2196887	70.4079284	226.6916106	120
11	.2946301	3.3940861	6.0031479	20.3752005	.2763152	3.6190557	73.9082379	267.4780311	132
12	.2636511	3.7928912	6.2667990	23.7692866	.2458235	4.0679599	77.0222841	313.3235593	144
13	.2359294	4.2385559	6.5027284	27.5621777	.2186966	4.5725456	79.7926916	364.8557219	156
14	.2111225	4.7365862	6.7138509	31.8007336	.1945631	5.1397197	82.2573815	422.7798835	168
15	.1889240	5.2931351	6.9027749	36.5373198	.1730929	5.7772455	84.4500899	487.8889015	180
16	.1690595	5.9150784	7.0718343	41.8304549	.1539919	6.4938494	86.4008304	561.0739783	192
17	.1512836	6.6101002	7.2231180	47.7455333	.1369987	7.2993401	88.1363044	643.3368604	204
18	.1353769	7.3867869	7.3584948	54.3556335	.1218807	8.2047431	89.6802668	735.8035500	216
19	.1211426	8.2547344	7.4796374	61.7424204	.1084310	9.2224514	91.0538512	839.7397172	228
20	.1084050	9.2246657	7.5880424	69.9971548	.0964655	10.3663952	92.2758589	956.5680248	240
21	.0970067	10.3085639	7.6850492	79.2218205	.0858205	11.6522328	93.3630166	1087.8876015	252
22	.0868069	11.5198202	7.7718561	89.5303844	.0763501	13.0975643	94.3302052	1235.4959299	264
23	.0776796	12.8733990	7.8495356	101.0502046	.0679248	14.7221734	95.1906635	1401.4134509	276
24	.0695119	14.3860234	7.9190476	113.9236037	.0604292	16.5482974	95.9561691	1587.9112188	288
25	.0622031	16.0763842	7.9812506	128.3096271	.0537607	18.6009320	96.6372003	1797.5419874	300
26	.0556627	17.9653560	8.0369133	144.3860083	.0478282	20.9081734	97.2430789	2033.1751513	312
27	.0498100	20.0762853	8.0867233	162.3513642	.0425503	23.5016027	97.7820981	2298.0360223	324
28	.0445727	22.4352488	8.1312960	182.4276495	.0378548	26.4167185	98.2616359	2595.7499765	336
29	.0398861	25.0713906	8.1711821	204.8628984	.0336775	29.6934224	98.6882561	2930.3920783	348
30	.0356923	28.0172789	8.2068744	229.9342889	.0299611	33.3765655	99.0677983	3306.5428589	360
31	.0319394	31.3093092	8.2388138	257.9515679	.0266549	37.5165620	99.4054576	3729.3510142	372
32	.0285811	34.9881531	8.2673949	289.2608771	.0237135	42.1700797	99.7058558	4204.6038793	384
33	.0255759	39.0992610	8.2929708	324.2490302	.0210967	47.4008151	99.9731046	4738.8066447	396
34	.0228867	43.6934242	8.3158575	363.3482912	.0187686	53.2803658	100.2108623	5339.2713983	408
35	.0204803	48.8274016	8.3363378	407.0417154	.0166975	59.8892102	100.4223831	6014.2172123	420
36	.0183269	54.5646212	8.3546647	455.8691170	.0148549	67.3178092	100.6105624	6772.8826446	432
37	.0163999	60.9759642	8.3710646	510.4337382	.0132157	75.6678444	100.7779758	7625.6521947	444
38	.0146755	68.1406400	8.3857402	571.4097025	.0117573	85.0536098	100.9269150	8584.1984452	456
39	.0131325	76.1471652	8.3988726	639.5503425	.0104599	95.6035763	101.0594186	9661.6418345	468
40	.0117516	85.0944572	8.4106243	715.6975078	.0093056	107.4621503	101.1773002	10872.7302475	480
41	.0105160	95.0930559	8.4211403	800.7919649	.0082787	120.7916503	101.2821735	12234.0408820	492
42	.0094103	106.2664899	8.4305506	895.8850208	.0073652	135.7745284	101.3754739	13764.2071554	504
43	.0084209	118.7528025	8.4389715	1002.1515107	.0065524	152.6158680	101.4584784	15484.1737558	516
44	.0075354	132.7062568	8.4465069	1120.9043133	.0058293	171.5461909	101.5323234	17417.4833302	528
45	.0067431	148.2992420	8.4532500	1253.6105701	.0051861	192.8246126	101.5980194	19590.5987322	540
46	.0060341	165.7244029	8.4592841	1401.9098120	.0046138	216.7423888	101.6564658	22033.2652420	552
47	.0053997	185.1970203	8.4646838	1567.6342150	.0041046	243.6269026	101.7084626	24778.9177153	564
48	.0048319	206.9576701	8.4695157	1752.8312352	.0036517	273.8461452	101.7547215	27865.1382343	576
49	.0043239	231.2751964	8.4738395	1959.7889054	.0032487	307.8137531	101.7958756	31334.1705262	588
50	.0038692	258.4500320	8.4777088	2191.0641017	.0028902	345.9946698	101.8324884	35233.4981888	600

Present and Future Value

	Annual Payments				Monthly Payments				
Years	Present Value	Future Value	Present Value of 1 per Period	Future Value of 1 per Period	Present Value	Future Value	Present Value of 1 per Period	Future Value of 1 per Period	Months
					.9900990	1.0100000	0.9900990	1.0000000	1
					.9802960	1.0201000	1.9703951	2.0100000	2
					.9705901	1.0303010	2.9409852	3.0301000	3
					.9609803	1.0406040	3.9019656	4.0604010	4
					.9514657	1.0510101	4.8534312	5.1010050	5
					.9420452	1.0615202	5.7954765	6.1520151	6
					.9327181	1.0721354	6.7281945	7.2135352	7
					.9234832	1.0828567	7.6516778	8.2856706	8
					.9143398	1.0936853	8.5660176	9.3685273	9
					.9052870	1.1046221	9.4713045	10.4622125	10
					.8963237	1.1156683	10.3676282	11.5668347	11
1	.8928571	1.1200000	0.8928571	1.0000000	.8874492	1.1268250	11.2550775	12.6825030	12
2	.7971939	1.2544000	1.6900510	2.1200000	.7875661	1.2697346	21.2433873	26.9734649	24
3	.7117802	1.4049280	2.4018313	3.3744000	.6989249	1.4307688	30.1075050	43.0768784	36
4	.6355181	1.5735194	3.0373493	4.7793280	.6202604	1.6122261	37.9739595	61.2226078	48
5	.5674269	1.7623417	3.6047762	6.3528474	.5504496	1.8166967	44.9550384	81.6696699	60
6	.5066311	1.9738227	4.1114073	8.1151890	.4884961	2.0470993	51.1503915	104.7099312	72
7	.4523492	2.2106814	4.5637565	10.0890117	.4335155	2.3067227	56.6484528	130.6722744	84
8	.4038832	2.4759632	4.9676398	12.2996931	.3847230	2.5992729	61.5277030	159.9272926	96
9	.3606100	2.7730788	5.3282498	14.7756563	.3414221	2.9289258	65.8577898	192.8925793	108
10	.3219732	3.1058482	5.6502230	17.5487351	.3029948	3.3003869	69.7005220	230.0386895	120
11	.2874761	3.4785500	5.9376991	20.6545833	.2688925	3.7189586	73.1107518	271.8958562	132
12	.2566751	3.8959760	6.1943742	24.1331333	.2386284	4.1906156	76.1371575	319.0615594	144
13	.2291742	4.3634931	6.4235484	28.0291093	.2117706	4.7220905	78.8229389	372.2090543	156
14	.2046198	4.8871123	6.6281682	32.3926024	.1879357	5.3209698	81.2064335	432.0969818	168
15	.1826963	5.4735658	6.8108645	37.2797147	.1667834	5.9958020	83.3216640	499.5801975	180
16	.1631217	6.1303937	6.9739862	42.7532804	.1480118	6.7562197	85.1988236	575.6219742	192
17	.1456443	6.8660409	7.1196305	48.8836741	.1313529	7.6130775	86.8647075	661.3077514	204
18	.1300396	7.6899658	7.2496701	55.7497150	.1165691	8.5786063	88.3430948	757.8606299	216
19	.1161068	8.6127617	7.3657769	63.4396808	.1034491	9.6665883	89.6550886	866.6588301	228
20	.1036668	9.6462931	7.4694436	72.0524424	.0918058	10.8925537	90.8194163	989.2553654	240
21	.0925596	10.8038483	7.5620032	81.6987355	.0814730	12.2740021	91.8526982	1127.4002099	252
22	.0826425	12.1003101	7.6446457	92.5025838	.0723032	13.8306528	92.7696833	1283.0652785	264
23	.0737880	13.5523473	7.7184337	104.6028939	.0641654	15.5847257	93.5834610	1458.4725742	276
24	.0658821	15.1786289	7.7843158	118.1552411	.0569435	17.5612591	94.3056475	1656.1259053	288
25	.0588220	17.0000644	7.8431391	133.3338701	.0505345	19.7884663	94.9465513	1878.8466262	300
26	.0525208	19.0400721	7.8956599	150.3339345	.0448468	22.2981391	95.5153208	2129.8139092	312
27	.0468936	21.3248808	7.9425535	169.3740066	.0397993	25.1261013	96.0200749	2412.6101254	324
28	.0418693	23.8838665	7.9844228	190.6988874	.0353198	28.3127198	96.4680186	2731.2719803	336
29	.0373833	26.7499305	8.0218060	214.5827539	.0313445	31.9034813	96.8655458	3090.3481345	348
30	.0333779	29.9599221	8.0551840	241.3326843	.0278167	35.9496413	97.2183311	3494.9641328	360
31	.0298017	33.5551128	8.0849857	271.2926065	.0246859	40.5089557	97.5314101	3950.8955672	372
32	.0266087	37.5817263	8.1115944	304.8477192	.0219075	45.6465052	97.8092518	4464.6505196	384
33	.0237577	42.0915335	8.1353521	342.4294455	.0194418	51.4356246	98.0558222	5043.5624593	396
34	.0212123	47.1425175	8.1565644	384.5209790	.0172536	57.9589492	98.2746409	5695.8949232	408
35	.0189395	52.7996196	8.1755039	431.6634965	.0153117	65.3095947	98.4688314	6430.9594715	420
36	.0169103	59.1355739	8.1924142	484.4631161	.0135883	73.5924860	98.6411656	7259.2486032	432
37	.0150985	66.2318428	8.2075127	543.5986900	.0120590	82.9258553	98.7941035	8192.5855291	444
38	.0134808	74.1796639	8.2209935	609.8305328	.0107017	93.4429294	98.9298281	9244.2929387	456
39	.0120364	83.0812236	8.2330299	684.0101967	.0094972	105.2938317	99.0502768	10429.3831722	468
40	.0107468	93.0509704	8.2437767	767.0914203	.0084283	118.6477251	99.1571688	11764.7725103	480
41	.0095954	104.2170869	8.2533720	860.1423908	.0074797	133.6952264	99.2520301	13269.5226414	492
42	.0085673	116.7231373	8.2619393	964.3594777	.0066379	150.6511275	99.3362147	14965.1127532	504
43	.0076494	130.7299138	8.2695887	1081.0826150	.0058908	169.7574613	99.4109243	16875.7461321	516
44	.0068298	146.4175035	8.2764185	1211.8125288	.0052277	191.2869565	99.4772252	19028.6956468	528
45	.0060980	163.9876039	8.2825165	1358.2300323	.0046394	215.5469305	99.5360639	21454.6930486	540
46	.0054447	183.6661163	8.2879611	1522.2176361	.0041172	242.8836764	99.5882803	24188.3676440	552
47	.0048613	205.7060503	8.2928225	1705.8837525	.0036538	273.6874060	99.6346197	27268.7406023	564
48	.0043405	230.3907763	8.2971629	1911.5898028	.0032426	308.3978195	99.6757435	30739.7819538	576
49	.0038754	258.0376695	8.3010383	2141.9805791	.0028776	347.5103823	99.7122388	34651.0382294	588
50	.0034602	289.0021898	8.3044985	2400.0182486	.0025537	391.5833970	99.7446266	39058.3396999	600

Present and Future Value

	Annual Payments				Monthly Payments				
Years	Present Value	Future Value	Present Value of 1 per Period	Future Value of 1 per Period	Present Value	Future Value	Present Value of 1 per Period	Future Value of 1 per Period	Months
					.9898948	1.0102083	0.9898948	1.0000000	1
					.9798918	1.0205209	1.9697866	2.0102083	2
					.9699898	1.0309387	2.9397764	3.0307292	3
					.9601879	1.0414629	3.8999642	4.0616679	4
					.9504850	1.0520945	4.8504492	5.1031308	5
					.9408802	1.0628346	5.7913294	6.1552252	6
					.9313724	1.0736844	6.7227018	7.2180598	7
					.9219607	1.0846449	7.6446626	8.2917442	8
					.9126442	1.0957173	8.5573067	9.3763891	9
					.9034217	1.1069028	9.4607285	10.4721064	10
					.8942925	1.1182024	10.3550210	11.5790091	11
1	.8908686	1.1225000	0.8908686	1.0000000	.8852555	1.1296174	11.2402765	12.6972115	12
2	.7936469	1.2600063	1.6845155	2.1225000	.7836773	1.2760354	21.1907931	27.0402021	24
3	.7070351	1.4143570	2.3915505	3.3825062	.6937547	1.4414317	29.9995429	43.2422935	36
4	.6298753	1.5876158	3.0214258	4.7968633	.6141501	1.6282663	37.7975371	61.5444572	48
5	.5611362	1.7820987	3.5825620	6.3844790	.5436798	1.8393179	44.7007545	82.2188992	60
6	.4998986	2.0004058	4.0824606	8.1665777	.4812955	2.0777255	50.8118657	105.5731080	72
7	.4453439	2.2454555	4.5278045	10.1669835	.4260695	2.3470348	56.2217606	131.9544279	84
8	.3967429	2.5205238	4.9245475	12.4124389	.3771804	2.6512513	61.0108999	161.7552249	96
9	.3534458	2.8292879	5.2779933	14.9329627	.3339010	2.9948995	65.2505118	195.4187229	108
10	.3148738	3.1758757	5.5928671	17.7622506	.2955877	3.3830904	69.0036517	233.4455948	120
11	.2805112	3.5649205	5.8733782	20.9381263	.2616707	3.8215977	72.3261394	276.4014097	132
12	.2498986	4.0016232	6.1232768	24.5030468	.2316454	4.3169432	75.2673900	324.9250443	144
13	.2226268	4.4918221	6.3459036	28.5046701	.2050654	4.8764940	77.8711482	379.7381847	156
14	.1983312	5.0420703	6.5442349	32.9964921	.1815352	5.5085723	80.1761396	441.6560600	168
15	.1766871	5.6597239	6.7209219	38.0385624	.1607051	6.2225789	82.2166459	511.5995674	180
16	.1574050	6.3530401	6.8783269	43.6982863	.1422651	7.0291332	84.0230153	590.6089680	192
17	.1402271	7.1312875	7.0185540	50.0513264	.1259409	7.9402310	85.6221139	679.8593591	204
18	.1249239	8.0048702	7.1434780	57.1826139	.1114899	8.9694228	87.0377246	780.6781510	216
19	.1112908	8.9854668	7.2547688	65.1874841	.0986970	10.1320158	88.2909019	894.5648093	228
20	.0991455	10.0861865	7.3539143	74.1729509	.0873721	11.4453010	89.4002839	1023.2131564	240
21	.0883256	11.3217243	7.4422399	84.2591374	.0773466	12.9288108	90.3823705	1168.5365636	252
22	.0786865	12.7086580	7.5209264	95.5808817	.0684715	14.6046092	91.2517681	1332.6964082	264
23	.0700993	14.2654686	7.5910258	108.2895397	.0606148	16.4976202	92.0214070	1518.1342198	276
24	.0624493	16.0129885	7.6534751	122.5550083	.0536596	18.6359983	92.7027342	1727.6079923	288
25	.0556341	17.9745796	7.7091092	138.5679968	.0475024	21.0515473	93.3058828	1964.2332038	300
26	.0495627	20.1764656	7.7586719	156.5425764	.0420518	23.7801934	93.8398234	2231.5291522	312
27	.0441538	22.6480826	7.8028257	176.7190420	.0372266	26.8625195	94.3124973	2533.4712978	324
28	.0393353	25.4224728	7.8421610	199.3671247	.0329550	30.3443686	94.7309345	2874.5503895	336
29	.0350426	28.5367257	7.8772036	224.7895975	.0291736	34.2775257	95.1013583	3259.8392551	348
30	.0312183	32.0324746	7.9084219	253.3263232	.0258261	38.7204884	95.4292780	3695.0682492	360
31	.0278114	35.9564527	7.9362333	285.3587977	.0228627	43.7393361	95.7195707	4186.7104797	372
32	.0247763	40.3611182	7.9610096	321.3152505	.0202393	49.4087138	95.9765540	4742.0780819	384
33	.0220724	45.3053552	7.9830821	361.6763686	.0179170	55.8129412	96.2040498	5369.4309707	396
34	.0196636	50.8552612	8.0027457	406.9817238	.0158611	63.0472677	96.4054417	6078.0996893	408
35	.0175177	57.0850307	8.0202635	457.8369850	.0140411	71.2192885	96.5837251	6878.6241817	420
36	.0156060	64.0779469	8.0358694	514.9220156	.0124300	80.4505452	96.7415514	7782.9105514	432
37	.0139029	71.9274954	8.0497723	578.9999625	.0110037	90.8783331	96.8812680	8804.4081397	444
38	.0123856	80.7386136	8.0621580	650.9274580	.0097411	102.6577434	97.0049528	9958.3095563	456
39	.0110340	90.6290938	8.0731920	731.6660716	.0086234	115.9639698	97.1144456	11261.7766369	468
40	.0098298	101.7311578	8.0830218	822.2951653	.0076339	130.9949143	97.2113746	12734.1956889	480
41	.0087571	114.1932246	8.0917789	924.0263231	.0067579	147.9741303	97.2971816	14397.4658223	492
42	.0078014	128.1818946	8.0995803	1038.2195476	.0059825	167.1541475	97.3731427	16276.3246518	504
43	.0069500	143.8841767	8.1065303	1166.4014422	.0052960	188.8202280	97.4403876	18398.7162165	516
44	.0061916	161.5099883	8.1127219	1310.2856189	.0046884	213.2946089	97.4999166	20796.2065886	528
45	.0055159	181.2949619	8.1182378	1471.7956072	.0041504	240.9412946	97.5526150	23504.4533513	540
46	.0049139	203.5035947	8.1231517	1653.0905691	.0036742	272.1714709	97.5992665	26563.7359297	552
47	.0043777	228.4327851	8.1275293	1856.5941638	.0032526	307.4496205	97.6405650	30019.5546622	564
48	.0038999	256.4158012	8.1314293	2085.0269489	.0028794	347.3004309	97.6771248	33923.3075213	576
49	.0034743	287.8267369	8.1349036	2341.4427501	.0025490	392.3165985	97.7094895	38333.0545492	588
50	.0030952	323.0855122	8.1379987	2629.2694870	.0022565	443.1676432	97.7381405	43314.3813779	600

Present and Future Value

12.500% Discount Rate   12.500% Discount Rate

| | Annual Payments | | | | Monthly Payments | | | | |
Years	Present Value	Future Value	Present Value of 1 per Period	Future Value of 1 per Period	Present Value	Future Value	Present Value of 1 per Period	Future Value of 1 per Period	Months
					.9896907	1.0104167	0.9896907	1.0000000	1
					.9794877	1.0209418	1.9691784	2.0104167	2
					.9693899	1.0315767	2.9385684	3.0313585	3
					.9593962	1.0423222	3.8979646	4.0629352	4
					.9495055	1.0531798	4.8474701	5.1052574	5
					.9397168	1.0641504	5.7871869	6.1584372	6
					.9300290	1.0752353	6.7172159	7.2225876	7
					.9204411	1.0864357	7.6376570	8.2978228	8
					.9109520	1.0977527	8.5486089	9.3842585	9
					.9015607	1.1091876	9.4501697	10.4820112	10
					.8922663	1.1207417	10.3424360	11.5911988	11
1	.8888889	1.1250000	0.8888889	1.0000000	.8830677	1.1324160	11.2255036	12.7119405	12
2	.7901235	1.2656250	1.6790123	2.1250000	.7798085	1.2823661	21.1383830	27.1071458	24
3	.7023320	1.4238281	2.3813443	3.3906250	.6886237	1.4521720	29.8921263	43.4085073	36
4	.6242951	1.6018066	3.0056394	4.8144531	.6081013	1.6444628	37.6222740	61.8684307	48
5	.5549290	1.8020325	3.5605683	6.4162598	.5369946	1.8622161	44.4485175	82.7727442	60
6	.4932702	2.0272865	4.0538385	8.2182922	.4742026	2.1088034	50.4765524	106.4451242	72
7	.4384624	2.2806973	4.4923009	10.2455788	.4187530	2.3880428	55.7997152	133.2521071	84
8	.3897443	2.5657845	4.8820453	12.5262761	.3697872	2.7042580	60.5004281	163.6087648	96
9	.3464394	2.8865076	5.2284847	15.0920606	.3265471	3.0623451	64.6514758	197.9851310	108
10	.3079461	3.2473210	5.5364308	17.9785682	.2883632	3.4678487	68.3171317	236.9134798	120
11	.2737299	3.6532362	5.8101607	21.2258892	.2546442	3.9270476	71.5541540	280.9965666	132
12	.2433155	4.1098907	6.0534762	24.8791254	.2248681	4.4470517	74.4126637	330.9169614	144
13	.2162804	4.6236270	6.2697566	28.9890161	.1985737	5.0359127	76.9369213	387.4476176	156
14	.1922493	5.2015804	6.4620059	33.6126431	.1753540	5.7027483	79.1660115	451.4638398	168
15	.1708882	5.8517779	6.6328941	38.8142234	.1548495	6.4578837	81.1344490	523.9568370	180
16	.1519007	6.5832502	6.7847948	44.6660014	.1367426	7.3130111	82.8727125	606.0490703	192
17	.1350228	7.4061564	6.9198176	51.2492515	.1207530	8.2813712	84.4077168	699.0116326	204
18	.1200203	8.3319260	7.0398378	58.6554080	.1066330	9.3779576	85.7632295	804.2839298	216
19	.1066847	9.3734167	7.1465225	66.9873340	.0941642	10.6197497	86.9602389	923.4959685	228
20	.0948308	10.5450938	7.2413534	76.3607507	.0831533	12.0259749	88.0172792	1058.4935939	240
21	.0842941	11.8632306	7.3256474	86.9058446	.0734300	13.6184070	88.9507174	1211.3670713	252
22	.0749281	13.3461344	7.4005755	98.7690752	.0648437	15.4217026	89.7750064	1384.4834500	264
23	.0666027	15.0144012	7.4671782	112.1152095	.0572614	17.4637835	90.5029094	1580.5232153	276
24	.0592024	16.8912013	7.5263806	127.1296107	.0505657	19.7762687	91.1456970	1802.5217912	288
25	.0526244	19.0026015	7.5790050	144.0208121	.0446529	22.3949640	91.7133220	2053.9165408	300
26	.0467772	21.3779267	7.6257822	163.0234136	.0394315	25.3604166	92.2145732	2338.5999892	312
27	.0415798	24.0501675	7.6673620	184.4013403	.0348207	28.7185427	92.6572120	2660.9800944	324
28	.0369598	27.0564385	7.7043218	208.4515078	.0307490	32.5213385	93.0480920	3026.0484986	336
29	.0328531	30.4384933	7.7371749	235.5079463	.0271535	36.8276856	93.3932655	3439.4578175	348
30	.0292028	34.2433050	7.7663777	265.9464396	.0239784	41.7042621	93.6980770	3907.6091639	360
31	.0259580	38.5237181	7.7923357	300.1897446	.0211745	47.2265756	93.9672462	4437.7512608	372
32	.0230738	43.3391828	7.8154095	338.7134626	.0186985	53.4801321	94.2049409	5038.0926782	384
33	.0205101	48.7565807	7.8359196	382.0526454	.0165121	60.5617597	94.4148413	5717.9289326	396
34	.0182312	54.8511533	7.8541507	430.8092261	.0145813	68.5811085	94.6001976	6487.7864160	408
35	.0162055	61.7075474	7.8703562	485.6603794	.0128763	77.6623477	94.7638798	7359.5853836	420
36	.0144049	69.4209909	7.8847611	547.3679268	.0113706	87.9460888	94.9084222	8346.8245238	432
37	.0128043	78.0986147	7.8975654	616.7889177	.0100410	99.5915622	95.0360629	9464.7899678	444
38	.0113816	87.8609415	7.9089470	694.8875324	.0088669	112.7790831	95.1487783	10730.7919760	456
39	.0101170	98.8435592	7.9190640	782.7484739	.0078301	127.7128434	95.2483137	12164.4329648	468
40	.0089929	111.1990041	7.9280569	881.5920332	.0069145	144.6240732	95.3362101	13787.9110253	480
41	.0079937	125.0988797	7.9360506	992.7910373	.0061060	163.7746212	95.4138286	15626.3636321	492
42	.0071055	140.7362396	7.9431561	1117.8899170	.0053920	185.4610090	95.4823710	17708.2568646	504
43	.0063160	158.3282696	7.9494721	1258.6261566	.0047615	210.0190226	95.5428985	20065.8261679	516
44	.0056142	178.1193033	7.9550863	1416.9544262	.0042047	237.8289112	95.5963485	22735.5754776	528
45	.0049904	200.3842162	7.9600767	1595.0737294	.0037130	269.3212754	95.6435484	25758.8424358	540
46	.0044359	225.4322432	7.9645126	1795.4579456	.0032789	304.9837339	95.6852291	29182.4384518	552
47	.0039430	253.6112736	7.9684557	2020.8901888	.0028955	345.3684741	95.7220360	33059.3735168	564
48	.0035049	285.3126828	7.9719606	2274.5014624	.0025569	391.1008020	95.7545390	37449.6769953	576
49	.0031155	320.9767682	7.9750761	2559.8141452	.0022579	442.8888240	95.7832413	42421.3271031	588
50	.0027693	361.0988642	7.9778454	2880.7909134	.0019939	501.5344111	95.8085874	48051.3034622	600

Present and Future Value

	Annual Payments				Monthly Payments				
Years	Present Value	Future Value	Present Value of 1 per Period	Future Value of 1 per Period	Present Value	Future Value	Present Value of 1 per Period	Future Value of 1 per Period	Months
					.9894867	1.0106250	0.9894867	1.0000000	1
					.9790839	1.0213629	1.9685706	2.0106250	2
					.9687905	1.0322149	2.9373612	3.0319879	3
					.9586054	1.0431822	3.8959665	4.0642028	4
					.9485273	1.0542660	4.8444938	5.1073849	5
					.9385551	1.0654675	5.7830489	6.1616509	6
					.9286878	1.0767881	6.7117367	7.2271184	7
					.9189242	1.0882290	7.6306609	8.3039066	8
					.9092633	1.0997914	8.5399242	9.3921356	9
					.8997040	1.1114767	9.4396282	10.4919270	10
					.8902451	1.1232862	10.3298733	11.6034037	11
1	.8869180	1.1275000	0.8869180	1.0000000	.8808857	1.1352211	11.2107590	12.7266899	12
2	.7866235	1.2712563	1.6735414	2.1275000	.7759596	1.2887269	21.0861561	27.1742965	24
3	.6976705	1.4333414	2.3712119	3.3987563	.6835317	1.4629899	29.7852520	43.5755242	36
4	.6187765	1.6160925	2.9899884	4.8320977	.6021133	1.6608170	37.4481611	62.1945435	48
5	.5488040	1.8221442	3.5387924	6.4481901	.5303930	1.8853945	44.1983080	83.3312467	60
6	.4867441	2.0544676	4.0255365	8.2703344	.4672156	2.1403396	50.1444159	107.3260778	72
7	.4317021	2.3164123	4.4572385	10.3248020	.4115635	2.4297586	55.3822571	134.5655159	84
8	.3828843	2.6117548	4.8401229	12.6412143	.3625404	2.7583132	59.9961965	165.4883002	96
9	.3395870	2.9447536	5.1797099	15.2529691	.3193567	3.1312953	64.0605497	200.5924967	108
10	.3011858	3.3202096	5.4808957	18.1977226	.2813167	3.5547124	67.6407802	240.4435207	120
11	.2671271	3.7435364	5.7480228	21.5179323	.2478079	4.0353845	70.7945540	285.6832432	132
12	.2369198	4.2208372	5.9849426	25.2614686	.2182904	4.5810535	73.5726683	337.0403297	144
13	.2101284	4.7589940	6.1950710	29.4823059	.1922889	5.2005085	76.0198693	395.3419771	156
14	.1863667	5.3657657	6.3814377	34.2412999	.1693845	5.9037269	78.1755737	461.5272361	168
15	.1652920	6.0499009	6.5467297	39.6070656	.1492084	6.7020352	80.0745028	536.6621374	180
16	.1466004	6.8212632	6.6933301	45.6569665	.1314356	7.6082916	81.7472423	621.9568611	192
17	.1300225	7.6909743	6.8233526	52.4782297	.1157797	8.6370931	83.2207346	718.7852295	204
18	.1153193	8.6715735	6.9386720	60.1692040	.1019887	9.8050101	84.5187128	828.7068345	216
19	.1022788	9.7771991	7.0409507	68.8407775	.0898404	11.1308542	85.6620833	953.4921576	228
20	.0907129	11.0237920	7.1316636	78.6179766	.0791391	12.6359803	86.6692620	1095.1510870	240
21	.0804549	12.4293255	7.2121185	89.6417686	.0697125	14.3446312	87.5564713	1255.9652897	252
22	.0713569	14.0140645	7.2834754	102.0710941	.0614087	16.2843277	88.3380012	1438.5249626	264
23	.0632877	15.8008577	7.3467631	116.0851586	.0540941	18.4863121	89.0264398	1645.7705517	276
24	.0561310	17.8154671	7.4028941	131.8860164	.0476507	20.9860512	89.6328754	1881.0401132	288
25	.0497836	20.0869391	7.4526777	149.7014835	.0419748	23.8238077	90.1670759	2148.1230789	300
26	.0441540	22.6480239	7.4968317	169.7884226	.0369750	27.0452887	90.6376455	2451.3212917	312
27	.0391609	25.5356469	7.5359926	192.4364465	.0325708	30.7023819	91.0521635	2795.5182943	324
28	.0347325	28.7914419	7.5707252	217.9720934	.0286911	34.8539911	91.4173065	3186.2579874	336
29	.0308049	32.4623508	7.6015301	246.7635353	.0252736	39.5669854	91.7389557	3629.8339238	348
30	.0273214	36.6013005	7.6288515	279.2258861	.0222631	44.9172759	92.0222919	4133.3906774	360
31	.0242319	41.2679663	7.6530834	315.8271865	.0196113	50.9910385	92.2718787	4705.0389192	372
32	.0214917	46.5296320	7.6745751	357.0951528	.0172753	57.8861018	92.4917361	5353.9860536	384
33	.0190614	52.4621601	7.6936364	403.6247848	.0152176	65.7135230	92.6854054	6090.6845205	396
34	.0169059	59.1510855	7.7105423	456.0869449	.0134049	74.5993766	92.8560059	6927.0001498	408
35	.0149941	66.6928489	7.7255364	515.2380303	.0118082	84.6867849	93.0062854	7876.4032817	420
36	.0132985	75.1961871	7.7388349	581.9308792	.0104017	96.1382234	93.1386645	8954.1857306	432
37	.0117947	84.7837010	7.7506296	657.1270663	.0091627	109.1381378	93.2552753	10177.7070864	444
38	.0104609	95.5936228	7.7610906	741.9107673	.0080713	123.8959147	93.3579961	11566.6743214	456
39	.0092780	107.7818097	7.7703686	837.5043901	.0071099	140.6492541	93.4484814	13143.4592062	468
40	.0082288	121.5239905	7.7785974	945.2861998	.0062630	159.6679981	93.5281886	14933.4586461	480
41	.0072983	137.0182993	7.7858957	1066.8101903	.0055170	181.2584773	93.5984016	16965.5037437	492
42	.0064730	154.4881324	7.7923687	1203.8284896	.0048598	205.7684444	93.6602511	19272.3241742	504
43	.0057410	174.1853693	7.7981097	1358.3166220	.0042810	233.5926756	93.7147335	21891.0753549	516
44	.0050918	196.3940039	7.8032015	1532.5019913	.0037710	265.1793295	93.7627263	24863.9368987	528
45	.0045160	221.4342394	7.8077175	1728.8959952	.0033218	301.0371649	93.8050024	28238.7919915	540
46	.0040053	249.6671049	7.8117229	1950.3302346	.0029262	341.7437355	93.8422429	32069.9986350	552
47	.0035524	281.4996608	7.8152753	2199.9973395	.0025776	387.9546925	93.8750475	36419.2651790	564
48	.0031507	317.3908675	7.8184260	2481.4970003	.0022706	440.4143451	93.9039446	41356.6442427	576
49	.0027944	357.8582031	7.8212204	2798.8878678	.0020001	499.9676485	93.9293996	46961.6610363	588
50	.0024784	403.4851240	7.8236988	3156.7460710	.0017619	567.5738140	93.9518226	53324.5942546	600

Present and Future Value

13.000% Discount Rate   13.000% Discount Rate

| | Annual Payments | | | | Monthly Payments | | | | |
Years	Present Value	Future Value	Present Value of 1 per Period	Future Value of 1 per Period	Present Value	Future Value	Present Value of 1 per Period	Future Value of 1 per Period	Months
					.9892828	1.0108333	0.9892828	1.0000000	1
					.9786804	1.0217840	1.9679632	2.0108333	2
					.9681917	1.0328534	2.9361548	3.0326174	3
					.9578153	1.0440426	3.8939701	4.0654707	4
					.9475502	1.0553531	4.8415203	5.1095133	5
					.9373951	1.0667861	5.7789154	6.1648664	6
					.9273488	1.0783429	6.7062642	7.2316524	7
					.9174102	1.0900249	7.6236744	8.3099953	8
					.9075781	1.1018336	8.5312525	9.4000203	9
					.8978514	1.1137701	9.4291039	10.5018538	10
					.8882289	1.1258359	10.3173328	11.6156239	11
1	.8849558	1.1300000	0.8849558	1.0000000	.8787095	1.1380325	11.1960423	12.7414598	12
2	.7831467	1.2769000	1.6681024	2.1300000	.7721305	1.2951179	21.0341116	27.2416550	24
3	.6930502	1.4428970	2.3611526	3.4069000	.6784784	1.4738863	29.6789169	43.7433481	36
4	.6133187	1.6304736	2.9744713	4.8497970	.5961854	1.6773305	37.2751898	62.5228108	48
5	.5427599	1.8424352	3.5172313	6.4802706	.5238738	1.9088565	43.9501072	83.8944494	60
6	.4803185	2.0819518	3.9975498	8.3227058	.4603329	2.1723407	49.8154209	108.2160683	72
7	.4250606	2.3526055	4.4226104	10.4046575	.4044989	2.4721943	54.9693280	135.8948606	84
8	.3761599	2.6584442	4.7987703	12.7572630	.3554371	2.8134374	59.4981153	167.3942253	96
9	.3328848	3.0040419	5.1316551	15.4157072	.3123260	3.2017832	63.4776040	203.2415254	108
10	.2945883	3.3945674	5.4262435	18.4197492	.2744438	3.6437333	66.9744186	244.0369174	120
11	.2606977	3.8358612	5.6869411	21.8143165	.2411564	4.1466868	70.0471030	290.4633985	132
12	.2307059	4.3345231	5.9176470	25.6501777	.2119064	4.7190643	72.7471001	343.2982421	144
13	.2041645	4.8980111	6.1218115	29.9847008	.1862042	5.3704484	75.1196133	403.4260102	156
14	.1806766	5.5347525	6.3024881	34.8827119	.1636194	6.1117448	77.2043633	471.8533634	168
15	.1598908	6.2542704	6.4623788	40.4174644	.1437739	6.9553641	79.0362530	549.7259140	180
16	.1414962	7.0673255	6.6038751	46.6717348	.1263355	7.9154302	80.6459519	638.3474059	192
17	.1252179	7.9860778	6.7290930	53.7390603	.1110122	9.0080167	82.0604098	739.2015423	204
18	.1108123	9.0242680	6.8399053	61.7251382	.0975475	10.2514156	83.3033074	853.9768255	216
19	.0980640	10.1974228	6.9379693	70.7494062	.0857159	11.6664439	84.3954533	984.5948258	228
20	.0867823	11.5230878	7.0247516	80.9468290	.0753194	13.2767922	85.3551324	1133.2423528	240
21	.0767985	13.0210892	7.1015501	92.4699167	.0661839	15.1094207	86.1984116	1302.4080669	252
22	.0679633	14.7138308	7.1695133	105.4910059	.0581564	17.1950116	86.9394091	1494.9241443	264
23	.0601445	16.6266288	7.2296578	120.2048367	.0511026	19.5684817	87.5905306	1714.0136936	276
24	.0532252	18.7880905	7.2828830	136.8314654	.0449043	22.2695678	88.1626773	1963.3447171	288
25	.0471020	21.2305423	7.3299850	155.6195559	.0394579	25.3434915	88.6654281	2247.0915205	300
26	.0416831	23.9905128	7.3716681	176.8500982	.0346720	28.8417165	89.1072000	2570.0045993	312
27	.0368877	27.1092794	7.4085559	200.8406110	.0304666	32.8228102	89.4953892	2937.4901717	324
28	.0326440	30.6334858	7.4411999	227.9498904	.0267713	37.3534241	89.8364947	3355.7006897	336
29	.0288885	34.6158389	7.4700884	258.5833762	.0235242	42.5094100	90.1362274	3831.6378433	348
30	.0255651	39.1158980	7.4956534	293.1992151	.0206709	48.3770893	90.3996054	4373.2697833	360
31	.0226239	44.2009647	7.5182774	332.3151130	.0181638	55.0546990	90.6310381	4989.6645240	372
32	.0200212	49.9470901	7.5382986	376.5160777	.0159607	62.6540357	90.8344003	5691.1417606	384
33	.0177179	56.4402118	7.5560164	426.4631678	.0140248	71.3023278	91.0130965	6489.4456408	396
34	.0156795	63.7774394	7.5716960	482.9033796	.0123237	81.1443650	91.1701186	7397.9413868	408
35	.0138757	72.0685065	7.5855716	546.6808190	.0108290	92.3449231	91.3080955	8431.8390551	420
36	.0122794	81.4374123	7.5978510	618.7493254	.0095155	105.0915220	91.4293370	9608.4481842	432
37	.0108667	92.0242759	7.6087177	700.1867377	.0083614	119.5975656	91.5358732	10947.4675914	444
38	.0096165	103.9874318	7.6183343	792.2110137	.0073472	136.1059143	91.6294874	12471.3151703	456
39	.0085102	117.5057979	7.6268445	896.1984454	.0064561	154.8929515	91.7117472	14205.5032121	468
40	.0075312	132.7815516	7.6343756	1013.7042433	.0056730	176.2732099	91.7840297	16179.0655328	480
41	.0066647	150.0431533	7.6410404	1146.4857950	.0049849	200.6046385	91.8475450	18425.0435584	492
42	.0058980	169.5487633	7.6469384	1296.5289483	.0043803	228.2945946	91.9033564	20981.0395044	504
43	.0052195	191.5901025	7.6521579	1466.0777116	.0038490	259.8066641	91.9523985	23889.8459139	516
44	.0046190	216.4968158	7.6567769	1657.6678141	.0033822	295.6684226	91.9954923	27200.1620906	528
45	.0040876	244.6414019	7.6608645	1874.1646299	.0029719	336.4802688	92.0333592	30967.4094241	540
46	.0036174	276.4447841	7.6644819	2118.8060318	.0026115	382.9254753	92.0666332	35254.6592559	552
47	.0032012	312.3826061	7.6676831	2395.2508160	.0022947	435.7816289	92.0958713	40133.6888213	564
48	.0028329	352.9923449	7.6705160	2707.6334220	.0020164	495.9336486	92.1215632	45686.1829455	576
49	.0025070	398.8813497	7.6730230	3060.6257669	.0017718	564.3886008	92.1441389	52005.1016127	588
50	.0022186	450.7359252	7.6752416	3459.5071166	.0015569	642.2925600	92.1639763	59196.2363048	600

Present and Future Value

13.250% Discount Rate

13.250% Discount Rate

Annual Payments

Monthly Payments

Years	Present Value	Future Value	Present Value of 1 per Period	Future Value of 1 per Period	Present Value	Future Value	Present Value of 1 per Period	Future Value of 1 per Period	Months
					.9890789	1.0110417	0.9890789	1.0000000	1
					.9782771	1.0222053	1.9673560	2.0110417	2
					.9675933	1.0334921	2.9349493	3.0332469	3
					.9570261	1.0449036	3.8919754	4.0667390	4
					.9465743	1.0564411	4.8385498	5.1116426	5
					.9362367	1.0681059	5.7747865	6.1680837	6
					.9260120	1.0798996	6.7007985	7.2361896	7
					.9158990	1.0918235	7.6166975	8.3160892	8
					.9058964	1.1038790	8.5225938	9.4079127	9
					.8960030	1.1160677	9.4185968	10.5117917	10
					.8862177	1.1283909	10.3048145	11.6278594	11
1	.8830022	1.1325000	0.8830022	1.0000000	.8765392	1.1408503	11.1813537	12.7562503	12
2	.7796929	1.2825563	1.6626951	2.1325000	.7683210	1.3015393	20.9822488	27.3092219	24
3	.6884706	1.4524950	2.3511657	3.4150563	.6734635	1.4848615	29.5731177	43.9119833	36
4	.6079210	1.6449505	2.9590867	4.8675512	.5903172	1.6940046	37.1033512	62.8532481	48
5	.5367956	1.8629065	3.4958823	6.5125017	.5174361	1.9326056	43.7038962	84.4623951	60
6	.4739917	2.1097416	3.9698740	8.3754082	.4535531	2.2048136	49.4895328	109.1151961	72
7	.4185357	2.3892823	4.3884097	10.4851498	.3975571	2.5153622	54.5608701	137.2403506	84
8	.3695680	2.7058623	4.7579776	12.8744322	.3484744	2.8696516	59.0060962	169.3269405	96
9	.3263293	3.0643890	5.0843070	15.5802944	.3054514	3.2738428	62.9025112	205.9329352	108
10	.2881495	3.4704206	5.3724565	18.6446834	.2677402	3.7349645	66.3178718	247.6948938	120
11	.2544367	3.9302513	5.6268931	22.1151040	.2346848	4.2610352	69.3115693	295.3390353	132
12	.2246681	4.4510096	5.8515613	26.0453553	.2057104	4.8612031	71.9356626	349.6938668	144
13	.1983825	5.0407683	6.0499437	30.4963648	.1803132	5.5459049	74.2357832	411.7045906	156
14	.1751721	5.7086701	6.2251159	35.5371332	.1580516	6.3270470	76.2519292	482.4495413	168
15	.1546774	6.4650689	6.3797933	41.2458033	.1385384	7.2182133	78.0191602	563.1589369	180
16	.1365805	7.3216906	6.5163737	47.7108723	.1214344	8.2349005	79.5682075	655.2362723	192
17	.1206009	8.2918146	6.6369746	55.0325628	.1064420	9.3947884	80.9260082	760.2827246	204
18	.1064908	9.3904800	6.7434654	63.3243774	.0933006	10.7180468	82.1161738	880.1249975	216
19	.0940316	10.6347186	6.8374971	72.7148574	.0817816	12.2276866	83.1594006	1016.8470862	228
20	.0830301	12.0438188	6.9205272	83.3495760	.0716848	13.9499595	84.0738298	1172.8265172	240
21	.0733158	13.6396248	6.9938430	95.3933948	.0628345	15.9148149	84.8753628	1350.7756922	252
22	.0647380	15.4468751	7.0585810	109.0330197	.0550769	18.1564208	85.5779380	1553.7890556	264
23	.0571638	17.4935861	7.1157448	124.4798948	.0482771	20.7137575	86.1937727	1785.3969047	276
24	.0504758	19.8114862	7.1662206	141.9734808	.0423168	23.6312957	86.7335759	2049.6267806	288
25	.0445702	22.4365081	7.2107908	161.7849670	.0370923	26.9597699	87.2067347	2351.0735044	300
26	.0393556	25.4093455	7.2501464	184.2214752	.0325129	30.7570607	87.6214769	2694.9790787	312
27	.0347511	28.7760837	7.2848975	209.6308206	.0284988	35.0892008	87.9850146	3087.3238441	324
28	.0306853	32.5889148	7.3155828	238.4069043	.0249803	40.0315240	88.3036698	3534.9304732	336
29	.0270952	36.9069460	7.3426780	270.9958192	.0218962	45.6699747	88.5829835	4045.5826143	348
30	.0239251	41.7971164	7.3666031	307.9027652	.0191929	52.1026027	88.8278129	4628.1602443	360
31	.0211259	47.3352343	7.3877290	349.6998816	.0168233	59.4412680	89.0424155	5292.7940874	372
32	.0186542	53.6071529	7.4063832	397.0351159	.0147463	67.8135864	89.2305231	6051.0417828	384
33	.0164717	60.7101006	7.4228549	450.6422688	.0129257	77.3651479	89.3954068	6916.0888664	396
34	.0145446	68.7541889	7.4373995	511.3523694	.0113299	88.2620494	89.5399338	7902.9780602	408
35	.0128429	77.8641190	7.4502424	580.1065583	.0099311	100.6937824	89.6666174	9028.8708575	420
36	.0113403	88.1811147	7.4615827	657.9706773	.0087050	114.8765282	89.7776605	10313.3459527	432
37	.0100135	99.8651124	7.4715962	746.1517920	.0076303	131.0569176	89.8749942	11778.7397044	444
38	.0088419	113.0972398	7.4804381	846.0169045	.0066882	149.5163190	89.9603110	13450.5345529	456
39	.0078075	128.0826241	7.4882456	959.1141443	.0058625	170.5757320	90.0350945	15357.8021474	468
40	.0068940	145.0535718	7.4951396	1087.1967684	.0051387	194.6013690	90.1006451	17533.7088864	480
41	.0060874	164.2731701	7.5012270	1232.2503403	.0045043	222.0110232	90.1581029	20016.0926641	492
42	.0053752	186.0393651	7.5066022	1396.5235103	.0039482	253.2813344	90.2084668	22848.1208526	504
43	.0047463	210.6895810	7.5113485	1582.5628755	.0034607	288.9560773	90.2526128	26079.0409594	516
44	.0041910	238.6059505	7.5155395	1793.2524565	.0030335	329.6556171	90.2913085	29765.0370166	528
45	.0037007	270.2212389	7.5192402	2031.8584069	.0026590	376.0876978	90.3252268	33970.2065919	540
46	.0032677	306.0255531	7.5225079	2302.0796459	.0023307	429.0597493	90.3549575	38767.6754126	552
47	.0028854	346.5739389	7.5253933	2608.1051989	.0020429	489.4929284	90.3810176	44240.8689836	564
48	.0025478	392.4949858	7.5279411	2954.6791378	.0017907	558.4381366	90.4038603	50484.9633147	576
49	.0022497	444.5005714	7.5301908	3347.1741236	.0015696	637.0942956	90.4238829	57608.5399814	588
50	.0019865	503.3968971	7.5321773	3791.6746949	.0013758	726.8291954	90.4414334	65735.4743030	600

Present and Future Value

Annual Payments   Monthly Payments

Years	Present Value	Future Value	Present Value of 1 per Period	Future Value of 1 per Period	Present Value	Future Value	Present Value of 1 per Period	Future Value of 1 per Period	Months
					.9888752	1.0112500	0.9888752	1.0000000	1
					.9778741	1.0226266	1.9667492	2.0112500	2
					.9669954	1.0341311	2.9337446	3.0338766	3
					.9562377	1.0457651	3.8899823	4.0680077	4
					.9455997	1.0575299	4.8355820	5.1137728	5
					.9350801	1.0694272	5.7706621	6.1713027	6
					.9246774	1.0814582	6.6953395	7.2407299	7
					.9143905	1.0936246	7.6097300	8.3221881	8
					.9042181	1.1059279	8.5139481	9.4158127	9
					.8941588	1.1183696	9.4081069	10.5217406	10
					.8842114	1.1309512	10.2923183	11.6401102	11
1	.8810573	1.1350000	0.8810573	1.0000000	.8743747	1.1436744	11.1666930	12.7710614	12
2	.7762619	1.2882250	1.6573192	2.1350000	.7645311	1.3079912	20.9305669	27.3769979	24
3	.6839312	1.4621354	2.3412504	3.4232250	.6684867	1.4959161	29.4678513	44.0814342	36
4	.6025826	1.6595237	2.9438329	4.8853604	.5845078	1.7108410	36.9326367	63.1858710	48
5	.5309097	1.8835593	3.4747427	6.5448840	.5110789	1.9566452	43.4596563	85.0351270	60
6	.4677619	2.1378399	3.9425046	8.4284434	.4468744	2.2377651	49.1667171	110.0235628	72
7	.4121250	2.4264482	4.3546296	10.5662832	.3907357	2.5592747	54.1568267	138.6021980	84
8	.3631057	2.7540187	4.7177353	12.9927315	.3416494	2.9269771	58.5200523	171.2868527	96
9	.3199169	3.1258113	5.0376522	15.7467502	.2987296	3.3475089	62.3351464	208.6674569	108
10	.2818652	3.5477958	5.3195174	18.8725615	.2612016	3.8284604	65.6709682	251.4186984	120
11	.2483393	4.0267482	5.5678567	22.4203573	.2283881	4.3785123	68.5877264	300.3122007	132
12	.2188012	4.5703592	5.7866579	26.4471055	.1996968	5.0075926	71.1380659	356.2304496	144
13	.1927764	5.1873577	5.9794343	31.0174648	.1746098	5.7270556	73.3680183	420.1827216	156
14	.1698470	5.8876510	6.1492813	36.2048225	.1526744	6.5498871	75.3178323	493.3233005	168
15	.1496450	6.6824839	6.2989263	42.0924735	.1334946	7.4909385	77.0227003	576.9723113	180
16	.1318458	7.5846193	6.4307720	48.7749575	.1167243	8.5671949	78.5133938	672.6395468	192
17	.1161637	8.6085429	6.5469357	56.3595767	.1020608	9.7980818	79.8168184	782.0517189	204
18	.1023469	9.7706961	6.6492826	64.9681196	.0892394	11.2058158	80.9565000	907.1836237	216
19	.0901734	11.0897401	6.7394560	74.7388157	.0780287	12.8158051	81.9530087	1050.2937848	228
20	.0794480	12.5868550	6.8189040	85.8285559	.0682263	14.6571087	82.8243307	1213.9652184	240
21	.0699982	14.2860805	6.8889022	98.4154109	.0596553	16.7629606	83.5861926	1401.1520536	252
22	.0616724	16.2147013	6.9505746	112.7014914	.0521611	19.1713696	84.2523454	1615.2328527	264
23	.0543369	18.4036860	7.0049115	128.9161927	.0456084	21.9258054	84.8348125	1860.0715909	276
24	.0478740	20.8881836	7.0527855	147.3198787	.0398788	25.0759832	85.3441071	2140.0873979	288
25	.0421797	23.7080884	7.0949652	168.2080623	.0348690	28.6787611	85.7894214	2460.3343193	300
26	.0371627	26.9086804	7.1321279	191.9161508	.0304886	32.7991661	86.1787929	2826.5925381	312
27	.0327425	30.5413522	7.1648704	218.8248311	.0266584	37.5115679	86.5192495	3245.4727016	324
28	.0288480	34.6644347	7.1937184	249.3661833	.0233095	42.9010214	86.8169361	3724.5352383	336
29	.0254167	39.3441334	7.2191352	284.0306181	.0203812	49.0648017	87.0772258	4272.4268171	348
30	.0223936	44.6555915	7.2415288	323.3747515	.0178208	56.1141596	87.3048165	4899.0364121	360
31	.0197301	50.6840963	7.2612589	368.0303430	.0155821	64.1763301	87.5038161	5615.6737901	372
32	.0173833	57.5264493	7.2786422	418.7144393	.0136246	73.3968285	87.6778163	6435.2736427	384
33	.0153157	65.2925200	7.2939579	476.2408886	.0119130	83.9420768	87.8299576	7372.6290458	396
34	.0134940	74.1070101	7.3074519	541.5334085	.0104164	96.0024077	87.9629862	8444.6584621	408
35	.0118890	84.1114565	7.3193408	615.6404187	.0091078	109.7954999	88.0793030	9670.7111053	420
36	.0104749	95.4665031	7.3298157	699.7518752	.0079563	125.5703070	88.1810075	11072.9161764	432
37	.0092290	108.3544811	7.3390447	795.2183783	.0069632	143.6115506	88.2699353	12676.5822768	444
38	.0081312	122.9823360	7.3471759	903.5728594	.0060885	164.2448598	88.3476915	14510.6542074	456
39	.0071641	139.5849514	7.3543400	1026.5551954	.0053236	187.8426482	88.4156796	16608.2353968	468
40	.0063120	158.4289198	7.3606520	1166.1401468	.0046548	214.8308356	88.4751266	19007.1853906	480
41	.0055612	179.8168240	7.3662132	1324.5690666	.0040701	245.6965358	88.5271056	21750.8031831	492
42	.0048997	204.0920952	7.3711130	1504.3858906	.0035588	280.9968482	88.5725548	24888.6087275	504
43	.0043170	231.6445281	7.3754299	1708.4779859	.0031117	321.3689132	88.6122943	28477.2367287	516
44	.0038035	262.9165394	7.3792334	1940.1225140	.0027208	367.5414121	88.6470416	32581.4588510	528
45	.0033511	298.4102722	7.3825845	2203.0390533	.0023790	420.3477189	88.6774237	37275.3527914	540
46	.0029525	338.6956589	7.3855305	2501.4493255	.0020801	480.7409423	88.7039891	42643.6393185	552
47	.0026013	384.4195729	7.3881383	2840.1449845	.0018188	549.8111284	88.7272172	48783.2114103	564
48	.0022919	436.3162152	7.3904303	3224.5645574	.0015903	628.8049347	88.7475273	55804.8830887	576
49	.0020193	495.2189043	7.3924496	3660.8807726	.0013905	719.1481321	88.7652859	63835.3895185	588
50	.0017791	562.0734564	7.3942287	4156.0996769	.0012158	822.4713378	88.7808135	73019.6744686	600

Present and Future Value

| | Annual Payments | | | | Monthly Payments | | | | |
Years	Present Value	Future Value	Present Value of 1 per Period	Future Value of 1 per Period	Present Value	Future Value	Present Value of 1 per Period	Future Value of 1 per Period	Months
					.9886715	1.0114583	0.9886715	1.0000000	1
					.9774713	1.0230480	1.9661428	2.0114583	2
					.9663980	1.0347704	2.9325407	3.0345063	3
					.9554501	1.0466271	3.8879908	4.0692767	4
					.9446263	1.0586197	4.8326171	5.1159038	5
					.9339250	1.0707497	5.7665421	6.1745235	6
					.9233450	1.0830188	6.6898872	7.2452733	7
					.9128849	1.0954283	7.6027721	8.3282920	8
					.9025433	1.1079801	8.5053153	9.4237204	9
					.8923188	1.1206757	9.3976341	10.5317005	10
					.8822101	1.1335168	10.2798442	11.6523763	11
1	.8791209	1.1375000	0.8791209	1.0000000	.8722160	1.1465050	11.1520602	12.7858931	12
2	.7728535	1.2939063	1.6519744	2.1375000	.7607607	1.3144738	20.8790653	27.4449837	24
3	.6794317	1.4718184	2.3314061	3.4314063	.6635476	1.5070508	29.3631145	44.2517048	36
4	.5973026	1.6741934	2.9287086	4.9032246	.5787569	1.7278413	36.7630378	63.5206950	48
5	.5251012	1.9043950	3.4538098	6.5774180	.5048010	1.9809787	43.2173692	85.6126890	60
6	.4616274	2.1662493	3.9154372	8.4818130	.4402955	2.2712021	48.8469401	110.9412712	72
7	.4058263	2.4641086	4.3212634	10.6480623	.3840328	2.6039446	53.7571418	139.9806179	84
8	.3567704	2.8029235	4.6780338	13.1121708	.3349595	2.9854355	58.0398981	173.2743749	96
9	.3136443	3.1883255	4.9916781	15.9150943	.2921570	3.4228169	61.7753866	211.4458345	108
10	.2757312	3.6267202	5.2674093	19.1034198	.2548240	3.9242767	65.0335394	255.2096048	120
11	.2424011	4.1253942	5.5098104	22.7301400	.2222616	4.4992030	67.8753523	305.3849873	132
12	.2130998	4.6926360	5.7229102	26.8555342	.1938601	5.1583588	70.3540269	362.9113155	144
13	.1873405	5.3378734	5.9102507	31.5481702	.1690879	5.9140843	72.5159665	428.8655398	156
14	.1646950	6.0718310	6.0749457	36.8860436	.1474812	6.7805274	74.4016448	504.4823894	168
15	.1447868	6.9067078	6.2197325	42.9578746	.1286354	7.7739087	76.0463635	591.1774874	180
16	.1272851	7.8563801	6.3470176	49.8645823	.1121979	8.9128254	77.4809134	690.5738528	192
17	.1118990	8.9366323	6.4589165	57.7209624	.0978608	10.2185991	78.7321508	804.5322853	204
18	.0983727	10.1654193	6.5572893	66.6575947	.0853557	11.7156752	79.8235000	935.1862007	216
19	.0864815	11.5631644	6.6437708	76.8230140	.0744486	13.4320805	80.7753922	1084.9815711	228
20	.0760277	13.1530995	6.7197985	88.3861784	.0649353	15.3999478	81.6056478	1256.7227161	240
21	.0668375	14.9616507	6.7866360	101.5392780	.0566376	17.6561175	82.3298101	1453.6248017	252
22	.0587583	17.0188777	6.8453943	116.5009287	.0494002	20.2428275	82.9614359	1679.3740323	264
23	.0516556	19.3589734	6.8970500	133.5198064	.0430877	23.2085034	83.5123501	1938.1966594	276
24	.0454115	22.0208322	6.9424615	152.8787798	.0375817	26.6086658	83.9928662	2234.9381020	288
25	.0399222	25.0486966	6.9823837	174.8996120	.0327794	30.5069690	84.4119800	2575.1536569	300
26	.0350965	28.4928924	7.0174802	199.9483086	.0285907	34.9763932	84.7775378	2965.2125001	312
27	.0308540	32.4106651	7.0483342	228.4412011	.0249373	40.1006106	85.0963832	3412.4169237	324
28	.0271244	36.8671316	7.0754587	260.8518662	.0217507	45.9755515	85.3744852	3925.1390425	336
29	.0238457	41.9363622	7.0993043	297.7189978	.0189713	52.7112008	85.6170502	4512.9775280	348
30	.0209632	47.7026120	7.1202675	339.6553600	.0165471	60.4336566	85.8286193	5186.9373053	360
31	.0184292	54.2617211	7.1386967	387.3579720	.0144326	69.2874910	86.0131532	5959.6355764	372
32	.0162015	61.7227078	7.1548982	441.6196931	.0125884	79.4384566	86.1741066	6845.5380268	384
33	.0142431	70.2095801	7.1691413	503.3424010	.0109798	91.0765896	86.3144928	7861.2296376	396
34	.0125214	79.8633974	7.1816627	573.5519811	.0095767	104.4197676	86.4369399	9025.7251729	408
35	.0110078	90.8446145	7.1926705	653.4153785	.0083530	119.7177882	86.5437401	10360.8251554	420
36	.0096772	103.3357490	7.2023477	744.2599930	.0072856	137.2570458	86.6368930	11891.5239938	432
37	.0085074	117.5444145	7.2108551	847.5957421	.0063546	157.3658926	86.7181425	13646.4779034	444
38	.0074791	133.7067715	7.2183342	965.1401566	.0055426	180.4207866	86.7890096	15658.5413788	456
39	.0065750	152.0914526	7.2249092	1098.8469281	.0048343	206.8533384	86.8508210	17965.3822634	468
40	.0057802	173.0040274	7.2306894	1250.9383807	.0042166	237.1583919	86.9047339	20610.1869289	480
41	.0050815	196.7920811	7.2357709	1423.9424081	.0036778	271.9032880	86.9517575	23642.4687671	492
42	.0044673	223.8509923	7.2402381	1620.7344892	.0032078	311.7384859	86.9927723	27118.9951310	504
43	.0039273	254.6305037	7.2441654	1844.5854815	.0027979	357.4097405	87.0285461	31104.8500757	516
44	.0034525	289.6421980	7.2476179	2099.2159852	.0024404	409.7720633	87.0597486	35674.6527975	528
45	.0030352	329.4680002	7.2506531	2388.8581831	.0021285	469.8057296	87.0869638	40913.9545800	540
46	.0026683	374.7698502	7.2533214	2718.3261833	.0018565	538.6346296	87.1107014	46920.8403996	552
47	.0023458	426.3007046	7.2556672	3093.0960335	.0016193	617.5473093	87.1314057	53807.7651746	564
48	.0020622	484.9170515	7.2577294	3519.3967381	.0014124	708.0210931	87.1494644	61703.6590339	576
49	.0018129	551.5931461	7.2595423	4004.3137896	.0012319	811.7497408	87.1652154	70756.3410181	588
50	.0015938	627.4372037	7.2611361	4555.9069357	.0010745	930.6751567	87.1789537	81135.2864000	600

Present and Future Value

14.000% Discount Rate   14.000% Discount Rate

	Annual Payments					Monthly Payments			
Years	Present Value	Future Value	Present Value of 1 per Period	Future Value of 1 per Period	Present Value	Future Value	Present Value of 1 per Period	Future Value of 1 per Period	Months
					.9884679	1.011667	0.988468	1.000000	1
					.9770687	1.023469	1.965537	2.011667	2
					.9658011	1.035410	2.931338	3.035136	3
					.9546633	1.047490	3.886001	4.070546	4
					.9436540	1.059710	4.829655	5.118036	5
					.9327717	1.072074	5.762427	6.177746	6
					.9220148	1.084581	6.684442	7.249820	7
					.9113821	1.097235	7.595824	8.334401	8
					.9008719	1.110036	8.496696	9.431636	9
					.8904829	1.122986	9.387178	10.541672	10
					.8802138	1.136088	10.267392	11.664658	11
1	.8771930	1.1400000	0.8771930	1.0000000	.8700630	1.149342	11.137455	12.800745	12
2	.7694675	1.2996000	1.6466605	2.1400000	.7570097	1.320987	20.827743	27.513180	24
3	.6749715	1.4815440	2.3216320	3.4396000	.6586461	1.518266	29.258904	44.422800	36
4	.5920803	1.6889602	2.9137123	4.9211440	.5730636	1.745007	36.594546	63.857736	48
5	.5193687	1.9254146	3.4330810	6.6101042	.4986015	2.005610	42.977016	86.195125	60
6	.4555865	2.1949726	3.8886675	8.5355187	.4338147	2.305132	48.530168	111.868425	72
7	.3996373	2.5022688	4.2883048	10.7304914	.3774461	2.649385	53.361760	141.375828	84
8	.3505591	2.8525864	4.6388639	13.2327602	.3284019	3.045049	57.565549	175.289927	96
9	.3075079	3.2519485	4.9463718	16.0853466	.2857304	3.499803	61.223111	214.268826	108
10	.2697438	3.7072213	5.2161156	19.3372951	.2486034	4.022471	64.405420	259.068912	120
11	.2366174	4.2262323	5.4527330	23.0445164	.2163007	4.623195	67.174230	310.559534	132
12	.2075591	4.8179048	5.6602921	27.2707487	.1881952	5.313632	69.583269	369.739871	144
13	.1820694	5.4924115	5.8423615	32.0886535	.1637417	6.107180	71.679284	437.758319	156
14	.1597100	6.2613491	6.0020715	37.5810650	.1424656	7.019239	73.502950	515.934780	168
15	.1400965	7.1379380	6.1421680	43.8424141	.1239540	8.067507	75.089654	605.786272	180
16	.1228917	8.1372493	6.2650596	50.9803521	.1078478	9.272324	76.470187	709.056369	192
17	.1077997	9.2764642	6.3728593	59.1176014	.0938344	10.657072	77.671337	827.749031	204
18	.0945611	10.5751692	6.4674205	68.3940656	.0816418	12.248621	78.716413	964.167496	216
19	.0829484	12.0556929	6.5503688	78.9692348	.0710336	14.077855	79.625696	1120.958972	228
20	.0727617	13.7434899	6.6231306	91.0249277	.0618037	16.180270	80.416829	1301.166005	240
21	.0638261	15.6675785	6.6869566	104.7684175	.0537731	18.596664	81.105164	1508.285522	252
22	.0559878	17.8610394	6.7429444	120.4359960	.0467860	21.373928	81.704060	1746.336688	264
23	.0491121	20.3615850	6.7920565	138.2970354	.0407067	24.565954	82.225136	2019.938898	276
24	.0430808	23.2122069	6.8351373	158.6586204	.0354174	28.234683	82.678506	2334.401417	288
25	.0377902	26.4619158	6.8729274	181.8708272	.0308154	32.451308	83.072966	2695.826407	300
26	.0331493	30.1665840	6.9060767	208.3327430	.0268111	37.297652	83.416171	3111.227338	312
27	.0290783	34.3899058	6.9351550	238.4993271	.0233276	42.867759	83.714781	3588.665088	324
28	.0255073	39.2044926	6.9606623	272.8892329	.0202964	49.269718	83.974591	4137.404359	336
29	.0223748	44.6931216	6.9830371	312.0937255	.0176592	56.627757	84.200641	4768.093467	348
30	.0196270	50.9501586	7.0026641	356.7868470	.0153646	65.084661	84.397320	5492.970967	360
31	.0172167	58.0831808	7.0198808	407.7370056	.0133682	74.804537	84.568442	6326.103143	372
32	.0151024	66.2148261	7.0349832	465.8201864	.0116312	85.975998	84.717330	7283.656968	384
33	.0132477	75.4849017	7.0482308	532.0350125	.0101198	98.815828	84.846871	8384.213825	396
34	.0116208	86.0527880	7.0598516	607.5199142	.0088049	113.573184	84.959580	9649.130077	408
35	.0101937	98.1001783	7.0700453	693.5727022	.0076608	130.534434	85.057645	11102.951488	420
36	.0089418	111.8342033	7.0789871	791.6728805	.0066654	150.028711	85.142966	12773.889538	432
37	.0078437	127.4909917	7.0868308	903.5070838	.0057993	172.434303	85.217202	14694.368868	444
38	.0068804	145.3397306	7.0937112	1030.9980755	.0050458	198.185992	85.281792	16901.656478	456
39	.0060355	165.6872929	7.0997467	1176.3378061	.0043901	227.783490	85.337989	19438.584899	468
40	.0052943	188.8835139	7.1050409	1342.0250990	.0038197	261.801139	85.386883	22354.383358	480
41	.0046441	215.3272058	7.1096850	1530.9086128	.0033234	300.899053	85.429425	25705.633076	492
42	.0040738	245.4730146	7.1137588	1746.2358186	.0028915	345.835928	85.466439	29557.365227	504
43	.0035735	279.8392367	7.1173323	1991.7088332	.0025158	397.483767	85.498643	33984.322874	516
44	.0031346	319.0167298	7.1204669	2271.5480699	.0021889	456.844799	85.526663	39072.411358	528
45	.0027497	363.6790720	7.1232166	2590.5647997	.0019045	525.070929	85.551042	44920.365302	540
46	.0024120	414.5941420	7.1256286	2954.2438716	.0016570	603.486086	85.572254	51641.664554	552
47	.0021158	472.6373219	7.1277444	3368.8380137	.0014417	693.611923	85.590709	59366.736276	564
48	.0018560	538.8065470	7.1296003	3841.4753356	.0012544	797.197335	85.606766	68245.485884	576
49	.0016280	614.2394636	7.1312284	4380.2818826	.0010914	916.252403	85.620737	78450.205975	588
50	.0014281	700.2329885	7.1326565	4994.5213461	.0009496	1053.087396	85.632892	90178.919673	600

Present and Future Value

	Annual Payments				Monthly Payments				
Years	Present Value	Future Value	Present Value of 1 per Period	Future Value of 1 per Period	Present Value	Future Value	Present Value of 1 per Period	Future Value of 1 per Period	Months
					.9882644	1.011875	0.988264	1.000000	1
					.9766664	1.023891	1.964931	2.011875	2
					.9652046	1.036050	2.930135	3.035766	3
					.9538773	1.048353	3.884013	4.071816	4
					.9426830	1.060802	4.826696	5.120169	5
					.9316200	1.073399	5.758316	6.180971	6
					.9206868	1.086146	6.679003	7.254370	7
					.9098820	1.099044	7.588885	8.340515	8
					.8992039	1.112095	8.488089	9.439559	9
					.8886512	1.125301	9.376740	10.551654	10
					.8782223	1.138664	10.254962	11.676954	11
1	.8752735	1.1425000	0.8752735	1.0000000	.8679158	1.152185	11.122878	12.815618	12
2	.7661037	1.3053063	1.6413773	2.1425000	.7532779	1.327531	20.776600	27.581587	24
3	.6705503	1.4913124	2.3119276	3.4478063	.6537818	1.529562	29.155218	44.594723	36
4	.5869149	1.7038244	2.8988425	4.9391186	.5674276	1.762339	36.427153	64.197010	48
5	.5137111	1.9466194	3.4125536	6.6429430	.4924794	2.030542	42.738580	86.782480	60
6	.4496377	2.2240126	3.8621914	8.5895624	.4274306	2.339561	48.216368	112.805130	72
7	.3935560	2.5409344	4.2557474	10.8135751	.3709738	2.695608	52.970627	142.788050	84
8	.3444691	2.9030176	4.6002165	13.3545095	.3219740	3.105840	57.096923	177.333935	96
9	.3015047	3.3166976	4.9017212	16.2575271	.2794464	3.578504	60.678201	217.137201	108
10	.2638991	3.7893270	5.1656203	19.5742248	.2425359	4.123101	63.786449	262.997946	120
11	.2309839	4.3293061	5.3966042	23.3635518	.2105008	4.750577	66.484146	315.838029	132
12	.2021741	4.9462323	5.5987783	27.6928579	.1826969	5.473545	68.825521	376.719606	144
13	.1769576	5.6510703	5.7757359	32.6390902	.1585656	6.306539	70.857636	446.866473	156
14	.1548863	6.4563479	5.9306223	38.2901605	.1376216	7.266303	72.621342	527.688675	168
15	.1355679	7.3763774	6.0661902	44.7465084	.1194439	8.372129	74.152090	620.810841	180
16	.1186590	8.4275112	6.1848492	52.1228858	.1036673	9.646245	75.480650	728.104847	192
17	.1038591	9.6284316	6.2887082	60.5503970	.0899745	11.114263	76.633729	851.727442	204
18	.0909051	11.0004831	6.3796133	70.1788286	.0780903	12.805693	77.634504	994.163599	216
19	.0795668	12.5680519	6.4591802	81.1793117	.0677758	14.754533	78.503092	1158.276469	228
20	.0696427	14.3589993	6.5288229	93.7473636	.0588237	16.999959	79.256954	1347.364934	240
21	.0609564	16.4051567	6.5897793	108.1063629	.0510540	19.587105	79.911242	1565.229914	252
22	.0533536	18.7428916	6.6431329	124.5115197	.0443106	22.567978	80.479110	1816.250779	264
23	.0466990	21.4137536	6.6898319	143.2544112	.0384578	26.002496	80.971971	2105.473371	276
24	.0408744	24.4652135	6.7307062	164.6681648	.0333782	29.959698	81.399733	2438.711438	288
25	.0357762	27.9515064	6.7664825	189.1333783	.0289694	34.519129	81.770994	2822.663497	300
26	.0313140	31.9345961	6.7977965	217.0848847	.0251430	39.772439	82.093218	3265.047479	312
27	.0274083	36.4852760	6.8252048	249.0194808	.0218220	45.825226	82.372881	3774.755874	324
28	.0239898	41.6844278	6.8491946	285.5047568	.0189397	52.799159	82.615605	4362.034480	336
29	.0209976	47.6244588	6.8701922	327.1891846	.0164381	60.834424	82.826269	5038.688355	348
30	.0183787	54.4109442	6.8885708	374.8136434	.0142669	70.092540	83.009107	5818.319116	360
31	.0160864	62.1645037	6.9046572	429.2245876	.0123824	80.759605	83.167796	6716.598349	372
32	.0140800	71.0229455	6.9187371	491.3890914	.0107469	93.050044	83.305524	7751.582627	384
33	.0123238	81.1437153	6.9310610	562.4120369	.0093274	107.210908	83.425060	8944.076471	396
34	.0107867	92.7066947	6.9418477	643.5557521	.0080954	123.526850	83.528808	10318.050549	408
35	.0094413	105.9173987	6.9512890	736.2624468	.0070261	142.325842	83.618852	11901.123513	420
36	.0082637	121.0106280	6.9595527	842.1798455	.0060981	163.985766	83.697003	13725.117177	432
37	.0072330	138.2546425	6.9667858	963.1904735	.0052926	188.942017	83.764831	15826.696169	444
38	.0063309	157.9559290	6.9731166	1101.4451159	.0045936	217.696246	83.823701	18248.104943	456
39	.0055413	180.4646489	6.9786579	1259.4010450	.0039868	250.826451	83.874794	21038.016943	468
40	.0048501	206.1808614	6.9835080	1439.8656939	.0034602	288.998592	83.919139	24252.513005	480
41	.0042452	235.5616341	6.9877532	1646.0465552	.0030032	332.979978	83.957627	27956.208652	492
42	.0037157	269.1291670	6.9914689	1881.6081894	.0026065	383.654691	83.991031	32223.552953	504
43	.0032522	307.4800733	6.9947211	2150.7373504	.0022622	442.041360	84.020023	37140.325042	516
44	.0028466	351.2959837	6.9975677	2458.2174296	.0019634	509.313631	84.045185	42805.358390	528
45	.0024916	401.3556614	7.0000593	2809.5134134	.0017041	586.823764	84.067024	49332.527485	540
46	.0021808	458.5488432	7.0022401	3210.8690748	.0014790	676.129813	84.085978	56853.036861	552
47	.0019088	523.8920533	7.0041488	3669.4179179	.0012837	779.026944	84.102429	65518.058472	564
48	.0016707	598.5466709	7.0058196	4193.3099712	.0011141	897.583524	84.116707	75501.770448	576
49	.0014623	683.8395715	7.0072819	4791.8566421	.0009669	1034.182692	84.129099	87004.858298	588
50	.0012799	781.2867104	7.0085618	5475.6962136	.0008392	1191.570269	84.139854	100258.548950	600

Present and Future Value

14.500% Discount Rate   14.500% Discount Rate

	Annual Payments				Monthly Payments				
Years	Present Value	Future Value	Present Value of 1 per Period	Future Value of 1 per Period	Present Value	Future Value	Present Value of 1 per Period	Future Value of 1 per Period	Months
					.9880609	1.012083	0.988061	1.000000	1
					.9762644	1.024313	1.964325	2.012083	2
					.9646087	1.036690	2.928934	3.036396	3
					.9530922	1.049216	3.882026	4.073086	4
					.9417131	1.061894	4.823739	5.122302	5
					.9304700	1.074726	5.754209	6.184197	6
					.9193610	1.087712	6.673570	7.258922	7
					.9083847	1.100855	7.581955	8.346634	8
					.8975394	1.114157	8.479495	9.447490	9
					.8868237	1.127620	9.366318	10.561647	10
					.8762358	1.141245	10.242554	11.689267	11
1	.8733624	1.1450000	0.8733624	1.0000000	.8657744	1.155035	11.108328	12.830512	12
2	.7627620	1.3110250	1.6361244	2.1450000	.7495653	1.334107	20.725634	27.650207	24
3	.6661677	1.5011236	2.3022921	3.4560250	.6489544	1.540940	29.052051	44.767478	36
4	.5818058	1.7187866	2.8840979	4.9571486	.5618481	1.779841	36.260850	64.538532	48
5	.5081273	1.9680106	3.3922252	6.6759352	.4864337	2.055779	42.502042	87.374798	60
6	.4437793	2.2533721	3.8360046	8.6439458	.4211418	2.374497	47.905507	113.751493	72
7	.3875802	2.5801111	4.2235848	10.8973179	.3646138	2.742628	52.583688	144.217508	84
8	.3384980	2.9542272	4.5620828	13.4774290	.3156733	3.167833	56.633938	179.406832	96
9	.2956314	3.3825902	4.8577142	16.4316562	.2733018	3.658959	60.140540	220.051745	108
10	.2581934	3.8730657	5.1159076	19.8142464	.2366177	4.226227	63.176466	266.998057	120
11	.2254964	4.4346603	5.3414040	23.6873121	.2048575	4.881441	65.804893	321.222707	132
12	.1969401	5.0776860	5.5383441	28.1219723	.1773604	5.638237	68.080518	383.854095	144
13	.1720001	5.8139505	5.7103442	33.1996583	.1535541	6.512363	70.050696	456.195562	156
14	.1502184	6.6569733	5.8605626	39.0136088	.1329432	7.522010	71.756425	539.752513	168
15	.1311951	7.6222344	5.9917578	45.6705821	.1150988	8.688187	73.233202	636.263747	180
16	.1145809	8.7274584	6.1063386	53.2928165	.0996496	10.035163	74.511757	747.737633	192
17	.1000077	9.9929399	6.2064093	62.0202749	.0862747	11.590968	75.618688	876.493913	204
18	.0873979	11.4419161	6.2938072	72.0132147	.0746939	13.387978	76.577058	1025.211968	216
19	.0763301	13.1009940	6.3701373	83.4551308	.0646680	15.463588	77.406782	1196.986579	228
20	.0666638	15.0006381	6.4368012	96.5561248	.0559879	17.860991	78.125136	1395.392327	240
21	.0582217	17.1757306	6.4950229	111.5567629	.0484729	20.630076	78.747069	1624.557981	252
22	.0508486	19.6662116	6.5458715	128.7324935	.0419666	23.828467	79.285522	1889.252413	264
23	.0444093	22.5178122	6.5902808	148.3987051	.0363336	27.522721	79.751701	2194.983839	276
24	.0387854	25.7828950	6.6290662	170.9165173	.0314567	31.789716	80.155306	2548.114445	288
25	.0338737	29.5214148	6.6629399	196.6994124	.0272344	36.718246	80.504738	2955.992779	300
26	.0295840	33.8020199	6.6925239	226.2208272	.0235789	42.410872	80.807267	3427.106674	312
27	.0258376	38.7033128	6.7183615	260.0228471	.0204140	48.986057	81.069189	3971.259878	324
28	.0225656	44.3152932	6.7409271	298.7261599	.0176739	56.580627	81.295954	4599.776067	336
29	.0197079	50.7410107	6.7606350	343.0414531	.0153016	65.352625	81.492281	5325.734484	348
30	.0172122	58.0984573	6.7778472	393.7824638	.0132477	75.484592	81.662256	6164.242121	360
31	.0150325	66.5227336	6.7928796	451.8809211	.0114696	87.187373	81.809416	7132.748085	372
32	.0131288	76.1685299	6.8060084	518.4036546	.0099300	100.704498	81.936824	8251.406712	384
33	.0114662	87.2129668	6.8174746	594.5721845	.0085972	116.317255	82.047130	9543.496975	396
34	.0100141	99.8588469	6.8274887	681.7851513	.0074442	134.350542	82.142630	11035.906907	408
35	.0087460	114.3383797	6.8362347	781.6439982	.0064441	155.179625	82.225312	12759.693140	420
36	.0076384	130.9174448	6.8438731	895.9823780	.0055792	179.237953	82.296896	14750.727180	432
37	.0066711	149.9004743	6.8505442	1026.8998228	.0048303	207.026173	82.358871	17050.441884	444
38	.0058263	171.6360431	6.8563705	1176.8002971	.0041820	239.122549	82.412528	19706.693669	456
39	.0050885	196.5232693	6.8614589	1348.4363402	.0036206	276.194997	82.458982	22774.758387	468
40	.0044441	225.0191434	6.8659030	1544.9596095	.0031346	319.014986	82.499201	26318.481600	480
41	.0038813	257.6469192	6.8697843	1769.9787529	.0027139	368.473587	82.534022	30411.607192	492
42	.0033898	295.0057224	6.8731740	2027.6256720	.0023496	425.600019	82.564169	35139.311955	504
43	.0029605	337.7815522	6.8761345	2322.6313945	.0020342	491.583069	82.590269	40599.978093	516
44	.0025856	386.7598773	6.8787201	2660.4129467	.0017612	567.795823	82.612866	46907.240532	528
45	.0022582	442.8400595	6.8809783	3047.1728239	.0015248	655.824249	82.632430	54192.351629	540
46	.0019722	507.0518681	6.8829504	3490.0128834	.0013201	757.500193	82.649368	62606.912495	552
47	.0017224	580.5743890	6.8846729	3997.0647515	.0011429	874.939502	82.664033	72326.027774	564
48	.0015043	664.7576754	6.8861772	4577.6391404	.0009895	1010.586057	82.676729	83551.949519	576
49	.0013138	761.1475383	6.8874910	5242.3968158	.0008567	1167.262623	82.687721	96518.286002	588
50	.0011474	871.5139313	6.8886384	6003.5443541	.0007417	1348.229595	82.697238	111494.863036	600

Present and Future Value

	Annual Payments				Monthly Payments				
Years	Present Value	Future Value	Present Value of 1 per Period	Future Value of 1 per Period	Present Value	Future Value	Present Value of 1 per Period	Future Value of 1 per Period	Months
					.9878576	1.012292	0.987858	1.000000	1
					.9758626	1.024734	1.963720	2.012292	2
					.9640133	1.037330	2.927733	3.037026	3
					.9523078	1.050081	3.880041	4.074356	4
					.9407445	1.062988	4.820786	5.124437	5
					.9293216	1.076054	5.750107	6.187425	6
					.9180374	1.089280	6.668145	7.263478	7
					.9068902	1.102669	7.575035	8.352759	8
					.8958784	1.116223	8.470913	9.455428	9
					.8850002	1.129943	9.355914	10.571651	10
					.8742542	1.143832	10.230168	11.701594	11
1	.8714597	1.1475000	0.8714597	1.0000000	.8636386	1.157892	11.093806	12.845426	12
2	.7594420	1.3167563	1.6309017	2.1475000	.7458717	1.340713	20.674846	27.719039	24
3	.6618231	1.5109778	2.2927248	3.4642562	.6441636	1.552401	28.949402	44.941071	36
4	.5767522	1.7338470	2.8694769	4.9752340	.5563246	1.797512	36.095628	64.882320	48
5	.5026163	1.9895895	3.3720932	6.7090811	.4804634	2.081324	42.267385	87.972126	60
6	.4380098	2.2830539	3.8101030	8.6986705	.4149467	2.409948	47.597553	114.707620	72
7	.3817079	2.6198044	4.1918109	10.9817244	.3583640	2.790459	52.200892	145.664428	84
8	.3326430	3.0062255	4.5244539	13.6015288	.3094970	3.231049	56.176513	181.509058	96
9	.2898850	3.4496438	4.8143389	16.6077543	.2672936	3.741205	59.610013	223.013257	108
10	.2526231	3.9584662	5.0669620	20.0573980	.2308451	4.331910	62.575317	271.070626	120
11	.2201508	4.5423400	5.2871129	24.0158642	.1993667	5.015882	65.136267	326.715854	132
12	.1918526	5.2123351	5.4789655	28.5582042	.1721808	5.807849	67.348003	391.147001	144
13	.1671918	5.9811546	5.6461573	33.7705393	.1487020	6.724860	69.258143	465.751291	156
14	.1457009	6.8633748	5.7918582	39.7516939	.1284248	7.786659	70.907814	552.134980	168
15	.1269725	7.8757226	5.9188307	46.6150687	.1109126	9.016108	72.332534	652.157936	180
16	.1106514	9.0373997	6.0294821	54.4907914	.0957884	10.439677	73.562977	767.973687	192
17	.0964282	10.3704070	6.1259103	63.5281831	.0827266	12.088015	74.625635	902.075783	204
18	.0840333	11.9000420	6.2099436	73.8985901	.0714459	13.996612	75.543388	1057.351487	216
19	.0732316	13.6552982	6.2831753	85.7986322	.0617034	16.206561	76.335994	1237.143935	228
20	.0638184	15.6694547	6.3469937	99.4539304	.0532894	18.765442	77.020520	1445.324119	240
21	.0556152	17.9806993	6.4026089	115.1233851	.0460228	21.728350	77.611703	1686.374225	252
22	.0484664	20.6328523	6.4510753	133.1040845	.0397471	25.159076	78.122271	1965.484142	264
23	.0422365	23.6761982	6.4933118	153.7369369	.0343271	29.131485	78.563217	2288.663198	276
24	.0368074	27.1684374	6.5301192	177.4131351	.0296462	33.731105	78.944036	2662.869543	288
25	.0320762	31.1757819	6.5621954	204.5815725	.0256036	39.056966	79.272925	3096.159965	300
26	.0279531	35.7742098	6.5901485	235.7573545	.0221123	45.223737	79.556967	3597.863346	312
27	.0243600	41.0509057	6.6145085	271.5315643	.0190970	52.364190	79.802276	4178.781527	324
28	.0212288	47.1059143	6.6357372	312.5824700	.0164929	60.632060	80.014135	4851.421866	336
29	.0185000	54.0540367	6.6542372	359.6883843	.0142439	70.205359	80.197104	5630.266531	348
30	.0161220	62.0270071	6.6703593	413.7424210	.0123016	81.290203	80.355124	6532.084302	360
31	.0140497	71.1759906	6.6844089	475.7694281	.0106241	94.125251	80.491595	7576.291614	372
32	.0122437	81.6744493	6.6966627	546.9454188	.0091754	108.986847	80.609457	8785.370591	384
33	.0106699	93.7214305	6.7073226	628.6198680	.0079242	126.194965	80.711248	10185.353101	396
34	.0092984	107.5453415	6.7166210	722.3412986	.0068437	146.120103	80.799158	11806.381228	408
35	.0081032	123.4082794	6.7247242	829.8866401	.0059105	169.191254	80.875080	13683.356239	420
36	.0070616	141.6110006	6.7317858	953.2949195	.0051045	195.905148	80.940650	15856.690022	432
37	.0061539	162.4986232	6.7379397	1094.9059201	.0044085	226.836945	80.997278	18373.175168	444
38	.0053629	186.4671701	6.7433025	1257.4045434	.0038073	262.652615	81.046185	21286.992427	456
39	.0046735	213.9710777	6.7479761	1443.8717135	.0032881	304.123283	81.088422	24660.877243	468
40	.0040728	245.5318117	6.7520489	1657.8427912	.0028398	352.141824	81.124900	28567.470462	480
41	.0035493	281.7477539	6.7555981	1903.3746030	.0024525	407.742095	81.156404	33090.882320	492
42	.0030930	323.3055476	6.7586912	2185.1223569	.0021181	472.121187	81.183612	38328.503359	504
43	.0026955	370.9931159	6.7613867	2508.4279045	.0018293	546.665203	81.207110	44393.101279	516
44	.0023490	425.7146005	6.7637357	2879.4210205	.0015798	632.979101	81.227404	51415.248866	528
45	.0020471	488.5075041	6.7657827	3305.1356210	.0013644	732.921246	81.244930	59546.135262	540
46	.0017839	560.5623609	6.7675666	3793.6431251	.0011784	848.643426	81.260066	68960.821120	552
47	.0015546	643.2453092	6.7691212	4354.2054860	.0010177	982.637178	81.273139	79862.007720	564
48	.0013548	738.1239923	6.7704760	4997.4507952	.0008789	1137.787431	81.284429	92484.401186	576
49	.0011806	846.9972812	6.7716567	5735.5747875	.0007591	1317.434621	81.294179	107099.765795	588
50	.0010289	971.9293801	6.7726856	6582.5720686	.0006555	1525.446611	81.302600	124022.775146	600

Present and Future Value

15.000% Discount Rate   15.000% Discount Rate

	Annual Payments				Monthly Payments				
Years	Present Value	Future Value	Present Value of 1 per Period	Future Value of 1 per Period	Present Value	Future Value	Present Value of 1 per Period	Future Value of 1 per Period	Months
					.9876543	1.012500	0.987654	1.000000	1
					.9754611	1.025156	1.963115	2.012500	2
					.9634183	1.037971	2.926534	3.037656	3
					.9515243	1.050945	3.878058	4.075627	4
					.9397771	1.064082	4.817835	5.126572	5
					.9281749	1.077383	5.746010	6.190654	6
					.9167159	1.090850	6.662726	7.268038	7
					.9053984	1.104486	7.568124	8.358888	8
					.8942207	1.118292	8.462345	9.463374	9
					.8831809	1.132271	9.345526	10.581666	10
					.8722775	1.146424	10.217803	11.713937	11
1	.8695652	1.1500000	0.8695652	1.0000000	.8615086	1.160755	11.079312	12.860361	12
2	.7561437	1.3225000	1.6257089	2.1500000	.7421971	1.347351	20.624235	27.788084	24
3	.6575162	1.5208750	2.2832251	3.4725000	.6394092	1.563944	28.847267	45.115505	36
4	.5717532	1.7490062	2.8549784	4.9933750	.5508565	1.815355	35.931481	65.228388	48
5	.4971767	2.0113572	3.3521551	6.7423812	.4745676	2.107181	42.034592	88.574508	60
6	.4323276	2.3130608	3.7844827	8.7537384	.4088441	2.445920	47.292474	115.673621	72
7	.3759370	2.6600199	4.1604197	11.0667992	.3522227	2.839113	51.822185	147.129040	84
8	.3269018	3.0590229	4.4873215	13.7268191	.3034429	3.295513	55.724570	183.641059	96
9	.2842624	3.5178763	4.7715839	16.7858419	.2614186	3.825282	59.086509	226.022551	108
10	.2471847	4.0455577	5.0187686	20.3037182	.2252144	4.440213	61.982847	275.217058	120
11	.2149432	4.6523914	5.2337118	24.3492760	.1940242	5.153998	64.478068	332.319805	132
12	.1869072	5.3502501	5.4206190	29.0016674	.1671535	5.982526	66.627722	398.602077	144
13	.1625280	6.1527876	5.5831470	34.3519175	.1440042	6.944244	68.479668	475.539523	156
14	.1413287	7.0757058	5.7244756	40.5047051	.1240608	8.060563	70.075134	564.845011	168
15	.1228945	8.1370616	5.8473701	47.5804109	.1068795	9.356334	71.449643	668.506759	180
16	.1068648	9.3576209	5.9542349	55.7174725	.0920776	10.860408	72.633794	788.832603	192
17	.0929259	10.7612640	6.0471608	65.0750934	.0793256	12.606267	73.653950	928.501369	204
18	.0808051	12.3754536	6.1279659	75.8363574	.0683397	14.632781	74.532823	1090.622520	216
19	.0702653	14.2317716	6.1982312	88.2118110	.0588752	16.985067	75.289980	1278.805378	228
20	.0611003	16.3665374	6.2593315	102.4435826	.0507215	19.715494	75.942278	1497.239481	240
21	.0531307	18.8215180	6.3124622	118.8101200	.0436970	22.884848	76.504237	1750.787854	252
22	.0462006	21.6447457	6.3586627	137.6316380	.0376454	26.563691	76.988370	2045.095272	264
23	.0401744	24.8914576	6.3988372	159.2763837	.0324318	30.833924	77.405455	2386.713938	276
24	.0349343	28.6251762	6.4337714	184.1678413	.0279403	35.790617	77.764777	2783.249347	288
25	.0303776	32.9189526	6.4641491	212.7930175	.0240708	41.544120	78.074336	3243.529615	300
26	.0264153	37.8567955	6.4905644	245.7119701	.0207372	48.222525	78.341024	3777.802015	312
27	.0229699	43.5353148	6.5135343	283.5687656	.0178653	55.974514	78.570778	4397.961118	324
28	.0199738	50.0656121	6.5335081	327.1040804	.0153911	64.972670	78.768713	5117.813598	336
29	.0173685	57.5754539	6.5508766	377.1696925	.0132596	75.417320	78.939236	5953.385616	348
30	.0151031	66.2117720	6.5659796	434.7451464	.0114232	87.540995	79.086142	6923.279611	360
31	.0131331	76.1435378	6.5791127	500.9569183	.0098412	101.613606	79.212704	8049.088447	372
32	.0114201	87.5650684	6.5905328	577.1004561	.0084783	117.948452	79.321738	9355.876140	384
33	.0099305	100.6998287	6.6004633	664.6655245	.0073041	136.909198	79.415671	10872.735858	396
34	.0086352	115.8048030	6.6090985	765.3653532	.0062926	158.917970	79.496596	12633.437629	408
35	.0075089	133.1755234	6.6166074	881.1701561	.0054211	184.464752	79.566313	14677.180163	420
36	.0065295	153.1518519	6.6231369	1014.3456796	.0046703	214.118294	79.626375	17049.463544	432
37	.0056778	176.1246297	6.6288147	1167.4975315	.0040235	248.538777	79.678119	19803.102194	444
38	.0049372	202.5433242	6.6337519	1343.6221612	.0034663	288.492509	79.722696	22999.400699	456
39	.0042932	232.9248228	6.6380451	1546.1654854	.0029862	334.868983	79.761101	26709.518627	468
40	.0037332	267.8635462	6.6417784	1779.0903082	.0025727	388.700685	79.794186	31016.054774	480
41	.0032463	308.0430782	6.6450247	2046.9538545	.0022164	451.186076	79.822690	36014.886062	492
42	.0028229	354.2495399	6.6478475	2354.9969326	.0019094	523.716276	79.847246	41817.302064	504
43	.0024547	407.3869709	6.6503022	2709.2464725	.0016450	607.906033	79.868401	48552.482651	516
44	.0021345	468.4950165	6.6524367	3116.6334434	.0014172	705.629674	79.886626	56370.373945	528
45	.0018561	538.7692690	6.6542928	3585.1284599	.0012209	819.062832	79.902327	65445.026584	540
46	.0016140	619.5846593	6.6559068	4123.8977289	.0010518	950.730883	79.915854	75978.470631	552
47	.0014035	712.5223582	6.6573102	4743.4823882	.0009062	1103.565167	79.927508	88205.213396	564
48	.0012204	819.4007120	6.6585306	5456.0047465	.0007807	1280.968254	79.937547	102397.460298	576
49	.0010612	942.3108188	6.6595919	6275.4054585	.0006725	1486.889688	79.946196	118871.175005	588
50	.0009228	%1083.6574416	6.6605147	7217.7162772	.0005794	1725.913922	79.953648	137993.113776	600

Present Value of a Series of Payments Increasing at Constant Rate

Annual Rate of Growth 3%

Holding					Discount Rate						
Period	5.50%	5.75%	6.00%	6.25%	6.50%	6.75%	7.00%	7.25%	7.50%	7.75%	
1	0.94787	0.94563	0.94340	0.94118	0.93897	0.93677	0.93458	0.93240	0.93023	0.92807	1
2	1.87327	1.86666	1.86009	1.85356	1.84708	1.84063	1.83422	1.82785	1.82153	1.81524	2
3	2.77675	2.76375	2.75084	2.73804	2.72534	2.71274	2.70023	2.68782	2.67551	2.66329	3
4	3.65882	3.63750	3.61639	3.59547	3.57474	3.55421	3.53387	3.51371	3.49374	3.47396	4
5	4.51998	4.48854	4.45743	4.42667	4.39623	4.36612	4.33634	4.30688	4.27772	4.24889	5
6	5.36074	5.31744	5.27468	5.23244	5.19072	5.14952	5.10881	5.06861	5.02889	4.98965	6
7	6.18158	6.12479	6.06879	6.01356	5.95910	5.90539	5.85241	5.80016	5.74861	5.69777	7
8	6.98296	6.91114	6.84043	6.77080	6.70223	6.63471	6.56821	6.50271	6.43820	6.37466	8
9	7.76536	7.67704	7.59023	7.50487	7.42093	7.33841	7.25724	7.17743	7.09893	7.02172	9
10	8.52921	8.42303	8.31881	8.21648	8.11602	8.01738	7.92052	7.82541	7.73200	7.64025	10
11	9.27497	9.14962	9.02676	8.90633	8.78826	8.67251	8.55901	8.44772	8.33856	8.23152	11
12	10.00305	9.85731	9.71469	9.57508	9.43841	9.30463	9.17363	9.04536	8.91974	8.79672	12
13	10.71388	10.54660	10.38314	10.22337	10.06720	9.91453	9.76527	9.61932	9.47659	9.33700	13
14	11.40786	11.21797	11.03267	10.85183	10.67532	10.50302	10.33479	10.17054	10.01013	9.85347	14
15	12.08540	11.87187	11.66383	11.46107	11.26345	11.07083	10.88302	10.69991	10.52133	10.34717	15
16	12.74689	12.50877	12.27711	12.05167	11.83226	11.61869	11.41076	11.20830	11.01113	10.81910	16
17	13.39270	13.12911	12.87305	12.62421	12.38237	12.14731	11.91876	11.69655	11.48043	11.27023	17
18	14.02320	13.73332	13.45211	13.17923	12.91440	12.65736	12.40778	12.16546	11.93009	11.70147	18
19	14.63877	14.32182	14.01479	13.71728	13.42895	13.14949	12.87852	12.61578	12.36092	12.11371	19
20	15.23975	14.89501	14.56154	14.23887	13.92659	13.62433	13.33166	13.04825	12.77372	12.50777	20
21	15.82648	15.45329	15.09282	14.74450	14.40788	14.08249	13.76786	13.46359	13.16924	12.88445	21
22	16.39932	15.99706	15.60606	15.23467	14.87335	14.52456	14.18775	13.86247	13.54820	13.24454	22
23	16.95858	16.52669	16.11069	15.70985	15.32352	14.95110	14.59194	14.24554	13.91130	13.58875	23
24	17.50458	17.04254	16.59813	16.17049	15.75889	15.36265	14.98103	14.61343	14.25920	13.91778	24
25	18.03765	17.54498	17.07176	16.61704	16.17996	15.75975	15.35557	14.96675	14.59253	14.23231	25
30	20.51940	19.86786	19.24631	18.65306	18.08661	17.54554	17.02843	16.53408	16.06123	15.60880	30
35	22.72071	21.90401	21.13008	20.39618	19.69988	19.03894	18.41112	17.81452	17.24720	16.70749	35
40	24.67327	23.68883	22.76194	21.88851	21.06493	20.28783	19.55398	18.86059	18.20488	17.58443	40
45	26.40519	25.25334	24.17558	23.16615	22.21993	21.33224	20.49861	19.71519	18.97820	18.28439	45
50	27.94141	26.62473	25.40019	24.25998	23.19722	22.20564	21.27939	20.41335	19.60267	18.84309	50

Annual Rate of Growth 4%

Holding					Discount Rate						
Period	5.50%	5.75%	6.00%	6.25%	6.50%	6.75%	7.00%	7.25%	7.50%	7.75%	
1	0.94787	0.94563	0.94340	0.94118	0.93897	0.93677	0.93458	0.93240	0.93023	0.92807	1
2	1.88226	1.87560	1.86899	1.86242	1.85589	1.84940	1.84296	1.83655	1.83018	1.82385	2
3	2.80336	2.79019	2.77713	2.76416	2.75129	2.73853	2.72586	2.71330	2.70082	2.68845	3
4	3.71137	3.68965	3.66812	3.64680	3.62568	3.60475	3.58402	3.56348	3.54312	3.52296	4
5	4.60647	4.57421	4.54231	4.51075	4.47953	4.44866	4.41811	4.38789	4.35800	4.32842	5
6	5.48885	5.44414	5.40000	5.35641	5.31335	5.27082	5.22882	5.18733	5.14634	5.10586	6
7	6.35867	6.29968	6.24151	6.18415	6.12759	6.07181	6.01679	5.96254	5.90902	5.85623	7
8	7.21613	7.14105	7.06714	6.99437	6.92271	6.85216	6.78268	6.71425	6.64686	6.58049	8
9	8.06140	7.96851	7.87720	7.78743	7.69918	7.61241	7.52709	7.44319	7.36069	7.27955	9
10	8.89465	8.78227	8.67197	8.56370	8.45741	8.35307	8.25063	8.15004	8.05127	7.95427	10
11	9.71606	9.58256	9.45174	9.32352	9.19785	9.07466	8.95388	8.83547	8.71937	8.60552	11
12	10.52578	10.36961	10.21681	10.06726	9.92090	9.77765	9.63742	9.50013	9.36571	9.23410	12
13	11.32399	11.14364	10.96743	10.79525	10.62698	10.46254	10.30179	10.14465	9.99101	9.84080	13
14	12.11086	11.90485	11.70390	11.50782	11.31649	11.12978	10.94753	10.76964	10.59596	10.42639	14
15	12.88653	12.65347	12.42647	12.20530	11.98981	11.77983	11.57517	11.37569	11.18121	10.99159	15
16	13.65118	13.38970	13.13540	12.88801	12.64733	12.41314	12.18521	11.96337	11.74740	11.53713	16
17	14.40496	14.11375	13.83096	13.55627	13.28941	13.03013	12.77815	12.53325	12.29516	12.06368	17
18	15.14802	14.82582	14.51340	14.21037	13.91642	13.63123	13.35446	13.08585	12.82508	12.57190	18
19	15.88051	15.52610	15.18295	14.85062	14.52871	14.21684	13.91462	13.62171	13.33775	13.06244	19
20	16.60259	16.21479	15.83988	15.47731	15.12662	14.78737	14.45906	14.14134	13.83373	13.53591	20
21	17.31440	16.89209	16.48441	16.09073	15.71050	15.34320	14.98825	14.64521	14.31356	13.99289	21
22	18.01610	17.55817	17.11678	16.69117	16.28068	15.88471	15.50260	15.13382	14.77777	14.43398	22
23	18.70781	18.21324	17.73722	17.27888	16.83747	16.41227	16.00252	15.60762	15.22687	14.85971	23
24	19.38969	18.85747	18.34595	17.85415	17.38119	16.92624	16.48843	16.06706	15.66134	15.27062	24
25	20.06188	19.49103	18.94320	18.41724	17.91215	17.42697	16.96072	16.51258	16.08167	15.66724	25
30	23.28214	22.50501	21.76460	21.05879	20.38573	19.74365	19.13079	18.54568	17.98673	17.45262	30
35	26.27990	25.27772	24.32968	23.43225	22.58229	21.77691	21.01324	20.28884	19.60121	18.94821	35
40	29.07051	27.82849	26.66174	25.56481	24.53287	23.56142	22.64618	21.78341	20.96943	20.20104	40
45	31.66831	30.17506	28.78194	27.48094	26.26500	25.12762	24.06269	23.06485	22.12896	21.25051	45
50	34.08661	32.33380	30.70953	29.20260	27.80315	26.50222	25.29144	24.16355	23.11162	22.12964	50

Present Value of a Series of Payments Increasing at Constant Rate

Annual Rate of Growth 5%

Holding Period	5.50%	5.75%	6.00%	6.25%	Discount Rate 6.50%	6.75%	7.00%	7.25%	7.50%	7.75%	
1	0.94787	0.94563	0.94340	0.94118	0.93897	0.93677	0.93458	0.93240	0.93023	0.92807	1
2	1.89124	1.88455	1.87789	1.87128	1.86471	1.85818	1.85169	1.84524	1.83883	1.83246	2
3	2.83015	2.81681	2.80357	2.79044	2.77741	2.76449	2.75166	2.73893	2.72630	2.71377	3
4	3.76460	3.74246	3.72052	3.69879	3.67726	3.65593	3.63480	3.61387	3.59313	3.57258	4
5	4.69463	4.66154	4.62882	4.59645	4.56444	4.53277	4.50144	4.47046	4.43980	4.40948	5
6	5.62025	5.57411	5.52855	5.48355	5.43911	5.39523	5.35188	5.30907	5.26678	5.22501	6
7	6.54148	6.48020	6.41979	6.36022	6.30147	6.24355	6.18643	6.13009	6.07453	6.01973	7
8	7.45834	7.37987	7.30262	7.22657	7.15169	7.07797	7.00537	6.93389	6.86350	6.79417	8
9	8.37086	8.27315	8.17712	8.08272	7.98993	7.89870	7.80901	7.72083	7.63411	7.54884	9
10	9.27906	9.16011	9.04338	8.92881	8.81636	8.70598	8.59763	8.49125	8.38681	8.28426	10
11	10.18295	10.04077	9.90146	9.76494	9.63115	9.50003	9.37150	9.24552	9.12200	9.00090	11
12	11.08256	10.91518	10.75145	10.59124	10.43447	10.28106	10.13091	9.98396	9.84009	9.69925	12
13	11.97790	11.78340	11.59341	11.40781	11.22647	11.04929	10.87613	10.70690	10.54148	10.37978	13
14	12.86900	12.64545	12.42744	12.21478	12.00732	11.80492	11.60742	11.41468	11.22656	11.04294	14
15	13.75588	13.50139	13.25360	13.01225	12.77717	12.54817	12.32503	12.10762	11.89571	11.68918	15
16	14.63856	14.35127	14.07196	13.80034	13.53617	13.27923	13.02924	12.78601	12.54930	12.31892	16
17	15.51705	15.19511	14.88260	14.57916	14.28449	13.99830	13.72028	13.45018	13.18769	12.93259	17
18	16.39138	16.03297	15.68560	15.34882	15.02227	14.70559	14.39840	14.10041	13.81123	13.53060	18
19	17.26156	16.86489	16.48102	16.10942	15.74965	15.40129	15.06385	14.73699	14.42027	14.11335	19
20	18.12762	17.69090	17.26893	16.86107	16.46679	16.08557	15.71687	15.36023	15.01515	14.68122	20
21	18.98958	18.51106	18.04942	17.60388	17.17383	16.75865	16.35767	15.97039	15.59619	15.23460	21
22	19.84745	19.32541	18.82254	18.33796	17.87091	17.42068	16.98650	16.56775	16.16372	15.77386	22
23	20.70125	20.13397	19.58836	19.06339	18.55818	18.07187	17.60357	17.15257	16.71805	16.29935	23
24	21.55101	20.93680	20.34696	19.78029	19.23576	18.71237	18.20911	17.72513	17.25949	16.81143	24
25	22.39674	21.73394	21.09841	20.48876	19.90380	19.34238	18.80333	18.28568	17.78834	17.31044	25
30	26.56566	25.63563	24.75062	23.90802	23.10549	22.34085	21.61193	20.91687	20.25372	19.62085	30
35	30.63672	29.40091	28.23379	27.13082	26.08796	25.10147	24.16767	23.28340	22.44546	21.65109	35
40	34.61222	33.03454	31.55572	30.16845	28.86624	27.64311	26.49332	25.41189	24.39392	23.43514	40
45	38.49440	36.54114	34.72389	33.03155	31.45430	29.98314	28.60959	27.32629	26.12611	25.00286	45
50	42.28546	39.92515	37.74541	35.73016	33.86516	32.13754	30.53534	29.04813	27.66604	26.38048	50

Annual Rate of Growth 6%

Holding Period	5.50%	5.75%	6.00%	6.25%	Discount Rate 6.50%	6.75%	7.00%	7.25%	7.50%	7.75%	
1	0.94787	0.94563	0.94340	0.94118	0.93897	0.93677	0.93458	0.93240	0.93023	0.92807	1
2	1.90023	1.89349	1.88679	1.88014	1.87353	1.86695	1.86042	1.85393	1.84749	1.84108	2
3	2.85710	2.84359	2.83019	2.81689	2.80370	2.79061	2.77762	2.76473	2.75194	2.73925	3
4	3.81851	3.79594	3.77359	3.75144	3.72950	3.70777	3.68624	3.66491	3.64377	3.62283	4
5	4.78447	4.75054	4.71698	4.68379	4.65096	4.61849	4.58637	4.55459	4.52316	4.49207	5
6	5.75502	5.70740	5.66038	5.61394	5.56809	5.52281	5.47808	5.43391	5.39028	5.34719	6
7	6.73016	6.66652	6.60377	6.54191	6.48092	6.42077	6.36146	6.30298	6.24530	6.18841	7
8	7.70992	7.62790	7.54717	7.46770	7.38946	7.31243	7.23659	7.16192	7.08839	7.01598	8
9	8.69433	8.59156	8.49057	8.39130	8.29373	8.19782	8.10354	8.01085	7.91971	7.83011	9
10	9.68341	9.55750	9.43397	9.31273	9.19376	9.07700	8.96238	8.84988	8.73944	8.63101	10
11	10.67717	10.52572	10.37736	10.23200	10.08956	9.94999	9.81320	9.67914	9.54772	9.41891	11
12	11.67564	11.49623	11.32076	11.14910	10.98116	10.81685	10.65607	10.49873	10.34473	10.19400	12
13	12.67884	12.46903	12.26416	12.06404	11.86857	11.67763	11.49106	11.30877	11.13062	10.95652	13
14	13.68680	13.44414	13.20755	12.97683	12.75182	12.53235	12.31824	12.10937	11.90554	11.70664	14
15	14.69953	14.42155	14.15095	13.88748	13.63092	13.38107	13.13770	12.90063	12.66965	12.44458	15
16	15.71707	15.40127	15.09435	14.79598	14.50589	14.22383	13.94949	13.68268	13.42309	13.17054	16
17	16.73943	16.38330	16.03774	15.70234	15.37675	15.06066	14.75370	14.45561	14.16603	13.88471	17
18	17.76663	17.36766	16.98114	16.60657	16.24353	15.89162	15.55040	15.21953	14.89859	14.58728	18
19	18.79870	18.35435	17.92454	17.50867	17.10623	16.71674	16.33964	15.97454	15.62094	15.27844	19
20	19.83566	19.34336	18.86794	18.40865	17.96489	17.53606	17.12152	16.72076	16.33320	15.95837	20
21	20.87754	20.33472	19.81133	19.30651	18.81951	18.34962	17.89608	17.45828	17.03553	16.62726	21
22	21.92435	21.32842	20.75473	20.20226	19.67012	19.15747	18.66341	18.18721	17.72806	17.28529	22
23	22.97613	22.32446	21.69813	21.09590	20.51674	19.95964	19.42356	18.90764	18.41092	17.93263	23
24	24.03289	23.32287	22.64152	21.98744	21.35938	20.75618	20.17661	19.61967	19.08426	18.56945	24
25	25.09466	24.32363	23.58492	22.87688	22.19807	21.54712	20.92262	20.32341	19.74819	19.19593	25
30	30.47947	29.36305	28.30191	27.29280	26.33281	25.41925	24.54939	23.72094	22.93149	22.17899	30
35	35.99310	34.46231	33.01890	31.65700	30.37140	29.15725	28.00983	26.92505	25.89880	24.92754	35
40	41.63863	39.62213	37.73589	35.97010	34.31607	32.76577	31.31155	29.94674	28.66479	27.46003	40
45	47.41921	44.84324	42.45288	40.23270	38.16901	36.24930	34.46185	32.79640	31.24311	29.79343	45
50	53.33809	50.12635	47.16988	44.44539	41.93235	39.61217	37.46766	35.48382	33.64650	31.94341	50

Present Value of a Series of Payments Increasing at Constant Rate

Annual Rate of Growth 7%

Holding Period	5.50%	5.75%	6.00%	6.25%	Discount Rate 6.50%	6.75%	7.00%	7.25%	7.50%	7.75%	
1	0.94787	0.94563	0.94340	0.94118	0.93897	0.93677	0.93458	0.93240	0.93023	0.92807	1
2	1.90921	1.90243	1.89569	1.88900	1.88234	1.87573	1.86916	1.86263	1.85614	1.84969	2
3	2.88422	2.87054	2.85697	2.84351	2.83015	2.81689	2.80374	2.79069	2.77774	2.76489	3
4	3.87310	3.85010	3.82732	3.80476	3.78240	3.76026	3.73832	3.71658	3.69505	3.67372	4
5	4.87604	4.84124	4.80683	4.77279	4.73913	4.70583	4.67290	4.64032	4.60810	4.57622	5
6	5.89323	5.84409	5.79557	5.74766	5.70034	5.65362	5.60748	5.56191	5.51690	5.47244	6
7	6.92489	6.85879	6.79364	6.72940	6.66607	6.60363	6.54205	6.48134	6.42147	6.36242	7
8	7.97121	7.88549	7.80113	7.71808	7.63633	7.55586	7.47663	7.39864	7.32183	7.24621	8
9	9.03242	8.92433	8.81812	8.71374	8.61115	8.51033	8.41121	8.31379	8.21801	8.12385	9
10	10.10871	9.97544	9.84471	9.71642	9.59055	9.46702	9.34579	9.22681	9.11002	8.99538	10
11	11.20030	11.03898	10.88098	10.72619	10.57454	10.42596	10.28037	10.13771	9.99788	9.86084	11
12	12.30742	12.11509	11.92703	11.74308	11.56315	11.38715	11.21495	11.04648	10.88161	10.72028	12
13	13.43027	13.20393	12.98294	12.76715	12.55640	12.35059	12.14953	11.95313	11.76123	11.57373	13
14	14.56909	14.30563	14.04882	13.79844	13.55432	13.31628	13.08411	12.85767	12.63676	12.42125	14
15	15.72410	15.42035	15.12475	14.83702	14.55692	14.28423	14.01869	13.76010	13.50821	13.26286	15
16	16.89554	16.54825	16.21084	15.88293	15.56423	15.25445	14.95326	14.66042	14.37562	14.09862	16
17	18.08363	17.68948	17.30717	16.93622	16.57627	16.22695	15.88784	15.55865	15.23899	14.92856	17
18	19.28861	18.84420	18.41384	17.99695	17.59306	17.20172	16.82242	16.45479	16.09834	15.75272	18
19	20.51073	20.01258	19.53095	19.06516	18.61462	18.17877	17.75700	17.34883	16.95369	16.57115	19
20	21.75022	21.19476	20.65860	20.14092	19.64098	19.15811	18.69158	18.24079	17.80507	17.38388	20
21	23.00733	22.39091	21.79689	21.22426	20.67216	20.13975	19.62616	19.13067	18.65249	18.19095	21
22	24.28232	23.60121	22.94592	22.31526	21.70818	21.12368	20.56074	20.01848	19.49597	18.99241	22
23	25.57543	24.82581	24.10579	23.41395	22.74906	22.10992	21.49531	20.90422	20.33552	19.78829	23
24	26.88694	26.06488	25.27660	24.52041	23.79483	23.09847	22.42989	21.78790	21.17117	20.57862	24
25	28.21708	27.31860	26.45846	25.63467	24.84551	24.08934	23.36447	22.66951	22.00293	21.36346	25
30	35.15694	33.81304	32.53710	31.32507	30.17336	29.07857	28.03736	27.04685	26.10406	25.20645	30
35	42.60439	40.70048	38.90794	37.21917	35.62745	34.12650	32.71025	31.37341	30.11070	28.91755	35
40	50.59656	48.00473	45.58501	43.32425	41.21078	39.23383	37.38314	35.64978	34.02503	32.50127	40
45	59.17327	55.75099	52.58304	49.64788	46.92641	44.40123	42.05603	39.87654	37.84916	35.96200	45
50	68.37730	63.96602	59.91745	56.19786	52.77748	49.62943	46.72891	44.05427	41.58519	39.30395	50

Annual Rate of Growth 8%

Holding Period	5.50%	5.75%	6.00%	6.25%	Discount Rate 6.50%	6.75%	7.00%	7.25%	7.50%	7.75%	
1	0.94787	0.94563	0.94340	0.94118	0.93897	0.93677	0.93458	0.93240	0.93023	0.92807	1
2	1.91820	1.91137	1.90459	1.89785	1.89116	1.88451	1.87789	1.87132	1.86479	1.85830	2
3	2.91152	2.89767	2.88392	2.87029	2.85676	2.84334	2.83002	2.81681	2.80370	2.79069	3
4	3.92838	3.90495	3.88173	3.85874	3.83597	3.81340	3.79105	3.76891	3.74697	3.72524	4
5	4.96934	4.93366	4.89837	4.86347	4.82896	4.79482	4.76106	4.72767	4.69463	4.66195	5
6	6.03496	5.98425	5.93419	5.88475	5.83594	5.78774	5.74014	5.69313	5.64670	5.60085	6
7	7.12584	7.05720	6.98955	6.92286	6.85710	6.79228	6.72836	6.66534	6.60319	6.54191	7
8	8.24256	8.15298	8.06483	7.97806	7.89265	7.80858	7.72582	7.64435	7.56414	7.48517	8
9	9.38575	9.27208	9.16039	9.05064	8.94278	8.83679	8.73260	8.63021	8.52955	8.43061	9
10	10.55603	10.41498	10.27663	10.14088	10.00770	9.87703	9.74880	9.62296	9.49946	9.37824	10
11	11.75404	11.58220	11.41392	11.24908	11.08762	10.92945	10.77449	10.62266	10.47387	10.32808	11
12	12.98044	12.77426	12.57267	12.37554	12.18275	11.99420	11.80976	11.62934	11.45282	11.28011	12
13	14.23591	13.99168	13.75329	13.52055	13.29331	13.07142	12.85471	12.64307	12.43632	12.23436	13
14	15.52112	15.23500	14.95618	14.68442	14.41950	14.16125	13.90943	13.66388	13.42440	13.19082	14
15	16.83679	16.50478	16.18177	15.86745	15.56156	15.26384	14.97400	14.69184	14.41707	14.14950	15
16	18.18363	17.80157	17.43049	17.06998	16.71970	16.37934	16.04852	15.72698	15.41436	15.11041	16
17	19.56239	19.12595	18.70276	18.29231	17.89416	17.50791	17.13309	16.76936	16.41628	16.07354	17
18	20.97383	20.47851	19.99904	19.53477	19.08515	18.64969	18.22779	17.81903	17.42287	17.03891	18
19	22.41871	21.85985	21.31978	20.79769	20.29293	19.80483	19.33272	18.87604	18.43414	18.00651	19
20	23.89782	23.27058	22.66544	22.08142	21.51771	20.97351	20.44798	19.94044	19.45011	18.97637	20
21	25.41199	24.71133	24.03648	23.38629	22.75974	22.15587	21.57366	21.01229	20.47081	19.94847	21
22	26.96204	26.18273	25.43340	24.71265	24.01927	23.35208	22.70986	22.09163	21.49625	20.92283	22
23	28.54882	27.68543	26.85667	26.06086	25.29653	24.56229	23.85668	23.17852	22.52647	21.89945	23
24	30.17320	29.22011	28.30680	27.43128	26.59179	25.78667	25.01422	24.27300	23.56147	22.87833	24
25	31.83608	30.78744	29.78429	28.82426	27.90528	27.02539	26.18258	25.37515	24.60129	23.85949	25
30	40.76054	39.13872	37.60056	36.14099	34.75554	33.44000	32.19020	31.00256	29.87339	28.79953	30
35	50.79371	48.41706	46.18257	44.08045	42.10199	40.23907	38.48384	36.82950	35.26923	33.79714	35
40	62.07335	58.72536	55.60535	52.69565	49.98057	47.44564	45.07714	42.86306	40.79174	38.85300	40
45	74.75430	70.17795	65.95125	62.04409	58.42983	55.08414	51.98433	49.11055	46.44387	43.96778	45
50	89.01065	82.90186	77.31071	72.18819	67.49110	63.18046	59.22039	55.57956	52.22868	49.14218	50

Present Value of a Series of Payments Increasing at Constant Rate

Annual Rate of Growth 9%

Holding Period	5.50%	5.75%	6.00%	6.25%	Discount Rate 6.50%	6.75%	7.00%	7.25%	7.50%	7.75%	
1	0.94787	0.94563	0.94340	0.94118	0.93897	0.93677	0.93458	0.93240	0.93023	0.92807	1
2	1.92718	1.92031	1.91349	1.90671	1.89998	1.89328	1.88663	1.88002	1.87344	1.86692	2
3	2.93898	2.92496	2.91104	2.89724	2.88354	2.86995	2.85647	2.84309	2.82982	2.81665	3
4	3.98435	3.96048	3.93683	3.91340	3.89020	3.86721	3.84444	3.82189	3.79954	3.77740	4
5	5.06440	5.02782	4.99164	4.95587	4.92048	4.88549	4.85088	4.81665	4.78279	4.74929	5
6	6.18028	6.12797	6.07631	6.02531	5.97496	5.92523	5.87613	5.82764	5.77975	5.73246	6
7	7.33318	7.26192	7.19168	7.12244	7.05418	6.98689	6.92054	6.85513	6.79063	6.72704	7
8	8.52433	8.43073	8.33862	8.24796	8.15874	8.07092	7.98448	7.89939	7.81562	7.73315	8
9	9.75500	9.63545	9.51801	9.40261	9.28922	9.17780	9.06830	8.96069	8.85491	8.75094	9
10	11.02649	10.87721	10.73079	10.58715	10.44625	10.30802	10.17238	10.03930	9.90870	9.78053	10
11	12.34017	12.15712	11.97789	11.80235	11.63043	11.46205	11.29710	11.13551	10.97719	10.82207	11
12	13.69743	13.47637	13.26028	13.04900	12.84241	12.64041	12.44284	12.24961	12.06059	11.87569	12
13	15.09971	14.83616	14.57897	14.32791	14.08284	13.84360	13.60999	13.38189	13.15911	12.94154	13
14	16.54852	16.23775	15.93498	15.63993	15.35239	15.07216	14.79896	14.53264	14.27296	14.01974	14
15	18.04539	17.68241	17.32936	16.98591	16.65174	16.32660	16.01016	15.70217	15.40235	15.11046	15
16	19.59192	19.17146	18.76321	18.36672	17.98160	17.60749	17.24399	16.89079	16.54750	16.21383	16
17	21.18976	20.70628	20.23765	19.78327	19.34267	18.91538	18.50089	18.09880	17.70862	17.33000	17
18	22.84061	22.28827	21.75381	21.23648	20.73569	20.25083	19.78128	19.32652	18.88595	18.45912	18
19	24.54622	23.91888	23.31288	22.72731	22.16141	21.61444	21.08560	20.57427	20.07971	19.60134	19
20	26.30842	25.59960	24.91607	24.25672	23.62059	23.00678	22.41430	21.84238	21.29012	20.75680	20
21	28.12908	27.33198	26.56464	25.82572	25.11403	24.42847	23.76784	23.13119	22.51743	21.92568	21
22	30.01015	29.11759	28.25987	27.43533	26.64253	25.88012	25.14667	24.44102	23.76185	23.10811	22
23	31.95361	30.95809	30.00308	29.08659	28.20691	27.36237	26.55128	25.77223	25.02365	24.30426	23
24	33.96156	32.85514	31.79562	30.78060	29.80801	28.87587	27.98215	27.12515	26.30304	25.51429	24
25	36.03611	34.81050	33.63889	32.51845	31.44669	30.42126	29.43976	28.50016	27.60030	26.73835	25
30	47.48808	45.52650	43.66795	41.90614	40.23549	38.65077	37.14680	35.71913	34.36317	33.07500	30
35	60.96966	57.99354	55.19885	52.57324	50.10542	47.78490	45.60157	43.54660	41.61122	39.78783	35
40	76.84157	72.49774	68.45651	64.69413	61.18947	57.92309	54.87659	52.03385	49.37927	46.89918	40
45	95.52649	89.37198	83.69949	78.46692	73.63698	69.17570	65.05145	61.23651	57.70460	54.43270	45
50	117.52340	109.00355	101.22510	94.11676	87.61569	81.66525	76.21345	71.21488	66.62720	62.41346	50

Annual Rate of Growth 10%

Holding Period	5.50%	5.75%	6.00%	6.25%	Discount Rate 6.50%	6.75%	7.00%	7.25%	7.50%	7.75%	
1	0.94787	0.94563	0.94340	0.94118	0.93897	0.93677	0.93458	0.93240	0.93023	0.92807	1
2	1.93617	1.92926	1.92239	1.91557	1.90879	1.90206	1.89536	1.88871	1.88210	1.87553	2
3	2.96662	2.95242	2.93833	2.92436	2.91049	2.89673	2.88308	2.86954	2.85610	2.84277	3
4	4.04102	4.01670	3.99261	3.96874	3.94511	3.92169	3.89850	3.87552	3.85275	3.83020	4
5	5.16126	5.12375	5.08667	5.04999	5.01372	4.97786	4.94238	4.90729	4.87259	4.83826	5
6	6.32927	6.27530	6.22202	6.16941	6.11746	6.06617	6.01553	5.96552	5.91613	5.86736	6
7	7.54711	7.47312	7.40021	7.32833	7.25747	7.18763	7.11877	7.05088	6.98395	6.91796	7
8	8.81689	8.71909	8.62286	8.52815	8.43495	8.34322	8.25294	8.16408	8.07660	7.99049	8
9	10.14084	10.01513	9.89164	9.77032	9.65112	9.53400	9.41891	9.30581	9.19466	9.08542	9
10	11.52125	11.36325	11.20831	11.05633	10.90726	10.76103	10.61757	10.47683	10.33872	10.20321	10
11	12.96055	12.76556	12.57466	12.38773	12.20468	12.02542	11.84984	11.67786	11.50939	11.34435	11
12	14.46124	14.22422	13.99257	13.76612	13.54474	13.32830	13.11665	12.90970	12.70728	12.50931	12
13	16.02594	15.74151	15.46399	15.19316	14.92884	14.67085	14.41899	14.17312	13.93303	13.69860	13
14	17.65738	17.31977	16.99094	16.67057	16.35842	16.05427	15.75784	15.46893	15.18729	14.91272	14
15	19.35840	18.96147	18.57550	18.20012	17.83499	17.47981	17.13423	16.79797	16.47071	16.15220	15
16	21.13199	20.66914	20.21986	19.78365	19.36008	18.94875	18.54920	18.16109	17.78398	17.41756	16
17	22.98122	22.44544	21.92627	21.42307	20.93529	20.46242	20.00385	19.55916	19.12780	18.70934	17
18	24.90933	24.29313	23.69708	23.12036	22.56228	22.02216	21.49929	20.99308	20.50286	20.02810	18
19	26.91968	26.21507	25.53470	24.87755	24.24272	23.62940	23.03665	22.46377	21.90990	21.37440	19
20	29.01579	28.21426	27.44167	26.69675	25.97840	25.28556	24.61711	23.97216	23.34967	22.74880	20
21	31.20130	30.29379	29.42061	28.58017	27.77112	26.99215	26.24189	25.51923	24.82291	24.15191	21
22	33.48003	32.45690	31.47422	30.53006	29.62275	28.75069	27.91222	27.10598	26.33042	25.58432	22
23	35.85596	34.70694	33.60532	32.54877	31.53523	30.56277	29.62939	28.73340	27.87299	27.04664	23
24	38.33323	37.04741	35.81684	34.63872	33.51057	32.43003	31.39470	30.40256	29.45143	28.53949	24
25	40.91617	39.48193	38.11182	36.80244	35.55082	34.35413	33.20950	32.11451	31.06658	30.06352	25
30	55.58049	53.20325	50.95299	48.82189	46.80300	44.88981	43.07589	41.35568	39.72352	38.17452	30
35	73.65071	69.91252	66.40692	63.11752	60.02972	57.12996	54.40517	51.84395	49.43500	47.16849	35
40	95.91787	90.26039	85.00521	80.12038	75.57747	71.35033	67.41427	63.74762	60.32948	57.14155	40
45	123.35673	115.03920	107.38765	100.34316	93.85074	87.87128	82.35223	77.25770	72.55107	68.20029	45
50	157.16845	145.21383	134.32417	124.39562	115.33669	107.06499	99.50507	92.59097	86.26142	80.46289	50

Present Value of a Series of Payments Increasing at Constant Rate

Annual Rate of Growth 3%

Holding Period					Discount Rate						
	8.00%	8.25%	8.50%	8.75%	9.00%	9.25%	9.50%	9.75%	10.00%	10.25%	
1	0.92593	0.92379	0.92166	0.91954	0.91743	0.91533	0.91324	0.91116	0.90909	0.90703	1
2	1.80898	1.80277	1.79660	1.79046	1.78436	1.77830	1.77227	1.76628	1.76033	1.75441	2
3	2.65116	2.63913	2.62718	2.61533	2.60357	2.59190	2.58031	2.56881	2.55740	2.54607	3
4	3.45435	3.43492	3.41567	3.39659	3.37769	3.35895	3.34038	3.32198	3.30375	3.28567	4
5	4.22035	4.19212	4.16418	4.13654	4.10919	4.08212	4.05534	4.02883	4.00260	3.97664	5
6	4.95089	4.91259	4.87475	4.83737	4.80043	4.76392	4.72785	4.69221	4.65698	4.62217	6
7	5.64761	5.59813	5.54931	5.50114	5.45361	5.40672	5.36045	5.31478	5.26972	5.22524	7
8	6.31207	6.25041	6.18966	6.12982	6.07085	6.01274	5.95549	5.89907	5.84346	5.78866	8
9	6.94577	6.87106	6.79756	6.72525	6.65410	6.58410	6.51521	6.44742	6.38070	6.31503	9
10	7.55013	7.46161	7.37464	7.28920	7.20525	7.12276	7.04170	6.96204	6.88374	6.80679	10
11	8.12651	8.02352	7.92247	7.82334	7.72606	7.63062	7.53694	7.44501	7.35478	7.26621	11
12	8.67621	8.55817	8.44253	8.32923	8.21821	8.10941	8.00279	7.89828	7.79584	7.69541	12
13	9.20046	9.06690	8.93623	8.80838	8.68326	8.56082	8.44098	8.32367	8.20883	8.09639	13
14	9.70044	9.55095	9.40490	9.26219	9.12271	8.98640	8.85316	8.72290	8.59554	8.47101	14
15	10.17727	10.01153	9.84981	9.69200	9.53798	9.38764	9.24087	9.09757	8.95764	8.82099	15
16	10.63203	10.44977	10.27217	10.09909	9.93038	9.76592	9.60557	9.44920	9.29670	9.14795	16
17	11.06573	10.86676	10.67312	10.48466	10.30118	10.12256	9.94861	9.77921	9.61418	9.45342	17
18	11.47935	11.26352	11.05374	10.84984	10.65158	10.45880	10.27130	10.08892	9.91146	9.73879	18
19	11.87383	11.64104	11.41507	11.19571	10.98268	10.77580	10.57483	10.37957	10.18982	10.00540	19
20	12.25004	12.00025	11.75809	11.52329	11.29556	11.07467	10.86034	10.65236	10.45047	10.25448	20
21	12.60883	12.34204	12.08371	11.83356	11.59122	11.35644	11.12891	10.90836	10.69453	10.48718	21
22	12.95102	12.66725	12.39283	12.12741	11.87060	11.62209	11.38153	11.14862	10.92306	10.70458	22
23	13.27736	12.97669	12.68628	12.40573	12.13460	11.87254	11.61915	11.37411	11.13705	10.90768	23
24	13.58859	13.27113	12.96486	12.66934	12.38407	12.10867	11.84267	11.58572	11.33742	11.09742	24
25	13.88541	13.55128	13.22931	12.91901	12.61981	12.33128	12.05293	11.78432	11.52504	11.27469	25
30	15.17570	14.76095	14.36358	13.98275	13.61757	13.26729	12.93115	12.60846	12.29853	12.00077	30
35	16.19371	15.70439	15.23807	14.79348	14.36932	13.96450	13.57787	13.20847	12.85530	12.51751	35
40	16.99690	16.44019	15.91227	15.41138	14.93573	14.48382	14.05412	13.64531	13.25608	12.88527	40
45	17.63060	17.01405	16.43206	15.88231	15.36250	14.87065	14.40484	13.96335	13.54456	13.14701	45
50	18.13059	17.46161	16.83281	16.24123	15.68404	15.15879	14.66310	14.19491	13.75222	13.33328	50

Annual Rate of Growth 4%

Holding Period					Discount Rate						
	8.00%	8.25%	8.50%	8.75%	9.00%	9.25%	9.50%	9.75%	10.00%	10.25%	
1	0.92593	0.92379	0.92166	0.91954	0.91743	0.91533	0.91324	0.91116	0.90909	0.90703	1
2	1.81756	1.81131	1.80509	1.79892	1.79278	1.78668	1.78061	1.77459	1.76859	1.76264	2
3	2.67617	2.66398	2.65189	2.63988	2.62797	2.61615	2.60442	2.59277	2.58122	2.56975	3
4	3.50298	3.48318	3.46356	3.44412	3.42485	3.40576	3.38684	3.36810	3.34951	3.33110	4
5	4.29916	4.27021	4.24157	4.21323	4.18518	4.15743	4.12997	4.10280	4.07590	4.04929	5
6	5.06586	5.02635	4.98731	4.94874	4.91063	4.87298	4.83577	4.79901	4.76267	4.72677	6
7	5.80416	5.75280	5.70212	5.65213	5.60280	5.55414	5.50612	5.45874	5.41198	5.36584	7
8	6.51512	6.45072	6.38729	6.32480	6.26323	6.20257	6.14280	6.08391	6.02587	5.96868	8
9	7.19974	7.12125	7.04403	6.96808	6.89335	6.81984	6.74750	6.67632	6.60628	6.53735	9
10	7.85901	7.76545	7.67354	7.58327	7.49457	7.40744	7.32183	7.23770	7.15503	7.07379	10
11	8.49386	8.38436	8.27694	8.17159	8.06822	7.96681	7.86730	7.76967	7.67385	7.57981	11
12	9.10520	8.97897	8.85532	8.73421	8.61555	8.49930	8.38538	8.27376	8.16436	8.05714	12
13	9.69390	9.55023	9.40971	9.27225	9.13777	9.00620	8.87744	8.75145	8.62812	8.50742	13
14	10.26079	10.09907	9.94110	9.78680	9.63604	9.48874	9.34479	9.20410	9.06659	8.93217	14
15	10.80669	10.62636	10.45046	10.27887	10.11145	9.94809	9.78865	9.63305	9.48114	9.33284	15
16	11.33236	11.13294	10.93868	10.74945	10.56505	10.38536	10.21023	10.03952	9.87308	9.71080	16
17	11.83857	11.61964	11.40667	11.19947	10.99785	10.80163	10.61063	10.42469	10.24364	10.06733	17
18	12.32603	12.08723	11.85524	11.62984	11.41079	11.19789	10.99092	10.78968	10.59398	10.40365	18
19	12.79544	12.53646	12.28520	12.04141	11.80479	11.57511	11.35210	11.13556	10.92522	10.72090	19
20	13.24746	12.96806	12.69734	12.43501	12.18071	11.93420	11.69515	11.46331	11.23839	11.02017	20
21	13.68274	13.38270	13.09238	12.81141	12.53940	12.27603	12.02096	11.77388	11.53448	11.30247	21
22	14.10189	13.78107	13.47103	13.17137	12.88163	12.60144	12.33041	12.06819	11.81442	11.56877	22
23	14.50553	14.16380	13.83399	13.51561	13.20816	12.91121	12.62432	12.34708	12.07908	11.81998	23
24	14.89421	14.53151	14.18188	13.84481	13.51971	13.20610	12.90346	12.61136	12.32932	12.05694	24
25	15.26850	14.88477	14.51535	14.15964	13.81697	13.48681	13.16858	12.86179	12.56590	12.28047	25
30	16.94199	16.45364	15.98636	15.53912	15.11082	14.70054	14.30733	13.93035	13.56876	13.22181	30
35	18.32769	17.73778	17.17660	16.64254	16.13392	15.64936	15.18741	14.74683	14.32636	13.92492	35
40	19.47510	18.78887	18.13966	17.52512	16.94293	16.39108	15.86759	15.37069	14.89869	14.45009	40
45	20.42520	19.64920	18.91889	18.23108	17.58265	16.97091	16.39326	15.84738	15.33106	14.84234	45
50	21.21191	20.35340	19.54940	18.79576	18.08850	17.42419	16.79953	16.21161	15.65769	15.13532	50

Present Value of a Series of Payments Increasing at Constant Rate

Annual Rate of Growth 5%

Holding Period	\	\	\	\	Discount Rate	\	\	\	\	\	
	8.00%	8.25%	8.50%	8.75%	9.00%	9.25%	9.50%	9.75%	10.00%	10.25%	
1	0.92593	0.92379	0.92166	0.91954	0.91743	0.91533	0.91324	0.91116	0.90909	0.90703	1
2	1.82613	1.81984	1.81359	1.80737	1.80120	1.79506	1.78895	1.78289	1.77686	1.77087	2
3	2.70133	2.68899	2.67674	2.66459	2.65253	2.64056	2.62868	2.61689	2.60518	2.59357	3
4	3.55222	3.53205	3.51206	3.49225	3.47262	3.45317	3.43389	3.41479	3.39586	3.37710	4
5	4.37947	4.34979	4.32042	4.29137	4.26261	4.23417	4.20601	4.17816	4.15059	4.12331	5
6	5.18375	5.14298	5.10271	5.06293	5.02362	4.98478	4.94641	4.90849	4.87102	4.83399	6
7	5.96568	5.91236	5.85977	5.80788	5.75670	5.70620	5.65637	5.60721	5.55870	5.51083	7
8	6.72589	6.65864	6.59240	6.52715	6.46287	6.39955	6.33716	6.27569	6.21512	6.15544	8
9	7.46499	7.38252	7.30140	7.22162	7.14313	7.06593	6.98997	6.91524	6.84171	6.76936	9
10	8.18355	8.08466	7.98753	7.89214	7.79843	7.70638	7.61595	7.52711	7.43981	7.35403	10
11	8.88216	8.76572	8.65153	8.53954	8.42968	8.32193	8.21621	8.11250	8.01073	7.91087	11
12	9.56136	9.42633	9.29410	9.16461	9.03777	8.91352	8.79180	8.67255	8.55570	8.44119	12
13	10.22169	10.06711	9.91595	9.76813	9.62354	9.48210	9.34373	9.20836	9.07589	8.94626	13
14	10.86368	10.68866	10.51774	10.35084	10.18781	10.02857	9.87299	9.72098	9.57244	9.42728	14
15	11.48784	11.29154	11.10012	10.91345	10.73137	10.55377	10.38049	10.21142	10.04642	9.88539	15
16	12.09465	11.87632	11.66371	11.45667	11.25499	11.05854	10.86714	10.68063	10.49886	10.32169	16
17	12.68462	12.44354	12.20912	11.98115	11.75940	11.54368	11.33378	11.12953	10.93073	10.73721	17
18	13.25819	12.99374	12.73693	12.48755	12.24529	12.00995	11.78125	11.55901	11.34297	11.13294	18
19	13.81583	13.52741	13.24772	12.97648	12.71335	12.45807	12.21033	11.96989	11.73647	11.50983	19
20	14.35799	14.04506	13.74204	13.44856	13.16424	12.88876	12.62178	12.36300	12.11208	11.86878	20
21	14.88508	14.54718	14.22040	13.90436	13.59858	13.30270	13.01632	12.73908	12.47062	12.21063	21
22	15.39753	15.03421	14.68334	14.34444	14.01698	13.70054	13.39464	13.09890	12.81287	12.53620	22
23	15.89575	15.50663	15.13134	14.76934	14.42002	14.08290	13.75742	13.44314	13.13956	12.84627	23
24	16.38012	15.96486	15.56489	15.17960	14.80828	14.45038	14.10529	13.77248	13.45139	13.14157	24
25	16.85105	16.40933	15.98446	15.57570	15.18229	14.80357	14.43886	14.08756	13.74906	13.42281	25
30	19.01656	18.43936	17.88779	17.36053	16.85625	16.37381	15.91202	15.46987	15.04631	14.64044	30
35	20.89755	20.18242	19.50331	18.85814	18.24479	17.66147	17.10636	16.57784	16.07435	15.59448	35
40	22.53141	21.67906	20.87454	20.11474	19.39658	18.71742	18.07464	17.46592	16.88904	16.34200	40
45	23.95061	22.96412	22.03841	21.16912	20.35199	19.58335	18.85965	18.17775	17.53465	16.92769	45
50	25.18335	24.06752	23.02630	22.05382	21.14449	20.29345	19.49609	18.74831	18.04628	17.38661	50

Annual Rate of Growth 6%

Holding Period	\	\	\	\	Discount Rate	\	\	\	\	\	
	8.00%	8.25%	8.50%	8.75%	9.00%	9.25%	9.50%	9.75%	10.00%	10.25%	
1	0.92593	0.92379	0.92166	0.91954	0.91743	0.91533	0.91324	0.91116	0.90909	0.90703	1
2	1.83470	1.82837	1.82208	1.81583	1.80961	1.80343	1.79729	1.79119	1.78512	1.77909	2
3	2.72665	2.71416	2.70176	2.68945	2.67724	2.66512	2.65309	2.64115	2.62930	2.61754	3
4	3.60209	3.58153	3.56116	3.54098	3.52098	3.50117	3.48153	3.46207	3.44278	3.42367	4
5	4.46131	4.43088	4.40077	4.37098	4.34151	4.31234	4.28349	4.25494	4.22668	4.19872	5
6	5.30462	5.26257	5.22103	5.17999	5.13945	5.09939	5.05981	5.02071	4.98207	4.94389	6
7	6.13231	6.07697	6.02238	5.96854	5.91542	5.86303	5.81133	5.76032	5.71000	5.66034	7
8	6.94467	6.87445	6.80528	6.73715	6.67005	6.60394	6.53882	6.47466	6.41145	6.34917	8
9	7.74199	7.65535	7.57013	7.48633	7.40390	7.32282	7.24306	7.16460	7.08740	7.01145	9
10	8.52455	8.42002	8.31737	8.21656	8.11755	8.02031	7.92479	7.83095	7.73877	7.64820	10
11	9.29261	9.16879	9.04738	8.92833	8.81156	8.69705	8.58472	8.47454	8.36645	8.26040	11
12	10.04645	9.90201	9.76057	9.62209	9.48647	9.35366	9.22357	9.09614	8.97130	8.84900	12
13	10.78633	10.61998	10.45733	10.29832	10.14281	9.99074	9.84199	9.69650	9.55417	9.41491	13
14	11.51251	11.32303	11.13804	10.95744	10.78108	10.60886	10.44065	10.27635	10.11583	9.95901	14
15	12.22524	12.01146	11.80306	11.59990	11.40178	11.20860	11.02017	10.83638	10.65707	10.48213	15
16	12.92477	12.68559	12.45276	12.22611	12.00540	11.79049	11.58117	11.37728	11.17864	10.98509	16
17	13.61135	13.34571	13.08749	12.83648	12.59241	12.35508	12.12424	11.89970	11.68123	11.46866	17
18	14.28522	13.99210	13.70759	13.43142	13.16326	12.90287	12.64995	12.40426	12.16555	11.93358	18
19	14.94660	14.62506	14.31341	14.01132	13.71840	13.43436	13.15885	12.89159	12.63226	12.38059	19
20	15.59574	15.24486	14.90526	14.57655	14.25826	13.95005	13.65149	13.36227	13.08199	12.81036	20
21	16.23285	15.85178	15.48348	15.12749	14.78326	14.45039	14.12839	13.81686	13.51537	13.22357	21
22	16.85817	16.44609	16.04838	15.66449	15.29381	14.93585	14.59004	14.25592	13.93300	13.62085	22
23	17.47191	17.02804	16.60026	16.18792	15.79031	15.40686	15.03693	14.67998	14.33543	14.00281	23
24	18.07428	17.59789	17.13942	16.69811	16.27315	15.86387	15.46954	15.08955	14.72323	14.37005	24
25	18.66549	18.15591	17.66616	17.19540	16.74269	16.30728	15.88832	15.48512	15.09694	14.72313	25
30	21.46135	20.77674	20.12331	19.49946	18.90354	18.33414	17.78980	17.26925	16.77122	16.29458	30
35	24.00774	23.13628	22.31012	21.52658	20.78295	20.07693	19.40620	18.76871	18.16243	17.58560	35
40	26.32693	25.26059	24.25634	23.31002	22.41757	21.57547	20.78027	20.02891	19.31844	18.64625	40
45	28.43918	27.17312	25.98844	24.87910	23.83929	22.86399	21.94833	21.08803	20.27900	19.51763	45
50	30.36296	28.89499	27.52997	26.25957	25.07584	23.97192	22.94128	21.97816	21.07717	20.23352	50

Present Value of a Series of Payments Increasing at Constant Rate

Annual Rate of Growth 7%

Holding Period	8.00%	8.25%	8.50%	8.75%	Discount Rate 9.00%	9.25%	9.50%	9.75%	10.00%	10.25%	
1	0.92593	0.92379	0.92166	0.91954	0.91743	0.91533	0.91324	0.91116	0.90909	0.90703	1
2	1.84328	1.83691	1.83058	1.82428	1.81803	1.81181	1.80563	1.79949	1.79339	1.78732	2
3	2.75214	2.73948	2.72693	2.71447	2.70210	2.68983	2.67765	2.66556	2.65357	2.64166	3
4	3.65258	3.63164	3.61089	3.59033	3.56995	3.54977	3.52976	3.50994	3.49029	3.47082	4
5	4.54469	4.51349	4.48263	4.45209	4.42188	4.39199	4.36241	4.33315	4.30419	4.27554	5
6	5.42853	5.38516	5.34231	5.29999	5.25818	5.21687	5.17606	5.13574	5.09589	5.05653	6
7	6.30419	6.24676	6.19011	6.13424	6.07913	6.02476	5.97112	5.91821	5.86601	5.81450	7
8	7.17175	7.09842	7.02620	6.95507	6.88501	6.81601	6.74804	6.68108	6.61512	6.55013	8
9	8.03127	7.94024	7.85072	7.76269	7.67611	7.59097	7.50722	7.42484	7.34379	7.26407	9
10	8.88283	8.77233	8.66384	8.55731	8.45270	8.34996	8.24906	8.14995	8.05260	7.95697	10
11	9.72651	9.59483	9.46572	9.33915	9.21503	9.09333	8.97397	8.85690	8.74207	8.62944	11
12	10.56237	10.40782	10.25652	10.10841	9.96338	9.82138	9.68232	9.54614	9.41274	9.28208	12
13	11.39050	11.21142	11.03638	10.86528	10.69800	10.53445	10.37451	10.21810	10.06512	9.91549	13
14	12.21096	12.00575	11.80546	11.60998	11.41913	11.23282	11.05089	10.87323	10.69971	10.53023	14
15	13.02382	12.79090	12.56391	12.34269	12.12704	11.91681	11.71183	11.51194	11.31699	11.12684	15
16	13.82915	13.56699	13.31188	13.06362	12.82196	12.58672	12.35768	12.13465	11.91744	11.70587	16
17	14.62703	14.33411	14.04950	13.77294	13.50412	13.24283	12.98878	12.74176	12.50151	12.26783	17
18	15.41752	15.09238	14.77692	14.47085	14.17377	13.88542	13.60547	13.33365	13.06965	12.81322	18
19	16.20069	15.84189	15.49429	15.15752	14.83113	14.51479	14.20809	13.91071	13.62229	13.34254	19
20	16.97661	16.58275	16.20174	15.83315	15.47643	15.13119	14.79694	14.47331	14.15987	13.85625	20
21	17.74534	17.31505	16.89942	16.49790	16.10989	15.73489	15.37236	15.02182	14.68278	14.35482	21
22	18.50696	18.03889	17.58744	17.15196	16.73173	16.32617	15.93463	15.55658	15.19143	14.83869	22
23	19.26152	18.75438	18.26595	17.79549	17.34215	16.90526	16.48407	16.07794	15.68621	15.30830	23
24	20.00910	19.46160	18.93509	18.42867	17.94138	17.47243	17.02096	16.58624	16.16749	15.76407	24
25	20.74976	20.16066	19.59497	19.05166	18.52961	18.02792	17.54560	17.08180	16.63565	16.20640	25
30	24.35143	23.53672	22.76004	22.01941	21.31277	20.63839	19.99448	19.37946	18.79175	18.22998	30
35	27.78941	26.72230	25.71229	24.75594	23.84980	22.99090	22.17629	21.40332	20.66944	19.97237	35
40	31.07115	29.72815	28.46603	27.27926	26.16245	25.11094	24.12015	23.18602	22.30468	21.47265	40
45	34.20375	32.56442	31.03461	29.60599	28.27058	27.02147	25.85201	24.75629	23.72876	22.76446	45
50	37.19398	35.24068	33.43048	31.75143	30.19227	28.74321	27.39499	26.13944	24.96895	23.87677	50

Annual Rate of Growth 8%

Holding Period	8.00%	8.25%	8.50%	8.75%	Discount Rate 9.00%	9.25%	9.50%	9.75%	10.00%	10.25%	
1	0.92593	0.92379	0.92166	0.91954	0.91743	0.91533	0.91324	0.91116	0.90909	0.90703	1
2	1.85185	1.84544	1.83907	1.83274	1.82645	1.82019	1.81397	1.80779	1.80165	1.79555	2
3	2.77778	2.76497	2.75225	2.73964	2.72712	2.71470	2.70237	2.69013	2.67799	2.66593	3
4	3.70370	3.68237	3.66123	3.64029	3.61953	3.59897	3.57859	3.55840	3.53839	3.51856	4
5	4.62963	4.59765	4.56602	4.53472	4.50376	4.47312	4.44281	4.41282	4.38314	4.35378	5
6	5.55555	5.51082	5.46663	5.42299	5.37987	5.33727	5.29519	5.25362	5.21254	5.17196	6
7	6.48148	6.42188	6.36310	6.30513	6.24794	6.19154	6.13590	6.08101	6.02686	5.97344	7
8	7.40741	7.33084	7.25544	7.18118	7.10805	7.03603	6.96509	6.89521	6.82637	6.75856	8
9	8.33333	8.23770	8.14366	8.05120	7.96027	7.87086	7.78291	7.69642	7.61134	7.52766	9
10	9.25926	9.14246	9.02779	8.91522	8.80467	8.69613	8.58954	8.48486	8.38205	8.28106	10
11	10.18518	10.04513	9.90785	9.77327	9.64133	9.51197	9.38512	9.26073	9.13874	9.01909	11
12	11.11111	10.94572	10.78385	10.62541	10.47031	10.31847	10.16980	10.02423	9.88167	9.74206	12
13	12.03703	11.84423	11.65581	11.47167	11.29168	11.11574	10.94373	10.77555	10.61109	10.45027	13
14	12.96296	12.74066	12.52375	12.31210	12.10552	11.90389	11.70705	11.51489	11.32725	11.14403	14
15	13.88889	13.63503	13.38770	13.14673	12.91189	12.68302	12.45993	12.24245	12.03040	11.82363	15
16	14.81481	14.52733	14.24766	13.97560	13.71086	13.45324	13.20248	12.95840	12.72075	12.48936	16
17	15.74074	15.41756	15.10366	14.79876	14.50250	14.21464	13.93487	13.66293	13.39856	13.14151	17
18	16.66666	16.30574	15.95572	15.61624	15.28688	14.96734	14.65722	14.35624	14.06404	13.78034	18
19	17.59259	17.19187	16.80385	16.42808	16.06407	15.71142	15.36968	15.03848	14.71742	14.40614	19
20	18.51851	18.07596	17.64807	17.23433	16.83412	16.44698	16.07238	15.70985	15.35892	15.01917	20
21	19.44444	18.95800	18.48840	18.03501	17.59711	17.17414	16.76545	16.37052	15.98876	15.61968	21
22	20.37036	19.83800	19.32486	18.83017	18.35310	17.89297	17.44903	17.02065	16.60714	16.20795	22
23	21.29629	20.71598	20.15746	19.61985	19.10215	18.60357	18.12324	17.66041	17.21429	16.78420	23
24	22.22221	21.59192	20.98623	20.40408	19.84433	19.30605	18.78822	18.28997	17.81039	17.34870	24
25	23.14814	22.46584	21.81117	21.18290	20.57970	20.00049	19.44409	18.90949	18.39565	17.90167	25
30	27.77776	26.80527	25.87923	24.99719	24.15660	23.35531	22.59110	21.86204	21.16618	20.50181	30
35	32.40739	31.09482	29.85442	28.68175	27.57239	26.52254	25.52839	24.58658	23.69383	22.84723	35
40	37.03701	35.33507	33.73885	32.24100	30.83435	29.51268	28.26993	27.10072	25.99991	24.96290	40
45	41.66664	39.52658	37.53460	35.67920	33.94939	32.33563	30.82877	29.42071	28.10382	26.87132	45
50	46.29626	43.66991	41.24368	39.00046	36.92415	35.00074	33.21708	31.56154	30.02330	28.59278	50

Present Value of a Series of Payments Increasing at Constant Rate

Annual Rate of Growth 9%

Holding Period	8.00%	8.25%	8.50%	8.75%	Discount Rate 9.00%	9.25%	9.50%	9.75%	10.00%	10.25%	
1	0.92593	0.92379	0.92166	0.91954	0.91743	0.91533	0.91324	0.91116	0.90909	0.90703	1
2	1.86043	1.85398	1.84757	1.84119	1.83486	1.82857	1.82231	1.81610	1.80992	1.80378	2
3	2.80358	2.79061	2.77774	2.76497	2.75229	2.73972	2.72723	2.71485	2.70255	2.69035	3
4	3.75546	3.73373	3.71220	3.69086	3.66972	3.64878	3.62802	3.60746	3.58708	3.56688	4
5	4.71616	4.68339	4.65096	4.61889	4.58716	4.55576	4.52470	4.49397	4.46356	4.43347	5
6	5.68575	5.63962	5.59405	5.54905	5.50459	5.46067	5.41728	5.37442	5.33207	5.29023	6
7	6.66433	6.60248	6.54149	6.48134	6.42202	6.36350	6.30579	6.24885	6.19269	6.13728	7
8	7.65196	7.57202	7.49330	7.41578	7.33945	7.26427	7.19023	7.11731	7.04548	6.97473	8
9	8.64874	8.54827	8.44949	8.35237	8.25688	8.16298	8.07064	7.97984	7.89052	7.80268	9
10	9.65474	9.53128	9.41008	9.29111	9.17431	9.05964	8.94703	8.83647	8.72788	8.62124	10
11	10.67006	10.52110	10.37511	10.23201	10.09174	9.95424	9.81942	9.68724	9.55763	9.43053	11
12	11.69479	11.51779	11.34458	11.17508	11.00917	10.84679	10.68783	10.53221	10.37983	10.23063	12
13	12.72900	12.52137	12.31851	12.12031	11.92660	11.73730	11.55226	11.37139	11.19456	11.02167	13
14	13.77278	13.53191	13.29694	13.06771	12.84403	12.62577	12.41276	12.20485	12.00188	11.80374	14
15	14.82623	14.54946	14.27987	14.01729	13.76146	13.51221	13.26932	13.03260	12.80186	12.57694	15
16	15.88944	15.57405	15.26734	14.96906	14.67889	14.39663	14.12197	13.85471	13.59457	13.34137	16
17	16.96249	16.60574	16.25935	15.92301	15.59632	15.27901	14.97073	14.67119	14.38008	14.09714	17
18	18.04547	17.64458	17.25594	16.87916	16.51375	16.15938	15.81561	15.48209	15.15844	14.84434	18
19	19.13849	18.69062	18.25712	17.83750	17.43119	17.03774	16.65663	16.28745	15.92973	15.58307	19
20	20.24162	19.74390	19.26291	18.79805	18.34862	17.91408	17.49382	17.08731	16.69400	16.31342	20
21	21.35497	20.80448	20.27333	19.76080	19.26605	18.78842	18.32718	17.88171	17.45133	17.03549	21
22	22.47863	21.87241	21.28842	20.72577	20.18348	19.66076	19.15674	18.67067	18.20177	17.74937	22
23	23.61269	22.94774	22.30818	21.69296	21.10091	20.53110	19.98250	19.45424	18.94539	18.45516	23
24	24.75725	24.03052	23.33264	22.66237	22.01834	21.39945	20.80450	20.23246	19.68225	19.15295	24
25	25.91241	25.12080	24.36182	23.63400	22.93577	22.26581	21.62275	21.00536	20.41241	19.84283	25
30	31.85063	30.68657	29.57931	28.52581	27.52292	26.56798	25.65826	24.79135	23.96485	23.17664	30
35	38.06892	36.44783	34.91812	33.47409	32.11007	30.82115	29.60248	28.44973	27.35872	26.32570	35
40	44.58046	42.41147	40.38109	38.47952	36.69721	35.02588	33.45746	31.98481	30.60110	29.30025	40
45	51.39910	48.58457	45.97110	43.54275	41.28436	39.18272	37.22524	35.40075	33.69876	32.10995	45
50	58.53932	54.97452	51.69110	48.66445	45.87151	43.29222	40.90777	38.70155	36.65815	34.76395	50

Annual Rate of Growth 10%

Holding Period	8.00%	8.25%	8.50%	8.75%	Discount Rate 9.00%	9.25%	9.50%	9.75%	10.00%	10.25%	
1	0.92593	0.92379	0.92166	0.91954	0.91743	0.91533	0.91324	0.91116	0.90909	0.90703	1
2	1.86900	1.86251	1.85606	1.84965	1.84328	1.83695	1.83065	1.82440	1.81818	1.81200	2
3	2.82954	2.81641	2.80338	2.79045	2.77762	2.76489	2.75226	2.73972	2.72727	2.71492	3
4	3.80786	3.78573	3.76379	3.74207	3.72053	3.69920	3.67806	3.65712	3.63636	3.61580	4
5	4.80430	4.77071	4.73749	4.70462	4.67210	4.63993	4.60810	4.57661	4.54545	4.51463	5
6	5.81920	5.77163	5.72464	5.67823	5.63239	5.58711	5.54238	5.49820	5.45455	5.41142	6
7	6.85288	6.78872	6.72544	6.66304	6.60150	6.54080	6.48093	6.42189	6.36364	6.30618	7
8	7.90572	7.82226	7.74008	7.65917	7.57949	7.50104	7.42377	7.34768	7.27273	7.19891	8
9	8.97804	8.87250	8.76874	8.66675	8.56646	8.46786	8.37091	8.27558	8.18182	8.08961	9
10	10.07023	9.93972	9.81163	9.68590	9.56248	9.44133	9.32237	9.20559	9.09091	8.97830	10
11	11.18264	11.02420	10.86893	10.71678	10.56764	10.42147	10.27818	10.13772	10.00000	9.86497	11
12	12.31565	12.12621	11.94085	11.75950	11.58202	11.40835	11.23836	11.07197	10.90909	10.74963	12
13	13.46965	13.24603	13.02759	12.81421	12.60571	12.40200	12.20292	12.00836	11.81818	11.63229	13
14	14.64501	14.38396	14.12935	13.88104	13.63879	13.40247	13.17188	12.94687	12.72727	12.51294	14
15	15.84214	15.54028	15.24635	14.96013	14.68135	14.40981	14.14527	13.88753	13.63636	13.39159	15
16	17.06144	16.71530	16.37879	16.05163	15.73347	15.42407	15.12310	14.83032	14.54545	14.26826	16
17	18.30331	17.90931	17.52688	17.15567	16.79524	16.44528	16.10540	15.77527	15.45454	15.14293	17
18	19.56819	19.12262	18.69084	18.27240	17.86676	17.47351	17.09218	16.72237	16.36363	16.01563	18
19	20.85649	20.35555	19.87090	19.40197	18.94810	18.50880	18.08347	17.67162	17.27272	16.88634	19
20	22.16865	21.60841	21.06727	20.54452	20.03937	19.55120	19.07928	18.62304	18.18182	17.75508	20
21	23.50510	22.88153	22.28018	21.70021	21.14065	20.60075	20.07964	19.57662	19.09091	18.62185	21
22	24.86631	24.17523	23.50986	22.86918	22.25203	21.65750	21.08457	20.53238	20.00000	19.48665	22
23	26.25272	25.48984	24.75654	24.05158	23.37361	22.72151	22.09409	21.49031	20.90909	20.34949	23
24	27.66480	26.82570	26.02045	25.24758	24.50547	23.79283	23.10822	22.45042	21.81818	21.21038	24
25	29.10304	28.18316	27.30184	26.45732	25.64772	24.87150	24.12698	23.41273	22.72727	22.06931	25
30	36.70373	35.30682	33.97945	32.71784	31.51810	30.37694	29.29098	28.25722	27.27272	26.33486	30
35	45.03475	43.02521	41.13158	39.34653	37.66275	36.07398	34.57395	33.15714	31.81817	30.55226	35
40	54.16625	51.38800	48.79196	46.36503	44.09449	41.96927	39.97865	38.11313	36.36363	34.72206	40
45	64.17516	60.44897	56.99670	53.79628	50.82671	48.06971	45.50788	43.12582	40.90908	38.84480	45
50	75.14579	70.26642	65.78449	61.66455	57.87347	54.38244	51.16450	48.19586	45.45453	42.92101	50

Present Value of a Series of Payments Increasing at Constant Rate

Annual Rate of Growth 3%

Holding Period	10.50%	10.75%	11.00%	11.25%	Discount Rate 11.50%	11.75%	12.00%	12.25%	15.00%	18.00%	
1	0.90498	0.90293	0.90090	0.89888	0.89686	0.89485	0.89286	0.89087	0.86957	0.84746	1
2	1.74853	1.74268	1.73687	1.73109	1.72535	1.71964	1.71397	1.70832	1.64839	1.58719	2
3	2.53483	2.52367	2.51259	2.50160	2.49068	2.47985	2.46909	2.45842	2.34595	2.23288	3
4	3.26776	3.25000	3.23241	3.21496	3.19767	3.18053	3.16354	3.14670	2.97072	2.79650	4
5	3.95094	3.92551	3.90034	3.87543	3.85076	3.82635	3.80219	3.77826	3.53030	3.28847	5
6	4.58776	4.55375	4.52014	4.48691	4.45407	4.42160	4.38951	4.35778	4.03149	3.71790	6
7	5.18135	5.13802	5.09526	5.05305	5.01138	4.97025	4.92964	4.88955	4.48037	4.09275	7
8	5.73465	5.68141	5.62894	5.57721	5.52621	5.47593	5.42636	5.37749	4.88242	4.41994	8
9	6.25040	6.18678	6.12415	6.06249	6.00179	5.94203	5.88317	5.82522	5.24252	4.70554	9
10	6.73114	6.65678	6.58367	6.51179	6.44112	6.37162	6.30328	6.23606	5.56504	4.95484	10
11	7.17925	7.09389	7.01007	6.92777	6.84695	6.76758	6.68962	6.61305	5.85390	5.17244	11
12	7.59695	7.50041	7.40574	7.31290	7.22185	7.13253	7.04492	6.95896	6.11263	5.36239	12
13	7.98630	7.87849	7.77290	7.66948	7.56816	7.46891	7.37167	7.27638	6.34435	5.52818	13
14	8.34922	8.23010	8.11359	7.99960	7.88808	7.77895	7.67216	7.56763	6.55190	5.67291	14
15	8.68751	8.55712	8.42973	8.30525	8.18361	8.06472	7.94850	7.83489	6.73779	5.79923	15
16	9.00283	8.86125	8.72308	8.58823	8.45661	8.32811	8.20264	8.08012	6.90428	5.90950	16
17	9.29676	9.14410	8.99529	8.85023	8.70879	8.57087	8.43636	8.30514	7.05340	6.00575	17
18	9.57074	9.40715	9.24788	9.09280	8.94175	8.79463	8.65129	8.51162	7.18696	6.08977	18
19	9.82612	9.65180	9.48227	9.31738	9.15696	9.00087	8.84896	8.70109	7.30658	6.16310	19
20	10.06416	9.87932	9.69976	9.52530	9.35575	9.19096	9.03074	8.87494	7.41372	6.22711	20
21	10.28605	10.09093	9.90158	9.71781	9.53940	9.36616	9.19791	9.03446	7.50968	6.28299	21
22	10.49288	10.28773	10.08885	9.89604	9.70904	9.52765	9.35165	9.18084	7.59562	6.33176	22
23	10.68567	10.47075	10.26263	10.06105	9.86575	9.67649	9.49303	9.31516	7.67260	6.37433	23
24	10.86538	10.64097	10.42388	10.21383	10.01051	9.81368	9.62306	9.43841	7.74155	6.41150	24
25	11.03288	10.79928	10.57351	10.35528	10.14424	9.94013	9.74263	9.55150	7.80330	6.44393	25
30	11.71456	11.43936	11.17463	10.91989	10.67464	10.43847	10.21092	9.99161	8.02784	6.55380	30
35	12.19423	11.88471	11.58818	11.30398	11.03144	10.76996	10.51896	10.27791	8.15726	6.60948	35
40	12.53177	12.19457	11.87269	11.56527	11.27145	10.99047	10.72160	10.46415	8.23185	6.63769	40
45	12.76929	12.41016	12.06843	11.74302	11.43290	11.13715	10.85489	10.58530	8.27484	6.65198	45
50	12.93643	12.56017	12.20309	11.86394	11.54151	11.23472	10.94257	10.66411	8.29962	6.65923	50

Annual Rate of Growth 4%

Holding Period	10.50%	10.75%	11.00%	11.25%	Discount Rate 11.50%	11.75%	12.00%	12.25%	15.00%	18.00%	
1	0.90498	0.90293	0.90090	0.89888	0.89686	0.89485	0.89286	0.89087	0.86957	0.84746	1
2	1.75672	1.75084	1.74499	1.73917	1.73340	1.72765	1.72194	1.71626	1.65595	1.59437	2
3	2.55836	2.54706	2.53584	2.52471	2.51366	2.50269	2.49180	2.48099	2.36712	2.25266	3
4	3.31285	3.29476	3.27683	3.25906	3.24144	3.22398	3.20667	3.18951	3.01027	2.83286	4
5	4.02295	3.99688	3.97108	3.94555	3.92027	3.89525	3.87048	3.84596	3.59190	3.34421	5
6	4.69128	4.65622	4.62155	4.58730	4.55343	4.51996	4.48688	4.45417	4.11789	3.79490	6
7	5.32030	5.27536	5.23101	5.18723	5.14401	5.10135	5.05924	5.01767	4.59357	4.19212	7
8	5.91232	5.85677	5.80202	5.74806	5.69486	5.64242	5.59072	5.53975	5.03375	4.54220	8
9	6.46952	6.40275	6.33703	6.27234	6.20866	6.14597	6.08424	6.02347	5.41278	4.85076	9
10	6.99393	6.91545	6.83830	6.76246	6.68790	6.61459	6.54251	6.47163	5.76460	5.12270	10
11	7.48750	7.39690	7.30796	7.22064	7.13490	7.05072	6.96805	6.88686	6.08277	5.36238	11
12	7.95204	7.84901	7.74799	7.64896	7.55184	7.45660	7.36319	7.27156	6.37051	5.57362	12
13	8.38925	8.27356	8.16028	8.04936	7.94073	7.83433	7.73010	7.62800	6.63072	5.75980	13
14	8.80074	8.67224	8.54657	8.42367	8.30346	8.18586	8.07081	7.95823	6.86604	5.92390	14
15	9.18803	9.04662	8.90850	8.77359	8.64179	8.51302	8.38718	8.26420	7.07885	6.06852	15
16	9.55253	9.39818	9.24760	9.10071	8.95736	8.81748	8.68095	8.54767	7.27131	6.19598	16
17	9.89560	9.72831	9.56532	9.40650	9.25171	9.10084	8.95374	8.81032	7.44536	6.30832	17
18	10.21848	10.03832	9.86300	9.69237	9.52626	9.36454	9.20705	9.05366	7.60276	6.40734	18
19	10.52237	10.32944	10.14191	9.95961	9.78234	9.60995	9.44226	9.27911	7.74511	6.49460	19
20	10.80838	10.60282	10.40323	10.20944	10.02120	9.83834	9.66067	9.48799	7.87383	6.57151	20
21	11.07757	10.85953	10.64808	10.44298	10.24399	10.05090	9.86348	9.68153	7.99025	6.63930	21
22	11.33093	11.10060	10.87748	10.66130	10.45179	10.24871	10.05180	9.86083	8.09553	6.69904	22
23	11.56938	11.32697	11.09241	10.86540	10.64562	10.43281	10.22667	10.02696	8.19074	6.75170	23
24	11.79381	11.53955	11.29379	11.05619	10.82641	10.60413	10.38905	10.18088	8.27684	6.79811	24
25	12.00503	11.73917	11.48247	11.23455	10.99503	10.76358	10.53983	10.32349	8.35471	6.83901	25
30	12.88876	12.56895	12.26170	11.96644	11.68254	11.40950	11.14678	10.89389	8.64559	6.98127	30
35	13.54141	13.17486	12.82433	12.48896	12.16791	11.86043	11.56579	11.28331	8.82154	7.05692	35
40	14.02339	13.61731	13.23056	12.86202	12.51057	12.17524	11.85506	11.54916	8.92797	7.09716	40
45	14.37934	13.94038	13.52387	13.12836	12.75248	12.39501	12.05476	11.73067	8.99235	7.11856	45
50	14.64221	14.17630	13.73564	13.31851	12.92326	12.54843	12.19262	11.85458	9.03129	7.12993	50

Present Value of a Series of Payments Increasing at Constant Rate

Annual Rate of Growth 5%

Holding Period	10.50%	10.75%	11.00%	11.25%	11.50%	11.75%	12.00%	12.25%	15.00%	18.00%	
1	0.90498	0.90293	0.90090	0.89888	0.89686	0.89485	0.89286	0.89087	0.86957	0.84746	1
2	1.76491	1.75899	1.75310	1.74725	1.74144	1.73566	1.72991	1.72420	1.66352	1.60155	2
3	2.58204	2.57060	2.55924	2.54797	2.53678	2.52567	2.51465	2.50370	2.38843	2.27257	3
4	3.35850	3.34007	3.32181	3.30370	3.28576	3.26797	3.25034	3.23286	3.05030	2.86966	4
5	4.09631	4.06959	4.04315	4.01698	3.99107	3.96543	3.94005	3.91493	3.65463	3.40097	5
6	4.79740	4.76124	4.72550	4.69018	4.65527	4.62076	4.58665	4.55294	4.20640	3.87374	6
7	5.46359	5.41698	5.37097	5.32557	5.28075	5.23651	5.19285	5.14974	4.71019	4.29443	7
8	6.09663	6.03867	5.98155	5.92525	5.86976	5.81507	5.76115	5.70800	5.17017	4.66877	8
9	6.69815	6.62808	6.55912	6.49125	6.42444	6.35868	6.29394	6.23020	5.59016	5.00187	9
10	7.26974	7.18690	7.10548	7.02545	6.94678	6.86945	6.79342	6.71867	5.97362	5.29828	10
11	7.81287	7.71670	7.62230	7.52964	7.43867	7.34937	7.26169	7.17559	6.32374	5.56203	11
12	8.32897	8.21899	8.11118	8.00550	7.90189	7.80031	7.70069	7.60300	6.64342	5.79672	12
13	8.81939	8.69521	8.57364	8.45463	8.33810	8.22400	8.11226	8.00281	6.93529	6.00556	13
14	9.28539	9.14670	9.01110	8.87853	8.74889	8.62211	8.49810	8.37679	7.20179	6.19139	14
15	9.72820	9.57475	9.42492	9.27861	9.13572	8.99616	8.85982	8.72662	7.44511	6.35674	15
16	10.14897	9.98057	9.81636	9.65622	9.50001	9.34762	9.19894	9.05385	7.66728	6.50388	16
17	10.54879	10.36533	10.18665	10.01261	9.84306	9.67786	9.51686	9.35995	7.87012	6.63481	17
18	10.92872	10.73011	10.53692	10.34898	10.16611	9.98814	9.81492	9.64628	8.05533	6.75131	18
19	11.28973	11.07595	10.86826	10.66646	10.47033	10.27969	10.09434	9.91411	8.22443	6.85498	19
20	11.63278	11.40384	11.18169	10.96609	10.75681	10.55362	10.35630	10.16465	8.37883	6.94723	20
21	11.95875	11.71470	11.47817	11.24890	11.02659	10.81101	10.60189	10.39900	8.51980	7.02932	21
22	12.26849	12.00942	11.75863	11.51582	11.28065	11.05285	10.83213	10.61822	8.64851	7.10236	22
23	12.56282	12.28884	12.02393	11.76774	11.51989	11.28009	11.04798	10.82328	8.76603	7.16735	23
24	12.84250	12.55376	12.27489	12.00550	11.74519	11.49359	11.25034	11.01509	8.87333	7.22519	24
25	13.10826	12.80491	12.51228	12.22992	11.95735	11.69421	11.44005	11.19452	8.97131	7.27665	25
30	14.25132	13.87814	13.52009	13.17644	12.84645	12.52949	12.22489	11.93208	9.34725	7.46042	30
35	15.13685	14.70023	14.28341	13.88533	13.50490	13.14120	12.79328	12.46029	9.58581	7.56295	35
40	15.82287	15.32995	14.86156	14.41625	13.99254	13.58917	13.20456	12.83858	9.73718	7.62014	40
45	16.35433	15.81231	15.29946	14.81387	14.35367	13.91724	13.50299	13.10950	9.83323	7.65205	45
50	16.76606	16.18180	15.63113	15.11166	14.62112	14.15750	13.71887	13.30353	9.89418	7.66985	50

Annual Rate of Growth 6%

Holding Period	10.50%	10.75%	11.00%	11.25%	11.50%	11.75%	12.00%	12.25%	15.00%	18.00%	
1	0.90498	0.90293	0.90090	0.89888	0.89686	0.89485	0.89286	0.89087	0.86957	0.84746	1
2	1.77310	1.76714	1.76122	1.75533	1.74948	1.74367	1.73788	1.73213	1.67108	1.60873	2
3	2.60587	2.59429	2.58279	2.57137	2.56005	2.54880	2.53764	2.52656	2.40986	2.29259	3
4	3.40473	3.38595	3.36735	3.34891	3.33063	3.31251	3.29455	3.27675	3.09083	2.90690	4
5	4.17105	4.14367	4.11657	4.08974	4.06320	4.03692	4.01091	3.98517	3.71850	3.45874	5
6	4.90617	4.86888	4.83204	4.79562	4.75963	4.72406	4.68890	4.65415	4.29706	3.95447	6
7	5.61134	5.56299	5.51528	5.46819	5.42171	5.37584	5.33057	5.28588	4.83033	4.39977	7
8	6.28780	6.22733	6.16774	6.10902	6.05113	5.99409	5.93786	5.88243	5.32187	4.79980	8
9	6.93672	6.86318	6.79082	6.71960	6.64951	6.58052	6.51262	6.44577	5.77494	5.15914	9
10	7.55920	7.47176	7.38582	7.30137	7.21837	7.13678	7.05658	6.97774	6.19255	5.48194	10
11	8.15634	8.05423	7.95403	7.85569	7.75917	7.66442	7.57141	7.48009	6.57748	5.77191	11
12	8.72916	8.61173	8.49664	8.38385	8.27329	8.16491	8.05865	7.95448	6.93229	6.03240	12
13	9.27865	9.14531	9.01481	8.88708	8.76205	8.63965	8.51980	8.40244	7.25933	6.26639	13
14	9.80576	9.65601	9.50964	9.36657	9.22670	9.08996	8.95624	8.82547	7.56077	6.47659	14
15	10.31141	10.14480	9.98218	9.82343	9.66843	9.51710	9.36930	9.22494	7.83862	6.66541	15
16	10.79647	10.61263	10.43343	10.25873	10.08838	9.92226	9.76023	9.60217	8.09473	6.83503	16
17	11.26177	11.06040	10.86436	10.67349	10.48761	10.30657	10.13021	9.95840	8.33080	6.98740	17
18	11.70812	11.48896	11.27587	11.06867	10.86714	10.67111	10.48038	10.29479	8.54839	7.12427	18
19	12.13630	11.89914	11.66885	11.44521	11.22795	11.01689	10.81179	10.61245	8.74895	7.24723	19
20	12.54704	12.29173	12.04413	11.80397	11.57097	11.34488	11.12544	10.91242	8.93381	7.35768	20
21	12.94105	12.66748	12.40250	12.14581	11.89707	11.65600	11.42230	11.19570	9.10421	7.45690	21
22	13.31902	13.02711	12.74473	12.47151	12.20708	11.95110	11.70324	11.46320	9.26127	7.54603	22
23	13.68159	13.37132	13.07154	12.78185	12.50179	12.23103	11.96914	11.71580	9.40604	7.62609	23
24	14.02940	13.70077	13.38364	13.07754	12.78198	12.49654	12.22079	11.95434	9.53948	7.69802	24
25	14.36304	14.01609	13.68167	13.35927	13.04834	12.74840	12.45897	12.17960	9.66248	7.76263	25
30	15.83819	15.40105	14.98216	14.58063	14.19555	13.82613	13.47157	13.13116	10.14729	7.99950	30
35	17.03645	16.51342	16.01497	15.53975	15.08638	14.65369	14.24049	13.84570	10.46984	8.13806	35
40	18.00981	17.40685	16.83521	16.29293	15.77814	15.28916	14.82436	14.38228	10.68445	8.21911	40
45	18.80047	18.12443	17.48661	16.88440	16.31530	15.77712	15.26772	14.78520	10.82724	8.26652	45
50	19.44272	18.70077	18.00394	17.34887	16.73243	16.15181	15.60438	15.08771	10.92224	8.29425	50

Present Value of a Series of Payments Increasing at Constant Rate

Annual Rate of Growth 7%

Holding Period	10.50%	10.75%	11.00%	11.25%	Discount Rate 11.50%	11.75%	12.00%	12.25%	15.00%	18.00%	
1	0.90498	0.90293	0.90090	0.89888	0.89686	0.89485	0.89286	0.89087	0.86957	0.84746	1
2	1.78129	1.77530	1.76934	1.76341	1.75753	1.75167	1.74585	1.74007	1.67864	1.61592	2
3	2.62985	2.61812	2.60648	2.59492	2.58346	2.57207	2.56077	2.54955	2.43143	2.31274	3
4	3.45153	3.43240	3.41345	3.39467	3.37605	3.35760	3.33931	3.32118	3.13185	2.94460	4
5	4.24718	4.21912	4.19135	4.16386	4.13666	4.10974	4.08309	4.05671	3.78355	3.51756	5
6	5.01763	4.97919	4.94121	4.90367	4.86657	4.82991	4.79367	4.75785	4.38991	4.03711	6
7	5.76368	5.71353	5.66405	5.61521	5.56702	5.51946	5.47252	5.42619	4.95409	4.50823	7
8	6.48610	6.42301	6.36084	6.29958	6.23921	6.17971	6.12107	6.06327	5.47902	4.93543	8
9	7.18563	7.10846	7.03252	6.95780	6.88426	6.81189	6.74066	6.67056	5.96744	5.32280	9
10	7.86301	7.77070	7.68000	7.59087	7.50328	7.41720	7.33260	7.24944	6.42188	5.67407	10
11	8.51893	8.41052	8.30414	8.19976	8.09732	7.99679	7.89811	7.80124	6.84470	5.99259	11
12	9.15408	9.02867	8.90579	8.78539	8.66738	8.55173	8.43837	8.32724	7.23812	6.28141	12
13	9.76911	9.62590	9.48576	9.34864	9.21444	9.08309	8.95451	8.82864	7.60416	6.54332	13
14	10.36466	10.20290	10.04484	9.89038	9.73942	9.59186	9.44762	9.30659	7.94474	6.78080	14
15	10.94134	10.76036	10.58376	10.41142	10.24321	10.07901	9.91871	9.76218	8.26163	6.99615	15
16	11.49976	11.29895	11.10326	10.91256	10.72667	10.54545	10.36876	10.19647	8.55647	7.19143	16
17	12.04049	11.81930	11.60405	11.39455	11.19061	10.99207	10.79873	10.61044	8.83080	7.36850	17
18	12.56410	12.32203	12.08678	11.85813	11.63583	11.41970	11.20950	11.00505	9.08605	7.52906	18
19	13.07112	12.80774	12.55213	12.30400	12.06309	11.82915	11.60193	11.38121	9.32354	7.67466	19
20	13.56208	13.27701	13.00070	12.73284	12.47310	12.22120	11.97685	11.73977	9.54452	7.80668	20
21	14.03748	13.73038	13.43310	13.14529	12.86656	12.59659	12.33502	12.08156	9.75011	7.92640	21
22	14.49784	14.16841	13.84993	13.54199	13.24414	12.95602	12.67721	12.40737	9.94141	8.03495	22
23	14.94361	14.59160	14.25173	13.92353	13.60649	13.30017	13.00412	12.71793	10.11940	8.13339	23
24	15.37526	15.00046	14.63906	14.29050	13.95421	13.62969	13.31644	13.01398	10.28501	8.22265	24
25	15.79323	15.39548	15.01243	14.64345	14.28789	13.94521	13.61481	13.29617	10.43909	8.30359	25
30	17.69273	17.17877	16.68688	16.21595	15.76487	15.33267	14.91837	14.52110	11.06290	8.60823	30
35	19.30986	18.67992	18.08061	17.51017	16.96690	16.44929	15.95581	15.48514	11.49788	8.79500	35
40	20.68660	19.94356	19.24067	18.57537	17.94518	17.34792	16.78145	16.24386	11.80121	8.90950	40
45	21.85869	21.00727	20.20624	19.45206	18.74135	18.07113	17.43853	16.84099	12.01272	8.97969	45
50	22.85655	21.90269	21.00993	20.17361	19.38932	18.65316	17.96147	17.31095	12.16021	9.02273	50

Annual Rate of Growth 8%

Holding Period	10.50%	10.75%	11.00%	11.25%	Discount Rate 11.50%	11.75%	12.00%	12.25%	15.00%	18.00%	
1	0.90498	0.90293	0.90090	0.89888	0.89686	0.89485	0.89286	0.89087	0.86957	0.84746	1
2	1.78948	1.78345	1.77745	1.77149	1.76557	1.75968	1.75383	1.74801	1.68620	1.62310	2
3	2.65397	2.64210	2.63031	2.61862	2.60701	2.59549	2.58405	2.57269	2.45313	2.33300	3
4	3.49890	3.47943	3.46013	3.44100	3.42204	3.40324	3.38462	3.36615	3.17337	2.98275	4
5	4.32472	4.29597	4.26751	4.23935	4.21148	4.18390	4.15659	4.12957	3.84978	3.57743	5
6	5.13185	5.09223	5.05307	5.01438	4.97614	4.93835	4.90100	4.86409	4.48501	4.12172	6
7	5.92073	5.86872	5.81740	5.76677	5.71680	5.66749	5.61882	5.57079	5.08157	4.61988	7
8	6.69175	6.62593	6.56108	6.49718	6.43421	6.37216	6.31101	6.25074	5.64182	5.07582	8
9	7.44533	7.36434	7.28465	7.20625	7.12910	7.05318	6.97847	6.90494	6.16797	5.49312	9
10	8.18186	8.08441	7.98867	7.89461	7.80218	7.71136	7.62210	7.53438	6.66210	5.87506	10
11	8.90173	8.78661	8.67366	8.56286	8.45413	8.34744	8.24274	8.13998	7.12614	6.22463	11
12	9.60531	9.47136	9.34014	9.21158	9.08561	8.96218	8.84121	8.72265	7.56194	6.54458	12
13	10.29297	10.13912	9.98860	9.84136	9.69728	9.55629	9.41831	9.28326	7.97122	6.83741	13
14	10.96508	10.79029	10.61954	10.45273	10.28974	10.13047	9.97480	9.82265	8.35558	7.10543	14
15	11.62198	11.42529	11.23343	11.04625	10.86360	10.68537	10.51141	10.34161	8.71654	7.35073	15
16	12.26401	12.04453	11.83072	11.62243	11.41945	11.22166	11.02886	10.84093	9.05553	7.57525	16
17	12.89152	12.64839	12.41187	12.18177	11.95786	11.73995	11.52783	11.32134	9.37389	7.78073	17
18	13.50484	13.23726	12.97732	12.72478	12.47936	12.24084	12.00898	11.78356	9.67287	7.96881	18
19	14.10427	13.81150	13.52748	13.25192	12.98449	12.72493	12.47295	12.22828	9.95366	8.14094	19
20	14.69015	14.37149	14.06278	13.76366	13.47377	13.19278	12.92034	12.65616	10.21735	8.29849	20
21	15.26277	14.91757	14.58360	14.26046	13.94769	13.64492	13.35176	13.06784	10.46499	8.44269	21
22	15.82244	15.45009	15.09035	14.74273	14.40673	14.08189	13.76777	13.46393	10.69755	8.57466	22
23	16.36944	15.96939	15.58340	15.21093	14.85136	14.50420	14.16892	13.84503	10.91596	8.69545	23
24	16.90407	16.47579	16.06313	15.66544	15.28203	14.91234	14.55574	14.21170	11.12108	8.80601	24
25	17.42660	16.96962	16.52989	16.10667	15.69919	15.30678	14.92875	14.56448	11.31371	8.90720	25
30	19.86719	19.26082	18.68116	18.12687	17.59658	17.08911	16.60324	16.13789	12.11462	9.29814	30
35	22.04391	21.28133	20.55701	19.86872	19.21429	18.59179	17.99931	17.43514	12.69969	9.54923	35
40	23.98529	23.06314	22.19270	21.37059	20.59355	19.85872	19.16327	18.50472	13.12710	9.71049	40
45	25.71677	24.63445	23.61898	22.66553	21.76951	20.92686	20.13371	19.38658	13.43933	9.81406	45
50	27.26104	26.02013	24.86267	23.78206	22.77212	21.82742	20.94280	20.11367	13.66742	9.88058	50

Present Value of a Series of Payments Increasing at Constant Rate

Annual Rate of Growth 9%

Holding Period	10.50%	10.75%	11.00%	11.25%	Discount Rate 11.50%	11.75%	12.00%	12.25%	15.00%	18.00%	
1	0.90498	0.90293	0.90090	0.89888	0.89686	0.89485	0.89286	0.89087	0.86957	0.84746	1
2	1.79767	1.79160	1.78557	1.77957	1.77361	1.76769	1.76180	1.75594	1.69376	1.63028	2
3	2.67824	2.66623	2.65430	2.64246	2.63071	2.61904	2.60746	2.59597	2.47496	2.35339	3
4	3.54687	3.52703	3.50737	3.48789	3.46858	3.44945	3.43048	3.41168	3.21539	3.02135	4
5	4.40370	4.37423	4.34508	4.31623	4.28767	4.25942	4.23145	4.20377	3.91720	3.63837	5
6	5.24889	5.20805	5.16769	5.12781	5.08840	5.04945	5.01096	4.97292	4.58239	4.20833	6
7	6.08262	6.02869	5.97548	5.92298	5.87117	5.82005	5.76960	5.71981	5.21287	4.73481	7
8	6.90503	6.83636	6.76871	6.70206	6.63639	6.57168	6.50791	6.44507	5.81046	5.22114	8
9	7.71627	7.63127	7.54766	7.46539	7.38445	7.30482	7.22645	7.14933	6.37687	5.67037	9
10	8.51650	8.41362	8.31256	8.21328	8.11574	8.01991	7.92574	7.83320	6.91373	6.08534	10
11	9.30587	9.18361	9.06369	8.94605	8.83064	8.71741	8.60630	8.49728	7.42258	6.46867	11
12	10.08452	9.94143	9.80128	9.66400	9.52950	9.39774	9.26863	9.14212	7.90488	6.82275	12
13	10.85261	10.68728	10.52558	10.36742	10.21270	10.06133	9.91322	9.76829	8.36202	7.14983	13
14	11.61026	11.42134	11.23683	11.05662	10.88057	10.70859	10.54055	10.37634	8.79530	7.45196	14
15	12.35764	12.14380	11.93527	11.73188	11.53348	11.33993	11.15107	10.96678	9.20598	7.73105	15
16	13.09486	12.85485	12.62112	12.39348	12.17174	11.95572	11.74524	11.54012	9.59524	7.98885	16
17	13.82208	13.55466	13.29461	13.04171	12.79569	12.55637	12.32349	12.09687	9.96418	8.22699	17
18	14.53943	14.24341	13.95597	13.67682	13.40565	13.14223	12.88625	12.63749	10.31388	8.44697	18
19	15.24704	14.92128	14.60541	14.29909	14.00194	13.71367	13.43394	13.16246	10.64533	8.65016	19
20	15.94504	15.58844	15.24315	14.90877	14.58486	14.27106	13.96696	13.67223	10.95948	8.83786	20
21	16.63357	16.24506	15.86940	15.50612	15.15470	14.81472	14.48570	14.16725	11.25725	9.01125	21
22	17.31275	16.89130	16.48437	16.09139	15.71177	15.34501	14.99055	14.64793	11.53948	9.17141	22
23	17.98272	17.52733	17.08825	16.66482	16.25635	15.86225	15.48188	15.11469	11.80698	9.31935	23
24	18.64358	18.15331	17.68126	17.22666	16.78872	16.36676	15.96004	15.56794	12.06053	9.45601	24
25	19.29548	18.76940	18.26358	17.77713	17.30915	16.85885	16.42540	16.00806	12.30085	9.58225	25
30	22.42460	21.70685	21.02152	20.36694	19.74143	19.14353	18.57175	18.02476	13.32696	10.08288	30
35	25.34703	24.41945	23.53980	22.70523	21.91298	21.16059	20.44563	19.76594	14.11190	10.41958	35
40	28.07642	26.92440	25.83923	24.81645	23.85177	22.94139	22.08164	21.26923	14.71235	10.64603	40
45	30.62551	29.23760	27.93884	26.72263	25.58273	24.51360	23.50997	22.56713	15.17168	10.79832	45
50	33.00623	31.37372	29.85599	28.44369	27.12814	25.90165	24.75698	23.68772	15.52305	10.90075	50

Annual Rate of Growth 10%

Holding Period	10.50%	10.75%	11.00%	11.25%	Discount Rate 11.50%	11.75%	12.00%	12.25%	15.00%	18.00%	
1	0.90498	0.90293	0.90090	0.89888	0.89686	0.89485	0.89286	0.89087	0.86957	0.84746	1
2	1.80586	1.79975	1.79369	1.78765	1.78166	1.77570	1.76977	1.76388	1.70132	1.63746	2
3	2.70267	2.69050	2.67843	2.66644	2.65455	2.64274	2.63102	2.61939	2.49692	2.37390	3
4	3.59541	3.57522	3.55520	3.53536	3.51570	3.49621	3.47690	3.45776	3.25792	3.06042	4
5	4.48412	4.45394	4.42407	4.39451	4.36526	4.33632	4.30767	4.27932	3.98584	3.70039	5
6	5.36881	5.32671	5.28511	5.24401	5.20340	5.16327	5.12360	5.08441	4.68211	4.29697	6
7	6.24949	6.19357	6.13840	6.08397	6.03026	5.97726	5.92497	5.87336	5.34810	4.85311	7
8	7.12619	7.05457	6.98400	6.91449	6.84600	6.77852	6.71202	6.64650	5.98514	5.37155	8
9	7.99892	7.90973	7.82198	7.73567	7.65076	7.56722	7.48502	7.40414	6.59448	5.85483	9
10	8.86771	8.75910	8.65242	8.54763	8.44469	8.34357	8.24422	8.14660	7.17733	6.30535	10
11	9.73256	9.60271	9.47537	9.35047	9.22795	9.10777	8.98986	8.87417	7.73484	6.72533	11
12	10.59350	10.44062	10.29090	10.14428	10.00067	9.86000	9.72218	9.58716	8.26811	7.11683	12
13	11.45054	11.27285	11.09909	10.92918	10.76299	10.60044	10.44143	10.28586	8.77819	7.48179	13
14	12.30371	12.09945	11.90000	11.70526	11.51506	11.32930	11.14783	10.97055	9.26609	7.82201	14
15	13.15301	12.92044	12.69370	12.47262	12.25701	12.04674	11.84162	11.64152	9.73278	8.13916	15
16	13.99847	13.73588	13.48024	13.23135	12.98898	12.75294	12.52302	12.29904	10.17919	8.43481	16
17	14.84011	14.54580	14.25970	13.98156	13.71110	13.44808	13.19225	12.94338	10.60618	8.71042	17
18	15.67794	15.35023	15.03213	14.72334	14.42351	14.13234	13.84953	13.57480	11.01460	8.96734	18
19	16.51197	16.14921	15.79761	15.45679	15.12633	14.80589	14.49508	14.19357	11.40527	9.20684	19
20	17.34223	16.94278	16.55619	16.18199	15.81970	15.46888	15.12909	14.79993	11.77896	9.43011	20
21	18.16874	17.73098	17.30794	16.89905	16.50374	16.12150	15.75179	15.39414	12.13639	9.63824	21
22	18.99151	18.51384	18.05291	17.60805	17.17857	16.76389	16.36336	15.97644	12.47829	9.83225	22
23	19.81055	19.29140	18.79117	18.30909	17.84433	17.39622	16.96402	16.54707	12.80532	10.01312	23
24	20.62589	20.06369	19.52278	19.00224	18.50114	18.01866	17.55395	17.10625	13.11813	10.18172	24
25	21.43753	20.83076	20.24780	19.68761	19.14910	18.63134	18.13334	17.65423	13.41734	10.33889	25
30	25.44101	24.58886	23.77609	23.00066	22.26051	21.55381	20.87876	20.23371	14.72921	10.97865	30
35	29.35473	28.22142	27.14829	26.13173	25.16818	24.25451	23.38765	22.56483	15.77964	11.42902	35
40	33.18070	31.73264	30.37130	29.09080	27.88546	26.75027	25.68040	24.67149	16.62072	11.74607	40
45	36.92089	35.12657	33.45173	31.88732	30.42481	29.05664	27.77561	26.57531	17.29419	11.96926	45
50	40.57722	38.40712	36.39587	34.53023	32.79789	31.18799	29.69032	28.29582	17.83343	12.12637	50

Present Value of a Series of Payments Decreasing at Constant Rate

Annual Rate of Decline   1%

Holding Period	5.50%	5.75%	6.00%	6.25%	Discount Rate 6.50%	6.75%	7.00%	7.25%	7.50%	7.75%
1	0.94787	0.94563	0.94340	0.94118	0.93897	0.93677	0.93458	0.93240	0.93023	0.92807
2	1.83733	1.83089	1.82449	1.81813	1.81181	1.80553	1.79928	1.79308	1.78691	1.78078
3	2.67200	2.65965	2.64740	2.63525	2.62318	2.61121	2.59934	2.58755	2.57585	2.56425
4	3.45524	3.43552	3.41597	3.39661	3.37742	3.35841	3.33957	3.32091	3.30241	3.28409
5	4.19023	4.16185	4.13378	4.10601	4.07854	4.05136	4.02446	3.99785	3.97152	3.94547
6	4.87993	4.84183	4.80419	4.76702	4.73029	4.69400	4.65815	4.62273	4.58773	4.55315
7	5.52714	5.47840	5.43033	5.38291	5.33614	5.28999	5.24446	5.19954	5.15521	5.11148
8	6.13447	6.07434	6.01512	5.95679	5.89932	5.84270	5.78693	5.73197	5.67782	5.62447
9	6.70439	6.63225	6.56129	6.49150	6.42284	6.35529	6.28884	6.22345	6.15911	6.09580
10	7.23919	7.15454	7.07140	6.98973	6.90949	6.83067	6.75323	6.67713	6.60235	6.52885
11	7.74104	7.64349	7.54781	7.45396	7.36188	7.27154	7.18289	7.09590	7.01053	6.92674
12	8.21197	8.10124	7.99277	7.88651	7.78240	7.68039	7.58043	7.48246	7.38644	7.29232
13	8.65389	8.52976	8.40834	8.28955	8.17331	8.05957	7.94825	7.83929	7.73263	7.62821
14	9.06857	8.93094	8.79647	8.66509	8.53670	8.41122	8.28857	8.16867	8.05145	7.93682
15	9.45772	9.30650	9.15897	9.01500	8.87449	8.73733	8.60344	8.47271	8.34505	8.22038
16	9.82288	9.65810	9.49753	9.34103	9.18849	9.03978	8.89477	8.75337	8.61544	8.48090
17	10.16555	9.98725	9.81373	9.64482	9.48038	9.32026	9.16432	9.01243	8.86446	8.72027
18	10.48710	10.29539	10.10905	9.92788	9.75172	9.58038	9.41372	9.25157	9.09378	8.94020
19	10.78884	10.58387	10.38487	10.19162	10.00394	9.82162	9.64447	9.47231	9.30497	9.14228
20	11.07199	10.85393	10.64247	10.43737	10.23841	10.04534	9.85797	9.67607	9.49946	9.32794
21	11.33770	11.10675	10.88306	10.66635	10.45636	10.25282	10.05550	9.86416	9.67857	9.49852
22	11.58704	11.34343	11.10776	10.87971	10.65896	10.44524	10.23827	10.03778	9.84352	9.65526
23	11.82101	11.56501	11.31763	11.07850	10.84730	10.62369	10.40737	10.19804	9.99543	9.79926
24	12.04057	11.77245	11.51363	11.26374	11.02237	10.78918	10.56383	10.34598	10.13532	9.93157
25	12.24660	11.96664	11.69670	11.43633	11.18512	10.94266	10.70859	10.48253	10.26416	10.05314
30	13.10129	12.76676	12.44587	12.13791	11.84224	11.55824	11.28535	11.02301	10.77071	10.52798
35	13.72319	13.34211	12.97825	12.63064	12.29835	11.98054	11.67641	11.38522	11.10627	10.83889
40	14.17570	13.75583	13.35659	12.97669	12.61494	12.27025	11.94157	11.62797	11.32854	11.04246
45	14.50497	14.05333	13.62544	13.21972	12.83469	12.46899	12.12136	11.79065	11.47578	11.17576
50	14.74455	14.26725	13.81650	13.39041	12.98722	12.60533	12.24327	11.89968	11.57332	11.26304

Annual Rate of Decline   2%

Holding Period	5.50%	5.75%	6.00%	6.25%	Discount Rate 6.50%	6.75%	7.00%	7.25%	7.50%	7.75%
1	0.94787	0.94563	0.94340	0.94118	0.93897	0.93677	0.93458	0.93240	0.93023	0.92807
2	1.82835	1.82195	1.81559	1.80927	1.80299	1.79675	1.79055	1.78438	1.77826	1.77217
3	2.64624	2.63405	2.62196	2.60996	2.59806	2.58625	2.57452	2.56289	2.55134	2.53988
4	3.40599	3.38664	3.36747	3.34849	3.32967	3.31103	3.29255	3.27425	3.25611	3.23813
5	4.11172	4.08407	4.05672	4.02966	4.00289	3.97640	3.95019	3.92425	3.89859	3.87320
6	4.76729	4.73039	4.69395	4.65795	4.62238	4.58723	4.55251	4.51820	4.48430	4.45080
7	5.37625	5.32935	5.28309	5.23745	5.19242	5.14800	5.10417	5.06092	5.01824	4.97613
8	5.94192	5.88441	5.82776	5.77195	5.71697	5.66280	5.60942	5.55683	5.50500	5.45393
9	6.46737	6.39879	6.33132	6.26495	6.19965	6.13540	6.07218	6.00997	5.94875	5.88849
10	6.95547	6.87547	6.79688	6.71967	6.64381	6.56927	6.49602	6.42403	6.35328	6.28373
11	7.40888	7.31722	7.22731	7.13909	7.05252	6.96757	6.88420	6.80238	6.72206	6.64321
12	7.83005	7.72660	7.62525	7.52593	7.42861	7.33323	7.23974	7.14809	7.05825	6.97016
13	8.22127	8.10597	7.99315	7.88274	7.77468	7.66891	7.56537	7.46399	7.36473	7.26752
14	8.58469	8.45755	8.33329	8.21185	8.09314	7.97708	7.86361	7.75264	7.64412	7.53798
15	8.92227	8.78335	8.64776	8.51540	8.38617	8.25999	8.13676	8.01640	7.89883	7.78396
16	9.23585	9.08528	8.93849	8.79538	8.65582	8.51971	8.38694	8.25741	8.13102	8.00769
17	9.52714	9.36508	9.20729	9.05362	8.90395	8.75814	8.61608	8.47763	8.34270	8.21117
18	9.79773	9.62438	9.45580	9.29181	9.13227	8.97703	8.82594	8.67886	8.53567	8.39623
19	10.04907	9.86467	9.68555	9.51151	9.34237	9.17798	9.01815	8.86274	8.71159	8.56456
20	10.28255	10.08736	9.89796	9.71414	9.53570	9.36245	9.19419	9.03075	8.87196	8.71765
21	10.49943	10.29372	10.09434	9.90104	9.71361	9.53180	9.35543	9.18428	9.01816	8.85689
22	10.70089	10.48496	10.27590	10.07343	9.87731	9.68728	9.50310	9.32456	9.15144	8.98353
23	10.88803	10.66219	10.44375	10.23244	10.02795	9.83001	9.63836	9.45275	9.27294	9.09871
24	11.06187	10.82642	10.59894	10.37909	10.16656	9.96104	9.76223	9.56988	9.38370	9.20346
25	11.22335	10.97862	10.74242	10.51437	10.29411	10.08133	9.87569	9.67690	9.48468	9.29874
30	11.87402	11.58779	11.31282	11.04856	10.79448	10.55008	10.31490	10.08850	9.87047	9.66039
35	12.32404	12.00415	11.69811	11.40516	11.12459	10.85574	10.59797	10.35070	10.11337	9.88547
40	12.63529	12.28872	11.95835	11.64321	11.34239	11.05505	10.78040	10.51772	10.26631	10.02555
45	12.85055	12.48322	12.13414	11.80212	11.48608	11.18501	10.89797	10.62411	10.36261	10.11273
50	12.99943	12.61616	12.25287	11.90820	11.58088	11.26975	10.97375	10.69188	10.42324	10.16699

Present Value of a Series of Payments Decreasing at Constant Rate

Annual Rate of Decline 3%

Holding Period	5.50%	5.75%	6.00%	6.25%	Discount Rate 6.50%	6.75%	7.00%	7.25%	7.50%	7.75%
1	0.94787	0.94563	0.94340	0.94118	0.93897	0.93677	0.93458	0.93240	0.93023	0.92807
2	1.81937	1.81301	1.80669	1.80042	1.79418	1.78798	1.78181	1.77569	1.76961	1.76356
3	2.62065	2.60862	2.59669	2.58485	2.57310	2.56144	2.54987	2.53839	2.52699	2.51568
4	3.35737	3.33841	3.31961	3.30099	3.28254	3.26426	3.24614	3.22819	3.21040	3.19277
5	4.03474	4.00780	3.98115	3.95479	3.92870	3.90289	3.87734	3.85207	3.82706	3.80231
6	4.65753	4.62182	4.58653	4.55167	4.51722	4.48318	4.44956	4.41632	4.38349	4.35104
7	5.23015	5.18502	5.14050	5.09658	5.05324	5.01048	4.96829	4.92665	4.88556	4.84502
8	5.75663	5.70163	5.64744	5.59405	5.54145	5.48962	5.43854	5.38821	5.33860	5.28971
9	6.24069	6.17549	6.11134	6.04822	5.98611	5.92499	5.86485	5.80565	5.74739	5.69004
10	6.68576	6.61014	6.53585	6.46284	6.39110	6.32060	6.25131	6.18320	6.11625	6.05043
11	7.09496	7.00883	6.92431	6.84137	6.75997	6.68008	6.60165	6.52467	6.44908	6.37487
12	7.47120	7.37453	7.27979	7.18695	7.09594	7.00672	6.91926	6.83350	6.74940	6.66694
13	7.81712	7.70997	7.60510	7.50244	7.40193	7.30353	7.20718	7.11281	7.02039	6.92986
14	8.13517	8.01766	7.90278	7.79046	7.68063	7.57323	7.46819	7.36544	7.26491	7.16656
15	8.42760	8.29988	8.17518	8.05341	7.93447	7.81830	7.70481	7.59391	7.48555	7.37964
16	8.69646	8.55876	8.42446	8.29346	8.16567	8.04099	7.91931	7.80056	7.68463	7.57146
17	8.94367	8.79621	8.65257	8.51262	8.37625	8.24333	8.11377	7.98745	7.86427	7.74415
18	9.17096	9.01402	8.86132	8.71270	8.56804	8.42720	8.29005	8.15648	8.02637	7.89960
19	9.37993	9.21381	9.05234	8.89536	8.74272	8.59427	8.44986	8.30936	8.17263	8.03955
20	9.57207	9.39706	9.22714	9.06212	8.90182	8.74608	8.59473	8.44762	8.30461	8.16553
21	9.74873	9.56515	9.38710	9.21435	9.04673	8.88402	8.72607	8.57268	8.42369	8.27895
22	9.91115	9.71934	9.53348	9.35334	9.17871	9.00937	8.84512	8.68578	8.53114	8.38105
23	10.06049	9.86076	9.66743	9.48023	9.29892	9.12327	8.95306	8.78807	8.62810	8.47296
24	10.19780	9.99049	9.79000	9.59606	9.40840	9.22676	9.05090	8.88059	8.71559	8.55571
25	10.32404	10.10948	9.90217	9.70182	9.50812	9.32081	9.13960	8.96426	8.79453	8.63020
30	10.81812	10.57206	10.33534	10.10751	9.88814	9.67683	9.47321	9.27691	9.08759	8.90493
35	11.14276	10.87242	10.61330	10.36479	10.12632	9.89738	9.67746	9.46611	9.26288	9.06736
40	11.35606	11.06746	10.79167	10.52795	10.27561	10.03400	9.80252	9.58061	9.36773	9.16340
45	11.49620	11.19409	10.90613	10.63143	10.36918	10.11864	9.87909	9.64990	9.43045	9.22019
50	11.58829	11.27632	10.97957	10.69705	10.42783	10.17106	9.92597	9.69183	9.46797	9.25376

Annual Rate of Decline 4%

Holding Period	5.50%	5.75%	6.00%	6.25%	Discount Rate 6.50%	6.75%	7.00%	7.25%	7.50%	7.75%
1	0.94787	0.94563	0.94340	0.94118	0.93897	0.93677	0.93458	0.93240	0.93023	0.92807
2	1.81038	1.80407	1.79779	1.79156	1.78536	1.77920	1.77308	1.76700	1.76095	1.75494
3	2.59523	2.58336	2.57159	2.55990	2.54831	2.53680	2.52538	2.51405	2.50280	2.49164
4	3.30940	3.29081	3.27238	3.25412	3.23603	3.21811	3.20034	3.18274	3.16530	3.14801
5	3.95927	3.93303	3.90706	3.88137	3.85595	3.83080	3.80592	3.78129	3.75691	3.73280
6	4.55061	4.51603	4.48187	4.44811	4.41476	4.38180	4.34923	4.31705	4.28525	4.25381
7	5.08871	5.04529	5.00245	4.96018	4.91847	4.87731	4.83669	4.79661	4.75706	4.71802
8	5.57835	5.52575	5.47391	5.42284	5.37251	5.32292	5.27404	5.22587	5.17840	5.13160
9	6.02390	5.96191	5.90090	5.84087	5.78180	5.72366	5.66643	5.61011	5.55466	5.50008
10	6.42933	6.35785	6.28761	6.21858	6.15073	6.08404	6.01848	5.95403	5.89067	5.82837
11	6.79826	6.71730	6.63784	6.55984	6.48329	6.40813	6.33434	6.26189	6.19074	6.12087
12	7.13396	7.04360	6.95502	6.86819	6.78306	6.69958	6.61772	6.53745	6.45871	6.38147
13	7.43943	7.33981	7.24228	7.14679	7.05327	6.96168	6.87198	6.78410	6.69801	6.61366
14	7.71740	7.60872	7.50245	7.39851	7.29685	7.19739	7.10009	7.00488	6.91171	6.82052
15	7.97033	7.85283	7.73806	7.62595	7.51641	7.40936	7.30475	7.20251	7.10255	7.00482
16	8.20049	8.07444	7.95145	7.83144	7.71432	7.59999	7.48838	7.37940	7.27298	7.16903
17	8.40993	8.27561	8.14471	8.01712	7.89272	7.77142	7.65312	7.53774	7.42517	7.31533
18	8.60050	8.45824	8.31974	8.18488	8.05353	7.92559	7.80093	7.67947	7.56108	7.44568
19	8.77392	8.62403	8.47826	8.33645	8.19849	8.06423	7.93355	7.80633	7.68245	7.56181
20	8.93172	8.77453	8.62182	8.47341	8.32915	8.18891	8.05253	7.91988	7.79084	7.66528
21	9.07531	8.91116	8.75183	8.59715	8.44694	8.30103	8.15928	8.02153	7.88764	7.75747
22	9.20597	9.03519	8.86959	8.70895	8.55311	8.40187	8.25505	8.11251	7.97408	7.83960
23	9.32486	9.14779	8.97623	8.80997	8.64881	8.49254	8.34098	8.19395	8.05127	7.91277
24	9.43305	9.25000	9.07281	8.90125	8.73508	8.57409	8.41808	8.26685	8.12020	7.97797
25	9.53149	9.34279	9.16028	8.98371	8.81284	8.64743	8.48725	8.33209	8.18176	8.03606
30	9.90568	9.69314	9.48836	9.29100	9.10069	8.91712	8.73997	8.56895	8.40379	8.24421
35	10.13912	9.90913	9.68826	9.47603	9.27200	9.07575	8.88689	8.70505	8.52989	8.36107
40	10.28476	10.04230	9.81006	9.58746	9.37395	9.16906	8.97230	8.78325	8.60150	8.42667
45	10.37561	10.12441	9.88427	9.65455	9.43463	9.22394	9.02196	8.82819	8.64218	8.46350
50	10.43230	10.17503	9.92949	9.69495	9.47073	9.25622	9.05082	8.85401	8.66528	8.48417

Present Value of a Series of Payments Decreasing at Constant Rate

Annual Rate of Decline 5%

Holding Period	Discount Rate									
	5.50%	5.75%	6.00%	6.25%	6.50%	6.75%	7.00%	7.25%	7.50%	7.75%
1	0.94787	0.94563	0.94340	0.94118	0.93897	0.93677	0.93458	0.93240	0.93023	0.92807
2	1.80140	1.79513	1.78889	1.78270	1.77654	1.77043	1.76435	1.75830	1.75230	1.74633
3	2.56998	2.55827	2.54665	2.53512	2.52368	2.51232	2.50106	2.48987	2.47878	2.46776
4	3.26207	3.24384	3.22577	3.20787	3.19014	3.17256	3.15514	3.13788	3.12078	3.10383
5	3.88527	3.85971	3.83442	3.80939	3.78463	3.76012	3.73588	3.71188	3.68813	3.66463
6	4.44646	4.41298	4.37990	4.34722	4.31493	4.28301	4.25148	4.22031	4.18951	4.15907
7	4.95178	4.91001	4.86878	4.82810	4.78796	4.74835	4.70926	4.67067	4.63259	4.59500
8	5.40682	5.35651	5.30693	5.25807	5.20992	5.16247	5.11570	5.06959	5.02415	4.97935
9	5.81657	5.75762	5.69960	5.64251	5.58631	5.53100	5.47655	5.42295	5.37018	5.31822
10	6.18554	6.11795	6.05153	5.98624	5.92206	5.85897	5.79694	5.73595	5.67597	5.61700
11	6.51778	6.44166	6.36694	6.29358	6.22156	6.15084	6.08139	6.01319	5.94621	5.88041
12	6.81696	6.73246	6.64962	6.56838	6.48872	6.41058	6.33395	6.25877	6.18502	6.11266
13	7.08636	6.99370	6.90296	6.81408	6.72702	6.64174	6.55818	6.47630	6.39607	6.31743
14	7.32895	7.22838	7.13001	7.03377	6.93960	6.84745	6.75726	6.66899	6.58257	6.49796
15	7.54740	7.43921	7.33350	7.23019	7.12922	7.03052	6.93402	6.83966	6.74739	6.65714
16	7.74410	7.62861	7.51587	7.40582	7.29836	7.19343	7.09095	6.99084	6.89304	6.79748
17	7.92123	7.79875	7.67932	7.56285	7.44925	7.33842	7.23028	7.12476	7.02176	6.92121
18	8.08073	7.95159	7.82580	7.70325	7.58383	7.46745	7.35399	7.24337	7.13551	7.03030
19	8.22435	8.08890	7.95709	7.82879	7.70389	7.58227	7.46382	7.34844	7.23603	7.12648
20	8.35368	8.21225	8.07475	7.94104	7.81098	7.68446	7.56134	7.44151	7.32486	7.21128
21	8.47014	8.32306	8.18020	8.04140	7.90651	7.77539	7.64792	7.52395	7.40337	7.28605
22	8.57501	8.42261	8.27471	8.13113	7.99172	7.85632	7.72479	7.59697	7.47274	7.35197
23	8.66944	8.51204	8.35941	8.21137	8.06773	7.92834	7.79303	7.66165	7.53405	7.41009
24	8.75447	8.59237	8.43532	8.28310	8.13554	7.99244	7.85363	7.71895	7.58823	7.46133
25	8.83104	8.66454	8.50335	8.34724	8.19602	8.04948	7.90743	7.76970	7.63611	7.50651
30	9.11366	8.92917	8.75118	8.57937	8.41348	8.25322	8.09836	7.94865	7.80387	7.66380
35	9.28098	9.08400	8.89447	8.71202	8.53629	8.36695	8.20370	8.04624	7.89429	7.74759
40	9.38004	9.17459	8.97733	8.78782	8.60565	8.43044	8.26182	8.09945	7.94302	7.79223
45	9.43869	9.22759	9.02523	8.83113	8.64482	8.46587	8.29388	8.12847	7.96929	7.81602
50	9.47342	9.25860	9.05293	8.85588	8.66694	8.48565	8.31157	8.14429	7.98345	7.82869

Annual Rate of Decline 6%

Holding Period	Discount Rate									
	5.50%	5.75%	6.00%	6.25%	6.50%	6.75%	7.00%	7.25%	7.50%	7.75%
1	0.94787	0.94563	0.94340	0.94118	0.93897	0.93677	0.93458	0.93240	0.93023	0.92807
2	1.79241	1.78618	1.77999	1.77384	1.76773	1.76165	1.75561	1.74961	1.74365	1.73772
3	2.54490	2.53335	2.52188	2.51050	2.49921	2.48801	2.47689	2.46586	2.45491	2.44404
4	3.21536	3.19749	3.17978	3.16223	3.14485	3.12762	3.11054	3.09362	3.07685	3.06023
5	3.81274	3.78784	3.76320	3.73882	3.71470	3.69083	3.66720	3.64383	3.62069	3.59779
6	4.34500	4.31259	4.28058	4.24894	4.21767	4.18677	4.15624	4.12606	4.09623	4.06675
7	4.81924	4.77904	4.73938	4.70024	4.66161	4.62348	4.58585	4.54871	4.51205	4.47586
8	5.24179	5.19367	5.14624	5.09950	5.05344	5.00803	4.96327	4.91915	4.87565	4.83277
9	5.61828	5.56222	5.50704	5.45274	5.39928	5.34665	5.29484	5.24382	5.19360	5.14414
10	5.95372	5.88982	5.82700	5.76524	5.70453	5.64482	5.58612	5.52839	5.47161	5.41577
11	6.25261	6.18102	6.11074	6.04172	5.97395	5.90739	5.84201	5.77779	5.71471	5.65273
12	6.51891	6.43987	6.36235	6.28632	6.21175	6.13859	6.06681	5.99639	5.92728	5.85946
13	6.75619	6.66995	6.58548	6.50272	6.42164	6.34218	6.26430	6.18798	6.11316	6.03981
14	6.96760	6.87447	6.78335	6.69417	6.60689	6.52145	6.43780	6.35590	6.27569	6.19714
15	7.15596	7.05627	6.95882	6.86355	6.77040	6.67931	6.59022	6.50307	6.41781	6.33440
16	7.32380	7.21787	7.11443	7.01340	6.91472	6.81831	6.72412	6.63206	6.54209	6.45414
17	7.47334	7.36151	7.25242	7.14597	7.04210	6.94072	6.84175	6.74512	6.65076	6.55860
18	7.60657	7.48919	7.37478	7.26326	7.15453	7.04850	6.94509	6.84420	6.74578	6.64973
19	7.72529	7.60268	7.48330	7.36703	7.25376	7.14341	7.03587	6.93105	6.82887	6.72923
20	7.83106	7.70357	7.57953	7.45883	7.34135	7.22698	7.11562	7.00717	6.90152	6.79859
21	7.92531	7.79324	7.66487	7.54005	7.41866	7.30058	7.18569	7.07388	6.96505	6.85909
22	8.00928	7.87295	7.74054	7.61190	7.48689	7.36538	7.24724	7.13235	7.02060	6.91188
23	8.08410	7.94381	7.80765	7.67547	7.54711	7.42244	7.30131	7.18360	7.06918	6.95792
24	8.15076	8.00679	7.86716	7.73171	7.60027	7.47269	7.34882	7.22852	7.11165	6.99810
25	8.21015	8.06277	7.91994	7.78146	7.64719	7.51693	7.39055	7.26788	7.14879	7.03314
30	8.42303	8.26210	8.10662	7.95633	7.81101	7.67044	7.53441	7.40273	7.27520	7.15166
35	8.54256	8.37272	8.20900	8.05111	7.89877	7.75171	7.60969	7.47246	7.33982	7.21155
40	8.60969	8.43410	8.26515	8.10248	7.94577	7.79473	7.64907	7.50853	7.37286	7.24182
45	8.64738	8.46817	8.29594	8.13032	7.97095	7.81751	7.66969	7.52719	7.38975	7.25711
50	8.66855	8.48707	8.31283	8.14541	7.98444	7.82957	7.68047	7.53683	7.39838	7.26484

Present Value of a Series of Payments Decreasing at Constant Rate

Annual Rate of Decline   7%

Holding Period	5.50%	5.75%	6.00%	6.25%	Discount Rate 6.50%	6.75%	7.00%	7.25%	7.50%	7.75%
1	0.94787	0.94563	0.94340	0.94118	0.93897	0.93677	0.93458	0.93240	0.93023	0.92807
2	1.78343	1.77724	1.77109	1.76498	1.75891	1.75288	1.74688	1.74092	1.73499	1.72910
3	2.51999	2.50859	2.49728	2.48606	2.47492	2.46386	2.45289	2.44201	2.43120	2.42048
4	3.16928	3.15176	3.13441	3.11721	3.10016	3.08327	3.06653	3.04995	3.03351	3.01721
5	3.74164	3.71739	3.69339	3.66965	3.64615	3.62290	3.59988	3.57711	3.55457	3.53226
6	4.24618	4.21482	4.18383	4.15320	4.12293	4.09302	4.06345	4.03423	4.00535	3.97680
7	4.69095	4.65228	4.61411	4.57645	4.53927	4.50258	4.46636	4.43061	4.39532	4.36048
8	5.08302	5.03699	4.99163	4.94691	4.90284	4.85939	4.81656	4.77433	4.73270	4.69165
9	5.42863	5.37532	5.32284	5.27118	5.22032	5.17024	5.12094	5.07238	5.02457	4.97748
10	5.73330	5.67286	5.61344	5.55501	5.49756	5.44105	5.38549	5.33083	5.27707	5.22418
11	6.00186	5.93452	5.86839	5.80344	5.73965	5.67698	5.61542	5.55494	5.49551	5.43711
12	6.23861	6.16464	6.09208	6.02090	5.95106	5.88253	5.81527	5.74927	5.68449	5.62089
13	6.44730	6.36701	6.28834	6.21123	6.13566	6.06159	5.98898	5.91778	5.84798	5.77952
14	6.63127	6.54498	6.46052	6.37783	6.29687	6.21759	6.13995	6.06391	5.98941	5.91643
15	6.79344	6.70150	6.61159	6.52365	6.43764	6.35350	6.27117	6.19061	6.11177	6.03460
16	6.93640	6.83914	6.74413	6.65129	6.56057	6.47190	6.38523	6.30048	6.21762	6.13659
17	7.06242	6.96019	6.86042	6.76301	6.66792	6.57505	6.48435	6.39576	6.30920	6.22462
18	7.17351	7.06665	6.96244	6.86080	6.76166	6.66492	6.57051	6.47837	6.38842	6.30060
19	7.27143	7.16027	7.05195	6.94640	6.84351	6.74321	6.64540	6.55001	6.45696	6.36618
20	7.35776	7.24260	7.13049	7.02132	6.91499	6.81141	6.71049	6.61213	6.51626	6.42278
21	7.43385	7.31500	7.19939	7.08689	6.97741	6.87083	6.76706	6.66600	6.56755	6.47164
22	7.50093	7.37868	7.25984	7.14429	7.03192	6.92260	6.81623	6.71271	6.61193	6.51380
23	7.56006	7.43468	7.31288	7.19453	7.07951	6.96770	6.85897	6.75321	6.65032	6.55019
24	7.61219	7.48392	7.35941	7.23851	7.12108	7.00699	6.89611	6.78833	6.68353	6.58161
25	7.65814	7.52723	7.40024	7.27700	7.15737	7.04122	6.92839	6.81879	6.71227	6.60872
30	7.81803	7.67696	7.54047	7.40837	7.28045	7.15654	7.03648	6.92010	6.80725	6.69778
35	7.90314	7.75572	7.61338	7.47586	7.34294	7.21442	7.09009	6.96977	6.85328	6.74044
40	7.94844	7.79716	7.65127	7.51053	7.37467	7.24347	7.11669	6.99412	6.87558	6.76087
45	7.97256	7.81895	7.67098	7.52835	7.39079	7.25804	7.12988	7.00606	6.88639	6.77066
50	7.98539	7.83041	7.68122	7.53750	7.39897	7.26536	7.13642	7.01191	6.89163	6.77535

Annual Rate of Decline   8%

Holding Period	5.50%	5.75%	6.00%	6.25%	Discount Rate 6.50%	6.75%	7.00%	7.25%	7.50%	7.75%
1	0.94787	0.94563	0.94340	0.94118	0.93897	0.93677	0.93458	0.93240	0.93023	0.92807
2	1.77444	1.76830	1.76219	1.75612	1.75009	1.74410	1.73814	1.73222	1.72634	1.72049
3	2.49525	2.48401	2.47285	2.46177	2.45079	2.43988	2.42906	2.41832	2.40766	2.39708
4	3.12382	3.10665	3.08964	3.07278	3.05608	3.03952	3.02312	3.00685	2.99074	2.97477
5	3.67196	3.64834	3.62497	3.60184	3.57896	3.55631	3.53389	3.51171	3.48975	3.46801
6	4.14995	4.11960	4.08960	4.05995	4.03065	4.00169	3.97307	3.94477	3.91681	3.88916
7	4.56678	4.52958	4.49286	4.45662	4.42084	4.38553	4.35067	4.31626	4.28229	4.24875
8	4.93028	4.88625	4.84286	4.80008	4.75791	4.71634	4.67535	4.63493	4.59508	4.55578
9	5.24725	5.19655	5.14663	5.09748	5.04909	5.00143	4.95450	4.90828	4.86276	4.81793
10	5.52367	5.46650	5.41028	5.35500	5.30062	5.24714	5.19453	5.14277	5.09185	5.04176
11	5.76472	5.70135	5.63911	5.57797	5.51791	5.45889	5.40090	5.34392	5.28791	5.23287
12	5.97492	5.90567	5.83772	5.77105	5.70561	5.64139	5.57835	5.51646	5.45570	5.39605
13	6.15822	6.08342	6.01010	5.93822	5.86776	5.79867	5.73091	5.66447	5.59930	5.53537
14	6.31807	6.23806	6.15971	6.08298	6.00783	5.93421	5.86209	5.79143	5.72219	5.65433
15	6.45747	6.37259	6.28956	6.20832	6.12883	6.05103	5.97488	5.90034	5.82736	5.75590
16	6.57902	6.48963	6.40226	6.31685	6.23335	6.15171	6.07186	5.99377	5.91737	5.84263
17	6.68502	6.59145	6.50007	6.41083	6.32365	6.23847	6.15525	6.07391	5.99440	5.91667
18	6.77746	6.68003	6.58497	6.49220	6.40165	6.31325	6.22694	6.14265	6.06032	5.97990
19	6.85807	6.75710	6.65865	6.56266	6.46903	6.37770	6.28858	6.20162	6.11674	6.03388
20	6.92837	6.82414	6.72260	6.62367	6.52724	6.43324	6.34159	6.25221	6.16503	6.07997
21	6.98966	6.88247	6.77811	6.67649	6.57752	6.48110	6.38716	6.29560	6.20635	6.11933
22	7.04312	6.93321	6.82628	6.72223	6.62096	6.52236	6.42634	6.33282	6.24171	6.15293
23	7.08974	6.97736	6.86810	6.76184	6.65848	6.55791	6.46003	6.36475	6.27198	6.18162
24	7.13039	7.01576	6.90438	6.79613	6.69089	6.58855	6.48900	6.39214	6.29788	6.20612
25	7.16583	7.04917	6.93588	6.82583	6.71889	6.61496	6.51391	6.41564	6.32004	6.22703
30	7.28559	7.16132	7.04092	6.92423	6.81109	6.70135	6.59488	6.49154	6.39121	6.29376
35	7.34597	7.21721	7.09265	6.97212	6.85544	6.74243	6.63293	6.52680	6.42388	6.32405
40	7.37643	7.24506	7.11813	6.99544	6.87678	6.76196	6.65082	6.54318	6.43888	6.33779
45	7.39179	7.25894	7.13068	7.00678	6.88704	6.77125	6.65922	6.55078	6.44577	6.34403
50	7.39953	7.26586	7.13686	7.01231	6.89198	6.77566	6.66317	6.55431	6.44893	6.34686

Present Value of a Series of Payments Decreasing at Constant Rate

Annual Rate of Decline 9%

Holding Period					Discount Rate					
	5.50%	5.75%	6.00%	6.25%	6.50%	6.75%	7.00%	7.25%	7.50%	7.75%
1	0.94787	0.94563	0.94340	0.94118	0.93897	0.93677	0.93458	0.93240	0.93023	0.92807
2	1.76546	1.75936	1.75329	1.74727	1.74128	1.73532	1.72941	1.72353	1.71769	1.71188
3	2.47068	2.45959	2.44858	2.43766	2.42682	2.41606	2.40538	2.39479	2.38427	2.37384
4	3.07898	3.06215	3.04548	3.02896	3.01259	2.99636	2.98028	2.96434	2.94855	2.93289
5	3.60367	3.58067	3.55791	3.53539	3.51310	3.49104	3.46921	3.44760	3.42621	3.40504
6	4.05624	4.02686	3.99783	3.96913	3.94077	3.91274	3.88503	3.85764	3.83056	3.80379
7	4.44662	4.41082	4.37550	4.34062	4.30620	4.27222	4.23867	4.20555	4.17285	4.14056
8	4.78334	4.74123	4.69972	4.65879	4.61844	4.57866	4.53943	4.50075	4.46260	4.42497
9	5.07378	5.02555	4.97806	4.93130	4.88524	4.83989	4.79522	4.75122	4.70787	4.66517
10	5.32430	5.27021	5.21701	5.16469	5.11321	5.06257	5.01275	4.96373	4.91550	4.86804
11	5.54039	5.48075	5.42215	5.36458	5.30800	5.25240	5.19776	5.14405	5.09126	5.03936
12	5.72678	5.66192	5.59826	5.53578	5.47444	5.41423	5.35511	5.29705	5.24004	5.18406
13	5.88756	5.81782	5.74945	5.68241	5.61666	5.55218	5.48892	5.42687	5.36599	5.30626
14	6.02624	5.95198	5.87925	5.80799	5.73818	5.66977	5.60273	5.53702	5.47261	5.40946
15	6.14585	6.06743	5.99067	5.91555	5.84201	5.77002	5.69952	5.63048	5.56286	5.49662
16	6.24903	6.16677	6.08633	6.00767	5.93073	5.85547	5.78183	5.70978	5.63926	5.57023
17	6.33802	6.25225	6.16846	6.08657	6.00654	5.92832	5.85184	5.77706	5.70393	5.63240
18	6.41479	6.32582	6.23896	6.15415	6.07132	5.99041	5.91138	5.83415	5.75867	5.68490
19	6.48100	6.38912	6.29948	6.21202	6.12667	6.04335	5.96201	5.88259	5.80502	5.72925
20	6.53812	6.44359	6.35144	6.26159	6.17396	6.08848	6.00508	5.92369	5.84425	5.76669
21	6.58738	6.49047	6.39605	6.30404	6.21437	6.12695	6.04170	5.95856	5.87746	5.79832
22	6.62987	6.53080	6.43434	6.34040	6.24890	6.15974	6.07285	5.98815	5.90557	5.82503
23	6.66653	6.56551	6.46722	6.37155	6.27840	6.18769	6.09934	6.01325	5.92936	5.84759
24	6.69814	6.59538	6.49544	6.39822	6.30361	6.21152	6.12187	6.03456	5.94951	5.86664
25	6.72541	6.62109	6.51967	6.42106	6.32515	6.23184	6.14103	6.05263	5.96656	5.88273
30	6.81484	6.70484	6.59812	6.49456	6.39401	6.29637	6.20151	6.10934	6.01973	5.93259
35	6.85754	6.74436	6.63470	6.52843	6.42538	6.32542	6.22843	6.13427	6.04284	5.95401
40	6.87792	6.76300	6.65176	6.54404	6.43966	6.33850	6.24040	6.14524	6.05288	5.96322
45	6.88766	6.77180	6.65972	6.55123	6.44617	6.34439	6.24573	6.15006	6.05725	5.96717
50	6.89230	6.77595	6.66343	6.55454	6.44913	6.34704	6.24810	6.15218	6.05915	5.96887

Annual Rate of Decline 10%

Holding Period					Discount Rate					
	5.50%	5.75%	6.00%	6.25%	6.50%	6.75%	7.00%	7.25%	7.50%	7.75%
1	0.94787	0.94563	0.94340	0.94118	0.93897	0.93677	0.93458	0.93240	0.93023	0.92807
2	1.75647	1.75042	1.74439	1.73841	1.73246	1.72655	1.72067	1.71484	1.70903	1.70326
3	2.44628	2.43534	2.42449	2.41371	2.40302	2.39241	2.38188	2.37142	2.36105	2.35075
4	3.03474	3.01826	3.00192	2.98573	2.96969	2.95379	2.93803	2.92241	2.90693	2.89158
5	3.53675	3.51436	3.49220	3.47027	3.44856	3.42708	3.40582	3.38477	3.36394	3.34332
6	3.96500	3.93657	3.90847	3.88070	3.85324	3.82611	3.79929	3.77277	3.74655	3.72064
7	4.33033	4.29590	4.26191	4.22836	4.19523	4.16253	4.13024	4.09836	4.06688	4.03580
8	4.64199	4.60171	4.56200	4.52284	4.48423	4.44616	4.40861	4.37158	4.33506	4.29904
9	4.90786	4.86197	4.81679	4.77229	4.72846	4.68529	4.64276	4.60086	4.55959	4.51892
10	5.13466	5.08348	5.03312	4.98359	4.93485	4.88689	4.83970	4.79327	4.74756	4.70258
11	5.32815	5.27199	5.21680	5.16257	5.10926	5.05687	5.00536	4.95472	4.90494	4.85598
12	5.49321	5.43243	5.37276	5.31417	5.25665	5.20017	5.14469	5.09021	5.03669	4.98412
13	5.63402	5.56897	5.50517	5.44260	5.38121	5.32098	5.26189	5.20391	5.14700	5.09114
14	5.75414	5.68517	5.61760	5.55138	5.48647	5.42284	5.36047	5.29931	5.23935	5.18054
15	5.85661	5.78407	5.71306	5.64352	5.57542	5.50872	5.44339	5.37938	5.31666	5.25520
16	5.94403	5.86824	5.79410	5.72157	5.65059	5.58112	5.51313	5.44656	5.38139	5.31757
17	6.01860	5.93987	5.86292	5.78768	5.71411	5.64216	5.57179	5.50294	5.43558	5.36967
18	6.08222	6.00084	5.92135	5.84368	5.76779	5.69363	5.62113	5.55026	5.48095	5.41318
19	6.13649	6.05272	5.97095	5.89112	5.81316	5.73702	5.66263	5.58996	5.51894	5.44952
20	6.18279	6.09688	6.01307	5.93130	5.85150	5.77360	5.69754	5.62328	5.55074	5.47988
21	6.22228	6.13446	6.04884	5.96534	5.88389	5.80444	5.72691	5.65123	5.57736	5.50524
22	6.25598	6.16644	6.07920	5.99417	5.91127	5.83044	5.75160	5.67469	5.59965	5.52642
23	6.28472	6.19366	6.10498	6.01859	5.93441	5.85236	5.77238	5.69438	5.61831	5.54411
24	6.30924	6.21683	6.12687	6.03928	5.95396	5.87084	5.78985	5.71090	5.63394	5.55888
25	6.33016	6.23655	6.14546	6.05680	5.97048	5.88643	5.80455	5.72477	5.64702	5.57122
30	6.39674	6.29890	6.20387	6.11153	6.02176	5.93449	5.84960	5.76700	5.68662	5.60836
35	6.42682	6.32675	6.22965	6.13539	6.04387	5.95496	5.86856	5.78458	5.70291	5.62346
40	6.44041	6.33918	6.24102	6.14580	6.05339	5.96368	5.87655	5.79189	5.70960	5.62960
45	6.44655	6.34473	6.24604	6.15034	6.05750	5.96739	5.87991	5.79493	5.71236	5.63209
50	6.44933	6.34721	6.24825	6.15232	6.05927	5.96898	5.88132	5.79620	5.71349	5.63311

Present Value of a Series of Payments Decreasing at Constant Rate

Annual Rate of Decline 1%

Holding Period	Discount Rate 8.00%	8.25%	8.50%	8.75%	9.00%	9.25%	9.50%	9.75%	10.00%	10.25%
1	0.92593	0.92379	0.92166	0.91954	0.91743	0.91533	0.91324	0.91116	0.90909	0.90703
2	1.77469	1.76864	1.76262	1.75664	1.75069	1.74479	1.73891	1.73308	1.72727	1.72150
3	2.55273	2.54129	2.52995	2.51869	2.50751	2.49642	2.48541	2.47448	2.46364	2.45287
4	3.26592	3.24793	3.23009	3.21241	3.19490	3.17753	3.16032	3.14327	3.12636	3.10961
5	3.91969	3.89418	3.86893	3.84394	3.81922	3.79474	3.77052	3.74655	3.72282	3.69933
6	4.51898	4.48521	4.45183	4.41886	4.38626	4.35405	4.32221	4.29074	4.25963	4.22888
7	5.06832	5.02573	4.98370	4.94222	4.90128	4.86088	4.82099	4.78162	4.74276	4.70439
8	5.57189	5.52007	5.46900	5.41867	5.36906	5.32015	5.27195	5.22442	5.17757	5.13138
9	6.03349	5.97216	5.91181	5.85240	5.79391	5.73634	5.67966	5.62385	5.56890	5.51480
10	6.45662	6.38563	6.31584	6.24724	6.17979	6.11348	6.04828	5.98416	5.92111	5.85909
11	6.84450	6.76376	6.68450	6.60668	6.53027	6.45524	6.38155	6.30917	6.23809	6.16826
12	7.20005	7.10958	7.02088	6.93390	6.84859	6.76493	6.68286	6.60235	6.52337	6.44587
13	7.52597	7.42585	7.32781	7.23178	7.13771	7.04556	6.95528	6.86681	6.78012	6.69516
14	7.82473	7.71510	7.60786	7.50295	7.40031	7.29987	7.20158	7.10537	7.01120	6.91901
15	8.09860	7.97963	7.86339	7.74981	7.63881	7.53032	7.42426	7.32056	7.21917	7.12002
16	8.34964	8.22156	8.09655	7.97454	7.85544	7.73914	7.62558	7.51468	7.40635	7.30051
17	8.57976	8.44281	8.30930	8.17913	8.05219	7.92838	7.80761	7.68978	7.57480	7.46259
18	8.79071	8.64516	8.50342	8.36536	8.23088	8.09986	7.97217	7.84773	7.72641	7.60813
19	8.98407	8.83021	8.68054	8.53491	8.39319	8.25525	8.12096	7.99020	7.86286	7.73882
20	9.16133	8.99945	8.84215	8.68925	8.54060	8.39606	8.25548	8.11873	7.98567	7.85618
21	9.32381	9.15424	8.98961	8.82975	8.67449	8.52366	8.37710	8.23466	8.09619	7.96156
22	9.47275	9.29579	9.12416	8.95766	8.79610	8.63929	8.48706	8.33924	8.19566	8.05618
23	9.60928	9.42525	9.24693	9.07410	8.90655	8.74407	8.58647	8.43357	8.28519	8.14115
24	9.73443	9.54365	9.35895	9.18010	9.00686	8.83902	8.67635	8.51867	8.36576	8.21745
25	9.84916	9.65193	9.46116	9.27660	9.09798	8.92506	8.75762	8.59542	8.43827	8.28597
30	10.29434	10.06937	9.85266	9.64382	9.44248	9.24830	9.06096	8.88013	8.70554	8.53689
35	10.58247	10.33645	10.10026	9.87341	9.65541	9.44582	9.24420	9.05017	8.86335	8.68338
40	10.76896	10.50732	10.25686	10.01695	9.78702	9.56650	9.35490	9.15173	8.95654	8.76891
45	10.88966	10.61664	10.35590	10.10670	9.86836	9.64025	9.42177	9.21238	9.01156	8.81884
50	10.96778	10.68658	10.41853	10.16281	9.91864	9.68531	9.46217	9.24861	9.04406	8.84799

Annual Rate of Decline 2%

Holding Period	Discount Rate 8.00%	8.25%	8.50%	8.75%	9.00%	9.25%	9.50%	9.75%	10.00%	10.25%
1	0.92593	0.92379	0.92166	0.91954	0.91743	0.91533	0.91324	0.91116	0.90909	0.90703
2	1.76612	1.76010	1.75412	1.74818	1.74228	1.73641	1.73057	1.72477	1.71901	1.71328
3	2.52851	2.51723	2.50603	2.49491	2.48388	2.47293	2.46207	2.45128	2.44057	2.42994
4	3.22032	3.20266	3.18517	3.16783	3.15065	3.13361	3.11673	3.10000	3.08342	3.06698
5	3.84807	3.82320	3.79859	3.77423	3.75012	3.72626	3.70265	3.67927	3.65614	3.63323
6	4.41769	4.38497	4.35264	4.32068	4.28910	4.25788	4.22703	4.19653	4.16638	4.13657
7	4.93457	4.89356	4.85308	4.81312	4.77369	4.73476	4.69633	4.65840	4.62095	4.58398
8	5.40359	5.35398	5.30508	5.25688	5.20937	5.16253	5.11635	5.07083	5.02594	4.98168
9	5.82918	5.77081	5.71335	5.65678	5.60108	5.54625	5.49226	5.43910	5.38675	5.33519
10	6.21537	6.14817	6.08210	6.01714	5.95327	5.89046	5.82869	5.76794	5.70819	5.64942
11	6.56580	6.48980	6.41517	6.34188	6.26991	6.19922	6.12979	6.06158	5.99457	5.92874
12	6.88378	6.79908	6.71601	6.63453	6.55460	6.47619	6.39926	6.32378	6.24971	6.17702
13	7.17232	7.07907	6.98773	6.89824	6.81056	6.72464	6.64043	6.55791	6.47701	6.39771
14	7.43414	7.33256	7.23316	7.13588	7.04068	6.94750	6.85628	6.76697	6.67952	6.59388
15	7.67172	7.56204	7.45483	7.35004	7.24759	7.14741	7.04946	6.95365	6.85994	6.76826
16	7.88730	7.76979	7.65506	7.54302	7.43361	7.32674	7.22234	7.12034	7.02067	6.92326
17	8.08292	7.95787	7.83590	7.71693	7.60086	7.48760	7.37708	7.26919	7.16387	7.06104
18	8.26043	8.12814	7.99925	7.87365	7.75123	7.63190	7.51556	7.40210	7.29145	7.18351
19	8.42150	8.28229	8.14679	8.01487	7.88643	7.76134	7.63949	7.52078	7.40511	7.29237
20	8.56766	8.42184	8.28005	8.14214	8.00798	7.87745	7.75041	7.62676	7.50637	7.38914
21	8.70028	8.54818	8.40041	8.25682	8.11727	7.98160	7.84969	7.72139	7.59658	7.47515
22	8.82063	8.66255	8.50913	8.36017	8.21553	8.07503	7.93853	7.80589	7.67696	7.55161
23	8.92983	8.76610	8.60732	8.45331	8.30387	8.15884	8.01805	7.88134	7.74856	7.61957
24	9.02892	8.85984	8.69601	8.53723	8.38329	8.23401	8.08921	7.94871	7.81235	7.67998
25	9.11883	8.94471	8.77612	8.61286	8.45470	8.30145	8.15290	8.00887	7.86919	7.73368
30	9.45791	9.26267	9.07434	8.89260	8.71715	8.54771	8.38401	8.22579	8.07283	7.92488
35	9.66651	9.45603	9.25361	9.05884	8.87133	8.69073	8.51671	8.34894	8.18712	8.03098
40	9.79484	9.57362	9.36138	9.15763	8.96191	8.77380	8.59290	8.41884	8.25127	8.08985
45	9.87379	9.64513	9.42617	9.21634	9.01512	8.82205	8.63665	8.45853	8.28727	8.12253
50	9.92236	9.68862	9.46511	9.25122	9.04639	8.85007	8.66178	8.48106	8.30748	8.14066

Present Value of a Series of Payments Decreasing at Constant Rate

Annual Rate of Decline 3%

Holding Period	Discount Rate									
	8.00%	8.25%	8.50%	8.75%	9.00%	9.25%	9.50%	9.75%	10.00%	10.25%
1	0.92593	0.92379	0.92166	0.91954	0.91743	0.91533	0.91324	0.91116	0.90909	0.90703
2	1.75754	1.75157	1.74563	1.73973	1.73386	1.72803	1.72223	1.71647	1.71074	1.70505
3	2.50446	2.49332	2.48227	2.47130	2.46041	2.44960	2.43887	2.42822	2.41766	2.40716
4	3.17530	3.15799	3.14083	3.12382	3.10697	3.09026	3.07370	3.05729	3.04102	3.02490
5	3.77782	3.75358	3.72959	3.70585	3.68235	3.65909	3.63607	3.61328	3.59072	3.56839
6	4.31897	4.28727	4.25595	4.22499	4.19438	4.16413	4.13423	4.10467	4.07545	4.04657
7	4.80500	4.76550	4.72651	4.68803	4.65005	4.61255	4.57553	4.53898	4.50290	4.46727
8	5.24153	5.19403	5.14721	5.10105	5.05555	5.01068	4.96645	4.92284	4.87983	4.83742
9	5.63359	5.57802	5.52331	5.46944	5.41640	5.36418	5.31275	5.26210	5.21221	5.16308
10	5.98573	5.92211	5.85955	5.79803	5.73753	5.67803	5.61951	5.56194	5.50532	5.44960
11	6.30200	6.23043	6.16015	6.09112	6.02331	5.95670	5.89126	5.82696	5.76378	5.70169
12	6.58605	6.50672	6.42889	6.35254	6.27762	6.20412	6.13198	6.06118	5.99170	5.92349
13	6.84118	6.75429	6.66915	6.58571	6.50394	6.42379	6.34522	6.26820	6.19268	6.11862
14	7.07032	6.97613	6.88394	6.79369	6.70534	6.61884	6.53413	6.45116	6.36991	6.29031
15	7.27612	7.17491	7.07596	6.97920	6.88457	6.79201	6.70146	6.61287	6.52619	6.44136
16	7.46096	7.35304	7.24763	7.14467	7.04407	6.94577	6.84970	6.75580	6.66400	6.57426
17	7.62697	7.51265	7.40111	7.29225	7.18600	7.08228	6.98101	6.88212	6.78553	6.69118
18	7.77607	7.65568	7.53832	7.42390	7.31232	7.20349	7.09733	6.99376	6.89270	6.79406
19	7.90999	7.78384	7.66099	7.54131	7.42472	7.31111	7.20038	7.09244	6.98720	6.88457
20	8.03027	7.89869	7.77065	7.64605	7.52475	7.40666	7.29166	7.17965	7.07053	6.96420
21	8.13830	8.00159	7.86869	7.73946	7.61377	7.49150	7.37252	7.25673	7.14401	7.03426
22	8.23533	8.09381	7.95634	7.82278	7.69299	7.56682	7.44415	7.32485	7.20881	7.09590
23	8.32247	8.17644	8.03470	7.89710	7.76349	7.63370	7.50760	7.38506	7.26595	7.15014
24	8.40074	8.25048	8.10476	7.96339	7.82622	7.69308	7.56381	7.43828	7.31634	7.19785
25	8.47103	8.31683	8.16739	8.02252	7.88205	7.74580	7.61361	7.48531	7.36077	7.23983
30	8.72863	8.55840	8.39396	8.23507	8.08146	7.93292	7.78923	7.65016	7.51553	7.38515
35	8.87918	8.69796	8.52336	8.35506	8.19276	8.03617	7.88502	7.73906	7.59805	7.46175
40	8.96716	8.77858	8.59726	8.42281	8.25488	8.09314	7.93728	7.78701	7.64205	7.50214
45	9.01859	8.82516	8.63946	8.46105	8.28955	8.12457	7.96579	7.81287	7.66551	7.52343
50	9.04864	8.85207	8.66356	8.48264	8.30889	8.14192	7.98134	7.82681	7.67802	7.53465

Annual Rate of Decline 4%

Holding Period	Discount Rate									
	8.00%	8.25%	8.50%	8.75%	9.00%	9.25%	9.50%	9.75%	10.00%	10.25%
1	0.92593	0.92379	0.92166	0.91954	0.91743	0.91533	0.91324	0.91116	0.90909	0.90703
2	1.74897	1.74304	1.73714	1.73127	1.72544	1.71965	1.71389	1.70817	1.70248	1.69682
3	2.48057	2.46957	2.45866	2.44784	2.43709	2.42642	2.41583	2.40532	2.39489	2.38454
4	3.13088	3.11390	3.09707	3.08039	3.06386	3.04747	3.03123	3.01514	2.99918	2.98336
5	3.70893	3.68530	3.66192	3.63878	3.61588	3.59320	3.57076	3.54855	3.52656	3.50479
6	4.22275	4.19205	4.16170	4.13171	4.10206	4.07275	4.04377	4.01513	3.98681	3.95882
7	4.67948	4.64145	4.60390	4.56684	4.53025	4.49413	4.45847	4.42326	4.38849	4.35416
8	5.08546	5.03999	4.99516	4.95096	4.90738	4.86441	4.82204	4.78025	4.73905	4.69841
9	5.44634	5.39343	5.34134	5.29004	5.23952	5.18978	5.14078	5.09252	5.04499	4.99816
10	5.76712	5.70688	5.64763	5.58937	5.53206	5.47568	5.42023	5.36567	5.31199	5.25917
11	6.05225	5.98485	5.91864	5.85360	5.78970	5.72692	5.66522	5.60459	5.54501	5.48644
12	6.30571	6.23137	6.15843	6.08686	6.01662	5.94768	5.88001	5.81359	5.74837	5.68434
13	6.53100	6.44999	6.37059	6.29277	6.21647	6.14167	6.06832	5.99639	5.92585	5.85666
14	6.73126	6.64387	6.55831	6.47454	6.39249	6.31213	6.23341	6.15630	6.08074	6.00671
15	6.90927	6.81581	6.72441	6.63499	6.54751	6.46192	6.37815	6.29617	6.21592	6.13736
16	7.06750	6.96830	6.87136	6.77664	6.68405	6.59354	6.50505	6.41852	6.33389	6.25112
17	7.20814	7.10352	7.00139	6.90167	6.80430	6.70920	6.61630	6.52554	6.43685	6.35018
18	7.33317	7.22345	7.11644	7.01205	6.91021	6.81083	6.71383	6.61915	6.52671	6.43644
19	7.44430	7.32980	7.21823	7.10949	7.00349	6.90013	6.79934	6.70103	6.60513	6.51155
20	7.54308	7.42412	7.30830	7.19550	7.08564	6.97861	6.87431	6.77266	6.67357	6.57695
21	7.63088	7.50776	7.38799	7.27143	7.15799	7.04756	6.94003	6.83531	6.73329	6.63390
22	7.70893	7.58194	7.45849	7.33846	7.22172	7.10816	6.99765	6.89011	6.78542	6.68349
23	7.77831	7.64773	7.52088	7.39763	7.27785	7.16140	7.04817	6.93805	6.83091	6.72666
24	7.83998	7.70607	7.57608	7.44986	7.32728	7.20819	7.09246	6.97998	6.87061	6.76426
25	7.89480	7.75781	7.62492	7.49597	7.37081	7.24930	7.13129	7.01665	6.90526	6.79700
30	8.08998	7.94085	7.79661	7.65704	7.52194	7.39112	7.26439	7.14160	7.02257	6.90715
35	8.19829	8.04126	7.88971	7.74338	7.60202	7.46541	7.33333	7.20558	7.08196	6.96228
40	8.25839	8.09634	7.94019	7.78966	7.64446	7.50434	7.36904	7.23834	7.11203	6.98988
45	8.29175	8.12655	7.96757	7.81447	7.66695	7.52473	7.38754	7.25512	7.12725	7.00370
50	8.31026	8.14313	7.98241	7.82777	7.67887	7.53541	7.39712	7.26371	7.13495	7.01061

Present Value of a Series of Payments Decreasing at Constant Rate

Annual Rate of Decline 5%

Holding Period	8.00%	8.25%	8.50%	8.75%	Discount Rate 9.00%	9.25%	9.50%	9.75%	10.00%	10.25%
1	0.92593	0.92379	0.92166	0.91954	0.91743	0.91533	0.91324	0.91116	0.90909	0.90703
2	1.74040	1.73450	1.72864	1.72282	1.71703	1.71127	1.70555	1.69987	1.69422	1.68860
3	2.45683	2.44598	2.43522	2.42453	2.41392	2.40340	2.39295	2.38257	2.37228	2.36206
4	3.08703	3.07038	3.05388	3.03752	3.02131	3.00524	2.98931	2.97353	2.95788	2.94236
5	3.64137	3.61835	3.59556	3.57301	3.55068	3.52859	3.50671	3.48506	3.46362	3.44240
6	4.12898	4.09924	4.06985	4.04079	4.01206	3.98367	3.95559	3.92784	3.90040	3.87327
7	4.55790	4.52127	4.48512	4.44942	4.41418	4.37939	4.34504	4.31111	4.27762	4.24454
8	4.93519	4.89165	4.84872	4.80639	4.76466	4.72350	4.68291	4.64288	4.60340	4.56446
9	5.26707	5.21669	5.16708	5.11823	5.07011	5.02272	4.97604	4.93005	4.88475	4.84012
10	5.55899	5.50195	5.44583	5.39064	5.33634	5.28291	5.23035	5.17863	5.12774	5.07766
11	5.81578	5.75228	5.68990	5.62860	5.56837	5.50917	5.45099	5.39381	5.33759	5.28233
12	6.04166	5.97198	5.90360	5.83648	5.77059	5.70592	5.64241	5.58006	5.51883	5.45870
13	6.24035	6.16479	6.09071	6.01807	5.94685	5.87700	5.80849	5.74128	5.67535	5.61067
14	6.41512	6.33399	6.25454	6.17671	6.10047	6.02576	5.95257	5.88084	5.81053	5.74162
15	6.56886	6.48249	6.39798	6.31529	6.23435	6.15513	6.07757	6.00164	5.92728	5.85446
16	6.70409	6.61281	6.52358	6.43634	6.35104	6.26762	6.18602	6.10620	6.02810	5.95169
17	6.82304	6.72718	6.63355	6.54209	6.45274	6.36543	6.28011	6.19671	6.11518	6.03547
18	6.92767	6.82754	6.72984	6.63447	6.54138	6.45049	6.36174	6.27506	6.19038	6.10766
19	7.01971	6.91563	6.81414	6.71517	6.61863	6.52445	6.43256	6.34287	6.25533	6.16987
20	7.10067	6.99293	6.88796	6.78567	6.68597	6.58877	6.49400	6.40158	6.31142	6.22347
21	7.17189	7.06077	6.95259	6.84725	6.74465	6.64470	6.54731	6.45239	6.35986	6.26965
22	7.23453	7.12031	7.00918	6.90104	6.79579	6.69333	6.59355	6.49637	6.40170	6.30945
23	7.28963	7.17256	7.05873	6.94804	6.84037	6.73562	6.63368	6.53445	6.43783	6.34375
24	7.33810	7.21841	7.10211	6.98909	6.87922	6.77239	6.66849	6.56740	6.46904	6.37330
25	7.38074	7.25865	7.14010	7.02495	6.91308	6.80437	6.69869	6.59593	6.49599	6.39876
30	7.52823	7.39698	7.26985	7.14668	7.02730	6.91156	6.79930	6.69038	6.58466	6.48203
35	7.60590	7.46898	7.33662	7.20861	7.08475	6.96485	6.84875	6.73627	6.62727	6.52158
40	7.64680	7.50647	7.37098	7.24011	7.11363	6.99135	6.87305	6.75858	6.64774	6.54037
45	7.66834	7.52598	7.38866	7.25613	7.12816	7.00452	6.88500	6.76941	6.65757	6.54930
50	7.67969	7.53614	7.39776	7.26429	7.13547	7.01107	6.89088	6.77468	6.66230	6.55354

Annual Rate of Decline 6%

Holding Period	8.00%	8.25%	8.50%	8.75%	Discount Rate 9.00%	9.25%	9.50%	9.75%	10.00%	10.25%
1	0.92593	0.92379	0.92166	0.91954	0.91743	0.91533	0.91324	0.91116	0.90909	0.90703
2	1.73182	1.72597	1.72015	1.71436	1.70861	1.70289	1.69721	1.69156	1.68595	1.68037
3	2.43325	2.42255	2.41192	2.40138	2.39091	2.38052	2.37021	2.35997	2.34981	2.33973
4	3.04376	3.02743	3.01125	2.99522	2.97932	2.96356	2.94794	2.93246	2.91711	2.90190
5	3.57512	3.55269	3.53049	3.50851	3.48675	3.46522	3.44390	3.42279	3.40190	3.38121
6	4.03761	4.00880	3.98033	3.95218	3.92435	3.89684	3.86965	3.84275	3.81617	3.78988
7	4.44014	4.40487	4.37005	4.33568	4.30174	4.26822	4.23513	4.20245	4.17018	4.13831
8	4.79049	4.74880	4.70770	4.66716	4.62719	4.58776	4.54888	4.51053	4.47270	4.43538
9	5.09543	5.04746	5.00022	4.95368	4.90785	4.86270	4.81822	4.77439	4.73121	4.68867
10	5.36084	5.30680	5.25364	5.20135	5.14989	5.09925	5.04943	5.00039	4.95213	4.90463
11	5.59184	5.53200	5.47320	5.41542	5.35862	5.30279	5.24791	5.19396	5.14091	5.08875
12	5.79290	5.72756	5.66342	5.60045	5.53863	5.47792	5.41830	5.35974	5.30223	5.24574
13	5.96789	5.89737	5.82822	5.76039	5.69386	5.62860	5.56457	5.50174	5.44009	5.37959
14	6.12020	6.04483	5.97099	5.89864	5.82773	5.75824	5.69013	5.62336	5.55789	5.49371
15	6.25277	6.17288	6.09468	6.01813	5.94318	5.86979	5.79792	5.72752	5.65856	5.59101
16	6.36815	6.28407	6.20184	6.12142	6.04274	5.96577	5.89045	5.81674	5.74459	5.67396
17	6.46858	6.38063	6.29469	6.21070	6.12861	6.04835	5.96989	5.89315	5.81811	5.74470
18	6.55598	6.46447	6.37512	6.28787	6.20265	6.11941	6.03808	5.95860	5.88093	5.80500
19	6.63206	6.53728	6.44480	6.35457	6.26651	6.18054	6.09661	6.01466	5.93461	5.85642
20	6.69827	6.60050	6.50518	6.41223	6.32157	6.23314	6.14686	6.06267	5.98048	5.90026
21	6.75590	6.65540	6.55748	6.46206	6.36906	6.27840	6.19000	6.10379	6.01969	5.93763
22	6.80607	6.70307	6.60279	6.50514	6.41002	6.31734	6.22703	6.13901	6.05319	5.96950
23	6.84972	6.74447	6.64205	6.54237	6.44534	6.35085	6.25882	6.16917	6.08181	5.99667
24	6.88772	6.78042	6.67606	6.57456	6.47580	6.37968	6.28611	6.19501	6.10628	6.01984
25	6.92080	6.81163	6.70553	6.60238	6.50206	6.40448	6.30954	6.21714	6.12718	6.03959
30	7.03194	6.91588	6.80332	6.69412	6.58815	6.48528	6.38538	6.28833	6.19403	6.10237
35	7.08746	6.96735	6.85105	6.73839	6.62922	6.52338	6.42074	6.32115	6.22450	6.13065
40	7.11519	6.99276	6.87434	6.75975	6.64880	6.54135	6.43722	6.33627	6.23838	6.14340
45	7.12904	7.00531	6.88571	6.77005	6.65815	6.54982	6.44490	6.34325	6.24470	6.14914
50	7.13595	7.01150	6.89126	6.77503	6.66260	6.55381	6.44848	6.34646	6.24759	6.15173

Present Value of a Series of Payments Decreasing at Constant Rate

Annual Rate of Decline   7%

Holding Period	8.00%	8.25%	8.50%	8.75%	9.00%	9.25%	9.50%	9.75%	10.00%	10.25%
					Discount Rate					
1	0.92593	0.92379	0.92166	0.91954	0.91743	0.91533	0.91324	0.91116	0.90909	0.90703
2	1.72325	1.71743	1.71165	1.70591	1.70019	1.69452	1.68887	1.68326	1.67769	1.67214
3	2.40984	2.39927	2.38879	2.37838	2.36806	2.35780	2.34763	2.33753	2.32750	2.31754
4	3.00106	2.98506	2.96919	2.95347	2.93788	2.92243	2.90712	2.89193	2.87688	2.86197
5	3.51017	3.48832	3.46668	3.44527	3.42406	3.40308	3.38230	3.36173	3.34137	3.32120
6	3.94858	3.92068	3.89310	3.86584	3.83888	3.81223	3.78588	3.75983	3.73406	3.70859
7	4.32609	4.29213	4.25860	4.22550	4.19281	4.16053	4.12865	4.09717	4.06607	4.03536
8	4.65117	4.61125	4.57189	4.53307	4.49478	4.45702	4.41976	4.38302	4.34677	4.31101
9	4.93110	4.88542	4.84042	4.79610	4.75243	4.70940	4.66701	4.62525	4.58409	4.54353
10	5.17215	5.12096	5.07059	5.02103	4.97225	4.92425	4.87701	4.83051	4.78473	4.73967
11	5.37972	5.32332	5.26788	5.21339	5.15981	5.10714	5.05536	5.00444	4.95436	4.90511
12	5.55846	5.49717	5.43699	5.37788	5.31984	5.26283	5.20683	5.15182	5.09778	5.04468
13	5.71238	5.64653	5.58193	5.51856	5.45638	5.39536	5.33548	5.27672	5.21903	5.16240
14	5.84492	5.77485	5.70617	5.63886	5.57287	5.50818	5.44475	5.38255	5.32154	5.26171
15	5.95905	5.88509	5.81266	5.74174	5.67227	5.60422	5.53755	5.47223	5.40822	5.34548
16	6.05733	5.97980	5.90394	5.82972	5.75707	5.68597	5.61637	5.54822	5.48149	5.41614
17	6.14196	6.06117	5.98218	5.90495	5.82943	5.75556	5.68331	5.61261	5.54344	5.47575
18	6.21484	6.13107	6.04924	5.96929	5.89116	5.81480	5.74016	5.66718	5.59582	5.52603
19	6.27759	6.19113	6.10672	6.02431	5.94384	5.86523	5.78845	5.71342	5.64010	5.56844
20	6.33163	6.24273	6.15599	6.07137	5.98878	5.90816	5.82946	5.75260	5.67754	5.60422
21	6.37816	6.28705	6.19823	6.11161	6.02712	5.94471	5.86429	5.78580	5.70919	5.63440
22	6.41823	6.32514	6.23442	6.14602	6.05984	5.97581	5.89387	5.81394	5.73595	5.65985
23	6.45274	6.35785	6.26545	6.17544	6.08775	6.00229	5.91899	5.83778	5.75858	5.68133
24	6.48245	6.38596	6.29205	6.20061	6.11157	6.02484	5.94033	5.85798	5.77771	5.69944
25	6.50804	6.41011	6.31484	6.22213	6.13189	6.04403	5.95846	5.87510	5.79388	5.71472
30	6.59156	6.48845	6.38833	6.29109	6.19660	6.10476	6.01546	5.92862	5.84414	5.76192
35	6.63111	6.52512	6.42234	6.32262	6.22585	6.13190	6.04066	5.95201	5.86584	5.78208
40	6.64983	6.54228	6.43807	6.33705	6.23908	6.14404	6.05179	5.96222	5.87522	5.79068
45	6.65869	6.55031	6.44535	6.34365	6.24506	6.14946	6.05671	5.96669	5.87927	5.79438
50	6.66289	6.55407	6.44871	6.34666	6.24777	6.15189	6.05888	5.96864	5.88102	5.79593

Annual Rate of Decline   8%

Holding Period	8.00%	8.25%	8.50%	8.75%	9.00%	9.25%	9.50%	9.75%	10.00%	10.25%
					Discount Rate					
1	0.92593	0.92379	0.92166	0.91954	0.91743	0.91533	0.91324	0.91116	0.90909	0.90703
2	1.71468	1.70890	1.70316	1.69745	1.69178	1.68614	1.68053	1.67496	1.66942	1.66392
3	2.38658	2.37616	2.36581	2.35554	2.34535	2.33524	2.32520	2.31523	2.30533	2.29551
4	2.95894	2.94325	2.92769	2.91228	2.89699	2.88185	2.86683	2.85195	2.83719	2.82256
5	3.44650	3.42521	3.40413	3.38326	3.36260	3.34215	3.32190	3.30186	3.28201	3.26236
6	3.86183	3.83482	3.80811	3.78170	3.75559	3.72977	3.70425	3.67901	3.65405	3.62936
7	4.21564	4.18294	4.15065	4.11877	4.08729	4.05619	4.02549	3.99516	3.96520	3.93561
8	4.51702	4.47880	4.44111	4.40393	4.36725	4.33107	4.29539	4.26018	4.22544	4.19117
9	4.77376	4.73025	4.68739	4.64516	4.60355	4.56255	4.52215	4.48234	4.44310	4.40442
10	4.99246	4.94396	4.89622	4.84924	4.80300	4.75748	4.71267	4.66856	4.62514	4.58238
11	5.17877	5.12558	5.07329	5.02189	4.97134	4.92163	4.87275	4.82467	4.77739	4.73087
12	5.33747	5.27994	5.22344	5.16794	5.11342	5.05986	5.00724	4.95554	4.90472	4.85479
13	5.47266	5.41113	5.35075	5.29150	5.23335	5.17627	5.12024	5.06523	5.01122	4.95819
14	5.58782	5.52262	5.45870	5.39603	5.33457	5.27430	5.21518	5.15719	5.10030	5.04448
15	5.68592	5.61738	5.55023	5.48445	5.42000	5.35684	5.29494	5.23427	5.17479	5.11648
16	5.76949	5.69791	5.62785	5.55926	5.49211	5.42636	5.36196	5.29889	5.23710	5.17656
17	5.84067	5.76635	5.69366	5.62255	5.55298	5.48490	5.41827	5.35305	5.28921	5.22670
18	5.90132	5.82452	5.74946	5.67609	5.60435	5.53419	5.46558	5.39846	5.33279	5.26854
19	5.95297	5.87396	5.79678	5.72138	5.64771	5.57570	5.50533	5.43652	5.36925	5.30345
20	5.99698	5.91597	5.83690	5.75970	5.68430	5.61066	5.53872	5.46843	5.39973	5.33259
21	6.03446	5.95168	5.87092	5.79211	5.71519	5.64010	5.56678	5.49518	5.42523	5.35690
22	6.06639	5.98203	5.89977	5.81953	5.74126	5.66489	5.59035	5.51760	5.44656	5.37718
23	6.09359	6.00782	5.92423	5.84273	5.76327	5.68577	5.61016	5.53639	5.46439	5.39411
24	6.11677	6.02974	5.94497	5.86236	5.78184	5.70334	5.62680	5.55214	5.47931	5.40824
25	6.13650	6.04837	5.96255	5.87896	5.79752	5.71815	5.64078	5.56535	5.49179	5.42003
30	6.19909	6.10708	6.01763	5.93064	5.84601	5.76367	5.68351	5.60547	5.52946	5.45541
35	6.22716	6.13311	6.04177	5.95303	5.86679	5.78294	5.70140	5.62208	5.54488	5.46972
40	6.23976	6.14465	6.05235	5.96273	5.87569	5.79111	5.70889	5.62895	5.55119	5.47552
45	6.24541	6.14977	6.05699	5.96694	5.87950	5.79456	5.71203	5.63179	5.55377	5.47786
50	6.24794	6.15204	6.05902	5.96876	5.88113	5.79603	5.71334	5.63297	5.55482	5.47881

Present Value of a Series of Payments Decreasing at Constant Rate

Annual Rate of Decline 9%

Holding Period	8.00%	8.25%	8.50%	8.75%	Discount Rate 9.00%	9.25%	9.50%	9.75%	10.00%	10.25%
1	0.92593	0.92379	0.92166	0.91954	0.91743	0.91533	0.91324	0.91116	0.90909	0.90703
2	1.70610	1.70037	1.69466	1.68899	1.68336	1.67776	1.67219	1.66666	1.66116	1.65569
3	2.36348	2.35319	2.34299	2.33286	2.32281	2.31282	2.30292	2.29308	2.28332	2.27363
4	2.91737	2.90199	2.88675	2.87163	2.85665	2.84180	2.82708	2.81249	2.79802	2.78368
5	3.38408	3.36334	3.34280	3.32247	3.30234	3.28242	3.26269	3.24316	3.22382	3.20467
6	3.77733	3.75117	3.72530	3.69972	3.67443	3.64943	3.62470	3.60025	3.57607	3.55215
7	4.10868	4.07719	4.04610	4.01540	3.98508	3.95513	3.92555	3.89633	3.86747	3.83896
8	4.38787	4.35127	4.31516	4.27955	4.24442	4.20976	4.17557	4.14183	4.10855	4.07570
9	4.62311	4.58166	4.54083	4.50059	4.46094	4.42186	4.38335	4.34539	4.30798	4.27110
10	4.82132	4.77535	4.73010	4.68555	4.64170	4.59853	4.55603	4.51418	4.47296	4.43238
11	4.98834	4.93817	4.88884	4.84032	4.79261	4.74569	4.69953	4.65412	4.60945	4.56550
12	5.12906	5.07504	5.02197	4.96983	4.91860	4.86826	4.81879	4.77016	4.72237	4.67538
13	5.24764	5.19010	5.13364	5.07821	5.02379	4.97036	4.91790	4.86638	4.81577	4.76607
14	5.34754	5.28683	5.22729	5.16889	5.11160	5.05540	5.00026	4.94615	4.89305	4.84093
15	5.43173	5.36815	5.30584	5.24477	5.18492	5.12624	5.06871	5.01230	4.95698	4.90272
16	5.50266	5.43650	5.37172	5.30827	5.24612	5.18524	5.12559	5.06715	5.00986	4.95372
17	5.56243	5.49396	5.42697	5.36140	5.29722	5.23439	5.17287	5.11262	5.05361	4.99581
18	5.61278	5.54227	5.47331	5.40586	5.33988	5.27533	5.21216	5.15033	5.08981	5.03056
19	5.65522	5.58288	5.51218	5.44307	5.37550	5.30943	5.24481	5.18159	5.11975	5.05924
20	5.69097	5.61702	5.54478	5.47420	5.40523	5.33783	5.27194	5.20752	5.14452	5.08291
21	5.72109	5.64571	5.57212	5.50025	5.43006	5.36149	5.29449	5.22901	5.16501	5.10244
22	5.74648	5.66984	5.59505	5.52205	5.45078	5.38119	5.31323	5.24683	5.18197	5.11857
23	5.76787	5.69012	5.61428	5.54029	5.46808	5.39761	5.32880	5.26161	5.19599	5.13188
24	5.78589	5.70717	5.63041	5.55555	5.48253	5.41128	5.34174	5.27387	5.20759	5.14287
25	5.80107	5.72150	5.64394	5.56832	5.49459	5.42267	5.35250	5.28402	5.21719	5.15194
30	5.84783	5.76536	5.68509	5.60694	5.53083	5.45668	5.38443	5.31401	5.24535	5.17838
35	5.86769	5.78378	5.70217	5.62278	5.54553	5.47032	5.39709	5.32576	5.25626	5.18851
40	5.87613	5.79151	5.70926	5.62928	5.55149	5.47579	5.40211	5.33037	5.26048	5.19239
45	5.87971	5.79475	5.71220	5.63195	5.55391	5.47798	5.40410	5.33217	5.26212	5.19388
50	5.88123	5.79612	5.71342	5.63304	5.55489	5.47886	5.40489	5.33288	5.26276	5.19445

Annual Rate of Decline 10%

Holding Period	8.00%	8.25%	8.50%	8.75%	Discount Rate 9.00%	9.25%	9.50%	9.75%	10.00%	10.25%
1	0.92593	0.92379	0.92166	0.91954	0.91743	0.91533	0.91324	0.91116	0.90909	0.90703
2	1.69753	1.69183	1.68617	1.68054	1.67494	1.66938	1.66385	1.65836	1.65289	1.64746
3	2.34054	2.33039	2.32032	2.31033	2.30041	2.29057	2.28079	2.27109	2.26146	2.25190
4	2.87637	2.86130	2.84635	2.83154	2.81685	2.80230	2.78787	2.77356	2.75937	2.74531
5	3.32290	3.30269	3.28269	3.26288	3.24327	3.22386	3.20464	3.18561	3.16676	3.14810
6	3.69501	3.66968	3.64463	3.61986	3.59536	3.57114	3.54719	3.52350	3.50008	3.47691
7	4.00510	3.97479	3.94485	3.91528	3.88608	3.85723	3.82874	3.80060	3.77279	3.74532
8	4.26351	4.22846	4.19389	4.15978	4.12612	4.09292	4.06015	4.02782	3.99592	3.96443
9	4.47885	4.43937	4.40046	4.36211	4.32432	4.28707	4.25035	4.21416	4.17848	4.14330
10	4.65830	4.61472	4.57181	4.52957	4.48797	4.44702	4.40668	4.36697	4.32785	4.28932
11	4.80784	4.76050	4.71394	4.66815	4.62310	4.57878	4.53517	4.49227	4.45006	4.40851
12	4.93246	4.88171	4.83184	4.78283	4.73467	4.68732	4.64078	4.59503	4.55005	4.50582
13	5.03631	4.98249	4.92964	4.87775	4.82679	4.77674	4.72758	4.67930	4.63186	4.58525
14	5.12285	5.06627	5.01076	4.95630	4.90285	4.85040	4.79893	4.74840	4.69879	4.65009
15	5.19497	5.13593	5.07805	5.02130	4.96566	4.91109	4.85757	4.80506	4.75356	4.70302
16	5.25507	5.19384	5.13387	5.07510	5.01752	4.96108	4.90576	4.85153	4.79836	4.74623
17	5.30515	5.24200	5.18017	5.11962	5.06033	5.00226	4.94538	4.88964	4.83503	4.78150
18	5.34688	5.28203	5.21857	5.15647	5.09569	5.03619	4.97793	4.92089	4.86502	4.81030
19	5.38166	5.31531	5.25043	5.18696	5.12488	5.06414	5.00469	4.94652	4.88956	4.83380
20	5.41064	5.34298	5.27685	5.21220	5.14898	5.08716	5.02669	4.96753	4.90964	4.85299
21	5.43480	5.36599	5.29877	5.23309	5.16889	5.10613	5.04477	4.98476	4.92607	4.86865
22	5.45492	5.38512	5.31695	5.25037	5.18532	5.12175	5.05963	4.99889	4.93951	4.88144
23	5.47170	5.40102	5.33204	5.26467	5.19889	5.13463	5.07184	5.01048	4.95051	4.89188
24	5.48567	5.41425	5.34455	5.27651	5.21009	5.14523	5.08188	5.01999	4.95951	4.90040
25	5.49732	5.42524	5.35492	5.28631	5.21934	5.15396	5.09013	5.02778	4.96687	4.90736
30	5.53215	5.45792	5.38558	5.31508	5.24634	5.17931	5.11392	5.05012	4.98785	4.92706
35	5.54615	5.47090	5.39762	5.32625	5.25670	5.18893	5.12285	5.05841	4.99555	4.93421
40	5.55178	5.47605	5.40235	5.33058	5.26068	5.19257	5.12620	5.06148	4.99837	4.93680
45	5.55404	5.47810	5.40421	5.33227	5.26221	5.19396	5.12745	5.06262	4.99940	4.93774
50	5.55495	5.47892	5.40493	5.33292	5.26279	5.19448	5.12792	5.06304	4.99978	4.93808

Present Value of a Series of Payments Decreasing at Constant Rate

Annual Rate of Decline 1%

Holding Period					Discount Rate					
	10.50%	10.75%	11.00%	11.25%	11.50%	11.75%	12.00%	12.25%	15.00%	18.00%
1	0.90498	0.90293	0.90090	0.89888	0.89686	0.89485	0.89286	0.89087	0.86957	0.84746
2	1.71577	1.71007	1.70441	1.69878	1.69318	1.68761	1.68208	1.67658	1.61815	1.55846
3	2.44218	2.43158	2.42105	2.41060	2.40022	2.38992	2.37969	2.36954	2.26258	2.15498
4	3.09300	3.07653	3.06021	3.04404	3.02800	3.01210	2.99634	2.98071	2.81735	2.65545
5	3.67608	3.65306	3.63028	3.60773	3.58540	3.56329	3.54141	3.51974	3.29494	3.07533
6	4.19848	4.16843	4.13872	4.10935	4.08031	4.05160	4.02321	3.99513	3.70608	3.42761
7	4.66651	4.62911	4.59219	4.55573	4.51974	4.48419	4.44908	4.41442	4.06001	3.72317
8	5.08583	5.04092	4.99664	4.95297	4.90990	4.86742	4.82553	4.78421	4.36471	3.97113
9	5.46152	5.40904	5.35736	5.30646	5.25632	5.20693	5.15828	5.11035	4.62701	4.17917
10	5.79810	5.73811	5.67909	5.62103	5.56391	5.50771	5.45241	5.39799	4.85282	4.35371
11	6.09965	6.03226	5.96603	5.90096	5.83701	5.77417	5.71240	5.65168	5.04721	4.50015
12	6.36983	6.29520	6.22196	6.15007	6.07950	6.01022	5.94221	5.87542	5.21455	4.62300
13	6.61188	6.53025	6.45022	6.37175	6.29480	6.21935	6.14534	6.07276	5.35861	4.72608
14	6.82874	6.74036	6.65380	6.56902	6.48597	6.40461	6.32490	6.24680	5.48263	4.81256
15	7.02304	6.92817	6.83537	6.74456	6.65570	6.56874	6.48362	6.40029	5.58940	4.88511
16	7.19711	7.09607	6.99731	6.90078	6.80641	6.71414	6.62391	6.53567	5.68131	4.94598
17	7.35307	7.24614	7.14174	7.03979	6.94022	6.84295	6.74792	6.65507	5.76043	4.99705
18	7.49279	7.38030	7.27057	7.16350	7.05903	6.95707	6.85754	6.76037	5.82854	5.03990
19	7.61798	7.50022	7.38546	7.27359	7.16452	7.05816	6.95443	6.85325	5.88718	5.07585
20	7.73013	7.60742	7.48793	7.37155	7.25818	7.14772	7.04008	6.93516	5.93766	5.10601
21	7.83062	7.70325	7.57933	7.45873	7.34135	7.22707	7.11578	7.00740	5.98112	5.13131
22	7.92064	7.78891	7.66084	7.53631	7.41519	7.29736	7.18270	7.07111	6.01853	5.15254
23	8.00130	7.86548	7.73354	7.60534	7.48075	7.35963	7.24185	7.12731	6.05073	5.17035
24	8.07356	7.93393	7.79838	7.66678	7.53896	7.41479	7.29414	7.17687	6.07846	5.18530
25	8.13831	7.99511	7.85622	7.72145	7.59065	7.46366	7.34035	7.22058	6.10232	5.19783
30	8.37392	8.21640	8.06407	7.91671	7.77411	7.63607	7.50239	7.37289	6.18018	5.23600
35	8.50993	8.34269	8.18137	8.02567	7.87535	7.73014	7.58982	7.45417	6.21699	5.25187
40	8.58845	8.41478	8.24757	8.08648	7.93121	7.78148	7.63701	7.49754	6.23439	5.25847
45	8.63377	8.45593	8.28493	8.12042	7.96204	7.80949	7.66247	7.52069	6.24262	5.26121
50	8.65993	8.47941	8.30602	8.13935	7.97905	7.82478	7.67620	7.53304	6.24651	5.26235

Annual Rate of Decline 2%

Holding Period					Discount Rate					
	10.50%	10.75%	11.00%	11.25%	11.50%	11.75%	12.00%	12.25%	15.00%	18.00%
1	0.90498	0.90293	0.90090	0.89888	0.89686	0.89485	0.89286	0.89087	0.86957	0.84746
2	1.70758	1.70192	1.69629	1.69070	1.68513	1.67960	1.67411	1.66864	1.61059	1.55128
3	2.41939	2.40892	2.39853	2.38821	2.37796	2.36780	2.35770	2.34768	2.24206	2.13581
4	3.05068	3.03453	3.01852	3.00265	2.98691	2.97131	2.95585	2.94051	2.78019	2.62126
5	3.61056	3.58812	3.56590	3.54390	3.52213	3.50057	3.47922	3.45809	3.23877	3.02444
6	4.10710	4.07797	4.04917	4.02070	3.99254	3.96470	3.93718	3.90996	3.62956	3.35928
7	4.54748	4.51143	4.47585	4.44070	4.40600	4.37173	4.33789	4.30446	3.96258	3.63737
8	4.93803	4.89499	4.85255	4.81069	4.76940	4.72868	4.68851	4.64888	4.24638	3.86832
9	5.28441	5.23440	5.18513	5.13661	5.08880	5.04170	4.99530	4.94958	4.48822	4.06013
10	5.59160	5.53473	5.47877	5.42371	5.36953	5.31621	5.26375	5.21211	4.69431	4.21943
11	5.86405	5.80048	5.73801	5.67661	5.61627	5.55695	5.49863	5.44130	4.86993	4.35173
12	6.10567	6.03564	5.96689	5.89940	5.83313	5.76806	5.70416	5.64141	5.01959	4.46161
13	6.31996	6.24373	6.16897	6.09565	6.02374	5.95320	5.88400	5.81611	5.14713	4.55286
14	6.51001	6.42786	6.34738	6.26853	6.19127	6.11556	6.04136	5.96863	5.25582	4.62865
15	6.67856	6.59079	6.50489	6.42082	6.33851	6.25794	6.17904	6.10178	5.34843	4.69159
16	6.82805	6.73496	6.64396	6.55497	6.46793	6.38280	6.29952	6.21804	5.42736	4.74386
17	6.96062	6.86254	6.76674	6.67314	6.58168	6.49230	6.40494	6.31954	5.49462	4.78728
18	7.07820	6.97543	6.87514	6.77724	6.68166	6.58833	6.49718	6.40815	5.55194	4.82333
19	7.18247	7.07533	6.97084	6.86894	6.76953	6.67254	6.57789	6.48551	5.60078	4.85327
20	7.27495	7.16372	7.05534	6.94971	6.84676	6.74639	6.64851	6.55305	5.64241	4.87814
21	7.35697	7.24194	7.12994	7.02087	6.91464	6.81115	6.71030	6.61202	5.67788	4.89880
22	7.42971	7.31115	7.19580	7.08356	6.97430	6.86794	6.76437	6.66350	5.70810	4.91595
23	7.49423	7.37239	7.25395	7.13877	7.02674	6.91775	6.81168	6.70844	5.73386	4.93020
24	7.55144	7.42659	7.30529	7.18741	7.07283	6.96143	6.85308	6.74768	5.75581	4.94203
25	7.60218	7.47454	7.35062	7.23026	7.11334	6.99973	6.88930	6.78194	5.77452	4.95185
30	7.78173	7.64317	7.50901	7.37907	7.25317	7.13113	7.01281	6.89804	5.83389	4.98098
35	7.88024	7.73465	7.59398	7.45800	7.32651	7.19929	7.07615	6.95693	5.86057	4.99248
40	7.93429	7.78428	7.63956	7.49987	7.36497	7.23464	7.10864	6.98680	5.87257	4.99703
45	7.96395	7.81121	7.66401	7.52208	7.38515	7.25297	7.12531	7.00195	5.87795	4.99883
50	7.98022	7.82582	7.67713	7.53386	7.39573	7.26248	7.13386	7.00963	5.88038	4.99954

Present Value of a Series of Payments Decreasing at Constant Rate

Annual Rate of Decline 3%

Holding Period	10.50%	10.75%	11.00%	11.25%	11.50%	11.75%	12.00%	12.25%	15.00%	18.00%
1	0.90498	0.90293	0.90090	0.89888	0.89686	0.89485	0.89286	0.89087	0.86957	0.84746
2	1.69939	1.69377	1.68817	1.68262	1.67709	1.67160	1.66614	1.66071	1.60302	1.54410
3	2.39675	2.38641	2.37615	2.36597	2.35585	2.34582	2.33585	2.32596	2.22168	2.11676
4	3.00891	2.99307	2.97736	2.96179	2.94635	2.93104	2.91587	2.90083	2.74351	2.58750
5	3.54629	3.52440	3.50274	3.48129	3.46005	3.43903	3.41821	3.39760	3.18365	2.97447
6	4.01801	3.98977	3.96185	3.93425	3.90695	3.87996	3.85327	3.82688	3.55491	3.29258
7	4.43210	4.39736	4.36306	4.32919	4.29573	4.26269	4.23006	4.19783	3.86805	3.55407
8	4.79560	4.75435	4.71366	4.67354	4.63396	4.59491	4.55639	4.51840	4.13218	3.76902
9	5.11469	5.06701	5.02005	4.97378	4.92819	4.88328	4.83902	4.79541	4.35497	3.94572
10	5.39479	5.34086	5.28779	5.23557	5.18417	5.13358	5.08379	5.03478	4.54289	4.09097
11	5.64068	5.58071	5.52176	5.46382	5.40686	5.35085	5.29579	5.24164	4.70139	4.21038
12	5.85652	5.79078	5.72623	5.66284	5.60058	5.53944	5.47939	5.42039	4.83509	4.30853
13	6.04600	5.97477	5.90490	5.83636	5.76912	5.70314	5.63840	5.57486	4.94786	4.38922
14	6.21232	6.13591	6.06104	5.98766	5.91573	5.84523	5.77611	5.70834	5.04298	4.45554
15	6.35833	6.27705	6.19748	6.11958	6.04328	5.96857	5.89538	5.82369	5.12321	4.51006
16	6.48650	6.40067	6.31672	6.23460	6.15425	6.07562	5.99868	5.92337	5.19088	4.55488
17	6.59901	6.50894	6.42092	6.33488	6.25078	6.16855	6.08814	6.00950	5.24796	4.59173
18	6.69777	6.60377	6.51197	6.42233	6.33476	6.24921	6.16562	6.08393	5.29610	4.62201
19	6.78447	6.68682	6.59154	6.49857	6.40782	6.31923	6.23273	6.14826	5.33671	4.64691
20	6.86057	6.75956	6.66108	6.56504	6.47138	6.38000	6.29084	6.20384	5.37097	4.66737
21	6.92738	6.82327	6.72184	6.62300	6.52667	6.43275	6.34118	6.25187	5.39986	4.68420
22	6.98603	6.87907	6.77494	6.67354	6.57477	6.47854	6.38477	6.29337	5.42423	4.69803
23	7.03751	6.92795	6.82135	6.71760	6.61662	6.51829	6.42252	6.32924	5.44478	4.70939
24	7.08270	6.97075	6.86190	6.75602	6.65302	6.55279	6.45522	6.36024	5.46212	4.71874
25	7.12237	7.00824	6.89734	6.78952	6.68469	6.58273	6.48354	6.38702	5.47675	4.72642
30	7.25883	7.13641	7.01773	6.90264	6.79098	6.68263	6.57743	6.47529	5.52191	4.74859
35	7.32996	7.20247	7.07909	6.95964	6.84395	6.73185	6.62319	6.51782	5.54119	4.75691
40	7.36704	7.23652	7.11036	6.98837	6.87034	6.75610	6.64548	6.53832	5.54942	4.76003
45	7.38637	7.25407	7.12630	7.00284	6.88349	6.76805	6.65634	6.54819	5.55294	4.76120
50	7.39644	7.26311	7.13442	7.01013	6.89004	6.77394	6.66164	6.55295	5.55444	4.76164

Annual Rate of Decline 4%

Holding Period	10.50%	10.75%	11.00%	11.25%	11.50%	11.75%	12.00%	12.25%	15.00%	18.00%
1	0.90498	0.90293	0.90090	0.89888	0.89686	0.89485	0.89286	0.89087	0.86957	0.84746
2	1.69120	1.68561	1.68006	1.67454	1.66905	1.66359	1.65816	1.65277	1.59546	1.53691
3	2.37426	2.36405	2.35392	2.34387	2.33389	2.32398	2.31414	2.30437	2.20143	2.09783
4	2.96768	2.95214	2.93673	2.92145	2.90631	2.89129	2.87641	2.86165	2.70728	2.55417
5	3.48323	3.46190	3.44077	3.41986	3.39915	3.37865	3.35835	3.33825	3.12956	2.92542
6	3.93114	3.90377	3.87671	3.84995	3.82349	3.79732	3.77144	3.74585	3.48206	3.22746
7	4.32026	4.28679	4.25373	4.22108	4.18883	4.15698	4.12552	4.09445	3.77633	3.47319
8	4.65833	4.61880	4.57980	4.54133	4.50339	4.46595	4.42902	4.39258	4.02198	3.67310
9	4.95203	4.90659	4.86181	4.81769	4.77422	4.73138	4.68916	4.64755	4.22705	3.83575
10	5.20720	5.15605	5.10571	5.05616	5.00740	4.95939	4.91214	4.86561	4.39823	3.96806
11	5.42888	5.37228	5.31665	5.26195	5.20816	5.15527	5.10326	5.05210	4.54113	4.07571
12	5.62147	5.55972	5.49908	5.43952	5.38102	5.32355	5.26708	5.21160	4.66042	4.16329
13	5.78879	5.72220	5.65687	5.59276	5.52985	5.46810	5.40750	5.34800	4.76000	4.23454
14	5.93415	5.86303	5.79333	5.72499	5.65798	5.59228	5.52785	5.46466	4.84313	4.29251
15	6.06044	5.98511	5.91134	5.83909	5.76831	5.69896	5.63102	5.56443	4.91253	4.33967
16	6.17015	6.09093	6.01342	5.93755	5.86330	5.79061	5.71944	5.64976	4.97046	4.37804
17	6.26547	6.18266	6.10169	6.02252	5.94508	5.86934	5.79524	5.72274	5.01882	4.40925
18	6.34828	6.26217	6.17804	6.09583	6.01550	5.93697	5.86020	5.78515	5.05919	4.43464
19	6.42023	6.33109	6.24407	6.15910	6.07612	5.99507	5.91589	5.83852	5.09289	4.45530
20	6.48273	6.39083	6.30118	6.21370	6.12832	6.04498	5.96362	5.88417	5.12102	4.47211
21	6.53703	6.44262	6.35057	6.26081	6.17326	6.08786	6.00453	5.92321	5.14450	4.48579
22	6.58421	6.48751	6.39328	6.30146	6.21196	6.12469	6.03960	5.95660	5.16411	4.49691
23	6.62520	6.52642	6.43023	6.33654	6.24527	6.15634	6.06966	5.98515	5.18047	4.50596
24	6.66080	6.56014	6.46218	6.36681	6.27396	6.18352	6.09542	6.00957	5.19413	4.51332
25	6.69174	6.58938	6.48981	6.39294	6.29865	6.20687	6.11750	6.03046	5.20554	4.51931
30	6.79518	6.68654	6.58109	6.47870	6.37924	6.28261	6.18870	6.09739	5.23980	4.53614
35	6.84638	6.73409	6.62526	6.51973	6.41737	6.31805	6.22164	6.12802	5.25369	4.54213
40	6.87172	6.75736	6.64663	6.53936	6.43541	6.33463	6.23688	6.14203	5.25932	4.54427
45	6.88426	6.76875	6.65697	6.54876	6.44395	6.34239	6.24393	6.14844	5.26160	4.54503
50	6.89047	6.77432	6.66198	6.55325	6.44799	6.34602	6.24719	6.15137	5.26253	4.54530

Present Value of a Series of Payments Decreasing at Constant Rate

Annual Rate of Decline 5%

Holding Period	10.50%	10.75%	11.00%	11.25%	11.50%	11.75%	12.00%	12.25%	15.00%	18.00%
					Discount Rate					
1	0.90498	0.90293	0.90090	0.89888	0.89686	0.89485	0.89286	0.89087	0.86957	0.84746
2	1.68301	1.67746	1.67194	1.66646	1.66100	1.65558	1.65019	1.64483	1.58790	1.52973
3	2.35191	2.34184	2.33184	2.32192	2.31207	2.30228	2.29257	2.28293	2.18131	2.07902
4	2.92698	2.91174	2.89662	2.88164	2.86678	2.85205	2.83745	2.82297	2.67152	2.52125
5	3.42139	3.40059	3.37999	3.35960	3.33941	3.31942	3.29962	3.28002	3.07647	2.87728
6	3.84644	3.81992	3.79369	3.76775	3.74210	3.71673	3.69165	3.66683	3.41100	3.16391
7	4.21187	4.17961	4.14775	4.11628	4.08520	4.05449	4.02416	3.99420	3.68735	3.39467
8	4.52605	4.48816	4.45078	4.41390	4.37752	4.34163	4.30621	4.27126	3.91563	3.58046
9	4.79615	4.75282	4.71013	4.66805	4.62659	4.58572	4.54545	4.50575	4.10422	3.73003
10	5.02836	4.97985	4.93209	4.88508	4.83880	4.79323	4.74837	4.70419	4.26001	3.85045
11	5.22800	5.17459	5.12206	5.07040	5.01960	4.96964	4.92049	4.87215	4.38870	3.94739
12	5.39964	5.34163	5.28464	5.22866	5.17365	5.11960	5.06649	5.01429	4.49501	4.02544
13	5.54720	5.48492	5.42379	5.36380	5.30491	5.24709	5.19033	5.13459	4.58284	4.08828
14	5.67407	5.60783	5.54289	5.47920	5.41674	5.35547	5.29537	5.23640	4.65539	4.13887
15	5.78313	5.71326	5.64481	5.57774	5.51202	5.44760	5.38446	5.32256	4.71532	4.17960
16	5.87690	5.80370	5.73205	5.66189	5.59320	5.52593	5.46003	5.39549	4.76483	4.21239
17	5.95752	5.88128	5.80671	5.73375	5.66237	5.59251	5.52414	5.45721	4.80573	4.23879
18	6.02683	5.94783	5.87061	5.79511	5.72130	5.64911	5.57851	5.50944	4.83952	4.26004
19	6.08641	6.00491	5.92529	5.84751	5.77151	5.69723	5.62463	5.55365	4.86743	4.27715
20	6.13764	6.05387	5.97210	5.89226	5.81429	5.73814	5.66375	5.59106	4.89048	4.29093
21	6.18168	6.09587	6.01216	5.93047	5.85074	5.77292	5.69693	5.62272	4.90953	4.30202
22	6.21954	6.13190	6.04644	5.96310	5.88180	5.80248	5.72507	5.64952	4.92526	4.31095
23	6.25210	6.16280	6.07578	5.99096	5.90826	5.82761	5.74895	5.67220	4.93826	4.31814
24	6.28008	6.18931	6.10089	6.01475	5.93080	5.84897	5.76920	5.69139	4.94900	4.32392
25	6.30414	6.21205	6.12239	6.03507	5.95001	5.86714	5.78637	5.70764	4.95787	4.32858
30	6.38235	6.28551	6.19140	6.09991	6.01095	5.92441	5.84021	5.75826	4.98379	4.34132
35	6.41908	6.31963	6.22309	6.12936	6.03831	5.94984	5.86385	5.78024	4.99376	4.34562
40	6.43633	6.33547	6.23764	6.14273	6.05060	5.96113	5.87423	5.78978	4.99760	4.34708
45	6.44444	6.34283	6.24433	6.14880	6.05611	5.96615	5.87879	5.79392	4.99908	4.34757
50	6.44824	6.34624	6.24739	6.15155	6.05859	5.96837	5.88079	5.79572	4.99965	4.34774

Annual Rate of Decline 6%

Holding Period	10.50%	10.75%	11.00%	11.25%	11.50%	11.75%	12.00%	12.25%	15.00%	18.00%
					Discount Rate					
1	0.90498	0.90293	0.90090	0.89888	0.89686	0.89485	0.89286	0.89087	0.86957	0.84746
2	1.67482	1.66931	1.66383	1.65838	1.65296	1.64757	1.64222	1.63690	1.58034	1.52255
3	2.32971	2.31977	2.30991	2.30011	2.29039	2.28073	2.27115	2.26163	2.16132	2.06034
4	2.88681	2.87186	2.85704	2.84234	2.82777	2.81332	2.79900	2.78480	2.63621	2.48874
5	3.36073	3.34045	3.32037	3.30050	3.28081	3.26132	3.24202	3.22290	3.02438	2.83002
6	3.76388	3.73817	3.71275	3.68761	3.66275	3.63816	3.61384	3.58978	3.34167	3.10188
7	4.10683	4.07574	4.04503	4.01470	3.98474	3.95514	3.92590	3.89701	3.60102	3.31844
8	4.39857	4.36225	4.32642	4.29107	4.25619	4.22177	4.18781	4.15429	3.81300	3.49096
9	4.64675	4.60543	4.56472	4.52459	4.48504	4.44605	4.40762	4.36974	3.98628	3.62840
10	4.85787	4.81184	4.76652	4.72190	4.67797	4.63471	4.59211	4.55016	4.12792	3.73787
11	5.03746	4.98702	4.93741	4.88862	4.84062	4.79340	4.74695	4.70125	4.24369	3.82509
12	5.19024	5.13571	5.08213	5.02948	4.97774	4.92689	4.87691	4.82777	4.33832	3.89456
13	5.32020	5.26191	5.20469	5.14851	5.09334	5.03917	4.98598	4.93372	4.41567	3.94990
14	5.43076	5.36903	5.30848	5.24908	5.19080	5.13362	5.07751	5.02245	4.47890	3.99399
15	5.52481	5.45994	5.39637	5.33405	5.27296	5.21307	5.15434	5.09675	4.53058	4.02911
16	5.60482	5.53711	5.47080	5.40585	5.34223	5.27990	5.21882	5.15897	4.57282	4.05709
17	5.67288	5.60260	5.53383	5.46652	5.40062	5.33611	5.27294	5.21108	4.60735	4.07938
18	5.73077	5.65819	5.58721	5.51778	5.44985	5.38340	5.31836	5.25471	4.63557	4.09713
19	5.78002	5.70537	5.63241	5.56109	5.49136	5.42317	5.35648	5.29125	4.65864	4.11127
20	5.82192	5.74542	5.67069	5.59768	5.52635	5.45663	5.38848	5.32185	4.67750	4.12254
21	5.85756	5.77940	5.70311	5.62860	5.55584	5.48477	5.41533	5.34747	4.69291	4.13151
22	5.88788	5.80825	5.73056	5.65473	5.58071	5.50844	5.43787	5.36893	4.70551	4.13866
23	5.91367	5.83274	5.75381	5.67681	5.60168	5.52835	5.45678	5.38690	4.71581	4.14436
24	5.93561	5.85352	5.77349	5.69546	5.61935	5.54510	5.47265	5.40195	4.72423	4.14890
25	5.95428	5.87116	5.79017	5.71122	5.63425	5.55919	5.48598	5.41455	4.73111	4.15251
30	6.01324	5.92655	5.84220	5.76011	5.68020	5.60238	5.52658	5.45272	4.75067	4.16213
35	6.03950	5.95094	5.86487	5.78117	5.69977	5.62057	5.54349	5.46845	4.75780	4.16521
40	6.05121	5.96169	5.87474	5.79024	5.70810	5.62823	5.55053	5.47492	4.76041	4.16620
45	6.05642	5.96642	5.87904	5.79415	5.71165	5.63146	5.55346	5.47759	4.76136	4.16652
50	6.05874	5.96851	5.88091	5.79583	5.71317	5.63281	5.55468	5.47868	4.76171	4.16662

Present Value of a Series of Payments Decreasing at Constant Rate

Annual Rate of Decline 7%

Holding Period	10.50%	10.75%	11.00%	11.25%	11.50%	11.75%	12.00%	12.25%	15.00%	18.00%
					Discount Rate					
1	0.90498	0.90293	0.90090	0.89888	0.89686	0.89485	0.89286	0.89087	0.86957	0.84746
2	1.66663	1.66115	1.65571	1.65030	1.64492	1.63957	1.63425	1.62896	1.57278	1.51537
3	2.30766	2.29785	2.28812	2.27845	2.26885	2.25933	2.24987	2.24047	2.14146	2.04177
4	2.84717	2.83251	2.81797	2.80356	2.78927	2.77510	2.76105	2.74712	2.60136	2.45665
5	3.30124	3.28148	3.26190	3.24253	3.22334	3.20433	3.18551	3.16688	2.97327	2.78363
6	3.68340	3.65849	3.63385	3.60948	3.58538	3.56155	3.53797	3.51465	3.27404	3.04134
7	4.00503	3.97507	3.94548	3.91624	3.88736	3.85883	3.83064	3.80279	3.51727	3.24444
8	4.27573	4.24092	4.20657	4.17268	4.13923	4.10623	4.07365	4.04151	3.71396	3.40452
9	4.50355	4.46416	4.42532	4.38705	4.34932	4.31212	4.27545	4.23929	3.87303	3.53068
10	4.69530	4.65162	4.60861	4.56625	4.52454	4.48346	4.44300	4.40315	4.00167	3.63011
11	4.85668	4.80903	4.76216	4.71606	4.67069	4.62606	4.58214	4.53891	4.10570	3.70848
12	4.99250	4.94122	4.89082	4.84129	4.79260	4.74473	4.69767	4.65139	4.18982	3.77024
13	5.10681	5.05222	4.99862	4.94598	4.89427	4.84349	4.79360	4.74459	4.25786	3.81892
14	5.20301	5.14543	5.08893	5.03349	4.97908	4.92568	4.87326	4.82179	4.31288	3.85728
15	5.28399	5.22370	5.16460	5.10665	5.04982	4.99408	4.93940	4.88576	4.35737	3.88752
16	5.35213	5.28943	5.22800	5.16780	5.10881	5.05100	4.99432	4.93876	4.39335	3.91135
17	5.40949	5.34462	5.28112	5.21893	5.15803	5.09837	5.03993	4.98267	4.42245	3.93013
18	5.45776	5.39097	5.32562	5.26167	5.19907	5.13779	5.07780	5.01905	4.44598	3.94493
19	5.49839	5.42989	5.36291	5.29739	5.23331	5.17060	5.10924	5.04919	4.46501	3.95660
20	5.53258	5.46257	5.39415	5.32726	5.26186	5.19791	5.13535	5.07416	4.48040	3.96580
21	5.56135	5.49001	5.42032	5.35223	5.28568	5.22063	5.15704	5.09485	4.49285	3.97304
22	5.58557	5.51306	5.44225	5.37310	5.30554	5.23954	5.17504	5.11199	4.50291	3.97875
23	5.60596	5.53241	5.46062	5.39054	5.32211	5.25528	5.18999	5.12619	4.51105	3.98326
24	5.62311	5.54866	5.47602	5.40513	5.33593	5.26837	5.20240	5.13796	4.51763	3.98680
25	5.63755	5.56231	5.48892	5.41732	5.34746	5.27927	5.21271	5.14771	4.52295	3.98960
30	5.68188	5.60395	5.52804	5.45409	5.38201	5.31175	5.24324	5.17642	4.53767	3.99684
35	5.70060	5.62134	5.54420	5.46910	5.39596	5.32472	5.25530	5.18763	4.54276	3.99904
40	5.70851	5.62860	5.55087	5.47523	5.40159	5.32989	5.26005	5.19200	4.54452	3.99971
45	5.71185	5.63163	5.55362	5.47773	5.40387	5.33196	5.26193	5.19371	4.54513	3.99991
50	5.71326	5.63290	5.55476	5.47875	5.40478	5.33279	5.26267	5.19438	4.54534	3.99997

Annual Rate of Decline 8%

Holding Period	10.50%	10.75%	11.00%	11.25%	11.50%	11.75%	12.00%	12.25%	15.00%	18.00%
					Discount Rate					
1	0.90498	0.90293	0.90090	0.89888	0.89686	0.89485	0.89286	0.89087	0.86957	0.84746
2	1.65844	1.65300	1.64759	1.64222	1.63687	1.63156	1.62628	1.62102	1.56522	1.50819
3	2.28576	2.27608	2.26647	2.25693	2.24746	2.23806	2.22873	2.21946	2.12174	2.02333
4	2.80806	2.79368	2.77942	2.76529	2.75127	2.73737	2.72360	2.70993	2.56696	2.42497
5	3.24291	3.22364	3.20456	3.18567	3.16697	3.14844	3.13010	3.11193	2.92313	2.73811
6	3.60495	3.58081	3.55694	3.53332	3.50996	3.48686	3.46401	3.44140	3.20807	2.98226
7	3.90639	3.87751	3.84899	3.82081	3.79298	3.76547	3.73829	3.71144	3.43602	3.17261
8	4.15735	4.12398	4.09106	4.05856	4.02649	3.99484	3.96360	3.93276	3.61838	3.32102
9	4.36630	4.32873	4.29169	4.25517	4.21917	4.18367	4.14867	4.11416	3.76427	3.43672
10	4.54027	4.49881	4.45797	4.41776	4.37815	4.33913	4.30069	4.26283	3.88098	3.52694
11	4.68511	4.64009	4.59580	4.55221	4.50932	4.46711	4.42557	4.38468	3.97435	3.59727
12	4.80570	4.75746	4.71003	4.66340	4.61756	4.57248	4.52815	4.48455	4.04905	3.65211
13	4.90611	4.85495	4.80471	4.75535	4.70686	4.65922	4.61241	4.56640	4.10880	3.69487
14	4.98970	4.93594	4.88318	4.83139	4.78055	4.73063	4.68162	4.63349	4.15661	3.72820
15	5.05930	5.00322	4.94822	4.89428	4.84135	4.78943	4.73847	4.68847	4.19485	3.75419
16	5.11724	5.05911	5.00213	4.94628	4.89152	4.83783	4.78517	4.73353	4.22545	3.77445
17	5.16549	5.10554	5.04681	4.98928	4.93291	4.87767	4.82354	4.77047	4.24992	3.79025
18	5.20565	5.14410	5.08384	5.02484	4.96707	4.91048	4.85505	4.80074	4.26950	3.80257
19	5.23910	5.17614	5.11454	5.05425	4.99525	4.93749	4.88093	4.82555	4.28517	3.81217
20	5.26694	5.20275	5.13998	5.07857	5.01850	4.95972	4.90219	4.84589	4.29770	3.81966
21	5.29012	5.22486	5.16106	5.09869	5.03769	4.97802	4.91966	4.86255	4.30772	3.82550
22	5.30942	5.24322	5.17854	5.11532	5.05352	4.99309	4.93401	4.87621	4.31575	3.83005
23	5.32549	5.25848	5.19302	5.12907	5.06658	5.00550	4.94579	4.88741	4.32216	3.83360
24	5.33887	5.27115	5.20503	5.14045	5.07736	5.01571	4.95547	4.89658	4.32729	3.83636
25	5.35001	5.28168	5.21498	5.14985	5.08625	5.02412	4.96342	4.90410	4.33140	3.83852
30	5.38324	5.31290	5.24431	5.17742	5.11216	5.04848	4.98632	4.92564	4.34244	3.84395
35	5.39654	5.32525	5.25579	5.18808	5.12207	5.05769	4.99488	4.93360	4.34606	3.84552
40	5.40186	5.33014	5.26028	5.19220	5.12586	5.06117	4.99809	4.93654	4.34725	3.84597
45	5.40399	5.33207	5.26203	5.19380	5.12731	5.06249	4.99928	4.93763	4.34764	3.84610
50	5.40484	5.33283	5.26272	5.19442	5.12786	5.06299	4.99973	4.93804	4.34776	3.84614

Present Value of a Series of Payments Decreasing at Constant Rate

Annual Rate of Decline　9%

Holding Period	10.50%	10.75%	11.00%	11.25%	Discount Rate 11.50%	11.75%	12.00%	12.25%	15.00%	18.00%
1	0.90498	0.90293	0.90090	0.89888	0.89686	0.89485	0.89286	0.89087	0.86957	0.84746
2	1.65025	1.64485	1.63948	1.63414	1.62883	1.62355	1.61830	1.61309	1.55766	1.50101
3	2.26401	2.25446	2.24498	2.23556	2.22622	2.21694	2.20773	2.19858	2.10215	2.00501
4	2.76946	2.75536	2.74138	2.72752	2.71377	2.70015	2.68664	2.67324	2.53300	2.39370
5	3.18571	3.16693	3.14834	3.12992	3.11169	3.09363	3.07575	3.05804	2.87394	2.69344
6	3.52850	3.50511	3.48197	3.45908	3.43645	3.41405	3.39190	3.36999	3.14373	2.92460
7	3.81080	3.78298	3.75549	3.72833	3.70150	3.67498	3.64878	3.62289	3.35721	3.10287
8	4.04328	4.01129	3.97972	3.94857	3.91781	3.88746	3.85749	3.82791	3.52614	3.24035
9	4.23474	4.19890	4.16356	4.12871	4.09436	4.06048	4.02707	3.99412	3.65982	3.34637
10	4.39241	4.35304	4.31427	4.27607	4.23844	4.20137	4.16485	4.12886	3.76559	3.42814
11	4.52226	4.47970	4.43782	4.39661	4.35604	4.31611	4.27680	4.23810	3.84930	3.49119
12	4.62919	4.58377	4.53912	4.49520	4.45201	4.40954	4.36776	4.32665	3.91553	3.53982
13	4.71725	4.66929	4.62216	4.57585	4.53034	4.48562	4.44166	4.39844	3.96794	3.57731
14	4.78977	4.73955	4.69024	4.64182	4.59427	4.54757	4.50170	4.45665	4.00941	3.60623
15	4.84950	4.79728	4.74605	4.69578	4.64645	4.59802	4.55049	4.50383	4.04223	3.62854
16	4.89868	4.84472	4.79181	4.73992	4.68903	4.63911	4.59013	4.54208	4.06820	3.64574
17	4.93918	4.88370	4.82932	4.77602	4.72378	4.67256	4.62234	4.57309	4.08875	3.65900
18	4.97254	4.91572	4.86007	4.80556	4.75214	4.69980	4.64851	4.59823	4.10501	3.66923
19	5.00001	4.94204	4.88529	4.82971	4.77529	4.72199	4.66977	4.61861	4.11788	3.67712
20	5.02263	4.96366	4.90595	4.84947	4.79418	4.74005	4.68705	4.63513	4.12806	3.68320
21	5.04126	4.98143	4.92290	4.86564	4.80960	4.75476	4.70108	4.64852	4.13612	3.68789
22	5.05661	4.99603	4.93679	4.87886	4.82219	4.76674	4.71249	4.65938	4.14249	3.69151
23	5.06924	5.00802	4.94818	4.88967	4.83246	4.77650	4.72175	4.66819	4.14754	3.69430
24	5.07965	5.01788	4.95752	4.89852	4.84084	4.78444	4.72928	4.67532	4.15153	3.69645
25	5.08822	5.02598	4.96517	4.90575	4.84768	4.79091	4.73540	4.68111	4.15469	3.69811
30	5.11306	5.04932	4.98710	4.92636	4.86705	4.80912	4.75252	4.69721	4.16295	3.70218
35	5.12247	5.05806	4.99522	4.93391	4.87407	4.81564	4.75858	4.70284	4.16551	3.70329
40	5.12603	5.06133	4.99823	4.93667	4.87661	4.81797	4.76073	4.70482	4.16631	3.70359
45	5.12738	5.06256	4.99935	4.93769	4.87753	4.81881	4.76149	4.70551	4.16656	3.70367
50	5.12789	5.06302	4.99976	4.93806	4.87786	4.81911	4.76176	4.70575	4.16663	3.70370

Annual Rate of Decline 10%

Holding Period	10.50%	10.75%	11.00%	11.25%	Discount Rate 11.50%	11.75%	12.00%	12.25%	15.00%	18.00%
1	0.90498	0.90293	0.90090	0.89888	0.89686	0.89485	0.89286	0.89087	0.86957	0.84746
2	1.64206	1.63670	1.63136	1.62606	1.62078	1.61554	1.61033	1.60515	1.55009	1.49382
3	2.24240	2.23298	2.22363	2.21434	2.20512	2.19596	2.18687	2.17785	2.08268	1.98681
4	2.73137	2.71755	2.70384	2.69025	2.67678	2.66342	2.65017	2.63703	2.49949	2.36282
5	3.12962	3.11132	3.09320	3.07526	3.05749	3.03989	3.02246	3.00519	2.82569	2.64961
6	3.45399	3.43133	3.40890	3.38673	3.36479	3.34309	3.32162	3.30038	3.08097	2.86835
7	3.71818	3.69137	3.66488	3.63870	3.61283	3.58727	3.56201	3.53705	3.28076	3.03518
8	3.93336	3.90269	3.87242	3.84254	3.81305	3.78393	3.75519	3.72681	3.43712	3.16243
9	4.10862	4.07442	4.04070	4.00745	3.97466	3.94232	3.91042	3.87896	3.55948	3.25948
10	4.25137	4.21398	4.17715	4.14086	4.10511	4.06988	4.03516	4.00095	3.65525	3.33350
11	4.36763	4.32739	4.28778	4.24879	4.21040	4.17261	4.13540	4.09875	3.73019	3.38996
12	4.46232	4.41955	4.37748	4.33610	4.29539	4.25534	4.21594	4.17717	3.78885	3.43302
13	4.53945	4.49444	4.45021	4.40673	4.36399	4.32198	4.28067	4.24005	3.83475	3.46586
14	4.60227	4.55530	4.50918	4.46387	4.41937	4.37564	4.33268	4.29046	3.87067	3.49091
15	4.65343	4.60476	4.55699	4.51010	4.46406	4.41886	4.37448	4.33088	3.89879	3.51002
16	4.69510	4.64495	4.59576	4.54750	4.50014	4.45367	4.40806	4.36329	3.92079	3.52459
17	4.72904	4.67761	4.62719	4.57775	4.52926	4.48170	4.43505	4.38928	3.93801	3.53570
18	4.75669	4.70416	4.65268	4.60222	4.55277	4.50428	4.45674	4.41011	3.95149	3.54418
19	4.77920	4.72572	4.67334	4.62202	4.57174	4.52246	4.47416	4.42681	3.96203	3.55065
20	4.79754	4.74325	4.69010	4.63804	4.58705	4.53711	4.48817	4.44021	3.97029	3.55558
21	4.81247	4.75750	4.70368	4.65100	4.59942	4.54890	4.49942	4.45095	3.97675	3.55934
22	4.82464	4.76907	4.71470	4.66148	4.60939	4.55840	4.50846	4.45956	3.98180	3.56221
23	4.83455	4.77848	4.72363	4.66996	4.61745	4.56605	4.51573	4.46646	3.98576	3.56440
24	4.84262	4.78612	4.73087	4.67682	4.62395	4.57221	4.52157	4.47199	3.98885	3.56606
25	4.84919	4.79233	4.73674	4.68238	4.62920	4.57717	4.52626	4.47643	3.99128	3.56734
30	4.86771	4.80973	4.75309	4.69774	4.64364	4.59074	4.53902	4.48843	3.99744	3.57037
35	4.87434	4.81589	4.75882	4.70306	4.64858	4.59534	4.54330	4.49241	3.99925	3.57116
40	4.87672	4.81808	4.76082	4.70490	4.65028	4.59690	4.54473	4.49373	3.99978	3.57136
45	4.87757	4.81885	4.76153	4.70554	4.65086	4.59743	4.54521	4.49417	3.99994	3.57141
50	4.87788	4.81913	4.76177	4.70577	4.65106	4.59761	4.54537	4.49431	3.99998	3.57142

Present Value of a Series of Payments Increasing by Constant Amount

Amount of 1st Year Growth 3.0%

Holding Period	5.50%	5.75%	6.00%	Discount Rate 6.25%	6.50%	6.75%	7.00%	7.25%	7.50%	7.75%	
1	0.94787	0.94563	0.94340	0.94118	0.93897	0.93677	0.93458	0.93240	0.93023	0.92807	1
2	1.87327	1.86666	1.86009	1.85356	1.84708	1.84063	1.83422	1.82785	1.82153	1.81524	2
3	2.77598	2.76299	2.75009	2.73729	2.72460	2.71200	2.69950	2.68709	2.67478	2.66257	3
4	3.65585	3.63456	3.61347	3.59258	3.57188	3.55137	3.53105	3.51092	3.49098	3.47121	4
5	4.51280	4.48143	4.45040	4.41971	4.38934	4.35931	4.32960	4.30020	4.27112	4.24235	5
6	5.34683	5.30370	5.26110	5.21903	5.17748	5.13643	5.09589	5.05584	5.01628	4.97719	6
7	6.15801	6.10155	6.04587	5.99097	5.93682	5.88341	5.83074	5.77878	5.72753	5.67697	7
8	6.94644	6.87519	6.80504	6.73596	6.66794	6.60094	6.53497	6.46998	6.40598	6.34293	8
9	7.71230	7.62491	7.53900	7.45452	7.37145	7.28977	7.20944	7.13044	7.05274	6.97631	9
10	8.45580	8.35102	8.24816	8.14717	8.04802	7.95066	7.85505	7.76115	7.66894	7.57836	10
11	9.17718	9.05386	8.93298	8.81448	8.69829	8.58437	8.47267	8.36312	8.25568	8.15030	11
12	9.87674	9.73383	9.59395	9.45702	9.32297	9.19172	9.06320	8.93735	8.81409	8.69336	12
13	10.55478	10.39133	10.23157	10.07541	9.92275	9.77350	9.62756	9.48484	9.34525	9.20872	13
14	11.21165	11.02679	10.84637	10.67027	10.49835	10.33051	10.16662	10.00658	9.85026	9.69757	14
15	11.84772	11.64067	11.43889	11.24221	11.05049	10.86356	10.68130	10.50354	10.33017	10.16105	15
16	12.46336	12.23343	12.00967	11.79188	11.57987	11.37346	11.17246	10.97671	10.78603	10.60028	16
17	13.05898	12.80556	12.55929	12.31993	12.08724	11.86100	11.64099	11.42701	11.21886	11.01635	17
18	13.63500	13.35755	13.08831	12.82698	12.57329	12.32696	12.08775	11.85539	11.62966	11.41032	18
19	14.19183	13.88990	13.59730	13.31369	13.03875	12.77214	12.51357	12.26274	12.01938	11.78322	19
20	14.72991	14.40310	14.08683	13.78070	13.48431	13.19729	12.91929	12.64996	12.38898	12.13604	20
21	15.24969	14.89768	14.55748	14.22863	13.91067	13.60317	13.30571	13.01790	12.73937	12.46974	21
22	15.75161	15.37413	15.00982	14.65812	14.31852	13.99051	13.67362	13.36740	13.07141	12.78525	22
23	16.23612	15.83297	15.44440	15.06978	14.70852	14.36004	14.02379	13.69927	13.38598	13.08345	23
24	16.70367	16.27470	15.86179	15.46423	15.08133	14.71245	14.35697	14.01430	13.68389	13.36521	24
25	17.15471	16.69983	16.26255	15.84207	15.43761	15.04845	14.67388	14.31325	13.96593	13.63134	25
30	19.17798	18.59370	18.03560	17.50227	16.99241	16.50478	16.03820	15.59158	15.16389	14.75415	30
35	20.85457	20.14461	19.47053	18.83016	18.22147	17.64259	17.09173	16.56727	16.06765	15.59145	35
40	22.23572	21.40721	20.62500	19.88600	19.18733	18.52631	17.90049	17.30758	16.74546	16.21217	40
45	23.36773	22.42987	21.54912	20.72128	19.94249	19.20921	18.51820	17.86646	17.25123	16.66999	45
50	24.29144	23.25455	22.28558	21.37914	20.53031	19.73460	18.98790	18.28649	17.62695	17.00616	50

Amount of 1st Year Growth 4.0%

Holding Period	5.50%	5.75%	6.00%	Discount Rate 6.25%	6.50%	6.75%	7.00%	7.25%	7.50%	7.75%	
1	0.94787	0.94563	0.94340	0.94118	0.93897	0.93677	0.93458	0.93240	0.93023	0.92807	1
2	1.88226	1.87560	1.86899	1.86242	1.85589	1.84940	1.84296	1.83655	1.83018	1.82385	2
3	2.80200	2.78884	2.77578	2.76283	2.74997	2.73721	2.72456	2.71200	2.69954	2.68717	3
4	3.70608	3.68440	3.66293	3.64165	3.62057	3.59969	3.57900	3.55850	3.53819	3.51807	4
5	4.59364	4.56152	4.52975	4.49832	4.46723	4.43648	4.40606	4.37597	4.34620	4.31675	5
6	5.46393	5.41954	5.37570	5.33240	5.28963	5.24740	5.20567	5.16446	5.12375	5.08354	6
7	6.31636	6.25796	6.20037	6.14358	6.08758	6.03235	5.97788	5.92416	5.87117	5.81890	7
8	7.15040	7.07636	7.00346	6.93168	6.86100	6.79140	6.72286	6.65535	6.58887	6.52339	8
9	7.96567	7.87445	7.78476	7.69659	7.60990	7.52467	7.44085	7.35842	7.27736	7.19763	9
10	8.76186	8.65201	8.54418	8.43833	8.33441	8.23238	8.13220	8.03383	7.93722	7.84234	10
11	9.53873	9.40892	9.28168	9.15697	9.03471	8.91485	8.79733	8.68210	8.56910	8.45828	11
12	10.29615	10.14512	9.99732	9.85266	9.71105	9.57243	9.43671	9.30382	9.17369	9.04625	12
13	11.03402	10.86063	10.69120	10.52561	10.36376	10.20554	10.05086	9.89962	9.75173	9.60709	13
14	11.75232	11.55553	11.36350	11.17610	10.99319	10.81465	10.64034	10.47015	10.30396	10.14166	14
15	12.45110	12.22993	12.01443	11.80443	11.59976	11.40025	11.20576	11.01612	10.83119	10.65083	15
16	13.13043	12.88401	12.64427	12.41097	12.18391	11.96290	11.74773	11.53823	11.33421	11.13550	16
17	13.79044	13.51800	13.25330	12.99610	12.74612	12.50314	12.26691	12.03722	11.81383	11.59655	17
18	14.43130	14.13213	13.84188	13.56024	13.28690	13.02157	12.76396	12.51382	12.27087	12.03488	18
19	15.05322	14.72670	14.41036	14.10384	13.80676	13.51878	13.23956	12.96879	12.70615	12.45136	19
20	15.65642	15.30201	14.95914	14.62736	14.30624	13.99538	13.69438	13.40286	13.12048	12.84688	20
21	16.24117	15.85841	15.48862	15.13128	14.78590	14.45199	14.12910	13.81680	13.51466	13.22229	21
22	16.80776	16.39624	15.99923	15.61610	15.24629	14.88923	14.54441	14.21132	13.88949	13.57845	22
23	17.35648	16.91589	16.49141	16.08232	15.68798	15.30774	14.94099	14.58718	14.24575	13.91617	23
24	17.88766	17.41774	16.96561	16.53046	16.11153	15.70811	15.31951	14.94508	14.58420	14.23627	24
25	18.40163	17.90219	17.42228	16.96102	16.51752	16.09099	15.68064	15.28574	14.90560	14.53954	25
30	20.72605	20.07792	19.45918	18.86826	18.30366	17.76398	17.24791	16.75422	16.28172	15.82933	30
35	22.67591	21.88159	21.12796	20.41252	19.73298	19.08717	18.47308	17.88885	17.33270	16.80301	35
40	24.29892	23.36528	22.48457	21.65322	20.86793	20.12560	19.42342	18.75875	18.12915	17.53236	40
45	25.64107	24.57777	23.58022	22.64353	21.76324	20.93524	20.15576	19.42133	18.72876	18.07513	45
50	26.74475	25.56311	24.46016	23.42956	22.46558	21.56297	20.71695	19.92318	19.17767	18.47678	50

Present Value of a Series of Payments Increasing by Constant Amount

Amount of 1st Year Growth 5.0%

Holding Period	5.50%	5.75%	6.00%	Discount Rate 6.25%	6.50%	6.75%	7.00%	7.25%	7.50%	7.75%	
1	0.94787	0.94563	0.94340	0.94118	0.93897	0.93677	0.93458	0.93240	0.93023	0.92807	1
2	1.89124	1.88455	1.87789	1.87128	1.86471	1.85818	1.85169	1.84524	1.83883	1.83246	2
3	2.82802	2.81469	2.80147	2.78836	2.77534	2.76243	2.74962	2.73690	2.72429	2.71177	3
4	3.75632	3.73425	3.71238	3.69072	3.66926	3.64801	3.62695	3.60608	3.58541	3.56493	4
5	4.67448	4.64160	4.60909	4.57693	4.54512	4.51366	4.48253	4.45174	4.42128	4.39114	5
6	5.58104	5.53538	5.49029	5.44577	5.40179	5.35836	5.31546	5.27309	5.23123	5.18989	6
7	6.47470	6.41436	6.35487	6.29620	6.23835	6.18130	6.12503	6.06954	6.01481	5.96083	7
8	7.35436	7.27752	7.20187	7.12739	7.05406	6.98185	6.91075	6.84072	6.77176	6.70384	8
9	8.21904	8.12398	8.03053	7.93867	7.84835	7.75956	7.67225	7.58640	7.50198	7.41895	9
10	9.06792	8.95300	8.84020	8.72949	8.62081	8.51411	8.40936	8.30651	8.20551	8.10633	10
11	9.90028	9.76397	9.63038	9.49946	9.37113	9.24533	9.12200	9.00108	8.88252	8.76626	11
12	10.71555	10.55641	10.40069	10.24829	10.09913	9.95314	9.81022	9.67030	9.53330	9.39915	12
13	11.51325	11.32994	11.15083	10.97581	10.80476	10.63758	10.47416	10.31440	10.15820	10.00546	13
14	12.29299	12.08426	11.88063	11.68193	11.48803	11.29878	11.11406	10.93373	10.75766	10.58574	14
15	13.05448	12.81919	12.58998	12.36665	12.14903	11.93694	11.73022	11.52869	11.33221	11.14061	15
16	13.79749	13.53459	13.27886	13.03005	12.78795	12.55234	12.32300	12.09975	11.88238	11.67072	16
17	14.52190	14.23043	13.94731	13.67227	13.40501	13.14529	12.89284	12.64742	12.40880	12.17675	17
18	15.22761	14.90671	14.59545	14.29349	14.00051	13.71617	13.44018	13.17225	12.91209	12.65943	18
19	15.91461	15.56350	15.22342	14.89398	14.57477	14.26541	13.96555	13.67483	13.39292	13.11950	19
20	16.58293	16.20092	15.83144	15.47402	15.12817	14.79347	14.46947	14.15577	13.85198	13.55772	20
21	17.23265	16.81914	16.41975	16.03393	15.66113	15.30081	14.95249	14.61569	14.28996	13.97485	21
22	17.86390	17.41836	16.98864	16.57409	16.17406	15.78796	15.41521	15.05525	14.70756	14.37165	22
23	18.47683	17.99881	17.53841	17.09487	16.66744	16.25544	15.85819	15.47509	15.10551	14.74889	23
24	19.07165	18.56078	18.06942	17.59668	17.14173	16.70378	16.28206	15.87586	15.48451	15.10734	24
25	19.64856	19.10455	18.58202	18.07996	17.59744	17.13354	16.68741	16.25824	15.84526	15.44774	25
30	22.27413	21.56215	20.88277	20.23424	19.61490	19.02319	18.45763	17.91686	17.39956	16.90451	30
35	24.49725	23.61858	22.78538	21.99488	21.24448	20.53175	19.85444	19.21042	18.59775	18.01457	35
40	26.36212	25.32334	24.34414	23.42045	22.54853	21.72490	20.94635	20.20991	19.51283	18.85256	40
45	27.91440	26.72567	25.61131	24.56579	23.58400	22.66127	21.79332	20.97620	20.20630	19.48027	45
50	29.19806	27.87168	26.63473	25.47997	24.40084	23.39134	22.44600	21.55987	20.72838	19.94740	50

Amount of 1st Year Growth 6.0%

Holding Period	5.50%	5.75%	6.00%	Discount Rate 6.25%	6.50%	6.75%	7.00%	7.25%	7.50%	7.75%	
1	0.94787	0.94563	0.94340	0.94118	0.93897	0.93677	0.93458	0.93240	0.93023	0.92807	1
2	1.90023	1.89349	1.88679	1.88014	1.87353	1.86695	1.86042	1.85393	1.84749	1.84108	2
3	2.85403	2.84055	2.82717	2.81389	2.80072	2.78765	2.77468	2.76181	2.74904	2.73637	3
4	3.80655	3.78409	3.76184	3.73979	3.71796	3.69633	3.67489	3.65366	3.63263	3.61178	4
5	4.75532	4.72169	4.68844	4.65554	4.62301	4.59083	4.55900	4.52751	4.49636	4.46554	5
6	5.69814	5.65122	5.60489	5.55913	5.51394	5.46932	5.42524	5.38171	5.33871	5.29623	6
7	6.63305	6.57077	6.50936	6.44882	6.38911	6.33024	6.27218	6.21492	6.15846	6.10276	7
8	7.55832	7.47868	7.40029	7.32311	7.24712	7.17230	7.09863	7.02609	6.95465	6.88430	8
9	8.47241	8.37351	8.27630	8.18074	8.08680	7.99445	7.90366	7.81438	7.72660	7.64027	9
10	9.37397	9.25399	9.13623	9.02065	8.90720	8.79584	8.68651	8.57918	8.47379	8.37031	10
11	10.26183	10.11902	9.97909	9.84195	9.70754	9.57580	9.44666	9.32006	9.19594	9.07424	11
12	11.13496	10.96770	10.80406	10.64392	10.48722	10.33384	10.18372	10.03677	9.89290	9.75204	12
13	11.99249	11.79924	11.61046	11.42601	11.24576	11.06962	10.89746	10.72918	10.56467	10.40383	13
14	12.83366	12.61300	12.39775	12.18776	11.98286	11.78292	11.58778	11.39730	11.21137	11.02983	14
15	13.65786	13.40845	13.16552	12.92887	12.69830	12.47363	12.25468	12.04126	11.83322	11.63039	15
16	14.46456	14.18518	13.91345	13.64913	13.39198	13.14177	12.89827	12.66127	12.43056	12.20594	16
17	15.25336	14.94286	14.64132	14.34843	14.06390	13.78743	13.51876	13.25762	13.00377	12.75695	17
18	16.02392	15.68128	15.34902	15.02675	14.71411	14.41078	14.11640	13.83068	13.55331	13.28399	18
19	16.77600	16.40030	16.03649	15.68412	15.34278	15.01205	14.69154	14.38087	14.07969	13.78764	19
20	17.50944	17.09983	16.70375	16.32068	15.95011	15.59156	15.24456	14.90867	14.58347	14.26856	20
21	18.22414	17.77987	17.35089	16.93658	16.53636	16.14964	15.77589	15.41459	15.06525	14.72740	21
22	18.92005	18.44047	17.97805	17.53207	17.10183	16.68669	16.28600	15.89917	15.52564	15.16485	22
23	19.59719	19.08174	18.58542	18.10741	17.64690	17.20314	16.77540	16.36299	15.96527	15.58161	23
24	20.25564	19.70382	19.17323	18.66290	18.17193	17.69944	17.24460	16.80664	16.38481	15.97840	24
25	20.89549	20.30691	19.74175	19.19891	18.67735	18.17608	17.69417	17.23073	16.78492	16.35594	25
30	23.82221	23.04637	22.30636	21.60023	20.92615	20.28240	19.66735	19.07949	18.51739	17.97969	30
35	26.31859	25.35556	24.44281	23.57725	22.75599	21.97634	21.23579	20.53200	19.86280	19.22612	35
40	28.42532	27.28141	26.20371	25.18767	24.22912	23.32419	22.46927	21.66108	20.89652	20.17275	40
45	30.18774	28.87357	27.64241	26.48804	25.40475	24.38730	23.43088	22.53108	21.68383	20.88541	45
50	31.65136	30.18025	28.80930	27.53039	26.33610	25.21971	24.17505	23.19655	22.27910	21.41802	50

Present Value of a Series of Payments Increasing by Constant Amount

Amount of 1st Year Growth 7.0%

Holding Period	Discount Rate 5.50%	5.75%	6.00%	6.25%	6.50%	6.75%	7.00%	7.25%	7.50%	7.75%	
1	0.94787	0.94563	0.94340	0.94118	0.93897	0.93677	0.93458	0.93240	0.93023	0.92807	1
2	1.90921	1.90243	1.89569	1.88900	1.88234	1.87573	1.86916	1.86263	1.85614	1.84969	2
3	2.88005	2.86640	2.85286	2.83942	2.82609	2.81286	2.79974	2.78672	2.77379	2.76097	3
4	3.85678	3.83393	3.81129	3.78887	3.76665	3.74464	3.72284	3.70124	3.67984	3.65864	4
5	4.83616	4.80178	4.76778	4.73416	4.70090	4.66800	4.63546	4.60328	4.57144	4.53994	5
6	5.81524	5.76706	5.71948	5.67250	5.62610	5.58028	5.53503	5.49033	5.44619	5.40258	6
7	6.79140	6.72718	6.66386	6.60143	6.53988	6.47918	6.41933	6.36031	6.30210	6.24469	7
8	7.76228	7.67985	7.59870	7.51882	7.44018	7.36276	7.28652	7.21146	7.13754	7.06475	8
9	8.72578	8.62304	8.52207	8.42282	8.32525	8.22935	8.13506	8.04236	7.95121	7.86159	9
10	9.68003	9.55497	9.43225	9.31181	9.19360	9.07757	8.96367	8.85186	8.74208	8.63430	10
11	10.62338	10.47408	10.32779	10.18444	10.04396	9.90628	9.77133	9.63904	9.50936	9.38222	11
12	11.55437	11.37900	11.20742	11.03956	10.87530	10.71455	10.55723	10.40324	10.25251	10.10494	12
13	12.47172	12.26855	12.07009	11.87620	11.68677	11.50166	11.32076	11.14396	10.97114	10.80219	13
14	13.37433	13.14174	12.91488	12.69359	12.47770	12.26705	12.06149	11.86088	11.66507	11.47392	14
15	14.26123	13.99771	13.74107	13.49109	13.24758	13.01032	12.77914	12.55384	12.33424	12.12018	15
16	15.13163	14.83576	14.54804	14.26822	13.99602	13.73121	13.47354	13.22279	12.97873	12.74116	16
17	15.98481	15.65530	15.33534	15.02460	14.72278	14.42957	14.14468	13.86783	13.59873	13.33715	17
18	16.82022	16.45586	16.10259	15.76000	15.42772	15.10538	14.79262	14.48911	14.19452	13.90854	18
19	17.63739	17.23710	16.84955	16.47427	16.11079	15.75869	15.41753	15.08692	14.76646	14.45578	19
20	18.43595	17.99873	17.57605	17.16734	16.77204	16.38964	16.01965	15.66158	15.31497	14.97940	20
21	19.21562	18.74060	18.28203	17.83923	17.41158	16.99846	16.59928	16.21349	15.84055	15.47995	21
22	19.97619	19.46258	18.96746	18.49005	18.02961	17.58541	17.15679	16.74310	16.34371	15.95804	22
23	20.71755	20.16466	19.63243	19.11995	18.62636	18.15084	17.69260	17.25090	16.82504	16.41433	23
24	21.43962	20.84686	20.27704	19.72913	19.20213	18.69510	18.20715	17.73743	17.28512	16.84947	24
25	22.14241	21.50927	20.90148	20.31785	19.75726	19.21863	18.70094	18.20323	17.72458	17.26414	25
30	25.37029	24.53059	23.72995	22.96621	22.23739	21.54160	20.87707	20.24213	19.63523	19.05487	30
35	28.13993	27.09254	26.10024	25.15961	24.26749	23.42092	22.61714	21.85358	21.12784	20.43768	35
40	30.48852	29.23948	28.06328	26.95490	25.90972	24.92348	23.99220	23.11224	22.28020	21.49295	40
45	32.46108	31.02147	29.67351	28.41029	27.22550	26.11333	25.06844	24.08595	23.16137	22.29055	45
50	34.10467	32.48882	30.98388	29.58080	28.27137	27.04808	25.90410	24.83324	23.82981	22.88863	50

Amount of 1st Year Growth 8.0%

Holding Period	Discount Rate 5.50%	5.75%	6.00%	6.25%	6.50%	6.75%	7.00%	7.25%	7.50%	7.75%	
1	0.94787	0.94563	0.94340	0.94118	0.93897	0.93677	0.93458	0.93240	0.93023	0.92807	1
2	1.91820	1.91137	1.90459	1.89785	1.89116	1.88451	1.87789	1.87132	1.86479	1.85830	2
3	2.90607	2.89225	2.87855	2.86495	2.85146	2.83808	2.82480	2.81162	2.79855	2.78557	3
4	3.90702	3.88377	3.86075	3.83794	3.81534	3.79296	3.77079	3.74882	3.72706	3.70550	4
5	4.91699	4.88187	4.84713	4.81277	4.77879	4.74518	4.71193	4.67905	4.64652	4.61434	5
6	5.93234	5.88289	5.83407	5.78586	5.73826	5.69124	5.64481	5.59895	5.55366	5.50893	6
7	6.94974	6.88358	6.81836	6.75405	6.69064	6.62813	6.56648	6.50569	6.44574	6.38662	7
8	7.96624	7.88101	7.79712	7.71454	7.63325	7.55321	7.47441	7.39683	7.32044	7.24521	8
9	8.97915	8.87257	8.76783	8.66489	8.56370	8.46424	8.36646	8.27034	8.17583	8.08291	9
10	9.98609	9.85596	9.72827	9.60297	9.47999	9.35930	9.24083	9.12455	9.01037	8.89828	10
11	10.98493	10.82913	10.67649	10.52693	10.38038	10.23675	10.09599	9.95803	9.82278	9.69020	11
12	11.97378	11.79029	11.61079	11.43519	11.26338	11.09526	10.93074	10.76972	10.61211	10.45783	12
13	12.95095	12.73786	12.52972	12.32640	12.12777	11.93370	11.74407	11.55874	11.37761	11.20056	13
14	13.91500	13.67048	13.43201	13.19942	12.97254	12.75119	12.53521	12.32446	12.11877	11.91800	14
15	14.86461	14.58697	14.31661	14.05331	13.79685	13.54701	13.30360	13.06641	12.83526	12.60996	15
16	15.79869	15.48634	15.18264	14.88730	14.60006	14.32065	14.04881	13.78431	13.52691	13.27637	16
17	16.71627	16.36773	16.02935	15.70077	15.38167	15.07172	14.77060	14.47803	14.19370	13.91735	17
18	17.61653	17.23044	16.85616	16.49326	16.14133	15.79999	15.46884	15.14754	14.83574	14.53309	18
19	18.49878	18.07390	17.66261	17.26441	16.87881	16.50533	16.14352	15.79296	15.45323	15.12392	19
20	19.36246	18.89764	18.44836	18.01400	17.59397	17.18773	16.79474	16.41448	16.04647	15.69023	20
21	20.20710	19.70133	19.21316	18.74189	18.28681	17.84728	17.42267	17.01238	16.61584	16.23250	21
22	21.03234	20.48470	19.95687	19.44804	18.95738	18.48414	18.02758	17.58702	17.16179	16.75124	22
23	21.83791	21.24758	20.67944	20.13249	19.60582	19.09854	18.60980	18.13881	17.68480	17.24705	23
24	22.62361	21.98990	21.38085	20.79535	20.23233	19.69076	19.16969	18.66821	18.18543	17.72053	24
25	23.38934	22.71163	22.06121	21.43680	20.83717	20.26117	19.70770	19.17572	18.66425	18.17234	25
30	26.91836	26.01482	25.15353	24.33220	23.54864	22.80081	22.08679	21.40477	20.75306	20.13005	30
35	29.96127	28.82952	27.75767	26.74198	25.77900	24.86551	23.99849	23.17516	22.39289	21.64924	35
40	32.55172	31.19755	29.92284	28.72212	27.59032	26.52277	25.51513	24.56341	23.66389	22.81314	40
45	34.73441	33.16937	31.70460	30.33255	29.04626	27.83935	26.70600	25.64082	24.63890	23.69570	45
50	36.55798	34.79739	33.15845	31.63122	30.20663	28.87645	27.63316	26.46993	25.38053	24.35925	50

Present Value of a Series of Payments Increasing by Constant Amount

Amount of 1st Year Growth 9.0%

Holding Period	5.50%	5.75%	6.00%	6.25%	Discount Rate 6.50%	6.75%	7.00%	7.25%	7.50%	7.75%	
1	0.94787	0.94563	0.94340	0.94118	0.93897	0.93677	0.93458	0.93240	0.93023	0.92807	1
2	1.92718	1.92031	1.91349	1.90671	1.89998	1.89328	1.88663	1.88002	1.87345	1.86692	2
3	2.93208	2.91811	2.90424	2.89049	2.87684	2.86330	2.84986	2.83653	2.82330	2.81017	3
4	3.95725	3.93361	3.91020	3.88701	3.86404	3.84128	3.81874	3.79640	3.77428	3.75235	4
5	4.99783	4.96195	4.92647	4.89138	4.85668	4.82235	4.78840	4.75481	4.72160	4.68873	5
6	6.04944	5.99873	5.94867	5.89923	5.85041	5.80220	5.75459	5.70758	5.66114	5.61528	6
7	7.10809	7.03999	6.97285	6.90667	6.84141	6.77707	6.71363	6.65107	6.58938	6.52855	7
8	8.17020	8.08217	7.99554	7.91026	7.82631	7.74366	7.66230	7.58220	7.50333	7.42566	8
9	9.23252	9.12211	9.01360	8.90696	8.80215	8.69914	8.59787	8.49832	8.40045	8.30423	9
10	10.29215	10.15695	10.02430	9.89413	9.76639	9.64102	9.51798	9.39721	9.27865	9.16226	10
11	11.34648	11.18419	11.02519	10.86942	10.71679	10.56723	10.42066	10.27701	10.13620	9.99818	11
12	12.39318	12.20158	12.01416	11.83082	11.65146	11.47597	11.30424	11.13619	10.97171	10.81072	12
13	13.43019	13.20716	12.98935	12.77660	12.56878	12.36574	12.16737	11.97352	11.78408	11.59893	13
14	14.45566	14.19921	13.94914	13.70525	13.46737	13.23532	13.00893	12.78803	12.57247	12.36209	14
15	15.46799	15.17623	14.89216	14.61553	14.34612	14.08370	13.82806	13.57898	13.33628	13.09974	15
16	16.46576	16.13692	15.81723	15.50638	15.20410	14.91009	14.62409	14.34583	14.07509	13.81159	16
17	17.44773	17.08016	16.72336	16.37694	16.04056	15.71386	15.39653	15.08823	14.78867	14.49755	17
18	18.41284	18.00502	17.60973	17.22651	16.85494	16.49459	16.14506	15.80597	15.47696	15.15765	18
19	19.36017	18.91070	18.47567	18.05455	17.64682	17.25197	16.86951	16.49901	16.14000	15.79206	19
20	20.28897	19.79655	19.32066	18.86066	18.41591	17.98582	17.56983	17.16738	16.77797	16.40107	20
21	21.19858	20.66206	20.14430	19.64454	19.16204	18.69611	18.24607	17.81128	17.39114	16.98505	21
22	22.08849	21.50681	20.94629	20.40602	19.88515	19.38287	18.89838	18.43094	17.97986	17.54444	22
23	22.95827	22.33051	21.72644	21.14503	20.58528	20.04624	19.52700	19.02671	18.54456	18.07977	23
24	23.80760	23.13294	22.48467	21.86158	21.26253	20.68643	20.13224	19.59899	19.08574	18.59160	24
25	24.63626	23.91399	23.22094	22.55574	21.91708	21.30372	20.71447	20.14822	19.60391	19.08054	25
30	28.46644	27.49904	26.57712	25.69818	24.85988	24.06002	23.29651	22.56741	21.87089	21.20523	30
35	31.78260	30.56651	29.41509	28.32434	27.29050	26.31009	25.37985	24.49674	23.65794	22.86079	35
40	34.61492	33.15562	31.78241	30.48935	29.27092	28.12206	27.03806	26.01457	25.04757	24.13333	40
45	37.00775	35.31726	33.73570	32.25480	30.86701	29.56538	28.34355	27.19569	26.11643	25.10084	45
50	39.01129	37.10595	35.33303	33.68163	32.14189	30.70482	29.36221	28.10662	26.93124	25.82987	50

Amount of 1st Year Growth 10.0%

Holding Period	5.50%	5.75%	6.00%	6.25%	Discount Rate 6.50%	6.75%	7.00%	7.25%	7.50%	7.75%	
1	0.94787	0.94563	0.94340	0.94118	0.93897	0.93677	0.93458	0.93240	0.93023	0.92807	1
2	1.93616	1.92926	1.92239	1.91557	1.90879	1.90206	1.89536	1.88871	1.88210	1.87553	2
3	2.95810	2.94396	2.92994	2.91602	2.90221	2.88851	2.87492	2.86143	2.84805	2.83477	3
4	4.00748	3.98346	3.95966	3.93608	3.91273	3.88960	3.86668	3.84398	3.82149	3.79921	4
5	5.07867	5.04204	5.00582	4.96999	4.93456	4.89952	4.86486	4.83058	4.79667	4.76313	5
6	6.16654	6.11457	6.06326	6.01259	5.96257	5.91316	5.86438	5.81620	5.76862	5.72162	6
7	7.26644	7.19640	7.12735	7.05928	6.99218	6.92601	6.86078	6.79645	6.73302	6.67048	7
8	8.37416	8.28334	8.19395	8.10597	8.01937	7.93412	7.85019	7.76757	7.68622	7.60612	8
9	9.48589	9.37164	9.25937	9.14904	9.04060	8.93403	8.82927	8.72630	8.62507	8.52555	9
10	10.59821	10.45794	10.32032	10.18529	10.05278	9.92275	9.79514	9.66988	9.54694	9.42625	10
11	11.70803	11.53924	11.37389	11.21191	11.05321	10.89770	10.74532	10.59599	10.44962	10.30616	11
12	12.81259	12.61287	12.41753	12.22646	12.03954	11.85667	11.67775	11.50266	11.33132	11.16362	12
13	13.90942	13.67647	13.44898	13.22680	13.00978	12.79778	12.59067	12.38830	12.19055	11.99729	13
14	14.99633	14.72795	14.46627	14.21108	13.96221	13.71946	13.48265	13.25161	13.02617	12.80618	14
15	16.07137	15.76549	15.46770	15.17775	14.89539	14.62039	14.35252	14.09156	13.83729	13.58952	15
16	17.13283	16.78750	16.45182	16.12547	15.80813	15.49952	15.19936	14.90736	14.62326	14.34681	16
17	18.17919	17.79260	17.41737	17.05311	16.69944	16.35601	16.02245	15.69843	15.38364	15.07775	17
18	19.20914	18.77960	18.36330	17.95977	17.56855	17.18919	16.82128	16.46441	16.11817	15.78220	18
19	20.22157	19.74750	19.28873	18.84470	18.41483	17.99860	17.59551	17.20505	16.82677	16.46020	19
20	21.21548	20.69546	20.19297	19.70731	19.23784	18.78391	18.34492	17.92029	17.50946	17.11191	20
21	22.19006	21.62279	21.07543	20.54719	20.03727	19.54493	19.06946	18.61018	18.16643	17.73760	21
22	23.14463	22.52892	21.93570	21.36400	20.81293	20.28159	19.76917	19.27487	18.79793	18.33764	22
23	24.07863	23.41343	22.77345	22.15757	21.56474	20.99394	20.44420	19.91462	19.40433	18.91249	23
24	24.99159	24.27598	23.58848	22.92780	22.29273	21.68209	21.09478	20.52977	19.98604	19.46266	24
25	25.88319	25.11635	24.38067	23.67469	22.99699	22.34626	21.72123	21.12071	20.54357	19.98874	25
30	30.01452	28.98327	28.00071	27.06417	26.17113	25.31922	24.50622	23.73005	22.98873	22.28041	30
35	33.60394	32.30349	31.07252	29.90670	28.80201	27.75468	26.76120	25.81832	24.92298	24.07235	35
40	36.67812	35.11369	33.64198	32.25657	30.95152	29.72135	28.56099	27.46573	26.43126	25.45353	40
45	39.28108	37.46516	35.76680	34.17706	32.68776	31.29141	29.98111	28.75057	27.59397	26.50598	45
50	41.46459	39.41452	37.50760	35.73205	34.07716	32.53319	31.09126	29.74330	28.48195	27.30048	50

Present Value of a Series of Payments Increasing by Constant Amount

Amount of 1st Year Growth 3.0%

Holding Period				Discount Rate							
	8.00%	8.25%	8.50%	8.75%	9.00%	9.25%	9.50%	9.75%	10.00%	10.25%	
1	0.92593	0.92379	0.92166	0.91954	0.91743	0.91533	0.91324	0.91116	0.90909	0.90703	1
2	1.80898	1.80277	1.79660	1.79046	1.78436	1.77830	1.77227	1.76628	1.76033	1.75441	2
3	2.65045	2.63842	2.62648	2.61463	2.60288	2.59121	2.57963	2.56813	2.55672	2.54540	3
4	3.45163	3.43223	3.41300	3.39394	3.37506	3.35635	3.33780	3.31942	3.30121	3.28316	4
5	4.21388	4.18572	4.15785	4.13027	4.10298	4.07598	4.04926	4.02281	3.99664	3.97074	5
6	4.93858	4.90043	4.86273	4.82549	4.78869	4.75233	4.71639	4.68088	4.64579	4.61110	6
7	5.62710	5.57789	5.52935	5.48145	5.43419	5.38756	5.34154	5.29613	5.25131	5.20708	7
8	6.28082	6.21964	6.15936	6.09997	6.04145	5.98379	5.92697	5.87097	5.81579	5.76140	8
9	6.90113	6.82717	6.75441	6.68282	6.61238	6.54307	6.47486	6.40773	6.34167	6.27664	9
10	7.48939	7.40198	7.31611	7.23174	7.14884	7.06738	6.98732	6.90864	6.83131	6.75529	10
11	8.04693	7.94553	7.84604	7.74842	7.65263	7.55863	7.46638	7.37583	7.28695	7.19970	11
12	8.57510	8.45924	8.34572	8.23449	8.12549	8.01867	7.91397	7.81134	7.71073	7.61209	12
13	9.07516	8.94450	8.81665	8.69154	8.56910	8.44928	8.33195	8.21711	8.10467	7.99458	13
14	9.54841	9.40267	9.26025	9.12108	8.98505	8.85208	8.72209	8.59499	8.47070	8.34916	14
15	9.99605	9.83505	9.67793	9.52458	9.37489	9.22876	9.08607	8.94673	8.81064	8.67771	15
16	10.41929	10.24292	10.07102	9.90346	9.74011	9.58082	9.42549	9.27399	9.12620	8.98202	16
17	10.81929	10.62750	10.44081	10.25906	10.08209	9.90975	9.74188	9.57835	9.41901	9.26374	17
18	11.19716	10.98997	10.78854	10.59268	10.40220	10.21693	10.03668	9.86129	9.69060	9.52446	18
19	11.55400	11.33147	11.11540	10.90555	10.70172	10.50368	10.31125	10.12421	9.94240	9.76563	19
20	11.89084	11.65309	11.42252	11.19886	10.98186	10.77127	10.56688	10.36845	10.17577	9.98864	20
21	12.20869	11.95588	11.71098	11.47371	11.24377	11.02089	10.80480	10.59524	10.39198	10.19478	21
22	12.50851	12.24083	11.98184	11.73119	11.48857	11.25365	11.02614	10.80576	10.59222	10.38527	22
23	12.79124	12.50891	12.23606	11.97231	11.71729	11.47063	11.23201	11.00110	10.77761	10.56122	23
24	13.05775	12.76104	12.47461	12.19804	11.93091	11.67283	11.42341	11.18231	10.94918	10.72370	24
25	13.30890	12.99808	12.69837	12.40929	12.13037	11.86119	11.60131	11.35035	11.10793	10.87369	25
30	14.36146	13.98494	13.62377	13.27720	12.94449	12.62497	12.31798	12.02292	11.73921	11.46631	30
35	15.13733	14.70402	14.29035	13.89521	13.51759	13.15651	12.81107	12.48043	12.16377	11.86037	35
40	15.70588	15.22490	14.76766	14.33269	13.91865	13.52425	13.14834	12.78980	12.44763	12.12086	40
45	16.12039	15.60030	15.10771	14.64080	14.19788	13.77738	13.37784	12.99795	12.63644	12.29218	45
50	16.42127	15.86965	15.34891	14.85684	14.39144	13.95083	13.53333	13.13736	12.76148	12.40435	50

Amount of 1st Year Growth 4.0%

Holding Period				Discount Rate							
	8.00%	8.25%	8.50%	8.75%	9.00%	9.25%	9.50%	9.75%	10.00%	10.25%	
1	0.92593	0.92379	0.92166	0.91954	0.91743	0.91533	0.91324	0.91116	0.90909	0.90703	1
2	1.81756	1.81131	1.80509	1.79892	1.79278	1.78668	1.78061	1.77459	1.76860	1.76264	2
3	2.67490	2.66272	2.65063	2.63864	2.62674	2.61492	2.60320	2.59156	2.58002	2.56855	3
4	3.49813	3.47837	3.45880	3.43940	3.42017	3.40112	3.38224	3.36353	3.34499	3.32661	4
5	4.28761	4.25878	4.23025	4.20202	4.17409	4.14646	4.11911	4.09204	4.06526	4.03875	5
6	5.04381	5.00456	4.96578	4.92747	4.88961	4.85221	4.81525	4.77872	4.74263	4.70696	6
7	5.76734	5.71647	5.66629	5.61678	5.56794	5.51974	5.47218	5.42525	5.37894	5.33324	7
8	6.45888	6.39534	6.33275	6.27108	6.21033	6.15046	6.09148	6.03335	5.97607	5.91962	8
9	7.11921	7.04207	6.96619	6.89154	6.81809	6.74582	6.67472	6.60474	6.53588	6.46811	9
10	7.74915	7.65762	7.56770	7.47936	7.39257	7.30729	7.22350	7.14115	7.06022	6.98068	10
11	8.34959	8.24298	8.13839	8.03578	7.93511	7.83634	7.73940	7.64428	7.55091	7.45927	11
12	8.92143	8.79917	8.67940	8.56206	8.44708	8.33442	8.22401	8.11581	8.00974	7.90577	12
13	9.46563	9.32725	9.19188	9.05943	8.92983	8.80300	8.67888	8.55738	8.43844	8.32201	13
14	9.98313	9.82827	9.67697	9.52914	9.38468	9.24350	9.10550	8.97060	8.83871	8.70975	14
15	10.47491	10.30328	10.13583	9.97243	9.81296	9.65731	9.50536	9.35702	9.21216	9.07070	15
16	10.94193	10.75334	10.56959	10.39050	10.21595	10.04580	9.87990	9.71813	9.56037	9.40648	16
17	11.38517	11.17950	10.97935	10.78455	10.59491	10.41028	10.23049	10.05539	9.88483	9.71866	17
18	11.80559	11.58278	11.36623	11.15573	10.95106	10.75204	10.55848	10.37019	10.18699	10.00873	18
19	12.20413	11.96420	11.73129	11.50517	11.28559	11.07232	10.86514	10.66385	10.46823	10.27809	19
20	12.58174	12.32474	12.07558	11.83396	11.59963	11.37229	11.15171	10.93764	10.72984	10.52809	20
21	12.93932	12.66537	12.40010	12.14318	11.89428	11.65311	11.41937	11.19278	10.97308	10.76000	21
22	13.27777	12.98704	12.70585	12.43383	12.17062	11.91586	11.66923	11.43042	11.19911	10.97503	22
23	13.59796	13.29065	12.99377	12.70691	12.42965	12.16159	11.90238	11.65165	11.40907	11.17430	23
24	13.90075	13.57708	13.26478	12.96335	12.67234	12.39131	12.11983	11.85752	11.60400	11.35889	24
25	14.18694	13.84721	13.51977	13.20408	12.89964	12.60595	12.32256	12.04901	11.78490	11.52981	25
30	15.39602	14.98079	14.58275	14.20101	13.83477	13.48326	13.14574	12.82153	12.50998	12.21048	30
35	16.29825	15.81698	15.35787	14.91966	14.50118	14.10134	13.71910	13.35350	13.00365	12.66868	35
40	16.96630	16.42902	15.91870	15.43369	14.97241	14.53342	14.11537	13.71700	13.33715	12.97473	40
45	17.45773	16.87406	16.32185	15.79896	15.30344	14.83349	14.38745	13.96375	13.56099	13.17782	45
50	17.81720	17.19587	16.61001	16.05706	15.53469	15.04073	14.57321	14.13032	13.71037	13.31183	50

Present Value of a Series of Payments Increasing by Constant Amount

Amount of 1st Year Growth   5.0%

Holding Period	8.00%	8.25%	8.50%	8.75%	9.00%	9.25%	9.50%	9.75%	10.00%	10.25%	
					Discount Rate						
1	0.92593	0.92379	0.92166	0.91954	0.91743	0.91533	0.91324	0.91116	0.90909	0.90703	1
2	1.82613	1.81984	1.81359	1.80737	1.80120	1.79506	1.78895	1.78289	1.77686	1.77087	2
3	2.69935	2.68702	2.67479	2.66265	2.65060	2.63864	2.62677	2.61500	2.60331	2.59170	3
4	3.54463	3.52452	3.50460	3.48485	3.46529	3.44590	3.42668	3.40764	3.38877	3.37007	4
5	4.36133	4.33183	4.30265	4.27378	4.24520	4.21693	4.18896	4.16127	4.13388	4.10677	5
6	5.14904	5.10869	5.06883	5.02945	4.99054	4.95209	4.91410	4.87656	4.83947	4.80281	6
7	5.90758	5.85505	5.80324	5.75212	5.70168	5.65192	5.60283	5.55438	5.50657	5.45940	7
8	6.63694	6.57105	6.50614	6.44220	6.37920	6.31714	6.25599	6.19573	6.13636	6.07785	8
9	7.33729	7.25698	7.17797	7.10026	7.02380	6.94858	6.87457	6.80175	6.73010	6.65958	9
10	8.00892	7.91326	7.81929	7.72698	7.63630	7.54720	7.45967	7.37366	7.28913	7.20607	10
11	8.65225	8.54042	8.43074	8.32315	8.21760	8.11404	8.01243	7.91272	7.81488	7.71884	11
12	9.26777	9.13911	9.01308	8.88962	8.76867	8.65017	8.53406	8.42027	8.30875	8.19945	12
13	9.85609	9.71000	9.56711	9.42732	9.29056	9.15675	9.02580	8.89765	8.77222	8.64944	13
14	10.41785	10.25387	10.09369	9.93721	9.78432	9.63492	9.48891	9.34621	9.20671	9.07034	14
15	10.95376	10.77151	10.59373	10.42028	10.25103	10.08587	9.92466	9.76730	9.61368	9.46368	15
16	11.46457	11.26377	11.06815	10.87755	10.69180	10.51077	10.33431	10.16227	9.99453	9.83095	16
17	11.95105	11.73150	11.51790	11.31003	11.10774	10.91082	10.71911	10.53244	10.35065	10.17359	17
18	12.41402	12.17559	11.94392	11.71877	11.49992	11.28716	11.08028	10.87909	10.68339	10.49300	18
19	12.85427	12.59692	12.34718	12.10478	11.86945	11.64095	11.41904	11.20348	10.99405	10.79055	19
20	13.27264	12.99639	12.72864	12.46907	12.21739	11.97331	11.73654	11.50683	11.28391	11.06754	20
21	13.66995	13.37487	13.08922	12.81264	12.54479	12.28533	12.03394	11.79032	11.55417	11.32522	21
22	14.04703	13.73324	13.42986	13.13647	12.85266	12.57807	12.31232	12.05508	11.80601	11.56479	22
23	14.40469	14.07238	13.75148	13.44150	13.14200	12.85256	12.57275	12.30220	12.04053	11.78738	23
24	14.74374	14.39313	14.05495	13.72867	13.41378	13.10979	12.81626	12.53273	12.25881	11.99409	24
25	15.06498	14.69633	14.34116	13.99887	13.66890	13.35072	13.04380	12.74767	12.46186	12.18593	25
30	16.43057	15.97665	15.54172	15.12483	14.72505	14.34155	13.97349	13.62013	13.28074	12.95465	30
35	17.45917	16.92994	16.42539	15.94410	15.48477	15.04616	14.62713	14.22658	13.84352	13.47698	35
40	18.22672	17.63313	17.06975	16.53468	16.02617	15.54258	15.08240	14.64420	14.22668	13.82860	40
45	18.79506	18.14783	17.53598	16.95711	16.40900	15.88961	15.39705	14.92956	14.48553	14.06346	45
50	19.21312	18.52209	17.87111	17.25728	16.67794	16.13062	15.61309	15.12327	14.65926	14.21932	50

Amount of 1st Year Growth   6.0%

Holding Period	8.00%	8.25%	8.50%	8.75%	9.00%	9.25%	9.50%	9.75%	10.00%	10.25%	
					Discount Rate						
1	0.92593	0.92379	0.92166	0.91954	0.91743	0.91533	0.91324	0.91116	0.90909	0.90703	1
2	1.83471	1.82837	1.82208	1.81583	1.80961	1.80343	1.79729	1.79119	1.78512	1.77909	2
3	2.72380	2.71132	2.69894	2.68665	2.67446	2.66236	2.65035	2.63843	2.62660	2.61486	3
4	3.59113	3.57067	3.55040	3.53031	3.51040	3.49067	3.47112	3.45175	3.43255	3.41353	4
5	4.43506	4.40489	4.37505	4.34553	4.31631	4.28741	4.25881	4.23050	4.20249	4.17478	5
6	5.25428	5.21283	5.17188	5.13143	5.09146	5.05197	5.01296	4.97441	4.93631	4.89867	6
7	6.04782	5.99363	5.94018	5.88745	5.83543	5.78410	5.73347	5.68351	5.63421	5.58556	7
8	6.81500	6.74676	6.67953	6.61331	6.54808	6.48381	6.42050	6.35811	6.29665	6.23608	8
9	7.55537	7.47188	7.38975	7.30897	7.22951	7.15134	7.07443	6.99876	6.92431	6.85105	9
10	8.26869	8.16889	8.07087	7.97460	7.88002	7.78712	7.69584	7.60617	7.51805	7.43146	10
11	8.95490	8.83787	8.72309	8.61051	8.50008	8.39174	8.28545	8.18117	8.07884	7.97842	11
12	9.61411	9.47904	9.34676	9.21719	9.09026	8.96592	8.84410	8.72474	8.60777	8.49313	12
13	10.24655	10.09276	9.94234	9.79521	9.65129	9.51049	9.37272	9.23792	9.10599	8.97687	13
14	10.85257	10.67947	10.51041	10.34527	10.18395	10.02633	9.87232	9.72182	9.57472	9.43093	14
15	11.43262	11.23975	11.05163	10.86813	10.68910	10.51442	10.34396	10.17759	10.01520	9.85667	15
16	11.98721	11.77420	11.56671	11.36459	11.16765	10.97575	10.78872	10.60642	10.42869	10.25541	16
17	12.51694	12.28351	12.05644	11.83552	11.62056	11.41135	11.20772	11.00949	10.81647	10.62851	17
18	13.02244	12.76840	12.52161	12.28182	12.04878	11.82228	11.60209	11.38799	11.17978	10.97728	18
19	13.50440	13.22965	12.96308	12.70440	12.45332	12.20959	11.97293	11.74311	11.51988	11.30301	19
20	13.96354	13.66803	13.38170	13.10418	12.83516	12.57433	12.32138	12.07602	11.83798	11.60699	20
21	14.40058	14.08436	13.77834	13.48211	13.19530	12.91755	12.64851	12.38786	12.13527	11.89044	21
22	14.81628	14.47945	14.15388	13.83911	13.53471	13.24028	12.95541	12.67974	12.41290	12.15455	22
23	15.21141	14.85412	14.50918	14.17609	13.85436	13.54352	13.24313	12.95275	12.67199	12.40046	23
24	15.58674	15.20918	14.84512	14.49398	14.15521	13.82827	13.51268	13.20794	12.91362	12.62928	24
25	15.94302	15.54546	15.16255	14.79366	14.43817	14.09548	13.76505	13.44633	13.13882	12.84205	25
30	17.46513	16.97251	16.50070	16.04864	15.61533	15.19983	14.80125	14.41874	14.05151	13.69882	30
35	18.62009	18.04290	17.49291	16.96855	16.46836	15.99099	15.53515	15.09966	14.68339	14.28529	35
40	19.48715	18.83725	18.22080	17.63568	17.07993	16.55175	16.04943	15.57140	15.11620	14.68247	40
45	20.13239	19.42159	18.75011	18.11526	17.51456	16.94573	16.40665	15.89536	15.41008	14.94911	45
50	20.60905	19.84831	19.13222	18.45751	17.82119	17.22051	16.65296	16.11622	15.60815	15.12680	50

Present Value of a Series of Payments Increasing by Constant Amount

Amount of 1st Year Growth 7.0%

Holding Period	8.00%	8.25%	8.50%	Discount Rate 8.75%	9.00%	9.25%	9.50%	9.75%	10.00%	10.25%	
1	0.92593	0.92379	0.92166	0.91954	0.91743	0.91533	0.91324	0.91116	0.90909	0.90703	1
2	1.84328	1.83691	1.83058	1.82428	1.81803	1.81181	1.80563	1.79949	1.79339	1.78732	2
3	2.74825	2.73562	2.72309	2.71066	2.69832	2.68607	2.67392	2.66186	2.64989	2.63801	3
4	3.63763	3.61682	3.59620	3.57576	3.55551	3.53545	3.51556	3.49586	3.47633	3.45698	4
5	4.50878	4.47795	4.44745	4.41728	4.38742	4.35788	4.32866	4.29973	4.27111	4.24279	5
6	5.35951	5.31696	5.27493	5.23341	5.19239	5.15186	5.11181	5.07225	5.03315	4.99452	6
7	6.18807	6.13222	6.07713	6.02278	5.96917	5.91629	5.86411	5.81263	5.76184	5.71172	7
8	6.99307	6.92246	6.85292	6.78443	6.71696	6.65049	6.58501	6.52050	6.45693	6.39430	8
9	7.77345	7.68678	7.60154	7.51769	7.43522	7.35410	7.27429	7.19578	7.11853	7.04252	9
10	8.52846	8.42453	8.32246	8.22222	8.12375	8.02703	7.93202	7.83867	7.74696	7.65685	10
11	9.25756	9.13532	9.01544	8.89787	8.78256	8.66944	8.55848	8.44961	8.34280	8.23799	11
12	9.96045	9.81898	9.68043	9.54475	9.41185	9.28168	9.15415	9.02920	8.90678	8.78681	12
13	10.63702	10.47551	10.31757	10.16311	10.01202	9.86423	9.71965	9.57818	9.43976	9.30429	13
14	11.28730	11.10508	10.92713	10.75334	10.58358	10.41775	10.25574	10.09743	9.94272	9.79152	14
15	11.91148	11.70798	11.50953	11.31597	11.12717	10.94298	10.76326	10.58788	10.41672	10.24965	15
16	12.50985	12.28462	12.06528	11.85163	11.64350	11.44072	11.24313	11.05056	10.86286	10.67988	16
17	13.08282	12.83551	12.59498	12.36100	12.13338	11.91189	11.69634	11.48653	11.28229	11.08343	17
18	13.63087	13.36121	13.09930	12.84486	12.59764	12.35740	12.12389	11.89689	11.67618	11.46155	18
19	14.15454	13.86237	13.57897	13.30401	13.03719	12.77822	12.52683	12.28274	12.04571	11.81548	19
20	14.65443	14.33968	14.03476	13.73929	13.45293	13.17535	12.90621	12.64521	12.39205	12.14644	20
21	15.13121	14.79386	14.46746	14.15158	13.84581	13.54977	13.26308	12.98539	12.71636	12.45566	21
22	15.58554	15.22566	14.87789	14.54174	14.21676	13.90249	13.59850	13.30440	13.01979	12.74431	22
23	16.01814	15.63586	15.26689	14.91069	14.56672	14.23449	13.91350	13.60330	13.30345	13.01354	23
24	16.42974	16.02523	15.63530	15.25930	14.89664	14.54675	14.20910	13.88316	13.56844	13.26447	24
25	16.82106	16.39458	15.98395	15.58845	15.20743	14.84025	14.48629	14.14499	13.81579	13.49817	25
30	18.49969	17.96837	17.45968	16.97246	16.50561	16.05812	15.62900	15.21734	14.82228	14.44299	30
35	19.78101	19.15587	18.56043	17.99299	17.45195	16.93581	16.44318	15.97274	15.52326	15.09360	35
40	20.74757	20.04137	19.37184	18.73667	18.13369	17.56091	17.01646	16.49860	16.00573	15.53634	40
45	21.46972	20.69536	19.96425	19.27341	18.62012	18.00184	17.41625	16.86117	16.33462	15.83475	45
50	22.00498	21.17453	20.39332	19.65773	18.96444	18.31040	17.69284	17.10917	16.55704	16.03428	50

Amount of 1st Year Growth 8.0%

Holding Period	8.00%	8.25%	8.50%	Discount Rate 8.75%	9.00%	9.25%	9.50%	9.75%	10.00%	10.25%	
1	0.92593	0.92379	0.92166	0.91954	0.91743	0.91533	0.91324	0.91116	0.90909	0.90703	1
2	1.85185	1.84544	1.83907	1.83274	1.82645	1.82019	1.81397	1.80779	1.80165	1.79555	2
3	2.77270	2.75992	2.74724	2.73466	2.72218	2.70979	2.69749	2.68529	2.67318	2.66116	3
4	3.68413	3.66297	3.64200	3.62122	3.60063	3.58022	3.56000	3.53997	3.52011	3.50044	4
5	4.58250	4.55101	4.51986	4.48903	4.45854	4.42836	4.39850	4.36896	4.33973	4.31080	5
6	5.46474	5.42109	5.37798	5.33539	5.29331	5.25174	5.21067	5.17009	5.12999	5.09038	6
7	6.32831	6.27080	6.21407	6.15812	6.10292	6.04847	5.99475	5.94176	5.88947	5.83788	7
8	7.17113	7.09817	7.02631	6.95554	6.88583	6.81716	6.74952	6.68288	6.61722	6.55253	8
9	7.99154	7.90168	7.81332	7.72641	7.64093	7.55685	7.47415	7.39279	7.31274	7.23399	9
10	8.78823	8.68017	8.57405	8.46983	8.36748	8.26695	8.16819	8.07118	7.97587	7.88224	10
11	9.56022	9.43277	9.30779	9.18524	9.06504	8.94715	8.83150	8.71806	8.60676	8.49757	11
12	10.30679	10.15891	10.01411	9.87232	9.73344	9.59743	9.46419	9.33367	9.20579	9.08049	12
13	11.02748	10.85826	10.69280	10.53100	10.37275	10.21798	10.06657	9.91845	9.77353	9.63172	13
14	11.72202	11.53068	11.34385	11.16140	10.98322	10.80917	10.63915	10.47304	10.31073	10.15212	14
15	12.39033	12.17621	11.96743	11.76382	11.56524	11.37153	11.18255	10.99817	10.81824	10.64264	15
16	13.03249	12.79505	12.56384	12.33867	12.11935	11.90570	11.69754	11.49470	11.29702	11.10434	16
17	13.64870	13.38751	13.13352	12.88649	12.64620	12.41242	12.18495	11.96358	11.74811	11.53835	17
18	14.23929	13.95402	13.67699	13.40791	13.14650	12.89252	12.64569	12.40579	12.17258	11.94582	18
19	14.80467	14.49510	14.19486	13.90362	13.62106	13.34686	13.08073	12.82238	12.57154	12.32794	19
20	15.34533	15.01133	14.68782	14.37440	14.07070	13.77637	13.49104	13.21440	12.94612	12.68589	20
21	15.86184	15.50335	15.15657	14.82104	14.49632	14.18199	13.87766	13.58293	13.29746	13.02088	21
22	16.35480	15.97187	15.60190	15.24438	14.89881	14.56469	14.24159	13.92906	13.62668	13.33407	22
23	16.82487	16.41759	16.02460	15.64528	15.27908	14.92545	14.58387	14.25385	13.93492	13.62662	23
24	17.27273	16.84128	16.42547	16.02461	15.63807	15.26524	14.90552	14.55837	14.22325	13.89966	24
25	17.69911	17.24371	16.80534	16.38325	15.97670	15.58501	15.20754	14.84365	14.49275	14.15430	25
30	19.53425	18.96423	18.41865	17.89627	17.39589	16.91641	16.45676	16.01595	15.59304	15.18715	30
35	20.94193	20.26883	19.62795	19.01744	18.43554	17.88064	17.35121	16.84582	16.36313	15.90190	35
40	22.00799	21.24548	20.52289	19.83766	19.18746	18.57007	17.98349	17.42580	16.89525	16.39021	40
45	22.80705	21.96912	21.17838	20.43156	19.72568	19.05796	18.42585	17.82698	17.25916	16.72039	45
50	23.40091	22.50075	21.65442	20.85795	20.10769	19.40030	18.73271	18.10212	17.50593	16.94176	50

Present Value of a Series of Payments Increasing by Constant Amount

Amount of 1st Year Growth 9.0%

Holding Period	8.00%	8.25%	8.50%	Discount Rate 8.75%	9.00%	9.25%	9.50%	9.75%	10.00%	10.25%	
1	0.92593	0.92379	0.92166	0.91954	0.91743	0.91533	0.91324	0.91116	0.90909	0.90703	1
2	1.86043	1.85398	1.84757	1.84119	1.83486	1.82857	1.82231	1.81610	1.80992	1.80378	2
3	2.79715	2.78422	2.77140	2.75867	2.74604	2.73350	2.72107	2.70872	2.69647	2.68431	3
4	3.73064	3.70912	3.68780	3.66667	3.64574	3.62500	3.60444	3.58408	3.56390	3.54390	4
5	4.65623	4.62407	4.59226	4.56078	4.52965	4.49884	4.46835	4.43819	4.40835	4.37882	5
6	5.56997	5.52523	5.48103	5.43737	5.39423	5.35162	5.30952	5.26793	5.22684	5.18623	6
7	6.46855	6.40938	6.35102	6.29345	6.23667	6.18065	6.12540	6.07088	6.01710	5.96404	7
8	7.34919	7.27388	7.19971	7.12666	7.05471	6.98384	6.91403	6.84526	6.77751	6.71076	8
9	8.20962	8.11658	8.02510	7.93513	7.84664	7.75961	7.67401	7.58980	7.50695	7.42545	9
10	9.04800	8.93580	8.82564	8.71745	8.61121	8.50686	8.40437	8.30369	8.20479	8.10762	10
11	9.86287	9.73022	9.60015	9.47260	9.34752	9.22485	9.10453	8.98651	8.87073	8.75714	11
12	10.65313	10.49885	10.34779	10.19988	10.05503	9.91318	9.77423	9.63813	9.50480	9.37417	12
13	11.41794	11.24101	11.06803	10.89889	10.73349	10.57172	10.41350	10.25872	10.10730	9.95915	13
14	12.15674	11.95628	11.76057	11.56947	11.38285	11.20059	11.02256	10.84865	10.67873	10.51271	14
15	12.86919	12.64444	12.42532	12.21167	12.00331	11.80008	11.60185	11.40846	11.21976	11.03562	15
16	13.55513	13.30547	13.06240	12.82571	12.59520	12.37068	12.15195	11.93885	11.73119	11.52881	16
17	14.21459	13.93951	13.67206	13.41197	13.15902	12.91296	12.67357	12.44063	12.21393	11.99327	17
18	14.84772	14.54563	14.25468	13.97095	13.69536	13.42763	13.16750	12.91469	12.66897	12.43010	18
19	15.45480	15.12782	14.81076	14.50324	14.20493	13.91549	13.63462	13.36201	13.09736	12.84040	19
20	16.03623	15.68298	15.34088	15.00951	14.68847	14.37738	14.07587	13.78359	13.50019	13.22535	20
21	16.59246	16.21285	15.84569	15.49051	15.14683	14.81421	14.49223	14.18047	13.87855	13.58610	21
22	17.12405	16.71807	16.32592	15.94702	15.58085	15.22690	14.88468	14.55372	14.23358	13.92383	22
23	17.63159	17.19933	16.78230	16.37988	15.99144	15.61642	15.25425	14.90440	14.56638	14.23970	23
24	18.11573	17.65733	17.21564	16.78993	16.37951	15.98372	15.60194	15.23358	14.87806	14.53485	24
25	18.57715	18.09283	17.62673	17.17804	16.74596	16.32978	15.92878	15.54230	15.16972	14.81042	25
30	20.56881	19.96008	19.37763	18.82008	18.28617	17.77469	17.28451	16.81455	16.36381	15.93132	30
35	22.10285	21.38179	20.69547	20.04188	19.41913	18.82546	18.25923	17.71889	17.20300	16.71021	35
40	23.26841	22.44960	21.67393	20.93866	20.24122	19.57924	18.95052	18.35300	17.78478	17.24408	40
45	24.14438	23.24289	22.39251	21.58972	20.83124	20.11408	19.43545	18.79278	18.18371	17.60604	45
50	24.79684	23.82697	22.91552	22.05817	21.25094	20.49019	19.77259	19.09507	18.45481	17.84924	50

Amount of 1st Year Growth 10.0%

Holding Period	8.00%	8.25%	8.50%	Discount Rate 8.75%	9.00%	9.25%	9.50%	9.75%	10.00%	10.25%	
1	0.92593	0.92379	0.92166	0.91954	0.91743	0.91533	0.91324	0.91116	0.90909	0.90703	1
2	1.86900	1.86251	1.85606	1.84965	1.84328	1.83695	1.83065	1.82440	1.81818	1.81200	2
3	2.82160	2.80852	2.79555	2.78268	2.76990	2.75722	2.74464	2.73215	2.71976	2.70746	3
4	3.77714	3.75527	3.73360	3.71213	3.69085	3.66977	3.64889	3.62819	3.60768	3.58735	4
5	4.72995	4.69713	4.66466	4.63254	4.60076	4.56931	4.53820	4.50742	4.47697	4.44683	5
6	5.67521	5.62936	5.58408	5.53935	5.49516	5.45150	5.40838	5.36577	5.32368	5.28209	6
7	6.60879	6.54796	6.48796	6.42878	6.37041	6.31283	6.25604	6.20001	6.14473	6.09020	7
8	7.52725	7.44958	7.37310	7.29777	7.22358	7.15051	7.07854	7.00764	6.93779	6.86899	8
9	8.42770	8.33149	8.23688	8.14385	8.05235	7.96237	7.87386	7.78681	7.70117	7.61692	9
10	9.30776	9.19144	9.07722	8.96507	8.85494	8.74677	8.64054	8.53620	8.43370	8.33301	10
11	10.16553	10.02766	9.89250	9.75996	9.63000	9.50255	9.37755	9.25495	9.13469	9.01671	11
12	10.99947	10.83878	10.68147	10.52744	10.37662	10.22893	10.08428	9.94260	9.80381	9.66785	12
13	11.80840	11.62377	11.44326	11.26678	11.09422	10.92546	10.76042	10.59899	10.44108	10.28658	13
14	12.59147	12.38188	12.17729	11.97753	11.78248	11.59201	11.40597	11.22426	11.04674	10.87330	14
15	13.34805	13.11267	12.88322	12.65951	12.44138	12.22864	12.02115	11.81874	11.62128	11.42861	15
16	14.07777	13.81590	13.56097	13.31275	13.07105	12.83565	12.60636	12.38299	12.16535	11.95327	16
17	14.78047	14.49151	14.21060	13.93746	13.67184	13.41349	13.16218	12.91767	12.67975	12.44819	17
18	15.45614	15.13964	14.83237	14.53400	14.24422	13.96275	13.68930	13.42359	13.16537	12.91437	18
19	16.10494	15.76055	15.42665	15.10285	14.78879	14.48413	14.18852	13.90164	13.62319	13.35286	19
20	16.72713	16.35462	15.99394	15.64462	15.30624	14.97840	14.66071	14.35278	14.05426	13.76480	20
21	17.32309	16.92235	16.53481	16.15997	15.79734	15.44643	15.10680	14.77801	14.45965	14.15132	21
22	17.89331	17.46428	17.04993	16.64966	16.26290	15.88911	15.52777	15.17838	14.84047	14.51359	22
23	18.43832	17.98106	17.54001	17.11447	16.70380	16.30738	15.92462	15.55495	15.19784	14.85278	23
24	18.95873	18.47338	18.00581	17.55524	17.12094	16.70220	16.29836	15.90879	15.53287	15.17004	24
25	19.45519	18.94196	18.44813	17.97283	17.51523	17.07454	16.65003	16.24096	15.84668	15.46654	25
30	21.60336	20.95594	20.33660	19.74390	19.17645	18.63298	18.11227	17.61316	17.13457	16.67549	30
35	23.26377	22.49475	21.76300	21.06632	20.40272	19.77029	19.16726	18.59197	18.04288	17.51851	35
40	24.52883	23.65372	22.82498	22.03965	21.29498	20.58840	19.91755	19.28020	18.67431	18.09795	40
45	25.48171	24.51665	23.60664	22.74787	21.93681	21.17020	20.44505	19.75859	19.10825	18.49168	45
50	26.19276	25.15319	24.17663	23.25839	22.39419	21.58008	20.81246	20.08802	19.40370	18.75672	50

Present Value of a Series of Payments Increasing by Constant Amount

Amount of 1st Year Growth 3.0%

Holding Period	10.50%	10.75%	11.00%	11.25%	11.50%	11.75%	12.00%	12.25%	15.00%	18.00%	
				Discount Rate							
1	0.90498	0.90293	0.90090	0.89888	0.89686	0.89485	0.89286	0.89087	0.86957	0.84746	1
2	1.74853	1.74268	1.73687	1.73109	1.72535	1.71964	1.71397	1.70832	1.64839	1.58719	2
3	2.53416	2.52301	2.51193	2.50094	2.49003	2.47920	2.46845	2.45778	2.34536	2.23234	3
4	3.26526	3.24753	3.22995	3.21253	3.19526	3.17814	3.16117	3.14435	2.96857	2.79455	4
5	3.94510	3.91973	3.89462	3.86976	3.84515	3.82080	3.79669	3.77282	3.52541	3.28411	5
6	4.57682	4.54294	4.50945	4.47635	4.44363	4.41129	4.37931	4.34770	4.02259	3.71010	6
7	5.16343	5.12034	5.07781	5.03583	4.99439	4.95347	4.91308	4.87321	4.46619	4.08054	7
8	5.70779	5.65495	5.60286	5.55152	5.50089	5.45099	5.40178	5.35327	4.86174	4.40244	8
9	6.21264	6.14963	6.08761	6.02655	5.96643	5.90723	5.84894	5.79154	5.21423	4.68201	9
10	6.68057	6.60711	6.53488	6.46387	6.39404	6.32538	6.25785	6.19143	5.52815	4.92466	10
11	7.11404	7.02993	6.94735	6.86626	6.78661	6.70839	6.63156	6.55609	5.80758	5.13515	11
12	7.51537	7.42053	7.32752	7.23630	7.14682	7.05905	6.97294	6.88846	6.05617	5.31766	12
13	7.88676	7.78117	7.67774	7.57642	7.47717	7.37991	7.28462	7.19123	6.27720	5.47581	13
14	8.23027	8.11398	8.00021	7.88890	7.77997	7.67338	7.56904	7.46691	6.47365	5.61279	14
15	8.54785	8.42098	8.29700	8.17584	8.05741	7.94165	7.82847	7.71781	6.64816	5.73138	15
16	8.84133	8.70403	8.57002	8.43921	8.31149	8.18678	8.06500	7.94604	6.80311	5.83401	16
17	9.11241	8.96490	8.82108	8.68084	8.54408	8.41068	8.28055	8.15358	6.94064	5.92278	17
18	9.36271	9.20522	9.05184	8.90245	8.75691	8.61510	8.47691	8.34222	7.06266	5.99953	18
19	9.59372	9.42652	9.26386	9.10560	8.95158	8.80166	8.65571	8.51360	7.17087	6.06587	19
20	9.80686	9.63024	9.45860	9.29176	9.12957	8.97186	8.81847	8.66926	7.26680	6.12319	20
21	10.00342	9.81769	9.63738	9.46230	9.29226	9.12707	8.96657	8.81058	7.35181	6.17268	21
22	10.18465	9.99013	9.80147	9.61847	9.44090	9.26856	9.10127	8.93884	7.42711	6.21542	22
23	10.35167	10.14869	9.95202	9.76142	9.57666	9.39751	9.22376	9.05521	7.49380	6.25230	23
24	10.50556	10.29445	10.09010	9.89225	9.70062	9.51499	9.33510	9.16075	7.55284	6.28412	24
25	10.64729	10.42840	10.21671	10.01193	9.81377	9.62198	9.43628	9.25644	7.60509	6.31157	25
30	11.20369	10.95089	10.70742	10.47287	10.24681	10.02886	9.81865	9.61582	7.78856	6.40140	30
35	11.56951	11.29055	11.02285	10.76585	10.51898	10.28175	10.05366	9.83426	7.88737	6.44394	35
40	11.80861	11.51006	11.22442	10.95097	10.68904	10.43800	10.19725	9.96624	7.94027	6.46396	40
45	11.96409	11.65119	11.35256	11.06735	10.79476	10.53405	10.28454	10.04559	7.96845	6.47334	45
50	12.06475	11.74154	11.43367	11.14019	10.86019	10.59284	10.33737	10.09308	7.98339	6.47771	50

Amount of 1st Year Growth 4.0%

Holding Period	10.50%	10.75%	11.00%	11.25%	11.50%	11.75%	12.00%	12.25%	15.00%	18.00%	
				Discount Rate							
1	0.90498	0.90293	0.90090	0.89888	0.89686	0.89485	0.89286	0.89087	0.86957	0.84746	1
2	1.75672	1.75084	1.74499	1.73917	1.73340	1.72765	1.72194	1.71626	1.65595	1.59437	2
3	2.55718	2.54588	2.53467	2.52355	2.51251	2.50154	2.49066	2.47986	2.36607	2.25169	3
4	3.30840	3.29035	3.27245	3.25472	3.23714	3.21971	3.20244	3.18532	3.00644	2.82937	4
5	4.01252	3.98655	3.96086	3.93542	3.91025	3.88533	3.86066	3.83624	3.58316	3.33642	5
6	4.67170	4.63686	4.60243	4.56839	4.53475	4.50149	4.46861	4.43612	4.10195	3.78094	6
7	5.28814	5.24362	5.19968	5.15631	5.11350	5.07124	5.02953	4.98834	4.56812	4.17021	7
8	5.86399	5.80916	5.75511	5.70183	5.64931	5.59754	5.54650	5.49617	4.98655	4.51073	8
9	6.40141	6.33576	6.27113	6.20751	6.14488	6.08322	6.02250	5.96272	5.36178	4.80834	9
10	6.90250	6.82565	6.75010	6.67583	6.60280	6.53099	6.46039	6.39095	5.69795	5.06818	10
11	7.36931	7.28100	7.19430	7.10916	7.02557	6.94348	6.86285	6.78367	5.99887	5.29487	11
12	7.80384	7.70390	7.60591	7.50981	7.41557	7.32313	7.23247	7.14352	6.26801	5.49247	12
13	8.20800	8.09636	7.98703	7.87995	7.77506	7.67231	7.57164	7.47301	6.50856	5.66457	13
14	8.58364	8.46030	8.33966	8.22165	8.10619	7.99322	7.88267	7.77447	6.72338	5.81437	14
15	8.93253	8.79756	8.66571	8.53687	8.41098	8.28794	8.16767	8.05010	6.91509	5.94465	15
16	9.25636	9.10990	8.96698	8.82749	8.69134	8.55843	8.42867	8.30195	7.08607	6.05789	16
17	9.55675	9.39897	9.24517	9.09525	8.94908	8.80654	8.66752	8.53192	7.23847	6.15626	17
18	9.83523	9.66634	9.50191	9.34180	9.18587	9.03397	8.88599	8.74180	7.37423	6.24166	18
19	10.09324	9.91351	9.73872	9.56870	9.40329	9.24234	9.08569	8.93322	7.49508	6.31575	19
20	10.33217	10.14188	9.95702	9.77739	9.60282	9.43313	9.26815	9.10771	7.60262	6.38000	20
21	10.55331	10.35277	10.15816	9.96925	9.78584	9.60774	9.43475	9.26670	7.69825	6.43569	21
22	10.75788	10.54742	10.34339	10.14553	9.95363	9.76747	9.58682	9.41148	7.78326	6.48393	22
23	10.94704	10.72700	10.51389	10.30744	10.10739	9.91350	9.72554	9.54327	7.85879	6.52570	23
24	11.12187	10.89260	10.67076	10.45607	10.24823	10.04697	9.85203	9.66317	7.92586	6.56185	24
25	11.28338	11.04523	10.81503	10.59245	10.37716	10.16889	9.96733	9.77221	7.98540	6.59312	25
30	11.92245	11.64534	11.37863	11.12184	10.87451	10.63619	10.40647	10.18495	8.19608	6.69626	30
35	12.34780	12.04027	11.74539	11.46249	11.19097	10.93022	10.67971	10.43892	8.31095	6.74571	35
40	12.62872	12.29817	11.98221	11.67999	11.39076	11.11379	10.84841	10.59399	8.37310	6.76923	40
45	12.81303	12.46548	12.13412	11.81795	11.51608	11.22765	10.95189	10.68804	8.40650	6.78034	45
50	12.93328	12.57341	12.23102	11.90497	11.59424	11.29788	11.01500	10.74477	8.42435	6.78557	50

Present Value of a Series of Payments Increasing by Constant Amount

Amount of 1st Year Growth   5.0%

Holding Period	10.50%	10.75%	11.00%	Discount Rate 11.25%	11.50%	11.75%	12.00%	12.25%	15.00%	18.00%	
1	0.90498	0.90293	0.90090	0.89888	0.89686	0.89485	0.89286	0.89087	0.86957	0.84746	1
2	1.76491	1.75899	1.75310	1.74725	1.74144	1.73566	1.72991	1.72420	1.66352	1.60155	2
3	2.58019	2.56876	2.55741	2.54615	2.53498	2.52388	2.51287	2.50194	2.38678	2.27105	3
4	3.35153	3.33316	3.31496	3.29691	3.27902	3.26129	3.24371	3.22629	3.04430	2.86420	4
5	4.07993	4.05338	4.02710	4.00108	3.97534	3.94985	3.92463	3.89966	3.64091	3.38873	5
6	4.76659	4.73078	4.69540	4.66043	4.62586	4.59169	4.55792	4.52453	4.18132	3.85177	6
7	5.41285	5.36690	5.32155	5.27680	5.23262	5.18902	5.14597	5.10348	4.67004	4.25988	7
8	6.02019	5.96336	5.90735	5.85215	5.79773	5.74409	5.69121	5.63908	5.11136	4.61903	8
9	6.59018	6.52188	6.45465	6.38847	6.32333	6.25920	6.19607	6.13390	5.50932	4.93467	9
10	7.12443	7.04419	6.96532	6.88778	6.81156	6.73661	6.66293	6.59047	5.86774	5.21171	10
11	7.62459	7.53207	7.44124	7.35207	7.26452	7.17856	7.09414	7.01124	6.19016	5.45459	11
12	8.09231	7.98727	7.88430	7.78333	7.68432	7.58722	7.49199	7.39858	6.47986	5.66728	12
13	8.52924	8.41155	8.29632	8.18347	8.07296	7.96471	7.85867	7.75478	6.73991	5.85334	13
14	8.93700	8.80662	8.67911	8.55440	8.43240	8.31306	8.19629	8.08203	6.97310	6.01594	14
15	9.31720	9.17415	9.03442	8.89791	8.76455	8.63423	8.50687	8.38240	7.18202	6.15792	15
16	9.67140	9.51577	9.36393	9.21577	9.07119	8.93008	8.79234	8.65786	7.36903	6.28178	16
17	10.00110	9.83304	9.66927	9.50966	9.35407	9.20239	9.05450	8.91027	7.53630	6.38974	17
18	10.30775	10.12747	9.95199	9.78116	9.61482	9.45284	9.29507	9.14137	7.68579	6.48378	18
19	10.59277	10.40050	10.21358	10.03180	9.85500	9.68301	9.51567	9.35283	7.81929	6.56563	19
20	10.85749	10.65353	10.45544	10.26302	10.07607	9.89440	9.71782	9.54616	7.93844	6.63681	20
21	11.10320	10.88785	10.67893	10.47620	10.27943	10.08841	9.90294	9.72281	8.04470	6.69869	21
22	11.33112	11.11047	10.88530	10.67260	10.46637	10.26637	10.07236	9.88412	8.13941	6.75243	22
23	11.54241	11.30531	11.07575	10.85345	10.63812	10.42950	10.22731	10.03133	8.22378	6.79909	23
24	11.73818	11.49074	11.25142	11.01988	10.79583	10.57895	10.36896	10.16559	8.29889	6.83957	24
25	11.91947	11.66207	11.41335	11.17296	10.94055	10.71579	10.49837	10.28799	8.36572	6.87468	25
30	12.64120	12.33979	12.04984	11.77082	11.50221	11.24352	10.99429	10.75408	8.60361	6.99113	30
35	13.12609	12.79000	12.46793	12.15914	11.86295	11.57869	11.30576	11.04359	8.73454	7.04748	35
40	13.44883	13.08629	12.73999	12.40901	12.09248	11.78959	11.49957	11.22173	8.80593	7.07450	40
45	13.66197	13.27977	12.91567	12.56855	12.23740	11.92126	11.61923	11.33049	8.84455	7.08735	45
50	13.80182	13.40529	13.02836	12.66975	12.32830	12.00292	11.69262	11.39646	8.86531	7.09342	50

Amount of 1st Year Growth   6.0%

Holding Period	10.50%	10.75%	11.00%	Discount Rate 11.25%	11.50%	11.75%	12.00%	12.25%	15.00%	18.00%	
1	0.90498	0.90293	0.90090	0.89888	0.89686	0.89485	0.89286	0.89087	0.86957	0.84746	1
2	1.77310	1.76714	1.76122	1.75533	1.74948	1.74367	1.73788	1.73213	1.67108	1.60873	2
3	2.60320	2.59164	2.58016	2.56876	2.55745	2.54622	2.53508	2.52401	2.40750	2.29040	3
4	3.39467	3.37598	3.35746	3.33910	3.32090	3.30287	3.28499	3.26727	3.08216	2.89903	4
5	4.14735	4.12020	4.09334	4.06675	4.04043	4.01438	3.98860	3.96308	3.69866	3.44105	5
6	4.86147	4.82470	4.78837	4.75246	4.71697	4.68189	4.64722	4.61294	4.26069	3.92261	6
7	5.53755	5.49018	5.44343	5.39728	5.35174	5.30679	5.26241	5.21861	4.77196	4.34955	7
8	6.17639	6.11757	6.05960	6.00247	5.94615	5.89064	5.83593	5.78199	5.23616	4.72732	8
9	6.77895	6.70800	6.63817	6.56944	6.50179	6.43519	6.36963	6.30509	5.65687	5.06099	9
10	7.34636	7.26273	7.18053	7.09974	7.02031	6.94223	6.86547	6.78999	6.03754	5.35523	10
11	7.87986	7.78313	7.68819	7.59498	7.50348	7.41364	7.32543	7.23881	6.38145	5.61430	11
12	8.38078	8.27064	8.16268	8.05684	7.95306	7.85130	7.75151	7.65364	6.69171	5.84209	12
13	8.85047	8.72674	8.60561	8.48700	8.37085	8.25710	8.14569	8.03656	6.97126	6.04210	13
14	9.29037	9.15294	9.01856	8.88715	8.75862	8.63290	8.50991	8.38959	7.22283	6.21752	14
15	9.70188	9.55074	9.40313	9.25895	9.11811	8.98052	8.84608	8.71469	7.44895	6.37119	15
16	10.08643	9.92163	9.76088	9.60406	9.45105	9.30173	9.15601	9.01376	7.65199	6.50566	16
17	10.44544	10.26710	10.09336	9.92406	9.75907	9.59825	9.44147	9.28861	7.83413	6.62323	17
18	10.78027	10.58859	10.40206	10.22051	10.04378	9.87171	9.70415	9.54095	7.99736	6.72590	18
19	11.09229	10.88750	10.68843	10.49490	10.30671	10.12369	9.94565	9.77244	8.14351	6.81550	19
20	11.38280	11.16517	10.95386	10.74865	10.54933	10.35567	10.16750	9.98461	8.27426	6.89362	20
21	11.65309	11.42293	11.19970	10.98314	10.77302	10.56909	10.37113	10.17893	8.39115	6.96169	21
22	11.90435	11.66201	11.42721	11.19967	10.97911	10.76527	10.55790	10.35676	8.49556	7.02094	22
23	12.13778	11.88361	11.63762	11.39946	11.16885	10.94549	10.72909	10.51939	8.58877	7.07248	23
24	12.35450	12.08889	11.83207	11.58370	11.34343	11.11093	10.88589	10.66802	8.67191	7.11730	24
25	12.55556	12.27890	12.01168	11.75348	11.50394	11.26270	11.02942	10.80377	8.74603	7.15623	25
30	13.35995	13.03424	12.72105	12.41980	12.12991	11.85084	11.58211	11.32322	9.01113	7.28599	30
35	13.90437	13.53972	13.19047	12.85579	12.53493	12.22716	11.93182	11.64825	9.15813	7.34925	35
40	14.26893	13.87440	13.49778	13.13804	12.79420	12.46538	12.15073	11.84947	9.23876	7.37977	40
45	14.51091	14.09406	13.69722	13.31915	12.95872	12.61486	12.28657	11.97294	9.28260	7.39435	45
50	14.67036	14.23717	13.82570	13.43453	13.06235	12.70796	12.37024	12.04816	9.30626	7.40128	50

Present Value of a Series of Payments Increasing by Constant Amount

Amount of 1st Year Growth   7.0%

Holding Period	10.50%	10.75%	11.00%	11.25%	11.50%	11.75%	12.00%	12.25%	15.00%	18.00%	
				Discount Rate							
1	0.90498	0.90293	0.90090	0.89888	0.89686	0.89485	0.89286	0.89087	0.86957	0.84746	1
2	1.78129	1.77530	1.76934	1.76341	1.75753	1.75167	1.74585	1.74007	1.67864	1.61591	2
3	2.62622	2.61451	2.60290	2.59137	2.57992	2.56856	2.55728	2.54609	2.42821	2.30975	3
4	3.43780	3.41880	3.39996	3.38129	3.36278	3.34444	3.32626	3.30824	3.12003	2.93386	4
5	4.21476	4.18703	4.15958	4.13241	4.10552	4.07891	4.05257	4.02649	3.75642	3.49336	5
6	4.95635	4.91862	4.88134	4.84450	4.80808	4.77209	4.73652	4.70136	4.34006	3.99344	6
7	5.66226	5.61346	5.56530	5.51777	5.47086	5.42456	5.37886	5.33375	4.87389	4.43921	7
8	6.33259	6.27178	6.21185	6.15278	6.09457	6.03720	5.98064	5.92489	5.36097	4.83561	8
9	6.96772	6.89412	6.82169	6.75040	6.68024	6.61118	6.54319	6.47627	5.80442	5.18732	9
10	7.56830	7.48127	7.39575	7.31169	7.22907	7.14785	7.06801	6.98951	6.20733	5.49876	10
11	8.13514	8.03420	7.93513	7.83789	7.74243	7.64872	7.55672	7.46638	6.57274	5.77402	11
12	8.66924	8.55402	8.44107	8.33035	8.22181	8.11539	8.01103	7.90870	6.90356	6.01690	12
13	9.17171	9.04194	8.91490	8.79052	8.66874	8.54950	8.43271	8.31834	7.20261	6.23087	13
14	9.64373	9.49926	9.35801	9.21989	9.08483	8.95274	8.82354	8.69715	7.47255	6.41910	14
15	10.08656	9.92732	9.77184	9.61999	9.47168	9.32681	9.18528	9.04699	7.71588	6.58446	15
16	10.50147	10.32750	10.15784	9.99234	9.83090	9.67338	9.51968	9.36967	7.93495	6.72955	16
17	10.88978	10.70117	10.51746	10.33847	10.16407	9.99410	9.82844	9.66695	8.13196	6.85671	17
18	11.25279	11.04972	10.85214	10.65987	10.47274	10.29058	10.11323	9.94053	8.30892	6.96803	18
19	11.59181	11.37449	11.16329	10.95800	10.75842	10.56436	10.37563	10.19205	8.46772	7.06538	19
20	11.90812	11.67682	11.45229	11.23428	11.02258	10.81694	10.61717	10.42306	8.61008	7.15044	20
21	12.20297	11.95800	11.72047	11.49009	11.26660	11.04976	10.83932	10.63504	8.73760	7.22469	21
22	12.47759	12.21930	11.96912	11.72673	11.49185	11.26417	11.04344	10.82940	8.85171	7.28944	22
23	12.73315	12.46192	12.19948	11.94548	11.69958	11.46148	11.23087	11.00745	8.95376	7.34588	23
24	12.97081	12.68703	12.41273	12.14752	11..89103	11.64291	11.40282	11.17044	9.04493	7.39502	24
25	13.19165	12.89574	12.61000	12.33400	12.06733	11.80961	11.56046	11.31954	9.12635	7.43779	25
30	14.07870	13.72869	13.39226	13.06877	12.75760	12.45817	12.16993	11.89235	9.41866	7.58086	30
35	14.68266	14.28945	13.91300	13.55244	13.20691	12.87563	12.55787	12.25292	9.58171	7.65103	35
40	15.08904	14.66252	14.25557	13.86706	13.49592	13.14117	12.80189	12.47721	9.67159	7.68504	40
45	15.35985	14.90835	14.47877	14.06975	13.68004	13.30846	12.95391	12.61539	9.72065	7.70136	45
50	15.53889	15.06904	14.62304	14.19931	13.79641	13.41301	13.04787	12.69985	9.74722	7.70913	50

Amount of 1st Year Growth   8.0%

Holding Period	10.50%	10.75%	11.00%	11.25%	11.50%	11.75%	12.00%	12.25%	15.00%	18.00%	
				Discount Rate							
1	0.90498	0.90293	0.90090	0.89888	0.89686	0.89485	0.89286	0.89087	0.86957	0.84746	1
2	1.78948	1.78345	1.77745	1.77149	1.76557	1.75968	1.75383	1.74801	1.68620	1.62310	2
3	2.64923	2.63739	2.62564	2.61397	2.60239	2.59090	2.57949	2.56817	2.44892	2.32911	3
4	3.48094	3.46161	3.44246	3.42348	3.40467	3.38602	3.36753	3.34921	3.15789	2.96869	4
5	4.28218	4.25385	4.22582	4.19807	4.17061	4.14344	4.11654	4.08991	3.81417	3.54567	5
6	5.05123	5.01254	4.97431	4.93653	4.89920	4.86229	4.82582	4.78977	4.41943	4.06428	6
7	5.78697	5.73674	5.68717	5.63825	5.58997	5.54233	5.49530	5.44888	4.97581	4.52888	7
8	6.48879	6.42599	6.36409	6.30310	6.24299	6.18375	6.12536	6.06780	5.48578	4.94390	8
9	7.15650	7.08025	7.00521	6.93137	6.85869	6.78716	6.71676	6.64745	5.95197	5.31365	9
10	7.79023	7.69982	7.61097	7.52365	7.43783	7.35347	7.27055	7.18903	6.37714	5.64228	10
11	8.39042	8.28527	8.18208	8.08080	7.98139	7.88381	7.78801	7.69395	6.76440	5.93374	11
12	8.95771	8.83739	8.71946	8.60387	8.49056	8.37947	8.27056	8.16376	7.11541	6.19171	12
13	9.49295	9.35713	9.22419	9.09405	8.96664	8.84189	8.71974	8.60011	7.43396	6.41963	13
14	9.99710	9.84558	9.69746	9.55264	9.41105	9.27258	9.13716	9.00471	7.72228	6.62067	14
15	10.47123	10.30391	10.14055	9.98103	9.82525	9.67310	9.52448	9.37928	7.98281	6.79773	15
16	10.91651	10.73337	10.55479	10.38063	10.21075	10.04503	9.88335	9.72557	8.21791	6.95344	16
17	11.33412	11.13524	10.94155	10.75288	10.56906	10.38996	10.21542	10.04529	8.42979	7.09019	17
18	11.72531	11.51084	11.30221	11.09922	10.90170	10.70945	10.52231	10.34011	8.62049	7.21015	18
19	12.09134	11.86148	11.63814	11.42110	11.21013	11.00504	10.80561	10.61166	8.79193	7.31526	19
20	12.43344	12.18846	11.95071	11.71991	11.49583	11.27822	11.06685	10.86151	8.94591	7.40725	20
21	12.75286	12.49308	12.24124	11.99704	11.76019	11.53043	11.30751	11.09116	9.08405	7.48769	21
22	13.05082	12.77660	12.51103	12.25380	12.00458	11.76308	11.52899	11.30204	9.20786	7.55795	22
23	13.32852	13.04023	12.76134	12.49149	12.23031	11.97747	11.73264	11.49551	9.31874	7.61927	23
24	13.58712	13.28518	12.99339	12.71134	12.43863	12.17489	11.91975	11.67287	9.41796	7.67275	24
25	13.82774	13.51257	13.20832	12.91452	12.63072	12.35652	12.09151	11.83532	9.50666	7.71934	25
30	14.79745	14.42314	14.06347	13.71775	13.38530	13.06550	12.75775	12.46148	9.82619	7.87572	30
35	15.46095	15.03917	14.63554	14.24908	13.87889	13.52410	13.18392	12.85758	10.00530	7.95280	35
40	15.90915	15.45064	15.01336	14.59608	14.19764	13.81696	13.45305	13.10495	10.10442	7.99031	40
45	16.20879	15.72264	15.26032	14.82036	14.40136	14.00206	13.62125	13.25784	10.15870	8.00837	45
50	16.40743	15.90092	15.42038	14.96409	14.53046	14.11805	13.72549	13.35154	10.18818	8.01699	50

Present Value of a Series of Payments Increasing by Constant Amount

Amount of 1st Year Growth 9.0%

Holding Period	Discount Rate 10.50%	10.75%	11.00%	11.25%	11.50%	11.75%	12.00%	12.25%	15.00%	18.00%	
1	0.90498	0.90293	0.90090	0.89888	0.89686	0.89485	0.89286	0.89087	0.86957	0.84746	1
2	1.79767	1.79160	1.78557	1.77957	1.77361	1.76769	1.76180	1.75594	1.69376	1.63028	2
3	2.67224	2.66026	2.64838	2.63658	2.62486	2.61324	2.60170	2.59025	2.46963	2.34846	3
4	3.52407	3.50443	3.48496	3.46567	3.44655	3.42759	3.40881	3.39019	3.19576	3.00351	4
5	4.34959	4.32068	4.29206	4.26374	4.23571	4.20796	4.18051	4.15333	3.87192	3.59798	5
6	5.14611	5.10646	5.06729	5.02857	4.99031	4.95250	4.91512	4.87818	4.49879	4.13511	6
7	5.91168	5.86002	5.80904	5.75873	5.70909	5.66010	5.61174	5.56401	5.07774	4.61855	7
8	6.64499	6.58019	6.51634	6.45342	6.39141	6.33030	6.27007	6.21071	5.61059	5.05220	8
9	7.34527	7.26637	7.18873	7.11233	7.03715	6.96315	6.89032	6.81863	6.09952	5.43998	9
10	8.01216	7.91836	7.82619	7.73561	7.64659	7.55909	7.47309	7.38855	6.54692	5.78581	10
11	8.64569	8.53634	8.42902	8.32371	8.22034	8.11889	8.01930	7.92152	6.95531	6.09345	11
12	9.24618	9.12076	8.99785	8.87738	8.75930	8.64355	8.53008	8.41882	7.32726	6.36652	12
13	9.81419	9.67232	9.53348	9.39757	9.26453	9.13429	9.00676	8.88189	7.66532	6.60840	13
14	10.35046	10.19190	10.03691	9.88539	9.73726	9.59242	9.45079	9.31227	7.97200	6.82225	14
15	10.85591	10.68050	10.50926	10.34207	10.17882	10.01939	9.86368	9.71158	8.24974	7.01100	15
16	11.33154	11.13924	10.95174	10.76891	10.59060	10.41668	10.24702	10.08148	8.50087	7.17732	16
17	11.77846	11.56931	11.36565	11.16728	10.97406	10.78581	10.60239	10.42363	8.72761	7.32367	17
18	12.19783	11.97197	11.75229	11.53858	11.33065	11.12832	10.93139	10.73969	8.93205	7.45227	18
19	12.59086	12.34847	12.11300	11.88420	11.66184	11.44571	11.23559	11.03127	9.11615	7.56513	19
20	12.95875	12.70011	12.44913	12.20554	11.96908	11.73949	11.51653	11.29996	9.28173	7.66406	20
21	13.30275	13.02816	12.76201	12.50398	12.25378	12.01111	11.77569	11.54727	9.43049	7.75069	21
22	13.62406	13.33389	13.05294	12.78087	12.51732	12.26198	12.01453	11.77467	9.56401	7.82646	22
23	13.92390	13.61854	13.32321	13.03750	12.76104	12.49346	12.23442	11.98357	9.68373	7.89267	23
24	14.20343	13.88332	13.57404	13.27515	12.98623	12.70687	12.43668	12.17529	9.79098	7.95047	24
25	14.46383	14.12941	13.80664	13.49503	13.19411	12.90343	12.62256	12.35109	9.88697	8.00090	25
30	15.51620	15.11759	14.73468	14.36673	14.01300	13.67283	13.34557	13.03061	10.23371	8.17058	30
35	16.23923	15.78890	15.35808	14.94573	14.55087	14.17257	13.80997	13.46225	10.42889	8.25457	35
40	16.72925	16.23875	15.77115	15.32510	14.89936	14.49276	14.10421	13.73269	10.53725	8.29557	40
45	17.05774	16.53693	16.04187	15.57096	15.12268	14.69566	14.28860	13.90030	10.59675	8.31537	45
50	17.27596	16.73280	16.21772	15.72886	15.26452	14.82309	14.40312	14.00324	10.62914	8.32485	50

Amount of 1st Year Growth 10.0%

Holding Period	Discount Rate 10.50%	10.75%	11.00%	11.25%	11.50%	11.75%	12.00%	12.25%	15.00%	18.00%	
1	0.90498	0.90293	0.90090	0.89888	0.89686	0.89485	0.89286	0.89087	0.86957	0.84746	1
2	1.80586	1.79975	1.79369	1.78765	1.78166	1.77570	1.76977	1.76388	1.70132	1.63746	2
3	2.69525	2.68314	2.67112	2.65918	2.64734	2.63558	2.62391	2.61232	2.49034	2.36782	3
4	3.56721	3.54725	3.52747	3.50786	3.48843	3.46917	3.45008	3.43116	3.23362	3.03834	4
5	4.41701	4.38750	4.35830	4.32940	4.30080	4.27249	4.24448	4.21675	3.92967	3.65030	5
6	5.24099	5.20038	5.16026	5.12061	5.08142	5.04270	5.00442	4.96660	4.57816	4.20594	6
7	6.03639	5.98330	5.93091	5.87922	5.82821	5.77787	5.72818	5.67915	5.17966	4.70822	7
8	6.80119	6.73440	6.66859	6.60374	6.53983	6.47685	6.41478	6.35361	5.73539	5.16049	8
9	7.53404	7.45249	7.37225	7.29330	7.21560	7.13914	7.06388	6.98981	6.24707	5.56631	9
10	8.23409	8.13690	8.04140	7.94756	7.85534	7.76471	7.67563	7.58807	6.71672	5.92933	10
11	8.90097	8.78740	8.67597	8.56662	8.45930	8.35397	8.25058	8.14910	7.14660	6.25317	11
12	9.53465	9.40413	9.27623	9.15089	9.02805	8.90764	8.78960	8.67388	7.53911	6.54133	12
13	10.13543	9.98751	9.84277	9.70110	9.56243	9.42668	9.29379	9.16366	7.89667	6.79716	13
14	10.70383	10.53822	10.37635	10.21814	10.06348	9.91226	9.76441	9.61982	8.22173	7.02383	14
15	11.24059	11.05708	10.87796	10.70311	10.53239	10.36568	10.20288	10.04387	8.51667	7.22426	15
16	11.74658	11.54510	11.34870	11.15719	10.97045	10.78833	10.61069	10.43739	8.78383	7.40121	16
17	12.22280	12.00338	11.78974	11.58169	11.37906	11.18167	10.98936	10.80198	9.02544	7.55715	17
18	12.67036	12.43309	12.20236	11.97793	11.75961	11.54719	11.34047	11.13927	9.24362	7.69440	18
19	13.09038	12.83547	12.58786	12.34730	12.11356	11.88639	11.66557	11.45089	9.44036	7.81501	19
20	13.48407	13.21176	12.94756	12.69117	12.44233	12.20076	11.96620	11.73841	9.61755	7.92088	20
21	13.85263	13.56324	13.28278	13.01093	12.74737	12.49178	12.24388	12.00338	9.77694	8.01369	21
22	14.19729	13.89118	13.59486	13.30793	13.03006	12.76088	12.50007	12.24731	9.92016	8.09496	22
23	14.51927	14.19685	13.88507	13.58352	13.29177	13.00946	12.73619	12.47163	10.04872	8.16606	23
24	14.81975	14.48147	14.15470	13.83897	13.53383	13.23885	12.95360	12.67771	10.16400	8.22820	24
25	15.09992	14.74625	14.40497	14.07555	13.75750	13.45034	13.15360	12.86687	10.26729	8.28245	25
30	16.23495	15.81204	15.40589	15.01570	14.64070	14.28016	13.93339	13.59975	10.64124	8.46545	30
35	17.01752	16.53862	16.08062	15.64238	15.22285	14.82104	14.43602	14.06691	10.85247	8.55635	35
40	17.54936	17.02687	16.52894	16.05412	15.60108	15.16855	14.75537	14.36043	10.97008	8.60084	40
45	17.90668	17.35122	16.82342	16.32156	15.84400	15.38926	14.95594	14.54275	11.03481	8.62238	45
50	18.14450	17.56467	17.01506	16.49364	15.99857	15.52813	15.08074	14.65493	11.07010	8.63270	50

Present Value of a Series of Payments Decreasing by a Constant Amount

Amount of 1st Year Decline   3.00%

Holding Period	5.50%	5.75%	6.00%	6.25%	Discount Rate 6.50%	6.75%	7.00%	7.25%	7.50%	7.75%	
1	0.94787	0.94563	0.94340	0.94118	0.93897	0.93677	0.93458	0.93240	0.93023	0.92807	1
2	1.81937	1.81301	1.80669	1.80042	1.79418	1.78798	1.78182	1.77569	1.76961	1.76356	2
3	2.61988	2.60786	2.59593	2.58410	2.57235	2.56070	2.54914	2.53766	2.52627	2.51496	3
4	3.35445	3.33551	3.31674	3.29814	3.27972	3.26146	3.24337	3.22544	3.20768	3.19007	4
5	4.02777	4.00090	3.97433	3.94803	3.92201	3.89627	3.87080	3.84559	3.82065	3.79596	5
6	4.64423	4.60867	4.57354	4.53884	4.50455	4.47067	4.43719	4.40411	4.37142	4.33911	6
7	5.20793	5.16311	5.11889	5.07527	5.03222	4.98975	4.94784	4.90649	4.86567	4.82540	7
8	5.72269	5.66821	5.61455	5.56167	5.50957	5.45822	5.40763	5.35777	5.30863	5.26020	8
9	6.19209	6.12772	6.06439	6.00207	5.94075	5.88041	5.82102	5.76257	5.70503	5.64840	9
10	6.61945	6.54509	6.47202	6.40021	6.32964	6.26029	6.19212	6.12510	6.05922	5.99446	10
11	7.00789	6.92354	6.84077	6.75953	6.67979	6.60152	6.52468	6.44924	6.37516	6.30243	11
12	7.36030	7.26608	7.17374	7.08322	6.99448	6.90748	6.82217	6.73851	6.65647	6.57600	12
13	7.67938	7.57549	7.47380	7.37423	7.27673	7.18125	7.08775	6.99615	6.90643	6.81852	13
14	7.96764	7.85436	7.74360	7.63528	7.52933	7.42570	7.32431	7.22512	7.12805	7.03305	14
15	8.22744	8.10510	7.98561	7.86889	7.75485	7.64342	7.53453	7.42810	7.32407	7.22236	15
16	8.46096	8.32994	8.20212	8.07739	7.95565	7.83683	7.72084	7.60758	7.49698	7.38896	16
17	8.67024	8.53096	8.39523	8.26291	8.13392	8.00813	7.88546	7.76579	7.64906	7.53515	17
18	8.85715	8.71009	8.56690	8.42746	8.29164	8.15934	8.03043	7.90480	7.78236	7.66300	18
19	9.02348	8.86910	8.71893	8.57284	8.43067	8.29231	8.15762	8.02648	7.89877	7.77438	19
20	9.17085	9.00966	8.85301	8.70074	8.55271	8.40875	8.26874	8.13253	8.00000	7.87101	20
21	9.30080	9.13330	8.97067	8.81273	8.65930	8.51022	8.36535	8.22452	8.08760	7.95444	21
22	9.41473	9.24145	9.07335	8.91022	8.75188	8.59815	8.44886	8.30385	8.16297	8.02606	22
23	9.51397	9.33543	9.16236	8.99453	8.83176	8.67383	8.52058	8.37183	8.22740	8.08713	23
24	9.59973	9.41646	9.23892	9.06689	8.90014	8.73848	8.58170	8.42961	8.28204	8.13882	24
25	9.67316	9.48567	9.30416	9.12840	8.95814	8.79318	8.63329	8.47828	8.32796	8.18214	25
30	9.88951	9.68835	9.49407	9.30636	9.12494	8.94954	8.77989	8.61575	8.45688	8.30308	30
35	9.92653	9.72271	9.52596	9.33598	9.15244	8.97508	8.80361	8.63779	8.47737	8.32212	35
40	9.85653	9.65879	9.46759	9.28266	9.10373	8.93056	8.76293	8.60059	8.44335	8.29100	40
45	9.72772	9.54248	9.36254	9.18775	9.01797	8.85305	8.69284	8.53722	8.38603	8.23914	45
50	9.57160	9.40314	9.23814	9.07666	8.91873	8.76438	8.61359	8.46637	8.32267	8.18246	50

Amount of 1st Year Decline   4.0%

Holding Period	5.50%	5.75%	6.00%	6.25%	Discount Rate 6.50%	6.75%	7.00%	7.25%	7.50%	7.75%	
1	0.94787	0.94563	0.94340	0.94118	0.93897	0.93677	0.93458	0.93240	0.93023	0.92807	1
2	1.81038	1.80407	1.79779	1.79156	1.78536	1.77920	1.77308	1.76700	1.76095	1.75494	2
3	2.59387	2.58201	2.57024	2.55857	2.54698	2.53548	2.52407	2.51275	2.50152	2.49036	3
4	3.30422	3.28567	3.26728	3.24907	3.23103	3.21314	3.19542	3.17786	3.16046	3.14321	4
5	3.94693	3.92082	3.89498	3.86942	3.84413	3.81910	3.79433	3.76982	3.74557	3.72157	5
6	4.52713	4.49283	4.45895	4.42547	4.39239	4.35971	4.32740	4.29548	4.26394	4.23276	6
7	5.04958	5.00670	4.96439	4.92265	4.88146	4.84081	4.80069	4.76111	4.72203	4.68347	7
8	5.51873	5.46705	5.41613	5.36596	5.31650	5.26777	5.21974	5.17240	5.12574	5.07974	8
9	5.93872	5.87819	5.81862	5.76000	5.70230	5.64552	5.58962	5.53459	5.48041	5.42708	9
10	6.31339	6.24410	6.17599	6.10905	6.04325	5.97856	5.91496	5.85243	5.79094	5.73047	10
11	6.64634	6.56849	6.49207	6.41704	6.34338	6.27104	6.20002	6.13026	6.06174	5.99445	11
12	6.94089	6.85479	6.77037	6.68759	6.60640	6.52677	6.44866	6.37204	6.29686	6.22310	12
13	7.20014	7.10619	7.01417	6.92403	6.83573	6.74921	6.66444	6.58137	6.49996	6.42015	13
14	7.42697	7.32563	7.22647	7.12945	7.03450	6.94156	6.85060	6.76154	6.67435	6.58896	14
15	7.62406	7.51584	7.41007	7.30667	7.20558	7.10673	7.01007	6.91553	6.82305	6.73258	15
16	7.79390	7.67936	7.56753	7.45830	7.35162	7.24740	7.14557	7.04606	6.94881	6.85374	16
17	7.93878	7.81850	7.70122	7.58675	7.47503	7.36599	7.25953	7.15559	7.05409	6.95495	17
18	8.06085	7.93551	7.81333	7.69420	7.57803	7.46473	7.35421	7.24637	7.14114	7.03844	18
19	8.16209	8.03230	7.90587	7.78269	7.66266	7.54567	7.43163	7.32044	7.21200	7.10624	19
20	8.24434	8.11075	7.98070	7.85408	7.73077	7.61067	7.49365	7.37963	7.26850	7.16018	20
21	8.30932	8.17257	8.03953	7.91007	7.78407	7.66140	7.54195	7.42562	7.31230	7.20189	21
22	8.35858	8.21934	8.08394	7.95223	7.82410	7.69942	7.57807	7.45993	7.34489	7.23286	22
23	8.39361	8.25251	8.11535	7.98199	7.85230	7.72613	7.60338	7.48392	7.36763	7.25441	23
24	8.41574	8.27342	8.13511	8.00066	7.86994	7.74282	7.61915	7.49883	7.38174	7.26775	24
25	8.42623	8.28331	8.14443	8.00945	7.87823	7.75063	7.62652	7.50579	7.38830	7.27394	25
30	8.34144	8.20413	8.07048	7.94037	7.81370	7.69033	7.57017	7.45311	7.33905	7.22790	30
35	8.10520	7.98573	7.86854	7.75361	7.64094	7.53049	7.42226	7.31621	7.21232	7.11056	35
40	7.79333	7.70072	7.60802	7.51543	7.42313	7.33127	7.24000	7.14943	7.05967	6.97081	40
45	7.45438	7.39459	7.33145	7.26550	7.19722	7.12702	7.05528	6.98234	6.90849	6.83400	45
50	7.11829	7.09457	7.06357	7.02624	6.98347	6.93601	6.88454	6.82968	6.77196	6.71185	50

Present Value of a Series of Payments Decreasing by a Constant Amount

Amount of 1st Year Decline 5.0%

Holding Period	5.50%	5.75%	6.00%	6.25%	6.50%	6.75%	7.00%	7.25%	7.50%	7.75%	
1	0.94787	0.94563	0.94340	0.94118	0.93897	0.93677	0.93458	0.93240	0.93023	0.92807	1
2	1.80140	1.79513	1.78889	1.78270	1.77654	1.77043	1.76435	1.75830	1.75230	1.74633	2
3	2.56785	2.55615	2.54455	2.53303	2.52161	2.51027	2.49901	2.48785	2.47676	2.46576	3
4	3.25398	3.23582	3.21783	3.20000	3.18233	3.16482	3.14748	3.13028	3.11324	3.09636	4
5	3.86609	3.84073	3.81564	3.79081	3.76624	3.74192	3.71786	3.69405	3.67049	3.64717	5
6	4.41003	4.37699	4.34436	4.31211	4.28024	4.24874	4.21762	4.18686	4.15646	4.12641	6
7	4.89123	4.85029	4.80990	4.77003	4.73069	4.69187	4.65355	4.61572	4.57839	4.54154	7
8	5.31477	5.26589	5.21771	5.17024	5.12344	5.07732	5.03185	4.98703	4.94285	4.89928	8
9	5.68535	5.62866	5.57285	5.51793	5.46385	5.41062	5.35821	5.30661	5.25580	5.20576	9
10	6.00733	5.94311	5.87997	5.81789	5.75685	5.69683	5.63780	5.57975	5.52265	5.46649	10
11	6.28479	6.21344	6.14336	6.07455	6.00696	5.94057	5.87535	5.81128	5.74832	5.68647	11
12	6.52148	6.44350	6.36700	6.29195	6.21832	6.14606	6.07516	6.00557	5.93726	5.87021	12
13	6.72091	6.63688	6.55454	6.47383	6.39472	6.31717	6.24114	6.16659	6.09348	6.02179	13
14	6.88631	6.79689	6.70934	6.62361	6.53966	6.45743	6.37688	6.29796	6.22064	6.14488	14
15	7.02069	6.92658	6.83452	6.74445	6.65631	6.57004	6.48561	6.40296	6.32203	6.24279	15
16	7.12683	7.02878	6.93293	6.83922	6.74758	6.65796	6.57030	6.48454	6.40063	6.31852	16
17	7.20732	7.10610	7.00721	6.91058	6.81614	6.72384	6.63361	6.54539	6.45912	6.37475	17
18	7.26454	7.16093	7.05976	6.96095	6.86443	6.77013	6.67799	6.58794	6.49993	6.41389	18
19	7.30070	7.19550	7.09281	6.99255	6.89465	6.79904	6.70564	6.61439	6.52524	6.43810	19
20	7.31783	7.21184	7.10840	7.00742	6.90884	6.81258	6.71856	6.62673	6.53701	6.44934	20
21	7.31783	7.21184	7.10840	7.00742	6.90884	6.81258	6.71856	6.62673	6.53701	6.44934	21
22	7.30244	7.19723	7.09452	6.99425	6.89633	6.80070	6.70728	6.61601	6.52682	6.43966	22
23	7.27325	7.16959	7.06834	6.96945	6.87284	6.77843	6.68618	6.59601	6.50787	6.42169	23
24	7.23175	7.13038	7.03130	6.93444	6.83975	6.74715	6.65661	6.56805	6.48143	6.39669	24
25	7.17931	7.08095	6.98470	6.89051	6.79832	6.70809	6.61976	6.53329	6.44863	6.36574	25
30	6.79336	6.71990	6.64689	6.57439	6.50245	6.43112	6.36045	6.29047	6.22122	6.15272	30
35	6.28386	6.24875	6.21111	6.17125	6.12943	6.08591	6.04091	5.99463	5.94728	5.89900	35
40	5.73013	5.74265	5.74846	5.74821	5.74253	5.73198	5.71707	5.69827	5.67599	5.65062	40
45	5.18105	5.24669	5.30035	5.34324	5.37646	5.40099	5.41773	5.42747	5.43096	5.42885	45
50	4.66498	4.78600	4.88899	4.97583	5.04820	5.10764	5.15549	5.19299	5.22124	5.24123	50

Amount of 1st Year Decline 6.0%

Holding Period	5.50%	5.75%	6.00%	6.25%	6.50%	6.75%	7.00%	7.25%	7.50%	7.75%	
1	0.94787	0.94563	0.94340	0.94118	0.93897	0.93677	0.93458	0.93240	0.93023	0.92807	1
2	1.79241	1.78618	1.77999	1.77384	1.76773	1.76165	1.75561	1.74961	1.74365	1.73772	2
3	2.54183	2.53030	2.51886	2.50750	2.49623	2.48505	2.47395	2.46294	2.45201	2.44116	3
4	3.20375	3.18598	3.16837	3.15093	3.13364	3.11651	3.09953	3.08270	3.06603	3.04950	4
5	3.78525	3.76064	3.73629	3.71219	3.68835	3.66475	3.64140	3.61829	3.59541	3.57277	5
6	4.29292	4.26116	4.22976	4.19874	4.16808	4.13778	4.10784	4.07824	4.04898	4.02007	6
7	4.73288	4.69389	4.65540	4.61742	4.57993	4.54292	4.50640	4.47034	4.43475	4.39961	7
8	5.11081	5.06472	5.01930	4.97452	4.93038	4.88686	4.84396	4.80166	4.75996	4.71883	8
9	5.43198	5.37912	5.32709	5.27585	5.22540	5.17573	5.12681	5.07863	5.03118	4.98444	9
10	5.70128	5.64212	5.58395	5.52673	5.47046	5.41510	5.36065	5.30708	5.25437	5.20251	10
11	5.92324	5.85838	5.79466	5.73206	5.67054	5.61009	5.55069	5.49230	5.43490	5.37849	11
12	6.10207	6.03221	5.96363	5.89632	5.83024	5.76536	5.70165	5.63909	5.57766	5.51731	12
13	6.24167	6.16757	6.09491	6.02363	5.95372	5.88513	5.81784	5.75181	5.68701	5.62342	13
14	6.34564	6.26815	6.19221	6.11778	6.04482	5.97329	5.90316	5.83439	5.76694	5.70079	14
15	6.41731	6.33732	6.25898	6.18223	6.10703	6.03336	5.96115	5.89038	5.82102	5.75301	15
16	6.45976	6.37820	6.29834	6.22014	6.14354	6.06852	5.99502	5.92302	5.85245	5.78330	16
17	6.47586	6.39366	6.31320	6.23441	6.15726	6.08170	6.00769	5.93519	5.86415	5.79455	17
18	6.46823	6.38635	6.30619	6.22769	6.15082	6.07553	6.00177	5.92951	5.85871	5.78933	18
19	6.43931	6.35870	6.27975	6.20241	6.12664	6.05240	5.97965	5.90835	5.83847	5.76996	19
20	6.39132	6.31294	6.23609	6.16076	6.08691	6.01449	5.94347	5.87382	5.80551	5.73850	20
21	6.32635	6.25111	6.17726	6.10477	6.03361	5.96375	5.89517	5.82783	5.76171	5.69679	21
22	6.24629	6.17511	6.10511	6.03627	5.96856	5.90197	5.83648	5.77208	5.70875	5.64646	22
23	6.15289	6.08666	6.02134	5.95691	5.89338	5.83073	5.76898	5.70811	5.64811	5.58898	23
24	6.04776	5.98734	5.92749	5.86822	5.80955	5.75149	5.69406	5.63727	5.58112	5.52562	24
25	5.93238	5.87859	5.82497	5.77156	5.71841	5.66554	5.61299	5.56080	5.50897	5.45754	25
30	5.24528	5.23568	5.22330	5.20840	5.19120	5.17192	5.15073	5.12783	5.10338	5.07754	30
35	4.46252	4.51176	4.55368	4.58888	4.61793	4.64132	4.65956	4.67306	4.68223	4.68745	35
40	3.66693	3.78459	3.88889	3.98098	4.06193	4.13269	4.19414	4.24710	4.29230	4.33042	40
45	2.90771	3.09879	3.26925	3.42099	3.55571	3.67496	3.78017	3.87260	3.95343	4.02371	45
50	2.21167	2.47744	2.71442	2.92541	3.11294	3.27927	3.42644	3.55630	3.67053	3.77061	50

Present Value of a Series of Payments Decreasing by a Constant Amount

Amount of 1st Year Decline 7.0%

Holding Period	5.50%	5.75%	6.00%	6.25%	6.50%	6.75%	7.00%	7.25%	7.50%	7.75%	
1	0.94787	0.94563	0.94340	0.94118	0.93897	0.93677	0.93458	0.93240	0.93023	0.92807	1
2	1.78343	1.77724	1.77109	1.76498	1.75891	1.75288	1.74688	1.74092	1.73499	1.72910	2
3	2.51582	2.50445	2.49317	2.48197	2.47086	2.45984	2.44889	2.43803	2.42726	2.41656	3
4	3.15352	3.13614	3.11892	3.10186	3.08495	3.06819	3.05158	3.03512	3.01881	3.00264	4
5	3.70441	3.68056	3.65695	3.63358	3.61046	3.58758	3.56493	3.54252	3.52033	3.49837	5
6	4.17582	4.14532	4.11517	4.08537	4.05593	4.02682	3.99805	3.96962	3.94151	3.91372	6
7	4.57454	4.53748	4.50090	4.46480	4.42916	4.39398	4.35925	4.32496	4.29111	4.25768	7
8	4.90685	4.86356	4.82088	4.77881	4.73732	4.69641	4.65607	4.61629	4.57706	4.53837	8
9	5.17861	5.12959	5.08132	5.03378	4.98695	4.94083	4.89540	4.85065	4.80656	4.76312	9
10	5.39522	5.34113	5.28792	5.23557	5.18406	5.13337	5.08349	5.03440	4.98608	4.93852	10
11	5.56169	5.50333	5.44596	5.38957	5.33413	5.27962	5.22602	5.17332	5.12149	5.07051	11
12	5.68267	5.62092	5.56026	5.50068	5.44215	5.38465	5.32814	5.27262	5.21805	5.16442	12
13	5.76244	5.69827	5.63528	5.57344	5.51272	5.45309	5.39454	5.33703	5.28054	5.22505	13
14	5.80497	5.73941	5.67509	5.61195	5.54999	5.48916	5.42944	5.37081	5.31324	5.25670	14
15	5.81393	5.74806	5.68343	5.62001	5.55776	5.49667	5.43669	5.37781	5.32000	5.26323	15
16	5.79270	5.72762	5.66375	5.60105	5.53951	5.47908	5.41975	5.36149	5.30428	5.24809	16
17	5.74440	5.68123	5.61918	5.55824	5.49837	5.43955	5.38176	5.32498	5.26919	5.21435	17
18	5.67193	5.61178	5.55262	5.49444	5.43721	5.38092	5.32555	5.27108	5.21750	5.16478	18
19	5.57792	5.52190	5.46669	5.41226	5.35863	5.30576	5.25366	5.20231	5.15170	5.10182	19
20	5.46481	5.41403	5.36379	5.31410	5.26497	5.21640	5.16838	5.12092	5.07401	5.02766	20
21	5.33487	5.29038	5.24613	5.20212	5.15838	5.11493	5.07177	5.02893	4.98642	4.94423	21
22	5.19015	5.15300	5.11570	5.07828	5.04078	5.00324	4.96569	4.92816	4.89067	4.85326	22
23	5.03253	5.00374	4.97433	4.94437	4.91392	4.88303	4.85178	4.82020	4.78834	4.75626	23
24	4.86377	4.84430	4.82367	4.80199	4.77935	4.75583	4.73152	4.70649	4.68081	4.65456	24
25	4.68545	4.67623	4.66523	4.65261	4.63849	4.62300	4.60623	4.58830	4.56931	4.54934	25
30	3.69720	3.75145	3.79972	3.84242	3.87996	3.91271	3.94101	3.96519	3.98555	4.00236	30
35	2.64118	2.77478	2.89626	3.00652	3.10642	3.19674	3.27820	3.35148	3.41718	3.47589	35
40	1.60373	1.82652	2.02932	2.21376	2.38133	2.53340	2.67122	2.79594	2.90862	3.01023	40
45	0.63437	0.95089	1.23816	1.49874	1.73496	1.94894	2.14261	2.31773	2.47589	2.61857	45
50	-0.24164	0.16887	0.53984	0.87500	1.17768	1.45090	1.69739	1.91962	2.11981	2.30000	50

Amount of 1st Year Decline 8.0%

Holding Period	5.50%	5.75%	6.00%	6.25%	6.50%	6.75%	7.00%	7.25%	7.50%	7.75%	
1	0.94787	0.94563	0.94340	0.94118	0.93897	0.93677	0.93458	0.93240	0.93023	0.92807	1
2	1.77444	1.76830	1.76219	1.75612	1.75009	1.74410	1.73814	1.73222	1.72634	1.72049	2
3	2.48980	2.47859	2.46747	2.45644	2.44549	2.43462	2.42383	2.41313	2.40251	2.39196	3
4	3.10328	3.08630	3.06946	3.05278	3.03625	3.01987	3.00363	2.98754	2.97159	2.95579	4
5	3.62358	3.60047	3.57760	3.55497	3.53257	3.51040	3.48846	3.46675	3.44525	3.42398	5
6	4.05872	4.02948	4.00058	3.97201	3.94377	3.91586	3.88827	3.86099	3.83403	3.80737	6
7	4.41619	4.38107	4.34641	4.31218	4.27840	4.24504	4.21210	4.17958	4.14746	4.11575	7
8	4.70289	4.66240	4.62247	4.58309	4.54426	4.50596	4.46818	4.43092	4.39417	4.35792	8
9	4.92524	4.88006	4.83555	4.79170	4.74850	4.70594	4.66400	4.62267	4.58194	4.54180	9
10	5.08916	5.04014	4.99190	4.94441	4.89767	4.85165	4.80634	4.76173	4.71780	4.67454	10
11	5.20014	5.14827	5.09726	5.04708	4.99771	4.94914	4.90136	4.85434	4.80807	4.76253	11
12	5.26326	5.20963	5.15690	5.10505	5.05407	5.00394	4.95464	4.90615	4.85845	4.81153	12
13	5.28320	5.22896	5.17565	5.12324	5.07171	5.02105	4.97124	4.92225	4.87407	4.82668	13
14	5.26430	5.21068	5.15796	5.10612	5.05515	5.00502	4.95572	4.90723	4.85954	4.81262	14
15	5.21055	5.15880	5.10788	5.05779	5.00849	4.95998	4.91223	4.86524	4.81898	4.77345	15
16	5.12563	5.07704	5.02916	4.98197	4.93547	4.88964	4.84448	4.79997	4.75610	4.71287	16
17	5.01295	4.96880	4.92517	4.88207	4.83948	4.79741	4.75584	4.71478	4.67422	4.63415	17
18	4.87562	4.83720	4.79905	4.76118	4.72360	4.68632	4.64933	4.61265	4.57628	4.54022	18
19	4.71652	4.68510	4.65362	4.62212	4.59062	4.55912	4.52767	4.49626	4.46493	4.43368	19
20	4.53831	4.51512	4.49149	4.46745	4.44304	4.41831	4.39329	4.36801	4.34251	4.31682	20
21	4.34339	4.32965	4.31499	4.29947	4.28315	4.26611	4.24838	4.23004	4.21112	4.19168	21
22	4.13400	4.13089	4.12629	4.12030	4.11301	4.10452	4.09490	4.08423	4.07260	4.06006	22
23	3.91218	3.92082	3.92732	3.93183	3.93446	3.93533	3.93458	3.93229	3.92858	3.92354	23
24	3.67978	3.70126	3.71986	3.73577	3.74915	3.76017	3.76897	3.77571	3.78051	3.78349	24
25	3.43853	3.47387	3.50550	3.53367	3.55858	3.58045	3.59946	3.61581	3.62965	3.64114	25
30	2.14913	2.26723	2.37613	2.47643	2.56871	2.65350	2.73130	2.80255	2.86771	2.92718	30
35	0.81984	1.03780	1.23883	1.42416	1.59492	1.75216	1.89685	2.02990	2.15213	2.26433	35
40	-0.45947	-0.13155	0.16975	0.44654	0.70073	0.93411	1.14829	1.34477	1.52493	1.69003	40
45	-1.63896	-1.19701	-0.79294	-0.42352	-0.08580	0.22291	0.50505	0.76285	0.99836	1.21343	45
50	-2.69494	-2.13970	-1.63473	-1.17542	-0.75759	-0.37747	-0.03166	0.28293	0.56910	0.82938	50

Present Value of a Series of Payments Decreasing by a Constant Amount

Amount of 1st Year Decline 9.0%

Holding Period	5.50%	5.75%	6.00%	6.25%	6.50%	6.75%	7.00%	7.25%	7.50%	7.75%	
1	0.94787	0.94563	0.94340	0.94118	0.93897	0.93677	0.93458	0.93240	0.93023	0.92807	1
2	1.76546	1.75936	1.75329	1.74727	1.74128	1.73532	1.72941	1.72353	1.71769	1.71188	2
3	2.46378	2.45274	2.44178	2.43091	2.42011	2.40940	2.39877	2.38822	2.37775	2.36736	3
4	3.05305	3.03646	3.02001	3.00371	2.98756	2.97155	2.95569	2.93996	2.92438	2.90893	4
5	3.54274	3.52038	3.49825	3.47636	3.45468	3.43323	3.41200	3.39098	3.37017	3.34958	5
6	3.94162	3.91364	3.88598	3.85864	3.83162	3.80490	3.77849	3.75237	3.72655	3.70103	6
7	4.25784	4.22467	4.19191	4.15957	4.12763	4.09609	4.06495	4.03420	4.00382	3.97382	7
8	4.49893	4.46124	4.42405	4.38737	4.35120	4.31550	4.28029	4.24556	4.21128	4.17746	8
9	4.67187	4.63053	4.58978	4.54963	4.51005	4.47105	4.43260	4.39469	4.35732	4.32048	9
10	4.78310	4.73916	4.69588	4.65325	4.61127	4.56992	4.52918	4.48905	4.44951	4.41055	10
11	4.83859	4.79322	4.74856	4.70459	4.66129	4.61867	4.57669	4.53536	4.49465	4.45455	11
12	4.84385	4.79833	4.75353	4.70942	4.66599	4.62323	4.58113	4.53967	4.49884	4.45863	12
13	4.80397	4.75966	4.71602	4.67304	4.63071	4.58901	4.54793	4.50747	4.46760	4.42832	13
14	4.72363	4.68194	4.64083	4.60029	4.56031	4.52089	4.48201	4.44366	4.40584	4.36853	14
15	4.60717	4.56954	4.53234	4.49557	4.45922	4.42329	4.38777	4.35266	4.31796	4.28367	15
16	4.45857	4.42646	4.39456	4.36289	4.33143	4.30021	4.26921	4.23845	4.20793	4.17765	16
17	4.28149	4.25636	4.23116	4.20590	4.18060	4.15526	4.12992	4.10458	4.07925	4.05395	17
18	4.07931	4.06262	4.04548	4.02793	4.00999	3.99171	3.97311	3.95422	3.93506	3.91567	18
19	3.85513	3.84830	3.84056	3.83198	3.82260	3.81249	3.80168	3.79022	3.77816	3.76554	19
20	3.61180	3.61621	3.61918	3.62079	3.62111	3.62022	3.61820	3.61511	3.61102	3.60598	20
21	3.35191	3.36893	3.38386	3.39682	3.40793	3.41728	3.42499	3.43114	3.43583	3.43913	21
22	3.07785	3.10823	3.13688	3.16231	3.18524	3.20579	3.22410	3.24031	3.25452	3.26686	22
23	2.79182	2.83790	2.88032	2.91928	2.95500	2.98763	3.01738	3.04438	3.06882	3.09082	23
24	2.49579	2.55822	2.61605	2.66954	2.71895	2.76451	2.80643	2.84493	2.88020	2.91243	24
25	2.19160	2.27151	2.34577	2.41472	2.47867	2.53791	2.59270	2.64331	2.68998	2.73294	25
30	0.60105	0.78301	0.95254	1.11045	1.25747	1.39430	1.52158	1.63992	1.74988	1.85200	30
35	-1.00150	-0.69919	-0.41860	-0.15821	0.08341	0.30757	0.51550	0.70832	0.88709	1.05278	35
40	-2.52267	-2.08962	-1.68982	-1.32069	-0.97987	-0.66519	-0.37464	-0.10639	0.14125	0.36984	40
45	-3.91230	-3.34491	-2.82404	-2.34577	-1.90655	-1.50312	-1.13251	-0.79202	-0.47917	-0.19171	45
50	-5.14825	-4.44827	-3.80930	-3.22583	-2.69285	-2.20584	-1.76071	-1.35376	-0.98161	-0.64124	50

Amount of 1st Year Decline 10.0%

Holding Period	5.50%	5.75%	6.00%	6.25%	6.50%	6.75%	7.00%	7.25%	7.50%	7.75%	
1	0.94787	0.94563	0.94340	0.94118	0.93897	0.93677	0.93458	0.93240	0.93023	0.92807	1
2	1.75647	1.75041	1.74439	1.73841	1.73246	1.72655	1.72067	1.71484	1.70903	1.70326	2
3	2.43777	2.42689	2.41609	2.40537	2.39474	2.38419	2.37371	2.36332	2.35300	2.34276	3
4	3.00282	2.98661	2.97055	2.95464	2.93887	2.92323	2.90774	2.89238	2.87716	2.86207	4
5	3.46190	3.44029	3.41891	3.39774	3.37679	3.35606	3.33553	3.31521	3.29510	3.27518	5
6	3.82452	3.79780	3.77139	3.74528	3.71946	3.69394	3.66870	3.64375	3.61908	3.59468	6
7	4.09950	4.06826	4.03741	4.00695	3.97686	3.94715	3.91780	3.88881	3.86018	3.83189	7
8	4.29498	4.26007	4.22564	4.19166	4.15813	4.12505	4.09240	4.06019	4.02839	3.99701	8
9	4.41850	4.38099	4.34402	4.30756	4.27160	4.23615	4.20119	4.16671	4.13271	4.09916	9
10	4.47704	4.43817	4.39985	4.36209	4.32488	4.28819	4.25203	4.21637	4.18123	4.14657	10
11	4.47704	4.43817	4.39985	4.36209	4.32488	4.28819	4.25203	4.21637	4.18123	4.14657	11
12	4.42445	4.38704	4.35016	4.31378	4.27791	4.24253	4.20763	4.17320	4.13924	4.10574	12
13	4.32473	4.29035	4.25639	4.22284	4.18970	4.15697	4.12463	4.09269	4.06113	4.02995	13
14	4.18296	4.15320	4.12370	4.09446	4.06547	4.03675	4.00829	3.98008	3.95213	3.92444	14
15	4.00379	3.98028	3.95679	3.93335	3.90994	3.88660	3.86331	3.84009	3.81695	3.79389	15
16	3.79150	3.77588	3.75997	3.74380	3.72740	3.71077	3.69394	3.67693	3.65975	3.64243	16
17	3.55003	3.54393	3.53715	3.52973	3.52171	3.51312	3.50400	3.49437	3.48428	3.47375	17
18	3.28301	3.28804	3.29191	3.29467	3.29639	3.29711	3.29689	3.29579	3.29385	3.29111	18
19	2.99374	3.01150	3.02750	3.04184	3.05459	3.06585	3.07569	3.08418	3.09139	3.09740	19
20	2.68529	2.71730	2.74688	2.77413	2.79917	2.82213	2.84311	2.86221	2.87952	2.89515	20
21	2.36042	2.40820	2.45272	2.49417	2.53270	2.56846	2.60160	2.63224	2.66053	2.68658	21
22	2.02171	2.08666	2.14747	2.20433	2.25744	2.30706	2.35331	2.39638	2.43645	2.47366	22
23	1.67146	1.75497	1.83331	1.90674	1.97553	2.03993	2.10017	2.15648	2.20905	2.25810	23
24	1.31181	1.41518	1.51224	1.60332	1.68875	1.76884	1.84388	1.91415	1.97989	2.04136	24
25	0.94468	1.06915	1.18604	1.29578	1.39876	1.49536	1.58593	1.67082	1.75032	1.82474	25
30	-0.94703	-0.70122	-0.47105	-0.25554	-0.05378	0.13509	0.31186	0.47728	0.63205	0.77682	30
35	-2.82284	-2.43617	-2.07603	-1.74057	-1.42809	-1.13701	-0.86586	-0.61326	-0.37796	-0.15878	35
40	-4.58587	-4.04769	-3.54939	-3.08791	-2.66047	-2.26448	-1.89757	-1.55756	-1.24244	-0.95036	40
45	-6.18563	-5.49281	-4.85513	-4.26803	-3.72731	-3.22915	-2.77007	-2.34689	-1.95671	-1.59686	45
50	-7.60156	-6.75684	-5.98388	-5.27625	-4.62811	-4.03421	-3.48977	-2.99045	-2.53233	-2.11186	50

Present Value of a Series of Payments Decreasing by a Constant Amount

Amount of 1st Year Decline 3.0%

Holding Perio	8.00%	8.25%	8.50%	8.75%	Discount Rate 9.00%	9.25%	9.50%	9.75%	10.00%	10.25%	
1	0.92593	0.92379	0.92166	0.91954	0.91743	0.91533	0.91324	0.91116	0.90909	0.90703	1
2	1.75754	1.75157	1.74563	1.73973	1.73386	1.72803	1.72223	1.71647	1.71074	1.70505	2
3	2.50375	2.49261	2.48156	2.47060	2.45971	2.44891	2.43819	2.42754	2.41698	2.40649	3
4	3.17262	3.15533	3.13820	3.12121	3.10438	3.08770	3.07116	3.05477	3.03852	3.02242	4
5	3.77154	3.74736	3.72344	3.69976	3.67632	3.65312	3.63016	3.60743	3.58493	3.56266	5
6	4.30718	4.27563	4.24444	4.21362	4.18315	4.15303	4.12326	4.09383	4.06474	4.03597	6
7	4.78564	4.74641	4.70768	4.66945	4.63172	4.59446	4.55768	4.52137	4.48553	4.45013	7
8	5.21246	5.16540	5.11901	5.07328	5.02819	4.98374	4.93991	4.89669	4.85407	4.81204	8
9	5.59265	5.53776	5.48372	5.43051	5.37811	5.32652	5.27571	5.22567	5.17638	5.12783	9
10	5.93078	5.86816	5.80659	5.74603	5.68647	5.62790	5.57028	5.51359	5.45783	5.40296	10
11	6.23099	6.16084	6.09193	6.02424	5.95775	5.89242	5.82823	5.76516	5.70317	5.64226	11
12	6.49706	6.41962	6.34365	6.26911	6.19596	6.12417	6.05371	5.98455	5.91666	5.85000	12
13	6.73239	6.64798	6.56526	6.48419	6.40471	6.32680	6.25040	6.17550	6.10204	6.03000	13
14	6.94007	6.84905	6.75994	6.67269	6.58725	6.50357	6.42162	6.34133	6.26267	6.18560	14
15	7.12291	7.02566	6.93054	6.83750	6.74648	6.65743	6.57028	6.48500	6.40152	6.31980	15
16	7.28345	7.18037	7.07964	6.98121	6.88501	6.79097	6.69903	6.60913	6.52122	6.43523	16
17	7.42399	7.31549	7.20957	7.10616	7.00517	6.90654	6.81019	6.71607	6.62410	6.53421	17
18	7.54661	7.43311	7.32241	7.21442	7.10905	7.00622	6.90586	6.80788	6.71223	6.61882	18
19	7.65320	7.53512	7.42004	7.30787	7.19851	7.09187	6.98787	6.88642	6.78744	6.69085	19
20	7.74545	7.62321	7.50416	7.38820	7.27524	7.16516	7.05788	6.95331	6.85136	6.75193	20
21	7.82492	7.69890	7.57627	7.45692	7.34072	7.22757	7.11736	7.01001	6.90541	6.80347	21
22	7.89297	7.76358	7.63776	7.51536	7.39628	7.28040	7.16761	7.05780	6.95086	6.84671	22
23	7.95088	7.81849	7.68983	7.56475	7.44313	7.32484	7.20977	7.09781	6.98883	6.88275	23
24	7.99977	7.86474	7.73358	7.60615	7.48231	7.36193	7.24488	7.13105	7.02031	6.91255	24
25	8.04065	7.90333	7.77001	7.64054	7.51479	7.39260	7.27384	7.15840	7.04615	6.93697	25
30	8.15411	8.00979	7.86992	7.73432	7.60281	7.47525	7.35146	7.23129	7.11462	7.00129	30
35	8.17181	8.02624	7.88522	7.74855	7.61605	7.48756	7.36292	7.24196	7.12454	7.01053	35
40	8.14335	8.00020	7.86138	7.72673	7.59607	7.46927	7.34616	7.22660	7.11047	6.99764	40
45	8.09641	7.95771	7.82291	7.69189	7.56452	7.44067	7.32024	7.20311	7.08917	6.97832	45
50	8.04570	7.91233	7.78229	7.65551	7.53193	7.41148	7.29408	7.17966	7.06815	6.95946	50

Amount of 1st Year Decline 4.0%

Holding Period	8.00%	8.25%	8.50%	8.75%	Discount Rate 9.00%	9.25%	9.50%	9.75%	10.00%	10.25%	
1	0.92593	0.92379	0.92166	0.91954	0.91743	0.91533	0.91324	0.91116	0.90909	0.90703	1
2	1.74897	1.74304	1.73714	1.73127	1.72544	1.71965	1.71389	1.70817	1.70248	1.69682	2
3	2.47930	2.46831	2.45741	2.44659	2.43585	2.42519	2.41461	2.40411	2.39369	2.38334	3
4	3.12612	3.10918	3.09240	3.07576	3.05927	3.04292	3.02672	3.01066	2.99474	2.97896	4
5	3.69781	3.67430	3.65104	3.62800	3.60521	3.58265	3.56031	3.53820	3.51631	3.49465	5
6	4.20195	4.17149	4.14139	4.11164	4.08222	4.05315	4.02440	3.99599	3.96789	3.94012	6
7	4.64540	4.60783	4.57074	4.53412	4.49797	4.46228	4.42704	4.39225	4.35789	4.32397	7
8	5.03440	4.98969	4.94562	4.90216	4.85931	4.81706	4.77539	4.73430	4.69378	4.65381	8
9	5.37456	5.32286	5.27194	5.22179	5.17240	5.12376	5.07585	5.02866	4.98217	4.93636	9
10	5.67101	5.61252	5.55500	5.49841	5.44275	5.38798	5.33410	5.28108	5.22891	5.17757	10
11	5.92834	5.86339	5.79958	5.73688	5.67527	5.61472	5.55520	5.49671	5.43921	5.38268	11
12	6.15072	6.07969	6.00997	5.94154	5.87437	5.80842	5.74366	5.68008	5.61764	5.55632	12
13	6.34192	6.26523	6.19003	6.11629	6.04398	5.97305	5.90348	5.83523	5.76827	5.70257	13
14	6.50535	6.42345	6.34322	6.26462	6.18762	6.11216	6.03820	5.96572	5.89467	5.82501	14
15	6.64405	6.55742	6.47264	6.38965	6.30841	6.22887	6.15099	6.07471	6.00000	5.92682	15
16	6.76081	6.66994	6.58108	6.49417	6.40916	6.32599	6.24462	6.16499	6.08705	6.01076	16
17	6.85811	6.76349	6.67103	6.58067	6.49235	6.40600	6.32158	6.23902	6.15828	6.07929	17
18	6.93818	6.84030	6.74472	6.65137	6.56019	6.47110	6.38405	6.29898	6.21583	6.13454	18
19	7.00306	6.90239	6.80415	6.70826	6.61464	6.52324	6.43397	6.34679	6.26161	6.17839	19
20	7.05456	6.95156	6.85110	6.75309	6.65747	6.56414	6.47305	6.38412	6.29729	6.21248	20
21	7.09429	6.98941	6.88716	6.78745	6.69021	6.59535	6.50279	6.41247	6.32431	6.23825	21
22	7.12372	7.01738	6.91374	6.81272	6.71424	6.61819	6.52452	6.43314	6.34397	6.25695	22
23	7.14416	7.03676	6.93212	6.83015	6.73077	6.63388	6.53940	6.44726	6.35737	6.26967	23
24	7.15677	7.04869	6.94341	6.84084	6.74088	6.64345	6.54846	6.45583	6.36549	6.27736	24
25	7.16261	7.05420	6.94862	6.84575	6.74552	6.64783	6.55260	6.45974	6.36918	6.28085	25
30	7.11955	7.01393	6.91094	6.81050	6.71253	6.61696	6.52370	6.43269	6.34385	6.25712	30
35	7.01089	6.91328	6.81770	6.72410	6.63246	6.54274	6.45489	6.36888	6.28467	6.20223	35
40	6.88293	6.79608	6.71034	6.62573	6.54231	6.46010	6.37913	6.29941	6.22095	6.14377	40
45	6.75908	6.68395	6.60878	6.53374	6.45895	6.38455	6.31064	6.23731	6.16463	6.09268	45
50	6.64977	6.58611	6.52118	6.45529	6.38868	6.32159	6.25421	6.18671	6.11926	6.05198	50

Present Value of a Series of Payments Decreasing by a Constant Amount

Amount of 1st Year Decline 5.0%

Holding Period	8.00%	8.25%	8.50%	8.75%	Discount Rate 9.00%	9.25%	9.50%	9.75%	10.00%	10.25%	
1	0.92593	0.92379	0.92166	0.91954	0.91743	0.91533	0.91324	0.91116	0.90909	0.90703	1
2	1.74040	1.73450	1.72864	1.72282	1.71703	1.71127	1.70555	1.69987	1.69421	1.68860	2
3	2.45485	2.44401	2.43326	2.42259	2.41199	2.40148	2.39104	2.38068	2.37040	2.36019	3
4	3.07962	3.06304	3.04660	3.03030	3.01415	2.99815	2.98228	2.96655	2.95096	2.93550	4
5	3.62409	3.60124	3.57863	3.55625	3.53410	3.51217	3.49046	3.46897	3.44770	3.42663	5
6	4.09672	4.06736	4.03834	4.00966	3.98130	3.95326	3.92555	3.89815	3.87105	3.84426	6
7	4.50516	4.46925	4.43379	4.39879	4.36422	4.33010	4.29640	4.26312	4.23026	4.19781	7
8	4.85633	4.81398	4.77223	4.73105	4.69044	4.65039	4.61088	4.57192	4.53349	4.49558	8
9	5.15648	5.10795	5.06015	5.01307	4.96669	4.92100	4.87599	4.83165	4.78795	4.74490	9
10	5.41124	5.35689	5.30341	5.25079	5.19902	5.14807	5.09793	5.04858	5.00000	4.95218	10
11	5.62568	5.56594	5.50723	5.44952	5.39279	5.33701	5.28218	5.22826	5.17525	5.12311	11
12	5.80438	5.73975	5.67629	5.61398	5.55278	5.49267	5.43362	5.37562	5.31863	5.26264	12
13	5.95146	5.88248	5.81480	5.74840	5.68325	5.61931	5.55656	5.49496	5.43450	5.37514	13
14	6.07062	5.99784	5.92650	5.85656	5.78798	5.72074	5.65479	5.59011	5.52666	5.46442	14
15	6.16520	6.08919	6.01474	5.94181	5.87035	5.80032	5.73169	5.66442	5.59848	5.53383	15
16	6.23817	6.15951	6.08252	6.00713	5.93331	5.86102	5.79021	5.72085	5.65289	5.58630	16
17	6.29222	6.21149	6.13249	6.05519	5.97953	5.90547	5.83297	5.76197	5.69246	5.62437	17
18	6.32976	6.24749	6.16703	6.08833	6.01133	5.93598	5.86225	5.79008	5.71944	5.65027	18
19	6.35293	6.26967	6.18826	6.10864	6.03078	5.95460	5.88008	5.80715	5.73579	5.66593	19
20	6.36366	6.27991	6.19804	6.11798	6.03970	5.96313	5.88822	5.81493	5.74322	5.67303	20
21	6.36366	6.27991	6.19804	6.11798	6.03970	5.96313	5.88822	5.81493	5.74322	5.67303	21
22	6.35446	6.27117	6.18973	6.11009	6.03219	5.95599	5.88143	5.80848	5.73708	5.66719	22
23	6.33743	6.25502	6.17441	6.09556	6.01841	5.94291	5.86903	5.79671	5.72591	5.65659	23
24	6.31377	6.23264	6.15324	6.07553	5.99945	5.92497	5.85204	5.78062	5.71068	5.64217	24
25	6.28457	6.20508	6.12722	6.05096	5.97626	5.90307	5.83135	5.76108	5.69222	5.62473	25
30	6.08499	6.01807	5.95196	5.88669	5.82225	5.75867	5.69595	5.63408	5.57309	5.51295	30
35	5.84997	5.80032	5.75017	5.69966	5.64887	5.59791	5.54686	5.49580	5.44480	5.39392	35
40	5.62250	5.59197	5.55929	5.52474	5.48855	5.45094	5.41210	5.37221	5.33142	5.28990	40
45	5.42175	5.41018	5.39465	5.37558	5.35339	5.32844	5.30104	5.27150	5.24009	5.20704	45
50	5.25385	5.25989	5.26008	5.25507	5.24543	5.23169	5.21433	5.19376	5.17037	5.14450	50

Amount of 1st Year Decline 6.0%

Holding Period	8.00%	8.25%	8.50%	8.75%	Discount Rate 9.00%	9.25%	9.50%	9.75%	10.00%	10.25%	
1	0.92593	0.92379	0.92166	0.91954	0.91743	0.91533	0.91324	0.91116	0.90909	0.90703	1
2	1.73182	1.72597	1.72015	1.71436	1.70861	1.70289	1.69721	1.69156	1.68595	1.68037	2
3	2.43040	2.41971	2.40911	2.39858	2.38813	2.37776	2.36747	2.35725	2.34711	2.33704	3
4	3.03312	3.01689	3.00080	2.98485	2.96904	2.95337	2.93784	2.92244	2.90718	2.89205	4
5	3.55036	3.52819	3.50623	3.48450	3.46299	3.44169	3.42061	3.39974	3.37908	3.35862	5
6	3.99148	3.96323	3.93529	3.90768	3.88038	3.85338	3.82669	3.80030	3.77421	3.74841	6
7	4.36492	4.33067	4.29685	4.26345	4.23048	4.19791	4.16576	4.13400	4.10263	4.07165	7
8	4.67827	4.63828	4.59883	4.55993	4.52156	4.48371	4.44637	4.40954	4.37321	4.33736	8
9	4.93840	4.89305	4.84837	4.80435	4.76098	4.71825	4.67614	4.63464	4.59374	4.55343	9
10	5.15147	5.10125	5.05182	5.00318	4.95529	4.90816	4.86175	4.81607	4.77109	4.72680	10
11	5.32302	5.26849	5.21488	5.16215	5.11030	5.05931	5.00915	4.95982	4.91128	4.86354	11
12	5.45804	5.39982	5.34262	5.28641	5.23119	5.17691	5.12358	5.07115	5.01962	4.96896	12
13	5.56100	5.49973	5.43957	5.38051	5.32252	5.26556	5.20963	5.15469	5.10072	5.04771	13
14	5.63590	5.57224	5.50978	5.44850	5.38835	5.32932	5.27138	5.21450	5.15866	5.10383	14
15	5.68634	5.62096	5.55684	5.49396	5.43228	5.37176	5.31239	5.25413	5.19696	5.14085	15
16	5.71553	5.64909	5.58395	5.52009	5.45746	5.39604	5.33580	5.27670	5.21872	5.16183	16
17	5.72634	5.65948	5.59395	5.52970	5.46671	5.40493	5.34435	5.28493	5.22664	5.16945	17
18	5.72133	5.65468	5.58934	5.52528	5.46247	5.40086	5.34045	5.28118	5.22304	5.16600	18
19	5.70280	5.63694	5.57236	5.50903	5.44691	5.38597	5.32618	5.26752	5.20996	5.15347	19
20	5.67276	5.60826	5.54498	5.48287	5.42193	5.36211	5.30339	5.24574	5.18915	5.13358	20
21	5.63303	5.57041	5.50892	5.44852	5.38919	5.33091	5.27365	5.21739	5.16212	5.10781	21
22	5.58520	5.52496	5.46572	5.40745	5.35014	5.29378	5.23834	5.18382	5.13018	5.07743	22
23	5.53070	5.47328	5.41671	5.36097	5.30605	5.25195	5.19866	5.14616	5.09445	5.04351	23
24	5.47078	5.41659	5.36307	5.31021	5.25802	5.20649	5.15562	5.10541	5.05587	5.00698	24
25	5.40653	5.35595	5.30583	5.25617	5.20699	5.15830	5.11011	5.06243	5.01526	4.96861	25
30	5.05044	5.02221	4.99299	4.96287	4.93197	4.90038	4.86819	4.83548	4.80232	4.76878	30
35	4.68905	4.68735	4.68265	4.67521	4.66528	4.65309	4.63884	4.62272	4.60493	4.58562	35
40	4.36208	4.38785	4.40825	4.42375	4.43479	4.44177	4.44507	4.44501	4.44190	4.43603	40
45	4.08442	4.13642	4.18051	4.21743	4.24783	4.27232	4.29144	4.30570	4.31554	4.32139	45
50	3.85792	3.93367	3.99898	4.05484	4.10218	4.14180	4.17445	4.20081	4.22148	4.23702	50

Present Value of a Series of Payments Decreasing by a Constant Amount

Amount of 1st Year Decline 7.0%

Holding Period	8.00%	8.25%	8.50%	8.75%	Discount Rate 9.00%	9.25%	9.50%	9.75%	10.00%	10.25%	
1	0.92593	0.92379	0.92166	0.91954	0.91743	0.91533	0.91324	0.91116	0.90909	0.90703	1
2	1.72325	1.71743	1.71165	1.70591	1.70019	1.69452	1.68887	1.68326	1.67769	1.67214	2
3	2.40595	2.39541	2.38495	2.37457	2.36427	2.35405	2.34389	2.33382	2.32382	2.31389	3
4	2.98662	2.97074	2.95500	2.93939	2.92393	2.90860	2.89340	2.87833	2.86340	2.84859	4
5	3.47664	3.45513	3.43383	3.41275	3.39188	3.37122	3.35076	3.33051	3.31046	3.29061	5
6	3.88625	3.85909	3.83224	3.80570	3.77945	3.75350	3.72784	3.70246	3.67737	3.65255	6
7	4.22467	4.19208	4.15990	4.12812	4.09673	4.06573	4.03511	4.00487	3.97500	3.94549	7
8	4.50021	4.46257	4.42544	4.38882	4.35268	4.31704	4.28186	4.24716	4.21292	4.17913	8
9	4.72032	4.67815	4.63659	4.59563	4.55527	4.51549	4.47628	4.43763	4.39952	4.36196	9
10	4.89170	4.84561	4.80024	4.75556	4.71156	4.66824	4.62558	4.58356	4.54217	4.50141	10
11	5.02037	4.97105	4.92253	4.87479	4.82782	4.78161	4.73613	4.69137	4.64732	4.60396	11
12	5.11170	5.05988	5.00894	4.95885	4.90960	4.86116	4.81353	4.76669	4.72061	4.67528	12
13	5.17054	5.11697	5.06434	5.01262	4.96179	4.91182	4.86271	4.81442	4.76695	4.72028	13
14	5.20118	5.14664	5.09306	5.04043	4.98872	4.93790	4.88797	4.83889	4.79065	4.74324	14
15	5.20748	5.15273	5.09895	5.04611	4.99421	4.94321	4.89309	4.84384	4.79544	4.74786	15
16	5.19289	5.13866	5.08539	5.03305	4.98161	4.93107	4.88139	4.83256	4.78456	4.73737	16
17	5.16046	5.10748	5.05541	5.00422	4.95389	4.90440	4.85574	4.80788	4.76082	4.71453	17
18	5.11291	5.06187	5.01165	4.96224	4.91361	4.86575	4.81864	4.77228	4.72664	4.68172	18
19	5.05266	5.00422	4.95647	4.90942	4.86304	4.81733	4.77229	4.72789	4.68413	4.64100	19
20	4.98186	4.93662	4.89192	4.84777	4.80416	4.76109	4.71856	4.67655	4.63508	4.59413	20
21	4.90240	4.86092	4.81980	4.77905	4.73868	4.69868	4.65908	4.61986	4.58103	4.54259	21
22	4.81595	4.77875	4.74170	4.70481	4.66809	4.63157	4.59525	4.55915	4.52329	4.48767	22
23	4.72398	4.69155	4.65900	4.62637	4.59369	4.56099	4.52828	4.49561	4.46298	4.43043	23
24	4.62778	4.60054	4.57290	4.54490	4.51658	4.48800	4.45920	4.43020	4.40105	4.37178	24
25	4.52849	4.50683	4.48444	4.46138	4.43773	4.41354	4.38886	4.36377	4.33829	4.31249	25
30	4.01588	4.02635	4.03401	4.03906	4.04169	4.04210	4.04044	4.03687	4.03155	4.02462	30
35	3.52813	3.57439	3.61513	3.65077	3.68169	3.70826	3.73081	3.74965	3.76506	3.77731	35
40	3.10166	3.18373	3.25720	3.32275	3.38103	3.43261	3.47804	3.51781	3.55237	3.58216	40
45	2.74709	2.86265	2.96638	3.05928	3.14227	3.21620	3.28184	3.33989	3.39100	3.43575	45
50	2.46199	2.60745	2.73787	2.85462	2.95893	3.05191	3.13458	3.20786	3.27259	3.32954	50

Amount of 1st Year Decline 8.0%

Holding Period	8.00%	8.25%	8.50%	8.75%	Discount Rate 9.00%	9.25%	9.50%	9.75%	10.00%	10.25%	
1	0.92593	0.92379	0.92166	0.91954	0.91743	0.91533	0.91324	0.91116	0.90909	0.90703	1
2	1.71468	1.70890	1.70316	1.69745	1.69178	1.68614	1.68053	1.67496	1.66942	1.66392	2
3	2.38150	2.37111	2.36080	2.35057	2.34041	2.33033	2.32032	2.31039	2.30053	2.29074	3
4	2.94012	2.92459	2.90920	2.89394	2.87881	2.86382	2.84896	2.83422	2.81962	2.80513	4
5	3.40292	3.38207	3.36143	3.34100	3.32077	3.30074	3.28091	3.26128	3.24184	3.22260	5
6	3.78102	3.75496	3.72920	3.70372	3.67853	3.65362	3.62898	3.60462	3.58053	3.55670	6
7	4.08443	4.05350	4.02296	3.99279	3.96299	3.93355	3.90447	3.87575	3.84737	3.81933	7
8	4.32215	4.28687	4.25205	4.21770	4.18381	4.15036	4.11735	4.08478	4.05263	4.02090	8
9	4.50224	4.46325	4.42481	4.38692	4.34956	4.31273	4.27642	4.24061	4.20531	4.17049	9
10	4.63193	4.58998	4.54865	4.50794	4.46784	4.42833	4.38940	4.35105	4.31326	4.27602	10
11	4.71771	4.67360	4.63018	4.58743	4.54534	4.50391	4.46310	4.42293	4.38336	4.34439	11
12	4.76537	4.71995	4.67526	4.63128	4.58801	4.54541	4.50349	4.46222	4.42159	4.38160	12
13	4.78007	4.73422	4.68911	4.64473	4.60105	4.55808	4.51578	4.47415	4.43318	4.39285	13
14	4.76645	4.72104	4.67634	4.63237	4.58908	4.54649	4.50456	4.46328	4.42265	4.38264	14
15	4.72863	4.68450	4.64105	4.59827	4.55614	4.51465	4.47380	4.43356	4.39392	4.35488	15
16	4.67025	4.62824	4.58683	4.54601	4.50577	4.46609	4.42698	4.38842	4.35039	4.31290	16
17	4.59457	4.55548	4.51687	4.47873	4.44106	4.40386	4.36712	4.33084	4.29500	4.25961	17
18	4.50448	4.46906	4.43397	4.39919	4.36475	4.33063	4.29684	4.26338	4.23025	4.19745	18
19	4.40253	4.37149	4.34058	4.30980	4.27917	4.24870	4.21839	4.18826	4.15831	4.12854	19
20	4.29096	4.26497	4.23886	4.21266	4.18639	4.16007	4.13372	4.10736	4.08101	4.05468	20
21	4.17177	4.15142	4.13068	4.10959	4.08817	4.06646	4.04450	4.02232	3.99993	3.97737	21
22	4.04669	4.03255	4.01769	4.00217	3.98605	3.96936	3.95216	3.93449	3.91640	3.89791	22
23	3.91725	3.90981	3.90130	3.89178	3.88133	3.87002	3.85791	3.84506	3.83152	3.81735	23
24	3.78478	3.78449	3.78273	3.77958	3.77515	3.76952	3.76278	3.75499	3.74624	3.73659	24
25	3.65045	3.65770	3.66304	3.66659	3.66846	3.66877	3.66762	3.66511	3.66133	3.65636	25
30	2.98132	3.03050	3.07504	3.11525	3.15141	3.18381	3.21268	3.23827	3.26079	3.28045	30
35	2.36721	2.46143	2.54761	2.62632	2.69810	2.76344	2.82278	2.87657	2.92519	2.96900	35
40	1.84124	1.97962	2.10615	2.22176	2.32727	2.42344	2.51101	2.59061	2.66285	2.72829	40
45	1.40975	1.58889	1.75225	1.90113	2.03671	2.16009	2.27224	2.37409	2.46645	2.55011	45
50	1.06606	1.28123	1.47677	1.65440	1.81568	1.96202	2.09470	2.21491	2.32370	2.42206	50

Present Value of a Series of Payments Decreasing by a Constant Amount

Amount of 1st Year Decline 9.0%

Holding Period	8.00%	8.25%	8.50%	8.75%	9.00%	9.25%	9.50%	9.75%	10.00%	10.25%	
1	0.92593	0.92379	0.92166	0.91954	0.91743	0.91533	0.91324	0.91116	0.90909	0.90703	1
2	1.70610	1.70037	1.69466	1.68899	1.68336	1.67776	1.67219	1.66666	1.66116	1.65569	2
3	2.35705	2.34681	2.33665	2.32656	2.31655	2.30661	2.29675	2.28696	2.27724	2.26759	3
4	2.89362	2.87844	2.86340	2.84848	2.83370	2.81905	2.80452	2.79011	2.77583	2.76168	4
5	3.32919	3.30901	3.28903	3.26924	3.24966	3.23026	3.21106	3.19205	3.17322	3.15458	5
6	3.67579	3.65083	3.62615	3.60174	3.57760	3.55373	3.53013	3.50678	3.48369	3.46084	6
7	3.94419	3.91492	3.88601	3.85745	3.82924	3.80137	3.77383	3.74662	3.71974	3.69317	7
8	4.14409	4.11116	4.07866	4.04659	4.01493	3.98369	3.95284	3.92240	3.89235	3.86268	8
9	4.28416	4.24834	4.21303	4.17820	4.14385	4.10997	4.07656	4.04360	4.01109	3.97902	9
10	4.37217	4.33434	4.29706	4.26032	4.22411	4.18841	4.15323	4.11854	4.08435	4.05063	10
11	4.41505	4.37615	4.33782	4.30006	4.26286	4.22620	4.19008	4.15448	4.11940	4.08482	11
12	4.41903	4.38001	4.34158	4.30372	4.26642	4.22966	4.19345	4.15776	4.12258	4.08792	12
13	4.38961	4.35147	4.31388	4.27683	4.24032	4.20433	4.16886	4.13389	4.09941	4.06542	13
14	4.33173	4.29543	4.25963	4.22430	4.18945	4.15507	4.12114	4.08767	4.05464	4.02205	14
15	4.24977	4.21626	4.18315	4.15042	4.11807	4.08610	4.05450	4.02327	3.99240	3.96189	15
16	4.14761	4.11781	4.08827	4.05897	4.02992	4.00112	3.97257	3.94427	3.91623	3.88844	16
17	4.02869	4.00348	3.97833	3.95325	3.92824	3.90333	3.87851	3.85379	3.82918	3.80468	17
18	3.89606	3.87625	3.85628	3.83615	3.81589	3.79551	3.77504	3.75448	3.73385	3.71318	18
19	3.75240	3.73877	3.72469	3.71019	3.69530	3.68006	3.66450	3.64863	3.63248	3.61608	19
20	3.60007	3.59332	3.58580	3.57755	3.56862	3.55905	3.54889	3.53817	3.52694	3.51523	20
21	3.44114	3.44193	3.44156	3.44012	3.43766	3.43424	3.42993	3.42478	3.41884	3.41216	21
22	3.27743	3.28634	3.29368	3.29953	3.30400	3.30715	3.30907	3.30983	3.30950	3.30815	22
23	3.11053	3.12808	3.14359	3.15718	3.16897	3.17906	3.18754	3.19451	3.20006	3.20427	23
24	2.94179	2.96845	2.99256	3.01427	3.03372	3.05104	3.06635	3.07978	3.09143	3.10140	24
25	2.77241	2.80858	2.84165	2.87180	2.89920	2.92400	2.94638	2.96645	2.98436	3.00024	25
30	1.94676	2.03464	2.11606	2.19143	2.26113	2.32552	2.38493	2.43966	2.49002	2.53628	30
35	1.20629	1.34847	1.48009	1.60188	1.71451	1.81861	1.91476	2.00349	2.08532	2.16070	35
40	0.58082	0.77550	0.95511	1.12076	1.27350	1.41428	1.54398	1.66341	1.77332	1.87442	40
45	0.07242	0.31512	0.53811	0.74297	0.93115	1.10397	1.26264	1.40828	1.54191	1.66446	45
50	-0.32987	-0.04499	0.21567	0.45418	0.67243	0.87212	1.05483	1.22196	1.37482	1.51458	50

Amount of 1st Year Decline 10.0%

Holding Period	8.00%	8.25%	8.50%	8.75%	9.00%	9.25%	9.50%	9.75%	10.00%	10.25%	
1	0.92593	0.92379	0.92166	0.91954	0.91743	0.91533	0.91324	0.91116	0.90909	0.90703	1
2	1.69753	1.69183	1.68617	1.68054	1.67494	1.66938	1.66385	1.65836	1.65289	1.64746	2
3	2.33260	2.32251	2.31250	2.30256	2.29269	2.28290	2.27317	2.26352	2.25394	2.24443	3
4	2.84712	2.83229	2.81760	2.80303	2.78859	2.77427	2.76008	2.74601	2.73205	2.71822	4
5	3.25547	3.23595	3.21662	3.19749	3.17855	3.15979	3.14121	3.12282	3.10461	3.08657	5
6	3.57055	3.54669	3.52310	3.49976	3.47668	3.45385	3.43127	3.40894	3.38684	3.36499	6
7	3.80395	3.77634	3.74907	3.72212	3.69549	3.66918	3.64319	3.61750	3.59211	3.56702	7
8	3.96603	3.93545	3.90527	3.87547	3.84605	3.81701	3.78833	3.76002	3.73206	3.70445	8
9	4.06608	4.03344	4.00124	3.96948	3.93814	3.90722	3.87670	3.84659	3.81688	3.78755	9
10	4.11240	4.07870	4.04547	4.01270	3.98038	3.94850	3.91705	3.88603	3.85543	3.82524	10
11	4.11240³	4.07870	4.04547	4.01270	3.98038	3.94850	3.91705	3.88603	3.85543	3.82524	11
12	4.07269	4.04008	4.00790	3.97615	3.94483	3.91391	3.88340	3.85329	3.82357	3.79424	12
13	3.99915	3.96872	3.93865	3.90894	3.87959	3.85059	3.82193	3.79362	3.76564	3.73799	13
14	3.89701	3.86983	3.84291	3.81624	3.78982	3.76365	3.73773	3.71206	3.68664	3.66146	14
15	3.77091	3.74803	3.72525	3.70257	3.68000	3.65754	3.63520	3.61298	3.59088	3.56891	15
16	3.62497	3.60739	3.58970	3.57192	3.55407	3.53614	3.51816	3.50013	3.48207	3.46397	16
17	3.46281	3.45148	3.43979	3.42776	3.41542	3.40279	3.38989	3.37674	3.36336	3.34976	17
18	3.28763	3.28344	3.27859	3.27310	3.26703	3.26039	3.25323	3.24558	3.23746	3.22890	18
19	3.10226	3.10604	3.10879	3.11057	3.11144	3.11143	3.11060	3.10899	3.10665	3.10362	19
20	2.90917	2.92167	2.93274	2.94244	2.95085	2.95803	2.96406	2.96898	2.97287	2.97578	20
21	2.71051	2.73243	2.75245	2.77065	2.78715	2.80202	2.81536	2.82724	2.83774	2.84694	21
22	2.50818	2.54013	2.56966	2.59689	2.62195	2.64494	2.66598	2.68517	2.70261	2.71839	22
23	2.30380	2.34634	2.38588	2.42259	2.45661	2.48809	2.51717	2.54396	2.56860	2.59119	23
24	2.09879	2.15240	2.20239	2.24895	2.29229	2.33256	2.36993	2.40457	2.43661	2.46621	24
25	1.89437	1.95945	2.02025	2.07701	2.12993	2.17924	2.22513	2.26779	2.30740	2.34412	25
30	0.91220	1.03878	1.15708	1.26762	1.37085	1.46723	1.55717	1.64106	1.71926	1.79211	30
35	0.04537	0.23550	0.41257	0.57744	0.73092	0.87379	1.00673	1.13041	1.24544	1.35239	35
40	-0.67961	-0.42862	-0.19594	0.01977	0.21974	0.40512	0.57695	0.73621	0.88380	1.02055	40
45	-1.26491	-0.95864	-0.67602	-0.41518	-0.17441	0.04785	0.25304	0.44247	0.61736	0.77882	45
50	-1.72579	-1.37121	-1.04544	-0.74604	-0.47082	-0.21777	0.01495	0.22901	0.42593	0.60709	50

Present Value of a Series of Payments Decreasing by a Constant Amount

Amount of 1st Year Decline 3.0%

Holding Period	10.50%	10.75%	11.00%	11.25%	11.50%	11.75%	12.00%	12.25%	15.00%	18.00%	
1	0.90498	0.90293	0.90090	0.89888	0.89686	0.89485	0.89286	0.89087	0.86957	0.84746	1
2	1.69939	1.69377	1.68817	1.68262	1.67709	1.67160	1.66614	1.66071	1.60302	1.54410	2
3	2.39608	2.38575	2.37549	2.36531	2.35520	2.34517	2.33521	2.32532	2.22109	2.11621	3
4	3.00645	2.99063	2.97494	2.95939	2.94397	2.92868	2.91353	2.89851	2.74139	2.58558	4
5	3.54061	3.51879	3.49718	3.47578	3.45460	3.43363	3.41287	3.39231	3.17890	2.97023	5
6	4.00754	3.97942	3.95162	3.92413	3.89696	3.87008	3.84350	3.81722	3.54638	3.28510	6
7	4.41518	4.38066	4.34658	4.31292	4.27968	4.24685	4.21443	4.18240	3.85465	3.54252	7
8	4.77059	4.72971	4.68938	4.64961	4.61038	4.57168	4.53350	4.49583	4.11290	3.75269	8
9	5.08001	5.03290	4.98649	4.94076	4.89570	4.85131	4.80756	4.76445	4.32894	3.92404	9
10	5.34898	5.29586	5.24358	5.19213	5.14150	5.09166	5.04260	4.99430	4.50938	4.06351	10
11	5.58238	5.52353	5.46568	5.40880	5.35288	5.29790	5.24383	5.19066	4.65984	4.17686	11
12	5.78456	5.72030	5.65719	5.59522	5.53434	5.47455	5.41581	5.35809	4.78507	4.26879	12
13	5.95933	5.89001	5.82200	5.75527	5.68980	5.62554	5.56248	5.50058	4.88909	4.34322	13
14	6.11008	6.03607	5.96352	5.89240	5.82269	5.75433	5.68730	5.62156	4.97530	4.40333	14
15	6.23980	6.16146	6.08474	6.00960	5.93600	5.86390	5.79326	5.72404	5.04658	4.45177	15
16	6.35111	6.26882	6.18830	6.10950	6.03238	5.95689	5.88298	5.81061	5.10536	4.49070	16
17	6.44636	6.36048	6.27651	6.19440	6.11410	6.03555	5.95871	5.88353	5.15368	4.52189	17
18	6.52758	6.43846	6.35139	6.26631	6.18316	6.10189	6.02243	5.94474	5.19327	4.54679	18
19	6.59659	6.50457	6.41473	6.32700	6.24131	6.15761	6.07584	5.99593	5.22559	4.56661	19
20	6.65496	6.56036	6.46806	6.37798	6.29006	6.20423	6.12042	6.03857	5.25187	4.58231	20
21	6.70410	6.60723	6.51276	6.42062	6.33073	6.24303	6.15744	6.07390	5.27312	4.59468	21
22	6.74524	6.64637	6.55000	6.45607	6.36447	6.27515	6.18802	6.10301	5.29021	4.60438	22
23	6.77945	6.67884	6.58084	6.48535	6.39228	6.30156	6.21311	6.12684	5.30387	4.61194	23
24	6.80768	6.70558	6.60617	6.50934	6.41502	6.32311	6.23353	6.14620	5.31470	4.61777	24
25	6.83075	6.72739	6.62678	6.52883	6.43344	6.34053	6.25000	6.16178	5.32321	4.62224	25
30	6.89119	6.78419	6.68016	6.57901	6.48062	6.38489	6.29172	6.20102	5.34340	4.63221	30
35	6.89979	6.79220	6.68763	6.58596	6.48710	6.39093	6.29735	6.20627	5.34585	4.63330	35
40	6.88797	6.78136	6.67769	6.57684	6.47873	6.38325	6.29030	6.19980	5.34329	4.63234	40
45	6.87045	6.76546	6.66326	6.56375	6.46684	6.37245	6.28049	6.19089	5.34014	4.63130	45
50	6.85353	6.75028	6.64963	6.55151	6.45585	6.36258	6.27163	6.18292	5.33764	4.63057	50

Amount of 1st Year Decline 4.0%

Holding Period	10.50%	10.75%	11.00%	11.25%	11.50%	11.75%	12.00%	12.25%	15.00%	18.00%	
1	0.90498	0.90293	0.90090	0.89888	0.89686	0.89485	0.89286	0.89087	0.86957	0.84746	1
2	1.69120	1.68561	1.68006	1.67454	1.66905	1.66359	1.65816	1.65277	1.59546	1.53691	2
3	2.37307	2.36288	2.35275	2.34271	2.33273	2.32283	2.31300	2.30324	2.20038	2.09686	3
4	2.96332	2.94781	2.93244	2.91720	2.90209	2.88711	2.87226	2.85753	2.70352	2.55075	4
5	3.47320	3.45196	3.43094	3.41012	3.38951	3.36910	3.34890	3.32889	3.12115	2.91792	5
6	3.91265	3.88550	3.85865	3.83210	3.80584	3.77988	3.75420	3.72881	3.46701	3.21427	6
7	4.29047	4.25738	4.22471	4.19244	4.16057	4.12908	4.09799	4.06727	3.75272	3.45285	7
8	4.61439	4.57550	4.53714	4.49929	4.46196	4.42512	4.38878	4.35292	3.98809	3.64440	8
9	4.89124	4.84674	4.80297	4.75979	4.71725	4.67532	4.63400	4.59326	4.18139	3.79771	9
10	5.12705	5.07731	5.02836	4.98018	4.93274	4.88604	4.84006	4.79478	4.33959	3.91999	10
11	5.32711	5.27247	5.21873	5.16590	5.11393	5.06282	5.01255	4.96309	4.46856	4.01714	11
12	5.49609	5.43693	5.37880	5.32170	5.26560	5.21046	5.15628	5.10303	4.57322	4.09398	12
13	5.63809	5.57482	5.51271	5.45175	5.39190	5.33315	5.27545	5.21880	4.65774	4.15445	13
14	5.75672	5.68975	5.62407	5.55966	5.49647	5.43449	5.37367	5.31400	4.72558	4.20176	14
15	5.85512	5.78487	5.71603	5.64857	5.58244	5.51761	5.45406	5.39174	4.77965	4.23850	15
16	5.93608	5.86295	5.79135	5.72122	5.65253	5.58524	5.51931	5.45470	4.82240	4.26681	16
17	6.00202	5.92641	5.85242	5.78000	5.70910	5.63970	5.57174	5.50518	4.85585	4.28841	17
18	6.05506	5.97734	5.90132	5.82696	5.75421	5.68302	5.61335	5.54516	4.88171	4.30467	18
19	6.09706	6.01757	5.93987	5.86389	5.78960	5.71694	5.64586	5.57632	4.90138	4.31673	19
20	6.12965	6.04872	5.96964	5.89235	5.81681	5.74296	5.67074	5.60012	4.91604	4.32549	20
21	6.15422	6.07215	5.99199	5.91367	5.83715	5.76236	5.68925	5.61778	4.92667	4.33168	21
22	6.17201	6.08907	6.00809	5.92900	5.85174	5.77625	5.70248	5.63037	4.93406	4.33588	22
23	6.18408	6.10054	6.01898	5.93933	5.86155	5.78557	5.71133	5.63878	4.93888	4.33854	23
24	6.19136	6.10744	6.02551	5.94553	5.86742	5.79113	5.71660	5.64378	4.94168	4.34005	24
25	6.19466	6.11055	6.02846	5.94831	5.87005	5.79362	5.71895	5.64601	4.94289	4.34069	25
30	6.17244	6.08974	6.00895	5.93003	5.85292	5.77756	5.70390	5.63189	4.93588	4.33735	30
35	6.12151	6.04247	5.96509	5.88932	5.81512	5.74246	5.67130	5.60162	4.92226	4.33153	35
40	6.06787	5.99324	5.91990	5.84782	5.77701	5.70746	5.63914	5.57206	4.91046	4.32708	40
45	6.02151	5.95117	5.88170	5.81314	5.74552	5.67885	5.61315	5.54843	4.90209	4.32430	45
50	5.98500	5.91840	5.85229	5.78673	5.72180	5.65754	5.59400	5.53123	4.89668	4.32272	50

Present Value of a Series of Payments Decreasing by a Constant Amount

Amount of 1st Year Decline   5.0%

Holding Period	10.50%	10.75%	11.00%	11.25%	11.50%	11.75%	12.00%	12.25%	15.00%	18.00%	
1	0.90498	0.90293	0.90090	0.89888	0.89686	0.89485	0.89286	0.89087	0.86957	0.84746	1
2	1.68301	1.67746	1.67194	1.66646	1.66100	1.65558	1.65019	1.64483	1.58790	1.52973	2
3	2.35006	2.34000	2.33001	2.32010	2.31026	2.30049	2.29079	2.28116	2.17967	2.07750	3
4	2.92018	2.90499	2.88994	2.87501	2.86021	2.84553	2.83098	2.81656	2.66566	2.51592	4
5	3.40578	3.38514	3.36470	3.34446	3.32442	3.30457	3.28493	3.26547	3.06340	2.86561	5
6	3.81777	3.79158	3.76568	3.74006	3.71473	3.68968	3.66490	3.64039	3.38764	3.14343	6
7	4.16576	4.13410	4.10284	4.07196	4.04145	4.01131	3.98154	3.95213	3.65080	3.36318	7
8	4.45819	4.42129	4.38489	4.34898	4.31354	4.27857	4.24407	4.21002	3.86329	3.53610	8
9	4.70247	4.66065	4.61945	4.57883	4.53880	4.49933	4.46043	4.42208	4.03384	3.67138	9
10	4.90511	4.85877	4.81315	4.76822	4.72399	4.68042	4.63752	4.59526	4.16979	3.77646	10
11	5.07183	5.02140	4.97179	4.92299	4.87497	4.82774	4.78126	4.73552	4.27727	3.85742	11
12	5.20762	5.15355	5.10042	5.04819	4.99685	4.94638	4.89676	4.84797	4.36137	3.91917	12
13	5.31685	5.25962	5.20342	5.14823	5.09401	5.04075	4.98843	4.93702	4.42639	3.96569	13
14	5.40335	5.34343	5.28462	5.22691	5.17026	5.11464	5.06005	5.00644	4.47585	4.00018	14
15	5.47044	5.40828	5.34732	5.28753	5.22887	5.17132	5.11486	5.05945	4.51272	4.02523	15
16	5.52104	5.45709	5.39440	5.33294	5.27268	5.21359	5.15564	5.09880	4.53944	4.04293	16
17	5.55768	5.49234	5.42832	5.36559	5.30411	5.24384	5.18477	5.12684	4.55802	4.05492	17
18	5.58254	5.51621	5.45125	5.38760	5.32525	5.26415	5.20427	5.14558	4.57014	4.06255	18
19	5.59754	5.53058	5.46501	5.40079	5.33789	5.27626	5.21588	5.15671	4.57717	4.06686	19
20	5.60433	5.53707	5.47121	5.40672	5.34356	5.28168	5.22107	5.16167	4.58022	4.06868	20
21	5.60433	5.53707	5.47121	5.40672	5.34356	5.28168	5.22107	5.16167	4.58022	4.06868	21
22	5.59877	5.53178	5.46618	5.40193	5.33900	5.27734	5.21693	5.15773	4.57791	4.06737	22
23	5.58871	5.52223	5.45711	5.39332	5.33082	5.26958	5.20955	5.15072	4.57390	4.06515	23
24	5.57505	5.50929	5.44486	5.38171	5.31982	5.25915	5.19967	5.14136	4.56866	4.06232	24
25	5.55857	5.49372	5.43013	5.36779	5.30666	5.24671	5.18791	5.13023	4.56258	4.05913	25
30	5.45369	5.39529	5.33774	5.28106	5.22522	5.17023	5.11608	5.06276	4.52835	4.04248	30
35	5.34322	5.29275	5.24255	5.19267	5.14314	5.09399	5.04525	4.99694	4.49868	4.02975	35
40	5.24776	5.20513	5.16211	5.11880	5.07529	5.03166	4.98798	4.94432	4.47763	4.02181	40
45	5.17257	5.13688	5.10015	5.06254	5.02420	4.98525	4.94581	4.90598	4.46404	4.01729	45
50	5.11646	5.08653	5.05495	5.02196	4.98774	4.95250	4.91638	4.87953	4.45572	4.01486	50

Amount of 1st Year Decline   6.0%

Holding Period	10.50%	10.75%	11.00%	11.25%	11.50%	11.75%	12.00%	12.25%	15.00%	18.00%	
1	0.90498	0.90293	0.90090	0.89888	0.89686	0.89485	0.89286	0.89087	0.86957	0.84746	1
2	1.67482	1.66931	1.66383	1.65838	1.65296	1.64757	1.64222	1.63690	1.58034	1.52255	2
3	2.32704	2.31712	2.30727	2.29750	2.28779	2.27815	2.26859	2.25909	2.15895	2.05815	3
4	2.87705	2.86218	2.84743	2.83282	2.81833	2.80396	2.78971	2.77559	2.62779	2.48109	4
5	3.33837	3.31831	3.29846	3.27880	3.25933	3.24005	3.22096	3.20205	3.00565	2.81330	5
6	3.72289	3.69766	3.67271	3.64803	3.62362	3.59948	3.57560	3.55198	3.30828	3.07260	6
7	4.04105	4.01082	3.98097	3.95147	3.92233	3.89354	3.86510	3.83700	3.54888	3.27351	7
8	4.30198	4.26708	4.23264	4.19866	4.16512	4.13202	4.09935	4.06711	3.73848	3.42781	8
9	4.51370	4.47453	4.43593	4.39787	4.36034	4.32335	4.28687	4.25090	3.88630	3.54505	9
10	4.68318	4.64023	4.59793	4.55627	4.51523	4.47480	4.43498	4.39574	4.00000	3.63294	10
11	4.81656	4.77033	4.72484	4.68008	4.63602	4.59265	4.54997	4.50795	4.08598	3.69771	11
12	4.91915	4.87018	4.82203	4.77467	4.72810	4.68230	4.63724	4.59291	4.14953	3.74436	12
13	4.99562	4.94443	4.89413	4.84470	4.79611	4.74836	4.70141	4.65525	4.19503	3.77692	13
14	5.04998	4.99711	4.94517	4.89416	4.84404	4.79480	4.74642	4.69888	4.22613	3.79860	14
15	5.08577	5.03170	4.97861	4.92649	4.87530	4.82503	4.77565	4.72715	4.24579	3.81197	15
16	5.10601	5.05122	4.99744	4.94465	4.89282	4.84194	4.79197	4.74289	4.25648	3.81904	16
17	5.11333	5.05827	5.00423	4.95118	4.89911	4.84799	4.79779	4.74850	4.26019	3.82144	17
18	5.11002	5.05509	5.00117	4.94825	4.89629	4.84528	4.79519	4.74600	4.25858	3.82043	18
19	5.09802	5.04359	4.99016	4.93769	4.88618	4.83559	4.78590	4.73710	4.25296	3.81698	19
20	5.07901	5.02542	4.97279	4.92109	4.87031	4.82041	4.77139	4.72322	4.24440	3.81187	20
21	5.05444	5.00199	4.95044	4.89978	4.84997	4.80101	4.75288	4.70555	4.23377	3.80568	21
22	5.02554	4.97449	4.92427	4.87487	4.82626	4.77844	4.73139	4.68509	4.22176	3.79886	22
23	4.99334	4.94392	4.89525	4.84731	4.80009	4.75358	4.70778	4.66266	4.20891	3.79175	23
24	4.95874	4.91115	4.86420	4.81789	4.77222	4.72717	4.68274	4.63893	4.19563	3.78460	24
25	4.92248	4.87688	4.83181	4.78728	4.74327	4.69980	4.65686	4.61445	4.18227	3.77758	25
30	4.73494	4.70084	4.66653	4.63208	4.59752	4.56291	4.52826	4.49363	4.12082	3.74762	30
35	4.56493	4.54302	4.52001	4.49602	4.47116	4.44552	4.41919	4.39228	4.07509	3.72798	35
40	4.42765	4.41701	4.40432	4.38978	4.37357	4.35587	4.33682	4.31658	4.04480	3.71654	40
45	4.32363	4.32259	4.31860	4.31194	4.30288	4.29165	4.27846	4.26353	4.02599	3.71028	45
50	4.24792	4.25465	4.25761	4.25718	4.25369	4.24745	4.23875	4.22784	4.01476	3.70700	50

Present Value of a Series of Payments Decreasing by a Constant Amount

Amount of 1st Year Decline 7.0%

Holding Period				Discount Rate						
	10.50%	10.75%	11.00%	11.25%	11.50%	11.75%	12.00%	12.25%	15.00%	18.00%
1	0.90498	0.90293	0.90090	0.89888	0.89686	0.89485	0.89286	0.89087	0.86957	0.84746	1
2	1.66663	1.66115	1.65571	1.65030	1.64492	1.63957	1.63425	1.62896	1.57278	1.51537	2
3	2.30403	2.29425	2.28453	2.27489	2.26532	2.25581	2.24638	2.23701	2.13824	2.03879	3
4	2.83391	2.81936	2.80493	2.79063	2.77644	2.76238	2.74844	2.73461	2.58993	2.44626	4
5	3.27095	3.25149	3.23222	3.21313	3.19423	3.17552	3.15699	3.13863	2.94790	2.76098	5
6	3.62801	3.60374	3.57973	3.55599	3.53250	3.50927	3.48630	3.46356	3.22891	3.00176	6
7	3.91634	3.88755	3.85910	3.83099	3.80321	3.77577	3.74866	3.72186	3.44695	3.18384	7
8	4.14578	4.11288	4.08040	4.04834	4.01670	3.98547	3.95464	3.92420	3.61367	3.31952	8
9	4.32492	4.28841	4.25240	4.21690	4.18189	4.14736	4.11331	4.07972	3.73875	3.41872	9
10	4.46125	4.42169	4.38271	4.34431	4.30647	4.26918	4.23244	4.19622	3.83021	3.48941	10
11	4.56128	4.51926	4.47790	4.43717	4.39706	4.35757	4.31868	4.28038	3.89469	3.53799	11
12	4.63068	4.58681	4.54364	4.50116	4.45936	4.41821	4.37771	4.33785	3.93768	3.56955	12
13	4.67438	4.62924	4.58484	4.54118	4.49822	4.45596	4.41438	4.37347	3.96368	3.58816	13
14	4.69662	4.65079	4.60572	4.56141	4.51783	4.47496	4.43280	4.39132	3.97640	3.59703	14
15	4.70109	4.65511	4.60990	4.56545	4.52173	4.47874	4.43645	4.39486	3.97886	3.59870	15
16	4.69097	4.64535	4.60049	4.55637	4.51297	4.47029	4.42830	4.38699	3.97352	3.59516	16
17	4.66899	4.62420	4.58013	4.53678	4.49411	4.45213	4.41082	4.37016	3.96236	3.58796	17
18	4.63750	4.59396	4.55110	4.50889	4.46733	4.42641	4.38611	4.34642	3.94701	3.57830	18
19	4.59850	4.55660	4.51530	4.47459	4.43447	4.39491	4.35592	4.31749	3.92874	3.56710	19
20	4.55370	4.51378	4.47437	4.43546	4.39706	4.35914	4.32171	4.28477	3.90858	3.55506	20
21	4.50456	4.46691	4.42967	4.39283	4.35638	4.32034	4.28469	4.24944	3.88733	3.54268	21
22	4.45230	4.41719	4.38236	4.34780	4.31352	4.27954	4.24585	4.21246	3.86561	3.53036	22
23	4.39797	4.36561	4.33338	4.30129	4.26936	4.23759	4.20600	4.17460	3.84392	3.51836	23
24	4.34242	4.31300	4.28354	4.25407	4.22462	4.19519	4.16581	4.13651	3.82261	3.50687	24
25	4.28639	4.26005	4.23349	4.20676	4.17988	4.15289	4.12581	4.09868	3.80195	3.49602	25
30	4.01619	4.00639	3.99532	3.98311	3.96983	3.95558	3.94044	3.92449	3.71330	3.45276	30
35	3.78665	3.79330	3.79748	3.79937	3.79917	3.79705	3.79314	3.78761	3.65150	3.42621	35
40	3.60755	3.62889	3.64653	3.66076	3.67186	3.68008	3.68567	3.68883	3.61197	3.41127	40
45	3.47469	3.50830	3.53705	3.56134	3.58156	3.59804	3.61112	3.62108	3.58793	3.40328	45
50	3.37939	3.42277	3.46027	3.49240	3.51963	3.54241	3.56113	3.57615	3.57381	3.39915	50

Amount of 1st Year Decline 8.0%

Holding Period				Discount Rate						
	10.50%	10.75%	11.00%	11.25%	11.50%	11.75%	12.00%	12.25%	15.00%	18.00%
1	0.90498	0.90293	0.90090	0.89888	0.89686	0.89485	0.89286	0.89087	0.86957	0.84746	1
2	1.65844	1.65300	1.64759	1.64222	1.63687	1.63156	1.62628	1.62102	1.56522	1.50819	2
3	2.28102	2.27137	2.26179	2.25229	2.24285	2.23348	2.22417	2.21493	2.11753	2.01944	3
4	2.79078	2.77654	2.76243	2.74844	2.73456	2.72081	2.70716	2.69364	2.55206	2.41144	4
5	3.20354	3.18467	3.16598	3.14747	3.12914	3.11099	3.09301	3.07521	2.89014	2.70867	5
6	3.53313	3.50982	3.48676	3.46395	3.44139	3.41907	3.39699	3.37515	3.14954	2.93093	6
7	3.79163	3.76427	3.73722	3.71050	3.68410	3.65800	3.63222	3.60673	3.34503	3.09417	7
8	3.98958	3.95867	3.92815	3.89802	3.86828	3.83892	3.80992	3.78130	3.48886	3.21123	8
9	4.13615	4.10229	4.06888	4.03594	4.00344	3.97137	3.93974	3.90854	3.59120	3.29239	9
10	4.23932	4.20315	4.16750	4.13235	4.09771	4.06356	4.02990	3.99670	3.66041	3.34589	10
11	4.30601	4.26820	4.23095	4.19426	4.15811	4.12249	4.08739	4.05280	3.70340	3.37827	11
12	4.34222	4.30344	4.26525	4.22765	4.19061	4.15413	4.11819	4.08279	3.72583	3.39474	12
13	4.35314	4.31405	4.27555	4.23765	4.20033	4.16357	4.12736	4.09170	3.73233	3.39939	13
14	4.34325	4.30447	4.26627	4.22866	4.19161	4.15512	4.11917	4.08376	3.72668	3.39545	14
15	4.31642	4.27853	4.24119	4.20441	4.16817	4.13245	4.09725	4.06256	3.71193	3.38543	15
16	4.27594	4.23948	4.20354	4.16808	4.13312	4.09864	4.06463	4.03108	3.69056	3.37127	16
17	4.22465	4.19013	4.15604	4.12237	4.08912	4.05628	4.02385	3.99182	3.66454	3.35448	17
18	4.16498	4.13284	4.10102	4.06954	4.03838	4.00754	3.97703	3.94684	3.63545	3.33618	18
19	4.09897	4.06961	4.04044	4.01149	3.98276	3.95424	3.92594	3.89788	3.60453	3.31723	19
20	4.02838	4.00213	3.97595	3.94983	3.92380	3.89787	3.87204	3.84632	3.57276	3.29824	20
21	3.95467	3.93184	3.90890	3.88588	3.86280	3.83967	3.81650	3.79332	3.54088	3.27968	21
22	3.87907	3.85990	3.84045	3.82073	3.80079	3.78064	3.76031	3.73982	3.50946	3.26185	22
23	3.80260	3.78731	3.77152	3.75528	3.73863	3.72160	3.70423	3.68654	3.47893	3.24497	23
24	3.72611	3.71486	3.70289	3.69026	3.67702	3.66321	3.64889	3.63408	3.44959	3.22915	24
25	3.65030	3.64321	3.63517	3.62624	3.61649	3.60598	3.59477	3.58290	3.42164	3.21447	25
30	3.29744	3.31194	3.32411	3.33413	3.34213	3.34825	3.35262	3.35536	3.30577	3.15789	30
35	3.00836	3.04358	3.07494	3.10273	3.12719	3.14857	3.16709	3.18295	3.22792	3.12444	35
40	2.78744	2.84078	2.88874	2.93174	2.97014	3.00429	3.03451	3.06109	3.17914	3.10600	40
45	2.62575	2.69401	2.75550	2.81074	2.86024	2.90444	2.94378	2.97863	3.14988	3.09627	45
50	2.51085	2.59090	2.66293	2.72762	2.78558	2.83737	2.88351	2.92445	3.13285	3.09129	50

Present Value of a Series of Payments Decreasing by a Constant Amount

Amount of 1st Year Decline 9.0%

Holding Period	10.50%	10.75%	11.00%	11.25%	Discount Rate 11.50%	11.75%	12.00%	12.25%	15.00%	18.00%	
1	0.90498	0.90293	0.90090	0.89888	0.89686	0.89485	0.89286	0.89087	0.86957	0.84746	1
2	1.65025	1.64485	1.63948	1.63414	1.62883	1.62355	1.61830	1.61309	1.55766	1.50101	2
3	2.25801	2.24850	2.23905	2.22968	2.22038	2.21114	2.20196	2.19286	2.09682	2.00008	3
4	2.74764	2.73373	2.71993	2.70625	2.69268	2.67923	2.66589	2.65266	2.51420	2.37661	4
5	3.13612	3.11784	3.09974	3.08181	3.06405	3.04646	3.02904	3.01179	2.83239	2.65636	5
6	3.43825	3.41590	3.39379	3.37192	3.35028	3.32887	3.30769	3.28674	3.07017	2.86010	6
7	3.66693	3.64099	3.61535	3.59002	3.56498	3.54023	3.51577	3.49159	3.24310	3.00450	7
8	3.83338	3.80446	3.77590	3.74771	3.71986	3.69237	3.66521	3.63839	3.36406	3.10294	8
9	3.94738	3.91616	3.88536	3.85497	3.82498	3.79539	3.76618	3.73735	3.44365	3.16606	9
10	4.01739	3.98461	3.95228	3.92040	3.88896	3.85794	3.82736	3.79718	3.49062	3.20237	10
11	4.05073	4.01713	3.98401	3.95135	3.91915	3.88741	3.85610	3.82523	3.51211	3.21856	11
12	4.05375	4.02007	3.98687	3.95413	3.92186	3.89004	3.85867	3.82773	3.51398	3.21993	12
13	4.03190	3.99885	3.96626	3.93413	3.90243	3.87117	3.84034	3.80992	3.50098	3.21063	13
14	3.98989	3.95815	3.92683	3.89591	3.86540	3.83528	3.80555	3.77620	3.47695	3.19387	14
15	3.93174	3.90194	3.87248	3.84337	3.81460	3.78616	3.75805	3.73027	3.44500	3.17216	15
16	3.86090	3.83362	3.80658	3.77980	3.75327	3.72699	3.70096	3.67517	3.40760	3.14739	16
17	3.78031	3.75606	3.73194	3.70796	3.68412	3.66042	3.63687	3.61347	3.36671	3.12100	17
18	3.69246	3.67171	3.65095	3.63018	3.60942	3.58867	3.56795	3.54726	3.32388	3.09406	18
19	3.59945	3.58261	3.56559	3.54839	3.53105	3.51356	3.49597	3.47826	3.28032	3.06735	19
20	3.50307	3.49049	3.47752	3.46420	3.45055	3.43660	3.42236	3.40787	3.23694	3.04143	20
21	3.40478	3.39676	3.38813	3.37893	3.36921	3.35899	3.34831	3.33721	3.19443	3.01668	21
22	3.30583	3.30261	3.29853	3.29367	3.28805	3.28173	3.27476	3.26718	3.15331	2.99335	22
23	3.20723	3.20900	3.20966	3.20927	3.20790	3.20561	3.20245	3.19848	3.11394	2.97157	23
24	3.10980	3.11671	3.12223	3.12644	3.12941	3.13123	3.13196	3.13166	3.07656	2.95142	24
25	3.01421	3.02638	3.03685	3.04572	3.05310	3.05907	3.06372	3.06713	3.04132	2.93291	25
30	2.57868	2.61749	2.65290	2.68515	2.71443	2.74092	2.76480	2.78623	2.89825	2.86303	30
35	2.23008	2.29385	2.35240	2.40608	2.45521	2.50010	2.54104	2.57828	2.80433	2.82266	35
40	1.96733	2.05266	2.13095	2.20272	2.26842	2.32849	2.38335	2.43335	2.74631	2.80073	40
45	1.77681	1.87973	1.97395	2.06014	2.13892	2.21084	2.27644	2.33618	2.71183	2.78927	45
50	1.64232	1.75902	1.86559	1.96284	2.05152	2.13233	2.20588	2.27276	2.69189	2.78344	50

Amount of 1st Year Decline 10.0%

Holding Period	10.50%	10.75%	11.00%	11.25%	Discount Rate 11.50%	11.75%	12.00%	12.25%	15.00%	18.00%	
1	0.90498	0.90293	0.90090	0.89888	0.89686	0.89485	0.89286	0.89087	0.86957	0.84746	1
2	1.64206	1.63670	1.63136	1.62606	1.62078	1.61554	1.61033	1.60515	1.55009	1.49382	2
3	2.23499	2.22562	2.21631	2.20708	2.19790	2.18880	2.17976	2.17078	2.07611	1.98073	3
4	2.70451	2.69091	2.67743	2.66406	2.65080	2.63765	2.62462	2.61169	2.47633	2.34178	4
5	3.06871	3.05102	3.03350	3.01614	2.99896	2.98194	2.96507	2.94837	2.77464	2.60405	5
6	3.34337	3.32198	3.30082	3.27988	3.25917	3.23867	3.21839	3.19832	2.99080	2.78926	6
7	3.54222	3.51771	3.49348	3.46953	3.44586	3.42246	3.39933	3.37646	3.14118	2.91483	7
8	3.67718	3.65025	3.62366	3.59739	3.57144	3.54581	3.52049	3.49548	3.23925	2.99464	8
9	3.75861	3.73004	3.70184	3.67401	3.64653	3.61940	3.59262	3.56617	3.29610	3.03973	9
10	3.79545	3.76606	3.73706	3.70844	3.68020	3.65233	3.62481	3.59766	3.32082	3.05884	10
11	3.79545	3.76606	3.73706	3.70844	3.68020	3.65233	3.62481	3.59766	3.32082	3.05884	11
12	3.76528	3.73670	3.70848	3.68062	3.65312	3.62596	3.59915	3.57267	3.30213	3.04512	12
13	3.71066	3.68366	3.65697	3.63060	3.60454	3.57877	3.55331	3.52814	3.26962	3.02186	13
14	3.63652	3.61183	3.58738	3.56316	3.53918	3.51544	3.49193	3.46864	3.22723	2.99230	14
15	3.54706	3.52535	3.50377	3.48233	3.46103	3.43987	3.41885	3.39797	3.17807	2.95889	15
16	3.44587	3.42775	3.40963	3.39152	3.37342	3.35534	3.33729	3.31927	3.12464	2.92350	16
17	3.33597	3.32199	3.30785	3.29356	3.27912	3.26457	3.24990	3.23513	3.06888	2.88751	17
18	3.21994	3.21058	3.20087	3.19083	3.18046	3.16980	3.15887	3.14768	3.01232	2.85193	18
19	3.09993	3.09562	3.09073	3.08529	3.07933	3.07289	3.06599	3.05865	2.95610	2.81747	19
20	2.97775	2.97884	2.97910	2.97857	2.97730	2.97533	2.97269	2.96942	2.90111	2.78462	20
21	2.85489	2.86168	2.86736	2.87199	2.87562	2.87832	2.88013	2.88110	2.84798	2.75368	21
22	2.73260	2.74531	2.75662	2.76660	2.77531	2.78283	2.78922	2.79454	2.79716	2.72484	22
23	2.61186	2.63069	2.64779	2.66326	2.67717	2.68962	2.70067	2.71042	2.74895	2.69818	23
24	2.49348	2.51857	2.54158	2.56262	2.58181	2.59925	2.61503	2.62924	2.70354	2.67370	24
25	2.37812	2.40954	2.43852	2.46521	2.48971	2.51217	2.53268	2.55135	2.66101	2.65136	25
30	1.85993	1.92304	1.98169	2.03618	2.08673	2.13359	2.17698	2.21710	2.49072	2.56816	30
35	1.45179	1.54413	1.62986	1.70943	1.78323	1.85163	1.91499	1.97362	2.38074	2.52089	35
40	1.14723	1.26455	1.37316	1.47369	1.56670	1.65270	1.73219	1.80561	2.31348	2.49546	40
45	0.92787	1.06544	1.19240	1.30954	1.41760	1.51724	1.60910	1.69373	2.27378	2.48226	45
50	0.77378	0.92714	1.06825	1.19806	1.31747	1.42729	1.52826	1.62107	2.25093	2.47558	50

Hoskold Present Value of 1 per Period

Safe Rate 5.50%

						Speculative Rate						
Year	5.50%		5.75%		6.00%		6.25%		6.50%		6.75%	
	Annual	Monthly	Annual	Monthly	Annual	Monthly	Annual	Monthly	Annual	Monthly	Annual	Monthly
1	0.94787	0.97083	0.94563	0.96848	0.94340	0.96614	0.94118	0.96382	0.93897	0.96150	0.93677	0.95919
2	1.84632	1.88983	1.83784	1.88094	1.82943	1.87214	1.82110	1.86342	1.81285	1.85478	1.80467	1.84622
3	2.69793	2.75976	2.67986	2.74085	2.66202	2.72219	2.64442	2.70379	2.62706	2.68564	2.60992	2.66773
4	3.50515	3.58323	3.47470	3.55142	3.44478	3.52016	3.41536	3.48946	3.38645	3.45928	3.35802	3.42962
5	4.27028	4.36274	4.22518	4.31567	4.18101	4.26960	4.13776	4.22451	4.09540	4.18036	4.05389	4.13712
6	4.99553	5.10062	4.93391	5.03640	4.87379	4.97377	4.81512	4.91269	4.75785	4.85308	4.70192	4.79491
7	5.68297	5.79910	5.60336	5.71623	5.52595	5.63569	5.45065	5.55739	5.37737	5.48124	5.30604	5.40714
8	6.33457	6.46029	6.23581	6.35761	6.14009	6.25814	6.04726	6.16174	5.95720	6.06826	5.86978	5.97758
9	6.95220	7.08617	6.83343	6.96282	6.71865	6.84369	6.60766	6.72857	6.50028	6.61726	6.39634	6.50957
10	7.53763	7.67863	7.39821	7.53400	7.26386	7.39472	7.13431	7.26050	7.00929	7.13106	6.88858	7.00616
11	8.09254	8.23946	7.93206	8.07316	7.77782	7.91345	7.62947	7.75993	7.48667	7.61225	7.34912	7.47009
12	8.61852	8.77034	8.43674	8.58217	8.26247	8.40190	8.09525	8.22905	7.93467	8.06317	7.78033	7.90385
13	9.11708	9.27287	8.91391	9.06278	8.71959	8.86199	8.53357	8.66991	8.35532	8.48598	8.18436	8.30969
14	9.58965	9.74858	9.36513	9.51664	9.15088	9.29549	8.94622	9.08438	8.75051	8.88264	8.56317	8.68968
15	10.03758	10.19888	9.79186	9.94530	9.55789	9.70403	9.33484	9.47418	9.12196	9.25497	8.91857	9.04568
16	10.46216	10.62513	10.19549	10.35020	9.94208	10.08914	9.70096	9.84092	9.47126	9.60463	9.25219	9.37941
17	10.86461	11.02863	10.57731	10.73271	10.30482	10.45226	10.04601	10.18609	9.79989	9.93314	9.56554	9.69245
18	11.24607	11.41058	10.93854	11.09410	10.64737	10.79471	10.37130	10.51105	10.10919	10.24192	9.86000	9.98622
19	11.60765	11.77214	11.28031	11.43558	10.97092	11.11774	10.67805	10.81709	10.40041	10.53226	10.13684	10.26206
20	11.95038	12.11439	11.60371	11.75828	11.27658	11.42250	10.96740	11.10538	10.67471	10.80538	10.39724	10.52117
21	12.27524	12.43836	11.90976	12.06325	11.56540	11.71009	11.24040	11.37703	10.93317	11.06238	10.64229	10.76468
22	12.58317	12.74504	12.19940	12.35149	11.83835	11.98152	11.49805	11.63306	11.17678	11.30430	10.87297	10.99361
23	12.87504	13.03534	12.47355	12.62395	12.09634	12.23773	11.74127	11.87444	11.40646	11.53209	11.09021	11.20894
24	13.15170	13.31014	12.73305	12.88151	12.34022	12.47962	11.97091	12.10204	11.62307	11.74665	11.29487	11.41153
25	13.41393	13.57027	12.97869	13.12500	12.57081	12.70801	12.18779	12.31671	11.82741	11.94879	11.48774	11.60221
26	13.66250	13.81651	13.21125	13.35520	12.78886	12.92371	12.39264	12.51922	12.02023	12.13928	11.66955	11.78173
27	13.89810	14.04960	13.43142	13.57286	12.99507	13.12742	12.58617	12.71029	12.20222	12.31885	11.84101	11.95080
28	14.12142	14.27024	13.63989	13.77868	13.19011	13.31985	12.76904	12.89060	12.37403	12.48815	12.00273	12.11007
29	14.33310	14.47910	13.83727	13.97330	13.37460	13.50165	12.94187	13.06079	12.53627	12.64781	12.15531	12.26015
30	14.53375	14.67681	14.02419	14.15735	13.54915	13.67340	13.10523	13.22145	12.68949	12.79841	12.29931	12.40161
31	14.72393	14.86397	14.20119	14.33141	13.71429	13.83570	13.25967	13.37313	12.83423	12.94050	12.43524	12.53497
32	14.90420	15.04113	14.36881	14.49603	13.87055	13.98907	13.40569	13.51637	12.97098	13.07456	12.56357	12.66073
33	15.07507	15.20883	14.52756	14.65174	14.01843	14.13402	13.54377	13.65164	13.10020	13.20109	12.68477	12.77934
34	15.23703	15.36757	14.67791	14.79901	14.15837	14.27102	13.67436	13.77940	13.22234	13.32053	12.79925	12.89123
35	15.39055	15.51784	14.82032	14.93832	14.29083	14.40052	13.79788	13.90010	13.33779	13.43329	12.90740	12.99681
36	15.53607	15.66009	14.95521	15.07009	14.41621	14.52293	13.91472	14.01412	13.44694	13.53975	13.00959	13.09644
37	15.67400	15.79474	15.08297	15.19474	14.53490	14.63867	14.02526	14.12185	13.55015	13.64029	13.10617	13.19048
38	15.80474	15.92220	15.20400	15.31267	14.64726	14.74809	14.12985	14.22366	13.64775	13.73524	13.19746	13.27926
39	15.92866	16.04285	15.31865	15.42423	14.75363	14.85155	14.22882	14.31987	13.74005	13.82494	13.28376	13.36308
40	16.04612	16.15706	15.42726	15.52977	14.85435	14.94937	14.32247	14.41079	13.82737	13.90967	13.36535	13.44223
41	16.15746	16.26518	15.53014	15.62963	14.94972	15.04188	14.41111	14.49674	13.90997	13.98972	13.44250	13.51698
42	16.26300	16.36752	15.62762	15.72411	15.04002	15.12937	14.49501	14.57798	13.98811	14.06537	13.51547	13.58758
43	16.36303	16.46439	15.71997	15.81350	15.12553	15.21210	14.57442	14.65478	14.06205	14.13685	13.58449	13.65428
44	16.45785	16.55610	15.80746	15.89807	15.20652	15.29035	14.64959	14.72739	14.13202	14.20440	13.64978	13.71729
45	16.54773	16.64290	15.89035	15.97810	15.28321	15.36437	14.72076	14.79604	14.19824	14.26825	13.71154	13.77682
46	16.63292	16.72508	15.96889	16.05382	15.35585	15.43437	14.78814	14.86095	14.26091	14.32861	13.76998	13.83308
47	16.71366	16.80286	16.04331	16.12548	15.42465	15.50059	14.85194	14.92233	14.32023	14.38566	13.82528	13.88625
48	16.79020	16.87649	16.11382	16.19328	15.48982	15.56323	14.91234	14.98037	14.37638	14.43959	13.87761	13.93650
49	16.86275	16.94619	16.18063	16.25744	15.55154	15.62248	14.96954	15.03526	14.42953	14.49059	13.92713	13.98400
50	16.93152	17.01217	16.24393	16.31815	15.61001	15.67854	15.02371	15.08718	14.47986	14.53880	13.97400	14.02889
51	16.99670	17.07462	16.30392	16.37560	15.66540	15.73157	15.07501	15.13628	14.52750	14.58439	14.01837	14.07134
52	17.05848	17.13374	16.36076	16.42997	15.71787	15.78174	15.12359	15.18272	14.57262	14.62750	14.06037	14.11146
53	17.11705	17.18970	16.41462	16.48143	15.76757	15.82921	15.16960	15.22664	14.61533	14.66827	14.10014	14.14940
54	17.17255	17.24268	16.46566	16.53012	15.81466	15.87412	15.21319	15.26820	14.65578	14.70683	14.13778	14.18528
55	17.22517	17.29283	16.51403	16.57620	15.85928	15.91661	15.25446	15.30750	14.69409	14.74329	14.17342	14.21920
56	17.27504	17.34029	16.55986	16.61981	15.90154	15.95682	15.29357	15.34468	14.73037	14.77778	14.20717	14.25128
57	17.32232	17.38523	16.60330	16.66109	15.94159	15.99486	15.33060	15.37986	14.76472	14.81041	14.23913	14.28161
58	17.36712	17.42776	16.64446	16.70015	15.97953	16.03085	15.36569	15.41314	14.79726	14.84126	14.26939	14.31031
59	17.40960	17.46803	16.68347	16.73712	16.01548	16.06491	15.39893	15.44462	14.82809	14.87045	14.29805	14.33744
60	17.44985	17.50614	16.72043	16.77210	16.04954	16.09715	15.43042	15.47441	14.85728	14.89806	14.32520	14.36311
61	17.48801	17.54222	16.75546	16.80522	16.08182	16.12765	15.46025	15.50259	14.88493	14.92419	14.35090	14.38739
62	17.52418	17.57637	16.78866	16.83656	16.11240	16.15651	15.48851	15.52926	14.91113	14.94890	14.37525	14.41035
63	17.55847	17.60870	16.82013	16.86622	16.14138	16.18382	15.51528	15.55449	14.93594	14.97228	14.39831	14.43207
64	17.59096	17.63930	16.84995	16.89429	16.16884	16.20967	15.54065	15.57837	14.95945	14.99439	14.42016	14.45262
65	17.62177	17.66827	16.87821	16.92086	16.19486	16.23412	15.56469	15.60096	14.98172	15.01532	14.44085	14.47207

Hoskold Present Value of 1 per Period

Safe Rate 5.50%

Year	Speculative Rate										
	7.00%		7.25%		7.50%		7.75%		8.00%		8.25%	
	Annual	Monthly	Annual	Monthly	Annual	Monthly	Annual	Monthly	Annual	Monthly	Annual	Monthly
1	0.93458	0.95690	0.93240	0.95462	0.93023	0.95234	0.92807	0.95008	0.92593	0.94783	0.92379	0.94559
2	1.79656	1.83774	1.78853	1.82933	1.78057	1.82100	1.77268	1.81275	1.76486	1.80457	1.75710	1.79647
3	2.59300	2.65005	2.57630	2.63261	2.55981	2.61540	2.54353	2.59841	2.52746	2.58164	2.51159	2.56508
4	3.33006	3.40046	3.30257	3.37180	3.27553	3.34361	3.24892	3.31590	3.22274	3.28863	3.19699	3.26182
5	4.01322	4.09477	3.97336	4.05328	3.93428	4.01262	3.89596	3.97276	3.85838	3.93369	3.82151	3.89539
6	4.64729	4.73811	4.59392	4.68264	4.54176	4.62846	4.49077	4.57551	4.44091	4.52377	4.39215	4.47318
7	5.23658	5.33503	5.16891	5.26481	5.10297	5.19641	5.03869	5.12977	4.97601	5.06482	4.91486	5.00149
8	5.78489	5.88956	5.70242	5.80410	5.62227	5.72109	5.54434	5.64042	5.46854	5.56199	5.39479	5.48571
9	6.29566	6.40533	6.19811	6.30438	6.10354	6.20656	6.01180	6.11172	5.92279	6.01975	5.83637	5.93050
10	6.77196	6.88556	6.65922	6.76904	6.55017	6.65639	6.44464	6.54744	6.34245	6.44199	6.24345	6.33989
11	7.21654	7.33314	7.08865	7.20112	6.96521	7.07378	6.84600	6.95086	6.73080	6.83213	6.61942	6.71740
12	7.63188	7.75070	7.48900	7.60337	7.35136	7.46154	7.21869	7.32490	7.09073	7.19318	6.96722	7.06611
13	8.02026	8.14058	7.86261	7.97821	7.71104	7.82219	7.56520	7.67216	7.42477	7.52777	7.28947	7.38872
14	8.38370	8.50491	8.21159	8.32784	8.04640	8.15800	7.88773	7.99494	7.73520	7.83828	7.58846	7.68763
15	8.72405	8.84564	8.53784	8.65426	8.35941	8.47099	8.18829	8.29531	8.02403	8.12678	7.86624	7.96495
16	9.04302	9.16452	8.84310	8.95925	8.65183	8.76298	8.46865	8.57512	8.29307	8.39514	8.12463	8.22257
17	9.34213	9.46315	9.12892	9.24444	8.92523	9.03562	8.73042	8.83602	8.54394	8.64505	8.36526	8.46216
18	9.62279	9.74298	9.39674	9.51131	9.18106	9.29040	8.97506	9.07952	8.77810	8.87800	8.58960	8.68523
19	9.88630	10.00537	9.64785	9.76121	9.42063	9.52868	9.20386	9.30697	8.99685	9.09535	8.79894	8.89313
20	10.13383	10.25152	9.88344	9.99535	9.64512	9.75168	9.41803	9.51960	9.20138	9.29831	8.99448	9.08707
21	10.36648	10.48257	10.10461	10.21488	9.85564	9.96051	9.61864	9.71851	9.39278	9.48799	9.17728	9.26815
22	10.58523	10.69955	10.31234	10.42080	10.05316	10.15621	9.80669	9.90473	9.57201	9.66539	9.34831	9.43735
23	10.79102	10.90340	10.50755	10.61408	10.23860	10.33971	9.98306	10.07917	9.73998	9.83144	9.50845	9.59559
24	10.98469	11.09500	10.69109	10.79556	10.41278	10.51186	10.14860	10.24268	9.89748	9.98695	9.65849	9.74368
25	11.16703	11.27516	10.86374	10.96605	10.57649	10.67344	10.30404	10.39604	10.04527	10.13269	9.79918	9.88235
26	11.33876	11.44463	11.02620	11.12629	10.73041	10.82518	10.45008	10.53994	10.18402	10.26935	9.93117	10.01230
27	11.50056	11.60410	11.17914	11.27696	10.87521	10.96775	10.58736	10.67505	10.31435	10.39756	10.05507	10.13413
28	11.65306	11.75421	11.32318	11.41867	11.01147	11.10175	10.71646	10.80195	10.43684	10.51791	10.17145	10.24843
29	11.79682	11.89555	11.45888	11.55201	11.13976	11.22775	10.83793	10.92120	10.55202	10.63094	10.28081	10.35571
30	11.93241	12.02867	11.58676	11.67751	11.26058	11.34627	10.95226	11.03330	10.66037	10.73714	10.38363	10.45646
31	12.06030	12.15410	11.70732	11.79568	11.37441	11.45780	11.05991	11.13874	10.76233	10.83696	10.48035	10.55111
32	12.18098	12.27229	11.82100	11.90698	11.48169	11.56278	11.16131	11.23793	10.85833	10.93083	10.57136	10.64007
33	12.29488	12.38370	11.92824	12.01183	11.58283	11.66163	11.25686	11.33128	10.94874	11.01913	10.65704	10.72371
34	12.40240	12.48875	12.02941	12.11063	11.67821	11.75474	11.34693	11.41916	11.03393	11.10222	10.73773	10.80239
35	12.50392	12.58781	12.12490	12.20376	11.76818	11.84245	11.43185	11.50193	11.11421	11.18044	10.81374	10.87643
36	12.59980	12.68125	12.21503	12.29156	11.85307	11.92512	11.51194	11.57989	11.18989	11.25409	10.88538	10.94612
37	12.69037	12.76940	12.30013	12.37436	11.93318	12.00304	11.58749	11.65335	11.26127	11.32346	10.95291	11.01173
38	12.77593	12.85258	12.38050	12.45246	12.00881	12.07651	11.65879	11.72259	11.32860	11.38882	11.01659	11.07353
39	12.85679	12.93108	12.45642	12.52614	12.08023	12.14579	11.72609	11.78786	11.39213	11.45042	11.07666	11.13176
40	12.93321	13.00518	12.52813	12.59566	12.14767	12.21114	11.78962	11.84940	11.45209	11.50848	11.13334	11.18663
41	13.00544	13.07514	12.59590	12.66127	12.21137	12.27279	11.84962	11.90745	11.50869	11.56323	11.18682	11.23835
42	13.07373	13.14119	12.65995	12.72319	12.27155	12.33097	11.90628	11.96221	11.56213	11.61486	11.23731	11.28711
43	13.13830	13.20356	12.72048	12.78166	12.32842	12.38588	11.95981	12.01387	11.61260	11.66356	11.28498	11.33310
44	13.19936	13.26248	12.77771	12.83685	12.38217	12.43770	12.01039	12.06262	11.66027	11.70951	11.33000	11.37647
45	13.25710	13.31812	12.83182	12.88898	12.43298	12.48663	12.05818	12.10864	11.70532	11.75286	11.37252	11.41739
46	13.31172	13.37069	12.88299	12.93821	12.48101	12.53283	12.10335	12.15208	11.74788	11.79378	11.41269	11.45601
47	13.36339	13.42036	12.93138	12.98471	12.52642	12.57645	12.14605	12.19309	11.78810	11.83240	11.45065	11.49245
48	13.41228	13.46728	12.97715	13.02863	12.56936	12.61766	12.18642	12.23181	11.82613	11.86887	11.48652	11.52684
49	13.45853	13.51163	13.02044	13.07013	12.60997	12.65658	12.22459	12.26839	11.86207	11.90330	11.52043	11.55932
50	13.50230	13.55354	13.06140	13.10935	12.64839	12.69334	12.26069	12.30293	11.89606	11.93582	11.55249	11.58998
51	13.54372	13.59315	13.10016	13.14640	12.68473	12.72808	12.29484	12.33556	11.92820	11.96652	11.58279	11.61893
52	13.58292	13.63060	13.13683	13.18142	12.71911	12.76090	12.32713	12.36639	11.95860	11.99553	11.61145	11.64627
53	13.62003	13.66599	13.17153	13.21452	12.75164	12.79192	12.35769	12.39551	11.98735	12.02294	11.63856	11.67210
54	13.65515	13.69945	13.20438	13.24580	12.78242	12.82123	12.38659	12.42304	12.01454	12.04883	11.66419	11.69650
55	13.68840	13.73109	13.23547	13.27537	12.81155	12.84894	12.41394	12.44904	12.04028	12.07329	11.68845	11.71956
56	13.71987	13.76100	13.26489	13.30333	12.83912	12.87513	12.43983	12.47363	12.06462	12.09641	11.71139	11.74134
57	13.74967	13.78928	13.29275	13.32976	12.86521	12.89988	12.46432	12.49686	12.08766	12.11826	11.73310	11.76193
58	13.77789	13.81603	13.31912	13.35475	12.88991	12.92328	12.48750	12.51882	12.10946	12.13891	11.75364	11.78138
59	13.80461	13.84132	13.34408	13.37838	12.91329	12.94541	12.50945	12.53959	12.13009	12.15843	11.77307	11.79976
60	13.82991	13.86524	13.36772	13.40073	12.93543	12.96633	12.53022	12.55921	12.14962	12.17688	11.79147	11.81714
61	13.85386	13.88786	13.39010	13.42186	12.95638	12.98611	12.54988	12.57777	12.16811	12.19433	11.80888	11.83357
62	13.87655	13.90926	13.41130	13.44184	12.97623	13.00482	12.56850	12.59532	12.18561	12.21082	11.82536	11.84910
63	13.89804	13.92949	13.43137	13.46074	12.99502	13.02251	12.58612	12.61191	12.20218	12.22642	11.84096	11.86379
64	13.91839	13.94864	13.45038	13.47862	13.01281	13.03924	12.60281	12.62760	12.21786	12.24116	11.85573	11.87767
65	13.93767	13.96675	13.46838	13.49552	13.02966	13.05506	12.61862	12.64244	12.23272	12.25511	11.86972	11.89080

Hoskold Present Value of 1 per Period

Safe Rate 5.50%

Year	8.50% Annual	8.50% Monthly	8.75% Annual	8.75% Monthly	9.00% Annual	9.00% Monthly	9.25% Annual	9.25% Monthly	9.50% Annual	9.50% Monthly	9.75% Annual	9.75% Monthly
1	0.92166	0.94336	0.91954	0.94114	0.91743	0.93893	0.91533	0.93673	0.91324	0.93454	0.91116	0.93236
2	1.74942	1.78844	1.74180	1.78048	1.73425	1.77258	1.72676	1.76476	1.71934	1.75701	1.71198	1.74933
3	2.49592	2.54874	2.48044	2.53260	2.46515	2.51667	2.45006	2.50093	2.43514	2.48539	2.42040	2.47005
4	3.17164	3.23543	3.14669	3.20947	3.12213	3.18393	3.09795	3.15878	3.07414	3.13403	3.05069	3.10967
5	3.78535	3.85782	3.74986	3.82097	3.71504	3.78481	3.68085	3.74934	3.64729	3.71452	3.61433	3.68034
6	4.34445	4.42371	4.29777	4.37532	4.25208	4.32798	4.20736	4.28165	4.16356	4.23631	4.12067	4.19191
7	4.85521	4.93972	4.79698	4.87946	4.74014	4.82066	4.68462	4.76325	4.63039	4.70720	4.57740	4.65245
8	5.32300	5.41149	5.25309	5.33926	5.18500	5.26893	5.11865	5.20043	5.05398	5.13368	4.99092	5.06863
9	5.75243	5.84385	5.67088	5.75971	5.59161	5.67795	5.51452	5.59848	5.43953	5.52120	5.36655	5.44603
10	6.14750	6.24097	6.05445	6.14509	5.96418	6.05211	5.87655	5.96191	5.79147	5.87435	5.70881	5.78933
11	6.51166	6.60645	6.40735	6.49911	6.30634	6.39520	6.20846	6.29457	6.11357	6.19705	6.02153	6.10250
12	6.84794	6.94345	6.73268	6.82498	6.62123	6.71048	6.51342	6.59976	6.40906	6.49264	6.30798	6.38893
13	7.15900	7.25471	7.03313	7.12548	6.91160	7.00077	6.79420	6.88035	6.68073	6.76400	6.57098	6.65153
14	7.44717	7.54267	7.31106	7.40307	7.17983	7.26855	7.05322	7.13882	6.93101	7.01365	6.81296	6.89279
15	7.71453	7.80945	7.56856	7.65990	7.42801	7.51597	7.29258	7.37735	7.16201	7.24375	7.03603	7.11490
16	7.96289	8.05695	7.80747	7.89787	7.65799	7.74495	7.51413	7.59783	7.37558	7.45621	7.24205	7.31976
17	8.19390	8.28685	8.02942	8.11866	7.87141	7.95715	7.71951	7.80195	7.57335	7.65268	7.43262	7.50902
18	8.40902	8.50066	8.23588	8.32376	8.06973	8.15408	7.91015	7.99118	7.75675	7.83466	7.60920	7.68415
19	8.60955	8.69971	8.42815	8.51453	8.25423	8.33706	8.08734	8.16684	7.92707	8.00344	7.77302	7.84644
20	8.79667	8.88522	8.60738	8.69214	8.42607	8.50727	8.25223	8.33011	8.08543	8.16017	7.92523	7.99703
21	8.97144	9.05826	8.77464	8.85768	8.58629	8.66578	8.40585	8.48202	8.23284	8.30589	8.06681	8.13693
22	9.13482	9.21983	8.93087	9.01210	8.73582	8.81353	8.54911	8.62352	8.37022	8.44153	8.19865	8.26707
23	9.28767	9.37080	9.07691	9.15629	8.87550	8.95139	8.68284	8.75545	8.49837	8.56791	8.32157	8.38824
24	9.43078	9.51197	9.21355	9.29103	9.00610	9.08012	8.80779	8.87858	8.61803	8.68578	8.43627	8.50118
25	9.56486	9.64409	9.34149	9.41704	9.12831	9.20044	8.92464	8.99357	8.72986	8.79581	8.54340	8.60656
26	9.69057	9.76780	9.46136	9.53496	9.24274	9.31297	9.03399	9.10107	8.83446	8.89860	8.64356	8.70495
27	9.80851	9.88373	9.57375	9.64540	9.34996	9.41829	9.13640	9.20163	8.93238	8.99471	8.73727	8.79690
28	9.91922	9.99242	9.67919	9.74888	9.45051	9.51693	9.23238	9.29576	9.02410	9.08464	8.82500	8.88290
29	10.02320	10.09438	9.77818	9.84591	9.54485	9.60937	9.32240	9.38394	9.11008	9.16884	8.90721	8.96338
30	10.12091	10.19008	9.87114	9.93693	9.63341	9.69606	9.40686	9.46659	9.19072	9.24773	8.98429	9.03876
31	10.21277	10.27994	9.95851	10.02237	9.71660	9.77739	9.48617	9.54410	9.26641	9.32168	9.05660	9.10939
32	10.29917	10.36437	10.04065	10.10260	9.79478	9.85373	9.56067	9.61683	9.33749	9.39105	9.12449	9.17563
33	10.38048	10.44372	10.11791	10.17799	9.86829	9.92543	9.63069	9.68511	9.40427	9.45615	9.18825	9.23776
34	10.45702	10.51833	10.19061	10.24883	9.93744	9.99280	9.69654	9.74924	9.46705	9.51728	9.24816	9.29609
35	10.52909	10.58851	10.25905	10.31545	10.00251	10.05612	9.75848	9.80950	9.52608	9.57470	9.30450	9.35087
36	10.59700	10.65455	10.32350	10.37812	10.06377	10.11566	9.81678	9.86616	9.58163	9.62866	9.35748	9.40233
37	10.66099	10.71671	10.38422	10.43708	10.12146	10.17167	9.87168	9.91943	9.63392	9.67940	9.40734	9.45070
38	10.72131	10.77523	10.44145	10.49258	10.17582	10.22438	9.92338	9.96955	9.68315	9.72712	9.45428	9.49619
39	10.77819	10.83036	10.49539	10.54485	10.22705	10.27400	9.97209	10.01672	9.72953	9.77201	9.49849	9.53898
40	10.83185	10.88229	10.54626	10.59407	10.27534	10.32072	10.01800	10.06113	9.77323	9.81427	9.54013	9.57924
41	10.88247	10.93123	10.59424	10.64044	10.32089	10.36473	10.06128	10.10295	9.81442	9.85406	9.57938	9.61714
42	10.93024	10.97736	10.63951	10.68415	10.36385	10.40619	10.10210	10.14234	9.85326	9.89153	9.61638	9.65282
43	10.97534	11.02085	10.68224	10.72534	10.40438	10.44527	10.14061	10.17945	9.88989	9.92683	9.65126	9.68644
44	11.01791	11.06186	10.72256	10.76418	10.44263	10.48210	10.17695	10.21443	9.92445	9.96009	9.68417	9.71811
45	11.05812	11.10055	10.76064	10.80081	10.47875	10.51683	10.21124	10.24741	9.95706	9.99144	9.71522	9.74795
46	11.09610	11.13704	10.79660	10.83536	10.51284	10.54958	10.24362	10.27850	9.98784	10.02100	9.74452	9.77608
47	11.13198	11.17148	10.83057	10.86795	10.54504	10.58048	10.27419	10.30782	10.01690	10.04887	9.77218	9.80261
48	11.16588	11.20398	10.86265	10.89870	10.57546	10.60963	10.30306	10.33549	10.04434	10.07516	9.79830	9.82762
49	11.19792	11.23465	10.89297	10.92773	10.60419	10.63713	10.33033	10.36159	10.07026	10.09996	9.82296	9.85122
50	11.22820	11.26361	10.92163	10.95513	10.63135	10.66309	10.35610	10.38622	10.09474	10.12336	9.84626	9.87348
51	11.25683	11.29096	10.94871	10.98099	10.65701	10.68759	10.38045	10.40946	10.11788	10.14544	9.86826	9.89448
52	11.28390	11.31678	10.97432	11.00541	10.68127	10.71072	10.40346	10.43140	10.13974	10.16628	9.88906	9.91430
53	11.30949	11.34117	10.99852	11.02848	10.70420	10.73257	10.42521	10.45212	10.16040	10.18596	9.90871	9.93302
54	11.33370	11.36420	11.02141	11.05026	10.72588	10.75319	10.44578	10.47168	10.17994	10.20454	9.92729	9.95068
55	11.35659	11.38596	11.04306	11.07083	10.74638	10.77268	10.46522	10.49016	10.19840	10.22208	9.94485	9.96736
56	11.37825	11.40652	11.06354	11.09027	10.76577	10.79108	10.48361	10.50761	10.21586	10.23865	9.96145	9.98311
57	11.39874	11.42595	11.08291	11.10863	10.78411	10.80846	10.50100	10.52409	10.23238	10.25430	9.97715	9.99799
58	11.41812	11.44430	11.10124	11.12598	10.80146	10.82489	10.51745	10.53966	10.24800	10.26908	9.99200	10.01204
59	11.43647	11.46165	11.11857	11.14238	10.81788	10.84041	10.53301	10.55437	10.26277	10.28305	10.00605	10.02532
60	11.45383	11.47805	11.13498	11.15787	10.83341	10.85507	10.54774	10.56828	10.27675	10.29624	10.01933	10.03786
61	11.47025	11.49355	11.15051	11.17252	10.84810	10.86894	10.56167	10.58141	10.28997	10.30871	10.03190	10.04971
62	11.48580	11.50820	11.16520	11.18636	10.86201	10.88204	10.57485	10.59383	10.30248	10.32050	10.04379	10.06091
63	11.50052	11.52205	11.17911	11.19945	10.87517	10.89442	10.58732	10.60557	10.31432	10.33163	10.05504	10.07150
64	11.51445	11.53514	11.19227	11.21182	10.88763	10.90613	10.59913	10.61666	10.32553	10.34216	10.06569	10.08150
65	11.52764	11.54753	11.20473	11.22352	10.89942	10.91719	10.61031	10.62715	10.33613	10.35211	10.07577	10.09096

Table 49 - 4

Hoskold Present Value of 1 per Period

Safe Rate 5.50%

Year	10.00% Annual	Monthly	10.25% Annual	Monthly	10.50% Annual	Monthly	10.75% Annual	Monthly	11.00% Annual	Monthly	11.25% Annual	Monthly
1	0.90909	0.93020	0.90703	0.92804	0.90498	0.92589	0.90293	0.92375	0.90090	0.92162	0.89888	0.91951
2	1.70469	1.74171	1.69745	1.73416	1.69028	1.72667	1.68317	1.71925	1.67611	1.71190	1.66912	1.70460
3	2.40585	2.45489	2.39146	2.43991	2.37725	2.42512	2.36321	2.41051	2.34933	2.39607	2.33561	2.38180
4	3.02760	3.08568	3.00486	3.06206	2.98245	3.03880	2.96038	3.01588	2.93863	2.99332	2.91720	2.97108
5	3.58196	3.64679	3.55017	3.61384	3.51894	3.58148	3.48825	3.54970	3.45810	3.51848	3.42846	3.48780
6	4.07865	4.14844	4.03748	4.10585	3.99714	4.06414	3.95759	4.02326	3.91882	3.98320	3.88080	3.94392
7	4.52562	4.59896	4.47499	4.54668	4.42548	4.49558	4.37705	4.44562	4.32967	4.39675	4.28331	4.34895
8	4.92941	5.00521	4.86940	4.94335	4.81084	4.88301	4.75366	4.82412	4.69783	4.76663	4.64330	4.71050
9	5.29550	5.37288	5.22631	5.30167	5.15891	5.23232	5.09322	5.16476	5.02918	5.09892	4.96674	5.03474
10	5.62848	5.70674	5.55038	5.62646	5.47442	5.54842	5.40051	5.47251	5.32857	5.39865	5.25851	5.32676
11	5.93223	6.01080	5.84554	5.92181	5.76134	5.83542	5.67954	5.75152	5.60002	5.66999	5.52271	5.59074
12	6.21005	6.28849	6.11511	6.19116	6.02304	6.09679	5.93369	6.00526	5.84695	5.91644	5.76272	5.83020
13	6.46478	6.54273	6.36196	6.43743	6.26236	6.33547	6.16583	6.23669	6.07223	6.14094	5.98142	6.04809
14	6.69886	6.77603	6.58852	6.66315	6.48176	6.55398	6.37840	6.44832	6.27829	6.34602	6.18127	6.24691
15	6.91441	6.99056	6.79691	6.87049	6.68335	6.75447	6.57352	6.64231	6.46723	6.53381	6.36434	6.42880
16	7.11326	7.18822	6.98897	7.06133	6.86896	6.93883	6.75299	6.82052	6.64088	6.70617	6.53242	6.59559
17	7.29703	7.37066	7.16630	7.23730	7.04017	7.10868	6.91841	6.98455	6.80078	6.86469	6.68709	6.74886
18	7.46715	7.53932	7.33031	7.39985	7.19839	7.26544	7.07114	7.13583	6.94831	7.01076	6.82967	6.89000
19	7.62485	7.69548	7.48223	7.55023	7.34484	7.41035	7.21240	7.27557	7.08466	7.14560	6.96136	7.02019
20	7.77126	7.84028	7.62315	7.68956	7.48059	7.54452	7.34326	7.40486	7.21088	7.27027	7.08319	7.14049
21	7.90734	7.97471	7.75406	7.81883	7.60660	7.66892	7.46465	7.52466	7.32790	7.38572	7.19607	7.25182
22	8.03398	8.09967	7.87580	7.93891	7.72372	7.78441	7.57741	7.63581	7.43653	7.49278	7.30080	7.35500
23	8.15198	8.21595	7.98916	8.05059	7.83272	7.89176	7.68228	7.73907	7.53752	7.59218	7.39811	7.45076
24	8.26202	8.32427	8.09482	8.15457	7.93425	7.99165	7.77993	7.83511	7.63150	7.68458	7.48863	7.53973
25	8.36475	8.42527	8.19341	8.25147	8.02895	8.08470	7.87096	7.92453	7.71907	7.77058	7.57293	7.62250
26	8.46073	8.51954	8.28548	8.34187	8.11734	8.17146	7.95589	8.00787	7.80073	7.85070	7.65152	7.69958
27	8.55050	8.60760	8.37154	8.42627	8.19993	8.25243	8.03521	8.08562	7.87698	7.92541	7.72485	7.77143
28	8.63450	8.68992	8.45206	8.50514	8.27716	8.32807	8.10935	8.15821	7.94822	7.99515	7.79336	7.83847
29	8.71319	8.76693	8.52743	8.57890	8.34944	8.39877	8.17872	8.22605	8.01484	8.06029	7.85740	7.90108
30	8.78693	8.83902	8.59805	8.64792	8.41713	8.46491	8.24366	8.28949	8.07719	8.12119	7.91732	7.95959
31	8.85609	8.90656	8.66426	8.71256	8.48057	8.52684	8.30450	8.34886	8.13559	8.17817	7.97342	8.01431
32	8.92099	8.96987	8.72637	8.77313	8.54006	8.58484	8.36154	8.40446	8.19033	8.23151	8.02599	8.06553
33	8.98193	9.02924	8.78467	8.82992	8.59589	8.63921	8.41505	8.45657	8.24167	8.28148	8.07528	8.11351
34	9.03917	9.08496	8.83942	8.88320	8.64831	8.69020	8.46528	8.50542	8.28984	8.32833	8.12153	8.15846
35	9.09298	9.13726	8.89087	8.93320	8.69755	8.73805	8.51245	8.55125	8.33507	8.37227	8.16494	8.20062
36	9.14358	9.18640	8.93924	8.98016	8.74383	8.78298	8.55678	8.59427	8.37757	8.41350	8.20571	8.24018
37	9.19118	9.23257	8.98473	9.02427	8.78735	8.82517	8.59846	8.63467	8.41751	8.45221	8.24403	8.27731
38	9.23598	9.27597	9.02754	9.06574	8.82829	8.86482	8.63765	8.67262	8.45507	8.48858	8.28005	8.31218
39	9.27817	9.31679	9.06783	9.10473	8.86683	8.90210	8.67454	8.70829	8.49041	8.52275	8.31394	8.34494
40	9.31790	9.35520	9.10578	9.14140	8.90311	8.93715	8.70926	8.74184	8.52367	8.55487	8.34583	8.37574
41	9.35533	9.39134	9.14153	9.17591	8.93728	8.97014	8.74195	8.77339	8.55499	8.58509	8.37585	8.40470
42	9.39062	9.42537	9.17521	9.20839	8.96947	9.00117	8.77278	8.80308	8.58448	8.61352	8.40412	8.43194
43	9.42388	9.45742	9.20697	9.23897	8.99982	9.03040	8.80178	8.83103	8.61227	8.64027	8.43075	8.45758
44	9.45526	9.48760	9.23691	9.26778	9.02843	9.05791	8.82914	8.85734	8.63847	8.66546	8.45585	8.48171
45	9.48485	9.51605	9.26516	9.29492	9.05541	9.08383	8.85494	8.88213	8.66316	8.68918	8.47952	8.50444
46	9.51278	9.54285	9.29180	9.32049	9.08086	9.10826	8.87928	8.90548	8.68646	8.71153	8.50183	8.52584
47	9.53914	9.56813	9.31695	9.34460	9.10487	9.13128	8.90224	8.92748	8.70843	8.73258	8.52288	8.54601
48	9.56402	9.59196	9.34068	9.36733	9.12754	9.15298	8.92391	8.94822	8.72916	8.75243	8.54273	8.56502
49	9.58752	9.61443	9.36309	9.38876	9.14894	9.17344	8.94436	8.96778	8.74873	8.77114	8.56147	8.58293
50	9.60971	9.63563	9.38426	9.40898	9.16914	9.19274	8.96367	8.98622	8.76720	8.78878	8.57917	8.59982
51	9.63067	9.65564	9.40425	9.42805	9.18822	9.21095	8.98191	9.00362	8.78465	8.80542	8.59587	8.61575
52	9.65047	9.67451	9.42313	9.44605	9.20625	9.22813	8.99913	9.02003	8.80112	8.82111	8.61164	8.63078
53	9.66919	9.69233	9.44097	9.46303	9.22328	9.24434	9.01540	9.03552	8.81669	8.83592	8.62654	8.64496
54	9.68688	9.70915	9.45783	9.47907	9.23937	9.25963	9.03078	9.05013	8.83139	8.84990	8.64062	8.65834
55	9.70360	9.72503	9.47377	9.49420	9.25458	9.27408	9.04531	9.06393	8.84529	8.86309	8.65392	8.67096
56	9.71940	9.74002	9.48884	9.50849	9.26896	9.28771	9.05904	9.07695	8.85842	8.87554	8.66649	8.68288
57	9.73435	9.75419	9.50308	9.52199	9.28255	9.30059	9.07202	9.08925	8.87083	8.88730	8.67837	8.69413
58	9.74848	9.76756	9.51655	9.53473	9.29540	9.31275	9.08430	9.10086	8.88257	8.89840	8.68960	8.70476
59	9.76185	9.78019	9.52929	9.54677	9.30756	9.32423	9.09590	9.11183	8.89366	8.90889	8.70022	8.71479
60	9.77450	9.79213	9.54134	9.55814	9.31905	9.33508	9.10688	9.12219	8.90416	8.91879	8.71027	8.72427
61	9.78646	9.80341	9.55274	9.56889	9.32992	9.34533	9.11726	9.13198	8.91408	8.92815	8.71976	8.73322
62	9.79777	9.81407	9.56352	9.57904	9.34021	9.35501	9.12709	9.14122	8.92347	8.93698	8.72875	8.74167
63	9.80848	9.82414	9.57372	9.58864	9.34994	9.36416	9.13638	9.14996	8.93235	8.94533	8.73724	8.74966
64	9.81861	9.83366	9.58338	9.59770	9.35915	9.37281	9.14517	9.15821	8.94076	8.95323	8.74528	8.75721
65	9.82820	9.84265	9.59251	9.60627	9.36786	9.38098	9.15349	9.16602	8.94871	8.96068	8.75289	8.76435

Hoskold Present Value of 1 per Period

Safe Rate 5.50%

Speculative Rate

Year	11.50% Annual	Monthly	11.75% Annual	Monthly	12.00% Annual	Monthly	12.25% Annual	Monthly	12.50% Annual	Monthly	13.00% Annual	Monthly
1	0.89686	0.91740	0.89485	0.91530	0.89286	0.91321	0.89087	0.91113	0.88889	0.90906	0.88496	0.90494
2	1.66218	1.69737	1.65531	1.69019	1.64848	1.68308	1.64172	1.67603	1.63501	1.66904	1.62175	1.65522
3	2.32205	2.36770	2.30865	2.35377	2.29540	2.34000	2.28230	2.32639	2.26935	2.31294	2.24389	2.28649
4	2.89608	2.94918	2.87526	2.92759	2.85474	2.90632	2.83451	2.88536	2.81457	2.86469	2.77551	2.82424
5	3.39932	3.45765	3.37068	3.42802	3.34251	3.39889	3.31481	3.37025	3.28757	3.34209	3.23440	3.28716
6	3.84351	3.90542	3.80693	3.86765	3.77104	3.83062	3.73582	3.79428	3.70125	3.75863	3.63400	3.68929
7	4.23793	4.30218	4.19350	4.25640	4.14999	4.21158	4.10738	4.16770	4.06563	4.12472	3.98463	4.04138
8	4.59002	4.65567	4.53795	4.60211	4.48704	4.54976	4.43727	4.49859	4.38858	4.44856	4.29435	4.35176
9	4.90582	4.97216	4.84638	4.91111	4.78837	4.85154	4.73172	4.79341	4.67641	4.73664	4.56956	4.62706
10	5.19028	5.25675	5.12380	5.18856	5.05899	5.12212	4.99581	5.05736	4.93418	4.99422	4.81538	4.87255
11	5.44749	5.51368	5.37430	5.43871	5.30305	5.36575	5.23367	5.29473	5.16607	5.22556	5.03599	5.09250
12	5.68087	5.74644	5.60132	5.66506	5.52397	5.58595	5.44872	5.50901	5.37550	5.43417	5.23480	5.29043
13	5.89330	5.95800	5.80773	5.87056	5.72461	5.78565	5.64384	5.70316	5.56532	5.62299	5.41465	5.46922
14	6.08720	6.15085	5.99595	6.05770	5.90740	5.96733	5.82143	5.87962	5.73792	5.79444	5.57789	5.63129
15	6.26466	6.32711	6.16806	6.22859	6.07439	6.13309	5.98352	6.04047	5.89534	5.95061	5.72654	5.77868
16	6.42746	6.48860	6.32581	6.38502	6.22733	6.28470	6.13186	6.18749	6.03928	6.09323	5.86226	5.91308
17	6.57713	6.63688	6.47073	6.52856	6.36772	6.42372	6.26794	6.32219	6.17124	6.22382	5.98652	6.03598
18	6.71502	6.77333	6.60415	6.66054	6.49689	6.55145	6.39305	6.44588	6.29248	6.34365	6.10054	6.14863
19	6.84228	6.89910	6.72721	6.78213	6.61594	6.66905	6.50830	6.55968	6.40410	6.45385	6.20540	6.25210
20	6.95994	7.01526	6.84091	6.89434	6.72588	6.77753	6.61466	6.66460	6.50706	6.55538	6.30202	6.34733
21	7.06890	7.12269	6.94614	6.99808	6.82758	6.87775	6.71300	6.76149	6.60220	6.64909	6.39121	6.43515
22	7.16994	7.22220	7.04368	7.09412	6.92179	6.97049	6.80405	6.85110	6.69025	6.73574	6.47370	6.51628
23	7.26377	7.31451	7.13421	7.18316	7.00920	7.05644	6.88849	6.93411	6.77187	6.81596	6.55009	6.59133
24	7.35101	7.40024	7.21835	7.26582	7.09040	7.13620	6.96690	7.01111	6.84764	6.89034	6.62095	6.66086
25	7.43222	7.47996	7.29664	7.34266	7.16592	7.21030	7.03981	7.08263	6.91805	6.95940	6.68676	6.72538
26	7.50790	7.55417	7.36957	7.41415	7.23625	7.27923	7.10767	7.14913	6.98358	7.02360	6.74795	6.78531
27	7.57850	7.62332	7.43758	7.48075	7.30181	7.34342	7.17091	7.21103	7.04462	7.08334	6.80493	6.84105
28	7.64442	7.68782	7.50107	7.54285	7.36299	7.40325	7.22991	7.26872	7.10155	7.13899	6.85803	6.89294
29	7.70603	7.74803	7.56037	7.60080	7.42013	7.45907	7.28499	7.32252	7.15468	7.19088	6.90758	6.94131
30	7.76365	7.80429	7.61583	7.65494	7.47354	7.51119	7.33647	7.37275	7.20433	7.23931	6.95384	6.98643
31	7.81759	7.85689	7.66773	7.70554	7.52351	7.55991	7.38462	7.41967	7.25076	7.28455	6.99709	7.02855
32	7.86812	7.90611	7.71634	7.75288	7.57030	7.60547	7.42969	7.46356	7.29420	7.32685	7.03754	7.06792
33	7.91548	7.95220	7.76188	7.79719	7.61413	7.64811	7.47190	7.50462	7.33489	7.36641	7.07540	7.10473
34	7.95991	7.99539	7.80460	7.83871	7.65523	7.68804	7.51148	7.54307	7.37302	7.40345	7.11088	7.13918
35	8.00161	8.03588	7.84468	7.87762	7.69379	7.72547	7.54860	7.57909	7.40878	7.43815	7.14414	7.17144
36	8.04076	8.07385	7.88231	7.91411	7.72999	7.76056	7.58344	7.61286	7.44234	7.47068	7.17533	7.20167
37	8.07755	8.10950	7.91766	7.94835	7.76398	7.79349	7.61615	7.64455	7.47385	7.50119	7.20461	7.23002
38	8.11213	8.14296	7.95088	7.98050	7.79592	7.82440	7.64689	7.67428	7.50344	7.52981	7.23211	7.25661
39	8.14465	8.17441	7.98213	8.01070	7.82596	7.85342	7.67578	7.70220	7.53126	7.55669	7.25795	7.28157
40	8.17526	8.20395	8.01151	8.03907	7.85420	7.88069	7.70295	7.72843	7.55742	7.58194	7.28224	7.30501
41	8.20406	8.23174	8.03917	8.06575	7.88079	7.90632	7.72852	7.75308	7.58202	7.60566	7.30509	7.32703
42	8.23118	8.25787	8.06521	8.09084	7.90581	7.93043	7.75258	7.77625	7.60518	7.62796	7.32658	7.34772
43	8.25673	8.28246	8.08974	8.11444	7.92937	7.95310	7.77524	7.79805	7.62699	7.64894	7.34682	7.36718
44	8.28080	8.30562	8.11285	8.13665	7.95157	7.97444	7.79659	7.81857	7.64752	7.66867	7.36587	7.38549
45	8.30349	8.32739	8.13463	8.15756	7.97249	7.99452	7.81670	7.83787	7.66687	7.68724	7.38382	7.40271
46	8.32489	8.34791	8.15516	8.17725	7.99222	8.01343	7.83565	7.85605	7.68511	7.70473	7.40073	7.41892
47	8.34507	8.36724	8.17452	8.19580	8.01081	8.03125	7.85353	7.87317	7.70230	7.72119	7.41668	7.43419
48	8.36410	8.38546	8.19279	8.21328	8.02835	8.04803	7.87039	7.88930	7.71852	7.73670	7.43171	7.44857
49	8.38207	8.40263	8.21003	8.22975	8.04490	8.06385	7.88629	7.90449	7.73381	7.75132	7.44589	7.46211
50	8.39902	8.41882	8.22629	8.24528	8.06052	8.07875	7.90130	7.91882	7.74825	7.76509	7.45927	7.47488
51	8.41503	8.43409	8.24165	8.25993	8.07526	8.09281	7.91547	7.93232	7.76187	7.77808	7.47189	7.48691
52	8.43015	8.44849	8.25615	8.27374	8.08918	8.10607	7.92884	7.94506	7.77473	7.79032	7.48381	7.49825
53	8.44443	8.46207	8.26984	8.28676	8.10233	8.11857	7.94147	7.95707	7.78687	7.80187	7.49506	7.50895
54	8.45791	8.47489	8.28278	8.29906	8.11475	8.13037	7.95340	7.96841	7.79834	7.81277	7.50568	7.51904
55	8.47063	8.48699	8.29500	8.31066	8.12648	8.14150	7.96466	7.97910	7.80917	7.82305	7.51571	7.52856
56	8.48270	8.49840	8.30655	8.32160	8.13756	8.15201	7.97531	7.98919	7.81940	7.83275	7.52519	7.53755
57	8.49408	8.50918	8.31746	8.33194	8.14803	8.16193	7.98537	7.99871	7.82908	7.84190	7.53415	7.54603
58	8.50484	8.51936	8.32778	8.34170	8.15793	8.17129	7.99488	8.00771	7.83822	7.85054	7.54261	7.55403
59	8.51502	8.52897	8.33753	8.35091	8.16729	8.18013	8.00387	8.01620	7.84686	7.85870	7.55061	7.56158
60	8.52464	8.53805	8.34675	8.35961	8.17614	8.18848	8.01237	8.02421	7.85502	7.86641	7.55818	7.56872
61	8.53373	8.54662	8.35547	8.36783	8.18451	8.19636	8.02040	8.03178	7.86275	7.87369	7.56533	7.57545
62	8.54234	8.55472	8.36372	8.37559	8.19242	8.20381	8.02800	8.03894	7.87005	7.88056	7.57209	7.58181
63	8.55047	8.56237	8.37152	8.38292	8.19991	8.21085	8.03519	8.04569	7.87696	7.88705	7.57848	7.58782
64	8.55817	8.56960	8.37890	8.38985	8.20699	8.21749	8.04199	8.05208	7.88349	7.89318	7.58453	7.59350
65	8.56546	8.57643	8.38589	8.39640	8.21369	8.22378	8.04842	8.05811	7.88967	7.89898	7.59025	7.59886

Hoskold Present Value of 1 per Period

Safe Rate 7.00%

Year	_Speculative Rate_ 5.50% Annual	5.50% Monthly	5.75% Annual	5.75% Monthly	6.00% Annual	6.00% Monthly	6.25% Annual	6.25% Monthly	6.50% Annual	6.50% Monthly	6.75% Annual	6.75% Monthly
1	0.94787	0.97721	0.94563	0.97483	0.94340	0.97246	0.94118	0.97010	0.93897	0.96775	0.93677	0.96542
2	1.85842	1.91471	1.84982	1.90559	1.84131	1.89656	1.83287	1.88761	1.82451	1.87874	1.81623	1.86996
3	2.73185	2.81274	2.71332	2.79310	2.69504	2.77373	2.67701	2.75463	2.65921	2.73579	2.64165	2.71721
4	3.56852	3.67168	3.53697	3.63828	3.50597	3.60549	3.47550	3.57328	3.44557	3.54164	3.41614	3.51056
5	4.36890	4.49207	4.32169	4.44219	4.27550	4.39340	4.23028	4.34566	4.18601	4.29896	4.14266	4.25325
6	5.13358	5.27459	5.06853	5.20595	5.00511	5.13906	4.94326	5.07387	4.88291	5.01032	4.82402	4.94834
7	5.86327	6.02003	5.77857	5.93077	5.69628	5.84412	5.61630	5.75997	5.53853	5.67820	5.46289	5.59872
8	6.55876	6.72927	6.45296	6.61793	6.35051	6.51022	6.25126	6.40596	6.15507	6.30499	6.06179	6.20715
9	7.22092	7.40328	7.09288	7.26875	6.96930	7.13902	6.84995	7.01384	6.73462	6.89297	6.62311	6.77620
10	7.85068	8.04310	7.69956	7.88456	7.55415	7.73215	7.41413	7.58552	7.27921	7.44434	7.14911	7.30833
11	8.44902	8.64983	8.27425	8.46674	8.10656	8.29124	7.94553	8.12287	7.79078	7.96120	7.64194	7.80584
12	9.01697	9.22460	8.81819	9.01667	8.62798	8.81790	8.44580	8.62770	8.27116	8.44554	8.10360	8.27091
13	9.55558	9.76859	9.33264	9.53572	9.11986	9.31368	8.91656	9.10176	8.72213	8.89926	8.53600	8.70558
14	10.06594	10.28298	9.81885	10.02526	9.58360	9.78014	9.35936	9.54672	9.14537	9.32418	8.94095	9.11178
15	10.54912	10.76897	10.27806	10.48664	10.02058	10.21874	9.77568	9.96419	9.54247	9.72201	9.32013	9.49132
16	11.00623	11.22776	10.71150	10.92121	10.43214	10.63095	10.16698	10.35572	9.91496	10.09439	9.67514	9.84592
17	11.43835	11.66055	11.12035	11.33025	10.81956	11.01816	10.53461	10.72279	10.26429	10.44285	10.00749	10.17716
18	11.84657	12.06851	11.50581	11.71505	11.18411	11.38171	10.87990	11.06681	10.59181	10.76887	10.31858	10.48655
19	12.23196	12.45282	11.86901	12.07684	11.52698	11.72291	11.20410	11.38912	10.89882	11.07382	10.60974	10.77550
20	12.59558	12.81462	12.21107	12.41683	11.84933	12.04299	11.50842	11.69100	11.18657	11.35901	10.88223	11.04535
21	12.93845	13.15502	12.53306	12.73616	12.15229	12.34315	11.79398	11.97367	11.45620	11.62566	11.13722	11.29732
22	13.26158	13.47511	12.83602	13.03596	12.43692	12.62453	12.06189	12.23827	11.70881	11.87495	11.37582	11.53258
23	13.56596	13.77594	13.12096	13.31730	12.70423	12.88821	12.31316	12.48591	11.94544	12.10796	11.59905	11.75222
24	13.85252	14.05854	13.38885	13.58121	12.95521	13.13523	12.54878	12.71761	12.16708	12.32572	11.80791	11.95727
25	14.12220	14.32388	13.64061	13.82868	13.19078	13.36657	12.76968	12.93435	12.37463	12.52921	12.00329	12.14867
26	14.37587	14.57290	13.87713	14.06064	13.41183	13.58317	12.97673	13.13706	12.56897	12.71933	12.18605	12.32734
27	14.61438	14.80652	14.09925	14.27801	13.61920	13.78592	13.17076	13.32662	12.75092	12.89694	12.35701	12.49410
28	14.83857	15.02561	14.30780	14.48162	13.81369	13.97565	13.35257	13.50384	12.92124	13.06284	12.51691	12.64974
29	15.04921	15.23099	14.50355	14.67231	13.99607	14.15316	13.52290	13.66949	13.08068	13.21779	12.66646	12.79499
30	15.24706	15.42346	14.68722	14.85083	14.16703	14.31920	13.68244	13.82432	13.22989	13.36250	12.80633	12.93054
31	15.43284	15.60377	14.85952	15.01793	14.32728	14.47449	13.83185	13.96900	13.36954	13.49763	12.93713	13.05703
32	15.60722	15.77264	15.02112	15.17429	14.47745	14.61968	13.97177	14.10418	13.50021	13.62380	13.05945	13.17507
33	15.77086	15.93075	15.17265	15.32058	14.61816	14.75542	14.10277	14.23048	13.62248	13.74161	13.17383	13.28521
34	15.92439	16.07874	15.31470	15.45740	14.74997	14.88230	14.22541	14.34846	13.73688	13.85158	13.28079	13.38797
35	16.06840	16.21724	15.44784	15.58536	14.87344	15.00088	14.34022	14.45865	13.84390	13.95425	13.38080	13.48386
36	16.20343	16.34682	15.57261	15.70501	14.98906	15.11168	14.44767	14.56156	13.94402	14.05008	13.47431	13.57332
37	16.33004	16.46803	15.68951	15.81685	15.09734	15.21521	14.54824	14.65766	14.03768	14.13953	13.56174	13.65678
38	16.44871	16.58139	15.79902	15.92139	15.19871	15.31193	14.64235	14.74740	14.12528	14.22302	13.64349	13.73465
39	16.55992	16.68739	15.90160	16.01909	15.29362	15.40227	14.73041	14.83118	14.20722	14.30093	13.71991	13.80729
40	16.66413	16.78648	15.99766	16.11039	15.38245	15.48665	14.81281	14.90941	14.28385	14.37365	13.79136	13.87506
41	16.76175	16.87910	16.08761	16.19568	15.46560	15.56545	14.88990	14.98243	14.35552	14.44151	13.85817	13.93828
42	16.85320	16.96567	16.17183	16.27536	15.54342	15.63904	14.96202	15.05059	14.42254	14.50483	13.92061	13.99726
43	16.93885	17.04656	16.25068	16.34979	15.61624	15.70775	15.02948	15.11422	14.48522	14.56391	13.97900	14.05227
44	17.01905	17.12214	16.32448	16.41931	15.68438	15.77190	15.09259	15.17361	14.54383	14.61905	14.03357	14.10359
45	17.09414	17.19275	16.39356	16.48422	15.74814	15.83179	15.15161	15.22903	14.59863	14.67049	14.08459	14.15147
46	17.16445	17.25870	16.45821	16.54485	15.80779	15.88770	15.20682	15.28076	14.64988	14.71848	14.13229	14.19612
47	17.23026	17.32030	16.51870	16.60145	15.86359	15.93988	15.25845	15.32903	14.69779	14.76326	14.17687	14.23777
48	17.29186	17.37783	16.57531	16.65429	15.91579	15.98860	15.30674	15.37407	14.74259	14.80504	14.21854	14.27662
49	17.34951	17.43156	16.62827	16.70363	15.96461	16.03406	15.35190	15.41611	14.78447	14.84401	14.25750	14.31286
50	17.40346	17.48172	16.67783	16.74969	16.01029	16.07649	15.39412	15.45533	14.82363	14.88037	14.29391	14.34666
51	17.45394	17.52855	16.72418	16.79268	16.05300	16.11609	15.43361	15.49192	14.86024	14.91429	14.32795	14.37819
52	17.50118	17.57228	16.76755	16.83280	16.09295	16.15305	15.47053	15.52607	14.89447	14.94594	14.35977	14.40760
53	17.54537	17.61310	16.80811	16.87025	16.13031	16.18753	15.50506	15.55792	14.92647	14.97545	14.38951	14.43503
54	17.58672	17.65120	16.84605	16.90520	16.16525	16.21971	15.53734	15.58764	14.95638	15.00299	14.41730	14.46061
55	17.62539	17.68676	16.88153	16.93782	16.19792	16.24974	15.56752	15.61537	14.98434	15.02868	14.44329	14.48447
56	17.66157	17.71995	16.91472	16.96826	16.22847	16.27775	15.59573	15.64124	15.01048	15.05263	14.46757	14.50672
57	17.69541	17.75093	16.94576	16.99667	16.25704	16.30389	15.62211	15.66537	15.03492	15.07498	14.49027	14.52748
58	17.72706	17.77984	16.97478	17.02317	16.28375	16.32827	15.64678	15.68788	15.05776	15.09583	14.51149	14.54684
59	17.75666	17.80682	17.00192	17.04790	16.30872	16.35103	15.66983	15.70888	15.07911	15.11527	14.53132	14.56489
60	17.78435	17.83200	17.02730	17.07098	16.33207	16.37225	15.69139	15.72847	15.09907	15.13341	14.54985	14.58173
61	17.81023	17.85549	17.05103	17.09251	16.35390	16.39205	15.71154	15.74675	15.11773	15.15033	14.56717	14.59744
62	17.83444	17.87741	17.07322	17.11259	16.37431	16.41053	15.73038	15.76380	15.13517	15.16611	14.58337	14.61209
63	17.85708	17.89787	17.09396	17.13133	16.39339	16.42776	15.74798	15.77970	15.15147	15.18082	14.59850	14.62575
64	17.87825	17.91695	17.11336	17.14881	16.41123	16.44383	15.76445	15.79453	15.16671	15.19455	14.61264	14.63849
65	17.89804	17.93476	17.13149	17.16512	16.42791	16.45883	15.77983	15.80836	15.18095	15.20735	14.62586	14.65037

Hoskold Present Value of 1 per Period

Safe Rate 7.00%

Year	7.00% Annual	7.00% Monthly	7.25% Annual	7.25% Monthly	Speculative Rate 7.50% Annual	7.50% Monthly	7.75% Annual	7.75% Monthly	8.00% Annual	8.00% Monthly	8.25% Annual	8.25% Monthly
1	0.93458	0.96309	0.93240	0.96078	0.93023	0.95848	0.92807	0.95619	0.92593	0.95391	0.92379	0.95164
2	1.80802	1.86126	1.79988	1.85264	1.79182	1.84410	1.78383	1.83563	1.77591	1.82725	1.76806	1.81894
3	2.62432	2.69887	2.60721	2.68078	2.59033	2.66294	2.57366	2.64533	2.55721	2.62795	2.54096	2.61079
4	3.38721	3.48002	3.35877	3.45000	3.33080	3.42050	3.30329	3.39150	3.27624	3.36298	3.24962	3.33495
5	4.10020	4.20850	4.05859	4.16468	4.01783	4.12177	3.97787	4.07973	3.93870	4.03854	3.90030	3.99817
6	4.76654	4.88787	4.71041	4.82886	4.65558	4.77126	4.60202	4.71502	4.54968	4.66009	4.49851	4.60643
7	5.38929	5.52144	5.31764	5.44626	5.24788	5.37310	5.17992	5.30189	5.11370	5.23253	5.04915	5.16496
8	5.97130	6.11230	5.88347	6.02030	5.79819	5.93104	5.71534	5.84438	5.63483	5.76022	5.55655	5.67844
9	6.51523	6.66332	6.41081	6.55414	6.30969	6.44848	6.21170	6.34617	6.11671	6.24706	6.02459	6.15100
10	7.02358	7.17720	6.90238	7.05069	6.78530	6.92856	6.67212	6.81059	6.56265	6.69657	6.45672	6.58631
11	7.49867	7.65643	7.36069	7.51263	7.22768	7.37413	7.09940	7.24065	6.97560	7.11191	6.85603	6.98767
12	7.94269	8.10335	7.78804	7.94245	7.63930	7.78781	7.49614	7.63908	7.35824	7.49593	7.22533	7.35804
13	8.35765	8.52014	8.18660	8.34245	8.02241	8.17201	7.86467	8.00840	7.71302	7.85121	7.56711	7.70007
14	8.74547	8.90884	8.55835	8.71474	8.37907	8.52893	8.20715	8.35087	8.04214	8.18009	7.88364	8.01616
15	9.10791	9.27133	8.90515	9.06130	8.71121	8.86058	8.52554	8.66856	8.34762	8.48469	8.17697	8.30845
16	9.44665	9.60938	9.22870	9.38395	9.02058	9.16885	8.82164	8.96339	8.63128	8.76693	8.44897	8.57891
17	9.76322	9.92464	9.53060	9.68436	9.30880	9.45544	9.09710	9.23708	8.89480	9.02859	8.70131	8.82930
18	10.05909	10.21865	9.81233	9.96410	9.57739	9.72193	9.35343	9.49124	9.13972	9.27126	8.93554	9.06123
19	10.33560	10.49284	10.07526	10.22463	9.82772	9.96978	9.59205	9.72733	9.36742	9.49640	9.15307	9.27617
20	10.59401	10.74854	10.32067	10.46727	10.06108	10.20035	9.81422	9.94670	9.57919	9.70536	9.35516	9.47545
21	10.83553	10.98701	10.54975	10.69329	10.27865	10.41487	10.02114	10.15057	9.77622	9.89936	9.54299	9.66029
22	11.06124	11.20939	10.76359	10.90383	10.48155	10.61448	10.21390	10.34010	9.95959	10.07954	9.71763	9.83179
23	11.27219	11.41679	10.96324	11.09997	10.67077	10.80027	10.39351	10.51632	10.13028	10.24692	9.88006	9.99098
24	11.46933	11.61020	11.14964	11.28271	10.84728	10.97320	10.56089	10.68021	10.28923	10.40246	10.03119	10.13878
25	11.65358	11.79058	11.32368	11.45298	11.01194	11.13418	10.71691	10.83265	10.43727	10.54702	10.17185	10.27607
26	11.82578	11.95879	11.48620	11.61164	11.16557	11.28407	10.86236	10.97448	10.57518	10.68142	10.30280	10.40361
27	11.98671	12.11566	11.63796	11.75948	11.30893	11.42364	10.99799	11.10645	10.70369	10.80640	10.42473	10.52213
28	12.13711	12.26196	11.77968	11.89725	11.44270	11.55361	11.12447	11.22926	10.82346	10.92263	10.53830	10.63230
29	12.27767	12.39839	11.91204	12.02565	11.56756	11.67466	11.24244	11.34358	10.93510	11.03076	10.64411	10.73473
30	12.40904	12.52563	12.03566	12.14531	11.68410	11.78741	11.35249	11.44999	11.03918	11.13136	10.74271	10.82998
31	12.53181	12.64429	12.15113	12.25684	11.79288	11.89243	11.45516	11.54907	11.13624	11.22497	10.83460	10.91857
32	12.64656	12.75495	12.25897	12.36080	11.89444	11.99027	11.55096	11.64132	11.22676	11.31210	10.92026	11.00099
33	12.75379	12.85815	12.35971	12.45769	11.98925	12.08142	11.64035	11.72722	11.31119	11.39319	11.00012	11.07767
34	12.85401	12.95439	12.45381	12.54801	12.07777	12.16635	11.72378	11.80722	11.38994	11.46869	11.07460	11.14903
35	12.94767	13.04414	12.54171	12.63220	12.16043	12.24548	11.80164	11.88174	11.46343	11.53898	11.14405	11.21544
36	13.03521	13.12784	12.62382	12.71069	12.23761	12.31922	11.87433	11.95115	11.53199	11.60443	11.20884	11.27727
37	13.11702	13.20590	12.70053	12.78385	12.30968	12.38794	11.94217	12.01581	11.59597	11.66538	11.26928	11.33482
38	13.19347	13.27870	12.77220	12.85205	12.37700	12.45197	12.00552	12.07605	11.65568	11.72215	11.32566	11.38841
39	13.26493	13.34659	12.83915	12.91564	12.43986	12.51165	12.06465	12.13217	11.71142	11.77503	11.37828	11.43831
40	13.33171	13.40990	12.90170	12.97492	12.49857	12.56727	12.11987	12.18446	11.76344	11.82428	11.42738	11.48478
41	13.39412	13.46895	12.96015	13.03019	12.55341	12.61912	12.17143	12.23319	11.81201	11.87016	11.47320	11.52806
42	13.45245	13.52401	13.01475	13.08172	12.60463	12.66744	12.21957	12.27859	11.85735	11.91291	11.51597	11.56838
43	13.50696	13.57536	13.06576	13.12976	12.65248	12.71248	12.26454	12.32091	11.89968	11.95274	11.55590	11.60593
44	13.55791	13.62325	13.11343	13.17455	12.69717	12.75447	12.30653	12.36034	11.93920	11.98985	11.59317	11.64091
45	13.60552	13.66791	13.15797	13.21631	12.73892	12.79360	12.34574	12.39709	11.97611	12.02442	11.62796	11.67351
46	13.65002	13.70956	13.19958	13.25525	12.77793	12.83009	12.38237	12.43135	12.01057	12.05665	11.66045	11.70388
47	13.69161	13.74840	13.23847	13.29156	12.81436	12.86410	12.41659	12.46328	12.04276	12.08668	11.69079	11.73217
48	13.73047	13.78463	13.27480	13.32541	12.84840	12.89581	12.44854	12.49304	12.07282	12.11467	11.71911	11.75854
49	13.76680	13.81841	13.30875	13.35698	12.88020	12.92537	12.47839	12.52078	12.10089	12.14075	11.74556	11.78311
50	13.80075	13.84991	13.34048	13.38641	12.90991	12.95293	12.50628	12.54664	12.12711	12.16506	11.77027	11.80601
51	13.83247	13.87929	13.37012	13.41386	12.93767	12.97862	12.53233	12.57075	12.15161	12.18772	11.79334	11.82735
52	13.86212	13.90669	13.39782	13.43945	12.96361	13.00258	12.55666	12.59322	12.17448	12.20885	11.81488	11.84724
53	13.88984	13.93225	13.42370	13.46331	12.98784	13.02491	12.57939	12.61417	12.19585	12.22854	11.83501	11.86578
54	13.91573	13.95608	13.44789	13.48556	13.01048	13.04574	12.60063	12.63370	12.21581	12.24689	11.85380	11.88306
55	13.93994	13.97830	13.47049	13.50631	13.03164	13.06516	12.62047	12.65191	12.23446	12.26400	11.87136	11.89917
56	13.96256	13.99902	13.49162	13.52566	13.05140	13.08326	12.63901	12.66888	12.25188	12.27995	11.88776	11.91419
57	13.98370	14.01835	13.51135	13.54370	13.06987	13.10014	12.65633	12.68471	12.26816	12.29482	11.90309	11.92818
58	14.00346	14.03638	13.52980	13.56052	13.08713	13.11588	12.67252	12.69947	12.28336	12.30868	11.91740	11.94123
59	14.02192	14.05319	13.54704	13.57621	13.10326	13.13055	12.68764	12.71323	12.29757	12.32161	11.93077	11.95339
60	14.03918	14.06886	13.56314	13.59084	13.11833	13.14424	12.70176	12.72605	12.31084	12.33366	11.94326	11.96473
61	14.05531	14.08348	13.57820	13.60448	13.13241	13.15700	12.71496	12.73801	12.32324	12.34489	11.95493	11.97531
62	14.07038	14.09711	13.59226	13.61721	13.14557	13.16890	12.72730	12.74917	12.33483	12.35536	11.96583	11.98516
63	14.08447	14.10983	13.60541	13.62907	13.15786	13.17999	12.73882	12.75957	12.34565	12.36513	11.97602	11.99435
64	14.09764	14.12169	13.61769	13.64013	13.16935	13.19034	12.74959	12.76926	12.35576	12.37424	11.98554	12.00292
65	14.10994	14.13275	13.62917	13.65045	13.18009	13.19999	12.75965	12.77830	12.36522	12.38273	11.99443	12.01091

Hoskold Present Value of 1 per Period

Safe Rate 7.00%

Speculative Rate

Year	8.50% Annual	8.50% Monthly	8.75% Annual	8.75% Monthly	9.00% Annual	9.00% Monthly	9.25% Annual	9.25% Monthly	9.50% Annual	9.50% Monthly	9.75% Annual	9.75% Monthly
1	0.92166	0.94938	0.91954	0.94713	0.91743	0.94489	0.91533	0.94267	0.91324	0.94045	0.91116	0.93824
2	1.76028	1.81071	1.75257	1.80255	1.74492	1.79446	1.73734	1.78644	1.72983	1.77850	1.72238	1.77063
3	2.52492	2.59386	2.50908	2.57715	2.49344	2.56065	2.47800	2.54437	2.46274	2.52828	2.44767	2.51240
4	3.22343	3.30737	3.19767	3.28025	3.17231	3.25357	3.14735	3.22732	3.12277	3.20149	3.09858	3.17607
5	3.86263	3.95860	3.82569	3.91981	3.78945	3.88177	3.75388	3.84446	3.71898	3.80786	3.68472	3.77196
6	4.44848	4.55398	4.39955	4.50272	4.35169	4.45260	4.30486	4.40358	4.25902	4.35563	4.21415	4.30871
7	4.98621	5.09912	4.92482	5.03494	4.86492	4.97235	4.80646	4.91130	4.74939	4.85173	4.69366	4.79358
8	5.48042	5.59896	5.40635	5.52167	5.33425	5.44649	5.26405	5.37332	5.19568	5.30210	5.12905	5.23274
9	5.93519	6.05784	5.84842	5.96747	5.76414	5.87975	5.68226	5.79457	5.60267	5.71183	5.52527	5.63141
10	6.35415	6.47961	6.25479	6.37632	6.15849	6.27628	6.06511	6.17932	5.97452	6.08531	5.88659	5.99412
11	6.74050	6.86770	6.62880	6.75177	6.52074	6.63970	6.41614	6.53129	6.31485	6.42635	6.21671	6.32474
12	7.09713	7.22513	6.97340	7.09694	6.85392	6.97322	6.73845	6.85374	6.62682	6.73828	6.51882	6.62665
13	7.42661	7.55464	7.29124	7.41461	7.16072	7.27967	7.03478	7.14955	6.91320	7.02401	6.79575	6.90279
14	7.73127	7.85867	7.58467	7.70724	7.44353	7.56155	7.30754	7.42126	7.17644	7.28608	7.04995	7.15573
15	8.01317	8.13939	7.85579	7.97706	7.70448	7.82109	7.55889	7.67110	7.41869	7.52675	7.28361	7.38774
16	8.27420	8.39878	8.10651	8.22605	7.94548	8.06029	7.79073	7.90108	7.64189	7.74804	7.49863	7.60081
17	8.51606	8.63862	8.33853	8.45600	8.16825	8.28094	8.00479	8.11298	7.84774	7.95170	7.69674	7.79671
18	8.74030	8.86051	8.55340	8.66850	8.37433	8.48462	8.20260	8.30839	8.03777	8.13933	7.87944	7.97701
19	8.94830	9.06593	8.75250	8.86501	8.56509	8.67279	8.38553	8.48874	8.21335	8.31234	8.04809	8.14312
20	9.14136	9.25618	8.93712	9.04684	8.74180	8.84675	8.55484	8.65532	8.37571	8.47200	8.20392	8.29629
21	9.32062	9.43248	9.10838	9.21518	8.90559	9.00766	8.71164	8.80928	8.52595	8.61946	8.34801	8.43764
22	9.48715	9.59593	9.26734	9.37111	9.05750	9.15660	8.85694	8.95168	8.66508	8.75573	8.48135	8.56818
23	9.64191	9.74751	9.41496	9.51563	9.19845	9.29452	8.99168	9.08345	8.79400	8.88176	8.60482	8.68883
24	9.78579	9.88815	9.55210	9.64961	9.32931	9.42230	9.11668	9.20546	8.91353	8.99838	8.71923	8.80040
25	9.91960	10.01868	9.67956	9.77388	9.45086	9.54076	9.23271	9.31849	9.02441	9.10635	8.82531	8.90365
26	10.04409	10.13988	9.79806	9.88919	9.56379	9.65060	9.34047	9.42325	9.12733	9.20636	8.92371	8.99924
27	10.15994	10.25244	9.90828	9.99622	9.66877	9.75250	9.44058	9.52038	9.22290	9.29906	9.01504	9.08779
28	10.26779	10.35700	10.01082	10.09560	9.76639	9.84707	9.53362	9.61048	9.31169	9.38500	9.09985	9.16985
29	10.36821	10.45417	10.10625	10.18791	9.85720	9.93487	9.62013	9.69409	9.39420	9.46471	9.17864	9.24594
30	10.46174	10.54449	10.19509	10.27366	9.94170	10.01640	9.70060	9.77170	9.47092	9.53868	9.25186	9.31651
31	10.54887	10.62845	10.27782	10.35335	10.02035	10.09213	9.77547	9.84377	9.54227	9.60734	9.31993	9.38200
32	10.63005	10.70653	10.35487	10.42743	10.09358	10.16250	9.84514	9.91071	9.60865	9.67109	9.38325	9.44279
33	10.70571	10.77915	10.42665	10.49630	10.16177	10.22791	9.91001	9.97290	9.67043	9.73031	9.44215	9.49923
34	10.77624	10.84670	10.49354	10.56034	10.22529	10.28871	9.97041	10.03070	9.72794	9.78532	9.49697	9.55165
35	10.84199	10.90956	10.55588	10.61991	10.28447	10.34525	10.02668	10.08443	9.78149	9.83644	9.54800	9.60036
36	10.90331	10.96804	10.61399	10.67532	10.33962	10.39782	10.07909	10.13439	9.83136	9.88397	9.59552	9.64562
37	10.96048	11.02248	10.66816	10.72689	10.39103	10.44673	10.12793	10.18084	9.87783	9.92815	9.63978	9.68770
38	11.01382	11.07315	10.71868	10.77487	10.43895	10.49228	10.17345	10.22405	9.92112	9.96924	9.68101	9.72682
39	11.06357	11.12032	10.76580	10.81952	10.48364	10.53458	10.21589	10.26425	9.96147	10.00746	9.71942	9.76319
40	11.10998	11.16423	10.80974	10.86109	10.52530	10.57398	10.25545	10.30166	9.99909	10.04301	9.75523	9.79703
41	11.15329	11.20513	10.85074	10.89979	10.56417	10.61066	10.29234	10.33647	10.03415	10.07609	9.78860	9.82851
42	11.19371	11.24321	10.88899	10.93583	10.60042	10.64480	10.32675	10.36887	10.06685	10.10687	9.81972	9.85780
43	11.23143	11.27868	10.92468	10.96938	10.63424	10.67659	10.35884	10.39903	10.09735	10.13553	9.84873	9.88505
44	11.26663	11.31172	10.95798	11.00063	10.66579	10.70619	10.38878	10.42710	10.12579	10.16220	9.87579	9.91042
45	11.29949	11.34249	10.98906	11.02973	10.69524	10.73375	10.41671	10.45325	10.15233	10.18703	9.90103	9.93403
46	11.33017	11.37116	11.01807	11.05684	10.72271	10.75942	10.44278	10.47759	10.17708	10.21015	9.92458	9.95602
47	11.35880	11.39787	11.04515	11.08209	10.74836	10.78333	10.46710	10.50026	10.20018	10.23167	9.94654	9.97648
48	11.38554	11.42275	11.07043	11.10561	10.77230	10.80560	10.48980	10.52138	10.22174	10.25172	9.96704	9.99554
49	11.41051	11.44594	11.09404	11.12753	10.79464	10.82635	10.51099	10.54105	10.24186	10.27040	9.98617	10.01330
50	11.43382	11.46755	11.11607	11.14795	10.81551	10.84568	10.53077	10.55937	10.26064	10.28779	10.00402	10.02983
51	11.45559	11.48768	11.13664	11.16697	10.83498	10.86369	10.54923	10.57644	10.27816	10.30399	10.02068	10.04523
52	11.47592	11.50644	11.15586	11.18470	10.85317	10.88047	10.56647	10.59234	10.29452	10.31908	10.03623	10.05957
53	11.49490	11.52393	11.17380	11.20123	10.87015	10.89610	10.58256	10.60716	10.30980	10.33315	10.05075	10.07293
54	11.51263	11.54023	11.19055	11.21662	10.88600	10.91067	10.59759	10.62097	10.32406	10.34625	10.06430	10.08538
55	11.52919	11.55542	11.20620	11.23097	10.90081	10.92425	10.61162	10.63383	10.33738	10.35846	10.07696	10.09699
56	11.54466	11.56958	11.22081	11.24435	10.91463	10.93690	10.62472	10.64582	10.34981	10.36983	10.08877	10.10779
57	11.55911	11.58278	11.23446	11.25682	10.92755	10.94870	10.63696	10.65700	10.36142	10.38044	10.09980	10.11787
58	11.57261	11.59508	11.24721	11.26844	10.93961	10.95969	10.64839	10.66741	10.37227	10.39032	10.11011	10.12725
59	11.58522	11.60655	11.25912	11.27927	10.95088	10.96993	10.65906	10.67712	10.38240	10.39952	10.11973	10.13600
60	11.59700	11.61724	11.27024	11.28936	10.96140	10.97948	10.66903	10.68616	10.39185	10.40811	10.12871	10.14415
61	11.60800	11.62721	11.28064	11.29877	10.97123	10.98839	10.67834	10.69460	10.40069	10.41611	10.13711	10.15175
62	11.61828	11.63650	11.29034	11.30755	10.98041	10.99668	10.68704	10.70246	10.40894	10.42356	10.14494	10.15883
63	11.62788	11.64516	11.29941	11.31573	10.98899	11.00442	10.69517	10.70978	10.41665	10.43051	10.15226	10.16543
64	11.63685	11.65324	11.30788	11.32335	10.99700	11.01163	10.70276	10.71661	10.42385	10.43699	10.15910	10.17159
65	11.64524	11.66077	11.31580	11.33046	11.00449	11.01835	10.70985	10.72298	10.43057	10.44303	10.16549	10.17732

Hoskold Present Value of 1 per Period

Safe Rate 7.00%

Speculative Rate

Year	10.00% Annual	Monthly	10.25% Annual	Monthly	10.50% Annual	Monthly	10.75% Annual	Monthly	11.00% Annual	Monthly	11.25% Annual	Monthly
1	0.90909	0.93605	0.90703	0.93386	0.90498	0.93169	0.90293	0.92952	0.90090	0.92737	0.89888	0.92522
2	1.71500	1.76283	1.70767	1.75509	1.70041	1.74742	1.69322	1.73982	1.68608	1.73229	1.67900	1.72482
3	2.43278	2.49672	2.41808	2.48123	2.40355	2.46594	2.38919	2.45083	2.37501	2.43590	2.36099	2.42116
4	3.07476	3.15105	3.05131	3.12642	3.02821	3.10217	3.00546	3.07830	2.98304	3.05479	2.96096	3.03164
5	3.65109	3.73672	3.61807	3.70214	3.58563	3.66819	3.55378	3.63485	3.52248	3.60212	3.49173	3.56997
6	4.17021	4.26279	4.12719	4.21784	4.08504	4.17383	4.04374	4.13073	4.00327	4.08851	3.96360	4.04714
7	4.63923	4.73682	4.58604	4.68138	4.53405	4.62723	4.48323	4.57431	4.43354	4.52259	4.38494	4.47203
8	5.06412	5.16517	5.00081	5.09932	4.93906	5.03513	4.87882	4.97254	4.82003	4.91148	4.76264	4.85191
9	5.44999	5.55323	5.37674	5.47719	5.30542	5.40321	5.23597	5.33119	5.16832	5.26107	5.10239	5.19277
10	5.80122	5.90562	5.71829	5.81970	5.63769	5.73624	5.55934	5.65514	5.48313	5.57631	5.40899	5.49964
11	6.12157	6.22629	6.02929	6.13086	5.93976	6.03831	5.85285	5.94851	5.76845	5.86135	5.68644	5.77670
12	6.41429	6.51866	6.31305	6.41413	6.21496	6.31290	6.11988	6.21482	6.02766	6.11974	5.93812	6.02752
13	6.68222	6.78569	6.57242	6.67250	6.46618	6.56302	6.36331	6.45707	6.26367	6.35450	6.16710	6.25513
14	6.92785	7.02997	6.80990	6.90856	6.69591	6.79126	6.58567	6.67788	6.47899	6.56823	6.37572	6.46212
15	7.15335	7.25377	7.02767	7.12457	6.90633	6.99989	6.78911	6.87950	6.67581	6.76318	6.56622	6.65073
16	7.36065	7.45907	7.22765	7.32252	7.09937	7.19088	6.97556	7.06389	6.85600	6.94131	6.74047	6.82291
17	7.55143	7.64764	7.41151	7.50417	7.27669	7.36598	7.14668	7.23279	7.02123	7.10433	6.90011	6.98035
18	7.72722	7.82104	7.58078	7.67105	7.43978	7.52671	7.30393	7.38769	7.17295	7.25372	7.04659	7.12452
19	7.88936	7.98065	7.73676	7.82454	7.58996	7.67442	7.44862	7.52995	7.31245	7.39081	7.18117	7.25673
20	8.03904	8.12771	7.88066	7.96585	7.72840	7.81031	7.58191	7.66073	7.44087	7.51677	7.30498	7.37812
21	8.17735	8.26333	8.01353	8.09608	7.85614	7.93546	7.70481	7.78110	7.55921	7.63262	7.41900	7.48971
22	8.30525	8.38850	8.13631	8.21619	7.97411	8.05082	7.81826	7.89198	7.66837	7.73929	7.52413	7.59239
23	8.42361	8.50410	8.24988	8.32707	8.08316	8.15725	7.92306	7.99422	7.76917	7.83759	7.62114	7.68697
24	8.53322	8.61095	8.35499	8.42949	8.18404	8.25551	8.01995	8.08858	7.86231	7.92826	7.71075	7.77417
25	8.63479	8.70978	8.45233	8.52417	8.27743	8.34630	8.10961	8.17571	7.94846	8.01195	7.79359	7.85463
26	8.72897	8.80123	8.54255	8.61174	8.36393	8.43025	8.19262	8.25624	8.02819	8.08927	7.87023	7.92892
27	8.81634	8.88590	8.62621	8.69280	8.44411	8.50790	8.26954	8.33071	8.10204	8.16075	7.94119	7.99758
28	8.89744	8.96435	8.70383	8.76785	8.51847	8.57979	8.34085	8.39962	8.17047	8.22686	8.00692	8.06107
29	8.97274	9.03705	8.77588	8.83739	8.58748	8.64636	8.40699	8.46342	8.23393	8.28805	8.06786	8.11981
30	9.04270	9.10446	8.84280	8.90184	8.65154	8.70805	8.46838	8.52251	8.29281	8.34472	8.12437	8.17419
31	9.10772	9.16699	8.90496	8.96161	8.71104	8.76523	8.52537	8.57728	8.34746	8.39722	8.17682	8.22456
32	9.16818	9.22501	8.96275	9.01706	8.76632	8.81827	8.57832	8.62806	8.39822	8.44588	8.22552	8.27123
33	9.22441	9.27887	9.01648	9.06851	8.81772	8.86747	8.62753	8.67516	8.44537	8.49100	8.27075	8.31451
34	9.27672	9.32889	9.06645	9.11628	8.86550	8.91314	8.67327	8.71886	8.48920	8.53287	8.31278	8.35464
35	9.32540	9.37534	9.11295	9.16063	8.90996	8.95554	8.71582	8.75942	8.52995	8.57172	8.35185	8.39188
36	9.37073	9.41850	9.15623	9.20184	8.95132	8.99491	8.75539	8.79709	8.56786	8.60778	8.38818	8.42645
37	9.41293	9.45862	9.19651	9.24012	8.98983	9.03149	8.79223	8.83207	8.60312	8.64127	8.42199	8.45854
38	9.45224	9.49590	9.23403	9.27570	9.02567	9.06548	8.82651	8.86457	8.63595	8.67238	8.45344	8.48835
39	9.48886	9.53057	9.26898	9.30878	9.05906	9.09707	8.85843	8.89478	8.66651	8.70129	8.48272	8.51604
40	9.52298	9.56281	9.30153	9.33953	9.09015	9.12644	8.88817	8.92285	8.69496	8.72815	8.50998	8.54177
41	9.55478	9.59280	9.33187	9.36813	9.11913	9.15375	8.91586	8.94896	8.72147	8.75313	8.53536	8.56569
42	9.58443	9.62070	9.36015	9.39474	9.14613	9.17915	8.94167	8.97323	8.74616	8.77635	8.55901	8.58793
43	9.61207	9.64666	9.38651	9.41949	9.17129	9.20278	8.96572	8.99581	8.76917	8.79795	8.58105	8.60860
44	9.63784	9.67081	9.41108	9.44252	9.19475	9.22476	8.98814	9.01681	8.79061	8.81804	8.60158	8.62784
45	9.66188	9.69330	9.43400	9.46396	9.21663	9.24522	9.00904	9.03636	8.81061	8.83673	8.62072	8.64573
46	9.68430	9.71423	9.45537	9.48391	9.23702	9.26425	9.02853	9.05454	8.82925	8.85412	8.63857	8.66237
47	9.70521	9.73371	9.47531	9.50248	9.25605	9.28197	9.04671	9.07147	8.84663	8.87030	8.65520	8.67787
48	9.72472	9.75186	9.49391	9.51977	9.27380	9.29847	9.06366	9.08723	8.86284	8.88537	8.67072	8.69228
49	9.74293	9.76875	9.51126	9.53587	9.29035	9.31383	9.07947	9.10190	8.87796	8.89939	8.68519	8.70570
50	9.75992	9.78449	9.52745	9.55086	9.30580	9.32813	9.09423	9.11555	8.89206	8.91245	8.69869	8.71820
51	9.77578	9.79914	9.54256	9.56482	9.32022	9.34145	9.10799	9.12827	8.90522	8.92461	8.71128	8.72983
52	9.79058	9.81279	9.55666	9.57783	9.33367	9.35385	9.12084	9.14011	8.91750	8.93593	8.72303	8.74066
53	9.80439	9.82551	9.56983	9.58994	9.34622	9.36541	9.13283	9.15115	8.92896	8.94647	8.73400	8.75075
54	9.81729	9.83735	9.58211	9.60122	9.35794	9.37617	9.14402	9.16142	8.93966	8.95629	8.74423	8.76014
55	9.82933	9.84839	9.59358	9.61174	9.36888	9.38619	9.15446	9.17099	8.94964	8.96544	8.75378	8.76889
56	9.84057	9.85867	9.60429	9.62153	9.37909	9.39553	9.16421	9.17991	8.95896	8.97396	8.76270	8.77705
57	9.85107	9.86825	9.61429	9.63066	9.38863	9.40424	9.17332	9.18822	8.96766	8.98190	8.77102	8.78464
58	9.86087	9.87718	9.62363	9.63916	9.39753	9.41234	9.18181	9.19596	8.97578	8.98929	8.77879	8.79171
59	9.87002	9.88550	9.63234	9.64709	9.40584	9.41990	9.18975	9.20317	8.98336	8.99618	8.78604	8.79831
60	9.87857	9.89326	9.64048	9.65447	9.41361	9.42694	9.19716	9.20989	8.99044	9.00261	8.79281	8.80445
61	9.88655	9.90048	9.64809	9.66135	9.42085	9.43350	9.20408	9.21615	8.99705	9.00859	8.79914	8.81017
62	9.89401	9.90722	9.65519	9.66777	9.42762	9.43962	9.21054	9.22199	9.00323	9.01417	8.80504	8.81550
63	9.90097	9.91350	9.66182	9.67375	9.43395	9.44532	9.21657	9.22743	9.00899	9.01936	8.81056	8.82048
64	9.90748	9.91935	9.66801	9.67932	9.43985	9.45063	9.22221	9.23250	9.01438	9.02421	8.81571	8.82511
65	9.91355	9.92480	9.67380	9.68451	9.44537	9.45558	9.22747	9.23722	9.01941	9.02872	8.82052	8.82942

Hoskold Present Value of 1 per Period

Safe Rate 7.00%

					Speculative Rate							
Year	11.50%		12.00%		12.50%		13.00%		14.00%		15.00%	
	Annual	Monthly	Annual	Monthly	Annual	Monthly	Annual	Monthly	Annual	Monthly	Annual	Monthly
1	0.89686	0.92309	0.89286	0.91885	0.88889	0.91464	0.88496	0.91048	0.87719	0.90227	0.86957	0.89420
2	1.67198	1.71741	1.65812	1.70279	1.64449	1.68842	1.63108	1.67428	1.60490	1.64671	1.57955	1.62003
3	2.34713	2.40659	2.31991	2.37798	2.29331	2.35004	2.26731	2.32274	2.21704	2.27002	2.16895	2.21963
4	2.93920	3.00883	2.89664	2.96424	2.85528	2.92095	2.81509	2.87890	2.73801	2.79834	2.66505	2.72216
5	3.46152	3.53839	3.40263	3.47688	3.34570	3.41747	3.29066	3.36005	3.18582	3.25082	3.08746	3.14847
6	3.92471	4.00660	3.84918	3.92791	3.77649	3.85226	3.70651	3.77946	3.57404	3.64182	3.45071	3.51385
7	4.33739	4.42258	4.24533	4.32690	4.15708	4.23528	4.07244	4.14745	3.91308	3.98228	3.76572	3.82977
8	4.70660	4.79376	4.59838	4.68155	4.49503	4.57447	4.39623	4.47218	4.21110	4.28074	4.04093	4.10501
9	5.03813	5.12623	4.91433	4.99812	4.79647	4.87626	4.68414	4.76020	4.47454	4.54390	4.28290	4.34640
10	5.33682	5.42505	5.19811	5.28178	5.06643	5.14588	4.94126	5.01680	4.70860	4.77714	4.49686	4.55934
11	5.60674	5.69446	5.45384	5.53682	5.30907	5.38766	5.17178	5.24634	4.91746	4.98482	4.68698	4.74813
12	5.85131	5.93804	5.68498	5.76682	5.52786	5.60520	5.37918	5.45239	5.10452	5.17048	4.85668	4.91628
13	6.07346	6.15882	5.89446	5.97483	5.72571	5.80151	5.56635	5.63797	5.27285	5.33707	5.00874	5.06665
14	6.27569	6.35938	6.08476	6.16340	5.90511	5.97914	5.73576	5.80558	5.42461	5.48703	5.14549	5.20161
15	6.46017	6.54196	6.25803	6.33475	6.06816	6.14027	5.88947	5.95737	5.56190	5.62242	5.26885	5.32313
16	6.62877	6.70848	6.41611	6.49077	6.21668	6.28674	6.02927	6.09515	5.68642	5.74498	5.38046	5.43286
17	6.78310	6.86063	6.56060	6.63309	6.35222	6.42016	6.15668	6.22048	5.79962	5.85620	5.48170	5.53222
18	6.92460	6.99985	6.69288	6.76314	6.47616	6.54192	6.27303	6.33472	5.90275	5.95734	5.57374	5.62239
19	7.05452	7.12743	6.81417	6.88217	6.58965	6.65322	6.37946	6.43902	5.99689	6.04949	5.65761	5.70441
20	7.17397	7.24449	6.92555	6.99125	6.69376	6.75512	6.47698	6.53442	6.08299	6.13362	5.73418	5.77915
21	7.28390	7.35204	7.02795	7.09136	6.78937	6.84854	6.56646	6.62179	6.16185	6.21054	5.80420	5.84739
22	7.38521	7.45096	7.12221	7.18335	6.87731	6.93429	6.64868	6.70192	6.23419	6.28098	5.86835	5.90979
23	7.47865	7.54203	7.20908	7.26795	6.95827	7.01310	6.72432	6.77551	6.30064	6.34557	5.92719	5.96693
24	7.56492	7.62595	7.28921	7.34586	7.03289	7.08561	6.79399	6.84317	6.36177	6.40487	5.98125	6.01934
25	7.64465	7.70336	7.36320	7.41765	7.10174	7.15238	6.85822	6.90543	6.41805	6.45938	6.03098	6.06746
26	7.71837	7.77481	7.43157	7.48388	7.16532	7.21394	6.91749	6.96279	6.46994	6.50955	6.07677	6.11170
27	7.78660	7.84081	7.49481	7.54502	7.22409	7.27073	6.97225	7.01568	6.51781	6.55575	6.11899	6.15242
28	7.84979	7.90183	7.55333	7.60150	7.27845	7.32316	7.02287	7.06449	6.56203	6.59835	6.15794	6.18992
29	7.90835	7.95826	7.60753	7.65371	7.32876	7.37161	7.06970	7.10956	6.60290	6.63766	6.19392	6.22449
30	7.96265	8.01049	7.65777	7.70201	7.37537	7.41640	7.11306	7.15122	6.64071	6.67395	6.22718	6.25640
31	8.01302	8.05886	7.70434	7.74671	7.41857	7.45784	7.15323	7.18974	6.67571	6.70749	6.25794	6.28587
32	8.05978	8.10367	7.74756	7.78810	7.45863	7.49620	7.19047	7.22538	6.70813	6.73850	6.28643	6.31309
33	8.10320	8.14520	7.78767	7.82646	7.49580	7.53173	7.22501	7.25838	6.73818	6.76720	6.31281	6.33827
34	8.14354	8.18371	7.82493	7.86201	7.53031	7.56464	7.25707	7.28895	6.76605	6.79376	6.33727	6.36157
35	8.18103	8.21944	7.85954	7.89498	7.56235	7.59516	7.28683	7.31728	6.79191	6.81836	6.35995	6.38314
36	8.21589	8.25260	7.89171	7.92557	7.59213	7.62346	7.31447	7.34355	6.81592	6.84116	6.38100	6.40312
37	8.24832	8.28338	7.92162	7.95395	7.61981	7.64972	7.34016	7.36791	6.83822	6.86230	6.40054	6.42163
38	8.27848	8.31196	7.94944	7.98030	7.64555	7.67409	7.36404	7.39051	6.85894	6.88191	6.41869	6.43879
39	8.30656	8.33851	7.97532	8.00477	7.66949	7.69672	7.38625	7.41150	6.87821	6.90010	6.43555	6.45472
40	8.33270	8.36318	7.99942	8.02750	7.69177	7.71773	7.40691	7.43098	6.89612	6.91698	6.45123	6.46949
41	8.35704	8.38611	8.02184	8.04862	7.71250	7.73725	7.42613	7.44908	6.91278	6.93266	6.46581	6.48320
42	8.37971	8.40742	8.04273	8.06825	7.73180	7.75539	7.44403	7.46589	6.92828	6.94722	6.47937	6.49593
43	8.40083	8.42724	8.06218	8.08650	7.74978	7.77225	7.46069	7.48151	6.94271	6.96074	6.49199	6.50775
44	8.42051	8.44567	8.08031	8.10347	7.76653	7.78792	7.47621	7.49603	6.95615	6.97331	6.50374	6.51874
45	8.43885	8.46281	8.09719	8.11925	7.78213	7.80250	7.49066	7.50953	6.96866	6.98499	6.51468	6.52895
46	8.45595	8.47876	8.11293	8.13393	7.79667	7.81605	7.50413	7.52209	6.98032	6.99585	6.52486	6.53844
47	8.47189	8.49360	8.12761	8.14759	7.81022	7.82866	7.51668	7.53377	6.99118	7.00596	6.53435	6.54726
48	8.48675	8.50741	8.14129	8.16030	7.82285	7.84040	7.52838	7.54463	7.00130	7.01535	6.54319	6.55546
49	8.50062	8.52027	8.15404	8.17212	7.83462	7.85131	7.53929	7.55474	7.01073	7.02409	6.55143	6.56309
50	8.51355	8.53223	8.16594	8.18313	7.84561	7.86147	7.54946	7.56415	7.01952	7.03222	6.55910	6.57019
51	8.52561	8.54337	8.17704	8.19338	7.85585	7.87093	7.55894	7.57290	7.02772	7.03979	6.56626	6.57679
52	8.53687	8.55375	8.18739	8.20292	7.86541	7.87974	7.56779	7.58105	7.03537	7.04683	6.57294	6.58294
53	8.54737	8.56341	8.19705	8.21180	7.87432	7.88793	7.57604	7.58864	7.04250	7.05338	6.57916	6.58866
54	8.55717	8.57240	8.20606	8.22008	7.88264	7.89556	7.58374	7.59570	7.04915	7.05949	6.58496	6.59398
55	8.56631	8.58078	8.21447	8.22778	7.89040	7.90267	7.59092	7.60228	7.05535	7.06517	6.59038	6.59894
56	8.57485	8.58859	8.22232	8.23496	7.89764	7.90929	7.59762	7.60841	7.06114	7.07046	6.59543	6.60356
57	8.58282	8.59586	8.22965	8.24164	7.90440	7.91546	7.60388	7.61411	7.06655	7.07538	6.60014	6.60785
58	8.59026	8.60263	8.23649	8.24787	7.91071	7.92120	7.60972	7.61943	7.07159	7.07997	6.60454	6.61186
59	8.59720	8.60895	8.24288	8.25367	7.91660	7.92655	7.61517	7.62438	7.07629	7.08425	6.60865	6.61558
60	8.60369	8.61483	8.24884	8.25907	7.92210	7.93154	7.62025	7.62899	7.08069	7.08823	6.61248	6.61906
61	8.60974	8.62031	8.25440	8.26411	7.92723	7.93618	7.62500	7.63329	7.08479	7.09194	6.61605	6.62229
62	8.61540	8.62541	8.25960	8.26880	7.93202	7.94051	7.62944	7.63729	7.08862	7.09539	6.61939	6.62530
63	8.62068	8.63017	8.26445	8.27318	7.93650	7.94454	7.63358	7.64102	7.09219	7.09861	6.62251	6.62811
64	8.62561	8.63460	8.26898	8.27725	7.94067	7.94830	7.63744	7.64450	7.09553	7.10161	6.62542	6.63073
65	8.63021	8.63874	8.27321	8.28105	7.94458	7.95180	7.64105	7.64774	7.09864	7.10441	6.62813	6.63316

Hoskold Present Value of 1 per Period

Safe Rate 8.50%

Speculative Rate

Year	5.50% Annual	5.50% Monthly	5.75% Annual	5.75% Monthly	6.00% Annual	6.00% Monthly	6.25% Annual	6.25% Monthly	6.50% Annual	6.50% Monthly	6.75% Annual	6.75% Monthly
1	0.94787	0.98363	0.94563	0.98122	0.94340	0.97882	0.94118	0.97643	0.93897	0.97405	0.93677	0.97169
2	1.87050	1.93998	1.86179	1.93062	1.85317	1.92135	1.84462	1.91216	1.83616	1.90307	1.82776	1.89405
3	2.76595	2.86689	2.74696	2.84649	2.72822	2.82637	2.70974	2.80654	2.69151	2.78699	2.67352	2.76770
4	3.63256	3.76252	3.59987	3.72745	3.56776	3.69304	3.53622	3.65926	3.50523	3.62608	3.47478	3.59351
5	4.46896	4.62538	4.41958	4.57251	4.37128	4.52083	4.32403	4.47031	4.27779	4.42090	4.23252	4.37257
6	5.27406	5.45433	5.20543	5.38096	5.13856	5.30953	5.07338	5.23997	5.00984	5.17222	4.94787	5.10619
7	6.04707	6.24852	5.95702	6.15241	5.86960	6.05922	5.78472	5.96880	5.70225	5.88104	5.62211	5.79583
8	6.78745	7.00744	6.67420	6.88679	6.56467	6.77023	6.45867	6.65754	6.35604	6.54855	6.25662	6.44307
9	7.49492	7.73083	7.35707	7.58425	7.22420	7.44312	7.09604	7.30715	6.97235	7.17606	6.85290	7.04959
10	8.16942	8.41873	8.00591	8.24519	7.84882	8.07867	7.69777	7.91873	7.55243	7.76501	7.41248	7.61714
11	8.81112	9.07139	8.62121	8.87023	8.43932	8.67779	8.26495	8.49353	8.09763	8.31693	7.93695	8.14752
12	9.42038	9.68930	9.20362	9.46014	8.99662	9.24157	8.79872	9.03288	8.60934	8.83340	8.42795	8.64254
13	9.99771	10.27311	9.75392	10.01588	9.52174	9.77121	9.30035	9.53821	9.08902	9.31606	8.88708	9.10403
14	10.54380	10.82366	10.27301	10.53849	10.01578	10.26797	9.77112	10.01099	9.53812	9.76656	9.31598	9.53378
15	11.05944	11.34189	10.76189	11.02916	10.47993	10.73321	10.21237	10.45273	9.95813	10.18654	9.71624	9.93357
16	11.54554	11.82887	11.22164	11.48911	10.91542	11.16833	10.62546	10.86497	10.35052	10.57765	10.08944	10.30514
17	12.00308	12.28576	11.65338	11.91965	11.32349	11.57474	11.01176	11.24922	10.71674	10.94151	10.43711	10.65019
18	12.43311	12.71377	12.05830	12.32212	11.70543	11.95387	11.37263	11.60700	11.05823	11.27969	10.76074	10.97034
19	12.83674	13.11416	12.43759	12.69785	12.06252	12.30717	11.70941	11.93980	11.37638	11.59374	11.06178	11.26716
20	13.21511	13.48822	12.79247	13.04822	12.39603	12.63603	12.02343	12.24908	11.67256	11.88512	11.34160	11.54217
21	13.56937	13.83725	13.12415	13.37458	12.70722	12.94185	12.31597	12.53624	11.94809	12.15529	11.60155	11.79681
22	13.90068	14.16255	13.43383	13.67826	12.99732	13.22598	12.58829	12.80266	12.20421	12.40560	11.84288	12.03243
23	14.21021	14.46542	13.72271	13.96056	13.26754	13.48975	12.84160	13.04965	12.44216	12.63737	12.06681	12.25034
24	14.49911	14.74711	13.99193	14.22275	13.51904	13.73440	13.07707	13.27847	12.66308	12.85184	12.27449	12.45177
25	14.76850	15.00887	14.24264	14.46608	13.75295	13.96117	13.29581	13.49032	12.86808	13.05019	12.46701	12.63787
26	15.01949	15.25190	14.47594	14.69171	13.97035	14.17121	13.49889	13.68633	13.05821	13.23354	12.64540	12.80974
27	15.25314	15.47735	14.69286	14.90079	14.17228	14.36564	13.68733	13.86760	13.23447	13.40294	12.81062	12.96840
28	15.47050	15.68635	14.89444	15.09441	14.35974	14.54552	13.86210	14.03515	13.39780	13.55938	12.96359	13.11481
29	15.67256	15.87996	15.08164	15.27360	14.53367	14.71184	14.02411	14.18994	13.54908	13.70380	13.10517	13.24987
30	15.86028	16.05920	15.25540	15.43934	14.69495	14.86555	14.17423	14.33289	13.68915	13.83707	13.23617	13.37442
31	16.03457	16.22503	15.41658	15.59256	14.84445	15.00754	14.31327	14.46484	13.81879	13.96001	13.35733	13.48924
32	16.19631	16.37838	15.56603	15.73413	14.98296	15.13865	14.44200	14.58660	13.93875	14.07339	13.46938	13.59507
33	16.34631	16.52012	15.70453	15.86490	15.11125	15.25966	14.56115	14.69891	14.04970	14.17791	13.57296	13.69258
34	16.48537	16.65106	15.83285	15.98562	15.23001	15.37132	14.67140	14.80248	14.15231	14.27425	13.66870	13.78241
35	16.61423	16.77198	15.95167	16.09703	15.33992	15.47430	14.77337	14.89796	14.24717	14.36301	13.75717	13.86515
36	16.73358	16.88359	16.06166	16.19981	15.44162	15.56926	14.86766	14.98596	14.33485	14.44479	13.83890	13.94134
37	16.84409	16.98657	16.16345	16.29460	15.53567	15.65680	14.95484	15.06704	14.41587	14.52010	13.91440	14.01148
38	16.94638	17.08157	16.25761	16.38199	15.62264	15.73747	15.03541	15.14173	14.49073	14.58946	13.98413	14.07606
39	17.04102	17.16917	16.34470	16.46255	15.70304	15.81179	15.10986	15.21053	14.55987	14.65331	14.04851	14.13549
40	17.12857	17.24992	16.42521	16.53677	15.77735	15.88025	15.17865	15.27387	14.62373	14.71209	14.10795	14.19018
41	17.20952	17.32434	16.49964	16.60516	15.84601	15.94330	15.24219	15.33219	14.68270	14.76619	14.16283	14.24050
42	17.28436	17.39291	16.56843	16.66814	15.90944	16.00136	15.30087	15.38587	14.73714	14.81598	14.21348	14.28680
43	17.35354	17.45608	16.63198	16.72615	15.96803	16.05481	15.35506	15.43528	14.78740	14.86179	14.26022	14.32939
44	17.41747	17.51425	16.69069	16.77955	16.02214	16.10401	15.40509	15.48075	14.83380	14.90394	14.30336	14.36857
45	17.47653	17.56782	16.74492	16.82871	16.07210	16.14928	15.45127	15.52259	14.87661	14.94271	14.34317	14.40460
46	17.53108	17.61714	16.79500	16.87396	16.11823	16.19095	15.49390	15.56108	14.91612	14.97838	14.37989	14.43774
47	17.58147	17.66254	16.84123	16.91561	16.16081	16.22928	15.53324	15.59649	14.95258	15.01118	14.41378	14.46822
48	17.62799	17.70432	16.88392	16.95392	16.20012	16.26455	15.56955	15.62905	14.98622	15.04135	14.44503	14.49624
49	17.67095	17.74277	16.92332	16.98918	16.23639	16.29700	15.60305	15.65901	15.01726	15.06909	14.47386	14.52201
50	17.71061	17.77814	16.95969	17.02161	16.26986	16.32684	15.63396	15.68656	15.04589	15.09460	14.50046	14.54570
51	17.74721	17.81069	16.99325	17.05145	16.30075	16.35428	15.66247	15.71189	15.07230	15.11806	14.52499	14.56748
52	17.78099	17.84063	17.02422	17.07889	16.32924	16.37953	15.68878	15.73519	15.09666	15.13963	14.54761	14.58750
53	17.81217	17.86817	17.05280	17.10412	16.35553	16.40274	15.71304	15.75661	15.11912	15.15945	14.56847	14.60591
54	17.84094	17.89350	17.07917	17.12733	16.37978	16.42408	15.73543	15.77630	15.13985	15.17768	14.58771	14.62283
55	17.86748	17.91680	17.10349	17.14867	16.40215	16.44370	15.75607	15.79441	15.15896	15.19444	14.60545	14.63838
56	17.89197	17.93822	17.12592	17.16829	16.42279	16.46174	15.77511	15.81105	15.17658	15.20984	14.62180	14.65268
57	17.91455	17.95791	17.14662	17.18634	16.44182	16.47833	15.79267	15.82635	15.19283	15.22400	14.63689	14.66582
58	17.93539	17.97603	17.16571	17.20292	16.45937	16.49358	15.80886	15.84042	15.20781	15.23702	14.65080	14.67790
59	17.95461	17.99268	17.18331	17.21817	16.47555	16.50760	15.82379	15.85335	15.22163	15.24898	14.66362	14.68900
60	17.97234	18.00799	17.19955	17.23219	16.49048	16.52048	15.83756	15.86523	15.23437	15.25997	14.67544	14.69920
61	17.98869	18.02206	17.21452	17.24508	16.50424	16.53233	15.85025	15.87615	15.24611	15.27008	14.68634	14.70857
62	18.00377	18.03500	17.22833	17.25693	16.51693	16.54321	15.86195	15.88619	15.25694	15.27936	14.69639	14.71719
63	18.01767	18.04689	17.24106	17.26781	16.52863	16.55322	15.87275	15.89542	15.26693	15.28790	14.70565	14.72511
64	18.03049	18.05782	17.25280	17.27782	16.53942	16.56242	15.88270	15.90390	15.27613	15.29574	14.71419	14.73239
65	18.04232	18.06787	17.26363	17.28702	16.54937	16.57087	15.89187	15.91169	15.28462	15.30295	14.72206	14.73907

Hoskold Present Value of 1 per Period

Safe Rate 8.50%

Year	7.00% Annual	7.00% Monthly	7.25% Annual	7.25% Monthly	7.50% Annual	7.50% Monthly	7.75% Annual	7.75% Monthly	8.00% Annual	8.00% Monthly	8.25% Annual	8.25% Monthly
1	0.93458	0.96933	0.93240	0.96699	0.93023	0.96466	0.92807	0.96234	0.92593	0.96003	0.92379	0.95773
2	1.81945	1.88513	1.81121	1.87628	1.80305	1.86752	1.79496	1.85885	1.78694	1.85025	1.77899	1.84173
3	2.65577	2.74868	2.63825	2.72992	2.62096	2.71142	2.60390	2.69316	2.58706	2.67515	2.57043	2.65738
4	3.44486	3.56151	3.41544	3.53008	3.38653	3.49920	3.35809	3.46885	3.33014	3.43903	3.30264	3.40972
5	4.18821	4.32529	4.14481	4.27902	4.10230	4.23373	4.06065	4.18939	4.01985	4.14596	3.97985	4.10343
6	4.88742	5.04183	4.82842	4.97907	4.77083	4.91786	4.71460	4.85813	4.65968	4.79983	4.60602	4.74292
7	5.54418	5.71305	5.46839	5.63260	5.39464	5.55439	5.32285	5.47832	5.25295	5.40430	5.18486	5.33226
8	6.16027	6.34093	6.06683	6.24198	5.97619	6.14607	5.88822	6.05307	5.80280	5.96283	5.71982	5.87525
9	6.73747	6.92750	6.62586	6.80957	6.51790	6.69558	6.41339	6.58535	6.31219	6.47869	6.21412	6.37543
10	7.27761	7.47480	7.14757	7.33768	7.02209	7.20550	6.90094	7.07800	6.78391	6.95493	6.67077	6.83607
11	7.78253	7.98488	7.63400	7.82860	7.49103	7.67833	7.35332	7.53371	7.22059	7.39444	7.09255	7.26023
12	8.25404	8.45976	8.08716	8.28455	7.92689	8.11644	7.77285	7.95503	7.62469	7.79991	7.48207	7.65072
13	8.69392	8.90143	8.50898	8.70765	8.33175	8.52213	8.16174	8.34436	7.99854	8.17384	7.84173	8.01016
14	9.10395	9.31183	8.90136	9.09999	8.70758	8.89757	8.52207	8.70396	8.34429	8.51860	8.17378	8.34096
15	9.48582	9.69286	9.26608	9.46354	9.05629	9.24481	8.85759	9.03597	8.66398	8.83636	8.48029	8.64538
16	9.84121	10.04632	9.60490	9.80018	9.37967	9.56582	9.16477	9.34240	8.95949	9.12918	8.76320	8.92547
17	10.17170	10.37398	9.91946	10.11173	9.67942	9.86241	9.45073	9.62510	9.23259	9.39893	9.02429	9.18315
18	10.47884	10.67750	10.21133	10.39989	9.95714	10.13634	9.71530	9.88583	9.48493	9.64740	9.26523	9.42020
19	10.76410	10.95849	10.48203	10.66627	10.21436	10.38924	9.96002	10.12623	9.71804	9.87620	9.48754	9.63823
20	11.02889	11.21846	10.73296	10.91241	10.45249	10.62261	10.18631	10.34781	9.93335	10.08687	9.69265	9.83876
21	11.27454	11.45886	10.96546	11.13974	10.67288	10.83791	10.39551	10.55201	10.13218	10.28080	9.88187	10.02318
22	11.50233	11.68105	11.18081	11.34961	10.87679	11.03646	10.58885	10.74013	10.31577	10.45929	10.05642	10.19277
23	11.71345	11.88631	11.38020	11.54329	11.06538	11.21952	10.76752	10.91341	10.48527	10.62356	10.21743	10.34871
24	11.90905	12.07585	11.56474	11.72197	11.23977	11.38824	10.93258	11.07299	10.64172	10.77472	10.36594	10.49209
25	12.09019	12.25081	11.73548	11.88675	11.40099	11.54371	11.08504	11.21991	10.78613	10.91378	10.50291	10.62392
26	12.25788	12.41225	11.89341	12.03868	11.54999	11.68694	11.22584	11.35517	10.91940	11.04172	10.62923	10.74511
27	12.41307	12.56115	12.03945	12.17871	11.68767	11.81886	11.35586	11.47967	11.04237	11.15940	10.74573	10.85652
28	12.55664	12.69846	12.17446	12.30774	11.81487	11.94034	11.47590	11.59425	11.15584	11.26765	10.85315	10.95894
29	12.68943	12.82504	12.29925	12.42661	11.93235	12.05219	11.58671	11.69968	11.26053	11.36719	10.95221	11.05309
30	12.81221	12.94170	12.41456	12.53610	12.04086	12.15516	11.68899	11.79668	11.35711	11.45874	11.04355	11.13963
31	12.92570	13.04918	12.52109	12.63693	12.14104	12.24992	11.78339	11.88592	11.44620	11.54292	11.12777	11.21917
32	13.03060	13.14819	12.61950	12.72976	12.23354	12.33714	11.87050	11.96801	11.52838	11.62033	11.20543	11.29228
33	13.12752	13.23938	12.71038	12.81521	12.31893	12.41739	11.95088	12.04351	11.60418	11.69150	11.27702	11.35947
34	13.21705	13.32334	12.79430	12.89387	12.39774	12.49122	12.02504	12.11296	11.67408	11.75693	11.34303	11.42123
35	13.29975	13.40065	12.87177	12.96626	12.47048	12.55914	12.09345	12.17682	11.73855	11.81708	11.40389	11.47799
36	13.37613	13.47180	12.94330	13.03286	12.53760	12.62162	12.15657	12.23554	11.79801	11.87238	11.46000	11.53015
37	13.44665	13.53729	13.00932	13.09414	12.59954	12.67909	12.21479	12.28954	11.85284	11.92321	11.51172	11.57809
38	13.51175	13.59756	13.07025	13.15052	12.65668	12.73194	12.26849	12.33918	11.90339	11.96994	11.55940	11.62215
39	13.57185	13.65301	13.12647	13.20238	12.70940	12.78054	12.31801	12.38483	11.95001	12.01289	11.60336	11.66263
40	13.62732	13.70402	13.17835	13.25007	12.75803	12.82523	12.36369	12.42679	11.99300	12.05236	11.64388	11.69984
41	13.67851	13.75095	13.22622	13.29394	12.80289	12.86633	12.40581	12.46537	12.03263	12.08865	11.68124	11.73402
42	13.72575	13.79411	13.27039	13.33428	12.84427	12.90411	12.44466	12.50083	12.06917	12.12199	11.71567	11.76544
43	13.76934	13.83382	13.31113	13.37137	12.88243	12.93885	12.48048	12.53343	12.10286	12.15264	11.74741	11.79431
44	13.80955	13.87033	13.34871	13.40548	12.91762	12.97078	12.51351	12.56339	12.13392	12.18081	11.77667	11.82084
45	13.84666	13.90390	13.38337	13.43684	12.95008	13.00014	12.54397	12.59093	12.16255	12.20670	11.80364	11.84522
46	13.88088	13.93478	13.41534	13.46567	12.98001	13.02713	12.57205	12.61624	12.18895	12.23049	11.82850	11.86762
47	13.91245	13.96316	13.44482	13.49218	13.00761	13.05193	12.59794	12.63951	12.21328	12.25235	11.85142	11.88820
48	13.94157	13.98926	13.47201	13.51655	13.03306	13.07473	12.62181	12.66089	12.23572	12.27244	11.87254	11.90712
49	13.96842	14.01326	13.49709	13.53895	13.05653	13.09569	12.64382	12.68054	12.25640	12.29090	11.89201	11.92449
50	13.99319	14.03532	13.52021	13.55953	13.07816	13.11495	12.66410	12.69860	12.27546	12.30787	11.90996	11.94046
51	14.01603	14.05559	13.54153	13.57846	13.09811	13.13266	12.68281	12.71520	12.29303	12.32346	11.92650	11.95514
52	14.03709	14.07423	13.56119	13.59585	13.11650	13.14892	12.70005	12.73045	12.30923	12.33778	11.94175	11.96862
53	14.05651	14.09137	13.57932	13.61184	13.13346	13.16388	12.71595	12.74446	12.32417	12.35095	11.95580	11.98101
54	14.07442	14.10712	13.59603	13.62654	13.14909	13.17762	12.73060	12.75735	12.33793	12.36305	11.96876	11.99239
55	14.09094	14.12159	13.61144	13.64004	13.16351	13.19025	12.74411	12.76918	12.35062	12.37416	11.98070	12.00285
56	14.10616	14.13489	13.62565	13.65245	13.17679	13.20186	12.75656	12.78006	12.36231	12.38438	11.99170	12.01246
57	14.12020	14.14712	13.63874	13.66386	13.18904	13.21253	12.76804	12.79005	12.37309	12.39376	12.00184	12.02129
58	14.13314	14.15836	13.65082	13.67434	13.20033	13.22233	12.77863	12.79924	12.38303	12.40239	12.01119	12.02940
59	14.14507	14.16869	13.66195	13.68398	13.21074	13.23133	12.78838	12.80768	12.39219	12.41031	12.01981	12.03686
60	14.15607	14.17818	13.67221	13.69283	13.22033	13.23961	12.79737	12.81543	12.40063	12.41759	12.02775	12.04371
61	14.16621	14.18690	13.68167	13.70097	13.22918	13.24722	12.80566	12.82256	12.40841	12.42428	12.03507	12.05000
62	14.17556	14.19492	13.69039	13.70844	13.23733	13.25421	12.81330	12.82911	12.41558	12.43043	12.04182	12.05578
63	14.18418	14.20228	13.69843	13.71531	13.24485	13.26063	12.82034	12.83512	12.42220	12.43608	12.04804	12.06109
64	14.19213	14.20905	13.70584	13.72162	13.25177	13.26653	12.82683	12.84065	12.42829	12.44127	12.05377	12.06598
65	14.19945	14.21527	13.71267	13.72743	13.25816	13.27195	12.83281	12.84573	12.43390	12.44604	12.05905	12.07046

Hoskold Present Value of 1 per Period

Safe Rate 8.50%

						Speculative Rate						
	8.50%		8.75%		9.00%		9.25%		9.50%		9.75%	
Year	Annual	Monthly	Annual	Monthly	Annual	Monthly	Annual	Monthly	Annual	Monthly	Annual	Monthly
1	0.92166	0.95544	0.91954	0.95316	0.91743	0.95090	0.91533	0.94864	0.91324	0.94640	0.91116	0.94416
2	1.77111	1.83329	1.76331	1.82492	1.75557	1.81664	1.74790	1.80842	1.74029	1.80028	1.73275	1.79222
3	2.55402	2.63984	2.53782	2.62254	2.52182	2.60545	2.50602	2.58859	2.49042	2.57195	2.47501	2.55552
4	3.27560	3.38090	3.24899	3.35256	3.22281	3.32469	3.19705	3.29729	3.17170	3.27033	3.14675	3.24381
5	3.94064	4.06177	3.90220	4.02093	3.86450	3.98092	3.82752	3.94169	3.79124	3.90323	3.75565	3.86551
6	4.55359	4.68734	4.50233	4.63305	4.45222	4.58000	4.40321	4.52815	4.35527	4.47747	4.30836	4.42790
7	5.11851	5.26211	5.05384	5.19378	4.99079	5.12721	4.92928	5.06232	4.86928	4.99905	4.81072	4.93735
8	5.63918	5.79020	5.56079	5.70758	5.48454	5.62729	5.41036	5.54922	5.33815	5.47329	5.26785	5.39941
9	6.11906	6.27541	6.02687	6.17848	5.93741	6.08449	5.85056	5.99333	5.76622	5.90485	5.68428	5.81895
10	6.56135	6.72121	6.45546	6.61014	6.35293	6.50268	6.25361	6.39866	6.15734	6.29791	6.06400	6.20029
11	6.96898	7.13080	6.84965	7.00591	6.73433	6.88531	6.62283	6.76880	6.51496	6.65616	6.41055	6.54721
12	7.34469	7.50713	7.21226	7.36883	7.08452	7.23554	6.96123	7.10698	6.84215	6.98292	6.72708	6.86310
13	7.69095	7.85290	7.54587	7.70170	7.40615	7.55621	7.27152	7.41611	7.14169	7.28112	7.01642	7.15095
14	8.01010	8.17059	7.85284	8.00703	7.70164	7.84990	7.55616	7.69881	7.41606	7.55343	7.28107	7.41344
15	8.30424	8.46247	8.13534	8.28715	7.97318	8.11894	7.81736	7.95743	7.66751	7.80221	7.52330	7.65294
16	8.57533	8.73066	8.39535	8.54417	8.22277	8.36548	8.05714	8.19411	7.89805	8.02962	7.74512	7.87160
17	8.82519	8.97706	8.63469	8.78001	8.45223	8.59143	8.27732	8.41078	8.10951	8.23757	7.94837	8.07135
18	9.05548	9.20345	8.85501	8.99645	8.66323	8.79857	8.47958	8.60919	8.30355	8.42780	8.13468	8.25390
19	9.26772	9.41146	9.05786	9.19511	8.85729	8.98848	8.66541	8.79094	8.48166	8.60189	8.30555	8.42081
20	9.46334	9.60257	9.24462	9.37745	9.03579	9.16265	8.83619	8.95746	8.64521	8.76126	8.46231	8.57348
21	9.64363	9.77816	9.41660	9.54484	9.20002	9.32238	8.99318	9.11006	8.79543	8.90720	8.60619	8.71318
22	9.80980	9.93949	9.57497	9.69850	9.35113	9.46891	9.13752	9.24995	8.93344	9.04088	8.73829	8.84105
23	9.96295	10.08772	9.72083	9.83958	9.49019	9.60334	9.27025	9.37819	9.06028	9.16335	8.85960	8.95813
24	10.10410	10.22392	9.85515	9.96911	9.61818	9.72669	9.39234	9.49579	9.17686	9.27559	8.97104	9.06537
25	10.23419	10.34905	9.97888	10.08804	9.73599	9.83988	9.50465	9.60363	9.28404	9.37847	9.07345	9.16361
26	10.35409	10.46402	10.09284	10.19726	9.84444	9.94376	9.60798	9.70256	9.38261	9.47278	9.16757	9.25364
27	10.46460	10.56965	10.19781	10.29755	9.94429	10.03910	9.70306	9.79331	9.47326	9.55927	9.25410	9.33615
28	10.56645	10.66670	10.29451	10.38964	10.03622	10.12661	9.79057	9.87657	9.55665	9.63858	9.33366	9.41179
29	10.66033	10.75587	10.38359	10.47423	10.12087	10.20695	9.87111	9.95298	9.63338	9.71133	9.40683	9.48115
30	10.74684	10.83780	10.46566	10.55190	10.19882	10.28070	9.94524	10.02309	9.70397	9.77808	9.47413	9.54475
31	10.82658	10.91308	10.54127	10.62325	10.27061	10.34841	10.01349	10.08744	9.76894	9.83931	9.53605	9.60309
32	10.90008	10.98224	10.61093	10.68878	10.33672	10.41058	10.07633	10.14651	9.82874	9.89550	9.59302	9.65660
33	10.96781	11.04579	10.67511	10.74896	10.39762	10.46767	10.13419	10.20073	9.88378	9.94706	9.64545	9.70570
34	11.03024	11.10417	10.73424	10.80424	10.45371	10.52009	10.18747	10.25050	9.93445	9.99438	9.69370	9.75075
35	11.08778	11.15782	10.78872	10.85502	10.50537	10.56823	10.23653	10.29619	9.98110	10.03782	9.73811	9.79209
36	11.14081	11.20710	10.83893	10.90166	10.55297	10.61243	10.28171	10.33815	10.02405	10.07769	9.77899	9.83003
37	11.18969	11.25239	10.88518	10.94451	10.59681	10.65303	10.32333	10.37667	10.06360	10.11429	9.81663	9.86485
38	11.23474	11.29399	10.92781	10.98387	10.63721	10.69031	10.36166	10.41204	10.10003	10.14789	9.85128	9.89681
39	11.27625	11.33222	10.96709	11.02002	10.67442	10.72456	10.39696	10.44452	10.13357	10.17874	9.88319	9.92615
40	11.31452	11.36735	11.00328	11.05323	10.70870	10.75601	10.42949	10.47435	10.16446	10.20707	9.91257	9.95309
41	11.34979	11.39962	11.03663	11.08374	10.74029	10.78490	10.45944	10.50175	10.19291	10.23308	9.93963	9.97782
42	11.38229	11.42927	11.06736	11.11177	10.76939	10.81143	10.48704	10.52690	10.21912	10.25697	9.96455	10.00053
43	11.41225	11.45651	11.09569	11.13752	10.79621	10.83581	10.51247	10.55001	10.24326	10.27890	9.98750	10.02138
44	11.43986	11.48154	11.12178	11.16117	10.82091	10.85819	10.53589	10.57123	10.26550	10.29905	10.00864	10.04053
45	11.46531	11.50453	11.14584	11.18290	10.84368	10.87876	10.55748	10.59072	10.28599	10.31755	10.02812	10.05811
46	11.48877	11.52566	11.16800	11.20286	10.86466	10.89765	10.57736	10.60863	10.30486	10.33454	10.04606	10.07426
47	11.51038	11.54508	11.18843	11.22120	10.88399	10.91500	10.59568	10.62507	10.32225	10.35014	10.06258	10.08909
48	11.53031	11.56291	11.20725	11.23805	10.90180	10.93095	10.61256	10.64018	10.33827	10.36448	10.07781	10.10270
49	11.54867	11.57930	11.22460	11.25353	10.91822	10.94559	10.62812	10.65405	10.35303	10.37764	10.09183	10.11521
50	11.56560	11.59436	11.24059	11.26775	10.93334	10.95904	10.64245	10.66680	10.36663	10.38974	10.10475	10.12670
51	11.58119	11.60819	11.25532	11.28082	10.94728	10.97140	10.65565	10.67851	10.37916	10.40084	10.11666	10.13725
52	11.59557	11.62090	11.26890	11.29282	10.96013	10.98276	10.66782	10.68926	10.39071	10.41105	10.12763	10.14695
53	11.60882	11.63258	11.28141	11.30385	10.97196	10.99319	10.67904	10.69914	10.40135	10.42042	10.13773	10.15585
54	11.62103	11.64331	11.29294	11.31398	10.98287	11.00277	10.68937	10.70822	10.41115	10.42903	10.14704	10.16403
55	11.63229	11.65317	11.30357	11.32329	10.99292	11.01157	10.69889	10.71656	10.42018	10.43694	10.15562	10.17154
56	11.64266	11.66223	11.31337	11.33184	11.00219	11.01966	10.70767	10.72422	10.42851	10.44420	10.16353	10.17844
57	11.65222	11.67055	11.32240	11.33970	11.01073	11.02709	10.71576	10.73125	10.43618	10.45088	10.17082	10.18478
58	11.66104	11.67820	11.33072	11.34692	11.01859	11.03392	10.72321	10.73772	10.44324	10.45701	10.17753	10.19060
59	11.66916	11.68522	11.33838	11.35355	11.02585	11.04019	10.73007	10.74366	10.44976	10.46264	10.18371	10.19595
60	11.67664	11.69168	11.34545	11.35965	11.03253	11.04595	10.73640	10.74911	10.45576	10.46782	10.18942	10.20086
61	11.68354	11.69761	11.35196	11.36524	11.03869	11.05124	10.74224	10.75413	10.46129	10.47257	10.19467	10.20538
62	11.68990	11.70306	11.35797	11.37039	11.04436	11.05611	10.74761	10.75873	10.46639	10.47694	10.19951	10.20952
63	11.69576	11.70806	11.36350	11.37511	11.04959	11.06058	10.75256	10.76296	10.47109	10.48095	10.20397	10.21333
64	11.70116	11.71266	11.36860	11.37946	11.05441	11.06469	10.75713	10.76685	10.47542	10.48463	10.20808	10.21684
65	11.70614	11.71689	11.37330	11.38344	11.05886	11.06845	10.76134	10.77042	10.47941	10.48802	10.21187	10.22005

Hoskold Present Value of 1 per Period

Safe Rate 8.50%

Year	_	_	_	_	Speculative Rate		_	_	_	_	_	_
	10.00%		10.25%		10.50%		10.75%		11.00%		11.25%	
	Annual	Monthly	Annual	Monthly	Annual	Monthly	Annual	Monthly	Annual	Monthly	Annual	Monthly
1	0.90909	0.94194	0.90703	0.93973	0.90498	0.93753	0.90293	0.93533	0.90090	0.93315	0.89888	0.93098
2	1.72528	1.78422	1.71787	1.77630	1.71052	1.76845	1.70324	1.76066	1.69602	1.75295	1.68886	1.74530
3	2.45979	2.53929	2.44475	2.52327	2.42990	2.50746	2.41523	2.49184	2.40073	2.47641	2.38641	2.46117
4	3.12219	3.21771	3.09801	3.19204	3.07420	3.16677	3.05075	3.14189	3.02766	3.11740	3.00492	3.09330
5	3.72071	3.82851	3.68642	3.79221	3.65276	3.75660	3.61970	3.72165	3.58724	3.68734	3.55536	3.65366
6	4.26245	4.37942	4.21750	4.33199	4.17350	4.28558	4.13040	4.24015	4.08819	4.19568	4.04683	4.15212
7	4.75355	4.87715	4.69772	4.81840	4.64319	4.76105	4.58991	4.70504	4.53784	4.65034	4.48694	4.59690
8	5.19938	5.32749	5.13266	5.25747	5.06764	5.18926	5.00424	5.12281	4.94240	5.05803	4.88208	4.99487
9	5.60464	5.73552	5.52719	5.65444	5.45186	5.57562	5.37855	5.49897	5.30719	5.42440	5.23769	5.35182
10	5.97344	6.10565	5.88555	6.01385	5.80020	5.92477	5.71730	5.83830	5.63673	5.75431	5.55841	5.67270
11	6.30943	6.44178	6.21145	6.33968	6.11647	6.24077	6.02435	6.14490	5.93497	6.05192	5.84819	5.96172
12	6.61582	6.74733	6.50818	6.63541	6.40398	6.52713	6.30307	6.42233	6.20529	6.32085	6.11050	6.22252
13	6.89546	7.02536	6.77861	6.90410	6.66565	6.78695	6.55639	6.67372	6.45066	6.56420	6.34828	6.45822
14	7.15091	7.27854	7.02531	7.14846	6.90405	7.02295	6.78691	6.90178	6.67368	6.78471	6.56416	6.67155
15	7.38441	7.50927	7.25056	7.37089	7.12147	7.23753	6.99690	7.10890	6.87661	6.98476	6.76039	6.86489
16	7.59800	7.71969	7.45637	7.57352	7.31992	7.43279	7.18837	7.29720	7.06147	7.16646	6.93897	7.04032
17	7.79350	7.91170	7.64456	7.75825	7.50120	7.61064	7.36312	7.46854	7.23003	7.33164	7.10167	7.19968
18	7.97255	8.08702	7.81675	7.92676	7.66692	7.77273	7.52273	7.62457	7.38387	7.48196	7.25003	7.34458
19	8.13660	8.24719	7.97439	8.08058	7.81852	7.92057	7.66863	7.76678	7.52438	7.61885	7.38545	7.47644
20	8.28700	8.39357	8.11880	8.22106	7.95729	8.05550	7.80208	7.89647	7.65281	7.74361	7.50914	7.59655
21	8.42493	8.52742	8.25114	8.34943	8.08437	8.17871	7.92422	8.01483	7.77028	7.85739	7.62222	7.70602
22	8.55147	8.64987	8.37248	8.46677	8.20083	8.29127	8.03607	8.12290	7.87780	7.96123	7.72565	7.80587
23	8.66762	8.76191	8.48378	8.57409	8.30758	8.39416	8.13856	8.22163	7.97627	8.05605	7.82032	7.89700
24	8.77426	8.86447	8.58592	8.67228	8.40550	8.48825	8.23250	8.31187	8.06648	8.14267	7.90703	7.98022
25	8.87219	8.95839	8.67968	8.76215	8.49533	8.57433	8.31866	8.39438	8.14918	8.22184	7.98648	8.05625
26	8.96217	9.04440	8.76577	8.84442	8.57779	8.65309	8.39770	8.46987	8.22503	8.29424	8.05931	8.12575
27	9.04484	9.12321	8.84484	8.91977	8.65349	8.72520	8.47025	8.53894	8.29461	8.36047	8.12610	8.18930
28	9.12083	9.19543	8.91749	8.98879	8.72302	8.79123	8.53686	8.60217	8.35847	8.42107	8.18738	8.24744
29	9.19069	9.26162	8.98426	9.05203	8.78690	8.85172	8.59803	8.66007	8.41710	8.47655	8.24363	8.30065
30	9.25493	9.32230	9.04563	9.10999	8.84560	8.90713	8.65422	8.71311	8.47095	8.52736	8.29527	8.34936
31	9.31400	9.37795	9.10206	9.16312	8.89955	8.95791	8.70585	8.76170	8.52041	8.57389	8.34270	8.39397
32	9.36834	9.42897	9.15395	9.21183	8.94915	9.00446	8.75331	8.80622	8.56586	8.61652	8.38627	8.43483
33	9.41834	9.47578	9.20167	9.25650	8.99476	9.04713	8.79694	8.84703	8.60764	8.65559	8.42631	8.47226
34	9.46433	9.51871	9.24558	9.29746	9.03670	9.08626	8.83706	8.88445	8.64604	8.69140	8.46311	8.50657
35	9.50666	9.55810	9.28597	9.33504	9.07529	9.12215	8.87395	8.91876	8.68136	8.72423	8.49694	8.53801
36	9.54562	9.59425	9.32313	9.36951	9.11078	9.15507	8.90789	8.95022	8.71383	8.75434	8.52805	8.56684
37	9.58148	9.62742	9.35734	9.40114	9.14344	9.18526	8.93911	8.97908	8.74371	8.78194	8.55666	8.59328
38	9.61449	9.65786	9.38882	9.43017	9.17350	9.21297	8.96783	9.00555	8.77119	8.80726	8.58298	8.61752
39	9.64488	9.68580	9.41780	9.45681	9.20116	9.23839	8.99427	9.02984	8.79647	8.83049	8.60719	8.63976
40	9.67286	9.71144	9.44448	9.48125	9.22662	9.26172	9.01860	9.05213	8.81974	8.85181	8.62947	8.66016
41	9.69863	9.73499	9.46904	9.50369	9.25006	9.28313	9.04099	9.07258	8.84116	8.87136	8.64997	8.67888
42	9.72235	9.75660	9.49165	9.52429	9.27164	9.30279	9.06160	9.09135	8.86087	8.88931	8.66883	8.69605
43	9.74420	9.77645	9.51247	9.54320	9.29151	9.32083	9.08058	9.10858	8.87901	8.90578	8.68620	8.71182
44	9.76433	9.79467	9.53165	9.56056	9.30981	9.33739	9.09805	9.12439	8.89572	8.92090	8.70219	8.72628
45	9.78286	9.81140	9.54931	9.57650	9.32665	9.35259	9.11414	9.13891	8.91110	8.93477	8.71691	8.73956
46	9.79993	9.82676	9.56558	9.59114	9.34217	9.36655	9.12896	9.15224	8.92526	8.94751	8.73046	8.75175
47	9.81565	9.84087	9.58056	9.60458	9.35646	9.37937	9.14260	9.16447	8.93830	8.95921	8.74293	8.76294
48	9.83014	9.85383	9.59436	9.61692	9.36962	9.39114	9.15517	9.17571	8.95031	8.96995	8.75442	8.77321
49	9.84348	9.86573	9.60707	9.62825	9.38174	9.40194	9.16674	9.18603	8.96137	8.97980	8.76501	8.78264
50	9.85578	9.87666	9.61878	9.63866	9.39290	9.41187	9.17740	9.19550	8.97156	8.98886	8.77475	8.79130
51	9.86710	9.88669	9.62956	9.64822	9.40319	9.42098	9.18722	9.20420	8.98094	8.99717	8.78373	8.79925
52	9.87754	9.89591	9.63950	9.65700	9.41267	9.42935	9.19626	9.21219	8.98959	9.00480	8.79199	8.80655
53	9.88715	9.90438	9.64865	9.66506	9.42139	9.43704	9.20459	9.21953	8.99755	9.01182	8.79961	8.81326
54	9.89601	9.91216	9.65709	9.67247	9.42944	9.44410	9.21227	9.22627	9.00488	9.01825	8.80663	8.81941
55	9.90417	9.91930	9.66486	9.67927	9.43685	9.45059	9.21934	9.23245	9.01164	9.02417	8.81309	8.82507
56	9.91169	9.92586	9.67202	9.68552	9.44367	9.45654	9.22586	9.23814	9.01786	9.02960	8.81904	8.83026
57	9.91861	9.93189	9.67862	9.69126	9.44996	9.46201	9.23186	9.24336	9.02360	9.03459	8.82453	8.83503
58	9.92500	9.93743	9.68470	9.69653	9.45576	9.46704	9.23739	9.24816	9.02888	9.03917	8.82958	8.83942
59	9.93088	9.94252	9.69030	9.70138	9.46110	9.47166	9.24249	9.25256	9.03375	9.04338	8.83423	8.84344
60	9.93630	9.94719	9.69546	9.70582	9.46602	9.47590	9.24718	9.25661	9.03824	9.04724	8.83852	8.84714
61	9.94130	9.95148	9.70022	9.70991	9.47055	9.47979	9.25151	9.26033	9.04237	9.05079	8.84248	8.85053
62	9.94590	9.95542	9.70460	9.71367	9.47473	9.48337	9.25549	9.26374	9.04618	9.05405	8.84612	8.85365
63	9.95014	9.95905	9.70864	9.71711	9.47858	9.48666	9.25917	9.26688	9.04969	9.05705	8.84947	8.85652
64	9.95405	9.96238	9.71236	9.72028	9.48212	9.48968	9.26255	9.26976	9.05292	9.05980	8.85257	8.85915
65	9.95765	9.96543	9.71579	9.72319	9.48539	9.49245	9.26567	9.27241	9.05590	9.06233	8.85541	8.86157

Hoskold Present Value of 1 per Period

Safe Rate 8.50%

Year	11.50% Annual	Monthly	12.00% Annual	Monthly	13.00% Annual	Monthly	14.00% Annual	Monthly	15.00% Annual	Monthly	16.00% Annual	Monthly
					Speculative Rate							
1	0.89686	0.92882	0.89286	0.92452	0.88496	0.91606	0.87719	0.90774	0.86957	0.89957	0.86207	0.89155
2	1.68176	1.73772	1.66773	1.72275	1.64038	1.69357	1.61390	1.66537	1.58827	1.63809	1.56344	1.61169
3	2.37226	2.44612	2.34445	2.41657	2.29074	2.35955	2.23944	2.30515	2.19039	2.25321	2.14344	2.20356
4	2.98251	3.06956	2.93869	3.02316	2.85479	2.93445	2.77556	2.85079	2.70060	2.77178	2.62959	2.69702
5	3.52403	3.62059	3.46301	3.55621	3.34710	3.43409	3.23870	3.32007	3.13710	3.21338	3.04168	3.11334
6	4.00630	4.10947	3.92762	4.02673	3.77919	3.87086	3.64157	3.72661	3.51362	3.59272	3.39435	3.46812
7	4.43716	4.54467	4.34086	4.44370	4.16027	4.25463	3.99410	4.08100	3.84070	3.92099	3.69865	3.77305
8	4.82321	4.93326	4.70964	4.81451	4.49781	4.59336	4.30421	4.39164	4.12659	4.20689	3.96305	4.03705
9	5.17000	5.28116	5.03972	5.14530	4.79792	4.89351	4.57826	4.66522	4.37783	4.45728	4.19421	4.26708
10	5.48222	5.59338	5.33596	5.44120	5.06566	5.16042	4.82142	4.90718	4.59965	4.67764	4.39739	4.46862
11	5.76392	5.87417	5.60246	5.70657	5.30524	5.39850	5.03796	5.12199	4.79633	4.87242	4.57681	4.64605
12	6.01855	6.12720	5.84273	5.94507	5.52020	5.61146	5.23142	5.31331	4.97134	5.04524	4.73591	4.80292
13	6.24911	6.35560	6.05977	6.15985	5.71354	5.80243	5.40474	5.48422	5.12760	5.19909	4.87750	4.94214
14	6.45818	6.56210	6.25616	6.35363	5.88781	5.97406	5.56042	5.63729	5.26753	5.33646	5.00394	5.06611
15	6.64803	6.74906	6.43416	6.52875	6.04520	6.12862	5.70059	5.77471	5.39315	5.45945	5.11717	5.17682
16	6.82065	6.91855	6.59572	6.68722	6.18760	6.26806	5.82705	5.89835	5.50620	5.56982	5.21884	5.27596
17	6.97778	7.07238	6.74254	6.83083	6.31664	6.39406	5.94135	6.00979	5.60815	5.66909	5.31034	5.36495
18	7.12096	7.21215	6.87614	6.96113	6.43375	6.50809	6.04484	6.11042	5.70027	5.75855	5.39286	5.44500
19	7.25156	7.33926	6.99783	7.07947	6.54016	6.61142	6.13868	6.20142	5.78364	5.83930	5.46743	5.51714
20	7.37077	7.45497	7.10879	7.18707	6.63698	6.70516	6.22390	6.28382	5.85923	5.91230	5.53492	5.58226
21	7.47969	7.56037	7.21004	7.28498	6.72516	6.79031	6.30138	6.35854	5.92784	5.97840	5.59611	5.64115
22	7.57926	7.65646	7.30253	7.37416	6.80555	6.86772	6.37191	6.42637	5.99021	6.03833	5.65167	5.69448
23	7.67036	7.74411	7.38706	7.45543	6.87891	6.93816	6.43617	6.48801	6.04698	6.09272	5.70217	5.74282
24	7.75376	7.82412	7.46437	7.52956	6.94590	7.00232	6.49478	6.54408	6.09869	6.14213	5.74813	5.78671
25	7.83014	7.89719	7.53513	7.59721	7.00713	7.06079	6.54829	6.59512	6.14584	6.18708	5.79000	5.82658
26	7.90013	7.96396	7.59993	7.65899	7.06314	7.11412	6.59717	6.64162	6.18888	6.22798	5.82818	5.86285
27	7.96430	8.02500	7.65930	7.71542	7.11439	7.16278	6.64186	6.68402	6.22819	6.26525	5.86303	5.89586
28	8.02316	8.08083	7.71372	7.76701	7.16132	7.20722	6.68274	6.72270	6.26413	6.29923	5.89487	5.92594
29	8.07717	8.13190	7.76363	7.81418	7.20431	7.24782	6.72017	6.75801	6.29700	6.33022	5.92397	5.95336
30	8.12674	8.17865	7.80941	7.85733	7.24372	7.28493	6.75445	6.79027	6.32709	6.35851	5.95059	5.97837
31	8.17226	8.22144	7.85144	7.89683	7.27986	7.31887	6.78586	6.81974	6.35464	6.38434	5.97496	6.00121
32	8.21406	8.26063	7.89002	7.93298	7.31302	7.34991	6.81466	6.84668	6.37989	6.40795	5.99727	6.02206
33	8.25247	8.29654	7.92545	7.96608	7.34344	7.37832	6.84107	6.87133	6.40304	6.42953	6.01772	6.04112
34	8.28776	8.32943	7.95799	7.99640	7.37138	7.40432	6.86531	6.89388	6.42426	6.44927	6.03647	6.05854
35	8.32020	8.35958	7.98790	8.02418	7.39703	7.42814	6.88756	6.91452	6.44374	6.46733	6.05366	6.07448
36	8.35003	8.38721	8.01539	8.04964	7.42060	7.44995	6.90798	6.93341	6.46162	6.48386	6.06943	6.08905
37	8.37746	8.41255	8.04065	8.07298	7.44225	7.46993	6.92674	6.95072	6.47803	6.49899	6.08391	6.10240
38	8.40268	8.43578	8.06389	8.09437	7.46215	7.48825	6.94398	6.96657	6.49310	6.51285	6.09720	6.11461
39	8.42588	8.45709	8.08526	8.11399	7.48044	7.50503	6.95982	6.98110	6.50695	6.52554	6.10941	6.12580
40	8.44723	8.47664	8.10491	8.13198	7.49726	7.52042	6.97438	6.99441	6.51967	6.53717	6.12063	6.13605
41	8.46687	8.49457	8.12299	8.14848	7.51273	7.53453	6.98776	7.00662	6.53136	6.54783	6.13093	6.14544
42	8.48495	8.51102	8.13963	8.16362	7.52696	7.54747	7.00007	7.01781	6.54212	6.55761	6.14040	6.15405
43	8.50159	8.52612	8.15494	8.17751	7.54005	7.55934	7.01139	7.02807	6.55200	6.56656	6.14911	6.16194
44	8.51690	8.53998	8.16902	8.19025	7.55209	7.57023	7.02180	7.03748	6.56109	6.57478	6.15712	6.16917
45	8.53100	8.55269	8.18199	8.20195	7.56317	7.58022	7.03138	7.04611	6.56946	6.58231	6.16448	6.17580
46	8.54397	8.56436	8.19393	8.21268	7.57337	7.58939	7.04019	7.05403	6.57715	6.58923	6.17126	6.18189
47	8.55592	8.57508	8.20492	8.22253	7.58276	7.59780	7.04831	7.06130	6.58423	6.59557	6.17749	6.18747
48	8.56693	8.58491	8.21504	8.23158	7.59140	7.60552	7.05577	7.06797	6.59074	6.60138	6.18322	6.19259
49	8.57706	8.59394	8.22436	8.23988	7.59936	7.61261	7.06264	7.07409	6.59674	6.60672	6.18850	6.19728
50	8.58639	8.60224	8.23294	8.24750	7.60668	7.61911	7.06897	7.07970	6.60226	6.61162	6.19336	6.20159
51	8.59499	8.60985	8.24084	8.25450	7.61343	7.62509	7.07479	7.08486	6.60734	6.61612	6.19783	6.20555
52	8.60290	8.61684	8.24811	8.26092	7.61964	7.63057	7.08016	7.08959	6.61201	6.62024	6.20194	6.20918
53	8.61019	8.62326	8.25482	8.26682	7.62536	7.63560	7.08509	7.09394	6.61632	6.62403	6.20573	6.21251
54	8.61691	8.62915	8.26099	8.27224	7.63062	7.64022	7.08964	7.09793	6.62029	6.62751	6.20922	6.21557
55	8.62310	8.63457	8.26668	8.27722	7.63548	7.64447	7.09383	7.10159	6.62394	6.63070	6.21243	6.21838
56	8.62880	8.63954	8.27191	8.28179	7.63994	7.64836	7.09768	7.10495	6.62730	6.63364	6.21539	6.22096
57	8.63405	8.64411	8.27674	8.28598	7.64406	7.65194	7.10124	7.10804	6.63040	6.63633	6.21811	6.22333
58	8.63888	8.64830	8.28118	8.28984	7.64785	7.65523	7.10451	7.11088	6.63325	6.63880	6.22062	6.22550
59	8.64334	8.65215	8.28528	8.29338	7.65134	7.65825	7.10752	7.11348	6.63588	6.64107	6.22293	6.22750
60	8.64745	8.65569	8.28905	8.29663	7.65456	7.66102	7.11030	7.11587	6.63830	6.64315	6.22506	6.22933
61	8.65123	8.65894	8.29253	8.29961	7.65753	7.66357	7.11286	7.11807	6.64053	6.64507	6.22702	6.23101
62	8.65472	8.66193	8.29573	8.30236	7.66026	7.66590	7.11521	7.12009	6.64258	6.64683	6.22882	6.23256
63	8.65793	8.66467	8.29868	8.30487	7.66277	7.66805	7.11738	7.12194	6.64447	6.64844	6.23049	6.23398
64	8.66089	8.66719	8.30140	8.30719	7.66509	7.67003	7.11938	7.12364	6.64621	6.64992	6.23202	6.23528
65	8.66361	8.66950	8.30391	8.30931	7.66723	7.67184	7.12123	7.12520	6.64782	6.65129	6.23343	6.23648

Mortgage-Equity Capitalization Rates

5.50% Equity Yield 5.50% Mortgage Rate

Mortgage Term	Loan to Value Ratio								
	50.00%	60.00%	67.00%	70.00%	75.00%	80.00%	85.00%	90.00%	100.00%
10	9.26158	10.01389	10.51544	10.76621	11.14237	11.51852	11.89468	12.27084	13.02315
12	8.45103	9.04124	9.43471	9.63145	9.92655	10.22165	10.51676	10.81186	11.40207
15	7.65250	8.08300	8.37000	8.51350	8.72875	8.94400	9.15925	9.37450	9.80500
18	7.13190	7.45828	7.67586	7.78466	7.94785	8.11104	8.27423	8.43742	8.76380
20	6.87732	7.15279	7.33643	7.42825	7.56599	7.70372	7.84145	7.97918	8.25465
23	6.58573	6.80287	6.94763	7.02002	7.12859	7.23716	7.34573	7.45431	7.67145
25	6.43452	6.62143	6.74603	6.80833	6.90179	6.99524	7.08869	7.18214	7.36905
27	6.30882	6.47058	6.57843	6.63235	6.71323	6.79411	6.87500	6.95588	7.11764
28	6.25379	6.40455	6.50506	6.55531	6.63069	6.70607	6.78145	6.85683	7.00759
29	6.20325	6.34390	6.43767	6.48455	6.55488	6.62520	6.69553	6.76585	6.90650
30	6.15673	6.28808	6.37565	6.41943	6.48510	6.55077	6.61645	6.68212	6.81347
35	5.97210	6.06652	6.12946	6.16094	6.20815	6.25536	6.30257	6.34978	6.44420

5.50% Equity Yield 6.00% Mortgage Rate

Mortgage Term	Loan to Value Ratio								
	50.00%	60.00%	67.00%	70.00%	75.00%	80.00%	85.00%	90.00%	100.00%
10	9.41123	10.19348	10.71497	10.97572	11.36685	11.75797	12.14909	12.54021	13.32246
12	8.60510	9.22612	9.64014	9.84714	10.15765	10.46816	10.77867	11.08918	11.71020
15	7.81314	8.27577	8.58419	8.73840	8.96971	9.20103	9.43234	9.66365	10.12628
18	7.29897	7.65877	7.89863	8.01856	8.19846	8.37836	8.55826	8.73815	9.09795
20	7.04859	7.35830	7.56478	7.66802	7.82288	7.97774	8.13260	8.28746	8.59717
23	6.76308	7.01570	7.18411	7.26832	7.39462	7.52093	7.64724	7.77355	8.02617
25	6.61581	6.83897	6.98774	7.06213	7.17371	7.28529	7.39687	7.50846	7.73162
27	6.49391	6.69269	6.82522	6.89148	6.99087	7.09026	7.18965	7.28904	7.48782
28	6.44074	6.62889	6.75433	6.81704	6.91112	7.00519	7.09926	7.19334	7.38149
29	6.39203	6.57043	6.68937	6.74884	6.83804	6.92724	7.01645	7.10565	7.28406
30	6.34730	6.51676	6.62974	6.68622	6.77095	6.85569	6.94042	7.02515	7.19461
35	6.17114	6.30537	6.39485	6.43959	6.50671	6.57382	6.64094	6.70805	6.84228

5.50% Equity Yield 6.50% Mortgage Rate

Mortgage Term	Loan to Value Ratio								
	50.00%	60.00%	67.00%	70.00%	75.00%	80.00%	85.00%	90.00%	100.00%
10	9.56288	10.37545	10.91717	11.18803	11.59432	12.00061	12.40689	12.81318	13.62576
12	8.76153	9.41383	9.84870	10.06614	10.39229	10.71844	11.04460	11.37075	12.02305
15	7.97664	8.47197	8.80219	8.96730	9.21497	9.46263	9.71030	9.95796	10.45329
18	7.46937	7.86324	8.12582	8.25711	8.45405	8.65099	8.84793	9.04486	9.43874
20	7.22344	7.56813	7.79792	7.91281	8.08516	8.25750	8.42985	8.60219	8.94688
23	6.94439	7.23327	7.42585	7.52214	7.66658	7.81102	7.95546	8.09990	8.38878
25	6.80124	7.06149	7.23499	7.32174	7.45186	7.58199	7.71211	7.84224	8.10249
27	6.68333	6.92000	7.07777	7.15666	7.27499	7.39333	7.51166	7.62999	7.86666
28	6.63210	6.85852	7.00946	7.08494	7.19814	7.31135	7.42456	7.53777	7.76419
29	6.58528	6.80233	6.94703	7.01939	7.12791	7.23644	7.34497	7.45350	7.67055
30	6.54241	6.75089	6.88988	6.95937	7.06361	7.16785	7.27209	7.37633	7.58482
35	6.37493	6.54991	6.66657	6.72490	6.81239	6.89988	6.98737	7.07487	7.24985

5.50% Equity Yield 7.00% Mortgage Rate

Mortgage Term	Loan to Value Ratio								
	50.00%	60.00%	67.00%	70.00%	75.00%	80.00%	85.00%	90.00%	100.00%
10	9.71651	10.55981	11.12201	11.40311	11.82476	12.24641	12.66806	13.08972	13.93302
12	8.92029	9.60434	10.06038	10.28840	10.63043	10.97246	11.31449	11.65652	12.34057
15	8.14297	8.67156	9.02396	9.20016	9.46445	9.72875	9.99305	10.25735	10.78594
18	7.64301	8.07162	8.35735	8.50022	8.71452	8.92882	9.14312	9.35742	9.78603
20	7.40179	7.78215	8.03572	8.16251	8.35269	8.54287	8.73305	8.92323	9.30359
23	7.12952	7.45542	7.67269	7.78132	7.94427	8.10722	8.27018	8.43313	8.75903
25	6.99068	7.28881	7.48757	7.58695	7.73601	7.88508	8.03415	8.18322	8.48135
27	6.87689	7.15227	7.33585	7.42765	7.56533	7.70302	7.84071	7.97840	8.25378
28	6.82765	7.09318	7.27020	7.35871	7.49148	7.62424	7.75701	7.88977	8.15530
29	6.78278	7.03934	7.21037	7.29589	7.42417	7.55245	7.68073	7.80900	8.06556
30	6.74181	6.99018	7.15575	7.23854	7.36272	7.48690	7.61109	7.73527	7.98363
35	6.58314	6.79977	6.94418	7.01639	7.12471	7.23302	7.34133	7.44965	7.66628

Mortgage-Equity Capitalization Rates

5.50% Equity Yield   7.50% Mortgage Rate

Mortgage Term	\	\	\	Loan to Value Ratio	\	\	\	\	\
	50.00%	60.00%	67.00%	70.00%	75.00%	80.00%	85.00%	90.00%	100.00%
10	9.87211	10.74653	11.32947	11.62095	12.05816	12.49537	12.93258	13.36979	14.24421
12	9.08136	9.79763	10.27514	10.51390	10.87204	11.23017	11.58831	11.94644	12.66272
15	8.31207	8.87449	9.24943	9.43690	9.71811	9.99932	10.28053	10.56173	11.12415
18	7.81984	8.28381	8.59312	8.74778	8.97976	9.21174	9.44373	9.67571	10.13968
20	7.58356	8.00027	8.27808	8.41698	8.62534	8.83369	9.04205	9.25041	9.66712
23	7.31834	7.68200	7.92445	8.04567	8.22750	8.40934	8.59117	8.77300	9.13667
25	7.18395	7.52074	7.74526	7.85753	8.02592	8.19432	8.36271	8.53110	8.86789
27	7.07440	7.38928	7.59920	7.70416	7.86160	8.01904	8.17649	8.33393	8.64881
28	7.02721	7.33265	7.53627	7.63809	7.79081	7.94353	8.09625	8.24897	8.55441
29	6.98432	7.28118	7.47909	7.57805	7.72648	7.87491	8.02334	8.17178	8.46864
30	6.94529	7.23434	7.42705	7.52340	7.66793	7.81246	7.95699	8.10152	8.39057
35	6.79546	7.05455	7.22727	7.31364	7.44318	7.57273	7.70227	7.83182	8.09091

5.50% Equity Yield   8.00% Mortgage Rate

Mortgage Term	\	\	\	Loan to Value Ratio	\	\	\	\	\
	50.00%	60.00%	67.00%	70.00%	75.00%	80.00%	85.00%	90.00%	100.00%
10	10.02966	10.93559	11.53954	11.84152	12.29448	12.74745	13.20041	13.65338	14.55931
12	9.24472	9.99366	10.49295	10.74260	11.11707	11.49154	11.86602	12.24049	12.98943
15	8.48391	9.08069	9.47855	9.67748	9.97587	10.27426	10.57265	10.87104	11.46782
18	7.99978	8.49973	8.83303	8.99969	9.24966	9.49964	9.74962	9.99960	10.49955
20	7.76864	8.22237	8.52485	8.67610	8.90296	9.12982	9.35669	9.58355	10.03728
23	7.51072	7.91286	8.18095	8.31500	8.51607	8.71714	8.91822	9.11929	9.52143
25	7.38090	7.75708	8.00786	8.13326	8.32135	8.50944	8.69753	8.88562	9.26179
27	7.27568	7.63081	7.86757	7.98595	8.16352	8.34109	8.51865	8.69622	9.05136
28	7.23055	7.57666	7.80740	7.92277	8.09583	8.26888	8.44194	8.61499	8.96110
29	7.18967	7.52761	7.75290	7.86554	8.03451	8.20348	8.37245	8.54141	8.87935
30	7.15259	7.48310	7.70345	7.81362	7.97888	8.14414	8.30940	8.47466	8.80517
35	7.01157	7.31388	7.51542	7.61619	7.76735	7.91850	8.06966	8.22082	8.52313

5.50% Equity Yield   8.50% Mortgage Rate

Mortgage Term	\	\	\	Loan to Value Ratio	\	\	\	\	\
	50.00%	60.00%	67.00%	70.00%	75.00%	80.00%	85.00%	90.00%	100.00%
10	10.18914	11.12697	11.75219	12.06480	12.53371	13.00263	13.47154	13.94045	14.87828
12	9.41033	10.19240	10.71378	10.97447	11.36550	11.75653	12.14757	12.53860	13.32067
15	8.65844	9.29012	9.71125	9.92181	10.23766	10.55350	10.86934	11.18519	11.81687
18	8.18274	8.71929	9.07699	9.25584	9.52412	9.79239	10.06067	10.32894	10.86549
20	7.95694	8.44833	8.77592	8.93972	9.18541	9.43110	9.67680	9.92249	10.41388
23	7.70652	8.14782	8.44203	8.58913	8.80978	9.03043	9.25108	9.47173	9.91304
25	7.58136	7.99763	8.27515	8.41391	8.62204	8.83018	9.03832	9.24645	9.66272
27	7.48053	7.87663	8.14070	8.27274	8.47079	8.66884	8.86689	9.06495	9.46105
28	7.43748	7.82498	8.08331	8.21248	8.40623	8.59997	8.79372	8.98747	9.37497
29	7.39862	7.77835	8.03150	8.15807	8.34793	8.53780	8.72766	8.91752	9.29725
30	7.36348	7.73618	7.98464	8.10887	8.29522	8.48157	8.66792	8.85427	9.22696
35	7.23116	7.57740	7.80822	7.92363	8.09675	8.26986	8.44298	8.61609	8.96233

5.50% Equity Yield   9.00% Mortgage Rate

Mortgage Term	\	\	\	Loan to Value Ratio	\	\	\	\	\
	50.00%	60.00%	67.00%	70.00%	75.00%	80.00%	85.00%	90.00%	100.00%
10	10.35055	11.32066	11.96740	12.29076	12.77582	13.26087	13.74593	14.23098	15.20109
12	9.57818	10.39382	10.93758	11.20946	11.61728	12.02509	12.43291	12.84073	13.65637
15	8.83560	9.50272	9.94747	10.16984	10.50340	10.83696	11.17052	11.50408	12.17120
18	8.36867	8.94240	9.32489	9.51614	9.80300	10.08987	10.37674	10.66360	11.23734
20	8.14836	8.67803	9.03114	9.20770	9.47253	9.73737	10.00220	10.26704	10.79671
23	7.90561	8.38673	8.70748	8.86785	9.10841	9.34897	9.58954	9.83010	10.31122
25	7.78518	8.24221	8.54690	8.69925	8.92777	9.15629	9.38480	9.61332	10.07036
27	7.68875	8.12650	8.41834	8.56425	8.78313	9.00200	9.22088	9.43975	9.87750
28	7.64780	8.07736	8.36373	8.50692	8.72170	8.93648	9.15126	9.36604	9.79560
29	7.61095	8.03313	8.31459	8.45532	8.66642	8.87751	9.08861	9.29970	9.72189
30	7.57774	7.99328	8.27031	8.40883	8.61660	8.82438	9.03215	9.23992	9.65547
35	7.45396	7.84475	8.10528	8.23554	8.43094	8.62633	8.82173	9.01712	9.40792

Mortgage-Equity Capitalization Rates

5.50% Equity Yield 9.50% Mortgage Rate

Mortgage Term	Loan to Value Ratio								
	50.00%	60.00%	67.00%	70.00%	75.00%	80.00%	85.00%	90.00%	100.00%
10	10.51385	11.51662	12.18514	12.51939	13.02078	13.52217	14.02355	14.52494	15.52771
12	9.74824	10.59789	11.16432	11.44754	11.87236	12.29718	12.72201	13.14683	13.99648
15	9.01535	9.71842	10.18713	10.42149	10.77302	11.12456	11.47609	11.82763	12.53070
18	8.55747	9.16896	9.57662	9.78046	10.08620	10.39195	10.69770	11.00344	11.61494
20	8.34279	8.91134	9.29038	9.47990	9.76418	10.04846	10.33274	10.61702	11.18557
23	8.10785	8.62941	8.97713	9.15098	9.41177	9.67255	9.93334	10.19412	10.71569
25	7.99218	8.49062	8.82291	8.98905	9.23827	9.48749	9.73671	9.98592	10.48436
27	7.90017	8.38020	8.70022	8.86024	9.10025	9.34027	9.58029	9.82030	10.30034
28	7.86129	8.33355	8.64839	8.80581	9.04194	9.27806	9.51419	9.75032	10.22258
29	7.82643	8.29171	8.60190	8.75700	8.98964	9.22229	9.45493	9.68757	10.15286
30	7.79513	8.25415	8.56017	8.71318	8.94269	9.17220	9.40171	9.63123	10.09025
35	7.67967	8.11560	8.40623	8.55154	8.76950	8.98747	9.20544	9.42341	9.85934

5.50% Equity Yield 10.00% Mortgage Rate

Mortgage Term	Loan to Value Ratio								
	50.00%	60.00%	67.00%	70.00%	75.00%	80.00%	85.00%	90.00%	100.00%
10	10.67904	11.71485	12.40539	12.75066	13.26857	13.78647	14.30438	14.82228	15.85809
12	9.92047	10.80456	11.39396	11.68866	12.13070	12.57275	13.01480	13.45685	14.34094
15	9.19763	9.93716	10.43017	10.67668	11.04645	11.41621	11.78597	12.15574	12.89526
18	8.74906	9.39887	9.83208	10.04869	10.37359	10.69850	11.02341	11.34831	11.99812
20	8.54013	9.14816	9.55351	9.75618	10.06019	10.36421	10.66822	10.97223	11.58026
23	8.31309	8.87571	9.25079	9.43833	9.71963	10.00094	10.28225	10.56356	11.12618
25	8.20220	8.74265	9.10294	9.28309	9.55331	9.82353	10.09375	10.36397	10.90441
27	8.11459	8.63750	8.98611	9.16042	9.42188	9.68334	9.94480	10.20625	10.72917
28	8.07776	8.59331	8.93702	9.10887	9.36664	9.62442	9.88220	10.13997	10.65552
29	8.04486	8.55383	8.89315	9.06281	9.31729	9.57178	9.82627	10.08075	10.58972
30	8.01543	8.51852	8.85391	9.02160	9.27314	9.52469	9.77623	10.02777	10.53086
35	7.90803	8.38964	8.71071	8.87125	9.11205	9.35286	9.59366	9.83446	10.31607

5.50% Equity Yield 10.50% Mortgage Rate

Mortgage Term	Loan to Value Ratio								
	50.00%	60.00%	67.00%	70.00%	75.00%	80.00%	85.00%	90.00%	100.00%
10	10.84610	11.91532	12.62813	12.98454	13.51915	14.05376	14.58837	15.12298	16.19220
12	10.09484	11.01381	11.62646	11.93278	12.39227	12.85175	13.31123	13.77072	14.68969
15	9.38239	10.15887	10.67652	10.93535	11.32359	11.71183	12.10007	12.48831	13.26479
18	8.94337	9.63204	10.09116	10.32071	10.66505	11.00939	11.35372	11.69806	12.38673
20	8.74028	9.38834	9.82037	10.03639	10.36042	10.68445	11.00847	11.33250	11.98056
23	8.52120	9.12544	9.52827	9.72968	10.03181	10.33393	10.63605	10.93817	11.54241
25	8.41509	8.99811	9.38679	9.58113	9.87264	10.16414	10.45565	10.74716	11.33018
27	8.33182	8.89819	9.27576	9.46455	9.74773	10.03092	10.31410	10.59728	11.16365
28	8.29702	8.85643	9.22936	9.41583	9.69553	9.97523	10.25494	10.53464	11.09404
29	8.26604	8.81925	9.18806	9.37246	9.64907	9.92567	10.20227	10.47888	11.03209
30	8.23844	8.78612	9.15125	9.33381	9.60765	9.88150	10.15534	10.42918	10.97687
35	8.13880	8.66656	9.01841	9.19433	9.45821	9.72209	9.98597	10.24985	10.77761

5.50% Equity Yield 11.00% Mortgage Rate

Mortgage Term	Loan to Value Ratio								
	50.00%	60.00%	67.00%	70.00%	75.00%	80.00%	85.00%	90.00%	100.00%
10	11.01500	12.11800	12.85333	13.22100	13.77250	14.32400	14.87550	15.42700	16.53000
12	10.27133	11.22560	11.86178	12.17986	12.65700	13.13413	13.61126	14.08840	15.04266
15	9.56958	10.38350	10.92611	11.19741	11.60437	12.01133	12.41829	12.82525	13.63916
18	9.14030	9.86836	10.35373	10.59642	10.96045	11.32448	11.68851	12.05254	12.78060
20	8.94313	9.63176	10.09084	10.32038	10.66470	11.00901	11.35332	11.69763	12.38626
23	8.73205	9.37846	9.80940	10.02487	10.34807	10.67128	10.99448	11.31769	11.96410
25	8.63068	9.25681	9.67424	9.88295	10.19602	10.50909	10.82215	11.13522	11.76136
27	8.55170	9.16204	9.56893	9.77238	10.07755	10.38272	10.68789	10.99306	11.60340
28	8.51888	9.12266	9.52517	9.72643	10.02832	10.33021	10.63210	10.93398	11.53776
29	8.48978	9.08773	9.48637	9.68569	9.98466	10.28364	10.58262	10.88160	11.47955
30	8.46394	9.05673	9.45192	9.64952	9.94591	10.24230	10.53870	10.83509	11.42788
35	8.37175	8.94610	9.32899	9.52044	9.80762	10.09479	10.38197	10.66914	11.24349

Mortgage-Equity Capitalization Rates

7.00% Equity Yield   6.00% Mortgage Rate

Mortgage Term	Loan to Value Ratio								
	50.00%	60.00%	67.00%	70.00%	75.00%	80.00%	85.00%	90.00%	100.00%
10	10.16123	10.79348	11.21497	11.42572	11.74185	12.05797	12.37409	12.69021	13.32246
12	9.35510	9.82612	10.14014	10.29714	10.53265	10.76816	11.00367	11.23918	11.71020
15	8.56314	8.87577	9.08419	9.18840	9.34471	9.50103	9.65734	9.81365	10.12628
18	8.04897	8.25877	8.39863	8.46856	8.57346	8.67836	8.78326	8.88815	9.09795
20	7.79859	7.95830	8.06478	8.11802	8.19788	8.27774	8.35760	8.43746	8.59717
23	7.51308	7.61570	7.68411	7.71832	7.76962	7.82093	7.87224	7.92355	8.02617
25	7.36581	7.43897	7.48774	7.51213	7.54871	7.58529	7.62187	7.65846	7.73162
27	7.24391	7.29269	7.32522	7.34148	7.36587	7.39026	7.41465	7.43904	7.48782
28	7.19074	7.22889	7.25433	7.26704	7.28612	7.30519	7.32426	7.34334	7.38149
29	7.14203	7.17043	7.18937	7.19884	7.21304	7.22724	7.24145	7.25565	7.28406
30	7.09730	7.11676	7.12974	7.13622	7.14595	7.15569	7.16542	7.17515	7.19461
35	6.92114	6.90537	6.89485	6.88959	6.88171	6.87382	6.86594	6.85805	6.84228

7.00% Equity Yield   6.50% Mortgage Rate

Mortgage Term	Loan to Value Ratio								
	50.00%	60.00%	67.00%	70.00%	75.00%	80.00%	85.00%	90.00%	100.00%
10	10.31288	10.97545	11.41717	11.63803	11.96932	12.30061	12.63189	12.96318	13.62576
12	9.51153	10.01383	10.34870	10.51614	10.76729	11.01844	11.26960	11.52075	12.02305
15	8.72664	9.07197	9.30219	9.41730	9.58997	9.76263	9.93530	10.10796	10.45329
18	8.21937	8.46324	8.62582	8.70711	8.82905	8.95099	9.07293	9.19486	9.43874
20	7.97344	8.16813	8.29792	8.36281	8.46016	8.55750	8.65485	8.75219	8.94688
23	7.69439	7.83327	7.92585	7.97214	8.04158	8.11102	8.18046	8.24990	8.38878
25	7.55124	7.66149	7.73499	7.77174	7.82686	7.88199	7.93711	7.99224	8.10249
27	7.43333	7.52000	7.57777	7.60666	7.64999	7.69333	7.73666	7.77999	7.86666
28	7.38210	7.45852	7.50946	7.53494	7.57314	7.61135	7.64956	7.68777	7.76419
29	7.33528	7.40233	7.44703	7.46939	7.50291	7.53644	7.56997	7.60350	7.67055
30	7.29241	7.35089	7.38988	7.40937	7.43861	7.46785	7.49709	7.52633	7.58482
35	7.12493	7.14991	7.16657	7.17490	7.18739	7.19988	7.21237	7.22487	7.24985

7.00% Equity Yield   7.00% Mortgage Rate

Mortgage Term	Loan to Value Ratio								
	50.00%	60.00%	67.00%	70.00%	75.00%	80.00%	85.00%	90.00%	100.00%
10	10.46651	11.15981	11.62201	11.85311	12.19976	12.54641	12.89306	13.23972	13.93302
12	9.67029	10.20434	10.56038	10.73840	11.00543	11.27246	11.53949	11.80652	12.34057
15	8.89297	9.27156	9.52396	9.65016	9.83945	10.02875	10.21805	10.40735	10.78594
18	8.39301	8.67162	8.85735	8.95022	9.08952	9.22882	9.36812	9.50742	9.78603
20	8.15179	8.38215	8.53572	8.61251	8.72769	8.84287	8.95805	9.07323	9.30359
23	7.87952	8.05542	8.17269	8.23132	8.31927	8.40722	8.49518	8.58313	8.75903
25	7.74068	7.88881	7.98757	8.03695	8.11101	8.18508	8.25915	8.33322	8.48135
27	7.62689	7.75227	7.83565	7.87765	7.94033	8.00302	8.06571	8.12840	8.25378
28	7.57765	7.69318	7.77020	7.80871	7.86648	7.92424	7.98201	8.03977	8.15530
29	7.53278	7.63934	7.71037	7.74589	7.79917	7.85245	7.90573	7.95900	8.06556
30	7.49181	7.59018	7.65575	7.68854	7.73772	7.78690	7.83609	7.88527	7.98363
35	7.33314	7.39977	7.44418	7.46639	7.49971	7.53302	7.56633	7.59965	7.66628

7.00% Equity Yield   7.50% Mortgage Rate

Mortgage Term	Loan to Value Ratio								
	50.00%	60.00%	67.00%	70.00%	75.00%	80.00%	85.00%	90.00%	100.00%
10	10.62211	11.34653	11.82947	12.07095	12.43316	12.79537	13.15758	13.51979	14.24421
12	9.83136	10.39763	10.77514	10.96390	11.24704	11.53017	11.81331	12.09644	12.66272
15	9.06207	9.47449	9.74943	9.88690	10.09311	10.29932	10.50553	10.71173	11.12415
18	8.56984	8.88381	9.09312	9.19778	9.35476	9.51174	9.66873	9.82571	10.13968
20	8.33356	8.60027	8.77808	8.86698	9.00034	9.13369	9.26705	9.40041	9.66712
23	8.06834	8.28200	8.42445	8.49567	8.60250	8.70934	8.81617	8.92300	9.13667
25	7.93395	8.12074	8.24526	8.30753	8.40092	8.49432	8.58771	8.68110	8.86789
27	7.82440	7.98928	8.09920	8.15416	8.23660	8.31904	8.40149	8.48393	8.64881
28	7.77721	7.93265	8.03627	8.08809	8.16581	8.24353	8.32125	8.39897	8.55441
29	7.73432	7.88118	7.97909	8.02805	8.10148	8.17491	8.24834	8.32178	8.46864
30	7.69529	7.83434	7.92705	7.97340	8.04293	8.11246	8.18199	8.25152	8.39057
35	7.54546	7.65455	7.72727	7.76364	7.81818	7.87273	7.92727	7.98182	8.09091

Mortgage-Equity Capitalization Rates

7.00% Equity Yield   8.00% Mortgage Rate

| Mortgage Term | Loan to Value Ratio | | | | | | | | |
	50.00%	60.00%	67.00%	70.00%	75.00%	80.00%	85.00%	90.00%	100.00%
10	10.77966	11.53559	12.03954	12.29152	12.66948	13.04745	13.42541	13.80338	14.55931
12	9.99472	10.59366	10.99295	11.19260	11.49207	11.79154	12.09102	12.39049	12.98943
15	9.23391	9.68069	9.97855	10.12748	10.35087	10.57426	10.79765	11.02104	11.46782
18	8.74978	9.09973	9.33303	9.44969	9.62466	9.79964	9.97462	10.14960	10.49955
20	8.51864	8.82237	9.02485	9.12610	9.27796	9.42982	9.58169	9.73355	10.03728
23	8.26072	8.51286	8.68095	8.76500	8.89107	9.01714	9.14322	9.26929	9.52143
25	8.13090	8.35708	8.50786	8.58326	8.69635	8.80944	8.92253	9.03562	9.26179
27	8.02568	8.23081	8.36757	8.43595	8.53852	8.64109	8.74365	8.84622	9.05136
28	7.98055	8.17666	8.30740	8.37277	8.47083	8.56888	8.66694	8.76499	8.96110
29	7.93967	8.12761	8.25290	8.31554	8.40951	8.50348	8.59745	8.69141	8.87935
30	7.90259	8.08310	8.20345	8.26362	8.35388	8.44414	8.53440	8.62466	8.80517
35	7.76157	7.91388	8.01542	8.06619	8.14235	8.21850	8.29466	8.37082	8.52313

7.00% Equity Yield   8.50% Mortgage Rate

| Mortgage Term | Loan to Value Ratio | | | | | | | | |
	50.00%	60.00%	67.00%	70.00%	75.00%	80.00%	85.00%	90.00%	100.00%
10	10.93914	11.72697	12.25219	12.51480	12.90871	13.30263	13.69654	14.09045	14.87828
12	10.16033	10.79240	11.21378	11.42447	11.74050	12.05653	12.37257	12.68860	13.32067
15	9.40844	9.89012	10.21125	10.37181	10.61266	10.85350	11.09434	11.33519	11.81687
18	8.93274	9.31929	9.57699	9.70584	9.89912	10.09239	10.28567	10.47894	10.86549
20	8.70694	9.04833	9.27592	9.38972	9.56041	9.73110	9.90180	10.07249	10.41388
23	8.45652	8.74782	8.94203	9.03913	9.18478	9.33043	9.47608	9.62173	9.91304
25	8.33136	8.59763	8.77515	8.86391	8.99704	9.13018	9.26332	9.39645	9.66272
27	8.23053	8.47663	8.64070	8.72274	8.84579	8.96884	9.09189	9.21495	9.46105
28	8.18748	8.42498	8.58331	8.66248	8.78123	8.89997	9.01872	9.13747	9.37497
29	8.14862	8.37835	8.53150	8.60807	8.72293	8.83780	8.95266	9.06752	9.29725
30	8.11348	8.33618	8.48464	8.55887	8.67022	8.78157	8.89292	9.00427	9.22696
35	7.98116	8.17740	8.30822	8.37363	8.47175	8.56986	8.66798	8.76609	8.96233

7.00% Equity Yield   9.00% Mortgage Rate

| Mortgage Term | Loan to Value Ratio | | | | | | | | |
	50.00%	60.00%	67.00%	70.00%	75.00%	80.00%	85.00%	90.00%	100.00%
10	11.10055	11.92066	12.46740	12.74076	13.15082	13.56087	13.97093	14.38098	15.20109
12	10.32818	10.99382	11.43758	11.65946	11.99228	12.32509	12.65791	12.99073	13.65637
15	9.58560	10.10272	10.44747	10.61984	10.87840	11.13696	11.39552	11.65408	12.17120
18	9.11867	9.54240	9.82489	9.96614	10.17800	10.38987	10.60174	10.81360	11.23734
20	8.89836	9.27803	9.53114	9.65770	9.84753	10.03737	10.22720	10.41704	10.79671
23	8.65561	8.98673	9.20748	9.31785	9.48341	9.64897	9.81454	9.98010	10.31122
25	8.53518	8.84221	9.04690	9.14925	9.30277	9.45629	9.60980	9.76332	10.07036
27	8.43875	8.72650	8.91834	9.01425	9.15813	9.30200	9.44588	9.58975	9.87750
28	8.39780	8.67736	8.86373	8.95692	9.09670	9.23648	9.37626	9.51604	9.79560
29	8.36095	8.63313	8.81459	8.90532	9.04142	9.17751	9.31361	9.44970	9.72189
30	8.32774	8.59328	8.77031	8.85883	8.99160	9.12438	9.25715	9.38992	9.65547
35	8.20396	8.44475	8.60528	8.68554	8.80594	8.92633	9.04673	9.16712	9.40792

7.00% Equity Yield   9.50% Mortgage Rate

| Mortgage Term | Loan to Value Ratio | | | | | | | | |
	50.00%	60.00%	67.00%	70.00%	75.00%	80.00%	85.00%	90.00%	100.00%
10	11.26385	12.11662	12.68514	12.96939	13.39578	13.82217	14.24855	14.67494	15.52771
12	10.49824	11.19789	11.66432	11.89754	12.24736	12.59718	12.94701	13.29683	13.99648
15	9.76535	10.31842	10.68713	10.87149	11.14802	11.42456	11.70109	11.97763	12.53070
18	9.30747	9.76896	10.07662	10.23046	10.46120	10.69195	10.92270	11.15344	11.61494
20	9.09279	9.51134	9.79038	9.92990	10.13918	10.34846	10.55774	10.76702	11.18557
23	8.85785	9.22941	9.47713	9.60098	9.78677	9.97255	10.15834	10.34412	10.71569
25	8.74218	9.09062	9.32291	9.43905	9.61327	9.78749	9.96171	10.13592	10.48436
27	8.65017	8.98020	9.20022	9.31024	9.47525	9.64027	9.80529	9.97030	10.30034
28	8.61129	8.93355	9.14839	9.25581	9.41694	9.57806	9.73919	9.90032	10.22258
29	8.57643	8.89171	9.10190	9.20700	9.36464	9.52229	9.67993	9.83757	10.15286
30	8.54513	8.85415	9.06017	9.16318	9.31769	9.47220	9.62671	9.78123	10.09025
35	8.42967	8.71560	8.90623	9.00154	9.14450	9.28747	9.43044	9.57341	9.85934

Mortgage-Equity Capitalization Rates

7.00% Equity Yield 10.00% Mortgage Rate

Mortgage Term	Loan to Value Ratio								
	50.00%	60.00%	67.00%	70.00%	75.00%	80.00%	85.00%	90.00%	100.00%
10	11.42904	12.31485	12.90539	13.20066	13.64357	14.08647	14.52938	14.97228	15.85809
12	10.67047	11.40456	11.89396	12.13866	12.50570	12.87275	13.23980	13.60685	14.34094
15	9.94763	10.53716	10.93017	11.12668	11.42145	11.71621	12.01097	12.30574	12.89526
18	9.49906	9.99887	10.33208	10.49869	10.74859	10.99850	11.24841	11.49831	11.99812
20	9.29013	9.74816	10.05351	10.20618	10.43519	10.66421	10.89322	11.12223	11.58026
23	9.06309	9.47571	9.75079	9.88833	10.09463	10.30094	10.50725	10.71356	11.12618
25	8.95220	9.34265	9.60294	9.73309	9.92831	10.12353	10.31875	10.51397	10.90441
27	8.86459	9.23750	9.48611	9.61042	9.79688	9.98334	10.16980	10.35625	10.72917
28	8.82776	9.19331	9.43702	9.55887	9.74164	9.92442	10.10720	10.28997	10.65552
29	8.79486	9.15383	9.39315	9.51281	9.69229	9.87178	10.05127	10.23075	10.58972
30	8.76543	9.11852	9.35391	9.47160	9.64814	9.82469	10.00123	10.17777	10.53086
35	8.65803	8.98964	9.21071	9.32125	9.48705	9.65286	9.81866	9.98446	10.31607

7.00% Equity Yield 10.50% Mortgage Rate

Mortgage Term	Loan to Value Ratio								
	50.00%	60.00%	67.00%	70.00%	75.00%	80.00%	85.00%	90.00%	100.00%
10	11.59610	12.51532	13.12813	13.43454	13.89415	14.35376	14.81337	15.27298	16.19220
12	10.84484	11.61381	12.12646	12.38278	12.76727	13.15175	13.53623	13.92072	14.68969
15	10.13239	10.75887	11.17652	11.38535	11.69859	12.01183	12.32507	12.63831	13.26479
18	9.69337	10.23204	10.59116	10.77071	11.04005	11.30939	11.57872	11.84806	12.38673
20	9.49028	9.98834	10.32037	10.48639	10.73542	10.98445	11.23347	11.48250	11.98056
23	9.27120	9.72544	10.02827	10.17968	10.40681	10.63393	10.86105	11.08817	11.54241
25	9.16509	9.59811	9.88679	10.03113	10.24764	10.46414	10.68065	10.89716	11.33018
27	9.08182	9.49819	9.77576	9.91455	10.12273	10.33092	10.53910	10.74728	11.16365
28	9.04702	9.45643	9.72936	9.86583	10.07053	10.27523	10.47994	10.68464	11.09404
29	9.01604	9.41925	9.68806	9.82246	10.02407	10.22567	10.42727	10.62888	11.03209
30	8.98844	9.38612	9.65125	9.78381	9.98265	10.18150	10.38034	10.57918	10.97687
35	8.88880	9.26656	9.51841	9.64433	9.83321	10.02209	10.21097	10.39985	10.77761

7.00% Equity Yield 11.00% Mortgage Rate

Mortgage Term	Loan to Value Ratio								
	50.00%	60.00%	67.00%	70.00%	75.00%	80.00%	85.00%	90.00%	100.00%
10	11.76500	12.71800	13.35333	13.67100	14.14750	14.62400	15.10050	15.57700	16.53000
12	11.02133	11.82560	12.36178	12.62986	13.03200	13.43413	13.83626	14.23840	15.04266
15	10.31958	10.98350	11.42611	11.64741	11.97937	12.31133	12.64329	12.97525	13.63916
18	9.89030	10.46836	10.85373	11.04642	11.33545	11.62448	11.91351	12.20254	12.78060
20	9.69313	10.23176	10.59084	10.77038	11.03970	11.30901	11.57832	11.84763	12.38626
23	9.48205	9.97846	10.30940	10.47487	10.72307	10.97128	11.21948	11.46769	11.96410
25	9.38068	9.85681	10.17424	10.33295	10.57102	10.80909	11.04715	11.28522	11.76136
27	9.30170	9.76204	10.06893	10.22238	10.45255	10.68272	10.91289	11.14306	11.60340
28	9.26888	9.72266	10.02517	10.17643	10.40332	10.63021	10.85710	11.08398	11.53776
29	9.23978	9.68773	9.98637	10.13569	10.35966	10.58364	10.80762	11.03160	11.47955
30	9.21394	9.65673	9.95192	10.09952	10.32091	10.54230	10.76370	10.98509	11.42788
35	9.12175	9.54610	9.82899	9.97044	10.18262	10.39479	10.60697	10.81914	11.24349

7.00% Equity Yield 11.50% Mortgage Rate

Mortgage Term	Loan to Value Ratio								
	50.00%	60.00%	67.00%	70.00%	75.00%	80.00%	85.00%	90.00%	100.00%
10	11.93573	12.92287	13.58097	13.91002	14.40359	14.89716	15.39074	15.88431	16.87145
12	11.19990	12.03988	12.59987	12.87986	13.29985	13.71984	14.13983	14.55982	15.39980
15	10.50914	11.21097	11.67885	11.91279	12.26371	12.61462	12.96554	13.31645	14.01828
18	10.08977	10.70773	11.11970	11.32568	11.63466	11.94363	12.25261	12.56159	13.17954
20	9.89858	10.47829	10.86477	11.05801	11.34787	11.63772	11.92758	12.21744	12.79716
23	9.69549	10.23459	10.59398	10.77368	11.04323	11.31278	11.58233	11.85188	12.39098
25	9.59881	10.11858	10.46509	10.63834	10.89822	11.15810	11.41798	11.67786	12.19763
27	9.52405	10.02886	10.36540	10.53367	10.78607	11.03847	11.29088	11.54328	12.04809
28	9.49316	9.99179	10.32421	10.49042	10.73973	10.98905	11.23837	11.48768	11.98631
29	9.46587	9.95905	10.28783	10.45222	10.69881	10.94540	11.19198	11.43857	11.93175
30	9.44175	9.93010	10.25566	10.41845	10.66262	10.90680	11.15097	11.39515	11.88350
35	9.35664	9.82797	10.14219	10.29930	10.53497	10.77063	11.00629	11.24196	11.71329

Mortgage-Equity Capitalization Rates

8.50% Equity Yield   6.00% Mortgage Rate

Mortgage Term	Loan to Value Ratio 50.00%	60.00%	67.00%	70.00%	75.00%	80.00%	85.00%	90.00%	100.00%
10	10.91123	11.39348	11.71497	11.87572	12.11685	12.35797	12.59909	12.84021	13.32246
12	10.10510	10.42612	10.64014	10.74714	10.90765	11.06816	11.22867	11.38918	11.71020
15	9.31314	9.47577	9.58419	9.63840	9.71971	9.80103	9.88234	9.96365	10.12628
18	8.79897	8.85877	8.89863	8.91856	8.94846	8.97836	9.00826	9.03815	9.09795
20	8.54859	8.55830	8.56478	8.56802	8.57288	8.57774	8.58260	8.58746	8.59717
23	8.26308	8.21570	8.18411	8.16832	8.14462	8.12093	8.09724	8.07355	8.02617
25	8.11581	8.03897	7.98774	7.96213	7.92371	7.88529	7.84687	7.80846	7.73162
27	7.99391	7.89269	7.82522	7.79148	7.74087	7.69026	7.63965	7.58904	7.48782
28	7.94074	7.82889	7.75433	7.71704	7.66112	7.60519	7.54926	7.49334	7.38149
29	7.89203	7.77043	7.68937	7.64884	7.58804	7.52724	7.46645	7.40565	7.28406
30	7.84730	7.71676	7.62974	7.58622	7.52095	7.45569	7.39042	7.32515	7.19461
35	7.67114	7.50537	7.39485	7.33959	7.25671	7.17382	7.09094	7.00805	6.84228

8.50% Equity Yield   6.50% Mortgage Rate

Mortgage Term	Loan to Value Ratio 50.00%	60.00%	67.00%	70.00%	75.00%	80.00%	85.00%	90.00%	100.00%
10	11.06288	11.57545	11.91717	12.08803	12.34432	12.60061	12.85689	13.11318	13.62576
12	10.26153	10.61383	10.84870	10.96614	11.14229	11.31844	11.49460	11.67075	12.02305
15	9.47664	9.67197	9.80219	9.86730	9.96497	10.06263	10.16030	10.25796	10.45329
18	8.96937	9.06324	9.12582	9.15711	9.20405	9.25099	9.29793	9.34486	9.43874
20	8.72344	8.76813	8.79792	8.81281	8.83516	8.85750	8.87985	8.90219	8.94688
23	8.44439	8.43327	8.42585	8.42214	8.41658	8.41102	8.40546	8.39990	8.38878
25	8.30124	8.26149	8.23499	8.22174	8.20186	8.18199	8.16211	8.14224	8.10249
27	8.18333	8.12000	8.07777	8.05666	8.02499	7.99333	7.96166	7.92999	7.86666
28	8.13210	8.05852	8.00946	7.98494	7.94814	7.91135	7.87456	7.83777	7.76419
29	8.08528	8.00233	7.94703	7.91939	7.87791	7.83644	7.79497	7.75350	7.67055
30	8.04241	7.95089	7.88988	7.85937	7.81361	7.76785	7.72209	7.67633	7.58482
35	7.87493	7.74991	7.66657	7.62490	7.56239	7.49988	7.43737	7.37487	7.24985

8.50% Equity Yield   7.00% Mortgage Rate

Mortgage Term	Loan to Value Ratio 50.00%	60.00%	67.00%	70.00%	75.00%	80.00%	85.00%	90.00%	100.00%
10	11.21651	11.75981	12.12201	12.30311	12.57476	12.84641	13.11806	13.38972	13.93302
12	10.42029	10.80434	11.06038	11.18840	11.38043	11.57246	11.76449	11.95652	12.34057
15	9.64297	9.87156	10.02396	10.10016	10.21445	10.32875	10.44305	10.55735	10.78594
18	9.14301	9.27162	9.35735	9.40022	9.46452	9.52882	9.59312	9.65742	9.78603
20	8.90179	8.98215	9.03572	9.06251	9.10269	9.14287	9.18305	9.22323	9.30359
23	8.62952	8.65542	8.67269	8.68132	8.69427	8.70722	8.72018	8.73313	8.75903
25	8.49068	8.48881	8.48757	8.48695	8.48601	8.48508	8.48415	8.48322	8.48135
27	8.37689	8.35227	8.33585	8.32765	8.31533	8.30302	8.29071	8.27840	8.25378
28	8.32765	8.29318	8.27020	8.25871	8.24148	8.22424	8.20701	8.18977	8.15530
29	8.28278	8.23934	8.21037	8.19589	8.17417	8.15245	8.13073	8.10900	8.06556
30	8.24181	8.19018	8.15575	8.13854	8.11272	8.08690	8.06109	8.03527	7.98363
35	8.08314	7.99977	7.94418	7.91639	7.87471	7.83302	7.79133	7.74965	7.66628

8.50% Equity Yield   7.50% Mortgage Rate

Mortgage Term	Loan to Value Ratio 50.00%	60.00%	67.00%	70.00%	75.00%	80.00%	85.00%	90.00%	100.00%
10	11.37211	11.94653	12.32947	12.52095	12.80816	13.09537	13.38258	13.66979	14.24421
12	10.58136	10.99763	11.27514	11.41390	11.62204	11.83017	12.03831	12.24644	12.66272
15	9.81207	10.07449	10.24943	10.33690	10.46811	10.59932	10.73053	10.86173	11.12415
18	9.31984	9.48381	9.59312	9.64778	9.72976	9.81174	9.89373	9.97571	10.13968
20	9.08356	9.20027	9.27808	9.31698	9.37534	9.43369	9.49205	9.55041	9.66712
23	8.81834	8.88200	8.92445	8.94567	8.97750	9.00934	9.04117	9.07300	9.13667
25	8.68395	8.72074	8.74526	8.75753	8.77592	8.79432	8.81271	8.83110	8.86789
27	8.57440	8.58928	8.59920	8.60416	8.61160	8.61904	8.62649	8.63393	8.64881
28	8.52721	8.53265	8.53627	8.53809	8.54081	8.54353	8.54625	8.54897	8.55441
29	8.48432	8.48118	8.47909	8.47805	8.47648	8.47491	8.47334	8.47178	8.46864
30	8.44529	8.43434	8.42705	8.42340	8.41793	8.41246	8.40699	8.40152	8.39057
35	8.29546	8.25455	8.22727	8.21364	8.19318	8.17273	8.15227	8.13182	8.09091

Mortgage-Equity Capitalization Rates

8.50% Equity Yield   8.00% Mortgage Rate

Mortgage Term	50.00%	60.00%	67.00%	70.00%	75.00%	80.00%	85.00%	90.00%	100.00%
10	11.52966	12.13559	12.53954	12.74152	13.04448	13.34745	13.65041	13.95338	14.55931
12	10.74472	11.19366	11.49295	11.64260	11.86707	12.09154	12.31602	12.54049	12.98943
15	9.98391	10.28069	10.47855	10.57748	10.72587	10.87426	11.02265	11.17104	11.46782
18	9.49978	9.69973	9.83303	9.89969	9.99966	10.09964	10.19962	10.29960	10.49955
20	9.26864	9.42237	9.52485	9.57610	9.65296	9.72982	9.80669	9.88355	10.03728
23	9.01072	9.11286	9.18095	9.21500	9.26607	9.31714	9.36822	9.41929	9.52143
25	8.88090	8.95708	9.00786	9.03326	9.07135	9.10944	9.14753	9.18562	9.26179
27	8.77568	8.83081	8.86757	8.88595	8.91352	8.94109	8.96865	8.99622	9.05136
28	8.73055	8.77666	8.80740	8.82277	8.84583	8.86888	8.89194	8.91499	8.96110
29	8.68967	8.72761	8.75290	8.76554	8.78451	8.80348	8.82245	8.84141	8.87935
30	8.65259	8.68310	8.70345	8.71362	8.72888	8.74414	8.75940	8.77466	8.80517
35	8.51157	8.51388	8.51542	8.51619	8.51735	8.51850	8.51966	8.52082	8.52313

8.50% Equity Yield   8.50% Mortgage Rate

Mortgage Term	50.00%	60.00%	67.00%	70.00%	75.00%	80.00%	85.00%	90.00%	100.00%
10	11.68914	12.32697	12.75219	12.96480	13.28371	13.60263	13.92154	14.24045	14.87828
12	10.91033	11.39240	11.71378	11.87447	12.11550	12.35653	12.59757	12.83860	13.32067
15	10.15844	10.49012	10.71125	10.82181	10.98766	11.15350	11.31934	11.48519	11.81687
18	9.68274	9.91929	10.07699	10.15584	10.27412	10.39239	10.51067	10.62894	10.86549
20	9.45694	9.64833	9.77592	9.83972	9.93541	10.03110	10.12680	10.22249	10.41388
23	9.20652	9.34782	9.44203	9.48913	9.55978	9.63043	9.70108	9.77173	9.91304
25	9.08136	9.19763	9.27515	9.31391	9.37204	9.43018	9.48832	9.54645	9.66272
27	8.98053	9.07663	9.14070	9.17274	9.22079	9.26884	9.31689	9.36495	9.46105
28	8.93748	9.02498	9.08331	9.11248	9.15623	9.19997	9.24372	9.28747	9.37497
29	8.89862	8.97835	9.03150	9.05807	9.09793	9.13780	9.17766	9.21752	9.29725
30	8.86348	8.93618	8.98464	9.00887	9.04522	9.08157	9.11792	9.15427	9.22696
35	8.73116	8.77740	8.80822	8.82363	8.84675	8.86986	8.89298	8.91609	8.96233

8.50% Equity Yield   9.00% Mortgage Rate

Mortgage Term	50.00%	60.00%	67.00%	70.00%	75.00%	80.00%	85.00%	90.00%	100.00%
10	11.85055	12.52066	12.96740	13.19076	13.52582	13.86087	14.19593	14.53098	15.20109
12	11.07818	11.59382	11.93758	12.10946	12.36728	12.62509	12.88291	13.14073	13.65637
15	10.33560	10.70272	10.94747	11.06984	11.25340	11.43696	11.62052	11.80408	12.17120
18	9.86867	10.14240	10.32489	10.41614	10.55300	10.68987	10.82674	10.96360	11.23734
20	9.64836	9.87803	10.03114	10.10770	10.22253	10.33737	10.45220	10.56704	10.79671
23	9.40561	9.58673	9.70748	9.76785	9.85841	9.94897	10.03954	10.13010	10.31122
25	9.28518	9.44221	9.54690	9.59925	9.67677	9.75629	9.83480	9.91332	10.07036
27	9.18875	9.32650	9.41834	9.46425	9.53313	9.60200	9.67088	9.73975	9.87750
28	9.14780	9.27736	9.36373	9.40692	9.47170	9.53648	9.60126	9.66604	9.79560
29	9.11095	9.23313	9.31459	9.35532	9.41642	9.47751	9.53861	9.59970	9.72189
30	9.07774	9.19328	9.27031	9.30883	9.36660	9.42438	9.48215	9.53992	9.65547
35	8.95396	9.04475	9.10528	9.13554	9.18094	9.22633	9.27173	9.31712	9.40792

8.50% Equity Yield   9.50% Mortgage Rate

Mortgage Term	50.00%	60.00%	67.00%	70.00%	75.00%	80.00%	85.00%	90.00%	100.00%
10	12.01385	12.71662	13.18514	13.41939	13.77078	14.12217	14.47355	14.82494	15.52771
12	11.24824	11.79789	12.16432	12.34754	12.62236	12.89718	13.17201	13.44683	13.99648
15	10.51535	10.91842	11.18713	11.32149	11.52302	11.72456	11.92609	12.12763	12.53070
18	10.05747	10.36896	10.57662	10.68046	10.83620	10.99195	11.14770	11.30344	11.61494
20	9.84279	10.11134	10.29038	10.37990	10.51418	10.64846	10.78274	10.91702	11.18557
23	9.60785	9.82941	9.97713	10.05098	10.16177	10.27255	10.38334	10.49412	10.71569
25	9.49218	9.69062	9.82291	9.88905	9.98827	10.08749	10.18671	10.28592	10.48436
27	9.40017	9.58020	9.70022	9.76024	9.85025	9.94027	10.03029	10.12030	10.30034
28	9.36129	9.53355	9.64839	9.70581	9.79194	9.87806	9.96419	10.05032	10.22258
29	9.32643	9.49171	9.60190	9.65700	9.73964	9.82229	9.90493	9.98757	10.15286
30	9.29513	9.45415	9.56017	9.61318	9.69269	9.77220	9.85171	9.93123	10.09025
35	9.17967	9.31560	9.40623	9.45154	9.51950	9.58747	9.65544	9.72341	9.85934

Mortgage-Equity Capitalization Rates

8.50% Equity Yield 10.00% Mortgage Rate

Mortgage Term	50.00%	60.00%	67.00%	70.00%	Loan to Value Ratio 75.00%	80.00%	85.00%	90.00%	100.00%
10	12.17904	12.91485	13.40539	13.65066	14.01857	14.38647	14.75438	15.12228	15.85809
12	11.42047	12.00456	12.39396	12.58866	12.88070	13.17275	13.46480	13.75685	14.34094
15	10.69763	11.13716	11.43017	11.57668	11.79645	12.01621	12.23597	12.45574	12.89526
18	10.24906	10.59887	10.83208	10.94869	11.12359	11.29850	11.47341	11.64831	11.99812
20	10.04013	10.34816	10.55351	10.65618	10.81019	10.96421	11.11822	11.27223	11.58026
23	9.81309	10.07571	10.25079	10.33833	10.46963	10.60094	10.73225	10.86356	11.12618
25	9.70220	9.94265	10.10294	10.18309	10.30331	10.42353	10.54375	10.66397	10.90441
27	9.61459	9.83750	9.98611	10.06042	10.17188	10.28334	10.39480	10.50625	10.72917
28	9.57776	9.79331	9.93702	10.00887	10.11664	10.22442	10.33220	10.43997	10.65552
29	9.54486	9.75383	9.89315	9.96281	10.06729	10.17178	10.27627	10.38075	10.58972
30	9.51543	9.71852	9.85391	9.92160	10.02314	10.12469	10.22623	10.32777	10.53086
35	9.40803	9.58964	9.71071	9.77125	9.86205	9.95286	10.04366	10.13446	10.31607

8.50% Equity Yield 10.50% Mortgage Rate

Mortgage Term	50.00%	60.00%	67.00%	70.00%	Loan to Value Ratio 75.00%	80.00%	85.00%	90.00%	100.00%
10	12.34610	13.11532	13.62813	13.88454	14.26915	14.65376	15.03837	15.42298	16.19220
12	11.59484	12.21381	12.62646	12.83278	13.14227	13.45175	13.76123	14.07072	14.68969
15	10.88239	11.35887	11.67652	11.83535	12.07359	12.31183	12.55007	12.78831	13.26479
18	10.44337	10.83204	11.09116	11.22071	11.41505	11.60939	11.80372	11.99806	12.38673
20	10.24028	10.58834	10.82037	10.93639	11.11042	11.28445	11.45847	11.63250	11.98056
23	10.02120	10.32544	10.52827	10.62968	10.78181	10.93393	11.08605	11.23817	11.54241
25	9.91509	10.19811	10.38679	10.48113	10.62264	10.76414	10.90565	11.04716	11.33018
27	9.83182	10.09819	10.27576	10.36455	10.49773	10.63092	10.76410	10.89728	11.16365
28	9.79702	10.05643	10.22936	10.31583	10.44553	10.57523	10.70494	10.83464	11.09404
29	9.76604	10.01925	10.18806	10.27246	10.39907	10.52567	10.65227	10.77888	11.03209
30	9.73844	9.98612	10.15125	10.23381	10.35765	10.48150	10.60534	10.72918	10.97687
35	9.63880	9.86656	10.01841	10.09433	10.20821	10.32209	10.43597	10.54985	10.77761

8.50% Equity Yield 11.00% Mortgage Rate

Mortgage Term	50.00%	60.00%	67.00%	70.00%	Loan to Value Ratio 75.00%	80.00%	85.00%	90.00%	100.00%
10	12.51500	13.31800	13.85333	14.12100	14.52250	14.92400	15.32550	15.72700	16.53000
12	11.77133	12.42560	12.86178	13.07986	13.40700	13.73413	14.06126	14.38840	15.04266
15	11.06958	11.58350	11.92611	12.09741	12.35437	12.61133	12.86829	13.12525	13.63916
18	10.64030	11.06836	11.35373	11.49642	11.71045	11.92448	12.13851	12.35254	12.78060
20	10.44313	10.83176	11.09084	11.22038	11.41470	11.60901	11.80332	11.99763	12.38626
23	10.23205	10.57846	10.80940	10.92487	11.09807	11.27128	11.44448	11.61769	11.96410
25	10.13068	10.45681	10.67424	10.78295	10.94602	11.10909	11.27215	11.43522	11.76136
27	10.05170	10.36204	10.56893	10.67238	10.82755	10.98272	11.13789	11.29306	11.60340
28	10.01888	10.32266	10.52517	10.62643	10.77832	10.93021	11.08210	11.23398	11.53776
29	9.98978	10.28773	10.48637	10.58569	10.73466	10.88364	11.03262	11.18160	11.47955
30	9.96394	10.25673	10.45192	10.54952	10.69591	10.84230	10.98870	11.13509	11.42788
35	9.87175	10.14610	10.32899	10.42044	10.55762	10.69479	10.83197	10.96914	11.24349

8.50% Equity Yield 11.50% Mortgage Rate

Mortgage Term	50.00%	60.00%	67.00%	70.00%	Loan to Value Ratio 75.00%	80.00%	85.00%	90.00%	100.00%
10	12.68573	13.52287	14.08097	14.36002	14.77859	15.19716	15.61574	16.03431	16.87145
12	11.94990	12.63988	13.09987	13.32986	13.67485	14.01984	14.36483	14.70982	15.39980
15	11.25914	11.81097	12.17885	12.36279	12.63871	12.91462	13.19054	13.46645	14.01828
18	10.83977	11.30773	11.61970	11.77568	12.00966	12.24363	12.47761	12.71159	13.17954
20	10.64858	11.07829	11.36477	11.50801	11.72287	11.93772	12.15258	12.36744	12.79716
23	10.44549	10.83459	11.09398	11.22368	11.41823	11.61278	11.80733	12.00188	12.39098
25	10.34881	10.71858	10.96509	11.08834	11.27322	11.45810	11.64298	11.82786	12.19763
27	10.27405	10.62886	10.86540	10.98367	11.16107	11.33847	11.51588	11.69328	12.04809
28	10.24316	10.59179	10.82421	10.94042	11.11473	11.28905	11.46337	11.63768	11.98631
29	10.21587	10.55905	10.78783	10.90222	11.07381	11.24540	11.41698	11.58857	11.93175
30	10.19175	10.53010	10.75566	10.86845	11.03762	11.20680	11.37597	11.54515	11.88350
35	10.10664	10.42797	10.64219	10.74930	10.90997	11.07063	11.23129	11.39196	11.71329

Mortgage Equity Capitalization Rates

10.00% Equity Yield 10.00% Mortgage Rate

Mortgage Term				Loan to Value Ratio					
	50%	60%	67%	70%	75%	80%	85%	90%	100%
10	12.92904	13.51485	13.90539	14.10066	14.39357	14.68647	14.97938	15.27228	15.85809
12	12.17047	12.60456	12.89396	13.03866	13.25570	13.47275	13.68980	13.90685	14.34094
15	11.44763	11.73716	11.93017	12.02668	12.17145	12.31621	12.46097	12.60574	12.89526
18	10.99906	11.19887	11.33208	11.39869	11.49859	11.59850	11.69841	11.79831	11.99812
20	10.79013	10.94816	11.05351	11.10618	11.18519	11.26421	11.34322	11.42223	11.58026
23	10.56309	10.67571	10.75079	10.78833	10.84464	10.90094	10.95725	11.01356	11.12618
25	10.45220	10.54265	10.60294	10.63309	10.67831	10.72353	10.76875	10.81397	10.90441
27	10.36459	10.43750	10.48611	10.51042	10.54688	10.58334	10.61980	10.65625	10.72917
28	10.32776	10.39331	10.43702	10.45887	10.49164	10.52442	10.55720	10.58997	10.65552
29	10.29486	10.35383	10.39315	10.41281	10.44229	10.47178	10.50127	10.53075	10.58972
30	10.26543	10.31852	10.35391	10.37160	10.39814	10.42469	10.45123	10.47777	10.53086
35	10.15803	10.18964	10.21071	10.22125	10.23705	10.25286	10.26866	10.28446	10.31607

10.00% Equity Yield 10.50% Mortgage Rate

Term	50%	60%	67%	70%	75%	80%	85%	90%	100%
10	13.09610	13.71532	14.12813	14.33454	14.64415	14.95376	15.26337	15.57298	16.19220
12	12.34484	12.81381	13.12646	13.28278	13.51727	13.75175	13.98624	14.22072	14.68969
15	11.63239	11.95887	12.17652	12.28535	12.44859	12.61183	12.77507	12.93831	13.26479
18	11.19337	11.43204	11.59116	11.67071	11.79005	11.90939	12.02872	12.14806	12.38673
20	10.99028	11.18834	11.32037	11.38639	11.48542	11.58445	11.68347	11.78250	11.98056
23	10.77120	10.92544	11.02827	11.07968	11.15681	11.23393	11.31105	11.38817	11.54241
25	10.66509	10.79811	10.88679	10.93113	10.99764	11.06414	11.13065	11.19716	11.33018
27	10.58182	10.69819	10.77576	10.81455	10.87273	10.93092	10.98910	11.04728	11.16365
28	10.54702	10.65643	10.72936	10.76583	10.82053	10.87523	10.92994	10.98464	11.09404
29	10.51604	10.61925	10.68806	10.72246	10.77407	10.82567	10.87727	10.92888	11.03209
30	10.48844	10.58612	10.65125	10.68381	10.73265	10.78150	10.83034	10.87918	10.97687
35	10.38880	10.46657	10.51841	10.54433	10.58321	10.62209	10.66097	10.69985	10.77761

10.00% Equity Yield 11.00% Mortgage Rate

Term	50%	60%	67%	70%	75%	80%	85%	90%	100%
10	13.26500	13.91800	14.35333	14.57100	14.89750	15.22400	15.55050	15.87700	16.53000
12	12.52133	13.02560	13.36178	13.52986	13.78200	14.03413	14.28626	14.53840	15.04266
15	11.81958	12.18350	12.42611	12.54741	12.72937	12.91133	13.09329	13.27525	13.63916
18	11.39030	11.66836	11.85373	11.94642	12.08545	12.22448	12.36351	12.50254	12.78060
20	11.19313	11.43176	11.59084	11.67038	11.78970	11.90901	12.02832	12.14763	12.38626
23	10.98205	11.17846	11.30940	11.37487	11.47307	11.57128	11.66948	11.76769	11.96410
25	10.88068	11.05681	11.17424	11.23295	11.32102	11.40909	11.49715	11.58522	11.76136
27	10.80170	10.96204	11.06893	11.12238	11.20255	11.28272	11.36289	11.44306	11.60340
28	10.76888	10.92266	11.02517	11.07643	11.15332	11.23021	11.30710	11.38398	11.53776
29	10.73978	10.88773	10.98637	11.03569	11.10967	11.18364	11.25762	11.33160	11.47955
30	10.71394	10.85673	10.95192	10.99952	11.07091	11.14230	11.21370	11.28509	11.42788
35	10.62175	10.74610	10.82899	10.87044	10.93262	10.99479	11.05697	11.11914	11.24349

10.00% Equity Yield 11.50% Mortgage Rate

Term	50%	60%	67%	70%	75%	80%	85%	90%	100%
10	13.43573	14.12287	14.58097	14.81002	15.15359	15.49716	15.84074	16.18431	16.87145
12	12.69990	13.23988	13.59987	13.77986	14.04985	14.31984	14.58983	14.85982	15.39980
15	12.00914	12.41097	12.67885	12.81279	13.01371	13.21462	13.41554	13.61645	14.01828
18	11.58977	11.90773	12.11970	12.22568	12.38466	12.54363	12.70261	12.86159	13.17954
20	11.39858	11.67829	11.86477	11.95801	12.09787	12.23772	12.37758	12.51744	12.79716
23	11.19549	11.43459	11.59398	11.67368	11.79323	11.91278	12.03233	12.15188	12.39098
25	11.09881	11.31858	11.46509	11.53834	11.64822	11.75810	11.86798	11.97786	12.19763
27	11.02405	11.22886	11.36540	11.43367	11.53607	11.63847	11.74088	11.84328	12.04809
28	10.99316	11.19179	11.32421	11.39042	11.48973	11.58905	11.68837	11.78768	11.98631
29	10.96587	11.15905	11.28783	11.35222	11.44881	11.54540	11.64198	11.73857	11.93175
30	10.94175	11.13010	11.25566	11.31845	11.41262	11.50680	11.60097	11.69515	11.88350
35	10.85664	11.02797	11.14219	11.19930	11.28497	11.37063	11.45629	11.54196	11.71329

Capitalization Rate to Account for Growth or Decline in Value

Equity Yield 7.50%			25% Growth over Term						Mortgage Ratio 67%			
Time to Sale	Mortgage Term	5.50%	6.50%	7.50%	8.00%	8.50%	9.00%	9.50%	10.00%	10.50%	11.00%	12.00%	12.50%
10 Years	15	4.5729	5.0873	5.6166	5.8867	6.1602	6.4371	6.7173	7.0007	7.2872	7.5767	8.1643	8.4623
	20	4.5105	5.0793	5.6634	5.9607	6.2614	6.5653	6.8721	7.1818	7.4942	7.8091	8.4457	8.7672
	25	4.4748	5.0748	5.6890	6.0009	6.3156	6.6330	6.9529	7.2749	7.5990	7.9250	8.5817	8.9121
	30	4.4524	5.0720	5.7043	6.0245	6.3471	6.6717	6.9982	7.3264	7.6560	7.9868	8.6516	8.9852
12 Years	15	5.0404	5.5218	6.0190	6.2733	6.5312	6.7928	7.0579	7.3265	7.5984	7.8736	8.4334	8.7179
	20	4.9573	5.5045	6.0689	6.3571	6.6490	6.9446	7.2436	7.5460	7.8514	8.1597	8.7847	9.1009
	25	4.9099	5.4948	6.0962	6.4025	6.7121	7.0248	7.3405	7.6588	7.9795	8.3025	8.9544	9.2829
	30	4.8801	5.4889	6.1126	6.4292	6.7487	7.0707	7.3949	7.7211	8.0491	8.3787	9.0416	9.3747
15 Years	15	5.5270	5.9592	6.4064	6.6356	6.8683	7.1045	7.3441	7.5872	7.8335	8.0831	8.5917	8.8505
	20	5.4127	5.9276	6.4613	6.7348	7.0126	7.2945	7.5803	7.8698	8.1630	8.4596	9.0625	9.3685
	25	5.3473	5.9098	6.4913	6.7886	7.0899	7.3949	7.7034	8.0151	8.3298	8.6474	9.2899	9.6145
	30	5.3064	5.8989	6.5093	6.8203	7.1347	7.4522	7.7725	8.0954	8.4205	8.7476	9.4069	9.7386
20 Years	15	6.9199	7.3521	7.7993	8.0284	8.2611	8.4973	8.7370	8.9801	9.2264	9.4760	9.9846	10.2434
	20	5.8863	6.3478	6.8280	7.0747	7.3258	7.5810	7.8403	8.1034	8.3703	8.6407	9.1919	9.4723
	25	5.7908	6.3161	6.8629	7.1437	7.4292	7.7192	8.0132	8.3112	8.6129	8.9181	9.5379	9.8522
	30	5.7310	6.2967	6.8838	7.1844	7.4893	7.7980	8.1104	8.4261	8.7448	9.0661	9.7158	10.0437

Equity Yield 7.50%			25% Growth over Term						Mortgage Ratio 70%			
10 Years	15	4.5149	5.0551	5.6108	5.8944	6.1816	6.4723	6.7665	7.0641	7.3649	7.6689	8.2859	8.5987
	20	4.4494	5.0466	5.6599	5.9721	6.2879	6.6069	6.9291	7.2543	7.5822	7.9129	8.5814	8.9190
	25	4.4119	5.0419	5.6868	6.0143	6.3448	6.6780	7.0139	7.3520	7.6923	8.0346	8.7241	9.0711
	30	4.3884	5.0389	5.7029	6.0391	6.3778	6.7187	7.0615	7.4061	7.7521	8.0995	8.7975	9.1478
12 Years	15	4.9852	5.4908	6.0128	6.2798	6.5506	6.8253	7.1037	7.3856	7.6711	7.9601	8.5479	8.8466
	20	4.8980	5.4726	6.0652	6.3678	6.6743	6.9847	7.2987	7.6161	7.9368	8.2606	8.9168	9.2488
	25	4.8482	5.4624	6.0939	6.4155	6.7406	7.0689	7.4003	7.7345	8.0713	8.4105	9.0949	9.4399
	30	4.8169	5.4562	6.1110	6.4435	6.7790	7.1170	7.4575	7.8000	8.1444	8.4904	9.1865	9.5363
15 Years	15	5.4762	5.9300	6.3996	6.6402	6.8845	7.1326	7.3842	7.6394	7.8981	8.1601	8.6941	8.9659
	20	5.3561	5.8968	6.4572	6.7444	7.0361	7.3320	7.6321	7.9362	8.2440	8.5554	9.1885	9.5097
	25	5.2876	5.8782	6.4888	6.8009	7.1172	7.4375	7.7614	8.0887	8.4192	8.7526	9.4273	9.7681
	30	5.2445	5.8667	6.5076	6.8342	7.1643	7.4977	7.8340	8.1730	8.5144	8.8578	9.5501	9.8984
20 Years	15	6.9197	7.3735	7.8431	8.0837	8.3281	8.5761	8.8277	9.0829	9.3416	9.6037	10.1377	10.4094
	20	5.8345	6.3191	6.8232	7.0823	7.3460	7.6139	7.8861	8.1624	8.4426	8.7266	9.3054	9.5998
	25	5.7343	6.2858	6.8599	7.1548	7.4546	7.7590	8.0678	8.3807	8.6974	9.0179	9.6687	9.9986
	30	5.6714	6.2654	6.8818	7.1975	7.5176	7.8418	8.1698	8.5013	8.8359	9.1733	9.8555	10.1998

Equity Yield 7.50%			25% Growth over Term						Mortgage Ratio 75%			
10 Years	15	4.4279	5.0066	5.6021	5.9059	6.2136	6.5251	6.8403	7.1591	7.4815	7.8071	8.4682	8.8034
	20	4.3577	4.9976	5.6547	5.9892	6.3275	6.6693	7.0145	7.3629	7.7143	8.0686	8.7848	9.1465
	25	4.3175	4.9925	5.6835	6.0344	6.3885	6.7455	7.1054	7.4677	7.8323	8.1990	8.9378	9.3095
	30	4.2924	4.9894	5.7007	6.0610	6.4238	6.7891	7.1564	7.5256	7.8964	8.2686	9.0164	9.3918
12 Years	15	4.9025	5.4442	6.0035	6.2896	6.5798	6.8740	7.1723	7.4744	7.7803	8.0899	8.7197	9.0397
	20	4.8091	5.4247	6.0596	6.3838	6.7123	7.0448	7.3812	7.7213	8.0649	8.4118	9.1149	9.4707
	25	4.7557	5.4138	6.0904	6.4349	6.7832	7.1351	7.4901	7.8482	8.2091	8.5724	9.3058	9.6754
	30	4.7222	5.4071	6.1088	6.4650	6.8244	7.1866	7.5514	7.9184	8.2874	8.6581	9.4039	9.7786
15 Years	15	5.4000	5.8862	6.3894	6.6471	6.9089	7.1747	7.4443	7.7177	7.9949	8.2756	8.8478	9.1390
	20	5.2714	5.8506	6.4511	6.7588	7.0713	7.3884	7.7099	8.0357	8.3655	8.6992	9.3774	9.7217
	25	5.1979	5.8307	6.4849	6.8193	7.1582	7.5014	7.8484	8.1991	8.5532	8.9104	9.6333	9.9985
	30	5.1518	5.8185	6.5051	6.8550	7.2087	7.5659	7.9263	8.2895	8.6552	9.0232	9.7649	10.1381
20 Years	15	6.9195	7.4057	7.9089	8.1666	8.4284	8.6942	8.9638	9.2372	9.5144	9.7952	10.3673	10.6585
	20	5.7568	6.2759	6.8161	7.0937	7.3762	7.6633	7.9550	8.2510	8.5512	8.8555	9.4756	9.7910
	25	5.6494	6.2403	6.8554	7.1714	7.4926	7.8187	8.1495	8.4848	8.8242	9.1675	9.8648	10.2183
	30	5.5820	6.2185	6.8789	7.2171	7.5601	7.9075	8.2589	8.6140	8.9725	9.3340	10.0650	10.4339

Equity Yield 7.50%			25% Growth over Term						Mortgage Ratio 80%			
10 Years	15	4.3409	4.9582	5.5934	5.9175	6.2457	6.5779	6.9142	7.2542	7.5980	7.9454	8.6506	9.0081
	20	4.2660	4.9486	5.6495	6.0063	6.3671	6.7318	7.1000	7.4716	7.8464	8.2243	8.9883	9.3741
	25	4.2232	4.9431	5.6802	6.0545	6.4322	6.8131	7.1969	7.5833	7.9723	8.3634	9.1514	9.5480
	30	4.1963	4.9398	5.6986	6.0828	6.4699	6.8595	7.2513	7.6451	8.0406	8.4376	9.2353	9.6357
12 Years	15	4.8198	5.3976	5.9942	6.2993	6.6089	6.9228	7.2409	7.5631	7.8894	8.2197	8.8915	9.2328
	20	4.7201	5.3768	6.0540	6.3999	6.7502	7.1049	7.4638	7.8265	8.1930	8.5631	9.3130	9.6925
	25	4.6632	5.3652	6.0869	6.4544	6.8259	7.2012	7.5800	7.9619	8.3468	8.7344	9.5166	9.9109
	30	4.6275	5.3580	6.1065	6.4865	6.8698	7.2562	7.6453	8.0367	8.4303	8.8258	9.6213	10.0210
15 Years	15	5.3238	5.8425	6.3792	6.6541	6.9333	7.2168	7.5044	7.7960	8.0917	8.3912	9.0015	9.3121
	20	5.1866	5.8045	6.4450	6.7732	7.1065	7.4448	7.7877	8.1352	8.4870	8.8430	9.5664	9.9336
	25	5.1082	5.7832	6.4810	6.8378	7.1993	7.5653	7.9355	8.3095	8.6872	9.0683	9.8393	10.2288
	30	5.0591	5.7702	6.5026	6.8758	7.2531	7.6341	8.0185	8.4059	8.7960	9.1885	9.9797	10.3778
20 Years	15	6.9193	7.4380	7.9746	8.2496	8.5288	8.8123	9.0999	9.3915	9.6871	9.9867	10.5969	10.9075
	20	5.6790	6.2328	6.8090	7.1051	7.4064	7.7127	8.0238	8.3395	8.6598	8.9843	9.6457	9.9823
	25	5.5645	6.1948	6.8509	7.1880	7.5306	7.8784	8.2313	8.5889	8.9510	9.3172	10.0610	10.4380
	30	5.4926	6.1715	6.8760	7.2367	7.6026	7.9731	8.3480	8.7268	9.1092	9.4948	10.2745	10.6680

Capitalization Rate to Account for Growth or Decline in Value
25% Decline over Term

Equity Yield 7.50% **Mortgage Ratio 67%**

Time to Sale	Mortgage Term	5.50%	6.50%	7.50%	8.00%	8.50%	9.00%	9.50%	10.00%	10.50%	11.00%	12.00%	12.50%
10 Years	15	8.1072	8.6216	9.1509	9.4210	9.6945	9.9714	10.2516	10.5350	10.8215	11.1110	11.6986	11.9966
	20	8.0448	8.6136	9.1977	9.4950	9.7957	10.0996	10.4064	10.7161	11.0285	11.3434	11.9800	12.3015
	25	8.0091	8.6091	9.2233	9.5352	9.8499	10.1673	10.4872	10.8092	11.1333	11.4593	12.1160	12.4464
	30	7.9867	8.6063	9.2386	9.5588	9.8814	10.2060	10.5325	10.8607	11.1903	11.5211	12.1859	12.5195
12 Years	15	7.7542	8.2357	8.7329	8.9872	9.2451	9.5067	9.7718	10.0404	10.3123	10.5874	11.1473	11.4318
	20	7.6712	8.2184	8.7828	9.0710	9.3629	9.6585	9.9575	10.2598	10.5653	10.8736	11.4986	11.8148
	25	7.6237	8.2087	8.8101	9.1164	9.4260	9.7387	10.0544	10.3727	10.6934	11.0164	11.6682	11.9968
	30	7.5940	8.2028	8.8265	9.1431	9.4626	9.7846	10.1088	10.4350	10.7630	11.0925	11.7555	12.0886
15 Years	15	7.4414	7.8736	8.3208	8.5499	8.7826	9.0188	9.2585	9.5015	9.7479	9.9975	10.5060	10.7649
	20	7.3270	7.8419	8.3756	8.6492	8.9270	9.2088	9.4946	9.7842	10.0774	10.3740	10.9769	11.2828
	25	7.2617	7.8242	8.4057	8.7030	9.0042	9.3092	9.6177	9.9295	10.2442	10.5617	11.2043	11.5289
	30	7.2207	7.8133	8.4237	8.7347	9.0491	9.3666	9.6869	10.0097	10.3348	10.6619	11.3212	11.6530
20 Years	15	8.0745	8.5067	8.9539	9.1830	9.4157	9.6520	9.8916	10.1347	10.3810	10.6306	11.1392	11.3980
	20	7.0409	7.5024	7.9826	8.2293	8.4804	8.7356	8.9949	9.2580	9.5249	9.7953	10.3465	10.6269
	25	6.9455	7.4707	8.0175	8.2984	8.5839	8.8738	9.1678	9.4658	9.7675	10.0727	10.6925	11.0068
	30	6.8856	7.4513	8.0384	8.3390	8.6439	8.9527	9.2650	9.5807	9.8994	10.2207	10.8705	11.1984

Equity Yield 7.50% -25% Decline over Term **Mortgage Ratio 70%**

Time to Sale	Mortgage Term	5.50%	6.50%	7.50%	8.00%	8.50%	9.00%	9.50%	10.00%	10.50%	11.00%	12.00%	12.50%
10 Years	15	8.0492	8.5893	9.1451	9.4287	9.7159	10.0066	10.3008	10.5984	10.8992	11.2031	11.8202	12.1330
	20	7.9837	8.5809	9.1942	9.5064	9.8222	10.1412	10.4634	10.7886	11.1165	11.4472	12.1157	12.4533
	25	7.9462	8.5761	9.2211	9.5486	9.8791	10.2123	10.5482	10.8863	11.2266	11.5689	12.2584	12.6054
	30	7.9227	8.5732	9.2372	9.5734	9.9121	10.2530	10.5958	10.9404	11.2864	11.6338	12.3318	12.6821
12 Years	15	7.6991	8.2047	8.7267	8.9937	9.2645	9.5392	9.8175	10.0995	10.3850	10.6740	11.2618	11.5605
	20	7.6119	8.1865	8.7791	9.0817	9.3882	9.6986	10.0126	10.3300	10.6507	10.9745	11.6306	11.9627
	25	7.5621	8.1763	8.8078	9.1293	9.4544	9.7828	10.1142	10.4484	10.7852	11.1243	11.8088	12.1538
	30	7.5308	8.1700	8.8249	9.1574	9.4929	9.8309	10.1714	10.5139	10.8583	11.2043	11.9004	12.2502
15 Years	15	7.3906	7.8444	8.3140	8.5546	8.7989	9.0469	9.2986	9.5538	9.8124	10.0745	10.6085	10.8803
	20	7.2705	7.8112	8.3716	8.6588	8.9504	9.2464	9.5465	9.8505	10.1584	10.4698	11.1028	11.4241
	25	7.2019	7.7925	8.4031	8.7153	9.0316	9.3518	9.6757	10.0031	10.3336	10.6670	11.3416	11.6825
	30	7.1589	7.7811	8.4220	8.7485	9.0787	9.4120	9.7484	10.0874	10.4287	10.7722	11.4644	11.8128
20 Years	15	8.0744	8.5282	8.9978	9.2383	9.4827	9.7307	9.9823	10.2375	10.4962	10.7583	11.2923	11.5640
	20	6.9891	7.4737	7.9778	8.2369	8.5006	8.7685	9.0408	9.3170	9.5972	9.8812	10.4600	10.7544
	25	6.8889	7.4404	8.0145	8.3094	8.6092	8.9136	9.2224	9.5353	9.8521	10.1725	10.8233	11.1532
	30	6.8260	7.4200	8.0364	8.3521	8.6722	8.9964	9.3244	9.6559	9.9905	10.3279	11.0101	11.3544

Equity Yield 7.50% -25% Decline over Term **Mortgage Ratio 75%**

Time to Sale	Mortgage Term	5.50%	6.50%	7.50%	8.00%	8.50%	9.00%	9.50%	10.00%	10.50%	11.00%	12.00%	12.50%
10 Years	15	7.9622	8.5409	9.1364	9.4402	9.7479	10.0594	10.3746	10.6934	11.0157	11.3414	12.0025	12.3377
	20	7.8920	8.5319	9.1890	9.5235	9.8618	10.2036	10.5488	10.8972	11.2486	11.6029	12.3191	12.6808
	25	7.8518	8.5268	9.2178	9.5687	9.9228	10.2798	10.6397	11.0020	11.3666	11.7333	12.4721	12.8438
	30	7.8267	8.5237	9.2350	9.5953	9.9581	10.3234	10.6907	11.0599	11.4307	11.8029	12.5507	12.9260
12 Years	15	7.6164	8.1581	8.7174	9.0034	9.2936	9.5879	9.8862	10.1883	10.4942	10.8038	11.4336	11.7536
	20	7.5230	8.1386	8.7735	9.0977	9.4262	9.7587	10.0951	10.4352	10.7788	11.1257	11.8288	12.1845
	25	7.4696	8.1277	8.8043	9.1488	9.4971	9.8490	10.2040	10.5621	10.9230	11.2863	12.0197	12.3893
	30	7.4361	8.1210	8.8227	9.1789	9.5383	9.9005	10.2653	10.6323	11.0013	11.3720	12.1178	12.4925
15 Years	15	7.3144	7.8006	8.3037	8.5615	8.8233	9.0890	9.3587	9.6321	9.9092	10.1900	10.7622	11.0533
	20	7.1857	7.7650	8.3654	8.6732	8.9857	9.3028	9.6243	9.9501	10.2799	10.6136	11.2918	11.6360
	25	7.1123	7.7451	8.3993	8.7337	9.0726	9.4157	9.7628	10.1135	10.4676	10.8248	11.5477	11.9128
	30	7.0662	7.7328	8.4195	8.7693	9.1230	9.4803	9.8406	10.2038	10.5695	10.9375	11.6792	12.0525
20 Years	15	8.0741	8.5604	9.0635	9.3213	9.5830	9.8488	10.1184	10.3918	10.6690	10.9498	11.5219	11.8131
	20	6.9114	7.4305	7.9707	8.2484	8.5308	8.8179	9.1096	9.4056	9.7058	10.0101	10.6302	10.9457
	25	6.8040	7.3949	8.0100	8.3260	8.6472	8.9733	9.3042	9.6394	9.9788	10.3221	11.0194	11.3729
	30	6.7366	7.3731	8.0335	8.3717	8.7147	9.0621	9.4135	9.7686	10.1271	10.4886	11.2196	11.5885

Equity Yield 7.50% -25% Decline over Term **Mortgage Ratio 80%**

Time to Sale	Mortgage Term	5.50%	6.50%	7.50%	8.00%	8.50%	9.00%	9.50%	10.00%	10.50%	11.00%	12.00%	12.50%
10 Years	15	7.8752	8.4925	9.1277	9.4517	9.7800	10.1122	10.4485	10.7885	11.1323	11.4797	12.1849	12.5424
	20	7.8003	8.4829	9.1838	9.5406	9.9014	10.2661	10.6343	11.0059	11.3807	11.7586	12.5226	12.9084
	25	7.7575	8.4774	9.2145	9.5888	9.9665	10.3474	10.7312	11.1176	11.5066	11.8977	12.6857	13.0823
	30	7.7306	8.4741	9.2329	9.6171	10.0042	10.3938	10.7856	11.1794	11.5749	11.9719	12.7696	13.1700
12 Years	15	7.5337	8.1115	8.7081	9.0132	9.3228	9.6367	9.9548	10.2770	10.6033	10.9335	11.6054	11.9467
	20	7.4340	8.0907	8.7679	9.1138	9.4641	9.8188	10.1777	10.5404	10.9069	11.2770	12.0269	12.4064
	25	7.3771	8.0791	8.8008	9.1683	9.5398	9.9151	10.2938	10.6758	11.0607	11.4483	12.2305	12.6247
	30	7.3414	8.0719	8.8204	9.2004	9.5837	9.9701	10.3591	10.7506	11.1442	11.5397	12.3352	12.7349
15 Years	15	7.2382	7.7568	8.2935	8.5685	8.8477	9.1312	9.4188	9.7104	10.0060	10.3055	10.9158	11.2264
	20	7.1010	7.7189	8.3593	8.6876	9.0209	9.3592	9.7021	10.0496	10.4014	10.7573	11.4808	11.8479
	25	7.0226	7.6976	8.3954	8.7521	9.1136	9.4796	9.8498	10.2239	10.6016	10.9826	11.7537	12.1432
	30	6.9734	7.6845	8.4170	8.7901	9.1674	9.5485	9.9328	10.3203	10.7104	11.1029	11.8940	12.2922
20 Years	15	8.0739	8.5926	9.1292	9.4042	9.6834	9.9669	10.2545	10.5461	10.8418	11.1413	11.7515	12.0621
	20	6.8336	7.3874	7.9636	8.2598	8.5610	8.8673	9.1784	9.4941	9.8144	10.1389	10.8004	11.1369
	25	6.7191	7.3494	8.0055	8.3426	8.6852	9.0331	9.3859	9.7435	10.1056	10.4718	11.2156	11.5927
	30	6.6472	7.3261	8.0306	8.3913	8.7572	9.1277	9.5026	9.8814	10.2638	10.6494	11.4291	11.8226

Capitalization Rate to Account for Growth or Decline in Value

| Equity Yield 7.50% | | | | | 50% Growth over Term | | | | | | Mortgage Ratio 67% | |

Time to Sale	Mortgage Term	5.50%	6.50%	7.50%	8.00%	8.50%	9.00%	9.50%	10.00%	10.50%	11.00%	12.00%	12.50%
10 Years	15	2.8058	3.3202	3.8495	4.1195	4.3931	4.6699	4.9501	5.2335	5.5200	5.8095	6.3972	6.6951
	20	2.7433	3.3121	3.8962	4.1936	4.4943	4.7981	5.1050	5.4147	5.7270	6.0419	6.6786	7.0001
	25	2.7077	3.3076	3.9218	4.2337	4.5485	4.8659	5.1857	5.5078	5.8319	6.1578	6.8145	7.1450
	30	2.6853	3.3048	3.9371	4.2574	4.5799	4.9046	5.2311	5.5592	5.8888	6.2197	6.8844	7.2181
12 Years	15	3.6834	4.1649	4.6621	4.9163	5.1743	5.4359	5.7010	5.9695	6.2414	6.5166	7.0765	7.3609
	20	3.6003	4.1476	4.7119	5.0001	5.2921	5.5877	5.8867	6.1890	6.4944	6.8028	7.4277	7.7440
	25	3.5529	4.1379	4.7393	5.0455	5.3552	5.6679	5.9835	6.3018	6.6226	6.9455	7.5974	7.9259
	30	3.5231	4.1319	4.7556	5.0723	5.3917	5.7137	6.0379	6.3642	6.6922	7.0217	7.6847	8.0177
15 Years	15	4.5698	5.0020	5.4493	5.6784	5.9111	6.1473	6.3870	6.6300	6.8763	7.1259	7.6345	7.8933
	20	4.4555	4.9704	5.5041	5.7776	6.0554	6.3373	6.6231	6.9126	7.2058	7.5024	8.1053	8.4113
	25	4.3902	4.9526	5.5342	5.8314	6.1327	6.4377	6.7462	7.0579	7.3727	7.6902	8.3327	8.6573
	30	4.3492	4.9418	5.5521	5.8631	6.1775	6.4950	6.8154	7.1382	7.4633	7.7904	8.4497	8.7814
20 Years	15	6.3426	6.7748	7.2220	7.4511	7.6838	7.9200	8.1597	8.4028	8.6491	8.8987	9.4073	9.6661
	20	5.3090	5.7705	6.2507	6.4974	6.7485	7.0037	7.2630	7.5261	7.7930	8.0634	8.6146	8.8950
	25	5.2135	5.7388	6.2856	6.5664	6.8519	7.1418	7.4359	7.7339	8.0356	8.3408	8.9606	9.2748
	30	5.1536	5.7194	6.3065	6.6071	6.9119	7.2207	7.5331	7.8488	8.1675	8.4888	9.1385	9.4664

| Equity Yield 7.50% | | | | | 50% Growth over Term | | | | | | Mortgage Ratio 70% | |

Time to Sale	Mortgage Term	5.50%	6.50%	7.50%	8.00%	8.50%	9.00%	9.50%	10.00%	10.50%	11.00%	12.00%	12.50%
10 Years	15	2.7478	3.2879	3.8437	4.1272	4.4144	4.7052	4.9994	5.2969	5.5977	5.9017	6.5187	6.8316
	20	2.6822	3.2794	3.8927	4.2050	4.5207	4.8398	5.1620	5.4871	5.8151	6.1457	6.8142	7.1518
	25	2.6448	3.2747	3.9196	4.2471	4.5776	4.9109	5.2467	5.5849	5.9252	6.2674	6.9570	7.3039
	30	2.6213	3.2718	3.9357	4.2719	4.6106	4.9515	5.2944	5.6389	5.9850	6.3324	7.0304	7.3807
12 Years	15	3.6283	4.1338	4.6559	4.9228	5.1937	5.4684	5.7467	6.0287	6.3142	6.6031	7.1910	7.4897
	20	3.5411	4.1157	4.7082	5.0108	5.3174	5.6277	5.9417	6.2592	6.5798	6.9036	7.5598	7.8919
	25	3.4912	4.1055	4.7369	5.0585	5.3836	5.7120	6.0434	6.3776	6.7144	7.0535	7.7380	8.0829
	30	3.4600	4.0992	4.7541	5.0866	5.4220	5.7601	6.1005	6.4431	6.7875	7.1335	7.8296	8.1793
15 Years	15	4.5190	4.9728	5.4424	5.6830	5.9273	6.1754	6.4270	6.6822	6.9409	7.2029	7.7369	8.0087
	20	4.3990	4.9396	5.5000	5.7872	6.0789	6.3749	6.6750	6.9790	7.2868	7.5983	8.2313	8.5526
	25	4.3304	4.9210	5.5316	5.8437	6.1600	6.4803	6.8042	7.1315	7.4620	7.7954	8.4701	8.8109
	30	4.2874	4.9096	5.5504	5.8770	6.2071	6.5405	6.8768	7.2158	7.5572	7.9006	8.5929	8.9412
20 Years	15	6.3424	6.7962	7.2658	7.5064	7.7507	7.9988	8.2504	8.5056	8.7643	9.0264	9.5603	9.8321
	20	5.2572	5.7418	6.2459	6.5050	6.7687	7.0366	7.3088	7.5851	7.8653	8.1493	8.7281	9.0225
	25	5.1569	5.7085	6.2826	6.5775	6.8773	7.1817	7.4904	7.8034	8.1201	8.4406	9.0914	9.4213
	30	5.0941	5.6881	6.3045	6.6202	6.9403	7.2645	7.5925	7.9240	8.2586	8.5960	9.2782	9.6225

| Equity Yield 7.50% | | | | | 50% Growth over Term | | | | | | Mortgage Ratio 75% | |

Time to Sale	Mortgage Term	5.50%	6.50%	7.50%	8.00%	8.50%	9.00%	9.50%	10.00%	10.50%	11.00%	12.00%	12.50%
10 Years	15	2.6608	3.2395	3.8350	4.1388	4.4465	4.7580	5.0732	5.3920	5.7143	6.0400	6.7011	7.0363
	20	2.5905	3.2304	3.8875	4.2221	4.5604	4.9022	5.2474	5.5958	5.9472	6.3014	7.0177	7.3794
	25	2.5504	3.2253	3.9164	4.2672	4.6213	4.9784	5.3382	5.7005	6.0651	6.4318	7.1706	7.5424
	30	2.5252	3.2222	3.9336	4.2938	4.6567	5.0219	5.3893	5.7584	6.1292	6.5014	7.2493	7.6246
12 Years	15	3.5456	4.0873	4.6466	4.9326	5.2228	5.5171	5.8153	6.1174	6.4233	6.7329	7.3627	7.6828
	20	3.4521	4.0678	4.7027	5.0269	5.3553	5.6879	6.0243	6.3644	6.7080	7.0549	7.7579	8.1137
	25	3.3988	4.0568	4.7334	5.0780	5.4263	5.7781	6.1332	6.4913	6.8521	7.2155	7.9488	8.3184
	30	3.3653	4.0501	4.7518	5.1081	5.4674	5.8297	6.1944	6.5614	6.9304	7.3012	8.0470	8.4217
15 Years	15	4.4428	4.9291	5.4322	5.6900	5.9518	6.2175	6.4871	6.7605	7.0377	7.3185	7.8906	8.1818
	20	4.3142	4.8935	5.4939	5.8016	6.1141	6.4312	6.7528	7.0785	7.4083	7.7420	8.4203	8.7645
	25	4.2407	4.8735	5.5277	5.8622	6.2011	6.5442	6.8912	7.2419	7.5960	7.9533	8.6761	9.0413
	30	4.1946	4.8613	5.5479	5.8978	6.2515	6.6087	6.9691	7.3323	7.6980	8.0660	8.8077	9.1809
20 Years	15	6.3422	6.8284	7.3316	7.5893	7.8511	8.1169	8.3865	8.6599	8.9371	9.2178	9.7900	10.0812
	20	5.1795	5.6986	6.2388	6.5164	6.7989	7.0860	7.3777	7.6737	7.9739	8.2782	8.8983	9.2137
	25	5.0721	5.6630	6.2781	6.5941	6.9153	7.2414	7.5722	7.9075	8.2469	8.5902	9.2875	9.6410
	30	5.0047	5.6412	6.3016	6.6398	6.9828	7.3302	7.6816	8.0367	8.3952	8.7567	9.4877	9.8566

| Equity Yield 7.50% | | | | | 50% Growth over Term | | | | | | Mortgage Ratio 80% | |

Time to Sale	Mortgage Term	5.50%	6.50%	7.50%	8.00%	8.50%	9.00%	9.50%	10.00%	10.50%	11.00%	12.00%	12.50%
10 Years	15	2.5738	3.1911	3.8263	4.1503	4.4785	4.8108	5.1470	5.4871	5.8309	6.1783	6.8835	7.2410
	20	2.4989	3.1814	3.8823	4.2392	4.6000	4.9646	5.3328	5.7045	6.0793	6.4571	7.2212	7.6070
	25	2.4560	3.1760	3.9131	4.2873	4.6650	5.0459	5.4297	5.8162	6.2051	6.5962	7.3843	7.7808
	30	2.4292	3.1727	3.9314	4.3157	4.7028	5.0923	5.4842	5.8779	6.2735	6.6705	7.4682	7.8685
12 Years	15	3.4629	4.0407	4.6372	4.9424	5.2519	5.5658	5.8839	6.2062	6.5325	6.8627	7.5345	7.8759
	20	3.3632	4.0199	4.6971	5.0429	5.3933	5.7480	6.1068	6.4696	6.8361	7.2061	7.9561	8.3355
	25	3.3063	4.0082	4.7299	5.0974	5.4690	5.8442	6.2230	6.6050	6.9898	7.3774	8.1597	8.5539
	30	3.2705	4.0011	4.7495	5.1295	5.5129	5.8992	6.2883	6.6798	7.0734	7.4688	8.2644	8.6641
15 Years	15	4.3667	4.8853	5.4220	5.6969	5.9762	6.2596	6.5472	6.8389	7.1345	7.4340	8.0443	8.3549
	20	4.2294	4.8473	5.4878	5.8160	6.1494	6.4876	6.8306	7.1780	7.5298	7.8858	8.6092	8.9764
	25	4.1511	4.8260	5.5239	5.8806	6.2421	6.6081	6.9783	7.3524	7.7301	8.1111	8.8822	9.2717
	30	4.1019	4.8130	5.5454	5.9186	6.2959	6.6769	7.0613	7.4487	7.8388	8.2313	9.0225	9.4206
20 Years	15	6.3420	6.8606	7.3973	7.6723	7.9515	8.2350	8.5226	8.8142	9.1098	9.4093	10.0196	10.3302
	20	5.1017	5.6555	6.2317	6.5278	6.8291	7.1354	7.4465	7.7622	8.0825	8.4070	9.0684	9.4050
	25	4.9872	5.6175	6.2736	6.6106	6.9532	7.3011	7.6540	8.0116	8.3737	8.7399	9.4837	9.8607
	30	4.9153	5.5942	6.2987	6.6594	7.0253	7.3958	7.7707	8.1495	8.5319	8.9175	9.6972	10.0906

Capitalization Rate to Account for Growth or Decline in Value

Equity Yield 7.50% · **50% Decline over Term** · **Mortgage Ratio 67%**

Time to Sale	Mortgage Term	5.50%	6.50%	7.50%	8.00%	8.50%	9.00%	9.50%	10.00%	10.50%	11.00%	12.00%	12.50%
10 Years	15	9.8744	10.3888	10.9181	11.1881	11.4616	11.7385	12.0187	12.3021	12.5886	12.8781	13.4658	13.7637
	20	9.8119	10.3807	10.9648	11.2622	11.5629	11.8667	12.1736	12.4833	12.7956	13.1105	13.7472	14.0687
	25	9.7763	10.3762	10.9904	11.3023	11.6171	11.9345	12.2543	12.5764	12.9005	13.2264	13.8831	14.2136
	30	9.7539	10.3734	11.0057	11.3260	11.6485	11.9732	12.2997	12.6278	12.9574	13.2883	13.9530	14.2867
12 Years	15	9.1112	9.5927	10.0898	10.3441	10.6021	10.8636	11.1287	11.3973	11.6692	11.9444	12.5042	12.7887
	20	9.0281	9.5754	10.1397	10.4279	10.7199	11.0155	11.3145	11.6168	11.9222	12.2306	12.8555	13.1718
	25	8.9807	9.5657	10.1671	10.4733	10.7829	11.0957	11.4113	11.7296	12.0503	12.3733	13.0252	13.3537
	30	8.9509	9.5597	10.1834	10.5001	10.8195	11.1415	11.4657	11.7920	12.1199	12.4495	13.1125	13.4455
15 Years	15	8.3985	8.8307	9.2780	9.5071	9.7398	9.9760	10.2157	10.4587	10.7051	10.9547	11.4632	11.7221
	20	8.2842	8.7991	9.3328	9.6063	9.8841	10.1660	10.4518	10.7414	11.0345	11.3311	11.9340	12.2400
	25	8.2189	8.7814	9.3629	9.6602	9.9614	10.2664	10.5749	10.8866	11.2014	11.5189	12.1615	12.4861
	30	8.1779	8.7705	9.3808	9.6918	10.0062	10.3238	10.6441	10.9669	11.2920	11.6191	12.2784	12.6102
20 Years	15	8.6518	9.0840	9.5312	9.7603	9.9930	10.2293	10.4689	10.7120	10.9583	11.2079	11.7165	11.9753
	20	7.6182	8.0797	8.5599	8.8067	9.0577	9.3129	9.5722	9.8353	10.1022	10.3726	10.9238	11.2043
	25	7.5228	8.0480	8.5948	8.8757	9.1612	9.4511	9.7451	10.0431	10.3448	10.6500	11.2698	11.5841
	30	7.4629	8.0286	8.6157	8.9163	9.2212	9.5300	9.8424	10.1580	10.4767	10.7980	11.4478	11.7757

Equity Yield 7.50% · **-50% Decline over Term** · **Mortgage Ratio 70%**

Time to Sale	Mortgage Term	5.50%	6.50%	7.50%	8.00%	8.50%	9.00%	9.50%	10.00%	10.50%	11.00%	12.00%	12.50%
10 Years	15	9.8164	10.3565	10.9123	11.1958	11.4830	11.7738	12.0680	12.3655	12.6663	12.9703	13.5873	13.9002
	20	9.7508	10.3480	10.9613	11.2736	11.5893	11.9084	12.2305	12.5557	12.8837	13.2143	13.8828	14.2204
	25	9.7133	10.3433	10.9882	11.3157	11.6462	11.9795	12.3153	12.6535	12.9938	13.3360	14.0256	14.3725
	30	9.6898	10.3404	11.0043	11.3405	11.6792	12.0201	12.3629	12.7075	13.0536	13.4010	14.0990	14.4493
12 Years	15	9.0561	9.5616	10.0836	10.3506	10.6215	10.8961	11.1745	11.4565	11.7420	12.0309	12.6188	12.9174
	20	8.9688	9.5434	10.1360	10.4386	10.7452	11.0555	11.3695	11.6869	12.0076	12.3314	12.9876	13.3197
	25	8.9190	9.5332	10.1647	10.4863	10.8114	11.1398	11.4712	11.8054	12.1422	12.4813	13.1658	13.5107
	30	8.8878	9.5270	10.1819	10.5144	10.8498	11.1879	11.5283	11.8709	12.2152	12.5613	13.2574	13.6071
15 Years	15	8.3478	8.8016	9.2712	9.5117	9.7561	10.0041	10.2557	10.5109	10.7696	11.0317	11.5657	11.8374
	20	8.2277	8.7683	9.3287	9.6159	9.9076	10.2036	10.5037	10.8077	11.1155	11.4270	12.0600	12.3813
	25	8.1591	8.7497	9.3603	9.6724	9.9888	10.3090	10.6329	10.9602	11.2907	11.6241	12.2988	12.6396
	30	8.1161	8.7383	9.3792	9.7057	10.0358	10.3692	10.7056	11.0446	11.3859	11.7294	12.4216	12.7700
20 Years	15	8.6517	9.1055	9.5751	9.8156	10.0600	10.3080	10.5596	10.8148	11.0735	11.3356	11.8696	12.1413
	20	7.5664	8.0510	8.5551	8.8143	9.0779	9.3459	9.6181	9.8943	10.1745	10.4585	11.0373	11.3317
	25	7.4662	8.0177	8.5918	8.8867	9.1865	9.4909	9.7997	10.1126	10.4294	10.7498	11.4006	11.7305
	30	7.4033	7.9973	8.6137	8.9294	9.2495	9.5737	9.9017	10.2332	10.5678	10.9052	11.5874	11.9317

Equity Yield 7.50% · **-50% Decline over Term** · **Mortgage Ratio 75%**

Time to Sale	Mortgage Term	5.50%	6.50%	7.50%	8.00%	8.50%	9.00%	9.50%	10.00%	10.50%	11.00%	12.00%	12.50%
10 Years	15	9.7294	10.3081	10.9036	11.2074	11.5151	11.8266	12.1418	12.4606	12.7829	13.1086	13.7697	14.1049
	20	9.6591	10.2990	10.9561	11.2907	11.6289	11.9708	12.3160	12.6644	13.0158	13.3700	14.0863	14.4480
	25	9.6190	10.2939	10.9850	11.3358	11.6899	12.0470	12.4068	12.7691	13.1337	13.5004	14.2392	14.6110
	30	9.5938	10.2908	11.0022	11.3624	11.7253	12.0905	12.4579	12.8270	13.1978	13.5700	14.3179	14.6932
12 Years	15	8.9734	9.5150	10.0743	10.3604	10.6506	10.9449	11.2431	11.5452	11.8511	12.1607	12.7905	13.1106
	20	8.8799	9.4955	10.1304	10.4547	10.7831	11.1156	11.4521	11.7922	12.1358	12.4827	13.1857	13.5415
	25	8.8265	9.4846	10.1612	10.5057	10.8541	11.2059	11.5610	11.9191	12.2799	12.6432	13.3766	13.7462
	30	8.7931	9.4779	10.1796	10.5358	10.8952	11.2574	11.6222	11.9892	12.3582	12.7289	13.4748	13.8495
15 Years	15	8.2716	8.7578	9.2609	9.5187	9.7805	10.0462	10.3158	10.5893	10.8664	11.1472	11.7193	12.0105
	20	8.1429	8.7222	9.3226	9.6303	9.9429	10.2600	10.5815	10.9072	11.2371	11.5707	12.2490	12.5932
	25	8.0694	8.7022	9.3565	9.6909	10.0298	10.3729	10.7200	11.0707	11.4248	11.7820	12.5048	12.8700
	30	8.0233	8.6900	9.3767	9.7265	10.0802	10.4374	10.7978	11.1610	11.5267	11.8947	12.6364	13.0096
20 Years	15	8.6514	9.1377	9.6408	9.8986	10.1604	10.4261	10.6957	10.9691	11.2463	11.5271	12.0992	12.3904
	20	7.4887	8.0079	8.5480	8.8257	9.1081	9.3952	9.6869	9.9829	10.2831	10.5874	11.2075	11.5230
	25	7.3813	7.9722	8.5873	8.9033	9.2245	9.5506	9.8815	10.2167	10.5561	10.8994	11.5967	11.9502
	30	7.3139	7.9504	8.6108	8.9490	9.2920	9.6394	9.9908	10.3459	10.7044	11.0660	11.7969	12.1658

Equity Yield 7.50% · **-50% Decline over Term** · **Mortgage Ratio 80%**

Time to Sale	Mortgage Term	5.50%	6.50%	7.50%	8.00%	8.50%	9.00%	9.50%	10.00%	10.50%	11.00%	12.00%	12.50%
10 Years	15	9.6424	10.2597	10.8948	11.2189	11.5471	11.8794	12.2156	12.5557	12.8995	13.2469	13.9520	14.3096
	20	9.5674	10.2500	10.9509	11.3078	11.6686	12.0332	12.4014	12.7731	13.1479	13.5257	14.2898	14.6756
	25	9.5246	10.2446	10.9817	11.3559	11.7336	12.1145	12.4983	12.8848	13.2737	13.6648	14.4529	14.8494
	30	9.4978	10.2413	11.0000	11.3843	11.7714	12.1609	12.5528	12.9465	13.3420	13.7391	14.5368	14.9371
12 Years	15	8.8906	9.4684	10.0650	10.3702	10.6797	10.9936	11.3117	11.6340	11.9603	12.2905	12.9623	13.3037
	20	8.7910	9.4477	10.1249	10.4707	10.8211	11.1758	11.5346	11.8974	12.2639	12.6339	13.3838	13.7633
	25	8.7340	9.4360	10.1577	10.5252	10.8967	11.2720	11.6508	12.0327	12.4176	12.8052	13.5875	13.9817
	30	8.6983	9.4289	10.1773	10.5573	10.9406	11.3270	11.7161	12.1076	12.5012	12.8966	13.6922	14.0918
15 Years	15	8.1954	8.7140	9.2507	9.5256	9.8049	10.0883	10.3759	10.6676	10.9632	11.2627	11.8730	12.1836
	20	8.0582	8.6760	9.3165	9.6447	9.9781	10.3163	10.6593	11.0068	11.3586	11.7145	12.4380	12.8051
	25	7.9798	8.6548	9.3526	9.7093	10.0708	10.4368	10.8070	11.1811	11.5588	11.9398	12.7109	13.1004
	30	7.9306	8.6417	9.3741	9.7473	10.1246	10.5056	10.8900	11.2774	11.6676	12.0601	12.8512	13.2493
20 Years	15	8.6512	9.1699	9.7066	9.9815	10.2607	10.5442	10.8318	11.1234	11.4191	11.7186	12.3288	12.6394
	20	7.4110	7.9647	8.5409	8.8371	9.1383	9.4446	9.7557	10.0714	10.3917	10.7162	11.3777	11.7142
	25	7.2964	7.9267	8.5829	8.9199	9.2625	9.6104	9.9632	10.3209	10.6829	11.0491	11.7929	12.1700
	30	7.2245	7.9034	8.6079	8.9686	9.3345	9.7050	10.0799	10.4587	10.8411	11.2267	12.0064	12.3999

Capitalization Rate to Account for Growth or Decline in Value

| Equity Yield 7.50% | | | | | 67% Growth over Term | | | | | | Mortgage Ratio 67% | |

Time to Sale	Mortgage Term	5.50%	6.50%	7.50%	8.00%	8.50%	9.00%	9.50%	10.00%	10.50%	11.00%	12.00%	12.50%
10 Years	15	1.6277	2.1421	2.6714	2.9414	3.2150	3.4918	3.7720	4.0554	4.3419	4.6314	5.2191	5.5170
	20	1.5652	2.1340	2.7181	3.0155	3.3162	3.6200	3.9269	4.2366	4.5489	4.8638	5.5005	5.8220
	25	1.5296	2.1295	2.7437	3.0556	3.3704	3.6878	4.0076	4.3297	4.6538	4.9797	5.6364	5.9669
	30	1.5072	2.1267	2.7590	3.0793	3.4018	3.7265	4.0530	4.3811	4.7107	5.0416	5.7063	6.0400
12 Years	15	2.7788	3.2603	3.7574	4.0117	4.2697	4.5312	4.7963	5.0649	5.3368	5.6120	6.1718	6.4563
	20	2.6957	3.2429	3.8073	4.0955	4.3875	4.6830	4.9821	5.2844	5.5898	5.8982	6.5231	6.8393
	25	2.6483	3.2332	3.8347	4.1409	4.4505	4.7633	5.0789	5.3972	5.7179	6.0409	6.6928	7.0213
	30	2.6185	3.2273	3.8510	4.1677	4.4871	4.8091	5.1333	5.4595	5.7875	6.1171	6.7800	7.1131
15 Years	15	3.9317	4.3639	4.8111	5.0403	5.2730	5.5092	5.7488	5.9919	6.2382	6.4878	6.9964	7.2552
	20	3.8174	4.3323	4.8660	5.1395	5.4173	5.6992	5.9850	6.2745	6.5677	6.8643	7.4672	7.7732
	25	3.7520	4.3145	4.8960	5.1933	5.4946	5.7996	6.1081	6.4198	6.7345	7.0521	7.6946	8.0192
	30	3.7111	4.3036	4.9140	5.2250	5.5394	5.8569	6.1772	6.5001	6.8252	7.1523	7.8116	8.1433
20 Years	15	5.9577	6.3899	6.8371	7.0663	7.2990	7.5352	7.7748	8.0179	8.2642	8.5138	9.0224	9.2812
	20	4.9241	5.3856	5.8658	6.1126	6.3636	6.6188	6.8781	7.1412	7.4081	7.6785	8.2297	8.5102
	25	4.8287	5.3540	5.9007	6.1816	6.4671	6.7570	7.0511	7.3491	7.6508	7.9559	8.5757	8.8900
	30	4.7688	5.3345	5.9216	6.2222	6.5271	6.8359	7.1483	7.4639	7.7826	8.1039	8.7537	9.0816

| Equity Yield 7.50% | | | | | 67% Growth over Term | | | | | | Mortgage Ratio 70% | |

Time to Sale	Mortgage Term	5.50%	6.50%	7.50%	8.00%	8.50%	9.00%	9.50%	10.00%	10.50%	11.00%	12.00%	12.50%
10 Years	15	1.5697	2.1098	2.6656	2.9491	3.2363	3.5271	3.8213	4.1188	4.4196	4.7236	5.3406	5.6535
	20	1.5041	2.1013	2.7146	3.0269	3.3426	3.6617	3.9839	4.3090	4.6370	4.9676	5.6361	5.9737
	25	1.4667	2.0966	2.7416	3.0690	3.3995	3.7328	4.0686	4.4068	4.7471	5.0893	5.7789	6.1258
	30	1.4432	2.0937	2.7576	3.0938	3.4325	3.7734	4.1163	4.4608	4.8069	5.1543	5.8523	6.2026
12 Years	15	2.7236	3.2292	3.7512	4.0182	4.2891	4.5637	4.8421	5.1241	5.4096	5.6985	6.2863	6.5850
	20	2.6364	3.2110	3.8036	4.1062	4.4128	4.7231	5.0371	5.3545	5.6752	5.9990	6.6552	6.9872
	25	2.5866	3.2008	3.8323	4.1539	4.4790	4.8074	5.1388	5.4730	5.8097	6.1489	6.8333	7.1783
	30	2.5554	3.1946	3.8495	4.1820	4.5174	4.8555	5.1959	5.5384	5.8828	6.2289	6.9250	7.2747
15 Years	15	3.8809	4.3347	4.8043	5.0449	5.2892	5.5373	5.7889	6.0441	6.3028	6.5648	7.0988	7.3706
	20	3.7608	4.3015	4.8619	5.1491	5.4408	5.7367	6.0368	6.3409	6.6487	6.9601	7.5932	7.9144
	25	3.6923	4.2829	4.8935	5.2056	5.5219	5.8422	6.1661	6.4934	6.8239	7.1573	7.8320	8.1728
	30	3.6492	4.2714	4.9123	5.2389	5.5690	5.9024	6.2387	6.5777	6.9191	7.2625	7.9548	8.3031
20 Years	15	5.9576	6.4114	6.8810	7.1215	7.3659	7.6139	7.8656	8.1208	8.3794	8.6415	9.1755	9.4473
	20	4.8723	5.3569	5.8610	6.1202	6.3838	6.6518	6.9240	7.2002	7.4805	7.7644	8.3432	8.6376
	25	4.7721	5.3236	5.8977	6.1926	6.4924	6.7968	7.1056	7.4185	7.7353	8.0557	8.7065	9.0364
	30	4.7092	5.3032	5.9196	6.2353	6.5554	6.8796	7.2076	7.5391	7.8737	8.2111	8.8933	9.2376

| Equity Yield 7.50% | | | | | 67% Growth over Term | | | | | | Mortgage Ratio 75% | |

Time to Sale	Mortgage Term	5.50%	6.50%	7.50%	8.00%	8.50%	9.00%	9.50%	10.00%	10.50%	11.00%	12.00%	12.50%
10 Years	15	1.4827	2.0614	2.6569	2.9607	3.2684	3.5799	3.8951	4.2139	4.5362	4.8619	5.5230	5.8582
	20	1.4124	2.0523	2.7094	3.0440	3.3823	3.7241	4.0693	4.4177	4.7691	5.1233	5.8396	6.2013
	25	1.3723	2.0472	2.7383	3.0891	3.4432	3.8003	4.1601	4.5224	4.8870	5.2537	5.9925	6.3643
	30	1.3471	2.0441	2.7555	3.1157	3.4786	3.8438	4.2112	4.5803	4.9511	5.3233	6.0712	6.4465
12 Years	15	2.6409	3.1826	3.7419	4.0280	4.3182	4.6125	4.9107	5.2128	5.5187	5.8283	6.4581	6.7781
	20	2.5475	3.1631	3.7980	4.1222	4.4507	4.7832	5.1196	5.4597	5.8033	6.1503	6.8533	7.2091
	25	2.4941	3.1522	3.8288	4.1733	4.5217	4.8735	5.2286	5.5866	5.9475	6.3108	7.0442	7.4138
	30	2.4606	3.1455	3.8472	4.2034	4.5628	4.9250	5.2898	5.6568	6.0258	6.3965	7.1424	7.5171
15 Years	15	3.8047	4.2909	4.7941	5.0518	5.3136	5.5794	5.8490	6.1224	6.3996	6.6803	7.2525	7.5437
	20	3.6761	4.2553	4.8558	5.1635	5.4760	5.7931	6.1146	6.4404	6.7702	7.1039	7.7821	8.1264
	25	3.6026	4.2354	4.8896	5.2240	5.5629	5.9061	6.2531	6.6038	6.9579	7.3151	8.0380	8.4032
	30	3.5565	4.2232	4.9098	5.2597	5.6134	5.9706	6.3310	6.6942	7.0599	7.4279	8.1696	8.5428
20 Years	15	5.9574	6.4436	6.9467	7.2045	7.4663	7.7320	8.0016	8.2751	8.5522	8.8330	9.4051	9.6963
	20	4.7946	5.3138	5.8539	6.1316	6.4140	6.7011	6.9928	7.2888	7.5890	7.8933	8.5134	8.8289
	25	4.6872	5.2781	5.8932	6.2092	6.5304	6.8565	7.1874	7.5226	7.8620	8.2053	8.9026	9.2562
	30	4.6198	5.2563	5.9167	6.2549	6.5979	6.9453	7.2967	7.6519	8.0103	8.3719	9.1028	9.4717

| Equity Yield 7.50% | | | | | 67% Growth over Term | | | | | | Mortgage Ratio 80% | |

Time to Sale	Mortgage Term	5.50%	6.50%	7.50%	8.00%	8.50%	9.00%	9.50%	10.00%	10.50%	11.00%	12.00%	12.50%
10 Years	15	1.3957	2.0130	2.6482	2.9722	3.3004	3.6327	3.9689	4.3090	4.6528	5.0002	5.7054	6.0629
	20	1.3208	2.0033	2.7042	3.0611	3.4219	3.7865	4.1547	4.5264	4.9012	5.2790	6.0431	6.4289
	25	1.2779	1.9979	2.7350	3.1092	3.4869	3.8678	4.2516	4.6381	5.0270	5.4181	6.2062	6.6027
	30	1.2511	1.9946	2.7533	3.1376	3.5247	3.9142	4.3061	4.6998	5.0954	5.4924	6.2901	6.6904
12 Years	15	2.5582	3.1360	3.7326	4.0377	4.3473	4.6612	4.9793	5.3016	5.6279	5.9581	6.6299	6.9713
	20	2.4586	3.1152	3.7925	4.1383	4.4887	4.8434	5.2022	5.5650	5.9315	6.3015	7.0514	7.4309
	25	2.4016	3.1036	3.8253	4.1928	4.5643	4.9396	5.3184	5.7003	6.0852	6.4728	7.2550	7.6493
	30	2.3659	3.0964	3.8449	4.2249	4.6082	4.9946	5.3837	5.7751	6.1687	6.5642	7.3597	7.7594
15 Years	15	3.7285	4.2472	4.7839	5.0588	5.3380	5.6215	5.9091	6.2007	6.4964	6.7959	7.4062	7.7168
	20	3.5913	4.2092	4.8497	5.1779	5.5112	5.8495	6.1924	6.5399	6.8917	7.2476	7.9711	8.3383
	25	3.5129	4.1879	4.8857	5.2425	5.6040	5.9700	6.3402	6.7142	7.0919	7.4730	8.2440	8.6335
	30	3.4638	4.1749	4.9073	5.2805	5.6578	6.0388	6.4232	6.8106	7.2007	7.5932	8.3844	8.7825
20 Years	15	5.9571	6.4758	7.0125	7.2874	7.5666	7.8501	8.1377	8.4294	8.7250	9.0245	9.6348	9.9454
	20	4.7169	5.2706	5.8468	6.1430	6.4442	6.7505	7.0616	7.3774	7.6976	8.0222	8.6836	9.0201
	25	4.6023	5.2326	5.8888	6.2258	6.5684	6.9163	7.2692	7.6268	7.9888	8.3550	9.0988	9.4759
	30	4.5304	5.2093	5.9138	6.2745	6.6404	7.0109	7.3858	7.7646	8.1470	8.5326	9.3123	9.7058

Capitalization Rate to Account for Growth or Decline in Value
100% Growth over Term

Equity Yield 7.50%													Mortgage Ratio 67%

Time to Sale	Mortgage Term	Mortgage Interest Rate											
		5.50%	6.50%	7.50%	8.00%	8.50%	9.00%	9.50%	10.00%	10.50%	11.00%	12.00%	12.50%
10 Years	15	-0.7285	-0.2141	0.3152	0.5852	0.8588	1.1357	1.4158	1.6992	1.9857	2.2752	2.8629	3.1608
	20	-0.7910	-0.2222	0.3619	0.6593	0.9600	1.2638	1.5707	1.8804	2.1927	2.5076	3.1443	3.4658
	25	-0.8266	-0.2267	0.3875	0.6994	1.0142	1.3316	1.6514	1.9735	2.2976	2.6235	3.2802	3.6107
	30	-0.8490	-0.2295	0.4029	0.7231	1.0456	1.3703	1.6968	2.0249	2.3545	2.6854	3.3501	3.6838
12 Years	15	0.9695	1.4510	1.9482	2.2024	2.4604	2.7220	2.9871	3.2556	3.5275	3.8027	4.3626	4.6470
	20	0.8865	1.4337	1.9980	2.2862	2.5782	2.8738	3.1728	3.4751	3.7805	4.0889	4.7138	5.0301
	25	0.8390	1.4240	2.0254	2.3316	2.6413	2.9540	3.2696	3.5879	3.9087	4.2316	4.8835	5.2121
	30	0.8092	1.4180	2.0417	2.3584	2.6778	2.9998	3.3240	3.6503	3.9783	4.3078	4.9708	5.3038
15 Years	15	2.6555	3.0877	3.5349	3.7640	3.9967	4.2329	4.4726	4.7156	4.9620	5.2116	5.7201	5.9790
	20	2.5411	3.0560	3.5897	3.8633	4.1410	4.4229	4.7087	4.9983	5.2914	5.5881	6.1909	6.4969
	25	2.4758	3.0383	3.6198	3.9171	4.2183	4.5233	4.8318	5.1435	5.4583	5.7758	6.4184	6.7430
	30	2.4348	3.0274	3.6378	3.9487	4.2632	4.5807	4.9010	5.2238	5.5489	5.8760	6.5353	6.8671
20 Years	15	5.1880	5.6202	6.0674	6.2965	6.5292	6.7654	7.0051	7.2481	7.4945	7.7441	8.2526	8.5115
	20	4.1544	4.6159	5.0960	5.3428	5.5939	5.8491	6.1084	6.3715	6.6383	6.9088	7.4600	7.7404
	25	4.0589	4.5842	5.1310	5.4118	5.6973	5.9872	6.2813	6.5793	6.8810	7.1862	7.8060	8.1202
	30	3.9990	4.5648	5.1519	5.4525	5.7573	6.0661	6.3785	6.6942	7.0128	7.3342	7.9839	8.3118

Equity Yield 7.50%						100% Growth over Term							Mortgage Ratio 70%
10 Years	15	-0.7865	-0.2464	0.3094	0.5929	0.8801	1.1709	1.4651	1.7626	2.0634	2.3674	2.9844	3.2973
	20	-0.8521	-0.2549	0.3584	0.6707	0.9864	1.3055	1.6277	1.9528	2.2808	2.6114	3.2799	3.6175
	25	-0.8895	-0.2596	0.3854	0.7128	1.0433	1.3766	1.7124	2.0506	2.3909	2.7331	3.4227	3.7696
	30	-0.9130	-0.2625	0.4014	0.7376	1.0763	1.4172	1.7601	2.1046	2.4507	2.7981	3.4961	3.8464
12 Years	15	0.9144	1.4200	1.9420	2.2089	2.4798	2.7545	3.0328	3.3148	3.6003	3.8892	4.4771	4.7758
	20	0.8272	1.4018	1.9943	2.2969	2.6035	2.9139	3.2278	3.5453	3.8660	4.1897	4.8459	5.1780
	25	0.7774	1.3916	2.0231	2.3446	2.6697	2.9981	3.3295	3.6637	4.0005	4.3396	5.0241	5.3690
	30	0.7461	1.3853	2.0402	2.3727	2.7081	3.0462	3.3866	3.7292	4.0736	4.4196	5.1157	5.4654
15 Years	15	2.6047	3.0585	3.5281	3.7686	4.0130	4.2610	4.5127	4.7679	5.0265	5.2886	5.8226	6.0944
	20	2.4846	3.0252	3.5856	3.8729	4.1645	4.4605	4.7606	5.0646	5.3725	5.6839	6.3169	6.6382
	25	2.4160	3.0066	3.6172	3.9294	4.2457	4.5659	4.8898	5.2172	5.5476	5.8811	6.5557	6.8966
	30	2.3730	2.9952	3.6361	3.9626	4.2927	4.6261	4.9625	5.3015	5.6428	5.9863	6.6785	7.0269
20 Years	15	5.1878	5.6416	6.1112	6.3518	6.5961	6.8442	7.0958	7.3510	7.6097	7.8717	8.4057	8.6775
	20	4.1026	4.5871	5.0913	5.3504	5.6140	5.8820	6.1542	6.4305	6.7107	6.9947	7.5735	7.8679
	25	4.0023	4.5539	5.1280	5.4229	5.7227	6.0271	6.3358	6.6487	6.9655	7.2859	7.9368	8.2667
	30	3.9395	4.5335	5.1499	5.4655	5.7857	6.1099	6.4379	6.7694	7.1039	7.4414	8.1236	8.4679

Equity Yield 7.50%						100% Growth over Term							Mortgage Ratio 75%
10 Years	15	-0.8735	-0.2948	0.3007	0.6045	0.9122	1.2237	1.5389	1.8577	2.1800	2.5057	3.1668	3.5020
	20	-0.9438	-0.3039	0.3532	0.6878	1.0261	1.3679	1.7131	2.0615	2.4129	2.7671	3.4834	3.8451
	25	-0.9839	-0.3090	0.3821	0.7329	1.0870	1.4441	1.8039	2.1662	2.5309	2.8975	3.6363	4.0081
	30	-1.0091	-0.3121	0.3993	0.7595	1.1224	1.4876	1.8550	2.2241	2.5949	2.9671	3.7150	4.0903
12 Years	15	0.8317	1.3734	1.9327	2.2187	2.5089	2.8032	3.1014	3.4036	3.7095	4.0190	4.6489	4.9689
	20	0.7382	1.3539	1.9888	2.3130	2.6414	2.9740	3.3104	3.6505	3.9941	4.3410	5.0440	5.3998
	25	0.6849	1.3429	2.0195	2.3641	2.7124	3.0642	3.4193	3.7774	4.1382	4.5016	5.2349	5.6045
	30	0.6514	1.3363	2.0379	2.3942	2.7536	3.1158	3.4805	3.8475	4.2165	4.5873	5.3331	5.7078
15 Years	15	2.5285	3.0147	3.5178	3.7756	4.0374	4.3031	4.5728	4.8462	5.1233	5.4041	5.9762	6.2674
	20	2.3998	2.9791	3.5795	3.8873	4.1998	4.5169	4.8384	5.1642	5.4940	5.8277	6.5059	6.8501
	25	2.3264	2.9591	3.6134	3.9478	4.2867	4.6298	4.9769	5.3276	5.6817	6.0389	6.7618	7.1269
	30	2.2803	2.9469	3.6336	3.9834	4.3371	4.6943	5.0547	5.4179	5.7836	6.1516	6.8933	7.2666
20 Years	15	5.1876	5.6738	6.1770	6.4347	6.6965	6.9623	7.2319	7.5053	7.7825	8.0632	8.6354	8.9266
	20	4.0249	4.5440	5.0842	5.3618	5.6443	5.9314	6.2230	6.5191	6.8193	7.1236	7.7436	8.0591
	25	3.9175	4.5084	5.1235	5.4395	5.7606	6.0868	6.4176	6.7529	7.0923	7.4356	8.1329	8.4864
	30	3.8501	4.4866	5.1470	5.4852	5.8282	6.1756	6.5270	6.8821	7.2406	7.6021	8.3331	8.7020

Equity Yield 7.50%						100% Growth over Term							Mortgage Ratio 80%
10 Years	15	-0.9605	-0.3432	0.2920	0.6160	0.9442	1.2765	1.6127	1.9528	2.2966	2.6440	3.3492	3.7067
	20	-1.0354	-0.3529	0.3480	0.7049	1.0657	1.4303	1.7986	2.1702	2.5450	2.9229	3.6869	4.0727
	25	-1.0782	-0.3583	0.3788	0.7530	1.1307	1.5116	1.8954	2.2819	2.6708	3.0619	3.8500	4.2465
	30	-1.1051	-0.3616	0.3971	0.7814	1.1685	1.5580	1.9499	2.3437	2.7392	3.1362	3.9339	4.3342
12 Years	15	0.7490	1.3268	1.9234	2.2285	2.5380	2.8519	3.1700	3.4923	3.8186	4.1488	4.8206	5.1620
	20	0.6493	1.3060	1.9832	2.3290	2.6794	3.0341	3.3929	3.7557	4.1222	4.4922	5.2422	5.6217
	25	0.5924	1.2943	2.0160	2.3835	2.7551	3.1304	3.5091	3.8911	4.2760	4.6635	5.4458	5.8400
	30	0.5567	1.2872	2.0356	2.4156	2.7990	3.1853	3.5744	3.9659	4.3595	4.7549	5.5505	5.9502
15 Years	15	2.4523	2.9709	3.5076	3.7826	4.0618	4.3453	4.6329	4.9245	5.2201	5.5196	6.1299	6.4405
	20	2.3151	2.9330	3.5734	3.9017	4.2350	4.5732	4.9162	5.2637	5.6155	5.9714	6.6949	7.0620
	25	2.2367	2.9117	3.6095	3.9662	4.3277	4.6937	5.0639	5.4380	5.8157	6.1967	6.9678	7.3573
	30	2.1875	2.8986	3.6311	4.0042	4.3815	4.7626	5.1469	5.5344	5.9245	6.3170	7.1081	7.5062
20 Years	15	5.1874	5.7060	6.2427	6.5177	6.7969	7.0804	7.3680	7.6596	7.9552	8.2547	8.8650	9.1756
	20	3.9471	4.5009	5.0771	5.3732	5.6745	5.9808	6.2919	6.6076	6.9279	7.2524	7.9138	8.2504
	25	3.8326	4.4629	5.1190	5.4560	5.7986	6.1465	6.4994	6.8570	7.2191	7.5853	8.3290	8.7061
	30	3.7607	4.4396	5.1441	5.5048	5.8706	6.2412	6.6161	6.9949	7.3773	7.7629	8.5426	8.9360

Capitalization Rate to Account for Growth or Decline in Value

Equity Yield 7.50%			150% Growth over Term							Mortgage Ratio 67%		

Time to Sale	Mortgage Term	5.50%	6.50%	7.50%	8.00%	Mortgage Interest Rate 8.50%	9.00%	9.50%	10.00%	10.50%	11.00%	12.00%	12.50%
10 Years	15	-4.2628	-3.7484	-3.2191	-2.9491	-2.6755	-2.3986	-2.1185	-1.8351	-1.5486	-1.2591	-0.6714	-0.3735
	20	-4.3253	-3.7565	-3.1724	-2.8750	-2.5743	-2.2705	-1.9636	-1.6539	-1.3416	-1.0267	-0.3900	-0.0685
	25	-4.3609	-3.7610	-3.1468	-2.8349	-2.5201	-2.2027	-1.8829	-1.5608	-1.2367	-0.9108	-0.2541	0.0764
	30	-4.3833	-3.7638	-3.1314	-2.8112	-2.4887	-2.1640	-1.8375	-1.5094	-1.1798	-0.8489	-0.1842	0.1495
12 Years	15	-1.7444	-1.2629	-0.7657	-0.5115	-0.2535	0.0081	0.2732	0.5417	0.8136	1.0888	1.6487	1.9331
	20	-1.8274	-1.2802	-0.7159	-0.4277	-0.1357	0.1599	0.4589	0.7612	1.0666	1.3750	1.9999	2.3162
	25	-1.8749	-1.2899	-0.6885	-0.3822	-0.0726	0.2401	0.5557	0.8740	1.1948	1.5178	2.1696	2.4982
	30	-1.9046	-1.2959	-0.6722	-0.3555	-0.0360	0.2859	0.6102	0.9364	1.2644	1.5939	2.2569	2.5900
15 Years	15	0.7411	1.1733	1.6205	1.8496	2.0823	2.3186	2.5582	2.8013	3.0476	3.2972	3.8058	4.0646
	20	0.6268	1.1416	1.6754	1.9489	2.2267	2.5086	2.7944	3.0839	3.3771	3.6737	4.2766	4.5826
	25	0.5614	1.1239	1.7054	2.0027	2.3040	2.6090	2.9175	3.2292	3.5439	3.8615	4.5040	4.8286
	30	0.5205	1.1130	1.7234	2.0344	2.3488	2.6663	2.9866	3.3095	3.6346	3.9617	4.6210	4.9527
20 Years	15	4.0334	4.4656	4.9128	5.1419	5.3746	5.6108	5.8505	6.0935	6.3399	6.5895	7.0980	7.3569
	20	2.9998	3.4613	3.9414	4.1882	4.4393	4.6945	4.9537	5.2169	5.4837	5.7542	6.3054	6.5858
	25	2.9043	3.4296	3.9764	4.2572	4.5427	4.8326	5.1267	5.4247	5.7264	6.0316	6.6514	6.9656
	30	2.8444	3.4102	3.9972	4.2979	4.6027	4.9115	5.2239	5.5396	5.8582	6.1796	6.8293	7.1572

Equity Yield 7.50%			150% Growth over Term							Mortgage Ratio 70%		

Time to Sale	Mortgage Term	5.50%	6.50%	7.50%	8.00%	8.50%	9.00%	9.50%	10.00%	10.50%	11.00%	12.00%	12.50%
10 Years	15	-4.3208	-3.7807	-3.2249	-2.9414	-2.6542	-2.3634	-2.0692	-1.7717	-1.4709	-1.1669	-0.5499	-0.2370
	20	-4.3864	-3.7891	-3.1759	-2.8636	-2.5479	-2.2288	-1.9066	-1.5815	-1.2535	-0.9229	-0.2544	0.0832
	25	-4.4238	-3.7939	-3.1489	-2.8215	-2.4910	-2.1577	-1.8219	-1.4837	-1.1434	-0.8012	-0.1116	0.2353
	30	-4.4473	-3.7968	-3.1329	-2.7967	-2.4580	-2.1171	-1.7742	-1.4297	-1.0836	-0.7362	-0.0382	0.3121
12 Years	15	-1.7995	-1.2939	-0.7719	-0.5049	-0.2341	0.0406	0.3189	0.6009	0.8864	1.1754	1.7632	2.0619
	20	-1.8867	-1.3121	-0.7196	-0.4170	-0.1104	0.2000	0.5139	0.8314	1.1521	1.4758	2.1320	2.4641
	25	-1.9365	-1.3223	-0.6908	-0.3693	-0.0442	0.2842	0.6156	0.9498	1.2866	1.6257	2.3102	2.6552
	30	-1.9678	-1.3286	-0.6737	-0.3412	-0.0058	0.3323	0.6727	1.0153	1.3597	1.7057	2.4018	2.7515
15 Years	15	0.6903	1.1441	1.6137	1.8543	2.0986	2.3466	2.5983	2.8535	3.1122	3.3742	3.9082	4.1800
	20	0.5702	1.1109	1.6713	1.9585	2.2502	2.5461	2.8462	3.1503	3.4581	3.7695	4.4026	4.7238
	25	0.5017	1.0923	1.7029	2.0150	2.3313	2.6516	2.9755	3.3028	3.6333	3.9667	4.6414	4.9822
	30	0.4586	1.0808	1.7217	2.0483	2.3784	2.7118	3.0481	3.3871	3.7285	4.0719	4.7642	5.1125
20 Years	15	4.0332	4.4870	4.9566	5.1972	5.4415	5.6896	5.9412	6.1964	6.4551	6.7171	7.2511	7.5229
	20	2.9480	3.4325	3.9367	4.1958	4.4594	4.7274	4.9996	5.2759	5.5561	5.8401	6.4188	6.7133
	25	2.8477	3.3993	3.9734	4.2683	4.5680	4.8724	5.1812	5.4941	5.8109	6.1313	6.7822	7.1121
	30	2.7848	3.3789	3.9953	4.3109	4.6311	4.9553	5.2833	5.6148	5.9493	6.2868	6.9690	7.3133

Equity Yield 7.50%			150% Growth over Term							Mortgage Ratio 75%		

Time to Sale	Mortgage Term	5.50%	6.50%	7.50%	8.00%	8.50%	9.00%	9.50%	10.00%	10.50%	11.00%	12.00%	12.50%
10 Years	15	-4.4078	-3.8291	-3.2336	-2.9298	-2.6221	-2.3106	-1.9954	-1.6766	-1.3543	-1.0286	-0.3675	-0.0323
	20	-4.4781	-3.8382	-3.1811	-2.8465	-2.5082	-2.1664	-1.8212	-1.4728	-1.1214	-0.7672	-0.0509	0.3108
	25	-4.5182	-3.8432	-3.1522	-2.8014	-2.4473	-2.0902	-1.7304	-1.3681	-1.0034	-0.6368	0.1020	0.4738
	30	-4.5434	-3.8464	-3.1350	-2.7748	-2.4119	-2.0467	-1.6793	-1.3102	-0.9394	-0.5672	0.1807	0.5560
12 Years	15	-1.8822	-1.3405	-0.7812	-0.4952	-0.2050	0.0893	0.3875	0.6897	0.9956	1.3051	1.9350	2.2550
	20	-1.9757	-1.3600	-0.7251	-0.4009	-0.0725	0.2601	0.5965	0.9366	1.2802	1.6271	2.3301	2.6859
	25	-2.0290	-1.3709	-0.6943	-0.3498	-0.0015	0.3503	0.7054	1.0635	1.4243	1.7877	2.5210	2.8906
	30	-2.0625	-1.3776	-0.6760	-0.3197	0.0397	0.4019	0.7666	1.1336	1.5026	1.8734	2.6192	2.9939
15 Years	15	0.6141	1.1003	1.6035	1.8612	2.1230	2.3888	2.6584	2.9318	3.2090	3.4897	4.0619	4.3531
	20	0.4855	1.0647	1.6652	1.9729	2.2854	2.6025	2.9240	3.2498	3.5796	3.9133	4.5915	4.9358
	25	0.4120	1.0448	1.6990	2.0334	2.3723	2.7155	3.0625	3.4132	3.7673	4.1245	4.8474	5.2126
	30	0.3659	1.0326	1.7192	2.0691	2.4228	2.7800	3.1403	3.5035	3.8693	4.2373	4.9790	5.3522
20 Years	15	4.0330	4.5192	5.0224	5.2801	5.5419	5.8077	6.0773	6.3507	6.6278	6.9086	7.4808	7.7720
	20	2.8702	3.3894	3.9296	4.2072	4.4897	4.7768	5.0684	5.3645	5.6647	5.9690	6.5890	6.9045
	25	2.7628	3.3538	3.9689	4.2849	4.6060	4.9322	5.2630	5.5983	5.9377	6.2810	6.9783	7.3318
	30	2.6955	3.3319	3.9924	4.3306	4.6735	5.0209	5.3724	5.7275	6.0860	6.4475	7.1785	7.5473

Equity Yield 7.50%			150% Growth over Term							Mortgage Ratio 80%		

Time to Sale	Mortgage Term	5.50%	6.50%	7.50%	8.00%	8.50%	9.00%	9.50%	10.00%	10.50%	11.00%	12.00%	12.50%
10 Years	15	-4.4948	-3.8775	-3.2423	-2.9183	-2.5901	-2.2578	-1.9216	-1.5815	-1.2377	-0.8903	-0.1851	0.1724
	20	-4.5697	-3.8872	-3.1863	-2.8294	-2.4686	-2.1040	-1.7357	-1.3641	-0.9893	-0.6114	0.1526	0.5384
	25	-4.6125	-3.8926	-3.1555	-2.7813	-2.4036	-2.0227	-1.6389	-1.2524	-0.8635	-0.4724	0.3157	0.7122
	30	-4.6394	-3.8959	-3.1372	-2.7529	-2.3658	-1.9762	-1.5844	-1.1906	-0.7951	-0.3981	0.3996	0.7999
12 Years	15	-1.9649	-1.3871	-0.7905	-0.4854	-0.1759	0.1380	0.4562	0.7784	1.1047	1.4349	2.1067	2.4481
	20	-2.0646	-1.4079	-0.7307	-0.3849	-0.0345	0.3202	0.6790	1.0418	1.4083	1.7784	2.5283	2.9078
	25	-2.1215	-1.4196	-0.6979	-0.3304	0.0412	0.4165	0.7952	1.1772	1.5621	1.9496	2.7319	3.1261
	30	-2.1572	-1.4267	-0.6783	-0.2983	0.0851	0.4715	0.8605	1.2520	1.6456	2.0410	2.8366	3.2363
15 Years	15	0.5379	1.0566	1.5933	1.8682	2.1474	2.4309	2.7185	3.0101	3.3058	3.6053	4.2155	4.5261
	20	0.4007	1.0186	1.6591	1.9873	2.3206	2.6589	3.0018	3.3493	3.7011	4.0570	4.7805	5.1477
	25	0.3223	0.9973	1.6951	2.0519	2.4134	2.7794	3.1496	3.5236	3.9013	4.2824	5.0534	5.4429
	30	0.2732	0.9843	1.7167	2.0899	2.4672	2.8482	3.2326	3.6200	4.0101	4.4026	5.1938	5.5919
20 Years	15	4.0328	4.5514	5.0881	5.3631	5.6423	5.9258	6.2134	6.5050	6.8006	7.1001	7.7104	8.0210
	20	2.7925	3.3463	3.9225	4.2186	4.5199	4.8262	5.1373	5.4530	5.7732	6.0978	6.7592	7.0957
	25	2.6780	3.3083	3.9644	4.3014	4.6440	4.9919	5.3448	5.7024	6.0645	6.4306	7.1744	7.5515
	30	2.6061	3.2850	3.9895	4.3502	4.7160	5.0866	5.4615	5.8403	6.2226	6.6083	7.3879	7.7814

Capitalization Rate to Account for Growth or Decline in Value

| Equity Yield 9.00% | | | | | 25% Growth over Term | | | | | Mortgage Ratio 67% | | |

| Time to | Mortgage | | | | | Mortgage Interest Rate | | | | | | | |
Sale	Term	5.50%	6.50%	7.50%	8.00%	8.50%	9.00%	9.50%	10.00%	10.50%	11.00%	12.00%	12.50%
10	15	5.3802	5.8889	6.4126	6.6798	6.9505	7.2246	7.5020	7.7826	8.0664	8.3531	8.9353	9.2306
Years	20	5.2509	5.8123	6.3892	6.6831	6.9804	7.2809	7.5845	7.8910	8.2002	8.5120	9.1428	9.4615
	25	5.1770	5.7694	6.3764	6.6849	6.9964	7.3107	7.6275	7.9467	8.2680	8.5913	9.2430	9.5712
	30	5.1307	5.7430	6.3688	6.6860	7.0057	7.3277	7.6516	7.9774	8.3048	8.6336	9.2946	9.6265
12	15	5.8810	6.3583	6.8512	7.1034	7.3592	7.6186	7.8815	8.1479	8.4176	8.6906	9.2461	9.5284
Years	20	5.7169	6.2569	6.8140	7.0987	7.3872	7.6793	7.9750	8.2739	8.5761	8.8812	9.4998	9.8130
	25	5.6232	6.2000	6.7936	7.0962	7.4022	7.7114	8.0237	8.3387	8.6563	8.9763	9.6224	9.9483
	30	5.5644	6.1651	6.7815	7.0947	7.4109	7.7298	8.0511	8.3745	8.6999	9.0270	9.6855	10.0165
15	15	6.4146	6.8468	7.2940	7.5232	7.7559	7.9921	8.2317	8.4748	8.7211	8.9707	9.4793	9.7381
Years	20	6.1987	6.7077	7.2355	7.5061	7.7810	8.0599	8.3427	8.6294	8.9197	9.2134	9.8106	10.1137
	25	6.0754	6.6298	7.2034	7.4969	7.7944	8.0957	8.4006	8.7089	9.0202	9.3344	9.9706	10.2921
	30	5.9981	6.5820	7.1843	7.4914	7.8022	8.1162	8.4331	8.7528	9.0748	9.3990	10.0529	10.3821
20	15	7.7449	8.1771	8.6243	8.8535	9.0862	9.3224	9.5620	9.8051	10.0514	10.3010	10.8096	11.0684
Years	20	6.7113	7.1728	7.6530	7.8998	8.1508	8.4060	8.6653	8.9284	9.1953	9.4657	10.0169	10.2974
	25	6.5399	7.0596	7.6007	7.8788	8.1615	8.4486	8.7399	9.0352	9.3341	9.6366	10.2510	10.5626
	30	6.4323	6.9902	7.5695	7.8664	8.1677	8.4729	8.7819	9.0942	9.4095	9.7277	10.3714	10.6964

Equity Yield 9.00%					25% Growth over Term					Mortgage Ratio 70%		
10	15	5.2815	5.8157	6.3655	6.6461	6.9303	7.2181	7.5094	7.8040	8.1020	8.4031	9.0144	9.3244
Years	20	5.1457	5.7352	6.3410	6.6496	6.9617	7.2772	7.5960	7.9178	8.2425	8.5699	9.2322	9.5668
	25	5.0682	5.6901	6.3275	6.6514	6.9785	7.3085	7.6411	7.9763	8.3137	8.6531	9.3375	9.6820
	30	5.0195	5.6624	6.3195	6.6525	6.9882	7.3263	7.6665	8.0086	8.3523	8.6975	9.3916	9.7401
12	15	5.7872	6.2883	6.8059	7.0706	7.3392	7.6116	7.8876	8.1673	8.4506	8.7372	9.3205	9.6169
Years	20	5.6149	6.1818	6.7668	7.0657	7.3686	7.6754	7.9858	8.2997	8.6169	8.9373	9.5869	9.9158
	25	5.5164	6.1221	6.7454	7.0630	7.3844	7.7091	8.0369	8.3677	8.7012	9.0371	9.7156	10.0577
	30	5.4547	6.0855	6.7326	7.0615	7.3935	7.7283	8.0657	8.4053	8.7470	9.0904	9.7818	10.1294
15	15	6.3279	6.7817	7.2513	7.4919	7.7362	7.9842	8.2359	8.4911	8.7498	9.0118	9.5458	9.8176
Years	20	6.1012	6.6357	7.1899	7.4740	7.7626	8.0555	8.3525	8.6534	8.9582	9.2666	9.8937	10.2120
	25	5.9718	6.5539	7.1562	7.4643	7.7767	8.0931	8.4132	8.7369	9.0638	9.3937	10.0617	10.3993
	30	5.8906	6.5037	7.1361	7.4586	7.7849	8.1146	8.4474	8.7830	9.1211	9.4615	10.1481	10.4938
20	15	7.7066	8.1604	8.6300	8.8706	9.1149	9.3629	9.6146	9.8698	10.1284	10.3905	10.9245	11.1963
Years	20	6.6213	7.1059	7.6101	7.8692	8.1328	8.4008	8.6730	8.9493	9.2295	9.5135	10.0922	10.3867
	25	6.4413	6.9870	7.5552	7.8472	8.1440	8.4455	8.7513	9.0614	9.3753	9.6928	10.3380	10.6652
	30	6.3284	6.9141	7.5225	7.8342	8.1505	8.4710	8.7954	9.1233	9.4544	9.7885	10.4644	10.8057

Equity Yield 9.00%					25% Growth over Term					Mortgage Ratio 75%		
10	15	5.1334	5.7057	6.2949	6.5955	6.9000	7.2084	7.5205	7.8362	8.1554	8.4779	9.1329	9.4651
Years	20	4.9880	5.6195	6.2686	6.5992	6.9336	7.2717	7.6132	7.9580	8.3059	8.6567	9.3664	9.7249
	25	4.9049	5.5712	6.2542	6.6012	6.9516	7.3052	7.6616	8.0207	8.3822	8.7459	9.4791	9.8483
	30	4.8527	5.5416	6.2456	6.6024	6.9621	7.3243	7.6888	8.0553	8.4236	8.7934	9.5371	9.9105
12	15	5.6463	6.1833	6.7378	7.0214	7.3092	7.6011	7.8969	8.1965	8.5000	8.8071	9.4320	9.7496
Years	20	5.4617	6.0691	6.6960	7.0162	7.3407	7.6694	8.0020	8.3383	8.6782	9.0215	9.7175	10.0698
	25	5.3563	6.0052	6.6730	7.0134	7.3576	7.7055	8.0568	8.4112	8.7685	9.1284	9.8554	10.2220
	30	5.2901	5.9659	6.6593	7.0117	7.3674	7.7261	8.0876	8.4515	8.8175	9.1855	9.9263	10.2987
15	15	6.1979	6.6841	7.1872	7.4450	7.7068	7.9725	8.2421	8.5156	8.7927	9.0735	9.6456	9.9368
Years	20	5.9550	6.5276	7.1214	7.4258	7.7350	8.0488	8.3670	8.6895	9.0160	9.3465	10.0183	10.3594
	25	5.8163	6.4399	7.0853	7.4154	7.7501	8.0891	8.4321	8.7789	9.1292	9.4826	10.1983	10.5601
	30	5.7293	6.3862	7.0638	7.4093	7.7589	8.1121	8.4687	8.8283	9.1906	9.5553	10.2909	10.6613
20	15	7.6491	8.1353	8.6385	8.8962	9.1580	9.4238	9.6934	9.9668	10.2439	10.5247	11.0969	11.3881
Years	20	6.4863	7.0055	7.5457	7.8233	8.1058	8.3929	8.6845	8.9805	9.2808	9.5850	10.2051	10.5206
	25	6.2934	6.8781	7.4869	7.7997	8.1178	8.4408	8.7685	9.1006	9.4370	9.7772	10.4685	10.8190
	30	6.1724	6.8000	7.4518	7.7858	8.1247	8.4681	8.8157	9.1670	9.5218	9.8798	10.6039	10.9696

Equity Yield 9.00%					25% Growth over Term					Mortgage Ratio 80%		
10	15	4.9853	5.5958	6.2242	6.5449	6.8697	7.1987	7.5315	7.8683	8.2087	8.5528	9.2515	9.6058
Years	20	4.8302	5.5039	6.1962	6.5489	6.9056	7.2662	7.6305	7.9983	8.3693	8.7435	9.5005	9.8829
	25	4.7416	5.4523	6.1808	6.5510	6.9248	7.3019	7.6821	8.0651	8.4507	8.8386	9.6207	10.0145
	30	4.6859	5.4207	6.1716	6.5523	6.9359	7.3223	7.7111	8.1020	8.4949	8.8894	9.6826	10.0809
12	15	5.5055	6.0783	6.6697	6.9723	7.2793	7.5905	7.9061	8.2257	8.5494	8.8770	9.5436	9.8823
Years	20	5.3086	5.9565	6.6251	6.9667	7.3129	7.6634	8.0182	8.3770	8.7395	9.1057	9.8481	10.2239
	25	5.1961	5.8883	6.6006	6.9637	7.3309	7.7020	8.0767	8.4547	8.8358	9.2198	9.9952	10.3862
	30	5.1256	5.8464	6.5860	6.9619	7.3413	7.7240	8.1095	8.4977	8.8881	9.2806	10.0708	10.4680
15	15	6.0678	6.5864	7.1231	7.3981	7.6773	7.9608	8.2484	8.5400	8.8356	9.1351	9.7454	10.0560
Years	20	5.8088	6.4196	7.0529	7.3776	7.7074	8.0422	8.3816	8.7256	9.0739	9.4263	10.1430	10.5067
	25	5.6608	6.3260	7.0144	7.3666	7.7236	8.0852	8.4510	8.8209	9.1945	9.5716	10.3350	10.7209
	30	5.5680	6.2687	6.9914	7.3600	7.7329	8.1097	8.4901	8.8736	9.2601	9.6491	10.4337	10.8289
20	15	7.5916	8.1103	8.6469	8.9219	9.2011	9.4846	9.7722	10.0638	10.3594	10.6590	11.2692	11.5798
Years	20	6.3513	6.9051	7.4813	7.7774	8.0787	8.3850	8.6961	9.0118	9.3321	9.6566	10.3180	10.6546
	25	6.1456	6.7692	7.4186	7.7523	8.0915	8.4361	8.7856	9.1399	9.4987	9.8616	10.5990	10.9729
	30	6.0165	6.6859	7.3812	7.7375	8.0989	8.4652	8.8360	9.2107	9.5892	9.9710	10.7434	11.1334

Capitalization Rate to Account for Growth or Decline in Value

| Equity Yield 9.00% | | | | | 25% Decline over Term | | | | | | Mortgage Ratio 67% | | |

Time to Sale	Mortgage Term	5.50%	6.50%	7.50%	8.00%	8.50%	9.00%	9.50%	10.00%	10.50%	11.00%	12.00%	12.50%
10 Years	15	8.6712	9.1799	9.7036	9.9708	10.2415	10.5156	10.7930	11.0736	11.3574	11.6441	12.2263	12.5216
	20	8.5419	9.1033	9.6802	9.9741	10.2714	10.5719	10.8755	11.1820	11.4912	11.8030	12.4338	12.7525
	25	8.4680	9.0604	9.6674	9.9759	10.2874	10.6017	10.9185	11.2377	11.5590	11.8823	12.5340	12.8622
	30	8.4217	9.0340	9.6598	9.9770	10.2967	10.6187	10.9426	11.2684	11.5958	11.9246	12.5856	12.9175
12 Years	15	8.3636	8.8409	9.3338	9.5859	9.8417	10.1011	10.3640	10.6304	10.9002	11.1732	11.7286	12.0109
	20	8.1995	8.7394	9.2966	9.5812	9.8697	10.1619	10.4575	10.7565	11.0586	11.3637	11.9824	12.2956
	25	8.1058	8.6825	9.2762	9.5787	9.8847	10.1940	10.5062	10.8212	11.1388	11.4588	12.1050	12.4308
	30	8.0469	8.6477	9.2640	9.5772	9.8934	10.2123	10.5336	10.8570	11.1824	11.5095	12.1680	12.4990
15 Years	15	8.1175	8.5497	8.9970	9.2261	9.4588	9.6950	9.9347	10.1777	10.4241	10.6737	11.1822	11.4411
	20	7.9017	8.4107	8.9385	9.2091	9.4839	9.7628	10.0457	10.3323	10.6226	10.9163	11.5135	11.8166
	25	7.7784	8.3327	8.9064	9.1998	9.4973	9.7987	10.1036	10.4118	10.7231	11.0373	11.6735	11.9951
	30	7.7010	8.2849	8.8872	9.1944	9.5051	9.8191	10.1361	10.4557	10.7778	11.1019	11.7558	12.0851
20 Years	15	8.7222	9.1544	9.6017	9.8308	10.0635	10.2997	10.5394	10.7824	11.0288	11.2783	11.7869	12.0457
	20	7.6887	8.1501	8.6303	8.8771	9.1281	9.3834	9.6426	9.9057	10.1726	10.4431	10.9943	11.2747
	25	7.5172	8.0369	8.5781	8.8561	9.1388	9.4259	9.7172	10.0125	10.3114	10.6139	11.2283	11.5399
	30	7.4096	7.9675	8.5469	8.8438	9.1450	9.4503	9.7592	10.0715	10.3869	10.7050	11.3487	11.6737

| Equity Yield 9.00% | | | | | -25% Decline over Term | | | | | | Mortgage Ratio 70% | | |

Time to Sale	Mortgage Term	5.50%	6.50%	7.50%	8.00%	8.50%	9.00%	9.50%	10.00%	10.50%	11.00%	12.00%	12.50%
10 Years	15	8.5725	9.1067	9.6565	9.9371	10.2213	10.5091	10.8004	11.0951	11.3930	11.6941	12.3054	12.6154
	20	8.4367	9.0262	9.6320	9.9406	10.2527	10.5682	10.8870	11.2088	11.5335	11.8609	12.5232	12.8578
	25	8.3592	8.9811	9.6185	9.9424	10.2695	10.5995	10.9321	11.2673	11.6047	11.9441	12.6285	12.9730
	30	8.3105	8.9534	9.6105	9.9436	10.2792	10.6173	10.9575	11.2996	11.6433	11.9885	12.6826	13.0311
12 Years	15	8.2697	8.7708	9.2884	9.5531	9.8217	10.0941	10.3702	10.6499	10.9331	11.2197	11.8030	12.0994
	20	8.0974	8.6643	9.2493	9.5482	9.8511	10.1579	10.4683	10.7822	11.0995	11.4199	12.0694	12.3983
	25	7.9990	8.6046	9.2279	9.5456	9.8669	10.1916	10.5195	10.8502	11.1837	11.5197	12.1981	12.5403
	30	7.9372	8.5680	9.2151	9.5440	9.8760	10.2108	10.5482	10.8878	11.2295	11.5729	12.2643	12.6119
15 Years	15	8.0309	8.4847	8.9543	9.1948	9.4392	9.6872	9.9388	10.1940	10.4527	10.7148	11.2488	11.5205
	20	7.8042	8.3386	8.8928	9.1769	9.4655	9.7584	10.0554	10.3564	10.6612	10.9696	11.5966	11.9149
	25	7.6747	8.2568	8.8591	9.1672	9.4796	9.7960	10.1162	10.4398	10.7667	11.0966	11.7646	12.1023
	30	7.5935	8.2066	8.8390	9.1615	9.4878	9.8175	10.1503	10.4859	10.8241	11.1645	11.8510	12.1968
20 Years	15	8.6839	9.1377	9.6073	9.8479	10.0922	10.3402	10.5919	10.8471	11.1058	11.3678	11.9018	12.1736
	20	7.5987	8.0832	8.5874	8.8465	9.1101	9.3781	9.6503	9.9266	10.2068	10.4908	11.0695	11.3640
	25	7.4186	7.9643	8.5325	8.8245	9.1213	9.4228	9.7287	10.0387	10.3526	10.6701	11.3153	11.6425
	30	7.3057	7.8914	8.4998	8.8115	9.1278	9.4483	9.7727	10.1006	10.4318	10.7659	11.4417	11.7830

| Equity Yield 9.00% | | | | | -25% Decline over Term | | | | | | Mortgage Ratio 75% | | |

Time to Sale	Mortgage Term	5.50%	6.50%	7.50%	8.00%	8.50%	9.00%	9.50%	10.00%	10.50%	11.00%	12.00%	12.50%
10 Years	15	8.4244	8.9968	9.5859	9.8865	10.1910	10.4994	10.8115	11.1272	11.4464	11.7690	12.4239	12.7561
	20	8.2790	8.9105	9.5596	9.8902	10.2247	10.5627	10.9042	11.2490	11.5969	11.9477	12.6574	13.0159
	25	8.1959	8.8622	9.5452	9.8922	10.2426	10.5962	10.9526	11.3117	11.6732	12.0369	12.7701	13.1393
	30	8.1437	8.8326	9.5366	9.8934	10.2531	10.6153	10.9798	11.3463	11.7146	12.0845	12.8281	13.2015
12 Years	15	8.1289	8.6658	9.2203	9.5040	9.7918	10.0836	10.3794	10.6791	10.9825	11.2896	11.9145	12.2321
	20	7.9443	8.5517	9.1785	9.4987	9.8233	10.1519	10.4845	10.8209	11.1608	11.5040	12.2000	12.5524
	25	7.8388	8.4877	9.1555	9.4959	9.8401	10.1880	10.5393	10.8937	11.2510	11.6110	12.3379	12.7045
	30	7.7727	8.4485	9.1418	9.4942	9.8499	10.2087	10.5701	10.9340	11.3001	11.6680	12.4088	12.7812
15 Years	15	7.9008	8.3870	8.8902	9.1479	9.4097	9.6755	9.9451	10.2185	10.4956	10.7764	11.3486	11.6398
	20	7.6580	8.2306	8.8244	9.1288	9.4380	9.7517	10.0700	10.3924	10.7190	11.0494	11.7213	12.0623
	25	7.5192	8.1429	8.7883	9.1184	9.4531	9.7921	10.1351	10.4818	10.8321	11.1856	11.9013	12.2630
	30	7.4322	8.0891	8.7667	9.1123	9.4618	9.8151	10.1717	10.5313	10.8935	11.2582	11.9938	12.3643
20 Years	15	8.6264	9.1126	9.6158	9.8735	10.1353	10.4011	10.6707	10.9441	11.2213	11.5020	12.0742	12.3654
	20	7.4637	7.9828	8.5230	8.8006	9.0831	9.3702	9.6619	9.9579	10.2581	10.5624	11.1825	11.4979
	25	7.2708	7.8554	8.4642	8.7770	9.0951	9.4181	9.7458	10.0780	10.4143	10.7545	11.4458	11.7963
	30	7.1498	7.7773	8.4291	8.7632	9.1020	9.4454	9.7930	10.1443	10.4991	10.8571	11.5812	11.9469

| Equity Yield 9.00% | | | | | -25% Decline over Term | | | | | | Mortgage Ratio 80% | | |

Time to Sale	Mortgage Term	5.50%	6.50%	7.50%	8.00%	8.50%	9.00%	9.50%	10.00%	10.50%	11.00%	12.00%	12.50%
10 Years	15	8.2763	8.8868	9.5152	9.8359	10.1607	10.4897	10.8225	11.1593	11.4997	11.8439	12.5425	12.8968
	20	8.1212	8.7949	9.4872	9.8399	10.1966	10.5572	10.9215	11.2893	11.6603	12.0345	12.7915	13.1739
	25	8.0326	8.7433	9.4718	9.8420	10.2158	10.5929	10.9731	11.3561	11.7417	12.1296	12.9118	13.3055
	30	7.9770	8.7117	9.4626	9.8433	10.2269	10.6133	11.0021	11.3930	11.7859	12.1804	12.9736	13.3719
12 Years	15	7.9880	8.5608	9.1523	9.4548	9.7618	10.0731	10.3886	10.7082	11.0319	11.3595	12.0261	12.3648
	20	7.7911	8.4390	9.1076	9.4492	9.7954	10.1460	10.5007	10.8595	11.2221	11.5882	12.3306	12.7064
	25	7.6786	8.3708	9.0832	9.4462	9.8134	10.1845	10.5592	10.9372	11.3184	11.7023	12.4777	12.8687
	30	7.6081	8.3289	9.0685	9.4444	9.8238	10.2065	10.5921	10.9802	11.3707	11.7632	12.5533	12.9506
15 Years	15	7.7708	8.2894	8.8261	9.1010	9.3803	9.6637	9.9513	10.2430	10.5386	10.8381	11.4484	11.7590
	20	7.5117	8.1225	8.7559	9.0806	9.4104	9.7451	10.0845	10.4285	10.7768	11.1293	11.8459	12.2097
	25	7.3638	8.0290	8.7174	9.0695	9.4265	9.7881	10.1540	10.5239	10.8975	11.2745	12.0379	12.4238
	30	7.2709	7.9716	8.6944	9.0630	9.4359	9.8127	10.1930	10.5766	10.9630	11.3520	12.1367	12.5318
20 Years	15	8.5689	9.0876	9.6243	9.8992	10.1784	10.4619	10.7495	11.0412	11.3368	11.6363	12.2466	12.5572
	20	7.3287	7.8824	8.4586	8.7548	9.0560	9.3623	9.6734	9.9892	10.3094	10.6340	11.2954	11.6319
	25	7.1229	7.7466	8.3960	8.7296	9.0688	9.4134	9.7630	10.1172	10.4760	10.8389	11.5763	11.9502
	30	6.9938	7.6632	8.3585	8.7148	9.0763	9.4426	9.8133	10.1880	10.5665	10.9483	11.7207	12.1108

Capitalization Rate to Account for Growth or Decline in Value

Equity Yield 9.00%				50% Growth over Term						Mortgage Ratio 67%		

Time to Sale	Mortgage Term	5.50%	6.50%	7.50%	8.00%	Mortgage Interest Rate 8.50%	9.00%	9.50%	10.00%	10.50%	11.00%	12.00%	12.50%
10 Years	15	3.7347	4.2434	4.7671	5.0343	5.3050	5.5791	5.8565	6.1371	6.4209	6.7076	7.2898	7.5851
	20	3.6054	4.1668	4.7437	5.0376	5.3349	5.6354	5.9390	6.2455	6.5547	6.8665	7.4973	7.8160
	25	3.5315	4.1238	4.7309	5.0394	5.3509	5.6652	5.9820	6.3012	6.6225	6.9458	7.5975	7.9257
	30	3.4852	4.0975	4.7233	5.0405	5.3602	5.6822	6.0061	6.3319	6.6593	6.9881	7.6491	7.9810
12 Years	15	4.6398	5.1171	5.6100	5.8621	6.1179	6.3773	6.6402	6.9066	7.1764	7.4494	8.0048	8.2871
	20	4.4757	5.0156	5.5728	5.8574	6.1459	6.4381	6.7337	7.0327	7.3348	7.6399	8.2586	8.5718
	25	4.3820	4.9587	5.5524	5.8549	6.1609	6.4702	6.7824	7.0974	7.4150	7.7350	8.3812	8.7070
	30	4.3231	4.9239	5.5402	5.8534	6.1696	6.4885	6.8098	7.1333	7.4586	7.7857	8.4442	8.7752
15 Years	15	5.5631	5.9953	6.4426	6.6717	6.9044	7.1406	7.3803	7.6233	7.8697	8.1192	8.6278	8.8866
	20	5.3473	5.8563	6.3841	6.6546	6.9295	7.2084	7.4913	7.7779	8.0682	8.3619	8.9591	9.2622
	25	5.2240	5.7783	6.3520	6.6454	6.9429	7.2442	7.5491	7.8574	8.1687	8.4829	9.1191	9.4407
	30	5.1466	5.7305	6.3328	6.6400	6.9507	7.2647	7.5817	7.9013	8.2233	8.5475	9.2014	9.5307
20 Years	15	7.2562	7.6884	8.1357	8.3648	8.5975	8.8337	9.0734	9.3164	9.5628	9.8124	10.3209	10.5798
	20	6.2227	6.6842	7.1643	7.4111	7.6622	7.9174	8.1766	8.4398	8.7066	8.9771	9.5283	9.8087
	25	6.0512	6.5709	7.1121	7.3901	7.6728	7.9600	8.2513	8.5465	8.8455	9.1479	9.7624	10.0740
	30	5.9436	6.5015	7.0809	7.3778	7.6790	7.9843	8.2932	8.6055	8.9209	9.2391	9.8827	10.2078

Equity Yield 9.00%				50% Growth over Term						Mortgage Ratio 70%		

Time to Sale	Mortgage Term	5.50%	6.50%	7.50%	8.00%	8.50%	9.00%	9.50%	10.00%	10.50%	11.00%	12.00%	12.50%
10 Years	15	3.6360	4.1702	4.7200	5.0006	5.2848	5.5726	5.8639	6.1585	6.4565	6.7576	7.3689	7.6789
	20	3.5002	4.0897	4.6955	5.0041	5.3162	5.6317	5.9505	6.2723	6.5970	6.9244	7.5867	7.9213
	25	3.4227	4.0446	4.6820	5.0059	5.3330	5.6630	5.9956	6.3308	6.6682	7.0076	7.6920	8.0365
	30	3.3740	4.0169	4.6740	5.0070	5.3427	5.6808	6.0210	6.3631	6.7068	7.0520	7.7461	8.0946
12 Years	15	4.5459	5.0470	5.5646	5.8293	6.0979	6.3703	6.6464	6.9261	7.2093	7.4959	8.0792	8.3756
	20	4.3736	4.9405	5.5255	5.8244	6.1273	6.4341	6.7445	7.0584	7.3757	7.6961	8.3456	8.6745
	25	4.2752	4.8808	5.5041	5.8218	6.1431	6.4678	6.7957	7.1264	7.4599	7.7959	8.4743	8.8165
	30	4.2134	4.8442	5.4913	5.8202	6.1522	6.4870	6.8244	7.1640	7.5057	7.8491	8.5405	8.8881
15 Years	15	5.4764	5.9302	6.3998	6.6404	6.8847	7.1328	7.3844	7.6396	7.8983	8.1603	8.6943	8.9661
	20	5.2498	5.7842	6.3384	6.6225	6.9111	7.2040	7.5010	7.8020	8.1067	8.4151	9.0422	9.3605
	25	5.1203	5.7024	6.3047	6.6128	6.9252	7.2416	7.5618	7.8854	8.2123	8.5422	9.2102	9.5478
	30	5.0391	5.6522	6.2846	6.6071	6.9334	7.2631	7.5959	7.9315	8.2697	8.6100	9.2966	9.6423
20 Years	15	7.2179	7.6717	8.1413	8.3819	8.6262	8.8743	9.1259	9.3811	9.6398	9.9018	10.4358	10.7076
	20	6.1327	6.6172	7.1214	7.3805	7.6441	7.9121	8.1843	8.4606	8.7408	9.0248	9.6035	9.8980
	25	5.9526	6.4983	7.0666	7.3585	7.6553	7.9568	8.2627	8.5727	8.8866	9.2042	9.8493	10.1765
	30	5.8397	6.4254	7.0338	7.3455	7.6618	7.9823	8.3067	8.6346	8.9658	9.2999	9.9757	10.3170

Equity Yield 9.00%				50% Growth over Term						Mortgage Ratio 75%		

Time to Sale	Mortgage Term	5.50%	6.50%	7.50%	8.00%	8.50%	9.00%	9.50%	10.00%	10.50%	11.00%	12.00%	12.50%
10 Years	15	3.4879	4.0602	4.6494	4.9500	5.2545	5.5629	5.8750	6.1907	6.5099	6.8324	7.4874	7.8196
	20	3.3424	3.9740	4.6231	4.9537	5.2881	5.6262	5.9677	6.3125	6.6604	7.0112	7.7208	8.0794
	25	3.2594	3.9257	4.6087	4.9557	5.3061	5.6597	6.0161	6.3752	6.7367	7.1004	7.8336	8.2028
	30	3.2072	3.8961	4.6001	4.9569	5.3166	5.6788	6.0433	6.4098	6.7781	7.1479	7.8916	8.2650
12 Years	15	4.4051	4.9420	5.4965	5.7802	6.0680	6.3598	6.6556	6.9553	7.2587	7.5658	8.1907	8.5083
	20	4.2205	4.8279	5.4547	5.7749	6.0995	6.4281	6.7607	7.0971	7.4370	7.7802	8.4762	8.8286
	25	4.1150	4.7639	5.4317	5.7721	6.1163	6.4642	6.8155	7.1699	7.5272	7.8872	8.6141	8.9807
	30	4.0489	4.7247	5.4180	5.7704	6.1261	6.4849	6.8463	7.2102	7.5763	7.9442	8.6850	9.0574
15 Years	15	5.3464	5.8326	6.3358	6.5935	6.8553	7.1210	7.3907	7.6641	7.9412	8.2220	8.7942	9.0853
	20	5.1035	5.6762	6.2699	6.5743	6.8835	7.1973	7.5156	7.8380	8.1646	8.4950	9.1668	9.5079
	25	4.9648	5.5885	6.2338	6.5640	6.8987	7.2376	7.5807	7.9274	8.2777	8.6312	9.3469	9.7086
	30	4.8778	5.5347	6.2123	6.5578	6.9074	7.2607	7.6173	7.9768	8.3391	8.7038	9.4394	9.8099
20 Years	15	7.1604	7.6467	8.1498	8.4076	8.6693	8.9351	9.2047	9.4781	9.7553	10.0361	10.6082	10.8994
	20	5.9977	6.5168	7.0570	7.3347	7.6171	7.9042	8.1959	8.4919	8.7921	9.0964	9.7165	10.0320
	25	5.8048	6.3895	6.9983	7.3111	7.6291	7.9521	8.2798	8.6120	8.9483	9.2886	9.9798	10.3304
	30	5.6838	6.3113	6.9632	7.2972	7.6361	7.9795	8.3270	8.6783	9.0332	9.3911	10.1152	10.4809

Equity Yield 9.00%				50% Growth over Term						Mortgage Ratio 80%		

Time to Sale	Mortgage Term	5.50%	6.50%	7.50%	8.00%	8.50%	9.00%	9.50%	10.00%	10.50%	11.00%	12.00%	12.50%
10 Years	15	3.3398	3.9503	4.5787	4.8994	5.2242	5.5532	5.8860	6.2228	6.5632	6.9073	7.6060	7.9603
	20	3.1847	3.8584	4.5507	4.9034	5.2601	5.6207	5.9850	6.3528	6.7238	7.0980	7.8550	8.2374
	25	3.0960	3.8068	4.5353	4.9055	5.2793	5.6564	6.0366	6.4196	6.8052	7.1931	7.9752	8.3690
	30	3.0404	3.7752	4.5261	4.9068	5.2904	5.6768	6.0656	6.4565	6.8494	7.2439	8.0371	8.4354
12 Years	15	4.2642	4.8370	5.4285	5.7310	6.0380	6.3493	6.6648	6.9844	7.3081	7.6357	8.3023	8.6410
	20	4.0673	4.7152	5.3838	5.7254	6.0716	6.4222	6.7769	7.1357	7.4983	7.8644	8.6068	8.9826
	25	3.9548	4.6470	5.3594	5.7224	6.0896	6.4607	6.8354	7.2134	7.5946	7.9785	8.7539	9.1449
	30	3.8843	4.6051	5.3447	5.7206	6.1000	6.4827	6.8683	7.2564	7.6469	8.0394	8.8295	9.2268
15 Years	15	5.2163	5.7350	6.2717	6.5466	6.8258	7.1093	7.3969	7.6886	7.9842	8.2837	8.8940	9.2046
	20	4.9573	5.5681	6.2015	6.5262	6.8560	7.1907	7.5301	7.8741	8.2224	8.5749	9.2915	9.6553
	25	4.8093	5.4746	6.1630	6.5151	6.8721	7.2337	7.5996	7.9694	8.3431	8.7201	9.4835	9.8694
	30	4.7165	5.4172	6.1400	6.5086	6.8814	7.2582	7.6386	8.0222	8.4086	8.7976	9.5823	9.9774
20 Years	15	7.1030	7.6216	8.1583	8.4332	8.7125	8.9959	9.2835	9.5752	9.8708	10.1703	10.7806	11.0912
	20	5.8627	6.4165	6.9927	7.2888	7.5901	7.8963	8.2074	8.5232	8.8434	9.1680	9.8294	10.1659
	25	5.6569	6.2806	6.9300	7.2636	7.6029	7.9474	8.2970	8.6513	9.0100	9.3729	10.1103	10.4842
	30	5.5278	6.1973	6.8925	7.2488	7.6103	7.9766	8.3473	8.7221	9.1005	9.4823	10.2547	10.6448

Capitalization Rate to Account for Growth or Decline in Value

| Equity Yield 9.00% | | | | | 50% Decline over Term | | | | | | Mortgage Ratio 67% | |

Time to Sale	Mortgage Term	5.50%	6.50%	7.50%	8.00%	8.50%	9.00%	9.50%	10.00%	10.50%	11.00%	12.00%	12.50%
10 Years	15	10.3167	10.8254	11.3491	11.6163	11.8870	12.1611	12.4385	12.7191	13.0029	13.2896	13.8718	14.1671
	20	10.1874	10.7488	11.3258	11.6196	11.9169	12.2174	12.5210	12.8275	13.1367	13.4485	14.0793	14.3980
	25	10.1135	10.7059	11.3129	11.6214	11.9329	12.2472	12.5640	12.8832	13.2045	13.5278	14.1795	14.5077
	30	10.0672	10.6795	11.3053	11.6225	11.9422	12.2642	12.5882	12.9139	13.2413	13.5701	14.2311	14.5630
12 Years	15	9.6048	10.0821	10.5750	10.8272	11.0830	11.3424	11.6053	11.8717	12.1414	12.4144	12.9699	13.2522
	20	9.4407	9.9807	10.5378	10.8225	11.1110	11.4031	11.6988	11.9977	12.2999	12.6050	13.2236	13.5368
	25	9.3470	9.9238	10.5174	10.8200	11.1260	11.4352	11.7475	12.0625	12.3801	12.7001	13.3462	13.6721
	30	9.2882	9.8889	10.5053	10.8185	11.1347	11.4536	11.7749	12.0983	12.4237	12.7508	13.4093	13.7403
15 Years	15	8.9690	9.4012	9.8485	10.0776	10.3103	10.5465	10.7861	11.0292	11.2755	11.5251	12.0337	12.2925
	20	8.7532	9.2622	9.7900	10.0605	10.3354	10.6143	10.8972	11.1838	11.4741	11.7678	12.3650	12.6681
	25	8.6298	9.1842	9.7579	10.0513	10.3488	10.6501	10.9550	11.2633	11.5746	11.8888	12.5250	12.8465
	30	8.5525	9.1364	9.7387	10.0459	10.3566	10.6706	10.9876	11.3072	11.6292	11.9534	12.6073	12.9366
20 Years	15	9.2109	9.6431	10.0903	10.3194	10.5521	10.7884	11.0280	11.2711	11.5174	11.7670	12.2756	12.5344
	20	8.1773	8.6388	9.1190	9.3657	9.6168	9.8720	10.1313	10.3944	10.6613	10.9317	11.4829	11.7633
	25	8.0059	8.5256	9.0667	9.3448	9.6275	9.9146	10.2059	10.5011	10.8001	11.1025	11.7170	12.0286
	30	7.8983	8.4561	9.0355	9.3324	9.6337	9.9389	10.2478	10.5601	10.8755	11.1937	11.8374	12.1624

| Equity Yield 9.00% | | | | | -50% Decline over Term | | | | | | Mortgage Ratio 70% | |

Time to Sale	Mortgage Term	5.50%	6.50%	7.50%	8.00%	8.50%	9.00%	9.50%	10.00%	10.50%	11.00%	12.00%	12.50%
10 Years	15	10.2180	10.7522	11.3020	11.5826	11.8668	12.1546	12.4459	12.7406	13.0385	13.3396	13.9509	14.2609
	20	10.0822	10.6717	11.2775	11.5861	11.8982	12.2137	12.5325	12.8543	13.1790	13.5064	14.1687	14.5033
	25	10.0047	10.6266	11.2640	11.5879	11.9150	12.2450	12.5776	12.9128	13.2502	13.5896	14.2740	14.6185
	30	9.9560	10.5990	11.2560	11.5891	11.9248	12.2628	12.6030	12.9451	13.2888	13.6340	14.3281	14.6766
12 Years	15	9.5110	10.0121	10.5297	10.7944	11.0630	11.3354	11.6114	11.8911	12.1744	12.4610	13.0443	13.3407
	20	9.3387	9.9056	10.4906	10.7895	11.0924	11.3992	11.7096	12.0235	12.3407	12.6611	13.3107	13.6396
	25	9.2402	9.8459	10.4692	10.7868	11.1082	11.4329	11.7607	12.0915	12.4250	12.7609	13.4394	13.7815
	30	9.1785	9.8093	10.4564	10.7853	11.1173	11.4521	11.7895	12.1291	12.4708	12.8142	13.5056	13.8532
15 Years	15	8.8823	9.3361	9.8057	10.0463	10.2906	10.5387	10.7903	11.0455	11.3042	11.5662	12.1002	12.3720
	20	8.6557	9.1901	9.7443	10.0284	10.3170	10.6099	10.9069	11.2079	11.5126	11.8210	12.4481	12.7664
	25	8.5262	9.1083	9.7106	10.0187	10.3311	10.6475	10.9676	11.2913	11.6182	11.9481	12.6161	12.9537
	30	8.4450	9.0581	9.6905	10.0130	10.3393	10.6690	11.0018	11.3374	11.6755	12.0159	12.7025	13.0482
20 Years	15	9.1726	9.6264	10.0960	10.3365	10.5809	10.8289	11.0806	11.3358	11.5944	11.8565	12.3905	12.6623
	20	8.0873	8.5719	9.0761	9.3352	9.5988	9.8668	10.1390	10.4153	10.6955	10.9795	11.5582	11.8527
	25	7.9073	8.4530	9.0212	9.3131	9.6100	9.9115	10.2173	10.5273	10.8412	11.1588	11.8040	12.1312
	30	7.7943	8.3801	8.9884	9.3002	9.6165	9.9370	10.2614	10.5893	10.9204	11.2545	11.9304	12.2717

| Equity Yield 9.00% | | | | | -50% Decline over Term | | | | | | Mortgage Ratio 75% | |

Time to Sale	Mortgage Term	5.50%	6.50%	7.50%	8.00%	8.50%	9.00%	9.50%	10.00%	10.50%	11.00%	12.00%	12.50%
10 Years	15	10.0699	10.6423	11.2314	11.5320	11.8365	12.1449	12.4570	12.7727	13.0919	13.4145	14.0694	14.4016
	20	9.9245	10.5560	11.2051	11.5357	11.8702	12.2082	12.5498	12.8945	13.2424	13.5932	14.3029	14.6614
	25	9.8414	10.5077	11.1907	11.5377	11.8882	12.2417	12.5981	12.9572	13.3187	13.6824	14.4156	14.7848
	30	9.7892	10.4781	11.1821	11.5389	11.8986	12.2608	12.6253	12.9918	13.3601	13.7300	14.4736	14.8470
12 Years	15	9.3701	9.9071	10.4616	10.7452	11.0330	11.3249	11.6207	11.9203	12.2238	12.5309	13.1558	13.4734
	20	9.1855	9.7929	10.4198	10.7400	11.0645	11.3932	11.7258	12.0621	12.4020	12.7453	13.4413	13.7936
	25	9.0801	9.7290	10.3968	10.7372	11.0814	11.4293	11.7806	12.1350	12.4923	12.8522	13.5792	13.9458
	30	9.0139	9.6897	10.3831	10.7355	11.0912	11.4499	11.8114	12.1753	12.5413	12.9093	13.6501	14.0225
15 Years	15	8.7523	9.2385	9.7416	9.9994	10.2612	10.5269	10.7966	11.0700	11.3471	11.6279	12.2000	12.4912
	20	8.5094	9.0821	9.6758	9.9802	10.2894	10.6032	10.9214	11.2439	11.5705	11.9009	12.5727	12.9138
	25	8.3707	8.9944	9.6397	9.9698	10.3045	10.6435	10.9865	11.3333	11.6836	12.0371	12.7527	13.1145
	30	8.2837	8.9406	9.6182	9.9637	10.3133	10.6666	11.0231	11.3827	11.7450	12.1097	12.8453	13.2158
20 Years	15	9.1151	9.6013	10.1044	10.3622	10.6240	10.8897	11.1594	11.4328	11.7099	11.9907	12.5629	12.8540
	20	7.9523	8.4715	9.0117	9.2893	9.5717	9.8589	10.1505	10.4465	10.7468	11.0510	11.6711	11.9866
	25	7.7594	8.3441	8.9529	9.2657	9.5837	9.9068	10.2345	10.5666	10.9030	11.2432	11.9345	12.2850
	30	7.6384	8.2660	8.9178	9.2518	9.5907	9.9341	10.2817	10.6330	10.9878	11.3457	12.0699	12.4355

| Equity Yield 9.00% | | | | | -50% Decline over Term | | | | | | Mortgage Ratio 80% | |

Time to Sale	Mortgage Term	5.50%	6.50%	7.50%	8.00%	8.50%	9.00%	9.50%	10.00%	10.50%	11.00%	12.00%	12.50%
10 Years	15	9.9218	10.5323	11.1607	11.4814	11.8063	12.1352	12.4680	12.8048	13.1452	13.4894	14.1880	14.5423
	20	9.7667	10.4404	11.1327	11.4854	11.8421	12.2027	12.5670	12.9348	13.3059	13.6800	14.4370	14.8194
	25	9.6781	10.3888	11.1173	11.4875	11.8613	12.2384	12.6186	13.0016	13.3872	13.7751	14.5573	14.9510
	30	9.6225	10.3572	11.1081	11.4888	11.8724	12.2588	12.6476	13.0385	13.4314	13.8259	14.6191	15.0174
12 Years	15	9.2293	9.8020	10.3935	10.6961	11.0030	11.3143	11.6299	11.9495	12.2732	12.6008	13.2674	13.6061
	20	9.0324	9.6803	10.3489	10.6905	11.0367	11.3872	11.7420	12.1008	12.4633	12.8295	13.5719	13.9477
	25	8.9199	9.6121	10.3244	10.6875	11.0547	11.4258	11.8005	12.1785	12.5596	12.9436	13.7190	14.1100
	30	8.8494	9.5702	10.3098	10.6857	11.0651	11.4478	11.8333	12.2215	12.6119	13.0044	13.7946	14.1918
15 Years	15	8.6222	9.1409	9.6776	9.9525	10.2317	10.5152	10.8028	11.0944	11.3901	11.6896	12.2998	12.6104
	20	8.3632	8.9740	9.6074	9.9321	10.2619	10.5966	10.9360	11.2800	11.6283	11.9808	12.6974	13.0612
	25	8.2152	8.8805	9.5688	9.9210	10.2780	10.6396	11.0055	11.3753	11.7489	12.1260	12.8894	13.2753
	30	8.1224	8.8231	9.5459	9.9144	10.2873	10.6641	11.0445	11.4280	11.8145	12.2035	12.9881	13.3833
20 Years	15	9.0576	9.5762	10.1129	10.3879	10.6671	10.9506	11.2382	11.5298	11.8254	12.1249	12.7352	13.0458
	20	7.8173	8.3711	8.9473	9.2434	9.5447	9.8510	10.1621	10.4778	10.7981	11.1226	11.7840	12.1206
	25	7.6116	8.2352	8.8846	9.2183	9.5575	9.9021	10.2516	10.6059	10.9647	11.3276	12.0649	12.4389
	30	7.4825	8.1519	8.8472	9.2035	9.5649	9.9312	10.3019	10.6767	11.0552	11.4370	12.2094	12.5994

Capitalization Rate to Account for Growth or Decline in Value

Equity Yield 9.00%					67% Growth over Term						Mortgage Ratio 67%	

Time to Sale	Mortgage Term					Mortgage Interest Rate							
		5.50%	6.50%	7.50%	8.00%	8.50%	9.00%	9.50%	10.00%	10.50%	11.00%	12.00%	12.50%
10 Years	15	2.6377	3.1464	3.6701	3.9373	4.2080	4.4821	4.7595	5.0401	5.3239	5.6106	6.1928	6.4881
	20	2.5084	3.0698	3.6467	3.9406	4.2379	4.5384	4.8420	5.1485	5.4577	5.7695	6.4003	6.7190
	25	2.4345	3.0268	3.6339	3.9424	4.2539	4.5682	4.8850	5.2042	5.5255	5.8488	6.5005	6.8287
	30	2.3882	3.0005	3.6263	3.9435	4.2632	4.5852	4.9091	5.2349	5.5623	5.8911	6.5521	6.8840
12 Years	15	3.8123	4.2896	4.7825	5.0346	5.2904	5.5498	5.8127	6.0791	6.3488	6.6218	7.1773	7.4596
	20	3.6482	4.1881	4.7453	5.0299	5.3184	5.6105	5.9062	6.2052	6.5073	6.8124	7.4311	7.7443
	25	3.5544	4.1312	4.7249	5.0274	5.3334	5.6426	5.9549	6.2699	6.5875	6.9075	7.5536	7.8795
	30	3.4956	4.0964	4.7127	5.0259	5.3421	5.6610	5.9823	6.3057	6.6311	6.9582	7.6167	7.9477
15 Years	15	4.9955	5.4277	5.8749	6.1040	6.3367	6.5729	6.8126	7.0557	7.3020	7.5516	8.0602	8.3190
	20	4.7796	5.2886	5.8164	6.0870	6.3618	6.6408	6.9236	7.2103	7.5005	7.7943	8.3914	8.6946
	25	4.6563	5.2107	5.7843	6.0778	6.3753	6.6766	6.9815	7.2897	7.6011	7.9153	8.5515	8.8730
	30	4.5790	5.1629	5.7652	6.0723	6.3831	6.6971	7.0140	7.3337	7.6557	7.9799	8.6337	8.9630
20 Years	15	6.9305	7.3627	7.8099	8.0390	8.2717	8.5079	8.7476	8.9906	9.2370	9.4866	9.9951	10.2540
	20	5.8969	6.3584	6.8385	7.0853	7.3364	7.5916	7.8509	8.1140	8.3808	8.6513	9.2025	9.4829
	25	5.7254	6.2451	6.7863	7.0644	7.3471	7.6342	7.9255	8.2207	8.5197	8.8221	9.4366	9.7482
	30	5.6179	6.1757	6.7551	7.0520	7.3532	7.6585	7.9674	8.2797	8.5951	8.9133	9.5570	9.8820

Equity Yield 9.00%					67% Growth over Term						Mortgage Ratio 70%	

10 Years	15	2.5390	3.0732	3.6230	3.9036	4.1878	4.4756	4.7669	5.0615	5.3595	5.6605	6.2719	6.5819
	20	2.4032	2.9927	3.5985	3.9071	4.2192	4.5347	4.8535	5.1753	5.5000	5.8274	6.4897	6.8243
	25	2.3257	2.9476	3.5850	3.9089	4.2360	4.5660	4.8986	5.2338	5.5712	5.9106	6.5950	6.9395
	30	2.2770	2.9199	3.5770	3.9100	4.2457	4.5838	4.9240	5.2661	5.6098	5.9550	6.6491	6.9976
12 Years	15	3.7184	4.2195	4.7371	5.0018	5.2704	5.5428	5.8189	6.0986	6.3818	6.6684	7.2517	7.5481
	20	3.5461	4.1130	4.6980	4.9969	5.2998	5.6066	5.9170	6.2309	6.5482	6.8685	7.5181	7.8470
	25	3.4477	4.0533	4.6766	4.9943	5.3156	5.6403	5.9681	6.2989	6.6324	6.9684	7.6468	7.9890
	30	3.3859	4.0167	4.6638	4.9927	5.3247	5.6595	5.9969	6.3365	6.6782	7.0216	7.7130	8.0606
15 Years	15	4.9088	5.3626	5.8322	6.0728	6.3171	6.5651	6.8168	7.0720	7.3306	7.5927	8.1267	8.3985
	20	4.6821	5.2166	5.7708	6.0549	6.3435	6.6363	6.9333	7.2343	7.5391	7.8475	8.4745	8.7928
	25	4.5527	5.1347	5.7371	6.0452	6.3576	6.6740	6.9941	7.3178	7.6447	7.9746	8.6426	8.9802
	30	4.4714	5.0846	5.7170	6.0395	6.3658	6.6955	7.0283	7.3639	7.7020	8.0424	8.7290	9.0747
20 Years	15	6.8921	7.3460	7.8156	8.0561	8.3005	8.5485	8.8001	9.0553	9.3140	9.5761	10.1101	10.3818
	20	5.8069	6.2915	6.7956	7.0547	7.3184	7.5863	7.8586	8.1348	8.4150	8.6990	9.2778	9.5722
	25	5.6269	6.1726	6.7408	7.0327	7.3296	7.6310	7.9369	8.2469	8.5608	8.8784	9.5236	9.8507
	30	5.5139	6.0997	6.7080	7.0198	7.3361	7.6566	7.9809	8.3089	8.6400	8.9741	9.6500	9.9912

Equity Yield 9.00%					67% Growth over Term						Mortgage Ratio 75%	

10 Years	15	2.3909	2.9632	3.5524	3.8530	4.1575	4.4659	4.7780	5.0937	5.4128	5.7354	6.3904	6.7226
	20	2.2454	2.8770	3.5261	3.8567	4.1911	4.5292	4.8707	5.2155	5.5634	5.9142	6.6238	6.9824
	25	2.1624	2.8287	3.5117	3.8587	4.2091	4.5627	4.9191	5.2782	5.6397	6.0034	6.7366	7.1058
	30	2.1102	2.7991	3.5031	3.8599	4.2196	4.5818	4.9463	5.3128	5.6811	6.0509	6.7946	7.1680
12 Years	15	3.5775	4.1145	4.6690	4.9527	5.2404	5.5323	5.8281	6.1278	6.4312	6.7383	7.3632	7.6808
	20	3.3929	4.0004	4.6272	4.9474	5.2720	5.6006	5.9332	6.2696	6.6095	6.9527	7.6487	8.0010
	25	3.2875	3.9364	4.6042	4.9446	5.2888	5.6367	5.9880	6.3424	6.6997	7.0597	7.7866	8.1532
	30	3.2213	3.8972	4.5905	4.9429	5.2986	5.6574	6.0188	6.3827	6.7488	7.1167	7.8575	8.2299
15 Years	15	4.7787	5.2650	5.7681	6.0259	6.2876	6.5534	6.8230	7.0964	7.3736	7.6544	8.2265	8.5177
	20	4.5359	5.1085	5.7023	6.0067	6.3159	6.6297	6.9479	7.2704	7.5969	7.9274	8.5992	8.9402
	25	4.3972	5.0208	5.6662	5.9963	6.3310	6.6700	7.0130	7.3598	7.7100	8.0635	8.7792	9.1410
	30	4.3101	4.9671	5.6446	5.9902	6.3398	6.6930	7.0496	7.4092	7.7715	8.1362	8.8718	9.2422
20 Years	15	6.8347	7.3209	7.8240	8.0818	8.3436	8.6093	8.8789	9.1524	9.4295	9.7103	10.2824	10.5736
	20	5.6719	6.1911	6.7313	7.0089	7.2913	7.5784	7.8701	8.1661	8.4663	8.7706	9.3907	9.7062
	25	5.4790	6.0637	6.6725	6.9853	7.3033	7.6263	7.9540	8.2862	8.6225	8.9628	9.6540	10.0046
	30	5.3580	5.9856	6.6374	6.9714	7.3103	7.6537	8.0012	8.3526	8.7074	9.0653	9.7895	10.1551

Equity Yield 9.00%					67% Growth over Term						Mortgage Ratio 80%	

10 Years	15	2.2428	2.8533	3.4817	3.8024	4.1272	4.4562	4.7890	5.1258	5.4662	5.8103	6.5090	6.8633
	20	2.0877	2.7614	3.4537	3.8064	4.1631	4.5237	4.8880	5.2558	5.6268	6.0010	6.7580	7.1404
	25	1.9990	2.7098	3.4383	3.8085	4.1823	4.5594	4.9396	5.3226	5.7082	6.0961	6.8782	7.2720
	30	1.9434	2.6782	3.4291	3.8098	4.1934	4.5798	4.9686	5.3595	5.7524	6.1469	6.9401	7.3384
12 Years	15	3.4367	4.0095	4.6010	4.9035	5.2105	5.5218	5.8373	6.1569	6.4806	6.8082	7.4748	7.8135
	20	3.2398	3.8877	4.5563	4.8979	5.2441	5.5947	5.9494	6.3082	6.6708	7.0369	7.7793	8.1551
	25	3.1273	3.8195	4.5319	4.8949	5.2621	5.6332	6.0079	6.3859	6.7670	7.1510	7.9264	8.3174
	30	3.0568	3.7776	4.5172	4.8931	5.2725	5.6552	6.0407	6.4289	6.8194	7.2119	8.0020	8.3993
15 Years	15	4.6487	5.1673	5.7040	5.9790	6.2582	6.5417	6.8293	7.1209	7.4165	7.7160	8.3263	8.6369
	20	4.3897	5.0005	5.6338	5.9585	6.2883	6.6230	6.9625	7.3064	7.6548	8.0072	8.7238	9.0876
	25	4.2417	4.9069	5.5953	5.9474	6.3044	6.6660	7.0319	7.4018	7.7754	8.1525	8.9159	9.3017
	30	4.1489	4.8496	5.5723	5.9409	6.3138	6.6906	7.0710	7.4545	7.8409	8.2300	9.0146	9.4097
20 Years	15	6.7772	7.2958	7.8325	8.1074	8.3867	8.6701	8.9577	9.2494	9.5450	9.8445	10.4548	10.7654
	20	5.5369	6.0907	6.6669	6.9630	7.2643	7.5706	7.8816	8.1974	8.5176	8.8422	9.5036	9.8401
	25	5.3311	5.9548	6.6042	6.9378	7.2771	7.6216	7.9712	8.3255	8.6842	9.0472	9.7845	10.1584
	30	5.2021	5.8715	6.5668	6.9230	7.2845	7.6508	8.0215	8.3963	8.7747	9.1566	9.9290	10.3190

Capitalization Rate to Account for Growth or Decline in Value

Equity Yield 9.00%					100% Growth over Term						Mortgage Ratio 67%		

Time to Mortgage Sale	Term	5.50%	6.50%	7.50%	8.00%	8.50%	9.00%	9.50%	10.00%	10.50%	11.00%	12.00%	12.50%
10 Years	15	0.4437	0.9524	1.4761	1.7433	2.0140	2.2881	2.5655	2.8461	3.1299	3.4166	3.9988	4.2941
	20	0.3144	0.8758	1.4527	1.7466	2.0439	2.3444	2.6480	2.9545	3.2637	3.5755	4.2063	4.5250
	25	0.2405	0.8328	1.4399	1.7484	2.0599	2.3742	2.6910	3.0101	3.3315	3.6548	4.3065	4.6347
	30	0.1942	0.8065	1.4323	1.7495	2.0692	2.3911	2.7151	3.0409	3.3683	3.6971	4.3581	4.6900
12 Years	15	2.1572	2.6345	3.1274	3.3796	3.6354	3.8948	4.1577	4.4241	4.6938	4.9668	5.5223	5.8046
	20	1.9931	2.5331	3.0902	3.3749	3.6634	3.9555	4.2512	4.5501	4.8523	5.1574	5.7760	6.0892
	25	1.8994	2.4762	3.0698	3.3724	3.6784	3.9876	4.2999	4.6149	4.9325	5.2525	5.8986	6.2245
	30	1.8406	2.4413	3.0577	3.3709	3.6871	4.0060	4.3273	4.6507	4.9761	5.3032	5.9617	6.2927
15 Years	15	3.8602	4.2924	4.7396	4.9687	5.2014	5.4377	5.6773	5.9204	6.1667	6.4163	6.9249	7.1837
	20	3.6443	4.1533	4.6811	4.9517	5.2265	5.5055	5.7883	6.0750	6.3652	6.6590	7.2561	7.5593
	25	3.5210	4.0754	4.6490	4.9425	5.2400	5.5413	5.8462	6.1544	6.4658	6.7800	7.4162	7.7377
	30	3.4437	4.0276	4.6299	4.9370	5.2478	5.5618	5.8787	6.1984	6.5204	6.8446	7.4984	7.8277
20 Years	15	6.2789	6.7111	7.1584	7.3875	7.6202	7.8564	8.0961	8.3391	8.5854	8.8350	9.3436	9.6024
	20	5.2454	5.7068	6.1870	6.4338	6.6848	6.9401	7.1993	7.4624	7.7293	7.9998	8.5509	8.8314
	25	5.0739	5.5936	6.1348	6.4128	6.6955	6.9826	7.2739	7.5692	7.8681	8.1706	8.7850	9.0966
	30	4.9663	5.5242	6.1036	6.4005	6.7017	7.0069	7.3159	7.6282	7.9436	8.2617	8.9054	9.2304

Equity Yield 9.00%					100% Growth over Term						Mortgage Ratio 70%		

		5.50%	6.50%	7.50%	8.00%	8.50%	9.00%	9.50%	10.00%	10.50%	11.00%	12.00%	12.50%
10 Years	15	0.3450	0.8792	1.4290	1.7096	1.9938	2.2816	2.5729	2.8675	3.1655	3.4665	4.0779	4.3879
	20	0.2092	0.7987	1.4045	1.7131	2.0252	2.3407	2.6595	2.9813	3.3060	3.6334	4.2957	4.6303
	25	0.1317	0.7536	1.3910	1.7149	2.0420	2.3720	2.7046	3.0398	3.3771	3.7166	4.4010	4.7455
	30	0.0830	0.7259	1.3830	1.7160	2.0517	2.3898	2.7300	3.0721	3.4158	3.7610	4.4551	4.8036
12 Years	15	2.0634	2.5645	3.0821	3.3468	3.6154	3.8878	4.1638	4.4435	4.7268	5.0134	5.5967	5.8931
	20	1.8911	2.4580	3.0430	3.3419	3.6448	3.9516	4.2620	4.5759	4.8931	5.2135	5.8631	6.1920
	25	1.7926	2.3983	3.0216	3.3392	3.6606	3.9853	4.3131	4.6439	4.9774	5.3133	5.9918	6.3339
	30	1.7309	2.3617	3.0088	3.3377	3.6697	4.0045	4.3419	4.6815	5.0232	5.3666	6.0580	6.4056
15 Years	15	3.7735	4.2273	4.6969	4.9375	5.1818	5.4298	5.6815	5.9367	6.1953	6.4574	6.9914	7.2632
	20	3.5468	4.0813	4.6355	4.9196	5.2082	5.5010	5.7980	6.0990	6.4038	6.7122	7.3392	7.6575
	25	3.4174	3.9994	4.6018	4.9099	5.2223	5.5387	5.8588	6.1825	6.5094	6.8393	7.5073	7.8449
	30	3.3361	3.9493	4.5817	4.9042	5.2305	5.5602	5.8930	6.2286	6.5667	6.9071	7.5937	7.9394
20 Years	15	6.2406	6.6944	7.1640	7.4046	7.6489	7.8969	8.1486	8.4038	8.6625	8.9245	9.4585	9.7303
	20	5.1554	5.6399	6.1441	6.4032	6.6668	6.9348	7.2070	7.4833	7.7635	8.0475	8.6262	8.9207
	25	4.9753	5.5210	6.0892	6.3812	6.6780	6.9795	7.2854	7.5954	7.9093	8.2268	8.8720	9.1992
	30	4.8624	5.4481	6.0565	6.3682	6.6845	7.0050	7.3294	7.6573	7.9885	8.3225	8.9984	9.3397

Equity Yield 9.00%					100% Growth over Term						Mortgage Ratio 75%		

		5.50%	6.50%	7.50%	8.00%	8.50%	9.00%	9.50%	10.00%	10.50%	11.00%	12.00%	12.50%
10 Years	15	0.1969	0.7692	1.3584	1.6590	1.9635	2.2719	2.5840	2.8997	3.2188	3.5414	4.1964	4.5286
	20	0.0514	0.6830	1.3321	1.6627	1.9971	2.3352	2.6767	3.0215	3.3694	3.7202	4.4298	4.7884
	25	-0.0316	0.6347	1.3177	1.6647	2.0151	2.3687	2.7251	3.0842	3.4457	3.8094	4.5426	4.9118
	30	-0.0838	0.6051	1.3091	1.6659	2.0256	2.3878	2.7523	3.1188	3.4871	3.8569	4.6006	4.9740
12 Years	15	1.9225	2.4595	3.0140	3.2976	3.5854	3.8773	4.1731	4.4727	4.7762	5.0833	5.7082	6.0258
	20	1.7379	2.3453	2.9722	3.2924	3.6169	3.9456	4.2782	4.6145	4.9544	5.2977	5.9937	6.3460
	25	1.6325	2.2814	2.9492	3.2896	3.6638	3.9817	4.3330	4.6874	5.0447	5.4046	6.1316	6.4982
	30	1.5663	2.2421	2.9355	3.2879	3.6436	4.0023	4.3638	4.7277	5.0937	5.4617	6.2025	6.5749
15 Years	15	3.6434	4.1297	4.6328	4.8906	5.1524	5.4181	5.6877	5.9611	6.2383	6.5191	7.0912	7.3824
	20	3.4006	3.9732	4.5670	4.8714	5.1806	5.4944	5.8126	6.1351	6.4616	6.7921	7.4639	7.8049
	25	3.2619	3.8855	4.5309	4.8610	5.1957	5.5347	5.8777	6.2245	6.5747	6.9282	7.6439	8.0057
	30	3.1749	3.8318	4.5093	4.8549	5.2045	5.5577	5.9143	6.2739	6.6362	7.0009	7.7365	8.1069
20 Years	15	6.1831	6.6693	7.1725	7.4302	7.6920	7.9578	8.2274	8.5008	8.7780	9.0587	9.6309	9.9221
	20	5.0204	5.5395	6.0797	6.3573	6.6398	6.9269	7.2185	7.5146	7.8148	8.1191	8.7391	9.0546
	25	4.8275	5.4121	6.0209	6.3337	6.6518	6.9748	7.3025	7.6347	7.9710	8.3112	9.0025	9.3530
	30	4.7064	5.3340	5.9858	6.3198	6.6587	7.0021	7.3497	7.7010	8.0558	8.4138	9.1379	9.5036

Equity Yield 9.00%					100% Growth over Term						Mortgage Ratio 80%		

		5.50%	6.50%	7.50%	8.00%	8.50%	9.00%	9.50%	10.00%	10.50%	11.00%	12.00%	12.50%
10 Years	15	0.0488	0.6593	1.2877	1.6084	1.9332	2.2622	2.5950	2.9318	3.2722	3.6163	4.3150	4.6693
	20	-0.1063	0.5674	1.2597	1.6124	1.9691	2.3297	2.6940	3.0618	3.4328	3.8070	4.5640	4.9464
	25	-0.1950	0.5158	1.2443	1.6145	1.9883	2.3654	2.7456	3.1286	3.5142	3.9021	4.6842	5.0780
	30	-0.2506	0.4842	1.2351	1.6158	1.9994	2.3858	2.7746	3.1655	3.5584	3.9529	4.7461	5.1444
12 Years	15	1.7817	2.3545	2.9459	3.2485	3.5555	3.8667	4.1823	4.5019	4.8256	5.1532	5.8198	6.1585
	20	1.5848	2.2327	2.9013	3.2429	3.5891	3.9396	4.2944	4.6532	5.0157	5.3819	6.1243	6.5001
	25	1.4723	2.1645	2.8768	3.2399	3.6071	3.9782	4.3529	4.7309	5.1120	5.4960	6.2714	6.6624
	30	1.4018	2.1226	2.8622	3.2381	3.6175	4.0002	4.3857	4.7739	5.1643	5.5568	6.3470	6.7442
15 Years	15	3.5134	4.0320	4.5687	4.8437	5.1229	5.4064	5.6940	5.9856	6.2812	6.5807	7.1910	7.5016
	20	3.2544	3.8652	4.4985	4.8232	5.1530	5.4877	5.8272	6.1711	6.5195	6.8719	7.5885	7.9523
	25	3.1064	3.7716	4.4600	4.8121	5.1691	5.5307	5.8966	6.2665	6.6401	7.0172	7.7806	8.1664
	30	3.0136	3.7143	4.4370	4.8056	5.1785	5.5553	5.9357	6.3192	6.7056	7.0947	7.8793	8.2744
20 Years	15	6.1256	6.6443	7.1810	7.4559	7.7351	8.0186	8.3062	8.5978	8.8935	9.1930	9.8032	10.1138
	20	4.8854	5.4391	6.0153	6.3115	6.6127	6.9190	7.2301	7.5458	7.8661	8.1906	8.8521	9.1886
	25	4.6796	5.3032	5.9526	6.2863	6.6255	6.9701	7.3196	7.6739	8.0327	8.3956	9.1330	9.5069
	30	4.5505	5.2199	5.9152	6.2715	6.6330	6.9993	7.3700	7.7447	8.1232	8.5050	9.2774	9.6674

Capitalization Rate to Account for Growth or Decline in Value

Equity Yield 9.00%		150% Growth over Term										Mortgage Ratio 67%	

Time to Sale	Mortgage Term	5.50%	6.50%	7.50%	8.00%	8.50%	9.00%	9.50%	10.00%	10.50%	11.00%	12.00%	12.50%
10 Years	15	-2.8473	-2.3386	-1.8149	-1.5477	-1.2770	-1.0029	-0.7255	-0.4449	-0.1611	0.1256	0.7078	1.0031
	20	-2.9766	-2.4152	-1.8383	-1.5444	-1.2471	-0.9466	-0.6430	-0.3365	-0.0273	0.2845	0.9153	1.2340
	25	-3.0505	-2.4582	-1.8511	-1.5426	-1.2311	-0.9168	-0.6000	-0.2809	0.0405	0.3638	1.0155	1.3437
	30	-3.0968	-2.4845	-1.8587	-1.5415	-1.2218	-0.8999	-0.5759	-0.2501	0.0773	0.4061	1.0671	1.3990
12 Years	15	-0.3253	0.1520	0.6449	0.8970	1.1528	1.4122	1.6752	1.9416	2.2113	2.4843	3.0398	3.3220
	20	-0.4894	0.0505	0.6077	0.8924	1.1808	1.4730	1.7686	2.0676	2.3697	2.6749	3.2935	3.6067
	25	-0.5831	-0.0063	0.5873	0.8898	1.1958	1.5051	1.8173	2.1324	2.4500	2.7699	3.4161	3.7419
	30	-0.6419	-0.0412	0.5751	0.8884	1.2046	1.5234	1.8447	2.1682	2.4936	2.8206	3.4791	3.8102
15 Years	15	2.1572	2.5894	3.0367	3.2658	3.4985	3.7347	3.9744	4.2174	4.4638	4.7134	5.2219	5.4808
	20	1.9414	2.4504	2.9782	3.2488	3.5236	3.8025	4.0854	4.3720	4.6623	4.9560	5.5532	5.8563
	25	1.8181	2.3724	2.9461	3.2395	3.5370	3.8384	4.1433	4.4515	4.7628	5.0770	5.7132	6.0348
	30	1.7407	2.3246	2.9269	3.2341	3.5448	3.8588	4.1758	4.4954	4.8174	5.1416	5.7955	6.1248
20 Years	15	5.3016	5.7338	6.1810	6.4101	6.6428	6.8791	7.1187	7.3618	7.6081	7.8577	8.3663	8.6251
	20	4.2680	4.7295	5.2097	5.4565	5.7075	5.9627	6.2220	6.4851	6.7520	7.0224	7.5736	7.8541
	25	4.0966	4.6163	5.1574	5.4355	5.7182	6.0053	6.2966	6.5918	6.8908	7.1933	7.8077	8.1193
	30	3.9890	4.5468	5.1262	5.4231	5.7244	6.0296	6.3385	6.6508	6.9662	7.2844	7.9281	8.2531

Equity Yield 9.00%		150% Growth over Term										Mortgage Ratio 70%	

		5.50%	6.50%	7.50%	8.00%	8.50%	9.00%	9.50%	10.00%	10.50%	11.00%	12.00%	12.50%
10 Years	15	-2.9460	-2.4118	-1.8620	-1.5814	-1.2972	-1.0094	-0.7181	-0.4235	-0.1255	0.1755	0.7869	1.0969
	20	-3.0818	-2.4923	-1.8865	-1.5779	-1.2658	-0.9503	-0.6315	-0.3097	0.0150	0.3424	1.0047	1.3393
	25	-3.1593	-2.5374	-1.9000	-1.5761	-1.2490	-0.9190	-0.5864	-0.2512	0.0861	0.4256	1.1100	1.4545
	30	-3.2080	-2.5651	-1.9080	-1.5750	-1.2393	-0.9012	-0.5610	-0.2189	0.1248	0.4700	1.1641	1.5126
12 Years	15	-0.4192	0.0820	0.5995	0.8643	1.1329	1.4052	1.6813	1.9610	2.2442	2.5309	3.1141	3.4105
	20	-0.5915	-0.0246	0.5605	0.8594	1.1623	1.4690	1.7794	2.0934	2.4106	2.7310	3.3806	3.7094
	25	-0.6899	-0.0843	0.5391	0.8567	1.1780	1.5027	1.8306	2.1614	2.4949	2.8308	3.5093	3.8514
	30	-0.7516	-0.1209	0.5263	0.8552	1.1872	1.5220	1.8593	2.1990	2.5406	2.8841	3.5755	3.9230
15 Years	15	2.0705	2.5243	2.9939	3.2345	3.4789	3.7269	3.9785	4.2337	4.4924	4.7545	5.2885	5.5602
	20	1.8439	2.3783	2.9325	3.2166	3.5052	3.7981	4.0951	4.3961	4.7008	5.0093	5.6363	5.9546
	25	1.7144	2.2965	2.8988	3.2069	3.5193	3.8357	4.1559	4.4795	4.8064	5.1363	5.8043	6.1419
	30	1.6332	2.2463	2.8787	3.2012	3.5275	3.8572	4.1900	4.5256	4.8638	5.2042	5.8907	6.2365
20 Years	15	5.2633	5.7171	6.1867	6.4273	6.6716	6.9196	7.1713	7.4265	7.6851	7.9472	8.4812	8.7530
	20	4.1780	4.6626	5.1668	5.4259	5.6895	5.9575	6.2297	6.5060	6.7862	7.0702	7.6489	7.9434
	25	3.9980	4.5437	5.1119	5.4039	5.7007	6.0022	6.3080	6.6180	6.9319	7.2495	7.8947	8.2219
	30	3.8850	4.4708	5.0791	5.3909	5.7072	6.0277	6.3521	6.6800	7.0111	7.3452	8.0211	8.3624

Equity Yield 9.00%		150% Growth over Term										Mortgage Ratio 75%	

		5.50%	6.50%	7.50%	8.00%	8.50%	9.00%	9.50%	10.00%	10.50%	11.00%	12.00%	12.50%
10 Years	15	-3.0941	-2.5218	-1.9326	-1.6320	-1.3275	-1.0191	-0.7070	-0.3914	-0.0722	0.2504	0.9054	1.2376
	20	-3.2396	-2.6080	-1.9589	-1.6283	-1.2939	-0.9558	-0.6143	-0.2695	0.0784	0.4292	1.1388	1.4974
	25	-3.3227	-2.6563	-1.9733	-1.6263	-1.2759	-0.9223	-0.5659	-0.2068	0.1547	0.5184	1.2516	1.6208
	30	-3.3748	-2.6859	-1.9819	-1.6251	-1.2654	-0.9032	-0.5387	-0.1722	0.1961	0.5659	1.3096	1.6830
12 Years	15	-0.5600	-0.0231	0.5315	0.8151	1.1029	1.3947	1.6905	1.9902	2.2936	2.6008	3.2257	3.5432
	20	-0.7446	-0.1372	0.4896	0.8099	1.1344	1.4631	1.7957	2.1320	2.4719	2.8152	3.5112	3.8635
	25	-0.8501	-0.2012	0.4667	0.8070	1.1513	1.4992	1.8505	2.2049	2.5622	2.9221	3.6491	4.0156
	30	-0.9162	-0.2404	0.4530	0.8054	1.1611	1.5198	1.8813	2.2452	2.6112	2.9792	3.7200	4.0924
15 Years	15	1.9405	2.4267	2.9299	3.1876	3.4494	3.7152	3.9848	4.2582	4.5353	4.8161	5.3883	5.6795
	20	1.6977	2.2703	2.8641	3.1685	3.4776	3.7914	4.1097	4.4321	4.7587	5.0891	5.7609	6.1020
	25	1.5589	2.1826	2.8280	3.1581	3.4928	3.8318	4.1748	4.5215	4.8718	5.2253	5.9410	6.3027
	30	1.4719	2.1288	2.8064	3.1520	3.5015	3.8548	4.2114	4.5709	4.9332	5.2979	6.0335	6.4040
20 Years	15	5.2058	5.6920	6.1952	6.4529	6.7147	6.9804	7.2501	7.5235	7.8006	8.0814	8.6536	8.9447
	20	4.0430	4.5622	5.1024	5.3800	5.6625	5.9496	6.2412	6.5372	6.8375	7.1417	7.7618	8.0773
	25	3.8501	4.4348	5.0436	5.3564	5.6745	5.9975	6.3252	6.6573	6.9937	7.3339	8.0252	8.3757
	30	3.7291	4.3567	5.0085	5.3425	5.6814	6.0248	6.3724	6.7237	7.0785	7.4365	8.1606	8.5262

Equity Yield 9.00%		150% Growth over Term										Mortgage Ratio 80%	

		5.50%	6.50%	7.50%	8.00%	8.50%	9.00%	9.50%	10.00%	10.50%	11.00%	12.00%	12.50%
10 Years	15	-3.2422	-2.6317	-2.0033	-1.6826	-1.3578	-1.0289	-0.6960	-0.3592	-0.0188	0.3253	1.0240	1.3783
	20	-3.3973	-2.7236	-2.0313	-1.6787	-1.3219	-0.9613	-0.5970	-0.2292	0.1418	0.5160	1.2730	1.6554
	25	-3.4860	-2.7752	-2.0467	-1.6765	-1.3027	-0.9256	-0.5454	-0.1624	0.2232	0.6111	1.3932	1.7870
	30	-3.5416	-2.8068	-2.0559	-1.6752	-1.2916	-0.9052	-0.5164	-0.1255	0.2674	0.6619	1.4551	1.8534
12 Years	15	-0.7008	-0.1281	0.4634	0.7659	1.0729	1.3842	1.6997	2.0194	2.3431	2.6707	3.3372	3.6760
	20	-0.8977	-0.2498	0.4188	0.7604	1.1065	1.4571	1.8119	2.1706	2.5332	2.8994	3.6417	4.0176
	25	-1.0102	-0.3181	0.3943	0.7573	1.1245	1.4956	1.8703	2.2484	2.6295	3.0134	3.7888	4.1798
	30	-1.0808	-0.3599	0.3797	0.7555	1.1350	1.5176	1.9032	2.2913	2.6818	3.0743	3.8645	4.2617
15 Years	15	1.8105	2.3291	2.8658	3.1407	3.4200	3.7034	3.9910	4.2827	4.5783	4.8778	5.4881	5.7987
	20	1.5514	2.1622	2.7956	3.1203	3.4501	3.7848	4.1242	4.4682	4.8165	5.1690	5.8856	6.2494
	25	1.4035	2.0687	2.7571	3.1092	3.4662	3.8278	4.1937	4.5636	4.9372	5.3142	6.0776	6.4635
	30	1.3106	2.0113	2.7341	3.1027	3.4756	3.8524	4.2327	4.6163	5.0027	5.3917	6.1764	6.5715
20 Years	15	5.1483	5.6669	6.2036	6.4786	6.7578	7.0413	7.3289	7.6205	7.9161	8.2156	8.8259	9.1365
	20	3.9080	4.4618	5.0380	5.3341	5.6354	5.9417	6.2528	6.5685	6.8888	7.2133	7.8747	8.2113
	25	3.7023	4.3259	4.9753	5.3090	5.6482	5.9928	6.3423	6.6966	7.0554	7.4183	8.1556	8.5296
	30	3.5732	4.2426	4.9379	5.2942	5.6556	6.0219	6.3926	6.7674	7.1459	7.5277	8.3001	8.6901

Capitalization Rate to Account for Growth or Decline in Value

Equity Yield 10.50%					25% Growth over Term						Mortgage Ratio 67%	

Time to Sale	Mortgage Term	5.50%	6.50%	7.50%	8.00%	Mortgage Interest Rate 8.50%	9.00%	9.50%	10.00%	10.50%	11.00%	12.00%	12.50%
10 Years	15	6.1683	6.6718	7.1901	7.4547	7.7228	7.9943	8.2690	8.5470	8.8282	9.1124	9.6895	9.9822
	20	5.9763	6.5308	7.1011	7.3917	7.6858	7.9831	8.2836	8.5871	8.8934	9.2023	9.8276	10.1436
	25	5.8667	6.4518	7.0522	7.3575	7.6659	7.9772	8.2912	8.6077	8.9264	9.2472	9.8944	10.2203
	30	5.7979	6.4034	7.0230	7.3374	7.6544	7.9739	8.2955	8.6191	8.9444	9.2712	9.9287	10.2590
12 Years	15	6.6957	7.1691	7.6581	7.9082	8.1621	8.4195	8.6804	8.9448	9.2125	9.4835	10.0349	10.3152
	20	6.4568	6.9899	7.5405	7.8219	8.1071	8.3961	8.6886	8.9845	9.2836	9.5858	10.1986	10.5090
	25	6.3203	6.8895	7.4760	7.7751	8.0778	8.3838	8.6929	9.0049	9.3196	9.6368	10.2777	10.6010
	30	6.2347	6.8279	7.4375	7.7475	8.0607	8.3767	8.6953	9.0162	9.3392	9.6640	10.3183	10.6475
15 Years	15	7.2639	7.6961	8.1434	8.3725	8.6052	8.8414	9.0811	9.3241	9.5705	9.8200	10.3286	10.5874
	20	6.9566	7.4603	7.9827	8.2506	8.5228	8.7991	9.0793	9.3633	9.6510	9.9421	10.5341	10.8347
	25	6.7810	7.3280	7.8946	8.1846	8.4787	8.7767	9.0784	9.3835	9.6918	10.0030	10.6334	10.9522
	30	6.6709	7.2470	7.8420	8.1457	8.4531	8.7640	9.0779	9.3946	9.7139	10.0355	10.6845	11.0115
20 Years	15	8.5248	8.9570	9.4042	9.6333	9.8660	10.1023	10.3419	10.5850	10.8313	11.0809	11.5895	11.8483
	20	7.4912	7.9527	8.4329	8.6796	8.9307	9.1859	9.4452	9.7083	9.9752	10.2456	10.7968	11.0772
	25	7.2543	7.7692	8.3056	8.5812	8.8615	9.1462	9.4351	9.7280	10.0246	10.3247	10.9345	11.2438
	30	7.1057	7.6567	8.2295	8.5232	8.8213	9.1235	9.4295	9.7389	10.0514	10.3669	11.0053	11.3279

Equity Yield 10.50%					25% Growth over Term						Mortgage Ratio 70%	

Time to Sale	Mortgage Term	5.50%	6.50%	7.50%	8.00%	8.50%	9.00%	9.50%	10.00%	10.50%	11.00%	12.00%	12.50%
10 Years	15	6.0283	6.5569	7.1012	7.3790	7.6605	7.9455	8.2341	8.5260	8.8212	9.1196	9.7255	10.0329
	20	5.8267	6.4089	7.0077	7.3128	7.6216	7.9339	8.2494	8.5680	8.8896	9.2140	9.8706	10.2024
	25	5.7116	6.3260	6.9564	7.2770	7.6008	7.9277	8.2574	8.5896	8.9243	9.2612	9.9406	10.2829
	30	5.6394	6.2751	6.9257	7.2558	7.5887	7.9241	8.2618	8.6016	8.9431	9.2863	9.9767	10.3236
12 Years	15	6.5622	7.0593	7.5727	7.8354	8.1019	8.3722	8.6461	8.9237	9.2048	9.4894	10.0684	10.3627
	20	6.3113	6.8712	7.4492	7.7447	8.0442	8.3476	8.6548	8.9654	9.2795	9.5968	10.2402	10.5661
	25	6.1680	6.7657	7.3815	7.6956	8.0134	8.3347	8.6593	8.9869	9.3173	9.6503	10.3233	10.6628
	30	6.0781	6.7011	7.3411	7.6666	7.9955	8.3273	8.6618	8.9987	9.3379	9.6789	10.3660	10.7116
15 Years	15	7.1399	7.5937	8.0633	8.3039	8.5483	8.7963	9.0479	9.3031	9.5618	9.8239	10.3579	10.6296
	20	6.8172	7.3461	7.8947	8.1760	8.4618	8.7519	9.0461	9.3443	9.6463	9.9520	10.5736	10.8893
	25	6.6329	7.2073	7.8022	8.1066	8.4155	8.7284	9.0451	9.3655	9.6891	10.0159	10.6779	11.0126
	30	6.5172	7.1221	7.7469	8.0658	8.3886	8.7150	9.0446	9.3772	9.7124	10.0500	10.7315	11.0749
20 Years	15	8.4466	8.9004	9.3700	9.6106	9.8550	10.1030	10.3546	10.6098	10.8685	11.1306	11.6646	11.9363
	20	7.3614	7.8460	8.3501	8.6092	8.8729	9.1408	9.4130	9.6893	9.9695	10.2535	10.8323	11.1267
	25	7.1126	7.6533	8.2165	8.5059	8.8002	9.0991	9.4025	9.7100	10.0214	10.3365	10.9769	11.3017
	30	6.9566	7.5352	8.1366	8.4450	8.7580	9.0753	9.3966	9.7214	10.0496	10.3808	11.0512	11.3899

Equity Yield 10.50%					25% Growth over Term						Mortgage Ratio 75%	

Time to Sale	Mortgage Term	5.50%	6.50%	7.50%	8.00%	8.50%	9.00%	9.50%	10.00%	10.50%	11.00%	12.00%	12.50%
10 Years	15	5.8183	6.3847	6.9678	7.2655	7.5671	7.8725	8.1816	8.4944	8.8106	9.1303	9.7796	10.1089
	20	5.6023	6.2261	6.8676	7.1946	7.5254	7.8599	8.1980	8.5394	8.8840	9.2316	9.9350	10.2905
	25	5.4789	6.1372	6.8126	7.1561	7.5031	7.8533	8.2066	8.5626	8.9211	9.2821	10.0101	10.3768
	30	5.4015	6.0827	6.7798	7.1335	7.4902	7.8495	8.2114	8.5754	8.9413	9.3090	10.0487	10.4203
12 Years	15	6.3620	6.8946	7.4447	7.7261	8.0116	8.3012	8.5948	8.8922	9.1934	9.4982	10.1186	10.4339
	20	6.0932	6.6930	7.3124	7.6289	7.9498	8.2749	8.6040	8.9369	9.2734	9.6133	10.3027	10.6519
	25	5.9396	6.5800	7.2398	7.5763	7.9168	8.2610	8.6088	8.9598	9.3139	9.6707	10.3917	10.7555
	30	5.8433	6.5107	7.1964	7.5453	7.8976	8.2531	8.6115	8.9725	9.3359	9.7013	10.4374	10.8077
15 Years	15	6.9540	7.4402	7.9433	8.2011	8.4629	8.7286	8.9982	9.2716	9.5488	9.8296	10.4017	10.6929
	20	6.6082	7.1748	7.7626	8.0640	8.3702	8.6810	8.9963	9.3158	9.6394	9.9669	10.6329	10.9711
	25	6.4107	7.0261	7.6635	7.9897	8.3206	8.6559	8.9952	9.3385	9.6852	10.0354	10.7446	11.1033
	30	6.2867	6.9349	7.6043	7.9459	8.2918	8.6415	8.9947	9.3510	9.7102	10.0719	10.8020	11.1699
20 Years	15	8.3294	8.8156	9.3188	9.5765	9.8383	10.1041	10.3737	10.6471	10.9243	11.2050	11.7772	12.0684
	20	7.1667	7.6858	8.2260	8.5036	8.7861	9.0732	9.3649	9.6609	9.9611	10.2654	10.8854	11.2009
	25	6.9001	7.4794	8.0828	8.3929	8.7082	9.0285	9.3535	9.6830	10.0167	10.3543	11.0404	11.3884
	30	6.7329	7.3529	7.9973	8.3277	8.6630	9.0030	9.3472	9.6953	10.0469	10.4018	11.1200	11.4829

Equity Yield 10.50%					25% Growth over Term						Mortgage Ratio 80%	

Time to Sale	Mortgage Term	5.50%	6.50%	7.50%	8.00%	8.50%	9.00%	9.50%	10.00%	10.50%	11.00%	12.00%	12.50%
10 Years	15	5.6083	6.2124	6.8344	7.1519	7.4736	7.7994	8.1291	8.4627	8.8001	9.1411	9.8336	10.1849
	20	5.3779	6.0433	6.7276	7.0763	7.4292	7.7860	8.1466	8.5108	8.8784	9.2491	9.9994	10.3787
	25	5.2463	5.9485	6.6689	7.0353	7.4054	7.7790	8.1558	8.5355	8.9180	9.3030	10.0795	10.4707
	30	5.1637	5.8904	6.6339	7.0111	7.3916	7.7749	8.1609	8.5492	8.9395	9.3317	10.1207	10.5171
12 Years	15	6.1617	6.7298	7.3166	7.6168	7.9214	8.2303	8.5434	8.8606	9.1819	9.5071	10.1688	10.5051
	20	5.8750	6.5148	7.1755	7.5132	7.8555	8.2022	8.5532	8.9083	9.2672	9.6298	10.3652	10.7376
	25	5.7112	6.3943	7.0981	7.4570	7.8202	8.1874	8.5584	8.9328	9.3104	9.6910	10.4601	10.8481
	30	5.6085	6.3204	7.0518	7.4239	7.7997	8.1789	8.5613	8.9463	9.3339	9.7237	10.5089	10.9038
15 Years	15	6.7680	7.2866	7.8233	8.0982	8.3775	8.6609	8.9485	9.2402	9.5358	9.8353	10.4456	10.7562
	20	6.3991	7.0035	7.6305	7.9520	8.2786	8.6102	8.9464	9.2872	9.6324	9.9818	10.6922	11.0529
	25	6.1884	6.8449	7.5248	7.8728	8.2257	8.5833	8.9453	9.3114	9.6813	10.0548	10.8113	11.1939
	30	6.0563	6.7476	7.4616	7.8261	8.1950	8.5680	8.9447	9.3248	9.7079	10.0938	10.8726	11.2650
20 Years	15	8.2122	8.7308	9.2675	9.5425	9.8217	10.1052	10.3928	10.6844	10.9800	11.2795	11.8898	12.2004
	20	6.9719	7.5257	8.1019	8.3980	8.6993	9.0056	9.3167	9.6324	9.9527	10.2772	10.9386	11.2752
	25	6.6876	7.3055	7.9491	8.2799	8.6162	8.9579	9.3046	9.6560	10.0120	10.3721	11.1039	11.4751
	30	6.5093	7.1705	7.8579	8.2103	8.5681	8.9307	9.2978	9.6691	10.0442	10.4227	11.1889	11.5759

Capitalization Rate to Account for Growth or Decline in Value

Equity Yield 10.50%						25% Decline over Term					Mortgage Ratio 67%		

Time to Sale	Term	5.50%	6.50%	7.50%	8.00%	8.50%	9.00%	9.50%	10.00%	10.50%	11.00%	12.00%	12.50%
10 Years	15	9.2312	9.7346	10.2530	10.5176	10.7857	11.0571	11.3319	11.6099	11.8911	12.1752	12.7523	13.0451
	20	9.0392	9.5937	10.1639	10.4545	10.7486	11.0460	11.3465	11.6500	11.9563	12.2652	12.8905	13.2065
	25	8.9295	9.5147	10.1151	10.4204	10.7288	11.0401	11.3541	11.6706	11.9893	12.3101	12.9572	13.2832
	30	8.8608	9.4663	10.0859	10.4002	10.7173	11.0367	11.3584	11.6819	12.0072	12.3340	12.9915	13.3219
12 Years	15	8.9645	9.4380	9.9269	10.1771	10.4309	10.6883	10.9492	11.2136	11.4813	11.7523	12.3037	12.5840
	20	8.7256	9.2588	9.8093	10.0907	10.3760	10.6650	10.9575	11.2533	11.5524	11.8546	12.4674	12.7778
	25	8.5891	9.1584	9.7448	10.0439	10.3466	10.6526	10.9617	11.2738	11.5884	11.9056	12.5465	12.8699
	30	8.5035	9.0968	9.7063	10.0164	10.3295	10.6456	10.9641	11.2850	11.6080	11.9328	12.5872	12.9163
15 Years	15	8.7763	9.2085	9.6558	9.8849	10.1176	10.3538	10.5935	10.8365	11.0829	11.3324	11.8410	12.0998
	20	8.4690	8.9727	9.4951	9.7630	10.0352	10.3115	10.5917	10.8757	11.1634	11.4545	12.0465	12.3471
	25	8.2934	8.8404	9.4070	9.6970	9.9911	10.2891	10.5908	10.8959	11.2042	11.5154	12.1458	12.4646
	30	8.1833	8.7594	9.3544	9.6581	9.9655	10.2764	10.5903	10.9070	11.2263	11.5479	12.1969	12.5239
20 Years	15	9.3494	9.7816	10.2289	10.4580	10.6907	10.9269	11.1666	11.4096	11.6560	11.9056	12.4141	12.6730
	20	8.3159	8.7774	9.2575	9.5043	9.7554	10.0106	10.2698	10.5330	10.7998	11.0703	11.6215	11.9019
	25	8.0790	8.5939	9.1302	9.4059	9.6861	9.9709	10.2598	10.5526	10.8492	11.1493	11.7592	12.0685
	30	7.9304	8.4814	9.0542	9.3479	9.6460	9.9482	10.2541	10.5635	10.8761	11.1915	11.8300	12.1525

Equity Yield 10.50%						-25% Decline over Term					Mortgage Ratio 70%		

Time to Sale	Term	5.50%	6.50%	7.50%	8.00%	8.50%	9.00%	9.50%	10.00%	10.50%	11.00%	12.00%	12.50%
10 Years	15	9.0912	9.6198	10.1641	10.4419	10.7234	11.0084	11.2969	11.5888	11.8840	12.1824	12.7884	13.0957
	20	8.8896	9.4718	10.0705	10.3757	10.6845	10.9967	11.3122	11.6309	11.9525	12.2769	12.9334	13.2653
	25	8.7745	9.3889	10.0192	10.3398	10.6637	10.9905	11.3202	11.6525	11.9872	12.3240	13.0035	13.3458
	30	8.7022	9.3380	9.9886	10.3187	10.6516	10.9870	11.3247	11.6645	12.0060	12.3492	13.0395	13.3864
12 Years	15	8.8311	9.3281	9.8416	10.1042	10.3707	10.6410	10.9150	11.1926	11.4737	11.7582	12.3372	12.6315
	20	8.5802	9.1400	9.7181	10.0135	10.3131	10.6165	10.9236	11.2343	11.5483	11.8656	12.5091	12.8350
	25	8.4369	9.0346	9.6503	9.9644	10.2822	10.6035	10.9281	11.2557	11.5862	11.9192	12.5921	12.9316
	30	8.3470	8.9699	9.6099	9.9355	10.2643	10.5961	10.9306	11.2676	11.6067	11.9477	12.6348	12.9804
15 Years	15	8.6523	9.1061	9.5757	9.8163	10.0607	10.3087	10.5603	10.8155	11.0742	11.3363	11.8703	12.1420
	20	8.3296	8.8585	9.4071	9.6884	9.9742	10.2643	10.5585	10.8567	11.1587	11.4644	12.0860	12.4017
	25	8.1453	8.7197	9.3146	9.6190	9.9279	10.2408	10.5575	10.8779	11.2015	11.5283	12.1903	12.5250
	30	8.0296	8.6345	9.2593	9.5782	9.9010	10.2274	10.5570	10.8896	11.2248	11.5624	12.2439	12.5873
20 Years	15	9.2713	9.7251	10.1947	10.4353	10.6796	10.9276	11.1793	11.4345	11.6932	11.9552	12.4892	12.7610
	20	8.1861	8.6706	9.1748	9.4339	9.6975	9.9655	10.2377	10.5140	10.7942	11.0782	11.6569	11.9514
	25	7.9373	8.4780	9.0411	9.3305	9.6248	9.9238	10.2271	10.5347	10.8461	11.1612	11.8015	12.1263
	30	7.7813	8.3598	8.9613	9.2697	9.5827	9.9000	10.2212	10.5461	10.8743	11.2055	11.8759	12.2146

Equity Yield 10.50%						-25% Decline over Term					Mortgage Ratio 75%		

Time to Sale	Term	5.50%	6.50%	7.50%	8.00%	8.50%	9.00%	9.50%	10.00%	10.50%	11.00%	12.00%	12.50%
10 Years	15	8.8812	9.4475	10.0307	10.3284	10.6299	10.9353	11.2445	11.5572	11.8735	12.1932	12.8424	13.1718
	20	8.6652	9.2890	9.9305	10.2574	10.5883	10.9228	11.2609	11.6023	11.9469	12.2944	12.9979	13.3534
	25	8.5418	9.2001	9.8755	10.2190	10.5660	10.9162	11.2694	11.6254	11.9840	12.3449	13.0729	13.4397
	30	8.4644	9.1456	9.8427	10.1964	10.5530	10.9124	11.2742	11.6382	12.0042	12.3719	13.1115	13.4832
12 Years	15	8.6308	9.1634	9.7135	9.9949	10.2805	10.5700	10.8636	11.1610	11.4622	11.7671	12.3874	12.7027
	20	8.3620	8.9618	9.5812	9.8978	10.2187	10.5438	10.8728	11.2057	11.5422	11.8821	12.5716	12.9207
	25	8.2085	8.8488	9.5086	9.8451	10.1856	10.5299	10.8777	11.2287	11.5827	11.9395	12.6605	13.0243
	30	8.1121	8.7796	9.4653	9.8141	10.1664	10.5219	10.8804	11.2414	11.6047	11.9701	12.7062	13.0765
15 Years	15	8.4664	8.9526	9.4557	9.7135	9.9753	10.2410	10.5106	10.7840	11.0612	11.3420	11.9141	12.2053
	20	8.1206	8.6872	9.2750	9.5764	9.8826	10.1934	10.5087	10.8282	11.1518	11.4793	12.1453	12.4835
	25	7.9231	8.5385	9.1759	9.5021	9.8330	10.1683	10.5076	10.8509	11.1976	11.5478	12.2570	12.6157
	30	7.7991	8.4473	9.1167	9.4583	9.8042	10.1539	10.5071	10.8634	11.2226	11.5843	12.3144	12.6823
20 Years	15	9.1541	9.6403	10.1434	10.4012	10.6630	10.9287	11.1984	11.4718	11.7489	12.0297	12.6018	12.8930
	20	7.9913	8.5105	9.0507	9.3283	9.6107	9.8979	10.1895	10.4855	10.7858	11.0900	11.7101	12.0256
	25	7.7248	8.3041	8.9075	9.2175	9.5329	9.8532	10.1782	10.5077	10.8414	11.1790	11.8650	12.2130
	30	7.5576	8.1775	8.8219	9.1523	9.4877	9.8277	10.1719	10.5199	10.8716	11.2264	11.9447	12.3076

Equity Yield 10.50%						-25% Decline over Term					Mortgage Ratio 80%		

Time to Sale	Term	5.50%	6.50%	7.50%	8.00%	8.50%	9.00%	9.50%	10.00%	10.50%	11.00%	12.00%	12.50%
10 Years	15	8.6712	9.2753	9.8973	10.2148	10.5365	10.8623	11.1920	11.5256	11.8630	12.2040	12.8965	13.2478
	20	8.4408	9.1061	9.7904	10.1392	10.4921	10.8489	11.2095	11.5737	11.9412	12.3120	13.0623	13.4415
	25	8.3092	9.0113	9.7318	10.0982	10.4683	10.8418	11.2186	11.5984	11.9809	12.3658	13.1424	13.5336
	30	8.2266	8.9532	9.6968	10.0740	10.4545	10.8378	11.2238	11.6120	12.0024	12.3946	13.1836	13.5800
12 Years	15	8.4306	8.9987	9.5854	9.8856	10.1902	10.4991	10.8122	11.1294	11.4507	11.7759	12.4376	12.7739
	20	8.1439	8.7837	9.4443	9.7820	10.1243	10.4711	10.8221	11.1771	11.5360	11.8986	12.6340	13.0065
	25	7.9801	8.6631	9.3669	9.7258	10.0890	10.4562	10.8272	11.2016	11.5793	11.9598	12.7289	13.1169
	30	7.8773	8.5893	9.3207	9.6927	10.0686	10.4478	10.8301	11.2152	11.6027	11.9925	12.7777	13.1727
15 Years	15	8.2804	8.7990	9.3357	9.6106	9.8899	10.1733	10.4609	10.7526	11.0482	11.3477	11.9580	12.2686
	20	7.9115	8.5159	9.1429	9.4644	9.7910	10.1226	10.4588	10.7996	11.1448	11.4942	12.2046	12.5653
	25	7.7008	8.3573	9.0372	9.3852	9.7381	10.0957	10.4577	10.8238	11.1937	11.5672	12.3237	12.7063
	30	7.5687	8.2600	8.9740	9.3385	9.7074	10.0804	10.4571	10.8372	11.2203	11.6062	12.3850	12.7774
20 Years	15	9.0369	9.5555	10.0922	10.3671	10.6464	10.9298	11.2174	11.5091	11.8047	12.1042	12.7145	13.0251
	20	7.7966	8.3504	8.9266	9.2227	9.5240	9.8302	10.1413	10.4571	10.7773	11.1019	11.7633	12.0998
	25	7.5123	8.1302	8.7738	9.1046	9.4409	9.7826	10.1293	10.4807	10.8366	11.1967	11.9286	12.2997
	30	7.3340	7.9952	8.6826	9.0350	9.3927	9.7553	10.1225	10.4938	10.8688	11.2474	12.0135	12.4006

Capitalization Rate to Account for Growth or Decline in Value

| Equity Yield 10.50% | | | | | 50% Growth over Term | | | | | | Mortgage Ratio 67% | |

| Time to | Mortgage | | | | Mortgage Interest Rate | | | | | | | | |
Sale	Term	5.50%	6.50%	7.50%	8.00%	8.50%	9.00%	9.50%	10.00%	10.50%	11.00%	12.00%	12.50%
10	15	4.6369	5.1403	5.6587	5.9233	6.1914	6.4628	6.7376	7.0156	7.2968	7.5809	8.1580	8.4508
Years	20	4.4449	4.9994	5.5696	5.8602	6.1543	6.4517	6.7522	7.0557	7.3620	7.6709	8.2962	8.6122
	25	4.3353	4.9204	5.5208	5.8261	6.1345	6.4458	6.7598	7.0763	7.3950	7.7158	8.3629	8.6889
	30	4.2665	4.8720	5.4916	5.8059	6.1230	6.4424	6.7641	7.0876	7.4129	7.7397	8.3972	8.7276
12	15	5.5613	6.0347	6.5237	6.7738	7.0276	7.2851	7.5460	7.8104	8.0781	8.3491	8.9005	9.1808
Years	20	5.3224	5.8555	6.4061	6.6875	6.9727	7.2617	7.5542	7.8501	8.1492	8.4513	9.0642	9.3745
	25	5.1859	5.7551	6.3416	6.6407	6.9433	7.2494	7.5585	7.8705	8.1852	8.5023	9.1432	9.4666
	30	5.1003	5.6935	6.3030	6.6131	6.9263	7.2423	7.5609	7.8818	8.2048	8.5296	9.1839	9.5130
15	15	6.5077	6.9399	7.3872	7.6163	7.8490	8.0852	8.3249	8.5679	8.8143	9.0638	9.5724	9.8312
Years	20	6.2004	6.7041	7.2265	7.4944	7.7666	8.0429	8.3231	8.6071	8.8948	9.1859	9.7779	10.0785
	25	6.0248	6.5718	7.1384	7.4284	7.7225	8.0205	8.3222	8.6273	8.9356	9.2468	9.8772	10.1960
	30	5.9147	6.4908	7.0858	7.3895	7.6969	8.0078	8.3217	8.6384	8.9577	9.2793	9.9283	10.2553
20	15	8.1125	8.5446	8.9919	9.2210	9.4537	9.6899	9.9296	10.1726	10.4190	10.6686	11.1771	11.4360
Years	20	7.0789	7.5404	8.0205	8.2673	8.5184	8.7736	9.0328	9.2960	9.5628	9.8333	10.3845	10.6649
	25	6.8420	7.3569	7.8932	8.1689	8.4492	8.7339	9.0228	9.3157	9.6122	9.9124	10.5222	10.8315
	30	6.6934	7.2444	7.8172	8.1109	8.4090	8.7112	9.0171	9.3265	9.6391	9.9545	10.5930	10.9156

| Equity Yield 10.50% | | | | | 50% Growth over Term | | | | | | Mortgage Ratio 70% | |

		5.50%	6.50%	7.50%	8.00%	8.50%	9.00%	9.50%	10.00%	10.50%	11.00%	12.00%	12.50%
10	15	4.4969	5.0255	5.5698	5.8476	6.1291	6.4141	6.7026	6.9945	7.2897	7.5881	8.1941	8.5014
Years	20	4.2953	4.8775	5.4762	5.7814	6.0902	6.4024	6.7179	7.0366	7.3582	7.6826	8.3391	8.6710
	25	4.1802	4.7946	5.4249	5.7455	6.0694	6.3962	6.7259	7.0582	7.3929	7.7297	8.4092	8.7515
	30	4.1079	4.7437	5.3943	5.7244	6.0573	6.3927	6.7304	7.0702	7.4117	7.7549	8.4452	8.7921
12	15	5.4278	5.9249	6.4383	6.7010	6.9675	7.2377	7.5117	7.7893	8.0704	8.3550	8.9340	9.2282
Years	20	5.1769	5.7367	6.3148	6.6103	6.9098	7.2132	7.5204	7.8310	8.1451	8.4623	9.1058	9.4317
	25	5.0336	5.6313	6.2471	6.5611	6.8789	7.2003	7.5248	7.8525	8.1829	8.5159	9.1888	9.5284
	30	4.9437	5.5666	6.2066	6.5322	6.8610	7.1929	7.5274	7.8643	8.2034	8.5445	9.2315	9.5771
15	15	6.3837	6.8375	7.3071	7.5477	7.7921	8.0401	8.2917	8.5469	8.8056	9.0677	9.6017	9.8734
Years	20	6.0610	6.5899	7.1385	7.4198	7.7056	7.9957	8.2899	8.5881	8.8901	9.1958	9.8174	10.1331
	25	5.8767	6.4511	7.0460	7.3504	7.6593	7.9722	8.2889	8.6093	8.9329	9.2597	9.9217	10.2564
	30	5.7610	6.3659	6.9907	7.3096	7.6324	7.9588	8.2884	8.6210	8.9562	9.2938	9.9753	10.3187
20	15	8.0343	8.4881	8.9577	9.1983	9.4426	9.6906	9.9423	10.1975	10.4562	10.7182	11.2522	11.5240
Years	20	6.9491	7.4336	7.9378	8.1969	8.4605	8.7285	9.0007	9.2770	9.5572	9.8412	10.4199	10.7144
	25	6.7003	7.2410	7.8041	8.0935	8.3878	8.6868	8.9902	9.2977	9.6091	9.9242	10.5645	10.8893
	30	6.5443	7.1229	7.7243	8.0327	8.3457	8.6630	8.9842	9.3091	9.6373	9.9685	10.6389	10.9776

| Equity Yield 10.50% | | | | | 50% Growth over Term | | | | | | Mortgage Ratio 75% | |

		5.50%	6.50%	7.50%	8.00%	8.50%	9.00%	9.50%	10.00%	10.50%	11.00%	12.00%	12.50%
10	15	4.2869	4.8532	5.4364	5.7341	6.0356	6.3410	6.6502	6.9629	7.2792	7.5989	8.2481	8.5775
Years	20	4.0709	4.6947	5.3362	5.6631	5.9940	6.3285	6.6666	7.0080	7.3526	7.7001	8.4036	8.7591
	25	3.9475	4.6058	5.2812	5.6247	5.9717	6.3219	6.6751	7.0311	7.3897	7.7506	8.4786	8.8454
	30	3.8701	4.5513	5.2484	5.6021	5.9587	6.3181	6.6799	7.0439	7.4099	7.7776	8.5173	8.8889
12	15	5.2276	5.7601	6.3102	6.5917	6.8772	7.1668	7.4603	7.7578	8.0589	8.3638	8.9842	9.2995
Years	20	4.9588	5.5586	6.1779	6.4945	6.8154	7.1405	7.4696	7.8024	8.1389	8.4789	9.1683	9.5175
	25	4.8052	5.4456	6.1054	6.4418	6.7824	7.1266	7.4744	7.8254	8.1794	8.5362	9.2572	9.6210
	30	4.7089	5.3763	6.0620	6.4108	6.7632	7.1187	7.4771	7.8381	8.2015	8.5669	9.3030	9.6733
15	15	6.1978	6.6840	7.1871	7.4449	7.7067	7.9724	8.2420	8.5154	8.7926	9.0734	9.6455	9.9367
Years	20	5.8520	6.4186	7.0064	7.3078	7.6140	7.9248	8.2401	8.5596	8.8832	9.2107	9.8767	10.2149
	25	5.6545	6.2699	6.9073	7.2335	7.5644	7.8997	8.2390	8.5823	8.9290	9.2792	9.9884	10.3471
	30	5.5305	6.1787	6.8481	7.1897	7.5356	7.8853	8.2385	8.5948	8.9540	9.3157	10.0458	10.4137
20	15	7.9171	8.4033	8.9065	9.1642	9.4260	9.6917	9.9614	10.2348	10.5119	10.7927	11.3649	11.6560
Years	20	6.7543	7.2735	7.8137	8.0913	8.3738	8.6609	8.9525	9.2485	9.5488	9.8530	10.4731	10.7886
	25	6.4878	7.0671	7.6705	7.9805	8.2959	8.6162	8.9412	9.2707	9.6044	9.9420	10.6280	10.9760
	30	6.3206	6.9405	7.5849	7.9153	8.2507	8.5907	8.9349	9.2829	9.6346	9.9894	10.7077	11.0706

| Equity Yield 10.50% | | | | | 50% Growth over Term | | | | | | Mortgage Ratio 80% | |

		5.50%	6.50%	7.50%	8.00%	8.50%	9.00%	9.50%	10.00%	10.50%	11.00%	12.00%	12.50%
10	15	4.0769	4.6810	5.3030	5.6205	5.9422	6.2680	6.5977	6.9313	7.2687	7.6097	8.3022	8.6535
Years	20	3.8465	4.5118	5.1961	5.5449	5.8978	6.2546	6.6152	6.9794	7.3469	7.7177	8.4680	8.8472
	25	3.7149	4.4170	5.1375	5.5039	5.8740	6.2475	6.6243	7.0041	7.3866	7.7715	8.5481	8.9393
	30	3.6323	4.3589	5.1025	5.4797	5.8602	6.2435	6.6295	7.0177	7.4081	7.8003	8.5893	8.9857
12	15	5.0273	5.5954	6.1822	6.4824	6.7869	7.0958	7.4089	7.7262	8.0475	8.3726	9.0344	9.3707
Years	20	4.7406	5.3804	6.0411	6.3787	6.7210	7.0678	7.4188	7.7739	8.1328	8.4954	9.2308	9.6032
	25	4.5768	5.2599	5.9636	6.3226	6.6858	7.0530	7.4239	7.7984	8.1760	8.5566	9.3257	9.7137
	30	4.4741	5.1860	5.9174	6.2895	6.6653	7.0445	7.4268	7.8119	8.1995	8.5892	9.3744	9.7694
15	15	6.0118	6.5304	7.0671	7.3420	7.6213	7.9047	8.1923	8.4840	8.7796	9.0791	9.6894	10.0000
Years	20	5.6429	6.2473	6.8743	7.1958	7.5224	7.8540	8.1902	8.5310	8.8762	9.2256	9.9360	10.2967
	25	5.4322	6.0887	6.7686	7.1166	7.4695	7.8271	8.1891	8.5552	8.9251	9.2986	10.0551	10.4377
	30	5.3001	5.9914	6.7054	7.0699	7.4388	7.8118	8.1885	8.5686	8.9517	9.3376	10.1164	10.5088
20	15	7.7999	8.3185	8.8552	9.1301	9.4094	9.6928	9.9804	10.2721	10.5677	10.8672	11.4775	11.7881
Years	20	6.5596	7.1134	7.6896	7.9857	8.2870	8.5932	8.9043	9.2201	9.5403	9.8649	10.5263	10.8628
	25	6.2753	6.8932	7.5368	7.8676	8.2039	8.5456	8.8923	9.2437	9.5996	9.9598	10.6916	11.0627
	30	6.0970	6.7582	7.4456	7.7980	8.1557	8.5184	8.8855	9.2568	9.6319	10.0104	10.7765	11.1636

Capitalization Rate to Account for Growth or Decline in Value

Equity Yield 10.50%					50% Decline over Term						Mortgage Ratio 67%		

Time to Sale	Mortgage Term	| Mortgage Interest Rate												
		5.50%	6.50%	7.50%	8.00%	8.50%	9.00%	9.50%	10.00%	10.50%	11.00%	12.00%	12.50%
10 Years	15	10.7626	11.2661	11.7844	12.0490	12.3171	12.5886	12.8633	13.1413	13.4225	13.7067	14.2838	14.5765
	20	10.5706	11.1251	11.6954	11.9860	12.2801	12.5774	12.8779	13.1814	13.4877	13.7966	14.4219	14.7379
	25	10.4610	11.0461	11.6465	11.9518	12.2602	12.5715	12.8855	13.2020	13.5207	13.8415	14.4887	14.8146
	30	10.3922	10.9977	11.6173	11.9317	12.2487	12.5682	12.8898	13.2134	13.5387	13.8655	14.5230	14.8533
12 Years	15	10.0990	10.5724	11.0614	11.3115	11.5653	11.8227	12.0837	12.3480	12.6157	12.8867	13.4382	13.7184
	20	9.8600	10.3932	10.9438	11.2251	11.5104	11.7994	12.0919	12.3878	12.6869	12.9890	13.6018	13.9122
	25	9.7236	10.2928	10.8792	11.1783	11.4810	11.7870	12.0962	12.4082	12.7229	13.0400	13.6809	14.0043
	30	9.6379	10.2312	10.8407	11.1508	11.4640	11.7800	12.0986	12.4195	12.7424	13.0672	13.7216	14.0507
15 Years	15	9.5325	9.9647	10.4120	10.6411	10.8738	11.1100	11.3497	11.5927	11.8391	12.0886	12.5972	12.8560
	20	9.2252	9.7289	10.2513	10.5192	10.7914	11.0677	11.3479	11.6319	11.9196	12.2107	12.8027	13.1033
	25	9.0496	9.5966	10.1632	10.4532	10.7473	11.0453	11.3470	11.6521	11.9604	12.2716	12.9020	13.2208
	30	8.9395	9.5156	10.1106	10.4143	10.7217	11.0326	11.3465	11.6632	11.9825	12.3041	12.9531	13.2801
20 Years	15	9.7618	10.1940	10.6412	10.8703	11.1030	11.3392	11.5789	11.8220	12.0683	12.3179	12.8265	13.0853
	20	8.7282	9.1897	9.6699	9.9166	10.1677	10.4229	10.6822	10.9453	11.2122	11.4826	12.0338	12.3142
	25	8.4913	9.0062	9.5426	9.8182	10.0985	10.3832	10.6721	10.9650	11.2616	11.5617	12.1715	12.4808
	30	8.3427	8.8937	9.4665	9.7602	10.0583	10.3605	10.6665	10.9759	11.2884	11.6039	12.2423	12.5649

Equity Yield 10.50%					-50% Decline over Term						Mortgage Ratio 70%		
10 Years	15	10.6226	11.1512	11.6955	11.9733	12.2548	12.5398	12.8284	13.1203	13.4155	13.7138	14.3198	14.6272
	20	10.4210	11.0032	11.6020	11.9071	12.2159	12.5282	12.8437	13.1623	13.4839	13.8083	14.4649	14.7967
	25	10.3059	10.9203	11.5507	11.8713	12.1951	12.5220	12.8517	13.1839	13.5186	13.8555	14.5349	14.8772
	30	10.2336	10.8694	11.5200	11.8501	12.1830	12.5184	12.8561	13.1959	13.5374	13.8806	14.5710	14.9179
12 Years	15	9.9655	10.4626	10.9760	11.2386	11.5051	11.7754	12.0494	12.3270	12.6081	12.8926	13.4716	13.7659
	20	9.7146	10.2744	10.8525	11.1480	11.4475	11.7509	12.0580	12.3687	12.6828	13.0000	13.6435	13.9694
	25	9.5713	10.1690	10.7848	11.0988	11.4166	11.7379	12.0625	12.3901	12.7206	13.0536	13.7265	14.0661
	30	9.4814	10.1043	10.7443	11.0699	11.3987	11.7305	12.0651	12.4020	12.7411	13.0822	13.7692	14.1148
15 Years	15	9.4085	9.8623	10.3319	10.5725	10.8169	11.0649	11.3165	11.5717	11.8304	12.0925	12.6265	12.8982
	20	9.0858	9.6147	10.1633	10.4446	10.7304	11.0205	11.3147	11.6129	11.9149	12.2206	12.8422	13.1579
	25	8.9015	9.4759	10.0708	10.3752	10.6841	10.9970	11.3137	11.6341	11.9577	12.2845	12.9465	13.2812
	30	8.7858	9.3907	10.0155	10.3344	10.6572	10.9836	11.3132	11.6458	11.9810	12.3186	13.0001	13.3435
20 Years	15	9.6836	10.1374	10.6070	10.8476	11.0919	11.3400	11.5916	11.8468	12.1055	12.3675	12.9015	13.1733
	20	8.5984	9.0829	9.5871	9.8462	10.1098	10.3778	10.6500	10.9263	11.2065	11.4905	12.0693	12.3637
	25	8.3496	8.8903	9.4534	9.7429	10.0372	10.3361	10.6395	10.9470	11.2584	11.5735	12.2139	12.5386
	30	8.1936	8.7722	9.3736	9.6820	9.9950	10.3123	10.6335	10.9584	11.2866	11.6178	12.2882	12.6269

Equity Yield 10.50%					-50% Decline over Term						Mortgage Ratio 75%		
10 Years	15	10.4126	10.9790	11.5621	11.8598	12.1614	12.4668	12.7759	13.0887	13.4049	13.7246	14.3739	14.7032
	20	10.1966	10.8204	11.4619	11.7889	12.1197	12.4542	12.7923	13.1337	13.4783	13.8259	14.5293	14.8848
	25	10.0732	10.7315	11.4069	11.7504	12.0974	12.4476	12.8009	13.1569	13.5154	13.8764	14.6044	14.9711
	30	9.9958	10.6770	11.3741	11.7278	12.0845	12.4438	12.8057	13.1697	13.5356	13.9033	14.6430	15.0146
12 Years	15	9.7652	10.2978	10.8479	11.1293	11.4149	11.7045	11.9980	12.2954	12.5966	12.9015	13.5218	13.8371
	20	9.4964	10.0963	10.7156	11.0322	11.3531	11.6782	12.0073	12.3401	12.6766	13.0165	13.7060	14.0551
	25	9.3429	9.9833	10.6430	10.9795	11.3200	11.6643	12.0121	12.3631	12.7171	13.0739	13.7949	14.1587
	30	9.2466	9.9140	10.5997	10.9485	11.3008	11.6564	12.0148	12.3758	12.7391	13.1045	13.8407	14.2110
15 Years	15	9.2226	9.7088	10.2119	10.4697	10.7315	10.9972	11.2668	11.5402	11.8174	12.0982	12.6703	12.9615
	20	8.8768	9.4434	10.0312	10.3326	10.6388	10.9496	11.2649	11.5844	11.9080	12.2355	12.9015	13.2397
	25	8.6793	9.2947	9.9321	10.2583	10.5892	10.9245	11.2638	11.6071	11.9538	12.3040	13.0132	13.3719
	30	8.5553	9.2035	9.8729	10.2145	10.5604	10.9101	11.2633	11.6196	11.9788	12.3405	13.0706	13.4385
20 Years	15	9.5664	10.0526	10.5558	10.8135	11.0753	11.3411	11.6107	11.8841	12.1613	12.4420	13.0142	13.3054
	20	8.4037	8.9228	9.4630	9.7406	10.0231	10.3102	10.6018	10.8979	11.1981	11.5024	12.1224	12.4379
	25	8.1371	8.7164	9.3198	9.6299	9.9452	10.2655	10.5905	10.9200	11.2537	11.5913	12.2774	12.6254
	30	7.9699	8.5899	9.2343	9.5647	9.9000	10.2400	10.5842	10.9323	11.2839	11.6388	12.3570	12.7199

Equity Yield 10.50%					-50% Decline over Term						Mortgage Ratio 80%		
10 Years	15	10.2026	10.8067	11.4287	11.7462	12.0679	12.3937	12.7234	13.0570	13.3944	13.7354	14.4279	14.7792
	20	9.9722	10.6376	11.3219	11.6706	12.0235	12.3803	12.7409	13.1051	13.4727	13.8434	14.5937	14.9730
	25	9.8406	10.5428	11.2632	11.6296	11.9997	12.3733	12.7501	13.1298	13.5123	13.8973	14.6738	15.0650
	30	9.7580	10.4847	11.2282	11.6054	11.9859	12.3692	12.7552	13.1435	13.5338	13.9260	14.7150	15.1114
12 Years	15	9.5650	10.1331	10.7199	11.0200	11.3246	11.6335	11.9466	12.2639	12.5851	12.9103	13.5720	13.9084
	20	9.2783	9.9181	10.5787	10.9164	11.2587	11.6055	11.9565	12.3115	12.6705	13.0330	13.7684	14.1409
	25	9.1145	9.7976	10.5013	10.8602	11.2234	11.5907	11.9616	12.3360	12.7137	13.0943	13.8633	14.2514
	30	9.0117	9.7237	10.4551	10.8272	11.2030	11.5822	11.9645	12.3496	12.7372	13.1269	13.9121	14.3071
15 Years	15	9.0366	9.5552	10.0919	10.3668	10.6461	10.9295	11.2171	11.5088	11.8044	12.1039	12.7142	13.0248
	20	8.6677	9.2721	9.8991	10.2206	10.5472	10.8788	11.2150	11.5558	11.9010	12.2504	12.9608	13.3215
	25	8.4570	9.1135	9.7934	10.1414	10.4943	10.8519	11.2139	11.5800	11.9499	12.3234	13.0799	13.4625
	30	8.3249	9.0162	9.7302	10.0947	10.4636	10.8366	11.2133	11.5934	11.9765	12.3624	13.1412	13.5336
20 Years	15	9.4492	9.9678	10.5045	10.7795	11.0587	11.3422	11.6298	11.9214	12.2170	12.5165	13.1268	13.4374
	20	8.2089	8.7627	9.3389	9.6350	9.9363	10.2426	10.5537	10.8694	11.1896	11.5142	12.1756	12.5122
	25	7.9246	8.5425	9.1861	9.5169	9.8532	10.1949	10.5416	10.8930	11.2490	11.6091	12.3409	12.7121
	30	7.7463	8.4075	9.0949	9.4473	9.8051	10.1677	10.5348	10.9061	11.2812	11.6597	12.4259	12.8129

Capitalization Rate to Account for Growth or Decline in Value

Equity Yield 10.50% 67% Growth over Term Mortgage Ratio 67%

Time to Sale	Mortgage Term	5.50%	6.50%	7.50%	8.00%	8.50%	9.00%	9.50%	10.00%	10.50%	11.00%	12.00%	12.50%
10 Years	15	3.6159	4.1194	4.6377	4.9023	5.1704	5.4419	5.7167	5.9947	6.2758	6.5600	7.1371	7.4298
	20	3.4240	3.9784	4.5487	4.8393	5.1334	5.4307	5.7312	6.0347	6.3410	6.6500	7.2752	7.5913
	25	3.3143	3.8994	4.4998	4.8051	5.1135	5.4249	5.7388	6.0553	6.3740	6.6948	7.3420	7.6680
	30	3.2455	3.8510	4.4706	4.7850	5.1020	5.4215	5.7431	6.0667	6.3920	6.7188	7.3763	7.7066
12 Years	15	4.8050	5.2784	5.7674	6.0175	6.2714	6.5288	6.7897	7.0541	7.3218	7.5928	8.1442	8.4245
	20	4.5661	5.0993	5.6498	5.9312	6.2165	6.5054	6.7979	7.0938	7.3929	7.6951	8.3079	8.6183
	25	4.4296	4.9988	5.5853	5.8844	6.1871	6.4931	6.8022	7.1142	7.4289	7.7461	8.3870	8.7103
	30	4.3440	4.9372	5.5468	5.8568	6.1700	6.4860	6.8046	7.1255	7.4485	7.7733	8.4276	8.7568
15 Years	15	6.0036	6.4358	6.8830	7.1121	7.3448	7.5811	7.8207	8.0638	8.3101	8.5597	9.0683	9.3271
	20	5.6962	6.1999	6.7224	6.9903	7.2625	7.5388	7.8190	8.1030	8.3906	8.6818	9.2738	9.5744
	25	5.5207	6.0677	6.6343	6.9243	7.2184	7.5164	7.8181	8.1232	8.4314	8.7426	9.3731	9.6919
	30	5.4105	5.9867	6.5817	6.8854	7.1928	7.5036	7.8176	8.1343	8.4536	8.7751	9.4241	9.7511
20 Years	15	7.8376	8.2698	8.7170	8.9461	9.1788	9.4150	9.6547	9.8977	10.1441	10.3937	10.9022	11.1611
	20	6.8040	7.2655	7.7456	7.9924	8.2435	8.4987	8.7579	9.0211	9.2879	9.5584	10.1096	10.3900
	25	6.5671	7.0820	7.6183	7.8940	8.1743	8.4590	8.7479	9.0408	9.3374	9.6375	10.2473	10.5566
	30	6.4185	6.9695	7.5423	7.8360	8.1341	8.4363	8.7422	9.0516	9.3642	9.6797	10.3181	10.6407

Equity Yield 10.50% 67% Growth over Term Mortgage Ratio 70%

Time to Sale	Mortgage Term	5.50%	6.50%	7.50%	8.00%	8.50%	9.00%	9.50%	10.00%	10.50%	11.00%	12.00%	12.50%
10 Years	15	3.4759	4.0045	4.5488	4.8266	5.1081	5.3932	5.6817	5.9736	6.2688	6.5672	7.1731	7.4805
	20	3.2744	3.8566	4.4553	4.7604	5.0692	5.3815	5.6970	6.0156	6.3372	6.6616	7.3182	7.6500
	25	3.1592	3.7736	4.4040	4.7246	5.0484	5.3753	5.7050	6.0373	6.3719	6.7088	7.3883	7.7305
	30	3.0870	3.7227	4.3733	4.7034	5.0363	5.3718	5.7095	6.0492	6.3908	6.7339	7.4243	7.7712
12 Years	15	4.6715	5.1686	5.6820	5.9447	6.2112	6.4815	6.7554	7.0330	7.3141	7.5987	8.1777	8.4720
	20	4.4206	4.9805	5.5585	5.8540	6.1535	6.4569	6.7641	7.0748	7.3888	7.7061	8.3495	8.6754
	25	4.2773	4.8750	5.4908	5.8049	6.1227	6.4440	6.7686	7.0962	7.4266	7.7596	8.4326	8.7721
	30	4.1874	4.8104	5.4504	5.7759	6.1048	6.4366	6.7711	7.1080	7.4472	7.7882	8.4753	8.8209
15 Years	15	5.8796	6.3334	6.8030	7.0436	7.2879	7.5359	7.7876	8.0428	8.3015	8.5635	9.0975	9.3693
	20	5.5569	6.0857	6.6343	6.9157	7.2014	7.4915	7.7858	8.0840	8.3860	8.6917	9.3133	9.6289
	25	5.3725	5.9469	6.5418	6.8463	7.1551	7.4681	7.7848	8.1051	8.4288	8.7556	9.4175	9.7523
	30	5.2569	5.8618	6.4866	6.8055	7.1283	7.4546	7.7843	8.1168	8.4521	8.7897	9.4712	9.8145
20 Years	15	7.7594	8.2132	8.6828	8.9234	9.1677	9.4158	9.6674	9.9226	10.1813	10.4433	10.9773	11.2491
	20	6.6742	7.1587	7.6629	7.9220	8.1856	8.4536	8.7258	9.0021	9.2823	9.5663	10.1450	10.4395
	25	6.4254	6.9661	7.5292	7.8186	8.1130	8.4119	8.7153	9.0228	9.3342	9.6493	10.2896	10.6144
	30	6.2694	6.8480	7.4494	7.7578	8.0708	8.3881	8.7093	9.0342	9.3624	9.6936	10.3640	10.7027

Equity Yield 10.50% 67% Growth over Term Mortgage Ratio 75%

Time to Sale	Mortgage Term	5.50%	6.50%	7.50%	8.00%	8.50%	9.00%	9.50%	10.00%	10.50%	11.00%	12.00%	12.50%
10 Years	15	3.2659	3.8323	4.4154	4.7131	5.0147	5.3201	5.6292	5.9420	6.2582	6.5779	7.2272	7.5565
	20	3.0499	3.6737	4.3152	4.6422	4.9730	5.3076	5.6456	5.9870	6.3316	6.6792	7.3826	7.7381
	25	2.9266	3.5848	4.2603	4.6037	4.9507	5.3009	5.6542	6.0102	6.3688	6.7297	7.4577	7.8244
	30	2.8492	3.5304	4.2274	4.5811	4.9378	5.2972	5.6590	6.0230	6.3889	6.7566	7.4963	7.8680
12 Years	15	4.4713	5.0039	5.5540	5.8354	6.1209	6.4105	6.7041	7.0015	7.3027	7.6075	8.2279	8.5432
	20	4.2025	4.8023	5.4217	5.7382	6.0591	6.3842	6.7133	7.0462	7.3827	7.7226	8.4120	8.7612
	25	4.0489	4.6893	5.3491	5.6856	6.0261	6.3703	6.7181	7.0691	7.4232	7.7800	8.5010	8.8648
	30	3.9526	4.6200	5.3057	5.6546	6.0069	6.3624	6.7208	7.0818	7.4452	7.8106	8.5467	8.9170
15 Years	15	5.6936	6.1798	6.6830	6.9407	7.2025	7.4683	7.7379	8.0113	8.2885	8.5692	9.1414	9.4326
	20	5.3478	5.9145	6.5023	6.8037	7.1099	7.4207	7.7359	8.0554	8.3790	8.7065	9.3726	9.7108
	25	5.1503	5.7657	6.4031	6.7294	7.0603	7.3955	7.7349	8.0781	8.4249	8.7750	9.4843	9.8429
	30	5.0264	5.6746	6.3439	6.6856	7.0315	7.3812	7.7343	8.0907	8.4498	8.8116	9.5417	9.9096
20 Years	15	7.6422	8.1284	8.6316	8.8893	9.1511	9.4169	9.6865	9.9599	10.2370	10.5178	11.0900	11.3812
	20	6.4794	6.9986	7.5388	7.8164	8.0989	8.3860	8.6776	8.9736	9.2739	9.5781	10.1982	10.5137
	25	6.2129	6.7922	7.3956	7.7057	8.0210	8.3413	8.6663	8.9958	9.3295	9.6671	10.3532	10.7011
	30	6.0457	6.6656	7.3100	7.6404	7.9758	8.3158	8.6600	9.0080	9.3597	9.7146	10.4328	10.7957

Equity Yield 10.50% 67% Growth over Term Mortgage Ratio 80%

Time to Sale	Mortgage Term	5.50%	6.50%	7.50%	8.00%	8.50%	9.00%	9.50%	10.00%	10.50%	11.00%	12.00%	12.50%
10 Years	15	3.0559	3.6600	4.2821	4.5996	4.9212	5.2470	5.5767	5.9104	6.2477	6.5887	7.2812	7.6325
	20	2.8255	3.4909	4.1752	4.5239	4.8768	5.2336	5.5942	5.9584	6.3260	6.6967	7.4470	7.8263
	25	2.6939	3.3961	4.1165	4.4829	4.8530	5.2266	5.6034	5.9831	6.3656	6.7506	7.5271	7.9183
	30	2.6114	3.3380	4.0815	4.4588	4.8392	5.2226	5.6085	5.9968	6.3871	6.7793	7.5683	7.9647
12 Years	15	4.2710	4.8391	5.4259	5.7261	6.0307	6.3396	6.6527	6.9699	7.2912	7.6164	8.2781	8.6144
	20	3.9843	4.6241	5.2848	5.6225	5.9648	6.3115	6.6625	7.0176	7.3765	7.7391	8.4745	8.8469
	25	3.8205	4.5036	5.2074	5.5663	5.9295	6.2967	6.6677	7.0421	7.4197	7.8003	8.5694	8.9574
	30	3.7178	4.4297	5.1611	5.5332	5.9090	6.2883	6.6706	7.0556	7.4432	7.8330	8.6182	9.0131
15 Years	15	5.5076	6.0263	6.5629	6.8379	7.1171	7.4006	7.6882	7.9798	8.2755	8.5750	9.1852	9.4958
	20	5.1388	5.7432	6.3702	6.6917	7.0183	7.3498	7.6861	8.0269	8.3721	8.7214	9.4319	9.7926
	25	4.9281	5.5846	6.2644	6.6124	6.9654	7.3230	7.6850	8.0511	8.4210	8.7945	9.5510	9.9336
	30	4.7959	5.4873	6.2013	6.5658	6.9347	7.3077	7.6844	8.0645	8.4476	8.8334	9.6122	10.0047
20 Years	15	7.5250	8.0436	8.5803	8.8552	9.1345	9.4179	9.7055	9.9972	10.2928	10.5923	11.2026	11.5132
	20	6.2847	6.8385	7.4147	7.7108	8.0121	8.3184	8.6294	8.9452	9.2654	9.5900	10.2514	10.5879
	25	6.0004	6.6183	7.2619	7.5927	7.9290	8.2707	8.6174	8.9688	9.3247	9.6849	10.4167	10.7879
	30	5.8221	6.4833	7.1707	7.5231	7.8808	8.2435	8.6106	8.9819	9.3570	9.7355	10.5017	10.8887

Capitalization Rate to Account for Growth or Decline in Value

Equity Yield 10.50%		100% Growth over Term									Mortgage Ratio 67%		

Time to Sale	Mortgage Term	5.50%	6.50%	7.50%	8.00%	8.50%	9.00%	9.50%	10.00%	10.50%	11.00%	12.00%	12.50%
10 Years	15	1.5740	2.0775	2.5958	2.8604	3.1285	3.4000	3.6747	3.9527	4.2339	4.5181	5.0952	5.3879
	20	1.3821	1.9365	2.5068	2.7974	3.0915	3.3888	3.6893	3.9928	4.2991	4.6080	5.2333	5.5493
	25	1.2724	1.8575	2.4579	2.7632	3.0716	3.3829	3.6969	4.0134	4.3321	4.6529	5.3001	5.6260
	30	1.2036	1.8091	2.4287	2.7431	3.0601	3.3796	3.7012	4.0248	4.3501	4.6769	5.3344	5.6647
12 Years	15	3.2925	3.7659	4.2548	4.5050	4.7588	5.0162	5.2771	5.5415	5.8092	6.0802	6.6317	6.9119
	20	3.0535	3.5867	4.1372	4.4186	4.7039	4.9929	5.2854	5.5812	5.8803	6.1825	6.7953	7.1057
	25	2.9170	3.4863	4.0727	4.3718	4.6745	4.9805	5.2896	5.6017	5.9164	6.2335	6.8744	7.1978
	30	2.8314	3.4247	4.0342	4.3443	4.6574	4.9735	5.2921	5.6130	5.9359	6.2607	6.9151	7.2442
15 Years	15	4.9953	5.4275	5.8748	6.1039	6.3366	6.5728	6.8125	7.0555	7.3019	7.5514	8.0600	8.3188
	20	4.6880	5.1917	5.7141	5.9820	6.2542	6.5305	6.8107	7.0947	7.3824	7.6735	8.2655	8.5661
	25	4.5124	5.0594	5.6260	5.9160	6.2101	6.5081	6.8098	7.1149	7.4232	7.7344	8.3648	8.6836
	30	4.4023	4.9784	5.5734	5.8771	6.1845	6.4954	6.8093	7.1260	7.4453	7.7669	8.4159	8.7429
20 Years	15	7.2878	7.7200	8.1672	8.3963	8.6290	8.8653	9.1049	9.3480	9.5943	9.8439	10.3525	10.6113
	20	6.2542	6.7157	7.1959	7.4426	7.6937	7.9489	8.2082	8.4713	8.7382	9.0086	9.5598	9.8402
	25	6.0173	6.5322	7.0686	7.3442	7.6245	7.9092	8.1981	8.4910	8.7876	9.0877	9.6975	10.0068
	30	5.8687	6.4197	6.9925	7.2862	7.5843	7.8865	8.1925	8.5019	8.8144	9.1299	9.7683	10.0909

Equity Yield 10.50%		100% Growth over Term									Mortgage Ratio 70%		

Time to Sale	Mortgage Term	5.50%	6.50%	7.50%	8.00%	8.50%	9.00%	9.50%	10.00%	10.50%	11.00%	12.00%	12.50%
10 Years	15	1.4340	1.9626	2.5069	2.7847	3.0662	3.3512	3.6398	3.9317	4.2269	4.5253	5.1312	5.4386
	20	1.2324	1.8146	2.4134	2.7185	3.0273	3.3396	3.6551	3.9737	4.2953	4.6197	5.2763	5.6081
	25	1.1173	1.7317	2.3621	2.6827	3.0065	3.3334	3.6631	3.9953	4.3300	4.6669	5.3463	5.6886
	30	1.0451	1.6808	2.3314	2.6615	2.9944	3.3298	3.6675	4.0073	4.3488	4.6920	5.3824	5.7293
12 Years	15	3.1590	3.6560	4.1695	4.4321	4.6986	4.9689	5.2429	5.5205	5.8016	6.0861	6.6651	6.9594
	20	2.9081	3.4679	4.0460	4.3414	4.6410	4.9444	5.2515	5.5622	5.8762	6.1935	6.8370	7.1629
	25	2.7648	3.3625	3.9783	4.2923	4.6101	4.9314	5.2560	5.5836	5.9141	6.2471	6.9200	7.2595
	30	2.6749	3.2978	3.9378	4.2634	4.5922	4.9240	5.2585	5.5955	5.9346	6.2757	6.9627	7.3083
15 Years	15	4.8713	5.3251	5.7947	6.0353	6.2797	6.5277	6.7793	7.0345	7.2932	7.5553	8.0893	8.3610
	20	4.5486	5.0775	5.6261	5.9074	6.1932	6.4833	6.7775	7.0757	7.3777	7.6834	8.3050	8.6207
	25	4.3643	4.9387	5.5336	5.8380	6.1469	6.4598	6.7765	7.0969	7.4205	7.7473	8.4093	8.7440
	30	4.2486	4.8535	5.4783	5.7972	6.1200	6.4464	6.7760	7.1086	7.4438	7.7814	8.4629	8.8063
20 Years	15	7.2096	7.6634	8.1330	8.3736	8.6180	8.8660	9.1176	9.3728	9.6315	9.8936	10.4276	10.6993
	20	6.1244	6.6090	7.1131	7.3722	7.6359	7.9038	8.1760	8.4523	8.7325	9.0165	9.5953	9.8897
	25	5.8757	6.4163	6.9795	7.2689	7.5632	7.8621	8.1655	8.4730	8.7844	9.0995	9.7399	10.0647
	30	5.7196	6.2982	6.8996	7.2080	7.5210	7.8383	8.1596	8.4844	8.8126	9.1438	9.8142	10.1529

Equity Yield 10.50%		100% Growth over Term									Mortgage Ratio 75%		

Time to Sale	Mortgage Term	5.50%	6.50%	7.50%	8.00%	8.50%	9.00%	9.50%	10.00%	10.50%	11.00%	12.00%	12.50%
10 Years	15	1.2240	1.7904	2.3735	2.6712	2.9728	3.2782	3.5873	3.9001	4.2163	4.5360	5.1853	5.5146
	20	1.0080	1.6318	2.2733	2.6003	2.9311	3.2656	3.6037	3.9451	4.2897	4.6373	5.3407	5.6962
	25	0.8846	1.5429	2.2184	2.5618	2.9088	3.2590	3.6123	3.9683	4.3268	4.6878	5.4158	5.7825
	30	0.8072	1.4884	2.1855	2.5392	2.8959	3.2552	3.6171	3.9811	4.3470	4.7147	5.4544	5.8260
12 Years	15	2.9587	3.4913	4.0414	4.3228	4.6084	4.8980	5.1915	5.4889	5.7901	6.0950	6.7153	7.0306
	20	2.6899	3.2897	3.9091	4.2257	4.5466	4.8717	5.2007	5.5336	5.8701	6.2100	6.8995	7.2486
	25	2.5364	3.1768	3.8365	4.1730	4.5135	4.8578	5.2056	5.5566	5.9106	6.2674	6.9884	7.3522
	30	2.4401	3.1075	3.7932	4.1420	4.4943	4.8499	5.2083	5.5693	5.9326	6.2980	7.0341	7.4044
15 Years	15	4.6854	5.1716	5.6747	5.9325	6.1943	6.4600	6.7296	7.0030	7.2802	7.5610	8.1331	8.4243
	20	4.3396	4.9062	5.4940	5.7954	6.1016	6.4124	6.7277	7.0472	7.3708	7.6983	8.3643	8.7025
	25	4.1421	4.7575	5.3949	5.7211	6.0520	6.3873	6.7266	7.0699	7.4166	7.7668	8.4760	8.8347
	30	4.0181	4.6663	5.3357	5.6773	6.0232	6.3729	6.7261	7.0824	7.4416	7.8033	8.5334	8.9013
20 Years	15	7.0924	7.5786	8.0818	8.3395	8.6013	8.8671	9.1367	9.4101	9.6873	9.9681	10.5402	10.8314
	20	5.9297	6.4488	6.9890	7.2666	7.5491	7.8362	8.1279	8.4239	8.7241	9.0284	9.6485	9.9639
	25	5.6632	6.2424	6.8458	7.1559	7.4712	7.7915	8.1165	8.4460	8.7797	9.1173	9.8034	10.1514
	30	5.4960	6.1159	6.7603	7.0907	7.4260	7.7660	8.1102	8.4583	8.8099	9.1648	9.8831	10.2459

Equity Yield 10.50%		100% Growth over Term									Mortgage Ratio 80%		

Time to Sale	Mortgage Term	5.50%	6.50%	7.50%	8.00%	8.50%	9.00%	9.50%	10.00%	10.50%	11.00%	12.00%	12.50%
10 Years	15	1.0140	1.6181	2.2402	2.5577	2.8793	3.2051	3.5348	3.8684	4.2058	4.5468	5.2393	5.5906
	20	0.7836	1.4490	2.1333	2.4820	2.8349	3.1917	3.5523	3.9165	4.2841	4.6548	5.4051	5.7844
	25	0.6520	1.3542	2.0746	2.4410	2.8111	3.1847	3.5615	3.9412	4.3237	4.7087	5.4852	5.8764
	30	0.5694	1.2961	2.0396	2.4168	2.7973	3.1806	3.5666	3.9549	4.3452	4.7374	5.5264	5.9228
12 Years	15	2.7585	3.3266	3.9133	4.2135	4.5181	4.8270	5.1401	5.4574	5.7786	6.1038	6.7655	7.1018
	20	2.4718	3.1116	3.7722	4.1099	4.4522	4.7990	5.1500	5.5050	5.8639	6.2265	6.9619	7.3344
	25	2.3080	2.9910	3.6948	4.0537	4.4169	4.7842	5.1551	5.5295	5.9072	6.2877	7.0568	7.4449
	30	2.2052	2.9172	3.6486	4.0206	4.3965	4.7757	5.1580	5.5431	5.9306	6.3204	7.1056	7.5006
15 Years	15	4.4994	5.0180	5.5547	5.8296	6.1089	6.3923	6.6799	6.9716	7.2672	7.5667	8.1770	8.4876
	20	4.1305	4.7349	5.3619	5.6834	6.0100	6.3416	6.6778	7.0186	7.3638	7.7132	8.4236	8.7843
	25	3.9198	4.5763	5.2562	5.6042	5.9571	6.3147	6.6767	7.0428	7.4127	7.7862	8.5427	8.9253
	30	3.7877	4.4790	5.1930	5.5575	5.9264	6.2994	6.6761	7.0562	7.4393	7.8252	8.6040	8.9964
20 Years	15	6.9752	7.4938	8.0305	8.3055	8.5847	8.8682	9.1558	9.4474	9.7430	10.0425	10.6528	10.9634
	20	5.7349	6.2887	6.8649	7.1610	7.4623	7.7686	8.0797	8.3954	8.7157	9.0402	9.7016	10.0382
	25	5.4506	6.0685	6.7121	7.0429	7.3793	7.7209	8.0676	8.4191	8.7750	9.1351	9.8669	10.2381
	30	5.2723	5.9335	6.6209	6.9733	7.3311	7.6937	8.0608	8.4321	8.8072	9.1857	9.9519	10.3389

Capitalization Rate to Account for Growth or Decline in Value

Equity Yield 10.50%   150% Growth over Term   Mortgage Ratio 67%

Time to Sale	Mortgage Term	5.50%	6.50%	7.50%	8.00%	8.50%	9.00%	9.50%	10.00%	10.50%	11.00%	12.00%	12.50%
10 Years	15	-1.4888	-0.9854	-0.4670	-0.2024	0.0656	0.3371	0.6119	0.8899	1.1710	1.4552	2.0323	2.3250
	20	-1.6808	-1.1263	-0.5561	-0.2655	0.0286	0.3260	0.6265	0.9299	1.2362	1.5452	2.1705	2.4865
	25	-1.7905	-1.2053	-0.6050	-0.2997	0.0088	0.3201	0.6341	0.9505	1.2692	1.5901	2.2372	2.5632
	30	-1.8593	-1.2538	-0.6342	-0.3198	-0.0027	0.3167	0.6383	0.9619	1.2872	1.6140	2.2715	2.6019
12 Years	15	1.0236	1.4970	1.9860	2.2361	2.4900	2.7474	3.0083	3.2727	3.5404	3.8114	4.3628	4.6431
	20	0.7847	1.3179	1.8684	2.1498	2.4351	2.7240	3.0165	3.3124	3.6115	3.9137	4.5265	4.8369
	25	0.6482	1.2174	1.8039	2.1030	2.4057	2.7117	3.0208	3.3328	3.6475	3.9647	4.6056	4.9289
	30	0.5626	1.1559	1.7654	2.0754	2.3886	2.7046	3.0232	3.3441	3.6671	3.9919	4.6462	4.9754
15 Years	15	3.4829	3.9151	4.3624	4.5915	4.8242	5.0604	5.3001	5.5431	5.7895	6.0390	6.5476	6.8064
	20	3.1756	3.6793	4.2017	4.4696	4.7418	5.0181	5.2983	5.5823	5.8700	6.1611	6.7531	7.0537
	25	3.0000	3.5470	4.1136	4.4036	4.6977	4.9957	5.2974	5.6025	5.9108	6.2220	6.8524	7.1712
	30	2.8899	3.4660	4.0610	4.3647	4.6721	4.9830	5.2969	5.6136	5.9329	6.2545	6.9035	7.2305
20 Years	15	6.4631	6.8953	7.3426	7.5717	7.8044	8.0406	8.2803	8.5233	8.7697	9.0192	9.5278	9.7866
	20	5.4296	5.8910	6.3712	6.6180	6.8690	7.1243	7.3835	7.6466	7.9135	8.1840	8.7351	9.0156
	25	5.1927	5.7076	6.2439	6.5195	6.7998	7.0845	7.3735	7.6663	7.9629	8.2630	8.8729	9.1822
	30	5.0440	5.5951	6.1679	6.4616	6.7597	7.0619	7.3678	7.6772	7.9898	8.3052	8.9437	9.2662

Equity Yield 10.50%   150% Growth over Term   Mortgage Ratio 70%

Time to Sale	Mortgage Term	5.50%	6.50%	7.50%	8.00%	8.50%	9.00%	9.50%	10.00%	10.50%	11.00%	12.00%	12.50%
10 Years	15	-1.6288	-1.1002	-0.5560	-0.2781	0.0033	0.2884	0.5769	0.8688	1.1640	1.4624	2.0683	2.3757
	20	-1.8304	-1.2482	-0.6495	-0.3443	-0.0356	0.2767	0.5922	0.9109	1.2325	1.5569	2.2134	2.5452
	25	-1.9456	-1.3312	-0.7008	-0.3802	-0.0564	0.2705	0.6002	0.9325	1.2671	1.6040	2.2835	2.6258
	30	-2.0178	-1.3820	-0.7314	-0.4013	-0.0684	0.2670	0.6047	0.9444	1.2860	1.6291	2.3195	2.6664
12 Years	15	0.8901	1.3872	1.9006	2.1633	2.4298	2.7001	2.9741	3.2516	3.5327	3.8173	4.3963	4.6906
	20	0.6392	1.1991	1.7771	2.0726	2.3721	2.6755	2.9827	3.2934	3.6074	3.9247	4.5681	4.8940
	25	0.4959	1.0936	1.7094	2.0235	2.3413	2.6626	2.9872	3.3148	3.6452	3.9782	4.6512	4.9907
	30	0.4060	1.0290	1.6690	1.9945	2.3234	2.6552	2.9897	3.3266	3.6658	4.0068	4.6939	5.0395
15 Years	15	3.3589	3.8127	4.2823	4.5229	4.7673	5.0153	5.2669	5.5221	5.7808	6.0429	6.5769	6.8486
	20	3.0362	3.5651	4.1137	4.3950	4.6808	4.9709	5.2651	5.5633	5.8653	6.1710	6.7926	7.1083
	25	2.8519	3.4263	4.0212	4.3256	4.6345	4.9474	5.2641	5.5845	5.9081	6.2349	6.8969	7.2316
	30	2.7362	3.3411	3.9659	4.2848	4.6076	4.9340	5.2636	5.5962	5.9314	6.2690	6.9505	7.2939
20 Years	15	6.3850	6.8388	7.3084	7.5490	7.7933	8.0413	8.2930	8.5482	8.8068	9.0689	9.6029	9.8747
	20	5.2997	5.7843	6.2885	6.5476	6.8112	7.0792	7.3514	7.6277	7.9079	8.1919	8.7706	9.0651
	25	5.0510	5.5916	6.1548	6.4442	6.7385	7.0375	7.3408	7.6483	7.9598	8.2749	8.9152	9.2400
	30	4.8949	5.4735	6.0750	6.3833	6.6964	7.0136	7.3349	7.6598	7.9880	8.3192	8.9896	9.3282

Equity Yield 10.50%   150% Growth over Term   Mortgage Ratio 75%

Time to Sale	Mortgage Term	5.50%	6.50%	7.50%	8.00%	8.50%	9.00%	9.50%	10.00%	10.50%	11.00%	12.00%	12.50%
10 Years	15	-1.8389	-1.2725	-0.6893	-0.3917	-0.0901	0.2153	0.5244	0.8372	1.1535	1.4732	2.1224	2.4517
	20	-2.0548	-1.4311	-0.7895	-0.4626	-0.1318	0.2028	0.5408	0.8823	1.2268	1.5744	2.2778	2.6334
	25	-2.1782	-1.5199	-0.8445	-0.5010	-0.1541	0.1962	0.5494	0.9054	1.2640	1.6249	2.3529	2.7196
	30	-2.2556	-1.5744	-0.8773	-0.5237	-0.1670	0.1924	0.5542	0.9182	1.2842	1.6518	2.3915	2.7632
12 Years	15	0.6899	1.2225	1.7726	2.0540	2.3395	2.6291	2.9227	3.2201	3.5213	3.8261	4.4465	4.7618
	20	0.4211	1.0209	1.6403	1.9568	2.2778	2.6028	2.9319	3.2648	3.6013	3.9412	4.6306	4.9798
	25	0.2675	0.9079	1.5677	1.9042	2.2447	2.5890	2.9367	3.2877	3.6418	3.9986	4.7196	5.0834
	30	0.1712	0.8386	1.5244	1.8732	2.2255	2.5810	2.9394	3.3004	3.6638	4.0292	4.7653	5.1356
15 Years	15	3.1730	3.6592	4.1623	4.4201	4.6819	4.9476	5.2172	5.4906	5.7678	6.0486	6.6207	6.9119
	20	2.8272	3.3938	3.9816	4.2830	4.5892	4.9000	5.2153	5.5348	5.8584	6.1859	6.8519	7.1901
	25	2.6297	3.2451	3.8825	4.2087	4.5396	4.8749	5.2142	5.5575	5.9042	6.2544	6.9636	7.3223
	30	2.5057	3.1539	3.8233	4.1649	4.5108	4.8605	5.2137	5.5700	5.9292	6.2909	7.0210	7.3889
20 Years	15	6.2678	6.7540	7.2571	7.5149	7.7767	8.0424	8.3120	8.5855	8.8626	9.1434	9.7155	10.0067
	20	5.1050	5.6242	6.1644	6.4420	6.7244	7.0115	7.3032	7.5992	7.8994	8.2037	8.8238	9.1393
	25	4.8385	5.4178	6.0211	6.3312	6.6466	6.9669	7.2919	7.6214	7.9550	8.2927	8.9787	9.3267
	30	4.6713	5.2912	5.9356	6.2660	6.6014	6.9413	7.2855	7.6336	7.9852	8.3401	9.0584	9.4213

Equity Yield 10.50%   150% Growth over Term   Mortgage Ratio 80%

Time to Sale	Mortgage Term	5.50%	6.50%	7.50%	8.00%	8.50%	9.00%	9.50%	10.00%	10.50%	11.00%	12.00%	12.50%
10 Years	15	-2.0489	-1.4448	-0.8227	-0.5052	-0.1835	0.1422	0.4720	0.8056	1.1429	1.4840	2.1765	2.5278
	20	-2.2793	-1.6139	-0.9296	-0.5809	-0.2280	0.1289	0.4895	0.8536	1.2212	1.5919	2.3423	2.7215
	25	-2.4109	-1.7087	-0.9882	-0.6219	-0.2518	0.1218	0.4986	0.8783	1.2608	1.6458	2.4223	2.8135
	30	-2.4934	-1.7668	-1.0233	-0.6460	-0.2656	0.1178	0.5037	0.8920	1.2823	1.6745	2.4635	2.8600
12 Years	15	0.4896	1.0577	1.6445	1.9447	2.2493	2.5582	2.8713	3.1885	3.5098	3.8350	4.4967	4.8330
	20	0.2029	0.8427	1.5034	1.8411	2.1834	2.5301	2.8811	3.2362	3.5951	3.9577	4.6931	5.0655
	25	0.0391	0.7222	1.4260	1.7849	2.1481	2.5153	2.8863	3.2607	3.6383	4.0189	4.7880	5.1760
	30	-0.0636	0.6483	1.3797	1.7518	2.1276	2.5069	2.8892	3.2742	3.6618	4.0516	4.8368	5.2317
15 Years	15	2.9870	3.5056	4.0423	4.3172	4.5965	4.8799	5.1675	5.4592	5.7548	6.0543	6.6646	6.9752
	20	2.6181	3.2225	3.8495	4.1710	4.4976	4.8292	5.1654	5.5062	5.8514	6.2008	6.9112	7.2719
	25	2.4074	3.0639	3.7438	4.0918	4.4447	4.8023	5.1643	5.5304	5.9003	6.2738	7.0303	7.4129
	30	2.2753	2.9666	3.6806	4.0451	4.4140	4.7870	5.1637	5.5438	5.9269	6.3128	7.0916	7.4840
20 Years	15	6.1506	6.6692	7.2059	7.4808	7.7600	8.0435	8.3311	8.6228	8.9184	9.2179	9.8282	10.1388
	20	4.9103	5.4641	6.0402	6.3364	6.6377	6.9439	7.2550	7.5708	7.8910	8.2156	8.8770	9.2135
	25	4.6260	5.2439	5.8875	6.2182	6.5546	6.8963	7.2429	7.5944	7.9503	8.3104	9.0422	9.4134
	30	4.4476	5.1089	5.7962	6.1487	6.5064	6.8690	7.2362	7.6074	7.9825	8.3611	9.1272	9.5143

Deposit to Create a Sinking Fund

End of Year	5.50% Annual	Interest Monthly	5.75% Annual	Interest Monthly	6.00% Annual	Interest Monthly	6.25% Annual	Interest Monthly	
1	100.000000	97.504141	100.000000	97.391877	100.000000	97.279716	100.000000	97.167657	1
2	48.661800	47.414787	48.602673	47.299657	48.543689	47.184732	48.484848	47.070014	2
3	31.565407	30.735082	31.488067	30.620549	31.410981	30.506325	31.334149	30.392410	3
4	23.029449	22.407770	22.944120	22.294697	22.859149	22.182035	22.774534	22.069784	4
5	17.917644	17.421395	17.828414	17.310122	17.739640	17.199362	17.651321	17.089114	5
6	14.517895	14.105465	14.426803	13.996158	14.336263	13.887465	14.246273	13.779385	6
7	12.096442	11.744051	12.004648	11.636802	11.913502	11.530265	11.822999	11.424440	7
8	10.286401	9.979187	10.194628	9.874046	10.103594	9.769716	10.013296	9.666194	8
9	8.883946	8.611996	8.792670	8.508995	8.702224	8.406900	8.612603	8.305708	9
10	7.766777	7.523153	7.676327	7.422306	7.586796	7.322460	7.498179	7.223612	10
11	6.857065	6.636719	6.767676	6.538034	6.679294	6.440442	6.591911	6.343939	11
12	6.102923	5.902066	6.014767	5.805542	5.927703	5.710203	5.841722	5.616041	12
13	5.468426	5.284142	5.381631	5.189776	5.296011	5.096681	5.211555	5.004852	13
14	4.927912	4.757908	4.842574	4.665691	4.758491	4.574831	4.675653	4.485321	14
15	4.462560	4.305001	4.378751	4.214921	4.296276	4.126282	4.215123	4.039074	15
16	4.058254	3.911647	3.976029	3.823690	3.895214	3.737254	3.815795	3.652330	16
17	3.704197	3.567310	3.623597	3.481460	3.544480	3.397209	3.466831	3.314545	17
18	3.391992	3.263796	3.313045	3.180035	3.235654	3.097948	3.159799	3.017520	18
19	3.115006	2.994635	3.037734	2.912942	2.962086	2.832996	2.888040	2.754779	19
20	2.867933	2.754648	2.792350	2.675002	2.718456	2.597173	2.646227	2.521138	20
21	2.646478	2.539643	2.572590	2.462022	2.500455	2.386283	2.430045	2.312402	21
22	2.447123	2.346189	2.374934	2.270569	2.304557	2.196893	2.235962	2.125136	22
23	2.266965	2.171452	2.196472	2.097807	2.127848	2.026166	2.061061	1.956500	23
24	2.103580	2.013067	2.034779	1.941372	1.967900	1.871737	1.902909	1.804128	24
25	1.954935	1.869050	1.887817	1.799277	1.822672	1.731617	1.759462	1.666033	25
26	1.819307	1.737719	1.753860	1.669840	1.690435	1.604124	1.628989	1.540529	26
27	1.695228	1.617641	1.631439	1.551629	1.569717	1.487824	1.510015	1.426183	27
28	1.581440	1.507590	1.519293	1.443414	1.459255	1.381488	1.401276	1.321765	28
29	1.476857	1.406505	1.416336	1.344135	1.357961	1.284055	1.301680	1.226212	29
30	1.380539	1.313468	1.321624	1.252874	1.264891	1.194606	1.210284	1.138606	30
31	1.291665	1.227679	1.234336	1.168831	1.179222	1.112340	1.126261	1.058145	31
32	1.209519	1.148438	1.153754	1.091303	1.100234	1.036555	1.048892	0.984127	32
33	1.133469	1.075129	1.079246	1.019676	1.027293	0.966635	0.977543	0.915936	33
34	1.062958	1.007209	1.010253	0.953405	0.959843	0.902036	0.911653	0.853027	34
35	0.997493	0.944195	0.946282	0.892009	0.897386	0.842276	0.850726	0.794918	35
36	0.936635	0.885661	0.886893	0.835059	0.839483	0.786927	0.794324	0.741180	36
37	0.879993	0.831223	0.831694	0.782173	0.785743	0.735606	0.742051	0.691432	37
38	0.827217	0.780540	0.780335	0.733009	0.735812	0.687971	0.693557	0.645331	38
39	0.777991	0.733306	0.732500	0.687261	0.689377	0.643716	0.648526	0.602571	39
40	0.732034	0.689243	0.687907	0.644652	0.646154	0.602564	0.606675	0.562875	40
41	0.689090	0.648104	0.646299	0.604932	0.605886	0.564266	0.567746	0.525995	41
42	0.648927	0.609662	0.607445	0.567878	0.568342	0.528597	0.531509	0.491706	42
43	0.611337	0.573713	0.571135	0.533283	0.533312	0.495353	0.497754	0.459804	43
44	0.576128	0.540071	0.537179	0.500963	0.500606	0.464349	0.466290	0.430103	44
45	0.543127	0.508567	0.505404	0.470749	0.470050	0.435415	0.436944	0.402437	45
46	0.512175	0.479046	0.475650	0.442486	0.441485	0.408398	0.409557	0.376650	46
47	0.483129	0.451368	0.447773	0.416033	0.414768	0.383157	0.383985	0.352603	47
48	0.455854	0.425402	0.421641	0.391262	0.389765	0.359564	0.360096	0.330168	48
49	0.430230	0.401031	0.397131	0.368053	0.366356	0.337500	0.337769	0.309227	49
50	0.406145	0.378146	0.374133	0.346299	0.344429	0.316858	0.316893	0.289673	50

Entries are one year's periodic deposits as a percentage of desired future fund.
Entries under "Monthly" are the sum of 12 monthly payments.

Deposit to Create a Sinking Fund

End of Year	6.50% Annual	Interest Monthly	6.75% Annual	Interest Monthly	7.00% Annual	Interest Monthly	7.25% Annual	Interest Monthly	
1	100.000000	97.055700	100.000000	96.943847	100.000000	96.832095	100.000000	96.720447	1
2	48.426150	46.955502	48.367594	46.841195	48.309179	46.727095	48.250905	46.613200	2
3	31.257570	30.278803	31.181243	30.165506	31.105167	30.052516	31.029340	29.939835	3
4	22.690274	21.957944	22.606367	21.846514	22.522812	21.735494	22.439607	21.624883	4
5	17.563454	16.979378	17.476037	16.870153	17.389069	16.761438	17.302548	16.653234	5
6	14.156831	13.671916	14.067934	13.565057	13.979580	13.458808	13.891766	13.353167	6
7	11.733137	11.319324	11.643912	11.214916	11.555322	11.111216	11.467363	11.008221	7
8	9.923730	9.563479	9.834891	9.461568	9.746776	9.360460	9.659381	9.260153	8
9	8.523803	8.205418	8.435820	8.106027	8.348647	8.007532	8.262281	7.909930	9
10	7.410469	7.125757	7.323662	7.028894	7.237750	6.933018	7.152729	6.838125	10
11	6.505521	6.248521	6.420116	6.154183	6.335690	6.060921	6.252237	5.968730	11
12	5.756817	5.523053	5.672978	5.431232	5.590199	5.340573	5.508470	5.251070	12
13	5.128256	4.914282	5.046102	4.824964	4.965085	4.736890	4.885194	4.650053	13
14	4.594048	4.397153	4.513666	4.310318	4.434494	4.224807	4.356522	4.140610	14
15	4.135278	3.953288	4.056729	3.868914	3.979462	3.785939	3.903465	3.704355	15
16	3.737757	3.568903	3.661086	3.486963	3.585765	3.406496	3.511780	3.327490	16
17	3.390633	3.233453	3.315868	3.153919	3.242519	3.075928	3.170570	2.999464	17
18	3.085461	2.938735	3.012621	2.861576	2.941260	2.786026	2.871358	2.712067	18
19	2.815575	2.678272	2.744670	2.603455	2.675301	2.530309	2.607449	2.458812	19
20	2.575640	2.446878	2.506670	2.374368	2.439293	2.303587	2.373484	2.234512	20
21	2.361333	2.240355	2.294294	2.170116	2.228900	2.101661	2.165124	2.034961	21
22	2.169120	2.055268	2.104002	1.987262	2.040577	1.921089	1.978816	1.856720	22
23	1.996078	1.888776	1.932866	1.822964	1.871393	1.759031	1.811624	1.696944	23
24	1.839770	1.738512	1.778446	1.674853	1.718902	1.613115	1.661101	1.553263	24
25	1.698148	1.602486	1.638691	1.540938	1.581052	1.481350	1.525190	1.423682	25
26	1.569480	1.479014	1.511865	1.419535	1.456103	1.362051	1.402149	1.306517	26
27	1.452288	1.366660	1.396489	1.309207	1.342573	1.253779	1.290494	1.200328	27
28	1.345305	1.264193	1.291294	1.208723	1.239193	1.155303	1.188951	1.103883	28
29	1.247440	1.170552	1.195186	1.117020	1.144865	1.065561	1.096425	1.016120	29
30	1.157744	1.084816	1.107215	1.033177	1.058640	0.983630	1.011962	0.936115	30
31	1.075393	1.006184	1.026557	0.956393	0.979691	0.908709	0.934734	0.863068	31
32	0.999665	0.933953	0.952486	0.885964	0.907292	0.840094	0.864017	0.796275	32
33	0.929924	0.867507	0.884368	0.821275	0.840807	0.777170	0.799172	0.735120	33
34	0.865610	0.806300	0.821641	0.761780	0.779674	0.719391	0.739637	0.679058	34
35	0.806226	0.749852	0.763808	0.706998	0.723396	0.666276	0.684915	0.627607	35
36	0.751332	0.697733	0.710428	0.656500	0.671531	0.617397	0.634563	0.580340	36
37	0.700534	0.649561	0.661106	0.609903	0.623685	0.572370	0.588187	0.536875	37
38	0.653480	0.604994	0.615492	0.566867	0.579505	0.530857	0.545435	0.496873	38
39	0.609854	0.563726	0.573268	0.527085	0.538676	0.492550	0.505991	0.460026	39
40	0.569373	0.525482	0.534150	0.490282	0.500914	0.457175	0.469571	0.426063	40
41	0.531779	0.490012	0.497884	0.456210	0.465962	0.424485	0.435920	0.394736	41
42	0.496842	0.457092	0.464236	0.424644	0.433591	0.394256	0.404807	0.365821	42
43	0.464352	0.426518	0.432999	0.395383	0.403590	0.366286	0.376023	0.339119	43
44	0.434119	0.398107	0.403981	0.368241	0.375769	0.340391	0.349379	0.314446	44
45	0.405968	0.371689	0.377010	0.343052	0.349957	0.316406	0.324704	0.291637	45
46	0.379743	0.347113	0.351928	0.319663	0.325996	0.294179	0.301840	0.270542	46
47	0.355300	0.324239	0.328591	0.297936	0.303744	0.273571	0.280646	0.251024	47
48	0.332505	0.302938	0.306869	0.277744	0.283070	0.254457	0.260992	0.232957	48
49	0.311240	0.283095	0.286642	0.258970	0.263853	0.236723	0.242758	0.216228	49
50	0.291393	0.264603	0.267798	0.241509	0.245985	0.220261	0.225837	0.200733	50

Entries are one year's periodic deposits as a percentage of desired future fund.
Entries under "Monthly" are the sum of 12 monthly payments.

Deposit to Create a Sinking Fund

End of Year	7.50% Annual	Interest Monthly	7.75% Annual	Interest Monthly	8.00% Annual	Interest Monthly	8.25% Annual	Interest Monthly	
1	100.000000	96.608900	100.000000	96.497456	100.000000	96.386115	100.000000	96.274876	1
2	48.192771	46.499511	48.134777	46.386028	48.076923	46.272750	48.019208	46.159677	2
3	30.953763	29.827462	30.878434	29.715396	30.803351	29.603639	30.728515	29.492188	3
4	22.356751	21.514682	22.274243	21.404890	22.192080	21.295507	22.110263	21.186532	4
5	17.216472	16.545538	17.130838	16.438352	17.045645	16.331673	16.960892	16.225502	5
6	13.804489	13.248135	13.717748	13.143709	13.631539	13.039889	13.545860	12.936673	6
7	11.380032	10.905931	11.293325	10.804344	11.207240	10.703457	11.121774	10.603271	7
8	9.572702	9.160645	9.486735	9.061933	9.401476	8.964015	9.316921	8.866890	8
9	8.176716	7.813219	8.091948	7.717396	8.007971	7.622458	7.924781	7.528401	9
10	7.068593	6.744212	6.985335	6.651276	6.902949	6.559311	6.821430	6.468315	10
11	6.169747	5.877606	6.088216	5.787543	6.007634	5.698536	5.927996	5.610580	11
12	5.427783	5.162716	5.348130	5.075505	5.269502	4.989431	5.191890	4.904487	12
13	4.806420	4.564445	4.728752	4.480059	4.652181	4.396887	4.576696	4.314920	13
14	4.279737	4.057720	4.204129	3.976126	4.129685	3.895818	4.056394	3.816787	14
15	3.828724	3.624148	3.755225	3.545309	3.682954	3.467825	3.611900	3.391684	15
16	3.439116	3.249931	3.367757	3.173806	3.297687	3.099100	3.228892	3.025801	16
17	3.100003	2.924513	3.030800	2.851057	2.962943	2.779082	2.896415	2.708570	17
18	2.802896	2.639680	2.735853	2.568848	2.670210	2.499551	2.605946	2.431772	18
19	2.541090	2.388946	2.476202	2.320688	2.412763	2.254017	2.350750	2.188910	19
20	2.309219	2.167118	2.246473	2.101383	2.185221	2.037281	2.125437	1.974788	20
21	2.102937	1.969992	2.042314	1.906726	1.983225	1.845135	1.925643	1.785193	21
22	1.918687	1.794125	1.860161	1.733273	1.803207	1.674135	1.747794	1.616679	22
23	1.753528	1.636671	1.697070	1.578178	1.642217	1.521431	1.588936	1.466396	23
24	1.605008	1.495259	1.550585	1.439067	1.497796	1.384649	1.446605	1.331969	24
25	1.471067	1.367894	1.418643	1.313945	1.367878	1.261795	1.318733	1.211402	25
26	1.349961	1.252889	1.299497	1.201124	1.250713	1.151177	1.203567	1.103004	26
27	1.240204	1.148806	1.191658	1.099165	1.144810	1.051358	1.099614	1.005337	27
28	1.140520	1.054411	1.093849	1.006835	1.048891	0.961104	1.005595	0.917165	28
29	1.049811	0.968641	1.004971	0.923069	0.961854	0.879350	0.920406	0.837427	29
30	0.967124	0.890574	0.924069	0.846947	0.882743	0.805175	0.843091	0.765199	30
31	0.891628	0.819408	0.850313	0.777665	0.810728	0.737777	0.772818	0.699681	31
32	0.822599	0.754440	0.782974	0.714521	0.745081	0.676454	0.708859	0.640171	32
33	0.759397	0.695053	0.721416	0.656900	0.685163	0.620589	0.650575	0.586054	33
34	0.701461	0.640704	0.665075	0.604257	0.630411	0.569642	0.597402	0.536788	34
35	0.648291	0.590911	0.613452	0.556111	0.580326	0.523131	0.548844	0.491894	35
36	0.599447	0.545247	0.566106	0.512037	0.534467	0.480630	0.504458	0.450947	36
37	0.554533	0.503332	0.522643	0.471654	0.492440	0.441761	0.463850	0.413570	37
38	0.513197	0.464824	0.482710	0.434624	0.453894	0.406186	0.426671	0.379426	38
39	0.475124	0.429421	0.445993	0.400643	0.418513	0.373603	0.392606	0.348215	39
40	0.440031	0.396849	0.412208	0.369438	0.386016	0.343740	0.361373	0.319666	40
41	0.407663	0.366861	0.381102	0.340766	0.356149	0.316355	0.332722	0.293537	41
42	0.377789	0.339237	0.352444	0.314405	0.328684	0.291227	0.306422	0.269612	42
43	0.350201	0.313776	0.326028	0.290156	0.303414	0.268160	0.282270	0.247693	43
44	0.324710	0.290297	0.301665	0.267840	0.280152	0.246974	0.260079	0.227603	44
45	0.301146	0.268635	0.279186	0.247292	0.258728	0.227508	0.239682	0.209183	45
46	0.279354	0.248641	0.258436	0.228366	0.238991	0.209615	0.220926	0.192288	46
47	0.259190	0.230179	0.239274	0.210927	0.220799	0.193163	0.203673	0.176786	47
48	0.240527	0.213126	0.221572	0.194852	0.204027	0.178030	0.187797	0.162557	48
49	0.223247	0.197368	0.205213	0.180030	0.188557	0.164106	0.173184	0.149494	49
50	0.207241	0.182803	0.190091	0.166359	0.174286	0.151291	0.159730	0.137498	50

Entries are one year's periodic deposits as a percentage of desired future fund.
Entries under "Monthly" are the sum of 12 monthly payments.

684 Table 52, page 4

Deposit to Create a Sinking Fund

End of Year	8.50% Annual	Interest Monthly	8.75% Annual	Interest Monthly	9.00% Annual	Interest Monthly	9.25% Annual	Interest Monthly	
1	100.000000	96.163739	100.000000	96.052704	100.000000	95.941772	100.000000	95.830942	1
2	47.961631	46.046810	47.904192	45.934148	47.846890	45.821691	47.789725	45.709439	2
3	30.653925	29.381045	30.579579	29.270209	30.505476	29.159679	30.431615	29.049456	3
4	22.028789	21.077964	21.947657	20.969804	21.866866	20.862051	21.786414	20.754704	4
5	16.876575	16.119838	16.792694	16.014679	16.709246	15.910026	16.626229	15.805878	5
6	13.460708	12.834062	13.376082	12.732052	13.291978	12.630645	13.208395	12.529837	6
7	11.036922	10.503783	10.952683	10.404991	10.869052	10.306894	10.786026	10.209490	7
8	9.233065	8.770554	9.149906	8.675006	9.067438	8.580244	8.985658	8.486264	8
9	7.842372	7.435223	7.760740	7.342921	7.679880	7.251490	7.599786	7.160929	9
10	6.740771	6.378283	6.660966	6.289210	6.582009	6.201093	6.503894	6.113927	10
11	5.849293	5.523670	5.771519	5.437800	5.694666	5.352965	5.618726	5.269158	11
12	5.115286	4.820667	5.039681	4.737963	4.965066	4.656368	4.891432	4.575876	12
13	4.502287	4.234149	4.428944	4.154568	4.356656	4.076166	4.285414	3.998935	13
14	3.984244	3.739022	3.913222	3.662514	3.843317	3.587250	3.774517	3.513221	14
15	3.542046	3.316875	3.473380	3.243384	3.405888	3.171199	3.339556	3.100307	15
16	3.161354	2.953892	3.095059	2.883360	3.029991	2.814190	2.966133	2.746367	16
17	2.831198	2.639505	2.767274	2.571870	2.704625	2.505647	2.643232	2.440819	17
18	2.543041	2.365489	2.481476	2.300685	2.421229	2.237338	2.362281	2.175429	18
19	2.290140	2.125348	2.230912	2.063305	2.173041	2.002761	2.116506	1.943693	19
20	2.067097	1.913879	2.010176	1.854529	1.954648	1.796711	1.900487	1.740402	20
21	1.869541	1.726870	1.814890	1.670140	1.761663	1.614972	1.709832	1.561339	21
22	1.693892	1.560874	1.641471	1.506689	1.590499	1.454092	1.540947	1.403052	22
23	1.537193	1.413038	1.486954	1.361324	1.438188	1.311218	1.390860	1.262685	23
24	1.396975	1.280988	1.348871	1.231668	1.302256	1.183972	1.257095	1.137861	24
25	1.271168	1.162725	1.225145	1.115724	1.180625	1.070356	1.137569	1.026582	25
26	1.158017	1.056560	1.114020	1.011800	1.071536	0.968681	1.030523	0.927157	26
27	1.056025	0.961052	1.013999	0.918458	0.973491	0.877505	0.934456	0.838147	27
28	0.963914	0.874969	0.923799	0.834462	0.885205	0.795596	0.848083	0.758318	28
29	0.880577	0.797245	0.842315	0.758752	0.805572	0.721891	0.770298	0.686611	29
30	0.805058	0.726962	0.768590	0.690405	0.733635	0.655471	0.700142	0.622105	30
31	0.736524	0.663316	0.701789	0.628622	0.668560	0.595537	0.636781	0.564004	31
32	0.674247	0.605609	0.641186	0.572703	0.609619	0.541390	0.579488	0.511610	32
33	0.617588	0.553225	0.586140	0.522035	0.556173	0.492419	0.527625	0.464314	33
34	0.565984	0.505623	0.536090	0.476079	0.507660	0.448086	0.480631	0.421579	34
35	0.518937	0.462327	0.490538	0.434358	0.463584	0.407916	0.438010	0.382932	35
36	0.476006	0.422912	0.449044	0.396450	0.423505	0.371488	0.399323	0.347955	36
37	0.436799	0.387003	0.411216	0.361981	0.387033	0.338431	0.364182	0.316278	37
38	0.400966	0.354263	0.376705	0.330617	0.353820	0.308412	0.332240	0.287572	38
39	0.368193	0.324395	0.345200	0.302061	0.323555	0.281135	0.303188	0.261542	39
40	0.338201	0.297129	0.316421	0.276046	0.295961	0.256338	0.276750	0.237927	40
41	0.310737	0.272225	0.290118	0.252334	0.270789	0.233783	0.252678	0.216493	41
42	0.285576	0.249468	0.266065	0.230712	0.247814	0.213258	0.230750	0.197029	42
43	0.262512	0.228664	0.244060	0.210985	0.226837	0.194573	0.210768	0.179349	43
44	0.241363	0.209635	0.223921	0.192981	0.207675	0.177557	0.192551	0.163283	44
45	0.221961	0.192225	0.205481	0.176544	0.190165	0.162055	0.175938	0.148678	45
46	0.204154	0.176290	0.188592	0.161532	0.174160	0.147929	0.160783	0.135399	46
47	0.187807	0.161701	0.173118	0.147818	0.159525	0.135052	0.146953	0.123321	47
48	0.172795	0.148340	0.158936	0.135286	0.146139	0.123311	0.134330	0.112334	48
49	0.159005	0.136100	0.145934	0.123831	0.133893	0.112603	0.122806	0.102336	49
50	0.146334	0.124884	0.134013	0.113358	0.122687	0.102836	0.112282	0.093237	50

Entries are one year's periodic deposits as a percentage of desired future fund.
Entries under "Monthly" are the sum of 12 monthly payments.

Deposit to Create a Sinking Fund

End of Year	9.50% Annual	Interest Monthly	9.75% Annual	Interest Monthly	10.00% Annual	Interest Monthly	10.25% Annual	Interest Monthly	
1	100.000000	95.720214	100.000000	95.609588	100.000000	95.499065	100.000000	95.388643	1
2	47.732697	45.597392	47.675805	45.485549	47.619048	45.373912	47.562426	45.262479	2
3	30.357997	28.939540	30.284619	28.829929	30.211480	28.720625	30.138581	28.611626	3
4	21.706300	20.647764	21.626523	20.541229	21.547080	20.435100	21.467972	20.329376	4
5	16.543642	15.702234	16.461482	15.599092	16.379748	15.496454	16.298438	15.394317	5
6	13.125328	12.429629	13.042777	12.330019	12.960738	12.231005	12.879209	12.132587	6
7	10.703603	10.112778	10.621779	10.016755	10.540550	9.921421	10.459914	9.826772	7
8	8.904561	8.393065	8.824144	8.300643	8.744402	8.208997	8.665331	8.118123	8
9	7.520454	7.071233	7.441878	6.982399	7.364054	6.894423	7.286976	6.807303	9
10	6.426615	6.027707	6.350166	5.942429	6.274539	5.858088	6.199730	5.774680	10
11	5.543693	5.186375	5.469558	5.104608	5.396314	5.023853	5.323954	4.944103	11
12	4.818771	4.496479	4.747074	4.418169	4.676332	4.340939	4.606535	4.264781	12
13	4.215206	3.922866	4.146022	3.847950	4.077852	3.774177	4.010686	3.701538	13
14	3.706809	3.440416	3.640182	3.368823	3.574622	3.298432	3.510119	3.229231	14
15	3.274370	3.030696	3.210315	2.962352	3.147378	2.895261	3.085544	2.829411	15
16	2.903470	2.679875	2.841985	2.614699	2.781662	2.550823	2.722486	2.488232	16
17	2.583078	2.377368	2.524145	2.315276	2.466413	2.254525	2.409866	2.195098	17
18	2.304610	2.114937	2.248198	2.055843	2.193022	1.998124	2.139064	1.941761	18
19	2.061284	1.886076	2.007352	1.829889	1.954687	1.775107	1.903267	1.721708	19
20	1.847670	1.685574	1.796170	1.632202	1.745962	1.580260	1.697023	1.529721	20
21	1.659370	1.509212	1.610248	1.458562	1.562439	1.409360	1.515916	1.361577	21
22	1.492784	1.353536	1.445981	1.305513	1.400506	1.258952	1.356331	1.213820	22
23	1.344938	1.215691	1.300389	1.170201	1.257181	1.126180	1.215282	1.083593	23
24	1.213351	1.093298	1.170990	1.050245	1.129978	1.008665	1.090278	0.968519	24
25	1.095939	0.984360	1.055698	0.943649	1.016807	0.904409	0.979231	0.866599	25
26	0.990940	0.887185	0.952747	0.848722	0.915904	0.811724	0.880372	0.776147	26
27	0.896852	0.800336	0.860635	0.764026	0.825764	0.729172	0.792197	0.695727	27
28	0.812389	0.722580	0.778076	0.688332	0.745101	0.655525	0.713420	0.624111	28
29	0.736444	0.652857	0.703963	0.620579	0.672807	0.589725	0.642933	0.560244	29
30	0.668058	0.590250	0.637336	0.559853	0.607925	0.530859	0.579778	0.503216	30
31	0.606399	0.533963	0.577363	0.505359	0.549621	0.478134	0.523125	0.452235	31
32	0.550739	0.483301	0.523318	0.456404	0.497172	0.430860	0.472249	0.406614	32
33	0.500441	0.437655	0.474565	0.412381	0.449941	0.388434	0.426517	0.365753	33
34	0.454945	0.396491	0.430543	0.372761	0.407371	0.350325	0.385372	0.329125	34
35	0.413756	0.359339	0.390762	0.337073	0.368971	0.316069	0.348326	0.296267	35
36	0.376437	0.325783	0.354784	0.304904	0.334306	0.285255	0.314947	0.266773	36
37	0.342600	0.295454	0.322224	0.275890	0.302994	0.257520	0.284853	0.240281	37
38	0.311901	0.268026	0.292739	0.249705	0.274692	0.232543	0.257704	0.216475	38
39	0.284032	0.243207	0.266023	0.226062	0.249098	0.210038	0.233200	0.195071	39
40	0.258719	0.220739	0.241804	0.204703	0.225941	0.189751	0.211073	0.175818	40
41	0.235716	0.200389	0.219838	0.185399	0.204980	0.171457	0.191083	0.158495	41
42	0.214803	0.181950	0.199907	0.167947	0.185999	0.154953	0.173018	0.142902	42
43	0.195783	0.165236	0.181817	0.152162	0.168805	0.140059	0.156687	0.128862	43
44	0.178478	0.150082	0.165390	0.137882	0.153224	0.126615	0.141918	0.116217	44
45	0.162729	0.136337	0.150471	0.124959	0.139100	0.114476	0.128558	0.104825	45
46	0.148390	0.123867	0.136915	0.113261	0.126295	0.103513	0.116470	0.094560	46
47	0.135333	0.112551	0.124597	0.102669	0.114682	0.093610	0.105531	0.085309	47
48	0.123439	0.102280	0.113399	0.093078	0.104148	0.084661	0.095628	0.076969	48
49	0.112603	0.092955	0.103218	0.084390	0.094590	0.076575	0.086662	0.069451	49
50	0.102728	0.084488	0.093960	0.076519	0.085917	0.069267	0.078543	0.062671	50

Entries are one year's periodic deposits as a percentage of desired future fund.
Entries under "Monthly" are the sum of 12 monthly payments.

Deposit to Create a Sinking Fund

End of Year	10.50% Annual	Interest Monthly	10.75% Annual	Interest Monthly	11.00% Annual	Interest Monthly	11.25% Annual	Interest Monthly	
1	100.000000	95.278323	100.000000	95.168106	100.000000	95.057990	100.000000	94.947976	1
2	47.505938	45.151250	47.449585	45.040226	47.393365	44.929406	47.337278	44.818790	2
3	30.065920	28.502932	29.993495	28.394544	29.921307	28.286461	29.849354	28.178682	3
4	21.389196	20.224056	21.310751	20.119140	21.232635	20.014627	21.154848	19.910518	4
5	16.217550	15.292680	16.137081	15.191544	16.057031	15.090908	15.977397	14.990769	5
6	12.798187	12.034764	12.717671	11.937534	12.637656	11.840895	12.558142	11.744847	6
7	10.379867	9.732808	10.300405	9.639526	10.221527	9.546924	10.143228	9.455000	7
8	8.586928	8.028019	8.509187	7.938683	8.432105	7.850111	8.355678	7.762300	8
9	7.210638	6.721033	7.135037	6.635611	7.060166	6.551033	6.986022	6.467295	9
10	6.125732	5.692200	6.052538	5.610642	5.980143	5.530001	5.908539	5.450274	10
11	5.252470	4.865351	5.181855	4.787592	5.112101	4.710819	5.043200	4.635025	11
12	4.537675	4.189688	4.469742	4.115651	4.402729	4.042663	4.336625	3.970715	12
13	3.944512	3.630024	3.879320	3.559624	3.815099	3.490328	3.751840	3.422128	13
14	3.446659	3.161208	3.384230	3.094352	3.322820	3.028651	3.262417	2.964092	14
15	3.024800	2.764787	2.965131	2.701376	2.906524	2.639163	2.848964	2.578135	15
16	2.664440	2.426909	2.607508	2.366839	2.551675	2.308005	2.496923	2.250390	16
17	2.354485	2.136975	2.300252	2.080138	2.247148	2.024568	2.195157	1.970247	17
18	2.086302	1.886733	2.034716	1.833018	1.984287	1.780596	1.934994	1.729444	18
19	1.853069	1.669667	1.804071	1.618961	1.756250	1.569567	1.709585	1.521460	19
20	1.649327	1.480559	1.602848	1.432747	1.557564	1.386261	1.513448	1.341072	20
21	1.470652	1.315184	1.426620	1.270152	1.383793	1.226451	1.342145	1.184054	21
22	1.313426	1.170085	1.271762	1.127716	1.231310	1.086681	1.192041	1.046950	22
23	1.174659	1.042407	1.135282	1.002586	1.097118	0.964096	1.060138	0.926904	23
24	1.051858	0.929771	1.014684	0.892383	0.978721	0.856319	0.943938	0.821543	24
25	0.942932	0.830180	0.907875	0.795113	0.874024	0.761357	0.841345	0.728875	25
26	0.846112	0.741950	0.813086	0.709091	0.781258	0.677528	0.750589	0.647220	26
27	0.759894	0.663646	0.728813	0.632886	0.698916	0.603402	0.670165	0.575152	27
28	0.682990	0.594043	0.653768	0.565274	0.625715	0.537759	0.598788	0.511454	28
29	0.614293	0.532088	0.586846	0.505206	0.560547	0.479553	0.535355	0.455081	29
30	0.552848	0.476872	0.527090	0.451776	0.502460	0.427881	0.478914	0.405137	30
31	0.497824	0.427608	0.473674	0.404200	0.450627	0.381961	0.428639	0.360842	31
32	0.448499	0.383611	0.425875	0.361796	0.404329	0.341117	0.383815	0.321524	32
33	0.404241	0.344283	0.383064	0.323969	0.362938	0.304757	0.343816	0.286596	33
34	0.364495	0.309102	0.344690	0.290201	0.325905	0.272366	0.308096	0.255546	34
35	0.328776	0.277608	0.310266	0.260035	0.292749	0.243492	0.276175	0.227927	35
36	0.296652	0.249397	0.279368	0.233071	0.263044	0.217738	0.247633	0.203345	36
37	0.267744	0.224113	0.251616	0.208956	0.236416	0.194755	0.222097	0.181456	37
38	0.241717	0.201439	0.226678	0.187378	0.212535	0.174236	0.199240	0.161957	38
39	0.218271	0.181099	0.204257	0.168063	0.191107	0.155908	0.178772	0.144580	39
40	0.197141	0.162843	0.184091	0.150767	0.171873	0.139533	0.160436	0.129088	40
41	0.178090	0.146453	0.165947	0.135272	0.154601	0.124897	0.144004	0.115273	41
42	0.160908	0.131733	0.149615	0.121388	0.139086	0.111811	0.129275	0.102950	42
43	0.145407	0.118509	0.134910	0.108943	0.125146	0.100109	0.116067	0.091955	43
44	0.131417	0.106626	0.121667	0.097786	0.112617	0.089641	0.104221	0.082143	44
45	0.118788	0.095945	0.109737	0.087780	0.101354	0.080276	0.093594	0.073384	45
46	0.107385	0.086343	0.098987	0.078806	0.091227	0.071896	0.084059	0.065565	46
47	0.097087	0.077709	0.089299	0.070755	0.082119	0.064395	0.075502	0.058583	47
48	0.087784	0.069944	0.080566	0.063531	0.073926	0.057681	0.067821	0.052348	48
49	0.079380	0.062959	0.072693	0.057049	0.066556	0.051671	0.060925	0.046780	49
50	0.071785	0.056676	0.065594	0.051231	0.059924	0.046289	0.054734	0.041806	50

Entries are one year's periodic deposits as a percentage of desired future fund.
Entries under "Monthly" are the sum of 12 monthly payments.

Deposit to Create a Sinking Fund

End of Year	11.50% Annual	Interest Monthly	11.75% Annual	Interest Monthly	12.00% Annual	Interest Monthly	12.25% Annual	Interest Monthly	
1	100.000000	94.838065	100.000000	94.728255	100.000000	94.618546	100.000000	94.508940	1
2	47.281324	44.708378	47.225502	44.598171	47.169811	44.488167	47.114252	44.378366	2
3	29.777636	28.071208	29.706150	27.964038	29.634898	27.857172	29.563877	27.750610	3
4	21.077388	19.806811	21.000254	19.703506	20.923444	19.600603	20.846957	19.498100	4
5	15.898177	14.891129	15.819370	14.791985	15.740973	14.693337	15.662985	14.595184	5
6	12.479125	11.649387	12.400602	11.554516	12.322572	11.460231	12.245031	11.366531	6
7	10.065505	9.363753	9.988354	9.273180	9.911774	9.183279	9.835759	9.094049	7
8	8.279902	7.675249	8.204772	7.588953	8.130284	7.503410	8.056434	7.418617	8
9	6.912597	6.384392	6.839888	6.302322	6.767889	6.221079	6.696595	6.140660	9
10	5.837721	5.371453	5.767682	5.293535	5.698416	5.216514	5.629917	5.140384	10
11	4.975144	4.560204	4.907927	4.486350	4.841540	4.413455	4.775977	4.341512	11
12	4.271422	3.899799	4.207110	3.829907	4.143681	3.761030	4.081125	3.693159	12
13	3.689530	3.355012	3.628160	3.288971	3.567720	3.223995	3.508197	3.160072	13
14	3.203008	2.900665	3.144582	2.838356	3.087125	2.777154	3.030625	2.717046	14
15	2.792436	2.518278	2.736928	2.459576	2.682424	2.402017	2.628911	2.345584	15
16	2.443238	2.193980	2.390603	2.138755	2.339002	2.084702	2.288419	2.031801	16
17	2.144259	1.917155	2.094437	1.865275	2.045673	1.814586	1.997949	1.765071	17
18	1.886817	1.679543	1.839736	1.630870	1.793731	1.583405	1.748783	1.537125	18
19	1.664053	1.474617	1.619632	1.429014	1.576300	1.384628	1.534037	1.341434	19
20	1.470478	1.297156	1.428629	1.254485	1.387878	1.213034	1.348200	1.172776	20
21	1.301648	1.142932	1.262278	1.103055	1.224009	1.064396	1.186815	1.026926	21
22	1.153927	1.008489	1.116939	0.971270	1.081051	0.935260	1.046234	0.900430	22
23	1.024311	0.890976	0.989607	0.856278	0.955996	0.822779	0.923450	0.790444	23
24	0.910302	0.788018	0.877781	0.755710	0.846344	0.724583	0.815960	0.694602	24
25	0.809803	0.697628	0.779365	0.667578	0.749997	0.638690	0.721667	0.610925	25
26	0.721044	0.618127	0.692588	0.590210	0.665186	0.563430	0.638804	0.537748	26
27	0.642521	0.548093	0.615948	0.522185	0.590409	0.497387	0.565870	0.473658	27
28	0.572951	0.486313	0.548163	0.462294	0.524387	0.439356	0.501587	0.417457	28
29	0.511230	0.431746	0.488131	0.409502	0.466021	0.388306	0.444860	0.368116	29
30	0.456410	0.383497	0.434907	0.362917	0.414366	0.343351	0.394748	0.324757	30
31	0.407667	0.340795	0.387670	0.321772	0.368606	0.303729	0.350436	0.286621	31
32	0.364289	0.302968	0.345709	0.285401	0.328033	0.268778	0.311221	0.253054	32
33	0.325653	0.269436	0.308405	0.253228	0.292031	0.237927	0.276490	0.223487	33
34	0.291215	0.239690	0.275218	0.224750	0.260064	0.210678	0.245711	0.197430	34
35	0.260499	0.213288	0.245675	0.199527	0.231662	0.186597	0.218418	0.174453	35
36	0.233086	0.189841	0.219361	0.177177	0.206414	0.165306	0.194204	0.154184	36
37	0.208610	0.169009	0.195912	0.157364	0.183959	0.146474	0.172712	0.136295	37
38	0.186745	0.150492	0.175006	0.139792	0.163980	0.129810	0.153627	0.120502	38
39	0.167204	0.134027	0.156360	0.124202	0.146197	0.115060	0.136674	0.106555	39
40	0.149734	0.119382	0.139724	0.110368	0.130363	0.101999	0.121611	0.094234	40
41	0.134111	0.106352	0.124876	0.098087	0.116260	0.090433	0.108222	0.083348	41
42	0.120134	0.094756	0.111621	0.087183	0.103696	0.080186	0.096319	0.073727	42
43	0.107628	0.084433	0.099785	0.077498	0.092500	0.071108	0.085734	0.065222	43
44	0.096434	0.075242	0.089214	0.068896	0.082521	0.063063	0.076319	0.057703	44
45	0.086413	0.067058	0.079770	0.061254	0.073625	0.055932	0.067944	0.051054	45
46	0.077441	0.059768	0.071331	0.054463	0.065694	0.049611	0.060493	0.045174	46
47	0.069405	0.053275	0.063790	0.048428	0.058621	0.044006	0.053862	0.039974	47
48	0.062208	0.047489	0.057051	0.043065	0.052312	0.039037	0.047961	0.035374	48
49	0.055761	0.042335	0.051026	0.038297	0.046686	0.034631	0.042709	0.031305	49
50	0.049985	0.037741	0.045640	0.034058	0.041666	0.030723	0.038033	0.027704	50

Entries are one year's periodic deposits as a percentage of desired future fund.
Entries under "Monthly" are the sum of 12 monthly payments.

Deposit to Complete Partial Sinking Fund

Starting from Partial Fund of 10%

Years to Complete	Interest Rate											
	5.50%	5.75%	6.00%	6.25%	6.50%	6.75%	7.00%	7.25%	7.50%	7.75%	8.00%	8.25%
1	7.26698	7.25647	7.24598	7.23549	7.22501	7.21454	7.20407	7.19362	7.18317	7.17273	7.16229	7.15187
2	3.51028	3.49956	3.48885	3.47817	3.46750	3.45684	3.44620	3.43557	3.42496	3.41437	3.40379	3.39323
3	2.25930	2.24862	2.23797	2.22735	2.21674	2.20616	2.19561	2.18507	2.17456	2.16407	2.15361	2.14316
4	1.63475	1.62419	1.61365	1.60315	1.59268	1.58224	1.57183	1.56145	1.55110	1.54078	1.53050	1.52024
5	1.26077	1.25034	1.23995	1.22960	1.21929	1.20901	1.19877	1.18858	1.17842	1.16829	1.15821	1.14816
7.5	0.76431	0.75427	0.74427	0.73434	0.72446	0.71464	0.70488	0.69517	0.68552	0.67593	0.66639	0.65690
10	0.51840	0.50876	0.49918	0.48969	0.48027	0.47092	0.46164	0.45244	0.44332	0.43426	0.42528	0.41637
12.5	0.37269	0.36344	0.35430	0.34524	0.33627	0.32740	0.31861	0.30991	0.30131	0.29279	0.28436	0.27602
15	0.27704	0.26820	0.25947	0.25085	0.24233	0.23392	0.22561	0.21741	0.20931	0.20131	0.19342	0.18563
17.5	0.20998	0.20154	0.19322	0.18502	0.17694	0.16898	0.16114	0.15342	0.14581	0.13832	0.13094	0.12367
20	0.16077	0.15271	0.14479	0.13700	0.12935	0.12183	0.11444	0.10717	0.10003	0.09302	0.08613	0.07936
22.5	0.12341	0.11573	0.10820	0.10082	0.09357	0.08647	0.07951	0.07268	0.06599	0.05944	0.05301	0.04671
25	0.09435	0.08703	0.07987	0.07287	0.06602	0.05932	0.05277	0.04636	0.04009	0.03396	0.02797	0.02211
27.5	0.07127	0.06431	0.05751	0.05088	0.04440	0.03809	0.03192	0.02591	0.02004	0.01431	0.00872	0.00326
30	0.05268	0.04605	0.03960	0.03331	0.02719	0.02124	0.01544	0.00979	0.00429	-0.00106	-0.00628	-0.01136

Starting from Partial Fund of 20%

Years to Complete	5.50%	5.75%	6.00%	6.25%	6.50%	6.75%	7.00%	7.25%	7.50%	7.75%	8.00%	8.25%
1	6.40861	6.39696	6.38531	6.37368	6.36205	6.35042	6.33881	6.32720	6.31559	6.30400	6.29241	6.28083
2	3.06932	3.05748	3.04565	3.03383	3.02203	3.01025	2.99847	2.98671	2.97497	2.96324	2.95152	2.93981
3	1.95734	1.94554	1.93375	1.92199	1.91025	1.89853	1.88683	1.87516	1.86350	1.85186	1.84024	1.82865
4	1.40218	1.39048	1.37880	1.36715	1.35553	1.34393	1.33237	1.32083	1.30931	1.29783	1.28637	1.27494
5	1.06976	1.05817	1.04662	1.03511	1.02363	1.01218	1.00076	0.98938	0.97804	0.96672	0.95544	0.94420
7.5	0.62846	0.61722	0.60602	0.59488	0.58378	0.57274	0.56174	0.55080	0.53991	0.52906	0.51827	0.50753
10	0.40988	0.39899	0.38816	0.37741	0.36672	0.35609	0.34553	0.33504	0.32461	0.31425	0.30395	0.29372
12.5	0.28035	0.26982	0.25937	0.24901	0.23872	0.22852	0.21839	0.20835	0.19838	0.18850	0.17869	0.16896
15	0.19533	0.18516	0.17509	0.16510	0.15522	0.14543	0.13573	0.12612	0.11661	0.10719	0.09786	0.08861
17.5	0.13573	0.12591	0.11619	0.10659	0.09710	0.08771	0.07842	0.06924	0.06016	0.05119	0.04231	0.03354
20	0.09198	0.08250	0.07314	0.06391	0.05479	0.04579	0.03691	0.02813	0.01947	0.01093	0.00249	-0.00585
22.5	0.05878	0.04963	0.04062	0.03174	0.02299	0.01436	0.00586	-0.00252	-0.01078	-0.01893	-0.02696	-0.03487
25	0.03294	0.02412	0.01544	0.00690	-0.00150	-0.00977	-0.01791	-0.02592	-0.03381	-0.04157	-0.04921	-0.05674
27.5	0.01243	0.00392	-0.00443	-0.01265	-0.02072	-0.02865	-0.03644	-0.04410	-0.05164	-0.05904	-0.06633	-0.07349
30	-0.00410	-0.01231	-0.02036	-0.02826	-0.03601	-0.04362	-0.05109	-0.05843	-0.06563	-0.07270	-0.07966	-0.08649

Starting from Partial Fund of 25%

Years to Complete	5.50%	5.75%	6.00%	6.25%	6.50%	6.75%	7.00%	7.25%	7.50%	7.75%	8.00%	8.25%
1	5.97943	5.96720	5.95498	5.94277	5.93056	5.91837	5.90617	5.89399	5.88181	5.86963	5.85747	5.84530
2	2.84884	2.83644	2.82405	2.81167	2.79930	2.78695	2.77461	2.76228	2.74997	2.73767	2.72538	2.71310
3	1.80636	1.79399	1.78165	1.76932	1.75701	1.74472	1.73245	1.72020	1.70797	1.69575	1.68356	1.67139
4	1.28590	1.27363	1.26138	1.24915	1.23695	1.22478	1.21264	1.20051	1.18842	1.17635	1.16430	1.15228
5	0.97425	0.96209	0.94996	0.93786	0.92579	0.91376	0.90176	0.88979	0.87785	0.86594	0.85406	0.84222
7.5	0.56054	0.54869	0.53690	0.52514	0.51344	0.50179	0.49018	0.47861	0.46710	0.45563	0.44421	0.43284
10	0.35561	0.34410	0.33265	0.32127	0.30994	0.29868	0.28748	0.27634	0.26526	0.25425	0.24329	0.23239
12.5	0.23418	0.22301	0.21191	0.20089	0.18995	0.17908	0.16829	0.15757	0.14692	0.13635	0.12585	0.11543
15	0.15448	0.14364	0.13289	0.12223	0.11166	0.10118	0.09079	0.08048	0.07026	0.06012	0.05007	0.04011
17.5	0.09860	0.08809	0.07768	0.06738	0.05717	0.04707	0.03706	0.02715	0.01734	0.00762	-0.00200	-0.01153
20	0.05758	0.04740	0.03732	0.02736	0.01751	0.00777	-0.00186	-0.01138	-0.02081	-0.03012	-0.03934	-0.04845
22.5	0.02646	0.01658	0.00683	-0.00279	-0.01230	-0.02169	-0.03096	-0.04012	-0.04917	-0.05811	-0.06694	-0.07566
25	0.00223	-0.00734	-0.01677	-0.02608	-0.03526	-0.04432	-0.05325	-0.06206	-0.07076	-0.07934	-0.08780	-0.09616
27.5	-0.01699	-0.02627	-0.03541	-0.04441	-0.05328	-0.06201	-0.07062	-0.07911	-0.08747	-0.09572	-0.10385	-0.11187
30	-0.03249	-0.04149	-0.05034	-0.05905	-0.06762	-0.07605	-0.08436	-0.09253	-0.10059	-0.10852	-0.11634	-0.12405

Starting from Partial Fund of 33.3%

Years to Complete	5.50%	5.75%	6.00%	6.25%	6.50%	6.75%	7.00%	7.25%	7.50%	7.75%	8.00%	8.25%
1	5.26412	5.25094	5.23776	5.22459	5.21143	5.19827	5.18512	5.17197	5.15883	5.14569	5.13256	5.11944
2	2.48138	2.46804	2.45471	2.44139	2.42808	2.41479	2.40151	2.38823	2.37497	2.36172	2.34849	2.33526
3	1.55473	1.54142	1.52813	1.51486	1.50160	1.48836	1.47514	1.46194	1.44875	1.43558	1.42242	1.40929
4	1.09210	1.07887	1.06567	1.05249	1.03933	1.02620	1.01308	0.99999	0.98693	0.97388	0.96086	0.94786
5	0.81508	0.80195	0.78885	0.77578	0.76274	0.74973	0.73675	0.72379	0.71086	0.69796	0.68509	0.67225
7.5	0.44733	0.43449	0.42168	0.40892	0.39621	0.38353	0.37090	0.35831	0.34576	0.33325	0.32078	0.30835
10	0.26518	0.25263	0.24014	0.22770	0.21532	0.20299	0.19072	0.17851	0.16635	0.15424	0.14218	0.13018
12.5	0.15724	0.14499	0.13281	0.12070	0.10866	0.09668	0.08477	0.07293	0.06115	0.04944	0.03780	0.02622
15	0.08639	0.07444	0.06257	0.05078	0.03907	0.02744	0.01589	0.00441	-0.00699	-0.01832	-0.02957	-0.04074
17.5	0.03672	0.02506	0.01350	0.00202	-0.00936	-0.02066	-0.03187	-0.04299	-0.05403	-0.06498	-0.07585	-0.08664
20	0.00026	-0.01111	-0.02238	-0.03355	-0.04462	-0.05559	-0.06647	-0.07725	-0.08794	-0.09853	-0.10904	-0.11946
22.5	-0.02741	-0.03850	-0.04948	-0.06035	-0.07112	-0.08178	-0.09234	-0.10280	-0.11315	-0.12341	-0.13357	-0.14364
25	-0.04894	-0.05976	-0.07047	-0.08105	-0.09153	-0.10189	-0.11215	-0.12230	-0.13234	-0.14228	-0.15212	-0.16187
27.5	-0.06603	-0.07659	-0.08703	-0.09734	-0.10754	-0.11762	-0.12759	-0.13745	-0.14720	-0.15684	-0.16638	-0.17583
30	-0.07981	-0.09012	-0.10030	-0.11036	-0.12029	-0.13010	-0.13980	-0.14938	-0.15886	-0.16823	-0.17749	-0.18666

Entry is the percentage of desired fund to be added monthly to complete fund.

Deposit to Complete Partial Sinking Fund

Starting from Partial Fund of 40%

Years to Complete	5.50%	5.75%	6.00%	6.25%	6.50%	6.75%	7.00%	7.25%	7.50%	7.75%	8.00%	8.25%
					Interest Rate							
1	4.69187	4.67793	4.66399	4.65005	4.63612	4.62219	4.60827	4.59436	4.58045	4.56654	4.55264	4.53874
2	2.18741	2.17332	2.15924	2.14517	2.13111	2.11706	2.10302	2.08899	2.07498	2.06097	2.04697	2.03298
3	1.35342	1.33936	1.32532	1.31129	1.29727	1.28328	1.26929	1.25533	1.24137	1.22744	1.21352	1.19961
4	0.93706	0.92307	0.90910	0.89516	0.88123	0.86733	0.85344	0.83958	0.82573	0.81191	0.79811	0.78433
5	0.68774	0.67384	0.65997	0.64612	0.63230	0.61851	0.60474	0.59100	0.57728	0.56358	0.54992	0.53628
7.5	0.35676	0.34312	0.32952	0.31595	0.30242	0.28893	0.27547	0.26206	0.24868	0.23534	0.22204	0.20877
10	0.19282	0.17945	0.16612	0.15285	0.13962	0.12644	0.11332	0.10024	0.08721	0.07423	0.06130	0.04842
12.5	0.09568	0.08257	0.06953	0.05655	0.04363	0.03076	0.01796	0.00522	-0.00746	-0.02009	-0.03265	-0.04516
15	0.03192	0.01908	0.00631	-0.00638	-0.01900	-0.03155	-0.04404	-0.05645	-0.06879	-0.08107	-0.09328	-0.10542
17.5	-0.01279	-0.02536	-0.03785	-0.05026	-0.06259	-0.07485	-0.08702	-0.09911	-0.11113	-0.12307	-0.13493	-0.14672
20	-0.04560	-0.05792	-0.07014	-0.08228	-0.09432	-0.10628	-0.11815	-0.12994	-0.14164	-0.15326	-0.16480	-0.17626
22.5	-0.07050	-0.08257	-0.09453	-0.10640	-0.11817	-0.12985	-0.14144	-0.15293	-0.16434	-0.17565	-0.18688	-0.19803
25	-0.08988	-0.10170	-0.11342	-0.12503	-0.13654	-0.14795	-0.15927	-0.17048	-0.18161	-0.19264	-0.20358	-0.21443
27.5	-0.10526	-0.11685	-0.12833	-0.13969	-0.15095	-0.16211	-0.17316	-0.18412	-0.19498	-0.20574	-0.21641	-0.22699
30	-0.11766	-0.12902	-0.14027	-0.15140	-0.16243	-0.17334	-0.18415	-0.19486	-0.20547	-0.21599	-0.22641	-0.23674

Starting from Partial Fund of 50%

Years to Complete	5.50%	5.75%	6.00%	6.25%	6.50%	6.75%	7.00%	7.25%	7.50%	7.75%	8.00%	8.25%
1	3.83351	3.81841	3.80332	3.78824	3.77315	3.75808	3.74300	3.72794	3.71287	3.69781	3.68275	3.66770
2	1.74645	1.73124	1.71603	1.70083	1.68565	1.67047	1.65530	1.64013	1.62498	1.60983	1.59470	1.57957
3	1.05146	1.03627	1.02110	1.00593	0.99078	0.97565	0.96052	0.94541	0.93031	0.91522	0.90015	0.88509
4	0.70449	0.68936	0.67425	0.65916	0.64408	0.62902	0.61398	0.59895	0.58395	0.56895	0.55398	0.53902
5	0.49672	0.48167	0.46664	0.45163	0.43664	0.42167	0.40673	0.39180	0.37690	0.36201	0.34715	0.33231
7.5	0.22092	0.20607	0.19126	0.17649	0.16174	0.14702	0.13234	0.11769	0.10307	0.08848	0.07392	0.05939
10	0.08430	0.06968	0.05510	0.04057	0.02607	0.01162	-0.00279	-0.01716	-0.03149	-0.04578	-0.06003	-0.07424
12.5	0.00334	-0.01105	-0.02539	-0.03968	-0.05392	-0.06811	-0.08225	-0.09634	-0.11039	-0.12438	-0.13832	-0.15221
15	-0.04979	-0.06396	-0.07807	-0.09212	-0.10611	-0.12005	-0.13392	-0.14774	-0.16149	-0.17520	-0.18884	-0.20243
17.5	-0.08705	-0.10100	-0.11488	-0.12869	-0.14244	-0.15612	-0.16974	-0.18329	-0.19677	-0.21019	-0.22355	-0.23685
20	-0.11439	-0.12812	-0.14178	-0.15537	-0.16888	-0.18232	-0.19568	-0.20898	-0.22220	-0.23536	-0.24845	-0.26147
22.5	-0.13514	-0.14867	-0.16211	-0.17547	-0.18876	-0.20196	-0.21509	-0.22814	-0.24111	-0.25402	-0.26685	-0.27961
25	-0.15129	-0.16461	-0.17785	-0.19100	-0.20406	-0.21704	-0.22994	-0.24276	-0.25550	-0.26817	-0.28076	-0.29327
27.5	-0.16411	-0.17724	-0.19027	-0.20322	-0.21607	-0.22884	-0.24153	-0.25413	-0.26665	-0.27909	-0.29145	-0.30374
30	-0.17444	-0.18738	-0.20022	-0.21297	-0.22563	-0.23820	-0.25068	-0.26308	-0.27539	-0.28763	-0.29978	-0.31187

Starting from Partial Fund of 60%

Years to Complete	5.50%	5.75%	6.00%	6.25%	6.50%	6.75%	7.00%	7.25%	7.50%	7.75%	8.00%	8.25%
1	2.97514	2.95890	2.94266	2.92642	2.91019	2.89396	2.87774	2.86151	2.84530	2.82908	2.81287	2.79666
2	1.30549	1.28916	1.27282	1.25650	1.24018	1.22387	1.20757	1.19127	1.17498	1.15870	1.14242	1.12616
3	0.74950	0.73318	0.71688	0.70058	0.68429	0.66802	0.65175	0.63549	0.61925	0.60301	0.58679	0.57057
4	0.47193	0.45566	0.43940	0.42316	0.40693	0.39072	0.37452	0.35833	0.34216	0.32600	0.30985	0.29372
5	0.30571	0.28950	0.27331	0.25714	0.24098	0.22484	0.20871	0.19261	0.17652	0.16045	0.14439	0.12835
7.5	0.08507	0.06903	0.05301	0.03702	0.02106	0.00512	-0.01079	-0.02668	-0.04255	-0.05839	-0.07420	-0.08999
10	-0.02423	-0.04009	-0.05592	-0.07171	-0.08747	-0.10320	-0.11890	-0.13456	-0.15019	-0.16579	-0.18136	-0.19689
12.5	-0.08899	-0.10467	-0.12031	-0.13591	-0.15147	-0.16699	-0.18247	-0.19791	-0.21331	-0.22867	-0.24399	-0.25927
15	-0.13150	-0.14700	-0.16246	-0.17786	-0.19322	-0.20854	-0.22380	-0.23902	-0.25420	-0.26932	-0.28441	-0.29944
17.5	-0.16130	-0.17663	-0.19190	-0.20712	-0.22229	-0.23740	-0.25246	-0.26746	-0.28242	-0.29732	-0.31218	-0.32698
20	-0.18318	-0.19833	-0.21343	-0.22846	-0.24344	-0.25835	-0.27321	-0.28802	-0.30276	-0.31745	-0.33209	-0.34667
22.5	-0.19978	-0.21477	-0.22969	-0.24455	-0.25934	-0.27407	-0.28874	-0.30334	-0.31789	-0.33238	-0.34681	-0.36119
25	-0.21270	-0.22752	-0.24228	-0.25697	-0.27158	-0.28614	-0.30062	-0.31504	-0.32940	-0.34370	-0.35794	-0.37212
27.5	-0.22295	-0.23762	-0.25222	-0.26674	-0.28119	-0.29557	-0.30989	-0.32413	-0.33832	-0.35244	-0.36650	-0.38050
30	-0.23122	-0.24574	-0.26018	-0.27455	-0.28884	-0.30306	-0.31721	-0.33130	-0.34531	-0.35927	-0.37316	-0.38699

Starting from Partial Fund of 66.7%

Years to Complete	5.50%	5.75%	6.00%	6.25%	6.50%	6.75%	7.00%	7.25%	7.50%	7.75%	8.00%	8.25%
1	2.40289	2.38589	2.36888	2.35188	2.33488	2.31788	2.30089	2.28390	2.26691	2.24993	2.23295	2.21597
2	1.01152	0.99443	0.97735	0.96028	0.94321	0.92614	0.90909	0.89203	0.87499	0.85795	0.84091	0.82388
3	0.54820	0.53113	0.51406	0.49701	0.47997	0.46293	0.44590	0.42888	0.41187	0.39487	0.37788	0.36089
4	0.31688	0.29985	0.28283	0.26583	0.24883	0.23185	0.21487	0.19791	0.18096	0.16402	0.14710	0.13018
5	0.17837	0.16139	0.14443	0.12748	0.11054	0.09362	0.07671	0.05981	0.04293	0.02607	0.00921	-0.00762
7.5	-0.00550	-0.02234	-0.03916	-0.05595	-0.07273	-0.08948	-0.10622	-0.12293	-0.13962	-0.15629	-0.17294	-0.18957
10	-0.09658	-0.11327	-0.12993	-0.14657	-0.16317	-0.17975	-0.19631	-0.21283	-0.22933	-0.24580	-0.26224	-0.27866
12.5	-0.15055	-0.16709	-0.18359	-0.20007	-0.21650	-0.23291	-0.24928	-0.26562	-0.28192	-0.29820	-0.31443	-0.33064
15	-0.18597	-0.20236	-0.21871	-0.23503	-0.25130	-0.26753	-0.28372	-0.29988	-0.31600	-0.33207	-0.34812	-0.36412
17.5	-0.21081	-0.22705	-0.24325	-0.25941	-0.27552	-0.29158	-0.30760	-0.32358	-0.33951	-0.35541	-0.37126	-0.38707
20	-0.22904	-0.24514	-0.26119	-0.27719	-0.29314	-0.30905	-0.32490	-0.34071	-0.35647	-0.37218	-0.38785	-0.40348
22.5	-0.24287	-0.25883	-0.27474	-0.29059	-0.30639	-0.32214	-0.33784	-0.35348	-0.36908	-0.38462	-0.40012	-0.41557
25	-0.25364	-0.26946	-0.28523	-0.30094	-0.31660	-0.33220	-0.34774	-0.36323	-0.37867	-0.39406	-0.40939	-0.42468
27.5	-0.26218	-0.27788	-0.29351	-0.30909	-0.32460	-0.34006	-0.35546	-0.37081	-0.38610	-0.40134	-0.41652	-0.43166
30	-0.26907	-0.28464	-0.30015	-0.31559	-0.33098	-0.34630	-0.36157	-0.37677	-0.39193	-0.40703	-0.42208	-0.43708

Entry is the percentage of desired fund to be added monthly to complete fund.

Deposit to Complete Partial Sinking Fund

Starting from Partial Fund of 10%

Years to Complete	Interest Rate 8.50%	8.75%	9.00%	9.25%	9.50%	9.75%	10.00%	10.25%	10.50%	11.00%	11.50%	12.00%
1	7.14145	7.13104	7.12063	7.11024	7.09985	7.08947	7.07910	7.06873	7.05837	7.03768	7.01702	6.99639
2	3.38268	3.37214	3.36163	3.35112	3.34064	3.33017	3.31971	3.30927	3.29884	3.27804	3.25730	3.23661
3	2.13275	2.12235	2.11198	2.10163	2.09130	2.08099	2.07071	2.06046	2.05022	2.02982	2.00951	1.98929
4	1.51001	1.49982	1.48965	1.47952	1.46942	1.45934	1.44930	1.43929	1.42930	1.40943	1.38968	1.37005
5	1.13815	1.12818	1.11825	1.10836	1.09850	1.08868	1.07890	1.06916	1.05945	1.04015	1.02100	1.00200
7.5	0.64748	0.63811	0.62879	0.61953	0.61033	0.60118	0.59208	0.58304	0.57405	0.55625	0.53865	0.52128
10	0.40754	0.39877	0.39008	0.38146	0.37291	0.36443	0.35602	0.34768	0.33941	0.32308	0.30703	0.29124
12.5	0.26776	0.25959	0.25151	0.24351	0.23560	0.22777	0.22003	0.21236	0.20478	0.18987	0.17527	0.16099
15	0.17793	0.17034	0.16284	0.15544	0.14814	0.14093	0.13381	0.12679	0.11986	0.10627	0.09304	0.08015
17.5	0.11651	0.10946	0.10252	0.09568	0.08895	0.08233	0.07580	0.06938	0.06305	0.05069	0.03871	0.02709
20	0.07271	0.06617	0.05975	0.05345	0.04725	0.04117	0.03519	0.02931	0.02354	0.01230	0.00145	-0.00902
22.5	0.04053	0.03448	0.02854	0.02273	0.01702	0.01143	0.00596	0.00058	-0.00468	-0.01491	-0.02475	-0.03422
25	0.01637	0.01076	0.00528	-0.00009	-0.00534	-0.01048	-0.01550	-0.02042	-0.02524	-0.03456	-0.04351	-0.05210
27.5	-0.00207	-0.00726	-0.01234	-0.01730	-0.02214	-0.02687	-0.03149	-0.03600	-0.04041	-0.04895	-0.05712	-0.06494
30	-0.01631	-0.02114	-0.02584	-0.03043	-0.03490	-0.03926	-0.04352	-0.04768	-0.05173	-0.05958	-0.06707	-0.07425

Starting from Partial Fund of 20%

Years to Complete	8.50%	8.75%	9.00%	9.25%	9.50%	9.75%	10.00%	10.25%	10.50%	11.00%	11.50%	12.00%
1	6.26925	6.25768	6.24612	6.23456	6.22301	6.21147	6.19994	6.18841	6.17689	6.15387	6.13087	6.10790
2	2.92812	2.91644	2.90478	2.89313	2.88149	2.86987	2.85826	2.84667	2.83508	2.81196	2.78889	2.76588
3	1.81707	1.80551	1.79398	1.78246	1.77097	1.75950	1.74804	1.73661	1.72520	1.70243	1.67975	1.65714
4	1.26353	1.25215	1.24080	1.22948	1.21818	1.20692	1.19567	1.18446	1.17327	1.15098	1.12879	1.10671
5	0.93299	0.92181	0.91067	0.89956	0.88848	0.87744	0.86643	0.85545	0.84451	0.82273	0.80108	0.77956
7.5	0.49683	0.48619	0.47559	0.46505	0.45455	0.44410	0.43370	0.42335	0.41305	0.39259	0.37232	0.35224
10	0.28355	0.27345	0.26341	0.25343	0.24351	0.23366	0.22387	0.21415	0.20448	0.18533	0.16643	0.14777
12.5	0.15931	0.14973	0.14023	0.13081	0.12146	0.11219	0.10299	0.09386	0.08481	0.06692	0.04931	0.03199
15	0.07946	0.07039	0.06141	0.05252	0.04371	0.03499	0.02635	0.01779	0.00932	-0.00739	-0.02378	-0.03987
17.5	0.02486	0.01628	0.00779	-0.00060	-0.00889	-0.01710	-0.02521	-0.03324	-0.04118	-0.05679	-0.07207	-0.08703
20	-0.01407	-0.02220	-0.03022	-0.03814	-0.04596	-0.05369	-0.06132	-0.06885	-0.07630	-0.09092	-0.10519	-0.11913
22.5	-0.04268	-0.05037	-0.05796	-0.06545	-0.07283	-0.08011	-0.08730	-0.09439	-0.10138	-0.11511	-0.12848	-0.14153
25	-0.06415	-0.07145	-0.07864	-0.08573	-0.09271	-0.09959	-0.10637	-0.11306	-0.11965	-0.13258	-0.14516	-0.15742
27.5	-0.08054	-0.08748	-0.09430	-0.10102	-0.10764	-0.11416	-0.12058	-0.12691	-0.13314	-0.14536	-0.15725	-0.16884
30	-0.09320	-0.09981	-0.10630	-0.11269	-0.11898	-0.12518	-0.13128	-0.13729	-0.14321	-0.15481	-0.16610	-0.17711

Starting from Partial Fund of 25%

Years to Complete	8.50%	8.75%	9.00%	9.25%	9.50%	9.75%	10.00%	10.25%	10.50%	11.00%	11.50%	12.00%
1	5.83315	5.82100	5.80886	5.79673	5.78460	5.77247	5.76036	5.74825	5.73615	5.71196	5.68780	5.66366
2	2.70084	2.68859	2.67636	2.66413	2.65192	2.63972	2.62754	2.61536	2.60320	2.57892	2.55469	2.53051
3	1.65923	1.64710	1.63498	1.62288	1.61080	1.59875	1.58671	1.57468	1.56268	1.53874	1.51487	1.49107
4	1.14029	1.12832	1.11638	1.10446	1.09257	1.08070	1.06886	1.05704	1.04525	1.02175	0.99834	0.97504
5	0.83041	0.81863	0.80688	0.79516	0.78347	0.77182	0.76020	0.74860	0.73704	0.71402	0.69111	0.66833
7.5	0.42151	0.41023	0.39899	0.38780	0.37666	0.36556	0.35451	0.34351	0.33254	0.31076	0.28916	0.26773
10	0.22156	0.21078	0.20007	0.18941	0.17882	0.16828	0.15780	0.14738	0.13701	0.11646	0.09613	0.07603
12.5	0.10508	0.09480	0.08459	0.07446	0.06439	0.05439	0.04447	0.03461	0.02482	0.00544	-0.01366	-0.03251
15	0.03022	0.02042	0.01070	0.00106	-0.00850	-0.01798	-0.02738	-0.03670	-0.04595	-0.06422	-0.08219	-0.09987
17.5	-0.02097	-0.03031	-0.03957	-0.04874	-0.05782	-0.06681	-0.07572	-0.08455	-0.09329	-0.11054	-0.12747	-0.14409
20	-0.05747	-0.06638	-0.07521	-0.08393	-0.09257	-0.10111	-0.10957	-0.11793	-0.12622	-0.14253	-0.15851	-0.17419
22.5	-0.08428	-0.09280	-0.10121	-0.10953	-0.11776	-0.12589	-0.13393	-0.14187	-0.14974	-0.16520	-0.18035	-0.19518
25	-0.10441	-0.11256	-0.12060	-0.12855	-0.13639	-0.14415	-0.15181	-0.15938	-0.16686	-0.18158	-0.19598	-0.21008
27.5	-0.11978	-0.12758	-0.13528	-0.14289	-0.15039	-0.15780	-0.16513	-0.17236	-0.17951	-0.19357	-0.20732	-0.22079
30	-0.13165	-0.13914	-0.14653	-0.15383	-0.16103	-0.16813	-0.17515	-0.18209	-0.18895	-0.20242	-0.21561	-0.22854

Starting from Partial Fund of 33.3%

Years to Complete	8.50%	8.75%	9.00%	9.25%	9.50%	9.75%	10.00%	10.25%	10.50%	11.00%	11.50%	12.00%
1	5.10632	5.09321	5.08010	5.06700	5.05390	5.04081	5.02773	5.01465	5.00157	4.97544	4.94934	4.92325
2	2.32204	2.30884	2.29565	2.28247	2.26930	2.25614	2.24300	2.22986	2.21674	2.19052	2.16435	2.13823
3	1.39617	1.38307	1.36998	1.35691	1.34386	1.33083	1.31781	1.30481	1.29183	1.26591	1.24007	1.21429
4	0.93489	0.92193	0.90900	0.89609	0.88321	0.87035	0.85751	0.84469	0.83189	0.80637	0.78093	0.75559
5	0.65944	0.64665	0.63389	0.62116	0.60846	0.59578	0.58314	0.57052	0.55793	0.53283	0.50784	0.48296
7.5	0.29597	0.28363	0.27133	0.25907	0.24685	0.23467	0.22253	0.21043	0.19837	0.17438	0.15055	0.12687
10	0.11824	0.10635	0.09451	0.08272	0.07098	0.05930	0.04767	0.03609	0.02457	0.00167	-0.02103	-0.04353
12.5	0.01470	0.00325	-0.00814	-0.01947	-0.03073	-0.04193	-0.05307	-0.06414	-0.07516	-0.09701	-0.11863	-0.14001
15	-0.05184	-0.06287	-0.07382	-0.08471	-0.09552	-0.10626	-0.11693	-0.12753	-0.13807	-0.15894	-0.17954	-0.19989
17.5	-0.09734	-0.10796	-0.11851	-0.12897	-0.13936	-0.14967	-0.15990	-0.17006	-0.18015	-0.20011	-0.21978	-0.23919
20	-0.12978	-0.14003	-0.15018	-0.16026	-0.17025	-0.18016	-0.18999	-0.19974	-0.20941	-0.22854	-0.24738	-0.26594
22.5	-0.15362	-0.16351	-0.17330	-0.18301	-0.19264	-0.20218	-0.21164	-0.22102	-0.23032	-0.24870	-0.26679	-0.28461
25	-0.17152	-0.18107	-0.19054	-0.19991	-0.20920	-0.21841	-0.22753	-0.23658	-0.24555	-0.26326	-0.28069	-0.29785
27.5	-0.18517	-0.19442	-0.20359	-0.21266	-0.22164	-0.23055	-0.23937	-0.24812	-0.25679	-0.27391	-0.29076	-0.30736
30	-0.19572	-0.20470	-0.21358	-0.22238	-0.23110	-0.23973	-0.24829	-0.25677	-0.26517	-0.28178	-0.29814	-0.31426

Entry is the percentage of desired fund to be added monthly to complete fund.

Deposit to Complete Partial Sinking Fund

Starting from Partial Fund of 40%

Years to Complete	Interest Rate											
	8.50%	8.75%	9.00%	9.25%	9.50%	9.75%	10.00%	10.25%	10.50%	11.00%	11.50%	12.00%
1	4.52485	4.51097	4.49709	4.48321	4.46934	4.45548	4.44162	4.42777	4.41392	4.38623	4.35857	4.33093
2	2.01901	2.00504	1.99108	1.97714	1.96320	1.94928	1.93536	1.92146	1.90756	1.87980	1.85209	1.82441
3	1.18572	1.17184	1.15798	1.14414	1.13031	1.11650	1.10270	1.08891	1.07515	1.04766	1.02023	0.99286
4	0.77056	0.75682	0.74310	0.72940	0.71572	0.70206	0.68842	0.67480	0.66120	0.63406	0.60701	0.58003
5	0.52266	0.50907	0.49550	0.48196	0.46845	0.45495	0.44149	0.42805	0.41463	0.38788	0.36122	0.33467
7.5	0.19554	0.18235	0.16919	0.15608	0.14299	0.12995	0.11694	0.10397	0.09104	0.06527	0.03966	0.01418
10	0.03558	0.02279	0.01005	-0.00264	-0.01528	-0.02788	-0.04043	-0.05293	-0.06539	-0.09017	-0.11476	-0.13917
12.5	-0.05760	-0.06999	-0.08233	-0.09460	-0.10682	-0.11899	-0.13109	-0.14315	-0.15514	-0.17898	-0.20260	-0.22601
15	-0.11749	-0.12950	-0.14144	-0.15332	-0.16513	-0.17688	-0.18857	-0.20020	-0.21176	-0.23471	-0.25742	-0.27990
17.5	-0.15844	-0.17008	-0.18165	-0.19316	-0.20459	-0.21595	-0.22724	-0.23847	-0.24963	-0.27176	-0.29364	-0.31527
20	-0.18764	-0.19894	-0.21016	-0.22131	-0.23239	-0.24339	-0.25432	-0.26518	-0.27597	-0.29735	-0.31848	-0.33935
22.5	-0.20909	-0.22007	-0.23097	-0.24179	-0.25254	-0.26321	-0.27381	-0.28433	-0.29479	-0.31550	-0.33594	-0.35615
25	-0.22520	-0.23588	-0.24648	-0.25700	-0.26745	-0.27782	-0.28811	-0.29834	-0.30849	-0.32860	-0.34845	-0.36807
27.5	-0.23749	-0.24790	-0.25823	-0.26848	-0.27865	-0.28874	-0.29877	-0.30872	-0.31861	-0.33819	-0.35752	-0.37663
30	-0.24699	-0.25715	-0.26723	-0.27723	-0.28715	-0.29701	-0.30679	-0.31651	-0.32616	-0.34527	-0.36416	-0.38283

Starting from Partial Fund of 50%

Years to Complete	8.50%	8.75%	9.00%	9.25%	9.50%	9.75%	10.00%	10.25%	10.50%	11.00%	11.50%	12.00%
1	3.65266	3.63761	3.62257	3.60754	3.59251	3.57748	3.56246	3.54744	3.53243	3.50242	3.47242	3.44244
2	1.56445	1.54934	1.53424	1.51914	1.50406	1.48898	1.47391	1.45885	1.44380	1.41373	1.38368	1.35367
3	0.87004	0.85501	0.83999	0.82498	0.80998	0.79500	0.78003	0.76507	0.75012	0.72027	0.69047	0.66072
4	0.52408	0.50916	0.49425	0.47936	0.46449	0.44963	0.43480	0.41997	0.40517	0.37561	0.34612	0.31669
5	0.31749	0.30269	0.28792	0.27316	0.25843	0.24371	0.22902	0.21435	0.19970	0.17045	0.14130	0.11222
7.5	0.04489	0.03043	0.01599	0.00159	-0.01278	-0.02712	-0.04144	-0.05572	-0.06997	-0.09838	-0.12667	-0.15485
10	-0.08840	-0.10253	-0.11662	-0.13067	-0.14468	-0.15865	-0.17258	-0.18647	-0.20033	-0.22792	-0.25536	-0.28265
12.5	-0.16606	-0.17986	-0.19361	-0.20731	-0.22096	-0.23457	-0.24813	-0.26165	-0.27512	-0.30193	-0.32855	-0.35501
15	-0.21596	-0.22944	-0.24287	-0.25624	-0.26955	-0.28282	-0.29603	-0.30919	-0.32230	-0.34837	-0.37424	-0.39992
17.5	-0.25009	-0.26326	-0.27638	-0.28944	-0.30243	-0.31537	-0.32826	-0.34109	-0.35386	-0.37925	-0.40442	-0.42939
20	-0.27442	-0.28731	-0.30014	-0.31290	-0.32560	-0.33824	-0.35082	-0.36334	-0.37581	-0.40057	-0.42512	-0.44946
22.5	-0.29230	-0.30492	-0.31748	-0.32997	-0.34239	-0.35476	-0.36706	-0.37931	-0.39149	-0.41569	-0.43968	-0.46345
25	-0.30572	-0.31809	-0.33040	-0.34264	-0.35482	-0.36693	-0.37898	-0.39098	-0.40291	-0.42661	-0.45010	-0.47339
27.5	-0.31596	-0.32811	-0.34019	-0.35220	-0.36415	-0.37604	-0.38786	-0.39963	-0.41134	-0.43460	-0.45766	-0.48052
30	-0.32388	-0.33582	-0.34769	-0.35950	-0.37124	-0.38292	-0.39455	-0.40612	-0.41763	-0.44050	-0.46319	-0.48569

Starting from Partial Fund of 60%

Years to Complete	8.50%	8.75%	9.00%	9.25%	9.50%	9.75%	10.00%	10.25%	10.50%	11.00%	11.50%	12.00%
1	2.78046	2.76426	2.74806	2.73186	2.71567	2.69949	2.68330	2.66712	2.65094	2.61860	2.58627	2.55395
2	1.10989	1.09364	1.07739	1.06115	1.04491	1.02868	1.01246	0.99625	0.98004	0.94765	0.91528	0.88294
3	0.55437	0.53817	0.52199	0.50582	0.48965	0.47350	0.45735	0.44122	0.42510	0.39288	0.36071	0.32857
4	0.27760	0.26149	0.24540	0.22932	0.21326	0.19721	0.18117	0.16515	0.14914	0.11715	0.08523	0.05335
5	0.11233	0.09632	0.08033	0.06436	0.04841	0.03247	0.01655	0.00064	-0.01524	-0.04697	-0.07863	-0.11022
7.5	-0.10575	-0.12149	-0.13720	-0.15289	-0.16856	-0.18420	-0.19982	-0.21541	-0.23098	-0.26204	-0.29301	-0.32388
10	-0.21239	-0.22786	-0.24330	-0.25870	-0.27408	-0.28942	-0.30473	-0.32001	-0.33526	-0.36567	-0.39595	-0.42612
12.5	-0.27451	-0.28972	-0.30488	-0.32001	-0.33510	-0.35016	-0.36517	-0.38015	-0.39510	-0.42487	-0.45451	-0.48400
15	-0.31444	-0.32939	-0.34429	-0.35916	-0.37398	-0.38875	-0.40349	-0.41819	-0.43284	-0.46203	-0.49106	-0.51993
17.5	-0.34174	-0.35644	-0.37110	-0.38572	-0.40028	-0.41480	-0.42927	-0.44370	-0.45809	-0.48673	-0.51520	-0.54351
20	-0.36120	-0.37568	-0.39011	-0.40449	-0.41881	-0.43309	-0.44732	-0.46151	-0.47565	-0.50379	-0.53176	-0.55957
22.5	-0.37551	-0.38977	-0.40398	-0.41814	-0.43225	-0.44631	-0.46032	-0.47428	-0.48819	-0.51589	-0.54341	-0.57076
25	-0.38624	-0.40031	-0.41432	-0.42828	-0.44219	-0.45605	-0.46985	-0.48361	-0.49733	-0.52462	-0.55175	-0.57871
27.5	-0.39444	-0.40832	-0.42215	-0.43593	-0.44965	-0.46333	-0.47696	-0.49054	-0.50407	-0.53101	-0.55779	-0.58442
30	-0.40077	-0.41449	-0.42815	-0.44176	-0.45532	-0.46884	-0.48230	-0.49573	-0.50910	-0.53574	-0.56222	-0.58855

Starting from Partial Fund of 66.7%

Years to Complete	8.50%	8.75%	9.00%	9.25%	9.50%	9.75%	10.00%	10.25%	10.50%	11.00%	11.50%	12.00%
1	2.19899	2.18202	2.16505	2.14808	2.13112	2.11416	2.09720	2.08024	2.06329	2.02939	1.99550	1.96163
2	0.80686	0.78984	0.77282	0.75582	0.73882	0.72182	0.70483	0.68785	0.67087	0.63693	0.60301	0.56912
3	0.34392	0.32695	0.30999	0.29304	0.27610	0.25916	0.24224	0.22532	0.20841	0.17462	0.14087	0.10714
4	0.11328	0.09638	0.07950	0.06263	0.04577	0.02892	0.01209	-0.00474	-0.02155	-0.05515	-0.08870	-0.12221
5	-0.02445	-0.04126	-0.05805	-0.07484	-0.09160	-0.10836	-0.12510	-0.14182	-0.15854	-0.19192	-0.22525	-0.25852
7.5	-0.20618	-0.22277	-0.23934	-0.25588	-0.27241	-0.28892	-0.30540	-0.32187	-0.33831	-0.37114	-0.40389	-0.43656
10	-0.29505	-0.31141	-0.32775	-0.34406	-0.36034	-0.37660	-0.39283	-0.40904	-0.42522	-0.45750	-0.48968	-0.52176
12.5	-0.34682	-0.36296	-0.37907	-0.39515	-0.41120	-0.42721	-0.44320	-0.45916	-0.47508	-0.50684	-0.53848	-0.57000
15	-0.38009	-0.39602	-0.41191	-0.42777	-0.44359	-0.45938	-0.47513	-0.49085	-0.50653	-0.53780	-0.56894	-0.59994
17.5	-0.40284	-0.41856	-0.43425	-0.44990	-0.46551	-0.48108	-0.49662	-0.51211	-0.52757	-0.55839	-0.58906	-0.61960
20	-0.41906	-0.43460	-0.45009	-0.46554	-0.48096	-0.49633	-0.51166	-0.52695	-0.54221	-0.57260	-0.60286	-0.63297
22.5	-0.43098	-0.44634	-0.46165	-0.47692	-0.49215	-0.50734	-0.52249	-0.53759	-0.55266	-0.58268	-0.61256	-0.64230
25	-0.43992	-0.45512	-0.47027	-0.48537	-0.50043	-0.51545	-0.53043	-0.54537	-0.56027	-0.58996	-0.61951	-0.64893
27.5	-0.44675	-0.46180	-0.47679	-0.49175	-0.50666	-0.52152	-0.53635	-0.55114	-0.56589	-0.59529	-0.62455	-0.65368
30	-0.45203	-0.46693	-0.48179	-0.49661	-0.51138	-0.52612	-0.54081	-0.55547	-0.57009	-0.59923	-0.62824	-0.65713

Entry is the percentage of desired fund to be added monthly to complete fund.

Balance Accumulated on a Sinking Fund

3 Year Funding

	5.50%		5.75%		6.00%		6.25%		6.50%	
	Annual	Monthly	Annual	Monthly	Annual	Monthly	Annual	Monthly	Annual	Monthly
1	31.565	31.522	31.488	31.441	31.411	31.359	31.334	31.278	31.258	31.197
2	64.867	64.822	64.787	64.737	64.707	64.653	64.627	64.569	64.547	64.484
3	100.000	100.000	100.000	100.000	100.000	100.000	100.000	100.000	100.000	100.000

5 Year Funding

	Annual	Monthly	Annual	Monthly	Annual	Monthly	Annual	Monthly	Annual	Monthly
1	17.918	17.867	17.828	17.774	17.740	17.680	17.651	17.587	17.563	17.494
2	36.821	36.743	36.682	36.597	36.544	36.451	36.406	36.306	36.269	36.161
3	56.764	56.682	56.620	56.531	56.476	56.380	56.333	56.228	56.189	56.077
4	77.803	77.747	77.704	77.642	77.604	77.537	77.505	77.432	77.405	77.327
5	100.000	100.000	100.000	100.000	100.000	100.000	100.000	100.000	100.000	100.000

7 Year Funding

	Annual	Monthly	Annual	Monthly	Annual	Monthly	Annual	Monthly	Annual	Monthly
1	12.096	12.045	12.005	11.948	11.914	11.853	11.823	11.757	11.733	11.663
2	24.858	24.769	24.700	24.602	24.542	24.436	24.385	24.271	24.229	24.106
3	38.322	38.211	38.124	38.003	37.928	37.796	37.732	37.590	37.537	37.384
4	52.526	52.411	52.321	52.195	52.117	51.980	51.913	51.765	51.710	51.550
5	67.511	67.412	67.334	67.225	67.158	67.039	66.981	66.852	66.804	66.665
6	83.321	83.259	83.211	83.143	83.100	83.026	82.990	82.910	82.880	82.793
7	100.000	100.000	100.000	100.000	100.000	100.000	100.000	100.000	100.000	100.000

10 Year Funding

	Annual	Monthly	Annual	Monthly	Annual	Monthly	Annual	Monthly	Annual	Monthly
1	7.767	7.716	7.676	7.621	7.587	7.527	7.498	7.434	7.410	7.342
2	15.961	15.867	15.794	15.692	15.629	15.519	15.465	15.347	15.303	15.176
3	24.605	24.477	24.379	24.240	24.153	24.003	23.930	23.768	23.708	23.534
4	33.725	33.574	33.457	33.292	33.189	33.011	32.924	32.731	32.659	32.452
5	43.347	43.183	43.057	42.878	42.767	42.574	42.479	42.270	42.193	41.967
6	53.498	53.335	53.209	53.031	52.920	52.727	52.633	52.423	52.346	52.120
7	64.207	64.059	63.945	63.783	63.682	63.506	63.420	63.229	63.158	62.952
8	75.505	75.388	75.298	75.170	75.090	74.951	74.882	74.731	74.674	74.510
9	87.425	87.357	87.304	87.229	87.182	87.101	87.061	86.972	86.939	86.842
10	100.000	100.000	100.000	100.000	100.000	100.000	100.000	100.000	100.000	100.000

12 Year Funding

	Annual	Monthly	Annual	Monthly	Annual	Monthly	Annual	Monthly	Annual	Monthly
1	6.103	6.053	6.015	5.961	5.928	5.870	5.842	5.780	5.757	5.691
2	12.542	12.448	12.375	12.274	12.211	12.102	12.049	11.931	11.888	11.762
3	19.334	19.203	19.102	18.960	18.871	18.718	18.643	18.478	18.417	18.241
4	26.501	26.339	26.215	26.040	25.931	25.742	25.650	25.447	25.371	25.153
5	34.061	33.878	33.737	33.538	33.415	33.200	33.095	32.863	32.777	32.528
6	42.037	41.842	41.692	41.480	41.348	41.118	41.005	40.757	40.665	40.397
7	50.452	50.256	50.104	49.889	49.756	49.524	49.410	49.158	49.065	48.793
8	59.330	59.144	58.999	58.796	58.669	58.448	58.340	58.100	58.011	57.752
9	68.696	68.533	68.407	68.228	68.117	67.923	67.828	67.617	67.538	67.310
10	78.577	78.452	78.355	78.217	78.132	77.982	77.909	77.746	77.685	77.508
11	89.002	88.930	88.875	88.796	88.747	88.662	88.620	88.526	88.491	88.390
12	100.000	100.000	100.000	100.000	100.000	100.000	100.000	100.000	100.000	100.000

15 Year Funding

	Annual	Monthly	Annual	Monthly	Annual	Monthly	Annual	Monthly	Annual	Monthly
1	4.463	4.415	4.379	4.328	4.296	4.242	4.215	4.157	4.135	4.073
2	9.171	9.079	9.009	8.911	8.850	8.745	8.694	8.581	8.539	8.419
3	14.138	14.007	13.906	13.765	13.678	13.526	13.452	13.290	13.230	13.056
4	19.378	19.212	19.084	18.905	18.795	18.602	18.508	18.301	18.225	18.004
5	24.906	24.711	24.561	24.349	24.219	23.991	23.880	23.635	23.545	23.283
6	30.738	30.520	30.352	30.115	29.968	29.712	29.588	29.312	29.210	28.915
7	36.892	36.657	36.475	36.221	36.062	35.787	35.652	35.355	35.244	34.925
8	43.383	43.140	42.952	42.687	42.522	42.235	42.095	41.786	41.671	41.337
9	50.232	49.988	49.800	49.535	49.370	49.082	48.941	48.630	48.514	48.179
10	57.457	57.223	57.042	56.787	56.628	56.351	56.215	55.915	55.803	55.479
11	65.080	64.866	64.701	64.468	64.322	64.068	63.944	63.668	63.566	63.268
12	73.122	72.941	72.800	72.602	72.478	72.262	72.155	71.920	71.833	71.578
13	81.606	81.470	81.365	81.216	81.123	80.960	80.880	80.703	80.637	80.445
14	90.557	90.481	90.422	90.339	90.287	90.195	90.150	90.051	90.014	89.906
15	100.000	100.000	100.000	100.000	100.000	100.000	100.000	100.000	100.000	100.000

Entry is percentage of final plan accumulated at selected time, including interest.

Balance Accumulated on a Sinking Fund

25 Year Funding

	5.50%		5.75%		6.00%		6.25%		6.50%	
	Annual	Monthly	Annual	Monthly	Annual	Monthly	Annual	Monthly	Annual	Monthly
1	1.955	1.917	1.888	1.847	1.823	1.780	1.759	1.715	1.698	1.651
2	4.017	3.942	3.884	3.804	3.755	3.670	3.629	3.539	3.507	3.413
3	6.193	6.081	5.995	5.876	5.803	5.676	5.615	5.482	5.433	5.292
4	8.489	8.341	8.228	8.070	7.973	7.806	7.726	7.549	7.484	7.298
5	10.911	10.728	10.589	10.394	10.275	10.068	9.968	9.749	9.669	9.438
6	13.466	13.251	13.085	12.856	12.714	12.469	12.350	12.091	11.995	11.721
7	16.161	15.915	15.726	15.462	15.299	15.018	14.882	14.583	14.473	14.157
8	19.005	18.729	18.518	18.222	18.040	17.724	17.571	17.236	17.112	16.756
9	22.005	21.703	21.470	21.146	20.945	20.598	20.429	20.059	19.922	19.530
10	25.170	24.844	24.593	24.241	24.024	23.648	23.465	23.064	22.916	22.489
11	28.510	28.162	27.895	27.520	27.288	26.887	26.691	26.262	26.103	25.646
12	32.033	31.668	31.386	30.992	30.748	30.325	30.119	29.666	29.498	29.014
13	35.750	35.371	35.079	34.670	34.416	33.975	33.761	33.288	33.114	32.609
14	39.671	39.283	38.984	38.564	38.304	37.851	37.630	37.144	36.964	36.444
15	43.807	43.416	43.113	42.688	42.424	41.966	41.742	41.248	41.065	40.536
16	48.172	47.782	47.480	47.056	46.793	46.334	46.110	45.616	45.432	44.901
17	52.776	52.394	52.098	51.682	51.423	50.972	50.751	50.264	50.084	49.560
18	57.634	57.266	56.981	56.580	56.331	55.896	55.683	55.212	55.037	54.530
19	62.759	62.413	62.146	61.768	61.533	61.123	60.922	60.478	60.313	59.833
20	68.165	67.851	67.607	67.263	67.048	66.673	66.489	66.083	65.931	65.491
21	73.869	73.595	73.382	73.081	72.894	72.565	72.405	72.048	71.915	71.528
22	79.887	79.663	79.489	79.243	79.090	78.821	78.689	78.397	78.287	77.970
23	86.236	86.074	85.948	85.769	85.658	85.463	85.367	85.154	85.074	84.843
24	92.934	92.846	92.777	92.681	92.620	92.514	92.462	92.346	92.302	92.176
25	100.000	100.000	100.000	100.000	100.000	100.000	100.000	100.000	100.000	100.000

30 Year Funding

	5.50%		5.75%		6.00%		6.25%		6.50%	
	Annual	Monthly	Annual	Monthly	Annual	Monthly	Annual	Monthly	Annual	Monthly
1	1.381	1.347	1.322	1.286	1.265	1.228	1.210	1.172	1.158	1.118
2	2.837	2.770	2.719	2.649	2.606	2.532	2.496	2.419	2.391	2.310
3	4.374	4.274	4.197	4.092	4.027	3.916	3.863	3.746	3.704	3.583
4	5.995	5.862	5.760	5.620	5.533	5.385	5.314	5.159	5.102	4.940
5	7.705	7.539	7.413	7.238	7.130	6.946	6.857	6.663	6.592	6.389
6	9.509	9.312	9.161	8.952	8.823	8.602	8.495	8.263	8.178	7.935
7	11.413	11.184	11.009	10.766	10.617	10.361	10.237	9.966	9.867	9.584
8	13.421	13.162	12.964	12.689	12.519	12.228	12.087	11.779	11.666	11.343
9	15.540	15.252	15.031	14.724	14.535	14.210	14.052	13.709	13.582	13.221
10	17.775	17.459	17.217	16.880	16.672	16.314	16.141	15.762	15.623	15.224
11	20.133	19.791	19.528	19.163	18.937	18.549	18.360	17.948	17.796	17.361
12	22.621	22.254	21.973	21.581	21.339	20.921	20.718	20.274	20.111	19.642
13	25.246	24.857	24.558	24.141	23.884	23.439	23.223	22.750	22.576	22.075
14	28.015	27.606	27.292	26.853	26.582	26.113	25.885	25.385	25.201	24.671
15	30.936	30.510	30.183	29.725	29.442	28.951	28.713	28.190	27.997	27.441
16	34.018	33.578	33.240	32.766	32.473	31.965	31.718	31.175	30.974	30.396
17	37.270	36.820	36.473	35.987	35.686	35.164	34.910	34.352	34.145	33.550
18	40.700	40.244	39.892	39.398	39.092	38.561	38.303	37.733	37.523	36.914
19	44.319	43.861	43.507	43.011	42.703	42.168	41.907	41.332	41.119	40.504
20	48.137	47.682	47.330	46.836	46.530	45.996	45.736	45.162	44.950	44.335
21	52.165	51.719	51.373	50.888	50.586	50.061	49.805	49.239	49.029	48.422
22	56.415	55.983	55.649	55.179	54.887	54.377	54.128	53.578	53.374	52.782
23	60.898	60.488	60.170	59.723	59.445	58.959	58.721	58.196	58.001	57.435
24	65.628	65.247	64.952	64.536	64.276	63.823	63.602	63.111	62.929	62.399
25	70.618	70.275	70.008	69.632	69.398	68.988	68.787	68.342	68.177	67.696
26	75.883	75.586	75.355	75.030	74.826	74.471	74.297	73.910	73.766	73.347
27	81.437	81.196	81.010	80.746	80.581	80.292	80.150	79.836	79.719	79.377
28	87.296	87.124	86.989	86.799	86.681	86.472	86.370	86.143	86.058	85.811
29	93.478	93.385	93.313	93.210	93.146	93.034	92.979	92.856	92.810	92.676
30	100.000	100.000	100.000	100.000	100.000	100.000	100.000	100.000	100.000	100.000

Entry is percentage of final plan accumulated at selected time, including interest.

Balance Accumulated on a Sinking Fund

3 Year Funding

	6.75%		7.00%		7.25%		7.50%		7.75%	
	Annual	Monthly	Annual	Monthly	Annual	Monthly	Annual	Monthly	Annual	Monthly
1	31.181	31.116	31.105	31.036	31.029	30.955	30.954	30.874	30.878	30.794
2	64.467	64.400	64.388	64.315	64.308	64.230	64.229	64.146	64.150	64.061
3	100.000	100.000	100.000	100.000	100.000	100.000	100.000	100.000	100.000	100.000

5 Year Funding

	Annual	Monthly	Annual	Monthly	Annual	Monthly	Annual	Monthly	Annual	Monthly
1	17.476	17.402	17.389	17.310	17.303	17.218	17.216	17.126	17.131	17.035
2	36.132	36.016	35.995	35.871	35.860	35.726	35.724	35.582	35.589	35.438
3	56.047	55.925	55.904	55.774	55.762	55.622	55.620	55.471	55.478	55.319
4	77.306	77.221	77.206	77.116	77.107	77.010	77.008	76.903	76.909	76.797
5	100.000	100.000	100.000	100.000	100.000	100.000	100.000	100.000	100.000	100.000

7 Year Funding

	Annual	Monthly	Annual	Monthly	Annual	Monthly	Annual	Monthly	Annual	Monthly
1	11.644	11.568	11.555	11.475	11.467	11.381	11.380	11.289	11.293	11.197
2	24.074	23.942	23.920	23.779	23.766	23.616	23.614	23.454	23.462	23.292
3	37.343	37.178	37.149	36.973	36.957	36.768	36.765	36.563	36.574	36.359
4	51.507	51.335	51.305	51.120	51.103	50.905	50.902	50.691	50.701	50.476
5	66.628	66.478	66.452	66.290	66.276	66.103	66.100	65.915	65.924	65.726
6	82.769	82.675	82.659	82.557	82.548	82.439	82.437	82.321	82.326	82.202
7	100.000	100.000	100.000	100.000	100.000	100.000	100.000	100.000	100.000	100.000

10 Year Funding

	Annual	Monthly	Annual	Monthly	Annual	Monthly	Annual	Monthly	Annual	Monthly
1	7.324	7.250	7.238	7.160	7.153	7.070	7.069	6.981	6.985	6.893
2	15.142	15.006	14.982	14.837	14.824	14.670	14.667	14.504	14.512	14.339
3	23.487	23.301	23.269	23.070	23.052	22.840	22.836	22.611	22.622	22.383
4	32.396	32.174	32.135	31.897	31.875	31.622	31.617	31.347	31.361	31.074
5	41.907	41.665	41.622	41.363	41.339	41.062	41.057	40.762	40.776	40.462
6	52.059	51.816	51.774	51.513	51.489	51.210	51.205	50.907	50.922	50.604
7	62.897	62.675	62.636	62.397	62.375	62.118	62.114	61.840	61.854	61.561
8	74.466	74.289	74.258	74.067	74.050	73.845	73.841	73.622	73.633	73.398
9	86.816	86.712	86.694	86.581	86.571	86.450	86.448	86.318	86.325	86.185
10	100.000	100.000	100.000	100.000	100.000	100.000	100.000	100.000	100.000	100.000

12 Year Funding

	Annual	Monthly	Annual	Monthly	Annual	Monthly	Annual	Monthly	Annual	Monthly
1	5.673	5.602	5.590	5.515	5.508	5.429	5.428	5.344	5.348	5.260
2	11.729	11.595	11.572	11.429	11.416	11.265	11.263	11.103	11.111	10.942
3	18.194	18.005	17.972	17.771	17.752	17.539	17.535	17.309	17.320	17.080
4	25.095	24.861	24.820	24.571	24.548	24.283	24.278	23.996	24.010	23.712
5	32.461	32.194	32.148	31.862	31.836	31.532	31.527	31.203	31.219	30.876
6	40.326	40.038	39.988	39.681	39.653	39.325	39.319	38.969	38.987	38.615
7	48.721	48.429	48.378	48.065	48.036	47.701	47.696	47.339	47.357	46.977
8	57.682	57.403	57.354	57.055	57.027	56.706	56.701	56.358	56.375	56.009
9	67.249	67.002	66.959	66.694	66.670	66.386	66.381	66.077	66.092	65.767
10	77.461	77.270	77.237	77.031	77.012	76.791	76.787	76.550	76.562	76.309
11	88.363	88.253	88.233	88.115	88.104	87.976	87.974	87.837	87.844	87.697
12	100.000	100.000	100.000	100.000	100.000	100.000	100.000	100.000	100.000	100.000

15 Year Funding

	Annual	Monthly	Annual	Monthly	Annual	Monthly	Annual	Monthly	Annual	Monthly
1	4.057	3.991	3.979	3.910	3.903	3.830	3.829	3.751	3.755	3.674
2	8.387	8.260	8.237	8.102	8.090	7.947	7.945	7.794	7.801	7.643
3	13.010	12.826	12.794	12.598	12.580	12.373	12.369	12.150	12.161	11.931
4	17.945	17.710	17.669	17.418	17.395	17.130	17.126	16.845	16.859	16.563
5	23.213	22.933	22.885	22.587	22.560	22.244	22.239	21.904	21.921	21.567
6	28.837	28.521	28.466	28.130	28.099	27.741	27.735	27.356	27.375	26.973
7	34.840	34.498	34.438	34.073	34.040	33.651	33.644	33.231	33.252	32.814
8	41.248	40.891	40.828	40.446	40.411	40.003	39.996	39.562	39.584	39.123
9	48.089	47.729	47.666	47.280	47.244	46.832	46.825	46.385	46.407	45.939
10	55.392	55.043	54.982	54.607	54.573	54.172	54.165	53.737	53.759	53.303
11	63.188	62.866	62.810	62.465	62.433	62.063	62.056	61.660	61.680	61.258
12	71.510	71.235	71.186	70.890	70.863	70.545	70.539	70.198	70.216	69.851
13	80.393	80.185	80.149	79.925	79.904	79.663	79.659	79.400	79.413	79.135
14	89.877	89.759	89.739	89.612	89.600	89.464	89.462	89.315	89.322	89.165
15	100.000	100.000	100.000	100.000	100.000	100.000	100.000	100.000	100.000	100.000

Entry is percentage of final plan accumulated at selected time, including interest.

Balance Accumulated on a Sinking Fund

25 Year Funding

	6.75%		7.00%		7.25%		7.50%		7.75%	
	Annual	Monthly	Annual	Monthly	Annual	Monthly	Annual	Monthly	Annual	Monthly
1	1.639	1.590	1.581	1.530	1.525	1.472	1.471	1.416	1.419	1.362
2	3.388	3.290	3.273	3.170	3.161	3.054	3.052	2.942	2.947	2.833
3	5.255	5.108	5.083	4.929	4.915	4.755	4.752	4.586	4.594	4.422
4	7.249	7.053	7.020	6.815	6.797	6.584	6.580	6.358	6.369	6.139
5	9.377	9.134	9.092	8.838	8.815	8.549	8.545	8.267	8.281	7.993
6	11.648	11.360	11.310	11.007	10.979	10.662	10.656	10.325	10.342	9.997
7	14.073	13.740	13.682	13.332	13.300	12.933	12.927	12.543	12.562	12.161
8	16.662	16.286	16.221	15.826	15.790	15.374	15.367	14.932	14.954	14.500
9	19.425	19.010	18.938	18.499	18.460	17.999	17.991	17.507	17.532	17.026
10	22.375	21.923	21.845	21.367	21.323	20.820	20.811	20.282	20.309	19.755
11	25.524	25.039	24.955	24.441	24.394	23.852	23.843	23.273	23.301	22.703
12	28.886	28.372	28.283	27.738	27.688	27.112	27.103	26.496	26.526	25.888
13	32.474	31.937	31.843	31.273	31.221	30.616	30.606	29.968	30.000	29.329
14	36.305	35.750	35.653	35.063	35.009	34.383	34.373	33.711	33.744	33.046
15	40.394	39.829	39.730	39.128	39.073	38.433	38.422	37.744	37.778	37.062
16	44.760	44.191	44.092	43.486	43.431	42.785	42.775	42.090	42.124	41.400
17	49.420	48.858	48.760	48.159	48.105	47.465	47.454	46.773	46.808	46.086
18	54.394	53.849	53.754	53.171	53.117	52.494	52.484	51.820	51.854	51.149
19	59.704	59.188	59.098	58.544	58.494	57.901	57.891	57.259	57.291	56.619
20	65.373	64.899	64.816	64.306	64.260	63.713	63.704	63.120	63.150	62.528
21	71.425	71.007	70.934	70.485	70.444	69.961	69.953	69.437	69.463	68.911
22	77.884	77.541	77.481	77.110	77.076	76.677	76.671	76.243	76.265	75.807
23	84.780	84.529	84.485	84.214	84.189	83.897	83.892	83.578	83.594	83.257
24	92.142	92.004	91.980	91.832	91.818	91.658	91.655	91.482	91.491	91.305
25	100.000	100.000	100.000	100.000	100.000	100.000	100.000	100.000	100.000	100.000

30 Year Funding

	Annual	Monthly	Annual	Monthly	Annual	Monthly	Annual	Monthly	Annual	Monthly
1	1.107	1.066	1.059	1.016	1.012	0.968	0.967	0.922	0.924	0.878
2	2.289	2.206	2.191	2.105	2.097	2.008	2.007	1.915	1.920	1.826
3	3.551	3.425	3.403	3.273	3.261	3.127	3.124	2.986	2.993	2.850
4	4.898	4.729	4.700	4.525	4.510	4.329	4.326	4.139	4.149	3.957
5	6.336	6.124	6.088	5.868	5.849	5.621	5.617	5.383	5.394	5.152
6	7.870	7.616	7.573	7.308	7.285	7.010	7.006	6.722	6.736	6.444
7	9.509	9.213	9.161	8.853	8.825	8.504	8.498	8.166	8.182	7.839
8	11.258	10.920	10.861	10.508	10.476	10.109	10.103	9.722	9.741	9.346
9	13.125	12.746	12.680	12.284	12.248	11.835	11.828	11.398	11.420	10.975
10	15.118	14.699	14.627	14.188	14.148	13.690	13.682	13.205	13.229	12.734
11	17.246	16.788	16.709	16.229	16.186	15.684	15.675	15.152	15.178	14.634
12	19.517	19.023	18.937	18.418	18.371	17.827	17.818	17.250	17.278	16.687
13	21.942	21.413	21.322	20.765	20.715	20.131	20.121	19.511	19.542	18.905
14	24.530	23.970	23.873	23.282	23.229	22.608	22.598	21.948	21.980	21.301
15	27.293	26.705	26.603	25.981	25.925	25.271	25.260	24.573	24.608	23.889
16	30.243	29.630	29.523	28.875	28.816	28.133	28.121	27.403	27.439	26.686
17	33.391	32.759	32.649	31.978	31.917	31.209	31.198	30.452	30.489	29.706
18	36.753	36.105	35.993	35.306	35.243	34.517	34.504	33.738	33.776	32.970
19	40.341	39.685	39.571	38.874	38.810	38.072	38.059	37.279	37.318	36.496
20	44.171	43.514	43.399	42.700	42.636	41.894	41.881	41.095	41.134	40.304
21	48.260	47.609	47.496	46.803	46.739	46.002	45.989	45.207	45.246	44.419
22	52.624	51.990	51.879	51.202	51.140	50.418	50.405	49.638	49.677	48.864
23	57.284	56.676	56.570	55.919	55.859	55.165	55.153	54.414	54.451	53.666
24	62.257	61.688	61.588	60.977	60.921	60.268	60.257	59.560	59.595	58.854
25	67.567	67.049	66.958	66.401	66.350	65.753	65.743	65.105	65.138	64.458
26	73.235	72.783	72.704	72.217	72.172	71.650	71.641	71.082	71.110	70.513
27	79.286	78.916	78.852	78.453	78.417	77.988	77.981	77.522	77.545	77.054
28	85.745	85.477	85.430	85.140	85.114	84.802	84.797	84.462	84.479	84.120
29	92.640	92.494	92.469	92.311	92.297	92.126	92.124	91.941	91.950	91.753
30	100.000	100.000	100.000	100.000	100.000	100.000	100.000	100.000	100.000	100.000

Entry is percentage of final plan accumulated at selected time, including interest.

Balance Accumulated on a Sinking Fund

3 Year Funding

	8.00%		8.25%		8.50%		8.75%		9.00%	
	Annual	Monthly	Annual	Monthly	Annual	Monthly	Annual	Monthly	Annual	Monthly
1	30.803	30.714	30.729	30.633	30.654	30.553	30.580	30.473	30.505	30.393
2	64.071	63.976	63.992	63.892	63.913	63.807	63.835	63.722	63.756	63.637
3	100.000	100.000	100.000	100.000	100.000	100.000	100.000	100.000	100.000	100.000

5 Year Funding

	Annual	Monthly	Annual	Monthly	Annual	Monthly	Annual	Monthly	Annual	Monthly
1	17.046	16.944	16.961	16.853	16.877	16.763	16.793	16.673	16.709	16.583
2	35.455	35.294	35.321	35.151	35.188	35.008	35.055	34.864	34.922	34.722
3	55.337	55.168	55.196	55.016	55.055	54.865	54.915	54.713	54.775	54.562
4	76.810	76.691	76.710	76.584	76.611	76.477	76.512	76.370	76.414	76.263
5	100.000	100.000	100.000	100.000	100.000	100.000	100.000	100.000	100.000	100.000

7 Year Funding

	Annual	Monthly	Annual	Monthly	Annual	Monthly	Annual	Monthly	Annual	Monthly
1	11.207	11.105	11.122	11.014	11.037	10.923	10.953	10.833	10.869	10.743
2	23.311	23.131	23.161	22.971	23.012	22.811	22.864	22.652	22.716	22.493
3	36.383	36.156	36.194	35.953	36.005	35.750	35.817	35.548	35.630	35.346
4	50.501	50.262	50.301	50.047	50.102	49.833	49.904	49.619	49.706	49.405
5	65.748	65.538	65.573	65.349	65.398	65.161	65.223	64.972	65.048	64.782
6	82.216	82.082	82.105	81.963	81.994	81.843	81.883	81.723	81.772	81.602
7	100.000	100.000	100.000	100.000	100.000	100.000	100.000	100.000	100.000	100.000

10 Year Funding

	Annual	Monthly	Annual	Monthly	Annual	Monthly	Annual	Monthly	Annual	Monthly
1	6.903	6.805	6.821	6.719	6.741	6.633	6.661	6.548	6.582	6.463
2	14.358	14.175	14.206	14.013	14.055	13.852	13.905	13.692	13.756	13.533
3	22.410	22.157	22.199	21.932	21.990	21.709	21.782	21.487	21.576	21.266
4	31.105	30.801	30.852	30.530	30.600	30.260	30.349	29.992	30.100	29.724
5	40.497	40.163	40.219	39.865	39.942	39.568	39.666	39.272	39.391	38.976
6	50.640	50.302	50.358	50.000	50.077	49.698	49.798	49.397	49.519	49.096
7	61.594	61.282	61.334	61.003	61.075	60.724	60.816	60.444	60.557	60.165
8	73.424	73.174	73.215	72.949	73.007	72.724	72.798	72.498	72.590	72.272
9	86.201	86.052	86.077	85.919	85.953	85.785	85.829	85.650	85.705	85.515
10	100.000	100.000	100.000	100.000	100.000	100.000	100.000	100.000	100.000	100.000

12 Year Funding

	Annual	Monthly	Annual	Monthly	Annual	Monthly	Annual	Monthly	Annual	Monthly
1	5.270	5.177	5.192	5.094	5.115	5.013	5.040	4.933	4.965	4.853
2	10.961	10.783	10.812	10.625	10.665	10.469	10.520	10.315	10.377	10.162
3	17.107	16.854	16.896	16.630	16.687	16.407	16.481	16.187	16.276	15.969
4	23.745	23.430	23.482	23.149	23.221	22.871	22.962	22.594	22.706	22.320
5	30.914	30.551	30.611	30.227	30.310	29.905	30.011	29.585	29.714	29.267
6	38.657	38.263	38.328	37.912	38.002	37.562	37.677	37.213	37.354	36.866
7	47.019	46.615	46.682	46.254	46.347	45.895	46.013	45.535	45.681	45.177
8	56.050	55.661	55.725	55.312	55.402	54.964	55.079	54.616	54.757	54.268
9	65.803	65.457	65.515	65.146	65.226	64.836	64.938	64.524	64.650	64.213
10	76.337	76.066	76.111	75.823	75.886	75.579	75.660	75.335	75.434	75.089
11	87.713	87.556	87.583	87.415	87.451	87.273	87.320	87.130	87.188	86.987
12	100.000	100.000	100.000	100.000	100.000	100.000	100.000	100.000	100.000	100.000

15 Year Funding

	Annual	Monthly	Annual	Monthly	Annual	Monthly	Annual	Monthly	Annual	Monthly
1	3.683	3.598	3.612	3.523	3.542	3.449	3.473	3.377	3.406	3.305
2	7.661	7.494	7.522	7.348	7.385	7.203	7.251	7.061	7.118	6.921
3	11.956	11.714	11.754	11.500	11.555	11.289	11.358	11.081	11.165	10.875
4	16.596	16.284	16.336	16.009	16.079	15.736	15.826	15.467	15.576	15.201
5	21.606	21.234	21.295	20.903	20.988	20.576	20.684	20.253	20.383	19.932
6	27.018	26.594	26.664	26.218	26.314	25.844	25.967	25.474	25.624	25.107
7	32.862	32.399	32.476	31.987	32.093	31.578	31.713	31.171	31.336	30.768
8	39.174	38.686	38.767	38.251	38.363	37.818	37.961	37.388	37.562	36.959
9	45.991	45.495	45.577	45.052	45.165	44.610	44.756	44.170	44.348	43.732
10	53.353	52.869	52.949	52.435	52.547	52.003	52.145	51.571	51.745	51.139
11	61.305	60.855	60.930	60.452	60.555	60.048	60.181	59.645	59.808	59.242
12	69.892	69.503	69.568	69.155	69.244	68.805	68.921	68.455	68.597	68.105
13	79.166	78.870	78.919	78.604	78.672	78.336	78.425	78.068	78.177	77.799
14	89.182	89.014	89.042	88.862	88.901	88.710	88.760	88.556	88.618	88.402
15	100.000	100.000	100.000	100.000	100.000	100.000	100.000	100.000	100.000	100.000

Entry is percentage of final plan accumulated at selected time, including interest.

Balance Accumulated on a Sinking Fund

25 Year Funding

	8.00% Annual	8.00% Monthly	8.25% Annual	8.25% Monthly	8.50% Annual	8.50% Monthly	8.75% Annual	8.75% Monthly	9.00% Annual	9.00% Monthly
1	1.368	1.309	1.319	1.258	1.271	1.209	1.225	1.162	1.181	1.116
2	2.845	2.727	2.746	2.624	2.650	2.525	2.557	2.429	2.468	2.336
3	4.441	4.262	4.292	4.108	4.147	3.957	4.006	3.812	3.870	3.671
4	6.164	5.925	5.964	5.718	5.770	5.516	5.582	5.321	5.399	5.131
5	8.025	7.726	7.775	7.466	7.532	7.213	7.296	6.967	7.066	6.728
6	10.035	9.676	9.735	9.364	9.444	9.060	9.159	8.763	8.882	8.474
7	12.205	11.789	11.857	11.425	11.517	11.070	11.186	10.723	10.862	10.385
8	14.550	14.076	14.154	13.662	13.768	13.257	13.390	12.861	13.020	12.475
9	17.081	16.554	16.641	16.091	16.209	15.638	15.786	15.195	15.373	14.761
10	19.816	19.237	19.332	18.728	18.858	18.229	18.393	17.740	17.937	17.261
11	22.769	22.142	22.246	21.591	21.732	21.050	21.227	20.518	20.732	19.996
12	25.958	25.289	25.400	24.700	24.850	24.120	24.310	23.549	23.779	22.987
13	29.403	28.697	28.814	28.075	28.234	27.461	27.662	26.855	27.099	26.259
14	33.123	32.388	32.510	31.739	31.905	31.097	31.308	30.463	30.719	29.838
15	37.141	36.386	36.511	35.717	35.888	35.055	35.272	34.400	34.664	33.752
16	41.480	40.715	40.842	40.036	40.210	39.362	39.584	38.695	38.965	38.034
17	46.166	45.403	45.530	44.725	44.899	44.051	44.273	43.382	43.652	42.718
18	51.227	50.481	50.605	49.816	49.986	49.154	49.372	48.495	48.761	47.841
19	56.693	55.980	56.098	55.343	55.506	54.708	54.917	54.075	54.331	53.444
20	62.597	61.935	62.045	61.343	61.495	60.752	60.947	60.162	60.401	59.573
21	68.972	68.385	68.483	67.858	67.994	67.331	67.505	66.804	67.018	66.277
22	75.858	75.370	75.451	74.931	75.044	74.492	74.637	74.051	74.230	73.610
23	83.295	82.935	82.995	82.611	82.694	82.285	82.393	81.959	82.091	81.631
24	91.326	91.127	91.161	90.948	90.994	90.768	90.827	90.586	90.660	90.404
25	100.000	100.000	100.000	100.000	100.000	100.000	100.000	100.000	100.000	100.000

30 Year Funding

	8.00% Annual	8.00% Monthly	8.25% Annual	8.25% Monthly	8.50% Annual	8.50% Monthly	8.75% Annual	8.75% Monthly	9.00% Annual	9.00% Monthly
1	0.883	0.835	0.843	0.795	0.805	0.756	0.769	0.719	0.734	0.683
2	1.836	1.740	1.756	1.658	1.679	1.579	1.604	1.503	1.533	1.430
3	2.866	2.720	2.744	2.595	2.626	2.474	2.513	2.359	2.405	2.248
4	3.978	3.781	3.813	3.612	3.655	3.449	3.502	3.292	3.355	3.142
5	5.179	4.930	4.971	4.716	4.770	4.510	4.577	4.311	4.391	4.120
6	6.476	6.175	6.224	5.915	5.981	5.664	5.746	5.423	5.519	5.190
7	7.877	7.523	7.581	7.217	7.294	6.921	7.017	6.635	6.750	6.360
8	9.389	8.982	9.049	8.630	8.719	8.289	8.400	7.959	8.091	7.639
9	11.023	10.563	10.639	10.164	10.265	9.777	9.904	9.402	9.553	9.039
10	12.788	12.275	12.359	11.830	11.943	11.397	11.539	10.978	11.146	10.570
11	14.694	14.130	14.222	13.639	13.763	13.161	13.317	12.696	12.883	12.245
12	16.752	16.138	16.239	15.602	15.738	15.080	15.251	14.572	14.776	14.077
13	18.975	18.312	18.421	17.734	17.881	17.169	17.354	16.618	16.839	16.081
14	21.376	20.668	20.784	20.048	20.206	19.443	19.641	18.851	19.089	18.272
15	23.968	23.218	23.342	22.561	22.729	21.917	22.128	21.287	21.540	20.670
16	26.769	25.981	26.111	25.289	25.466	24.610	24.833	23.944	24.212	23.292
17	29.793	28.973	29.108	28.251	28.435	27.542	27.774	26.844	27.125	26.160
18	33.059	32.213	32.353	31.467	31.657	30.732	30.973	30.009	30.300	29.297
19	36.586	35.722	35.865	34.958	35.153	34.204	34.452	33.461	33.761	32.728
20	40.396	39.522	39.667	38.748	38.946	37.984	38.235	37.228	37.533	36.482
21	44.510	43.638	43.782	42.864	43.062	42.097	42.349	41.338	41.644	40.587
22	48.954	48.095	48.237	47.332	47.527	46.574	46.823	45.823	46.126	45.078
23	53.753	52.922	53.060	52.182	52.372	51.447	51.689	50.716	51.011	49.990
24	58.936	58.150	58.281	57.449	57.629	56.750	56.980	56.054	56.336	55.362
25	64.534	63.812	63.932	63.166	63.332	62.522	62.735	61.880	62.140	61.239
26	70.579	69.944	70.049	69.374	69.520	68.805	68.992	68.235	68.466	67.666
27	77.108	76.584	76.672	76.114	76.235	75.642	75.798	75.170	75.361	74.697
28	84.160	83.776	83.840	83.431	83.520	83.084	83.199	82.736	82.877	82.387
29	91.775	91.565	91.600	91.375	91.424	91.184	91.247	90.992	91.070	90.799
30	100.000	100.000	100.000	100.000	100.000	100.000	100.000	100.000	100.000	100.000

Entry is percentage of final plan accumulated at selected time, including interest.

Balance Accumulated on a Sinking Fund

3 Year Funding

| | 9.25% | | 9.50% | | 9.75% | | 10.00% | | 10.25% | |
	Annual	Monthly	Annual	Monthly	Annual	Monthly	Annual	Monthly	Annual	Monthly
1	30.432	30.313	30.358	30.233	30.285	30.154	30.211	30.074	30.139	29.995
2	63.678	63.552	63.600	63.468	63.522	63.383	63.444	63.298	63.366	63.213
3	100.000	100.000	100.000	100.000	100.000	100.000	100.000	100.000	100.000	100.000

5 Year Funding

	Annual	Monthly	Annual	Monthly	Annual	Monthly	Annual	Monthly	Annual	Monthly
1	16.626	16.494	16.544	16.404	16.461	16.315	16.380	16.227	16.298	16.139
2	34.790	34.579	34.659	34.437	34.528	34.295	34.397	34.153	34.267	34.011
3	54.635	54.410	54.495	54.259	54.356	54.107	54.217	53.956	54.078	53.804
4	76.315	76.156	76.216	76.048	76.117	75.940	76.018	75.833	75.920	75.724
5	100.000	100.000	100.000	100.000	100.000	100.000	100.000	100.000	100.000	100.000

7 Year Funding

	Annual	Monthly	Annual	Monthly	Annual	Monthly	Annual	Monthly	Annual	Monthly
1	10.786	10.654	10.704	10.565	10.622	10.477	10.541	10.389	10.460	10.302
2	22.570	22.336	22.424	22.178	22.279	22.022	22.135	21.866	21.992	21.711
3	35.443	35.145	35.258	34.945	35.073	34.744	34.889	34.545	34.706	34.345
4	49.508	49.191	49.311	48.978	49.115	48.764	48.919	48.551	48.723	48.338
5	64.874	64.593	64.699	64.403	64.525	64.214	64.351	64.024	64.177	63.834
6	81.660	81.481	81.549	81.360	81.438	81.239	81.327	81.117	81.215	80.995
7	100.000	100.000	100.000	100.000	100.000	100.000	100.000	100.000	100.000	100.000

10 Year Funding

	Annual	Monthly	Annual	Monthly	Annual	Monthly	Annual	Monthly	Annual	Monthly
1	6.504	6.380	6.427	6.297	6.350	6.215	6.275	6.134	6.200	6.054
2	13.609	13.376	13.464	13.219	13.319	13.064	13.177	12.911	13.035	12.758
3	21.372	21.047	21.169	20.829	20.968	20.612	20.769	20.397	20.571	20.183
4	29.853	29.458	29.607	29.193	29.363	28.929	29.120	28.667	28.879	28.406
5	39.118	38.681	38.846	38.388	38.576	38.095	38.307	37.803	38.039	37.512
6	49.241	48.795	48.963	48.495	48.687	48.195	48.412	47.895	48.138	47.596
7	60.299	59.885	60.042	59.605	59.784	59.325	59.528	59.045	59.271	58.765
8	72.381	72.045	72.172	71.818	71.964	71.590	71.755	71.362	71.546	71.133
9	85.580	85.379	85.455	85.243	85.330	85.106	85.205	84.969	85.080	84.831
10	100.000	100.000	100.000	100.000	100.000	100.000	100.000	100.000	100.000	100.000

12 Year Funding

	Annual	Monthly	Annual	Monthly	Annual	Monthly	Annual	Monthly	Annual	Monthly
1	4.891	4.775	4.819	4.698	4.747	4.621	4.676	4.546	4.607	4.471
2	10.235	10.011	10.095	9.861	9.957	9.713	9.820	9.567	9.685	9.422
3	16.074	15.752	15.873	15.537	15.675	15.325	15.479	15.114	15.285	14.906
4	22.452	22.047	22.200	21.777	21.950	21.509	21.703	21.243	21.458	20.978
5	29.420	28.950	29.128	28.636	28.837	28.323	28.549	28.012	28.264	27.704
6	37.033	36.520	36.714	36.175	36.396	35.833	36.081	35.491	35.767	35.151
7	45.350	44.820	45.020	44.463	44.692	44.108	44.365	43.753	44.040	43.400
8	54.436	53.921	54.116	53.574	53.796	53.227	53.478	52.880	53.161	52.534
9	64.363	63.901	64.076	63.588	63.789	63.276	63.502	62.963	63.216	62.650
10	75.208	74.843	74.981	74.597	74.755	74.350	74.529	74.102	74.302	73.853
11	87.056	86.843	86.923	86.698	86.791	86.553	86.658	86.407	86.525	86.260
12	100.000	100.000	100.000	100.000	100.000	100.000	100.000	100.000	100.000	100.000

15 Year Funding

	Annual	Monthly	Annual	Monthly	Annual	Monthly	Annual	Monthly	Annual	Monthly
1	3.340	3.235	3.274	3.166	3.210	3.098	3.147	3.032	3.086	2.966
2	6.988	6.783	6.860	6.647	6.734	6.513	6.609	6.381	6.487	6.251
3	10.974	10.673	10.786	10.473	10.600	10.275	10.418	10.081	10.238	9.889
4	15.329	14.938	15.085	14.678	14.844	14.421	14.607	14.168	14.373	13.918
5	20.086	19.615	19.792	19.301	19.502	18.991	19.215	18.683	18.932	18.380
6	25.284	24.743	24.947	24.383	24.614	24.026	24.284	23.671	23.958	23.321
7	30.962	30.367	30.591	29.969	30.224	29.574	29.860	29.182	29.499	28.793
8	37.165	36.533	36.772	36.110	36.381	35.688	35.993	35.269	35.608	34.853
9	43.943	43.295	43.540	42.860	43.139	42.426	42.740	41.994	42.343	41.564
10	51.347	50.709	50.950	50.279	50.555	49.851	50.161	49.423	49.769	48.997
11	59.436	58.839	59.065	58.436	58.694	58.033	58.325	57.630	57.956	57.228
12	68.274	67.753	67.950	67.402	67.627	67.049	67.304	66.697	66.982	66.344
13	77.928	77.528	77.680	77.257	77.431	76.985	77.182	76.712	76.933	76.439
14	88.476	88.247	88.334	88.091	88.191	87.934	88.048	87.777	87.904	87.619
15	100.000	100.000	100.000	100.000	100.000	100.000	100.000	100.000	100.000	100.000

Entry is percentage of final plan accumulated at selected time, including interest.

Balance Accumulated on a Sinking Fund

25 Year Funding

	9.25% Annual	9.25% Monthly	9.50% Annual	9.50% Monthly	9.75% Annual	9.75% Monthly	10.00% Annual	10.00% Monthly	10.25% Annual	10.25% Monthly
1	1.138	1.071	1.096	1.028	1.056	0.987	1.017	0.947	0.979	0.908
2	2.380	2.246	2.296	2.159	2.214	2.075	2.135	1.993	2.059	1.915
3	3.738	3.534	3.610	3.401	3.486	3.273	3.366	3.149	3.249	3.029
4	5.221	4.946	5.049	4.767	4.881	4.594	4.719	4.426	4.561	4.263
5	6.842	6.495	6.625	6.269	6.413	6.049	6.208	5.836	6.008	5.629
6	8.612	8.193	8.350	7.919	8.094	7.653	7.845	7.394	7.603	7.143
7	10.547	10.055	10.239	9.734	9.939	9.421	9.647	9.116	9.362	8.819
8	12.660	12.097	12.308	11.728	11.964	11.368	11.628	11.017	11.301	10.675
9	14.968	14.336	14.573	13.921	14.186	13.515	13.808	13.118	13.438	12.730
10	17.491	16.791	17.053	16.331	16.625	15.880	16.205	15.439	15.795	15.007
11	20.246	19.483	19.769	18.980	19.301	18.486	18.843	18.002	18.393	17.528
12	23.256	22.435	22.743	21.892	22.239	21.358	21.744	20.834	21.257	20.320
13	26.545	25.671	26.000	25.093	25.463	24.523	24.935	23.963	24.416	23.412
14	30.138	29.221	29.566	28.612	29.001	28.011	28.445	27.419	27.897	26.836
15	34.063	33.112	33.470	32.480	32.885	31.855	32.306	31.238	31.736	30.628
16	38.352	37.380	37.746	36.732	37.146	36.090	36.554	35.456	35.968	34.828
17	43.037	42.059	42.428	41.405	41.824	40.758	41.226	40.115	40.634	39.479
18	48.156	47.190	47.554	46.543	46.958	45.901	46.366	45.263	45.778	44.630
19	53.747	52.816	53.168	52.191	52.592	51.569	52.019	50.950	51.450	50.334
20	59.857	58.985	59.315	58.399	58.775	57.814	58.238	57.232	57.703	56.651
21	66.531	65.750	66.046	65.223	65.561	64.697	65.078	64.172	64.597	63.647
22	73.823	73.168	73.416	72.725	73.009	72.282	72.603	71.838	72.197	71.394
23	81.789	81.302	81.486	80.971	81.183	80.640	80.880	80.308	80.576	79.975
24	90.492	90.220	90.323	90.036	90.154	89.850	89.985	89.664	89.815	89.477
25	100.000	100.000	100.000	100.000	100.000	100.000	100.000	100.000	100.000	100.000

30 Year Funding

	9.25% Annual	9.25% Monthly	9.50% Annual	9.50% Monthly	9.75% Annual	9.75% Monthly	10.00% Annual	10.00% Monthly	10.25% Annual	10.25% Monthly
1	0.700	0.649	0.668	0.617	0.637	0.586	0.608	0.556	0.580	0.528
2	1.465	1.361	1.400	1.294	1.337	1.231	1.277	1.170	1.219	1.112
3	2.301	2.142	2.201	2.040	2.104	1.942	2.012	1.848	1.924	1.759
4	3.214	2.997	3.078	2.859	2.947	2.726	2.821	2.598	2.701	2.475
5	4.211	3.936	4.038	3.759	3.872	3.589	3.711	3.426	3.557	3.269
6	5.301	4.965	5.090	4.749	4.887	4.541	4.691	4.340	4.502	4.148
7	6.491	6.093	6.241	5.837	6.000	5.589	5.767	5.351	5.543	5.121
8	7.792	7.331	7.502	7.033	7.223	6.745	6.952	6.467	6.691	6.199
9	9.213	8.687	8.883	8.347	8.564	8.018	8.255	7.700	7.956	7.392
10	10.765	10.175	10.395	9.792	10.037	9.421	9.689	9.062	9.352	8.714
11	12.461	11.807	12.051	11.381	11.652	10.968	11.266	10.567	10.890	10.178
12	14.314	13.595	13.864	13.127	13.426	12.672	13.000	12.229	12.586	11.799
13	16.338	15.557	15.849	15.046	15.372	14.549	14.908	14.066	14.456	13.595
14	18.549	17.708	18.022	17.156	17.508	16.619	17.007	16.094	16.517	15.583
15	20.965	20.066	20.403	19.476	19.853	18.899	19.315	18.335	18.790	17.785
16	23.605	22.652	23.009	22.025	22.426	21.412	21.855	20.811	21.296	20.224
17	26.488	25.488	25.863	24.828	25.250	24.181	24.648	23.546	24.059	22.925
18	29.638	28.597	28.988	27.909	28.349	27.232	27.721	26.568	27.104	25.915
19	33.080	32.006	32.410	31.295	31.750	30.595	31.101	29.906	30.462	29.228
20	36.840	35.745	36.157	35.018	35.483	34.300	34.819	33.593	34.164	32.896
21	40.948	39.844	40.260	39.110	39.580	38.384	38.909	37.667	38.246	36.958
22	45.436	44.339	44.753	43.608	44.076	42.884	43.408	42.167	42.746	41.457
23	50.339	49.268	49.672	48.553	49.011	47.842	48.356	47.138	47.707	46.440
24	55.695	54.673	55.059	53.988	54.427	53.307	53.800	52.630	53.177	51.957
25	61.547	60.600	60.958	59.963	60.371	59.329	59.788	58.697	59.207	58.068
26	67.940	67.098	67.417	66.531	66.895	65.964	66.374	65.399	65.856	64.835
27	74.925	74.224	74.489	73.750	74.054	73.277	73.620	72.803	73.186	72.329
28	82.556	82.037	82.234	81.687	81.912	81.335	81.590	80.982	81.267	80.629
29	90.892	90.605	90.714	90.410	90.535	90.215	90.356	90.018	90.177	89.821
30	100.000	100.000	100.000	100.000	100.000	100.000	100.000	100.000	100.000	100.000

Entry is percentage of final plan accumulated at selected time, including interest.

Balance Accumulated on a Sinking Fund

3 Year Funding

	10.50% Annual	Monthly	10.75% Annual	Monthly	11.00% Annual	Monthly	11.25% Annual	Monthly	11.50% Annual	Monthly
1	30.066	29.915	29.993	29.836	29.921	29.757	29.849	29.678	29.778	29.599
2	63.289	63.128	63.211	63.043	63.134	62.958	63.057	62.872	62.980	62.787
3	100.000	100.000	100.000	100.000	100.000	100.000	100.000	100.000	100.000	100.000

5 Year Funding

	Annual	Monthly	Annual	Monthly	Annual	Monthly	Annual	Monthly	Annual	Monthly
1	16.218	16.051	16.137	15.963	16.057	15.875	15.977	15.788	15.898	15.702
2	34.138	33.870	34.009	33.729	33.880	33.588	33.752	33.448	33.625	33.307
3	53.940	53.653	53.802	53.502	53.664	53.350	53.527	53.199	53.390	53.048
4	75.821	75.616	75.723	75.508	75.624	75.399	75.526	75.291	75.428	75.182
5	100.000	100.000	100.000	100.000	100.000	100.000	100.000	100.000	100.000	100.000

7 Year Funding

	Annual	Monthly	Annual	Monthly	Annual	Monthly	Annual	Monthly	Annual	Monthly
1	10.380	10.215	10.300	10.129	10.222	10.043	10.143	9.958	10.066	9.873
2	21.850	21.556	21.708	21.402	21.567	21.249	21.428	21.096	21.289	20.944
3	34.524	34.147	34.342	33.949	34.161	33.751	33.981	33.554	33.802	33.357
4	48.529	48.125	48.334	47.912	48.141	47.700	47.948	47.487	47.755	47.275
5	64.004	63.644	63.831	63.453	63.658	63.263	63.485	63.072	63.312	62.881
6	81.104	80.872	80.993	80.750	80.882	80.627	80.770	80.503	80.659	80.380
7	100.000	100.000	100.000	100.000	100.000	100.000	100.000	100.000	100.000	100.000

10 Year Funding

	Annual	Monthly	Annual	Monthly	Annual	Monthly	Annual	Monthly	Annual	Monthly
1	6.126	5.974	6.053	5.896	5.980	5.818	5.909	5.740	5.838	5.664
2	12.895	12.607	12.756	12.457	12.618	12.308	12.482	12.161	12.347	12.014
3	20.374	19.971	20.180	19.760	19.986	19.550	19.795	19.342	19.604	19.135
4	28.639	28.146	28.401	27.887	28.165	27.630	27.930	27.374	27.697	27.119
5	37.772	37.222	37.507	36.933	37.243	36.645	36.981	36.358	36.719	36.071
6	47.864	47.298	47.592	47.000	47.320	46.703	47.049	46.406	46.780	46.109
7	59.016	58.485	58.760	58.205	58.505	57.924	58.251	57.644	57.997	57.364
8	71.338	70.904	71.129	70.675	70.921	70.445	70.713	70.215	70.505	69.984
9	84.954	84.692	84.828	84.553	84.703	84.414	84.577	84.274	84.450	84.134
10	100.000	100.000	100.000	100.000	100.000	100.000	100.000	100.000	100.000	100.000

12 Year Funding

	Annual	Monthly	Annual	Monthly	Annual	Monthly	Annual	Monthly	Annual	Monthly
1	4.538	4.397	4.470	4.325	4.403	4.253	4.337	4.182	4.271	4.112
2	9.552	9.279	9.420	9.138	9.290	8.998	9.161	8.859	9.034	8.723
3	15.092	14.699	14.902	14.495	14.714	14.292	14.528	14.091	14.344	13.893
4	21.215	20.716	20.974	20.456	20.736	20.199	20.499	19.943	20.265	19.689
5	27.980	27.397	27.699	27.092	27.419	26.789	27.142	26.488	26.867	26.189
6	35.456	34.813	35.146	34.477	34.838	34.142	34.532	33.808	34.229	33.476
7	43.716	43.047	43.394	42.696	43.073	42.345	42.754	41.996	42.436	41.648
8	52.844	52.188	52.528	51.843	52.214	51.498	51.900	51.154	51.588	50.810
9	62.930	62.337	62.645	62.024	62.360	61.710	62.076	61.397	61.792	61.083
10	74.076	73.604	73.849	73.354	73.622	73.104	73.396	72.853	73.169	72.602
11	86.391	86.113	86.258	85.965	86.124	85.817	85.990	85.668	85.855	85.518
12	100.000	100.000	100.000	100.000	100.000	100.000	100.000	100.000	100.000	100.000

15 Year Funding

	Annual	Monthly	Annual	Monthly	Annual	Monthly	Annual	Monthly	Annual	Monthly
1	3.025	2.902	2.965	2.839	2.907	2.776	2.849	2.715	2.792	2.655
2	6.367	6.123	6.249	5.998	6.133	5.874	6.018	5.752	5.906	5.633
3	10.061	9.700	9.886	9.514	9.714	9.330	9.544	9.149	9.378	8.971
4	14.142	13.671	13.914	13.427	13.689	13.186	13.467	12.949	13.248	12.714
5	18.651	18.079	18.375	17.782	18.101	17.488	17.831	17.198	17.565	16.911
6	23.635	22.973	23.315	22.629	22.999	22.289	22.686	21.951	22.377	21.617
7	29.141	28.407	28.787	28.024	28.435	27.644	28.087	27.267	27.743	26.894
8	35.226	34.439	34.846	34.028	34.470	33.619	34.096	33.214	33.725	32.810
9	41.949	41.136	41.557	40.710	41.168	40.286	40.781	39.864	40.396	39.444
10	49.379	48.572	48.990	48.147	48.603	47.724	48.218	47.303	47.834	46.883
11	57.588	56.826	57.221	56.425	56.856	56.023	56.491	55.623	56.128	55.223
12	66.660	65.990	66.338	65.637	66.016	65.283	65.695	64.929	65.375	64.575
13	76.684	76.164	76.434	75.889	76.185	75.614	75.935	75.337	75.685	75.060
14	87.760	87.460	87.616	87.300	87.472	87.140	87.327	86.979	87.182	86.817
15	100.000	100.000	100.000	100.000	100.000	100.000	100.000	100.000	100.000	100.000

Entry is percentage of final plan accumulated at selected time, including interest.

Balance Accumulated on a Sinking Fund

25 Year Funding

	10.50% Annual	Monthly	10.75% Annual	Monthly	11.00% Annual	Monthly	11.25% Annual	Monthly	11.50% Annual	Monthly
1	0.943	0.871	0.908	0.835	0.874	0.801	0.841	0.768	0.810	0.736
2	1.985	1.839	1.913	1.765	1.844	1.695	1.777	1.626	1.713	1.560
3	3.136	2.913	3.027	2.800	2.921	2.692	2.819	2.587	2.720	2.485
4	4.408	4.105	4.260	3.952	4.116	3.804	3.977	3.661	3.842	3.522
5	5.814	5.429	5.626	5.234	5.443	5.045	5.266	4.862	5.094	4.685
6	7.368	6.898	7.139	6.661	6.916	6.430	6.700	6.206	6.489	5.989
7	9.084	8.530	8.814	8.248	8.551	7.975	8.295	7.709	8.045	7.450
8	10.981	10.341	10.669	10.016	10.365	9.699	10.069	9.390	9.780	9.089
9	13.077	12.352	12.724	11.983	12.380	11.622	12.043	11.270	11.715	10.927
10	15.393	14.585	15.000	14.172	14.615	13.768	14.239	13.373	13.872	12.988
11	17.952	17.063	17.520	16.608	17.097	16.162	16.683	15.725	16.277	15.298
12	20.780	19.815	20.312	19.319	19.852	18.833	19.401	18.356	18.959	17.889
13	23.905	22.870	23.403	22.337	22.910	21.813	22.425	21.299	21.949	20.794
14	27.358	26.261	26.827	25.696	26.304	25.138	25.789	24.590	25.283	24.051
15	31.173	30.027	30.618	29.434	30.071	28.848	29.532	28.271	29.000	27.703
16	35.389	34.207	34.818	33.594	34.253	32.988	33.695	32.389	33.145	31.797
17	40.048	38.848	39.468	38.224	38.895	37.606	38.327	36.994	37.766	36.389
18	45.196	44.001	44.619	43.377	44.047	42.759	43.481	42.145	42.919	41.537
19	50.885	49.721	50.324	49.113	49.766	48.507	49.213	47.906	48.665	47.309
20	57.171	56.072	56.641	55.496	56.115	54.922	55.591	54.350	55.071	53.781
21	64.117	63.123	63.638	62.600	63.161	62.078	62.687	61.558	62.214	61.038
22	71.792	70.950	71.387	70.506	70.983	70.063	70.580	69.619	70.178	69.175
23	80.273	79.641	79.969	79.306	79.665	78.971	79.362	78.635	79.058	78.299
24	89.644	89.289	89.474	89.100	89.303	88.910	89.131	88.720	88.960	88.529
25	100.000	100.000	100.000	100.000	100.000	100.000	100.000	100.000	100.000	100.000

30 Year Funding

	10.50% Annual	Monthly	10.75% Annual	Monthly	11.00% Annual	Monthly	11.25% Annual	Monthly	11.50% Annual	Monthly
1	0.553	0.501	0.527	0.475	0.502	0.450	0.479	0.427	0.456	0.404
2	1.164	1.056	1.111	1.003	1.060	0.952	1.012	0.904	0.965	0.858
3	1.839	1.673	1.757	1.591	1.679	1.513	1.604	1.438	1.533	1.366
4	2.585	2.358	2.473	2.246	2.366	2.138	2.264	2.035	2.165	1.936
5	3.409	3.118	3.266	2.974	3.129	2.835	2.997	2.703	2.871	2.575
6	4.320	3.962	4.145	3.785	3.976	3.614	3.814	3.449	3.657	3.292
7	5.326	4.900	5.117	4.687	4.916	4.482	4.722	4.285	4.534	4.096
8	6.438	5.940	6.194	5.691	5.959	5.451	5.732	5.219	5.512	4.997
9	7.667	7.095	7.387	6.808	7.117	6.532	6.855	6.264	6.603	6.007
10	9.025	8.378	8.709	8.052	8.402	7.737	8.105	7.433	7.818	7.140
11	10.525	9.801	10.172	9.436	9.829	9.083	9.496	8.741	9.174	8.410
12	12.184	11.382	11.792	10.977	11.412	10.584	11.043	10.203	10.685	9.834
13	14.016	13.137	13.587	12.692	13.170	12.259	12.765	11.839	12.370	11.431
14	16.040	15.085	15.575	14.600	15.121	14.128	14.680	13.668	14.249	13.221
15	18.277	17.248	17.776	16.724	17.287	16.213	16.810	15.714	16.344	15.229
16	20.749	19.649	20.214	19.088	19.691	18.539	19.180	18.003	18.681	17.480
17	23.481	22.315	22.914	21.719	22.360	21.134	21.817	20.563	21.285	20.003
18	26.499	25.275	25.905	24.647	25.322	24.030	24.750	23.426	24.189	22.833
19	29.834	28.561	29.217	27.905	28.610	27.261	28.013	26.628	27.428	26.007
20	33.520	32.209	32.885	31.532	32.259	30.866	31.644	30.210	31.038	29.564
21	37.592	36.259	36.947	35.569	36.310	34.888	35.683	34.216	35.064	33.554
22	42.092	40.755	41.446	40.061	40.807	39.375	40.176	38.697	39.553	38.027
23	47.065	45.747	46.428	45.061	45.798	44.382	45.175	43.709	44.558	43.042
24	52.559	51.289	51.946	50.626	51.338	49.967	50.736	49.314	50.138	48.666
25	58.631	57.442	58.058	56.819	57.488	56.200	56.922	55.584	56.361	54.972
26	65.340	64.273	64.826	63.712	64.314	63.153	63.805	62.596	63.298	62.042
27	72.753	71.856	72.322	71.384	71.891	70.911	71.462	70.440	71.034	69.969
28	80.945	80.276	80.623	79.922	80.302	79.567	79.980	79.213	79.660	78.858
29	89.997	89.623	89.818	89.424	89.637	89.225	89.457	89.025	89.277	88.825
30	100.000	100.000	100.000	100.000	100.000	100.000	100.000	100.000	100.000	100.000

Entry is percentage of final plan accumulated at selected time, including interest.

Balance Accumulated on a Sinking Fund

3 Year Funding

| | 11.75% | | 12.00% | | 12.25% | | 12.50% | | 15.00% | |
	Annual	Monthly	Annual	Monthly	Annual	Monthly	Annual	Monthly	Annual	Monthly
1	29.706	29.520	29.635	29.442	29.564	29.363	29.493	29.284	28.798	28.505
2	62.903	62.702	62.826	62.617	62.749	62.532	62.673	62.447	61.915	61.593
3	100.000	100.000	100.000	100.000	100.000	100.000	100.000	100.000	100.000	100.000

5 Year Funding

	Annual	Monthly	Annual	Monthly	Annual	Monthly	Annual	Monthly	Annual	Monthly
1	15.819	15.615	15.741	15.529	15.663	15.443	15.585	15.358	14.832	14.519
2	33.498	33.167	33.371	33.028	33.245	32.888	33.119	32.749	31.888	31.373
3	53.253	52.896	53.116	52.745	52.980	52.594	52.844	52.443	51.503	50.935
4	75.329	75.073	75.231	74.964	75.133	74.854	75.035	74.745	74.060	73.642
5	100.000	100.000	100.000	100.000	100.000	100.000	100.000	100.000	100.000	100.000

7 Year Funding

	Annual	Monthly	Annual	Monthly	Annual	Monthly	Annual	Monthly	Annual	Monthly
1	9.988	9.789	9.912	9.706	9.836	9.622	9.760	9.540	9.036	8.741
2	21.150	20.793	21.013	20.642	20.876	20.492	20.741	20.343	19.427	18.887
3	33.624	33.161	33.446	32.966	33.270	32.771	33.094	32.576	31.378	30.664
4	47.563	47.064	47.372	46.852	47.181	46.641	46.991	46.430	45.120	44.334
5	63.140	62.691	62.968	62.500	62.796	62.309	62.625	62.117	60.924	60.202
6	80.547	80.256	80.436	80.132	80.324	80.007	80.213	79.883	79.099	78.621
7	100.000	100.000	100.000	100.000	100.000	100.000	100.000	100.000	100.000	100.000

10 Year Funding

	Annual	Monthly	Annual	Monthly	Annual	Monthly	Annual	Monthly	Annual	Monthly
1	5.768	5.588	5.698	5.513	5.630	5.439	5.562	5.366	4.925	4.673
2	12.213	11.869	12.081	11.726	11.949	11.583	11.820	11.442	10.589	10.097
3	19.416	18.930	19.229	18.726	19.043	18.523	18.859	18.323	17.103	16.393
4	27.465	26.866	27.235	26.614	27.006	26.364	26.779	26.114	24.593	23.701
5	36.460	35.787	36.201	35.503	35.944	35.220	35.688	34.938	33.208	32.184
6	46.511	45.814	46.244	45.518	45.977	45.224	45.712	44.930	43.114	42.030
7	57.744	57.084	57.491	56.804	57.239	56.525	56.988	56.245	54.506	53.459
8	70.297	69.753	70.089	69.522	69.881	69.290	69.673	69.058	67.607	66.726
9	84.324	83.993	84.198	83.852	84.071	83.711	83.945	83.569	82.674	82.125
10	100.000	100.000	100.000	100.000	100.000	100.000	100.000	100.000	100.000	100.000

12 Year Funding

	Annual	Monthly	Annual	Monthly	Annual	Monthly	Annual	Monthly	Annual	Monthly
1	4.207	4.043	4.144	3.975	4.081	3.908	4.019	3.841	3.448	3.226
2	8.909	8.588	8.785	8.454	8.662	8.322	8.541	8.192	7.413	6.971
3	14.162	13.696	13.982	13.501	13.804	13.308	13.628	13.118	11.973	11.318
4	20.034	19.438	19.804	19.188	19.577	18.941	19.351	18.696	17.218	16.364
5	26.595	25.892	26.324	25.597	26.056	25.304	25.790	25.013	23.248	22.221
6	33.927	33.146	33.627	32.818	33.329	32.492	33.033	32.167	30.184	29.020
7	42.120	41.301	41.806	40.955	41.493	40.611	41.181	40.268	38.159	36.911
8	51.276	50.467	50.966	50.124	50.657	49.782	50.349	49.441	47.331	46.071
9	61.508	60.770	61.226	60.456	60.943	60.143	60.662	59.829	57.879	56.704
10	72.943	72.351	72.716	72.099	72.490	71.846	72.264	71.593	70.009	69.046
11	85.721	85.368	85.586	85.217	85.451	85.066	85.316	84.915	83.958	83.371
12	100.000	100.000	100.000	100.000	100.000	100.000	100.000	100.000	100.000	100.000

15 Year Funding

	Annual	Monthly	Annual	Monthly	Annual	Monthly	Annual	Monthly	Annual	Monthly
1	2.737	2.596	2.682	2.539	2.629	2.482	2.576	2.426	2.102	1.924
2	5.795	5.515	5.687	5.399	5.580	5.285	5.475	5.174	4.519	4.157
3	9.213	8.795	9.052	8.623	8.892	8.452	8.736	8.285	7.298	6.749
4	13.033	12.483	12.820	12.255	12.611	12.030	12.404	11.808	10.495	9.757
5	17.301	16.628	17.041	16.348	16.784	16.071	16.531	15.798	14.170	13.250
6	22.071	21.287	21.768	20.960	21.469	20.636	21.173	20.316	18.398	17.303
7	27.401	26.524	27.063	26.156	26.728	25.793	26.396	25.432	23.259	22.009
8	33.358	32.410	32.993	32.012	32.631	31.618	32.272	31.226	28.850	27.470
9	40.014	39.027	39.635	38.611	39.257	38.198	38.883	37.787	35.279	33.810
10	47.453	46.464	47.073	46.046	46.695	45.631	46.320	45.216	42.672	41.169
11	55.765	54.824	55.404	54.425	55.044	54.027	54.686	53.630	51.175	49.711
12	65.055	64.220	64.735	63.866	64.416	63.512	64.098	63.157	60.953	59.626
13	75.436	74.783	75.186	74.504	74.936	74.226	74.687	73.946	72.198	71.135
14	87.036	86.655	86.891	86.492	86.745	86.328	86.599	86.164	85.129	84.494
15	100.000	100.000	100.000	100.000	100.000	100.000	100.000	100.000	100.000	100.000

Entry is percentage of final plan accumulated at selected time, including interest.

Balance Accumulated on a Sinking Fund

25 Year Funding

	11.75%		12.00%		12.25%		12.50%		15.00%	
	Annual	Monthly	Annual	Monthly	Annual	Monthly	Annual	Monthly	Annual	Monthly
1	0.779	0.705	0.750	0.675	0.722	0.646	0.694	0.619	0.470	0.396
2	1.650	1.497	1.590	1.436	1.532	1.377	1.475	1.320	1.010	0.857
3	2.624	2.387	2.531	2.293	2.441	2.201	2.354	2.113	1.632	1.391
4	3.711	3.388	3.584	3.259	3.462	3.133	3.343	3.012	2.347	2.011
5	4.927	4.513	4.765	4.347	4.607	4.186	4.455	4.030	3.169	2.731
6	6.285	5.778	6.086	5.573	5.894	5.375	5.706	5.183	4.114	3.566
7	7.803	7.199	7.567	6.955	7.337	6.718	7.114	6.488	5.201	4.536
8	9.499	8.797	9.225	8.512	8.958	8.235	8.698	7.966	6.451	5.662
9	11.394	10.593	11.082	10.267	10.777	9.949	10.479	9.639	7.888	6.968
10	13.513	12.611	13.161	12.244	12.818	11.885	12.483	11.535	9.542	8.485
11	15.880	14.880	15.491	14.471	15.110	14.072	14.738	13.681	11.443	10.246
12	18.525	17.431	18.100	16.982	17.683	16.542	17.275	16.112	13.629	12.289
13	21.481	20.297	21.022	19.811	20.571	19.333	20.128	18.864	16.143	14.661
14	24.784	23.520	24.294	22.998	23.812	22.485	23.339	21.981	19.035	17.415
15	28.476	27.142	27.960	26.590	27.451	26.046	26.950	25.510	22.360	20.610
16	32.601	31.213	32.065	30.637	31.536	30.068	31.014	29.507	26.184	24.320
17	37.211	35.790	36.663	35.198	36.120	34.612	35.585	34.033	30.581	28.626
18	42.363	40.934	41.812	40.336	41.267	39.745	40.727	39.159	35.639	33.625
19	48.120	46.716	47.580	46.127	47.044	45.543	46.512	44.963	41.454	39.426
20	54.553	53.215	54.039	52.652	53.528	52.092	53.021	51.535	48.142	46.161
21	61.743	60.521	61.274	60.005	60.807	59.491	60.343	58.978	55.834	53.978
22	69.777	68.733	69.377	68.290	68.978	67.848	68.580	67.407	64.679	63.052
23	78.755	77.963	78.452	77.626	78.149	77.289	77.847	76.952	74.850	73.584
24	88.788	88.338	88.616	88.146	88.444	87.953	88.272	87.760	86.548	85.809
25	100.000	100.000	100.000	100.000	100.000	100.000	100.000	100.000	100.000	100.000

30 Year Funding

	Annual	Monthly	Annual	Monthly	Annual	Monthly	Annual	Monthly	Annual	Monthly
1	0.435	0.383	0.414	0.363	0.395	0.344	0.376	0.325	0.230	0.186
2	0.921	0.814	0.878	0.772	0.838	0.732	0.799	0.694	0.495	0.401
3	1.464	1.298	1.398	1.233	1.335	1.170	1.275	1.111	0.799	0.652
4	2.071	1.842	1.980	1.752	1.894	1.666	1.810	1.583	1.149	0.942
5	2.749	2.453	2.632	2.337	2.520	2.225	2.413	2.118	1.551	1.279
6	3.507	3.141	3.363	2.996	3.224	2.857	3.090	2.724	2.014	1.671
7	4.354	3.914	4.181	3.739	4.013	3.571	3.852	3.410	2.546	2.125
8	5.301	4.782	5.097	4.576	4.900	4.378	4.710	4.187	3.157	2.653
9	6.358	5.758	6.123	5.519	5.895	5.289	5.675	5.067	3.861	3.265
10	7.540	6.856	7.272	6.582	7.012	6.318	6.760	6.063	4.670	3.975
11	8.861	8.089	8.559	7.780	8.265	7.480	7.981	7.191	5.601	4.800
12	10.337	9.476	10.000	9.129	9.673	8.793	9.355	8.469	6.671	5.757
13	11.987	11.034	11.614	10.650	11.252	10.277	10.900	9.915	7.902	6.869
14	13.830	12.786	13.422	12.363	13.025	11.953	12.639	11.553	9.317	8.159
15	15.890	14.755	15.447	14.294	15.016	13.845	14.595	13.409	10.944	9.656
16	18.192	16.969	17.715	16.470	17.250	15.984	16.795	15.509	12.816	11.394
17	20.765	19.456	20.256	18.922	19.758	18.399	19.271	17.888	14.969	13.411
18	23.640	22.253	23.101	21.684	22.573	21.128	22.055	20.583	17.444	15.753
19	26.852	25.396	26.287	24.797	25.733	24.210	25.188	23.633	20.290	18.471
20	30.442	28.930	29.856	28.305	29.280	27.691	28.713	27.088	23.564	21.626
21	34.454	32.901	33.853	32.258	33.261	31.624	32.678	31.000	27.329	25.288
22	38.937	37.365	38.330	36.712	37.730	36.067	37.139	35.430	31.658	29.539
23	43.947	42.383	43.344	41.731	42.747	41.085	42.157	40.447	36.637	34.474
24	49.546	48.023	48.959	47.386	48.378	46.754	47.803	46.129	42.362	40.201
25	55.803	54.363	55.249	53.759	54.699	53.158	54.154	52.562	48.947	46.850
26	62.794	61.489	62.293	60.940	61.795	60.392	61.299	59.847	56.519	54.567
27	70.608	69.500	70.183	69.031	69.759	68.564	69.338	68.097	65.226	63.524
28	79.339	78.503	79.019	78.149	78.700	77.794	78.381	77.440	75.240	73.922
29	89.096	88.624	88.916	88.423	88.735	88.221	88.555	88.019	86.757	85.991
30	100.000	100.000	100.000	100.000	100.000	100.000	100.000	100.000	100.000	100.000

Entry is percentage of final plan accumulated at selected time, including interest.

Number of Monthly Deposits to Build a Sinking Fund

Monthly Deposit	Annual Total	Interest Rate on Deposit										
		5.50%	5.75%	6.00%	6.25%	6.50%	6.75%	7.00%	7.25%	7.50%	7.75%	8.00%
10.00%	120.00%	9.8	9.7	9.7	9.7	9.7	9.7	9.7	9.7	9.7	9.7	9.7
9.00	108.00	10.8	10.8	10.8	10.8	10.8	10.7	10.7	10.7	10.7	10.7	10.7
8.00	96.00	12.1	12.1	12.1	12.1	12.1	12.0	12.0	12.0	12.0	12.0	12.0
7.00	84.00	13.8	13.8	13.8	13.7	13.7	13.7	13.7	13.7	13.6	13.6	13.6
6.00	72.00	16.0	16.0	16.0	15.9	15.9	15.9	15.9	15.8	15.8	15.8	15.8
5.00	60.00	19.1	19.1	19.0	19.0	18.9	18.9	18.9	18.8	18.8	18.8	18.7
4.1667	50.00	22.7	22.7	22.6	22.6	22.5	22.5	22.4	22.4	22.3	22.3	22.2
4.00	48.00	23.6	23.6	23.5	23.4	23.4	23.3	23.3	23.2	23.2	23.1	23.1
3.3333	40.00	28.1	28.0	27.9	27.8	27.7	27.7	27.6	27.5	27.4	27.3	27.3
3.00	36.00	31.0	30.9	30.8	30.7	30.6	30.5	30.4	30.3	30.2	30.1	30.0
2.50	30.00	36.7	36.5	36.4	36.3	36.1	36.0	35.9	35.7	35.6	35.5	35.4
2.0833	25.00	43.3	43.1	42.9	42.8	42.6	42.4	42.2	42.1	41.9	41.7	41.5
2.00	24.00	44.9	44.7	44.5	44.3	44.2	44.0	43.8	43.6	43.4	43.2	43.0
1.75	21.00	50.7	50.4	50.2	49.9	49.7	49.4	49.2	49.0	48.8	48.5	48.3
1.6667	20.00	52.9	52.6	52.4	52.1	51.8	51.6	51.3	51.1	50.8	50.6	50.4
1.50	18.00	58.1	57.8	57.4	57.1	56.8	56.5	56.2	55.9	55.6	55.3	55.0
1.25	15.00	68.0	67.6	67.2	66.8	66.3	65.9	65.5	65.1	64.7	64.4	64.0
1.00	12.00	82.2	81.6	81.0	80.4	79.8	79.2	78.6	78.1	77.5	77.0	76.5
0.9917	11.90	82.8	82.1	81.5	80.9	80.3	79.7	79.2	78.6	78.1	77.5	77.0
0.9833	11.80	83.4	82.7	82.1	81.5	80.9	80.3	79.7	79.1	78.6	78.0	77.5
0.9750	11.70	83.9	83.3	82.7	82.0	81.4	80.8	80.2	79.7	79.1	78.6	78.0
0.9667	11.60	84.5	83.9	83.2	82.6	82.0	81.4	80.8	80.2	79.6	79.1	78.5
0.9583	11.50	85.2	84.5	83.8	83.2	82.6	82.0	81.4	80.8	80.2	79.6	79.1
0.95	11.40	85.8	85.1	84.4	83.8	83.2	82.5	81.9	81.3	80.7	80.2	79.6
0.9417	11.30	86.4	85.7	85.0	84.4	83.8	83.1	82.5	81.9	81.3	80.7	80.2
0.9333	11.20	87.0	86.3	85.7	85.0	84.4	83.7	83.1	82.5	81.9	81.3	80.7
0.9250	11.10	87.7	87.0	86.3	85.6	85.0	84.3	83.7	83.1	82.4	81.9	81.3
0.9167	11.00	88.3	87.6	86.9	86.2	85.6	84.9	84.3	83.7	83.0	82.4	81.8
0.9083	10.90	89.0	88.3	87.6	86.9	86.2	85.5	84.9	84.3	83.6	83.0	82.4
0.90	10.80	89.7	88.9	88.2	87.5	86.8	86.2	85.5	84.9	84.2	83.6	83.0
0.8917	10.70	90.4	89.6	88.9	88.2	87.5	86.8	86.1	85.5	84.8	84.2	83.6
0.8833	10.60	91.1	90.3	89.6	88.9	88.1	87.5	86.8	86.1	85.5	84.8	84.2
0.8750	10.50	91.8	91.0	90.3	89.5	88.8	88.1	87.4	86.8	86.1	85.4	84.8
0.8667	10.40	92.5	91.7	91.0	90.2	89.5	88.8	88.1	87.4	86.7	86.1	85.4
0.8583	10.30	93.2	92.4	91.7	90.9	90.2	89.5	88.8	88.1	87.4	86.7	86.1
0.85	10.20	94.0	93.2	92.4	91.6	90.9	90.1	89.4	88.7	88.0	87.4	86.7
0.8417	10.10	94.7	93.9	93.1	92.3	91.6	90.8	90.1	89.4	88.7	88.0	87.4
0.8333	10.00	95.5	94.7	93.9	93.1	92.3	91.6	90.8	90.1	89.4	88.7	88.0
0.8250	9.90	96.3	95.4	94.6	93.8	93.0	92.3	91.5	90.8	90.1	89.4	88.7
0.8167	9.80	97.1	96.2	95.4	94.6	93.8	93.0	92.3	91.5	90.8	90.1	89.4
0.8083	9.70	97.9	97.0	96.2	95.3	94.5	93.8	93.0	92.2	91.5	90.8	90.1
0.80	9.60	98.7	97.8	97.0	96.1	95.3	94.5	93.7	93.0	92.2	91.5	90.8
0.7917	9.50	99.5	98.6	97.8	96.9	96.1	95.3	94.5	93.7	93.0	92.2	91.5
0.7833	9.40	100.4	99.5	98.6	97.7	96.9	96.1	95.3	94.5	93.7	93.0	92.2
0.7750	9.30	101.2	100.3	99.4	98.6	97.7	96.9	96.0	95.3	94.5	93.7	93.0
0.7667	9.20	102.1	101.2	100.3	99.4	98.5	97.7	96.8	96.0	95.2	94.5	93.7
0.7583	9.10	103.0	102.1	101.1	100.2	99.4	98.5	97.7	96.8	96.0	95.2	94.5
0.75	9.00	103.9	103.0	102.0	101.1	100.2	99.3	98.5	97.6	96.8	96.0	95.2
0.7417	8.90	104.8	103.9	102.9	102.0	101.1	100.2	99.3	98.5	97.6	96.8	96.0
0.7333	8.80	105.8	104.8	103.8	102.9	102.0	101.1	100.2	99.3	98.5	97.7	96.8
0.7250	8.70	106.7	105.7	104.8	103.8	102.9	101.9	101.0	100.2	99.3	98.5	97.7
0.7167	8.60	107.7	106.7	105.7	104.7	103.8	102.8	101.9	101.0	100.2	99.3	98.5
0.7083	8.50	108.7	107.7	106.7	105.7	104.7	103.8	102.8	101.9	101.1	100.2	99.3
0.70	8.40	109.7	108.7	107.7	106.6	105.7	104.7	103.8	102.8	101.9	101.1	100.2
0.6917	8.30	110.8	109.7	108.7	107.6	106.6	105.7	104.7	103.8	102.8	102.0	101.1
0.6833	8.20	111.8	110.7	109.7	108.6	107.6	106.6	105.6	104.7	103.8	102.9	102.0
0.6750	8.10	112.9	111.8	110.7	109.7	108.6	107.6	106.6	105.7	104.7	103.8	102.9
0.6667	8.00	114.0	112.9	111.8	110.7	109.6	108.6	107.6	106.6	105.7	104.7	103.8
0.6583	7.90	115.1	114.0	112.9	111.8	110.7	109.6	108.6	107.6	106.6	105.7	104.8
0.65	7.80	116.3	115.1	114.0	112.8	111.8	110.7	109.6	108.6	107.6	106.7	105.7
0.6417	7.70	117.5	116.3	115.1	113.9	112.8	111.8	110.7	109.7	108.7	107.7	106.7
0.6333	7.60	118.6	117.4	116.2	115.1	113.9	112.8	111.8	110.7	109.7	108.7	107.7
0.6250	7.50	119.9	118.6	117.4	116.2	115.1	114.0	112.9	111.8	110.8	109.7	108.7

Entry is time in months to accumulate desired fund with selected deposit.

Number of Monthly Deposits to Build a Sinking Fund

Monthly Deposit	Annual Total	8.50%	8.75%	9.00%	Interest Rate on Deposit 9.25%	9.50%	9.75%	10.00%	10.25%	10.50%	11.00%	12.00%
10.00%	120.00%	9.6	9.6	9.6	9.6	9.6	9.6	9.6	9.6	9.5	9.5	9.5
9.00	108.00	10.7	10.6	10.6	10.6	10.6	10.6	10.6	10.6	10.6	10.5	10.5
8.00	96.00	11.9	11.9	11.9	11.9	11.9	11.9	11.8	11.8	11.8	11.8	11.7
7.00	84.00	13.6	13.5	13.5	13.5	13.5	13.5	13.4	13.4	13.4	13.4	13.3
6.00	72.00	15.7	15.7	15.7	15.6	15.6	15.6	15.5	15.5	15.5	15.4	15.3
5.00	60.00	18.6	18.6	18.6	18.5	18.5	18.5	18.4	18.4	18.4	18.3	18.2
4.1667	50.00	22.1	22.0	22.0	21.9	21.9	21.9	21.8	21.8	21.7	21.6	21.4
4.00	48.00	22.9	22.9	22.8	22.8	22.7	22.7	22.6	22.6	22.5	22.4	22.2
3.3333	40.00	27.1	27.1	27.0	26.9	26.8	26.8	26.7	26.6	26.5	26.4	26.1
3.00	36.00	29.8	29.8	29.7	29.6	29.5	29.4	29.3	29.2	29.2	29.0	28.7
2.50	30.00	35.1	35.0	34.9	34.8	34.6	34.5	34.4	34.3	34.2	34.0	33.5
2.0833	25.00	41.2	41.0	40.9	40.7	40.6	40.4	40.3	40.1	40.0	39.7	39.1
2.00	24.00	42.7	42.5	42.3	42.2	42.0	41.8	41.7	41.5	41.4	41.0	40.4
1.75	21.00	47.9	47.6	47.4	47.2	47.0	46.8	46.6	46.4	46.2	45.8	45.1
1.6667	20.00	49.9	49.6	49.4	49.2	49.0	48.7	48.5	48.3	48.1	47.7	46.9
1.50	18.00	54.5	54.2	53.9	53.7	53.4	53.1	52.9	52.6	52.4	51.9	50.9
1.25	15.00	63.2	62.9	62.5	62.2	61.8	61.5	61.2	60.8	60.5	59.9	58.6
1.00	12.00	75.5	75.0	74.5	74.0	73.5	73.0	72.6	72.1	71.7	70.8	69.2
0.9917	11.90	75.9	75.4	74.9	74.5	74.0	73.5	73.0	72.6	72.1	71.3	69.6
0.9833	11.80	76.4	75.9	75.4	74.9	74.5	74.0	73.5	73.0	72.6	71.7	70.0
0.9750	11.70	76.9	76.4	75.9	75.4	74.9	74.5	74.0	73.5	73.0	72.2	70.4
0.9667	11.60	77.5	76.9	76.4	75.9	75.4	74.9	74.5	74.0	73.5	72.6	70.9
0.9583	11.50	78.0	77.4	76.9	76.4	75.9	75.4	74.9	74.5	74.0	73.1	71.3
0.95	11.40	78.5	78.0	77.4	76.9	76.4	75.9	75.4	74.9	74.5	73.5	71.8
0.9417	11.30	79.0	78.5	78.0	77.4	76.9	76.4	75.9	75.4	74.9	74.0	72.2
0.9333	11.20	79.6	79.0	78.5	78.0	77.4	76.9	76.4	75.9	75.4	74.5	72.7
0.9250	11.10	80.1	79.6	79.0	78.5	78.0	77.4	76.9	76.4	75.9	75.0	73.1
0.9167	11.00	80.7	80.1	79.6	79.0	78.5	78.0	77.4	76.9	76.4	75.5	73.6
0.9083	10.90	81.2	80.7	80.1	79.6	79.0	78.5	78.0	77.5	76.9	76.0	74.1
0.90	10.80	81.8	81.2	80.7	80.1	79.6	79.0	78.5	78.0	77.5	76.5	74.6
0.8917	10.70	82.4	81.8	81.2	80.7	80.1	79.6	79.0	78.5	78.0	77.0	75.1
0.8833	10.60	83.0	82.4	81.8	81.2	80.7	80.1	79.6	79.0	78.5	77.5	75.6
0.8750	10.50	83.6	83.0	82.4	81.8	81.2	80.7	80.1	79.6	79.1	78.0	76.1
0.8667	10.40	84.2	83.6	83.0	82.4	81.8	81.3	80.7	80.1	79.6	78.6	76.6
0.8583	10.30	84.8	84.2	83.6	83.0	82.4	81.8	81.3	80.7	80.2	79.1	77.1
0.85	10.20	85.4	84.8	84.2	83.6	83.0	82.4	81.8	81.3	80.7	79.7	77.6
0.8417	10.10	86.1	85.4	84.8	84.2	83.6	83.0	82.4	81.9	81.3	80.2	78.2
0.8333	10.00	86.7	86.1	85.4	84.8	84.2	83.6	83.0	82.5	81.9	80.8	78.7
0.8250	9.90	87.4	86.7	86.1	85.4	84.8	84.2	83.6	83.0	82.5	81.4	79.2
0.8167	9.80	88.0	87.4	86.7	86.1	85.5	84.8	84.2	83.7	83.1	81.9	79.8
0.8083	9.70	88.7	88.0	87.4	86.7	86.1	85.5	84.9	84.3	83.7	82.5	80.4
0.80	9.60	89.4	88.7	88.0	87.4	86.7	86.1	85.5	84.9	84.3	83.1	80.9
0.7917	9.50	90.1	89.4	88.7	88.1	87.4	86.8	86.1	85.5	84.9	83.8	81.5
0.7833	9.40	90.8	90.1	89.4	88.7	88.1	87.4	86.8	86.2	85.6	84.4	82.1
0.7750	9.30	91.5	90.8	90.1	89.4	88.8	88.1	87.5	86.8	86.2	85.0	82.7
0.7667	9.20	92.2	91.5	90.8	90.1	89.4	88.8	88.1	87.5	86.9	85.6	83.3
0.7583	9.10	93.0	92.2	91.5	90.8	90.1	89.5	88.8	88.2	87.5	86.3	84.0
0.75	9.00	93.7	93.0	92.3	91.6	90.9	90.2	89.5	88.9	88.2	87.0	84.6
0.7417	8.90	94.5	93.7	93.0	92.3	91.6	90.9	90.2	89.6	88.9	87.6	85.2
0.7333	8.80	95.3	94.5	93.8	93.0	92.3	91.6	90.9	90.3	89.6	88.3	85.9
0.7250	8.70	96.1	95.3	94.5	93.8	93.1	92.4	91.7	91.0	90.3	89.0	86.5
0.7167	8.60	96.9	96.1	95.3	94.6	93.8	93.1	92.4	91.7	91.0	89.7	87.2
0.7083	8.50	97.7	96.9	96.1	95.4	94.6	93.9	93.2	92.5	91.8	90.4	87.9
0.70	8.40	98.5	97.7	96.9	96.2	95.4	94.7	93.9	93.2	92.5	91.2	88.6
0.6917	8.30	99.4	98.6	97.8	97.0	96.2	95.5	94.7	94.0	93.3	91.9	89.3
0.6833	8.20	100.3	99.4	98.6	97.8	97.0	96.3	95.5	94.8	94.1	92.7	90.0
0.6750	8.10	101.1	100.3	99.5	98.7	97.9	97.1	96.3	95.6	94.9	93.4	90.7
0.6667	8.00	102.0	101.2	100.4	99.5	98.7	97.9	97.2	96.4	95.7	94.2	91.5
0.6583	7.90	103.0	102.1	101.2	100.4	99.6	98.8	98.0	97.2	96.5	95.0	92.2
0.65	7.80	103.9	103.0	102.1	101.3	100.5	99.7	98.9	98.1	97.3	95.8	93.0
0.6417	7.70	104.9	104.0	103.1	102.2	101.4	100.5	99.7	98.9	98.2	96.7	93.8
0.6333	7.60	105.8	104.9	104.0	103.1	102.3	101.4	100.6	99.8	99.0	97.5	94.6
0.6250	7.50	106.8	105.9	105.0	104.1	103.2	102.4	101.5	100.7	99.9	98.4	95.4

Entry is time in months to accumulate desired fund with selected deposit.

Number of Deposits to Complete Partial Sinking Fund

Starting from Partial Fund of 10%

Monthly Deposit	Annual Total	5.50%	5.75%	6.00%	6.25%	6.50%	6.75%	7.00%	7.25%	7.50%	7.75%	8.00%	8.25%
4.17%	50.00%	20.4	20.4	20.3	20.3	20.2	20.2	20.1	20.1	20.0	20.0	19.9	19.9
3.00	36.00	27.8	27.7	27.6	27.5	27.4	27.3	27.2	27.2	27.1	27.0	26.9	26.8
2.50	30.00	32.8	32.7	32.6	32.5	32.3	32.2	32.1	32.0	31.9	31.7	31.6	31.5
2.0833	25.00	38.7	38.6	38.4	38.2	38.0	37.9	37.7	37.5	37.4	37.2	37.0	36.9
1.50	18.00	51.7	51.4	51.1	50.8	50.5	50.2	49.9	49.6	49.4	49.1	48.8	48.5
1.25	15.00	60.4	60.0	59.6	59.2	58.8	58.4	58.0	57.6	57.2	56.9	56.5	56.2
1.00	12.00	72.7	72.1	71.5	70.9	70.4	69.8	69.3	68.7	68.2	67.7	67.2	66.7
0.9167	11.00	78.0	77.3	76.6	76.0	75.3	74.7	74.1	73.5	72.9	72.3	71.7	71.1
0.8333	10.00	84.1	83.3	82.6	81.8	81.0	80.3	79.6	78.9	78.2	77.5	76.9	76.2
0.7917	9.50	87.6	86.7	85.9	85.1	84.2	83.5	82.7	81.9	81.2	80.5	79.8	79.1
0.75	9.00	91.3	90.4	89.5	88.6	87.7	86.9	86.0	85.2	84.4	83.7	82.9	82.2
0.7083	8.50	95.4	94.4	93.4	92.4	91.5	90.6	89.7	88.8	87.9	87.1	86.3	85.5
0.6667	8.00	99.9	98.8	97.7	96.7	95.6	94.6	93.7	92.7	91.8	90.9	90.0	89.1
0.5833	7.00	110.3	108.9	107.6	106.4	105.1	103.9	102.8	101.7	100.5	99.5	98.4	97.4
0.5417	6.50	116.3	114.8	113.4	112.0	110.7	109.4	108.1	106.8	105.6	104.4	103.3	102.2
0.50	6.00	123.1	121.5	119.9	118.3	116.8	115.4	114.0	112.6	111.2	110.0	108.7	107.4

Starting from Partial Fund of 20%

Monthly Deposit	Annual Total	5.50%	5.75%	6.00%	6.25%	6.50%	6.75%	7.00%	7.25%	7.50%	7.75%	8.00%	8.25%
4.17%	50.00%	18.1	18.0	18.0	17.9	17.9	17.8	17.8	17.7	17.7	17.6	17.6	17.6
3.00	36.00	24.5	24.4	24.3	24.2	24.2	24.1	24.0	23.9	23.8	23.7	23.7	23.6
2.50	30.00	28.9	28.8	28.7	28.6	28.5	28.3	28.2	28.1	28.0	27.9	27.8	27.6
2.0833	25.00	34.1	33.9	33.7	33.6	33.4	33.2	33.1	32.9	32.8	32.6	32.4	32.3
1.50	18.00	45.3	45.0	44.7	44.4	44.2	43.9	43.6	43.3	43.1	42.8	42.5	42.3
1.25	15.00	52.8	52.4	52.0	51.6	51.3	50.9	50.5	50.1	49.8	49.4	49.1	48.7
1.00	12.00	63.3	62.8	62.2	61.6	61.1	60.6	60.0	59.5	59.0	58.5	58.0	57.6
0.9167	11.00	67.8	67.2	66.5	65.9	65.3	64.7	64.1	63.5	62.9	62.4	61.8	61.3
0.8333	10.00	73.0	72.3	71.5	70.8	70.1	69.4	68.7	68.0	67.4	66.7	66.1	65.5
0.7917	9.50	75.9	75.1	74.3	73.5	72.8	72.0	71.3	70.6	69.9	69.2	68.5	67.9
0.75	9.00	79.1	78.2	77.3	76.5	75.7	74.9	74.1	73.3	72.5	71.8	71.1	70.4
0.7083	8.50	82.5	81.5	80.6	79.7	78.8	77.9	77.1	76.2	75.4	74.6	73.9	73.1
0.6667	8.00	86.3	85.2	84.2	83.2	82.2	81.3	80.3	79.5	78.6	77.7	76.9	76.1
0.5833	7.00	94.9	93.6	92.4	91.2	90.0	88.9	87.8	86.8	85.7	84.7	83.7	82.8
0.5417	6.50	99.9	98.5	97.1	95.8	94.6	93.3	92.1	91.0	89.8	88.7	87.6	86.6
0.50	6.00	105.5	103.9	102.4	101.0	99.6	98.2	96.9	95.6	94.3	93.1	91.9	90.8

Starting from Partial Fund of 25%

Monthly Deposit	Annual Total	5.50%	5.75%	6.00%	6.25%	6.50%	6.75%	7.00%	7.25%	7.50%	7.75%	8.00%	8.25%
4.17%	50.00%	16.9	16.8	16.8	16.7	16.7	16.7	16.6	16.6	16.5	16.5	16.4	16.4
3.00	36.00	22.9	22.8	22.7	22.6	22.6	22.5	22.4	22.3	22.2	22.1	22.1	22.0
2.50	30.00	27.0	26.9	26.8	26.7	26.5	26.4	26.3	26.2	26.1	26.0	25.9	25.8
2.0833	25.00	31.8	31.6	31.4	31.3	31.1	31.0	30.8	30.7	30.5	30.4	30.2	30.1
1.50	18.00	42.2	41.9	41.6	41.3	41.1	40.8	40.5	40.3	40.0	39.7	39.5	39.2
1.25	15.00	49.1	48.7	48.4	48.0	47.6	47.2	46.9	46.5	46.2	45.8	45.5	45.2
1.00	12.00	58.8	58.2	57.7	57.1	56.6	56.1	55.6	55.1	54.6	54.1	53.7	53.2
0.9167	11.00	62.9	62.3	61.7	61.0	60.4	59.9	59.3	58.7	58.2	57.6	57.1	56.6
0.8333	10.00	67.7	66.9	66.2	65.5	64.8	64.2	63.5	62.9	62.2	61.6	61.0	60.4
0.7917	9.50	70.3	69.5	68.8	68.0	67.3	66.6	65.8	65.2	64.5	63.8	63.2	62.6
0.75	9.00	73.2	72.3	71.5	70.7	69.9	69.1	68.4	67.6	66.9	66.2	65.5	64.8
0.7083	8.50	76.3	75.4	74.5	73.6	72.8	71.9	71.1	70.3	69.5	68.8	68.0	67.3
0.6667	8.00	79.7	78.7	77.7	76.8	75.9	75.0	74.1	73.2	72.4	71.5	70.7	70.0
0.5833	7.00	87.6	86.4	85.2	84.0	82.9	81.9	80.8	79.8	78.8	77.8	76.9	76.0
0.5417	6.50	92.1	90.8	89.5	88.2	87.0	85.8	84.7	83.6	82.5	81.4	80.4	79.4
0.50	6.00	97.1	95.7	94.2	92.8	91.5	90.2	88.9	87.7	86.5	85.4	84.2	83.1

Starting from Partial Fund of 33.3%

Monthly Deposit	Annual Total	5.50%	5.75%	6.00%	6.25%	6.50%	6.75%	7.00%	7.25%	7.50%	7.75%	8.00%	8.25%
4.17%	50.00%	14.9	14.9	14.9	14.8	14.8	14.7	14.7	14.6	14.6	14.6	14.5	14.5
3.00	36.00	20.2	20.1	20.1	20.0	19.9	19.8	19.8	19.7	19.6	19.5	19.4	19.4
2.50	30.00	23.8	23.7	23.6	23.5	23.4	23.3	23.2	23.1	23.0	22.9	22.8	22.7
2.0833	25.00	28.0	27.9	27.7	27.5	27.4	27.2	27.1	27.0	26.8	26.7	26.5	26.4
1.50	18.00	37.1	36.8	36.6	36.3	36.0	35.8	35.5	35.3	35.0	34.8	34.6	34.3
1.25	15.00	43.1	42.7	42.4	42.0	41.7	41.3	41.0	40.7	40.3	40.0	39.7	39.4
1.00	12.00	51.4	50.9	50.4	49.9	49.4	48.9	48.5	48.0	47.6	47.1	46.7	46.3
0.9167	11.00	55.0	54.4	53.8	53.2	52.7	52.1	51.6	51.1	50.6	50.1	49.6	49.1
0.8333	10.00	59.0	58.3	57.7	57.0	56.4	55.8	55.2	54.6	54.0	53.4	52.9	52.3
0.7917	9.50	61.3	60.6	59.8	59.2	58.5	57.8	57.2	56.5	55.9	55.3	54.7	54.1
0.75	9.00	63.7	63.0	62.2	61.4	60.7	60.0	59.3	58.6	57.9	57.3	56.7	56.0
0.7083	8.50	66.4	65.6	64.7	63.9	63.1	62.3	61.6	60.9	60.1	59.4	58.8	58.1
0.6667	8.00	69.3	68.4	67.5	66.6	65.7	64.9	64.1	63.3	62.5	61.8	61.0	60.3
0.5833	7.00	75.9	74.8	73.7	72.7	71.7	70.7	69.7	68.8	67.9	67.0	66.1	65.3
0.5417	6.50	79.7	78.5	77.3	76.2	75.1	74.0	72.9	71.9	70.9	70.0	69.0	68.1
0.50	6.00	84.0	82.6	81.3	80.0	78.8	77.6	76.5	75.3	74.3	73.2	72.2	71.2

Entry is number of monthly deposits to take fund from starting balance to 100%.

Number of Deposits to Complete Partial Sinking Fund

Starting from Partial Fund of 40%

Monthly Deposit	Annual Total	5.50%	5.75%	6.00%	6.25%	6.50%	6.75%	7.00%	7.25%	7.50%	7.75%	8.00%	8.25%
						Interest Rate on Deposit							
4.17%	50.00%	13.4	13.4	13.3	13.3	13.2	13.2	13.2	13.1	13.1	13.0	13.0	13.0
3.00	36.00	18.1	18.0	18.0	17.9	17.8	17.7	17.7	17.6	17.5	17.5	17.4	17.3
2.50	30.00	21.3	21.2	21.1	21.0	20.9	20.8	20.7	20.6	20.5	20.4	20.3	20.2
2.0833	25.00	25.0	24.9	24.8	24.6	24.5	24.3	24.2	24.1	23.9	23.8	23.7	23.5
1.50	18.00	33.1	32.8	32.6	32.3	32.1	31.9	31.6	31.4	31.2	30.9	30.7	30.5
1.25	15.00	38.4	38.0	37.7	37.4	37.1	36.7	36.4	36.1	35.8	35.5	35.2	34.9
1.00	12.00	45.7	45.2	44.7	44.3	43.8	43.4	42.9	42.5	42.1	41.7	41.3	40.9
0.9167	11.00	48.8	48.2	47.7	47.2	46.7	46.2	45.7	45.2	44.7	44.3	43.8	43.4
0.8333	10.00	52.4	51.7	51.1	50.5	49.9	49.3	48.8	48.2	47.7	47.2	46.7	46.2
0.7917	9.50	54.3	53.7	53.0	52.3	51.7	51.1	50.5	49.9	49.4	48.8	48.3	47.7
0.75	9.00	56.5	55.7	55.0	54.3	53.7	53.0	52.3	51.7	51.1	50.5	49.9	49.4
0.7083	8.50	58.8	58.0	57.2	56.5	55.7	55.0	54.3	53.7	53.0	52.4	51.7	51.1
0.6667	8.00	61.3	60.4	59.6	58.8	58.0	57.2	56.5	55.8	55.0	54.4	53.7	53.0
0.5833	7.00	67.0	66.0	65.0	64.0	63.1	62.2	61.3	60.5	59.6	58.8	58.0	57.3
0.5417	6.50	70.3	69.2	68.1	67.0	66.0	65.0	64.1	63.1	62.2	61.4	60.5	59.7
0.50	6.00	74.0	72.7	71.5	70.4	69.2	68.1	67.1	66.1	65.1	64.1	63.2	62.3

Starting from Partial Fund of 50%

Monthly Deposit	Annual Total	5.50%	5.75%	6.00%	6.25%	6.50%	6.75%	7.00%	7.25%	7.50%	7.75%	8.00%	8.25%
4.17%	50.00%	11.1	11.1	11.0	11.0	11.0	10.9	10.9	10.9	10.8	10.8	10.8	10.7
3.00	36.00	15.0	14.9	14.9	14.8	14.7	14.7	14.6	14.5	14.5	14.4	14.3	14.3
2.50	30.00	17.6	17.5	17.5	17.4	17.4	17.3	17.2	17.1	17.0	16.9	16.8	16.7
2.0833	25.00	20.7	20.5	20.4	20.3	20.2	20.0	19.9	19.8	19.7	19.6	19.4	19.3
1.50	18.00	27.2	27.0	26.8	26.6	26.3	26.1	25.9	25.7	25.5	25.3	25.1	25.0
1.25	15.00	31.5	31.2	30.9	30.6	30.3	30.1	29.8	29.5	29.3	29.0	28.8	28.5
1.00	12.00	37.4	37.0	36.6	36.2	35.8	35.4	35.0	34.6	34.3	33.9	33.6	33.2
0.9167	11.00	39.9	39.4	38.9	38.5	38.0	37.6	37.2	36.8	36.4	36.0	35.6	35.2
0.8333	10.00	42.7	42.2	41.6	41.1	40.6	40.1	39.6	39.2	38.7	38.3	37.8	37.4
0.7917	9.50	44.3	43.7	43.1	42.6	42.0	41.5	41.0	40.5	40.0	39.5	39.1	38.6
0.75	9.00	46.0	45.4	44.7	44.1	43.6	43.0	42.4	41.9	41.4	40.9	40.4	39.9
0.7083	8.50	47.8	47.1	46.5	45.8	45.2	44.6	44.0	43.4	42.9	42.3	41.8	41.3
0.6667	8.00	49.8	49.1	48.4	47.7	47.0	46.3	45.7	45.1	44.5	43.9	43.3	42.7
0.5833	7.00	54.3	53.5	52.6	51.8	51.0	50.2	49.5	48.7	48.0	47.3	46.7	46.0
0.5417	6.50	56.9	56.0	55.0	54.1	53.3	52.4	51.6	50.8	50.0	49.3	48.6	47.9
0.50	6.00	59.8	58.7	57.7	56.7	55.7	54.8	53.9	53.1	52.2	51.4	50.6	49.9

Starting from Partial Fund of 60%

Monthly Deposit	Annual Total	5.50%	5.75%	6.00%	6.25%	6.50%	6.75%	7.00%	7.25%	7.50%	7.75%	8.00%	8.25%
4.17%	50.00%	8.8	8.8	8.8	8.8	8.7	8.7	8.7	8.6	8.6	8.6	8.5	8.5
3.00	36.00	11.9	11.9	11.8	11.7	11.7	11.6	11.6	11.5	11.5	11.4	11.4	11.3
2.50	30.00	14.0	13.9	13.8	13.8	13.7	13.6	13.5	13.5	13.4	13.3	13.2	13.2
2.0833	25.00	16.4	16.3	16.2	16.1	15.9	15.8	15.7	15.6	15.5	15.4	15.4	15.3
1.50	18.00	21.5	21.3	21.1	20.9	20.8	20.6	20.4	20.3	20.1	19.9	19.8	19.6
1.25	15.00	24.8	24.6	24.3	24.1	23.9	23.6	23.4	23.2	23.0	22.8	22.5	22.3
1.00	12.00	29.4	29.0	28.7	28.4	28.0	27.7	27.4	27.1	26.8	26.5	26.2	26.0
0.9167	11.00	31.3	30.9	30.5	30.1	29.8	29.4	29.1	28.7	28.4	28.1	27.8	27.4
0.8333	10.00	33.5	33.0	32.6	32.2	31.7	31.3	30.9	30.6	30.2	29.8	29.5	29.1
0.7917	9.50	34.7	34.2	33.7	33.3	32.8	32.4	32.0	31.6	31.2	30.8	30.4	30.0
0.75	9.00	36.0	35.5	35.0	34.5	34.0	33.5	33.1	32.6	32.2	31.8	31.4	31.0
0.7083	8.50	37.4	36.8	36.3	35.8	35.2	34.7	34.3	33.8	33.3	32.9	32.4	32.0
0.6667	8.00	38.9	38.3	37.7	37.1	36.6	36.0	35.5	35.0	34.5	34.0	33.6	33.1
0.5833	7.00	42.3	41.6	40.9	40.3	39.6	39.0	38.4	37.8	37.2	36.7	36.1	35.6
0.5417	6.50	44.3	43.5	42.7	42.0	41.3	40.6	40.0	39.3	38.7	38.1	37.5	37.0
0.50	6.00	46.4	45.6	44.7	43.9	43.2	42.4	41.7	41.0	40.3	39.7	39.1	38.4

Starting from Partial Fund of 66.7%

Monthly Deposit	Annual Total	5.50%	5.75%	6.00%	6.25%	6.50%	6.75%	7.00%	7.25%	7.50%	7.75%	8.00%	8.25%
4.17%	50.00%	7.3	7.3	7.3	7.3	7.2	7.2	7.2	7.2	7.1	7.1	7.1	7.1
3.00	36.00	9.9	9.8	9.8	9.7	9.7	9.6	9.6	9.5	9.5	9.5	9.4	9.4
2.50	30.00	11.6	11.5	11.5	11.4	11.3	11.3	11.2	11.1	11.1	11.0	11.0	10.9
2.0833	25.00	13.6	13.5	13.4	13.3	13.2	13.1	13.0	12.9	12.8	12.8	12.7	12.6
1.50	18.00	17.8	17.6	17.4	17.3	17.1	17.0	16.8	16.7	16.6	16.4	16.3	16.2
1.25	15.00	20.5	20.3	20.1	19.9	19.7	19.5	19.3	19.1	18.9	18.7	18.5	18.4
1.00	12.00	24.2	23.9	23.6	23.3	23.1	22.8	22.5	22.3	22.0	21.8	21.5	21.3
0.9167	11.00	25.8	25.4	25.1	24.8	24.5	24.2	23.9	23.6	23.3	23.0	22.8	22.5
0.8333	10.00	27.5	27.1	26.8	26.4	26.1	25.7	25.4	25.1	24.7	24.4	24.1	23.8
0.7917	9.50	28.5	28.1	27.7	27.3	26.9	26.6	26.2	25.9	25.5	25.2	24.9	24.6
0.75	9.00	29.6	29.1	28.7	28.3	27.9	27.5	27.1	26.7	26.4	26.0	25.7	25.3
0.7083	8.50	30.7	30.2	29.8	29.3	28.9	28.5	28.1	27.7	27.3	26.9	26.5	26.2
0.6667	8.00	31.9	31.4	30.9	30.4	30.0	29.5	29.1	28.6	28.2	27.8	27.4	27.1
0.5833	7.00	34.7	34.1	33.5	32.9	32.4	31.9	31.3	30.9	30.4	29.9	29.5	29.0
0.5417	6.50	36.3	35.6	35.0	34.3	33.8	33.2	32.6	32.1	31.6	31.1	30.6	30.1
0.50	6.00	38.0	37.3	36.6	35.9	35.2	34.6	34.0	33.4	32.9	32.3	31.8	31.3

Entry is number of monthly deposits to take fund from starting balance to 100%.

Number of Deposits to Complete Partial Sinking Fund

Starting from Partial Fund of 10%

Monthly Deposit	Annual Total	Interest Rate on Deposit											
		8.50%	8.75%	9.00%	9.25%	9.50%	9.75%	10.00%	10.25%	10.50%	11.00%	11.50%	12.00%
4.17%	50.00%	19.9	19.8	19.8	19.7	19.7	19.6	19.6	19.5	19.5	19.4	19.3	19.2
3.00	36.00	26.7	26.6	26.6	26.5	26.4	26.3	26.2	26.2	26.1	25.9	25.8	25.6
2.50	30.00	31.4	31.3	31.2	31.0	30.9	30.8	30.7	30.6	30.5	30.3	30.1	29.9
2.0833	25.00	36.7	36.6	36.4	36.3	36.1	36.0	35.8	35.7	35.5	35.2	35.0	34.7
1.50	18.00	48.3	48.0	47.7	47.5	47.2	47.0	46.7	46.5	46.2	45.8	45.3	44.9
1.25	15.00	55.8	55.4	55.1	54.8	54.4	54.1	53.8	53.5	53.1	52.5	51.9	51.3
1.00	12.00	66.2	65.7	65.2	64.7	64.3	63.8	63.4	63.0	62.5	61.7	60.9	60.1
0.9167	11.00	70.6	70.0	69.5	69.0	68.4	67.9	67.4	66.9	66.5	65.5	64.6	63.7
0.8333	10.00	75.6	75.0	74.4	73.8	73.2	72.6	72.0	71.5	70.9	69.9	68.8	67.9
0.7917	9.50	78.4	77.7	77.1	76.4	75.8	75.2	74.6	74.0	73.4	72.3	71.2	70.1
0.75	9.00	81.4	80.7	80.0	79.3	78.7	78.0	77.3	76.7	76.1	74.9	73.7	72.6
0.7083	8.50	84.7	83.9	83.2	82.4	81.7	81.0	80.3	79.6	79.0	77.7	76.4	75.2
0.6667	8.00	88.3	87.4	86.6	85.8	85.0	84.3	83.5	82.8	82.1	80.7	79.3	78.0
0.5833	7.00	96.4	95.4	94.4	93.5	92.6	91.7	90.8	90.0	89.1	87.5	85.9	84.5
0.5417	6.50	101.1	100.0	99.0	97.9	96.9	96.0	95.0	94.1	93.2	91.4	89.7	88.1
0.50	6.00	106.2	105.1	103.9	102.8	101.7	100.7	99.6	98.6	97.6	95.7	93.8	92.1

Starting from Partial Fund of 20%

Monthly Deposit	Annual Total	8.50%	8.75%	9.00%	9.25%	9.50%	9.75%	10.00%	10.25%	10.50%	11.00%	11.50%	12.00%
4.17%	50.00%	17.5	17.5	17.4	17.4	17.3	17.3	17.2	17.2	17.2	17.1	17.0	16.9
3.00	36.00	23.5	23.4	23.3	23.3	23.2	23.1	23.0	22.9	22.9	22.7	22.6	22.4
2.50	30.00	27.5	27.4	27.3	27.2	27.1	27.0	26.9	26.8	26.7	26.5	26.3	26.1
2.0833	25.00	32.1	32.0	31.8	31.7	31.6	31.4	31.3	31.1	31.0	30.7	30.5	30.2
1.50	18.00	42.0	41.8	41.5	41.3	41.0	40.8	40.5	40.3	40.1	39.6	39.2	38.8
1.25	15.00	48.4	48.1	47.7	47.4	47.1	46.8	46.5	46.2	45.9	45.3	44.7	44.2
1.00	12.00	57.1	56.6	56.2	55.7	55.3	54.9	54.5	54.1	53.6	52.9	52.1	51.3
0.9167	11.00	60.8	60.2	59.7	59.2	58.7	58.3	57.8	57.3	56.9	56.0	55.1	54.3
0.8333	10.00	64.9	64.3	63.7	63.2	62.6	62.1	61.6	61.0	60.5	59.5	58.6	57.6
0.7917	9.50	67.2	66.6	66.0	65.4	64.8	64.2	63.6	63.1	62.5	61.5	60.4	59.4
0.75	9.00	69.7	69.0	68.4	67.7	67.1	66.5	65.9	65.3	64.7	63.5	62.4	61.4
0.7083	8.50	72.4	71.6	70.9	70.2	69.6	68.9	68.3	67.6	67.0	65.8	64.6	63.5
0.6667	8.00	75.3	74.5	73.7	73.0	72.2	71.5	70.8	70.1	69.5	68.2	66.9	65.7
0.5833	7.00	81.8	80.9	80.0	79.1	78.3	77.5	76.6	75.8	75.1	73.6	72.1	70.7
0.5417	6.50	85.6	84.6	83.6	82.6	81.7	80.8	79.9	79.1	78.2	76.6	75.0	73.5
0.50	6.00	89.7	88.6	87.5	86.5	85.5	84.5	83.5	82.6	81.7	79.9	78.2	76.6

Starting from Partial Fund of 25%

Monthly Deposit	Annual Total	8.50%	8.75%	9.00%	9.25%	9.50%	9.75%	10.00%	10.25%	10.50%	11.00%	11.50%	12.00%
4.17%	50.00%	16.3	16.3	16.3	16.2	16.2	16.1	16.1	16.0	16.0	15.9	15.8	15.8
3.00	36.00	21.9	21.8	21.8	21.7	21.6	21.5	21.4	21.4	21.3	21.2	21.0	20.9
2.50	30.00	25.6	25.5	25.4	25.3	25.2	25.1	25.0	24.9	24.8	24.6	24.4	24.2
2.0833	25.00	29.9	29.8	29.6	29.5	29.3	29.2	29.1	28.9	28.8	28.5	28.3	28.0
1.50	18.00	39.0	38.7	38.5	38.3	38.0	37.8	37.6	37.3	37.1	36.7	36.3	35.8
1.25	15.00	44.8	44.5	44.2	43.9	43.6	43.3	43.0	42.7	42.4	41.8	41.3	40.7
1.00	12.00	52.8	52.3	51.9	51.5	51.1	50.6	50.2	49.8	49.4	48.7	47.9	47.2
0.9167	11.00	56.1	55.6	55.1	54.6	54.2	53.7	53.2	52.8	52.4	51.5	50.7	49.9
0.8333	10.00	59.9	59.3	58.7	58.2	57.7	57.1	56.6	56.1	55.6	54.7	53.8	52.9
0.7917	9.50	61.9	61.3	60.7	60.2	59.6	59.0	58.5	58.0	57.4	56.4	55.4	54.5
0.75	9.00	64.2	63.5	62.9	62.3	61.7	61.1	60.5	59.9	59.4	58.3	57.2	56.2
0.7083	8.50	66.6	65.9	65.2	64.6	63.9	63.3	62.6	62.0	61.4	60.3	59.2	58.1
0.6667	8.00	69.2	68.4	67.7	67.0	66.3	65.6	64.9	64.3	63.7	62.4	61.2	60.1
0.5833	7.00	75.1	74.2	73.3	72.5	71.7	70.9	70.1	69.4	68.6	67.2	65.8	64.5
0.5417	6.50	78.4	77.5	76.5	75.6	74.7	73.9	73.0	72.2	71.4	69.9	68.4	67.0
0.50	6.00	82.1	81.0	80.0	79.0	78.1	77.1	76.2	75.3	74.5	72.8	71.2	69.7

Starting from Partial Fund of 33.3%

Monthly Deposit	Annual Total	8.50%	8.75%	9.00%	9.25%	9.50%	9.75%	10.00%	10.25%	10.50%	11.00%	11.50%	12.00%
4.17%	50.00%	14.4	14.4	14.4	14.3	14.3	14.2	14.2	14.2	14.1	14.0	14.0	13.9
3.00	36.00	19.3	19.2	19.2	19.1	19.0	18.9	18.9	18.8	18.7	18.6	18.5	18.3
2.50	30.00	22.6	22.5	22.4	22.3	22.2	22.1	22.0	21.9	21.8	21.6	21.4	21.2
2.0833	25.00	26.3	26.1	26.0	25.9	25.7	25.6	25.5	25.3	25.2	25.0	24.7	24.5
1.50	18.00	34.1	33.9	33.6	33.4	33.2	33.0	32.8	32.6	32.4	31.9	31.6	31.2
1.25	15.00	39.1	38.8	38.5	38.2	37.9	37.6	37.4	37.1	36.8	36.3	35.8	35.3
1.00	12.00	45.8	45.4	45.0	44.6	44.3	43.9	43.5	43.1	42.8	42.1	41.4	40.7
0.9167	11.00	48.6	48.2	47.7	47.3	46.9	46.4	46.0	45.6	45.2	44.4	43.7	43.0
0.8333	10.00	51.8	51.3	50.8	50.3	49.8	49.3	48.9	48.4	48.0	47.1	46.2	45.4
0.7917	9.50	53.6	53.0	52.5	51.9	51.4	50.9	50.4	49.9	49.4	48.5	47.6	46.8
0.75	9.00	55.4	54.8	54.3	53.7	53.1	52.6	52.1	51.6	51.0	50.1	49.1	48.2
0.7083	8.50	57.4	56.8	56.2	55.6	55.0	54.4	53.8	53.3	52.7	51.7	50.7	49.7
0.6667	8.00	59.6	58.9	58.3	57.6	57.0	56.4	55.7	55.2	54.6	53.4	52.4	51.3
0.5833	7.00	64.5	63.7	62.9	62.1	61.4	60.7	60.0	59.3	58.6	57.3	56.1	54.9
0.5417	6.50	67.2	66.4	65.5	64.7	63.9	63.1	62.4	61.6	60.9	59.5	58.2	56.9
0.50	6.00	70.2	69.3	68.4	67.5	66.6	65.8	64.9	64.1	63.4	61.9	60.4	59.1

Entry is number of monthly deposits to take fund from starting balance to 100%.

Number of Deposits to Complete Partial Sinking Fund

Starting from Partial Fund of 40%

Monthly Deposit	Annual Total	Interest Rate on Deposit											
		8.50%	8.75%	9.00%	9.25%	9.50%	9.75%	10.00%	10.25%	10.50%	11.00%	11.50%	12.00%
4.17%	50.00%	12.9	12.9	12.8	12.8	12.8	12.7	12.7	12.7	12.6	12.5	12.5	12.4
3.00	36.00	17.2	17.2	17.1	17.0	17.0	16.9	16.8	16.8	16.7	16.6	16.5	16.3
2.50	30.00	20.1	20.0	19.9	19.9	19.8	19.7	19.6	19.5	19.4	19.2	19.1	18.9
2.0833	25.00	23.4	23.3	23.1	23.0	22.9	22.8	22.7	22.5	22.4	22.2	22.0	21.7
1.50	18.00	30.3	30.1	29.9	29.7	29.5	29.3	29.1	28.9	28.7	28.3	27.9	27.6
1.25	15.00	34.7	34.4	34.1	33.8	33.6	33.3	33.1	32.8	32.6	32.1	31.6	31.2
1.00	12.00	40.5	40.2	39.8	39.4	39.1	38.7	38.4	38.0	37.7	37.1	36.4	35.8
0.9167	11.00	43.0	42.5	42.1	41.7	41.3	40.9	40.5	40.2	39.8	39.1	38.4	37.7
0.8333	10.00	45.7	45.2	44.7	44.3	43.8	43.4	43.0	42.6	42.1	41.3	40.6	39.8
0.7917	9.50	47.2	46.7	46.2	45.7	45.2	44.8	44.3	43.9	43.4	42.6	41.8	41.0
0.75	9.00	48.8	48.3	47.7	47.2	46.7	46.2	45.7	45.3	44.8	43.9	43.0	42.2
0.7083	8.50	50.5	50.0	49.4	48.8	48.3	47.8	47.2	46.7	46.2	45.3	44.4	43.5
0.6667	8.00	52.4	51.8	51.2	50.6	50.0	49.4	48.9	48.3	47.8	46.8	45.8	44.9
0.5833	7.00	56.5	55.8	55.1	54.4	53.7	53.1	52.5	51.8	51.2	50.1	48.9	47.9
0.5417	6.50	58.9	58.1	57.3	56.6	55.9	55.2	54.5	53.8	53.1	51.9	50.7	49.5
0.50	6.00	61.4	60.6	59.7	58.9	58.1	57.4	56.6	55.9	55.2	53.9	52.6	51.3

Starting from Partial Fund of 50%

Monthly Deposit	Annual Total	8.50%	8.75%	9.00%	9.25%	9.50%	9.75%	10.00%	10.25%	10.50%	11.00%	11.50%	12.00%
4.17%	50.00%	10.7	10.7	10.6	10.6	10.6	10.5	10.5	10.5	10.4	10.4	10.3	10.2
3.00	36.00	14.2	14.2	14.1	14.0	14.0	13.9	13.9	13.8	13.8	13.6	13.5	13.4
2.50	30.00	16.6	16.5	16.4	16.3	16.2	16.2	16.1	16.0	15.9	15.8	15.6	15.5
2.0833	25.00	19.2	19.1	19.0	18.9	18.8	18.7	18.6	18.5	18.4	18.2	18.0	17.8
1.50	18.00	24.8	24.6	24.4	24.2	24.0	23.9	23.7	23.5	23.4	23.0	22.7	22.4
1.25	15.00	28.3	28.0	27.8	27.6	27.3	27.1	26.9	26.7	26.5	26.0	25.6	25.3
1.00	12.00	32.9	32.6	32.3	32.0	31.7	31.4	31.1	30.8	30.5	30.0	29.4	28.9
0.9167	11.00	34.8	34.5	34.1	33.8	33.4	33.1	32.8	32.4	32.1	31.5	30.9	30.4
0.8333	10.00	37.0	36.6	36.2	35.8	35.4	35.0	34.7	34.3	34.0	33.3	32.6	32.0
0.7917	9.50	38.2	37.7	37.3	36.9	36.5	36.1	35.7	35.3	35.0	34.2	33.5	32.9
0.75	9.00	39.4	39.0	38.5	38.1	37.6	37.2	36.8	36.4	36.0	35.2	34.5	33.8
0.7083	8.50	40.8	40.3	39.8	39.3	38.9	38.4	38.0	37.5	37.1	36.3	35.5	34.8
0.6667	8.00	42.2	41.7	41.2	40.6	40.2	39.7	39.2	38.8	38.3	37.5	36.6	35.8
0.5833	7.00	45.4	44.8	44.2	43.6	43.1	42.5	42.0	41.4	40.9	40.0	39.0	38.1
0.5417	6.50	47.2	46.5	45.9	45.3	44.7	44.1	43.5	42.9	42.4	41.3	40.4	39.4
0.50	6.00	49.1	48.4	47.7	47.1	46.4	45.8	45.2	44.5	44.0	42.8	41.8	40.7

Starting from Partial Fund of 60%

Monthly Deposit	Annual Total	8.50%	8.75%	9.00%	9.25%	9.50%	9.75%	10.00%	10.25%	10.50%	11.00%	11.50%	12.00%
4.17%	50.00%	8.5	8.5	8.4	8.4	8.4	8.3	8.3	8.3	8.3	8.2	8.2	8.1
3.00	36.00	11.3	11.2	11.2	11.1	11.1	11.0	11.0	10.9	10.9	10.8	10.7	10.6
2.50	30.00	13.1	13.0	13.0	12.9	12.8	12.8	12.7	12.6	12.6	12.4	12.3	12.2
2.0833	25.00	15.2	15.1	15.0	14.9	14.8	14.7	14.6	14.5	14.5	14.3	14.1	14.0
1.50	18.00	19.5	19.3	19.2	19.0	18.9	18.7	18.6	18.4	18.3	18.0	17.8	17.5
1.25	15.00	22.1	21.9	21.8	21.6	21.4	21.2	21.0	20.8	20.7	20.3	20.0	19.7
1.00	12.00	25.7	25.4	25.2	24.9	24.7	24.4	24.2	23.9	23.7	23.3	22.8	22.4
0.9167	11.00	27.1	26.8	26.6	26.3	26.0	25.7	25.5	25.2	24.9	24.5	24.0	23.5
0.8333	10.00	28.8	28.4	28.1	27.8	27.5	27.2	26.9	26.6	26.3	25.8	25.2	24.7
0.7917	9.50	29.7	29.3	29.0	28.6	28.3	28.0	27.7	27.4	27.1	26.5	25.9	25.4
0.75	9.00	30.6	30.2	29.9	29.5	29.2	28.8	28.5	28.2	27.8	27.2	26.6	26.1
0.7083	8.50	31.6	31.2	30.8	30.4	30.1	29.7	29.4	29.0	28.7	28.0	27.4	26.8
0.6667	8.00	32.7	32.3	31.8	31.4	31.0	30.7	30.3	29.9	29.6	28.9	28.2	27.6
0.5833	7.00	35.1	34.6	34.1	33.6	33.2	32.8	32.3	31.9	31.5	30.7	30.0	29.3
0.5417	6.50	36.4	35.9	35.4	34.9	34.4	33.9	33.5	33.0	32.6	31.7	30.9	30.2
0.50	6.00	37.9	37.3	36.7	36.2	35.7	35.2	34.7	34.2	33.7	32.8	32.0	31.2

Starting from Partial Fund of 66.7%

Monthly Deposit	Annual Total	8.50%	8.75%	9.00%	9.25%	9.50%	9.75%	10.00%	10.25%	10.50%	11.00%	11.50%	12.00%
4.17%	50.00%	7.0	7.0	7.0	7.0	6.9	6.9	6.9	6.9	6.8	6.8	6.7	6.7
3.00	36.00	9.3	9.3	9.2	9.2	9.1	9.1	9.1	9.0	9.0	8.9	8.8	8.7
2.50	30.00	10.8	10.8	10.7	10.7	10.6	10.5	10.5	10.4	10.4	10.3	10.2	10.1
2.0833	25.00	12.5	12.4	12.4	12.3	12.2	12.1	12.1	12.0	11.9	11.8	11.6	11.5
1.50	18.00	16.0	15.9	15.8	15.6	15.5	15.4	15.3	15.2	15.0	14.8	14.6	14.4
1.25	15.00	18.2	18.0	17.9	17.7	17.6	17.4	17.2	17.1	16.9	16.7	16.4	16.1
1.00	12.00	21.1	20.8	20.6	20.4	20.2	20.0	19.8	19.6	19.4	19.0	18.7	18.3
0.9167	11.00	22.2	22.0	21.8	21.5	21.3	21.1	20.8	20.6	20.4	20.0	19.6	19.2
0.8333	10.00	23.6	23.3	23.0	22.7	22.5	22.2	22.0	21.7	21.5	21.0	20.6	20.2
0.7917	9.50	24.3	24.0	23.7	23.4	23.1	22.9	22.6	22.3	22.1	21.6	21.1	20.7
0.75	9.00	25.0	24.7	24.4	24.1	23.8	23.5	23.2	23.0	22.7	22.2	21.7	21.2
0.7083	8.50	25.8	25.5	25.2	24.8	24.5	24.2	23.9	23.7	23.4	22.8	22.3	21.8
0.6667	8.00	26.7	26.3	26.0	25.6	25.3	25.0	24.7	24.4	24.1	23.5	22.9	22.4
0.5833	7.00	28.6	28.2	27.8	27.4	27.0	26.7	26.3	26.0	25.6	25.0	24.3	23.8
0.5417	6.50	29.7	29.2	28.8	28.4	28.0	27.6	27.2	26.8	26.5	25.8	25.1	24.5
0.50	6.00	30.8	30.3	29.9	29.4	29.0	28.6	28.2	27.8	27.4	26.6	25.9	25.3

Entry is number of monthly deposits to take fund from starting balance to 100%.

Time When a Given Sinking Fund Balance Occurs

5.50% Interest Rate

Monthly Payment	Annual Constant	20%	25%	33.3%	40%	50%	60%	66.7%	70%	75%	80%	90%	100%
2.50%	30.00%	7.84	9.76	12.91	15.41	19.10	22.72	25.11	26.29	28.05	29.80	33.26	36.66
2.0833	25.00	9.37	11.66	15.41	18.36	22.72	27.00	29.80	31.19	33.26	35.30	39.34	43.30
2.00	24.00	9.76	12.13	16.03	19.10	23.62	28.05	30.96	32.40	34.54	36.66	40.84	44.94
1.6667	20.00	11.66	14.48	19.10	22.72	28.05	33.26	36.66	38.34	40.83	43.30	48.16	52.91
1.50	18.00	12.91	16.03	21.12	25.11	30.96	36.66	40.38	42.21	44.94	47.63	52.91	58.07
1.25	15.00	15.41	19.10	25.11	29.80	36.66	43.30	47.63	49.76	52.91	56.02	62.12	68.04
1.00	12.00	19.10	23.62	30.96	36.66	44.94	52.91	58.07	60.61	64.36	68.04	75.23	82.19
0.9167	11.00	20.75	25.65	33.57	39.70	48.60	57.14	62.66	65.37	69.37	73.29	80.94	88.33
0.8333	10.00	22.72	28.05	36.66	43.30	52.91	62.12	68.04	70.95	75.23	79.44	87.61	95.48
0.75	9.00	25.11	30.96	40.38	47.63	58.07	68.04	74.44	77.58	82.19	86.71	95.48	103.92
0.6667	8.00	28.05	34.54	44.94	52.91	64.36	75.23	82.19	85.59	90.59	95.48	104.95	114.02
0.6250	7.50	29.80	36.66	47.63	56.02	68.04	79.44	86.71	90.26	95.48	100.58	110.43	119.86
0.5833	7.00	31.78	39.05	50.66	59.53	72.18	84.14	91.77	95.48	100.94	106.27	116.54	126.36
0.50	6.00	36.66	44.94	58.07	68.04	82.19	95.48	103.92	108.01	114.02	119.86	131.10	141.79

5.75% Interest

Monthly Payment	Annual Constant	20%	25%	33.3%	40%	50%	60%	66.7%	70%	75%	80%	90%	100%
2.50%	30.00%	7.83	9.75	12.90	15.38	19.06	22.67	25.04	26.22	27.97	29.71	33.14	36.52
2.0833	25.00	9.36	11.64	15.38	18.33	22.67	26.92	29.71	31.09	33.14	35.18	39.19	43.12
2.00	24.00	9.75	12.11	16.00	19.06	23.56	27.97	30.86	32.29	34.42	36.52	40.67	44.74
1.6667	20.00	11.64	14.45	19.06	22.67	27.97	33.14	36.52	38.19	40.67	43.12	47.93	52.64
1.50	18.00	12.90	16.00	21.07	25.04	30.86	36.52	40.21	42.04	44.74	47.41	52.64	57.75
1.25	15.00	15.38	19.06	25.04	29.71	36.52	43.12	47.41	49.52	52.64	55.72	61.75	67.61
1.00	12.00	19.06	23.56	30.86	36.52	44.74	52.64	57.75	60.26	63.97	67.61	74.71	81.57
0.9167	11.00	20.71	25.58	33.45	39.55	48.37	56.83	62.29	64.97	68.92	72.79	80.34	87.63
0.8333	10.00	22.67	27.97	36.52	43.12	52.64	61.75	67.61	70.48	74.71	78.85	86.91	94.67
0.75	9.00	25.04	30.86	40.21	47.41	57.75	67.61	73.93	77.02	81.57	86.03	94.67	102.96
0.6667	8.00	27.97	34.42	44.74	52.64	63.97	74.71	81.57	84.92	89.85	94.67	103.97	112.88
0.6250	7.50	29.71	36.52	47.41	55.72	67.61	78.85	86.03	89.53	94.67	99.68	109.37	118.62
0.5833	7.00	31.68	38.90	50.41	59.19	71.69	83.49	91.01	94.67	100.03	105.27	115.35	124.99
0.50	6.00	36.52	44.74	57.75	67.61	81.57	94.67	102.96	106.99	112.88	118.62	129.64	140.11

6.00% Interest

Monthly Payment	Annual Constant	20%	25%	33.3%	40%	50%	60%	66.7%	70%	75%	80%	90%	100%
2.50%	30.00%	7.83	9.73	12.88	15.36	19.02	22.62	24.98	26.15	27.89	29.62	33.03	36.39
2.0833	25.00	9.35	11.63	15.36	18.29	22.62	26.85	29.62	30.99	33.03	35.05	39.03	42.94
2.00	24.00	9.73	12.10	15.97	19.02	23.50	27.89	30.76	32.19	34.30	36.39	40.51	44.54
1.6667	20.00	11.63	14.43	19.02	22.61	27.89	33.03	36.39	38.05	40.51	42.94	47.71	52.37
1.50	18.00	12.88	15.97	21.02	24.98	30.76	36.39	40.05	41.86	44.54	47.19	52.37	57.43
1.25	15.00	15.36	19.02	24.98	29.62	36.39	42.94	47.19	49.28	52.37	55.42	61.39	67.18
1.00	12.00	19.02	23.50	30.76	36.39	44.54	52.37	57.43	59.91	63.58	67.18	74.19	80.96
0.9167	11.00	20.66	25.51	33.34	39.39	48.14	56.52	61.92	64.57	68.47	72.30	79.75	86.93
0.8333	10.00	22.62	27.89	36.39	42.94	52.37	61.39	67.18	70.01	74.19	78.28	86.22	93.86
0.75	9.00	24.98	30.76	40.05	47.19	57.43	67.18	73.42	76.47	80.96	85.35	93.86	102.02
0.6667	8.00	27.89	34.30	44.54	52.37	63.58	74.19	80.96	84.27	89.12	93.86	103.02	111.77
0.6250	7.50	29.62	36.39	47.19	55.42	67.18	78.28	85.35	88.80	93.86	98.80	108.32	117.41
0.5833	7.00	31.58	38.75	50.17	58.85	71.21	82.86	90.26	93.86	99.14	104.29	114.21	123.66
0.50	6.00	36.39	44.54	57.43	67.18	80.96	93.86	102.02	105.98	111.77	117.41	128.22	138.48

6.25% Interest

Monthly Payment	Annual Constant	20%	25%	33.3%	40%	50%	60%	66.7%	70%	75%	80%	90%	100%
2.50%	30.00%	7.82	9.72	12.86	15.33	18.98	22.56	24.91	26.08	27.81	29.53	32.92	36.26
2.0833	25.00	9.34	11.61	15.33	18.26	22.56	26.77	29.53	30.90	32.92	34.93	38.88	42.76
2.00	24.00	9.72	12.08	15.94	18.98	23.45	27.81	30.67	32.08	34.18	36.26	40.34	44.35
1.6667	20.00	11.61	14.41	18.98	22.56	27.81	32.92	36.26	37.90	40.34	42.76	47.49	52.11
1.50	18.00	12.86	15.94	20.98	24.91	30.67	36.26	39.89	41.69	44.35	46.97	52.11	57.12
1.25	15.00	15.33	18.98	24.91	29.53	36.26	42.76	46.97	49.04	52.11	55.13	61.03	66.76
1.00	12.00	18.98	23.45	30.67	36.26	44.35	52.11	57.12	59.57	63.20	66.76	73.68	80.37
0.9167	11.00	20.62	25.44	33.23	39.24	47.91	56.22	61.56	64.17	68.03	71.82	79.17	86.25
0.8333	10.00	22.56	27.81	36.26	42.76	52.11	61.03	66.76	69.56	73.68	77.72	85.55	93.08
0.75	9.00	24.91	30.67	39.89	46.97	57.12	66.76	72.92	75.94	80.37	84.70	93.08	101.11
0.6667	8.00	27.81	34.18	44.35	52.11	63.20	73.68	80.37	83.62	88.41	93.08	102.09	110.70
0.6250	7.50	29.53	36.26	46.97	55.13	66.76	77.72	84.70	88.09	93.08	97.94	107.30	116.23
0.5833	7.00	31.48	38.60	49.92	58.52	70.74	82.23	89.53	93.08	98.28	103.34	113.09	122.36
0.50	6.00	36.26	44.35	57.12	66.76	80.37	93.08	101.11	105.00	110.70	116.23	126.84	136.89

6.50% Interest

Monthly Payment	Annual Constant	20%	25%	33.3%	40%	50%	60%	66.7%	70%	75%	80%	90%	100%
2.50%	30.00%	7.81	9.71	12.84	15.31	18.94	22.51	24.85	26.01	27.73	29.44	32.81	36.13
2.0833	25.00	9.33	11.60	15.31	18.22	22.51	26.70	29.44	30.80	32.81	34.81	38.73	42.58
2.00	24.00	9.71	12.06	15.92	18.94	23.39	27.73	30.57	31.98	34.06	36.13	40.18	44.15
1.6667	20.00	11.60	14.39	18.94	22.51	27.73	32.81	36.13	37.76	40.18	42.58	47.27	51.85
1.50	18.00	12.84	15.92	20.93	24.85	30.57	36.13	39.74	41.52	44.15	46.76	51.85	56.81
1.25	15.00	15.31	18.94	24.85	29.44	36.13	42.58	46.76	48.81	51.85	54.84	60.68	66.34
1.00	12.00	18.94	23.39	30.57	36.13	44.15	51.85	56.81	59.24	62.82	66.34	73.18	79.78
0.9167	11.00	20.57	25.38	33.12	39.09	47.69	55.92	61.20	63.79	67.60	71.34	78.60	85.58
0.8333	10.00	22.51	27.73	36.13	42.58	51.85	60.68	66.34	69.11	73.18	77.17	84.89	92.31
0.75	9.00	24.85	30.57	39.74	46.76	56.81	66.34	72.43	75.41	79.78	84.05	92.31	100.21
0.6667	8.00	27.73	34.06	44.15	51.85	62.82	73.18	79.78	82.99	87.71	92.31	101.18	109.64
0.6250	7.50	29.44	36.13	46.76	54.84	66.34	77.17	84.05	87.40	92.31	97.09	106.30	115.08
0.5833	7.00	31.38	38.46	49.68	58.20	70.28	81.62	88.81	92.31	97.43	102.41	111.99	121.10
0.50	6.00	36.13	44.15	56.81	66.34	79.78	92.31	100.21	104.04	109.64	115.08	125.49	135.35

Entry is months until percentage selected is achieved.

Time When a Given Sinking Fund Balance Occurs

6.75% Interest Rate

Monthly Payment	Annual Constant	Percentage of Total Fund											
		20%	25%	33.3%	40%	50%	60%	66.7%	70%	75%	80%	90%	100%
2.50%	30.00%	7.80	9.70	12.82	15.28	18.91	22.46	24.79	25.94	27.66	29.36	32.71	36.00
2.0833	25.00	9.33	11.58	15.28	18.19	22.46	26.63	29.36	30.70	32.71	34.69	38.59	42.40
2.00	24.00	9.70	12.05	15.89	18.91	23.33	27.66	30.48	31.88	33.95	36.00	40.03	43.97
1.6667	20.00	11.58	14.36	18.91	22.46	27.66	32.71	36.00	37.62	40.02	42.40	47.05	51.59
1.50	18.00	12.82	15.89	20.89	24.79	30.48	36.00	39.58	41.35	43.97	46.54	51.59	56.50
1.25	15.00	15.28	18.91	24.79	29.36	36.00	42.40	46.54	48.58	51.59	54.55	60.33	65.93
1.00	12.00	18.91	23.33	30.48	36.00	43.97	51.59	56.50	58.91	62.45	65.93	72.69	79.20
0.9167	11.00	20.53	25.31	33.01	38.94	47.47	55.62	60.85	63.41	67.18	70.87	78.04	84.93
0.8333	10.00	22.46	27.66	36.00	42.40	51.59	60.33	65.93	68.67	72.69	76.63	84.25	91.56
0.75	9.00	24.79	30.48	39.58	46.54	56.50	65.93	71.95	74.89	79.20	83.42	91.56	99.34
0.6667	8.00	27.66	33.95	43.97	51.59	62.45	72.69	79.20	82.37	87.02	91.56	100.29	108.61
0.6250	7.50	29.36	36.00	46.54	54.55	65.93	76.63	83.42	86.72	91.56	96.27	105.33	113.96
0.5833	7.00	31.28	38.31	49.45	57.88	69.83	81.02	88.11	91.56	96.60	101.50	110.92	119.87
0.50	6.00	36.00	43.97	56.50	65.93	79.20	91.56	99.34	103.11	108.62	113.96	124.18	133.85

7.00% Interest

Monthly Payment	Annual Constant	20%	25%	33.3%	40%	50%	60%	66.7%	70%	75%	80%	90%	100%
2.50%	30.00%	7.80	9.69	12.81	15.26	18.87	22.40	24.72	25.87	27.58	29.27	32.60	35.87
2.0833	25.00	9.32	11.57	15.26	18.15	22.40	26.56	29.27	30.61	32.60	34.57	38.44	42.22
2.00	24.00	9.69	12.03	15.86	18.87	23.28	27.58	30.39	31.77	33.83	35.87	39.87	43.78
1.6667	20.00	11.57	14.34	18.87	22.40	27.58	32.60	35.87	37.48	39.87	42.22	46.84	51.34
1.50	18.00	12.81	15.86	20.84	24.72	30.39	35.87	39.43	41.18	43.78	46.33	51.34	56.20
1.25	15.00	15.26	18.87	24.72	29.27	35.87	42.22	46.33	48.35	51.34	54.27	59.99	65.53
1.00	12.00	18.87	23.28	30.39	35.87	43.78	51.34	56.20	58.58	62.09	65.53	72.21	78.64
0.9167	11.00	20.48	25.25	32.90	38.79	47.25	55.33	60.50	63.03	66.76	70.41	77.49	84.28
0.8333	10.00	22.40	27.58	35.87	42.22	51.34	59.99	65.53	68.23	72.21	76.10	83.61	90.82
0.75	9.00	24.72	30.39	39.43	46.33	56.20	65.53	71.48	74.38	78.64	82.79	90.82	98.48
0.6667	8.00	27.58	33.83	43.78	51.34	62.09	72.21	78.64	81.76	86.35	90.82	99.42	107.61
0.6250	7.50	29.27	35.87	46.33	54.27	65.53	76.10	82.79	86.05	90.82	95.46	104.38	112.86
0.5833	7.00	31.18	38.16	49.21	57.56	69.38	80.43	87.43	90.82	95.79	100.61	109.88	118.67
0.50	6.00	35.87	43.78	56.20	65.53	78.64	90.82	98.48	102.19	107.61	112.86	122.90	132.39

7.25% Interest

Monthly Payment	Annual Constant	20%	25%	33.3%	40%	50%	60%	66.7%	70%	75%	80%	90%	100%
2.50%	30.00%	7.79	9.68	12.79	15.23	18.83	22.35	24.66	25.80	27.50	29.18	32.49	35.74
2.0833	25.00	9.31	11.55	15.23	18.12	22.35	26.48	29.18	30.52	32.49	34.45	38.29	42.05
2.00	24.00	9.68	12.02	15.84	18.83	23.22	27.50	30.29	31.67	33.72	35.74	39.71	43.59
1.6667	20.00	11.55	14.32	18.83	22.35	27.50	32.49	35.74	37.34	39.71	42.05	46.63	51.09
1.50	18.00	12.79	15.84	20.80	24.66	30.29	35.74	39.28	41.02	43.59	46.13	51.09	55.90
1.25	15.00	15.23	18.83	24.66	29.18	35.74	42.05	46.13	48.13	51.09	53.99	59.66	65.13
1.00	12.00	18.83	23.22	30.29	35.74	43.59	51.09	55.90	58.26	61.73	65.13	71.74	78.09
0.9167	11.00	20.44	25.18	32.79	38.64	47.04	55.04	60.16	62.67	66.35	69.96	76.95	83.65
0.8333	10.00	22.35	27.50	35.74	42.05	51.09	59.66	65.13	67.81	71.74	75.57	83.00	90.10
0.75	9.00	24.66	30.29	39.28	46.13	55.90	65.13	71.02	73.86	78.09	82.19	90.10	97.65
0.6667	8.00	27.50	33.72	43.59	51.09	61.73	71.74	78.09	81.17	85.69	90.10	98.57	106.63
0.6250	7.50	29.18	35.74	46.13	53.99	65.13	75.57	82.19	85.40	90.10	94.67	103.45	111.79
0.5833	7.00	31.08	38.02	48.98	57.25	68.94	79.86	86.75	90.10	94.99	99.75	108.86	117.51
0.50	6.00	35.74	43.59	55.90	65.13	78.09	90.10	97.65	101.30	106.63	111.79	121.66	130.98

7.50% Interest

Monthly Payment	Annual Constant	20%	25%	33.3%	40%	50%	60%	66.7%	70%	75%	80%	90%	100%
2.50%	30.00%	7.78	9.67	12.77	15.21	18.79	22.30	24.60	25.73	27.42	29.10	32.39	35.61
2.0833	25.00	9.30	11.54	15.21	18.08	22.30	26.41	29.10	30.42	32.39	34.33	38.15	41.88
2.00	24.00	9.67	12.00	15.81	18.79	23.17	27.42	30.20	31.57	33.61	35.61	39.56	43.41
1.6667	20.00	11.54	14.30	18.79	22.30	27.42	32.39	35.61	37.20	39.56	41.88	46.42	50.84
1.50	18.00	12.77	15.81	20.75	24.60	30.20	35.61	39.13	40.85	43.41	45.92	50.84	55.61
1.25	15.00	15.21	18.79	24.60	29.10	35.61	41.88	45.92	47.91	50.84	53.72	59.33	64.74
1.00	12.00	18.79	23.17	30.20	35.61	43.41	50.84	55.61	57.94	61.38	64.74	71.27	77.54
0.9167	11.00	20.40	25.12	32.68	38.49	46.83	54.75	59.83	62.30	65.95	69.52	76.42	83.03
0.8333	10.00	22.30	27.42	35.61	41.88	50.84	59.33	64.74	67.39	71.27	75.06	82.39	89.39
0.75	9.00	24.60	30.20	39.13	45.92	55.61	64.74	70.56	73.39	77.54	81.59	89.39	96.83
0.6667	8.00	27.42	33.61	43.41	50.84	61.38	71.27	77.54	80.59	85.05	89.39	97.74	105.67
0.6250	7.50	29.10	35.61	45.92	53.72	64.74	75.06	81.59	84.75	89.39	93.90	102.54	110.75
0.5833	7.00	30.99	37.88	48.75	56.95	68.51	79.29	86.09	89.39	94.21	98.89	107.87	116.37
0.50	6.00	35.61	43.41	55.61	64.74	77.54	89.39	96.83	100.43	105.67	110.75	120.45	129.60

7.75% Interest

Monthly Payment	Annual Constant	20%	25%	33.3%	40%	50%	60%	66.7%	70%	75%	80%	90%	100%
2.50%	30.00%	7.78	9.66	12.75	15.18	18.76	22.25	24.54	25.67	27.35	29.01	32.28	35.49
2.0833	25.00	9.29	11.52	15.18	18.05	22.25	26.34	29.01	30.33	32.28	34.22	38.01	41.71
2.00	24.00	9.66	11.99	15.78	18.76	23.11	27.35	30.11	31.47	33.49	35.49	39.41	43.23
1.6667	20.00	11.52	14.28	18.76	22.25	27.35	32.28	35.49	37.07	39.41	41.71	46.22	50.60
1.50	18.00	12.75	15.78	20.71	24.54	30.11	35.49	38.98	40.69	43.23	45.72	50.60	55.32
1.25	15.00	15.18	18.76	24.54	29.01	35.49	41.71	45.72	47.69	50.60	53.45	59.00	64.36
1.00	12.00	18.76	23.11	30.11	35.49	43.23	50.60	55.32	57.63	61.03	64.36	70.81	77.01
0.9167	11.00	20.35	25.05	32.58	38.35	46.62	54.47	59.50	61.95	65.55	69.08	75.90	82.43
0.8333	10.00	22.25	27.35	35.49	41.71	50.60	59.00	64.36	66.97	70.81	74.56	81.79	88.70
0.75	9.00	24.54	30.11	38.98	45.72	55.32	64.36	70.11	72.90	77.01	81.00	88.70	96.03
0.6667	8.00	27.35	33.49	43.23	50.60	61.03	70.81	77.01	80.01	84.42	88.70	96.92	104.74
0.6250	7.50	29.01	35.49	45.72	53.45	64.36	74.56	81.00	84.13	88.70	93.14	101.66	109.73
0.5833	7.00	30.89	37.74	48.53	56.65	68.08	78.73	85.45	88.70	93.45	98.06	106.90	115.26
0.50	6.00	35.49	43.23	55.32	64.36	77.01	88.70	96.03	99.57	104.74	109.73	119.27	128.26

Entry is months until percentage selected is achieved.

Time When a Given Sinking Fund Balance Occurs

8.00% Interest Rate

Monthly Payment	Annual Constant	Percentage of Total Fund											
		20%	25%	33.3%	40%	50%	60%	66.7%	70%	75%	80%	90%	100%
2.50%	30.00%	7.77	9.65	12.73	15.16	18.72	22.20	24.48	25.60	27.27	28.93	32.18	35.37
2.0833	25.00	9.28	11.51	15.16	18.01	22.20	26.27	28.93	30.24	32.18	34.10	37.87	41.54
2.00	24.00	9.65	11.97	15.76	18.72	23.06	27.27	30.02	31.37	33.38	35.37	39.26	43.05
1.6667	20.00	11.51	14.25	18.72	22.20	27.27	32.18	35.37	36.93	39.26	41.54	46.01	50.35
1.50	18.00	12.73	15.76	20.66	24.48	30.02	35.37	38.83	40.53	43.05	45.52	50.35	55.04
1.25	15.00	15.16	18.72	24.48	28.93	35.37	41.54	45.52	47.47	50.35	53.18	58.68	63.98
1.00	12.00	18.72	23.06	30.02	35.37	43.05	50.35	55.04	57.32	60.69	63.98	70.36	76.48
0.9167	11.00	20.31	24.99	32.47	38.21	46.41	54.20	59.17	61.60	65.16	68.65	75.39	81.84
0.8333	10.00	22.20	27.27	35.37	41.54	50.35	58.68	63.98	66.57	70.36	74.06	81.20	88.02
0.75	9.00	24.48	30.02	38.83	45.52	55.04	63.98	69.67	72.43	76.48	80.43	88.02	95.25
0.6667	8.00	27.27	33.38	43.05	50.35	60.69	70.36	76.48	79.45	83.79	88.02	96.13	103.82
0.6250	7.50	28.93	35.37	45.52	53.18	63.98	74.06	80.43	83.51	88.02	92.40	100.79	108.74
0.5833	7.00	30.80	37.60	48.30	56.35	67.66	78.18	84.81	88.02	92.71	97.25	105.95	114.17
0.50	6.00	35.37	43.05	55.04	63.98	76.48	88.02	95.25	98.74	103.82	108.74	118.12	126.95

8.25% Interest

Monthly Payment	Annual Constant	20%	25%	33.3%	40%	50%	60%	66.7%	70%	75%	80%	90%	100%
2.50%	30.00%	7.76	9.64	12.72	15.13	18.68	22.15	24.41	25.53	27.20	28.84	32.08	35.24
2.0833	25.00	9.27	11.49	15.13	17.98	22.15	26.20	28.84	30.15	32.08	33.99	37.73	41.38
2.00	24.00	9.64	11.95	15.73	18.68	23.00	27.20	29.93	31.28	33.27	35.24	39.11	42.87
1.6667	20.00	11.49	14.23	18.68	22.15	27.20	32.08	35.24	36.80	39.11	41.37	45.81	50.11
1.50	18.00	12.72	15.73	20.62	24.41	29.93	35.24	38.68	40.37	42.87	45.32	50.12	54.75
1.25	15.00	15.13	18.68	24.41	28.84	35.24	41.38	45.32	47.26	50.12	52.92	58.36	63.61
1.00	12.00	18.68	23.00	29.93	35.24	42.87	50.12	54.75	57.02	60.35	63.61	69.92	75.96
0.9167	11.00	20.27	24.92	32.37	38.06	46.21	53.92	58.85	61.25	64.78	68.22	74.88	81.25
0.8333	10.00	22.15	27.20	35.24	41.38	50.12	58.36	63.61	66.17	69.92	73.57	80.63	87.35
0.75	9.00	24.41	29.93	38.68	45.32	54.75	63.61	69.23	71.96	75.96	79.86	87.35	94.48
0.6667	8.00	27.20	33.27	42.87	50.11	60.35	69.92	75.96	78.89	83.18	87.35	95.34	102.92
0.6250	7.50	28.84	35.24	45.32	52.92	63.61	73.57	79.86	82.90	87.35	91.67	99.94	107.77
0.5833	7.00	30.70	37.46	48.08	56.05	67.25	77.65	84.19	87.35	91.97	96.45	105.02	113.11
0.50	6.00	35.24	42.87	54.75	63.61	75.96	87.35	94.48	97.91	102.92	107.77	116.99	125.67

8.50% Interest

Monthly Payment	Annual Constant	20%	25%	33.3%	40%	50%	60%	66.7%	70%	75%	80%	90%	100%
2.50%	30.00%	7.76	9.63	12.70	15.11	18.65	22.10	24.35	25.47	27.12	28.76	31.98	35.12
2.0833	25.00	9.26	11.48	15.11	17.95	22.10	26.13	28.76	30.06	31.98	33.87	37.59	41.21
2.00	24.00	9.63	11.94	15.70	18.65	22.95	27.12	29.84	31.18	33.17	35.12	38.96	42.69
1.6667	20.00	11.48	14.21	18.65	22.10	27.12	31.98	35.12	36.67	38.96	41.21	45.61	49.88
1.50	18.00	12.70	15.70	20.58	24.35	29.84	35.12	38.54	40.22	42.69	45.13	49.88	54.48
1.25	15.00	15.11	18.65	24.35	28.76	35.12	41.21	45.13	47.05	49.88	52.66	58.05	63.25
1.00	12.00	18.65	22.95	29.84	35.12	42.69	49.88	54.48	56.72	60.02	63.25	69.48	75.46
0.9167	11.00	20.23	24.86	32.27	37.92	46.01	53.65	58.53	60.91	64.40	67.81	74.39	80.68
0.8333	10.00	22.10	27.12	35.12	41.21	49.88	58.05	63.25	65.77	69.48	73.10	80.06	86.70
0.75	9.00	24.35	29.84	38.54	45.13	54.48	63.25	68.80	71.50	75.46	79.31	86.70	93.73
0.6667	8.00	27.12	33.17	42.69	49.88	60.02	69.48	75.46	78.35	82.59	86.70	94.58	102.05
0.6250	7.50	28.76	35.12	45.13	52.66	63.25	73.10	79.31	82.31	86.70	90.96	99.11	106.82
0.5833	7.00	30.61	37.33	47.86	55.76	66.84	77.12	83.58	86.70	91.26	95.67	104.11	112.08
0.50	6.00	35.12	42.69	54.48	63.25	75.46	86.70	93.73	97.12	102.05	106.82	115.90	124.43

8.75% Interest

Monthly Payment	Annual Constant	20%	25%	33.3%	40%	50%	60%	66.7%	70%	75%	80%	90%	100%
2.50%	30.00%	7.75	9.62	12.68	15.08	18.61	22.05	24.29	25.40	27.05	28.68	31.88	35.00
2.0833	25.00	9.25	11.47	15.08	17.91	22.05	26.06	28.68	29.97	31.88	33.76	37.45	41.05
2.00	24.00	9.62	11.92	15.68	18.61	22.90	27.05	29.75	31.08	33.06	35.00	38.81	42.52
1.6667	20.00	11.47	14.19	18.61	22.05	27.05	31.88	35.00	36.54	38.81	41.05	45.41	49.65
1.50	18.00	12.68	15.68	20.53	24.29	29.75	35.00	38.39	40.06	42.52	44.94	49.65	54.20
1.25	15.00	15.08	18.61	24.29	28.68	35.00	41.05	44.94	46.84	49.65	52.40	57.74	62.88
1.00	12.00	18.61	22.90	29.75	35.00	42.52	49.65	54.20	56.42	59.69	62.88	69.05	74.96
0.9167	11.00	20.18	24.80	32.16	37.78	45.81	53.39	58.22	60.57	64.03	67.40	73.90	80.11
0.8333	10.00	22.05	27.05	35.00	41.05	49.65	57.74	62.88	65.38	69.05	72.63	79.51	86.06
0.75	9.00	24.29	29.75	38.39	44.94	54.20	62.88	68.38	71.05	74.96	78.76	86.06	92.99
0.6667	8.00	27.05	33.06	42.52	49.65	59.69	69.05	74.96	77.82	82.00	86.06	93.83	101.19
0.6250	7.50	28.68	35.00	44.94	52.40	62.88	72.63	78.76	81.72	86.06	90.26	98.29	105.89
0.5833	7.00	30.51	37.19	47.65	55.48	66.44	76.60	82.98	86.06	90.55	94.91	103.22	111.06
0.50	6.00	35.00	42.52	54.20	62.88	74.96	86.06	92.99	96.33	101.19	105.89	114.82	123.21

9.00% Interest

Monthly Payment	Annual Constant	20%	25%	33.3%	40%	50%	60%	66.7%	70%	75%	80%	90%	100%
2.50%	30.00%	7.74	9.61	12.66	15.06	18.57	22.00	24.23	25.34	26.98	28.60	31.78	34.88
2.0833	25.00	9.24	11.45	15.06	17.88	22.00	26.00	28.60	29.88	31.78	33.65	37.32	40.89
2.00	24.00	9.61	11.91	15.65	18.57	22.84	26.98	29.66	30.99	32.95	34.88	38.67	42.35
1.6667	20.00	11.45	14.17	18.57	22.00	26.98	31.78	34.88	36.41	38.67	40.89	45.22	49.42
1.50	18.00	12.66	15.65	20.49	24.23	29.66	34.88	38.25	39.91	42.35	44.75	49.42	53.93
1.25	15.00	15.06	18.57	24.23	28.60	34.88	40.89	44.75	46.63	49.42	52.14	57.44	62.53
1.00	12.00	18.57	22.84	29.66	34.88	42.35	49.42	53.93	56.13	59.37	62.53	68.63	74.47
0.9167	11.00	20.14	24.74	32.06	37.65	45.61	53.12	57.91	60.24	63.66	66.99	73.42	79.56
0.8333	10.00	22.00	26.98	34.88	40.89	49.42	57.44	62.53	65.00	68.63	72.16	78.96	85.43
0.75	9.00	24.23	29.66	38.25	44.75	53.93	62.53	67.97	70.60	74.47	78.22	85.43	92.27
0.6667	8.00	26.98	32.95	42.35	49.42	59.37	68.63	74.47	77.29	81.42	85.43	93.10	100.35
0.6250	7.50	28.60	34.88	44.75	52.14	62.53	72.16	78.22	81.15	85.43	89.57	97.50	104.98
0.5833	7.00	30.42	37.06	47.44	55.19	66.05	76.09	82.39	85.43	89.86	94.16	102.35	110.07
0.50	6.00	34.88	42.35	53.93	62.53	74.47	85.43	92.27	95.56	100.35	104.98	113.77	122.03

Entry is months until percentage selected is achieved.

Time When a Given Sinking Fund Balance Occurs

9.25% Interest Rate

Monthly Payment	Annual Constant	Percentage of Total Fund											
		20%	25%	33.3%	40%	50%	60%	66.7%	70%	75%	80%	90%	100%
2.50%	30.00%	7.74	9.60	12.65	15.04	18.54	21.95	24.18	25.27	26.90	28.51	31.68	34.76
2.0833	25.00	9.23	11.44	15.04	17.85	21.95	25.93	28.51	29.79	31.68	33.54	37.18	40.73
2.00	24.00	9.60	11.89	15.63	18.54	22.79	26.90	29.58	30.89	32.84	34.76	38.52	42.18
1.6667	20.00	11.44	14.15	18.54	21.95	26.90	31.68	34.76	36.28	38.52	40.73	45.03	49.19
1.50	18.00	12.65	15.63	20.44	24.18	29.58	34.76	38.11	39.75	42.18	44.56	49.19	53.67
1.25	15.00	15.04	18.54	24.18	28.51	34.76	40.73	44.56	46.43	49.19	51.89	57.14	62.18
1.00	12.00	18.54	22.79	29.58	34.76	42.18	49.19	53.67	55.85	59.05	62.18	68.21	73.99
0.9167	11.00	20.10	24.68	31.96	37.51	45.41	52.86	57.60	59.91	63.30	66.60	72.95	79.02
0.8333	10.00	21.95	26.90	34.76	40.73	49.19	57.14	62.18	64.63	68.21	71.71	78.42	84.81
0.75	9.00	24.18	29.58	38.11	44.56	53.67	62.18	67.56	70.17	73.99	77.69	84.81	91.56
0.6667	8.00	26.90	32.84	42.18	49.19	59.05	68.21	73.98	76.78	80.86	84.81	92.38	99.53
0.6250	7.50	28.51	34.76	44.56	51.89	62.18	71.71	77.69	80.59	84.81	88.90	96.72	104.09
0.5833	7.00	30.33	36.93	47.23	54.92	65.66	75.59	81.81	84.81	89.19	93.42	101.50	109.11
0.50	6.00	34.76	42.18	53.67	62.18	73.99	84.81	91.56	94.81	99.53	104.09	112.75	120.87

9.50% Interest

Monthly Payment	Annual Constant	20%	25%	33.3%	40%	50%	60%	66.7%	70%	75%	80%	90%	100%
2.50%	30.00%	7.73	9.59	12.63	15.01	18.50	21.90	24.12	25.21	26.83	28.43	31.58	34.65
2.0833	25.00	9.22	11.42	15.01	17.81	21.90	25.86	28.43	29.70	31.58	33.43	37.05	40.57
2.00	24.00	9.59	11.88	15.60	18.50	22.74	26.83	29.49	30.80	32.74	34.65	38.38	42.01
1.6667	20.00	11.42	14.12	18.50	21.90	26.83	31.58	34.65	36.15	38.38	40.57	44.84	48.97
1.50	18.00	12.63	15.60	20.40	24.12	29.49	34.65	37.97	39.60	42.01	44.37	48.97	53.40
1.25	15.00	15.01	18.50	24.12	28.43	34.65	40.57	44.37	46.23	48.97	51.65	56.84	61.83
1.00	12.00	18.50	22.74	29.49	34.65	42.01	48.97	53.40	55.56	58.74	61.83	67.81	73.51
0.9167	11.00	20.06	24.61	31.86	37.37	45.22	52.61	57.30	59.59	62.94	66.20	72.49	78.48
0.8333	10.00	21.90	26.83	34.65	40.57	48.97	56.84	61.83	64.26	67.81	71.26	77.90	84.20
0.75	9.00	24.12	29.49	37.97	44.37	53.40	61.83	67.16	69.74	73.51	77.18	84.20	90.86
0.6667	8.00	26.83	32.74	42.01	48.97	58.74	67.81	73.51	76.27	80.30	84.20	91.67	98.72
0.6250	7.50	28.43	34.65	44.37	51.65	61.83	71.26	77.18	80.04	84.20	88.24	95.95	103.22
0.5833	7.00	30.24	36.79	47.02	54.64	65.28	75.10	81.24	84.20	88.53	92.70	100.67	108.16
0.50	6.00	34.65	42.01	53.40	61.83	73.51	84.20	90.86	94.07	98.72	103.22	111.75	119.75

9.75% Interest

Monthly Payment	Annual Constant	20%	25%	33.3%	40%	50%	60%	66.7%	70%	75%	80%	90%	100%
2.50%	30.00%	7.72	9.58	12.61	14.99	18.47	21.85	24.06	25.15	26.76	28.35	31.48	34.53
2.0833	25.00	9.21	11.41	14.99	17.78	21.85	25.79	28.35	29.61	31.48	33.32	36.92	40.41
2.00	24.00	9.58	11.86	15.58	18.47	22.68	26.76	29.41	30.71	32.63	34.53	38.24	41.84
1.6667	20.00	11.41	14.10	18.47	21.85	26.76	31.48	34.53	36.03	38.24	40.41	44.65	48.74
1.50	18.00	12.61	15.58	20.36	24.06	29.41	34.53	37.83	39.45	41.84	44.19	48.75	53.14
1.25	15.00	14.99	18.47	24.06	28.35	34.53	40.41	44.19	46.03	48.75	51.40	56.55	61.49
1.00	12.00	18.47	22.68	29.41	34.53	41.84	48.75	53.14	55.28	58.43	61.49	67.40	73.04
0.9167	11.00	20.02	24.55	31.76	37.24	45.03	52.35	57.01	59.27	62.59	65.82	72.04	77.96
0.8333	10.00	21.85	26.76	34.53	40.41	48.75	56.55	61.49	63.89	67.40	70.82	77.38	83.61
0.75	9.00	24.06	29.41	37.83	44.19	53.14	61.49	66.76	69.31	73.04	76.67	83.61	90.18
0.6667	8.00	26.76	32.63	41.84	48.74	58.43	67.40	73.04	75.77	79.75	83.61	90.98	97.94
0.6250	7.50	28.35	34.53	44.19	51.40	61.49	70.82	76.67	79.49	83.61	87.60	95.20	102.36
0.5833	7.00	30.15	36.66	46.81	54.37	64.90	74.61	80.68	83.61	87.88	92.00	99.85	107.24
0.50	6.00	34.53	41.84	53.14	61.49	73.04	83.61	90.18	93.34	97.94	102.36	110.77	118.64

10.00% Interest

Monthly Payment	Annual Constant	20%	25%	33.3%	40%	50%	60%	66.7%	70%	75%	80%	90%	100%
2.50%	30.00%	7.71	9.57	12.60	14.96	18.43	21.80	24.00	25.08	26.69	28.28	31.38	34.42
2.0833	25.00	9.20	11.39	14.96	17.75	21.80	25.73	28.28	29.53	31.38	33.21	36.79	40.26
2.00	24.00	9.57	11.85	15.55	18.43	22.63	26.69	29.32	30.61	32.53	34.42	38.10	41.68
1.6667	20.00	11.39	14.08	18.43	21.80	26.69	31.38	34.42	35.90	38.10	40.26	44.46	48.53
1.50	18.00	12.60	15.55	20.32	24.00	29.32	34.42	37.70	39.31	41.68	44.00	48.53	52.88
1.25	15.00	14.96	18.43	24.00	28.28	34.42	40.26	44.00	45.83	48.53	51.16	56.26	61.16
1.00	12.00	18.43	22.63	29.32	34.42	41.68	48.53	52.88	55.01	58.12	61.16	67.01	72.59
0.9167	11.00	19.98	24.49	31.66	37.11	44.84	52.10	56.71	58.96	62.24	65.44	71.59	77.44
0.8333	10.00	21.80	26.69	34.42	40.26	48.53	56.26	61.16	63.53	67.01	70.39	76.87	83.03
0.75	9.00	24.00	29.32	37.70	44.00	52.88	61.16	66.37	68.90	72.59	76.17	83.03	89.51
0.6667	8.00	26.69	32.53	41.68	48.53	58.12	67.01	72.59	75.28	79.22	83.03	90.30	97.16
0.6250	7.50	28.28	34.42	44.00	51.16	61.16	70.39	76.17	78.96	83.03	86.96	94.46	101.53
0.5833	7.00	30.06	36.54	46.61	54.10	64.53	74.13	80.13	83.03	87.24	91.31	99.05	106.33
0.50	6.00	34.42	41.68	52.88	61.16	72.59	83.03	89.51	92.63	97.16	101.53	109.81	117.57

10.25% Interest

Monthly Payment	Annual Constant	20%	25%	33.3%	40%	50%	60%	66.7%	70%	75%	80%	90%	100%
2.50%	30.00%	7.71	9.56	12.58	14.94	18.40	21.76	23.94	25.02	26.62	28.20	31.29	34.30
2.0833	25.00	9.19	11.38	14.94	17.71	21.76	25.66	28.20	29.44	31.29	33.11	36.66	40.11
2.00	24.00	9.56	11.83	15.52	18.40	22.58	26.62	29.24	30.52	32.43	34.30	37.96	41.51
1.6667	20.00	11.38	14.06	18.40	21.76	26.62	31.29	34.30	35.78	37.96	40.11	44.28	48.31
1.50	18.00	12.58	15.52	20.27	23.94	29.24	34.30	37.56	39.16	41.51	43.82	48.31	52.63
1.25	15.00	14.94	18.40	23.94	28.20	34.30	40.11	43.82	45.64	48.31	50.92	55.98	60.82
1.00	12.00	18.40	22.58	29.24	34.30	41.51	48.31	52.63	54.73	57.82	60.82	66.62	72.13
0.9167	11.00	19.94	24.43	31.57	36.98	44.65	51.86	56.43	58.65	61.90	65.06	71.15	76.94
0.8333	10.00	21.76	26.62	34.30	40.11	48.31	55.98	60.82	63.17	66.62	69.96	76.37	82.45
0.75	9.00	23.94	29.24	37.56	43.82	52.63	60.82	65.99	68.48	72.13	75.67	82.45	88.86
0.6667	8.00	26.62	32.43	41.51	48.31	57.82	66.61	72.13	74.80	78.69	82.45	89.63	96.40
0.6250	7.50	28.20	34.30	43.82	50.92	60.82	69.96	75.67	78.43	82.45	86.34	93.74	100.71
0.5833	7.00	29.97	36.41	46.41	53.84	64.17	73.66	79.59	82.45	86.61	90.63	98.27	105.45
0.50	6.00	34.30	41.51	52.63	60.82	72.13	82.45	88.86	91.93	96.40	100.71	108.88	116.51

Entry is months until percentage selected is achieved.

Time When a Given Sinking Fund Balance Occurs

10.50% Interest Rate

Monthly Payment	Annual Constant	20%	25%	33.3%	40%	50%	60%	66.7%	70%	75%	80%	90%	100%
2.50%	30.00%	7.70	9.55	12.56	14.92	18.36	21.71	23.88	24.96	26.55	28.12	31.19	34.19
2.0833	25.00	9.18	11.37	14.92	17.68	21.71	25.60	28.12	29.36	31.19	33.00	36.53	39.96
2.00	24.00	9.55	11.82	15.50	18.36	22.53	26.55	29.15	30.43	32.33	34.19	37.83	41.35
1.6667	20.00	11.37	14.04	18.36	21.71	26.55	31.19	34.19	35.66	37.83	39.95	44.10	48.09
1.50	18.00	12.56	15.50	20.23	23.88	29.15	34.19	37.43	39.01	41.35	43.64	48.10	52.38
1.25	15.00	14.92	18.36	23.88	28.12	34.19	39.96	43.64	45.45	48.10	50.69	55.70	60.50
1.00	12.00	18.36	22.53	29.15	34.19	41.35	48.10	52.38	54.46	57.52	60.50	66.23	71.69
0.9167	11.00	19.90	24.37	31.47	36.85	44.47	51.61	56.14	58.34	61.56	64.69	70.72	76.44
0.8333	10.00	21.71	26.55	34.19	39.96	48.10	55.70	60.50	62.83	66.23	69.54	75.88	81.89
0.75	9.00	23.88	29.15	37.43	43.64	52.38	60.50	65.61	68.08	71.69	75.19	81.89	88.21
0.6667	8.00	26.55	32.33	41.35	48.10	57.52	66.23	71.69	74.32	78.17	81.89	88.98	95.66
0.6250	7.50	28.12	34.19	43.64	50.69	60.50	69.54	75.19	77.92	81.89	85.72	93.04	99.91
0.5833	7.00	29.89	36.28	46.21	53.58	63.81	73.20	79.06	81.89	85.99	89.96	97.50	104.58
0.50	6.00	34.19	41.35	52.38	60.50	71.69	81.89	88.21	91.25	95.66	99.91	107.96	115.48

10.75% Interest

Monthly Payment	Annual Constant	20%	25%	33.3%	40%	50%	60%	66.7%	70%	75%	80%	90%	100%
2.50%	30.00%	7.69	9.54	12.55	14.89	18.33	21.66	23.83	24.90	26.48	28.04	31.10	34.08
2.0833	25.00	9.17	11.35	14.89	17.65	21.66	25.53	28.04	29.27	31.10	32.90	36.40	39.81
2.00	24.00	9.54	11.80	15.47	18.33	22.48	26.48	29.07	30.34	32.23	34.08	37.69	41.19
1.6667	20.00	11.35	14.02	18.33	21.66	26.48	31.10	34.08	35.54	37.69	39.80	43.92	47.88
1.50	18.00	12.55	15.47	20.19	23.83	29.07	34.08	37.30	38.87	41.19	43.47	47.88	52.13
1.25	15.00	14.89	18.33	23.83	28.04	34.08	39.81	43.47	45.26	47.88	50.45	55.42	60.18
1.00	12.00	18.33	22.48	29.07	34.08	41.19	47.88	52.13	54.20	57.23	60.18	65.85	71.25
0.9167	11.00	19.85	24.31	31.37	36.72	44.28	51.37	55.86	58.04	61.23	64.33	70.29	75.95
0.8333	10.00	21.66	26.48	34.08	39.81	47.88	55.42	60.18	62.48	65.85	69.12	75.39	81.33
0.75	9.00	23.83	29.07	37.30	43.47	52.13	60.18	65.23	67.68	71.25	74.71	81.33	87.58
0.6667	8.00	26.48	32.22	41.19	47.88	57.23	65.85	71.25	73.86	77.66	81.33	88.34	94.93
0.6250	7.50	28.04	34.08	43.47	50.45	60.18	69.12	74.71	77.41	81.33	85.12	92.34	99.12
0.5833	7.00	29.80	36.16	46.01	53.32	63.45	72.75	78.54	81.33	85.39	89.30	96.75	103.73
0.50	6.00	34.08	41.19	52.13	60.18	71.25	81.33	87.58	90.58	94.93	99.12	107.06	114.47

11.00% Interest

Monthly Payment	Annual Constant	20%	25%	33.3%	40%	50%	60%	66.7%	70%	75%	80%	90%	100%
2.50%	30.00%	7.69	9.53	12.53	14.87	18.29	21.61	23.77	24.83	26.41	27.96	31.01	33.97
2.0833	25.00	9.16	11.34	14.87	17.62	21.61	25.47	27.96	29.19	31.01	32.79	36.28	39.66
2.00	24.00	9.53	11.79	15.45	18.29	22.43	26.41	28.99	30.25	32.13	33.97	37.56	41.03
1.6667	20.00	11.34	14.00	18.29	21.61	26.41	31.00	33.97	35.42	37.56	39.66	43.74	47.67
1.50	18.00	12.53	15.45	20.15	23.77	28.99	33.97	37.16	38.73	41.03	43.29	47.67	51.89
1.25	15.00	14.87	18.29	23.77	27.96	33.97	39.66	43.29	45.07	47.67	50.22	55.15	59.86
1.00	12.00	18.29	22.43	28.99	33.97	41.03	47.67	51.89	53.94	56.94	59.86	65.48	70.82
0.9167	11.00	19.81	24.26	31.28	36.59	44.10	51.13	55.58	57.74	60.90	63.97	69.87	75.46
0.8333	10.00	21.61	26.41	33.97	39.66	47.67	55.15	59.86	62.14	65.48	68.71	74.92	80.79
0.75	9.00	23.77	28.99	37.16	43.29	51.89	59.86	64.87	67.29	70.82	74.24	80.79	86.96
0.6667	8.00	26.41	32.12	41.03	47.67	56.94	65.48	70.82	73.40	77.15	80.79	87.71	94.22
0.6250	7.50	27.96	33.97	43.29	50.22	59.86	68.71	74.24	76.91	80.79	84.53	91.66	98.35
0.5833	7.00	29.71	36.03	45.82	53.06	63.10	72.30	78.03	80.79	84.79	88.66	96.01	102.89
0.50	6.00	33.97	41.03	51.89	59.86	70.82	80.79	86.96	89.92	94.22	98.35	106.18	113.49

11.25% Interest

Monthly Payment	Annual Constant	20%	25%	33.3%	40%	50%	60%	66.7%	70%	75%	80%	90%	100%
2.50%	30.00%	7.68	9.52	12.51	14.85	18.26	21.57	23.71	24.77	26.34	27.89	30.91	33.86
2.0833	25.00	9.15	11.32	14.85	17.59	21.57	25.40	27.89	29.11	30.91	32.69	36.15	39.51
2.00	24.00	9.52	11.77	15.42	18.26	22.38	26.34	28.90	30.16	32.03	33.86	37.42	40.88
1.6667	20.00	11.32	13.98	18.26	21.56	26.34	30.91	33.86	35.30	37.42	39.51	43.56	47.47
1.50	18.00	12.51	15.42	20.11	23.71	28.90	33.86	37.03	38.59	40.88	43.12	47.47	51.65
1.25	15.00	14.85	18.26	23.71	27.89	33.86	39.51	43.12	44.88	47.47	49.99	54.88	59.54
1.00	12.00	18.26	22.38	28.90	33.86	40.88	47.47	51.65	53.68	56.65	59.54	65.11	70.40
0.9167	11.00	19.77	24.20	31.18	36.46	43.92	50.90	55.31	57.45	60.58	63.62	69.45	74.99
0.8333	10.00	21.57	26.34	33.86	39.51	47.47	54.88	59.54	61.80	65.11	68.31	74.45	80.25
0.75	9.00	23.71	28.90	37.03	43.12	51.65	59.54	64.50	66.90	70.40	73.78	80.25	86.35
0.6667	8.00	26.34	32.03	40.88	47.47	56.65	65.11	70.40	72.95	76.66	80.25	87.09	93.52
0.6250	7.50	27.89	33.86	43.12	49.99	59.54	68.31	73.78	76.42	80.25	83.95	90.99	97.60
0.5833	7.00	29.63	35.91	45.63	52.81	62.76	71.86	77.53	80.25	84.21	88.03	95.28	102.08
0.50	6.00	33.86	40.88	51.65	59.54	70.40	80.25	86.35	89.27	93.52	97.60	105.32	112.52

11.50% Interest

Monthly Payment	Annual Constant	20%	25%	33.3%	40%	50%	60%	66.7%	70%	75%	80%	90%	100%
2.50%	30.00%	7.67	9.51	12.49	14.82	18.23	21.52	23.66	24.71	26.27	27.81	30.82	33.75
2.0833	25.00	9.14	11.31	14.82	17.55	21.52	25.34	27.81	29.02	30.82	32.59	36.03	39.36
2.00	24.00	9.51	11.76	15.40	18.23	22.33	26.27	28.82	30.08	31.93	33.75	37.29	40.72
1.6667	20.00	11.31	13.96	18.22	21.52	26.27	30.82	33.75	35.18	37.29	39.36	43.39	47.26
1.50	18.00	12.49	15.40	20.07	23.66	28.82	33.75	36.90	38.45	40.72	42.95	47.26	51.41
1.25	15.00	14.82	18.23	23.66	27.81	33.75	39.36	42.95	44.70	47.26	49.77	54.61	59.24
1.00	12.00	18.23	22.33	28.82	33.75	40.72	47.26	51.41	53.42	56.37	59.24	64.74	69.98
0.9167	11.00	19.73	24.14	31.09	36.34	43.75	50.67	55.04	57.16	60.26	63.27	69.05	74.52
0.8333	10.00	21.52	26.27	33.75	39.36	47.26	54.61	59.24	61.47	64.74	67.92	73.99	79.72
0.75	9.00	23.66	28.82	36.90	42.95	51.41	59.24	64.15	66.52	69.98	73.33	79.72	85.75
0.6667	8.00	26.27	31.93	40.72	47.26	56.37	64.74	69.98	72.50	76.17	79.72	86.48	92.83
0.6250	7.50	27.81	33.75	42.95	49.77	59.24	67.92	73.33	75.93	79.72	83.38	90.33	96.86
0.5833	7.00	29.54	35.79	45.44	52.56	62.42	71.43	77.03	79.72	83.64	87.41	94.57	101.28
0.50	6.00	33.75	40.72	51.41	59.24	69.98	79.72	85.75	88.64	92.83	96.86	104.47	111.58

Entry is months until percentage selected is achieved.

Time When a Given Sinking Fund Balance Occurs

11.75% Interest Rate

Monthly Payment	Annual Constant	Percentage of Total Fund											
		20%	25%	33.3%	40%	50%	60%	66.7%	70%	75%	80%	90%	100%
2.50%	30.00%	7.67	9.50	12.48	14.80	18.19	21.47	23.60	24.65	26.21	27.74	30.73	33.64
2.0833	25.00	9.13	11.30	14.80	17.52	21.47	25.28	27.74	28.94	30.73	32.48	35.91	39.22
2.00	24.00	9.50	11.74	15.37	18.19	22.28	26.21	28.74	29.99	31.83	33.64	37.16	40.57
1.6667	20.00	11.30	13.94	18.19	21.47	26.20	30.73	33.64	35.06	37.16	39.22	43.22	47.06
1.50	18.00	12.48	15.37	20.03	23.60	28.74	33.64	36.78	38.31	40.57	42.78	47.06	51.17
1.25	15.00	14.80	18.19	23.60	27.74	33.64	39.22	42.78	44.51	47.06	49.55	54.35	58.93
1.00	12.00	18.19	22.28	28.74	33.64	40.57	47.06	51.17	53.17	56.09	58.93	64.39	69.57
0.9167	11.00	19.70	24.08	31.00	36.21	43.57	50.44	54.77	56.87	59.94	62.93	68.65	74.06
0.8333	10.00	21.47	26.21	33.64	39.22	47.06	54.35	58.93	61.15	64.39	67.53	73.53	79.21
0.75	9.00	23.60	28.74	36.78	42.78	51.17	58.93	63.80	66.14	69.57	72.88	79.21	85.16
0.6667	8.00	26.21	31.83	40.57	47.06	56.09	64.39	69.57	72.06	75.70	79.21	85.88	92.15
0.6250	7.50	27.74	33.64	42.78	49.55	58.93	67.53	72.88	75.46	79.21	82.82	89.69	96.13
0.5833	7.00	29.46	35.67	45.25	52.32	62.08	71.00	76.54	79.21	83.07	86.80	93.88	100.49
0.50	6.00	33.64	40.57	51.17	58.93	69.57	79.21	85.16	88.02	92.15	96.13	103.65	110.65

12.00% Interest

Monthly Payment	Annual Constant	20%	25%	33.3%	40%	50%	60%	66.7%	70%	75%	80%	90%	100%
2.50%	30.00%	7.66	9.49	12.46	14.78	18.16	21.43	23.55	24.59	26.14	27.66	30.64	33.53
2.0833	25.00	9.13	11.28	14.78	17.49	21.43	25.21	27.66	28.86	30.64	32.38	35.79	39.08
2.00	24.00	9.49	11.73	15.35	18.16	22.23	26.14	28.66	29.90	31.73	33.53	37.03	40.42
1.6667	20.00	11.28	13.92	18.16	21.43	26.14	30.64	33.53	34.95	37.03	39.08	43.04	46.86
1.50	18.00	12.46	15.35	19.99	23.55	28.66	33.53	36.65	38.17	40.42	42.61	46.86	50.94
1.25	15.00	14.78	18.16	23.55	27.66	33.53	39.08	42.61	44.33	46.86	49.33	54.09	58.63
1.00	12.00	18.16	22.23	28.66	33.53	40.42	46.86	50.94	52.92	55.81	58.63	64.03	69.16
0.9167	11.00	19.66	24.02	30.90	36.09	43.40	50.21	54.51	56.59	59.63	62.59	68.25	73.61
0.8333	10.00	21.43	26.14	33.53	39.08	46.86	54.09	58.63	60.83	64.03	67.14	73.08	78.70
0.75	9.00	23.55	28.66	36.65	42.61	50.94	58.63	63.45	65.77	69.16	72.44	78.70	84.58
0.6667	8.00	26.14	31.73	40.42	46.86	55.81	64.03	69.16	71.63	75.23	78.70	85.30	91.49
0.6250	7.50	27.66	33.53	42.61	49.33	58.63	67.14	72.44	74.99	78.70	82.27	89.06	95.41
0.5833	7.00	29.37	35.55	45.06	52.07	61.75	70.58	76.06	78.70	82.52	86.20	93.19	99.72
0.50	6.00	33.53	40.42	50.94	58.63	69.16	78.70	84.58	87.40	91.49	95.41	102.83	109.74

12.25% Interest

Monthly Payment	Annual Constant	20%	25%	33.3%	40%	50%	60%	66.7%	70%	75%	80%	90%	100%
2.50%	30.00%	7.65	9.48	12.45	14.76	18.12	21.38	23.49	24.53	26.07	27.59	30.55	33.42
2.0833	25.00	9.12	11.27	14.76	17.46	21.38	25.15	27.59	28.78	30.55	32.28	35.67	38.94
2.00	24.00	9.48	11.71	15.33	18.12	22.18	26.07	28.58	29.82	31.64	33.42	36.90	40.27
1.6667	20.00	11.27	13.90	18.12	21.38	26.07	30.55	33.42	34.83	36.90	38.93	42.87	46.66
1.50	18.00	12.45	15.33	19.95	23.49	28.58	33.42	36.52	38.04	40.27	42.44	46.66	50.71
1.25	15.00	14.76	18.12	23.49	27.59	33.42	38.94	42.44	44.15	46.66	49.11	53.83	58.33
1.00	12.00	18.12	22.18	28.58	33.42	40.27	46.66	50.71	52.67	55.54	58.33	63.69	68.76
0.9167	11.00	19.62	23.97	30.81	35.97	43.23	49.99	54.25	56.31	59.33	62.25	67.86	73.16
0.8333	10.00	21.38	26.07	33.42	38.94	46.66	53.83	58.33	60.51	63.69	66.76	72.64	78.19
0.75	9.00	23.49	28.58	36.52	42.44	50.71	58.33	63.10	65.41	68.76	72.01	78.19	84.01
0.6667	8.00	26.07	31.64	40.27	46.66	55.54	63.68	68.76	71.21	74.76	78.19	84.72	90.84
0.6250	7.50	27.59	33.42	42.44	49.11	58.33	66.76	72.01	74.53	78.19	81.73	88.43	94.71
0.5833	7.00	29.29	35.43	44.88	51.83	61.43	70.17	75.59	78.19	81.97	85.62	92.52	98.97
0.50	6.00	33.42	40.27	50.71	58.33	68.76	78.19	84.01	86.80	90.84	94.71	102.04	108.86

12.50% Interest

Monthly Payment	Annual Constant	20%	25%	33.3%	40%	50%	60%	66.7%	70%	75%	80%	90%	100%
2.50%	30.00%	7.65	9.47	12.43	14.73	18.09	21.33	23.44	24.47	26.00	27.51	30.46	33.32
2.0833	25.00	9.11	11.26	14.73	17.43	21.33	25.09	27.51	28.70	30.46	32.18	35.55	38.80
2.00	24.00	9.47	11.70	15.30	18.09	22.13	26.00	28.50	29.73	31.54	33.32	36.78	40.12
1.6667	20.00	11.26	13.88	18.09	21.33	26.00	30.46	33.32	34.72	36.78	38.79	42.71	46.47
1.50	18.00	12.43	15.30	19.91	23.44	28.50	33.32	36.40	37.90	40.12	42.28	46.47	50.48
1.25	15.00	14.73	18.09	23.44	27.51	33.32	38.80	42.28	43.98	46.47	48.90	53.58	58.04
1.00	12.00	18.09	22.13	28.50	33.32	40.12	46.47	50.48	52.43	55.27	58.04	63.34	68.37
0.9167	11.00	19.58	23.91	30.72	35.85	43.06	49.76	53.99	56.04	59.03	61.92	67.47	72.72
0.8333	10.00	21.33	26.00	33.32	38.80	46.47	53.58	58.04	60.20	63.34	66.39	72.21	77.70
0.75	9.00	23.44	28.50	36.40	42.28	50.48	58.04	62.77	65.05	68.37	71.58	77.70	83.45
0.6667	8.00	26.00	31.54	40.12	46.47	55.27	63.34	68.37	70.79	74.31	77.70	84.15	90.20
0.6250	7.50	27.51	33.32	42.28	48.90	58.04	66.39	71.58	74.08	77.70	81.19	87.82	94.03
0.5833	7.00	29.21	35.31	44.70	51.60	61.10	69.76	75.13	77.70	81.44	85.04	91.86	98.22
0.50	6.00	33.32	40.12	50.48	58.04	68.37	77.70	83.45	86.21	90.20	94.03	101.26	107.99

15.00% Interest

Monthly Payment	Annual Constant	20%	25%	33.3%	40%	50%	60%	66.7%	70%	75%	80%	90%	100%
2.50%	30.00%	7.58	9.37	12.27	14.51	17.76	20.89	22.91	23.90	25.36	26.80	29.60	32.31
2.0833	25.00	9.02	11.12	14.51	17.12	20.89	24.49	26.80	27.93	29.60	31.24	34.41	37.46
2.00	24.00	9.37	11.55	15.06	17.76	21.65	25.36	27.75	28.91	30.63	32.31	35.57	38.70
1.6667	20.00	11.12	13.68	17.76	20.89	25.36	29.60	32.31	33.63	35.57	37.46	41.12	44.62
1.50	18.00	12.27	15.06	19.52	22.91	27.75	32.31	35.21	36.62	38.70	40.72	44.62	48.34
1.25	15.00	14.51	17.76	22.91	26.80	32.31	37.46	40.72	42.30	44.62	46.87	51.20	55.30
1.00	12.00	17.76	21.65	27.75	32.31	38.70	44.62	48.34	50.14	52.76	55.30	60.15	64.72
0.9167	11.00	19.20	23.36	29.85	34.69	41.45	47.68	51.58	53.46	56.20	58.86	63.91	68.67
0.8333	10.00	20.89	25.36	32.31	37.46	44.62	51.20	55.30	57.27	60.15	62.93	68.21	73.16
0.75	9.00	22.91	27.75	35.21	40.72	48.34	55.30	59.62	61.70	64.72	67.64	73.16	78.33
0.6667	8.00	25.36	30.63	38.70	44.62	52.76	60.15	64.72	66.92	70.10	73.16	78.96	84.36
0.6250	7.50	26.80	32.31	40.72	46.87	55.30	62.93	67.64	69.89	73.16	76.30	82.24	87.77
0.5833	7.00	28.41	34.19	42.97	49.37	58.11	65.99	70.84	73.16	76.52	79.75	85.84	91.50
0.50	6.00	32.31	38.70	48.34	55.30	64.72	73.16	78.33	80.80	84.36	87.77	94.19	100.13

Entry is months until percentage selected is achieved.

Deposit to Obtain a Number of Payments of 1
Loan Amortized by a Number of Payments of 1

Draw Delay of 1 Month — Interest Rate

Term	5.50%	6.00%	6.50%	6.75%	7.00%	7.25%	7.50%	7.75%	8.00%	8.25%	8.50%	8.75%
6	5.90491	5.89638	5.88787	5.88362	5.87938	5.87514	5.87091	5.86668	5.86245	5.85823	5.85402	5.84980
12	11.65002	11.61893	11.58797	11.57253	11.55712	11.54174	11.52639	11.51107	11.49578	11.48052	11.46529	11.45009
24	22.67797	22.56287	22.44858	22.39174	22.33510	22.27866	22.22242	22.16638	22.11054	22.05490	21.99945	21.94420
30	27.96912	27.79405	27.62051	27.53430	27.44847	27.36301	27.27792	27.19320	27.10885	27.02486	26.94124	26.85798
36	33.11708	32.87102	32.62749	32.50667	32.38646	32.26688	32.14791	32.02956	31.91181	31.79466	31.67811	31.56216
48	42.99878	42.58032	42.16749	41.96316	41.76020	41.55861	41.35837	41.15948	40.96191	40.76567	40.57074	40.37712
60	52.35284	51.72556	51.10868	50.80407	50.50199	50.20241	49.90531	49.61066	49.31843	49.02862	48.74118	48.45611
72	61.20743	60.33951	59.48865	59.06949	58.65444	58.24347	57.83652	57.43356	57.03452	56.63938	56.24808	55.86058
84	69.58922	68.45304	67.34262	66.79686	66.25729	65.72382	65.19638	64.67488	64.15926	63.64943	63.14532	62.64686
90	73.61075	72.33130	71.08276	70.46982	69.86428	69.26605	68.67502	68.09110	67.51418	66.94416	66.38096	65.82447
96	77.52345	76.09522	74.70362	74.02122	73.34757	72.68255	72.02602	71.37787	70.73797	70.10619	69.48243	68.86655
120	92.14358	90.07345	88.06850	87.08972	86.12635	85.17812	84.24474	83.32595	82.42148	81.53107	80.65447	79.79142
150	108.30065	105.34998	102.51298	101.13553	99.78461	98.45964	97.16003	95.88522	94.63465	93.40779	92.20411	91.02310
180	122.38652	118.50351	114.79641	113.00591	111.25596	109.54548	107.87343	106.23879	104.64059	103.07787	101.54969	100.05517
240	145.37265	139.58077	134.12500	131.51596	128.98251	126.52206	124.13213	121.81031	119.55429	117.36185	115.23084	113.15920
300	162.84325	155.20686	148.10269	144.73633	141.48690	138.34954	135.31961	132.39268	129.56452	126.83110	124.18857	121.63325
360	176.12176	166.79161	158.21082	154.17868	150.30757	146.58968	143.01763	139.58444	136.28349	133.10854	130.05364	127.11319

Term	9.00%	9.25%	9.50%	9.75%	10.00%	10.25%	10.50%	10.75%	11.00%	11.25%	11.50%	12.00%
6	5.84560	5.84140	5.83720	5.83301	5.82882	5.82463	5.82045	5.81628	5.81211	5.80794	5.80378	5.79548
12	11.43491	11.41977	11.40465	11.38957	11.37451	11.35948	11.34448	11.32951	11.31456	11.29965	11.28476	11.25508
24	21.88915	21.83428	21.77962	21.72514	21.67085	21.61676	21.56286	21.50914	21.45562	21.40228	21.34913	21.24339
30	26.77508	26.69254	26.61035	26.52852	26.44704	26.36592	26.28513	26.20471	26.12462	26.04488	25.96548	25.80771
36	31.44681	31.33204	31.21786	31.10426	30.99124	30.87879	30.76692	30.65561	30.54487	30.43470	30.32508	30.10751
48	40.18478	39.99373	39.80395	39.61543	39.42816	39.24214	39.05734	38.87378	38.69142	38.51027	38.33032	37.97396
60	48.17337	47.89295	47.61483	47.33897	47.06537	46.79399	46.52483	46.25785	45.99303	45.73037	45.46982	44.95504
72	55.47685	55.09683	54.72049	54.34778	53.97867	53.61310	53.25106	52.89248	52.53735	52.18561	51.83722	51.15039
84	62.15396	61.66657	61.18460	60.70799	60.23667	59.77056	59.30961	58.85375	58.40290	57.95701	57.51602	56.64845
90	65.27461	64.73128	64.19439	63.66385	63.13958	62.62149	62.10949	61.60350	61.10344	60.60923	60.12078	59.16088
96	68.25844	67.65799	67.06509	66.47963	65.90149	65.33057	64.76677	64.20998	63.66010	63.11703	62.58068	61.52770
120	78.94169	78.10503	77.28121	76.47000	75.67116	74.88449	74.10976	73.34676	72.59528	71.85511	71.12606	69.70052
150	89.86425	88.72707	87.61110	86.51585	85.44089	84.38575	83.35003	82.33328	81.33509	80.35507	79.39283	77.52012
180	98.59341	97.16357	95.76483	94.39638	93.05744	91.74725	90.46508	89.21021	87.98194	86.77960	85.60253	83.32166
240	111.14495	109.18618	107.28104	105.42775	103.62462	101.86999	100.16227	98.49995	96.88154	95.30562	93.77084	90.81942
300	119.16162	116.77034	114.45620	112.21614	110.04723	107.94668	105.91182	103.94009	102.02904	100.17636	98.37979	94.94655
360	124.28187	121.55462	118.92668	116.39351	113.95082	111.59453	109.32077	107.12587	105.00635	102.95890	100.98037	97.21833

Draw Delay of 12 Months — Interest Rate

Term	5.50%	6.00%	6.50%	6.75%	7.00%	7.25%	7.50%	7.75%	8.00%	8.25%	8.50%	8.75%
6	5.61524	5.58161	5.54819	5.53157	5.51500	5.49848	5.48202	5.46561	5.44925	5.43295	5.41669	5.40050
12	11.07850	10.99865	10.91944	10.88007	10.84085	10.80179	10.76288	10.72413	10.68553	10.64708	10.60878	10.57064
24	21.56545	21.35834	21.15349	21.05189	20.95085	20.85035	20.75041	20.65100	20.55213	20.45380	20.35600	20.25873
30	26.59703	26.31026	26.02704	25.88674	25.74731	25.60874	25.47102	25.33416	25.19814	25.06296	24.92861	24.79509
36	31.49244	31.11619	30.74516	30.56158	30.37927	30.19822	30.01843	29.83988	29.66257	29.48649	29.31162	29.13796
48	40.88937	40.30716	39.73478	39.45222	39.17205	38.89425	38.61878	38.34564	38.07480	37.80624	37.53993	37.27586
60	49.78455	48.96418	48.16014	47.76413	47.37206	46.98389	46.59957	46.21907	45.84233	45.46932	45.10000	44.73432
72	58.20475	57.11828	56.05666	55.53497	55.01925	54.50943	54.00542	53.50716	53.01457	52.52757	52.04610	51.57008
84	66.17536	64.79607	63.45753	62.79906	62.15089	61.51020	60.87776	60.25344	59.63714	59.02873	58.42809	57.83512
90	69.99961	68.46988	66.98189	66.25314	65.53434	64.82533	64.12597	63.43611	62.75559	62.08427	61.42201	60.76867
96	73.72036	72.03286	70.39386	69.59203	68.80175	68.02280	67.25501	66.49819	65.75216	65.01675	64.29178	63.57709
120	87.62327	85.26487	82.98770	81.87856	80.78855	79.71727	78.66435	77.62944	76.61218	75.61222	74.62923	73.66286
150	102.98771	99.72585	96.59886	95.08392	93.60031	92.14729	90.72413	89.33011	87.96454	86.62674	85.31606	84.03186
180	116.38257	112.17719	108.17364	106.22440	104.36071	102.52241	100.72787	98.97587	97.26523	95.59481	93.96349	92.37020
240	138.24106	132.12923	126.38713	123.64648	120.98863	118.41061	115.90959	113.48285	111.12777	108.84182	106.62259	104.46775
300	154.85459	146.92112	139.55843	136.07580	132.71805	129.47982	126.35601	123.34177	120.43245	117.62364	114.91114	112.29092
360	167.48170	157.88742	149.08340	144.95315	140.99204	137.19167	133.54411	130.04187	126.67785	123.44536	120.33807	117.34997

Term	9.00%	9.25%	9.50%	9.75%	10.00%	10.25%	10.50%	10.75%	11.00%	11.25%	11.50%	12.00%
6	5.38435	5.36826	5.35221	5.33623	5.32029	5.30440	5.28857	5.27278	5.25705	5.24137	5.22573	5.19462
12	10.53264	10.49479	10.45710	10.41955	10.38215	10.34490	10.30779	10.27083	10.23401	10.19734	10.16082	10.08819
24	20.16198	20.06576	19.97006	19.87487	19.78020	19.68604	19.59238	19.49924	19.40659	19.31444	19.22278	19.04095
30	24.66239	24.53051	24.39943	24.26916	24.13969	24.01102	23.88313	23.75603	23.62970	23.50414	23.37936	23.13206
36	28.96549	28.79422	28.62412	28.45520	28.28743	28.12082	27.95535	27.79102	27.62781	27.46572	27.30474	26.98607
48	37.01400	36.75433	36.49684	36.24150	35.98828	35.73718	35.48818	35.24124	34.99636	34.75350	34.51267	34.03696
60	44.37225	44.01374	43.65875	43.30725	42.95919	42.61454	42.27326	41.93531	41.60066	41.26926	40.94109	40.29427
72	51.09944	50.63412	50.17404	49.71914	49.26934	48.82460	48.38483	47.94998	47.51998	47.09478	46.67430	45.84731
84	57.24970	56.67173	56.10108	55.53767	54.98137	54.43210	53.88974	53.35420	52.82537	52.30317	51.78750	50.77535
90	60.12411	59.48820	58.86080	58.24179	57.63102	57.02839	56.43375	55.84700	55.26801	54.69666	54.13283	53.02730
96	62.87250	62.17786	61.49299	60.81775	60.15197	59.49551	58.84821	58.20992	57.58051	56.95982	56.34772	55.14874
120	72.71279	71.77871	70.86031	69.95727	69.06930	68.19611	67.33740	66.49291	65.66236	64.84547	64.04200	62.47423
150	82.77350	81.54039	80.33193	79.14755	77.98667	76.84876	75.73327	74.63969	73.56752	72.51625	71.48540	69.48312
180	90.81389	89.29356	87.80822	86.35691	84.93872	83.55275	82.19813	80.87401	79.57958	78.31404	77.07663	74.68318
240	102.37505	100.34236	98.36760	96.44878	94.58398	92.77137	91.00917	89.29568	87.62646	86.00834	84.43138	81.40360
300	109.75917	107.31222	104.94661	102.65901	100.44625	98.30531	96.23330	94.22747	92.28518	90.40392	88.58129	85.10285
360	114.47540	111.70899	109.04567	106.48061	104.00928	101.62735	99.33073	97.11556	94.97814	92.91501	90.92286	87.13910

Entry is the multiple of the desired payment which will fund the number of payments selected.

Deposit to Obtain a Number of Payments of 1
Loan Amortized by a Number of Payments of 1

Draw Delay of 24 Months

Term	5.50%	6.00%	6.50%	6.75%	7.00%	Interest Rate 7.25%	7.50%	7.75%	8.00%	8.25%	8.50%	8.75%
6	5.31540	5.25734	5.19994	5.17149	5.14320	5.11506	5.08709	5.05928	5.03163	5.00413	4.97679	4.94961
12	10.48695	10.35969	10.23405	10.17182	10.11000	10.04857	9.98752	9.92687	9.86660	9.80672	9.74722	9.68809
24	20.41394	20.11754	19.82572	19.68151	19.53842	19.39643	19.25555	19.11576	18.97705	18.83941	18.70284	18.56732
30	25.17686	24.78178	24.39337	24.20163	24.01151	23.82301	23.63609	23.45076	23.26699	23.08478	22.90410	22.72494
36	29.81087	29.30851	28.81534	28.57216	28.33120	28.09246	27.85590	27.62152	27.38928	27.15916	26.93115	26.70522
48	38.70605	37.96553	37.24070	36.88406	36.53121	36.18210	35.83669	35.49494	35.15681	34.82225	34.49122	34.16369
60	47.12625	46.11963	45.13722	44.65490	44.17840	43.70764	43.24254	42.78303	42.32904	41.88050	41.43732	40.99945
72	55.09686	53.80001	52.53809	51.91989	51.31004	50.70841	50.11487	49.52931	48.95161	48.38165	47.81931	47.26449
84	62.64186	61.03421	59.47442	58.71197	57.96090	57.22101	56.49212	55.77406	55.06663	54.36967	53.68300	53.00645
90	66.26192	64.49215	62.77756	61.94036	61.11624	60.30498	59.50634	58.72012	57.94609	57.18405	56.43378	55.69508
96	69.78400	67.84814	65.97536	65.06191	64.16337	63.27948	62.40996	61.55456	60.71301	59.88507	59.07049	58.26903
120	82.94454	80.31144	77.77871	76.54864	75.34206	74.15847	72.99738	71.85829	70.74074	69.64426	68.56840	67.51273
150	97.48859	93.93231	90.53553	88.89438	87.29010	85.72174	84.18837	82.68910	81.22306	79.78942	78.38733	77.01602
180	110.16821	105.66029	101.38378	99.32801	97.32507	95.37338	93.47144	91.61777	89.81096	88.04964	86.33248	84.65819
240	130.85955	124.45323	118.45405	115.59766	112.83199	110.15368	107.55947	105.04627	102.61110	100.25109	97.96351	95.74571
300	146.58599	138.38579	130.79861	127.21788	123.77065	120.45102	117.25333	114.17225	111.20268	108.33978	105.57892	102.91573
360	158.53887	148.71501	139.72571	135.51736	131.48684	127.62511	123.92360	120.37425	116.96945	113.70200	110.56512	107.55239

Term	9.00%	9.25%	9.50%	9.75%	10.00%	10.25%	10.50%	10.75%	11.00%	11.25%	11.50%	12.00%
6	4.92258	4.89570	4.86898	4.84241	4.81599	4.78972	4.76360	4.73763	4.71180	4.68613	4.66059	4.60996
12	9.62934	9.57097	9.51296	9.45532	9.39805	9.34114	9.28460	9.22841	9.17257	9.11710	9.06197	8.95276
24	18.43285	18.29942	18.16702	18.03565	17.90528	17.77592	17.64756	17.52019	17.39380	17.26838	17.14392	16.89788
30	22.54730	22.37115	22.19649	22.02329	21.85155	21.68126	21.51239	21.34494	21.17890	21.01425	20.85098	20.52853
36	26.48136	26.25954	26.03974	25.82195	25.60614	25.39229	25.18039	24.97041	24.76234	24.55616	24.35185	23.94877
48	33.83961	33.51895	33.20165	32.88770	32.57704	32.26965	31.96547	31.66448	31.36664	31.07192	30.78027	30.20607
60	40.56680	40.13933	39.71694	39.29959	38.88719	38.47970	38.07704	37.67915	37.28597	36.89743	36.51349	35.75912
72	46.71706	46.17693	45.64398	45.11812	44.59922	44.08720	43.58195	43.08337	42.59136	42.10583	41.62668	40.68716
84	52.33986	51.68306	51.03589	50.39820	49.76982	49.15061	48.54042	47.93909	47.34649	46.76248	46.18690	45.06055
90	54.96776	54.25161	53.54645	52.85208	52.16832	51.49499	50.83190	50.17889	49.53578	48.90241	48.27860	47.05904
96	57.48044	56.70450	55.94098	55.18966	54.45031	53.72272	53.00060	52.30199	51.60844	50.92582	50.25396	48.94171
120	66.47681	65.46022	64.46255	63.48341	62.52239	61.57911	60.65321	59.74431	58.85207	57.97612	57.11613	55.44271
150	75.67469	74.36261	73.07902	71.82321	70.59450	69.39221	68.21567	67.06425	65.93733	64.83430	63.75457	61.66275
180	83.02552	81.43328	79.88029	78.36542	76.88759	75.44557	74.03800	72.66583	71.32584	70.01791	68.74112	66.27703
240	93.59518	91.50949	89.48630	87.52338	85.61859	83.76986	81.97522	80.23275	78.54063	76.89711	75.30049	72.24156
300	100.34602	97.86581	95.47132	93.15893	90.92520	88.76686	86.68078	84.66399	82.71365	80.82705	79.00160	75.52445
360	104.65778	101.87554	99.20028	96.62687	94.15049	91.76656	89.47075	87.25896	85.12731	83.07213	81.08995	77.33152

Draw Delay of 36 Months

Term	5.50%	6.00%	6.50%	6.75%	7.00%	Interest Rate 7.25%	7.50%	7.75%	8.00%	8.25%	8.50%	8.75%
6	5.03158	4.95192	4.87355	4.83485	4.79646	4.75838	4.72062	4.68316	4.64601	4.60916	4.57261	4.53636
12	9.92699	9.75785	9.59167	9.50968	9.42842	9.34787	9.26802	9.18888	9.11044	9.03269	8.95562	8.87923
24	19.32392	18.94882	18.58130	18.40033	18.22120	18.04389	17.86838	17.69465	17.52267	17.35244	17.18393	17.01713
30	23.83252	23.34209	22.86224	22.62621	22.39274	22.16180	21.93335	21.70738	21.48384	21.26273	21.04400	20.82763
36	28.21910	27.60584	27.00666	26.71224	26.42121	26.13353	25.84916	25.56807	25.29020	25.01553	24.74400	24.47560
48	36.63930	35.75994	34.90317	34.48308	34.06840	33.65907	33.25502	32.85616	32.46244	32.07378	31.69010	31.31136
60	44.60991	43.44032	42.30404	41.74807	41.20004	40.65984	40.12735	39.60244	39.08501	38.57493	38.07209	37.57639
72	52.15491	50.67452	49.24037	48.54014	47.85090	47.17244	46.50460	45.84719	45.20003	44.56295	43.93579	43.31836
84	59.29704	57.48845	55.74132	54.89008	54.05337	53.23091	52.42243	51.62768	50.84641	50.07835	49.32327	48.58093
90	62.72380	60.74550	58.83713	57.90832	56.99600	56.09983	55.21951	54.35473	53.50519	52.67059	51.85065	51.04509
96	66.05782	63.90653	61.83421	60.82667	59.83770	58.86691	57.91395	56.97845	56.06005	55.15843	54.27323	53.40413
120	78.51564	75.64577	72.89669	71.56567	70.26276	68.98730	67.73665	66.51618	65.31927	64.14734	62.99980	61.87608
150	92.28310	88.47535	84.85278	83.10776	81.40531	79.74424	78.12344	76.54180	74.99825	73.49175	72.02131	70.58594
180	104.28568	99.52199	95.02011	92.86221	90.76375	88.72287	86.73776	84.80669	82.92798	81.10001	79.32121	77.59006
240	123.87219	117.22316	111.01891	108.07277	105.22525	102.47251	99.81089	97.23689	94.74713	92.33842	90.00765	87.75188
300	138.75890	130.34632	122.58862	118.93657	115.42647	112.05180	108.80641	105.68442	102.68027	99.78867	97.00460	94.32327
360	150.07354	140.07546	130.95539	126.69579	122.62245	118.72564	114.99615	111.42535	108.00508	104.72766	101.58585	98.57282

Term	9.00%	9.25%	9.50%	9.75%	10.00%	10.25%	10.50%	10.75%	11.00%	11.25%	11.50%	12.00%
6	4.50041	4.46475	4.42938	4.39429	4.35949	4.32498	4.29075	4.25679	4.22311	4.18971	4.15657	4.09111
12	8.80351	8.72846	8.65406	8.58032	8.50723	8.43478	8.36297	8.29178	8.22122	8.15128	8.08196	7.94512
24	16.85202	16.68857	16.52678	16.36662	16.20808	16.05115	15.89579	15.74200	15.58977	15.43907	15.28988	14.99601
30	20.61360	20.40188	20.19244	19.98525	19.78030	19.57755	19.37698	19.17857	18.98229	18.78812	18.59604	18.21803
36	24.21027	23.94798	23.68869	23.43238	23.17899	22.92850	22.68088	22.43608	22.19407	21.95482	21.71830	21.25332
48	30.93746	30.56836	30.20398	29.84426	29.48914	29.13856	28.79244	28.45074	28.11339	27.78034	27.45152	26.80636
60	37.08772	36.60597	36.13102	35.66279	35.20117	34.74606	34.29735	33.85494	33.41879	32.98873	32.56471	31.73440
72	42.71052	42.11210	41.52309	40.94288	40.37177	39.80947	39.25582	38.71068	38.17392	37.64538	37.12494	36.10779
84	47.85110	47.13354	46.42802	45.73434	45.05226	44.38158	43.72209	43.07358	42.43586	41.80873	41.19199	39.98895
90	50.25362	49.47598	48.71191	47.96113	47.22341	46.49848	45.78611	45.08606	44.39809	43.72197	43.05748	41.76251
96	52.55081	51.71295	50.89025	50.08240	49.28910	48.51007	47.74502	46.99368	46.25577	45.53104	44.81923	43.43328
120	60.77564	59.69793	58.64243	57.60864	56.59604	55.60416	54.63252	53.68065	52.74812	51.83446	50.93927	49.20259
150	69.18469	67.81666	66.48094	65.17668	63.90302	62.65916	61.44430	60.25766	59.09852	57.96613	56.85979	54.72256
180	75.90510	74.26492	72.66815	71.11347	69.59960	68.12531	66.68940	65.29072	63.92815	62.60061	61.30707	58.81795
240	85.56829	83.45415	81.40686	79.42395	77.50301	75.64177	73.83801	72.08960	70.39465	68.75107	67.15707	64.11072
300	91.74016	89.25094	86.85151	84.53798	82.30662	80.15391	78.07648	76.07115	74.13485	72.26470	70.45792	67.02412
360	95.68213	92.90770	90.24380	87.68500	85.22620	82.86255	80.58951	78.40274	76.29817	74.27195	72.32042	68.62780

Entry is the multiple of the desired payment which will fund the number of payments selected.

Deposit to Obtain a Number of Payments of 1
Loan Amortized by a Number of Payments of 1

Draw Delay of 48 Months — Interest Rate

Term	5.50%	6.00%	6.50%	6.75%	7.00%	7.25%	7.50%	7.75%	8.00%	8.25%	8.50%	8.75%
6	4.76292	4.66424	4.56765	4.52012	4.47310	4.42658	4.38055	4.33500	4.28995	4.24537	4.20126	4.15762
12	9.39693	9.19097	8.98962	8.89065	8.79279	8.69603	8.60036	8.50576	8.41223	8.31975	8.22831	8.13790
24	18.29210	17.84799	17.41498	17.20255	16.99279	16.78567	16.58114	16.37918	16.17976	15.98284	15.78838	15.59637
30	22.55996	21.98604	21.42722	21.15335	20.88310	20.61642	20.35327	20.09360	19.83735	19.58449	19.33496	19.08873
36	26.71231	26.00209	25.31150	24.97339	24.63998	24.31121	23.98699	23.66728	23.35200	23.04109	22.73448	22.43213
48	34.68291	33.68247	32.71237	32.23838	31.77163	31.31198	30.85933	30.41356	29.97456	29.54224	29.11647	28.69716
60	42.22792	40.91667	39.64869	39.03046	38.42248	37.82458	37.23658	36.65830	36.08959	35.53026	34.98016	34.43913
72	49.37005	47.73060	46.14964	45.38040	44.62496	43.88305	43.15441	42.43880	41.73597	41.04566	40.36765	39.70170
84	56.13082	54.14868	52.24254	51.31699	50.40928	49.51905	48.64593	47.78956	46.94961	46.12574	45.31761	44.52490
90	59.37461	57.21651	55.14403	54.13875	53.15352	52.18791	51.24150	50.31387	49.40463	48.51338	47.63973	46.78332
96	62.53060	60.19390	57.95299	56.86713	55.80365	54.76204	53.74183	52.74253	51.76369	50.80485	49.86557	48.94541
120	74.32323	71.25116	68.32110	66.90707	65.52589	64.17673	62.85876	61.57121	60.31330	59.08428	57.88343	56.71003
150	87.35556	83.33540	79.52673	77.69782	75.91724	74.18357	72.49543	70.85150	69.25049	67.69115	66.17228	64.69270
180	98.71725	93.74030	89.05587	86.81730	84.64477	82.53610	80.48918	78.50196	76.57250	74.69890	72.87934	71.11205
240	117.25792	110.41312	104.05045	101.03773	98.13133	95.32697	92.62052	90.00807	87.48585	85.05028	82.69791	80.42546
300	131.34974	122.77389	114.89396	111.19434	107.64481	104.23828	100.96800	97.82759	94.81101	91.91249	89.12662	86.44820
360	142.06022	131.93782	122.73556	118.44847	114.35567	110.44674	106.71183	103.14173	99.72773	96.46165	93.33581	90.34296

Term	9.00%	9.25%	9.50%	9.75%	10.00%	10.25%	10.50%	10.75%	11.00%	11.25%	11.50%	12.00%
6	4.11445	4.07173	4.02946	3.98764	3.94627	3.90533	3.86483	3.82475	3.78510	3.74587	3.70706	3.63065
12	8.04851	7.96011	7.87272	7.78630	7.70085	7.61636	7.53282	7.45022	7.36854	7.28778	7.20793	7.05089
24	15.40676	15.21952	15.03463	14.85205	14.67176	14.49372	14.31791	14.14429	13.97285	13.80354	13.63635	13.30820
30	18.84574	18.60595	18.36932	18.13581	17.90537	17.67796	17.45354	17.23207	17.01351	16.79782	16.58496	16.16757
36	22.13395	21.83990	21.54992	21.26394	20.98191	20.70378	20.42948	20.15896	19.89217	19.62906	19.36956	18.86124
48	28.28421	27.87751	27.47696	27.08247	26.69394	26.31128	25.93439	25.56318	25.19756	24.83745	24.48276	23.78928
60	33.90701	33.38364	32.86887	32.36255	31.86454	31.37469	30.89285	30.41890	29.95269	29.49410	29.04298	28.16267
72	39.04759	38.40508	37.77396	37.15401	36.54503	35.94680	35.35912	34.78180	34.21464	33.65745	33.11003	32.04383
84	43.74730	42.98450	42.23618	41.50207	40.78187	40.07529	39.38205	38.70190	38.03455	37.37975	36.73726	35.48816
90	45.94378	45.12074	44.31386	43.52280	42.74722	41.98679	41.24119	40.51012	39.79326	39.09032	38.40100	37.06210
96	48.04396	47.16080	46.29553	45.44776	44.61710	43.80319	43.00565	42.22413	41.45827	40.70774	39.97221	38.54483
120	55.56341	54.44288	53.34779	52.27752	51.23144	50.20895	49.20947	48.23242	47.27725	46.34342	45.43041	43.66480
150	63.25129	61.84694	60.47859	59.14521	57.84581	56.57901	55.34508	54.14190	52.96900	51.82553	50.71065	48.56349
180	69.39534	67.72757	66.10717	64.53261	63.00242	61.51518	60.06953	58.66413	57.29772	55.96907	54.67698	52.19794
240	78.22979	76.10790	74.05690	72.07404	70.15669	68.30233	66.50854	64.77302	63.09354	61.46798	59.89433	56.89500
300	83.87235	81.39441	79.00997	76.71481	74.50498	72.37666	70.32628	68.35042	66.44582	64.60939	62.83821	59.48050
360	87.47626	84.72928	82.09597	79.57061	77.14781	74.82249	72.58985	70.44537	68.38477	66.40401	64.49928	60.90369

Draw Delay of 60 Months — Interest Rate

Term	5.50%	6.00%	6.50%	6.75%	7.00%	7.25%	7.50%	7.75%	8.00%	8.25%	8.50%	8.75%
6	4.50860	4.39327	4.28095	4.22588	4.17154	4.11790	4.06497	4.01273	3.96117	3.91029	3.86007	3.81050
12	8.89517	8.65702	8.42536	8.31191	8.20001	8.08964	7.98079	7.87342	7.76753	7.66309	7.56007	7.45847
24	17.31538	16.81112	16.32188	16.08275	15.84720	15.61518	15.38664	15.16152	14.93977	14.72133	14.50617	14.29422
30	21.35535	20.70877	20.08227	19.77636	19.47523	19.17881	18.88702	18.59979	18.31705	18.03871	17.76472	17.49501
36	25.28598	24.49151	23.72274	23.34774	22.97884	22.61595	22.25897	21.90780	21.56233	21.22249	20.88816	20.55926
48	32.83099	31.72570	30.65907	30.13981	29.62969	29.12855	28.63622	28.15254	27.67736	27.21051	26.75185	26.30123
60	39.97312	38.53963	37.16002	36.48975	35.83217	35.18702	34.55406	33.93304	33.32373	32.72591	32.13934	31.56380
72	46.73389	44.95771	43.25291	42.42634	41.61650	40.82302	40.04557	39.28380	38.53738	37.80599	37.08930	36.38700
84	53.13367	51.00293	48.96337	47.97648	47.01086	46.06602	45.14148	44.23677	43.35146	42.48510	41.63725	40.80751
90	56.20424	53.89254	51.68294	50.61457	49.57010	48.54878	47.55006	46.57342	45.61833	44.68428	43.77079	42.87737
96	59.19172	56.69695	54.31539	53.16534	52.04156	50.94341	49.87027	48.82153	47.79660	46.79490	45.81586	44.85895
120	70.35467	67.11184	64.03271	62.55172	61.10836	59.70160	58.33042	56.99386	55.69097	54.42084	53.18257	51.97530
150	82.69113	78.49406	74.53498	72.64005	70.79917	69.01065	67.27287	65.58423	63.94323	62.34838	60.79826	59.29149
180	93.44615	88.29449	83.46600	81.16589	78.93832	76.78075	74.69074	72.66594	70.70410	68.80302	66.96063	65.17489
240	110.99682	103.99871	97.51940	94.46063	91.51566	88.67969	85.94814	83.31666	80.78106	78.33738	75.98181	73.71072
300	124.33620	115.64138	107.68228	103.95609	100.38777	96.96960	93.69427	90.55486	87.54483	84.65797	81.88842	79.23062
360	134.47479	124.27294	115.03168	110.73801	106.64621	102.74514	99.02432	95.47393	92.08474	88.84807	85.75578	82.80020

Term	9.00%	9.25%	9.50%	9.75%	10.00%	10.25%	10.50%	10.75%	11.00%	11.25%	11.50%	12.00%
6	3.76158	3.71330	3.66565	3.61863	3.57221	3.52640	3.48119	3.43657	3.39252	3.34906	3.30615	3.22202
12	7.35825	7.25941	7.16191	7.06575	6.97091	6.87736	6.78508	6.69407	6.60430	6.51576	6.42842	6.25731
24	14.08545	13.87979	13.67720	13.47764	13.28106	13.08741	12.89665	12.70874	12.52363	12.34127	12.16164	11.81035
30	17.22949	16.96812	16.71082	16.45752	16.20816	15.96269	15.72103	15.48313	15.24892	15.01835	14.79137	14.34790
36	20.23570	19.91739	19.60424	19.29617	18.99309	18.69491	18.40156	18.11296	17.82902	17.54967	17.27483	16.73839
48	25.85850	25.42352	24.99615	24.57625	24.16369	23.75832	23.36003	22.96868	22.58415	22.20631	21.83505	21.11178
60	30.99908	30.44496	29.90124	29.36771	28.84418	28.33044	27.82630	27.33158	26.84610	26.36966	25.90211	24.99294
72	35.69879	35.02438	34.36347	33.71577	33.08101	32.45892	31.84923	31.25167	30.66601	30.09197	29.52933	28.43727
84	39.99545	39.20068	38.42281	37.66146	36.91625	36.18683	35.47282	34.77390	34.08973	33.41996	32.76428	31.49394
90	42.00355	41.14888	40.31290	39.49519	38.69531	37.91286	37.14742	36.39860	35.66603	34.94932	34.24810	32.89074
96	43.92362	43.00936	42.11565	41.24201	40.38796	39.55301	38.73673	37.93865	37.15835	36.39540	35.64939	34.20658
120	50.79819	49.65041	48.53119	47.43975	46.37534	45.33723	44.32473	43.33714	42.37380	41.43407	40.51731	38.75029
150	57.82674	56.40271	55.01817	53.67190	52.36275	51.08957	49.85129	48.64685	47.47523	46.33543	45.22651	43.09763
180	63.44387	61.76569	60.13857	58.56075	57.03058	55.54643	54.10677	52.71010	51.35498	50.04003	48.76390	46.32302
240	71.52066	69.40832	67.37053	65.40429	63.50671	61.67503	59.90663	58.19898	56.54967	54.95642	53.41702	50.49143
300	76.67931	74.22948	71.87641	69.61561	67.44283	65.35404	63.34540	61.41330	59.55427	57.76505	56.04253	52.78593
360	79.97413	77.27079	74.68379	72.20713	69.83516	67.56255	65.38428	63.29562	61.29212	59.36955	57.52396	54.04893

Entry is the multiple of the desired payment which will fund the number of payments selected.

Deposit to Obtain a Number of Payments of 1
Loan Amortized by a Number of Payments of 1

Draw Delay of 72 Months — Interest Rate

Term	5.50%	6.00%	6.50%	6.75%	7.00%	7.25%	7.50%	7.75%	8.00%	8.25%	8.50%	8.75%
6	4.26786	4.13805	4.01224	3.95080	3.89031	3.83076	3.77213	3.71441	3.65759	3.60165	3.54658	3.49236
12	8.42021	8.15410	7.89652	7.77084	7.64719	7.52554	7.40585	7.28809	7.17224	7.05825	6.94610	6.83576
24	16.39081	15.83448	15.29738	15.03583	14.77883	14.52631	14.27818	14.03437	13.79480	13.55940	13.32809	13.10080
30	20.21506	19.50570	18.82175	18.48901	18.16228	17.84145	17.52640	17.21704	16.91326	16.61494	16.32201	16.03435
36	23.93582	23.06868	22.23371	21.82791	21.42969	21.03891	20.65544	20.27912	19.90983	19.54743	19.19178	18.84277
48	31.07795	29.88261	28.73466	28.17785	27.63216	27.09738	26.57327	26.05962	25.55621	25.06282	24.57927	24.10534
60	37.83872	36.30069	34.82755	34.11443	33.41649	32.73338	32.06478	31.41038	30.76985	30.14290	29.52922	28.92853
72	44.23849	42.34591	40.53801	39.66458	38.81086	37.97638	37.16069	36.36335	35.58393	34.82201	34.07718	33.34904
84	50.29655	48.03993	45.89003	44.85343	43.84155	42.85377	41.88949	40.94811	40.02907	39.13181	38.25579	37.40048
90	53.20317	50.76167	48.43871	47.31979	46.22825	45.16341	44.12456	43.11104	42.12221	41.15742	40.21606	39.29753
96	56.03112	53.40316	50.90611	49.70452	48.53310	47.39106	46.27762	45.19202	44.13354	43.10144	42.09504	41.11366
120	66.59802	63.21300	60.01349	58.47989	56.98865	55.53852	54.12830	52.75680	51.42290	50.12548	48.86348	47.63587
150	78.27576	73.93397	69.85656	67.91151	66.02613	64.19844	62.42653	60.70855	59.04272	57.42732	55.86069	54.34123
180	88.45651	83.16505	78.22699	75.88235	73.61657	71.42672	69.31002	67.26379	65.28544	63.37250	61.52259	59.73342
240	105.07005	97.95694	91.39829	88.31167	85.34599	82.49593	79.75644	77.12270	74.59012	72.15432	69.81114	67.55660
300	117.69716	108.92324	100.92326	97.18902	93.61998	90.20778	86.94454	83.82280	80.83552	77.97604	75.23806	72.61564
360	127.29439	117.05334	107.81135	103.52946	99.45649	95.58058	91.89061	88.37617	85.02750	81.83542	78.79134	75.88720

Term	9.00%	9.25%	9.50%	9.75%	10.00%	10.25%	10.50%	10.75%	11.00%	11.25%	11.50%	12.00%
6	3.43898	3.38643	3.33469	3.28376	3.23361	3.18424	3.13563	3.08778	3.04066	2.99428	2.94861	2.85938
12	6.72719	6.62038	6.51529	6.41189	6.31015	6.21005	6.11157	6.01467	5.91932	5.82552	5.73322	5.55304
24	12.87745	12.65799	12.44233	12.23042	12.02218	11.81755	11.61648	11.41888	11.22472	11.03391	10.84641	10.48108
30	15.75186	15.47446	15.20205	14.93454	14.67183	14.41385	14.16049	13.91169	13.66735	13.42740	13.19174	12.73303
36	18.50025	18.16412	17.83424	17.51050	17.19278	16.88096	16.57495	16.27461	15.97985	15.69056	15.40663	14.85447
48	23.64083	23.18556	22.73933	22.30196	21.87327	21.45308	21.04121	20.63751	20.24179	19.85391	19.47369	18.73563
60	28.34054	27.76497	27.20155	26.65002	26.11011	25.58156	25.06414	24.55760	24.06170	23.57621	23.10091	22.17996
72	32.63720	31.94128	31.26090	30.59571	29.94534	29.30947	28.68774	28.07983	27.48542	26.90420	26.33586	25.23663
84	36.56537	35.74995	34.95374	34.17626	33.41705	32.67566	31.95164	31.24458	30.55405	29.87964	29.22097	27.94927
90	38.40125	37.52665	36.67318	35.84030	35.02748	34.23421	33.46001	32.70438	31.96686	31.24699	30.54432	29.18886
96	40.15665	39.22336	38.31316	37.42547	36.55968	35.71523	34.89156	34.08812	33.30440	32.53988	31.79406	30.35660
120	46.44164	45.27982	44.14946	43.04966	41.97953	40.93821	39.92487	38.93870	37.97892	37.04478	36.13554	34.38892
150	52.86741	51.43773	50.05075	48.70509	47.39941	46.13241	44.90284	43.70951	42.55125	41.42692	40.33546	38.24696
180	58.00280	56.32862	54.70885	53.14153	51.62479	50.15663	48.73591	47.36037	46.02861	44.73908	43.49029	41.10933
240	65.38692	63.29849	61.28786	59.35176	57.48706	55.69077	53.96004	52.29216	50.68452	49.13465	47.64020	44.80858
300	70.10315	67.69525	65.38691	63.17336	61.05009	59.01281	57.05747	55.18024	53.37749	51.64575	49.98177	46.84483
360	73.11540	70.46884	67.94082	65.52506	63.21565	61.00703	58.89396	56.87153	54.93509	53.08029	51.30300	47.96568

Draw Delay of 84 Months — Interest Rate

Term	5.50%	6.00%	6.50%	6.75%	7.00%	7.25%	7.50%	7.75%	8.00%	8.25%	8.50%	8.75%
6	4.03997	3.89765	3.76040	3.69362	3.62804	3.56363	3.50039	3.43828	3.37728	3.31738	3.25855	3.20078
12	7.97060	7.68039	7.40087	7.26499	7.13164	7.00077	6.87233	6.74628	6.62257	6.50115	6.38199	6.26504
24	15.51561	14.91458	14.33719	14.05707	13.78250	13.51337	13.24958	12.99103	12.73759	12.48918	12.24568	12.00701
30	19.13566	18.37252	17.64034	17.28546	16.93784	16.59734	16.26380	15.93709	15.61705	15.30355	14.99646	14.69563
36	22.65774	21.72851	20.83814	20.40701	19.98497	19.57184	19.16742	18.77152	18.38397	18.00458	17.63317	17.26958
48	29.41851	28.14659	26.93104	26.34360	25.76930	25.20784	24.65893	24.12228	23.59761	23.08465	22.58313	22.09278
60	35.81829	34.19181	32.64149	31.89374	31.16366	30.45084	29.75484	29.07526	28.41170	27.76376	27.13108	26.51328
72	41.87634	39.88583	37.99351	37.08259	36.19436	35.32823	34.48363	33.66001	32.85683	32.07356	31.30969	30.56472
84	47.61092	45.24907	43.00960	41.93368	40.88591	39.86552	38.87177	37.90393	36.96130	36.04319	35.14894	34.27791
90	50.36234	47.81269	45.39830	44.23948	43.11170	42.01410	40.94583	39.90607	38.89402	37.90892	36.95001	36.01657
96	53.03929	50.30072	47.71083	46.46898	45.26116	44.08642	42.94378	41.83234	40.75121	39.69951	38.67640	37.68108
120	63.04196	59.54067	56.24656	54.67311	53.14667	51.66655	50.22980	48.83474	47.48192	46.16915	44.89516	43.65874
150	74.09616	69.63881	65.47179	63.49078	61.57488	59.72180	57.92933	56.19533	54.51777	52.89466	51.32410	49.80427
180	83.73330	78.33360	73.31683	70.94276	68.65359	66.44604	64.31693	62.26324	60.28206	58.37060	56.52619	54.74627
240	99.45974	92.26616	85.66139	82.56298	79.59226	76.74338	74.01079	71.38922	68.87364	66.45928	64.14160	61.91628
300	111.41261	102.59538	94.58849	90.86245	87.30844	83.91747	80.68106	77.59122	74.64040	71.82150	69.12780	66.55295
360	120.49739	110.25317	101.04423	96.79017	92.75148	88.91562	85.27082	81.80608	78.51111	75.37627	72.39250	69.55136

Term	9.00%	9.25%	9.50%	9.75%	10.00%	10.25%	10.50%	10.75%	11.00%	11.25%	11.50%	12.00%
6	3.14405	3.08833	3.03361	2.97988	2.92710	2.87528	2.82438	2.77439	2.72529	2.67708	2.62973	2.53755
12	6.15026	6.03761	5.92704	5.81853	5.71203	5.60750	5.50491	5.40422	5.30539	5.20839	5.11319	4.92804
24	11.77306	11.54374	11.31859	11.09861	10.88263	10.67091	10.46338	10.25994	10.06052	9.86504	9.67342	9.30143
30	14.40095	14.11228	13.82950	13.55249	13.28112	13.01529	12.75486	12.49974	12.24982	12.00497	11.76511	11.29992
36	16.91364	16.56518	16.22404	15.89007	15.56312	15.24302	14.92965	14.62284	14.32247	14.02839	13.74047	13.18259
48	21.61335	21.14459	20.68627	20.23813	19.79995	19.37151	18.95258	18.54294	18.14238	17.75070	17.36769	16.62692
60	25.91001	25.32090	24.74656	24.18362	23.65319	23.09941	22.57517	22.06517	21.56610	21.07869	20.60264	19.68359
72	29.83817	29.12957	28.43845	27.76437	27.10690	26.46560	25.84008	25.22991	24.63472	24.05413	23.48775	22.39623
84	33.42945	32.60298	31.79788	31.01358	30.24953	29.50518	28.77999	28.07346	27.38508	26.71436	26.06085	24.80356
90	35.10789	34.22328	33.36207	32.52363	31.70731	30.91251	30.13863	29.38510	28.65136	27.93686	27.24108	25.90363
96	36.71274	35.77063	34.85399	33.96211	33.09428	32.24982	31.42808	30.62840	29.85017	29.09279	28.35567	26.93994
120	42.45872	41.29395	40.16335	39.06584	38.00039	36.96602	35.96176	34.98668	34.03987	33.12047	32.22764	30.51842
150	48.33340	46.90980	45.53183	44.19791	42.90653	41.65623	40.44560	39.27328	38.13796	37.03839	35.97336	33.94223
180	53.02838	51.37016	49.76936	48.22380	46.73140	45.29016	43.89818	42.55360	41.25466	39.99968	38.78701	36.48244
240	59.77921	57.72649	55.75437	53.85934	52.03800	50.28716	48.60374	46.98484	45.42768	43.92967	42.48812	39.76534
300	64.09097	61.73621	59.48334	57.32729	55.26330	53.28686	51.39371	49.57981	47.84134	46.17470	44.57646	41.57241
360	66.84489	64.26565	61.90666	59.46136	57.22360	55.08759	53.04790	51.09944	49.23740	47.45727	45.75480	42.56711

Entry is the multiple of the desired payment which will fund the number of payments selected.

Deposit to Obtain a Number of Payments of 1
Loan Amortized by a Number of Payments of 1

Draw Delay of 96 Months

Term	5.50%	6.00%	6.50%	6.75%	7.00%	7.25%	7.50%	7.75%	8.00%	8.25%	8.50%	8.75%
6	3.82425	3.67122	3.52436	3.45318	3.38345	3.31514	3.24822	3.18267	3.11845	3.05554	2.99392	2.93355
12	7.54501	7.23420	6.93633	6.79207	6.65085	6.51260	6.37725	6.24475	6.11502	5.98802	5.86369	5.74197
24	14.68714	14.04813	13.43728	13.14202	12.85333	12.57107	12.29509	12.02524	11.76140	11.50342	11.25118	11.00454
30	18.11389	17.30518	16.53309	16.16025	15.79595	15.43998	15.09216	14.75229	14.42018	14.09566	13.77856	13.46869
36	21.44791	20.46620	19.53017	19.07860	18.63765	18.20707	17.78660	17.37600	16.97505	16.58350	16.20114	15.82774
48	27.84768	26.51142	25.24063	24.62875	24.03202	23.45006	22.88250	22.32898	21.78913	21.26261	20.74909	20.24825
60	33.90574	32.20545	30.59265	29.81760	29.06272	28.32746	27.61130	26.91373	26.23426	25.57241	24.92770	24.29968
72	39.64031	37.56868	35.60873	34.66868	33.75426	32.86475	31.99944	31.15765	30.33873	29.54204	28.76695	28.01287
84	45.06869	42.62034	40.30996	39.20398	38.12952	37.08564	36.07145	35.08606	34.12864	33.19835	32.29441	31.41604
90	47.67319	45.03502	42.54874	41.35969	40.20526	39.08440	37.99609	36.93936	35.91324	34.91682	33.94921	33.00954
96	50.20721	47.37862	44.71611	43.44406	42.20981	41.01221	39.85011	38.72243	37.62809	36.56608	35.53539	34.53507
120	59.67578	56.08167	52.71606	51.11414	49.56371	48.06302	46.61041	45.20425	43.84298	42.52508	41.24911	40.01366
150	70.13972	65.59316	61.36225	59.35781	57.42371	55.55732	53.75610	52.01764	50.33961	48.71976	47.15595	45.64610
180	79.26228	73.78284	68.71486	66.32470	64.02521	61.81267	59.68354	57.63445	55.66213	53.76349	51.93556	50.17549
240	94.14899	86.90599	80.28458	77.18850	74.22642	71.39196	68.67906	66.08198	63.59527	61.21375	58.93250	56.74688
300	105.46363	96.63513	88.65135	84.94772	81.42241	78.06579	74.86880	71.82290	68.92007	66.15273	63.51376	60.99643
360	114.06332	103.84805	94.70187	90.48956	86.49850	82.71541	79.12791	75.72443	72.49414	69.42692	66.51333	63.74450

Term	9.00%	9.25%	9.50%	9.75%	10.00%	10.25%	10.50%	10.75%	11.00%	11.25%	11.50%	12.00%
6	2.87441	2.81647	2.75972	2.70412	2.64965	2.59629	2.54402	2.49280	2.44264	2.39349	2.34533	2.25195
12	5.62280	5.50613	5.39191	5.28008	5.17060	5.06341	4.95847	4.85572	4.75513	4.65665	4.56022	4.37339
24	10.76338	10.52757	10.29700	10.07154	9.85109	9.63552	9.42474	9.21862	9.01708	8.82000	8.62728	8.25455
30	13.16590	12.87002	12.58088	12.29834	12.02224	11.75243	11.48876	11.23110	10.97930	10.73324	10.49277	10.02811
36	15.46309	15.10699	14.75922	14.41960	14.08793	13.76401	13.44767	13.13872	12.83699	12.54230	12.25450	11.69888
48	19.75975	19.28329	18.81857	18.36529	17.92317	17.49191	17.07126	16.66095	16.26071	15.87029	15.48945	14.75555
60	23.68792	23.09196	22.51141	21.94584	21.39487	20.85810	20.33517	19.82569	19.32933	18.84573	18.37456	17.46819
72	27.27920	26.56537	25.87083	25.19505	24.53750	23.89768	23.27508	22.66924	22.07969	21.50597	20.94765	19.87552
84	30.56248	29.73302	28.92695	28.14358	27.38225	26.64232	25.92317	25.22418	24.54478	23.88440	23.24248	22.01190
90	32.09697	31.21069	30.34992	29.51388	28.70185	27.91310	27.14694	26.40270	25.67973	24.97739	24.29508	22.98816
96	33.56419	32.62183	31.70713	30.81925	29.95735	29.12066	28.30839	27.51982	26.75421	26.01087	25.28913	23.90783
120	38.81738	37.65896	36.53713	35.45068	34.39843	33.37925	32.39204	31.43576	30.50936	29.61188	28.74236	27.08355
150	44.18824	42.78045	41.42090	40.10783	38.83953	37.61437	36.43080	35.28730	34.18242	33.11476	32.08299	30.12201
180	48.48057	46.84818	45.27584	43.76116	42.30184	40.89511	39.54066	38.23469	36.97586	35.76234	34.59326	32.37632
240	54.65244	52.64497	50.72049	48.87518	47.10545	45.40785	43.77913	42.21619	40.71607	39.27596	37.89321	35.28972
300	58.59441	56.30174	54.11277	52.02221	50.02502	48.11650	46.29215	44.54778	42.87939	41.28322	39.75571	36.89340
360	61.11215	58.60852	56.22633	53.95879	51.79951	49.74250	47.78214	45.91318	44.13065	42.42992	40.80662	37.77615

Draw Delay of 120 Months

Term	5.50%	6.00%	6.50%	6.75%	7.00%	7.25%	7.50%	7.75%	8.00%	8.25%	8.50%	8.75%
6	3.42676	3.25705	3.09581	3.01824	2.94262	2.86892	2.79707	2.72704	2.65878	2.59224	2.52738	2.46415
12	6.76077	6.41808	6.09289	5.93659	5.78433	5.63600	5.49151	5.35076	5.21365	5.08008	4.94996	4.82320
24	13.16055	12.46330	11.80335	11.48673	11.17869	10.87900	10.58742	10.30373	10.02773	9.75919	9.49791	9.24371
30	16.23112	15.35290	14.52272	14.12481	13.73793	13.36176	12.99601	12.64038	12.29459	11.95837	11.63145	11.31357
36	19.21860	18.15732	17.15537	16.67559	16.20939	15.75639	15.31622	14.88849	14.47286	14.06899	13.67652	13.29514
48	24.95318	23.52055	22.17145	21.52667	20.90094	20.29368	19.70435	19.13241	18.57733	18.03862	17.51577	17.00833
60	30.38155	28.57221	26.87269	26.06197	25.27619	24.51458	23.77636	23.06082	22.36724	21.69493	21.04323	20.41150
72	35.52007	33.33039	31.27883	30.30204	29.35649	28.44114	27.55503	26.69719	25.86669	25.06266	24.28421	23.53053
84	40.38422	37.81215	35.40841	34.26610	33.16170	32.09391	31.06148	30.06322	29.09795	28.16457	27.26199	26.38916
90	42.71801	39.95443	37.37496	36.15029	34.96700	33.82363	32.71881	31.65120	30.61950	29.62247	28.65892	27.72769
96	44.98864	42.03354	39.27879	37.97212	36.71038	35.49196	34.31533	33.17901	32.08158	31.02166	29.99793	29.00912
120	53.47303	49.75485	46.30598	44.67613	43.10615	41.59373	40.13668	38.73290	37.38036	36.07711	34.82129	33.61109
150	62.84935	58.19331	53.90081	51.88149	49.94209	48.07929	46.28991	44.57090	42.91937	41.33251	39.80766	38.34228
180	71.02370	65.45908	60.35938	57.97087	55.68349	53.49267	51.39409	49.38362	47.45733	45.61147	43.84247	42.14692
240	84.36308	77.10175	70.52226	67.46634	64.55560	61.78258	59.14022	56.62182	54.22109	51.93206	49.74908	47.66682
300	94.50167	85.73331	77.87166	74.24825	70.81404	67.55812	64.47026	61.54089	58.76100	56.12216	53.61644	51.23640
360	102.20750	92.13250	83.18646	79.09208	75.22877	71.58189	68.13782	64.88388	61.80824	58.89990	56.14859	53.54476

Term	9.00%	9.25%	9.50%	9.75%	10.00%	10.25%	10.50%	10.75%	11.00%	11.25%	11.50%	12.00%
6	2.40252	2.34245	2.28388	2.22680	2.17115	2.11690	2.06402	2.01248	1.96223	1.91324	1.86549	1.77356
12	4.69971	4.57942	4.46223	4.34806	4.23684	4.12849	4.02293	3.92009	3.81991	3.72231	3.62722	3.44433
24	8.99637	8.75572	8.52157	8.29375	8.07208	7.85639	7.64653	7.44232	7.24363	7.05030	6.86217	6.50100
30	11.00447	10.70392	10.41166	10.12748	9.85114	9.58242	9.32112	9.06702	8.81993	8.57965	8.34599	7.89780
36	12.92454	12.56439	12.21441	11.87430	11.54378	11.22258	10.91043	10.60707	10.31225	10.02574	9.74728	9.21364
48	16.51582	16.03780	15.57383	15.12351	14.68641	14.26215	13.85034	13.45062	13.06261	12.68597	12.32037	11.62097
60	19.79910	19.20545	18.62995	18.07203	17.53116	17.00680	16.49843	16.00556	15.52771	15.06440	14.61520	13.75735
72	22.80081	22.09426	21.41013	20.74770	20.10626	19.48513	18.88365	18.30119	17.73713	17.19088	16.66185	15.65328
84	25.54506	24.72728	23.93931	23.17576	22.43728	21.72300	21.03211	20.36383	19.71740	19.09208	18.48716	17.33583
90	26.82766	25.95775	25.11693	24.30419	23.51857	22.75914	22.02499	21.31527	20.62913	19.96577	19.32440	18.10469
96	28.05400	27.13138	26.24013	25.37913	24.54734	23.74373	22.96731	22.21713	21.49228	20.79188	20.11508	18.82900
120	32.44479	31.32073	30.23732	29.19304	28.18640	27.21600	26.28048	25.37852	24.50889	23.67036	22.86179	21.33008
150	36.93392	35.58025	34.27903	33.02812	31.82548	30.66914	29.55722	28.48793	27.45954	26.47040	25.51895	23.72307
180	40.52158	38.96335	37.46929	36.03658	34.66253	33.34460	32.08033	30.86739	29.70358	28.58676	27.51491	25.49849
240	45.68022	43.78451	41.97516	40.24789	38.59865	37.02360	35.51910	34.08171	32.70817	31.39538	30.14042	27.79299
300	48.97505	46.82582	44.78254	42.83942	40.99098	39.23211	37.55798	35.96404	34.44602	32.99989	31.62186	29.05599
360	51.07945	48.74435	46.53168	44.43416	42.44501	40.55789	38.76685	37.06635	35.45119	33.91651	32.45775	29.75121

Entry is the multiple which, with interest, will fund the number of payments selected.

Deposit to Obtain a Number of Payments of 1
Loan Amortized by a Number of Payments of 1

Draw Delay of 144 Months

Term	5.50%	6.00%	6.50%	6.75%	7.00%	Interest Rate 7.25%	7.50%	7.75%	8.00%	8.25%	8.50%	8.75%
6	3.07058	2.88961	2.71937	2.63808	2.55923	2.48276	2.40859	2.33665	2.26687	2.19919	2.13354	2.06986
12	6.05805	5.69403	5.35202	5.18885	5.03070	4.87739	4.72880	4.58476	4.44514	4.30980	4.17861	4.05144
24	11.79263	11.05726	10.36810	10.03994	9.72224	9.41468	9.11693	8.82867	8.54960	8.27943	8.01786	7.76462
30	14.54405	13.62088	12.75681	12.34574	11.94804	11.56326	11.19099	10.83081	10.48233	10.14516	9.81893	9.50329
36	17.22100	16.10892	15.06934	14.57524	14.09750	13.63558	13.18894	12.75709	12.33951	11.93574	11.54532	11.16779
48	22.35953	20.86710	19.47548	18.81531	18.17779	17.56215	16.96761	16.39345	15.83897	15.30347	14.78630	14.28683
60	27.22367	25.34886	23.60506	22.77937	21.98301	21.21491	20.47406	19.75948	19.07023	18.40538	17.76408	17.14546
72	31.82809	29.57025	27.47544	26.48539	25.53169	24.61296	23.72791	22.87527	22.05385	21.26247	20.50002	19.76542
84	36.18665	33.54640	31.10288	29.95017	28.84113	27.77406	26.74735	25.75943	24.80881	23.89405	23.01377	22.16664
90	38.27787	35.44700	32.83030	31.59704	30.41121	29.27096	28.17449	27.12008	26.10607	25.13089	24.19302	23.29099
96	40.31249	37.29156	34.50263	33.18940	31.92745	30.71473	29.54927	28.42917	27.35264	26.31792	25.32337	24.36738
120	47.91501	44.14179	40.67533	39.04902	37.48993	35.99520	34.56209	33.18798	31.87036	30.60683	29.39510	28.23298
150	56.31675	51.62827	47.34667	45.34683	43.43523	41.60780	39.86070	38.19023	36.59290	35.06536	33.60445	32.20714
180	63.64145	58.07436	53.01989	50.66924	48.42859	46.29254	44.25596	42.31396	40.46195	38.69552	37.01052	35.40300
240	75.59432	68.40357	61.94700	58.96871	56.14478	53.46663	50.92622	48.51596	46.22871	44.05774	41.99671	40.03966
300	84.67910	76.06136	68.40274	64.89643	61.58782	58.46478	55.51598	52.73082	50.09942	47.61250	45.26142	43.03807
360	91.58398	81.73864	73.07128	69.13016	65.42736	61.94695	58.67415	55.59524	52.69748	49.96906	47.39899	44.97707

Term	9.00%	9.25%	9.50%	9.75%	10.00%	10.25%	10.50%	10.75%	11.00%	11.25%	11.50%	12.00%
6	2.00810	1.94820	1.89009	1.83373	1.77906	1.72603	1.67459	1.62470	1.57630	1.52936	1.48382	1.39680
12	3.92817	3.80867	3.69284	3.58055	3.47171	3.36619	3.26390	3.16475	3.06862	2.97544	2.88511	2.71264
24	7.51945	7.28208	7.05226	6.82976	6.61434	6.40576	6.20382	6.00829	5.81898	5.63568	5.45820	5.11997
30	9.19788	8.90238	8.61646	8.33981	8.07212	7.81309	7.56246	7.31993	7.08526	6.85818	6.63844	6.22004
36	10.80273	10.44973	10.10838	9.77829	9.45908	9.15041	8.85190	8.56324	8.28408	8.01411	7.75303	7.25635
48	13.80444	13.33854	12.88856	12.45396	12.03419	11.62874	11.23713	10.85887	10.49350	10.14058	9.79968	9.15228
60	16.54871	15.97306	15.41774	14.88202	14.36520	13.86661	13.38559	12.92151	12.47377	12.04179	11.62499	10.83483
72	19.05763	18.37567	17.71856	17.08539	16.47526	15.88734	15.32078	14.77481	14.24865	13.74159	13.25291	12.32800
84	21.35138	20.56678	19.81164	19.08485	18.38532	17.71200	17.06388	16.44001	15.83945	15.26132	14.70477	13.65311
90	22.42340	21.58891	20.78622	20.01409	19.27134	18.55682	17.86943	17.20811	16.57187	15.95971	15.37071	14.25864
96	23.44842	22.56501	21.71575	20.89929	20.11432	19.35961	18.63395	17.93620	17.26526	16.62007	15.99962	14.82908
120	27.11837	26.04926	25.02375	24.03998	23.09621	22.19075	21.32201	20.48843	19.68857	18.92099	18.18436	16.79885
150	30.87053	29.59188	28.36857	27.19811	26.07810	25.00629	23.98051	22.99870	22.05889	21.15921	20.29788	18.68349
180	33.86921	32.40559	31.00876	29.67552	28.40281	27.18774	26.02757	24.91968	23.86158	22.85093	21.88547	20.08175
240	38.18097	36.41532	34.73772	33.14347	31.62811	30.18745	28.81754	27.51464	26.27524	25.09601	23.97381	21.88882
300	40.93488	38.94476	37.06105	35.27754	33.58840	31.98817	30.47173	29.03427	27.67130	26.37858	25.15216	22.88352
360	42.69381	40.54039	38.50860	36.59079	34.77985	33.06915	31.45251	29.92418	28.47877	27.11128	25.81703	23.43105

Draw Delay of 180 Months

Term	5.50%	6.00%	6.50%	6.75%	7.00%	Interest Rate 7.25%	7.50%	7.75%	8.00%	8.25%	8.50%	8.75%
6	2.60451	2.41469	2.23877	2.15571	2.07574	1.99876	1.92464	1.85329	1.78460	1.71847	1.65480	1.59350
12	5.13852	4.75818	4.40615	4.24007	4.08029	3.92657	3.77867	3.63637	3.49945	3.36773	3.24098	3.11904
24	10.00267	9.23994	8.53573	8.20414	7.88551	7.57933	7.28512	7.00240	6.73072	6.46964	6.21876	5.97767
30	12.33646	11.38222	10.50227	10.08832	9.69080	9.30905	8.94245	8.59037	8.25226	7.92754	7.61569	7.31619
36	14.60709	13.46133	12.40610	11.91016	11.43419	10.97738	10.53896	10.11819	9.71434	9.32673	8.95470	8.59763
48	18.96565	17.43748	16.03354	15.37493	14.74363	14.13848	13.55840	13.00234	12.46930	11.95831	11.46845	10.99885
60	23.09148	21.18264	19.43329	18.61416	17.82995	17.07915	16.36032	15.67208	15.01312	14.38218	13.77805	13.19959
72	26.99701	24.71023	22.61964	21.64254	20.70821	19.81477	18.96039	18.14335	17.36199	16.61474	15.90009	15.21659
84	30.69400	28.03288	25.60600	24.47378	23.39243	22.35962	21.37315	20.43090	19.53085	18.67109	17.84979	17.06519
90	32.46780	29.62110	27.02813	25.81952	24.66590	23.56471	22.51355	21.51008	20.55213	19.63758	18.76443	17.93078
96	34.19359	31.16250	28.40490	27.12072	25.89569	24.72702	23.61210	22.54838	21.53349	20.56513	19.64115	18.75945
120	40.64215	36.88687	33.48669	31.90890	30.40729	28.97809	27.61772	26.32280	25.09009	23.91654	22.79924	21.73542
150	47.76862	43.14290	38.97898	37.05516	35.22940	33.49654	31.85171	30.29029	28.80793	27.40049	26.06406	24.79496
180	53.98153	48.52954	43.64957	41.40437	39.27941	37.26801	35.36385	33.56100	31.85385	30.23713	28.70585	27.25533
240	64.12012	57.16110	50.99897	48.18629	45.53785	43.04354	40.69390	38.48007	36.39376	34.42723	32.57321	30.82490
300	71.82595	63.56029	56.31377	53.03011	49.95258	47.06732	44.36146	41.82306	39.44100	37.20497	35.10536	33.13326
360	77.68276	68.30448	60.15723	56.48971	53.06676	49.87066	46.88508	44.09494	41.48633	39.04641	36.76329	34.62601

Term	9.00%	9.25%	9.50%	9.75%	10.00%	10.25%	10.50%	10.75%	11.00%	11.25%	11.50%	12.00%
6	1.53449	1.47767	1.42297	1.37031	1.31960	1.27078	1.22378	1.17852	1.13495	1.09299	1.05260	0.97625
12	3.00171	2.88881	2.78019	2.67567	2.57510	2.47834	2.38523	2.29563	2.20943	2.12647	2.04665	1.89593
24	5.74598	5.52333	5.30936	5.10373	4.90612	4.71620	4.53368	4.35828	4.18970	4.02768	3.87196	3.57847
30	7.02855	6.75230	6.48698	6.23215	5.98741	5.75234	5.52656	5.30971	5.10142	4.90136	4.70920	4.34734
36	8.25490	7.92593	7.61018	7.30710	7.01618	6.73693	6.46888	6.21157	5.96458	5.72748	5.49988	5.07165
48	10.54865	10.11705	9.70327	9.30657	8.92623	8.56159	8.21198	7.87677	7.55538	7.24722	6.95174	6.39676
60	12.64568	12.11728	11.60738	11.11210	10.65524	10.20920	9.78205	9.37296	8.98118	8.60596	8.24659	7.57273
72	14.56287	13.93762	13.33957	12.76753	12.22036	11.69695	11.19627	10.71730	10.25911	9.82077	9.40141	8.61634
84	16.31564	15.59953	14.91537	14.26169	13.63712	13.04034	12.47010	11.92520	11.40449	10.90688	10.43134	9.54250
90	17.13482	16.37480	15.64908	14.95609	14.29432	13.66234	13.05879	12.48237	11.93183	11.40600	10.90375	9.96572
96	17.91808	17.11516	16.34889	15.61758	14.91959	14.25339	13.61749	13.01050	12.43108	11.87794	11.34988	10.36442
120	20.72247	19.75790	18.83934	17.96454	17.13137	16.33780	15.58190	14.86184	14.17587	13.52235	12.89971	11.74114
150	23.58968	22.44492	21.35753	20.32454	19.34316	18.41072	17.52470	16.68272	15.88252	15.12195	14.39900	13.05836
180	25.88112	24.57906	23.34521	22.17586	21.06749	20.01680	19.02067	18.07616	17.18047	16.33098	15.52522	14.03563
240	29.17595	27.62037	26.15260	24.76738	23.45982	22.22532	21.05955	19.95848	18.91831	17.93549	17.00666	15.29864
300	31.28035	29.53891	27.90173	26.36213	24.91385	23.55109	22.26842	21.06079	19.92348	18.85210	17.84255	15.99386
360	32.62443	30.74916	28.99153	27.34349	25.79759	24.34695	22.98516	21.70630	20.50487	19.37575	18.31421	16.37654

Entry is the multiple of the desired payment which will fund the number of payments selected.

Number of Installments Available from a Deposit
Number of Payments to Amortize a Loan

Monthly Payment	Annual Constant	5.50%	5.75%	6.00%	6.25%	6.50%	6.75%	7.00%	7.25%	7.50%	7.75%	8.00%
10.00%	120.00%	10.3	10.3	10.3	10.3	10.3	10.3	10.3	10.3	10.4	10.4	10.4
9.00	108.00	11.4	11.4	11.5	11.5	11.5	11.5	11.5	11.5	11.6	11.6	11.6
8.00	96.00	12.9	12.9	12.9	13.0	13.0	13.0	13.0	13.0	13.1	13.1	13.1
7.00	84.00	14.8	14.8	14.9	14.9	14.9	14.9	15.0	15.0	15.0	15.0	15.1
6.00	72.00	17.4	17.4	17.4	17.5	17.5	17.5	17.6	17.6	17.7	17.7	17.7
5.00	60.00	21.0	21.1	21.1	21.2	21.2	21.3	21.3	21.4	21.4	21.5	21.5
4.1667	50.00	25.5	25.6	25.6	25.7	25.8	25.9	25.9	26.0	26.1	26.2	26.2
4.00	48.00	26.6	26.7	26.8	26.9	26.9	27.0	27.1	27.2	27.3	27.4	27.4
3.3333	40.00	32.3	32.5	32.6	32.7	32.8	33.0	33.1	33.2	33.3	33.5	33.6
3.00	36.00	36.3	36.4	36.6	36.7	36.9	37.0	37.2	37.3	37.5	37.7	37.8
2.50	30.00	44.3	44.5	44.7	45.0	45.2	45.4	45.7	45.9	46.2	46.4	46.7
2.0833	25.00	54.3	54.7	55.0	55.4	55.7	56.1	56.5	56.9	57.2	57.6	58.0
2.00	24.00	56.9	57.3	57.7	58.1	58.5	58.9	59.3	59.7	60.1	60.6	61.0
1.75	21.00	66.4	66.9	67.5	68.0	68.6	69.1	69.7	70.3	70.9	71.5	72.2
1.6667	20.00	70.3	70.9	71.5	72.1	72.8	73.4	74.1	74.7	75.4	76.1	76.9
1.50	18.00	79.7	80.5	81.3	82.1	82.9	83.8	84.7	85.6	86.5	87.5	88.5
1.25	15.00	99.9	101.1	102.4	103.8	105.1	106.6	108.1	109.6	111.2	112.9	114.7
1.00	12.00	134.1	136.5	139.0	141.6	144.4	147.4	150.5	153.9	157.4	161.2	165.3
0.9917	11.90	135.6	138.1	140.7	143.4	146.3	149.3	152.6	156.0	159.7	163.6	167.9
0.9833	11.80	137.2	139.8	142.4	145.2	148.2	151.3	154.6	158.2	162.0	166.1	170.5
0.9750	11.70	138.9	141.5	144.2	147.1	150.1	153.4	156.8	160.5	164.4	168.7	173.3
0.9667	11.60	140.5	143.2	146.0	149.0	152.1	155.5	159.0	162.8	166.9	171.3	176.1
0.9583	11.50	142.3	145.0	147.9	150.9	154.2	157.6	161.3	165.3	169.5	174.1	179.0
0.95	11.40	144.0	146.8	149.8	153.0	156.3	159.9	163.7	167.8	172.2	176.9	182.1
0.9417	11.30	145.8	148.7	151.8	155.0	158.5	162.2	166.1	170.3	174.9	179.9	185.2
0.9333	11.20	147.7	150.7	153.8	157.2	160.7	164.6	168.6	173.0	177.8	182.9	188.5
0.9250	11.10	149.6	152.7	155.9	159.4	163.1	167.0	171.2	175.8	180.7	186.1	192.0
0.9167	11.00	151.6	154.7	158.1	161.7	165.5	169.5	173.9	178.7	183.8	189.4	195.5
0.9083	10.90	153.6	156.9	160.3	164.0	167.9	172.2	176.7	181.6	187.0	192.8	199.3
0.90	10.80	155.7	159.0	162.6	166.4	170.5	174.9	179.6	184.7	190.3	196.4	203.2
0.8917	10.70	157.8	161.3	164.9	168.9	173.1	177.7	182.6	187.9	193.7	200.1	207.2
0.8833	10.60	160.0	163.6	167.4	171.5	175.8	180.6	185.7	191.2	197.3	204.0	211.5
0.8750	10.50	162.2	165.9	169.9	174.1	178.7	183.6	188.9	194.7	201.1	208.1	216.0
0.8667	10.40	164.6	168.4	172.5	176.9	181.6	186.7	192.2	198.3	205.0	212.4	220.7
0.8583	10.30	167.0	170.9	175.1	179.7	184.6	189.9	195.7	202.0	209.1	216.9	225.6
0.85	10.20	169.4	173.5	177.9	182.6	187.7	193.3	199.3	206.0	213.3	221.6	230.9
0.8417	10.10	172.0	176.2	180.8	185.7	191.0	196.7	203.1	210.0	217.8	226.5	236.4
0.8333	10.00	174.6	179.0	183.7	188.8	194.3	200.4	207.0	214.3	222.5	231.7	242.2
0.8250	9.90	177.3	181.9	186.8	192.1	197.8	204.2	211.1	218.8	227.4	237.2	248.4
0.8167	9.80	180.1	184.9	189.9	195.5	201.5	208.1	215.4	223.5	232.6	243.0	255.0
0.8083	9.70	183.0	187.9	193.2	199.0	205.3	212.2	219.9	228.4	238.1	249.2	262.1
0.80	9.60	186.0	191.1	196.7	202.7	209.2	216.5	224.6	233.6	243.9	255.8	269.7
0.7917	9.50	189.2	194.5	200.2	206.5	213.4	221.0	229.5	239.1	250.1	262.8	277.8
0.7833	9.40	192.4	197.9	203.9	210.5	217.7	225.7	234.7	244.9	256.6	270.3	286.6
0.7750	9.30	195.7	201.5	207.7	214.6	222.2	230.7	240.2	251.0	263.6	278.3	296.1
0.7667	9.20	199.2	205.2	211.7	219.0	226.9	235.9	246.0	257.6	271.0	287.0	306.6
0.7583	9.10	202.8	209.1	215.9	223.5	231.9	241.4	252.1	264.5	279.0	296.4	318.0
0.75	9.00	206.5	213.1	220.3	228.2	237.1	247.1	258.6	271.9	287.6	306.7	330.7
0.7417	8.90	210.4	217.3	224.8	233.2	242.6	253.3	265.5	279.8	296.9	317.9	344.9
0.7333	8.80	214.5	221.7	229.6	238.4	248.4	259.7	272.8	288.3	306.9	330.2	360.9
0.7250	8.70	218.7	226.3	234.6	243.9	254.5	266.6	280.7	297.5	317.9	344.0	379.3
0.7167	8.60	223.1	231.0	239.8	249.7	261.0	273.9	289.1	307.4	330.1	359.5	400.7
0.7083	8.50	227.7	236.1	245.4	255.9	267.8	281.8	298.2	318.2	343.5	377.1	426.4
0.70	8.40	232.6	241.3	251.2	262.3	275.2	290.1	308.1	330.1	358.5	397.5	458.2
0.6917	8.30	237.6	246.9	257.3	269.2	282.9	299.2	318.7	343.2	375.5	421.6	499.7
0.6833	8.20	242.9	252.7	263.8	276.5	291.3	308.9	330.4	357.8	395.0	450.9	558.9
0.6750	8.10	248.5	258.9	270.7	284.3	300.2	319.4	343.3	374.3	417.7	488.0	661.4
0.6667	8.00	254.4	265.4	278.0	292.6	309.9	330.9	357.5	393.0	445.0	538.4	unl
0.6583	7.90	260.5	272.3	285.7	301.5	320.3	343.6	373.5	414.7	478.8	615.8	unl
0.65	7.80	267.1	279.6	294.0	311.1	331.7	357.5	391.5	440.3	522.9	784.4	unl
0.6417	7.70	274.0	287.3	302.9	321.4	344.1	373.1	412.3	471.4	585.9	unl	unl
0.6333	7.60	281.3	295.6	312.4	332.7	357.8	390.6	436.5	511.0	695.1	unl	unl
0.6250	7.50	289.0	304.4	322.7	344.9	373.0	410.5	465.6	564.7	unl	unl	unl

Entries are numbers of monthly installments at end of month.

Number of Installments Available from a Deposit
Number of Payments to Amortize a Loan

Monthly Payment	Annual Constant	8.50%	8.75%	9.00%	9.25%	9.50%	9.75%	10.00%	10.25%	10.50%	11.00%	12.00%
10.00%	120.00%	10.4	10.4	10.4	10.4	10.5	10.5	10.5	10.5	10.5	10.5	10.6
9.00	108.00	11.6	11.6	11.6	11.7	11.7	11.7	11.7	11.7	11.7	11.8	11.8
8.00	96.00	13.1	13.2	13.2	13.2	13.2	13.2	13.3	13.3	13.3	13.3	13.4
7.00	84.00	15.1	15.1	15.2	15.2	15.2	15.2	15.3	15.3	15.3	15.4	15.5
6.00	72.00	17.8	17.8	17.9	17.9	17.9	18.0	18.0	18.1	18.1	18.2	18.3
5.00	60.00	21.6	21.7	21.8	21.8	21.9	21.9	22.0	22.0	22.1	22.2	22.4
4.1667	50.00	26.4	26.5	26.6	26.6	26.7	26.8	26.9	27.0	27.1	27.2	27.6
4.00	48.00	27.6	27.7	27.8	27.9	28.0	28.1	28.2	28.2	28.3	28.5	28.9
3.3333	40.00	33.8	34.0	34.1	34.2	34.4	34.5	34.7	34.8	35.0	35.2	35.8
3.00	36.00	38.2	38.3	38.5	38.7	38.9	39.0	39.2	39.4	39.6	40.0	40.7
2.50	30.00	47.2	47.5	47.7	48.0	48.3	48.6	48.9	49.2	49.4	50.1	51.3
2.0833	25.00	58.9	59.3	59.7	60.2	60.6	61.1	61.6	62.0	62.5	63.5	65.7
2.00	24.00	61.9	62.4	62.9	63.4	63.9	64.4	64.9	65.5	66.0	67.2	69.7
1.75	21.00	73.5	74.2	74.9	75.6	76.4	77.1	77.9	78.7	79.6	81.3	85.2
1.6667	20.00	78.4	79.2	80.0	80.9	81.7	82.6	83.5	84.5	85.5	87.5	92.1
1.50	18.00	90.5	91.6	92.8	93.9	95.2	96.4	97.7	99.1	100.5	103.5	110.4
1.25	15.00	118.5	120.5	122.6	124.9	127.2	129.7	132.4	135.2	138.2	144.9	161.7
1.00	12.00	174.6	179.8	185.5	191.9	198.9	206.9	215.9	226.4	238.7	272.3	unl
0.9917	11.90	177.5	182.9	188.9	195.6	203.0	211.4	221.1	232.3	245.6	283.0	unl
0.9833	11.80	180.5	186.2	192.5	199.5	207.4	216.3	226.6	238.7	253.2	294.9	unl
0.9750	11.70	183.7	189.6	196.2	203.6	211.9	221.4	232.4	245.5	261.4	308.6	unl
0.9667	11.60	187.0	193.2	200.1	207.9	216.7	226.9	238.7	252.9	270.4	324.6	unl
0.9583	11.50	190.4	196.9	204.2	212.5	221.8	232.7	245.4	260.9	280.3	343.6	unl
0.95	11.40	193.9	200.8	208.5	217.2	227.2	238.9	252.7	269.7	291.4	367.1	unl
0.9417	11.30	197.7	204.9	213.0	222.3	233.0	245.5	260.6	279.4	303.9	397.7	unl
0.9333	11.20	201.6	209.2	217.8	227.7	239.1	252.6	269.1	290.1	318.3	441.1	unl
0.9250	11.10	205.6	213.7	222.8	233.3	245.6	260.4	278.6	302.1	334.9	516.1	unl
0.9167	11.00	209.9	218.4	228.2	239.4	252.7	268.7	288.9	315.8	354.8	unl	unl
0.9083	10.90	214.4	223.4	233.8	245.9	260.3	277.9	300.5	331.5	379.4	unl	unl
0.90	10.80	219.1	228.7	239.8	252.8	268.5	288.0	313.6	350.1	411.3	unl	unl
0.8917	10.70	224.1	234.3	246.2	260.3	277.5	299.2	328.6	372.6	456.8	unl	unl
0.8833	10.60	229.4	240.3	253.1	268.4	287.3	311.8	346.0	401.0	535.3	unl	unl
0.8750	10.50	234.9	246.6	260.4	277.2	298.2	326.1	366.9	439.4	unl	unl	unl
0.8667	10.40	240.8	253.4	268.4	286.8	310.3	342.6	392.6	498.4	unl	unl	unl
0.8583	10.30	247.1	260.7	277.0	297.4	324.1	362.1	426.1	626.4	unl	unl	unl
0.85	10.20	253.9	268.5	286.4	309.1	339.7	385.7	473.8	unl	unl	unl	unl
0.8417	10.10	261.0	277.0	296.7	322.3	358.0	415.5	556.1	unl	unl	unl	unl
0.8333	10.00	268.8	286.2	308.2	337.3	379.9	455.9	unl	unl	unl	unl	unl
0.8250	9.90	277.1	296.3	320.9	354.7	406.9	517.7	unl	unl	unl	unl	unl
0.8167	9.80	286.2	307.4	335.3	375.1	442.1	652.3	unl	unl	unl	unl	unl
0.8083	9.70	296.1	319.8	351.8	399.9	492.2	unl	unl	unl	unl	unl	unl
0.80	9.60	306.9	333.7	371.1	431.3	578.8	unl	unl	unl	unl	unl	unl
0.7917	9.50	319.0	349.5	394.1	473.7	unl	unl	unl	unl	unl	unl	unl
0.7833	9.40	332.4	367.7	422.5	538.9	unl	unl	unl	unl	unl	unl	unl
0.7750	9.30	347.6	389.2	459.6	680.5	unl	unl	unl	unl	unl	unl	unl
0.7667	9.20	364.9	415.4	512.4	unl	unl	unl	unl	unl	unl	unl	unl
0.7583	9.10	385.2	448.4	603.7	unl	unl	unl	unl	unl	unl	unl	unl
0.75	9.00	409.5	493.2	unl	unl	unl	unl	unl	unl	unl	unl	unl

Entries are numbers of monthly installments at end of month.

Amount of Series of Deposits to Get Series of Withdrawals

Years of Deposit	Withdrawal	Interest on Deposits (compounded monthly)										
		5.50%	5.75%	6.00%	6.25%	6.50%	6.75%	7.00%	7.25%	7.50%	8.00%	8.25%
1	1	94.6604	94.4252	94.1905	93.9565	93.7232	93.4905	93.2584	93.0269	92.7960	92.3361	92.1072
	2	184.2663	183.5863	182.9091	182.2349	181.5635	180.8951	180.2296	179.5669	178.9070	177.5958	176.9444
	3	269.0877	267.7768	266.4736	265.1781	263.8903	262.6101	261.3374	260.0723	258.8146	256.3212	255.0856
	4	349.3799	347.2738	345.1835	343.1087	341.0496	339.0058	336.9773	334.9640	332.9656	329.0133	327.0592
	5	425.3849	422.3390	419.3207	416.3297	413.3657	410.4286	407.5179	404.6333	401.7748	396.1344	393.3520
	7	565.4364	560.1483	554.9244	549.7637	544.6654	539.6288	534.6526	529.7365	524.8792	515.3385	510.6535
	10	748.6985	739.3685	730.1933	721.1701	712.2958	703.5678	694.9830	686.5388	678.2327	662.0238	654.1161
	12	855.1446	842.8152	830.7261	818.8717	807.2467	795.8460	784.6646	773.6974	762.9398	742.0350	731.8786
	15	994.4328	977.3472	960.6657	944.3770	928.4704	912.9357	897.7623	882.9406	868.4611	840.4916	826.9841
2	1	46.0319	45.8588	45.6864	45.5145	45.3432	45.1726	45.0026	44.8331	44.6643	44.3285	44.1614
	2	89.6059	89.1611	88.7186	88.2783	87.8404	87.4047	86.9712	86.5400	86.1110	85.2596	84.8373
	3	130.8533	130.0493	129.2508	128.4578	127.6700	126.8876	126.1105	125.3386	124.5719	123.0539	122.3026
	4	169.8982	168.6581	167.4284	166.2090	164.9996	163.8004	162.6111	161.4316	160.2620	157.9517	156.8109
	5	206.8582	205.1145	203.3881	201.6787	199.9862	198.3103	196.6510	195.0079	193.3810	190.1750	188.5954
	7	274.9631	272.0435	269.1615	266.3169	263.5089	260.7371	258.0009	255.2998	252.6333	247.4021	244.8365
	10	364.0807	359.0841	354.1743	349.3497	344.6084	339.9489	335.3695	330.8687	326.4450	317.8224	313.6207
	12	415.8438	409.3244	402.9370	396.6784	390.5456	384.5358	378.6461	372.8737	367.2160	356.2339	350.9044
	15	483.5776	474.6616	465.9631	457.4757	449.1936	441.1110	433.2223	425.5221	418.0052	403.5007	396.5034
3	1	29.8387	29.6878	29.5376	29.3880	29.2391	29.0909	28.9434	28.7965	28.6503	28.3598	28.2155
	2	58.0841	57.7205	57.3592	57.0000	56.6430	56.2882	55.9355	55.5850	55.2365	54.5460	54.2039
	3	84.8213	84.1905	83.5645	82.9433	82.3268	81.7150	81.1079	80.5054	79.9076	78.7255	78.1412
	4	110.1309	109.1848	108.2474	107.3187	106.3984	105.4867	104.5833	103.6882	102.8013	101.0518	100.1891
	5	134.0891	132.7857	131.4964	130.2209	128.9591	127.7109	126.4760	125.2543	124.0457	121.6671	120.4968
	7	178.2359	176.1138	174.0209	171.9569	169.9212	167.9134	165.9332	163.9800	162.0535	158.2790	156.4301
	10	236.0034	232.4616	228.9842	225.5699	222.2174	218.9255	215.6928	212.5182	209.4006	203.3313	200.3775
	12	269.5571	264.9859	260.5107	256.1293	251.8396	247.6392	243.5261	239.4982	235.5534	227.9056	224.1987
	15	313.4633	307.2834	301.2589	295.3853	289.6582	284.0734	278.6268	273.3145	268.1326	258.1452	253.3327
4	1	21.7542	21.6156	21.4776	21.3404	21.2040	21.0683	20.9333	20.7991	20.6656	20.4007	20.2694
	2	42.3469	42.0261	41.7075	41.3912	41.0771	40.7651	40.4554	40.1478	39.8424	39.2379	38.9389
	3	61.8400	61.2988	60.7622	60.2302	59.7027	59.1798	58.6613	58.1473	57.6377	56.6315	56.1349
	4	80.2922	79.4970	78.7098	77.9306	77.1593	76.3957	75.6399	74.8917	74.1510	72.6921	71.9736
	5	97.7592	96.6808	95.6148	94.5614	93.5201	92.4910	91.4738	90.4684	89.4747	87.5218	86.5622
	7	129.9449	128.2277	126.5357	124.8684	123.2255	121.6066	120.0112	118.4392	116.8900	113.8587	112.3759
	10	172.0610	169.2543	166.5010	163.8001	161.1503	158.5506	155.9999	153.4972	151.0416	146.2673	143.9467
	12	196.5238	192.9351	189.4249	185.9911	182.6320	179.3457	176.1303	172.9843	169.9058	163.9449	161.0594
	15	228.5341	223.7318	219.0541	214.4973	210.0578	205.7321	201.5169	197.4090	193.4052	185.6979	181.9885
5	1	16.9133	16.7828	16.6532	16.5244	16.3964	16.2692	16.1428	16.0173	15.8925	15.6454	15.5231
	2	32.9235	32.6300	32.3389	32.0501	31.7636	31.4793	31.1974	30.9176	30.6402	30.0918	29.8210
	3	48.0788	47.5938	47.1134	46.6375	46.1662	45.6994	45.2370	44.7790	44.3254	43.4311	42.9904
	4	62.4249	61.7233	61.0295	60.3434	59.6648	58.9937	58.3301	57.6738	57.0247	55.7480	55.1203
	5	76.0050	75.0652	74.1372	73.2209	72.3161	71.4227	70.5405	69.6694	68.8092	67.1211	66.2928
	7	101.0284	99.5590	98.1124	96.6883	95.2863	93.9061	92.5473	91.2095	89.8924	87.3190	86.0620
	10	133.7725	131.4130	129.1005	126.8340	124.6124	122.4347	120.3001	118.2076	116.1562	112.1734	110.2402
	12	152.7916	149.7993	146.8750	144.0170	141.2235	138.4930	135.8238	133.2145	130.6634	125.7305	123.3458
	15	177.6787	173.7106	169.8487	166.0899	162.4310	158.8689	155.4008	152.0239	148.7353	142.4130	139.3742
7	1	11.4015	11.2823	11.1641	11.0469	10.9307	10.8154	10.7011	10.5878	10.4755	10.2537	10.1443
	2	22.1943	21.9357	21.6797	21.4262	21.1752	20.9268	20.6808	20.4374	20.1964	19.7216	19.4878
	3	32.4107	31.9951	31.5843	31.1782	30.7768	30.3800	29.9878	29.6001	29.2169	28.4639	28.0939
	4	42.0817	41.4938	40.9135	40.3408	39.7756	39.2178	38.6672	38.1239	37.5876	36.5362	36.0208
	5	51.2362	50.4629	49.7008	48.9498	48.2096	47.4803	46.7615	46.0533	45.3553	43.9898	43.3220
	7	68.1049	66.9289	65.7735	64.6382	63.5227	62.4268	61.3499	60.2919	59.2523	57.2272	56.2410
	10	90.1782	88.3429	86.5476	84.7912	83.0730	81.3920	79.7474	78.1383	76.5640	73.5162	72.0413
	12	102.9993	100.7032	98.4634	96.2784	94.1468	92.0672	90.0381	88.0582	86.1263	82.4013	80.6057
	15	119.7761	116.7777	113.8648	111.0347	108.2848	105.6127	103.0158	100.4917	98.0383	93.3347	91.0802
10	1	7.3037	7.1962	7.0899	6.9849	6.8811	6.7785	6.6771	6.5770	6.4780	6.2837	6.1883
	2	14.2175	13.9912	13.7680	13.5477	13.3303	13.1158	12.9041	12.6954	12.4894	12.0858	11.8882
	3	20.7621	20.4075	20.0581	19.7138	19.3746	19.0405	18.7113	18.3871	18.0677	17.4433	17.1382
	4	26.9572	26.4660	25.9827	25.5073	25.0396	24.5795	24.1270	23.6819	23.2441	22.3902	21.9738
	5	32.8215	32.1868	31.5632	30.9507	30.3490	29.7580	29.1776	28.6075	28.0477	26.9579	26.4277
	7	43.6275	42.6893	41.7704	40.8704	39.9889	39.1257	38.2802	37.4523	36.6415	35.0701	34.3087
	10	57.7675	56.3478	54.9633	53.6130	52.2962	51.0120	49.7596	48.5382	47.3470	45.0523	43.9474
	12	65.9806	64.2316	62.5306	60.8763	59.2675	57.7027	56.1807	54.7003	53.2604	50.4973	49.1719
	15	76.7277	74.4844	72.3114	70.2066	68.1676	66.1922	64.2783	62.4238	60.6268	57.1975	55.5617
12	1	5.7299	5.6287	5.5289	5.4304	5.3334	5.2378	5.1435	5.0505	4.9590	4.7798	4.6922
	2	11.1539	10.9436	10.7365	10.5327	10.3321	10.1346	9.9402	9.7489	9.5607	9.1933	9.0140
	3	16.2883	15.9622	15.6417	15.3266	15.0169	14.7126	14.4135	14.1196	13.8309	13.2685	12.9947
	4	21.1485	20.7010	20.2619	19.8308	19.4078	18.9926	18.5853	18.1856	17.7935	17.0314	16.6612
	5	25.7492	25.1757	24.6136	24.0628	23.5230	22.9941	22.4758	21.9680	21.4706	20.5059	20.0384
	7	34.2267	33.3905	32.5734	31.7749	30.9947	30.2324	29.4877	28.7600	28.0492	26.6765	26.0140
	10	45.3198	44.0739	42.8615	41.6818	40.5339	39.4170	38.3303	37.2730	36.2443	34.2697	33.3223
	12	51.7631	50.2403	48.7626	47.3287	45.9372	44.5869	43.2765	42.0050	40.7710	38.4115	37.2838
	15	60.1944	58.2598	56.3899	54.5826	52.8356	51.1468	49.5142	47.9359	46.4100	43.5081	42.1287
15	1	4.1794	4.0865	3.9952	3.9056	3.8175	3.7311	3.6462	3.5629	3.4811	3.3221	3.2449
	2	8.1357	7.9452	7.7584	7.5752	7.3955	7.2193	7.0466	6.8773	6.7114	6.3896	6.2336
	3	11.8808	11.5888	11.3029	11.0229	10.7488	10.4805	10.2178	9.9607	9.7091	9.2220	8.9865
	4	15.4258	15.0293	14.6415	14.2624	13.8917	13.5293	13.1751	12.8290	12.4907	11.8374	11.5220
	5	18.7816	18.2780	17.7862	17.3060	16.8373	16.3797	15.9331	15.4973	15.0720	14.2523	13.8575
	7	24.9651	24.2421	23.5380	22.8526	22.1854	21.5359	20.9038	20.2887	19.6901	18.5411	17.9899
	10	33.0565	31.9984	30.9724	29.9777	29.0133	28.0786	27.1724	26.2942	25.4430	23.8186	23.0440
	12	37.7563	36.4753	35.2366	34.0389	32.8809	31.7613	30.6788	29.6323	28.6206	26.6973	25.7835
	15	43.9062	42.2976	40.7482	39.2560	37.8186	36.4342	35.1007	33.8163	32.5791	30.2396	29.1340

Entry is percentage of desired withdrawal that must be deposited monthly.

Amount of Series of Deposits to Get Series of Withdrawals

Years of Deposit	Withdrawal	8.50%	8.75%	9.00%	9.25%	9.50%	9.75%	10.00%	10.50%	11.00%	11.50%	12.00%
						Interest on Deposits (compounded monthly)						
1	1	91.8788	91.6510	91.4238	91.1973	90.9713	90.7460	90.5213	90.0736	89.6283	89.1854	88.7449
	2	176.2958	175.6500	175.0070	174.3667	173.7291	173.0943	172.4622	171.2061	169.9607	168.7259	167.5015
	3	253.8572	252.6359	251.4219	250.2149	249.0150	247.8221	246.6362	244.2850	241.9612	239.6643	237.3940
	4	325.1195	323.1943	321.2833	319.3864	317.5036	315.6346	313.7794	310.1099	306.4941	302.9311	299.4201
	5	390.5945	387.8617	385.1533	382.4689	379.8085	377.1716	374.5582	369.4006	364.3338	359.3558	354.4650
	7	506.0242	501.4500	496.9302	492.4638	488.0503	483.6888	479.3788	470.9101	462.6386	454.5590	446.6662
	10	646.3363	638.6818	631.1505	623.7399	616.4479	609.2721	602.2105	588.4211	575.0635	562.1215	549.5801
	12	721.9138	712.1365	702.5424	693.1275	683.8878	674.8196	665.9192	648.6068	631.9226	615.8396	600.3323
	15	813.7831	800.8808	788.2690	775.9397	763.8859	752.1000	740.5749	718.2801	696.9489	676.5315	656.9812
2	1	43.9950	43.8292	43.6639	43.4993	43.3352	43.1717	43.0088	42.6848	42.3631	42.0436	41.7265
	2	84.4171	83.9990	83.5831	83.1694	82.7578	82.3483	81.9410	81.1325	80.3324	79.5404	78.7566
	3	121.5563	120.8151	120.0788	119.3475	118.6211	117.8995	117.1828	115.7637	114.3636	112.9821	111.6190
	4	155.6794	154.5574	153.4446	152.3409	151.2464	150.1608	149.0842	146.9573	144.8652	142.8072	140.7827
	5	187.0313	185.4825	183.9488	182.4300	180.9260	179.4366	177.9617	175.0545	172.2033	169.4069	166.6639
	7	242.3034	239.8025	237.3333	234.8954	232.4882	230.1114	227.7644	223.1586	218.6673	214.2873	210.0155
	10	309.4901	305.4293	301.4368	297.5114	293.6518	289.8567	286.1247	278.8457	271.8052	264.9942	258.4040
	12	345.6795	340.5566	335.5335	330.6079	325.7776	321.0404	316.3943	307.3670	298.6799	290.3179	282.2669
	15	389.6700	382.9957	376.4764	370.1077	363.8856	357.8060	351.8650	340.3843	329.4147	318.9292	308.9023
3	1	28.0718	27.9289	27.7865	27.6448	27.5038	27.3634	27.2236	26.9459	26.6707	26.3981	26.1279
	2	53.8639	53.5260	53.1900	52.8562	52.5243	52.1945	51.8667	51.2171	50.5753	49.9413	49.3151
	3	77.5613	76.9859	76.4149	75.8482	75.2859	74.7278	74.1740	73.0790	72.0005	70.9385	69.8925
	4	99.3342	98.4872	97.6480	96.8163	95.9923	95.1758	94.3668	92.7707	91.2036	89.6649	88.1539
	5	119.3389	118.1934	117.0600	115.9387	114.8293	113.7316	112.6456	110.5078	108.4150	106.3661	104.3600
	7	154.6063	152.8072	151.0325	149.2817	147.5545	145.8506	144.1696	140.8748	137.6676	134.5454	131.5055
	10	197.4760	194.6260	191.8262	189.0757	186.3736	183.7187	181.1103	176.0288	171.1220	166.3829	161.8050
	12	220.5674	217.0099	213.5244	210.1094	206.7630	203.4838	200.2702	194.0336	188.0416	182.2830	176.7472
	15	248.6363	244.0530	239.5794	235.2124	230.9492	226.7868	222.7223	214.8767	207.3915	200.2472	193.4255
4	1	20.1387	20.0088	19.8796	19.7512	19.6234	19.4963	19.3699	19.1193	18.8714	18.6263	18.3839
	2	38.6420	38.3471	38.0544	37.7637	37.4750	37.1884	36.9038	36.3407	35.7855	35.2382	34.6986
	3	55.6425	55.1544	54.6704	54.1906	53.7149	53.2433	52.7758	51.8527	50.9454	50.0536	49.1771
	4	71.2624	70.5584	69.8614	69.1715	68.4885	67.8125	67.1432	65.8248	64.5329	63.2668	62.0260
	5	85.6137	84.6763	83.7496	82.8337	81.9283	81.0334	80.1488	78.4101	76.7111	75.0510	73.4288
	7	110.9146	109.4744	108.0549	106.6560	105.2771	103.9181	102.5785	99.9567	97.4094	94.9341	92.5287
	10	141.6693	139.4342	137.2405	135.0873	132.9737	130.8990	128.8623	124.9000	121.0806	117.3984	113.8477
	12	158.2351	155.4705	152.7643	150.1150	147.5211	144.9815	142.4949	137.6752	133.0524	128.6173	124.3612
	15	178.3717	174.8448	171.4051	168.0501	164.7775	161.5848	158.4698	152.4642	146.7438	141.2928	136.0962
5	1	15.4016	15.2808	15.1608	15.0416	14.9232	14.8056	14.6887	14.4573	14.2289	14.0036	13.7812
	2	29.5523	29.2858	29.0214	28.7592	28.4991	28.2410	27.9851	27.4795	26.9821	26.4927	26.0114
	3	42.5538	42.1215	41.6933	41.2692	40.8492	40.4332	40.0212	39.2091	38.4125	37.6312	36.8650
	4	54.4995	53.8856	53.2784	52.6780	52.0842	51.4971	50.9164	49.7743	48.6574	47.5651	46.4970
	5	65.4750	64.6674	63.8700	63.0825	62.3049	61.5371	60.7789	59.2908	57.8397	56.4248	55.0450
	7	84.8244	83.6058	82.4059	81.2245	80.0612	78.9158	77.7879	75.5836	73.4461	71.3732	69.3629
	10	108.3448	106.4862	104.6637	102.8766	101.1240	99.4052	97.7196	94.4447	91.2941	88.2623	85.3444
	12	121.0138	118.7331	116.5026	114.3210	112.1870	110.0996	108.0575	104.1049	100.3207	96.6969	93.2257
	15	136.4137	133.5293	130.7186	127.9796	125.3102	122.7082	120.1711	115.2878	110.6440	106.2265	102.0228
7	1	10.0357	9.9282	9.8215	9.7158	9.6111	9.5072	9.4043	9.2011	9.0016	8.8056	8.6132
	2	19.2565	19.0274	18.8008	18.5764	18.3544	18.1346	17.9171	17.4889	17.0696	16.6590	16.2570
	3	27.7283	27.3670	27.0099	26.6570	26.3083	25.9636	25.6231	24.9540	24.3008	23.6630	23.0405
	4	35.5122	35.0103	34.5150	34.0263	33.5440	33.0682	32.5986	31.6781	30.7820	29.9096	29.0605
	5	42.6639	42.0154	41.3765	40.7469	40.1265	39.5152	38.9129	37.7348	36.5910	35.4807	34.4029
	7	55.2721	54.3200	53.3845	52.4654	51.5622	50.6748	49.8028	48.1041	46.4640	44.8805	43.3515
	10	70.5981	69.1858	67.8036	66.4511	65.1273	63.8310	62.5638	60.1080	57.7551	55.5006	53.3399
	12	78.8533	77.1428	75.4732	73.8433	72.2523	70.6990	69.1825	66.2561	63.4657	60.8044	58.2657
	15	88.8880	86.7561	84.6827	82.6659	80.7040	78.7955	76.9385	73.3733	69.9964	66.7967	63.7638
10	1	6.0941	6.0010	5.9091	5.8183	5.7287	5.6401	5.5527	5.3813	5.2141	5.0513	4.8927
	2	11.6932	11.5010	11.3114	11.1244	10.9401	10.7583	10.5791	10.2283	9.8875	9.5563	9.2347
	3	16.8377	16.5418	16.2504	15.9635	15.6810	15.4029	15.1291	14.5943	14.0761	13.5741	13.0880
	4	21.5643	21.1617	20.7658	20.3766	19.9939	19.6177	19.2478	18.5269	17.8303	17.1575	16.5076
	5	25.9071	25.3959	24.8940	24.4012	23.9174	23.4424	22.9761	22.0691	21.1951	20.3533	19.5424
	7	33.5632	32.8333	32.1185	31.4187	30.7336	30.0627	29.4060	28.1335	26.9140	25.7454	24.6256
	10	42.8697	41.8188	40.7937	39.7940	38.8190	37.8681	36.9407	35.1540	33.4543	31.8375	30.2995
	12	47.8826	46.6283	45.4081	44.2209	43.0659	41.9421	40.8487	38.7496	36.7621	34.8800	33.0975
	15	53.9761	52.4390	50.9489	49.5042	48.1035	46.7453	45.4282	42.9121	40.5450	38.3175	36.2207
12	1	4.6059	4.5208	4.4371	4.3546	4.2734	4.1934	4.1147	3.9608	3.8117	3.6674	3.5276
	2	8.8377	8.6642	8.4937	8.3259	8.1610	7.9988	7.8393	7.5285	7.2282	6.9381	6.6581
	3	12.7258	12.4617	12.2023	11.9476	11.6975	11.4520	11.2109	10.7420	10.2902	9.8551	9.4363
	4	16.2982	15.9421	15.5929	15.2505	14.9148	14.5856	14.2629	13.6365	13.0347	12.4567	11.9001
	5	19.5804	19.1319	18.6927	18.2627	17.8416	17.4293	17.0257	16.2437	15.4945	14.7769	14.0898
	7	25.3669	24.7349	24.1176	23.5149	22.9263	22.3515	21.7903	20.7074	19.6753	18.6917	17.7547
	10	32.4007	31.5041	30.6318	29.7832	28.9578	28.1548	27.3737	25.8747	24.4565	23.1148	21.8455
	12	36.1894	35.1273	34.0967	33.0965	32.1258	31.1838	30.2696	28.5213	26.8747	25.3237	23.8628
	15	40.7948	39.5048	38.2573	37.0507	35.8837	34.7549	33.6631	31.5850	29.6401	27.8194	26.1146
15	1	3.1691	3.0948	3.0219	2.9504	2.8803	2.8117	2.7443	2.6138	2.4884	2.3682	2.2529
	2	6.0808	5.9311	5.7846	5.6411	5.5006	5.3631	5.2286	4.9681	4.7187	4.4803	4.2522
	3	8.7560	8.5307	8.3103	8.0949	7.8843	7.6785	7.4773	7.0887	6.7177	6.3639	6.0266
	4	11.2140	10.9132	10.6195	10.3327	10.0528	9.7796	9.5129	8.9988	8.5094	8.0439	7.6012
	5	13.4724	13.0968	12.7306	12.3736	12.0255	11.6862	11.3555	10.7193	10.1153	9.5421	8.9986
	7	17.4538	16.9323	16.4252	15.9321	15.4527	14.9865	14.5334	13.6649	12.8446	12.0701	11.3392
	10	22.2934	21.5662	20.8617	20.1791	19.5180	18.8776	18.2573	17.0748	15.9659	14.9263	13.9518
	12	24.9002	24.0465	23.2214	22.4240	21.6533	20.9085	20.1888	18.8213	17.5445	16.3527	15.2402
	15	28.0690	27.0431	26.0549	25.1031	24.1862	23.3029	22.4521	20.8431	19.3499	17.9642	16.6783

Entry is percentage of desired withdrawal that must be deposited monthly.

Amount of Series of Withdrawals from Series of Given Deposits

Years of Deposit	Withdrawal	5.50%	5.75%	6.00%	6.25%	6.50%	6.75%	7.00%	7.25%	7.50%	8.00%	8.25%
						Interest on Deposits (compounded monthly)						
1	1	105.6408	105.9040	106.1678	106.4322	106.6972	106.9628	107.2290	107.4958	107.7633	108.3000	108.5692
	2	54.2693	54.4703	54.6720	54.8742	55.0771	55.2807	55.4848	55.6896	55.8950	56.3077	56.5149
	3	37.1626	37.3445	37.5272	37.7105	37.8945	38.0793	38.2647	38.4509	38.6377	39.0135	39.2025
	4	28.6221	28.7957	28.9701	29.1453	29.3212	29.4980	29.6756	29.8540	30.0331	30.3939	30.5755
	5	23.5081	23.6777	23.8481	24.0194	24.1917	24.3648	24.5388	24.7137	24.8896	25.2440	25.4225
	7	17.6855	17.8524	18.0205	18.1896	18.3599	18.5313	18.7037	18.8773	19.0520	19.4047	19.5828
	10	13.3565	13.5251	13.6950	13.8664	14.0391	14.2133	14.3888	14.5658	14.7442	15.1052	15.2878
	12	11.6939	11.8650	12.0377	12.2119	12.3878	12.5652	12.7443	12.9250	13.1072	13.4765	13.6635
	15	10.0560	10.2318	10.4094	10.5890	10.7704	10.9537	11.1388	11.3258	11.5146	11.8978	12.0921
2	1	217.2406	218.0605	218.8838	219.7103	220.5401	221.3732	222.2096	223.0494	223.8925	225.5887	226.4420
	2	111.5998	112.1565	112.7160	113.2781	113.8429	114.4104	114.9806	115.5535	116.1292	117.2888	117.8727
	3	76.4215	76.8939	77.3689	77.8466	78.3269	78.8099	79.2956	79.7839	80.2750	81.2652	81.7644
	4	58.8588	59.2915	59.7270	60.1652	60.6062	61.0499	61.4964	61.9457	62.3978	63.3105	63.7711
	5	48.3423	48.7533	49.1671	49.5838	50.0035	50.4260	50.8515	51.2800	51.7114	52.5832	53.0236
	7	36.3685	36.7588	37.1524	37.5493	37.9494	38.3528	38.7596	39.1696	39.5831	40.4200	40.8436
	10	27.4664	27.8486	28.2347	28.6246	29.0184	29.4162	29.8179	30.2235	30.6330	31.4641	31.8857
	12	24.0475	24.4305	24.8178	25.2093	25.6052	26.0054	26.4099	26.8187	27.2319	28.0714	28.4978
	15	20.6792	21.0676	21.4609	21.8591	22.2621	22.6700	23.0828	23.5005	23.9232	24.7831	25.2205
3	1	335.1354	336.8388	338.5518	340.2746	342.0073	343.7497	345.5021	347.2646	349.0371	352.6124	354.4154
	2	172.1641	173.2485	174.3400	175.4386	176.5443	177.6572	178.7774	179.9048	181.0396	183.3314	184.4884
	3	117.8949	118.7783	119.6681	120.5644	121.4672	122.3766	123.2926	124.2153	125.1446	127.0237	127.9735
	4	90.8010	91.5878	92.3810	93.1805	93.9864	94.7987	95.6176	96.4430	97.2751	98.9591	99.8113
	5	74.5773	75.3093	76.0477	76.7926	77.5440	78.3019	79.0664	79.8376	80.6154	82.1915	82.9898
	7	56.1054	56.7815	57.4644	58.1541	58.8508	59.5545	60.2652	60.9830	61.7080	63.1796	63.9263
	10	42.3723	43.0179	43.6711	44.3322	45.0010	45.6776	46.3622	47.0548	47.7554	49.1808	49.9058
	12	37.0979	37.7379	38.3861	39.0428	39.7078	40.3813	41.0634	41.7540	42.4532	43.8778	44.6033
	15	31.9017	32.5432	33.1940	33.8541	34.5235	35.2022	35.8903	36.5879	37.2950	38.7379	39.4738
4	1	459.6804	462.6296	465.6008	468.5939	471.6093	474.6471	477.7075	480.7908	483.8970	490.1791	493.3553
	2	236.1448	237.9474	239.7649	241.5974	243.4449	245.3078	247.1860	249.0797	250.9891	254.8554	256.8126
	3	161.7077	163.1354	164.5761	166.0298	167.4966	168.9766	170.4701	171.9771	173.4976	176.5802	178.1424
	4	124.5451	125.7909	127.0489	128.3193	129.6020	130.8974	132.2054	133.5262	134.8599	137.5666	138.9398
	5	102.2922	103.4332	104.5863	105.7514	106.9289	108.1186	109.3209	110.5358	111.7634	114.2573	115.5239
	7	76.9557	77.9663	79.0291	80.0843	81.1521	82.2324	83.3255	84.4315	85.5506	87.8282	88.9871
	10	58.1189	59.0827	60.0597	61.0500	62.0539	63.0714	64.1026	65.1478	66.2069	68.3680	69.4701
	12	50.8844	51.8309	52.7914	53.7660	54.7549	55.7582	56.7761	57.8087	58.8562	60.9961	62.0889
	15	43.7571	44.6964	45.6508	46.6206	47.6060	48.6069	49.6236	50.6563	51.7049	53.8509	54.9485
5	1	591.2508	595.8473	600.4858	605.1670	609.8910	614.6586	619.4701	624.3259	629.2264	639.1636	644.2011
	2	303.7345	306.4661	309.2250	312.0116	314.8260	317.6687	320.5399	323.4399	326.3690	332.3159	335.3343
	3	207.9918	210.1115	212.2540	214.4196	216.6087	218.8214	221.0581	223.3190	225.6044	230.2498	232.6103
	4	160.1925	162.0133	163.8551	165.7183	167.6030	169.5095	171.4381	173.3890	175.3626	179.3785	181.4214
	5	131.5704	133.2176	134.8850	136.5730	138.2817	140.0115	141.7625	143.5351	145.3295	148.9846	150.8459
	7	98.9820	100.4430	101.9239	103.4252	104.9469	106.4894	108.0529	109.6377	111.2441	114.5226	116.1953
	10	74.7538	76.0960	77.4590	78.8432	80.2489	81.6762	83.1254	84.5969	86.0910	89.1477	90.7110
	12	65.4486	66.7560	68.0851	69.4363	70.8097	72.2058	73.6248	75.0669	76.5325	79.5352	81.0729
	15	56.2814	57.5670	58.8759	60.2084	61.5646	62.9450	64.3497	65.7791	67.2335	70.2183	71.7493
7	1	877.0750	886.3422	895.7272	905.2318	914.8577	924.6065	934.4800	944.4799	954.6081	975.2561	985.7796
	2	450.5667	455.8783	461.2620	466.7188	472.2500	477.8564	483.5393	489.2997	495.1390	507.0582	513.1406
	3	308.5399	312.5477	316.6131	320.7370	324.9205	329.1644	333.4695	337.8369	342.2676	351.3224	355.9486
	4	237.6333	241.0000	244.4179	247.8877	251.4103	254.9864	258.6170	262.3029	266.0450	273.7014	277.6175
	5	195.1745	198.1655	201.2041	204.2911	207.4274	210.6137	213.8509	217.1398	220.4813	227.3254	230.8298
	7	146.8322	149.4122	152.0370	154.7073	157.4239	160.1877	162.9994	165.8599	168.7699	174.7422	177.8062
	10	110.8915	113.1953	115.5434	117.9368	120.3761	122.8622	125.3960	127.9782	130.6098	136.0244	138.8092
	12	97.0880	99.3017	101.5606	103.8654	106.2171	108.6164	111.0641	113.5612	116.1085	121.3574	124.0607
	15	83.4891	85.6328	87.8235	90.0620	92.3491	94.6856	97.0725	99.5107	102.0009	107.1413	109.7933
10	1	1369.1620	1389.6200	1410.4510	1431.6610	1453.2590	1475.2510	1497.6470	1520.4530	1543.6780	1591.4190	1615.9520
	2	703.3592	714.7328	726.3233	738.1351	750.1730	762.4414	774.9454	787.6896	800.6793	827.4154	841.1723
	3	481.6476	490.0168	498.5527	507.2589	516.1389	525.1966	534.4357	543.8602	553.4740	573.2864	583.4934
	4	370.9584	377.8434	384.8711	392.0447	399.3673	406.8423	414.4731	422.2632	430.2161	446.6247	455.0881
	5	304.6780	310.6867	316.8247	323.0948	329.5001	336.0437	342.7287	349.5583	356.5359	370.9486	378.3907
	7	229.2131	234.2507	239.4040	244.6760	250.0692	255.5867	261.2314	267.0063	272.9145	285.1436	291.4711
	10	173.1076	177.4692	181.9397	186.5218	191.2184	196.0322	200.9661	206.0232	211.2065	221.9640	227.5448
	12	151.5597	155.6867	159.9217	164.2674	168.7267	173.3023	177.9972	182.8143	187.7568	198.0304	203.3681
	15	130.3310	134.2564	138.2907	142.4367	146.6972	151.0752	155.5735	160.1953	164.9436	174.8328	179.9802
12	1	1745.2220	1776.6110	1808.6870	1841.4690	1874.9720	1909.2140	1944.2130	1979.9860	2016.5530	2092.1450	2131.2090
	2	896.5468	913.7760	931.3982	949.4234	967.8614	986.7226	1006.0170	1025.7570	1045.9520	1087.7540	1109.3860
	3	613.9389	626.4798	639.3175	652.4598	665.9144	679.6893	693.7929	708.2335	723.0199	753.6659	769.5440
	4	472.8475	483.0677	493.5383	504.2660	515.2575	526.5198	538.0601	549.8858	562.0042	587.1513	600.1959
	5	388.3622	397.2088	406.2791	415.5795	425.1160	434.8949	444.9231	455.2070	465.7537	487.6643	499.0430
	7	292.1697	299.4863	306.9990	314.7135	322.6354	330.7706	339.1250	347.7048	356.5165	374.8615	384.4086
	10	220.6541	226.8919	233.3098	239.9130	246.7070	253.6974	260.8899	268.2906	275.9054	291.8031	300.0990
	12	193.1877	199.0433	205.0751	211.2884	217.6886	224.2812	231.0721	238.0671	245.2724	260.3389	268.2133
	15	166.1283	171.6449	177.3366	183.2087	189.2665	195.5157	201.9622	208.6119	215.4709	229.8423	237.3680
15	1	2392.6620	2447.0660	2502.9730	2560.4300	2619.4830	2680.1800	2742.5720	2806.7090	2872.6450	3010.1320	3081.7980
	2	1229.1470	1258.6160	1288.9260	1320.1050	1352.1780	1385.1740	1419.1220	1454.0510	1489.9920	1565.0370	1604.2080
	3	841.6973	862.8999	884.7269	907.1982	930.3345	954.1569	978.6876	1003.9490	1029.9650	1084.3580	1112.7860
	4	648.2639	665.3671	682.9886	701.1454	719.8550	739.1355	759.0057	779.4849	800.5931	844.7804	867.9030
	5	532.4364	547.1069	562.2341	577.8333	593.9202	610.5113	627.6234	645.2740	663.4811	701.6408	721.6327
	7	400.5585	412.5060	424.8441	437.5864	450.7469	464.3401	478.3811	492.8854	507.8692	539.3426	555.8676
	10	302.5122	312.5161	322.8684	333.5817	344.6690	356.1437	368.0201	380.3126	393.0361	419.8399	433.9530
	12	264.8563	274.1580	283.7955	293.7812	304.1279	314.8489	325.9581	337.4696	349.3984	374.5700	387.8453
	15	227.7584	236.4201	245.4094	254.7384	264.4201	274.4676	284.8947	295.7156	306.9452	330.6922	343.2420

Entry is percentage of desired deposit that may be withdrawn.

Amount of Series of Withdrawals from Series of Given Deposits

Years of Deposit	Withdrawal	8.50%	8.75%	9.00%	9.25%	9.50%	9.75%	10.00%	10.50%	11.00%	11.50%	12.00%
					Interest on Deposits (compounded monthly)							
1	1	108.8391	109.1096	109.3807	109.6524	109.9248	110.1977	110.4713	111.0203	111.5719	112.1259	112.6825
	2	56.7228	56.9314	57.1406	57.3504	57.5609	57.7720	57.9837	58.4091	58.8371	59.2677	59.7009
	3	39.3922	39.5827	39.7738	39.9656	40.1582	40.3515	40.5456	40.9358	41.3289	41.7250	42.1241
	4	30.7579	30.9411	31.1252	31.3100	31.4957	31.6822	31.8695	32.2466	32.6271	33.0108	33.3979
	5	25.6020	25.7824	25.9637	26.1459	26.3291	26.5131	26.6981	27.0709	27.4474	27.8276	28.2115
	7	19.7619	19.9422	20.1236	20.3061	20.4897	20.6745	20.8603	21.2355	21.6151	21.9993	22.3881
	10	15.4718	15.6572	15.8441	16.0323	16.2220	16.4130	16.6055	16.9946	17.3894	17.7897	18.1957
	12	13.8521	14.0423	14.2340	14.4274	14.6223	14.8188	15.0168	15.4177	15.8247	16.2380	16.6574
	15	12.2883	12.4863	12.6860	12.8876	13.0910	13.2961	13.5030	13.9221	14.3483	14.7813	15.2211
2	1	227.2986	228.1586	229.0220	229.8890	230.7593	231.6331	232.5104	234.2755	236.0547	237.8482	239.6560
	2	118.4595	119.0490	119.6414	120.2365	120.8345	121.4354	122.0391	123.2552	124.4829	125.7223	126.9735
	3	82.2664	82.7711	83.2786	83.7889	84.3021	84.8180	85.3368	86.3828	87.4404	88.5096	89.5905
	4	64.2346	64.7009	65.1701	65.6423	66.1173	66.5953	67.0762	68.0470	69.0297	70.0245	71.0315
	5	53.4670	53.9134	54.3630	54.8156	55.2712	55.7300	56.1919	57.1251	58.0709	59.0295	60.0010
	7	41.2706	41.7010	42.1348	42.5722	43.0129	43.4572	43.9050	44.8112	45.7316	46.6663	47.6155
	10	32.3112	32.7408	33.1744	33.6122	34.0539	34.4998	34.9498	35.8621	36.7911	37.7367	38.6991
	12	28.9285	29.3637	29.8033	30.2473	30.6958	31.1487	31.6061	32.5344	33.4807	34.4450	35.4275
	15	25.6627	26.1100	26.5621	27.0192	27.4812	27.9481	28.4200	29.3786	30.3569	31.3549	32.3727
3	1	356.2288	358.0525	359.8866	361.7312	363.5864	365.4521	367.3286	371.1138	374.9426	378.8154	382.7329
	2	185.6531	186.8253	188.0051	189.1926	190.3879	191.5910	192.8019	195.2475	197.7250	200.2350	202.7778
	3	128.9302	129.8939	130.8645	131.8422	132.8271	133.8190	134.8182	136.8383	138.8879	140.9672	143.0769
	4	100.6702	101.5360	102.4087	103.2883	104.1750	105.0687	105.9695	107.7926	109.6448	111.5264	113.4379
	5	83.7950	84.6071	85.4263	86.2525	87.0858	87.9263	88.7740	90.4913	92.2382	94.0149	95.8221
	7	64.6804	65.4419	66.2109	66.9875	67.7716	68.5633	69.3628	70.9860	72.6387	74.3244	76.0425
	10	50.6391	51.3806	52.1305	52.8889	53.6557	54.4310	55.2150	56.8089	58.4379	60.1023	61.8028
	12	45.3376	46.0809	46.8331	47.5943	48.3646	49.1440	49.9325	51.5375	53.1797	54.8598	56.5780
	15	40.2194	40.9747	41.7398	42.5148	43.2996	44.0943	44.8990	46.5383	48.2180	49.9383	51.6995
4	1	496.5553	499.7792	503.0271	506.2994	509.5962	512.9177	516.2641	523.0322	529.9024	536.8763	543.9555
	2	258.7860	260.7757	262.7819	264.8047	266.8444	268.9009	270.9745	275.1736	279.4426	283.7831	288.1961
	3	179.7187	181.3093	182.9143	184.5338	186.1681	187.8171	189.4810	192.8542	196.2887	199.7859	203.3467
	4	140.3265	141.7267	143.1405	144.5682	146.0098	147.4655	148.9354	151.9184	154.9598	158.0608	161.2226
	5	116.8037	118.0969	119.4035	120.7239	122.0579	123.4059	124.7679	127.5347	130.3592	133.2427	136.1863
	7	90.1595	91.3456	92.5455	93.7594	94.9874	96.2297	97.4863	100.0433	102.6595	105.3363	108.0746
	10	70.5869	71.7184	72.8648	74.0262	75.2029	76.3948	77.6022	80.0641	82.5896	85.1801	87.8367
	12	63.1971	64.3209	65.4603	66.6156	67.7869	68.9743	70.1780	72.6347	75.1583	77.7500	80.4110
	15	56.0627	57.1936	58.3413	59.5061	60.6879	61.8870	63.1035	65.5892	68.1460	70.7750	73.4774
5	1	649.2853	654.4166	659.5952	664.8220	670.0971	675.4213	680.7950	691.6925	702.7939	714.1035	725.6251
	2	338.3831	341.4627	344.5732	347.7152	350.8889	354.0946	357.3328	363.9078	370.6166	377.4622	384.4475
	3	234.9965	237.4085	239.8467	242.3115	244.8030	247.3216	249.8677	255.0431	260.3320	265.7368	271.2602
	4	183.4880	185.5785	187.6933	189.8326	191.9967	194.1859	196.4004	200.9070	205.5186	210.2380	215.0676
	5	152.7301	154.6374	156.5681	158.5225	160.5010	162.5036	164.5309	168.6603	172.8916	177.2272	181.6697
	7	117.8907	119.6090	121.3505	123.1155	124.9044	126.7173	128.5547	132.3039	136.1543	140.1086	144.1693
	10	92.2980	93.9089	95.5441	97.2039	98.8885	100.5984	102.3337	105.8820	109.5362	113.2987	117.1723
	12	82.6352	84.2225	85.8350	87.4730	89.1369	90.8269	92.5434	96.0570	99.6803	103.4159	107.2665
	15	73.3064	74.8899	76.5002	78.1374	79.8020	81.4942	83.2143	86.7395	90.3800	94.1385	98.0173
7	1	996.4385	1007.2350	1018.1710	1029.2480	1040.4680	1051.8340	1063.3460	1086.8220	1110.9130	1135.6350	1161.0070
	2	519.3064	525.5569	531.8935	538.3171	544.8295	551.4315	558.1248	571.7903	585.8370	600.2762	615.1198
	3	360.6419	365.4036	370.2345	375.1358	380.1086	385.1539	390.2730	400.7367	411.5091	422.5999	434.0189
	4	281.5935	285.6303	289.7289	293.8903	298.1156	302.4056	306.7615	315.6752	324.8651	334.3404	344.1102
	5	234.3902	238.0077	241.6832	245.4175	249.2118	253.0669	256.9839	265.0076	273.2913	281.8435	290.6733
	7	180.9232	184.0943	187.3202	190.6020	193.9406	197.3369	200.7920	207.8825	215.2204	222.8140	230.6723
	10	141.6469	144.5384	147.4847	150.4867	153.5454	156.6618	159.8369	166.3672	173.1448	180.1783	187.4768
	12	126.8178	129.6298	132.4974	135.4218	138.4039	141.4447	144.5452	150.9296	157.5656	164.4618	171.6275
	15	112.5011	115.2657	118.0880	120.9689	123.9095	126.9109	129.9739	136.2894	142.8645	149.7079	156.8287
10	1	1640.9390	1666.3890	1692.3110	1718.7140	1745.6090	1773.0050	1800.9130	1858.3030	1917.8650	1979.6890	2043.8660
	2	855.1959	869.4916	884.0651	898.9221	914.0688	929.5113	945.2556	977.6758	1011.3810	1046.4280	1082.8720
	3	593.9066	604.5308	615.3703	626.4298	637.7141	649.2282	660.9771	685.1996	710.4241	736.6946	764.0576
	4	463.7293	472.5523	481.5611	490.7600	500.1531	509.7450	519.5397	539.7572	560.8430	582.8369	605.7801
	5	385.9948	393.7646	401.7038	409.8165	418.1065	426.5780	435.2350	453.1233	471.8065	491.3220	511.7084
	7	297.9451	304.5691	311.3466	318.2814	325.3771	332.6376	340.0669	355.4480	371.5537	388.4192	406.0812
	10	233.2648	239.1272	245.1357	251.2940	257.6055	264.0744	270.7041	284.4630	298.9150	314.0948	330.0387
	12	208.8441	214.4620	220.2252	226.1374	232.2024	238.4239	244.8058	258.0670	272.0191	286.6971	302.1373
	15	185.2673	190.6978	196.2751	202.0029	207.8850	213.9252	220.1275	233.0345	246.6394	260.9774	276.0851
12	1	2171.1470	2211.9780	2253.7260	2296.4110	2340.0580	2384.6890	2430.3280	2524.7300	2623.4690	2726.7570	2834.8240
	2	1131.5200	1154.1700	1177.3490	1201.0690	1225.3450	1250.1910	1275.6210	1328.2910	1383.4790	1441.3150	1501.9340
	3	785.8051	802.4590	819.5158	836.9861	854.8809	873.2107	891.9873	930.9269	971.7965	1014.6990	1059.7410
	4	613.5659	627.2696	641.3163	655.7149	670.4750	685.6059	701.1180	733.3256	767.1831	802.7800	840.2114
	5	510.7144	522.6862	534.9668	547.5646	560.4882	573.7465	587.3488	615.6230	645.3892	676.7305	709.7348
	7	394.2148	404.2875	414.6341	425.2626	436.1808	447.3970	458.9196	482.9192	508.2522	534.9956	563.2308
	10	308.6354	317.4193	326.4581	335.7592	345.3304	355.1795	365.3147	386.4775	408.8889	432.6237	457.7606
	12	276.3242	284.6785	293.2837	302.1471	311.2764	320.6796	330.3649	350.6153	372.0979	394.8870	419.0616
	15	245.1295	253.1338	261.3883	269.9004	278.6780	287.7290	297.0616	316.6056	337.3807	359.4616	382.9275
15	1	3155.4930	3231.2760	3309.2150	3389.3720	3471.8170	3556.6200	3643.8530	3825.9120	4018.6220	4222.6510	4438.7100
	2	1644.5240	1686.0220	1728.7370	1772.7090	1817.9780	1864.5840	1912.5700	2012.8590	2119.2100	2232.0170	2351.6980
	3	1142.0700	1172.2390	1203.3200	1235.3440	1268.3400	1302.3410	1337.3790	1410.7030	1488.5950	1571.3600	1659.3210
	4	891.7419	916.3208	941.6644	967.7977	994.7472	1022.5400	1051.2040	1111.2630	1175.1690	1243.1840	1315.5860
	5	742.2601	763.5445	785.5082	808.1740	831.5658	855.7083	880.6271	932.8994	988.6053	1047.9830	1111.2890
	7	572.9424	590.5866	608.8200	627.6633	647.1377	667.2656	688.0700	731.8035	778.5393	828.4930	881.8956
	10	448.5633	463.6889	479.3485	495.5614	512.3479	529.7287	547.7256	585.6581	626.3350	669.9600	716.7525
	12	401.6029	415.8608	430.6374	445.9518	461.8239	478.2743	495.3245	531.3136	569.9785	611.5211	656.1582
	15	356.2653	369.7800	383.8044	398.3575	413.4594	429.1304	445.3920	479.7761	516.7988	556.6613	599.5802

Entry is percentage of desired deposit that may be withdrawn.

Amount of Succeeding Payments to Match Prior Series

Prior Payments	5.75%	6.00%	6.25%	6.50%	6.75%	7.00%	7.25%	7.50%	7.75%	8.00%	8.25%
						Interest Rate on Deposits					
12	105.9040	106.1678	106.4322	106.6972	106.9628	107.2290	107.4958	107.7633	108.0313	108.3000	108.5692
15	107.4337	107.7683	108.1039	108.4404	108.7780	109.1165	109.4560	109.7965	110.1380	110.4804	110.8239
18	108.9854	109.3929	109.8018	110.2121	110.6239	111.0372	111.4519	111.8681	112.2857	112.7048	113.1254
24	112.1565	112.7160	113.2781	113.8429	114.4104	114.9806	115.5535	116.1292	116.7076	117.2888	117.8727
25	112.6940	113.2796	113.8681	114.4595	115.0540	115.6513	116.2517	116.8550	117.4614	118.0707	118.6831
30	115.4199	116.1400	116.8644	117.5933	118.3265	119.0641	119.8061	120.5527	121.3037	122.0592	122.8193
36	118.7782	119.6681	120.5643	121.4672	122.3766	123.2926	124.2152	125.1446	126.0808	127.0237	127.9735
48	125.7909	127.0489	128.3193	129.6020	130.8974	132.2054	133.5262	134.8599	136.2067	137.5666	138.9398
50	126.9993	128.3226	129.6594	131.0099	132.3741	133.7523	135.1445	136.5509	137.9717	139.4069	140.8568
60	133.2176	134.8850	136.5730	138.2817	140.0115	141.7625	143.5351	145.3294	147.1458	148.9846	150.8459
72	141.0827	143.2044	145.3576	147.5427	149.7602	152.0106	154.2942	156.6117	158.9636	161.3502	163.7722
75	143.1205	145.3633	147.6407	149.9533	152.3016	154.6863	157.1077	159.5666	162.0634	164.5988	167.1733
84	149.4122	152.0370	154.7073	157.4239	160.1877	162.9994	165.8599	168.7699	171.7304	174.7422	177.8062
90	153.7596	156.6555	159.6053	162.6100	165.6706	168.7882	171.9638	175.1985	178.4933	181.8494	185.2679
96	158.2335	161.4143	164.6583	167.9669	171.3412	174.7826	178.2924	181.8720	185.5226	189.2457	193.0428
100	161.2881	164.6668	168.1156	171.6359	175.2291	178.8967	182.6404	186.4616	190.3619	194.3430	198.4064
108	167.5755	171.3699	175.2495	179.2160	183.2714	187.4177	191.6569	195.9912	200.4225	204.9530	209.5850
120	177.4692	181.9397	186.5218	191.2184	196.0322	200.9661	206.0232	211.2065	216.5190	221.9640	227.5448
144	199.0433	205.0751	211.2884	217.6885	224.2812	231.0721	238.0671	245.2724	252.6942	260.3389	268.2133
150	204.8348	211.3048	217.9777	224.8599	231.9579	239.2785	246.8284	254.6150	262.6455	270.9276	279.4690
180	236.4201	245.4094	254.7384	264.4201	274.4676	284.8947	295.7156	306.9452	318.5987	330.6921	343.2420
200	260.1387	271.1517	282.6286	294.5887	307.0523	320.0404	333.5751	347.6792	362.3765	377.6919	393.6512
210	272.8759	285.0184	297.6986	310.9402	324.7678	339.2072	354.2854	370.0306	386.4720	403.6403	421.5675
240	314.9531	331.0204	347.9039	365.6447	384.2862	403.8739	424.4557	446.0817	468.8048	492.6803	517.7664
250	330.3742	347.9489	366.4545	385.9402	406.4577	428.0613	450.8084	474.7592	499.9770	526.5287	554.4845
300	419.5728	446.4970	475.1427	505.6198	538.0448	572.5418	609.2428	648.2880	689.8268	734.0176	781.0293
360	558.9447	602.2575	648.9166	699.1798	753.3245	811.6497	874.4772	942.1534	1015.0514	1093.5730	1178.1506

Prior Payments	8.50%	8.75%	9.00%	9.25%	9.50%	9.75%	10.00%	10.25%	10.50%	11.00%	12.00%
						Interest Rate on Deposits					
12	108.8391	109.1096	109.3807	109.6524	109.9248	110.1977	110.4713	110.7455	111.0203	111.5719	112.6825
15	111.1683	111.5138	111.8603	112.2077	112.5562	112.9057	113.2562	113.6077	113.9602	114.6683	116.0969
18	113.5474	113.9710	114.3960	114.8226	115.2506	115.6802	116.1112	116.5438	116.9779	117.8507	119.6147
24	118.4595	119.0490	119.6414	120.2365	120.8345	121.4354	122.0391	122.6457	123.2552	124.4829	126.9735
25	119.2986	119.9171	120.5387	121.1633	121.7911	122.4220	123.0561	123.6933	124.3337	125.6239	128.2432
30	123.5840	124.3533	125.1272	125.9057	126.6890	127.4769	128.2696	129.0670	129.8693	131.4882	134.7849
36	128.9302	129.8939	130.8645	131.8422	132.8271	133.8190	134.8182	135.8246	136.8383	138.8879	143.0769
48	140.3265	141.7267	143.1405	144.5682	146.0098	147.4655	148.9354	150.4196	151.9184	154.9598	161.2226
50	142.3215	143.8010	145.2957	146.8056	148.3308	149.8716	151.4280	153.0003	154.5886	157.8138	164.4632
60	152.7301	154.6374	156.5681	158.5225	160.5009	162.5036	164.5309	166.5830	168.6603	172.8916	181.6697
72	166.2300	168.7242	171.2553	173.8238	176.4303	179.0753	181.7594	184.4832	187.2472	192.8984	204.7099
75	169.7875	172.4420	175.1375	177.8745	180.6538	183.4758	186.3414	189.2511	192.2056	198.2519	210.9128
84	180.9232	184.0943	187.3202	190.6020	193.9406	197.3369	200.7920	204.3069	207.8825	215.2204	230.6723
90	188.7499	192.2966	195.9092	199.5890	203.3370	207.1546	211.0431	215.0038	219.0379	227.3321	244.8633
96	196.9152	200.8645	204.8921	208.9997	213.1887	217.4608	221.8176	226.2607	230.7919	240.1254	259.9273
100	202.5540	206.7874	211.1084	215.5187	220.0203	224.6149	229.3044	234.0909	238.9763	249.0518	270.4814
108	214.3207	219.1624	224.1124	229.1732	234.3472	239.6368	245.0448	250.5736	256.2260	267.9124	292.8926
120	233.2647	239.1272	245.1357	251.2939	257.6055	264.0743	270.7041	277.4990	284.4630	298.9150	330.0387
144	276.3242	284.6785	293.2837	302.1471	311.2764	320.6797	330.3649	340.3406	350.6153	372.0979	419.0616
150	288.2779	297.3625	306.7314	316.3935	326.3578	336.6338	347.2311	358.1598	369.4300	393.0380	444.8423
180	356.2653	369.7800	383.8043	398.3575	413.4593	429.1304	445.3920	462.2662	479.7761	516.7988	599.5802
200	410.2813	427.6104	445.6675	464.4832	484.0891	504.5183	525.8052	547.9855	571.0966	620.2681	731.6018
210	440.2870	459.8335	480.2435	501.5549	523.8074	547.0422	571.3025	596.6333	623.0817	679.5296	808.1435
240	544.1243	571.8180	600.9152	631.4864	663.6061	697.3525	732.8074	770.0570	809.1918	893.5015	1089.2554
250	583.9184	614.9082	647.5357	681.8871	718.0533	756.1295	796.2163	838.4194	882.8500	978.8683	1203.2156
300	831.0413	884.2444	940.8415	1001.0482	1065.0941	1133.2231	1205.6945	1282.7841	1364.7852	1544.7889	1978.8466
360	1269.2499	1367.3723	1473.0576	1586.8870	1709.4862	1841.5288	1983.7399	2136.9005	2301.8509	2670.8098	3594.9641

Entry is percentage of prior series to make succeeding series of equal value.

Number of Succeeding Payments to Match Prior Series

Number of Prior Payments	Interest Rate on Deposits										
	5.50%	5.75%	6.00%	6.25%	6.50%	6.75%	7.00%	7.25%	7.50%	7.75%	8.00%
12	12.70	12.73	12.76	12.80	12.83	12.87	12.90	12.94	12.97	13.01	13.04
13	13.82	13.86	13.90	13.94	13.98	14.02	14.06	14.11	14.15	14.19	14.23
14	14.96	15.00	15.05	15.10	15.15	15.19	15.24	15.29	15.34	15.39	15.44
15	16.11	16.16	16.21	16.27	16.32	16.38	16.43	16.49	16.55	16.61	16.66
16	17.26	17.33	17.39	17.45	17.51	17.58	17.64	17.71	17.77	17.84	17.91
17	18.43	18.51	18.58	18.65	18.72	18.79	18.87	18.94	19.02	19.09	19.17
18	19.62	19.70	19.78	19.86	19.94	20.02	20.11	20.19	20.28	20.36	20.45
19	20.81	20.90	20.99	21.08	21.18	21.27	21.36	21.46	21.56	21.65	21.75
20	22.01	22.12	22.22	22.32	22.43	22.53	22.64	22.74	22.85	22.96	23.07
21	23.23	23.35	23.46	23.57	23.69	23.81	23.93	24.05	24.17	24.29	24.41
22	24.46	24.59	24.71	24.84	24.97	25.10	25.23	25.37	25.50	25.64	25.78
23	25.71	25.85	25.98	26.13	26.27	26.41	26.56	26.71	26.86	27.01	27.16
24	26.96	27.12	27.27	27.42	27.58	27.74	27.90	28.07	28.23	28.40	28.57
25	28.23	28.40	28.57	28.74	28.91	29.09	29.26	29.44	29.63	29.81	30.00
26	29.51	29.70	29.88	30.07	30.26	30.45	30.64	30.84	31.04	31.24	31.45
27	30.81	31.01	31.21	31.41	31.62	31.83	32.04	32.26	32.48	32.70	32.93
28	32.12	32.34	32.55	32.78	33.00	33.23	33.46	33.70	33.94	34.18	34.43
29	33.44	33.68	33.92	34.16	34.40	34.65	34.90	35.16	35.42	35.69	35.96
30	34.78	35.03	35.29	35.55	35.82	36.09	36.36	36.64	36.93	37.22	37.51
33	38.88	39.20	39.52	39.85	40.19	40.53	40.88	41.23	41.59	41.96	42.33
36	43.12	43.51	43.91	44.32	44.73	45.16	45.59	46.03	46.48	46.94	47.41
42	52.03	52.61	53.19	53.80	54.41	55.05	55.70	56.36	57.04	57.74	58.46
48	61.59	62.40	63.23	64.09	64.98	65.89	66.83	67.80	68.79	69.83	70.90
50	64.93	65.84	66.76	67.73	68.72	69.74	70.79	71.89	73.02	74.19	75.40
60	82.96	84.46	86.02	87.64	89.33	91.10	92.95	94.89	96.92	99.05	101.29
72	108.06	110.67	113.42	116.34	119.43	122.72	126.23	129.98	134.01	138.36	143.07
75	115.06	118.04	121.19	124.56	128.14	131.98	136.09	140.53	145.33	150.56	156.28
80	127.46	131.17	135.14	139.40	143.98	148.95	154.35	160.25	166.74	173.95	182.00
84	138.14	142.56	147.31	152.47	158.07	164.20	170.94	178.42	186.79	196.25	207.10
90	155.62	161.36	167.61	174.50	182.11	190.61	200.19	211.12	223.78	238.73	256.83
96	175.18	182.65	190.93	200.22	210.74	222.80	236.85	253.60	274.09	300.21	335.60
100	189.59	198.54	208.59	220.04	233.25	248.79	267.47	290.70	320.94	363.41	432.28
108	222.59	235.61	250.77	268.79	290.81	318.77	356.38	412.35	516.27	Unl	Unl
120	287.20	311.77	343.14	385.79	450.30	575.30	Unl	Unl	Unl	Unl	Unl

	8.25%	8.50%	8.75%	9.00%	9.25%	9.50%	10.00%	10.50%	11.00%	11.50%	12.00%
12	13.08	13.11	13.15	13.18	13.22	13.26	13.33	13.40	13.48	13.55	13.63
13	14.27	14.31	14.36	14.40	14.44	14.49	14.57	14.66	14.75	14.84	14.94
14	15.49	15.54	15.59	15.64	15.69	15.74	15.84	15.95	16.05	16.16	16.27
15	16.72	16.78	16.84	16.90	16.96	17.02	17.14	17.26	17.38	17.51	17.64
16	17.97	18.04	18.11	18.18	18.24	18.31	18.45	18.60	18.74	18.89	19.04
17	19.24	19.32	19.40	19.48	19.56	19.64	19.80	19.96	20.13	20.30	20.47
18	20.54	20.62	20.71	20.80	20.89	20.98	21.17	21.36	21.55	21.74	21.94
19	21.85	21.95	22.05	22.15	22.25	22.36	22.57	22.78	23.00	23.22	23.45
20	23.18	23.30	23.41	23.52	23.64	23.76	23.99	24.24	24.48	24.74	24.99
21	24.54	24.66	24.79	24.92	25.05	25.18	25.45	25.72	26.00	26.29	26.58
22	25.91	26.06	26.20	26.34	26.49	26.63	26.93	27.24	27.55	27.88	28.21
23	27.31	27.47	27.63	27.79	27.95	28.12	28.45	28.79	29.15	29.51	29.88
24	28.74	28.91	29.09	29.27	29.45	29.63	30.00	30.38	30.77	31.18	31.59
25	30.19	30.38	30.57	30.77	30.97	31.17	31.58	32.01	32.44	32.89	33.35
26	31.66	31.87	32.08	32.30	32.52	32.74	33.20	33.67	34.15	34.65	35.17
27	33.15	33.39	33.62	33.86	34.10	34.35	34.85	35.37	35.91	36.46	37.03
28	34.68	34.93	35.19	35.45	35.72	35.99	36.54	37.11	37.70	38.32	38.95
29	36.23	36.51	36.79	37.07	37.37	37.66	38.27	38.90	39.55	40.22	40.93
30	37.80	38.11	38.42	38.73	39.05	39.37	40.04	40.73	41.44	42.19	42.96
33	42.71	43.10	43.49	43.90	44.31	44.73	45.60	46.50	47.44	48.43	49.46
36	47.89	48.38	48.88	49.40	49.92	50.46	51.57	52.74	53.97	55.26	56.63
42	59.20	59.96	60.74	61.55	62.38	63.23	65.02	66.93	68.97	71.15	73.51
48	72.00	73.15	74.33	75.56	76.84	78.17	80.99	84.05	87.41	91.11	95.21
50	76.66	77.96	79.32	80.73	82.20	83.74	87.02	90.61	94.58	99.01	103.98
60	103.66	106.16	108.80	111.61	114.61	117.80	124.90	133.18	143.05	155.13	170.51
72	148.19	153.81	159.98	166.85	174.55	183.27	205.03	236.39	289.85	456.76	Unl
75	162.58	169.58	177.40	186.27	196.44	208.32	239.89	292.91	443.47	Unl	Unl
80	191.10	201.52	213.64	228.05	245.65	268.03	343.85	Unl	Unl	Unl	Unl
84	219.71	234.72	253.05	276.39	307.95	355.53	Unl	Unl	Unl	Unl	Unl
90	279.52	309.54	352.85	427.79	715.51	Unl	Unl	Unl	Unl	Unl	Unl
96	389.02	492.86	Unl	Unl	Unl	Unl	Unl	Unl	Unl	Unl	Unl
100	604.13	Unl	Unl	Unl	Unl	Unl	Unl	Unl	Unl	Unl	Unl
108	Unl	Unl	Unl	Unl	Unl	Unl	Unl	Unl	Unl	Unl	Unl
120	Unl	Unl	Unl	Unl	Unl	Unl	Unl	Unl	Unl	Unl	Unl

Entry is number of deferred payments with same present value as prior series. Unl means unlimited series.

Partitions of Payment Series into Segments of Equal Value

Two Party Partition

Total Payments	Sequence	5.50%	5.75%	6.00%	6.25%	Interest Rate 6.50%	6.75%	7.00%	7.25%	7.50%	7.75%	8.00%
12	1st Party	5.9177	5.9138	5.9103	5.9064	5.9028	5.8990	5.8954	5.8915	5.8879	5.8840	5.8803
	2nd Party	6.0823	6.0862	6.0897	6.0936	6.0972	6.1010	6.1046	6.1085	6.1121	6.1160	6.1197
18	1st Party	8.8149	8.8063	8.7981	8.7896	8.7813	8.7728	8.7646	8.7561	8.7478	8.7393	8.7309
	2nd Party	9.1851	9.1937	9.2019	9.2104	9.2187	9.2272	9.2354	9.2439	9.2522	9.2607	9.2691
24	1st Party	11.6710	11.6558	11.6412	11.6261	11.6113	11.5962	11.5816	11.5665	11.5518	11.5368	11.5219
	2nd Party	12.3290	12.3442	12.3588	12.3739	12.3887	12.4038	12.4184	12.4335	12.4482	12.4632	12.4781
25	1st Party	12.1430	12.1265	12.1107	12.0943	12.0783	12.0619	12.0461	12.0297	12.0138	11.9974	11.9813
	2nd Party	12.8570	12.8735	12.8893	12.9057	12.9217	12.9381	12.9539	12.9703	12.9862	13.0026	13.0187
30	1st Party	14.4860	14.4624	14.4395	14.4160	14.3929	14.3694	14.3466	14.3231	14.3001	14.2766	14.2535
	2nd Party	15.5140	15.5376	15.5605	15.5840	15.6071	15.6306	15.6534	15.6769	15.6999	15.7234	15.7465
36	1st Party	17.2601	17.2262	17.1932	17.1594	17.1262	17.0925	17.0596	17.0259	16.9928	16.9591	16.9259
	2nd Party	18.7399	18.7738	18.8068	18.8406	18.8738	18.9075	18.9404	18.9741	19.0072	19.0409	19.0741
48	1st Party	22.6858	22.6258	22.5672	22.5075	22.4485	22.3889	22.3305	22.2709	22.2123	22.1529	22.0941
	2nd Party	25.3142	25.3742	25.4328	25.4925	25.5515	25.6111	25.6695	25.7291	25.7877	25.8471	25.9059
50	1st Party	23.5742	23.5092	23.4456	23.3808	23.3169	23.2523	23.1889	23.1243	23.0608	22.9965	22.9327
	2nd Party	26.4258	26.4908	26.5544	26.6192	26.6831	26.7477	26.8111	26.8757	26.9392	27.0035	27.0673
60	1st Party	27.9488	27.8556	27.7641	27.6713	27.5796	27.4871	27.3960	27.3036	27.2125	27.1204	27.0291
	2nd Party	32.0512	32.1444	32.2359	32.3287	32.4204	32.5129	32.6040	32.6964	32.7875	32.8796	32.9709
72	1st Party	33.0503	32.9168	32.7855	32.6527	32.5212	32.3890	32.2585	32.1264	31.9961	31.8646	31.7342
	2nd Party	38.9497	39.0832	39.2145	39.3473	39.4788	39.6110	39.7415	39.8736	40.0039	40.1354	40.2658
75	1st Party	34.3006	34.1559	34.0136	33.8697	33.7273	33.5840	33.4427	33.2997	33.1585	33.0162	32.8750
	2nd Party	40.6994	40.8441	40.9864	41.1303	41.2727	41.4160	41.5573	41.7003	41.8415	41.9838	42.1250
84	1st Party	37.9916	37.8109	37.6330	37.4535	37.2756	37.0969	36.9205	36.7423	36.5663	36.3892	36.2134
	2nd Party	46.0084	46.1891	46.3670	46.5465	46.7244	46.9031	47.0795	47.2577	47.4337	47.6108	47.7866
90	1st Party	40.4026	40.1958	39.9923	39.7868	39.5834	39.3791	39.1773	38.9737	38.7726	38.5703	38.3696
	2nd Party	49.5974	49.8042	50.0077	50.2132	50.4166	50.6209	50.8227	51.0263	51.2274	51.4297	51.6304
96	1st Party	42.7741	42.5397	42.3087	42.0759	41.8453	41.6138	41.3852	41.1547	40.9270	40.6981	40.4711
	2nd Party	53.2259	53.4603	53.6913	53.9241	54.1547	54.3862	54.6148	54.8453	55.0730	55.3019	55.5289
100	1st Party	44.3334	44.0796	43.8294	43.5775	43.3279	43.0775	42.8302	42.5810	42.3347	42.0874	41.8420
	2nd Party	55.6666	55.9204	56.1706	56.4225	56.6721	56.9225	57.1698	57.4190	57.6653	57.9126	58.1580
108	1st Party	47.3998	47.1052	46.8147	46.5225	46.2329	45.9427	45.6560	45.3675	45.0823	44.7962	44.5124
	2nd Party	60.6002	60.8948	61.1853	61.4775	61.7671	62.0573	62.3440	62.6325	62.9177	63.2038	63.4876
120	1st Party	51.8705	51.5096	51.1536	50.7961	50.4418	50.0872	49.7369	49.3848	49.0370	48.6884	48.3428
	2nd Party	68.1295	68.4904	68.8464	69.2039	69.5582	69.9128	70.2631	70.6152	70.9630	71.3116	71.6572
144	1st Party	60.3558	59.8451	59.3414	58.8367	58.3371	57.8382	57.3457	56.8521	56.3648	55.8778	55.3956
	2nd Party	83.6442	84.1549	84.6586	85.1633	85.6629	86.1618	86.6543	87.1479	87.6352	88.1222	88.6044
150	1st Party	62.3839	61.8323	61.2884	60.7438	60.2048	59.6669	59.1360	58.6043	58.0796	57.5555	57.0368
	2nd Party	87.6161	88.1677	88.7116	89.2562	89.7952	90.3331	90.8640	91.3957	91.9204	92.4445	92.9632
180	1st Party	71.9810	71.2071	70.4450	69.6842	68.9326	68.1847	67.4477	66.7121	65.9875	65.2661	64.5539
	2nd Party	108.0190	108.7929	109.5550	110.3158	111.0674	111.8153	112.5523	113.2879	114.0125	114.7339	115.4461
200	1st Party	77.8915	76.9547	76.0330	75.1149	74.2092	73.3097	72.4245	71.5431	70.6762	69.8149	68.9661
	2nd Party	122.1085	123.0453	123.9670	124.8851	125.7908	126.6903	127.5755	128.4569	129.3238	130.1851	131.0339
240	1st Party	88.6070	87.3160	86.0495	84.7932	83.5580	82.3362	81.1381	79.9504	78.7863	77.6348	76.5045
	2nd Party	151.3930	152.6840	153.9505	155.2068	156.4420	157.6638	158.8619	160.0496	161.2137	162.3652	163.4955
250	1st Party	91.0666	89.6824	88.3256	86.9811	85.6604	84.3556	83.0770	81.8111	80.5715	79.3468	78.1457
	2nd Party	158.9334	160.3176	161.6744	163.0189	164.3396	165.6444	166.9230	168.1889	169.4285	170.6532	171.8543
300	1st Party	102.1472	100.2792	98.4564	96.6600	94.9042	93.1785	91.4962	89.8396	88.2258	86.6401	85.0933
	2nd Party	197.8528	199.7208	201.5436	203.3400	205.0958	206.8215	208.5038	210.1604	211.7742	213.3599	214.9067
360	1st Party	113.0301	110.5665	108.1771	105.8378	103.5654	101.3468	99.1974	97.0949	95.0594	93.0721	91.1457
	2nd Party	246.9699	249.4335	251.8229	254.1622	256.4346	258.6532	260.8026	262.9051	264.9406	266.9279	268.8543

Entries are sequences of payments that have equal present value.

Partitions of Payment Series into Segments of Equal Value

Two Party Partition

Total Payments	Sequence	8.25%	8.50%	8.75%	9.00%	Interest Rate 9.25%	9.50%	9.75%	10.00%	10.50%	11.00%	12.00%
12	1st Party	5.8768	5.8729	5.8693	5.8656	5.8618	5.8581	5.8544	5.8506	5.8432	5.8358	5.8209
	2nd Party	6.1232	6.1271	6.1307	6.1344	6.1382	6.1419	6.1456	6.1494	6.1568	6.1642	6.1791
18	1st Party	8.7227	8.7141	8.7060	8.6976	8.6893	8.6809	8.6725	8.6641	8.6475	8.6309	8.5975
	2nd Party	9.2773	9.2859	9.2940	9.3024	9.3107	9.3191	9.3275	9.3359	9.3525	9.3691	9.4025
24	1st Party	11.5073	11.4921	11.4776	11.4628	11.4479	11.4330	11.4182	11.4034	11.3738	11.3443	11.2852
	2nd Party	12.4927	12.5079	12.5224	12.5372	12.5521	12.5670	12.5818	12.5966	12.6262	12.6557	12.7148
25	1st Party	11.9655	11.9490	11.9332	11.9171	11.9010	11.8849	11.8688	11.8527	11.8207	11.7887	11.7245
	2nd Party	13.0345	13.0510	13.0668	13.0829	13.0990	13.1151	13.1312	13.1473	13.1793	13.2113	13.2755
30	1st Party	14.2307	14.2071	14.1843	14.1612	14.1380	14.1149	14.0918	14.0686	14.0226	13.9766	13.8846
	2nd Party	15.7693	15.7929	15.8157	15.8388	15.8620	15.8851	15.9082	15.9314	15.9774	16.0234	16.1154
36	1st Party	16.8930	16.8592	16.8265	16.7932	16.7599	16.7267	16.6936	16.6604	16.5943	16.5284	16.3964
	2nd Party	19.1070	19.1408	19.1735	19.2068	19.2401	19.2733	19.3064	19.3396	19.4057	19.4716	19.6036
48	1st Party	22.0358	21.9763	21.9183	21.8595	21.8009	21.7423	21.6838	21.6254	21.5089	21.3928	21.1609
	2nd Party	25.9642	26.0237	26.0817	26.1405	26.1991	26.2577	26.3162	26.3746	26.4911	26.6072	26.8391
50	1st Party	22.8695	22.8051	22.7421	22.6785	22.6149	22.5515	22.4881	22.4248	22.2986	22.1729	21.9219
	2nd Party	27.1305	27.1949	27.2579	27.3215	27.3851	27.4485	27.5119	27.5752	27.7014	27.8271	28.0781
60	1st Party	26.9385	26.8465	26.7564	26.6654	26.5746	26.4840	26.3935	26.3032	26.1233	25.9441	25.5871
	2nd Party	33.0615	33.1535	33.2436	33.3346	33.4254	33.5160	33.6065	33.6968	33.8767	34.0559	34.4129
72	1st Party	31.6048	31.4737	31.3451	31.2155	31.0862	30.9572	30.8286	30.7002	30.4446	30.1904	29.6852
	2nd Party	40.3952	40.5263	40.6549	40.7845	40.9138	41.0428	41.1714	41.2998	41.5554	41.8096	42.3148
75	1st Party	32.7349	32.5931	32.4538	32.3137	32.1738	32.0343	31.8952	31.7564	31.4801	31.2055	30.6599
	2nd Party	42.2651	42.4069	42.5462	42.6863	42.8262	42.9657	43.1048	43.2436	43.5199	43.7945	44.3401
84	1st Party	36.0389	35.8626	35.6894	35.5152	35.3415	35.1684	34.9957	34.8236	34.4813	34.1414	33.4676
	2nd Party	47.9611	48.1374	48.3106	48.4848	48.6585	48.8316	49.0043	49.1764	49.5187	49.8586	50.5324
90	1st Party	38.1704	37.9694	37.7716	37.5731	37.3751	37.1779	36.9813	36.7854	36.3959	36.0095	35.2446
	2nd Party	51.8296	52.0306	52.2284	52.4269	52.6249	52.8221	53.0187	53.2146	53.6041	53.9905	54.7554
96	1st Party	40.2458	40.0186	39.7951	39.5708	39.3473	39.1247	38.9029	38.6819	38.2430	37.8079	36.9478
	2nd Party	55.7542	55.9814	56.2049	56.4292	56.6527	56.8753	57.0971	57.3181	57.7570	58.1921	59.0522
100	1st Party	41.5985	41.3531	41.1117	40.8696	40.6284	40.3882	40.1489	39.9107	39.4376	38.9689	38.0432
	2nd Party	58.4015	58.6469	58.8883	59.1304	59.3716	59.6118	59.8511	60.0893	60.5624	61.0311	61.9568
108	1st Party	44.2309	43.9475	43.6687	43.3893	43.1111	42.8342	42.5586	42.2844	41.7402	41.2018	40.1405
	2nd Party	63.7691	64.0525	64.3313	64.6107	64.8889	65.1658	65.4414	65.7156	66.2598	66.7982	67.8595
120	1st Party	48.0003	47.6560	47.3173	46.9783	46.6411	46.3058	45.9724	45.6409	44.9841	44.3356	43.0615
	2nd Party	71.9997	72.3440	72.6827	73.0217	73.3589	73.6942	74.0276	74.3591	75.0159	75.6644	76.9385
144	1st Party	54.9183	54.4401	53.9700	53.5006	53.0348	52.5725	52.1138	51.6587	50.7600	49.8764	48.1527
	2nd Party	89.0817	89.5599	90.0300	90.4994	90.9652	91.4275	91.8862	92.3413	93.2400	94.1236	95.8473
150	1st Party	56.5236	56.0097	55.5047	55.0010	54.5012	54.0054	53.5139	53.0264	52.0646	51.1202	49.2811
	2nd Party	93.4764	93.9903	94.4953	94.9990	95.4988	95.9946	96.4861	96.9736	97.9354	98.8798	100.7189
180	1st Party	63.8508	63.1494	62.4614	61.7773	61.1007	60.4314	59.7698	59.1157	57.8308	56.5768	54.1577
	2nd Party	116.1492	116.8506	117.5386	118.2227	118.8993	119.5686	120.2302	120.8843	122.1692	123.4232	125.8423
200	1st Party	68.1297	67.2973	66.4821	65.6734	64.8750	64.0871	63.3097	62.5427	61.0409	59.5815	56.7839
	2nd Party	131.8703	132.7027	133.5179	134.3266	135.1250	135.9129	136.6903	137.4573	138.9591	140.4185	143.2161
240	1st Party	75.3952	74.2962	73.2239	72.1648	71.1238	70.1007	69.0956	68.1082	66.1870	64.3359	60.8322
	2nd Party	164.6048	165.7038	166.7761	167.8352	168.8762	169.8993	170.9044	171.8918	173.8130	175.6641	179.1678
250	1st Party	76.9683	75.8030	74.6672	73.5466	72.4464	71.3662	70.3062	69.2659	67.2452	65.3021	61.6357
	2nd Party	173.0317	174.1970	175.3328	176.4534	177.5536	178.6338	179.6938	180.7341	182.7548	184.6979	188.3643
300	1st Party	83.5848	82.1000	80.6604	79.2477	77.8679	76.5204	75.2050	73.9206	71.4448	69.0880	64.7044
	2nd Party	216.4152	217.9000	219.3396	220.7523	222.1321	223.4796	224.7950	226.0794	228.5552	230.9120	235.2956
360	1st Party	89.2789	87.4524	85.6926	83.9759	82.3093	80.6910	79.1203	77.5953	74.6797	71.9338	66.9011
	2nd Party	270.7211	272.5476	274.3074	276.0241	277.6907	279.3090	280.8797	282.4047	285.3203	288.0662	293.0989

Entries are sequences of payments that have equal present value.

Partitions of Payment Series into Segments of Equal Value

Three Party Partition

Total Payments	Sequence	5.50%	5.75%	6.00%	6.25%	Interest Rate 6.50%	6.75%	7.00%	7.25%	7.50%	7.75%	8.00%
24	1st Party	7.7111	7.6977	7.6853	7.6721	7.6594	7.6463	7.6338	7.6207	7.6081	7.5951	7.5824
	2nd Party	7.9928	7.9924	7.9914	7.9909	7.9901	7.9894	7.9884	7.9877	7.9868	7.9860	7.9851
	3rd Party	8.2961	8.3099	8.3233	8.3370	8.3505	8.3643	8.3777	8.3915	8.4051	8.4189	8.4326
30	1st Party	9.5500	9.5294	9.5100	9.4896	9.4699	9.4496	9.4303	9.4100	9.3905	9.3704	9.3507
	2nd Party	9.9860	9.9850	9.9834	9.9822	9.9806	9.9792	9.9774	9.9760	9.9742	9.9726	9.9708
	3rd Party	10.4640	10.4856	10.5066	10.5282	10.5495	10.5711	10.5923	10.6140	10.6353	10.6570	10.6785
36	1st Party	11.3542	11.3248	11.2969	11.2679	11.2397	11.2108	11.1831	11.1542	11.1264	11.0977	11.0697
	2nd Party	11.9759	11.9740	11.9714	11.9691	11.9665	11.9641	11.9611	11.9585	11.9554	11.9527	11.9495
	3rd Party	12.6699	12.7012	12.7318	12.7630	12.7938	12.8251	12.8559	12.8872	12.9182	12.9496	12.9808
48	1st Party	14.8596	14.8084	14.7592	14.7087	14.6592	14.6090	14.5604	14.5103	14.4616	14.4120	14.3631
	2nd Party	15.9430	15.9382	15.9323	15.9269	15.9208	15.9149	15.9081	15.9018	15.8948	15.8880	15.8807
	3rd Party	17.1974	17.2534	17.3084	17.3644	17.4200	17.4761	17.5315	17.5879	17.6437	17.7001	17.7562
60	1st Party	18.2304	18.1519	18.0760	17.9985	17.9225	17.8457	17.7709	17.6944	17.6198	17.5441	17.4695
	2nd Party	19.8890	19.8794	19.8682	19.8575	19.8458	19.8341	19.8213	19.8089	19.7953	19.7820	19.7679
	3rd Party	21.8806	21.9687	22.0558	22.1440	22.2317	22.3202	22.4078	22.4967	22.5849	22.6739	22.7626
72	1st Party	21.4697	21.3588	21.2511	21.1416	21.0342	20.9258	20.8200	20.7124	20.6072	20.5008	20.3959
	2nd Party	23.8089	23.7920	23.7731	23.7545	23.7344	23.7144	23.6925	23.6711	23.6481	23.6252	23.6010
	3rd Party	26.7214	26.8492	26.9758	27.1039	27.2314	27.3599	27.4874	27.6165	27.7447	27.8741	28.0031
75	1st Party	22.2594	22.1396	22.0232	21.9050	21.7889	21.6719	21.5577	21.4416	21.3280	21.2133	21.1002
	2nd Party	24.7842	24.7650	24.7437	24.7227	24.7002	24.6775	24.6529	24.6287	24.6028	24.5769	24.5498
	3rd Party	27.9564	28.0953	28.2330	28.3723	28.5109	28.6506	28.7894	28.9297	29.0691	29.2098	29.3500
84	1st Party	24.5810	24.4328	24.2885	24.1423	23.9987	23.8543	23.7131	23.5700	23.4299	23.2887	23.1494
	2nd Party	27.6975	27.6706	27.6411	27.6116	27.5802	27.5484	27.5144	27.4805	27.4446	27.4084	27.3706
	3rd Party	31.7214	31.8966	32.0705	32.2461	32.4211	32.5973	32.7725	32.9495	33.1255	33.3029	33.4799
90	1st Party	26.0897	25.9210	25.7567	25.5906	25.4273	25.2633	25.1029	24.9406	24.7816	24.6215	24.4637
	2nd Party	29.6287	29.5956	29.5595	29.5233	29.4849	29.4460	29.4045	29.3630	29.3191	29.2748	29.2287
	3rd Party	34.2817	34.4834	34.6838	34.8861	35.0877	35.2907	35.4926	35.6965	35.8993	36.1036	36.3076
96	1st Party	27.5675	27.3774	27.1921	27.0049	26.8210	26.6364	26.4558	26.2733	26.0945	25.9147	25.7375
	2nd Party	31.5502	31.5101	31.4666	31.4228	31.3766	31.3295	31.2795	31.2294	31.1765	31.1232	31.0677
	3rd Party	36.8822	37.1125	37.3413	37.5722	37.8025	38.0341	38.2647	38.4974	38.7290	38.9621	39.1949
100	1st Party	28.5359	28.3308	28.1309	27.9292	27.7309	27.5321	27.3376	27.1411	26.9487	26.7553	26.5647
	2nd Party	32.8257	32.7803	32.7314	32.6821	32.6300	32.5769	32.5207	32.4643	32.4049	32.3448	32.2824
	3rd Party	38.6384	38.8888	39.1377	39.3887	39.6391	39.8910	40.1417	40.3946	40.6464	40.8999	41.1529
108	1st Party	30.4326	30.1964	29.9660	29.7339	29.5057	29.2772	29.0536	28.8281	28.6074	28.3858	28.1674
	2nd Party	35.3624	35.3055	35.2444	35.1826	35.1175	35.0511	34.9811	34.9105	34.8365	34.7616	34.6839
	3rd Party	42.2050	42.4981	42.7897	43.0836	43.3768	43.6717	43.9653	44.2613	44.5561	44.8527	45.1487
120	1st Party	33.1798	32.8936	32.6143	32.3336	32.0577	31.7820	31.5122	31.2407	30.9749	30.7086	30.4464
	2nd Party	39.1294	39.0519	38.9693	38.8852	38.7972	38.7072	38.6128	38.5173	38.4176	38.3164	38.2119
	3rd Party	47.6907	48.0545	48.4164	48.7811	49.1450	49.5108	49.8750	50.2420	50.6075	50.9750	51.3417
144	1st Party	38.3341	37.9376	37.5507	37.1635	36.7832	36.4045	36.0341	35.6628	35.2998	34.9373	34.5809
	2nd Party	46.5119	46.3804	46.2416	46.0998	45.9522	45.8010	45.6437	45.4840	45.3185	45.1503	44.9772
	3rd Party	59.1540	59.6820	60.2077	60.7367	61.2646	61.7945	62.3222	62.8531	63.3818	63.9125	64.4418
150	1st Party	39.5544	39.1284	38.7129	38.2972	37.8893	37.4832	37.0863	36.6888	36.3001	35.9124	35.5315
	2nd Party	48.3230	48.1753	48.0194	47.8604	47.6949	47.5254	47.3493	47.1705	46.9854	46.7973	46.6040
	3rd Party	62.1225	62.6964	63.2677	63.8424	64.4159	64.9914	65.5645	66.1407	66.7145	67.2902	67.8644
180	1st Party	45.2676	44.6846	44.1168	43.5511	42.9971	42.4477	41.9116	41.3771	40.8556	40.3374	39.8296
	2nd Party	57.1499	56.9026	56.6439	56.3797	56.1062	55.8266	55.5378	55.2447	54.9432	54.6372	54.3245
	3rd Party	77.5824	78.4128	79.2393	80.0692	80.8967	81.7256	82.5505	83.3781	84.2012	85.0254	85.8460
200	1st Party	48.7356	48.0407	47.3648	46.6932	46.0366	45.3869	44.7540	44.1246	43.5115	42.9037	42.3094
	2nd Party	62.8060	62.4751	62.1306	61.7789	61.4161	61.0459	60.6649	60.2787	59.8828	59.4819	59.0733
	3rd Party	88.4585	89.4842	90.5046	91.5279	92.5473	93.5672	94.5811	95.5967	96.6057	97.6144	98.6173
240	1st Party	54.9237	53.9936	53.0916	52.2000	51.3312	50.4758	49.6453	48.8236	48.0259	47.2389	46.4724
	2nd Party	73.5165	72.9772	72.4200	71.8528	71.2716	70.6810	70.0776	69.4682	68.8481	68.2230	67.5901
	3rd Party	111.5598	113.0292	114.4883	115.9472	117.3971	118.8432	120.2771	121.7083	123.1260	124.5381	125.9376
300	1st Party	62.5591	61.2638	60.0147	58.7884	57.6008	56.4391	55.3179	54.2160	53.1526	52.1103	51.1012
	2nd Party	87.9629	87.0146	86.0452	85.0652	84.0711	83.0690	82.0559	81.0405	80.0183	78.9964	77.9723
	3rd Party	149.4781	151.7216	153.9401	156.1463	158.3281	160.4919	162.6263	164.7435	166.8291	168.8933	170.9265
360	1st Party	68.5462	66.8919	65.3062	63.7596	62.2708	60.8236	59.4350	58.0789	56.7779	55.5100	54.2896
	2nd Party	100.3896	98.9401	97.4738	96.0040	94.5279	93.0535	91.5784	90.1128	88.6525	87.2058	85.7703
	3rd Party	191.0642	194.1680	197.2200	200.2363	203.2013	206.1229	208.9867	211.8083	214.5697	217.2842	219.9400

Entries are sequences of payments that have equal present value.

Partitions of Payment Series into Segments of Equal Value

Three Party Partition

Total Payments	Sequence	8.25%	8.50%	8.75%	9.00%	Interest Rate 9.25%	9.50%	9.75%	10.00%	10.50%	11.00%	12.00%
24	1st Party	7.5700	7.5568	7.5445	7.5317	7.5190	7.5063	7.4937	7.4810	7.4559	7.4309	7.3809
	2nd Party	7.9840	7.9832	7.9820	7.9810	7.9800	7.9789	7.9778	7.9766	7.9742	7.9717	7.9664
	3rd Party	8.4461	8.4600	8.4735	8.4873	8.5010	8.5148	8.5285	8.5423	8.5698	8.5974	8.6527
30	1st Party	9.3314	9.3112	9.2921	9.2724	9.2528	9.2332	9.2137	9.1942	9.1555	9.1170	9.0400
	2nd Party	9.9688	9.9671	9.9649	9.9629	9.9609	9.9588	9.9566	9.9544	9.9497	9.9448	9.9346
	3rd Party	10.6998	10.7217	10.7430	10.7647	10.7863	10.8080	10.8297	10.8514	10.8948	10.9382	11.0254
36	1st Party	11.0421	11.0135	10.9861	10.9582	10.9303	10.9025	10.8748	10.8471	10.7921	10.7375	10.6285
	2nd Party	11.9461	11.9432	11.9395	11.9360	11.9325	11.9289	11.9252	11.9214	11.9133	11.9049	11.8872
	3rd Party	13.0118	13.0434	13.0744	13.1057	13.1372	13.1686	13.2000	13.2316	13.2945	13.3576	13.4843
48	1st Party	14.3150	14.2655	14.2179	14.1695	14.1212	14.0731	14.0251	13.9773	13.8825	13.7883	13.6012
	2nd Party	15.8728	15.8656	15.8572	15.8491	15.8408	15.8323	15.8235	15.8145	15.7958	15.7762	15.7348
	3rd Party	17.8121	17.8689	17.9249	17.9814	18.0380	18.0946	18.1513	18.2081	18.3217	18.4355	18.6640
60	1st Party	17.3960	17.3207	17.2479	17.1743	17.1009	17.0279	16.9552	16.8828	16.7391	16.5968	16.3150
	2nd Party	19.7530	19.7386	19.7228	19.7071	19.6910	19.6745	19.6576	19.6403	19.6043	19.5668	19.4874
	3rd Party	22.8511	22.9407	23.0293	23.1186	23.2080	23.2976	23.3872	23.4769	23.6565	23.8364	24.1977
72	1st Party	20.2924	20.1870	20.0849	19.9818	19.8792	19.7771	19.6756	19.5746	19.3745	19.1767	18.7863
	2nd Party	23.5758	23.5510	23.5243	23.4976	23.4701	23.4420	23.4133	23.3839	23.3229	23.2594	23.1252
	3rd Party	28.1317	28.2620	28.3908	28.5207	28.6507	28.7808	28.9111	29.0415	29.3026	29.5640	30.0885
75	1st Party	20.9886	20.8751	20.7649	20.6539	20.5434	20.4335	20.3242	20.2155	20.0002	19.7875	19.3681
	2nd Party	24.5214	24.4934	24.4634	24.4332	24.4024	24.3708	24.3384	24.3053	24.2368	24.1653	24.0147
	3rd Party	29.4900	29.6315	29.7717	29.9129	30.0543	30.1958	30.3374	30.4792	30.7630	31.0471	31.6171
84	1st Party	23.0121	22.8727	22.7373	22.6010	22.4655	22.3309	22.1972	22.0642	21.8012	21.5417	21.0315
	2nd Party	27.3313	27.2922	27.2507	27.2089	27.1661	27.1223	27.0775	27.0317	26.9370	26.8385	26.6312
	3rd Party	33.6566	33.8351	34.0120	34.1901	34.3684	34.5468	34.7254	34.9041	35.2618	35.6198	36.3373
90	1st Party	24.3081	24.1503	23.9971	23.8430	23.6899	23.5378	23.3868	23.2368	22.9403	22.6480	22.0745
	2nd Party	29.1808	29.1331	29.0825	29.0316	28.9794	28.9261	28.8715	28.8158	28.7008	28.5813	28.3301
	3rd Party	36.5111	36.7166	36.9204	37.1254	37.3307	37.5362	37.7417	37.9474	38.3589	38.7707	39.5954
96	1st Party	25.5628	25.3859	25.2140	25.0414	24.8699	24.6997	24.5308	24.3631	24.0319	23.7058	23.0670
	2nd Party	31.0101	30.9525	30.8918	30.8306	30.7679	30.7039	30.6384	30.5716	30.4338	30.2908	29.9908
	3rd Party	39.4272	39.6616	39.8942	40.1281	40.3622	40.5964	40.8308	41.0653	41.5344	42.0034	42.9422
100	1st Party	26.3768	26.1868	26.0021	25.8166	25.6325	25.4500	25.2688	25.0890	24.7340	24.3848	23.7016
	2nd Party	32.2178	32.1530	32.0849	32.0162	31.9459	31.8740	31.8006	31.7257	31.5714	31.4114	31.0761
	3rd Party	41.4054	41.6602	41.9130	42.1672	42.4216	42.6760	42.9306	43.1853	43.6946	44.2038	45.2224
108	1st Party	27.9522	27.7350	27.5238	27.3120	27.1020	26.8937	26.6873	26.4825	26.0788	25.6824	24.9085
	2nd Party	34.6036	34.5229	34.4384	34.3530	34.2658	34.1767	34.0858	33.9931	33.8023	33.6049	33.1924
	3rd Party	45.4442	45.7421	46.0378	46.3350	46.6322	46.9296	47.2270	47.5244	48.1188	48.7127	49.8991
120	1st Party	30.1882	29.9282	29.6753	29.4222	29.1715	28.9232	28.6773	28.4338	27.9544	27.4848	26.5714
	2nd Party	38.1040	37.9954	37.8824	37.7680	37.6512	37.5321	37.4107	37.2872	37.0336	36.7718	36.2272
	3rd Party	51.7077	52.0764	52.4423	52.8098	53.1773	53.5447	53.9120	54.2790	55.0120	55.7434	57.2013
144	1st Party	34.2307	33.8793	33.5378	33.1972	32.8606	32.5280	32.1996	31.8750	31.2384	30.6178	29.4201
	2nd Party	44.7995	44.6203	44.4351	44.2477	44.0570	43.8630	43.6660	43.4660	43.0575	42.6387	41.7755
	3rd Party	64.9698	65.5004	66.0271	66.5552	67.0825	67.6090	68.1345	68.6590	69.7041	70.7435	72.8044
150	1st Party	35.1573	34.7822	34.4178	34.0545	33.6958	33.3416	32.9921	32.6468	31.9703	31.3116	30.0429
	2nd Party	46.4058	46.2057	45.9994	45.7907	45.5784	45.3628	45.1438	44.9218	44.4689	44.0053	43.0522
	3rd Party	68.4369	69.0120	69.5828	70.1548	70.7258	71.2956	71.8641	72.4314	73.5608	74.6831	76.9049
180	1st Party	39.3320	38.8353	38.3537	37.8755	37.4048	36.9414	36.4854	36.0366	35.1612	34.3143	32.6981
	2nd Party	54.0052	53.6833	53.3537	53.0211	52.6842	52.3434	51.9989	51.6511	50.9463	50.2314	48.7813
	3rd Party	86.6629	87.4814	88.2926	89.1034	89.9110	90.7152	91.5157	92.3123	93.8925	95.4544	98.5205
200	1st Party	41.7281	41.1494	40.5891	40.0341	39.4889	38.9533	38.4275	37.9109	36.9066	35.9389	34.1037
	2nd Party	58.6576	58.2392	57.8126	57.3831	56.9493	56.5118	56.0709	55.6271	54.7321	53.8300	52.0175
	3rd Party	99.6143	100.6114	101.5983	102.5829	103.5618	104.5349	105.5016	106.4619	108.3612	110.2311	113.8788
240	1st Party	45.7257	44.9858	44.2721	43.5682	42.8797	42.2062	41.5475	40.9032	39.6580	38.4677	36.2369
	2nd Party	66.9506	66.3096	65.6613	65.0120	64.3604	63.7073	63.0533	62.3993	61.0929	59.7929	57.2304
	3rd Party	127.3238	128.7046	130.0666	131.4198	132.7599	134.0865	135.3991	136.6975	139.2491	141.7393	146.5327
300	1st Party	50.1242	49.1621	48.2395	47.3351	46.4557	45.6003	44.7688	43.9600	42.4096	40.9440	38.2391
	2nd Party	76.9479	75.9295	74.9110	73.8997	72.8946	71.8968	70.9072	69.9269	67.9963	66.1108	62.4928
	3rd Party	172.9280	174.9084	176.8496	178.7653	180.6497	182.5028	184.3239	186.1132	189.5940	192.9452	199.2681
360	1st Party	53.1151	51.9644	50.8675	49.7977	48.7631	47.7619	46.7935	45.8562	44.0727	42.4023	39.3583
	2nd Party	84.3483	82.9471	81.5597	80.1943	78.8497	77.5268	76.2265	74.9493	72.4664	70.0810	65.6083
	3rd Party	222.5366	225.0885	227.5728	230.0079	232.3873	234.7112	236.9800	239.1944	243.4609	247.5167	255.0334

Entries are sequences of payments that have equal present value.

Partitions of Payment Series into Segments of Equal Value

Four Party Partition

Total	Sequence					Interest Rate						
Payments		5.50%	5.75%	6.00%	6.25%	6.50%	6.75%	7.00%	7.25%	7.50%	7.75%	8.00%
24	1st Party	5.7577	5.7465	5.7362	5.7251	5.7146	5.7036	5.6934	5.6824	5.6720	5.6611	5.6506
	2nd Party	5.9133	5.9093	5.9050	5.9009	5.8967	5.8926	5.8882	5.8841	5.8798	5.8757	5.8714
	3rd Party	6.0777	6.0811	6.0842	6.0876	6.0907	6.0940	6.0971	6.1004	6.1034	6.1067	6.1098
	4th Party	6.2514	6.2632	6.2746	6.2864	6.2980	6.3097	6.3213	6.3331	6.3447	6.3566	6.3683
36	1st Party	8.4599	8.4354	8.4125	8.3884	8.3651	8.3411	8.3185	8.2945	8.2716	8.2480	8.2249
	2nd Party	8.8002	8.7907	8.7807	8.7711	8.7611	8.7514	8.7411	8.7313	8.7211	8.7112	8.7010
	3rd Party	9.1693	9.1764	9.1830	9.1899	9.1965	9.2032	9.2095	9.2162	9.2224	9.2289	9.2351
	4th Party	9.5706	9.5974	9.6238	9.6507	9.6773	9.7043	9.7309	9.7580	9.7848	9.8120	9.8390
48	1st Party	11.0490	11.0066	10.9664	10.9247	10.8842	10.8428	10.8031	10.7619	10.7222	10.6815	10.6417
	2nd Party	11.6368	11.6192	11.6008	11.5828	11.5643	11.5461	11.5273	11.5090	11.4901	11.4714	11.4525
	3rd Party	12.2910	12.3027	12.3135	12.3246	12.3352	12.3460	12.3561	12.3666	12.3765	12.3866	12.3962
	4th Party	13.0232	13.0716	13.1194	13.1680	13.2163	13.2650	13.3134	13.3625	13.4112	13.4605	13.5096
60	1st Party	13.5284	13.4638	13.4021	13.3385	13.2766	13.2138	13.1531	13.0907	13.0302	12.9686	12.9082
	2nd Party	14.4204	14.3918	14.3621	14.3328	14.3030	14.2733	14.2429	14.2129	14.1822	14.1518	14.1210
	3rd Party	15.4389	15.4554	15.4708	15.4865	15.5014	15.5163	15.5303	15.5446	15.5580	15.5715	15.5844
	4th Party	16.6122	16.6890	16.7651	16.8422	16.9190	16.9966	17.0737	17.1518	17.2296	17.3081	17.3865
72	1st Party	15.9016	15.8108	15.7236	15.6343	15.5473	15.4593	15.3741	15.2868	15.2021	15.1161	15.0317
	2nd Party	17.1487	17.1059	17.0619	17.0184	16.9740	16.9297	16.8844	16.8396	16.7940	16.7486	16.7025
	3rd Party	18.6088	18.6303	18.6500	18.6701	18.6889	18.7077	18.7250	18.7426	18.7588	18.7750	18.7903
	4th Party	20.3409	20.4530	20.5644	20.6772	20.7898	20.9034	21.0165	21.1310	21.2451	21.3603	21.4755
84	1st Party	18.1720	18.0514	17.9351	17.8167	17.7011	17.5845	17.4714	17.3561	17.2441	17.1307	17.0195
	2nd Party	19.8195	19.7595	19.6979	19.6368	19.5746	19.5124	19.4491	19.3862	19.3222	19.2584	19.1939
	3rd Party	21.7965	21.8224	21.8461	21.8698	21.8919	21.9135	21.9333	21.9530	21.9709	21.9885	22.0046
	4th Party	24.2120	24.3667	24.5208	24.6767	24.8325	24.9896	25.1462	25.3047	25.4628	25.6224	25.7820
96	1st Party	20.3432	20.1893	20.0407	19.8899	19.7426	19.5945	19.4507	19.3046	19.1625	19.0192	18.8785
	2nd Party	22.4309	22.3504	22.2680	22.1859	22.1026	22.0193	21.9345	21.8501	21.7644	21.6790	21.5926
	3rd Party	24.9975	25.0271	25.0538	25.0800	25.1041	25.1272	25.1478	25.1681	25.1858	25.2029	25.2179
	4th Party	28.2283	28.4332	28.6375	28.8441	29.0507	29.2590	29.4670	29.6772	29.8872	30.0990	30.3110
100	1st Party	21.0454	20.8798	20.7197	20.5576	20.3991	20.2398	20.0852	19.9282	19.7756	19.6218	19.4708
	2nd Party	23.2879	23.1998	23.1097	23.0199	22.9288	22.8377	22.7450	22.6527	22.5591	22.4656	22.3712
	3rd Party	26.0668	26.0973	26.1246	26.1515	26.1757	26.1990	26.2195	26.2394	26.2567	26.2730	26.2871
	4th Party	29.5998	29.8231	30.0459	30.2711	30.4964	30.7235	30.9504	31.1796	31.4086	31.6396	31.8709
120	1st Party	24.4013	24.1720	23.9502	23.7266	23.5079	23.2892	23.0766	22.8619	22.6530	22.4433	22.2377
	2nd Party	27.4692	27.3376	27.2034	27.0695	26.9339	26.7980	26.6603	26.5229	26.3839	26.2451	26.1051
	3rd Party	31.4222	31.4547	31.4826	31.5088	31.5310	31.5511	31.5669	31.5811	31.5911	31.5991	31.6036
	4th Party	36.7073	37.0357	37.3638	37.6952	38.0272	38.3617	38.6963	39.0341	39.3719	39.7124	40.0536
150	1st Party	28.9754	28.6382	28.3119	27.9848	27.6654	27.3473	27.0385	26.7283	26.4270	26.1258	25.8312
	2nd Party	33.4085	33.1941	32.9765	32.7590	32.5395	32.3196	32.0975	31.8760	31.6526	31.4297	31.2056
	3rd Party	39.4491	39.4730	39.4889	39.5007	39.5054	39.5053	39.4979	39.4864	39.4677	39.4446	39.4151
	4th Party	48.1670	48.6947	49.2227	49.7555	50.2897	50.8277	51.3661	51.9093	52.4527	52.9999	53.5481
180	1st Party	33.0427	32.5862	32.1450	31.7048	31.2758	30.8505	30.4381	30.0259	29.6263	29.2286	28.8406
	2nd Party	38.9382	38.6209	38.3000	37.9795	37.6568	37.3342	37.0096	36.6862	36.3613	36.0375	35.7133
	3rd Party	47.4066	47.4026	47.3860	47.3615	47.3258	47.2815	47.2258	47.1626	47.0884	47.0066	46.9148
	4th Party	60.6124	61.3903	62.1690	62.9543	63.7416	64.5338	65.3266	66.1252	66.9240	67.7273	68.5314
200	1st Party	35.4966	34.9562	34.4343	33.9153	33.4103	32.9109	32.4274	31.9455	31.4790	31.0159	30.5650
	2nd Party	42.3949	41.9985	41.5987	41.1996	40.7989	40.3988	39.9972	39.5976	39.1972	38.7989	38.4010
	3rd Party	52.6397	52.6037	52.5513	52.4879	52.4101	52.3206	52.2165	52.1024	51.9742	51.8360	51.6863
	4th Party	69.4688	70.4416	71.4156	72.3971	73.3807	74.3697	75.3590	76.3545	77.3496	78.3491	79.3486
240	1st Party	39.8469	39.1321	38.4441	37.7634	37.1035	36.4540	35.8274	35.2061	34.6067	34.0147	33.4405
	2nd Party	48.7601	48.1839	47.6054	47.0298	46.4545	45.8822	45.3107	44.7442	44.1795	43.6201	43.0640
	3rd Party	62.8488	62.7111	62.5484	62.3674	62.1643	61.9430	61.7001	61.4416	61.1632	60.8698	60.5591
	4th Party	88.5441	89.9729	91.4021	92.8394	94.2777	95.7208	97.1618	98.6081	100.0506	101.4953	102.9363
300	1st Party	45.1639	44.1838	43.2453	42.3235	41.4352	40.5666	39.7333	38.9129	38.1258	37.3533	36.6085
	2nd Party	56.9833	56.0955	55.2111	54.3365	53.4690	52.6120	51.7629	50.9267	50.1001	49.2868	48.4848
	3rd Party	77.2743	76.8802	76.4470	75.9840	75.4878	74.9641	74.4102	73.8342	73.2321	72.6110	71.9690
	4th Party	120.5786	122.8406	125.0965	127.3559	129.6081	131.8574	134.0937	136.3262	138.5420	140.7488	142.9377
360	1st Party	49.2934	48.0573	46.8806	45.7323	44.6320	43.5629	42.5430	41.5450	40.5929	39.6636	38.7727
	2nd Party	63.7367	62.5092	61.2965	60.1055	58.9334	57.7840	56.6544	55.5499	54.4666	53.4085	52.3730
	3rd Party	90.3292	89.5547	88.7302	87.8682	86.9670	86.0346	85.0699	84.0836	83.0728	82.0466	81.0040
	4th Party	156.6407	159.8788	163.0928	166.2940	169.4676	172.6185	175.7327	178.8215	181.8678	184.8813	187.8502

Entries are sequences of payments that have equal present value.

Partitions of Payment Series into Segments of Equal Value

Four Party Partition

Total Payments	Sequence	8.25%	8.50%	8.75%	9.00%	Interest Rate 9.25%	9.50%	9.75%	10.00%	10.50%	11.00%	12.00%
24	1st Party	5.6404	5.6293	5.6193	5.6087	5.5982	5.5877	5.5772	5.5667	5.5460	5.5254	5.4842
	2nd Party	5.8670	5.8628	5.8583	5.8540	5.8497	5.8453	5.8410	5.8366	5.8278	5.8189	5.8010
	3rd Party	6.1127	6.1160	6.1189	6.1219	6.1249	6.1279	6.1309	6.1338	6.1396	6.1453	6.1565
	4th Party	6.3800	6.3919	6.4035	6.4154	6.4272	6.4391	6.4509	6.4628	6.4866	6.5104	6.5584
36	1st Party	8.2024	8.1786	8.1564	8.1334	8.1105	8.0877	8.0650	8.0423	7.9974	7.9529	7.8641
	2nd Party	8.6906	8.6806	8.6701	8.6598	8.6494	8.6390	8.6286	8.6181	8.5969	8.5755	8.5324
	3rd Party	9.2411	9.2474	9.2532	9.2591	9.2650	9.2709	9.2766	9.2822	9.2932	9.3039	9.3245
	4th Party	9.8659	9.8934	9.9204	9.9477	9.9750	10.0024	10.0299	10.0574	10.1125	10.1677	10.2790
48	1st Party	10.6026	10.5619	10.5234	10.4840	10.4447	10.4057	10.3668	10.3280	10.2512	10.1752	10.0244
	2nd Party	11.4332	11.4144	11.3948	11.3755	11.3561	11.3366	11.3170	11.2974	11.2577	11.2176	11.1366
	3rd Party	12.4055	12.4152	12.4240	12.4330	12.4418	12.4505	12.4589	12.4672	12.4830	12.4981	12.5262
	4th Party	13.5587	13.6085	13.6577	13.7074	13.7573	13.8072	13.8573	13.9075	14.0081	14.1091	14.3128
60	1st Party	12.8489	12.7876	12.7292	12.6698	12.6106	12.5518	12.4933	12.4351	12.3199	12.2061	11.9812
	2nd Party	14.0896	14.0589	14.0272	13.9957	13.9640	13.9322	13.9003	13.8682	13.8034	13.7380	13.6059
	3rd Party	15.5966	15.6092	15.6206	15.6321	15.6432	15.6540	15.6643	15.6743	15.6931	15.7104	15.7407
	4th Party	17.4649	17.5443	17.6230	17.7025	17.7821	17.8620	17.9421	18.0225	18.1836	18.3456	18.6723
72	1st Party	14.9489	14.8639	14.7824	14.6998	14.6177	14.5362	14.4552	14.3747	14.2157	14.0588	13.7502
	2nd Party	16.6559	16.6099	16.5627	16.5157	16.4685	16.4211	16.3734	16.3255	16.2290	16.1316	15.9350
	3rd Party	18.8045	18.8190	18.8319	18.8446	18.8567	18.8682	18.8790	18.8891	18.9074	18.9229	18.9466
	4th Party	21.5907	21.7072	21.8231	21.9399	22.0570	22.1746	22.2925	22.4107	22.6480	22.8866	23.3682
84	1st Party	16.9103	16.7986	16.6914	16.5831	16.4755	16.3688	16.2629	16.1578	15.9505	15.7465	15.3467
	2nd Party	19.1287	19.0640	18.9980	18.9321	18.8660	18.7996	18.7329	18.6658	18.5309	18.3949	18.1209
	3rd Party	22.0193	22.0340	22.0466	22.0587	22.0698	22.0798	22.0888	22.0968	22.1095	22.1180	22.1231
	4th Party	25.9418	26.1033	26.2641	26.4261	26.5887	26.7518	26.9155	27.0796	27.4092	27.7406	28.4093
96	1st Party	18.7404	18.5999	18.4646	18.3283	18.1931	18.0592	17.9265	17.7950	17.5358	17.2816	16.7850
	2nd Party	21.5053	21.4187	21.3305	21.2425	21.1542	21.0654	20.9763	20.8870	20.7072	20.5264	20.1628
	3rd Party	25.2309	25.2435	25.2533	25.2623	25.2697	25.2756	25.2799	25.2826	25.2835	25.2781	25.2498
	4th Party	30.5233	30.7379	30.9516	31.1669	31.3830	31.5998	31.8173	32.0354	32.4735	32.9140	33.8024
100	1st Party	19.3226	19.1719	19.0269	18.8808	18.7361	18.5928	18.4507	18.3100	18.0330	17.7614	17.2317
	2nd Party	22.2759	22.1812	22.0849	21.9888	21.8923	21.7954	21.6982	21.6007	21.4046	21.2075	20.8115
	3rd Party	26.2989	26.3103	26.3185	26.3258	26.3313	26.3350	26.3370	26.3373	26.3325	26.3208	26.2777
	4th Party	32.1026	32.3366	32.5697	32.8046	33.0404	33.2768	33.5141	33.7520	34.2299	34.7103	35.6791
120	1st Party	22.0362	21.8322	21.6357	21.4385	21.2435	21.0507	20.8602	20.6718	20.3020	19.9409	19.2413
	2nd Party	25.9641	25.8238	25.6816	25.5398	25.3976	25.2550	25.1122	24.9691	24.6822	24.3947	23.8202
	3rd Party	31.6044	31.6038	31.5985	31.5912	31.5809	31.5677	31.5516	31.5326	31.4859	31.4278	31.2797
	4th Party	40.3953	40.7402	41.0842	41.4305	41.7780	42.1265	42.4761	42.8266	43.5300	44.2366	45.6588
150	1st Party	25.5431	25.2531	24.9738	24.6948	24.4199	24.1490	23.8821	23.6189	23.1048	22.6060	21.6489
	2nd Party	30.9805	30.7567	30.5310	30.3061	30.0812	29.8565	29.6318	29.4075	28.9599	28.5142	27.6322
	3rd Party	39.3793	39.3398	39.2928	39.2415	39.1850	39.1232	39.0562	38.9842	38.8251	38.6468	38.2373
	4th Party	54.0972	54.6504	55.2025	55.7575	56.3139	56.8714	57.4299	57.9894	59.1103	60.2330	62.4816
180	1st Party	28.4620	28.0828	27.7181	27.3555	26.9992	26.6492	26.3054	25.9675	25.3106	24.6772	23.4732
	2nd Party	35.3888	35.0666	34.7433	34.4218	34.1015	33.7823	33.4645	33.1481	32.5202	31.8996	30.6845
	3rd Party	46.8133	46.7053	46.5865	46.4607	46.3269	46.1853	46.0361	45.8795	45.5449	45.1837	44.3908
	4th Party	69.3359	70.1453	70.9521	71.7619	72.5724	73.3833	74.1941	75.0049	76.6243	78.2395	81.4516
200	1st Party	30.1260	29.6874	29.2662	28.8483	28.4387	28.0370	27.6434	27.2574	26.5091	25.7905	24.4327
	2nd Party	38.0038	37.6099	37.2159	36.8250	36.4363	36.0500	35.6663	35.2853	34.5319	33.7910	32.3512
	3rd Party	51.5224	51.3512	51.1668	50.9737	50.7709	50.5586	50.3373	50.1073	49.6227	49.1080	48.0021
	4th Party	80.3478	81.3515	82.3511	83.3529	84.3541	85.3543	86.3530	87.3500	89.3363	91.3106	95.2140
240	1st Party	32.8834	32.3297	31.7998	31.2764	30.7654	30.2664	29.7794	29.3036	28.3867	27.5131	25.8808
	2nd Party	42.5118	41.9664	41.4241	40.8884	40.3584	39.8342	39.3162	38.8045	37.8004	36.8228	34.9514
	3rd Party	60.2320	59.8932	59.5374	59.1704	58.7912	58.4007	57.9996	57.5887	56.7405	55.8621	54.0395
	4th Party	104.3727	105.8107	107.2387	108.6648	110.0850	111.4986	112.9048	114.3031	117.0725	119.8020	125.1283
300	1st Party	35.8903	35.1806	34.5053	33.8422	33.1985	32.5734	31.9666	31.3771	30.2501	29.1875	27.2309
	2nd Party	47.6945	46.9194	46.1551	45.4055	44.6694	43.9470	43.2384	42.5435	41.1948	39.9005	37.4735
	3rd Party	71.3081	70.6349	69.9441	69.2432	68.5318	67.8116	67.0841	66.3508	64.8722	63.3863	60.4297
	4th Party	145.1071	147.2651	149.3955	151.5091	153.6003	155.6680	157.7110	159.7285	163.6829	167.5257	174.8659
360	1st Party	37.9185	37.0783	36.2837	35.5071	34.7570	34.0322	33.3320	32.6549	31.3692	30.1678	27.9817
	2nd Party	51.3604	50.3741	49.4089	48.4688	47.5522	46.6588	45.7883	44.9404	43.3105	41.7659	38.9194
	3rd Party	79.9486	78.8886	77.8186	76.7480	75.6767	74.6071	73.5410	72.4806	70.3824	68.3242	64.3635
	4th Party	190.7725	193.6590	196.4887	199.2761	202.0141	204.7020	207.3387	209.9241	214.9378	219.7420	228.7354

Entries are sequences of payments that have equal present value.

Partitions of Payment Series into Segments of Equal Value

Five Party Partition

Total Payments	Sequence	Interest Rate										
		5.50%	5.75%	6.00%	6.25%	6.50%	6.75%	7.00%	7.25%	7.50%	7.75%	8.00%
25	1st Party	4.7767	4.7663	4.7570	4.7467	4.7372	4.7270	4.7177	4.7076	4.6982	4.6881	4.6785
	2nd Party	4.8832	4.8779	4.8724	4.8671	4.8616	4.8563	4.8507	4.8454	4.8398	4.8344	4.8290
	3rd Party	4.9948	4.9944	4.9937	4.9933	4.9927	4.9922	4.9915	4.9910	4.9903	4.9898	4.9891
	4th Party	5.1115	5.1166	5.1213	5.1263	5.1311	5.1361	5.1408	5.1457	5.1505	5.1554	5.1601
	5th Party	5.2338	5.2448	5.2556	5.2665	5.2774	5.2884	5.2992	5.3103	5.3212	5.3323	5.3433
50	1st Party	9.1273	9.0885	9.0521	9.0141	8.9775	8.9398	8.9041	8.8666	8.8309	8.7939	8.7580
	2nd Party	9.5245	9.5025	9.4799	9.4577	9.4352	9.4129	9.3901	9.3678	9.3451	9.3227	9.3000
	3rd Party	9.9583	9.9547	9.9505	9.9465	9.9420	9.9377	9.9328	9.9282	9.9231	9.9181	9.9128
	4th Party	10.4335	10.4522	10.4702	10.4886	10.5065	10.5245	10.5420	10.5599	10.5772	10.5948	10.6120
	5th Party	10.9563	11.0020	11.0472	11.0931	11.1388	11.1850	11.2309	11.2774	11.3238	11.3706	11.4174
60	1st Party	10.7550	10.7006	10.6491	10.5957	10.5440	10.4913	10.4409	10.3885	10.3382	10.2866	10.2363
	2nd Party	11.3110	11.2790	11.2462	11.2139	11.1812	11.1487	11.1157	11.0832	11.0501	11.0175	10.9845
	3rd Party	11.9282	11.9219	11.9147	11.9077	11.9001	11.8926	11.8843	11.8763	11.8676	11.8590	11.8498
	4th Party	12.6165	12.6426	12.6677	12.6932	12.7180	12.7430	12.7672	12.7918	12.8156	12.8397	12.8632
	5th Party	13.3892	13.4560	13.5223	13.5896	13.6567	13.7244	13.7919	13.8603	13.9284	13.9973	14.0662
72	1st Party	12.6275	12.5513	12.4788	12.4041	12.3316	12.2580	12.1874	12.1145	12.0443	11.9726	11.9027
	2nd Party	13.4011	13.3544	13.3068	13.2597	13.2122	13.1650	13.1171	13.0698	13.0219	12.9744	12.9266
	3rd Party	14.2763	14.2654	14.2531	14.2411	14.2282	14.2152	14.2012	14.1873	14.1725	14.1576	14.1421
	4th Party	15.2738	15.3097	15.3444	15.3794	15.4135	15.4476	15.4806	15.5139	15.5462	15.5785	15.6101
	5th Party	16.4213	16.5192	16.6168	16.7157	16.8144	16.9142	17.0137	17.1145	17.2151	17.3168	17.4186
75	1st Party	13.0822	13.0001	12.9218	12.8413	12.7633	12.6841	12.6079	12.5295	12.4540	12.3769	12.3016
	2nd Party	13.9144	13.8636	13.8119	13.7607	13.7090	13.6576	13.6056	13.5542	13.5021	13.4505	13.3986
	3rd Party	14.8603	14.8479	14.8342	14.8206	14.8061	14.7913	14.7755	14.7599	14.7432	14.7265	14.7090
	4th Party	15.9443	15.9828	16.0200	16.0575	16.0940	16.1305	16.1658	16.2014	16.2358	16.2702	16.3038
	5th Party	17.1988	17.3056	17.4121	17.5199	17.6276	17.7365	17.8451	17.9550	18.0649	18.1759	18.2870
90	1st Party	15.2777	15.1634	15.0540	14.9423	14.8337	14.7240	14.6183	14.5100	14.4055	14.2995	14.1958
	2nd Party	16.4252	16.3512	16.2762	16.2018	16.1269	16.0523	15.9769	15.9023	15.8270	15.7522	15.6771
	3rd Party	17.7598	17.7384	17.7151	17.6918	17.6670	17.6419	17.6152	17.5884	17.5602	17.5317	17.5020
	4th Party	19.3307	19.3830	19.4334	19.4838	19.5328	19.5814	19.6282	19.6750	19.7202	19.7650	19.8085
	5th Party	21.2066	21.3640	21.5212	21.6803	21.8396	22.0005	22.1614	22.3242	22.4871	22.6516	22.8166
100	1st Party	16.6713	16.5333	16.4011	16.2664	16.1354	16.0035	15.8762	15.7463	15.6208	15.4938	15.3696
	2nd Party	18.0473	17.9555	17.8626	17.7703	17.6775	17.5851	17.4920	17.3995	17.3065	17.2140	17.1212
	3rd Party	19.6718	19.6425	19.6110	19.5791	19.5456	19.5114	19.4753	19.4389	19.4008	19.3621	19.3220
	4th Party	21.6178	21.6797	21.7392	21.7984	21.8557	21.9122	21.9666	22.0206	22.0725	22.1238	22.1732
	5th Party	23.9918	24.1890	24.3862	24.5857	24.7858	24.9878	25.1900	25.3946	25.5995	25.8063	26.0139
120	1st Party	19.2985	19.1085	18.9259	18.7412	18.5614	18.3811	18.2070	18.0303	17.8594	17.6873	17.5192
	2nd Party	21.1671	21.0340	20.8997	20.7663	20.6324	20.4990	20.3650	20.2319	20.0983	19.9655	19.8326
	3rd Party	23.4376	23.3877	23.3345	23.2805	23.2239	23.1661	23.1055	23.0442	22.9803	22.9155	22.8485
	4th Party	26.2545	26.3353	26.4124	26.4883	26.5612	26.6323	26.7000	26.7664	26.8294	26.8908	26.9491
	5th Party	29.8423	30.1346	30.4274	30.7236	31.0211	31.3215	31.6226	31.9272	32.2325	32.5409	32.8506
150	1st Party	22.8652	22.5876	22.3208	22.0524	21.7915	21.5314	21.2801	21.0268	20.7820	20.5368	20.2977
	2nd Party	25.5371	25.3289	25.1197	24.9119	24.7039	24.4970	24.2898	24.0843	23.8787	23.6746	23.4710
	3rd Party	28.9185	28.8236	28.7237	28.6218	28.5159	28.4075	28.2950	28.1809	28.0629	27.9430	27.8200
	4th Party	33.3340	33.4393	33.5381	33.6634	33.7229	33.8082	33.8871	33.9626	34.0316	34.0967	34.1558
	5th Party	39.3452	39.8206	40.2977	40.7804	41.2658	41.7559	42.2479	42.7455	43.2448	43.7489	44.2554
180	1st Party	26.0230	25.6494	25.2906	24.9318	24.5835	24.2378	23.9044	23.5700	23.2474	22.9256	22.6128
	2nd Party	29.5418	29.2444	28.9464	28.6509	28.3561	28.0635	27.7714	27.4823	27.1941	26.9087	26.6249
	3rd Party	34.1654	34.0073	33.8422	33.6737	33.4995	33.3216	33.1381	32.9521	32.7610	32.5673	32.3695
	4th Party	40.5098	40.6294	40.7381	40.8397	40.9314	41.0150	41.0881	41.1540	41.2094	41.2571	41.2949
	5th Party	49.7600	50.4696	51.1826	51.9038	52.6295	53.3621	54.0980	54.8416	55.5881	56.3413	57.0979
240	1st Party	31.2758	30.6970	30.1432	29.5941	29.0638	28.5415	28.0401	27.5415	27.0627	26.5889	26.1307
	2nd Party	36.5056	35.9959	35.4892	34.9891	34.4934	34.0041	33.5194	33.0421	32.5699	32.1050	31.6460
	3rd Party	43.8454	43.5038	43.1515	42.7934	42.4272	42.0557	41.6768	41.2948	40.9069	40.5164	40.1218
	4th Party	54.8989	54.9917	55.0600	55.1094	55.1360	55.1430	55.1269	55.0929	55.0367	54.9624	54.8677
	5th Party	73.4743	74.8116	76.1561	77.5140	78.8795	80.2557	81.6368	83.0287	84.4239	85.8273	87.2337
300	1st Party	35.3544	34.5674	33.8181	33.0808	32.3727	31.6800	31.0185	30.3654	29.7417	29.1283	28.5387
	2nd Party	42.1913	41.4414	40.7013	39.9752	39.2608	38.5602	37.8713	37.1974	36.5354	35.8881	35.2536
	3rd Party	52.3256	51.7308	51.1243	50.5124	49.8930	49.2700	48.6417	48.0131	47.3818	46.7518	46.1219
	4th Party	68.9209	68.8791	68.7940	68.6732	68.5128	68.3176	68.0847	67.8210	67.5225	67.1955	66.8380
	5th Party	101.2078	103.3813	105.5623	107.7585	109.9607	112.1722	114.3838	116.6031	118.8186	121.0362	123.2478
360	1st Party	38.5062	37.5202	36.5868	35.6743	34.8029	33.9556	33.1511	32.3614	31.6115	30.8779	30.1766
	2nd Party	46.7640	45.7644	44.7851	43.8308	42.8987	41.9908	41.1044	40.2430	39.4030	38.5868	37.7923
	3rd Party	59.5633	58.6632	57.7551	56.8470	55.9374	55.0310	54.1264	53.2296	52.3380	51.4567	50.5840
	4th Party	82.1229	81.8161	81.4457	81.0222	80.5435	80.0167	79.4405	78.8248	78.1669	77.4756	76.7505
	5th Party	133.0436	136.2362	139.4272	142.6256	145.8175	149.0060	152.1776	155.3413	158.4807	161.6030	164.6966

Entries are sequences of payments that have equal present value.

Partitions of Payment Series into Segments of Equal Value

Five Party Partition

Total Payments	Sequence	8.25%	8.50%	8.75%	9.00%	Interest Rate 9.25%	9.50%	9.75%	10.00%	10.50%	11.00%	12.00%
25	1st Party	4.6693	4.6591	4.6500	4.6403	4.6307	4.6211	4.6116	4.6020	4.5832	4.5645	4.5269
	2nd Party	4.8234	4.8180	4.8124	4.8070	4.8015	4.7960	4.7905	4.7850	4.7739	4.7628	4.7407
	3rd Party	4.9883	4.9877	4.9868	4.9861	4.9853	4.9845	4.9837	4.9829	4.9811	4.9793	4.9754
	4th Party	5.1648	5.1697	5.1743	5.1790	5.1838	5.1885	5.1932	5.1979	5.2072	5.2163	5.2346
	5th Party	5.3543	5.3655	5.3765	5.3876	5.3987	5.4099	5.4210	5.4322	5.4546	5.4771	5.5223
50	1st Party	8.7229	8.6860	8.6515	8.6160	8.5806	8.5455	8.5105	8.4757	8.4068	8.3388	8.2040
	2nd Party	9.2771	9.2547	9.2317	9.2090	9.1862	9.1634	9.1406	9.1177	9.0719	9.0260	8.9342
	3rd Party	9.9071	9.9017	9.8957	9.8898	9.8837	9.8775	9.8711	9.8645	9.8509	9.8367	9.8066
	4th Party	10.6288	10.6461	10.6626	10.6793	10.6959	10.7123	10.7286	10.7447	10.7764	10.8075	10.8680
	5th Party	11.4641	11.5115	11.5585	11.6059	11.6536	11.7014	11.7493	11.7974	11.8939	11.9910	12.1873
60	1st Party	10.1871	10.1359	10.0875	10.0381	9.9889	9.9400	9.8914	9.8432	9.7478	9.6537	9.4678
	2nd Party	10.9514	10.9187	10.8854	10.8523	10.8193	10.7862	10.7530	10.7199	10.6535	10.5869	10.4540
	3rd Party	11.8402	11.8309	11.8207	11.8106	11.8002	11.7896	11.7787	11.7675	11.7443	11.7201	11.6690
	4th Party	12.8862	12.9096	12.9321	12.9546	12.9770	12.9990	13.0208	13.0423	13.0844	13.1253	13.2041
	5th Party	14.1351	14.2050	14.2743	14.3444	14.4147	14.4852	14.5561	14.6272	14.7701	14.9139	15.2051
72	1st Party	11.8342	11.7634	11.6962	11.6278	11.5599	11.4925	11.4256	11.3592	11.2281	11.0991	10.8454
	2nd Party	12.8785	12.8310	12.7828	12.7349	12.6870	12.6391	12.5911	12.5432	12.4472	12.3512	12.1597
	3rd Party	14.1258	14.1098	14.0926	14.0754	14.0577	14.0396	14.0211	14.0022	13.9630	13.9222	13.8361
	4th Party	15.6409	15.6720	15.7018	15.7316	15.7609	15.7897	15.8180	15.8458	15.8998	15.9518	16.0497
	5th Party	17.5205	17.6237	17.7265	17.8302	17.9344	18.0390	18.1441	18.2496	18.4619	18.6758	19.1091
75	1st Party	12.2280	12.1519	12.0797	12.0063	11.9334	11.8610	11.7892	11.7180	11.5774	11.4391	11.1676
	2nd Party	13.3463	13.2947	13.2424	13.1903	13.1383	13.0863	13.0342	12.9822	12.8780	12.7739	12.5662
	3rd Party	14.6907	14.6726	14.6533	14.6339	14.6141	14.5937	14.5729	14.5516	14.5076	14.4617	14.3651
	4th Party	16.3366	16.3696	16.4013	16.4328	16.4638	16.4942	16.5240	16.5533	16.6101	16.6644	16.7663
	5th Party	18.3983	18.5111	18.6233	18.7367	18.8505	18.9648	19.0796	19.1950	19.4270	19.6609	20.1348
90	1st Party	14.0944	13.9903	13.8911	13.7907	13.6911	13.5925	13.4947	13.3979	13.2073	13.0203	12.6551
	2nd Party	15.6017	15.5270	15.4515	15.3765	15.3016	15.2266	15.1518	15.0770	14.9276	14.7785	14.4823
	3rd Party	17.4713	17.4405	17.4080	17.3753	17.3418	17.3076	17.2726	17.2369	17.1632	17.0867	16.9263
	4th Party	19.8507	19.8928	19.9329	19.9725	20.0111	20.0487	20.0853	20.1208	20.1885	20.2519	20.3662
	5th Party	22.9820	23.1494	23.3164	23.4849	23.6543	23.8246	23.9956	24.1675	24.5134	24.8625	25.5702
100	1st Party	15.2482	15.1239	15.0054	14.8856	14.7670	14.6497	14.5335	14.4185	14.1925	13.9714	13.5407
	2nd Party	17.0282	16.9360	16.8431	16.7506	16.6584	16.5662	16.4742	16.3823	16.1990	16.0164	15.6545
	3rd Party	19.2806	19.2390	19.1953	19.1513	19.1062	19.0601	19.0132	18.9653	18.8667	18.7645	18.5510
	4th Party	22.2209	22.2682	22.3129	22.3568	22.3993	22.4404	22.4799	22.5180	22.5896	22.6551	22.7684
	5th Party	26.2222	26.4329	26.6433	26.8556	27.0691	27.2836	27.4992	27.7159	28.1522	28.5925	29.4855
120	1st Party	17.3549	17.1878	17.0280	16.8673	16.7084	16.5516	16.3968	16.2438	15.9440	15.6519	15.0868
	2nd Party	19.6995	19.5678	19.4352	19.3036	19.1723	19.0415	18.9110	18.7810	18.5224	18.2658	17.7598
	3rd Party	22.7796	22.7101	22.6379	22.5649	22.4904	22.4145	22.3372	22.2586	22.0974	21.9313	21.5866
	4th Party	27.0044	27.0585	27.1085	27.1567	27.2024	27.2453	27.2856	27.3233	27.3905	27.4470	27.5286
	5th Party	33.1615	33.4759	33.7904	34.1075	34.4265	34.7471	35.0694	35.3933	36.0457	36.7040	38.0382
150	1st Party	20.0645	19.8288	19.6035	19.3779	19.1558	18.9371	18.7219	18.5100	18.0966	17.6963	16.9297
	2nd Party	23.2679	23.0669	22.8657	22.6662	22.4679	22.2708	22.0748	21.8802	21.4948	21.1148	20.3727
	3rd Party	27.6941	27.5670	27.4361	27.3038	27.1694	27.0330	26.8947	26.7546	26.4692	26.1778	25.5807
	4th Party	34.2092	34.2590	34.3018	34.3403	34.3737	34.4018	34.4246	34.4423	34.4620	34.4612	34.4005
	5th Party	44.7643	45.2783	45.7930	46.3117	46.8332	47.3574	47.8839	48.4130	49.4774	50.5499	52.7164
180	1st Party	22.3085	22.0024	21.7102	21.4188	21.1329	20.8523	20.5770	20.3067	19.7820	19.2772	18.3191
	2nd Party	26.3428	26.0641	25.7864	25.5118	25.2397	24.9701	24.7030	24.4386	23.9176	23.4075	22.4217
	3rd Party	32.1680	31.9650	31.7574	31.5483	31.3367	31.1229	30.9071	30.6895	30.2495	29.8044	28.9050
	4th Party	41.3230	41.3441	41.3541	41.3565	41.3501	41.3351	41.3114	41.2794	41.1902	41.0686	40.7352
	5th Party	57.8577	58.6244	59.3919	60.1646	60.9406	61.7196	62.5014	63.2858	64.8607	66.4423	69.6191
240	1st Party	25.6877	25.2455	24.8252	24.4091	24.0034	23.6074	23.2213	22.8446	22.1195	21.4301	20.1435
	2nd Party	31.1929	30.7480	30.3082	29.8761	29.4508	29.0323	28.6207	28.2160	27.4270	26.6652	25.2225
	3rd Party	39.7239	39.3256	38.9236	38.5216	38.1188	37.7158	37.3130	36.9107	36.1091	35.3139	33.7532
	4th Party	54.7532	54.6229	54.4719	54.3052	54.1218	53.9224	53.7076	53.4780	52.9771	52.4253	51.1928
	5th Party	88.6423	90.0581	91.4711	92.8880	94.3052	95.7220	97.1374	98.5507	101.3672	104.1655	109.6880
300	1st Party	27.9719	27.4094	26.8779	26.3546	25.8471	25.3547	24.8771	24.4134	23.5282	22.6949	21.1619
	2nd Party	34.6318	34.0250	33.4298	32.8487	32.2807	31.7256	31.1833	30.6536	29.6310	28.6562	26.8437
	3rd Party	45.4930	44.8690	44.2461	43.6288	43.0164	42.4095	41.8086	41.2142	40.0465	38.9094	36.7361
	4th Party	66.4519	66.0430	65.6065	65.1496	64.6718	64.1750	63.6607	63.1307	62.0293	60.8830	58.5022
	5th Party	125.4515	127.6536	129.8397	132.0183	134.1840	136.3353	138.4704	140.5881	144.7650	148.8564	156.7561
360	1st Party	29.5064	28.8439	28.2219	27.6121	27.0238	26.4555	25.9070	25.3769	24.3715	23.4332	21.7267
	2nd Party	37.0191	36.2691	35.5385	34.8297	34.1410	33.4722	32.8226	32.1918	30.9845	29.8463	27.7619
	3rd Party	49.7212	48.8727	48.0341	47.2103	46.4004	45.6047	44.8239	44.0582	42.5725	41.1486	38.4876
	4th Party	75.9949	75.2174	74.4136	73.5927	72.7555	71.9048	71.0434	70.1737	68.4184	66.6560	63.1667
	5th Party	167.7584	170.7968	173.7919	176.7552	179.6794	182.5627	185.4032	188.1995	193.6532	198.9159	208.8571

Entries are sequences of payments that have equal present value.

Payments in a Rising Series

Annual Rate of Increase 3.0%

Plan	Year of Plan	6.00%	6.50%	7.00%	7.50%	Interest Rate 8.00%	8.50%	9.00%	9.50%	10.00%	11.00%	12.00%	12.50%
3 Year Plan	1	35.36358	35.61231	35.86066	36.10862	36.35618	36.60334	36.85007	37.09637	37.34224	37.83263	38.32115	38.56470
	2	36.42449	36.68068	36.93648	37.19188	37.44687	37.70144	37.95557	38.20927	38.46251	38.96761	39.47079	39.72164
	3	37.51722	37.78110	38.04458	38.30764	38.57027	38.83248	39.09424	39.35554	39.61638	40.13663	40.65491	40.91329
	Level	36.32470	36.58066	36.83763	37.09561	37.35461	37.61461	37.87561	38.13762	38.40062	38.92961	39.46255	39.73049
4 Year Plan	1	26.89970	27.15040	27.40116	27.65198	27.90283	28.15371	28.40458	28.65545	28.90628	29.40781	29.90905	30.15952
	2	27.70669	27.96491	28.22320	28.48154	28.73992	28.99832	29.25672	29.51511	29.77347	30.29005	30.80632	31.06431
	3	28.53789	28.80386	29.06989	29.33599	29.60212	29.86827	30.13442	30.40056	30.66668	31.19875	31.73051	31.99624
	4	29.39403	29.66797	29.94199	30.21607	30.49018	30.76432	31.03845	31.31258	31.58668	32.13471	32.68243	32.95613
	Level	28.04183	28.30463	28.56884	28.83447	29.10150	29.36993	29.63975	29.91097	30.18357	30.73291	31.28773	31.56717
5 Year Plan	1	21.82416	22.07703	22.33037	22.58418	22.83841	23.09306	23.34810	23.60350	23.85926	24.37171	24.88530	25.14247
	2	22.47888	22.73934	23.00028	23.26170	23.52356	23.78585	24.04854	24.31161	24.57503	25.10287	25.63186	25.89674
	3	23.15325	23.42152	23.69029	23.95955	24.22927	24.49943	24.77000	25.04096	25.31229	25.85595	26.40082	26.67364
	4	23.84785	24.12416	24.40100	24.67834	24.95615	25.23441	25.51310	25.79219	26.07165	26.63163	27.19284	27.47385
	5	24.56328	24.84789	25.13303	25.41869	25.70483	25.99144	26.27849	26.56595	26.85380	27.43058	28.00863	28.29807
	Level	23.08394	23.35288	23.62363	23.89619	24.17054	24.44667	24.72459	25.00428	25.28574	25.85391	26.42905	26.71920
6 Year Plan	1	18.44279	18.69792	18.95393	19.21078	19.46844	19.72689	19.98609	20.24602	20.50665	21.02990	21.55560	21.81931
	2	18.99607	19.25886	19.52255	19.78710	20.05249	20.31869	20.58567	20.85340	21.12185	21.66079	22.20227	22.47389
	3	19.56595	19.83663	20.10822	20.38072	20.65407	20.92826	21.20324	21.47900	21.75551	22.31062	22.86834	23.14811
	4	20.15293	20.43173	20.71147	20.99214	21.27369	21.55610	21.83934	22.12337	22.40817	22.97994	23.55439	23.84255
	5	20.75752	21.04468	21.33282	21.62190	21.91190	22.20279	22.49452	22.78708	23.08042	23.66933	24.26102	24.55783
	6	21.38025	21.67602	21.97280	22.27056	22.56926	22.86887	23.16936	23.47069	23.77283	24.37941	24.98885	25.29456
	Level	19.78852	20.06324	20.34016	20.61926	20.90055	21.18401	21.46962	21.75738	22.04728	22.63342	23.22795	23.52833
7 Year Plan	1	16.02951	16.28697	16.54568	16.80561	17.06671	17.32897	17.59233	17.85676	18.12224	18.65616	19.19381	19.46395
	2	16.51040	16.77558	17.04205	17.30978	17.57872	17.84883	18.12010	18.39246	18.66590	19.21584	19.76962	20.04786
	3	17.00571	17.27885	17.55331	17.82907	18.10608	18.38430	18.66370	18.94424	19.22588	19.79232	20.36271	20.64930
	4	17.51588	17.79721	18.07991	18.36394	18.64926	18.93583	19.22361	19.51257	19.80266	20.38609	20.97359	21.26878
	5	18.04136	18.33113	18.62231	18.91486	19.20874	19.50390	19.80032	20.09794	20.39674	20.99767	21.60280	21.90684
	6	18.58260	18.88106	19.18098	19.48230	19.78500	20.08902	20.39433	20.70088	21.00864	21.62760	22.25088	22.56405
	7	19.14008	19.44750	19.75641	20.06677	20.37855	20.69169	21.00616	21.32191	21.63890	22.27643	22.91841	23.24097
	Level	17.44305	17.72332	18.00618	18.29161	18.57959	18.87012	19.16317	19.45873	19.75678	20.36029	20.97354	21.28378
10 Year Plan	1	11.69395	11.95853	12.22546	12.49469	12.76615	13.03978	13.31553	13.59333	13.87313	14.43845	15.01101	15.29985
	2	12.04477	12.31729	12.59223	12.86953	13.14913	13.43098	13.71500	14.00113	14.28932	14.87161	15.46134	15.75884
	3	12.40612	12.68681	12.96999	13.25561	13.54361	13.83390	14.12645	14.42117	14.71800	15.31775	15.92518	16.23161
	4	12.77830	13.06741	13.35909	13.65328	13.94991	14.24892	14.55024	14.85380	15.15954	15.77729	16.40294	16.71856
	5	13.16165	13.45943	13.75987	14.06288	14.36841	14.67639	14.98675	15.29942	15.61433	16.25061	16.89502	17.22011
	6	13.55650	13.86322	14.17266	14.48477	14.79946	15.11668	15.43635	15.75840	16.08276	16.73812	17.40187	17.73672
	7	13.96319	14.27911	14.59784	14.91931	15.24345	15.57018	15.89944	16.23115	16.56524	17.24027	17.92393	18.26882
	8	14.38209	14.70749	15.03578	15.36689	15.70075	16.03729	16.37642	16.71809	17.06220	17.75748	18.46165	18.81688
	9	14.81355	15.14871	15.48685	15.82790	16.17177	16.51841	16.86772	17.21963	17.57406	18.29020	19.01550	19.38139
	10	15.25796	15.60317	15.95145	16.30273	16.65693	17.01396	17.37375	17.73622	18.10129	18.83891	19.58596	19.96283
	Level	13.25618	13.55235	13.85221	14.15574	14.46289	14.77364	15.08793	15.40574	15.72703	16.37985	17.04605	17.38406
12 Year Plan	1	10.01368	10.28305	10.55549	10.83091	11.10924	11.39039	11.67429	11.96086	12.25001	12.83572	13.43075	13.73156
	2	10.31409	10.59154	10.87215	11.15583	11.44251	11.73210	12.02452	12.31968	12.61751	13.22079	13.83367	14.14350
	3	10.62351	10.90929	11.19831	11.49051	11.78579	12.08407	12.38526	12.68928	12.99603	13.61741	14.24868	14.56781
	4	10.94222	11.23657	11.53426	11.83522	12.13936	12.44659	12.75682	13.06995	13.38591	14.02593	14.67614	15.00484
	5	11.27048	11.57366	11.88029	12.19028	12.50354	12.81999	13.13952	13.46205	13.78749	14.44671	15.11643	15.45499
	6	11.60860	11.92087	12.23670	12.55599	12.87865	13.20459	13.53371	13.86591	14.20112	14.88011	15.56992	15.91864
	7	11.95686	12.27850	12.60380	12.93267	13.26501	13.60072	13.93972	14.28189	14.62715	15.32652	16.03702	16.39620
	8	12.31556	12.64685	12.98192	13.32065	13.66296	14.00874	14.35791	14.71035	15.06596	15.78631	16.51813	16.88808
	9	12.68503	13.02626	13.37137	13.72027	14.07285	14.42901	14.78865	15.15166	15.51794	16.25990	17.01367	17.39472
	10	13.06558	13.41705	13.77251	14.13188	14.49503	14.86188	15.23230	15.60621	15.98348	16.74770	17.52408	17.91657
	11	13.45755	13.81956	14.18569	14.55583	14.92988	15.30773	15.68927	16.07439	16.46298	17.25013	18.04981	18.45406
	12	13.86127	14.23415	14.61126	14.99251	15.37778	15.76697	16.15995	16.55663	16.95687	17.76763	18.59130	19.00769
	Level	11.65194	11.95828	12.26900	12.58407	12.90341	13.22698	13.55471	13.88654	14.22242	14.90602	15.60498	15.96004
15 Year Plan	1	8.34030	8.61687	8.89754	9.18219	9.47072	9.76300	10.05892	10.35836	10.66118	11.27652	11.90395	12.22188
	2	8.59050	8.87537	9.16446	9.45766	9.75484	10.05589	10.36069	10.66911	10.98102	11.61482	12.26107	12.58853
	3	8.84822	9.14163	9.43940	9.74139	10.04749	10.35757	10.67151	10.98918	11.31045	11.96326	12.62890	12.96619
	4	9.11367	9.41588	9.72258	10.03363	10.34891	10.66830	10.99166	11.31885	11.64976	12.32216	13.00776	13.35518
	5	9.38708	9.69836	10.01426	10.33464	10.65938	10.98835	11.32140	11.65842	11.99925	12.69183	13.39800	13.75583
	6	9.66869	9.98931	10.31468	10.64468	10.97916	11.31800	11.66105	12.00817	12.35923	13.07258	13.79994	14.16851
	7	9.95875	10.28899	10.62412	10.96402	11.30854	11.65754	12.01088	12.36842	12.73001	13.46476	14.21394	14.59356
	8	10.25751	10.59766	10.94285	11.29294	11.64779	12.00726	12.37120	12.73947	13.11191	13.86870	14.64035	15.03137
	9	10.56524	10.91559	11.27113	11.63173	11.99723	12.36748	12.74234	13.12165	13.50527	14.28476	15.07956	15.48231
	10	10.88219	11.24306	11.60927	11.98068	12.35714	12.73850	13.12461	13.51530	13.91043	14.71330	15.53195	15.94678
	11	11.20866	11.58035	11.95755	12.34010	12.72786	13.12066	13.51835	13.92076	14.32774	15.15470	15.99791	16.42518
	12	11.54492	11.92776	12.31627	12.71030	13.10969	13.51428	13.92390	14.33839	14.75757	15.60934	16.47785	16.91794
	13	11.89127	12.28559	12.68576	13.09161	13.50298	13.91971	14.34162	14.76854	15.20030	16.07762	16.97218	17.42548
	14	12.24801	12.65416	13.06633	13.48436	13.90807	14.33730	14.77187	15.21159	15.65631	16.55995	17.48135	17.94824
	15	12.61545	13.03378	13.45832	13.88889	14.32531	14.76742	15.21502	15.66794	16.12600	17.05675	18.00579	18.48669
	Level	10.07590	10.39697	10.72339	11.05505	11.39188	11.73376	12.08059	12.43227	12.78869	13.51527	14.25942	14.63779

Entries are annual percentages of initial cost or value. Divide by 12 for monthly figures.

Payments in a Rising Series

Annual Rate of Increase 3.0%

Plan	Year of Plan	6.00%	6.50%	7.00%	7.50%	8.00%	8.50%	9.00%	9.50%	10.00%	11.00%	12.00%	12.50%
	1	5.69828	5.99851	6.30599	6.62043	6.94153	7.26899	7.60247	7.94166	8.28623	8.99020	9.71180	10.07843
	2	5.86923	6.17846	6.49517	6.81904	7.14978	7.48706	7.83054	8.17991	8.53481	9.25991	10.00316	10.38078
	3	6.04531	6.36382	6.69002	7.02362	7.36427	7.71167	8.06546	8.42530	8.79086	9.53770	10.30325	10.69220
	4	6.22667	6.55473	6.89072	7.23432	7.58520	7.94302	8.30742	8.67806	9.05458	9.82383	10.61235	11.01297
	5	6.41347	6.75137	7.09745	7.45135	7.81276	8.18131	8.55665	8.93840	9.32622	10.11855	10.93072	11.34336
	6	6.60587	6.95392	7.31037	7.67489	8.04714	8.42675	8.81334	9.20656	9.60601	10.42211	11.25864	11.68366
	7	6.80405	7.16253	7.52968	7.90514	8.28856	8.67955	9.07774	9.48275	9.89419	10.73477	11.59640	12.03417
	8	7.00817	7.37741	7.75557	8.14230	8.53721	8.93994	9.35008	9.76724	10.19101	11.05681	11.94429	12.39519
	9	7.21842	7.59873	7.98824	8.38656	8.79333	9.20813	9.63058	10.06025	10.49674	11.38852	12.30262	12.76705
	10	7.43497	7.82669	8.22788	8.63816	9.05713	9.48438	9.91950	10.36206	10.81164	11.73017	12.67170	13.15006
	11	7.65802	8.06149	8.47472	8.89731	9.32884	9.76891	10.21708	10.67292	11.13599	12.08208	13.05185	13.54456
25 Year	12	7.88776	8.30334	8.72896	9.16422	9.60871	10.06198	10.52359	10.99311	11.47007	12.44454	13.44341	13.95090
Plan	13	8.12439	8.55244	8.99083	9.43915	9.89697	10.36384	10.83930	11.32290	11.81418	12.81788	13.84671	14.36942
	14	8.36812	8.80901	9.26056	9.72233	10.19388	10.67475	11.16448	11.66259	12.16860	13.20241	14.26211	14.80051
	15	8.61917	9.07328	9.53837	10.01400	10.49969	10.99499	11.49942	12.01247	12.53366	13.59848	14.68997	15.24452
	16	8.87774	9.34548	9.82452	10.31442	10.81468	11.32484	11.84440	12.37284	12.90967	14.00644	15.13067	15.70186
	17	9.14407	9.62585	10.11926	10.62385	11.13913	11.66459	12.19973	12.74403	13.29696	14.42663	15.58459	16.17291
	18	9.41840	9.91462	10.42284	10.94256	11.47330	12.01453	12.56572	13.12635	13.69587	14.85943	16.05213	16.65810
	19	9.70095	10.21206	10.73552	11.27084	11.81750	12.37496	12.94269	13.52014	14.10674	15.30521	16.53370	17.15784
	20	9.99198	10.51842	11.05759	11.60897	12.17202	12.74621	13.33097	13.92574	14.52995	15.76437	17.02971	17.67258
	21	10.29174	10.83397	11.38932	11.95724	12.53718	13.12860	13.73090	14.34352	14.96584	16.23730	17.54060	18.20276
	22	10.60049	11.15899	11.73100	12.31595	12.91330	13.52246	14.14283	14.77382	15.41482	16.72442	18.06682	18.74884
	23	10.91850	11.49376	12.08293	12.68543	13.30070	13.92813	14.56712	15.21704	15.87726	17.22615	18.60882	19.31130
	24	11.24606	11.83858	12.44541	13.06599	13.69972	14.34597	15.00413	15.67355	16.35358	17.74294	19.16708	19.89064
	25	11.58344	12.19373	12.81878	13.45797	14.11071	14.77635	15.45425	16.14375	16.84419	18.27522	19.74210	20.48736
	Level	7.69315	8.05883	8.43216	8.81281	9.20046	9.59476	9.99539	10.40201	10.81429	11.65452	12.51355	12.94936
	1	5.05446	5.36616	5.68649	6.01504	6.35134	6.69497	7.04544	7.40230	7.76508	8.50659	9.26641	9.65212
	2	5.20610	5.52714	5.85709	6.19549	6.54188	6.89581	7.25680	7.62437	7.99803	8.76179	9.54440	9.94168
	3	5.36228	5.69296	6.03280	6.38135	6.73814	7.10269	7.47450	7.85310	8.23797	9.02464	9.83073	10.23993
	4	5.52315	5.86375	6.21378	6.57279	6.94029	7.31577	7.69874	8.08869	8.48511	9.29538	10.12565	10.54713
	5	5.68884	6.03966	6.40020	6.76998	7.14849	7.53524	7.92970	8.33135	8.73967	9.57424	10.42942	10.86354
	6	5.85951	6.22085	6.59220	6.97307	7.36295	7.76130	8.16759	8.58129	9.00186	9.86147	10.74230	11.18945
	7	6.03529	6.40748	6.78997	7.18227	7.58384	7.99414	8.41262	8.83873	9.27191	10.15731	11.06457	11.52513
	8	6.21635	6.59970	6.99367	7.39774	7.81135	8.23396	8.66500	9.10389	9.55007	10.46203	11.39651	11.87088
	9	6.40284	6.79769	7.20348	7.61967	8.04569	8.48098	8.92495	9.37701	9.83657	10.77589	11.73841	12.22701
	10	6.59493	7.00162	7.41958	7.84826	8.28706	8.73541	9.19270	9.65832	10.13167	11.09917	12.09056	12.59382
	11	6.79278	7.21167	7.64217	8.08370	8.53568	8.99747	9.46848	9.94807	10.43562	11.43215	12.45327	12.97164
	12	6.99656	7.42802	7.87144	8.32622	8.79175	9.26740	9.75253	10.24651	10.74869	11.77511	12.82687	13.36079
	13	7.20646	7.65086	8.10758	8.57600	9.05550	9.54542	10.04511	10.55391	11.07115	12.12836	13.21168	13.76161
	14	7.42265	7.88039	8.35081	8.83328	9.32716	9.83178	10.34646	10.87052	11.40328	12.49221	13.60803	14.17446
30 Year	15	7.64533	8.11680	8.60133	9.09828	9.60698	10.12674	10.65686	11.19664	11.74538	12.86698	14.01627	14.59969
Plan	16	7.87469	8.36030	8.85937	9.37123	9.89519	10.43054	10.97656	11.53254	12.09774	13.25299	14.43676	15.03768
	17	8.11093	8.61111	9.12515	9.65237	10.19204	10.74345	11.30586	11.87851	12.46067	13.65058	14.86986	15.48881
	18	8.35426	8.86944	9.39891	9.94194	10.49780	11.06576	11.64503	12.23487	12.83449	14.06010	15.31596	15.95348
	19	8.60489	9.13553	9.68087	10.24020	10.81274	11.39773	11.99439	12.60191	13.21953	14.48190	15.77543	16.43208
	20	8.86303	9.40959	9.97130	10.54740	11.13712	11.73966	12.35422	12.97997	13.61611	14.91636	16.24870	16.92504
	21	9.12892	9.69188	10.27044	10.86382	11.47123	12.09185	12.72484	13.36937	14.02460	15.36385	16.73616	17.43279
	22	9.40279	9.98264	10.57855	11.18974	11.81537	12.45461	13.10659	13.77045	14.44534	15.82476	17.23824	17.95578
	23	9.68487	10.28212	10.89591	11.52543	12.16983	12.82825	13.49979	14.18357	14.87870	16.29951	17.75539	18.49445
	24	9.97542	10.59058	11.22279	11.87119	12.53493	13.21309	13.90478	14.60907	15.32506	16.78849	18.28805	19.04929
	25	10.27468	10.90830	11.55947	12.22733	12.91098	13.60949	14.32192	15.04735	15.78481	17.29215	18.83669	19.62076
	26	10.58292	11.23555	11.90625	12.59415	13.29830	14.01777	14.75158	15.49877	16.25835	17.81091	19.40180	20.20939
	27	10.90041	11.57261	12.26344	12.97197	13.69725	14.43830	15.19413	15.96373	16.74610	18.34524	19.98385	20.81567
	28	11.22742	11.91979	12.63134	13.36113	14.10817	14.87145	15.64995	16.44264	17.24849	18.89560	20.58336	21.44014
	29	11.56425	12.27739	13.01028	13.76197	14.53142	15.31760	16.11945	16.93592	17.76594	19.46246	21.20087	22.08334
	30	11.91117	12.64571	13.40059	14.17483	14.96736	15.77712	16.60304	17.44400	18.29892	20.04634	21.83689	22.74584
	Level	7.15881	7.54395	7.93733	8.33846	8.74686	9.16206	9.58359	10.01100	10.44383	11.32408	12.22114	12.67506

Entries are annual percentages of initial cost or value. Divide by 12 for monthly figures.

Payments in a Rising Series

Annual Rate of Increase 4.0%

Plan	Year of Plan	6.00%	6.50%	7.00%	7.50%	Interest Rate 8.00%	8.50%	9.00%	9.50%	10.00%	11.00%	12.00%	12.50%
3 Year Plan	1	35.02893	35.27638	35.52346	35.77016	36.01648	36.26240	36.50791	36.75301	36.99769	37.48573	37.97196	38.21438
	2	36.43009	36.68743	36.94440	37.20097	37.45714	37.71289	37.96823	38.22313	38.47759	38.98516	39.49084	39.74295
	3	37.88729	38.15493	38.42217	38.68900	38.95542	39.22141	39.48696	39.75206	40.01670	40.54456	41.07047	41.33267
	Level	36.32470	36.58066	36.83763	37.09561	37.35461	37.61461	37.87561	38.13762	38.40062	38.92961	39.46255	39.73049
4 Year Plan	1	26.52030	26.76899	27.01776	27.26660	27.51549	27.76443	28.01339	28.26236	28.51132	29.00915	29.50678	29.75547
	2	27.58111	27.83975	28.09847	28.35726	28.61611	28.87501	29.13393	29.39285	29.65177	30.16952	30.68705	30.94569
	3	28.68436	28.95334	29.22241	29.49155	29.76076	30.03001	30.29928	30.56857	30.83784	31.37630	31.91453	32.18352
	4	29.83173	30.11147	30.39130	30.67121	30.95119	31.23121	31.51125	31.79131	32.07135	32.63135	33.19111	33.47086
	Level	28.04183	28.30463	28.56884	28.83447	29.10150	29.36993	29.63975	29.91097	30.18357	30.73291	31.28773	31.56717
5 Year Plan	1	21.41636	21.66647	21.91709	22.16819	22.41975	22.67174	22.92416	23.17697	23.43015	23.93756	24.44620	24.70093
	2	22.27301	22.53313	22.79377	23.05491	23.31653	23.57861	23.84112	24.10405	24.36736	24.89506	25.42405	25.68897
	3	23.16393	23.43445	23.70552	23.97711	24.24920	24.52176	24.79477	25.06821	25.34205	25.89086	26.44101	26.71653
	4	24.09049	24.37183	24.65374	24.93619	25.21916	25.50263	25.78656	26.07094	26.35574	26.92649	27.49865	27.78519
	5	25.05411	25.34671	25.63989	25.93364	26.22793	26.52273	26.81802	27.11378	27.40996	28.00355	28.59860	28.89660
	Level	23.08394	23.35288	23.62363	23.89619	24.17054	24.44667	24.72459	25.00428	25.28574	25.85391	26.42905	26.71920
6 Year Plan	1	18.01476	18.26639	18.51893	18.77234	19.02661	19.28169	19.53756	19.79420	20.05157	20.56840	21.08785	21.34848
	2	18.73535	18.99705	19.25969	19.52324	19.78767	20.05295	20.31906	20.58596	20.85363	21.39114	21.93136	22.20242
	3	19.48476	19.75693	20.03007	20.30417	20.57918	20.85507	21.13182	21.40940	21.68778	22.24679	22.80862	23.09052
	4	20.26415	20.54721	20.83128	21.11633	21.40234	21.68928	21.97710	22.26578	22.55529	23.13666	23.72096	24.01414
	5	21.07472	21.36909	21.66453	21.96099	22.25844	22.55685	22.85618	23.15641	23.45750	24.06212	24.66980	24.97470
	6	21.91771	22.22386	22.53111	22.83943	23.14878	23.45912	23.77043	24.08267	24.39580	25.02461	25.65659	25.97369
	Level	19.78852	20.06324	20.34016	20.61926	20.90055	21.18401	21.46962	21.75738	22.04728	22.63342	23.22795	23.52833
7 Year Plan	1	15.58593	15.83913	16.09364	16.34940	16.60638	16.86455	17.12388	17.38433	17.64586	18.17203	18.70212	18.96855
	2	16.20936	16.47270	16.73738	17.00337	17.27064	17.53914	17.80884	18.07970	18.35169	18.89891	19.45021	19.72729
	3	16.85774	17.13161	17.40688	17.68351	17.96146	18.24070	18.52119	18.80289	19.08576	19.65487	20.22822	20.51639
	4	17.53205	17.81687	18.10315	18.39085	18.67992	18.97033	19.26204	19.55500	19.84919	20.44106	21.03734	21.33704
	5	18.23333	18.52955	18.82728	19.12648	19.42712	19.72914	20.03252	20.33720	20.64316	21.25870	21.87884	22.19052
	6	18.96266	19.27073	19.58037	19.89154	20.20420	20.51831	20.83382	21.15069	21.46888	22.10905	22.75399	23.07814
	7	19.72117	20.04156	20.36358	20.68720	21.01237	21.33904	21.66717	21.99672	22.32764	22.99342	23.66415	24.00127
	Level	17.44305	17.72332	18.00618	18.29161	18.57959	18.87012	19.16317	19.45873	19.75678	20.36029	20.97354	21.28378
10 Year Plan	1	11.21772	11.47581	11.73633	11.99921	12.26441	12.53185	12.80149	13.07327	13.34712	13.90082	14.46211	14.74545
	2	11.66643	11.93485	12.20578	12.47918	12.75498	13.03313	13.31355	13.59620	13.88101	14.45686	15.04060	15.33527
	3	12.13309	12.41224	12.69401	12.97835	13.26518	13.55445	13.84610	14.14005	14.43625	15.03513	15.64222	15.94868
	4	12.61841	12.90873	13.20177	13.49748	13.79579	14.09663	14.39994	14.70565	15.01370	15.63654	16.26791	16.58663
	5	13.12315	13.42508	13.72985	14.03738	14.34762	14.66049	14.97594	15.29388	15.61425	16.26200	16.91863	17.25010
	6	13.64808	13.96208	14.27904	14.59888	14.92153	15.24691	15.57497	15.90563	16.23882	16.91248	17.59537	17.94010
	7	14.19400	14.52057	14.85020	15.18283	15.51839	15.85679	16.19797	16.54186	16.88837	17.58898	18.29919	18.65770
	8	14.76176	15.10139	15.44421	15.79014	16.13912	16.49106	16.84589	17.20353	17.56391	18.29254	19.03115	19.40401
	9	15.35223	15.70544	16.06198	16.42175	16.78469	17.15071	17.51973	17.89167	18.26646	19.02424	19.79240	20.18017
	10	15.96632	16.33366	16.70446	17.07862	17.45607	17.83673	18.22052	18.60734	18.99712	19.78521	20.58410	20.98830
	Level	13.25618	13.55235	13.85221	14.15574	14.46289	14.77364	15.08793	15.40574	15.72703	16.37985	17.04605	17.38406
12 Year Plan	1	9.52154	9.78295	10.04751	10.31517	10.58583	10.85943	11.13589	11.41512	11.69706	12.26872	12.85022	13.14445
	2	9.90240	10.17427	10.44941	10.72777	11.00926	11.29381	11.58132	11.87173	12.16494	12.75947	13.36423	13.67023
	3	10.29850	10.58124	10.86739	11.15688	11.44963	11.74556	12.04457	12.34660	12.65154	13.26985	13.89880	14.21704
	4	10.71044	11.00449	11.30209	11.60316	11.90762	12.21538	12.52636	12.84046	13.15760	13.80064	14.45475	14.78572
	5	11.13886	11.44467	11.75417	12.06729	12.38392	12.70400	13.02741	13.35408	13.68391	14.35267	15.03294	15.37715
	6	11.58441	11.90245	12.22434	12.54998	12.87928	13.21216	13.54851	13.88824	14.23126	14.92678	15.63425	15.99223
	7	12.04779	12.37855	12.71331	13.05198	13.39445	13.74064	14.09045	14.44377	14.80052	15.52385	16.25962	16.63192
	8	12.52970	12.87369	13.22184	13.57405	13.93023	14.29027	14.65407	15.02152	15.39254	16.14480	16.91001	17.29720
	9	13.03089	13.38864	13.75072	14.11702	14.48744	14.86188	15.24023	15.62238	16.00824	16.79059	17.58641	17.98909
	10	13.55212	13.92419	14.30075	14.68170	15.06694	15.45635	15.84984	16.24728	16.64857	17.46222	18.28987	18.70865
	11	14.09421	14.48115	14.87278	15.26897	15.66961	16.07461	16.48383	16.89717	17.31451	18.16070	19.02146	19.45700
	12	14.65798	15.06040	15.46769	15.87974	16.29640	16.71759	17.14318	17.57306	18.00709	18.88713	19.78232	20.23528
	Level	11.65194	11.95828	12.26900	12.58407	12.90341	13.22698	13.55471	13.88654	14.22242	14.90602	15.60498	15.96004
5 Year Plan	1	7.82843	8.09484	8.36550	8.64029	8.91912	9.20187	9.48843	9.77869	10.07253	10.67048	11.28133	11.59129
	2	8.14157	8.41864	8.70012	8.98590	9.27588	9.56994	9.86797	10.16984	10.47543	11.09730	11.73258	12.05494
	3	8.46723	8.75538	9.04812	9.34534	9.64692	9.95274	10.26268	10.57663	10.89445	11.54119	12.20189	12.53714
	4	8.80592	9.10560	9.41005	9.71915	10.03279	10.35085	10.67319	10.99969	11.33023	12.00284	12.68996	13.03862
	5	9.15816	9.46982	9.78645	10.10792	10.43411	10.76488	11.10012	11.43968	11.78343	12.48296	13.19756	13.56017
	6	9.52449	9.84862	10.17791	10.51224	10.85147	11.19548	11.54412	11.89727	12.25477	12.98227	13.72546	14.10257
	7	9.90547	10.24256	10.58502	10.93273	11.28553	11.64330	12.00589	12.37316	12.74496	13.50156	14.27448	14.66668
	8	10.30168	10.65226	11.00843	11.37003	11.73695	12.10903	12.48612	12.86809	13.25476	14.04163	14.84546	15.25334
	9	10.71375	11.07835	11.44876	11.82484	12.20643	12.59339	12.98557	13.38281	13.78495	14.60329	15.43928	15.86348
	10	11.14230	11.52149	11.90671	12.29783	12.69469	13.09713	13.50499	13.91812	14.33635	15.18742	16.05685	16.49802
	11	11.58799	11.98235	12.38298	12.78974	13.20247	13.62101	14.04519	14.47485	14.90980	15.79492	16.69913	17.15794
	12	12.05151	12.46164	12.87830	13.30133	13.73057	14.16585	14.60700	15.05384	15.50624	16.42672	17.36709	17.84425
	13	12.53357	12.96011	13.39343	13.83339	14.27979	14.73249	15.19128	15.65599	16.12644	17.08379	18.06177	18.55802
	14	13.03492	13.47851	13.92917	14.38672	14.85099	15.32179	15.79893	16.28223	16.77150	17.76714	18.78425	19.30035
	15	13.55631	14.01765	14.48634	14.96219	15.44503	15.93466	16.43089	16.93352	17.44236	18.47782	19.53561	20.07236
	Level	10.07590	10.39697	10.72339	11.05505	11.39188	11.73376	12.08059	12.43227	12.78869	13.51527	14.25942	14.63779

Entries are annual percentages of initial cost or value. Divide by 12 for monthly figures.

Payments in a Rising Series

Annual Rate of Increase 4.0%

Plan	Year of Plan	6.00%	6.50%	7.00%	7.50%	8.00%	8.50%	9.00%	9.50%	10.00%	11.00%	12.00%	12.50%
								Interest Rate					
	1	5.13534	5.41843	5.70919	6.00739	6.31274	6.62496	6.94376	7.26883	7.59986	8.27853	8.97723	9.33330
	2	5.34075	5.63516	5.93756	6.24769	6.56525	6.88996	7.22151	7.55958	7.90385	8.60967	9.33632	9.70663
	3	5.55438	5.86057	6.17506	6.49759	6.82786	7.16556	7.51037	7.86197	8.22001	8.95406	9.70978	10.09490
	4	5.77656	6.09499	6.42207	6.75750	7.10098	7.45218	7.81079	8.17645	8.54881	9.31222	10.09817	10.49870
	5	6.00762	6.33879	6.67895	7.02780	7.38501	7.75027	8.12322	8.50350	8.89076	9.68471	10.50209	10.91864
	6	6.24793	6.59234	6.94611	7.30891	7.68041	8.06028	8.44815	8.84364	9.24639	10.07210	10.92218	11.35539
	7	6.49784	6.85604	7.22395	7.60126	7.98763	8.38269	8.78607	9.19739	9.61625	10.47498	11.35906	11.80960
	8	6.75776	7.13028	7.51291	7.90532	8.30714	8.71800	9.13752	9.56528	10.00090	10.89398	11.81343	12.28199
	9	7.02807	7.41549	7.81343	8.22153	8.63942	9.06672	9.50302	9.94790	10.40093	11.32974	12.28596	12.77327
	10	7.30919	7.71211	8.12596	8.55039	8.98500	9.42939	9.88314	10.34581	10.81697	11.78293	12.77740	13.28420
25 Year Plan	11	7.60156	8.02059	8.45100	8.89240	9.34440	9.80656	10.27846	10.75964	11.24965	12.25425	13.28850	13.81557
	12	7.90562	8.34142	8.78904	9.24810	9.71818	10.19883	10.68960	11.19003	11.69963	12.74442	13.82004	14.36819
	13	8.22184	8.67507	9.14060	9.61802	10.10690	10.60678	11.11719	11.63763	12.16762	13.25420	14.37284	14.94292
	14	8.55072	9.02208	9.50623	10.00275	10.51118	11.03105	11.56187	12.10314	12.65432	13.78436	14.94775	15.54063
	15	8.89275	9.38296	9.88648	10.40286	10.93163	11.47229	12.02435	12.58726	13.16050	14.33574	15.54566	16.16226
	16	9.24846	9.75828	10.28194	10.81897	11.36889	11.93118	12.50532	13.09075	13.68692	14.90917	16.16749	16.80875
	17	9.61840	10.14861	10.69321	11.25173	11.82365	12.40843	13.00553	13.61438	14.23439	15.50553	16.81419	17.48110
	18	10.00313	10.55455	11.12094	11.70180	12.29659	12.90477	13.52576	14.15896	14.80377	16.12576	17.48676	18.18034
	19	10.40326	10.97674	11.56578	12.16987	12.78846	13.42096	14.06679	14.72532	15.39592	16.77079	18.18623	18.90756
	20	10.81939	11.41581	12.02841	12.65666	13.29999	13.95780	14.62946	15.31433	16.01176	17.44162	18.91368	19.66386
	21	11.25216	11.87244	12.50955	13.16293	13.83199	14.51611	15.21464	15.92690	16.65223	18.13928	19.67022	20.45041
	22	11.70225	12.34734	13.00993	13.68945	14.38527	15.09676	15.82322	16.56398	17.31832	18.86485	20.45703	21.26843
	23	12.17034	12.84123	13.53033	14.23703	14.96068	15.70063	16.45615	17.22654	18.01105	19.61945	21.27531	22.11917
	24	12.65715	13.35488	14.07154	14.80651	15.55911	16.32865	17.11440	17.91560	18.73149	20.40423	22.12633	23.00393
	25	13.16344	13.88907	14.63440	15.39877	16.18148	16.98180	17.79897	18.63222	19.48075	21.22039	23.01138	23.92409
	Level	7.69315	8.05883	8.43216	8.81281	9.20046	9.59476	9.99539	10.40201	10.81429	11.65452	12.51355	12.94936
	1	4.46963	4.76096	5.06158	5.37112	5.68918	6.01536	6.34921	6.69029	7.03816	7.75243	8.48842	8.86347
	2	4.64842	4.95140	5.26404	5.58596	5.91675	6.25597	6.60317	6.95790	7.31968	8.06253	8.82796	9.21800
	3	4.83436	5.14945	5.47460	5.80940	6.15342	6.50621	6.86730	7.23622	7.61247	8.38503	9.18108	9.58673
	4	5.02773	5.35543	5.69359	6.04178	6.39956	6.76646	7.14199	7.52567	7.91697	8.72043	9.54832	9.97019
	5	5.22884	5.56965	5.92133	6.28345	6.65554	7.03712	7.42767	7.82669	8.23365	9.06925	9.93025	10.36900
	6	5.43799	5.79244	6.15818	6.53479	6.92176	7.31860	7.72478	8.13976	8.56299	9.43202	10.32746	10.78376
	7	5.65551	6.02413	6.40451	6.79618	7.19863	7.61134	8.03377	8.46535	8.90551	9.80930	10.74056	11.21511
	8	5.88173	6.26510	6.66069	7.06803	7.48658	7.91580	8.35512	8.80397	9.26173	10.20167	11.17018	11.66372
	9	6.11700	6.51570	6.92712	7.35075	7.78604	8.23243	8.68933	9.15612	9.63220	10.60973	11.61699	12.13027
	10	6.36168	6.77633	7.20421	7.64478	8.09748	8.56173	9.03690	9.52237	10.01749	11.03412	12.08167	12.61548
	11	6.61615	7.04738	7.49237	7.95057	8.42138	8.90420	9.39838	9.90326	10.41819	11.47549	12.56494	13.12010
	12	6.88080	7.32928	7.79207	8.26859	8.75824	9.26036	9.77431	10.29939	10.83492	11.93451	13.06754	13.64490
	13	7.15603	7.62245	8.10375	8.59933	9.10857	9.63078	10.16528	10.71137	11.26832	12.41189	13.59024	14.19070
	14	7.44227	7.92735	8.42790	8.94331	9.47291	10.01601	10.57190	11.13982	11.71905	12.90836	14.13385	14.75832
30 Year Plan	15	7.73996	8.24444	8.76502	9.30104	9.85182	10.41665	10.99477	11.58542	12.18781	13.42470	14.69920	15.34866
	16	8.04956	8.57422	9.11562	9.67308	10.24590	10.83332	11.43456	12.04883	12.67532	13.96169	15.28717	15.96260
	17	8.37154	8.91719	9.48024	10.06000	10.65573	11.26665	11.89194	12.53079	13.18234	14.52015	15.89866	16.60111
	18	8.70640	9.27388	9.85945	10.46240	11.08196	11.71732	12.36762	13.03202	13.70963	15.10096	16.53460	17.26515
	19	9.05466	9.64483	10.25383	10.88090	11.52524	12.18601	12.86233	13.55330	14.25802	15.70500	17.19599	17.95576
	20	9.41684	10.03063	10.66398	11.31614	11.98625	12.67345	13.37682	14.09543	14.82834	16.33320	17.88383	18.67399
	21	9.79352	10.43185	11.09054	11.76878	12.46570	13.18039	13.91189	14.65925	15.42147	16.98653	18.59918	19.42095
	22	10.18526	10.84912	11.53416	12.23953	12.96433	13.70760	14.46837	15.24562	16.03833	17.66599	19.34315	20.19778
	23	10.59267	11.28309	11.99553	12.72912	13.48290	14.25591	15.04710	15.85544	16.67986	18.37263	20.11687	21.00570
	24	11.01638	11.73441	12.47535	13.23828	14.02222	14.82614	15.64899	16.48966	17.34706	19.10753	20.92155	21.84592
	25	11.45703	12.20379	12.97437	13.76781	14.58311	15.41919	16.27495	17.14925	18.04094	19.87183	21.75841	22.71976
	26	11.91531	12.69194	13.49334	14.31852	15.16643	16.03596	16.92595	17.83522	18.76258	20.66671	22.62874	23.62855
	27	12.39193	13.19962	14.03308	14.89126	15.77309	16.67739	17.60298	18.54863	19.51308	21.49338	23.53389	24.57369
	28	12.88760	13.72760	14.59440	15.48691	16.40401	17.34449	18.30710	19.29057	20.29360	22.35311	24.47525	25.55664
	29	13.40311	14.27671	15.17817	16.10639	17.06017	18.03827	19.03939	20.06220	21.10535	23.24724	25.45426	26.57891
	30	13.93923	14.84778	15.78530	16.75065	17.74258	18.75980	19.80096	20.86468	21.94956	24.17712	26.47243	27.64206
	Level	7.15881	7.54395	7.93733	8.33846	8.74686	9.16206	9.58359	10.01100	10.44383	11.32408	12.22114	12.67506

Entries are annual percentages of initial cost or value. Divide by 12 for monthly figures.

Payments in a Rising Series

Annual Rate of Increase 5.0%

Plan	Year of Plan	6.00%	6.50%	7.00%	7.50%	8.00%	8.50%	9.00%	9.50%	10.00%	11.00%	12.00%	12.50%
3 Year Plan	1	34.69848	34.94464	35.19045	35.43589	35.68096	35.92565	36.16994	36.41384	36.65732	37.14301	37.62695	37.86824
	2	36.43341	36.69187	36.94997	37.20769	37.46501	37.72193	37.97844	38.23453	38.49019	39.00016	39.50830	39.76165
	3	38.25508	38.52647	38.79747	39.06807	39.33826	39.60803	39.87736	40.14626	40.41469	40.95017	41.48371	41.74973
	Level	36.32470	36.58066	36.83763	37.09561	37.35461	37.61461	37.87561	38.13762	38.40062	38.92961	39.46255	39.73049
4 Year Plan	1	26.14681	26.39347	26.64024	26.88711	27.13404	27.38104	27.62808	27.87515	28.12222	28.61635	29.11035	29.35727
	2	27.45415	27.71315	27.97226	28.23146	28.49075	28.75009	29.00948	29.26890	29.52833	30.04717	30.56587	30.82513
	3	28.82685	29.09880	29.37087	29.64304	29.91528	30.18760	30.45996	30.73235	31.00475	31.54953	32.09416	32.36639
	4	30.26820	30.55374	30.83941	31.12519	31.41105	31.69698	31.98296	32.26897	32.55499	33.12701	33.69887	33.98470
	Level	28.04183	28.30463	28.56884	28.83447	29.10150	29.36993	29.63975	29.91097	30.18357	30.73291	31.28773	31.56717
5 Year Plan	1	21.01611	21.26346	21.51134	21.75973	22.00861	22.25795	22.50773	22.75794	23.00854	23.51087	24.01455	24.26684
	2	22.06691	22.32663	22.58691	22.84772	23.10904	23.37085	23.63312	23.89584	24.15897	24.68642	25.21528	25.48018
	3	23.17026	23.44296	23.71625	23.99010	24.26449	24.53939	24.81477	25.09063	25.36692	25.92074	26.47604	26.75419
	4	24.32877	24.61511	24.90206	25.18961	25.47771	25.76636	26.05551	26.34516	26.63527	27.21677	27.79984	28.09190
	5	25.54521	25.84587	26.14717	26.44909	26.75160	27.05467	27.35829	27.66242	27.96703	28.57761	29.18983	29.49650
	Level	23.08394	23.35288	23.62363	23.89619	24.17054	24.44667	24.72459	25.00428	25.28574	25.85391	26.42905	26.71920
6 Year Plan	1	17.59590	17.84402	18.09308	18.34305	18.59391	18.84561	19.09814	19.35147	19.60556	20.11595	20.62910	20.88663
	2	18.47569	18.73622	18.99774	19.26021	19.52360	19.78789	20.05305	20.31904	20.58584	21.12175	21.66055	21.93096
	3	19.39948	19.67303	19.94762	20.22322	20.49978	20.77728	21.05570	21.33499	21.61513	22.17784	22.74358	23.02751
	4	20.36945	20.65669	20.94501	21.23438	21.52477	21.81615	22.10848	22.40174	22.69589	23.28673	23.88076	24.17889
	5	21.38792	21.68952	21.99226	22.29610	22.60101	22.90696	23.21391	23.52183	23.83068	24.45107	25.07480	25.38783
	6	22.45732	22.77400	23.09187	23.41090	23.73106	24.05230	24.37460	24.69792	25.02222	25.67362	26.32854	26.65722
	Level	19.78852	20.06324	20.34016	20.61926	20.90055	21.18401	21.46962	21.75738	22.04728	22.63342	23.22795	23.52833
7 Year Plan	1	15.15311	15.40206	15.65234	15.90392	16.15677	16.41084	16.66611	16.92255	17.18011	17.69847	18.22094	18.48363
	2	15.91077	16.17216	16.43496	16.69912	16.96461	17.23139	17.49942	17.76867	18.03911	18.58340	19.13199	19.40781
	3	16.70630	16.98077	17.25671	17.53407	17.81284	18.09295	18.37439	18.65711	18.94107	19.51257	20.08859	20.37820
	4	17.54162	17.82981	18.11954	18.41078	18.70348	18.99760	19.29311	19.58996	19.88812	20.48820	21.09302	21.39711
	5	18.41870	18.72130	19.02552	19.33132	19.63865	19.94748	20.25777	20.56946	20.88253	21.51261	22.14767	22.46697
	6	19.33964	19.65736	19.97679	20.29788	20.62058	20.94486	21.27065	21.59794	21.92666	22.58824	23.25505	23.59031
	7	20.30662	20.64023	20.97563	21.31278	21.65161	21.99210	22.33419	22.67783	23.02299	23.71765	24.41780	24.76983
	Level	17.44305	17.72332	18.00618	18.29161	18.57959	18.87012	19.16317	19.45873	19.75678	20.36029	20.97354	21.28378
10 Year Plan	1	10.75701	11.00859	11.26265	11.51915	11.77803	12.03923	12.30270	12.56838	12.83622	13.37813	13.92797	14.20571
	2	11.29487	11.55902	11.82578	12.09511	12.36693	12.64119	12.91783	13.19680	13.47803	14.04704	14.62436	14.91600
	3	11.85961	12.13697	12.41707	12.69986	12.98527	13.27325	13.56373	13.85664	14.15193	14.74939	15.35558	15.66179
	4	12.45259	12.74382	13.03793	13.33486	13.63454	13.93691	14.24191	14.54947	14.85953	15.48686	16.12336	16.44488
	5	13.07522	13.38101	13.68982	14.00160	14.31626	14.63376	14.95401	15.27695	15.60251	16.26120	16.92953	17.26713
	6	13.72898	14.05006	14.37431	14.70168	15.03208	15.36545	15.70171	16.04079	16.38263	17.07426	17.77601	18.13049
	7	14.41543	14.75256	15.09303	15.43676	15.78368	16.13372	16.48679	16.84283	17.20176	17.92797	18.66481	19.03701
	8	15.13620	15.49019	15.84768	16.20860	16.57287	16.94040	17.31113	17.68498	18.06185	18.82437	19.59805	19.98886
	9	15.89301	16.26470	16.64007	17.01903	17.40151	17.78742	18.17669	18.56922	18.96494	19.76559	20.57795	20.98830
	10	16.68766	17.07793	17.47207	17.86998	18.27158	18.67680	19.08552	19.49769	19.91319	20.75387	21.60685	22.03772
	Level	13.25618	13.55235	13.85221	14.15574	14.46289	14.77364	15.08793	15.40574	15.72703	16.37985	17.04605	17.38406
12 Year Plan	1	9.04806	9.30145	9.55808	9.81789	10.08080	10.34674	10.61565	10.88744	11.16204	11.71938	12.28702	12.57451
	2	9.50046	9.76652	10.03598	10.30878	10.58484	10.86408	11.14643	11.43181	11.72015	12.30534	12.90137	13.20324
	3	9.97549	10.25485	10.53778	10.82422	11.11408	11.40728	11.70375	12.00340	12.30615	12.92061	13.54644	13.86340
	4	10.47426	10.76759	11.06467	11.36543	11.66978	11.97765	12.28894	12.60357	12.92146	13.56664	14.22376	14.55657
	5	10.99798	11.30597	11.61791	11.93370	12.25327	12.57653	12.90339	13.23375	13.56753	14.24497	14.93495	15.28440
	6	11.54787	11.87127	12.19880	12.53039	12.86594	13.20536	13.54856	13.89544	14.24591	14.95722	15.68170	16.04862
	7	12.12527	12.46483	12.80874	13.15691	13.50923	13.86563	14.22599	14.59021	14.95821	15.70508	16.46578	16.85105
	8	12.73153	13.08807	13.44918	13.81475	14.18469	14.55891	14.93728	15.31972	15.70612	16.49034	17.28907	17.69360
	9	13.36811	13.74248	14.12164	14.50549	14.89393	15.28685	15.68415	16.08571	16.49142	17.31485	18.15352	18.57828
	10	14.03651	14.42960	14.82772	15.23076	15.63863	16.05119	16.46836	16.88999	17.31599	18.18060	19.06120	19.50719
	11	14.73834	15.15108	15.56910	15.99230	16.42056	16.85375	17.29177	17.73449	18.18179	19.08963	20.01426	20.48255
	12	15.47526	15.90863	16.34756	16.79192	17.24158	17.69644	18.15636	18.62122	19.09088	20.04411	21.01497	21.50668
	Level	11.65194	11.95828	12.26900	12.58407	12.90341	13.22698	13.55471	13.88654	14.22242	14.90602	15.60498	15.96004
15 Year Plan	1	7.33988	7.59602	7.85654	8.12132	8.39027	8.66330	8.94030	9.22116	9.50578	10.08582	10.67951	10.98118
	2	7.70687	7.97582	8.24936	8.52738	8.80979	9.09647	9.38732	9.68222	9.98107	10.59011	11.21348	11.53024
	3	8.09221	8.37462	8.66183	8.95375	9.25028	9.55129	9.85668	10.16633	10.48012	11.11961	11.77416	12.10675
	4	8.49682	8.79335	9.09492	9.40144	9.71279	10.02886	10.34952	10.67465	11.00413	11.67560	12.36287	12.71209
	5	8.92167	9.23301	9.54967	9.87151	10.19843	10.53030	10.86699	11.20838	11.55433	12.25937	12.98101	13.34769
	6	9.36775	9.69466	10.02715	10.36509	10.70835	11.05682	11.41034	11.76880	12.13205	12.87234	13.63006	14.01508
	7	9.83614	10.17940	10.52851	10.88334	11.24377	11.60966	11.98086	12.35724	12.73865	13.51596	14.31156	14.71583
	8	10.32794	10.68837	11.05493	11.42751	11.80596	12.19014	12.57990	12.97510	13.37558	14.19176	15.02714	15.45162
	9	10.84434	11.22279	11.60768	11.99889	12.39626	12.79965	13.20890	13.62386	14.04436	14.90135	15.77850	16.22420
	10	11.38656	11.78393	12.18806	12.59883	13.01607	13.43963	13.86934	14.30505	14.74658	15.64641	16.56742	17.03541
	11	11.95588	12.37312	12.79747	13.22877	13.66687	14.11161	14.56281	15.02030	15.48391	16.42873	17.39579	17.88718
	12	12.55368	12.99178	13.43734	13.89021	14.35022	14.81719	15.29095	15.77132	16.25811	17.25017	18.26558	18.78154
	13	13.18136	13.64137	14.10921	14.58472	15.06773	15.55805	16.05550	16.55989	17.07101	18.11268	19.17886	19.72062
	14	13.84043	14.32344	14.81467	15.31396	15.82111	16.33595	16.85827	17.38788	17.92456	19.01831	20.13780	20.70665
	15	14.53245	15.03961	15.55540	16.07965	16.61217	17.15275	17.70119	18.25727	18.82079	19.96923	21.14469	21.74198
	Level	10.07590	10.39697	10.72339	11.05505	11.39188	11.73376	12.08059	12.43227	12.78869	13.51527	14.25942	14.63779

Entries are annual percentages of initial cost or value. Divide by 12 for monthly figures.

Payments in a Rising Series

Annual Rate of Increase 5.0%

Plan	Year of Plan	6.00%	6.50%	7.00%	7.50%	8.00%	8.50%	9.00%	9.50%	10.00%	11.00%	12.00%	12.50%
	1	4.61076	4.87624	5.14973	5.43102	5.71989	6.01607	6.31932	6.62934	6.94586	7.59717	8.27082	8.61523
	2	4.84130	5.12005	5.40721	5.70257	6.00588	6.31688	6.63529	6.96081	7.29315	7.97703	8.68436	9.04600
	3	5.08337	5.37605	5.67757	5.98770	6.30618	6.63272	6.96705	7.30885	7.65781	8.37589	9.11858	9.49830
	4	5.33754	5.64485	5.96145	6.28709	6.62148	6.96436	7.31540	7.67430	8.04070	8.79468	9.57450	9.97321
	5	5.60441	5.92710	6.25953	6.60144	6.95256	7.31258	7.68117	8.05801	8.44274	9.23441	10.05323	10.47187
	6	5.88463	6.22345	6.57250	6.93151	7.30019	7.67821	8.06523	8.46091	8.86487	9.69613	10.55589	10.99546
	7	6.17886	6.53462	6.90113	7.27809	7.66520	8.06212	8.46849	8.88396	9.30812	10.18094	11.08369	11.54524
	8	6.48781	6.86136	7.24618	7.64199	8.04846	8.46522	8.89192	9.32815	9.77352	10.68999	11.63787	12.12250
	9	6.81220	7.20442	7.60849	8.02409	8.45088	8.88848	9.33651	9.79456	10.26220	11.22449	12.21976	12.72862
	10	7.15281	7.56464	7.98892	8.42530	8.87342	9.33291	9.80334	10.28429	10.77531	11.78571	12.83075	13.36506
25 Year Plan	11	7.51045	7.94288	8.38836	8.84656	9.31709	9.79955	10.29351	10.79850	11.31408	12.37500	13.47229	14.03331
	12	7.88597	8.34002	8.80778	9.28889	9.78295	10.28953	10.80818	11.33843	11.87978	12.99375	14.14590	14.73497
	13	8.28027	8.75702	9.24817	9.75333	10.27210	10.80401	11.34859	11.90535	12.47377	13.64343	14.85320	15.47172
	14	8.69428	9.19487	9.71058	10.24100	10.78570	11.34421	11.91602	12.50062	13.09746	14.32561	15.59586	16.24531
	15	9.12900	9.65462	10.19611	10.75305	11.32499	11.91142	12.51182	13.12565	13.75233	15.04189	16.37565	17.05757
	16	9.58545	10.13735	10.70591	11.29070	11.89123	12.50699	13.13741	13.78193	14.43995	15.79398	17.19443	17.91045
	17	10.06472	10.64421	11.24121	11.85524	12.48580	13.13234	13.79428	14.47103	15.16194	16.58368	18.05416	18.80597
	18	10.56796	11.17642	11.80327	12.44800	13.11009	13.78895	14.48400	15.19458	15.92004	17.41286	18.95686	19.74627
	19	11.09635	11.73525	12.39343	13.07040	13.76559	14.47840	15.20820	15.95431	16.71604	18.28351	19.90471	20.73359
	20	11.65117	12.32201	13.01310	13.72392	14.45387	15.20232	15.96861	16.75202	17.55185	19.19768	20.89994	21.77027
	21	12.23373	12.93811	13.66376	14.41012	15.17656	15.96244	16.76704	17.58963	18.42944	20.15757	21.94494	22.85878
	22	12.84542	13.58501	14.34695	15.13062	15.93539	16.76056	17.60539	18.46911	19.35091	21.16544	23.04219	24.00172
	23	13.48769	14.26426	15.06429	15.88715	16.73216	17.59859	18.48566	19.39256	20.31846	22.22372	24.19430	25.20180
	24	14.16207	14.97748	15.81751	16.68151	17.56877	18.47852	19.40994	20.36219	21.33438	23.33490	25.40401	26.46189
	25	14.87017	15.72635	16.60839	17.51559	18.44721	19.40244	20.38044	21.38030	22.40110	24.50165	26.67421	27.78499
	Level	7.69315	8.05883	8.43216	8.81281	9.20046	9.59476	9.99539	10.40201	10.81429	11.65452	12.51355	12.94936
	1	3.93040	4.20054	4.48049	4.76993	5.06853	5.37594	5.69176	6.01559	6.34701	7.03087	7.73983	8.10261
	2	4.12692	4.41057	4.70451	5.00843	5.32196	5.64474	5.97635	6.31637	6.66436	7.38241	8.12682	8.50774
	3	4.33326	4.63110	4.93974	5.25885	5.58806	5.92697	6.27517	6.63219	6.99758	7.75153	8.53316	8.93313
	4	4.54993	4.86266	5.18673	5.52179	5.86746	6.22332	6.58892	6.96380	7.34745	8.13911	8.95982	9.37978
	5	4.77742	5.10579	5.44606	5.79788	6.16084	6.53449	6.91837	7.31199	7.71483	8.54607	9.40781	9.84877
	6	5.01629	5.36108	5.71837	6.08777	6.46888	6.86121	7.26429	7.67759	8.10057	8.97337	9.87820	10.34121
	7	5.26711	5.62913	6.00428	6.39216	6.79232	7.20427	7.62750	8.06147	8.50560	9.42204	10.37211	10.85827
	8	5.53046	5.91059	6.30450	6.71177	7.13194	7.56449	8.00888	8.46454	8.93088	9.89314	10.89071	11.40119
	9	5.80699	6.20612	6.61972	7.04736	7.48853	7.94271	8.40932	8.88777	9.37742	10.38780	11.43525	11.97125
	10	6.09734	6.51642	6.95071	7.39973	7.86296	8.33985	8.82979	9.33215	9.84629	10.90719	12.00701	12.56981
	11	6.40220	6.84225	7.29825	7.76971	8.25611	8.75684	9.27128	9.79876	10.33861	11.45255	12.60736	13.19830
	12	6.72231	7.18436	7.66316	8.15820	8.66891	9.19468	9.73484	10.28870	10.85554	12.02517	13.23773	13.85821
	13	7.05843	7.54358	8.04632	8.56611	9.10236	9.65442	10.22158	10.80313	11.39831	12.62643	13.89962	14.55112
	14	7.41135	7.92075	8.44863	8.99442	9.55748	10.13714	10.73266	11.34329	11.96823	13.25775	14.59460	15.27868
30 Year	15	7.78192	8.31679	8.87106	9.44414	10.03535	10.64399	11.26930	11.91046	12.56664	13.92064	15.32433	16.04261
Plan	16	8.17101	8.73263	9.31462	9.91634	10.53712	11.17619	11.83276	12.50598	13.19497	14.61667	16.09054	16.84475
	17	8.57956	9.16926	9.78035	10.41216	11.06398	11.73500	12.42440	13.13128	13.85472	15.34751	16.89507	17.68698
	18	9.00854	9.62773	10.26936	10.93277	11.61717	12.32175	13.04562	13.78784	14.54746	16.11488	17.73982	18.57133
	19	9.45897	10.10911	10.78283	11.47941	12.19803	12.93784	13.69790	14.47723	15.27483	16.92063	18.62681	19.49990
	20	9.93192	10.61457	11.32197	12.05338	12.80794	13.58473	14.38279	15.20109	16.03857	17.76666	19.55815	20.47489
	21	10.42851	11.14530	11.88807	12.65605	13.44833	14.26397	15.10193	15.96115	16.84050	18.65499	20.53606	21.49864
	22	10.94994	11.70256	12.48248	13.28885	14.12075	14.97717	15.85703	16.75921	17.68252	19.58774	21.56287	22.57357
	23	11.49744	12.28769	13.10660	13.95329	14.82679	15.72603	16.64988	17.59717	18.56665	20.56713	22.64101	23.70225
	24	12.07231	12.90207	13.76193	14.65096	15.56813	16.51233	17.48238	18.47703	19.49498	21.59548	23.77306	24.88736
	25	12.67592	13.54718	14.45003	15.38350	16.34653	17.33794	18.35650	19.40088	20.46973	22.67526	24.96171	26.13173
	26	13.30972	14.22454	15.17253	16.15268	17.16386	18.20484	19.27432	20.37092	21.49322	23.80902	26.20980	27.43832
	27	13.97521	14.93576	15.93115	16.96031	18.02205	19.11508	20.23804	21.38947	22.56788	24.99947	27.52029	28.81023
	28	14.67397	15.68255	16.72771	17.80833	18.92315	20.07084	21.24994	22.45894	23.69627	26.24945	28.89630	30.25074
	29	15.40767	16.46668	17.56410	18.69875	19.86931	21.07438	22.31243	23.58189	24.88109	27.56192	30.34112	31.76328
	30	16.17805	17.29001	18.44230	19.63368	20.86278	22.12810	23.42806	24.76098	26.12514	28.94001	31.85817	33.35144
	Level	7.15881	7.54395	7.93733	8.33846	8.74686	9.16206	9.58359	10.01100	10.44383	11.32408	12.22114	12.67506

Entries are annual percentages of initial cost or value. Divide by 12 for monthly figures.

Payments in a Rising Series

Annual Rate of Increase   6.0%

Plan	Year of Plan	6.00%	6.50%	7.00%	7.50%	8.00%	8.50%	9.00%	9.50%	10.00%	11.00%	12.00%	12.50%
3 Year Plan	1	34.37217	34.61704	34.86157	35.10576	35.34958	35.59304	35.83611	36.07879	36.32108	36.80442	37.28606	37.52621
	2	36.43450	36.69406	36.95327	37.21210	37.47056	37.72862	37.98628	38.24352	38.50035	39.01269	39.52322	39.77778
	3	38.62057	38.89571	39.17047	39.44483	39.71879	39.99234	40.26545	40.53813	40.81037	41.35345	41.89461	42.16445
	Level	36.32470	36.58066	36.83763	37.09561	37.35461	37.61461	37.87561	38.13762	38.40062	38.92961	39.46255	39.73049
4 Year Plan	1	25.77912	26.02377	26.26855	26.51343	26.75841	27.00346	27.24857	27.49374	27.73893	28.22935	28.71971	28.96483
	2	27.32587	27.58520	27.84466	28.10424	28.36391	28.62367	28.88349	29.14336	29.40326	29.92311	30.44289	30.70274
	3	28.96542	29.24031	29.51534	29.79049	30.06575	30.34109	30.61650	30.89196	31.16746	31.71849	32.26946	32.54488
	4	30.70335	30.99473	31.28626	31.57792	31.86969	32.16155	32.45349	32.74548	33.03751	33.62160	34.20563	34.49758
	Level	28.04183	28.30463	28.56884	28.83447	29.10150	29.36993	29.63975	29.91097	30.18357	30.73291	31.28773	31.56717
5 Year Plan	1	20.62330	20.86789	21.11303	21.35871	21.60490	21.85158	22.09873	22.34632	22.59434	23.09158	23.59027	23.84011
	2	21.86070	22.11996	22.37982	22.64023	22.90119	23.16268	23.42465	23.68710	23.95000	24.47707	25.00568	25.27051
	3	23.17234	23.44716	23.72260	23.99865	24.27527	24.55244	24.83013	25.10833	25.38701	25.94570	26.50602	26.78674
	4	24.56268	24.85399	25.14596	25.43857	25.73178	26.02558	26.31994	26.61483	26.91023	27.50244	28.09639	28.39395
	5	26.03644	26.34523	26.65472	26.96488	27.27569	27.58712	27.89914	28.21172	28.52484	29.15259	29.78217	30.09758
	Level	23.08394	23.35288	23.62363	23.89619	24.17054	24.44667	24.72459	25.00428	25.28574	25.85391	26.42905	26.71920
6 Year Plan	1	17.18608	17.43070	17.67628	17.92280	18.17023	18.41855	18.66772	18.91773	19.16854	19.67245	20.17926	20.43368
	2	18.21725	18.47654	18.73685	18.99817	19.26044	19.52366	19.78779	20.05279	20.31865	20.85280	21.39001	21.65970
	3	19.31028	19.58513	19.86106	20.13806	20.41607	20.69508	20.97505	21.25596	21.53777	22.10397	22.67341	22.95928
	4	20.46890	20.76024	21.05273	21.34634	21.64104	21.93679	22.23356	22.53132	22.83004	23.43021	24.03382	24.33683
	5	21.69703	22.00585	22.31589	22.62712	22.93950	23.25299	23.56757	23.88320	24.19984	24.83602	25.47585	25.79704
	6	22.99886	23.32620	23.65485	23.98475	24.31587	24.64817	24.98163	25.31619	25.65183	26.32618	27.00440	27.34487
	Level	19.78852	20.06324	20.34016	20.61926	20.90055	21.18401	21.46962	21.75738	22.04728	22.63342	23.22795	23.52833
7 Year Plan	1	14.73093	14.97561	15.22167	15.46906	15.71775	15.96771	16.21891	16.47132	16.72489	17.23540	17.75018	18.00910
	2	15.61478	15.87415	16.13497	16.39720	16.66082	16.92578	17.19205	17.45959	17.72838	18.26952	18.81519	19.08964
	3	16.55167	16.82660	17.10307	17.38103	17.66047	17.94132	18.22357	18.50717	18.79208	19.36569	19.94411	20.23502
	4	17.54477	17.83619	18.12925	18.42390	18.72010	19.01780	19.31699	19.61760	19.91961	20.52763	21.14075	21.44912
	5	18.59746	18.90637	19.21700	19.52933	19.84330	20.15887	20.47601	20.79466	21.11478	21.75929	22.40920	22.73607
	6	19.71331	20.04075	20.37002	20.70109	21.03390	21.36840	21.70457	22.04234	22.38167	23.06485	23.75375	24.10023
	7	20.89610	21.24319	21.59223	21.94315	22.29593	22.65051	23.00684	23.36488	23.72457	24.44874	25.17897	25.54625
	Level	17.44305	17.72332	18.00618	18.29161	18.57959	18.87012	19.16317	19.45873	19.75678	20.36029	20.97354	21.28378
10 Year Plan	1	10.31165	10.55669	10.80428	11.05436	11.30689	11.56180	11.81905	12.07858	12.34035	12.87033	13.40855	13.68061
	2	10.93035	11.19009	11.45254	11.71762	11.98530	12.25551	12.52819	12.80330	13.08077	13.64255	14.21306	14.50145
	3	11.58617	11.86150	12.13969	12.42068	12.70442	12.99084	13.27989	13.57150	13.86561	14.46110	15.06585	15.37153
	4	12.28134	12.57319	12.86807	13.16592	13.46668	13.77029	14.07668	14.38579	14.69755	15.32877	15.96980	16.29382
	5	13.01822	13.32758	13.64015	13.95588	14.27468	14.59651	14.92128	15.24894	15.57940	16.24849	16.92799	17.27145
	6	13.79931	14.12723	14.45856	14.79323	15.13116	15.47230	15.81656	16.16387	16.51417	17.22340	17.94367	18.30774
	7	14.62727	14.97487	15.32608	15.68082	16.03903	16.40063	16.76555	17.13370	17.50502	18.25681	19.02028	19.40621
	8	15.50491	15.87336	16.24564	16.62167	17.00138	17.38467	17.77148	18.16173	18.55532	19.35222	20.16150	20.57058
	9	16.43520	16.82576	17.22038	17.61897	18.02146	18.42775	18.83777	19.25143	19.66864	20.51335	21.37119	21.80481
	10	17.42132	17.83531	18.25360	18.67611	19.10274	19.53342	19.96804	20.40652	20.84875	21.74415	22.65346	23.11310
	Level	13.25618	13.55235	13.85221	14.15574	14.46289	14.77364	15.08793	15.40574	15.72703	16.37985	17.04605	17.38406
12 Year Plan	1	8.59304	8.83838	9.08704	9.33895	9.59404	9.85226	10.11353	10.37778	10.64495	11.18771	11.74123	12.02184
	2	9.10862	9.36868	9.63226	9.89928	10.16969	10.44340	10.72034	11.00045	11.28364	11.85898	12.44571	12.74315
	3	9.65514	9.93080	10.21019	10.49324	10.77987	11.07000	11.36356	11.66048	11.96066	12.57051	13.19245	13.50742
	4	10.23445	10.52665	10.82281	11.12283	11.42666	11.73420	12.04538	12.36011	12.67830	13.32474	13.98400	14.31820
	5	10.84852	11.15825	11.47217	11.79020	12.11226	12.43825	12.76810	13.10171	13.43900	14.12423	14.82304	15.17729
	6	11.49943	11.82775	12.16050	12.49762	12.83899	13.18455	13.53419	13.88782	14.24534	14.97168	15.71242	16.08793
	7	12.18939	12.53741	12.89013	13.24747	13.60933	13.97562	14.34624	14.72108	15.10006	15.86998	16.65516	17.05321
	8	12.92076	13.28966	13.66354	14.04232	14.42589	14.81416	15.20701	15.60435	16.00606	16.82218	17.65447	18.07640
	9	13.69600	14.08704	14.48336	14.88486	15.29145	15.70301	16.11943	16.54061	16.96643	17.83151	18.71374	19.16098
	10	14.51776	14.93226	15.35236	15.77795	16.20893	16.64519	17.08660	17.53305	17.98441	18.90141	19.83657	20.31064
	11	15.38883	15.82819	16.27350	16.72463	17.18147	17.64390	18.11179	18.58503	19.06348	20.03549	21.02676	21.52928
	12	16.31216	16.77788	17.24991	17.72811	18.21236	18.70253	19.19850	19.70013	20.20729	21.23762	22.28837	22.82104
	Level	11.65194	11.95828	12.26900	12.58407	12.90341	13.22698	13.55471	13.88654	14.22242	14.90602	15.60498	15.96004
15 Year Plan	1	6.87443	7.12026	7.37055	7.62522	7.88419	8.14735	8.41463	8.68591	8.96109	9.52277	10.09879	10.39190
	2	7.28690	7.54748	7.81278	8.08274	8.35724	8.63619	8.91950	9.20706	9.49876	10.09414	10.70472	11.01541
	3	7.72411	8.00032	8.28155	8.56770	8.85867	9.15437	9.45467	9.75949	10.06869	10.69978	11.34700	11.67634
	4	8.18756	8.48034	8.77844	9.08176	9.39019	9.70363	10.02195	10.34505	10.67281	11.34177	12.02782	12.37692
	5	8.67881	8.98916	9.30515	9.62667	9.95360	10.28585	10.62327	10.96576	11.31318	12.02228	12.74949	13.11953
	6	9.19954	9.52851	9.86346	10.20427	10.55082	10.90300	11.26067	11.62370	11.99197	12.74361	13.51446	13.90671
	7	9.75151	10.10022	10.45527	10.81652	11.18387	11.55718	11.93631	12.32113	12.71148	13.50823	14.32533	14.74111
	8	10.33661	10.70624	11.08258	11.46551	11.85490	12.25061	12.65249	13.06039	13.47417	14.31873	15.18484	15.62557
	9	10.95680	11.34861	11.74754	12.15345	12.56620	12.98564	13.41164	13.84402	14.28262	15.17785	16.09594	16.56311
	10	11.61421	12.02953	12.45239	12.88265	13.32017	13.76478	14.21633	14.67466	15.13958	16.08852	17.06169	17.55689
	11	12.31106	12.75130	13.19953	13.65561	14.11938	14.59067	15.06931	15.55514	16.04796	17.05383	18.08539	18.61031
	12	13.04973	13.51638	13.99151	14.47495	14.96654	15.46611	15.97347	16.48844	17.01083	18.07706	19.17052	19.72693
	13	13.83271	14.32736	14.83100	15.34344	15.86453	16.39407	16.93188	17.47775	18.03148	19.16168	20.32075	20.91054
	14	14.66267	15.18700	15.72086	16.26405	16.81640	17.37772	17.94779	18.52642	19.11337	20.31139	21.53999	22.16518
	15	15.54243	16.09822	16.66411	17.23989	17.82539	18.42038	19.02466	19.63800	20.26017	21.53007	22.83239	23.49509
	Level	10.07590	10.39697	10.72339	11.05505	11.39188	11.73376	12.08059	12.43227	12.78869	13.51527	14.25942	14.63779

Entries are annual percentages of initial cost or value. Divide by 12 for monthly figures.

Payments in a Rising Series

Annual Rate of Increase 6.0%

Plan	Year of Plan	6.00%	6.50%	7.00%	7.50%	Interest Rate 8.00%	8.50%	9.00%	9.50%	10.00%	11.00%	12.00%	12.50%
	1	4.12466	4.37226	4.62810	4.89203	5.16386	5.44338	5.73036	6.02456	6.32572	6.94783	7.59441	7.92614
	2	4.37214	4.63459	4.90579	5.18556	5.47370	5.76999	6.07419	6.38604	6.70527	7.36470	8.05008	8.40171
	3	4.63447	4.91267	5.20014	5.49669	5.80212	6.11619	6.43864	6.76920	7.10758	7.80659	8.53308	8.90581
	4	4.91254	5.20743	5.51214	5.82649	6.15024	6.48316	6.82496	7.17535	7.53404	8.27498	9.04507	9.44016
	5	5.20729	5.51987	5.84287	6.17608	6.51926	6.87215	7.23445	7.60587	7.98608	8.77148	9.58777	10.00657
	6	5.51973	5.85106	6.19344	6.54665	6.91042	7.28447	7.66852	8.06223	8.46525	9.29777	10.16304	10.60696
	7	5.85091	6.20213	6.56505	6.93944	7.32504	7.72154	8.12863	8.54596	8.97316	9.85564	10.77282	11.24338
	8	6.20196	6.57426	6.95895	7.35581	7.76454	8.18484	8.61635	9.05872	9.51155	10.44697	11.41919	11.91798
	9	6.57408	6.96871	7.37649	7.79716	8.23042	8.67593	9.13333	9.60224	10.08224	11.07379	12.10434	12.63306
	10	6.96853	7.38683	7.81908	8.26499	8.72424	9.19648	9.68133	10.17837	10.68718	11.73822	12.83060	13.39104
	11	7.38664	7.83004	8.28823	8.76089	9.24769	9.74827	10.26221	10.78908	11.32841	12.44251	13.60044	14.19450
25 Year	12	7.82984	8.29985	8.78552	9.28654	9.80256	10.33317	10.87794	11.43642	12.00811	13.18906	14.41646	15.04617
Plan	13	8.29963	8.79784	9.31265	9.84373	10.39071	10.95316	11.53062	12.12261	12.72860	13.98041	15.28145	15.94894
	14	8.79760	9.32571	9.87141	10.43436	11.01415	11.61035	12.22246	12.84996	13.49232	14.81923	16.19834	16.90588
	15	9.32546	9.88525	10.46369	11.06042	11.67500	12.30697	12.95580	13.62096	14.30185	15.70839	17.17024	17.92023
	16	9.88499	10.47836	11.09152	11.72405	12.37550	13.04538	13.73315	14.43822	15.15997	16.65089	18.20045	18.99545
	17	10.47809	11.10707	11.75701	12.42749	13.11803	13.82811	14.55714	15.30451	16.06956	17.64994	19.29248	20.13518
	18	11.10677	11.77349	12.46243	13.17314	13.90511	14.65779	15.43057	16.22278	17.03374	18.70894	20.45003	21.34329
	19	11.77318	12.47990	13.21017	13.96353	14.73942	15.53726	16.35640	17.19615	18.05576	19.83148	21.67703	22.62388
	20	12.47957	13.22869	14.00278	14.80134	15.62378	16.46950	17.33779	18.22792	19.13911	21.02136	22.97765	23.98132
	21	13.22834	14.02242	14.84295	15.68942	16.56121	17.45767	18.37805	19.32159	20.28745	22.28265	24.35631	25.42019
	22	14.02204	14.86376	15.73353	16.63078	17.55488	18.50513	19.48074	20.48089	21.50470	23.61960	25.81769	26.94541
	23	14.86337	15.75559	16.67754	17.62863	18.60818	19.61543	20.64958	21.70974	22.79498	25.03678	27.36675	28.56213
	24	15.75517	16.70092	17.67819	18.68635	19.72467	20.79236	21.88856	23.01233	24.16268	26.53899	29.00876	30.27586
	25	16.70048	17.70298	18.73888	19.80753	20.90815	22.03990	23.20187	24.39306	25.61244	28.13133	30.74929	32.09241
	Level	7.69315	8.05883	8.43216	8.81281	9.20046	9.59476	9.99539	10.40201	10.81429	11.65452	12.51355	12.94936
	1	3.43722	3.68573	3.94438	4.21293	4.49115	4.77872	5.07533	5.38062	5.69422	6.34474	7.02357	7.37253
	2	3.64345	3.90687	4.18104	4.46571	4.76062	5.06544	5.37985	5.70346	6.03588	6.72543	7.44499	7.81488
	3	3.86206	4.14129	4.43190	4.73365	5.04625	5.36937	5.70264	6.04567	6.39803	7.12895	7.89169	8.28377
	4	4.09378	4.38976	4.69781	5.01767	5.34903	5.69153	6.04480	6.40841	6.78191	7.55669	8.36519	8.78080
	5	4.33941	4.65315	4.97968	5.31873	5.66997	6.03303	6.40749	6.79291	7.18882	8.01009	8.86710	9.30765
	6	4.59977	4.93234	5.27846	5.63786	6.01017	6.39501	6.79194	7.20049	7.62015	8.49070	9.39912	9.86610
	7	4.87576	5.22828	5.59517	5.97613	6.37078	6.77871	7.19945	7.63252	8.07736	9.00014	9.96307	10.45807
	8	5.16830	5.54197	5.93088	6.33469	6.75302	7.18543	7.63142	8.09047	8.56201	9.54015	10.56086	11.08556
	9	5.47840	5.87449	6.28673	6.71478	7.15821	7.61656	8.08931	8.57590	9.07573	10.11256	11.19451	11.75069
	10	5.80711	6.22696	6.66394	7.11766	7.58770	8.07355	8.57466	9.09045	9.62027	10.71931	11.86618	12.45573
	11	6.15553	6.60058	7.06378	7.54472	8.04296	8.55796	9.08914	9.63588	10.19749	11.36247	12.57815	13.20307
	12	6.52486	6.99662	7.48760	7.99741	8.52554	9.07144	9.63449	10.21403	10.80933	12.04422	13.33284	13.99526
	13	6.91636	7.41641	7.93686	8.47725	9.03707	9.61573	10.21256	10.82687	11.45789	12.76687	14.13281	14.83497
	14	7.33134	7.86140	8.41307	8.98589	9.57929	10.19267	10.82532	11.47648	12.14537	13.53288	14.98078	15.72507
30 Year	15	7.77122	8.33308	8.91785	9.52504	10.15405	10.80423	11.47483	12.16507	12.87409	14.34486	15.87962	16.66858
Plan	16	8.23749	8.83307	9.45292	10.09654	10.76330	11.45248	12.16332	12.89498	13.64654	15.20555	16.83240	17.66869
	17	8.73174	9.36305	10.02010	10.70233	11.40909	12.13963	12.89312	13.66868	14.46533	16.11788	17.84234	18.72881
	18	9.25564	9.92483	10.62131	11.34447	12.09364	12.86801	13.66671	14.48880	15.33325	17.08495	18.91288	19.85254
	19	9.81098	10.52032	11.25858	12.02514	12.81926	13.64009	14.48671	15.35812	16.25324	18.11005	20.04766	21.04369
	20	10.39964	11.15154	11.93410	12.74665	13.58841	14.45850	15.35592	16.27961	17.22844	19.19666	21.25052	22.30632
	21	11.02362	11.82063	12.65015	13.51145	14.40372	15.32601	16.27727	17.25639	18.26214	20.34845	22.52555	23.64469
	22	11.68504	12.52987	13.40915	14.32214	15.26794	16.24557	17.25391	18.29177	19.35787	21.56936	23.87708	25.06338
	23	12.38614	13.28166	14.21370	15.18146	16.18402	17.22030	18.28914	19.38928	20.51934	22.86352	25.30971	26.56718
	24	13.12931	14.07856	15.06653	16.09235	17.15506	18.25352	19.38649	20.55263	21.75050	24.23533	26.82829	28.16121
	25	13.91707	14.92328	15.97052	17.05789	18.18436	19.34873	20.54968	21.78579	23.05554	25.68945	28.43799	29.85088
	26	14.75209	15.81867	16.92875	18.08137	19.27542	20.50965	21.78266	23.09294	24.43887	27.23082	30.14426	31.64194
	27	15.63721	16.76780	17.94447	19.16625	20.43195	21.74023	23.08962	24.47852	25.90520	28.86467	31.95292	33.54045
	28	16.57545	17.77386	19.02114	20.31622	21.65786	23.04465	24.47500	25.94723	27.45951	30.59655	33.87010	35.55288
	29	17.56997	18.84029	20.16241	21.53520	22.95734	24.42732	25.94350	27.50406	29.10708	32.43234	35.90230	37.68605
	30	18.62417	19.97071	21.37216	22.82731	24.33478	25.89296	27.50011	29.15430	30.85351	34.37829	38.05644	39.94721
	Level	7.15881	7.54395	7.93733	8.33846	8.74686	9.16206	9.58359	10.01100	10.44383	11.32408	12.22114	12.67506

Entries are annual percentages of initial cost or value. Divide by 12 for monthly figures.

Payments in a Rising Series

Annual Rate of Increase 7.0%

Plan	Year of Plan	6.00%	6.50%	7.00%	7.50%	8.00%	8.50%	9.00%	9.50%	10.00%	11.00%	12.00%	12.50%
3 Year Plan	1	34.04993	34.29352	34.53678	34.77970	35.02228	35.26450	35.50635	35.74783	35.98892	36.46990	36.94923	37.18825
	2	36.43343	36.69407	36.95436	37.21428	37.47384	37.73301	37.99180	38.25018	38.50814	39.02279	39.53568	39.79143
	3	38.98377	39.26265	39.54116	39.81928	40.09701	40.37433	40.65122	40.92769	41.20371	41.75439	42.30317	42.57683
	Level	36.32470	36.58066	36.83763	37.09561	37.35461	37.61461	37.87561	38.13762	38.40062	38.92961	39.46255	39.73049
4 Year Plan	1	25.41718	25.65981	25.90259	26.14549	26.38850	26.63161	26.87480	27.11805	27.36136	27.84805	28.33477	28.57810
	2	27.19638	27.45600	27.71577	27.97567	28.23570	28.49582	28.75604	29.01632	29.27665	29.79742	30.31820	30.57856
	3	29.10013	29.37792	29.65587	29.93397	30.21219	30.49053	30.76896	31.04746	31.32602	31.88324	32.44048	32.71906
	4	31.13714	31.43437	31.73178	32.02935	32.32705	32.62487	32.92279	33.22078	33.51884	34.11506	34.71131	35.00940
	Level	28.04183	28.30463	28.56884	28.83447	29.10150	29.36993	29.63975	29.91097	30.18357	30.73291	31.28773	31.56717
5 Year Plan	1	20.23783	20.47966	20.72207	20.96503	21.20853	21.45255	21.69705	21.94203	22.18746	22.67959	23.17327	23.42065
	2	21.65448	21.91324	22.17261	22.43258	22.69313	22.95422	23.21585	23.47797	23.74058	24.26716	24.79540	25.06009
	3	23.17030	23.44716	23.72470	24.00287	24.28165	24.56102	24.84096	25.12143	25.40242	25.96586	26.53108	26.81430
	4	24.79222	25.08847	25.38542	25.68307	25.98136	26.28029	26.57982	26.87993	27.18059	27.78347	28.38825	28.69130
	5	26.52767	26.84466	27.16240	27.48088	27.80006	28.11991	28.44041	28.76153	29.08324	29.72832	30.37543	30.69969
	Level	23.08394	23.35288	23.62363	23.89619	24.17054	24.44667	24.72459	25.00428	25.28574	25.85391	26.42905	26.71920
6 Year Plan	1	16.78519	17.02629	17.26839	17.51146	17.75547	18.00039	18.24621	18.49288	18.74039	19.23781	19.73824	19.98953
	2	17.96015	18.21813	18.47718	18.73726	18.99835	19.26042	19.52344	19.78738	20.05222	20.58446	21.11992	21.38879
	3	19.21737	19.49340	19.77058	20.04887	20.32824	20.60865	20.89008	21.17250	21.45587	22.02537	22.59831	22.88601
	4	20.56258	20.85794	21.15452	21.45229	21.75121	22.05126	22.35239	22.65458	22.95779	23.56714	24.18020	24.48803
	5	22.00196	22.31800	22.63534	22.95395	23.27380	23.59484	23.91706	24.24040	24.56483	25.21684	25.87281	26.20219
	6	23.54210	23.88026	24.21981	24.56073	24.90296	25.24648	25.59125	25.93722	26.28437	26.98202	27.68391	28.03635
	Level	19.78852	20.06324	20.34016	20.61926	20.90055	21.18401	21.46962	21.75738	22.04728	22.63342	23.22795	23.52833
7 Year Plan	1	14.31923	14.55965	14.80148	15.04467	15.28921	15.53505	15.78216	16.03052	16.28008	16.78270	17.28976	17.54487
	2	15.32158	15.57883	15.83758	16.09780	16.35945	16.62250	16.88691	17.15265	17.41969	17.95749	18.50004	18.77301
	3	16.39409	16.66935	16.94621	17.22465	17.50461	17.78608	18.06900	18.35334	18.63907	19.21451	19.79504	20.08712
	4	17.54168	17.83620	18.13245	18.43037	18.72994	19.03110	19.33383	19.63807	19.94380	20.55953	21.18070	21.49322
	5	18.76960	19.08474	19.40172	19.72050	20.04103	20.36328	20.68720	21.01274	21.33987	21.99870	22.66335	22.99774
	6	20.08347	20.42067	20.75984	21.10093	21.44390	21.78871	22.13530	22.48363	22.83366	23.53861	24.24978	24.60758
	7	21.48931	21.85011	22.21303	22.57800	22.94498	23.31392	23.68477	24.05748	24.43201	25.18631	25.94726	26.33012
	Level	17.44305	17.72332	18.00618	18.29161	18.57959	18.87012	19.16317	19.45873	19.75678	20.36029	20.97354	21.28378
10 Year Plan	1	9.88143	10.11993	10.36103	10.60468	10.85083	11.09943	11.35043	11.60377	11.85941	12.37735	12.90382	13.17012
	2	10.57313	10.82833	11.08631	11.34701	11.61039	11.87639	12.14496	12.41604	12.68957	13.24376	13.80709	14.09203
	3	11.31324	11.58631	11.86235	12.14130	12.42312	12.70774	12.99511	13.28516	13.57784	14.17083	14.77359	15.07847
	4	12.10517	12.39735	12.69271	12.99119	13.29274	13.59728	13.90476	14.21512	14.52828	15.16279	15.80774	16.13396
	5	12.95253	13.26517	13.58120	13.90058	14.22323	14.54909	14.87810	15.21018	15.54526	16.22418	16.91428	17.26334
	6	13.85921	14.19373	14.53189	14.87362	15.21886	15.56753	15.91956	16.27489	16.63343	17.35987	18.09828	18.47178
	7	14.82936	15.18729	15.54912	15.91477	16.28418	16.65725	17.03393	17.41413	17.79777	18.57506	19.36516	19.76480
	8	15.86741	16.25040	16.63756	17.02881	17.42407	17.82326	18.22631	18.63312	19.04362	19.87532	20.72072	21.14834
	9	16.97813	17.38793	17.80219	18.22082	18.64375	19.07089	19.50215	19.93744	20.37667	21.26659	22.17117	22.62872
	10	18.16660	18.60508	19.04834	19.49628	19.94882	20.40585	20.86730	21.33306	21.80304	22.75525	23.72315	24.21273
	Level	13.25618	13.55235	13.85221	14.15574	14.46289	14.77364	15.08793	15.40574	15.72703	16.37985	17.04605	17.38406
12 Year Plan	1	8.15625	8.39353	8.63420	8.87818	9.12542	9.37586	9.62944	9.88608	10.14572	10.67373	11.21289	11.48648
	2	8.72718	8.98108	9.23859	9.49965	9.76420	10.03217	10.30350	10.57810	10.85592	11.42089	11.99780	12.29053
	3	9.33809	9.60975	9.88529	10.16463	10.44770	10.73443	11.02474	11.31857	11.61583	12.22035	12.83764	13.15087
	4	9.99175	10.28244	10.57726	10.87615	11.17903	11.48583	11.79647	12.11087	12.42894	13.07577	13.73628	14.07143
	5	10.69117	11.00221	11.31767	11.63748	11.96157	12.28984	12.62223	12.95863	13.29897	13.99108	14.69782	15.05643
	6	11.43956	11.77236	12.10991	12.45211	12.79888	13.15013	13.50578	13.86573	14.22990	14.97045	15.72666	16.11038
	7	12.24032	12.59643	12.95760	13.32375	13.69480	14.07064	14.45119	14.83634	15.22599	16.01838	16.82753	17.23811
	8	13.09715	13.47818	13.86463	14.25642	14.65343	15.05559	15.46277	15.87488	16.29181	17.13967	18.00546	18.44478
	9	14.01395	14.42165	14.83515	15.25436	15.67917	16.10948	16.54516	16.98612	17.43223	18.33945	19.26584	19.73591
	10	14.99492	15.43116	15.87362	16.32217	16.77672	17.23714	17.70333	18.17515	18.65249	19.62321	20.61445	21.11743
	11	16.04457	16.51135	16.98477	17.46472	17.95109	18.44374	18.94256	19.44741	19.95816	20.99683	22.05746	22.59565
	12	17.16769	17.66714	18.17370	18.68725	19.20766	19.73480	20.26854	20.80873	21.35524	22.46661	23.60148	24.17734
	Level	11.65194	11.95828	12.26900	12.58407	12.90341	13.22698	13.55471	13.88654	14.22242	14.90602	15.60498	15.96004
15 Year Plan	1	6.43182	6.66732	6.90736	7.15186	7.40076	7.65396	7.91139	8.17295	8.43855	8.98149	9.53941	9.82371
	2	6.88205	7.13403	7.39087	7.65249	7.91881	8.18974	8.46519	8.74506	9.02925	9.61020	10.20716	10.51137
	3	7.36380	7.63341	7.90823	8.18817	8.47313	8.76302	9.05775	9.35721	9.66130	10.28291	10.92166	11.24717
	4	7.87926	8.16775	8.46181	8.76134	9.06624	9.37643	9.69179	10.01222	10.33759	11.00272	11.68618	12.03447
	5	8.43081	8.73950	9.05413	9.37463	9.70088	10.03278	10.37022	10.71307	11.06122	11.77291	12.50421	12.87688
	6	9.02097	9.35126	9.68792	10.03085	10.37994	10.73508	11.09613	11.46299	11.83551	12.59701	13.37951	13.77826
	7	9.65243	10.00585	10.36608	10.73301	11.10654	11.48653	11.87286	12.26540	12.66400	13.47880	14.31607	14.74274
	8	10.32810	10.70626	11.09170	11.48433	11.88400	12.29059	12.70396	13.12397	13.55048	14.42232	15.31820	15.77473
	9	11.05107	11.45570	11.86812	12.28823	12.71588	13.15093	13.59324	14.04265	14.49901	15.43188	16.39047	16.87897
	10	11.82465	12.25760	12.69889	13.14840	13.60599	14.07150	14.54477	15.02564	15.51394	16.51211	17.53781	18.06049
	11	12.65237	13.11563	13.58781	14.06879	14.55841	15.05650	15.56290	16.07743	16.59991	17.66796	18.76545	19.32473
	12	13.53804	14.03372	14.53896	15.05361	15.57750	16.11046	16.65230	17.20285	17.76191	18.90472	20.07904	20.67646
	13	14.48570	15.01608	15.55669	16.10736	16.66792	17.23819	17.81797	18.40705	19.00524	20.22805	21.48457	22.12488
	14	15.49970	16.07211	16.64566	17.23488	17.83468	18.44486	19.06522	19.69555	20.33561	21.64401	22.98849	23.67362
	15	16.58468	17.19191	17.81085	18.44132	19.08310	19.73600	20.39979	21.07424	21.75910	23.15909	24.59768	25.33078
	Level	10.07590	10.39697	10.72339	11.05505	11.39188	11.73376	12.08059	12.43227	12.78869	13.51527	14.25942	14.63779

Entries are annual percentages of initial cost or value. Divide by 12 for monthly figures.

Payments in a Rising Series

Annual Rate of Increase 7.0%

Plan	Year of Plan	6.00%	6.50%	7.00%	7.50%	8.00%	8.50%	9.00%	9.50%	10.00%	11.00%	12.00%	12.50%
							Interest Rate						
	1	3.67670	3.90637	4.14441	4.39073	4.64517	4.90757	5.17775	5.45551	5.74063	6.33195	6.94968	7.26775
	2	3.93407	4.17981	4.43452	4.69808	4.97033	5.25110	5.54019	5.83740	6.14247	6.77519	7.43616	7.77649
	3	4.20945	4.47240	4.74494	5.02694	5.31825	5.61868	5.92801	6.24601	6.57244	7.24945	7.95669	8.32085
	4	4.50411	4.78547	5.07708	5.37883	5.69053	6.01198	6.34297	6.68324	7.03251	7.75692	8.51365	8.90330
	5	4.81940	5.12045	5.43248	5.75535	6.08887	6.43282	6.78698	7.15106	7.52479	8.29990	9.10961	9.52654
	6	5.15676	5.47888	5.81275	6.15822	6.51509	6.88312	7.26206	7.65164	8.05152	8.88089	9.74728	10.19339
	7	5.51773	5.86240	6.21965	6.58930	6.97114	7.36494	7.77041	8.18725	8.61513	9.50256	10.42959	10.90693
	8	5.90398	6.27277	6.65502	7.05055	7.45912	7.88048	8.31434	8.76036	9.21819	10.16773	11.15966	11.67042
	9	6.31725	6.71186	7.12087	7.54409	7.98126	8.43212	8.89634	9.37358	9.86346	10.87948	11.94084	12.48735
	10	6.75946	7.18169	7.61934	8.07217	8.53995	9.02237	9.51909	10.02973	10.55390	11.64104	12.77670	13.36146
25 Year Plan	11	7.23262	7.68441	8.15269	8.63722	9.13775	9.65393	10.18542	10.73182	11.29268	12.45591	13.67107	14.29676
	12	7.73891	8.22232	8.72338	9.24183	9.77739	10.32971	10.89840	11.48304	12.08317	13.32783	14.62804	15.29754
	13	8.28063	8.79788	9.33401	9.88876	10.46180	11.05279	11.66129	12.28686	12.92899	14.26077	15.65201	16.36836
	14	8.86028	9.41374	9.98739	10.58097	11.19413	11.82648	12.47758	13.14694	13.83402	15.25903	16.74765	17.51415
	15	9.48049	10.07270	10.68651	11.32164	11.97772	12.65434	13.35101	14.06722	14.80240	16.32716	17.91998	18.74014
	16	10.14413	10.77779	11.43457	12.11415	12.81616	13.54014	14.28558	15.05193	15.83857	17.47006	19.17438	20.05195
	17	10.85422	11.53223	12.23499	12.96215	13.71329	14.48795	15.28557	16.10556	16.94727	18.69296	20.51659	21.45558
	18	11.61401	12.33949	13.09144	13.86950	14.67322	15.50210	16.35556	17.23295	18.13357	20.00147	21.95275	22.95748
	19	12.42699	13.20325	14.00784	14.84036	15.70035	16.58725	17.50045	18.43926	19.40292	21.40157	23.48944	24.56450
	20	13.29688	14.12748	14.98839	15.87919	16.79937	17.74836	18.72548	19.73001	20.76113	22.89968	25.13370	26.28401
	21	14.22767	15.11640	16.03757	16.99073	17.97533	18.99074	20.03627	21.11111	22.21441	24.50266	26.89306	28.12389
	22	15.22360	16.17455	17.16020	18.18008	19.23360	20.32010	21.43880	22.58888	23.76942	26.21785	28.77558	30.09257
	23	16.28925	17.30677	18.36142	19.45268	20.57995	21.74250	22.93952	24.17011	25.43328	28.05310	30.78987	32.19905
	24	17.42950	18.51824	19.64672	20.81437	22.02055	23.26448	24.54529	25.86201	27.21360	30.01682	32.94516	34.45298
	25	18.64957	19.81452	21.02199	22.27138	23.56199	24.89299	26.26346	27.67235	29.11856	32.11799	35.25132	36.86469
	Level	7.69315	8.05883	8.43216	8.81281	9.20046	9.59476	9.99539	10.40201	10.81429	11.65452	12.51355	12.94936
	1	2.98981	3.21660	3.45368	3.70091	3.95813	4.22511	4.50161	4.78733	5.08197	5.69657	6.34242	6.67605
	2	3.19910	3.44176	3.69544	3.95998	4.23520	4.52087	4.81672	5.12244	5.43770	6.09533	6.78639	7.14337
	3	3.42304	3.68269	3.95412	4.23717	4.53166	4.83733	5.15389	5.48102	5.81834	6.52200	7.26143	7.64341
	4	3.66265	3.94047	4.23090	4.53378	4.84888	5.17594	5.51466	5.86469	6.22563	6.97854	7.76973	8.17845
	5	3.91903	4.21631	4.52707	4.85114	5.18830	5.53826	5.90069	6.27521	6.66142	7.46704	8.31361	8.74934
	6	4.19337	4.51145	4.84396	5.19072	5.55148	5.92594	6.31374	6.71448	7.12772	7.98973	8.89557	9.36350
	7	4.48690	4.82725	5.18304	5.55407	5.94008	6.34075	6.75570	7.18449	7.62666	8.54902	9.51826	10.01895
	8	4.80098	5.16516	5.54585	5.94286	6.35589	6.78460	7.22860	7.68741	8.16053	9.14745	10.18454	10.72027
	9	5.13705	5.52672	5.93406	6.35886	6.80080	7.25953	7.73460	8.22553	8.73176	9.78777	10.89745	11.47069
	10	5.49665	5.91359	6.34945	6.80398	7.27686	7.76769	8.27602	8.80131	9.34299	10.47291	11.66027	12.27364
	11	5.88141	6.32754	6.79391	7.28025	7.78624	8.31143	8.85534	9.41740	9.99700	11.20602	12.47649	13.13280
	12	6.29311	6.77047	7.26948	7.78987	8.33127	8.89323	9.47522	10.07662	10.69679	11.99044	13.34985	14.05209
	13	6.73363	7.24440	7.77834	8.33516	8.91446	9.51576	10.13848	10.78199	11.44556	12.82977	14.28434	15.03574
	14	7.20498	7.75151	8.32283	8.91862	9.53847	10.18186	10.84817	11.53673	12.24675	13.72785	15.28424	16.08824
30 Year Plan	15	7.70933	8.29411	8.90543	9.54293	10.20617	10.89459	11.60755	12.34430	13.10402	14.68880	16.35414	17.21442
	16	8.24898	8.87470	9.52881	10.21093	10.92060	11.65721	12.42007	13.20840	14.02130	15.71702	17.49893	18.41943
	17	8.82641	9.49593	10.19582	10.92570	11.68504	12.47322	13.28948	14.13298	15.00280	16.81721	18.72385	19.70879
	18	9.44426	10.16065	10.90953	11.69050	12.50299	13.34634	14.21974	15.12229	16.05299	17.99441	20.03452	21.08840
	19	10.10536	10.87189	11.67320	12.50883	13.37820	14.28059	15.21513	16.18085	17.17670	19.25402	21.43694	22.56459
	20	10.81274	11.63292	12.49032	13.38445	14.31468	15.28023	16.28018	17.31351	18.37907	20.60180	22.93752	24.14411
	21	11.56963	12.44723	13.36464	14.32136	15.31671	16.34984	17.41980	18.52546	19.66560	22.04393	24.54315	25.83420
	22	12.37950	13.31853	14.30017	15.32386	16.38888	17.49433	18.63918	19.82224	21.04220	23.58700	26.26117	27.64259
	23	13.24607	14.25083	15.30118	16.39653	17.53610	18.71894	19.94393	21.20980	22.51515	25.23809	28.09945	29.57758
	24	14.17329	15.24839	16.37226	17.54429	18.76362	20.02926	21.34000	22.69449	24.09121	27.00476	30.06642	31.64801
	25	15.16542	16.31578	17.51832	18.77238	20.07708	21.43131	22.83380	24.28310	25.77760	28.89509	32.17106	33.86337
	26	16.22700	17.45788	18.74461	20.08645	21.48247	22.93150	24.43217	25.98292	27.58203	30.91775	34.42304	36.23380
	27	17.36289	18.67993	20.05673	21.49250	22.98625	24.53671	26.14242	27.80172	29.51277	33.08199	36.83265	38.77017
	28	18.57829	19.98753	21.46070	22.99698	24.59528	26.25428	27.97239	29.74784	31.57866	35.39773	39.41094	41.48408
	29	19.87877	21.38666	22.96295	24.60677	26.31695	28.09207	29.93045	31.83019	33.78917	37.87557	42.16970	44.38797
	30	21.27029	22.88372	24.57035	26.32924	28.15914	30.05852	32.02559	34.05830	36.15441	40.52686	45.12158	47.49512
	Level	7.15881	7.54395	7.93733	8.33846	8.74686	9.16206	9.58359	10.01100	10.44383	11.32408	12.22114	12.67506

Entries are annual percentages of initial cost or value. Divide by 12 for monthly figures.

Payments in a Rising Series

Annual Rate of Increase 8.0%

Plan	Year of Plan	Interest Rate 6.00%	6.50%	7.00%	7.50%	8.00%	8.50%	9.00%	9.50%	10.00%	11.00%	12.00%	12.50%
3 Year Plan	1	33.73172	33.97402	34.21601	34.45767	34.69900	34.93999	35.18061	35.42088	35.66077	36.13940	36.61642	36.85430
	2	36.43025	36.69194	36.95329	37.21429	37.47492	37.73518	37.99506	38.25455	38.51363	39.03055	39.54573	39.80265
	3	39.34467	39.62730	39.90955	40.19143	40.47292	40.75400	41.03467	41.31491	41.59472	42.15299	42.70939	42.98686
	Level	36.32470	36.58066	36.83763	37.09561	37.35461	37.61461	37.87561	38.13762	38.40062	38.92961	39.46255	39.73049
4 Year Plan	1	25.06089	25.30150	25.54228	25.78320	26.02425	26.26542	26.50668	26.74802	26.98944	27.47241	27.95547	28.19700
	2	27.06576	27.32562	27.58566	27.84586	28.10619	28.36665	28.62721	28.88787	29.14859	29.67020	30.19191	30.45276
	3	29.23102	29.51167	29.79252	30.07353	30.35469	30.63598	30.91739	31.19889	31.48048	32.04382	32.60726	32.88898
	4	31.56950	31.87261	32.17592	32.47941	32.78306	33.08686	33.39078	33.69481	33.99892	34.60732	35.21584	35.52010
	Level	28.04183	28.30463	28.56884	28.83447	29.10150	29.36993	29.63975	29.91097	30.18357	30.73291	31.28773	31.56717
5 Year Plan	1	19.85961	20.09867	20.33834	20.57859	20.81940	21.06075	21.30261	21.54497	21.78780	22.27481	22.76348	23.00838
	2	21.44838	21.70657	21.96541	22.22488	22.48495	22.74561	23.00682	23.26857	23.53083	24.05680	24.58455	24.84905
	3	23.16425	23.44309	23.72264	24.00287	24.28375	24.56526	24.84736	25.13005	25.41329	25.98134	26.55132	26.83697
	4	25.01738	25.31854	25.62045	25.92310	26.22645	26.53048	26.83515	27.14046	27.44636	28.05985	28.67542	28.98393
	5	27.01878	27.34402	27.67009	27.99695	28.32456	28.65291	28.98197	29.31169	29.64207	30.30464	30.96946	31.30264
	Level	23.08394	23.35288	23.62363	23.89619	24.17054	24.44667	24.72459	25.00428	25.28574	25.85391	26.42905	26.71920
6 Year Plan	1	16.39309	16.63069	16.86930	17.10892	17.34950	17.59103	17.83348	18.07682	18.32102	18.81192	19.30596	19.55409
	2	17.70454	17.96114	18.21885	18.47763	18.73746	18.99831	19.26016	19.52296	19.78670	20.31687	20.85044	21.11842
	3	19.12090	19.39803	19.67635	19.95584	20.23646	20.51818	20.80097	21.08480	21.36964	21.94222	22.51847	22.80790
	4	20.65058	20.94987	21.25046	21.55231	21.85537	22.15963	22.46505	22.77158	23.07921	23.69760	24.31995	24.63253
	5	22.30262	22.62586	22.95050	23.27649	23.60380	23.93240	24.26225	24.59331	24.92555	25.59341	26.26554	26.60313
	6	24.08683	24.43593	24.78654	25.13861	25.49211	25.84699	26.20323	26.56077	26.91959	27.64088	28.36679	28.73138
	Level	19.78852	20.06324	20.34016	20.61926	20.90055	21.18401	21.46962	21.75738	22.04728	22.63342	23.22795	23.52833
7 Year Plan	1	13.91788	14.15404	14.39163	14.63063	14.87100	15.11271	15.35574	15.60004	15.84558	16.34028	16.83957	17.09085
	2	15.03131	15.28636	15.54296	15.80108	16.06068	16.32173	16.58419	16.84804	17.11323	17.64750	18.18673	18.45812
	3	16.23381	16.50927	16.78640	17.06517	17.34554	17.62747	17.91093	18.19588	18.48228	19.05930	19.64167	19.93477
	4	17.53252	17.83001	18.12931	18.43038	18.73318	19.03767	19.34381	19.65155	19.96087	20.58404	21.21300	21.52955
	5	18.93512	19.25641	19.57965	19.90481	20.23183	20.56068	20.89131	21.22368	21.55774	22.23077	22.91004	23.25192
	6	20.44993	20.79692	21.14603	21.49719	21.85038	22.20553	22.56261	22.92157	23.28236	24.00923	24.74285	25.11207
	7	22.08592	22.46068	22.83771	23.21697	23.59841	23.98198	24.36762	24.75530	25.14494	25.92996	26.72227	27.12104
	Level	17.44305	17.72332	18.00618	18.29161	18.57959	18.87012	19.16317	19.45873	19.75678	20.36029	20.97354	21.28378
10 Year Plan	1	9.46612	9.69810	9.93272	10.16994	10.40970	10.65197	10.89669	11.14381	11.39329	11.89910	12.41371	12.67419
	2	10.22341	10.47395	10.72734	10.98353	11.24248	11.50412	11.76842	12.03531	12.30475	12.85103	13.40681	13.68812
	3	11.04128	11.31186	11.58552	11.86221	12.14187	12.42445	12.70989	12.99814	13.28913	13.87911	14.47936	14.78317
	4	11.92458	12.21681	12.51237	12.81119	13.11322	13.41841	13.72669	14.03799	14.35226	14.98944	15.63770	15.96583
	5	12.87855	13.19416	13.51336	13.83609	14.16228	14.49188	14.82482	15.16103	15.50044	16.18859	16.88872	17.24309
	6	13.90883	14.24969	14.59442	14.94297	15.29527	15.65123	16.01081	16.37391	16.74047	17.48368	18.23982	18.62254
	7	15.02154	15.38966	15.76198	16.13841	16.51889	16.90333	17.29167	17.68382	18.07971	18.88238	19.69900	20.11235
	8	16.22326	16.62084	17.02294	17.42948	17.84040	18.25560	18.67500	19.09853	19.52609	20.39297	21.27492	21.72133
	9	17.52112	17.95050	18.38477	18.82384	19.26763	19.71605	20.16900	20.63024	21.08818	22.02440	22.97692	23.45904
	10	18.92281	19.38654	19.85555	20.32975	20.80904	21.29333	21.78252	22.27652	22.77523	23.78636	24.81507	25.33576
	Level	13.25618	13.55235	13.85221	14.15574	14.46289	14.77364	15.08793	15.40574	15.72703	16.37985	17.04605	17.38406
12 Year Plan	1	7.73740	7.96665	8.19932	8.43538	8.67475	8.91739	9.16322	9.41220	9.66426	10.17736	10.70199	10.96845
	2	8.35639	8.60398	8.85527	9.11021	9.36873	9.63078	9.89628	10.16518	10.43740	10.99155	11.55815	11.84593
	3	9.02490	9.29230	9.56369	9.83902	10.11823	10.40124	10.68798	10.97839	11.27240	11.87088	12.48280	12.79360
	4	9.74689	10.03568	10.32879	10.62615	10.92769	11.23334	11.54302	11.85667	12.17419	12.82055	13.48142	13.81709
	5	10.52664	10.83853	11.15509	11.47624	11.80190	12.13200	12.46646	12.80520	13.14812	13.84619	14.55994	14.92246
	6	11.36877	11.70562	12.04750	12.39434	12.74605	13.10256	13.46378	13.82962	14.19997	14.95389	15.72473	16.11626
	7	12.27827	12.64207	13.01130	13.38588	13.76574	14.15077	14.54088	14.93598	15.33597	16.15020	16.98271	17.40556
	8	13.26054	13.65343	14.05220	14.45676	14.86700	15.28283	15.70415	16.13086	16.56285	17.44221	18.34133	18.79800
	9	14.32138	14.74571	15.17638	15.61330	16.05636	16.50546	16.96049	17.42133	17.88788	18.83759	19.80863	20.30184
	10	15.46709	15.92536	16.39049	16.86236	17.34087	17.82589	18.31733	18.81504	19.31891	20.34460	21.39333	21.92599
	11	16.70446	17.19939	17.70173	18.21135	18.72814	19.25197	19.78271	20.32024	20.86642	21.97216	23.10479	23.68007
	12	18.04081	18.57534	19.11787	19.66826	20.22639	20.79212	21.36533	21.94586	22.53357	23.72994	24.95318	25.57447
	Level	11.65194	11.95828	12.26900	12.58407	12.90341	13.22698	13.55471	13.88654	14.22242	14.90602	15.60498	15.96004
15 Year Plan	1	6.01169	6.23689	6.46668	6.70101	6.93980	7.18299	7.43050	7.68225	7.93815	8.46206	9.00151	9.27680
	2	6.49262	6.73584	6.98401	7.23709	7.49498	7.75763	8.02494	8.29682	8.57320	9.13903	9.72163	10.01895
	3	7.01203	7.27470	7.54273	7.81605	8.09458	8.37824	8.66693	8.96057	9.25906	9.87015	10.49936	10.82046
	4	7.57299	7.85668	8.14615	8.44134	8.74215	9.04850	9.36029	9.67742	9.99978	10.65976	11.33930	11.68610
	5	8.17883	8.48521	8.79785	9.11665	9.44152	9.77238	10.10911	10.45161	10.79976	11.51254	12.24645	12.62099
	6	8.83314	9.16403	9.50167	9.84598	10.19684	10.55417	10.91784	11.28774	11.66374	12.43355	13.22616	13.63067
	7	9.53979	9.89715	10.26181	10.63365	11.01259	11.39850	11.79127	12.19076	12.59684	13.42823	14.28426	14.72112
	8	10.30297	10.68893	11.08275	11.48435	11.89360	12.31038	12.73457	13.16602	13.60459	14.50249	15.42700	15.89881
	9	11.12721	11.54404	11.96937	12.40309	12.84509	13.29521	13.75333	14.21930	14.69296	15.66269	16.66116	17.17072
	10	12.01739	12.46756	12.92692	13.39534	13.87269	14.35883	14.85360	15.35684	15.86839	16.91570	17.99405	18.54437
	11	12.97878	13.46497	13.96107	14.46697	14.98251	15.50754	16.04189	16.58539	17.13787	18.26896	19.43357	20.02792
	12	14.01708	14.54216	15.07796	15.62433	16.18111	16.74814	17.32524	17.91222	18.50889	19.73048	20.98826	21.63016
	13	15.13845	15.70554	16.28420	16.87427	17.47560	18.08799	18.71126	19.34520	19.98961	21.30892	22.66732	23.36057
	14	16.34953	16.96198	17.58693	18.22242	18.87365	19.53503	20.20816	20.89282	21.58877	23.01363	24.48071	25.22941
	15	17.65749	18.31894	18.99389	19.68215	20.38354	21.09783	21.81841	22.56424	23.31588	24.85472	26.43916	27.24777
	Level	10.07590	10.39697	10.72339	11.05505	11.39188	11.73376	12.08059	12.43227	12.78869	13.51527	14.25942	14.63779

Entries are annual percentages of initial cost or value. Divide by 12 for monthly figures.

Payments in a Rising Series

Annual Rate of Increase 8.0%

Plan	Year of Plan	6.00%	6.50%	7.00%	7.50%	8.00%	8.50%	9.00%	9.50%	10.00%	11.00%	12.00%	12.50%
							Interest Rate						
	1	3.26614	3.47804	3.69834	3.92698	4.16388	4.40892	4.66196	4.92284	5.19139	5.75067	6.33801	6.64158
	2	3.52744	3.75628	3.99421	4.24114	4.49699	4.76163	5.03491	5.31667	5.60670	6.21072	6.84505	7.17290
	3	3.80963	4.05678	4.31374	4.58043	4.85675	5.14256	5.43771	5.74200	6.05524	6.70758	7.39265	7.74674
	4	4.11440	4.38133	4.65884	4.94687	5.24529	5.55397	5.87272	6.20136	6.53966	7.24419	7.98406	8.36647
	5	4.44355	4.73183	5.03155	5.34262	5.66491	5.99828	6.34254	6.69747	7.06283	7.82372	8.62279	9.03579
	6	4.79904	5.11038	5.43407	5.77003	6.11811	6.47815	6.84995	7.23327	7.62786	8.44962	9.31261	9.75866
	7	5.18296	5.51921	5.86880	6.23163	6.60755	6.99640	7.39794	7.81193	8.23809	9.12559	10.05762	10.53935
	8	5.59760	5.96075	6.33830	6.73016	7.13616	7.55611	7.98978	8.43689	8.89713	9.85564	10.86223	11.38250
	9	6.04541	6.43761	6.84537	7.26857	7.70705	8.16060	8.62896	9.11184	9.60890	10.64409	11.73121	12.29310
	10	6.52904	6.95261	7.39300	7.85006	8.32362	8.81345	9.31928	9.84079	10.37762	11.49562	12.66971	13.27654
	11	7.05136	7.50882	7.98444	8.47806	8.98950	9.51852	10.06482	10.62805	11.20783	12.41527	13.68328	14.33867
25 Year	12	7.61547	8.10953	8.62319	9.15631	9.70867	10.28000	10.87000	11.47829	12.10445	13.40849	14.77795	15.48576
Plan	13	8.22471	8.75829	9.31305	9.88881	10.48536	11.10240	11.73960	12.39656	13.07281	14.48117	15.96018	16.72462
	14	8.88268	9.45895	10.05809	10.67992	11.32419	11.99060	12.67877	13.38828	14.11863	15.63966	17.23700	18.06259
	15	9.59330	10.21567	10.86274	11.53431	12.23012	12.94984	13.69307	14.45934	15.24812	16.89083	18.61596	19.50760
	16	10.36076	11.03292	11.73176	12.45705	13.20853	13.98583	14.78852	15.61609	16.46797	18.24210	20.10523	21.06821
	17	11.18962	11.91556	12.67030	13.45362	14.26521	15.10470	15.97160	16.86538	17.78541	19.70147	21.71365	22.75366
	18	12.08479	12.86880	13.68392	14.52991	15.40643	16.31307	17.24933	18.21461	19.20824	21.27759	23.45074	24.57396
	19	13.05158	13.89831	14.77863	15.69230	16.63895	17.61812	18.62928	19.67178	20.74490	22.97979	25.32680	26.53987
	20	14.09570	15.01017	15.96092	16.94768	17.97006	19.02757	20.11962	21.24552	22.40450	24.81818	27.35295	28.66306
	21	15.22336	16.21099	17.23780	18.30350	19.40767	20.54978	21.72919	22.94516	24.19685	26.80363	29.54118	30.95611
	22	16.44123	17.50786	18.61682	19.76778	20.96028	22.19376	23.46752	24.78077	26.13260	28.94792	31.90448	33.43260
	23	17.75653	18.90849	20.10617	21.34920	22.63710	23.96926	25.34492	26.76323	28.22321	31.26376	34.45684	36.10720
	24	19.17705	20.42117	21.71466	23.05714	24.44807	25.88680	27.37252	28.90429	30.48107	33.76486	37.21338	38.99578
	25	20.71121	22.05487	23.45183	24.90171	26.40392	27.95774	29.56232	31.21664	32.91955	36.46605	40.19046	42.11544
	Level	7.69315	8.05883	8.43216	8.81281	9.20046	9.59476	9.99539	10.40201	10.81429	11.65452	12.51355	12.94936
	1	2.58719	2.79252	3.00812	3.23394	3.46990	3.71586	3.97166	4.23707	4.51187	5.08844	5.69880	6.01575
	2	2.79417	3.01592	3.24877	3.49266	3.74749	4.01313	4.28939	4.57604	4.87282	5.49552	6.15471	6.49701
	3	3.01770	3.25720	3.50867	3.77207	4.04729	4.33418	4.63254	4.94212	5.26264	5.93516	6.64708	7.01677
	4	3.25911	3.51777	3.78937	4.07384	4.37107	4.68092	5.00314	5.33749	5.68366	6.40997	7.17885	7.57811
	5	3.51984	3.79920	4.09252	4.39974	4.72076	5.05539	5.40340	5.76449	6.13835	6.92277	7.75316	8.18436
	6	3.80143	4.10313	4.41992	4.75172	5.09842	5.45982	5.83567	6.22565	6.62942	7.47659	8.37341	8.83911
	7	4.10555	4.43138	4.77351	5.13186	5.50630	5.89661	6.30252	6.72371	7.15977	8.07472	9.04328	9.54624
	8	4.43399	4.78589	5.15539	5.54241	5.94680	6.36833	6.80672	7.26160	7.73255	8.72069	9.76674	10.30994
	9	4.78871	5.16876	5.56782	5.98580	6.42254	6.87780	7.35126	7.84253	8.35116	9.41835	10.54808	11.13473
	10	5.17181	5.58227	6.01325	6.46467	6.93635	7.42803	7.93936	8.46993	9.01925	10.17182	11.39193	12.02551
	11	5.58555	6.02885	6.49431	6.98184	7.49125	8.02227	8.57451	9.14753	9.74079	10.98556	12.30329	12.98755
	12	6.03239	6.51115	7.01385	7.54039	8.09055	8.66405	9.26047	9.87933	10.52005	11.86441	13.28755	14.02655
	13	6.51499	7.03205	7.57496	8.14362	8.73780	9.35717	10.00131	10.66968	11.36166	12.81356	14.35055	15.14868
	14	7.03618	7.59461	8.18096	8.79511	9.43682	10.10575	10.80141	11.52325	12.27059	13.83865	15.49860	16.36057
30 Year	15	7.59908	8.20218	8.83543	9.49872	10.19177	10.91421	11.66553	12.44511	13.25223	14.94574	16.73848	17.66942
Plan	16	8.20701	8.85835	9.54227	10.25861	11.00711	11.78734	12.59877	13.44072	14.31241	16.14140	18.07756	19.08297
	17	8.86357	9.56702	10.30565	11.07930	11.88768	12.73033	13.60667	14.51598	15.45741	17.43271	19.52377	20.60961
	18	9.57265	10.33238	11.13010	11.96565	12.83869	13.74876	14.69520	15.67725	16.69400	18.82733	21.08567	22.25838
	19	10.33846	11.15897	12.02051	12.92290	13.86579	14.84866	15.87082	16.93143	18.02952	20.33351	22.77252	24.03905
	20	11.16554	12.05169	12.98215	13.95673	14.97505	16.03655	17.14048	18.28595	19.47188	21.96019	24.59433	25.96217
	21	12.05878	13.01583	14.02072	15.07327	16.17306	17.31947	18.51172	19.74882	21.02963	23.71701	26.56187	28.03914
	22	13.02349	14.05709	15.14238	16.27913	17.46690	18.70503	19.99266	21.32873	22.71200	25.61437	28.68682	30.28228
	23	14.06536	15.18166	16.35377	17.58146	18.86425	20.20143	21.59207	23.03503	24.52896	27.66352	30.98177	32.70486
	24	15.19059	16.39619	17.66208	18.98798	20.37339	21.81755	23.31944	24.87783	26.49128	29.87660	33.46031	35.32125
	25	16.40584	17.70789	19.07504	20.50702	22.00326	23.56295	25.18499	26.86806	28.61058	32.26673	36.13713	38.14695
	26	17.71831	19.12452	20.60104	22.14758	23.76353	25.44799	27.19979	29.01750	30.89943	34.84807	39.02810	41.19870
	27	19.13577	20.65448	22.24913	23.91939	25.66461	27.48383	29.37578	31.33890	33.37138	37.63591	42.15035	44.49460
	28	20.66664	22.30684	24.02906	25.83294	27.71778	29.68253	31.72584	33.84601	36.04109	40.64678	45.52238	48.05417
	29	22.31997	24.09139	25.95138	27.89957	29.93520	32.05714	34.26391	36.55370	38.92438	43.89853	49.16417	51.89850
	30	24.10556	26.01870	28.02749	30.13154	32.33001	34.62171	37.00502	39.47799	42.03833	47.41041	53.09730	56.05038
	Level	7.15881	7.54395	7.93733	8.33846	8.74686	9.16206	9.58359	10.01100	10.44383	11.32408	12.22114	12.67506

Entries are annual percentages of initial cost or value. Divide by 12 for monthly figures.

Payments in a Rising Series

Annual Rate of Increase 10.0%

Plan	Year of Plan	6.00%	6.50%	7.00%	7.50%	8.00%	8.50%	9.00%	9.50%	10.00%	11.00%	12.00%	12.50%
3 Year Plan	1	33.10713	33.34686	33.58631	33.82545	34.06429	34.30280	34.54099	34.77883	35.01632	35.49023	35.96262	36.19823
	2	36.41784	36.68155	36.94494	37.20800	37.47072	37.73308	37.99508	38.25671	38.51796	39.03925	39.55889	39.81806
	3	40.05962	40.34970	40.63943	40.92880	41.21779	41.50639	41.79459	42.08238	42.36975	42.94318	43.51478	43.79986
	Level	36.32470	36.58066	36.83763	37.09561	37.35461	37.61463	37.87561	38.13762	38.40062	38.92961	39.46255	39.73049
4 Year Plan	1	24.36495	24.60154	24.83832	25.07528	25.31241	25.54968	25.78709	26.02461	26.26224	26.73775	27.21349	27.45141
	2	26.80145	27.06169	27.32215	27.58281	27.84365	28.10465	28.36580	28.62708	28.88847	29.41152	29.93484	30.19655
	3	29.48159	29.76786	30.05437	30.34109	30.62801	30.91512	31.20238	31.48978	31.77731	32.35268	32.92832	33.21620
	4	32.42975	32.74465	33.05981	33.37520	33.69081	34.00663	34.32262	34.63876	34.95505	35.58794	36.22115	36.53782
	Level	28.04183	28.30463	28.56884	28.83447	29.10150	29.36993	29.63975	29.91097	30.18357	30.73291	31.28773	31.56717
5 Year Plan	1	19.12444	19.35800	19.59220	19.82703	20.06246	20.29847	20.53504	20.77216	21.00979	21.48655	21.96514	22.20508
	2	21.03689	21.29380	21.55142	21.80973	22.06870	22.32832	22.58855	22.84937	23.11077	23.63520	24.16165	24.42558
	3	23.14058	23.42318	23.70657	23.99071	24.27557	24.56115	24.84740	25.13431	25.42185	25.99872	26.57782	26.86814
	4	25.45463	25.76550	26.07722	26.38978	26.70313	27.01726	27.33214	27.64774	27.96404	28.59869	29.23560	29.55496
	5	28.00010	28.34205	28.68494	29.02875	29.37345	29.71899	30.06536	30.41252	30.76044	31.45845	32.15916	32.51045
	Level	23.08394	23.35288	23.62363	23.89619	24.17054	24.44667	24.72459	25.00428	25.28574	25.85391	26.42905	26.71920
6 Year Plan	1	15.63476	15.86535	16.09702	16.32973	16.56347	16.79821	17.03392	17.27058	17.50816	17.98598	18.46719	18.70899
	2	17.19824	17.45189	17.70672	17.96271	18.21982	18.47803	18.73732	18.99764	19.25898	19.78458	20.31391	20.57989
	3	18.91806	19.19708	19.47739	19.75898	20.04180	20.32584	20.61105	20.89740	21.18488	21.76304	22.34530	22.63788
	4	20.80987	21.11678	21.42513	21.73488	22.04598	22.35842	22.67215	22.98714	23.30336	23.93935	24.57983	24.90167
	5	22.89085	23.22846	23.56764	23.90836	24.25058	24.59426	24.93937	25.28586	25.63370	26.33328	27.03781	27.39184
	6	25.17994	25.55131	25.92441	26.29920	26.67564	27.05369	27.43330	27.81444	28.19707	28.96661	29.74159	30.13102
	Level	19.78852	20.06324	20.34016	20.61926	20.90055	21.18401	21.46962	21.75738	22.04728	22.63342	23.22795	23.52833
7 Year Plan	1	13.14554	13.37321	13.60237	13.83299	14.06504	14.29850	14.53333	14.76951	15.00700	15.48579	15.96946	16.21305
	2	14.46010	14.71053	14.96260	15.21628	15.47154	15.72835	15.98667	16.24646	16.50770	17.03437	17.56641	17.83436
	3	15.90611	16.18158	16.45886	16.73791	17.01870	17.30118	17.58533	17.87110	18.15847	18.73780	19.32305	19.61779
	4	17.49672	17.79974	18.10475	18.41170	18.72057	19.03130	19.34386	19.65821	19.97434	20.61158	21.25535	21.57957
	5	19.24639	19.57971	19.91522	20.25287	20.59263	20.93443	21.27825	21.62404	21.97174	22.67274	23.38089	23.73753
	6	21.17103	21.53769	21.90674	22.27816	22.65189	23.02788	23.40608	23.78644	24.16892	24.94002	25.71898	26.11129
	7	23.28813	23.69145	24.09742	24.50598	24.91708	25.33066	25.74668	26.16508	26.58581	27.43402	28.29088	28.72241
	Level	17.44305	17.72332	18.00618	18.29161	18.57959	18.87012	19.16317	19.45873	19.75678	20.36029	20.97354	21.28378
10 Year Plan	1	8.67925	8.89827	9.11999	9.34437	9.57139	9.80099	10.03314	10.26779	10.50490	10.98629	11.47696	11.72565
	2	9.54718	9.78809	10.03198	10.27881	10.52853	10.78109	11.03646	11.29457	11.55539	12.08492	12.62466	12.89821
	3	10.50190	10.76690	11.03518	11.30669	11.58138	11.85920	12.14010	12.42403	12.71093	13.29342	13.88712	14.18803
	4	11.55208	11.84359	12.13870	12.43736	12.73952	13.04512	13.35411	13.66643	13.98202	14.62276	15.27583	15.60684
	5	12.70729	13.02795	13.35257	13.68110	14.01347	14.34964	14.68952	15.03307	15.38022	16.08503	16.80342	17.16752
	6	13.97802	14.33074	14.68783	15.04921	15.41482	15.78460	16.15848	16.53638	16.91824	17.69354	18.48376	18.88456
	7	15.37582	15.76382	16.15661	16.55413	16.95630	17.36306	17.77432	18.19002	18.61007	19.46289	20.33213	20.77270
	8	16.91341	17.34020	17.77227	18.20954	18.65193	19.09937	19.55176	20.00902	20.47107	21.40918	22.36535	22.84997
	9	18.60475	19.07422	19.54950	20.03050	20.51713	21.00930	21.50693	22.00992	22.51818	23.55010	24.60188	25.13497
	10	20.46522	20.98164	21.50445	22.03354	22.56884	23.11023	23.65763	24.21092	24.77000	25.90511	27.06207	27.64846
	Level	13.25618	13.55235	13.85221	14.15574	14.46289	14.77364	15.08793	15.40574	15.72703	16.37985	17.04605	17.38406
12 Year Plan	1	6.95224	7.16556	7.38238	7.60264	7.82631	8.05334	8.28368	8.51728	-8.75408	9.23709	9.73224	9.98421
	2	7.64747	7.88212	8.12061	8.36290	8.60894	8.85867	9.11204	9.36900	9.62949	10.16080	10.70546	10.98263
	3	8.41221	8.67033	8.93267	9.19919	9.46983	9.74454	10.02325	10.30590	10.59244	11.17688	11.77600	12.08089
	4	9.25343	9.53736	9.82594	10.11911	10.41682	10.71899	11.02557	11.33649	11.65168	12.29456	12.95361	13.28898
	5	10.17878	10.49110	10.80854	11.13102	11.45850	11.79089	12.12813	12.47014	12.81685	13.52402	14.24897	14.61788
	6	11.19665	11.54021	11.88939	12.24413	12.60435	12.96998	13.34094	13.71716	14.09853	14.87642	15.67386	16.07967
	7	12.31632	12.69423	13.07833	13.46854	13.86478	14.26698	14.67504	15.08887	15.50839	16.36406	17.24125	17.68764
	8	13.54795	13.96365	14.38616	14.81539	15.25126	15.69338	16.14254	16.59776	17.05923	18.00047	18.96537	19.45640
	9	14.90275	15.36002	15.82478	16.29693	16.77639	17.26304	17.75680	18.25754	18.76515	19.80052	20.86191	21.40204
	10	16.39302	16.89602	17.40726	17.92663	18.45403	18.98935	19.53248	20.08329	20.64166	21.78057	22.94810	23.54225
	11	18.03232	18.58562	19.14798	19.71929	20.29943	20.88828	21.48573	22.09162	22.70693	23.95863	25.24291	25.89647
	12	19.83556	20.44419	21.06278	21.69122	22.32937	22.97711	23.63430	24.30078	24.97641	26.35449	27.76720	28.48612
	Level	11.65194	11.95828	12.26900	12.58407	12.90341	13.22698	13.55471	13.88654	14.22242	14.90602	15.60498	15.96004
15 Year Plan	1	5.23699	5.44187	5.65138	5.86549	6.08416	6.30733	6.53494	6.76694	7.00326	7.48860	7.99034	8.24716
	2	5.76069	5.98605	6.21652	6.45204	6.69258	6.93806	7.18843	7.44364	7.70359	8.23746	8.78937	9.07187
	3	6.33676	6.58466	6.83817	7.09725	7.36183	7.63187	7.90728	8.18800	8.47395	9.06120	9.66831	9.97906
	4	6.97044	7.24313	7.52199	7.80697	8.09802	8.39505	8.69801	9.00680	9.32135	9.96732	10.63514	10.97697
	5	7.66748	7.96744	8.27419	8.58767	8.90782	9.23456	9.56781	9.90748	10.25348	10.96406	11.69866	12.07467
	6	8.43423	8.76418	9.10161	9.44644	9.79860	10.15801	10.52459	10.89823	11.27883	12.06046	12.86852	13.28213
	7	9.27765	9.64060	10.01177	10.39108	10.77846	11.17381	11.57705	11.98805	12.40671	13.26651	14.15537	14.61035
	8	10.20542	10.60646	11.01295	11.43019	11.85631	12.29120	12.73475	13.18685	13.64738	14.59316	15.57091	16.07138
	9	11.22596	11.66513	12.11424	12.57321	13.04194	13.52031	14.00823	14.50554	15.01212	16.05247	17.12800	17.67852
	10	12.34855	12.83164	13.32566	13.83053	14.34613	14.87235	15.40905	15.95609	16.51333	17.65772	18.84080	19.44637
	11	13.58341	14.11480	14.65823	15.21358	15.78074	16.35959	16.94995	17.55170	18.16467	19.42349	20.72488	21.39101
	12	14.94175	15.52628	16.12405	16.73494	17.35882	17.99554	18.64495	19.30687	19.98113	21.36584	22.79737	23.53011
	13	16.43593	17.07891	17.73646	18.40843	19.09470	19.79509	20.50944	21.23756	21.97924	23.50243	25.07711	25.88312
	14	18.07952	18.78680	19.51010	20.24928	21.00417	21.77460	22.56039	23.36132	24.17717	25.85267	27.58482	28.47143
	15	19.88747	20.66549	21.46111	22.27421	23.10459	23.95206	24.81643	25.69745	26.59489	28.43794	30.34330	31.31857
	Level	10.07590	10.39697	10.72339	11.05505	11.39188	11.73376	12.08059	12.43227	12.78869	13.51527	14.25942	14.63779

Entries are annual percentages of initial cost or value. Divide by 12 for monthly figures.

Payments in a Rising Series

Annual Rate of Increase 10.0%

Plan	Year of Plan	6.00%	6.50%	7.00%	7.50%	Interest Rate 8.00%	8.50%	9.00%	9.50%	10.00%	11.00%	12.00%	12.50%
	1	2.55248	2.73005	2.91579	3.10974	3.31189	3.52224	3.74075	3.96735	4.20196	4.69473	5.21793	5.49050
	2	2.80773	3.00306	3.20737	3.42071	3.64308	3.87447	4.11482	4.36409	4.62215	5.16420	5.73973	6.03956
	3	3.08850	3.30336	3.52811	3.76278	4.00739	4.26191	4.52631	4.80049	5.08437	5.68062	6.31370	6.64351
	4	3.39736	3.63370	3.88092	4.13906	4.40813	4.68810	4.97894	5.28054	5.59281	6.24869	6.94507	7.30786
	5	3.73709	3.99707	4.26901	4.55296	4.84894	5.15691	5.47683	5.80860	6.15209	6.87356	7.63958	8.03865
	6	4.11080	4.39678	4.69591	5.00826	5.33383	5.67260	6.02451	6.38946	6.76730	7.56091	8.40353	8.84251
	7	4.52188	4.83646	5.16551	5.50909	5.86722	6.23987	6.62697	7.02840	7.44403	8.31700	9.24389	9.72676
	8	4.97407	5.32010	5.68206	6.05999	6.45394	6.86385	7.28966	7.73125	8.18843	9.14870	10.16828	10.69944
	9	5.47147	5.85211	6.25026	6.66599	7.09933	7.55024	8.01863	8.50437	9.00727	10.06357	11.18510	11.76939
	10	6.01862	6.43732	6.87529	7.33259	7.80926	8.30526	8.82049	9.35481	9.90800	11.06993	12.30361	12.94632
25 Year Plan	11	6.62048	7.08106	7.56282	8.06585	8.59019	9.13579	9.70254	10.29029	10.89880	12.17692	13.53397	14.24096
	12	7.28253	7.78916	8.31910	8.87244	9.44921	10.04937	10.67280	11.31932	11.98868	13.39462	14.88737	15.66505
	13	8.01079	8.56808	9.15101	9.75968	10.39413	11.05430	11.74007	12.45125	13.18755	14.73408	16.37611	17.23156
	14	8.81187	9.42489	10.06611	10.73565	11.43354	12.15973	12.91408	13.69637	14.50630	16.20749	18.01372	18.95471
	15	9.69305	10.36737	11.07272	11.80922	12.57690	13.37571	14.20549	15.06601	15.95693	17.82823	19.81509	20.85018
	16	10.66236	11.40411	12.17999	12.99014	13.83459	14.71328	15.62604	16.57261	17.55262	19.61106	21.79660	22.93520
	17	11.72859	12.54452	13.39799	14.28915	15.21805	16.18460	17.18864	18.22987	19.30789	21.57216	23.97626	25.22872
	18	12.90145	13.79897	14.73779	15.71807	16.73985	17.80306	18.90751	20.05286	21.23868	23.72938	26.37389	27.75159
	19	14.19160	15.17887	16.21157	17.28987	18.41384	19.58337	20.79826	22.05814	23.36254	26.10232	29.01128	30.52675
	20	15.61076	16.69676	17.83273	19.01886	20.25522	21.54171	22.87808	24.26396	25.69880	28.71255	31.91240	33.57943
	21	17.17183	18.36643	19.61600	20.92075	22.28074	23.69588	25.16589	26.69035	28.26868	31.58380	35.10364	36.93737
	22	18.88902	20.20308	21.57760	23.01282	24.50881	26.06547	27.68248	29.35939	31.09555	34.74218	38.61401	40.63111
	23	20.77792	22.22339	23.73536	25.31410	26.95970	28.67201	30.45073	32.29533	34.20510	38.21640	42.47541	44.69422
	24	22.85571	24.44572	26.10889	27.84551	29.65567	31.53921	33.49580	35.52486	37.62561	42.03804	46.72295	49.16364
	25	25.14128	26.89030	28.71978	30.63006	32.62123	34.69314	36.84538	39.07735	41.38817	46.24185	51.39525	54.08001
	Level	7.69315	8.05883	8.43216	8.81281	9.20046	9.59476	9.99539	10.40201	10.81429	11.65452	12.51355	12.94936
	1	1.90921	2.07370	2.24794	2.43203	2.62606	2.83005	3.04402	3.26791	3.50163	3.99805	4.53181	4.81209
	2	2.10013	2.28108	2.47273	2.67523	2.88866	3.11306	3.34842	3.59470	3.85180	4.39785	4.98499	5.29330
	3	2.31014	2.50918	2.72001	2.94276	3.17753	3.42436	3.68326	3.95417	4.23698	4.83764	5.48349	5.82262
	4	2.54115	2.76010	2.99201	3.23703	3.49528	3.76680	4.05159	4.34958	4.66067	5.32140	6.03184	6.40489
	5	2.79527	3.03611	3.29121	3.56074	3.84481	4.14348	4.45675	4.78454	5.12674	5.85354	6.63502	7.04538
	6	3.07480	3.33972	3.62033	3.91681	4.22929	4.55783	4.90242	5.26300	5.63941	6.43890	7.29852	7.74991
	7	3.38228	3.67369	3.98236	4.30849	4.65222	5.01361	5.39266	5.78930	6.20336	7.08279	8.02838	8.52491
	8	3.72050	4.04106	4.38060	4.73934	5.11744	5.51497	5.93193	6.36823	6.82369	7.79107	8.83121	9.37740
	9	4.09255	4.44517	4.81866	5.21327	5.62918	6.06647	6.52512	7.00505	7.50606	8.57017	9.71433	10.31514
	10	4.50181	4.88969	5.30053	5.73460	6.19210	6.67312	7.17764	7.70555	8.25667	9.42719	10.68577	11.34665
	11	4.95199	5.37866	5.83058	6.30806	6.81131	7.34043	7.89540	8.47611	9.08233	10.36991	11.75435	12.48131
	12	5.44719	5.91652	6.41364	6.93887	7.49244	8.07447	8.68494	9.32372	9.99057	11.40690	12.92978	13.72945
	13	5.99191	6.50817	7.05500	7.63276	8.24169	8.88192	9.55343	10.25609	10.98962	12.54759	14.22276	15.10239
	14	6.59110	7.15899	7.76050	8.39603	9.06586	9.77011	10.50878	11.28170	12.08858	13.80235	15.64503	16.61263
30 Year Plan	15	7.25021	7.87489	8.53655	9.23563	9.97244	10.74712	11.55966	12.40987	13.29744	15.18258	17.20954	18.27389
	16	7.97523	8.66238	9.39020	10.15920	10.96969	11.82184	12.71562	13.65086	14.62719	16.70084	18.93049	20.10128
	17	8.77275	9.52862	10.32922	11.17512	12.06666	13.00402	13.98718	15.01595	16.08991	18.37093	20.82354	22.11141
	18	9.65003	10.48148	11.36215	12.29263	13.27332	14.30442	15.38590	16.51754	17.69890	20.20802	22.90589	24.32255
	19	10.61503	11.52963	12.49836	13.52189	14.60066	15.73486	16.92449	18.16929	19.46879	22.22882	25.19648	26.75480
	20	11.67654	12.68259	13.74820	14.87408	16.06072	17.30835	18.61694	19.98622	21.41567	24.45170	27.71613	29.43028
	21	12.84419	13.95085	15.12302	16.36149	17.66679	19.03918	20.47864	21.98485	23.55723	26.89687	30.48774	32.37331
	22	14.12861	15.34593	16.63532	17.99764	19.43347	20.94310	22.52650	24.18333	25.91295	29.58656	33.53652	35.61064
	23	15.54147	16.88053	18.29885	19.79740	21.37682	23.03741	24.77915	26.60166	28.50425	32.54522	36.89017	39.17171
	24	17.09562	18.56858	20.12874	21.77714	23.51450	25.34115	27.25706	29.26183	31.35468	35.79974	40.57919	43.08888
	25	18.80518	20.42544	22.14161	23.95486	25.86595	27.87527	29.98277	32.18801	34.49014	39.37971	44.63711	47.39777
	26	20.68570	22.46798	24.35577	26.35034	28.45255	30.66280	32.98105	35.40681	37.93916	43.31768	49.10082	52.13754
	27	22.75427	24.71478	26.79135	28.98537	31.29780	33.72908	36.27915	38.94750	41.73307	47.64945	54.01090	57.35130
	28	25.02969	27.18626	29.47048	31.88391	34.42758	37.10198	39.90707	42.84225	45.90638	52.41440	59.41199	63.08643
	29	27.53266	29.90489	32.41753	35.07230	37.87034	40.81218	43.89778	47.12647	50.49702	57.65584	65.35319	69.39507
	30	30.28593	32.89537	35.65928	38.57953	41.65737	44.89340	48.28755	51.83912	55.54672	63.42142	71.88851	76.33458
	Level	7.15881	7.54395	7.93733	8.33846	8.74686	9.16206	9.58359	10.01100	10.44383	11.32408	12.22114	12.67506

Entries are annual percentages of initial cost or value. Divide by 12 for monthly figures.

Graduated Rental Payments
Graduated Sales Prices

Annual Rate of Increase 3.0%

Plan	Year of Plan	6.00%	6.50%	7.00%	7.50%	8.00%	8.50%	9.00%	9.50%	10.00%	11.00%	12.00%	12.50%
3 Year Plan	1	97.3541	97.3528	97.3479	97.3393	97.3272	97.3115	97.2923	97.2698	97.2439	97.1821	97.1077	97.0657
	2	100.2747	100.2734	100.2683	100.2595	100.2470	100.2308	100.2111	100.1879	100.1612	100.0976	100.0209	99.9777
	3	103.2829	103.2816	103.2764	103.2673	103.2544	103.2378	103.2174	103.1935	103.1660	103.1005	103.0215	102.9770
4 Year Plan	1	95.9271	95.9221	95.9128	95.8991	95.8811	95.8590	95.8327	95.8025	95.7683	95.6883	95.5936	95.5408
	2	98.8049	98.7998	98.7901	98.7760	98.7575	98.7347	98.7077	98.6765	98.6413	98.5590	98.4614	98.4070
	3	101.7690	101.7638	101.7538	101.7393	101.7203	101.6968	101.6689	101.6368	101.6006	101.5158	101.4152	101.3592
	4	104.8221	104.8167	104.8065	104.7915	104.7719	104.7477	104.7190	104.6859	104.6486	104.5612	104.4577	104.4000
5 Year Plan	1	94.5426	94.5366	94.5256	94.5095	94.4886	94.4630	94.4327	94.3978	94.3586	94.2670	94.1589	94.0989
	2	97.3789	97.3727	97.3613	97.3448	97.3233	97.2969	97.2657	97.2298	97.1893	97.0950	96.9837	96.9218
	3	100.3002	100.2939	100.2822	100.2652	100.2430	100.2158	100.1836	100.1467	100.1050	100.0079	99.8932	99.8295
	4	103.3093	103.3027	103.2906	103.2731	103.2503	103.2223	103.1892	103.1511	103.1081	103.0081	102.8900	102.8244
	5	106.4085	106.4018	106.3894	106.3713	106.3478	106.3189	106.2848	106.2456	106.2014	106.0984	105.9767	105.9091
6 Year Plan	1	93.1994	93.1949	93.1848	93.1691	93.1480	93.1216	93.0901	93.0536	93.0122	92.9152	92.8003	92.7363
	2	95.9954	95.9908	95.9803	95.9642	95.9424	95.9153	95.8828	95.8452	95.8025	95.7027	95.5843	95.5184
	3	98.8753	98.8705	98.8597	98.8431	98.8207	98.7927	98.7593	98.7205	98.6766	98.5738	98.4518	98.3840
	4	101.8415	101.8366	101.8255	101.8084	101.7853	101.7565	101.7221	101.6821	101.6369	101.5310	101.4054	101.3355
	5	104.8968	104.8917	104.8803	104.8626	104.8389	104.8092	104.7737	104.7326	104.6860	104.5769	104.4475	104.3756
	6	108.0437	108.0385	108.0267	108.0085	107.9840	107.9535	107.9169	107.8746	107.8266	107.7142	107.5810	107.5068
7 Year Plan	1	91.8963	91.8957	91.8889	91.8760	91.8573	91.8328	91.8028	91.7674	91.7267	91.6301	91.5144	91.4497
	2	94.6532	94.6526	94.6456	94.6323	94.6130	94.5878	94.5569	94.5204	94.4785	94.3790	94.2598	94.1932
	3	97.4928	97.4921	97.4849	97.4713	97.4514	97.4255	97.3936	97.3560	97.3128	97.2104	97.0876	97.0190
	4	100.4175	100.4169	100.4095	100.3954	100.3750	100.3482	100.3154	100.2767	100.2322	100.1267	100.0002	99.9295
	5	103.4301	103.4294	103.4218	103.4073	103.3862	103.3587	103.3249	103.2850	103.2392	103.1305	103.0002	102.9274
	6	106.5330	106.5323	106.5244	106.5095	106.4878	106.4594	106.4246	106.3835	106.3363	106.2244	106.0902	106.0152
	7	109.7290	109.7283	109.7202	109.7048	109.6824	109.6532	109.6173	109.5750	109.5264	109.4112	109.2730	109.1957
10 Year Plan	1	88.2151	88.2396	88.2564	88.2659	88.2683	88.2639	88.2528	88.2355	88.2120	88.1476	88.0615	88.0108
	2	90.8616	90.8867	90.9041	90.9139	90.9163	90.9118	90.9004	90.8825	90.8584	90.7921	90.7033	90.6511
	3	93.5874	93.6133	93.6312	93.6413	93.6438	93.6391	93.6274	93.6090	93.5841	93.5158	93.4244	93.3707
	4	96.3950	96.4217	96.4401	96.4505	96.4531	96.4483	96.4363	96.4173	96.3916	96.3213	96.2272	96.1718
	5	99.2869	99.3144	99.3333	99.3440	99.3467	99.3418	99.3294	99.3098	99.2834	99.2109	99.1140	99.0569
	6	102.2655	102.2938	102.3133	102.3243	102.3271	102.3220	102.3092	102.2891	102.2619	102.1873	102.0874	102.0286
	7	105.3335	105.3626	105.3827	105.3941	105.3969	105.3917	105.3785	105.3578	105.3298	105.2529	105.1500	105.0895
	8	108.4935	108.5235	108.5442	108.5559	108.5589	108.5534	108.5399	108.5185	108.4896	108.4105	108.3045	108.2422
	9	111.7483	111.7792	111.8005	111.8126	111.8156	111.8100	111.7961	111.7741	111.7443	111.6628	111.5537	111.4895
	10	115.1007	115.1326	115.1546	115.1669	115.1701	115.1643	115.1499	115.1273	115.0967	115.0127	114.9003	114.8341
12 Year Plan	1	85.9400	85.9911	86.0338	86.0684	86.0954	86.1149	86.1272	86.1327	86.1317	86.1109	86.0671	86.0371
	2	88.5182	88.5708	88.6148	88.6505	88.6782	88.6983	88.7110	88.7167	88.7156	88.6942	88.6491	88.6182
	3	91.1737	91.2279	91.2732	91.3100	91.3386	91.3593	91.3724	91.3782	91.3771	91.3551	91.3086	91.2768
	4	93.9089	93.9647	94.0114	94.0493	94.0787	94.1000	94.1135	94.1196	94.1184	94.0957	94.0478	94.0151
	5	96.7262	96.7837	96.8318	96.8708	96.9011	96.9230	96.9369	96.9431	96.9420	96.9186	96.8693	96.8355
	6	99.6280	99.6872	99.7367	99.7769	99.8081	99.8307	99.8451	99.8502	99.8490	99.8262	99.7753	99.7406
	7	102.6168	102.6778	102.7288	102.7702	102.8024	102.8256	102.8404	102.8470	102.8457	102.8209	102.7686	102.7328
	8	105.6953	105.7581	105.8107	105.8533	105.8864	105.9104	105.9256	105.9324	105.9311	105.9056	105.8517	105.8148
	9	108.8662	108.9309	108.9850	109.0289	109.0630	109.0877	109.1034	109.1104	109.1090	109.0827	109.0272	108.9892
	10	112.1322	112.1988	112.2545	112.2998	112.3349	112.3604	112.3765	112.3837	112.3823	112.3552	112.2980	112.2589
	11	115.4962	115.5648	115.6222	115.6688	115.7050	115.7312	115.7478	115.7552	115.7538	115.7259	115.6670	115.6267
	12	118.9610	119.0317	119.0908	119.1388	119.1761	119.2031	119.2202	119.2278	119.2264	119.1977	119.1370	119.0955
15 Year Plan	1	82.7747	82.8786	82.9732	83.0588	83.1357	83.2044	83.2651	83.3183	83.3642	83.4354	83.4813	83.4954
	2	85.2579	85.3650	85.4624	85.5505	85.6298	85.7005	85.7631	85.8178	85.8651	85.9385	85.9857	86.0003
	3	87.8157	87.9259	88.0263	88.1171	88.1987	88.2715	88.3360	88.3924	88.4410	88.5166	88.5653	88.5803
	4	90.4501	90.5637	90.6671	90.7606	90.8446	90.9197	90.9860	91.0441	91.0943	91.1721	91.2222	91.2377
	5	93.1636	93.2806	93.3871	93.4834	93.5700	93.6473	93.7156	93.7754	93.8271	93.9073	93.9589	93.9748
	6	95.9585	96.0790	96.1887	96.2879	96.3771	96.4567	96.5271	96.5887	96.6419	96.7245	96.7777	96.7940
	7	98.8373	98.9614	99.0743	99.1765	99.2684	99.3504	99.4229	99.4864	99.5412	99.6262	99.6810	99.6979
	8	101.8024	101.9303	102.0466	102.1518	102.2464	102.3309	102.4056	102.4710	102.5274	102.6150	102.6714	102.6888
	9	104.8565	104.9882	105.1080	105.2164	105.3138	105.4008	105.4778	105.5451	105.6032	105.6935	105.7516	105.7695
	10	108.0022	108.1378	108.2612	108.3729	108.4733	108.5628	108.6421	108.7114	108.7713	108.8643	108.9241	108.9425
	11	111.2422	111.3819	111.5090	111.6240	111.7275	111.8197	111.9014	111.9728	112.0345	112.1302	112.1918	112.2108
	12	114.5795	114.7234	114.8543	114.9728	115.0793	115.1743	115.2584	115.3320	115.3955	115.4941	115.5576	115.5771
	13	118.0169	118.1651	118.2999	118.4220	118.5317	118.6296	118.7162	118.7919	118.8574	118.9589	119.0243	119.0445
	14	121.5574	121.7101	121.8489	121.9746	122.0876	122.1884	122.2776	122.3557	122.4231	122.5277	122.5951	122.6158
	15	125.2041	125.3614	125.5044	125.6339	125.7502	125.8541	125.9460	126.0264	126.0958	126.2035	126.2729	126.2943

Entries are percentages of standard rent or price. The present value of a graduated series equals that of a normal series.

Graduated Rental Payments
Graduated Sales Prices

Annual Rate of Increase   3.0%

Plan	Year of Plan	6.00%	6.50%	7.00%	7.50%	Interest Rate 8.00%	8.50%	9.00%	9.50%	10.00%	11.00%	12.00%	12.50%
	1	74.0696	74.4340	74.7849	75.1228	75.4477	75.7599	76.0597	76.3473	76.6229	77.1391	77.6103	77.8295
	2	76.2917	76.6670	77.0285	77.3765	77.7111	78.0327	78.3415	78.6377	78.9216	79.4533	79.9386	80.1644
	3	78.5804	78.9670	79.3393	79.6978	80.0425	80.3737	80.6918	80.9969	81.2893	81.8369	82.3367	82.5693
	4	80.9378	81.3360	81.7195	82.0887	82.4437	82.7849	83.1125	83.4268	83.7279	84.2920	84.8068	85.0464
	5	83.3660	83.7761	84.1711	84.5514	84.9171	85.2685	85.6059	85.9296	86.2398	86.8208	87.3510	87.5978
	6	85.8669	86.2894	86.6962	87.0879	87.4646	87.8265	88.1741	88.5075	88.8270	89.4254	89.9716	90.2257
	7	88.4430	88.8780	89.2971	89.7005	90.0885	90.4613	90.8193	91.1627	91.4918	92.1082	92.6707	92.9325
	8	91.0962	91.5444	91.9760	92.3915	92.7912	93.1752	93.5439	93.8976	94.2365	94.8714	95.4508	95.7205
	9	93.8291	94.2907	94.7353	95.1633	95.5749	95.9704	96.3502	96.7145	97.0636	97.7176	98.3144	98.5921
	10	96.6440	97.1194	97.5774	98.0182	98.4421	98.8495	99.2407	99.6159	99.9755	100.6491	101.2638	101.5499
25 Year Plan	11	99.5433	100.0330	100.5047	100.9587	101.3954	101.8150	102.2179	102.6044	102.9748	103.6686	104.3017	104.5964
	12	102.5296	103.0340	103.5199	103.9875	104.4373	104.8695	105.2845	105.6826	106.0641	106.7786	107.4308	107.7343
	13	105.6055	106.1250	106.6254	107.1071	107.5704	108.0156	108.4430	108.8530	109.2460	109.9820	110.6537	110.9663
	14	108.7737	109.3088	109.8242	110.3203	110.7975	111.2560	111.6963	112.1186	112.5234	113.2814	113.9733	114.2953
	15	112.0369	112.5880	113.1189	113.6299	114.1214	114.5937	115.0472	115.4822	115.8991	116.6799	117.3925	117.7241
	16	115.3980	115.9657	116.5125	117.0388	117.5451	118.0315	118.4986	118.9466	119.3760	120.1803	120.9143	121.2559
	17	118.8599	119.4446	120.0079	120.5500	121.0714	121.5725	122.0536	122.5150	122.9573	123.7857	124.5417	124.8935
	18	122.4257	123.0280	123.6081	124.1665	124.7036	125.2196	125.7152	126.1905	126.6460	127.4992	128.2780	128.6403
	19	126.0985	126.7188	127.3164	127.8915	128.4447	128.9762	129.4866	129.9762	130.4454	131.3242	132.1263	132.4995
	20	129.8815	130.5204	131.1359	131.7283	132.2980	132.8455	133.3712	133.8755	134.3588	135.2640	136.0901	136.4745
	21	133.7779	134.4360	135.0699	135.6801	136.2669	136.8309	137.3724	137.8918	138.3895	139.3219	140.1728	140.5688
	22	137.7912	138.4691	139.1220	139.7505	140.3550	140.9358	141.4935	142.0285	142.5412	143.5015	144.3780	144.7858
	23	141.9250	142.6232	143.2957	143.9430	144.5656	145.1639	145.7383	146.2894	146.8175	147.8066	148.7093	149.1294
	24	146.1827	146.9018	147.5946	148.2613	148.9026	149.5188	150.1105	150.6780	151.2220	152.2408	153.1706	153.6033
	25	150.5682	151.3089	152.0224	152.7091	153.3697	154.0044	154.6138	155.1984	155.7586	156.8080	157.7657	158.2114
	1	70.6048	71.1319	71.6424	72.1361	72.6128	73.0727	73.5156	73.9417	74.3509	75.1195	75.8228	76.1504
	2	72.7229	73.2659	73.7917	74.3001	74.7912	75.2649	75.7211	76.1599	76.5814	77.3731	78.0974	78.4350
	3	74.9046	75.4639	76.0054	76.5291	77.0350	77.5228	77.9927	78.4447	78.8789	79.6943	80.4404	80.7880
	4	77.1517	77.7278	78.2856	78.8250	79.3460	79.8485	80.3325	80.7980	81.2452	82.0851	82.8536	83.2116
	5	79.4663	80.0596	80.6342	81.1898	81.7264	82.2439	82.7425	83.2220	83.6826	84.5477	85.3392	85.7080
	6	81.8503	82.4614	83.0532	83.6255	84.1782	84.7113	85.2247	85.7186	86.1931	87.0841	87.8994	88.2792
	7	84.3058	84.9353	85.5448	86.1342	86.7035	87.2526	87.7815	88.2902	88.7789	89.6966	90.5363	90.9276
	8	86.8350	87.4833	88.1111	88.7183	89.3046	89.8702	90.4149	90.9389	91.4422	92.3875	93.2524	93.6554
	9	89.4400	90.1078	90.7545	91.3798	91.9838	92.5663	93.1274	93.6671	94.1855	95.1591	96.0500	96.4651
	10	92.1232	92.8110	93.4771	94.1212	94.7433	95.3433	95.9212	96.4771	97.0111	98.0139	98.9315	99.3591
	11	94.8869	95.5954	96.2814	96.9448	97.5856	98.2036	98.7988	99.3714	99.9214	100.9543	101.8994	102.3398
	12	97.7335	98.4632	99.1698	99.8532	100.5131	101.1497	101.7628	102.3525	102.9190	103.9830	104.9564	105.4100
	13	100.6655	101.4171	102.1449	102.8488	103.5285	104.1842	104.8157	105.4231	106.0066	107.1024	108.1051	108.5723
	14	103.6855	104.4596	105.2093	105.9342	106.6344	107.3097	107.9601	108.5858	109.1868	110.3155	111.3483	111.8295
30 Year Plan	15	106.7961	107.5934	108.3656	109.1123	109.8334	110.5290	111.1990	111.8434	112.4624	113.6250	114.6887	115.1844
	16	109.9999	110.8212	111.6165	112.3856	113.1284	113.8449	114.5349	115.1987	115.8363	117.0337	118.1294	118.6399
	17	113.2999	114.1459	114.9650	115.7572	116.5223	117.2602	117.9710	118.6546	119.3114	120.5447	121.6733	122.1991
	18	116.6989	117.5703	118.4140	119.2299	120.0179	120.7780	121.5101	122.2143	122.8907	124.1611	125.3235	125.8651
	19	120.1999	121.0974	121.9664	122.8068	123.6185	124.4013	125.1554	125.8807	126.5774	127.8859	129.0832	129.6410
	20	123.8059	124.7303	125.6254	126.4910	127.3270	128.1334	128.9101	129.6571	130.3748	131.7225	132.9557	133.5303
	21	127.5201	128.4722	129.3941	130.2857	131.1469	131.9774	132.7774	133.5469	134.2860	135.6742	136.9443	137.5362
	22	131.3457	132.3264	133.2760	134.1943	135.0813	135.9367	136.7607	137.5533	138.3146	139.7444	141.0527	141.6623
	23	135.2860	136.2961	137.2743	138.2201	139.1337	140.0148	140.8635	141.6799	142.4640	143.9367	145.2842	145.9121
	24	139.3446	140.3850	141.3925	142.3668	143.3077	144.2153	145.0894	145.9303	146.7379	148.2548	149.6428	150.2895
	25	143.5250	144.5966	145.6343	146.6378	147.6069	148.5417	149.4421	150.3082	151.1401	152.7025	154.1321	154.7982
	26	147.8307	148.9345	150.0033	151.0369	152.0351	152.9980	153.9254	154.8174	155.6743	157.2836	158.7560	159.4421
	27	152.2656	153.4025	154.5034	155.5680	156.5962	157.5879	158.5431	159.4619	160.3445	162.0021	163.5187	164.2254
	28	156.8336	158.0046	159.1385	160.2350	161.2941	162.3155	163.2994	164.2458	165.1548	166.8621	168.4243	169.1521
	29	161.5386	162.7447	163.9126	165.0421	166.1329	167.1850	168.1984	169.1732	170.1095	171.8680	173.4770	174.2267
	30	166.3848	167.6271	168.8300	169.9933	171.1169	172.2006	173.2443	174.2484	175.2128	177.0240	178.6813	179.4535

Entries are percentages of standard rent or price. The present value of a graduated series equals that of a normal series.

Graduated Rental Payments
Graduated Sales Prices

Annual Rate of Increase 4.0%

Plan	Year of Plan	Interest Rate											
		6.00%	6.50%	7.00%	7.50%	8.00%	8.50%	9.00%	9.50%	10.00%	11.00%	12.00%	12.50%
3 Year Plan	1	96.4328	96.4345	96.4325	96.4269	96.4178	96.4051	96.3890	96.3695	96.3466	96.2911	96.2228	96.1840
	2	100.2901	100.2919	100.2898	100.2840	100.2745	100.2613	100.2445	100.2242	100.2005	100.1427	100.0717	100.0314
	3	104.3017	104.3036	104.3014	104.2954	104.2855	104.2717	104.2543	104.2332	104.2085	104.1484	104.0746	104.0326
4 Year Plan	1	94.5741	94.5746	94.5707	94.5625	94.5501	94.5335	94.5129	94.4883	94.4597	94.3912	94.3078	94.2608
	2	98.3571	98.3576	98.3535	98.3450	98.3321	98.3149	98.2934	98.2678	98.2381	98.1668	98.0802	98.0312
	3	102.2913	102.2919	102.2877	102.2788	102.2654	102.2475	102.2252	102.1985	102.1676	102.0935	102.0034	101.9525
	4	106.3830	106.3836	106.3792	106.3700	106.3560	106.3374	106.3142	106.2865	106.2543	106.1772	106.0835	106.0306
5 Year Plan	1	92.7760	92.7786	92.7761	92.7687	92.7565	92.7396	92.7180	92.6920	92.6615	92.5877	92.4975	92.4464
	2	96.4870	96.4897	96.4871	96.4795	96.4668	96.4492	96.4268	96.3997	96.3680	96.2913	96.1974	96.1442
	3	100.3465	100.3493	100.3466	100.3386	100.3254	100.3071	100.2838	100.2557	100.2227	100.1429	100.0453	99.9900
	4	104.3604	104.3633	104.3605	104.3522	104.3385	104.3194	104.2952	104.2659	104.2316	104.1486	104.0471	103.9896
	5	108.5348	108.5378	108.5349	108.5263	108.5120	108.4922	108.4670	108.4365	108.4009	108.3146	108.2090	108.1492
6 Year Plan	1	91.0364	91.0441	91.0461	91.0427	91.0340	91.0200	91.0009	90.9769	90.9480	90.8762	90.7865	90.7352
	2	94.6779	94.6858	94.6880	94.6845	94.6753	94.6608	94.6410	94.6160	94.5860	94.5113	94.4180	94.3646
	3	98.4650	98.4733	98.4755	98.4718	98.4624	98.4472	98.4266	98.4006	98.3694	98.2917	98.1947	98.1392
	4	102.4036	102.4122	102.4145	102.4107	102.4009	102.3851	102.3637	102.3367	102.3042	102.2234	102.1225	102.0648
	5	106.4997	106.5087	106.5111	106.5071	106.4969	106.4805	106.4582	106.4301	106.3963	106.3124	106.2074	106.1474
	6	110.7597	110.7690	110.7716	110.7674	110.7568	110.7398	110.7166	110.6873	110.6522	110.5648	110.4557	110.3933
7 Year Plan	1	89.3532	89.3689	89.3784	89.3820	89.3797	89.3717	89.3583	89.3395	89.3154	89.2523	89.1701	89.1221
	2	92.9273	92.9436	92.9535	92.9572	92.9549	92.9466	92.9326	92.9131	92.8881	92.8224	92.7369	92.6870
	3	96.6444	96.6614	96.6717	96.6755	96.6731	96.6645	96.6499	96.6296	96.6036	96.5353	96.4463	96.3945
	4	100.5102	100.5278	100.5385	100.5425	100.5400	100.5311	100.5159	100.4948	100.4677	100.3967	100.3042	100.2502
	5	104.5306	104.5489	104.5601	104.5642	104.5616	104.5523	104.5366	104.5146	104.4864	104.4126	104.3164	104.2603
	6	108.7118	108.7309	108.7425	108.7468	108.7441	108.7344	108.7180	108.6951	108.6659	108.5891	108.4890	108.4307
	7	113.0603	113.0801	113.0922	113.0967	113.0938	113.0838	113.0667	113.0429	113.0125	112.9327	112.8286	112.7679
10 Year Plan	1	84.6226	84.6777	84.7253	84.7657	84.7991	84.8258	84.8459	84.8597	84.8674	84.8654	84.8414	84.8217
	2	88.0075	88.0648	88.1143	88.1563	88.1911	88.2188	88.2397	88.2541	88.2621	88.2600	88.2351	88.2146
	3	91.5278	91.5874	91.6389	91.6826	91.7187	91.7476	91.7693	91.7843	91.7926	91.7904	91.7645	91.7432
	4	95.1889	95.2509	95.3044	95.3499	95.3875	95.4175	95.4401	95.4556	95.4643	95.4620	95.4351	95.4129
	5	98.9965	99.0609	99.1166	99.1639	99.2030	99.2342	99.2577	99.2739	99.2829	99.2805	99.2525	99.2294
	6	102.9563	103.0233	103.0813	103.1304	103.1711	103.2035	103.2280	103.2448	103.2542	103.2517	103.2226	103.1986
	7	107.0746	107.1443	107.2045	107.2557	107.2979	107.3317	107.3571	107.3746	107.3844	107.3818	107.3515	107.3265
	8	111.3576	111.4300	111.4927	111.5459	111.5899	111.6249	111.6514	111.6696	111.6797	111.6770	111.6455	111.6196
	9	115.8119	115.8872	115.9524	116.0077	116.0535	116.0899	116.1175	116.1364	116.1469	116.1441	116.1113	116.0844
	10	120.4443	120.5227	120.5905	120.6480	120.6956	120.7335	120.7622	120.7818	120.7928	120.7899	120.7558	120.7277
12 Year Plan	1	81.7164	81.8090	81.8935	81.9701	82.0390	82.1006	82.1551	82.2028	82.2438	82.3071	82.3469	82.3585
	2	84.9850	85.0814	85.1692	85.2489	85.3206	85.3846	85.4413	85.4909	85.5336	85.5994	85.6408	85.6529
	3	88.3844	88.4846	88.5760	88.6588	88.7334	88.8000	88.8590	88.9105	88.9549	89.0234	89.0664	89.0790
	4	91.9198	92.0240	92.1190	92.2052	92.2827	92.3520	92.4133	92.4669	92.5131	92.5843	92.6291	92.6421
	5	95.5966	95.7050	95.8038	95.8934	95.9740	96.0461	96.1099	96.1656	96.2136	96.2877	96.3342	96.3478
	6	99.4204	99.5332	99.6359	99.7291	99.8130	99.8880	99.9543	100.0122	100.0622	100.1392	100.1876	100.2017
	7	103.3973	103.5145	103.6214	103.7183	103.8055	103.8835	103.9524	104.0127	104.0647	104.1448	104.1951	104.2098
	8	107.5331	107.6551	107.7662	107.8670	107.9578	108.0388	108.1105	108.1732	108.2273	108.3106	108.3629	108.3782
	9	111.8345	111.9613	112.0769	112.1817	112.2761	112.3604	112.4349	112.5002	112.5564	112.6430	112.6974	112.7133
	10	116.3079	116.4397	116.5600	116.6690	116.7671	116.8548	116.9323	117.0002	117.0586	117.1487	117.2053	117.2219
	11	120.9602	121.0973	121.2224	121.3357	121.4378	121.5290	121.6096	121.6802	121.7410	121.8347	121.8935	121.9107
	12	125.7986	125.9412	126.0712	126.1891	126.2953	126.3901	126.4740	126.5474	126.6106	126.7081	126.7693	126.7872
15 Year Plan	1	77.6946	77.8577	78.0117	78.1569	78.2936	78.4221	78.5427	78.6557	78.7612	78.9513	79.1149	79.1874
	2	80.8024	80.9720	81.1322	81.2832	81.4254	81.5590	81.6844	81.8019	81.9117	82.1093	82.2795	82.3549
	3	84.0345	84.2109	84.3775	84.5345	84.6824	84.8214	84.9518	85.0740	85.1881	85.3937	85.5707	85.6491
	4	87.3959	87.5793	87.7526	87.9159	88.0697	88.2143	88.3499	88.4769	88.5957	88.8095	88.9935	89.0751
	5	90.8917	91.0825	91.2627	91.4326	91.5925	91.7428	91.8839	92.0160	92.1395	92.3618	92.5533	92.6381
	6	94.5274	94.7258	94.9132	95.0899	95.2562	95.4125	95.5592	95.6966	95.8251	96.0563	96.2554	96.3436
	7	98.3085	98.5149	98.7097	98.8935	99.0664	99.2290	99.3816	99.5245	99.6581	99.8986	100.1056	100.1974
	8	102.2408	102.4554	102.6581	102.8492	103.0291	103.1982	103.3569	103.5055	103.6444	103.8945	104.1098	104.2052
	9	106.3304	106.5537	106.7644	106.9632	107.1503	107.3261	107.4911	107.6457	107.7902	108.0503	108.2742	108.3735
	10	110.5837	110.8158	111.0350	111.2417	111.4363	111.6192	111.7908	111.9515	112.1018	112.3723	112.6052	112.7084
	11	115.0070	115.2484	115.4764	115.6914	115.8937	116.0839	116.2624	116.4296	116.5859	116.8672	117.1094	117.2167
	12	119.6073	119.8584	120.0955	120.3190	120.5295	120.7273	120.9129	121.0868	121.2493	121.5419	121.7938	121.9054
	13	124.3916	124.6527	124.8993	125.1318	125.3506	125.5564	125.7494	125.9303	126.0993	126.4036	126.6655	126.7816
	14	129.3672	129.6388	129.8953	130.1370	130.3647	130.5786	130.7794	130.9675	131.1432	131.4597	131.7322	131.8529
	15	134.5419	134.8244	135.0911	135.3425	135.5793	135.8018	136.0106	136.2062	136.3890	136.7181	137.0014	137.1270

Entries are percentages of standard rent or price. The present value of a graduated series equals that of a normal series.

Graduated Rental Payments
Graduated Sales Prices

Annual Rate of Increase 4.0%

Plan	Year of Plan	6.00%	6.50%	7.00%	7.50%	8.00%	8.50%	9.00%	9.50%	10.00%	11.00%	12.00%	12.50%
	1	66.7521	67.2359	67.7074	68.1665	68.6133	69.0477	69.4696	69.8791	70.2761	71.0328	71.7401	72.0754
	2	69.4222	69.9253	70.4156	70.8932	71.3579	71.8096	72.2484	72.6743	73.0871	73.8741	74.6097	74.9584
	3	72.1991	72.7223	73.2323	73.7289	74.2122	74.6820	75.1384	75.5812	76.0106	76.8290	77.5941	77.9567
	4	75.0870	75.6312	76.1616	76.6781	77.1807	77.6693	78.1439	78.6045	79.0510	79.9022	80.6978	81.0750
	5	78.0905	78.6564	79.2080	79.7452	80.2679	80.7761	81.2696	81.7486	82.2131	83.0983	83.9257	84.3180
	6	81.2141	81.8027	82.3764	82.9350	83.4786	84.0071	84.5204	85.0186	85.5016	86.4222	87.2828	87.6907
	7	84.4627	85.0748	85.6714	86.2524	86.8178	87.3674	87.9012	88.4193	88.9217	89.8791	90.7741	91.1984
	8	87.8412	88.4778	89.0983	89.7025	90.2905	90.8621	91.4173	91.9561	92.4785	93.4743	94.4050	94.8463
	9	91.3549	92.0169	92.6622	93.2906	93.9021	94.4966	95.0740	95.6344	96.1777	97.2133	98.1812	98.6401
	10	95.0091	95.6976	96.3687	97.0222	97.6582	98.2764	98.8769	99.4597	100.0248	101.1018	102.1085	102.5858
25 Year Plan	11	98.8094	99.5255	100.2234	100.9031	101.5645	102.2075	102.8320	103.4381	104.0258	105.1459	106.1928	106.6892
	12	102.7618	103.5065	104.2324	104.9392	105.6271	106.2958	106.9453	107.5756	108.1868	109.3517	110.4406	110.9568
	13	106.8723	107.6468	108.4017	109.1368	109.8522	110.5476	111.2231	111.8787	112.5143	113.7258	114.8582	115.3950
	14	111.1472	111.9526	112.7377	113.5023	114.2462	114.9695	115.6720	116.3538	117.0148	118.2748	119.4525	120.0108
	15	115.5930	116.4307	117.2472	118.0424	118.8161	119.5683	120.2989	121.0080	121.6954	123.0058	124.2306	124.8113
	16	120.2168	121.0880	121.9371	122.7641	123.5687	124.3510	125.1109	125.8483	126.5632	127.9260	129.1998	129.8037
	17	125.0254	125.9315	126.8146	127.6746	128.5115	129.3251	130.1153	130.8822	131.6258	133.0431	134.3678	134.9959
	18	130.0264	130.9688	131.8872	132.7816	133.6519	134.4981	135.3199	136.1175	136.8908	138.3648	139.7425	140.3957
	19	135.2275	136.2075	137.1627	138.0929	138.9980	139.8780	140.7327	141.5622	142.3664	143.8994	145.3322	146.0115
	20	140.6366	141.6558	142.6492	143.6166	144.5579	145.4731	146.3620	147.2247	148.0611	149.6553	151.1455	151.8520
	21	146.2621	147.3220	148.3552	149.3613	150.3403	151.2920	152.2165	153.1137	153.9835	155.6416	157.1913	157.9261
	22	152.1126	153.2149	154.2894	155.3357	156.3539	157.3437	158.3052	159.2382	160.1429	161.8672	163.4790	164.2431
	23	158.1971	159.3435	160.4609	161.5492	162.6080	163.6375	164.6374	165.6078	166.5486	168.3419	170.0182	170.8128
	24	164.5249	165.7173	166.8794	168.0111	169.1124	170.1830	171.2229	172.2321	173.2105	175.0756	176.8189	177.6453
	25	171.1059	172.3459	173.5545	174.7316	175.8768	176.9903	178.0718	179.1214	180.1390	182.0786	183.8916	184.7511
	1	62.4354	63.1096	63.7693	64.4138	65.0426	65.6550	66.2508	66.8294	67.3906	68.4597	69.4569	69.9284
	2	64.9328	65.6340	66.3201	66.9904	67.6443	68.2812	68.9008	69.5026	70.0862	71.1981	72.2352	72.7255
	3	67.5301	68.2594	68.9729	69.6700	70.3500	71.0125	71.6568	72.2827	72.8897	74.0460	75.1246	75.6345
	4	70.2313	70.9897	71.7318	72.4568	73.1640	73.8530	74.5231	75.1740	75.8053	77.0079	78.1295	78.6599
	5	73.0406	73.8293	74.6011	75.3550	76.0906	76.8071	77.5040	78.1810	78.8375	80.0882	81.2547	81.8063
	6	75.9622	76.7825	77.5851	78.3692	79.1342	79.8794	80.6042	81.3082	81.9910	83.2917	84.5049	85.0786
	7	79.0007	79.8538	80.6885	81.5040	82.2996	83.0746	83.8284	84.5605	85.2706	86.6234	87.8851	88.4817
	8	82.1607	83.0480	83.9160	84.7642	85.5916	86.3977	87.1815	87.9429	88.6814	90.0883	91.4005	92.0210
	9	85.4472	86.3699	87.2727	88.1547	89.0152	89.8535	90.6688	91.4607	92.2287	93.6918	95.0565	95.7018
	10	88.8651	89.8247	90.7636	91.6809	92.5758	93.4476	94.2955	95.1191	95.9178	97.4395	98.8588	99.5299
	11	92.4197	93.4177	94.3941	95.3482	96.2789	97.1855	98.0673	98.9239	99.7545	101.3371	102.8131	103.5111
	12	96.1165	97.1544	98.1699	99.1621	100.1300	101.0729	101.9900	102.8808	103.7447	105.3906	106.9257	107.6515
	13	99.9611	101.0405	102.0967	103.1286	104.1352	105.1158	106.0696	106.9960	107.8945	109.6062	111.2027	111.9576
	14	103.9596	105.0822	106.1806	107.2537	108.3006	109.3205	110.3124	111.2759	112.2103	113.9904	115.6508	116.4359
30 Year Plan	15	108.1179	109.2854	110.4278	111.5439	112.6327	113.6933	114.7249	115.7269	116.6987	118.5501	120.2768	121.0933
	16	112.4427	113.6569	114.8449	116.0056	117.1380	118.2410	119.3139	120.3560	121.3667	123.2921	125.0879	125.9371
	17	116.9404	118.2031	119.4387	120.6459	121.8235	122.9707	124.0865	125.1702	126.2213	128.2237	130.0914	130.9746
	18	121.6180	122.9313	124.2163	125.4717	126.6964	127.8895	129.0499	130.1770	131.2702	133.3527	135.2951	136.2135
	19	126.4827	127.8485	129.1849	130.4906	131.7643	133.0051	134.2119	135.3841	136.5210	138.6868	140.7069	141.6621
	20	131.5420	132.9625	134.3523	135.7102	137.0349	138.3253	139.5804	140.7995	141.9818	144.2343	146.3352	147.3286
	21	136.8037	138.2810	139.7264	141.1386	142.5163	143.8583	145.1636	146.4315	147.6611	150.0036	152.1886	153.2217
	22	142.2758	143.8122	145.3154	146.7841	148.2169	149.6126	150.9702	152.2887	153.5675	156.0038	158.2761	159.3506
	23	147.9669	149.5647	151.1281	152.6555	154.1456	155.5971	157.0090	158.3803	159.7102	162.2439	164.6072	165.7246
	24	153.8855	155.5473	157.1732	158.7617	160.3114	161.8210	163.2893	164.7155	166.0987	168.7337	171.1914	172.3536
	25	160.0410	161.7692	163.4601	165.1122	166.7239	168.2938	169.8209	171.3041	172.7426	175.4830	178.0391	179.2477
	26	166.4426	168.2399	169.9985	171.7167	173.3928	175.0256	176.6137	178.1563	179.6523	182.5024	185.1607	186.4176
	27	173.1003	174.9695	176.7985	178.5853	180.3285	182.0266	183.6783	185.2825	186.8384	189.8025	192.5671	193.8743
	28	180.0243	181.9683	183.8704	185.7287	187.5417	189.3077	191.0254	192.6938	194.3119	197.3946	200.2698	201.6293
	29	187.2253	189.2470	191.2252	193.1579	195.0433	196.8800	198.6664	200.4016	202.0844	205.2903	208.2806	209.6945
	30	194.7143	196.8169	198.8742	200.8842	202.8451	204.7552	206.6131	208.4176	210.1678	213.5020	216.6118	218.0823

Entries are percentages of standard rent or price. The present value of a graduated series equals that of a normal series.

Graduated Rental Payments
Graduated Sales Prices

Annual Rate of Increase   5.0%

Plan	Year of Plan	6.00%	6.50%	7.00%	7.50%	8.00%	8.50%	9.00%	9.50%	10.00%	11.00%	12.00%	12.50%
3 Year Plan	1	95.5231	95.5276	95.5285	95.5258	95.5196	95.5098	95.4967	95.4801	95.4602	95.4107	95.3485	95.3128
	2	100.2993	100.3040	100.3050	100.3021	100.2956	100.2853	100.2715	100.2541	100.2332	100.1812	100.1159	100.0784
	3	105.3142	105.3192	105.3202	105.3172	105.3103	105.2996	105.2851	105.2668	105.2449	105.1903	105.1217	105.0823
4 Year Plan	1	93.2422	93.2479	93.2493	93.2464	93.2393	93.2282	93.2129	93.1937	93.1706	93.1131	93.0408	92.9993
	2	97.9043	97.9103	97.9118	97.9087	97.9013	97.8896	97.8736	97.8534	97.8292	97.7687	97.6929	97.6493
	3	102.7995	102.8058	102.8073	102.8042	102.7964	102.7840	102.7672	102.7461	102.7206	102.6572	102.5775	102.5318
	4	107.9395	107.9461	107.9477	107.9444	107.9362	107.9232	107.9056	107.8834	107.8567	107.7900	107.7064	107.6584
5 Year Plan	1	91.0421	91.0528	91.0586	91.0594	91.0555	91.0469	91.0338	91.0162	90.9942	90.9374	90.8642	90.8217
	2	95.5942	95.6055	95.6115	95.6124	95.6083	95.5993	95.5855	95.5670	95.5439	95.4843	95.4074	95.3628
	3	100.3739	100.3857	100.3921	100.3930	100.3887	100.3792	100.3648	100.3453	100.3211	100.2585	100.1778	100.1310
	4	105.3926	105.4050	105.4117	105.4127	105.4081	105.3982	105.3830	105.3626	105.3371	105.2714	105.1867	105.1375
	5	110.6622	110.6753	110.6822	110.6833	110.6785	110.6681	110.6521	110.6307	110.6040	110.5350	110.4460	110.3944
6 Year Plan	1	88.9197	88.9389	88.9525	88.9608	88.9637	88.9615	88.9542	88.9421	88.9251	88.8772	88.8115	88.7723
	2	93.3657	93.3858	93.4002	93.4088	93.4119	93.4096	93.4020	93.3892	93.3713	93.3211	93.2521	93.2109
	3	98.0340	98.0551	98.0702	98.0792	98.0825	98.0800	98.0720	98.0586	98.0399	97.9871	97.9147	97.8714
	4	102.9357	102.9579	102.9737	102.9832	102.9866	102.9840	102.9757	102.9616	102.9419	102.8865	102.8104	102.7650
	5	108.0825	108.1058	108.1224	108.1324	108.1359	108.1333	108.1244	108.1096	108.0890	108.0308	107.9510	107.9033
	6	113.4866	113.5111	113.5285	113.5390	113.5427	113.5399	113.5307	113.5151	113.4935	113.4323	113.3485	113.2984
7 Year Plan	1	86.8719	86.9028	86.9276	86.9465	86.9597	86.9674	86.9695	86.9664	86.9580	86.9264	86.8758	86.8437
	2	91.2155	91.2479	91.2740	91.2939	91.3077	91.3157	91.3180	91.3147	91.3059	91.2728	91.2196	91.1859
	3	95.7763	95.8103	95.8377	95.8586	95.8731	95.8815	95.8839	95.8804	95.8712	95.8364	95.7806	95.7452
	4	100.5651	100.6008	100.6296	100.6515	100.6668	100.6756	100.6781	100.6744	100.6648	100.6282	100.5696	100.5325
	5	105.5933	105.6309	105.6611	105.6841	105.7001	105.7094	105.7120	105.7081	105.6980	105.6596	105.5981	105.5591
	6	110.8730	110.9124	110.9441	110.9683	110.9851	110.9948	110.9976	110.9936	110.9829	110.9426	110.8780	110.8370
	7	116.4167	116.4580	116.4913	116.5167	116.5344	116.5446	116.5475	116.5432	116.5321	116.4898	116.4219	116.3789
10 Year Plan	1	81.1472	81.2301	81.3058	81.3744	81.4362	81.4913	81.5400	81.5824	81.6188	81.6743	81.7079	81.7169
	2	85.2045	85.2916	85.3711	85.4431	85.5080	85.5659	85.6170	85.6616	85.6998	85.7580	85.7933	85.8027
	3	89.4648	89.5562	89.6396	89.7153	89.7834	89.8442	89.8978	89.9446	89.9848	90.0459	90.0829	90.0929
	4	93.9380	94.0340	94.1216	94.2011	94.2726	94.3364	94.3927	94.4419	94.4840	94.5482	94.5871	94.5975
	5	98.6349	98.7357	98.8277	98.9111	98.9862	99.0532	99.1124	99.1640	99.2082	99.2756	99.3164	99.3274
	6	103.5666	103.6725	103.7691	103.8567	103.9355	104.0058	104.0680	104.1222	104.1686	104.2394	104.2822	104.2938
	7	108.7450	108.8561	108.9575	109.0495	109.1323	109.2061	109.2714	109.3283	109.3771	109.4514	109.4964	109.5084
	8	114.1822	114.2989	114.4054	114.5020	114.5889	114.6664	114.7350	114.7947	114.8459	114.9239	114.9712	114.9839
	9	119.8913	120.0139	120.1257	120.2271	120.3183	120.3998	120.4717	120.5344	120.5882	120.6701	120.7197	120.7331
	10	125.8859	126.0146	126.1320	126.2384	126.3342	126.4198	126.4953	126.5611	126.6176	126.7036	126.7557	126.7697
12 Year Plan	1	77.6528	77.7825	77.9043	78.0184	78.1251	78.2246	78.3171	78.4028	78.4820	78.6217	78.7378	78.7875
	2	81.5355	81.6716	81.7995	81.9193	82.0313	82.1358	82.2329	82.3230	82.4061	82.5528	82.6747	82.7269
	3	85.6122	85.7552	85.8895	86.0153	86.1329	86.2426	86.3446	86.4391	86.5264	86.6805	86.8084	86.8632
	4	89.8928	90.0430	90.1839	90.3160	90.4395	90.5547	90.6618	90.7611	90.8528	91.0145	91.1489	91.2064
	5	94.3875	94.5451	94.6931	94.8318	94.9615	95.0824	95.1949	95.2991	95.3954	95.5652	95.7063	95.7667
	6	99.1069	99.2724	99.4278	99.5734	99.7096	99.8366	99.9546	100.0641	100.1652	100.3435	100.4916	100.5550
	7	104.0622	104.2360	104.3992	104.5521	104.6951	104.8284	104.9524	105.0673	105.1734	105.3606	105.5162	105.5828
	8	109.2653	109.4478	109.6191	109.7797	109.9298	110.0698	110.2000	110.3206	110.4321	110.6287	110.7920	110.8619
	9	114.7286	114.9202	115.1001	115.2687	115.4263	115.5733	115.7100	115.8367	115.9537	116.1601	116.3316	116.4050
	10	120.4650	120.6662	120.8551	121.0321	121.1976	121.3520	121.4955	121.6285	121.7514	121.9681	122.1482	122.2252
	11	126.4883	126.6995	126.8979	127.0837	127.2575	127.4196	127.5702	127.7099	127.8390	128.0665	128.2556	128.3365
	12	132.8127	133.0345	133.2428	133.4379	133.6204	133.7905	133.9488	134.0954	134.2309	134.4698	134.6684	134.7533
15 Year Plan	1	72.8458	73.0600	73.2654	73.4625	73.6514	73.8323	74.0055	74.1712	74.3296	74.6253	74.8944	75.0194
	2	76.4881	76.7130	76.9287	77.1356	77.3339	77.5239	77.7058	77.8797	78.0461	78.3566	78.6391	78.7704
	3	80.3125	80.5486	80.7751	80.9924	81.2006	81.4001	81.5911	81.7737	81.9484	82.2744	82.5711	82.7089
	4	84.3282	84.5760	84.8139	85.0420	85.2607	85.4701	85.6706	85.8624	86.0458	86.3882	86.6996	86.8443
	5	88.5446	88.8048	89.0546	89.2941	89.5237	89.7436	89.9541	90.1555	90.3481	90.7076	91.0346	91.1865
	6	92.9718	93.2451	93.5073	93.7588	93.9999	94.2308	94.4518	94.6633	94.8655	95.2429	95.5863	95.7459
	7	97.6204	97.9073	98.1827	98.4468	98.6999	98.9423	99.1744	99.3965	99.6087	100.0051	100.3656	100.5332
	8	102.5014	102.8027	103.0918	103.3691	103.6349	103.8894	104.1332	104.3663	104.5892	105.0053	105.3839	105.5598
	9	107.6265	107.9428	108.2464	108.5376	108.8166	109.0839	109.3398	109.5846	109.8186	110.2556	110.6531	110.8378
	10	113.0078	113.3400	113.6587	113.9644	114.2574	114.5381	114.8068	115.0638	115.3096	115.7684	116.1858	116.3797
	11	118.6582	119.0070	119.3417	119.6627	119.9703	120.2650	120.5471	120.8170	121.0750	121.5568	121.9951	122.1987
	12	124.5911	124.9573	125.3088	125.6458	125.9688	126.2783	126.5745	126.8579	127.1288	127.6346	128.0948	128.3086
	13	130.8207	131.2052	131.5742	131.9281	132.2673	132.5922	132.9032	133.2008	133.4852	134.0164	134.4996	134.7240
	14	137.3617	137.7655	138.1529	138.5245	138.8806	139.2218	139.5484	139.8608	140.1595	140.7172	141.2245	141.4602
	15	144.2298	144.6537	145.0605	145.4507	145.8247	146.1829	146.5258	146.8539	147.1675	147.7531	148.2858	148.5333

Entries are percentages of standard rent or price. The present value of a graduated series equals that of a normal series.

Graduated Rental Payments
Graduated Sales Prices

Annual Rate of Increase 5.0%

Plan	Year of Plan	6.00%	6.50%	7.00%	7.50%	8.00%	8.50%	9.00%	9.50%	10.00%	11.00%	12.00%	12.50%
						Interest Rate							
	1	59.9334	60.5080	61.0724	61.6264	62.1696	62.7017	63.2223	63.7314	64.2285	65.1865	66.0949	66.5302
	2	62.9300	63.5334	64.1261	64.7077	65.2781	65.8367	66.3835	66.9179	67.4400	68.4458	69.3996	69.8567
	3	66.0765	66.7100	67.3324	67.9431	68.5420	69.1286	69.7026	70.2638	70.8120	71.8681	72.8696	73.3495
	4	69.3804	70.0455	70.6990	71.3403	71.9691	72.5850	73.1878	73.7770	74.3526	75.4615	76.5131	77.0170
	5	72.8494	73.5478	74.2339	74.9073	75.5675	76.2143	76.8471	77.4659	78.0702	79.2346	80.3387	80.8679
	6	76.4918	77.2252	77.9456	78.6527	79.3459	80.0250	80.6895	81.3392	81.9737	83.1963	84.3557	84.9113
	7	80.3164	81.0865	81.8429	82.5853	83.3132	84.0262	84.7240	85.4061	86.0724	87.3561	88.5734	89.1568
	8	84.3323	85.1408	85.9351	86.7146	87.4789	88.2275	88.9602	89.6765	90.3760	91.7239	93.0021	93.6147
	9	88.5489	89.3978	90.2318	91.0503	91.8528	92.6389	93.4082	94.1603	94.8948	96.3101	97.6522	98.2954
	10	92.9763	93.8677	94.7434	95.6028	96.4454	97.2709	98.0786	98.8683	99.6396	101.1256	102.5348	103.2102
25 Year Plan	11	97.6251	98.5611	99.4806	100.3829	101.2677	102.1344	102.9825	103.8117	104.6215	106.1819	107.6616	108.3707
	12	102.5064	103.4892	104.4546	105.4021	106.3311	107.2411	108.1317	109.0023	109.8526	111.4910	113.0446	113.7892
	13	107.6317	108.6636	109.6773	110.6722	111.6477	112.6032	113.5382	114.4524	115.3452	117.0656	118.6969	119.4787
	14	113.0133	114.0968	115.1612	116.2058	117.2300	118.2333	119.2152	120.1750	121.1125	122.9188	124.6317	125.4526
	15	118.6640	119.8016	120.9192	122.0161	123.0915	124.1450	125.1759	126.1838	127.1681	129.0648	130.8633	131.7252
	16	124.5972	125.7917	126.9652	128.1169	129.2461	130.3522	131.4347	132.4930	133.5265	135.5180	137.4065	138.3115
	17	130.8270	132.0813	133.3135	134.5227	135.7084	136.8699	138.0064	139.1176	140.2029	142.2939	144.2768	145.2271
	18	137.3684	138.6854	139.9791	141.2489	142.4938	143.7133	144.9068	146.0735	147.2130	149.4086	151.4906	152.4884
	19	144.2368	145.6197	146.9781	148.3113	149.6185	150.8990	152.1521	153.3772	154.5737	156.8791	159.0652	160.1128
	20	151.4486	152.9006	154.3270	155.7269	157.0995	158.4440	159.7597	161.0460	162.3023	164.7230	167.0184	168.1185
	21	159.0211	160.5457	162.0434	163.5132	164.9544	166.3662	167.7477	169.0983	170.4175	172.9592	175.3694	176.5244
	22	166.9721	168.5729	170.1455	171.6889	173.2022	174.6845	176.1351	177.5532	178.9383	181.6071	184.1378	185.3506
	23	175.3207	177.0016	178.6528	180.2733	181.8623	183.4187	184.9418	186.4309	187.8853	190.6875	193.3447	194.6181
	24	184.0867	185.8517	187.5854	189.2870	190.9554	192.5896	194.1889	195.7524	197.2795	200.2218	203.0119	204.3490
	25	193.2911	195.1443	196.9647	198.7514	200.5031	202.2191	203.8984	205.5401	207.1435	210.2329	213.1625	214.5665
	1	54.9029	55.6810	56.4483	57.2040	57.9469	58.6761	59.3907	60.0898	60.7728	62.0878	63.3315	63.9256
	2	57.6481	58.4650	59.2707	60.0642	60.8442	61.6099	62.3602	63.0943	63.8114	65.1922	66.4980	67.1219
	3	60.5305	61.3882	62.2343	63.0674	63.8864	64.6904	65.4782	66.2490	67.0020	68.4518	69.8229	70.4780
	4	63.5570	64.4577	65.3460	66.2208	67.0808	67.9249	68.7521	69.5615	70.3521	71.8744	73.3141	74.0019
	5	66.7349	67.6805	68.6133	69.5318	70.4348	71.3211	72.1897	73.0395	73.8697	75.4681	76.9798	77.7020
	6	70.0716	71.0646	72.0440	73.0084	73.9565	74.8872	75.7992	76.6915	77.5632	79.2415	80.8288	81.5871
	7	73.5752	74.6178	75.6462	76.6588	77.6544	78.6316	79.5892	80.5261	81.4414	83.2036	84.8702	85.6664
	8	77.2539	78.3487	79.4285	80.4918	81.5371	82.5631	83.5686	84.5524	85.5134	87.3638	89.1137	89.9498
	9	81.1166	82.2661	83.3999	84.5163	85.6140	86.6913	87.7471	88.7800	89.7891	91.7320	93.5694	94.4472
	10	85.1725	86.3794	87.5699	88.7422	89.8946	91.0259	92.1344	93.2190	94.2786	96.3186	98.2479	99.1696
	11	89.4311	90.6984	91.9484	93.1793	94.3894	95.5772	96.7411	97.8800	98.9925	101.1345	103.1603	104.1281
	12	93.9026	95.2333	96.5458	97.8382	99.1088	100.3560	101.5782	102.7740	103.9421	106.1912	108.3183	109.3345
	13	98.5978	99.9950	101.3731	102.7301	104.0643	105.3738	106.6571	107.9127	109.1392	111.5008	113.7342	114.8012
	14	103.5277	104.9947	106.4417	107.8667	109.2675	110.6425	111.9899	113.3083	114.5962	117.0758	119.4209	120.5413
30 Year Plan	15	108.7040	110.2445	111.7638	113.2600	114.7309	116.1746	117.5894	118.9737	120.3260	122.9296	125.3920	126.5683
	16	114.1392	115.7567	117.3520	118.9230	120.4674	121.9834	123.4689	124.9224	126.3423	129.0761	131.6616	132.8968
	17	119.8462	121.5445	123.2196	124.8691	126.4908	128.0825	129.6424	131.1685	132.6594	135.5299	138.2446	139.5416
	18	125.8385	127.6218	129.3806	131.1126	132.8153	134.4867	136.1245	137.7270	139.2924	142.3064	145.1569	146.5187
	19	132.1304	134.0028	135.8496	137.6682	139.4561	141.2110	142.9307	144.6133	146.2570	149.4217	152.4147	153.8446
	20	138.7370	140.7030	142.6421	144.5516	146.4289	148.2715	150.0772	151.8440	153.5699	156.8928	160.0354	161.5368
	21	145.6738	147.7381	149.7742	151.7792	153.7504	155.6851	157.5811	159.4362	161.2484	164.7374	168.0372	169.6137
	22	152.9575	155.1250	157.2629	159.3682	161.4379	163.4694	165.4602	167.4080	169.3108	172.9743	176.4391	178.0944
	23	160.6054	162.8813	165.1261	167.3366	169.5098	171.6428	173.7332	175.7784	177.7763	181.6230	185.2610	186.9991
	24	168.6356	171.0254	173.3824	175.7034	177.9853	180.2250	182.4198	184.5673	186.6651	190.7041	194.5241	196.3490
	25	177.0674	179.5766	182.0515	184.4886	186.8845	189.2362	191.5408	193.7957	195.9984	200.2394	204.2503	206.1665
	26	185.9208	188.5555	191.1541	193.7130	196.2287	198.6980	201.1179	203.4854	205.7983	210.2513	214.4628	216.4748
	27	195.2168	197.9832	200.7118	203.3987	206.0402	208.6329	211.1738	213.6597	216.0882	220.7639	225.1859	227.2986
	28	204.9777	207.8824	210.7474	213.5686	216.3422	219.0646	221.7324	224.3427	226.8926	231.8021	236.4452	238.6635
	29	215.2266	218.2765	221.2848	224.2470	227.1593	230.0178	232.8191	235.5598	238.2373	243.3922	248.2675	250.5967
	30	225.9879	229.1903	232.3490	235.4594	238.5173	241.5187	244.4600	247.3378	250.1491	255.5618	260.6809	263.1265

Entries are percentages of standard rent or price. The present value of a graduated series equals that of a normal series.

Graduated Rental Payments
Graduated Sales Prices

Annual Rate of Increase   6.0%

Plan	Year of Plan	6.00%	6.50%	7.00%	7.50%	Interest Rate 8.00%	8.50%	9.00%	9.50%	10.00%	11.00%	12.00%	12.50%
3 Year Plan	1	94.6248	94.6321	94.6358	94.6359	94.6325	94.6256	94.6153	94.6016	94.5846	94.5410	94.4847	94.4519
	2	100.3023	100.3100	100.3139	100.3140	100.3104	100.3031	100.2922	100.2777	100.2597	100.2134	100.1537	100.1190
	3	106.3204	106.3286	106.3286	106.3328	106.3290	106.3213	106.3097	106.2944	106.2753	106.2262	106.1630	106.1262
4 Year Plan	1	91.9310	91.9418	91.9482	91.9505	91.9486	91.9425	91.9325	91.9186	91.9008	91.8538	91.7923	91.7562
	2	97.4468	97.4583	97.4651	97.4675	97.4655	97.4591	97.4485	97.4337	97.4148	97.3650	97.2998	97.2615
	3	103.2936	103.3058	103.3130	103.3156	103.3134	103.3066	103.2954	103.2797	103.2597	103.2069	103.1378	103.0972
	4	109.4913	109.5041	109.5118	109.5145	109.5122	109.5050	109.4931	109.4765	109.4553	109.3994	109.3260	109.2831
5 Year Plan	1	89.3405	89.3589	89.3725	89.3813	89.3853	89.3847	89.3795	89.3700	89.3561	89.3156	89.2589	89.2246
	2	94.7009	94.7205	94.7349	94.7441	94.7484	94.7478	94.7423	94.7322	94.7174	94.6745	94.6144	94.5781
	3	100.3829	100.4037	100.4189	100.4288	100.4333	100.4326	100.4269	100.4161	100.4005	100.3550	100.2913	100.2528
	4	106.4059	106.4279	106.4441	106.4545	106.4593	106.4586	106.4525	106.4411	106.4245	106.3763	106.3087	106.2679
	5	112.7903	112.8136	112.8307	112.8418	112.8469	112.8461	112.8396	112.8275	112.8100	112.7589	112.6873	112.6440
6 Year Plan	1	86.8487	86.8788	86.9033	86.9226	86.9366	86.9455	86.9495	86.9486	86.9429	86.9177	86.8749	86.8471
	2	92.0597	92.0915	92.1175	92.1379	92.1528	92.1623	92.1664	92.1655	92.1594	92.1328	92.0874	92.0579
	3	97.5832	97.6170	97.6446	97.6662	97.6820	97.6920	97.6964	97.6954	97.6890	97.6608	97.6126	97.5814
	4	103.4382	103.4740	103.5033	103.5262	103.5429	103.5535	103.5582	103.5571	103.5504	103.5204	103.4694	103.4363
	5	109.6445	109.6824	109.7135	109.7378	109.7555	109.7667	109.7717	109.7705	109.7634	109.7316	109.6776	109.6425
	6	116.2232	116.2634	116.2963	116.3220	116.3408	116.3527	116.3580	116.3568	116.3492	116.3155	116.2582	116.2210
7 Year Plan	1	84.4516	84.4966	84.5358	84.5692	84.5969	84.6190	84.6359	84.6474	84.6539	84.6520	84.6313	84.6142
	2	89.5187	89.5664	89.6079	89.6433	89.6727	89.6962	89.7140	89.7263	89.7331	89.7312	89.7092	89.6910
	3	94.8898	94.9404	94.9844	95.0219	95.0530	95.0780	95.0969	95.1099	95.1171	95.1150	95.0917	95.0725
	4	100.5832	100.6369	100.6835	100.7232	100.7562	100.7826	100.8027	100.8164	100.8241	100.8219	100.7972	100.7768
	5	106.6182	106.6751	106.7245	106.7666	106.8016	106.8296	106.8508	106.8654	106.8736	106.8712	106.8451	106.8234
	6	113.0152	113.0756	113.1280	113.1726	113.2097	113.2394	113.2619	113.2774	113.2860	113.2835	113.2558	113.2329
	7	119.7962	119.8601	119.9156	119.9630	120.0023	120.0337	120.0576	120.0740	120.0832	120.0805	120.0511	120.0268
10 Year Plan	1	77.7875	77.8957	77.9968	78.0910	78.1786	78.2597	78.3345	78.4031	78.4658	78.5741	78.6607	78.6963
	2	82.4547	82.5694	82.6766	82.7765	82.8693	82.9553	83.0345	83.1073	83.1738	83.2886	83.3804	83.4181
	3	87.4020	87.5236	87.6372	87.7431	87.8415	87.9326	88.0166	88.0937	88.1642	88.2859	88.3832	88.4232
	4	92.6462	92.7750	92.8954	93.0077	93.1120	93.2085	93.2976	93.3794	93.4541	93.5831	93.6862	93.7286
	5	98.2049	98.3415	98.4691	98.5881	98.6987	98.8010	98.8955	98.9821	99.0613	99.1980	99.3074	99.3523
	6	104.0972	104.2420	104.3773	104.5034	104.6206	104.7291	104.8292	104.9211	105.0050	105.1499	105.2658	105.3134
	7	110.3430	110.4965	110.6399	110.7736	110.8978	111.0129	111.1189	111.2163	111.3053	111.4589	111.5818	111.6322
	8	116.9636	117.1263	117.2783	117.4200	117.5517	117.6736	117.7861	117.8893	117.9836	118.1465	118.2767	118.3301
	9	123.9814	124.1538	124.3150	124.4652	124.6048	124.7340	124.8532	124.9627	125.0626	125.2352	125.3733	125.4299
	10	131.4203	131.6031	131.7739	131.9331	132.0811	132.2181	132.3444	132.4604	132.5664	132.7494	132.8957	132.9557
12 Year Plan	1	73.7477	73.9101	74.0650	74.2125	74.3528	74.4861	74.6127	74.7327	74.8462	75.0550	75.2403	75.3246
	2	78.1726	78.3447	78.5089	78.6652	78.8139	78.9553	79.0894	79.2166	79.3370	79.5583	79.7547	79.8441
	3	82.8629	83.0454	83.2194	83.3851	83.5428	83.6926	83.8348	83.9696	84.0972	84.3318	84.5400	84.6347
	4	87.8347	88.0282	88.2126	88.3882	88.5553	88.7142	88.8649	89.0078	89.1431	89.3917	89.6124	89.7128
	5	93.1048	93.3098	93.5053	93.6915	93.8687	94.0370	94.1968	94.3483	94.4917	94.7552	94.9891	95.0956
	6	98.6911	98.9084	99.1157	99.3130	99.5008	99.6792	99.8486	100.0092	100.1612	100.4405	100.6885	100.8013
	7	104.6125	104.8429	105.0626	105.2718	105.4708	105.6600	105.8395	106.0097	106.1708	106.4669	106.7298	106.8494
	8	110.8893	111.1335	111.3664	111.5881	111.7991	111.9996	112.1899	112.3703	112.5411	112.8549	113.1336	113.2604
	9	117.5427	117.8015	118.0483	118.2834	118.5070	118.7196	118.9213	119.1125	119.2935	119.6262	119.9216	120.0560
	10	124.5952	124.8696	125.1312	125.3804	125.6175	125.8427	126.0566	126.2593	126.4512	126.8038	127.1169	127.2594
	11	132.0709	132.3618	132.6391	132.9032	133.1545	133.3933	133.6200	133.8348	134.0382	134.4120	134.7439	134.8949
	12	139.9952	140.3035	140.5975	140.8774	141.1438	141.3969	141.6371	141.8649	142.0805	142.4767	142.8286	142.9886
15 Year Plan	1	68.2265	68.4840	68.7334	68.9750	69.2088	69.4351	69.6541	69.8658	70.0705	70.4593	70.8219	70.9936
	2	72.3201	72.5930	72.8574	73.1135	73.3614	73.6012	73.8333	74.0577	74.2747	74.6869	75.0712	75.2533
	3	76.6593	76.9486	77.2289	77.5003	77.7630	78.0173	78.2633	78.5012	78.7312	79.1681	79.5754	79.7685
	4	81.2588	81.5655	81.8626	82.1503	82.4288	82.6984	82.9591	83.2113	83.4551	83.9182	84.3500	84.5546
	5	86.1344	86.4594	86.7744	87.0793	87.3746	87.6603	87.9367	88.2040	88.4624	88.9533	89.4110	89.6278
	6	91.3024	91.6470	91.9808	92.3041	92.6170	92.9199	93.2129	93.4962	93.7701	94.2905	94.7756	95.0055
	7	96.7806	97.1458	97.4997	97.8423	98.1741	98.4951	98.8056	99.1060	99.3963	99.9479	100.4622	100.7058
	8	102.5874	102.9746	103.3497	103.7129	104.0645	104.4048	104.7340	105.0523	105.3601	105.9448	106.4899	106.7482
	9	108.7426	109.1531	109.5506	109.9356	110.3084	110.6691	111.0180	111.3555	111.6817	112.3015	112.8793	113.1531
	10	115.2672	115.7022	116.1237	116.5318	116.9269	117.3092	117.6791	118.0368	118.3826	119.0395	119.6521	119.9423
	11	122.1832	122.6444	123.0911	123.5237	123.9425	124.3478	124.7398	125.1190	125.4855	126.1819	126.8312	127.1388
	12	129.5142	130.0030	130.4766	130.9351	131.3790	131.8086	132.2242	132.6261	133.0147	133.7528	134.4410	134.7671
	13	137.2851	137.8032	138.3052	138.7912	139.2618	139.7171	140.1577	140.5837	140.9956	141.7780	142.5075	142.8532
	14	145.5222	146.0714	146.6035	147.1187	147.6175	148.1002	148.5671	149.0187	149.4553	150.2847	151.0580	151.4243
	15	154.2535	154.8357	155.3997	155.9458	156.4745	156.9862	157.4812	157.9599	158.4226	159.3018	160.1214	160.5098

Entries are percentages of standard rent or price. The present value of a graduated series equals that of a normal series.

Graduated Rental Payments
Graduated Sales Prices

Annual Rate of Increase 6.0%

Plan	Year of Plan	6.00%	6.50%	7.00%	7.50%	8.00%	8.50%	9.00%	9.50%	10.00%	11.00%	12.00%	12.50%
							Interest Rate						
	1	53.6147	54.2542	54.8863	55.5105	56.1262	56.7329	57.3301	57.9173	58.4941	59.6149	60.6895	61.2087
	2	56.8316	57.5094	58.1795	58.8411	59.4937	60.1368	60.7699	61.3923	62.0038	63.1918	64.3309	64.8812
	3	60.2415	60.9600	61.6702	62.3716	63.0634	63.7450	64.4161	65.0759	65.7240	66.9833	68.1907	68.7741
	4	63.8560	64.6176	65.3705	66.1139	66.8472	67.5697	68.2810	68.9804	69.6674	71.0023	72.2822	72.9006
	5	67.6873	68.4947	69.2927	70.0807	70.8580	71.6239	72.3779	73.1193	73.8475	75.2625	76.6191	77.2746
	6	71.7486	72.6044	73.4503	74.2855	75.1095	75.9214	76.7206	77.5064	78.2783	79.7782	81.2162	81.9111
	7	76.0535	76.9606	77.8573	78.7427	79.6160	80.4766	81.3238	82.1568	82.9750	84.5649	86.0892	86.8257
	8	80.6167	81.5782	82.5287	83.4672	84.3930	85.3052	86.2032	87.0862	87.9535	89.6388	91.2546	92.0353
	9	85.4537	86.4729	87.4804	88.4753	89.4566	90.4236	91.3754	92.3114	93.2307	95.0171	96.7298	97.5574
	10	90.5809	91.6613	92.7293	93.7838	94.8240	95.8490	96.8579	97.8501	98.8246	100.7181	102.5336	103.4108
25 Year Plan	11	96.0158	97.1610	98.2930	99.4108	100.5134	101.5999	102.6694	103.7211	104.7541	106.7612	108.6857	109.6155
	12	101.7767	102.9907	104.1906	105.3754	106.5442	107.6959	108.8296	109.9443	111.0393	113.1669	115.2068	116.1924
	13	107.8833	109.1701	110.4420	111.6980	112.9369	114.1577	115.3594	116.5410	117.7017	119.9569	122.1192	123.1640
	14	114.3563	115.7203	117.0685	118.3999	119.7131	121.0071	122.2809	123.5334	124.7638	127.1543	129.4464	130.5538
	15	121.2177	122.6635	124.0927	125.5038	126.8959	128.2675	129.6178	130.9455	132.2496	134.7836	137.2131	138.3870
	16	128.4908	130.0233	131.5382	133.0341	134.5096	135.9636	137.3948	138.8022	140.1846	142.8706	145.4459	146.6902
	17	136.2002	137.8247	139.4305	141.0161	142.5802	144.1214	145.6385	147.1303	148.5956	151.4428	154.1727	155.4917
	18	144.3722	146.0942	147.7963	149.4771	151.1350	152.7687	154.3768	155.9581	157.5114	160.5294	163.4230	164.8212
	19	153.0345	154.8599	156.6641	158.4457	160.2031	161.9348	163.6394	165.3156	166.9621	170.1612	173.2284	174.7104
	20	162.2166	164.1515	166.0640	167.9525	169.8153	171.6509	173.4578	175.2346	176.9798	180.3709	183.6221	185.1931
	21	171.9496	174.0006	176.0278	178.0296	180.0042	181.9500	183.8653	185.7486	187.5986	191.1931	194.6395	196.3046
	22	182.2666	184.4406	186.5895	188.7114	190.8045	192.8670	194.8972	196.8935	198.8545	202.6647	206.3178	208.0829
	23	193.2026	195.5070	197.7848	200.0341	202.2527	204.4390	206.5910	208.7072	210.7858	214.8246	218.6969	220.5679
	24	204.7947	207.2374	209.6519	212.0361	214.3879	216.7053	218.9865	221.2296	223.4329	227.7140	231.8187	233.8020
	25	217.0824	219.6717	222.2310	224.7583	227.2512	229.7076	232.1257	234.5034	236.8389	241.3769	245.7278	247.8301
	1	48.0138	48.8567	49.6940	50.5241	51.3458	52.1577	52.9585	53.7471	54.5224	56.0288	57.4707	58.1656
	2	50.8946	51.7881	52.6756	53.5556	54.4266	55.2872	56.1360	56.9720	57.7937	59.3905	60.9189	61.6556
	3	53.9483	54.8954	55.8362	56.7689	57.6921	58.6044	59.5042	60.3903	61.2613	62.9540	64.5741	65.3549
	4	57.1852	58.1892	59.1863	60.1750	61.1537	62.1206	63.0745	64.0137	64.9370	66.7312	68.4485	69.2762
	5	60.6163	61.6805	62.7375	63.7856	64.8229	65.8479	66.8589	67.8545	68.8332	70.7351	72.5554	73.4328
	6	64.2533	65.3813	66.5018	67.6127	68.7123	69.7988	70.8705	71.9258	72.9632	74.9792	76.9087	77.8387
	7	68.1085	69.3042	70.4919	71.6694	72.8350	73.9867	75.1227	76.2413	77.3410	79.4779	81.5233	82.5090
	8	72.1950	73.4625	74.7214	75.9696	77.2051	78.4259	79.6300	80.8158	81.9815	84.2466	86.4147	87.4596
	9	76.5267	77.8702	79.2047	80.5278	81.8374	83.1314	84.4078	85.6648	86.9004	89.3014	91.5995	92.7072
	10	81.1183	82.5424	83.9569	85.3595	86.7477	88.1193	89.4723	90.8046	92.1144	94.6595	97.0955	98.2696
	11	85.9854	87.4950	88.9944	90.4810	91.9525	93.4065	94.8407	96.2529	97.6413	100.3390	102.9212	104.1658
	12	91.1445	92.7447	94.3340	95.9099	97.4697	99.0109	100.5311	102.0281	103.4997	106.3594	109.0965	110.4157
	13	96.6132	98.3094	99.9941	101.6645	103.3178	104.9515	106.5630	108.1498	109.7097	112.7410	115.6423	117.0406
30 Year Plan	14	102.4100	104.2079	105.9937	107.7643	109.5169	111.2486	112.9567	114.6388	116.2923	119.5054	122.5808	124.0631
	15	108.5546	110.4604	112.3533	114.2302	116.0879	117.9235	119.7341	121.5171	123.2699	126.6757	129.9357	131.5069
	16	115.0678	117.0880	119.0945	121.0840	123.0532	124.9989	126.9182	128.8081	130.6660	134.2763	137.7318	139.3973
	17	121.9719	124.1133	126.2402	128.3491	130.4364	132.4989	134.5333	136.5366	138.5060	142.3329	145.9957	147.7611
	18	129.2902	131.5601	133.8146	136.0500	138.2626	140.4488	142.6053	144.7288	146.8164	150.8728	154.7555	156.6268
	19	137.0476	139.4537	141.8435	144.2130	146.5583	148.8757	151.1616	153.4125	155.6254	159.9252	164.0408	166.0244
	20	145.2705	147.8209	150.3541	152.8658	155.3518	157.8083	160.2313	162.6173	164.9629	169.5207	173.8833	175.9859
	21	153.9867	156.6902	159.3754	162.0377	164.6730	167.2768	169.8452	172.3743	174.8606	179.6920	184.3163	186.5450
	22	163.2259	166.0916	168.9379	171.7600	174.5533	177.3134	180.0359	182.7168	185.3523	190.4735	195.3752	197.7377
	23	173.0195	176.0571	179.0741	182.0656	185.0265	187.9522	190.8380	193.6798	196.4734	201.9019	207.0978	209.6020
	24	183.4006	186.6205	189.8186	192.9895	196.1281	199.2293	202.2883	205.3006	208.2618	214.0160	219.5236	222.1781
	25	194.4047	197.8177	201.2077	204.5689	207.8958	211.1831	214.4256	217.6186	220.7575	226.8569	232.6950	235.5088
	26	206.0690	209.6868	213.2802	216.8430	220.3696	223.8541	227.2912	230.6757	234.0030	240.4684	246.6567	249.6393
	27	218.4331	222.2680	226.0770	229.8536	233.5917	237.2853	240.9286	244.5163	248.0432	254.8965	261.4561	264.6177
	28	231.5391	235.6041	239.6416	243.6448	247.6072	251.5224	255.3843	259.1872	262.9258	270.1903	277.1435	280.4947
	29	245.4314	249.7403	254.0201	258.2635	262.4637	266.6138	270.7074	274.7385	278.7013	286.4017	293.7721	297.3244
	30	260.1573	264.7248	269.2613	273.7593	278.2115	282.6106	286.9498	291.2228	295.4234	303.5858	311.3985	315.1639

Entries are percentages of standard rent or price. The present value of a graduated series equals that of a normal series.

Graduated Rental Payments
Graduated Sales Prices

Annual Rate of Increase 7.0%

Plan	Year of Plan	6.00%	6.50%	7.00%	7.50%	8.00%	8.50%	9.00%	9.50%	10.00%	11.00%	12.00%	12.50%
							Interest Rate						
3 Year Plan	1	93.7377	93.7477	93.7541	93.7569	93.7563	93.7521	93.7446	93.7338	93.7196	93.6817	93.6311	93.6013
	2	100.2993	100.3100	100.3169	100.3199	100.3192	100.3148	100.3068	100.2951	100.2800	100.2394	100.1853	100.1534
	3	107.3203	107.3317	107.3390	107.3423	107.3415	107.3368	107.3282	107.3158	107.2996	107.2561	107.1983	107.1641
4 Year Plan	1	90.6402	90.6559	90.6673	90.6744	90.6775	90.6765	90.6715	90.6626	90.6498	90.6131	90.5619	90.5311
	2	96.9851	97.0018	97.0140	97.0216	97.0249	97.0238	97.0185	97.0090	96.9953	96.9561	96.9013	96.8682
	3	103.7740	103.7919	103.8049	103.8132	103.8166	103.8155	103.8098	103.7996	103.7850	103.7430	103.6844	103.6490
	4	111.0382	111.0574	111.0713	111.0801	111.0838	111.0826	111.0765	111.0656	111.0500	111.0050	110.9423	110.9044
5 Year Plan	1	87.6706	87.6965	87.7175	87.7338	87.7454	87.7524	87.7549	87.7531	87.7469	87.7221	87.6811	87.6547
	2	93.8076	93.8353	93.8578	93.8752	93.8876	93.8951	93.8978	93.8958	93.8892	93.8626	93.8187	93.7906
	3	100.3741	100.4037	100.4278	100.4464	100.4597	100.4677	100.4706	100.4685	100.4615	100.4330	100.3861	100.3559
	4	107.4003	107.4320	107.4577	107.4777	107.4919	107.5005	107.5036	107.5013	107.4938	107.4633	107.4131	107.3808
	5	114.9183	114.9522	114.9798	115.0011	115.0163	115.0255	115.0288	115.0264	115.0183	114.9857	114.9320	114.8975
6 Year Plan	1	84.8229	84.8631	84.8980	84.9277	84.9521	84.9716	84.9862	84.9959	85.0009	84.9973	84.9763	84.9594
	2	90.7605	90.8035	90.8409	90.8726	90.8988	90.9196	90.9352	90.9456	90.9510	90.9472	90.9246	90.9066
	3	97.1137	97.1598	97.1997	97.2337	97.2617	97.2840	97.3007	97.3118	97.3176	97.3135	97.2893	97.2700
	4	103.9117	103.9610	104.0037	104.0400	104.0700	104.0939	104.1117	104.1236	104.1298	104.1254	104.0996	104.0789
	5	111.1855	111.2382	111.2840	111.3228	111.3549	111.3805	111.3995	111.4123	111.4189	111.4142	111.3865	111.3644
	6	118.9684	119.0249	119.0739	119.1154	119.1498	119.1771	119.1975	119.2111	119.2182	119.2132	119.1836	119.1600
7 Year Plan	1	82.0913	82.1497	82.2022	82.2490	82.2903	82.3262	82.3567	82.3821	82.4025	82.4286	82.4360	82.4330
	2	87.8377	87.9002	87.9564	88.0065	88.0506	88.0890	88.1217	88.1489	88.1707	88.1986	88.2066	88.2034
	3	93.9864	94.0532	94.1133	94.1669	94.2142	94.2552	94.2902	94.3193	94.3426	94.3725	94.3810	94.3776
	4	100.5654	100.6369	100.7012	100.7586	100.8092	100.8531	100.8905	100.9217	100.9466	100.9786	100.9877	100.9840
	5	107.6050	107.6815	107.7503	107.8117	107.8658	107.9128	107.9529	107.9862	108.0129	108.0471	108.0568	108.0529
	6	115.1374	115.2192	115.2928	115.3585	115.4164	115.4667	115.5096	115.5452	115.5738	115.6104	115.6208	115.6166
	7	123.1970	123.2845	123.3633	123.4336	123.4956	123.5494	123.5953	123.6334	123.6639	123.7031	123.7143	123.7098
10 Year Plan	1	74.5420	74.6729	74.7970	74.9144	75.0253	75.1300	75.2285	75.3211	75.4078	75.5645	75.6998	75.7598
	2	79.7600	79.9000	80.0327	80.1584	80.2771	80.3891	80.4945	80.5935	80.6863	80.8540	80.9988	81.0630
	3	85.3432	85.4930	85.6350	85.7695	85.8965	86.0163	86.1291	86.2351	86.3344	86.5138	86.6687	86.7374
	4	91.3172	91.4775	91.6295	91.7733	91.9093	92.0375	92.1582	92.2715	92.3778	92.5697	92.7355	92.8090
	5	97.7094	97.8809	98.0436	98.1975	98.3429	98.4801	98.6092	98.7306	98.8442	99.0496	99.2270	99.3056
	6	104.5491	104.7326	104.9066	105.0713	105.2269	105.3737	105.5119	105.6417	105.7633	105.9831	106.1728	106.2570
	7	111.8675	112.0639	112.2501	112.4263	112.5928	112.7499	112.8977	113.0366	113.1668	113.4019	113.6049	113.6950
	8	119.6982	119.9084	120.1076	120.2961	120.4743	120.6424	120.8006	120.9492	121.0885	121.3400	121.5573	121.6536
	9	128.0771	128.3019	128.5151	128.7169	128.9075	129.0873	129.2566	129.4156	129.5646	129.8338	130.0663	130.1694
	10	137.0425	137.2831	137.5112	137.7270	137.9310	138.1234	138.3046	138.4747	138.6342	138.9222	139.1709	139.2813
12 Year Plan	1	69.9990	70.1901	70.3741	70.5510	70.7210	70.8844	71.0413	71.1918	71.3361	71.6068	71.8546	71.9703
	2	74.8989	75.1034	75.3002	75.4895	75.6715	75.8463	76.0142	76.1752	76.3296	76.6193	76.8844	77.0082
	3	80.1419	80.3607	80.5713	80.7738	80.9685	81.1556	81.3351	81.5075	81.6727	81.9826	82.2663	82.3988
	4	85.7518	85.9859	86.2112	86.4280	86.6363	86.8364	87.0286	87.2130	87.3898	87.7214	88.0250	88.1667
	5	91.7544	92.0049	92.2460	92.4779	92.7008	92.9150	93.1206	93.3179	93.5071	93.8619	94.1867	94.3383
	6	98.1772	98.4453	98.7032	98.9514	99.1899	99.4190	99.6391	99.8502	100.0526	100.4322	100.7798	100.9420
	7	105.0496	105.3365	105.6125	105.8780	106.1332	106.3784	106.6138	106.8397	107.0562	107.4625	107.8344	108.0080
	8	112.4031	112.7100	113.0053	113.2894	113.5625	113.8249	114.0767	114.3184	114.5502	114.9849	115.3828	115.5685
	9	120.2713	120.5997	120.9157	121.2197	121.5119	121.7926	122.0621	122.3207	122.5687	123.0338	123.4596	123.6583
	10	128.6903	129.0417	129.3798	129.7051	130.0177	130.3181	130.6065	130.8832	131.1485	131.6462	132.1017	132.3144
	11	137.6987	138.0746	138.4364	138.7844	139.1190	139.4403	139.7489	140.0450	140.3289	140.8614	141.3488	141.5764
	12	147.3376	147.7398	148.1270	148.4993	148.8573	149.2012	149.5313	149.8482	150.1519	150.7217	151.2433	151.4868
15 Year Plan	1	63.8337	64.1275	64.4139	64.6931	64.9652	65.2302	65.4884	65.7398	65.9845	66.4544	66.8990	67.1120
	2	68.3021	68.6164	68.9229	69.2217	69.5128	69.7964	70.0726	70.3416	70.6034	71.1062	71.5819	71.8098
	3	73.0832	73.4196	73.7475	74.0672	74.3787	74.6821	74.9777	75.2655	75.5457	76.0837	76.5926	76.8365
	4	78.1991	78.5590	78.9099	79.2519	79.5852	79.9099	80.2261	80.5341	80.8339	81.4095	81.9541	82.2151
	5	83.6730	84.0581	84.4335	84.7995	85.1561	85.5036	85.8420	86.1715	86.4922	87.1082	87.6909	87.9701
	6	89.5301	89.9422	90.3439	90.7355	91.1170	91.4888	91.8509	92.2035	92.5467	93.2057	93.8293	94.1280
	7	95.7972	96.2381	96.6680	97.0869	97.4952	97.8930	98.2804	98.6577	99.0250	99.7301	100.3973	100.7170
	8	102.5030	102.9748	103.4347	103.8830	104.3199	104.7455	105.1601	105.5637	105.9567	106.7113	107.4251	107.7672
	9	109.6782	110.1830	110.6752	111.1548	111.6223	112.0777	112.5213	112.9532	113.3737	114.1810	114.9449	115.3109
	10	117.3557	117.8958	118.4224	118.9357	119.4359	119.9232	120.3978	120.8599	121.3098	122.1737	122.9910	123.3827
	11	125.5706	126.1485	126.7120	127.2612	127.7964	128.3178	128.8256	129.3201	129.8015	130.7259	131.6004	132.0195
	12	134.3606	134.9789	135.5818	136.1695	136.7421	137.3000	137.8434	138.3725	138.8876	139.8767	140.8124	141.2608
	13	143.7658	144.4275	145.0725	145.7013	146.3141	146.9110	147.4925	148.0586	148.6098	149.6681	150.6693	151.1491
	14	153.8294	154.5374	155.2276	155.9004	156.5560	157.1948	157.8169	158.4227	159.0125	160.1448	161.2161	161.7295
	15	164.5975	165.3550	166.0936	166.8135	167.5150	168.1984	168.8641	169.5123	170.1433	171.3550	172.5012	173.0506

Entries are percentages of standard rent or price. The present value of a graduated series equals that of a normal series.

Graduated Rental Payments
Graduated Sales Prices

Annual Rate of Increase 7.0%

Plan	Year of Plan	6.00%	6.50%	7.00%	7.50%	8.00%	8.50%	9.00%	9.50%	10.00%	11.00%	12.00%	12.50%
							Interest Rate						
	1	47.7919	48.4731	49.1501	49.8221	50.4884	51.1484	51.8014	52.4467	53.0837	54.3304	55.5372	56.1244
	2	51.1373	51.8662	52.5906	53.3096	54.0226	54.7288	55.4275	56.1180	56.7996	58.1336	59.4248	60.0531
	3	54.7169	55.4968	56.2719	57.0413	57.8042	58.5598	59.3074	60.0462	60.7755	62.2029	63.5845	64.2568
	4	58.5471	59.3816	60.2109	61.0342	61.8505	62.6590	63.4589	64.2495	65.0298	66.5571	68.0355	68.7548
	5	62.6454	63.5383	64.4257	65.3066	66.1800	67.0451	67.9011	68.7469	69.5819	71.2161	72.7979	73.5676
	6	67.0305	67.9860	68.9355	69.8780	70.8126	71.7383	72.6541	73.5592	74.4526	76.2012	77.8938	78.7174
	7	71.7227	72.7450	73.7610	74.7695	75.7695	76.7600	77.7399	78.7083	79.6643	81.5353	83.3464	84.2276
	8	76.7433	77.8372	78.9243	80.0034	81.0734	82.1332	83.1817	84.2179	85.2408	87.2428	89.1806	90.1235
	9	82.1153	83.2858	84.4490	85.6036	86.7485	87.8825	89.0044	90.1132	91.2077	93.3498	95.4233	96.4321
	10	87.8634	89.1158	90.3604	91.5959	92.8209	94.0343	95.2348	96.4211	97.5922	99.8843	102.1029	103.1824
25 Year Plan	11	94.0138	95.3539	96.6856	98.0076	99.3184	100.6167	101.9012	103.1706	104.4237	106.8762	109.2501	110.4052
	12	100.5948	102.0287	103.4536	104.8681	106.2707	107.6599	109.0343	110.3925	111.7333	114.3575	116.8976	118.1335
	13	107.6364	109.1707	110.6954	112.2089	113.7096	115.1960	116.6667	118.1200	119.5547	122.3626	125.0804	126.4029
	14	115.1710	116.8126	118.4440	120.0635	121.6693	123.2598	124.8333	126.3884	127.9235	130.9279	133.8361	135.2511
	15	123.2329	124.9895	126.7351	128.4679	130.1861	131.8879	133.5717	135.2356	136.8781	140.0929	143.2046	144.7186
	16	131.8592	133.7388	135.6066	137.4607	139.2992	141.1201	142.9217	144.7021	146.4596	149.8994	153.2289	154.8489
	17	141.0894	143.1005	145.0990	147.0829	149.0501	150.9985	152.9262	154.8312	156.7118	160.3923	163.9549	165.6884
	18	150.9656	153.1175	155.2560	157.3787	159.4836	161.5684	163.6310	165.6694	167.6816	171.6198	175.4318	177.2866
	19	161.5332	163.8358	166.1239	168.3952	170.6475	172.8782	175.0852	177.2663	179.4193	183.6332	187.7120	189.6966
	20	172.8405	175.3043	177.7526	180.1829	182.5928	184.9797	187.3412	189.6749	191.9787	196.4875	200.8518	202.9754
	21	184.9394	187.5756	190.1953	192.7957	195.3743	197.9282	200.4551	202.9522	205.4172	210.2416	214.9115	217.1837
	22	197.8851	200.7059	203.5089	206.2914	209.0505	211.7832	214.4869	217.1588	219.7964	224.9586	229.9553	232.3865
	23	211.7371	214.7553	217.7545	220.7318	223.6840	226.6081	229.5010	232.3599	235.1821	240.7057	246.0521	248.6536
	24	226.5587	229.7881	232.9974	236.1830	239.3419	242.4706	245.5661	248.6251	251.6449	257.5551	263.2758	266.0593
	25	242.4178	245.8733	249.3072	252.7159	256.0958	259.4436	262.7557	266.0289	269.2600	275.5839	281.7051	284.6835
	1	41.7641	42.6381	43.5118	44.3836	45.2520	46.1153	46.9720	47.8207	48.6600	50.3049	51.8971	52.6707
	2	44.6876	45.6228	46.5577	47.4905	48.4196	49.3433	50.2600	51.1682	52.0662	53.8263	55.5299	56.3577
	3	47.8157	48.8164	49.8167	50.8148	51.8090	52.7974	53.7783	54.7499	55.7108	57.5941	59.4170	60.3027
	4	51.1628	52.2335	53.3039	54.3719	55.4356	56.4932	57.5427	58.5824	59.6106	61.6257	63.5762	64.5239
	5	54.7442	55.8899	57.0352	58.1779	59.3161	60.4477	61.5707	62.6832	63.7833	65.9395	68.0265	69.0406
	6	58.5763	59.8022	61.0276	62.2504	63.4682	64.6790	65.8807	67.0710	68.2482	70.5553	72.7884	73.8734
	7	62.6766	63.9883	65.2995	66.6079	67.9110	69.2066	70.4923	71.7660	73.0255	75.4942	77.8835	79.0446
	8	67.0640	68.4675	69.8705	71.2704	72.6648	74.0510	75.4268	76.7896	78.1373	80.7787	83.3354	84.5777
	9	71.7585	73.2602	74.7614	76.2594	77.7513	79.2346	80.7067	82.1649	83.6069	86.4333	89.1689	90.4981
	10	76.7815	78.3885	79.9947	81.5975	83.1939	84.7810	86.3561	87.9164	89.4594	92.4836	95.4107	96.8330
	11	82.1563	83.8756	85.5944	87.3094	89.0175	90.7157	92.4010	94.0706	95.7216	98.9574	102.0894	103.6113
	12	87.9072	89.7469	91.5860	93.4210	95.2487	97.0658	98.8691	100.6555	102.4221	105.8845	109.2357	110.8641
	13	94.0607	96.0292	97.9970	99.9605	101.9161	103.8604	105.7900	107.7014	109.5916	113.2964	116.8822	118.6246
30 Year Plan	14	100.6449	102.7513	104.8568	106.9577	109.0502	111.1306	113.1953	115.2405	117.2631	121.2271	125.0640	126.9283
	15	107.6901	109.9439	112.1968	114.4448	116.6838	118.9098	121.1189	123.3074	125.4715	129.7130	133.8184	135.8133
	16	115.2284	117.6399	120.0505	122.4559	124.8516	127.2335	129.5972	131.9389	134.2545	138.7929	143.1857	145.3202
	17	123.2944	125.8747	128.4541	131.0278	133.5912	136.1398	138.6691	141.1746	143.6523	148.5084	153.2087	155.4926
	18	131.9250	134.6860	137.4459	140.1997	142.9426	145.6696	148.3759	151.0568	153.7079	158.9040	163.9333	166.3771
	19	141.1597	144.1140	147.0671	150.0137	152.9486	155.8665	158.7622	161.6308	164.4675	170.0273	175.4087	178.0235
	20	151.0409	154.2020	157.3618	160.5147	163.6550	166.7771	169.8756	172.9450	175.9802	181.9292	187.6873	190.4852
	21	161.6138	164.9961	168.3771	171.7507	175.1109	178.4515	181.7668	185.0511	188.2988	194.6642	200.8254	203.8191
	22	172.9268	176.5458	180.1635	183.7733	187.3686	190.9431	194.4905	198.0047	201.4798	208.2907	214.8832	218.0865
	23	185.0316	188.9040	192.7749	196.6374	200.4844	204.3092	208.1049	211.8650	215.5833	222.8711	229.9250	233.3525
	24	197.9838	202.1273	206.2692	210.4020	214.5183	218.6108	222.6722	226.6956	230.6742	238.4721	246.0197	249.6872
	25	211.8427	216.2762	220.7080	225.1302	229.5346	233.9136	238.2593	242.5642	246.8214	255.1651	263.2411	267.1653
	26	226.6717	231.4156	236.1576	240.8893	245.6020	250.2875	254.9374	259.5437	264.0989	273.0267	281.6680	285.8669
	27	242.5387	247.6147	252.6886	257.7515	262.7942	267.8076	272.7830	277.7118	282.5858	292.1385	301.3847	305.8776
	28	259.5164	264.9477	270.3768	275.7941	281.1898	286.5542	291.8778	297.1516	302.3668	312.5882	322.4817	327.2890
	29	277.6826	283.4940	289.3032	295.0997	300.8731	306.6130	312.3093	317.9523	323.5325	334.4694	345.0554	350.1992
	30	297.1204	303.3386	309.5544	315.7567	321.9342	328.0759	334.1709	340.2089	346.1797	357.8823	369.2093	374.7132

Entries are percentages of standard rent or price. The present value of a graduated series equals that of a normal series.

Graduated Rental Payments
Graduated Sales Prices

Annual Rate of Increase   8.0%

Plan	Year of Plan	6.00%	6.50%	7.00%	7.50%	8.00%	8.50%	9.00%	9.50%	10.00%	11.00%	12.00%	12.50%
3 Year Plan	1	92.8616	92.8743	92.8833	92.8888	92.8908	92.8894	92.8846	92.8765	92.8651	92.8327	92.7878	92.7608
	2	100.2906	100.3042	100.3140	100.3199	100.3221	100.3206	100.3154	100.3066	100.2943	100.2593	100.2108	100.1816
	3	108.3138	108.3286	108.3391	108.3455	108.3479	108.3462	108.3406	108.3311	108.3178	108.2800	108.2277	108.1961
4 Year Plan	1	89.3697	89.3900	89.4061	89.4180	89.4258	89.4296	89.4295	89.4255	89.4176	89.3908	89.3496	89.3238
	2	96.5193	96.5412	96.5586	96.5714	96.5799	96.5840	96.5838	96.5795	96.5711	96.5421	96.4976	96.4697
	3	104.2408	104.2645	104.2832	104.2971	104.3063	104.3107	104.3105	104.3059	104.2967	104.2655	104.2174	104.1873
	4	112.5801	112.6056	112.6259	112.6409	112.6508	112.6556	112.6554	112.6503	112.6405	112.6067	112.5548	112.5223
5 Year Plan	1	86.0321	86.0651	86.0932	86.1166	86.1355	86.1497	86.1596	86.1651	86.1664	86.1564	86.1305	86.1118
	2	92.9147	92.9503	92.9807	93.0060	93.0263	93.0417	93.0524	93.0583	93.0597	93.0490	93.0210	93.0007
	3	100.3479	100.3863	100.4191	100.4464	100.4684	100.4851	100.4966	100.5030	100.5045	100.4929	100.4626	100.4408
	4	108.3757	108.4172	108.4526	108.4822	108.5059	108.5239	108.5363	108.5432	108.5448	108.5323	108.4997	108.4760
	5	117.0458	117.0906	117.1289	117.1607	117.1863	117.2058	117.2192	117.2267	117.2284	117.2149	117.1796	117.1541
6 Year Plan	1	82.8414	82.8913	82.9359	82.9754	83.0098	83.0392	83.0638	83.0836	83.0988	83.1157	83.1152	83.1087
	2	89.4687	89.5226	89.5708	89.6134	89.6506	89.6823	89.7089	89.7303	89.7467	89.7649	89.7644	89.7574
	3	96.6262	96.6844	96.7365	96.7825	96.8226	96.8569	96.8856	96.9087	96.9264	96.9461	96.9456	96.9380
	4	104.3563	104.4192	104.4754	104.5251	104.5684	104.6055	104.6364	104.6614	104.6805	104.7018	104.7012	104.6931
	5	112.7048	112.7727	112.8334	112.8871	112.9339	112.9739	113.0073	113.0343	113.0550	113.0779	113.0773	113.0685
	6	121.7212	121.7946	121.8601	121.9181	121.9686	122.0118	122.0479	122.0771	122.0994	122.1242	122.1235	122.1140
7 Year Plan	1	79.7904	79.8611	79.9261	79.9855	80.0394	80.0881	80.1315	80.1699	80.2032	80.2556	80.2896	80.2999
	2	86.1736	86.2500	86.3201	86.3843	86.4426	86.4951	86.5420	86.5834	86.6195	86.6761	86.7127	86.7239
	3	93.0675	93.1500	93.2258	93.2950	93.3580	93.4147	93.4654	93.5101	93.5491	93.6102	93.6497	93.6618
	4	100.5129	100.6020	100.6838	100.7587	100.8266	100.8879	100.9426	100.9909	101.0330	101.0990	101.1417	101.1547
	5	108.5539	108.6501	108.7385	108.8193	108.8928	108.9589	109.0180	109.0702	109.1156	109.1869	109.2331	109.2471
	6	117.2383	117.3421	117.4376	117.5249	117.6042	117.6756	117.7395	117.7958	117.8449	117.9218	117.9717	117.9869
	7	126.6173	126.7295	126.8326	126.9269	127.0125	127.0897	127.1586	127.2195	127.2725	127.3556	127.4094	127.4258
10 Year Plan	1	71.4091	71.5603	71.7049	71.8432	71.9752	72.1012	72.2212	72.3354	72.4440	72.6447	72.8246	72.9070
	2	77.1218	77.2851	77.4413	77.5907	77.7333	77.8693	77.9989	78.1222	78.2395	78.4563	78.6505	78.7395
	3	83.2916	83.4679	83.6366	83.7979	83.9519	84.0988	84.2388	84.3720	84.4987	84.7328	84.9426	85.0387
	4	89.9549	90.1453	90.3276	90.5017	90.6681	90.8267	90.9779	91.1218	91.2585	91.5114	91.7380	91.8418
	5	97.1513	97.3570	97.5538	97.7419	97.9215	98.0929	98.2561	98.4115	98.5592	98.8324	99.0770	99.1891
	6	104.9234	105.1455	105.3581	105.5612	105.7552	105.9403	106.1166	106.2844	106.4440	106.7389	107.0032	107.1243
	7	113.3173	113.5572	113.7867	114.0061	114.2157	114.4155	114.6060	114.7872	114.9595	115.2781	115.5634	115.6942
	8	122.3826	122.6417	122.8897	123.1266	123.3529	123.5688	123.7744	123.9702	124.1562	124.5003	124.8085	124.9497
	9	132.1733	132.4531	132.7208	132.9768	133.2211	133.4543	133.6764	133.8878	134.0887	134.4603	134.7932	134.9457
	10	142.7471	143.0493	143.3385	143.6149	143.8788	144.1306	144.3705	144.5988	144.8158	145.2171	145.5766	145.7414
12 Year Plan	1	66.4043	66.6203	66.8296	67.0322	67.2284	67.4182	67.6018	67.7793	67.9509	68.2768	68.5806	68.7245
	2	71.7167	71.9500	72.1760	72.3948	72.6066	72.8116	73.0099	73.2017	73.3870	73.7390	74.0670	74.2224
	3	77.4540	77.7060	77.9500	78.1864	78.4152	78.6366	78.8507	79.0578	79.2579	79.6381	79.9924	80.1602
	4	83.6503	83.9224	84.1860	84.4413	84.6884	84.9275	85.1588	85.3824	85.5986	86.0092	86.3918	86.5731
	5	90.3424	90.6362	90.9209	91.1966	91.4634	91.7217	91.9715	92.2130	92.4465	92.8899	93.3032	93.4989
	6	97.5698	97.8871	98.1946	98.4923	98.7805	99.0594	99.3292	99.5900	99.8422	100.3211	100.7674	100.9788
	7	105.3753	105.7181	106.0502	106.3717	106.6830	106.9842	107.2755	107.5573	107.8296	108.3468	108.8288	109.0571
	8	113.8054	114.1756	114.5342	114.8814	115.2176	115.5429	115.8576	116.1618	116.4559	117.0145	117.5351	117.7817
	9	122.9098	123.3096	123.6969	124.0720	124.4350	124.7863	125.1262	125.4548	125.7724	126.3757	126.9379	127.2042
	10	132.7426	133.1744	133.5927	133.9977	134.3898	134.7692	135.1363	135.4912	135.8342	136.4857	137.0929	137.3806
	11	143.3620	143.8283	144.2801	144.7175	145.1410	145.5508	145.9472	146.3305	146.7009	147.4046	148.0604	148.3710
	12	154.8309	155.3346	155.8225	156.2949	156.7523	157.1948	157.6229	158.0369	158.4370	159.1970	159.9052	160.2407
15 Year Plan	1	59.6640	59.9875	60.3044	60.6149	60.9188	61.2164	61.5077	61.7928	62.0716	62.6111	63.1267	63.3757
	2	64.4371	64.7865	65.1288	65.4641	65.7923	66.1137	66.4283	66.7362	67.0374	67.6200	68.1769	68.4458
	3	69.5921	69.9694	70.3391	70.7012	71.0557	71.4028	71.7426	72.0751	72.4003	73.0296	73.6310	73.9214
	4	75.1595	75.5670	75.9662	76.3573	76.7402	77.1151	77.4820	77.8411	78.1924	78.8720	79.5215	79.8352
	5	81.1722	81.6124	82.0435	82.4659	82.8794	83.2843	83.6806	84.0684	84.4478	85.1817	85.8832	86.2220
	6	87.6660	88.1413	88.6070	89.0631	89.5098	89.9470	90.3750	90.7938	91.2036	91.9963	92.7539	93.1197
	7	94.6793	95.1927	95.6956	96.1882	96.6705	97.1428	97.6050	98.0573	98.4999	99.3560	100.1742	100.5693
	8	102.2536	102.8081	103.3512	103.8832	104.4042	104.9142	105.4134	105.9019	106.3799	107.3045	108.1881	108.6148
	9	110.4339	111.0327	111.6193	112.1939	112.7565	113.3073	113.8465	114.3741	114.8903	115.8888	116.8431	117.3040
	10	119.2686	119.9153	120.5489	121.1694	121.7770	122.3719	122.9542	123.5240	124.0815	125.1599	126.1906	126.6884
	11	128.8101	129.5086	130.1928	130.8629	131.5192	132.1617	132.7905	133.4059	134.0080	135.1727	136.2858	136.8234
	12	139.1149	139.8692	140.6082	141.3320	142.0407	142.7346	143.4138	144.0784	144.7286	145.9865	147.1887	147.7693
	13	150.2441	151.0588	151.8569	152.6385	153.4040	154.1534	154.8869	155.6047	156.3069	157.6654	158.9638	159.5908
	14	162.2636	163.1435	164.0054	164.8496	165.6763	166.4857	167.2778	168.0531	168.8115	170.2787	171.6809	172.3581
	15	175.2447	176.1950	177.1258	178.0376	178.9304	179.8045	180.6601	181.4973	182.3164	183.9010	185.4154	186.1468

Entries are percentages of standard rent or price. The present value of a graduated series equals that of a normal series.

Graduated Rental Payments
Graduated Sales Prices

Annual Rate of Increase   8.0%

Plan	Year of Plan	6.00%	6.50%	7.00%	7.50%	8.00%	8.50%	9.00%	9.50%	10.00%	11.00%	12.00%	12.50%
							Interest Rate						
	1	42.4552	43.1581	43.8599	44.5599	45.2573	45.9513	46.6411	47.3259	48.0049	49.3428	50.6491	51.2888
	2	45.8516	46.6107	47.3687	48.1247	48.8779	49.6274	50.3724	51.1119	51.8453	53.2903	54.7011	55.3920
	3	49.5198	50.3396	51.1582	51.9747	52.7881	53.5976	54.4022	55.2009	55.9929	57.5535	59.0772	59.8233
	4	53.4814	54.3667	55.2509	56.1327	57.0112	57.8854	58.7543	59.6170	60.4724	62.1577	63.8033	64.6092
	5	57.7599	58.7161	59.6709	60.6233	61.5721	62.5162	63.4547	64.3863	65.3102	67.1304	68.9076	69.7779
	6	62.3806	63.4134	64.4446	65.4731	66.4978	67.5175	68.5310	69.5372	70.5350	72.5008	74.4202	75.3601
	7	67.3711	68.4864	69.6002	70.7110	71.8177	72.9189	74.0135	75.1002	76.1778	78.3009	80.3738	81.3889
	8	72.7608	73.9654	75.1682	76.3679	77.5631	78.7524	79.9346	81.1082	82.2720	84.5649	86.8037	87.9001
	9	78.5817	79.8826	81.1816	82.4773	83.7681	85.0526	86.3294	87.5969	88.8538	91.3301	93.7480	94.9321
	10	84.8682	86.2732	87.6762	89.0755	90.4696	91.8569	93.2357	94.6046	95.9621	98.6365	101.2479	102.5266
25 Year Plan	11	91.6576	93.1751	94.6902	96.2015	97.7071	99.2054	100.6946	102.1730	103.6390	106.5275	109.3477	110.7288
	12	98.9903	100.6291	102.2655	103.8976	105.5237	107.1418	108.7502	110.3469	111.9302	115.0497	118.0955	119.5871
	13	106.9095	108.6794	110.4467	112.2095	113.9656	115.7132	117.4502	119.1746	120.8846	124.2536	127.5432	129.1540
	14	115.4622	117.3737	119.2824	121.1862	123.0829	124.9702	126.8462	128.7086	130.5553	134.1939	137.7466	139.4864
	15	124.6992	126.7636	128.8250	130.8811	132.9295	134.9679	136.9939	139.0053	140.9998	144.9294	148.7663	150.6453
	16	134.6751	136.9047	139.1310	141.3516	143.5638	145.7653	147.9534	150.1257	152.2797	156.5238	160.6677	162.6969
	17	145.4492	147.8571	150.2615	152.6597	155.0490	157.4265	159.7897	162.1357	164.4621	169.0457	173.5211	175.7126
	18	157.0851	159.6857	162.2824	164.8725	167.4529	170.0206	172.5728	175.1066	177.6191	182.5693	187.4028	189.7696
	19	169.6519	172.4605	175.2650	178.0623	180.8491	183.6223	186.3787	189.1151	191.8286	197.1749	202.3950	204.9512
	20	183.2240	186.2574	189.2862	192.3073	195.3170	198.3121	201.2890	204.2443	207.1749	212.9489	218.5866	221.3473
	21	197.8820	201.1580	204.4291	207.6919	210.9424	214.1770	217.3921	220.5839	223.7489	229.9848	236.0735	239.0551
	22	213.7125	217.2506	220.7835	224.3072	227.8178	231.3112	234.7834	238.2306	241.6488	248.3836	254.9594	258.1795
	23	230.8095	234.6306	238.4462	242.2518	246.0432	249.8161	253.5661	257.2890	260.9807	268.2543	275.3561	278.8339
	24	249.2743	253.4011	257.5218	261.6319	265.7267	269.8014	273.8514	277.8722	281.8592	289.7146	297.3846	301.1406
	25	269.2162	273.6732	278.1236	282.5625	286.9848	291.3855	295.7595	300.1019	304.4079	312.8918	321.1754	325.2318
	1	36.1399	37.0167	37.8984	38.7835	39.6702	40.5570	41.4422	42.3242	43.2013	44.9347	46.6307	47.4613
	2	39.0311	39.9780	40.9303	41.8861	42.8438	43.8016	44.7576	45.7101	46.6574	48.5295	50.3611	51.2582
	3	42.1536	43.1763	44.2047	45.2370	46.2714	47.3057	48.3382	49.3670	50.3900	52.4119	54.3900	55.3589
	4	45.5259	46.6304	47.7411	48.8560	49.9731	51.0902	52.2053	53.3163	54.4212	56.6048	58.7412	59.7876
	5	49.1680	50.3608	51.5604	52.7645	53.9709	55.1774	56.3817	57.5816	58.7749	61.1332	63.4405	64.5706
	6	53.1014	54.3897	55.6852	56.9856	58.2886	59.5916	60.8923	62.1881	63.4769	66.0238	68.5158	69.7362
	7	57.3495	58.7408	60.1400	61.5445	62.9517	64.3589	65.7636	67.1632	68.5550	71.3057	73.9970	75.3151
	8	61.9375	63.4401	64.9512	66.4680	67.9878	69.5076	71.0247	72.5363	74.0394	77.0102	79.9168	81.3403
	9	66.8925	68.5153	70.1473	71.7855	73.4268	75.0682	76.7067	78.3392	79.9626	83.1710	86.3102	87.8475
	10	72.2439	73.9966	75.7591	77.5283	79.3010	81.0737	82.8432	84.6063	86.3596	89.8247	93.2150	94.8753
	11	78.0234	79.9163	81.8198	83.7306	85.6450	87.5596	89.4707	91.3748	93.2684	97.0107	100.6722	102.4654
	12	84.2653	86.3096	88.3654	90.4290	92.4966	94.5644	96.6284	98.6848	100.7298	104.7715	108.7259	110.6626
	13	91.0065	93.2143	95.4346	97.6634	99.8964	102.1295	104.3586	106.5796	108.7882	113.1533	117.4240	119.5156
	14	98.2870	100.6715	103.0694	105.4764	107.8881	110.2999	112.7073	115.1059	117.4913	122.2055	126.8179	129.0769
30 Year Plan	15	106.1500	108.7252	111.3150	113.9145	116.5191	119.1239	121.7239	124.3144	126.8906	131.9820	136.9634	139.4030
	16	114.6420	117.4232	120.2202	123.0277	125.8407	128.6538	131.4618	134.2595	137.0418	142.5405	147.9204	150.5553
	17	123.8134	126.8171	129.8378	132.8699	135.9079	138.9461	141.9788	145.0003	148.0052	153.9438	159.7541	162.5997
	18	133.7184	136.9625	140.2248	143.4995	146.7806	150.0618	153.3371	156.6003	159.8456	166.2593	172.5344	175.6076
	19	144.4159	147.9194	151.4428	154.9795	158.5230	162.0667	165.6040	169.1284	172.6333	179.5600	186.3371	189.6563
	20	155.9692	159.7530	163.5582	167.3778	171.2048	175.0321	178.8523	182.6586	186.4439	193.9248	201.2441	204.8288
	21	168.4467	172.5332	176.6429	180.7681	184.9012	189.0346	193.1605	197.2713	201.3594	209.4388	217.3436	221.2151
	22	181.9224	186.3359	190.7743	195.2295	199.6933	204.1574	208.6134	213.0530	217.4682	226.1939	234.7311	238.9123
	23	196.4762	201.2428	206.0362	210.8479	215.6688	220.4900	225.3024	230.0973	234.8656	244.2894	253.5096	258.0252
	24	212.1943	217.3422	222.5191	227.7157	232.9223	238.1292	243.3266	248.5050	253.6549	263.8325	273.7904	278.6673
	25	229.1699	234.7296	240.3207	245.9330	251.5561	257.1795	262.7928	268.3854	273.9473	284.9391	295.6936	300.9606
	26	247.5035	253.5079	259.5463	265.6076	271.6806	277.7539	283.8162	289.8563	295.8631	307.7343	319.3491	325.0375
	27	267.3037	273.7886	280.3100	286.8562	293.4150	299.9742	306.5215	313.0448	319.5321	332.3530	344.8971	351.0405
	28	288.6880	295.6917	302.7348	309.8047	316.8882	323.9721	331.0432	338.0884	345.0947	358.9413	372.4888	379.1237
	29	311.7831	319.3470	326.9536	334.5891	342.2393	349.8899	357.5267	365.1354	372.7023	387.6566	402.2879	409.4536
	30	336.7257	344.8948	353.1099	361.3562	369.6184	377.8811	386.1288	394.3463	402.5184	418.6691	434.4710	442.2099

Entries are percentages of standard rent or price. The present value of a graduated series equals that of a normal series.

Graduated Rental Payments
Graduated Sales Prices

Annual Rate of Increase 10.0%

Plan	Year of Plan	6.00%	6.50%	7.00%	7.50%	8.00%	8.50%	9.00%	9.50%	10.00%	11.00%	12.00%	12.50%
3 Year Plan	1	91.1422	91.1598	91.1739	91.1845	91.1917	91.1954	91.1958	91.1930	91.1869	91.1651	91.1310	91.1095
	2	100.2564	100.2758	100.2913	100.3030	100.3108	100.3150	100.3154	100.3123	100.3056	100.2816	100.2441	100.2204
	3	110.2820	110.3034	110.3204	110.3333	110.3419	110.3465	110.3470	110.3435	110.3361	110.3098	110.2685	110.2424
4 Year Plan	1	86.8879	86.9170	86.9420	86.9629	86.9797	86.9927	87.0017	87.0069	87.0084	87.0004	86.9782	86.9619
	2	95.5767	95.6087	95.6362	95.6592	95.6777	95.6919	95.7019	95.7076	95.7092	95.7004	95.6760	95.6581
	3	105.1344	105.1696	105.1998	105.2251	105.2455	105.2611	105.2721	105.2784	105.2802	105.2705	105.2436	105.2239
	4	115.6478	115.6866	115.7198	115.7476	115.7700	115.7872	115.7993	115.8062	115.8082	115.7975	115.7679	115.7463
5 Year Plan	1	82.8474	82.8934	82.9348	82.9715	83.0038	83.0316	83.0551	83.0744	83.0895	83.1075	83.1098	83.1053
	2	91.1321	91.1828	91.2282	91.2687	91.3042	91.3348	91.3607	91.3818	91.3984	91.4183	91.4208	91.4159
	3	100.2453	100.3010	100.3511	100.3955	100.4346	100.4683	100.4967	100.5200	100.5383	100.5601	100.5629	100.5574
	4	110.2699	110.3311	110.3862	110.4351	110.4780	110.5151	110.5464	110.5720	110.5921	110.6161	110.6192	110.6132
	5	121.2969	121.3642	121.4248	121.4786	121.5258	121.5666	121.6010	121.6292	121.6513	121.6777	121.6811	121.6745
6 Year Plan	1	79.0092	79.0767	79.1391	79.1965	79.2490	79.2967	79.3397	79.3780	79.4119	79.4665	79.5042	79.5169
	2	86.9102	86.9844	87.0530	87.1161	87.1739	87.2263	87.2736	87.3158	87.3531	87.4131	87.4546	87.4686
	3	95.6012	95.6828	95.7583	95.8278	95.8913	95.9490	96.0010	96.0474	96.0884	96.1544	96.2000	96.2154
	4	105.1613	105.2511	105.3342	105.4105	105.4804	105.5439	105.6011	105.6522	105.6972	105.7699	105.8200	105.8370
	5	115.6774	115.7762	115.8676	115.9516	116.0284	116.0983	116.1612	116.2174	116.2670	116.3469	116.4020	116.4207
	6	127.2452	127.3538	127.4543	127.5467	127.6313	127.7081	127.7773	127.8391	127.8937	127.9816	128.0423	128.0627
7 Year Plan	1	75.3626	75.4554	75.5428	75.6248	75.7016	75.7732	75.8399	75.9017	75.9587	76.0588	76.1410	76.1756
	2	82.8989	83.0010	83.0970	83.1872	83.2717	83.3506	83.4239	83.4919	83.5546	83.6647	83.7551	83.7932
	3	91.1888	91.3011	91.4067	91.5060	91.5989	91.6856	91.7663	91.8411	91.9100	92.0311	92.1306	92.1725
	4	100.3077	100.4312	100.5474	100.6566	100.7588	100.8542	100.9429	101.0252	101.1010	101.2342	101.3436	101.3898
	5	110.3385	110.4743	110.6022	110.7222	110.8346	110.9396	111.0372	111.1277	111.2111	111.3577	111.4780	111.5287
	6	121.3723	121.5217	121.6624	121.7944	121.9181	122.0336	122.1409	122.2405	122.3323	122.4934	122.6258	122.6816
	7	133.5095	133.6739	133.8286	133.9739	134.1099	134.2369	134.3550	134.4645	134.5655	134.7428	134.8884	134.9498
10 Year Plan	1	65.4733	65.6585	65.8377	66.0112	66.1790	66.3411	66.4978	66.6491	66.7952	67.0720	67.3291	67.4506
	2	72.0206	72.2243	72.4215	72.6123	72.7969	72.9752	73.1476	73.3140	73.4747	73.7792	74.0620	74.1956
	3	79.2226	79.4468	79.6637	79.8736	80.0765	80.2727	80.4623	80.6454	80.8222	81.1571	81.4682	81.6152
	4	87.1449	87.3914	87.6300	87.8609	88.0842	88.3000	88.5086	88.7100	88.9044	89.2728	89.6151	89.7767
	5	95.8594	96.1306	96.3930	96.6470	96.8926	97.1300	97.3594	97.5810	97.7948	98.2001	98.5766	98.7544
	6	105.4453	105.7436	106.0324	106.3117	106.5819	106.8430	107.0954	107.3391	107.5743	108.0201	108.4342	108.6298
	7	115.9899	116.3180	116.6356	116.9429	117.2401	117.5273	117.8049	118.0730	118.3317	118.8221	119.2777	119.4928
	8	127.5889	127.9498	128.2991	128.6372	128.9641	129.2801	129.5854	129.8803	130.1649	130.7043	131.2054	131.4421
	9	140.3477	140.7448	141.1291	141.5009	141.8605	142.2081	142.5439	142.8683	143.1814	143.7748	144.3260	144.5863
	10	154.3825	154.8192	155.2420	155.6510	156.0465	156.4289	156.7983	157.1551	157.4995	158.1523	158.7586	159.0449
12 Year Plan	1	59.6659	59.9214	60.1709	60.4148	60.6530	60.8857	61.1129	61.3347	61.5513	61.9688	62.3662	62.5576
	2	65.6325	65.9135	66.1880	66.4563	66.7183	66.9743	67.2242	67.4682	67.7064	68.1657	68.6028	68.8133
	3	72.1958	72.5048	72.8068	73.1019	73.3902	73.6717	73.9466	74.2150	74.4770	74.9823	75.4631	75.6947
	4	79.4154	79.7553	80.0875	80.4121	80.7292	81.0389	81.3413	81.6365	81.9248	82.4805	83.0094	83.2641
	5	87.3569	87.7309	88.0963	88.4533	88.8021	89.1428	89.4754	89.8002	90.1172	90.7286	91.3104	91.5905
	6	96.0926	96.5039	96.9059	97.2987	97.6823	98.0570	98.4230	98.7802	99.1290	99.8014	100.4414	100.7496
	7	105.7019	106.1543	106.5965	107.0285	107.4506	107.8627	108.2653	108.6582	109.0418	109.7815	110.4856	110.8245
	8	116.2720	116.7698	117.2562	117.7314	118.1956	118.6490	119.0918	119.5241	119.9460	120.7597	121.5341	121.9070
	9	127.8992	128.4467	128.9818	129.5045	130.0152	130.5139	131.0010	131.4765	131.9406	132.8357	133.6875	134.0977
	10	140.6892	141.2914	141.8799	142.4550	143.0167	143.5653	144.1011	144.6241	145.1347	146.1192	147.0563	147.5075
	11	154.7581	155.4206	156.0679	156.7005	157.3184	157.9218	158.5112	159.0865	159.6482	160.7312	161.7619	162.2582
	12	170.2339	170.9626	171.6747	172.3705	173.0502	173.7140	174.3623	174.9952	175.6130	176.8043	177.9381	178.4840
15 Year Plan	1	51.9754	52.3409	52.7015	53.0571	53.4079	53.7537	54.0945	54.4304	54.7614	55.4084	56.0355	56.3416
	2	57.1730	57.5750	57.9716	58.3628	58.7487	59.1290	59.5040	59.8735	60.2375	60.9492	61.6391	61.9757
	3	62.8903	63.3325	63.7688	64.1991	64.6235	65.0419	65.4544	65.8608	66.2613	67.0442	67.8030	68.1733
	4	69.1793	69.6657	70.1457	70.6190	71.0859	71.5461	71.9998	72.4469	72.8874	73.7486	74.5833	74.9906
	5	76.0972	76.6323	77.1602	77.6809	78.1945	78.7007	79.1998	79.6916	80.1762	81.1234	82.0416	82.4897
	6	83.7069	84.2955	84.8762	85.4490	86.0139	86.5708	87.1198	87.6608	88.1938	89.2358	90.2457	90.7387
	7	92.0776	92.7251	93.3639	93.9939	94.6153	95.2279	95.8318	96.4268	97.0132	98.1594	99.2703	99.8125
	8	101.2854	101.9976	102.7003	103.3933	104.0768	104.7507	105.4149	106.0695	106.7145	107.9753	109.1973	109.7938
	9	111.4139	112.1974	112.9703	113.7327	114.4845	115.2258	115.9564	116.6765	117.3859	118.7728	120.1171	120.7732
	10	122.5553	123.4171	124.2673	125.1059	125.9330	126.7483	127.5521	128.3441	129.1245	130.6501	132.1288	132.8505
	11	134.8109	135.7588	136.6940	137.6165	138.5262	139.4232	140.3073	141.1785	142.0370	143.7151	145.3417	146.1355
	12	148.2919	149.3347	150.3634	151.3782	152.3789	153.3655	154.3380	155.2964	156.2407	158.0866	159.8758	160.7491
	13	163.1211	164.2682	165.3998	166.5160	167.6168	168.7020	169.7718	170.8260	171.8647	173.8953	175.8634	176.8240
	14	179.4332	180.6950	181.9398	183.1676	184.3784	185.5722	186.7490	187.9086	189.0512	191.2848	193.4497	194.5064
	15	197.3766	198.7645	200.1337	201.4844	202.8163	204.1295	205.4239	206.6995	207.9563	210.4133	212.7947	213.9570

Entries are percentages of standard rent or price. The present value of a graduated series equals that of a normal series.

Graduated Rental Payments
Graduated Sales Prices

Annual Rate of Increase 10.0%

Plan	Year of Plan	6.00%	6.50%	7.00%	7.50%	8.00%	8.50%	9.00%	9.50%	10.00%	11.00%	12.00%	12.50%
							Interest Rate						
	1	33.1786	33.8765	34.5794	35.2865	35.9970	36.7100	37.4247	38.1402	38.8556	40.2825	41.6982	42.3998
	2	36.4965	37.2642	38.0374	38.8152	39.5967	40.3810	41.1672	41.9543	42.7412	44.3107	45.8681	46.6398
	3	40.1462	40.9906	41.8411	42.6967	43.5564	44.4192	45.2839	46.1497	47.0153	48.7418	50.4549	51.3038
	4	44.1608	45.0897	46.0252	46.9664	47.9120	48.8611	49.8123	50.7647	51.7168	53.6160	55.5004	56.4342
	5	48.5769	49.5986	50.6277	51.6630	52.7032	53.7472	54.7936	55.8411	56.8885	58.9776	61.0504	62.0776
	6	53.4345	54.5585	55.6905	56.8293	57.9735	59.1219	60.2729	61.4252	62.5774	64.8753	67.1554	68.2853
	7	58.7780	60.0143	61.2596	62.5122	63.7709	65.0341	66.3002	67.5678	68.8351	71.3629	73.8710	75.1139
	8	64.6558	66.0158	67.3855	68.7634	70.1480	71.5375	72.9302	74.3245	75.7186	78.4992	81.2581	82.6252
	9	71.1214	72.6174	74.1241	75.6398	77.1628	78.6912	80.2233	81.7570	83.2905	86.3491	89.3839	90.8878
	10	78.2335	79.8791	81.5365	83.2038	84.8791	86.5604	88.2456	89.9327	91.6195	94.9840	98.3223	99.9765
25 Year Plan	11	86.0569	87.8670	89.6901	91.5242	93.3670	95.2164	97.0702	98.9259	100.7815	104.4824	108.1545	109.9742
	12	94.6626	96.6537	98.6591	100.6766	102.7037	104.7380	106.7772	108.8185	110.8596	114.9306	118.9700	120.9716
	13	104.1288	106.3191	108.5250	110.7442	112.9740	115.2118	117.4549	119.7004	121.9456	126.4237	130.8670	133.0688
	14	114.5417	116.9510	119.3775	121.8186	124.2715	126.7330	129.2004	131.6704	134.1401	139.0660	143.9537	146.3757
	15	125.9959	128.6461	131.3153	134.0005	136.6986	139.4063	142.1204	144.8375	147.5541	152.9727	158.3490	161.0132
	16	138.5954	141.5107	144.4468	147.4006	150.3685	153.3470	156.3324	159.3212	162.3095	168.2699	174.1839	177.1146
	17	152.4550	155.6618	158.8915	162.1406	165.4053	168.6817	171.9657	175.2533	178.5405	185.0969	191.6023	194.8260
	18	167.7005	171.2279	174.7807	178.3547	181.9458	185.5498	189.1623	192.7787	196.3946	203.6066	210.7626	214.3086
	19	184.4705	188.3507	192.2587	196.1901	200.1404	204.1048	208.0785	212.0565	216.0340	223.9673	231.8388	235.7395
	20	202.9176	207.1858	211.4846	215.8092	220.1545	224.5153	228.8863	233.2622	237.6374	246.3640	255.0227	259.3134
	21	223.2093	227.9044	232.6331	237.3901	242.1699	246.9668	251.7750	256.5884	261.4011	271.0004	280.5250	285.2448
	22	245.5303	250.6948	255.8964	261.1291	266.3869	271.6635	276.9525	282.2473	287.5413	298.1004	308.5775	313.7692
	23	270.0833	275.7643	281.4860	287.2420	293.0256	298.8298	304.6477	310.4720	316.2954	327.9105	339.4352	345.1462
	24	297.0916	303.3407	309.6346	315.9662	322.3281	328.7128	335.1125	341.5192	347.9249	360.7015	373.3787	379.6608
	25	326.8008	333.6748	340.5981	347.5628	354.5610	361.5841	368.6237	375.6711	382.7174	396.7717	410.7166	417.6269
	1	26.6693	27.4883	28.3211	29.1664	30.0228	30.8888	31.7628	32.6432	33.5282	35.3057	37.0817	37.9650
	2	29.3363	30.2371	31.1532	32.0831	33.0251	33.9777	34.9391	35.9075	36.8811	38.8363	40.7899	41.7615
	3	32.2699	33.2609	34.2686	35.2914	36.3276	37.3755	38.4330	39.4982	40.5692	42.7199	44.8689	45.9376
	4	35.4969	36.5869	37.6954	38.8205	39.9604	41.1130	42.2763	43.4481	44.6261	46.9919	49.3558	50.5314
	5	39.0466	40.2456	41.4649	42.7026	43.9564	45.2243	46.5039	47.7929	49.0887	51.6911	54.2913	55.5846
	6	42.9512	44.2702	45.6114	46.9728	48.3521	49.7468	51.1543	52.5722	53.9976	56.8602	59.7205	61.1430
	7	47.2463	48.6972	50.1726	51.6701	53.1873	54.7214	56.2698	57.8294	59.3973	62.5463	65.6925	67.2573
	8	51.9710	53.5669	55.1898	56.8371	58.5060	60.1936	61.8967	63.6123	65.3371	68.8009	72.2618	73.9830
	9	57.1681	58.9236	60.7088	62.5208	64.3566	66.2129	68.0864	69.9735	71.8708	75.6810	79.4880	81.3813
	10	62.8849	64.8160	66.7797	68.7729	70.7923	72.8342	74.8950	76.9709	79.0579	83.2491	87.4368	89.5195
	11	69.1734	71.2976	73.4577	75.6502	77.8715	80.1176	82.3845	84.6680	86.9636	91.5740	96.1804	98.4714
	12	76.0907	78.4273	80.8035	83.2152	85.6587	88.1294	90.6230	93.1348	95.6600	100.7314	105.7985	108.3186
	13	83.6998	86.2701	88.8838	91.5368	94.2245	96.9423	99.6853	102.4483	105.2260	110.8045	116.3783	119.1504
	14	92.0697	94.8971	97.7722	100.6904	103.6470	106.6366	109.6538	112.6931	115.7486	121.8850	128.0162	131.0655
30 Year Plan	15	101.2767	104.3868	107.5494	110.7595	114.0117	117.3002	120.6192	123.9624	127.3235	134.0735	140.8178	144.1720
	16	111.4044	114.8255	118.3043	121.8354	125.4128	129.0303	132.6811	136.3586	140.0558	147.4808	154.8996	158.5892
	17	122.5448	126.3080	130.1348	134.0190	137.9541	141.9333	145.9492	149.9945	154.0614	162.2289	170.3895	174.4481
	18	134.7993	138.9388	143.1482	147.4209	151.7495	156.1266	160.5442	164.9940	169.4675	178.4518	187.4285	191.8930
	19	148.2793	152.8327	157.4631	162.1630	166.9245	171.7393	176.5986	181.4934	186.4143	196.2970	206.1713	211.0822
	20	163.1072	168.1160	173.2094	178.3793	183.6169	188.9132	194.2585	199.6427	205.0557	215.9267	226.7884	232.1905
	21	179.4179	184.9276	190.5303	196.2172	201.9786	207.8045	213.6843	219.6070	225.5613	237.5193	249.4673	255.4095
	22	197.3597	203.4203	209.5833	215.8389	222.1765	228.5850	235.0527	241.5677	248.1174	261.2713	274.4140	280.9505
	23	217.0957	223.7624	230.5417	237.4228	244.3941	251.4435	258.5580	265.7244	272.9292	287.3984	301.8554	309.0455
	24	238.8052	246.1386	253.5958	261.1651	268.8335	276.5878	284.4138	292.2969	300.2221	316.1383	332.0409	339.9501
	25	262.6857	270.7525	278.9554	287.2816	295.7169	304.2466	312.8552	321.5266	330.2443	347.7521	365.2450	373.9451
	26	288.9543	297.8277	306.8510	316.0097	325.2886	334.6713	344.1407	353.6792	363.2687	382.5273	401.7695	411.3396
	27	317.8497	327.6105	337.5361	347.6107	357.8175	368.1384	378.5548	389.0471	399.5956	420.7800	441.9465	452.4735
	28	349.6347	360.3715	371.2897	382.3718	393.5992	404.9522	416.4102	427.9518	439.5552	462.8580	486.1411	497.7209
	29	384.5982	396.4087	408.4186	420.6089	432.9591	445.4475	458.0513	470.7470	483.5107	509.1438	534.7553	547.4930
	30	423.0580	436.0496	449.2605	462.6698	476.2550	489.9922	503.8564	517.8217	531.8617	560.0582	588.2308	602.2423

Entries are percentages of standard rent or price. The present value of a graduated series equals that of a normal series.

Time When Given Mortgage Balance Occurs

5.50% Interest Rate

Amortization of Loan	90%	80%	75%	70%	60%	50%	40%	30%	25%	20%	10%	
5	0Y 7m	1Y 2m	1Y 5m	1Y 8m	2Y 3m	2Y 9m	3Y 2m	3Y 8m	3Y11m	4Y 2m	4Y 7m	5
7	0Y11m	1Y 8m	2Y 1m	2Y 5m	3Y 2m	3Y11m	4Y 7m	5Y 3m	5Y 6m	5Y10m	6Y 5m	7
10	1Y 4m	2Y 6m	3Y 1m	3Y 8m	4Y 9m	5Y 9m	6Y 8m	7Y 7m	7Y12m	8Y 5m	9Y 3m	10
12	1Y 8m	3Y 2m	3Y10m	4Y 6m	5Y10m	6Y12m	8Y 2m	9Y 2m	9Y 8m	10Y 2m	11Y 2m	12
15	2Y 3m	4Y 2m	5Y 1m	5Y11m	7Y 7m	9Y 1m	10Y 5m	11Y 8m	12Y 3m	12Y10m	13Y12m	15
18	2Y11m	5Y 4m	6Y 5m	7Y 6m	9Y 5m	11Y 2m	12Y 9m	14Y 3m	14Y11m	15Y 7m	16Y10m	18
20	3Y 4m	6Y 2m	7Y 5m	8Y 7m	10Y 9m	12Y 8m	14Y 5m	15Y12m	16Y 9m	17Y 5m	18Y 9m	20
22	3Y11m	7Y 1m	8Y 5m	9Y 9m	12Y 1m	14Y 2m	16Y 1m	17Y 9m	18Y 6m	19Y 3m	20Y 9m	22
25	4Y 9m	8Y 6m	10Y 1m	11Y 7m	14Y 3m	16Y 6m	18Y 7m	20Y 5m	21Y 3m	22Y 1m	23Y 8m	25
27	5Y 5m	9Y 6m	11Y 3m	12Y10m	15Y 8m	18Y 2m	20Y 4m	22Y 3m	23Y 2m	23Y12m	25Y 7m	27
30	6Y 5m	11Y 2m	13Y 1m	14Y10m	17Y12m	20Y 7m	22Y11m	24Y12m	25Y11m	26Y10m	28Y 6m	30
35	8Y 5m	14Y 1m	16Y 5m	18Y 6m	21Y12m	24Y11m	27Y 5m	29Y 8m	30Y 8m	31Y 8m	33Y 5m	35

5.75% Interest Rate

Amortization of Loan	90%	80%	75%	70%	60%	50%	40%	30%	25%	20%	10%	
5	0Y 7m	1Y 2m	1Y 5m	1Y 8m	2Y 3m	2Y 9m	3Y 3m	3Y 8m	3Y11m	4Y 2m	4Y 7m	5
7	0Y11m	1Y 8m	2Y 1m	2Y 5m	3Y 2m	3Y11m	4Y 7m	5Y 3m	5Y 6m	5Y10m	6Y 5m	7
10	1Y 4m	2Y 7m	3Y 2m	3Y 8m	4Y 9m	5Y 9m	6Y 8m	7Y 7m	7Y12m	8Y 5m	9Y 3m	10
12	1Y 8m	3Y 2m	3Y11m	4Y 7m	5Y10m	7Y 1m	8Y 2m	9Y 3m	9Y 9m	10Y 3m	11Y 2m	12
15	2Y 3m	4Y 3m	5Y 2m	5Y12m	7Y 8m	9Y 1m	10Y 6m	11Y 9m	12Y 4m	12Y11m	13Y12m	15
18	2Y11m	5Y 5m	6Y 7m	7Y 7m	9Y 6m	11Y 3m	12Y10m	14Y 4m	14Y12m	15Y 8m	16Y11m	18
20	3Y 5m	6Y 3m	7Y 6m	8Y 9m	10Y10m	12Y 9m	14Y 6m	16Y 1m	16Y 9m	17Y 6m	18Y10m	20
22	3Y12m	7Y 2m	8Y 7m	9Y11m	12Y 3m	14Y 4m	16Y 2m	17Y10m	18Y 7m	19Y 4m	20Y 9m	22
25	4Y11m	8Y 8m	10Y 3m	11Y 9m	14Y 5m	16Y 8m	18Y 8m	20Y 6m	21Y 4m	22Y 2m	23Y 8m	25
27	5Y 6m	9Y 9m	11Y 6m	13Y 1m	15Y11m	18Y 4m	20Y 5m	22Y 4m	23Y 3m	24Y 1m	25Y 7m	27
30	6Y 8m	11Y 5m	13Y 4m	15Y 2m	18Y 3m	20Y10m	23Y 1m	25Y 1m	25Y12m	26Y11m	28Y 7m	30
35	8Y 9m	14Y 6m	16Y 9m	18Y10m	22Y 3m	25Y 2m	27Y 8m	29Y10m	30Y 9m	31Y 9m	33Y 6m	35

6.00% Interest Rate

Amortization of Loan	90%	80%	75%	70%	60%	50%	40%	30%	25%	20%	10%	
5	0Y 7m	1Y 2m	1Y 5m	1Y 8m	2Y 3m	2Y 9m	3Y 3m	3Y 8m	3Y11m	4Y 2m	4Y 7m	5
7	0Y11m	1Y 8m	2Y 1m	2Y 6m	3Y 2m	3Y11m	4Y 7m	5Y 3m	5Y 7m	5Y10m	6Y 6m	7
10	1Y 4m	2Y 7m	3Y 2m	3Y 9m	4Y 9m	5Y 9m	6Y 9m	7Y 7m	8Y 1m	8Y 6m	9Y 3m	10
12	1Y 9m	3Y 3m	3Y11m	4Y 7m	5Y11m	7Y 1m	8Y 3m	9Y 3m	9Y 9m	10Y 3m	11Y 2m	12
15	2Y 4m	4Y 4m	5Y 3m	6Y 1m	7Y 8m	9Y 2m	10Y 6m	11Y 9m	12Y 4m	12Y11m	13Y12m	15
18	2Y12m	5Y 6m	6Y 8m	7Y 8m	9Y 8m	11Y 4m	12Y11m	14Y 4m	14Y12m	15Y 8m	16Y11m	18
20	3Y 6m	6Y 5m	7Y 8m	8Y10m	10Y12m	12Y10m	14Y 7m	16Y 1m	16Y10m	17Y 6m	18Y10m	20
22	4Y 1m	7Y 4m	8Y 9m	9Y12m	12Y 5m	14Y 5m	16Y 3m	17Y11m	18Y 8m	19Y 5m	20Y 9m	22
25	4Y12m	8Y10m	10Y 6m	11Y11m	14Y 7m	16Y10m	18Y10m	20Y 7m	21Y 5m	22Y 3m	23Y 8m	25
27	5Y 8m	9Y11m	11Y 8m	13Y 3m	16Y 1m	18Y 6m	20Y 7m	22Y 5m	23Y 4m	24Y 1m	25Y 8m	27
30	6Y10m	11Y 8m	13Y 8m	15Y 5m	18Y 5m	20Y12m	23Y 3m	25Y 3m	26Y 2m	26Y12m	28Y 7m	30
35	8Y12m	14Y10m	17Y 2m	19Y 2m	22Y 7m	25Y 5m	27Y10m	29Y11m	30Y11m	31Y10m	33Y 6m	35

6.25% Interest Rate

Amortization of Loan	90%	80%	75%	70%	60%	50%	40%	30%	25%	20%	10%	
5	0Y 7m	1Y 2m	1Y 5m	1Y 9m	2Y 3m	2Y 9m	3Y 3m	3Y 8m	3Y11m	4Y 2m	4Y 7m	5
7	0Y11m	1Y 8m	2Y 1m	2Y 6m	3Y 3m	3Y11m	4Y 7m	5Y 3m	5Y 7m	5Y10m	6Y 6m	7
10	1Y 4m	2Y 7m	3Y 2m	3Y 9m	4Y10m	5Y10m	6Y 9m	7Y 8m	8Y 1m	8Y 6m	9Y 3m	10
12	1Y 9m	3Y 3m	3Y12m	4Y 8m	5Y11m	7Y 2m	8Y 3m	9Y 3m	9Y 9m	10Y 3m	11Y 2m	12
15	2Y 4m	4Y 4m	5Y 3m	6Y 2m	7Y 9m	9Y 3m	10Y 7m	11Y10m	12Y 5m	12Y12m	13Y12m	15
18	3Y 1m	5Y 7m	6Y 9m	7Y10m	9Y 9m	11Y 5m	12Y12m	14Y 5m	15Y 1m	15Y 9m	16Y11m	18
20	3Y 7m	6Y 6m	7Y 9m	8Y12m	11Y 1m	12Y12m	14Y 8m	16Y 2m	16Y11m	17Y 7m	18Y10m	20
22	4Y 2m	7Y 6m	8Y11m	10Y 2m	12Y 6m	14Y 7m	16Y 4m	17Y12m	18Y 9m	19Y 5m	20Y10m	22
25	5Y 2m	8Y12m	10Y 8m	12Y 2m	14Y 9m	16Y12m	18Y11m	20Y 8m	21Y 6m	22Y 3m	23Y 9m	25
27	5Y10m	10Y 2m	11Y11m	13Y 6m	16Y 3m	18Y 8m	20Y 9m	22Y 7m	23Y 5m	24Y 2m	25Y 8m	27
30	7Y 1m	11Y11m	13Y11m	15Y 8m	18Y 8m	21Y 3m	23Y 5m	25Y 4m	26Y 3m	27Y 1m	28Y 7m	30
35	9Y 4m	15Y 2m	17Y 6m	19Y 6m	22Y10m	25Y 8m	27Y12m	30Y 1m	30Y12m	31Y11m	33Y 7m	35

6.50% Interest Rate

Amortization of Loan	90%	80%	75%	70%	60%	50%	40%	30%	25%	20%	10%	
5	0Y 7m	1Y 2m	1Y 5m	1Y 9m	2Y 3m	2Y 9m	3Y 3m	3Y 8m	3Y11m	4Y 2m	4Y 7m	5
7	0Y11m	1Y 9m	2Y 1m	2Y 6m	3Y 3m	3Y11m	4Y 7m	5Y 3m	5Y 7m	5Y10m	6Y 6m	7
10	1Y 5m	2Y 8m	3Y 3m	3Y 9m	4Y10m	5Y10m	6Y 9m	7Y 8m	8Y 1m	8Y 6m	9Y 3m	10
12	1Y 9m	3Y 4m	3Y12m	4Y 8m	5Y12m	7Y 2m	8Y 3m	9Y 4m	9Y10m	10Y 3m	11Y 2m	12
15	2Y 5m	4Y 5m	5Y 4m	6Y 3m	7Y10m	9Y 4m	10Y 8m	11Y10m	12Y 5m	12Y12m	14Y 1m	15
18	3Y 1m	5Y 8m	6Y10m	7Y11m	9Y10m	11Y 6m	13Y 1m	14Y 6m	15Y 2m	15Y 9m	16Y11m	18
20	3Y 8m	6Y 7m	7Y11m	9Y 1m	11Y 3m	13Y 1m	14Y 9m	16Y 3m	16Y11m	17Y 7m	18Y11m	20
22	4Y 3m	7Y 7m	8Y12m	10Y 4m	12Y 8m	14Y 8m	16Y 5m	18Y 1m	18Y10m	19Y 6m	20Y10m	22
25	5Y 4m	9Y 2m	10Y10m	12Y 4m	14Y11m	17Y 2m	19Y 1m	20Y10m	21Y 7m	22Y 4m	23Y 9m	25
27	6Y 1m	10Y 4m	12Y 2m	13Y 9m	16Y 6m	18Y10m	20Y10m	22Y 8m	23Y 6m	24Y 3m	25Y 9m	27
30	7Y 3m	12Y 2m	14Y 2m	15Y11m	18Y11m	21Y 5m	23Y 7m	25Y 5m	26Y 4m	27Y 2m	28Y 8m	30
35	9Y 8m	15Y 7m	17Y10m	19Y10m	23Y 2m	25Y10m	28Y 2m	30Y 3m	31Y 2m	31Y12m	33Y 7m	35

Entry is the month when balance will pass though selected percentage balance.

Time When Given Mortgage Balance Occurs

6.75% Interest Rate

Amortization of Loan	Unpaid Balance of Loan 90%	80%	75%	70%	60%	50%	40%	30%	25%	20%	10%	
5	0Y 7m	1Y 2m	1Y 5m	1Y 9m	2Y 3m	2Y 9m	3Y 3m	3Y 9m	3Y11m	4Y 2m	4Y 7m	5
7	0Y11m	1Y 9m	2Y 1m	2Y 6m	3Y 3m	3Y11m	4Y 7m	5Y 3m	5Y 7m	5Y11m	6Y 6m	7
10	1Y 5m	2Y 8m	3Y 3m	3Y10m	4Y10m	5Y10m	6Y10m	7Y 8m	8Y 1m	8Y 6m	9Y 4m	10
12	1Y 9m	3Y 4m	4Y 1m	4Y 9m	5Y12m	7Y 3m	8Y 4m	9Y 4m	9Y10m	10Y 4m	11Y 2m	12
15	2Y 5m	4Y 6m	5Y 5m	6Y 4m	7Y11m	9Y 4m	10Y 8m	11Y11m	12Y 6m	12Y12m	14Y 1m	15
18	3Y 2m	5Y 9m	6Y11m	7Y12m	9Y11m	11Y 7m	13Y 2m	14Y 6m	15Y 2m	15Y10m	16Y12m	18
20	3Y 9m	6Y 9m	7Y12m	9Y 2m	11Y 4m	13Y 2m	14Y10m	16Y 4m	16Y12m	17Y 8m	18Y11m	20
22	4Y 5m	7Y 9m	9Y 2m	10Y 6m	12Y 9m	14Y 9m	16Y 7m	18Y 1m	18Y10m	19Y 7m	20Y10m	22
25	5Y 5m	9Y 5m	10Y12m	12Y 6m	15Y 1m	17Y 3m	19Y 2m	20Y11m	21Y 8m	22Y 5m	23Y 9m	25
27	6Y 3m	10Y 7m	12Y 4m	13Y11m	16Y 8m	18Y12m	20Y12m	22Y 9m	23Y 7m	24Y 4m	25Y 9m	27
30	7Y 6m	12Y 6m	14Y 5m	16Y 2m	19Y 2m	21Y 7m	23Y 9m	25Y 7m	26Y 5m	27Y 3m	28Y 8m	30
35	9Y12m	15Y11m	18Y 2m	20Y 1m	23Y 5m	26Y 1m	28Y 4m	30Y 4m	31Y 3m	32Y 1m	33Y 8m	35

7.00% Interest Rate

Amortization of Loan	90%	80%	75%	70%	60%	50%	40%	30%	25%	20%	10%	
5	0Y 8m	1Y 2m	1Y 6m	1Y 9m	2Y 3m	2Y 9m	3Y 3m	3Y 9m	3Y11m	4Y 2m	4Y 7m	5
7	0Y11m	1Y 9m	2Y 2m	2Y 6m	3Y 3m	3Y12m	4Y 8m	5Y 3m	5Y 7m	5Y11m	6Y 6m	7
10	1Y 5m	2Y 8m	3Y 3m	3Y10m	4Y11m	5Y11m	6Y10m	7Y 8m	8Y 1m	8Y 6m	9Y 4m	10
12	1Y10m	3Y 5m	4Y 1m	4Y10m	6Y 1m	7Y 3m	8Y 4m	9Y 4m	9Y10m	10Y 4m	11Y 2m	12
15	2Y 6m	4Y 7m	5Y 6m	6Y 4m	7Y12m	9Y 5m	10Y 7m	11Y11m	12Y 6m	13Y 1m	14Y 1m	15
18	3Y 3m	5Y10m	6Y12m	8Y 1m	9Y12m	11Y 8m	13Y 3m	14Y 7m	15Y 3m	15Y10m	16Y12m	18
20	3Y10m	6Y10m	8Y 2m	9Y 4m	11Y 5m	13Y 3m	14Y11m	16Y 5m	17Y 1m	17Y 8m	18Y11m	20
22	4Y 6m	7Y11m	9Y 4m	10Y 7m	12Y11m	14Y11m	16Y 8m	18Y 2m	18Y11m	19Y 7m	20Y10m	22
25	5Y 7m	9Y 7m	11Y 3m	12Y 8m	15Y 3m	17Y 5m	19Y 4m	20Y12m	21Y 9m	22Y 5m	23Y10m	25
27	6Y 5m	10Y 9m	12Y 7m	14Y 2m	16Y10m	19Y 2m	21Y 1m	22Y10m	23Y 8m	24Y 5m	25Y 9m	27
30	7Y 9m	12Y 9m	14Y 8m	16Y 5m	19Y 4m	21Y 9m	23Y10m	25Y 9m	26Y 6m	27Y 3m	28Y 9m	30
35	10Y 4m	16Y 3m	18Y 6m	20Y 5m	23Y 8m	26Y 4m	28Y 6m	30Y 5m	31Y 4m	32Y 2m	33Y 8m	35

7.25% Interest Rate

Amortization of Loan	90%	80%	75%	70%	60%	50%	40%	30%	25%	20%	10%	
5	0Y 8m	1Y 2m	1Y 6m	1Y 9m	2Y 3m	2Y 9m	3Y 3m	3Y 9m	3Y11m	4Y 2m	4Y 7m	5
7	0Y11m	1Y 9m	2Y 2m	2Y 6m	3Y 3m	3Y12m	4Y 8m	5Y 3m	5Y 7m	5Y11m	6Y 6m	7
10	1Y 5m	2Y 8m	3Y 4m	3Y10m	4Y11m	5Y11m	6Y10m	7Y 9m	8Y 2m	8Y 6m	9Y 4m	10
12	1Y10m	3Y 5m	4Y 2m	4Y10m	6Y 2m	7Y 4m	8Y 5m	9Y 5m	9Y10m	10Y 4m	11Y 3m	12
15	2Y 6m	4Y 7m	5Y 7m	6Y 5m	7Y12m	9Y 6m	10Y 9m	11Y12m	12Y 6m	13Y 1m	14Y 1m	15
18	3Y 4m	5Y12m	7Y 1m	8Y 2m	10Y 1m	11Y 9m	13Y 3m	14Y 8m	15Y 3m	15Y10m	16Y12m	18
20	3Y11m	6Y12m	8Y 3m	9Y 5m	11Y 7m	13Y 5m	14Y12m	16Y 5m	17Y 1m	17Y 9m	18Y11m	20
22	4Y 7m	7Y12m	9Y 6m	10Y 9m	13Y 1m	14Y12m	16Y 9m	18Y 3m	18Y12m	19Y 8m	20Y11m	22
25	5Y 9m	9Y 9m	11Y 5m	12Y10m	15Y 5m	17Y 7m	19Y 5m	21Y 1m	21Y10m	22Y 6m	23Y10m	25
27	6Y 7m	10Y12m	12Y 9m	14Y 4m	16Y12m	19Y 3m	21Y 3m	22Y11m	23Y 8m	24Y 5m	25Y10m	27
30	7Y12m	12Y12m	14Y11m	16Y 8m	19Y 7m	21Y11m	23Y12m	25Y 9m	26Y 7m	27Y 4m	28Y 9m	30
35	10Y 8m	16Y 7m	18Y10m	20Y 9m	23Y11m	26Y 6m	28Y 8m	30Y 7m	31Y 5m	32Y 3m	33Y 8m	35

7.50% Interest Rate

Amortization of Loan	90%	80%	75%	70%	60%	50%	40%	30%	25%	20%	10%	
5	0Y 8m	1Y 2m	1Y 6m	1Y 9m	2Y 3m	2Y 9m	3Y 3m	3Y 9m	3Y11m	4Y 2m	4Y 7m	5
7	0Y11m	1Y 9m	2Y 2m	2Y 7m	3Y 4m	3Y12m	4Y 8m	5Y 4m	5Y 7m	5Y11m	6Y 6m	7
10	1Y 5m	2Y 9m	3Y 4m	3Y11m	4Y12m	5Y11m	6Y11m	7Y 9m	8Y 2m	8Y 7m	9Y 4m	10
12	1Y10m	3Y 5m	4Y 2m	4Y11m	6Y 2m	7Y 4m	8Y 5m	9Y 5m	9Y11m	10Y 4m	11Y 3m	12
15	2Y 7m	4Y 8m	5Y 7m	6Y 6m	8Y 1m	9Y 6m	10Y10m	11Y12m	12Y 7m	13Y 1m	14Y 1m	15
18	3Y 5m	6Y 1m	7Y 3m	8Y 3m	10Y 2m	11Y10m	13Y 4m	14Y 8m	15Y 4m	15Y11m	16Y12m	18
20	3Y12m	7Y 1m	8Y 5m	9Y 7m	11Y 8m	13Y 6m	15Y 1m	16Y 6m	17Y 2m	17Y 9m	18Y12m	20
22	4Y 9m	8Y 2m	9Y 7m	10Y11m	13Y 2m	15Y 2m	16Y10m	18Y 4m	18Y12m	19Y 8m	20Y11m	22
25	5Y11m	9Y11m	11Y 7m	13Y 1m	15Y 7m	17Y 8m	19Y 6m	21Y 2m	21Y10m	22Y 7m	23Y10m	25
27	6Y 9m	11Y 3m	12Y12m	14Y 7m	17Y 3m	19Y 5m	21Y 4m	22Y12m	23Y 9m	24Y 6m	25Y10m	27
30	8Y 3m	13Y 3m	15Y 2m	16Y11m	19Y 9m	22Y 1m	24Y 1m	25Y10m	26Y 8m	27Y 5m	28Y 9m	30
35	10Y12m	16Y11m	19Y 2m	21Y 1m	24Y 2m	26Y 6m	28Y10m	30Y 8m	31Y 6m	32Y 4m	33Y 9m	35

7.75% Interest Rate

Amortization of Loan	90%	80%	75%	70%	60%	50%	40%	30%	25%	20%	10%	
5	0Y 8m	1Y 2m	1Y 6m	1Y 9m	2Y 3m	2Y 9m	3Y 3m	3Y 9m	3Y12m	4Y 2m	4Y 7m	5
7	0Y11m	1Y 9m	2Y 2m	2Y 7m	3Y 4m	3Y12m	4Y 8m	5Y 4m	5Y 7m	5Y11m	6Y 6m	7
10	1Y 6m	2Y 9m	3Y 4m	3Y11m	4Y12m	5Y12m	6Y11m	7Y 9m	8Y 2m	8Y 7m	9Y 4m	10
12	1Y11m	3Y 6m	4Y 3m	4Y11m	6Y 3m	7Y 5m	8Y 6m	9Y 5m	9Y11m	10Y 4m	11Y 3m	12
15	2Y 7m	4Y 9m	5Y 8m	6Y 7m	8Y 2m	9Y 7m	10Y11m	12Y 1m	12Y 7m	13Y 2m	14Y 1m	15
18	3Y 5m	6Y 2m	7Y 4m	8Y 5m	10Y 3m	11Y11m	13Y 5m	14Y 9m	15Y 4m	15Y11m	16Y12m	18
20	4Y 1m	7Y 2m	8Y 6m	9Y 8m	11Y 9m	13Y 7m	15Y 2m	16Y 7m	17Y 2m	17Y10m	18Y12m	20
22	4Y10m	8Y 4m	9Y 9m	11Y 1m	13Y 4m	15Y 3m	16Y11m	18Y 5m	19Y 1m	19Y 9m	20Y11m	22
25	6Y 1m	10Y 2m	11Y 9m	13Y 3m	15Y 9m	17Y10m	19Y 7m	21Y 2m	21Y11m	22Y 7m	23Y11m	25
27	6Y11m	11Y 5m	13Y 2m	14Y 9m	17Y 5m	19Y 7m	21Y 6m	23Y 1m	23Y10m	24Y 7m	25Y10m	27
30	8Y 5m	13Y 6m	15Y 5m	17Y 2m	19Y12m	22Y 3m	24Y 3m	25Y12m	26Y 9m	27Y 6m	28Y10m	30
35	11Y 4m	17Y 3m	19Y 6m	21Y 4m	24Y 5m	26Y11m	28Y12m	30Y 9m	31Y 7m	32Y 4m	33Y 9m	35

Entry is the month when balance will pass though selected percentage balance.

Time When Given Mortgage Balance Occurs

8.00% Interest Rate

Amortization of Loan	90%	80%	75%	70%	60%	50%	40%	30%	25%	20%	10%	
5	0Y 8m	1Y 3m	1Y 6m	1Y 9m	2Y 3m	2Y 9m	3Y 3m	3Y 9m	3Y12m	4Y 2m	4Y 7m	5
7	0Y11m	1Y 9m	2Y 2m	2Y 7m	3Y 4m	3Y12m	4Y 8m	5Y 4m	5Y 7m	5Y11m	6Y 6m	7
10	1Y 6m	2Y 9m	3Y 5m	3Y11m	4Y12m	5Y12m	6Y11m	7Y 9m	8Y 2m	8Y 7m	9Y 4m	10
12	1Y11m	3Y 6m	4Y 3m	4Y12m	6Y 3m	7Y 5m	8Y 6m	9Y 6m	9Y11m	10Y 5m	11Y 3m	12
15	2Y 8m	4Y10m	5Y 9m	6Y 8m	8Y 3m	9Y 8m	10Y11m	12Y 1m	12Y 8m	13Y 2m	14Y 2m	15
18	3Y 6m	6Y 3m	7Y 5m	8Y 6m	10Y 5m	11Y12m	13Y 6m	14Y 9m	15Y 5m	15Y12m	17Y 1m	18
20	4Y 2m	7Y 4m	8Y 7m	9Y10m	11Y11m	13Y 8m	15Y 3m	16Y 7m	17Y 3m	17Y10m	18Y12m	20
22	4Y11m	8Y 5m	9Y11m	11Y 2m	13Y 5m	15Y 4m	16Y12m	18Y 6m	19Y 2m	19Y 9m	20Y12m	22
25	6Y 2m	10Y 4m	11Y11m	13Y 5m	15Y11m	17Y11m	19Y 9m	21Y 3m	21Y12m	22Y 8m	23Y11m	25
27	7Y 2m	11Y 8m	13Y 5m	14Y11m	17Y 7m	19Y 9m	21Y 7m	23Y 2m	23Y11m	24Y 7m	25Y11m	27
30	8Y 8m	13Y 9m	15Y 8m	17Y 4m	20Y 2m	22Y 5m	24Y 5m	26Y 1m	26Y10m	27Y 6m	28Y10m	30
35	11Y 8m	17Y 7m	19Y 9m	21Y 7m	24Y 8m	27Y 1m	29Y 2m	30Y11m	31Y 8m	32Y 5m	33Y10m	35

8.25% Interest Rate

Amortization of Loan	90%	80%	75%	70%	60%	50%	40%	30%	25%	20%	10%	
5	0Y 8m	1Y 3m	1Y 6m	1Y 9m	2Y 4m	2Y10m	3Y 3m	3Y 9m	3Y12m	4Y 2m	4Y 7m	5
7	0Y11m	1Y10m	2Y 2m	2Y 7m	3Y 4m	3Y12m	4Y 8m	5Y 4m	5Y 8m	5Y11m	6Y 6m	7
10	1Y 6m	2Y10m	3Y 5m	3Y12m	5Y 1m	5Y12m	6Y11m	7Y10m	8Y 2m	8Y 7m	9Y 4m	10
12	1Y11m	3Y 7m	4Y 4m	4Y12m	6Y 4m	7Y 6m	8Y 6m	9Y 6m	9Y11m	10Y 5m	11Y 3m	12
15	2Y 8m	4Y10m	5Y10m	6Y 8m	8Y 4m	9Y 9m	10Y12m	12Y 2m	12Y 8m	13Y 2m	14Y 2m	15
18	3Y 7m	6Y 4m	7Y 6m	8Y 7m	10Y 6m	12Y 1m	13Y 7m	14Y10m	15Y 5m	15Y12m	17Y 1m	18
20	4Y 3m	7Y 5m	8Y 9m	9Y11m	11Y12m	13Y 9m	15Y 4m	16Y 8m	17Y 4m	17Y11m	18Y12m	20
22	5Y 1m	8Y 7m	10Y 1m	11Y 4m	13Y 7m	15Y 5m	17Y 1m	18Y 6m	19Y 2m	19Y10m	20Y12m	22
25	6Y 4m	10Y 6m	12Y 2m	13Y 7m	15Y12m	18Y 1m	19Y10m	21Y 4m	22Y 1m	22Y 9m	23Y11m	25
27	7Y 4m	11Y10m	13Y 7m	15Y 2m	17Y 9m	19Y10m	21Y 8m	23Y 3m	23Y12m	24Y 8m	25Y11m	27
30	8Y11m	13Y12m	15Y11m	17Y 7m	20Y 4m	22Y 7m	24Y 6m	26Y 2m	26Y11m	27Y 7m	28Y10m	30
35	11Y12m	17Y11m	20Y 1m	21Y11m	24Y11m	27Y 3m	29Y 3m	30Y12m	31Y 9m	32Y 6m	33Y10m	35

8.50% Interest Rate

Amortization of Loan	90%	80%	75%	70%	60%	50%	40%	30%	25%	20%	10%	
5	0Y 8m	1Y 3m	1Y 6m	1Y 9m	2Y 4m	2Y10m	3Y 3m	3Y 9m	3Y12m	4Y 2m	4Y 8m	5
7	0Y12m	1Y10m	2Y 3m	2Y 7m	3Y 4m	4Y 1m	4Y 9m	5Y 4m	5Y 8m	5Y11m	6Y 6m	7
10	1Y 6m	2Y10m	3Y 5m	3Y12m	5Y 1m	6Y 1m	6Y12m	7Y10m	8Y 3m	8Y 7m	9Y 4m	10
12	1Y12m	3Y 7m	4Y 4m	5Y 1m	6Y 4m	7Y 6m	8Y 7m	9Y 6m	9Y12m	10Y 5m	11Y 3m	12
15	2Y 9m	4Y11m	5Y11m	6Y 9m	8Y 4m	9Y 9m	10Y12m	12Y 2m	12Y 8m	13Y 2m	14Y 2m	15
18	3Y 8m	6Y 5m	7Y 7m	8Y 8m	10Y 7m	12Y 2m	13Y 7m	14Y11m	15Y 6m	15Y12m	17Y 1m	18
20	4Y 5m	7Y 7m	8Y10m	9Y12m	12Y 1m	13Y10m	15Y 5m	16Y 9m	17Y 4m	17Y11m	18Y12m	20
22	5Y 2m	8Y 9m	10Y 2m	11Y 6m	13Y 8m	15Y 7m	17Y 2m	18Y 7m	19Y 3m	19Y10m	20Y12m	22
25	6Y 6m	10Y 8m	12Y 4m	13Y 9m	16Y 2m	18Y 2m	19Y11m	21Y 5m	22Y 1m	22Y 9m	23Y11m	25
27	7Y 6m	12Y 1m	13Y10m	15Y 4m	17Y11m	19Y12m	21Y 9m	23Y 4m	23Y12m	24Y 8m	25Y11m	27
30	9Y 2m	14Y 3m	16Y 2m	17Y10m	20Y 7m	22Y 9m	24Y 7m	26Y 3m	26Y11m	27Y 8m	28Y11m	30
35	12Y 4m	18Y 3m	20Y 4m	22Y 2m	25Y 1m	27Y 5m	29Y 5m	31Y 1m	31Y10m	32Y 7m	33Y10m	35

8.75% Interest Rate

Amortization of Loan	90%	80%	75%	70%	60%	50%	40%	30%	25%	20%	10%	
5	0Y 8m	1Y 3m	1Y 6m	1Y 9m	2Y 4m	2Y10m	3Y 4m	3Y 9m	3Y12m	4Y 2m	4Y 8m	5
7	0Y12m	1Y10m	2Y 3m	2Y 7m	3Y 4m	4Y 1m	4Y 9m	5Y 4m	5Y 8m	5Y11m	6Y 6m	7
10	1Y 6m	2Y10m	3Y 6m	4Y 1m	5Y 1m	6Y 1m	6Y12m	7Y10m	8Y 3m	8Y 7m	9Y 4m	10
12	1Y12m	3Y 8m	4Y 5m	5Y 1m	6Y 5m	7Y 7m	8Y 7m	9Y 7m	9Y12m	10Y 5m	11Y 3m	12
15	2Y 9m	4Y12m	5Y11m	6Y10m	8Y 5m	9Y10m	11Y 1m	12Y 2m	12Y 9m	13Y 3m	14Y 2m	15
18	3Y 9m	6Y 6m	7Y 8m	8Y 9m	10Y 8m	12Y 3m	13Y 8m	14Y11m	15Y 6m	16Y 1m	17Y 1m	18
20	4Y 6m	7Y 8m	8Y12m	10Y 2m	12Y 2m	13Y11m	15Y 5m	16Y 9m	17Y 5m	17Y12m	19Y 1m	20
22	5Y 4m	8Y11m	10Y 4m	11Y 7m	13Y10m	15Y 8m	17Y 3m	18Y 8m	19Y 3m	19Y11m	20Y12m	22
25	6Y 8m	10Y10m	12Y 6m	13Y11m	16Y 4m	18Y 4m	19Y12m	21Y 6m	22Y 2m	22Y10m	23Y12m	25
27	7Y 9m	12Y 3m	13Y12m	15Y 6m	18Y 1m	20Y 2m	21Y11m	23Y 5m	24Y 1m	24Y 9m	25Y11m	27
30	9Y 5m	14Y 6m	16Y 5m	17Y12m	20Y 9m	22Y11m	24Y 9m	26Y 4m	26Y12m	27Y 8m	28Y11m	30
35	12Y 8m	18Y 7m	20Y 8m	22Y 5m	25Y 4m	27Y 7m	29Y 7m	31Y 2m	31Y11m	32Y 7m	33Y11m	35

9.00% Interest Rate

Amortization of Loan	90%	80%	75%	70%	60%	50%	40%	30%	25%	20%	10%	
5	0Y 8m	1Y 3m	1Y 6m	1Y 9m	2Y 4m	2Y10m	3Y 4m	3Y 9m	3Y12m	4Y 2m	4Y 8m	5
7	0Y12m	1Y10m	2Y 3m	2Y 8m	3Y 5m	4Y 1m	4Y 9m	5Y 4m	5Y 8m	5Y11m	6Y 6m	7
10	1Y 7m	2Y11m	3Y 6m	4Y 1m	5Y 2m	6Y 2m	6Y12m	7Y10m	8Y 3m	8Y 8m	9Y 4m	10
12	1Y12m	3Y 8m	4Y 5m	5Y 2m	6Y 5m	7Y 7m	8Y 8m	9Y 7m	9Y12m	10Y 6m	11Y 3m	12
15	2Y10m	5Y 1m	5Y12m	6Y11m	8Y 6m	9Y11m	11Y 2m	12Y 3m	12Y 9m	13Y 3m	14Y 2m	15
18	3Y10m	6Y 8m	7Y10m	8Y10m	10Y 9m	12Y 4m	13Y 9m	14Y12m	15Y 7m	16Y 1m	17Y 1m	18
20	4Y 7m	7Y 9m	9Y 1m	10Y 3m	12Y 4m	13Y12m	15Y 6m	16Y10m	17Y 5m	17Y12m	19Y 1m	20
22	5Y 5m	8Y12m	10Y 6m	11Y 9m	13Y11m	15Y 9m	17Y 4m	18Y 9m	19Y 4m	19Y11m	20Y12m	22
25	6Y10m	11Y 1m	12Y 8m	14Y 1m	16Y 6m	18Y 5m	20Y 1m	21Y 7m	22Y 3m	22Y10m	23Y12m	25
27	7Y11m	12Y 6m	14Y 3m	15Y 9m	18Y 3m	20Y 4m	21Y12m	23Y 6m	24Y 2m	24Y10m	25Y12m	27
30	9Y 8m	14Y 9m	16Y 8m	18Y 3m	20Y11m	23Y 1m	24Y10m	26Y 5m	27Y 1m	27Y 9m	28Y11m	30
35	12Y12m	18Y11m	20Y11m	22Y 8m	25Y 6m	27Y 9m	29Y 8m	31Y 3m	31Y12m	32Y 8m	33Y11m	35

Entry is the month when balance will pass though selected percentage balance.

Time When Given Mortgage Balance Occurs

9.25% Interest Rate

Amortization of Loan	90%	80%	75%	Unpaid Balance of Loan 70%	60%	50%	40%	30%	25%	20%	10%	
5	0Y 8m	1Y 3m	1Y 6m	1Y10m	2Y 4m	2Y10m	3Y 4m	3Y 9m	3Y12m	4Y 3m	4Y 8m	5
7	0Y12m	1Y10m	2Y 3m	2Y 8m	3Y 5m	4Y 1m	4Y 9m	5Y 4m	5Y 8m	5Y11m	6Y 6m	7
10	1Y 7m	2Y11m	3Y 6m	4Y 1m	5Y 2m	6Y 2m	7Y 1m	7Y11m	8Y 3m	8Y 8m	9Y 4m	10
12	1Y12m	3Y 9m	4Y 6m	5Y 2m	6Y 6m	7Y 7m	8Y 8m	9Y 7m	10Y 1m	10Y 6m	11Y 3m	12
15	2Y11m	5Y 1m	6Y 1m	6Y12m	8Y 7m	9Y11m	11Y 2m	12Y 3m	12Y10m	13Y 3m	14Y 2m	15
18	3Y11m	6Y 9m	7Y11m	8Y12m	10Y10m	12Y 5m	13Y10m	14Y12m	15Y 7m	16Y 1m	17Y 2m	18
20	4Y 8m	7Y11m	9Y 3m	10Y 5m	12Y 5m	14Y 1m	15Y 7m	16Y11m	17Y 6m	17Y12m	19Y 1m	20
22	5Y 6m	9Y 2m	10Y 7m	11Y11m	14Y 1m	15Y10m	17Y 5m	18Y 9m	19Y 5m	19Y12m	21Y 1m	22
25	6Y12m	11Y 3m	12Y10m	14Y 3m	16Y 7m	18Y 7m	20Y 2m	21Y 8m	22Y 3m	22Y11m	23Y12m	25
27	8Y 1m	12Y 8m	14Y 5m	15Y11m	18Y 4m	20Y 5m	22Y 1m	23Y 7m	24Y 3m	24Y10m	25Y12m	27
30	9Y11m	14Y12m	16Y11m	18Y 5m	21Y 1m	23Y 2m	24Y11m	26Y 6m	27Y 2m	27Y 9m	28Y12m	30
35	13Y 4m	19Y 2m	21Y 3m	22Y11m	25Y 9m	27Y11m	29Y 9m	31Y 4m	32Y 1m	32Y 9m	33Y11m	35

9.50% Interest Rate

Amortization of Loan	90%	80%	75%	70%	60%	50%	40%	30%	25%	20%	10%	
5	0Y 8m	1Y 3m	1Y 6m	1Y10m	2Y 4m	2Y10m	3Y 4m	3Y 9m	3Y12m	4Y 3m	4Y 8m	5
7	0Y12m	1Y10m	2Y 3m	2Y 8m	3Y 5m	4Y 1m	4Y 9m	5Y 5m	5Y 8m	5Y12m	6Y 6m	7
10	1Y 7m	2Y11m	3Y 7m	4Y 2m	5Y 2m	6Y 2m	7Y 1m	7Y11m	8Y 3m	8Y 8m	9Y 4m	10
12	2Y 1m	3Y 9m	4Y 6m	5Y 3m	6Y 6m	7Y 8m	8Y 8m	9Y 8m	10Y 1m	10Y 6m	11Y 4m	12
15	2Y11m	5Y 2m	6Y 2m	7Y 1m	8Y 8m	9Y12m	11Y 3m	12Y 4m	12Y10m	13Y 4m	14Y 3m	15
18	3Y12m	6Y10m	7Y12m	9Y 1m	10Y11m	12Y 6m	13Y10m	15Y 1m	15Y 7m	16Y 2m	17Y 2m	18
20	4Y 9m	7Y12m	9Y 4m	10Y 6m	12Y 6m	14Y 2m	15Y 8m	16Y11m	17Y 6m	18Y 1m	19Y 1m	20
22	5Y 8m	9Y 4m	10Y 9m	11Y12m	14Y 2m	15Y12m	17Y 6m	18Y10m	19Y 5m	19Y12m	21Y 1m	22
25	7Y 2m	11Y 5m	12Y12m	14Y 5m	16Y 9m	18Y 8m	20Y 3m	21Y 8m	22Y 4m	22Y11m	23Y12m	25
27	8Y 4m	12Y11m	14Y 7m	16Y 1m	18Y 6m	20Y 6m	22Y 2m	23Y 7m	24Y 3m	24Y11m	25Y12m	27
30	10Y 2m	15Y 3m	17Y 1m	18Y 8m	21Y 3m	23Y 4m	25Y 1m	26Y 6m	27Y 2m	27Y10m	28Y12m	30
35	13Y 8m	19Y 6m	21Y 6m	23Y 2m	25Y11m	28Y 1m	29Y11m	31Y 5m	32Y 2m	32Y 9m	33Y12m	35

9.75% Interest Rate

Amortization of Loan	90%	80%	75%	70%	60%	50%	40%	30%	25%	20%	10%	
5	0Y 8m	1Y 3m	1Y 6m	1Y10m	2Y 4m	2Y10m	3Y 4m	3Y 9m	3Y12m	4Y 3m	4Y 8m	5
7	0Y12m	1Y10m	2Y 3m	2Y 8m	3Y 5m	4Y 2m	4Y 9m	5Y 5m	5Y 8m	5Y12m	6Y 6m	7
10	1Y 7m	2Y12m	3Y 7m	4Y 2m	5Y 3m	6Y 3m	7Y 1m	7Y11m	8Y 4m	8Y 8m	9Y 5m	10
12	2Y 1m	3Y10m	4Y 7m	5Y 3m	6Y 7m	7Y 8m	8Y 9m	9Y 8m	10Y 1m	10Y 6m	11Y 4m	12
15	2Y12m	5Y 3m	6Y 3m	7Y 1m	8Y 8m	10Y 1m	11Y 3m	12Y 4m	12Y10m	13Y 4m	14Y 3m	15
18	3Y12m	6Y11m	8Y 1m	9Y 2m	10Y12m	12Y 7m	13Y11m	15Y 1m	15Y 8m	16Y 2m	17Y 2m	18
20	4Y10m	8Y 2m	9Y 5m	10Y 7m	12Y 7m	14Y 3m	15Y 9m	16Y12m	17Y 7m	18Y 1m	19Y 1m	20
22	5Y 9m	9Y 5m	10Y11m	12Y 2m	14Y 3m	16Y 1m	17Y 7m	18Y11m	19Y 6m	20Y 1m	21Y 1m	22
25	7Y 4m	11Y 7m	13Y 2m	14Y 7m	16Y11m	18Y 9m	20Y 4m	21Y 9m	22Y 5m	22Y12m	24Y 1m	25
27	8Y 6m	13Y 1m	14Y10m	16Y 3m	18Y 8m	20Y 8m	22Y 3m	23Y 8m	24Y 4m	24Y11m	25Y12m	27
30	10Y 5m	15Y 6m	17Y 4m	18Y10m	21Y 5m	23Y 5m	25Y 2m	26Y 7m	27Y 3m	27Y11m	28Y12m	30
35	13Y12m	19Y 9m	21Y 9m	23Y 5m	26Y 1m	28Y 3m	29Y12m	31Y 6m	32Y 2m	32Y10m	33Y12m	35

10.00% Interest Rate

Amortization of Loan	90%	80%	75%	70%	60%	50%	40%	30%	25%	20%	10%	
5	0Y 8m	1Y 3m	1Y 7m	1Y10m	2Y 4m	2Y10m	3Y 4m	3Y 9m	3Y12m	4Y 3m	4Y 8m	5
7	0Y12m	1Y11m	2Y 4m	2Y 8m	3Y 5m	4Y 2m	4Y 9m	5Y 5m	5Y 8m	5Y12m	6Y 6m	7
10	1Y 7m	2Y12m	3Y 7m	4Y 2m	5Y 3m	6Y 3m	7Y 1m	7Y11m	8Y 4m	8Y 8m	9Y 5m	10
12	2Y 1m	3Y10m	4Y 7m	5Y 4m	6Y 7m	7Y 9m	8Y 9m	9Y 8m	10Y 1m	10Y 6m	11Y 4m	12
15	2Y12m	5Y 4m	6Y 4m	7Y 2m	8Y 9m	10Y 1m	11Y 4m	12Y 5m	12Y11m	13Y 4m	14Y 3m	15
18	4Y 1m	6Y12m	8Y 2m	9Y 3m	11Y 1m	12Y 8m	13Y12m	15Y 2m	15Y 8m	16Y 3m	17Y 2m	18
20	4Y12m	8Y 3m	9Y 7m	10Y 9m	12Y 9m	14Y 4m	15Y 9m	16Y12m	17Y 7m	18Y 2m	19Y 2m	20
22	5Y11m	9Y 7m	10Y12m	12Y 3m	14Y 5m	16Y 2m	17Y 8m	18Y11m	19Y 6m	20Y 1m	21Y 1m	22
25	7Y 6m	11Y 9m	13Y 4m	14Y 9m	16Y12m	18Y11m	20Y 5m	21Y10m	22Y 5m	22Y12m	24Y 1m	25
27	8Y 9m	13Y 4m	14Y12m	16Y 5m	18Y10m	20Y 9m	22Y 4m	23Y 9m	24Y 5m	24Y12m	26Y 1m	27
30	10Y 8m	15Y 9m	17Y 6m	19Y 1m	21Y 7m	23Y 7m	25Y 3m	26Y 8m	27Y 4m	27Y11m	28Y12m	30
35	14Y 4m	19Y12m	21Y12m	23Y 8m	26Y 4m	28Y 5m	30Y 1m	31Y 7m	32Y 3m	32Y11m	33Y12m	35

10.25% Interest Rate

Amortization of Loan	90%	80%	75%	70%	60%	50%	40%	30%	25%	20%	10%	
5	0Y 8m	1Y 3m	1Y 7m	1Y10m	2Y 4m	2Y10m	3Y 4m	3Y 9m	3Y12m	4Y 3m	4Y 8m	5
7	0Y12m	1Y11m	2Y 4m	2Y 9m	3Y 5m	4Y 2m	4Y10m	5Y 5m	5Y 8m	5Y12m	6Y 6m	7
10	1Y 8m	2Y12m	3Y 8m	4Y 3m	5Y 4m	6Y 3m	7Y 2m	7Y11m	8Y 4m	8Y 8m	9Y 5m	10
12	2Y 2m	3Y11m	4Y 8m	5Y 4m	6Y 8m	7Y 9m	8Y 9m	9Y 9m	10Y 2m	10Y 7m	11Y 4m	12
15	3Y 1m	5Y 5m	6Y 4m	7Y 3m	8Y10m	10Y 2m	11Y 4m	12Y 5m	12Y11m	13Y 4m	14Y 3m	15
18	4Y 2m	7Y 1m	8Y 3m	9Y 4m	11Y 2m	12Y 8m	13Y12m	15Y 2m	15Y 9m	16Y 3m	17Y 2m	18
20	5Y 1m	8Y 4m	9Y 8m	10Y10m	12Y10m	14Y 5m	15Y10m	17Y 1m	17Y 8m	18Y 2m	19Y 2m	20
22	5Y12m	9Y 9m	11Y 2m	12Y 5m	14Y 6m	16Y 3m	17Y 8m	18Y12m	19Y 7m	20Y 1m	21Y 1m	22
25	7Y 8m	11Y11m	13Y 6m	14Y11m	17Y 2m	18Y12m	20Y 6m	21Y10m	22Y 5m	23Y 1m	24Y 1m	25
27	8Y11m	13Y 6m	15Y 2m	16Y 7m	18Y11m	20Y10m	22Y 5m	23Y 9m	24Y 5m	24Y12m	26Y 1m	27
30	10Y11m	15Y11m	17Y 9m	19Y 3m	21Y 9m	23Y 8m	25Y 4m	26Y 9m	27Y 4m	27Y12m	29Y 1m	30
35	14Y 8m	20Y 4m	22Y 3m	23Y10m	26Y 6m	28Y 6m	30Y 3m	31Y 8m	32Y 4m	32Y11m	33Y12m	35

Entry is the month when balance will pass though selected percentage balance.

Time When Given Mortgage Balance Occurs

10.50% Interest Rate

Amortization of Loan	90%	80%	75%	70%	60%	50%	40%	30%	25%	20%	10%	
5	0Y 8m	1Y 3m	1Y 7m	1Y10m	2Y 4m	2Y10m	3Y 4m	3Y10m	3Y12m	4Y 3m	4Y 8m	5
7	0Y12m	1Y11m	2Y 4m	2Y 9m	3Y 6m	4Y 2m	4Y10m	5Y 5m	5Y 9m	5Y12m	6Y 6m	7
10	1Y 8m	3Y 1m	3Y 8m	4Y 3m	5Y 4m	6Y 4m	7Y 2m	7Y12m	8Y 4m	8Y 9m	9Y 5m	10
12	2Y 2m	3Y11m	4Y 8m	5Y 5m	6Y 8m	7Y10m	8Y10m	9Y 9m	10Y 2m	10Y 7m	11Y 4m	12
15	3Y 1m	5Y 5m	6Y 5m	7Y 4m	8Y11m	10Y 3m	11Y 5m	12Y 5m	12Y11m	13Y 5m	14Y 3m	15
18	4Y 3m	7Y 2m	8Y 5m	9Y 5m	11Y 3m	12Y 9m	14Y 1m	15Y 3m	15Y 9m	16Y 3m	17Y 2m	18
20	5Y 2m	8Y 6m	9Y10m	10Y11m	12Y11m	14Y 6m	15Y11m	17Y 1m	17Y 8m	18Y 2m	19Y 2m	20
22	6Y 2m	9Y10m	11Y 4m	12Y 6m	14Y 7m	16Y 4m	17Y 9m	18Y12m	19Y 7m	20Y 2m	21Y 2m	22
25	7Y10m	12Y 1m	13Y 8m	14Y12m	17Y 3m	19Y 1m	20Y 7m	21Y11m	22Y 6m	23Y 1m	24Y 1m	25
27	9Y 1m	13Y 8m	15Y 4m	16Y 9m	19Y 1m	20Y12m	22Y 6m	23Y10m	24Y 6m	25Y 1m	26Y 1m	27
30	11Y 2m	16Y 2m	17Y11m	19Y 5m	21Y11m	23Y10m	25Y 5m	26Y10m	27Y 5m	27Y12m	29Y 1m	30
35	14Y12m	20Y 7m	22Y 6m	24Y 1m	26Y 8m	28Y 8m	30Y 4m	31Y 9m	32Y 4m	32Y12m	34Y 1m	35

10.75% Interest Rate

Amortization of Loan	90%	80%	75%	70%	60%	50%	40%	30%	25%	20%	10%	
5	0Y 8m	1Y 3m	1Y 7m	1Y10m	2Y 4m	2Y10m	3Y 4m	3Y10m	3Y12m	4Y 3m	4Y 8m	5
7	0Y12m	1Y11m	2Y 4m	2Y 9m	3Y 6m	4Y 2m	4Y10m	5Y 5m	5Y 9m	5Y12m	6Y 6m	7
10	1Y 8m	3Y 1m	3Y 8m	4Y 3m	5Y 4m	6Y 4m	7Y 2m	7Y12m	8Y 4m	8Y 9m	9Y 5m	10
12	2Y 3m	3Y12m	4Y 9m	5Y 5m	6Y 9m	7Y10m	8Y10m	9Y 9m	10Y 2m	10Y 7m	11Y 4m	12
15	3Y 2m	5Y 6m	6Y 6m	7Y 5m	8Y11m	10Y 3m	11Y 5m	12Y 6m	12Y12m	13Y 5m	14Y 3m	15
18	4Y 4m	7Y 4m	8Y 6m	9Y 6m	11Y 4m	12Y10m	14Y 2m	15Y 3m	15Y10m	16Y 3m	17Y 2m	18
20	5Y 3m	8Y 7m	9Y11m	11Y 1m	12Y12m	14Y 7m	15Y12m	17Y 2m	17Y 9m	18Y 3m	19Y 2m	20
22	6Y 4m	9Y12m	11Y 5m	12Y 8m	14Y 9m	16Y 5m	17Y10m	19Y 1m	19Y 8m	20Y 2m	21Y 2m	22
25	7Y12m	12Y 3m	13Y10m	15Y 2m	17Y 5m	19Y 2m	20Y 8m	21Y12m	22Y 7m	23Y 1m	24Y 2m	25
27	9Y 4m	13Y11m	15Y 6m	16Y11m	19Y 3m	21Y 1m	22Y 7m	23Y11m	24Y 6m	25Y 1m	26Y 1m	27
30	11Y 5m	16Y 5m	18Y 2m	19Y 8m	21Y12m	23Y11m	25Y 6m	26Y10m	27Y 6m	28Y 1m	29Y 1m	30
35	15Y 4m	20Y10m	22Y 9m	24Y 4m	26Y10m	28Y 9m	30Y 5m	31Y10m	32Y 5m	32Y12m	34Y 1m	35

11.00% Interest Rate

Amortization of Loan	90%	80%	75%	70%	60%	50%	40%	30%	25%	20%	10%	
5	0Y 8m	1Y 3m	1Y 7m	1Y10m	2Y 5m	2Y10m	3Y 4m	3Y10m	3Y12m	4Y 3m	4Y 8m	5
7	0Y12m	1Y11m	2Y 4m	2Y 9m	3Y 6m	4Y 2m	4Y10m	5Y 5m	5Y 9m	5Y12m	6Y 6m	7
10	1Y 8m	3Y 1m	3Y 9m	4Y 4m	5Y 5m	6Y 4m	7Y 3m	7Y12m	8Y 5m	8Y 9m	9Y 5m	10
12	2Y 3m	3Y12m	4Y 9m	5Y 6m	6Y 9m	7Y11m	8Y11m	9Y 9m	10Y 2m	10Y 7m	11Y 4m	12
15	3Y 3m	5Y 7m	6Y 7m	7Y 5m	8Y12m	10Y 4m	11Y 6m	12Y 6m	12Y12m	13Y 5m	14Y 3m	15
18	4Y 5m	7Y 5m	8Y 7m	9Y 7m	11Y 5m	12Y11m	14Y 2m	15Y 4m	15Y10m	16Y 4m	17Y 3m	18
20	5Y 5m	8Y 9m	9Y12m	11Y 2m	13Y 1m	14Y 8m	15Y12m	17Y 3m	17Y 9m	18Y 3m	19Y 2m	20
22	6Y 5m	10Y 2m	11Y 7m	12Y 9m	14Y10m	16Y 6m	17Y11m	19Y 2m	19Y 8m	20Y 2m	21Y 2m	22
25	8Y 2m	12Y 5m	13Y12m	15Y 4m	17Y 6m	19Y 3m	20Y 9m	21Y12m	22Y 7m	23Y 2m	24Y 2m	25
27	9Y 6m	14Y 1m	15Y 8m	17Y 1m	19Y 4m	21Y 2m	22Y 8m	23Y12m	24Y 7m	25Y 1m	26Y 2m	27
30	11Y 8m	16Y 7m	18Y 4m	19Y10m	22Y 2m	24Y 1m	25Y 7m	26Y11m	27Y 6m	28Y 1m	29Y 1m	30
35	15Y 8m	21Y 1m	22Y11m	24Y 6m	26Y12m	28Y11m	30Y 6m	31Y10m	32Y 6m	33Y 1m	34Y 1m	35

11.25% Interest Rate

Amortization of Loan	90%	80%	75%	70%	60%	50%	40%	30%	25%	20%	10%	
5	0Y 8m	1Y 3m	1Y 7m	1Y10m	2Y 5m	2Y11m	3Y 4m	3Y10m	3Y12m	4Y 3m	4Y 8m	5
7	1Y 1m	1Y11m	2Y 4m	2Y 9m	3Y 6m	4Y 3m	4Y10m	5Y 5m	5Y 9m	5Y12m	6Y 7m	7
10	1Y 9m	3Y 2m	3Y 9m	4Y 4m	5Y 5m	6Y 4m	7Y 3m	7Y12m	8Y 5m	8Y 9m	9Y 5m	10
12	2Y 3m	4Y 1m	4Y10m	5Y 6m	6Y10m	7Y11m	8Y11m	9Y10m	10Y 3m	10Y 7m	11Y 4m	12
15	3Y 3m	5Y 8m	6Y 8m	7Y 6m	9Y 1m	10Y 5m	11Y 6m	12Y 7m	12Y12m	13Y 5m	14Y 3m	15
18	4Y 6m	7Y 6m	8Y 8m	9Y 8m	11Y 6m	12Y12m	14Y 3m	15Y 4m	15Y10m	16Y 4m	17Y 3m	18
20	5Y 6m	8Y10m	10Y 2m	11Y 3m	13Y 2m	14Y 9m	16Y 1m	17Y 3m	17Y 9m	18Y 3m	19Y 2m	20
22	6Y 7m	10Y 3m	11Y 8m	12Y11m	14Y11m	16Y 7m	17Y12m	19Y 2m	19Y 9m	20Y 3m	21Y 2m	22
25	8Y 5m	12Y 7m	14Y 2m	15Y 6m	17Y 8m	19Y 5m	20Y10m	22Y 1m	22Y 8m	23Y 2m	24Y 2m	25
27	9Y 9m	14Y 3m	15Y11m	17Y 3m	19Y 6m	21Y 3m	22Y 9m	23Y12m	24Y 7m	25Y 2m	26Y 2m	27
30	11Y11m	16Y10m	18Y 7m	19Y12m	22Y 4m	24Y 2m	25Y 8m	26Y11m	27Y 7m	28Y 2m	29Y 2m	30
35	15Y11m	21Y 4m	23Y 2m	24Y 8m	27Y 1m	28Y12m	30Y 7m	31Y11m	32Y 6m	33Y 1m	34Y 1m	35

11.50% Interest Rate

Amortization of Loan	90%	80%	75%	70%	60%	50%	40%	30%	25%	20%	10%	
5	0Y 8m	1Y 4m	1Y 7m	1Y10m	2Y 5m	2Y11m	3Y 4m	3Y10m	3Y12m	4Y 3m	4Y 8m	5
7	1Y 1m	1Y12m	2Y 5m	2Y 9m	3Y 6m	4Y 3m	4Y10m	5Y 6m	5Y 9m	5Y12m	6Y 7m	7
10	1Y 9m	3Y 2m	3Y 9m	4Y 5m	5Y 5m	6Y 5m	7Y 3m	8Y 1m	8Y 5m	8Y 9m	9Y 5m	10
12	2Y 4m	4Y 1m	4Y10m	5Y 7m	6Y10m	7Y11m	8Y11m	9Y10m	10Y 3m	10Y 8m	11Y 4m	12
15	3Y 4m	5Y 9m	6Y 8m	7Y 7m	9Y 1m	10Y 5m	11Y 7m	12Y 7m	12Y12m	13Y 6m	14Y 4m	15
18	4Y 7m	7Y 7m	8Y 9m	9Y10m	11Y 7m	12Y12m	14Y 3m	15Y 5m	15Y11m	16Y 4m	17Y 3m	18
20	5Y 7m	8Y11m	10Y 3m	11Y 5m	13Y 3m	14Y10m	16Y 2m	17Y 4m	17Y10m	18Y 4m	19Y 3m	20
22	6Y 8m	10Y 5m	11Y10m	12Y12m	14Y12m	16Y 8m	17Y12m	19Y 3m	19Y 9m	20Y 3m	21Y 2m	22
25	8Y 7m	12Y 9m	14Y 4m	15Y 7m	17Y 9m	19Y 6m	20Y11m	22Y 2m	22Y 8m	23Y 3m	24Y 2m	25
27	9Y11m	14Y 5m	16Y 1m	17Y 5m	19Y 7m	21Y 4m	22Y10m	24Y 1m	24Y 8m	25Y 2m	26Y 2m	27
30	12Y 2m	16Y12m	18Y 9m	20Y 2m	22Y 5m	24Y 3m	25Y 9m	27Y 1m	27Y 7m	28Y 2m	29Y 2m	30
35	16Y 3m	21Y 7m	23Y 5m	24Y11m	27Y 3m	29Y 2m	30Y 8m	31Y12m	32Y 7m	33Y 2m	34Y 2m	35

Entry is the month when balance will pass though selected percentage balance.

Time When Given Mortgage Balance Occurs

11.75% Interest Rate

Amortization of Loan	90%	80%	75%	70%	60%	50%	40%	30%	25%	20%	10%	
5	0Y 8m	1Y 4m	1Y 7m	1Y10m	2Y 5m	2Y11m	3Y 4m	3Y10m	3Y12m	4Y 3m	4Y 8m	5
7	1Y 1m	1Y12m	2Y 5m	2Y10m	3Y 7m	4Y 3m	4Y11m	5Y 6m	5Y 9m	5Y12m	6Y 7m	7
10	1Y 9m	3Y 2m	3Y10m	4Y 5m	5Y 6m	6Y 5m	7Y 3m	8Y 1m	8Y 5m	8Y 9m	9Y 5m	10
12	2Y 4m	4Y 2m	4Y11m	5Y 7m	6Y11m	7Y12m	8Y12m	9Y10m	10Y 3m	10Y 8m	11Y 4m	12
15	3Y 5m	5Y 9m	6Y 9m	7Y 8m	9Y 2m	10Y 6m	11Y 7m	12Y 7m	13Y 1m	13Y 6m	14Y 4m	15
18	4Y 8m	7Y 8m	8Y10m	9Y11m	11Y 8m	13Y 1m	14Y 4m	15Y 5m	15Y11m	16Y 5m	17Y 3m	18
20	5Y 8m	9Y 1m	10Y 4m	11Y 6m	13Y 4m	14Y11m	16Y 2m	17Y 4m	17Y10m	18Y 4m	19Y 3m	20
22	6Y10m	10Y 7m	11Y11m	13Y 2m	15Y 2m	16Y 9m	18Y 1m	19Y 3m	19Y10m	20Y 4m	21Y 3m	22
25	8Y 9m	12Y11m	14Y 6m	15Y 9m	17Y10m	19Y 7m	20Y12m	22Y 2m	22Y 9m	23Y 3m	24Y 2m	25
27	10Y 1m	14Y 7m	16Y 3m	17Y 7m	19Y 9m	21Y 6m	22Y11m	24Y 2m	24Y 8m	25Y 3m	26Y 2m	27
30	12Y 5m	17Y 3m	18Y11m	20Y 4m	22Y 7m	24Y 4m	25Y10m	27Y 1m	27Y 8m	28Y 2m	29Y 2m	30
35	16Y 7m	21Y10m	23Y 7m	25Y 1m	27Y 5m	29Y 3m	30Y 9m	32Y 1m	32Y 8m	33Y 2m	34Y 2m	35

12.00% Interest Rate

Amortization of Loan	90%	80%	75%	70%	60%	50%	40%	30%	25%	20%	10%	
5	0Y 8m	1Y 4m	1Y 7m	1Y11m	2Y 5m	2Y11m	3Y 5m	3Y10m	4Y 1m	4Y 3m	4Y 8m	5
7	1Y 1m	1Y12m	2Y 5m	2Y10m	3Y 7m	4Y 3m	4Y11m	5Y 6m	5Y 9m	5Y12m	6Y 7m	7
10	1Y 9m	3Y 3m	3Y10m	4Y 5m	5Y 6m	6Y 5m	7Y 4m	8Y 1m	8Y 5m	8Y 9m	9Y 5m	10
12	2Y 4m	4Y 2m	4Y11m	5Y 8m	6Y11m	7Y12m	8Y12m	9Y10m	10Y 3m	10Y 8m	11Y 5m	12
15	3Y 5m	5Y10m	6Y10m	7Y 9m	9Y 3m	10Y 6m	11Y 8m	12Y 8m	13Y 1m	13Y 6m	14Y 4m	15
18	4Y 9m	7Y 9m	8Y11m	9Y12m	11Y 9m	13Y 2m	14Y 5m	15Y 6m	15Y11m	16Y 5m	17Y 3m	18
20	5Y10m	9Y 2m	10Y 6m	11Y 7m	13Y 5m	14Y12m	16Y 3m	17Y 5m	17Y11m	18Y 4m	19Y 3m	20
22	6Y11m	10Y 8m	12Y 1m	13Y 3m	15Y 3m	16Y10m	18Y 2m	19Y 4m	19Y10m	20Y 4m	21Y 3m	22
25	8Y11m	13Y 1m	14Y 7m	15Y11m	17Y12m	19Y 8m	21Y 1m	22Y 3m	22Y 9m	23Y 3m	24Y 2m	25
27	10Y 4m	14Y10m	16Y 5m	17Y 8m	19Y10m	21Y 7m	22Y12m	24Y 2m	24Y 9m	25Y 3m	26Y 2m	27
30	12Y 8m	17Y 5m	19Y 1m	20Y 6m	22Y 9m	24Y 6m	25Y11m	27Y 2m	27Y 9m	28Y 3m	29Y 2m	30
35	16Y10m	22Y 1m	23Y10m	25Y 3m	27Y 7m	29Y 4m	30Y10m	32Y 1m	32Y 8m	33Y 2m	34Y 2m	35

12.25% Interest Rate

Amortization of Loan	90%	80%	75%	70%	60%	50%	40%	30%	25%	20%	10%	
5	0Y 8m	1Y 4m	1Y 7m	1Y11m	2Y 5m	2Y11m	3Y 5m	3Y10m	4Y 1m	4Y 3m	4Y 8m	5
7	1Y 1m	1Y12m	2Y 5m	2Y10m	3Y 7m	4Y 3m	4Y11m	5Y 6m	5Y 9m	5Y12m	6Y 7m	7
10	1Y10m	3Y 3m	3Y11m	4Y 6m	5Y 6m	6Y 6m	7Y 4m	8Y 1m	8Y 5m	8Y10m	9Y 5m	10
12	2Y 5m	4Y 3m	4Y12m	5Y 9m	6Y12m	8Y 1m	8Y12m	9Y11m	10Y 3m	10Y 8m	11Y 5m	12
15	3Y 6m	5Y11m	6Y11m	7Y 9m	9Y 4m	10Y 7m	11Y 8m	12Y 8m	13Y 1m	13Y 6m	14Y 4m	15
18	4Y10m	7Y10m	8Y12m	10Y 1m	11Y10m	13Y 3m	14Y 5m	15Y 6m	15Y12m	16Y 5m	17Y 3m	18
20	5Y11m	9Y 4m	10Y 7m	11Y 8m	13Y 6m	15Y 1m	16Y 4m	17Y 5m	17Y11m	18Y 5m	19Y 3m	20
22	7Y 1m	10Y10m	12Y 2m	13Y 5m	15Y 4m	16Y11m	18Y 3m	19Y 4m	19Y10m	20Y 4m	21Y 3m	22
25	9Y 1m	13Y 3m	14Y 9m	15Y12m	18Y 1m	19Y 9m	21Y 1m	22Y 3m	22Y10m	23Y 4m	24Y 3m	25
27	10Y 6m	14Y12m	16Y 6m	17Y10m	19Y12m	21Y 8m	23Y 1m	24Y 3m	24Y 9m	25Y 3m	26Y 3m	27
30	12Y10m	17Y 8m	19Y 3m	20Y 8m	22Y10m	24Y 7m	25Y12m	27Y 2m	27Y 9m	28Y 3m	29Y 2m	30
35	17Y 2m	22Y 3m	23Y12m	25Y 5m	27Y 8m	29Y 6m	30Y11m	32Y 2m	32Y 9m	33Y 3m	34Y 2m	35

12.50% Interest Rate

Amortization of Loan	90%	80%	75%	70%	60%	50%	40%	30%	25%	20%	10%	
5	0Y 8m	1Y 4m	1Y 7m	1Y11m	2Y 5m	2Y11m	3Y 5m	3Y10m	4Y 1m	4Y 3m	4Y 8m	5
7	1Y 1m	1Y12m	2Y 5m	2Y10m	3Y 7m	4Y 3m	4Y11m	5Y 6m	5Y 9m	6Y 1m	6Y 7m	7
10	1Y10m	3Y 3in	3Y11m	4Y 6m	5Y 7m	6Y 6m	7Y 4m	8Y 1m	8Y 6m	8Y10m	9Y 5m	10
12	2Y 5m	4Y 3m	4Y12m	5Y 9m	6Y12m	8Y 1m	9Y 1m	9Y11m	10Y 4m	10Y 8m	11Y 5m	12
15	3Y 7m	5Y12m	6Y12m	7Y10m	9Y 4m	10Y 8m	11Y 9m	12Y 8m	13Y 2m	13Y 7m	14Y 4m	15
18	4Y11m	7Y11m	9Y 2m	10Y 2m	11Y10m	13Y 3m	14Y 6m	15Y 6m	15Y12m	16Y 6m	17Y 3m	18
20	5Y12m	9Y 5m	10Y 8m	11Y 9m	13Y 7m	15Y 1m	16Y 4m	17Y 5m	17Y11m	18Y 5m	19Y 3m	20
22	7Y 3m	10Y11m	12Y 4m	13Y 6m	15Y 5m	16Y12m	18Y 3m	19Y 5m	19Y11m	20Y 5m	21Y 3m	22
25	9Y 3m	13Y 5m	14Y11m	16Y 2m	18Y 2m	19Y10m	21Y 2m	22Y 4m	22Y10m	23Y 4m	24Y 3m	25
27	10Y 9m	15Y 2m	16Y 8m	17Y12m	20Y 1m	21Y 9m	23Y 1m	24Y 4m	24Y10m	25Y 4m	26Y 3m	27
30	13Y 1m	17Y10m	19Y 5m	20Y10m	22Y11m	24Y 8m	26Y 1m	27Y 3m	27Y10m	28Y 4m	29Y 3m	30
35	17Y 5m	22Y 6m	24Y 2m	25Y 7m	27Y10m	29Y 7m	30Y12m	32Y 3m	32Y 9m	33Y 3m	34Y 2m	35

12.75% Interest Rate

Amortization of Loan	90%	80%	75%	70%	60%	50%	40%	30%	25%	20%	10%	
5	0Y 9m	1Y 4m	1Y 7m	1Y11m	2Y 5m	2Y11m	3Y 5m	3Y10m	4Y 1m	4Y 3m	4Y 8m	5
7	1Y 1m	1Y12m	2Y 5m	2Y10m	3Y 7m	4Y 4m	4Y11m	5Y 6m	5Y 9m	6Y 1m	6Y 7m	7
10	1Y10m	3Y 4m	3Y11m	4Y 6m	5Y 7m	6Y 6m	7Y 4m	8Y 2m	8Y 6m	8Y10m	9Y 5m	10
12	2Y 5m	4Y 4m	5Y 1m	5Y10m	7Y 1m	8Y 2m	9Y 1m	9Y11m	10Y 4m	10Y 8m	11Y 5m	12
15	3Y 7m	6Y 1m	6Y12m	7Y11m	9Y 5m	10Y 8m	11Y 9m	12Y 9m	13Y 2m	13Y 7m	14Y 4m	15
18	4Y12m	8Y 1m	9Y 3m	10Y 3m	11Y11m	13Y 4m	14Y 6m	15Y 7m	15Y12m	16Y 6m	17Y 4m	18
20	6Y 2m	9Y 6m	10Y 9m	11Y11m	13Y 8m	15Y 2m	16Y 5m	17Y 6m	17Y12m	18Y 5m	19Y 3m	20
22	7Y 4m	11Y 1m	12Y 5m	13Y 7m	15Y 6m	17Y 1m	18Y 4m	19Y 5m	19Y11m	20Y 5m	21Y 3m	22
25	9Y 5m	13Y 7m	15Y 1m	16Y 3m	18Y 4m	19Y11m	21Y 3m	22Y 4m	22Y11m	23Y 4m	24Y 3m	25
27	10Y11m	15Y 4m	16Y10m	18Y 2m	20Y 2m	21Y10m	23Y 2m	24Y 4m	24Y10m	25Y 4m	26Y 3m	27
30	13Y 4m	17Y12m	19Y 7m	20Y11m	23Y 1m	24Y 9m	26Y 2m	27Y 4m	27Y10m	28Y 4m	29Y 3m	30
35	17Y 8m	22Y 9m	24Y 5m	25Y 9m	27Y11m	29Y 8m	31Y 1m	32Y 3m	32Y10m	33Y 4m	34Y 3m	35

Entry is the month when balance will pass though selected percentage balance.

Time When Compounded Profit Will Be Achieved

Interest Rate	20%	25%	33.3%	40%	50%	60%	66.7%	70%	75%	80%	90%
5.50%	3Y 4m	4Y 1m	5Y 3m	6Y 2m	7Y 5m	8Y 7m	9Y 4m	9Y 9m	10Y 3m	10Y 9m	11Y 9m
.75	3Y 3m	3Y11m	5Y 1m	5Y11m	7Y 1m	8Y 3m	8Y11m	9Y 4m	9Y10m	10Y 3m	11Y 3m
6.00%	3Y 1m	3Y 9m	4Y10m	5Y 8m	6Y10m	7Y11m	8Y 7m	8Y11m	9Y 5m	9Y10m	10Y 9m
.25	2Y12m	3Y 7m	4Y 8m	5Y 5m	6Y 7m	7Y 7m	8Y 3m	8Y 7m	8Y12m	9Y 6m	10Y 4m
.50	2Y10m	3Y 6m	4Y 6m	5Y 3m	6Y 4m	7Y 4m	7Y11m	8Y 3m	8Y 8m	9Y 1m	9Y11m
.75	2Y 9m	3Y 4m	4Y 4m	4Y12m	6Y 1m	6Y12m	7Y 8m	7Y11m	8Y 4m	8Y 9m	9Y 7m
7.00%	2Y 8m	3Y 3m	4Y 2m	4Y10m	5Y10m	6Y 9m	7Y 4m	7Y 8m	8Y 1m	8Y 6m	9Y 3m
.25	2Y 7m	3Y 2m	3Y12m	4Y 8m	5Y 8m	6Y 7m	7Y 1m	7Y 5m	7Y 9m	8Y 2m	8Y11m
.50	2Y 6m	2Y12m	3Y11m	4Y 7m	5Y 6m	6Y 4m	6Y10m	7Y 2m	7Y 6m	7Y11m	8Y 8m
.75	2Y 5m	2Y11m	3Y 9m	4Y 5m	5Y 3m	6Y 2m	6Y 8m	6Y11m	7Y 3m	7Y 8m	8Y 4m
8.00%	2Y 4m	2Y10m	3Y 8m	4Y 3m	5Y 2m	5Y11m	6Y 5m	6Y 8m	7Y 1m	7Y 5m	8Y 1m
.25	2Y 3m	2Y 9m	3Y 6m	4Y 2m	4Y12m	5Y 9m	6Y 3m	6Y 6m	6Y10m	7Y 2m	7Y10m
.50	2Y 2m	2Y 8m	3Y 5m	3Y12m	4Y10m	5Y 7m	6Y 1m	6Y 4m	6Y 8m	6Y12m	7Y 7m
.75	2Y 2m	2Y 7m	3Y 4m	3Y11m	4Y 8m	5Y 5m	5Y11m	6Y 2m	6Y 6m	6Y 9m	7Y 5m
9.00%	2Y 1m	2Y 6m	3Y 3m	3Y10m	4Y 7m	5Y 3m	5Y 9m	5Y12m	6Y 3m	6Y 7m	7Y 2m
.25	1Y12m	2Y 6m	3Y 2m	3Y 8m	4Y 5m	5Y 2m	5Y 7m	5Y10m	6Y 1m	6Y 5m	6Y12m
.50	1Y12m	2Y 5m	3Y 1m	3Y 7m	4Y 4m	4Y12m	5Y 5m	5Y 8m	5Y11m	6Y 3m	6Y10m
.75	1Y11m	2Y 4m	2Y12m	3Y 6m	4Y 3m	4Y11m	5Y 4m	5Y 6m	5Y10m	6Y 1m	6Y 8m
10.00%	1Y10m	2Y 3m	2Y11m	3Y 5m	4Y 1m	4Y 9m	5Y 2m	5Y 4m	5Y 8m	5Y11m	6Y 6m
.25	1Y10m	2Y 3m	2Y10m	3Y 4m	3Y12m	4Y 8m	5Y 1m	5Y 3m	5Y 6m	5Y10m	6Y 4m
.50	1Y 9m	2Y 2m	2Y10m	3Y 3m	3Y11m	4Y 6m	4Y11m	5Y 1m	5Y 5m	5Y 8m	6Y 2m
.75	1Y 9m	2Y 2m	2Y 9m	3Y 2m	3Y10m	4Y 5m	4Y10m	4Y12m	5Y 3m	5Y 6m	5Y12m
11.00%	1Y 8m	2Y 1m	2Y 8m	3Y 1m	3Y 9m	4Y 4m	4Y 8m	4Y11m	5Y 2m	5Y 5m	5Y11m
.25	1Y 8m	1Y12m	2Y 7m	3Y 1m	3Y 8m	4Y 3m	4Y 7m	4Y 9m	4Y12m	5Y 3m	5Y 9m
.50	1Y 8m	1Y12m	2Y 7m	2Y12m	3Y 7m	4Y 2m	4Y 6m	4Y 8m	4Y11m	5Y 2m	5Y 8m
.75	1Y 7m	1Y11m	2Y 6m	2Y11m	3Y 6m	4Y 1m	4Y 5m	4Y 7m	4Y10m	5Y 1m	5Y 6m
12.00%	1Y 7m	1Y11m	2Y 5m	2Y10m	3Y 5m	3Y12m	4Y 4m	4Y 6m	4Y 9m	4Y12m	5Y 5m
.25	1Y 6m	1Y10m	2Y 5m	2Y10m	3Y 4m	3Y11m	4Y 3m	4Y 5m	4Y 8m	4Y10m	5Y 4m
.50	1Y 6m	1Y10m	2Y 4m	2Y 9m	3Y 4m	3Y10m	4Y 2m	4Y 4m	4Y 7m	4Y 9m	5Y 2m

Interest Rate	100%	125%	150%	175%	200%	250%	300%	400%	500%	750%	1000%
5.50%	12Y 8m	14Y10m	16Y 9m	18Y 6m	20Y 1m	22Y10m	25Y 4m	29Y 4m	32Y 8m	38Y12m	43Y 9m
.75	12Y 2m	14Y 2m	15Y12m	17Y 8m	19Y 2m	21Y11m	24Y 3m	28Y 1m	31Y 3m	37Y 4m	41Y10m
6.00%	11Y 7m	13Y 7m	15Y 4m	16Y11m	18Y 5m	20Y12m	23Y 2m	26Y11m	29Y12m	35Y10m	40Y 1m
.25	11Y 2m	13Y 1m	14Y 9m	16Y 3m	17Y 8m	20Y 2m	22Y 3m	25Y10m	28Y 9m	34Y 4m	38Y 6m
.50	10Y 9m	12Y 7m	14Y 2m	15Y 8m	16Y12m	19Y 4m	21Y 5m	24Y10m	27Y 8m	33Y 1m	36Y12m
.75	10Y 4m	12Y 1m	13Y 8m	15Y 1m	16Y 4m	18Y 8m	20Y 8m	23Y11m	26Y 8m	31Y10m	35Y 8m
7.00%	9Y12m	11Y 8m	13Y 2m	14Y 6m	15Y 9m	17Y12m	19Y11m	23Y 1m	25Y 9m	30Y 8m	34Y 5m
.25	9Y 8m	11Y 3m	12Y 9m	13Y12m	15Y 3m	17Y 4m	19Y 3m	22Y 4m	24Y10m	29Y 8m	33Y 3m
.50	9Y 4m	10Y11m	12Y 4m	13Y 7m	14Y 9m	16Y10m	18Y 7m	21Y 7m	23Y12m	28Y 8m	32Y 1m
.75	8Y12m	10Y 6m	11Y11m	13Y 2m	14Y 3m	16Y 3m	17Y12m	20Y11m	23Y 3m	27Y 9m	31Y 1m
8.00%	8Y 9m	10Y 3m	11Y 6m	12Y 9m	13Y10m	15Y 9m	17Y 5m	20Y 3m	22Y 6m	26Y11m	30Y 1m
.25	8Y 6m	9Y11m	11Y 2m	12Y 4m	13Y 5m	15Y 3m	16Y11m	19Y 7m	21Y10m	26Y 1m	29Y 2m
.50	8Y 3m	9Y 7m	10Y10m	11Y12m	12Y12m	14Y10m	16Y 5m	19Y 1m	21Y 2m	25Y 4m	28Y 4m
.75	7Y12m	9Y 4m	10Y 7m	11Y 8m	12Y 8m	14Y 5m	15Y11m	18Y 6m	20Y 7m	24Y 7m	27Y 7m
9.00%	7Y 9m	9Y 1m	10Y 3m	11Y 4m	12Y 4m	13Y12m	15Y 6m	17Y12m	19Y12m	23Y11m	26Y 9m
.25	7Y 7m	8Y10m	9Y12m	10Y12m	11Y12m	13Y 8m	15Y 1m	17Y 6m	19Y 6m	23Y 3m	26Y 1m
.50	7Y 4m	8Y 7m	9Y 9m	10Y 9m	11Y 8m	13Y 3m	14Y 8m	17Y 1m	18Y12m	22Y 9m	25Y 5m
.75	7Y 2m	8Y 5m	9Y 6m	10Y 6m	11Y 4m	12Y11m	14Y 4m	16Y 7m	18Y 6m	22Y 1m	24Y 9m
10.00%	6Y12m	8Y 2m	9Y 3m	10Y 2m	11Y 1m	12Y 7m	13Y12m	16Y 2m	17Y12m	21Y 6m	24Y 1m
.25	6Y10m	7Y12m	8Y12m	9Y11m	10Y10m	12Y 4m	13Y 7m	15Y10m	17Y 7m	20Y12m	23Y 6m
.50	6Y 8m	7Y10m	8Y10m	9Y 9m	10Y 7m	11Y12m	13Y 4m	15Y 5m	17Y 2m	20Y 6m	22Y12m
.75	6Y 6m	7Y 7m	8Y 7m	9Y 6m	10Y 4m	11Y 9m	12Y12m	15Y 1m	16Y 9m	19Y12m	22Y 5m
11.00%	6Y 4m	7Y 5m	8Y 5m	9Y 3m	10Y 1m	11Y 6m	12Y 8m	14Y 9m	16Y 5m	19Y 7m	21Y11m
.25	6Y 3m	7Y 3m	8Y 3m	9Y 1m	9Y10m	11Y 3m	12Y 5m	14Y 5m	16Y 1m	19Y 2m	21Y 5m
.50	6Y 1m	7Y 2m	8Y 1m	8Y11m	9Y 8m	10Y12m	12Y 2m	14Y 1m	15Y 8m	18Y 9m	20Y12m
.75	5Y12m	6Y12m	7Y11m	8Y 8m	9Y 5m	10Y 9m	11Y11m	13Y10m	15Y 4m	18Y 4m	20Y 7m
12.00%	5Y10m	6Y10m	7Y 9m	8Y 6m	9Y 3m	10Y 6m	11Y 8m	13Y 6m	15Y 1m	17Y12m	20Y 1m
.25	5Y 9m	6Y 8m	7Y 7m	8Y 4m	9Y 1m	10Y 4m	11Y 5m	13Y 3m	14Y 9m	17Y 7m	19Y 9m
.50	5Y 7m	6Y 7m	7Y 5m	8Y 2m	8Y11m	10Y 1m	11Y 2m	12Y12m	14Y 5m	17Y 3m	19Y 4m

Entry is time until the investment will reach the selected increase by compounding.

Time When Income on Deferred Tax Equals Tax

Deferred Taxation of Interest

Total Tax Bracket	5.50%	6.00%	6.50%	7.00%	7.50%	8.00%	8.50%	9.00%	9.50%	10.00%	10.50%	11.00%	12.00%
12.5	13Y11m	12Y 9m	11Y10m	10Y12m	10Y 3m	9Y 7m	8Y12m	8Y 6m	8Y 1m	7Y 8m	7Y 4m	6Y12m	6Y 5m
15.0	14Y 3m	12Y12m	11Y12m	11Y 2m	10Y 5m	9Y10m	9Y 3m	8Y 9m	8Y 3m	7Y10m	7Y 6m	7Y 2m	6Y 7m
17.5	14Y 6m	13Y 4m	12Y 3m	11Y 5m	10Y 8m	9Y12m	9Y 5m	8Y11m	8Y 5m	7Y12m	7Y 8m	7Y 4m	6Y 8m
20.0	14Y10m	13Y 7m	12Y 7m	11Y 8m	10Y11m	10Y 3m	9Y 7m	9Y 1m	8Y 7m	8Y 2m	7Y10m	7Y 5m	6Y10m
22.5	15Y 2m	13Y11m	12Y10m	11Y11m	11Y 2m	10Y 5m	9Y10m	9Y 3m	8Y10m	8Y 4m	7Y12m	7Y 7m	6Y12m
25.0	15Y 6m	14Y 2m	13Y 1m	12Y 2m	11Y 4m	10Y 8m	10Y 1m	9Y 6m	8Y12m	8Y 7m	8Y 2m	7Y 9m	7Y 2m
26.0	15Y 7m	14Y 4m	13Y 3m	12Y 3m	11Y 6m	10Y 9m	10Y 2m	9Y 7m	9Y 1m	8Y 8m	8Y 3m	7Y10m	7Y 2m
27.0	15Y 9m	14Y 5m	13Y 4m	12Y 5m	11Y 7m	10Y10m	10Y 3m	9Y 8m	9Y 2m	8Y 8m	8Y 4m	7Y11m	7Y 3m
27.5	15Y10m	14Y 6m	13Y 5m	12Y 6m	11Y 8m	10Y11m	10Y 3m	9Y 9m	9Y 2m	8Y 9m	8Y 4m	7Y11m	7Y 4m
28.0	15Y11m	14Y 7m	13Y 6m	12Y 6m	11Y 8m	10Y12m	10Y 4m	9Y 9m	9Y 3m	8Y 9m	8Y 4m	7Y12m	7Y 4m
29.0	16Y 1m	14Y 9m	13Y 7m	12Y 8m	11Y10m	11Y 1m	10Y 5m	9Y10m	9Y 4m	8Y10m	8Y 5m	8Y 1m	7Y 5m
30.0	16Y 3m	14Y10m	13Y 9m	12Y 9m	11Y11m	11Y 2m	10Y 6m	9Y11m	9Y 5m	8Y11m	8Y 6m	8Y 2m	7Y 6m
31.0	16Y 4m	14Y12m	13Y10m	12Y11m	11Y12m	11Y 3m	10Y 7m	9Y12m	9Y 6m	8Y12m	8Y 7m	8Y 3m	7Y 7m
32.0	16Y 6m	15Y 2m	13Y12m	12Y12m	12Y 2m	11Y 5m	10Y 9m	10Y 2m	9Y 7m	9Y 1m	8Y 8m	8Y 4m	7Y 7m
32.5	16Y 7m	15Y 3m	14Y 1m	13Y 1m	12Y 2m	11Y 5m	10Y 9m	10Y 2m	9Y 8m	9Y 2m	8Y 9m	8Y 4m	7Y 8m
33.0	16Y 8m	15Y 4m	14Y 2m	13Y 2m	12Y 3m	11Y 6m	10Y10m	10Y 3m	9Y 8m	9Y 3m	8Y 9m	8Y 5m	7Y 8m
34.0	16Y10m	15Y 5m	14Y 3m	13Y 3m	12Y 5m	11Y 7m	10Y11m	10Y 4m	9Y 9m	9Y 4m	8Y10m	8Y 6m	7Y 9m
35.0	16Y12m	15Y 7m	14Y 5m	13Y 5m	12Y 6m	11Y 9m	10Y12m	10Y 5m	9Y11m	9Y 5m	8Y11m	8Y 7m	7Y10m
37.5	17Y 5m	15Y12m	14Y 9m	13Y 9m	12Y10m	11Y12m	11Y 4m	10Y 8m	10Y 2m	9Y 8m	9Y 2m	8Y 9m	8Y 1m
40.0	17Y11m	16Y 5m	15Y 2m	14Y 1m	13Y 2m	12Y 4m	11Y 7m	10Y12m	10Y 5m	9Y11m	9Y 5m	8Y12m	8Y 3m
42.5	18Y 5m	16Y11m	15Y 7m	14Y 6m	13Y 6m	12Y 8m	11Y11m	11Y 3m	10Y 8m	10Y 2m	9Y 8m	9Y 3m	8Y 6m
45.0	18Y11m	17Y 4m	15Y12m	14Y11m	13Y11m	12Y12m	12Y 3m	11Y 7m	10Y12m	10Y 5m	9Y11m	9Y 6m	8Y 9m
50.0	20Y 1m	18Y 5m	16Y12m	15Y 9m	14Y 9m	13Y10m	12Y12m	12Y 4m	11Y 8m	11Y 1m	10Y 7m	10Y 1m	9Y 3m
52.5	20Y 8m	18Y12m	17Y 6m	16Y 3m	15Y 2m	14Y 3m	13Y 5m	12Y 8m	11Y12m	11Y 5m	10Y11m	10Y 5m	9Y 6m
55.0	21Y 4m	19Y 7m	18Y 1m	16Y10m	15Y 8m	14Y 9m	13Y10m	13Y 1m	12Y 5m	11Y 9m	11Y 3m	10Y 9m	9Y10m
57.5	22Y 1m	20Y 3m	18Y 8m	17Y 5m	16Y 3m	15Y 3m	14Y 4m	13Y 6m	12Y10m	12Y 2m	11Y 7m	11Y 1m	10Y 2m
60.0	22Y10m	20Y12m	19Y 4m	17Y12m	16Y10m	15Y 9m	14Y10m	13Y12m	13Y 3m	12Y 7m	11Y12m	11Y 6m	10Y 6m

Current Taxation of Interest

Total Tax Bracket	5.50%	6.00%	6.50%	7.00%	7.50%	8.00%	8.50%	9.00%	9.50%	10.00%	10.50%	11.00%	12.00%
12.5	14Y 6m	13Y 3m	12Y 3m	11Y 5m	10Y 8m	9Y12m	9Y 5m	8Y10m	8Y 5m	7Y12m	7Y 7m	7Y 3m	6Y 8m
15.0	14Y11m	13Y 8m	12Y 7m	11Y 9m	10Y11m	10Y 3m	9Y 8m	9Y 2m	8Y 8m	8Y 3m	7Y10m	7Y 6m	6Y10m
17.5	15Y 4m	14Y 1m	12Y12m	12Y 1m	11Y 3m	10Y 7m	9Y11m	9Y 5m	8Y11m	8Y 6m	8Y 1m	7Y 9m	7Y 1m
20.0	15Y10m	14Y 6m	13Y 5m	12Y 5m	11Y 7m	10Y11m	10Y 3m	9Y 8m	9Y 2m	8Y 9m	8Y 4m	7Y11m	7Y 3m
22.5	16Y 4m	14Y12m	13Y10m	12Y10m	11Y12m	11Y 3m	10Y 7m	9Y12m	9Y 6m	8Y12m	8Y 7m	8Y 2m	7Y 6m
25.0	16Y10m	15Y 6m	14Y 3m	13Y 3m	12Y 5m	11Y 7m	10Y11m	10Y 4m	9Y10m	9Y 4m	8Y10m	8Y 6m	7Y 9m
26.0	17Y 1m	15Y 8m	14Y 6m	13Y 5m	12Y 7m	11Y 9m	11Y 1m	10Y 6m	9Y11m	9Y 5m	8Y12m	8Y 7m	7Y11m
27.0	17Y 4m	15Y11m	14Y 8m	13Y 8m	12Y 9m	11Y11m	11Y 3m	10Y 7m	10Y 1m	9Y 7m	9Y 1m	8Y 8m	7Y12m
27.5	17Y 5m	15Y12m	14Y 9m	13Y 9m	12Y10m	11Y12m	11Y 4m	10Y 8m	10Y 2m	9Y 8m	9Y 2m	8Y 9m	7Y12m
28.0	17Y 7m	16Y 1m	14Y11m	13Y10m	12Y11m	12Y 1m	11Y 5m	10Y 9m	10Y 2m	9Y 8m	9Y 3m	8Y10m	8Y 1m
29.0	17Y10m	16Y 4m	15Y 1m	13Y12m	13Y 1m	12Y 3m	11Y 7m	10Y11m	10Y 4m	9Y10m	9Y 4m	8Y11m	8Y 2m
30.0	18Y 1m	16Y 7m	15Y 4m	14Y 3m	13Y 3m	12Y 5m	11Y 9m	11Y 1m	10Y 6m	9Y12m	9Y 6m	9Y 1m	8Y 4m
31.0	18Y 4m	16Y10m	15Y 6m	14Y 5m	13Y 6m	12Y 8m	11Y11m	11Y 3m	10Y 8m	10Y 1m	9Y 8m	9Y 2m	8Y 5m
32.0	18Y 7m	17Y 1m	15Y 9m	14Y 8m	13Y 8m	12Y10m	12Y 1m	11Y 5m	10Y10m	10Y 3m	9Y 9m	9Y 4m	8Y 7m
32.5	18Y 9m	17Y 2m	15Y10m	14Y 9m	13Y 9m	12Y11m	12Y 2m	11Y 6m	10Y11m	10Y 4m	9Y10m	9Y 5m	8Y 8m
33.0	18Y11m	17Y 4m	15Y12m	14Y10m	13Y10m	12Y12m	12Y 3m	11Y 7m	10Y12m	10Y 5m	9Y11m	9Y 6m	8Y 8m
34.0	19Y 2m	17Y 7m	16Y 3m	15Y 1m	14Y 1m	13Y 2m	12Y 5m	11Y 9m	11Y 2m	10Y 7m	10Y 1m	9Y 7m	8Y10m
35.0	19Y 6m	17Y10m	16Y 6m	15Y 4m	14Y 3m	13Y 5m	12Y 7m	11Y11m	11Y 4m	10Y 9m	10Y 3m	9Y 9m	8Y11m
37.5	20Y 3m	18Y 7m	17Y 2m	15Y11m	14Y10m	13Y11m	13Y 1m	12Y 5m	11Y 9m	11Y 2m	10Y 8m	10Y 2m	9Y 4m
40.0	21Y 1m	19Y 4m	17Y10m	16Y 7m	15Y 6m	14Y 6m	13Y 8m	12Y11m	12Y 3m	11Y 7m	11Y 1m	10Y 7m	9Y 8m
42.5	21Y12m	20Y 2m	18Y 7m	17Y 3m	16Y 2m	15Y 2m	14Y 3m	13Y 6m	12Y 9m	12Y 2m	11Y 7m	10Y12m	10Y 1m
45.0	22Y12m	21Y 1m	19Y 6m	18Y 1m	16Y10m	15Y10m	14Y11m	14Y 1m	13Y 4m	12Y 8m	12Y 1m	11Y 6m	10Y 7m
50.0	25Y 3m	23Y 2m	21Y 5m	19Y10m	18Y 7m	17Y 5m	16Y 5m	15Y 6m	14Y 8m	13Y11m	13Y 3m	12Y 8m	11Y 7m
52.5	26Y 7m	24Y 5m	22Y 6m	20Y11m	19Y 6m	18Y 4m	17Y 3m	16Y 3m	15Y 5m	14Y 8m	13Y12m	13Y 4m	12Y 3m
55.0	28Y 1m	25Y 9m	23Y 9m	22Y 1m	20Y 7m	19Y 4m	18Y 2m	17Y 2m	16Y 3m	15Y 6m	14Y 9m	14Y 1m	12Y11m
57.5	29Y 9m	27Y 3m	25Y 2m	23Y 4m	21Y10m	20Y 5m	19Y 3m	18Y 2m	17Y 3m	16Y 5m	15Y 7m	14Y11m	13Y 8m
60.0	31Y 7m	28Y11m	26Y 9m	24Y10m	23Y 2m	21Y 9m	20Y 5m	19Y 4m	18Y 4m	17Y 5m	16Y 7m	15Y10m	14Y 7m

At time of the entries, the account balance, net after-tax, will equal the originally deferred tax.

Cost of Providing Leasehold Improvements

Equity Yield of 7.50%   Includes 3.5% Management Fee

Improvement Cost per square foot of Rented Area	Term of Lease in Years									
	1	2	3	4	5	6	7	8	9	10
$5.00	5.361	2.781	1.922	1.494	1.238	1.068	0.948	0.858	0.789	0.733
6.00	6.433	3.337	2.306	1.793	1.486	1.282	1.137	1.029	0.946	0.880
7.00	7.505	3.893	2.691	2.092	1.733	1.496	1.327	1.201	1.104	1.027
8.00	8.577	4.449	3.075	2.390	1.981	1.709	1.516	1.373	1.262	1.174
9.00	9.649	5.005	3.460	2.689	2.229	1.923	1.706	1.544	1.419	1.320
10.00	10.721	5.561	3.844	2.988	2.476	2.137	1.896	1.716	1.577	1.467
11.00	11.794	6.117	4.229	3.287	2.724	2.350	2.085	1.887	1.735	1.614
12.00	12.866	6.673	4.613	3.586	2.972	2.564	2.275	2.059	1.892	1.760
13.00	13.938	7.229	4.997	3.884	3.219	2.778	2.464	2.230	2.050	1.907
14.00	15.010	7.785	5.382	4.183	3.467	2.991	2.654	2.402	2.208	2.054
15.00	16.082	8.342	5.766	4.482	3.714	3.205	2.843	2.574	2.366	2.200
16.00	17.154	8.898	6.151	4.781	3.962	3.419	3.033	2.745	2.523	2.347
17.00	18.227	9.454	6.535	5.080	4.210	3.632	3.222	2.917	2.681	2.494
18.00	19.299	10.010	6.919	5.378	4.457	3.846	3.412	3.088	2.839	2.640
19.00	20.371	10.566	7.304	5.677	4.705	4.060	3.601	3.260	2.996	2.787
20.00	21.443	11.122	7.688	5.976	4.953	4.273	3.791	3.432	3.154	2.934
21.00	22.515	11.678	8.073	6.275	5.200	4.487	3.981	3.603	3.312	3.081
22.00	23.587	12.234	8.457	6.574	5.448	4.701	4.170	3.775	3.469	3.227
23.00	24.659	12.790	8.841	6.872	5.695	4.914	4.360	3.946	3.627	3.374
24.00	25.732	13.347	9.226	7.171	5.943	5.128	4.549	4.118	3.785	3.521
25.00	26.804	13.903	9.610	7.470	6.191	5.342	4.739	4.289	3.943	3.667
26.00	27.876	14.459	9.995	7.769	6.438	5.555	4.928	4.461	4.100	3.814
27.00	28.948	15.015	10.379	8.068	6.686	5.769	5.118	4.633	4.258	3.961
28.00	30.020	15.571	10.763	8.366	6.934	5.983	5.307	4.804	4.416	4.107
29.00	31.092	16.127	11.148	8.665	7.181	6.196	5.497	4.976	4.573	4.254
30.00	32.164	16.683	11.532	8.964	7.429	6.410	5.687	5.147	4.731	4.401
31.00	33.237	17.239	11.917	9.263	7.676	6.624	5.876	5.319	4.889	4.547
32.00	34.309	17.795	12.301	9.562	7.924	6.837	6.066	5.490	5.046	4.694
33.00	35.381	18.351	12.686	9.860	8.172	7.051	6.255	5.662	5.204	4.841
34.00	36.453	18.908	13.070	10.159	8.419	7.265	6.445	5.834	5.362	4.988
35.00	37.525	19.464	13.454	10.458	8.667	7.478	6.634	6.005	5.520	5.134
36.00	38.597	20.020	13.839	10.757	8.915	7.692	6.824	6.177	5.677	5.281
37.00	39.669	20.576	14.223	11.056	9.162	7.906	7.013	6.348	5.835	5.428
38.00	40.742	21.132	14.608	11.355	9.410	8.120	7.203	6.520	5.993	5.574
39.00	41.814	21.688	14.992	11.653	9.658	8.333	7.392	6.691	6.150	5.721
40.00	42.886	22.244	15.376	11.952	9.905	8.547	7.582	6.863	6.308	5.868
41.00	43.958	22.800	15.761	12.251	10.153	8.761	7.772	7.035	6.466	6.014
42.00	45.030	23.356	16.145	12.550	10.400	8.974	7.961	7.206	6.623	6.161
43.00	46.102	23.913	16.530	12.849	10.648	9.188	8.151	7.378	6.781	6.308
44.00	47.175	24.469	16.914	13.147	10.896	9.402	8.340	7.549	6.939	6.454
45.00	48.247	25.025	17.298	13.446	11.143	9.615	8.530	7.721	7.097	6.601
46.00	49.319	25.581	17.683	13.745	11.391	9.829	8.719	7.893	7.254	6.748
47.00	50.391	26.137	18.067	14.044	11.639	10.043	8.909	8.064	7.412	6.895
48.00	51.463	26.693	18.452	14.343	11.886	10.256	9.098	8.236	7.570	7.041
49.00	52.535	27.249	18.836	14.641	12.134	10.470	9.288	8.407	7.727	7.188
50.00	53.607	27.805	19.221	14.940	12.381	10.684	9.478	8.579	7.885	7.335
51.00	54.680	28.361	19.605	15.239	12.629	10.897	9.667	8.750	8.043	7.481
52.00	55.752	28.917	19.989	15.538	12.877	11.111	9.857	8.922	8.200	7.628
53.00	56.824	29.474	20.374	15.837	13.124	11.325	10.046	9.094	8.358	7.775
54.00	57.896	30.030	20.758	16.135	13.372	11.538	10.236	9.265	8.516	7.921
55.00	58.968	30.586	21.143	16.434	13.620	11.752	10.425	9.437	8.674	8.068
56.00	60.040	31.142	21.527	16.733	13.867	11.966	10.615	9.608	8.831	8.215
57.00	61.112	31.698	21.911	17.032	14.115	12.179	10.804	9.780	8.989	8.361
58.00	62.185	32.254	22.296	17.331	14.362	12.393	10.994	9.951	9.147	8.508
59.00	63.257	32.810	22.680	17.629	14.610	12.607	11.183	10.123	9.304	8.655
60.00	64.329	33.366	23.065	17.928	14.858	12.820	11.373	10.295	9.462	8.801
61.00	65.401	33.922	23.449	18.227	15.105	13.034	11.563	10.466	9.620	8.948
62.00	66.473	34.478	23.833	18.526	15.353	13.248	11.752	10.638	9.777	9.095
63.00	67.545	35.035	24.218	18.825	15.601	13.461	11.942	10.809	9.935	9.242
64.00	68.617	35.591	24.602	19.123	15.848	13.675	12.131	10.981	10.093	9.388
65.00	69.690	36.147	24.987	19.422	16.096	13.889	12.321	11.152	10.251	9.535

Entry is rental that repays cost with interest and management fee on rent.

Cost of Providing Leasehold Improvements

Equity Yield of 9.00%   Includes 3.5% Management Fee

Improvement Cost per square foot of Rented Area	Term of Lease in Years									
	1	2	3	4	5	6	7	8	9	10
$5.00	5.397	2.819	1.962	1.536	1.281	1.112	0.993	0.904	0.836	0.782
6.00	6.476	3.383	2.355	1.843	1.537	1.335	1.191	1.085	1.003	0.938
7.00	7.556	3.947	2.747	2.150	1.793	1.557	1.390	1.266	1.170	1.094
8.00	8.635	4.511	3.140	2.457	2.050	1.780	1.589	1.447	1.337	1.251
9.00	9.714	5.075	3.532	2.764	2.306	2.002	1.787	1.627	1.504	1.407
10.00	10.794	5.639	3.925	3.071	2.562	2.225	1.986	1.808	1.672	1.564
11.00	11.873	6.203	4.317	3.379	2.818	2.447	2.184	1.989	1.839	1.720
12.00	12.953	6.766	4.710	3.686	3.075	2.670	2.383	2.170	2.006	1.876
13.00	14.032	7.330	5.102	3.993	3.331	2.892	2.582	2.351	2.173	2.033
14.00	15.111	7.894	5.495	4.300	3.587	3.115	2.780	2.532	2.340	2.189
15.00	16.191	8.458	5.887	4.607	3.843	3.337	2.979	2.712	2.507	2.345
16.00	17.270	9.022	6.280	4.914	4.099	3.560	3.177	2.893	2.674	2.502
17.00	18.350	9.586	6.672	5.222	4.356	3.782	3.376	3.074	2.842	2.658
18.00	19.429	10.150	7.065	5.529	4.612	4.005	3.574	3.255	3.009	2.814
19.00	20.508	10.714	7.457	5.836	4.868	4.227	3.773	3.436	3.176	2.971
20.00	21.588	11.277	7.850	6.143	5.124	4.450	3.972	3.616	3.343	3.127
21.00	22.667	11.841	8.242	6.450	5.380	4.672	4.170	3.797	3.510	3.283
22.00	23.746	12.405	8.635	6.757	5.637	4.895	4.369	3.978	3.677	3.440
23.00	24.826	12.969	9.027	7.064	5.893	5.117	4.567	4.159	3.845	3.596
24.00	25.905	13.533	9.420	7.372	6.149	5.340	4.766	4.340	4.012	3.752
25.00	26.985	14.097	9.812	7.679	6.405	5.562	4.965	4.521	4.179	3.909
26.00	28.064	14.661	10.205	7.986	6.662	5.785	5.163	4.701	4.346	4.065
27.00	29.143	15.225	10.597	8.293	6.918	6.007	5.362	4.882	4.513	4.221
28.00	30.223	15.788	10.990	8.600	7.174	6.230	5.560	5.063	4.680	4.378
29.00	31.302	16.352	11.382	8.907	7.430	6.452	5.759	5.244	4.848	4.534
30.00	32.382	16.916	11.775	9.214	7.686	6.674	5.957	5.425	5.015	4.691
31.00	33.461	17.480	12.167	9.522	7.943	6.897	6.156	5.605	5.182	4.847
32.00	34.540	18.044	12.560	9.829	8.199	7.119	6.355	5.786	5.349	5.003
33.00	35.620	18.608	12.952	10.136	8.455	7.342	6.553	5.967	5.516	5.160
34.00	36.699	19.172	13.345	10.443	8.711	7.564	6.752	6.148	5.683	5.316
35.00	37.778	19.735	13.737	10.750	8.967	7.787	6.950	6.329	5.850	5.472
36.00	38.858	20.299	14.130	11.057	9.224	8.009	7.149	6.510	6.018	5.629
37.00	39.937	20.863	14.522	11.364	9.480	8.232	7.348	6.690	6.185	5.785
38.00	41.017	21.427	14.915	11.672	9.736	8.454	7.546	6.871	6.352	5.941
39.00	42.096	21.991	15.307	11.979	9.992	8.677	7.745	7.052	6.519	6.098
40.00	43.175	22.555	15.700	12.286	10.249	8.899	7.943	7.233	6.686	6.254
41.00	44.255	23.119	16.092	12.593	10.505	9.122	8.142	7.414	6.853	6.410
42.00	45.334	23.683	16.485	12.900	10.761	9.344	8.340	7.595	7.021	6.567
43.00	46.414	24.246	16.877	13.207	11.017	9.567	8.539	7.775	7.188	6.723
44.00	47.493	24.810	17.270	13.514	11.273	9.789	8.738	7.956	7.355	6.879
45.00	48.572	25.374	17.662	13.822	11.530	10.012	8.936	8.137	7.522	7.036
46.00	49.652	25.938	18.055	14.129	11.786	10.234	9.135	8.318	7.689	7.192
47.00	50.731	26.502	18.447	14.436	12.042	10.457	9.333	8.499	7.856	7.349
48.00	51.810	27.066	18.840	14.743	12.298	10.679	9.532	8.679	8.023	7.505
49.00	52.890	27.630	19.232	15.050	12.554	10.902	9.731	8.860	8.191	7.661
50.00	53.969	28.194	19.625	15.357	12.811	11.124	9.929	9.041	8.358	7.818
51.00	55.049	28.757	20.017	15.665	13.067	11.347	10.128	9.222	8.525	7.974
52.00	56.128	29.321	20.410	15.972	13.323	11.569	10.326	9.403	8.692	8.130
53.00	57.207	29.885	20.802	16.279	13.579	11.792	10.525	9.584	8.859	8.287
54.00	58.287	30.449	21.195	16.586	13.836	12.014	10.723	9.764	9.026	8.443
55.00	59.366	31.013	21.587	16.893	14.092	12.237	10.922	9.945	9.194	8.599
56.00	60.446	31.577	21.980	17.200	14.348	12.459	11.121	10.126	9.361	8.756
57.00	61.525	32.141	22.372	17.507	14.604	12.682	11.319	10.307	9.528	8.912
58.00	62.604	32.705	22.765	17.815	14.860	12.904	11.518	10.488	9.695	9.068
59.00	63.684	33.268	23.157	18.122	15.117	13.127	11.716	10.669	9.862	9.225
60.00	64.763	33.832	23.550	18.429	15.373	13.349	11.915	10.849	10.029	9.381
61.00	65.842	34.396	23.942	18.736	15.629	13.571	12.114	11.030	10.196	9.537
62.00	66.922	34.960	24.335	19.043	15.885	13.794	12.312	11.211	10.364	9.694
63.00	68.001	35.524	24.727	19.350	16.141	14.016	12.511	11.392	10.531	9.850
64.00	69.081	36.088	25.120	19.657	16.398	14.239	12.709	11.573	10.698	10.007
65.00	70.160	36.652	25.512	19.965	16.654	14.461	12.908	11.753	10.865	10.163

Entry is rental that repays cost with interest and management fee on rent.

Cost of Providing Leasehold Improvements

Equity Yield of 10.50%   Includes 3.5% Management Fee

Improvement Cost per square foot of Rented Area	Term of Lease in Years									
	1	2	3	4	5	6	7	8	9	10
$5.00	5.433	2.858	2.003	1.578	1.325	1.157	1.039	0.952	0.885	0.832
6.00	6.520	3.430	2.404	1.894	1.590	1.389	1.247	1.142	1.061	0.998
7.00	7.606	4.002	2.805	2.209	1.855	1.620	1.455	1.332	1.238	1.164
8.00	8.693	4.574	3.205	2.525	2.120	1.852	1.663	1.523	1.415	1.331
9.00	9.780	5.145	3.606	2.841	2.385	2.083	1.871	1.713	1.592	1.497
10.00	10.866	5.717	4.007	3.156	2.650	2.315	2.078	1.903	1.769	1.663
11.00	11.953	6.289	4.407	3.472	2.915	2.546	2.286	2.094	1.946	1.830
12.00	13.040	6.860	4.808	3.787	3.180	2.778	2.494	2.284	2.123	1.996
13.00	14.126	7.432	5.209	4.103	3.445	3.009	2.702	2.474	2.300	2.162
14.00	15.213	8.004	5.609	4.419	3.709	3.241	2.910	2.665	2.477	2.329
15.00	16.300	8.575	6.010	4.734	3.974	3.472	3.118	2.855	2.654	2.495
16.00	17.386	9.147	6.411	5.050	4.239	3.704	3.326	3.045	2.831	2.661
17.00	18.473	9.719	6.811	5.366	4.504	3.935	3.533	3.236	3.007	2.828
18.00	19.560	10.291	7.212	5.681	4.769	4.167	3.741	3.426	3.184	2.994
19.00	20.646	10.862	7.613	5.997	5.034	4.398	3.949	3.616	3.361	3.160
20.00	21.733	11.434	8.013	6.312	5.299	4.630	4.157	3.807	3.538	3.327
21.00	22.819	12.006	8.414	6.628	5.564	4.861	4.365	3.997	3.715	3.493
22.00	23.906	12.577	8.815	6.944	5.829	5.093	4.573	4.187	3.892	3.659
23.00	24.993	13.149	9.215	7.259	6.094	5.324	4.780	4.378	4.069	3.826
24.00	26.079	13.721	9.616	7.575	6.359	5.556	4.988	4.568	4.246	3.992
25.00	27.166	14.292	10.017	7.891	6.624	5.787	5.196	4.758	4.423	4.158
26.00	28.253	14.864	10.417	8.206	6.889	6.019	5.404	4.949	4.600	4.325
27.00	29.339	15.436	10.818	8.522	7.154	6.250	5.612	5.139	4.777	4.491
28.00	30.426	16.007	11.219	8.837	7.419	6.482	5.820	5.329	4.953	4.658
29.00	31.513	16.579	11.619	9.153	7.684	6.713	6.028	5.520	5.130	4.824
30.00	32.599	17.151	12.020	9.469	7.949	6.945	6.235	5.710	5.307	4.990
31.00	33.686	17.723	12.421	9.784	8.214	7.176	6.443	5.900	5.484	5.157
32.00	34.772	18.294	12.821	10.100	8.479	7.408	6.651	6.091	5.661	5.323
33.00	35.859	18.866	13.222	10.416	8.744	7.639	6.859	6.281	5.838	5.489
34.00	36.946	19.438	13.623	10.731	9.009	7.871	7.067	6.471	6.015	5.656
35.00	38.032	20.009	14.023	11.047	9.274	8.102	7.275	6.662	6.192	5.822
36.00	39.119	20.581	14.424	11.362	9.539	8.334	7.483	6.852	6.369	5.988
37.00	40.206	21.153	14.825	11.678	9.804	8.565	7.690	7.042	6.546	6.155
38.00	41.292	21.724	15.225	11.994	10.069	8.797	7.898	7.233	6.723	6.321
39.00	42.379	22.296	15.626	12.309	10.334	9.028	8.106	7.423	6.899	6.487
40.00	43.466	22.868	16.027	12.625	10.599	9.260	8.314	7.613	7.076	6.654
41.00	44.552	23.439	16.427	12.941	10.863	9.491	8.522	7.804	7.253	6.820
42.00	45.639	24.011	16.828	13.256	11.128	9.723	8.730	7.994	7.430	6.986
43.00	46.726	24.583	17.229	13.572	11.393	9.954	8.937	8.184	7.607	7.153
44.00	47.812	25.155	17.629	13.887	11.658	10.186	9.145	8.375	7.784	7.319
45.00	48.899	25.726	18.030	14.203	11.923	10.417	9.353	8.565	7.961	7.485
46.00	49.985	26.298	18.431	14.519	12.188	10.649	9.561	8.755	8.138	7.652
47.00	51.072	26.870	18.831	14.834	12.453	10.880	9.769	8.946	8.315	7.818
48.00	52.159	27.441	19.232	15.150	12.718	11.112	9.977	9.136	8.492	7.984
49.00	53.245	28.013	19.633	15.465	12.983	11.343	10.185	9.326	8.669	8.151
50.00	54.332	28.585	20.033	15.781	13.248	11.575	10.392	9.517	8.845	8.317
51.00	55.419	29.156	20.434	16.097	13.513	11.806	10.600	9.707	9.022	8.483
52.00	56.505	29.728	20.835	16.412	13.778	12.038	10.808	9.897	9.199	8.650
53.00	57.592	30.300	21.235	16.728	14.043	12.269	11.016	10.088	9.376	8.816
54.00	58.679	30.872	21.636	17.044	14.308	12.501	11.224	10.278	9.553	8.982
55.00	59.765	31.443	22.037	17.359	14.573	12.732	11.432	10.468	9.730	9.149
56.00	60.852	32.015	22.437	17.675	14.838	12.964	11.639	10.659	9.907	9.315
57.00	61.938	32.587	22.838	17.990	15.103	13.195	11.847	10.849	10.084	9.481
58.00	63.025	33.158	23.239	18.306	15.368	13.427	12.055	11.039	10.261	9.648
59.00	64.112	33.730	23.640	18.622	15.633	13.658	12.263	11.230	10.438	9.814
60.00	65.198	34.302	24.040	18.937	15.898	13.890	12.471	11.420	10.615	9.980
61.00	66.285	34.873	24.441	19.253	16.163	14.121	12.679	11.610	10.791	10.147
62.00	67.372	35.445	24.842	19.569	16.428	14.353	12.887	11.801	10.968	10.313
63.00	68.458	36.017	25.242	19.884	16.693	14.584	13.094	11.991	11.145	10.479
64.00	69.545	36.588	25.643	20.200	16.958	14.816	13.302	12.181	11.322	10.646
65.00	70.632	37.160	26.044	20.515	17.223	15.047	13.510	12.372	11.499	10.812

Entry is rental that repays cost with interest and management fee on rent.

Cost of Providing Leasehold Improvements

Equity Yield of 7.50%   Includes 5.0% Management Fee

Improvement Cost per square foot of Rented Area	\multicolumn{10}{c}{Term of Lease in Years}									
	1	2	3	4	5	6	7	8	9	10
$5.00	5.445	2.824	1.952	1.518	1.258	1.085	0.963	0.871	0.801	0.745
6.00	6.534	3.389	2.343	1.821	1.509	1.302	1.155	1.046	0.961	0.894
7.00	7.624	3.954	2.733	2.125	1.761	1.519	1.348	1.220	1.121	1.043
8.00	8.713	4.519	3.124	2.428	2.012	1.736	1.540	1.394	1.282	1.192
9.00	9.802	5.084	3.514	2.732	2.264	1.953	1.733	1.569	1.442	1.341
10.00	10.891	5.649	3.905	3.035	2.515	2.170	1.925	1.743	1.602	1.490
11.00	11.980	6.214	4.295	3.339	2.767	2.387	2.118	1.917	1.762	1.639
12.00	13.069	6.779	4.686	3.642	3.018	2.605	2.311	2.091	1.922	1.788
13.00	14.158	7.344	5.076	3.946	3.270	2.822	2.503	2.266	2.082	1.937
14.00	15.247	7.908	5.467	4.249	3.522	3.039	2.696	2.440	2.243	2.086
15.00	16.336	8.473	5.857	4.553	3.773	3.256	2.888	2.614	2.403	2.235
16.00	17.425	9.038	6.248	4.856	4.025	3.473	3.081	2.789	2.563	2.384
17.00	18.514	9.603	6.638	5.160	4.276	3.690	3.273	2.963	2.723	2.533
18.00	19.603	10.168	7.029	5.463	4.528	3.907	3.466	3.137	2.883	2.682
19.00	20.692	10.733	7.419	5.767	4.779	4.124	3.658	3.311	3.044	2.831
20.00	21.782	11.298	7.810	6.070	5.031	4.341	3.851	3.486	3.204	2.980
21.00	22.871	11.863	8.200	6.374	5.282	4.558	4.043	3.660	3.364	3.129
22.00	23.960	12.427	8.591	6.677	5.534	4.775	4.236	3.834	3.524	3.278
23.00	25.049	12.992	8.981	6.981	5.785	4.992	4.428	4.009	3.684	3.427
24.00	26.138	13.557	9.372	7.284	6.037	5.209	4.621	4.183	3.845	3.576
25.00	27.227	14.122	9.762	7.588	6.288	5.426	4.814	4.357	4.005	3.725
26.00	28.316	14.687	10.152	7.892	6.540	5.643	5.006	4.531	4.165	3.874
27.00	29.405	15.252	10.543	8.195	6.792	5.860	5.199	4.706	4.325	4.023
28.00	30.494	15.817	10.933	8.499	7.043	6.077	5.391	4.880	4.485	4.172
29.00	31.583	16.382	11.324	8.802	7.295	6.294	5.584	5.054	4.646	4.321
30.00	32.672	16.947	11.714	9.106	7.546	6.511	5.776	5.229	4.806	4.470
31.00	33.761	17.511	12.105	9.409	7.798	6.728	5.969	5.403	4.966	4.619
32.00	34.850	18.076	12.495	9.713	8.049	6.945	6.161	5.577	5.126	4.768
33.00	35.940	18.641	12.886	10.016	8.301	7.162	6.354	5.751	5.286	4.917
34.00	37.029	19.206	13.276	10.320	8.552	7.380	6.546	5.926	5.446	5.066
35.00	38.118	19.771	13.667	10.623	8.804	7.597	6.739	6.100	5.607	5.215
36.00	39.207	20.336	14.057	10.927	9.055	7.814	6.932	6.274	5.767	5.364
37.00	40.296	20.901	14.448	11.230	9.307	8.031	7.124	6.449	5.927	5.513
38.00	41.385	21.466	14.838	11.534	9.558	8.248	7.317	6.623	6.087	5.662
39.00	42.474	22.031	15.229	11.837	9.810	8.465	7.509	6.797	6.247	5.811
40.00	43.563	22.595	15.619	12.141	10.062	8.682	7.702	6.971	6.408	5.960
41.00	44.652	23.160	16.010	12.444	10.313	8.899	7.894	7.146	6.568	6.109
42.00	45.741	23.725	16.400	12.748	10.565	9.116	8.087	7.320	6.728	6.258
43.00	46.830	24.290	16.791	13.051	10.816	9.333	8.279	7.494	6.888	6.407
44.00	47.919	24.855	17.181	13.355	11.068	9.550	8.472	7.669	7.048	6.556
45.00	49.008	25.420	17.572	13.658	11.319	9.767	8.664	7.843	7.209	6.705
46.00	50.098	25.985	17.962	13.962	11.571	9.984	8.857	8.017	7.369	6.854
47.00	51.187	26.550	18.353	14.265	11.822	10.201	9.050	8.191	7.529	7.003
48.00	52.276	27.114	18.743	14.569	12.074	10.418	9.242	8.366	7.689	7.152
49.00	53.365	27.679	19.134	14.873	12.325	10.635	9.435	8.540	7.849	7.301
50.00	54.454	28.244	19.524	15.176	12.577	10.852	9.627	8.714	8.010	7.450
51.00	55.543	28.809	19.914	15.480	12.828	11.069	9.820	8.889	8.170	7.599
52.00	56.632	29.374	20.305	15.783	13.080	11.286	10.012	9.063	8.330	7.748
53.00	57.721	29.939	20.695	16.087	13.332	11.503	10.205	9.237	8.490	7.897
54.00	58.810	30.504	21.086	16.390	13.583	11.720	10.397	9.411	8.650	8.046
55.00	59.899	31.069	21.476	16.694	13.835	11.937	10.590	9.586	8.810	8.195
56.00	60.988	31.634	21.867	16.997	14.086	12.155	10.782	9.760	8.971	8.344
57.00	62.077	32.198	22.257	17.301	14.338	12.372	10.975	9.934	9.131	8.493
58.00	63.166	32.763	22.648	17.604	14.589	12.589	11.168	10.109	9.291	8.642
59.00	64.256	33.328	23.038	17.908	14.841	12.806	11.360	10.283	9.451	8.791
60.00	65.345	33.893	23.429	18.211	15.092	13.023	11.553	10.457	9.611	8.940
61.00	66.434	34.458	23.819	18.515	15.344	13.240	11.745	10.631	9.772	9.089
62.00	67.523	35.023	24.210	18.818	15.595	13.457	11.938	10.806	9.932	9.238
63.00	68.612	35.588	24.600	19.122	15.847	13.674	12.130	10.980	10.092	9.387
64.00	69.701	36.153	24.991	19.425	16.098	13.891	12.323	11.154	10.252	9.536
65.00	70.790	36.718	25.381	19.729	16.350	14.108	12.515	11.329	10.412	9.686

Entry is rental that repays cost with interest and management fee on rent.

Cost of Providing Leasehold Improvements

Equity Yield of 9.00%   Includes 5.0% Management Fee

Improvement Cost per square foot of Rented Area	Term of Lease in Years									
	1	2	3	4	5	6	7	8	9	10
$5.00	5.482	2.864	1.993	1.560	1.301	1.130	1.009	0.918	0.849	0.794
6.00	6.579	3.437	2.392	1.872	1.562	1.356	1.210	1.102	1.019	0.953
7.00	7.675	4.009	2.791	2.184	1.822	1.582	1.412	1.286	1.189	1.112
8.00	8.771	4.582	3.190	2.496	2.082	1.808	1.614	1.469	1.358	1.271
9.00	9.868	5.155	3.588	2.808	2.342	2.034	1.815	1.653	1.528	1.429
10.00	10.964	5.728	3.987	3.120	2.603	2.260	2.017	1.837	1.698	1.588
11.00	12.061	6.301	4.386	3.432	2.863	2.486	2.219	2.020	1.868	1.747
12.00	13.157	6.873	4.784	3.744	3.123	2.712	2.421	2.204	2.038	1.906
13.00	14.254	7.446	5.183	4.056	3.383	2.938	2.622	2.388	2.207	2.065
14.00	15.350	8.019	5.582	4.368	3.644	3.164	2.824	2.571	2.377	2.223
15.00	16.446	8.592	5.980	4.680	3.904	3.390	3.026	2.755	2.547	2.382
16.00	17.543	9.164	6.379	4.992	4.164	3.616	3.227	2.939	2.717	2.541
17.00	18.639	9.737	6.778	5.304	4.424	3.842	3.429	3.123	2.887	2.700
18.00	19.736	10.310	7.176	5.616	4.685	4.068	3.631	3.306	3.056	2.859
19.00	20.832	10.883	7.575	5.928	4.945	4.294	3.833	3.490	3.226	3.018
20.00	21.929	11.455	7.974	6.240	5.205	4.520	4.034	3.674	3.396	3.176
21.00	23.025	12.028	8.373	6.552	5.465	4.746	4.236	3.857	3.566	3.335
22.00	24.121	12.601	8.771	6.864	5.726	4.972	4.438	4.041	3.735	3.494
23.00	25.218	13.174	9.170	7.176	5.986	5.198	4.640	4.225	3.905	3.653
24.00	26.314	13.747	9.569	7.488	6.246	5.424	4.841	4.408	4.075	3.812
25.00	27.411	14.319	9.967	7.800	6.506	5.650	5.043	4.592	4.245	3.971
26.00	28.507	14.892	10.366	8.112	6.767	5.876	5.245	4.776	4.415	4.129
27.00	29.604	15.465	10.765	8.424	7.027	6.102	5.446	4.959	4.584	4.288
28.00	30.700	16.038	11.163	8.736	7.287	6.328	5.648	5.143	4.754	4.447
29.00	31.796	16.610	11.562	9.048	7.548	6.554	5.850	5.327	4.924	4.606
30.00	32.893	17.183	11.961	9.360	7.808	6.780	6.052	5.510	5.094	4.765
31.00	33.989	17.756	12.359	9.672	8.068	7.006	6.253	5.694	5.264	4.923
32.00	35.086	18.329	12.758	9.984	8.328	7.232	6.455	5.878	5.433	5.082
33.00	36.182	18.902	13.157	10.296	8.589	7.458	6.657	6.061	5.603	5.241
34.00	37.279	19.474	13.555	10.608	8.849	7.684	6.858	6.245	5.773	5.400
35.00	38.375	20.047	13.954	10.920	9.109	7.910	7.060	6.429	5.943	5.559
36.00	39.471	20.620	14.353	11.232	9.369	8.136	7.262	6.612	6.113	5.718
37.00	40.568	21.193	14.752	11.544	9.630	8.362	7.464	6.796	6.282	5.876
38.00	41.664	21.765	15.150	11.856	9.890	8.588	7.665	6.980	6.452	6.035
39.00	42.761	22.338	15.549	12.168	10.150	8.814	7.867	7.163	6.622	6.194
40.00	43.857	22.911	15.948	12.480	10.410	9.040	8.069	7.347	6.792	6.353
41.00	44.954	23.484	16.346	12.792	10.671	9.266	8.270	7.531	6.962	6.512
42.00	46.050	24.057	16.745	13.104	10.931	9.492	8.472	7.714	7.131	6.670
43.00	47.146	24.629	17.144	13.416	11.191	9.718	8.674	7.898	7.301	6.829
44.00	48.243	25.202	17.542	13.728	11.451	9.944	8.876	8.082	7.471	6.988
45.00	49.339	25.775	17.941	14.040	11.712	10.170	9.077	8.265	7.641	7.147
46.00	50.436	26.348	18.340	14.352	11.972	10.396	9.279	8.449	7.811	7.306
47.00	51.532	26.920	18.738	14.664	12.232	10.622	9.481	8.633	7.980	7.465
48.00	52.628	27.493	19.137	14.976	12.492	10.848	9.682	8.817	8.150	7.623
49.00	53.725	28.066	19.536	15.288	12.753	11.074	9.884	9.000	8.320	7.782
50.00	54.821	28.639	19.935	15.600	13.013	11.300	10.086	9.184	8.490	7.941
51.00	55.918	29.212	20.333	15.912	13.273	11.526	10.288	9.368	8.660	8.100
52.00	57.014	29.784	20.732	16.224	13.533	11.752	10.489	9.551	8.829	8.259
53.00	58.111	30.357	21.131	16.536	13.794	11.978	10.691	9.735	8.999	8.417
54.00	59.207	30.930	21.529	16.848	14.054	12.204	10.893	9.919	9.169	8.576
55.00	60.303	31.503	21.928	17.160	14.314	12.430	11.094	10.102	9.339	8.735
56.00	61.400	32.075	22.327	17.472	14.574	12.656	11.296	10.286	9.509	8.894
57.00	62.496	32.648	22.725	17.784	14.835	12.882	11.498	10.470	9.678	9.053
58.00	63.593	33.221	23.124	18.096	15.095	13.108	11.700	10.653	9.848	9.212
59.00	64.689	33.794	23.523	18.408	15.355	13.334	11.901	10.837	10.018	9.370
60.00	65.786	34.366	23.921	18.720	15.616	13.560	12.103	11.021	10.188	9.529
61.00	66.882	34.939	24.320	19.032	15.876	13.786	12.305	11.204	10.357	9.688
62.00	67.978	35.512	24.719	19.344	16.136	14.012	12.506	11.388	10.527	9.847
63.00	69.075	36.085	25.118	19.656	16.396	14.238	12.708	11.572	10.697	10.006
64.00	70.171	36.658	25.516	19.968	16.657	14.464	12.910	11.755	10.867	10.165
65.00	71.268	37.230	25.915	20.280	16.917	14.690	13.112	11.939	11.037	10.323

Entry is rental that repays cost with interest and management fee on rent.

Cost of Providing Leasehold Improvements

Equity Yield of 10.50%   Includes 5.0% Management Fee

Improvement Cost per square foot of Rented Area	Term of Lease in Years									
	1	2	3	4	5	6	7	8	9	10
$5.00	5.519	2.904	2.035	1.603	1.346	1.176	1.056	0.967	0.899	0.845
6.00	6.623	3.484	2.442	1.924	1.615	1.411	1.267	1.160	1.078	1.014
7.00	7.727	4.065	2.849	2.244	1.884	1.646	1.478	1.353	1.258	1.183
8.00	8.830	4.646	3.256	2.565	2.153	1.881	1.689	1.547	1.438	1.352
9.00	9.934	5.226	3.663	2.885	2.422	2.116	1.900	1.740	1.617	1.521
10.00	11.038	5.807	4.070	3.206	2.691	2.352	2.111	1.933	1.797	1.690
11.00	12.142	6.388	4.477	3.527	2.961	2.587	2.322	2.127	1.977	1.859
12.00	13.246	6.969	4.884	3.847	3.230	2.822	2.534	2.320	2.156	2.028
13.00	14.349	7.549	5.291	4.168	3.499	3.057	2.745	2.513	2.336	2.197
14.00	15.453	8.130	5.698	4.488	3.768	3.292	2.956	2.707	2.516	2.366
15.00	16.557	8.711	6.105	4.809	4.037	3.527	3.167	2.900	2.696	2.534
16.00	17.661	9.292	6.512	5.130	4.306	3.762	3.378	3.093	2.875	2.703
17.00	18.765	9.872	6.919	5.450	4.575	3.998	3.589	3.287	3.055	2.872
18.00	19.868	10.453	7.326	5.771	4.845	4.233	3.800	3.480	3.235	3.041
19.00	20.972	11.034	7.733	6.092	5.114	4.468	4.011	3.673	3.414	3.210
20.00	22.076	11.614	8.140	6.412	5.383	4.703	4.223	3.867	3.594	3.379
21.00	23.180	12.195	8.547	6.733	5.652	4.938	4.434	4.060	3.774	3.548
22.00	24.284	12.776	8.954	7.053	5.921	5.173	4.645	4.253	3.953	3.717
23.00	25.387	13.357	9.361	7.374	6.190	5.408	4.856	4.447	4.133	3.886
24.00	26.491	13.937	9.768	7.695	6.460	5.644	5.067	4.640	4.313	4.055
25.00	27.595	14.518	10.175	8.015	6.729	5.879	5.278	4.834	4.493	4.224
26.00	28.699	15.099	10.582	8.336	6.998	6.114	5.489	5.027	4.672	4.393
27.00	29.803	15.679	10.989	8.656	7.267	6.349	5.700	5.220	4.852	4.562
28.00	30.906	16.260	11.396	8.977	7.536	6.584	5.912	5.414	5.032	4.731
29.00	32.010	16.841	11.803	9.298	7.805	6.819	6.123	5.607	5.211	4.900
30.00	33.114	17.422	12.210	9.618	8.074	7.055	6.334	5.800	5.391	5.069
31.00	34.218	18.002	12.617	9.939	8.344	7.290	6.545	5.994	5.571	5.238
32.00	35.322	18.583	13.024	10.259	8.613	7.525	6.756	6.187	5.750	5.407
33.00	36.425	19.164	13.431	10.580	8.882	7.760	6.967	6.380	5.930	5.576
34.00	37.529	19.745	13.838	10.901	9.151	7.995	7.178	6.574	6.110	5.745
35.00	38.633	20.325	14.245	11.221	9.420	8.230	7.390	6.767	6.290	5.914
36.00	39.737	20.906	14.652	11.542	9.689	8.465	7.601	6.960	6.469	6.083
37.00	40.841	21.487	15.059	11.862	9.958	8.701	7.812	7.154	6.649	6.252
38.00	41.944	22.067	15.466	12.183	10.228	8.936	8.023	7.347	6.829	6.421
39.00	43.048	22.648	15.873	12.504	10.497	9.171	8.234	7.540	7.008	6.590
40.00	44.152	23.229	16.280	12.824	10.766	9.406	8.445	7.734	7.188	6.759
41.00	45.256	23.810	16.687	13.145	11.035	9.641	8.656	7.927	7.368	6.928
42.00	46.360	24.390	17.094	13.465	11.304	9.876	8.867	8.120	7.547	7.097
43.00	47.463	24.971	17.501	13.786	11.573	10.111	9.079	8.314	7.727	7.266
44.00	48.567	25.552	17.908	14.107	11.842	10.347	9.290	8.507	7.907	7.434
45.00	49.671	26.132	18.315	14.427	12.112	10.582	9.501	8.700	8.087	7.603
46.00	50.775	26.713	18.722	14.748	12.381	10.817	9.712	8.894	8.266	7.772
47.00	51.878	27.294	19.129	15.068	12.650	11.052	9.923	9.087	8.446	7.941
48.00	52.982	27.875	19.536	15.389	12.919	11.287	10.134	9.280	8.626	8.110
49.00	54.086	28.455	19.943	15.710	13.188	11.522	10.345	9.474	8.805	8.279
50.00	55.190	29.036	20.350	16.030	13.457	11.758	10.556	9.667	8.985	8.448
51.00	56.294	29.617	20.757	16.351	13.726	11.993	10.768	9.860	9.165	8.617
52.00	57.397	30.198	21.164	16.672	13.996	12.228	10.979	10.054	9.344	8.786
53.00	58.501	30.778	21.571	16.992	14.265	12.463	11.190	10.247	9.524	8.955
54.00	59.605	31.359	21.978	17.313	14.534	12.698	11.401	10.440	9.704	9.124
55.00	60.709	31.940	22.385	17.633	14.803	12.933	11.612	10.634	9.884	9.293
56.00	61.813	32.520	22.792	17.954	15.072	13.168	11.823	10.827	10.063	9.462
57.00	62.916	33.101	23.199	18.275	15.341	13.404	12.034	11.020	10.243	9.631
58.00	64.020	33.682	23.606	18.595	15.611	13.639	12.246	11.214	10.423	9.800
59.00	65.124	34.263	24.013	18.916	15.880	13.874	12.457	11.407	10.602	9.969
60.00	66.228	34.843	24.420	19.236	16.149	14.109	12.668	11.600	10.782	10.138
61.00	67.332	35.424	24.827	19.557	16.418	14.344	12.879	11.794	10.962	10.307
62.00	68.435	36.005	25.234	19.878	16.687	14.579	13.090	11.987	11.142	10.476
63.00	69.539	36.585	25.641	20.198	16.956	14.814	13.301	12.180	11.321	10.645
64.00	70.643	37.166	26.048	20.519	17.225	15.050	13.512	12.374	11.501	10.814
65.00	71.747	37.747	26.455	20.839	17.495	15.285	13.723	12.567	11.681	10.983

Entry is rental that repays cost with interest and management fee on rent.

Cost of Assuming a Tenant's Lease Obligation

Interest Rate 7.50%   3.5% Management Fee

Old Rent	3/1	5/1	5/2	6/1	New Lease Term / Old Lease Term in Years 6/2	7/1	7/2	7/3	10/1	10/2	10/3	10/4
0.50	0.187	0.120	0.232	0.104	0.200	0.092	0.178	0.257	0.071	0.138	0.199	0.256
1.00	0.374	0.241	0.464	0.208	0.401	0.184	0.355	0.514	0.143	0.275	0.398	0.512
1.50	0.561	0.361	0.696	0.312	0.601	0.277	0.533	0.771	0.214	0.413	0.597	0.768
2.00	0.748	0.482	0.929	0.416	0.801	0.369	0.711	1.028	0.285	0.550	0.796	1.024
2.50	0.935	0.602	1.161	0.520	1.002	0.461	0.889	1.285	0.357	0.688	0.995	1.280
3.00	1.122	0.723	1.393	0.623	1.202	0.553	1.066	1.543	0.428	0.825	1.194	1.536
3.50	1.309	0.843	1.625	0.727	1.402	0.645	1.244	1.800	0.499	0.963	1.393	1.792
4.00	1.495	0.963	1.857	0.831	1.603	0.737	1.422	2.057	0.571	1.100	1.592	2.048
4.50	1.682	1.084	2.089	0.935	1.803	0.830	1.599	2.314	0.642	1.238	1.791	2.304
5.00	1.869	1.204	2.322	1.039	2.003	0.922	1.777	2.571	0.713	1.375	1.990	2.560
5.50	2.056	1.325	2.554	1.143	2.204	1.014	1.955	2.828	0.785	1.513	2.189	2.816
6.00	2.243	1.445	2.786	1.247	2.404	1.106	2.133	3.085	0.856	1.650	2.387	3.072
6.50	2.430	1.565	3.018	1.351	2.604	1.198	2.310	3.342	0.927	1.788	2.586	3.327
7.00	2.617	1.686	3.250	1.455	2.805	1.290	2.488	3.599	0.999	1.925	2.785	3.583
7.50	2.804	1.806	3.482	1.559	3.005	1.383	2.666	3.856	1.070	2.063	2.984	3.839
8.00	2.991	1.927	3.715	1.662	3.205	1.475	2.843	4.113	1.141	2.200	3.183	4.095
8.50	3.178	2.047	3.947	1.766	3.406	1.567	3.021	4.370	1.213	2.338	3.382	4.351
9.00	3.365	2.168	4.179	1.870	3.606	1.659	3.199	4.628	1.284	2.476	3.581	4.607
9.50	3.552	2.288	4.411	1.974	3.806	1.751	3.377	4.885	1.355	2.613	3.780	4.863
10.00	3.739	2.408	4.643	2.078	4.007	1.844	3.554	5.142	1.427	2.751	3.979	5.119
10.50	3.926	2.529	4.875	2.182	4.207	1.936	3.732	5.399	1.498	2.888	4.178	5.375
11.00	4.113	2.649	5.108	2.286	4.407	2.028	3.910	5.656	1.569	3.026	4.377	5.631
11.50	4.299	2.770	5.340	2.390	4.608	2.120	4.087	5.913	1.641	3.163	4.576	5.887
12.00	4.486	2.890	5.572	2.494	4.808	2.212	4.265	6.170	1.712	3.301	4.775	6.143
12.50	4.673	3.010	5.804	2.598	5.008	2.304	4.443	6.427	1.783	3.438	4.974	6.399
13.00	4.860	3.131	6.036	2.702	5.208	2.397	4.621	6.684	1.855	3.576	5.173	6.655
13.50	5.047	3.251	6.268	2.805	5.409	2.489	4.798	6.941	1.926	3.713	5.372	6.911
14.00	5.234	3.372	6.501	2.909	5.609	2.581	4.976	7.198	1.997	3.851	5.571	7.167
14.50	5.421	3.492	6.733	3.013	5.809	2.673	5.154	7.455	2.069	3.988	5.770	7.423
15.00	5.608	3.613	6.965	3.117	6.010	2.765	5.331	7.713	2.140	4.126	5.969	7.679
15.50	5.795	3.733	7.197	3.221	6.210	2.857	5.509	7.970	2.211	4.263	6.168	7.935
16.00	5.982	3.853	7.429	3.325	6.410	2.950	5.687	8.227	2.283	4.401	6.367	8.191
16.50	6.169	3.974	7.661	3.429	6.611	3.042	5.865	8.484	2.354	4.538	6.566	8.447
17.00	6.356	4.094	7.894	3.533	6.811	3.134	6.042	8.741	2.425	4.676	6.765	8.703
17.50	6.543	4.215	8.126	3.637	7.011	3.226	6.220	8.998	2.497	4.814	6.963	8.959
18.00	6.730	4.335	8.358	3.741	7.212	3.318	6.398	9.255	2.568	4.951	7.162	9.215
18.50	6.917	4.456	8.590	3.845	7.412	3.411	6.575	9.512	2.639	5.089	7.361	9.470
19.00	7.104	4.576	8.822	3.948	7.612	3.503	6.753	9.769	2.711	5.226	7.560	9.726
19.50	7.290	4.696	9.054	4.052	7.813	3.595	6.931	10.026	2.782	5.364	7.759	9.982
20.00	7.477	4.817	9.287	4.156	8.013	3.687	7.108	10.283	2.853	5.501	7.958	10.238
20.50	7.664	4.937	9.519	4.260	8.213	3.779	7.286	10.541	2.925	5.639	8.157	10.494
21.00	7.851	5.058	9.751	4.364	8.414	3.871	7.464	10.798	2.996	5.776	8.356	10.750
21.50	8.038	5.178	9.983	4.468	8.614	3.964	7.642	11.055	3.067	5.914	8.555	11.006
22.00	8.225	5.298	10.215	4.572	8.814	4.056	7.819	11.312	3.139	6.051	8.754	11.262
22.50	8.412	5.419	10.447	4.676	9.015	4.148	7.997	11.569	3.210	6.189	8.953	11.518
23.00	8.599	5.539	10.680	4.780	9.215	4.240	8.175	11.826	3.281	6.326	9.152	11.774
23.50	8.786	5.660	10.912	4.884	9.415	4.332	8.352	12.083	3.353	6.464	9.351	12.030
24.00	8.973	5.780	11.144	4.987	9.616	4.424	8.530	12.340	3.424	6.601	9.550	12.286
24.50	9.160	5.901	11.376	5.091	9.816	4.517	8.708	12.597	3.495	6.739	9.749	12.542
25.00	9.347	6.021	11.608	5.195	10.016	4.609	8.886	12.854	3.567	6.877	9.948	12.798
25.50	9.534	6.141	11.840	5.299	10.217	4.701	9.063	13.111	3.638	7.014	10.147	13.054
26.00	9.721	6.262	12.072	5.403	10.417	4.793	9.241	13.368	3.709	7.152	10.346	13.310
26.50	9.908	6.382	12.305	5.507	10.617	4.885	9.419	13.626	3.781	7.289	10.545	13.566
27.00	10.094	6.503	12.537	5.611	10.818	4.978	9.596	13.883	3.852	7.427	10.744	13.822
27.50	10.281	6.623	12.769	5.715	11.018	5.070	9.774	14.140	3.923	7.564	10.943	14.078
28.00	10.468	6.743	13.001	5.819	11.218	5.162	9.952	14.397	3.995	7.702	11.142	14.334
28.50	10.655	6.864	13.233	5.923	11.419	5.254	10.130	14.654	4.066	7.839	11.341	14.590
29.00	10.842	6.984	13.465	6.027	11.619	5.346	10.307	14.911	4.137	7.977	11.540	14.846
29.50	11.029	7.105	13.698	6.130	11.819	5.438	10.485	15.168	4.209	8.114	11.738	15.102
30.00	11.216	7.225	13.930	6.234	12.020	5.531	10.663	15.425	4.280	8.252	11.937	15.358

Entry is annual rent per square foot to pay back lease assumption, interest and management fee.

Cost of Assuming a Tenant's Lease Obligation

Interest Rate 7.50%   3.5% Management Fee

Old Rent	12/1	12/2	12/3	12/4	15/1	New Lease Term / Old Lease Term in Years 15/2	15/3	15/4	20/1	20/2	20/3	20/4
0.50	0.063	0.122	0.177	0.228	0.056	0.107	0.155	0.200	0.048	0.093	0.135	0.174
1.00	0.127	0.245	0.354	0.455	0.111	0.215	0.311	0.400	0.097	0.187	0.270	0.347
1.50	0.190	0.367	0.531	0.683	0.167	0.322	0.466	0.600	0.145	0.280	0.405	0.521
2.00	0.254	0.489	0.707	0.910	0.223	0.430	0.622	0.800	0.194	0.373	0.540	0.695
2.50	0.317	0.611	0.884	1.138	0.279	0.537	0.777	0.999	0.242	0.467	0.675	0.869
3.00	0.380	0.734	1.061	1.365	0.334	0.644	0.932	1.199	0.290	0.560	0.810	1.042
3.50	0.444	0.856	1.238	1.593	0.390	0.752	1.088	1.399	0.339	0.653	0.945	1.216
4.00	0.507	0.978	1.415	1.820	0.446	0.859	1.243	1.599	0.387	0.747	1.080	1.390
4.50	0.571	1.100	1.592	2.048	0.501	0.967	1.398	1.799	0.436	0.840	1.215	1.563
5.00	0.634	1.223	1.769	2.275	0.557	1.074	1.554	1.999	0.484	0.933	1.350	1.737
5.50	0.698	1.345	1.946	2.503	0.613	1.181	1.709	2.199	0.533	1.027	1.485	1.911
6.00	0.761	1.467	2.122	2.730	0.669	1.289	1.865	2.399	0.581	1.120	1.620	2.085
6.50	0.824	1.589	2.299	2.958	0.724	1.396	2.020	2.599	0.629	1.213	1.755	2.258
7.00	0.888	1.712	2.476	3.186	0.780	1.504	2.175	2.799	0.678	1.307	1.890	2.432
7.50	0.951	1.834	2.653	3.413	0.836	1.611	2.331	2.998	0.726	1.400	2.025	2.606
8.00	1.015	1.956	2.830	3.641	0.891	1.718	2.486	3.198	0.775	1.493	2.160	2.779
8.50	1.078	2.078	3.007	3.868	0.947	1.826	2.641	3.398	0.823	1.587	2.295	2.953
9.00	1.141	2.201	3.184	4.096	1.003	1.933	2.797	3.598	0.871	1.680	2.430	3.127
9.50	1.205	2.323	3.360	4.323	1.058	2.041	2.952	3.798	0.920	1.773	2.565	3.301
10.00	1.268	2.445	3.537	4.551	1.114	2.148	3.108	3.998	0.968	1.867	2.701	3.474
10.50	1.332	2.567	3.714	4.778	1.170	2.256	3.263	4.198	1.017	1.960	2.836	3.648
11.00	1.395	2.690	3.891	5.006	1.226	2.363	3.418	4.398	1.065	2.053	2.971	3.822
11.50	1.459	2.812	4.068	5.233	1.281	2.470	3.574	4.598	1.113	2.147	3.106	3.995
12.00	1.522	2.934	4.245	5.461	1.337	2.578	3.729	4.797	1.162	2.240	3.241	4.169
12.50	1.585	3.057	4.422	5.689	1.393	2.685	3.884	4.997	1.210	2.333	3.376	4.343
13.00	1.649	3.179	4.599	5.916	1.448	2.793	4.040	5.197	1.259	2.427	3.511	4.517
13.50	1.712	3.301	4.775	6.144	1.504	2.900	4.195	5.397	1.307	2.520	3.646	4.690
14.00	1.776	3.423	4.952	6.371	1.560	3.007	4.351	5.597	1.356	2.613	3.781	4.864
14.50	1.839	3.546	5.129	6.599	1.616	3.115	4.506	5.797	1.404	2.707	3.916	5.038
15.00	1.902	3.668	5.306	6.826	1.671	3.222	4.661	5.997	1.452	2.800	4.051	5.211
15.50	1.966	3.790	5.483	7.054	1.727	3.330	4.817	6.197	1.501	2.893	4.186	5.385
16.00	2.029	3.912	5.660	7.281	1.783	3.437	4.972	6.397	1.549	2.987	4.321	5.559
16.50	2.093	4.035	5.837	7.509	1.838	3.544	5.127	6.596	1.598	3.080	4.456	5.732
17.00	2.156	4.157	6.013	7.736	1.894	3.652	5.283	6.796	1.646	3.173	4.591	5.906
17.50	2.220	4.279	6.190	7.964	1.950	3.759	5.438	6.996	1.694	3.267	4.726	6.080
18.00	2.283	4.401	6.367	8.191	2.006	3.867	5.594	7.196	1.743	3.360	4.861	6.254
18.50	2.346	4.524	6.544	8.419	2.061	3.974	5.749	7.396	1.791	3.453	4.996	6.427
19.00	2.410	4.646	6.721	8.647	2.117	4.081	5.904	7.596	1.840	3.547	5.131	6.601
19.50	2.473	4.768	6.898	8.874	2.173	4.189	6.060	7.796	1.888	3.640	5.266	6.775
20.00	2.537	4.890	7.075	9.102	2.228	4.296	6.215	7.996	1.937	3.734	5.401	6.948
20.50	2.600	5.013	7.252	9.329	2.284	4.404	6.370	8.196	1.985	3.827	5.536	7.122
21.00	2.663	5.135	7.428	9.557	2.340	4.511	6.526	8.396	2.033	3.920	5.671	7.296
21.50	2.727	5.257	7.605	9.784	2.396	4.618	6.681	8.595	2.082	4.014	5.806	7.470
22.00	2.790	5.379	7.782	10.012	2.451	4.726	6.837	8.795	2.130	4.107	5.941	7.643
22.50	2.854	5.502	7.959	10.239	2.507	4.833	6.992	8.995	2.179	4.200	6.076	7.817
23.00	2.917	5.624	8.136	10.467	2.563	4.941	7.147	9.195	2.227	4.294	6.211	7.991
23.50	2.980	5.746	8.313	10.694	2.618	5.048	7.303	9.395	2.275	4.387	6.346	8.164
24.00	3.044	5.869	8.490	10.922	2.674	5.155	7.458	9.595	2.324	4.480	6.481	8.338
24.50	3.107	5.991	8.667	11.149	2.730	5.263	7.613	9.795	2.372	4.574	6.616	8.512
25.00	3.171	6.113	8.843	11.377	2.785	5.370	7.769	9.995	2.421	4.667	6.751	8.686
25.50	3.234	6.235	9.020	11.605	2.841	5.478	7.924	10.195	2.469	4.760	6.886	8.859
26.00	3.298	6.358	9.197	11.832	2.897	5.585	8.080	10.394	2.517	4.854	7.021	9.033
26.50	3.361	6.480	9.374	12.060	2.953	5.692	8.235	10.594	2.566	4.947	7.156	9.207
27.00	3.424	6.602	9.551	12.287	3.008	5.800	8.390	10.794	2.614	5.040	7.291	9.380
27.50	3.488	6.724	9.728	12.515	3.064	5.907	8.546	10.994	2.663	5.134	7.426	9.554
28.00	3.551	6.847	9.905	12.742	3.120	6.015	8.701	11.194	2.711	5.227	7.561	9.728
28.50	3.615	6.969	10.081	12.970	3.175	6.122	8.857	11.394	2.760	5.320	7.696	9.902
29.00	3.678	7.091	10.258	13.197	3.231	6.230	9.012	11.594	2.808	5.414	7.832	10.075
29.50	3.741	7.213	10.435	13.425	3.287	6.337	9.167	11.794	2.856	5.507	7.967	10.249
30.00	3.805	7.336	10.612	13.652	3.343	6.444	9.323	11.994	2.905	5.600	8.102	10.423

Entry is annual rent per square foot to pay back lease assumption, interest and management fee.

Cost of Assuming a Tenant's Lease Obligation

Interest Rate 7.50%   5.0% Management Fee

Old Rent	3/1	5/1	5/2	New Lease Term / Old Lease Term in Years 6/1	6/2	7/1	7/2	7/3	10/1	10/2	10/3	10/4
0.50	0.190	0.122	0.236	0.106	0.203	0.094	0.181	0.261	0.072	0.140	0.202	0.260
1.00	0.380	0.245	0.472	0.211	0.407	0.187	0.361	0.522	0.145	0.279	0.404	0.520
1.50	0.570	0.367	0.707	0.317	0.610	0.281	0.542	0.783	0.217	0.419	0.606	0.780
2.00	0.760	0.489	0.943	0.422	0.814	0.375	0.722	1.045	0.290	0.559	0.808	1.040
2.50	0.949	0.612	1.179	0.528	1.017	0.468	0.903	1.306	0.362	0.699	1.010	1.300
3.00	1.139	0.734	1.415	0.633	1.221	0.562	1.083	1.567	0.435	0.838	1.213	1.560
3.50	1.329	0.856	1.651	0.739	1.424	0.655	1.264	1.828	0.507	0.978	1.415	1.820
4.00	1.519	0.979	1.887	0.844	1.628	0.749	1.444	2.089	0.580	1.118	1.617	2.080
4.50	1.709	1.101	2.122	0.950	1.831	0.843	1.625	2.350	0.652	1.257	1.819	2.340
5.00	1.899	1.223	2.358	1.055	2.035	0.936	1.805	2.611	0.725	1.397	2.021	2.600
5.50	2.089	1.346	2.594	1.161	2.238	1.030	1.986	2.873	0.797	1.537	2.223	2.860
6.00	2.279	1.468	2.830	1.267	2.442	1.124	2.166	3.134	0.870	1.676	2.425	3.120
6.50	2.469	1.590	3.066	1.372	2.645	1.217	2.347	3.395	0.942	1.816	2.627	3.380
7.00	2.658	1.712	3.302	1.478	2.849	1.311	2.527	3.656	1.014	1.956	2.829	3.640
7.50	2.848	1.835	3.537	1.583	3.052	1.404	2.708	3.917	1.087	2.096	3.031	3.900
8.00	3.038	1.957	3.773	1.689	3.256	1.498	2.888	4.178	1.159	2.235	3.234	4.160
8.50	3.228	2.079	4.009	1.794	3.459	1.592	3.069	4.439	1.232	2.375	3.436	4.420
9.00	3.418	2.202	4.245	1.900	3.663	1.685	3.249	4.701	1.304	2.515	3.638	4.680
9.50	3.608	2.324	4.481	2.005	3.866	1.779	3.430	4.962	1.377	2.654	3.840	4.940
10.00	3.798	2.446	4.717	2.111	4.070	1.873	3.610	5.223	1.449	2.794	4.042	5.200
10.50	3.988	2.569	4.952	2.216	4.273	1.966	3.791	5.484	1.522	2.934	4.244	5.460
11.00	4.177	2.691	5.188	2.322	4.477	2.060	3.971	5.745	1.594	3.073	4.446	5.720
11.50	4.367	2.813	5.424	2.428	4.680	2.154	4.152	6.006	1.667	3.213	4.648	5.980
12.00	4.557	2.936	5.660	2.533	4.884	2.247	4.332	6.267	1.739	3.353	4.850	6.240
12.50	4.747	3.058	5.896	2.639	5.087	2.341	4.513	6.529	1.812	3.493	5.052	6.500
13.00	4.937	3.180	6.132	2.744	5.291	2.434	4.693	6.790	1.884	3.632	5.255	6.760
13.50	5.127	3.303	6.367	2.850	5.494	2.528	4.874	7.051	1.956	3.772	5.457	7.020
14.00	5.317	3.425	6.603	2.955	5.698	2.622	5.055	7.312	2.029	3.912	5.659	7.280
14.50	5.507	3.547	6.839	3.061	5.901	2.715	5.235	7.573	2.101	4.051	5.861	7.540
15.00	5.697	3.670	7.075	3.166	6.105	2.809	5.416	7.834	2.174	4.191	6.063	7.800
15.50	5.886	3.792	7.311	3.272	6.308	2.903	5.596	8.095	2.246	4.331	6.265	8.060
16.00	6.076	3.914	7.547	3.377	6.512	2.996	5.777	8.357	2.319	4.470	6.467	8.320
16.50	6.266	4.037	7.782	3.483	6.715	3.090	5.957	8.618	2.391	4.610	6.669	8.580
17.00	6.456	4.159	8.018	3.589	6.919	3.183	6.138	8.879	2.464	4.750	6.871	8.840
17.50	6.646	4.281	8.254	3.694	7.122	3.277	6.318	9.140	2.536	4.890	7.073	9.100
18.00	6.836	4.404	8.490	3.800	7.326	3.371	6.499	9.401	2.609	5.029	7.276	9.360
18.50	7.026	4.526	8.726	3.905	7.529	3.464	6.679	9.662	2.681	5.169	7.478	9.620
19.00	7.216	4.648	8.962	4.011	7.733	3.558	6.860	9.924	2.754	5.309	7.680	9.880
19.50	7.406	4.771	9.197	4.116	7.936	3.652	7.040	10.185	2.826	5.448	7.882	10.140
20.00	7.595	4.893	9.433	4.222	8.140	3.745	7.221	10.446	2.898	5.588	8.084	10.400
20.50	7.785	5.015	9.669	4.327	8.343	3.839	7.401	10.707	2.971	5.728	8.286	10.660
21.00	7.975	5.137	9.905	4.433	8.547	3.933	7.582	10.968	3.043	5.867	8.488	10.920
21.50	8.165	5.260	10.141	4.539	8.750	4.026	7.762	11.229	3.116	6.007	8.690	11.180
22.00	8.355	5.382	10.376	4.644	8.954	4.120	7.943	11.490	3.188	6.147	8.892	11.440
22.50	8.545	5.504	10.612	4.750	9.157	4.213	8.123	11.752	3.261	6.287	9.094	11.700
23.00	8.735	5.627	10.848	4.855	9.361	4.307	8.304	12.013	3.333	6.426	9.297	11.960
23.50	8.925	5.749	11.084	4.961	9.564	4.401	8.484	12.274	3.406	6.566	9.499	12.220
24.00	9.115	5.871	11.320	5.066	9.767	4.494	8.665	12.535	3.478	6.706	9.701	12.480
24.50	9.304	5.994	11.556	5.172	9.971	4.588	8.845	12.796	3.551	6.845	9.903	12.740
25.00	9.494	6.116	11.791	5.277	10.174	4.682	9.026	13.057	3.623	6.985	10.105	13.000
25.50	9.684	6.238	12.027	5.383	10.378	4.775	9.206	13.318	3.696	7.125	10.307	13.260
26.00	9.874	6.361	12.263	5.488	10.581	4.869	9.387	13.580	3.768	7.264	10.509	13.520
26.50	10.064	6.483	12.499	5.594	10.785	4.962	9.567	13.841	3.840	7.404	10.711	13.780
27.00	10.254	6.605	12.735	5.700	10.988	5.056	9.748	14.102	3.913	7.544	10.913	14.040
27.50	10.444	6.728	12.971	5.805	11.192	5.150	9.928	14.363	3.985	7.684	11.115	14.300
28.00	10.634	6.850	13.206	5.911	11.395	5.243	10.109	14.624	4.058	7.823	11.318	14.560
28.50	10.824	6.972	13.442	6.016	11.599	5.337	10.290	14.885	4.130	7.963	11.520	14.820
29.00	11.013	7.095	13.678	6.122	11.802	5.431	10.470	15.146	4.203	8.103	11.722	15.080
29.50	11.203	7.217	13.914	6.227	12.006	5.524	10.651	15.408	4.275	8.242	11.924	15.340
30.00	11.393	7.339	14.150	6.333	12.209	5.618	10.831	15.669	4.348	8.382	12.126	15.600

Entry is annual rent per square foot to pay back lease assumption, interest and management fee.

Cost of Assuming a Tenant's Lease Obligation

Interest Rate 7.50%   5.0% Management Fee

Old Rent	New Lease Term / Old Lease Term in Years											
	12/1	12/2	12/3	12/4	15/1	15/2	15/3	15/4	20/1	20/2	20/3	20/4
0.50	0.064	0.124	0.180	0.231	0.057	0.109	0.158	0.203	0.049	0.095	0.137	0.176
1.00	0.129	0.248	0.359	0.462	0.113	0.218	0.316	0.406	0.098	0.190	0.274	0.353
1.50	0.193	0.373	0.539	0.693	0.170	0.327	0.473	0.609	0.148	0.284	0.411	0.529
2.00	0.258	0.497	0.719	0.925	0.226	0.436	0.631	0.812	0.197	0.379	0.549	0.706
2.50	0.322	0.621	0.898	1.156	0.283	0.546	0.789	1.015	0.246	0.474	0.686	0.882
3.00	0.386	0.745	1.078	1.387	0.340	0.655	0.947	1.218	0.295	0.569	0.823	1.059
3.50	0.451	0.869	1.258	1.618	0.396	0.764	1.105	1.421	0.344	0.664	0.960	1.235
4.00	0.515	0.994	1.437	1.849	0.453	0.873	1.263	1.624	0.393	0.758	1.097	1.412
4.50	0.580	1.118	1.617	2.080	0.509	0.982	1.420	1.827	0.443	0.853	1.234	1.588
5.00	0.644	1.242	1.797	2.311	0.566	1.091	1.578	2.030	0.492	0.948	1.372	1.765
5.50	0.709	1.366	1.976	2.542	0.622	1.200	1.736	2.234	0.541	1.043	1.509	1.941
6.00	0.773	1.490	2.156	2.774	0.679	1.309	1.894	2.437	0.590	1.138	1.646	2.117
6.50	0.837	1.614	2.336	3.005	0.736	1.418	2.052	2.640	0.639	1.233	1.783	2.294
7.00	0.902	1.739	2.515	3.236	0.792	1.527	2.210	2.843	0.688	1.327	1.920	2.470
7.50	0.966	1.863	2.695	3.467	0.849	1.637	2.367	3.046	0.738	1.422	2.057	2.647
8.00	1.031	1.987	2.875	3.698	0.905	1.746	2.525	3.249	0.787	1.517	2.195	2.823
8.50	1.095	2.111	3.054	3.929	0.962	1.855	2.683	3.452	0.836	1.612	2.332	3.000
9.00	1.159	2.235	3.234	4.160	1.019	1.964	2.841	3.655	0.885	1.707	2.469	3.176
9.50	1.224	2.360	3.414	4.392	1.075	2.073	2.999	3.858	0.934	1.801	2.606	3.353
10.00	1.288	2.484	3.593	4.623	1.132	2.182	3.157	4.061	0.984	1.896	2.743	3.529
10.50	1.353	2.608	3.773	4.854	1.188	2.291	3.314	4.264	1.033	1.991	2.880	3.706
11.00	1.417	2.732	3.953	5.085	1.245	2.400	3.472	4.467	1.082	2.086	3.017	3.882
11.50	1.482	2.856	4.132	5.316	1.302	2.509	3.630	4.670	1.131	2.181	3.155	4.058
12.00	1.546	2.981	4.312	5.547	1.358	2.618	3.788	4.873	1.180	2.275	3.292	4.235
12.50	1.610	3.105	4.492	5.778	1.415	2.728	3.946	5.076	1.229	2.370	3.429	4.411
13.00	1.675	3.229	4.671	6.009	1.471	2.837	4.104	5.279	1.279	2.465	3.566	4.588
13.50	1.739	3.353	4.851	6.241	1.528	2.946	4.261	5.482	1.328	2.560	3.703	4.764
14.00	1.804	3.477	5.030	6.472	1.584	3.055	4.419	5.685	1.377	2.655	3.840	4.941
14.50	1.868	3.602	5.210	6.703	1.641	3.164	4.577	5.888	1.426	2.750	3.978	5.117
15.00	1.932	3.726	5.390	6.934	1.698	3.273	4.735	6.091	1.475	2.844	4.115	5.294
15.50	1.997	3.850	5.569	7.165	1.754	3.382	4.893	6.295	1.524	2.939	4.252	5.470
16.00	2.061	3.974	5.749	7.396	1.811	3.491	5.051	6.498	1.574	3.034	4.389	5.647
16.50	2.126	4.098	5.929	7.627	1.867	3.600	5.208	6.701	1.623	3.129	4.526	5.823
17.00	2.190	4.222	6.108	7.859	1.924	3.709	5.366	6.904	1.672	3.224	4.663	5.999
17.50	2.255	4.347	6.288	8.090	1.981	3.819	5.524	7.107	1.721	3.318	4.801	6.176
18.00	2.319	4.471	6.468	8.321	2.037	3.928	5.682	7.310	1.770	3.413	4.938	6.352
18.50	2.383	4.595	6.647	8.552	2.094	4.037	5.840	7.513	1.820	3.508	5.075	6.529
19.00	2.448	4.719	6.827	8.783	2.150	4.146	5.998	7.716	1.869	3.603	5.212	6.705
19.50	2.512	4.843	7.007	9.014	2.207	4.255	6.155	7.919	1.918	3.698	5.349	6.882
20.00	2.577	4.968	7.186	9.245	2.264	4.364	6.313	8.122	1.967	3.792	5.486	7.058
20.50	2.641	5.092	7.366	9.476	2.320	4.473	6.471	8.325	2.016	3.887	5.623	7.235
21.00	2.705	5.216	7.546	9.708	2.377	4.582	6.629	8.528	2.065	3.982	5.761	7.411
21.50	2.770	5.340	7.725	9.939	2.433	4.691	6.787	8.731	2.115	4.077	5.898	7.588
22.00	2.834	5.464	7.905	10.170	2.490	4.800	6.945	8.934	2.164	4.172	6.035	7.764
22.50	2.899	5.589	8.085	10.401	2.547	4.910	7.102	9.137	2.213	4.267	6.172	7.940
23.00	2.963	5.713	8.264	10.632	2.603	5.019	7.260	9.340	2.262	4.361	6.309	8.117
23.50	3.028	5.837	8.444	10.863	2.660	5.128	7.418	9.543	2.311	4.456	6.446	8.293
24.00	3.092	5.961	8.624	11.094	2.716	5.237	7.576	9.746	2.361	4.551	6.584	8.470
24.50	3.156	6.085	8.803	11.326	2.773	5.346	7.734	9.949	2.410	4.646	6.721	8.646
25.00	3.221	6.210	8.983	11.557	2.829	5.455	7.892	10.152	2.459	4.741	6.858	8.823
25.50	3.285	6.334	9.163	11.788	2.886	5.564	8.049	10.356	2.508	4.835	6.995	8.999
26.00	3.350	6.458	9.342	12.019	2.943	5.673	8.207	10.559	2.557	4.930	7.132	9.176
26.50	3.414	6.582	9.522	12.250	2.999	5.782	8.365	10.762	2.606	5.025	7.269	9.352
27.00	3.478	6.706	9.702	12.481	3.056	5.891	8.523	10.965	2.656	5.120	7.407	9.529
27.50	3.543	6.831	9.881	12.712	3.112	6.001	8.681	11.168	2.705	5.215	7.544	9.705
28.00	3.607	6.955	10.061	12.943	3.169	6.110	8.839	11.371	2.754	5.309	7.681	9.881
28.50	3.672	7.079	10.241	13.175	3.226	6.219	8.996	11.574	2.803	5.404	7.818	10.058
29.00	3.736	7.203	10.420	13.406	3.282	6.328	9.154	11.777	2.852	5.499	7.955	10.234
29.50	3.801	7.327	10.600	13.637	3.339	6.437	9.312	11.980	2.901	5.594	8.092	10.411
30.00	3.865	7.451	10.780	13.868	3.395	6.546	9.470	12.183	2.951	5.689	8.229	10.587

Entry is annual rent per square foot to pay back lease assumption, interest and management fee.

Cost of Assuming a Tenant's Lease Obligation

Interest Rate 10.00%   3.5% Management Fee

Old Rent	3/1	5/1	5/2	New Lease Term / Old Lease Term in Years 6/1	6/2	7/1	7/2	7/3	10/1	10/2	10/3	10/4
0.50	0.192	0.126	0.241	0.110	0.210	0.099	0.188	0.269	0.079	0.150	0.214	0.272
1.00	0.384	0.253	0.481	0.220	0.419	0.197	0.376	0.538	0.157	0.299	0.428	0.544
1.50	0.575	0.379	0.722	0.330	0.629	0.296	0.564	0.806	0.236	0.449	0.642	0.817
2.00	0.767	0.505	0.962	0.440	0.839	0.395	0.752	1.075	0.314	0.598	0.856	1.089
2.50	0.959	0.631	1.203	0.550	1.049	0.493	0.940	1.344	0.393	0.748	1.070	1.361
3.00	1.151	0.758	1.443	0.661	1.258	0.592	1.128	1.613	0.471	0.898	1.284	1.633
3.50	1.342	0.884	1.684	0.771	1.468	0.691	1.316	1.882	0.550	1.047	1.498	1.906
4.00	1.534	1.010	1.924	0.881	1.678	0.789	1.504	2.150	0.628	1.197	1.712	2.178
4.50	1.726	1.136	2.165	0.991	1.888	0.888	1.692	2.419	0.707	1.347	1.926	2.450
5.00	1.918	1.263	2.406	1.101	2.097	0.987	1.880	2.688	0.785	1.496	2.140	2.722
5.50	2.109	1.389	2.646	1.211	2.307	1.085	2.068	2.957	0.864	1.646	2.354	2.994
6.00	2.301	1.515	2.887	1.321	2.517	1.184	2.255	3.226	0.942	1.795	2.568	3.267
6.50	2.493	1.641	3.127	1.431	2.727	1.283	2.443	3.494	1.021	1.945	2.782	3.539
7.00	2.685	1.768	3.368	1.541	2.936	1.381	2.631	3.763	1.099	2.095	2.996	3.811
7.50	2.876	1.894	3.608	1.651	3.146	1.480	2.819	4.032	1.178	2.244	3.210	4.083
8.00	3.068	2.020	3.849	1.761	3.356	1.578	3.007	4.301	1.257	2.394	3.424	4.356
8.50	3.260	2.146	4.089	1.872	3.566	1.677	3.195	4.570	1.335	2.544	3.638	4.628
9.00	3.452	2.273	4.330	1.982	3.775	1.776	3.383	4.838	1.414	2.693	3.851	4.900
9.50	3.643	2.399	4.571	2.092	3.985	1.874	3.571	5.107	1.492	2.843	4.065	5.172
10.00	3.835	2.525	4.811	2.202	4.195	1.973	3.759	5.376	1.571	2.992	4.279	5.444
10.50	4.027	2.652	5.052	2.312	4.405	2.072	3.947	5.645	1.649	3.142	4.493	5.717
11.00	4.219	2.778	5.292	2.422	4.614	2.170	4.135	5.914	1.728	3.292	4.707	5.989
11.50	4.410	2.904	5.533	2.532	4.824	2.269	4.323	6.182	1.806	3.441	4.921	6.261
12.00	4.602	3.030	5.773	2.642	5.034	2.368	4.511	6.451	1.885	3.591	5.135	6.533
12.50	4.794	3.157	6.014	2.752	5.244	2.466	4.699	6.720	1.963	3.741	5.349	6.806
13.00	4.986	3.283	6.255	2.862	5.453	2.565	4.887	6.989	2.042	3.890	5.563	7.078
13.50	5.177	3.409	6.495	2.972	5.663	2.664	5.075	7.258	2.120	4.040	5.777	7.350
14.00	5.369	3.535	6.736	3.083	5.873	2.762	5.263	7.526	2.199	4.189	5.991	7.622
14.50	5.561	3.662	6.976	3.193	6.083	2.861	5.451	7.795	2.277	4.339	6.205	7.894
15.00	5.753	3.788	7.217	3.303	6.292	2.960	5.639	8.064	2.356	4.489	6.419	8.167
15.50	5.944	3.914	7.457	3.413	6.502	3.058	5.827	8.333	2.435	4.638	6.633	8.439
16.00	6.136	4.040	7.698	3.523	6.712	3.157	6.015	8.602	2.513	4.788	6.847	8.711
16.50	6.328	4.167	7.938	3.633	6.922	3.256	6.203	8.870	2.592	4.937	7.061	8.983
17.00	6.520	4.293	8.179	3.743	7.131	3.354	6.391	9.139	2.670	5.087	7.275	9.256
17.50	6.711	4.419	8.420	3.853	7.341	3.453	6.579	9.408	2.749	5.237	7.489	9.528
18.00	6.903	4.545	8.660	3.963	7.551	3.552	6.766	9.677	2.827	5.386	7.703	9.800
18.50	7.095	4.672	8.901	4.073	7.761	3.650	6.954	9.945	2.906	5.536	7.917	10.072
19.00	7.287	4.798	9.141	4.184	7.970	3.749	7.142	10.214	2.984	5.686	8.131	10.344
19.50	7.478	4.924	9.382	4.294	8.180	3.848	7.330	10.483	3.063	5.835	8.345	10.617
20.00	7.670	5.051	9.622	4.404	8.390	3.946	7.518	10.752	3.141	5.985	8.559	10.889
20.50	7.862	5.177	9.863	4.514	8.600	4.045	7.706	11.021	3.220	6.134	8.773	11.161
21.00	8.054	5.303	10.103	4.624	8.809	4.144	7.894	11.289	3.298	6.284	8.987	11.433
21.50	8.245	5.429	10.344	4.734	9.019	4.242	8.082	11.558	3.377	6.434	9.201	11.706
22.00	8.437	5.556	10.585	4.844	9.229	4.341	8.270	11.827	3.455	6.583	9.415	11.978
22.50	8.629	5.682	10.825	4.954	9.439	4.439	8.458	12.096	3.534	6.733	9.629	12.250
23.00	8.821	5.808	11.066	5.064	9.648	4.538	8.646	12.365	3.612	6.883	9.843	12.522
23.50	9.012	5.934	11.306	5.174	9.858	4.637	8.834	12.633	3.691	7.032	10.057	12.794
24.00	9.204	6.061	11.547	5.284	10.068	4.735	9.022	12.902	3.770	7.182	10.271	13.067
24.50	9.396	6.187	11.787	5.395	10.278	4.834	9.210	13.171	3.848	7.331	10.485	13.339
25.00	9.588	6.313	12.028	5.505	10.487	4.933	9.398	13.440	3.927	7.481	10.699	13.611
25.50	9.779	6.439	12.268	5.615	10.697	5.031	9.586	13.709	4.005	7.631	10.913	13.883
26.00	9.971	6.566	12.509	5.725	10.907	5.130	9.774	13.977	4.084	7.780	11.126	14.156
26.50	10.163	6.692	12.750	5.835	11.117	5.229	9.962	14.246	4.162	7.930	11.340	14.428
27.00	10.355	6.818	12.990	5.945	11.326	5.327	10.150	14.515	4.241	8.080	11.554	14.700
27.50	10.546	6.944	13.231	6.055	11.536	5.426	10.338	14.784	4.319	8.229	11.768	14.972
28.00	10.738	7.071	13.471	6.165	11.746	5.525	10.526	15.053	4.398	8.379	11.982	15.244
28.50	10.930	7.197	13.712	6.275	11.956	5.623	10.714	15.321	4.476	8.528	12.196	15.517
29.00	11.122	7.323	13.952	6.385	12.165	5.722	10.902	15.590	4.555	8.678	12.410	15.789
29.50	11.313	7.450	14.193	6.495	12.375	5.821	11.090	15.859	4.633	8.828	12.624	16.061
30.00	11.505	7.576	14.434	6.606	12.585	5.919	11.277	16.128	4.712	8.977	12.838	16.333

Entry is annual rent per square foot to pay back lease assumption, interest and management fee.

Cost of Assuming a Tenant's Lease Obligation

Interest Rate 10.00%   3.5% Management Fee

Old Rent	12/1	12/2	12/3	12/4	15/1	15/2	15/3	15/4	20/1	20/2	20/3	20/4
0.50	0.071	0.135	0.194	0.246	0.064	0.122	0.174	0.221	0.057	0.109	0.156	0.199
1.00	0.142	0.271	0.387	0.492	0.128	0.243	0.348	0.443	0.115	0.219	0.313	0.398
1.50	0.213	0.406	0.581	0.739	0.192	0.365	0.522	0.664	0.172	0.328	0.469	0.596
2.00	0.284	0.541	0.774	0.985	0.255	0.487	0.696	0.885	0.229	0.437	0.625	0.795
2.50	0.355	0.677	0.968	1.231	0.319	0.608	0.870	1.107	0.287	0.546	0.781	0.994
3.00	0.426	0.812	1.161	1.477	0.383	0.730	1.044	1.328	0.344	0.656	0.938	1.193
3.50	0.497	0.947	1.355	1.723	0.447	0.852	1.218	1.550	0.401	0.765	1.094	1.392
4.00	0.568	1.082	1.548	1.969	0.511	0.973	1.392	1.771	0.459	0.874	1.250	1.590
4.50	0.639	1.218	1.742	2.216	0.575	1.095	1.566	1.992	0.516	0.983	1.406	1.789
5.00	0.710	1.353	1.935	2.462	0.639	1.217	1.740	2.214	0.573	1.093	1.563	1.988
5.50	0.781	1.488	2.129	2.708	0.702	1.338	1.914	2.435	0.631	1.202	1.719	2.187
6.00	0.852	1.624	2.322	2.954	0.766	1.460	2.088	2.656	0.688	1.311	1.875	2.385
6.50	0.923	1.759	2.516	3.200	0.830	1.582	2.262	2.878	0.746	1.420	2.031	2.584
7.00	0.994	1.894	2.709	3.446	0.894	1.703	2.436	3.099	0.803	1.530	2.188	2.783
7.50	1.065	2.030	2.903	3.693	0.958	1.825	2.610	3.320	0.860	1.639	2.344	2.982
8.00	1.136	2.165	3.096	3.939	1.022	1.947	2.784	3.542	0.918	1.748	2.500	3.181
8.50	1.207	2.300	3.290	4.185	1.086	2.068	2.958	3.763	0.975	1.857	2.656	3.379
9.00	1.278	2.436	3.483	4.431	1.149	2.190	3.132	3.985	1.032	1.967	2.813	3.578
9.50	1.349	2.571	3.677	4.677	1.213	2.312	3.306	4.206	1.090	2.076	2.969	3.777
10.00	1.420	2.706	3.870	4.924	1.277	2.433	3.480	4.427	1.147	2.185	3.125	3.976
10.50	1.491	2.841	4.064	5.170	1.341	2.555	3.654	4.649	1.204	2.294	3.281	4.175
11.00	1.562	2.977	4.257	5.416	1.405	2.677	3.828	4.870	1.262	2.404	3.438	4.373
11.50	1.633	3.112	4.451	5.662	1.469	2.798	4.002	5.091	1.319	2.513	3.594	4.572
12.00	1.704	3.247	4.644	5.908	1.533	2.920	4.176	5.313	1.376	2.622	3.750	4.771
12.50	1.775	3.383	4.838	6.154	1.596	3.042	4.350	5.534	1.434	2.731	3.906	4.970
13.00	1.846	3.518	5.031	6.401	1.660	3.163	4.524	5.755	1.491	2.841	4.063	5.168
13.50	1.918	3.653	5.225	6.647	1.724	3.285	4.698	5.977	1.548	2.950	4.219	5.367
14.00	1.989	3.789	5.418	6.893	1.788	3.407	4.872	6.198	1.606	3.059	4.375	5.566
14.50	2.060	3.924	5.612	7.139	1.852	3.528	5.046	6.419	1.663	3.169	4.531	5.765
15.00	2.131	4.059	5.805	7.385	1.916	3.650	5.220	6.641	1.720	3.278	4.688	5.964
15.50	2.202	4.194	5.999	7.632	1.980	3.772	5.394	6.862	1.778	3.387	4.844	6.162
16.00	2.273	4.330	6.192	7.878	2.044	3.893	5.568	7.084	1.835	3.496	5.000	6.361
16.50	2.344	4.465	6.386	8.124	2.107	4.015	5.742	7.305	1.892	3.606	5.156	6.560
17.00	2.415	4.600	6.579	8.370	2.171	4.137	5.916	7.526	1.950	3.715	5.313	6.759
17.50	2.486	4.736	6.773	8.616	2.235	4.258	6.090	7.748	2.007	3.824	5.469	6.958
18.00	2.557	4.871	6.966	8.862	2.299	4.380	6.264	7.969	2.065	3.933	5.625	7.156
18.50	2.628	5.006	7.160	9.109	2.363	4.502	6.438	8.190	2.122	4.043	5.781	7.355
19.00	2.699	5.142	7.353	9.355	2.427	4.623	6.612	8.412	2.179	4.152	5.938	7.554
19.50	2.770	5.277	7.547	9.601	2.491	4.745	6.786	8.633	2.237	4.261	6.094	7.753
20.00	2.841	5.412	7.740	9.847	2.554	4.867	6.960	8.854	2.294	4.370	6.250	7.952
20.50	2.912	5.548	7.934	10.093	2.618	4.988	7.134	9.076	2.351	4.480	6.406	8.150
21.00	2.983	5.683	8.127	10.339	2.682	5.110	7.308	9.297	2.409	4.589	6.563	8.349
21.50	3.054	5.818	8.321	10.586	2.746	5.232	7.482	9.519	2.466	4.698	6.719	8.548
22.00	3.125	5.953	8.514	10.832	2.810	5.353	7.656	9.740	2.523	4.807	6.875	8.747
22.50	3.196	6.089	8.708	11.078	2.874	5.475	7.830	9.961	2.581	4.917	7.031	8.945
23.00	3.267	6.224	8.901	11.324	2.938	5.597	8.004	10.183	2.638	5.026	7.188	9.144
23.50	3.338	6.359	9.095	11.570	3.001	5.718	8.178	10.404	2.695	5.135	7.344	9.343
24.00	3.409	6.495	9.288	11.817	3.065	5.840	8.352	10.625	2.753	5.244	7.500	9.542
24.50	3.480	6.630	9.482	12.063	3.129	5.962	8.526	10.847	2.810	5.354	7.656	9.741
25.00	3.551	6.765	9.675	12.309	3.193	6.083	8.700	11.068	2.867	5.463	7.813	9.939
25.50	3.622	6.901	9.869	12.555	3.257	6.205	8.874	11.289	2.925	5.572	7.969	10.138
26.00	3.693	7.036	10.062	12.801	3.321	6.327	9.048	11.511	2.982	5.681	8.125	10.337
26.50	3.764	7.171	10.256	13.047	3.385	6.448	9.222	11.732	3.039	5.791	8.281	10.536
27.00	3.835	7.307	10.449	13.294	3.448	6.570	9.396	11.954	3.097	5.900	8.438	10.735
27.50	3.906	7.442	10.643	13.540	3.512	6.692	9.570	12.175	3.154	6.009	8.594	10.933
28.00	3.977	7.577	10.836	13.786	3.576	6.813	9.744	12.396	3.211	6.119	8.750	11.132
28.50	4.048	7.712	11.030	14.032	3.640	6.935	9.918	12.618	3.269	6.228	8.906	11.331
29.00	4.119	7.848	11.223	14.278	3.704	7.057	10.092	12.839	3.326	6.337	9.063	11.530
29.50	4.190	7.983	11.417	14.524	3.768	7.178	10.266	13.060	3.384	6.446	9.219	11.728
30.00	4.261	8.118	11.610	14.771	3.832	7.300	10.440	13.282	3.441	6.556	9.375	11.927

Entry is annual rent per square foot to pay back lease assumption, interest and management fee.

Cost of Assuming a Tenant's Lease Obligation

Interest Rate 10.00%   5.0% Management Fee

| Old Rent | 3/1 | 5/1 | 5/2 | New Lease Term / Old Lease Term in Years |||||||||
				6/1	6/2	7/1	7/2	7/3	10/1	10/2	10/3	10/4
0.50	0.195	0.128	0.244	0.112	0.213	0.100	0.191	0.273	0.080	0.152	0.217	0.277
1.00	0.390	0.257	0.489	0.224	0.426	0.200	0.382	0.546	0.160	0.304	0.435	0.553
1.50	0.584	0.385	0.733	0.335	0.639	0.301	0.573	0.819	0.239	0.456	0.652	0.830
2.00	0.779	0.513	0.977	0.447	0.852	0.401	0.764	1.092	0.319	0.608	0.869	1.106
2.50	0.974	0.641	1.222	0.559	1.065	0.501	0.955	1.365	0.399	0.760	1.087	1.383
3.00	1.169	0.770	1.466	0.671	1.278	0.601	1.146	1.638	0.479	0.912	1.304	1.659
3.50	1.363	0.898	1.710	0.783	1.491	0.701	1.336	1.911	0.558	1.064	1.521	1.936
4.00	1.558	1.026	1.955	0.895	1.704	0.802	1.527	2.184	0.638	1.216	1.739	2.212
4.50	1.753	1.154	2.199	1.006	1.918	0.902	1.718	2.457	0.718	1.368	1.956	2.489
5.00	1.948	1.283	2.444	1.118	2.131	1.002	1.909	2.730	0.798	1.520	2.173	2.765
5.50	2.143	1.411	2.688	1.230	2.344	1.102	2.100	3.003	0.877	1.672	2.391	3.042
6.00	2.337	1.539	2.932	1.342	2.557	1.203	2.291	3.276	0.957	1.824	2.608	3.318
6.50	2.532	1.667	3.177	1.454	2.770	1.303	2.482	3.550	1.037	1.976	2.826	3.595
7.00	2.727	1.796	3.421	1.566	2.983	1.403	2.673	3.823	1.117	2.128	3.043	3.871
7.50	2.922	1.924	3.665	1.677	3.196	1.503	2.864	4.096	1.197	2.280	3.260	4.148
8.00	3.116	2.052	3.910	1.789	3.409	1.603	3.055	4.369	1.276	2.432	3.478	4.424
8.50	3.311	2.180	4.154	1.901	3.622	1.704	3.246	4.642	1.356	2.584	3.695	4.701
9.00	3.506	2.309	4.398	2.013	3.835	1.804	3.437	4.915	1.436	2.736	3.912	4.977
9.50	3.701	2.437	4.643	2.125	4.048	1.904	3.628	5.188	1.516	2.888	4.130	5.254
10.00	3.896	2.565	4.887	2.237	4.261	2.004	3.819	5.461	1.595	3.040	4.347	5.530
10.50	4.090	2.693	5.131	2.348	4.474	2.104	4.009	5.734	1.675	3.192	4.564	5.807
11.00	4.285	2.822	5.376	2.460	4.687	2.205	4.200	6.007	1.755	3.344	4.782	6.083
11.50	4.480	2.950	5.620	2.572	4.900	2.305	4.391	6.280	1.835	3.496	4.999	6.360
12.00	4.675	3.078	5.865	2.684	5.113	2.405	4.582	6.553	1.915	3.648	5.216	6.636
12.50	4.869	3.206	6.109	2.796	5.327	2.505	4.773	6.826	1.994	3.800	5.434	6.913
13.00	5.064	3.335	6.353	2.908	5.540	2.606	4.964	7.099	2.074	3.952	5.651	7.190
13.50	5.259	3.463	6.598	3.019	5.753	2.706	5.155	7.372	2.154	4.104	5.868	7.466
14.00	5.454	3.591	6.842	3.131	5.966	2.806	5.346	7.645	2.234	4.256	6.086	7.743
14.50	5.649	3.719	7.086	3.243	6.179	2.906	5.537	7.918	2.313	4.408	6.303	8.019
15.00	5.843	3.848	7.331	3.355	6.392	3.006	5.728	8.191	2.393	4.559	6.520	8.296
15.50	6.038	3.976	7.575	3.467	6.605	3.107	5.919	8.464	2.473	4.711	6.738	8.572
16.00	6.233	4.104	7.819	3.579	6.818	3.207	6.110	8.737	2.553	4.863	6.955	8.849
16.50	6.428	4.232	8.064	3.690	7.031	3.307	6.301	9.010	2.632	5.015	7.173	9.125
17.00	6.623	4.361	8.308	3.802	7.244	3.407	6.491	9.283	2.712	5.167	7.390	9.402
17.50	6.817	4.489	8.552	3.914	7.457	3.507	6.682	9.556	2.792	5.319	7.607	9.678
18.00	7.012	4.617	8.797	4.026	7.670	3.608	6.873	9.829	2.872	5.471	7.825	9.955
18.50	7.207	4.746	9.041	4.138	7.883	3.708	7.064	10.103	2.952	5.623	8.042	10.231
19.00	7.402	4.874	9.286	4.250	8.096	3.808	7.255	10.376	3.031	5.775	8.259	10.508
19.50	7.596	5.002	9.530	4.361	8.309	3.908	7.446	10.649	3.111	5.927	8.477	10.784
20.00	7.791	5.130	9.774	4.473	8.522	4.008	7.637	10.922	3.191	6.079	8.694	11.061
20.50	7.986	5.259	10.019	4.585	8.736	4.109	7.828	11.195	3.271	6.231	8.911	11.337
21.00	8.181	5.387	10.263	4.697	8.949	4.209	8.019	11.468	3.350	6.383	9.129	11.614
21.50	8.376	5.515	10.507	4.809	9.162	4.309	8.210	11.741	3.430	6.535	9.346	11.890
22.00	8.570	5.643	10.752	4.921	9.375	4.409	8.401	12.014	3.510	6.687	9.563	12.167
22.50	8.765	5.772	10.996	5.032	9.588	4.510	8.592	12.287	3.590	6.839	9.781	12.443
23.00	8.960	5.900	11.240	5.144	9.801	4.610	8.783	12.560	3.670	6.991	9.998	12.720
23.50	9.155	6.028	11.485	5.256	10.014	4.710	8.974	12.833	3.749	7.143	10.215	12.996
24.00	9.349	6.156	11.729	5.368	10.227	4.810	9.164	13.106	3.829	7.295	10.433	13.273
24.50	9.544	6.285	11.973	5.480	10.440	4.910	9.355	13.379	3.909	7.447	10.650	13.549
25.00	9.739	6.413	12.218	5.592	10.653	5.011	9.546	13.652	3.989	7.599	10.867	13.826
25.50	9.934	6.541	12.462	5.703	10.866	5.111	9.737	13.925	4.068	7.751	11.085	14.103
26.00	10.129	6.669	12.707	5.815	11.079	5.211	9.928	14.198	4.148	7.903	11.302	14.379
26.50	10.323	6.798	12.951	5.927	11.292	5.311	10.119	14.471	4.228	8.055	11.520	14.656
27.00	10.518	6.926	13.195	6.039	11.505	5.411	10.310	14.744	4.308	8.207	11.737	14.932
27.50	10.713	7.054	13.440	6.151	11.718	5.512	10.501	15.017	4.387	8.359	11.954	15.209
28.00	10.908	7.182	13.684	6.263	11.931	5.612	10.692	15.290	4.467	8.511	12.172	15.485
28.50	11.102	7.311	13.928	6.374	12.144	5.712	10.883	15.563	4.547	8.663	12.389	15.762
29.00	11.297	7.439	14.173	6.486	12.358	5.812	11.074	15.836	4.627	8.815	12.606	16.038
29.50	11.492	7.567	14.417	6.598	12.571	5.913	11.265	16.109	4.707	8.967	12.824	16.315
30.00	11.687	7.695	14.661	6.710	12.784	6.013	11.456	16.382	4.786	9.119	13.041	16.591

Entry is annual rent per square foot to pay back lease assumption, interest and management fee.

Cost of Assuming a Tenant's Lease Obligation

Interest Rate 10.00%   5.0% Management Fee

Old Rent	New Lease Term / Old Lease Term in Years											
	12/1	12/2	12/3	12/4	15/1	15/2	15/3	15/4	20/1	20/2	20/3	20/4
0.50	0.072	0.137	0.197	0.250	0.065	0.124	0.177	0.225	0.058	0.111	0.159	0.202
1.00	0.144	0.275	0.393	0.500	0.130	0.247	0.353	0.450	0.117	0.222	0.317	0.404
1.50	0.216	0.412	0.590	0.750	0.195	0.371	0.530	0.675	0.175	0.333	0.476	0.606
2.00	0.289	0.550	0.786	1.000	0.259	0.494	0.707	0.899	0.233	0.444	0.635	0.808
2.50	0.361	0.687	0.983	1.250	0.324	0.618	0.884	1.124	0.291	0.555	0.794	1.010
3.00	0.433	0.825	1.179	1.500	0.389	0.742	1.060	1.349	0.350	0.666	0.952	1.212
3.50	0.505	0.962	1.376	1.750	0.454	0.865	1.237	1.574	0.408	0.777	1.111	1.413
4.00	0.577	1.100	1.572	2.001	0.519	0.989	1.414	1.799	0.466	0.888	1.270	1.615
4.50	0.649	1.237	1.769	2.251	0.584	1.112	1.591	2.024	0.524	0.999	1.428	1.817
5.00	0.721	1.374	1.966	2.501	0.649	1.236	1.767	2.249	0.583	1.110	1.587	2.019
5.50	0.794	1.512	2.162	2.751	0.714	1.359	1.944	2.473	0.641	1.221	1.746	2.221
6.00	0.866	1.649	2.359	3.001	0.778	1.483	2.121	2.698	0.699	1.332	1.905	2.423
6.50	0.938	1.787	2.555	3.251	0.843	1.607	2.298	2.923	0.757	1.443	2.063	2.625
7.00	1.010	1.924	2.752	3.501	0.908	1.730	2.474	3.148	0.816	1.554	2.222	2.827
7.50	1.082	2.062	2.948	3.751	0.973	1.854	2.651	3.373	0.874	1.665	2.381	3.029
8.00	1.154	2.199	3.145	4.001	1.038	1.977	2.828	3.598	0.932	1.776	2.539	3.231
8.50	1.226	2.337	3.341	4.251	1.103	2.101	3.005	3.823	0.990	1.887	2.698	3.433
9.00	1.299	2.474	3.538	4.501	1.168	2.225	3.181	4.047	1.049	1.998	2.857	3.635
9.50	1.371	2.611	3.735	4.751	1.232	2.348	3.358	4.272	1.107	2.109	3.016	3.837
10.00	1.443	2.749	3.931	5.001	1.297	2.472	3.535	4.497	1.165	2.220	3.174	4.039
10.50	1.515	2.886	4.128	5.251	1.362	2.595	3.712	4.722	1.223	2.331	3.333	4.240
11.00	1.587	3.024	4.324	5.501	1.427	2.719	3.888	4.947	1.282	2.442	3.492	4.442
11.50	1.659	3.161	4.521	5.751	1.492	2.843	4.065	5.172	1.340	2.553	3.651	4.644
12.00	1.731	3.299	4.717	6.002	1.557	2.966	4.242	5.397	1.398	2.664	3.809	4.846
12.50	1.804	3.436	4.914	6.252	1.622	3.090	4.419	5.621	1.456	2.775	3.968	5.048
13.00	1.876	3.574	5.110	6.502	1.687	3.213	4.595	5.846	1.515	2.886	4.127	5.250
13.50	1.948	3.711	5.307	6.752	1.751	3.337	4.772	6.071	1.573	2.997	4.285	5.452
14.00	2.020	3.848	5.504	7.002	1.816	3.460	4.949	6.296	1.631	3.108	4.444	5.654
14.50	2.092	3.986	5.700	7.252	1.881	3.584	5.125	6.521	1.689	3.219	4.603	5.856
15.00	2.164	4.123	5.897	7.502	1.946	3.708	5.302	6.746	1.748	3.330	4.762	6.058
15.50	2.236	4.261	6.093	7.752	2.011	3.831	5.479	6.971	1.806	3.441	4.920	6.260
16.00	2.308	4.398	6.290	8.002	2.076	3.955	5.656	7.195	1.864	3.552	5.079	6.462
16.50	2.381	4.536	6.486	8.252	2.141	4.078	5.832	7.420	1.922	3.662	5.238	6.664
17.00	2.453	4.673	6.683	8.502	2.206	4.202	6.009	7.645	1.981	3.773	5.396	6.865
17.50	2.525	4.810	6.879	8.752	2.270	4.326	6.186	7.870	2.039	3.884	5.555	7.067
18.00	2.597	4.948	7.076	9.002	2.335	4.449	6.363	8.095	2.097	3.995	5.714	7.269
18.50	2.669	5.085	7.273	9.252	2.400	4.573	6.539	8.320	2.155	4.106	5.873	7.471
19.00	2.741	5.223	7.469	9.502	2.465	4.696	6.716	8.545	2.214	4.217	6.031	7.673
19.50	2.813	5.360	7.666	9.753	2.530	4.820	6.893	8.769	2.272	4.328	6.190	7.875
20.00	2.886	5.498	7.862	10.003	2.595	4.943	7.070	8.994	2.330	4.439	6.349	8.077
20.50	2.958	5.635	8.059	10.253	2.660	5.067	7.246	9.219	2.388	4.550	6.507	8.279
21.00	3.030	5.773	8.255	10.503	2.724	5.191	7.423	9.444	2.447	4.661	6.666	8.481
21.50	3.102	5.910	8.452	10.753	2.789	5.314	7.600	9.669	2.505	4.772	6.825	8.683
22.00	3.174	6.047	8.648	11.003	2.854	5.438	7.777	9.894	2.563	4.883	6.984	8.885
22.50	3.246	6.185	8.845	11.253	2.919	5.561	7.953	10.119	2.621	4.994	7.142	9.087
23.00	3.318	6.322	9.042	11.503	2.984	5.685	8.130	10.343	2.680	5.105	7.301	9.289
23.50	3.391	6.460	9.238	11.753	3.049	5.809	8.307	10.568	2.738	5.216	7.460	9.491
24.00	3.463	6.597	9.435	12.003	3.114	5.932	8.484	10.793	2.796	5.327	7.618	9.692
24.50	3.535	6.735	9.631	12.253	3.179	6.056	8.660	11.018	2.854	5.438	7.777	9.894
25.00	3.607	6.872	9.828	12.503	3.243	6.179	8.837	11.243	2.913	5.549	7.936	10.096
25.50	3.679	7.010	10.024	12.753	3.308	6.303	9.014	11.468	2.971	5.660	8.095	10.298
26.00	3.751	7.147	10.221	13.003	3.373	6.427	9.191	11.693	3.029	5.771	8.253	10.500
26.50	3.823	7.284	10.417	13.253	3.438	6.550	9.367	11.917	3.087	5.882	8.412	10.702
27.00	3.896	7.422	10.614	13.504	3.503	6.674	9.544	12.142	3.146	5.993	8.571	10.904
27.50	3.968	7.559	10.811	13.754	3.568	6.797	9.721	12.367	3.204	6.104	8.729	11.106
28.00	4.040	7.697	11.007	14.004	3.633	6.921	9.898	12.592	3.262	6.215	8.888	11.308
28.50	4.112	7.834	11.204	14.254	3.697	7.044	10.074	12.817	3.320	6.326	9.047	11.510
29.00	4.184	7.972	11.400	14.504	3.762	7.168	10.251	13.042	3.379	6.437	9.206	11.712
29.50	4.256	8.109	11.597	14.754	3.827	7.292	10.428	13.267	3.437	6.548	9.364	11.914
30.00	4.328	8.247	11.793	15.004	3.892	7.415	10.604	13.491	3.495	6.659	9.523	12.116

Entry is annual rent per square foot to pay back lease assumption, interest and management fee.

Cost of Replacing a Capital Asset

Time to Replacement 3 Years

Salvage Ratio	Maintenance	7.00%	7.50%	8.00%	8.50%	9.00%	9.50%	10.00%	10.50%	11.00%	11.50%	12.00%	12.50%
0%	0%	5.2932	4.9770	4.7005	4.4566	4.2400	4.0463	3.8721	3.7146	3.5715	3.4410	3.3214	3.2115
	5%	6.0075	5.6437	5.3255	5.0448	4.7955	4.5726	4.3721	4.1908	4.0260	3.8758	3.7381	3.6115
	10%	6.7218	6.3103	5.9505	5.6331	5.3511	5.0989	4.8721	4.6669	4.4806	4.3105	4.1548	4.0115
	15%	7.4361	6.9770	6.5755	6.2213	5.9066	5.6252	5.3721	5.1431	4.9351	4.7453	4.5714	4.4115
	20%	8.1504	7.6437	7.2005	6.8095	6.4622	6.1515	5.8721	5.6193	5.3897	5.1801	4.9881	4.8115
10%	0%	4.8639	4.5793	4.3304	4.1109	3.9160	3.7416	3.5849	3.4431	3.3143	3.1969	3.0893	2.9904
	5%	5.5782	5.2460	4.9554	4.6992	4.4715	4.2680	4.0849	3.9193	3.7689	3.6317	3.5060	3.3904
	10%	6.2925	5.9126	5.5804	5.2874	5.0271	4.7943	4.5849	4.3955	4.2234	4.0664	3.9226	3.7904
	15%	7.0068	6.5793	6.2054	5.8756	5.5826	5.3206	5.0849	4.8717	4.6780	4.5012	4.3393	4.1904
	20%	7.7210	7.2460	6.8304	6.4639	6.1382	5.8469	5.5849	5.3479	5.1325	4.9360	4.7560	4.5904
15%	0%	4.6492	4.3804	4.1454	3.9381	3.7540	3.5893	3.4413	3.3074	3.1858	3.0748	2.9732	2.8798
	5%	5.3635	5.0471	4.7704	4.5263	4.3095	4.1156	3.9413	3.7836	3.6403	3.5096	3.3899	3.2798
	10%	6.0778	5.7138	5.3954	5.1146	4.8651	4.6420	4.4413	4.2598	4.0949	3.9444	3.8065	3.6798
	15%	6.7921	6.3804	6.0204	5.7028	5.4206	5.1683	4.9413	4.7360	4.5494	4.3792	4.2232	4.0798
	20%	7.5064	7.0471	6.6454	6.2910	5.9762	5.6946	5.4413	5.2121	5.0040	4.8140	4.6399	4.4798
20%	0%	4.4346	4.1816	3.9604	3.7653	3.5920	3.4370	3.2976	3.1717	3.0572	2.9528	2.8571	2.7692
	5%	5.1489	4.8483	4.5854	4.3535	4.1475	3.9633	3.7976	3.6478	3.5117	3.3876	3.2738	3.1692
	10%	5.8631	5.5149	5.2104	4.9417	4.7031	4.4896	4.2976	4.1240	3.9663	3.8223	3.6905	3.5692
	15%	6.5774	6.1816	5.8354	5.5300	5.2586	5.0160	4.7976	4.6002	4.4208	4.2571	4.1071	3.9692
	20%	7.2917	6.8483	6.4604	6.1182	5.8142	5.5423	5.2976	5.0764	4.8754	4.6919	4.5238	4.3692
25%	0%	4.2199	3.9827	3.7753	3.5924	3.4300	3.2847	3.1540	3.0359	2.9286	2.8307	2.7411	2.6587
	5%	4.9342	4.6494	4.4003	4.1807	3.9855	3.8110	3.6540	3.5121	3.3832	3.2655	3.1577	3.0587
	10%	5.6485	5.3161	5.0253	4.7689	4.5411	4.3373	4.1540	3.9883	3.8377	3.7003	3.5744	3.4587
	15%	6.3628	5.9827	5.6503	5.3572	5.0966	4.8636	4.6540	4.4645	4.2923	4.1351	3.9911	3.8587
	20%	7.0771	6.6494	6.2753	5.9454	5.6522	5.3900	5.1540	4.9407	4.7468	4.5699	4.4077	4.2587
33%	0%	3.8621	3.6513	3.4670	3.3044	3.1600	3.0308	2.9147	2.8097	2.7143	2.6273	2.5476	2.4744
	5%	4.5764	4.3180	4.0920	3.8926	3.7155	3.5572	3.4147	3.2859	3.1689	3.0621	2.9643	2.8744
	10%	5.2907	4.9847	4.7170	4.4809	4.2711	4.0835	3.9147	3.7621	3.6234	3.4969	3.3810	3.2744
	15%	6.0050	5.6513	5.3420	5.0691	4.8266	4.6098	4.4147	4.2383	4.0780	3.9317	3.7976	3.6744
	20%	6.7193	6.3180	5.9670	5.6573	5.3822	5.1361	4.9147	4.7145	4.5325	4.3664	4.2143	4.0744
40%	0%	3.5759	3.3862	3.2203	3.0740	2.9440	2.8278	2.7232	2.6287	2.5429	2.4646	2.3929	2.3269
	5%	4.2902	4.0529	3.8453	3.6622	3.4995	3.3541	3.2232	3.1049	2.9974	2.8994	2.8095	2.7269
	10%	5.0045	4.7195	4.4703	4.2504	4.0551	3.8804	3.7232	3.5811	3.4520	3.3341	3.2262	3.1269
	15%	5.7188	5.3862	5.0953	4.8387	4.6106	4.4067	4.2232	4.0573	3.9065	3.7689	3.6429	3.5269
	20%	6.4331	6.0529	5.7203	5.4269	5.1662	4.9330	4.7232	4.5335	4.3611	4.2037	4.0595	3.9269

Time to Replacement 4 Years

Salvage Ratio	Maintenance	7.00%	7.50%	8.00%	8.50%	9.00%	9.50%	10.00%	10.50%	11.00%	11.50%	12.00%	12.50%
0%	0%	4.1051	3.8686	3.6619	3.4798	3.3180	3.1734	3.0435	2.9261	2.8195	2.7223	2.6334	2.5517
	5%	4.8194	4.5353	4.2869	4.0680	3.8736	3.6998	3.5435	3.4023	3.2741	3.1571	3.0501	2.9517
	10%	5.5336	5.2020	4.9119	4.6562	4.4291	4.2261	4.0435	3.8785	3.7286	3.5919	3.4667	3.3517
	15%	6.2479	5.8686	5.5369	5.2445	4.9847	4.7524	4.5435	4.3547	4.1831	4.0267	3.8834	3.7517
	20%	6.9622	6.5353	6.1619	5.8327	5.5402	5.2787	5.0435	4.8309	4.6377	4.4615	4.3001	4.1517
10%	0%	3.7946	3.5818	3.3957	3.2318	3.0862	2.9561	2.8392	2.7335	2.6376	2.5501	2.4700	2.3965
	5%	4.5088	4.2484	4.0207	3.8200	3.6418	3.4824	3.3392	3.2097	3.0921	2.9849	2.8867	2.7965
	10%	5.2231	4.9151	4.6457	4.4083	4.1973	4.0087	3.8392	3.6859	3.5467	3.4197	3.3034	3.1965
	15%	5.9374	5.5818	5.2707	4.9965	4.7529	4.5351	4.3392	4.1621	4.0012	3.8544	3.7200	3.5965
	20%	6.6517	6.2484	5.8957	5.5847	5.3084	5.0614	4.8392	4.6383	4.4557	4.2892	4.1367	3.9965
15%	0%	3.6393	3.4383	3.2626	3.1078	2.9703	2.8474	2.7370	2.6372	2.5466	2.4640	2.3884	2.3189
	5%	4.3536	4.1050	3.8876	3.6960	3.5259	3.3737	3.2370	3.1134	3.0011	2.8988	2.8050	2.7189
	10%	5.0679	4.7717	4.5126	4.2843	4.0814	3.9001	3.7370	3.5896	3.4557	3.3335	3.2217	3.1189
	15%	5.7822	5.4383	5.1376	4.8725	4.6370	4.4264	4.2370	4.0658	3.9102	3.7683	3.6384	3.5189
	20%	6.4965	6.1050	5.7626	5.4607	5.1925	4.9527	4.7370	4.5419	4.3648	4.2031	4.0550	3.9189
20%	0%	3.4841	3.2949	3.1296	2.9838	2.8544	2.7388	2.6348	2.5409	2.4556	2.3779	2.3067	2.2413
	5%	4.1983	3.9616	3.7546	3.5720	3.4100	3.2651	3.1348	3.0171	2.9102	2.8126	2.7234	2.6413
	10%	4.9126	4.6282	4.3796	4.1603	3.9655	3.7914	3.6348	3.4933	3.3647	3.2474	3.1400	3.0413
	15%	5.6269	5.2949	5.0046	4.7485	4.5211	4.3177	4.1348	3.9695	3.8192	3.6822	3.5567	3.4413
	20%	6.3412	5.9616	5.6296	5.3367	5.0766	4.8440	4.6348	4.4456	4.2738	4.1170	3.9734	3.8413
25%	0%	3.3288	3.1515	2.9965	2.8598	2.7385	2.6301	2.5326	2.4446	2.3646	2.2917	2.2250	2.1638
	5%	4.0431	3.8181	3.6215	3.4481	3.2941	3.1564	3.0326	2.9208	2.8192	2.7265	2.6417	2.5638
	10%	4.7574	4.4848	4.2465	4.0363	3.8496	3.6827	3.5326	3.3970	3.2737	3.1613	3.0584	2.9638
	15%	5.4717	5.1515	4.8715	4.6245	4.4052	4.2090	4.0326	3.8731	3.7283	3.5961	3.4750	3.3638
	20%	6.1859	5.8181	5.4965	5.2128	4.9607	4.7353	4.5326	4.3493	4.1828	4.0309	3.8917	3.7638
33%	0%	3.0700	2.9124	2.7746	2.6532	2.5453	2.4490	2.3623	2.2841	2.2130	2.1482	2.0889	2.0345
	5%	3.7843	3.5791	3.3996	3.2414	3.1009	2.9753	2.8623	2.7603	2.6676	2.5830	2.5056	2.4345
	10%	4.4986	4.2457	4.0246	3.8296	3.6564	3.5016	3.3623	3.2364	3.1221	3.0178	2.9223	2.8345
	15%	5.2129	4.9124	4.6496	4.4179	4.2120	4.0279	3.8623	3.7126	3.5766	3.4526	3.3389	3.2345
	20%	5.9272	5.5791	5.2746	5.0061	4.7676	4.5542	4.3623	4.1888	4.0312	3.8874	3.7556	3.6345
40%	0%	2.8630	2.7212	2.5972	2.4879	2.3908	2.3041	2.2261	2.1557	2.0917	2.0334	1.9800	1.9310
	5%	3.5773	3.3878	3.2222	3.0761	2.9464	2.8304	2.7261	2.6319	2.5463	2.4682	2.3967	2.3310
	10%	4.2916	4.0545	3.8472	3.6643	3.5019	3.3567	3.2261	3.1080	3.0008	2.9030	2.8134	2.7310
	15%	5.0059	4.7212	4.4722	4.2526	4.0575	3.8830	3.7261	3.5842	3.4553	3.3377	3.2300	3.1310
	20%	5.7202	5.3878	5.0972	4.8408	4.6130	4.4093	4.2261	4.0604	3.9099	3.7725	3.6467	3.5310

Entry is an index of effective cost as percentage of original purchase price.

Cost of Replacing a Capital Asset

Time to Replacement 5 Years

Salvage Ratio	Maint- enance					Interest Rate							
		7.00%	7.50%	8.00%	8.50%	9.00%	9.50%	10.00%	10.50%	11.00%	11.50%	12.00%	12.50%
0%	0%	3.3945	3.2061	3.0415	2.8965	2.7678	2.6529	2.5496	2.4564	2.3719	2.2949	2.2244	2.1598
	5%	4.1088	3.8727	3.6665	3.4847	3.3233	3.1792	3.0496	2.9326	2.8264	2.7297	2.6411	2.5598
	10%	4.8231	4.5394	4.2915	4.0729	3.8789	3.7055	3.5496	3.4088	3.2810	3.1644	3.0578	2.9598
	15%	5.5373	5.2061	4.9165	4.6612	4.4344	4.2318	4.0496	3.8850	3.7355	3.5992	3.4744	3.3598
	20%	6.2516	5.8727	5.5415	5.2494	4.9900	4.7581	4.5496	4.3612	4.1901	4.0340	3.8911	3.7598
10%	0%	3.1550	2.9855	2.8373	2.7068	2.5910	2.4876	2.3947	2.3108	2.2347	2.1654	2.1020	2.0438
	5%	3.8693	3.6521	3.4623	3.2950	3.1466	3.0139	2.8947	2.7870	2.6893	2.6002	2.5187	2.4438
	10%	4.5836	4.3188	4.0873	3.8833	3.7021	3.5402	3.3947	3.2632	3.1438	3.0350	2.9353	2.8438
	15%	5.2979	4.9855	4.7123	4.4715	4.2577	4.0665	3.8947	3.7394	3.5983	3.4697	3.3520	3.2438
	20%	6.0122	5.6521	5.3373	5.0597	4.8132	4.5928	4.3947	4.2156	4.0529	3.9045	3.7687	3.6438
15%	0%	3.0353	2.8752	2.7352	2.6120	2.5026	2.4049	2.3172	2.2380	2.1661	2.1006	2.0408	1.9858
	5%	3.7496	3.5418	3.3602	3.2002	3.0582	2.9313	2.8172	2.7142	2.6207	2.5354	2.4574	2.3858
	10%	4.4639	4.2085	3.9852	3.7885	3.6137	3.4576	3.3172	3.1904	3.0752	2.9702	2.8741	2.7858
	15%	5.1782	4.8752	4.6102	4.3767	4.1693	3.9839	3.8172	3.6666	3.5298	3.4050	3.2908	3.1858
	20%	5.8925	5.5418	5.2352	4.9649	4.7248	4.5102	4.3172	4.1427	3.9843	3.8398	3.7074	3.5858
20%	0%	2.9156	2.7649	2.6332	2.5172	2.4142	2.3223	2.2397	2.1652	2.0975	2.0359	1.9796	1.9278
	5%	3.6299	3.4315	3.2582	3.1054	2.9698	2.8486	2.7397	2.6413	2.5521	2.4707	2.3962	2.3278
	10%	4.3442	4.0982	3.8832	3.6936	3.5253	3.3749	3.2397	3.1175	3.0066	2.9055	2.8129	2.7278
	15%	5.0585	4.7649	4.5082	4.2819	4.0809	3.9012	3.7397	3.5937	3.4612	3.3403	3.2296	3.1278
	20%	5.7727	5.4315	5.1332	4.8701	4.6364	4.4276	4.2397	4.0699	3.9157	3.7750	3.6462	3.5278
25%	0%	2.7959	2.6546	2.5311	2.4223	2.3258	2.2397	2.1622	2.0923	2.0289	1.9712	1.9183	1.8699
	5%	3.5102	3.3212	3.1561	3.0106	2.8814	2.7660	2.6622	2.5685	2.4835	2.4059	2.3350	2.2699
	10%	4.2244	3.9879	3.7811	3.5988	3.4369	3.2923	3.1622	3.0447	2.9380	2.8407	2.7517	2.6699
	15%	4.9387	4.6546	4.4061	4.1870	3.9925	3.8186	3.6622	3.5209	3.3926	3.2755	3.1683	3.0699
	20%	5.6530	5.3212	5.0311	4.7753	4.5481	4.3449	4.1622	3.9971	3.8471	3.7103	3.5850	3.4699
33%	0%	2.5963	2.4707	2.3610	2.2643	2.1785	2.1019	2.0331	1.9710	1.9146	1.8633	1.8163	1.7732
	5%	3.3106	3.1374	2.9860	2.8525	2.7341	2.6282	2.5331	2.4472	2.3691	2.2980	2.2330	2.1732
	10%	4.0249	3.8040	3.6110	3.4408	3.2896	3.1545	3.0331	2.9233	2.8237	2.7328	2.6496	2.5732
	15%	4.7392	4.4707	4.2360	4.0290	3.8452	3.6809	3.5331	3.3995	3.2782	3.1676	3.0663	2.9732
	20%	5.4535	5.1374	4.8610	4.6172	4.4007	4.2072	4.0331	3.8757	3.7328	3.6024	3.4830	3.3732
40%	0%	2.4367	2.3236	2.2249	2.1379	2.0607	1.9917	1.9298	1.8739	1.8231	1.7769	1.7347	1.6959
	5%	3.1510	2.9903	2.8499	2.7261	2.6162	2.5180	2.4298	2.3501	2.2777	2.2117	2.1513	2.0959
	10%	3.8653	3.6570	3.4749	3.3143	3.1718	3.0444	2.9298	2.8262	2.7322	2.6465	2.5680	2.4959
	15%	4.5796	4.3236	4.0999	3.9026	3.7273	3.5707	3.4298	3.3024	3.1868	3.0813	2.9847	2.8959
	20%	5.2938	4.9903	4.7249	4.4908	4.2829	4.0970	3.9298	3.7786	3.6413	3.5161	3.4013	3.2959

Time to Replacement 6 Years

Salvage Ratio	Maint- enance	7.00%	7.50%	8.00%	8.50%	9.00%	9.50%	10.00%	10.50%	11.00%	11.50%	12.00%	12.50%
0%	0%	2.9227	2.7664	2.6300	2.5099	2.4034	2.3084	2.2231	2.1462	2.0764	2.0130	1.9550	1.9019
	5%	3.6370	3.4331	3.2550	3.0981	2.9590	2.8347	2.7231	2.6224	2.5310	2.4478	2.3717	2.3019
	10%	4.3513	4.0998	3.8800	3.6864	3.5145	3.3610	3.2231	3.0985	2.9855	2.8826	2.7884	2.7019
	15%	5.0655	4.7664	4.5050	4.2746	4.0701	3.8873	3.7231	3.5747	3.4401	3.3173	3.2050	3.1019
	20%	5.7798	5.4331	5.1300	4.8628	4.6256	4.4136	4.2231	4.0509	3.8946	3.7521	3.6217	3.5019
10%	0%	2.7304	2.5898	2.4670	2.3589	2.2631	2.1775	2.1008	2.0316	1.9688	1.9117	1.8595	1.8117
	5%	3.4447	3.2564	3.0920	2.9471	2.8186	2.7039	2.6008	2.5077	2.4233	2.3465	2.2762	2.2117
	10%	4.1590	3.9231	3.7170	3.5354	3.3742	3.2302	3.1008	2.9839	2.8779	2.7813	2.6929	2.6117
	15%	4.8733	4.5898	4.3420	4.1236	3.9297	3.7565	3.6008	3.4601	3.3324	3.2160	3.1095	3.0117
	20%	5.5876	5.2564	4.9670	4.7118	4.4853	4.2828	4.1008	3.9363	3.7870	3.6508	3.5262	3.4117
15%	0%	2.6343	2.5015	2.3855	2.2834	2.1929	2.1121	2.0396	1.9742	1.9150	1.8610	1.8118	1.7666
	5%	3.3486	3.1681	3.0105	2.8716	2.7484	2.6384	2.5396	2.4504	2.3695	2.2958	2.2284	2.1666
	10%	4.0629	3.8348	3.6355	3.4599	3.3040	3.1648	3.0396	2.9266	2.8241	2.7306	2.6451	2.5666
	15%	4.7771	4.5015	4.2605	4.0481	3.8596	3.6911	3.5396	3.4028	3.2786	3.1654	3.0618	2.9666
	20%	5.4914	5.1681	4.8855	4.6363	4.4151	4.2174	4.0396	3.8790	3.7332	3.6002	3.4784	3.3666
20%	0%	2.5381	2.4131	2.3040	2.2079	2.1227	2.0467	1.9785	1.9169	1.8612	1.8104	1.7640	1.7215
	5%	3.2524	3.0798	2.9290	2.7961	2.6783	2.5730	2.4785	2.3931	2.3157	2.2452	2.1807	2.1215
	10%	3.9667	3.7465	3.5540	3.3844	3.2338	3.0993	2.9785	2.8693	2.7702	2.6800	2.5973	2.5215
	15%	4.6810	4.4131	4.1790	3.9726	3.7894	3.6257	3.4785	3.3455	3.2248	3.1147	3.0140	2.9215
	20%	5.3953	5.0798	4.8040	4.5609	4.3449	4.1520	3.9785	3.8217	3.6793	3.5495	3.4307	3.3215
25%	0%	2.4420	2.3248	2.2225	2.1324	2.0526	1.9813	1.9173	1.8596	1.8073	1.7597	1.7163	1.6764
	5%	3.1563	2.9915	2.8475	2.7207	2.6081	2.5076	2.4173	2.3358	2.2619	2.1945	2.1329	2.0764
	10%	3.8706	3.6581	3.4725	3.3089	3.1637	3.0339	2.9173	2.8120	2.7164	2.6293	2.5496	2.4764
	15%	4.5849	4.3248	4.0975	3.8971	3.7192	3.5602	3.4173	3.2882	3.1710	3.0641	2.9663	2.8764
	20%	5.2992	4.9915	4.7225	4.4854	4.2748	4.0865	3.9173	3.7644	3.6255	3.4989	3.3829	3.2764
33%	0%	2.2818	2.1776	2.0867	2.0066	1.9356	1.8723	1.8154	1.7641	1.7176	1.6753	1.6367	1.6012
	5%	2.9961	2.8443	2.7117	2.5948	2.4912	2.3986	2.3154	2.2403	2.1722	2.1101	2.0533	2.0012
	10%	3.7104	3.5109	3.3367	3.1831	3.0467	2.9249	2.8154	2.7165	2.6267	2.5449	2.4700	2.4012
	15%	4.4246	4.1776	3.9617	3.7713	3.6023	3.4512	3.3154	3.1927	3.0813	2.9797	2.8867	2.8012
	20%	5.1389	4.8443	4.5867	4.3595	4.1578	3.9775	3.8154	3.6689	3.5358	3.4145	3.3033	3.2012
40%	0%	2.1536	2.0599	1.9780	1.9059	1.8420	1.7850	1.7339	1.6877	1.6459	1.6078	1.5730	1.5411
	5%	2.8679	2.7265	2.6030	2.4942	2.3976	2.3113	2.2339	2.1639	2.1004	2.0426	1.9897	1.9411
	10%	3.5822	3.3932	3.2280	3.0824	2.9532	2.8377	2.7339	2.6401	2.5550	2.4774	2.4063	2.3411
	15%	4.2965	4.0599	3.8530	3.6706	3.5087	3.3640	3.2339	3.1163	3.0095	2.9121	2.8230	2.7411
	20%	5.0108	4.7265	4.4780	4.2589	4.0643	3.8903	3.7339	3.5925	3.4640	3.3469	3.2397	3.1411

Entry is an index of effective cost as percentage of original purchase price.

Cost of Replacing a Capital Asset

Time to Replacement 7 Years

Salvage Ratio	Maintenance	7.00%	7.50%	8.00%	8.50%	9.00%	9.50%	10.00%	10.50%	11.00%	11.50%	12.00%	12.50%
0%	0%	2.5873	2.4541	2.3379	2.2357	2.1452	2.0645	1.9921	1.9269	1.8679	1.8142	1.7653	1.7204
	5%	3.3016	3.1208	2.9629	2.8240	2.7008	2.5908	2.4921	2.4031	2.3224	2.2490	2.1819	2.1204
	10%	4.0159	3.7875	3.5879	3.4122	3.2563	3.1171	2.9921	2.8793	2.7770	2.6838	2.5986	2.5204
	15%	4.7302	4.4541	4.2129	4.0004	3.8119	3.6435	3.4921	3.3555	3.2315	3.1186	3.0153	2.9204
	20%	5.4445	5.1208	4.8379	4.5887	4.3674	4.1698	3.9921	3.8317	3.6861	3.5534	3.4319	3.3204
10%	0%	2.4286	2.3087	2.2041	2.1122	2.0307	1.9581	1.8929	1.8342	1.7811	1.7328	1.6887	1.6484
	5%	3.1429	2.9754	2.8291	2.7004	2.5862	2.4844	2.3929	2.3104	2.2357	2.1676	2.1054	2.0484
	10%	3.8572	3.6420	3.4541	3.2886	3.1418	3.0107	2.8929	2.7866	2.6902	2.6024	2.5221	2.4484
	15%	4.5714	4.3087	4.0791	3.8769	3.6974	3.5370	3.3929	3.2628	3.1447	3.0372	2.9387	2.8484
	20%	5.2857	4.9754	4.7041	4.4651	4.2529	4.0633	3.8929	3.7390	3.5993	3.4719	3.3554	3.2484
15%	0%	2.3492	2.2360	2.1372	2.0504	1.9734	1.9048	1.8433	1.7879	1.7377	1.6921	1.6505	1.6124
	5%	3.0635	2.9027	2.7622	2.6386	2.5290	2.4311	2.3433	2.2641	2.1923	2.1269	2.0671	2.0124
	10%	3.7778	3.5693	3.3872	3.2268	3.0845	2.9575	2.8433	2.7403	2.6468	2.5617	2.4838	2.4124
	15%	4.4921	4.2360	4.0122	3.8151	3.6401	3.4838	3.3433	3.2165	3.1014	2.9965	2.9005	2.8124
	20%	5.2064	4.9027	4.6372	4.4033	4.1957	4.0101	3.8433	3.6927	3.5559	3.4312	3.3171	3.2124
20%	0%	2.2699	2.1633	2.0703	1.9886	1.9162	1.8516	1.7937	1.7415	1.6943	1.6514	1.6122	1.5764
	5%	2.9841	2.8300	2.6953	2.5768	2.4717	2.3779	2.2937	2.2177	2.1489	2.0862	2.0289	1.9764
	10%	3.6984	3.4966	3.3203	3.1651	3.0273	2.9042	2.7937	2.6939	2.6034	2.5210	2.4456	2.3764
	15%	4.4127	4.1633	3.9453	3.7533	3.5828	3.4305	3.2937	3.1701	3.0580	2.9557	2.8622	2.7764
	20%	5.1270	4.8300	4.5703	4.3415	4.1384	3.9569	3.7937	3.6463	3.5125	3.3905	3.2789	3.1764
25%	0%	2.1905	2.0906	2.0034	1.9268	1.8589	1.7984	1.7441	1.6952	1.6509	1.6107	1.5740	1.5403
	5%	2.9048	2.7573	2.6284	2.5150	2.4145	2.3247	2.2441	2.1714	2.1055	2.0455	1.9906	1.9403
	10%	3.6191	3.4239	3.2534	3.1033	2.9700	2.8510	2.7441	2.6476	2.5600	2.4802	2.4073	2.3403
	15%	4.3333	4.0906	3.8784	3.6915	3.5256	3.3773	3.2441	3.1238	3.0146	2.9150	2.8240	2.7403
	20%	5.0476	4.7573	4.5034	4.2797	4.0811	3.9036	3.7441	3.6000	3.4691	3.3498	3.2406	3.1403
33%	0%	2.0582	1.9694	1.8920	1.8238	1.7635	1.7097	1.6614	1.6180	1.5786	1.5428	1.5102	1.4803
	5%	2.7725	2.6361	2.5170	2.4121	2.3190	2.2360	2.1614	2.0941	2.0331	1.9776	1.9268	1.8803
	10%	3.4868	3.3027	3.1420	3.0003	2.8746	2.7623	2.6614	2.5703	2.4877	2.4124	2.3435	2.2803
	15%	4.2011	3.9694	3.7670	3.5885	3.4301	3.2886	3.1614	3.0465	2.9422	2.8472	2.7602	2.6803
	20%	4.9154	4.6361	4.3920	4.1768	3.9857	3.8149	3.6614	3.5227	3.3968	3.2820	3.1768	3.0803
40%	0%	1.9524	1.8725	1.8028	1.7414	1.6871	1.6387	1.5953	1.5562	1.5207	1.4885	1.4592	1.4323
	5%	2.6667	2.5391	2.4278	2.3297	2.2427	2.1650	2.0953	2.0324	1.9753	1.9233	1.8758	1.8323
	10%	3.3810	3.2058	3.0528	2.9179	2.7982	2.6913	2.5953	2.5085	2.4298	2.3581	2.2925	2.2323
	15%	4.0952	3.8725	3.6778	3.5061	3.3538	3.2176	3.0953	2.9847	2.8844	2.7929	2.7092	2.6323
	20%	4.8095	4.5391	4.3028	4.0944	3.9093	3.7440	3.5953	3.4609	3.3389	3.2277	3.1258	3.0323

Time to Replacement 10 Years

Salvage Ratio	Maintenance	7.00%	7.50%	8.00%	8.50%	9.00%	9.50%	10.00%	10.50%	11.00%	11.50%	12.00%	12.50%
0%	0%	1.9904	1.8992	1.8199	1.7504	1.6890	1.6345	1.5858	1.5421	1.5027	1.4671	1.4347	1.4052
	5%	2.7047	2.5659	2.4449	2.3386	2.2446	2.1608	2.0858	2.0183	1.9573	1.9019	1.8514	1.8052
	10%	3.4190	3.2326	3.0699	2.9269	2.8001	2.6871	2.5858	2.4945	2.4118	2.3366	2.2680	2.2052
	15%	4.1333	3.8992	3.6949	3.5151	3.3557	3.2134	3.0858	2.9707	2.8664	2.7714	2.6847	2.6052
	20%	4.8476	4.5659	4.3199	4.1033	3.9112	3.7398	3.5858	3.4469	3.3209	3.2062	3.1014	3.0052
10%	0%	1.8914	1.8093	1.7379	1.6753	1.6201	1.5710	1.5272	1.4879	1.4525	1.4204	1.3912	1.3647
	5%	2.6057	2.4760	2.3629	2.2636	2.1757	2.0974	2.0272	1.9641	1.9070	1.8552	1.8079	1.7647
	10%	3.3200	3.1426	2.9879	2.8518	2.7312	2.6237	2.5272	2.4403	2.3615	2.2899	2.2246	2.1647
	15%	4.0342	3.8093	3.6129	3.4401	3.2868	3.1500	3.0272	2.9165	2.8161	2.7247	2.6412	2.5647
	20%	4.7485	4.4760	4.2379	4.0283	3.8423	3.6763	3.5272	3.3927	3.2706	3.1595	3.0579	2.9647
15%	0%	1.8419	1.7643	1.6969	1.6378	1.5857	1.5393	1.4979	1.4608	1.4273	1.3970	1.3695	1.3444
	5%	2.5562	2.4310	2.3219	2.2261	2.1412	2.0656	1.9979	1.9370	1.8819	1.8318	1.7862	1.7444
	10%	3.2704	3.0977	2.9469	2.8143	2.6968	2.5920	2.4979	2.4132	2.3364	2.2666	2.2028	2.1444
	15%	3.9847	3.7643	3.5719	3.4025	3.2523	3.1183	2.9979	2.8894	2.7910	2.7014	2.6195	2.5444
	20%	4.6990	4.4310	4.1969	3.9908	3.8079	3.6446	3.4979	3.3656	3.2455	3.1362	3.0362	2.9444
20%	0%	1.7923	1.7194	1.6559	1.6003	1.5512	1.5076	1.4686	1.4337	1.4022	1.3737	1.3478	1.3242
	5%	2.5066	2.3860	2.2809	2.1885	2.1068	2.0339	1.9686	1.9099	1.8567	1.8084	1.7644	1.7242
	10%	3.2209	3.0527	2.9059	2.7768	2.6623	2.5602	2.4686	2.3861	2.3113	2.2432	2.1811	2.1242
	15%	3.9352	3.7194	3.5309	3.3650	3.2179	3.0865	2.9686	2.8623	2.7658	2.6780	2.5978	2.5242
	20%	4.6495	4.3860	4.1559	3.9533	3.7734	3.6129	3.4686	3.3385	3.2204	3.1128	3.0144	2.9242
25%	0%	1.7428	1.6744	1.6149	1.5628	1.5168	1.4759	1.4394	1.4066	1.3770	1.3503	1.3260	1.3039
	5%	2.4571	2.3411	2.2399	2.1510	2.0723	2.0022	1.9394	1.8828	1.8316	1.7851	1.7427	1.7039
	10%	3.1714	3.0078	2.8649	2.7393	2.6279	2.5285	2.4394	2.3590	2.2861	2.2199	2.1594	2.1039
	15%	3.8857	3.6744	3.4899	3.3275	3.1834	3.0548	2.9394	2.8352	2.7407	2.6547	2.5760	2.5039
	20%	4.6000	4.3411	4.1149	3.9157	3.7390	3.5811	3.4394	3.3113	3.1952	3.0894	2.9927	2.9039
33%	0%	1.6603	1.5995	1.5466	1.5003	1.4593	1.4230	1.3905	1.3614	1.3352	1.3114	1.2898	1.2701
	5%	2.3746	2.2662	2.1716	2.0885	2.0149	1.9493	1.8905	1.8376	1.7897	1.7462	1.7065	1.6701
	10%	3.0889	2.9328	2.7966	2.6767	2.5705	2.4756	2.3905	2.3138	2.2442	2.1810	2.1231	2.0701
	15%	3.8031	3.5995	3.4216	3.2650	3.1260	3.0019	2.8905	2.7900	2.6988	2.6157	2.5398	2.4701
	20%	4.5174	4.2662	4.0466	3.8532	3.6816	3.5283	3.3905	3.2662	3.1533	3.0505	2.9565	2.8701
40%	0%	1.5943	1.5395	1.4919	1.4502	1.4134	1.3807	1.3515	1.3253	1.3016	1.2802	1.2608	1.2431
	5%	2.3085	2.2062	2.1169	2.0385	1.9690	1.9070	1.8515	1.8015	1.7562	1.7150	1.6775	1.6431
	10%	3.0228	2.8729	2.7419	2.6267	2.5245	2.4333	2.3515	2.2776	2.2107	2.1498	2.0942	2.0431
	15%	3.7371	3.5395	3.3669	3.2149	3.0801	2.9596	2.8515	2.7538	2.6653	2.5846	2.5108	2.4431
	20%	4.4514	4.2062	3.9919	3.8032	3.6356	3.4860	3.3515	3.2300	3.1198	3.0194	2.9275	2.8431

Entry is an index of effective cost as percentage of original purchase price.

Cost of Replacing a Capital Asset

Time to Replacement 12 Years

Salvage Ratio	Maint-enance	7.00%	7.50%	8.00%	8.50%	9.00%	9.50%	10.00%	10.50%	11.00%	11.50%	12.00%	12.50%
0%	0%	1.7629	1.6884	1.6237	1.5671	1.5174	1.4733	1.4341	1.3990	1.3675	1.3391	1.3134	1.2901
	5%	2.4772	2.3550	2.2487	2.1554	2.0729	1.9996	1.9341	1.8752	1.8221	1.7739	1.7301	1.6901
	10%	3.1915	3.0217	2.8737	2.7436	2.6285	2.5259	2.4341	2.3514	2.2766	2.2087	2.1468	2.0901
	15%	3.9058	3.6884	3.4987	3.3318	3.1840	3.0523	2.9341	2.8276	2.7312	2.6435	2.5634	2.4901
	20%	4.6201	4.3550	4.1237	3.9201	3.7396	3.5786	3.4341	3.3038	3.1857	3.0782	2.9801	2.8901
10%	0%	1.6866	1.6195	1.5613	1.5104	1.4656	1.4260	1.3907	1.3591	1.3308	1.3052	1.2821	1.2611
	5%	2.4009	2.2862	2.1863	2.0987	2.0212	1.9523	1.8907	1.8353	1.7853	1.7400	1.6987	1.6611
	10%	3.1152	2.9529	2.8113	2.6869	2.5767	2.4786	2.3907	2.3115	2.2399	2.1748	2.1154	2.0611
	15%	3.8295	3.6195	3.4363	3.2751	3.1323	3.0049	2.8907	2.7877	2.6944	2.6095	2.5321	2.4611
	20%	4.5438	4.2862	4.0613	3.8634	3.6879	3.5312	3.3907	3.2639	3.1489	3.0443	2.9487	2.8611
15%	0%	1.6485	1.5851	1.5301	1.4821	1.4398	1.4023	1.3690	1.3392	1.3124	1.2882	1.2664	1.2466
	5%	2.3628	2.2518	2.1551	2.0703	1.9953	1.9286	1.8690	1.8154	1.7669	1.7230	1.6831	1.6466
	10%	3.0771	2.9184	2.7801	2.6585	2.5509	2.4549	2.3690	2.2915	2.2215	2.1578	2.0997	2.0466
	15%	3.7914	3.5851	3.4051	3.2468	3.1064	2.9813	2.8690	2.7677	2.6760	2.5926	2.5164	2.4466
	20%	4.5056	4.2518	4.0301	3.8350	3.6620	3.5076	3.3690	3.2439	3.1306	3.0274	2.9331	2.8466
20%	0%	1.6104	1.5507	1.4989	1.4537	1.4139	1.3787	1.3473	1.3192	1.2940	1.2713	1.2507	1.2321
	5%	2.3246	2.2174	2.1239	2.0419	1.9695	1.9050	1.8473	1.7954	1.7486	1.7061	1.6674	1.6321
	10%	3.0389	2.8840	2.7489	2.6302	2.5250	2.4313	2.3473	2.2716	2.2031	2.1409	2.0841	2.0321
	15%	3.7532	3.5507	3.3739	3.2184	3.0806	2.9576	2.8473	2.7478	2.6576	2.5756	2.5007	2.4321
	20%	4.4675	4.2174	3.9989	3.8067	3.6361	3.4839	3.3473	3.2240	3.1122	3.0104	2.9174	2.8321
25%	0%	1.5722	1.5163	1.4678	1.4254	1.3880	1.3550	1.3256	1.2993	1.2756	1.2543	1.2351	1.2176
	5%	2.2865	2.1829	2.0928	2.0136	1.9436	1.8813	1.8256	1.7755	1.7302	1.6891	1.6517	1.6176
	10%	3.0008	2.8496	2.7178	2.6018	2.4991	2.4076	2.3256	2.2516	2.1847	2.1239	2.0684	2.0176
	15%	3.7151	3.5163	3.3428	3.1901	3.0547	2.9339	2.8256	2.7278	2.6393	2.5587	2.4851	2.4176
	20%	4.4293	4.1829	3.9678	3.7783	3.6103	3.4602	3.3256	3.2040	3.0938	2.9935	2.9017	2.8176
33%	0%	1.5086	1.4589	1.4158	1.3781	1.3449	1.3155	1.2894	1.2660	1.2450	1.2261	1.2089	1.1934
	5%	2.2229	2.1256	2.0408	1.9663	1.9005	1.8419	1.7894	1.7422	1.6996	1.6609	1.6256	1.5934
	10%	2.9372	2.7922	2.6658	2.5546	2.4560	2.3682	2.2894	2.2184	2.1541	2.0956	2.0423	1.9934
	15%	3.6515	3.4589	3.2908	3.1428	3.0116	2.8945	2.7894	2.6946	2.6086	2.5304	2.4589	2.3934
	20%	4.3658	4.1256	3.9158	3.7310	3.5671	3.4208	3.2894	3.1708	3.0632	2.9652	2.8756	2.7934
40%	0%	1.4578	1.4130	1.3742	1.3403	1.3104	1.2840	1.2605	1.2394	1.2205	1.2035	1.1881	1.1741
	5%	2.1720	2.0797	1.9992	1.9285	1.8660	1.8103	1.7605	1.7156	1.6751	1.6383	1.6047	1.5741
	10%	2.8863	2.7464	2.6242	2.5168	2.4215	2.3366	2.2605	2.1918	2.1296	2.0730	2.0214	1.9741
	15%	3.6006	3.4130	3.2492	3.1050	2.9771	2.8629	2.7605	2.6680	2.5841	2.5078	2.4381	2.3741
	20%	4.3149	4.0797	3.8742	3.6932	3.5326	3.3893	3.2605	3.1442	3.0387	2.9426	2.8547	2.7741

Time to Replacement 15 Years

Salvage Ratio	Maint-enance	7.00%	7.50%	8.00%	8.50%	9.00%	9.50%	10.00%	10.50%	11.00%	11.50%	12.00%	12.50%
0%	0%	1.5408	1.4832	1.4335	1.3902	1.3524	1.3190	1.2895	1.2633	1.2399	1.2190	1.2002	1.1832
	5%	2.2551	2.1499	2.0585	1.9785	1.9079	1.8453	1.7895	1.7395	1.6945	1.6538	1.6168	1.5832
	10%	2.9694	2.8166	2.6835	2.5667	2.4635	2.3717	2.2895	2.2157	2.1490	2.0885	2.0335	1.9832
	15%	3.6837	3.4832	3.3085	3.1549	3.0190	2.8980	2.7895	2.6919	2.6036	2.5233	2.4502	2.3832
	20%	4.3980	4.1499	3.9335	3.7432	3.5746	3.4243	3.2895	3.1681	3.0581	2.9581	2.8668	2.7832
10%	0%	1.4868	1.4349	1.3901	1.3512	1.3171	1.2871	1.2606	1.2370	1.2159	1.1971	1.1802	1.1649
	5%	2.2010	2.1016	2.0151	1.9394	1.8727	1.8134	1.7606	1.7132	1.6705	1.6319	1.5968	1.5649
	10%	2.9153	2.7682	2.6401	2.5277	2.4282	2.3398	2.2606	2.1894	2.1250	2.0666	2.0135	1.9649
	15%	3.6296	3.4349	3.2651	3.1159	2.9838	2.8661	2.7606	2.6656	2.5796	2.5014	2.4302	2.3649
	20%	4.3439	4.1016	3.8901	3.7041	3.5393	3.3924	3.2606	3.1417	3.0341	2.9362	2.8468	2.7649
15%	0%	1.4597	1.4107	1.3685	1.3317	1.2995	1.2712	1.2461	1.2238	1.2039	1.1861	1.1701	1.1557
	5%	2.1740	2.0774	1.9935	1.9199	1.8551	1.7975	1.7461	1.7000	1.6585	1.6209	1.5868	1.5557
	10%	2.8883	2.7441	2.6185	2.5082	2.4106	2.3238	2.2461	2.1762	2.1130	2.0557	2.0035	1.9557
	15%	3.6026	3.4107	3.2435	3.0964	2.9662	2.8501	2.7461	2.6524	2.5676	2.4905	2.4201	2.3557
	20%	4.3169	4.0774	3.8685	3.6846	3.5217	3.3764	3.2461	3.1286	3.0221	2.9253	2.8368	2.7557
20%	0%	1.4327	1.3866	1.3468	1.3122	1.2819	1.2552	1.2316	1.2107	1.1919	1.1752	1.1601	1.1466
	5%	2.1470	2.0532	1.9718	1.9004	1.8374	1.7815	1.7316	1.6868	1.6465	1.6100	1.5768	1.5466
	10%	2.8613	2.7199	2.5968	2.4886	2.3930	2.3078	2.2316	2.1630	2.1010	2.0447	1.9935	1.9466
	15%	3.5755	3.3866	3.2218	3.0769	2.9486	2.8342	2.7316	2.6392	2.5556	2.4795	2.4101	2.3466
	20%	4.2898	4.0532	3.8468	3.6651	3.5041	3.3605	3.2316	3.1154	3.0101	2.9143	2.8268	2.7466
25%	0%	1.4056	1.3624	1.3251	1.2927	1.2643	1.2393	1.2171	1.1975	1.1799	1.1642	1.1501	1.1374
	5%	2.1199	2.0291	1.9501	1.8809	1.8198	1.7656	1.7171	1.6737	1.6345	1.5990	1.5668	1.5374
	10%	2.8342	2.6957	2.5751	2.4691	2.3754	2.2919	2.2171	2.1499	2.0890	2.0338	1.9835	1.9374
	15%	3.5485	3.3624	3.2001	3.0574	2.9309	2.8182	2.7171	2.6261	2.5436	2.4686	2.4001	2.3374
	20%	4.2628	4.0291	3.8251	3.6456	3.4865	3.3445	3.2171	3.1022	2.9981	2.9034	2.8168	2.7374
33%	0%	1.3606	1.3221	1.2890	1.2601	1.2349	1.2127	1.1930	1.1755	1.1599	1.1460	1.1334	1.1221
	5%	2.0749	1.9888	1.9140	1.8484	1.7905	1.7390	1.6930	1.6517	1.6145	1.5808	1.5501	1.5221
	10%	2.7891	2.6555	2.5390	2.4366	2.3460	2.2653	2.1930	2.1279	2.0690	2.0156	1.9668	1.9221
	15%	3.5034	3.3221	3.1640	3.0249	2.9016	2.7916	2.6930	2.6041	2.5236	2.4503	2.3834	2.3221
	20%	4.2177	3.9888	3.7890	3.6131	3.4571	3.3179	3.1930	3.0803	2.9781	2.8851	2.8001	2.7221
40%	0%	1.3245	1.2899	1.2601	1.2341	1.2114	1.1914	1.1737	1.1580	1.1440	1.1314	1.1201	1.1099
	5%	2.0388	1.9566	1.8851	1.8224	1.7670	1.7177	1.6737	1.6342	1.5985	1.5662	1.5368	1.5099
	10%	2.7531	2.6233	2.5101	2.4106	2.3225	2.2440	2.1737	2.1104	2.0530	2.0010	1.9534	1.9099
	15%	3.4674	3.2899	3.1351	2.9988	2.8781	2.7704	2.6737	2.5866	2.5076	2.4357	2.3701	2.3099
	20%	4.1817	3.9566	3.7601	3.5871	3.4336	3.2967	3.1737	3.0627	2.9621	2.8705	2.7868	2.7099

Entry is an index of effective cost as percentage of original purchase price.

Create Value by Buying in Below-Market Leases

Capitalization Rate 8.50%

Ratio of Target Rent to Old Rent

Years Left	1.25 times Non-Discounted Pay to Tenant	Value Added	1.25 times Discounted Pay to Tenant	Value Added	1.33 times Non-Discounted Pay to Tenant	Value Added	1.33 times Discounted Pay to Tenant	Value Added
1	0.25000	2.69118	0.23886	2.70232	0.33333	3.58824	0.31848	3.60309
2	0.50000	2.44118	0.45832	2.48285	0.66667	3.25490	0.61110	3.31047
3	0.75000	2.19118	0.65996	2.28122	1.00000	2.92157	0.87995	3.04162
4	1.00000	1.94118	0.84522	2.09595	1.33333	2.58824	1.12697	2.79460
5	1.25000	1.69118	1.01544	1.92574	1.66667	2.25490	1.35392	2.56765
6	1.50000	1.44118	1.17183	1.76934	2.00000	1.92157	1.56245	2.35912
7	1.75000	1.19118	1.31553	1.62565	2.33333	1.58824	1.75404	2.16753
8	2.00000	0.94118	1.44755	1.49363	2.66667	1.25490	1.93007	1.99150
9	2.25000	0.69118	1.56885	1.37232	3.00000	0.92157	2.09180	1.82977
10	2.50000	0.44118	1.68030	1.26088	3.33333	0.58824	2.24040	1.68117
12	3.00000	-0.05882	1.87678	1.06439	4.00000	-0.07843	2.50238	1.41919
15	3.75000	-0.80882	2.11562	0.82556	5.00000	-1.07843	2.82082	1.10074
20	5.00000	-2.05882	2.40064	0.54053	6.66667	-2.74510	3.20086	0.72071

Years Left	1.50 times Non-Discounted Pay to Tenant	Value Added	1.50 times Discounted Pay to Tenant	Value Added	1.67 times Non-Discounted Pay to Tenant	Value Added	1.67 times Discounted Pay to Tenant	Value Added
1	0.50000	5.38235	0.47772	5.40463	0.66667	7.17647	0.63696	7.20618
2	1.00000	4.88235	0.91664	4.96571	1.33333	6.50980	1.22219	6.62095
3	1.50000	4.38235	1.31992	4.56243	2.00000	5.84314	1.75990	6.08324
4	2.00000	3.88235	1.69045	4.19191	2.66667	5.17647	2.25393	5.58921
5	2.50000	3.38235	2.03088	3.85147	3.33333	4.50980	2.70784	5.13529
6	3.00000	2.88235	2.34367	3.53868	4.00000	3.84314	3.12489	4.71824
7	3.50000	2.38235	2.63106	3.25130	4.66667	3.17647	3.50807	4.33506
8	4.00000	1.88235	2.89510	2.98725	5.33333	2.50980	3.86013	3.98300
9	4.50000	1.38235	3.13770	2.74465	6.00000	1.84314	4.18360	3.65953
10	5.00000	0.88235	3.36060	2.52175	6.66667	1.17647	4.48080	3.36233
12	6.00000	-0.11765	3.75357	2.12879	8.00000	-0.15686	5.00475	2.83838
15	7.50000	-1.61765	4.23124	1.65112	10.00000	-2.15686	5.64165	2.20149
20	10.00000	-4.11765	4.80128	1.08107	13.33333	-5.49020	6.40171	1.44142

Years Left	1.75 times Non-Discounted Pay to Tenant	Value Added	1.75 times Discounted Pay to Tenant	Value Added	2.00 times Non-Discounted Pay to Tenant	Value Added	2.00 times Discounted Pay to Tenant	Value Added
1	0.75000	8.07353	0.71658	8.10695	1.00000	10.76471	0.95544	10.80927
2	1.50000	7.32353	1.37497	7.44856	2.00000	9.76471	1.83329	9.93142
3	2.25000	6.57353	1.97988	6.84365	3.00000	8.76471	2.63984	9.12486
4	3.00000	5.82353	2.53567	6.28786	4.00000	7.76471	3.38090	8.38381
5	3.75000	5.07353	3.04632	5.77721	5.00000	6.76471	4.06177	7.70294
6	4.50000	4.32353	3.51550	5.30802	6.00000	5.76471	4.68734	7.07737
7	5.25000	3.57353	3.94658	4.87695	7.00000	4.76471	5.26211	6.50260
8	6.00000	2.82353	4.34265	4.48088	8.00000	3.76471	5.79020	5.97450
9	6.75000	2.07353	4.70655	4.11697	9.00000	2.76471	6.27541	5.48930
10	7.50000	1.32353	5.04090	3.78263	10.00000	1.76471	6.72121	5.04350
12	9.00000	-0.17647	5.63035	3.19318	12.00000	-0.23529	7.50713	4.25757
15	11.25000	-2.42647	6.34686	2.47667	15.00000	-3.23529	8.46247	3.30223
20	15.00000	-6.17647	7.20193	1.62160	20.00000	-8.23529	9.60257	2.16214

Years Left	2.25 times Non-Discounted Pay to Tenant	Value Added	2.25 times Discounted Pay to Tenant	Value Added	2.50 times Non-Discounted Pay to Tenant	Value Added	2.50 times Discounted Pay to Tenant	Value Added
1	1.25000	13.45588	1.19430	13.51158	1.50000	16.14706	1.43316	16.21390
2	2.50000	12.20588	2.29161	12.41427	3.00000	14.64706	2.74993	14.89713
3	3.75000	10.95588	3.29980	11.40608	4.50000	13.14706	3.95976	13.68729
4	5.00000	9.70588	4.22612	10.47976	6.00000	11.64706	5.07134	12.57572
5	6.25000	8.45588	5.07721	9.62868	7.50000	10.14706	6.09265	11.55441
6	7.50000	7.20588	5.85917	8.84671	9.00000	8.64706	7.03101	10.61605
7	8.75000	5.95588	6.57764	8.12824	10.50000	7.14706	7.89317	9.75389
8	10.00000	4.70588	7.23775	7.46813	12.00000	5.64706	8.68530	8.96176
9	11.25000	3.45588	7.84426	6.86162	13.50000	4.14706	9.41311	8.23395
10	12.50000	2.20588	8.40151	6.30438	15.00000	2.64706	10.08181	7.56525
12	15.00000	-0.29412	9.38391	5.32197	18.00000	-0.35294	11.26070	6.38636
15	18.75000	-4.04412	10.57809	4.12779	22.50000	-4.85294	12.69371	4.95335
20	25.00000	-10.29412	12.00321	2.70267	30.00000	-12.35294	14.40385	3.24320

Entries are multiples of present annual rent. Negative entries indicate unprofitable programs.

Create Value by Buying in Below-Market Leases

Capitalization Rate 8.50%

Ratio of Target Rent to Old Rent

	2.75 times				3.00 times			
	Non-Discounted		Discounted		Non-Discounted		Discounted	
Years Left	Pay to Tenant	Value Added	Pay to Tenant	Value Added	Pay to Tenant	Value Added	Pay to Tenant	Value Added
1	1.75000	18.83824	1.67202	18.91621	2.00000	21.52941	1.91088	21.61853
2	3.50000	17.08824	3.20825	17.37998	4.00000	19.52941	3.66658	19.86284
3	5.25000	15.33824	4.61972	15.96851	6.00000	17.52941	5.27969	18.24973
4	7.00000	13.58824	5.91657	14.67167	8.00000	15.52941	6.76179	16.76762
5	8.75000	11.83824	7.10809	13.48015	10.00000	13.52941	8.12353	15.40588
6	10.50000	10.08824	8.20284	12.38539	12.00000	11.52941	9.37468	14.15473
7	12.25000	8.33824	9.20869	11.37954	14.00000	9.52941	10.52422	13.00519
8	14.00000	6.58824	10.13285	10.45538	16.00000	7.52941	11.58040	11.94901
9	15.75000	4.83824	10.98196	9.60627	18.00000	5.52941	12.55081	10.97860
10	17.50000	3.08824	11.76211	8.82613	20.00000	3.52941	13.44241	10.08700
12	21.00000	-0.41176	13.13748	7.45075	24.00000	-0.47059	15.01426	8.51515
15	26.25000	-5.66176	14.80933	5.77891	30.00000	-6.47059	16.92495	6.60446
20	35.00000	-14.41176	16.80450	3.78374	40.00000	-16.47059	19.20514	4.32427

	3.33 times				3.50 times			
1	2.33333	25.11765	2.22936	25.22162	2.50000	26.91176	2.38860	27.02316
2	4.66667	22.78431	4.27767	23.17331	5.00000	24.41176	4.58322	24.82855
3	7.00000	20.45098	6.15963	21.29135	7.50000	21.91176	6.59961	22.81216
4	9.33333	18.11765	7.88876	19.56222	10.00000	19.41176	8.45224	20.95953
5	11.66667	15.78431	9.47745	17.97353	12.50000	16.91176	10.15441	19.25735
6	14.00000	13.45098	10.93713	16.51385	15.00000	14.41176	11.71835	17.69341
7	16.33333	11.11765	12.27826	15.17272	17.50000	11.91176	13.15528	16.25649
8	18.66667	8.78431	13.51047	13.94051	20.00000	9.41176	14.47551	14.93626
9	21.00000	6.45098	14.64261	12.80837	22.50000	6.91176	15.68852	13.72325
10	23.33333	4.11765	15.68281	11.76817	25.00000	4.41176	16.80301	12.60875
12	28.00000	-0.54902	17.51664	9.93434	30.00000	-0.58824	18.76783	10.64394
15	35.00000	-7.54902	19.74577	7.70521	37.50000	-8.08824	21.15619	8.25558
20	46.66667	-19.21569	22.40600	5.04498	50.00000	-20.58824	24.00642	5.40534

	4.00 times				4.50 times			
1	3.00000	32.29412	2.86632	32.42780	3.50000	37.67647	3.34404	37.83243
2	6.00000	29.29412	5.49986	29.79425	7.00000	34.17647	6.41651	34.75996
3	9.00000	26.29412	7.91953	27.37459	10.50000	30.67647	9.23945	31.93702
4	12.00000	23.29412	10.14269	25.15143	14.00000	27.17647	11.83313	29.34334
5	15.00000	20.29412	12.18530	23.10882	17.50000	23.67647	14.21618	26.96029
6	18.00000	17.29412	14.06202	21.23210	21.00000	20.17647	16.40569	24.77078
7	21.00000	14.29412	15.78633	19.50779	24.50000	16.67647	18.41739	22.75908
8	24.00000	11.29412	17.37061	17.92351	28.00000	13.17647	20.26571	20.91076
9	27.00000	8.29412	18.82622	16.46790	31.50000	9.67647	21.96392	19.21255
10	30.00000	5.29412	20.16362	15.13050	35.00000	6.17647	23.52422	17.65225
12	36.00000	-0.70588	22.52140	12.77272	42.00000	-0.82353	26.27496	14.90151
15	45.00000	-9.70588	25.38742	9.90669	52.50000	-11.32353	29.61866	11.55781
20	60.00000	-24.70588	28.80771	6.48641	70.00000	-28.82353	33.60899	7.56748

	5.00 times				6.00 times			
1	4.00000	43.05882	3.82176	43.23706	5.00000	53.82353	4.77720	54.04633
2	8.00000	39.05882	7.33315	39.72567	10.00000	48.82353	9.16644	49.65709
3	12.00000	35.05882	10.55937	36.49945	15.00000	43.82353	13.19921	45.62432
4	16.00000	31.05882	13.52358	33.53524	20.00000	38.82353	16.90448	41.91905
5	20.00000	27.05882	16.24706	30.81176	25.00000	33.82353	20.30883	38.51470
6	24.00000	23.05882	18.74936	28.30946	30.00000	28.82353	23.43670	35.38683
7	28.00000	19.05882	21.04844	26.01038	35.00000	23.82353	26.31055	32.51298
8	32.00000	15.05882	23.16081	23.89802	40.00000	18.82353	28.95101	29.87252
9	36.00000	11.05882	25.10163	21.95720	45.00000	13.82353	31.37703	27.44650
10	40.00000	7.05882	26.88482	20.17400	50.00000	8.82353	33.60603	25.21750
12	48.00000	-0.94118	30.02853	17.03030	60.00000	-1.17647	37.53566	21.28787
15	60.00000	-12.94118	33.84990	13.20893	75.00000	-16.17647	42.31237	16.51116
20	80.00000	-32.94118	38.41028	8.64854	100.00000	-41.17647	48.01285	10.81068

Entries are multiples of present annual rent. Negative entries indicate unprofitable programs.

Create Value by Buying in Below-Market Leases

Capitalization Rate 10.00%

Ratio of Target Rent to Old Rent

	1.25 times				1.33 times			
	Non-Discounted		Discounted		Non-Discounted		Discounted	
Years Left	Pay to Tenant	Value Added	Pay to Tenant	Value Added	Pay to Tenant	Value Added	Pay to Tenant	Value Added
1	0.25000	2.25000	0.23697	2.26303	0.33333	3.00000	0.31596	3.01737
2	0.50000	2.00000	0.45148	2.04852	0.66667	2.66667	0.60197	2.73137
3	0.75000	1.75000	0.64565	1.85435	1.00000	2.33333	0.86087	2.47247
4	1.00000	1.50000	0.82142	1.67858	1.33333	2.00000	1.09523	2.23811
5	1.25000	1.25000	0.98053	1.51947	1.66667	1.66667	1.30737	2.02596
6	1.50000	1.00000	1.12456	1.37544	2.00000	1.33333	1.49941	1.83393
7	1.75000	0.75000	1.25493	1.24507	2.33333	1.00000	1.67324	1.66009
8	2.00000	0.50000	1.37295	1.12705	2.66667	0.66667	1.83060	1.50274
9	2.25000	0.25000	1.47978	1.02022	3.00000	0.33333	1.97304	1.36030
10	2.50000	0.00000	1.57648	0.92352	3.33333	0.00000	2.10198	1.23136
12	3.00000	-0.50000	1.74326	0.75674	4.00000	-0.66667	2.32435	1.00899
15	3.75000	-1.25000	1.93870	0.56130	5.00000	-1.66667	2.58493	0.74840
20	5.00000	-2.50000	2.15885	0.34115	6.66667	-3.33333	2.87846	0.45487

	1.50 times				1.67 times			
	Non-Discounted		Discounted		Non-Discounted		Discounted	
Years Left	Pay to Tenant	Value Added	Pay to Tenant	Value Added	Pay to Tenant	Value Added	Pay to Tenant	Value Added
1	0.50000	4.50000	0.47394	4.52606	0.66667	6.00000	0.63192	6.03475
2	1.00000	4.00000	0.90295	4.09705	1.33333	5.33333	1.20394	5.46273
3	1.50000	3.50000	1.29130	3.70870	2.00000	4.66667	1.72174	4.94493
4	2.00000	3.00000	1.64284	3.35716	2.66667	4.00000	2.19045	4.47621
5	2.50000	2.50000	1.96106	3.03894	3.33333	3.33333	2.61474	4.05192
6	3.00000	2.00000	2.24911	2.75089	4.00000	2.66667	2.99881	3.66785
7	3.50000	1.50000	2.50986	2.49014	4.66667	2.00000	3.34648	3.32019
8	4.00000	1.00000	2.74590	2.25410	5.33333	1.33333	3.66119	3.00547
9	4.50000	0.50000	2.95956	2.04044	6.00000	0.66667	3.94608	2.72059
10	5.00000	0.00000	3.15297	1.84703	6.66667	0.00000	4.20395	2.46271
12	6.00000	-1.00000	3.48652	1.51348	8.00000	-1.33333	4.64870	2.01797
15	7.50000	-2.50000	3.87739	1.12261	10.00000	-3.33333	5.16986	1.49681
20	10.00000	-5.00000	4.31769	0.68231	13.33333	-6.66667	5.75692	0.90974

	1.75 times				2.00 times			
	Non-Discounted		Discounted		Non-Discounted		Discounted	
Years Left	Pay to Tenant	Value Added	Pay to Tenant	Value Added	Pay to Tenant	Value Added	Pay to Tenant	Value Added
1	0.75000	6.75000	0.71091	6.78909	1.00000	9.00000	0.94788	9.05212
2	1.50000	6.00000	1.35443	6.14557	2.00000	8.00000	1.80590	8.19410
3	2.25000	5.25000	1.93695	5.56305	3.00000	7.00000	2.58260	7.41740
4	3.00000	4.50000	2.46426	5.03574	4.00000	6.00000	3.28568	6.71432
5	3.75000	3.75000	2.94159	4.55841	5.00000	5.00000	3.92211	6.07789
6	4.50000	3.00000	3.37367	4.12633	6.00000	4.00000	4.49822	5.50178
7	5.25000	2.25000	3.76479	3.73521	7.00000	3.00000	5.01972	4.98028
8	6.00000	1.50000	4.11884	3.38116	8.00000	2.00000	5.49179	4.50821
9	6.75000	0.75000	4.43933	3.06067	9.00000	1.00000	5.91911	4.08089
10	7.50000	0.00000	4.72945	2.77055	10.00000	0.00000	6.30593	3.69407
12	9.00000	-1.50000	5.22978	2.27022	12.00000	-2.00000	6.97304	3.02696
15	11.25000	-3.75000	5.81609	1.68391	15.00000	-5.00000	7.75479	2.24521
20	15.00000	-7.50000	6.47654	1.02346	20.00000	-10.00000	8.63538	1.36462

	2.25 times				2.50 times			
	Non-Discounted		Discounted		Non-Discounted		Discounted	
Years Left	Pay to Tenant	Value Added	Pay to Tenant	Value Added	Pay to Tenant	Value Added	Pay to Tenant	Value Added
1	1.25000	11.25000	1.18484	11.31516	1.50000	13.50000	1.42181	13.57819
2	2.50000	10.00000	2.25738	10.24262	3.00000	12.00000	2.70886	12.29114
3	3.75000	8.75000	3.22825	9.27175	4.50000	10.50000	3.87390	11.12610
4	5.00000	7.50000	4.10710	8.39290	6.00000	9.00000	4.92852	10.07148
5	6.25000	6.25000	4.90264	7.59736	7.50000	7.50000	5.88317	9.11683
6	7.50000	5.00000	5.62278	6.87722	9.00000	6.00000	6.74733	8.25267
7	8.75000	3.75000	6.27465	6.22535	10.50000	4.50000	7.52958	7.47042
8	10.00000	2.50000	6.86474	5.63526	12.00000	3.00000	8.23769	6.76231
9	11.25000	1.25000	7.39889	5.10111	13.50000	1.50000	8.87867	6.12133
10	12.50000	0.00000	7.88241	4.61759	15.00000	0.00000	9.45890	5.54110
12	15.00000	-2.50000	8.71631	3.78370	18.00000	-3.00000	10.45957	4.54043
15	18.75000	-6.25000	9.69348	2.80652	22.50000	-7.50000	11.63218	3.36782
20	25.00000	-12.50000	10.79423	1.70577	30.00000	-15.00000	12.95308	2.04692

Entries are multiples of present annual rent. Negative entries indicate unprofitable programs.

Create Value by Buying in Below-Market Leases

Capitalization Rate 10.00%

- -

			Ratio of Target Rent to Old Rent				
			2.75 times			3.00 times	
	Non-Discounted		Discounted		Non-Discounted		Discounted
Years Left	Pay to Tenant	Value Added	Pay to Tenant	Value Added	Pay to Tenant	Value Added	Pay to Tenant	Value Added

Years Left	Pay to Tenant	Value Added	Pay to Tenant	Value Added	Pay to Tenant	Value Added	Pay to Tenant	Value Added
1	1.75000	15.75000	1.65878	15.84122	2.00000	18.00000	1.89575	18.10425
2	3.50000	14.00000	3.16033	14.33967	4.00000	16.00000	3.61181	16.38819
3	5.25000	12.25000	4.51956	12.98044	6.00000	14.00000	5.16521	14.83479
4	7.00000	10.50000	5.74994	11.75006	8.00000	12.00000	6.57136	13.42864
5	8.75000	8.75000	6.86370	10.63630	10.00000	10.00000	7.84423	12.15577
6	10.50000	7.00000	7.87189	9.62811	12.00000	8.00000	8.99644	11.00356
7	12.25000	5.25000	8.78451	8.71549	14.00000	6.00000	10.03944	9.96056
8	14.00000	3.50000	9.61063	7.88937	16.00000	4.00000	10.98358	9.01642
9	15.75000	1.75000	10.35845	7.14155	18.00000	2.00000	11.83823	8.16177
10	17.50000	0.00000	11.03538	6.46462	20.00000	0.00000	12.61186	7.38814
12	21.00000	-3.50000	12.20283	5.29717	24.00000	-4.00000	13.94609	6.05391
15	26.25000	-8.75000	13.57088	3.92912	30.00000	-10.00000	15.50957	4.49043
20	35.00000	-17.50000	15.11192	2.38808	40.00000	-20.00000	17.27077	2.72923

	3.33 times				3.50 times			
1	2.33333	21.00000	2.21171	21.12162	2.50000	22.50000	2.36969	22.63031
2	4.66667	18.66667	4.21378	19.11956	5.00000	20.00000	4.51476	20.48524
3	7.00000	16.33333	6.02607	17.30726	7.50000	17.50000	6.45651	18.54349
4	9.33333	14.00000	7.66659	15.66675	10.00000	15.00000	8.21420	16.78580
5	11.66667	11.66667	9.15160	14.18173	12.50000	12.50000	9.80529	15.19471
6	14.00000	9.33333	10.49585	12.83748	15.00000	10.00000	11.24556	13.75444
7	16.33333	7.00000	11.71269	11.62065	17.50000	7.50000	12.54931	12.45069
8	18.66667	4.66667	12.81418	10.51916	20.00000	5.00000	13.72948	11.27052
9	21.00000	2.33333	13.81126	9.52207	22.50000	2.50000	14.79778	10.20222
10	23.33333	0.00000	14.71384	8.61950	25.00000	0.00000	15.76483	9.23517
12	28.00000	-4.66667	16.27044	7.06290	30.00000	-5.00000	17.43261	7.56739
15	35.00000	-11.66667	18.09450	5.23883	37.50000	-12.50000	19.38697	5.61303
20	46.66667	-23.33333	20.14923	3.18410	50.00000	-25.00000	21.58846	3.41154

	4.00 times				4.50 times			
1	3.00000	27.00000	2.84363	27.15637	3.50000	31.50000	3.31756	31.68244
2	6.00000	24.00000	5.41771	24.58229	7.00000	28.00000	6.32067	28.67933
3	9.00000	21.00000	7.74781	22.25219	10.50000	24.50000	9.03911	25.96089
4	12.00000	18.00000	9.85704	20.14296	14.00000	21.00000	11.49988	23.50012
5	15.00000	15.00000	11.76634	18.23366	17.50000	17.50000	13.72740	21.27260
6	18.00000	12.00000	13.49467	16.50533	21.00000	14.00000	15.74378	19.25622
7	21.00000	9.00000	15.05917	14.94083	24.50000	10.50000	17.56903	17.43097
8	24.00000	6.00000	16.47537	13.52463	28.00000	7.00000	19.22127	15.77873
9	27.00000	3.00000	17.75734	12.24266	31.50000	3.50000	20.71690	14.28310
10	30.00000	0.00000	18.91779	11.08221	35.00000	0.00000	22.07076	12.92924
12	36.00000	-6.00000	20.91913	9.08087	42.00000	-7.00000	24.40565	10.59435
15	45.00000	-15.00000	23.26436	6.73564	52.50000	-17.50000	27.14175	7.85825
20	60.00000	-30.00000	25.90615	4.09385	70.00000	-35.00000	30.22385	4.77615

	5.00 times				6.00 times			
1	4.00000	36.00000	3.79150	36.20850	5.00000	45.00000	4.73938	45.26062
2	8.00000	32.00000	7.22362	32.77638	10.00000	40.00000	9.02952	40.97048
3	12.00000	28.00000	10.33041	29.66959	15.00000	35.00000	12.91301	37.08699
4	16.00000	24.00000	13.14272	26.85728	20.00000	30.00000	16.42840	33.57160
5	20.00000	20.00000	15.68846	24.31154	25.00000	25.00000	19.61057	30.38943
6	24.00000	16.00000	17.99289	22.00711	30.00000	20.00000	22.49111	27.50889
7	28.00000	12.00000	20.07889	19.92111	35.00000	15.00000	25.09861	24.90139
8	32.00000	8.00000	21.96716	18.03284	40.00000	10.00000	27.45895	22.54105
9	36.00000	4.00000	23.67645	16.32355	45.00000	5.00000	29.59556	20.40444
10	40.00000	0.00000	25.22372	14.77628	50.00000	0.00000	31.52965	18.47035
12	48.00000	-8.00000	27.89218	12.10782	60.00000	-10.00000	34.86522	15.13478
15	60.00000	-20.00000	31.01915	8.98085	75.00000	-25.00000	38.77393	11.22607
20	80.00000	-40.00000	34.54154	5.45846	100.00000	-50.00000	43.17692	6.82308

Entries are multiples of present annual rent. Negative entries indicate unprofitable programs.

Create Value by Buying in Below-Market Leases

Capitalization Rate 11.50%

	Ratio of Target Rent to Old Rent							
	1.25 times				1.33 times			
	Non-Discounted		Discounted		Non-Discounted		Discounted	
Years Left	Pay to Tenant	Value Added	Pay to Tenant	Value Added	Pay to Tenant	Value Added	Pay to Tenant	Value Added
1	0.25000	1.92391	0.23510	1.93881	0.33333	2.56522	0.31347	2.58509
2	0.50000	1.67391	0.44477	1.72914	0.66667	2.23188	0.59303	2.30552
3	0.75000	1.42391	0.63177	1.54214	1.00000	1.89855	0.84236	2.05619
4	1.00000	1.17391	0.79855	1.37536	1.33333	1.56522	1.06473	1.83382
5	1.25000	0.92391	0.94729	1.22663	1.66667	1.23188	1.26305	1.63550
6	1.50000	0.67391	1.07994	1.09397	2.00000	0.89855	1.43992	1.45863
7	1.75000	0.42391	1.19825	0.97566	2.33333	0.56522	1.59767	1.30088
8	2.00000	0.17391	1.30376	0.87015	2.66667	0.23188	1.73835	1.16020
9	2.25000	-0.07609	1.39787	0.77605	3.00000	-0.10145	1.86382	1.03473
10	2.50000	-0.32609	1.48179	0.69212	3.33333	-0.43478	1.97572	0.92283
12	3.00000	-0.82609	1.62340	0.55052	4.00000	-1.10145	2.16453	0.73402
15	3.75000	-1.57609	1.78339	0.39053	5.00000	-2.10145	2.37785	0.52070
20	5.00000	-2.82609	1.95356	0.22035	6.66667	-3.76812	2.60475	0.29381

	1.50 times				1.67 times			
1	0.50000	3.84783	0.47020	3.87763	0.66667	5.13043	0.62693	5.17017
2	1.00000	3.34783	0.88955	3.45828	1.33333	4.46377	1.18606	4.61104
3	1.50000	2.84783	1.26354	3.08428	2.00000	3.79710	1.68473	4.11237
4	2.00000	2.34783	1.59710	2.75073	2.66667	3.13043	2.12946	3.66764
5	2.50000	1.84783	1.89458	2.45325	3.33333	2.46377	2.52610	3.27100
6	3.00000	1.34783	2.15988	2.18794	4.00000	1.79710	2.87985	2.91726
7	3.50000	0.84783	2.39650	1.95133	4.66667	1.13043	3.19533	2.60177
8	4.00000	0.34783	2.60753	1.74030	5.33333	0.46377	3.47670	2.32040
9	4.50000	-0.15217	2.79573	1.55209	6.00000	-0.20290	3.72765	2.06946
10	5.00000	-0.65217	2.96359	1.38424	6.66667	-0.86957	3.95145	1.84565
12	6.00000	-1.65217	3.24680	1.10103	8.00000	-2.20290	4.32906	1.46804
15	7.50000	-3.15217	3.56677	0.78105	10.00000	-4.20290	4.75570	1.04141
20	10.00000	-5.65217	3.90712	0.44071	13.33333	-7.53623	5.20949	0.58761

	1.75 times				2.00 times			
1	0.75000	5.77174	0.70530	5.81644	1.00000	7.69565	0.94040	7.75526
2	1.50000	5.02174	1.33432	5.18742	2.00000	6.69565	1.77909	6.91656
3	2.25000	4.27174	1.89532	4.62642	3.00000	5.69565	2.52709	6.16856
4	3.00000	3.52174	2.39564	4.12609	4.00000	4.69565	3.19419	5.50146
5	3.75000	2.77174	2.84186	3.67988	5.00000	3.69565	3.78915	4.90650
6	4.50000	2.02174	3.23983	3.28191	6.00000	2.69565	4.31977	4.37588
7	5.25000	1.27174	3.59475	2.92699	7.00000	1.69565	4.79300	3.90265
8	6.00000	0.52174	3.91129	2.61045	8.00000	0.69565	5.21506	3.48060
9	6.75000	-0.22826	4.19360	2.32814	9.00000	-0.30435	5.59147	3.10418
10	7.50000	-0.97826	4.44538	2.07636	10.00000	-1.30435	5.92717	2.76848
12	9.00000	-2.47826	4.87019	1.65155	12.00000	-3.30435	6.49359	2.20206
15	11.25000	-4.72826	5.35016	1.17158	15.00000	-6.30435	7.13354	1.56211
20	15.00000	-8.47826	5.86068	0.66106	20.00000	-11.30435	7.81424	0.88142

	2.25 times				2.50 times			
1	1.25000	9.61957	1.17550	9.69407	1.50000	11.54348	1.41060	11.63288
2	2.50000	8.36957	2.22387	8.64570	3.00000	10.04348	2.66864	10.37484
3	3.75000	7.11957	3.15886	7.71070	4.50000	8.54348	3.79063	9.25284
4	5.00000	5.86957	3.99274	6.87682	6.00000	7.04348	4.79129	8.25219
5	6.25000	4.61957	4.73644	6.13313	7.50000	5.54348	5.68373	7.35975
6	7.50000	3.36957	5.39971	5.46985	9.00000	4.04348	6.47965	6.56383
7	8.75000	2.11957	5.99125	4.87831	10.50000	2.54348	7.18950	5.85398
8	10.00000	0.86957	6.51882	4.35074	12.00000	1.04348	7.82258	5.22089
9	11.25000	-0.38043	6.98933	3.88023	13.50000	-0.45652	8.38720	4.65628
10	12.50000	-1.63043	7.40896	3.46060	15.00000	-1.95652	8.89076	4.15272
12	15.00000	-4.13043	8.11699	2.75258	18.00000	-4.95652	9.74039	3.30309
15	18.75000	-7.88043	8.91693	1.95264	22.50000	-9.45652	10.70032	2.34316
20	25.00000	-14.13043	9.76780	1.10177	30.00000	-16.95652	11.72135	1.32212

Entries are multiples of present annual rent. Negative entries indicate unprofitable programs.

Create Value by Buying in Below-Market Leases

Capitalization Rate 11.50%

Ratio of Target Rent to Old Rent

Years Left	2.75 times Non-Discounted Pay to Tenant	Value Added	Discounted Pay to Tenant	Value Added	3.00 times Non-Discounted Pay to Tenant	Value Added	Discounted Pay to Tenant	Value Added
1	1.75000	13.46739	1.64569	13.57170	2.00000	15.39130	1.88079	15.51051
2	3.50000	11.71739	3.11341	12.10398	4.00000	13.39130	3.55819	13.83312
3	5.25000	9.96739	4.42241	10.79498	6.00000	11.39130	5.05418	12.33712
4	7.00000	8.21739	5.58984	9.62755	8.00000	9.39130	6.38839	11.00292
5	8.75000	6.46739	6.63102	8.58638	10.00000	7.39130	7.57830	9.81300
6	10.50000	4.71739	7.55960	7.65780	12.00000	5.39130	8.63954	8.75177
7	12.25000	2.96739	8.38775	6.82964	14.00000	3.39130	9.58600	7.80530
8	14.00000	1.21739	9.12635	6.09104	16.00000	1.39130	10.43011	6.96119
9	15.75000	-0.53261	9.78507	5.43232	18.00000	-0.60870	11.18294	6.20837
10	17.50000	-2.28261	10.37255	4.84484	20.00000	-2.60870	11.85434	5.53696
12	21.00000	-5.78261	11.36378	3.85361	24.00000	-6.60870	12.98718	4.40412
15	26.25000	-11.03261	12.48370	2.73369	30.00000	-12.60870	14.26709	3.12422
20	35.00000	-19.78261	13.67491	1.54248	40.00000	-22.60870	15.62847	1.76283

Years Left	3.33 times Non-Discounted Pay to Tenant	Value Added	Discounted Pay to Tenant	Value Added	3.50 times Non-Discounted Pay to Tenant	Value Added	Discounted Pay to Tenant	Value Added
1	2.33333	17.95652	2.19426	18.09560	2.50000	19.23913	2.35099	19.38814
2	4.66667	15.62319	4.15122	16.13864	5.00000	16.73913	4.44774	17.29140
3	7.00000	13.28986	5.89654	14.39331	7.50000	14.23913	6.31772	15.42141
4	9.33333	10.95652	7.45312	12.83674	10.00000	11.73913	7.98548	13.75365
5	11.66667	8.62319	8.84135	11.44850	12.50000	9.23913	9.47288	12.26625
6	14.00000	6.28986	10.07946	10.21039	15.00000	6.73913	10.79942	10.93971
7	16.33333	3.95652	11.18367	9.10618	17.50000	4.23913	11.98250	9.75663
8	18.66667	1.62319	12.16846	8.12139	20.00000	1.73913	13.03764	8.70149
9	21.00000	-0.71014	13.04676	7.24310	22.50000	-0.76087	13.97867	7.76046
10	23.33333	-3.04348	13.83007	6.45979	25.00000	-3.26087	14.81793	6.92120
12	28.00000	-7.71014	15.15171	5.13814	30.00000	-8.26087	16.23398	5.50515
15	35.00000	-14.71014	16.64494	3.64492	37.50000	-15.76087	17.83386	3.90527
20	46.66667	-26.37681	18.23322	2.05664	50.00000	-28.26087	19.53559	2.20354

Years Left	4.00 times Non-Discounted Pay to Tenant	Value Added	Discounted Pay to Tenant	Value Added	4.50 times Non-Discounted Pay to Tenant	Value Added	Discounted Pay to Tenant	Value Added
1	3.00000	23.08696	2.82119	23.26577	3.50000	26.93478	3.29139	27.14339
2	6.00000	20.08696	5.33728	20.74967	7.00000	23.43478	6.22683	24.20795
3	9.00000	17.08696	7.58127	18.50569	10.50000	19.93478	8.84481	21.58997
4	12.00000	14.08696	9.58258	16.50438	14.00000	16.43478	11.17968	19.25511
5	15.00000	11.08696	11.36746	14.71950	17.50000	12.93478	13.26203	17.17275
6	18.00000	8.08696	12.95931	13.12765	21.00000	9.43478	15.11919	15.31559
7	21.00000	5.08696	14.37900	11.70795	24.50000	5.93478	16.77551	13.65928
8	24.00000	2.08696	15.64517	10.44179	28.00000	2.43478	18.25270	12.18209
9	27.00000	-0.91304	16.77440	9.31255	31.50000	-1.06522	19.57014	10.86465
10	30.00000	-3.91304	17.78152	8.30544	35.00000	-4.56522	20.74510	9.68968
12	36.00000	-9.91304	19.48077	6.60618	42.00000	-11.56522	22.72757	7.70721
15	45.00000	-18.91304	21.40063	4.68632	52.50000	-22.06522	24.96740	5.46738
20	60.00000	-33.91304	23.44271	2.64425	70.00000	-39.56522	27.34983	3.08495

Years Left	5.00 times Non-Discounted Pay to Tenant	Value Added	Discounted Pay to Tenant	Value Added	6.00 times Non-Discounted Pay to Tenant	Value Added	Discounted Pay to Tenant	Value Added
1	4.00000	30.78261	3.76159	31.02102	5.00000	38.47826	4.70199	38.77628
2	8.00000	26.78261	7.11638	27.66623	10.00000	33.47826	8.89547	34.58279
3	12.00000	22.78261	10.10836	24.67425	15.00000	28.47826	12.63545	30.84281
4	16.00000	18.78261	12.77677	22.00584	20.00000	23.47826	15.97097	27.50730
5	20.00000	14.78261	15.15661	19.62600	25.00000	18.47826	18.94576	24.53250
6	24.00000	10.78261	17.27907	17.50353	30.00000	13.47826	21.59884	21.87942
7	28.00000	6.78261	19.17201	15.61060	35.00000	8.47826	23.96501	19.51325
8	32.00000	2.78261	20.86023	13.92238	40.00000	3.47826	26.07528	17.40298
9	36.00000	-1.21739	22.36587	12.41674	45.00000	-1.52174	27.95734	15.52092
10	40.00000	-5.21739	23.70869	11.07392	50.00000	-6.52174	29.63586	13.84240
12	48.00000	-13.21739	25.97437	8.80824	60.00000	-16.52174	32.46796	11.01030
15	60.00000	-25.21739	28.53418	6.24843	75.00000	-31.52174	35.66772	7.81054
20	80.00000	-45.21739	31.25695	3.52566	100.00000	-56.52174	39.07118	4.40708

Entries are multiples of present annual rent. Negative entries indicate unprofitable programs.

Spreading Average Prices or Rents to Typical Unit Values

Distribution of Types		20% Premium A over B — Spread High to Low						25% Premium A over B — Spread High to Low					
		5%	10%	15%	20%	25%	30%	5%	10%	15%	20%	25%	30%
10% Type A	Low	114.7	111.8	108.8	105.9	102.9	100.0	118.9	115.9	112.8	109.8	106.7	103.7
	Mid	117.6	117.6	117.6	117.6	117.6	117.6	122.0	122.0	122.0	122.0	122.0	122.0
	High	120.6	123.5	126.5	129.4	132.4	135.3	125.0	128.0	131.1	134.1	137.2	140.2
90% Type B	Low	95.6	93.1	90.7	88.2	85.8	83.3	95.1	92.7	90.2	87.8	85.4	82.9
	Mid	98.0	98.0	98.0	98.0	98.0	98.0	97.6	97.6	97.6	97.6	97.6	97.6
	High	100.5	102.9	105.4	107.8	110.3	112.7	100.0	102.4	104.9	107.3	109.8	112.2
20% Type A	Low	112.5	109.6	106.7	103.8	101.0	98.1	116.1	113.1	110.1	107.1	104.2	101.2
	Mid	115.4	115.4	115.4	115.4	115.4	115.4	119.0	119.0	119.0	119.0	119.0	119.0
	High	118.3	121.2	124.0	126.9	129.8	132.7	122.0	125.0	128.0	131.0	133.9	136.9
80% Type B	Low	93.8	91.3	88.9	86.5	84.1	81.7	92.9	90.5	88.1	85.7	83.3	81.0
	Mid	96.2	96.2	96.2	96.2	96.2	96.2	95.2	95.2	95.2	95.2	95.2	95.2
	High	98.6	101.0	103.4	105.8	108.2	110.6	97.6	100.0	102.4	104.8	107.1	109.5
25% Type A	Low	111.4	108.6	105.7	102.9	100.0	97.1	114.7	111.8	108.8	105.9	102.9	100.0
	Mid	114.3	114.3	114.3	114.3	114.3	114.3	117.6	117.6	117.6	117.6	117.6	117.6
	High	117.1	120.0	122.9	125.7	128.6	131.4	120.6	123.5	126.5	129.4	132.4	135.3
75% Type B	Low	92.9	90.5	88.1	85.7	83.3	81.0	91.8	89.4	87.1	84.7	82.4	80.0
	Mid	95.2	95.2	95.2	95.2	95.2	95.2	94.1	94.1	94.1	94.1	94.1	94.1
	High	97.6	100.0	102.4	104.8	107.1	109.5	96.5	98.8	101.2	103.5	105.9	108.2
30% Type A	Low	110.4	107.5	104.7	101.9	99.1	96.2	113.4	110.5	107.6	104.7	101.7	98.8
	Mid	113.2	113.2	113.2	113.2	113.2	113.2	116.3	116.3	116.3	116.3	116.3	116.3
	High	116.0	118.9	121.7	124.5	127.4	130.2	119.2	122.1	125.0	127.9	130.8	133.7
70% Type B	Low	92.0	89.6	87.3	84.9	82.5	80.2	90.7	88.4	86.0	83.7	81.4	79.1
	Mid	94.3	94.3	94.3	94.3	94.3	94.3	93.0	93.0	93.0	93.0	93.0	93.0
	High	96.7	99.1	101.4	103.8	106.1	108.5	95.3	97.7	100.0	102.3	104.7	107.0
33% Type A	Low	109.7	106.6	104.1	101.3	98.4	95.6	112.5	109.6	106.7	103.8	101.0	98.1
	Mid	112.5	112.5	112.5	112.5	112.5	112.5	115.4	115.4	115.4	115.4	115.4	115.4
	High	115.3	118.1	120.9	123.8	126.6	129.4	118.3	121.2	124.0	126.9	129.8	132.7
67% Type B	Low	91.4	89.1	86.7	84.4	82.0	79.7	90.0	87.7	85.4	83.1	80.8	78.5
	Mid	93.8	93.8	93.8	93.8	93.8	93.8	92.3	92.3	92.3	92.3	92.3	92.3
	High	96.1	98.4	100.8	103.1	105.5	107.8	94.6	96.9	99.2	101.5	103.8	106.2
40% Type A	Low	108.3	105.6	102.8	100.0	97.2	94.4	110.8	108.0	105.1	102.3	99.4	96.6
	Mid	111.1	111.1	111.1	111.1	111.1	111.1	113.6	113.6	113.6	113.6	113.6	113.6
	High	113.9	116.7	119.4	122.2	125.0	127.8	116.5	119.3	122.2	125.0	127.8	130.7
60% Type B	Low	90.3	88.0	85.6	83.3	81.0	78.7	88.6	86.4	84.1	81.8	79.5	77.3
	Mid	92.6	92.6	92.6	92.6	92.6	92.6	90.9	90.9	90.9	90.9	90.9	90.9
	High	94.9	97.2	99.5	101.9	104.2	106.5	93.2	95.5	97.7	100.0	102.3	104.5
50% Type A	Low	106.4	103.6	100.9	98.2	95.5	92.7	108.3	105.6	102.8	100.0	97.2	94.4
	Mid	109.1	109.1	109.1	109.1	109.1	109.1	111.1	111.1	111.1	111.1	111.1	111.1
	High	111.8	114.5	117.3	120.0	122.7	125.5	113.9	116.7	119.4	122.2	125.0	127.8
50% Type B	Low	88.6	86.4	84.1	81.8	79.5	77.3	86.7	84.4	82.2	80.0	77.8	75.6
	Mid	90.9	90.9	90.9	90.9	90.9	90.9	88.9	88.9	88.9	88.9	88.9	88.9
	High	93.2	95.5	97.7	100.0	102.3	104.5	91.1	93.3	95.6	97.8	100.0	102.2
60% Type A	Low	104.5	101.8	99.1	96.4	93.8	91.1	106.0	103.3	100.5	97.8	95.1	92.4
	Mid	107.1	107.1	107.1	107.1	107.1	107.1	108.7	108.7	108.7	108.7	108.7	108.7
	High	109.8	112.5	115.2	117.9	120.5	123.2	111.4	114.1	116.8	119.6	122.3	125.0
40% Type B	Low	87.1	84.8	82.6	80.4	78.1	75.9	84.8	82.6	80.4	78.3	76.1	73.9
	Mid	89.3	89.3	89.3	89.3	89.3	89.3	87.0	87.0	87.0	87.0	87.0	87.0
	High	91.5	93.8	96.0	98.2	100.4	102.7	89.1	91.3	93.5	95.7	97.8	100.0
67% Type A	Low	103.2	100.6	97.9	95.3	92.6	90.0	104.5	101.8	99.1	96.4	93.7	91.1
	Mid	105.9	105.9	105.9	105.9	105.9	105.9	107.1	107.1	107.1	107.1	107.1	107.1
	High	108.5	111.2	113.8	116.5	119.1	121.8	109.8	112.5	115.2	117.9	120.5	123.2
33% Type B	Low	86.0	83.8	81.6	79.4	77.2	75.0	83.6	81.4	79.3	77.1	75.0	72.9
	Mid	88.2	88.2	88.2	88.2	88.2	88.2	85.7	85.7	85.7	85.7	85.7	85.7
	High	90.4	92.6	94.9	97.1	99.3	101.5	87.9	90.0	92.1	94.3	96.4	98.6
75% Type A	Low	101.7	99.1	96.5	93.9	91.3	88.7	102.6	100.0	97.4	94.7	92.1	89.5
	Mid	104.3	104.3	104.3	104.3	104.3	104.3	105.3	105.3	105.3	105.3	105.3	105.3
	High	107.0	109.6	112.2	114.8	117.4	120.0	107.9	110.5	113.2	115.8	118.4	121.1
25% Type B	Low	84.8	82.6	80.4	78.3	76.1	73.9	82.1	80.0	77.9	75.8	73.7	71.6
	Mid	87.0	87.0	87.0	87.0	87.0	87.0	84.2	84.2	84.2	84.2	84.2	84.2
	High	89.1	91.3	93.5	95.7	97.8	100.0	86.3	88.4	90.5	92.6	94.7	96.8

Rule: There must be as many units at the Low figure as at the High. There may be any number of units at the Mid figure or an equal amount above and below the Mid figure.

Spreading Average Prices or Rents to Typical Unit Values

Distribution of Types		30% Premium A over B — Spread High to Low						33% Premium A over B — Spread High to Low					
		5%	10%	15%	20%	25%	30%	5%	10%	15%	20%	25%	30%
10% Type A	Low	123.1	119.9	116.7	113.6	110.4	107.3	125.8	122.6	119.4	116.1	112.9	109.7
	Mid	126.2	126.2	126.2	126.2	126.2	126.2	129.0	129.0	129.0	129.0	129.0	129.0
	High	129.4	132.5	135.7	138.8	142.0	145.1	132.3	135.5	138.7	141.9	145.2	148.4
90% Type B	Low	94.7	92.2	89.8	87.4	85.0	82.5	94.4	91.9	89.5	87.1	84.7	82.3
	Mid	97.1	97.1	97.1	97.1	97.1	97.1	96.8	96.8	96.8	96.8	96.8	96.8
	High	99.5	101.9	104.4	106.8	109.2	111.7	99.2	101.6	104.0	106.5	108.9	111.3
20% Type A	Low	119.6	116.5	113.4	110.4	107.3	104.2	121.9	118.7	115.6	112.5	109.4	106.2
	Mid	122.6	122.6	122.6	122.6	122.6	122.6	125.0	125.0	125.0	125.0	125.0	125.0
	High	125.7	128.8	131.8	134.9	138.0	141.0	128.1	131.2	134.4	137.5	140.6	143.7
80% Type B	Low	92.0	89.6	87.3	84.9	82.5	80.2	91.4	89.1	86.7	84.4	82.0	79.7
	Mid	94.3	94.3	94.3	94.3	94.3	94.3	93.8	93.8	93.8	93.8	93.8	93.8
	High	96.7	99.1	101.4	103.8	106.1	108.5	96.1	98.4	100.8	103.1	105.5	107.8
25% Type A	Low	117.9	114.9	111.9	108.8	105.8	102.8	120.0	116.9	113.8	110.8	107.7	104.6
	Mid	120.9	120.9	120.9	120.9	120.9	120.9	123.1	123.1	123.1	123.1	123.1	123.1
	High	124.0	127.0	130.0	133.0	136.0	139.1	126.2	129.2	132.3	135.4	138.5	141.5
75% Type B	Low	90.7	88.4	86.0	83.7	81.4	79.1	90.0	87.7	85.4	83.1	80.8	78.5
	Mid	93.0	93.0	93.0	93.0	93.0	93.0	92.3	92.3	92.3	92.3	92.3	92.3
	High	95.3	97.7	100.0	102.3	104.7	107.0	94.6	96.9	99.2	101.5	103.8	106.2
30% Type A	Low	116.3	113.3	110.3	107.3	104.4	101.4	118.2	115.2	112.1	109.1	106.1	103.0
	Mid	119.3	119.3	119.3	119.3	119.3	119.3	121.2	121.2	121.2	121.2	121.2	121.2
	High	122.2	125.2	128.2	131.2	134.2	137.2	124.2	127.3	130.3	133.3	136.4	139.4
70% Type B	Low	89.4	87.2	84.9	82.6	80.3	78.0	88.6	86.4	84.1	81.8	79.5	77.3
	Mid	91.7	91.7	91.7	91.7	91.7	91.7	90.9	90.9	90.9	90.9	90.9	90.9
	High	94.0	96.3	98.6	100.9	103.2	105.5	93.2	95.5	97.7	100.0	102.3	104.5
33% Type A	Low	115.2	112.3	109.3	106.4	103.4	100.5	117.0	114.0	111.0	108.0	105.0	102.0
	Mid	118.2	118.2	118.2	118.2	118.2	118.2	120.0	120.0	120.0	120.0	120.0	120.0
	High	121.1	124.1	127.0	130.0	133.0	135.9	123.0	126.0	129.0	132.0	135.0	138.0
67% Type B	Low	88.6	86.4	84.1	81.8	79.5	77.3	87.8	85.5	83.3	81.0	78.8	76.5
	Mid	90.9	90.9	90.9	90.9	90.9	90.9	90.0	90.0	90.0	90.0	90.0	90.0
	High	93.2	95.5	97.7	100.0	102.3	104.5	92.3	94.5	96.8	99.0	101.3	103.5
40% Type A	Low	113.2	110.3	107.4	104.5	101.6	98.7	114.7	111.8	108.8	105.9	102.9	100.0
	Mid	116.1	116.1	116.1	116.1	116.1	116.1	117.6	117.6	117.6	117.6	117.6	117.6
	High	119.0	121.9	124.8	127.7	130.6	133.5	120.6	123.5	126.5	129.4	132.4	135.3
60% Type B	Low	87.1	84.8	82.6	80.4	78.1	75.9	86.0	83.8	81.6	79.4	77.2	75.0
	Mid	89.3	89.3	89.3	89.3	89.3	89.3	88.2	88.2	88.2	88.2	88.2	88.2
	High	91.5	93.7	96.0	98.2	100.4	102.7	90.4	92.6	94.9	97.1	99.3	101.5
50% Type A	Low	110.2	107.4	104.6	101.7	98.9	96.1	111.4	108.6	105.7	102.9	100.0	97.1
	Mid	113.0	113.0	113.0	113.0	113.0	113.0	114.3	114.3	114.3	114.3	114.3	114.3
	High	115.9	118.7	121.5	124.3	127.2	130.0	117.1	120.0	122.9	125.7	128.6	131.4
50% Type B	Low	84.8	82.6	80.4	78.3	76.1	73.9	83.6	81.4	79.3	77.1	75.0	72.9
	Mid	87.0	87.0	87.0	87.0	87.0	87.0	85.7	85.7	85.7	85.7	85.7	85.7
	High	89.1	91.3	93.5	95.7	97.8	100.0	87.9	90.0	92.1	94.3	96.4	98.6
60% Type A	Low	107.4	104.7	101.9	99.2	96.4	93.6	108.3	105.6	102.8	100.0	97.2	94.4
	Mid	110.2	110.2	110.2	110.2	110.2	110.2	111.1	111.1	111.1	111.1	111.1	111.1
	High	112.9	115.7	118.4	121.2	123.9	126.7	113.9	116.7	119.4	122.2	125.0	127.8
40% Type B	Low	82.6	80.5	78.4	76.3	74.2	72.0	81.3	79.2	77.1	75.0	72.9	70.8
	Mid	84.7	84.7	84.7	84.7	84.7	84.7	83.3	83.3	83.3	83.3	83.3	83.3
	High	86.9	89.0	91.1	93.2	95.3	97.5	85.4	87.5	89.6	91.7	93.8	95.8
67% Type A	Low	105.6	102.9	100.2	97.5	94.8	92.1	106.4	103.6	100.9	98.2	95.5	92.7
	Mid	108.3	108.3	108.3	108.3	108.3	108.3	109.1	109.1	109.1	109.1	109.1	109.1
	High	111.0	113.7	116.5	119.2	121.9	124.6	111.8	114.5	117.3	120.0	122.7	125.5
33% Type B	Low	81.2	79.2	77.1	75.0	72.9	70.8	79.8	77.7	75.7	73.6	71.6	69.5
	Mid	83.3	83.3	83.3	83.3	83.3	83.3	81.8	81.8	81.8	81.8	81.8	81.8
	High	85.4	87.5	89.6	91.7	93.7	95.8	83.9	85.9	88.0	90.0	92.0	94.1
75% Type A	Low	103.5	100.8	98.2	95.5	92.9	90.2	104.0	101.3	98.7	96.0	93.3	90.7
	Mid	106.1	106.1	106.1	106.1	106.1	106.1	106.7	106.7	106.7	106.7	106.7	106.7
	High	108.8	111.4	114.1	116.7	119.4	122.0	109.3	112.0	114.7	117.3	120.0	122.7
25% Type B	Low	79.6	77.6	75.5	73.5	71.4	69.4	78.0	76.0	74.0	72.0	70.0	68.0
	Mid	81.6	81.6	81.6	81.6	81.6	81.6	80.0	80.0	80.0	80.0	80.0	80.0
	High	83.7	85.7	87.8	89.8	91.8	93.9	82.0	84.0	86.0	88.0	90.0	92.0

Rule: There must be as many units at the Low figure as at the High. There may be any number of units at the Mid figure or an equal amount above and below the Mid figure.

Table 74, page 3

Spreading Average Prices or Rents to Typical Unit Values

Distribution of Types		40% Premium A over B Spread High to Low 5%	10%	15%	20%	25%	30%	50% Premium A over B Spread High to Low 5%	10%	15%	20%	25%	30%
10%	Low	131.3	127.9	124.5	121.2	117.8	114.4	139.3	135.7	132.1	128.6	125.0	121.4
Type A	Mid	134.6	134.6	134.6	134.6	134.6	134.6	142.9	142.9	142.9	142.9	142.9	142.9
	High	138.0	141.3	144.7	148.1	151.4	154.8	146.4	150.0	153.6	157.1	160.7	164.3
90%	Low	93.8	91.3	88.9	86.5	84.1	81.7	92.9	90.5	88.1	85.7	83.3	81.0
Type B	Mid	96.2	96.2	96.2	96.2	96.2	96.2	95.2	95.2	95.2	95.2	95.2	95.2
	High	98.6	101.0	103.4	105.8	108.2	110.6	97.6	100.0	102.4	104.8	107.1	109.5
20%	Low	126.4	123.1	119.9	116.7	113.4	110.2	133.0	129.5	126.1	122.7	119.3	115.9
Type A	Mid	129.6	129.6	129.6	129.6	129.6	129.6	136.4	136.4	136.4	136.4	136.4	136.4
	High	132.9	136.1	139.4	142.6	145.8	149.1	139.8	143.2	146.6	150.0	153.4	156.8
80%	Low	90.3	88.0	85.6	83.3	81.0	78.7	88.6	86.4	84.1	81.8	79.5	77.3
Type B	Mid	92.6	92.6	92.6	92.6	92.6	92.6	90.9	90.9	90.9	90.9	90.9	90.9
	High	94.9	97.2	99.5	101.9	104.2	106.5	93.2	95.5	97.7	100.0	102.3	104.5
25%	Low	124.1	120.9	117.7	114.5	111.4	108.2	130.0	126.7	123.3	120.0	116.7	113.3
Type A	Mid	127.3	127.3	127.3	127.3	127.3	127.3	133.3	133.3	133.3	133.3	133.3	133.3
	High	130.5	133.6	136.8	140.0	143.2	146.4	136.7	140.0	143.3	146.7	150.0	153.3
75%	Low	88.6	86.4	84.1	81.8	79.5	77.3	86.7	84.4	82.2	80.0	77.8	75.6
Type B	Mid	90.9	90.9	90.9	90.9	90.9	90.9	88.9	88.9	88.9	88.9	88.9	88.9
	High	93.2	95.5	97.7	100.0	102.3	104.5	91.1	93.3	95.6	97.8	100.0	102.2
30%	Low	121.9	118.8	115.6	112.5	109.4	106.3	127.2	123.9	120.7	117.4	114.1	110.9
Type A	Mid	125.0	125.0	125.0	125.0	125.0	125.0	130.4	130.4	130.4	130.4	130.4	130.4
	High	128.1	131.2	134.4	137.5	140.6	143.8	133.7	137.0	140.2	143.5	146.7	150.0
70%	Low	87.1	84.8	82.6	80.4	78.1	75.9	84.8	82.6	80.4	78.3	76.1	73.9
Type B	Mid	89.3	89.3	89.3	89.3	89.3	89.3	87.0	87.0	87.0	87.0	87.0	87.0
	High	91.5	93.8	96.0	98.2	100.4	102.7	89.1	91.3	93.5	95.7	97.8	100.0
33%	Low	120.4	117.4	114.3	111.2	108.1	105.0	125.4	122.1	118.9	115.7	112.5	109.3
Type A	Mid	123.5	123.5	123.5	123.5	123.5	123.5	128.6	128.6	128.6	128.6	128.6	128.6
	High	126.6	129.7	132.8	135.9	139.0	142.1	131.8	135.0	138.2	141.4	144.6	147.9
67%	Low	86.0	83.8	81.6	79.4	77.2	75.0	83.6	81.4	79.3	77.1	75.0	72.9
Type B	Mid	88.2	88.2	88.2	88.2	88.2	88.2	85.7	85.7	85.7	85.7	85.7	85.7
	High	90.4	92.6	94.9	97.1	99.3	101.5	87.9	90.0	92.1	94.3	96.4	98.6
40%	Low	117.7	114.7	111.6	108.6	105.6	102.6	121.9	118.8	115.6	112.5	109.4	106.3
Type A	Mid	120.7	120.7	120.7	120.7	120.7	120.7	125.0	125.0	125.0	125.0	125.0	125.0
	High	123.7	126.7	129.7	132.8	135.8	138.8	128.1	131.2	134.4	137.5	140.6	143.8
60%	Low	84.1	81.9	79.7	77.6	75.4	73.3	81.3	79.2	77.1	75.0	72.9	70.8
Type B	Mid	86.2	86.2	86.2	86.2	86.2	86.2	83.3	83.3	83.3	83.3	83.3	83.3
	High	88.4	90.5	92.7	94.8	97.0	99.1	85.4	87.5	89.6	91.7	93.8	95.8
50%	Low	113.8	110.8	107.9	105.0	102.1	99.2	117.0	114.0	111.0	108.0	105.0	102.0
Type A	Mid	116.7	116.7	116.7	116.7	116.7	116.7	120.0	120.0	120.0	120.0	120.0	120.0
	High	119.6	122.5	125.4	128.3	131.2	134.2	123.0	126.0	129.0	132.0	135.0	138.0
50%	Low	81.3	79.2	77.1	75.0	72.9	70.8	78.0	76.0	74.0	72.0	70.0	68.0
Type B	Mid	83.3	83.3	83.3	83.3	83.3	83.3	80.0	80.0	80.0	80.0	80.0	80.0
	High	85.4	87.5	89.6	91.7	93.8	95.8	82.0	84.0	86.0	88.0	90.0	92.0
60%	Low	110.1	107.3	104.4	101.6	98.8	96.0	112.5	109.6	106.7	103.8	101.0	98.1
Type A	Mid	112.9	112.9	112.9	112.9	112.9	112.9	115.4	115.4	115.4	115.4	115.4	115.4
	High	115.7	118.5	121.4	124.2	127.0	129.8	118.3	121.2	124.0	126.9	129.8	132.7
40%	Low	78.6	76.6	74.6	72.6	70.6	68.5	75.0	73.1	71.2	69.2	67.3	65.4
Type B	Mid	80.6	80.6	80.6	80.6	80.6	80.6	76.9	76.9	76.9	76.9	76.9	76.9
	High	82.7	84.7	86.7	88.7	90.7	92.7	78.8	80.8	82.7	84.6	86.5	88.5
67%	Low	107.8	105.0	102.2	99.5	96.7	93.9	109.7	106.9	104.1	101.2	98.4	95.6
Type A	Mid	110.5	110.5	110.5	110.5	110.5	110.5	112.5	112.5	112.5	112.5	112.5	112.5
	High	113.3	116.1	118.8	121.6	124.3	127.1	115.3	118.1	120.9	123.7	126.6	129.4
33%	Low	77.0	75.0	73.0	71.1	69.1	67.1	73.1	71.2	69.4	67.5	65.6	63.7
Type B	Mid	78.9	78.9	78.9	78.9	78.9	78.9	75.0	75.0	75.0	75.0	75.0	75.0
	High	80.9	82.9	84.9	86.8	88.8	90.8	76.9	78.7	80.6	82.5	84.4	86.2
75%	Low	105.0	102.3	99.6	96.9	94.2	91.5	106.4	103.6	100.9	98.2	95.5	92.7
Type A	Mid	107.7	107.7	107.7	107.7	107.7	107.7	109.1	109.1	109.1	109.1	109.1	109.1
	High	110.4	113.1	115.8	118.5	121.2	123.8	111.8	114.5	117.3	120.0	122.7	125.5
25%	Low	75.0	73.1	71.2	69.2	67.3	65.4	70.9	69.1	67.3	65.5	63.6	61.8
Type B	Mid	76.9	76.9	76.9	76.9	76.9	76.9	72.7	72.7	72.7	72.7	72.7	72.7
	High	78.8	80.8	82.7	84.6	86.5	88.5	74.5	76.4	78.2	80.0	81.8	83.6

Rule: There must be as many units at the Low figure as at the High. There may be any number of units at the Mid figure or an equal amount above and below the Mid figure.

Spreading Average Prices or Rents to Typical Unit Values

Distribution of Types		60% Premium A over B Spread High to Low						67% Premium A over B Spread High to Low					
		5%	10%	15%	20%	25%	30%	5%	10%	15%	20%	25%	30%
10%	Low	147.2	143.4	139.6	135.8	132.1	128.3	152.3	148.4	144.5	140.6	136.7	132.8
Type A	Mid	150.9	150.9	150.9	150.9	150.9	150.9	156.2	156.2	156.2	156.2	156.2	156.2
	High	154.7	158.5	162.3	166.0	169.8	173.6	160.2	164.1	168.0	171.9	175.8	179.7
90%	Low	92.0	89.6	87.3	84.9	82.5	80.2	91.4	89.1	86.7	84.4	82.0	79.7
Type B	Mid	94.3	94.3	94.3	94.3	94.3	94.3	93.8	93.8	93.8	93.8	93.8	93.8
	High	96.7	99.1	101.4	103.8	106.1	108.5	96.1	98.4	100.8	103.1	105.5	107.8
20%	Low	139.3	135.7	132.1	128.6	125.0	121.4	143.4	139.7	136.0	132.4	128.7	125.0
Type A	Mid	142.9	142.9	142.9	142.9	142.9	142.9	147.1	147.1	147.1	147.1	147.1	147.1
	High	146.4	150.0	153.6	157.1	160.7	164.3	150.7	154.4	158.1	161.8	165.4	169.1
80%	Low	87.1	84.8	82.6	80.4	78.1	75.9	86.0	83.8	81.6	79.4	77.2	75.0
Type B	Mid	89.3	89.3	89.3	89.3	89.3	89.3	88.2	88.2	88.2	88.2	88.2	88.2
	High	91.5	93.8	96.0	98.2	100.4	102.7	90.4	92.6	94.9	97.1	99.3	101.5
25%	Low	135.7	132.2	128.7	125.2	121.7	118.3	139.3	135.7	132.1	128.6	125.0	121.4
Type A	Mid	139.1	139.1	139.1	139.1	139.1	139.1	142.9	142.9	142.9	142.9	142.9	142.9
	High	142.6	146.1	149.6	153.0	156.5	160.0	146.4	150.0	153.6	157.1	160.7	164.3
75%	Low	84.8	82.6	80.4	78.3	76.1	73.9	83.6	81.4	79.3	77.1	75.0	72.9
Type B	Mid	87.0	87.0	87.0	87.0	87.0	87.0	85.7	85.7	85.7	85.7	85.7	85.7
	High	89.1	91.3	93.5	95.7	97.8	100.0	87.9	90.0	92.1	94.3	96.4	98.6
30%	Low	132.2	128.8	125.4	122.0	118.6	115.3	135.4	131.9	128.5	125.0	121.5	118.1
Type A	Mid	135.6	135.6	135.6	135.6	135.6	135.6	138.9	138.9	138.9	138.9	138.9	138.9
	High	139.0	142.4	145.8	149.2	152.5	155.9	142.4	145.8	149.3	152.8	156.2	159.7
70%	Low	82.6	80.5	78.4	76.3	74.2	72.0	81.3	79.2	77.1	75.0	72.9	70.8
Type B	Mid	84.7	84.7	84.7	84.7	84.7	84.7	83.3	83.3	83.3	83.3	83.3	83.3
	High	86.9	89.0	91.1	93.2	95.3	97.5	85.4	87.5	89.6	91.7	93.8	95.8
33%	Low	130.0	126.7	123.3	120.0	116.7	113.3	133.0	129.5	126.1	122.7	119.3	115.9
Type A	Mid	133.3	133.3	133.3	133.3	133.3	133.3	136.4	136.4	136.4	136.4	136.4	136.4
	High	136.7	140.0	143.3	146.7	150.0	153.3	139.8	143.2	146.6	150.0	153.4	156.8
67%	Low	81.3	79.2	77.1	75.0	72.9	70.8	79.8	77.7	75.7	73.6	71.6	69.5
Type B	Mid	83.3	83.3	83.3	83.3	83.3	83.3	81.8	81.8	81.8	81.8	81.8	81.8
	High	85.4	87.5	89.6	91.7	93.8	95.8	83.9	85.9	88.0	90.0	92.0	94.1
40%	Low	125.8	122.6	119.4	116.1	112.9	109.7	128.3	125.0	121.7	118.4	115.1	111.8
Type A	Mid	129.0	129.0	129.0	129.0	129.0	129.0	131.6	131.6	131.6	131.6	131.6	131.6
	High	132.3	135.5	138.7	141.9	145.2	148.4	134.9	138.2	141.4	144.7	148.0	151.3
60%	Low	78.6	76.6	74.6	72.6	70.6	68.5	77.0	75.0	73.0	71.1	69.1	67.1
Type B	Mid	80.6	80.6	80.6	80.6	80.6	80.6	78.9	78.9	78.9	78.9	78.9	78.9
	High	82.7	84.7	86.7	88.7	90.7	92.7	80.9	82.9	84.9	86.8	88.8	90.8
50%	Low	120.0	116.9	113.8	110.8	107.7	104.6	121.9	118.7	115.6	112.5	109.4	106.2
Type A	Mid	123.1	123.1	123.1	123.1	123.1	123.1	125.0	125.0	125.0	125.0	125.0	125.0
	High	126.2	129.2	132.3	135.4	138.5	141.5	128.1	131.2	134.4	137.5	140.6	143.7
50%	Low	75.0	73.1	71.2	69.2	67.3	65.4	73.1	71.3	69.4	67.5	65.6	63.8
Type B	Mid	76.9	76.9	76.9	76.9	76.9	76.9	75.0	75.0	75.0	75.0	75.0	75.0
	High	78.8	80.8	82.7	84.6	86.5	88.5	76.9	78.8	80.6	82.5	84.4	86.3
60%	Low	114.7	111.8	108.8	105.9	102.9	100.0	116.1	113.1	110.1	107.1	104.2	101.2
Type A	Mid	117.6	117.6	117.6	117.6	117.6	117.6	119.0	119.0	119.0	119.0	119.0	119.0
	High	120.6	123.5	126.5	129.4	132.4	135.3	122.0	125.0	128.0	131.0	133.9	136.9
40%	Low	71.7	69.9	68.0	66.2	64.3	62.5	69.6	67.9	66.1	64.3	62.5	60.7
Type B	Mid	73.5	73.5	73.5	73.5	73.5	73.5	71.4	71.4	71.4	71.4	71.4	71.4
	High	75.4	77.2	79.0	80.9	82.7	84.6	73.2	75.0	76.8	78.6	80.4	82.1
67%	Low	111.4	108.6	105.7	102.9	100.0	97.1	112.5	109.6	106.7	103.8	101.0	98.1
Type A	Mid	114.3	114.3	114.3	114.3	114.3	114.3	115.4	115.4	115.4	115.4	115.4	115.4
	High	117.1	120.0	122.9	125.7	128.6	131.4	118.3	121.2	124.0	126.9	129.8	132.7
33%	Low	69.6	67.9	66.1	64.3	62.5	60.7	67.5	65.8	64.0	62.3	60.6	58.8
Type B	Mid	71.4	71.4	71.4	71.4	71.4	71.4	69.2	69.2	69.2	69.2	69.2	69.2
	High	73.2	75.0	76.8	78.6	80.4	82.1	71.0	72.7	74.4	76.2	77.9	79.6
75%	Low	107.6	104.8	102.1	99.3	96.6	93.8	108.3	105.6	102.8	100.0	97.2	94.4
Type A	Mid	110.3	110.3	110.3	110.3	110.3	110.3	111.1	111.1	111.1	111.1	111.1	111.1
	High	113.1	115.9	118.6	121.4	124.1	126.9	113.9	116.7	119.4	122.2	125.0	127.8
25%	Low	67.2	65.5	63.8	62.1	60.3	58.6	65.0	63.3	61.7	60.0	58.3	56.7
Type B	Mid	69.0	69.0	69.0	69.0	69.0	69.0	66.7	66.7	66.7	66.7	66.7	66.7
	High	70.7	72.4	74.1	75.9	77.6	79.3	68.3	70.0	71.7	73.3	75.0	76.7

Rule: There must be as many units at the Low figure as at the High. There may be any number of units at the Mid figure or an equal amount above and below the Mid figure.

Spreading Average Prices or Rents to Typical Unit Values

Distribution of Types		75% Premium A over B — Spread High to Low						80% Premium A over B — Spread High to Low					
		5%	10%	15%	20%	25%	30%	5%	10%	15%	20%	25%	30%
10% Type A	Low	158.7	154.7	150.6	146.5	142.4	138.4	162.5	158.3	154.2	150.0	145.8	141.7
	Mid	162.8	162.8	162.8	162.8	162.8	162.8	166.7	166.7	166.7	166.7	166.7	166.7
	High	166.9	170.9	175.0	179.1	183.1	187.2	170.8	175.0	179.2	183.3	187.5	191.7
90% Type B	Low	90.7	88.4	86.0	83.7	81.4	79.1	90.3	88.0	85.6	83.3	81.0	78.7
	Mid	93.0	93.0	93.0	93.0	93.0	93.0	92.6	92.6	92.6	92.6	92.6	92.6
	High	95.3	97.7	100.0	102.3	104.7	107.0	94.9	97.2	99.5	101.9	104.2	106.5
20% Type A	Low	148.4	144.6	140.8	137.0	133.2	129.3	151.3	147.4	143.5	139.7	135.8	131.9
	Mid	152.2	152.2	152.2	152.2	152.2	152.2	155.2	155.2	155.2	155.2	155.2	155.2
	High	156.0	159.8	163.6	167.4	171.2	175.0	159.1	162.9	166.8	170.7	174.6	178.4
80% Type B	Low	84.8	82.6	80.4	78.3	76.1	73.9	84.1	81.9	79.7	77.6	75.4	73.3
	Mid	87.0	87.0	87.0	87.0	87.0	87.0	86.2	86.2	86.2	86.2	86.2	86.2
	High	89.1	91.3	93.5	95.7	97.8	100.0	88.4	90.5	92.7	94.8	97.0	99.1
25% Type A	Low	143.7	140.0	136.3	132.6	128.9	125.3	146.3	142.5	138.8	135.0	131.3	127.5
	Mid	147.4	147.4	147.4	147.4	147.4	147.4	150.0	150.0	150.0	150.0	150.0	150.0
	High	151.1	154.7	158.4	162.1	165.8	169.5	153.8	157.5	161.3	165.0	168.8	172.5
75% Type B	Low	82.1	80.0	77.9	75.8	73.7	71.6	81.3	79.2	77.1	75.0	72.9	70.8
	Mid	84.2	84.2	84.2	84.2	84.2	84.2	83.3	83.3	83.3	83.3	83.3	83.3
	High	86.3	88.4	90.5	92.6	94.7	96.8	85.4	87.5	89.6	91.7	93.8	95.8
30% Type A	Low	139.4	135.7	132.1	128.6	125.0	121.4	141.5	137.9	134.3	130.6	127.0	123.4
	Mid	142.9	142.9	142.9	142.9	142.9	142.9	145.2	145.2	145.2	145.2	145.2	145.2
	High	146.4	150.0	153.6	157.1	160.7	164.3	148.8	152.4	156.0	159.7	163.3	166.9
70% Type B	Low	79.6	77.6	75.5	73.5	71.4	69.4	78.6	76.6	74.6	72.6	70.6	68.5
	Mid	81.6	81.6	81.6	81.6	81.6	81.6	80.6	80.6	80.6	80.6	80.6	80.6
	High	83.7	85.7	87.8	89.8	91.8	93.9	82.7	84.7	86.7	88.7	90.7	92.7
33% Type A	Low	136.5	133.0	129.5	126.0	122.5	119.0	138.6	135.0	131.4	127.9	124.3	120.8
	Mid	140.0	140.0	140.0	140.0	140.0	140.0	142.1	142.1	142.1	142.1	142.1	142.1
	High	143.5	147.0	150.5	154.0	157.5	161.0	145.7	149.2	152.8	156.3	159.9	163.4
67% Type B	Low	78.0	76.0	74.0	72.0	70.0	68.0	77.0	75.0	73.0	71.1	69.1	67.1
	Mid	80.0	80.0	80.0	80.0	80.0	80.0	78.9	78.9	78.9	78.9	78.9	78.9
	High	82.0	84.0	86.0	88.0	90.0	92.0	80.9	82.9	84.9	86.8	88.8	90.8
40% Type A	Low	131.3	127.9	124.5	121.2	117.8	114.4	133.0	129.5	126.1	122.7	119.3	115.9
	Mid	134.6	134.6	134.6	134.6	134.6	134.6	136.4	136.4	136.4	136.4	136.4	136.4
	High	138.0	141.3	144.7	148.1	151.4	154.8	139.8	143.2	146.6	150.0	153.4	156.8
60% Type B	Low	75.0	73.1	71.2	69.2	67.3	65.4	73.9	72.0	70.1	68.2	66.3	64.4
	Mid	76.9	76.9	76.9	76.9	76.9	76.9	75.8	75.8	75.8	75.8	75.8	75.8
	High	78.8	80.8	82.7	84.6	86.5	88.5	77.7	79.5	81.4	83.3	85.2	87.1
50% Type A	Low	124.1	120.9	117.7	114.5	111.4	108.2	125.4	122.1	118.9	115.7	112.5	109.3
	Mid	127.3	127.3	127.3	127.3	127.3	127.3	128.6	128.6	128.6	128.6	128.6	128.6
	High	130.5	133.6	136.8	140.0	143.2	146.4	131.8	135.0	138.2	141.4	144.6	147.9
50% Type B	Low	70.9	69.1	67.3	65.5	63.6	61.8	69.6	67.9	66.1	64.3	62.5	60.7
	Mid	72.7	72.7	72.7	72.7	72.7	72.7	71.4	71.4	71.4	71.4	71.4	71.4
	High	74.5	76.4	78.2	80.0	81.8	83.6	73.2	75.0	76.8	78.6	80.4	82.1
60% Type A	Low	117.7	114.7	111.6	108.6	105.6	102.6	118.6	115.5	112.5	109.5	106.4	103.4
	Mid	120.7	120.7	120.7	120.7	120.7	120.7	121.6	121.6	121.6	121.6	121.6	121.6
	High	123.7	126.7	129.7	132.8	135.8	138.8	124.7	127.7	130.7	133.8	136.8	139.9
40% Type B	Low	67.2	65.5	63.8	62.1	60.3	58.6	65.9	64.2	62.5	60.8	59.1	57.4
	Mid	69.0	69.0	69.0	69.0	69.0	69.0	67.6	67.6	67.6	67.6	67.6	67.6
	High	70.7	72.4	74.1	75.9	77.6	79.3	69.3	70.9	72.6	74.3	76.0	77.7
67% Type A	Low	113.7	110.8	107.9	105.0	102.1	99.2	114.5	111.5	108.6	105.7	102.7	99.8
	Mid	116.7	116.7	116.7	116.7	116.7	116.7	117.4	117.4	117.4	117.4	117.4	117.4
	High	119.6	122.5	125.4	128.3	131.2	134.2	120.3	123.3	126.2	129.1	132.1	135.0
33% Type B	Low	65.0	63.3	61.7	60.0	58.3	56.7	63.6	62.0	60.3	58.7	57.1	55.4
	Mid	66.7	66.7	66.7	66.7	66.7	66.7	65.2	65.2	65.2	65.2	65.2	65.2
	High	68.3	70.0	71.7	73.3	75.0	76.7	66.8	68.5	70.1	71.7	73.4	75.0
75% Type A	Low	109.2	106.4	103.6	100.8	98.0	95.2	109.7	106.9	104.1	101.3	98.4	95.6
	Mid	112.0	112.0	112.0	112.0	112.0	112.0	112.5	112.5	112.5	112.5	112.5	112.5
	High	114.8	117.6	120.4	123.2	126.0	128.8	115.3	118.1	120.9	123.8	126.6	129.4
25% Type B	Low	62.4	60.8	59.2	57.6	56.0	54.4	60.9	59.4	57.8	56.3	54.7	53.1
	Mid	64.0	64.0	64.0	64.0	64.0	64.0	62.5	62.5	62.5	62.5	62.5	62.5
	High	65.6	67.2	68.8	70.4	72.0	73.6	64.1	65.6	67.2	68.8	70.3	71.9

Rule: There must be as many units at the Low figure as at the High. There may be any number of units at the Mid figure or an equal amount above and below the Mid figure.

Spreading Alteration & Other Costs in Income Projections

3.0% Inflation Rate

Year					Tenant Turnover during Year						
	10%	20%	25%	30%	33%	40%	50%	60%	67%	100%	
1	10.300	20.600	25.750	30.900	34.333	41.200	51.500	61.800	68.667	103.000	1
2	10.609	21.218	26.523	31.827	35.363	42.436	53.045	63.654	70.727	106.090	2
3	10.927	21.855	27.318	32.782	36.424	43.709	54.636	65.564	72.848	109.273	3
4	11.255	22.510	28.138	33.765	37.517	45.020	56.275	67.531	75.034	112.551	4
5	11.593	23.185	28.982	34.778	38.642	46.371	57.964	69.556	77.285	115.927	5
6	11.941	23.881	29.851	35.822	39.802	47.762	59.703	71.643	79.603	119.405	6
7	12.299	24.597	30.747	36.896	40.996	49.195	61.494	73.792	81.992	122.987	7
8	12.668	25.335	31.669	38.003	42.226	50.671	63.339	76.006	84.451	126.677	8
9	13.048	26.095	32.619	39.143	43.492	52.191	65.239	78.286	86.985	130.477	9
10	13.439	26.878	33.598	40.317	44.797	53.757	67.196	80.635	89.594	134.392	10
11	13.842	27.685	34.606	41.527	46.141	55.369	69.212	83.054	92.282	138.423	11
12	14.258	28.515	35.644	42.773	47.525	57.030	71.288	85.546	95.051	142.576	12
13	14.685	29.371	36.713	44.056	48.951	58.741	73.427	88.112	97.902	146.853	13
14	15.126	30.252	37.815	45.378	50.420	60.504	75.629	90.755	100.839	151.259	14
15	15.580	31.159	38.949	46.739	51.932	62.319	77.898	93.478	103.864	155.797	15

3.5% Inflation Rate

Year					Tenant Turnover during Year						
	10%	20%	25%	30%	33%	40%	50%	60%	67%	100%	
1	10.350	20.700	25.875	31.050	34.500	41.400	51.750	62.100	69.000	103.500	1
2	10.712	21.425	26.781	32.137	35.707	42.849	53.561	64.274	71.415	107.123	2
3	11.087	22.174	27.718	33.262	36.957	44.349	55.436	66.523	73.915	110.872	3
4	11.475	22.950	28.688	34.426	38.251	45.901	57.376	68.851	76.502	114.752	4
5	11.877	23.754	29.692	35.631	39.590	47.507	59.384	71.261	79.179	118.769	5
6	12.293	24.585	30.731	36.878	40.975	49.170	61.463	73.755	81.950	122.926	6
7	12.723	25.446	31.807	38.168	42.409	50.891	63.614	76.337	84.819	127.228	7
8	13.168	26.336	32.920	39.504	43.894	52.672	65.840	79.009	87.787	131.681	8
9	13.629	27.258	34.072	40.887	45.430	54.516	68.145	81.774	90.860	136.290	9
10	14.106	28.212	35.265	42.318	47.020	56.424	70.530	84.636	94.040	141.060	10
11	14.600	29.199	36.499	43.799	48.666	58.399	72.998	87.598	97.331	145.997	11
12	15.111	30.221	37.777	45.332	50.369	60.443	75.553	90.664	100.738	151.107	12
13	15.640	31.279	39.099	46.919	52.132	62.558	78.198	93.837	104.264	156.396	13
14	16.187	32.374	40.467	48.561	53.956	64.748	80.935	97.122	107.913	161.869	14
15	16.753	33.507	41.884	50.260	55.845	67.014	83.767	100.521	111.690	167.535	15

4.0% Inflation Rate

Year					Tenant Turnover during Year						
	10%	20%	25%	30%	33%	40%	50%	60%	67%	100%	
1	10.400	20.800	26.000	31.200	34.667	41.600	52.000	62.400	69.333	104.000	1
2	10.816	21.632	27.040	32.448	36.053	43.264	54.080	64.896	72.107	108.160	2
3	11.249	22.497	28.122	33.746	37.495	44.995	56.243	67.492	74.991	112.486	3
4	11.699	23.397	29.246	35.096	38.995	46.794	58.493	70.192	77.991	116.986	4
5	12.167	24.333	30.416	36.500	40.555	48.666	60.833	72.999	81.110	121.665	5
6	12.653	25.306	31.633	37.960	42.177	50.613	63.266	75.919	84.355	126.532	6
7	13.159	26.319	32.898	39.478	43.864	52.637	65.797	78.956	87.729	131.593	7
8	13.686	27.371	34.214	41.057	45.619	54.743	68.428	82.114	91.238	136.857	8
9	14.233	28.466	35.583	42.699	47.444	56.932	71.166	85.399	94.887	142.331	9
10	14.802	29.605	37.006	44.407	49.341	59.210	74.012	88.815	98.683	148.024	10
11	15.395	30.789	38.486	46.184	51.315	61.578	76.973	92.367	102.630	153.945	11
12	16.010	32.021	40.026	48.031	53.368	64.041	80.052	96.062	106.735	160.103	12
13	16.651	33.301	41.627	49.952	55.502	66.603	83.254	99.904	111.005	166.507	13
14	17.317	34.634	43.292	51.950	57.723	69.267	86.584	103.901	115.445	173.168	14
15	18.009	36.019	45.024	54.028	60.031	72.038	90.047	108.057	120.063	180.094	15

4.5% Inflation Rate

Year					Tenant Turnover during Year						
	10%	20%	25%	30%	33%	40%	50%	60%	67%	100%	
1	10.450	20.900	26.125	31.350	34.833	41.800	52.250	62.700	69.667	104.500	1
2	10.920	21.841	27.301	32.761	36.401	43.681	54.601	65.522	72.802	109.203	2
3	11.412	22.823	28.529	34.235	38.039	45.647	57.058	68.470	76.078	114.117	3
4	11.925	23.850	29.813	35.776	39.751	47.701	59.626	71.551	79.501	119.252	4
5	12.462	24.924	31.155	37.385	41.539	49.847	62.309	74.771	83.079	124.618	5
6	13.023	26.045	32.557	39.068	43.409	52.090	65.113	78.136	86.817	130.226	6
7	13.609	27.217	34.022	40.826	45.362	54.434	68.043	81.652	90.724	136.086	7
8	14.221	28.442	35.553	42.663	47.403	56.884	71.105	85.326	94.807	142.210	8
9	14.861	29.722	37.152	44.583	49.537	59.444	74.305	89.166	99.073	148.610	9
10	15.530	31.059	38.824	46.589	51.766	62.119	77.648	93.178	103.531	155.297	10
11	16.229	32.457	40.571	48.686	54.095	64.914	81.143	97.371	108.190	162.285	11
12	16.959	33.918	42.397	50.876	56.529	67.835	84.794	101.753	113.059	169.588	12
13	17.722	35.444	44.305	53.166	59.073	70.888	88.610	106.332	118.146	177.220	13
14	18.519	37.039	46.299	55.558	61.731	74.078	92.597	111.117	123.463	185.194	14
15	19.353	38.706	48.382	58.058	64.509	77.411	96.764	116.117	129.019	193.528	15

Entry is a percentage of today's cost for 100% of the space.

Spreading Alteration & Other Costs in Income Projections

5.0% Inflation Rate

Year	10%	20%	25%	30%	33%	40%	50%	60%	67%	100%	
				Tenant Turnover during Year							
1	10.500	21.000	26.250	31.500	35.000	42.000	52.500	63.000	70.000	105.000	1
2	11.025	22.050	27.562	33.075	36.750	44.100	55.125	66.150	73.500	110.250	2
3	11.576	23.152	28.941	34.729	38.587	46.305	57.881	69.457	77.175	115.762	3
4	12.155	24.310	30.388	36.465	40.517	48.620	60.775	72.930	81.034	121.551	4
5	12.763	25.526	31.907	38.288	42.543	51.051	63.814	76.577	85.085	127.628	5
6	13.401	26.802	33.502	40.203	44.670	53.604	67.005	80.406	89.340	134.010	6
7	14.071	28.142	35.178	42.213	46.903	56.284	70.355	84.426	93.807	140.710	7
8	14.775	29.549	36.936	44.324	49.249	59.098	73.873	88.647	98.497	147.746	8
9	15.513	31.027	38.783	46.540	51.711	62.053	77.566	93.080	103.422	155.133	9
10	16.289	32.578	40.722	48.867	54.296	65.156	81.445	97.734	108.593	162.889	10
11	17.103	34.207	42.758	51.310	57.011	68.414	85.517	102.620	114.023	171.034	11
12	17.959	35.917	44.896	53.876	59.862	71.834	89.793	107.751	119.724	179.586	12
13	18.856	37.713	47.141	56.569	62.855	75.426	94.282	113.139	125.710	188.565	13
14	19.799	39.599	49.498	59.398	65.998	79.197	98.997	118.796	131.995	197.993	14
15	20.789	41.579	51.973	62.368	69.298	83.157	103.946	124.736	138.595	207.893	15

5.5% Inflation Rate

Year	10%	20%	25%	30%	33%	40%	50%	60%	67%	100%	
				Tenant Turnover during Year							
1	10.550	21.100	26.375	31.650	35.167	42.200	52.750	63.300	70.333	105.500	1
2	11.130	22.260	27.826	33.391	37.101	44.521	55.651	66.782	74.202	111.302	2
3	11.742	23.485	29.356	35.227	39.141	46.970	58.712	70.454	78.283	117.424	3
4	12.388	24.776	30.971	37.165	41.294	49.553	61.941	74.329	82.588	123.882	4
5	13.070	26.139	32.674	39.209	43.565	52.278	65.348	78.418	87.131	130.696	5
6	13.788	27.577	34.471	41.365	45.961	55.154	68.942	82.731	91.923	137.884	6
7	14.547	29.094	36.367	43.640	48.489	58.187	72.734	87.281	96.979	145.468	7
8	15.347	30.694	38.367	46.041	51.156	61.387	76.734	92.081	102.312	153.469	8
9	16.191	32.382	40.477	48.573	53.970	64.764	80.955	97.146	107.940	161.909	9
10	17.081	34.163	42.704	51.244	56.938	68.326	85.407	102.489	113.876	170.814	10
11	18.021	36.042	45.052	54.063	60.070	72.084	90.105	108.126	120.139	180.209	11
12	19.012	38.024	47.530	57.036	63.374	76.048	95.060	114.072	126.747	190.121	12
13	20.058	40.115	50.144	60.173	66.859	80.231	100.289	120.346	133.718	200.577	13
14	21.161	42.322	52.902	63.483	70.536	84.644	105.805	126.965	141.073	211.609	14
15	22.325	44.650	55.812	66.974	74.416	89.299	111.624	133.949	148.832	223.248	15

6.0% Inflation Rate

Year	10%	20%	25%	30%	33%	40%	50%	60%	67%	100%	
				Tenant Turnover during Year							
1	10.600	21.200	26.500	31.800	35.333	42.400	53.000	63.600	70.667	106.000	1
2	11.236	22.472	28.090	33.708	37.453	44.944	56.180	67.416	74.907	112.360	2
3	11.910	23.820	29.775	35.730	39.701	47.641	59.551	71.461	79.401	119.102	3
4	12.625	25.250	31.562	37.874	42.083	50.499	63.124	75.749	84.165	126.248	4
5	13.382	26.765	33.456	40.147	44.608	53.529	66.911	80.294	89.215	133.823	5
6	14.185	28.370	35.463	42.556	47.284	56.741	70.926	85.111	94.568	141.852	6
7	15.036	30.073	37.591	45.109	50.121	60.145	75.182	90.218	100.242	150.363	7
8	15.938	31.877	39.846	47.815	53.128	63.754	79.692	95.631	106.257	159.385	8
9	16.895	33.790	42.237	50.684	56.316	67.579	84.474	101.369	112.632	168.948	9
10	17.908	35.817	44.771	53.725	59.695	71.634	89.542	107.451	119.390	179.085	10
11	18.983	37.966	47.457	56.949	63.277	75.932	94.915	113.898	126.553	189.830	11
12	20.122	40.244	50.305	60.366	67.073	80.488	100.610	120.732	134.146	201.220	12
13	21.329	42.659	53.323	63.988	71.098	85.317	106.646	127.976	142.195	213.293	13
14	22.609	45.218	56.523	67.827	75.363	90.436	113.045	135.654	150.727	226.090	14
15	23.966	47.931	59.914	71.897	79.885	95.862	119.828	143.793	159.771	239.656	15

6.5% Inflation Rate

Year	10%	20%	25%	30%	33%	40%	50%	60%	67%	100%	
				Tenant Turnover during Year							
1	10.650	21.300	26.625	31.950	35.500	42.600	53.250	63.900	71.000	106.500	1
2	11.342	22.685	28.356	34.027	37.807	45.369	56.711	68.054	75.615	113.423	2
3	12.079	24.159	30.199	36.238	40.265	48.318	60.397	72.477	80.530	120.795	3
4	12.865	25.729	32.162	38.594	42.882	51.459	64.323	77.188	85.764	128.647	4
5	13.701	27.402	34.252	41.103	45.670	54.803	68.504	82.205	91.339	137.009	5
6	14.591	29.183	36.479	43.774	48.638	58.366	72.957	87.549	97.276	145.914	6
7	15.540	31.080	38.850	46.620	51.800	62.159	77.699	93.239	103.599	155.399	7
8	16.550	33.100	41.375	49.650	55.167	66.200	82.750	99.300	110.333	165.500	8
9	17.626	35.251	44.064	52.877	58.752	70.503	88.129	105.754	117.505	176.257	9
10	18.771	37.543	46.928	56.314	62.571	75.085	93.857	112.628	125.142	187.714	10
11	19.992	39.983	49.979	59.975	66.638	79.966	99.958	119.949	133.277	199.915	11
12	21.291	42.582	53.227	63.873	70.970	85.164	106.455	127.746	141.940	212.910	12
13	22.675	45.350	56.687	68.025	75.583	90.699	113.374	136.049	151.166	226.749	13
14	24.149	48.297	60.372	72.446	80.496	96.595	120.744	144.892	160.992	241.487	14
15	25.718	51.437	64.296	77.155	85.728	102.874	128.592	154.310	171.456	257.184	15

Entry is a percentage of today's cost for 100% of the space.

Spreading Alteration & Other Costs in Income Projections

7.0% Inflation Rate

Year				Tenant Turnover during Year							
	10%	20%	25%	30%	33%	40%	50%	60%	67%	100%	
1	10.700	21.400	26.750	32.100	35.667	42.800	53.500	64.200	71.333	107.000	1
2	11.449	22.898	28.623	34.347	38.163	45.796	57.245	68.694	76.327	114.490	2
3	12.250	24.501	30.626	36.751	40.835	49.002	61.252	73.503	81.670	122.504	3
4	13.108	26.216	32.770	39.324	43.693	52.432	65.540	78.648	87.386	131.080	4
5	14.026	28.051	35.064	42.077	46.752	56.102	70.128	84.153	93.503	140.255	5
6	15.007	30.015	37.518	45.022	50.024	60.029	75.037	90.044	100.049	150.073	6
7	16.058	32.116	40.145	48.173	53.526	64.231	80.289	96.347	107.052	160.578	7
8	17.182	34.364	42.955	51.546	57.273	68.727	85.909	103.091	114.546	171.819	8
9	18.385	36.769	45.961	55.154	61.282	73.538	91.923	110.308	122.564	183.846	9
10	19.672	39.343	49.179	59.015	65.572	78.686	98.358	118.029	131.143	196.715	10
11	21.049	42.097	52.621	63.146	70.162	84.194	105.243	126.291	140.323	210.485	11
12	22.522	45.044	56.305	67.566	75.073	90.088	112.610	135.131	150.146	225.219	12
13	24.098	48.197	60.246	72.295	80.328	96.394	120.492	144.591	160.656	240.985	13
14	25.785	51.571	64.463	77.356	85.951	103.141	128.927	154.712	171.902	257.853	14
15	27.590	55.181	68.976	82.771	91.968	110.361	137.952	165.542	183.935	275.903	15

7.5% Inflation Rate

Year				Tenant Turnover during Year							
	10%	20%	25%	30%	33%	40%	50%	60%	67%	100%	
1	10.750	21.500	26.875	32.250	35.833	43.000	53.750	64.500	71.667	107.500	1
2	11.556	23.113	28.891	34.669	38.521	46.225	57.781	69.338	77.042	115.563	2
3	12.423	24.846	31.057	37.269	41.410	49.692	62.115	74.538	82.820	124.230	3
4	13.355	26.709	33.387	40.064	44.516	53.419	66.773	80.128	89.031	133.547	4
5	14.356	28.713	35.891	43.069	47.854	57.425	71.781	86.138	95.709	143.563	5
6	15.433	30.866	38.583	46.299	51.443	61.732	77.165	92.598	102.887	154.330	6
7	16.590	33.181	41.476	49.771	55.302	66.362	82.952	99.543	110.603	165.905	7
8	17.835	35.670	44.587	53.504	59.449	71.339	89.174	107.009	118.899	178.348	8
9	19.172	38.345	47.931	57.517	63.908	76.690	95.862	115.034	127.816	191.724	9
10	20.610	41.221	51.526	61.831	68.701	82.441	103.052	123.662	137.402	206.103	10
11	22.156	44.312	55.390	66.468	73.854	88.624	110.780	132.937	147.707	221.561	11
12	23.818	47.636	59.544	71.453	79.393	95.271	119.089	142.907	158.785	238.178	12
13	25.604	51.208	64.010	76.812	85.347	102.417	128.021	153.625	170.694	256.041	13
14	27.524	55.049	68.811	82.573	91.748	110.098	137.622	165.147	183.496	275.244	14
15	29.589	59.178	73.972	88.766	98.629	118.355	147.944	177.533	197.258	295.888	15

8.0% Inflation Rate

Year				Tenant Turnover during Year							
	10%	20%	25%	30%	33%	40%	50%	60%	67%	100%	
1	10.800	21.600	27.000	32.400	36.000	43.200	54.000	64.800	72.000	108.000	1
2	11.664	23.328	29.160	34.992	38.880	46.656	58.320	69.984	77.760	116.640	2
3	12.597	25.194	31.493	37.791	41.990	50.388	62.986	75.583	83.981	125.971	3
4	13.605	27.210	34.012	40.815	45.350	54.420	68.024	81.629	90.699	136.049	4
5	14.693	29.387	36.733	44.080	48.978	58.773	73.466	88.160	97.955	146.933	5
6	15.869	31.737	39.672	47.606	52.896	63.475	79.344	95.212	105.792	158.687	6
7	17.138	34.276	42.846	51.415	57.127	68.553	85.691	102.829	114.255	171.382	7
8	18.509	37.019	46.273	55.528	61.698	74.037	92.547	111.056	123.395	185.093	8
9	19.990	39.980	49.975	59.970	66.633	79.960	99.950	119.940	133.267	199.900	9
10	21.589	43.178	53.973	64.768	71.964	86.357	107.946	129.535	143.928	215.892	10
11	23.316	46.633	58.291	69.949	77.721	93.266	116.582	139.898	155.443	233.164	11
12	25.182	50.363	62.954	75.545	83.939	100.727	125.909	151.090	167.878	251.817	12
13	27.196	54.392	67.991	81.589	90.654	108.785	135.981	163.177	181.308	271.962	13
14	29.372	58.744	73.430	88.116	97.906	117.488	146.860	176.232	195.813	293.719	14
15	31.722	63.443	79.304	95.165	105.739	126.887	158.608	190.330	211.478	317.217	15

8.5% Inflation Rate

Year				Tenant Turnover during Year							
	10%	20%	25%	30%	33%	40%	50%	60%	67%	100%	
1	10.850	21.700	27.125	32.550	36.167	43.400	54.250	65.100	72.333	108.500	1
2	11.772	23.545	29.431	35.317	39.241	47.089	58.861	70.634	78.482	117.723	2
3	12.773	25.546	31.932	38.319	42.576	51.092	63.864	76.637	85.153	127.729	3
4	13.859	27.717	34.646	41.576	46.195	55.434	69.293	83.152	92.391	138.586	4
5	15.037	30.073	37.591	45.110	50.122	60.146	75.183	90.219	100.244	150.366	5
6	16.315	32.629	40.787	48.944	54.382	65.259	81.573	97.888	108.765	163.147	6
7	17.701	35.403	44.254	53.104	59.005	70.806	88.507	106.209	118.009	177.014	7
8	19.206	38.412	48.015	57.618	64.020	76.824	96.030	115.236	128.040	192.060	8
9	20.839	41.677	52.096	62.516	69.462	83.354	104.193	125.031	138.924	208.386	9
10	22.610	45.220	56.525	67.830	75.366	90.439	113.049	135.659	150.732	226.098	10
11	24.532	49.063	61.329	73.595	81.772	98.127	122.658	147.190	163.544	245.317	11
12	26.617	53.234	66.542	79.851	88.723	106.467	133.084	159.701	177.446	266.169	12
13	28.879	57.759	72.198	86.638	96.264	115.517	144.396	173.276	192.529	288.793	13
14	31.334	62.668	78.335	94.002	104.447	125.336	156.670	188.004	208.894	313.340	14
15	33.997	67.995	84.994	101.992	113.325	135.990	169.987	203.985	226.650	339.974	15

Entry is a percentage of today's cost for 100% of the space.

True Rent When Free Rent & Other Concessions Are Given

36 Month Lease Term　　　　　　　　Interest Rate 8.00%

Months No Other Free Concessions	plus Other Concession Package (in Months' Rent) 1	2	3	4	5	6	8	10	12
0	100.000	96.887	93.774	90.661	87.548	84.436	81.323	75.097	68.871	62.645
1	96.887	94.399	91.266	88.132	84.998	81.865	78.731	72.464	66.197	59.929
2	93.795	91.916	88.782	85.649	82.515	79.381	76.248	69.981	63.713	57.446
3	90.723	89.416	86.282	83.149	80.015	76.881	73.748	67.481	61.213	54.946
4	87.672	86.899	83.766	80.632	77.498	74.365	71.231	64.964	58.697	52.429
5	84.640	84.366	81.232	78.099	74.965	71.831	68.698	62.430	56.163	49.896
6	81.629	81.816	78.682	75.548	72.415	69.281	66.147	59.880	53.613	47.346
8	75.667	76.664	73.530	70.397	67.263	64.129	60.996	54.728	48.461	42.194
10	69.783	71.443	68.310	65.176	62.042	58.909	55.775	49.508	43.241	36.973
12	63.976	66.153	63.019	59.885	56.752	53.618	50.485	44.217	37.950	31.683
15	55.410	58.084	54.950	51.817	48.683	45.549	42.416	36.149	29.881	23.614
18	47.014	49.853	46.719	43.586	40.452	37.318	34.185	27.917	21.650	15.383
24	30.714	32.890	29.756	26.623	23.489	20.355	17.222	10.955	4.687	---

48 Month Lease Term

0	100.000	97.575	95.150	92.725	90.300	87.874	85.449	80.599	75.749	70.899
1	97.575	95.784	93.343	90.901	88.460	86.019	83.578	78.695	73.812	68.930
2	95.166	93.998	91.556	89.115	86.674	84.232	81.791	76.909	72.026	67.143
3	92.773	92.199	89.758	87.317	84.875	82.434	79.993	75.110	70.228	65.345
4	90.395	90.389	87.948	85.506	83.065	80.624	78.182	73.300	68.417	63.535
5	88.034	88.566	86.125	83.684	81.243	78.801	76.360	71.477	66.595	61.712
6	85.688	86.732	84.291	81.849	79.408	76.967	74.525	69.643	64.760	59.878
8	81.043	83.026	80.585	78.143	75.702	73.261	70.820	65.937	61.054	56.172
10	76.459	79.270	76.829	74.388	71.947	69.505	67.064	62.181	57.299	52.416
12	71.935	75.465	73.023	70.582	68.141	65.700	63.258	58.376	53.493	48.611
15	65.262	69.660	67.219	64.778	62.337	59.895	57.454	52.571	47.689	42.806
18	58.720	63.739	61.298	58.857	56.415	53.974	51.533	46.650	41.768	36.885
24	46.022	51.537	49.096	46.654	44.213	41.772	39.331	34.448	29.565	24.683

60 Month Lease Term

0	100.000	97.986	95.972	93.957	91.943	89.929	87.915	83.886	79.858	75.829
1	97.986	96.611	94.584	92.556	90.528	88.501	86.473	82.418	78.363	74.307
2	95.985	95.241	93.214	91.186	89.158	87.131	85.103	81.048	76.993	72.937
3	93.997	93.862	91.835	89.807	87.779	85.752	83.724	79.669	75.613	71.558
4	92.023	92.474	90.446	88.419	86.391	84.363	82.336	78.280	74.225	70.170
5	90.061	91.076	89.049	87.021	84.993	82.966	80.938	76.883	72.827	68.772
6	88.113	89.669	87.642	85.614	83.586	81.559	79.531	75.476	71.420	67.365
8	84.255	86.827	84.799	82.772	80.744	78.717	76.689	72.634	68.578	64.523
10	80.448	83.947	81.919	79.892	77.864	75.836	73.809	69.754	65.698	61.643
12	76.691	81.028	79.001	76.973	74.945	72.918	70.890	66.835	62.780	58.724
15	71.148	76.577	74.549	72.522	70.494	68.466	66.439	62.384	58.328	54.273
18	65.715	72.036	70.008	67.981	65.953	63.925	61.898	57.843	53.787	49.732
24	55.168	62.678	60.650	58.623	56.595	54.567	52.540	48.485	44.429	40.374

72 Month Lease Term

0	100.000	98.258	96.517	94.775	93.033	91.291	89.550	86.066	82.583	79.099
1	98.258	97.160	95.407	93.653	91.900	90.147	88.393	84.887	81.380	77.873
2	96.528	96.066	94.313	92.559	90.806	89.053	87.299	83.793	80.286	76.780
3	94.809	94.965	93.212	91.458	89.705	87.952	86.198	82.692	79.185	75.678
4	93.102	93.856	92.103	90.350	88.596	86.843	85.090	81.583	78.076	74.570
5	91.406	92.740	90.987	89.234	87.480	85.727	83.974	80.467	76.961	73.454
6	89.721	91.617	89.864	88.110	86.357	84.604	82.850	79.344	75.837	72.331
8	86.385	89.348	87.595	85.841	84.088	82.335	80.581	77.075	73.568	70.061
10	83.093	87.048	85.295	83.542	81.788	80.035	78.282	74.775	71.268	67.762
12	79.844	84.718	82.965	81.211	79.458	77.705	75.951	72.445	68.938	65.431
15	75.051	81.164	79.410	77.657	75.904	74.150	72.397	68.890	65.384	61.877
18	70.353	77.538	75.785	74.031	72.278	70.525	68.771	65.265	61.758	58.251
24	61.233	70.066	68.313	66.560	64.806	63.053	61.300	57.793	54.286	50.780

84 Month Lease Term

0	100.000	98.452	96.903	95.355	93.807	92.259	90.710	87.614	84.517	81.420
1	98.452	97.549	95.991	94.432	92.874	91.315	89.756	86.639	83.522	80.405
2	96.914	96.652	95.093	93.534	91.976	90.417	88.858	85.741	82.624	79.507
3	95.386	95.748	94.189	92.630	91.072	89.513	87.955	84.837	81.720	78.603
4	93.868	94.838	93.279	91.720	90.162	88.603	87.045	83.927	80.810	77.693
5	92.360	93.922	92.363	90.805	89.246	87.687	86.129	83.011	79.894	76.777
6	90.863	93.000	91.441	89.882	88.324	86.765	85.207	82.089	78.972	75.855
8	87.897	91.137	89.578	88.020	86.461	84.903	83.344	80.227	77.109	73.992
10	84.970	89.249	87.691	86.132	84.574	83.015	81.456	78.339	75.222	72.105
12	82.082	87.337	85.778	84.219	82.661	81.102	79.544	76.426	73.309	70.192
15	77.822	84.419	82.861	81.302	79.743	78.185	76.626	73.509	70.392	67.274
18	73.645	81.443	79.885	78.326	76.767	75.209	73.650	70.533	67.416	64.298
24	65.538	75.310	73.752	72.193	70.634	69.076	67.517	64.400	61.283	58.165

Entry is the ratio of present value of rent package to that of the full rent.

True Rent When Free Rent & Other Concessions Are Given

96 Month Lease Term   Interest Rate 8.00%

| Months No Other | | plus Other Concession Package (in Months' Rent) | | | | | | | | |
Free Concessions	1	2	3	4	5	6	8	10	12
0	100.000	98.596	97.191	95.787	94.383	92.978	91.574	88.766	85.957	83.148
1	98.596	97.839	96.426	95.012	93.598	92.185	90.771	87.944	85.116	82.289
2	97.201	97.087	95.674	94.260	92.846	91.433	90.019	87.192	84.364	81.537
3	95.815	96.330	94.917	93.503	92.089	90.676	89.262	86.435	83.607	80.780
4	94.438	95.568	94.155	92.741	91.327	89.914	88.500	85.673	82.845	80.018
5	93.071	94.801	93.388	91.974	90.560	89.147	87.733	84.906	82.078	79.251
6	91.712	94.029	92.615	91.202	89.788	88.374	86.961	84.133	81.306	78.479
8	89.023	92.469	91.055	89.642	88.228	86.814	85.401	82.573	79.746	76.919
10	86.368	90.888	89.475	88.061	86.647	85.234	83.820	80.993	78.165	75.338
12	83.749	89.286	87.873	86.459	85.045	83.632	82.218	79.391	76.563	73.736
15	79.884	86.843	85.429	84.016	82.602	81.188	79.775	76.947	74.120	71.293
18	76.096	84.351	82.937	81.523	80.110	78.696	77.282	74.455	71.628	68.800
24	68.743	79.214	77.801	76.387	74.973	73.560	72.146	69.319	66.491	63.664

120 Month Lease Term

	1	2	3	4	5	6	8	10	12
0	100.000	98.795	97.590	96.384	95.179	93.974	92.769	90.358	87.948	85.537
1	98.795	98.240	97.027	95.814	94.600	93.387	92.174	89.747	87.321	84.894
2	97.597	97.690	96.477	95.263	94.050	92.837	91.623	89.197	86.770	84.344
3	96.408	97.136	95.923	94.709	93.496	92.283	91.070	88.643	86.216	83.790
4	95.227	96.578	95.365	94.152	92.938	91.725	90.512	88.085	85.659	83.232
5	94.053	96.017	94.804	93.590	92.377	91.164	89.951	87.524	85.098	82.671
6	92.887	95.452	94.239	93.025	91.812	90.599	89.386	86.959	84.532	82.106
8	90.579	94.310	93.097	91.884	90.671	89.457	88.244	85.818	83.391	80.964
10	88.300	93.154	91.940	90.727	89.514	88.301	87.087	84.661	82.234	79.808
12	86.052	91.981	90.768	89.555	88.342	87.128	85.915	83.489	81.062	78.635
15	82.736	90.194	88.980	87.767	86.554	85.341	84.127	81.701	79.274	76.848
18	79.485	88.370	87.157	85.943	84.730	83.517	82.304	79.877	77.450	75.024
24	73.174	84.611	83.398	82.185	80.972	79.758	78.545	76.118	73.692	71.265

144 Month Lease Term

	1	2	3	4	5	6	8	10	12
0	100.000	98.925	97.849	96.774	95.699	94.624	93.548	91.398	89.247	87.097
1	98.925	98.502	97.419	96.337	95.254	94.172	93.089	90.925	88.760	86.595
2	97.857	98.083	97.001	95.918	94.836	93.753	92.671	90.506	88.341	86.176
3	96.795	97.662	96.579	95.497	94.414	93.332	92.250	90.085	87.920	85.755
4	95.741	97.238	96.155	95.073	93.990	92.908	91.825	89.661	87.496	85.331
5	94.694	96.811	95.728	94.646	93.563	92.481	91.398	89.234	87.069	84.904
6	93.654	96.381	95.298	94.216	93.134	92.051	90.969	88.804	86.639	84.474
8	91.594	95.513	94.430	93.348	92.265	91.183	90.100	87.935	85.771	83.606
10	89.562	94.633	93.550	92.468	91.385	90.303	89.220	87.056	84.891	82.726
12	87.556	93.741	92.659	91.576	90.494	89.411	88.329	86.164	83.999	81.834
15	84.597	92.381	91.299	90.216	89.134	88.051	86.969	84.804	82.639	80.474
18	81.697	90.994	89.911	88.829	87.746	86.664	85.582	83.417	81.252	79.087
24	76.066	88.135	87.052	85.970	84.888	83.805	82.723	80.558	78.393	76.228

180 Month Lease Term

	1	2	3	4	5	6	8	10	12
0	100.000	99.051	98.101	97.152	96.203	95.253	94.304	92.405	90.507	88.608
1	99.051	98.755	97.800	96.844	95.888	94.933	93.977	92.066	90.154	88.243
2	98.108	98.464	97.509	96.553	95.597	94.642	93.686	91.775	89.864	87.952
3	97.171	98.172	97.216	96.260	95.305	94.349	93.393	91.482	89.571	87.659
4	96.240	97.877	96.921	95.965	95.010	94.054	93.099	91.187	89.276	87.365
5	95.316	97.580	96.624	95.669	94.713	93.757	92.802	90.890	88.979	87.068
6	94.398	97.281	96.326	95.370	94.414	93.459	92.503	90.592	88.680	86.769
8	92.579	96.678	95.722	94.766	93.811	92.855	91.900	89.988	88.077	86.166
10	90.785	96.066	95.111	94.155	93.199	92.244	91.288	89.377	87.465	85.554
12	89.014	95.447	94.491	93.535	92.580	91.624	90.668	88.757	86.846	84.934
15	86.402	94.501	93.546	92.590	91.634	90.679	89.723	87.812	85.900	83.989
18	83.841	93.537	92.581	91.626	90.670	89.714	88.759	86.848	84.936	83.025
24	78.870	91.550	90.594	89.639	88.683	87.727	86.772	84.860	82.949	81.038

240 Month Lease Term

	1	2	3	4	5	6	8	10	12
0	100.000	99.169	98.338	97.507	96.676	95.845	95.015	93.353	91.691	90.029
1	99.169	98.994	98.157	97.321	96.484	95.648	94.812	93.139	91.466	89.793
2	98.344	98.823	97.986	97.150	96.314	95.477	94.641	92.968	91.295	89.622
3	97.524	98.651	97.814	96.978	96.142	95.305	94.469	92.796	91.123	89.450
4	96.709	98.478	97.641	96.805	95.968	95.132	94.295	92.623	90.950	89.277
5	95.900	98.303	97.467	96.630	95.794	94.958	94.121	92.448	90.775	89.102
6	95.096	98.128	97.291	96.455	95.618	94.782	93.946	92.273	90.600	88.927
8	93.505	97.773	96.937	96.100	95.264	94.427	93.591	91.918	90.245	88.572
10	91.934	97.414	96.578	95.741	94.905	94.068	93.232	91.559	89.886	88.213
12	90.384	97.050	96.213	95.377	94.541	93.704	92.868	91.195	89.522	87.849
15	88.098	96.495	95.658	94.822	93.985	93.149	92.312	90.640	88.967	87.294
18	85.857	95.928	95.092	94.255	93.419	92.582	91.746	90.073	88.400	86.727
24	81.506	94.761	93.924	93.088	92.251	91.415	90.579	88.906	87.233	85.560

Entry is the ratio of present value of rent package to that of the full rent.

True Rent When Free Rent & Other Concessions Are Given

36 Month Lease Term — Interest Rate 9.00%

Months No Other Free Concessions		plus Other Concession Package (in Months' Rent)								
		1	2	3	4	5	6	8	10	12
0	100.000	96.844	93.687	90.531	87.375	84.218	81.062	74.750	68.437	62.124
1	96.844	94.390	91.210	88.030	84.850	81.670	78.490	72.130	65.770	59.410
2	93.711	91.942	88.762	85.582	82.402	79.222	76.042	69.682	63.322	56.962
3	90.601	89.475	86.295	83.115	79.935	76.755	73.575	67.215	60.856	54.496
4	87.515	86.990	83.810	80.630	77.450	74.270	71.090	64.730	58.370	52.011
5	84.452	84.487	81.307	78.127	74.947	71.767	68.587	62.227	55.867	49.507
6	81.411	81.964	78.784	75.604	72.424	69.244	66.064	59.704	53.344	46.984
8	75.398	76.862	73.682	70.502	67.322	64.142	60.962	54.602	48.242	41.883
10	69.474	71.684	68.504	65.324	62.144	58.964	55.784	49.424	43.064	36.704
12	63.637	66.427	63.247	60.067	56.887	53.707	50.527	44.167	37.807	31.447
15	55.045	58.393	55.213	52.033	48.853	45.673	42.493	36.133	29.773	23.414
18	46.643	50.177	46.997	43.817	40.637	37.457	34.278	27.918	21.558	15.198
24	30.393	33.183	30.003	26.823	23.643	20.463	17.283	10.923	4.563	---

48 Month Lease Term

Months No Other Free Concessions		1	2	3	4	5	6	8	10	12
0	100.000	97.530	95.060	92.590	90.120	87.650	85.180	80.240	75.300	70.360
1	97.530	95.773	93.284	90.796	88.307	85.819	83.330	78.353	73.376	68.399
2	95.078	94.021	91.533	89.044	86.556	84.067	81.579	76.602	71.625	66.648
3	92.645	92.257	89.768	87.280	84.791	82.303	79.814	74.837	69.860	64.883
4	90.230	90.479	87.990	85.502	83.013	80.525	78.036	73.059	68.082	63.105
5	87.833	88.688	86.199	83.711	81.222	78.734	76.245	71.268	66.291	61.314
6	85.453	86.883	84.394	81.906	79.417	76.929	74.440	69.463	64.486	59.509
8	80.747	83.233	80.744	78.256	75.767	73.279	70.790	65.813	60.836	55.859
10	76.111	79.528	77.039	74.551	72.062	69.574	67.085	62.108	57.131	52.154
12	71.544	75.767	73.278	70.790	68.301	65.813	63.324	58.347	53.370	48.393
15	64.820	70.019	67.531	65.042	62.554	60.065	57.577	52.600	47.623	42.646
18	58.245	64.141	61.653	59.164	56.676	54.187	51.699	46.722	41.745	36.768
24	45.529	51.983	49.494	47.006	44.517	42.029	39.540	34.563	29.586	24.609

60 Month Lease Term

Months No Other Free Concessions		1	2	3	4	5	6	8	10	12
0	100.000	97.940	95.879	93.819	91.758	89.698	87.638	83.517	79.396	75.275
1	97.940	96.598	94.522	92.447	90.371	88.295	86.219	82.067	77.916	73.764
2	95.895	95.263	93.187	91.111	89.035	86.959	84.883	80.732	76.580	72.428
3	93.865	93.917	91.841	89.765	87.689	85.613	83.538	79.386	75.234	71.083
4	91.850	92.561	90.485	88.409	86.333	84.258	82.182	78.030	73.878	69.727
5	89.850	91.195	89.119	87.043	84.967	82.891	80.816	76.664	72.512	68.361
6	87.866	89.818	87.743	85.667	83.591	81.515	79.439	75.288	71.136	66.984
8	83.940	87.035	84.959	82.883	80.807	78.731	76.656	72.504	68.352	64.201
10	80.073	84.209	82.133	80.058	77.982	75.906	73.830	69.678	65.527	61.375
12	76.263	81.341	79.265	77.189	75.114	73.038	70.962	66.810	62.659	58.507
15	70.654	76.958	74.882	72.806	70.730	68.654	66.579	62.427	58.275	54.124
18	65.169	72.475	70.399	68.323	66.248	64.172	62.096	57.944	53.793	49.641
24	54.562	63.203	61.127	59.051	56.975	54.899	52.823	48.672	44.520	40.368

72 Month Lease Term

Months No Other Free Concessions		1	2	3	4	5	6	8	10	12
0	100.000	98.211	96.422	94.633	92.843	91.054	89.265	85.687	82.109	78.530
1	98.211	97.145	95.342	93.540	91.737	89.935	88.132	84.527	80.922	77.317
2	96.435	96.084	94.282	92.479	90.677	88.874	87.072	83.467	79.861	76.256
3	94.672	95.016	93.213	91.411	89.608	87.806	86.003	82.398	78.793	75.188
4	92.923	93.940	92.137	90.335	88.532	86.729	84.927	81.322	77.717	74.112
5	91.187	92.855	91.053	89.250	87.447	85.645	83.842	80.237	76.632	73.027
6	89.463	91.763	89.960	88.157	86.355	84.552	82.750	79.145	75.540	71.934
8	86.054	89.553	87.750	85.948	84.145	82.342	80.540	76.935	73.330	69.725
10	82.696	87.309	85.507	83.704	81.902	80.099	78.297	74.692	71.086	67.481
12	79.388	85.033	83.230	81.427	79.625	77.822	76.020	72.415	68.810	65.204
15	74.517	81.553	79.750	77.948	76.145	74.342	72.540	68.935	65.330	61.725
18	69.755	77.994	76.191	74.389	72.586	70.784	68.981	65.376	61.771	58.166
24	60.544	70.633	68.830	67.028	65.225	63.422	61.620	58.015	54.410	50.805

84 Month Lease Term

Months No Other Free Concessions		1	2	3	4	5	6	8	10	12
0	100.000	98.403	96.806	95.209	93.612	92.015	90.418	87.225	84.031	80.837
1	98.403	97.532	95.923	94.314	92.705	91.097	89.488	86.270	83.052	79.834
2	96.818	96.667	95.058	93.449	91.840	90.231	88.622	85.404	82.187	78.969
3	95.245	95.795	94.186	92.577	90.968	89.359	87.750	84.533	81.315	78.097
4	93.683	94.917	93.308	91.699	90.090	88.481	86.872	83.654	80.436	77.219
5	92.133	94.032	92.423	90.814	89.205	87.596	85.987	82.769	79.551	76.334
6	90.595	93.140	91.531	89.922	88.313	86.704	85.096	81.878	78.660	75.442
8	87.553	91.337	89.728	88.119	86.510	84.901	83.292	80.074	76.857	73.639
10	84.555	89.506	87.897	86.288	84.680	83.071	81.462	78.244	75.026	71.808
12	81.602	87.648	86.039	84.430	82.822	81.213	79.604	76.386	73.168	69.950
15	77.255	84.809	83.200	81.591	79.982	78.373	76.764	73.546	70.328	67.111
18	73.004	81.905	80.296	78.687	77.078	75.469	73.860	70.642	67.424	64.207
24	64.782	75.898	74.289	72.680	71.071	69.462	67.853	64.635	61.417	58.200

Entry is the ratio of present value of rent package to that of the full rent.

True Rent When Free Rent & Other Concessions Are Given

96 Month Lease Term   Interest Rate   9.00%

Months No Other	plus Other Concession Package (in Months' Rent)								
Free Concessions	1	2	3	4	5	6	8	10	12
0	100.000	98.546	97.092	95.638	94.184	92.729	91.275	88.367	85.459	82.551
1	98.546	97.820	96.355	94.890	93.425	91.960	90.495	87.565	84.635	81.705
2	97.103	97.100	95.635	94.170	92.705	91.239	89.774	86.844	83.914	80.984
3	95.670	96.374	94.909	93.444	91.979	90.514	89.049	86.119	83.189	80.259
4	94.248	95.643	94.178	92.713	91.248	89.782	88.317	85.387	82.457	79.527
5	92.837	94.906	93.441	91.976	90.511	89.046	87.581	84.651	81.721	78.791
6	91.436	94.164	92.699	91.234	89.769	88.304	86.839	83.908	80.978	78.048
8	88.666	92.662	91.197	89.732	88.267	86.802	85.337	82.407	79.477	76.547
10	85.936	91.139	89.674	88.209	86.744	85.278	83.813	80.883	77.953	75.023
12	83.248	89.592	88.127	86.662	85.197	83.732	82.267	79.337	76.407	73.477
15	79.289	87.228	85.763	84.298	82.833	81.368	79.903	76.973	74.043	71.113
18	75.418	84.810	83.345	81.880	80.415	78.950	77.485	74.555	71.625	68.695
24	67.932	79.810	78.345	76.880	75.415	73.950	72.485	69.555	66.625	63.694

120 Month Lease Term

Months No Other	plus Other Concession Package (in Months' Rent)								
Free Concessions	1	2	3	4	5	6	8	10	12
0	100.000	98.743	97.485	96.228	94.971	93.713	92.456	89.941	87.427	84.912
1	98.743	98.216	96.950	95.683	94.416	93.149	91.883	89.349	86.816	84.282
2	97.495	97.696	96.429	95.162	93.896	92.629	91.362	88.829	86.295	83.762
3	96.256	97.171	95.905	94.638	93.371	92.104	90.838	88.304	85.770	83.237
4	95.027	96.643	95.376	94.109	92.843	91.576	90.309	87.776	85.242	82.709
5	93.806	96.110	94.844	93.577	92.310	91.043	89.777	87.243	84.710	82.176
6	92.595	95.574	94.307	93.040	91.774	90.507	89.240	86.707	84.173	81.640
8	90.200	94.489	93.222	91.956	90.689	89.422	88.155	85.622	83.088	80.555
10	87.840	93.388	92.121	90.854	89.587	88.321	87.054	84.520	81.987	79.453
12	85.515	92.270	91.003	89.736	88.470	87.203	85.936	83.403	80.869	78.336
15	82.092	90.561	89.295	88.028	86.761	85.494	84.228	81.694	79.161	76.627
18	78.745	88.814	87.547	86.281	85.014	83.747	82.480	79.947	77.413	74.880
24	72.272	85.200	83.933	82.667	81.400	80.133	78.866	76.333	73.799	71.266

144 Month Lease Term

Months No Other	plus Other Concession Package (in Months' Rent)								
Free Concessions	1	2	3	4	5	6	8	10	12
0	100.000	98.870	97.741	96.611	95.482	94.352	93.223	90.964	88.704	86.445
1	98.870	98.474	97.336	96.198	95.060	93.922	92.784	90.508	88.232	85.956
2	97.749	98.083	96.945	95.807	94.669	93.531	92.393	90.117	87.841	85.565
3	96.636	97.689	96.551	95.413	94.275	93.137	91.999	89.723	87.447	85.171
4	95.532	97.292	96.154	95.016	93.878	92.740	91.602	89.326	87.050	84.774
5	94.436	96.892	95.754	94.616	93.478	92.340	91.202	88.926	86.650	84.374
6	93.348	96.490	95.352	94.214	93.076	91.938	90.800	88.523	86.247	83.971
8	91.195	95.675	94.537	93.399	92.261	91.123	89.985	87.709	85.433	83.157
10	89.075	94.848	93.710	92.572	91.434	90.296	89.158	86.882	84.606	82.330
12	86.987	94.009	92.871	91.733	90.595	89.457	88.318	86.042	83.766	81.490
15	83.912	92.726	91.588	90.450	89.312	88.174	87.036	84.760	82.484	80.207
18	80.905	91.414	90.276	89.138	88.000	86.862	85.724	83.448	81.172	78.895
24	75.089	88.700	87.562	86.424	85.286	84.148	83.010	80.734	78.458	76.182

180 Month Lease Term

Months No Other	plus Other Concession Package (in Months' Rent)								
Free Concessions	1	2	3	4	5	6	8	10	12
0	100.000	98.993	97.987	96.980	95.973	94.966	93.960	91.946	89.933	87.919
1	98.993	98.721	97.707	96.693	95.679	94.664	93.650	91.622	89.593	87.565
2	97.994	98.455	97.441	96.427	95.412	94.398	93.384	91.355	89.327	87.298
3	97.002	98.187	97.173	96.158	95.144	94.130	93.116	91.087	89.059	87.030
4	96.018	97.917	96.902	95.888	94.874	93.860	92.845	90.817	88.788	86.760
5	95.041	97.644	96.630	95.616	94.602	93.587	92.573	90.545	88.516	86.487
6	94.071	97.370	96.356	95.342	94.327	93.313	92.299	90.270	88.242	86.213
8	92.153	96.815	95.801	94.787	93.772	92.758	91.744	89.715	87.687	85.658
10	90.263	96.252	95.238	94.224	93.209	92.195	91.181	89.152	87.124	85.095
12	88.402	95.680	94.666	93.652	92.638	91.623	90.609	88.581	86.552	84.523
15	85.661	94.807	93.792	92.778	91.764	90.750	89.735	87.707	85.678	83.650
18	82.981	93.913	92.899	91.885	90.870	89.856	88.842	86.813	84.785	82.756
24	77.799	92.065	91.051	90.036	89.022	88.008	86.994	84.965	82.937	80.908

240 Month Lease Term

Months No Other	plus Other Concession Package (in Months' Rent)								
Free Concessions	1	2	3	4	5	6	8	10	12
0	100.000	99.107	98.214	97.321	96.428	95.535	94.642	92.856	91.070	89.284
1	99.107	98.951	98.051	97.151	96.251	95.352	94.452	92.652	90.853	89.054
2	98.221	98.800	97.900	97.000	96.101	95.201	94.301	92.502	90.702	88.903
3	97.341	98.648	97.748	96.848	95.949	95.049	94.149	92.350	90.550	88.751
4	96.468	98.495	97.595	96.695	95.795	94.896	93.996	92.197	90.397	88.598
5	95.601	98.340	97.441	96.541	95.641	94.741	93.842	92.042	90.243	88.443
6	94.741	98.185	97.285	96.385	95.486	94.586	93.686	91.887	90.087	88.288
8	93.039	97.871	96.971	96.071	95.171	94.272	93.372	91.572	89.773	87.974
10	91.363	97.551	96.652	95.752	94.852	93.953	93.053	91.253	89.454	87.654
12	89.712	97.228	96.328	95.428	94.528	93.629	92.729	90.929	89.130	87.331
15	87.281	96.733	95.833	94.933	94.033	93.134	92.234	90.434	88.635	86.836
18	84.903	96.226	95.327	94.427	93.527	92.627	91.728	89.928	88.129	86.329
24	80.306	95.179	94.279	93.380	92.480	91.580	90.681	88.881	87.082	85.282

Entry is the ratio of present value of rent package to that of the full rent.

True Rent When Free Rent & Other Concessions Are Given

36 Month Lease Term   Interest Rate 10.00%

Months No Other	plus Other Concession Package (in Months' Rent)									
Free Concessions	1	2	3	4	5	6	8	10	12
0	100.000	96.800	93.600	90.400	87.200	84.000	80.800	74.400	67.999	61.599
1	96.800	94.380	91.153	87.926	84.700	81.473	78.246	71.793	65.339	58.886
2	93.626	91.967	88.740	85.513	82.286	79.060	75.833	69.380	62.926	56.473
3	90.479	89.533	86.306	83.080	79.853	76.626	73.400	66.946	60.493	54.039
4	87.358	87.079	83.853	80.626	77.399	74.173	70.946	64.492	58.039	51.585
5	84.262	84.605	81.379	78.152	74.925	71.698	68.472	62.018	55.565	49.111
6	81.192	82.110	78.884	75.657	72.430	69.204	65.977	59.523	53.070	46.617
8	75.128	77.058	73.832	70.605	67.378	64.151	60.925	54.471	48.018	41.564
10	69.164	71.922	68.695	65.468	62.242	59.015	55.788	49.335	42.881	36.428
12	63.298	66.699	63.472	60.246	57.019	53.792	50.565	44.112	37.659	31.205
15	54.679	58.701	55.474	52.247	49.021	45.794	42.567	36.114	29.660	23.207
18	46.272	50.501	47.274	44.047	40.821	37.594	34.367	27.914	21.460	15.007
24	30.074	33.476	30.249	27.022	23.795	20.569	17.342	10.889	4.435	- - -

48 Month Lease Term

Months No Other	plus Other Concession Package (in Months' Rent)									
Free Concessions	1	2	3	4	5	6	8	10	12
0	100.000	97.485	94.969	92.454	89.939	87.424	84.908	79.878	74.847	69.816
1	97.485	95.761	93.225	90.688	88.152	85.616	83.080	78.007	72.934	67.862
2	94.990	94.044	91.507	88.971	86.435	83.899	81.362	76.290	71.217	66.145
3	92.516	92.312	89.776	87.240	84.704	82.167	79.631	74.558	69.486	64.413
4	90.063	90.566	88.030	85.494	82.958	80.421	77.885	72.813	67.740	62.668
5	87.630	88.806	86.270	83.734	81.197	78.661	76.125	71.052	65.980	60.907
6	85.217	87.031	84.495	81.958	79.422	76.886	74.350	69.277	64.205	59.132
8	80.450	83.436	80.900	78.364	75.828	73.291	70.755	65.682	60.610	55.537
10	75.762	79.781	77.245	74.709	72.173	69.636	67.100	62.028	56.955	51.883
12	71.151	76.066	73.529	70.993	68.457	65.920	63.384	58.312	53.239	48.167
15	64.377	70.375	67.838	65.302	62.766	60.230	57.693	52.621	47.548	42.476
18	57.769	64.540	62.004	59.468	56.932	54.395	51.859	46.786	41.714	36.641
24	45.037	52.427	49.890	47.354	44.818	42.282	39.745	34.673	29.600	24.528

60 Month Lease Term

Months No Other	plus Other Concession Package (in Months' Rent)									
Free Concessions	1	2	3	4	5	6	8	10	12
0	100.000	97.893	95.786	93.679	91.571	89.464	87.357	83.143	78.929	74.714
1	97.893	96.584	94.459	92.335	90.210	88.085	85.960	81.711	77.462	73.212
2	95.803	95.282	93.157	91.032	88.908	86.783	84.658	80.409	76.159	71.910
3	93.731	93.969	91.844	89.719	87.595	85.470	83.345	79.096	74.846	70.597
4	91.675	92.645	90.520	88.395	86.271	84.146	82.021	77.772	73.523	69.273
5	89.637	91.310	89.185	87.061	84.936	82.811	80.686	76.437	72.188	67.938
6	87.615	89.964	87.839	85.714	83.590	81.465	79.340	75.091	70.842	66.592
8	83.622	87.238	85.113	82.989	80.864	78.739	76.614	72.365	68.116	63.866
10	79.695	84.466	82.342	80.217	78.092	75.968	73.843	69.593	65.344	61.095
12	75.833	81.648	79.524	77.399	75.274	73.150	71.025	66.776	62.526	58.277
15	70.157	77.333	75.208	73.084	70.959	68.834	66.709	62.460	58.211	53.961
18	64.622	72.909	70.784	68.659	66.534	64.410	62.285	58.036	53.786	49.537
24	53.956	63.723	61.598	59.473	57.348	55.224	53.099	48.850	44.600	40.351

72 Month Lease Term

Months No Other	plus Other Concession Package (in Months' Rent)									
Free Concessions	1	2	3	4	5	6	8	10	12
0	100.000	98.163	96.325	94.488	92.651	90.814	88.976	85.302	81.627	77.953
1	98.163	97.128	95.276	93.423	91.570	89.718	87.865	84.160	80.455	76.750
2	96.341	96.100	94.248	92.395	90.543	88.690	86.838	83.132	79.427	75.722
3	94.534	95.064	93.212	91.359	89.506	87.654	85.801	82.096	78.391	74.686
4	92.742	94.019	92.167	90.314	88.461	86.609	84.756	81.051	77.346	73.641
5	90.964	92.966	91.113	89.260	87.408	85.555	83.703	79.997	76.292	72.587
6	89.202	91.903	90.050	88.198	86.345	84.493	82.640	78.935	75.230	71.525
8	85.720	89.752	87.899	86.046	84.194	82.341	80.489	76.783	73.078	69.373
10	82.296	87.564	85.711	83.859	82.006	80.154	78.301	74.596	70.891	67.186
12	78.928	85.340	83.487	81.635	79.782	77.930	76.077	72.372	68.667	64.962
15	73.980	81.934	80.081	78.229	76.376	74.523	72.671	68.966	65.261	61.555
18	69.153	78.442	76.589	74.737	72.884	71.031	69.179	65.474	61.769	58.063
24	59.853	71.191	69.339	67.486	65.634	63.781	61.928	58.223	54.518	50.813

84 Month Lease Term

Months No Other	plus Other Concession Package (in Months' Rent)									
Free Concessions	1	2	3	4	5	6	8	10	12
0	100.000	98.354	96.707	95.061	93.414	91.768	90.122	86.829	83.536	80.243
1	98.354	97.513	95.853	94.193	92.533	90.873	89.213	85.892	82.572	79.252
2	96.721	96.679	95.019	93.359	91.699	90.039	88.379	85.059	81.738	78.418
3	95.102	95.839	94.179	92.519	90.858	89.198	87.538	84.218	80.898	77.577
4	93.496	94.991	93.331	91.671	90.011	88.351	86.691	83.370	80.050	76.730
5	91.903	94.136	92.476	90.816	89.156	87.496	85.836	82.516	79.195	75.875
6	90.323	93.275	91.615	89.954	88.294	86.634	84.974	81.654	78.334	75.013
8	87.204	91.529	89.869	88.209	86.549	84.889	83.229	79.909	76.588	73.268
10	84.135	89.755	88.095	86.435	84.775	83.115	81.454	78.134	74.814	71.494
12	81.117	87.951	86.291	84.631	82.971	81.310	79.650	76.330	73.010	69.690
15	76.683	85.188	83.528	81.868	80.208	78.547	76.887	73.567	70.247	66.927
18	72.358	82.355	80.695	79.035	77.375	75.715	74.055	70.734	67.414	64.094
24	64.024	76.474	74.814	73.154	71.494	69.833	68.173	64.853	61.533	58.213

Entry is the ratio of present value of rent package to that of the full rent.

True Rent When Free Rent & Other Concessions Are Given

96 Month Lease Term							Interest Rate 10.00%			

Months No Other Free Concessions		plus Other Concession Package (in Months' Rent)								
		1	2	3	4	5	6	8	10	12
0	100.000	98.495	96.990	95.485	93.980	92.476	90.971	87.961	84.951	81.941
1	98.495	97.799	96.281	94.764	93.246	91.729	90.211	87.177	84.142	81.107
2	97.003	97.109	95.591	94.074	92.556	91.039	89.522	86.487	83.452	80.417
3	95.523	96.413	94.896	93.378	91.861	90.344	88.826	85.791	82.756	79.722
4	94.055	95.712	94.194	92.677	91.160	89.642	88.125	85.090	82.055	79.020
5	92.599	95.005	93.487	91.970	90.452	88.935	87.418	84.383	81.348	78.313
6	91.155	94.292	92.774	91.257	89.739	88.222	86.705	83.670	80.635	77.600
8	88.304	92.848	91.330	89.813	88.295	86.778	85.261	82.226	79.191	76.156
10	85.499	91.379	89.862	88.345	86.827	85.310	83.792	80.758	77.723	74.688
12	82.740	89.887	88.369	86.852	85.334	83.817	82.300	79.265	76.230	73.195
15	78.687	87.601	86.083	84.566	83.048	81.531	80.014	76.979	73.944	70.909
18	74.734	85.257	83.739	82.222	80.705	79.187	77.670	74.635	71.600	68.565
24	67.116	80.391	78.873	77.356	75.838	74.321	72.804	69.769	66.734	63.699

120 Month Lease Term										
0	100.000	98.689	97.379	96.068	94.758	93.447	92.136	89.515	86.894	84.273
1	98.689	98.190	96.869	95.547	94.226	92.904	91.583	88.940	86.297	83.654
2	97.390	97.698	96.377	95.055	93.734	92.412	91.091	88.448	85.805	83.161
3	96.101	97.202	95.880	94.559	93.237	91.916	90.594	87.951	85.308	82.665
4	94.822	96.701	95.380	94.058	92.737	91.415	90.094	87.451	84.808	82.165
5	93.554	96.197	94.875	93.554	92.232	90.911	89.589	86.946	84.303	81.660
6	92.297	95.688	94.366	93.045	91.723	90.402	89.080	86.437	83.794	81.151
8	89.814	94.657	93.336	92.014	90.693	89.371	88.050	85.407	82.764	80.121
10	87.371	93.610	92.288	90.967	89.645	88.324	87.002	84.359	81.716	79.073
12	84.969	92.544	91.223	89.901	88.580	87.258	85.937	83.294	80.651	78.008
15	81.439	90.913	89.591	88.270	86.948	85.627	84.305	81.662	79.019	76.376
18	77.996	89.240	87.919	86.597	85.276	83.954	82.633	79.990	77.347	74.704
24	71.362	85.768	84.446	83.125	81.803	80.482	79.160	76.517	73.874	71.231

144 Month Lease Term										
0	100.000	98.815	97.630	96.444	95.259	94.074	92.889	90.518	88.148	85.778
1	98.815	98.443	97.248	96.053	94.858	93.663	92.468	90.078	87.687	85.297
2	97.639	98.078	96.883	95.688	94.493	93.298	92.103	89.713	87.323	84.933
3	96.474	97.711	96.516	95.320	94.125	92.930	91.735	89.345	86.955	84.565
4	95.318	97.340	96.145	94.950	93.755	92.559	91.364	88.974	86.584	84.194
5	94.171	96.966	95.771	94.576	93.381	92.185	90.990	88.600	86.210	83.820
6	93.034	96.589	95.394	94.199	93.003	91.808	90.613	88.223	85.833	83.443
8	90.788	95.825	94.630	93.435	92.240	91.045	89.850	87.460	85.069	82.679
10	88.579	95.049	93.854	92.659	91.464	90.268	89.073	86.683	84.293	81.903
12	86.407	94.259	93.064	91.869	90.674	89.479	88.284	85.894	83.504	81.114
15	83.215	93.050	91.855	90.660	89.465	88.270	87.075	84.685	82.295	79.905
18	80.101	91.811	90.616	89.421	88.226	87.031	85.836	83.446	81.055	78.665
24	74.102	89.238	88.043	86.848	85.653	84.458	83.262	80.872	78.482	76.092

180 Month Lease Term										
0	100.000	98.934	97.869	96.803	95.737	94.671	93.606	91.474	89.343	87.211
1	98.934	98.684	97.610	96.535	95.460	94.386	93.311	91.162	89.013	86.863
2	97.877	98.441	97.366	96.292	95.217	94.142	93.068	90.919	88.769	86.620
3	96.829	98.196	97.121	96.046	94.972	93.897	92.823	90.673	88.524	86.375
4	95.790	97.948	96.874	95.799	94.724	93.650	92.575	90.426	88.277	86.128
5	94.759	97.699	96.624	95.550	94.475	93.400	92.326	90.177	88.027	85.878
6	93.736	97.447	96.373	95.298	94.223	93.149	92.074	89.925	87.776	85.627
8	91.717	96.938	95.863	94.789	93.714	92.640	91.565	89.416	87.267	85.117
10	89.730	96.420	95.346	94.271	93.196	92.122	91.047	88.898	86.749	84.600
12	87.777	95.894	94.819	93.744	92.670	91.595	90.521	88.371	86.222	84.073
15	84.907	95.087	94.013	92.938	91.864	90.789	89.714	87.565	85.416	83.267
18	82.107	94.261	93.186	92.112	91.037	89.962	88.888	86.739	84.589	82.440
24	76.712	92.545	91.470	90.395	89.321	88.246	87.171	85.022	82.873	80.724

240 Month Lease Term										
0	100.000	99.043	98.086	97.129	96.172	95.215	94.258	92.344	90.430	88.515
1	99.043	98.903	97.938	96.973	96.008	95.043	94.078	92.148	90.218	88.288
2	98.094	98.771	97.805	96.840	95.875	94.910	93.945	92.015	90.085	88.155
3	97.153	98.637	97.672	96.707	95.742	94.777	93.812	91.881	89.951	88.021
4	96.219	98.502	97.537	96.572	95.607	94.642	93.676	91.746	89.816	87.886
5	95.293	98.365	97.400	96.435	95.470	94.505	93.540	91.610	89.680	87.750
6	94.375	98.228	97.263	96.298	95.333	94.368	93.403	91.473	89.543	87.613
8	92.561	97.950	96.985	96.020	95.055	94.090	93.125	91.195	89.265	87.335
10	90.778	97.668	96.703	95.738	94.773	93.808	92.842	90.912	88.982	87.052
12	89.023	97.380	96.415	95.450	94.485	93.520	92.555	90.625	88.695	86.765
15	86.446	96.940	95.975	95.010	94.045	93.080	92.115	90.185	88.255	86.325
18	83.932	96.489	95.524	94.559	93.594	92.629	91.664	89.734	87.804	85.874
24	79.087	95.552	94.587	93.622	92.657	91.692	90.727	88.797	86.867	84.937

Entry is the ratio of present value of rent package to that of the full rent.

True Rent When Free Rent & Other Concessions Are Given

36 Month Lease Term   Interest Rate 11.00%

Months No Other Free Concessions		plus Other Concession Package (in Months' Rent)								
		1	2	3	4	5	6	8	10	12
0	100.000	96.756	93.512	90.268	87.023	83.779	80.535	74.047	67.559	61.070
1	96.756	94.369	91.095	87.821	84.547	81.273	78.000	71.452	64.904	58.356
2	93.541	91.990	88.716	85.442	82.168	78.895	75.621	69.073	62.525	55.978
3	90.356	89.589	86.316	83.042	79.768	76.494	73.220	66.672	60.125	53.577
4	87.199	87.167	83.893	80.619	77.345	74.071	70.798	64.250	57.702	51.154
5	84.071	84.722	81.448	78.174	74.900	71.627	68.353	61.805	55.257	48.709
6	80.972	82.255	78.981	75.707	72.433	69.159	65.885	59.338	52.790	46.242
8	74.857	77.252	73.978	70.705	67.431	64.157	60.883	54.335	47.787	41.240
10	68.853	72.158	68.884	65.610	62.336	59.062	55.788	49.240	42.693	36.145
12	62.958	66.969	63.695	60.421	57.147	53.874	50.600	44.052	37.504	30.956
15	54.314	59.007	55.733	52.459	49.185	45.911	42.637	36.089	29.542	22.994
18	45.903	50.823	47.549	44.275	41.002	37.728	34.454	27.906	21.358	14.811
24	29.757	33.769	30.495	27.221	23.947	20.673	17.399	10.851	4.304	---

48 Month Lease Term

Months No Other Free Concessions		plus Other Concession Package (in Months' Rent)								
		1	2	3	4	5	6	8	10	12
0	100.000	97.439	94.878	92.317	89.756	87.195	84.634	79.511	74.389	69.267
1	97.439	95.748	93.163	90.578	87.994	85.409	82.825	77.656	72.487	67.317
2	94.901	94.064	91.480	88.895	86.311	83.726	81.142	75.973	70.803	65.634
3	92.386	92.366	89.781	87.197	84.612	82.028	79.443	74.274	69.105	63.936
4	89.894	90.652	88.067	85.483	82.898	80.313	77.729	72.560	67.391	62.222
5	87.425	88.922	86.337	83.753	81.168	78.584	75.999	70.830	65.661	60.492
6	84.978	87.176	84.591	82.007	79.422	76.838	74.253	69.084	63.915	58.746
8	80.151	83.636	81.052	78.467	75.883	73.298	70.714	65.544	60.375	55.206
10	75.411	80.031	77.447	74.862	72.278	69.693	67.109	61.940	56.771	51.601
12	70.757	76.360	73.776	71.191	68.607	66.022	63.438	58.268	53.099	47.930
15	63.933	70.726	68.142	65.557	62.973	60.388	57.804	52.634	47.465	42.296
18	57.293	64.936	62.351	59.767	57.182	54.598	52.013	46.844	41.675	36.506
24	44.547	52.869	50.284	47.700	45.115	42.530	39.946	34.777	29.608	24.439

60 Month Lease Term

Months No Other Free Concessions		plus Other Concession Package (in Months' Rent)								
		1	2	3	4	5	6	8	10	12
0	100.000	97.846	95.691	93.537	91.382	89.228	87.073	82.764	78.455	74.146
1	97.846	96.568	94.394	92.220	90.045	87.871	85.697	81.348	77.000	72.652
2	95.711	95.299	93.125	90.951	88.776	86.602	84.428	80.079	75.731	71.382
3	93.595	94.018	91.844	89.670	87.496	85.321	83.147	78.799	74.450	70.102
4	91.499	92.726	90.552	88.377	86.203	84.029	81.855	77.506	73.158	68.809
5	89.421	91.422	89.247	87.073	84.899	82.725	80.550	76.202	71.853	67.505
6	87.363	90.105	87.931	85.757	83.583	81.408	79.234	74.886	70.537	66.189
8	83.302	87.436	85.262	83.088	80.914	78.739	76.565	72.217	67.868	63.520
10	79.315	84.718	82.544	80.370	78.196	76.021	73.847	69.499	65.150	60.802
12	75.399	81.950	79.776	77.602	75.428	73.253	71.079	66.731	62.382	58.034
15	69.659	77.702	75.528	73.354	71.180	69.005	66.831	62.483	58.134	53.786
18	64.073	73.336	71.162	68.988	66.814	64.639	62.465	58.117	53.768	49.420
24	53.350	64.238	62.063	59.889	57.715	55.541	53.367	49.018	44.670	40.321

72 Month Lease Term

Months No Other Free Concessions		plus Other Concession Package (in Months' Rent)								
		1	2	3	4	5	6	8	10	12
0	100.000	98.114	96.228	94.342	92.456	90.569	88.683	84.911	81.139	77.367
1	98.114	97.110	95.206	93.303	91.400	89.496	87.593	83.786	79.979	76.172
2	96.245	96.114	94.211	92.307	90.404	88.500	86.597	82.790	78.983	75.177
3	94.393	95.109	93.206	91.302	89.399	87.496	85.592	81.785	77.978	74.172
4	92.558	94.095	92.192	90.288	88.385	86.481	84.578	80.771	76.964	73.158
5	90.739	93.072	91.168	89.265	87.361	85.458	83.555	79.748	75.941	72.134
6	88.937	92.039	90.135	88.232	86.329	84.425	82.522	78.715	74.908	71.101
8	85.382	89.945	88.041	86.138	84.234	82.331	80.428	76.621	72.814	69.007
10	81.891	87.812	85.909	84.005	82.102	80.198	78.295	74.488	70.681	66.875
12	78.464	85.640	83.737	81.833	79.930	78.026	76.123	72.316	68.509	64.703
15	73.438	82.307	80.404	78.500	76.597	74.693	72.790	68.983	65.176	61.369
18	68.548	78.881	76.978	75.074	73.171	71.268	69.364	65.557	61.751	57.944
24	59.161	71.742	69.839	67.935	66.032	64.129	62.225	58.418	54.611	50.805

84 Month Lease Term

Months No Other Free Concessions		plus Other Concession Package (in Months' Rent)								
		1	2	3	4	5	6	8	10	12
0	100.000	98.303	96.607	94.910	93.213	91.517	89.820	86.426	83.033	79.640
1	98.303	97.492	95.780	94.068	92.355	90.643	88.931	85.506	82.082	78.657
2	96.622	96.689	94.977	93.265	91.553	89.840	88.128	84.704	81.279	77.855
3	94.956	95.879	94.167	92.455	90.742	89.030	87.318	83.893	80.469	77.044
4	93.305	95.061	93.349	91.637	89.925	88.212	86.500	83.076	79.651	76.227
5	91.669	94.236	92.524	90.812	89.100	87.387	85.675	82.251	78.826	75.402
6	90.048	93.404	91.691	89.979	88.267	86.555	84.842	81.418	77.993	74.569
8	86.850	91.715	90.003	88.291	86.578	84.866	83.154	79.729	76.305	72.880
10	83.710	89.996	88.283	86.571	84.859	83.147	81.434	78.010	74.585	71.161
12	80.627	88.244	86.532	84.820	83.108	81.396	79.683	76.259	72.834	69.410
15	76.106	85.557	83.845	82.133	80.420	78.708	76.996	73.571	70.147	66.722
18	71.707	82.795	81.083	79.371	77.658	75.946	74.234	70.809	67.385	63.960
24	63.263	77.039	75.327	73.615	71.902	70.190	68.478	65.053	61.629	58.204

Entry is the ratio of present value of rent package to that of the full rent.

True Rent When Free Rent & Other Concessions Are Given

96 Month Lease Term   Interest Rate 11.00%

Months No Other Free Concessions		plus Other Concession Package (in Months' Rent)								
		1	2	3	4	5	6	8	10	12
0	100.000	98.443	96.887	95.330	93.774	92.217	90.661	87.547	84.434	81.321
1	98.443	97.775	96.204	94.633	93.062	91.492	89.921	86.779	83.637	80.496
2	96.901	97.115	95.544	93.973	92.402	90.831	89.261	86.119	82.977	79.836
3	95.373	96.449	94.878	93.307	91.736	90.165	88.594	85.453	82.311	79.169
4	93.858	95.776	94.205	92.635	91.064	89.493	87.922	84.780	81.639	78.497
5	92.357	95.098	93.527	91.956	90.385	88.814	87.244	84.102	80.960	77.818
6	90.870	94.413	92.842	91.271	89.701	88.130	86.559	83.417	80.275	77.134
8	87.936	93.025	91.454	89.883	88.312	86.741	85.171	82.029	78.887	75.745
10	85.055	91.611	90.040	88.469	86.898	85.327	83.757	80.615	77.473	74.332
12	82.227	90.171	88.600	87.029	85.458	83.888	82.317	79.175	76.033	72.892
15	78.079	87.961	86.390	84.819	83.249	81.678	80.107	76.965	73.824	70.682
18	74.044	85.690	84.119	82.548	80.978	79.407	77.836	74.694	71.552	68.411
24	66.297	80.957	79.386	77.815	76.245	74.674	73.103	69.961	66.819	63.678

120 Month Lease Term

Months No Other Free Concessions		1	2	3	4	5	6	8	10	12
0	100.000	98.635	97.270	95.905	94.540	93.175	91.810	89.080	86.350	83.620
1	98.635	98.162	96.784	95.407	94.029	92.652	91.274	88.519	85.764	83.009
2	97.282	97.697	96.319	94.942	93.564	92.187	90.809	88.054	85.299	82.544
3	95.942	97.227	95.850	94.472	93.095	91.717	90.340	87.585	84.830	82.075
4	94.614	96.754	95.376	93.999	92.621	91.244	89.866	87.111	84.356	81.601
5	93.298	96.276	94.898	93.521	92.143	90.766	89.388	86.633	83.878	81.123
6	91.994	95.793	94.416	93.038	91.661	90.283	88.906	86.151	83.396	80.641
8	89.421	94.815	93.438	92.060	90.683	89.305	87.928	85.173	82.418	79.663
10	86.895	93.819	92.442	91.064	89.687	88.309	86.932	84.177	81.422	78.667
12	84.414	92.805	91.427	90.050	88.672	87.295	85.917	83.162	80.407	77.652
15	80.777	91.248	89.871	88.493	87.116	85.738	84.361	81.606	78.851	76.096
18	77.238	89.648	88.271	86.893	85.516	84.138	82.761	80.006	77.251	74.496
24	70.445	86.314	84.937	83.559	82.182	80.804	79.427	76.672	73.917	71.162

144 Month Lease Term

Months No Other Free Concessions		1	2	3	4	5	6	8	10	12
0	100.000	98.758	97.516	96.273	95.031	93.789	92.547	90.063	87.578	85.094
1	98.758	98.410	97.156	95.902	94.649	93.395	92.142	89.635	87.128	84.620
2	97.527	98.070	96.816	95.562	94.309	93.055	91.802	89.295	86.788	84.280
3	96.307	97.726	96.473	95.219	93.966	92.712	91.459	88.952	86.444	83.937
4	95.099	97.380	96.127	94.873	93.620	92.366	91.112	88.605	86.098	83.591
5	93.901	97.031	95.777	94.524	93.270	92.017	90.763	88.256	85.749	83.242
6	92.714	96.678	95.425	94.171	92.918	91.664	90.410	87.903	85.396	82.889
8	90.373	95.963	94.710	93.456	92.203	90.949	89.695	87.188	84.681	82.174
10	88.074	95.235	93.982	92.728	91.474	90.221	88.967	86.460	83.953	81.446
12	85.817	94.494	93.240	91.986	90.733	89.479	88.226	85.719	83.212	80.704
15	82.507	93.356	92.102	90.849	89.595	88.341	87.088	84.581	82.074	79.567
18	79.286	92.186	90.932	89.679	88.425	87.172	85.918	83.411	80.904	78.397
24	73.104	89.749	88.495	87.242	85.988	84.734	83.481	80.974	78.467	75.960

180 Month Lease Term

Months No Other Free Concessions		1	2	3	4	5	6	8	10	12
0	100.000	98.874	97.747	96.621	95.495	94.369	93.242	90.990	88.737	86.485
1	98.874	98.643	97.507	96.370	95.234	94.097	92.960	90.687	88.414	86.141
2	97.758	98.422	97.285	96.148	95.012	93.875	92.739	90.465	88.192	85.919
3	96.652	98.198	97.061	95.924	94.788	93.651	92.515	90.241	87.968	85.695
4	95.556	97.972	96.835	95.698	94.562	93.425	92.289	90.015	87.742	85.469
5	94.470	97.743	96.607	95.470	94.334	93.197	92.060	89.787	87.514	85.241
6	93.394	97.513	96.377	95.240	94.103	92.967	91.830	89.557	87.284	85.011
8	91.271	97.046	95.910	94.773	93.637	92.500	91.363	89.090	86.817	84.544
10	89.187	96.571	95.435	94.298	93.161	92.025	90.888	88.615	86.342	84.069
12	87.140	96.087	94.950	93.814	92.677	91.541	90.404	88.131	85.858	83.584
15	84.139	95.344	94.208	93.071	91.934	90.798	89.661	87.388	85.115	82.842
18	81.219	94.581	93.444	92.307	91.171	90.034	88.898	86.624	84.351	82.078
24	75.614	92.989	91.853	90.716	89.580	88.443	87.306	85.033	82.760	80.487

240 Month Lease Term

Months No Other Free Concessions		1	2	3	4	5	6	8	10	12
0	100.000	98.977	97.954	96.932	95.909	94.886	93.863	91.817	89.772	87.726
1	98.977	98.852	97.820	96.788	95.756	94.724	93.691	91.627	89.563	87.498
2	97.964	98.736	97.704	96.671	95.639	94.607	93.575	91.510	89.446	87.382
3	96.959	98.618	97.586	96.554	95.521	94.489	93.457	91.393	89.328	87.264
4	95.964	98.499	97.467	96.435	95.403	94.371	93.338	91.274	89.210	87.145
5	94.978	98.380	97.347	96.315	95.283	94.251	93.219	91.154	89.090	87.025
6	94.001	98.259	97.226	96.194	95.162	94.130	93.098	91.033	88.969	86.905
8	92.073	98.013	96.981	95.949	94.917	93.885	92.852	90.788	88.724	86.659
10	90.180	97.764	96.732	95.699	94.667	93.635	92.603	90.538	88.474	86.410
12	88.321	97.509	96.477	95.445	94.413	93.381	92.349	90.284	88.220	86.155
15	85.596	97.119	96.087	95.055	94.023	92.991	91.958	89.894	87.830	85.765
18	82.944	96.718	95.686	94.654	93.622	92.589	91.557	89.493	87.429	85.364
24	77.854	95.882	94.850	93.818	92.786	91.754	90.721	88.657	86.593	84.528

Entry is the ratio of present value of rent package to that of the full rent.

True Rent When Free Rent & Other Concessions Are Given

36 Month Lease Term   Interest Rate 12.00%

Months No Other Free Concessions		plus Other Concession Package (in Months' Rent)								
		1	2	3	4	5	6	8	10	12
0	100.000	96.711	93.423	90.134	86.846	83.557	80.269	73.692	67.115	60.537
1	96.711	94.357	91.036	87.714	84.393	81.071	77.750	71.107	64.464	57.821
2	93.455	92.012	88.691	85.370	82.048	78.727	75.405	68.762	62.120	55.477
3	90.232	89.644	86.323	83.002	79.680	76.359	73.037	66.394	59.752	53.109
4	87.040	87.253	83.931	80.610	77.288	73.967	70.645	64.003	57.360	50.717
5	83.880	84.837	81.516	78.194	74.873	71.551	68.230	61.587	54.944	48.301
6	80.751	82.397	79.076	75.754	72.433	69.111	65.790	59.147	52.504	45.861
8	74.585	77.444	74.123	70.801	67.480	64.158	60.837	54.194	47.551	40.908
10	68.542	72.391	69.070	65.748	62.427	59.106	55.784	49.141	42.498	35.856
12	62.617	67.237	63.916	60.594	57.273	53.951	50.630	43.987	37.344	30.701
15	53.948	59.311	55.989	52.668	49.346	46.025	42.704	36.061	29.418	22.775
18	45.534	51.144	47.823	44.501	41.180	37.859	34.537	27.894	21.251	14.609
24	29.442	34.062	30.740	27.419	24.097	20.776	17.454	10.812	4.169	---

48 Month Lease Term

Months No Other Free Concessions		plus Other Concession Package (in Months' Rent)								
		1	2	3	4	5	6	8	10	12
0	100.000	97.393	94.785	92.178	89.571	86.963	84.356	79.142	73.927	68.712
1	97.393	95.733	93.100	90.466	87.833	85.200	82.566	77.300	72.033	66.766
2	94.811	94.084	91.450	88.817	86.183	83.550	80.917	75.650	70.383	65.116
3	92.255	92.417	89.784	87.151	84.517	81.884	79.250	73.984	68.717	63.450
4	89.725	90.734	88.101	85.468	82.834	80.201	77.568	72.301	67.034	61.767
5	87.219	89.035	86.401	83.768	81.135	78.501	75.868	70.601	65.334	60.067
6	84.738	87.318	84.685	82.051	79.418	76.784	74.151	68.884	63.618	58.351
8	79.850	83.833	81.200	78.566	75.933	73.299	70.666	65.399	60.132	54.866
10	75.058	80.278	77.644	75.011	72.378	69.744	67.111	61.844	56.577	51.311
12	70.361	76.651	74.018	71.384	68.751	66.118	63.484	58.218	52.951	47.684
15	63.488	71.074	68.441	65.807	63.174	60.541	57.907	52.641	47.374	42.107
18	56.817	65.328	62.695	60.061	57.428	54.795	52.161	46.895	41.628	36.361
24	44.058	53.309	50.675	48.042	45.408	42.775	40.142	34.875	29.608	24.341

60 Month Lease Term

Months No Other Free Concessions		plus Other Concession Package (in Months' Rent)								
		1	2	3	4	5	6	8	10	12
0	100.000	97.798	95.595	93.393	91.190	88.988	86.785	82.381	77.976	73.571
1	97.798	96.551	94.327	92.102	89.878	87.653	85.429	80.980	76.531	72.082
2	95.617	95.314	93.090	90.866	88.641	86.417	84.192	79.743	75.294	70.846
3	93.458	94.065	91.841	89.616	87.392	85.168	82.943	78.494	74.045	69.596
4	91.320	92.804	90.579	88.355	86.130	83.906	81.682	77.233	72.784	68.335
5	89.204	91.530	89.305	87.081	84.856	82.632	80.407	75.959	71.510	67.061
6	87.108	90.243	88.018	85.794	83.569	81.345	79.121	74.672	70.223	65.774
8	82.979	87.630	85.406	83.181	80.957	78.732	76.508	72.059	67.610	63.161
10	78.932	84.965	82.741	80.516	78.292	76.067	73.843	69.394	64.945	60.496
12	74.964	82.247	80.022	77.798	75.573	73.349	71.124	66.675	62.227	57.778
15	69.158	78.066	75.841	73.617	71.392	69.168	66.944	62.495	58.046	53.597
18	63.523	73.758	71.534	69.309	67.085	64.861	62.636	58.187	53.738	49.289
24	52.745	64.748	62.524	60.299	58.075	55.850	53.626	49.177	44.728	40.279

72 Month Lease Term

Months No Other Free Concessions		plus Other Concession Package (in Months' Rent)								
		1	2	3	4	5	6	8	10	12
0	100.000	98.064	96.129	94.193	92.257	90.322	88.386	84.515	80.643	76.772
1	98.064	97.090	95.135	93.180	91.225	89.270	87.315	83.405	79.495	75.585
2	96.148	96.125	94.170	92.215	90.260	88.305	86.350	82.440	78.530	74.620
3	94.250	95.151	93.196	91.241	89.286	87.331	85.376	81.466	77.556	73.646
4	92.372	94.167	92.212	90.257	88.302	86.347	84.392	80.482	76.572	72.662
5	90.511	93.173	91.218	89.263	87.308	85.353	83.398	79.488	75.578	71.668
6	88.670	92.170	90.215	88.260	86.305	84.350	82.395	78.485	74.575	70.664
8	85.041	90.132	88.177	86.222	84.267	82.312	80.357	76.447	72.537	68.627
10	81.483	88.053	86.098	84.143	82.188	80.233	78.278	74.368	70.458	66.548
12	77.996	85.933	83.978	82.023	80.068	78.113	76.158	72.248	68.338	64.428
15	72.894	82.672	80.717	78.762	76.807	74.852	72.897	68.987	65.077	61.167
18	67.941	79.313	77.357	75.402	73.447	71.492	69.537	65.627	61.717	57.807
24	58.469	72.285	70.330	68.375	66.420	64.465	62.510	58.600	54.690	50.780

84 Month Lease Term

Months No Other Free Concessions		plus Other Concession Package (in Months' Rent)								
		1	2	3	4	5	6	8	10	12
0	100.000	98.252	96.504	94.757	93.009	91.261	89.513	86.018	82.522	79.026
1	98.252	97.469	95.704	93.939	92.174	90.408	88.643	85.113	81.582	78.051
2	96.522	96.697	94.931	93.166	91.401	89.635	87.870	84.340	80.809	77.279
3	94.808	95.916	94.151	92.385	90.620	88.855	87.090	83.559	80.028	76.498
4	93.112	95.127	93.362	91.597	89.832	88.066	86.301	82.770	79.240	75.709
5	91.432	94.331	92.566	90.801	89.035	87.270	85.505	81.974	78.444	74.913
6	89.769	93.527	91.761	89.996	88.231	86.466	84.700	81.170	77.639	74.109
8	86.493	91.894	90.129	88.363	86.598	84.833	83.068	79.537	76.006	72.476
10	83.281	90.228	88.463	86.698	84.932	83.167	81.402	77.871	74.341	70.810
12	80.132	88.529	86.764	84.999	83.233	81.468	79.703	76.172	72.642	69.111
15	75.524	85.916	84.151	82.386	80.620	78.855	77.090	73.559	70.029	66.498
18	71.053	83.224	81.459	79.694	77.928	76.163	74.398	70.867	67.337	63.806
24	62.500	77.593	75.827	74.062	72.297	70.532	68.766	65.236	61.705	58.175

Entry is the ratio of present value of rent package to that of the full rent.

True Rent When Free Rent & Other Concessions Are Given

96 Month Lease Term   Interest Rate 12.00%

Months No Other Free Concessions	plus Other Concession Package (in Months' Rent)								
	1	2	3	4	5	6	8	10	12
0	100.000	98.391	96.782	95.172	93.563	91.954	90.345	87.126	83.908	80.690
1	98.391	97.749	96.124	94.499	92.874	91.248	89.623	86.372	83.122	79.871
2	96.798	97.118	95.493	93.867	92.242	90.617	88.991	85.741	82.490	79.240
3	95.220	96.480	94.855	93.229	91.604	89.979	88.354	85.103	81.852	78.602
4	93.658	95.836	94.211	92.585	90.960	89.335	87.709	84.459	81.208	77.958
5	92.112	95.185	93.560	91.935	90.309	88.684	87.059	83.808	80.558	77.307
6	90.581	94.528	92.903	91.277	89.652	88.027	86.402	83.151	79.900	76.650
8	87.564	93.194	91.569	89.943	88.318	86.693	85.067	81.817	78.566	75.316
10	84.606	91.833	90.208	88.582	86.957	85.332	83.706	80.456	77.205	73.955
12	81.707	90.445	88.819	87.194	85.569	83.943	82.318	79.068	75.817	72.566
15	77.465	88.310	86.684	85.059	83.434	81.808	80.183	76.933	73.682	70.431
18	73.348	86.110	84.485	82.859	81.234	79.609	77.984	74.733	71.482	68.232
24	65.473	81.509	79.883	78.258	76.633	75.007	73.382	70.132	66.881	63.631

120 Month Lease Term

Months No Other Free Concessions	plus Other Concession Package (in Months' Rent)								
	1	2	3	4	5	6	8	10	12
0	100.000	98.579	97.159	95.738	94.318	92.897	91.477	88.636	85.795	82.954
1	98.579	98.131	96.696	95.261	93.826	92.392	90.957	88.088	85.218	82.349
2	97.173	97.692	96.257	94.822	93.387	91.953	90.518	87.649	84.779	81.910
3	95.781	97.248	95.813	94.379	92.944	91.509	90.075	87.205	84.336	81.466
4	94.402	96.800	95.365	93.931	92.496	91.061	89.627	86.757	83.888	81.018
5	93.037	96.348	94.913	93.478	92.044	90.609	89.174	86.305	83.435	80.566
6	91.685	95.891	94.456	93.022	91.587	90.152	88.717	85.848	82.979	80.109
8	89.022	94.963	93.529	92.094	90.659	89.225	87.790	84.920	82.051	79.182
10	86.411	94.017	92.583	91.148	89.713	88.278	86.844	83.974	81.105	78.235
12	83.852	93.052	91.617	90.183	88.748	87.313	85.879	83.009	80.140	77.270
15	80.108	91.568	90.133	88.698	87.264	85.829	84.394	81.525	78.655	75.786
18	76.473	90.039	88.604	87.169	85.734	84.300	82.865	79.996	77.126	74.257
24	69.522	86.840	85.405	83.970	82.536	81.101	79.666	76.797	73.927	71.058

144 Month Lease Term

Months No Other Free Concessions	plus Other Concession Package (in Months' Rent)								
	1	2	3	4	5	6	8	10	12
0	100.000	98.700	97.399	96.099	94.798	93.498	92.198	89.597	86.996	84.395
1	98.700	98.373	97.060	95.746	94.433	93.119	91.806	89.179	86.552	83.926
2	97.412	98.057	96.743	95.430	94.116	92.803	91.490	88.863	86.236	83.609
3	96.137	97.737	96.423	95.110	93.797	92.483	91.170	88.543	85.916	83.289
4	94.875	97.414	96.101	94.787	93.474	92.160	90.847	88.220	85.593	82.966
5	93.625	97.088	95.774	94.461	93.148	91.834	90.521	87.894	85.267	82.640
6	92.388	96.758	95.445	94.132	92.818	91.505	90.191	87.564	84.938	82.311
8	89.950	96.090	94.776	93.463	92.149	90.836	89.523	86.896	84.269	81.642
10	87.560	95.408	94.094	92.781	91.467	90.154	88.840	86.214	83.587	80.960
12	85.217	94.712	93.398	92.085	90.771	89.458	88.145	85.518	82.891	80.264
15	81.789	93.642	92.328	91.015	89.701	88.388	87.074	84.448	81.821	79.194
18	78.462	92.539	91.226	89.912	88.599	87.285	85.972	83.345	80.718	78.091
24	72.099	90.233	88.919	87.606	86.292	84.979	83.665	81.039	78.412	75.785

180 Month Lease Term

Months No Other Free Concessions	plus Other Concession Package (in Months' Rent)								
	1	2	3	4	5	6	8	10	12
0	100.000	98.812	97.623	96.435	95.247	94.059	92.870	90.494	88.117	85.741
1	98.812	98.600	97.399	96.199	94.999	93.799	92.599	90.198	87.798	85.398
2	97.635	98.397	97.197	95.997	94.797	93.597	92.397	89.996	87.596	85.196
3	96.470	98.193	96.993	95.793	94.593	93.393	92.192	89.792	87.392	84.991
4	95.317	97.987	96.787	95.587	94.387	93.186	91.986	89.586	87.186	84.785
5	94.175	97.779	96.579	95.378	94.178	92.978	91.778	89.378	86.977	84.577
6	93.044	97.568	96.368	95.168	93.968	92.768	91.568	89.167	86.767	84.367
8	90.817	97.141	95.941	94.741	93.541	92.341	91.140	88.740	86.340	83.939
10	88.633	96.706	95.505	94.305	93.105	91.905	90.705	88.304	85.904	83.504
12	86.492	96.261	95.061	93.861	92.661	91.461	90.260	87.860	85.460	83.059
15	83.360	95.578	94.378	93.177	91.977	90.777	89.577	87.177	84.776	82.376
18	80.319	94.874	93.673	92.473	91.273	90.073	88.873	86.472	84.072	81.672
24	74.504	93.401	92.200	91.000	89.800	88.600	87.400	84.999	82.599	80.199

240 Month Lease Term

Months No Other Free Concessions	plus Other Concession Package (in Months' Rent)								
	1	2	3	4	5	6	8	10	12
0	100.000	98.910	97.820	96.729	95.639	94.549	93.459	91.279	89.098	86.918
1	98.910	98.798	97.697	96.596	95.495	94.393	93.292	91.090	88.888	86.686
2	97.830	98.696	97.595	96.494	95.392	94.291	93.190	90.988	88.786	86.584
3	96.762	98.593	97.492	96.390	95.289	94.188	93.087	90.885	88.683	86.481
4	95.704	98.488	97.387	96.286	95.185	94.084	92.983	90.781	88.579	86.377
5	94.656	98.383	97.282	96.181	95.080	93.979	92.878	90.676	88.473	86.271
6	93.619	98.277	97.176	96.075	94.974	93.873	92.772	90.569	88.367	86.165
8	91.575	98.061	96.960	95.859	94.758	93.657	92.556	90.354	88.152	85.949
10	89.571	97.841	96.740	95.639	94.538	93.437	92.336	90.134	87.932	85.729
12	87.607	97.617	96.516	95.415	94.314	93.213	92.111	89.909	87.707	85.505
15	84.733	97.272	96.171	95.070	93.968	92.867	91.766	89.564	87.362	85.160
18	81.944	96.916	95.815	94.714	93.613	92.512	91.411	89.209	87.006	84.804
24	76.609	96.172	95.071	93.970	92.869	91.768	90.667	88.465	86.262	84.060

Entry is the ratio of present value of rent package to that of the full rent.

Actual Rent Increase from CPI Clause

Percent of CPI	Time	Annual Growth in Consumer Price Index											
		3.00%	3.25%	3.50%	3.75%	4.00%	4.25%	4.50%	4.75%	5.00%	5.25%	5.50%	5.75%
25%	1	7.50	8.13	8.75	9.38	10.00	10.63	11.25	11.88	12.50	13.13	13.75	14.38
	2	7.78	8.46	9.14	9.82	10.50	11.19	11.89	12.59	13.29	14.00	14.71	15.42
	3	8.08	8.81	9.54	10.28	11.04	11.80	12.57	13.35	14.14	14.93	15.74	16.55
	4	8.39	9.17	9.97	10.78	11.60	12.44	13.30	14.16	15.05	15.95	16.86	17.79
	5	8.71	9.55	10.42	11.30	12.20	13.13	14.07	15.04	16.03	17.04	18.07	19.13
	6	9.05	9.95	10.89	11.85	12.84	13.86	14.90	15.98	17.09	18.22	19.39	20.59
	7	9.40	10.38	11.39	12.43	13.52	14.64	15.79	16.99	18.23	19.51	20.83	22.19
	8	9.77	10.82	11.91	13.05	14.23	15.47	16.75	18.08	19.46	20.90	22.39	23.94
	10	10.46	11.65	12.90	14.22	15.60	17.05	18.57	20.16	21.83	23.58	25.42	27.34
	12	11.20	12.55	13.99	15.50	17.11	18.81	20.61	22.52	24.53	26.67	28.92	31.30
	15	12.37	13.98	15.71	17.56	19.54	21.67	23.95	26.40	29.01	31.81	34.80	38.00
30%	1	9.00	9.75	10.50	11.25	12.00	12.75	13.50	14.25	15.00	15.75	16.50	17.25
	2	9.35	10.17	10.98	11.80	12.63	13.46	14.30	15.14	15.99	16.84	17.69	18.56
	3	9.72	10.60	11.49	12.39	13.30	14.22	15.15	16.10	17.05	18.02	18.99	19.98
	4	10.11	11.06	12.03	13.01	14.01	15.03	16.07	17.12	18.20	19.29	20.41	21.54
	5	10.52	11.54	12.59	13.67	14.77	15.89	17.05	18.23	19.44	20.68	21.94	23.24
	6	10.94	12.05	13.19	14.36	15.57	16.82	18.10	19.42	20.78	22.18	23.63	25.11
	7	11.39	12.58	13.82	15.10	16.43	17.81	19.24	20.71	22.24	23.82	25.46	27.16
	8	11.86	13.14	14.49	15.89	17.35	18.87	20.46	22.10	23.82	25.61	27.47	29.41
	10	12.72	14.18	15.73	17.35	19.06	20.86	22.75	24.73	26.82	29.01	31.31	33.73
	12	13.65	15.32	17.09	18.97	20.97	23.09	25.34	27.73	30.26	32.94	35.78	38.80
	15	15.10	17.09	19.24	21.54	24.02	26.69	29.55	32.62	35.92	39.47	43.27	47.35
33.3%	1	10.00	10.83	11.67	12.50	13.33	14.17	15.00	15.83	16.67	17.50	18.33	19.17
	2	10.40	11.31	12.22	13.13	14.05	14.98	15.91	16.85	17.79	18.74	19.70	20.66
	3	10.83	11.80	12.80	13.80	14.82	15.85	16.89	17.94	19.01	20.09	21.18	22.29
	4	11.27	12.33	13.41	14.51	15.63	16.77	17.94	19.12	20.33	21.55	22.80	24.07
	5	11.73	12.88	14.06	15.26	16.50	17.77	19.06	20.39	21.75	23.15	24.57	26.04
	6	12.22	13.46	14.75	16.07	17.43	18.83	20.28	21.77	23.30	24.89	26.51	28.19
	7	12.73	14.08	15.47	16.92	18.42	19.97	21.59	23.26	24.99	26.78	28.64	30.57
	8	13.27	14.73	16.24	17.83	19.48	21.20	23.00	24.87	26.82	28.86	30.98	33.19
	10	14.25	15.91	17.66	19.50	21.44	23.48	25.63	27.89	30.27	32.77	35.40	38.17
	12	15.32	17.21	19.22	21.36	23.63	26.04	28.61	31.34	34.23	37.31	40.58	44.04
	15	16.97	19.23	21.67	24.30	27.12	30.17	33.44	36.97	40.76	44.84	49.22	53.93
35%	1	10.50	11.38	12.25	13.13	14.00	14.88	15.75	16.63	17.50	18.38	19.25	20.13
	2	10.93	11.88	12.83	13.80	14.76	15.74	16.72	17.70	18.70	19.70	20.70	21.71
	3	11.38	12.41	13.45	14.51	15.58	16.66	17.76	18.87	19.99	21.13	22.28	23.45
	4	11.85	12.97	14.11	15.26	16.45	17.65	18.88	20.12	21.40	22.69	24.01	25.35
	5	12.35	13.56	14.80	16.07	17.37	18.71	20.08	21.48	22.92	24.39	25.90	27.45
	6	12.87	14.18	15.53	16.93	18.36	19.85	21.38	22.95	24.58	26.25	27.98	29.76
	7	13.41	14.83	16.31	17.84	19.42	21.07	22.78	24.55	26.39	28.29	30.26	32.31
	8	13.99	15.53	17.13	18.81	20.56	22.39	24.29	26.28	28.35	30.52	32.77	35.13
	10	15.03	16.79	18.64	20.59	22.65	24.81	27.10	29.50	32.03	34.69	37.50	40.45
	12	16.17	18.17	20.30	22.57	24.98	27.55	30.28	33.19	36.27	39.55	43.04	46.74
	15	17.92	20.32	22.91	25.70	28.71	31.95	35.44	39.20	43.25	47.60	52.29	57.34
40%	1	12.00	13.00	14.00	15.00	16.00	17.00	18.00	19.00	20.00	21.00	22.00	23.00
	2	12.51	13.60	14.69	15.80	16.91	18.02	19.15	20.28	21.42	22.57	23.72	24.88
	3	13.04	14.23	15.43	16.64	17.88	19.12	20.39	21.67	22.96	24.28	25.61	26.95
	4	13.61	14.89	16.21	17.55	18.91	20.30	21.72	23.17	24.64	26.15	27.68	29.24
	5	14.20	15.60	17.03	18.51	20.02	21.57	23.17	24.80	26.47	28.19	29.95	31.76
	6	14.82	16.34	17.91	19.54	21.21	22.94	24.73	26.57	28.47	30.44	32.46	34.55
	7	15.48	17.13	18.85	20.64	22.49	24.42	26.42	28.50	30.66	32.90	35.23	37.65
	8	16.17	17.97	19.84	21.81	23.86	26.01	28.26	30.60	33.06	35.62	38.30	41.09
	10	17.41	19.46	21.64	23.93	26.35	28.91	31.61	34.46	37.47	40.64	43.99	47.52
	12	18.76	21.11	23.62	26.30	29.15	32.20	35.45	38.91	42.59	46.52	50.70	55.16
	15	20.84	23.66	26.72	30.03	33.60	37.46	41.63	46.13	50.99	56.24	61.90	68.01
50%	1	15.00	16.25	17.50	18.75	20.00	21.25	22.50	23.75	25.00	26.25	27.50	28.75
	2	15.68	17.05	18.43	19.82	21.22	22.62	24.04	25.47	26.91	28.35	29.81	31.28
	3	16.40	17.90	19.42	20.96	22.52	24.11	25.71	27.34	28.99	30.67	32.36	34.08
	4	17.16	18.80	20.48	22.19	23.93	25.71	27.53	29.39	31.28	33.21	35.19	37.20
	5	17.97	19.76	21.60	23.50	25.45	27.45	29.51	31.62	33.80	36.03	38.32	40.68
	6	18.82	20.78	22.81	24.91	27.09	29.34	31.66	34.07	36.56	39.14	41.81	44.56
	7	19.72	21.86	24.10	26.43	28.85	31.38	34.02	36.76	39.62	42.59	45.69	48.92
	8	20.68	23.02	25.48	28.06	30.77	33.61	36.59	39.72	42.99	46.43	50.03	53.81
	10	22.34	25.04	27.90	30.94	34.15	37.57	41.18	45.01	49.07	53.36	57.91	62.73
	12	24.16	27.27	30.60	34.17	37.99	42.09	46.47	51.17	56.19	61.57	67.33	73.49
	15	26.95	30.71	34.79	39.23	44.05	49.29	54.97	61.14	67.83	75.10	82.98	91.53
100%	1	30.00	32.50	35.00	37.50	40.00	42.50	45.00	47.50	50.00	52.50	55.00	57.50
	2	31.83	34.65	37.49	40.37	43.26	46.19	49.14	52.12	55.12	58.16	61.22	64.30
	3	33.79	36.97	40.21	43.51	46.87	50.29	53.77	57.31	60.92	64.59	68.33	72.13
	4	35.92	39.50	43.18	46.96	50.85	54.84	58.95	63.16	67.49	71.94	76.50	81.19
	5	38.21	42.24	46.42	50.76	55.26	59.93	64.76	69.78	74.97	80.35	85.92	91.69
	6	40.68	45.22	49.98	54.96	60.16	65.61	71.31	77.27	83.50	90.02	96.82	103.94
	7	43.36	48.47	53.88	59.59	65.61	71.98	78.70	85.79	93.27	101.17	109.49	118.27
	8	46.26	52.02	58.16	64.71	71.69	79.13	87.06	95.50	104.50	114.08	124.27	135.13
	10	50.89	57.71	65.08	73.04	81.62	90.89	100.89	111.68	123.31	135.86	149.39	163.97
	12	56.10	64.19	73.04	82.72	93.31	104.89	117.55	131.38	146.50	163.02	181.08	200.81
	15	63.85	73.92	85.12	97.58	111.43	126.82	143.93	162.95	184.09	207.59	233.70	262.74

Entry is rent increase, in cents per sf, at given time for each $10 per sf base rent

Actual Rent Increase from CPI Clause

Percent of CPI	Time	6.00%	6.25%	6.50%	6.75%	7.00%	7.25%	7.50%	7.75%	8.00%	8.25%	8.50%	9.00%
25%	1	15.00	15.63	16.25	16.87	17.50	18.12	18.75	19.37	20.00	20.62	21.25	22.50
	2	16.14	16.86	17.59	18.32	19.05	19.79	20.53	21.28	22.03	22.79	23.55	25.08
	3	17.38	18.21	19.05	19.91	20.77	21.64	22.52	23.41	24.31	25.22	26.14	28.00
	4	18.73	19.69	20.67	21.66	22.67	23.69	24.73	25.79	26.87	27.96	29.07	31.34
	5	20.21	21.31	22.44	23.60	24.77	25.98	27.21	28.46	29.75	31.06	32.39	35.16
	6	21.83	23.10	24.40	25.74	27.12	28.53	29.98	31.47	33.00	34.57	36.18	39.54
	7	23.60	25.06	26.57	28.12	29.73	31.38	33.10	34.86	36.69	38.57	40.51	44.59
	8	25.55	27.23	28.96	30.77	32.64	34.59	36.61	38.70	40.88	43.14	45.48	50.43
	10	29.36	31.47	33.68	36.00	38.42	40.96	43.62	46.40	49.32	52.36	55.55	62.39
	12	33.82	36.48	39.30	42.27	45.41	48.72	52.22	55.92	59.82	63.94	68.30	77.74
	15	41.43	45.09	49.01	53.20	57.67	62.46	67.57	73.03	78.87	85.11	91.78	106.53
30%	1	18.00	18.75	19.50	20.25	21.00	21.75	22.50	23.25	24.00	24.75	25.50	27.00
	2	19.42	20.30	21.17	22.05	22.94	23.83	24.73	25.63	26.54	27.45	28.37	30.22
	3	20.98	21.99	23.02	24.05	25.10	26.16	27.23	28.31	29.41	30.52	31.64	33.91
	4	22.69	23.86	25.06	26.27	27.50	28.76	30.03	31.33	32.65	33.99	35.36	38.15
	5	24.57	25.92	27.31	28.73	30.18	31.67	33.19	34.74	36.33	37.95	39.61	43.04
	6	26.63	28.20	29.82	31.48	33.19	34.94	36.75	38.61	40.52	42.48	44.50	48.70
	7	28.91	30.73	32.60	34.55	36.56	38.63	40.78	43.00	45.30	47.67	50.13	55.29
	8	31.43	33.53	35.71	37.98	40.35	42.81	45.36	48.02	50.79	53.66	56.65	63.00
	10	36.27	38.93	41.73	44.67	47.75	50.98	54.38	57.94	61.67	65.59	69.70	78.54
	12	41.99	45.38	48.96	52.76	56.78	61.04	65.55	70.33	75.39	80.75	86.42	98.78
	15	51.72	56.41	61.45	66.84	72.63	78.84	85.49	92.63	100.28	108.49	117.29	136.84
33.3%	1	20.00	20.83	21.67	22.50	23.33	24.17	25.00	25.83	26.67	27.50	28.33	30.00
	2	21.62	22.60	23.57	24.56	25.55	26.55	27.55	28.55	29.57	30.59	31.61	33.68
	3	23.41	24.54	25.69	26.85	28.02	29.21	30.41	31.62	32.85	34.10	35.35	37.91
	4	25.37	26.69	28.03	29.39	30.78	32.20	33.63	35.10	36.59	38.10	39.64	42.80
	5	27.53	29.06	30.63	32.24	33.88	35.56	37.28	39.04	40.84	42.68	44.56	48.46
	6	29.92	31.70	33.53	35.42	37.36	39.36	41.41	43.53	45.71	47.95	50.25	55.06
	7	32.56	34.63	36.77	38.99	41.28	43.66	46.12	48.66	51.30	54.02	56.85	62.79
	8	35.50	37.90	40.40	43.01	45.72	48.55	51.49	54.55	57.75	61.07	64.53	71.88
	10	41.09	44.15	47.37	50.75	54.30	58.04	61.97	66.10	70.43	74.99	79.77	90.08
	12	47.72	51.63	55.77	60.17	64.84	69.79	75.05	80.62	86.53	92.80	99.46	114.00
	15	59.00	64.44	70.29	76.58	83.33	90.59	98.39	106.77	115.78	125.46	135.87	159.07
35%	1	21.00	21.88	22.75	23.62	24.50	25.37	26.25	27.12	28.00	28.87	29.75	31.50
	2	22.73	23.75	24.78	25.82	26.86	27.91	28.96	30.02	31.09	32.16	33.24	35.42
	3	24.63	25.82	27.03	28.25	29.49	30.74	32.01	33.29	34.59	35.90	37.23	39.93
	4	26.72	28.11	29.53	30.97	32.44	33.93	35.45	37.00	38.58	40.18	41.81	45.15
	5	29.03	30.65	32.31	34.01	35.75	37.53	39.36	41.22	43.13	45.09	47.08	51.22
	6	31.59	33.48	35.42	37.42	39.48	41.61	43.79	46.04	48.36	50.74	53.19	58.32
	7	34.43	36.62	38.90	41.26	43.70	46.23	48.85	51.56	54.37	57.28	60.30	66.65
	8	37.58	40.14	42.80	45.58	48.48	51.50	54.64	57.92	61.33	64.89	68.60	76.48
	10	43.56	46.83	50.26	53.88	57.69	61.69	65.89	70.32	74.97	79.86	85.01	96.10
	12	50.68	54.86	59.30	64.01	69.02	74.34	79.98	85.98	92.34	99.10	106.28	121.99
	15	62.76	68.60	74.89	81.64	88.91	96.73	105.14	114.19	123.92	134.39	145.65	170.82
40%	1	24.00	25.00	26.00	27.00	28.00	29.00	30.00	31.00	32.00	33.00	34.00	36.00
	2	26.05	27.23	28.41	29.60	30.80	32.00	33.22	34.44	35.67	36.90	38.14	40.65
	3	28.32	29.70	31.09	32.51	33.94	35.39	36.86	38.35	39.85	41.37	42.91	46.05
	4	30.82	32.44	34.09	35.77	37.48	39.22	41.00	42.81	44.64	46.52	48.42	52.34
	5	33.61	35.50	37.45	39.44	41.48	43.57	45.72	47.91	50.16	52.46	54.82	59.71
	6	36.70	38.93	41.22	43.58	46.01	48.53	51.11	53.78	56.53	59.36	62.29	68.39
	7	40.16	42.76	45.46	48.26	51.17	54.19	57.31	60.56	63.92	67.41	71.03	78.68
	8	44.01	47.06	50.25	53.58	57.05	60.68	64.47	68.42	72.54	76.85	81.35	90.94
	10	51.24	55.16	59.30	63.66	68.26	73.10	78.21	83.59	89.26	95.23	101.53	115.15
	12	59.91	64.96	70.34	76.07	82.17	88.66	95.57	102.93	110.77	119.11	127.99	147.51
	15	74.60	81.71	89.38	97.66	106.59	116.23	126.62	137.84	149.95	163.01	177.11	208.78
50%	1	30.00	31.25	32.50	33.75	35.00	36.25	37.50	38.75	40.00	41.25	42.50	45.00
	2	32.75	34.24	35.74	37.24	38.76	40.29	41.82	43.37	44.93	46.50	48.07	51.26
	3	35.82	37.59	39.38	41.19	43.03	44.89	46.77	48.68	50.62	52.58	54.56	58.61
	4	39.25	41.35	43.48	45.66	47.88	50.15	52.46	54.82	57.22	59.67	62.16	67.30
	5	43.09	45.58	48.13	50.75	53.43	56.19	59.02	61.93	64.91	67.97	71.11	77.63
	6	47.41	50.36	53.40	56.54	59.80	63.16	66.63	70.21	73.92	77.74	81.70	90.00
	7	52.27	55.77	59.40	63.19	67.12	71.22	75.48	79.91	84.52	89.32	94.31	104.89
	8	57.77	61.92	66.26	70.82	75.59	80.60	85.84	91.33	97.08	103.10	109.42	122.96
	10	67.83	73.24	78.95	85.01	91.41	98.19	105.37	112.96	121.00	129.50	138.50	158.10
	12	80.08	87.13	94.68	102.75	111.39	120.63	130.52	141.10	152.41	164.52	177.48	206.20
	15	100.81	110.88	121.80	133.65	146.51	160.47	175.61	192.05	209.90	229.29	250.33	298.04
100%	1	60.00	62.50	65.00	67.50	70.00	72.50	75.00	77.50	80.00	82.50	85.00	90.00
	2	67.42	70.56	73.72	76.92	80.14	83.39	86.67	89.98	93.31	96.67	100.06	106.93
	3	76.01	79.94	83.95	88.03	92.18	96.39	100.68	105.05	109.48	114.00	118.58	127.99
	4	86.00	90.93	96.00	101.20	106.53	112.00	117.62	123.37	129.28	135.33	141.54	154.42
	5	97.67	103.86	110.27	116.90	123.76	130.87	138.22	145.82	153.69	161.82	170.24	187.94
	6	111.37	119.14	127.26	135.73	144.58	153.82	163.47	173.54	184.05	195.02	206.47	230.88
	7	127.54	137.30	147.60	158.45	169.89	181.94	194.65	208.02	222.14	237.00	252.65	286.51
	8	146.69	159.00	172.10	186.04	200.88	216.67	233.47	251.34	270.37	290.61	312.14	359.43
	10	179.70	196.65	214.92	234.61	255.84	278.71	303.37	329.95	358.59	389.47	422.75	497.29
	12	222.37	245.94	271.69	299.84	330.60	364.23	400.99	441.19	485.15	533.23	585.82	706.33
	15	295.02	330.91	370.84	415.25	464.67	519.60	580.93	649.15	725.15	809.85	904.29	1127.15

Entry is rent increase, in cents per sf, at given time for each $10 per sf base rent

Actual Rent Increase from Fixed Percent Increase Clause

Increase Every	Time	Fixed Rate of Rent Increase												
		0.50%	0.75%	1.00%	1.25%	1.50%	1.75%	2.00%	2.25%	2.50%	2.75%	3.00%	3.25%	3.50%
Year	1	5.00	7.50	10.00	12.50	15.00	17.50	20.00	22.50	25.00	27.50	30.00	32.50	35.00
	2	5.03	7.56	10.10	12.66	15.22	17.81	20.40	23.01	25.62	28.26	30.90	33.56	36.22
	3	5.05	7.61	10.20	12.81	15.45	18.12	20.81	23.52	26.27	29.03	31.83	34.65	37.49
	4	5.08	7.67	10.30	12.97	15.69	18.44	21.22	24.05	26.92	29.83	32.78	35.77	38.81
	5	5.10	7.73	10.41	13.14	15.92	18.76	21.65	24.59	27.60	30.65	33.77	36.94	40.16
	6	5.13	7.79	10.51	13.30	16.16	19.09	22.08	25.15	28.29	31.49	34.78	38.14	41.57
	7	5.15	7.84	10.62	13.47	16.40	19.42	22.52	25.71	28.99	32.36	35.82	39.38	43.02
	8	5.18	7.90	10.72	13.64	16.65	19.76	22.97	26.29	29.72	33.25	36.90	40.66	44.53
	9	5.20	7.96	10.83	13.81	16.90	20.11	23.43	26.88	30.46	34.17	38.00	41.98	46.09
	10	5.23	8.02	10.94	13.98	17.15	20.46	23.90	27.49	31.22	35.11	39.14	43.34	47.70
	11	5.26	8.08	11.05	14.15	17.41	20.82	24.38	28.11	32.00	36.07	40.32	44.75	49.37
	12	5.28	8.14	11.16	14.33	17.67	21.18	24.87	28.74	32.80	37.06	41.53	46.20	51.10
	13	5.31	8.20	11.27	14.51	17.93	21.55	25.36	29.39	33.62	38.08	42.77	47.70	52.89
	14	5.33	8.27	11.38	14.69	18.20	21.93	25.87	30.05	34.46	39.13	44.06	49.26	54.74
	15	5.36	8.33	11.49	14.87	18.48	22.31	26.39	30.72	35.32	40.20	45.38	50.86	56.65
	16	5.39	8.39	11.61	15.06	18.75	22.70	26.92	31.41	36.21	41.31	46.74	52.51	58.64
	17	5.42	8.45	11.73	15.25	19.03	23.10	27.46	32.12	37.11	42.45	48.14	54.22	60.69
	18	5.44	8.52	11.84	15.44	19.32	23.50	28.00	32.84	38.04	43.61	49.59	55.98	62.81
	19	5.47	8.58	11.96	15.63	19.61	23.91	28.56	33.58	38.99	44.81	51.07	57.80	65.01
	20	5.50	8.64	12.08	15.83	19.90	24.33	29.14	34.34	39.97	46.05	52.61	59.68	67.29
2 Years	2	5.00	7.50	10.00	12.50	15.00	17.50	20.00	22.50	25.00	27.50	30.00	32.50	35.00
	4	5.03	7.56	10.10	12.66	15.22	17.81	20.40	23.01	25.62	28.26	30.90	33.56	36.22
	6	5.05	7.61	10.20	12.81	15.45	18.12	20.81	23.52	26.27	29.03	31.83	34.65	37.49
	8	5.08	7.67	10.30	12.97	15.69	18.44	21.22	24.05	26.92	29.83	32.78	35.77	38.81
	10	5.10	7.73	10.41	13.14	15.92	18.76	21.65	24.59	27.60	30.65	33.77	36.94	40.16
	12	5.13	7.79	10.51	13.30	16.16	19.09	22.08	25.15	28.29	31.49	34.78	38.14	41.57
	14	5.15	7.84	10.62	13.47	16.40	19.42	22.52	25.71	28.99	32.36	35.82	39.38	43.02
	16	5.18	7.90	10.72	13.64	16.65	19.76	22.97	26.29	29.72	33.25	36.90	40.66	44.53
	18	5.20	7.96	10.83	13.81	16.90	20.11	23.43	26.88	30.46	34.17	38.00	41.98	46.09
	20	5.23	8.02	10.94	13.98	17.15	20.46	23.90	27.49	31.22	35.11	39.14	43.34	47.70
3 Years	3	5.00	7.50	10.00	12.50	15.00	17.50	20.00	22.50	25.00	27.50	30.00	32.50	35.00
	6	5.03	7.56	10.10	12.66	15.22	17.81	20.40	23.01	25.62	28.26	30.90	33.56	36.22
	9	5.05	7.61	10.20	12.81	15.45	18.12	20.81	23.52	26.27	29.03	31.83	34.65	37.49
	12	5.08	7.67	10.30	12.97	15.69	18.44	21.22	24.05	26.92	29.83	32.78	35.77	38.81
	15	5.10	7.73	10.41	13.14	15.92	18.76	21.65	24.59	27.60	30.65	33.77	36.94	40.16
	18	5.13	7.79	10.51	13.30	16.16	19.09	22.08	25.15	28.29	31.49	34.78	38.14	41.57
	21	5.15	7.84	10.62	13.47	16.40	19.42	22.52	25.71	28.99	32.36	35.82	39.38	43.02
4 Years	4	5.00	7.50	10.00	12.50	15.00	17.50	20.00	22.50	25.00	27.50	30.00	32.50	35.00
	8	5.03	7.56	10.10	12.66	15.22	17.81	20.40	23.01	25.62	28.26	30.90	33.56	36.22
	12	5.05	7.61	10.20	12.81	15.45	18.12	20.81	23.52	26.27	29.03	31.83	34.65	37.49
	16	5.08	7.67	10.30	12.97	15.69	18.44	21.22	24.05	26.92	29.83	32.78	35.77	38.81
	20	5.10	7.73	10.41	13.14	15.92	18.76	21.65	24.59	27.60	30.65	33.77	36.94	40.16
5 Years	5	5.00	7.50	10.00	12.50	15.00	17.50	20.00	22.50	25.00	27.50	30.00	32.50	35.00
	10	5.03	7.56	10.10	12.66	15.22	17.81	20.40	23.01	25.62	28.26	30.90	33.56	36.22
	15	5.05	7.61	10.20	12.81	15.45	18.12	20.81	23.52	26.27	29.03	31.83	34.65	37.49
	20	5.08	7.67	10.30	12.97	15.69	18.44	21.22	24.05	26.92	29.83	32.78	35.77	38.81
10 Years	10	5.00	7.50	10.00	12.50	15.00	17.50	20.00	22.50	25.00	27.50	30.00	32.50	35.00
	20	5.03	7.56	10.10	12.66	15.22	17.81	20.40	23.01	25.62	28.26	30.90	33.56	36.22

Entry is rent increase, in cents per s.f, at given time for each $10 per sf base rent

Actual Rent Increase from Fixed Percent Increase Clause

Increase Every	Time					Fixed Rate of Rent Increase								
		3.75%	4.00%	4.25%	4.50%	4.75%	5.00%	5.50%	6.00%	6.50%	7.00%	7.50%	8.00%	8.50%
	1	37.50	40.00	42.50	45.00	47.50	50.00	55.00	60.00	65.00	70.00	75.00	80.00	85.00
	2	38.91	41.60	44.31	47.02	49.76	52.50	58.02	63.60	69.23	74.90	80.63	86.40	92.23
	3	40.37	43.26	46.19	49.14	52.12	55.12	61.22	67.42	73.72	80.14	86.67	93.31	100.06
	4	41.88	44.99	48.15	51.35	54.60	57.88	64.58	71.46	78.52	85.75	93.17	100.78	108.57
	5	43.45	46.79	50.20	53.66	57.19	60.78	68.14	75.75	83.62	91.76	100.16	108.84	117.80
	6	45.08	48.67	52.33	56.08	59.91	63.81	71.88	80.29	89.06	98.18	107.67	117.55	127.81
	7	46.77	50.61	54.56	58.60	62.75	67.00	75.84	85.11	94.84	105.05	115.75	126.95	138.67
	8	48.52	52.64	56.87	61.24	65.73	70.35	80.01	90.22	101.01	112.40	124.43	137.11	150.46
Year	9	50.34	54.74	59.29	63.99	68.85	73.87	84.41	95.63	107.57	120.27	133.76	148.07	163.25
	10	52.23	56.93	61.81	66.87	72.12	77.57	89.05	101.37	114.57	128.69	143.79	159.92	177.13
	11	54.19	59.21	64.44	69.88	75.55	81.44	93.95	107.45	122.01	137.70	154.58	172.71	192.18
	12	56.22	61.58	67.18	73.03	79.14	85.52	99.11	113.90	129.94	147.34	166.17	186.53	208.52
	13	58.33	64.04	70.03	76.31	82.90	89.79	104.57	120.73	138.39	157.65	178.63	201.45	226.24
	14	60.52	66.60	73.01	79.75	86.84	94.28	110.32	127.98	147.39	168.69	192.03	217.57	245.47
	15	62.79	69.27	76.11	83.34	90.96	99.00	116.38	135.65	156.97	180.50	206.43	234.98	266.34
	16	65.14	72.04	79.35	87.09	95.28	103.95	122.79	143.79	167.17	193.13	221.92	253.77	288.98
	17	67.58	74.92	82.72	91.01	99.81	109.14	129.54	152.42	178.04	206.65	238.56	274.08	313.54
	18	70.12	77.92	86.23	95.10	104.55	114.60	136.66	161.57	189.61	221.12	256.45	296.00	340.19
	19	72.75	81.03	89.90	99.38	109.51	120.33	144.18	171.26	201.93	236.60	275.69	319.68	369.11
	20	75.48	84.27	93.72	103.85	114.72	126.35	152.11	181.54	215.06	253.16	296.36	345.26	400.48
	2	37.50	40.00	42.50	45.00	47.50	50.00	55.00	60.00	65.00	70.00	75.00	80.00	85.00
	4	38.91	41.60	44.31	47.02	49.76	52.50	58.02	63.60	69.23	74.90	80.63	86.40	92.23
	6	40.37	43.26	46.19	49.14	52.12	55.12	61.22	67.42	73.72	80.14	86.67	93.31	100.06
2	8	41.88	44.99	48.15	51.35	54.60	57.88	64.58	71.46	78.52	85.75	93.17	100.78	108.57
Years	10	43.45	46.79	50.20	53.66	57.19	60.78	68.14	75.75	83.62	91.76	100.16	108.84	117.80
	12	45.08	48.67	52.33	56.08	59.91	63.81	71.88	80.29	89.06	98.18	107.67	117.55	127.81
	14	46.77	50.61	54.56	58.60	62.75	67.00	75.84	85.11	94.84	105.05	115.75	126.95	138.67
	16	48.52	52.64	56.87	61.24	65.73	70.35	80.01	90.22	101.01	112.40	124.43	137.11	150.46
	18	50.34	54.74	59.29	63.99	68.85	73.87	84.41	95.63	107.57	120.27	133.76	148.07	163.25
	20	52.23	56.93	61.81	66.87	72.12	77.57	89.05	101.37	114.57	128.69	143.79	159.92	177.13
	3	37.50	40.00	42.50	45.00	47.50	50.00	55.00	60.00	65.00	70.00	75.00	80.00	85.00
	6	38.91	41.60	44.31	47.02	49.76	52.50	58.02	63.60	69.23	74.90	80.63	86.40	92.23
3	9	40.37	43.26	46.19	49.14	52.12	55.12	61.22	67.42	73.72	80.14	86.67	93.31	100.06
Years	12	41.88	44.99	48.15	51.35	54.60	57.88	64.58	71.46	78.52	85.75	93.17	100.78	108.57
	15	43.45	46.79	50.20	53.66	57.19	60.78	68.14	75.75	83.62	91.76	100.16	108.84	117.80
	18	45.08	48.67	52.33	56.08	59.91	63.81	71.88	80.29	89.06	98.18	107.67	117.55	127.81
	21	46.77	50.61	54.56	58.60	62.75	67.00	75.84	85.11	94.84	105.05	115.75	126.95	138.67
	4	37.50	40.00	42.50	45.00	47.50	50.00	55.00	60.00	65.00	70.00	75.00	80.00	85.00
4	8	38.91	41.60	44.31	47.02	49.76	52.50	58.02	63.60	69.23	74.90	80.63	86.40	92.23
Years	12	40.37	43.26	46.19	49.14	52.12	55.12	61.22	67.42	73.72	80.14	86.67	93.31	100.06
	16	41.88	44.99	48.15	51.35	54.60	57.88	64.58	71.46	78.52	85.75	93.17	100.78	108.57
	20	43.45	46.79	50.20	53.66	57.19	60.78	68.14	75.75	83.62	91.76	100.16	108.84	117.80
	5	37.50	40.00	42.50	45.00	47.50	50.00	55.00	60.00	65.00	70.00	75.00	80.00	85.00
5	10	38.91	41.60	44.31	47.02	49.76	52.50	58.02	63.60	69.23	74.90	80.63	86.40	92.23
Years	15	40.37	43.26	46.19	49.14	52.12	55.12	61.22	67.42	73.72	80.14	86.67	93.31	100.06
	20	41.88	44.99	48.15	51.35	54.60	57.88	64.58	71.46	78.52	85.75	93.17	100.78	108.57
10	10	37.50	40.00	42.50	45.00	47.50	50.00	55.00	60.00	65.00	70.00	75.00	80.00	85.00
Years	20	38.91	41.60	44.31	47.02	49.76	52.50	58.02	63.60	69.23	74.90	80.63	86.40	92.23

Entry is rent increase, in cents per s.f, at given time for each $10 per sf base rent

Cash Cost of Vacancy
Annual Rent per Square Foot

Time Vacant	$ 2.50	2.75	3.00	3.25	3.50	3.75	4.00	4.25	4.50	4.75	5.00	5.25	5.50	5.75	6.00
1 Day	0.007	0.008	0.008	0.009	0.010	0.010	0.011	0.012	0.013	0.013	0.014	0.015	0.015	0.016	0.017
2 Days	0.014	0.015	0.017	0.018	0.019	0.021	0.022	0.024	0.025	0.026	0.028	0.029	0.031	0.032	0.033
3	0.021	0.023	0.025	0.027	0.029	0.031	0.033	0.035	0.038	0.040	0.042	0.044	0.046	0.048	0.050
4	0.028	0.031	0.033	0.036	0.039	0.042	0.044	0.047	0.050	0.053	0.056	0.058	0.061	0.064	0.067
5	0.035	0.038	0.042	0.045	0.049	0.052	0.056	0.059	0.063	0.066	0.069	0.073	0.076	0.080	0.083
6	0.042	0.046	0.050	0.054	0.058	0.063	0.067	0.071	0.075	0.079	0.083	0.088	0.092	0.096	0.100
7	0.049	0.053	0.058	0.063	0.068	0.073	0.078	0.083	0.088	0.092	0.097	0.102	0.107	0.112	0.117
8	0.056	0.061	0.067	0.072	0.078	0.083	0.089	0.094	0.100	0.106	0.111	0.117	0.122	0.128	0.133
9	0.063	0.069	0.075	0.081	0.088	0.094	0.100	0.106	0.113	0.119	0.125	0.131	0.138	0.144	0.150
10	0.069	0.076	0.083	0.090	0.097	0.104	0.111	0.118	0.125	0.132	0.139	0.146	0.153	0.160	0.167
11	0.076	0.084	0.092	0.099	0.107	0.115	0.122	0.130	0.138	0.145	0.153	0.160	0.168	0.176	0.183
12	0.083	0.092	0.100	0.108	0.117	0.125	0.133	0.142	0.150	0.158	0.167	0.175	0.183	0.192	0.200
13	0.090	0.099	0.108	0.117	0.126	0.135	0.144	0.153	0.163	0.172	0.181	0.190	0.199	0.208	0.217
14	0.097	0.107	0.117	0.126	0.136	0.146	0.156	0.165	0.175	0.185	0.194	0.204	0.214	0.224	0.233
15 Days	0.104	0.115	0.125	0.135	0.146	0.156	0.167	0.177	0.188	0.198	0.208	0.219	0.229	0.240	0.250
16	0.111	0.122	0.133	0.144	0.156	0.167	0.178	0.189	0.200	0.211	0.222	0.233	0.244	0.256	0.267
17	0.118	0.130	0.142	0.153	0.165	0.177	0.189	0.201	0.213	0.224	0.236	0.248	0.260	0.272	0.283
18	0.125	0.138	0.150	0.163	0.175	0.188	0.200	0.213	0.225	0.238	0.250	0.263	0.275	0.288	0.300
19	0.132	0.145	0.158	0.172	0.185	0.198	0.211	0.224	0.238	0.251	0.264	0.277	0.290	0.303	0.317
20	0.139	0.153	0.167	0.181	0.194	0.208	0.222	0.236	0.250	0.264	0.278	0.292	0.306	0.319	0.333
21	0.146	0.160	0.175	0.190	0.204	0.219	0.233	0.248	0.263	0.277	0.292	0.306	0.321	0.335	0.350
22	0.153	0.168	0.183	0.199	0.214	0.229	0.244	0.260	0.275	0.290	0.306	0.321	0.336	0.351	0.367
23	0.160	0.176	0.192	0.208	0.224	0.240	0.256	0.272	0.288	0.303	0.319	0.335	0.351	0.367	0.383
24	0.167	0.183	0.200	0.217	0.233	0.250	0.267	0.283	0.300	0.317	0.333	0.350	0.367	0.383	0.400
25	0.174	0.191	0.208	0.226	0.243	0.260	0.278	0.295	0.313	0.330	0.347	0.365	0.382	0.399	0.417
26	0.181	0.199	0.217	0.235	0.253	0.271	0.289	0.307	0.325	0.343	0.361	0.379	0.397	0.415	0.433
27	0.188	0.206	0.225	0.244	0.263	0.281	0.300	0.319	0.338	0.356	0.375	0.394	0.413	0.431	0.450
28	0.194	0.214	0.233	0.253	0.272	0.292	0.311	0.331	0.350	0.369	0.389	0.408	0.428	0.447	0.467
29	0.201	0.222	0.242	0.262	0.282	0.302	0.322	0.342	0.363	0.383	0.403	0.423	0.443	0.463	0.483
30	0.208	0.229	0.250	0.271	0.292	0.313	0.333	0.354	0.375	0.396	0.417	0.438	0.458	0.479	0.500
31 Days	0.215	0.237	0.258	0.280	0.301	0.323	0.344	0.366	0.388	0.409	0.431	0.452	0.474	0.495	0.517
2 Months	0.417	0.458	0.500	0.542	0.583	0.625	0.667	0.708	0.750	0.792	0.833	0.875	0.917	0.958	1.000
3	0.625	0.688	0.750	0.813	0.875	0.938	1.000	1.063	1.125	1.188	1.250	1.313	1.375	1.438	1.500
4	0.833	0.917	1.000	1.083	1.167	1.250	1.333	1.417	1.500	1.583	1.667	1.750	1.833	1.917	2.000
5	1.042	1.146	1.250	1.354	1.458	1.563	1.667	1.771	1.875	1.979	2.083	2.188	2.292	2.396	2.500
6	1.250	1.375	1.500	1.625	1.750	1.875	2.000	2.125	2.250	2.375	2.500	2.625	2.750	2.875	3.000
7 Months	1.458	1.604	1.750	1.896	2.042	2.188	2.333	2.479	2.625	2.771	2.917	3.063	3.208	3.354	3.500
8	1.667	1.833	2.000	2.167	2.333	2.500	2.667	2.833	3.000	3.167	3.333	3.500	3.667	3.833	4.000
9	1.875	2.063	2.250	2.438	2.625	2.813	3.000	3.188	3.375	3.563	3.750	3.938	4.125	4.313	4.500
10	2.083	2.292	2.500	2.708	2.917	3.125	3.333	3.542	3.750	3.958	4.167	4.375	4.583	4.792	5.000
11	2.292	2.521	2.750	2.979	3.208	3.437	3.667	3.896	4.125	4.354	4.583	4.813	5.042	5.271	5.500
12 Months	2.500	2.750	3.000	3.250	3.500	3.750	4.000	4.250	4.500	4.750	5.000	5.250	5.500	5.750	6.000

Annual Rent per Square Foot

Time Vacant	$ 6.25	6.50	6.75	7.00	7.25	7.50	7.75	8.00	8.25	8.50	8.75	9.00	9.25	9.50	9.75
1 Day	0.017	0.018	0.019	0.019	0.020	0.021	0.022	0.022	0.023	0.024	0.024	0.025	0.026	0.026	0.027
2 Days	0.035	0.036	0.038	0.039	0.040	0.042	0.043	0.044	0.046	0.047	0.049	0.050	0.051	0.053	0.054
3	0.052	0.054	0.056	0.058	0.060	0.063	0.065	0.067	0.069	0.071	0.073	0.075	0.077	0.079	0.081
4	0.069	0.072	0.075	0.078	0.081	0.083	0.086	0.089	0.092	0.094	0.097	0.100	0.103	0.106	0.108
5	0.087	0.090	0.094	0.097	0.101	0.104	0.108	0.111	0.115	0.118	0.122	0.125	0.128	0.132	0.135
6	0.104	0.108	0.113	0.117	0.121	0.125	0.129	0.133	0.138	0.142	0.146	0.150	0.154	0.158	0.163
7	0.122	0.126	0.131	0.136	0.141	0.146	0.151	0.156	0.160	0.165	0.170	0.175	0.180	0.185	0.190
8	0.139	0.144	0.150	0.156	0.161	0.167	0.172	0.178	0.183	0.189	0.194	0.200	0.206	0.211	0.217
9	0.156	0.163	0.169	0.175	0.181	0.188	0.194	0.200	0.206	0.213	0.219	0.225	0.231	0.238	0.244
10	0.174	0.181	0.188	0.194	0.201	0.208	0.215	0.222	0.229	0.236	0.243	0.250	0.257	0.264	0.271
11	0.191	0.199	0.206	0.214	0.222	0.229	0.237	0.244	0.252	0.260	0.267	0.275	0.283	0.290	0.298
12	0.208	0.217	0.225	0.233	0.242	0.250	0.258	0.267	0.275	0.283	0.292	0.300	0.308	0.317	0.325
13	0.226	0.235	0.244	0.253	0.262	0.271	0.280	0.289	0.298	0.307	0.316	0.325	0.334	0.343	0.352
14	0.243	0.253	0.263	0.272	0.282	0.292	0.301	0.311	0.321	0.331	0.340	0.350	0.360	0.369	0.379
15 Days	0.260	0.271	0.281	0.292	0.302	0.313	0.323	0.333	0.344	0.354	0.365	0.375	0.385	0.396	0.406
16	0.278	0.289	0.300	0.311	0.322	0.333	0.344	0.356	0.367	0.378	0.389	0.400	0.411	0.422	0.433
17	0.295	0.307	0.319	0.331	0.342	0.354	0.366	0.378	0.390	0.401	0.413	0.425	0.437	0.449	0.460
18	0.313	0.325	0.338	0.350	0.363	0.375	0.388	0.400	0.413	0.425	0.438	0.450	0.463	0.475	0.488
19	0.330	0.343	0.356	0.369	0.383	0.396	0.409	0.422	0.435	0.449	0.462	0.475	0.488	0.501	0.515
20	0.347	0.361	0.375	0.389	0.403	0.417	0.431	0.444	0.458	0.472	0.486	0.500	0.514	0.528	0.542
21	0.365	0.379	0.394	0.408	0.423	0.438	0.452	0.467	0.481	0.496	0.510	0.525	0.540	0.554	0.569
22	0.382	0.397	0.413	0.428	0.443	0.458	0.474	0.489	0.504	0.519	0.535	0.550	0.565	0.581	0.596
23	0.399	0.415	0.431	0.447	0.463	0.479	0.495	0.511	0.527	0.543	0.559	0.575	0.591	0.607	0.623
24	0.417	0.433	0.450	0.467	0.483	0.500	0.517	0.533	0.550	0.567	0.583	0.600	0.617	0.633	0.650
25	0.434	0.451	0.469	0.486	0.503	0.521	0.538	0.556	0.573	0.590	0.608	0.625	0.642	0.660	0.677
26	0.451	0.469	0.488	0.506	0.524	0.542	0.560	0.578	0.596	0.614	0.632	0.650	0.668	0.686	0.704
27	0.469	0.488	0.506	0.525	0.544	0.563	0.581	0.600	0.619	0.638	0.656	0.675	0.694	0.713	0.731
28	0.486	0.506	0.525	0.544	0.564	0.583	0.603	0.622	0.642	0.661	0.681	0.700	0.719	0.739	0.758
29	0.503	0.524	0.544	0.564	0.584	0.604	0.624	0.644	0.665	0.685	0.705	0.725	0.745	0.765	0.785
30	0.521	0.542	0.563	0.583	0.604	0.625	0.646	0.667	0.688	0.708	0.729	0.750	0.771	0.792	0.813
31 Days	0.538	0.560	0.581	0.603	0.624	0.646	0.667	0.689	0.710	0.732	0.753	0.775	0.797	0.818	0.840
2 Months	1.042	1.083	1.125	1.167	1.208	1.250	1.292	1.333	1.375	1.417	1.458	1.500	1.542	1.583	1.625
3	1.563	1.625	1.688	1.750	1.813	1.875	1.938	2.000	2.063	2.125	2.188	2.250	2.313	2.375	2.438
4	2.083	2.167	2.250	2.333	2.417	2.500	2.583	2.667	2.750	2.833	2.917	3.000	3.083	3.167	3.250
5	2.604	2.708	2.813	2.917	3.021	3.125	3.229	3.333	3.438	3.542	3.646	3.750	3.854	3.958	4.063
6	3.125	3.250	3.375	3.500	3.625	3.750	3.875	4.000	4.125	4.250	4.375	4.500	4.625	4.750	4.875
7 Months	3.646	3.792	3.937	4.083	4.229	4.375	4.521	4.667	4.813	4.958	5.104	5.250	5.396	5.542	5.688
8	4.167	4.333	4.500	4.667	4.833	5.000	5.167	5.333	5.500	5.667	5.833	6.000	6.167	6.333	6.500
9	4.688	4.875	5.063	5.250	5.438	5.625	5.813	6.000	6.188	6.375	6.563	6.750	6.938	7.125	7.313
10	5.208	5.417	5.625	5.833	6.042	6.250	6.458	6.667	6.875	7.083	7.292	7.500	7.708	7.917	8.125
11	5.729	5.958	6.188	6.417	6.646	6.875	7.104	7.333	7.563	7.792	8.021	8.250	8.479	8.708	8.938
12 Months	6.250	6.500	6.750	7.000	7.250	7.500	7.750	8.000	8.250	8.500	8.750	9.000	9.250	9.500	9.750

Entry is lost rent in dollars and cents per square foot.

Cash Cost of Vacancy
Annual Rent per Square Foot

Time Vacant	$10.00	10.25	10.50	10.75	11.00	11.25	11.50	11.75	12.00	12.25	12.50	12.75	13.00	13.25	13.50
1 Day	0.028	0.028	0.029	0.030	0.031	0.031	0.032	0.033	0.033	0.034	0.035	0.035	0.036	0.037	0.038
2 Days	0.056	0.057	0.058	0.060	0.061	0.063	0.064	0.065	0.067	0.068	0.069	0.071	0.072	0.074	0.075
3	0.083	0.085	0.088	0.090	0.092	0.094	0.096	0.098	0.100	0.102	0.104	0.106	0.108	0.110	0.113
4	0.111	0.114	0.117	0.119	0.122	0.125	0.128	0.131	0.133	0.136	0.139	0.142	0.144	0.147	0.150
5	0.139	0.142	0.146	0.149	0.153	0.156	0.160	0.163	0.167	0.170	0.174	0.177	0.181	0.184	0.188
6	0.167	0.171	0.175	0.179	0.183	0.188	0.192	0.196	0.200	0.204	0.208	0.213	0.217	0.221	0.225
7	0.194	0.199	0.204	0.209	0.214	0.219	0.224	0.228	0.233	0.238	0.243	0.248	0.253	0.258	0.263
8	0.222	0.228	0.233	0.239	0.244	0.250	0.256	0.261	0.267	0.272	0.278	0.283	0.289	0.294	0.300
9	0.250	0.256	0.263	0.269	0.275	0.281	0.288	0.294	0.300	0.306	0.313	0.319	0.325	0.331	0.338
10	0.278	0.285	0.292	0.299	0.306	0.313	0.319	0.326	0.333	0.340	0.347	0.354	0.361	0.368	0.375
11	0.306	0.313	0.321	0.328	0.336	0.344	0.351	0.359	0.367	0.374	0.382	0.390	0.397	0.405	0.413
12	0.333	0.342	0.350	0.358	0.367	0.375	0.383	0.392	0.400	0.408	0.417	0.425	0.433	0.442	0.450
13	0.361	0.370	0.379	0.388	0.397	0.406	0.415	0.424	0.433	0.442	0.451	0.460	0.469	0.478	0.488
14	0.389	0.399	0.408	0.418	0.428	0.438	0.447	0.457	0.467	0.476	0.486	0.496	0.506	0.515	0.525
15 Days	0.417	0.427	0.438	0.448	0.458	0.469	0.479	0.490	0.500	0.510	0.521	0.531	0.542	0.552	0.563
16	0.444	0.456	0.467	0.478	0.489	0.500	0.511	0.522	0.533	0.544	0.556	0.567	0.578	0.589	0.600
17	0.472	0.484	0.496	0.508	0.519	0.531	0.543	0.555	0.567	0.578	0.590	0.602	0.614	0.626	0.638
18	0.500	0.513	0.525	0.538	0.550	0.563	0.575	0.588	0.600	0.613	0.625	0.638	0.650	0.663	0.675
19	0.528	0.541	0.554	0.567	0.581	0.594	0.607	0.620	0.633	0.647	0.660	0.673	0.686	0.699	0.713
20	0.556	0.569	0.583	0.597	0.611	0.625	0.639	0.653	0.667	0.681	0.694	0.708	0.722	0.736	0.750
21	0.583	0.598	0.613	0.627	0.642	0.656	0.671	0.685	0.700	0.715	0.729	0.744	0.758	0.773	0.788
22	0.611	0.626	0.642	0.657	0.672	0.688	0.703	0.718	0.733	0.749	0.764	0.779	0.794	0.810	0.825
23	0.639	0.655	0.671	0.687	0.703	0.719	0.735	0.751	0.767	0.783	0.799	0.815	0.831	0.847	0.863
24	0.667	0.683	0.700	0.717	0.733	0.750	0.767	0.783	0.800	0.817	0.833	0.850	0.867	0.883	0.900
25	0.694	0.712	0.729	0.747	0.764	0.781	0.799	0.816	0.833	0.851	0.868	0.885	0.903	0.920	0.938
26	0.722	0.740	0.758	0.776	0.794	0.813	0.831	0.849	0.867	0.885	0.903	0.921	0.939	0.957	0.975
27	0.750	0.769	0.788	0.806	0.825	0.844	0.863	0.881	0.900	0.919	0.938	0.956	0.975	0.994	1.013
28	0.778	0.797	0.817	0.836	0.856	0.875	0.894	0.914	0.933	0.953	0.972	0.992	1.011	1.031	1.050
29	0.806	0.826	0.846	0.866	0.886	0.906	0.926	0.947	0.967	0.987	1.007	1.027	1.047	1.067	1.088
30	0.833	0.854	0.875	0.896	0.917	0.938	0.958	0.979	1.000	1.021	1.042	1.063	1.083	1.104	1.125
31 Days	0.861	0.883	0.904	0.926	0.947	0.969	0.990	1.012	1.033	1.055	1.076	1.098	1.119	1.141	1.162
2 Months	1.667	1.708	1.750	1.792	1.833	1.875	1.917	1.958	2.000	2.042	2.083	2.125	2.167	2.208	2.250
3	2.500	2.563	2.625	2.688	2.750	2.813	2.875	2.938	3.000	3.063	3.125	3.188	3.250	3.313	3.375
4	3.333	3.417	3.500	3.583	3.667	3.750	3.833	3.917	4.000	4.083	4.167	4.250	4.333	4.417	4.500
5	4.167	4.271	4.375	4.479	4.583	4.688	4.792	4.896	5.000	5.104	5.208	5.313	5.417	5.521	5.625
6	5.000	5.125	5.250	5.375	5.500	5.625	5.750	5.875	6.000	6.125	6.250	6.375	6.500	6.625	6.750
7 Months	5.833	5.979	6.125	6.271	6.417	6.563	6.708	6.854	7.000	7.146	7.292	7.437	7.583	7.729	7.875
8	6.667	6.833	7.000	7.167	7.333	7.500	7.667	7.833	8.000	8.167	8.333	8.500	8.667	8.833	9.000
9	7.500	7.688	7.875	8.063	8.250	8.438	8.625	8.813	9.000	9.188	9.375	9.563	9.750	9.938	10.125
10	8.333	8.542	8.750	8.958	9.167	9.375	9.583	9.792	10.000	10.208	10.417	10.625	10.833	11.042	11.250
11	9.167	9.396	9.625	9.854	10.083	10.313	10.542	10.771	11.000	11.229	11.458	11.688	11.917	12.146	12.375
12 Months	10.000	10.250	10.500	10.750	11.000	11.250	11.500	11.750	12.000	12.250	12.500	12.750	13.000	13.250	13.500

Annual Rent per Square Foot

Time Vacant	$13.75	14.00	14.25	14.50	14.75	15.00	15.25	15.50	15.75	16.00	16.25	16.50	16.75	17.00	17.25
1 Day	0.038	0.039	0.040	0.040	0.041	0.042	0.042	0.043	0.044	0.044	0.045	0.046	0.047	0.047	0.048
2 Days	0.076	0.078	0.079	0.081	0.082	0.083	0.085	0.086	0.088	0.089	0.090	0.092	0.093	0.094	0.096
3	0.115	0.117	0.119	0.121	0.123	0.125	0.127	0.129	0.131	0.133	0.135	0.138	0.140	0.142	0.144
4	0.153	0.156	0.158	0.161	0.164	0.167	0.169	0.172	0.175	0.178	0.181	0.183	0.186	0.189	0.192
5	0.191	0.194	0.198	0.201	0.205	0.208	0.212	0.215	0.219	0.222	0.226	0.229	0.233	0.236	0.240
6	0.229	0.233	0.238	0.242	0.246	0.250	0.254	0.258	0.263	0.267	0.271	0.275	0.279	0.283	0.288
7	0.267	0.272	0.277	0.282	0.287	0.292	0.297	0.301	0.306	0.311	0.316	0.321	0.326	0.331	0.335
8	0.306	0.311	0.317	0.322	0.328	0.333	0.339	0.344	0.350	0.356	0.361	0.367	0.372	0.378	0.383
9	0.344	0.350	0.356	0.363	0.369	0.375	0.381	0.388	0.394	0.400	0.406	0.413	0.419	0.425	0.431
10	0.382	0.389	0.396	0.403	0.410	0.417	0.424	0.431	0.438	0.444	0.451	0.458	0.465	0.472	0.479
11	0.420	0.428	0.435	0.443	0.451	0.458	0.466	0.474	0.481	0.489	0.497	0.504	0.512	0.519	0.527
12	0.458	0.467	0.475	0.483	0.492	0.500	0.508	0.517	0.525	0.533	0.542	0.550	0.558	0.567	0.575
13	0.497	0.506	0.515	0.524	0.533	0.542	0.551	0.560	0.569	0.578	0.587	0.596	0.605	0.614	0.623
14	0.535	0.544	0.554	0.564	0.574	0.583	0.593	0.603	0.613	0.622	0.632	0.642	0.651	0.661	0.671
15 Days	0.573	0.583	0.594	0.604	0.615	0.625	0.635	0.646	0.656	0.667	0.677	0.688	0.698	0.708	0.719
16	0.611	0.622	0.633	0.644	0.656	0.667	0.678	0.689	0.700	0.711	0.722	0.733	0.744	0.756	0.767
17	0.649	0.661	0.673	0.685	0.697	0.708	0.720	0.732	0.744	0.756	0.767	0.779	0.791	0.803	0.815
18	0.688	0.700	0.713	0.725	0.738	0.750	0.763	0.775	0.788	0.800	0.813	0.825	0.838	0.850	0.863
19	0.726	0.739	0.752	0.765	0.778	0.792	0.805	0.818	0.831	0.844	0.858	0.871	0.884	0.897	0.910
20	0.764	0.778	0.792	0.806	0.819	0.833	0.847	0.861	0.875	0.889	0.903	0.917	0.931	0.944	0.958
21	0.802	0.817	0.831	0.846	0.860	0.875	0.890	0.904	0.919	0.933	0.948	0.963	0.977	0.992	1.006
22	0.840	0.856	0.871	0.886	0.901	0.917	0.932	0.947	0.963	0.978	0.993	1.008	1.024	1.039	1.054
23	0.878	0.894	0.910	0.926	0.942	0.958	0.974	0.990	1.006	1.022	1.038	1.054	1.070	1.086	1.102
24	0.917	0.933	0.950	0.967	0.983	1.000	1.017	1.033	1.050	1.067	1.083	1.100	1.117	1.133	1.150
25	0.955	0.972	0.990	1.007	1.024	1.042	1.059	1.076	1.094	1.111	1.128	1.146	1.163	1.181	1.198
26	0.993	1.011	1.029	1.047	1.065	1.083	1.101	1.119	1.138	1.156	1.174	1.192	1.210	1.228	1.246
27	1.031	1.050	1.069	1.088	1.106	1.125	1.144	1.163	1.181	1.200	1.219	1.238	1.256	1.275	1.294
28	1.069	1.089	1.108	1.128	1.147	1.167	1.186	1.206	1.225	1.244	1.264	1.283	1.303	1.322	1.342
29	1.108	1.128	1.148	1.168	1.188	1.208	1.228	1.249	1.269	1.289	1.309	1.329	1.349	1.369	1.390
30	1.146	1.167	1.188	1.208	1.229	1.250	1.271	1.292	1.313	1.333	1.354	1.375	1.396	1.417	1.438
31 Days	1.184	1.206	1.227	1.249	1.270	1.292	1.313	1.335	1.356	1.378	1.399	1.421	1.442	1.464	1.485
2 Months	2.292	2.333	2.375	2.417	2.458	2.500	2.542	2.583	2.625	2.667	2.708	2.750	2.792	2.833	2.875
3	3.438	3.500	3.563	3.625	3.688	3.750	3.813	3.875	3.938	4.000	4.063	4.125	4.188	4.250	4.313
4	4.583	4.667	4.750	4.833	4.917	5.000	5.083	5.167	5.250	5.333	5.417	5.500	5.583	5.667	5.750
5	5.729	5.833	5.938	6.042	6.146	6.250	6.354	6.458	6.563	6.667	6.771	6.875	6.979	7.083	7.188
6	6.875	7.000	7.125	7.250	7.375	7.500	7.625	7.750	7.875	8.000	8.125	8.250	8.375	8.500	8.625
7 Months	8.021	8.167	8.313	8.458	8.604	8.750	8.896	9.042	9.188	9.333	9.479	9.625	9.771	9.917	10.062
8	9.167	9.333	9.500	9.667	9.833	10.000	10.167	10.333	10.500	10.667	10.833	11.000	11.167	11.333	11.500
9	10.313	10.500	10.688	10.875	11.063	11.250	11.438	11.625	11.813	12.000	12.188	12.375	12.563	12.750	12.938
10	11.458	11.667	11.875	12.083	12.292	12.500	12.708	12.917	13.125	13.333	13.542	13.750	13.958	14.167	14.375
11	12.604	12.833	13.063	13.292	13.521	13.750	13.979	14.208	14.438	14.667	14.896	15.125	15.354	15.583	15.813
12 Months	13.750	14.000	14.250	14.500	14.750	15.000	15.250	15.500	15.750	16.000	16.250	16.500	16.750	17.000	17.250

Entry is lost rent in dollars and cents per square foot.

Cash Cost of Vacancy
Annual Rent per Square Foot

Time Vacant	$17.50	17.75	18.00	18.25	18.50	18.75	19.00	19.25	19.50	19.75	20.00	20.25	20.50	20.75	21.00
1 Day	0.049	0.049	0.050	0.051	0.051	0.052	0.053	0.053	0.054	0.055	0.056	0.056	0.057	0.058	0.058
2 Days	0.097	0.099	0.100	0.101	0.103	0.104	0.106	0.107	0.108	0.110	0.111	0.113	0.114	0.115	0.117
3	0.146	0.148	0.150	0.152	0.154	0.156	0.158	0.160	0.163	0.165	0.167	0.169	0.171	0.173	0.175
4	0.194	0.197	0.200	0.203	0.206	0.208	0.211	0.214	0.217	0.219	0.222	0.225	0.228	0.231	0.233
5	0.243	0.247	0.250	0.253	0.257	0.260	0.264	0.267	0.271	0.274	0.278	0.281	0.285	0.288	0.292
6	0.292	0.296	0.300	0.304	0.308	0.313	0.317	0.321	0.325	0.329	0.333	0.338	0.342	0.346	0.350
7	0.340	0.345	0.350	0.355	0.360	0.365	0.369	0.374	0.379	0.384	0.389	0.394	0.399	0.403	0.408
8	0.389	0.394	0.400	0.406	0.411	0.417	0.422	0.428	0.433	0.439	0.444	0.450	0.456	0.461	0.467
9	0.438	0.444	0.450	0.456	0.463	0.469	0.475	0.481	0.488	0.494	0.500	0.506	0.513	0.519	0.525
10	0.486	0.493	0.500	0.507	0.514	0.521	0.528	0.535	0.542	0.549	0.556	0.563	0.569	0.576	0.583
11	0.535	0.542	0.550	0.558	0.565	0.573	0.581	0.588	0.596	0.603	0.611	0.619	0.626	0.634	0.642
12	0.583	0.592	0.600	0.608	0.617	0.625	0.633	0.642	0.650	0.658	0.667	0.675	0.683	0.692	0.700
13	0.632	0.641	0.650	0.659	0.668	0.677	0.686	0.695	0.704	0.713	0.722	0.731	0.740	0.749	0.758
14	0.681	0.690	0.700	0.710	0.719	0.729	0.739	0.749	0.758	0.768	0.778	0.787	0.797	0.807	0.817
15 Days	0.729	0.740	0.750	0.760	0.771	0.781	0.792	0.802	0.813	0.823	0.833	0.844	0.854	0.865	0.875
16	0.778	0.789	0.800	0.811	0.822	0.833	0.844	0.856	0.867	0.878	0.889	0.900	0.911	0.922	0.933
17	0.826	0.838	0.850	0.862	0.874	0.885	0.897	0.909	0.921	0.933	0.944	0.956	0.968	0.980	0.992
18	0.875	0.888	0.900	0.913	0.925	0.938	0.950	0.963	0.975	0.988	1.000	1.013	1.025	1.038	1.050
19	0.924	0.937	0.950	0.963	0.976	0.990	1.003	1.016	1.029	1.042	1.056	1.069	1.082	1.095	1.108
20	0.972	0.986	1.000	1.014	1.028	1.042	1.056	1.069	1.083	1.097	1.111	1.125	1.139	1.153	1.167
21	1.021	1.035	1.050	1.065	1.079	1.094	1.108	1.123	1.138	1.152	1.167	1.181	1.196	1.210	1.225
22	1.069	1.085	1.100	1.115	1.131	1.146	1.161	1.176	1.192	1.207	1.222	1.238	1.253	1.268	1.283
23	1.118	1.134	1.150	1.166	1.182	1.198	1.214	1.230	1.246	1.262	1.278	1.294	1.310	1.326	1.342
24	1.167	1.183	1.200	1.217	1.233	1.250	1.267	1.283	1.300	1.317	1.333	1.350	1.367	1.383	1.400
25	1.215	1.233	1.250	1.267	1.285	1.302	1.319	1.337	1.354	1.372	1.389	1.406	1.424	1.441	1.458
26	1.264	1.282	1.300	1.318	1.336	1.354	1.372	1.390	1.408	1.426	1.444	1.463	1.481	1.499	1.517
27	1.313	1.331	1.350	1.369	1.388	1.406	1.425	1.444	1.463	1.481	1.500	1.519	1.538	1.556	1.575
28	1.361	1.381	1.400	1.419	1.439	1.458	1.478	1.497	1.517	1.536	1.556	1.575	1.594	1.614	1.633
29	1.410	1.430	1.450	1.470	1.490	1.510	1.531	1.551	1.571	1.591	1.611	1.631	1.651	1.672	1.692
30	1.458	1.479	1.500	1.521	1.542	1.563	1.583	1.604	1.625	1.646	1.667	1.688	1.708	1.729	1.750
31 Days	1.507	1.528	1.550	1.572	1.593	1.615	1.636	1.658	1.679	1.701	1.722	1.744	1.765	1.787	1.808
2 Months	2.917	2.958	3.000	3.042	3.083	3.125	3.167	3.208	3.250	3.292	3.333	3.375	3.417	3.458	3.500
3	4.375	4.438	4.500	4.563	4.625	4.688	4.750	4.813	4.875	4.938	5.000	5.063	5.125	5.188	5.250
4	5.833	5.917	6.000	6.083	6.167	6.250	6.333	6.417	6.500	6.583	6.667	6.750	6.833	6.917	7.000
5	7.292	7.396	7.500	7.604	7.708	7.813	7.917	8.021	8.125	8.229	8.333	8.438	8.542	8.646	8.750
6	8.750	8.875	9.000	9.125	9.250	9.375	9.500	9.625	9.750	9.875	10.000	10.125	10.250	10.375	10.500
7 Months	10.208	10.354	10.500	10.646	10.792	10.937	11.083	11.229	11.375	11.521	11.667	11.812	11.958	12.104	12.250
8	11.667	11.833	12.000	12.167	12.333	12.500	12.667	12.833	13.000	13.167	13.333	13.500	13.667	13.833	14.000
9	13.125	13.313	13.500	13.688	13.875	14.063	14.250	14.438	14.625	14.813	15.000	15.188	15.375	15.563	15.750
10	14.583	14.792	15.000	15.208	15.417	15.625	15.833	16.042	16.250	16.458	16.667	16.875	17.083	17.292	17.500
11	16.042	16.271	16.500	16.729	16.958	17.187	17.417	17.646	17.875	18.104	18.333	18.563	18.792	19.021	19.250
12 Months	17.500	17.750	18.000	18.250	18.500	18.750	19.000	19.250	19.500	19.750	20.000	20.250	20.500	20.750	21.000

Annual Rent per Square Foot

Time Vacant	$21.00	21.25	21.50	21.75	22.00	22.25	22.50	22.75	23.00	23.25	23.50	23.75	24.00	24.25	24.50
1 Day	0.058	0.059	0.060	0.060	0.061	0.062	0.063	0.063	0.064	0.065	0.065	0.066	0.067	0.067	0.068
2 Days	0.117	0.118	0.119	0.121	0.122	0.124	0.125	0.126	0.128	0.129	0.131	0.132	0.133	0.135	0.136
3	0.175	0.177	0.179	0.181	0.183	0.185	0.188	0.190	0.192	0.194	0.196	0.198	0.200	0.202	0.204
4	0.233	0.236	0.239	0.242	0.244	0.247	0.250	0.253	0.256	0.258	0.261	0.264	0.267	0.269	0.272
5	0.292	0.295	0.299	0.302	0.306	0.309	0.313	0.316	0.319	0.323	0.326	0.330	0.333	0.337	0.340
6	0.350	0.354	0.358	0.363	0.367	0.371	0.375	0.379	0.383	0.388	0.392	0.396	0.400	0.404	0.408
7	0.408	0.413	0.418	0.423	0.428	0.433	0.438	0.442	0.447	0.452	0.457	0.462	0.467	0.472	0.476
8	0.467	0.472	0.478	0.483	0.489	0.494	0.500	0.506	0.511	0.517	0.522	0.528	0.533	0.539	0.544
9	0.525	0.531	0.538	0.544	0.550	0.556	0.563	0.569	0.575	0.581	0.588	0.594	0.600	0.606	0.613
10	0.583	0.590	0.597	0.604	0.611	0.618	0.625	0.632	0.639	0.646	0.653	0.660	0.667	0.674	0.681
11	0.642	0.649	0.657	0.665	0.672	0.680	0.688	0.695	0.703	0.710	0.718	0.726	0.733	0.741	0.749
12	0.700	0.708	0.717	0.725	0.733	0.742	0.750	0.758	0.767	0.775	0.783	0.792	0.800	0.808	0.817
13	0.758	0.767	0.776	0.785	0.794	0.803	0.813	0.822	0.831	0.840	0.849	0.858	0.867	0.876	0.885
14	0.817	0.826	0.836	0.846	0.856	0.865	0.875	0.885	0.894	0.904	0.914	0.924	0.933	0.943	0.953
15 Days	0.875	0.885	0.896	0.906	0.917	0.927	0.938	0.948	0.958	0.969	0.979	0.990	1.000	1.010	1.021
16	0.933	0.944	0.956	0.967	0.978	0.989	1.000	1.011	1.022	1.033	1.044	1.056	1.067	1.078	1.089
17	0.992	1.003	1.015	1.027	1.039	1.051	1.063	1.074	1.086	1.098	1.110	1.122	1.133	1.145	1.157
18	1.050	1.063	1.075	1.088	1.100	1.113	1.125	1.138	1.150	1.163	1.175	1.188	1.200	1.213	1.225
19	1.108	1.122	1.135	1.148	1.161	1.174	1.188	1.201	1.214	1.227	1.240	1.253	1.267	1.280	1.293
20	1.167	1.181	1.194	1.208	1.222	1.236	1.250	1.264	1.278	1.292	1.306	1.319	1.333	1.347	1.361
21	1.225	1.240	1.254	1.269	1.283	1.298	1.313	1.327	1.342	1.356	1.371	1.385	1.400	1.415	1.429
22	1.283	1.299	1.314	1.329	1.344	1.360	1.375	1.390	1.406	1.421	1.436	1.451	1.467	1.482	1.497
23	1.342	1.358	1.374	1.390	1.406	1.422	1.438	1.453	1.469	1.485	1.501	1.517	1.533	1.549	1.565
24	1.400	1.417	1.433	1.450	1.467	1.483	1.500	1.517	1.533	1.550	1.567	1.583	1.600	1.617	1.633
25	1.458	1.476	1.493	1.510	1.528	1.545	1.563	1.580	1.597	1.615	1.632	1.649	1.667	1.684	1.701
26	1.517	1.535	1.553	1.571	1.589	1.607	1.625	1.643	1.661	1.679	1.697	1.715	1.733	1.751	1.769
27	1.575	1.594	1.613	1.631	1.650	1.669	1.688	1.706	1.725	1.744	1.763	1.781	1.800	1.819	1.838
28	1.633	1.653	1.672	1.692	1.711	1.731	1.750	1.769	1.789	1.808	1.828	1.847	1.867	1.886	1.906
29	1.692	1.712	1.732	1.752	1.772	1.792	1.813	1.833	1.853	1.873	1.893	1.913	1.933	1.953	1.974
30	1.750	1.771	1.792	1.813	1.833	1.854	1.875	1.896	1.917	1.938	1.958	1.979	2.000	2.021	2.042
31 Days	1.808	1.830	1.851	1.873	1.894	1.916	1.938	1.959	1.981	2.002	2.024	2.045	2.067	2.088	2.110
2 Months	3.500	3.542	3.583	3.625	3.667	3.708	3.750	3.792	3.833	3.875	3.917	3.958	4.000	4.042	4.083
3	5.250	5.313	5.375	5.438	5.500	5.563	5.625	5.688	5.750	5.813	5.875	5.938	6.000	6.063	6.125
4	7.000	7.083	7.167	7.250	7.333	7.417	7.500	7.583	7.667	7.750	7.833	7.917	8.000	8.083	8.167
5	8.750	8.854	8.958	9.063	9.167	9.271	9.375	9.479	9.583	9.688	9.792	9.896	10.000	10.104	10.208
6	10.500	10.625	10.750	10.875	11.000	11.125	11.250	11.375	11.500	11.625	11.750	11.875	12.000	12.125	12.250
7 Months	12.250	12.396	12.542	12.688	12.833	12.979	13.125	13.271	13.417	13.563	13.708	13.854	14.000	14.146	14.292
8	14.000	14.167	14.333	14.500	14.667	14.833	15.000	15.167	15.333	15.500	15.667	15.833	16.000	16.167	16.333
9	15.750	15.938	16.125	16.313	16.500	16.688	16.875	17.063	17.250	17.438	17.625	17.813	18.000	18.188	18.375
10	17.500	17.708	17.917	18.125	18.333	18.542	18.750	18.958	19.167	19.375	19.583	19.792	20.000	20.208	20.417
11	19.250	19.479	19.708	19.938	20.167	20.396	20.625	20.854	21.083	21.313	21.542	21.771	22.000	22.229	22.458
12 Months	21.000	21.250	21.500	21.750	22.000	22.250	22.500	22.750	23.000	23.250	23.500	23.750	24.000	24.250	24.500

Entry is lost rent in dollars and cents per square foot.

Annual Reserve for Vacancy Converted to Spot Cost

Interest Rate on Savings 5.50%

Annual Reserve	33 1/3% Turnover						50% Turnover					
	1	3	5	7	10	12	1	3	5	7	10	12
1.0%	0m/11	1m/ 6	2m/ 3	3m/ 3	4m/26	6m/ 6	0m/ 7	0m/24	1m/12	2m/ 2	3m/ 7	4m/ 4
1.5	0m/17	1m/23	3m/ 4	4m/20	7m/ 8	9m/ 8	0m/11	1m/ 6	2m/ 3	3m/ 3	4m/26	6m/ 6
2.0	0m/22	2m/11	4m/ 6	6m/ 6	9m/21	12m/11	0m/15	1m/18	2m/24	4m/ 4	6m/14	8m/ 7
2.5	0m/28	2m/29	5m/ 7	7m/23	12m/ 4	15m/14	0m/19	1m/29	3m/15	5m/ 5	8m/ 3	10m/ 9
3.0	1m/ 4	3m/17	6m/ 9	9m/10	14m/17	18m/17	0m/22	2m/11	4m/ 6	6m/ 6	9m/21	12m/11
3.5	1m/ 9	4m/ 5	7m/10	10m/26	16m/29	21m/19	0m/26	2m/23	4m/27	7m/ 8	11m/10	14m/13
4.0	1m/15	4m/23	8m/11	12m/13	19m/12	24m/22	0m/30	3m/ 5	5m/18	8m/ 9	12m/28	16m/15
5.0	1m/26	5m/28	10m/14	15m/16	24m/ 8	30m/28	1m/ 7	3m/29	6m/30	10m/11	16m/ 5	20m/18
7.0	2m/19	8m/ 9	14m/20	21m/23	33m/29	43m/ 9	1m/22	5m/16	9m/23	14m/15	22m/19	28m/26

	66 2/3% Turnover						100% Turnover					
1.0%	0m/ 6	0m/18	1m/ 1	1m/17	2m/13	3m/ 3	0m/ 4	0m/12	0m/21	1m/ 1	1m/19	2m/ 2
1.5	0m/ 8	0m/27	1m/17	2m/10	3m/19	4m/19	0m/ 6	0m/18	1m/ 1	1m/17	2m/13	3m/ 3
2.0	0m/11	1m/ 6	2m/ 3	3m/ 3	4m/26	6m/ 6	0m/ 7	0m/24	1m/12	2m/ 2	3m/ 7	4m/ 4
2.5	0m/14	1m/15	2m/19	3m/27	6m/ 2	7m/22	0m/ 9	0m/30	1m/22	2m/18	4m/ 1	5m/ 5
3.0	0m/17	1m/23	3m/ 4	4m/20	7m/ 8	9m/ 8	0m/11	1m/ 6	2m/ 3	3m/ 3	4m/26	6m/ 6
3.5	0m/20	2m/ 2	3m/20	5m/13	8m/15	10m/25	0m/13	1m/12	2m/13	3m/19	5m/20	7m/ 6
4.0	0m/22	2m/11	4m/ 6	6m/ 6	9m/21	12m/11	0m/15	1m/18	2m/24	4m/ 4	6m/14	8m/ 7
5.0	0m/28	2m/29	5m/ 7	7m/23	12m/ 4	15m/14	0m/19	1m/29	3m/15	5m/ 5	8m/ 3	10m/ 9
7.0	1m/ 9	4m/ 5	7m/10	10m/26	16m/29	21m/19	0m/26	2m/23	4m/27	7m/ 8	11m/10	14m/13

Interest Rate on Savings 6.50%

Annual Reserve	33 1/3% Turnover						50% Turnover					
1.0%	0m/11	1m/ 6	2m/ 4	3m/ 7	5m/ 4	6m/18	0m/ 8	0m/24	1m/13	2m/ 4	3m/12	4m/12
1.5	0m/17	1m/24	3m/ 7	4m/25	7m/21	9m/27	0m/11	1m/ 6	2m/ 4	3m/ 7	5m/ 4	6m/18
2.0	0m/23	2m/12	4m/ 9	6m/13	10m/ 7	13m/ 7	0m/15	1m/18	2m/26	4m/ 9	6m/25	8m/24
2.5	0m/28	3m/ 0	5m/11	8m/ 2	12m/24	16m/16	0m/19	2m/ 0	3m/17	5m/11	8m/16	11m/ 0
3.0	1m/ 4	3m/18	6m/13	9m/20	15m/11	19m/25	0m/23	2m/12	4m/ 9	6m/13	10m/ 7	13m/ 7
3.5	1m/ 9	4m/ 7	7m/16	11m/ 9	17m/28	23m/ 4	0m/26	2m/24	5m/ 0	7m/16	11m/29	15m/13
4.0	1m/15	4m/25	8m/18	12m/27	20m/15	26m/13	1m/ 0	3m/ 6	5m/22	8m/18	13m/20	17m/19
5.0	1m/26	6m/ 1	10m/22	16m/ 4	25m/18	33m/ 1	1m/ 8	4m/ 1	7m/ 5	10m/22	17m/ 2	22m/ 1
7.0	2m/19	8m/13	15m/ 1	22m/17	35m/26	46m/ 8	1m/23	5m/19	10m/ 1	15m/ 1	23m/27	30m/25

	66 2/3% Turnover						100% Turnover					
1.0%	0m/ 6	0m/18	1m/ 2	1m/18	2m/17	3m/ 9	0m/ 4	0m/12	0m/21	1m/ 2	1m/21	2m/ 6
1.5	0m/ 8	0m/27	1m/18	2m/13	3m/25	4m/29	0m/ 6	0m/18	1m/ 2	1m/18	2m/17	3m/ 9
2.0	0m/11	1m/ 6	2m/ 4	3m/ 7	5m/ 4	6m/18	0m/ 8	0m/24	1m/13	2m/ 4	3m/12	4m/12
2.5	0m/14	1m/15	2m/21	4m/ 1	6m/12	8m/ 8	0m/ 9	1m/ 0	1m/24	2m/21	4m/ 8	5m/15
3.0	0m/17	1m/24	3m/ 7	4m/25	7m/21	9m/27	0m/11	1m/ 6	2m/ 4	3m/ 7	5m/ 4	6m/18
3.5	0m/20	2m/ 3	3m/23	5m/19	8m/29	11m/17	0m/13	1m/12	2m/15	3m/23	5m/29	7m/21
4.0	0m/23	2m/12	4m/ 9	6m/13	10m/ 7	13m/ 7	0m/15	1m/18	2m/26	4m/ 9	6m/25	8m/24
5.0	0m/28	3m/ 0	5m/11	8m/ 2	12m/24	16m/16	0m/19	2m/ 0	3m/17	5m/11	8m/16	11m/ 0
7.0	1m/ 9	4m/ 7	7m/16	11m/ 9	17m/28	23m/ 4	0m/26	2m/24	5m/ 0	7m/16	11m/29	15m/13

Interest Rate on Savings 7.50%

Annual Reserve	33 1/3% Turnover						50% Turnover					
1.0%	0m/11	1m/ 7	2m/ 6	3m/10	5m/12	7m/ 2	0m/ 8	0m/24	1m/14	2m/ 7	3m/18	4m/21
1.5	0m/17	1m/25	3m/ 9	5m/ 1	8m/ 4	10m/18	0m/11	1m/ 7	2m/ 6	3m/10	5m/12	7m/ 2
2.0	0m/23	2m/13	4m/12	6m/21	10m/25	14m/ 4	0m/15	1m/19	2m/28	4m/14	7m/ 6	9m/13
2.5	0m/28	3m/ 2	5m/15	8m/11	13m/16	17m/20	0m/19	2m/ 1	3m/20	5m/17	9m/ 1	11m/23
3.0	1m/ 4	3m/20	6m/19	10m/ 1	16m/ 7	21m/ 6	0m/23	2m/13	4m/12	6m/21	10m/25	14m/ 4
3.5	1m/10	4m/ 8	7m/22	11m/21	18m/28	24m/22	0m/26	2m/26	5m/ 4	7m/24	12m/19	16m/15
4.0	1m/15	4m/27	8m/25	13m/12	21m/19	28m/ 8	1m/ 0	3m/ 8	5m/26	8m/28	14m/13	18m/26
5.0	1m/27	6m/ 4	11m/ 1	16m/22	27m/ 2	35m/10	1m/ 8	4m/ 2	7m/11	11m/ 5	18m/ 1	23m/17
7.0	2m/19	8m/17	15m/13	23m/13	37m/27	49m/15	1m/23	5m/21	10m/ 9	15m/19	25m/ 8	32m/30

	66 2/3% Turnover						100% Turnover					
1.0%	0m/ 6	0m/18	1m/ 3	1m/20	2m/21	3m/16	0m/ 4	0m/12	0m/22	1m/ 3	1m/24	2m/11
1.5	0m/ 9	0m/28	1m/20	2m/15	4m/ 2	5m/ 9	0m/ 6	0m/18	1m/ 3	1m/20	2m/21	3m/16
2.0	0m/11	1m/ 7	2m/ 6	3m/10	5m/12	7m/ 2	0m/ 8	0m/24	1m/14	2m/ 7	3m/18	4m/21
2.5	0m/14	1m/16	2m/23	4m/ 6	6m/23	8m/25	0m/ 9	1m/ 1	1m/25	2m/24	4m/15	5m/27
3.0	0m/17	1m/25	3m/ 9	5m/ 1	8m/ 4	10m/18	0m/11	1m/ 7	2m/ 6	3m/10	5m/12	7m/ 2
3.5	0m/20	2m/ 4	3m/26	5m/26	9m/14	12m/11	0m/13	1m/13	2m/17	3m/27	6m/ 9	8m/ 7
4.0	0m/23	2m/13	4m/12	6m/21	10m/25	14m/ 4	0m/15	1m/19	2m/28	4m/14	7m/ 6	9m/13
5.0	0m/28	3m/ 2	5m/15	8m/11	13m/16	17m/20	0m/19	2m/ 1	3m/20	5m/17	9m/ 1	11m/23
7.0	1m/10	4m/ 8	7m/22	11m/21	18m/28	24m/22	0m/26	2m/26	5m/ 4	7m/24	12m/19	16m/15

Entry is months / days of vacancy covered by reserve accumulated after selected years.

Annual Reserve for Vacancy Converted to Spot Cost

Interest Rate on Savings 8.50%

Annual Reserve	33 1/3% Turnover						50% Turnover					
	1	3	5	7	10	12	1	3	5	7	10	12
1.0%	0m/11	1m/ 7	2m/ 8	3m/14	5m/22	7m/17	0m/ 8	0m/25	1m/15	2m/ 9	3m/24	5m/ 1
1.5	0m/17	1m/26	3m/12	5m/ 6	8m/18	11m/11	0m/11	1m/ 7	2m/ 8	3m/14	5m/22	7m/17
2.0	0m/23	2m/15	4m/16	6m/28	11m/13	15m/ 4	0m/15	1m/20	3m/ 1	4m/19	7m/19	10m/ 3
2.5	0m/28	3m/ 3	5m/20	8m/21	14m/ 9	18m/28	0m/19	2m/ 2	3m/23	5m/24	9m/16	12m/19
3.0	1m/ 4	3m/22	6m/24	10m/13	17m/ 5	22m/21	0m/23	2m/15	4m/16	6m/28	11m/13	15m/ 4
3.5	1m/10	4m/10	7m/28	12m/ 5	20m/ 1	26m/15	0m/27	2m/27	5m/ 9	8m/ 3	13m/11	17m/20
4.0	1m/16	4m/29	9m/ 2	13m/27	22m/27	30m/ 9	1m/ 0	3m/ 9	6m/ 1	9m/ 8	15m/ 8	20m/ 6
5.0	1m/27	6m/ 6	11m/10	17m/11	28m/18	37m/26	1m/ 8	4m/ 4	7m/16	11m/17	19m/ 2	25m/ 7
7.0	2m/20	8m/21	15m/26	24m/10	40m/ 2	53m/ 0	1m/23	5m/24	10m/17	16m/ 6	26m/21	35m/10

Annual Reserve	66 2/3% Turnover						100% Turnover					
1.0%	0m/ 6	0m/19	1m/ 4	1m/22	2m/26	3m/24	0m/ 4	0m/12	0m/23	1m/ 5	1m/27	2m/16
1.5	0m/ 9	0m/28	1m/21	2m/18	4m/ 9	5m/20	0m/ 6	0m/19	1m/ 4	1m/22	2m/26	3m/24
2.0	0m/11	1m/ 7	2m/ 8	3m/14	5m/22	7m/17	0m/ 8	0m/25	1m/15	2m/ 9	3m/24	5m/ 1
2.5	0m/14	1m/17	2m/25	4m/10	7m/ 5	9m/14	0m/ 9	1m/ 1	1m/27	2m/27	4m/23	6m/ 9
3.0	0m/17	1m/26	3m/12	5m/ 6	8m/18	11m/11	0m/11	1m/ 7	2m/ 8	3m/14	5m/22	7m/17
3.5	0m/20	2m/ 5	3m/29	6m/ 2	10m/ 0	13m/ 8	0m/13	1m/13	2m/19	4m/ 2	6m/20	8m/25
4.0	0m/23	2m/15	4m/16	6m/28	11m/13	15m/ 4	0m/15	1m/20	3m/ 1	4m/19	7m/19	10m/ 3
5.0	0m/28	3m/ 3	5m/20	8m/21	14m/ 9	18m/28	0m/19	2m/ 2	3m/23	5m/24	9m/16	12m/19
7.0	1m/10	4m/10	7m/28	12m/ 5	20m/ 1	26m/15	0m/27	2m/27	5m/ 9	8m/ 3	13m/11	17m/20

Interest Rate on Savings 9.50%

Annual Reserve	33 1/3% Turnover						50% Turnover					
1.0%	0m/11	1m/ 8	2m/10	3m/18	6m/ 2	8m/ 4	0m/ 8	0m/25	1m/16	2m/12	4m/ 1	5m/12
1.5	0m/17	1m/27	3m/15	5m/12	9m/ 2	12m/ 5	0m/11	1m/ 8	2m/10	3m/18	6m/ 2	8m/ 4
2.0	0m/23	2m/16	4m/19	7m/ 7	12m/ 3	16m/ 7	0m/15	1m/20	3m/ 3	4m/24	8m/ 2	10m/25
2.5	0m/29	3m/ 5	5m/24	9m/ 1	15m/ 4	20m/ 9	0m/19	2m/ 3	3m/26	6m/ 0	10m/ 3	13m/16
3.0	1m/ 4	3m/24	6m/29	10m/25	18m/ 5	24m/11	0m/23	2m/16	4m/19	7m/ 7	12m/ 3	16m/ 7
3.5	1m/10	4m/12	8m/ 4	12m/19	21m/ 6	28m/12	0m/27	2m/28	5m/13	8m/13	14m/ 4	18m/28
4.0	1m/16	5m/ 1	9m/ 9	14m/13	24m/ 7	32m/14	1m/ 1	3m/11	6m/ 6	9m/19	16m/ 4	21m/19
5.0	1m/27	6m/ 9	11m/19	18m/ 1	30m/ 8	40m/18	1m/ 8	4m/ 6	7m/22	12m/ 1	20m/ 6	27m/ 2
7.0	2m/20	8m/25	16m/ 8	25m/ 8	42m/12	56m/25	1m/23	5m/27	10m/25	16m/25	28m/ 8	37m/26

Annual Reserve	66 2/3% Turnover						100% Turnover					
1.0%	0m/ 6	0m/19	1m/ 5	1m/24	3m/ 1	4m/ 2	0m/ 4	0m/13	0m/23	1m/ 6	2m/ 1	2m/21
1.5	0m/ 9	0m/28	1m/22	2m/21	4m/16	6m/ 3	0m/ 6	0m/19	1m/ 5	1m/24	3m/ 1	4m/ 2
2.0	0m/11	1m/ 8	2m/10	3m/18	6m/ 2	8m/ 4	0m/ 8	0m/25	1m/16	2m/12	4m/ 1	5m/12
2.5	0m/14	1m/17	2m/27	4m/15	7m/17	10m/ 4	0m/10	1m/ 2	1m/28	3m/ 0	5m/ 1	6m/23
3.0	0m/17	1m/27	3m/15	5m/12	9m/ 2	12m/ 5	0m/11	1m/ 8	2m/10	3m/18	6m/ 2	8m/ 4
3.5	0m/20	2m/ 6	4m/ 2	6m/ 9	10m/18	14m/ 6	0m/13	1m/14	2m/21	4m/ 6	7m/ 2	9m/ 4
4.0	0m/23	2m/16	4m/19	7m/ 7	12m/ 3	16m/ 7	0m/15	1m/20	3m/ 3	4m/24	8m/ 2	10m/25
5.0	0m/29	3m/ 5	5m/24	9m/ 1	15m/ 4	20m/ 9	0m/19	2m/ 3	3m/26	6m/ 0	10m/ 3	13m/16
7.0	1m/10	4m/12	8m/ 4	12m/19	21m/ 6	28m/12	0m/27	2m/28	5m/13	8m/13	14m/ 4	18m/28

Interest Rate on Savings 10.50%

Annual Reserve	33 1/3% Turnover						50% Turnover					
1.0%	0m/11	1m/ 8	2m/12	3m/23	6m/12	8m/21	0m/ 8	0m/26	1m/18	2m/15	4m/ 8	5m/24
1.5	0m/17	1m/28	3m/17	5m/19	9m/19	13m/ 2	0m/11	1m/ 8	2m/12	3m/23	6m/12	8m/21
2.0	0m/23	2m/17	4m/23	7m/15	12m/25	17m/13	0m/15	1m/21	3m/ 5	5m/ 0	8m/16	11m/18
2.5	0m/29	3m/ 6	5m/29	9m/11	16m/ 1	21m/23	0m/19	2m/ 4	3m/29	6m/ 8	10m/21	14m/16
3.0	1m/ 4	3m/25	7m/ 5	11m/ 8	19m/ 7	26m/ 4	0m/23	2m/17	4m/23	7m/15	12m/25	17m/13
3.5	1m/10	4m/14	8m/11	13m/ 4	22m/13	30m/15	0m/27	2m/30	5m/17	8m/23	14m/29	20m/10
4.0	1m/16	5m/ 4	9m/16	15m/ 0	25m/19	34m/25	1m/ 1	3m/12	6m/11	10m/ 0	17m/ 3	23m/ 7
5.0	1m/27	6m/12	11m/28	18m/23	32m/ 2	43m/17	1m/ 8	4m/ 8	7m/29	12m/15	21m/11	29m/ 1
7.0	2m/20	8m/29	16m/21	26m/ 8	44m/27	60m/29	1m/24	5m/29	11m/ 4	17m/15	29m/28	40m/20

Annual Reserve	66 2/3% Turnover						100% Turnover					
1.0%	0m/ 6	0m/19	1m/ 6	1m/26	3m/ 6	4m/11	0m/ 4	0m/13	0m/24	1m/ 8	2m/ 4	2m/27
1.5	0m/ 9	0m/29	1m/24	2m/24	4m/24	6m/16	0m/ 6	0m/19	1m/ 6	1m/26	3m/ 6	4m/11
2.0	0m/11	1m/ 8	2m/12	3m/23	6m/12	8m/21	0m/ 8	0m/26	1m/18	2m/15	3m/ 6	4m/11
2.5	0m/14	1m/18	2m/30	4m/21	8m/ 0	10m/27	0m/10	1m/ 2	1m/30	3m/ 4	5m/10	7m/ 8
3.0	0m/17	1m/28	3m/17	5m/19	9m/19	13m/ 2	0m/11	1m/ 8	2m/12	3m/23	6m/12	8m/21
3.5	0m/20	2m/ 7	4m/ 5	6m/17	11m/ 7	15m/ 7	0m/13	1m/15	2m/24	4m/11	7m/14	10m/ 5
4.0	0m/23	2m/17	4m/23	7m/15	12m/25	17m/13	0m/15	1m/21	3m/ 5	5m/ 0	8m/16	11m/18
5.0	0m/29	3m/ 6	5m/29	9m/11	16m/ 1	21m/23	0m/19	2m/ 4	3m/29	6m/ 8	10m/21	14m/16
7.0	1m/10	4m/14	8m/11	13m/ 4	22m/13	30m/15	0m/27	2m/30	5m/17	8m/23	14m/29	20m/10

Entry is months / days of vacancy covered by reserve accumulated after selected years.

Spot Vacancy Cost Converted to Annual Reserve

Time Span	Spot Vacancy 9 Months Percent Turnover at Time Span									Spot Vacancy 12 Months Percent Turnover at Time Span								
	20	30	40	50	60	70	80	90	100	20	30	40	50	60	70	80	90	100
Interest Rate on Savings 7.50%																		
6	7.0	10.5	13.9	17.4	20.9	24.4	27.9	31.4	34.9	9.3	13.9	18.6	23.2	27.9	32.5	37.2	41.8	46.5
9	4.5	6.7	8.9	11.2	13.4	15.7	17.9	20.1	22.4	6.0	8.9	11.9	14.9	17.9	20.9	23.9	26.8	29.8
12	3.2	4.8	6.5	8.1	9.7	11.3	12.9	14.5	16.1	4.3	6.5	8.6	10.8	12.9	15.1	17.2	19.4	21.5
15	2.5	3.7	5.0	6.2	7.4	8.7	9.9	11.2	12.4	3.3	5.0	6.6	8.3	9.9	11.6	13.2	14.9	16.5
18	2.0	3.0	4.0	5.0	6.0	7.0	7.9	8.9	9.9	2.6	4.0	5.3	6.6	7.9	9.3	10.6	11.9	13.2
21	1.6	2.5	3.3	4.1	4.9	5.7	6.5	7.4	8.2	2.2	3.3	4.4	5.5	6.5	7.6	8.7	9.8	10.9
24	1.4	2.1	2.7	3.4	4.1	4.8	5.5	6.2	6.9	1.8	2.7	3.7	4.6	5.5	6.4	7.3	8.2	9.2
27	1.2	1.8	2.3	2.9	3.5	4.1	4.7	5.3	5.9	1.6	2.3	3.1	3.9	4.7	5.5	6.3	7.0	7.8
30	1.0	1.5	2.0	2.5	3.0	3.5	4.0	4.6	5.1	1.3	2.0	2.7	3.4	4.0	4.7	5.4	6.1	6.7
33	0.9	1.3	1.8	2.2	2.6	3.1	3.5	4.0	4.4	1.2	1.8	2.4	2.9	3.5	4.1	4.7	5.3	5.9
36	0.8	1.2	1.5	1.9	2.3	2.7	3.1	3.5	3.9	1.0	1.5	2.1	2.6	3.1	3.6	4.1	4.6	5.2
39	0.7	1.0	1.4	1.7	2.1	2.4	2.7	3.1	3.4	0.9	1.4	1.8	2.3	2.7	3.2	3.7	4.1	4.6
42	0.6	0.9	1.2	1.5	1.8	2.1	2.4	2.7	3.0	0.8	1.2	1.6	2.0	2.4	2.8	3.2	3.7	4.1
45	0.5	0.8	1.1	1.4	1.6	1.9	2.2	2.4	2.7	0.7	1.1	1.4	1.8	2.2	2.5	2.9	3.3	3.6
Interest Rate on Savings 8.50%																		
6	6.9	10.4	13.8	17.3	20.7	24.2	27.6	31.1	34.5	9.2	13.8	18.4	23.0	27.6	32.2	36.8	41.4	46.0
9	4.4	6.6	8.8	11.0	13.2	15.4	17.6	19.8	22.0	5.9	8.8	11.8	14.7	17.6	20.6	23.5	26.4	29.4
12	3.2	4.7	6.3	7.9	9.5	11.1	12.6	14.2	15.8	4.2	6.3	8.4	10.5	12.6	14.8	16.9	19.0	21.1
15	2.4	3.6	4.8	6.0	7.3	8.5	9.7	10.9	12.1	3.2	4.8	6.4	8.1	9.7	11.3	12.9	14.5	16.1
18	1.9	2.9	3.9	4.8	5.8	6.7	7.7	8.7	9.6	2.6	3.9	5.1	6.4	7.7	9.0	10.3	11.6	12.8
21	1.6	2.4	3.2	3.9	4.7	5.5	6.3	7.1	7.9	2.1	3.2	4.2	5.3	6.3	7.4	8.4	9.5	10.5
24	1.3	2.0	2.6	3.3	3.9	4.6	5.3	5.9	6.6	1.8	2.6	3.5	4.4	5.3	6.1	7.0	7.9	8.8
27	1.1	1.7	2.2	2.8	3.3	3.9	4.5	5.0	5.6	1.5	2.2	3.0	3.7	4.5	5.2	5.9	6.7	7.4
30	1.0	1.4	1.9	2.4	2.9	3.3	3.8	4.3	4.8	1.3	1.9	2.6	3.2	3.8	4.5	5.1	5.7	6.4
33	0.8	1.2	1.7	2.1	2.5	2.9	3.3	3.7	4.1	1.1	1.7	2.2	2.8	3.3	3.9	4.4	5.0	5.5
36	0.7	1.1	1.4	1.8	2.2	2.5	2.9	3.3	3.6	1.0	1.4	1.9	2.4	2.9	3.4	3.9	4.3	4.8
39	0.6	1.0	1.3	1.6	1.9	2.2	2.5	2.9	3.2	0.8	1.3	1.7	2.1	2.5	3.0	3.4	3.8	4.2
42	0.6	0.8	1.1	1.4	1.7	2.0	2.2	2.5	2.8	0.7	1.1	1.5	1.9	2.2	2.6	3.0	3.4	3.7
45	0.5	0.7	1.0	1.2	1.5	1.7	2.0	2.2	2.5	0.7	1.0	1.3	1.7	2.0	2.3	2.7	3.0	3.3
Interest Rate on Savings 9.50%																		
6	6.8	10.3	13.7	17.1	20.5	23.9	27.4	30.8	34.2	9.1	13.7	18.2	22.8	27.4	31.9	36.5	41.0	45.6
9	4.3	6.5	8.7	10.9	13.0	15.2	17.4	19.5	21.7	5.8	8.7	11.6	14.5	17.4	20.3	23.2	26.0	28.9
12	3.1	4.6	6.2	7.7	9.3	10.8	12.4	13.9	15.5	4.1	6.2	8.3	10.3	12.4	14.5	16.5	18.6	20.6
15	2.4	3.5	4.7	5.9	7.1	8.2	9.4	10.6	11.8	3.1	4.7	6.3	7.9	9.4	11.0	12.6	14.1	15.7
18	1.9	2.8	3.7	4.7	5.6	6.5	7.5	8.4	9.3	2.5	3.7	5.0	6.2	7.5	8.7	9.9	11.2	12.4
21	1.5	2.3	3.0	3.8	4.6	5.3	6.1	6.8	7.6	2.0	3.0	4.0	5.1	6.1	7.1	8.1	9.1	10.1
24	1.3	1.9	2.5	3.1	3.8	4.4	5.0	5.7	6.3	1.7	2.5	3.4	4.2	5.0	5.9	6.7	7.6	8.4
27	1.1	1.6	2.1	2.7	3.2	3.7	4.2	4.8	5.3	1.4	2.1	2.8	3.5	4.2	4.9	5.7	6.4	7.1
30	0.9	1.4	1.8	2.3	2.7	3.2	3.6	4.1	4.5	1.2	1.8	2.4	3.0	3.6	4.2	4.8	5.4	6.0
33	0.8	1.2	1.6	1.9	2.3	2.7	3.1	3.5	3.9	1.0	1.6	2.1	2.6	3.1	3.6	4.1	4.7	5.2
36	0.7	1.0	1.3	1.7	2.0	2.4	2.7	3.0	3.4	0.9	1.3	1.8	2.2	2.7	3.1	3.6	4.0	4.5
39	0.6	0.9	1.2	1.5	1.8	2.1	2.4	2.6	2.9	0.8	1.2	1.6	2.0	2.4	2.7	3.1	3.5	3.9
42	0.5	0.8	1.0	1.3	1.5	1.8	2.1	2.3	2.6	0.7	1.0	1.4	1.7	2.1	2.4	2.8	3.1	3.4
45	0.5	0.7	0.9	1.1	1.4	1.6	1.8	2.0	2.3	0.6	0.9	1.2	1.5	1.8	2.1	2.4	2.7	3.0
Interest Rate on Savings 10.50%																		
6	6.8	10.2	13.5	16.9	20.3	23.7	27.1	30.5	33.9	9.0	13.5	18.1	22.6	27.1	31.6	36.1	40.6	45.2
9	4.3	6.4	8.6	10.7	12.8	15.0	17.1	19.2	21.4	5.7	8.6	11.4	14.3	17.1	20.0	22.8	25.7	28.5
12	3.0	4.6	6.1	7.6	9.1	10.6	12.1	13.7	15.2	4.0	6.1	8.1	10.1	12.1	14.2	16.2	18.2	20.2
15	2.3	3.4	4.6	5.7	6.9	8.0	9.2	10.3	11.5	3.1	4.6	6.1	7.6	9.2	10.7	12.2	13.8	15.3
18	1.8	2.7	3.6	4.5	5.4	6.3	7.2	8.1	9.0	2.4	3.6	4.8	6.0	7.2	8.4	9.6	10.8	12.0
21	1.5	2.2	2.9	3.6	4.4	5.1	5.8	6.6	7.3	1.9	2.9	3.9	4.9	5.8	6.8	7.8	8.8	9.7
24	1.2	1.8	2.4	3.0	3.6	4.2	4.8	5.4	6.0	1.6	2.4	3.2	4.0	4.8	5.6	6.4	7.2	8.0
27	1.0	1.5	2.0	2.5	3.0	3.5	4.0	4.5	5.0	1.3	2.0	2.7	3.4	4.0	4.7	5.4	6.0	6.7
30	0.9	1.3	1.7	2.1	2.6	3.0	3.4	3.8	4.3	1.1	1.7	2.3	2.8	3.4	4.0	4.6	5.1	5.7
33	0.7	1.1	1.5	1.8	2.2	2.6	2.9	3.3	3.6	1.0	1.5	1.9	2.4	2.9	3.4	3.9	4.4	4.9
36	0.6	0.9	1.3	1.6	1.9	2.2	2.5	2.8	3.1	0.8	1.3	1.7	2.1	2.5	2.9	3.4	3.8	4.2
39	0.5	0.8	1.1	1.4	1.6	1.9	2.2	2.5	2.7	0.7	1.1	1.5	1.8	2.2	2.5	2.9	3.3	3.6
42	0.5	0.7	0.9	1.2	1.4	1.7	1.9	2.1	2.4	0.6	0.9	1.3	1.6	1.9	2.2	2.5	2.8	3.2
45	0.4	0.6	0.8	1.0	1.2	1.5	1.7	1.9	2.1	0.6	0.8	1.1	1.4	1.7	1.9	2.2	2.5	2.8

Entry is reserve as annual percentage of gross income that covers the spot vacancy.

Spot Vacancy Cost Converted to Annual Reserve

Time Span	Spot Vacancy 15 Months — Percent Turnover at Time Span									Spot Vacancy 18 Months — Percent Turnover at Time Span								
	20	30	40	50	60	70	80	90	100	20	30	40	50	60	70	80	90	100
Interest Rate on Savings 7.50%																		
6	11.6	17.4	23.2	29.1	34.9	40.7	46.5	52.3	58.1	13.9	20.9	27.9	34.9	41.8	48.8	55.8	62.8	69.7
9	7.5	11.2	14.9	18.6	22.4	26.1	29.8	33.6	37.3	8.9	13.4	17.9	22.4	26.8	31.3	35.8	40.3	44.7
12	5.4	8.1	10.8	13.4	16.1	18.8	21.5	24.2	26.9	6.5	9.7	12.9	16.1	19.4	22.6	25.8	29.0	32.3
15	4.1	6.2	8.3	10.3	12.4	14.5	16.5	18.6	20.7	5.0	7.4	9.9	12.4	14.9	17.4	19.9	22.3	24.8
18	3.3	5.0	6.6	8.3	9.9	11.6	13.2	14.9	16.6	4.0	6.0	7.9	9.9	11.9	13.9	15.9	17.9	19.9
21	2.7	4.1	5.5	6.8	8.2	9.5	10.9	12.3	13.6	3.3	4.9	6.5	8.2	9.8	11.5	13.1	14.7	16.4
24	2.3	3.4	4.6	5.7	6.9	8.0	9.2	10.3	11.5	2.7	4.1	5.5	6.9	8.2	9.6	11.0	12.4	13.7
27	2.0	2.9	3.9	4.9	5.9	6.8	7.8	8.8	9.8	2.3	3.5	4.7	5.9	7.0	8.2	9.4	10.5	11.7
30	1.7	2.5	3.4	4.2	5.1	5.9	6.7	7.6	8.4	2.0	3.0	4.0	5.1	6.1	7.1	8.1	9.1	10.1
33	1.5	2.2	2.9	3.7	4.4	5.1	5.9	6.6	7.3	1.8	2.6	3.5	4.4	5.3	6.2	7.1	7.9	8.8
36	1.3	1.9	2.6	3.2	3.9	4.5	5.2	5.8	6.5	1.5	2.3	3.1	3.9	4.6	5.4	6.2	7.0	7.7
39	1.1	1.7	2.3	2.9	3.4	4.0	4.6	5.1	5.7	1.4	2.1	2.7	3.4	4.1	4.8	5.5	6.2	6.8
42	1.0	1.5	2.0	2.5	3.0	3.6	4.1	4.6	5.1	1.2	1.8	2.4	3.0	3.7	4.3	4.9	5.5	6.1
45	0.9	1.4	1.8	2.3	2.7	3.2	3.6	4.1	4.5	1.1	1.6	2.2	2.7	3.3	3.8	4.3	4.9	5.4
Interest Rate on Savings 8.50%																		
6	11.5	17.3	23.0	28.8	34.5	40.3	46.0	51.8	57.6	13.8	20.7	27.6	34.5	41.4	48.3	55.3	62.2	69.1
9	7.3	11.0	14.7	18.4	22.0	25.7	29.4	33.1	36.7	8.8	13.2	17.6	22.0	26.4	30.9	35.3	39.7	44.1
12	5.3	7.9	10.5	13.2	15.8	18.4	21.1	23.7	26.3	6.3	9.5	12.6	15.8	19.0	22.1	25.3	28.5	31.6
15	4.0	6.0	8.1	10.1	12.1	14.1	16.1	18.1	20.1	4.8	7.3	9.7	12.1	14.5	16.9	19.3	21.8	24.2
18	3.2	4.8	6.4	8.0	9.6	11.2	12.8	14.4	16.0	3.9	5.8	7.7	9.6	11.6	13.5	15.4	17.3	19.3
21	2.6	3.9	5.3	6.6	7.9	9.2	10.5	11.8	13.1	3.2	4.7	6.3	7.9	9.5	11.0	12.6	14.2	15.8
24	2.2	3.3	4.4	5.5	6.6	7.7	8.8	9.9	11.0	2.6	3.9	5.3	6.6	7.9	9.2	10.5	11.8	13.2
27	1.9	2.8	3.7	4.6	5.6	6.5	7.4	8.4	9.3	2.2	3.3	4.5	5.6	6.7	7.8	8.9	10.0	11.2
30	1.6	2.4	3.2	4.0	4.8	5.6	6.4	7.2	8.0	1.9	2.9	3.8	4.8	5.7	6.7	7.7	8.6	9.6
33	1.4	2.1	2.8	3.5	4.1	4.8	5.5	6.2	6.9	1.7	2.5	3.3	4.1	5.0	5.8	6.6	7.5	8.3
36	1.2	1.8	2.4	3.0	3.6	4.2	4.8	5.4	6.0	1.4	2.2	2.9	3.6	4.3	5.1	5.8	6.5	7.2
39	1.1	1.6	2.1	2.6	3.2	3.7	4.2	4.8	5.3	1.3	1.9	2.5	3.2	3.8	4.4	5.1	5.7	6.4
42	0.9	1.4	1.9	2.3	2.8	3.3	3.7	4.2	4.7	1.1	1.7	2.2	2.8	3.4	3.9	4.5	5.0	5.6
45	0.8	1.2	1.7	2.1	2.5	2.9	3.3	3.7	4.1	1.0	1.5	2.0	2.5	3.0	3.5	4.0	4.5	5.0
Interest Rate on Savings 9.50%																		
6	11.4	17.1	22.8	28.5	34.2	39.9	45.6	51.3	57.0	13.7	20.5	27.4	34.2	41.0	47.9	54.7	61.6	68.4
9	7.2	10.9	14.5	18.1	21.7	25.3	28.9	32.6	36.2	8.7	13.0	17.4	21.7	26.0	30.4	34.7	39.1	43.4
12	5.2	7.7	10.3	12.9	15.5	18.1	20.6	23.2	25.8	6.2	9.3	12.4	15.5	18.6	21.7	24.8	27.9	31.0
15	3.9	5.9	7.9	9.8	11.8	13.7	15.7	17.7	19.6	4.7	7.1	9.4	11.8	14.1	16.5	18.8	21.2	23.6
18	3.1	4.7	6.2	7.8	9.3	10.9	12.4	14.0	15.5	3.7	5.6	7.5	9.3	11.2	13.1	14.9	16.8	18.6
21	2.5	3.8	5.1	6.3	7.6	8.8	10.1	11.4	12.6	3.0	4.6	6.1	7.6	9.1	10.6	12.1	13.7	15.2
24	2.1	3.2	4.2	5.2	6.3	7.3	8.4	9.4	10.5	2.5	3.8	5.0	6.3	7.6	8.8	10.1	11.3	12.6
27	1.8	2.7	3.5	4.4	5.3	6.2	7.1	8.0	8.8	2.1	3.2	4.2	5.3	6.4	7.4	8.5	9.5	10.6
30	1.5	2.3	3.0	3.8	4.5	5.3	6.0	6.8	7.5	1.8	2.7	3.6	4.5	5.4	6.3	7.2	8.1	9.0
33	1.3	1.9	2.6	3.2	3.9	4.5	5.2	5.8	6.5	1.6	2.3	3.1	3.9	4.7	5.4	6.2	7.0	7.8
36	1.1	1.7	2.2	2.8	3.4	3.9	4.5	5.1	5.6	1.3	2.0	2.7	3.4	4.0	4.7	5.4	6.1	6.7
39	1.0	1.5	2.0	2.5	2.9	3.4	3.9	4.4	4.9	1.2	1.8	2.4	2.9	3.5	4.1	4.7	5.3	5.9
42	0.9	1.3	1.7	2.2	2.6	3.0	3.4	3.9	4.3	1.0	1.5	2.1	2.6	3.1	3.6	4.1	4.6	5.2
45	0.8	1.1	1.5	1.9	2.3	2.7	3.0	3.4	3.8	0.9	1.4	1.8	2.3	2.7	3.2	3.6	4.1	4.5
Interest Rate on Savings 10.50%																		
6	11.3	16.9	22.6	28.2	33.9	39.5	45.2	50.8	56.4	13.5	20.3	27.1	33.9	40.6	47.4	54.2	61.0	67.7
9	7.1	10.7	14.3	17.8	21.4	24.9	28.5	32.1	35.6	8.6	12.8	17.1	21.4	25.7	29.9	34.2	38.5	42.8
12	5.1	7.6	10.1	12.6	15.2	17.7	20.2	22.8	25.3	6.1	9.1	12.1	15.2	18.2	21.2	24.3	27.3	30.3
15	3.8	5.7	7.6	9.6	11.5	13.4	15.3	17.2	19.1	4.6	6.9	9.2	11.5	13.8	16.1	18.4	20.6	22.9
18	3.0	4.5	6.0	7.5	9.0	10.5	12.0	13.5	15.0	3.6	5.4	7.2	9.0	10.8	12.6	14.4	16.2	18.1
21	2.4	3.6	4.9	6.1	7.3	8.5	9.7	10.9	12.2	2.9	4.4	5.8	7.3	8.8	10.2	11.7	13.1	14.6
24	2.0	3.0	4.0	5.0	6.0	7.0	8.0	9.0	10.0	2.4	3.6	4.8	6.0	7.2	8.4	9.6	10.8	12.0
27	1.7	2.5	3.4	4.2	5.0	5.9	6.7	7.6	8.4	2.0	3.0	4.0	5.0	6.0	7.1	8.1	9.1	10.1
30	1.4	2.1	2.8	3.6	4.3	5.0	5.7	6.4	7.1	1.7	2.6	3.4	4.3	5.1	6.0	6.8	7.7	8.5
33	1.2	1.8	2.4	3.0	3.6	4.3	4.9	5.5	6.1	1.5	2.2	2.9	3.6	4.4	5.1	5.8	6.6	7.3
36	1.0	1.6	2.1	2.6	3.1	3.7	4.2	4.7	5.2	1.3	1.9	2.5	3.1	3.8	4.4	5.0	5.7	6.3
39	0.9	1.4	1.8	2.3	2.7	3.2	3.6	4.1	4.5	1.1	1.6	2.2	2.7	3.3	3.8	4.4	4.9	5.4
42	0.8	1.2	1.6	2.0	2.4	2.8	3.2	3.6	4.0	0.9	1.4	1.9	2.4	2.8	3.3	3.8	4.3	4.7
45	0.7	1.0	1.4	1.7	2.1	2.4	2.8	3.1	3.5	0.8	1.2	1.7	2.1	2.5	2.9	3.3	3.7	4.1

Entry is reserve as annual percentage of gross income that covers the spot vacancy.

Spot Vacancy Cost Converted to Annual Reserve

Time Span	Spot Vacancy 21 Months Percent Turnover at Time Span									Spot Vacancy 24 Months Percent Turnover at Time Span								
	20	30	40	50	60	70	80	90	100	20	30	40	50	60	70	80	90	100
Interest Rate on Savings 7.50%																		
6	16.3	24.4	32.5	40.7	48.8	57.0	65.1	73.2	81.4	18.6	27.9	37.2	46.5	55.8	65.1	74.4	83.7	93.0
9	10.4	15.7	20.9	26.1	31.3	36.5	41.8	47.0	52.2	11.9	17.9	23.9	29.8	35.8	41.8	47.7	53.7	59.7
12	7.5	11.3	15.1	18.8	22.6	26.4	30.1	33.9	37.7	8.6	12.9	17.2	21.5	25.8	30.1	34.4	38.7	43.0
15	5.8	8.7	11.6	14.5	17.4	20.3	23.2	26.1	29.0	6.6	9.9	13.2	16.5	19.9	23.2	26.5	29.8	33.1
18	4.6	7.0	9.3	11.6	13.9	16.2	18.5	20.9	23.2	5.3	7.9	10.6	13.2	15.9	18.5	21.2	23.8	26.5
21	3.8	5.7	7.6	9.5	11.5	13.4	15.3	17.2	19.1	4.4	6.5	8.7	10.9	13.1	15.3	17.4	19.6	21.8
24	3.2	4.8	6.4	8.0	9.6	11.2	12.8	14.4	16.0	3.7	5.5	7.3	9.2	11.0	12.8	14.7	16.5	18.3
27	2.7	4.1	5.5	6.8	8.2	9.6	10.9	12.3	13.7	3.1	4.7	6.3	7.8	9.4	10.9	12.5	14.1	15.6
30	2.4	3.5	4.7	5.9	7.1	8.3	9.4	10.6	11.8	2.7	4.0	5.4	6.7	8.1	9.4	10.8	12.1	13.5
33	2.1	3.1	4.1	5.1	6.2	7.2	8.2	9.3	10.3	2.4	3.5	4.7	5.9	7.1	8.2	9.4	10.6	11.8
36	1.8	2.7	3.6	4.5	5.4	6.3	7.2	8.1	9.0	2.1	3.1	4.1	5.2	6.2	7.2	8.3	9.3	10.3
39	1.6	2.4	3.2	4.0	4.8	5.6	6.4	7.2	8.0	1.8	2.7	3.7	4.6	5.5	6.4	7.3	8.2	9.1
42	1.4	2.1	2.8	3.6	4.3	5.0	5.7	6.4	7.1	1.6	2.4	3.2	4.1	4.9	5.7	6.5	7.3	8.1
45	1.3	1.9	2.5	3.2	3.8	4.4	5.1	5.7	6.3	1.4	2.2	2.9	3.6	4.3	5.1	5.8	6.5	7.2
Interest Rate on Savings 8.50%																		
6	16.1	24.2	32.2	40.3	48.3	56.4	64.5	72.5	80.6	18.4	27.6	36.8	46.0	55.3	64.5	73.7	82.9	92.1
9	10.3	15.4	20.6	25.7	30.9	36.0	41.1	46.3	51.4	11.8	17.6	23.5	29.4	35.3	41.1	47.0	52.9	58.8
12	7.4	11.1	14.8	18.4	22.1	25.8	29.5	33.2	36.9	8.4	12.6	16.9	21.1	25.3	29.5	33.7	37.9	42.2
15	5.6	8.5	11.3	14.1	16.9	19.7	22.6	25.4	28.2	6.4	9.7	12.9	16.1	19.3	22.6	25.8	29.0	32.2
18	4.5	6.7	9.0	11.2	13.5	15.7	18.0	20.2	22.5	5.1	7.7	10.3	12.8	15.4	18.0	20.5	23.1	25.7
21	3.7	5.5	7.4	9.2	11.0	12.9	14.7	16.5	18.4	4.2	6.3	8.4	10.5	12.6	14.7	16.8	18.9	21.0
24	3.1	4.6	6.1	7.7	9.2	10.7	12.3	13.8	15.3	3.5	5.3	7.0	8.8	10.5	12.3	14.0	15.8	17.5
27	2.6	3.9	5.2	6.5	7.8	9.1	10.4	11.7	13.0	3.0	4.5	5.9	7.4	8.9	10.4	11.9	13.4	14.9
30	2.2	3.3	4.5	5.6	6.7	7.8	8.9	10.0	11.2	2.6	3.8	5.1	6.4	7.7	8.9	10.2	11.5	12.8
33	1.9	2.9	3.9	4.8	5.8	6.8	7.7	8.7	9.7	2.2	3.3	4.4	5.5	6.6	7.7	8.8	9.9	11.0
36	1.7	2.5	3.4	4.2	5.1	5.9	6.7	7.6	8.4	1.9	2.9	3.9	4.8	5.8	6.7	7.7	8.7	9.6
39	1.5	2.2	3.0	3.7	4.4	5.2	5.9	6.7	7.4	1.7	2.5	3.4	4.2	5.1	5.9	6.8	7.6	8.5
42	1.3	2.0	2.6	3.3	3.9	4.6	5.2	5.9	6.5	1.5	2.2	3.0	3.7	4.5	5.2	6.0	6.7	7.5
45	1.2	1.7	2.3	2.9	3.5	4.1	4.6	5.2	5.8	1.3	2.0	2.7	3.3	4.0	4.6	5.3	6.0	6.6
Interest Rate on Savings 9.50%																		
6	16.0	23.9	31.9	39.9	47.9	55.9	63.8	71.8	79.8	18.2	27.4	36.5	45.6	54.7	63.8	73.0	82.1	91.2
9	10.1	15.2	20.3	25.3	30.4	35.5	40.5	45.6	50.6	11.6	17.4	23.2	28.9	34.7	40.5	46.3	52.1	57.9
12	7.2	10.8	14.5	18.1	21.7	25.3	28.9	32.5	36.1	8.3	12.4	16.5	20.6	24.8	28.9	33.0	37.2	41.3
15	5.5	8.2	11.0	13.7	16.5	19.2	22.0	24.7	27.5	6.3	9.4	12.6	15.7	18.8	22.0	25.1	28.3	31.4
18	4.4	6.5	8.7	10.9	13.1	15.2	17.4	19.6	21.8	5.0	7.5	9.9	12.4	14.9	17.4	19.9	22.4	24.9
21	3.5	5.3	7.1	8.8	10.6	12.4	14.2	15.9	17.7	4.0	6.1	8.1	10.1	12.1	14.2	16.2	18.2	20.2
24	2.9	4.4	5.9	7.3	8.8	10.3	11.8	13.2	14.7	3.4	5.0	6.7	8.4	10.1	11.8	13.4	15.1	16.8
27	2.5	3.7	4.9	6.2	7.4	8.7	9.9	11.1	12.4	2.8	4.2	5.7	7.1	8.5	9.9	11.3	12.7	14.1
30	2.1	3.2	4.2	5.3	6.3	7.4	8.4	9.5	10.5	2.4	3.6	4.8	6.0	7.2	8.4	9.6	10.8	12.1
33	1.8	2.7	3.6	4.5	5.4	6.4	7.3	8.2	9.1	2.1	3.1	4.1	5.2	6.2	7.3	8.3	9.3	10.4
36	1.6	2.4	3.1	3.9	4.7	5.5	6.3	7.1	7.9	1.8	2.7	3.6	4.5	5.4	6.3	7.2	8.1	9.0
39	1.4	2.1	2.7	3.4	4.1	4.8	5.5	6.2	6.9	1.6	2.4	3.1	3.9	4.7	5.5	6.3	7.1	7.8
42	1.2	1.8	2.4	3.0	3.6	4.2	4.8	5.4	6.0	1.4	2.1	2.8	3.4	4.1	4.8	5.5	6.2	6.9
45	1.1	1.6	2.1	2.7	3.2	3.7	4.2	4.8	5.3	1.2	1.8	2.4	3.0	3.6	4.2	4.8	5.5	6.1
Interest Rate on Savings 10.50%																		
6	15.8	23.7	31.6	39.5	47.4	55.3	63.2	71.1	79.0	18.1	27.1	36.1	45.2	54.2	63.2	72.2	81.3	90.3
9	10.0	15.0	20.0	24.9	29.9	34.9	39.9	44.9	49.9	11.4	17.1	22.8	28.5	34.2	39.9	45.6	51.3	57.0
12	7.1	10.6	14.2	17.7	21.2	24.8	28.3	31.9	35.4	8.1	12.1	16.2	20.2	24.3	28.3	32.4	36.4	40.4
15	5.4	8.0	10.7	13.4	16.1	18.7	21.4	24.1	26.8	6.1	9.2	12.2	15.3	18.4	21.4	24.5	27.5	30.6
18	4.2	6.3	8.4	10.5	12.6	14.7	16.8	19.0	21.1	4.8	7.2	9.6	12.0	14.4	16.8	19.3	21.7	24.1
21	3.4	5.1	6.8	8.5	10.2	11.9	13.6	15.3	17.0	3.9	5.8	7.8	9.7	11.7	13.6	15.6	17.5	19.5
24	2.8	4.2	5.6	7.0	8.4	9.8	11.2	12.6	14.0	3.2	4.8	6.4	8.0	9.6	11.2	12.8	14.5	16.1
27	2.4	3.5	4.7	5.9	7.1	8.2	9.4	10.6	11.8	2.7	4.0	5.4	6.7	8.1	9.4	10.8	12.1	13.4
30	2.0	3.0	4.0	5.0	6.0	7.0	8.0	9.0	10.0	2.3	3.4	4.6	5.7	6.8	8.0	9.1	10.2	11.4
33	1.7	2.6	3.4	4.3	5.1	6.0	6.8	7.7	8.5	1.9	2.9	3.9	4.9	5.8	6.8	7.8	8.8	9.7
36	1.5	2.2	2.9	3.7	4.4	5.1	5.9	6.6	7.3	1.7	2.5	3.4	4.2	5.0	5.9	6.7	7.5	8.4
39	1.3	1.9	2.5	3.2	3.8	4.4	5.1	5.7	6.4	1.5	2.2	2.9	3.6	4.4	5.1	5.8	6.5	7.3
42	1.1	1.7	2.2	2.8	3.3	3.9	4.4	5.0	5.5	1.3	1.9	2.5	3.2	3.8	4.4	5.1	5.7	6.3
45	1.0	1.5	1.9	2.4	2.9	3.4	3.9	4.4	4.8	1.1	1.7	2.2	2.8	3.3	3.9	4.4	5.0	5.5

Entry is reserve as annual percentage of gross income that covers the spot vacancy.

Spot Vacancy Cost Converted to Annual Reserve

Time Span	Spot Vacancy 27 Months — Percent Turnover at Time Span									Spot Vacancy 30 Months — Percent Turnover at Time Span								
	20	30	40	50	60	70	80	90	100	20	30	40	50	60	70	80	90	100
Interest Rate on Savings 7.50%																		
6	20.9	31.4	41.8	52.3	62.8	73.2	83.7	94.2	104.6	23.2	34.9	46.5	58.1	69.7	81.4	93.0	104.6	116.2
9	13.4	20.1	26.8	33.6	40.3	47.0	53.7	60.4	67.1	14.9	22.4	29.8	37.3	44.7	52.2	59.7	67.1	74.6
12	9.7	14.5	19.4	24.2	29.0	33.9	38.7	43.6	48.4	10.8	16.1	21.5	26.9	32.3	37.7	43.0	48.4	53.8
15	7.4	11.2	14.9	18.6	22.3	26.1	29.8	33.5	37.2	8.3	12.4	16.5	20.7	24.8	29.0	33.1	37.2	41.4
18	6.0	8.9	11.9	14.9	17.9	20.9	23.8	26.8	29.8	6.6	9.9	13.2	16.6	19.9	23.2	26.5	29.8	33.1
21	4.9	7.4	9.8	12.3	14.7	17.2	19.6	22.1	24.5	5.5	8.2	10.9	13.6	16.4	19.1	21.8	24.5	27.3
24	4.1	6.2	8.2	10.3	12.4	14.4	16.5	18.6	20.6	4.6	6.9	9.2	11.5	13.7	16.0	18.3	20.6	22.9
27	3.5	5.3	7.0	8.8	10.5	12.3	14.1	15.8	17.6	3.9	5.9	7.8	9.8	11.7	13.7	15.6	17.6	19.5
30	3.0	4.6	6.1	7.6	9.1	10.6	12.1	13.7	15.2	3.4	5.1	6.7	8.4	10.1	11.8	13.5	15.2	16.9
33	2.6	4.0	5.3	6.6	7.9	9.3	10.6	11.9	13.2	2.9	4.4	5.9	7.3	8.8	10.3	11.8	13.2	14.7
36	2.3	3.5	4.6	5.8	7.0	8.1	9.3	10.5	11.6	2.6	3.9	5.2	6.5	7.7	9.0	10.3	11.6	12.9
39	2.1	3.1	4.1	5.1	6.2	7.2	8.2	9.2	10.3	2.3	3.4	4.6	5.7	6.8	8.0	9.1	10.3	11.4
42	1.8	2.7	3.7	4.6	5.5	6.4	7.3	8.2	9.1	2.0	3.0	4.1	5.1	6.1	7.1	8.1	9.1	10.1
45	1.6	2.4	3.3	4.1	4.9	5.7	6.5	7.3	8.2	1.8	2.7	3.6	4.5	5.4	6.3	7.2	8.2	9.1
Interest Rate on Savings 8.50%																		
6	20.7	31.1	41.4	51.8	62.2	72.5	82.9	93.2	103.6	23.0	34.5	46.0	57.6	69.1	80.6	92.1	103.6	115.1
9	13.2	19.8	26.4	33.1	39.7	46.3	52.9	59.5	66.1	14.7	22.0	29.4	36.7	44.1	51.4	58.8	66.1	73.5
12	9.5	14.2	19.0	23.7	28.5	33.2	37.9	42.7	47.4	10.5	15.8	21.1	26.3	31.6	36.9	42.2	47.4	52.7
15	7.3	10.9	14.5	18.1	21.8	25.4	29.0	32.6	36.3	8.1	12.1	16.1	20.1	24.2	28.2	32.2	36.3	40.3
18	5.8	8.7	11.6	14.4	17.3	20.2	23.1	26.0	28.9	6.4	9.6	12.8	16.0	19.3	22.5	25.7	28.9	32.1
21	4.7	7.1	9.5	11.8	14.2	16.5	18.9	21.3	23.6	5.3	7.9	10.5	13.1	15.8	18.4	21.0	23.6	26.3
24	3.9	5.9	7.9	9.9	11.8	13.8	15.8	17.8	19.7	4.4	6.6	8.8	11.0	13.2	15.3	17.5	19.7	21.9
27	3.3	5.0	6.7	8.4	10.0	11.7	13.4	15.1	16.7	3.7	5.6	7.4	9.3	11.2	13.0	14.9	16.7	18.6
30	2.9	4.3	5.7	7.2	8.6	10.0	11.5	12.9	14.4	3.2	4.8	6.4	8.0	9.6	11.2	12.8	14.4	15.9
33	2.5	3.7	5.0	6.2	7.5	8.7	9.9	11.2	12.4	2.8	4.1	5.5	6.9	8.3	9.7	11.0	12.4	13.8
36	2.2	3.3	4.3	5.4	6.5	7.6	8.7	9.8	10.8	2.4	3.6	4.8	6.0	7.2	8.4	9.6	10.8	12.1
39	1.9	2.9	3.8	4.8	5.7	6.7	7.6	8.6	9.5	2.1	3.2	4.2	5.3	6.4	7.4	8.5	9.5	10.6
42	1.7	2.5	3.4	4.2	5.0	5.9	6.7	7.6	8.4	1.9	2.8	3.7	4.7	5.6	6.5	7.5	8.4	9.3
45	1.5	2.2	3.0	3.7	4.5	5.2	6.0	6.7	7.5	1.7	2.5	3.3	4.1	5.0	5.8	6.6	7.5	8.3
Interest Rate on Savings 9.50%																		
6	20.5	30.8	41.0	51.3	61.6	71.8	82.1	92.3	102.6	22.8	34.2	45.6	57.0	68.4	79.8	91.2	102.6	114.0
9	13.0	19.5	26.0	32.6	39.1	45.6	52.1	58.6	65.1	14.5	21.7	28.9	36.2	43.4	50.6	57.9	65.1	72.3
12	9.3	13.9	18.6	23.2	27.9	32.5	37.2	41.8	46.5	10.3	15.5	20.6	25.8	31.0	36.1	41.3	46.5	51.6
15	7.1	10.6	14.1	17.7	21.2	24.7	28.3	31.8	35.3	7.9	11.8	15.7	19.6	23.6	27.5	31.4	35.3	39.3
18	5.6	8.4	11.2	14.0	16.8	19.6	22.4	25.2	28.0	6.2	9.3	12.4	15.5	18.6	21.8	24.9	28.0	31.1
21	4.6	6.8	9.1	11.4	13.7	15.9	18.2	20.5	22.8	5.1	7.6	10.1	12.6	15.2	17.7	20.2	22.8	25.3
24	3.8	5.7	7.6	9.4	11.3	13.2	15.1	17.0	18.9	4.2	6.3	8.4	10.5	12.6	14.7	16.8	18.9	21.0
27	3.2	4.8	6.4	8.0	9.5	11.1	12.7	14.3	15.9	3.5	5.3	7.1	8.8	10.6	12.4	14.1	15.9	17.7
30	2.7	4.1	5.4	6.8	8.1	9.5	10.8	12.2	13.6	3.0	4.5	6.0	7.5	9.0	10.5	12.1	13.6	15.1
33	2.3	3.5	4.7	5.8	7.0	8.2	9.3	10.5	11.7	2.6	3.9	5.2	6.5	7.8	9.1	10.4	11.7	13.0
36	2.0	3.0	4.0	5.1	6.1	7.1	8.1	9.1	10.1	2.2	3.4	4.5	5.6	6.7	7.9	9.0	10.1	11.2
39	1.8	2.6	3.5	4.4	5.3	6.2	7.1	7.9	8.8	2.0	2.9	3.9	4.9	5.9	6.9	7.8	8.8	9.8
42	1.5	2.3	3.1	3.9	4.6	5.4	6.2	7.0	7.7	1.7	2.6	3.4	4.3	5.2	6.0	6.9	7.7	8.6
45	1.4	2.0	2.7	3.4	4.1	4.8	5.5	6.1	6.8	1.5	2.3	3.0	3.8	4.5	5.3	6.1	6.8	7.6
Interest Rate on Savings 10.50%																		
6	20.3	30.5	40.6	50.8	61.0	71.1	81.3	91.4	101.6	22.6	33.9	45.2	56.4	67.7	79.0	90.3	101.6	112.9
9	12.8	19.2	25.7	32.1	38.5	44.9	51.3	57.7	64.1	14.3	21.4	28.5	35.6	42.8	49.9	57.0	64.1	71.3
12	9.1	13.7	18.2	22.8	27.3	31.9	36.4	41.0	45.5	10.1	15.2	20.2	25.3	30.3	35.4	40.4	45.5	50.6
15	6.9	10.3	13.8	17.2	20.6	24.1	27.5	31.0	34.4	7.6	11.5	15.3	19.1	22.9	26.8	30.6	34.4	38.2
18	5.4	8.1	10.8	13.5	16.2	19.0	21.7	24.4	27.1	6.0	9.0	12.0	15.0	18.1	21.1	24.1	27.1	30.1
21	4.4	6.6	8.8	10.9	13.1	15.3	17.5	19.7	21.9	4.9	7.3	9.7	12.2	14.6	17.0	19.5	21.9	24.3
24	3.6	5.4	7.2	9.0	10.8	12.6	14.3	16.3	18.1	4.0	6.0	8.0	10.0	12.0	14.0	16.1	18.1	20.1
27	3.0	4.5	6.0	7.6	9.1	10.6	12.1	13.6	15.1	3.4	5.0	6.7	8.4	10.1	11.8	13.4	15.1	16.8
30	2.6	3.8	5.1	6.4	7.7	9.0	10.2	11.5	12.8	2.8	4.3	5.7	7.1	8.5	10.0	11.4	12.8	14.2
33	2.2	3.3	4.4	5.5	6.6	7.7	8.8	9.9	10.9	2.4	3.6	4.9	6.1	7.3	8.5	9.7	10.9	12.2
36	1.9	2.8	3.8	4.7	5.7	6.6	7.5	8.5	9.4	2.1	3.1	4.2	5.2	6.3	7.3	8.4	9.4	10.5
39	1.6	2.5	3.3	4.1	4.9	5.7	6.5	7.4	8.2	1.8	2.7	3.6	4.5	5.4	6.4	7.3	8.2	9.1
42	1.4	2.1	2.8	3.6	4.3	5.0	5.7	6.4	7.1	1.6	2.4	3.2	4.0	4.7	5.5	6.3	7.1	7.9
45	1.2	1.9	2.5	3.1	3.7	4.4	5.0	5.6	6.2	1.4	2.1	2.8	3.5	4.1	4.8	5.5	6.2	6.9

Entry is reserve as annual percentage of gross income that covers the spot vacancy.

Effect of Expense Variance on Cash on Cash Yield

7.00% Cash on Cash Yield before Variance

Debt Cover	Expense Ratio	-50%	-33%	-25%	-20%	-15%	-10%	10%	15%	20%	25%	33%	50%
						Percent Variance in Expenses							
1.10	10%	11.28	9.82	9.14	8.71	8.28	7.86	6.14	5.72	5.29	4.86	4.18	2.72
	20%	16.63	13.35	11.81	10.85	9.89	8.93	5.07	4.11	3.15	2.19	0.65	-2.63
	30%	23.50	17.89	15.25	13.60	11.95	10.30	3.70	2.05	0.40	-1.25	-3.89	-9.50
	40%	32.67	23.94	19.83	17.27	14.70	12.13	1.87	-0.70	-3.27	-5.83	-9.94	-18.67
	50%	45.50	32.41	26.25	22.40	18.55	14.70	-0.70	-4.55	-8.40	-12.25	-18.41	-31.50
	60%	64.75	45.12	35.88	30.10	24.33	18.55	-4.55	-10.33	-16.10	-21.88	-31.12	-50.75
1.15	10%	9.98	8.97	8.49	8.19	7.89	7.60	6.40	6.11	5.81	5.51	5.03	4.02
	20%	13.71	11.43	10.35	9.68	9.01	8.34	5.66	4.99	4.32	3.65	2.57	0.29
	30%	18.50	14.59	12.75	11.60	10.45	9.30	4.70	3.55	2.40	1.25	-0.59	-4.50
	40%	24.89	18.81	15.94	14.16	12.37	10.58	3.42	1.63	-0.16	-1.94	-4.81	-10.89
	50%	33.83	24.71	20.42	17.73	15.05	12.37	1.63	-1.05	-3.73	-6.42	-10.71	-19.83
	60%	47.25	33.56	27.12	23.10	19.07	15.05	-1.05	-5.07	-9.10	-13.12	-19.56	-33.25
1.20	10%	9.33	8.54	8.17	7.93	7.70	7.47	6.53	6.30	6.07	5.83	5.46	4.67
	20%	12.25	10.46	9.62	9.10	8.57	8.05	5.95	5.43	4.90	4.38	3.54	1.75
	30%	16.00	12.94	11.50	10.60	9.70	8.80	5.20	4.30	3.40	2.50	1.06	-2.00
	40%	21.00	16.24	14.00	12.60	11.20	9.80	4.20	2.80	1.40	0.00	-2.24	-7.00
	50%	28.00	20.86	17.50	15.40	13.30	11.20	2.80	0.70	-1.40	-3.50	-6.86	-14.00
	60%	38.50	27.79	22.75	19.60	16.45	13.30	0.70	-2.45	-5.60	-8.75	-13.79	-24.50
1.25	10%	8.94	8.28	7.97	7.78	7.58	7.39	6.61	6.42	6.22	6.03	5.72	5.06
	20%	11.38	9.89	9.19	8.75	8.31	7.88	6.12	5.69	5.25	4.81	4.11	2.62
	30%	14.50	11.95	10.75	10.00	9.25	8.50	5.50	4.75	4.00	3.25	2.05	-0.50
	40%	18.67	14.70	12.83	11.67	10.50	9.33	4.67	3.50	2.33	1.17	-0.70	-4.67
	50%	24.50	18.55	15.75	14.00	12.25	10.50	3.50	1.75	-0.00	-1.75	-4.55	-10.50
	60%	33.25	24.33	20.13	17.50	14.88	12.25	1.75	-0.88	-3.50	-6.13	-10.33	-19.25
1.30	10%	8.69	8.11	7.84	7.67	7.51	7.34	6.66	6.49	6.33	6.16	5.89	5.31
	20%	10.79	9.50	8.90	8.52	8.14	7.76	6.24	5.86	5.48	5.10	4.50	3.21
	30%	13.50	11.29	10.25	9.60	8.95	8.30	5.70	5.05	4.40	3.75	2.71	0.50
	40%	17.11	13.67	12.06	11.04	10.03	9.02	4.98	3.97	2.96	1.94	0.33	-3.11
	50%	22.17	17.01	14.58	13.07	11.55	10.03	3.97	2.45	0.93	-0.58	-3.01	-8.17
	60%	29.75	22.02	18.38	16.10	13.83	11.55	2.45	0.17	-2.10	-4.38	-8.02	-15.75

8.00% Cash on Cash Yield before Variance

Debt Cover	Expense Ratio	-50%	-33%	-25%	-20%	-15%	-10%	10%	15%	20%	25%	33%	50%
1.10	10%	12.89	11.23	10.44	9.96	9.47	8.98	7.02	6.53	6.04	5.56	4.77	3.11
	20%	19.00	15.26	13.50	12.40	11.30	10.20	5.80	4.70	3.60	2.50	0.74	-3.00
	30%	26.86	20.45	17.43	15.54	13.66	11.77	4.23	2.34	0.46	-1.43	-4.45	-10.86
	40%	37.33	27.36	22.67	19.73	16.80	13.87	2.13	-0.80	-3.73	-6.67	-11.36	-21.33
	50%	52.00	37.04	30.00	25.60	21.20	16.80	-0.80	-5.20	-9.60	-14.00	-21.04	-36.00
	60%	74.00	51.56	41.00	34.40	27.80	21.20	-5.20	-11.80	-18.40	-25.00	-35.56	-58.00
1.15	10%	11.41	10.25	9.70	9.36	9.02	8.68	7.32	6.98	6.64	6.30	5.75	4.59
	20%	15.67	13.06	11.83	11.07	10.30	9.53	6.47	5.70	4.93	4.17	2.94	0.33
	30%	21.14	16.67	14.57	13.26	11.94	10.63	5.37	4.06	2.74	1.43	-0.67	-5.14
	40%	28.44	21.49	18.22	16.18	14.13	12.09	3.91	1.87	-0.18	-2.22	-5.49	-12.44
	50%	38.67	28.24	23.33	20.27	17.20	14.13	1.87	-1.20	-4.27	-7.33	-12.24	-22.67
	60%	54.00	38.36	31.00	26.40	21.80	17.20	-1.20	-5.80	-10.40	-15.00	-22.36	-38.00
1.20	10%	10.67	9.76	9.33	9.07	8.80	8.53	7.47	7.20	6.93	6.67	6.24	5.33
	20%	14.00	11.96	11.00	10.40	9.80	9.20	6.80	6.20	5.60	5.00	4.04	2.00
	30%	18.29	14.79	13.14	12.11	11.09	10.06	5.94	4.91	3.89	2.86	1.21	-2.29
	40%	24.00	18.56	16.00	14.40	12.80	11.20	4.80	3.20	1.60	0.00	-2.56	-8.00
	50%	32.00	23.84	20.00	17.60	15.20	12.80	3.20	0.80	-1.60	-4.00	-7.84	-16.00
	60%	44.00	31.76	26.00	22.40	18.80	15.20	0.80	-2.80	-6.40	-10.00	-15.76	-28.00
1.25	10%	10.22	9.47	9.11	8.89	8.67	8.44	7.56	7.33	7.11	6.89	6.53	5.78
	20%	13.00	11.30	10.50	10.00	9.50	9.00	7.00	6.50	6.00	5.50	4.70	3.00
	30%	16.57	13.66	12.29	11.43	10.57	9.71	6.29	5.43	4.57	3.71	2.34	-0.57
	40%	21.33	16.80	14.67	13.33	12.00	10.67	5.33	4.00	2.67	1.33	-0.80	-5.33
	50%	28.00	21.20	18.00	16.00	14.00	12.00	4.00	2.00	-0.00	-2.00	-5.20	-12.00
	60%	38.00	27.80	23.00	20.00	17.00	14.00	2.00	-1.00	-4.00	-7.00	-11.80	-22.00
1.30	10%	9.93	9.27	8.96	8.77	8.58	8.39	7.61	7.42	7.23	7.04	6.73	6.07
	20%	12.33	10.86	10.17	9.73	9.30	8.87	7.13	6.70	6.27	5.83	5.14	3.67
	30%	15.43	12.90	11.71	10.97	10.23	9.49	6.51	5.77	5.03	4.29	3.10	0.57
	40%	19.56	15.63	13.78	12.62	11.47	10.31	5.69	4.53	3.38	2.22	0.37	-3.56
	50%	25.33	19.44	16.67	14.93	13.20	11.47	4.53	2.80	1.07	-0.67	-3.44	-9.33
	60%	34.00	25.16	21.00	18.40	15.80	13.20	2.80	0.20	-2.40	-5.00	-9.16	-18.00

Entry is annual percentage cash-on-cash return (negative = loss) from change in expenses.

Effect of Expense Variance on Cash on Cash Yield

9.00% Cash on Cash Yield before Variance

Debt Cover	Expense Ratio	Percent Variance in Expenses											
		-50%	-33%	-25%	-20%	-15%	-10%	10%	15%	20%	25%	33%	50%
1.10	10%	14.50	12.63	11.75	11.20	10.65	10.10	7.90	7.35	6.80	6.25	5.37	3.50
	20%	21.38	17.17	15.19	13.95	12.71	11.48	6.52	5.29	4.05	2.81	0.83	-3.38
	30%	30.21	23.00	19.61	17.49	15.36	13.24	4.76	2.64	0.51	-1.61	-5.00	-12.21
	40%	42.00	30.78	25.50	22.20	18.90	15.60	2.40	-0.90	-4.20	-7.50	-12.78	-24.00
	50%	58.50	41.67	33.75	28.80	23.85	18.90	-0.90	-5.85	-10.80	-15.75	-23.67	-40.50
	60%	83.25	58.01	46.13	38.70	31.28	23.85	-5.85	-13.28	-20.70	-28.13	-40.01	-65.25
1.15	10%	12.83	11.53	10.92	10.53	10.15	9.77	8.23	7.85	7.47	7.08	6.47	5.17
	20%	17.62	14.69	13.31	12.45	11.59	10.72	7.28	6.41	5.55	4.69	3.31	0.38
	30%	23.79	18.76	16.39	14.91	13.44	11.96	6.04	4.56	3.09	1.61	-0.76	-5.79
	40%	32.00	24.18	20.50	18.20	15.90	13.60	4.40	2.10	-0.20	-2.50	-6.18	-14.00
	50%	43.50	31.77	26.25	22.80	19.35	15.90	2.10	-1.35	-4.80	-8.25	-13.77	-25.50
	60%	60.75	43.15	34.87	29.70	24.52	19.35	-1.35	-6.52	-11.70	-16.87	-25.15	-42.75
1.20	10%	12.00	10.98	10.50	10.20	9.90	9.60	8.40	8.10	7.80	7.50	7.02	6.00
	20%	15.75	13.45	12.37	11.70	11.02	10.35	7.65	6.98	6.30	5.63	4.55	2.25
	30%	20.57	16.64	14.79	13.63	12.47	11.31	6.69	5.53	4.37	3.21	1.36	-2.57
	40%	27.00	20.88	18.00	16.20	14.40	12.60	5.40	3.60	1.80	0.00	-2.88	-9.00
	50%	36.00	26.82	22.50	19.80	17.10	14.40	3.60	0.90	-1.80	-4.50	-8.82	-18.00
	60%	49.50	35.73	29.25	25.20	21.15	17.10	0.90	-3.15	-7.20	-11.25	-17.73	-31.50
1.25	10%	11.50	10.65	10.25	10.00	9.75	9.50	8.50	8.25	8.00	7.75	7.35	6.50
	20%	14.63	12.71	11.81	11.25	10.69	10.13	7.87	7.31	6.75	6.19	5.29	3.37
	30%	18.64	15.36	13.82	12.86	11.89	10.93	7.07	6.11	5.14	4.18	2.64	-0.64
	40%	24.00	18.90	16.50	15.00	13.50	12.00	6.00	4.50	3.00	1.50	-0.90	-6.00
	50%	31.50	23.85	20.25	18.00	15.75	13.50	4.50	2.25	-0.00	-2.25	-5.85	-13.50
	60%	42.75	31.28	25.88	22.50	19.13	15.75	2.25	-1.13	-4.50	-7.88	-13.28	-24.75
1.30	10%	11.17	10.43	10.08	9.87	9.65	9.43	8.57	8.35	8.13	7.92	7.57	6.83
	20%	13.88	12.22	11.44	10.95	10.46	9.98	8.02	7.54	7.05	6.56	5.78	4.12
	30%	17.36	14.52	13.18	12.34	11.51	10.67	7.33	6.49	5.66	4.82	3.48	0.64
	40%	22.00	17.58	15.50	14.20	12.90	11.60	6.40	5.10	3.80	2.50	0.42	-4.00
	50%	28.50	21.87	18.75	16.80	14.85	12.90	5.10	3.15	1.20	-0.75	-3.87	-10.50
	60%	38.25	28.31	23.63	20.70	17.78	14.85	3.15	0.22	-2.70	-5.63	-10.31	-20.25

10.00% Cash on Cash Yield before Variance

Debt Cover	Expense Ratio	-50%	-33%	-25%	-20%	-15%	-10%	10%	15%	20%	25%	33%	50%
1.10	10%	16.11	14.03	13.06	12.44	11.83	11.22	8.78	8.17	7.56	6.94	5.97	3.89
	20%	23.75	19.08	16.88	15.50	14.13	12.75	7.25	5.87	4.50	3.12	0.92	-3.75
	30%	33.57	25.56	21.79	19.43	17.07	14.71	5.29	2.93	0.57	-1.79	-5.56	-13.57
	40%	46.67	34.20	28.33	24.67	21.00	17.33	2.67	-1.00	-4.67	-8.33	-14.20	-26.67
	50%	65.00	46.30	37.50	32.00	26.50	21.00	-1.00	-6.50	-12.00	-17.50	-26.30	-45.00
	60%	92.50	64.45	51.25	43.00	34.75	26.50	-6.50	-14.75	-23.00	-31.25	-44.45	-72.50
1.15	10%	14.26	12.81	12.13	11.70	11.28	10.85	9.15	8.72	8.30	7.87	7.19	5.74
	20%	19.58	16.32	14.79	13.83	12.87	11.92	8.08	7.13	6.17	5.21	3.68	0.42
	30%	26.43	20.84	18.21	16.57	14.93	13.29	6.71	5.07	3.43	1.79	-0.84	-6.43
	40%	35.56	26.87	22.78	20.22	17.67	15.11	4.89	2.33	-0.22	-2.78	-6.87	-15.56
	50%	48.33	35.30	29.17	25.33	21.50	17.67	2.33	-1.50	-5.33	-9.17	-15.30	-28.33
	60%	67.50	47.95	38.75	33.00	27.25	21.50	-1.50	-7.25	-13.00	-18.75	-27.95	-47.50
1.20	10%	13.33	12.20	11.67	11.33	11.00	10.67	9.33	9.00	8.67	8.33	7.80	6.67
	20%	17.50	14.95	13.75	13.00	12.25	11.50	8.50	7.75	7.00	6.25	5.05	2.50
	30%	22.86	18.49	16.43	15.14	13.86	12.57	7.43	6.14	4.86	3.57	1.51	-2.86
	40%	30.00	23.20	20.00	18.00	16.00	14.00	6.00	4.00	2.00	0.00	-3.20	-10.00
	50%	40.00	29.80	25.00	22.00	19.00	16.00	4.00	1.00	-2.00	-5.00	-9.80	-20.00
	60%	55.00	39.70	32.50	28.00	23.50	19.00	1.00	-3.50	-8.00	-12.50	-19.70	-35.00
1.25	10%	12.78	11.83	11.39	11.11	10.83	10.56	9.44	9.17	8.89	8.61	8.17	7.22
	20%	16.25	14.13	13.13	12.50	11.88	11.25	8.75	8.12	7.50	6.87	5.87	3.75
	30%	20.71	17.07	15.36	14.29	13.21	12.14	7.86	6.79	5.71	4.64	2.93	-0.71
	40%	26.67	21.00	18.33	16.67	15.00	13.33	6.67	5.00	3.33	1.67	-1.00	-6.67
	50%	35.00	26.50	22.50	20.00	17.50	15.00	5.00	2.50	-0.00	-2.50	-6.50	-15.00
	60%	47.50	34.75	28.75	25.00	21.25	17.50	2.50	-1.25	-5.00	-8.75	-14.75	-27.50
1.30	10%	12.41	11.59	11.20	10.96	10.72	10.48	9.52	9.28	9.04	8.80	8.41	7.59
	20%	15.42	13.58	12.71	12.17	11.63	11.08	8.92	8.37	7.83	7.29	6.42	4.58
	30%	19.29	16.13	14.64	13.71	12.79	11.86	8.14	7.21	6.29	5.36	3.87	0.71
	40%	24.44	19.53	17.22	15.78	14.33	12.89	7.11	5.67	4.22	2.78	0.47	-4.44
	50%	31.67	24.30	20.83	18.67	16.50	14.33	5.67	3.50	1.33	-0.83	-4.30	-11.67
	60%	42.50	31.45	26.25	23.00	19.75	16.50	3.50	0.25	-3.00	-6.25	-11.45	-22.50

Entry is annual percentage cash-on-cash return (negative = loss) from change in expenses.

Effect of Expense Variance on Cash on Cash Yield

11.00% Cash on Cash Yield before Variance

Debt Cover	Expense Ratio	-50%	-33%	-25%	-20%	-15%	-10%	10%	15%	20%	25%	33%	50%
	10%	17.72	15.44	14.36	13.69	13.02	12.34	9.66	8.98	8.31	7.64	6.56	4.28
	20%	26.13	20.98	18.56	17.05	15.54	14.03	7.97	6.46	4.95	3.44	1.02	-4.13
1.10	30%	36.93	28.11	23.96	21.37	18.78	16.19	5.81	3.22	0.63	-1.96	-6.11	-14.93
	40%	51.33	37.62	31.17	27.13	23.10	19.07	2.93	-1.10	-5.13	-9.17	-15.62	-29.33
	50%	71.50	50.93	41.25	35.20	29.15	23.10	-1.10	-7.15	-13.20	-19.25	-28.93	-49.50
	60%	101.75	70.90	56.38	47.30	38.23	29.15	-7.15	-16.23	-25.30	-34.38	-48.90	-79.75
	10%	15.69	14.09	13.34	12.87	12.41	11.94	10.06	9.59	9.13	8.66	7.91	6.31
	20%	21.54	17.96	16.27	15.22	14.16	13.11	8.89	7.84	6.78	5.73	4.04	0.46
1.15	30%	29.07	22.93	20.04	18.23	16.42	14.61	7.39	5.58	3.77	1.96	-0.93	-7.07
	40%	39.11	29.55	25.06	22.24	19.43	16.62	5.38	2.57	-0.24	-3.06	-7.55	-17.11
	50%	53.17	38.83	32.08	27.87	23.65	19.43	2.57	-1.65	-5.87	-10.08	-16.83	-31.17
	60%	74.25	52.74	42.62	36.30	29.97	23.65	-1.65	-7.97	-14.30	-20.62	-30.74	-52.25
	10%	14.67	13.42	12.83	12.47	12.10	11.73	10.27	9.90	9.53	9.17	8.58	7.33
	20%	19.25	16.44	15.12	14.30	13.47	12.65	9.35	8.53	7.70	6.88	5.56	2.75
1.20	30%	25.14	20.33	18.07	16.66	15.24	13.83	8.17	6.76	5.34	3.93	1.67	-3.14
	40%	33.00	25.52	22.00	19.80	17.60	15.40	6.60	4.40	2.20	0.00	-3.52	-11.00
	50%	44.00	32.78	27.50	24.20	20.90	17.60	4.40	1.10	-2.20	-5.50	-10.78	-22.00
	60%	60.50	43.67	35.75	30.80	25.85	20.90	1.10	-3.85	-8.80	-13.75	-21.67	-38.50
	10%	14.06	13.02	12.53	12.22	11.92	11.61	10.39	10.08	9.78	9.47	8.98	7.94
	20%	17.88	15.54	14.44	13.75	13.06	12.38	9.62	8.94	8.25	7.56	6.46	4.12
1.25	30%	22.79	18.78	16.89	15.71	14.54	13.36	8.64	7.46	6.29	5.11	3.22	-0.79
	40%	29.33	23.10	20.17	18.33	16.50	14.67	7.33	5.50	3.67	1.83	-1.10	-7.33
	50%	38.50	29.15	24.75	22.00	19.25	16.50	5.50	2.75	-0.00	-2.75	-7.15	-16.50
	60%	52.25	38.23	31.63	27.50	23.38	19.25	2.75	-1.38	-5.50	-9.63	-16.23	-30.25
	10%	13.65	12.75	12.32	12.06	11.79	11.53	10.47	10.21	9.94	9.68	9.25	8.35
	20%	16.96	14.93	13.98	13.38	12.79	12.19	9.81	9.21	8.62	8.02	7.07	5.04
1.30	30%	21.21	17.74	16.11	15.09	14.06	13.04	8.96	7.94	6.91	5.89	4.26	0.79
	40%	26.89	21.49	18.94	17.36	15.77	14.18	7.82	6.23	4.64	3.06	0.51	-4.89
	50%	34.83	26.73	22.92	20.53	18.15	15.77	6.23	3.85	1.47	-0.92	-4.73	-12.83
	60%	46.75	34.60	28.88	25.30	21.73	18.15	3.85	0.27	-3.30	-6.88	-12.60	-24.75

12.00% Cash on Cash Yield before Variance

Debt Cover	Expense Ratio	-50%	-33%	-25%	-20%	-15%	-10%	10%	15%	20%	25%	33%	50%
	10%	19.33	16.84	15.67	14.93	14.20	13.47	10.53	9.80	9.07	8.33	7.16	4.67
	20%	28.50	22.89	20.25	18.60	16.95	15.30	8.70	7.05	5.40	3.75	1.11	-4.50
1.10	30%	40.29	30.67	26.14	23.31	20.49	17.66	6.34	3.51	0.69	-2.14	-6.67	-16.29
	40%	56.00	41.04	34.00	29.60	25.20	20.80	3.20	-1.20	-5.60	-10.00	-17.04	-32.00
	50%	78.00	55.56	45.00	38.40	31.80	25.20	-1.20	-7.80	-14.40	-21.00	-31.56	-54.00
	60%	111.00	77.34	61.50	51.60	41.70	31.80	-7.80	-17.70	-27.60	-37.50	-53.34	-87.00
	10%	17.11	15.37	14.56	14.04	13.53	13.02	10.98	10.47	9.96	9.44	8.63	6.89
	20%	23.50	19.59	17.75	16.60	15.45	14.30	9.70	8.55	7.40	6.25	4.41	0.50
1.15	30%	31.71	25.01	21.86	19.89	17.91	15.94	8.06	6.09	4.11	2.14	-1.01	-7.71
	40%	42.67	32.24	27.33	24.27	21.20	18.13	5.87	2.80	-0.27	-3.33	-8.24	-18.67
	50%	58.00	42.36	35.00	30.40	25.80	21.20	2.80	-1.80	-6.40	-11.00	-18.36	-34.00
	60%	81.00	57.54	46.50	39.60	32.70	25.80	-1.80	-8.70	-15.60	-22.50	-33.54	-57.00
	10%	16.00	14.64	14.00	13.60	13.20	12.80	11.20	10.80	10.40	10.00	9.36	8.00
	20%	21.00	17.94	16.50	15.60	14.70	13.80	10.20	9.30	8.40	7.50	6.06	3.00
1.20	30%	27.43	22.18	19.71	18.17	16.63	15.09	8.91	7.37	5.83	4.29	1.82	-3.43
	40%	36.00	27.84	24.00	21.60	19.20	16.80	7.20	4.80	2.40	0.00	-3.84	-12.00
	50%	48.00	35.76	30.00	26.40	22.80	19.20	4.80	1.20	-2.40	-6.00	-11.76	-24.00
	60%	66.00	47.64	39.00	33.60	28.20	22.80	1.20	-4.20	-9.60	-15.00	-23.64	-42.00
	10%	15.33	14.20	13.67	13.33	13.00	12.67	11.33	11.00	10.67	10.33	9.80	8.67
	20%	19.50	16.95	15.75	15.00	14.25	13.50	10.50	9.75	9.00	8.25	7.05	4.50
1.25	30%	24.86	20.49	18.43	17.14	15.86	14.57	9.43	8.14	6.86	5.57	3.51	-0.86
	40%	32.00	25.20	22.00	20.00	18.00	16.00	8.00	6.00	4.00	2.00	-1.20	-8.00
	50%	42.00	31.80	27.00	24.00	21.00	18.00	6.00	3.00	-0.00	-3.00	-7.80	-18.00
	60%	57.00	41.70	34.50	30.00	25.50	21.00	3.00	-1.50	-6.00	-10.50	-17.70	-33.00
	10%	14.89	13.91	13.44	13.16	12.87	12.58	11.42	11.13	10.84	10.56	10.09	9.11
	20%	18.50	16.29	15.25	14.60	13.95	13.30	10.70	10.05	9.40	8.75	7.71	5.50
1.30	30%	23.14	19.35	17.57	16.46	15.34	14.23	9.77	8.66	7.54	6.43	4.65	0.86
	40%	29.33	23.44	20.67	18.93	17.20	15.47	8.53	6.80	5.07	3.33	0.56	-5.33
	50%	38.00	29.16	25.00	22.40	19.80	17.20	6.80	4.20	1.60	-1.00	-5.16	-14.00
	60%	51.00	37.74	31.50	27.60	23.70	19.80	4.20	0.30	-3.60	-7.50	-13.74	-27.00

Entry is annual percentage cash-on-cash return (negative = loss) from change in expenses.

Straight-Line Depreciation with Mid-month Convention

27.5 Year Property Life — Annual Percentage Recovery

Month When Property Placed in Service

Recovery Year	1	2	3	4	5	6	7	8	9	10	11	12
1	3.485	3.182	2.879	2.576	2.273	1.970	1.667	1.364	1.061	0.758	0.455	0.152
2	3.636	3.636	3.636	3.636	3.636	3.636	3.636	3.636	3.636	3.636	3.636	3.636
3	3.636	3.636	3.636	3.636	3.636	3.636	3.636	3.636	3.636	3.636	3.636	3.636
4	3.636	3.636	3.636	3.636	3.636	3.636	3.636	3.636	3.636	3.636	3.636	3.636
5	3.636	3.636	3.636	3.636	3.636	3.636	3.636	3.636	3.636	3.636	3.636	3.636
6	3.636	3.636	3.636	3.636	3.636	3.636	3.636	3.636	3.636	3.636	3.636	3.636
7	3.636	3.636	3.636	3.636	3.636	3.636	3.636	3.636	3.636	3.636	3.636	3.636
8	3.636	3.636	3.636	3.636	3.636	3.636	3.636	3.636	3.636	3.636	3.636	3.636
9	3.636	3.636	3.636	3.636	3.636	3.636	3.636	3.636	3.636	3.636	3.636	3.636
10	3.637	3.637	3.637	3.637	3.637	3.637	3.636	3.636	3.636	3.636	3.636	3.636
11	3.636	3.636	3.636	3.636	3.636	3.636	3.637	3.637	3.637	3.637	3.637	3.637
12	3.637	3.637	3.637	3.637	3.637	3.637	3.636	3.637	3.637	3.637	3.637	3.637
13	3.636	3.636	3.636	3.636	3.636	3.636	3.637	3.636	3.636	3.636	3.636	3.636
14	3.637	3.637	3.637	3.637	3.637	3.637	3.636	3.636	3.636	3.636	3.637	3.637
15	3.636	3.636	3.636	3.636	3.636	3.636	3.637	3.637	3.637	3.637	3.637	3.637
16	3.637	3.637	3.637	3.637	3.637	3.637	3.636	3.636	3.636	3.636	3.636	3.636
17	3.636	3.636	3.636	3.636	3.636	3.636	3.637	3.637	3.637	3.637	3.637	3.637
18	3.637	3.637	3.637	3.637	3.637	3.637	3.636	3.637	3.637	3.637	3.637	3.637
19	3.636	3.636	3.636	3.636	3.636	3.636	3.637	3.636	3.636	3.636	3.636	3.636
20	3.637	3.637	3.637	3.637	3.637	3.637	3.636	3.637	3.637	3.637	3.637	3.637
21	3.636	3.636	3.636	3.636	3.636	3.636	3.637	3.637	3.637	3.637	3.636	3.636
22	3.637	3.637	3.637	3.637	3.637	3.637	3.636	3.636	3.636	3.636	3.637	3.637
23	3.636	3.636	3.636	3.636	3.636	3.636	3.637	3.637	3.637	3.637	3.636	3.636
24	3.637	3.637	3.637	3.637	3.637	3.637	3.636	3.636	3.636	3.636	3.637	3.637
25	3.636	3.636	3.636	3.636	3.636	3.636	3.637	3.637	3.637	3.637	3.637	3.637
26	3.637	3.637	3.637	3.637	3.637	3.637	3.636	3.636	3.636	3.636	3.636	3.636
27	3.636	3.636	3.636	3.636	3.636	3.636	3.637	3.637	3.637	3.637	3.637	3.637
28	1.970	2.273	2.576	2.879	3.182	3.485	3.636	3.637	3.637	3.637	3.637	3.637
29	0.000	0.000	0.000	0.000	0.000	0.000	0.152	0.455	0.758	1.061	1.364	1.667

Accumulated Cost Recovery

Recovery Year	1	2	3	4	5	6	7	8	9	10	11	12
1	3.5	3.2	2.9	2.6	2.3	2.0	1.7	1.4	1.1	0.8	0.5	0.2
2	7.1	6.8	6.5	6.2	5.9	5.6	5.3	5.0	4.7	4.4	4.1	3.8
3	10.8	10.5	10.2	9.8	9.5	9.2	8.9	8.6	8.3	8.0	7.7	7.4
4	14.4	14.1	13.8	13.5	13.2	12.9	12.6	12.3	12.0	11.7	11.4	11.1
5	18.0	17.7	17.4	17.1	16.8	16.5	16.2	15.9	15.6	15.3	15.0	14.7
6	21.7	21.4	21.1	20.8	20.5	20.2	19.8	19.5	19.2	18.9	18.6	18.3
7	25.3	25.0	24.7	24.4	24.1	23.8	23.5	23.2	22.9	22.6	22.3	22.0
8	28.9	28.6	28.3	28.0	27.7	27.4	27.1	26.8	26.5	26.2	25.9	25.6
9	32.6	32.3	32.0	31.7	31.4	31.1	30.8	30.5	30.1	29.8	29.5	29.2
10	36.2	35.9	35.6	35.3	35.0	34.7	34.4	34.1	33.8	33.5	33.2	32.9
11	39.8	39.5	39.2	38.9	38.6	38.3	38.0	37.7	37.4	37.1	36.8	36.5
12	43.5	43.2	42.9	42.6	42.3	42.0	41.7	41.4	41.1	40.8	40.5	40.1
13	47.1	46.8	46.5	46.2	45.9	45.6	45.3	45.0	44.7	44.4	44.1	43.8
14	50.8	50.5	50.2	49.8	49.5	49.2	48.9	48.6	48.3	48.0	47.7	47.4
15	54.4	54.1	53.8	53.5	53.2	52.9	52.6	52.3	52.0	51.7	51.4	51.1
16	58.0	57.7	57.4	57.1	56.8	56.5	56.2	55.9	55.6	55.3	55.0	54.7
17	61.7	61.4	61.1	60.8	60.5	60.2	59.8	59.5	59.2	58.9	58.6	58.3
18	65.3	65.0	64.7	64.4	64.1	63.8	63.5	63.2	62.9	62.6	62.3	62.0
19	68.9	68.6	68.3	68.0	67.7	67.4	67.1	66.8	66.5	66.2	65.9	65.6
20	72.6	72.3	72.0	71.7	71.4	71.1	70.8	70.5	70.2	69.8	69.5	69.2
21	76.2	75.9	75.6	75.3	75.0	74.7	74.4	74.1	73.8	73.5	73.2	72.9
22	79.8	79.5	79.2	78.9	78.6	78.3	78.0	77.7	77.4	77.1	76.8	76.5
23	83.5	83.2	82.9	82.6	82.3	82.0	81.7	81.4	81.1	80.8	80.5	80.2
24	87.1	86.8	86.5	86.2	85.9	85.6	85.3	85.0	84.7	84.4	84.1	83.8
25	90.8	90.5	90.2	89.8	89.5	89.2	88.9	88.6	88.3	88.0	87.7	87.4
26	94.4	94.1	93.8	93.5	93.2	92.9	92.6	92.3	92.0	91.7	91.4	91.1
27	98.0	97.7	97.4	97.1	96.8	96.5	96.2	95.9	95.6	95.3	95.0	94.7
28	100.0	100.0	100.0	100.0	100.0	100.0	99.8	99.5	99.2	95.3	95.0	94.7
29							100.0	100.0	100.0	98.9	98.6	98.3
										100.0	100.0	100.0

Entry is annual percentage of depcreciable portion of asset that may be deducted.

Straight-Line Depreciation with Mid-month Convention

31.5 Year Property Life — Annual Percentage Recovery

Recovery Year	Month When Property Placed in Service											
	1	2	3	4	5	6	7	8	9	10	11	12
1	3.042	2.778	2.513	2.249	1.984	1.720	1.455	1.190	0.926	0.661	0.397	0.132
2	3.175	3.175	3.175	3.175	3.175	3.175	3.175	3.175	3.175	3.175	3.175	3.175
3	3.175	3.175	3.175	3.175	3.175	3.175	3.175	3.175	3.175	3.175	3.175	3.175
4	3.175	3.175	3.175	3.175	3.175	3.175	3.175	3.175	3.175	3.175	3.175	3.175
5	3.175	3.175	3.175	3.175	3.175	3.175	3.175	3.175	3.175	3.175	3.175	3.175
6	3.175	3.175	3.175	3.175	3.175	3.175	3.175	3.175	3.175	3.175	3.175	3.175
7	3.175	3.175	3.175	3.175	3.175	3.175	3.175	3.175	3.175	3.175	3.175	3.175
8	3.175	3.174	3.175	3.174	3.175	3.174	3.175	3.175	3.175	3.175	3.175	3.175
9	3.174	3.175	3.174	3.175	3.174	3.175	3.174	3.175	3.174	3.175	3.174	3.175
10	3.175	3.174	3.175	3.174	3.175	3.174	3.175	3.174	3.175	3.174	3.175	3.174
11	3.174	3.175	3.174	3.175	3.174	3.175	3.174	3.175	3.174	3.175	3.174	3.175
12	3.175	3.174	3.175	3.174	3.175	3.174	3.175	3.174	3.175	3.174	3.175	3.174
13	3.174	3.175	3.174	3.175	3.174	3.175	3.174	3.175	3.174	3.175	3.174	3.175
14	3.175	3.174	3.175	3.174	3.175	3.174	3.175	3.174	3.175	3.174	3.175	3.174
15	3.174	3.175	3.174	3.175	3.174	3.175	3.174	3.175	3.174	3.175	3.174	3.175
16	3.175	3.174	3.175	3.174	3.175	3.174	3.175	3.174	3.175	3.174	3.175	3.174
17	3.174	3.175	3.174	3.175	3.174	3.175	3.174	3.175	3.174	3.175	3.174	3.175
18	3.175	3.174	3.175	3.174	3.175	3.174	3.175	3.174	3.175	3.174	3.175	3.175
19	3.174	3.175	3.174	3.175	3.174	3.175	3.174	3.175	3.174	3.175	3.174	3.175
20	3.175	3.174	3.175	3.174	3.175	3.174	3.175	3.174	3.175	3.174	3.175	3.174
21	3.174	3.175	3.174	3.175	3.174	3.175	3.174	3.175	3.174	3.175	3.174	3.175
22	3.175	3.174	3.175	3.174	3.175	3.174	3.175	3.174	3.175	3.174	3.175	3.174
23	3.174	3.175	3.174	3.175	3.174	3.175	3.174	3.175	3.174	3.175	3.174	3.175
24	3.175	3.174	3.175	3.174	3.175	3.174	3.175	3.174	3.175	3.174	3.175	3.174
25	3.174	3.175	3.174	3.175	3.174	3.175	3.174	3.175	3.174	3.175	3.174	3.175
26	3.175	3.174	3.175	3.174	3.175	3.174	3.175	3.174	3.175	3.174	3.175	3.174
27	3.174	3.175	3.174	3.175	3.174	3.175	3.174	3.175	3.174	3.175	3.174	3.175
28	3.175	3.174	3.175	3.174	3.175	3.174	3.175	3.174	3.175	3.174	3.175	3.174
29	3.174	3.175	3.174	3.175	3.174	3.175	3.174	3.175	3.174	3.175	3.174	3.175
30	3.175	3.174	3.175	3.174	3.175	3.174	3.175	3.174	3.175	3.174	3.175	3.174
31	3.174	3.175	3.174	3.175	3.174	3.175	3.174	3.175	3.174	3.175	3.174	3.175
32	1.720	1.984	2.249	2.513	2.778	3.042	3.175	3.174	3.175	3.174	3.175	3.174
33	0.000	0.000	0.000	0.000	0.000	0.000	0.132	0.397	0.661	0.926	1.190	1.455

Accumulated Cost Recovery

	1	2	3	4	5	6	7	8	9	10	11	12
1	3.0	2.8	2.5	2.2	2.0	1.7	1.5	1.2	0.9	0.7	0.4	0.1
2	6.2	6.0	5.7	5.4	5.2	4.9	4.6	4.4	4.1	3.8	3.6	3.3
3	9.4	9.1	8.9	8.6	8.3	8.1	7.8	7.5	7.3	7.0	6.7	6.5
4	12.6	12.3	12.0	11.8	11.5	11.2	11.0	10.7	10.5	10.2	9.9	9.7
5	15.7	15.5	15.2	14.9	14.7	14.4	14.2	13.9	13.6	13.4	13.1	12.8
6	18.9	18.7	18.4	18.1	17.9	17.6	17.3	17.1	16.8	16.5	16.3	16.0
7	22.1	21.8	21.6	21.3	21.0	20.8	20.5	20.2	20.0	19.7	19.4	19.2
8	25.3	25.0	24.7	24.5	24.2	23.9	23.7	23.4	23.2	22.9	22.6	22.4
9	28.4	28.2	27.9	27.6	27.4	27.1	26.9	26.6	26.3	26.1	25.8	25.5
10	31.6	31.4	31.1	30.8	30.6	30.3	30.0	29.8	29.5	29.2	29.0	28.7
11	34.8	34.5	34.3	34.0	33.7	33.5	33.2	32.9	32.7	32.4	32.1	31.9
12	38.0	37.7	37.4	37.2	36.9	36.6	36.4	36.1	35.8	35.6	35.3	35.1
13	41.1	40.9	40.6	40.3	40.1	39.8	39.6	39.3	39.0	38.8	38.5	38.2
14	44.3	44.0	43.8	43.5	43.3	43.0	42.7	42.5	42.2	41.9	41.7	41.4
15	47.5	47.2	47.0	46.7	46.4	46.2	45.9	45.6	45.4	45.1	44.8	44.6
16	50.7	50.4	50.1	49.9	49.6	49.3	49.1	48.8	48.5	48.3	48.0	47.8
17	53.8	53.6	53.3	53.0	52.8	52.5	52.2	52.0	51.7	51.5	51.2	50.9
18	57.0	56.7	56.5	56.2	56.0	55.7	55.4	55.2	54.9	54.6	54.4	54.1
19	60.2	59.9	59.7	59.4	59.1	58.9	58.6	58.3	58.1	57.8	57.5	57.3
20	63.4	63.1	62.8	62.6	62.3	62.0	61.8	61.5	61.2	61.0	60.7	60.4
21	66.5	66.3	66.0	65.7	65.5	65.2	64.9	64.7	64.4	64.2	63.9	63.6
22	69.7	69.4	69.2	68.9	68.7	68.4	68.1	67.9	67.6	67.3	67.1	66.8
23	72.9	72.6	72.4	72.1	71.8	71.6	71.3	71.0	70.8	70.5	70.2	70.0
24	76.1	75.8	75.5	75.3	75.0	74.7	74.5	74.2	73.9	73.7	73.4	73.1
25	79.2	79.0	78.7	78.4	78.2	77.9	77.6	77.4	77.1	76.9	76.6	76.3
26	82.4	82.1	81.9	81.6	81.4	81.1	80.8	80.6	80.3	80.0	79.8	79.5
27	85.6	85.3	85.1	84.8	84.5	84.3	84.0	83.7	83.5	83.2	82.9	82.7
28	88.8	88.5	88.2	88.0	87.7	87.4	87.2	86.9	86.6	86.4	86.1	85.8
29	91.9	91.7	91.4	91.1	90.9	90.6	90.3	90.1	89.8	89.6	89.3	89.0
30	95.1	94.8	94.6	94.3	94.0	93.8	93.5	93.3	93.0	92.7	92.5	92.2
31	98.3	98.0	97.8	97.5	97.2	97.0	96.7	96.4	96.2	95.9	95.6	95.4
32	100.0	100.0	100.0	100.0	100.0	100.0	99.9	99.6	99.3	99.1	98.8	98.5
33							100.0	100.0	100.0	100.0	100.0	100.0

Entry is annual percentage of depcreciable portion of asset that may be deducted.

Straight-Line Depreciation with Mid-month Convention

40.0 Year Property Life				Annual Percentage Recovery							

Recovery Year	Month When Property Placed in Service											
	1	2	3	4	5	6	7	8	9	10	11	12
1	2.396	2.188	1.979	1.771	1.563	1.354	1.146	0.938	0.729	0.521	0.313	0.104
2	2.500	2.500	2.500	2.500	2.500	2.500	2.500	2.500	2.500	2.500	2.500	2.500
3	2.500	2.500	2.500	2.500	2.500	2.500	2.500	2.500	2.500	2.500	2.500	2.500
4	2.500	2.500	2.500	2.500	2.500	2.500	2.500	2.500	2.500	2.500	2.500	2.500
5	2.500	2.500	2.500	2.500	2.500	2.500	2.500	2.500	2.500	2.500	2.500	2.500
6	2.500	2.500	2.500	2.500	2.500	2.500	2.500	2.500	2.500	2.500	2.500	2.500
7	2.500	2.500	2.500	2.500	2.500	2.500	2.500	2.500	2.500	2.500	2.500	2.500
8	2.500	2.500	2.500	2.500	2.500	2.500	2.500	2.500	2.500	2.500	2.500	2.500
9	2.500	2.500	2.500	2.500	2.500	2.500	2.500	2.500	2.500	2.500	2.500	2.500
10	2.500	2.500	2.500	2.500	2.500	2.500	2.500	2.500	2.500	2.500	2.500	2.500
11 - 34	2.500	2.500	2.500	2.500	2.500	2.500	2.500	2.500	2.500	2.500	2.500	2.500
35	2.500	2.500	2.500	2.500	2.500	2.500	2.500	2.500	2.500	2.500	2.500	2.500
36	2.500	2.500	2.500	2.500	2.500	2.500	2.500	2.500	2.500	2.500	2.500	2.500
37	2.500	2.500	2.500	2.500	2.500	2.500	2.500	2.500	2.500	2.500	2.500	2.500
38	2.500	2.500	2.500	2.500	2.500	2.500	2.500	2.500	2.500	2.500	2.500	2.500
39	2.500	2.500	2.500	2.500	2.500	2.500	2.500	2.500	2.500	2.500	2.500	2.500
40	2.500	2.500	2.500	2.500	2.500	2.500	2.500	2.500	2.500	2.500	2.500	2.500
41	0.104	0.313	0.521	0.729	0.938	1.146	1.354	1.563	1.771	1.979	2.188	2.396

Accumulated Cost Recovery												
1	2.4	2.2	2.0	1.8	1.6	1.4	1.1	0.9	0.7	0.5	0.3	0.1
2	4.9	4.7	4.5	4.3	4.1	3.9	3.6	3.4	3.2	3.0	2.8	2.6
3	7.4	7.2	7.0	6.8	6.6	6.4	6.1	5.9	5.7	5.5	5.3	5.1
4	9.9	9.7	9.5	9.3	9.1	8.9	8.6	8.4	8.2	8.0	7.8	7.6
5	12.4	12.2	12.0	11.8	11.6	11.4	11.1	10.9	10.7	10.5	10.3	10.1
6	14.9	14.7	14.5	14.3	14.1	13.9	13.6	13.4	13.2	13.0	12.8	12.6
7	17.4	17.2	17.0	16.8	16.6	16.4	16.1	15.9	15.7	15.5	15.3	15.1
8	19.9	19.7	19.5	19.3	19.1	18.9	18.6	18.4	18.2	18.0	17.8	17.6
9	22.4	22.2	22.0	21.8	21.6	21.4	21.1	20.9	20.7	20.5	20.3	20.1
10	24.9	24.7	24.5	24.3	24.1	23.9	23.6	23.4	23.2	23.0	22.8	22.6
11	27.4	27.2	27.0	26.8	26.6	26.4	26.1	25.9	25.7	25.5	25.3	25.1
12	29.9	29.7	29.5	29.3	29.1	28.9	28.6	28.4	28.2	28.0	27.8	27.6
13	32.4	32.2	32.0	31.8	31.6	31.4	31.1	30.9	30.7	30.5	30.3	30.1
14	34.9	34.7	34.5	34.3	34.1	33.9	33.6	33.4	33.2	33.0	32.8	32.6
15	37.4	37.2	37.0	36.8	36.6	36.4	36.1	35.9	35.7	35.5	35.3	35.1
16	39.9	39.7	39.5	39.3	39.1	38.9	38.6	38.4	38.2	38.0	37.8	37.6
17	42.4	42.2	42.0	41.8	41.6	41.4	41.1	40.9	40.7	40.5	40.3	40.1
18	44.9	44.7	44.5	44.3	44.1	43.9	43.6	43.4	43.2	43.0	42.8	42.6
19	47.4	47.2	47.0	46.8	46.6	46.4	46.1	45.9	45.7	45.5	45.3	45.1
20	49.9	49.7	49.5	49.3	49.1	48.9	48.6	48.4	48.2	48.0	47.8	47.6
21	52.4	52.2	52.0	51.8	51.6	51.4	51.1	50.9	50.7	50.5	50.3	50.1
22	54.9	54.7	54.5	54.3	54.1	53.9	53.6	53.4	53.2	53.0	52.8	52.6
23	57.4	57.2	57.0	56.8	56.6	56.4	56.1	55.9	55.7	55.5	55.3	55.1
24	59.9	59.7	59.5	59.3	59.1	58.9	58.6	58.4	58.2	58.0	57.8	57.6
25	62.4	62.2	62.0	61.8	61.6	61.4	61.1	60.9	60.7	60.5	60.3	60.1
26	64.9	64.7	64.5	64.3	64.1	63.9	63.6	63.4	63.2	63.0	62.8	62.6
27	67.4	67.2	67.0	66.8	66.6	66.4	66.1	65.9	65.7	65.5	65.3	65.1
28	69.9	69.7	69.5	69.3	69.1	68.9	68.6	68.4	68.2	68.0	67.8	67.6
29	72.4	72.2	72.0	71.8	71.6	71.4	71.1	70.9	70.7	70.5	70.3	70.1
30	74.9	74.7	74.5	74.3	74.1	73.9	73.6	73.4	73.2	73.0	72.8	72.6
31	77.4	77.2	77.0	76.8	76.6	76.4	76.1	75.9	75.7	75.5	75.3	75.1
32	79.9	79.7	79.5	79.3	79.1	78.9	78.6	78.4	78.2	78.0	77.8	77.6
33	82.4	82.2	82.0	81.8	81.6	81.4	81.1	80.9	80.7	80.5	80.3	80.1
34	84.9	84.7	84.5	84.3	84.1	83.9	83.6	83.4	83.2	83.0	82.8	82.6
35	87.4	87.2	87.0	86.8	86.6	86.4	86.1	85.9	85.7	85.5	85.3	85.1
36	89.9	89.7	89.5	89.3	89.1	88.9	88.6	88.4	88.2	88.0	87.8	87.6
37	92.4	92.2	92.0	91.8	91.6	91.4	91.1	90.9	90.7	90.5	90.3	90.1
38	94.9	94.7	94.5	94.3	94.1	93.9	93.6	93.4	93.2	93.0	92.8	92.6
39	97.4	97.2	97.0	96.8	96.6	96.4	96.1	95.9	95.7	95.5	95.3	95.1
40	99.9	99.7	99.5	99.3	99.1	98.9	98.6	98.4	98.2	98.0	97.8	97.6
41	100.0	100.0	100.0	100.0	100.0	100.0	100.0	100.0	100.0	100.0	100.0	100.0

Entry is annual percentage of depreciable portion of asset that may be deducted.

Conversion of Asset-based Management Fee to Income-based Fee

Operating Expense Ratio 25%

Asset Based Fee	Capitalization Rate												
	5.50%	6.00%	6.50%	7.00%	7.50%	8.00%	8.50%	9.00%	9.50%	10.00%	10.50%	11.00%	11.50%
0.125%	1.70	1.56	1.44	1.34	1.25	1.17	1.10	1.04	0.99	0.94	0.89	0.85	0.82
0.150	2.05	1.88	1.73	1.61	1.50	1.41	1.32	1.25	1.18	1.13	1.07	1.02	0.98
0.200	2.73	2.50	2.31	2.14	2.00	1.87	1.76	1.67	1.58	1.50	1.43	1.36	1.30
0.250	3.41	3.13	2.88	2.68	2.50	2.34	2.21	2.08	1.97	1.88	1.79	1.70	1.63
0.300	4.09	3.75	3.46	3.21	3.00	2.81	2.65	2.50	2.37	2.25	2.14	2.05	1.96
0.333	4.55	4.17	3.85	3.57	3.33	3.12	2.94	2.78	2.63	2.50	2.38	2.27	2.17
0.350	4.77	4.38	4.04	3.75	3.50	3.28	3.09	2.92	2.76	2.63	2.50	2.39	2.28
0.375	5.11	4.69	4.33	4.02	3.75	3.52	3.31	3.13	2.96	2.81	2.68	2.56	2.45
0.400	5.45	5.00	4.62	4.29	4.00	3.75	3.53	3.33	3.16	3.00	2.86	2.73	2.61
0.500	6.82	6.25	5.77	5.36	5.00	4.69	4.41	4.17	3.95	3.75	3.57	3.41	3.26
0.600	8.18	7.50	6.92	6.43	6.00	5.63	5.29	5.00	4.74	4.50	4.29	4.09	3.91
0.625	8.52	7.81	7.21	6.70	6.25	5.86	5.51	5.21	4.93	4.69	4.46	4.26	4.08
0.667	9.09	8.33	7.69	7.14	6.67	6.25	5.88	5.56	5.26	5.00	4.76	4.55	4.35
0.700	9.55	8.75	8.08	7.50	7.00	6.56	6.18	5.83	5.53	5.25	5.00	4.77	4.57
0.750	10.23	9.38	8.65	8.04	7.50	7.03	6.62	6.25	5.92	5.63	5.36	5.11	4.89
0.800	10.91	10.00	9.23	8.57	8.00	7.50	7.06	6.67	6.32	6.00	5.71	5.45	5.22
0.850	11.59	10.63	9.81	9.11	8.50	7.97	7.50	7.08	6.71	6.38	6.07	5.80	5.54
1.000	13.64	12.50	11.54	10.71	10.00	9.38	8.82	8.33	7.89	7.50	7.14	6.82	6.52
1.100	15.00	13.75	12.69	11.79	11.00	10.31	9.71	9.17	8.68	8.25	7.86	7.50	7.17
1.250	17.05	15.63	14.42	13.39	12.50	11.72	11.03	10.42	9.87	9.38	8.93	8.52	8.15
1.333	18.18	16.67	15.38	14.29	13.33	12.50	11.76	11.11	10.53	10.00	9.52	9.09	8.70
1.500	20.45	18.75	17.31	16.07	15.00	14.06	13.24	12.50	11.84	11.25	10.71	10.23	9.78
1.600	21.82	20.00	18.46	17.14	16.00	15.00	14.12	13.33	12.63	12.00	11.43	10.91	10.43
1.667	22.73	20.83	19.23	17.86	16.67	15.63	14.71	13.89	13.16	12.50	11.91	11.36	10.87
1.750	23.86	21.88	20.19	18.75	17.50	16.41	15.44	14.58	13.82	13.13	12.50	11.93	11.41
1.800	24.55	22.50	20.77	19.29	18.00	16.87	15.88	15.00	14.21	13.50	12.86	12.27	11.74
2.000%	27.27	25.00	23.08	21.43	20.00	18.75	17.65	16.67	15.79	15.00	14.29	13.64	13.04

Entry is annual percentage of gross income equal to selected asset rate.

Conversion of Income-based Management Fee to Asset-based Fee

Operating Expense Ratio 25%

Income Based Fee	Capitalization Rate												
	5.50%	6.00%	6.50%	7.00%	7.50%	8.00%	8.50%	9.00%	9.50%	10.00%	10.50%	11.00%	11.50%
1.000%	0.073	0.080	0.087	0.093	0.100	0.107	0.113	0.120	0.127	0.133	0.140	0.147	0.153
1.250	0.092	0.100	0.108	0.117	0.125	0.133	0.142	0.150	0.158	0.167	0.175	0.183	0.192
1.500	0.110	0.120	0.130	0.140	0.150	0.160	0.170	0.180	0.190	0.200	0.210	0.220	0.230
1.750	0.128	0.140	0.152	0.163	0.175	0.187	0.198	0.210	0.222	0.233	0.245	0.257	0.268
2.000%	0.147	0.160	0.173	0.187	0.200	0.213	0.227	0.240	0.253	0.267	0.280	0.293	0.307
2.250	0.165	0.180	0.195	0.210	0.225	0.240	0.255	0.270	0.285	0.300	0.315	0.330	0.345
2.500	0.183	0.200	0.217	0.233	0.250	0.267	0.283	0.300	0.317	0.333	0.350	0.367	0.383
2.750	0.202	0.220	0.238	0.257	0.275	0.293	0.312	0.330	0.348	0.367	0.385	0.403	0.422
3.000	0.220	0.240	0.260	0.280	0.300	0.320	0.340	0.360	0.380	0.400	0.420	0.440	0.460
3.250%	0.238	0.260	0.282	0.303	0.325	0.347	0.368	0.390	0.412	0.433	0.455	0.477	0.498
3.500	0.257	0.280	0.303	0.327	0.350	0.373	0.397	0.420	0.443	0.467	0.490	0.513	0.537
3.750	0.275	0.300	0.325	0.350	0.375	0.400	0.425	0.450	0.475	0.500	0.525	0.550	0.575
4.000	0.293	0.320	0.347	0.373	0.400	0.427	0.453	0.480	0.507	0.533	0.560	0.587	0.613
4.250	0.312	0.340	0.368	0.397	0.425	0.453	0.482	0.510	0.538	0.567	0.595	0.623	0.652
4.500%	0.330	0.360	0.390	0.420	0.450	0.480	0.510	0.540	0.570	0.600	0.630	0.660	0.690
4.750	0.348	0.380	0.412	0.443	0.475	0.507	0.538	0.570	0.602	0.633	0.665	0.697	0.728
5.000	0.367	0.400	0.433	0.467	0.500	0.533	0.567	0.600	0.633	0.667	0.700	0.733	0.767
5.250	0.385	0.420	0.455	0.490	0.525	0.560	0.595	0.630	0.665	0.700	0.735	0.770	0.805
5.500	0.403	0.440	0.477	0.513	0.550	0.587	0.623	0.660	0.697	0.733	0.770	0.807	0.843
5.750%	0.422	0.460	0.498	0.537	0.575	0.613	0.652	0.690	0.728	0.767	0.805	0.843	0.882
6.000	0.440	0.480	0.520	0.560	0.600	0.640	0.680	0.720	0.760	0.800	0.840	0.880	0.920
6.250	0.458	0.500	0.542	0.583	0.625	0.667	0.708	0.750	0.792	0.833	0.875	0.917	0.958
6.500	0.477	0.520	0.563	0.607	0.650	0.693	0.737	0.780	0.823	0.867	0.910	0.953	0.997
6.750	0.495	0.540	0.585	0.630	0.675	0.720	0.765	0.810	0.855	0.900	0.945	0.990	1.035
7.000%	0.513	0.560	0.607	0.653	0.700	0.747	0.793	0.840	0.887	0.933	0.980	1.027	1.073
7.250%	0.532	0.580	0.628	0.677	0.725	0.773	0.822	0.870	0.918	0.967	1.015	1.063	1.112
7.500	0.550	0.600	0.650	0.700	0.750	0.800	0.850	0.900	0.950	1.000	1.050	1.100	1.150

Entry is annual percentage of assets equal to selected percentage of gross income.

Conversion of Asset-based Management Fee to Income-based Fee

Operating Expense Ratio 35%

Asset Based Fee	Capitalization Rate												
	5.50%	6.00%	6.50%	7.00%	7.50%	8.00%	8.50%	9.00%	9.50%	10.00%	10.50%	11.00%	11.50%
0.125%	1.48	1.35	1.25	1.16	1.08	1.02	0.96	0.90	0.86	0.81	0.77	0.74	0.71
0.150	1.77	1.63	1.50	1.39	1.30	1.22	1.15	1.08	1.03	0.98	0.93	0.89	0.85
0.200	2.36	2.17	2.00	1.86	1.73	1.63	1.53	1.44	1.37	1.30	1.24	1.18	1.13
0.250	2.95	2.71	2.50	2.32	2.17	2.03	1.91	1.81	1.71	1.62	1.55	1.48	1.41
0.300	3.55	3.25	3.00	2.79	2.60	2.44	2.29	2.17	2.05	1.95	1.86	1.77	1.70
0.333	3.94	3.61	3.33	3.10	2.89	2.71	2.55	2.41	2.28	2.17	2.06	1.97	1.88
0.350	4.14	3.79	3.50	3.25	3.03	2.84	2.68	2.53	2.39	2.27	2.17	2.07	1.98
0.375	4.43	4.06	3.75	3.48	3.25	3.05	2.87	2.71	2.57	2.44	2.32	2.22	2.12
0.400	4.73	4.33	4.00	3.71	3.47	3.25	3.06	2.89	2.74	2.60	2.48	2.36	2.26
0.500	5.91	5.42	5.00	4.64	4.33	4.06	3.82	3.61	3.42	3.25	3.10	2.95	2.83
0.600	7.09	6.50	6.00	5.57	5.20	4.88	4.59	4.33	4.11	3.90	3.71	3.55	3.39
0.625	7.39	6.77	6.25	5.80	5.42	5.08	4.78	4.51	4.28	4.06	3.87	3.69	3.53
0.667	7.88	7.22	6.67	6.19	5.78	5.42	5.10	4.81	4.56	4.33	4.13	3.94	3.77
0.700	8.27	7.58	7.00	6.50	6.07	5.69	5.35	5.06	4.79	4.55	4.33	4.14	3.96
0.750	8.86	8.13	7.50	6.96	6.50	6.09	5.74	5.42	5.13	4.87	4.64	4.43	4.24
0.800	9.45	8.67	8.00	7.43	6.93	6.50	6.12	5.78	5.47	5.20	4.95	4.73	4.52
0.850	10.05	9.21	8.50	7.89	7.37	6.91	6.50	6.14	5.82	5.52	5.26	5.02	4.80
1.000	11.82	10.83	10.00	9.29	8.67	8.13	7.65	7.22	6.84	6.50	6.19	5.91	5.65
1.100	13.00	11.92	11.00	10.21	9.53	8.94	8.41	7.94	7.53	7.15	6.81	6.50	6.22
1.250	14.77	13.54	12.50	11.61	10.83	10.16	9.56	9.03	8.55	8.13	7.74	7.39	7.07
1.333	15.76	14.44	13.33	12.38	11.56	10.83	10.20	9.63	9.12	8.67	8.25	7.88	7.54
1.500	17.73	16.25	15.00	13.93	13.00	12.19	11.47	10.83	10.26	9.75	9.29	8.86	8.48
1.600	18.91	17.33	16.00	14.86	13.87	13.00	12.24	11.56	10.95	10.40	9.90	9.45	9.04
1.667	19.70	18.06	16.67	15.48	14.44	13.54	12.75	12.04	11.40	10.83	10.32	9.85	9.42
1.750	20.68	18.96	17.50	16.25	15.17	14.22	13.38	12.64	11.97	11.37	10.83	10.34	9.89
1.800	21.27	19.50	18.00	16.71	15.60	14.62	13.76	13.00	12.32	11.70	11.14	10.64	10.17
2.000%	23.64	21.67	20.00	18.57	17.33	16.25	15.29	14.44	13.68	13.00	12.38	11.82	11.30

Entry is annual percentage of gross income equal to selected asset rate.

Conversion of Income-based Management Fee to Asset-based Fee

Operating Expense Ratio 35%

Income Based Fee	Capitalization Rate												
	5.50%	6.00%	6.50%	7.00%	7.50%	8.00%	8.50%	9.00%	9.50%	10.00%	10.50%	11.00%	11.50%
1.000%	0.085	0.092	0.100	0.108	0.115	0.123	0.131	0.138	0.146	0.154	0.162	0.169	0.177
1.250	0.106	0.115	0.125	0.135	0.144	0.154	0.163	0.173	0.183	0.192	0.202	0.212	0.221
1.500	0.127	0.138	0.150	0.162	0.173	0.185	0.196	0.208	0.219	0.231	0.242	0.254	0.265
1.750	0.148	0.162	0.175	0.188	0.202	0.215	0.229	0.242	0.256	0.269	0.283	0.296	0.310
2.000%	0.169	0.185	0.200	0.215	0.231	0.246	0.262	0.277	0.292	0.308	0.323	0.338	0.354
2.250	0.190	0.208	0.225	0.242	0.260	0.277	0.294	0.312	0.329	0.346	0.363	0.381	0.398
2.500	0.212	0.231	0.250	0.269	0.288	0.308	0.327	0.346	0.365	0.385	0.404	0.423	0.442
2.750	0.233	0.254	0.275	0.296	0.317	0.338	0.360	0.381	0.402	0.423	0.444	0.465	0.487
3.000	0.254	0.277	0.300	0.323	0.346	0.369	0.392	0.415	0.438	0.462	0.485	0.508	0.531
3.250%	0.275	0.300	0.325	0.350	0.375	0.400	0.425	0.450	0.475	0.500	0.525	0.550	0.575
3.500	0.296	0.323	0.350	0.377	0.404	0.431	0.458	0.485	0.512	0.538	0.565	0.592	0.619
3.750	0.317	0.346	0.375	0.404	0.433	0.462	0.490	0.519	0.548	0.577	0.606	0.635	0.663
4.000	0.338	0.369	0.400	0.431	0.462	0.492	0.523	0.554	0.585	0.615	0.646	0.677	0.708
4.250	0.360	0.392	0.425	0.458	0.490	0.523	0.556	0.588	0.621	0.654	0.687	0.719	0.752
4.500%	0.381	0.415	0.450	0.485	0.519	0.554	0.588	0.623	0.658	0.692	0.727	0.762	0.796
4.750	0.402	0.438	0.475	0.512	0.548	0.585	0.621	0.658	0.694	0.731	0.767	0.804	0.840
5.000	0.423	0.462	0.500	0.538	0.577	0.615	0.654	0.692	0.731	0.769	0.808	0.846	0.885
5.250	0.444	0.485	0.525	0.565	0.606	0.646	0.687	0.727	0.767	0.808	0.848	0.888	0.929
5.500	0.465	0.508	0.550	0.592	0.635	0.677	0.719	0.762	0.804	0.846	0.888	0.931	0.973
5.750%	0.487	0.531	0.575	0.619	0.663	0.708	0.752	0.796	0.840	0.885	0.929	0.973	1.017
6.000	0.508	0.554	0.600	0.646	0.692	0.738	0.785	0.831	0.877	0.923	0.969	1.015	1.062
6.250	0.529	0.577	0.625	0.673	0.721	0.769	0.817	0.865	0.913	0.962	1.010	1.058	1.106
6.500	0.550	0.600	0.650	0.700	0.750	0.800	0.850	0.900	0.950	1.000	1.050	1.100	1.150
6.750	0.571	0.623	0.675	0.727	0.779	0.831	0.883	0.935	0.987	1.038	1.090	1.142	1.194
7.000%	0.592	0.646	0.700	0.754	0.808	0.862	0.915	0.969	1.023	1.077	1.131	1.185	1.238
7.250%	0.613	0.669	0.725	0.781	0.837	0.892	0.948	1.004	1.060	1.115	1.171	1.227	1.283
7.500	0.635	0.692	0.750	0.808	0.865	0.923	0.981	1.038	1.096	1.154	1.212	1.269	1.327

Entry is annual percentage of assets equal to selected percentage of gross income.

Conversion of Asset-based Management Fee to Income-based Fee

Operating Expense Ratio 45%

Asset Based Fee	\multicolumn{13}{c}{Capitalization Rate}												
	5.50%	6.00%	6.50%	7.00%	7.50%	8.00%	8.50%	9.00%	9.50%	10.00%	10.50%	11.00%	11.50%
0.125%	1.25	1.15	1.06	0.98	0.92	0.86	0.81	0.76	0.72	0.69	0.65	0.62	0.60
0.150	1.50	1.37	1.27	1.18	1.10	1.03	0.97	0.92	0.87	0.83	0.79	0.75	0.72
0.200	2.00	1.83	1.69	1.57	1.47	1.37	1.29	1.22	1.16	1.10	1.05	1.00	0.96
0.250	2.50	2.29	2.12	1.96	1.83	1.72	1.62	1.53	1.45	1.37	1.31	1.25	1.20
0.300	3.00	2.75	2.54	2.36	2.20	2.06	1.94	1.83	1.74	1.65	1.57	1.50	1.43
0.333	3.33	3.06	2.82	2.62	2.44	2.29	2.16	2.04	1.93	1.83	1.75	1.67	1.59
0.350	3.50	3.21	2.96	2.75	2.57	2.41	2.26	2.14	2.03	1.93	1.83	1.75	1.67
0.375	3.75	3.44	3.17	2.95	2.75	2.58	2.43	2.29	2.17	2.06	1.96	1.87	1.79
0.400	4.00	3.67	3.38	3.14	2.93	2.75	2.59	2.44	2.32	2.20	2.10	2.00	1.91
0.500	5.00	4.58	4.23	3.93	3.67	3.44	3.24	3.06	2.89	2.75	2.62	2.50	2.39
0.600	6.00	5.50	5.08	4.71	4.40	4.12	3.88	3.67	3.47	3.30	3.14	3.00	2.87
0.625	6.25	5.73	5.29	4.91	4.58	4.30	4.04	3.82	3.62	3.44	3.27	3.12	2.99
0.667	6.67	6.11	5.64	5.24	4.89	4.58	4.31	4.07	3.86	3.67	3.49	3.33	3.19
0.700	7.00	6.42	5.92	5.50	5.13	4.81	4.53	4.28	4.05	3.85	3.67	3.50	3.35
0.750	7.50	6.87	6.35	5.89	5.50	5.16	4.85	4.58	4.34	4.12	3.93	3.75	3.59
0.800	8.00	7.33	6.77	6.29	5.87	5.50	5.18	4.89	4.63	4.40	4.19	4.00	3.83
0.850	8.50	7.79	7.19	6.68	6.23	5.84	5.50	5.19	4.92	4.68	4.45	4.25	4.07
1.000	10.00	9.17	8.46	7.86	7.33	6.87	6.47	6.11	5.79	5.50	5.24	5.00	4.78
1.100	11.00	10.08	9.31	8.64	8.07	7.56	7.12	6.72	6.37	6.05	5.76	5.50	5.26
1.250	12.50	11.46	10.58	9.82	9.17	8.59	8.09	7.64	7.24	6.87	6.55	6.25	5.98
1.333	13.33	12.22	11.28	10.48	9.78	9.17	8.63	8.15	7.72	7.33	6.98	6.67	6.38
1.500	15.00	13.75	12.69	11.79	11.00	10.31	9.71	9.17	8.68	8.25	7.86	7.50	7.17
1.600	16.00	14.67	13.54	12.57	11.73	11.00	10.35	9.78	9.26	8.80	8.38	8.00	7.65
1.667	16.67	15.28	14.10	13.10	12.22	11.46	10.78	10.19	9.65	9.17	8.73	8.33	7.97
1.750	17.50	16.04	14.81	13.75	12.83	12.03	11.32	10.69	10.13	9.62	9.17	8.75	8.37
1.800	18.00	16.50	15.23	14.14	13.20	12.37	11.65	11.00	10.42	9.90	9.43	9.00	8.61
2.000%	20.00	18.33	16.92	15.71	14.67	13.75	12.94	12.22	11.58	11.00	10.48	10.00	9.57

Entry is annual percentage of gross income equal to selected asset rate.

Conversion of Income-based Management Fee to Asset-based Fee

Operating Expense Ratio 45%

Income Based Fee	\multicolumn{13}{c}{Capitalization Rate}												
	5.50%	6.00%	6.50%	7.00%	7.50%	8.00%	8.50%	9.00%	9.50%	10.00%	10.50%	11.00%	11.50%
1.000%	0.100	0.109	0.118	0.127	0.136	0.145	0.155	0.164	0.173	0.182	0.191	0.200	0.209
1.250	0.125	0.136	0.148	0.159	0.170	0.182	0.193	0.205	0.216	0.227	0.239	0.250	0.261
1.500	0.150	0.164	0.177	0.191	0.205	0.218	0.232	0.245	0.259	0.273	0.286	0.300	0.314
1.750	0.175	0.191	0.207	0.223	0.239	0.255	0.270	0.286	0.302	0.318	0.334	0.350	0.366
2.000%	0.200	0.218	0.236	0.255	0.273	0.291	0.309	0.327	0.345	0.364	0.382	0.400	0.418
2.250	0.225	0.245	0.266	0.286	0.307	0.327	0.348	0.368	0.389	0.409	0.430	0.450	0.470
2.500	0.250	0.273	0.295	0.318	0.341	0.364	0.386	0.409	0.432	0.455	0.477	0.500	0.523
2.750	0.275	0.300	0.325	0.350	0.375	0.400	0.425	0.450	0.475	0.500	0.525	0.550	0.575
3.000	0.300	0.327	0.355	0.382	0.409	0.436	0.464	0.491	0.518	0.545	0.573	0.600	0.627
3.250%	0.325	0.355	0.384	0.414	0.443	0.473	0.502	0.532	0.561	0.591	0.620	0.650	0.680
3.500	0.350	0.382	0.414	0.445	0.477	0.509	0.541	0.573	0.605	0.636	0.668	0.700	0.732
3.750	0.375	0.409	0.443	0.477	0.511	0.545	0.580	0.614	0.648	0.682	0.716	0.750	0.784
4.000	0.400	0.436	0.473	0.509	0.545	0.582	0.618	0.655	0.691	0.727	0.764	0.800	0.836
4.250	0.425	0.464	0.502	0.541	0.580	0.618	0.657	0.695	0.734	0.773	0.811	0.850	0.889
4.500%	0.450	0.491	0.532	0.573	0.614	0.655	0.695	0.736	0.777	0.818	0.859	0.900	0.941
4.750	0.475	0.518	0.561	0.605	0.648	0.691	0.734	0.777	0.820	0.864	0.907	0.950	0.993
5.000	0.500	0.545	0.591	0.636	0.682	0.727	0.773	0.818	0.864	0.909	0.955	1.000	1.045
5.250	0.525	0.573	0.620	0.668	0.716	0.764	0.811	0.859	0.907	0.955	1.002	1.050	1.098
5.500	0.550	0.600	0.650	0.700	0.750	0.800	0.850	0.900	0.950	1.000	1.050	1.100	1.150
5.750%	0.575	0.627	0.680	0.732	0.784	0.836	0.889	0.941	0.993	1.045	1.098	1.150	1.202
6.000	0.600	0.655	0.709	0.764	0.818	0.873	0.927	0.982	1.036	1.091	1.145	1.200	1.255
6.250	0.625	0.682	0.739	0.795	0.852	0.909	0.966	1.023	1.080	1.136	1.193	1.250	1.307
6.500	0.650	0.709	0.768	0.827	0.886	0.945	1.005	1.064	1.123	1.182	1.241	1.300	1.359
6.750	0.675	0.736	0.798	0.859	0.920	0.982	1.043	1.105	1.166	1.227	1.289	1.350	1.411
7.000%	0.700	0.764	0.827	0.891	0.955	1.018	1.082	1.145	1.209	1.273	1.336	1.400	1.464
7.250%	0.725	0.791	0.857	0.923	0.989	1.055	1.120	1.186	1.252	1.318	1.384	1.450	1.516
7.500	0.750	0.818	0.886	0.955	1.023	1.091	1.159	1.227	1.295	1.364	1.432	1.500	1.568

Entry is annual percentage of assets equal to selected percentage of gross income.

Conversion of Asset-based Management Fee to Income-based Fee

Operating Expense Ratio 50%

Asset Based Fee	5.50%	6.00%	6.50%	7.00%	7.50%	8.00%	8.50%	9.00%	9.50%	10.00%	10.50%	11.00%	11.50%
						Capitalization Rate							
0.125%	1.14	1.04	0.96	0.89	0.83	0.78	0.74	0.69	0.66	0.63	0.60	0.57	0.54
0.150	1.36	1.25	1.15	1.07	1.00	0.94	0.88	0.83	0.79	0.75	0.71	0.68	0.65
0.200	1.82	1.67	1.54	1.43	1.33	1.25	1.18	1.11	1.05	1.00	0.95	0.91	0.87
0.250	2.27	2.08	1.92	1.79	1.67	1.56	1.47	1.39	1.32	1.25	1.19	1.14	1.09
0.300	2.73	2.50	2.31	2.14	2.00	1.88	1.76	1.67	1.58	1.50	1.43	1.36	1.30
0.333	3.03	2.78	2.56	2.38	2.22	2.08	1.96	1.85	1.75	1.67	1.59	1.52	1.45
0.350	3.18	2.92	2.69	2.50	2.33	2.19	2.06	1.94	1.84	1.75	1.67	1.59	1.52
0.375	3.41	3.13	2.88	2.68	2.50	2.34	2.21	2.08	1.97	1.88	1.79	1.70	1.63
0.400	3.64	3.33	3.08	2.86	2.67	2.50	2.35	2.22	2.11	2.00	1.90	1.82	1.74
0.500	4.55	4.17	3.85	3.57	3.33	3.13	2.94	2.78	2.63	2.50	2.38	2.27	2.17
0.600	5.45	5.00	4.62	4.29	4.00	3.75	3.53	3.33	3.16	3.00	2.86	2.73	2.61
0.625	5.68	5.21	4.81	4.46	4.17	3.91	3.68	3.47	3.29	3.13	2.98	2.84	2.72
0.667	6.06	5.56	5.13	4.76	4.44	4.17	3.92	3.70	3.51	3.33	3.17	3.03	2.90
0.700	6.36	5.83	5.38	5.00	4.67	4.38	4.12	3.89	3.68	3.50	3.33	3.18	3.04
0.750	6.82	6.25	5.77	5.36	5.00	4.69	4.41	4.17	3.95	3.75	3.57	3.41	3.26
0.800	7.27	6.67	6.15	5.71	5.33	5.00	4.71	4.44	4.21	4.00	3.81	3.64	3.48
0.850	7.73	7.08	6.54	6.07	5.67	5.31	5.00	4.72	4.47	4.25	4.05	3.86	3.70
1.000	9.09	8.33	7.69	7.14	6.67	6.25	5.88	5.56	5.26	5.00	4.76	4.55	4.35
1.100	10.00	9.17	8.46	7.86	7.33	6.88	6.47	6.11	5.79	5.50	5.24	5.00	4.78
1.250	11.36	10.42	9.62	8.93	8.33	7.81	7.35	6.94	6.58	6.25	5.95	5.68	5.43
1.333	12.12	11.11	10.26	9.52	8.89	8.33	7.84	7.41	7.02	6.67	6.35	6.06	5.80
1.500	13.64	12.50	11.54	10.71	10.00	9.38	8.82	8.33	7.89	7.50	7.14	6.82	6.52
1.600	14.55	13.33	12.31	11.43	10.67	10.00	9.41	8.89	8.42	8.00	7.62	7.27	6.96
1.667	15.15	13.89	12.82	11.91	11.11	10.42	9.80	9.26	8.77	8.33	7.94	7.58	7.25
1.750	15.91	14.58	13.46	12.50	11.67	10.94	10.29	9.72	9.21	8.75	8.33	7.95	7.61
1.800	16.36	15.00	13.85	12.86	12.00	11.25	10.59	10.00	9.47	9.00	8.57	8.18	7.83
2.000%	18.18	16.67	15.38	14.29	13.33	12.50	11.76	11.11	10.53	10.00	9.52	9.09	8.70

Entry is annual percentage of gross income equal to selected asset rate.

Conversion of Income-based Management Fee to Asset-based Fee

Operating Expense Ratio 50%

Income Based Fee	5.50%	6.00%	6.50%	7.00%	7.50%	8.00%	8.50%	9.00%	9.50%	10.00%	10.50%	11.00%	11.50%
						Capitalization Rate							
1.000%	0.110	0.120	0.130	0.140	0.150	0.160	0.170	0.180	0.190	0.200	0.210	0.220	0.230
1.250	0.138	0.150	0.163	0.175	0.188	0.200	0.213	0.225	0.238	0.250	0.263	0.275	0.288
1.500	0.165	0.180	0.195	0.210	0.225	0.240	0.255	0.270	0.285	0.300	0.315	0.330	0.345
1.750	0.192	0.210	0.228	0.245	0.263	0.280	0.298	0.315	0.332	0.350	0.368	0.385	0.402
2.000%	0.220	0.240	0.260	0.280	0.300	0.320	0.340	0.360	0.380	0.400	0.420	0.440	0.460
2.250	0.248	0.270	0.293	0.315	0.338	0.360	0.383	0.405	0.428	0.450	0.473	0.495	0.518
2.500	0.275	0.300	0.325	0.350	0.375	0.400	0.425	0.450	0.475	0.500	0.525	0.550	0.575
2.750	0.303	0.330	0.358	0.385	0.413	0.440	0.468	0.495	0.523	0.550	0.578	0.605	0.633
3.000	0.330	0.360	0.390	0.420	0.450	0.480	0.510	0.540	0.570	0.600	0.630	0.660	0.690
3.250%	0.358	0.390	0.423	0.455	0.488	0.520	0.553	0.585	0.618	0.650	0.683	0.715	0.748
3.500	0.385	0.420	0.455	0.490	0.525	0.560	0.595	0.630	0.665	0.700	0.735	0.770	0.805
3.750	0.413	0.450	0.488	0.525	0.563	0.600	0.638	0.675	0.713	0.750	0.788	0.825	0.863
4.000	0.440	0.480	0.520	0.560	0.600	0.640	0.680	0.720	0.760	0.800	0.840	0.880	0.920
4.250	0.468	0.510	0.552	0.595	0.638	0.680	0.722	0.765	0.808	0.850	0.892	0.935	0.978
4.500%	0.495	0.540	0.585	0.630	0.675	0.720	0.765	0.810	0.855	0.900	0.945	0.990	1.035
4.750	0.522	0.570	0.618	0.665	0.713	0.760	0.808	0.855	0.903	0.950	0.998	1.045	1.093
5.000	0.550	0.600	0.650	0.700	0.750	0.800	0.850	0.900	0.950	1.000	1.050	1.100	1.150
5.250	0.578	0.630	0.683	0.735	0.787	0.840	0.893	0.945	0.998	1.050	1.103	1.155	1.208
5.500	0.605	0.660	0.715	0.770	0.825	0.880	0.935	0.990	1.045	1.100	1.155	1.210	1.265
5.750%	0.633	0.690	0.748	0.805	0.863	0.920	0.978	1.035	1.093	1.150	1.208	1.265	1.323
6.000	0.660	0.720	0.780	0.840	0.900	0.960	1.020	1.080	1.140	1.200	1.260	1.320	1.380
6.250	0.688	0.750	0.813	0.875	0.938	1.000	1.063	1.125	1.188	1.250	1.313	1.375	1.438
6.500	0.715	0.780	0.845	0.910	0.975	1.040	1.105	1.170	1.235	1.300	1.365	1.430	1.495
6.750	0.743	0.810	0.877	0.945	1.012	1.080	1.148	1.215	1.282	1.350	1.417	1.485	1.553
7.000%	0.770	0.840	0.910	0.980	1.050	1.120	1.190	1.260	1.330	1.400	1.470	1.540	1.610
7.250%	0.798	0.870	0.943	1.015	1.088	1.160	1.233	1.305	1.378	1.450	1.523	1.595	1.668
7.500	0.825	0.900	0.975	1.050	1.125	1.200	1.275	1.350	1.425	1.500	1.575	1.650	1.725

Entry is annual percentage of assets equal to selected percentage of gross income.

Conversion of Asset-based Management Fee to Income-based Fee

Net Rentals

Asset Based Fee	\multicolumn{13}{c}{Capitalization Rate}

Asset Based Fee	5.50%	6.00%	6.50%	7.00%	7.50%	8.00%	8.50%	9.00%	9.50%	10.00%	10.50%	11.00%	11.50%
0.125%	2.27	2.08	1.92	1.79	1.67	1.56	1.47	1.39	1.32	1.25	1.19	1.14	1.09
0.150	2.73	2.50	2.31	2.14	2.00	1.88	1.76	1.67	1.58	1.50	1.43	1.36	1.30
0.200	3.64	3.33	3.08	2.86	2.67	2.50	2.35	2.22	2.11	2.00	1.90	1.82	1.74
0.250	4.55	4.17	3.85	3.57	3.33	3.13	2.94	2.78	2.63	2.50	2.38	2.27	2.17
0.300	5.45	5.00	4.62	4.29	4.00	3.75	3.53	3.33	3.16	3.00	2.86	2.73	2.61
0.333	6.06	5.56	5.13	4.76	4.44	4.17	3.92	3.70	3.51	3.33	3.17	3.03	2.90
0.350	6.36	5.83	5.38	5.00	4.67	4.38	4.12	3.89	3.68	3.50	3.33	3.18	3.04
0.375	6.82	6.25	5.77	5.36	5.00	4.69	4.41	4.17	3.95	3.75	3.57	3.41	3.26
0.400	7.27	6.67	6.15	5.71	5.33	5.00	4.71	4.44	4.21	4.00	3.81	3.64	3.48
0.500	9.09	8.33	7.69	7.14	6.67	6.25	5.88	5.56	5.26	5.00	4.76	4.55	4.35
0.600	10.91	10.00	9.23	8.57	8.00	7.50	7.06	6.67	6.32	6.00	5.71	5.45	5.22
0.625	11.36	10.42	9.62	8.93	8.33	7.81	7.35	6.94	6.58	6.25	5.95	5.68	5.43
0.667	12.12	11.11	10.26	9.52	8.89	8.33	7.84	7.41	7.02	6.67	6.35	6.06	5.80
0.700	12.73	11.67	10.77	10.00	9.33	8.75	8.24	7.78	7.37	7.00	6.67	6.36	6.09
0.750	13.64	12.50	11.54	10.71	10.00	9.38	8.82	8.33	7.89	7.50	7.14	6.82	6.52
0.800	14.55	13.33	12.31	11.43	10.67	10.00	9.41	8.89	8.42	8.00	7.62	7.27	6.96
0.850	15.45	14.17	13.08	12.14	11.33	10.63	10.00	9.44	8.95	8.50	8.10	7.73	7.39
1.000	18.18	16.67	15.38	14.29	13.33	12.50	11.76	11.11	10.53	10.00	9.52	9.09	8.70
1.100	20.00	18.33	16.92	15.71	14.67	13.75	12.94	12.22	11.58	11.00	10.48	10.00	9.57
1.250	22.73	20.83	19.23	17.86	16.67	15.63	14.71	13.89	13.16	12.50	11.90	11.36	10.87
1.333	24.24	22.22	20.51	19.05	17.78	16.67	15.69	14.81	14.04	13.33	12.70	12.12	11.59
1.500	27.27	25.00	23.08	21.43	20.00	18.75	17.65	16.67	15.79	15.00	14.29	13.64	13.04
1.600	29.09	26.67	24.62	22.86	21.33	20.00	18.82	17.78	16.84	16.00	15.24	14.55	13.91
1.667	30.30	27.78	25.64	23.81	22.22	20.83	19.61	18.52	17.54	16.67	15.87	15.15	14.49
1.750	31.82	29.17	26.92	25.00	23.33	21.88	20.59	19.44	18.42	17.50	16.67	15.91	15.22
1.800	32.73	30.00	27.69	25.71	24.00	22.50	21.18	20.00	18.95	18.00	17.14	16.36	15.65
2.000%	36.36	33.33	30.77	28.57	26.67	25.00	23.53	22.22	21.05	20.00	19.05	18.18	17.39

Entry is annual percentage of gross income equal to selected asset rate.

Conversion of Income-based Management Fee to Asset-based Fee

Net Rentals

Income Based Fee	5.50%	6.00%	6.50%	7.00%	7.50%	8.00%	8.50%	9.00%	9.50%	10.00%	10.50%	11.00%	11.50%
1.000%	0.055	0.060	0.065	0.070	0.075	0.080	0.085	0.090	0.095	0.100	0.105	0.110	0.115
1.250	0.069	0.075	0.081	0.088	0.094	0.100	0.106	0.113	0.119	0.125	0.131	0.138	0.144
1.500	0.083	0.090	0.098	0.105	0.113	0.120	0.128	0.135	0.143	0.150	0.158	0.165	0.173
1.750	0.096	0.105	0.114	0.123	0.131	0.140	0.149	0.158	0.166	0.175	0.184	0.192	0.201
2.000%	0.110	0.120	0.130	0.140	0.150	0.160	0.170	0.180	0.190	0.200	0.210	0.220	0.230
2.250	0.124	0.135	0.146	0.158	0.169	0.180	0.191	0.203	0.214	0.225	0.236	0.248	0.259
2.500	0.138	0.150	0.163	0.175	0.188	0.200	0.213	0.225	0.238	0.250	0.263	0.275	0.288
2.750	0.151	0.165	0.179	0.193	0.206	0.220	0.234	0.248	0.261	0.275	0.289	0.303	0.316
3.000	0.165	0.180	0.195	0.210	0.225	0.240	0.255	0.270	0.285	0.300	0.315	0.330	0.345
3.250%	0.179	0.195	0.211	0.228	0.244	0.260	0.276	0.293	0.309	0.325	0.341	0.358	0.374
3.500	0.192	0.210	0.228	0.245	0.263	0.280	0.298	0.315	0.332	0.350	0.368	0.385	0.402
3.750	0.206	0.225	0.244	0.263	0.281	0.300	0.319	0.338	0.356	0.375	0.394	0.413	0.431
4.000	0.220	0.240	0.260	0.280	0.300	0.320	0.340	0.360	0.380	0.400	0.420	0.440	0.460
4.250	0.234	0.255	0.276	0.298	0.319	0.340	0.361	0.382	0.404	0.425	0.446	0.468	0.489
4.500%	0.248	0.270	0.293	0.315	0.338	0.360	0.383	0.405	0.428	0.450	0.473	0.495	0.518
4.750	0.261	0.285	0.309	0.332	0.356	0.380	0.404	0.428	0.451	0.475	0.499	0.522	0.546
5.000	0.275	0.300	0.325	0.350	0.375	0.400	0.425	0.450	0.475	0.500	0.525	0.550	0.575
5.250	0.289	0.315	0.341	0.368	0.394	0.420	0.446	0.473	0.499	0.525	0.551	0.578	0.604
5.500	0.303	0.330	0.358	0.385	0.413	0.440	0.468	0.495	0.523	0.550	0.578	0.605	0.633
5.750%	0.316	0.345	0.374	0.402	0.431	0.460	0.489	0.518	0.546	0.575	0.604	0.633	0.661
6.000	0.330	0.360	0.390	0.420	0.450	0.480	0.510	0.540	0.570	0.600	0.630	0.660	0.690
6.250	0.344	0.375	0.406	0.438	0.469	0.500	0.531	0.563	0.594	0.625	0.656	0.688	0.719
6.500	0.358	0.390	0.423	0.455	0.488	0.520	0.553	0.585	0.618	0.650	0.683	0.715	0.748
6.750	0.371	0.405	0.439	0.473	0.506	0.540	0.574	0.608	0.641	0.675	0.709	0.743	0.776
7.000%	0.385	0.420	0.455	0.490	0.525	0.560	0.595	0.630	0.665	0.700	0.735	0.770	0.805
7.250%	0.399	0.435	0.471	0.508	0.544	0.580	0.616	0.653	0.689	0.725	0.761	0.798	0.834
7.500	0.413	0.450	0.488	0.525	0.563	0.600	0.638	0.675	0.713	0.750	0.788	0.825	0.863

Entry is annual percentage of assets equal to selected percentage of gross income.

Days Between Dates

	Jan	Feb	Mar	Apr	May	Jun	Jul	Aug	Sep	Oct	Nov	Dec
1	1	32	60	91	121	152	182	213	244	274	305	335
2	2	33	61	92	122	153	183	214	245	275	306	336
3	3	34	62	93	123	154	184	215	246	276	307	337
4	4	35	63	94	124	155	185	216	247	277	308	338
5	5	36	64	95	125	156	186	217	248	278	309	339
6	6	37	65	96	126	157	187	218	249	279	310	340
7	7	38	66	97	127	158	188	219	250	280	311	341
8	8	39	67	98	128	159	189	220	251	281	312	342
9	9	40	68	99	129	160	190	221	252	282	313	343
10	10	41	69	100	130	161	191	222	253	283	314	344
11	11	42	70	101	131	162	192	223	254	284	315	345
12	12	43	71	102	132	163	193	224	255	285	316	346
13	13	44	72	103	133	164	194	225	256	286	317	347
14	14	45	73	104	134	165	195	226	257	287	318	348
15	15	46	74	105	135	166	196	227	258	288	319	349
16	16	47	75	106	136	167	197	228	259	289	320	350
17	17	48	76	107	137	168	198	229	260	290	321	351
18	18	49	77	108	138	169	199	230	261	291	322	352
19	19	50	78	109	139	170	200	231	262	292	323	353
20	20	51	79	110	140	171	201	232	263	293	324	354
21	21	52	80	111	141	172	202	233	264	294	325	355
22	22	53	81	112	142	173	203	234	265	295	326	356
23	23	54	82	113	143	174	204	235	266	296	327	357
24	24	55	83	114	144	175	205	236	267	297	328	358
25	25	56	84	115	145	176	206	237	268	298	329	359
26	26	57	85	116	146	177	207	238	269	299	330	360
27	27	58	86	117	147	178	208	239	270	300	331	361
28	28	59	87	118	148	179	209	240	271	301	332	362
29	29	---	88	119	149	180	210	241	272	302	333	363
30	30	---	89	120	150	181	211	242	273	303	334	364
31	31	---	90	---	151	---	212	243	---	304	---	365

Days Between Dates

	Jan	Feb	Mar	Apr	May	Jun	Jul	Aug	Sep	Oct	Nov	Dec
1	366	397	425	456	486	517	547	578	609	639	670	700
2	367	398	426	457	487	518	548	579	610	640	671	701
3	368	399	427	458	488	519	549	580	611	641	672	702
4	369	400	428	459	489	520	550	581	612	642	673	703
5	370	401	429	460	490	521	551	582	613	643	674	704
6	371	402	430	461	491	522	552	583	614	644	675	705
7	372	403	431	462	492	523	553	584	615	645	676	706
8	373	404	432	463	493	524	554	585	616	646	677	707
9	374	405	433	464	494	525	555	586	617	647	678	708
10	375	406	434	465	495	526	556	587	618	648	679	709
11	376	407	435	466	496	527	557	588	619	649	680	710
12	377	408	436	467	497	528	558	589	620	650	681	711
13	378	409	437	468	498	529	559	590	621	651	682	712
14	379	410	438	469	499	530	560	591	622	652	683	713
15	380	411	439	470	500	531	561	592	623	653	684	714
16	381	412	440	471	501	532	562	593	624	654	685	715
17	382	413	441	472	502	533	563	594	625	655	686	716
18	383	414	442	473	503	534	564	595	626	656	687	717
19	384	415	443	474	504	535	565	596	627	657	688	718
20	385	416	444	475	505	536	566	597	628	658	689	719
21	386	417	445	476	506	537	567	598	629	659	690	720
22	387	418	446	477	507	538	568	599	630	660	691	721
23	388	419	447	478	508	539	569	600	631	661	692	722
24	389	420	448	479	509	540	570	601	632	662	693	723
25	390	421	449	480	510	541	571	602	633	663	694	724
26	391	422	450	481	511	542	572	603	634	664	695	725
27	392	423	451	482	512	543	573	604	635	665	696	726
28	393	424	452	483	513	544	574	605	636	666	697	727
29	394	---	453	484	514	545	575	606	637	667	698	728
30	395	---	454	485	515	546	576	607	638	668	699	729
31	396	---	455	---	516	---	577	608	---	669	---	730

Leap Year   Days Between Dates   Leap Year

Jan	Feb	Mar	Apr	May	Jun	Jul	Aug	Sep	Oct	Nov	Dec
1	32	61	92	122	153	183	214	245	275	306	336
2	33	62	93	123	154	184	215	246	276	307	337
3	34	63	94	124	155	185	216	247	277	308	338
4	35	64	95	125	156	186	217	248	278	309	339
5	36	65	96	126	157	187	218	249	279	310	340
6	37	66	97	127	158	188	219	250	280	311	341
7	38	67	98	128	159	189	220	251	281	312	342
8	39	68	99	129	160	190	221	252	282	313	343
9	40	69	100	130	161	191	222	253	283	314	344
10	41	70	101	131	162	192	223	254	284	315	345
11	42	71	102	132	163	193	224	255	285	316	346
12	43	72	103	133	164	194	225	256	286	317	347
13	44	73	104	134	165	195	226	257	287	318	348
14	45	74	105	135	166	196	227	258	288	319	349
15	46	75	106	136	167	197	228	259	289	320	350
16	47	76	107	137	168	198	229	260	290	321	351
17	48	77	108	138	169	199	230	261	291	322	352
18	49	78	109	139	170	200	231	262	292	323	353
19	50	79	110	140	171	201	232	263	293	324	354
20	51	80	111	141	172	202	233	264	294	325	355
21	52	81	112	142	173	203	234	265	295	326	356
22	53	82	113	143	174	204	235	266	296	327	357
23	54	83	114	144	175	205	236	267	297	328	358
24	55	84	115	145	176	206	237	268	298	329	359
25	56	85	116	146	177	207	238	269	299	330	360
26	57	86	117	147	178	208	239	270	300	331	361
27	58	87	118	148	179	209	240	271	301	332	362
28	59	88	119	149	180	210	241	272	302	333	363
29	60	89	120	150	181	211	242	273	303	334	364
30	---	90	121	151	182	212	243	274	304	335	365
31	---	91	---	152	---	213	244	---	305	---	366

Leap Year   Days Between Dates   Leap Year

Jan	Feb	Mar	Apr	May	Jun	Jul	Aug	Sep	Oct	Nov	Dec
366	397	426	457	487	518	548	579	610	640	671	701
367	398	427	458	488	519	549	580	611	641	672	702
368	399	428	459	489	520	550	581	612	642	673	703
369	400	429	460	490	521	551	582	613	643	674	704
370	401	430	461	491	522	552	583	614	644	675	705
371	402	431	462	492	523	553	584	615	645	676	706
372	403	432	463	493	524	554	585	616	646	677	707
373	404	433	464	494	525	555	586	617	647	678	708
374	405	434	465	495	526	556	587	618	648	679	709
375	406	435	466	496	527	557	588	619	649	680	710
376	407	436	467	497	528	558	589	620	650	681	711
377	408	437	468	498	529	559	590	621	651	682	712
378	409	438	469	499	530	560	591	622	652	683	713
379	410	439	470	500	531	561	592	623	653	684	714
380	411	440	471	501	532	562	593	624	654	685	715
381	412	441	472	502	533	563	594	625	655	686	716
382	413	442	473	503	534	564	595	626	656	687	717
383	414	443	474	504	535	565	596	627	657	688	718
384	415	444	475	505	536	566	597	628	658	689	719
385	416	445	476	506	537	567	598	629	659	690	720
386	417	446	477	507	538	568	599	630	660	691	721
387	418	447	478	508	539	569	600	631	661	692	722
388	419	448	479	509	540	570	601	632	662	693	723
389	420	449	480	510	541	571	602	633	663	694	724
390	421	450	481	511	542	572	603	634	664	695	725
391	422	451	482	512	543	573	604	635	665	696	726
392	423	452	483	513	544	574	605	636	666	697	727
393	424	453	484	514	545	575	606	637	667	698	728
394	425	454	485	515	546	576	607	638	668	699	729
395	---	455	486	516	547	577	608	639	669	700	730
396	---	456	---	517	---	578	609	---	670	---	731

Percentage of Year Elapsed

Date	Jan	Feb	Mar	Apr	May	Jun	Jul	Aug	Sep	Oct	Nov	Dec
1	0.27	8.77	16.44	24.93	33.15	41.64	49.86	58.36	66.85	75.07	83.56	91.78
2	0.55	9.04	16.71	25.21	33.42	41.92	50.14	58.63	67.12	75.34	83.84	92.05
3	0.82	9.32	16.99	25.48	33.70	42.19	50.41	58.90	67.40	75.62	84.11	92.33
4	1.10	9.59	17.26	25.75	33.97	42.47	50.68	59.18	67.67	75.89	84.38	92.60
5	1.37	9.86	17.53	26.03	34.25	42.74	50.96	59.45	67.95	76.16	84.66	92.88
6	1.64	10.14	17.81	26.30	34.52	43.01	51.23	59.73	68.22	76.44	84.93	93.15
7	1.92	10.41	18.08	26.58	34.79	43.29	51.51	60.00	68.49	76.71	85.21	93.42
8	2.19	10.68	18.36	26.85	35.07	43.56	51.78	60.27	68.77	76.99	85.48	93.70
9	2.47	10.96	18.63	27.12	35.34	43.84	52.05	60.55	69.04	77.26	85.75	93.97
10	2.74	11.23	18.90	27.40	35.62	44.11	52.33	60.82	69.32	77.53	86.03	94.25
11	3.01	11.51	19.18	27.67	35.89	44.38	52.60	61.10	69.59	77.81	86.30	94.52
12	3.29	11.78	19.45	27.95	36.16	44.66	52.88	61.37	69.86	78.08	86.58	94.79
13	3.56	12.05	19.73	28.22	36.44	44.93	53.15	61.64	70.14	78.36	86.85	95.07
14	3.84	12.33	20.00	28.49	36.71	45.21	53.42	61.92	70.41	78.63	87.12	95.34
15	4.11	12.60	20.27	28.77	36.99	45.48	53.70	62.19	70.68	78.90	87.40	95.62
16	4.38	12.88	20.55	29.04	37.26	45.75	53.97	62.47	70.96	79.18	87.67	95.89
17	4.66	13.15	20.82	29.32	37.53	46.03	54.25	62.74	71.23	79.45	87.95	96.16
18	4.93	13.42	21.10	29.59	37.81	46.30	54.52	63.01	71.51	79.73	88.22	96.44
19	5.21	13.70	21.37	29.86	38.08	46.58	54.79	63.29	71.78	80.00	88.49	96.71
20	5.48	13.97	21.64	30.14	38.36	46.85	55.07	63.56	72.05	80.27	88.77	96.99
21	5.75	14.25	21.92	30.41	38.63	47.12	55.34	63.84	72.33	80.55	89.04	97.26
22	6.03	14.52	22.19	30.68	38.90	47.40	55.62	64.11	72.60	80.82	89.32	97.53
23	6.30	14.79	22.47	30.96	39.18	47.67	55.89	64.38	72.88	81.10	89.59	97.81
24	6.58	15.07	22.74	31.23	39.45	47.95	56.16	64.66	73.15	81.37	89.86	98.08
25	6.85	15.34	23.01	31.51	39.73	48.22	56.44	64.93	73.42	81.64	90.14	98.36
26	7.12	15.62	23.29	31.78	40.00	48.49	56.71	65.21	73.70	81.92	90.41	98.63
27	7.40	15.89	23.56	32.05	40.27	48.77	56.99	65.48	73.97	82.19	90.68	98.90
28	7.67	16.16	23.84	32.33	40.55	49.04	57.26	65.75	74.25	82.47	90.96	99.18
29	7.95	---	24.11	32.60	40.82	49.32	57.53	66.03	74.52	82.74	91.23	99.45
30	8.22	---	24.38	32.88	41.10	49.59	57.81	66.30	74.79	83.01	91.51	99.73
31	8.49	---	24.66	---	41.37	---	58.08	66.58	---	83.29	---	100.00

Percentage of Year Remaining

Date	Jan	Feb	Mar	Apr	May	Jun	Jul	Aug	Sep	Oct	Nov	Dec
1	99.73	91.23	83.56	75.07	66.85	58.36	50.14	41.64	33.15	24.93	16.44	8.22
2	99.45	90.96	83.29	74.79	66.58	58.08	49.86	41.37	32.88	24.66	16.16	7.95
3	99.18	90.68	83.01	74.52	66.30	57.81	49.59	41.10	32.60	24.38	15.89	7.67
4	98.90	90.41	82.74	74.25	66.03	57.53	49.32	40.82	32.33	24.11	15.62	7.40
5	98.63	90.14	82.47	73.97	65.75	57.26	49.04	40.55	32.05	23.84	15.34	7.12
6	98.36	89.86	82.19	73.70	65.48	56.99	48.77	40.27	31.78	23.56	15.07	6.85
7	98.08	89.59	81.92	73.42	65.21	56.71	48.49	40.00	31.51	23.29	14.79	6.58
8	97.81	89.32	81.64	73.15	64.93	56.44	48.22	39.73	31.23	23.01	14.52	6.30
9	97.53	89.04	81.37	72.88	64.66	56.16	47.95	39.45	30.96	22.74	14.25	6.03
10	97.26	88.77	81.10	72.60	64.38	55.89	47.67	39.18	30.68	22.47	13.97	5.75
11	96.99	88.49	80.82	72.33	64.11	55.62	47.40	38.90	30.41	22.19	13.70	5.48
12	96.71	88.22	80.55	72.05	63.84	55.34	47.12	38.63	30.14	21.92	13.42	5.21
13	96.44	87.95	80.27	71.78	63.56	55.07	46.85	38.36	29.86	21.64	13.15	4.93
14	96.16	87.67	80.00	71.51	63.29	54.79	46.58	38.08	29.59	21.37	12.88	4.66
15	95.89	87.40	79.73	71.23	63.01	54.52	46.30	37.81	29.32	21.10	12.60	4.38
16	95.62	87.12	79.45	70.96	62.74	54.25	46.03	37.53	29.04	20.82	12.33	4.11
17	95.34	86.85	79.18	70.68	62.47	53.97	45.75	37.26	28.77	20.55	12.05	3.84
18	95.07	86.58	78.90	70.41	62.19	53.70	45.48	36.99	28.49	20.27	11.78	3.56
19	94.79	86.30	78.63	70.14	61.92	53.42	45.21	36.71	28.22	20.00	11.51	3.29
20	94.52	86.03	78.36	69.86	61.64	53.15	44.93	36.44	27.95	19.73	11.23	3.01
21	94.25	85.75	78.08	69.59	61.37	52.88	44.66	36.16	27.67	19.45	10.96	2.74
22	93.97	85.48	77.81	69.32	61.10	52.60	44.38	35.89	27.40	19.18	10.68	2.47
23	93.70	85.21	77.53	69.04	60.82	52.33	44.11	35.62	27.12	18.90	10.41	2.19
24	93.42	84.93	77.26	68.77	60.55	52.05	43.84	35.34	26.85	18.63	10.14	1.92
25	93.15	84.66	76.99	68.49	60.27	51.78	43.56	35.07	26.58	18.36	9.86	1.64
26	92.88	84.38	76.71	68.22	60.00	51.51	43.29	34.79	26.30	18.08	9.59	1.37
27	92.60	84.11	76.44	67.95	59.73	51.23	43.01	34.52	26.03	17.81	9.32	1.10
28	92.33	83.84	76.16	67.67	59.45	50.96	42.74	34.25	25.75	17.53	9.04	0.82
29	92.05	---	75.89	67.40	59.18	50.68	42.47	33.97	25.48	17.26	8.77	0.55
30	91.78	---	75.62	67.12	58.90	50.41	42.19	33.70	25.21	16.99	8.49	0.27
31	91.51	---	75.34	---	58.63	---	41.92	33.42	---	16.71	---	0.00

All figures are as of the end of the day.

Leap Year					Percentage of Year Elapsed						Leap Year
Date	Jan	Feb	Mar	Apr	May	Jun	Jul	Aug	Sep	Oct	Nov	Dec
1	0.27	8.74	16.67	25.14	33.33	41.80	50.00	58.47	66.94	75.14	83.61	91.80
2	0.55	9.02	16.94	25.41	33.61	42.08	50.27	58.74	67.21	75.41	83.88	92.08
3	0.82	9.29	17.21	25.68	33.88	42.35	50.55	59.02	67.49	75.68	84.15	92.35
4	1.09	9.56	17.49	25.96	34.15	42.62	50.82	59.29	67.76	75.96	84.43	92.62
5	1.37	9.84	17.76	26.23	34.43	42.90	51.09	59.56	68.03	76.23	84.70	92.90
6	1.64	10.11	18.03	26.50	34.70	43.17	51.37	59.84	68.31	76.50	84.97	93.17
7	1.91	10.38	18.31	26.78	34.97	43.44	51.64	60.11	68.58	76.78	85.25	93.44
8	2.19	10.66	18.58	27.05	35.25	43.72	51.91	60.38	68.85	77.05	85.52	93.72
9	2.46	10.93	18.85	27.32	35.52	43.99	52.19	60.66	69.13	77.32	85.79	93.99
10	2.73	11.20	19.13	27.60	35.79	44.26	52.46	60.93	69.40	77.60	86.07	94.26
11	3.01	11.48	19.40	27.87	36.07	44.54	52.73	61.20	69.67	77.87	86.34	94.54
12	3.28	11.75	19.67	28.14	36.34	44.81	53.01	61.48	69.95	78.14	86.61	94.81
13	3.55	12.02	19.95	28.42	36.61	45.08	53.28	61.75	70.22	78.42	86.89	95.08
14	3.83	12.30	20.22	28.69	36.89	45.36	53.55	62.02	70.49	78.69	87.16	95.36
15	4.10	12.57	20.49	28.96	37.16	45.63	53.83	62.30	70.77	78.96	87.43	95.63
16	4.37	12.84	20.77	29.23	37.43	45.90	54.10	62.57	71.04	79.23	87.70	95.90
17	4.64	13.11	21.04	29.51	37.70	46.17	54.37	62.84	71.31	79.51	87.98	96.17
18	4.92	13.39	21.31	29.78	37.98	46.45	54.64	63.11	71.58	79.78	88.25	96.45
19	5.19	13.66	21.58	30.05	38.25	46.72	54.92	63.39	71.86	80.05	88.52	96.72
20	5.46	13.93	21.86	30.33	38.52	46.99	55.19	63.66	72.13	80.33	88.80	96.99
21	5.74	14.21	22.13	30.60	38.80	47.27	55.46	63.93	72.40	80.60	89.07	97.27
22	6.01	14.48	22.40	30.87	39.07	47.54	55.74	64.21	72.68	80.87	89.34	97.54
23	6.28	14.75	22.68	31.15	39.34	47.81	56.01	64.48	72.95	81.15	89.62	97.81
24	6.56	15.03	22.95	31.42	39.62	48.09	56.28	64.75	73.22	81.42	89.89	98.09
25	6.83	15.30	23.22	31.69	39.89	48.36	56.56	65.03	73.50	81.69	90.16	98.36
26	7.10	15.57	23.50	31.97	40.16	48.63	56.83	65.30	73.77	81.97	90.44	98.63
27	7.38	15.85	23.77	32.24	40.44	48.91	57.10	65.57	74.04	82.24	90.71	98.91
28	7.65	16.12	24.04	32.51	40.71	49.18	57.38	65.85	74.32	82.51	90.98	99.18
29	7.92	16.39	24.32	32.79	40.98	49.45	57.65	66.12	74.59	82.79	91.26	99.45
30	8.20	---	24.59	33.06	41.26	49.73	57.92	66.39	74.86	83.06	91.53	99.73
31	8.47	---	24.86	---	41.53	---	58.20	66.67	---	83.33	---	100.00

Leap Year					Percentage of Year Remaining						Leap Year
Date	Jan	Feb	Mar	Apr	May	Jun	Jul	Aug	Sep	Oct	Nov	Dec
1	99.73	91.26	83.33	74.86	66.67	58.20	50.00	41.53	33.06	24.86	16.39	8.20
2	99.45	90.98	83.06	74.59	66.39	57.92	49.73	41.26	32.79	24.59	16.12	7.92
3	99.18	90.71	82.79	74.32	66.12	57.65	49.45	40.98	32.51	24.32	15.85	7.65
4	98.91	90.44	82.51	74.04	65.85	57.38	49.18	40.71	32.24	24.04	15.57	7.38
5	98.63	90.16	82.24	73.77	65.57	57.10	48.91	40.44	31.97	23.77	15.30	7.10
6	98.36	89.89	81.97	73.50	65.30	56.83	48.63	40.16	31.69	23.50	15.03	6.83
7	98.09	89.62	81.69	73.22	65.03	56.56	48.36	39.89	31.42	23.22	14.75	6.56
8	97.81	89.34	81.42	72.95	64.75	56.28	48.09	39.62	31.15	22.95	14.48	6.28
9	97.54	89.07	81.15	72.68	64.48	56.01	47.81	39.34	30.87	22.68	14.21	6.01
10	97.27	88.80	80.87	72.40	64.21	55.74	47.54	39.07	30.60	22.40	13.93	5.74
11	96.99	88.52	80.60	72.13	63.93	55.46	47.27	38.80	30.33	22.13	13.66	5.46
12	96.72	88.25	80.33	71.86	63.66	55.19	46.99	38.52	30.05	21.86	13.39	5.19
13	96.45	87.98	80.05	71.58	63.39	54.92	46.72	38.25	29.78	21.58	13.11	4.92
14	96.17	87.70	79.78	71.31	63.11	54.64	46.45	37.98	29.51	21.31	12.84	4.64
15	95.90	87.43	79.51	71.04	62.84	54.37	46.17	37.70	29.23	21.04	12.57	4.37
16	95.63	87.16	79.23	70.77	62.57	54.10	45.90	37.43	28.96	20.77	12.30	4.10
17	95.36	86.89	78.96	70.49	62.30	53.83	45.63	37.16	28.69	20.49	12.02	3.83
18	95.08	86.61	78.69	70.22	62.02	53.55	45.36	36.89	28.42	20.22	11.75	3.55
19	94.81	86.34	78.42	69.95	61.75	53.28	45.08	36.61	28.14	19.95	11.48	3.28
20	94.54	86.07	78.14	69.67	61.48	53.01	44.81	36.34	27.87	19.67	11.20	3.01
21	94.26	85.79	77.87	69.40	61.20	52.73	44.54	36.07	27.60	19.40	10.93	2.73
22	93.99	85.52	77.60	69.13	60.93	52.46	44.26	35.79	27.32	19.13	10.66	2.46
23	93.72	85.25	77.32	68.85	60.66	52.19	43.99	35.52	27.05	18.85	10.38	2.19
24	93.44	84.97	77.05	68.58	60.38	51.91	43.72	35.25	26.78	18.58	10.11	1.91
25	93.17	84.70	76.78	68.31	60.11	51.64	43.44	34.97	26.50	18.31	9.84	1.64
26	92.90	84.43	76.50	68.03	59.84	51.37	43.17	34.70	26.23	18.03	9.56	1.37
27	92.62	84.15	76.23	67.76	59.56	51.09	42.90	34.43	25.96	17.76	9.29	1.09
28	92.35	83.88	75.96	67.49	59.29	50.82	42.62	34.15	25.68	17.49	9.02	0.82
29	92.08	83.61	75.68	67.21	59.02	50.55	42.35	33.88	25.41	17.21	8.74	0.55
30	91.80	---	75.41	66.94	58.74	50.27	42.08	33.61	25.14	16.94	8.47	0.27
31	91.53	---	75.14	---	58.47	---	41.80	33.33	---	16.67	---	0.00

All figures are as of the end of the day.

Percentage of Month Elapsed

Date	Jan	Feb	Mar	Apr	May	Jun	Jul	Aug	Sep	Oct	Nov	Dec
1	3.23	3.57	3.23	3.33	3.23	3.33	3.23	3.23	3.33	3.23	3.33	3.23
2	6.45	7.14	6.45	6.67	6.45	6.67	6.45	6.45	6.67	6.45	6.67	6.45
3	9.68	10.71	9.68	10.00	9.68	10.00	9.68	9.68	10.00	9.68	10.00	9.68
4	12.90	14.29	12.90	13.33	12.90	13.33	12.90	12.90	13.33	12.90	13.33	12.90
5	16.13	17.86	16.13	16.67	16.13	16.67	16.13	16.13	16.67	16.13	16.67	16.13
6	19.35	21.43	19.35	20.00	19.35	20.00	19.35	19.35	20.00	19.35	20.00	19.35
7	22.58	25.00	22.58	23.33	22.58	23.33	22.58	22.58	23.33	22.58	23.33	22.58
8	25.81	28.57	25.81	26.67	25.81	26.67	25.81	25.81	26.67	25.81	26.67	25.81
9	29.03	32.14	29.03	30.00	29.03	30.00	29.03	29.03	30.00	29.03	30.00	29.03
10	32.26	35.71	32.26	33.33	32.26	33.33	32.26	32.26	33.33	32.26	33.33	32.26
11	35.48	39.29	35.48	36.67	35.48	36.67	35.48	35.48	36.67	35.48	36.67	35.48
12	38.71	42.86	38.71	40.00	38.71	40.00	38.71	38.71	40.00	38.71	40.00	38.71
13	41.94	46.43	41.94	43.33	41.94	43.33	41.94	41.94	43.33	41.94	43.33	41.94
14	45.16	50.00	45.16	46.67	45.16	46.67	45.16	45.16	46.67	45.16	46.67	45.16
15	48.39	53.57	48.39	50.00	48.39	50.00	48.39	48.39	50.00	48.39	50.00	48.39
16	51.61	57.14	51.61	53.33	51.61	53.33	51.61	51.61	53.33	51.61	53.33	51.61
17	54.84	60.71	54.84	56.67	54.84	56.67	54.84	54.84	56.67	54.84	56.67	54.84
18	58.06	64.29	58.06	60.00	58.06	60.00	58.06	58.06	60.00	58.06	60.00	58.06
19	61.29	67.86	61.29	63.33	61.29	63.33	61.29	61.29	63.33	61.29	63.33	61.29
20	64.52	71.43	64.52	66.67	64.52	66.67	64.52	64.52	66.67	64.52	66.67	64.52
21	67.74	75.00	67.74	70.00	67.74	70.00	67.74	67.74	70.00	67.74	70.00	67.74
22	70.97	78.57	70.97	73.33	70.97	73.33	70.97	70.97	73.33	70.97	73.33	70.97
23	74.19	82.14	74.19	76.67	74.19	76.67	74.19	74.19	76.67	74.19	76.67	74.19
24	77.42	85.71	77.42	80.00	77.42	80.00	77.42	77.42	80.00	77.42	80.00	77.42
25	80.65	89.29	80.65	83.33	80.65	83.33	80.65	80.65	83.33	80.65	83.33	80.65
26	83.87	92.86	83.87	86.67	83.87	86.67	83.87	83.87	86.67	83.87	86.67	83.87
27	87.10	96.43	87.10	90.00	87.10	90.00	87.10	87.10	90.00	87.10	90.00	87.10
28	90.32	100.00	90.32	93.33	90.32	93.33	90.32	90.32	93.33	90.32	93.33	90.32
29	93.55	---	93.55	96.67	93.55	96.67	93.55	93.55	96.67	93.55	96.67	93.55
30	96.77	---	96.77	100.00	96.77	100.00	96.77	96.77	100.00	96.77	100.00	96.77
31	100.00	---	100.00	---	100.00	---	100.00	100.00	---	100.00	---	100.00

Percentage of Month Remaining

Date	Jan	Feb	Mar	Apr	May	Jun	Jul	Aug	Sep	Oct	Nov	Dec
1	96.77	96.43	96.77	96.67	96.77	96.67	96.77	96.77	96.67	96.77	96.67	96.77
2	93.55	92.86	93.55	93.33	93.55	93.33	93.55	93.55	93.33	93.55	93.33	93.55
3	90.32	89.29	90.32	90.00	90.32	90.00	90.32	90.32	90.00	90.32	90.00	90.32
4	87.10	85.71	87.10	86.67	87.10	86.67	87.10	87.10	86.67	87.10	86.67	87.10
5	83.87	82.14	83.87	83.33	83.87	83.33	83.87	83.87	83.33	83.87	83.33	83.87
6	80.65	78.57	80.65	80.00	80.65	80.00	80.65	80.65	80.00	80.65	80.00	80.65
7	77.42	75.00	77.42	76.67	77.42	76.67	77.42	77.42	76.67	77.42	76.67	77.42
8	74.19	71.43	74.19	73.33	74.19	73.33	74.19	74.19	73.33	74.19	73.33	74.19
9	70.97	67.86	70.97	70.00	70.97	70.00	70.97	70.97	70.00	70.97	70.00	70.97
10	67.74	64.29	67.74	66.67	67.74	66.67	67.74	67.74	66.67	67.74	66.67	67.74
11	64.52	60.71	64.52	63.33	64.52	63.33	64.52	64.52	63.33	64.52	63.33	64.52
12	61.29	57.14	61.29	60.00	61.29	60.00	61.29	61.29	60.00	61.29	60.00	61.29
13	58.06	53.57	58.06	56.67	58.06	56.67	58.06	58.06	56.67	58.06	56.67	58.06
14	54.84	50.00	54.84	53.33	54.84	53.33	54.84	54.84	53.33	54.84	53.33	54.84
15	51.61	46.43	51.61	50.00	51.61	50.00	51.61	51.61	50.00	51.61	50.00	51.61
16	48.39	42.86	48.39	46.67	48.39	46.67	48.39	48.39	46.67	48.39	46.67	48.39
17	45.16	39.29	45.16	43.33	45.16	43.33	45.16	45.16	43.33	45.16	43.33	45.16
18	41.94	35.71	41.94	40.00	41.94	40.00	41.94	41.94	40.00	41.94	40.00	41.94
19	38.71	32.14	38.71	36.67	38.71	36.67	38.71	38.71	36.67	38.71	36.67	38.71
20	35.48	28.57	35.48	33.33	35.48	33.33	35.48	35.48	33.33	35.48	33.33	35.48
21	32.26	25.00	32.26	30.00	32.26	30.00	32.26	32.26	30.00	32.26	30.00	32.26
22	29.03	21.43	29.03	26.67	29.03	26.67	29.03	29.03	26.67	29.03	26.67	29.03
23	25.81	17.86	25.81	23.33	25.81	23.33	25.81	25.81	23.33	25.81	23.33	25.81
24	22.58	14.29	22.58	20.00	22.58	20.00	22.58	22.58	20.00	22.58	20.00	22.58
25	19.35	10.71	19.35	16.67	19.35	16.67	19.35	19.35	16.67	19.35	16.67	19.35
26	16.13	7.14	16.13	13.33	16.13	13.33	16.13	16.13	13.33	16.13	13.33	16.13
27	12.90	3.57	12.90	10.00	12.90	10.00	12.90	12.90	10.00	12.90	10.00	12.90
28	9.68	0.00	9.68	6.67	9.68	6.67	9.68	9.68	6.67	9.68	6.67	9.68
29	6.45	---	6.45	3.33	6.45	3.33	6.45	6.45	3.33	6.45	3.33	6.45
30	3.23	---	3.23	0.00	3.23	0.00	3.23	3.23	0.00	3.23	0.00	3.23
31	0.00	---	0.00	---	0.00	---	0.00	0.00	---	0.00	---	0.00

All figures are as of the end of the day.

The Consumer Price Index for Years 1960 through 1991

All Urban Consumers (CPI-U)   U.S. City Average 1982-1984 = 100

Year	Jan	Feb	Mar	Apr	May	Jun	Jul	Aug	Sep	Oct	Nov	Dec	Avge
1960	29.3	29.4	29.4	29.5	29.5	29.6	29.6	29.6	29.6	29.8	29.8	29.8	29.6
1961	29.8	29.8	29.8	29.8	29.8	29.8	30.0	29.9	30.0	30.0	30.0	30.0	29.9
1962	30.0	30.1	30.1	30.2	30.2	30.2	30.3	30.3	30.4	30.4	30.4	30.4	30.2
1963	30.4	30.4	30.5	30.5	30.5	30.6	30.7	30.7	30.7	30.8	30.8	30.9	30.6
1964	30.9	30.9	30.9	30.9	30.9	31.0	31.1	31.0	31.1	31.1	31.2	31.2	31.0
1965	31.2	31.2	31.3	31.4	31.4	31.6	31.6	31.6	31.6	31.7	31.7	31.8	31.5
1966	31.8	32.0	32.1	32.3	32.3	32.4	32.5	32.7	32.7	32.9	32.9	32.9	32.4
1967	32.9	32.9	33.0	33.1	33.2	33.3	33.4	33.5	33.6	33.7	33.8	33.9	33.4
1968	34.1	34.2	34.3	34.4	34.5	34.7	34.9	35.0	35.1	35.3	35.4	35.5	34.8
1969	35.6	35.8	36.1	36.3	36.4	36.6	36.8	37.0	37.1	37.3	37.5	37.7	36.7
1970	37.8	38.0	38.2	38.5	38.6	38.8	39.0	39.0	39.2	39.4	39.6	39.8	38.8
1971	39.8	39.9	40.0	40.1	40.3	40.6	40.7	40.8	40.8	40.9	40.9	41.1	40.5
1972	41.1	41.3	41.4	41.5	41.6	41.7	41.9	42.0	42.1	42.3	42.4	42.5	41.8
1973	42.6	42.9	43.3	43.6	43.9	44.2	44.3	45.1	45.2	45.6	45.9	46.2	44.4
1974	46.6	47.2	47.8	48.0	48.6	49.0	49.4	50.0	50.6	51.1	51.5	51.9	49.3
1975	52.1	52.5	52.7	52.9	53.2	53.6	54.2	54.3	54.6	54.9	55.3	55.5	53.8
1976	55.6	55.8	55.9	56.1	56.5	56.8	57.1	57.4	57.6	57.9	58.0	58.2	56.9
1977	58.5	59.1	59.5	60.0	60.3	60.7	61.0	61.2	61.4	61.6	61.9	62.1	60.6
1978	62.5	62.9	63.4	63.9	64.5	65.2	65.7	66.0	66.5	67.1	67.4	67.7	65.2
1979	68.3	69.1	69.8	70.6	71.5	72.3	73.1	73.8	74.6	75.2	75.9	76.7	72.6
1980	77.8	78.9	80.1	81.0	81.8	82.7	82.7	83.3	84.0	84.8	85.5	86.3	82.4
1981	87.0	87.9	88.5	89.1	89.8	90.6	91.6	92.3	93.2	93.4	93.7	94.0	90.0
1982	94.3	94.6	94.5	94.9	95.8	97.0	97.5	97.7	97.9	98.2	98.0	97.6	96.5
1983	97.8	97.9	97.9	98.6	99.2	99.5	99.9	100.2	100.7	101.0	101.2	101.3	99.6
1984	101.9	102.4	102.6	103.1	103.4	103.7	104.1	104.5	105.0	105.3	105.3	105.3	103.9
1985	105.5	106.0	106.4	106.9	107.3	107.6	107.8	108.0	108.3	108.7	109.0	109.3	107.6
1986	109.6	109.3	108.8	108.6	108.9	109.5	109.5	109.7	110.2	110.3	110.4	110.5	109.6
1987	111.2	111.6	112.1	112.7	113.1	113.5	113.8	114.4	115.0	115.3	115.4	115.4	113.6
1988	115.7	116.0	116.5	117.1	117.5	118.0	118.5	119.0	118.8	120.2	120.3	120.5	118.3
1989	121.1	121.6	122.3	123.1	123.8	124.1	124.4	124.6	125.0	125.6	125.9	126.1	124.0
1990	127.4	128.0	128.7	128.9	129.2	129.9	130.4	131.6	132.7	133.5	133.8	133.8	130.7
1991	134.6	134.8	135.0	135.2	135.6	136.0	136.2	136.6	137.2	137.4	137.8	137.9	136.2

Source: U.S. Department of Labor, Bureau of Labor Statistics

Percentage Change in CPI over 3 Years Earlier

Year	Jan	Feb	Mar	Apr	May	Jun	Jul	Aug	Sep	Oct	Nov	Dec	Avge
63/60	3.8	3.4	3.7	3.4	3.4	3.4	3.7	3.7	3.7	3.4	3.4	3.7	3.4
64/61	3.7	3.7	3.7	3.7	3.7	4.0	3.7	3.7	3.7	3.7	4.0	4.0	3.7
65/62	4.0	3.7	4.0	4.0	4.0	4.6	4.3	4.3	3.9	4.3	4.3	4.6	4.3
66/63	4.6	5.3	5.2	5.9	5.9	5.9	5.9	6.5	6.5	6.8	6.8	6.5	5.9
67/64	6.5	6.5	6.8	7.1	7.4	7.4	7.4	8.1	8.0	8.4	8.3	8.7	7.7
68/65	9.3	9.6	9.6	9.6	9.6	9.9	9.8	10.4	10.8	11.1	11.4	11.7	11.6	10.5
69/66	11.9	11.9	12.5	12.4	12.7	13.0	13.2	13.1	13.5	13.4	14.0	14.6	13.3
70/67	14.9	15.5	15.8	16.3	16.3	16.5	16.8	16.4	16.7	16.9	17.2	17.4	16.2
71/68	16.7	16.7	16.6	16.6	16.8	17.0	16.6	16.6	16.2	15.9	15.5	15.8	16.4
72/69	15.4	15.4	14.7	14.3	14.3	13.9	13.9	13.5	13.5	13.4	13.1	12.7	13.9
73/70	12.7	12.9	13.4	13.2	13.7	13.9	13.6	15.6	15.3	15.7	15.9	16.1	14.4
74/71	17.1	18.3	19.5	19.7	20.6	20.7	21.4	22.5	24.0	24.9	25.9	26.3	21.7
75/72	26.8	27.1	27.3	27.5	27.9	28.5	29.4	29.3	29.7	29.8	30.4	30.6	28.7
76/73	30.5	30.1	29.1	28.7	28.7	28.5	28.9	27.3	27.4	27.0	26.4	26.0	28.2
77/74	25.5	25.2	24.5	25.0	24.1	23.9	23.5	22.4	21.3	20.5	20.2	19.7	22.9
78/75	20.0	19.8	20.3	20.8	21.2	21.6	21.2	21.5	21.8	22.2	21.9	22.0	21.2
79/76	22.8	23.8	24.9	25.8	26.5	27.3	28.0	28.6	29.5	29.9	30.9	31.8	27.6
80/77	33.0	33.5	34.6	35.0	35.7	36.2	35.6	36.1	36.8	37.7	38.1	39.0	36.0
81/78	39.2	39.7	39.6	39.4	39.2	39.0	39.4	39.8	40.2	39.2	39.0	38.8	38.0
82/79	38.1	36.9	35.4	34.4	34.0	34.2	33.4	32.4	31.2	30.6	29.1	27.2	32.9
83/80	25.7	24.1	22.2	21.7	21.3	20.3	20.8	20.3	19.9	19.1	18.4	17.4	20.9
84/81	17.1	16.5	15.9	15.7	15.1	14.5	13.6	13.2	12.7	12.7	12.4	12.0	15.4
85/82	11.9	12.1	12.6	12.6	12.0	10.9	10.6	10.5	10.6	10.7	11.2	12.0	11.5
86/83	12.1	11.6	11.1	10.1	9.8	10.1	9.6	9.5	9.4	9.2	9.1	9.1	10.0
87/84	9.1	9.0	9.3	9.3	9.4	9.5	9.3	9.5	9.5	9.5	9.6	9.6	9.3
88/85	9.7	9.4	9.5	9.5	9.5	9.7	9.9	10.2	9.7	10.6	10.4	10.2	9.9
89/86	10.5	11.3	12.4	13.4	13.7	13.3	13.6	13.6	13.4	13.9	14.0	14.1	13.1
90/87	14.6	14.7	14.8	14.4	14.2	14.4	14.6	15.0	15.4	15.8	15.9	15.9	15.1
91/88	___	___	___	___	___	___	___	___	___	___	___	___	___

Entry is the total percentage change over the three-year period.

The Consumer Price Index for Years 1960 through 1990

Percentage Change in CPI over 5 Years Earlier

Year	Jan	Feb	Mar	Apr	May	Jun	Jul	Aug	Sep	Oct	Nov	Dec	Avge
65/60	6.5	6.1	6.5	6.4	6.4	6.8	6.8	6.8	6.8	6.4	6.4	6.7	6.4
66/61	6.7	7.4	7.7	8.4	8.4	8.7	8.3	9.4	9.0	9.7	9.7	9.7	8.4
67/62	9.7	9.3	9.6	9.6	9.9	10.3	10.2	10.6	10.5	10.9	11.2	11.5	10.6
68/63	12.2	12.5	12.5	12.8	13.1	13.4	13.7	14.0	14.3	14.6	14.9	14.9	13.7
69/64	15.2	15.9	16.8	17.5	17.8	18.1	18.3	19.4	19.3	19.9	20.2	20.8	18.4
70/65	21.2	21.8	22.0	22.6	22.9	22.8	23.4	23.4	24.1	24.3	24.9	25.2	23.2
71/66	25.2	24.7	24.6	24.1	24.8	25.3	25.2	24.8	24.8	24.3	24.3	24.9	25.0
72/67	24.9	25.5	25.5	25.4	25.3	25.2	25.4	25.4	25.3	25.5	25.4	25.4	25.1
73/68	24.9	25.4	26.2	26.7	27.2	27.4	26.9	28.9	28.8	29.2	29.7	30.1	27.6
74/69	30.9	31.8	32.4	32.2	33.5	33.9	34.2	35.1	36.4	37.0	37.3	37.7	34.3
75/70	37.8	38.2	38.0	37.4	37.8	38.1	39.0	39.2	39.3	39.3	39.6	39.4	38.7
76/71	39.7	39.8	39.8	39.9	40.2	39.9	40.3	40.7	41.2	41.6	41.8	41.6	40.5
77/72	42.3	43.1	43.7	44.6	45.0	45.6	45.6	45.7	45.8	45.6	46.0	46.1	45.0
78/73	46.7	46.6	46.4	46.6	46.9	47.5	48.3	46.3	47.1	47.1	46.8	46.5	46.8
79/74	46.6	46.4	46.0	47.1	47.1	47.6	48.0	47.6	47.4	47.2	47.4	47.8	47.3
80/75	49.3	50.3	52.0	53.1	53.8	54.3	52.6	53.4	53.8	54.5	54.6	55.5	53.2
81/76	56.5	57.5	58.3	58.8	58.9	59.5	60.4	60.8	61.8	61.3	61.6	61.5	58.2
82/77	61.2	60.1	58.8	58.2	58.9	59.8	59.8	59.6	59.4	59.4	58.3	57.2	59.2
83/78	56.5	55.6	54.4	54.3	53.8	52.6	52.1	51.8	51.4	50.5	50.1	49.6	52.8
84/79	49.2	48.2	47.0	46.0	44.6	43.4	42.4	41.6	40.8	40.0	38.7	37.3	43.1
85/80	35.6	34.3	32.8	32.0	31.2	30.1	30.4	29.7	28.9	28.2	27.5	26.7	30.6
86/81	26.0	24.3	22.9	21.9	21.3	20.9	19.5	18.9	18.2	18.1	17.8	17.6	21.8
87/82	17.9	18.0	18.6	18.8	18.1	17.0	16.7	17.1	17.5	17.4	17.8	18.2	17.7
88/83	18.3	18.5	19.0	18.8	18.4	18.6	18.6	18.8	18.0	19.0	17.8	18.2	17.7
89/84	18.8	18.7	19.2	19.4	19.7	19.7	19.5	19.2	19.0	19.3	18.9	19.0	18.8
90/85	20.8	20.8	21.0	20.6	20.4	20.7	21.0	21.9	22.5	22.8	22.8	22.4	21.5
91/86	___	___	___	___	___	___	___	___	___	___	___	___	___

Entry is the total percentage change over the five-year period.

Percentage Change in CPI over 10 Years Earlier

Year	Jan	Feb	Mar	Apr	May	Jun	Jul	Aug	Sep	Oct	Nov	Dec	Avge
70/60	29.0	29.3	29.9	30.5	30.8	31.1	31.8	31.8	32.4	32.2	32.9	33.6	31.1
71/61	33.6	33.9	34.2	34.6	35.2	36.2	36.5	36.5	36.0	36.3	36.3	37.0	35.5
72/62	37.0	37.2	37.5	37.4	37.7	38.1	38.3	38.6	38.5	39.1	39.5	39.8	38.4
73/63	40.1	41.1	42.0	43.0	43.9	44.4	44.3	46.9	47.2	48.1	49.0	49.5	45.1
74/64	50.8	52.8	54.7	55.3	57.3	58.1	58.8	61.3	62.7	64.3	65.1	66.3	59.0
75/65	67.0	68.3	68.4	68.5	69.4	69.6	71.5	71.8	72.8	73.2	74.4	74.5	70.8
76/66	74.8	74.4	74.1	73.7	74.9	75.3	75.7	75.5	76.1	76.0	76.3	76.9	75.6
77/67	77.8	79.6	80.3	81.3	81.6	82.3	82.6	82.7	82.7	82.8	83.1	83.2	81.4
78/68	83.3	83.9	84.8	85.8	87.0	87.9	88.3	88.6	89.5	90.1	90.4	90.7	87.4
79/69	91.9	93.0	93.4	94.5	96.4	97.5	98.6	99.5	101.1	101.6	102.4	103.4	97.8
80/70	105.8	107.6	109.7	110.4	111.9	113.1	112.1	113.6	114.3	115.2	115.9	116.8	112.4
81/71	118.6	120.3	121.3	122.2	122.8	123.2	125.1	126.2	128.4	128.4	129.1	128.7	122.2
82/72	129.4	129.1	128.3	128.7	130.3	132.6	132.7	132.6	132.5	132.2	131.1	129.6	130.9
83/73	129.6	128.2	126.1	126.1	126.0	125.1	125.5	122.2	122.8	121.5	120.5	119.3	124.3
84/74	118.7	116.9	114.6	114.8	112.8	111.6	110.7	109.0	107.5	106.1	104.5	102.9	110.8
85/75	102.5	101.9	101.9	102.1	101.7	100.7	98.9	98.9	98.4	98.0	97.1	96.9	100.0
86/76	97.1	95.9	94.6	93.6	92.7	92.8	91.8	91.1	91.3	90.5	90.3	89.9	92.6
87/77	90.1	88.8	88.4	87.8	87.6	87.0	86.6	86.9	87.3	87.2	86.4	85.8	87.5
88/78	85.1	84.4	83.8	83.3	82.2	81.0	80.4	80.3	78.6	79.1	78.5	78.0	81.4
89/79	77.3	76.0	75.2	74.4	73.1	71.6	70.2	68.8	67.6	67.0	65.9	64.4	70.8
90/80	63.8	62.2	60.7	59.1	57.9	57.1	57.7	58.0	58.0	57.4	56.5	55.0	58.6
91/81	___	___	___	___	___	___	___	___	___	___	___	___	

Entry is the total percentage change over the ten-year period.

Calendars for Years 1960 through 2020

Find the Letter below for the selected year. Follow the calendar for that Letter. Leap year calendars follow those for regular years.

1960	G leap yr	1970	E		1980	C leap yr	1990	B		2000	G leap yr	2010	F	
1961	A	1971	F		1981	E	1991	C		2001	B	2011	G	
1962	B	1972	G leap yr		1982	F	1992	D leap yr	2002	C	2012	A leap yr	
1963	C	1973	B		1983	G	1993	F		2003	D	2013	C	
1964	D leap yr	1974	C		1984	A leap yr	1994	G		2004	E leap yr	2014	D	
1965	F	1975	D		1985	C	1995	A		2005	G	2015	E	
1966	G	1976	E leap yr		1986	D	1996	B leap yr	2006	A	2016	F leap yr	
1967	A	1977	G		1987	E	1997	D		2007	B	2017	A	
1968	B leap yr	1978	A		1988	F leap yr	1998	E		2008	C leap yr	2018	B	
1969	D	1979	B		1989	A	1999	F		2009	D	2019	C	
													2020	D leap yr

Year A

```
   January              February              March                 April
S  M  T  W  T  F  S   S  M  T  W  T  F  S   S  M  T  W  T  F  S   S  M  T  W  T  F  S
1  2  3  4  5  6  7            1  2  3  4            1  2  3  4                        1
8  9 10 11 12 13 14   5  6  7  8  9 10 11   5  6  7  8  9 10 11   2  3  4  5  6  7  8
15 16 17 18 19 20 21  12 13 14 15 16 17 18  12 13 14 15 16 17 18  9 10 11 12 13 14 15
22 23 24 25 26 27 28  19 20 21 22 23 24 25  19 20 21 22 23 24 25  16 17 18 19 20 21 22
29 30 31              26 27 28              26 27 28 29 30 31      23 24 25 26 27 28 29
                                                                  30

   May                  June                  July                  August
S  M  T  W  T  F  S   S  M  T  W  T  F  S   S  M  T  W  T  F  S   S  M  T  W  T  F  S
   1  2  3  4  5  6            1  2  3                        1      1  2  3  4  5
7  8  9 10 11 12 13   4  5  6  7  8  9 10   2  3  4  5  6  7  8   6  7  8  9 10 11 12
14 15 16 17 18 19 20  11 12 13 14 15 16 17  9 10 11 12 13 14 15  13 14 15 16 17 18 19
21 22 23 24 25 26 27  18 19 20 21 22 23 24  16 17 18 19 20 21 22  20 21 22 23 24 25 26
28 29 30 31           25 26 27 28 29 30      23 24 25 26 27 28 29  27 28 29 30 31
                                             30 31

   September            October               November              December
S  M  T  W  T  F  S   S  M  T  W  T  F  S   S  M  T  W  T  F  S   S  M  T  W  T  F  S
               1  2   1  2  3  4  5  6  7            1  2  3  4                     1  2
3  4  5  6  7  8  9   8  9 10 11 12 13 14   5  6  7  8  9 10 11   3  4  5  6  7  8  9
10 11 12 13 14 15 16  15 16 17 18 19 20 21  12 13 14 15 16 17 18  10 11 12 13 14 15 16
17 18 19 20 21 22 23  22 23 24 25 26 27 28  19 20 21 22 23 24 25  17 18 19 20 21 22 23
24 25 26 27 28 29 30  29 30 31              26 27 28 29 30         24 25 26 27 28 29 30
                                                                  31
```

Year B

```
   January              February              March                 April
S  M  T  W  T  F  S   S  M  T  W  T  F  S   S  M  T  W  T  F  S   S  M  T  W  T  F  S
   1  2  3  4  5  6            1  2  3               1  2  3   1  2  3  4  5  6  7
7  8  9 10 11 12 13   4  5  6  7  8  9 10   4  5  6  7  8  9 10   8  9 10 11 12 13 14
14 15 16 17 18 19 20  11 12 13 14 15 16 17  11 12 13 14 15 16 17  15 16 17 18 19 20 21
21 22 23 24 25 26 27  18 19 20 21 22 23 24  18 19 20 21 22 23 24  22 23 24 25 26 27 28
28 29 30 31           25 26 27 28           25 26 27 28 29 30 31  29 30

   May                  June                  July                  August
S  M  T  W  T  F  S   S  M  T  W  T  F  S   S  M  T  W  T  F  S   S  M  T  W  T  F  S
   1  2  3  4  5               1  2   1  2  3  4  5  6  7            1  2  3  4
6  7  8  9 10 11 12   3  4  5  6  7  8  9   8  9 10 11 12 13 14   5  6  7  8  9 10 11
13 14 15 16 17 18 19  10 11 12 13 14 15 16  15 16 17 18 19 20 21  12 13 14 15 16 17 18
20 21 22 23 24 25 26  17 18 19 20 21 22 23  22 23 24 25 26 27 28  19 20 21 22 23 24 25
27 28 29 30 31        24 25 26 27 28 29 30  29 30 31              26 27 28 29 30 31

   September            October               November              December
S  M  T  W  T  F  S   S  M  T  W  T  F  S   S  M  T  W  T  F  S   S  M  T  W  T  F  S
                  1   1  2  3  4  5  6               1  2  3                        1
2  3  4  5  6  7  8   7  8  9 10 11 12 13   4  5  6  7  8  9 10   2  3  4  5  6  7  8
9 10 11 12 13 14 15  14 15 16 17 18 19 20  11 12 13 14 15 16 17   9 10 11 12 13 14 15
16 17 18 19 20 21 22  21 22 23 24 25 26 27  18 19 20 21 22 23 24  16 17 18 19 20 21 22
23 24 25 26 27 28 29  28 29 30 31          25 26 27 28 29 30      23 24 25 26 27 28 29
30                                                                30 31
```

Calendars for Years 1960 through 2020

Select the letter for the desired year from the chart above and follow the calendar for that letter.

Year C

```
        January                    February                    March                      April
S  M  T  W  T  F  S        S  M  T  W  T  F  S        S  M  T  W  T  F  S        S  M  T  W  T  F  S
         1  2  3  4  5                       1  2                       1  2                 1  2  3  4  5  6
 6  7  8  9 10 11 12        3  4  5  6  7  8  9        3  4  5  6  7  8  9        7  8  9 10 11 12 13
13 14 15 16 17 18 19       10 11 12 13 14 15 16       10 11 12 13 14 15 16       14 15 16 17 18 19 20
20 21 22 23 24 25 26       17 18 19 20 21 22 23       17 18 19 20 21 22 23       21 22 23 24 25 26 27
27 28 29 30 31             24 25 26 27 28             24 25 26 27 28 29 30       28 29 30
                                                      31

          May                        June                       July                       August
S  M  T  W  T  F  S        S  M  T  W  T  F  S        S  M  T  W  T  F  S        S  M  T  W  T  F  S
            1  2  3  4                          1           1  2  3  4  5  6                       1  2  3
 5  6  7  8  9 10 11        2  3  4  5  6  7  8        7  8  9 10 11 12 13        4  5  6  7  8  9 10
12 13 14 15 16 17 18        9 10 11 12 13 14 15       14 15 16 17 18 19 20       11 12 13 14 15 16 17
19 20 21 22 23 24 25       16 17 18 19 20 21 22       21 22 23 24 25 26 27       18 19 20 21 22 23 24
26 27 28 29 30 31          23 24 25 26 27 28 29       28 29 30 31                25 26 27 28 29 30 31
                           30

        September                    October                    November                    December
S  M  T  W  T  F  S        S  M  T  W  T  F  S        S  M  T  W  T  F  S        S  M  T  W  T  F  S
 1  2  3  4  5  6  7                 1  2  3  4  5                       1  2     1  2  3  4  5  6  7
 8  9 10 11 12 13 14        6  7  8  9 10 11 12        3  4  5  6  7  8  9        8  9 10 11 12 13 14
15 16 17 18 19 20 21       13 14 15 16 17 18 19       10 11 12 13 14 15 16       15 16 17 18 19 20 21
22 23 24 25 26 27 28       20 21 22 23 24 25 26       17 18 19 20 21 22 23       22 23 24 25 26 27 28
29 30                      27 28 29 30 31             24 25 26 27 28 29 30       29 30 31
```

Year D

```
        January                    February                    March                      April
S  M  T  W  T  F  S        S  M  T  W  T  F  S        S  M  T  W  T  F  S        S  M  T  W  T  F  S
            1  2  3  4                          1                          1                 1  2  3  4  5
 5  6  7  8  9 10 11        2  3  4  5  6  7  8        2  3  4  5  6  7  8        6  7  8  9 10 11 12
12 13 14 15 16 17 18        9 10 11 12 13 14 15        9 10 11 12 13 14 15       13 14 15 16 17 18 19
19 20 21 22 23 24 25       16 17 18 19 20 21 22       16 17 18 19 20 21 22       20 21 22 23 24 25 26
26 27 28 29 30 31          23 24 25 26 27 28          23 24 25 26 27 28 29       27 28 29 30

          May                        June                       July                       August
S  M  T  W  T  F  S        S  M  T  W  T  F  S        S  M  T  W  T  F  S        S  M  T  W  T  F  S
                  1  2  3  1  2  3  4  5  6  7              1  2  3  4  5                       1  2
 4  5  6  7  8  9 10        8  9 10 11 12 13 14        6  7  8  9 10 11 12        3  4  5  6  7  8  9
11 12 13 14 15 16 17       15 16 17 18 19 20 21       13 14 15 16 17 18 19       10 11 12 13 14 15 16
18 19 20 21 22 23 24       22 23 24 25 26 27 28       20 21 22 23 24 25 26       17 18 19 20 21 22 23
25 26 27 28 29 30 31       29 30                      27 28 29 30 31             24 25 26 27 28 29 30

        September                    October                    November                    December
S  M  T  W  T  F  S        S  M  T  W  T  F  S        S  M  T  W  T  F  S        S  M  T  W  T  F  S
    1  2  3  4  5  6                    1  2  3  4                          1     1  2  3  4  5  6
 7  8  9 10 11 12 13        5  6  7  8  9 10 11        2  3  4  5  6  7  8        7  8  9 10 11 12 13
14 15 16 17 18 19 20       12 13 14 15 16 17 18        9 10 11 12 13 14 15       14 15 16 17 18 19 20
21 22 23 24 25 26 27       19 20 21 22 23 24 25       16 17 18 19 20 21 22       21 22 23 24 25 26 27
28 29 30                   26 27 28 29 30 31          23 24 25 26 27 28 29       28 29 30 31
                                                      30
```

Year E

```
        January                    February                    March                      April
S  M  T  W  T  F  S        S  M  T  W  T  F  S        S  M  T  W  T  F  S        S  M  T  W  T  F  S
            1  2  3        1  2  3  4  5  6  7        1  2  3  4  5  6  7                    1  2  3  4
 4  5  6  7  8  9 10        8  9 10 11 12 13 14        8  9 10 11 12 13 14        5  6  7  8  9 10 11
11 12 13 14 15 16 17       15 16 17 18 19 20 21       15 16 17 18 19 20 21       12 13 14 15 16 17 18
18 19 20 21 22 23 24       22 23 24 25 26 27 28       22 23 24 25 26 27 28       19 20 21 22 23 24 25
25 26 27 28 29 30 31                                  29 30 31                   26 27 28 29 30

          May                        June                       July                       August
S  M  T  W  T  F  S        S  M  T  W  T  F  S        S  M  T  W  T  F  S        S  M  T  W  T  F  S
                  1  2         1  2  3  4  5  6              1  2  3  4                             1
 3  4  5  6  7  8  9        7  8  9 10 11 12 13        5  6  7  8  9 10 11        2  3  4  5  6  7  8
10 11 12 13 14 15 16       14 15 16 17 18 19 20       12 13 14 15 16 17 18        9 10 11 12 13 14 15
17 18 19 20 21 22 23       21 22 23 24 25 26 27       19 20 21 22 23 24 25       16 17 18 19 20 21 22
24 25 26 27 28 29 30       28 29 30                   26 27 28 29 30 31          23 24 25 26 27 28 29
31                                                                               30 31

        September                    October                    November                    December
S  M  T  W  T  F  S        S  M  T  W  T  F  S        S  M  T  W  T  F  S        S  M  T  W  T  F  S
       1  2  3  4  5                    1  2  3        1  2  3  4  5  6  7              1  2  3  4  5
 6  7  8  9 10 11 12        4  5  6  7  8  9 10        8  9 10 11 12 13 14        6  7  8  9 10 11 12
13 14 15 16 17 18 19       11 12 13 14 15 16 17       15 16 17 18 19 20 21       13 14 15 16 17 18 19
20 21 22 23 24 25 26       18 19 20 21 22 23 24       22 23 24 25 26 27 28       20 21 22 23 24 25 26
27 28 29 30                25 26 27 28 29 30 31       29 30                      27 28 29 30 31
```

Calendars for Years 1960 through 2020

Select the letter for the desired year from the chart above and follow the calendar for that letter.

Year F

```
     January                  February                 March                    April
S  M  T  W  T  F  S      S  M  T  W  T  F  S      S  M  T  W  T  F  S      S  M  T  W  T  F  S
            1  2                1  2  3  4  5  6             1  2  3  4  5  6                   1  2
3  4  5  6  7  8  9      7  8  9 10 11 12 13      7  8  9 10 11 12 13      4  5  6  7  8  9 10
10 11 12 13 14 15 16    14 15 16 17 18 19 20     14 15 16 17 18 19 20     11 12 13 14 15 16 17
17 18 19 20 21 22 23    21 22 23 24 25 26 27     21 22 23 24 25 26 27     18 19 20 21 22 23 24
24 25 26 27 28 29 30    28                       28 29 30 31              25 26 27 28 29 30
31

     May                      June                     July                     August
S  M  T  W  T  F  S      S  M  T  W  T  F  S      S  M  T  W  T  F  S      S  M  T  W  T  F  S
                  1                1  2  3  4  5                1  2  3      1  2  3  4  5  6  7
2  3  4  5  6  7  8      6  7  8  9 10 11 12      4  5  6  7  8  9 10      8  9 10 11 12 13 14
9 10 11 12 13 14 15     13 14 15 16 17 18 19     11 12 13 14 15 16 17     15 16 17 18 19 20 21
16 17 18 19 20 21 22    20 21 22 23 24 25 26     18 19 20 21 22 23 24     22 23 24 25 26 27 28
23 24 25 26 27 28 29    27 28 29 30              25 26 27 28 29 30 31     29 30 31
30 31

     September                October                  November                 December
S  M  T  W  T  F  S      S  M  T  W  T  F  S      S  M  T  W  T  F  S      S  M  T  W  T  F  S
         1  2  3  4                        1  2             1  2  3  4  5  6             1  2  3  4
5  6  7  8  9 10 11      3  4  5  6  7  8  9      7  8  9 10 11 12 13      5  6  7  8  9 10 11
12 13 14 15 16 17 18    10 11 12 13 14 15 16     14 15 16 17 18 19 20     12 13 14 15 16 17 18
19 20 21 22 23 24 25    17 18 19 20 21 22 23     21 22 23 24 25 26 27     19 20 21 22 23 24 25
26 27 28 29 30          24 25 26 27 28 29 30     28 29 30                 26 27 28 29 30 31
                        31
```

Year G

```
     January                  February                 March                    April
S  M  T  W  T  F  S      S  M  T  W  T  F  S      S  M  T  W  T  F  S      S  M  T  W  T  F  S
                  1                1  2  3  4  5             1  2  3  4  5                   1  2
2  3  4  5  6  7  8      6  7  8  9 10 11 12      6  7  8  9 10 11 12      3  4  5  6  7  8  9
9 10 11 12 13 14 15     13 14 15 16 17 18 19     13 14 15 16 17 18 19     10 11 12 13 14 15 16
16 17 18 19 20 21 22    20 21 22 23 24 25 26     20 21 22 23 24 25 26     17 18 19 20 21 22 23
23 24 25 26 27 28 29    27 28                    27 28 29 30 31           24 25 26 27 28 29 30
30 31

     May                      June                     July                     August
S  M  T  W  T  F  S      S  M  T  W  T  F  S      S  M  T  W  T  F  S      S  M  T  W  T  F  S
1  2  3  4  5  6  7                1  2  3  4                   1  2         1  2  3  4  5  6
8  9 10 11 12 13 14     5  6  7  8  9 10 11      3  4  5  6  7  8  9      7  8  9 10 11 12 13
15 16 17 18 19 20 21    12 13 14 15 16 17 18     10 11 12 13 14 15 16     14 15 16 17 18 19 20
22 23 24 25 26 27 28    19 20 21 22 23 24 25     17 18 19 20 21 22 23     21 22 23 24 25 26 27
29 30 31                26 27 28 29 30           24 25 26 27 28 29 30     28 29 30 31
                                                 31

     September                October                  November                 December
S  M  T  W  T  F  S      S  M  T  W  T  F  S      S  M  T  W  T  F  S      S  M  T  W  T  F  S
            1  2  3                           1             1  2  3  4  5                1  2  3
4  5  6  7  8  9 10      2  3  4  5  6  7  8      6  7  8  9 10 11 12      4  5  6  7  8  9 10
11 12 13 14 15 16 17    9 10 11 12 13 14 15     13 14 15 16 17 18 19     11 12 13 14 15 16 17
18 19 20 21 22 23 24    16 17 18 19 20 21 22     20 21 22 23 24 25 26     18 19 20 21 22 23 24
25 26 27 28 29 30       23 24 25 26 27 28 29     27 28 29 30              25 26 27 28 29 30 31
                        30 31
```

		English	French	Spanish	German	Dutch
S	Sun	Sunday	dimanche	domingo	sonntag	zondag
M	Mon	Monday	lundi	lunes	montag	maandag
T	Tue	Tuesday	mardi	martes	diensdag	dinsdag
W	Wed	Wednesday	mercredi	miercoles	mittwoch	woensdag
T	Thu	Thursday	jeudi	jueves	donnerstag	donderdag
F	Fri	Friday	vendredi	viernes	freitag	vrijdag
S	Sat	Saturday	samedi	sabado	samstag	zaterdag

Calendars for Years 1960 through 2020

Select the letter for the desired year from the chart above and follow the calendar for that letter.

Year A - Leap Year

```
        January                February                 March                   April
S  M  T  W  T  F  S     S  M  T  W  T  F  S     S  M  T  W  T  F  S     S  M  T  W  T  F  S
1  2  3  4  5  6  7              1  2  3  4                 1  2  3     1  2  3  4  5  6  7
8  9 10 11 12 13 14     5  6  7  8  9 10 11     4  5  6  7  8  9 10     8  9 10 11 12 13 14
15 16 17 18 19 20 21    12 13 14 15 16 17 18    11 12 13 14 15 16 17    15 16 17 18 19 20 21
22 23 24 25 26 27 28    19 20 21 22 23 24 25    18 19 20 21 22 23 24    22 23 24 25 26 27 28
29 30 31                26 27 28 29             25 26 27 28 29 30 31    29 30

          May                    June                    July                   August
S  M  T  W  T  F  S     S  M  T  W  T  F  S     S  M  T  W  T  F  S     S  M  T  W  T  F  S
      1  2  3  4  5                    1  2     1  2  3  4  5  6  7              1  2  3  4
6  7  8  9 10 11 12     3  4  5  6  7  8  9     8  9 10 11 12 13 14     5  6  7  8  9 10 11
13 14 15 16 17 18 19    10 11 12 13 14 15 16    15 16 17 18 19 20 21    12 13 14 15 16 17 18
20 21 22 23 24 25 26    17 18 19 20 21 22 23    22 23 24 25 26 27 28    19 20 21 22 23 24 25
27 28 29 30 31          24 25 26 27 28 29 30    29 30 31                26 27 28 29 30 31

       September                October                November                December
S  M  T  W  T  F  S     S  M  T  W  T  F  S     S  M  T  W  T  F  S     S  M  T  W  T  F  S
                  1              1  2  3  4  5  6              1  2  3                    1
2  3  4  5  6  7  8     7  8  9 10 11 12 13     4  5  6  7  8  9 10     2  3  4  5  6  7  8
9 10 11 12 13 14 15    14 15 16 17 18 19 20    11 12 13 14 15 16 17     9 10 11 12 13 14 15
16 17 18 19 20 21 22    21 22 23 24 25 26 27    18 19 20 21 22 23 24    16 17 18 19 20 21 22
23 24 25 26 27 28 29    28 29 30 31             25 26 27 28 29 30       23 24 25 26 27 28 29
30                                                                     30 31
```

Year B - Leap Year

```
        January                February                 March                   April
S  M  T  W  T  F  S     S  M  T  W  T  F  S     S  M  T  W  T  F  S     S  M  T  W  T  F  S
      1  2  3  4  5                    1  2  3                 1  2                 1  2  3  4  5  6
7  8  9 10 11 12 13     4  5  6  7  8  9 10     3  4  5  6  7  8  9     7  8  9 10 11 12 13
14 15 16 17 18 19 20    11 12 13 14 15 16 17    10 11 12 13 14 15 16    14 15 16 17 18 19 20
21 22 23 24 25 26 27    18 19 20 21 22 23 24    17 18 19 20 21 22 23    21 22 23 24 25 26 27
28 29 30 31             25 26 27 28 29          24 25 26 27 28 29 30    28 29 30

          May                    June                    July                   August
S  M  T  W  T  F  S     S  M  T  W  T  F  S     S  M  T  W  T  F  S     S  M  T  W  T  F  S
         1  2  3  4                       1              1  2  3  4  5  6                 1  2  3
5  6  7  8  9 10 11     2  3  4  5  6  7  8     7  8  9 10 11 12 13     4  5  6  7  8  9 10
12 13 14 15 16 17 18    9 10 11 12 13 14 15    14 15 16 17 18 19 20    11 12 13 14 15 16 17
19 20 21 22 23 24 25    16 17 18 19 20 21 22    21 22 23 24 25 26 27    18 19 20 21 22 23 24
26 27 28 29 30 31       23 24 25 26 27 28 29    28 29 30 31             25 26 27 28 29 30 31

       September                October                November                December
S  M  T  W  T  F  S     S  M  T  W  T  F  S     S  M  T  W  T  F  S     S  M  T  W  T  F  S
1  2  3  4  5  6  7              1  2  3  4  5                 1  2     1  2  3  4  5  6  7
8  9 10 11 12 13 14     6  7  8  9 10 11 12     3  4  5  6  7  8  9     8  9 10 11 12 13 14
15 16 17 18 19 20 21    13 14 15 16 17 18 19    10 11 12 13 14 15 16    15 16 17 18 19 20 21
22 23 24 25 26 27 28    20 21 22 23 24 25 26    17 18 19 20 21 22 23    22 23 24 25 26 27 28
29 30                   27 28 29 30 31          24 25 26 27 28 29 30    29 30 31
```

Year C - Leap Year

```
        January                February                 March                   April
S  M  T  W  T  F  S     S  M  T  W  T  F  S     S  M  T  W  T  F  S     S  M  T  W  T  F  S
         1  2  3  4  5                    1  2     1  2  3  4  5  6  7                 1  2  3  4  5
6  7  8  9 10 11 12     3  4  5  6  7  8  9     2  3  4  5  6  7  8     6  7  8  9 10 11 12
13 14 15 16 17 18 19    10 11 12 13 14 15 16    9 10 11 12 13 14 15    13 14 15 16 17 18 19
20 21 22 23 24 25 26    17 18 19 20 21 22 23    16 17 18 19 20 21 22    20 21 22 23 24 25 26
27 28 29 30 31          24 25 26 27 28 29       23 24 25 26 27 28 29    27 28 29 30
                                               30 31

          May                    June                    July                   August
S  M  T  W  T  F  S     S  M  T  W  T  F  S     S  M  T  W  T  F  S     S  M  T  W  T  F  S
            1  2  3     1  2  3  4  5  6  7              1  2  3  4  5                    1  2
4  5  6  7  8  9 10     8  9 10 11 12 13 14     6  7  8  9 10 11 12     3  4  5  6  7  8  9
11 12 13 14 15 16 17    15 16 17 18 19 20 21    13 14 15 16 17 18 19    10 11 12 13 14 15 16
18 19 20 21 22 23 24    22 23 24 25 26 27 28    20 21 22 23 24 25 26    17 18 19 20 21 22 23
25 26 27 28 29 30 31    29 30                   27 28 29 30 31          24 25 26 27 28 29 30
                                                                       31

       September                October                November                December
S  M  T  W  T  F  S     S  M  T  W  T  F  S     S  M  T  W  T  F  S     S  M  T  W  T  F  S
   1  2  3  4  5  6                 1  2  3  4                       1     1  2  3  4  5  6
7  8  9 10 11 12 13     5  6  7  8  9 10 11     2  3  4  5  6  7  8     7  8  9 10 11 12 13
14 15 16 17 18 19 20    12 13 14 15 16 17 18    9 10 11 12 13 14 15    14 15 16 17 18 19 20
21 22 23 24 25 26 27    19 20 21 22 23 24 25    16 17 18 19 20 21 22    21 22 23 24 25 26 27
28 29 30                26 27 28 29 30 31       23 24 25 26 27 28 29    28 29 30 31
```

Calendars for Years 1960 through 2020

Select the letter for the desired year from the chart above and follow the calendar for that letter.

Year D - Leap Year

January

S	M	T	W	T	F	S
			1	2	3	4
5	6	7	8	9	10	11
12	13	14	15	16	17	18
19	20	21	22	23	24	25
26	27	28	29	30	31	

February

S	M	T	W	T	F	S
						1
2	3	4	5	6	7	8
9	10	11	12	13	14	15
16	17	18	19	20	21	22
23	24	25	26	27	28	29

March

S	M	T	W	T	F	S
1	2	3	4	5	6	7
8	9	10	11	12	13	14
15	16	17	18	19	20	21
22	23	24	25	26	27	28
29	30	31				

April

S	M	T	W	T	F	S
			1	2	3	4
5	6	7	8	9	10	11
12	13	14	15	16	17	18
19	20	21	22	23	24	25
26	27	28	29	30		

May

S	M	T	W	T	F	S
					1	2
3	4	5	6	7	8	9
10	11	12	13	14	15	16
17	18	19	20	21	22	23
24	25	26	27	28	29	30
31						

June

S	M	T	W	T	F	S
	1	2	3	4	5	6
7	8	9	10	11	12	13
14	15	16	17	18	19	20
21	22	23	24	25	26	27
28	29	30				

July

S	M	T	W	T	F	S
			1	2	3	4
5	6	7	8	9	10	11
12	13	14	15	16	17	18
19	20	21	22	23	24	25
26	27	28	29	30	31	

August

S	M	T	W	T	F	S
						1
2	3	4	5	6	7	8
9	10	11	12	13	14	15
16	17	18	19	20	21	22
23	24	25	26	27	28	29
30	31					

September

S	M	T	W	T	F	S
		1	2	3	4	5
6	7	8	9	10	11	12
13	14	15	16	17	18	19
20	21	22	23	24	25	26
27	28	29	30			

October

S	M	T	W	T	F	S
				1	2	3
4	5	6	7	8	9	10
11	12	13	14	15	16	17
18	19	20	21	22	23	24
25	26	27	28	29	30	31

November

S	M	T	W	T	F	S
1	2	3	4	5	6	7
8	9	10	11	12	13	14
15	16	17	18	19	20	21
22	23	24	25	26	27	28
29	30					

December

S	M	T	W	T	F	S
		1	2	3	4	5
6	7	8	9	10	11	12
13	14	15	16	17	18	19
20	21	22	23	24	25	26
27	28	29	30	31		

Year E - Leap Year

January

S	M	T	W	T	F	S
				1	2	3
4	5	6	7	8	9	10
11	12	13	14	15	16	17
18	19	20	21	22	23	24
25	26	27	28	29	30	31

February

S	M	T	W	T	F	S
1	2	3	4	5	6	7
8	9	10	11	12	13	14
15	16	17	18	19	20	21
22	23	24	25	26	27	28
29						

March

S	M	T	W	T	F	S
	1	2	3	4	5	6
7	8	9	10	11	12	13
14	15	16	17	18	19	20
21	22	23	24	25	26	27
28	29	30	31			

April

S	M	T	W	T	F	S
				1	2	3
4	5	6	7	8	9	10
11	12	13	14	15	16	17
18	19	20	21	22	23	24
25	26	27	28	29	30	

May

S	M	T	W	T	F	S
						1
2	3	4	5	6	7	8
9	10	11	12	13	14	15
16	17	18	19	20	21	22
23	24	25	26	27	28	29

June

S	M	T	W	T	F	S
	1	2	3	4	5	
6	7	8	9	10	11	12
13	14	15	16	17	18	19
20	21	22	23	24	25	26
27	28	29	30			

July

S	M	T	W	T	F	S
				1	2	3
4	5	6	7	8	9	10
11	12	13	14	15	16	17
18	19	20	21	22	23	24
25	26	27	28	29	30	31

August

S	M	T	W	T	F	S
1	2	3	4	5	6	7
8	9	10	11	12	13	14
15	16	17	18	19	20	21
22	23	24	25	26	27	28
29	30	31				

September

S	M	T	W	T	F	S
			1	2	3	4
5	6	7	8	9	10	11
12	13	14	15	16	17	18
19	20	21	22	23	24	25
26	27	28	29	30		

October

S	M	T	W	T	F	S
					1	2
3	4	5	6	7	8	9
10	11	12	13	14	15	16
17	18	19	20	21	22	23
24	25	26	27	28	29	30
31						

November

S	M	T	W	T	F	S
	1	2	3	4	5	6
7	8	9	10	11	12	13
14	15	16	17	18	19	20
21	22	23	24	25	26	27
28	29	30				

December

S	M	T	W	T	F	S
			1	2	3	4
5	6	7	8	9	10	11
12	13	14	15	16	17	18
19	20	21	22	23	24	25
26	27	28	29	30	31	

Year F - Leap Year

January

S	M	T	W	T	F	S
					1	2
3	4	5	6	7	8	9
10	11	12	13	14	15	16
17	18	19	20	21	22	23
24	25	26	27	28	29	30
31						

February

S	M	T	W	T	F	S
	1	2	3	4	5	6
7	8	9	10	11	12	13
14	15	16	17	18	19	20
21	22	23	24	25	26	27
28	29					

March

S	M	T	W	T	F	S
		1	2	3	4	5
6	7	8	9	10	11	12
13	14	15	16	17	18	19
20	21	22	23	24	25	26
27	28	29	30	31		

April

S	M	T	W	T	F	S
					1	2
3	4	5	6	7	8	9
10	11	12	13	14	15	16
17	18	19	20	21	22	23
24	25	26	27	28	29	30

May

S	M	T	W	T	F	S
1	2	3	4	5	6	7
8	9	10	11	12	13	14
15	16	17	18	19	20	21
22	23	24	25	26	27	28
29	30	31				

June

S	M	T	W	T	F	S
			1	2	3	4
5	6	7	8	9	10	11
12	13	14	15	16	17	18
19	20	21	22	23	24	25
26	27	28	29	30		

July

S	M	T	W	T	F	S
					1	2
3	4	5	6	7	8	9
10	11	12	13	14	15	16
17	18	19	20	21	22	23
24	25	26	27	28	29	30
31						

August

S	M	T	W	T	F	S
	1	2	3	4	5	6
7	8	9	10	11	12	13
14	15	16	17	18	19	20
21	22	23	24	25	26	27
28	29	30	31			

September

S	M	T	W	T	F	S
			1	2	3	
4	5	6	7	8	9	10
11	12	13	14	15	16	17
18	19	20	21	22	23	24
25	26	27	28	29	30	

October

S	M	T	W	T	F	S
						1
2	3	4	5	6	7	8
9	10	11	12	13	14	15
16	17	18	19	20	21	22
23	24	25	26	27	28	29

November

S	M	T	W	T	F	S
		1	2	3	4	5
6	7	8	9	10	11	12
13	14	15	16	17	18	19
20	21	22	23	24	25	26
27	28	29	30			

December

S	M	T	W	T	F	S
				1	2	3
4	5	6	7	8	9	10
11	12	13	14	15	16	17
18	19	20	21	22	23	24
25	26	27	28	29	30	31

Calendars for Years 1960 through 2020

Select the letter for the desired year from the chart above and follow the calendar for that letter.

Year G - Leap Year

```
        January                    February                    March                      April
  S  M  T  W  T  F  S        S  M  T  W  T  F  S        S  M  T  W  T  F  S        S  M  T  W  T  F  S
                    1                 1  2  3  4  5                 1  2  3  4                             1
  2  3  4  5  6  7  8        6  7  8  9 10 11 12        5  6  7  8  9 10 11        2  3  4  5  6  7  8
  9 10 11 12 13 14 15       13 14 15 16 17 18 19       12 13 14 15 16 17 18        9 10 11 12 13 14 15
 16 17 18 19 20 21 22       20 21 22 23 24 25 26       19 20 21 22 23 24 25       16 17 18 19 20 21 22
 23 24 25 26 27 28 29       27 28 29                   26 27 28 29 30 31          23 24 25 26 27 28 29
 30 31                                                                            30

          May                        June                        July                     August
  S  M  T  W  T  F  S        S  M  T  W  T  F  S        S  M  T  W  T  F  S        S  M  T  W  T  F  S
     1  2  3  4  5  6                    1  2  3                          1              1  2  3  4  5
  7  8  9 10 11 12 13        4  5  6  7  8  9 10        2  3  4  5  6  7  8        6  7  8  9 10 11 12
 14 15 16 17 18 19 20       11 12 13 14 15 16 17        9 10 11 12 13 14 15       13 14 15 16 17 18 19
 21 22 23 24 25 26 27       18 19 20 21 22 23 24       16 17 18 19 20 21 22       20 21 22 23 24 25 26
 28 29 30 31                25 26 27 28 29 30          23 24 25 26 27 28 29       27 28 29 30 31
                                                       30 31

       September                    October                     November                   December
  S  M  T  W  T  F  S        S  M  T  W  T  F  S        S  M  T  W  T  F  S        S  M  T  W  T  F  S
                 1  2        1  2  3  4  5  6  7                 1  2  3  4                          1  2
  3  4  5  6  7  8  9        8  9 10 11 12 13 14        5  6  7  8  9 10 11        3  4  5  6  7  8  9
 10 11 12 13 14 15 16       15 16 17 18 19 20 21       12 13 14 15 16 17 18       10 11 12 13 14 15 16
 17 18 19 20 21 22 23       22 23 24 25 26 27 28       19 20 21 22 23 24 25       17 18 19 20 21 22 23
 24 25 26 27 28 29 30       29 30 31                   26 27 28 29 30             24 25 26 27 28 29 30
                                                                                  31
```

Measurements and Conversions
United States & International System (SI) Units

Common Measures, United States Measurement

	inches	feet	yards
inch	1.00	0.08333	0.0277
foot	12.00	1.00	0.3333
yard	36.00	3.00	1.0000
mile	63,360.00	5280.00	1760.00

Land Survey Measures, United States Measurement

	inches	links	feet	rods	chains	furlongs	miles
inch	1.00	0.12626	0.0833	0.0505	0.01263	--	--
link	7.920	1.00	0.6600	0.400	0.010	--	--
foot	36.00	1.51515	1.00	0.0606	0.01515	--	--
rod	198.00	2.50	16.50	1.00	0.250	0.025	0.003125
chain	792.00	100.00	66.00	4.00	1.00	0.100	0.012500
furlong	7920.00	1000.00	660.00	40.00	10.00	1.00	0.12500
mile	63,360	8000.00	5280.00	320.00	80.00	8.00	1.00

U.S. to International System (SI) Conversion

	cms	inches	meters	feet	kms	miles
inch	2.54		0.0254	0.0328	---	---
centimeter		0.3937				
foot	30.48		0.3048		---	
meter		39.3696		3.2808		
yard	91.44		0.9144		0.009144	0.62137
kilometer				3280.8	1.609344	
mile			1609.3			

Reciprocal Percentage Markups & Markdowns

Markdown	Markup	Markdown	Markup	Markdown	Markup	Markdown	Markup
0.5	100.50251	25.5	134.22819	50.5	202.02020	75.5	408.16327
1	101.01010	26	135.13514	51	204.08163	76.0	416.66667
1.5	101.52284	26.5	136.05442	51.5	206.18557	76.5	425.53191
2	102.04082	27	136.98630	52	208.33333	77.0	434.78261
2.5	102.56410	27.5	137.93103	52.5	210.52632	77.5	444.44444
3	103.09278	28	138.88889	53	212.76596	78.0	454.54545
3.5	103.62694	28.5	139.86014	53.5	215.05376	78.5	465.11628
4	104.16667	29	140.84507	54	217.39130	79.0	476.19048
4.5	104.71204	29.5	141.84397	54.5	219.78022	79.5	487.80488
5	105.26316	30	142.85714	55	222.22222	80.0	500.00000
5.5	105.82011	30.5	143.88489	55.5	224.71910	80.5	512.82051
6	106.38298	31	144.92754	56	227.27273	81.0	526.31579
6.5	106.95187	31.5	145.98540	56.5	229.88506	81.5	540.54054
7	107.52688	32	147.05882	57	232.55814	82.0	555.55556
7.5	108.10811	32.5	148.14815	57.5	235.29412	82.5	571.42857
8	108.69565	33	149.25373	58	238.09524	83.0	588.23529
8.5	109.28962	33.33	150.00000	58.5	240.96386	83.5	606.06061
9	109.89011	34	151.51515	59	243.90244	84.0	625.00000
9.5	110.49724	34.5	152.67176	59.5	246.91358	84.5	645.16129
10	111.11111	35	153.84615	60	250.00000	85.0	666.66667
10.5	111.73184	35.5	155.03876	60.5	253.16456	85.5	689.65517
11	112.35955	36	156.25000	61	256.41026	86.0	714.28571
11.5	112.99435	36.5	157.48031	61.5	259.74026	86.5	740.74074
12	113.63636	37	158.73016	62	263.15789	87.0	769.23077
12.5	114.28571	37.5	160.00000	62.5	266.66667	87.5	800.00000
13	114.94253	38	161.29032	63	270.27027	88.0	833.33333
13.5	115.60694	38.5	162.60163	63.5	273.97260	88.5	869.56522
14	116.27907	39	163.93443	64	277.77778	89.0	909.09091
14.5	116.95906	39.5	165.28926	64.5	281.69014	89.5	952.38095
15	117.64706	40	166.66667	65	285.71429	90.0	1000.00000
15.5	118.34320	40.5	168.06723	65.5	289.85507	90.5	1052.63158
16	119.04762	41	169.49153	66	294.11765	91.0	1111.11111
16.5	119.76048	41.5	170.94017	66.5	298.50746	91.5	1176.47059
17	120.48193	42	172.41379	66.67	300.00000	92.0	1250.00000
17.5	121.21212	42.5	173.91304	67.5	307.69231	92.5	1333.33333
18	121.95122	43	175.43860	68	312.50000	93.0	1428.57143
18.5	122.69939	43.5	176.99115	68.5	317.46032	93.5	1538.46154
19	123.45679	44	178.57143	69	322.58065	94.0	1666.66667
19.5	124.22360	44.5	180.18018	69.5	327.86885	94.5	1818.18182
20	125.00000	45	181.81818	70	333.33333	95.0	2000.00000
20.5	125.78616	45.5	183.48624	70.5	338.98305	95.5	2222.22222
21	126.58228	46	185.18519	71	344.82759	96.0	2500.00000
21.5	127.38854	46.5	186.91589	71.5	350.87719	96.5	2857.14286
22	128.20513	47	188.67925	72	357.14286	97.0	3333.33333
22.5	129.03226	47.5	190.47619	72.5	363.63636	97.5	4000.00000
23	129.87013	48	192.30769	73	370.37037	98.0	5000.00000
23.5	130.71895	48.5	194.17476	73.5	377.35849	98.5	6666.66667
24	131.57895	49	196.07843	74	384.61538	99.0	10000.00000
24.5	132.45033	49.5	198.01980	74.5	392.15686	99.5	20000.00000
25	133.33333	50	200.00000	75	400.00000	--	---

Entry is the percentage that restores a marked down number to its original value.

Reciprocal Percentage Markups & Markdowns

Markup	Markdown	Markup	Markdown	Markup	Markdown	Markup	Markdown
100.5	99.50249	125.5	79.68127	150.5	66.44518	175.5	56.98006
101	99.00990	126	79.36508	151	66.22517	176.0	56.81818
101.5	98.52217	126.5	79.05138	151.5	66.00660	176.5	56.65722
102	98.03922	127	78.74016	152	65.78947	177.0	56.49718
102.5	97.56098	127.5	78.43137	152.5	65.57377	177.5	56.33803
103	97.08738	128	78.12500	153	65.35948	178.0	56.17978
103.5	96.61836	128.5	77.82101	153.5	65.14658	178.5	56.02241
104	96.15385	129	77.51938	154	64.93506	179.0	55.86592
104.5	95.69378	129.5	77.22008	154.5	64.72492	179.5	55.71031
105	95.23810	130	76.92308	155	64.51613	180.0	55.55556
105.5	94.78673	130.5	76.62835	155.5	64.30868	180.5	55.40166
106	94.33962	131	76.33588	156	64.10256	181.0	55.24862
106.5	93.89671	131.5	76.04563	156.5	63.89776	181.5	55.09642
107	93.45794	132	75.75758	157	63.69427	182.0	54.94505
107.5	93.02326	132.5	75.47170	157.5	63.49206	182.5	54.79452
108	92.59259	133	75.18797	158	63.29114	183.0	54.64481
108.5	92.16590	133.33	75.00000	158.5	63.09148	183.5	54.49591
109	91.74312	134	74.62687	159	62.89308	184.0	54.34783
109.5	91.32420	134.5	74.34944	159.5	62.69592	184.5	54.20054
110	90.90909	135	74.07407	160	62.50000	185.0	54.05405
110.5	90.49774	135.5	73.80074	160.5	62.30530	185.5	53.90836
111	90.09009	136	73.52941	161	62.11180	186.0	53.76344
111.5	89.68610	136.5	73.26007	161.5	61.91950	186.5	53.61930
112	89.28571	137	72.99270	162	61.72840	187.0	53.47594
112.5	88.88889	137.5	72.72727	162.5	61.53846	187.5	53.33333
113	88.49558	138	72.46377	163	61.34969	188.0	53.19149
113.5	88.10573	138.5	72.20217	163.5	61.16208	188.5	53.05040
114	87.71930	139	71.94245	164	60.97561	189.0	52.91005
114.5	87.33624	139.5	71.68459	164.5	60.79027	189.5	52.77045
115	86.95652	140	71.42857	165	60.60606	190.0	52.63158
115.5	86.58009	140.5	71.17438	165.5	60.42296	190.5	52.49344
116	86.20690	141	70.92199	166	60.24096	191.0	52.35602
116.5	85.83691	141.5	70.67138	166.5	60.06006	191.5	52.21932
117	85.47009	142	70.42254	166.67	60.00000	192.0	52.08333
117.5	85.10638	142.5	70.17544	167.5	59.70149	192.5	51.94805
118	84.74576	143	69.93007	168	59.52381	193.0	51.81347
118.5	84.38819	143.5	69.68641	168.5	59.34718	193.5	51.67959
119	84.03361	144	69.44444	169	59.17160	194.0	51.54639
119.5	83.68201	144.5	69.20415	169.5	58.99705	194.5	51.41388
120	83.33333	145	68.96552	170	58.82353	195.0	51.28205
120.5	82.98755	145.5	68.72852	170.5	58.65103	195.5	51.15090
121	82.64463	146	68.49315	171	58.47953	196.0	51.02041
121.5	82.30453	146.5	68.25939	171.5	58.30904	196.5	50.89059
122	81.96721	147	68.02721	172	58.13953	197.0	50.76142
122.5	81.63265	147.5	67.79661	172.5	57.97101	197.5	50.63291
123	81.30081	148	67.56757	173	57.80347	198.0	50.50505
123.5	80.97166	148.5	67.34007	173.5	57.63689	198.5	50.37783
124	80.64516	149	67.11409	174	57.47126	199.0	50.25126
124.5	80.32129	149.5	66.88963	174.5	57.30659	199.5	50.12531
125	80.00000	150	66.66667	175	57.14286	--	---

Entry is the percentage which retores a marked up figure to its original value.

INDEX

About the Author

Dennis R. Kelley has 28 years of professional experience in real estate investment, finance, appraising, and management. He has brought his intimate knowledge of the real estate field gained over that time to bear in crafting this comprehensive and eminently practical volume.

At present, Mr. Kelley heads the real estate advisory division of LaSalle National Trust, subsidiary of ABN AMRD Holding, N.V., which is sixteenth in assets among the world's financial institutions. Within that capacity, he has bought, sold, or financed some $3.8 billion in real estate.